Longman Crossword Key

Longman

Longman Group Limited
Longman House, Burnt Mill, Harlow,
Essex CM20 2JE, England
and Associated Companies throughout the world.

First published 1982
Second impression, 1983

ISBN 0 582 55620 1 (Standard edition)
ISBN 0 582 55562 0 (De-luxe edition)

Printed in Great Britain
at the Pitman Press,
Bath

Author's preface

In these days of increased leisure, more and more people find the fascination of word games hard to resist.

The *Longman Crossword Key* has been compiled to alleviate the frustrating and time-wasting search for that elusive word which gets no further than 'the tip of one's tongue'. With the aid of this book not only can those sought-after words be found at a glance, but also arguments can be settled finally and tension eliminated.

Crosswords are available at all levels, ranging from those whose challenge is the speed at which they can be solved, to those whose intractable clues tease the brain for days. The *Longman Crossword Key* lists all words both by length and by letter position. It contains over 750,000 words from three to fifteen letters long. Previous crossword dictionaries listed words in alphabetical order only by length.

In this book, if, for instance, you wanted a six-letter word whose third letter was '**e**' (xx**e**xxx) you would turn to the section for six-letter words. Then you would find 'position = 3' and look through the letters printed in heavy type until you came to '**e**'. In an ordinary dictionary it would take hours to find all the possible words with '**e**' as the third letter, but this method provides a quick reference thus allowing you far more time to match the words available with the clue you have been given.

The solution to crossword problems you had previously thought insoluble will now be well within your reach. The *Crossword Key* will also prove to be an invaluable aid to compilers in their work. Then there are also the thousands of other word games, puzzles and competitions which can be solved with the aid of this book. Why not keep the children occupied on long journeys by using the *Longman Crossword Key* to invent guessing games for them?

Happy hours . . . Evelyn Marshall

A note on the author

Evelyn Marshall is a retired businesswoman who lives in Stourport-on-Severn. In addition to being a keen solver of crosswords she has also been a compiler of them for many years, in particular for the *Birmingham Mail*.

Six years ago she started working on her idea for a crossword dictionary based on first and last letters. This project became known and she was interviewed by the *Birmingham Mail* and ATV's 'Today People', which resulted in her being 'inundated with requests for copies of the book'. It was brought to the attention of the Longman Dictionary and Reference Book Department who used their unique and extensive computer-based text-processing facilities to extend her idea.

The result is the *Longman Crossword Key* which has a separate section for letters in all positions, thus making it the first truly comprehensive crossword dictionary.

How to use the Crossword Key

The words are arranged in sections, the first covering words of three letters and the last covering words of fifteen letters.

Each section contains words listed alphabetically with

- ☐ first letter in bold type in the first section
- ☐ second letter in bold type in the second section
- ☐ and so on, until the last letter is reached.

Thus, every word in the *Key* will appear as many times as it has letters – a three-letter word will appear three times, a ten-letter word ten times, etc.

So, if you need a six-letter word with 'p' as the fourth letter

- ☐ turn to the section for six-letter words
- ☐ look for 'position = 4' at the top of the page
- ☐ find 'p' in the bold letters.

Now comes the real display of skill. Which word is the one that will fit your requirements?

3 letter words

aba bit dim fie hen key mog pap rom ted wig fag pat odd ree bib sic cod
ABC biz din fig hep kid mol par rot tee win fah paw ode ref bid sin cog
abo boa dip fin her kif mom pas row teg wis fan pax bed rem big sip col
aby bob dit fir het kin moo pat rub ten wit far pay bee rep bin sir con
ace bod div fit hew kip mop paw rue tew wiz fat rad beg ret bio sis coo
act bog doe fix hex kit mor pax rug the woe fay rag bel rev bis sit cop
add bok dog flu hey koa mot pay rum tho wog gab rah ben Rex bit six cor
ado boo doh fly hic kob mow pea run thy won gad raj bet sea biz tic cos
adz bop Dom fob hid kop Mrs ped rut tic woo gag ram bey sec dib tie cot
aft bot don foe hie lab mud peg rye tie wop gal ran deb see did tig cow
aga bow dop fog him lac mug pen sac tig wot gam rap dee sei die til cox
age box dor fop hin lad mum pep sad til wow gan rat den sen dig tin coy
ago boy dot for hip lag nab per sag tin wry gap raw dew set dim tip coz
aha bra dow fou his lah nae pet sai tip wud gar rax dey sew din tit doe
aid bub dry fox hit lam nag pew sal tit wye gas ray eel sex dip via dog
ail bud dso foy hob lap nap phi sap tod yah gat sac een sez dit vie doh
aim bug dub Fra hod lar nay pie sat toe yak gay sad fed tea div vim Dom
ain bum dud fro hoe lat neb pig saw tog yam had sag fee tec fib vis don
air bun due fry hog law nee pin sax tom yap hae sai fen ted fid wig dop
ait bur dug fud hon lax net pip say ton yaw hag sal feu tee fie win dor
ala bus dun fug hop lay new pit sea too yea hah sap few teg fig wis dot
alb but duo fun hot lea nib pix sec top yen ham sat fey ten fin wit dow
ale buy dup fur how led nil ply see tor yep han saw fez tew fir wiz eon
all bye dux gab hoy lee nim pod sei tot yes hap sax ged vee fit yin fob
alp cab dye gad hub leg nip poe sen tow yet has say gee veg fix yip foe
alt cad dzo gag hue lei nit poi set toy yew hat tab gel vet gib zip fog
ama cam ear gal hug Leo nix pom sew try yin haw tag gem vex gid eke fop
amp can eat gam huh let nob pon sex tub yip hay tai gen web gie oke for
ana cap eau gan hum leu nod pop sez tug yob jab taj get wed gig ski fou
and car ebb gap Hun lev nog pot she tui yod jag tam gey wee gin sky fox
ane cat ecu gar hup lex Noh pow shy tum yon jam tan heh wen git ala foy
ani caw edh gas hut ley non pox sib tun you Jap tap hem wet hic alb Goa
ant cay eel gat hyp lib nor pro sic tup zap jar tar hen wey hid ale gob
any chi een gay Ibo lid not pry sin tut zax Jat tat hep yea hie all god
ape cob eff ged ice lie now psi sip tux zed jaw tau her yen him alp goo
apt cod eft gee icy lip nth pub sir twa zee jay taw het yep hin alt got
arc cog egg gel Ido lis nub pud sis Twi zel kai tax hew yes hip eld gov
are col ego gem ilk lit nun pug sit two Zen kat vac hex yet his elf goy
ark con eke gen ill lob nut pun six ufo zho lab van hey yew hit elk hob
arm coo eld get imp log oaf pup ski ugh zip lac vas jet zed jib ell hod
art cop elf gey Ind loo oak pur sky ule zoa lad vat jeu zee jig elm hoe
ash cor elk ghi ink lop oar pus sly ure zoo lag wad Jew zel kid flu hog
ask cos ell gib inn lor oat put sob urn —— lah wae kea Zen kif fly hon
asp cot elm gid ion lot obi puy soc use baa lam wag ked aft kin ilk hop
ass cow emu gie ire low oca pye sod vac bad lap wan kef eff kip ill hot
ate cox end gig irk lox och pyx soh van bag lar wap keg eft kit old how
auk coy eon gin ism loy odd qua sol vas bah lat war ken off lib ply hoy
ave coz era git ita lud ode rad son vat bam law was key oft lid sly ion
awe cru ere gnu its lug oer rag sop vee ban lax waw lea ufo lie ule job
awl cry erf Goa ivy lum off rah sot veg bap lay wax led aga lip ama jog
awn cub erg gob jab lur oft raj sou vet bar mac way lee age lis amp jot
axe cud erk god jag lux ohm ram sow vex bat mad yah leg ago lit emu jow
aye cue ern goo jam luz oho ran sox via bay mag yak lei egg mid imp joy
azo cum err got Jap lye oil rap soy vie cab mam yam Leo ego mil ana koa
baa cup ess gov jar mac oke rat spa vim cad man yap let ugh mim and kob
bad cur eta goy Jat mad old raw spy vis cam map yaw leu aha mir ane kop
bag cut eth gum jaw mag one rax sri voe can mar zap lev chi mix ani lob
bah cwm eve gun jay mam oof ray sty vow cap mat zax lex ghi nib ant log
bam dab ewe gup jet man ooh red sub vug car maw aba ley mho nil any loo
ban dad eye gut jeu map ope ree sue wad cat may ABC men ohm nim end lop
bap dag fab guv Jew mar opt ref sum wae caw nab abo met oho nip gnu lor
bar dak fad guy jib mat orb rem sun wag cay nae aby meu phi nit Ind lot
bat dal fag gym jig maw orc rep sup wan dab nag ebb mew rho nix ink low
bay dam fah gyp job may ore ret tab wap dad nap Ibo neb she oil inn lox
bed dan fan had jog men ort rev tag war dag nay obi nee shy pie one loy
bee dap far hae jot met our Rex tai was dak oaf ace net the pig boa moa
beg daw fat hag jow meu out rho taj waw dal oak act new tho pin bob mob
bel day fay hah joy mew ova ria tam wax dam oar ecu oer thy pip bod mod
ben deb fed ham jug mho owe rib tan way dan oat ice pea who pit bog mog
bet dee fee han jut mid owl rid tap web dap pad icy ped why pix bok mol
bey den fen hap kai mil own rig tar wed daw pah oca peg zho ria boo mom
bib dew feu has kat mim oxy rim tat wee day pal och pen aid rib bop moo
bid dey few hat kea mir pad rip tau wen ear pam add pep ail rid bot mop
big dib fey haw ked mix pah rob taw wet eat pan ado per aim rig bow mor
bin did fez hay kef moa pal roc tax wey eau pap adz pet ain rim box mot
bio die fib heh keg mob pam rod tea who fab par edh pew air rip boy mow
bis dig fid hem ken mod pan roe tec why fad pas Ido red ait sib cob nob

nod yon auk pub wye lib hid foe cog och arm fin Ibo sip pus out mew fay
nog you bub pud azo lob hod gee dag ooh bam fun Ido sop sis pat mow fey
Noh zoa bud pug dzo mob Ind gie dig pah bum gan Leo sup vas pet new fly
non zoo bug pun —— nab ked hae dog rah cam gen loo tap vis pit now foy
nor ape bum pup aba neb kid hie dug soh cum gin mho tip was pot paw fry
not apt bun pur aga nib lad hoe egg ugh cwm gun moo top wis put pew gay
now ope bur pus aha nob led hue erg yah dam han oho tup yes rat pow gey
oof opt bus put ala nub lid ice fag ani dim hen pro wap act ret raw goy
ooh spa but puy ama orb lud ire fig chi Dom hin rho wop aft rot row guy
pod spy buy qua ana pub mad lee fog ghi elm hon tho yap ait rut saw hay
poe arc cub rub baa rib mid lie fug kai gam Hun too yep alt sat sew hey
poi are cud rue boa rob mod lye gag lei gem inn two yip ant set sow hoy
pom ark cue rug bra rub mud nae gig obi gum ion ufo zap apt sit taw icy
pon arm cum rum era sib nod nee hag phi gym ken who zip art sot tew ivy
pop art cup run eta sob odd ode hog poi ham kin woo air bat tat tow jay
pot bra cur rut Fra sub old oke hug psi hem man zho bar bet tit vow joy
pow cru cut sub Goa tab pad one jag sai him men zoo bur bit tot waw key
pox cry dub sue ita tub ped ope jig sei hum non alp car bot tut wow lay
rob dry dud sum kea web pod ore jog ski ism nun amp cor but vat yaw ley
roc era due sun koa yob pud owe jug Sri jam own asp cur cat vet yew loy
rod ere dug sup lea ABC rad pie keg tai lam pan bap dor cot wet box may
roe erf dun tub moa arc red poe lag tui lum pen bop ear cut wit cox nay
rom erg duo tug oca hic rid pye leg Twi mam pin cap err dit wot dux oxy
rot erk dup tui ova lac rod ree log raj mim pon cop far dot yet fix pay
row ern dux tum pea mac sad roe lug taj mom pun cup fir eat cru fox ply
sob err fud tun qua orc sod rue mag ark mum ran dap for eft eau hex pry
soc Fra fug tup ria roc ted rye mog ask nim run dip fur fat ecu lax puy
sod fro fun tut sea sac tod see mug auk ohm sen dop gar fit emu lex ray
soh fry fur tux spa sec wad she nag bok pam sin dup her gat feu lox say
sol ire gum vug tea sic wed sue nog dak pom son fop jar get flu lux shy
son irk gun wud twa soc wud tee peg elk ram sun gap lar git fou mix sky
sop Mrs gup ave via tec yod the pig erk rem tan gup lor got gnu nix sly
sot orb gut eve yea tic zed tie pug ilk rim ten gyp lur gut jeu pax soy
sou orc guv ivy zoa vac ace toe rag ink rom tin hap mar hat leu pix spy
sow ore guy ova alb add age ule rig irk rum ton hep mir het meu pox sty
sox ort hub awe bib aid ale ure rug oak sum tun hip mor hit sou pyx thy
soy pro hue awl bob and ane use sag yak tam urn hop nor hot tau rax toy
tod pry hug awn bub bad ape vee tag ail tom van hup oar hut you Rex try
toe Sri huh cwm cab bed are vie teg all tum wan hyp oer Jat div sax way
tog try hum ewe cob bid ate voe tig awl vim wen imp our jet gov sex wey
tom ure Hun owe cub bod ave wae tog bel yam win Jap par jot guv six why
ton urn hup owl dab bud awe wee tug col ain won kip per jut lev sox wry
too wry hut own deb cad axe woe veg dal awn yen kop pur kat rev tax adz
top ash jug twa dib cod aye wye vug eel ban yin lap sir kit bow tux biz
tor ask jut Twi dub cud bee zee wag ell ben yon lip tar lat caw vex coz
tot asp lud two ebb dad bye eff wig gal bin Zen lop tor let cow wax fez
tow ass lug axe fab did cue elf wog gel bun abo map war lit daw zax luz
toy dso lum oxy fib dud dee erf ash ill can ado mop ass lot dew aby sez
voe ess lur aye fob eld die kef bah mil con ago nap bis mat dow any wiz
vow ism lux bye gab end doe kif doh mol dan azo nip bus met few bay
woe psi luz dye gib fad due oaf edh nil den bio pap cos mot haw bey
wog use mud eye gob fed dye off eth oil din boo pep ess net hew boy
won ate mug gym hob fid eke oof fah owl don coo pip gas nit how buy
woo eta mum gyp hub fud ere ref hah pal dun dso pop has not jaw cay
wop eth nub hyp jab gad eve bag heh sal een duo pup his nut Jew coy
wot ita nun lye jib ged ewe beg huh sol eon dzo rap its oat jow cry
wow its nut pye job gid eye big lah til ern ego rep lis oft law day
yob nth our pyx kob god fee bog Noh zel fan fro rip Mrs opt low dey
yod sty out rye lab had fie bug nth aim fen goo sap pas ort maw dry

4 letter words

abba Acts agio alas amir apse asci awry back bank bats Beeb best bint
abbe acyl agog alee ammo aqua ashy axel bade bant batt beef beta bird
abed Adam agon alfa amok Arab Asti axes bael barb baud been bevy birk
abet Adar ague alga amyl arak atom axil bail bard bawd beep bias birl
able adit ahem ally anew arch atop axis bait bare bawl beer bice bise
ably adze ahoy alms anil area auld axle bake bark bawn beet bide bisk
abut aeon aide aloe ankh Ares aunt axon bald barm bays bell bier bite
abye aero aine alow anna aria aura ayah bale barn bead belt biff bitt
ache aery Ainu also anoa arid auto baas balk base beak bema bigg blab
achy afar airy alto anon aril aver baba ball bash beam bend bike blae
acid Afro ajar alum anta arms avid babe balm bask bean bent bile blah
acme agar akee amah ante army avow Babi banc bass bear bere bilk blat
acne aged akin ambo anti arty away babu band bast beat berg bill bleb
acol agha alae amen apex arum awed baby bane bate beau berk bind bled
acre agin alar amid apod aryl awny bach bang bath beck berm bine blew

blin bund chop coup deed dost eery feet fore germ grow helm hwyl joss
blip bung chou cove deem dote egad feis fork gest grub help hyle jota
blob bunk chow cowl deep doth egal fell form geum grum heme hymn jowl
bloc bunt chub coxa deer doup eger felt fort ghat guan hemp hype juba
blot buoy chug coxy deft dour eggy feme foss ghee guar hent hypo judo
blow burd chum coze defy dove egis fend foul gibe guff herb iamb judy
blub burg chut crab deil down ekka fere four gift gula herd ibex juju
blue burk ciao crag dele doxy elan fern fowl gila gulf here ibid July
blur burl cine cram delf doze elmy fess foxy gild gull herl ibis jump
boar burn cire cran dell dozy else fest frae gill gulp herm icky June
boat burp cist crap deme drab emeu fete frap gilt gump hern icon junk
bock burr cite craw demo drag emir feud frat gimp gunk hero idea Juno
bode bury city cree demy dram emit fiat Frau gink guru Herr idem jury
body bush clad crew dene drat Emmy fico fray gird gush hers ides just
Boer busk clam crib dent draw enow fido free girl gust hest idle jute
bogy buss clan crit deny dray envy fief fret girn guts hewn idly kadi
boil bust clap crop derm dree epee fife frit giro gybe hick idol kago
boko busy claw crow derv dreg epha file froe girt gymp hide iffy kail
bold butt clay crud desk drew epic fill frog gist gyre hifi ikon kaka
bole buzz clef crux dewy drey epos film from give gyri high ilea kale
boll byre cleg cube dhal drib ergo fils frow glad gyro hike ilex kali
bolt byte clem cuff dhow drip Erin find fuci glam gyve hila ilia kame
boma cade clew cuit dial drop erne fine fuel glee haaf hill ilka kana
bomb cadi clip cull dice drub Eros fink full gleg haar hilt illy kaon
bond cafe clod culm dick drug Erse Finn fume glen hack hind imam kart
bone caff clog cult dido drum erst fino fumy gley hade hint impi kava
bong cage clop cups diet Druz esne fire fund glia hadj hipt inby kayo
bony cagy clot curb dike duad espy firm funk glib haem hire Inca keck
boob cake clou curd dill dual esse firn furl glim haet hiss inch keek
book calf cloy cure dime duce etch fisc fury glob haft hist info keel
boom calk club curl dine duck etna fish fuse glop haha hive inky keen
boon call clue curn ding duct etui fisk fuss glow haik hoar inly keep
boor calm coal curr dink dude euro fist fuze glue hail hoax into kelp
boot calp coat curt dint duds even fitz fuzz glum hair hobo iota Kelt
bora calx coax cush dire duel ever five fyrd glut hajj hock iris kemp
bore came coca cusk dirk dues evil fizz gaby Gman haka hoer iron kent
born camp cock cusp dirl duet ewer flab gade gnar hake hogg isle kepi
bort cane coco cuss dirt duff exam flag gadi gnat hale hoho isnt kept
bosh cang coda cute disc duke exes flak Gael gnaw half hold itch kerb
bosk cant code cyan dish dull exit flam gaff goad hall hole item kerf
boss cape coed cyma disk duly exon flan gaga goal halm holm iwis kern
both capo coho cyme diss duma expo flap gage goat halo holp jack khan
bott card coif cyst dite dumb eyas flat gain goby halt hols jade khat
bout care coil czar ditt dump eyed flaw gait goer hame holt jail kibe
bowl cark coin dace diva dune eyne flax gala goes hand holy Jain kick
boxy carl coir Dada dive dung eyot flay gale gogo hang home jake kier
boyg carp coke dado divi dunk eyra flea gall gold hank homo jamb kill
boyo cart cola daff dixy dupe eyre fled gamb golf hard homy jane kiln
bozo case cold daft doat dura eyry flee game gone hare hone jape kilo
brad cash cole dago dock durn face flew gamp gong hark hong jarl kilt
brae cask colt dahl dodo duro fact flex gamy gonk harl honk jato kind
brag cast coma Dail doer dusk fade fley gang good harm hood Java kine
bran cate comb dais does dust fado flic gaol goof harn hoof jazz king
brat caul come dale doff duty faff flip gape gook harp hook jean kink
braw cave comp dame doge dyad fail flit garb goon hart hoop jeep kino
bray cavy cone damn dogy Dyak fain floc garn goop hash hoot jeer kiri
bred cede conk damp doit dyer fair floe gash gory hasp hope jehu kirk
bree cedi conn Dane dojo dyke fake flog gasp Goth hast horn jell kiss
bren ceil cony dang dole dyne fall flop gast gout hate hose jerk kist
brer cell cook dank doll each falx flow gate gowk hath hoss jess kite
brew celt cool dare dolt earl fame flub gaud gown haul host jest kith
Brie cent coon darg dome earn fane flue Gaul grab have hour jete kiwi
brig cere coop dark domy ease fang flux gaum graf hawk hove jibe knag
brim cert coot darn dona east fard flys gaup gram haze howl jiff knap
brio cess cope dart done easy fare foal gaur gran hazy hued jill knar
brit chad Copt dash dong eath farl foam gave grat head huff jilt knee
brog cham copy data dont eats farm foci gawk gray heal huge jimp knew
brow chap cord date dook ebon faro fogy gawp gree heap hula jink knit
brut char core daub doom echo fash fohn gaze grew hear hulk jinn knob
bubo chat corf dawk door echt fast foil gean grey heat hull jinx knop
buck chaw cork dawn dope ecru fate foin gear grid heck hump jive knot
buff chef corm daze dopy Edam faun fold geat grig heed hung jock know
buhl chew corn dead dorm Edda fawn folk geck grim heel hunk joey knur
bulb chic cose deaf dorp eddy faze fond Geez grin heft hunt john knut
bulk chid cosh deal dorr Eden fear font geld grip heil hurl join koan
bull chin cost dean dort edge feat food gelt gris heir hurt joke koel
bumf chip cosy dear dory edgy feck fool gene grit held hush joky kohl
bump chit cote debt dose edit feed foot gens grog hele husk jolt kola
buna choc cott deck doss eely feel ford gent grot hell huss josh kolo

kook koto kris kudu Kurd kyat kyle lace lack lacy lade lady laic laid lain lair lake lakh laky lama lamb lame lamp land lane lang lank Lapp lard lark larn lase lash lass last late lath laud lava lave lawk lawn laze lazy lead leaf leak leal lean leap leat leek leer lees leet left lehr lend leno lens Lent less lest Lett leva levy lewd liar Lias lice lich lick lido lied lief lien lier lieu life

lift like lilo lilt lily lima limb lime limn limo limp limy line ling link linn lino lint liny lion lira lire lisp list live load loaf loam loan lobe loch loci lock loco lode loft loge logo loin loir loll lone long look loom loon loop loot lope lord lore lorn lory lose loss lost lota loth loud loup lour lout love lowe lown luau luce luck ludo lues luff luge lull lulu lump lune lung lunt lure

lurk lush lust lute luxe lyam lych lyme lynx Lyon lyre lyse maam mace Mach mack made mage magi maid mail maim main make mako male mali mall malm malt mama mana mane Manx many marc mare mark marl marm Mars mart mash mask mass mast mate math matt maty maud maul maun maxi maya maze mazy mead meal mean meat Mede meed meek meet meld mell melt memo mend menu meow mere mesa mesh mess mete mewl mews

mica mice mick midi mien miff mike mild mile milk mill milt mime mina mind mine Ming mini mink mint minx mire mirk miry mise miss mist mite mitt moan moat mock mode mods moho moil moke moko mole moll moly mome mona monk mono mood moon moor moot mope mora more morn Moro mort moss most mote moth moue move mown moxa much muck muff mule mull mump muon mure murk muse mush musk muss must mute mutt

myna myth Naga naif nail name nana nape nard nark nary nave navy naze Nazi neap near neat neck need neem neer nene neon ness nest nett neum neve news newt next nice nick nide nidi niff nigh nill nine nipa nisi nixy nock node nodi noel noil nome none nonU nook noon nope norm nose nosh nosy note noun nous nova nowt nude null numb nuts oary oast oath oats obey obit oboe obol odds odea odic ogam

ogee ogle ogre oily oink okay okra oleo olid olio olla omen omer omit once oner only onto onus onyx oont oops ooze oozy opah opal open opus oral orca orfe orgy orle orra orts oryx otic otto ouch ouph ours oust ouzo oval oven over ovum oxen oxer oyer oyes oyez paca pace pack pact page paid pail pain pair pale Pali pall palm palp paly pane pang pant papa para pard pare park parr part pash pass

past pate path paua paul pave pawl pawn peak peal pean pear peat peck peek peel peen peep peer peke pelf pelt pent peon pepo peri perk perm pern pert peso pest phew phiz phon phot pica pice pick Pict pied pier pika pike pile pili pill pimp pine ping pink pint piny pion pipa pipe pipy pirn pise pish piss pita pith pity pium pixy plan plat play plea pleb pled plie plod plop plot plow ploy plug

plum plus pock poco poem poet pogo poke poky pole poll polo poly pome pomp pond pone pong pons pony pood poof pooh pool poon poop poor pope pore pork porn port pose posh post posy pouf pour pout poxy pram prat prau pray pree prep prex prey prig prim proa prod prof prog prom prop prow puce puck puff puja puke pule pull pulp puma pump puna punk punt puny pupa pure purl purr push puss putt pyre

quad quag quay quid quin quip quit quiz quod rabi race rack racy raff raft raga rage ragi raid rail rain raja rake raki rale rami ramp rand rang rani rank rant rape rapt rare rase rash rasp rata rate rath rave raze razz read real ream reap rear reck redd rede redo reed reef reek reel refs reft rein reis rely rend rent repp rest rete rhea rhus rial rice rich rick ride rife riff rift rile rill

rima rime rimy rind ring rink riot ripe rise risk rite rive road roam roan roar robe rock rode roil role roll romp rood roof rook room root rope ropy rose rosy rota rote rotl roue roup rout roux rove ruby ruck rudd rude ruff ruin rule rump rune rung runt ruse rush rusk Russ rust ruth ryal ryot rype sack safe saga sage sago said sail sain sake saki sale salt same samp sand sane sang sank sans

sard sari sark sash sass sate sati save sawn saxe scab scad scan scar scat scot scow scry scud scug scum scup scut seal seam sear seat sect seed seek seel seem seen seep seer sego self sell seme semi send sent seps sept sera Serb sere serf seta sett sewn sext sexy shad shag shah sham Shan shaw shay shea shed shew shim shin ship shiv shod shoe shog shoo shop shot show Shri shun shut sial sice

sick side sift sigh sign sika sike Sikh sild silk sill silo silt sima sine sing sinh sink Sion sire site sith Siva size sizy skat skaw skep skew skid skim skin skip skit skua slab slag slam slap slat Slav slaw slay sled slew sley slid slim slip slit slob sloe slog slop slot slow slub slue slug slum slur slut smew smit smog smug smut snag snap sned snib snip snob snog snot snow snub snug soak

soap soar sock soda sofa soft soho soil soke sola sold sole soli solo soma some sone song soon soot soph sora sorb sore sori sorn sort soso souk soul soup sour sown soya spae span spar spat spay spec sped spew spin spit spiv spot spry spud spue spun spur stab stag stap star stay stem sten step stet stew stir stoa stob stop stot stow stub stud stum stun stye such suck sudd suds suer suet Sufi

suit sulk sumo sump sung sunk sunn sura surd sure surf swab swag swam swan swap swat sway swig swim swiz swob swop swot swum syce sync syne taal tabu tace tach tack taco tact tael tahr tail take tala talc tale tali talk tall tame tamp tana tang tank tapa tape taps tara tare tarn taro tarp tart tash task tass tata taut taws taxa taxi teak teal team tear teat teem teen teff tegg tele tell temp tend tent term tern test text Thai than thar that thaw thee them then thew they thig thin thir this thou thro thud thug thus tice tick tide tidy tied tier tiff tige tike tiki tile till tilt time tine ting tint tiny tire tirl tiro titi tizz toad toby toco todo tody toed toff toft tofu toga togs toil toko tola told tole toll tolu tomb tome tone tong tony took tool toom toon tope topi tops torc

tore tori torn torr tort Tory tosh toss tote tour tout town towy trad tram trap tray tree trek tret trey trig trim trio trip trod tron trot trow troy true trug tsar Tshi tuan tuba tube tuck tufa tuff tuft tule tump tuna tune tung Tupi turf Turk turn tush tusk tutu twae twee twig twin twit tyke type typo tyre tyro tzar udal ugli ugly ulna umbo unci unco undo unit unto upas upon Urdu urea urge

uric urim urus used user uvea vagi vail vain vair vale vali vamp vane vang vara vary vasa vase vast veal Veda veer vehm veil vein vela veld vena vend vent verb vert vest veto vial vice vide view vile vill vina vine vino vint viny viol virl visa vise viva vive vlei void vole volt vote Waac Waaf wade wadi wady waff waft wage waif wail wain wait wake wale walk wall wame wand wane want ward ware

warm warn warp wart wary wash wasp wast watt waul wave wavy wawl waxy ways weak weal wean wear weed week ween weep weet weft weir weka weld well wels welt wend went wept were wert west wham whap what whee when whet whew whey whid Whig whim whin whip whir whit whiz whoa whom whop wick wide wife wild wile will wilt wily wind wine wing wink wino winy wipe wire wiry wise wish wisp wist wite with

wits wive woad woes woke wold wolf womb wont wood woof wool word wore work worm worn wort wost wove wrap wren writ wynd Xmas Xray yack yang yank yapp yard yare yarn yaup yawl yawn yaws yeah yean year yegg yeld yell yelp yerk yeti yeuk yill ylem yoga yogh yogi yoke yolk yond yoni yore york your yowl yoyo yuan yuca yuga yule yurt ywis zack zany zati zeal zebu zein Zend zero zest zeta zinc zing

Zion zoea zoic zone zoom zoon zoot zori Zulu

———

baas baba babe Babi babu baby bach back bade bael bail bait bake bald bale balk ball balm banc band bane bang bank bant barb bard bare bark barm barn base bash bask bass bast bate bath bats batt baud bawd bawl bawn bays cade cadi cafe caff cage cagy cake calf calk call calm calp calx came camp cane cang cant cape capo card care cark carl carp

cart case cash cask cast cate caul cave cavy dace Dada dado daff daft dago dahl Dail dais dale dame damn damp Dane dang dank dare darg dark darn dart dash data date daub dawk dawn daze each earl earn ease east easy eath eats face fact fade fado faff fail fain fair fake fall falx fame fane fang fard fare farl farm faro fash fast fate faun fawn faze gaby gade gadi Gael gaff gaga gage gain gait

gala gale gall gamb game gamp gamy gang gaol gape garb garn gash gasp gast gate gaud Gaul gaum gaup gaur gave gawk gawp gaze haaf haar hack hade hadj haem haet haft haha haik hail hair hajj haka hake hale half hall halm halo halt hame hand hang hank hard hare hark harl harm harn harp hart hash hasp hast hate hath haul have hawk haze hazy iamb jack jade jail Jain jake jamb jane jape jarl jato

Java jazz kadi kago kail kaka kale kali kame kana kaon kart kava kayo lace lack lacy lade lady laic laid lain lair lake lakh laky lama lamb lame lamp land lane lang lank Lapp lard lark larn lase lash lass last late lath laud lava lave lawk lawn laze lazy maam mace Mach mack made mage magi maid mail maim main make mako male mali mall malm malt mama mana mane Manx many marc mare mark marl marm

Mars mart mash mask mass mast mate math matt maty maud maul maun maxi maya maze mazy Naga naif nail name nana nape nard nark nary nave navy naze Nazi oary oast oath oats paca pace pack pact page paid pail pain pair pale Pali pall palm palp paly pane pang pant papa para pard pare park parr part pash pass past pate path paua paul pave pawl pawn rabi race rack racy raff raft raga rage ragi raid

rail rain raja rake raki rale rami ramp rand rang rani rank rant rape rapt rare rase rash rasp rata rate rath rave raze razz sack safe saga sage sago said sail sain sake saki sale salt same samp sand sane sang sank sans sard sari sark sash sass sate sati save sawn saxe taal tabu tace tach tack taco tact tael tahr tail take tala talc tale tali talk tall tame tamp tana tang tank tapa tape taps

tara tare tarn taro tarp tart tash task tass tata taut taws taxa taxi vagi vail vain vair vale vali vamp vane vang vara vary vasa vase vast Waac Waaf wade wadi wady waff waft wage waif wail wain wait wake wale walk wall wame wand wane want ward ware warm warn warp wart wary wash wasp wast watt waul wave wavy wawl waxy ways yack yang yank yapp yard yare yarn yaup yawl yawn yaws zack zany zati

abba abbe abed abet able ably abut abye ebon ibex ibid ibis obey obit oboe obol ache achy acid acme acne acol acre Acts acyl echo echt ecru icky icon scab scad scan scar scat scot scow scry scud scug scum scup scut Adam Adar adit adze Edam Edda eddy Eden edge edgy edit idea idem ides idle idly idol odds odea odic udal aeon aero aery bead beak beam bean bear beat beau beck Beeb beef been beep

beer beet bell belt bema bend bent bere berg berk berm best beta bevy cede cedi ceil cell celt cent cere cert cess dead deaf deal dean dear debt deck deed deem deep deer deft defy deil dele delf dell deme demo demy dene dent deny derm derv desk dewy eely eery fear feat feck feed feel feet feis fell felt feme fend fere fern fess fest fete feud gean gear geat geck Geez geld gelt gene gens gent

germ mead reis weft khan bigg gird lint pixy vina blob olio ante boss
gest meal rely weir khat bike girl liny rial vine bloc olla anti both
geum mean rend weka phew bile girn lion rice vino blot plan enow bott
head meat rent weld phiz bilk giro lira rich vint blow plat envy bout
heal Mede repp well phon bill girt lire rick viny blub play gnar bowl
heap meed rest wels phot bind gist lisp ride viol blue plea gnat boxy
hear meek rete welt rhea bine give list rife virl blur pleb gnaw boyg
heat meet seal wend rhus bint hick live riff visa clad pled inby boyo
heck meld seam went shad bird hide mica rift vise clam plie Inca bozo
heed mell sear wept shag birk hifi mice rile viva clan plod inch coal
heel melt seat were shah birl high mick rill vive clap plop info coat
heft memo sect wert sham bise hike midi rima wick claw plot inky coax
heil mend seed west Shan bisk hila mien rime wide clay plow inly coca
heir menu seek yeah shaw bite hill miff rimy wife clef ploy into cock
held meow seel yean shay bitt hilt mike rind wild cleg plug knag coco
hele mere seem year shea ciao hind mild ring wile clem plum knap coda
hell mesa seen yegg shed cine hint mile rink will clew plus knar code
helm mesh seep yeld shew cire hipt milk riot wilt clip slab knee coed
help mess seer yell shim cist hire mill ripe wily clod slag knew coho
heme mete sego yelp shin cite hiss milt rise wind clog slam knit coif
hemp mewl self yerk ship city hist mime risk wine clop slap knob coil
hent mews sell yeti shiv dial hive mina rite wing clot slat knop coin
herb neap seme yeuk shod dice jibe mind rive wink clou Slav knot coir
herd near semi zeal shoe dick jiff mine sial wino cloy slaw know coke
here neat send zebu shog dido jill Ming sice winy club slay knur cola
herl neck sent zein shoo diet jilt mini sick wipe clue sled knut cold
herm need seps Zend shop dike jimp mink side wire elan slew once cole
hern neem sept zero shot dill jink mint sift wiry elmy sley oner colt
hero neer sera zest show dime jinn minx sigh wise else slid only coma
Herr nene Serb zeta Shri dine jinx mire sign wish flab slim onto comb
hers neon sere afar shun ding jive mirk sika wisp flag slip onus come
hest ness serf Afro shut dink kibe miry sike wist flak slit onyx comp
hewn nest seta iffy Thai dint kick mise Sikh wite flam slob snag cone
jean nett sett agar than dire kier miss sild with flan sloe snap conk
jeep neum sewn aged thar dirk kill mist silk wits flap slog sned conn
jeer neve sext agha that dirl kiln mite sill wive flat slop snib cony
jehu news sexy agin thaw dirt kilo mitt silo yill flaw slot snip cook
jell newt teak agio thee disc kilt nice silt zinc flax slow snob cool
jerk next teal agog them dish kind nick sima zing flay slub snog coon
jess peak team agon then disk kine nide sine Zion flea slue snot coop
jest peal tear ague thew diss king nidi sing ajar fled slug snow coot
jete pean teat egad they dite kink niff sinh akee flee slum snub cope
keck pear teem egal thig ditt kino nigh sink akin flew slur snug Copt
keek peat teen eger thin diva kiri nill Sion ekka flex slut unci copy
keel peck teff eggy thir dive kirk nine sire ikon fley ulna unco cord
keen peek tegg egis this divi kiss nipa site okay flic vlei undo core
keep peel tele ogam thou dixy kist nisi sith okra flip ylem unit corf
kelp peen tell ogee thro fiat kite nixy Siva skat flit amah unto cork
Kelt peep temp ogle thud fico kith oily size skaw floc ambo boar corm
kemp peer tend ogre thug fido kiwi oink sizy skep floe amen boat corn
kent peke tent ugli thus fief liar pica tice skew flog amid bock cose
kepi pelf term ugly wham fife Lias pice tick skid flop amir bode cosh
kept pelt tern ahem whap file lice pick tide skim flow ammo body cost
kerb pent test ahoy what fill lich Pict tidy skin flub amok Boer cosy
kerf peon text chad whee film lick pied tied skip flue amyl bogy cote
kern pepo veal cham when fils lido pier tier skit flux emeu boil cott
lead peri Veda chap whet find lied pika tiff skua flys emir boko coup
leaf perk veer char whew fine lief pike tige alae glad emit bold cove
leak perm vehm chat whey fink lien pile tike alar glam Emmy bole cowl
leal pern veil chaw whid Finn lier pili tiki alas glee Gman boll coxa
lean pert vein chef Whig fino lieu pill tile alee gleg imam bolt coxy
leap peso vela chew whim fire life pimp till alfa glen impi boma coze
leat pest veld chic whin firm lift pine tilt alga gley omen bomb doat
leek read vena chid whip firn like ping time ally glia omer bond dock
leer real vend chin whir fisc lilo pink tine alms glib omit bone dodo
lees ream vent chip whit fish lilt pint ting aloe glim smew bong doer
leet reap verb chit whiz fisk lily piny tint alow glob smit bony does
left rear vert choc whoa fist lima pion tiny also glop smog boob doff
lehr reck vest chop whom fitz limb pipa tire alto glow smug book doge
lend redd veto chou whop five lime pipe tirl alum glue smut boom dogy
leno rede weak chow aide fizz limn pipy tiro blab glum umbo boon doit
lens redo weal chub aine gibe limo pirn titi blae glut Xmas boor dojo
Lent reed wean chug Ainu gift limp pise tizz blah ilea anew boot dole
less reef wear chum airy gila limy pish vial blat ilex anil bora doll
lest reek weed chut bias gild line piss vice bleb ilia ankh bore dolt
Lett reel week dhal bice gill ling pita vide bled ilka anna born dome
leva refs ween dhow bide gilt link pith view blew illy anoa bort domy
levy reft weep ghat bier gimp linn pity vile blin oleo anon bosh dona
lewd rein weet ghee biff gink lino pium vill blip olid anta bosk done

dong holm lout pony soul york crap prau stot dunk lush suds axes alas
dont holp love pood soup your craw pray stow dupe lust suer axil amah
dook hols lowe poof sour yowl cree pree stub dura lute suet axis Arab
doom holt lown pooh sown yoyo crew prep stud durn luxe Sufi axle arak
door holy moan pool soya zoea crib prex stum duro much suit axon away
dope home moat poon toad zoic crit prey stun dusk muck sulk exam ayah
dopy homo mock poop toby zone crop prig stye dust muff sumo exes baas
dorm homy mode poor toco zoom crow prim auld duty mule sump exit bead
dorp hone mods pope todo zoon crud proa aunt euro mull sung exon beak
dorr hong moho pore tody zoot crux prod aura fuci mump sunk expo beam
dort honk moil pork toed zori drab prof auto fuel muon sunn oxen bean
dory hood moke porn toff apex drag prog bubo full mure sura oxer bear
dose hoof moko port toft apod dram prom buck fume murk surd ayah beat
doss hook mole pose tofu apse drat prop buff fumy muse sure byre beau
dost hoop moll posh toga epee draw prow buhl fund mush surf byte bias
dote hoot moly post togs epha dray trad bulb funk musk tuan cyan blab
doth hope mome posy toil epic dree tram bulk furl muss tuba cyma blae
doup horn mona pouf toko epos dreg trap bull fury must tube cyme blah
dour hose monk pour tola opah drew tray bumf fuse mute tuck cyst blat
dove hoss mono pout told opal drey tree bump fuss mutt tufa dyad boar
down host mood poxy tole open drib trek buna fuze nude tuff Dyak boat
doxy hour moon road toll opus drip tret bund fuzz null tuft dyer brad
doze hove moor roam tolu spae drop trey bung guan numb tule dyke brae
dozy howl moot roan tomb span drub trig bunk guar nuts tump dyne brag
foal iota mope roar tome spar drug trim bunt guff ouch tuna eyas bran
foam jock mora robe tone spat drum trio buoy gula ouph tune eyed brat
foci joey more rock tong spay Druz trip burd gulf ours tung eyne braw
fogy john morn rode tony spec ergo trod burg gull oust Tupi eyot bray
fohn join Moro roil took sped Erin tron burk gulp ouzo turf eyra chad
foil joke mort role tool spew erne trot burl gump puce Turk eyre cham
foin joky moss roll toom spin Eros trow burn gunk puck turn eyry chap
fold jolt most romp toon spit Erse troy burp guru puff tush fyrd char
folk josh mote rood tope spiv erst true burr gush puja tusk gybe chat
fond joss moth roof topi spot frae trug bury gust puke tutu gymp chaw
font jota moue rook tops spry frap Urdu bush guts pule yuan gyre ciao
food jowl move room torc spud frat urea busk hued pull yuca gyri clad
fool koan mown root tore spue Frau urge buss huff pulp yuga gyro clam
foot koel moxa rope tori spun fray uric bust huge puma yule gyve clan
ford kohl nock ropy torn spur free urim busy hula pump yurt hyle clap
fore kola node rose torr upas fret urus butt hulk puna Zulu hymn claw
fork kolo nodi rosy tort upon frit wrap buzz hull punk aver hype clay
form kook noel rota Tory aqua froe wren cube hump punt avid hypo coal
fort koto noil rote tosh Arab frog writ cuff hung puny avow kyat coat
foss load nome rotl toss arak from Xray cuit hunk pupa even kyle coax
foul loaf none roue tote arch frow asci cull hunt pure ever lyam crab
four loam nonU roup tour area grab ashy culm hurl purl evil lych crag
fowl loan nook rout tout Ares graf Asti cult hurt purr oval lyme cram
foxy lobe noon roux town aria gram esne cups hush push oven lynx cran
goad loch nope rove towy arid gran espy curb husk puss over Lyon crap
goal loci norm soak void aril grat esse curd huss putt ovum lyre craw
goat lock nose soap vole arms gray isle cure juba quad uvea lyse cyan
goby loco nosh soar volt army gree isnt curl judo quag away myna czar
goer lode nosy sock vote arty grew tsar curn judy quay awed myth dead
goes loft note soda woad arum grey Tshi curr juju quid awny oyer deaf
gogo loge noun sofa woes aryl grid used curt July quin awry oyes deal
gold logo nous soft woke brad grig user cush jump quip ewer oyez dean
golf loin nova soho wold brae grim atom cusk June quit hwyl pyre dear
gone loir nowt soil wolf brag grin atop cusp junk quiz iwis ryal dhal
gong loll oont soke womb bran grip etch cuss Juno quod swab ryot dial
gonk lone oops sola wont brat gris etna cute jury ruby swag rype doat
good long ooze sold wood braw grit etui duad just ruck swam syce drab
goof look oozy sole woof bray grog itch dual jute rudd swan sync drag
gook loom pock soli wool bred grot item duce kudu rude swap syne dram
goon loon poco solo word bree grow otic duck Kurd ruff swat tyke drat
goop loop poem soma wore bren grub otto duct luau ruin sway type draw
gory loot poet some work brer grum stab dude luce rule swig typo dray
Goth lope pogo sone worm brew iris stag duds luck rump swim tyre duad
gout lord poke song worn Brie iron stap duel ludo rune swiz tyro dual
gowk lore poky soon wort brig kris star dues lues rung swob wynd dyad
gown lorn pole soot wost brim oral stay duet luff runt swop czar Dyak
hoar lory poll soph wove brio orca stem duff luge ruse swot tzar Edam
hoax lose polo sora yoga brit orfe sten duke lull rush swum ——— egad
hobo loss poly sorb yogh brog orgy step dull lulu rusk twae Adam egal
hock lost pome sore yogi brow orle stet duly lump Russ twee Adar elan
hoer lota pomp sori yoke brut orra stew duma lune rust twig afar exam
hogg loth pond sorn yolk crab orts stir dumb lung ruth twin agar eyas
hoho loud pone sort yond crag oryx stoa dump lunt such twit ajar fear
hold loup pong soso yoni cram pram stob dune lure suck ywis alae feat
hole lour pons souk yore cran prat stop dung lurk sudd axel alar fiat

flab near swan back rack odds dyer ogee used alga amir Jain trig sike
flag neat swap beck racy redd Eden oleo user bigg anil join trim Sikh
flak ogam swat bice reck rede eger omen uvea bogy aria kail trio soke
flam okay sway bock rice redo emeu omer veer cage arid knit trip take
flan opah taal buck rich ride epee oner view cagy aril kris twig tike
flap opal teak coca rick rode even open vlei dago avid laic twin tiki
flat oral teal cock rock rudd ever oven weed doge axil laid twit toko
flaw oval team coco ruck rude ewer over week dogy axis lain unit tyke
flax peak tear dace sack side exes oxen ween edge bail lair uric wake
flay peal teat deck sect soda eyed oxer weep edgy bait loin urim weka
foal pean Thai dice sice sudd feed oyer weet eggy blin loir vail woke
foam pear than dick sick suds feel oyes whee ergo blip maid vain yoke
frae peat thar dock sock tide feet oyez when fogy boil mail vair able
frap plan that duce such tidy fief peek whet gaga Brie maim veil ably
frat plat thaw duck suck todo flea peel whew gage brig main vein ally
Frau play toad duct syce tody fled peen whey gogo brim moil void auld
fray pram trad each tace undo flee peep woes high brio naif waif axle
gean prat tram etch tach Urdu flew peer wren hogg brit nail wail bald
gear prau trap face tack Veda flex phew ylem huge ceil noil wain bale
geat pray tray fact taco vide fley pied zoea kago chic obit wait balk
ghat quad tsar feck tact wade free pier alfa loge chid odic weir ball
glad quag tuan fico tice wadi fret plea biff logo chin olid whid balm
glam quay twae foci tick wady fuel pleb buff luge chip olio Whig bell
Gman read tzar fuci toco wide Gael pled cafe mage chit omit whim belt
gnar real udal geck tuck abed Geez poem caff magi clip otic whin bile
gnat ream upas hack unci abet ghee poet cuff Naga coif paid whip bilk
gnaw reap veal heck unco aged glee pree daff nigh coil pail whir bill
goad rear vial hick vice ahem gleg prep daft orgy coin pain whit bold
goal rial Waac hock wick akee glen prex deft page coir pair whiz bole
goat road Waaf Inca yack alee gley prey defy pogo crib phiz writ boll
grab roam weak inch yuca amen goer reed doff raga crit plie ywis bolt
graf roan weal itch zack anew goes reef duff rage cuit prig zein bulb
gram roar wean jack aide apex gree reek faff ragi Dail prim zoic bulk
gran ryal wear jock bade area grew reel fife saga dais quid dojo bull
grat scab wham keck bide Ares grey rhea gaff sage deil quin hajj calf
gray scad whap kick bode aver haem seed gift sago doit quip juju calk
guan scan what lace body awed haet seek guff sego drib quit puja call
guar scar woad lack cade axel heed seel haft sigh drip quiz raja calm
haaf scat wrap lacy cadi axes heel seem heft sign edit raid ankh calp
haar seal Xmas lice cede bael hoer seen hifi tegg egis rail bake calx
head seam Xray lich cedi Beeb hued seep huff tige emir rain bike cell
heal sear yeah lick coda beef ibex seer iffy toga emit rein boko celt
heap seat yean loch code been idea shea info togs epic reis cake cola
hear shad year loci Dada beep idem shed jiff urge Erin roil coke cold
heat shag yuan lock dado beer ides shew left vagi evil ruin dike cole
hoar shah zeal loco dido beet ilea skep life wage exit said duke colt
hoax sham abba luce dodo bier ilex skew lift yegg fail sail dyke cull
imam Shan abbe luck dude bleb item sled loft yoga fain sain ekka culm
jean shaw ambo lych duds bled jeep slew luff yogh fair shim fake cult
khan shay baba mace Edda blew jeer sley miff yogi feis shin haka dale
khat sial babe Mach eddy Boer joey smew muff yuga flic ship hake dele
knag skat Babi mack fade bred keek sned niff ache flip shiv hike delf
knap skaw babu mica fado bree keel spec orfe achy flit skid icky dell
knar slab baby mice fido bren keen sped puff agha foil skim ilka dill
koan slag bubo mick gade brer keep spew raff ashy foin skin inky dole
kyat slam cube mock gadi brew kier stem raft buhl frit skip jake doll
lead slap debt much hade chef knee sten refs coho gain skit joke dolt
leaf slat gaby muck hadj chew knew step reft dahl gait slid joky dull
leak Slav gibe neck hide clef koel stet rife echo glia slim kaka duly
leal slaw goby nice jade cleg leek stew riff echt glib slip lake eely
lean slay gybe nick judo clem leer suer rift epha glim slit lakh fall
leap snag hobo nock judy clew lees suet ruff fohn grid smit laky falx
leat snap inby once kadi coed leet tael safe haha grig snib like fell
liar soak jibe orca kudu cree lied teem sift hoho grim snip make felt
Lias soap juba ouch lade crew lief teen sofa jehu grin soil mako file
load soar kibe paca lady deed lien thee soft john grip spin mike fill
loaf spae lobe pace lido deem lier them Sufi kohl gris spit moke film
loam span rabi pack lode deep lieu then teff lehr grit spiv moko fils
loan spar robe pact ludo deer lues thew tiff moho haik stir peke fold
luau spat ruby peck made diet meed they toff soho hail suit pika folk
lyam spay tabu pica Mede doer meek tied toft tahr hair swig pike full
maam stab toby pice midi does meet tier tofu Tshi heil swim poke gala
mead stag tuba pick mode dree mien toed tufa vehm heir swiz poky gale
meal stap tube Pict mods dreg need tree tuff acid ibid tail puke gall
mean star umbo pock nide drew neem trek tuft adit ibis thig rake geld
meat stay zebu poco nidi drey neer tret waff agin ilia thin raki gelt
moan swab arch puce node duel noel trey waft agio iris thir sake gila
moat swag asci puck nodi dues obey twee weft akin iwis this saki gild
neap swam bach race nude duet odea urea wife amid jail toil sika gill

gilt ogle wild limo Dane ling sone boot mood tron awry farm mire Tory
gold oily wile limp dang link song brog moon trot barb faro mirk turf
golf olla will limy dank linn sung brow moor trow bard fere miry Turk
gula only wilt lump dene lino sunk buoy moot troy bare fern mora turn
gulf orle wily lyme dent lint sunn choc muon upon bark fire more tyre
gull pale wold mama deny liny sync chop neon viol barm firm morn tyro
gulp Pali wolf memo dine lone syne chou nook whoa barn firn Moro vara
hale pall yeld mime ding long tana chow noon whom bere ford mort vary
half palm yell mome dink lune tang clod oboe whop berg fore mure verb
hall palp yelp mump dint lung tank clog obol wood berk fork murk vert
halm paly yill name dona lunt tend clop peon woof berm form nard virl
halo pelf yolk nome done lynx tent clot phon wool bird fort nark ward
halt pelt yule numb dong mana tine clou phot Zion birk furl nary ware
held pile Zulu pimp dont mane ting cloy pion zoom birl fury norm warm
hele pili acme pome dune Manx tint cook plod zoon bora fyrd oary warn
hell pill alms pomp dung many tiny cool plop zoot bore garb ogre warp
helm pole ammo puma dunk mend tone coon plot cape born garn okra wart
help poll arms pump dyne menu tong coop plow capo bort germ orra wary
hila polo army rami erne mina tony coot ploy cope burd gird ours were
hill poly bema ramp esne mind tuna crop pood Copt burg girl para wert
hilt pule boma rima etna mine tune crow poof copy burk girn pard wire
hold pull bomb rime eyne Ming tung dhow pooh cups burl giro pare wiry
hole pulp bumf rimy fane mini ulna dook pool dope burn girt park word
holm rale bump romp fang mink vane doom poon dopy burp gory parr wore
holp rely came rump fend mint vang door poop dupe burr guru part work
hols rile camp same find minx vena drop poor espy bury gyre peri worm
holt rill coma samp fine mona vend ebon proa expo byre gyri perk worn
holy role comb seme fink monk vent enow prod gape card gyro perm wort
hula roll come semi Finn mono vina epos prof hipt care hard pern yard
hulk rule comp sima fino myna vine Eros prog hope cark hare pert yare
hull sale cyma soma fond nana vino exon prom hype carl hark pirn yarn
hyle salt cyme some font nene vint eyot prop hypo carp harl pore yerk
idle self dame sumo fund nine viny floc prow impi cart harm pork yore
idly sell damn sump funk none wand floe quod jape cere harn porn york
illy sild damp tame gang nonU wane flog riot kepi cert harp port yurt
inly silk deme tamp gene oink want flop rood kept cire hart pure zero
isle sill demo temp gens oont wend flow roof Lapp cord herb purl zori
jell silo demy time gent pane went food rook lope core herd purr also
jill silt dime tomb gink pang wind fool room mope corf here pyre apse
jilt sola dome tome gone pant wine foot root nape cork herl rare base
jolt sold domy tump gong pent wing froe ryot nipa corm herm sard bash
July sole duma vamp gonk pine wink frog scot nope corn hern sari bask
kale soli dumb wame gunk ping wino from scow oops curb hero sark bass
kali solo dump womb hand pink winy frow shod ouph curd Herr scry bast
kelp sulk elmy acne hang pint wont gaol shoe papa cure hers sera best
Kelt tala Emmy aine hank piny wynd glob shog pepo curl hire Serb bise
kill talc fame Ainu hent pond yang glop shoo pipa curn horn sere bisk
kiln tale feme anna hind pone yank glow shop pipe curr hurl serf bosh
kilo tali fume aunt hint pong yond good shot pipy curt hurt Shri bosk
kilt talk fumy awny hone pons yoni goof show pope dare jarl sire boss
kola tall gamb banc hong pony zany gook Sion pupa darg jerk sora bush
kolo tele game band honk puna Zend goon slob rape dark jury sorb busk
kyle tell gamp bane hung punk zinc goop sloe rapt darn kart sore buss
lilo tile gamy bang hunk punt zing grog slog repp dart kerb sori bust
lilt till gimp bank hunt puny zone grot slop ripe derm kerf sorn busy
lily tilt gump bant isnt rand acol grow slot rope derv kern sort case
loll tola gymp bend jane rang aeon hood slow ropy dire kiri spry cash
lull told hame bent jink rani agog hoof smog rype dirk kirk sura cask
lulu tole heme bind jinn rank agon hook snob seps dirl Kurd surd cast
male toll hemp bine jinx rant ahoy hoop snog sept dirt lard sure cess
mali tolu home bint June rend aloe hoot snot soph dorm lark surf cist
mall tule homo bond junk rent alow icon snow tapa dorp larn tara cose
malm ugli homy bone Juno rind amok idol soon tape dorr lira tare cosh
malt ugly hump bong kana ring anoa ikon soot taps dort lire tarn cost
meld vale hymn bony kent rink anon iron spot tope dory lord taro cosy
mell vali iamb buna kind rune apod kaon stoa topi dura lore tarp cush
melt vela jamb bund kine rung atom knob stob tops durn lorn tart cusk
mild veld jimp bung king runt atop knop stop Tupi duro lory term cusp
mile vile jump bunk kink sand avow knot stot type earl lure tern cuss
milk vill kame bunt kino sane axon know stow typo earn lurk thro cyst
mill vole kemp cane land sang blob kook swob wept ecru lyre tire dash
milt volt lama cang lane sank bloc lion swop wipe eery marc tirl desk
mole wale lamb cant lang sans blot look swot yapp euro mare tiro disc
moll walk lame cent lank send blow loom thou acre eyra mark torc dish
moly wall lamp cine lend sent boob loon took aero eyre marl tore disk
mule weld lima cone leno sine book loop tool aery eyry marm tori diss
mull well limb conk lens sing boom loot toom Afro fard Mars torn dose
nill wels lime conn lent sinh boon Lyon toon airy fare mart torr doss
null welt limn cony line sink boor meow trod aura farl mere tort dost

dusk nisi cate tata opus lava poxy data sera limb dyad rood bice dude
dust nose cite titi ovum lave saxe diva seta numb egad rudd bide duke
ease nosh city tote paua leva sext dona shea pleb eyed said bike dune
east nosy cote tutu paul levy sexy duma sika scab fard sand bile dupe
easy oast cott unto pium live taxa dura sima Serb feed sard bine dyke
else oust cute veto plug love taxi Edda Siva slab fend scad bise dyne
Erse pash data vote plum move text ekka skua slob feud scud bite ease
erst pass date watt plus nave waxy epha soda slub find seed blae edge
esse past dite wite pouf navy abye etna sofa snib fled send blue else
fash peso ditt with pour neve acyl eyra sola snob fold shad bode epee
fast pest dote wits pout nova amyl flea soma snub fond shed bole erne
fess pise doth yeti rhus pave aryl gaga sora sorb food shod bone Erse
fest pish duty zati roue rave bays gala soya stab ford sild bore esne
fisc piss eath zeta roup rive boyg gila stoa stob fund skid brae esse
fish pose eats abut rout rove boyo glia sura stub fyrd sled bree eyne
fisk posh fate ague roux save flys gula tala swab gaud slid Brie eyre
fist post fete alum scud Siva hwyl haha tana swob geld sned byre face
foss posy fitz aqua scug viva kayo haka tapa tomb gild sold byte fade
fuse push gate arum scum vive maya hila tara verb gird sped cade fake
fuss puss Goth baud scup wave onyx hula tata womb glad spud cafe fame
gash rase guts blub scut wavy oryx idea taxa banc goad stud cage fane
gasp rash hate blue shun wive soya ilea toga bloc gold sudd cake fare
gast rasp hath blur shut wove stye ilia tola chic good surd came fate
gest rest into bout skua bawd ways ilka tuba choc grid tend cane faze
gist rise iota brut slub bawl yoyo Inca tufa disc hand thud cape feme
gush risk jato caul slue bawn adze iota tuna epic hard tied care fere
gust rose jete chub slug bowl bozo Java ulna fisc head toad case fete
hash rosy jota chug slum cowl buzz jota urea flic heed toed cate fife
hasp ruse jute chum slur dawk coze juba uvea floc held told cave file
hast rush kite chut slut dawn daze kaka vara laic herd trad cede fine
hest rusk kith club smug dewy doze kana vasa marc hind trod cere fire
hiss Russ koto clue smut down dozy kava Veda odic hold used cine five
hist rust late coup snub fawn faze kola vela otic hood veld cire flee
hose sash lath crud snug fowl fizz lama vena spec hued vend cite floe
hoss sass Lett crux souk gawk fuze lava vina sync ibid void clue flue
host soso lota daub soul gawp fuzz leva visa talc kind wand code fore
hush tash loth doup soup gowk gaze lima viva torc Kurd ward coke frae
husk task lute dour sour gown haze lira weka uric laid weed cole free
huss tass mate drub spud hawk hazy lota whoa Waac land weld come froe
jess test math drug spue hewn jazz mama yoga zinc lard wend cone fume
jest tosh matt drum spun howl laze mana yuca zoic laud whid cope fuse
josh toss maty Druz spur jowl lazy maya yuga abed lead wild core fuze
joss tush mete etui stub kiwi maze mesa zeta acid lend wind cose gade
just tusk mite faun stud lawk mazy mica zoea aged lewd woad cote gage
kiss vasa mitt feud stum lawn naze mina Arab amid lied wold cove gale
kist vase mote flub stun lewd Nazi mona barb apod load wood coze game
lase vast moth flue swum lowe ooze mora Beeb arid lord word cree gape
lash vest mute flux taut lown oozy moxa blab auld loud wynd cube gate
lass visa mutt foul thud mewl ouzo myna bleb avid maid yard cure gave
last vise myth four thug mews raze Naga blob awed maud yeld cute gaze
less wash nett gaud thus mown razz nana blub bald mead yond cyme gene
lest wasp note Gaul tour news size nipa bomb band meed Zend dace ghee
lisp wast nuts gaum tout newt sizy nova boob bard meld abbe dale gibe
list west oath gaup true nowt tizz odea bulb baud mend able dame give
lose wise oats gaur trug pawl —— okra chub bawd mild abye Dane glee
loss wish onto geum urus pawn abba olla club bead mind ache dare glue
lost wisp orts glue waul sawn agha orca comb bend mood acme date gone
lush wist otto glum yaup sewn alfa orra crab bind nard acne daze gree
lust wost pate glut yeuk sown alga paca crib bird need acre dele gybe
lyse zest path gout your taws anna papa curb bled olid adze deme gyre
mash Acts pita grub bevy town anoa para daub bold paid ague dene gyve
mask alto pith grum cave towy anta paua drab bond pard aide dice hade
mass anta pity haul cavy wawl aqua pica drib brad pied aine dike hake
mast ante putt hour cove yawl area pika drub bred pled akee dime hale
mesa anti rata knur diva yawn aria pipa dumb bund plod alae dine hame
mesh arty rate knut dive yaws aura pita flab burd pond alee dire hare
mess Asti rath laud divi yowl baba plea flub card pood aloe dite hate
mise auto rete loud dove boxy bema proa gamb chad prod ante dive have
miss bate rite loup envy coxa beta puja garb chid quad apse doge haze
mist bath rota lour five coxy boma puma glib clad quid axle dole hele
moss bats rote lout gave dixy bora puna glob clod quod babe dome heme
most batt rotl maud give doxy buna pupa grab coed raid bade done here
muse beta ruth maul gyve foxy coca raga grub cold rand bake dope hide
mush bite sate maun have luxe coda raja herb cord read bale dose hike
musk bitt sati moue hive maxi cola rata iamb crud redd bane dote hire
muss both seta neum hove moxa coma rhea jamb curd reed bare dove hive
must bott sett noun Java next coxa rima kerb dead rend base doze hole
ness butt site nous jive nixy cyma rota knob deed rind bate dree home
nest byte sith onus kava pixy Dada saga lamb duad road bere duce hone

hope mode rife twae muff rung mesh sati gawk rink dell opal corm trim
hose moke rile twee naif sang moth semi geck risk dhal oral cram urim
hove mole rime tyke niff scug much Shri gink rock dial oval culm vehm
huge mome ripe type pelf shag mush soli gonk rook dill pail deem warm
hyle mope rise tyre poof shog myth sori gook ruck dirl pall derm wham
hype more rite urge pouf sing nigh Sufi gowk rusk doll paul doom whim
idle mote rive vale prof slag nosh tali gunk sack dual pawl dorm whom
isle moue robe vane puff slog oath taxi hack sank duel peal dram worm
jade move rode vase raff slug opah Thai haik sark dull peel drum ylem
jake mule role vice reef smog ouch tiki hank seek earl pill Edam zoom
jane mure rope vide riff smug ouph titi hark sick egal poll exam aeon
jape muse rose vile roof snag pash topi hawk silk evil pool farm agin
jete mute rote vine ruff snog path tori heck sink fail pull film agon
jibe name roue vise self snug pish Tshi hick soak fall purl firm akin
jive nape rove vive serf song pith Tupi hock sock farl rail flam amen
joke nave rude vole surf stag pooh ugli honk souk feel real foam anon
June naze rule vote teff sung posh unci hook suck fell reel form axon
jute nene rune wade tiff swag push vagi hulk sulk fill rial from barn
kale neve ruse wage toff swig rash vali hunk sunk foal rill gaum bawn
kame nice rype wake tuff tang rath vlei husk tack foil roil germ bean
kibe nide safe wale turf tegg rich wadi jack talk fool roll geum been
kine nine sage wame Waaf thig rush yeti jerk tank foul rotl glam blin
kite node sake wane waff thug ruth yogi jink task fowl ryal glim boon
knee nome sale ware waif ting sash yoni jock teak fuel sail glum born
kyle none same wave wolf tong shah zati junk tick full seal gram bran
lace nope sane were woof trig sigh zori keck took furl seel grim bren
lade nose sate whee agog trug Sikh hadj keek trek Gael sell grum burn
lake note save wide bang tung sinh hajj kick tuck gall sial haem chin
lame nude saxe wife berg twig sith amok kink Turk gaol sill halm clan
lane oboe seme wile bigg vang soph arak kirk tusk Gaul soil harm coin
lase ogee sere wine bong Whig such back kook walk gill soul helm conn
late ogle shoe wipe boyg wing tach balk lack weak girl taal herm coon
lave ogre sice wire brag yang tash bank lank week goal tael holm corn
laze once side wise brig yegg tosh bark lark wick gull tail idem cran
lice ooze sike wite brog zing tush bask lawk wink hail tall imam curn
life orfe sine wive bung amah wash beak leak work hall teal item cyan
like orle sire woke burg ankh wish beck leek yack harl tell loam damn
lime pace site wore cang arch with berk lick yank haul till loom darn
line page size wove chug ayah yeah bilk link yerk heal tirl lyam dawn
lire pale sloe yare cleg bach yogh birk lock yeuk heel toil maam dean
live pane slue yoke clog bash anti bisk look yolk heil toll maim down
lobe pare soke yore crag bath asci bock luck york hell tool malm durn
lode pate sole yule dang blah Asti book lurk zack herl udal marm earn
loge pave some zone darg bosh Babi bosk mack acol hill vail neem ebon
lone peke sone beef ding both cadi buck mark acyl howl veal neum Eden
lope pice sore biff dong bush cedi bulk mask amyl hull veil norm elan
lore pike spae buff drag cash divi bunk meek anil hurl vial ogam Erin
lose pile spue bumf dreg cosh etui burk mick aril hwyl vill ovum even
love pine stye caff drug cush foci busk milk aryl idol viol palm exon
lowe pipe sure calf dung dash fuci calk mink axel jail virl perm fain
luce pise syce chef fang dish gadi cark mirk axil jarl wail pium faun
luge plie syne clef flag doth gyri cask mock bael jell wall plum fawn
lune poke tace coif flog each hifi cock monk bail jill waul poem fern
lure pole take corf frog eath impi conk muck ball jowl wawl pram Finn
lute pome tale cuff gang etch kadi cook murk bawl kail weal prim firn
luxe pone tame daff gleg fash kali cork musk bell keel well prom flan
lyme pope tape deaf gong fish kepi cusk nark bill kill will ream fohn
lyre pore tare delf grig gash kiri dank neck birl koel wool roam foin
lyse pose tele doff grog Goth kiwi dark nick boil kohl yawl room gain
mace pree thee duff hang gush loci dawk nock boll leal yell scum garn
made puce tice faff hogg hash magi deck nook bowl loll yill seam gean
mage puke tide fief hong hath mali desk oink buhl lull yowl seem girn
make pule tige gaff hung high maxi dick pack bull mail zeal sham glen
male pure tike golf king hush midi dink park burl mall Adam shim Gman
mane pyre tile goof knag inch mini dirk peak call marl ahem skim goon
mare race time graf lang itch Nazi disk peck carl maul alum slam gown
mate rage tine guff ling josh nidi dock peek caul meal arum slim gran
maze rake tire gulf long kith nisi dook perk ceil mell atom slum grin
Mede rale tole haaf lung lakh nodi duck pick cell mewl balm stem guan
mere rape tome half Ming lash Pali dunk pink coal mill barm stum harn
mete rare tone hoof pang lath peri dusk pock coil moil beam swam hern
mice rase tope huff ping lich pili Dyak pork cool moll berm swim hewn
mike rate tore jiff plug loch rabi feck puck cowl mull boom swum horn
mile rave tote kerf pong loth ragi fink punk cull nail brim team hymn
mime raze tree leaf prig lush raki fisk rack curl nill calm teem icon
mine rede true lief prog lych rami flak rank dahl noel cham term ikon
mire rete tube loaf quag Mach rani folk reck Dail noil chum them iron
mise rice tule luff rang mash saki fork reek deal null clam toom Jain
mite ride tune miff ring math sari funk rick deil obol clem tram jean

jinn tern kino drip sump moor foss aunt fest lunt skat jehu flax gamy
john than kolo drop swap near fuss bait fiat lust skit juju flex gley
join then koto dump swop neer gens bant fist malt slat kudu flux goby
kaon thin leno flap tamp omer goes bast flat mart slit lieu hoax gory
keen toon lido flip tarp oner gris batt flit mast slot luau ibex gray
kern torn lilo flop temp over guts beat font matt slut lulu ilex grey
khan town limo frap trap oxer hers beet foot meat smit menu jinx hazy
kiln tron lino gamp trip oyer hiss belt fort meet smut nonU lynx holy
koan tuan loco gasp tump pair hols bent frat melt snot prau Manx homy
lain turn logo gaup vamp parr hoss best fret milt soft tabu minx icky
larn twin ludo gawp warp pear huss bint frit mint soot thou onyx idly
lawn upon mako gimp wasp peer ibis bitt gait mist sort tofu oryx iffy
lean vain memo glop weep pier ides blat gast mitt spat tolu prex illy
lien vein moho goop whap poor iris blot geat moat spit tutu roux inby
limn wain moko grip whip pour iwis boat gelt moot spot Urdu ably inky
linn warn mono gulp whop purr jess bolt gent mort stet zebu achy inly
lion wean Moro gump wisp rear joss boot gest most stot Zulu aery joey
loan ween oleo gymp wrap roar kiss bort ghat must suet derv ahoy joky
loin when olio harp yapp scar kris bott gift mutt suit shiv airy judy
loon whin onto hasp yaup sear lass bout gilt neat swat Slav ally July
lorn worn otto heap yelp seer lees brat girt nest swot spiv army jury
lown wren ouzo help Adar slur lens brit gist nett tact alow arty lacy
Lyon yarn pepo hemp afar soar less brut glut newt tart anew ashy lady
main yawn peso holp agar sour Lias bunt gnat next taut avow away laky
maun yean poco hoop ajar spar loss bust goat nowt teat blew awny lazy
mean yuan pogo hump alar spur lues butt gout oast tent blow awry levy
mien zein polo jeep amir star Mars cant grat obit test braw baby lily
moan Zion redo jimp aver stir mass cart grit omit text brew bevy limy
moon zoon sago jump bear suer mess cast grot oont that brow body liny
morn aero sego keep beer tahr mews celt gust oust tilt chaw bogy lory
mown Afro shoo kelp bier tear miss cent haet pact tint chew bony many
muon agio silo kemp blur thar mods cert haft pant toft chow boxy maty
neon also soho knap boar thir moss chat halt part tort claw bray mazy
noon alto solo knop Boer tier muss chit hart past tout clew buoy miry
noun ambo soso lamp boor torr ness chut hast peat tret craw bury moly
omen ammo sumo Lapp brer tour news cist heat pelt trot crew busy nary
open auto taco leap burr tsar nous clot heft pent tuft crow cagy navy
oven boko taro limp char tzar nuts coat hent pert twit dhow cavy nixy
oxen boyo thro lisp coir user oats colt hest pest unit draw city nosy
pain bozo tiro loop curr vair odds coot hilt phot vast drew clay oary
pawn brio toco loup czar veer onus Copt hint Pict vent enow cloy obey
pean bubo todo lump dear wear oops cost hipt pint vert flaw cony oily
peen capo toko mump deer weir opus cott hist plat vest flew copy okay
peon ciao trio neap doer whir orts crit holt plot vint flow cosy only
pern coco typo palp door year ours cuit hoot poet volt frow coxy oozy
phon coho tyro peep dorr your oyes cult host port waft glow defy orgy
pion dado umbo pimp dour Acts pass curt hunt post wait gnaw demy paly
pirn dago unco plop dyer alas piss cyst hurt pout want grew deny piny
plan demo undo pomp eger alms plus daft isnt prat wart grow dewy pipy
poon dido unto poop emir Ares pons dart jest punt wast knew dixy pity
porn dodo veto prep ever arms puss debt jilt putt watt know dogy pixy
quin dojo vino prop ewer axes refs deft jolt quit weet meow domy play
rain duro wino pulp fair axis reis dent just raft weft phew dopy ploy
rein echo yoyo pump fear baas rhus diet kart rant welt plow dory poky
roan ergo zero quip four bass Russ dint Kelt rapt went prow doxy poly
ruin euro atop ramp gaur bats sans dirt kent reft wept scow dozy pony
sain expo beep rasp gear bays sass ditt kept rent wert shaw dray posy
sawn fado blip reap gnar bias seps doat khat rest west shew drey poxy
scan faro bump repp goer boss suds doit kilt rift what show duly pray
seen fico burp romp guar buss taps dolt kist riot whet skaw duty prey
sewn fido calp roup haar cess tass dont knit root whit skew easy puny
Shan fino camp rump hair cups taws dort knot rout wilt slaw eddy quay
shin giro carp samp hear cuss this dost knut runt wist slew edgy racy
shun gogo chap scup heir dais thus drat kyat rust wont slow eely rely
sign gyro chip seep Herr diss togs duct last ryot wort smew eery rimy
Sion halo chop ship hoar does tops duet leat salt wost snow eggy ropy
skin hero clap shop hoer doss toss dust leet scat writ spew elmy rosy
soon hobo clip skep hour duds upas east left scot yurt stew Emmy ruby
sorn hoho clop skip jeer dues urus echt lent scut zest stow envy scry
sown homo comp slap kier eats ways edit lest seat zoot thaw espy sexy
span hypo coop slip knar egis wels emit Lett sect Ainu thew eyry shay
spin info coup slop knur epos wits erst lift sent babu trow flay sizy
spun into crap snap lair Eros woes exit lilt sept beau view fley slay
sten jato crop snip leer exes Xmas eyot lint sett chou whew fogy sley
stun judo cusp soap lehr eyas yaws fact list sext clou apex foxy spay
sunn Juno damp soup liar feis ywis fast loft shot ecru calx fray spry
swan kago deep stap lier fess abet feat loot shut emeu coax fumy stay
tarn kayo dorp step loir fils abut feet lost sift Frau crux fury sway
teen kilo doup stop lour flys adit felt lout silt guru falx gaby they

tidy tody towy troy viny wavy wily Xray Druz fuzz oyez razz whiz
tiny tony tray ugly wady waxy winy zany fitz Geez phiz swiz
toby Tory trey vary wary whey wiry buzz fizz jazz quiz tizz

5 letter words

abaca again alway apply aunty bason bield boast brava bunko carat chimp
abaci agami amain appro aurae bassi bifid bobby brave bunny carer china
aback agape amass appui aural basso bight boche bravi bunty caret chine
abaft agate Amati appuy auras baste bigot bodge bravo bunya cargo chink
abase agave amaze April auric batch bijou bogey brawl buran Carib chirk
abash agaze amban apron auxin bated biker boggy brawn burgh carny chirp
abask agene amber apsis avail bathe bilbo bogie braxy burin carob chirr
abate agent ambit aptly avast baths bilge bogle braze burka carol chive
abaya aggro amble Araby avens batik bilgy bogus bread burke carom chivy
abbey agile ambos arbor avert baton billy bohea break burly carpi chizz
abbot aging ambry areal avian batty bimbo bolas bream burnt carry chock
abeam agist ameer areca avoid baulk binge bolus brede burro carve choir
abele aglet amend arena await bawdy bingo bombe breed burry caste choke
abhor agley ament argil awake bayou biome bonce breer bursa catch choky
abide aglow amice argol award beach biota boned brent burse cater choli
ablow agogo amide argon aware beady biped boner breve burst cates chomp
abode agone amido argot awash beamy bipod boney briar busby catty chops
aboil agony amigo argue awful beano birch bongo bribe bused cauli chord
Abomb agora amine Argus awned beard birth bonne brick bushy caulk chore
abort agree amino Arian awoke beast bison bonny bride busty cause chose
about agued Amish ariel axial beaus bitch bonus brief butch caver choux
above ahead amiss arise axile beaut biter bonze brier butte cavil chuck
abrim ahold amity armed axiom beaux bitsy booby brill butty cease chuff
abuse ahull amnia aroid ayrie bebop bitts booed brine butyl cedar chump
abuzz aider among aroma azoic bedad bitty boost bring buxom cello chunk
abysm ainee amort arose azote bedel bivvy booth brink buyer cense churl
abyss aioli amour arrah azoth bedew black boots briny bwana cento churn
acari airer ample arras Aztec bedim blade booty brisk byend ceorl churr
acerb aisle amply array azure beech blain booze brize bylaw cesti chuse
acini aitch amuck arris babel beefs blame boozy broad byway chafe chute
ackee akene amuse arrow baboo beefy bland borax broch Caaba chaff chyle
acock alack ancon arsis babul beery blank borer brock cabal chain chyme
acold alarm anele arson bacca befit blare boric broil cabby chair cider
acorn alary anent artel baccy befog blase borne broke caber chalk cigar
acred alate angel arval bacon begad blast boron bronc cabin champ cilia
acrid album anger Aryan baddy began blate bosky brood cable chant cimex
actin alder angle ascot badge begat blaze bosom brook cabob chaos cinch
acton aleph Anglo ascus badly beget bleak boson broom caboc chape circa
actor alert angst asdic bagel begin blear bossy brose cacao chaps cirri
acute algae anigh ashen baggy begot bleat bosun broth cache chard cisco
adage algal anile ashet Bahai begum bleed botch brown cacti chare cissy
adapt algid anima Asian bairn begun bleep botel bruin caddy charm civet
addax algin anion aside baize beige blend bothy bruit cadet charr civic
adder Algol anise asker baker being blent bough brule cadge chart civil
addle alias anker askew balas belay bless boule brume cadre chary civvy
adept alibi ankle aspen baler belch blest boult brunt caeca chase clack
adieu alien annal aspic balky belga blimp bound brush cagey chasm claim
adios align annex assai bally belie blimy bourg brute caird cheap clamp
adlib alike annoy assay balmy belle blind bourn bubal cairn cheat clang
adman aline annul asset balsa belly blink bouse bubby calid check clank
admit alive anode aster banal below bliss bousy bucko calif cheek clary
admix alkyd anomy astir banco bench blitz bowed buddy calix cheep clash
adobe alkyl antae aswim bandy bends bloat bowel budge calla cheer clasp
adopt Allah antic ataxy banjo bendy block bower buffi calpa cheka class
adore allay antra atilt banns benni bloke bowls buffo calve chela clave
adorn alley antre atlas Bantu benny blond bowse buggy calyx chert clean
adown allin anvil atman barbe beret blood boxer bugle camas chess clear
adoze allot Anzac atoll bardy berry bloom boyar build camel chest cleat
adult allow aorta atomy barge berth blown brace built cameo chevy cleek
adunc alloy apace atone baric beryl blowy brach buist campy chewy cleft
adust allyl apart atony barky beset blude bract bulge canal chiao clepe
adyta aloft apeak atria barmy besom blues braid bulgy candy chick clerk
aegis aloha apery atrip baron besot bluet brail bulky canna chide click
aerie alone aphid attar barre betel bluey brain bulla canny chief cliff
affix along aphis attic basal beton bluff brake bully canoe chiel climb
afire aloof apian audio basan bevel blunt braky bumbo canon child clime
afoot aloud apish audit bases bezel blurb brand bumph canst chile cline
afore alpha apode auger basic bhang blurt brank bumpy canto chili cling
Afric altar aport aught basil bible blush brant bunch canty chill clink
afrit alter appal augur basin biddy board brash bunco caper chimb cloak
after alula apple aulic basis bidet boart brass bunia capon chime clock

cloke clone clonk cloot close cloth cloud clout clove clown clubs cluck clump clung clunk cnida coach coact coapt coast coati cobby cobia coble Cobol cobra cocci cocky cocoa coder codex codon cogue cohoe coign coley colic colin colly colon colza comae comal combe combo comer comet comfy comic comma compo compt conch coney conga conge conic conky conte cooee cooey cooky cooly coomb coopt copal coper copra copse copsy coral cords corer corgi corky corno cornu corny corps

corse coset costa cotta couch coude cough could count coupe court couth coven cover covet covey covin cowed cower cowry coxae coxal coyly coypu cozen crack craft crake cramp crane crank crape craps crash crass crate crave crawl craze crazy creak cream credo creed creek creel creep creme crepe crept cress crest crick crier cries crime crimp crisp croak Croat crock croft crone cronk crony crook croon crore cross croup crowd crown cruck crude cruel cruet crumb crump cruse

crush crust crwth cryer crypt Cuban cubby cubeb cubic cubit cuddy Cufic cuish culch culet culex cully cumin cupel Cupid cuppa curch curds curdy curer curia curie curio curly curry curse curst curve curvy cusec cushy cutch cutey cutie cutin cutis cutty cycad cycle cyclo cyder cymar Cymry cynic Czech dacha daddy daffy dagga dagos daily dairy daisy dalek dally daman damar dance dandy daric darky darts dated dater datum dauby daunt davit dealt deary death debag debar debit

debug debut decal decay decor decoy decry deedy defer degas degum deice deify deign deism deist deity dekko delay delft delta delve demit demob demon demos demur denim dense depot depth derby derma desex deter deuce devil dewan dhobi dhole dhoti Diana diary diazo dicer dicey dicky dicot dicta didst diene dight digit diker dilly dimer dimly dinar diner dingo dingy dinky diode dippy dirge dirty disco dishy disme ditch ditto ditty divan diver Dives divot divvy dixie dizen

dizzy djinn dobby docht dodge dodgy dodos doest doeth doggo doggy dogie dogma doily doing dolce dolly domed donah donee donga donna donor donut doper dopey Doric dormy dorts dorty dotal doter dotty Douay doubt douce dough douma douse dowdy dowed dowel dower downa downy dowry dowse doyen dozen dozer Draco draff draft drail drain drake drama drank drape drawl drawn dread dream drear dregs dress dried drier drift drill drily drink drive droit droll drome drone drool droop

drops dross drove drown druid drunk drupe druse Druze dryad dryer dryly ducal ducat duchy ducks ducky duddy dulia dully dulse dumka dumky dummy dumps dumpy dunce dungy dunno dunny duomo duper duple duppy durra durst durum dusky dusty dutch duvet dwale dwarf dwell dwelt dying eager eagle eagre eared early earth easel eaten eater eaves ebony eclat Eddic edged edict edify educe educt eerie egest eggar egger egret eider eight eject eland elate elbow elder elect elegy elemi

elfin elide elite eloge eloin elope elude elute elvan elver elves embay embed ember embow embus emcee emeer emend emery emmer emmet emote empty enact enate ended endow endue enema enemy enjoy ennui enrol ensew ensky ensue enter entia entry enure envoi envoy Eolic eosin epact ephah ephod ephor epoch epode epoxy equal equip erase erect ergot erica Ernie erode erose error eruct erupt escot esker essay ester estoc estop ether ethic ethos ethyl etude etwee etyma evade evens

event evert every evict evite evoke exact exalt excel exeat exert exile exine exist exode expel extol extra exude exult exurb eying eyrie fable faced facer facet facia facta faddy faery fagin fagot faint fairy faith faker fakir falls false famed fancy fanny Fanti farad farce farci farcy farle fatal fated fatly fatso fatty faugh fault fauna favus fawny fayre feast feeze feign feint fella felly felon femur fence fenny feoff feral ferly fermi ferny ferry fesse fetal fetch

fetid fetor fetus fever fibre fiche fichu field fiend fiery fifer fifth fifty fight filch filet fille filly filmy filth final finch fines finis finny fiord firer firry first firth fishy fitch fitly fiver fives fixed fixer fizzy fjeld fjord flack flail flair flake flaky flame flamy flank flare flash flask flaxy fleam fleck fleer fleet flesh flews flick flied flier flimp fling flint flirt float flock flong flood floor flora flory floss flota flour flout flown fluff fluid

fluke fluky flume flump flung flunk fluor flush flute fluty flyby flyer foamy focal focus foehn fogey foggy foist folia folio folly foots footy foray forby force fordo forge forgo forme forte forth forty forum fossa fosse found fount fovea foyer frail frame franc frank fraud freak freer frena fresh friar frier frill frisk frith fritz frizz frock frond frons front frore frost froth frown froze fruit frump fryer fryup fubsy fucus fudge fugal fuggy fugle fugue fully fumet

fundi funds fungi funky funny fural furan furor furry furze furzy fusee fusil fussy fusty fuzzy fytte gabby gable gaffe gaily galah galea Galla gally galop gamba games gamic gamin gamma gammy gamut ganja gaper gappy garth gassy gaudy gauge gault gaumy gaunt gauss gauze gauzy gavel gawky gawsy gazer gecko geese geist gelid gelly gemma gemmy gemot genet genic genie genii genoa genre genro gents genus geode geoid gerah germy gesso geste getup ghast ghaut Ghazi ghost ghoul

ghyll giant giber giddy gigot gigue gilpy gimme ginny gipsy girly giron girth gismo given giver glace glade glady glair gland glare glary glass glaur glaze glazy gleam glean glebe glede gleed gleek gleet glial glide glint gloat globe gloom glory gloss glout glove gloze gluey glume glyph gnarl gnarr gnash gnawn gnome goaty godet godly goest goeth goety going golem golly gonad goner gonna goody gooey goofy goopy goose gopak goral gorge gorse gorsy gotta Gouda gouge gourd gouty gowan goyim graal grace grade graft grail grain graip grama grand grant grape graph grapy grasp grass grate grave gravy graze great grebe greed Greek green greet grege gride grief griff grift grike grill grime grimy grind gripe grise grist grith grits groan groat groin groom grope gross group grout grove growl grown gruel gruff grume grump grunt guana guano guard guava Guelf guess guest guide guild guile guilt guimp guise gular gulch gules gully gulph gumbo gummy

gunge gunny guppy gurry gushy gusto gusty gutsy gutta gutty guyot gypsy gyral gyron gyrus habit hadal Hades hadji hadst haick haiku haily hairy hajji hakim halal hallo halma halos halva halve hamal hammy handy hanky Hanse haply happy haram hardy harem harpy harry harsh haste hasty hatch hater haugh haulm haunt Hausa haven haver havoc hawse hazel hazer Hbomb heady heard heart heath heave heavy hedge hefty heigh heist helix hello helot helve heman hence henge henna henry

herby herma heron hertz hewer hexad hight hiker hilar hillo hilly hilum Hindi Hindu hinge hinny hippo hippy hirer hitch hives hoard hoary hobby hocus hodge hogan hohum hoick hoise hoist hokey hokku hokum holey holla hollo holly homer homey honey honky hooch hooey hooky hoots horal horde horme horny horse horst horsy hosen hosta hotch hotel hotly hough hound houri house hovel hover howdy howff hubby huffy hullo human humic humid humph humpy humus hunch hunks hunky hurly

hurry hurst husky hussy hutch hutia huzza huzzy hydra hydro hyena hying Hykos hylic hyoid hypha hyrax hyson iambi ichor icily icing icker ictus idead ideal idiom idiot idler idola idyll igloo ihram ileac ileal ileum ileus iliac Iliad ilial ilium image imago imaum imbed imbue imide immit immix impel imply inane inapt inarm incur incus index Indic indri indue inept inert infer infix infra ingle ingot injun inker inkle inlaw inlay inlet inner inoff input inset inter intro

inure inurn iodic ionic irade Iraqi irate Irish irony Islam islet issei issue istle itchy ivied ivory ixtle izard izzat jabot jacks jaded jaggy Jaina jakes jalap jammy japan jaspe jaunt jazzy jeans jehad jelly jemmy jenny jerky Jerry Jesse jetty jewel Jewry jibba jiber jiffy jihad jingo jinks jinni jocko joint joist joker jokey jokul jolly jolty Jonah jorum joule joust jowar judas judge juice juicy julep jumbo jumpy junky junta junto jural jurat juror Kaaba kabob Kafir

kalif kalpa kapok kappa kaput karma karoo karst kauri kayak kazoo kebab kebob kedge kefir kelpy kempt kenaf kendo kerne kerry ketch keyed khadi khaki Khmer kiang kiddy kinin kinky kiosk kitty kloof knack knave knead kneed kneel knell knelt knife knish knock knoll knout known knurl knurr koala koine kooky kopek kopje Koran kotow kraal krait krans kraut krill krona krone kudos kudzu Kufic kukri kulak kulan kumis kvass kwela kyang kylin kyloe kyrie label labia labra lacet

lacey laded laden Ladin ladle lagan lager lahar laigh laird lairy laity lance lanky lapel lapse larch lardy lares large largo larky larum larva laser lasso latch lated laten latex lathe lathi lathy Latin lauds laugh laura laver lawks lawny laxly layby layer layup lazar leach leads leady leafy leaky leant leapt learn lease leash least leave ledge ledgy leech leery lefty legal leger leges leggy legit leman lemma lemon lemur lento Lents leper lepta lethe letup levee level

lever levin lewis lexis liana liane liang liard libel liber libra licht licit liege liein lifer ligan liger light liken lilac limbo limen limey limit linen liner lines lingo linin links linny lipid lippy lisle lists lithe litho litre liven liver lives livid livre llama llano loach loamy loath lobar lobby lobed lobus local locum locus loden lodge loess lofty logan logia logic Logos lolly loner longa longe looby loofa looks loony loopy loose loppy loral loran lordy lorel

loris lorry losel loser lotah lotto lotus lough louis lound loupe loury louse lousy lover lovey lower lowly lowne loyal Lucan lucid lucky lucre luffa lumen lumme lumpy lunar lunch lunge lungi lupin lupus lurch lurid lushy lusty lyart lycee lying lymph lynch lyric lyses lysin lysis lysol lythe lytta macaw macer macho macle Macon macro madam madge madly Mafia magic magma magus Mahdi mains maize major makar maker malar Malay malic malty mamba mambo mamma mammy maned manes

mange mango mangy mania manic manly manna manor manse manta manto manul manus Maori maple marah march mardy mares marge maria marid marly marry marsh maser mashy mason massa masse massy match mater matey maths matin matlo matte matzo maund mauve mavis maxim Mayan maybe mayor mayst mazer McCoy mealy means meant meany meaty mecca medal media medic Medoc meiny melee melic melon mense mercy merge meril merit merle merry mesel mesic mesne meson messy mesto metal meter meths

metic metif metis metre metro mezzo miaow miaul micky micro middy midge midon midst might milch miler milky mille mimer mimic minar mince miner mingy minim minor minty minus mirky mirth misdo miser missy misty mitre mixed mixen mixer mixup mizen mneme mobby mocha modal model modus mogul mohur moire moist moksa molal molar molly molto momma monad monas monde money monte month mooch moody moola moony moose moped moper mopup mopus moral morat moray morel mores moron morph

morra morse mosey mossy motel motet mothy motif motor motte motto mould moult mound mount mourn mouse mousy mouth mover movie mower mucic mucin mucky mucro mucus muddy mudir mufti muggy mujik mulch mulct muley mulga mulla multi mummy mumps munch mungo mural murex murky murra murre muser mushy music musky mussy musth musty mutch muted muzzy myall mynah myoid myoma myope myrrh nabob nacre nadir naevi naiad naive naked naker namer nancy nanna nanny nappe nappy nares naris

narky
nasal
nasty
natal
nates
natty
naval
navel
navvy
nawab
neath
necks
neddy
needs
needy
Negro
negus
neigh
neive
nelly
nerka
nerve
nervy
netty
neume
never
newel
newly
newsy
nexus
niche
nidus
niece
nieve
niffy
nifty
night
nimbi
ninny
ninon
ninth
nippy
nisei
nisus
nitid
niton
nitre
nitro
nival
nixie
nizam
nobby
noble
nobly
nodal
noddy
nodus
nohow
noise
noisy
nomad
nomen
nonce
nones
nonet
nonny
nooky
noone
noose
nopal
noria
Norse
north
noser
nosey
notch
noted
notum
novae
novel
noway
Nowel
noyau
nucha
nudge
nulla
numen
nurse
nutty
nyala
nylon
nymph
oaken
oakum
oared
oases
oasis
oaten
oaves
obang
obeah
obeli
obese
occur
ocean
ochre
ochry
octal
octet
oddly
odeon
odeum
odium
odour
offal
offer
often
ogham
ogive
ogler
ohmic
ohone
oidia
oiled
oiler
okapi
olden
oldie
oleic
olein
oleum
olive
ology
omasa
ombre
omega
oncer
oneup
onion
onset
oomph
opera
opine
opium
optic
orach
oracy
orate
orbed
orbit
order
oread
organ
oribi
oriel
Oriya
orlop
ormer
orpin
orris
ortho
Osage
Oscan
Oscar
osier
ossia
ostia
otary
other
otter
ought
ounce
ouphe
ousel
outby
outdo
outer
outgo
outre
ouzel
ovary
ovate
overs
overt
ovine
ovoid
ovoli
ovolo
ovule
owing
owlet
owner
oxbow
oxeye
oxide
oxlip
oxter
ozone
pacer
pacha
paddy
padre
paean
paeon
pagan
paint
paisa
palay
palea
pally
palmy
palpi
palsy
pampa
panda
pandy
panel
panga
panic
panne
pansy
panto
pants
panty
papal
papaw
paper
pappy
parch
pardi
pardy
parer
parge
parka
parky
parle
parol
parry
parse
Parsi
parti
party
Pasch
pasha
pashm
passe
pasta
paste
pasty
patch
paten
pater
patio
patsy
patty
pause
pavan
paver
pavid
pavis
pawky
payee
payer
peace
peach
peaky
pearl
peart
pease
peaty
pecan
pedal
peeve
peggy
pekan
pekoe
pelta
penal
pence
penna
penny
peony
peppy
perai
perch
perdu
peril
perky
perry
perse
pesky
petal
peter
petit
petri
petty
pewit
phage
phase
phene
pheon
phial
phlox
phone
phono
phony
photo
phyla
phyle
piano
picky
picot
picul
pidog
piece
pieta
piety
piezo
piggy
pigmy
piker
pilaf
pilau
pilaw
pilch
pilea
pilei
pilot
pilus
pinch
piney
pinko
pinky
pinna
pinny
pinon
pinta
pinto
pinup
pious
pipal
piper
pipit
pipul
pique
piste
pitch
pithy
piton
pitta
pivot
pixie
pizza
place
plage
plaid
plain
plait
plane
plank
plant
plash
plasm
plate
playa
plaza
plead
pleat
plebs
plica
plonk
pluck
plumb
plume
plump
plumy
plunk
plush
Pluto
poach
pocky
poddy
podge
podgy
podia
poesy
poilu
poind
point
poise
poker
polar
polio
polka
polyp
pommy
ponce
poncy
pongo
pooch
pooja
pools
poort
poppy
popsy
porch
porgy
porky
porno
Porte
poser
posit
posse
potto
potty
pouch
poult
pound
pouty
powan
power
praam
prahu
prang
prank
prase
prate
prawn
preen
press
prest
prexy
price
prick
pricy
pride
prier
prima
prime
primo
primp
prink
print
prior
prise
prism
privy
prize
probe
proem
prole
prone
prong
proof
prose
prosy
proud
Provo
prowl
proxy
prude
prune
prunt
pryer
psalm
pseud
pshaw
psoas
psora
psych
pubic
pubis
pucka
pudge
pudgy
puffy
puggy
pukka
puler
pulpy
pulse
punch
Punic
punty
pupae
pupal
pupil
puppy
puree
purge
Purim
purin
purse
pursy
pushy
pussy
puton
putti
putto
putty
pygmy
pylon
pyxie
pyxis
Qboat
quack
quaff
quail
quake
quaky
qualm
quant
quark
quart
quash
quasi
quean
queen
queer
quell
quern
query
quest
queue
quick
quiet
quiff
quill
quilt
quins
quint
quipu
quire
quirk
quirt
quite
quits
quoin
quoit
quota
quote
quoth
Quran
rabbi
rabic
rabid
racer
races
radar
radii
radio
radix
radon
raggy
rainy
raise
rajah
raker
rally
ramal
ramie
ramus
ranch
randy
ranee
range
rangy
raper
raphe
rapid
raspy
rasse
ratan
ratch
ratel
rater
rathe
ratio
ratty
ravel
raven
raver
ravin
rawly
rayed
razee
razor
reach
react
ready
realm
reams
rearm
reata
reave
rebec
rebel
rebid
rebus
rebut
recap
recce
recto
recur
redan
reddy
redia
redid
redly
redox
reedy
reeky
reest
reeve
refel
refer
refit
regal
regie
Reich
reify
reign
reins
reive
rejig
relax
relay
relet
relic
relit
reman
remex
remit
renal
renew
rente
repay
repel
reply
repot
repro
reran
rerun
resat
reset
resin
resit
retch
retry
reuse
revel
revet
revue
rheum
rhine
rhino
rhomb
rhumb
rhyme
riant
riata
ribes
ricer
rider
ridge
ridgy
rifle
right
rigid
rigor
rille
rinse
ripen
risen
riser
rishi
risky
ritzy
rival
rived
rivel
riven
river
rivet
roach
roast
robin
roble
robot
rocks
rocky
rodeo
roger
rogue
roily
roker
rolls
roman
Romeo
rondo
rooky
roomy
roost
rooty
roper
ropey
rorty
roset
rosin
rotch
rotor
rouge
rough
round
roupy
rouse
roust
route
routh
rover
rowan
rowdy
rowel
rowen
rower
royal
rubin
ruble
rubus
ruche
ruddy
rugby
ruler
rumba
rumen
rumly
rummy
rumpy
runic
runny
runty
runup
rupee
rural
rushy
rusty
rutty
sable
sabot
sabra
sabre
sacra
sadhu
sadly
saggy
sahib
saiga
saint
saith
saker
Sakta
salad
salep
sales
salic
sally
salmi
salon
salse
salts
salty
salve
salvo
samba
sambo
samel
sandy
sapan
sapid
sapor
sappy
saree
sarge
sarky
saros
sasin
sassy
Satan
sated
satin
satyr
sauce
sauch
saucy
Saudi
saugh
sault
sauna
saury
saute
saver
savin
savoy
savvy
Saxon
sayer
sayso
sayst
scald
scale
scall
scalp
scaly
scamp
scant
scape
scare
scarf
scarp
scart
scary
scatt
scaup
scaur
sceat
scena
scend
scene
scent
schmo
schwa
scifi
scion
scoff
scold
scone
scoop
scoot
scopa
scope
score
scorn
Scots
scour
scout
scowl
scrag
scram
scran
scrap
scray
scree
screw
scrim
scrip
scrod
scrub
scrum
scuba
scudi
scudo
scuff
scull
sculp
scurf
scuta
scute
seamy
sebum
secco
sedan
Seder
sedge
sedgy
sedum
seedy
seely
seepy
segno
segue
seine
seise
seism
seize
sekos
selah
sells
selva
semee
semen
senna
senor
sensa
sense
sepal
sepia
sepoy
septa
serac
serai
seral
serge
Seric
serif
serin
serow
serra
serry
serum
serve
servo
setae
seton
setto
setup
seven
sever
sewer
sewin
sexed
sexto
shack
shade
shady
shaft
shake
shako
shaky
shale
shall
shalt
shaly
shame
shank
shant
shape
shard
share
shark
sharp
shave
shawl
shawm
sheaf
shear
sheen
sheep
sheer

sheet sizar smirk sower squid stoup sweal tatou those torse tufty unlit
sheik sizer smite space squit stour swear tatty thraw torsk tuism unman
shelf skald smith spade stack stout sweat taunt three torso tulip unpeg
shell skate smock spado staff stove swede taupe threw torte tulle unpin
shend skean smoke spahi stage strad sweep tawer thrid torus tumid unrig
shent skeet smoko spake stagy strap sweet tawie throb total tummy unrip
Sheol skein smoky spall staid straw swell tawny throe totem tuner unsay
sherd skelm smolt spang stain stray swept tawse throw touch tunic unset
sheva skelp smote spank stair strep swift taxer thrum tough tunny unsex
shewn skene snack spare stake strew swill taxis thuja touse tuque untie
Shiah skier snafu spark stale stria swine taxon thumb tousy turbo until
shiel skiey snail spasm stalk strip swing taxus thump towel turfy unzip
shier skiff snake spate stall strop swink tazza thuya tower Turki upend
shift skill snaky spawn stamp strow swipe teach thyme towny turps upped
shill skimp snare speak stand stroy swirl teary thymy toxic tusky upper
shily skink snark spean stane strum swish tease tiara toxin tutee upset
shine skint snarl spear stang strut Swiss techy tibia trace tutor uraei
shiny skirl snash speck stank stuck swith teens tical track tutti urate
shire skirr snath specs staph study swizz teeny tidal tract tutty urban
shirk skirt sneak speed stare stuff swoon teeth tiein trade twain ureal
shirr skite sneap speel stark stull swoop tehee tieup tragi twang uredo
shirt skive sneck speer start stump sword teind tiger trail tweak urger
Shiva skoal sneer speir stash stung swore telex tight train tweed urial
shoal skulk snell spell state stunk sworn telic tigon trait tween urine
shoat skull snick spelt stave stunt swung telly tilde tramp tweet urubu
shock skunk snide spend stays stupa sybil tempi tiler traps twere usage
shoer skyer sniff spent stead stupe sycee tempo tilth trash twerp usher
shoji skyey snipe sperm steak sturt sylph tempt timer trass twice usual
shone slack snips spica steal styes sylva tench times trawl twill usurp
shook slain snoek spice steam style synch tenet timid tread twine usury
shoon slake snood spick steed styli synod tenne tinct treat twink uteri
shoot slang snook spicy steek stylo syren tenon tinea treen twiny utile
shore slant snoop spiel steel suave syrup tenor tined trend twirl utter
shorn slash snoot spier steep suber tabby tense tinge tress twirp uveal
short slate snore spike steer sucre tabes tenth tinny trews twist uvula
shout slaty snort spiky stein sudor tabla tenty tinty triad twite Uzbeg
shove slave snout spile stela Sudra table tepee tippy trial twixt Uzbek
shown sleek snowy spill stele sudsy taboo tepid tipsy Trias twyer vacua
showy sleep snuff spilt steno suede tabor terai tipup tribe tying vagal
shred sleet soapy spine steps suety tache terce titan trice tyler vague
shrew slept sober spiny stere Sufic tacit terms tithe trick typal vagus
shrub slice socle spire stern sugar tacky terne title tried typic vails
shrug slick sodic spirt stich suint taffy terra titre trier Uboat valet
shuck slide Sodom spiry stick suite tafia terry tizzy trike udder valid
shunt slily softa spite sties sulci taiga terse toady trill Ugric valse
shush slime softy spitz stiff sulfa tails tesla toast trine uhlan value
shyer slimy soggy splat stile sulky taint testa today trior ukase valve
shyly sling solan splay still sully taken testy toddy tripe ulcer vaned
sibyl slink solar split stilt sumac taker tetra toffy trist ulema vapid
sided slips soldi Spode stime summa takin texas togue trite ulmin varan
sidle sloid soldo spoil sting Sunna tales thane toile troat ulnae varec
siege sloop solen spoke stink Sunni tally thank toils trode ulnar varix
sieve sloot solfa spoof stint sunny talon thawy Tokay troll ultra varus
sight slope solid spook stipe sunup taluk theca token tromp umbel varve
sigil slops solon spool stirk super talus theft toman trona umber vasal
sigla slosh solum spoom stirp supra tamer thegn tommy trone umbra vasty
sigma sloth solus spoon stoae surah Tamil their tonal troop umiak vatic
silex sloyd solve spoor stoat sural tamis thema tondi trope umpty vault
silks slubb sonar spore stock surat tammy theme tondo troth unapt vaunt
silky sluit sonde sport stoep surfy tango there toner trout unarm vealy
silly slump sonic spout stogy surge tangy therm tonga trove unbar Vedda
silty slung sonny sprag stoic surly tanka these tongs truce unbed Vedic
silva slunk sonsy sprat stoke surra tansy theta tonic truck uncap veena
simar slurp sooth spray stola sutor taper thews tonka trull uncle veery
since slush sooty spree stole sutra tapir thewy tonne truly uncus vegan
sinew slyer sophy sprig stoma swage tapis thick tonus trump uncut veiny
singe slyly sopor sprit stomp swain tardy thief tooth trunk under velar
Singh slype soppy sprue stone swale targe thigh topaz truss undid veldt
sinus smack sorel spume stonk swami tarok thill topee trust undue velum
Sioux small sorgo spumy stony swamp tarot thine toper truth unfit venae
siren smalt sorra spunk stood swank tarre thing tophi tryon unfix venal
sisal smarm sorry spurn stook sward tarry think topic tryst ungot venge
sissy smart sorus spurt stool sware tarsi third topoi tsade ungum venin
sitar smash sough sputa stoop swarf tarty thirl topos tubae Uniat venom
sitin smaze sound squab stope swarm tasse thole toque tubal unify venue
sixer smear soupy squad store swart taste tholi Torah tubby union Venus
sixte smell souse squat stork swash tasty thong torch tuber unite verge
sixth smelt south squaw storm swath Tatar thorn toric tucum unity verse
sixty smile sowar squib story swayl tater thorp torii Tudor unlay verso

verst
vertu
verve
vesta
vetch
viand
vibes
vicar
Vichy
video
viewy
vigil
villa
villi
vinal
vinca
vinyl
viola
viper
viral
vireo
vires
virga
Virgo
virid
virtu
virus
visit
visor
vista
vital
vitta
vivat
vives
vivid
vixen
vizor
Vlach
vocal
vodka
vogie
vogue
voice
voile
volar
volet
volta
volte
volti
volva
vomer
vomit
voter
vouch
vouge
vowel
vraic
vrouw
vuggy
vying
wacke
wacky
waddy
wader
wafer
wager
wages
wagon
wahoo
waist
waits
waive
waken
waker
wakes
waler
walla
wally
waltz

waney
wanly
wares
warty
washy
waste
watch
water
waved
waver
wavey
waxen
waxer
weald
weary
weave
webby
weber
wedge
weeds
weedy
weeny
weepy
weigh
weird
welch
wells
welsh
wench
wetly
whack
whale
whang
wharf
whaup
wheal
wheat
wheel
wheen
whelk
whelm
whelp
where
which
whiff
while
whine
whiny
whirl
whirr
whish
whisk
whist
white
whity
whizz
whole
whoop
whore
whorl
whose
whoso
widdy
widen
widow
width
wield
wigan
wight
wilco
wilds
wiles
willy
wince
winch
windy
winey
winge
wings

wingy
winze
wiper
wispy
witan
witch
withe
withy
witty
wives
wizen
wodge
woful
woken
woman
women
wonga
wonky
woods
woody
wooer
woozy
words
wordy
works
world
worms
wormy
worry
worse
worst
worth
would
wound
woven
wrack
wrapt
wrath
wreak
wreck
wrest
wrick
wring
wrist
write
wrong
wrote
wroth
wrung
wryly
xebec
xenia
xenon
xeric
Xhosa
Xrays
xylem
xylol
xysti
yacht
yager
yahoo
yamen
yapok
yauld
yawny
yearn
years
yeast
yerba
yield
yippy
yobbo
yodel
yogic
yokel
yolky
yonks
young

yours
youth
yucca
yucky
yukky
yulan
yummy
zambo
zanze
zebec
zebra
zesty
zibet
zinco
zincy
zingy
zinky
zippy
zloty
zombi
zonal
zonda
zooid
zooks
zoril
zygal
——
babel
baboo
babul
bacca
baccy
bacon
baddy
badge
badly
bagel
baggy
Bahai
bairn
baize
baker
balas
baler
balky
bally
balmy
balsa
banal
banco
bandy
banjo
banns
Bantu
barbe
bardy
barge
baric
barky
barmy
baron
barre
basal
basan
bases
basic
basil
basin
basis
bason
bassi
basso
baste
batch
bated
bathe
baths
batik
baton

batty
baulk
bawdy
bayou
Caaba
cabal
cabby
caber
cabin
cable
cabob
caboc
cacao
cache
cacti
caddy
cadet
cadge
cadre
caeca
cagey
caird
cairn
calid
calif
calix
calla
calpa
calve
calyx
camas
camel
cameo
campy
canal
candy
canna
canny
canoe
canon
canst
canto
canty
caper
capon
carat
carer
caret
cargo
Carib
carny
carob
carol
carom
carpi
carry
carve
caste
catch
cater
cates
catty
cauli
caulk
cause
caver
cavil
dacha
daddy
daffy
dagga
dagos
daily
dairy
daisy
dalek
dally
daman
damar

dance
dandy
daric
darky
darts
dated
dater
datum
dauby
daunt
davit
eager
eagle
eagre
eared
early
earth
easel
eaten
eater
eaves
fable
faced
facer
facet
facia
facta
faddy
faery
fagin
fagot
faint
fairy
faith
faker
fakir
falls
false
famed
fancy
fanny
Fanti
farad
farce
farci
farcy
farle
fatal
fated
fatly
fatso
fatty
faugh
fault
fauna
favus
fawny
fayre
gabby
gable
gaffe
gaily
galah
galea
Galla
gally
galop
gamba
games
gamic
gamin
gamma
gammy
gamut
ganja
gaper
gappy
garth
gassy

gaudy
gauge
gault
gaumy
gaunt
gauss
gauze
gauzy
gavel
gawky
gawsy
gazer
habit
hadal
Hades
hadji
hadst
haick
haiku
haily
hairy
hajji
hakim
halal
hallo
halma
halos
halva
halve
hamal
hammy
handy
hanky
Hanse
haply
happy
haram
hardy
harem
harpy
harry
harsh
haste
hasty
hatch
hater
haugh
haulm
haunt
Hausa
haven
haver
havoc
hawse
hazel
hazer
iambi
jabot
jacks
jaded
jaggy
Jaina
jakes
jalap
jammy
japan
jaspe
jaunt
jazzy
Kaaba
kabob
Kafir
kalif
kalpa
kapok
kappa
kaput
karma
karoo

karst
kauri
kayak
kazoo
label
labia
labra
lacet
lacey
laded
laden
Ladin
ladle
lagan
lager
lahar
laigh
laird
lairy
laity
lance
lanky
lapel
lapse
larch
lardy
lares
large
largo
larky
larum
larva
laser
lasso
latch
lated
laten
latex
lathe
lathi
lathy
Latin
lauds
laugh
laura
laver
lawks
lawny
laxly
layby
layer
layup
lazar
macaw
macer
macho
macle
Macon
macro
madam
madge
madly
Mafia
magic
magma
magus
Mahdi
mains
maize
major
makar
maker
malar
Malay
malic
malty
mamba
mambo
mamma

mammy
maned
manes
mange
mango
mangy
mania
manic
manly
manna
manor
manse
manta
manto
manul
manus
Maori
maple
marah
march
mardy
mares
marge
maria
marid
marly
marry
marsh
maser
mashy
mason
massa
masse
massy
match
mater
matey
maths
matin
matlo
matte
matzo
maund
mauve
mavis
maxim
Mayan
maybe
mayor
mayst
mazer
nabob
nacre
nadir
naevi
naiad
naive
naked
naker
namer
nancy
nanna
nanny
nappe
nappy
nares
naris
narky
nasal
nasty
natal
nates
natty
naval
navel
navvy
nawab
oaken
oakum

oared
oases
oasis
oaten
oaves
pacer
pacha
paddy
padre
paean
paeon
pagan
paint
paisa
palay
palea
pally
palmy
palpi
palsy
pampa
panda
pandy
panel
panga
panic
panne
pansy
panto
pants
panty
papal
papaw
paper
pappy
parch
pardi
pardy
parer
parge
parka
parky
parle
parol
parry
parse
Parsi
parti
party
Pasch
pasha
pashm
passe
pasta
paste
pasty
patch
paten
pater
patio
patsy
patty
pause
pavan
paver
pavid
pavis
pawky
payee
payer
rabbi
rabic
rabid
racer
races
radar
radii
radio
radix

radon
raggy
rainy
raise
rajah
raker
rally
ramal
ramie
ramus
ranch
randy
ranee
range
rangy
raper
raphe
rapid
raspy
rasse
ratan
ratch
ratel
rater
rathe
ratio
ratty
ravel
raven
raver
ravin
rawly
rayed
razee
razor
sable
sabot
sabra
sabre
sacra
sadhu
sadly
saggy
sahib
saiga
saint
saith
saker
Sakta
salad
salep
sales
salic
sally
salmi
salon
salse
salts
salty
salve
salvo
samba
sambo
samel
sandy
sapan
sapid
sapor
sappy
saree
sarge
sarky
saros
sasin
sassy
Satan
sated
satin
satyr

sauce
sauch
saucy
Saudi
saugh
sault
sauna
saury
saute
saver
savin
savoy
savvy
Saxon
sayer
sayso
sayst
tabby
tabes
tabla
table
taboo
tabor
tache
tacit
tacky
taffy
tafia
taiga
tails
taint
taken
taker
takin
tales
tally
talon
taluk
talus
tamer
Tamil
tamis
tammy
tango
tangy
tanka
tansy
taper
tapir
tapis
tardy
targe
tarok
tarot
tarre
tarry
tarsi
tarty
tasse
taste
tasty
Tatar
tater
tatou
tatty
taunt
taupe
tawer
tawie
tawny
tawse
taxer
taxis
taxon
taxus
tazza
vacua
vagal
vague

vagus
vails
valet
valid
valse
value
valve
vaned
vapid
varan
varec
varix
varus
varve
vasal
vasty
vatic
vault
vaunt
wacke
wacky
waddy
wader
wafer
wager
wages
wagon
wahoo
waist
waits
waive
waken
waker
wakes
waler
walla
wally
waltz
waney
wanly
wares
warty
washy
waste
watch
water
waved
waver
wavey
waxen
waxer
yacht
yager
yahoo
yamen
yapok
yauld
yawny
zambo
zanze
abaca
abaci
aback
abaft
abase
abash
abask
abate
abaya
abbey
abbot
abeam
abele
abhor
abide
ablow
abode
aboil
Abomb
abort
about
above
abrim
abuse
abuzz
abysm
abyss
ebony
Hbomb
obang
obeah
obeli
obese
Qboat
Uboat
acari
acerb
acini
ackee
acock
acold
acorn
acred
acrid
actin
acton
actor
acute
eclat
ichor
icily
icing
icker
ictus
McCoy
occur
ocean
ochre
ochry
octal
octet
scald
scale
scall
scalp
scaly
scamp
scant
scape
scare
scarf
scarp
scart
scary
scatt
scaup
scaur
sceat
scena
scend
scene
scent
schmo
schwa
scifi
scion
scoff
scold
scone
scoop
scoot
scopa
scope
score
scorn
Scots
scour
scout
scowl
scrag
scram
scran
scrap
scray
scree
screw
scrim
scrip
scrod
scrub
scrum
scuba
scudi
scudo
scuff
scull
sculp
scurf
scuta
scute
adage
adapt
addax
adder
addle
adept
adieu
adios
adlib
adman
admit
admix
adobe
adopt
adore
adorn
adown
adoze
adult
adunc
adust
adyta
Eddic
edged
edict
edify
educe
educt
idead
ideal
idiom
idiot
idler
idola
idyll
oddly
odeon
odeum
odium
odour
udder
aegis
aerie
beach
beady
beamy
beano
beard
beast
beaus
beaut
beaux
bebop
bedad
bedel
bedew
bedim
beech
beefs
beefy
beery
befit
befog
begad
began
begat
beget
begin
begot
begum
begun
beige
being
belay
belch
belga
belie
belle
belly
below
bench
bends
bendy
benni
benny
beret
berry
berth
beryl
beset
besom
besot
betel
beton
bevel
bezel
cease
cedar
cello
cense
cento
ceorl
cesti
dealt
deary
death
debag
debar
debit
debug
debut
decal
decay
decor
decoy
decry
deedy
defer
degas
degum
deice
deify
deign
deism
deist
deity
dekko
delay
delft
delta
delve
demit
demob
demon
demos
demur
denim
dense
depot
depth
derby
derma
desex
deter
deuce
devil
dewan
eerie
feast
feeze
feign
feint
fella
felly
felon
femur
fence
fenny
feoff
feral
ferly
fermi
ferny
ferry
fesse
fetal
fetch
fetid
fetor
fetus
fever
gecko
geese
geist
gelid
gelly
gemma
gemmy
gemot
genet
genic
genie
genii
genoa
genre
genro
gents
genus
geode
geoid
gerah
germy
gesso
geste
getup
heady
heard
heart
heath
heave
heavy
hedge
hefty
heigh
heist
helix
hello
helot
helve
heman
hence
henge
henna
henry
herby
herma
heron
hertz
hewer
hexad
jeans
jehad
jelly
jemmy
jenny
jerky
Jerry
Jesse
jetty
jewel
Jewry
kebab
kebob
kedge
kefir
kelpy
kempt
kenaf
kendo
kerne
kerry
ketch
keyed
leach
leads
leady
leafy
leaky
leant
leapt
learn
lease
leash
least
leave
ledge
ledgy
leech
leery
lefty
legal
leger
leges
leggy
legit
leman
lemma
lemon
lemur
lento
Lents
leper
lepta
lethe
letup
levee
level
lever
levin
lewis
lexis
mealy
means
meant
meany
meaty
mecca
medal
media
medic
Medoc
meiny
melee
melic
melon
mense
mercy
merge
meril
merit
merle
merry
mesel
mesic
mesne
meson
messy
mesto
metal
meter
meths
metic
metif
metis
metre
metro
mezzo
neath
necks
neddy
needs
needy
Negro
negus
neigh
neive
nelly
nerka
nerve
nervy
netty
neume
never
newel
newly
newsy
nexus
peace
peach
peaky
pearl
peart
pease
peaty
pecan
pedal
peeve
peggy
pekan
pekoe
pelta
penal
pence
penna
penny
peony
peppy
perai
perch
perdu
peril
perky
perry
perse
pesky
petal
peter
petit
petri
petty
pewit
reach
react
ready
realm
reams
rearm
reata
reave
rebec
rebel
rebid
rebus
rebut
recap
recce
recto
recur
redan
reddy
redia
redid
redly
redox
reedy
reeky
reest
reeve
refel
refer
refit
regal
regie
Reich
reify
reign
reins
reive
rejig
relax
relay
relet
relic
relit
reman
remex
remit
renal
renew
rente
repay
repel
reply
repot
repro
reran
rerun
resat
reset
resin
resit
retch
retry
reuse
revel
revet
revue
seamy
sebum
secco
sedan
Seder
sedge
sedgy
sedum
seedy
seely
seepy
segno
segue
seine
seise
seism
seize
sekos
selah
sells
selva
semee
semen
senna
senor
sensa
sense
sepal
sepia
sepoy
septa
serac
serai
seral
serge
Seric
serif
serin
serow
serra
serry
serum
serve
servo
setae
seton
setto
setup
seven
sever
sewer
sewin
sexed
sexto
teach
teary
tease
techy
teens
teeny
teeth
tehee
teind
telex
telic
telly
tempi
tempo
tempt
tench
tenet
tenne
tenon
tenor
tense
tenth
tenty
tepee
tepid
terai
terce
terms
terne
terra
terry
terse
tesla
testa
testy
tetra
texas
vealy
Vedda
Vedic
veena
veery
vegan
veiny
velar
veldt
velum
venae
venal
venge
venin
venom
venue
Venus
verge
verse
verso
verst
vertu
verve
vesta
vetch
weald
weary
weave
webby
weber
wedge
weeds
weedy
weeny
weepy
weigh
weird
welch
wells
welsh
wench
wetly
xebec
xenia
xenon
xeric
yearn
years
yeast
yerba
zebec
zebra
zesty
affix
afire
afoot
afore
Afric
afrit
after
offal
offer
often
again
agami
agape
agate
agave
agaze
agene
agent
aggro
agile
aging
agist
aglet
agley
aglow
agogo
agone
agony
agora
agree
agued
egest
eggar
egger
egret
igloo
ogham
ogive
ogler
Ugric
ahead
ahold
ahull
bhang
chafe
chaff
chain
chair
chalk
champ
chant
chaos
chape
chaps
chard
chare
charm
charr
chart
chary
chase
chasm
cheap
cheat
check
cheek
cheep
cheer
cheka
chela
chert
chess
chest
chevy
chewy
chiao
chick
chide
chief
chiel
child
chile
chili
chill
chimb
chime
chimp
china
chine
chink
chirk
chirp
chirr
chive
chivy
chizz
chock
choir
choke
choky
choli
chomp
chops
chord
chore
chose
choux
chuck
chuff
chump
chunk
churl
churn
churr
chuse
chute
chyle
chyme
dhobi
dhole
dhoti
ghast
ghaut
Ghazi
ghost
ghoul
ghyll
ihram
khadi
khaki
Khmer
ohmic
ohone
phage
phase
phene
pheon
phial
phlox
phone
phono
phony
photo
phyla
phyle
rheum
rhine
rhino
rhomb
rhumb
rhyme
shack
shade
shady
shaft
shake
shako
shaky
shale
shall
shalt
shaly
shame
shank
shant
shape
shard
share
shark
sharp
shave
shawl
shawm
sheaf
shear
sheen
sheep
sheer
sheet
sheik
shelf
shell
shend
shent
Sheol
sherd
sheva

shewn thump cirri fixed litho pilau sisal wilds aline cleek flota playa
Shiah thuya cisco fixer litre pilaw sissy wiles alive cleft flour plaza
shiel thyme cissy fizzy liven pilch sitar willy alkyd clepe flout plead
shier thymy civet giant liver pilea sitin wince alkyl clerk flown pleat
shift uhlan civic giber lives pilei sixer winch Allah click fluff plebs
shill whack civil giddy livid pilot sixte windy allay cliff fluid plica
shily whale civvy gigot livre pilus sixth winey alley climb fluke plonk
shine whang Diana gigue miaow pinch sixty winge allin clime fluky pluck
shiny wharf diary gilpy miaul piney sizar wings allot cline flume plumb
shire whaup diazo gimme micky pinko sizer wingy allow cling flump plume
shirk wheal dicer ginny micro pinky tiara winze alloy clink flung plump
shirr wheat dicey gipsy middy pinna tibia wiper allyl cloak flunk plumy
shirt wheel dicky girly midge pinny tical wispy aloft clock fluor plunk
Shiva wheen dicot giron midon pinon tidal witan aloha cloke flush plush
shoal whelk dicta girth midst pinta tiein witch alone clone flute Pluto
shoat whelm didst gismo might pinto tieup withe along clonk fluty slack
shock whelp diene given milch pinup tiger withy aloof cloot flyby slain
shoer where dight giver miler pious tight witty aloud close flyer slake
shoji which digit hight milky pipal tigon wives alpha cloth glace slang
shone whiff diker hiker mille piper tilde wizen altar cloud glade slant
shook while dilly hilar mimer pipit tiler yield alter clout glady slash
shoon whine dimer hillo mimic pipul tilth yippy alula clove glair slate
shoot whiny dimly hilly minar pique timer zibet alway clown gland slaty
shore whirl dinar hilum mince piste times zinco black clubs glare slave
shorn whirr diner Hindi miner pitch timid zincy blade cluck glary sleek
short whish dingo Hindu mingy pithy tinct zingy blain clump glass sleep
shout whisk dingy hinge minim piton tinea zinky blame clung glaur sleet
shove whist dinky hinny minor pitta tined zippy bland clunk glaze slept
shown white diode hippo minty pivot tinge djinn blank eland glazy slice
showy whity dippy hippy minus pixie tinny eject blare elate gleam slick
shred whizz dirge hirer mirky pizza tinty fjeld blase elbow glean slide
shrew whole dirty hitch mirth riant tippy fjord blast elder glebe slily
shrub whoop disco hives misdo riata tipsy akene blate elect glede slime
shrug whore dishy jibba miser ribes tipup okapi blaze elegy gleed slimy
shuck whorl disme jiber missy ricer titan skald bleak elemi gleek sling
shunt whose ditch jiffy misty rider tithe skate blear elfin gleet slink
shush whoso ditto jihad mitre ridge title skean bleat elide glial slips
shyer Xhosa ditty jingo mixed ridgy titre skeet bleed elite glide sloid
shyly aider divan jinks mixen rifle tizzy skein bleep eloge glint sloop
thane ainee diver jinni mixer right viand skelm blend eloin gloat sloot
thank aioli Dives kiang mixup rigid vibes skelp blent elope globe slope
thawy airer divot kiddy mizen rigor vicar skene bless elude gloom slops
theca aisle divvy kinin niche rille Vichy skier blest elute glory slosh
theft aitch dixie kinky nidus rinse video skiey blimp elvan gloss sloth
thegn bible dizen kiosk niece ripen viewy skiff blimy elver glout sloyd
their biddy dizzy kitty nieve risen vigil skill blind elves glove slubb
thema bidet eider liana niffy riser villa skimp blink flack gloze sluit
theme bield eight liane nifty rishi villi skink bliss flail gluey slump
there bifid fibre liang night risky vinal skint blitz flair glume slung
therm bight fiche liard nimbi ritzy vinca skirl bloat flake glyph slunk
these bigot fichu libel ninny rival vinyl skirr block flaky ileac slurp
theta bijou field liber ninon rived viola skirt bloke flame ileal slush
thews biker fiend libra ninth rivel viper skite blond flamy ileum slyer
thewy bilbo fiery licht nippy riven viral skive blood flank ileus slyly
thick bilge fifer licit nisei river vireo skoal bloom flare iliac slype
thief bilgy fifth liege nisus rivet vires skulk blown flash Iliad ulcer
thigh billy fifty liein nitid sibyl virga skull blowy flask ilial ulema
thill bimbo fight lifer niton sided Virgo skunk blude flaxy ilium ulmin
thine binge filch ligan nitre sidle virid skyer blues fleam kloof ulnae
thing bingo filet liger nitro siege virtu skyey bluet fleck llama ulnar
think biome fille light nival sieve virus ukase bluey fleer llano ultra
third biota filly liken nixie sight visit alack bluff fleet olden Vlach
thirl biped filmy lilac nizam sigil visor alarm blunt flesh oldie zloty
thole bipod filth limbo oidia sigla vista alary blurb flews oleic amain
tholi birch final limen oiled sigma vital alate blurt flick olein amass
thong birth finch limey oiler silex vitta album blush flied oleum Amati
thorn bison fines limit piano silks vivat alder clack flier olive amaze
thorp bitch finis linen picky silky vives aleph claim flimp ology amban
those biter finny liner picot silly vivid alert clamp fling place amber
thraw bitsy fiord lines picul silty vixen algae clang flint plage ambit
three bitts firer lingo pidog silva vizor algal clank flirt plaid amble
threw bitty firry linin piece simar widdy algid clary float plain ambos
thrid bivvy first links pieta since widen algin clash flock plait ambry
throb cider firth linny piety sinew widow Algol clasp flong plane ameer
throe cigar fishy lipid piezo singe width alias class flood plank amend
throw cilia fitch lippy piggy Singh wield alibi clave floor plant ament
thrum cimex fitly lisle pigmy sinus wigan alien clean flora plash amice
thuja cinch fiver lists piker Sioux wight align clear flory plasm amide
thumb circa fives lithe pilaf siren wilco alike cleat floss plate amido

amigo ankle knout bogey comae donah goose kotow moose polar soggy tousy
amine annal known boggy comal donee gopak loach moped polio solan towel
amino annex knurl bogie combe donga goral loamy moper polka solar tower
Amish annoy knurr bogle combo donna gorge loath mopup polyp soldi towny
amiss annul mneme bogus comer donor gorse lobar mopus pommy soldo toxic
amity anode oncer bohea comet donut gorsy lobby moral ponce solen toxin
amnia anomy oneup bolas comfy doper gotta lobed morat poncy solfa vocal
among antae onion bolus comic dopey Gouda lobus moray pongo solid vodka
amort antic onset bombe comma Doric gouge local morel pooch solon vogie
amour antra snack bonce compo dormy gourd locum mores pooja solum vogue
ample antre snafu boned compt dorts gouty locus moron pools solus voice
amply anvil snail boner conch dorty gowan loden morph poort solve voile
amuck Anzac snake boney coney dotal goyim lodge morra poppy sonar volar
amuse cnida snaky bongo conga doter hoard loess morse popsy sonde volet
embay enact snare bonne conge dotty hoary lofty mosey porch sonic volta
embed enate snark bonny conic Douay hobby logan mossy porgy sonny volte
ember ended snarl bonus conky doubt hocus logia motel porky sonsy volti
embow endow snash bonze conte douce hodge logic motet porno sooth volva
embus endue snath booby cooee dough hogan Logos mothy Porte sooty vomer
emcee enema sneak booed cooey douma hohum lolly motif poser sophy vomit
emeer enemy sneap boost cooky douse hoick loner motor posit sopor voter
emend enjoy sneck booth cooly dowdy hoise longa motte posse soppy vouch
emery ennui sneer boots coomb dowed hoist longe motto potto sorel vouge
emmer enrol snell booty coopt dowel hokey looby mould potty sorgo vowel
emmet ensew snick booze copal dower hokku loofa moult pouch sorra wodge
emote ensky snide boozy coper downa hokum looks mound poult sorry woful
empty ensue sniff borax copra downy holey loony mount pound sorus woken
image enter snipe borer copse dowry holla loopy mourn pouty sough woman
imago entia snips boric copsy dowse hollo loose mouse powan sound women
imaum entry snoek borne coral doyen holly loppy mousy power soupy wonga
imbed enure snood boron cords dozen homer loral mouth roach souse wonky
imbue envoi snook bosky corer dozer homey loran mover roast south woods
imide envoy snoop bosom corgi Eolic honey lordy movie robin sowar woody
immit gnarl snoot boson corky eosin honky lorel mower roble sower wooer
immix gnarr snore bossy corno foamy hooch loris nobby robot toady woozy
impel gnash snort bosun cornu focal hooey lorry noble rocks toast words
imply gnawn snout botch corny focus hooky losel nobly rocky today wordy
omasa gnome snowy botel corps foehn hoots loser nodal rodeo toddy works
ombre inane snuff bothy corse fogey horal lotah noddy roger toffy world
omega inapt unapt bough coset foggy horde lotto nodus rogue togue worms
smack inarm unarm boule costa foist horme lotus nohow roily toile wormy
small incur unbar boult cotta folia horny lough noise roker toils worry
smalt incus unbed bound couch folio horse louis noisy rolls Tokay worse
smarm index uncap bourg coude folly horst lound nomad roman token worst
smart Indic uncle bourn cough foots horsy loupe nomen Romeo toman worth
smash indri uncus bouse could footy hosen loury nonce rondo tommy would
smaze indue uncut bousy count foray hosta louse nones rooky tonal wound
smear inept under bowed coupe forby hotch lousy nonet roomy tondi woven
smell inert undid bowel court force hotel lover nonny roost tondo yobbo
smelt infer undue bower couth fordo hotly lovey nooky rooty toner yodel
smile infix unfit bowls coven forge hough lower noone roper tonga yogic
smirk infra unfix bowse cover forgo hound lowly noose ropey tongs yokel
smite ingle ungot boxer covet forme houri lowne nopal rorty tonic yolky
smith ingot ungum boyar covey forte house loyal noria roset tonka yonks
smock injun Uniat coach covin forth hovel mobby Norse rosin tonne young
smoke inker unify coact cowed forty hover mocha north rotch tonus yours
smoko inkle union coapt cower forum howdy modal noser rotor tooth youth
smoky inlaw unite coast cowry fossa howff model nosey rouge topaz zombi
smolt inlay unity coati coxae fosse iodic modus notch rough topee zonal
smote inlet unlay cobby coxal found ionic mogul noted round toper zonda
umbel inner unlit cobia coyly fount jocko mohur notum roupy tophi zooid
umber inoff unman coble coypu fovea joint moire novae rouse topic zooks
umbra input unpeg Cobol cozen foyer joist moist novel roust topoi zoril
umiak inset unpin cobra dobby goaty joker moksa noway route topos apace
umpty inter unrig cocci docht godet jokey molal Nowel routh toque apart
ancon intro unrip cocky dodge godly jokul molar noyau rover Torah apeak
anele inure unsay cocoa dodgy goest jolly molly oomph rowan torch apery
anent inurn unset coder dodos goeth jolty molto poach rowdy toric aphid
angel knack unsex codex doest goety Jonah momma pocky rowel torii aphis
anger knave untie codon doeth going jorum monad poddy rowen torse apian
angle knead until cogue doggo golem joule monas podge rower torsk apish
Anglo kneed unzip cohoe doggy golly joust monde podgy royal torso apode
angst kneel aorta coign dogie gonad jowar money podia soapy torte aport
anigh knell board coley dogma goner koala monte poesy sober torus appal
anile knelt boart colic doily gonna koine month poilu socle total apple
anima knife boast colin doing goody kooky mooch poind sodic totem apply
anion knish bobby colly dolce gooey kopek moody point Sodom touch appro
anise knock boche colon dolly goofy kopje moola poise softa tough appui
anker knoll bodge colza domed goopy Koran moony poker softy touse appuy

April sprig briar cruck frock krona trews aster stead stupe culet fussy
apron sprit bribe crude frond krone triad astir steak sturt culex fusty
apsis sprue brick cruel frons orach trial aswim steal styes cully fuzzy
aptly spume bride cruet front oracy Trias escot steam style cumin guana
epact spumy brief crumb frore orate tribe esker steed styli cupel guano
ephah spunk brier crump frost orbed trice essay steek stylo Cupid guard
ephod spurn brill cruse froth orbit trick ester steel uteri cuppa guava
ephor spurt brine crush frown order tried estoc steep utile curch Guelf
epoch sputa bring crust froze oread trier estop steer utter curds guess
epode upend brink crwth fruit organ trike Islam stein audio curdy guest
epoxy upped briny cryer frump oribi trill islet stela audit curer guide
opera upper brisk crypt fryer oriel trine issei stele auger curia guild
opine upset brize Draco fryup Oriya trior issue steno aught curie guile
opium equal broad draff graal orlop tripe istle steps augur curio guilt
optic equip broch draft grace ormer trist Osage stere aulic curly guimp
space squab brock drail grade orpin trite Oscan stern aunty curry guise
spade squad broil drain graft orris troat Oscar stich aurae curse gular
spado squat broke drake grail ortho trode osier stick aural curst gulch
spahi squaw bronc drama grain praam troll ossia sties auras curve gules
spake squib brood drank graip prahu tromp ostia stiff auric curvy gully
spall squid brook drape grama prang trona psalm stile auxin cusec gulph
spang squit broom drawl grand prank trone pseud still bubal cushy gumbo
spank Araby brose drawn grant prase troop pshaw stilt bubby cutch gummy
spare arbor broth dread grape prate trope psoas stime bucko cutey gunge
spark areal brown dream graph prawn troth psora sting buddy cutie gunny
spasm areca bruin drear grapy preen trout psych stink budge cutin guppy
spate arena bruit dregs grasp press trove tsade stint buffi cutis gurry
spawn argil brule dress grass prest truce usage stipe buffo cutty gushy
speak argol brume dried grate prexy truck usher stirk buggy ducal gusto
spean argon brunt drier grave price trull usual stirp bugle ducat gusty
spear argot brush drift gravy prick truly usurp stoae build duchy gutsy
speck argue brute drill graze pricy trump usury stoat built ducks gutta
specs Argus crack drily great pride trunk ataxy stock buist ducky gutty
speed Arian craft drink grebe prier truss atilt stoep bulge duddy guyot
speel ariel crake drive greed prima trust atlas stogy bulgy dulia hubby
speer arise cramp droit Greek prime truth atman stoic bulky dully huffy
speir armed crane droll green primo tryon atoll stoke bulla dulse hullo
spell aroid crank drome greet primp tryst atomy stola bully dumka human
spelt aroma crape drone grege prink uraei atone stole bumbo dumky humic
spend arose craps drool gride print urate atony stoma bumph dummy humid
spent arrah crash droop grief prior urban atria stomp bumpy dumps humph
sperm arras crass drops griff prise ureal atrip stone bunch dumpy humpy
spica array crate dross grift prism uredo attar stonk bunco dunce humus
spice arris crave drove grike privy urger attic stony bunia dungy hunch
spick arrow crawl drown grill prize urial ether stood bunko dunno hunks
spicy arsis craze druid grime probe urine ethic stook bunny dunny hunky
spiel arson crazy drunk grimy proem urubu ethos stool bunty duomo hurly
spier artel creak drupe grind prole vraic ethyl stoop bunya duper hurry
spike arval cream druse gripe prone vrouw etude stope buran duple hurst
spiky Aryan credo Druze grise prong wrack etwee store burgh duppy husky
spile brace creed dryad grist proof wrapt etyma stork burin durra hussy
spill brach creek dryer grith prose wrath itchy storm burka durst hutch
spilt bract creel dryly grits prosy wreak otary story burke durum hutia
spine braid creep erase groan proud wreck other stoup burly dusky huzza
spiny brail creme erect groat Provo wrest otter stour burnt dusty huzzy
spire brain crepe ergot groin prowl wrick stack stout burro dutch judas
spirt brake crept erica groom proxy wring staff stove burry duvet judge
spiry braky cress Ernie grope prude wrist stage strad bursa fubsy juice
spite brand crest erode gross prune write stagy strap burse fucus juicy
spitz brank crick erose group prunt wrong staid straw burst fudge julep
splat brant crier error grout pryer wrote stain stray busby fugal jumbo
splay brash cries eruct grove trace wroth stair strep bused fuggy jumpy
split brass crime erupt growl track wrung stake strew bushy fugle junky
Spode brava crimp frail grown tract wryly stale stria busty fugue junta
spoil brave crisp frame gruel trade Xrays stalk strip butch fully junto
spoke bravi croak franc gruff tragi ascot stall strop butte fumet jural
spoof bravo Croat frank grume trail ascus stamp strow butty fundi jurat
spook brawl crock fraud grump train asdic stand stroy butyl funds juror
spool brawn croft freak grunt trait ashen stane strum buxom fungi kudos
spoom braxy crone freer irade tramp ashet stang strut buyer funky kudzu
spoon braze cronk frena Iraqi traps Asian stank stuck Cuban funny Kufic
spoor bread crony fresh irate trash aside staph study cubby fural kukri
spore break crook friar Irish trass asker stare stuff cubeb furan kulak
sport bream croon frier irony trawl askew stark stull cubic furor kulan
spout brede crore frill kraal tread aspen start stump cubit furry kumis
sprag breed cross frisk krait treat aspic stash stung cuddy furze Lucan
sprat breer croup frith krans treen assai state stunk Cufic furzy lucid
spray brent crowd fritz kraut trend assay stave stunt cuish fusee lucky
spree breve crown frizz krill tress asset stays stupa culch fusil lucre

luffa lumen lumme lumpy lunar lunch lunge lungi lupin lupus lurch lurid lushy lusty mucic mucin mucky mucro mucus muddy mudir mufti muggy mujik mulch mulct muley mulga mulla multi mummy mumps munch mungo mural murex murky murra murre muser mushy music musky mussy musth musty mutch muted muzzy nucha nudge nulla numen nurse nutty ought ounce ouphe ousel outby outdo outer outgo outre ouzel pubic pubis pucka pudge pudgy puffy puggy pukka puler pulpy pulse punch Punic punty

pupae pupal pupil puppy puree purge Purim purin purse pursy pushy pussy puton putti putto putty quack quaff quail quake quaky qualm quant quark quart quash quasi quean queen queer quell quern query quest queue quick quiet quiff quill quilt quins quint quipu quire quirk quirt quite quits quoin quoit quota quote quoth Quran rubin ruble rubus ruche ruddy rugby ruler rumba rumen rumly rummy rumpy runic runny runty runup rupee rural rushy rusty rutty suave suber sucre sudor

Sudra sudsy suede suety Sufic sugar suint suite sulci sulfa sulky sully sumac summa Sunna Sunni sunny sunup super supra surah sural surat surfy surge surly surra sutor sutra tubae tubal tubby tuber tucum Tudor tufty tuism tulip tulle tumid tummy tuner tunic tunny tuque turbo turfy Turki turps tusky tutee tutor tutti tutty vuggy yucca yucky yukky yulan yummy avail avast avens avert avian avoid evade evens event evert every evict evite evoke ivied ivory kvass ovary ovate

overs overt ovine ovoid ovoli ovolo ovule uveal uvula await awake award aware awash awful awned awoke bwana dwale dwarf dwell dwelt kwela owing owlet owner swage swain swale swami swamp swank sward sware swarf swarm swart swash swath swayl sweal swear sweat swede sweep sweet swell swept swift swill swine swing swink swipe swirl swish Swiss swith swizz swoon swoop sword swore sworn swung twain twang tweak tweed tween tweet twere twerp twice twill twine twink twiny twirl

twirp twist twite twixt twyer axial axile axiom exact exalt excel exeat exert exile exine exist exode expel extol extra exude exult exurb ixtle oxbow oxeye oxide oxlip oxter ayrie byend bylaw byway cycad cycle cyclo cyder cymar Cymry cynic dying eying eyrie fytte gypsy gyral gyron gyrus hydra hydro hyena hying Hykos hylic hyoid hypha hyrax hyson kyang kylin kyloe kyrie lyart lycee lying lymph lynch lyric lyses lysin lysis lysol lythe lytta myall mynah myoid myoma myope

myrrh nyala nylon nymph pygmy pylon pyxie pyxis sybil sycee sylph sylva synch synod syren syrup tying tyler typal typic vying xylem xylol xysti zygal azoic azote azoth Aztec azure Czech izard izzat ozone Uzbeg Uzbek

———

abaca abaci aback abaft abase abash abask abate abaya acari adage adapt again agami agape agate agave agaze alack alarm alary alate amain amass Amati amaze apace apart Araby ataxy avail avast await awake award aware awash beach beady beamy beano beard

beast beaus beaut beaux bhang black blade blain blame bland blank blare blase blast blate blaze board boart boast brace brach bract braid brail brain brake braky brand brank brant brash brass brava brave bravi bravo brawl brawn braxy braze bwana Caaba cease chafe chaff chain chair chalk champ chant chaos chape chaps chard chare charm charr chart chary chase chasm clack claim clamp clang clank clary clash clasp class clave coach coact coapt coast coati crack craft crake

cramp crane crank crape craps crash crass crate crave crawl craze crazy dealt deary death Diana diary diazo Draco draff draft drail drain drake drama drank drape drawl drawn dwale dwarf eland elate enact enate epact erase evade exact exalt feast flack flail flair flake flaky flame flamy flank flare flash flask flaxy foamy frail frame franc frank fraud ghast ghaut Ghazi giant glace glade glady glair gland glare glary glass glaur glaze glazy gnarl gnarr gnash gnawn goaty

graal grace grade graft grail grain graip grama grand grant grape graph grapy grasp grass grate grave gravy graze guana guano guard guava heady heard heart heath heave heavy hoard hoary image imago imaum inane inapt inarm irade Iraqi irate izard jeans Kaaba khadi khaki kiang knack knave koala kraal krait krans kraut kvass kyang leach leads leady leafy leaky leant leapt learn lease leash least leave liana liane liang liard llama llano loach loamy loath lyart mealy means

meant meany meaty miaow miaul myall neath nyala obang okapi omasa orach oracy orate Osage otary ovary ovate peace peach peaky pearl peart pease peaty phage phase piano place plage plaid plain plait plane plank plant plash plasm plate playa plaza poach praam prahu prang prank prase prate prawn psalm quack quaff quail quake quaky qualm quant quark quart quash quasi reach react ready realm reams rearm reata reave riant riata roach roast scald scale scall scalp scaly scamp

scant scape scare scarf scarp scart scary scatt scaup scaur seamy shack shade shady shaft shake shako shaky shale shall shalt shaly shame shank shant shape shard share shark sharp shave shawl shawm skald skate slack slain slake slang slant slash slate slaty slave smack small smalt smarm smart smash smaze snack snafu snail snake snaky snare snark snarl snash snath soapy space spade spado spahi spake spall spang spank spare spark spasm spate spawn stack staff stage stagy

staid stain stair stake stale stalk stall stamp stand stane stang stank staph stare stark start stash state stave stays suave swage swain swale swami swamp swank sward sware swarf swarm swart swash swath swayl teach teary tease thane thank thawy tiara toady toast trace track tract trade tragi trail train trait tramp traps trash trass trawl tsade twain twang ukase unapt unarm uraei urate usage vealy viand Vlach vraic weald weary weave whack whale whang wharf whaup wrack

wrapt lobus cyclo picul endow reddy bless fleam piece spelt where begad
wrath mobby dacha pocky endue redia blest fleck pieta spend wield began
Xrays nabob decal pucka faddy redid bread fleer piety spent wreak begat
yearn nobby decay racer fudge redly break fleet piezo sperm wreck beget
years noble decor races giddy redox bream flesh plead stead wrest begin
yeast nobly decoy recap godet rider brede flews pleat steak yield begot
abbey ombre decry recce godly ridge breed foehn plebs steal affix begum
abbot orbed dicer recto hadal ridgy breer freak poesy steam awful begun
album orbit dicey recur Hades rodeo brent freer preen steed befit bight
amban oxbow dicky ricer hadji ruddy breve frena press steek befog bigot
amber pubic dicot rocks hadst sadhu byend fresh prest steel bifid bogey
ambit pubis dicta rocky hedge sadly caeca geese proxy steep buffi boggy
amble rabbi docht ruche hodge sedan cheap gleam pseud steer buffo bogie
ambos rabic ducal sacra hydra Seder cheat glean quean stein Cufic bogle
ambry rabid ducat secco hydro sedge check glebe queen stela daffy bogus
arbor rebec duchy socle index sedgy cheek glede queer stele defer buggy
babel rebel ducks sucre Indic sedum cheep gleed quell steno elfin bugle
baboo rebid ducky sycee indri sided cheer gleek quern steps fifer cagey
babul rebus emcee tache indue sidle cheka gleet query stere fifth cigar
bebop rebut escot tacit iodic sodic chela goest quest stern fifty cogue
bible ribes excel tacky jaded Sodom chert goeth queue suede gaffe dagga
bobby robin faced techy judas sudor chess goety reedy suety hefty dagos
bubal roble facer tical judge Sudra chest great reeky sweal huffy degas
bubby robot facet tucum kedge sudsy chevy grebe reest swear infer degum
cabal rubin facia ulcer kiddy tidal chewy greed reeve sweat infix dight
cabby ruble facta uncap kudos today clean Greek rheum swede infra digit
caber rubus fiche uncle kudzu toddy clear green sceat sweep jiffy doggo
cabin sable fichu uncus laded Tudor cleat greet scena sweet Kafir doggy
cable sabot focal uncut laden udder cleek grege scend swell kefir dogie
cabob sabra focus vacua Ladin under cleft Guelf scene swept Kufic dogma
caboc sabre fucus vicar ladle undid clepe guess scent teens lefty eager
cobby sebum gecko Vichy ledge undue clerk guest seedy teeny lifer eagle
cobia sibyl hocus vocal ledgy Vedda creak hyena seely teeth lofty eagre
coble sober incur wacke loden Vedic cream idead seepy theca luffa edged
Cobol suber incus wacky lodge video credo ideal sheaf theft Mafia eggar
cobra sybil itchy yacht madam vodka creed ileac shear thegn mufti egger
Cuban tabby jacks yucca madge waddy creek ileal sheen their niffy eight
cubby tabes jocko yucky madly wader creel ileum sheep thema nifty ergot
cubeb tabla lacet addax medal wedge creep ileus sheer theme offal fagin
cubic table lacey adder media widdy creme inept sheet there offer fagot
cubit taboo licht addle medic widen crepe inert sheik therm puffy fight
debag tabor licit aider Medoc widow crept knead shelf these refel fogey
debar tibia local alder middy width cress kneed shell theta refer foggy
debit tubae locum asdic midge wodge crest kneel shend thews refit fugal
debug tubal locus audio midon yodel Czech knell shent thewy rifle fuggy
debut tubby Lucan audit midst abeam deedy knelt Sheol tiein softa fugle
dobby tuber lucid baddy modal abele diene kwela sherd tieup softy fugue
elbow umbel lucky badge model acerb doest leech sheva tread Sufic gigot
embay umber lucre badly modus adept doeth leery shewn treat taffy gigue
embed umbra lycee bedad muddy agene dread liege siege treen tafia hight
ember unbar macaw bedel mudir agent dream liein sieve trend toffy hogan
embow unbed macer bedew nadir ahead drear loess skean tress tufty ingle
embus urban macho bedim neddy akene dregs mneme skeet trews unfit ingot
fable Uzbeg macle biddy nidus aleph dress naevi skein tweak unfix jaggy
fibre Uzbek Macon bidet nodal alert dwell needs skelm tweed wafer lagan
fubsy vibes macro bodge noddy ameer dwelt needy skelp tween woful lager
gabby webby McCoy buddy nodus amend egest niece skene tweet aegis legal
gable weber mecca budge nudge ament eject nieve sleek twere aggro leger
giber xebec micky caddy oddly anele elect obeah sleep twerp algae leges
habit yobbo micro cadet oidia anent elegy obeli sleet ulema algal leggy
hobby zebec mocha cadge olden apeak elemi obese slept upend algid legit
hubby zebra mucic cadre oldie apery emeer ocean smear ureal algin ligan
imbed zibet mucin cedar order areal emend odeon smell uredo Algol liger
imbue ancon mucky cider paddy areca emery odeum smelt uteri angel light
jabot ascot mucro coder padre arena enema oleic sneak uveal anger logan
jibba ascus mucus codex pedal avens enemy olein sneap veena angle logia
jiber bacca nacre codon pidog avert erect oleum sneck veery Anglo logic
kabob baccy necks cuddy poddy beech evens omega sneer viewy angst Logos
kebab bacon niche cyder podge beefs event oneup snell weeds argil magic
kebob boche nucha daddy podgy beefy evert opera speak weedy argol magma
label bucko occur didst podia beery every oread spean weeny argon magus
labia cacao oncer dodge pudge bield exeat overs spear weepy argot might
labra cache Oscan dodgy pudgy bleak exert overt speck wheal argue mogul
libel cacti Oscar dodos radar blear faery oxeye specs wheat Argus muggy
liber cocci pacer duddy radii bleat feeze paean speed wheel auger Negro
libra cocky pacha Eddic radio bleed field paeon speel wheen aught negus
lobar cocoa pecan eider radix bleep fiend peeve speer whelk augur night
lobby cycad picky elder radon blend fiery phene speir whelm bagel organ
lobed cycle picot ended redan blent fjeld pheon spell whelp baggy ought

pagan	usher	chili	fritz	opium	skiff	thigh	rejig	belay	gules	palsy	tilth
peggy	wahoo	chill	frizz	oribi	skill	thill	ackee	belch	gully	pelta	tulip
piggy	yahoo	chimb	gaily	oriel	skimp	thine	alkyd	belga	gulph	phlox	tulle
pigmy	abide	chime	geist	Oriya	skink	thing	alkyl	belie	halal	pilaf	tyler
puggy	acini	chimp	glial	osier	skint	think	anker	belle	hallo	pilau	uhlan
pygmy	adieu	china	glide	ovine	skirl	third	ankle	belly	halma	pilaw	unlay
raggy	adios	chine	glint	owing	skirr	thirl	asker	below	halos	pilch	unlit
regal	afire	chink	going	oxide	skirt	toile	askew	bilbo	halva	pilea	valet
regie	agile	chirk	gride	paint	skite	toils	baker	bilge	halve	pilei	valid
right	aging	chirp	grief	paisa	skive	triad	biker	bilgy	helix	pilot	valse
rigid	agist	chirr	griff	phial	slice	trial	dekko	billy	hello	pilus	value
rigor	alias	chive	grift	plica	slick	Trias	diker	bolas	helot	polar	valve
roger	alibi	chivy	grike	poilu	slide	tribe	esker	bolus	helve	polio	velar
rogue	alien	chizz	grill	poind	slily	trice	faker	bulge	hilar	polka	veldt
rugby	align	click	grime	point	slime	trick	fakir	bulgy	hillo	polyp	velum
saggy	alike	cliff	grimy	poise	slimy	tried	hakim	bulky	hilly	puler	villa
segno	aline	climb	grind	price	sling	trier	hiker	bulla	hilum	pulpy	villi
segue	alive	clime	gripe	prick	slink	trike	hokey	bully	holey	pulse	volar
sight	amice	cline	grise	pricy	slips	trill	hokku	bylaw	holla	pylon	volet
sigil	amide	cling	grist	pride	smile	trine	hokum	calid	hollo	rally	volta
sigla	amido	clink	grith	prier	smirk	trior	Hykos	calif	holly	relax	volte
sigma	amigo	cnida	grits	prima	smite	tripe	icker	calix	hullo	relay	volti
soggy	amine	coign	guide	prime	smith	trist	inker	calla	hylic	relet	volva
sugar	amino	crick	guild	primo	snick	trite	inkle	calpa	idler	relic	waler
tiger	Amish	crier	guile	primp	snide	tuism	jakes	calve	igloo	relit	walla
tight	amiss	cries	guilt	prink	sniff	twice	joker	calyx	inlaw	rille	wally
tigon	amity	crime	guimp	print	snipe	twill	jokey	cello	inlay	rolls	waltz
togue	anigh	crimp	guise	prior	snips	twine	jokul	cilia	inlet	ruler	welch
ungot	anile	crisp	haick	prise	spica	twink	kukri	coley	Islam	salad	wells
ungum	anima	cuish	haiku	prism	spice	twiny	liken	colic	islet	salep	welsh
urger	anion	daily	haily	privy	spick	twirl	makar	colin	jalap	sales	wilco
vagal	anise	dairy	hairy	prize	spicy	twirp	maker	colly	jelly	salic	wilds
vague	apian	daisy	heigh	quick	spiel	twist	moksa	colon	jolly	sally	wiles
vagus	apish	deice	heist	quiet	spier	twite	naked	colza	jolty	salmi	willy
vegan	Arian	deify	hoick	quiff	spike	twixt	naker	culch	julep	salon	xylem
vigil	ariel	deign	hoise	quill	spiky	tying	oaken	culet	kalif	salse	xylol
vogie	arise	deism	hoist	quilt	spile	umiak	oakum	culex	kalpa	salts	yolky
vogue	Asian	deist	hying	quins	spill	Uniat	pekan	cully	kelpy	salty	yulan
vuggy	aside	deity	icily	quint	spilt	unify	pekoe	dalek	kulak	salve	adman
wager	atilt	djinn	icing	quipu	spine	union	piker	dally	kulan	salvo	admit
wages	avian	doily	idiom	quire	spiny	unite	poker	delay	kylin	selah	admix
wagon	axial	doing	idiot	quirk	spire	unity	pukka	delft	kyloe	sells	armed
wigan	axile	dried	iliac	quirt	spirt	urial	raker	delta	lilac	selva	atman
wight	axiom	drier	Iliad	quite	spiry	urine	roker	delve	lolly	silex	bimbo
yager	bairn	drift	ilial	quits	spite	utile	saker	dilly	malar	silks	bombe
yogic	baize	drill	ilium	rainy	spitz	vails	Sakta	dolce	Malay	silky	bumbo
zygal	beige	drily	imide	raise	stich	veiny	sekos	dolly	malic	silly	bumph
abhor	being	drink	Irish	Reich	stick	voice	taken	dulia	malty	silty	bumpy
aphid	blimp	drive	ivied	reify	sties	voile	taker	dully	melee	silva	camas
aphis	blimy	dying	Jaina	reign	stiff	vying	takin	dulse	melic	solan	camel
ashen	blind	edict	joint	reins	stile	waist	Tokay	eclat	melon	solar	cameo
ashet	blink	edify	joist	reive	still	waits	token	Eolic	milch	soldi	campy
Bahai	bliss	elide	juice	rhine	stilt	waive	waken	falls	miler	soldo	cimex
bohea	blitz	elite	juicy	rhino	stime	weigh	waker	false	milky	solen	comae
cohoe	briar	erica	knife	roily	sting	weird	wakes	fella	mille	solfa	comal
ephah	bribe	evict	knish	saiga	stink	which	woken	felly	molal	solid	combe
ephod	brick	evite	koine	saint	stint	whiff	yokel	felon	molar	solon	combo
ephor	bride	exile	krill	saith	stipe	while	yukky	filch	molly	solum	comer
ether	brief	exine	laigh	scifi	stirk	whine	ablow	filet	molto	solus	comet
ethic	brier	exist	laird	scion	stirp	whiny	adlib	fille	mulch	solve	comfy
ethos	brill	eying	lairy	seine	suint	whirl	aglet	filly	mulct	splat	comic
ethyl	brine	faint	laity	seise	suite	whirr	agley	filmy	muley	splay	comma
hohum	bring	fairy	lying	seism	swift	whish	aglow	filth	mulga	split	compo
ichor	brink	faith	mains	seize	swill	whisk	Allah	folia	mulla	sulci	compt
jehad	briny	feign	maize	Shiah	swine	whist	allay	folio	multi	sulfa	cumin
jihad	brisk	feint	meiny	shiel	swing	white	alley	folly	nelly	sulky	cymar
lahar	brize	flick	moire	shier	swink	whity	allin	fully	nulla	sully	Cymry
Mahdi	build	flied	moist	shift	swipe	whizz	allot	galah	nylon	sylph	daman
mohur	built	flier	naiad	shill	swirl	wrick	allow	galea	ogler	sylva	damar
nohow	buist	flimp	naive	shily	swish	wring	alloy	Galla	oiled	tales	demit
ochre	caird	fling	neigh	shine	Swiss	wrist	allyl	gally	oiler	tally	demob
ochry	cairn	flint	neive	shiny	swith	write	atlas	galop	orlop	talon	demon
ogham	chiao	flirt	noise	shire	swizz	bijou	aulic	gelid	owlet	taluk	demos
other	chick	foist	noisy	shirk	taiga	enjoy	balas	gelly	oxlip	talus	demur
pshaw	chide	friar	odium	shirr	tails	hajji	baler	gilpy	palay	telex	dimer
sahib	chief	frier	ogive	shirt	taint	injun	balky	golem	palea	telic	dimly
schmo	chiel	frill	olive	Shiva	teind	major	bally	golly	pally	telly	domed
schwa	child	frisk	onion	skier	thick	mujik	balmy	gular	palmy	tilde	dumka
tehee	chile	frith	opine	skiey	thief	rajah	balsa	gulch	palpi	tiler	dumky

dummy dumps dumpy emmer emmet famed femur fumet gamba games gamic gamin gamma gammy gamut gemma gemmy gemot gimme gumbo gummy hamal hammy heman homer homey human humic humid humph humpy humus iambi immit immix jammy jemmy jumbo jumpy kempt Khmer kumis leman lemma lemon lemur limbo limen limey limit lumen lumme lumpy lymph mamba mambo mamma mammy mimer mimic momma mummy mumps namer nimbi nomad nomen numen nymph ohmic oomph ormer pampa pommy ramal ramie ramus reman remex

remit roman Romeo rumba rumen rumly rummy rumpy samba sambo samel semee semen simar sumac summa tamer Tamil tamis tammy tempi tempo tempt timer times timid toman tommy tumid tummy ulmin unman vomer vomit woman women yamen yummy zambo zombi ainee amnia annal annex annoy annul aunty awned banal banco bandy banjo banns Bantu bench bends bendy benni benny binge bingo bonce boned boner boney bongo bonne bonny bonus bonze bunch bunco bunia bunko bunny bunty bunya canal candy

canna canny canoe canon canst canto canty cense cento cinch conch coney conga conge conic conky conte cynic dance dandy denim dense dinar diner dingo dingy dinky donah donee donga donna donor donut dunce dungy dunno dunny ennui Ernie fancy fanny Fanti fence fenny final finch fines finis finny fundi funds fungi funky funny ganja genet genic genie genii genoa genre genro gents genus ginny gonad goner gonna gunge gunny handy hanky Hanse hence henge henna henry Hindi Hindu

hinge hinny honey honky hunch hunks hunky inner ionic jenny jingo jinks jinni Jonah junky junta junto kenaf kendo kinin kinky lance lanky lento Lents linen liner lines lingo linin links linny loner longa longe lunar lunch lunge lungi lynch maned manes mange mango mangy mania manic manly manna manor manse manta manto manul manus mense minar mince miner mingy minim minor minty minus monad monas monde money monte month munch mungo mynah nancy nanna nanny ninny ninon ninth

nonce nones nonet nonny ounce owner panda pandy panel panga panic panne pansy panto pants panty penal pence penna penny pinch piney pinko pinky pinna pinny pinon pinta pinto pinup ponce poncy pongo punch Punic punty ranch randy ranee range rangy renal renew rente rinse rondo runic runny runty runup sandy senna senor sensa sense since sinew singe Singh sinus sonar sonde sonic sonny sonsy Sunna Sunni sunny sunup synch synod tango tangy tanka tansy tench tenet tenne tenon

tenor tense tenth tenty tinct tinea tined tinge tinny tinty tonal tondi tondo toner tonga tongs tonic tonka tonne tonus tuner tunic tunny ulnae ulnar vaned venae venal venge venin venom venue Venus vinal vinca vinyl waney wanly wench wince winch windy winey winge wings wingy winze wonga wonky xenia xenon yonks zanze zinco zincy zingy zinky zonal zonda abode aboil Abomb abort about above acock acold acorn adobe adopt adore adorn adown adoze afoot afore agogo agone agony

agora ahold aioli aloft aloha alone along aloof aloud among amort amour anode anomy apode aport aroid aroma arose atoll atomy atone atony avoid awoke azoic azote azoth biome biota bloat block bloke blond blood bloom blown blowy booby booed boost booth boots booty booze boozy broad broch brock broil broke bronc brood brook broom brose broth brown ceorl chock choir choke choky choli chomp chops chord chore chose choux cloak clock cloke clone clonk cloot close cloth cloud

clout clove clown cooee cooey cooky cooly coomb coopt croak Croat crock croft crone cronk crony crook croon crore cross croup crowd crown dhobi dhole dhoti diode droit droll drome drone drool droop drops dross drove drown duomo ebony eloge eloin elope emote epoch epode epoxy erode erose evoke exode feoff fiord fjord float flock flong flood floor flora flory floss flota flour flout flown foots footy frock frond frons front frore frost froth frown froze geode geoid ghost

ghoul gloat globe gloom glory gloss glout glove gloze gnome goody gooey goofy goopy goose groan groat groin groom grope gross group grout grove growl grown Hbomb hooch hooey hooky hoots hyoid idola inoff irony ivory kiosk kloof knock knoll knout known kooky krona krone looby loofa looks loony loopy loose Maori mooch moody moola moony moose myoid myoma myope nooky noone noose odour ohone ology ovoid ovoli ovolo ozone peony phone phono phony photo pious plonk pooch pooja

pools poort probe proem prole prone prong proof prose prosy proud Provo prowl proxy psoas psora Qboat quoin quoit quota quote quoth rhomb rooky roomy roost rooty scoff scold scone scoop scoot scopa scope score scorn Scots scour scout scowl shoal shoat shock shoer shoji shone shook shoon shoot shore shorn short shout shove shown showy Sioux skoal sloid sloop sloot slope slops slosh sloth sloyd smock smoke smoko smoky smolt smote snoek snood snook snoop snoot snore snort

snout snowy sooth sooty Spode spoil spoke spoof spook spool spoom spoon spoor spore sport spout stoae stoat stock stoep stogy stoic stoke stola stole stoma stomp stone stonk stony stood stook stool stoop stope store stork storm story stoup stour stout stove swoon swoop sword swore sworn thole tholi thong thorn thorp those tooth troat trode troll tromp trona trone troop trope troth trout trove Uboat viola vrouw whole whoop whore whorl whose whoso woods woody wooer woozy

wrong wrote wroth Xhosa zloty zooid zooks alpha ample amply appal apple apply appro appui appuy aspen aspic biped bipod caper capon copal coper copra copse copsy cupel Cupid cuppa depot depth dippy doper dopey duper duple duppy empty expel gaper gappy gipsy gopak guppy gypsy haply happy hippo hippy hypha impel imply input japan kapok kappa kaput kopek kopje lapel lapse leper lepta lipid lippy loppy lupin lupus maple moped moper mopup mopus nappe nappy nippy nopal orpin

ouphe airer curry herma nares shrew varix ensky Pasch betel kitty peter
papal aorta curse heron naris shrub varus ensue pasha beton kotow petit
papaw April curst hertz narky shrug varve eosin pashm bitch latch petri
paper apron curve hirer nerka siren verge essay passe biter lated petty
pappy arrah curvy horal nerve sorel verse fesse pasta bitsy laten pitch
peppy arras daric horde nervy sorgo verso fishy paste bitts latex pithy
pipal array darky horme noria sorra verst fossa pasty bitty lathe piton
piper arris darts horny Norse sorry vertu fosse pesky botch lathi pitta
pipit arrow derby horse north sorus verve fusee piste botel lathy potto
pipul atria derma horst nurse sprag viral fusil poser bothy Latin potty
poppy atrip dirge horsy oared sprat vireo fussy posit butch lethe puton
popsy aurae dirty hurly orris spray vires fusty posse butte letup putti
pupae aural Doric hurry parch spree virga gassy pushy butty lithe putto
pupal auras dormy hurst pardi sprig Virgo gesso pussy butyl litho putty
pupil auric dorts hyrax pardy sprit virid geste raspy catch litre ratan
puppy ayrie dorty ihram parer sprue virtu gismo rasse cater lotah ratch
raper barbe durra jerky parge strad virus gushy resat cates lotto ratel
raphe bardy durst Jerry parka strap wares gusto reset catty lotus rater
rapid barge durum jorum parky straw warty gusty resin cotta lythe rathe
repay baric eared jural parle stray words haste resit cutch lytta ratio
repel barky early jurat parol strep wordy hasty risen cutey match ratty
reply barmy earth juror parry strew works hosen riser cutie mater retch
repot baron eerie karma parse stria world hosta rishi cutin matey retry
repro barre egret karoo Parsi strip worms husky risky cutis maths ritzy
ripen beret enrol karst parti strop wormy hussy roset cutty matin rotch
roper berry error kerne party strow worry hyson rosin dated matlo rotor
ropey berth eyrie kerry perai stroy worse inset rushy dater matte rutty
rupee beryl farad Koran perch strum worst issei rusty datum matzo Satan
sapan birch farce kyrie perdu strut worth issue sasin deter metal sated
sapid birth farci larch peril surah xeric jaspe sassy ditch meter satin
sapor borax farcy lardy perky sural yerba Jesse sisal ditto meths satyr
sappy borer farle lares perry surat zoril laser sissy ditty metic setae
sepal boric feral large perse surfy aisle lasso tasse dotal metif seton
sepia borne ferly largo porch surge apsis lisle taste doter metis setto
sepoy boron fermi larky porgy surly arsis lists tasty dotty metre setup
septa buran ferny larum porky surra arson losel tesla dutch metro sitar
sophy burgh ferry larva porno syren assai loser testa eaten mitre sitin
sopor burin firer loral Porte syrup assay lushy testy eater motel sutor
soppy burka firry loran puree tardy asset lusty tusky enter motet sutra
super burke first lordy purge targe basal lyses unsay entia mothy Tatar
supra burly firth lorel Purim tarok basan lysin unset entry motif tater
taper burnt foray loris purin tarot bases lysis unsex ester motor tatou
tapir burro forby lorry purse tarre basic lysol upset estoc motte tatty
tapis burry force lurch pursy tarry basil maser vasal estop motto tetra
tepee bursa fordo lurid Quran tarsi basin mashy vasty extol mutch titan
tepid burse forge lyric reran tarty basis mason vesta extra muted tithe
tippy burst forgo marah rerun terai bason massa visit fatal natal title
tipsy carat forme march rorty terce bassi masse visor fated nates titre
tipup carer forte mardy rural terms basso massy vista fatly natty tótal
topaz caret forth mares saree terne baste mesel washy fatso netty totem
topee cargo forty marge sarge terra beset mesic waste fatty nitid tutee
toper Carib forum maria sarky terry besom mesne wispy fetal niton tutor
tophi carny fural marid saros terse besot meson xysti fetch nitre tutti
topic carob furan marly scrag thraw bison messy zesty fetid nitro tutty
topoi carol furor marry scram three bosky mesto actin fetor notch ultra
topos carom furry marsh scran threw bosom misdo acton fetus noted untie
typal carpi furze mercy scrap thrid boson miser actor fitch notum until
typic carry furzy merge scray throb bossy missy after fitly nutty utter
umpty carve garth meril scree throe bosun misty aitch fytte oaten vatic
unpeg circa gerah merit screw throw busby mosey altar getup octal vetch
unpin cirri germy merle scrim thrum bused mossy alter gotta octet vital
upped coral girly merry scrip Torah bushy muser antae gutsy often vitta
upper cords giron mirky scrod torch busty mushy antic gutta optic voter
vapid corer girth mirth scrub toric caste music antra gutty ortho watch
viper corgi goral moral scrum torii cesti musky antre hatch ostia water
wiper corky gorge morat serac torse cisco mussy aptly hater otter wetly
yapok corno gorse moray serai torsk cissy musth artel hitch outby witan
yippy cornu gorsy morel seral torso coset musty aster hotch outdo witch
zippy corny gurry mores serge torte costa nasal astir hotel outer withe
pique corps gyral moron Seric torus cusec nasty attar hotly outgo withy
toque corse gyron morph serif turbo cushy nisei attic hutch outre witty
tuque curch gyrus morra serin turfy desex nisus Aztec hutia oxter abuse
abrim curds haram morse serow Turki disco noser batch ictus patch abuzz
acred curdy hardy mural serra turps dishy nosey bated inter paten acute
acrid curer harem murex serry Ugric disme oases bathe intro pater adult
aerie curia harpy murky serum unrig dusky oasis baths istle patio adunc
Afric curie harry murra serve unrip dusty onset batik ixtle patsy adust
afrit curio harsh murre servo varan easel ossia baton jetty patty agued
agree curly herby myrrh shred varec ensew ousel batty ketch petal ahull

alula elude mound squat envoi bowse nexus slyly aural elvan legal pupae
amuck elute mount squaw envoy byway nixie slype auras embay leman pupal
amuse enure mourn squib favus cowed pixie styes avian ephah ligan Qboat
azure equal mouse squid fever cower pyxie style axial equal lilac quean
baulk equip mousy squit fiver cowry pyxis styli Bahai essay lobar Quran
blude eruct mouth stuck fives crwth Saxon stylo balas exeat local radar
blues erupt neume study fovea dewan sexed thyme banal farad logan rajah
bluet etude ovule stuff gavel dowdy sexto thymy basal fatal loral ramal
bluey exude pause stull given dowed sixer tryon basan feral loran ratan
bluff exult pluck stump giver dowel sixte tryst bedad fetal lotah recap
blunt exurb plumb stung haven dower sixth twyer begad final loyal redan
blurb faugh plume stunk haver downa sixty wryly began fleam Lucan regal
blurt fault plump stunt havoc downy taxer Anzac begat float lunar relax
blush fauna plumy stupa hives dowry taxis bezel belay focal macaw relay
bough fluff plunk stupe hovel dowse taxon cozen bleak foray madam reman
boule fluid plush sturt hover etwee taxus dizen blear freak makar renal
boult fluke Pluto swung laver fawny texas dizzy bleat friar malar repay
bound fluky pouch taunt levee gawky toxic dozen bloat fugal Malay reran
bourg flume poult taupe level gawsy toxin dozer bolas fural marah resat
bourn flump pound thuja lever gowan vixen fizzy borax furan Mayan rival
bouse flung pouty thumb levin hawse waxen fuzzy boyar galah medal roman
bousy flunk prude thump liven hewer waxer gazer bread gerah metal rowan
bruin fluor prune thuya liver howdy abysm hazel break gleam minar royal
bruit flush prunt touch lives howff abyss hazer bream glean modal rural
brule flute reuse tough livid jewel adyta huzza briar glial molal salad
brume fluty rhumb touse livre Jewry Aryan huzzy broad gloat molar sapan
brunt found rouge tousy lover jowar bayou izzat bubal gonad monad Satan
brush fount rough truce lovey lawks boyar jazzy buran gopak monas sceat
brute fruit round truck mavis lawny buyer kazoo bylaw goral moral scrag
cauli frump roupy trull mover lewis chyle lazar byway gowan morat scram
caulk gaudy rouse truly movie lower chyme mazer cabal graal moray scran
cause gauge roust trump naval lowly coyly mezzo cacao great mural scrap
chuck gault route trunk navel lowne coypu mizen camas groan mynah scray
chuff gaumy routh truss navvy mower cryer muzzy canal groat naiad sedan
chump gaunt sauce trust never nawab crypt nizam carat gular nasal selah
chunk gauss sauch truth nival newel doyen ouzel cedar gyral natal sepal
churl gauze saucy urubu novae newly dryad pizza cheap hadal naval serac
churn gauzy Saudi usual novel newsy dryer razee cheat halal nawab serai
churr gluey saugh usurp oaves noway dryly razor chiao hamal nival seral
chuse glume sault usury pavan Nowel etyma sizar cigar haram nizam setae
chute Gouda sauna uvula paver pawky fayre sizer clean heman nodal sheaf
clubs gouge saury vault pavid pewit flyby tazza clear hexad nomad shear
cluck gourd saute vaunt pavis powan flyer tizzy cleat hilar nopal Shiah
clump gouty scuba vouch pivot power foyer unzip cloak hogan novae shoal
clung gruel scudi vouge ravel rawly fryer vizor comae horal noway shoat
clunk gruff scudo would raven rowan fryup wizen comal human noyau simar
couch grume scuff wound raver rowdy ghyll ——— copal hyrax obeah sisal
coude grump scull wrung ravin rowel glyph abeam coral idead ocean sitar
cough grunt sculp yauld revel rowen goyim addax coxae ideal octal sizar
could haugh scurf young revet rower guyot adman coxal ihram offal skean
count haulm scuta yours revue sewer idyll ahead creak ileac ogham skoal
coupe haunt scute youth rival sewin kayak algae cream ileal oread smear
court Hausa shuck anvil rived sowar keyed algal croak iliac organ sneak
couth hough shunt arval rivel sower layby alias Croat Iliad Oscan sneap
cruck hound shush bevel riven tawer layer Allah Cuban ilial Oscar solan
crude houri skulk bivvy river tawie layup allay cycad inlaw paean solar
cruel house skull caver rivet tawny loyal altar cymar inlay pagan sonar
cruet inure skunk cavil rover tawse Mayan alway daman Islam palay sowar
crumb inurn slubb civet saver towel maybe amban damar izzat papal speak
crump jaunt sluit civic savin tower mayor annal debag jalap papaw spean
cruse joule slump civil savoy towny mayst antae debar japan pavan spear
crush joust slung civvy savvy vowel noyau Anzaç decal jehad pecan splat
crust kauri slunk coven seven yawny payee apeak decay jihad pedal splay
dauby knurl slurp cover sever auxin payer apian degas Jonah pekan sprag
daunt knurr slush covet vivat boxer phyla appal delay jowar penal sprat
deuce lauds snuff covey vives buxom phyle areal dewan judas perai spray
Douay laugh sough covin vivid coxae pryer Arian dinar jural petal squab
doubt laura sound davit waved coxal psych arrah divan jurat phial squad
douce lough soupy devil waver dixie rayed arras donah kayak pilaf squat
dough louis souse divan wavey fixed rhyme array dotal kebab pilau squaw
douma lound south diver wives fixer royal arval Douay kenaf pilaw stead
douse loupe spume Dives woven hexad sayer Aryan dread knead pipal steak
druid loury spumy divot alway laxly sayso Asian dream Koran plead steal
drunk louse spunk divvy aswim lexis sayst assai drear kraal pleat steam
drupe lousy spurn duvet bawdy maxim shyer assay dryad kulak polar stoae
druse maund spurt eaves bowed mixed shyly atlas ducal kulan powan stoat
Druze mauve sputa elvan bowel mixen skyer atman ducat lagan praam strad
educe mould squab elver bower mixer skyey attar eclat lahar pshaw strap
educt moult squad elves bowls mixup slyer aurae eggar lazar psoas straw

stray	bombe	beech	flock	Reich	bardy	noddy	angel	codex	emcee	homey	maker
sugar	booby	belch	force	retch	bawdy	outdo	anger	coley	emeer	honey	maned
sumac	bribe	bench	frock	roach	beady	oxide	anker	comer	emmer	hooey	manes
surah	bubby	birch	glace	rotch	bends	paddy	annex	comet	emmet	hosen	mares
sural	bumbo	bitch	grace	sauce	bendy	panda	ariel	coney	ended	hotel	maser
surat	busby	black	gulch	sauch	biddy	pandy	armed	cooee	ensew	hovel	mater
sweal	Caaba	block	haick	saucy	blade	pardi	artel	cooey	enter	hover	matey
swear	cabby	bonce	hatch	secco	blude	pardy	ashen	coper	esker	icker	mazer
sweat	clubs	botch	hence	shack	brede	perdu	ashet	corer	ester	idler	melee
Tatar	cobby	brace	hitch	shock	bride	poddy	asker	coset	ether	imbed	mesel
terai	combe	brach	hoick	shuck	buddy	pride	askew	coven	etwee	impel	meter
texas	combo	bract	hooch	since	caddy	prude	aspen	cover	excel	index	miler
thraw	cubby	brick	hotch	slack	candy	randy	asset	covet	expel	infer	mimer
tical	dauby	broch	hunch	slice	chide	ready	aster	covey	faced	inker	miner
tidal	derby	brock	hutch	slick	cnida	reddy	auger	cowed	facer	inlet	miser
titan	dhobi	bunch	juice	smack	cords	reedy	awned	cower	facet	inner	mixed
today	dobby	bunco	juicy	smock	coude	rondo	Aztec	cozen	faker	inset	mixen
Tokay	doubt	butch	ketch	snack	credo	rowdy	babel	creed	famed	inter	mixer
toman	flyby	caeca	knack	sneck	crude	ruddy	bagel	creek	fated	islet	mizen
tonal	forby	catch	knock	snick	cuddy	sandy	baker	creel	fever	issei	model
topaz	gabby	check	lance	space	curds	Saudi	baler	creep	fifer	ivied	money
Torah	gamba	chick	larch	speck	curdy	scudi	bases	crier	filet	jaded	moped
total	glebe	chock	latch	specs	daddy	scudo	bated	cries	fines	jakes	moper
tread	globe	chuck	leach	spica	dandy	seedy	bedel	cruel	firer	jewel	morel
treat	grebe	cinch	leech	spice	deedy	shade	bedew	cruet	fiver	jiber	mores
triad	gumbo	circa	loach	spick	diode	shady	beget	cryer	fives	joker	mosey
trial	herby	cisco	lunch	spicy	dowdy	slide	beret	cubeb	fixed	jokey	motel
Trias	hobby	clack	lurch	stack	duddy	snide	beset	culet	fixer	julep	motet
troat	hubby	click	lynch	stich	elide	soldi	betel	culex	fleer	keyed	mover
tubae	iambi	clock	march	stick	elude	soldo	bevel	cupel	fleet	Khmer	mower
tubal	jibba	cluck	match	stock	epode	sonde	bezel	curer	flied	kneed	muley
tweak	jumbo	coach	mecca	stuck	erode	spade	bidet	cusec	flier	kneel	murex
typal	Kaaba	coact	mercy	sulci	etude	spado	biker	cutey	flyer	kopek	muser
Uboat	layby	cocci	milch	synch	evade	Spode	biped	cyder	fogey	label	muted
uhlan	limbo	conch	mince	teach	exode	study	biter	dalek	fovea	lacet	naked
ulnae	lobby	couch	mooch	tench	exude	suede	bleed	dated	foyer	lacey	naker
ulnar	looby	crack	mulch	terce	faddy	swede	bleep	dater	freer	laded	namer
umiak	mamba	crick	mulct	theca	fordo	tardy	blues	defer	frier	laden	nares
unbar	mambo	crock	munch	thick	fundi	tilde	bluet	desex	fryer	lager	nates
uncap	maybe	cruck	mutch	tinct	funds	toady	bluey	deter	fumet	lapel	navel
Uniat	mobby	culch	nancy	torch	gaudy	toddy	bogey	dicer	fusee	lares	never
unlay	nimbi	curch	niece	touch	geode	tondi	bohea	dicey	galea	laser	newel
unman	nobby	cutch	nonce	trace	giddy	tondo	boned	diker	games	lated	nisei
unsay	oribi	Czech	notch	track	glade	trade	boner	dimer	gaper	laten	nomen
urban	outby	dance	orach	tract	glady	trode	boney	diner	gavel	latex	nones
ureal	plebs	deice	oracy	trice	glede	tsade	booed	diver	gazer	laver	nonet
urial	probe	deuce	ounce	trick	glide	uredo	borer	Dives	genet	layer	noser
usual	rabbi	disco	parch	truce	goody	Vedda	botel	dizen	giber	leger	nosey
uveal	rugby	ditch	Pasch	truck	Gouda	veldt	bowed	domed	given	leges	noted
vagal	rumba	dolce	patch	twice	grade	waddy	bowel	donee	giver	leper	novel
varan	samba	douce	peace	vetch	gride	weeds	bower	doper	gleed	levee	Nowel
vasal	sambo	Draco	peach	vinca	guide	weedy	boxer	dopey	gleek	level	numen
vegan	scuba	dunce	pence	Vlach	handy	widdy	breed	doter	gleet	lever	oaken
velar	slubb	dutch	perch	voice	hardy	wilds	breer	dowed	gluey	libel	oared
venae	tabby	edict	piece	vouch	heady	windy	brief	dowel	godet	liber	oases
venal	tribe	educe	pilch	watch	Hindi	woods	brier	dower	golem	lifer	oaten
vicar	tubby	educt	pinch	welch	Hindu	woody	bused	doyen	goner	liger	oaves
vinal	turbo	eject	pitch	wench	horde	words	buyer	dozen	gooey	liken	octet
viral	urubu	elect	place	whack	howdy	wordy	caber	dozer	greed	limen	offer
vital	webby	enact	plica	which	imide	zonda	cadet	dried	Greek	limey	often
vivat	yerba	epact	pluck	wilco	irade	abbey	cagey	drier	green	linen	ogler
vocal	yobbo	epoch	poach	wince	kendo	ackee	camel	dryer	greet	liner	oiled
volar	zambo	erect	ponce	winch	khadi	acred	cameo	duper	grief	lines	oiler
wheal	zombi	erica	poncy	witch	kiddy	adder	caper	duvet	gruel	liven	olden
wheat	abaca	eruct	pooch	wrack	lardy	adieu	carer	eager	gules	liver	oncer
wigan	abaci	evict	porch	wreck	lauds	after	caret	eared	Hades	lives	onset
witan	aback	exact	pouch	wrick	leads	aglet	cater	easel	harem	lobed	orbed
woman	acock	fancy	price	yucca	leady	agley	cates	eaten	hater	loden	order
wreak	aitch	farce	prick	zinco	lordy	agree	caver	eater	haven	loner	oriel
yulan	alack	farci	pricy	zincy	Mahdi	agued	cheek	eaves	haver	lorel	ormer
zonal	amice	farcy	psych	abide	mardy	aider	cheep	edged	hazel	losel	osier
zygal	amuck	fence	punch	abode	middy	ainee	cheer	egger	hazer	loser	other
adobe	apace	fetch	quack	amide	misdo	airer	chief	egret	hewer	lover	otter
alibi	areca	filch	quick	amido	monde	alder	chiel	eider	hiker	lovey	ousel
Araby	bacca	finch	ranch	anode	moody	alien	cider	elder	hirer	lower	outer
barbe	baccy	fitch	ratch	apode	muddy	alley	cimex	elver	hives	lumen	ouzel
bilbo	banco	flack	reach	aside	neddy	alter	civet	elves	hokey	lycee	owlet
bimbo	batch	fleck	react	baddy	needs	amber	cleek	embed	holey	lyses	owner
bobby	beach	flick	recce	bandy	needy	ameer	coder	ember	homer	macer	oxter

pacer	samel	tepee	widen	toffy	ledge	usage	sophy	bunia	glair	music	scrip
palea	saree	thief	wiles	turfy	ledgy	venge	spahi	burin	goyim	myoid	sepia
panel	sated	three	winey	unify	leggy	verge	tache	cabin	grail	nadir	Seric
paper	saver	threw	wiper	whiff	liege	virga	techy	calid	grain	naris	serif
parer	sayer	tiger	wives	adage	lingo	Virgo	tight	calif	graip	nitid	serin
paten	scree	tiler	wizen	agogo	lodge	vouge	tithe	calix	groin	nixie	sewin
pater	screw	timer	woken	align	longa	vuggy	tophi	Carib	habit	noria	sheik
paver	Seder	times	women	amigo	longe	wedge	Vichy	cavil	hakim	oasis	sigil
payee	semee	tinea	wooer	anigh	lough,	weigh	washy	chain	helix	ohmic	sitin
payer	semen	tined	woven	badge	lunge	winge	wight	chair	humic	oidia	skein
peter	seven	token	xebec	baggy	lungi	wings	withe	choir	humid	oldie	slain
piker	sever	toner	xylem	barge	madge	wingy	withy	cilia	hutia	oleic	sloid
pilea	sewer	topee	yager	beige	mange	wodge	yacht	civic	hylic	olein	sluit
pilei	sexed	toper	yamen	belga	mango	wonga	aboil	civil	hyoid	optic	snail
piney	sheen	totem	yodel	bilge	mangy	zingy	abrim	claim	immit	orbit	sodic
piper	sheep	towel	yokel	bilgy	marge	aloha	acrid	cobia	immix	orpin	solid
poker	sheer	tower	zebec	binge	merge	alpha	actin	colic	Indic	orris	sonic
poser	sheet	treen	zibet	bingo	midge	aught	adlib	colin	infix	ossia	speir
power	shiel	tried	abaft	bodge	mingy	bathe	admit	comic	iodic	ostia	split
preen	shier	trier	aloft	boggy	muggy	baths	admix	conic	ionic	ovoid	spoil
prier	shoer	tuber	beefs	bongo	mulga	bight	aegis	covin	Kafir	oxlip	sprig
proem	shred	tuner	beefy	bough	mungo	boche	aerie	cubic	kalif	panic	sprit
pryer	shrew	tutee	bluff	budge	neigh	bothy	affix	cubit	kefir	patio	squib
puler	shyer	tweed	buffi	buggy	nudge	bushy	Afric	Cufic	kinin	pavid	squid
puree	sided	tween	buffo	bulge	ology	cache	afrit	cumin	krait	pavis	squit
queen	silex	tweet	chafe	bulgy	omega	cushy	again	Cupid	Kufic	peril	staid
queer	sinew	twyer	chaff	burgh	Osage	dacha	algid	curia	kumis	petit	stain
quiet	siren	tyler	chuff	cadge	outgo	dight	algin	curie	kylin	pewit	stair
racer	sixer	udder	cleft	cargo	panga	dishy	allin	curio	kyrie	pipit	stein
races	sizer	ulcer	cliff	coign	parge	docht	amain	cutie	labia	pixie	stoic
raker	skeet	umbel	comfy	conga	peggy	duchy	ambit	cutin	Ladin	plaid	stria
ranee	skier	umber	craft	conge	phage	eight	amnia	cutis	Latin	plain	strip
raper	skiey	unbed	croft	corgi	piggy	fiche	antic	cynic	legit	plait	Sufic
ratel	skyer	under	daffy	cough	plage	fichu	anvil	daric	levin	podia	swain
rater	skyey	unpeg	deify	dagga	podge	fight	aphid	davit	lewis	polio	sybil
ravel	sleek	unset	delft	deign	podgy	fishy	aphis	debit	lexis	posit	tacit
raven	sleep	unsex	draff	dingo	pongo	foehn	April	demit	licit	pubic	tafia
raver	sleet	upped	draft	dingy	porgy	gushy	apsis	denim	liein	pubis	takin
rayed	slyer	upper	drift	dirge	pudge	hight	argil	devil	limit	Punic	Tamil
razee	sneer	upset	edify	dodge	pudgy	hypha	aroid	digit	linin	pupil	tamis
rebec	snoek	uraei	feoff	dodgy	puggy	itchy	arris	dixie	lipid	Purim	tapir
rebel	sober	urger	fluff	doggo	purge	lathe	arsis	dogie	livid	purin	tapis
refel	solen	usher	gaffe	doggy	raggy	lathi	asdic	Doric	logia	pyxie	tawie
refer	sorel	utter	goofy	donga	range	lathy	aspic	drail	logic	pyxis	taxis
relet	sower	Uzbeg	graft	dough	rangy	lethe	astir	drain	loris	quail	telic
remex	speed	Uzbek	griff	dregs	reign	licht	aswim	droit	louis	quoin	tepid
renew	speel	valet	grift	dungy	ridge	light	atria	druid	lucid	quoit	their
repel	speer	vaned	gruff	elegy	ridgy	lithe	atrip	dulia	lupin	rabic	thrid
reset	spiel	varec	howff	eloge	rouge	litho	attic	Eddic	lurid	rabid	tibia
revel	spier	vibes	huffy	faugh	rough	lushy	audio	eerie	lyric	radii	tiein
revet	spree	video	inoff	feign	saggy	lythe	audit	elfin	lysin	radio	timid
ribes	steed	viper	jiffy	foggy	saiga	macho	aulic	eloin	lysis	radix	tonic
ricer	steek	vireo	knife	forge	sarge	mashy	auric	entia	Mafia	ramie	topic
rider	steel	vires	leafy	forgo	saugh	maths	auxin	Eolic	magic	rapid	toric
ripen	steep	vives	loofa	fudge	sedge	meths	avail	eosin	malic	ratio	torii
risen	steer	vixen	luffa	fuggy	sedgy	might	avoid	equip	mania	ravin	toxic
riser	sties	volet	niffy	fungi	serge	mocha	await	Ernie	manic	rebid	toxin
rived	stoep	vomer	puffy	gauge	siege	mothy	ayrie	ethic	maria	redia	trail
rivel	strep	voter	quaff	gorge	singe	mushy	azoic	eyrie	marid	redid	train
riven	strew	vowel	quiff	gouge	Singh	niche	baric	facia	matin	refit	trait
river	styes	wader	reify	grege	soggy	night	basic	fagin	mavis	regie	tulip
rivet	suber	wafer	scifi	gunge	sorgo	nucha	basil	fakir	maxim	rejig	tumid
rodeo	super	wager	scoff	haugh	sough	ortho	basin	fetid	media	relic	tunic
roger	sweep	wages	scuff	hedge	stage	ought	basis	finis	medic	relit	twain
roker	sweet	waken	shaft	heigh	stagy	ouphe	batik	flail	melic	remit	typic
Romeo	sycee	waker	shift	henge	stogy	pacha	bedim	flair	meril	resin	Ugric
roper	syren	wakes	skiff	hinge	surge	pasha	befit	fluid	merit	resit	ulmin
ropey	tabes	waler	snafu	hodge	swage	pashm	begin	folia	mesic	rigid	undid
roset	taken	waney	sniff	hough	taiga	pithy	belie	folio	metic	robin	unfit
rover	taker	wares	snuff	image	tango	prahu	bifid	frail	metif	rosin	unfix
rowel	tales	water	solfa	imago	tangy	pushy	blain	fruit	metis	rubin	unlit
rowen	tamer	waved	staff	jaggy	targe	raphe	bogie	fusil	mimic	runic	unpin
rower	taper	waver	stiff	jingo	thegn	rathe	boric	gamic	minim	sahib	unrig
ruler	tater	wavey	stuff	judge	thigh	right	braid	gamin	motif	salic	unrip
rumen	tawer	waxen	sulfa	kedge	tinge	rishi	brail	gelid	movie	sapid	untie
rupee	taxer	waxer	surfy	laigh	tonga	ruche	brain	genic	mucic	sasin	until
saker	tehee	weber	swift	large	tongs	rushy	broil	genie	mucin	satin	unzip
salep	telex	wheel	taffy	largo	tough	sadhu	bruin	genii	mudir	savin	valid
sales	tenet	wheen	theft	laugh	tragi	sight	bruit	geoid	mujik	scrim	vapid

varix jocko abele duple manly skulk world halma aging doing lawny scone
vatic junky acold dwale maple skull would hammy agone donna leant segno
Vedic khaki addle dwell marly slily wryly Hbomb agony downa liana seine
venin kinky adult dwelt matlo slyly yauld herma akene downy liane senna
vigil kooky agile eagle mealy small yield horme aline drank liang shank
virid lanky ahold early merle smalt Abomb jammy alone drink linny shant
visit larky ahull exalt mille smell agami jemmy along drone llano shend
vivid lawks aioli exile molly smelt anima karma amend drunk loony shent
vogie leaky aisle exult moola smile anomy lemma ament dunno lound shine
vomit links alula fable mould smolt aroma llama amine dunny lowne shiny
vraic looks amble falls moult snell atomy loamy amino dying lying shone
xenia lucky ample farle mulla socle balmy lumme among ebony mains shunt
xeric micky amply fatly myall spall barmy magma anent eland manna skene
yogic milky anele fault nelly spell beamy mamma arena emend maund skink
zooid mirky angle fella newly spelt biome mammy atone evens means skint
zoril mucky Anglo felly noble spile blame mneme atony event meant skunk
banjo murky anile ferly nobly spill blimp momma avens exine meany slang
ganja musky ankle field nulla spilt blimy mummy banns eying meiny slant
hadji narky apple fille nyala stale brume myoma beano faint mesne sling
hajji necks apply filly obeli stalk champ neume being fanny moony slink
kopje nerka aptly fitly oddly stall chimb palmy benni fauna mound slung
pooja nooky atilt fjeld ovoli stela chime pigmy benny fawny mount slunk
shoji parka atoll folly ovolo stele chimp plumb bhang feint nanna sonny
thuja parky axile frill ovule stile chomp plume bland fenny nanny sound
alike pawky badly fugle pally still chump plump blank ferny ninny spang
awake peaky bally fully parle stilt chyme plumy blend fiend nonny spank
awoke perky baulk gable phyla stola clamp pommy blent finny noone spend
balky pesky belle gaily phyle stole climb prima blind flank obang spent
barky picky belly Galla poilu stull clime prime blink fling ohone spine
bloke pinko bible gally pools style clump primo blond flint opine spiny
bosky pinky bield gault poult styli comma primp blunt flong ovine spunk
brake pocky billy gelly prole stylo coomb pygmy bonne flung owing stand
braky polka bogle ghyll psalm sully cramp reams bonny flunk ozone stane
broke porky boule girly qualm surly creme rhomb borne found paint stang
bucko pucka boult godly quell swale crime rhumb bound fount panne stank
bulky pukka bowls golly quill swell crimp rhyme brand franc penna steno
bunko quake brill grill quilt swill crumb roomy brank frank penny sting
burka quaky brule Guelf rally tabla crump rummy brant frena peony stink
burke reeky bugle guild rawly table derma salmi brent frond phene stint
cheka risky build guile realm tails disme scamp brine frons phone stone
choke rocks built guilt redly tally dogma schmo bring front phono stonk
choky rocky bulla gully reply telly dormy seamy brink funny phony stony
cloke rooky bully haily rifle tesla douma shame briny gaunt piano stung
cocky sarky burly hallo rille thill drama sigma bronc giant pinna stunk
conky shake cable haply roble thole drome skimp brunt ginny pinny stunt
cooky shako calla haulm roily tholi dummy slime bunny gland plane suint
corky shaky cauli hello rolls title duomo slimy burnt glint plank Sunna
crake silks caulk hillo ruble toile elemi slump bwana going plant Sunni
darky silky cello hilly rumly toils enema spume byend gonna plonk sunny
dekko slake chalk holla sable trill enemy spumy canna grand plunk swank
dicky smoke chela hollo sadly troll etyma stamp canny grant poind swine
dinky smoko child holly sally trull fermi stime carny grind point swing
drake smoky chile hotly sault truly filmy stoma chant grunt porno swink
ducks snake chili hullo scald tulle flame stomp china guana pound swung
ducky snaky chill hurly scale twill flamy stump chine guano prang taint
dumka spake choli icily scall uncle flimp summa chink gunny prank taunt
dumky spike chyle idola scalp utile flume swami chunk haunt prink tawny
dusky spiky coble idyll scaly uvula flump swamp clang henna print teens
ensky spoke colly imply scold vails foamy tammy clank hinny prone teeny
evoke stake cooly ingle scull vault forme terms cline horny prong teind
flake stoke could inkle sculp vealy frame thema cling hound prune tenne
flaky sulky coyly istle seely villa frump theme clink hyena prunt terne
fluke tacky cully ixtle sells villi gamma thumb clone hying quant thane
fluky tanka curly jelly shale viola gammy thump clonk icing quins thank
funky tonka cycle jolly shall voile gaumy thyme clung inane quint thine
gawky trike cyclo joule shalt walla gemma thymy clunk irony rainy thing
gecko Turki daily knell shaly wally gemmy tommy corno Jaina reins think
grike tusky dally knelt shelf wanly germy tramp cornu jaunt rhine thong
haiku vodka dealt knoll shell weald gimme tromp corny jeans rhino tinny
hanky wacke dhole koala shill wells gismo trump count jenny riant tonne
hokku wacky dilly krill shily wetly glume tummy crane jinni round towny
honky wonky dimly kwela shyly whale gnome ulema crank joint runny trend
hooky works doily ladle sidle whelk grama worms crone kerne saint trine
hunks yolky dolly laxly sigla whelm grime wormy cronk kiang sauna trona
hunky yonks drill lisle silly whelp grimy yummy crony koine scant trone
husky yucky drily lolly skald while grume acini daunt krans scena trunk
jacks yukky droll lowly skelm whole grump adunc Diana krona scend tunny
jerky zinky dryly macle skelp wield guimp agene diene krone scene twang
jinks zooks dully madly skill willy gummy agent djinn kyang scent twine

twink	carom	lysol	spoor	duppy	sylph	cobra	learn	shore	weird	crest	horst
twiny	chaos	Macon	stood	elope	taupe	copra	leery	shorn	wharf	crisp	horsy
tying	cloot	major	stook	erupt	tempi	court	liard	short	where	cross	house
upend	Cobol	manor	stool	gappy	tempo	cowry	libra	skirl	whirl	cruse	hurst
urine	cocoa	mason	stoop	gilpy	tempt	crore	litre	skirr	whirr	crush	hussy
vaunt	codon	mayor	strop	glyph	tippy	curry	livre	skirt	whore	crust	Irish
veena	cohoe	McCoy	strow	goopy	traps	Cymry	lorry	slurp	whorl	cuish	Jesse
veiny	colon	Medoc	stroy	grape	tripe	dairy	loury	smarm	worry	curse	joist
viand	crook	melon	sudor	graph	trope	deary	lucre	smart	yearn	curst	joust
vying	croon	meson	sutor	grapy	turps	decry	lyart	smirk	years	daisy	karst
weeny	dagos	miaow	swoon	gripe	unapt	diary	macro	snare	yours	deism	kiosk
whang	decor	midon	swoop	grope	weepy	dowry	Maori	snark	zebra	deist	knish
whine	decoy	minor	synod	gulph	wispy	durra	marry	snarl	abase	dense	kvass
whiny	demob	moron	taboo	guppy	wrapt	dwarf	merry	snore	abash	didst	lapse
wound	demon	motor	tabor	happy	yippy	eagre	metre	snort	abask	doest	lasso
wring	demos	nabob	talon	harpy	zippy	emery	metro	sorra	abuse	douse	lease
wrong	depot	ninon	tarok	hippo	Iraqi	entry	micro	sorry	abysm	dowse	leash
wrung	dicot	niton	tarot	hippy	abort	enure	mitre	spare	abyss	dress	least
yawny	divot	nohow	tatou	humph	acari	evert	moire	spark	adust	dross	loess
young	dodos	nylon	taxon	humpy	acerb	every	morra	sperm	agist	druse	loose
abbot	donor	odeon	tenon	inapt	acorn	exert	mourn	spire	amass	dulse	louse
abhor	drool	onion	tenor	inept	adore	extra	mucro	spirt	Amish	durst	lousy
ablow	droop	orlop	throb	jaspe	adorn	exurb	murra	spiry	amiss	egest	manse
acton	elbow	oxbow	throe	jumpy	afire	faery	murre	spore	amuse	erase	marsh
actor	embow	paeon	throw	kalpa	afore	fairy	myrrh	sport	angst	erose	massa
adios	endow	parol	tigon	kappa	aggro	fayre	nacre	spurn	anise	exist	masse
afoot	enjoy	pekoe	topoi	kelpy	agora	ferry	Negro	spurt	apish	false	massy
aglow	enrol	pheon	topos	kempt	alarm	fibre	nitre	stare	arise	fatso	mayst
Algol	envoi	phlox	trior	leapt	alary	fiery	nitro	stark	arose	feast	mense
allot	envoy	picot	troop	lippy	alert	fiord	ochre	start	avast	fesse	messy
allow	ephod	pidog	tryon	loopy	ambry	firry	ochry	stere	awash	first	midst
alloy	ephor	pilot	Tudor	loppy	amort	fjord	ombre	stern	balsa	flash	missy
aloof	ergot	pinon	tutor	loupe	antra	flare	opera	stirk	bassi	flask	moist
ambos	error	piton	ungot	lumpy	antre	flirt	otary	stirp	basso	flesh	moksa
ancon	escot	pivot	union	lymph	apart	flora	outre	store	beast	floss	moose
anion	estoc	prior	venom	morph	apery	flory	ovary	stork	bitsy	flush	morse
annoy	estop	proof	visor	mumps	aport	frore	overs	storm	blase	foist	mossy
apron	ethos	puton	vizor	myope	appro	furry	overt	story	blast	fossa	mouse
arbor	extol	pylon	wagon	nappe	avert	genre	padre	sturt	bless	fosse	mousy
argol	fagot	radon	wahoo	nappy	award	genro	parry	sucre	blest	fresh	mussy
argon	felon	razor	whoop	nippy	aware	glare	pearl	Sudra	bliss	frisk	newsy
argot	fetor	redox	widow	nymph	azure	glary	peart	supra	blush	frost	noise
arrow	flood	repot	xenon	okapi	bairn	glory	perry	surra	boast	fubsy	noisy
arson	floor	rigor	xylol	oomph	barre	gnarl	petri	sutra	boost	fussy	noose
ascot	fluor	robot	yahoo	palpi	beard	gnarr	poort	sward	bossy	gassy	Norse
axiom	furor	rotor	yapok	pampa	beery	gourd	psora	sware	bouse	gauss	nurse
baboo	galop	sabot	adapt	pappy	berry	guard	quark	swarf	bousy	gawsy	obese
bacon	gemot	salon	adept	peppy	blare	gurry	quart	swarm	bowse	geese	omasa
baron	genoa	sapor	adopt	poppy	blurb	hairy	quern	swart	brash	geist	paisa
bason	gigot	saros	agape	pulpy	blurt	harry	query	swirl	brass	gesso	palsy
baton	giron	savoy	aleph	puppy	board	heard	quire	sword	brisk	ghast	pansy
bayou	gloom	Saxon	bumph	quipu	boart	heart	quirk	swore	brose	ghost	parse
bebop	groom	scion	bumpy	raspy	bourg	henry	quirt	sworn	brush	gipsy	Parsi
befog	guyot	scoop	calpa	roupy	bourn	hoard	rearm	tarre	buist	glass	passe
begot	gyron	scoot	campy	rumpy	burro	hoary	repro	tarry	bursa	gloss	patsy
below	halos	scrod	carpi	sappy	burry	houri	retry	teary	burse	gnash	pause
besom	havoc	sekos	chape	scape	cadre	hurry	sabra	terra	burst	goest	pease
besot	helot	senor	chaps	scopa	caird	hydra	sabre	terry	canst	goose	perse
beton	heron	sepoy	chops	scope	cairn	hydro	sacra	tetra	cause	gorse	phase
bigot	Hykos	serow	clepe	seepy	carry	inarm	saury	there	cease	gorsy	plash
bijou	hyson	seton	coapt	shape	ceorl	indri	scare	therm	cense	grasp	plasm
bipod	ichor	Sheol	compo	slept	chard	inert	scarf	third	chase	grass	plush
bison	idiom	shook	compt	slips	chare	infra	scarp	thirl	chasm	grise	poesy
blood	idiot	shoon	coopt	slope	charm	intro	scart	thorn	chess	grist	poise
bloom	igloo	shoot	corps	slops	charr	inure	scary	thorp	chest	gross	popsy
boron	ingot	sloop	coupe	slype	chart	inurn	score	tiara	chose	guess	posse
bosom	jabot	sloot	coypu	snipe	chary	ivory	scorn	titre	chuse	guest	prase
boson	juror	snood	crape	snips	chert	izard	scurf	twere	cissy	guise	press
brood	kabob	snook	craps	soapy	chirk	Jerry	serra	twerp	clash	gutsy	prest
brook	kapok	snoop	crepe	soppy	chirp	Jewry	serry	twirl	clasp	gypsy	prise
broom	karoo	snoot	crept	soupy	chirr	kauri	shard	twirp	class	hadst	prism
buxom	kazoo	Sodom	crypt	staph	chord	kerry	share	ultra	close	Hanse	prose
cabob	kebob	solon	cuppa	steps	chore	knurl	shark	umbra	coast	harsh	prosy
caboc	kloof	sopor	dippy	stipe	churl	knurr	sharp	unarm	copse	Hausa	pulse
canoe	kotow	spoof	drape	stope	churn	kukri	sherd	usurp	copsy	hawse	purse
canon	kudos	spook	drops	stupa	churr	labra	shire	usury	corse	heist	pursy
capon	kyloe	spool	drupe	stupe	cirri	laird	shirk	uteri	crash	hoise	pussy
carob	lemon	spoom	dumps	swept	clary	lairy	shirr	veery	crass	hoist	quash
carol	Logos	spoon	dumpy	swipe	clerk	laura	shirt	weary	cress	horse	quasi

quest	agate	footy	pants	sputa	choux	mopus	undue	silva	vinyl	bunia	huzza
raise	alate	forte	panty	state	cloud	mucus	ungum	skive	Xrays	bunya	hydra
rasse	Amati	forth	parti	suety	clout	negus	vacua	slave	abuzz	burka	hyena
reest	amity	forty	party	suite	cogue	nexus	vague	solve	adoze	bursa	hypha
reuse	aorta	frith	pasta	swath	croup	nidus	vagus	stave	agaze	bwana	idola
rinse	aunty	fritz	paste	swith	datum	nisus	value	stove	amaze	Caaba	infra
roast	azote	froth	pasty	tarty	debug	nodus	varus	suave	baize	caeca	Jaina
roost	azoth	fusty	patty	taste	debut	notum	velum	sylva	blaze	calla	jibba
rouse	Bantu	fytte	peaty	tasty	degum	oakum	venue	trove	bonze	calpa	junta
roust	baste	garth	pelta	tatty	demur	occur	Venus	valve	booze	canna	Kaaba
salse	batty	gents	petty	teeth	donut	odeum	virus	varve	boozy	cheka	kalpa
sassy	berth	geste	photo	tenth	durum	odium	vogue	verve	braze	chela	kappa
sayso	biota	girth	pieta	tenty	embus	odour	vrouw	volva	brize	china	karma
sayst	birth	goaty	piety	testa	endue	oleum	whaup	waive	chizz	cilia	koala
seise	bitts	goeth	pinta	testy	ennui	oneup	woful	weave	colza	circa	krona
seism	bitty	goety	pinto	theta	ensue	opium	above	adown	craze	cnida	kwela
sensa	blate	gotta	piste	tilth	favus	picul	agave	blown	crazy	cobia	labia
sense	blitz	gouty	pitta	tinty	femur	pilus	alive	blowy	diazo	cobra	labra
shush	booth	grate	plate	tooth	fetus	pinup	bivvy	brawl	dizzy	cocoa	larva
sissy	boots	grith	Pluto	torte	flour	pious	brava	brawn	Druze	colza	laura
slash	booty	grits	Porte	trite	flout	pipul	brave	brown	feeze	comma	lemma
slosh	broth	gusto	potto	troth	focus	pique	bravi	chewy	fizzy	conga	lepta
slush	brute	gusty	potty	truth	forum	proud	bravo	clown	frizz	copra	liana
smash	bunty	gutta	pouty	tufty	fraud	pseud	breve	crawl	froze	costa	libra
snash	busty	gutty	prate	tutti	fryup	queue	calve	crowd	furze	cotta	llama
sonsy	butte	haste	punty	tutty	fucus	ramus	carve	crown	furzy	cuppa	logia
souse	butty	hasty	putti	twite	fugue	rebus	chevy	drawl	fuzzy	curia	longa
spasm	cacti	heath	putto	umpty	gamut	rebut	chive	drawn	gauze	dacha	loofa
stash	canto	hefty	putty	unite	genus	recur	chivy	drown	gauzy	dagga	luffa
sudsy	canty	hertz	quite	unity	getup	rerun	civvy	flews	Ghazi	delta	lytta
swash	caste	hoots	quits	urate	ghaut	revue	clave	flown	glaze	derma	Mafia
swish	catty	hosta	quota	vasty	ghoul	rheum	clove	frown	glazy	Diana	magma
Swiss	cento	irate	quote	vertu	gigue	rogue	crave	gnawn	gloze	dicta	mamba
tansy	cesti	jetty	quoth	vesta	glaur	rubus	curve	growl	graze	dogma	mamma
tarsi	chute	jolty	ratty	virtu	glout	runup	curvy	grown	huzza	donga	mania
tasse	cloth	junta	reata	vista	group	scaup	delve	known	huzzy	donna	manna
tawse	coati	junto	recto	vitta	grout	scaur	divvy	prawn	jazzy	douma	manta
tease	conte	kitty	rente	volta	gyrus	scour	drive	prowl	kudzu	downa	maria
tense	costa	laity	riata	volte	hilum	scout	drove	schwa	maize	drama	massa
terse	cotta	lefty	rooty	volti	hocus	scrub	glove	scowl	matzo	dulia	mecca
these	couth	lento	rorty	waits	hohum	scrum	grave	shawl	mezzo	dumka	media
those	crate	Lents	route	waltz	hokum	sebum	gravy	shawm	muzzy	durra	mocha
tipsy	crwth	lepta	routh	warty	humus	sedum	grove	shewn	piezo	enema	moksa
toast	cutty	lists	runty	waste	ictus	segue	guava	shown	pizza	entia	momma
torse	darts	loath	rusty	white	ileum	serum	halva	showy	plaza	erica	moola
torsk	death	lofty	rutty	whity	ileus	setup	halve	snowy	prize	etyma	morra
torso	deity	lotto	saith	width	ilium	shout	heave	spawn	ritzy	extra	mulga
touse	delta	lusty	Sakta	witty	imaum	shrub	heavy	thawy	seize	facia	mulla
tousy	depth	lytta	salts	worth	imbue	shrug	helve	thews	smaze	facta	murra
trash	dhoti	malty	salty	wrath	incur	sinus	knave	thewy	swizz	fauna	myoma
trass	dicta	manta	saute	write	incus	Sioux	larva	trawl	tazza	fella	nanna
tress	dirty	manto	scatt	wrote	indue	snout	leave	trews	tizzy	flora	nerka
trist	ditto	matte	Scots	wroth	injun	solum	mauve	viewy	whizz	flota	noria
truss	ditty	meaty	scuta	xysti	input	solus	naevi	ataxy	winze	folia	nucha
trust	doeth	mesto	scute	youth	issue	sorus	naive	braxy	woozy	fossa	nulla
tryst	dorts	minty	septa	zesty	jokul	spout	navvy	epoxy	zanze	fovea	nyala
tuism	dorty	mirth	setto	zloty	jorum	sprue	neive	flaxy	———	frena	oidia
twist	dotty	misty	sexto	about	kaput	stoup	nerve	prexy	abaca	galea	omasa
ukase	dusty	molto	silty	album	knout	stour	nervy	proxy	abaya	Galla	omega
valse	earth	monte	sixte	aloud	kraut	stout	nieve	twixt	adyta	gamba	opera
verse	elate	month	sixth	amour	larum	strum	ogive	abaya	agora	gamma	Oriya
verso	elite	motte	sixty	annul	layup	strut	olive	alkyd	aloha	ganja	ossia
verst	elute	motto	skate	appui	lemur	sunup	peeve	alkyl	alpha	gemma	ostia
waist	emote	mouth	skite	appuy	letup	syrup	privy	allyl	alula	genoa	pacha
welsh	empty	mufti	slate	argue	lobus	taluk	Provo	beryl	amnia	gonna	paisa
whish	enate	multi	slaty	Argus	locum	talus	reave	bunya	anima	gotta	palea
whisk	evite	musth	sloth	ascus	locus	taxus	reeve	butyl	antra	Gouda	pampa
whist	facta	musty	smite	augur	lotus	thrum	reive	calyx	aorta	grama	panda
whose	faith	nasty	smith	awful	lupus	tieup	salve	ethyl	areca	guana	panga
whoso	Fanti	natty	smote	babul	magus	tipup	salvo	Oriya	arena	guava	parka
worse	fatty	neath	snath	beaus	manul	togue	savvy	oxeye	aroma	gutta	pasha
worst	fifth	netty	softa	beaut	manus	tonus	selva	playa	atria	halma	pasta
wrest	fifty	nifty	softy	beaux	miaul	toque	serve	polyp	bacca	halva	pelta
wrist	filth	ninth	sooth	begum	minus	torus	servo	satyr	balsa	Hausa	penna
Xhosa	firth	north	sooty	begun	mixup	trout	shave	sibyl	belga	henna	phyla
yeast	flota	nutty	south	bogus	modus	tucum	sheva	sloyd	biota	herma	pieta
abate	flute	orate	spate	bolus	mogul	tuque	Shiva	stays	bohea	holla	pilea
acute	fluty	ovate	spite	bonus	mohur	uncus	shove	swayl	brava	hosta	pinna
adyta	foots	panto	spitz	bosun	mopup	uncut	sieve	thuya	bulla	hutia	pinta

pitta umbra Doric award grand sided akene bribe cutie fluke house monte
pizza uvula Eddic awned greed skald alate bride cycle flume image moose
playa vacua Eolic bated grind sloid algae brine dance flute imbue morse
plaza Vedda estoc beard guard sloyd alike brize deice force imide motte
plica veena ethic bedad guild snood aline broke delve forge inane mouse
podia vesta franc begad heard solid alive brose dense forme indue movie
polka villa gamic bield hexad sound alone brule deuce forte ingle murre
pooja vinca genic bifid hoard speed amaze brume dhole fosse inkle myope
prima viola havoc biped hound spend amble brute diene frame inure nacre
psora virga humic bipod humid squad amice budge diode frore irade naive
pucka vista hylic bland hyoid squid amide bugle dirge froze irate nappe
pukka vitta ileac bleed idead staid amine bulge disme fudge issue neive
quota vodka iliac blend Iliad stand ample burke dixie fugle istle nerve
reata volta Indic blind imbed stead amuse burse dodge fugue ixtle neume
redia volva iodic blond ivied steed anele butte dogie furze jaspe niche
riata walla ionic blood izard stood angle cable dolce fusee Jesse niece
rumba wonga Kufic board jaded strad anile cache donee fytte joule nieve
sabra xenia lilac boned jehad sward anise cadge douce gable judge nitre
sacra Xhosa logic booed jihad sword ankle cadre douse gaffe juice nixie
saiga yerba lyric bound keyed synod anode calve dowse gauge kedge noble
Sakta yucca magic bowed knead teind antae canoe drake gauze kerne noise
samba zebra malic braid kneed tepid antre carve drape geese knave nonce
sauna zonda manic brand laded third apace caste drive genie knife noone
scena Abomb medic bread laird thrid apode cause drome genre koine noose
schwa acerb Medoc breed lated timid apple cease drone geode kopje Norse
scopa adlib melic broad liard tined argue cense drove geste krone novae
scuba blurb mesic brood lipid tread arise chafe drupe gigue kyloe nudge
scuta cabob metic build livid trend arose chape druse gimme kyrie nurse
selva Carib mimic bused lobed triad aside chare Druze glace ladle obese
senna carob mucic byend lound tried atone chase dulse glade lance ochre
sensa chimb music caird lucid tumid aurae chide dunce glare lapse ogive
sepia climb ohmic calid lurid tweed awake chile duple glaze large ohone
septa coomb oleic chard maned unbed aware chime dwale glebe lathe oldie
serra crumb optic child marid undid awoke chine eagle glede lease olive
sheva cubeb panic chord maund upend axile chive eagre glide leave ombre
Shiva demob pubic cloud mixed upped ayrie choke educe globe ledge opine
sigla exurb Punic could monad valid azote chore eerie glove lethe orate
sigma Hbomb rabic cowed moped vaned azure chose elate gloze levee Osage
silva kabob rebec creed mould vapid badge chuse elide glume liane ounce
softa kebab relic crowd mound viand baize chute elite gnome liege ouphe
solfa kebob runic Cupid muted virid barbe chyle eloge goose lisle outre
sorra nabob salic cycad myoid vivid barge chyme elope gorge lithe ovate
spica nawab serac dated naiad waved barre clave elude gorse litre ovine
sputa plumb Seric domed naked weald baste clepe elute gouge livre ovule
stela rhomb sodic dowed nitid weird bathe clime emcee grace lodge oxeye
stola rhumb sonic dread nomad wield beige cline emote grade longe oxide
stoma sahib stoic dried noted world belie cloke enate grape loose ozone
stria scrub Sufic druid oared would belle clone endue grate loupe padre
stupa shrub sumac dryad oiled wound bible close ensue grave louse panne
Sudra slubb telic eared orbed yauld bilge clove enure graze lowne parge
sulfa squab tonic edged oread yield binge coble epode grebe lucre parle
summa squib topic eland ovoid zooid biome cogue erase grege lumme parse
Sunna throb toric embed pavid abase blade cohoe Ernie gride lunge passe
supra thumb toxic emend plaid abate blame comae erode grike lycee paste
surra adunc tunic ended plead abele blare combe erose grime lythe pause
sutra Afric typic ephod poind abide blase conge etude gripe macle payee
sylva antic Ugric faced pound abode blate conte etwee grise madge peace
tabla Anzac varec famed proud above blaze cooee evade grope maize pease
tafia asdic vatic farad pseud abuse bloke copse evite grove mange peeve
taiga aspic Vedic fated rabid ackee blude corse evoke grume manse pekoe
tanka attic vraic fetid rapid acute boche coude exile guide maple pence
tazza aulic xebec field rayed adage bodge coupe exine guile marge perse
terra auric xeric fiend rebid addle bogie coxae exode guise masse phage
tesla azoic yogic fiord redid adobe bogle crake exude gunge matte phase
testa Aztec zebec fixed rigid adore bombe crane eyrie halve mauve phene
tetra baric acold fjeld rived adoze bonce crape fable Hanse maybe phone
theca basic acred fjord round aerie bonne crate false haste melee phyle
thema boric acrid flied salad afire bonze crave farce hawse mense piece
theta bronc agued flood sapid afore booze craze farle heave merge pique
thuja caboc ahead fluid sated agape borne creme fayre hedge merle piste
thuya civic ahold found scald agate boule crepe feeze helve mesne pixie
tiara colic algid fraud scend agave bouse crime fence hence metre place
tibia comic alkyd frond scold agaze bowse crone fesse henge midge plage
tinea conic aloud gelid scrod agene brace crore fibre hinge mille plane
tonga cubic amend geoid sexed agile brake crude fiche hodge mince plate
tonka Cufic aphid gland shard agone brave cruse fille hoise mitre plume
trona cusec armed gleed shend agree braze curie flake horde mneme podge
ulema cynic aroid gonad sherd ainee brede curse flame horme moire poise
ultra daric avoid gourd shred aisle breve curve flare horse monde ponce

Porte semee stoke twere quiff aleph goeth rajah Bahai terai frisk thick
posse sense stole twice scarf Allah graph ranch bassi tholi frock think
prase serge stone twine scoff Amish grith ratch benni tondi gleek torsk
prate serve stope twite scuff anigh gulch reach bravi tophi gopak track
price setae store ukase scurf apish gulph Reich buffi topoi Greek trick
pride shade stove ulnae serif arrah harsh retch cacti torii haick truck
prime shake stupe uncle sheaf awash hatch roach carpi tragi hoick trunk
prise shale style undue shelf azoth haugh rotch cauli Turki kapok tweak
prize shame suave unite skiff batch heath rough cesti tutti kayak twink
probe shape sucre untie sniff beach heigh routh chili uraei kiosk umiak
prole share suede urate snuff beech hitch saith choli uteri knack Uzbek
prone shave suite urine spoof belch hooch sauch cirri villi knock whack
prose shine surge usage staff bench hotch saugh coati volti kopek whelk
prude shire swage utile stiff berth hough selah cocci xysti kulak whisk
prune shone swale vague stuff birch humph Shiah corgi zombi mujik wrack
pudge shore sware valse swarf birth hunch shush dhobi aback plank wreak
pulse shove swede value thief bitch hutch Singh dhoti abask plonk wreck
pupae sidle swine valve wharf blush Irish sixth elemi acock pluck wrick
puree siege swipe varve whiff booth Jonah slash ennui alack plunk yapok
purge sieve swore venae aging botch ketch slosh envoi amuck prank aboil
purse since sycee venge along bough knish sloth Fanti apeak prick ahull
pyxie singe table venue among brach laigh slush farci batik prink algal
quake sixte tache verge befog brash larch smash fermi baulk quack Algol
queue skate targe verse being broch latch smith fundi black quark alkyl
quire skene tarre verve bhang broth laugh snash fungi blank quick allyl
quite skite tasse vogie bourg brush leach snath genii bleak quirk angel
quote skive taste vogue bring bumph leash sooth Ghazi blink shack annal
raise slake taupe voice clang bunch leech sough hadji block shank annul
ramie slate tawie voile cling burgh loach south hajji brank shark anvil
ranee slave tawse volte clung butch loath staph Hindi break sheik appal
range slice tease vouge debag catch lotah stash houri brick shirk April
raphe slide tehee wacke debug cinch lough stich iambi brink shock areal
rasse slime tenne waive doing clash lunch surah indri brisk shook argil
rathe slope tense waste dying cloth lurch swash Iraqi brock shuck argol
razee slype tepee weave eying coach lymph swath issei brook skink ariel
reave smaze terce wedge fling conch lynch swish jinni caulk skulk artel
recce smile terne whale flong couch marah swith kauri chalk skunk arval
reeve smite terse where flung cough march sylph khadi check slack atoll
regie smoke thane while going couth marsh synch khaki cheek sleek aural
reive smote theme whine hying crash match teach kukri chick slick avail
rente snake there white icing crush milch teeth lathi chink slink awful
reuse snare these whole kiang crwth mirth tench lungi chirk slunk axial
revue snide thine whore kyang cuish month tenth Mahdi chock smack babel
rhine snipe thole whose liang culch mooch thigh Maori chuck smirk babul
rhyme snore those wince lying curch morph tilth mufti chunk smock bagel
ridge socle three winge obang cutch mouth tooth multi clack snack banal
rifle solve throe winze owing Czech mulch Torah naevi clank snark basal
rille sonde thyme withe pidog death munch torch nimbi cleek sneak basil
rinse souse tilde wodge prang depth musth touch nisei clerk sneck bedel
roble space tinge worse prong ditch mutch tough obeli click snick beryl
rogue spade tithe write rejig doeth mynah trash okapi clink snoek betel
rouge spake title wrote scrag donah myrrh troth oribi cloak snook bevel
rouse spare titre zanze shrug dough neath truth ovoli clock spank bezel
route spate togue aloof slang dutch neigh vetch palpi clonk spark botel
ruble spice toile bluff sling earth ninth Vlach pardi cluck speak bowel
ruche spike tonne brief slung ephah north vouch Parsi clunk speck brail
rupee spile topee calif spang epoch notch watch parti crack spick brawl
sable spine toque chaff sprag faith nymph weigh perai crank spook brill
sabre spire torse chief sprig faugh obeah welch petri creak spunk broil
salse spite torte chuff stang fetch oomph welsh pilei creek stack bubal
salve Spode touse cliff sting fifth orach wench putti crick stalk butyl
saree spoke trace draff stung filch parch which quasi croak stank cabal
sarge spore trade dwarf swing filth Pasch whish rabbi crock stark camel
sauce spree tribe feoff swung finch patch width radii cronk steak canal
saute sprue trice fluff thing firth peach winch rishi crook steek carol
scale spume trike grief thong fitch perch witch salmi cruck stick cavil
scape stage trine griff twang flash pilch worth Saudi dalek stink ceorl
scare stake tripe gruff tying flesh pinch wrath scifi drank stirk chiel
scene stale trite Guelf unpeg flush pitch wroth scudi drink stock chill
scone stane trode howff unrig forth plash youth serai drunk stonk churl
scope stare trone inoff Uzbeg fresh plush abaci shoji flack stook civil
score state trope kalif vying frith poach acari soldi flank stork Cobol
scree stave trove kenaf whang froth pooch acini spahi flask stuck comal
scute stele truce kloof wring galah porch agami styli fleck stunk copal
sedge stere tsade metif wrong garth pouch aioli sulci flick swank coral
segue stile tubae motif wrung gerah psych alibi Sunni flock swink coxal
seine stime tulle pilaf young girth punch Amati swami flunk taluk crawl
seise stipe tuque proof abash glyph quash appui tarsi frank tarok creel
seize stoae tutee quaff aitch gnash quoth assai tempi freak thank cruel

cupel	miaul	snail	bloom	strum	croon	Macon	scran	amino	macho	zambo	strep
decal	modal	snarl	bosom	swarm	crown	mason	sedan	Anglo	macro	zinco	strip
devil	model	snell	bream	therm	Cuban	matin	semen	appro	mambo	atrip	strop
dotal	mogul	sorel	broom	thrum	cumin	Mayan	serin	audio	mango	bebop	stump
dowel	molal	spall	buxom	totem	cutin	melon	seton	baboo	manto	bleep	sunup
drail	moral	speel	carom	tucum	daman	meson	seven	banco	matlo	blimp	swamp
drawl	morel	spell	charm	tuism	deign	midon	sewin	banjo	matzo	champ	sweep
drill	motel	spiel	chasm	unarm	demon	mixen	sheen	basso	mesto	cheap	swoop
droll	mural	spill	claim	ungum	dewan	mizen	shewn	beano	metro	cheep	syrup
drool	myall	spoil	cream	velum	divan	moron	shoon	bilbo	mezzo	chimp	thorp
ducal	nasal	spool	datum	venom	dizen	mourn	shorn	bimbo	micro	chirp	thump
dwell	natal	stall	degum	whelm	djinn	mucin	shown	bingo	misdo	chomp	tieup
easel	naval	steal	deism	xylem	doyen	ninon	siren	bongo	molto	chump	tipup
enrol	navel	steel	denim	acorn	dozen	niton	sitin	bravo	motto	clamp	tramp
equal	newel	still	dream	actin	drain	nomen	skean	bucko	mucro	clasp	tromp
ethyl	nival	stool	durum	acton	drawn	numen	skein	buffo	mungo	clump	troop
excel	nodal	stull	fleam	adman	drown	nylon	slain	bumbo	Negro	cramp	trump
expel	nopal	sural	forum	adorn	eaten	oaken	solan	bunco	nitro	creep	tulip
extol	novel	swayl	gleam	adown	elfin	oaten	solen	bunko	ortho	crimp	twerp
fatal	Nowel	sweal	gloom	again	eloin	ocean	solon	burro	outdo	crisp	twirp
feral	octal	swell	golem	algin	elvan	odeon	spawn	cacao	outgo	croup	uncap
fetal	offal	swill	goyim	alien	eosin	often	spean	cameo	ovolo	crump	unrip
final	oriel	swirl	groom	align	fagin	olden	spoon	canto	panto	droop	unzip
flail	ousel	sybil	hakim	allin	feign	olein	spurn	cargo	patio	equip	usurp
focal	ouzel	Tamil	haram	amain	felon	onion	stain	cello	phono	estop	whaup
frail	panel	thill	harem	amban	flown	organ	stein	cento	photo	flimp	whelp
frill	papal	thirl	haulm	ancon	foehn	orpin	stern	chiao	piano	flump	whoop
fugal	parol	tical	hilum	anion	frown	Oscan	swain	cisco	piezo	frump	abhor
fural	pearl	tidal	hohum	apian	furan	paean	swoon	combo	pinko	fryup	actor
fusil	pedal	tonal	hokum	apron	gamin	paeon	sworn	compo	pinto	galop	adder
gavel	penal	total	idiom	argon	giron	pagan	syren	corno	Pluto	getup	after
ghoul	peril	towel	ihram	Arian	given	paten	taken	credo	polio	graip	aider
ghyll	petal	trail	ileum	arson	glean	pavan	takin	curio	pongo	grasp	airer
glial	phial	trawl	ilium	Aryan	gnawn	pecan	talon	cyclo	porno	group	alder
gnarl	picul	trial	imaum	ashen	gowan	pekan	taxon	dekko	potto	grump	altar
goral	pipal	trill	inarm	Asian	grain	pheon	tenon	diazo	primo	guimp	alter
graal	pipul	troll	Islam	aspen	green	pinon	thegn	dingo	Provo	jalap	amber
grail	prowl	trull	jorum	atman	groan	piton	thorn	disco	putto	julep	ameer
grill	pupal	tubal	larum	auxin	groin	plain	tiein	ditto	radio	layup	amour
growl	pupil	twill	locum	avian	grown	powan	tigon	doggo	ratio	letup	anger
gruel	quail	twirl	madam	bacon	gyron	prawn	titan	Draco	recto	mixup	anker
gyral	quell	typal	maxim	bairn	haven	preen	token	dunno	repro	mopup	arbor
hadal	quill	umbel	minim	baron	heman	purin	toman	duomo	rhino	oneup	asker
halal	ramal	until	nizam	basan	heron	puton	toxin	fatso	rodeo	orlop	aster
hamal	ratel	ureal	notum	basin	hogan	pylon	train	folio	Romeo	oxlip	astir
hazel	ravel	urial	oakum	bason	hosen	quean	treen	fordo	rondo	pinup	attar
horal	rebel	usual	odeum	baton	human	queen	tryon	forgo	salvo	plump	auger
hotel	refel	uveal	odium	began	hyson	quern	twain	gecko	sambo	polyp	augur
hovel	regal	vagal	ogham	begin	injun	quoin	tween	genro	sayso	primp	baker
ideal	renal	vasal	oleum	begun	inurn	Quran	uhlan	gesso	schmo	recap	baler
idyll	repel	venal	opium	beton	japan	radon	ulmin	gismo	scudo	runup	biker
ileal	revel	vigil	pashm	bison	kinin	ratan	union	guano	secco	salep	biter
ilial	rival	vinal	plasm	blain	known	raven	unman	gumbo	segno	scalp	blear
impel	rivel	vinyl	praam	blown	Koran	ravin	unpin	gusto	servo	scamp	boner
jewel	rowel	viral	prism	boron	kulan	redan	urban	hallo	setto	scarp	borer
jokul	royal	vital	proem	boson	kylin	reign	varan	hello	sexto	scaup	bower
jural	rural	vocal	psalm	bosun	laden	reman	vegan	hillo	shako	scoop	boxer
kneel	samel	vowel	Purim	bourn	Ladin	reran	venin	hippo	smoko	scrap	boyar
knell	scall	wheal	qualm	brain	lagan	rerun	vixen	hollo	soldo	scrip	breer
knoll	scowl	wheel	realm	brawn	laten	resin	wagon	hullo	sorgo	sculp	briar
knurl	scull	whirl	rearm	brown	Latin	ripen	waken	hydro	spado	setup	brier
kraal	sepal	whorl	rheum	bruin	learn	risen	waxen	igloo	steno	sharp	buyer
krill	seral	woful	scram	buran	leman	riven	wheen	imago	stylo	sheep	caber
label	shall	xylol	scrim	burin	lemon	robin	widen	intro	taboo	skelp	caper
lapel	shawl	yodel	scrum	cabin	levin	roman	wigan	jingo	tango	skimp	carer
legal	shell	yokel	sebum	cairn	liein	rosin	witan	jocko	tempo	sleep	cater
level	Sheol	zonal	sedum	canon	ligan	rowan	wizen	jumbo	tondo	sloop	caver
libel	shiel	zoril	seism	capon	liken	rowen	woken	junto	torso	slump	cedar
local	shill	zygal	serum	chain	limen	rubin	woman	karoo	turbo	slurp	chair
loral	shoal	abeam	shawm	churn	linen	rumen	women	kazoo	uredo	sneap	charr
lorel	sibyl	abrim	skelm	clean	linin	salon	woven	kendo	verso	snoop	cheer
losel	sigil	abysm	smarm	clown	liven	sapan	xenon	largo	video	stamp	chirr
loyal	sisal	alarm	Sodom	codon	loden	sasin	yamen	lasso	vireo	steep	choir
lysol	skill	album	solum	coign	logan	Satan	yearn	lento	Virgo	stirp	churr
manul	skirl	aswim	spasm	colin	loran	satin	yulan	limbo	wahoo	stoep	cider
medal	skoal	axiom	sperm	colon	Lucan	savin	aggro	lingo	whoso	stomp	cigar
meril	skull	bedim	spoom	coven	lumen	Saxon	agogo	litho	wilco	stoop	clear
mesel	small	begum	steam	covin	lupin	scion	amido	llano	yahoo	stoup	coder
metal	smell	besom	storm	cozen	lysin	scorn	amigo	lotto	yobbo	strap	comer

coper	hater	offer	sneer	aegis	frons	needs	vails	blunt	egret	hurst	quirt
corer	haver	ogler	sober	alias	fucus	negus	varus	blurt	eight	idiot	quoit
cover	hazer	oiler	solar	amass	funds	nexus	Venus	boart	eject	immit	react
cower	hewer	oncer	sonar	ambos	games	nidus	vibes	boast	elect	inapt	rebut
crier	hiker	order	sopor	amiss	gauss	nisus	vires	boost	emmet	inept	reest
cryer	hilar	ormer	sowar	aphis	gents	nodus	virus	boult	enact	inert	refit
curer	hirer	Oscar	sower	apsis	genus	nones	vives	bract	epact	ingot	relet
cyder	homer	osier	spear	Argus	glass	oases	wages	brant	erect	inlet	relit
cymar	hover	other	speer	arras	gloss	oasis	waits	brent	ergot	input	remit
damar	ichor	otter	speir	arris	grass	oaves	wakes	bruit	eruct	inset	repot
dater	icker	outer	spier	arsis	grits	orris	wares	brunt	erupt	islet	resat
debar	idler	owner	spoor	ascus	gross	overs	weeds	built	escot	izzat	reset
decor	incur	oxter	stair	atlas	guess	pants	wells	buist	event	jabot	resit
defer	infer	pacer	steer	auras	gules	pavis	wilds	burnt	evert	jaunt	revet
demur	inker	paper	stour	avens	gyrus	pilus	wiles	burst	evict	joint	riant
deter	inner	parer	suber	balas	Hades	pious	wings	cadet	exact	joist	right
dicer	inter	pater	sudor	banns	halos	plebs	wives	canst	exalt	joust	rivet
diker	jiber	paver	sugar	bases	hives	pools	woods	carat	exeat	jurat	roast
dimer	joker	payer	super	basis	hocus	press	words	caret	exert	kaput	robot
dinar	jowar	peter	sutor	baths	hoots	psoas	works	chant	exist	karst	roost
diner	juror	piker	swear	beaus	humus	pubis	worms	chart	exult	kempt	roset
diver	Kafir	piper	tabor	beefs	hunks	pyxis	Xrays	cheat	facet	knelt	roust
donor	kefir	poker	taker	bends	Hykos	quins	years	chert	fagot	knout	sabot
doper	Khmer	polar	tamer	bitts	ictus	quits	yonks	chest	faint	krait	saint
doter	knurr	poser	taper	bless	ileus	races	yours	civet	fault	kraut	sault
dower	lager	power	tapir	bliss	incus	ramus	zooks	cleat	feast	lacet	sayst
dozer	lahar	prier	Tatar	blues	jacks	reams	abaft	cleft	feint	leant	scant
drear	laser	prior	tater	bogus	jakes	rebus	abbot	cloot	fight	leapt	scart
drier	laver	pryer	tawer	bolas	jeans	reins	abort	clout	filet	least	scatt
dryer	layer	puler	taxer	bolus	jinks	ribes	about	coact	first	legit	sceat
duper	lazar	queer	tenor	bonus	judas	rocks	adapt	coapt	fleet	licht	scent
eager	leger	racer	their	boots	krans	rolls	adept	coast	flint	licit	scoot
eater	lemur	radar	tiger	bowls	kudos	rubus	admit	comet	flirt	light	scout
eggar	leper	raker	tiler	brass	kumis	sales	adopt	compt	float	limit	shaft
egger	lever	raper	timer	camas	kvass	salts	adult	coopt	flout	lyart	shalt
eider	liber	rater	toner	cates	lares	saros	adust	coset	foist	mayst	shant
elder	lifer	raver	toper	chaos	lauds	Scots	afoot	count	fount	meant	sheet
elver	liger	razor	tower	chaps	lawks	sekos	afrit	court	front	merit	shent
ember	liner	recur	trier	chess	leads	sells	agent	covet	frost	midst	shift
emeer	liver	refer	trior	chops	leges	silks	agist	craft	fruit	might	shirt
emmer	lobar	ricer	tuber	class	Lents	sinus	aglet	crept	fumet	moist	shoat
enter	loner	rider	Tudor	clubs	lewis	slips	alert	crest	gamut	morat	shoot
ephor	loser	rigor	tuner	cords	lexis	slops	allot	Croat	gault	motet	short
error	lover	riser	tutor	corps	lines	snips	aloft	croft	gaunt	moult	shout
esker	lower	river	twyer	craps	links	solus	ambit	cruet	geist	mount	shunt
ester	lunar	roger	tyler	crass	lists	sorus	ament	crust	gemot	mulct	sight
ether	macer	roker	udder	cress	lives	specs	amort	crypt	genet	night	skeet
facer	major	roper	ulcer	cries	lobus	stays	anent	cubit	ghast	nonet	skint
faker	makar	rotor	ulnar	cross	locus	steps	angst	culet	ghaut	octet	skirt
fakir	maker	rover	umber	curds	loess	sties	apart	curst	ghost	onset	slant
femur	malar	rower	unbar	cutis	Logos	styes	aport	daunt	giant	orbit	sleet
fetor	manor	ruler	under	dagos	looks	Swiss	argot	davit	gigot	ought	slept
fever	maser	saker	upper	darts	loris	tabes	ascot	dealt	gleet	overt	sloot
fifer	mater	sapor	urger	degas	lotus	tails	ashet	debit	glint	owlet	sluit
firer	mayor	satyr	usher	demos	louis	tales	asset	debut	gloat	paint	smalt
fiver	mazer	saver	utter	Dives	lupus	talus	atilt	deist	glout	peart	smart
fixer	meter	sayer	velar	dodos	lyses	tamis	audit	delft	godet	petit	smelt
flair	miler	scaur	vicar	dorts	lysis	tapis	aught	demit	goest	pewit	smolt
fleer	mimer	scour	viper	dregs	magus	taxis	avast	depot	graft	picot	snoot
flier	minar	Seder	visor	dress	mains	taxus	avert	dicot	grant	pilot	snort
floor	miner	senor	vizor	drops	manes	teens	await	didst	great	pipit	snout
flour	minor	sever	volar	dross	manus	terms	beast	dight	greet	pivot	spelt
fluor	miser	sewer	vomer	ducks	mares	texas	beaut	digit	grift	plait	spent
flyer	mixer	shear	voter	dumps	maths	thews	befit	divot	grist	plant	spilt
foyer	mohur	sheer	wader	eaves	mavis	times	begat	docht	groat	pleat	spirt
freer	molar	shier	wafer	elves	means	toils	beget	doest	grout	point	splat
friar	moper	shirr	wager	embus	meths	tongs	begot	donut	grunt	poort	split
frier	motor	shoer	waker	ethos	metis	tonus	beret	doubt	guest	posit	sport
fryer	mover	shyer	waler	evens	minus	topos	beset	draft	guilt	poult	spout
furor	mower	simar	water	falls	modus	torus	besot	drift	guyot	prest	sprat
gaper	mudir	sitar	waver	favus	monas	traps	bidet	droit	habit	print	sprit
gazer	muser	sixer	waxer	fetus	mopus	trass	bight	ducat	hadst	prunt	spurt
giber	nadir	sizar	weber	fines	mores	tress	bigot	durst	haunt	Qboat	squat
giver	naker	sizer	whirr	finis	mucus	trews	blast	duvet	heart	quant	squit
glair	namer	skier	wiper	fives	mumps	Trias	bleat	dwelt	heist	quart	start
glaur	never	skirr	wooer	flews	nares	truss	blent	eclat	helot	quest	stilt
gnarr	noser	skyer	yager	floss	naris	turps	blest	edict	hight	quiet	stint
goner	occur	slyer	abyss	focus	nates	uncus	bloat	educt	hoist	quilt	stoat
gular	odour	smear	adios	foots	necks	vagus	bluet	egest	horst	quint	stout

strut	tatou	amity	cagey	doily	fully	homey	lovey	nosey	rally	snaky	unify
stunt	urubu	amply	campy	dolly	funky	honey	lowly	noway	randy	snowy	unity
sturt	vertu	annoy	candy	dopey	funny	honky	lucky	nutty	rangy	soapy	unlay
suint	virtu	anomy	canny	dormy	furry	hooey	lumpy	ochry	raspy	softy	unsay
surat	ablow	apery	canty	dorty	furzy	hooky	lushy	oddly	ratty	soggy	usury
swart	aglow	apply	carny	dotty	fussy	horny	lusty	ology	rawly	sonny	vasty
sweat	allow	appuy	carry	Douay	fusty	horsy	madly	oracy	ready	sonsy	vealy
sweet	arrow	aptly	catty	dowdy	fuzzy	hotly	Malay	otary	reddy	sooty	veery
swept	askew	Araby	chary	downy	gabby	howdy	malty	outby	redly	sophy	veiny
swift	bedew	array	chevy	dowry	gaily	hubby	mammy	ovary	reedy	soppy	Vichy
tacit	below	assay	chewy	drily	gally	huffy	mangy	paddy	reeky	sorry	viewy
taint	bylaw	ataxy	chivy	dryly	gammy	humpy	manly	palay	reify	soupy	vuggy
tarot	elbow	atomy	choky	duchy	gappy	hunky	mardy	pally	relay	spicy	wacky
taunt	embow	atony	cissy	ducky	gassy	hurly	marly	palmy	repay	spiky	waddy
tempt	endow	aunty	civvy	duddy	gaudy	hurry	marry	palsy	reply	spiny	wally
tenet	ensew	baccy	clary	dully	gaumy	husky	mashy	pandy	retry	spiry	waney
theft	inlaw	baddy	cobby	dumky	gauzy	hussy	massy	pansy	ridgy	splay	wanly
tight	kotow	badly	cocky	dummy	gawky	huzzy	matey	panty	risky	spray	warty
tinct	macaw	baggy	coley	dumpy	gawsy	icily	McCoy	pappy	ritzy	spumy	washy
toast	miaow	balky	colly	dungy	gelly	imply	mealy	pardy	rocky	stagy	wavey
tract	nohow	bally	comfy	dunny	gemmy	inlay	meany	parky	roily	stogy	weary
trait	oxbow	balmy	coney	duppy	germy	irony	meaty	parry	rooky	stony	webby
treat	papaw	bandy	conky	dusky	giddy	itchy	meiny	party	roomy	story	weedy
trist	pilaw	bardy	cooey	dusty	gilpy	ivory	mercy	pasty	rooty	stray	weeny
troat	pshaw	barky	cooky	early	ginny	jaggy	merry	patsy	ropey	stroy	weepy
trout	renew	barmy	cooly	ebony	gipsy	jammy	messy	patty	rorty	study	wetly
trust	screw	batty	copsy	edify	girly	jazzy	micky	pawky	roupy	sudsy	whiny
tryst	serow	bawdy	corky	elegy	glady	jelly	middy	peaky	rowdy	suety	whity
tweet	shrew	beady	corny	embay	glary	jemmy	milky	peaty	ruddy	sulky	widdy
twist	sinew	beamy	covey	emery	glazy	jenny	mingy	peggy	rugby	sully	willy
twixt	squaw	beefy	cowry	empty	glory	jerky	minty	penny	rumly	sunny	windy
Uboat	straw	beery	coyly	enemy	gluey	Jerry	mirky	peony	rummy	surfy	winey
unapt	strew	belay	crazy	enjoy	goaty	jetty	missy	peppy	rumpy	surly	wingy
uncut	strow	belly	crony	ensky	godly	Jewry	misty	perky	runny	tabby	wispy
unfit	thraw	bendy	cubby	entry	goety	jiffy	mobby	perry	runty	tacky	withy
ungot	threw	benny	cuddy	envoy	golly	jokey	molly	pesky	rushy	taffy	witty
Uniat	throw	berry	cully	epoxy	goody	jolly	money	petty	rusty	tally	wonky
unlit	vrouw	biddy	curdy	essay	gooey	jolty	moody	phony	rutty	tammy	woody
unset	widow	bilgy	curly	every	goofy	juicy	moony	picky	sadly	tangy	woozy
upset	addax	billy	curry	faddy	goopy	jumpy	moray	piety	saggy	tansy	wordy
valet	admix	bitsy	curvy	faery	gorsy	junky	mosey	piggy	sally	tardy	wormy
vault	affix	bitty	cushy	fairy	gouty	kelpy	mossy	pigmy	salty	tarry	worry
vaunt	annex	bivvy	cutey	fancy	grapy	kerry	mothy	piney	sandy	tarty	wryly
veldt	beaux	blimy	cutty	fanny	gravy	kiddy	mousy	pinky	sappy	tasty	yawny
verst	borax	blowy	Cymry	farcy	grimy	kinky	mucky	pinny	sarky	tatty	yippy
visit	calix	bluey	daddy	fatly	gully	kitty	muddy	pithy	sassy	tawny	yolky
vivat	calyx	bobby	daffy	fatty	gummy	kooky	muggy	plumy	saucy	teary	yucky
volet	choux	bogey	daily	fawny	gunny	lacey	muley	pocky	saury	techy	yukky
vomit	cimex	boggy	dairy	felly	guppy	lairy	mummy	poddy	savoy	teeny	yummy
waist	codex	boney	daisy	fenny	gurry	laity	murky	podgy	savvy	telly	zesty
wheat	culex	bonny	dally	ferly	gushy	lanky	mushy	poesy	scaly	tenty	zincy
whist	desex	booby	dandy	ferny	gusty	lardy	musky	pommy	scary	terry	zingy
wight	helix	booty	darky	ferry	gutsy	larky	mussy	poncy	scray	testy	zinky
worst	hyrax	boozy	dauby	fiery	gutty	lathy	musty	poppy	seamy	thawy	zippy
wrapt	immix	bosky	deary	fifty	gypsy	lawny	muzzy	popsy	sedgy	thewy	zloty
wrest	index	bossy	decay	filly	haily	laxly	nancy	porgy	seedy	thymy	abuzz
wrist	infix	bothy	decoy	filmy	hairy	layby	nanny	porky	seely	tinny	blitz
yacht	latex	bousy	decry	finny	hammy	leady	nappy	potty	seepy	tinty	chizz
yeast	murex	braky	deedy	firry	handy	leafy	narky	pouty	sepoy	tippy	fritz
zibet	phlox	braxy	deify	fishy	hanky	leaky	nasty	prexy	serry	tipsy	frizz
adieu	radix	briny	deity	fitly	haply	ledgy	natty	pricy	shady	tizzy	hertz
Bantu	redox	bubby	delay	fizzy	happy	leery	navvy	privy	shaky	toady	spitz
bayou	relax	buddy	derby	flaky	hardy	lefty	neddy	prosy	shaly	today	swizz
bijou	remex	buggy	diary	flamy	harpy	leggy	needy	proxy	shily	toddy	topaz
cornu	silex	bulgy	dicey	flaxy	harry	limey	nelly	pudgy	shiny	toffy	waltz
coypu	Sioux	bulky	dicky	flory	hasty	linny	nervy	puffy	showy	Tokay	whizz
fichu	telex	bully	dilly	fluky	heady	lippy	netty	puggy	shyly	tommy	
haiku	unfix	bumpy	dimly	fluty	heavy	loamy	newly	pulpy	silky	tousy	
Hindu	unsex	bunny	dingy	flyby	hefty	lobby	newsy	punty	silly	towny	
hokku	varix	bunty	dinky	foamy	henry	lofty	niffy	puppy	silty	truly	
kudzu	abbey	burly	dippy	fogey	herby	lolly	nifty	pursy	sissy	tubby	
noyau	agley	burry	dirty	foggy	hilly	looby	ninny	pushy	sixty	tufty	
perdu	agony	busby	dishy	folly	hinny	loony	nippy	pussy	skiey	tummy	
pilau	alary	bushy	ditty	footy	hippy	loopy	nobby	putty	skyey	tunny	
poilu	allay	busty	divvy	foray	hoary	loppy	nobly	pygmy	slaty	turfy	
prahu	alley	butty	dizzy	forby	hobby	lordy	noddy	quaky	slily	tusky	
quipu	alloy	byway	dobby	forty	hokey	lorry	noisy	query	slimy	tutty	
sadhu	alway	cabby	dodgy	fubsy	holey	loury	nonny	raggy	slyly	twiny	
snafu	ambry	caddy	doggy	fuggy	holly	lousy	nooky	rainy	smoky	umpty	

6 letter words

abacus
abater
abatis
abbacy
abbess
abduce
abduct
abject
abjure
ablate
ablaut
ablaze
abloom
ablush
aboard
aboral
abound
abrade
abroad
abrupt
abseil
absent
absorb
absurd
abulia
abuser
acacia
acajou
acarid
acarus
accede
accent
accept
access
accord
accost
accrue
accuse
acedia
acetal
acetic
acetyl
achene
acidic
acidly
acinar
acinus
ackack
acquit
across
acting
action
active
actual
acuity
acumen
adagio
Adamic
addend
addict
addled
adduce
adduct
adenyl
adhere
adieus
adieux
adipic
adjoin
adjure
adjust
admass
admire
adnate
adnexa
Adonic
Adonis
adorer
adrift
adroit
adsorb
advent
adverb
advert
advice
advise
adytum
aedile
Aegean
Aeolic
aerate
aerial
aerily
aerobe
aether
afeard
affair
affect
affeer
affine
affirm
afflux
afford
affray
Afghan
afield
aflame
afloat
afraid
afreet
afresh
afrite
afters
agamic
agamid
agaric
ageing
agency
agenda
ageold
aghast
agnail
agnate
agnise
agonal
agonic
agouti
agrafe
aguish
ahimsa
aikido
airbed
airbus
airgun
airily
airing
airman
airsac
airway
aisled
akimbo
alalia
alarum
alated
albata
albedo
albeit
albert
albino
albite
alcaic
alcove
Aldine
aldose
aldrin
alegar
alevin
alexia
alexin
algoid
alight
aliped
alkali
alkane
alkene
alkyne
allege
allele
allied
allium
allout
allred
allude
allure
almond
almost
alpaca
alpine
alsike
alulae
alumna
alumni
always
amadou
amatol
amazon
ambler
ambush
amends
amenta
amerce
amidst
amnion
amoeba
amoral
amount
ampere
amulet
amuser
amylum
anabas
anadem
ananas
anarch
anatta
anatto
anchor
angary
angina
angled
angler
angora
anicut
animal
animus
anklet
anlace
anlage
annals
anneal
annexe
annual
annuli
anodal
anodic
anoint
anomic
anomie
anonym
anorak
anoxia
anoxic
answer
anthem
anther
antiar
anting
antler
antral
antrum
anyhow
anyone
anyway
aorist
aortal
aortic
aoudad
apache
apathy
apexes
aphony
apiary
apical
apices
apiece
aplomb
apnoea
apodal
apogee
apozem
appeal
appear
append
appose
Arabic
arable
arbour
arcade
Arcady
arcana
arcane
arched
archer
archil
archly
archon
arctic
ardent
ardour
areola
areole
argala
argali
argand
argent
Argive
argosy
arguer
argufy
argute
argyle
aright
ariled
ariosi
arioso
arisen
arista
armada
armful
armlet
armour
armpit
arnica
aroint
around
arouse
arpent
arrack
arrant
arrest
arrive
arroba
arrowy
arroyo
arsine
artery
artful
artist
ascend
ascent
aseity
ashbin
ashcan
ashlar
ashore
ashpan
ashram
askant
askari
aslant
asleep
aslope
aspect
aspire
assail
assent
assert
assess
assign
assist
assize
assoil
assort
assume
assure
astern
asthma
astral
astray
astute
aswoon
asylum
ataman
ataxia
ataxic
athome
atomic
atonal
atonic
atrial
atrium
attach
attack
attain
attend
attest
attire
attorn
attune
aubade
auburn
audile
Augean
augite
augury
august
auklet
aumbry
auntie
aurist
aurora
aurous
Aussie
Austin
author
autism
autumn
avatar
avaunt
avenge
avenue
averse
Avesta
aviary
aviate
avidly
avocet
avouch
avowal
avowed
avulse
awaked
awaken
aweary
aweigh
awheel
awhile
awmous
awning
awoken
axilla
ayeaye
azalea
azonal
azotic
Baalim
babble
babbly
Babism
Babist
baboon
backer
backup
baddie
badger
baffle
bagful
bagged
bagman
bagnio
bagwig
bailee
bailer
bailey
bailie
bailor
baiter
bakery
balata
balboa
baldly
baleen
balker
ballad
ballet
ballon
ballot
balsam
Baltic
bamboo
banana
bandit
bandog
banger
bangle
bangup
banian
banish
banjax
banjos
banker
banket
banned
banner
bantam
banter
banyan
banzai
baobab
barbed
barbel
barber
barbet
bardic
barege
barely
barfly
bargee
barite
barium
barker
barley
barman
barney
barony
barque
barred
barrel
barren
barret
barrio
barrow
barter
barton
baryon
baryta
basalt
basely
bashaw
basher
basics
basket
basnet
Basque
basset
bassos
baster
Basuto
Basutu
batata
bateau
bather
bathos
bating
batman
batted
batten
batter
battle
battue
bauble
bawbee
bawble
bawdry
bawler
bawley
bayard
bazaar
beachy
beacon
beadle
beagle
beaked
beaker
beamer
beanie
bearer
beaten
beater
Beaune
beauty
beaver
becall
becalm
became
becket
beckon
become
bedaub
bedaze
bedbug
bedded
bedder
bedeck
bedell
bedlam
bedpan
bedsit
beduin
beeper
beetle
beeves
befall
befell
befool
before
befoul
beggar
begged
begird
begirt
begone
behalf
behave
behead
beheld
behest
behind
behold
behoof
behove
beigel
belaud
beldam
belfry
Belgic
belief
belike
belive
bellow
belong
belted
beluga
bemire
bemoan
bemock
bemuse
bender
benign
bennet
benumb
benzol
benzyl
berate
Berber
bereft
berlin
bertha
berthe
beseem
beside
bested
bestir
bestow
betake
bethel
betide
betony
betook
betray
betted
better
bettor
bewail
beware
bewray
beyond
bezant
bezoar
bharal
bhisti
bibbed
bibber
biceps
bicker
bidden
bidder
bieldy
biffin
biform
bigamy
bigger
biggin
bigwig
Bihari
bijoux
bikini
bilbos
bilker
billet
billon
billow
billyo
binary
binate
binder
binful
bionic
biopsy
biotic
biotin
birdie
bireme
birkie
birler
bisect
bishop
bisque
bister
bistre
bistro
bitchy
biting
bitted
bitten
bitter
bizone
bladed
blanch
blanky
blazer
blazes
blazon
bleach
bleary
blench
blende
blenny
blight
blimey
blintz
blithe
blonde
bloody
bloomy
blotch
blotto
blouse
blowed
blower
blowsy
blowup
blowzy
bluing
bluish
blunge
blurry
boatel
boater
bobbed
bobbin
bobble
bobcat
boblet
bobwig
bocage
bodega
bodger
bodice
bodily
boding
bodkin
boffin
bogged
boggle
bohunk
boiler
boldly
bolero
bolide
bollix
bolshy
bolter
bomber
bonbon
bonded
bonder
bongos
bonism
bonist
bonito
bonnet
bonnie
bonsai
bonxie
bonzer
booboo
boodle
boohoo
booing
booker
bookie
booksy
boomer
booted
bootee
boozer
bopeep
bopped
bopper
borage
borane
borate
bordel
border
boreal
Boreas
boride
boring
borrow

borsch bridle burbot cahoot carnal cerium chroma coated conger coulee
borzoi briefs burden caiman carnet cermet chrome coatee congou county
bosche briery bureau caique carney certes chromo cobalt conics couple
bosket bright burgee cajole carpal ceruse chubby cobber conker coupon
bosomy briner burger calami carpel cervix chuffy cobble conman course
boston briony burgle calash carper cesser chukar cobnut conned cousin
botany Briton burgoo calcar carpet cestus chukka cobweb conner covert
botchy broach burhel calces carpus cesura chummy coccal conoid coving
botfly broche burial calcic carrel cetane chunky coccid consul cowage
bother brogue burkha calico carrot chacha church coccus convex coward
bothie broken burlap caliph cartel chacma chypre coccyx convey cowboy
botone broker burler calker carter chafer cicada cochin convoy cowish
bottle brolly Burman calkin carton chaffy cicala cocked cooker cowled
bottom bromic burner caller carvel chaise cicely cocker cookie cowman
boucle bronco burnet callet carven chalet cigala cockle cooler cowpat
bought bronze burnup callow carver chalky cilice cocoon coolie cowpea
bougie bronzy burrel callup casbah chance cilium coddle coolly cowpox
boulle brooch burrow callus casein chancy cinder codger coolth cowrie
bounce broody bursae calmly casern change cinema codify coonty coyote
bouncy browny bursal calory cashew chanty cineol codlin cooper crabby
bounds browse bursar calpac casing chapel cinque coelom cootie cradle
bounty bruise bursas calque casino chappy cipher coerce copeck crafty
bourne brumal burton calves casket charas circle coeval copier craggy
bourse brumby busbar calxes Caslon charge circus coffee coping crambo
bovine brunch busboy camass casque Charon cirque coffer copita cranch
bovver brunet bushed camber cassia chaser cirrus coffin copout crania
bowels brushy bushel camera cassis chaste cistus coffle copped cranky
bowery brutal busily camion caster chatty cither cogent copper cranny
bowfin brutus busing camise castle chaunt citole cogged Coptic crappy
bowing bryony busker camlet castor cheeky citric cogito copula crases
bowleg bubble buskin camper casual cheers citron cognac coquet crasis
bowler bubbly busman campus catalo cheery citrus coheir corban cratch
bowman buccal bussed canape catchy cheese civics cohere corbel crater
bowsaw bucker busted canard catena cheesy claggy cohort corbie cravat
bowtie bucket bustee canary catgut chelae clammy coigne corded craven
bowwow buckle buster cancan Cathar chemic claque coiner corder craver
bowyer buckra bustle cancel cation cheque claret coinop cordon crawly
boxbed budded bustup cancer catkin cherry classy coital corium crayon
boxcar Buddha butane candid catnap cherty clause coitus corked crazed
boxful buddle butene candle catnip cherub claver coldly corker creaky
boxing budget butler canful catsup chesil clavis coleus cornea creamy
boyish budgie butter cangue cattle chesty clayey collar corned crease
bracer buffer button canine caucus chevet cleave collet cornel create
braces buffet buzzer canker caudal chiasm clench collie corner creche
Brahma bugged byblow canned caudex chiaus clergy collop cornet credal
Brahmi bugler byebye cannel caudle chichi cleric colony cornua credit
brains buglet byelaw canner caught chicle clever colour corody creeps
brainy bulbar byform cannon caulis chield clevis colter corona creepy
braird bulbed bygone cannot causal chigoe cliche colugo corozo creese
braise bulbil bylane canopy causer chilli client column corpse crenel
branch bulbul byline canter causey chilly cliffy colure corpus creole
brandy Bulgar byname canthi caveat chimer climax comate corral cresol
branle bulger bypass cantle cavern chintz clinch combat corrie Cretan
brassy bulimy bypast canton caviar chippy clingy combed corsac cretic
brawly bulker bypath cantor caving chirpy clinic comber corsak cretin
brawny bullae byplay cantus cavity chisel clipon comedo corset crewel
brayer buller byroad Canuck cavort chital clique comedy cortex crikey
brazen bullet byssus canvas cayman chitin cliquy comely corvee crimpy
brazil bumalo byword canyon cayuse chiton cloaca comeon corves cringe
breach bumble bywork capful cecity chitty cloche comfit Corvus cripes
breast bumkin cabala capias cedarn chives cloddy coming corymb crises
breath bummed cabana caplin celery chivvy cloggy comity coryza crisis
breech bummer cabman capote celiac choice clonal commie cosher crispy
breeks bummle cachet capped cellar choker clonic commis cosily crista
breese bumper cachou capric celled chokey clonus commit cosine critic
breeze bunchy cackle capsid Celtic choler closed commix cosmic croaky
breezy bunder cacoon captor cement choose closet common cosmos crocus
bregma bundle cactus carafe censer choosy clothe comose cosset croppy
brehon bungle caddie carbon censor chopin cloudy comous costae crosse
Breton bunion caddis carboy census choppy clough compel costal crotal
brevet bunker cadent carder cental choral cloven comply costar crotch
brewer bunkum cadger careen centre chorea clover comsat coster croton
brewis bunnia caecal career centum choric clumpy concha costly crouch
briard bunsen caecum caress cerate chorus clumsy conchy cottar croupy
briary bunted cafard carfax cercus chosen clunch concur cotted crouse
briber bunter Caffre carful cereal chough clutch condor cotter cruces
bricky bunyip caftan caries cereus chouse clypei confab cotton cruddy
bridal burble cagily carina ceriph chrism coaita confer coucal cruise
bridge burbly cahier carman cerise Christ coarse congee cougar cruive

crumby cygnet debris deride diploe dorado duffel elated enroll eunuch
crummy cymbal debtor derive diplon Dorian duffer elater enroot eureka
crunch cymose debunk dermal dipnet dormer duffle eldest ensate eutaxy
crural Cymric decade dermic dipody dormie dugong eleven ensign evader
cruset cypher decamp dermis dipole dorsal dugout elevon ensile evener
crusty cyprid decani derris dipped dorsum duiker elfish ensoul evenly
crutch cystic decant desalt dipper dorter dukery elicit ensure evilly
cruxes cystid deceit descry dipsas dosage dulcet elixir entail evince
crying dabbed decent desert dirdum dossal dumbly elodea entera evolue
crypto dabber decide design direct dossel dumdum eloign entice evolve
cubage dabble decker desire direly dosser dumose eloper entire evzone
cubism dacoit deckle desist dirham dotage dumper eluant entity examen
cubist dactyl decoct desman dirhem dotard dunite eluate entoil exarch
cuboid daedal decode desmid dirndl dotted Dunker eluent entomb exceed
cuckoo daemon decoke desorb disarm dottle dunlin elvish entrap except
cuddie daftly decree despot disbar douane dunned elytra entree excess
cuddle dagger dedans detach disbud double dupery embalm envier excide
cuddly dagoes deduce detail discal doubly duplet embank enwind excise
cudgel dahlia deduct detain discus douche duplex embark enwomb excite
cueing daimen deejay detect diseur dought durbar embers enwrap excuse
cueist daimio deepen detent dismal doughy duress emblem enzyme exedra
cuesta daimon deeply detest dismay dourly durgan emblic Eocene exempt
cuffed dainty deface detour disown douser Durham embody eolian exequy
cuisse damage defame deuced dispel dowlas durian emboli eolith exeunt
culler damask defeat devest distal downer during emboly eonian exhale
cullet dammar defect device distil dowser durned emboss eonism exhort
cullis dammed defend devise disuse doyley durrie embrue Eozoic exhume
cultch damned defier devoid dither dozily duster embryo Eozoon exilic
cultic dampen defile devoir dittos drably dustup emerge ephebe exodus
cultus damper define devote divers drachm duyker emeses ephebi exogen
culver damply deform devour divert drafty dyadic emesis epical exomis
cumber damsel defray devout divest dragee dybbuk emetic epimer exotic
cummer damson deftly dewily divide draggy dyeing emetin epizoa expand
cummin dancer defuse dewlap divine dragon dynamo emeute epodic expect
cumuli dander degras dexter diving draper dynast empery eponym expend
cunner dandle degree dharma djibba drawee eaglet empire epopee expert
cupful danger degust dhooti djinni drawer earful employ equate expire
cupola dangle dehorn dhurra doable dreamt earing empusa equine expiry
cupped Daniel deicer diacid dobbin dreamy earner emulge equity export
cupric Danish deific diadem docent dreary earthy enable eraser expose
cuptie dankly deject diaper docile dredge earwax enamel erbium exsect
cupule daphne delate diatom docker dreggy earwig encage eremic exsert
curacy dapper delete dibbed docket dreich easily encamp erenow extant
curare dapple delict dibber doctor drench easter encase ergate extasy
curari daring delude dibble dodder dressy eatery encash ermine extend
curate darken deluge dicast doddle drifty eating encode erotic extent
curdle darkey deluxe dicker dodgem drippy ecarte encore errand extern
curfew darkie delver dickey dodger drivel echoer encyst errant extort
curiae darkle demand dictum dodoes driven echoic endear errata eyalet
curial darkly demark diddle dogate driver eclair ending ersatz eyecup
curium darned demean didoes dogear droger eczema endive eryngo eyeful
curler darnel dement diesel dogend drogue Eddaic endure escape eyeing
curlew darner demise dieses dogfox droich Edenic energy escarp eyelet
currie darter demist diesis dogged drolly edgily enface eschar eyelid
cursed dartle demode dieter dogger drongo edging enfold eschew Eyetie
cursor dartre demote differ doggie droopy edible engage escort Fabian
cursus dasher demure digamy dogleg dropsy editor engild escrow fabled
curtal dassie denary digest dogood drosky eerily engine escudo fabler
curtly datary dengue digger doited drossy efface engird Eskimo fabric
curtsy dative denial diglot dolium drouth effect engirt espial facade
curule datura denier dikdik dollar drover effete englut esprit facete
curvet dauber denims diktat dollop drowse effigy engram Essene facial
cuscus dawdle denote dilate dolman drowsy efflux engulf essive facies
cushat daybed dental dilute dolmen drudge effort enhalo essoin facile
cusped dayfly dentel dimity dolour drupel effuse enigma estate facing
cuspid dazzle dentil dimmed domain drybob Egeria enisle esteem factor
cussed deacon denude dimmer domett dryfly egesta enjoin estray factum
custom deaden deodar dimple domino dryish eggcup enlace etcher facula
cutely deadly depart dimply donate dryrot eggler enlist eterne fadein
cutler deafen depend dimwit donjon dryrun eggnog enmesh ethane faerie
cutlet deafly depict dingey donkey dually egoism enmity ethene fagend
cutoff dealer deploy dinghy donned dubbed egoist ennead ethics fagged
cutout dearie depone dingle donsie dubbin egress ennuye Ethiop faggot
cutter dearly deport dingus doodad ducker eidola enosis ethnic failed
cuttle dearth depose dining doodah dudeen eighth enough ethyne faille
cyanic deasil depute dinkum doodle dudish eighty enrage etrier fainly
cyanin debark deputy dinned doolie duello either enrapt etymon fairly
cycler debase derail dinner dopant duende ejecta enrich euchre fakery
cyclic debate derate diplex Dopper duenna elapse enrobe eulogy falcon

fallal
fallen
fallow
falsie
falter
family
famine
famish
famous
famuli
fandom
fanged
fanion
fanjet
fanned
fanner
fantan
Fantee
fantod
fantom
faquir
fardel
farfel
farina
farmer
faroff
farout
farrow
fasces
fascia
fasten
faster
fathen
father
fathom
fatted
fatten
fatter
faucal
fauces
faucet
faulty
faunae
faunal
faunas
favour
fawner
fealty
featly
feckly
fecula
fecund
fedora
feeble
feebly
feeder
feeing
feeler
feirie
feisty
feline
fellah
feller
felloe
fellow
felony
female
femora
fencer
fender
Fenian
fenman
fennec
fennel
ferial
ferine
ferret
ferric
ferula
ferule
fervid
fescue
festal
fester
fetial
fetich
fetish
fetter
fettle
feudal
fezzed
fezzes
fiacre
fiance
fiasco
fibbed
fibber
fibred
fibril
fibrin
fibula
fickle
fiddle
fiddly
fidget
fierce
fiesta
figged
figure
filfot
filial
filing
filler
fillet
fillip
filmic
filose
filter
filthy
fimble
finale
finals
finder
finely
finery
finger
finial
fining
finish
finite
finnan
finned
finner
Finnic
fiorin
fipple
firing
firkin
firlot
firman
firmly
fiscal
fisher
fistic
fitful
fitted
fitter
fixate
fixity
fizgig
fizzle
flabby
flacon
flaggy
flagon
flambe
flamen
flanch
flange
flappy
flashy
flatly
flatus
flaunt
flavin
flaxen
fleche
fledge
fleece
fleech
fleecy
flench
flense
fleshy
fletch
fleury
flexor
flight
flimsy
flinch
flinty
flirty
flitch
floaty
flocci
floozy
floppy
florae
floral
floras
floret
florid
florin
flossy
floury
flower
fluent
fluffy
flukey
flunky
flurry
fluted
fluter
flying
flyman
flysch
flyway
fobbed
focsle
fodder
foeman
foetal
foetid
foetus
fogbow
fogdog
fogged
foible
foiled
foison
folder
foliar
folium
folksy
follow
foment
fondle
fondly
fondue
fontal
fooler
footed
footer
footle
foozle
forage
forbad
forbid
forbye
forced
forcer
fordid
forego
forest
forger
forget
forgot
forint
forked
formal
format
formed
former
formic
fornix
forrad
forrit
forsay
fossae
fossil
fossor
foster
fother
fought
foully
foulup
fourth
foveae
foveal
fowler
fracas
fraena
fraise
framer
frappe
fratch
frater
Frauen
frazil
freaky
freely
freest
freeze
french
frenum
frenzy
fresco
friary
Friday
fridge
friend
frieze
fright
frigid
frijol
frilly
fringe
fringy
frisky
frivol
frizzy
froggy
frolic
frosty
frothy
frowst
frowsy
frowzy
frozen
frugal
fruity
frumpy
frusta
frutex
fucoid
fuddle
fugato
fugged
fuhrer
fulcra
fulfil
fulgid
fulham
fullam
fuller
fulmar
fumble
fundus
fungal
fungus
funkia
funned
funnel
furfur
furore
furred
furrow
fusain
fusile
fusion
fusser
fustic
futile
future
fylfot
gabbed
gabber
gabble
gabbro
gabion
gabled
gablet
gadded
gadder
gadfly
gadget
Gadhel
gadoid
Gaelic
gaffer
gagged
gagger
gaggle
gagman
gaiety
gainer
gainly
gainst
gaited
gaiter
galago
galaxy
galena
galiot
galley
Gallic
Gallio
gallon
gallop
galoot
galore
galosh
gambir
gambit
gamble
gambol
gamely
gamete
gamily
gamine
gaming
gammer
gammon
gander
ganger
gangly
gangue
gannet
ganoid
gantry
gaoler
gapped
garage
garbed
garble
garcon
garden
garget
gargle
garial
garish
garlic
garner
garnet
garran
garret
garron
garrot
garter
garuda
garvie
gasbag
Gascon
gasify
gasket
gaskin
gasman
gasper
gassed
gasser
gateau
gather
gauche
gaucho
gauger
gavage
gavial
gazebo
gazump
geckos
geegee
geezer
geisha
gelled
Gemara
Gemini
gemmae
gemmed
gender
genera
geneva
genial
genius
genned
genome
gentes
gentle
gently
gentoo
gentry
geodic
George
gerbil
gerent
german
germen
gerund
getout
getter
gewgaw
geyser
gharry
ghetto
ghosty
giaour
gibber
gibbet
gibbon
giddap
gifted
gigged
giggle
giggly
giglet
giglot
gigman
gigolo
gilder
gilled
gillie
gimbal
gimlet
gimmal
gimmer
gingal
ginger
gingko
ginkgo
ginned
ginner
girder
girdle
girlie
glacis
gladly
glairy
glaive
glance
glassy
glazer
gleamy
gleety
glibly
glider
glitch
global
gloomy
gloria
glossy
glover
glower
glumly
glumpy
glutei
gluten
glycin
glycol
gnarly
gnawer
gneiss
gnomic
gnomon
gnosis
goalie
goanna
goatee
gobang
gobbet
gobble
goblet
goblin
gocart
goddam
godown
godson
godwit
goffer
goggle
goggly
goglet
Goidel
goitre
gokart
golden
golfer
gollop
golosh
goober
goodie
goodly
googly
googol
gooier
gooney
gooses
gopher
goramy
gorget
gorgio
gorgon
gorily
goslow
gospel
gossan
gossip
Gothic
gotten
gourde
govern
gowany
goyish
gozzan
grabby
graben
grader
gradin
gradus
grainy
gramme
Grammy
gramps
grange
granny
Granth
grappa
grassy
grater
gratin
gratis
graved
gravel
graven
graver
Graves
gravid
grazer
grease
greasy
greave
greedy
greens
greeny
greige
greyly
grieve
grigri
grille
grilse
grimly
gringo
griper
grippe
grippy
grisly
grison
gritty
grivet
groats
grocer
groggy
groove
groovy
groper
grotto
grotty
grouch
ground
grouse
grovel
grower
growly
growth
groyne
grubby
grudge
grugru
grumly
grumps
grumpy
grutch
guaiac
guanin
guddle
Guelph
guenon
guffaw
guggle
guider
guidon
guilty
guinea
guiser
guitar
gulden
Gullah
gullet
gulley
gummed
gundog
gunman
gunned
gunnel
gunner
gunsel
gunshy
gunter
gunyah
gurgle
gurjun
Gurkha
gurnet
gurrah
gusher
gusset
guttae
gutted
gutter
guvnor
guzzle
gypped
gypsum
gyrate
habile
hackle
hackly
haddie
hadron
haemal
haemin
haffet
haffit
hagbut
haggis
haggle
hailer
hairdo
haired
haleru
halide
halite
hallal
halloa
halloo
hallow
hallux
haloes
halter
halvah
halves
hamate
Hamite
hamlet
hammal
hammam
hammed
hammer
hamper
handed
handle
hangar
hanged
hanger
hangup
hanker
hankie
hansel
hansom
happed
happen
haptic
harass
harden
hardly
hardup
harken
harlot
harper
harrow
hartal
haslet
hassle
hasten
hatbox
hatful
hatpeg
hatpin
hatred
hatted
hatter
hauler
haunch
Havana
havers
hawhaw
hawked
hawker
hawser
haybox
haymow
hazard
hazily
headed
header
headon
healer
health
hearer
hearse
hearth
hearty
heated
heater
heathy
heaven
heaver
Hebrew
heckle
hectic
hector
heddle

hedera hedger heehaw heeled heeler hegira heifer height hejira helium heller helmet helper hemmed hempen henrun henrys hepcat heptad herald herbal herder herdic hereat hereby herein hereof hereon heresy hereto heriot hermit hernia heroic heroin herpes Herren hetero hetman hexact hexane hexose heyday hiatus hiccup hickey hidden hiding hieing higgle higher highly hijack hinder Hindoo hinged hipped hippie hirple hispid hisser hither hitman hoarse hoaxer hobbit hobble hobnob hocker hockey hodden hodman hoeing hogged hogget hoggin hogtie hoicks hoised

holden holder holdup holily holism holler holloa hollow holpen homage hombre homely homily homing hominy honest honied honour hooded hoodie hoodoo hoofed hoofer hookah hooked hooker hookey hookup hooper hoopla hoopoe hooray hootch hooter hooves hopped hopper hopple horary horned horner hornet horrid horror horsey hosier hostel hotbed hotdog hotpot hotter houdan hourly housel housey howdah howler hoyden hubbub hubcap hubris huckle huddle hugely hugged humane humble humbly humbug humect humeri humify hummed hummel hummer hummum humour humped hunger

hungry hunker hunter hurdle hurler hurley hurrah hurray hurter hurtle husker hussar hustle hutted huzoor hyaena hybrid hybris hydric hymnal hymnic hyphae hyphal hyphen hyssop iambic iambus ibexes ibices ibidem iceaxe icebag icebox icecap iceman icicle iconic ideaed ideate idiocy idolum ignite ignore iguana illume illuse imbibe imbrex imbrue immane immesh immune immure impact impair impala impale impark impart impawn impede impend impish impone import impose impost impugn impure impute inarch inborn inbred incase incept incest inches incise incite

inclip income incubi incult incuse indaba indeed indene indent Indian indict indign indigo indite indium indole indoor induce induct indult induna infamy infant infare infect infelt infest infirm inflow influx infold inform infula infuse ingest ingulf inhale inhere inhume inject injure injury inkpot inlaid inland inlaws inlier inmate inmost innate inning inroad inrush insane inseam insect insert inside insist insole inspan instal instar instep instil insult insure intact intake intend intent intern intine intoed intone intray intuit inulin invade

invent invert invest invite invoke inward inwick inwove inwrap inyala iodate iodide iodine iodise iodism iolite Ionian ionise ionium ireful irenic irides iritis ironer ironic irrupt isabel isatin ischia island isobar isohel isomer isopod italic itself izzard jabbed jabber jabiru jacana jackal jacket jaeger jagged jagger jaguar jailer jailor jalopy jammed jammer jangle jarful jargon jarrah jarred jarvey jasper jaunce jaunty jeerer jejune jennet jerbil jerboa jerker jerkin jersey jester Jesuit jetlag jetsam jetted Jewess Jewish jezail jibbah jibbed

jibber jigged jigger jiggle jiggly jigsaw jilter jingle jingly jinnee jitney jitter joanna jobber joblot jockey jocose jocund jogged jogger joggle johnny joiner jolter josher josser jostle jotted jotter jounce jouncy jovial Jovian joyful joyous Judaic judder Judean judger judoka jugate jugful jugged juggle jujube Julian jumbal jumble jumbly jumper jungle jungly junior junker junket junkie jurist justly Jutish jutted kabala kabuki Kabyle Kaffir kaftan kainit kaiser kakapo kalong kanaka kaolin kaputt karate karmic kaross karroo kasbah kation keenly

keeper kelpie kelson kelter Keltic kelvin kenned kennel kermes kermis kerned kernel kersey ketone kettle kewpie keyway kiaugh kibble kibitz kiblah kibosh kicker kidded kidder kiddie kidnap kidney kiekie killer kilted kilter kimono kincob kindle kindly kinema kingly kipper kirsch kirtle kismet kisser kitbag kitcat kitool kitsch kitten kittle kittul klepht knaggy knight knives knobby knotty knower kobold koedoe koodoo kookie koolah kopeck koppie Korean kosher kowhai kowtow kraken krantz kronen kroner kronor kronur kultur kumiss kummel kurgan laager

labial labile labium labour labret labrum laceup laches lacing lackey lactic lacuna ladder laddie ladify lading ladino ladyfy lagged lagger lagoon laguna laical lallan lambda lamber lamely lament lamina lamish Lammas lammed lanate lancer lancet landau landed lander langue langur lankly lanner lanugo lapdog lapful lapped lappet lappie lapsed lapsus larder lardon lariat larker larrup larvae larval larynx lascar lasher lashup lasque lassie lassos laster lastly lateen lately latent latest lather latish latria latron latten latter launce launch laurel

lavabo lavage laveer lavish lavolt lawful lawman lawyer laxity layday layman layoff layout lazily lazuli leaden leader leadin leadup leafed league lealty leanly leanto leaper learnt leaved leaven leaver leaves lecher lector ledged ledger leeway legacy legate legato legbye legend legged legion legist legman legume lemony lender length lenity lensed Lenten lentil Leonid lepton lesion lessee lessen lesser lesson lessor lethal letoff letter Lettic levant Levite levity lewdly liable liaise libber libido Libyan lichee lichen lictor lidded lieder lierne

lifter liftup ligate ligger lights lignin ligula ligule ligure likely liking lilied limbec limbed limber limbic limbus liming limner limper limpet limpid limply limuli linage linden lineal linear lineup linger lingua linhay lining linkup linnet linney linsey lintel lintie lionel lipase lipide lipoid lipoma lipped lippen lippie liquid liquor lisper lissom listed listel listen lister litany litchi lithia lithic litmus litter little livein lively livery living lizard loaded loader loafer loaner loathe loaves lobate lobbed lobose lobule locale locate

lochan
locker
locket
lockup
loculi
locust
lodger
lofter
loggat
logged
logger
loggia
logion
logjam
loiter
loller
lollop
loment
lonely
longan
loofah
looker
lookin
looper
loosen
looter
lopped
lopper
loquat
lorcha
lordly
lorica
loriot
lotion
lotted
louche
louden
loudly
lounge
loupen
loupit
louver
louvre
lovage
lovein
lovely
loving
lowboy
lowery
lowing
lowish
lowkey
lubber
lubric
lucent
lucern
luetic
lugged
lugger
luggie
lumbar
lumber
lumina
lummox
lumpen
lumper
lunacy
lunate
lunger
lunula
lunule
lupine
lurdan
lurker
lushly
lustra
lustre
luteal
lutein
luting
luxate
luxury
lyceum
lychee
Lydian
lyrate
lyrics
lyrism
lyrist
lysine
macaco
machan
mackle
macron
macula
macule
Madame
madcap
madden
madder
madman
madras
maduro
maenad
maggot
Magian
magilp
magnet
magnum
magpie
maguey
Magyar
mahout
maidan
maiden
maigre
mailed
mainly
Majlis
makedo
makeup
making
malady
Malaga
malate
maleic
malice
malign
malism
malkin
mallee
mallei
mallet
mallow
maltha
mammae
mammal
mammee
mammer
mammon
manage
manana
manche
Manchu
manday
manege
manful
mangel
manger
mangle
mangos
maniac
manila
manioc
manito
manned
manner
manque
mantel
mantes
mantic
mantid
mantis
mantle
mantra
mantua
manual
manuka
manure
Maoism
Maoist
mapped
mapper
maquis
maraca
maraud
marble
marbly
marcel
margay
margin
marina
marine
marish
Marist
marked
marker
market
markup
marlin
marmot
maroon
marque
marram
marred
marron
marrow
marrum
marshy
marten
martin
martyr
marvel
mascle
mascon
mascot
masher
mashie
masker
maslin
Masora
masque
massif
masted
master
mastic
matico
matins
matlow
matrix
matron
matted
matter
mature
matzoh
maugre
maundy
maxima
maxixe
maybug
mayday
mayest
mayfly
mayhap
mayhem
maying
mazard
mazily
meadow
meagre
mealie
meanie
meanly
measly
meatus
meddle
mediae
medial
median
medick
medico
medium
medius
medlar
medley
medusa
meekly
meetly
megilp
megohm
megrim
meinie
mellow
melody
melton
member
memoir
memory
menace
menage
mender
menhir
menial
meninx
mensal
menses
mental
mentor
mentum
mercer
merely
merest
merger
merils
merino
merism
merlin
merlon
merman
merrie
mescal
mesial
messan
Messrs
mestee
metage
metals
meteor
method
methyl
metier
metope
metred
metric
mettle
mezuza
miasma
mickey
mickle
micron
midage
midair
midday
midden
middle
midget
midgut
midoff
midrib
midway
miffed
mighty
mignon
mihrab
mikado
milady
milage
mildew
mildly
milieu
milker
milled
miller
millet
milord
milter
mimosa
mincer
minded
minder
mingle
minify
minima
mining
minion
minish
minium
minnow
Minoan
minter
minuet
minute
miosis
miotic
mirage
mirror
miscue
misdid
misere
misery
misfit
mishap
mishit
mishmi
Mishna
mislay
misled
missal
missel
missis
missus
mister
mistle
misuse
mitral
mitten
mizzen
mizzle
mizzly
moaner
moated
mobbed
mobcap
mobile
mocker
mockup
modena
modern
modest
modify
modish
modius
module
moduli
modulo
moggie
mohair
Mohawk
Mohock
mohole
moider
moiety
moiler
molest
moline
mollie
Moloch
molten
moment
Monday
moneys
monger
Mongol
monial
monied
monies
monism
monist
monkey
monody
moocow
mooing
moolah
mopish
mopoke
mopped
mopper
moppet
morale
morals
morass
morbid
morbus
moreen
morgen
morgue
morion
morish
Mormon
mornay
morose
morpho
morris
morrow
morsel
mortal
mortar
morula
mosaic
moshav
Moslem
mosque
mostly
motett
mother
motile
motion
motive
motley
motmot
motory
mottle
moujik
mouldy
moulin
mouser
mousse
mouthy
moving
mucker
muckle
mucoid
mucosa
mucous
muddle
muesli
muffin
muffle
muflon
mugged
mugger
mukluk
mulish
mullah
muller
mullet
mulley
multum
mumble
mummer
mumper
mundic
Munich
muntin
murder
murine
murmur
murphy
murrey
muscat
muscle
museum
musing
muskeg
musket
muskox
Muslim
muslin
mussel
muster
mutant
mutate
mutely
mutine
mutiny
mutism
mutter
mutton
mutual
mutule
mutuum
muumuu
muzhik
muzzle
myelin
mygale
myopia
myopic
myosin
myosis
myotic
myriad
myrica
myrtle
myself
mystic
mythic
mythos
myxoma
nabbed
naevus
nagana
nagged
nagger
nailer
namely
nanism
napalm
napkin
napped
nardoo
narrow
nastic
natant
nation
native
natron
natter
nature
naught
nausea
nautch
Nazify
Nazism
neaped
nearby
nearer
nearly
neaten
neatly
nebula
nebuly
nectar
needle
neednt
negate
nekton
nelson
Nepali
nephew
nereid
nerine
nerite
neroli
nestle
Nestor
netful
nether
netted
nettle
neural
neuron
neuter
newish
newton
niacin
nibbed
nibble
nicely
nicety
nicish
nickel
nicker
nidget
nidify
nielli
niello
nigger
niggle
nighty
nignog
nilgai
nimble
nimbly
nimbus
Nimrod
ninety
nipped
nipper
nipple
nitric
nitwit
nobble
nobbut
nobody
nocent
nodded
noddle
nodose
nodule
noesis
noetic
noggin
nomism
nonage
nonary
noncom
nonego
nonfat
nonius
nonuse
noodle
Nordic
normal
Norman
noshup
nosily
nosing
nostoc
notary
notate
notice
notify
notion
nougat
nought
nounal
novena
novice
Nowell
nowise
noyade
nozzle
nuance
nubble
nubbly
nubile
nuchal
nuclei
nudely
nudism
nudist
nudity
nugget
nullah
number
numbly
numina
nuncio
nuncle
nurser
nutant
nutate
nutmeg
nutria
nutter
nuzzle
nympho
oafish
oarage
obeche
obelus
obeyer
obital
object
objure
oblast
oblate
oblige
oblong
oboist
obsess
obtain
obtect
obtest
obtund
obtuse
obvert
occamy
occult
occupy
ocelli
ocelot
ochone
oclock
octane
octant
octave
octavo
octroi
ocular
oddity
oddjob
oddson
odious
oecist
oedema
oeuvre
offend
offent
office
offing
offish
offkey
offset
ogamic
ogival
ogress
ogrish
ohmage
oidium
oilcan
oilman
oilnut
oldish
oleate
olefin
oliver
omasum
omelet
omenta
onager
oncost
oneoff
oneway
onfall
online
onrush
onside
onward
oocyte
oodles
oogamy
oogeny
oolite
oology
oolong
oomiak
opaque
opener
openly
ophite
opiate
oppose
oppugn
optant
optics
optima
option
orache
oracle
orally
orange
orator
orcein
orchid
orchil
orchis
ordain
ordeal

ordure
orexis
orfray
orgasm
orgeat
orient
origan
origin
oriole
orison
ormolu
ornate
ornery
orphan
orphic
orpine
orrery
oscine
oscula
osmium
osmose
osprey
ossein
ossify
osteal
ostial
ostium
ostler
otiose
otitis
ottava
ouster
outact
outage
outbid
outbye
outcry
outdid
outfit
outfox
outgun
outing
outlaw
outlay
outlet
output
outran
outrun
outsat
outset
outsit
outtop
outvie
outwit
ovally
overdo
overly
ovisac
ovular
owlish
oxalic
oxalis
oxbird
oxford
oxgall
oxgang
oxgate
oxherd
oxhide
oxland
oxtail
oxygen
oxymel
oyster
ozonic
pacify
packer
packet
padauk

padded
paddle
paella
paeony
pagoda
paidup
pajama
pakeha
palace
palais
palate
paleae
palely
paling
palish
pallet
pallia
pallid
pallor
palmar
palmer
palolo
palpal
palpus
palter
paltry
pampas
pamper
panada
panama
panary
pander
pandit
panful
panned
pantry
panzer
papacy
papain
papaya
papers
papery
papism
papist
pappus
papula
papule
papyri
parade
paramo
parang
paraph
parcel
pardie
pardon
parent
parget
pariah
parian
paring
parish
parity
parkin
parlay
parley
parody
parole
parous
parpen
parral
parrel
parrot
parsec
Parsee
parson
partan
partly
parure
parvis

pascal
Pashto
passer
passim
pastel
pastil
pastor
pastry
patchy
patent
Pathan
pathic
pathos
patina
patois
patrol
patron
patted
patten
patter
paunch
pauper
pavage
pavane
paving
pavior
pavise
pawnee
pawner
pawpaw
payday
paynim
payoff
payola
peachy
peahen
peaked
peanut
pearly
peavey
pebble
pebbly
pecker
pecten
pectic
pectin
pedalo
pedant
pedate
peddle
pedlar
peeler
peeper
peepul
peewit
pegged
pegleg
pegtop
pelage
pelham
pellet
pelmet
pelota
peltae
pelter
peltry
pelves
pelvic
pelvis
pencil
penman
pennae
penned
pennon
pentad
pentup
pentyl
penult
penury

people
peplum
pepped
pepper
pepsin
peptic
perdue
period
perish
permit
perron
person
pertly
peruke
peruse
pesade
peseta
pesewa
pester
pestle
petara
petard
petite
petrel
petrol
petted
petter
pewter
peyote
peyotl
phalli
pharos
phasic
phasis
phatic
phenol
phenyl
phlegm
phloem
phobia
phobic
phoebe
phoney
phonic
phonon
phooey
photic
photon
phrase
phylum
physic
piaffe
piazza
picker
picket
pickle
pickup
picnic
picric
piddle
pidgin
piecer
piedog
pieman
pierce
piffle
pigeon
pigged
piggin
piglet
pignut
pigsty
pilaff
pileum
pileup
pileus
pilfer
pillar
pillow

pilose
pilous
pilule
pimple
pimply
pincer
pineal
pinery
pineta
pinger
pinion
pinkie
pinnae
pinned
pinner
pinole
pintle
piolet
pionic
piping
pipkin
pipped
pippin
piquet
piracy
pirate
piraya
Pisces
pissed
pistil
pistol
piston
pitchy
pithos
pitier
pitman
pitpan
pitsaw
pitted
pitter
pizzle
placed
placer
placet
placid
plagal
plague
plaguy
plaice
plaint
planar
planer
planet
plaque
plashy
plasma
platan
platen
plater
player
pleach
please
plebby
pledge
plenty
plenum
pleura
plexor
plexus
pliant
plicae
pliers
plight
plinth
plisse
ploidy
plotty
plough
plover

plucky
plumed
plummy
plumpy
plunge
plural
plushy
pluton
pneuma
pocked
pocket
podded
podite
podium
podsol
podzol
poetic
poetry
pogrom
pointe
points
poison
Polack
polder
police
policy
polish
polite
polity
pollan
polled
pollen
poller
pollex
polony
polypi
pomace
pomade
pomelo
pommel
pommie
pompom
poncho
ponder
pongee
pontie
pontil
ponton
poodle
pooped
poorly
popery
popgun
popish
poplar
poplin
popped
popper
poppet
popple
popply
porgie
porism
porker
porose
porous
portal
porter
portly
posada
poseur
posset
possum
postal
poster
postil
potage
potale
potash

potato
potboy
poteen
potent
potful
pother
potion
potman
potpie
potted
potter
pottle
pouchy
pouffe
pounce
pourer
pouter
powder
powwow
praise
prance
prater
pratie
praxis
prayer
preach
precis
prefab
prefer
prefix
prelim
premed
premix
prepay
preses
preset
presto
pretax
pretty
prewar
pricey
priest
primal
primer
primly
primus
prince
priory
prison
prissy
privet
prizer
prober
probit
profit
proleg
prolix
prompt
pronto
propel
proper
propyl
proser
prosit
protea
proton
proven
pruina
pruner
prying
pseudo
psyche
psycho
pterin
ptisan
ptosis
public
pucker
puddle

puddly
pueblo
puffed
puffer
puffin
pugdog
puisne
puller
pullet
pulley
pullin
pullon
pullup
pulper
pulpit
pulque
pulsar
pulser
pulvil
pumice
pummel
pumper
punchy
puncta
pundit
punily
punish
punkah
punned
punner
punnet
puntee
punter
pupate
pupped
puppet
purdah
purely
purfle
purger
purify
purine
purism
purist
purity
purler
purlin
purple
purply
purser
pursue
purvey
pusher
Pushtu
pushup
putlog
putoff
putrid
putsch
puttee
putter
puttie
puzzle
pycnic
pyedog
pyknic
pylori
pyrene
pyrite
pyrola
pyrope
python
quaere
quagga
quaggy
quahog
quaich
quaigh
quaint

Quaker
qualmy
quanta
quarry
quarte
quarto
quartz
quasar
quaver
queasy
queazy
quench
queuer
quiche
quince
quinoa
quinol
quinsy
quinta
quirky
quitch
quiver
quoits
quorum
quotes
quotha
rabato
rabbet
rabbin
rabbit
rabble
rabies
raceme
rachis
racial
racily
racism
racist
racker
racket
racoon
raddle
radial
radian
radish
radium
radius
radome
radula
raffia
raffle
rafter
ragbag
ragged
raggee
raggle
raglan
ragman
ragout
ragtag
raguly
raider
railer
raiser
raisin
Rajput
rakish
ramate
ramble
ramify
ramjet
rammed
rammer
ramose
ramous
ramper
ramrod
ramson
rancho

rancid
randan
randem
random
ranger
ranker
rankle
rankly
ransom
ranter
ranula
raphia
raphis
rapids
rapier
rapine
rapist
rapped
rappee
rappel
rapper
raptly
raptor
rarefy
rarely
raring
rarity
rascal
rasher
rashly
rasper
raster
rasure
ratbag
rather
ratify
ratine
rating
ration
ratite
ratlin
ratoon
rattan
rattat
ratted
ratter
rattle
ravage
ravine
raving
ravish
razzia
razzle
reader
really
realty
reamer
reaper
rearer
reason
reaver
rebate
rebato
rebeck
rebore
reborn
rebuff
rebuke
recall
recant
recast
recede
recent
recess
recipe
recite
reckon
recoil
recoin

record recoup rector rectum rectus redact redbud redcap redden redder reddle redeem redeye redhot rediae redone redraw redtop reduce reebok reecho reedit reefer reeler reface refect refill refine reflex reflow reflux reform refuel refuge refund refuse refute regain regale regard regent reggae regime regina region regius reglet regnal regret regulo rehash rehear reheat reheel reiver reject rejoin relaid relate relent relict relief reline relish relive reload reluct relume remade remain remake remand remark remedy remind remint remise remiss remora

remote remove remuda rename render renege rennet renown rental renter reopen repaid repair repand repass repast repeal repeat repent repine replay replum report repose repugn repute reread resale rescue reseat reseau resect reseda resell resent reship reside resign resile resist resold resole resorb resort rester result resume retail retain retake retard retell retene retest retial retina retire retold retook retool retort retral retrod retted returf return retuse revamp reveal reverb revere revers revert revery revest review revile revise revive

revoke revolt revved reward rewind rewire rewoke reword rework rhaphe rhebok rhesus rhetor rheumy rhinal rhombi rhumba rhymer rhythm ribald riband ribbed ribbon ribose richen riches richly ricker rickey ricrac rictal rictus ridded ridden riddle rident ridged riding rifely riffle rifler rigged rigger righto rigour rigout rillet rimmed rimose rimous ringed ringer rinser rioter ripely ripoff ripped ripper ripple ripply riprap ripsaw rising risker risque ritual rivage rizzar rizzer roadie roamer roarer robalo robbed robber robust rochet rocker rocket

rococo rodent rodman roller rollon Romaic Romany Romish romper rondel ronyon roofer rookie roomer rooted rooter ropery roping roquet rosace rosary rosery rosily rosiny roster rostra rosula rotary rotate rotche rotgut rotted rotten rotter rotund rouble roucou rouncy rouser router roving rowing royals rozzer rubato rubbed rubber rubble rubbly rubefy rubify rubric ruched ruckle ruckus rudder ruddle rudely rudish rueful ruelle ruffed ruffle rufous rugged rugger rugose ruiner ruling rumble rumbly rumina rummer rumour rumple rumpus rundle runlet runnel

runner runoff runrig runway rupiah rusher rushes russet russia rustic rustle rutile rutted sabbat Sabian Sabine sables sachem sachet sacque sacral sacred sacrum sadden sadder saddhu saddle sadism sadist saeter safari safely safety sagely saggar sagged sagger saidst sailed sailer sailor saithe salaam salade salami salary Salian salify salina saline saliva sallee sallet sallow salmon saloon saloop salter saltus saluki salute salver salvia salvor salvos samara sambar sambur Samian samite samlet Samoan sampan sample Samson sandal sander sandhi sanely

sangar sanies sanify sanity sanjak sannup santal santir sapele sapful sapota sappan sapped sapper sarape sardel sarong sarsen sashay sasine sateen satiny satire satori satrap Saturn satyra saucer sauger saurel savage savant savate savine saving savory savour sawder sawfly sawney sawpit sawset sawyer saxony sayest saying sayyid scabby scalar scaled scaler scales scampi scanty scarab scarce scarer scarry scarus scathe scatty scazon scenic schema scheme schism schist schizo schlep school schorl schuss scilla sclaff sclera scolex sconce scopae scopas

scorch scorer scoria scotch scoter scotia Scotic scouse scouth scrape scrawl screak scream screed screen screwy scribe scrimp script scroll scroop scruff scrump scryer sculpt scummy scurfy scurry scurvy scutal scutch scutum scyphi scythe seaair seabed seabee seacow seadog seaear seafan seafog seafox sealer seaman seamat seamer seamew seance seapen seapig search season seater seaway secant secede secern second secret sector secund secure sedate sedile seduce seeder seeing seeker seemly seesaw seethe seiche seiner seisin seizer seizin sejant seldom

select Seljuk seller selves semble Semite semmit semple sempre senary senate sendal sender sendup senega senhor senile senior sennet sennit senora senses sensor sensum sentry sephen sepsis septal septet septic septum sequel sequin serang serape seraph serein serene serial series seriph sermon serosa serous serrae serran serval server sesame seseli sestet setoff setose setout settee setter settle sevens severe severy Sevres sewage sewing sexily sexism sexist sexpot sextan sextet sexton sexual shabby shader shades shadow shaduf shaggy shaken shaker

Shakta Shakti shalom shaman shammy shamus shandy shanny shanty shaped shapen shaper sharer sharif sharps shaven shaver shavie shears sheass sheath sheave sheeny sheets sheikh sheila shekel shelly Shelta shelty shelve sheoak sherif Sherpa sherry sheugh shield shiest shifty Shiite shikar shiksa shimmy shindy shiner shinny Shinto shinty shirty shiver shoaly shoddy shofar shogun shoppy shoran shorts shorty should shovel shover shower shrank shrewd shriek shrift shrike shrill shrimp shrine shrink shrive shroff shroud shrove shrunk shucks shutin shyest

sialic sicken sicker sickle sickly siding sienna sierra siesta sifter sigher siglum signal signer signet signor silage sileni silent silica silken siller silvan silver simian simile simmer simnel simony simoom simper simple simply simurg sinewy sinful singer single singly sinker sinned sinner sinnet sinter Siouan siphon sipped sipper sippet sircar sirdar sirkar sirrah sirree siskin sissoo sister sistra sittar sitter sixain sixgun sizing sizzle skater skeely skeigh skerry sketch skewer skibob skiddy skiing skilly skimpy skinny skirun skiver

skivvy
skylab
skyman
skyway
slacks
slaggy
slalom
slangy
slapup
slater
slaver
slavey
Slavic
slayer
sleave
sleazy
sledge
sleepy
sleety
sleeve
sleigh
sleuth
slicer
slider
slight
slimly
slinky
slipon
slippy
slipup
sliver
slogan
sloppy
sloshy
slouch
slough
Slovak
sloven
slowly
sludge
sludgy
sluice
sluicy
slummy
slurry
slushy
slyest
smalls
smalto
smarmy
smarty
smatch
smeary
smeech
smelly
smilax
smiler
smirch
smirky
smiter
smithy
smoggy
smoker
smooch
smooth
smouch
smudge
smudgy
smugly
smutch
smutty
snaggy
snappy
snarer
snarly
snatch
snathe
snazzy
sneaky
sneesh
sneeze
sneezy
sniffy
sniper
snippy
snitch
snivel
snobby
snoopy
snooty
snooze
snorer
snotty
snouty
snubby
snuffy
snugly
soaker
sobbed
sobeit
socage
soccer
social
socket
sodden
sodium
sodomy
soever
soffit
soften
softie
softly
soigne
soiree
solace
solano
soldan
solder
solely
solemn
solidi
solids
solute
solver
sombre
somite
sonant
sonata
sonnet
sonsie
sooner
soothe
sophic
sopite
sopped
sorage
sorbet
sordid
sorely
sorgho
sorner
sorrel
sorrow
sorter
sortes
sortie
Sothic
sotted
souari
sought
souled
source
sourly
souter
soviet
sovran
sowans
sowens
spacer
spadix
sparer
sparge
sparks
sparry
sparse
spathe
spavin
specie
speech
speedo
speedy
speiss
spence
spewer
sphene
sphere
sphery
sphinx
spider
spiffy
spigot
spilth
spinal
spined
spinel
spinet
spiral
spirit
spital
splash
spleen
splent
splice
spline
splint
splits
splore
splosh
spoffy
spoilt
spoken
sponge
spongy
spooky
spoony
sports
sporty
spotty
spouse
sprain
sprang
sprawl
spread
sprent
spring
sprint
sprite
sprout
spruce
spruit
sprung
spryer
spryly
spunky
spurge
spurry
sputum
squail
squall
squama
square
squash
squawk
squeak
squeal
squill
squint
squire
squirm
squirt
squish
stable
stably
stacte
stadia
stager
stagey
stairs
staith
stakes
stalag
stalky
stamen
stance
stanch
stanza
stapes
staple
starch
starer
starry
starve
stases
stasis
statal
stated
stater
states
static
stator
statue
status
stayer
steady
steamy
steely
steeve
stelae
stelar
stemma
stench
stepin
steppe
stepup
stereo
steric
sterna
sterol
stewed
sticky
stifle
stigma
stilly
stingo
stingy
stinko
stipel
stipes
stirps
stitch
stithy
stiver
stocks
stocky
stodge
stodgy
stogie
stoker
stokes
stolen
stolid
stolon
stoned
stoner
stooge
stopgo
storax
stores
storey
stormy
stound
stover
strafe
strain
strait
strake
strand
strass
strata
strath
strati
strawy
strays
streak
stream
streek
street
stress
strewn
striae
strict
stride
strife
strike
Strine
string
stripe
stripy
strive
strobe
strode
stroke
stroll
stroma
stromb
strong
stroud
strout
strove
strown
struck
struma
strung
strunt
Stuart
stubby
stucco
studio
stuffy
stumer
stumpy
stupid
stupor
sturdy
stylar
stylet
stylus
stymie
styrax
suable
subbed
subdue
sublet
subman
submit
suborn
subset
subtil
subtle
subtly
suburb
subway
sucker
suckle
sudary
sudden
suffer
suffix
Sufism
sugary
suitor
sulcus
sullen
sultan
sultry
sumach
summae
summed
summer
summit
summon
sunbow
sundae
Sunday
sunder
sundew
sundog
sundry
sungod
sunhat
sunken
sunlit
sunned
sunray
sunset
suntan
superb
supine
supped
supper
supple
supply
surely
surety
surfer
surrey
surtax
survey
suslik
sutile
sutler
suttee
suture
svelte
swaddy
swampy
swanky
swaraj
swarth
swatch
swathe
swayer
sweaty
sweeny
sweets
swerve
sweven
swimmy
swinge
swiper
swipes
swirly
swishy
switch
swivel
swoosh
swound
sylvan
symbol
syndic
syntax
syphon
Syriac
Syrian
syrinx
syrupy
system
syzygy
tabard
tabbed
tablet
tabour
tacker
tacket
tackle
tactic
taenia
tagend
tagged
tagrag
tahini
tahsil
tailor
taipan
takahe
takein
taking
talbot
talcky
talcum
talent
talion
talker
talkie
tallow
Talmud
tamale
tamara
tamely
taming
tampan
tamper
tampon
tamtam
tandem
tangle
tangly
tanist
tanked
tanker
tanned
tanner
tannic
tannin
tanrec
tantra
Taoism
Taoist
tapeta
tapped
tapper
tappet
tappit
target
Targum
tariff
tarmac
tarpan
tarpon
tarras
tarred
tarsal
tarsia
tarsus
tartan
tartar
tartly
Tarzan
tassel
tassie
taster
tatami
tatted
tatter
tattle
tattoo
taught
Taurus
tauten
tautly
tautog
tavern
tawdry
tawery
tawpie
taxies
taxman
teabag
teacup
teapot
teapoy
teasel
teaser
teaset
teazel
teazle
tedded
tedder
tedium
teemer
teensy
teepee
teeter
teethe
tegmen
tegula
teledu
telega
teller
telson
Telugu
temper
temple
tenace
tenant
tender
tendon
tenner
tennis
tenour
tenpin
tenrec
tenson
tensor
tenter
tentie
tenues
tenuis
tenure
tenuto
tenzon
tepefy
teraph
tercel
tercet
teredo
terete
tergal
tergum
termer
termly
termor
terret
territ
terror
testae
tester
teston
tetany
tetchy
tether
tetrad
tetter
Teuton
thaler
thalli
thanks
thatch
Theban
thecae
thecal
theine
theirs
theism
theist
thenar
thence
theory
theses
thesis
thetic
thieve
things
thingy
thinly
thirst
thirty
tholoi
tholos
tholus
thorax
thoria
thorny
thoron
thorpe
though
thrall
thrash
thrawn
thread
threap
threat
thresh
thrice
thrift
thrill
thrips
thrive
throat
throes
throne
throng
throve
thrown
thrush
thrust
thulia
thwack
thwart
thymol
thymus
thyrse
thyrsi
tibiae
tibial
ticked
ticker
ticket
tickey
tickle
tickly
tictac
tidbit
tiddly
tidily
tiebar
tiedye
tiepin
tierce
tiered
tierod
tiewig
tiffin
tights
tiling
tiller
tilter
timbal
timber
timbre
timely
timing
timous
tincal
tindal
tinder
tinful
tingle
tingly
tinily
tinker
tinkle
tinkly
tinman
tinned
tinner
tinpot
tinsel
tinter
tipcat
tipoff
tipped
tipper
tippet
tipple
tiptoe
tiptop
tirade
tisane
tissue
titbit
titfer
tither
titian
titled
titter
tittle
tittup
tmeses
tmesis
tocher
tocsin
toddle
toecap
toeing
toffee
togaed
togged
toggle
toiler
toilet
Toledo
toluic
toluol
tomato
tombac
tombak
tomboy
tomcat
tomcod
tomtit
tomtom
toneme
tongue
tonish
tonsil
tooter
toothy
tootle
tootsy

Tophet triune tuxedo ungues unwrap vassal virago wangle whinge wonted
tophus trivet tuyere unguis unyoke vastly virgin wanion whinny wonton
topman trivia twangy ungula upbear vatful virile wanted whippy wooded
topped trocar tweeds unhair upbeat vatted virose wanton whirly wooden
topper troche tweedy unhand upcast vaudoo virtue wapiti whisht woodsy
topple trogon tweeny unholy update vaulty visage wapper whisky woofer
torero troika twelve unhook upheld vaward viscid warble whited wooled
Tories Trojan twenty Uniate uphill vector viscus warcry whiten woolly
toroid trolly twicer unific uphold Vedist Vishnu warden whites worker
torose trompe twiggy uniped uphroe vegete visile warder whitey wormer
torpid trophy twilit unipod upkeep veiled vision wardog wholly worrit
torpor tropic twiner unique upland veined visive wargod whomso worsen
torque troppo twinge unisex uplift veleta visual warily whoops worthy
torrid trough twirly unison upmost vellum vitals warmer whoosh wortle
torsel troupe twisty united upping veloce vitric warmly whydah woundy
torten trouty twitch uniter uppish velour vittae warmth wicked wowser
torula trover twoply unjoin uppity velure vivace warmup wicker wraith
tosher trowel twould unjust uprise velvet vivers warped wicket wrasse
tosser truant twoway unkind uproar vendee vivify warper widely wrathy
tossup trudge twyere unking uproot vender vizard warred widget wreath
tother truism tycoon unkink uprush vendor vizier warren widish wrench
totted trumps tymbal unknit upshot vendue vizsla warsle wieldy wretch
totter trusty tympan unknot upside veneer voiced warted wiener wright
toucan trying typhus unlace uptake venery voided washer wifely writer
touche tryout typify unlade uptown venial voider wasted wigeon writhe
touchy tsamba typing unlaid upturn venire volant waster wigged wyvern
toupee tsetse typist unlash upward Venite volley waters wiggle xenial
toupet Tshirt tyrant unless upwind venose volost watery wiggly xenium
tourer tsotsi Tyrian unlike uracil venous volume wattle wigwag xylene
tousle Tswana ubiety unlink uraeus venter volute waught wigwam xyloid
touter Tuareg uglify unload Uralic ventil volvox wavery wilder xylose
towage tubber uglily unlock Urania ventre voodoo wavily wildly xystus
toward tubful Ugrian unmade uranic venule vorant waxily wilful yabber
towery tubing ugsome unmake Uranus verbal vortex waylay wilily yaffle
towhee tubule ullage unmask uranyl verger votary wayout willed Yahveh
townee tuchun ulster unmeet urbane verify voting weaken willet Yahweh
toxoid tucker ultima unmoor urchin verily votive weakly willow yammer
tracer tucket ultimo unnail ureter verism voulge wealth Wilton Yankee
traces tuckin umbles unpack urgent verist voyage weaner wimble yaourt
tracks tuffet umbrae unpaid urinal verity voyeur weapon wimple yapock
trader tufted umbral unpick urnful vermin vulcan wearer wincey yapped
tragic tufter umbras unplug ursine vernal vulgar weasel winded yapper
tragus tugged umlaut unread usable versal vulgus weaver winder yarely
trance tuille umpire unreal usance versed wabain weazen window yarrow
trapan tulwar unable unreel useful verser wabble webbed windup yatter
trapes tumble unbend unrest ustion verset wadded wedded winery yaupon
trappy tumefy unbent unripe usurer versus waddie weeder winged yclept
trashy tumour unbind unrobe uterus vertex waddle weekly winger yearly
trauma tumtum unbitt unroll utmost vervet waders weeper winker yeasty
travel tumuli unbolt unroof utopia vesica wadmal weepie winkle yellow
treaty tumult unborn unroot uvulae vesper wadmol weever winner yelper
treble tundra unbred unrope uvular vessel wafery weevil winnow yenned
trebly tuning uncage unruly vacant vestal waffle weight winsey yeoman
tremie tunnel uncate unsafe vacate vested wafter weirdo winter yesman
tremor tupelo uncial unsaid vacuum vestee wagged weirdy wintle yester
trench turban uncini unseal vagary vestry waggle welder wintry yipped
trendy turbid unclad unseam vagile vetted waggly weldor wirily yippee
trepan turbit uncoil unseat vagrom viable waggon welkin wiring yippie
trepid turbot uncool unseen vainly viands Wahabi welter wisdom yogism
tressy tureen uncork unself Vaisya viator wahine Wendic wisely yogurt
triage turgid uncurl unship valeta vibist wailer wester wisent yoicks
tribal turgor undate unshod valgus vibrio waiter wether wisher yolked
tricar turion undies unshoe valine victim waiver wetted withal yonder
tricky turkey undine unstop valise victor walker wetter wither yoohoo
tricot Turkic undock unsung valley vicuna walkin whacky within yorker
trifid turner undoer untidy vallum vidual walkon whaler withit Yoruba
trifle turnip undone untied valour vielle wallah whatso witted yttria
trigon turnup unduly untold valuer viewer walled wheeze wittol yumyum
trilby turret unease untrue valuta vigour waller wheezy wivern zaffer
trimer turtle uneasy untuck valved vihara wallet whenas wizard zaffre
trimly turves uneath untune vamper Viking wallop whence wizier zander
trinal Tuscan uneven unused vandal vilely wallow wherry wobble zanily
triode tusked unfair unveil vanish vilify walnut wheyey wobbly zapped
triple tusker unfold unwary vanity villus walrus whidah woeful zarape
triply tussah unfurl unwell vanner vinery wamble whiles woggle zareba
tripod tusser ungird unwept vapour vinous wambly whilom wolves zariba
tripos tussle ungirt unwind varied vintry wampee whilst wombat zealot
triste tutsan unglue unwise varlet violet wampum whimsy womera zebeck
triton tutted ungual unworn varved violin wander whiner wonder zeloso

zenana
zenith
zephyr
zeugma
zigzag
zillah
zinced
zincic
zincky
zingel
zinked
zinnia
zipped
zipper
zircon
zither
zlotys
zodiac
zombie
zonary
zonate
zoning
zonked
Zouave
zounds
zufolo
zygoma
zygote
zymase
zythum

Baalim
babble
babbly
Babism
Babist
baboon
backer
backup
baddie
badger
baffle
bagful
bagged
bagman
bagnio
bagwig
bailee
bailer
bailey
bailie
bailor
baiter
bakery
balata
balboa
baldly
baleen
balker
ballad
ballet
ballon
ballot
balsam
Baltic
bamboo
banana
bandit
bandog
banger
bangle
bangup
banian
banish
banjax
banjos
banker
banket
banned
banner
bantam
banter
banyan
banzai
baobab
barbed
barbel
barber
barbet
bardic
barege
barely
barfly
bargee
barite
barium
barker
barley
barman
barney
barony
barque
barred
barrel
barren
barret
barrio
barrow
barter
barton
baryon
baryta
basalt
basely
bashaw
basher
basics
basket
basnet
Basque
basset
bassos
baster
Basuto
Basutu
batata
bateau
bather
bathos
bating
batman
batted
batten
batter
battle
battue
bauble
bawbee
bawble
bawdry
bawler
bawley
bayard
bazaar
cabala
cabana
cabman
cachet
cachou
cackle
cacoon
cactus
caddie
caddis
cadent
cadger
caecal
caecum
cafard
Caffre
caftan
cagily
cahier
cahoot
caiman
caique
cajole
calami
calash
calcar
calces
calcic
calico
caliph
calker
calkin
caller
callet
callow
callup
callus
calmly
calory
calpac
calque
calves
calxes
camass
camber
camera
camion
camise
camlet
camper
campus
canape
canard
canary
cancan
cancel
cancer
candid
candle
canful
cangue
canine
canker
canned
cannel
canner
cannon
cannot
canopy
canter
canthi
cantle
canton
cantor
cantus
Canuck
canvas
canyon
capful
capias
caplin
capote
capped
capric
capsid
captor
carafe
carbon
carboy
carder
careen
career
caress
carfax
carful
caries
carina
carman
carnal
carnet
carney
carpal
carpel
carper
carpet
carpus
carrel
carrot
cartel
carter
carton
carvel
carven
carver
casbah
casein
casern
cashew
casing
casino
casket
Caslon
casque
cassia
cassis
caster
castle
castor
casual
catalo
catchy
catena
catgut
Cathar
cation
catkin
catnap
catnip
catsup
cattle
caucus
caudal
caudex
caudle
caught
caulis
causal
causer
causey
caveat
cavern
caviar
caving
cavity
cavort
cayman
cayuse
dabbed
dabber
dabble
dacoit
dactyl
daedal
daemon
daftly
dagger
dagoes
dahlia
daimen
daimio
daimon
dainty
damage
damask
dammar
dammed
damned
dampen
damper
damply
damsel
damson
dancer
dander
dandle
danger
dangle
Daniel
Danish
dankly
daphne
dapper
dapple
daring
darken
darkey
darkie
darkle
darkly
darned
darnel
darner
darter
dartle
dartre
dasher
dassie
datary
dative
datura
dauber
dawdle
daybed
dayfly
dazzle
eaglet
earful
earing
earner
earthy
earwax
earwig
easily
easter
eatery
eating
Fabian
fabled
fabler
fabric
facade
facete
facial
facies
facile
facing
factor
factum
facula
fadein
faerie
fagend
fagged
faggot
failed
faille
fainly
fairly
fakery
falcon
fallal
fallen
fallow
falsie
falter
family
famine
famish
famous
famuli
fandom
fanged
fanion
fanjet
fanned
fanner
fantan
Fantee
fantod
fantom
faquir
fardel
farfel
farina
farmer
faroff
farout
farrow
fasces
fascia
fasten
faster
fathen
father
fathom
fatted
fatten
fatter
faucal
fauces
faucet
faulty
faunae
faunal
faunas
favour
fawner
gabbed
gabber
gabble
gabbro
gabion
gabled
gablet
gadded
gadder
gadfly
gadget
Gadhel
gadoid
Gaelic
gaffer
gagged
gagger
gaggle
gagman
gaiety
gainer
gainly
gainst
gaited
gaiter
galago
galaxy
galena
galiot
galley
Gallic
Gallio
gallon
gallop
galoot
galore
galosh
gambir
gambit
gamble
gambol
gamely
gamete
gamily
gamine
gaming
gammer
gammon
gander
ganger
gangly
gangue
gannet
ganoid
gantry
gaoler
gapped
garage
garbed
garble
garcon
garden
garget
gargle
garial
garish
garlic
garner
garnet
garran
garret
garron
garrot
garter
garuda
garvie
gasbag
Gascon
gasify
gasket
gaskin
gasman
gasper
gassed
gasser
gateau
gather
gauche
gaucho
gauger
gavage
gavial
gazebo
gazump
habile
hackle
hackly
haddie
hadron
haemal
haemin
haffet
haffit
hagbut
haggis
haggle
hailer
hairdo
haired
haleru
halide
halite
hallal
halloa
halloo
hallow
hallux
haloes
halter
halvah
halves
hamate
Hamite
hamlet
hammal
hammam
hammed
hammer
hamper
handed
handle
hangar
hanged
hanger
hangup
hanker
hankie
hansel
hansom
happed
happen
haptic
harass
harden
hardly
hardup
harken
harlot
harper
harrow
hartal
haslet
hassle
hasten
hatbox
hatful
hatpeg
hatpin
hatred
hatted
hatter
hauler
haunch
Havana
havers
hawhaw
hawked
hawker
hawser
haybox
haymow
hazard
hazily
iambic
iambus
jabbed
jabber
jabiru
jacana
jackal
jacket
jaeger
jagged
jagger
jaguar
jailer
jailor
jalopy
jammed
jammer
jangle
jarful
jargon
jarrah
jarred
jarvey
jasper
jaunce
jaunty
kabala
kabuki
Kabyle
Kaffir
kaftan
kainit
kaiser
kakapo
kalong
kanaka
kaolin
kaputt
karate
karmic
kaross
karroo
kasbah
kation
laager
labial
labile
labium
labour
labret
labrum
laceup
laches
lacing
lackey
lactic
lacuna
ladder
laddie
ladify
lading
ladino
ladyfy
lagged
lagger
lagoon
laguna
laical
lallan
lambda
lamber
lamely
lament
lamina
lamish
Lammas
lammed
lanate
lancer
lancet
landau
landed
lander
langue
langur
lankly
lanner
lanugo
lapdog
lapful
lapped
lappet
lappie
lapsed
lapsus
larder
lardon
lariat
larker
larrup
larvae
larval
larynx
lascar
lasher
lashup
lasque
lassie
lassos
laster
lastly
lateen
lately
latent
latest
lather
latish
latria
latron
latten
latter
launce
launch
laurel
lavabo
lavage
laveer
lavish
lavolt
lawful
lawman
lawyer
laxity
layday
layman
layoff
layout
lazily
lazuli
macaco
machan
mackle
macron
macula
macule
Madame
madcap
madden
madder
madman
madras
maduro
maenad
maggot
Magian
magilp
magnet
magnum
magpie
maguey
Magyar
mahout
maidan
maiden
maigre
mailed
mainly
Majlis
makedo
makeup
making
malady
Malaga
malate
maleic
malice

malign masher pallia patron ransom salify tabard Taurus wander absent
malism mashie pallid patted ranter salina tabbed tauten wangle absorb
malkin masker pallor patten ranula saline tablet tautly wanion absurd
mallee maslin palmar patter raphia saliva tabour tautog wanted abulia
mallei Masora palmer paunch raphis sallee tacker tavern wanton abuser
mallet masque palolo pauper rapids sallet tacket tawdry wapiti ibexes
mallow massif palpal pavage rapier sallow tackle tawery wapper ibices
maltha masted palpus pavane rapine salmon tactic tawpie warble ibidem
mammae master palter paving rapist saloon taenia taxies warcry obeche
mammal mastic paltry pavior rapped saloop tagend taxman warden obelus
mammee matico pampas pavise rappee salter tagged vacant warder obeyer
mammer matins pamper pawnee rappel saltus tagrag vacate wardog obital
mammon matlow panada pawner rapper saluki tahini vacuum wargod object
manage matrix panama pawpaw raptly salute tahsil vagary warily objure
manana matron panary payday raptor salver tailor vagile warmer oblast
manche matted pander paynim rarefy salvia taipan vagrom warmly oblate
Manchu matter pandit payoff rarely salvor takahe vainly warmth oblige
manday mature panful payola raring salvos takein Vaisya warmup oblong
manege matzoh panned rabato rarity samara taking valeta warped oboist
manful maugre pantry rabbet rascal sambar talbot valgus warper obsess
mangel maundy panzer rabbin rasher sambur talcky valine warred obtain
manger maxima papacy rabbit rashly Samian talcum valise warren obtect
mangle maxixe papain rabble rasper samite talent valley warsle obtest
mangos maybug papaya rabies raster samlet talion vallum warted obtund
maniac mayday papers raceme rasure Samoan talker valour washer obtuse
manila mayest papery rachis ratbag sampan talkie valuer wasted obvert
manioc mayfly papism racial rather sample tallow valuta waster ubiety
manito mayhap papist racily ratify Samson Talmud valved waters acacia
manned mayhem pappus racism ratine sandal tamale vamper watery acajou
manner maying papula racist rating sander tamara vandal wattle acarid
manque mazard papule racker ration sandhi tamely vanish waught acarus
mantel mazily papyri racket ratite sanely taming vanity wavery accede
mantes nabbed parade racoon ratlin sangar tampan vanner wavily accent
mantic naevus paramo raddle ratoon sanies tamper vapour waxily accept
mantid nagana parang radial rattan sanify tampon varied waylay access
mantis nagged paraph radian rattat sanity tamtam varlet wayout accord
mantle nagger parcel radish ratted sanjak tandem varved yabber accost
mantra nailer pardie radium ratter sannup tangle vassal yaffle accrue
mantua namely pardon radius rattle santal tangly vastly Yahveh accuse
manual nanism parent radome ravage santir tanist vatful Yahweh acedia
manuka napalm parget radula ravine sapele tanked vatted yammer acetal
manure napkin pariah raffia raving sapful tanker vaudoo Yankee acetic
Maoism napped parian raffle ravish sapota tanned vaulty yaourt acetyl
Maoist nardoo paring rafter razzia sappan tanner vaward yapock achene
mapped narrow parish ragbag razzle sapped tannic wabain yapped acidic
mapper nastic parity ragged sabbat sapper tannin wabble yapper acidly
maquis natant parkin raggee Sabian sarape tanrec wadded yarely acinar
maraca nation parlay raggle Sabine sardel tantra waddie yarrow acinus
maraud native parley raglan sables sarong Taoism waddle yatter ackack
marble natron parody ragman sachem sarsen Taoist waders yaupon acquit
marbly natter parole ragout sachet sashay tapeta wadmal zaffer across
marcel nature parous ragtag sacque sasine tapped wadmol zaffre acting
margay naught parpen raguly sacral sateen tapper wafery zander action
margin nausea parral raider sacred satiny tappet waffle zanily active
marina nautch parrel railer sacrum satire tappit wafter zapped actual
marine Nazify parrot raiser sadden satori target wagged zarape acuity
marish Nazism parsec raisin sadder satrap Targum waggle zareba acumen
Marist oafish Parsee Rajput saddhu Saturn tariff waggly zariba ecarte
marked oarage parson rakish saddle satyra tarmac waggon abacus echoer
marker pacify partan ramate sadism saucer tarpan Wahabi abater echoic
market packer partly ramble sadist sauger tarpon wahine abatis eclair
markup packet parure ramify saeter saurel tarras wailer abbacy eczema
marlin padauk parvis ramjet safari savage tarred waiter abbess iceaxe
marmot padded pascal rammed safely savant tarsal waiver abduce icebag
maroon paddle Pashto rammer safety savate tarsia walker abduct icebox
marque paella passer ramose sagely savine tarsus walkin abject icecap
marram paeony passim ramous saggar saving tartan walkon abjure iceman
marred pagoda pastel ramper sagged savory tartar wallah ablate icicle
marron paidup pastil ramrod sagger savour tartly walled ablaut iconic
marrow pajama pastor ramson saidst sawder Tarzan waller ablaze occamy
marrum pakeha pastry rancho sailed sawfly tassel wallet abloom occult
marshy palace patchy rancid sailer sawney tassie wallop ablush occupy
marten palais patent randan sailor sawpit taster wallow aboard ocelli
martin palate Pathan randem saithe sawset tatami walnut aboral ocelot
martyr paleae pathic random salaam sawyer tatted walrus abound ochone
marvel palely pathos ranger salade saxony tatter wamble abrade oclock
mascle paling patina ranker salami sayest tattle wambly abroad octane
mascon palish patois rankle salary saying tattoo wampee abrupt octant
mascot pallet patrol rankly Salian sayyid taught wampum abseil octave

octavo
octroi
ocular
scabby
scalar
scaled
scaler
scales
scampi
scanty
scarab
scarce
scarer
scarry
scarus
scathe
scatty
scazon
scenic
schema
scheme
schism
schist
schizo
schlep
school
schorl
schuss
scilla
sclaff
sclera
scolex
sconce
scopae
scopas
scorch
scorer
scoria
scotch
scoter
scotia
Scotic
scouse
scouth
scrape
scrawl
screak
scream
screed
screen
screwy
scribe
scrimp
script
scroll
scroop
scruff
scrump
scryer
sculpt
scummy
scurfy
scurry
scurvy
scutal
scutch
scutum
scyphi
scythe
yclept
adagio
Adamic
addend
addict
addled
adduce
adduct
adenyl
adhere

adieus
adieux
adipic
adjoin
adjure
adjust
admass
admire
adnate
adnexa
Adonic
Adonis
adorer
adrift
adroit
adsorb
advent
adverb
advert
advice
advise
adytum
Eddaic
Edenic
edgily
edging
edible
editor
ideaed
ideate
idiocy
idolum
oddity
oddjob
oddson
odious
aedile
Aegean
Aeolic
aerate
aerial
aerily
aerobe
aether
beachy
beacon
beadle
beagle
beaked
beaker
beamer
beanie
bearer
beaten
beater
Beaune
beauty
beaver
becall
becalm
became
becket
beckon
become
bedaub
bedaze
bedbug
bedded
bedder
bedeck
bedell
bedlam
bedpan
bedsit
beduin
beeper
beetle
beeves
befall

befell
befool
before
befoul
beggar
begged
begird
begirt
begone
behalf
behave
behead
beheld
behest
behind
behold
behoof
behove
beigel
belaud
beldam
belfry
Belgic
belief
belike
belive
bellow
belong
belted
beluga
bemire
bemoan
bemock
bemuse
bender
benign
bennet
benumb
benzol
benzyl
berate
Berber
bereft
berlin
bertha
berthe
beseem
beside
bested
bestir
bestow
betake
bethel
betide
betony
betook
betray
betted
better
bettor
bewail
beware
bewray
beyond
bezant
bezoar
cecity
cedarn
celery
celiac
cellar
celled
Celtic
cement
censer
censor
census
cental
centre

centum
cerate
cercus
cereal
cereus
ceriph
cerise
cerium
cermet
certes
ceruse
cervix
cesser
cestus
cesura
cetane
deacon
deaden
deadly
deafen
deafly
dealer
dearie
dearly
dearth
deasil
debark
debase
debate
debris
debtor
debunk
decade
decamp
decani
decant
deceit
decent
decide
decker
deckle
decoct
decode
decoke
decree
dedans
deduce
deduct
deejay
deepen
deeply
deface
defame
defeat
defect
defend
defier
defile
define
deform
defray
deftly
defuse
degras
degree
degust
dehorn
deicer
deific
deject
delate
delete
delict
delude
deluge
deluxe
delver
demand
demark

demean
dement
demise
demist
demode
demote
demure
denary
dengue
denial
denier
denims
denote
dental
dentel
dentil
denude
deodar
depart
depend
depict
deploy
depone
deport
depose
depute
deputy
derail
derate
deride
derive
dermal
dermic
dermis
derris
desalt
descry
desert
design
desire
desist
desman
desmid
desorb
despot
detach
detail
detain
detect
detent
detest
detour
deuced
devest
device
devise
devoid
devoir
devote
devour
devout
dewily
dewlap
dexter
eerily
fealty
featly
feckly
fecula
fecund
fedora
feeble
feebly
feeder
feeing
feeler
feirie
feisty
feline

fellah
feller
felloe
fellow
felony
female
femora
fencer
fender
Fenian
fenman
fennec
fennel
ferial
ferine
ferret
ferric
ferula
ferule
fervid
fescue
festal
fester
fetial
fetich
fetish
fetter
fettle
feudal
fezzed
fezzes
geckos
geegee
geezer
geisha
gelled
Gemara
Gemini
gemmae
gemmed
gender
genera
geneva
genial
genius
genned
genome
gentes
gentle
gently
gentoo
gentry
geodic
George
gerbil
gerent
german
germen
gerund
getout
getter
gewgaw
geyser
headed
header
headon
healer
health
hearer
hearse
hearth
hearty
heated
heater
heathy
heaven
heaver
Hebrew
heckle

hectic
hector
heddle
hedera
hedger
heehaw
heeled
heeler
hegira
heifer
height
hejira
helium
heller
helmet
helper
hemmed
hempen
henrun
henrys
hepcat
heptad
herald
herbal
herder
herdic
hereat
hereby
herein
hereof
hereon
heresy
hereto
heriot
hermit
hernia
heroic
heroin
herpes
Herren
hetero
hetman
hexact
hexane
hexose
heyday
jeerer
jejune
jennet
jerbil
jerboa
jerker
jerkin
jersey
jester
Jesuit
jetlag
jetsam
jetted
Jewess
Jewish
jezail
keenly
keeper
kelpie
kelson
kelter
Keltic
kelvin
kenned
kennel
kermes
kermis
kerned
kernel
kersey
ketone
kettle
kewpie

keyway
leaden
leader
leadin
leadup
leafed
league
lealty
leanly
leanto
leaper
learnt
leaved
leaven
leaver
leaves
lecher
lector
ledged
ledger
leeway
legacy
legate
legato
legbye
legend
legged
legion
legist
legman
legume
lemony
lender
length
lenity
lensed
Lenten
lentil
Leonid
lepton
lesion
lessee
lessen
lesser
lesson
lessor
lethal
letoff
letter
Lettic
levant
Levite
levity
lewdly
meadow
meagre
mealie
meanie
meanly
measly
meatus
meddle
mediae
medial
median
medick
medico
medium
medius
medlar
medley
medusa
meekly
meetly
megilp
megohm
megrim
meinie
mellow

melody
melton
member
memoir
memory
menace
menage
mender
menhir
menial
meninx
mensal
menses
mental
mentor
mentum
mercer
merely
merest
merger
merils
merino
merism
merlin
merlon
merman
merrie
mescal
mesial
messan
Messrs
mestee
metage
metals
meteor
method
methyl
metier
metope
metred
metric
mettle
mezuza
neaped
nearby
nearer
nearly
neaten
neatly
nebula
nebuly
nectar
needle
neednt
negate
nekton
nelson
Nepali
nephew
nereid
nerine
nerite
neroli
nestle
Nestor
netful
nether
netted
nettle
neural
neuron
neuter
newish
newton
oecist
oedema
oeuvre
peachy
peahen

peaked
peanut
pearly
peavey
pebble
pebbly
pecker
pecten
pectic
pectin
pedalo
pedant
pedate
peddle
pedlar
peeler
peeper
peepul
peewit
pegged
pegleg
pegtop
pelage
pelham
pellet
pelmet
pelota
peltae
pelter
peltry
pelves
pelvic
pelvis
pencil
penman
pennae
penned
pennon
pentad
pentup
pentyl
penult
penury
people
peplum
pepped
pepper
pepsin
peptic
perdue
period
perish
permit
perron
person
pertly
peruke
peruse
pesade
peseta
pesewa
pester
pestle
petara
petard
petite
petrel
petrol
petted
petter
pewter
peyote
peyotl
reader
really
realty
reamer
reaper
rearer

reason
reaver
rebate
rebato
rebeck
rebore
reborn
rebuff
rebuke
recall
recant
recast
recede
recent
recess
recipe
recite
reckon
recoil
recoin
record
recoup
rector
rectum
rectus
redact
redbud
redcap
redden
redder
reddle
redeem
redeye
redhot
rediae
redone
redraw
redtop
reduce
reebok
reecho
reedit
reefer
reeler
reface
refect
refill
refine
reflex
reflow
reflux
reform
refuel
refuge
refund
refuse
refute
regain
regale
regard
regent
reggae
regime
regina
region
regius
reglet
regnal
regret
regulo
rehash
rehear
reheat
reheel
reiver
reject
rejoin
relaid
relate
relent
relict
relief
reline
relish
relive
reload
reluct
relume
remade
remain
remake
remand
remark
remedy
remind
remint
remise
remiss
remora
remote
remove
remuda
rename
render
renege
rennet
renown
rental
renter
reopen
repaid
repair
repand
repass
repast
repeal
repeat
repent
repine
replay
replum
report
repose
repugn
repute
reread
resale
rescue
reseat
reseau
resect
reseda
resell
resent
reship
reside
resign
resile
resist
resold
resole
resorb
resort
rester
result
resume
retail
retain
retake
retard
retell
retene
retest
retial
retina
retire
retold
retook
retool
retort
retral
retrod
retted
returf
return
retuse
revamp
reveal
reverb
revere
revers
revert
revery
revest
review
revile
revise
revive
revoke
revolt
revved
reward
rewind
rewire
rewoke
reword
rework
seaair
seabed
seabee
seacow
seadog
seaear
seafan
seafog
seafox
sealer
seaman
seamat
seamer
seamew
seance
seapen
seapig
search
season
seater
seaway
secant
secede
secern
second
secret
sector
secund
secure
sedate
sedile
seduce
seeder
seeing
seeker
seemly
seesaw
seethe
seiche
seiner
seisin
seizer
seizin
sejant
seldom
select
Seljuk
seller
selves
semble
Semite
semmit
semple
sempre
senary
senate
sendal
sender
sendup
senega
senhor
senile
senior
sennet
sennit
senora
senses
sensor
sensum
sentry
sephen
sepsis
septal
septet
septic
septum
sequel
sequin
serang
serape
seraph
serein
serene
serial
series
seriph
sermon
serosa
serous
serrae
serran
serval
server
sesame
seseli
sestet
setoff
setose
setout
settee
setter
settle
sevens
severe
severy
Sevres
sewage
sewing
sexily
sexism
sexist
sexpot
sextan
sextet
sexton
sexual
teabag
teacup
teapot
teapoy
teasel
teaser
teaset
teazel
teazle
tedded
tedder
tedium
teemer
teensy
teepee
teeter
teethe
tegmen
tegula
teledu
telega
teller
telson
Telugu
temper
temple
tenace
tenant
tender
tendon
tenner
tennis
tenour
tenpin
tenrec
tenson
tensor
tenter
tentie
tenues
tenuis
tenure
tenuto
tenzon
tepefy
teraph
tercel
tercet
teredo
terete
tergal
tergum
termer
termly
termor
terret
territ
terror
testae
tester
teston
tetany
tetchy
tether
tetrad
tetter
Teuton
vector
Vedist
vegete
veiled
veined
veleta
vellum
veloce
velour
velure
velvet
vendee
vender
vendor
vendue
veneer
venery
venial
venire
Venite
venose
venous
venter
ventil
ventre
venule
verbal
verger
verify
verily
verism
verist
verity
vermin
vernal
versal
versed
verser
verset
versus
vertex
vervet
vesica
vesper
vessel
vestal
vested
vestee
vestry
vetted
weaken
weakly
wealth
weaner
weapon
wearer
weasel
weaver
weazen
webbed
wedded
weeder
weekly
weeper
weepie
weever
weevil
weight
weirdo
weirdy
welder
weldor
welkin
welter
Wendic
wester
wether
wetted
wetter
xenial
xenium
yearly
yeasty
yellow
yelper
yenned
yeoman
yesman
yester
zealot
zebeck
zeloso
zenana
zenith
zephyr
zeugma
afeard
affair
affect
affeer
affine
affirm
afflux
afford
affray
Afghan
afield
aflame
afloat
afraid
afreet
afresh
afrite
afters
efface
effect
effete
effigy
efflux
effort
effuse
offend
offent
office
offing
offish
offkey
offset
agamic
agamid
agaric
ageing
agency
agenda
ageold
aghast
agnail
agnate
agnise
agonal
agonic
agouti
agrafe
aguish
Egeria
egesta
eggcup
eggler
eggnog
egoism
egoist
egress
ignite
ignore
iguana
ogamic
ogival
ogress
ogrish
uglify
uglily
Ugrian
ugsome
ahimsa
bharal
bhisti
chacha
chacma
chafer
chaffy
chaise
chalet
chalky
chance
chancy
change
chanty
chapel
chappy
charas
charge
Charon
chaser
chaste
chatty
chaunt
cheeky
cheers
cheery
cheese
cheesy
chelae
chemic
cheque
cherry
cherty
cherub
chesil
chesty
chevet
chiasm
chiaus
chichi
chicle
chield
chigoe
chilli
chilly
chimer
chintz
chippy
chirpy
chisel
chital
chitin
chiton
chitty
chives
chivvy
choice
choker
chokey
choler
choose
choosy
chopin
choppy
choral
chorea
choric
chorus
chosen
chough
chouse
chrism
Christ
chroma
chrome
chromo
chubby
chuffy
chukar
chukka
chummy
chunky
church
chypre
dharma
dhooti
dhurra
gharry
ghetto
ghosty
ohmage
phalli
pharos
phasic
phasis
phatic
phenol
phenyl
phlegm
phloem
phobia
phobic
phoebe
phoney
phonic
phonon
phooey
photic
photon
phrase
phylum
physic
rhaphe
rhebok
rhesus
rhetor
rheumy
rhinal
rhombi
rhumba
rhymer
rhythm
shabby
shader
shades
shadow
shaduf
shaggy
shaken
shaker
Shakta
Shakti
shalom
shaman
shammy
shamus
shandy
shanny
shanty
shaped
shapen
shaper
sharer
sharif
sharps
shaven
shaver
shavie
shears
sheass
sheath
sheave
sheeny
sheets
sheikh
sheila
shekel
shelly
Shelta
shelty
shelve
sheoak
sherif
Sherpa
sherry
sheugh
shield
shiest
shifty
Shiite
shikar
shiksa
shimmy
shindy
shiner
shinny
Shinto
shinty
shirty
shiver
shoaly
shoddy
shofar
shogun
shoppy
shoran
shorts
shorty
should
shovel
shover
shower
shrank
shrewd
shriek
shrift
shrike
shrill
shrimp
shrine
shrink
shrive
shroff
shroud
shrove
shrunk
shucks
shutin
shyest
thaler
thalli
thanks
thatch
Theban
thecae
thecal
theine
theirs
theism
theist
thenar
thence
theory
theses
thesis
thetic
thieve
things
thingy
thinly
thirst
thirty
tholoi
tholos
tholus
thorax
thoria
thorny
thoron
thorpe
though
thrall
thrash
thrawn
thread
threap
threat
thresh
thrice
thrift
thrill
thrips
thrive
throat
throes
throne
throng

throve biotic dinner finnan jingle lingua Minoan piggin rillet sissoo
thrown biotin diplex finned jingly linhay minter piglet rimmed sister
thrush birdie diploe finner jinnee lining minuet pignut rimose sistra
thrust bireme diplon Finnic jitney linkup minute pigsty rimous sittar
thulia birkie dipnet fiorin jitter linnet miosis pilaff ringed sitter
thwack birler dipody fipple kiaugh linney miotic pileum ringer sixain
thwart bisect dipole firing kibble linsey mirage pileup rinser sixgun
thymol bishop dipped firkin kibitz lintel mirror pileus rioter sizing
thymus bisque dipper firlot kiblah lintie miscue pilfer ripely sizzle
thyrse bister dipsas firman kibosh lionel misdid pillar ripoff tibiae
thyrsi bistre dirdum firmly kicker lipase misere pillow ripped tibial
whacky bistro direct fiscal kidded lipide misery pilose ripper ticked
whaler bitchy direly fisher kidder lipoid misfit pilous ripple ticker
whatso biting dirham fistic kiddie lipoma mishap pilule ripply ticket
wheeze bitted dirhem fitful kidnap lipped mishit pimple riprap tickey
wheezy bitten dirndl fitted kidney lippen mishmi pimply ripsaw tickle
whenas bitter disarm fitter kiekie lippie Mishna pincer rising tickly
whence bizone disbar fixate killer liquid mislay pineal risker tictac
wherry cicada disbud fixity kilted liquor misled pinery risque tidbit
wheyey cicala discal fizgig kilter lisper missal pineta ritual tiddly
whidah cicely discus fizzle kimono lissom missel pinger rivage tidily
whiles cigala diseur giaour kincob listed missis pinion rizzar tiebar
whilom cilice dismal gibber kindle listel missus pinkie rizzer tiedye
whilst cilium dismay gibbet kindly listen mister pinnae sialic tiepin
whimsy cinder disown gibbon kinema lister mistle pinned sicken tierce
whiner cinema dispel giddap kingly litany misuse pinner sicker tiered
whinge cineol distal gifted kipper litchi mitral pinole sickle tierod
whinny cinque distil gigged kirsch lithia mitten pintle sickly tiewig
whippy cipher disuse giggle kirtle lithic mizzen piolet siding tiffin
whirly circle dither giggly kismet litmus mizzle pionic sienna tights
whisht circus dittos giglet kisser litter mizzly piping sierra tiling
whisky cirque divers giglot kitbag little niacin pipkin siesta tiller
whited cirrus divert gigman kitcat livein nibbed pipped sifter tilter
whiten cistus divest gigolo kitool lively nibble pippin sigher timbal
whites cither divide gilder kitsch livery nicely piquet siglum timber
whitey citole divine gilled kitten living nicety piracy signal timbre
wholly citric diving gillie kittle lizard nicish pirate signer timely
whomso citron eidola gimbal kittul miasma nickel piraya signet timing
whoops citrus eighth gimlet liable mickey nicker Pisces signor timous
whoosh civics eighty gimmal liaise mickle nidget pissed silage tincal
whydah diacid either gimmer libber micron nidify pistil sileni tindal
aikido diadem fiacre gingal libido midage nielli pistol silent tinder
airbed diaper fiance ginger Libyan midair niello piston silica tinful
airbus diatom fiasco gingko lichee midday nigger pitchy silken tingle
airgun dibbed fibbed ginkgo lichen midden niggle pithos siller tingly
airily dibber fibber ginned lictor middle nighty pitier silvan tinily
airing dibble fibred ginner lidded midget nignog pitman silver tinker
airman dicast fibril girder lieder midgut nilgai pitpan simian tinkle
airsac dicker fibrin girdle lierne midoff nimble pitsaw simile tinkly
airway dickey fibula girlie lifter midrib nimbly pitted simmer tinman
aisled dictum fickle hiatus liftup midway nimbus pitter simnel tinned
bibbed diddle fiddle hiccup ligate miffed Nimrod pizzle simony tinner
bibber didoes fiddly hickey ligger mighty ninety ribald simoom tinpot
biceps diesel fidget hidden lights mignon nipped riband simoon tinsel
bicker dieses fierce hiding lignin mihrab nipper ribbed simper tinter
bidden diesis fiesta hieing ligula mikado nipple ribbon simple tipcat
bidder dieter figged higgle ligule milady nitric ribose simply tipoff
bieldy differ figure higher ligure milage nitwit richen simurg tipped
biffin digamy filfot highly likely mildew oidium riches sinewy tipper
biform digest filial hijack liking mildly oilcan richly sinful tippet
bigamy digger filing hinder lilied milieu oilman ricker singer tipple
bigger diglot filler Hindoo limbec milker oilnut rickey single tiptoe
biggin dikdik fillet hinged limbed milled piaffe ricrac singly tiptop
bigwig diktat fillip hipped limber miller piazza rictal sinker tirade
Bihari dilate filmic hippie limbic millet picker rictus sinned tisane
bijoux dilute filose hirple limbus milord picket ridded sinner tissue
bikini dimity filter hispid liming milter pickle ridden sinnet titbit
bilbos dimmed filthy hisser limner mimosa pickup riddle sinter titfer
bilker dimmer fimble hither limper mincer picnic rident Siouan tither
billet dimple finale hitman limpet minded picric ridged siphon titian
billon dimply finals jibbah limpid minder piddle riding sipped titled
billow dimwit finder jibbed limply mingle pidgin rifely sipper titter
billyo dingey finely jibber limuli minify piecer riffle sippet tittle
binary dinghy finery jigged linage minima piedog rifler sircar tittup
binate dingle finger jigger linden mining pieman rigged sirdar viable
binder dingus finial jiggle lineal minion pierce rigger sirkar viands
binful dining fining jiggly linear minish piffle righto sirrah viator
bionic dinkum finish jigsaw lineup minium pigeon rigour sirree vibist
biopsy dinned finite jilter linger minnow pigged rigout siskin vibrio

victim wintry allele closet fluter plural embryo angina ensile inmate
victor wirily allied clothe flying plushy emerge angled ensoul inmost
vicuna wiring allium cloudy flyman pluton emeses angler ensure innate
vidual wisdom allout clough flysch slacks emesis angora entail inning
vielle wisely allred cloven flyway slaggy emetic anicut entera inroad
viewer wisent allude clover glacis slalom emetin animal entice inrush
vigour wisher allure clumpy gladly slangy emeute animus entire insane
vihara withal almond clumsy glairy slapup empery anklet entity inseam
Viking wither almost clunch glaive slater empire anlace entoil insect
vilely within alpaca clutch glance slaver employ anlage entomb insert
vilify withit alpine clypei glassy slavey empusa annals entrap inside
villus witted alsike elapse glazer Slavic emulge anneal entree insist
vinery wittol alulae elated gleamy slayer imbibe annexe envier insole
vinous wivern alumna elater gleety sleave imbrex annual enwind inspan
vintry wizard alumni eldest glibly sleazy imbrue annuli enwomb instal
violet wizier always eleven glider sledge immane anodal enwrap instar
violin yipped bladed elevon glitch sleepy immesh anodic enzyme instep
virago yippee blanch elfish global sleety immune anoint gnarly instil
virgin yippie blanky elicit gloomy sleeve immure anomic gnawer insult
virile zigzag blazer elixir gloria sleigh impact anomie gneiss insure
virose zillah blazes elodea glossy sleuth impair anonym gnomic intact
virtue zinced blazon eloign glover slicer impala anorak gnomon intake
visage zincic bleach eloper glower slider impale anoxia gnosis intend
viscid zincky bleary eluant glumly slight impark anoxic inarch intent
viscus zingel blench eluate glumpy slimly impart answer inborn intern
Vishnu zinked blende eluent glutei slinky impawn anthem inbred intine
visile zinnia blenny elvish gluten slipon impede anther incase intoed
vision zipped blight elytra glycin slippy impend antiar incept intone
visive zipper blimey flabby glycol slipup impish anting incest intray
visual zircon blintz flacon illume sliver impone antler inches intuit
vitals zither blithe flaggy illuse slogan import antral incise inulin
vitric djibba blonde flagon klepht sloppy impose antrum incite invade
vittae djinni bloody flambe oldish sloshy impost anyhow inclip invent
vivace ejecta bloomy flamen oleate slouch impugn anyone income invert
vivers akimbo blotch flanch olefin slough impure anyway incubi invest
vivify skater blotto flange oliver Slovak impute enable incult invite
vizard skeely blouse flappy placed sloven omasum enamel incuse invoke
vizier skeigh blowed flashy placer slowly omelet encage indaba inward
vizsla skerry blower flatly placet sludge omenta encamp indeed inwick
wicked sketch blowsy flatus placid sludgy smalls encase indene inwove
wicker skewer blowup flaunt plagal sluice smalto encash indent inwrap
wicket skibob blowzy flavin plague sluicy smarmy encode Indian inyala
widely skiddy bluing flaxen plaguy slummy smarty encore indict knaggy
widget skiing bluish fleche plaice slurry smatch encyst indign knight
widish skilly blunge fledge plaint slushy smeary endear indigo knives
wieldy skimpy blurry fleece planar slyest smeech ending indite knobby
wiener skinny claggy fleech planer ullage smelly endive indium knotty
wifely skirun clammy fleecy planet ulster smilax endure indole knower
wigeon skiver claque flench plaque ultima smiler energy indoor onager
wigged skivvy claret flense plashy ultimo smirch enface induce oncost
wiggle skylab classy fleshy plasma zlotys smirky enfold induct oneoff
wiggly skyman clause fletch platan amadou smiter engage indult oneway
wigwag skyway claver fleury platen amatol smithy engild induna onfall
wigwam alalia clavis flexor plater amazon smoggy engine infamy online
wilder alarum clayey flight player ambler smoker engird infant onrush
wildly alated cleave flimsy pleach ambush smooch engirt infare onside
wilful albata clench flinch please amends smooth englut infect onward
wilily albedo clergy flinty plebby amenta smouch engram infelt pneuma
willed albeit cleric flirty pledge amerce smudge engulf infest snaggy
willet albert clever flitch plenty amidst smudgy enhalo infirm snappy
willow albino clevis floaty plenum amnion smugly enigma inflow snarer
Wilton albite cliche flocci pleura amoeba smutch enisle influx snarly
wimble alcaic client floozy plexor amoral smutty enjoin infold snatch
wimple alcove cliffy floppy plexus amount tmeses enlace inform snathe
wincey Aldine climax florae pliant ampere tmesis enlist infula snazzy
winded aldose clinch floral plicae amulet umbles enmesh infuse sneaky
winder aldrin clingy floras pliers amuser umbrae enmity ingest sneesh
window alegar clinic floret plight amylum umbral ennead ingulf sneeze
windup alevin clipon florid plinth embalm umbras ennuye inhale sneezy
winery alexia clique florin plisse embank umlaut enosis inhere sniffy
winged alexin cliquy flossy ploidy embark umpire enough inhume sniper
winger algoid cloaca floury plotty embers anabas enrage inject snippy
winker alight cloche flower plough emblem anadem enrapt injure snitch
winkle aliped cloddy fluent plover emblic ananas enrich injury snivel
winner alkali cloggy fluffy plucky embody anarch enrobe inkpot snobby
winnow alkane clonal flukey plumed emboli anatta enroll inlaid snoopy
winsey alkene clonic flunky plummy emboly anatto enroot inland snooty
winter alkyne clonus flurry plumpy emboss anchor ensate inlaws snooze
wintle allege closed fluted plunge embrue angary ensign inlier snorer

snotty	unpaid	bonito	cobnut	conned	cousin	dowlas	gobbet	hooded	Korean
snouty	unpick	bonnet	cobweb	conner	covert	downer	gobble	hoodie	kosher
snubby	unplug	bonnie	coccal	conoid	coving	dowser	goblet	hoodoo	kowhai
snuffy	unread	bonsai	coccid	consul	cowage	doyley	goblin	hoofed	kowtow
snugly	unreal	bonxie	coccus	convex	coward	dozily	gocart	hoofer	loaded
unable	unreel	bonzer	coccyx	convey	cowboy	Eocene	goddam	hookah	loader
unbend	unrest	booboo	cochin	convoy	cowish	eolian	godown	hooked	loafer
unbent	unripe	boodle	cocked	cooker	cowled	eolith	godson	hooker	loaner
unbind	unrobe	boohoo	cocker	cookie	cowman	eonian	godwit	hookey	loathe
unbitt	unroll	booing	cockle	cooler	cowpat	eonism	goffer	hookup	loaves
unbolt	unroof	booker	cocoon	coolie	cowpea	Eozoic	goggle	hooper	lobate
unborn	unroot	bookie	coddle	coolly	cowpox	Eozoon	goggly	hoopla	lobbed
unbred	unrope	booksy	codger	coolth	cowrie	fobbed	goglet	hoopoe	lobose
uncage	unruly	boomer	codify	coonty	coyote	focsle	Goidel	hooray	lobule
uncate	unsafe	booted	codlin	cooper	doable	fodder	goitre	hootch	locale
uncial	unsaid	bootee	coelom	cootie	dobbin	foeman	gokart	hooter	locate
uncini	unseal	boozer	coerce	copeck	docent	foetal	golden	hooves	lochan
unclad	unseam	bopeep	coeval	copier	docile	foetid	golfer	hopped	locker
uncoil	unseat	bopped	coffee	coping	docker	foetus	gollop	hopper	locket
uncool	unseen	bopper	coffer	copita	docket	fogbow	golosh	hopple	lockup
uncork	unself	borage	coffin	copout	doctor	fogdog	goober	horary	loculi
uncurl	unship	borane	coffle	copped	dodder	fogged	goodie	horned	locust
undate	unshod	borate	cogent	copper	doddle	foible	goodly	horner	lodger
undies	unshoe	bordel	cogged	Coptic	dodgem	foiled	googly	hornet	lofter
undine	unstop	border	cogito	copula	dodger	foison	googol	horrid	loggat
undock	unsung	boreal	cognac	coquet	dodoes	folder	gooier	horror	logged
undoer	untidy	Boreas	coheir	corban	dogate	foliar	gooney	horsey	logger
undone	untied	boride	cohere	corbel	dogear	folium	gooses	hosier	loggia
unduly	untold	boring	cohort	corbie	dogend	folksy	gopher	hostel	logion
unease	untrue	borrow	coigne	corded	dogfox	follow	goramy	hotbed	logjam
uneasy	untuck	borsch	coiner	corder	dogged	foment	gorget	hotdog	loiter
uneath	untune	borzoi	coinop	cordon	dogger	fondle	gorgio	hotpot	loller
uneven	unused	bosche	coital	corium	doggie	fondly	gorgon	hotter	lollop
unfair	unveil	bosket	coitus	corked	dogleg	fondue	gorily	houdan	loment
unfold	unwary	bosomy	coldly	corker	dogood	fontal	goslow	hourly	lonely
unfurl	unwell	boston	coleus	cornea	doited	fooler	gospel	housel	longan
ungird	unwept	botany	collar	corned	dolium	footed	gossan	housey	loofah
ungirt	unwind	botchy	collet	cornel	dollar	footer	gossip	howdah	looker
unglue	unwise	botfly	collie	corner	dollop	footle	Gothic	howler	lookin
ungual	unworn	bother	collop	cornet	dolman	foozle	gotten	hoyden	looper
ungues	unwrap	bothie	colony	cornua	dolmen	forage	gourde	iodate	loosen
unguis	unyoke	botone	colour	corody	dolour	forbad	govern	iodide	looter
ungula	aorist	bottle	colter	corona	domain	forbid	gowany	iodine	lopped
unhair	aortal	bottom	colugo	corozo	domett	forbye	goyish	iodise	lopper
unhand	aortic	boucle	column	corpse	domino	forced	gozzan	iodism	loquat
unholy	aoudad	bought	colure	corpus	donate	forcer	hoarse	iolite	lorcha
unhook	boatel	bougie	comate	corral	donjon	fordid	hoaxer	Ionian	lordly
Uniate	boater	boulle	combat	corrie	donkey	forego	hobbit	ionise	lorica
unific	bobbed	bounce	combed	corsac	donned	forest	hobble	ionium	loriot
uniped	bobbin	bouncy	comber	corsak	donsie	forger	hobnob	joanna	lotion
unipod	bobble	bounds	comedo	corset	doodad	forget	hocker	jobber	lotted
unique	bobcat	bounty	comedy	cortex	doodah	forgot	hockey	joblot	louche
unisex	boblet	bourne	comely	corvee	doodle	forint	hodden	jockey	louden
unison	bobwig	bourse	comeon	corves	doolie	forked	hodman	jocose	loudly
united	bocage	bovine	comfit	Corvus	dopant	formal	hoeing	jocund	lounge
uniter	bodega	bovver	coming	corymb	Dopper	format	hogged	jogged	loupen
unjoin	bodger	bowels	comity	coryza	dorado	formed	hogget	jogger	loupit
unjust	bodice	bowery	commie	cosher	Dorian	former	hoggin	joggle	louver
unkind	bodily	bowfin	commis	cosily	dormer	formic	hogtie	johnny	louvre
unking	boding	bowing	commit	cosine	dormie	fornix	hoicks	joiner	lovage
unkink	bodkin	bowleg	commix	cosmic	dorsal	forrad	hoised	jolter	lovein
unknit	boffin	bowler	common	cosmos	dorsum	forrit	holden	josher	lovely
unknot	bogged	bowman	comose	cosset	dorter	forsay	holder	josser	loving
unlace	boggle	bowsaw	comous	costae	dosage	fossae	holdup	jostle	lowboy
unlade	bohunk	bowtie	compel	costal	dossal	fossil	holily	jotted	lowery
unlaid	boiler	bowwow	comply	costar	dossel	fossor	holism	jotter	lowing
unlash	boldly	bowyer	comsat	coster	dosser	foster	holler	jounce	lowish
unless	bolero	boxbed	concha	costly	dotage	fother	holloa	jouncy	lowkey
unlike	bolide	boxcar	conchy	cottar	dotard	fought	hollow	jovial	moaner
unlink	bollix	boxful	concur	cotted	dotted	foully	holpen	Jovian	moated
unload	bolshy	boxing	condor	cotter	dottle	foulup	homage	joyful	mobbed
unlock	bolter	boyish	confab	cotton	douane	fourth	hombre	joyous	mobcap
unmade	bomber	coaita	confer	coucal	double	foveae	homely	kobold	mobile
unmake	bonbon	coarse	congee	cougar	doubly	foveal	homily	koedoe	mocker
unmask	bonded	coated	conger	coulee	douche	fowler	homing	koodoo	mockup
unmeet	bonder	coatee	congou	county	dought	goalie	hominy	kookie	modena
unmoor	bongos	cobalt	conics	couple	doughy	goanna	honest	koolah	modern
unnail	bonism	cobber	conker	coupon	dourly	goatee	honied	kopeck	modest
unpack	bonist	cobble	conman	course	douser	gobang	honour	koppie	modify

modish
modius
module
moduli
modulo
moggie
mohair
Mohawk
Mohock
mohole
moider
moiety
moiler
molest
moline
mollie
Moloch
molten
moment
Monday
moneys
monger
Mongol
monial
monied
monies
monism
monist
monkey
monody
moocow
mooing
moolah
mopish
mopoke
mopped
mopper
moppet
morale
morals
morass
morbid
morbus
moreen
morgen
morgue
morion
morish
Mormon
mornay
morose
morpho
morris
morrow
morsel
mortal
mortar
morula
mosaic
moshav
Moslem
mosque
mostly
motett
mother
motile
motion
motive
motley
motmot
motory
mottle
moujik
mouldy
moulin
mouser
mousse
mouthy
moving
nobble
nobbut
nobody
nocent
nodded
noddle
nodose
nodule
noesis
noetic
noggin
nomism
nonage
nonary
noncom
nonego
nonfat
nonius
nonuse
noodle
Nordic
normal
Norman
noshup
nosily
nosing
nostoc
notary
notate
notice
notify
notion
nougat
nought
nounal
novena
novice
Nowell
nowise
noyade
nozzle
oocyte
oodles
oogamy
oogeny
oolite
oology
oolong
oomiak
pocked
pocket
podded
podite
podium
podsol
podzol
poetic
poetry
pogrom
pointe
points
poison
Polack
polder
police
policy
polish
polite
polity
pollan
polled
pollen
poller
pollex
polony
polypi
pomace
pomade
pomelo
pommel
pommie
pompom
poncho
ponder
pongee
pontie
pontil
ponton
poodle
pooped
poorly
popery
popgun
popish
poplar
poplin
popped
popper
poppet
popple
popply
porgie
porism
porker
porose
porous
portal
porter
portly
posada
poseur
posset
possum
postal
poster
postil
potage
potale
potash
potato
potboy
poteen
potent
potful
pother
potion
potman
potpie
potted
potter
pottle
pouchy
pouffe
pounce
pourer
pouter
powder
powwow
roadie
roamer
roarer
robalo
robbed
robber
robust
rochet
rocker
rocket
rococo
rodent
rodman
roller
rollon
Romaic
Romany
Romish
romper
rondel
ronyon
roofer
rookie
roomer
rooted
rooter
ropery
roping
roquet
rosace
rosary
rosery
rosily
rosiny
roster
rostra
rosula
rotary
rotate
rotche
rotgut
rotted
rotten
rotter
rotund
rouble
roucou
rouncy
rouser
router
roving
rowing
royals
rozzer
soaker
sobbed
sobeit
socage
soccer
social
socket
sodden
sodium
sodomy
soever
soffit
soften
softie
softly
soigne
soiree
solace
solano
soldan
solder
solely
solemn
solidi
solids
solute
solver
sombre
somite
sonant
sonata
sonnet
sonsie
sooner
soothe
sophic
sopite
sopped
sorage
sorbet
sordid
sorely
sorgho
sorner
sorrel
sorrow
sorter
sortes
sortie
Sothic
sotted
souari
sought
souled
source
sourly
souter
soviet
sovran
sowans
sowens
tocher
tocsin
toddle
toecap
toeing
toffee
togaed
togged
toggle
toiler
toilet
Toledo
toluic
toluol
tomato
tombac
tombak
tomboy
tomcat
tomcod
tomtit
tomtom
toneme
tongue
tonish
tonsil
tooter
toothy
tootle
tootsy
Tophet
tophus
topman
topped
topper
topple
torero
Tories
toroid
torose
torpid
torpor
torque
torrid
torsel
torten
torula
tosher
tosser
tossup
tother
totted
totter
toucan
touche
touchy
toupee
toupet
tourer
tousle
touter
towage
toward
towery
towhee
townee
toxoid
voiced
voided
voider
volant
volley
volost
volume
volute
volvox
voodoo
vorant
vortex
votary
voting
votive
voulge
voyage
voyeur
wobble
wobbly
woeful
woggle
wolves
wombat
womera
wonder
wonted
wonton
wooded
wooden
woodsy
woofer
wooled
woolly
worker
wormer
worrit
worsen
worthy
wortle
woundy
wowser
yogism
yogurt
yoicks
yolked
yonder
yoohoo
yorker
Yoruba
zodiac
zombie
zonary
zonate
zoning
zonked
Zouave
zounds
apache
apathy
apexes
aphony
apiary
apical
apices
apiece
aplomb
apnoea
apodal
apogee
apozem
appeal
appear
append
appose
ephebe
ephebi
epical
epimer
epizoa
epodic
eponym
epopee
opaque
opener
openly
ophite
opiate
oppose
oppugn
optant
optics
optima
option
spacer
spadix
sparer
sparge
sparks
sparry
sparse
spathe
spavin
specie
speech
speedo
speedy
speiss
spence
spewer
sphene
sphere
sphery
sphinx
spider
spiffy
spigot
spilth
spinal
spined
spinel
spinet
spiral
spirit
spital
splash
spleen
splent
splice
spline
splint
splits
splore
splosh
spoffy
spoilt
spoken
sponge
spongy
spooky
spoony
sports
sporty
spotty
spouse
sprain
sprang
sprawl
spread
sprent
spring
sprint
sprite
sprout
spruce
spruit
sprung
spryer
spryly
spunky
spurge
spurry
sputum
upbear
upbeat
upcast
update
upheld
uphill
uphold
uphroe
upkeep
upland
uplift
upmost
upping
uppish
uppity
uprise
uproar
uproot
uprush
upshot
upside
uptake
uptown
upturn
upward
upwind
equate
equine
equity
squail
squall
squama
square
squash
squawk
squeak
squeal
squill
squint
squire
squirm
squirt
squish
Arabic
arable
arbour
arcade
Arcady
arcana
arcane
arched
archer
archil
archly
archon
arctic
ardent
ardour
areola
areole
argala
argali
argand
argent
Argive
argosy
arguer
argufy
argute
argyle
aright
ariled
ariosi
arioso
arisen
arista
armada
armful
armlet
armour
armpit
arnica
aroint
around
arouse
arpent
arrack
arrant
arrest
arrive
arroba
arrowy
arroyo
arsine
artery
artful
artist
bracer
braces
Brahma
Brahmi
brains
brainy
braird
braise
branch
brandy
branle
brassy
brawly
brawny
brayer
brazen
brazil
breach
breast
breath
breech
breeks
breese
breeze
breezy
bregma
brehon
Breton
brevet
brewer
brewis
briard
briary
briber
bricky
bridal
bridge
bridle
briefs
briery
bright
briner
briony
Briton
broach
broche
brogue
broken
broker
brolly
bromic
bronco
bronze
bronzy
brooch
broody
browny
browse
bruise
brumal
brumby
brunch
brunet
brushy
brutal
brutus
bryony
crabby
cradle
crafty
craggy
crambo
cranch
crania
cranky
cranny
crappy
crases
crasis
cratch
crater
cravat
craven
craver
crawly
crayon
crazed
creaky
creamy
crease
create
creche
credal
credit
creeps
creepy
creese
crenel
creole
cresol
Cretan
cretic
cretin
crewel
crikey
crimpy
cringe
cripes
crises
crisis
crispy
crista
critic
croaky
crocus
croppy
crosse
crotal
crotch
croton
crouch
croupy
crouse
cruces
cruddy
cruise
cruive
crumby
crummy
crunch
crural

cruset crusty crutch cruxes crying crypto drably drachm drafty dragee draggy dragon draper drawee drawer dreamt dreamy dreary dredge dreggy dreich drench dressy drifty drippy drivel driven driver droger drogue droich drolly drongo droopy dropsy drosky drossy drouth drover drowse drowsy drudge drupel drybob dryfly dryish dryrot dryrun eraser erbium eremic erenow ergate ermine erotic errand errant errata ersatz eryngo fracas fraena fraise framer frappe fratch frater Frauen frazil freaky freely freest freeze french frenum frenzy fresco friary Friday

fridge friend frieze fright frigid frijol frilly fringe fringy frisky frivol frizzy froggy frolic frosty frothy frowst frowsy frowzy frozen frugal fruity frumpy frusta frutex grabby graben grader gradin gradus grainy gramme Grammy gramps grange granny Granth grappa grassy grater gratin gratis graved gravel graven graver Graves gravid grazer grease greasy greave greedy greens greeny greige greyly grieve grigri grille grilse grimly gringo griper grippe grippy grisly grison gritty grivet groats grocer groggy groove groovy groper grotto grotty grouch

ground grouse grovel grower growly growth groyne grubby grudge grugru grumly grumps grumpy grutch ireful irenic irides iritis ironer ironic irrupt kraken krantz kronen kroner kronor kronur orache oracle orally orange orator orcein orchid orchil orchis ordain ordeal ordure orexis orfray orgasm orgeat orient origan origin oriole orison ormolu ornate ornery orphan orphic orpine orrery praise prance prater pratie praxis prayer preach precis prefab prefer prefix prelim premed premix prepay preses preset presto pretax pretty prewar pricey priest primal

primer primly primus prince priory prison prissy privet prizer prober probit profit proleg prolix prompt pronto propel proper propyl proser prosit protea proton proven pruina pruner prying tracer traces tracks trader tragic tragus trance trapan trapes trappy trashy trauma travel treaty treble trebly tremie tremor trench trendy trepan trepid tressy triage tribal tricar tricky tricot trifid trifle trigon trilby trimer trimly trinal triode triple triply tripod tripos triste triton triune trivet trivia trocar troche trogon troika Trojan trolly trompe

trophy tropic troppo trough troupe trouty trover trowel truant trudge truism trumps trusty trying tryout uracil uraeus Uralic Urania uranic Uranus uranyl urbane urchin ureter urgent urinal urnful ursine wraith wrasse wrathy wreath wrench wretch wright writer writhe ascend ascent aseity ashbin ashcan ashlar ashore ashpan ashram askant askari aslant asleep aslope aspect aspire assail assent assert assess assign assist assize assoil assort assume assure astern asthma astral astray astute aswoon asylum escape escarp eschar eschew escort escrow escudo

Eskimo espial esprit Essene essive essoin estate esteem estray isabel isatin ischia island isobar isohel isomer isopod oscine oscula osmium osmose osprey ossein ossify osteal ostial ostium ostler pseudo psyche psycho tsamba tsetse Tshirt tsotsi Tswana usable usance useful ustion usurer ataman ataxia ataxic athome atomic atonal atonic atrial atrium attach attack attain attend attest attire attorn attune etcher eterne ethane ethene ethics Ethiop ethnic ethyne etrier etymon italic itself otiose otitis ottava pterin ptisan ptosis stable stably stacte

stadia stager stagey stairs staith stakes stalag stalky stamen stance stanch stanza stapes staple starch starer starry starve stases stasis statal stated stater states static stator statue status stayer steady steamy steely steeve stelae stelar stemma stench stepin steppe stepup stereo steric sterna sterol stewed sticky stifle stigma stilly stingo stingy stinko stipel stipes stirps stitch stithy stiver stocks stocky stodge stodgy stogie stoker stokes stolen stolid stolon stoned stoner stooge stopgo storax stores storey stormy stound stover strafe

strain strait strake strand strass strata strath strati strawy strays streak stream streek street stress strewn striae strict stride strife strike Strine string stripe stripy strive strobe strode stroke stroll stroma stromb strong stroud strout strove strown struck struma strung strunt Stuart stubby stucco studio stuffy stumer stumpy stupid stupor sturdy stylar stylet stylus stymie styrax uterus utmost utopia yttria aubade auburn audile Augean augite augury august auklet aumbry auntie aurist aurora aurous Aussie Austin author autism autumn bubble

bubbly buccal bucker bucket buckle buckra budded Buddha buddle budget budgie buffer buffet bugged bugler buglet bulbar bulbed bulbil bulbul Bulgar bulger bulimy bulker bullae buller bullet bumalo bumble bumkin bummed bummer bummle bumper bunchy bunder bundle bungle bunion bunker bunkum bunnia bunsen bunted bunter bunyip burble burbly burbot burden bureau burgee burger burgle burgoo burhel burial burkha burlap burler Burman burner burnet burnup burrel burrow bursae bursal bursar bursas burton busbar busboy bushed bushel busily busing busker buskin

busman bussed busted bustee buster bustle bustup butane butene butler butter button buzzer cubage cubism cubist cuboid cuckoo cuddie cuddle cuddly cudgel cueing cueist cuesta cuffed cuisse culler cullet cullis cultch cultic cultus culver cumber cummer cummin cumuli cunner cupful cupola cupped cupric cuptie cupule curacy curare curari curate curdle curfew curiae curial curium curler curlew currie cursed cursor cursus curtal curtly curtsy curule curvet cuscus cushat cusped cuspid cussed custom cutely cutler cutlet cutoff cutout cutter cuttle dually

dubbed
dubbin
ducker
dudeen
dudish
duello
duende
duenna
duffel
duffer
duffle
dugong
dugout
duiker
dukery
dulcet
dumbly
dumdum
dumose
dumper
dunite
Dunker
dunlin
dunned
dupery
duplet
duplex
durbar
duress
durgan
Durham
durian
during
durned
durrie
duster
dustup
duyker
euchre
eulogy
eunuch
eureka
eutaxy
fucoid
fuddle
fugato
fugged
fuhrer
fulcra
fulfil
fulgid
fulham
fullam
fuller
fulmar
fumble
fundus
fungal
fungus
funkia
funned
funnel
furfur
furore
furred
furrow
fusain
fusile
fusion
fusser
fustic
futile
future
guaiac
guanin
guddle
Guelph
guenon
guffaw
guggle
guider
guidon
guilty
guinea
guiser
guitar
gulden
Gullah
gullet
gulley
gummed
gundog
gunman
gunned
gunnel
gunner
gunsel
gunshy
gunter
gunyah
gurgle
gurjun
Gurkha
gurnet
gurrah
gusher
gusset
guttae
gutted
gutter
guvnor
guzzle
hubbub
hubcap
hubris
huckle
huddle
hugely
hugged
humane
humble
humbly
humbug
humect
humeri
humify
hummed
hummel
hummer
hummum
humour
humped
hunger
hungry
hunker
hunter
hurdle
hurler
hurley
hurrah
hurray
hurter
hurtle
husker
hussar
hustle
hutted
huzoor
Judaic
judder
Judean
judger
judoka
jugate
jugful
jugged
juggle
jujube
Julian
jumbal
jumble
jumbly
jumper
jungle
jungly
junior
junker
junket
junkie
jurist
justly
Jutish
jutted
kultur
kumiss
kummel
kurgan
lubber
lubric
lucent
lucern
luetic
lugged
lugger
luggie
lumbar
lumber
lumina
lummox
lumpen
lumper
lunacy
lunate
lunger
lunula
lunule
lupine
lurdan
lurker
lushly
lustra
lustre
luteal
lutein
luting
luxate
luxury
mucker
muckle
mucoid
mucosa
mucous
muddle
muesli
muffin
muffle
muflon
mugged
mugger
mukluk
mulish
mullah
muller
mullet
mulley
multum
mumble
mummer
mumper
mundic
Munich
muntin
murder
murine
murmur
murphy
murrey
muscat
muscle
museum
musing
muskeg
musket
muskox
Muslim
muslin
mussel
muster
mutant
mutate
mutely
mutine
mutiny
mutism
mutter
mutton
mutual
mutule
mutuum
muumuu
muzhik
muzzle
nuance
nubble
nubbly
nubile
nuchal
nuclei
nudely
nudism
nudist
nudity
nugget
nullah
number
numbly
numina
nuncio
nuncle
nurser
nutant
nutate
nutmeg
nutria
nutter
nuzzle
ouster
outact
outage
outbid
outbye
outcry
outdid
outfit
outfox
outgun
outing
outlaw
outlay
outlet
output
outran
outrun
outsat
outset
outsit
outtop
outvie
outwit
public
pucker
puddle
puddly
pueblo
puffed
puffer
puffin
pugdog
puisne
puller
pullet
pulley
pullin
pullon
pullup
pulper
pulpit
pulque
pulsar
pulser
pulvil
pumice
pummel
pumper
punchy
puncta
pundit
punily
punish
punkah
punned
punner
punnet
puntee
punter
pupate
pupped
puppet
purdah
purely
purfle
purger
purify
purine
purism
purist
purity
purler
purlin
purple
purply
purser
pursue
purvey
pusher
Pushtu
pushup
putlog
putoff
putrid
putsch
puttee
putter
puttie
puzzle
quaere
quagga
quaggy
quahog
quaich
quaigh
quaint
Quaker
qualmy
quanta
quarry
quarte
quarto
quartz
quasar
quaver
queasy
queazy
quench
queuer
quiche
quince
quinoa
quinol
quinsy
quinta
quirky
quitch
quiver
quoits
quorum
quotes
quotha
rubato
rubbed
rubber
rubble
rubbly
rubefy
rubify
rubric
ruched
ruckle
ruckus
rudder
ruddle
rudely
rudish
rueful
ruelle
ruffed
ruffle
rufous
rugged
rugger
rugose
ruiner
ruling
rumble
rumbly
rumina
rummer
rumour
rumple
rumpus
rundle
runlet
runnel
runner
runoff
runrig
runway
rupiah
rusher
rushes
russet
russia
rustic
rustle
rutile
rutted
suable
subbed
subdue
sublet
subman
submit
suborn
subset
subtil
subtle
subtly
suburb
subway
sucker
suckle
sudary
sudden
suffer
suffix
Sufism
sugary
suitor
sulcus
sullen
sultan
sultry
sumach
summae
summed
summer
summit
summon
sunbow
sundae
Sunday
sunder
sundew
sundog
sundry
sungod
sunhat
sunken
sunlit
sunned
sunray
sunset
suntan
superb
supine
supped
supper
supple
supply
surely
surety
surfer
surrey
surtax
survey
suslik
sutile
sutler
suttee
suture
Tuareg
tubber
tubful
tubing
tubule
tuchun
tucker
tucket
tuckin
tuffet
tufted
tufter
tugged
tuille
tulwar
tumble
tumefy
tumour
tumtum
tumuli
tumult
tundra
tuning
tunnel
tupelo
turban
turbid
turbit
turbot
tureen
turgid
turgor
turion
turkey
Turkic
turner
turnip
turnup
turret
turtle
turves
Tuscan
tusked
tusker
tussah
tusser
tussle
tutsan
tutted
tuxedo
tuyere
vulcan
vulgar
vulgus
yumyum
zufolo
avatar
avaunt
avenge
avenue
averse
Avesta
aviary
aviate
avidly
avocet
avouch
avowal
avowed
avulse
evader
evener
evenly
evilly
evince
evolue
evolve
evzone
ovally
overdo
overly
ovisac
ovular
svelte
uvulae
uvular
awaked
awaken
aweary
aweigh
awheel
awhile
awmous
awning
awoken
owlish
swaddy
swampy
swanky
swaraj
swarth
swatch
swathe
swayer
sweaty
sweeny
sweets
swerve
sweven
swimmy
swinge
swiper
swipes
swirly
swishy
switch
swivel
swoosh
swound
twangy
tweeds
tweedy
tweeny
twelve
twenty
twicer
twiggy
twilit
twiner
twinge
twirly
twisty
twitch
twoply
twould
twoway
twyere
axilla
examen
exarch
exceed
except
excess
excide
excise
excite
excuse
exedra
exempt
exequy
exeunt
exhale
exhort
exhume
exilic
exodus
exogen
exomis
exotic
expand
expect
expend
expert
expire
expiry
export
expose
exsect
exsert
extant
extasy
extend
extent
extern
extort
oxalic
oxalis
oxbird
oxford
oxgall
oxgang
oxgate
oxherd
oxhide
oxland
oxtail
oxygen
oxymel
ayeaye
byblow
byebye
byelaw
byform
bygone
bylane
byline
byname
bypass
bypast
bypath
byplay
byroad
byssus
byword
bywork
cyanic
cyanin
cycler
cyclic
cygnet
cymbal
cymose
Cymric
cypher
cyprid
cystic
cystid
dyadic
dybbuk
dyeing
dynamo
dynast
eyalet
eyecup
eyeful
eyeing
eyelet
eyelid
Eyetie
fylfot
gypped
gypsum
gyrate
hyaena
hybrid
hybris
hydric
hymnal
hymnic
hyphae
hyphal
hyphen
hyssop
lyceum
lychee
Lydian
lyrate
lyrics
lyrism
lyrist
lysine
myelin
mygale
myopia
myopic
myosin
myosis
myotic
myriad
myrica
myrtle
myself
mystic
mythic
mythos
myxoma
nympho
oyster
pycnic
pyedog

pyknic pylori pyrene pyrite pyrola pyrope python sylvan symbol syndic syntax syphon Syriac Syrian syrinx syrupy system syzygy tycoon tymbal tympan typhus typify typing typist tyrant Tyrian wyvern xylene xyloid xylose xystus zygoma zygote zymase zythum azalea azonal azotic izzard ozonic

abacus abater abatis acacia acajou acarid acarus adagio Adamic agamic agamid agaric alalia alarum alated amadou amatol amazon anabas anadem ananas anarch anatta anatto apache apathy Arabic arable ataman ataxia ataxic avatar avaunt awaked awaken azalea Baalim

beachy beacon beadle beagle beaked beaker beamer beanie bearer beaten beater Beaune beauty beaver bharal bladed blanch blanky blazer blazes blazon boatel boater bracer braces Brahma Brahmi brains brainy braird braise branch brandy branle brassy brawly brawny brayer brazen brazil chacha chacma chafer chaffy chaise chalet chalky chance chancy change chanty chapel chappy charas charge Charon chaser chaste chatty chaunt claggy clammy claque claret classy clause claver clavis clayey coaita coarse coated coatee crabby cradle crafty craggy crambo cranch

crania cranky cranny crappy crases crasis cratch crater cravat craven craver crawly crayon crazed cyanic cyanin deacon deaden deadly deafen deafly dealer dearie dearly dearth deasil dharma diacid diadem diaper diatom doable drably drachm drafty dragee draggy dragon draper drawee drawer dually dyadic ecarte elapse elated elater enable enamel eraser evader examen exarch eyalet fealty featly fiacre fiance fiasco flabby flacon flaggy flagon flambe flamen flanch flange flappy flashy flatly flatus flaunt flavin flaxen fracas fraena fraise framer frappe

fratch frater Frauen frazil gharry giaour glacis gladly glairy glaive glance glassy glazer gnarly gnawer goalie goanna goatee grabby graben grader gradin gradus grainy gramme Grammy gramps grange granny Granth grappa grassy grater gratin gratis graved gravel graven graver Graves gravid grazer guaiac guanin headed header headon healer health hearer hearse hearth hearty heated heater heathy heaven heaver hiatus hoarse hoaxer hyaena inarch isabel isatin italic joanna kiaugh knaggy kraken krantz laager leaden leader leadin leadup leafed league lealty

leanly leanto leaper learnt leaved leaven leaver leaves liable liaise loaded loader loafer loaner loathe loaves meadow meagre mealie meanie meanly measly meatus miasma moaner moated neaped nearby nearer nearly neaten neatly niacin nuance ogamic omasum onager opaque orache oracle orally orange orator ovally oxalic oxalis peachy peahen peaked peanut pearly peavey phalli pharos phasic phasis phatic piaffe piazza placed placer placet placid plagal plague plaguy plaice plaint planar planer planet plaque plashy plasma platan platen plater player praise

prance prater pratie praxis prayer quaere quagga quaggy quahog quaich quaigh quaint Quaker qualmy quanta quarry quarte quarto quartz quasar quaver reader really realty reamer reaper rearer reason reaver rhaphe roadie roamer roarer scabby scalar scaled scaler scales scampi scanty scarab scarce scarer scarry scarus scathe scatty scazon seaair seabed seabee seacow seadog seaear seafan seafog seafox sealer seaman seamat seamer seamew seance seapen seapig search season seater seaway shabby shader shades shadow shaduf shaggy shaken shaker Shakta Shakti

shalom shaman shammy shamus shandy shanny shanty shaped shapen shaper sharer sharif sharps shaven shaver shavie sialic skater slacks slaggy slalom slangy slapup slater slaver slavey Slavic slayer smalls smalto smarmy smarty smatch snaggy snappy snarer snarly snatch snathe snazzy soaker spacer spadix sparer sparge sparks sparry sparse spathe spavin stable stably stacte stadia stager stagey stairs staith stakes stalag stalky stamen stance stanch stanza stapes staple starch starer starry starve stases stasis statal stated stater states static stator

statue status stayer suable swaddy swampy swanky swaraj swarth swatch swathe swayer teabag teacup teapot teapoy teasel teaser teaset teazel teazle thaler thalli thanks thatch tracer traces tracks trader tragic tragus trance trapan trapes trappy trashy trauma travel tsamba Tuareg twangy unable uracil uraeus Uralic Urania uranic Uranus uranyl usable usance viable viands viator weaken weakly wealth weaner weapon wearer weasel weaver weazen whacky whaler whatso wraith wrasse wrathy yearly yeasty zealot abbacy abbess albata albedo albeit albert albino

albite ambler ambush arbour aubade auburn babble babbly Babism Babist baboon bibbed bibber bobbed bobbin bobble bobcat boblet bobwig bubble bubbly byblow cabala cabana cabman cobalt cobber cobble cobnut cobweb cubage cubism cubist cuboid dabbed dabber dabble debark debase debate debris debtor debunk dibbed dibber dibble dobbin dubbed dubbin dybbuk embalm embank embark embers emblem emblic embody emboli emboly emboss embrue embryo erbium Fabian fabled fabler fabric fibbed fibber fibred fibril fibrin fibula fobbed gabbed gabber gabble gabbro gabion

gabled gablet gibber gibbet gibbon gobang gobbet gobble goblet goblin habile Hebrew hobbit hobble hobnob hubbub hubcap hubris hybrid hybris imbibe imbrex imbrue inborn inbred jabbed jabber jabiru jibbah jibbed jibber jobber joblot kabala kabuki Kabyle kibble kibitz kiblah kibosh kobold labial labile labium labour labret labrum libber libido Libyan lobate lobbed lobose lobule lubber lubric mobbed mobcap mobile nabbed nebula nebuly nibbed nibble nobble nobbut nobody nubble nubbly nubile oxbird pebble pebbly public rabato rabbet rabbin rabbit rabble

rabies access docket lecher racoon uncoil dudeen lodger radian adenyl
rebate accord doctor lector recall uncool dudish Lydian radish afeard
rebato accost ducker lichee recant uncork Eddaic Madame radium ageing
rebeck accrue encage lichen recast uncurl eidola madcap radius agency
rebore accuse encamp lictor recede upcast eldest madden radome agenda
reborn alcaic encase locale recent urchin endear madder radula ageold
rebuff alcove encash locate recess vacant ending madman redact alegar
rebuke anchor encode lochan recipe vacate endive madras redbud alevin
ribald arcade encore locker recite vacuum endure maduro redcap alexia
riband Arcady encyst locket reckon vector fadein meddle redden alexin
ribbed arcana Eocene lockup recoil victim fedora mediae redder amends
ribbon arcane escape loculi recoin victor fiddle medial reddle amenta
ribose arched escarp locust record vicuna fiddly median redeem amerce
robalo archer eschar lucent recoup wicked fidget medick redeye apexes
robbed archil eschew lucern rector wicker fodder medico redhot areola
robber archly escort lyceum rectum wicket fuddle medium rediae areole
robust archon escrow lychee rectus abduce gadded medius redone aseity
rubato arctic escudo macaco richen abduct gadder medlar redraw avenge
rubbed ascend etcher machan riches addend gadfly medley redtop avenue
rubber ascent euchre mackle richly addict gadget medusa reduce averse
rubble backer exceed macron ricker addled Gadhel midage ridded Avesta
rubbly backup except macula rickey adduce gadoid midair ridden aweary
rubefy becall excess macule ricrac adduct giddap midday riddle aweigh
rubify becalm excide mickey rictal aedile goddam midden rident ayeaye
rubric became excise mickle rictus Aldine godown middle ridged beeper
sabbat becket excite micron rochet aldose godson midget riding beetle
Sabian beckon excuse mocker rocker aldrin godwit midgut rodent beeves
Sabine become facade mockup rocket ardent guddle midoff rodman bieldy
sables biceps facete mucker rococo ardour haddie midrib rudder bleach
sobbed bicker facial muckle ruched audile hadron midway ruddle bleary
sobeit bocage facies mucoid ruckle baddie heddle modena rudely blench
subbed buccal facile mucosa ruckus badger hedera modern rudish blende
subdue bucker facing mucous sachem bedaub hedger modest sadden blenny
sublet bucket factor nectar sachet bedaze hidden modify sadder breach
subman buckle factum nicely sacque bedbug hiding modish saddhu breast
submit buckra facula nicety sacral bedded hodden modius saddle breath
suborn cachet feckly nicish sacred bedder hodman module sadism breech
subset cachou fecula nickel sacrum bedeck huddle moduli sadist breeks
subtil cackle fecund nicker secant bedell hydric modulo sedate breese
subtle cacoon fickle nocent secede bedlam indaba muddle sedile breeze
subtly cactus focsle nuchal secern bedpan indeed nidget seduce breezy
suburb cecity fucoid nuclei second bedsit indene nidify siding bregma
subway cicada geckos occamy secret beduin indent nodded sodden brehon
tabard cicala gocart occult sector bidden Indian noddle sodium Breton
tabbed cicely hackle occupy secund bidder indict nodose sodomy brevet
tablet coccal hackly oecist secure bodega indign nodule sudary brewer
tabour coccid heckle oncost sicken bodger indigo nudely sudden brewis
tibiae coccus hectic oocyte sicker bodice indite nudism tedded byebye
tibial coccyx hector orcein sickle bodily indium nudist tedder byelaw
tubber cochin hiccup orchid sickly boding indole nudity tedium caecal
tubful cocked hickey orchil socage bodkin indoor oddity tidbit caecum
tubing cocker hocker orchis soccer budded induce oddjob tiddly cheeky
tubule cockle hockey oscine social Buddha induct oddson tidily cheers
umbles cocoon huckle oscula socket buddle indult oedema toddle cheery
umbrae cuckoo incase pacify sucker budget induna oidium undate cheese
umbral cycler incept packer suckle budgie iodate oldish undies cheesy
umbras cyclic incest packet tacker caddie iodide oodles undine chelae
unbend dacoit inches pecker tacket caddis iodine ordain undock chemic
unbent dactyl incise pecten tackle cadent iodise ordeal undoer cheque
unbind decade incite pectic tactic cadger iodism ordure undone cherry
unbitt decamp inclip pectin ticked cedarn Judaic padauk unduly cherty
unbolt decani income picker ticker coddle judder padded update cherub
unborn decant incubi picket ticket codger Judean paddle Vedist chesil
unbred deceit incult pickle tickey codify judger pedalo vidual chesty
upbear decent incuse pickup tickle codlin judoka pedant wadded chevet
upbeat decide ischia picnic tickly cuddie kidded pedate waddie cleave
urbane decker jacana picric tictac cuddle kidder peddle waddle clench
vibist deckle jackal pocked tocher cuddly kiddie pedlar waders clergy
vibrio decoct jacket pocket tocsin cudgel kidnap piddle wadmal cleric
wabain decode jockey pucker tuchun dedans kidney pidgin wadmol clever
wabble decoke jocose pycnic tucker deduce ladder podded wedded clevis
webbed decree jocund raceme tucket deduct laddie podite widely coelom
wobble dicast kicker rachis tuckin diddle ladify podium widget coerce
wobbly dicker laceup racial tycoon didoes lading podsol widish coeval
yabber dickey laches racily uncage dodder ladino podzol zodiac creaky
zebeck dictum lacing racism uncate doddle ladyfy puddle acedia creamy
accede docent lackey racist uncial dodgem ledged puddly acetal crease
accent docile lactic racker uncini dodger ledger raddle acetic create
accept docker lacuna racket unclad dodoes lidded radial acetyl creche

credal
credit
creeps
creepy
creese
crenel
creole
cresol
Cretan
cretic
cretin
crewel
cueing
cueist
cuesta
daedal
daemon
deejay
deepen
deeply
diesel
dieses
diesis
dieter
dreamt
dreamy
dreary
dredge
dreggy
dreich
drench
dressy
duello
duende
duenna
dyeing
Edenic
Egeria
egesta
ejecta
eleven
elevon
emerge
emeses
emesis
emetic
emetin
emeute
energy
eremic
erenow
eterne
evener
evenly
exedra
exempt
exequy
exeunt
eyecup
eyeful
eyeing
eyelet
eyelid
Eyetie
faerie
feeble
feebly
feeder
feeing
feeler
fierce
fiesta
fleche
fledge
fleece
fleech
fleecy
flench
flense

fleshy
fletch
fleury
flexor
foeman
foetal
foetid
foetus
freaky
freely
freest
freeze
french
frenum
frenzy
fresco
Gaelic
geegee
geezer
ghetto
gleamy
gleety
gneiss
grease
greasy
greave
greedy
greens
greeny
greige
greyly
Guelph
guenon
haemal
haemin
heehaw
heeled
heeler
hieing
hoeing
ibexes
iceaxe
icebag
icebox
icecap
iceman
ideaed
ideate
ireful
irenic
jaeger
jeerer
keenly
keeper
kiekie
klepht
koedoe
leeway
lieder
lierne
luetic
maenad
meekly
meetly
muesli
myelin
naevus
needle
neednt
nielli
niello
noesis
noetic
obeche
obelus
obeyer
ocelli
ocelot
oleate

olefin
omelet
omenta
oneoff
oneway
opener
openly
orexis
overdo
overly
paella
paeony
peeler
peeper
peepul
peewit
phenol
phenyl
piecer
piedog
pieman
pierce
pleach
please
plebby
pledge
plenty
plenum
pleura
plexor
plexus
pneuma
poetic
poetry
preach
precis
prefab
prefer
prefix
prelim
premed
premix
prepay
preses
preset
presto
pretax
pretty
prewar
pseudo
pterin
pueblo
pyedog
queasy
queazy
quench
queuer
reebok
reecho
reedit
reefer
reeler
rhebok
rhesus
rhetor
rheumy
rueful
ruelle
saeter
scenic
seeder
seeing
seeker
seemly
seesaw
seethe
shears
sheass
sheath

sheave
sheeny
sheets
sheikh
sheila
shekel
shelly
Shelta
shelty
shelve
sheoak
sherif
Sherpa
sherry
sheugh
sienna
sierra
siesta
skeely
skeigh
skerry
sketch
skewer
sleave
sleazy
sledge
sleepy
sleety
sleeve
sleigh
sleuth
smeary
smeech
smelly
sneaky
sneesh
sneeze
sneezy
soever
specie
speech
speedo
speedy
speiss
spence
spewer
steady
steamy
steely
steeve
stelae
stelar
stemma
stench
stepin
steppe
stepup
stereo
steric
sterna
sterol
stewed
svelte
sweaty
sweeny
sweets
swerve
sweven
taenia
teemer
teensy
teepee
teeter
teethe
Theban
thecae
thecal
theine
theirs

theism
theist
thenar
thence
theory
theses
thesis
thetic
tiebar
tiedye
tiepin
tierce
tiered
tierod
tiewig
tmeses
tmesis
toecap
toeing
treaty
treble
trebly
tremie
tremor
trench
trendy
trepan
trepid
tressy
tsetse
tweeds
tweedy
tweeny
twelve
twenty
unease
uneasy
uneath
uneven
ureter
useful
uterus
vielle
viewer
weeder
weekly
weeper
weepie
weever
weevil
wheeze
wheezy
whenas
whence
wherry
wheyey
wieldy
wiener
woeful
wreath
wrench
wretch
affair
affect
affeer
affine
affirm
afflux
afford
affray
baffle
befall
befell
befool
before
befoul
biffin
biform
boffin

buffer
buffet
byform
cafard
Caffre
caftan
coffee
coffer
coffin
coffle
cuffed
daftly
deface
defame
defeat
defect
defend
defier
defile
define
deform
defray
deftly
defuse
differ
duffel
duffer
duffle
efface
effect
effete
effigy
efflux
effort
effuse
elfish
enface
enfold
gaffer
gifted
goffer
guffaw
haffet
haffit
infamy
infant
infare
infect
infelt
infest
infirm
inflow
influx
infold
inform
infula
infuse
Kaffir
kaftan
lifter
liftup
lofter
miffed
muffin
muffle
muflon
oafish
offend
offent
office
offing
offish
offkey
offset
onfall
orfray
oxford
piffle
puffed

puffer
puffin
raffia
raffle
rafter
reface
refect
refill
refine
reflex
reflow
reflux
reform
refuel
refuge
refund
refuse
refute
rifely
riffle
rifler
ruffed
ruffle
rufous
safari
safely
safety
sifter
soffit
soften
softie
softly
suffer
suffix
Sufism
tiffin
toffee
tuffet
tufted
tufter
unfair
unfold
unfurl
wafery
waffle
wafter
wifely
yaffle
zaffer
zaffre
zufolo
Aegean
Afghan
algoid
angary
angina
angled
angler
angora
argala
argali
argand
argent
Argive
argosy
arguer
argufy
argute
argyle
Augean
augite
augury
august
bagful
bagged
bagman
bagnio
bagwig
beggar

begged
begird
begirt
begone
bigamy
bigger
biggin
bigwig
bogged
boggle
bugged
bugler
buglet
bygone
cagily
cigala
cogent
cogged
cogito
cognac
cygnet
dagger
dagoes
degras
degree
degust
digamy
digest
digger
diglot
dogate
dogear
dogend
dogfox
dogged
dogger
doggie
dogleg
dogood
dugong
dugout
eaglet
edgily
edging
eggcup
eggler
eggnog
eighth
eighty
engage
engild
engine
engird
engirt
englut
engram
engulf
ergate
fagend
fagged
faggot
figged
figure
fogbow
fogdog
fogged
fugato
fugged
gagged
gagger
gaggle
gagman
gigged
giggle
giggly
giglet
giglot
gigman
gigolo

goggle
goggly
goglet
guggle
hagbut
haggis
haggle
hegira
higgle
higher
highly
hogged
hogget
hoggin
hogtie
hugely
hugged
ingest
ingulf
jagged
jagger
jaguar
jigged
jigger
jiggle
jiggly
jigsaw
jogged
jogger
joggle
jugate
jugful
jugged
juggle
lagged
lagger
lagoon
laguna
legacy
legate
legato
legbye
legend
legged
legion
legist
legman
legume
ligate
ligger
lights
lignin
ligula
ligule
ligure
loggat
logged
logger
loggia
logion
logjam
lugged
lugger
luggie
maggot
Magian
magilp
magnet
magnum
magpie
maguey
Magyar
megilp
megohm
megrim
mighty
mignon
moggie
mugged

mugger
mygale
nagana
nagged
nagger
negate
nigger
niggle
nighty
nignog
noggin
nugget
oogamy
oogeny
orgasm
orgeat
oxgall
oxgang
oxgate
pagoda
pegged
pegleg
pegtop
pigeon
pigged
piggin
piglet
pignut
pigsty
pogrom
pugdog
ragbag
ragged
raggee
raggle
raglan
ragman
ragout
ragtag
raguly
regain
regale
regard
regent
reggae
regime
regina
region
regius
reglet
regnal
regret
regulo
rigged
rigger
righto
rigour
rigout
rugged
rugger
rugose
sagely
saggar
sagged
sagger
sigher
siglum
signal
signer
signet
signor
sugary
tagend
tagged
tagrag
tegmen
tegula
tights
togaed

togged inhere bailie drippy haired raisin stipes whidah taking calces
toggle inhume bailor drivel heifer reiver stirps whiles unkind calcic
tugged johnny baiter driven height rhinal stitch whilom unking calico
ungird mahout beigel driver hoicks ruiner stithy whilst unkink caliph
ungirt mihrab bhisti duiker hoised saidst stiver whimsy unknit calker
unglue mohair blight edible ibices sailed suitor whiner unknot calkin
ungual Mohawk blimey editor ibidem sailer swimmy whinge upkeep caller
ungues Mohock blintz elicit icicle sailor swinge whinny Viking callet
unguis mohole blithe elixir idiocy saithe swiper whippy ablate callow
ungula ochone boiler enigma irides scilla swipes whirly ablaut callup
urgent ophite briard enisle iritis seiche swirly whisht ablaze callus
vagary oxherd briary epical jailer seiner swishy whisky abloom calmly
vagile oxhide briber epimer jailor seisin switch whited ablush calory
vagrom rehash bricky epizoa joiner seizer swivel whiten aflame calpac
vegete rehear bridal evilly kainit seizin tailor whites afloat calque
vigour reheat bridge evince kaiser shield taipan whitey allege calves
wagged reheel bridle exilic knight shiest thieve wright allele calxes
waggle schema briefs failed knives shifty things writer allied celery
waggly scheme briery faille laical Shiite thingy writhe allium celiac
waggon schism bright fainly loiter shikar thinly yoicks allout cellar
wigeon schist briner fairly maidan shiksa thirst abject allred celled
wigged schizo briony feirie maiden shimmy thirty abjure allude Celtic
wiggle schlep Briton feisty maigre shindy toiler adjoin allure cilice
wiggly school caiman flight mailed shiner toilet adjure anlace cilium
wigwag schorl caique flimsy mainly shinny triage adjust anlage coldly
wigwam schuss chiasm flinch meinie Shinto tribal bijoux aplomb coleus
woggle sphene chiaus flinty moider shinty tricar cajole aslant collar
yogism sphere chichi flirty moiety shirty tricky deject asleep collet
yogurt sphery chicle flitch moiler shiver tricot enjoin aslope collie
zigzag sphinx chield foible nailer skibob trifid hejira balata collop
zygoma tahini chigoe foiled obital skiddy trifle hijack balboa colony
zygote tahsil chilli foison odious skiing trigon inject baldly colour
achene Tshirt chilly friary ogival skilly trilby injure baleen colter
adhere unhair chimer Friday oliver skimpy trimer injury balker colugo
aghast unhand chintz fridge opiate skinny trimly jejune ballad column
aphony unholy chippy friend orient skirun trinal jujube ballet colure
ashbin unhook chirpy frieze origan skiver triode Majlis ballon culler
ashcan upheld chisel fright origin skivvy triple object ballot cullet
ashlar uphill chital frigid oriole slicer triply objure balsam cullis
ashore uphold chitin frijol orison slider tripod pajama Baltic cultch
ashpan uphroe chiton frilly otiose slight tripos Rajput belaud cultic
ashram vihara chitty fringe otitis slimly triste reject beldam cultus
athome Wahabi chives fringy ovisac slinky triton rejoin belfry culver
awheel wahine chivvy frisky paidup slipon triune sejant Belgic delate
awhile Yahveh cliche frivol pliant slippy trivet unjoin belief delete
behalf Yahweh client frizzy plicae slipup trivia unjust belike delict
behave acidic cliffy gaiety pliers sliver tuille ackack belive delude
behead acidly climax gainer plight smilax twicer aikido bellow deluge
beheld acinar clinch gainly plinth smiler twiggy alkali belong deluxe
behest acinus clingy gainst plisse smirch twilit alkane belted delver
behind adieus clinic gaited pointe smirky twiner alkene beluga dilate
behold adieux clipon gaiter points smiter twinge alkyne bilbos dilute
behoof adipic clique geisha poison smithy twirly anklet bilker dolium
behove afield cliquy glibly pricey sniffy twisty askant billet dollar
Bihari ahimsa coigne glider priest sniper twitch askari billon dollop
bohunk akimbo coiner glitch primal snippy ubiety auklet billow dolman
cahier alight coinop Goidel primer snitch Uniate bakery billyo dolmen
cahoot aliped coital goitre primly snivel unific bikini boldly dolour
coheir amidst coitus grieve primus soigne uniped dikdik bolero dulcet
cohere anicut crikey grigri prince soiree unipod diktat bolide eclair
cohort animal crimpy grille priory spider unique dukery bollix enlace
dahlia animus cringe grilse prison spiffy unisex Eskimo bolshy enlist
dehorn apiary cripes grimly prissy spigot unison fakery bolter eolian
echoer apical crises gringo privet spilth united gokart bulbar eolith
echoic apices crisis griper prizer spinal uniter inkpot bulbed eulogy
enhalo apiece crispy grippe ptisan spined urinal kakapo bulbil falcon
ephebe aright crista grippy puisne spinel vainly likely bulbul fallal
ephebi ariled critic grisly quiche spinet Vaisya liking Bulgar fallen
ethane ariosi cuisse grison quince spiral veiled makedo bulger fallow
ethene arioso daimen gritty quinoa spirit veined makeup bulimy falsie
ethics arisen daimio grivet quinol spital voiced making bulker falter
Ethiop arista daimon guider quinsy sticky voided mikado bullae feline
ethnic aviary dainty guidon quinta stifle voider mukluk buller fellah
ethyne aviate deicer guilty quirky stigma wailer nekton bullet feller
exhale avidly deific guinea quitch stilly waiter pakeha bylane felloe
exhort axilla djibba guiser quiver stingo waiver pyknic byline fellow
exhume bailee djinni guitar raider stingy weight rakish calami felony
fuhrer bailer doited hailer railer stinko weirdo takahe calash filfot
inhale bailey drifty hairdo raiser stipel weirdy takein calcar filial

filing jilter pallet salary tulwar almond dimmed immesh pompom tamara
filler jolter pallia Salian uglify almost dimmer immune pumice tamely
fillet Julian pallid salify uglily armada dimple immure pummel taming
fillip kalong pallor salina ullage armful dimply inmate pumper tampan
filmic kelpie palmar saline umlaut armlet dimwit inmost ramate tamper
filose kelson palmer saliva unlace armour domain jammed ramble tampon
filter kelter palolo sallee unlade armpit domett jammer ramify tamtam
filthy Keltic palpal sallet unlaid aumbry domino jumbal ramjet temper
folder kelvin palpus sallow unlash awmous dumbly jumble rammed temple
foliar killer palter salmon unless bamboo dumdum jumbly rammer timbal
folium kilted paltry saloon unlike bemire dumose jumper ramose timber
folksy kilter pelage saloop unlink bemoan dumper kimono ramous timbre
follow kultur pelham salter unload bemock enmesh kumiss ramper timely
fulcra lallan pellet saltus unlock bemuse enmity kummel ramrod timing
fulfil lilied pelmet saluki upland bomber ermine lambda ramson timous
fulgid loller pelota salute uplift bumalo family lamber remade tomato
fulham lollop peltae salver valeta bumble famine lamely remain tombac
fullam malady pelter salvia valgus bumkin famish lament remake tombak
fuller Malaga peltry salvor valine bummed famous lamina remand tomboy
fulmar malate pelves salvos valise bummer famuli lamish remark tomcat
fylfot maleic pelvic sclaff valley bummle female Lammas remedy tomcod
galago malice pelvis sclera vallum bumper femora lammed remind tomtit
galaxy malign phlegm seldom valour camass fimble lemony remint tomtom
galena malism phloem select valuer camber foment limbec remise tumble
galiot malkin pilaff Seljuk valuta camera fumble limbed remiss tumefy
galley mallee pileum seller valved camion gambir limber remora tumour
Gallic mallei pileup selves veleta camise gambit limbic remote tumtum
Gallio mallet pileus silage vellum camlet gamble limbus remove tumuli
gallon mallow pilfer sileni veloce camper gambol liming remuda tumult
gallop maltha pillar silent velour campus gamely limner rimmed tymbal
galoot mellow pillow silica velure cement gamete limper rimose tympan
galore melody pilose silken velvet comate gamily limpet rimous unmade
galosh melton pilous siller vilely combat gamine limpid Romaic unmake
gelled milady pilule silvan vilify combed gaming limply Romany unmask
gilder milage Polack silver villus comber gammer limuli Romish unmeet
gilled mildew polder solace volant comedo gammon loment romper unmoor
gillie mildly police solano volley comedy Gemara lumbar rumble upmost
golden milieu policy soldan volost comely Gemini lumber rumbly utmost
golfer milker polish solder volume comeon gemmae lumina rumina vamper
gollop milled polite solely volute comfit gemmed lummox rummer wamble
golosh miller polity solemn volvox coming gimbal lumpen rumour wambly
gulden millet pollan solidi vulcan comity gimlet lumper rumple wampee
Gullah milord polled solids vulgar commie gimmal mammae rumpus wampum
gullet milter pollen solute vulgus commis gimmer mammal samara wimble
gulley molest poller solver walker commit gummed mammee sambar wimple
haleru moline pollex splash walkin commix hamate mammer sambur wombat
halide mollie polony spleen walkon common Hamite mammon Samian womera
halite Moloch polypi splent wallah comose hamlet member samite yammer
hallal molten puller splice walled comous hammal memoir samlet yumyum
halloa mulish pullet spline waller compel hammam memory Samoan zombie
halloo mullah pulley splint wallet comply hammed mimosa sampan zymase
hallow muller pullin splits wallop comsat hammer moment sample adnate
hallux mullet pullon splore wallow cumber hamper mumble Samson adnexa
haloes mulley pullup splosh walnut cummer hemmed mummer semble agnail
halter multum pulper sulcus walrus cummin hempen mumper Semite agnate
halvah nelson pulpit sullen welder cumuli homage namely semmit agnise
halves nilgai pulque sultan weldor cymbal hombre nimble semple amnion
helium nullah pulsar sultry welkin cymose homely nimbly sempre annals
heller oblast pulser sylvan welter Cymric homily nimbus simian anneal
helmet oblate pulvil talbot wilder damage homing Nimrod simile annexe
helper oblige pylori talcky wildly damask hominy nomism simmer annual
holden oblong relaid talcum wilful dammar humane number simnel annuli
holder oclock relate talent wilily dammed humble numbly simony apnoea
holdup oilcan relent talion willed damned humbly numina simoom arnica
holily oilman relict talker willet dampen humbug nympho simoon auntie
holism oilnut relief talkie willow damper humect ohmage simper awning
holler online reline tallow Wilton damply humeri oomiak simple banana
holloa oolite relish Talmud wolves damsel humify ormolu simply bandit
hollow oology relive teledu xylene damson hummed osmium simurg bandog
holpen oolong reload telega xyloid demand hummel osmose sombre banger
illume owlish reluct teller xylose demark hummer pampas somite bangle
illuse oxland relume telson yclept demean hummum pamper sumach bangup
inlaid palace rillet Telugu yellow dement humour pimple summae banian
inland palais roller tiling yelper demise humped pimply summed banish
inlaws palate rollon tiller yolked demist hymnal pomace summer banjax
inlier paleae ruling tilter zeloso demode hymnic pomade summit banjos
iolite palely salaam Toledo zillah demote iambic pomelo summon banker
island paling salade toluic admass demure iambus pommel symbol banket
jalopy palish salami toluol admire dimity immane pommie tamale banned

banner
bantam
banter
banyan
banzai
bender
benign
bennet
benumb
benzol
benzyl
binary
binate
binder
binful
bonbon
bonded
bonder
bongos
bonism
bonist
bonito
bonnet
bonnie
bonsai
bonxie
bonzer
bunchy
bunder
bundle
bungle
bunion
bunker
bunkum
bunnia
bunsen
bunted
bunter
bunyip
byname
canape
canard
canary
cancan
cancel
cancer
candid
candle
canful
cangue
canine
canker
canned
cannel
canner
cannon
cannot
canopy
canter
canthi
cantle
canton
cantor
cantus
Canuck
canvas
canyon
censer
censor
census
cental
centre
centum
cinder
cinema
cineol
cinque
concha
conchy
concur
condor
confab
confer
congee
conger
congou
conics
conker
conman
conned
conner
conoid
consul
convex
convey
convoy
cunner
dancer
dander
dandle
danger
dangle
Daniel
Danish
dankly
denary
dengue
denial
denier
denims
denote
dental
dentel
dentil
denude
dingey
dinghy
dingle
dingus
dining
dinkum
dinned
dinner
donate
donjon
donkey
donned
donsie
dunite
Dunker
dunlin
dunned
dynamo
dynast
ennead
ennuye
eonian
eonism
eunuch
fandom
fanged
fanion
fanjet
fanned
fanner
fantan
Fantee
fantod
fantom
fencer
fender
Fenian
fenman
fennec
fennel
finale
finals
finder
finely
finery
finger
finial
fining
finish
finite
finnan
finned
finner
Finnic
fondle
fondly
fondue
fontal
fundus
fungal
fungus
funkia
funned
funnel
gander
ganger
gangly
gangue
gannet
ganoid
gantry
gender
genera
geneva
genial
genius
genned
genome
gentes
gentle
gently
gentoo
gentry
gingal
ginger
gingko
ginkgo
ginned
ginner
gundog
gunman
gunned
gunnel
gunner
gunsel
gunshy
gunter
gunyah
handed
handle
hangar
hanged
hanger
hangup
hanker
hankie
hansel
hansom
henrun
henrys
hinder
Hindoo
hinged
honest
honied
honour
hunger
hungry
hunker
hunter
ignite
ignore
innate
inning
Ionian
ionise
ionium
jangle
jennet
jingle
jingly
jinnee
jungle
jungly
junior
junker
junket
junkie
kanaka
kenned
kennel
kincob
kindle
kindly
kinema
kingly
lanate
lancer
lancet
landau
landed
lander
langue
langur
lankly
lanner
lanugo
lender
length
lenity
lensed
Lenten
lentil
linage
linden
lineal
linear
lineup
linger
lingua
linhay
lining
linkup
linnet
linney
linsey
lintel
lintie
lonely
longan
lunacy
lunate
lunger
lunula
lunule
manage
manana
manche
Manchu
manday
manege
manful
mangel
manger
mangle
mangos
maniac
manila
manioc
manito
manned
manner
manque
mantel
mantes
mantic
mantid
mantis
mantle
mantra
mantua
manual
manuka
manure
menace
menage
mender
menhir
menial
meninx
mensal
menses
mental
mentor
mentum
mincer
minded
minder
mingle
minify
minima
mining
minion
minish
minium
minnow
Minoan
minter
minuet
minute
Monday
moneys
monger
Mongol
monial
monied
monies
monism
monist
monkey
monody
mundic
Munich
muntin
nanism
ninety
nonage
nonary
noncom
nonego
nonfat
nonius
nonuse
nuncio
nuncle
ornate
ornery
panada
panama
panary
pander
pandit
panful
panned
pantry
panzer
pencil
penman
pennae
penned
pennon
pentad
pentup
pentyl
penult
penury
pincer
pineal
pinery
pineta
pinger
pinion
pinkie
pinnae
pinned
pinner
pinole
pintle
poncho
ponder
pongee
pontie
pontil
ponton
punchy
puncta
pundit
punily
punish
punkah
punned
punner
punnet
puntee
punter
rancho
rancid
randan
randem
random
ranger
ranker
rankle
rankly
ransom
ranter
ranula
rename
render
renege
rennet
renown
rental
renter
ringed
ringer
rinser
rondel
ronyon
rundle
runlet
runnel
runner
runoff
runrig
runway
sandal
sander
sandhi
sanely
sangar
sanies
sanify
sanity
sanjak
sannup
santal
santir
senary
senate
sendal
sender
sendup
senega
senhor
senile
senior
sennet
sennit
senora
senses
sensor
sensum
sentry
sinewy
sinful
singer
single
singly
sinker
sinned
sinner
sinnet
sinter
sonant
sonata
sonnet
sonsie
sunbow
sundae
Sunday
sunder
sundew
sundog
sundry
sungod
sunhat
sunken
sunlit
sunned
sunray
sunset
suntan
syndic
syntax
tandem
tangle
tangly
tanist
tanked
tanker
tanned
tanner
tannic
tannin
tanrec
tantra
tenace
tenant
tender
tendon
tenner
tennis
tenour
tenpin
tenrec
tenson
tensor
tenter
tentie
tenues
tenuis
tenure
tenuto
tenzon
tincal
tindal
tinder
tinful
tingle
tingly
tinily
tinker
tinkle
tinkly
tinman
tinned
tinner
tinpot
tinsel
tinter
toneme
tongue
tonish
tonsil
tundra
tuning
tunnel
unnail
urnful
vandal
vanish
vanity
vanner
vendee
vender
vendor
vendue
veneer
venery
venial
venire
Venite
venose
venous
venter
ventil
ventre
venule
vinery
vinous
vintry
wander
wangle
wanion
wanted
wanton
Wendic
wincey
winded
winder
window
windup
winery
winged
winger
winker
winkle
winner
winnow
winsey
winter
wintle
wintry
wonder
wonted
wonton
xenial
xenium
Yankee
yenned
yonder
zander
zanily
zenana
zenith
zinced
zincic
zincky
zingel
zinked
zinnia
zonary
zonate
zoning
zonked
aboard
aboral
abound
Adonic
Adonis
adorer
Aeolic
agonal
agonic
agouti
amoeba
amoral
amount
anodal
anodic
anoint
anomic
anomie
anonym
anorak
anoxia
anoxic
apodal
apogee
apozem
aroint
around
arouse
atomic
atonal
atonic
avocet
avouch
avowal
avowed
awoken
azonal
azotic
baobab
bionic
biopsy
biotic
biotin
blonde
bloody
bloomy
blotch
blotto
blouse
blowed
blower
blowsy
blowup
blowzy
booboo
boodle
boohoo
booing
booker
bookie
booksy
boomer
booted
bootee
boozer
broach
broche
brogue
broken
broker
brolly
bromic
bronco
bronze
bronzy
brooch
broody
browny
browse
choice
choker
chokey
choler
choose
choosy
chopin
choppy
choral
chorea
choric
chorus
chosen
chough
chouse
cloaca
cloche
cloddy
cloggy
clonal
clonic
clonus
closed
closet
clothe
cloudy
clough
cloven
clover
cooker
cookie
cooler
coolie
coolly
coolth
coonty
cooper
cootie
croaky
crocus
croppy
crosse
crotal
crotch
croton
crouch
croupy
crouse
deodar
dhooti
doodad
doodah
doodle
doolie
droger
drogue
droich
drolly
drongo
droopy
dropsy
drosky
drossy
drouth
drover
drowse
drowsy
egoism
egoist
elodea

eloign eloper enosis enough epodic eponym epopee erotic evolue evolve exodus exogen exomis exotic fiorin floaty flocci floozy floppy florae floral floras floret florid florin flossy floury flower fooler footed footer footle foozle froggy frolic frosty frothy frowst frowsy frowzy frozen gaoler geodic George ghosty global gloomy gloria glossy glover glower gnomic gnomon gnosis goober goodie goodly googly googol gooier gooney gooses groats grocer groggy groove groovy groper grotto grotty grouch ground grouse grovel grower growly growth groyne hooded

hoodie hoodoo hoofed hoofer hookah hooked hooker hookey hookup hooper hoopla hoopoe hooray hootch hooter hooves iconic idolum ironer ironic isobar isohel isomer isopod kaolin knobby knotty knower koodoo kookie koolah kronen kroner kronor kronur Leonid lionel loofah looker lookin looper loosen looter Maoism Maoist miosis miotic moocow mooing moolah myopia myopic myosin myosis myotic noodle oboist ozonic people phobia phobic phoebe phoney phonic phonon phooey photic photon piolet pionic ploidy plotty plough plover poodle pooped poorly prober probit

profit proleg prolix prompt pronto propel proper propyl proser prosit protea proton proven ptosis quoits quorum quotes quotha reopen rhombi rioter roofer rookie roomer rooted rooter scolex sconce scopae scopas scorch scorer scoria scotch scoter scotia Scotic scouse scouth shoaly shoddy shofar shogun shoppy shoran shorts shorty should shovel shover shower Siouan slogan sloppy sloshy slouch slough Slovak sloven slowly smoggy smoker smooch smooth smouch snobby snoopy snooty snooze snorer snotty snouty sooner soothe spoffy spoilt spoken sponge spongy

spooky spoony sports sporty spotty spouse stocks stocky stodge stodgy stogie stoker stokes stolen stolid stolon stoned stoner stooge stopgo storax stores storey stormy stound stover swoosh swound Taoism Taoist tholoi tholos tholus thorax thoria thorny thoron thorpe though tooter toothy tootle tootsy trocar troche trogon troika Trojan trolly trompe trophy tropic troppo trough troupe trouty trover trowel tsotsi twoply twould twoway utopia violet violin voodoo wholly whomso whoops whoosh wooded wooden woodsy woofer wooled woolly yaourt yeoman yoohoo

zlotys alpaca alpine ampere appeal appear append appose arpent aspect aspire bopeep bopped bopper bypass bypast bypath byplay capful capias caplin capote capped capric capsid captor cipher copeck copier coping copita copout copped copper Coptic copula cupful cupola cupped cupric cuptie cupule cypher cyprid daphne dapper dapple depart depend depict deploy depone deport depose depute deputy diplex diploe diplon dipnet dipody dipole dipped dipper dipsas dopant Dopper dupery duplet duplex empery empire employ empusa espial esprit expand expect expend

expert expire expiry export expose fipple gapped gopher gypped gypsum happed happen haptic hepcat heptad hipped hippie hopped hopper hopple hyphae hyphal hyphen impact impair impala impale impark impart impawn impede impend impish impone import impose impost impugn impure impute kaputt kipper kopeck koppie lapdog lapful lapped lappet lappie lapsed lapsus lepton lipase lipide lipoid lipoma lipped lippen lippie lopped lopper lupine mapped mapper mopish mopoke mopped mopper moppet napalm napkin napped Nepali nephew nipped nipper nipple oppose oppugn

orphan orphic orpine osprey papacy papain papaya papers papery papism papist pappus papula papule papyri peplum pepped pepper pepsin peptic piping pipkin pipped pippin popery popgun popish poplar poplin popped popper poppet popple popply pupate pupped puppet raphia raphis rapids rapier rapine rapist rapped rappee rappel rapper raptly raptor repaid repair repand repass repast repeal repeat repent repine replay replum report repose repugn repute ripely ripoff ripped ripper ripple ripply riprap ripsaw ropery roping rupiah sapele sapful sapota sappan

sapped sapper sephen sepsis septal septet septic septum siphon sipped sipper sippet sophic sopite sopped superb supine supped supper supple supply syphon tapeta tapped tapper tappet tappit tepefy tipcat tipoff tipped tipper tippet tipple tiptoe tiptop Tophet tophus topman topped topper topple tupelo typhus typify typing typist umpire unpack unpaid unpick unplug upping uppish uppity vapour wapiti wapper yapock yapped yapper yipped yippee yippie zapped zephyr zipped zipper acquit coquet faquir liquid liquor loquat maquis piquet roquet sequel sequin

abrade abroad abrupt across adrift adroit aerate aerial aerily aerobe afraid afreet afresh afrite agrafe airbed airbus airgun airily airing airman airsac airway aorist aortal aortic arrack arrant arrest arrive arroba arrowy arroyo atrial atrium aurist aurora aurous barbed barbel barber barbet bardic barege barely barfly bargee barite barium barker barley barman barney barony barque barred barrel barren barret barrio barrow barter barton baryon baryta berate Berber bereft berlin bertha berthe birdie bireme birkie birler borage borane borate bordel

border boreal Boreas boride boring borrow borsch borzoi burble burbly burbot burden bureau burgee burger burgle burgoo burhel burial burkha burlap burler Burman burner burnet burnup burrel burrow bursae bursal bursar bursas burton byroad carafe carbon carboy carder careen career caress carfax carful caries carina carman carnal carnet carney carpal carpel carper carpet carpus carrel carrot cartel carter carton carvel carven carver cerate cercus cereal cereus ceriph cerise cerium cermet certes ceruse cervix chrism Christ chroma chrome chromo circle

circus dirndl furred hurray merest Parsee sermon strode torque warren
cirque dorado furrow hurter merger parson serosa stroke torrid warsle
cirrus Dorian garage hurtle merils partan serous stroll torsel warted
corban dormer garbed inroad merino partly serrae stroma torten wirily
corbel dormie garble inrush merism parure serran stromb torula wiring
corbie dorsal garcon irrupt merlin parvis serval strong turban worker
corded dorsum garden jarful merlon perdue server stroud turbid wormer
corder dorter garget jargon merman period shrank strout turbit worrit
cordon durbar gargle jarrah merrie perish shrewd strove turbot worsen
corium duress garial jarred mirage permit shriek strown tureen worthy
corked durgan garish jarvey mirror perron shrift struck turgid wortle
corker Durham garlic jerbil morale person shrike struma turgor yarely
cornea durian garner jerboa morals pertly shrill strung turion yarrow
corned during garnet jerker morass peruke shrimp strunt turkey yorker
cornel durned garran jerkin morbid peruse shrine surely Turkic Yoruba
corner durrie garret jersey morbus phrase shrink surety turner zarape
cornet earful garron jurist moreen piracy shrive surfer turnip zareba
cornua earing garrot karate morgen pirate shroff surrey turnup zariba
corody earner garter karmic morgue piraya shroud surtax turret zircon
corona earthy garuda kaross morion porgie shrove survey turtle ab**s**eil
corozo earwax garvie karroo morish porism shrunk Syriac turves ab**s**ent
corpse earwig gerbil kermes Mormon porker sircar Syrian tyrant ab**s**orb
corpus eerily gerent kermis mornay porose sirdar syrinx Tyrian ab**s**urd
corral egress german kerned morose porous sirkar syrupy Ugrian ad**s**orb
corrie enrage germen kernel morpho portal sirrah target unread ai**s**led
corsac enrapt gerund kersey morris porter sirree Targum unreal al**s**ike
corsak enrich girder kirsch morrow portly sorage tariff unreel an**s**wer
corset enrobe girdle kirtle morsel purdah sorbet tarmac unrest ar**s**ine
cortex enroll girlie Korean mortal purely sordid tarpan unripe as**s**ail
corvee enroot goramy kurgan mortar purfle sorely tarpon unrobe as**s**ent
corves errand gorget larder morula purger sorgho tarras unroll as**s**ert
Corvus errant gorgio lardon murder purify sorner tarred unroof as**s**ess
corymb errata gorgon lariat murine purine sorrel tarsal unroot as**s**ign
coryza etrier gorily larker murmur purism sorrow tarsia unrope as**s**ist
curacy eureka gurgle larrup murphy purist sorter tarsus unruly as**s**ize
curare fardel gurjun larvae murrey purity sortes tartan uprise as**s**oil
curari farfel Gurkha larval myriad purler sortie tartar uproar as**s**ort
curate farina gurnet larynx myrica purlin sprain tartly uproot as**s**ume
curdle farmer gurrah lorcha myrtle purple sprang Tarzan uprush as**s**ure
curfew faroff gyrate lordly nardoo purply sprawl teraph varied Au**s**sie
curiae farout harass lorica narrow purser spread tercel varlet Au**s**tin
curial farrow harden loriot nereid pursue sprent tercet varved ba**s**alt
curium ferial hardly lurdan nerine purvey spring teredo verbal ba**s**ely
curler ferine hardup lurker nerite pyrene sprint terete verger ba**s**haw
curlew ferret harken lyrate neroli pyrite sprite tergal verify ba**s**her
currie ferric harlot lyrics Nordic pyrola sprout tergum verily ba**s**ics
cursed ferula harper lyrism normal pyrope spruce termer verism ba**s**ket
cursor ferule harrow lyrist Norman rarefy spruit termly verist ba**s**net
cursus fervid hartal maraca nurser rarely sprung termor verity Ba**s**que
curtal firing herald maraud oarage raring spryer terret vermin ba**s**set
curtly firkin herbal marble ogress rarity spryly territ vernal ba**s**sos
curtsy firlot herder marbly ogrish reread strafe terror versal ba**s**ter
curule firman herdic marcel onrush sarape strain thrall versed Ba**s**uto
curvet firmly hereat margay orrery sardel strait thrash verser Ba**s**utu
daring forage hereby margin parade sarong strake thrawn verset be**s**eem
darken forbad herein marina paramo sarsen strand thread versus be**s**ide
darkey forbid hereof marine parang scrape strass threap vertex be**s**ted
darkie forbye hereon marish paraph scrawl strata threat vervet be**s**tir
darkle forced heresy Marist parcel screak strath thresh virago be**s**tow
darkly forcer hereto marked pardie scream strati thrice virgin bi**s**ect
darned fordid heriot marker pardon screed strawy thrift virile bi**s**hop
darnel forego hermit market parent screen strays thrill virose bi**s**que
darner forest hernia markup parget screwy streak thrips virtue bi**s**ter
darter forger heroic marlin pariah scribe stream thrive vorant bi**s**tre
dartle forget heroin marmot parian scrimp streek throat vortex bi**s**tro
dartre forgot herpes maroon paring script street throes warble bo**s**che
derail forint Herren marque parish scroll stress throne warcry bo**s**ket
derate forked hirple marram parity scroop strewn throng warden bo**s**omy
deride formal horary marred parkin scruff striae throve warder bo**s**ton
derive format horned marron parlay scrump strict thrown wardog bu**s**bar
dermal formed horner marrow parley scryer stride thrush wargod bu**s**boy
dermic former hornet marrum parody serang strife thrust warily bu**s**hed
dermis formic horrid marshy parole serape strike tirade warmer bu**s**hel
derris fornix horror marten parous seraph Strine torero warmly bu**s**ily
dirdum forrad horsey martin parpen serein string Tories warmth bu**s**ing
direct forrit hurdle martyr parral serene stripe toroid warmup bu**s**ker
direly forsay hurler marvel parrel serial stripy torose warped bu**s**kin
dirham furfur hurley mercer parrot series strive torpid warper bu**s**man
dirhem furore hurrah merely parsec seriph strobe torpor warred bu**s**sed

busted ensile kosher nastic rushes action cattle guttae matted outact
bustee ensoul lascar nestle russet active cetane gutted matter outage
buster ensure lasher Nestor russia actual cither gutter mature outbid
bustle ersatz lashup noshup rustic aether citole hatbox matzoh outbye
bustup Essene lasque nosily rustle afters citric hatful metage outcry
byssus essive lassie nosing sashay anthem citron hatpeg metals outdid
casbah essoin lassos nostoc sasine anther citrus hatpin meteor outfit
casein exsect laster obsess sesame antiar cottar hatred method outfox
casern exsert lastly onside seseli anting cotted hatted methyl outgun
cashew fasces lesion ossein sestet antler cotter hatter metier outing
casing fascia lessee ossify siskin antral cotton hetero metope outlaw
casino fasten lessen ouster sissoo antrum cutely hetman metred outlay
casket faster lesser oyster sister artery cutler hither metric outlet
Caslon fescue lesson pascal sistra artful cutlet hitman mettle output
casque festal lessor Pashto suslik artist cutoff hotbed mitral outran
cassia fester lisper passer system astern cutout hotdog mitten outrun
cassis fiscal lissom passim tassel asthma cutter hotpot motett outsat
caster fisher listed pastel tassie astral cuttle hotter mother outset
castle fistic listel pastil taster astray datary hutted motile outsit
castor fossae listen pastor testae astute dative intact motion outtop
casual fossil lister pastry tester attach datura intake motive outvie
cesser fossor lushly pesade teston attack detach intend motley outwit
cestus foster lustra peseta tisane attain detail intent motmot oxtail
cesura fusain lustre pesewa tissue attend detain intern motory patchy
cistus fusile lysine pester tosher attest detect intine mottle patent
cosher fusion mascle pestle tosser attire detent intoed mutant Pathan
cosily fusser mascon Pisces tossup attorn detest intone mutate pathic
cosine fustic mascot pissed Tuscan attune detour intray mutely pathos
cosmic gasbag masher pistil tusked author dither intuit mutine patina
cosmos Gascon mashie pistol tusker autism dittos jetlag mutiny patois
cosset gasify masker piston tussah autumn dotage jetsam mutism patrol
costae gasket maslin posada tusser batata dotard jetted mutter patron
costal gaskin Masora poseur tussle bateau dotted jitney mutton patted
costar gasman masque posset ugsome bather dottle jitter mutual patten
coster gasper massif possum ulster bathos eatery jotted mutule patter
costly gassed masted postal unsafe bating eating jotter mutuum petara
cuscus gasser master poster unsaid batman either Jutish mythic petard
cushat goslow mastic postil unseal batted entail jutted mythos petite
cusped gospel mescal pusher unseam batten entera kation natant petrel
cuspid gossan mesial Pushtu unseat batter entice ketone nation petrol
cussed gossip messan pushup unseen battle entire kettle native petted
custom gusher Messrs rascal unself battue entity kitbag natron petter
cystic gusset mestee rasher unship betake entoil kitcat natter pitchy
cystid haslet miscue rashly unshod bethel entomb kitool nature pithos
dasher hassle misdid rasper unshoe betide entrap kitsch netful pitier
dassie hasten misere raster unstop betony entree kitten nether pitman
desalt hispid misery rasure unsung betook estate kittle netted pitpan
descry hisser misfit resale upshot betray esteem kittul nettle pitsaw
desert hosier mishap rescue upside betted estray lateen nitric pitted
design hostel mishit reseat ursine better eutaxy lately nitwit pitter
desire husker mishmi reseau vassal bettor extant latent notary potage
desist hussar Mishna resect vastly bitchy extasy latest notate potale
desman hustle mislay reseda vesica biting extend lather notice potash
desmid hyssop misled resell vesper bitted extent latish notify potato
desorb insane missal resent vessel bitten extern latria notion potboy
despot inseam missel reship vestal bitter extort latron nutant poteen
disarm insect missis reside vested botany fathen latten nutate potent
disbar insert missus resign vestee botchy father latter nutmeg potful
disbud inside mister resile vestry botfly fathom lethal nutria pother
discal insist mistle resist visage bother fatted letoff nutter potion
discus insole misuse resold viscid bothie fatten letter obtain potman
diseur inspan mosaic resole viscus botone fatter Lettic obtect potpie
dismal instal moshav resorb Vishnu bottle fetial litany obtest potted
dismay instar Moslem resort visile bottom fetich litchi obtund potter
disown instep mosque rester vision butane fetish lithia obtuse pottle
dispel instil mostly result visive butene fetter lithic octane putlog
distal insult muscat resume visual butler fettle litmus octant putoff
distil insure muscle rising washer butter fitful litter octave putrid
disuse itself museum risker wasted button fitted little octavo putsch
dosage jasper musing risque waster catalo fitter lotion octroi puttee
dossal jester muskeg rosace wester catchy fother lotted optant putter
dossel Jesuit musket rosary wisdom catena futile luteal optics puttie
dosser josher muskox rosery wisely catgut future lutein optima python
duster josser Muslim rosily wisent Cathar gateau luting option ratbag
dustup jostle muslin rosiny wisher cation gather matico osteal rather
easily justly mussel roster xystus catkin getout matins ostial ratify
easter kasbah muster rostra yesman catnap getter matlow ostium ratine
ensate kismet myself rosula yester catnip Gothic matrix ostler rating
ensign kisser mystic rusher acting catsup gotten matron ottava ration

ratite totted caudle frusta rouble tourer lively bowyer tawery elytra
ratlin totter caught frutex roucou tousle livery byword tawpie eryngo
ratoon tutsan caulis gauche rouncy touter living bywork thwack etymon
rattan tutted causal gaucho rouser truant lovage cowage thwart flying
rattat ultima causer gauger router trudge lovein coward towage flyman
ratted ultimo causey glumly saucer truism lovely cowboy toward flysch
ratter untidy chubby glumpy sauger trumps loving cowish towery flyway
rattle untied chuffy glutei saurel trusty moving cowled towhee geyser
retail untold chukar gluten sculpt unused novena cowman townee glycin
retain untrue chukka gourde scummy usurer novice cowpat Tswana glycol
retake untuck chummy grubby scurfy uvulae obvert cowpea unwary goyish
retard untune chunky grudge scurry uvular pavage cowpox unwell haybox
retell uptake church grugru scurvy vaudoo pavane cowrie unwept haymow
retene uptown clumpy grumly scutal vaulty paving dawdle unwind heyday
retest upturn clumsy grumps scutch voulge pavior dewily unwise hoyden
retial ustion clunch grumpy scutum waught pavise dewlap unworn inyala
retina vatful clutch grutch shucks woundy ravage dowlas unwrap joyful
retire vatted coucal hauler shutin yaupon ravine downer upward joyous
retold vetted cougar haunch sludge zeugma raving dowser upwind keyway
retook vitals coulee houdan sludgy Zouave ravish enwind vaward layday
retool vitric county hourly sluice zounds revamp enwomb wowser layman
retort vittae couple housel sluicy advent reveal enwrap boxbed layoff
retral votary coupon housey slummy adverb reverb fawner boxcar layout
retrod voting course iguana slurry advert revere fowler boxful maybug
retted votive cousin inulin slushy advice revers gewgaw boxing mayday
returf waters cruces jaunce smudge advise revert gowany dexter mayest
return watery cruddy jaunty smudgy bovine revery hawhaw fixate mayfly
retuse wattle cruise jounce smugly bovver revest hawked fixity mayhap
ritual wether cruive jouncy smutch caveat review hawker hexact mayhem
rotary wetted crumby launce smutty cavern revile hawser hexane maying
rotate wetter crummy launch snubby caviar revise howdah hexose noyade
rotche withal crunch laurel snuffy caving revive howler laxity oxygen
rotgut wither crural louche snugly cavity revoke inward luxate oxymel
rotted within cruset louden souari cavort revolt inwick luxury payday
rotten withit crusty loudly sought civics revved inwove maxima paynim
rotter witted crutch lounge souled covert rivage inwrap maxixe payoff
rotund wittol cruxes loupen source coving roving Jewess myxoma payola
rutile yatter dauber loupit sourly devest savage Jewish saxony peyote
rutted yttria deuced louver souter device savant kewpie sexily peyotl
sateen zither dhurra louvre spunky devise savate kowhai sexism phylum
satiny zythum douane maugre spurge devoid savine kowtow sexist physic
satire abulia double maundy spurry devoir saving lawful sexpot prying
satori abuser doubly moujik sputum devote savory lawman sextan psyche
satrap acuity douche mouldy squail devour savour lawyer sextet psycho
Saturn acumen dought moulin squall devout sevens lewdly sexton rhymer
satyra aguish doughy mouser squama divers severe lowboy sexual rhythm
setoff alulae dourly mousse square divert severy lowery sixain royals
setose alumna douser mouthy squash divest Sevres lowing sixgun sayest
setout alumni drudge muumuu squawk divide soviet lowish taxies saying
settee amulet drupel naught squeak divine sovran lowkey taxman sayyid
setter amuser eluant nausea squeal diving tavern newish toxoid scyphi
settle aoudad eluate nautch squill elvish unveil newton tuxedo scythe
sittar avulse eluent neural squint envier vivace Nowell waxily shyest
sitter bauble emulge neuron squire favour vivers nowise adytum skylab
Sothic bluing equate neuter squirm foveae vivify onward amylum skyman
sotted bluish equine nougat squirt foveal wavery pawnee anyhow skyway
sutile blunge equity nought squish gavage wavily pawner anyone slyest
sutler blurry faucal nounal Stuart gavial wivern pawpaw anyway stylar
suttee boucle fauces ocular stubby govern wyvern pewter asylum stylet
suture bought faucet oeuvre stucco guvnor always powder bayard stylus
tatami bougie faulty ovular studio Havana aswoon powwow beyond stymie
tatted boulle faunae paunch stuffy havers bawbee reward boyish styrax
tatter bounce faunal pauper stumer invade bawble rewind bryony thymol
tattle bouncy faunas plucky stumpy invent bawdry rewire cayman thymus
tattoo bounds feudal plumed stupid invert bawler rewoke cayuse thyrse
tetany bounty fluent plummy stupor invest bawley reword chypre thyrsi
tetchy bourne fluffy plumpy sturdy invite bewail rework clypei trying
tether bourse flukey plunge taught invoke beware rowing coyote tryout
tetrad bruise flunky plural Taurus jovial bewray sawder crying tuyere
tetter brumal flurry plushy tauten Jovian bowels sawfly crypto twyere
titbit brumby fluted pluton tautly lavabo bowery sawney daybed unyoke
titfer brunch fluter pouchy tautog lavage bowfin sawpit dayfly voyage
tither brunet fought pouffe Teuton laveer bowing sawset doyley voyeur
titian brushy foully pounce thulia lavish bowleg sawyer drybob waylay
titled brutal foulup pourer toucan lavolt bowler sewage dryfly wayout
titter brutus fourth pouter touche levant bowman sewing dryish whydah
tittle caucus frugal pruina touchy Levite bowsaw sowans dryrot bazaar
tittup caudal fruity pruner toupee levity bowtie sowens dryrun bezant
tother caudex frumpy rhumba toupet livein bowwow tawdry duyker bezoar

bizone buzzer dazzle dozily eczema enzyme Eozoic Eozoon evzone fezzed fezzes fizgig fizzle gazebo gazump gozzan guzzle hazard hazily huzoor izzard jezail lazily lazuli lizard mazard mazily mezuza mizzen mizzle mizzly muzhik muzzle Nazify Nazism nozzle nuzzle pizzle puzzle razzia razzle rizzar rizzer rozzer sizing sizzle syzygy vizard vizier vizsla wizard wizier

---

abbacy ablate ablaut ablaze aboard abrade ackack admass adnate aerate afeard affair aflame afraid aghast agnail agnate agrafe albata alcaic alkali alkane alpaca always angary anlace

anlage annals apiary arcade Arcady arcana arcane argala argali argand armada arrack arrant askant askari aslant assail attach attack attain aubade aviary aviate aweary ayeaye balata banana basalt batata bayard bazaar becall becalm became bedaub bedaze befall behalf behave belaud berate betake bewail beware bezant bigamy Bihari binary binate bleach bleary bocage borage borane borate botany breach breast breath briard briary broach bumalo butane bylane byname bypass bypast bypath cabala cabana cafard calami calash camass canape canard canary carafe

catalo cedarn cerate cetane chiasm chiaus cicada cicala cigala cleave cloaca cobalt comate cowage coward creaky creamy crease create croaky cubage curacy curare curari curate damage damask datary debark debase debate decade decamp decani decant dedans deface defame delate demand demark denary depart derail derate desalt detach detail detain dicast digamy dilate disarm dogate domain donate dopant dorado dosage dotage dotard douane dreamt dreamy dreary dynamo dynast eclair Eddaic efface eluant eluate embalm embank embark encage encamp encase encash

enface engage enhalo enlace enrage enrapt ensate entail equate ergate errand errant errata ersatz escape escarp estate ethane eutaxy exhale expand extant extasy facade female finale finals fixate floaty forage freaky friary fugato fusain galago galaxy garage gavage Gemara gleamy gobang gocart gokart goramy gowany grease greasy greave groats gyrate hamate harass Havana hazard herald hexact hexane hijack homage horary humane iceaxe ideaed ideate iguana immane impact impair impala impale impark impart impawn incase indaba infamy infant infare inhale

inlaid inland inlaws inmate innate insane intact intake invade inward inyala iodate island izzard jacana jezail Judaic jugate kabala kakapo kanaka karate lanate lavabo lavage legacy legate legato levant ligate linage lipase litany lizard lobate locale locate lovage lunacy lunate luxate lyrate macaco Madame malady Malaga malate manage manana maraca maraud mazard menace menage metage metals midage midair mikado milady milage mirage mohair Mohawk morale morals morass mosaic mutant mutate mygale nagana napalm natant negate Nepali nonage nonary notary

notate noyade nutant nutate oarage oblast oblate obtain occamy octane octant octave octavo ohmage oleate onfall onward oogamy opiate optant ordain orgasm ornate ottava outact outage oxgall oxgang oxgate oxland oxtail padauk pajama palace palais palate panada panama panary papacy papain papaya parade paramo parang paraph pavage pavane pedalo pedant pedate pelage pesade petara petard phrase pilaff piracy pirate piraya pleach please pliant Polack pomace pomade posada potage potale potash potato preach pupate queasy queazy rabato ramate ravage rebate

rebato recall recant recast redact reface regain regale regard rehash relaid relate remade remain remake remand remark rename repaid repair repand repass repast resale retail retain retake retard revamp reward ribald riband rivage robalo Romaic Romany rosace rosary rotary rotate royals rubato safari salaam salade salami salary samara sarape savage savant savate sclaff scrape scrawl seaair secant sedate sejant senary senate serang serape seraph sesame sewage shears sheass sheath sheave shoaly shrank silage sixain sleave sleazy smeary sneaky socage

solace solano sonant sonata sorage souari sowans splash sprain sprang sprawl squail squall squama square squash squawk steady steamy strafe strain strait strake strand strass strata strath strati strawy strays Stuart sudary sugary sumach sweaty tabard takahe tamale tamara tatami tenace tenant teraph tetany thrall thrash thrawn thwack thwart tirade tisane togaed tomato towage toward treaty triage truant Tswana tyrant ullage umlaut uncage uncate undate unease uneasy uneath unfair unhair unhand Uniate unlace unlade unlaid unlash unmade unmake unmask

unnail unpack unpaid unsafe unsaid unwary upcast update upland uptake upward urbane vacant vacate vagary vaward vihara virago visage vitals vivace vizard volant vorant votary voyage wabain Wahabi wizard wreath zarape zenana zonary zonate Zouave zymase airbed airbus anabas Arabic arable ashbin aumbry babble babbly balboa bamboo baobab barbed barbel barber barbet bauble bawbee bawble bedbug Berber bibbed bibber bilbos bobbed bobbin bobble bomber bonbon booboo boxbed briber bubble bubbly bulbar bulbed bulbil bulbul bumble burble burbly burbot busbar

busboy byebye camber carbon carboy casbah chubby cobber cobble combat combed comber corban corbel corbie cowboy crabby cumber cymbal dabbed dabber dabble dauber daybed dibbed dibber dibble disbar disbud djibba doable dobbin double doubly drably drybob dubbed dubbin dumbly durbar dybbuk edible enable feeble feebly fibbed fibber fimble flabby fobbed fogbow foible forbad forbid forbye fumble gabbed gabber gabble gabbro gambir gambit gamble gambol garbed garble gasbag gerbil gibber gibbet gibbon gimbal glibly global gobbet gobble goober grabby graben

grubby
hagbut
hatbox
haybox
herbal
hobbit
hobble
hombre
hotbed
hubbub
humble
humbly
humbug
iambic
iambus
icebag
icebox
isabel
isobar
jabbed
jabber
jerbil
jerboa
jibbah
jibbed
jibber
jobber
jumbal
jumble
jumbly
kasbah
kibble
kitbag
knobby
lambda
lamber
legbye
liable
libber
limbec
limbed
limber
limbic
limbus
lobbed
lowboy
lubber
lumbar
lumber
marble
marbly
maybug
member
mobbed
morbid
morbus
mumble
nabbed
nibbed
nibble
nimble
nimbly
nimbus
nobble
nobbut
nubble
nubbly
number
numbly
outbid
outbye
pebble
pebbly
phobia
phobic
plebby
potboy
prober
probit
pueblo
rabbet
rabbin
rabbit
rabble
ragbag
ramble
ratbag
redbud
reebok
rhebok
ribbed
ribbon
robbed
robber
rouble
rubbed
rubber
rubble
rubbly
rumble
rumbly
sabbat
sambar
sambur
scabby
seabed
seabee
semble
shabby
skibob
snobby
snubby
sobbed
sombre
sorbet
stable
stably
stubby
suable
subbed
sunbow
symbol
tabbed
talbot
teabag
Theban
tidbit
tiebar
timbal
timber
timbre
titbit
tombac
tombak
tomboy
treble
trebly
tribal
tubber
tumble
turban
turbid
turbit
turbot
tymbal
unable
usable
verbal
viable
wabble
wamble
wambly
warble
webbed
wimble
wobble
wobbly
wombat
yabber
zombie
abacus
acacia
anicut
apache
apical
apices
ashcan
avocet
beachy
beacon
bitchy
bobcat
bosche
botchy
boucle
boxcar
bracer
braces
bricky
broche
buccal
bunchy
caecal
caecum
calcar
calces
calcic
cancan
cancel
cancer
catchy
caucus
cercus
chacha
chacma
chichi
chicle
circle
circus
cliche
cloche
coccal
coccid
coccus
coccyx
concha
conchy
concur
coucal
creche
crocus
cruces
cuscus
dancer
deacon
deicer
descry
deuced
diacid
discal
discus
douche
drachm
dulcet
eggcup
ejecta
elicit
epical
eyecup
falcon
fasces
fascia
faucal
fauces
faucet
fencer
fescue
fiacre
fiscal
flacon
fleche
flocci
forced
forcer
fracas
fulcra
garcon
Gascon
gauche
gaucho
glacis
glycin
glycol
grocer
hepcat
hiccup
hoicks
hubcap
ibices
icecap
icicle
kincob
kitcat
laical
lancer
lancet
lascar
litchi
lorcha
louche
madcap
manche
Manchu
marcel
mascle
mascon
mascot
mercer
mescal
mincer
miscue
mobcap
moocow
muscat
muscle
niacin
noncom
nuncio
nuncle
obeche
oilcan
orache
oracle
outcry
parcel
pascal
patchy
peachy
pencil
piecer
pincer
Pisces
pitchy
placed
placer
placet
placid
plicae
plucky
poncho
pouchy
precis
pricey
psyche
psycho
punchy
puncta
quiche
rancho
rancid
rascal
redcap
reecho
rescue
rotche
roucou
saucer
seacow
seiche
shucks
sircar
slacks
slicer
soccer
spacer
specie
stacte
sticky
stocks
stocky
stucco
sulcus
talcky
talcum
teacup
tercel
tercet
tetchy
thecae
thecal
tincal
tipcat
toecap
tomcat
tomcod
toucan
touche
touchy
tracer
traces
tracks
tricar
tricky
tricot
trocar
troche
Tuscan
twicer
uracil
viscid
viscus
voiced
vulcan
warcry
whacky
wincey
yoicks
zinced
zincic
zincky
zircon
acedia
acidic
acidly
amadou
amidst
anadem
anodal
anodic
aoudad
apodal
avidly
baddie
baldly
bandit
bandog
bardic
bawdry
beadle
bedded
bedder
beldam
bender
bidden
bidder
binder
birdie
bladed
boldly
bonded
bonder
boodle
bordel
border
bridal
bridge
bridle
budded
Buddha
buddle
bunder
bundle
burden
caddie
caddis
candid
candle
carder
caudal
caudex
caudle
cinder
cloddy
coddle
coldly
condor
corded
corder
cordon
cradle
credal
credit
cruddy
cuddie
cuddle
cuddly
curdle
daedal
dander
dandle
dawdle
deaden
deadly
deodar
diadem
diddle
dikdik
dirdum
dodder
doddle
doodad
doodah
doodle
dredge
drudge
dumdum
dyadic
elodea
epodic
evader
exedra
exodus
fandom
fardel
feeder
fender
feudal
fiddle
fiddly
finder
fledge
fodder
fogdog
folder
fondle
fondly
fondue
fordid
Friday
fridge
fuddle
fundus
gadded
gadder
gander
garden
gender
geodic
giddap
gilder
girder
girdle
gladly
glider
goddam
Goidel
golden
goodie
goodly
grader
gradin
gradus
grudge
guddle
guider
guidon
gulden
gundog
haddie
handed
handle
harden
hardly
hardup
headed
header
headon
heddle
herder
herdic
heyday
hidden
hinder
Hindoo
hodden
holden
holder
holdup
hooded
hoodie
hoodoo
hotdog
houdan
howdah
hoyden
huddle
hurdle
ibidem
irides
judder
kidded
kidder
kiddie
kindle
kindly
koedoe
koodoo
ladder
laddie
landau
landed
lander
lapdog
larder
lardon
layday
leaden
leader
leadin
leadup
lender
lewdly
lidded
lieder
linden
loaded
loader
lordly
louden
loudly
lurdan
madden
madder
maidan
maiden
manday
mayday
meadow
meddle
mender
midday
midden
middle
mildew
mildly
minded
minder
misdid
moider
Monday
muddle
mundic
murder
nardoo
needle
neednt
nodded
noddle
noodle
Nordic
outdid
padded
paddle
paidup
pander
pandit
pardie
pardon
payday
peddle
perdue
piddle
piedog
pledge
podded
polder
ponder
poodle
powder
puddle
puddly
pugdog
pundit
purdah
pyedog
raddle
raider
randan
randem
random
reader
redden
redder
reddle
reedit
render
ridded
ridden
riddle
roadie
rondel
rudder
ruddle
rundle
sadden
sadder
saddhu
saddle
saidst
sandal
sander
sandhi
sardel
sawder
seadog
seeder
seldom
sendal
sender
sendup
shader
shades
shadow
shaduf
shoddy
sirdar
skiddy
sledge
slider
sludge
sludgy
smudge
smudgy
sodden
soldan
solder
sordid
spadix
spider
stadia
stodge
stodgy
studio
subdue
sudden
sundae
Sunday
sunder
sundew
sundog
sundry
swaddy
syndic
tandem
tawdry
tedded
tedder
tender
tendon
tiddly
tiedye
tindal
tinder
toddle
trader
trudge
tundra
vandal
vaudoo
vendee
vender
vendor
vendue
voided
voider
voodoo
wadded
waddie
waddle
wander
warden
warder
wardog
wedded
weeder
welder
weldor
Wendic
whidah
whydah
wilder
wildly
winded
winder
window
windup
wisdom
wonder
wooded
wooden
woodsy
yonder
zander
abbess
abject
abseil
absent
accede
accent
accept
access
achene
addend
adhere
adieus
adieux
adnexa
advent
adverb
advert
Aegean
affect
affeer
afield
afreet
afresh
afters
albedo
albeit
albert
alkene
allege
allele
amoeba
ampere
anneal
annexe
apiece
appeal
appear

append ardent argent arpent arrest artery ascend ascent asleep aspect assent assert assess astern attend attest Augean awheel bakery baleen barege barely basely bateau bedeck bedell befell behead beheld behest bereft beseem biceps bireme bisect bodega bolero bopeep boreal Boreas bowels bowery breech breeks breese breeze breezy briefs briery bureau butene cadent camera careen career caress casein casern catena caveat cavern celery cement cereal cereus cheeky cheers cheery cheese cheesy chield cicely cinema cineol client cogent coheir cohere coleus

comedo comedy comely comeon copeck covert creeps creepy creese cutely deceit decent defeat defect defend deject delete demean dement depend desert detect detent detest devest digest direct direly diseur divers divert divest docent dogear dogend domett dudeen dukery dupery duress eatery eczema effect effete egress eldest eluent embers empery endear enmesh ennead entera Eocene ephebe ephebi Essene esteem ethene eureka exceed except excess expect expend expert exsect exsert extend extent extern facete fadein fagend fakery finely finery fleece fleech

fleecy fluent foment forego forest foveae foveal fraena freely freest freeze friend frieze gaiety galena gamely gamete gateau gazebo genera geneva gerent gleety govern greedy greens greeny grieve haleru havers hedera hereat hereby herein hereof hereon heresy hereto hetero homely honest hugely humect humeri hyaena immesh impede impend incept incest indeed indene indent infect infelt infest ingest inhere inject inseam insect insert intend intent intern invent invert invest itself Jewess Judean kinema kopeck Korean laceup lamely lament lateen lately

latent latest laveer legend likely lineal linear lineup livein lively livery loment lonely lovein lovely lowery lucent lucern luteal lutein lyceum makedo makeup maleic manege mayest merely merest meteor misere misery modena modern modest moiety molest moment moneys moreen motett museum mutely myself namely nereid nicely nicety ninety nocent nonego novena Nowell nudely object obsess obtect obtest obvert oedema offend offent ogress oogeny orcein ordeal orgeat orient ornery orrery ossein osteal oxherd pakeha paleae palely papers papery parent patent

peseta pesewa phlegm phoebe pigeon pileum pileup pileus pineal pinery pineta pliers pomelo popery poseur poteen potent priest purely pyrene quaere raceme rarefy rarely rebeck recede recent recess redeem redeye refect regent rehear reheat reheel reject relent remedy renege repeal repeat repent reread reseat reseau resect reseda resell resent retell retene retest reveal reverb revere revers revert revery revest rident rifely ripely rodent ropery rosery rubefy rudely safely safety sagely sanely sapele sateen sayest schema scheme sclera screak scream

screed screen screwy seaear secede secern select senega serein serene seseli sevens severe severy sheeny sheets shield shiest shrewd shyest sileni silent sinewy skeely sleepy sleety sleeve slyest smeech sneesh sneeze sneezy sobeit solely solemn sorely sowens speech speedo speedy sphene sphery spleen splent spread sprent squeak squeal steely steeve streak stream streek street stress strewn superb surely surety sweeny sweets tagend takein talent tamely tapeta tavern tawery teledu telega tepefy teredo terete thieve thread threap threat thresh

timely Toledo toneme torero towery tumefy tupelo tureen tuxedo tuyere tweeds tweedy tweeny twyere ubiety unbend unbent unless unmeet unread unreal unreel unrest unseal unseam unseat unseen unself unveil unwell unwept upbear upbeat upheld upkeep uraeus urgent valeta vegete veleta veneer venery vilely vinery vivers voyeur waders wafery waters watery wavery wheeze wheezy widely wifely wigeon winery wisely wisent wivern womera wyvern xylene yarely yclept zareba zebeck armful artful baffle bagful barfly belfry biffin binful boffin botfly bowfin boxful

buffer buffet Caffre canful capful carfax carful chafer chaffy chuffy cliffy coffee coffer coffin coffle comfit confab confer crafty cuffed cupful curfew dayfly deafen deafly deific differ dogfox drafty drifty dryfly duffel duffer duffle earful eyeful farfel filfot fitful fluffy fulfil furfur fylfot gadfly gaffer goffer golfer guffaw haffet haffit hatful heifer hoofed hoofer ireful jarful joyful jugful Kaffir lapful lawful leafed loafer loofah manful mayfly miffed misfit muffin muffle netful nonfat olefin outfit outfox panful piaffe piffle pilfer

potful pouffe prefab prefer prefix profit puffed puffer puffin purfle raffia raffle reefer riffle roofer rueful ruffed ruffle sapful sawfly seafan seafog seafox shifty shofar sinful sniffy snuffy soffit spiffy spoffy stifle stuffy suffer suffix surfer tiffin tinful titfer toffee trifid trifle tubful tuffet unific urnful useful vatful waffle wilful woeful woofer yaffle zaffer zaffre adagio airgun alegar alight apogee aright badger bagged banger bangle bangup bargee beagle beggar begged beigel Belgic bigger biggin blight bodger bogged boggle bongos

bought bougie bregma bright brogue budget budgie bugged Bulgar bulger bungle burgee burger burgle burgoo cadger cangue catgut caught chigoe claggy cloggy codger cogged coigne congee conger congou cougar craggy cudgel dagger danger dangle dengue digger dingey dinghy dingle dingus dodgem dodger dogged dogger doggie dought doughy dragee draggy dragon dreggy droger drogue durgan enigma exogen fagged faggot fanged fidget figged finger fizgig flaggy flagon flight fogged forger forget forgot fought fright frigid froggy frugal fugged fulgid fungal fungus gadget gagged gagger gaggle ganger gangly gangue garget gargle gauger geegee gewgaw gigged giggle giggly gingal ginger gingko goggle goggly googly googol gorget gorgio gorgon grigri groggy grugru guggle gurgle haggis haggle hangar hanged hanger hangup hedger height higgle hinged hogged hogget hoggin hugged hunger hungry jaeger jagged jagger jangle jargon jigged jigger jiggle jiggly jingle jingly jogged jogger joggle judger jugged juggle jungle jungly kingly knaggy knight kurgan laager lagged lagger langue langur league ledged ledger legged length

ligger linger lingua lodger loggat logged logger loggia longan lugged lugger luggie lunger maggot maigre mangel manger mangle mangos margay margin maugre meagre merger midget midgut mingle moggie monger Mongol morgen morgue mugged mugger nagged nagger naught nidget nigger niggle nilgai noggin nougat nought nugget onager origan origin outgun oxygen parget pegged pidgin pigged piggin pinger plagal plague plaguy plight pongee popgun porgie purger quagga quaggy ragged raggee raggle ranger reggae ridged rigged rigger ringed ringer rotgut rugged rugger

saggar sagged sagger sangar sauger shaggy shogun singer single singly sixgun slaggy slight slogan smoggy smugly snaggy snugly soigne sorgho sought spigot stager stagey stigma stogie sungod tagged tangle tangly target Targum taught tergal tergum tingle tingly togged toggle tongue tragic tragus trigon trogon tugged turgid turgor twiggy valgus verger virgin vulgar vulgus wagged waggle waggly waggon wangle wargod waught weight widget wigged wiggle wiggly winged winger woggle wright zeugma zingel aether Afghan anchor anthem anther anyhow arched archer

archil archly archon asthma author bashaw basher bather bathos bethel bishop boohoo bother bothie Brahma Brahmi brehon burhel bushed bushel cachet cachou cashew Cathar cipher cither cochin cosher cushat cypher daphne dasher dirham dirhem dither Durham eighth eighty either eschar eschew etcher euchre fathen father fathom fisher fother fulham Gadhel gather gopher Gothic gusher hawhaw heehaw higher highly hither hyphae hyphal hyphen inches ischia isohel josher kosher kowhai laches lasher lashup lather lecher lethal lichee lichen lights linhay lithia

lithic lochan lushly lychee machan masher mashie mayhap mayhem menhir method methyl mighty mishap mishit mishmi Mishna moshav mother muzhik mythic mythos nephew nether nighty noshup nuchal orchid orchil orchis orphan orphic Pashto Pathan pathic pathos peahen pelham pithos pother pusher Pushtu pushup python quahog rachis raphia raphis rasher rashly rather redhot reship richen riches richly righto rochet ruched rusher rushes sachem sachet sashay senhor sephen sigher siphon sophic Sothic sunhat syphon tether tights tither tocher Tophet tophus tosher

tother towhee tuchun typhus unship unshod unshoe upshot urchin Vishnu washer wether wisher withal wither within withit yoohoo zephyr zither zythum acting action active acuity addict admire adrift advice advise aedile aerial aerily affine affirm afrite ageing agnise aguish aikido airily airing albino albite Aldine allied allium alpine alsike amnion angina anoint antiar anting aorist Argive arnica aroint arrive arsine artist aseity aspire assign assist assize atrial atrium attire audile augite aurist autism aweigh awhile awning Babism Babist banian

banish barite barium basics bating begird begirt behind belief belike belive bemire benign beside betide bikini biting bluing bluish bodice bodily boding bolide bonism bonist bonito booing boride boring bovine bowing boxing boyish brains brainy braird braise bruise bulimy bunion burial busily busing byline cagily cahier calico caliph camion camise canine capias caries carina casing casino cation caviar caving cavity cecity celiac ceriph cerise cerium chaise choice chrism Christ cilice cilium civics coaita codify cogito coming comity conics copier

coping copita corium cosily cosine coving cowish cruise cruive crying cubism cubist cueing cueist curiae curial curium Daniel Danish daring dative decide defier defile define delict demise demist denial denier denims depict deride derive design desire desist device devise dewily dimity dining divide divine diving docile dolium domino Dorian dozily dreich droich dryish dudish dunite durian during dyeing earing easily eating edgily edging eerily effigy egoism egoist elfish eloign elvish empire ending endive engild engine engird engirt enlist enmity

enrich ensign ensile entice entire entity envier enwind eolian eolith eonian eonism equine equity erbium ermine Eskimo espial essive ethics Ethiop etrier excide excise excite expire expiry eyeing Fabian facial facies facile facing family famine famish fanion farina feeing feline Fenian ferial ferine fetial fetich fetish filial filing finial fining finish finite firing fixity flying foliar folium forint fraise fruity fusile fusion futile gabion galiot gamily gamine gaming garial garish gasify gavial Gemini genial genius glairy glaive gneiss gooier

gorily goyish grainy greige guaiac habile halide halite Hamite hazily hegira hejira helium heriot hiding hieing hoeing holily holism homily homing hominy honied hosier humify ignite imbibe impish incise incite Indian indict indign indigo indite indium infirm inlier inning inside insist intine invite inwick iodide iodine iodise iodism iolite Ionian ionise ionium jabiru Jewish jovial Jovian Julian junior jurist Jutish kation kibitz kumiss labial labile labium lacing ladify lading ladino lamina lamish lariat latish lavish laxity lazily legion legist lenity lesion Levite levity liaise libido liking lilied liming lining lipide living logion lorica loriot lotion loving lowing lowish lumina lupine luting Lydian lyrics lyrism lyrist lysine Magian magilp making malice malign malism maniac manila manioc manito Maoism Maoist marina marine marish Marist matico matins maxima maxixe maying mazily mediae medial median medick medico medium medius megilp menial meninx merils merino merism mesial metier milieu minify minima mining minion minish minium mobile modify modish modius moline monial monied monies

monism monist mooing mopish morion morish motile motion motive moving mulish Munich murine musing mutine mutiny mutism myriad myrica nanism nation native Nazify Nazism nerine nerite newish nicish nidify nomism nonius nosily nosing notice notify notion novice nowise nubile nudism nudist nudity numina oafish oblige oboist oddity oecist office offing offish ogrish oidium oldish online onside oolite oomiak ophite optics optima option orpine oscine osmium ossify ostial ostium outing owlish oxbird oxhide pacify paling palish papism papist pariah parian

paring parish parity patina paving pavior pavise period perish petite pinion piping pitier plaice plaint ploidy podite podium police policy polish polite polity popish porism potion praise pruina prying pumice punily punish purify purine purism purist purity pyrite quaich quaigh quaint quoits rabies racial racily racism racist radial radian radish radium radius rakish ramify rapids rapier rapine rapist raring rarity ratify ratine rating ration ratite ravine raving ravish recipe recite rediae refill refine regime regina region regius relict relief

reline relish relive remind remint remise remiss repine reside resign resile resist retial retina retire review revile revise revive rewind rewire riding rising Romish roping rosily rosiny roving rowing rubify rudish ruling rumina rupiah rutile Sabian Sabine sadism sadist Salian salify salina saline saliva Samian samite sanies sanify sanity sasine satiny satire savine saving saying schism schist schizo scribe scrimp script sedile seeing Semite senile senior serial series seriph sewing sexily sexism sexist sheikh sheila Shiite shriek shrift shrike

shrill shrimp shrine shrink shrive siding silica simian simile sizing skeigh skiing sleigh sluice sluicy social sodium solidi solids somite sopite soviet speiss sphinx splice spline splint splits spoilt spring sprint sprite squill squint squire squirm squirt squish stairs staith striae strict stride strife strike Strine string stripe stripy strive Sufism supine sutile Syriac Syrian syrinx tahini taking talion taming tanist Taoism Taoist tariff taxies tedium theine theirs theism theist thrice thrift thrill thrips thrive tibiae tibial tidily tiling

timing tinily titian toeing tonish Tories troika truism trying Tshirt tubing tuning turion typify typing typist Tyrian uglify uglily Ugrian ultima ultimo umpire unbind unbitt uncial uncini undies undine ungird ungirt unkind unking unkink unlike unlink unpick unripe untidy untied unwind unwise uphill uplift upping uppish uppity uprise upside upwind ursine ustion vagile valine valise vanish vanity varied Vedist venial venire Venite verify verily verism verist verity vesica vibist Viking vilify virile visile vision visive vivify vizier voting votive

wahine wanion wapiti warily wavily waxily widish wilily wirily wiring wizier wraith xenial xenium yogism zanily zariba zenith zodiac zoning acajou banjax banjos deejay donjon fanjet frijol gurjun logjam moujik oddjob ramjet sanjak Seljuk Trojan awaked awaken awoken backer backup balker banker banket barker basket beaked beaker becket beckon bicker bilker birkie bodkin booker bookie booksy bosket broken broker bucker bucket buckle buckra bulker bumkin bunker bunkum burkha busker buskin cackle calker calkin canker casket catkin choker chokey chukar

chukka cocked cocker cockle conker cooker cookie corked corker crikey cuckoo dankly darken darkey darkie darkle darkly decker deckle dicker dickey dinkum docker docket donkey ducker duiker Dunker duyker feckly fickle firkin flukey folksy forked funkia gasket gaskin geckos ginkgo Gurkha hackle hackly hanker hankie harken hawked hawker heckle hickey hocker hockey hookah hooked hooker hookey hookup huckle hunker husker jackal jacket jerker jerkin jockey junker junket junkie kicker kiekie kookie kraken lackey lankly larker linkup locker locket lockup

looker lookin lowkey lurker mackle malkin marked marker market markup masker meekly mickey mickle milker mocker mockup monkey mucker muckle muskeg musket muskox napkin nickel nicker offkey packer packet parkin peaked pecker picker picket pickle pickup pinkie pipkin pocked pocket porker pucker punkah Quaker racker racket ranker rankle rankly reckon ricker rickey risker rocker rocket rookie ruckle ruckus seeker shaken shaker Shakta Shakti shekel shikar shiksa sicken sicker sickle sickly silken sinker sirkar siskin smoker soaker socket spoken stakes

stoker stokes sucker suckle sunken tacker tacket tackle talker talkie tanked tanker ticked ticker ticket tickey tickle tickly tinker tinkle tinkly tucker tucket tuckin turkey Turkic tusked tusker walker walkin walkon weaken weakly weekly welkin wicked wicker wicket winker winkle worker Yankee yolked yorker zinked zonked abulia addled Aeolic afflux aisled alalia alulae ambler amulet amylum angled angler anklet antler ariled armlet ashlar asylum auklet avulse axilla azalea Baalim bailee bailer bailey bailie bailor ballad ballet ballon ballot barley

bawler
bawley
bedlam
bellow
berlin
bieldy
billet
billon
billow
billyo
birler
boblet
boiler
bollix
boulle
bowleg
bowler
brolly
bugler
buglet
bullae
buller
bullet
burlap
burler
butler
byblow
byelaw
byplay
caller
callet
callow
callup
callus
camlet
caplin
Caslon
caulis
cellar
celled
chalet
chalky
chelae
chilli
chilly
choler
codlin
coelom
collar
collet
collie
collop
cooler
coolie
coolly
coolth
coulee
cowled
culler
cullet
cullis
curler
curlew
cutler
cutlet
cycler
cyclic
dahlia
dealer
deploy
dewlap
diglot
diplex
diploe
diplon
dogleg
dollar
dollop
doolie
dowlas
doyley
drolly
dually
duello
dunlin
duplet
duplex
eaglet
efflux
eggler
emblem
emblic
employ
emulge
englut
evilly
evolue
evolve
exilic
eyalet
eyelet
eyelid
fabled
fabler
failed
faille
fallal
fallen
fallow
faulty
fealty
feeler
fellah
feller
felloe
fellow
filler
fillet
fillip
firlot
foiled
follow
fooler
foully
foulup
fowler
frilly
frolic
fullam
fuller
gabled
gablet
Gaelic
galley
Gallic
Gallio
gallon
gallop
gaoler
garlic
gelled
giglet
giglot
gilled
gillie
gimlet
girlie
goalie
goblet
goblin
goglet
gollop
goslow
grille
grilse
Guelph
guilty
Gullah
gullet
gulley
hailer
hallal
halloa
halloo
hallow
hallux
hamlet
harlot
haslet
hauler
healer
health
heeled
heeler
heller
holler
holloa
hollow
howler
hurler
hurley
idolum
inclip
inflow
influx
inulin
italic
jailer
jailor
jetlag
joblot
kaolin
kiblah
killer
koolah
lallan
lealty
loller
lollop
mailed
Majlis
mallee
mallei
mallet
mallow
marlin
maslin
matlow
mealie
medlar
medley
mellow
merlin
merlon
milled
miller
millet
mislay
misled
moiler
mollie
moolah
Moslem
motley
mouldy
moulin
muflon
mukluk
mullah
muller
mullet
mulley
Muslim
muslin
myelin
nailer
nielli
niello
nuclei
nullah
obelus
ocelli
ocelot
ocular
omelet
oodles
orally
ostler
outlaw
outlay
outlet
ovally
ovular
oxalic
oxalis
paella
pallet
pallia
pallid
pallor
parlay
parley
pedlar
peeler
pegleg
pellet
peplum
phalli
phylum
piglet
pillar
pillow
piolet
pollan
polled
pollen
poller
pollex
poplar
poplin
prelim
proleg
prolix
public
puller
pullet
pulley
pullin
pullon
pullup
purler
purlin
putlog
qualmy
raglan
railer
ratlin
really
realty
reeler
reflex
reflow
reflux
reglet
replay
replum
rifler
rillet
roller
rollon
ruelle
runlet
sables
sailed
sailer
sailor
sallee
sallet
sallow
samlet
scalar
scaled
scaler
scales
schlep
scilla
scolex
sculpt
sealer
seller
shalom
shelly
Shelta
shelty
shelve
sialic
siglum
siller
skilly
skylab
slalom
smalls
smalto
smelly
smilax
smiler
souled
spilth
stalag
stalky
stelae
stelar
stilly
stolen
stolid
stolon
stylar
stylet
stylus
sublet
sullen
sunlit
suslik
sutler
svelte
tablet
tailor
tallow
teller
thaler
thalli
tholoi
tholos
tholus
thulia
tiller
titled
toiler
toilet
trilby
trolly
tuille
twelve
twilit
umbles
unclad
unglue
unplug
Uralic
uvulae
uvular
valley
vallum
varlet
vaulty
veiled
vellum
vielle
villus
violet
violin
volley
voulge
wailer
wallah
walled
waller
wallet
wallop
wallow
waylay
wealth
whaler
whiles
whilom
whilst
wholly
wieldy
willed
willet
willow
wooled
woolly
yellow
zealot
zillah
acumen
Adamic
agamic
agamid
ahimsa
airman
akimbo
alumna
alumni
animal
animus
anomic
anomie
ataman
atomic
bagman
barman
batman
beamer
blimey
boomer
bowman
bromic
brumal
brumby
bummed
bummer
bummle
Burman
busman
cabman
caiman
calmly
carman
cayman
cermet
chemic
chimer
chummy
clammy
climax
clumpy
clumsy
commie
commis
commit
commix
common
conman
cosmic
cosmos
cowman
crambo
crimpy
crumby
crummy
cummer
cummin
daemon
daimen
daimio
daimon
dammar
dammed
dermal
dermic
dermis
desman
desmid
dimmed
dimmer
dismal
dismay
dolman
dolmen
dormer
dormie
enamel
epimer
eremic
etymon
examen
exempt
exomis
farmer
fenman
filmic
firman
firmly
flambe
flamen
flimsy
flyman
foeman
formal
format
formed
former
formic
framer
frumpy
fulmar
gagman
gammer
gammon
gasman
gemmae
gemmed
german
germen
gigman
gimmal
gimmer
glumly
glumpy
gnomic
gnomon
gramme
Grammy
gramps
grimly
grumly
grumps
grumpy
gummed
gunman
haemal
haemin
hammal
hammam
hammed
hammer
haymow
helmet
hemmed
hermit
hetman
hitman
hodman
hummed
hummel
hummer
hummum
iceman
isomer
jammed
jammer
karmic
kermes
kermis
kismet
kummel
Lammas
lammed
lawman
layman
legman
litmus
lummox
madman
mammae
mammal
mammee
mammer
mammon
marmot
merman
Mormon
motmot
mummer
murmur
muumuu
normal
Norman
nutmeg
ogamic
oilman
oxymel
palmar
palmer
pelmet
penman
permit
pieman
pitman
plumed
plummy
plumpy
pommel
pommie
potman
premed
premix
primal
primer
primly
primus
prompt
pummel
ragman
rammed
rammer
reamer
rhombi
rhumba
rhymer
rimmed
roamer
rodman
roomer
rummer
salmon
scampi
scummy
seaman
seamat
seamer
seamew
seemly
semmit
sermon
shaman
shammy
shamus
shimmy
simmer
skimpy
skyman
slimly
slummy
stamen
stemma
stumer
stumpy
stymie
subman
submit
summae
summed
summer
summit
summon
swampy
swimmy
Talmud
tarmac
taxman
teemer
tegmen
termer
termly
termor
thymol
thymus
tinman
topman
tremie
tremor
trimer
trimly
trompe
trumps
tsamba
vermin
wadmal
wadmol
warmer
warmly
warmth
warmup
whimsy
whomso
wormer
yammer
yeoman
yesman
acinar
acinus
adenyl
Adonic
Adonis
agency
agenda
agonal
agonic
amends
amenta
ananas
anonym
atonal
atonic
avenge
avenue
azonal
bagnio
banned
banner
barney
basnet
beanie
bennet
bionic
blanch
blanky
blench
blende
blenny
blintz
blonde
blunge
bonnet
bonnie
bounce
bouncy
bounds
bounty
branch
brandy
branle
briner
bronco
bronze
bronzy
brunch
brunet
bunnia
burner
burnet
burnup
canned
cannel
canner
cannon
cannot
carnal
carnet
carney
catnap
catnip
chance
chancy
change
chanty
chintz
chunky
clench
clinch
clingy
clinic
clonal
clonic
clonus
clunch
cobnut
cognac
coiner
coinop
conned
conner
coonty
cornea
corned
cornel
corner

cornet cornua county cranch crania cranky cranny crenel cringe crunch cunner cyanic cyanin cygnet dainty damned darned darnel darner dinned dinner dipnet dirndl djinni donned downer drench drongo duende duenna dunned durned earner Edenic eggnog eponym erenow eryngo ethnic evener evenly evince fainly fanned fanner faunae faunal faunas fawner fennec fennel fiance finnan finned finner Finnic flanch flange flench flense flinch flinty flunky fornix french frenum frenzy fringe fringy funned funnel gainer gainly gainst gannet garner garnet genned ginned

ginner glance goanna gooney grange granny Granth gringo guanin guenon guinea gunned gunnel gunner gurnet guvnor haunch hernia hobnob horned horner hornet hymnal hymnic iconic irenic ironer ironic jaunce jaunty jennet jinnee jitney joanna johnny joiner jounce jouncy kainit keenly kenned kennel kerned kernel kidnap kidney krantz kronen kroner kronor kronur lanner launce launch leanly leanto Leonid lignin limner linnet linney lionel loaner lounge maenad magnet magnum mainly manned manner maundy meanie meanly meinie mignon minnow moaner mornay nignog

nounal nuance oilnut omenta opener openly orange ozonic panned paunch pawnee pawner paynim peanut pennae penned pennon phenol phenyl phoney phonic phonon picnic pignut pinnae pinned pinner pionic planar planer planet plenty plenum plinth plunge pointe points pounce prance prince pronto pruner punned punner punnet pycnic pyknic quanta quench quince quinoa quinol quinsy quinta regnal rennet rhinal rouncy ruiner runnel runner sannup sawney scanty scenic sconce seance seiner sennet sennit shandy shanny shanty shindy shiner shinny Shinto shinty sienna

signal signer signet signor simnel sinned sinner sinnet skinny slangy slinky sonnet sooner sorner spence spinal spined spinel spinet sponge spongy spunky stance stanch stanza stench stingo stingy stinko stoned stoner sunned swanky swinge taenia tanned tanner tannic tannin teensy tenner tennis thanks thenar thence things thingy thinly tinned tinner townee trance trench trendy trinal tunnel turner turnip turnup twangy twenty twiner twinge unknit unknot Urania uranic Uranus uranyl urinal usance vainly vanner veined vernal viands walnut weaner whenas

whence whiner whinge whinny wiener winner winnow woundy wrench yenned zinnia zounds abloom abroad absorb accord accost across adjoin adroit adsorb aerobe afford afloat ageold alcove aldose algoid allout almond almost angora anyone aphony aplomb apnoea appose arbour ardour areola areole argosy ariosi arioso armour arroba arrowy arroyo ashore aslope assoil assort aswoon athome attorn aurora aurous awmous baboon barony become befool before befoul begone behold behoof behove belong bemoan bemock betony betook beyond bezoar biform bijoux bizone bloody

bloomy bosomy botone briony brooch broody bryony byform bygone byroad byword bywork cacoon cahoot cajole calory canopy capote cavort choose choosy chroma chrome chromo citole cocoon cohort colony colour comose comous conoid copout corody corona corozo coyote creole cuboid cupola cutoff cutout cymose dacoit dagoes decoct decode decoke deform dehorn demode demote denote depone deport depose desorb detour devoid devoir devote devour devout dhooti didoes dipody dipole disown dodoes dogood dolour droopy dugong dugout dumose echoer echoic effort eidola

embody emboli emboly emboss encode encore enfold enjoin enrobe enroll enroot ensoul entoil entomb enwomb Eozoic Eozoon escort essoin eulogy evzone exhort export expose extort famous faroff farout favour fedora felony femora filose floozy fucoid furore gadoid galoot galore galosh ganoid genome getout giaour gigolo gloomy godown golosh groove groovy haloes heroic heroin hexose honour humour huzoor idiocy ignore impone import impose impost inborn income indole indoor infold inform inmost inroad insole intoed intone invoke inwove jalopy jocose joyous

judoka kalong kaross ketone kibosh kimono kitool kobold labour lagoon lavolt layoff layout lemony letoff lipoid lipoma lobose mahout maroon Masora megohm melody memoir memory metope midoff milord mimosa Minoan Mohock mohole Moloch monody mopoke morose motory mucoid mucosa mucous myxoma neroli nobody nodose oblong ochone oclock odious oncost oneoff oology oolong oppose oriole ormolu osmose otiose oxford paeony pagoda palolo parody parole parous patois payoff payola pelota peyote peyotl phloem phooey pilose pilous pinole polony porose porous priory

putoff pylori pyrola pyrope racoon radome ragout ramose ramous ratoon rebore reborn recoil recoin record recoup redone reform rejoin reload remora remote remove renown report repose resold resole resorb resort retold retook retool retort revoke revolt rewoke reword rework ribose rigour rigout rimose rimous ripoff rococo rufous rugose rumour runoff saloon saloop Samoan sapota sarong satori savory savour saxony school schorl scroll scroop second senora serosa serous setoff setose setout sheoak shroff shroud shrove simony simoom simoon smooch smooth

snoopy snooty snooze sodomy splore splosh spooky spoony sprout stooge strobe strode stroke stroll stroma stromb strong stroud strout strove strown suborn swoosh tabour tenour theory throat throes throne throng throve thrown timous tipoff toroid torose toxoid triode tryout tumour tycoon ugsome unbolt unborn uncoil uncool uncork undock undoer undone unfold unholy unhook unjoin unload unlock unmoor unrobe unroll unroof unroot unrope untold unworn unyoke uphold upmost uproar uproot uptown utmost valour vapour veloce velour venose venous vigour vinous virose volost wayout whoops whoosh xyloid xylose yapock zeloso zufolo zygoma zygote adipic aliped armpit ashpan bedpan beeper biopsy bopped bopper bumper calpac camper campus capped carpal carpel carper carpet carpus chapel chappy chippy chopin choppy chypre clipon clypei compel comply cooper copped copper corpse corpus couple coupon cowpat cowpea cowpox crappy cripes croppy crypto cupped cusped cuspid dampen damper damply dapper dapple deepen deeply despot diaper dimple dimply dipped dipper dispel Dopper draper drippy dropsy drupel dumper elapse

eloper epopee fipple flappy floppy frappe gapped gasper gospel grappa griper grippe grippy groper gypped hamper happed happen harper hatpeg hatpin helper hempen herpes hipped hippie hirple hispid holpen hooper hoopla hoopoe hopped hopper hopple hotpot humped inkpot inspan isopod jasper jumper keeper kelpie kewpie kipper klepht koppie lapped lappet lappie leaper limper limpet limpid limply lipped lippen lippie lisper looper lopped lopper loupen loupit lumpen lumper magpie mapped mapper mopped mopper moppet morpho mumper murphy myopia myopic napped

neaped nipped nipper nipple nympho output palpal palpus pampas pamper pappus parpen pauper pawpaw peeper peepul people pepped pepper pimple pimply pipped pippin pitpan pompom pooped popped popper poppet popple popply potpie prepay propel proper propyl pulper pulpit pumper pupped puppet purple purply Rajput ramper rapped rappee rappel rapper rasper reaper reopen rhaphe ripped ripper ripple ripply romper rumple rumpus sampan sample sappan sapped sapper sawpit scopae scopas scyphi seapen seapig semple sempre sexpot shaped shapen shaper shoppy simper

simple simply sipped sipper sippet slapup slipon slippy slipup sloppy snappy sniper snippy sopped stapes staple stepin steppe stepup stipel stipes stopgo stupid stupor supped supper supple supply swiper swipes taipan tampan tamper tampon tapped tapper tappet tappit tarpan tarpon tawpie teapot teapoy teepee temper temple tenpin tiepin tinpot tipped tipper tippet tipple topped topper topple torpid torpor toupee toupet trapan trapes trappy trepan trepid triple triply tripod tripos trophy tropic troppo twoply tympan uniped unipod utopia vamper vesper

wampee wampum wapper warped warper weapon weeper weepie whippy wimple yapped yapper yaupon yelper yipped yippee yippie zapped zipped zipper barque Basque bisque caique calque casque cheque cinque cirque claque clique cliquy exequy lasque manque marque masque mosque opaque plaque pulque risque sacque torque unique aboral acarid acarus accrue adorer affray agaric alarum aldrin allred amerce amoral anarch anorak antral antrum ashram astral astray averse barred barrel barren barret barrio barrow bearer betray bewray bharal blurry borrow bourne bourse

burrel burrow capric carrel carrot charas charge Charon cherry cherty cherub chirpy choral chorea choric chorus church cirrus citric citron citrus claret clergy cleric coarse coerce corral corrie course cowrie crural cupric currie Cymric cyprid dearie dearly dearth debris decree defray degras degree derris dharma dhurra dourly dryrot dryrun durrie ecarte Egeria embrue embryo emerge energy engram entrap entree enwrap escrow esprit estray eterne exarch fabric faerie fairly farrow feirie ferret ferric fibred fibril fibrin fierce fiorin flirty florae

floral floras floret florid florin flurry forrad forrit fourth fuhrer furred furrow garran garret garron garrot George gharry gloria gnarly gourde gurrah hadron hairdo haired harrow hatred hearer hearse hearth hearty Hebrew henrun henrys Herren hoarse hooray horrid horror hourly hubris hurrah hurray hybrid hybris hydric imbrex imbrue inarch inbred intray inwrap jarrah jarred jeerer karroo labret labrum larrup latria latron laurel learnt lierne lubric macron madras marram marred marron marrow marrum matrix matron megrim merrie metred metric micron

midrib mihrab mirror mitral morris morrow murrey narrow natron nearby nearer nearly neural neuron Nimrod nitric nutria octroi orfray osprey outran outrun overdo overly parral parrel parrot patrol patron pearly perron petrel petrol pharos picric pierce plural pogrom poorly pourer pterin putrid quarry quarte quarto quartz quirky quorum ramrod rearer redraw regret retral retrod ricrac riprap roarer rubric runrig sacral sacred sacrum satrap saurel scarab scarce scarer scarry scarus scorch scorer scoria scurfy scurry scurvy search secret serrae serran

Sevres sharer sharif sharps sherif Sherpa sherry shirty shoran shorts shorty sierra sirrah sirree skerry skirun slurry smarmy smarty smirch smirky snarer snarly snorer soiree sorrel sorrow source sourly sovran sparer sparge sparks sparry sparse spiral spirit sports sporty spurge spurry starch starer starry starve stereo steric sterna sterol stirps storax stores storey stormy sturdy styrax sunray surrey swaraj swarth swerve swirly tagrag tanrec tarras tarred Taurus tenrec terret territ terror tetrad thirst thirty thorax thoria thorny thoron thorpe

thyrse thyrsi tierce tiered tierod torrid tourer Tuareg turret twirly umbrae umbral umbras unbred untrue unwrap uphroe usurer uterus vagrom vibrio vitric walrus warred warren wearer weirdo weirdy wherry whirly worrit yarrow yearly yttria abuser airsac amuser arisen arista Aussie Avesta balsam basset bassos bedsit bhisti bolshy bonsai borsch bowsaw brassy brushy bunsen bursae bursal bursar bursas bussed byssus capsid cassia cassis catsup causal causer causey censer censor census cesser chaser chaste chesil chesty chisel chosen classy closed closet

comsat grassy pepsin tmeses bettor cotted filthy instil mestee pistol
consul grisly person tmesis biotic cotter fistic iritis mettle piston
corsac grison phasic tocsin biotin cotton fitted isatin milter pitted
corsak guiser phasis tonsil bister cratch fitter jester minter pitter
corset gunsel physic torsel bistre crater flatly jetted miotic platan
cosset gunshy pigsty tosser bistro Cretan flatus jilter mister platen
cousin gusset pissed tossup bitted cretic fletch jitter mistle plater
crases gypsum pitsaw tousle bitten cretin flitch jolter mitten plotty
crasis hansel plashy trashy bitter critic fluted jostle moated pluton
cresol hansom plasma tressy blithe crotal fluter jotted molten poetic
crises hassle plisse triste blotch crotch foetal jotter mortal poetry
crisis hawser plushy trusty blotto croton foetid justly mortar pontie
crispy hisser podsol tussah boatel crutch foetus jutted mostly pontil
crista hoised poison tusser boater cultch fontal kaftan mottle ponton
crosse horsey posset tussle bolter cultic footed kelter mouthy portal
cruset housel possum tutsan booted cultus footer Keltic multum porter
crusty housey preses twisty bootee cuptie footle kettle muntin portly
cuesta hussar preset unisex boston curtal foster kilted muster postal
cuisse hyssop presto unison bottle curtly fratch kilter mutter poster
cursed jersey prison unused bottom curtsy frater kirtle mutton postil
cursor jetsam prissy Vaisya bowtie custom frothy kitten myotic potted
cursus jigsaw proser vassal Breton cutter frutex kittle myrtle potter
cussed josser prosit versal Briton cuttle fustic kittul mystic pottle
damsel kaiser ptisan versed brutal cystic gaited knotty nastic pouter
damson kelson ptosis verser brutus cystid gaiter kowtow natter prater
dassie kersey puisne verset bunted dactyl gantry kultur nautch pratie
deasil kirsch pulsar versus bunter daftly garter lactic neaten pretax
diesel kisser pulser vessel burton darter gentes laster neatly pretty
dieses kitsch purser vizsla busted dartle gentle lastly nectar protea
diesis lapsed pursue warsle bustee dartre gently latten nekton proton
dipsas lapsus putsch weasel buster debtor gentoo latter nestle puntee
donsie lassie quasar whisht bustle deftly gentry lector Nestor punter
dorsal lassos raiser whisky bustup dental getter Lenten netted puttee
dorsum lensed raisin winsey butter dentel ghetto lentil nettle putter
dossal lessee ramson worsen button dentil gifted lepton neuter puttie
dossel lessen ransom wowser cactus dexter glitch letter newton quitch
dosser lesser reason wrasse caftan diatom glutei Lettic noetic quotes
douser lesson rhesus yeasty canter dictum gluten lictor nostoc quotha
dowser lessor rinser abater canthi dieter goatee lifter nutter rafter
dressy linsey ripsaw abatis cantle diktat goitre liftup obital ragtag
drosky lissom rouser acetal canton distal gotten lintel orator ranter
drossy loosen russet acetic cantor distil grater lintie otitis raptly
egesta marshy russia acetyl cantus dittos gratin listed ouster raptor
emeses massif Samson adytum captor doctor gratis listel outtop raster
emesis measly sarsen alated cartel doited gritty listen oyster rattan
enisle mensal sawset amatol carter dorter grotto lister palter rattat
enosis menses season anatta carton dotted grotty litter paltry ratted
eraser messan seesaw anatto caster dottle grutch little pantry ratter
falsie Messrs seisin aortal castle duster guitar loathe partan rattle
feisty miasma senses aortic castor dustup gunter lofter partly rector
fiasco miosis sensor apathy cattle earthy guttae loiter pastel rectum
fiesta missal sensum arctic Celtic easter gutted looter pastil rectus
flashy missel sepsis auntie cental editor gutter lotted pastor redtop
fleshy missis siesta Austin centre elated halter luetic pastry rental
flossy missus sissoo avatar centum elater haptic lustra patted renter
flysch morsel sloshy azotic certes elytra hartal lustre patten rester
focsle mouser slushy baiter cestus emetic hasten maltha patter retted
foison mousse sonsie Baltic chatty emetin hatted mantel pecten rhetor
forsay muesli stases bantam chital erotic hatter mantes pectic rhythm
fossae mussel stasis banter chitin exotic heated mantic pectin rictal
fossil myosin subset barter chiton Eyetie heater mantid pegtop rictus
fossor myosis sunset barton chitty factor heathy mantis peltae rioter
fresco nausea swishy baster cistus factum hectic mantle pelter rooted
frisky nelson tahsil batted clothe falter hector mantra peltry rooter
frosty noesis tarsal batten clutch fantan heptad mantua pentad roster
frusta nurser tarsia batter coated Fantee hiatus marten pentup rostra
fusser oddson tarsus battle coatee fantod hogtie martin pentyl rotted
gassed offset tassel battue coital fantom hootch martyr peptic rotten
gasser omasum tassie beaten coitus fasten hooter masted pertly rotter
geisha orison teasel beater colter faster hostel master pester router
geyser outsat teaser beetle cootie fatted hotter mastic pestle rustic
ghosty outset teaset belted Coptic fatten hunter matted petted rustle
glassy outsit telson bertha cortex fatter hurter matter petter rutted
glossy ovisac tenson berthe costae featly hurtle meatus pewter saeter
gnosis parsec tensor bested costal festal hustle meetly phatic saithe
godson Parsee theses bestir costar fester hutted melton photic salter
gooses parson thesis bestow coster fetter instal mental photon saltus
gossan passer tinsel betted costly fettle instar mentor pintle santal
gossip passim tissue better cottar filter instep mentum pistil santir

scathe
scatty
scotch
scoter
scotia
Scotic
scutal
scutch
scutum
scythe
seater
sector
seethe
sentry
septal
septet
septic
septum
sestet
settee
setter
settle
sextan
sextet
sexton
shutin
sifter
sinter
sister
sistra
sittar
sitter
skater
sketch
slater
smatch
smiter
smithy
smutch
smutty
snatch
snathe
snitch
snotty
soften
softie
softly
soothe
sorter
sortes
sortie
sotted
souter
spathe
spital
spotty
sputum
statal
stated
stater
states
static
stator
statue
status
stitch
stithy
subtil
subtle
subtly
suitor
sultan
sultry
suntan
surtax
suttee
swatch
swathe
switch

syntax
system
tactic
tamtam
tantra
tartan
tartar
tartly
taster
tatted
tatter
tattle
tattoo
tauten
tautly
tautog
teeter
teethe
tenter
tentie
testae
tester
teston
tetter
Teuton
thatch
thetic
tictac
tilter
tinter
tiptoe
tiptop
titter
tittle
tittup
tomtit
tomtom
tooter
toothy
tootle
tootsy
torten
totted
totter
touter
triton
tsetse
tsotsi
tufted
tufter
tumtum
turtle
tutted
twitch
ulster
united
uniter
unstop
ureter
vastly
vatted
vector
venter
ventil
ventre
vertex
vestal
vested
vestee
vestry
vetted
viator
victim
victor
vintry
virtue
vittae
vortex
wafter

waiter
wanted
wanton
warted
wasted
waster
wattle
welter
wester
wetted
wetter
whatso
whited
whiten
whites
whitey
Wilton
winter
wintle
wintry
witted
wittol
wonted
wonton
worthy
wortle
wrathy
wretch
writer
writhe
xystus
yatter
yester
zlotys
abduce
abduct
abjure
ablush
abound
abrupt
absurd
accuse
acquit
actual
adduce
adduct
adjure
adjust
agouti
allude
allure
ambush
amount
annual
annuli
arguer
argufy
argute
around
arouse
assume
assure
astute
attune
auburn
augury
august
autumn
avaunt
avouch
Basuto
Basutu
Beaune
beauty
beduin
beluga
bemuse
benumb
blouse

bohunk
Canuck
casual
cayuse
ceruse
cesura
chaunt
chough
chouse
clause
cloudy
clough
colugo
column
colure
copula
coquet
crouch
croupy
crouse
cumuli
cupule
curule
datura
debunk
deduce
deduct
defuse
degust
delude
deluge
deluxe
demure
denude
depute
deputy
dilute
disuse
drouth
effuse
emeute
empusa
endure
engulf
ennuye
enough
ensure
escudo
eunuch
excuse
exeunt
exhume
facula
famuli
faquir
fecula
fecund
ferula
ferule
fibula
figure
flaunt
fleury
floury
Frauen
future
garuda
gazump
gerund
grouch
ground
grouse
illume
illuse
immune
immure
impugn
impure
impute

incubi
incult
incuse
induce
induct
indult
induna
infula
infuse
ingulf
inhume
injure
injury
inrush
insult
insure
intuit
irrupt
jaguar
jejune
Jesuit
jocund
jujube
kabuki
kaputt
kiaugh
lacuna
laguna
lanugo
lazuli
legume
ligula
ligule
ligure
limuli
liquid
liquor
lobule
loculi
locust
loquat
lunula
lunule
luxury
macula
macule
maduro
maguey
manual
manuka
manure
maquis
mature
medusa
mezuza
minuet
minute
misuse
module
moduli
modulo
morula
mutual
mutule
mutuum
nature
nebula
nebuly
nodule
nonuse
objure
obtund
obtuse
occult
occupy
onrush
oppugn
ordure
oscula

papula
papule
parure
penult
penury
peruke
peruse
pilule
piquet
pleura
plough
pneuma
pseudo
queuer
radula
raguly
ranula
rasure
rebuff
rebuke
reduce
refuel
refuge
refund
refuse
refute
regulo
reluct
relume
remuda
repugn
repute
result
resume
returf
return
retuse
rheumy
ritual
robust
roquet
rosula
rotund
saluki
salute
Saturn
schuss
scouse
scouth
scruff
scrump
secund
secure
seduce
sequel
sequin
sexual
sheugh
should
shrunk
simurg
Siouan
sleuth
slouch
slough
smouch
snouty
solute
spouse
spruce
spruit
sprung
stound
struck
struma
strung
strunt
suburb
suture

swound
syrupy
tegula
Telugu
tenues
tenuis
tenure
tenuto
though
thrush
thrust
toluic
toluol
torula
trauma
triune
trough
troupe
trouty
tubule
tumuli
tumult
twould
uncurl
unduly
unfurl
ungual
ungues
unguis
ungula
unjust
unruly
unsung
untuck
untune
uprush
upturn
vacuum
valuer
valuta
velure
venule
vicuna
vidual
visual
volume
volute
yaourt
yogurt
Yoruba
alevin
beaver
beeves
bovver
brevet
calves
canvas
carvel
carven
carver
cervix
chevet
chives
chivvy
claver
clavis
clever
clevis
cloven
clover
coeval
convex
convey
convoy
corvee
corves
Corvus
cravat
craven

craver
culver
curvet
delver
drivel
driven
driver
drover
eleven
elevon
fervid
flavin
frivol
garvie
glover
graved
gravel
graven
graver
Graves
gravid
grivet
grovel
halvah
halves
heaven
heaver
hooves
jarvey
kelvin
knives
larvae
larval
leaved
leaven
leaver
leaves
loaves
louver
louvre
marvel
naevus
oeuvre
ogival
oliver
outvie
parvis
peavey
pelves
pelvic
pelvis
plover
privet
proven
pulvil
purvey
quaver
quiver
reaver
reiver
revved
salver
salvia
salvor
salvos
selves
serval
server
shaven
shaver
shavie
shiver
shovel
shover
silvan
silver
skiver
skivvy
slaver

slavey
Slavic
sliver
Slovak
sloven
snivel
soever
solver
spavin
stiver
stover
survey
sweven
swivel
sylvan
travel
trivet
trivia
trover
turves
uneven
valved
varved
velvet
vervet
volvox
waiver
weaver
weever
weevil
wolves
Yahveh
airway
answer
anyway
avowal
avowed
bagwig
bigwig
blowed
blower
blowsy
blowup
blowzy
bobwig
bowwow
brawly
brawny
brewer
brewis
browny
browse
cobweb
crawly
crewel
dimwit
drawee
drawer
drowse
drowsy
earwax
earwig
flower
flyway
frowst
frowsy
frowzy
glower
gnawer
godwit
grower
growly
growth
keyway
knower
leeway
midway
nitwit
oneway

outwit
peewit
powwow
prewar
runway
seaway
shower
skewer
skyway
slowly
spewer
stewed
subway
tiewig
trowel
tulwar
twoway
viewer
wigwag
wigwam
Yahweh
alexia
alexin
anoxia
anoxic
apexes
ataxia
ataxic
bonxie
calxes
cruxes
elixir
flaxen
flexor
hoaxer
ibexes
orexis
plexor
plexus
praxis
alkyne
argyle
banyan
baryon
baryta
bowyer
brayer
bunyip
canyon
clayey
corymb
coryza
crayon
encyst
enzyme
ethyne
greyly
groyne
gunyah
Kabyle
ladyfy
larynx
lawyer
Libyan
Magyar
obeyer
oocyte
papyri
player
polypi
prayer
ronyon
satyra
sawyer
sayyid
scryer
slayer
spryer
spryly

stayer
swayer
syzygy
wheyey
yumyum
amazon
apozem
banzai
benzol
benzyl
blazer
blazes
blazon
bonzer
boozer
borzoi
brazen
brazil
buzzer
crazed
dazzle
epizoa
fezzed
fezzes
fizzle
foozle
frazil
frizzy
frozen
geezer
glazer
gozzan
grazer
guzzle
matzoh
mizzen
mizzle
mizzly
muzzle
nozzle
nuzzle
panzer
piazza
pizzle
podzol
prizer
puzzle
razzia
razzle
rizzar
rizzer
rozzer
scazon
seizer
seizin
sizzle
snazzy
Tarzan
teazel
teazle
tenzon
weazen
zigzag

---

aboral
abroad
acetal
acinar
actual
Aegean
aerial
affray
Afghan
afloat
agonal
airman
airsac
airway
alegar
alulae
amoral
anabas
ananas
animal
anneal
annual
anodal
anorak
antiar
antral
anyway
aortal
aoudad
apical
apodal
appeal
appear
ashcan
ashlar
ashpan
ashram
astral
astray
ataman
atonal
atrial
Augean
avatar
avowal
azonal
bagman
ballad
balsam
banian
banjax
bantam
banyan
banzai
baobab
barman
bashaw
bateau
batman
bazaar
bedlam
bedpan
beggar
behead
beldam
bemoan
betray
bewray
bezoar
bharal
bobcat
bonsai
boreal
Boreas
bowman
bowsaw
boxcar
bridal
brumal
brutal
buccal
bulbar
Bulgar
bullae
bureau
burial
burlap
Burman
bursae
bursal
bursar
bursas
busbar
busman
byelaw
byplay
byroad
cabman
caecal
caftan
caiman
calcar
calpac
cancan
canvas
capias
carfax
carman
carnal
carpal
casbah
casual
Cathar
catnap
caudal
causal
caveat
caviar
cayman
celiac
cellar
cental
cereal
charas
chelae
chital
choral
chukar
climax
clonal
coccal
coeval
cognac
coital
collar
combat
comsat
confab
conman
corban
corral
corsac
corsak
costae
costal
costar
cottar
coucal
cougar
cowman
cowpat
cravat
credal
Cretan
crotal
crural
curiae
curial
curtal
cushat
cymbal
daedal
dammar
deejay
defeat
defray
degras
demean
denial
dental
deodar
dermal
desman
dewlap
diktat
dipsas
dirham
disbar
discal
dismal
dismay
distal
dogear
dollar
dolman
doodad
doodah
Dorian
dorsal
dossal
dowlas
durbar
durgan
Durham
durian
earwax
endear
engram
ennead
entrap
enwrap
eolian
eonian
epical
eschar
espial
estray
Fabian
facial
fallal
fantan
faucal
faunae
faunal
faunas
fellah
Fenian
fenman
ferial
festal
fetial
feudal
filial
finial
finnan
firman
fiscal
florae
floral
floras
flyman
flyway
foeman
foetal
foliar
fontal
forbad
formal
format
forrad
forsay
fossae
foveae
foveal
fracas
Friday
frugal
fulham
fullam
fulmar
fungal
gagman
garial
garran
gasbag
gasman
gateau
gavial
gemmae
genial
german
gewgaw
giddap
gigman
gimbal
gimmal
gingal
global
goddam
gossan
gozzan
guaiac
guffaw
guitar
Gullah
gunman
gunyah
gurrah
guttae
haemal
hallal
halvah
hammal
hammam
hangar
hartal
hawhaw
heehaw
hepcat
heptad
herbal
hereat
hetman
heyday
hitman
hodman
hookah
hooray
houdan
howdah
hubcap
hurrah
hurray
hussar
hymnal
hyphae
hyphal
icebag
icecap
iceman
Indian
inroad
inseam
inspan
instal
instar
intray
inwrap
Ionian
isobar
jackal
jaguar
jarrah
jetlag
jetsam
jibbah
jigsaw
jovial
Jovian
Judean
Julian
jumbal
kaftan
kasbah
keyway
kiblah
kidnap
kitbag
kitcat
koolah
Korean
kowhai
kurgan
labial
laical
lallan
Lammas
landau
lariat
larvae
larval
lascar
lawman
layday
layman
leeway
legman
lethal
Libyan
lineal
linear
linhay
lochan
loggat
logjam
longan
loofah
loquat
lumbar
lurdan
luteal
Lydian
machan
madcap
madman
madras
maenad
Magian
Magyar
maidan
mammae
mammal
manday
maniac
manual
margay
marram
mayday
mayhap
mediae
medial
median
medlar
menial
mensal
mental
merman
mescal
mesial
messan
midday
midway
mihrab
Minoan
mishap
mislay
missal
mitral
mobcap
Monday
monial
moolah
mornay
mortal
mortar
moshav
mullah
muscat
mutual
myriad
nectar
neural
nilgai
nonfat
normal
Norman
nougat
nounal
nuchal
nullah
obital
ocular
ogival
oilcan
oilman
oneway
oomiak
ordeal
orfray
orgeat
origan
orphan
osteal
ostial
outlaw
outlay
outran
outsat
ovisac
ovular
paleae
palmar
palpal
pampas
pariah
parian
parlay
parral
partan
pascal
Pathan
pawpaw
payday
pedlar
pelham
peltae
penman
pennae
pentad
pieman
pillar
pineal
pinnae
pitman
pitpan
pitsaw
plagal
planar
platan
plicae
plural
pollan
poplar
portal
postal
potman
prefab
prepay
pretax
prewar
primal
ptisan
pulsar
punkah
purdah
quasar
racial
radial
radian
ragbag
raglan
ragman
ragtag
randan
rascal
ratbag
rattan
rattat
redcap
rediae
redraw
reggae
regnal
rehear
reheat
reload
rental
repeal
repeat
replay
reread
reseat
reseau
retial
retral
reveal
rhinal
ricrac
rictal
riprap
ripsaw
ritual
rizzar
rodman
runway
rupiah
sabbat
Sabian
sacral
saggar
salaam
Salian
sambar
Samian
Samoan
sampan
sandal
sangar
sanjak
santal
sappan
sashay
satrap
scalar
scarab
scopae
scopas
screak
scream
scutal
seaear
seafan
seaman
seamat
seaway
seesaw
sendal
septal
serial
serrae
serran
serval
sextan
sexual
shaman
sheoak
shikar
shofar
shoran
signal
silvan
simian
Siouan
sircar
sirdar
sirkar
sirrah
sittar
skylab
skyman
skyway
slogan
Slovak
smilax
social
soldan
sovran
spinal
spiral
spital
spread
squeak
squeal
stalag
statal
stelae
stelar
storax
streak
stream
striae
stylar
styrax
subman
subway
sultan
summae
sundae
Sunday
sunhat
sunray
suntan
surtax
swaraj
sylvan
syntax
Syriac
Syrian
tagrag
taipan
tampan
tamtam
tarmac
tarpan
tarras
tarsal
tartan
tartar
Tarzan
taxman
teabag
tergal
testae
tetrad
Theban
thecae
thecal
thenar
thorax
thread
threap
threat
throat
tibiae
tibial
tictac
tiebar
timbal
tincal
tindal
tinman
tipcat
titian
toecap
tombac
tombak
tomcat
topman
toucan
trapan
trepan
tribal
tricar
trinal
trocar
Trojan
tulwar
turban
Tuscan
tussah
tutsan
twoway
tymbal
tympan
Tyrian
Ugrian
umbrae
umbral
umbras
uncial
unclad
ungual
unload
unread
unreal
unseal
unseam
unseat
unwrap
upbear
upbeat
uproar
urinal
uvulae
uvular
vandal
vassal
venial
verbal
vernal
versal
vestal
vidual
visual
vittae
vulcan
vulgar
wadmal
wallah
waylay
whenas
whidah
whydah
wigwag
wigwam
withal

wombat xenial yeoman yesman zigzag zillah zodiac aerobe akimbo amoeba arroba brumby chubby crabby crambo crumby djibba enrobe ephebe ephebi flabby flambe gazebo grabby grubby hereby imbibe incubi indaba jujube knobby lavabo nearby phoebe plebby rhombi rhumba scabby scribe shabby snobby snubby strobe stubby trilby tsamba unrobe Wahabi Yoruba zareba zariba abbacy abduce abduct abject ackack addict adduce adduct advice affect agency alpaca amerce anarch anlace apiece arnica arrack aspect attach attack avouch basics bedeck bemock bisect blanch bleach

blench blotch bodice borsch bounce bouncy branch breach breech broach bronco brooch brunch calico Canuck chance chancy choice church cilice civics clench clinch cloaca clunch clutch coerce conics copeck cranch cratch crotch crouch crunch crutch cultch curacy decoct deduce deduct deface defect deject delict depict detach detect device direct dreich drench droich efface effect enface enlace enrich entice ethics eunuch evince exarch expect exsect fetich fiance fiasco fierce flanch fleece fleech fleecy flench fletch flinch flitch flocci flysch fratch

french fresco glance glitch grouch grutch haunch hexact hijack hootch humect idiocy impact inarch indict induce induct infect inject insect intact inwick jaunce jounce jouncy kirsch kitsch kopeck launce launch legacy lorica lunacy lyrics macaco malice maraca matico medick medico menace Mohock Moloch Munich myrica nautch notice novice nuance object obtect oclock office optics outact palace papacy paunch pierce piracy plaice pleach Polack police policy pomace pounce prance preach prince pumice putsch quaich quench quince quitch rebeck redact reduce

reface refect reject relict reluct resect rococo rosace rouncy scarce sconce scorch scotch scutch seance search seduce select silica sketch slouch sluice sluicy smatch smeech smirch smooch smouch smutch snatch snitch solace source speech spence splice spruce stance stanch starch stench stitch strict struck stucco sumach swatch switch tenace thatch thence thrice thwack tierce trance trench twitch undock unlace unlock unpack unpick untuck usance veloce vesica vivace whence wrench wretch yapock zebeck abrade accede agenda aikido albedo allude amends

arcade Arcady armada aubade beside betide bieldy blende blonde bloody bolide boride bounds brandy broody cicada cloddy cloudy comedo comedy corody cruddy decade decide decode delude demode denude deride dipody dirndl divide dorado duende embody encode escudo excide facade garuda gourde greedy hairdo halide impede inside invade iodide lambda libido lipide makedo malady maundy melody mikado milady monody mouldy nobody noyade onside overdo oxhide pagoda panada parade parody pesade ploidy pomade posada pseudo rapids recede remade remedy remuda reseda

reside salade secede shandy shindy shoddy skiddy solidi solids speedo speedy steady stride strode sturdy swaddy teledu teredo tirade Toledo trendy triode tuxedo tweeds tweedy unlade unmade untidy upside viands weirdo weirdy wieldy woundy zounds abater abuser acumen addled adorer aether affeer afreet airbed aisled alated aliped allied allred ambler amulet amuser anadem angled angler anklet answer anthem anther antler apexes apices apnoea apogee apozem arched archer arguer ariled arisen armlet asleep auklet avocet avowed awaked awaken awheel awoken

azalea backer badger bagged bailee bailer bailey baiter baleen balker ballet banger banker banket banned banner banter barbed barbel barber barbet bargee barker barley barney barred barrel barren barret barter basher basket basnet basset baster bather batted batten batter bawbee bawler bawley beaked beaker beamer bearer beaten beater beaver becket bedded bedder beeper beeves begged beigel belief belted bender bennet Berber beseem bested bethel betted better bibbed bibber bicker bidden bidder bigger bilker billet binder birler bister bitted bitten

bitter bladed blazer blazes blimey blowed blower boatel boater bobbed boblet bodger bogged boiler bolter bomber bonded bonder bonnet bonzer booker boomer booted bootee boozer bopeep bopped bopper bordel border bosket bother bovver bowleg bowler bowyer boxbed bracer braces brayer brazen brevet brewer briber briner broken broker brunet bucker bucket budded budget buffer buffet bugged bugler buglet bulbed bulger bulker buller bullet bummed bummer bumper bunder bunker bunsen bunted bunter burden burgee burger burhel burler burner burnet burrel bushed

bushel busker bussed busted bustee buster butler butter buzzer cachet cadger cahier calces calker caller callet calves calxes camber camlet camper cancel cancer canker canned cannel canner canter capped carder careen career caries carnet carney carpel carper carpet carrel cartel carter carvel carven carver cashew casket caster caudex causer causey celled censer cermet certes cesser chafer chalet chapel chaser chevet chimer chisel chives choker chokey choler chorea chosen cinder cipher cither claret claver clayey clever closed closet cloven clover

clypei coated coatee cobber cobweb cocked cocker codger coffee coffer cogged coiner collet colter combed comber compel confer congee conger conker conned conner convex convey cooker cooler cooper copier copped copper coquet corbel corded corder corked corker cornea corned cornel corner cornet corset cortex corvee corves cosher cosset coster cotted cotter coulee cowled cowpea crases crater craven craver crazed crenel crewel crikey cripes crises cruces cruset cruxes cudgel cuffed culler cullet culver cumber cummer cunner cupped curfew curler curlew

cursed dogger fanjet funnel gopher heifer isabel lagger lofter minded
curvet dogleg fanned furred gorget heller isohel lamber logged minder
cusped doited fanner fusser gospel helmet isomer lammed logger minter
cussed dolmen Fantee gabbed gotten helper jabbed lancer loiter minuet
cutler donkey fardel gabber graben hemmed jabber lancet loller misled
cutlet donned farfel gabled grader hempen jacket landed looker missel
cutter Dopper farmer gablet grater herder jaeger lander looper mister
cycler dormer fasces gadded graved herpes jagged lanner loosen mitten
cygnet dorter fasten gadder gravel Herren jagger lapped looter mizzen
cypher dossel faster gadget graven hickey jailer lappet lopped moaner
dabbed dosser fathen Gadhel graver hidden jammed lapsed lopper moated
dabber dotted father gaffer Graves higher jammer larder lotted mobbed
dagger douser fatted gagged grazer hinder jarred larker louden mocker
dagoes downer fatten gagger griper hinged jarvey lasher loupen moider
daimen dowser fatter gainer grivet hipped jasper laster louver moiler
dammed doyley fauces gaited grocer hisser jeerer lateen lowkey molten
damned dragee faucet gaiter groper hither jennet lather lubber monger
dampen draper fawner galley grovel hoaxer jerker latten lugged monied
damper drawee feeder gammer grower hocker jersey latter lugger monies
damsel drawer feeler gander guider hockey jester laurel lumber monkey
dancer drivel feller ganger guinea hodden jetted laveer lumpen mopped
dander driven fencer gannet guiser hogged jibbed lawyer lumper mopper
danger driver fender gaoler gulden hogget jibber leaden lunger moppet
Daniel droger fennec gapped gullet hoised jigged leader lurker moreen
dapper drover fennel garbed gulley holden jigger leafed lychee morgen
darken drupel ferret garden gummed holder jilter leaper madden morsel
darkey dubbed fester garget gunned holler jinnee leaved madder Moslem
darned ducker fetter garner gunnel holpen jitney leaven magnet mother
darnel dudeen fezzed garnet gunner honied jitter leaver maguey motley
darner duffel fezzes garret gunsel hooded jobber leaves maiden mouser
darter duffer fibbed garter gunter hoofed jockey lecher mailed mucker
dasher duiker fibber gasket gurnet hoofer jogged ledged mallee mugged
dauber dulcet fibred gasper gusher hooked jogger ledger mallei mugger
daybed dumper fidget gassed gusset hooker joiner legged mallet muller
deaden Dunker figged gasser gutted hookey jolter lender mammee mullet
deafen dunned filler gather gutter hooper josher lensed mammer mulley
dealer duplet fillet gauger gypped hooter josser Lenten mangel mummer
decker duplex filter geegee haffet hooves jotted lessee manger mumper
decree durned finder geezer hailer hopped jotter lessen manned murder
deepen duster finger gelled haired hopper judder lesser manner murrey
defier duyker finned gemmed haloes horned judger letter mantel muskeg
degree eaglet finner gender halter horner jugged libber mantes musket
deicer earner fisher genned halves hornet jumper lichee mapped mussel
delver easter fitted gentes hamlet horsey junker lichen mapper muster
denier echoer fitter germen hammed hosier junket lidded marcel mutter
dentel eggler flamen getter hammer hostel jutted lieder marked nabbed
deuced either flaxen geyser hamper hotbed kaiser lifter marker nagged
dexter elated floret gibber handed hotter keeper ligger market nagger
diadem elater flower gibbet hanged housel kelter lilied marred nailer
diaper eleven flukey gifted hanger housey kenned limbec marten napped
dibbed elodea fluted gigged hanker howler kennel limbed marvel natter
dibber eloper fluter giglet hansel hoyden kermes limber masher nausea
dicker emblem fobbed gilder happed hugged kerned limner masker neaped
dickey emeses fodder gilled happen hummed kernel limper masted nearer
didoes enamel fogged gimlet harden hummel kersey limpet master neaten
diesel entree foiled gimmer harken hummer kicker linden matted nephew
dieses envier folder ginger harper humped kidded linger matter nether
dieter epimer fooler ginned haslet hunger kidder linnet mayhem netted
differ epopee footed ginner hasten hunker kidney linney medley neuter
digger eraser footer girder hatpeg hunter killer linsey member nibbed
dimmed eschew forced glazer hatred hurler kilted lintel mender nickel
dimmer esteem forcer glider hatted hurley kilter lionel menses nicker
dingey etcher forger glover hatter hurter kipper lipped mercer nidget
dinned etrier forget glower hauler husker kismet lippen merger nigger
dinner evader forked glutei hawked hutted kisser lisper mestee nipped
diplex evener formed gluten hawker hyphen kitten listed metier nipper
dipnet examen former gnawer hawser ibexes knives listel metred nodded
dipped exceed foster goatee headed ibices knower listen mickey nuclei
dipper exogen fother gobbet header ibidem kosher lister midden nugget
dirhem eyalet fowler goblet healer ideaed kraken litter midget number
dispel eyelet framer goffer hearer imbrex kronen loaded miffed nurser
dither fabled frater goglet heated inbred kroner loader mildew nutmeg
docker fabler Frauen Goidel heater inches kummel loafer milieu nutter
docket facies frozen golden heaven indeed laager loaner milker obeyer
dodder fagged frutex golfer heaver inlier labret loaves milled offkey
dodgem failed fugged goober Hebrew instep laches lobbed miller offset
dodger fallen fuhrer gooier hedger intoed lackey locker millet oliver
dodoes falter fuller gooney heeled irides ladder locket milter omelet
dogged fanged funned gooses heeler ironer lagged lodger mincer onager

oodles opener osprey ostler ouster outlet outset oxygen oxymel oyster packer packet padded pallet palmer palter pamper pander panned panzer parcel parget parley parpen parrel parsec Parsee passer pastel patted patten patter pauper pawnee pawner peahen peaked peavey pecker pecten peeler peeper pegged pegleg pellet pelmet pelter pelves penned pepped pepper pester petrel petted petter pewter phloem phoney phooey picker picket piecer pigged piglet pilfer pincer pinger pinned pinner piolet pipped piquet Pisces pissed pitier pitted pitter placed placer

placet planer planet platen plater player plover plumed pocked pocket podded polder polled pollen poller pollex pommel ponder pongee pooped popped popper poppet porker porter posset poster poteen pother potted potter pourer pouter powder prater prayer prefer premed preses preset pricey primer privet prizer prober proleg propel proper proser protea proven pruner pucker puffed puffer puller pullet pulley pulper pulser pummel pumper punned punner punnet puntee punter pupped puppet purger purler purser purvey pusher puttee putter Quaker quaver queuer

quiver quotes rabbet rabies racker racket rafter ragged raggee raider railer raiser ramjet rammed rammer ramper random ranger ranker ranter rapier rapped rappee rappel rapper rasher rasper raster rather ratted ratter reader reamer reaper rearer reaver redden redder redeem reefer reeler reflex refuel reglet regret reheel reiver relief render rennet renter reopen rester retted review revved rhymer ribbed richen riches ricker rickey ridded ridden ridged rifler rigged rigger rillet rimmed ringed ringer rinser rioter ripped ripper risker rizzer roamer

roarer robbed robber rochet rocker rocket roller romper rondel roofer roomer rooted rooter roquet roster rotted rotten rotter rouser router rozzer rubbed rubber ruched rudder ruffed rugged rugger ruiner rummer runlet runnel runner rusher rushes russet rutted sables sachem sachet sacred sadden sadder saeter sagged sagger sailed sailer sallee sallet salter salver samlet sander sanies sapped sapper sardel sarsen sateen saucer sauger saurel sawder sawney sawset sawyer scaled scaler scales scarer schlep scolex scorer scoter screed screen scryer seabed

seabee sealer seamer seamew seapen seater secret seeder seeker seiner seizer seller selves sender sennet senses sephen septet sequel series server sestet settee setter Sevres sextet shader shades shaken shaker shaped shapen shaper sharer shaven shaver shekel shiner shiver shovel shover shower shriek sicken sicker sifter sigher signer signet silken siller silver simmer simnel simper singer sinker sinned sinner sinnet sinter sipped sipper sippet sirree sister sitter skater skewer skiver slater slaver slavey slayer slicer slider sliver sloven smiler

smiter smoker snarer sniper snivel snorer soaker sobbed soccer socket sodden soever soften soiree solder solver sonnet sooner sopped sorbet sorner sorrel sorter sortes sotted souled souter soviet spacer sparer spewer spider spined spinel spinet spleen spoken spryer stager stagey stakes stamen stapes starer stases stated stater states stayer stereo stewed stipel stipes stiver stoker stokes stolen stoned stoner stores storey stover streek street stumer stylet subbed sublet subset sucker sudden suffer sullen summed summer sunder sundew sunken sunned

sunset supped supper surfer surrey survey sutler suttee swayer sweven swiper swipes swivel system tabbed tablet tacker tacket tagged talker tamper tandem tanked tanker tanned tanner tanrec tapped tapper tappet target tarred tassel taster tatted tatter tauten taxies teasel teaser teaset teazel tedded tedder teemer teepee teeter tegmen teller temper tender tenner tenrec tenter tenues tercel tercet termer terret tester tether tetter thaler theses throes ticked ticker ticket tickey tiered tiller tilter timber tinder tinker tinned tinner tinsel tinter

tipped tipper tippet titfer tither titled titter tmeses tocher toffee togaed togged toiler toilet tooter Tophet topped topper Tories torsel torten tosher tosser tother totted totter toupee toupet tourer touter towhee townee tracer traces trader trapes travel trimer trivet trover trowel Tuareg tubber tucker tucket tuffet tufted tufter tugged tunnel tureen turkey turner turret turves tusked tusker tusser tutted twicer twiner ulster umbles unbred undies undoer uneven ungues uniped unisex united uniter unmeet unreel unseen untied unused upkeep ureter

usurer valley valuer valved vamper vanner varied varlet varved vatted veiled veined velvet vendee vender veneer venter verger versed verser verset vertex vervet vesper vessel vested vestee vetted viewer violet vizier voiced voided voider volley vortex wadded wafter wagged wailer waiter waiver walker walled waller wallet wampee wander wanted wapper warden warder warmer warped warper warred warren warted washer wasted waster weaken weaner wearer weasel weaver weazen webbed wedded weeder weeper weever welder welter wester wether wetted wetter whaler

wheyey whiles whiner whited whiten whites whitey wicked wicker wicket widget wiener wigged wilder willed willet wincey winded winder winged winger winker winner winsey winter wisher wither witted wizier wolves wonder wonted wooded wooden woofer wooled worker wormer worsen wowser writer yabber Yahveh Yahweh yammer Yankee yapped yapper yatter yelper yenned yester yipped yippee yolked yonder yorker zaffer zander zapped zinced zingel zinked zipped zipper zither zonked adrift agrafe argufy bereft briefs carafe chaffy chuffy cliffy codify cutoff faroff fluffy gasify humify ladify ladyfy layoff letoff midoff minify modify Nazify nidify notify oneoff ossify pacify payoff piaffe pilaff pouffe purify putoff ramify rarefy ratify rebuff ripoff rubefy rubify runoff salify sanify sclaff scruff scurfy setoff shrift shroff sniffy snuffy spiffy spoffy strafe strife stuffy tariff tepefy thrift tipoff tumefy typify uglify unsafe uplift verify vilify vivify allege anlage assign avenge aweigh barege beluga benign blunge bocage bodega borage bridge change charge chough claggy clergy clingy cloggy clough colugo

cowage craggy cringe cubage damage deluge design dosage dotage draggy dredge dreggy drongo drudge effigy eloign emerge emulge encage energy engage enough enrage ensign eryngo eulogy flaggy flange fledge forage forego fridge fringe fringy froggy galago garage gavage George ginkgo grange greige gringo groggy grudge homage impugn indign indigo kiaugh knaggy lanugo lavage linage lounge lovage Malaga malign manage manege menage metage midage milage mirage nonage nonego oarage oblige ohmage oology oppugn orange outage pavage pelage phlegm pledge plough

plunge potage quagga quaggy quaigh ravage refuge renege repugn resign rivage savage senega sewage shaggy sheugh silage skeigh slaggy slangy sledge sleigh slough sludge sludgy smoggy smudge smudgy snaggy socage sorage sparge sponge spongy spurge stingo stingy stodge stodgy stooge stopgo swinge syzygy telega Telugu things thingy though towage triage trough trudge twangy twiggy twinge ullage uncage virago visage voulge voyage whinge alight apache apathy aright beachy bertha berthe bitchy blight blithe bolshy bosche botchy bought bright broche brushy

Buddha bunchy burkha canthi catchy caught chacha chichi cliche cloche clothe concha conchy creche dinghy douche dought doughy drachm earthy filthy flashy fleche fleshy flight fought fright frothy gauche gaucho geisha gunshy Gurkha heathy height klepht knight litchi loathe lorcha louche maltha manche Manchu marshy megohm morpho mouthy murphy naught nought nympho obeche orache pakeha patchy peachy pitchy plashy plight plushy poncho pouchy psyche psycho punchy quiche quotha rancho reecho rhaphe rhythm rotche saddhu saithe sandhi scathe scyphi scythe

seethe seiche slight sloshy slushy smithy snathe soothe sorgho sought spathe stithy swathe swishy takahe taught teethe tetchy toothy touche touchy trashy troche trophy waught weight whisht worthy wrathy wright writhe abatis abseil abulia acacia acarid acedia acetic acidic acquit adagio Adamic adipic adjoin Adonic Adonis adroit Aeolic affair afraid agamic agamid agaric agnail agonic alalia albeit alcaic aldrin alevin alexia alexin algoid anodic anomic anomie anoxia anoxic aortic Arabic archil arctic armpit ashbin assail assoil ataxia ataxic atomic

atonic attain auntie Aussie Austin azotic Baalim baddie bagnio bagwig bailie Baltic bandit bardic barrio beanie bedsit beduin Belgic berlin bestir bewail biffin biggin bigwig bionic biotic biotin birdie birkie bobbin bobwig bodkin boffin bollix bonnie bonxie bookie bothie bougie bowfin bowtie brazil brewis bromic budgie bulbil bumkin bunnia bunyip buskin caddie caddis calcic calkin candid caplin capric capsid casein cassia cassis catkin catnip caulis Celtic cervix chemic chesil chitin chopin choric citric clavis cleric clevis clinic clonic coccid

cochin codlin coffin coheir collie comfit commie commis commit commix conoid cookie coolie cootie Coptic corbie corrie cosmic cousin cowrie crania crasis credit cretic cretin crisis critic cuboid cuddie cullis cultic cummin cupric cuptie currie cuspid cyanic cyanin cyclic Cymric cyprid cystic cystid dacoit dahlia daimio darkie dassie dearie deasil debris deceit deific dentil derail dermic dermis derris desmid detail detain devoid devoir diacid diesis dikdik dimwit distil dobbin doggie domain donsie doolie dormie dubbin dunlin durrie dyadic earwig

echoic eclair Eddaic Edenic Egeria elicit elixir emblic emesis emetic emetin enjoin enosis entail entoil Eozoic epodic eremic erotic esprit essoin ethnic exilic exomis exotic eyelid Eyetie fabric fadein faerie falsie faquir fascia feirie ferric fervid fibril fibrin fillip filmic Finnic fiorin firkin fistic fizgig flavin florid florin foetid forbid fordid formic fornix forrit fossil frazil frigid frolic fucoid fulfil fulgid funkia fusain fustic gadoid Gaelic Gallic Gallio gambir gambit ganoid garlic garvie gaskin geodic gerbil gillie girlie glacis

gloria glycin gnomic gnosis goalie goblin godwit goodie gorgio gossip Gothic gradin gratin gratis gravid guanin haddie haemin haffit haggis hankie haptic hatpin hectic herdic herein hermit hernia heroic heroin hippie hispid hobbit hoggin hogtie hoodie horrid hubris hybrid hybris hydric hymnic iambic iconic impair inclip inlaid instil intuit inulin irenic iritis ironic isatin ischia italic jerbil jerkin Jesuit jezail Judaic junkie Kaffir kainit kaolin karmic kelpie Keltic kelvin kermis kewpie kiddie kiekie kookie koppie lactic laddie lappie lassie

latria leadin lentil Leonid Lettic lignin limbic limpid lintie lipoid lippie liquid lithia lithic livein loggia lookin loupit lovein lubric luetic luggie lutein magpie Majlis maleic malkin mantic mantid mantis maquis margin marlin martin mashie maslin massif mastic matrix mealie meanie megrim meinie memoir menhir merlin merrie metric midair midrib miosis miotic misdid misfit mishit missis moggie mohair mollie morbid morris mosaic moujik moulin mucoid muffin mundic muntin Muslim muslin muzhik myelin myopia myopic myosin myosis myotic mystic mythic

napkin
nastic
nereid
niacin
nitric
nitwit
noesis
noetic
noggin
Nordic
nuncio
nutria
obtain
ogamic
olefin
orcein
orchid
orchil
orchis
ordain
orexis
origin
orphic
ossein
otitis
outbid
outdid
outfit
outsit
outvie
outwit
oxalic
oxalis
oxtail
ozonic
palais
pallia
pallid
pandit
papain
pardie
parkin
parvis
passim
pastil
pathic
patois
paynim
pectic
pectin
peewit
pelvic
pelvis
pencil
pepsin
peptic
permit
phasic
phasis
phatic
phobia
phobic
phonic
photic
physic
picnic
picric
pidgin
piggin
pinkie
pionic
pipkin
pippin
pistil
placid
poetic
pommie
pontie
pontil

poplin
porgie
postil
potpie
pratie
praxis
precis
prefix
prelim
premix
probit
profit
prolix
prosit
pterin
ptosis
public
puffin
pullin
pulpit
pulvil
pundit
purlin
putrid
puttie
pycnic
pyknic
rabbin
rabbit
rachis
raffia
raisin
rancid
raphia
raphis
ratlin
razzia
recoil
recoin
reedit
regain
rejoin
relaid
remain
repaid
repair
reship
retail
retain
roadie
Romaic
rookie
rubric
runrig
russia
rustic
salvia
santir
sawpit
sayyid
scenic
scoria
scotia
Scotic
seaair
seapig
seisin
seizin
semmit
sennit
sepsis
septic
sequin
serein
sharif
shavie
sherif
shutin
sialic

siskin
sixain
Slavic
sobeit
soffit
softie
sonsie
sophic
sordid
sortie
Sothic
spadix
spavin
specie
spirit
sprain
spruit
squail
stadia
stasis
static
stepin
steric
stogie
stolid
strain
strait
studio
stupid
stymie
submit
subtil
suffix
summit
sunlit
suslik
syndic
tactic
taenia
tahsil
takein
talkie
tannic
tannin
tappit
tarsia
tassie
tawpie
tennis
tenpin
tentie
tenuis
territ
thesis
thetic
thoria
thulia
tidbit
tiepin
tiewig
tiffin
titbit
tmesis
tocsin
toluic
tomtit
tonsil
toroid
torpid
torrid
toxoid
tragic
tremie
trepid
trifid
trivia
tropic
tuckin
turbid

turbit
turgid
Turkic
turnip
twilit
uncoil
unfair
unguis
unhair
unific
unjoin
unknit
unlaid
unnail
unpaid
unsaid
unship
unveil
uracil
Uralic
Urania
uranic
urchin
utopia
ventil
vermin
vibrio
victim
violin
virgin
viscid
vitric
wabain
waddie
walkin
weepie
weevil
welkin
Wendic
within
withit
worrit
xyloid
yippie
yttria
zincic
zinnia
zombie
alsike
belike
betake
blanky
breeks
bricky
chalky
cheeky
chukka
chunky
cranky
creaky
croaky
decoke
drosky
eureka
flunky
freaky
frisky
gingko
hoicks
intake
invoke
judoka
kabuki
kanaka
manuka
mopoke
peruke
plucky
quirky

rebuke
remake
retake
revoke
rewoke
saluki
sheikh
shrike
shucks
slacks
slinky
smirky
sneaky
sparks
spooky
spunky
stalky
sticky
stinko
stocks
stocky
strake
strike
stroke
swanky
talcky
thanks
tracks
tricky
troika
unlike
unmake
unyoke
uptake
whacky
whisky
yoicks
zincky
acidly
aedile
aerily
afield
ageold
airily
alkali
allele
annals
annuli
arable
archly
areola
areole
argala
argali
argyle
audile
avidly
awhile
axilla
babble
babbly
baffle
baldly
bangle
barely
barfly
basalt
basely
battle
bauble
bawble
beadle
beagle
becall
becalm
bedell
beetle
befall
befell

behalf
beheld
behold
bobble
bodily
boggle
boldly
boodle
botfly
bottle
boucle
boulle
bowels
branle
brawly
bridle
brolly
bubble
bubbly
buckle
buddle
bumalo
bumble
bummle
bundle
bungle
burble
burbly
burgle
busily
bustle
cabala
cackle
cagily
cajole
calmly
candle
cantle
castle
catalo
cattle
caudle
chicle
chield
chilli
chilly
cicala
cicely
cigala
circle
citole
cobalt
cobble
cockle
coddle
coffle
coldly
comely
comply
coolly
copula
cosily
costly
couple
cradle
crawly
creole
cuddle
cuddly
cumuli
cupola
cupule
curdle
curtly
curule
cutely
cuttle
dabble
daftly

damply
dandle
dangle
dankly
dapple
darkle
darkly
dartle
dawdle
dayfly
dazzle
deadly
deafly
dearly
deckle
deeply
defile
deftly
desalt
dewily
dibble
diddle
dimple
dimply
dingle
dipole
direly
doable
docile
doddle
doodle
dottle
double
doubly
dourly
dozily
drably
drolly
dryfly
dually
duello
duffle
dumbly
easily
edgily
edible
eerily
eidola
embalm
emboli
emboly
enable
enfold
engild
engulf
enhalo
enisle
enroll
ensile
evenly
evilly
exhale
facile
facula
faille
fainly
fairly
family
famuli
featly
feckly
fecula
feeble
feebly
female
ferula
ferule
fettle
fibula

fickle
fiddle
fiddly
fimble
finale
finals
finely
fipple
firmly
fizzle
flatly
focsle
foible
fondle
fondly
footle
foozle
foully
freely
frilly
fuddle
fumble
fusile
futile
gabble
gadfly
gaggle
gainly
gamble
gamely
gamily
gangly
garble
gargle
gentle
gently
giggle
giggly
gigolo
girdle
gladly
glibly
glumly
gnarly
gobble
goggle
goggly
goodly
googly
gorily
greyly
grille
grimly
grisly
growly
grumly
guddle
guggle
gurgle
guzzle
habile
hackle
hackly
haggle
handle
hardly
hassle
hazily
heckle
heddle
herald
higgle
highly
hirple
hobble
holily
homely
homily
hoopla

hopple
hourly
huckle
huddle
hugely
humble
humbly
hurdle
hurtle
hustle
icicle
impala
impale
incult
indole
indult
infelt
infold
infula
ingulf
inhale
insole
insult
inyala
itself
jangle
jiggle
jiggly
jingle
jingly
joggle
jostle
juggle
jumble
jumbly
jungle
jungly
justly
kabala
Kabyle
keenly
kettle
kibble
kindle
kindly
kingly
kirtle
kittle
kobold
labile
lamely
lankly
lastly
lately
lavolt
lazily
lazuli
leanly
lewdly
liable
ligula
ligule
likely
limply
limuli
little
lively
lobule
locale
loculi
lonely
lordly
loudly
lovely
lunula
lunule
lushly
mackle
macula

macule
magilp
mainly
mangle
manila
mantle
marble
marbly
mascle
mayfly
mazily
meanly
measly
meddle
meekly
meetly
megilp
merely
merils
metals
mettle
mickle
middle
mildly
mingle
mistle
mizzle
mizzly
mobile
module
moduli
modulo
mohole
morale
morals
morula
mostly
motile
mottle
muckle
muddle
muesli
muffle
mumble
muscle
mutely
mutule
muzzle
mygale
myrtle
myself
namely
napalm
nearly
neatly
nebula
nebuly
needle
Nepali
neroli
nestle
nettle
nibble
nicely
nielli
niello
niggle
nimble
nimbly
nipple
nobble
noddle
nodule
noodle
nosily
Nowell
nozzle
nubble
nubbly

nubile
nudely
numbly
nuncle
nuzzle
occult
ocelli
onfall
openly
oracle
orally
oriole
ormolu
oscula
ovally
overly
oxgall
paddle
paella
palely
palolo
papula
papule
parole
partly
payola
pearly
pebble
pebbly
pedalo
peddle
penult
people
pertly
pestle
phalli
pickle
piddle
piffle
pilule
pimple
pimply
pinole
pintle
pizzle
pomelo
poodle
poorly
popple
popply
portly
potale
pottle
primly
puddle
puddly
pueblo
punily
purely
purfle
purple
purply
puzzle
pyrola
rabble
racily
raddle
radula
raffle
raggle
raguly
ramble
rankle
rankly
ranula
raptly
rarely
rashly
rattle
razzle
really
recall
reddle
refill
regale
regulo
resale
resell
resile
resold
resole
result
retell
retold
revile
revolt
ribald
richly
riddle
rifely
riffle
ripely
ripple
ripply
robalo
rosily
rosula
rouble
royals
rubble
rubbly
ruckle
ruddle
rudely
ruelle
ruffle
rumble
rumbly
rumple
rundle
rustle
rutile
saddle
safely
sagely
sample
sanely
sapele
sawfly
scilla
scroll
sedile
seemly
semble
semple
senile
seseli
settle
sexily
sheila
shelly
shield
shoaly
should
shrill
sickle
sickly
simile
simple
simply
single
singly
sizzle
skeely
skilly
slimly
slowly
smalls
smelly
smugly
snarly
snugly
softly
solely
sorely
sourly
spoilt
spryly
squall
squill
stable
stably
staple
steely
stifle
stilly
stroll
suable
subtle
subtly
suckle
supple
supply
surely
sutile
swirly
tackle
tamale
tamely
tangle
tangly
tartly
tattle
tautly
teazle
tegula
temple
termly
thalli
thinly
thrall
thrill
tickle
tickly
tiddly
tidily
timely
tingle
tingly
tinily
tinkle
tinkly
tipple
tittle
toddle
toggle
tootle
topple
torula
tousle
treble
trebly
trifle
trimly
triple
triply
trolly
tubule
tuille
tumble
tumuli
tumult
tupelo
turtle
tussle
twirly
twoply
twould
uglily
unable
unbolt
unduly
unfold
ungula
unholy
unroll
unruly
unself
untold
unwell
upheld
uphill
uphold
usable
vagile
vainly
vastly
venule
verily
viable
vielle
vilely
virile
visile
vitals
vizsla
wabble
waddle
waffle
waggle
waggly
wamble
wambly
wangle
warble
warily
warmly
warsle
wattle
wavily
waxily
weakly
weekly
whirly
wholly
widely
wifely
wiggle
wiggly
wildly
wilily
wimble
wimple
winkle
wintle
wirily
wisely
wobble
wobbly
woggle
woolly
wortle
yaffle
yarely
yearly
zanily
zufolo
aflame
aplomb
assume
asthma
athome
autumn
became
become
benumb
bigamy
bireme
bloomy
bosomy
Brahma
Brahmi
bregma
bulimy
byname
calami
chacma
chroma
chrome
chromo
chummy
cinema
clammy
column
corymb
creamy
crummy
decamp
defame
denims
dharma
digamy
dreamt
dreamy
dynamo
eczema
encamp
enigma
entomb
enwomb
enzyme
Eskimo
exhume
gazump
genome
gleamy
gloomy
goramy
gramme
Grammy
illume
income
infamy
inhume
kinema
legume
lipoma
Madame
maxima
miasma
minima
mishmi
myxoma
occamy
oedema
oogamy
optima
pajama
panama
paramo
plasma
plummy
pneuma
qualmy
raceme
radome
regime
relume
rename
resume
revamp
rheumy
salami
schema
scheme
scrimp
scrump
scummy
sesame
shammy
shimmy
shrimp
slummy
smarmy
sodomy
solemn
squama
steamy
stemma
stigma
stormy
stroma
stromb
struma
swimmy
tatami
toneme
trauma
ugsome
ultima
ultimo
volume
zeugma
zygoma
abound
absent
accent
achene
acting
addend
advent
affine
ageing
airing
albino
Aldine
alkane
alkene
alkyne
almond
alpine
alumna
alumni
amount
angina
anoint
anting
anyone
aphony
append
arcana
arcane
ardent
argand
argent
aroint
around
arpent
arrant
arsine
ascend
ascent
askant
aslant
assent
attend
attune
avaunt
awning
banana
barony
bating
Beaune
begone
behind
belong
betony
beyond
bezant
bikini
biting
bizone
blenny
bluing
boding
bohunk
booing
borane
boring
botany
botone
bourne
bovine
bowing
boxing
brains
brainy
brawny
briony
browny
bryony
busing
butane
butene
bygone
bylane
byline
cabana
cadent
canine
carina
casing
casino
catena
caving
cement
cetane
chaunt
client
cogent
coigne
colony
coming
coping
corona
cosine
coving
cranny
crying
cueing
daphne
daring
debunk
decani
decant
decent
dedans
defend
define
demand
dement
depend
depone
detent
dining
divine
diving
djinni
docent
dogend
domino
dopant
douane
duenna
dugong
during
dyeing
earing
eating
edging
eluant
eluent
embank
ending
engine
enwind
Eocene
equine
ermine
errand
errant
Essene
eterne
ethane
ethene
ethyne
evzone
exeunt
expand
expend
extant
extend
extent
eyeing
facing
fagend
famine
farina
fecund
feeing
feline
felony
ferine
filing
fining
firing
flaunt
fluent
flying
foment
forint
fraena
friend
galena
gamine
gaming
Gemini
gerent
gerund
goanna
gobang
gowany
grainy
granny
greens
greeny
ground
groyne
Havana
hexane
hiding
hieing
hoeing
homing
hominy
humane
hyaena
iguana
immane
immune
impend
impone
indene
indent
induna
infant
inland
inning
insane
intend
intent
intine
intone
invent
iodine
island
jacana
jejune
joanna
jocund
johnny
kalong
ketone
kimono
lacing
lacuna
lading
ladino
laguna
lament
lamina
larynx
latent
learnt
legend
lemony
levant
lierne
liking
liming
lining
litany
living
loment
loving
lowing
lucent
lumina
lupine
luting
lysine
making
manana
marina
marine
matins
maying
meninx
merino
mining
Mishna
modena
moline
moment
mooing
moving
murine
musing
mutant
mutine
mutiny
nagana
natant
neednt
nerine
nocent
nosing
novena
numina
nutant
oblong
obtund
ochone
octane
octant
offend
offent
offing
online
oogeny
oolong
optant
orient
orpine
oscine
outing
oxgang
oxland
paeony
paling
parang
parent
paring
patent
patina
pavane
paving
pedant
piping
plaint
pliant
polony
potent
pruina
prying
puisne
purine
pyrene
quaint
rapine
raring
ratine
rating
ravine
raving
recant
recent
redone
refine
refund
regent
regina
relent
reline
remand
remind
remint
repand
repent
repine
resent
retene
retina
rewind
riband
rident
riding
rising
rodent
Romany
roping
rosiny
rotund
roving
rowing
ruling
rumina
Sabine
salina
saline

sarong
sasine
satiny
savant
savine
saving
saxony
saying
secant
second
secund
seeing
sejant
serang
serene
sevens
sewing
shanny
sheeny
shinny
shrank
shrine
shrink
shrunk
siding
sienna
sileni
silent
simony
sizing
skiing
skinny
soigne
solano
sonant
sowans
sowens
sphene
sphinx
splent
spline
splint
spoony
sprang
sprent
spring
sprint
sprung
squint
sterna
stound
strand
Strine
string
strong
strung
strunt
supine
sweeny
swound
syrinx
tagend
tahini
taking
talent
taming
tenant
tetany
theine
thorny
throne
throng
tiling
timing
tisane
toeing
triune
truant
trying
Tswana
tubing
tuning
tweeny
typing
tyrant
unbend
unbent
unbind
uncini
undine
undone
unhand
unkind
unking
unkink
unlink
unsung
untune
unwind
upland
upping
upwind
urbane
urgent
ursine
vacant
valine
vicuna
Viking
Vishnu
volant
vorant
voting
wahine
whinny
wiring
wisent
xylene
zenana
zoning
abloom
acajou
action
amadou
amatol
amazon
amnion
anchor
anyhow
archon
aswoon
author
baboon
bailor
balboa
ballon
ballot
bamboo
bandog
banjos
barrow
barton
baryon
bassos
bathos
beacon
beckon
befool
behoof
bellow
benzol
bestow
betook
bettor
bilbos
billon
billow
bishop
blazon
bonbon
bongos
booboo
boohoo
borrow
borzoi
boston
bottom
bowwow
brehon
Breton
Briton
bunion
burbot
burgoo
burrow
burton
busboy
button
byblow
cachou
cacoon
cahoot
callow
camion
cannon
cannot
canton
cantor
canyon
captor
carbon
carboy
carrot
carton
Caslon
castor
cation
censor
Charon
chigoe
chiton
cineol
citron
clipon
cocoon
coelom
coinop
collop
comeon
common
condor
congou
convoy
cordon
cosmos
cotton
coupon
cowboy
cowpox
crayon
cresol
croton
cuckoo
cursor
custom
daemon
daimon
damson
deacon
debtor
deploy
despot
diatom
diglot
diploe
diplon
dittos
doctor
dogfox
dogood
dollop
donjon
dragon
drybob
dryrot
editor
eggnog
elevon
employ
enroot
Eozoon
epizoa
erenow
escrow
Ethiop
etymon
factor
faggot
falcon
fallow
fandom
fanion
fantod
fantom
farrow
fathom
felloe
fellow
filfot
firlot
flacon
flagon
flexor
fogbow
fogdog
foison
follow
forgot
fossor
frijol
frivol
furrow
fusion
fylfot
gabion
galiot
gallon
gallop
galoot
gambol
gammon
garcon
garron
garrot
Gascon
geckos
gentoo
gibbon
giglot
glycol
gnomon
godson
gollop
googol
gorgon
goslow
grison
guenon
guidon
gundog
guvnor
hadron
halloa
halloo
hallow
hansom
harlot
harrow
hatbox
haybox
haymow
headon
hector
hereof
hereon
heriot
Hindoo
hobnob
holloa
hollow
hoodoo
hoopoe
horror
hotdog
hotpot
huzoor
hyssop
icebox
indoor
inflow
inkpot
isopod
jailor
jargon
jerboa
joblot
junior
karroo
kation
kelson
kincob
kitool
koedoe
koodoo
kowtow
kronor
lagoon
lapdog
lardon
lassos
latron
lector
legion
lepton
lesion
lesson
lessor
lictor
liquor
lissom
logion
lollop
loriot
lotion
lowboy
lummox
macron
maggot
mallow
mammon
mangos
manioc
marmot
maroon
marron
marrow
mascon
mascot
matlow
matron
matzoh
meadow
mellow
melton
mentor
merlon
meteor
method
micron
mignon
minion
minnow
mirror
Mongol
moocow
morion
Mormon
morrow
motion
motmot
muflon
muskox
mutton
mythos
nardoo
narrow
nation
natron
nekton
nelson
Nestor
neuron
newton
nignog
Nimrod
noncom
nostoc
notion
ocelot
octroi
oddjob
oddson
option
orator
orison
outfox
outtop
pallor
pardon
parrot
parson
pastor
pathos
patrol
patron
pavior
pegtop
pennon
period
perron
person
petrol
pharos
phenol
phonon
photon
piedog
pigeon
pillow
pinion
pistol
piston
pithos
plexor
pluton
podsol
podzol
pogrom
poison
pompom
ponton
potboy
potion
powwow
prison
proton
pugdog
pullon
putlog
pyedog
python
quahog
quinoa
quinol
racoon
ramrod
ramson
random
ransom
raptor
ration
ratoon
reason
reckon
rector
redhot
redtop
reebok
reflow
region
retook
retool
retrod
rhebok
rhetor
ribbon
rollon
ronyon
roucou
sailor
sallow
salmon
saloon
saloop
salvor
salvos
Samson
scazon
school
scroop
seacow
seadog
seafog
seafox
season
sector
seldom
senhor
senior
sensor
sermon
sexpot
sexton
shadow
shalom
signor
simoom
simoon
siphon
sissoo
skibob
slalom
slipon
sorrow
spigot
stator
sterol
stolon
stupor
suitor
summon
sunbow
sundog
sungod
symbol
syphon
tailor
talbot
talion
tallow
tampon
tarpon
tattoo
tautog
teapot
teapoy
telson
tendon
tenson
tensor
tenzon
termor
terror
teston
Teuton
tholoi
tholos
thoron
thymol
tierod
tinpot
tiptoe
tiptop
toluol
tomboy
tomcod
tomtom
torpor
tremor
tricot
trigon
tripod
tripos
triton
trogon
turbot
turgor
turion
tycoon
uncool
unhook
unipod
unison
unknot
unmoor
unroof
unroot
unshod
unshoe
unstop
uphroe
uproot
upshot
ustion
vagrom
vaudoo
vector
vendor
viator
victor
vision
volvox
voodoo
wadmol
waggon
walkon
wallop
wallow
wanion
wanton
wardog
wargod
weapon
weldor
whilom
wigeon
willow
Wilton
window
winnow
wisdom
wittol
wonton
yarrow
yaupon
yellow
yoohoo
zealot
zircon
abrupt
accept
aslope
biceps
caliph
canape
canopy
ceriph
chappy
chippy
chirpy
choppy
clumpy
crappy
creeps
creepy
crimpy
crispy
croppy
croupy
drippy
droopy
enrapt
escape
except
exempt
flappy
floppy
frappe
frumpy
glumpy
gramps
grappa
grippe
grippy
grumps
grumpy
Guelph
incept
irrupt
jalopy
kakapo
metope
occupy
paraph
plumpy
polypi
prompt
pyrope
recipe
sarape
scampi
scrape
script
sculpt
serape
seraph
seriph
sharps
Sherpa
shoppy
skimpy
sleepy
slippy
sloppy
snappy
snippy
snoopy
steppe
stirps
stripe
stripy
stumpy
swampy
syrupy
teraph
thorpe
thrips
trappy
trompe
troppo
troupe
trumps
unripe
unrope
unwept
whippy
whoops
yclept
zarape
abjure
aboard
absorb
absurd
accord
adhere
adjure
admire
adsorb
adverb
advert
afeard
affirm
afford
afters
albert
allure
ampere
angary
angora
apiary
artery
ashore
askari
aspire
assert
assort
assure
astern
attire
attorn
auburn
augury
aumbry
aurora
aviary
aweary
bakery
bawdry
bayard
before
begird
begirt
belfry
bemire
beware
biform
Bihari
binary
bistre
bistro

bleary expire maugre satori venire bruise eonism Maoism rakish unless
blurry expiry mazard Saturn ventre bypass excess Maoist ramose unmask
bolero export meagre satyra vestry bypast excise marish rapist unrest
bowery exsert memory savory vihara calash excuse Marist ravish unwise
braird extern Messrs scarry vinery camass expose mayest recast upcast
briard extort milord schorl vintry camise extasy medusa recess upmost
briary fakery misere sclera vivers caress famish merest refuse uppish
briery fedora misery scurry vizard cayuse fetish merism rehash uprise
buckra femora modern secern votary cerise filose mimosa relish uprush
byform fiacre motory secure waders ceruse finish minish remise utmost
byword figure nature sempre wafery chaise flense misuse remiss valise
bywork finery nonary senary warcry cheese flimsy modest repass vanish
cafard fleury notary senora waters cheesy flossy modish repast Vedist
Caffre floury objure sentry watery chiasm folksy molest repose venose
calory flurry obvert severe wavery choose forest monism resist verism
camera friary oeuvre severy wherry choosy fraise monist retest verist
canard fulcra onward shears winery chouse freest mopish retuse vibist
canary furore ordure sherry wintry chrism frowst morass revest virose
casern future ornery sierra wivern Christ frowsy morish revise volost
cavern gabbro orrery simurg wizard classy gainst morose ribose whatso
cavort galore outcry sistra womera clause galosh mousse rimose whilst
cedarn gantry oxbird skerry wyvern clumsy garish mucosa robust whimsy
celery Gemara oxford slurry yaourt coarse glassy mulish Romish whomso
centre genera oxherd smeary yogurt comose glossy mutism rudish whoosh
cesura gentry paltry sombre zaffre corpse gneiss nanism rugose widish
cheers gharry panary souari zonary course golosh Nazism sadism woodsy
cheery glairy pantry sparry abbess cowish goyish newish sadist wrasse
cherry gocart papers sphere ablush crease grassy nicish saidst xylose
chypre goitre papery sphery access creese grease nodose sayest yogism
cohere gokart papyri splore accost crosse greasy nomism schism zeloso
cohort govern parure spurry accuse crouse grilse nonuse schist zymase
colure grigri pastry square across cruise grouse nowise schuss ablate
covert grugru peltry squire adjust cubism harass nudism scouse acuity
coward haleru penury squirm admass cubist hearse nudist serosa adnate
curare havers petara squirt advise cueist heresy oafish setose aerate
curari hazard petard stairs afresh cuisse hexose oblast sexism afrite
dartre hedera pinery starry aghast curtsy hoarse oboist sexist agnate
datary hegira pleura Stuart agnise cymose holism obsess sheass agouti
datura hejira pliers suborn aguish damask honest obtest shiest albata
debark hetero poetry suburb ahimsa Danish illuse obtuse shiksa albite
deform hombre popery sudary aldose debase immesh oecist shyest amenta
dehorn horary priory sugary almost defuse impish offish slyest anatta
demark humeri pylori sultry ambush degust impose ogress sneesh anatto
demure hungry quaere sundry amidst demise impost ogrish sparse argute
denary ignore quarry superb aorist demist incase oldish speiss arista
depart immure rasure suture appose depose incest oncost splash aseity
deport impark rebore tabard argosy desist incise onrush splosh astute
descry impart reborn tamara ariosi detest incuse oppose spouse augite
desert import record tantra arioso devest infest orgasm squash Avesta
desire impure reform tavern arouse devise infuse osmose squish aviate
desorb inborn regard tawdry arrest dicast ingest otiose strass balata
dhurra infare remark tawery artist digest inmost owlish stress barite
disarm infirm remora tenure assess disuse inrush palish Sufism baryta
divers inform report theirs assist divest insist papism swoosh Basuto
divert inhere resorb theory attest dressy invest papist tanist Basutu
dotard injure resort thwart august dropsy iodise parish Taoism batata
dreary injury retard timbre aurist drossy iodism pavise Taoist beauty
dukery insert retire torero autism drowse ionise perish teensy berate
dupery insure retort toward averse drowsy Jewess peruse theism bhisti
eatery intern returf towery avulse dryish Jewish phrase theist binate
effort invert return Tshirt Babism dudish jocose pilose thirst blintz
elytra inward reverb tundra Babist dumose jurist please thrash blotto
embark izzard revere tuyere banish duress Jutish plisse thresh bonito
embers jabiru revers twyere behest dynast kaross polish thrush borate
empery ligure revert umpire bemuse effuse kibosh popish thrust bounty
empire livery revery unborn biopsy egoism kumiss porism thyrse breath
encore lizard reward uncork blouse egoist lamish porose thyrsi bypath
endure louvre rewire uncurl blowsy egress latest potash tonish capote
engird lowery reword unfurl bluish elapse latish praise tootsy cavity
engirt lucern rework ungird bonism eldest lavish priest torose cecity
ensure lustra ropery ungirt bonist elfish legist prissy tressy cerate
entera lustre rosary unwary booksy elvish liaise punish truism chanty
entire luxury rosery unworn bourse emboss lipase purism tsetse chaste
escarp maduro rostra upturn boyish empusa lobose purist tsotsi chatty
escort maigre rotary upward braise encase locust queasy typist cherty
euchre mantra safari vagary brassy encash lowish quinsy unease chesty
exedra manure salary vaward breast encyst lyrism racism uneasy chintz
exhort Masora samara velure breese enlist lyrist racist unjust chitty
expert mature satire venery browse enmesh malism radish unlash coaita

cogito groats peyote solute armful cornua humour oilnut sensum voyeur
comate grotto peyotl somite armour corpus iambus omasum septum vulgus
comity grotty pigsty sonata artful Corvus idolum opaque serous walnut
coolth growth pineta sopite asylum crocus imbrue osmium setout walrus
coonty guilty pirate spilth atrium cultus indium ostium shaduf wampum
copita gyrate plenty splits aurous cupful influx outgun shamus warmup
county halite plinth sports avenue curium ionium output shogun wayout
coyote hamate plotty sporty awmous cursus ireful outrun shroud wilful
crafty Hamite podite spotty backup cuscus jarful padauk siglum windup
create health pointe sprite bagful cutout joyful paidup sinful woeful
crista hearth points stacte bangup dengue joyous palpus sixgun xenium
crusty hearty polite staith barium detour jugful panful skirun xystus
crypto hereto polity strata barque devour kittul pappus slapup yumyum
cuesta ideate potato strath Basque devout kronur parous slipup zythum
curate ignite presto strati battue dictum kultur peanut sodium active
dainty impute pretty surety bedaub dingus labium peepul sprout alcove
dearth incite pronto svelte bedbug dinkum labour pentup sputum Argive
debate indite puncta swarth befoul dirdum labrum peplum statue arrive
delate inmate pupate sweaty belaud disbud laceup perdue status behave
delete innate purity sweets bijoux discus langue phylum stepup behove
demote invite Pushtu tapeta binful diseur langur pickup stroud belive
denote iodate pyrite tenuto bisque dolium lapful pignut strout chivvy
depute iolite quanta terete blowup dolour lapsus pileum stylus cleave
deputy jaunty quarte thirty boxful dorsum larrup pileup subdue cruive
derate jugate quarto tights brogue drogue lashup pileus sulcus dative
devote kaputt quartz tomato brutus dryrun lasque pilous tabour derive
dhooti karate quinta treaty bulbul dugout lawful plague talcum endive
dilate kibitz quoits triste bunkum dumdum layout plaguy Talmud essive
dilute knotty rabato trouty burnup dustup leadup plaque Targum evolve
dimity krantz ramate trusty bustup dybbuk league plenum tarsus geneva
dogate lanate rarity twenty byssus earful liftup plexus Taurus glaive
domett laxity ratite twisty cactus efflux limbus podium teacup greave
donate lealty realty ubiety caecum eggcup lineup popgun tedium grieve
drafty leanto rebate unbitt caique embrue lingua porous tenour groove
drifty legate rebato uncate callup englut linkup poseur tergum groovy
drouth legato recite undate callus ensoul litmus possum tholus inwove
dunite length refute uneath calque erbium lockup potful thymus motive
ecarte lenity relate Uniate campus evolue lyceum primus timous native
effete Levite remote update canful exequy magnum pullup tinful octave
egesta levity repute uppity cangue exodus mahout pulque tissue octavo
eighth ligate righto vacate cantus eyecup makeup pursue tittup ottava
eighty lights rotate valeta capful eyeful manful pushup tongue relive
ejecta lobate rubato valuta carful factum manque quorum tophus remove
eluate locate safety vanity carpus famous mantua radium torque revive
emeute lunate salute vaulty casque farout maraud radius tossup saliva
enmity luxate samite vegete catgut favour markup ragout tragus scurvy
ensate lyrate sanity veleta catsup fescue marque Rajput tryout sheave
entity malate sapota Venite caucus fitful marrum ramous tubful shelve
eolith manito savate verity census flatus masque recoup tuchun shrive
equate mighty scanty volute centum foetus maybug rectum tumour shrove
equity minute scatty wapiti cercus folium meatus rectus tumtum skivvy
ergate moiety scouth warmth cereus fondue medium redbud turnup sleave
errata motett sedate wealth cerium foulup medius reflux typhus sleeve
ersatz mutate Semite wraith cestus frenum mentum regius umlaut starve
estate negate senate wreath cheque fundus midgut replum unglue steeve
excite nerite Shakta yeasty cherub fungus minium rescue unique strive
facete nicety Shakti zenith chiaus furfur miscue rhesus unplug strove
faulty nighty shanty zonate chorus gangue missus rictus untrue swerve
fealty ninety sheath zygote cilium genius mockup rigour uraeus thieve
feisty notate sheets abacus cinque getout modius rigout Uranus thrive
fiesta nudity Shelta ablaut circus giaour morbus rimous urnful throve
finite nutate shelty acarus cirque gradus morgue risque useful twelve
fixate oblate shifty accrue cirrus gurjun mosque rotgut uterus visive
fixity oddity Shiite acinus cistus gypsum mucous ruckus vacuum votive
flinty oleate Shinto adieus citrus hagbut mukluk rueful valgus Zouave
flirty omenta shinty adieux claque hallux multum rufous vallum arrowy
floaty oocyte shirty adytum clique hangup murmur rumour valour disown
fourth oolite shorts afflux cliquy hardup museum rumpus vapour godown
frosty ophite shorty airbus clonus hatful mutuum sacque vatful impawn
fruity opiate siesta airgun cobnut helium muumuu sacrum vellum inlaws
frusta ornate sleety alarum coccus henrun naevus saltus velour Mohawk
fugato oxgate sleuth allium coitus hiatus netful sambur vendue pesewa
gaiety palate smalto allout coleus hiccup nimbus sannup venous renown
gamete parity smarty amylum colour holdup nobbut sapful versus scrawl
ghetto Pashto smooth anicut comous honour nonius savour vigour screwy
ghosty pedate smutty animus concur hookup noshup scarus villus shrewd
gleety pelota snooty antrum consul hubbub obelus scutum vinous sinewy
Granth peseta snotty arbour copout humbug odious Seljuk virtue sprawl
gritty petite snouty ardour corium hummum oidium sendup viscus squawk

strawy strewn strown thrawn thrown uptown adnexa annexe deluxe eutaxy galaxy iceaxe maxixe acetyl adenyl always anonym arroyo ayeaye benzyl billyo byebye coccyx dactyl embryo ennuye eponym forbye henrys legbye martyr methyl moneys outbye papaya pentyl phenyl piraya propyl redeye strays tiedye uranyl Vaisya zephyr zlotys ablaze assize bedaze blowzy breeze breezy bronze bronzy corozo coryza floozy freeze frenzy frieze frizzy frowzy mezuza piazza queazy schizo sleazy snazzy sneeze sneezy snooze stanza wheeze wheezy

---

abulia acacia acedia adnexa

agenda ahimsa alalia albata alexia alpaca alumna amenta amoeba anatta angina angora anoxia apnoea arcana areola argala arista armada arnica arroba asthma ataxia aurora Avesta axilla azalea balata balboa banana baryta batata beluga bertha bodega Brahma bregma buckra Buddha bunnia burkha cabala cabana camera carina cassia catena cesura chacha chacma chorea chroma chukka cicada cicala cigala cinema cloaca coaita concha copita copula cornea cornua corona coryza cowpea crania crista cuesta cupola dahlia datura dharma dhurra djibba duenna eczema Egeria

egesta eidola ejecta elodea elytra empusa enigma entera epizoa errata eureka exedra facula farina fascia fecula fedora femora ferula fibula fiesta fraena frusta fulcra funkia galena garuda geisha Gemara genera geneva gloria goanna grappa guinea Gurkha halloa Havana hedera hegira hejira hernia holloa hoopla hyaena iguana impala indaba induna infula inyala ischia jacana jerboa joanna judoka kabala kanaka kinema lacuna laguna lambda lamina latria ligula lingua lipoma lithia loggia lorcha lorica lumina lunula lustra macula Malaga maltha manana manila

mantra mantua manuka maraca marina Masora maxima medusa mezuza miasma mimosa minima Mishna modena morula mucosa myopia myrica myxoma nagana nausea nebula novena numina nutria oedema omenta optima oscula ottava paella pagoda pajama pakeha pallia panada panama papaya papula patina payola pelota peseta pesewa petara phobia piazza pineta piraya plasma pleura pneuma posada protea pruina puncta pyrola quagga quanta quinoa quinta quotha radula raffia ranula raphia razzia regina remora remuda reseda retina rhumba rostra rosula rumina russia salina saliva

salvia samara sapota satyra schema scilla sclera scoria scotia senega senora serosa Shakta sheila Shelta Sherpa shiksa sienna sierra siesta silica sistra sonata squama stadia stanza stemma sterna stigma strata stroma struma taenia tamara tantra tapeta tarsia tegula telega thoria thulia torula trauma trivia troika tsamba Tswana tundra ultima ungula Urania utopia Vaisya valeta valuta veleta vesica vicuna vihara vizsla womera Yoruba yttria zareba zariba zenana zeugma zinnia zygoma absorb adsorb adverb aplomb baobab bedaub benumb cherub cobweb confab

corymb desorb drybob entomb enwomb hobnob hubbub kincob midrib mihrab oddjob prefab resorb reverb scarab skibob skylab stromb suburb superb acetic acidic Adamic adipic Adonic Aeolic agamic agaric agonic airsac alcaic anodic anomic anoxic aortic Arabic arctic ataxic atomic atonic azotic Baltic bardic Belgic bionic biotic bromic calcic calpac capric celiac Celtic chemic choric citric cleric clinic clonic cognac Coptic corsac cosmic cretic critic cultic cupric cyanic cyclic Cymric cystic deific dermic dyadic echoic Eddaic Edenic emblic emetic Eozoic

epodic eremic erotic ethnic exilic exotic fabric fennec ferric filmic Finnic fistic formic frolic fustic Gaelic Gallic garlic geodic gnomic Gothic guaiac haptic hectic herdic heroic hydric hymnic iambic iconic irenic ironic italic Judaic karmic Keltic lactic Lettic limbec limbic lithic lubric luetic maleic maniac manioc mantic mastic metric miotic mosaic mundic myopic myotic mystic mythic nastic nitric noetic Nordic nostoc ogamic orphic ovisac oxalic ozonic parsec pathic pectic pelvic peptic phasic phatic phobic phonic photic physic picnic picric

pionic poetic public pycnic pyknic ricrac Romaic rubric rustic scenic Scotic septic sialic Slavic sophic Sothic static steric syndic Syriac tactic tannic tanrec tarmac tenrec thetic tictac toluic tombac tragic tropic Turkic unific Uralic uranic vitric Wendic zincic zodiac aboard abound abroad absurd acarid accord addend addled afeard afford afield afraid agamid ageold airbed aisled alated algoid aliped allied allred almond angled aoudad append arched argand ariled around ascend attend avowed awaked bagged ballad banned barbed barred batted bayard

beaked bedded begged begird behead beheld behind behold belaud belted bested betted beyond bibbed bitted bladed blowed bobbed bogged bonded booted bopped boxbed braird briard budded bugged bulbed bummed bunted bushed bussed busted byroad byword cafard canard candid canned capped capsid celled chield closed coated coccid cocked cogged combed conned conoid copped corded corked corned cotted coward cowled crazed cuboid cuffed cupped cursed cusped cuspid cussed cyprid cystid dabbed dammed damned darned daybed defend demand depend desmid deuced devoid

diacid dibbed dimmed dinned dipped disbud dogend dogged dogood doited donned doodad dotard dotted dubbed dunned durned elated enfold engild engird ennead enwind errand exceed expand expend extend eyelid fabled fagend fagged failed fanged fanned fantod fatted fecund fervid fezzed fibbed fibred figged finned fitted florid fluted fobbed foetid fogged foiled footed forbad forbid forced fordid forked formed forrad friend frigid fucoid fugged fulgid funned furred gabbed gabled gadded gadoid gagged gaited ganoid gapped garbed gassed gelled gemmed genned

gerund
gifted
gigged
gilled
ginned
graved
gravid
ground
gummed
gunned
gutted
gypped
haired
hammed
handed
hanged
happed
hatred
hatted
hawked
hazard
headed
heated
heeled
hemmed
heptad
herald
hinged
hipped
hispid
hogged
hoised
honied
hooded
hoofed
hooked
hopped
horned
horrid
hotbed
hugged
hummed
humped
hutted
hybrid
ideaed
impend
inbred
indeed
infold
inlaid
inland
inroad
intend
intoed
inward
island
isopod
izzard
jabbed
jagged
jammed
jarred
jetted
jibbed
jigged
jocund
jogged
jotted
jugged
jutted
kenned
kerned
kidded
kilted
kobold
lagged
lammed
landed

lapped
lapsed
leafed
leaved
ledged
legend
legged
lensed
Leonid
lidded
lilied
limbed
limpid
lipoid
lipped
liquid
listed
lizard
loaded
lobbed
logged
lopped
lotted
lugged
maenad
mailed
manned
mantid
mapped
maraud
marked
marred
masted
matted
mazard
method
metred
miffed
milled
milord
minded
misdid
misled
moated
mobbed
monied
mopped
morbid
mucoid
mugged
myriad
nabbed
nagged
napped
neaped
nereid
netted
nibbed
Nimrod
nipped
nodded
obtund
offend
onward
orchid
outbid
outdid
oxbird
oxford
oxherd
oxland
padded
pallid
panned
patted
peaked
pegged
penned
pentad

pepped
period
petard
petted
pigged
pinned
pipped
pissed
pitted
placed
placid
plumed
pocked
podded
polled
pooped
popped
potted
premed
puffed
punned
pupped
putrid
ragged
rammed
ramrod
rancid
rapped
ratted
record
redbud
refund
regard
relaid
reload
remand
remind
repaid
repand
reread
resold
retard
retold
retrod
retted
revved
reward
rewind
reword
ribald
riband
ribbed
ridded
ridged
rigged
rimmed
ringed
ripped
robbed
rooted
rotted
rotund
rubbed
ruched
ruffed
rugged
rutted
sacred
sagged
sailed
sapped
sayyid
scaled
screed
seabed
second
secund
shaped
shield

should
shrewd
shroud
sinned
sipped
sobbed
sopped
sordid
sotted
souled
spined
spread
stated
stewed
stolid
stoned
stound
strand
stroud
stupid
subbed
summed
sungod
sunned
supped
swound
tabard
tabbed
tagend
tagged
Talmud
tanked
tanned
tapped
tarred
tatted
tedded
tetrad
thread
ticked
tiered
tierod
tinned
tipped
titled
togaed
togged
tomcod
topped
toroid
torpid
torrid
totted
toward
toxoid
trepid
trifid
tripod
tufted
tugged
turbid
turgid
tusked
tutted
twould
unbend
unbind
unbred
unclad
unfold
ungird
unhand
uniped
unipod
united
unkind
unlaid
unload
unpaid

unread
unsaid
unshod
untied
untold
unused
unwind
upheld
uphold
upland
upward
upwind
valved
varied
varved
vatted
vaward
veiled
veined
versed
vested
vetted
viscid
vizard
voiced
voided
wadded
wagged
walled
wanted
wargod
warped
warred
warted
wasted
webbed
wedded
wetted
whited
wicked
wigged
willed
winded
winged
witted
wizard
wonted
wooded
wooled
xyloid
yapped
yenned
yipped
yolked
zapped
zinced
zinked
zipped
zonked
abduce
abjure
ablate
ablaze
abrade
accede
accrue
accuse
achene
active
adduce
adhere
adjure
admire
adnate
advice
advise
aedile
aerate
aerobe

affine
aflame
afrite
agnate
agnise
agrafe
albite
alcove
Aldine
aldose
alkane
alkene
alkyne
allege
allele
allude
allure
alpine
alsike
alulae
amerce
ampere
anlace
anlage
annexe
anomie
anyone
apache
apiece
apogee
appose
arable
arcade
arcane
areole
Argive
argute
argyle
arouse
arrive
arsine
ashore
aslope
aspire
assize
assume
assure
astute
athome
attire
attune
aubade
audile
augite
auntie
Aussie
avenge
avenue
averse
aviate
avulse
awhile
ayeaye
babble
baddie
baffle
bailee
bailie
bangle
barege
bargee
barite
barque
Basque
battle
battue
bauble
bawbee
bawble

beadle
beagle
beanie
Beaune
became
become
bedaze
beetle
before
begone
behave
behove
belike
belive
bemire
bemuse
berate
berthe
beside
betake
betide
beware
binate
birdie
bireme
birkie
bisque
bistre
bizone
blende
blithe
blonde
blouse
blunge
bobble
bocage
bodice
boggle
bolide
bonnie
bonxie
boodle
bookie
bootee
borage
borane
borate
boride
bosche
bothie
botone
bottle
boucle
bougie
boulle
bounce
bourne
bourse
bovine
bowtie
braise
branle
breese
breeze
bridge
bridle
broche
brogue
bronze
browse
bruise
bubble
buckle
buddle
budgie
bullae
bumble
bummle
bundle

bungle
burble
burgee
burgle
bursae
bustee
bustle
butane
butene
byebye
bygone
bylane
byline
byname
cackle
caddie
Caffre
caique
cajole
calque
camise
canape
candle
cangue
canine
cantle
capote
carafe
casque
castle
cattle
caudle
cayuse
centre
cerate
cerise
ceruse
cetane
chaise
chance
change
charge
chaste
cheese
chelae
cheque
chicle
chigoe
choice
choose
chouse
chrome
chypre
cilice
cinque
circle
cirque
citole
claque
clause
cleave
cliche
clique
cloche
clothe
coarse
coatee
cobble
cockle
coddle
coerce
coffee
coffle
cohere
coigne
collie
colure
comate
commie

comose
congee
cookie
coolie
cootie
corbie
corpse
corrie
corvee
cosine
costae
coulee
couple
course
cowage
cowrie
coyote
cradle
crease
create
creche
creese
creole
cringe
crosse
crouse
cruise
cruive
cubage
cuddie
cuddle
cuisse
cuptie
cupule
curare
curate
curdle
curiae
currie
curule
cuttle
cymose
dabble
damage
dandle
dangle
daphne
dapple
darkie
darkle
dartle
dartre
dassie
dative
dawdle
dazzle
dearie
debase
debate
decade
decide
deckle
decode
decoke
decree
deduce
deface
defame
defile
define
defuse
degree
delate
delete
delude
deluge
deluxe
demise
demode

demote
demure
dengue
denote
denude
depone
depose
depute
derate
deride
derive
desire
device
devise
devote
dibble
diddle
dilate
dilute
dimple
dingle
diploe
dipole
disuse
divide
divine
doable
docile
doddle
dogate
doggie
donate
donsie
doodle
doolie
dormie
dosage
dotage
dottle
douane
double
douche
dragee
drawee
dredge
drogue
drowse
drudge
duende
duffle
dumose
dunite
durrie
ecarte
edible
efface
effete
effuse
elapse
eluate
embrue
emerge
emeute
empire
emulge
enable
encage
encase
encode
encore
endive
endure
enface
engage
engine
enisle
enlace
ennuye
enrage

enrobe
ensate
ensile
ensure
entice
entire
entree
enzyme
Eocene
ephebe
epopee
equate
equine
ergate
ermine
escape
Essene
essive
estate
eterne
ethane
ethene
ethyne
euchre
evince
evolue
evolve
evzone
excide
excise
excite
excuse
exhale
exhume
expire
expose
Eyetie
facade
facete
facile
faerie
faille
falsie
famine
Fantee
faunae
feeble
feirie
feline
felloe
female
ferine
ferule
fescue
fettle
fiacre
fiance
fickle
fiddle
fierce
figure
filose
fimble
finale
finite
fipple
fixate
fizzle
flambe
flange
fleche
fledge
fleece
flense
florae
focsle
foible
fondle
fondue

footle
foozle
forage
forbye
fossae
foveae
fraise
frappe
freeze
fridge
frieze
fringe
fuddle
fumble
furore
fusile
futile
future
gabble
gaggle
galore
gamble
gamete
gamine
gangue
garage
garble
gargle
garvie
gauche
gavage
geegee
gemmae
genome
gentle
George
giggle
gillie
girdle
girlie
glaive
glance
goalie
goatee
gobble
goggle
goitre
goodie
gourde
gramme
grange
grease
greave
greige
grieve
grille
grilse
grippe
groove
grouse
groyne
grudge
guddle
guggle
gurgle
guttae
guzzle
gyrate
habile
hackle
haddie
haggle
halide
halite
hamate
Hamite
handle
hankie
hassle

hearse
heckle
heddle
hexane
hexose
higgle
hippie
hirple
hoarse
hobble
hogtie
homage
hombre
hoodie
hoopoe
hopple
huckle
huddle
humane
humble
hurdle
hurtle
hustle
hyphae
iceaxe
icicle
ideate
ignite
ignore
illume
illuse
imbibe
imbrue
immane
immune
immure
impale
impede
impone
impose
impure
impute
incase
incise
incite
income
incuse
indene
indite
indole
induce
infare
infuse
inhale
inhere
inhume
injure
inmate
innate
insane
inside
insole
insure
intake
intine
intone
invade
invite
invoke
inwove
iodate
iodide
iodine
iodise
iolite
ionise
jangle
jaunce
jejune

jiggle
jingle
jinnee
jocose
joggle
jostle
jounce
jugate
juggle
jujube
jumble
jungle
junkie
Kabyle
karate
kelpie
ketone
kettle
kewpie
kibble
kiddie
kiekie
kindle
kirtle
kittle
koedoe
kookie
koppie
labile
laddie
lanate
langue
lappie
larvae
lasque
lassie
launce
lavage
league
legate
legbye
legume
lessee
Levite
liable
liaise
lichee
lierne
ligate
ligule
ligure
linage
lintie
lipase
lipide
lippie
little
loathe
lobate
lobose
lobule
locale
locate
louche
lounge
louvre
lovage
luggie
lunate
lunule
lupine
lustre
luxate
lychee
lyrate
lysine
mackle
macule
Madame

magpie
maigre
malate
malice
mallee
mammae
mammee
manage
manche
manege
mangle
manque
mantle
manure
marble
marine
marque
mascle
mashie
masque
mature
maugre
maxixe
meagre
mealie
meanie
meddle
mediae
meinie
menace
menage
merrie
mestee
metage
metope
mettle
mickle
midage
middle
milage
mingle
minute
mirage
miscue
misere
mistle
misuse
mizzle
mobile
module
moggie
mohole
moline
mollie
mopoke
morale
morgue
morose
mosque
motile
motive
mottle
mousse
muckle
muddle
muffle
mumble
murine
muscle
mutate
mutine
mutule
muzzle
mygale
myrtle
native
nature
needle
negate

nerine
nerite
nestle
nettle
nibble
niggle
nimble
nipple
nobble
noddle
nodose
nodule
nonage
nonuse
noodle
notate
notice
novice
nowise
noyade
nozzle
nuance
nubble
nubile
nuncle
nutate
nuzzle
oarage
obeche
objure
oblate
oblige
obtuse
ochone
octane
octave
oeuvre
office
ohmage
oleate
online
onside
oocyte
oolite
opaque
ophite
opiate
oppose
orache
oracle
orange
ordure
oriole
ornate
orpine
oscine
osmose
otiose
outage
outbye
outvie
oxgate
oxhide
paddle
palace
palate
paleae
papule
parade
pardie
parole
Parsee
parure
pavage
pavane
pavise
pawnee
pebble
pedate

peddle
pelage
peltae
pennae
people
perdue
peruke
peruse
pesade
pestle
petite
peyote
phoebe
phrase
piaffe
pickle
piddle
pierce
piffle
pilose
pilule
pimple
pinkie
pinnae
pinole
pintle
pirate
pizzle
plague
plaice
plaque
please
pledge
plicae
plisse
plunge
podite
pointe
police
polite
pomace
pomade
pommie
pongee
pontie
poodle
popple
porgie
porose
potage
potale
potpie
pottle
pouffe
pounce
praise
prance
pratie
prince
psyche
puddle
puisne
pulque
pumice
puntee
pupate
purfle
purine
purple
pursue
puttee
puttie
puzzle
pyrene
pyrite
pyrope
quaere
quarte
quiche

quince
rabble
raceme
raddle
radome
raffle
raggee
raggle
ramate
ramble
ramose
rankle
rapine
rappee
rasure
ratine
ratite
rattle
ravage
ravine
razzle
rebate
rebore
rebuke
recede
recipe
recite
reddle
redeye
rediae
redone
reduce
reface
refine
refuge
refuse
refute
regale
reggae
regime
relate
reline
relive
relume
remade
remake
remise
remote
remove
rename
renege
repine
repose
repute
resale
rescue
reside
resile
resole
resume
retake
retene
retire
retuse
revere
revile
revise
revive
revoke
rewire
rewoke
rhaphe
ribose
riddle
riffle
rimose
ripple
risque
rivage

roadie
rookie
rosace
rotate
rotche
rouble
rubble
ruckle
ruddle
ruelle
ruffle
rugose
rumble
rumple
rundle
rustle
rutile
Sabine
sacque
saddle
saithe
salade
saline
sallee
salute
samite
sample
sapele
sarape
sasine
satire
savage
savate
savine
scarce
scathe
scheme
sconce
scopae
scouse
scrape
scribe
scythe
seabee
seance
secede
secure
sedate
sedile
seduce
seethe
seiche
semble
Semite
semple
sempre
senate
senile
serape
serene
serrae
sesame
setose
settee
settle
severe
sewage
shavie
sheave
shelve
Shiite
shrike
shrine
shrive
shrove
sickle
silage
simile
simple

single
sirree
sizzle
sleave
sledge
sleeve
sludge
sluice
smudge
snathe
sneeze
snooze
socage
softie
soigne
soiree
solace
solute
sombre
somite
sonsie
soothe
sopite
sorage
sortie
source
sparge
sparse
spathe
specie
spence
sphene
sphere
splice
spline
splore
sponge
spouse
sprite
spruce
spurge
square
squire
stable
stacte
stance
staple
starve
statue
steeve
stelae
steppe
stifle
stodge
stogie
stooge
strafe
strake
striae
stride
strife
strike
Strine
stripe
strive
strobe
strode
stroke
strove
stymie
suable
subdue
subtle
suckle
summae
sundae
supine
supple
sutile

suttee suture svelte swathe swerve swinge tackle takahe talkie tamale tangle tassie tattle tawpie teazle teepee teethe temple tenace tentie tenure terete testae thecae theine thence thieve thorpe thrice thrive throne throve thyrse tibiae tickle tiedye tierce timbre tingle tinkle tipple tiptoe tirade tisane tissue tittle toddle toffee toggle toneme tongue tootle topple torose torque touche toupee tousle towage towhee townee trance treble tremie triage trifle triode triple triste triune troche trompe troupe trudge tsetse tubule tuille tumble turtle

tussle tuyere twelve twinge twyere ugsome ullage umbrae umpire unable uncage uncate undate undine undone unease unglue Uniate unique unlace unlade unlike unmade unmake unripe unrobe unrope unsafe unshoe untrue untune unwise unyoke update uphroe uprise upside uptake urbane ursine usable usance uvulae vacate vagile valine valise vegete veloce velure vendee vendue venire Venite venose ventre venule vestee viable vielle virile virose virtue visage visile visive vittae vivace volume volute votive voulge voyage wabble waddie waddle waffle waggle wahine

wamble wampee wangle warble warsle wattle weepie wheeze whence whinge wiggle wimble wimple winkle wintle wobble woggle wortle wrasse writhe xylene xylose yaffle Yankee yippee yippie zaffre zarape zombie zonate Zouave zygote zymase behalf behoof belief cutoff engulf faroff hereof ingulf itself layoff letoff massif midoff myself oneoff payoff pilaff putoff rebuff relief returf ripoff runoff sclaff scruff setoff shaduf sharif sherif shroff tariff tipoff unroof unself acting ageing airing anting awning bagwig bandog bating bedbug belong bigwig biting

bluing bobwig boding booing boring bowing bowleg boxing busing casing caving coming coping coving crying cueing daring dining diving dogleg dugong during dyeing earing earwig eating edging eggnog ending eyeing facing feeing filing fining firing fizgig flying fogdog gaming gasbag gobang gundog hatpeg hiding hieing hoeing homing hotdog humbug icebag inning jetlag kalong kitbag lacing lading lapdog liking liming lining living loving lowing luting making maybug maying mining mooing moving musing muskeg nignog nosing nutmeg oblong offing oolong outing

oxgang paling parang paring paving pegleg piedog piping proleg prying pugdog putlog pyedog quahog ragbag ragtag raring ratbag rating raving riding rising roping roving rowing ruling runrig sarong saving saying seadog seafog seapig seeing serang sewing siding simurg sizing skiing sprang spring sprung stalag string strong strung sundog tagrag taking taming tautog teabag throng tiewig tiling timing toeing trying Tuareg tubing tuning typing unking unplug unsung upping Viking voting wardog wigwag wiring zigzag zoning ablush afresh aguish ambush anarch

attach avouch aweigh banish blanch bleach blench blotch bluish borsch boyish branch breach breath breech broach brooch brunch bypath calash caliph casbah ceriph chough church clench clinch clough clunch clutch coolth cowish cranch cratch crotch crouch crunch crutch cultch Danish dearth detach doodah dreich drench droich drouth dryish dudish eighth elfish elvish encash enmesh enough enrich eolith eunuch exarch famish fellah fetich fetish finish flanch fleech flench fletch flinch flitch flysch fourth fratch french galosh garish glitch golosh goyish

Granth grouch growth grutch Guelph Gullah gunyah gurrah halvah haunch health hearth hookah hootch howdah hurrah immesh impish inarch inrush jarrah Jewish jibbah Jutish kasbah kiaugh kiblah kibosh kirsch kitsch koolah lamish latish launch lavish length loofah lowish marish matzoh minish modish Moloch moolah mopish morish mulish mullah Munich nautch newish nicish nullah oafish offish ogrish oldish onrush owlish palish paraph pariah parish paunch perish pleach plinth plough polish popish potash preach punish punkah purdah putsch quaich quaigh quench

quitch radish rakish ravish rehash relish Romish rudish rupiah scorch scotch scouth scutch search seraph seriph sheath sheikh sheugh sirrah skeigh sketch sleigh sleuth slouch slough smatch smeech smirch smooch smooth smouch smutch snatch sneesh snitch speech spilth splash splosh squash squish staith stanch starch stench stitch strath sumach swarth swatch switch swoosh teraph thatch though thrash thresh thrush tonish trench trough tussah twitch uneath unlash uppish uprush vanish wallah warmth wealth whidah whoosh whydah widish wraith wreath wrench

wretch Yahveh Yahweh zenith zillah agouti alkali alumni annuli argali ariosi askari banzai bhisti Bihari bikini bonsai borzoi Brahmi calami canthi chichi chilli clypei cumuli curari decani dhooti djinni emboli ephebi famuli flocci Gemini glutei grigri humeri incubi kabuki kowhai lazuli limuli litchi loculi mallei mishmi moduli muesli Nepali neroli nielli nilgai nuclei ocelli octroi papyri phalli polypi pylori rhombi safari salami saluki sandhi satori scampi scyphi seseli Shakti sileni solidi souari strati tahini tatami thalli tholoi thyrsi tsotsi

tumuli uncini Wahabi wapiti swaraj ackack anorak arrack attack bedeck bemock betook bohunk bywork Canuck copeck corsak damask debark debunk demark dikdik dybbuk embank embark hijack impark inwick kopeck medick Mohawk Mohock moujik mukluk muzhik oclock oomiak padauk Polack rebeck reebok remark retook rework rhebok sanjak screak Seljuk sheoak shrank shriek shrink shrunk Slovak squawk squeak streak streek struck suslik thwack tombak uncork undock unhook unkink unlink unlock unmask unpack unpick untuck yapock zebeck aboral abseil acetal acetyl actual

adenyl
aerial
agnail
agonal
amatol
amoral
animal
anneal
annual
anodal
antral
aortal
apical
apodal
appeal
archil
armful
artful
assail
assoil
astral
atonal
atrial
avowal
awheel
azonal
bagful
barbel
barrel
becall
bedell
befall
befell
befool
befoul
beigel
benzol
benzyl
bethel
bewail
bharal
binful
boatel
bordel
boreal
boxful
brazil
bridal
brumal
brutal
buccal
bulbil
bulbul
burhel
burial
burrel
bursal
bushel
caecal
cancel
canful
cannel
capful
carful
carnal
carpal
carpel
carrel
cartel
carvel
casual
caudal
causal
cental
cereal
chapel
chesil
chisel
chital
choral
cineol
clonal
coccal
coeval
coital
compel
consul
corbel
cornel
corral
costal
coucal
credal
crenel
cresol
crewel
crotal
crural
cudgel
cupful
curial
curtal
cymbal
dactyl
daedal
damsel
Daniel
darnel
deasil
denial
dental
dentel
dentil
derail
dermal
detail
diesel
dirndl
discal
dismal
dispel
distal
distil
dorsal
dossal
dossel
drivel
drupel
duffel
earful
enamel
enroll
ensoul
entail
entoil
epical
espial
eyeful
facial
fallal
fardel
farfel
faucal
faunal
fennel
ferial
festal
fetial
feudal
fibril
filial
finial
fiscal
fitful
floral
foetal
fontal
formal
fossil
foveal
frazil
frijol
frivol
frugal
fulfil
fungal
funnel
Gadhel
gambol
garial
gavial
genial
gerbil
gimbal
gimmal
gingal
global
glycol
Goidel
googol
gospel
gravel
grovel
gunnel
gunsel
haemal
hallal
hammal
hansel
hartal
hatful
herbal
hostel
housel
hummel
hymnal
hyphal
instal
instil
ireful
isabel
isohel
jackal
jarful
jerbil
jezail
jovial
joyful
jugful
jumbal
kennel
kernel
kitool
kittul
kummel
labial
laical
lapful
larval
laurel
lawful
lentil
lethal
lineal
lintel
lionel
listel
luteal
mammal
manful
mangel
mantel
manual
marcel
marvel
medial
menial
mensal
mental
mescal
mesial
methyl
missal
missel
mitral
Mongol
monial
morsel
mortal
mussel
mutual
netful
neural
nickel
normal
nounal
Nowell
nuchal
obital
ogival
onfall
orchil
ordeal
osteal
ostial
oxgall
oxtail
oxymel
palpal
panful
parcel
parral
parrel
pascal
pastel
pastil
patrol
peepul
pencil
pentyl
petrel
petrol
peyotl
phenol
phenyl
pineal
pistil
pistol
plagal
plural
podsol
podzol
pommel
pontil
portal
postal
postil
potful
primal
propel
propyl
pulvil
pummel
quinol
racial
radial
rappel
rascal
recall
recoil
refill
refuel
regnal
reheel
rental
repeal
resell
retail
retell
retial
retool
retral
reveal
rhinal
rictal
ritual
rondel
rueful
runnel
sacral
sandal
santal
sapful
sardel
saurel
school
schorl
scrawl
scroll
scutal
sendal
septal
sequel
serial
serval
sexual
shekel
shovel
shrill
signal
simnel
sinful
snivel
social
sorrel
spinal
spinel
spiral
spital
sprawl
squail
squall
squeal
squill
statal
sterol
stipel
stroll
subtil
swivel
symbol
tahsil
tarsal
tassel
teasel
teazel
tercel
tergal
thecal
thrall
thrill
thymol
tibial
timbal
tincal
tindal
tinful
tinsel
toluol
tonsil
torsel
travel
tribal
trinal
trowel
tubful
tunnel
tymbal
umbral
uncial
uncoil
uncool
uncurl
unfurl
ungual
unnail
unreal
unreel
unroll
unseal
unveil
unwell
uphill
uracil
uranyl
urinal
urnful
useful
vandal
vassal
vatful
venial
ventil
verbal
vernal
versal
vessel
vestal
vidual
visual
wadmal
wadmol
weasel
weevil
wilful
withal
wittol
woeful
xenial
zingel
abloom
adytum
affirm
alarum
allium
amylum
anadem
anonym
anthem
antrum
apozem
ashram
asylum
atrium
autism
Baalim
Babism
balsam
bantam
barium
becalm
bedlam
beldam
beseem
biform
bonism
bottom
bunkum
byform
caecum
centum
cerium
chiasm
chrism
cilium
coelom
corium
cubism
curium
custom
deform
diadem
diatom
dictum
dinkum
dirdum
dirham
dirhem
disarm
dodgem
dolium
dorsum
drachm
dumdum
Durham
egoism
embalm
emblem
engram
eonism
eponym
erbium
esteem
factum
fandom
fantom
fathom
folium
frenum
fulham
fullam
goddam
gypsum
hammam
hansom
helium
holism
hummum
ibidem
idolum
indium
infirm
inform
inseam
iodism
ionium
jetsam
labium
labrum
lissom
logjam
lyceum
lyrism
magnum
malism
Maoism
marram
marrum
mayhem
medium
megohm
megrim
mentum
merism
minium
monism
Moslem
multum
museum
Muslim
mutism
mutuum
nanism
napalm
Nazism
nomism
noncom
nudism
oidium
omasum
orgasm
osmium
ostium
papism
passim
paynim
pelham
peplum
phlegm
phloem
phylum
pileum
plenum
podium
pogrom
pompom
porism
possum
prelim
purism
quorum
racism
radium
randem
random
ransom
rectum
redeem
reform
replum
rhythm
sachem
sacrum
sadism
salaam
schism
scream
scutum
seldom
sensum
septum
sexism
shalom
siglum
simoom
slalom
sodium
sputum
squirm
stream
Sufism
system
talcum
tamtam
tandem
Taoism
Targum
tedium
tergum
theism
tomtom
truism
tumtum
unseam
vacuum
vagrom
vallum
vellum
verism
victim
wampum
whilom
wigwam
wisdom
xenium
yogism
yumyum
zythum
action
acumen
adjoin
Aegean
Afghan
airgun
airman
aldrin
alevin
alexin
amazon
amnion
archon
arisen
ashbin
ashcan
ashpan
assign
astern
aswoon
ataman
attain
attorn
auburn
Augean
Austin
autumn
awaken
awoken
baboon
bagman
baleen
ballon
banian
banyan
barman
barren
barton
baryon
batman
batten
beacon
beaten
beckon
bedpan
beduin
bemoan
benign
berlin
bidden
biffin
biggin
billon
biotin
bitten
blazon
bobbin
bodkin
boffin
bonbon
boston
bowfin
bowman
brazen
brehon
Breton
Briton
broken
bumkin
bunion
bunsen
burden
Burman
burton
buskin
busman
button
cabman
cacoon
caftan
caiman
calkin
camion
cancan
cannon
canton
canyon
caplin
carbon
careen
carman
carton
carven
casein
casern
Caslon
cation
catkin
cavern
cayman
cedarn
Charon
chitin
chiton
chopin
chosen
citron
clipon
cloven
cochin
cocoon
codlin
coffin
column
comeon
common
conman
corban
cordon
cotton
coupon
cousin
cowman
craven
crayon
Cretan
cretin
croton
cummin
cyanin
daemon
daimen
daimon
dampen
damson
darken
deacon
deaden
deafen
deepen
dehorn
demean
design
desman
detain
diplon
disown
dobbin
dolman
dolmen
domain
donjon

Dorian
dragon
driven
dryrun
dubbin
dudeen
dunlin
durgan
durian
eleven
elevon
eloign
emetin
enjoin
ensign
eolian
eonian
Eozoon
essoin
etymon
examen
exogen
extern
Fabian
fadein
falcon
fallen
fanion
fantan
fasten
fathen
fatten
Fenian
fenman
fibrin
finnan
fiorin
firkin
firman
flacon
flagon
flamen
flavin
flaxen
florin
flyman
foeman
foison
Frauen
frozen
fusain
fusion
gabion
gagman
gallon
gammon
garcon
garden
garran
garron
Gascon
gaskin
gasman
german
germen
gibbon
gigman
gluten
glycin
gnomon
goblin
godown
godson
golden
gorgon
gossan
gotten
govern
gozzan
graben
gradin
gratin
graven
grison
guanin
guenon
guidon
gulden
gunman
gurjun
hadron
haemin
happen
harden
harken
hasten
hatpin
headon
heaven
hempen
henrun
herein
hereon
heroin
Herren
hetman
hidden
hitman
hodden
hodman
hoggin
holden
holpen
houdan
hoyden
hyphen
iceman
impawn
impugn
inborn
Indian
indign
inspan
intern
inulin
Ionian
isatin
jargon
jerkin
Jovian
Judean
Julian
kaftan
kaolin
kation
kelson
kelvin
kitten
Korean
kraken
kronen
kurgan
lagoon
lallan
lardon
lateen
latron
latten
lawman
layman
leaden
leadin
leaven
legion
legman
Lenten
lepton
lesion
lessen
lesson
Libyan
lichen
lignin
linden
lippen
listen
livein
lochan
logion
longan
lookin
loosen
lotion
louden
loupen
lovein
lucern
lumpen
lurdan
lutein
Lydian
machan
macron
madden
madman
Magian
maidan
maiden
malign
malkin
mammon
margin
marlin
maroon
marron
marten
martin
mascon
maslin
matron
median
melton
merlin
merlon
merman
messan
micron
midden
mignon
minion
Minoan
mitten
mizzen
modern
molten
moreen
morgen
morion
Mormon
motion
moulin
muffin
muflon
muntin
muslin
mutton
myelin
myosin
napkin
nation
natron
neaten
nekton
nelson
neuron
newton
niacin
noggin
Norman
notion
obtain
oddson
oilcan
oilman
olefin
oppugn
option
orcein
ordain
origan
origin
orison
orphan
ossein
outgun
outran
outrun
oxygen
papain
pardon
parian
parkin
parpen
parson
partan
Pathan
patron
patten
peahen
pecten
pectin
penman
pennon
pepsin
perron
person
phonon
photon
pidgin
pieman
pigeon
piggin
pinion
pipkin
pippin
piston
pitman
pitpan
platan
platen
pluton
poison
pollan
pollen
ponton
popgun
poplin
poteen
potion
potman
prison
proton
proven
pterin
ptisan
puffin
pullin
pullon
purlin
python
rabbin
racoon
radian
raglan
ragman
raisin
ramson
randan
ration
ratlin
ratoon
rattan
reason
reborn
reckon
recoin
redden
regain
region
rejoin
remain
renown
reopen
repugn
resign
retain
return
ribbon
richen
ridden
rodman
rollon
ronyon
rotten
Sabian
sadden
Salian
salmon
saloon
Samian
Samoan
sampan
Samson
sappan
sarsen
sateen
Saturn
scazon
screen
seafan
seaman
seapen
season
secern
seisin
seizin
sephen
sequin
serein
sermon
serran
sextan
sexton
shaken
shaman
shapen
shaven
shogun
shoran
shutin
sicken
silken
silvan
simian
simoon
Siouan
siphon
siskin
sixain
sixgun
skirun
skyman
slipon
slogan
sloven
sodden
soften
soldan
solemn
sovran
spavin
spleen
spoken
sprain
stamen
stepin
stolen
stolon
strain
strewn
strown
subman
suborn
sudden
sullen
sultan
summon
sunken
suntan
sweven
sylvan
syphon
Syrian
taipan
takein
talion
tampan
tampon
tannin
tarpan
tarpon
tartan
Tarzan
tauten
tavern
taxman
tegmen
telson
tendon
tenpin
tenson
tenzon
teston
Teuton
Theban
thoron
thrawn
thrown
tiepin
tiffin
tinman
titian
tocsin
topman
torten
toucan
trapan
trepan
trigon
triton
trogon
Trojan
tuchun
tuckin
turban
tureen
turion
Tuscan
tutsan
tycoon
tympan
Tyrian
Ugrian
unborn
uneven
unison
unjoin
unseen
unworn
uptown
upturn
urchin
ustion
vermin
violin
virgin
vision
vulcan
wabain
waggon
walkin
walkon
wanion
wanton
warden
warren
weaken
weapon
weazen
welkin
whiten
wigeon
Wilton
within
wivern
wonton
wooden
worsen
wyvern
yaupon
yeoman
yesman
zircon
adagio
aikido
akimbo
albedo
albino
anatto
arioso
arroyo
bagnio
bamboo
barrio
Basuto
billyo
bistro
blotto
bolero
bonito
booboo
boohoo
bronco
bumalo
burgoo
calico
casino
catalo
chromo
cogito
colugo
comedo
corozo
crambo
crypto
cuckoo
daimio
domino
dorado
drongo
duello
dynamo
embryo
enhalo
eryngo
escudo
Eskimo
fiasco
forego
fresco
fugato
gabbro
galago
Gallio
gaucho
gazebo
gentoo
ghetto
gigolo
gingko
ginkgo
gorgio
gringo
grotto
hairdo
halloo
hereto
hetero
Hindoo
hoodoo
indigo
kakapo
karroo
kimono
koodoo
ladino
lanugo
lavabo
leanto
legato
libido
macaco
maduro
makedo
manito
matico
medico
merino
mikado
modulo
morpho
nardoo
niello
nonego
nuncio
nympho
octavo
overdo
palolo
paramo
Pashto
pedalo
pomelo
poncho
potato
presto
pronto
pseudo
psycho
pueblo
quarto
rabato
rancho
rebato
reecho
regulo
righto
robalo
rococo
rubato
schizo
Shinto
sissoo
smalto
solano
sorgho
speedo
stereo
stingo
stinko
stopgo
stucco
studio
tattoo
tenuto
teredo
Toledo
tomato
torero
troppo
tupelo
tuxedo
ultimo
vaudoo
vibrio
virago
voodoo
weirdo
whatso
whomso
yoohoo
zeloso
zufolo
asleep
backup
bangup
bishop
blowup
bopeep
bunyip
burlap
burnup
bustup
callup
catnap
catnip
catsup
coinop
collop
decamp
dewlap
dollop
dustup
eggcup
encamp
entrap
enwrap
escarp
Ethiop
eyecup
fillip
foulup
gallop
gazump
giddap
gollop
gossip
hangup
hardup
hiccup
holdup
hookup
hubcap
hyssop
icecap
inclip
instep
inwrap
kidnap
laceup
larrup
lashup
leadup
liftup
lineup
linkup
lockup
lollop
madcap
magilp
makeup
markup
mayhap
megilp
mishap
mobcap
mockup
noshup
outtop
paidup
pegtop
pentup
pickup
pileup
pullup
pushup
recoup
redcap
redtop
reship
revamp
riprap
saloop
sannup
satrap
schlep
scrimp
scroop
scrump
sendup
shrimp
slapup
slipup
stepup
teacup
threap
tiptop
tittup
toecap
tossup
turnip
turnup
unship
unstop
unwrap
upkeep
wallop
warmup
windup
abater
abuser
acinar
adorer
aether
affair
affeer
alegar
ambler
amuser
anchor
angler
answer
anther
antiar
antler
appear
arbour
archer
ardour
arguer

armour bummer costar durbar ganger hooker larker mincer pitter reiver
ashlar bumper coster duster gaoler hooper lascar minder placer render
author bunder cottar duyker garner hooter lasher minter planar renter
avatar bunker cotter earner garter hopper laster mirror planer repair
backer bunter cougar easter gasper horner lather mister plater rester
badger burger crater echoer gasser horror latter moaner player rhetor
bailer burler craver eclair gather hosier laveer mocker plexor rhymer
bailor burner culler editor gauger hotter lawyer mohair plover ricker
baiter bursar culver eggler geezer howler leader moider polder rifler
balker busbar cumber either gender hummer leaper moiler poller rigger
banger busker cummer elater getter humour leaver monger ponder rigour
banker buster cunner elixir geyser hunger lecher mopper poplar ringer
banner butler curler eloper giaour hunker lector mortar popper rinser
banter butter cursor endear gibber hunter ledger mother porker rioter
barber buzzer cutler envier gilder hurler lender mouser porter ripper
barker cadger cutter epimer gimmer hurter lesser mucker poseur risker
barter cahier cycler eraser ginger husker lessor mugger poster rizzar
basher calcar cypher eschar ginner hussar letter muller pother rizzer
baster calker dabber etcher girder huzoor libber mummer potter roamer
bather caller dagger etrier glazer impair lictor mumper pourer roarer
batter camber dammar evader glider indoor lieder murder pouter robber
bawler camper damper evener glover inlier lifter murmur powder rocker
bazaar cancer dancer fabler glower instar ligger muster prater roller
beaker canker dander factor gnawer ironer limber mutter prayer romper
beamer canner danger falter goffer isobar limner nagger prefer roofer
bearer canter dapper fanner golfer isomer limper nailer prewar roomer
beater cantor darner faquir goober jabber linear natter primer rooter
beaver captor darter farmer gooier jaeger linger nearer prizer roster
bedder carder dasher faster gopher jagger liquor nectar prober rotter
beeper career dauber father grader jaguar lisper Nestor proper rouser
beggar carper dealer fatter grater jailer lister nether proser router
bender carter debtor favour graver jailor litter neuter pruner rozzer
Berber carver decker fawner grazer jammer loader nicker pucker rubber
bestir caster defier feeder griper jasper loafer nigger puffer rudder
better castor deicer feeler grocer jeerer loaner nipper puller rugger
bettor Cathar delver feller groper jerker locker number pulper ruiner
bezoar causer denier fencer grower jester lodger nurser pulsar rummer
bibber caviar deodar fender guider jibber lofter nutter pulser rumour
bicker cellar detour fester guiser jigger logger obeyer pumper runner
bidder censer devoir fetter guitar jilter loiter ocular punner rusher
bigger censor devour fibber gunner jitter loller oliver punter sadder
bilker cesser dexter filler gunter jobber looker onager purger saeter
binder chafer diaper filter gusher jogger looper opener purler saggar
birler chaser dibber finder gutter joiner looter orator purser sagger
bister chimer dicker finger guvnor jolter lopper ostler pusher sailer
bitter choker dieter finner hailer josher louver ouster putter sailor
blazer choler differ fisher halter josser lubber ovular Quaker salter
blower chukar digger fitter hammer jotter lugger oyster quasar salver
boater cinder dimmer flexor hamper judder lumbar packer quaver salvor
bodger cipher dinner flower hangar judger lumber pallor queuer sambar
boiler cither dipper fluter hanger jumper lumper palmar quiver sambur
bolter claver disbar fodder hanker junior lunger palmer racker sander
bomber clever diseur folder harper junker lurker palter rafter sangar
bonder clover dither foliar hatter Kaffir madder pamper raider santir
bonzer cobber docker fooler hauler kaiser Magyar pander railer sapper
booker cocker doctor footer hawker keeper mammer panzer raiser saucer
boomer codger dodder forcer hawser kelter manger passer rammer sauger
boozer coffer dodger forger header kicker manner pastor ramper savour
bopper coheir dogear former healer kidder mapper patter ranger sawder
border coiner dogger fossor hearer killer marker pauper ranker sawyer
bother collar dollar foster heater kilter martyr pavior ranter scalar
bovver colour dolour fother heaver kipper masher pawner rapier scaler
bowler colter Dopper fowler hector kisser masker pecker rapper scarer
bowyer comber dormer framer hedger knower master pedlar raptor scorer
boxcar concur dorter frater heeler kosher matter peeler rasher scoter
bracer condor dosser fuhrer heifer kroner medlar peeper rasper scryer
brayer confer douser fuller heller kronor member pelter raster seaair
brewer conger downer fulmar helper kronur memoir pepper rather seaear
briber conker dowser furfur herder kultur mender pester ratter sealer
briner conner draper fusser higher laager menhir petter reader seamer
broker cooker drawer gabber hinder labour mentor pewter reamer seater
bucker cooler driver gadder hisser ladder mercer picker reaper sector
buffer cooper droger gaffer hither lagger merger piecer rearer seeder
bugler copier drover gagger hoaxer lamber meteor pilfer reaver seeker
bulbar copper ducker gainer hocker lancer metier pillar rector seiner
Bulgar corder duffer gaiter holder lander midair pincer redder seizer
bulger corker duiker gambir holler langur milker pinger reefer seller
bulker corner dumper gammer honour lanner miller pinner reeler sender
buller cosher Dunker gander hoofer larder milter pitier rehear senhor

senior suitor twiner yammer cheers glacis odious shucks vivers basnet
sensor summer ulster yapper chiaus gneiss ogress slacks vulgus basset
server sunder undoer yatter chives gnosis oodles smalls waders becket
setter supper unfair yelper chorus gooses optics solids walrus bedsit
shader surfer unhair yester circus gradus orchis sortes waters begirt
shaker sutler uniter yonder cirrus gramps orexis sowans whenas behest
shaper swayer unmoor yorker cistus gratis otitis sowens whiles bennet
sharer swiper upbear zaffer citrus Graves oxalis sparks whites bereft
shaver tabour uproar zander civics greens palais speiss whoops bezant
shikar tacker ureter zephyr clavis groats palpus splits wolves billet
shiner tailor usurer zipper clevis grumps pampas sports xystus bisect
shiver talker uvular zither clonus haggis papers stairs yoicks blight
shofar tamper valour abacus coccus haloes pappus stakes zlotys bobcat
shover tanker valuer abatis coitus halves parous stapes zounds boblet
shower tanner vamper abbess coleus harass parvis stases abduct bonist
sicker tapper vanner acarus commis havers pathos stasis abject bonnet
sifter tartar vapour access comous henrys patois states ablaut bosket
sigher taster vector acinus conics herpes pelves status abrupt bought
signer tatter velour across corpus hiatus pelvis stipes absent breast
signor teaser vender adieus corves hoicks pharos stirps accent brevet
siller tedder vendor admass Corvus hooves phasis stocks accept bright
silver teemer veneer Adonis cosmos hubris pileus stokes accost brunet
simmer teeter venter afters crases hybris pilous stores acquit bucket
simper teller verger airbus crasis iambus Pisces strass addict budget
singer temper verser always creeps ibexes pithos strays adduct buffet
sinker tender vesper amends cripes ibices plexus stress adjust buglet
sinner tenner viator anabas crises inches pliers stylus adrift bullet
sinter tenour victor ananas crisis inlaws points sulcus adroit burbot
sipper tensor viewer animus crocus irides porous sweets advent burnet
sircar tenter vigour annals cruces iritis praxis swipes advert bypast
sirdar termer vizier apexes cruxes Jewess precis tarras affect cachet
sirkar termor voider apices cullis joyous preses tarsus afloat cadent
sister terror voyeur assess cultus kaross primus Taurus afreet cahoot
sittar tester vulgar aurous cursus kermes ptosis taxies aghast callet
sitter tether wafter awmous cuscus kermis quoits tennis albeit camlet
skater tetter wailer banjos dagoes knives quotes tenues albert cannot
skewer thaler waiter basics debris kumiss rabies tenuis alight carnet
skiver thenar waiver bassos dedans laches rachis thanks allout carpet
slater ticker walker bathos degras Lammas radius theirs almost carrot
slaver tiebar waller beeves denims lapsus ramous theses amidst casket
slayer tiller wander biceps dermis lassos raphis thesis amount catgut
slicer tilter wapper bilbos derris leaves rapids things amulet caught
slider timber warder blazes didoes lights recess tholos anicut caveat
sliver tinder warmer bongos dieses limbus rectus tholus anklet cavort
smiler tinker warper Boreas diesis litmus regius thrips anoint cement
smiter tinner washer bounds dingus loaves remiss throes aorist cermet
smoker tinter waster bowels dipsas lyrics repass thymus ardent chalet
snarer tipper weaner braces discus madras revers tights argent chaunt
sniper titfer wearer brains dittos Majlis rhesus timous aright chevet
snorer tither weaver breeks divers mangos riches tmeses armlet Christ
soaker titter weeder brewis dodoes mantes rictus tmesis armpit claret
soccer tocher weeper briefs dowlas mantis rimous tophus aroint client
soever toiler weever brutus duress maquis royals Tories arpent closet
solder tooter welder bursas egress matins ruckus traces arrant cobalt
solver topper weldor bypass embers meatus rufous tracks arrest cobnut
sooner torpor welter byssus emboss medius rumpus tragus artist cogent
sorner tosher wester cactus emeses menses rushes trapes ascent cohort
sorter tosser wether caddis emesis merils sables tripos askant collet
souter tother wetter calces enosis Messrs saltus trumps aslant combat
spacer totter whaler callus ethics metals salvos turves aspect comfit
sparer tourer whiner calves excess miosis sanies tweeds assent commit
spewer touter wicker calxes exodus missis scales typhus assert comsat
spider tracer wiener camass exomis missus scarus umbles assist copout
spryer trader wilder campus facies modius schuss umbras assort coquet
stager tremor winder cantus famous moneys scopas undies attest cornet
starer tricar winger canvas fasces monies selves ungues august corset
stater trimer winker capias fauces morals senses unguis auklet cosset
stator trocar winner caress faunas morass sepsis unless aurist covert
stayer trover winter caries fezzes morbus series uraeus avaunt cowpat
stelar tubber wisher carpus finals morris serous Uranus avocet cravat
stiver tucker wither cassis flatus mucous sevens uterus Babist credit
stoker tufter wizier caucus floras myosis Sevres valgus ballet cruset
stoner tulwar wonder caulis foetus mythos shades venous ballot cubist
stover tumour woofer census fracas naevus shamus versus bandit cueist
stumer turgor worker cercus fundus nimbus sharps viands banket cullet
stupor turner wormer cereus fungus noesis shears villus barbet curvet
stylar tusker wowser certes geckos nonius sheass vinous barret cushat
sucker tusser writer cestus genius obelus sheets viscus basalt cutlet
suffer twicer yabber charas gentes obsess shorts vitals basket cutout

cygnet farout indict motett prompt semmit tippet congou seesaw aphony
dacoit faucet induct motmot prosit sennet titbit gateau shadow apiary
decant ferret indult mullet pullet sennit toilet grugru sorrow Arcady
deceit fidget infant muscat pulpit septet tomcat haleru sunbow archly
decent filfot infect musket pundit sestet tomtit jabiru sundew argosy
decoct fillet infelt mutant punnet setout Tophet landau tallow argufy
deduct firlot infest natant puppet sexist toupet Manchu wallow arrowy
defeat flaunt ingest naught purist sexpot tricot milieu willow artery
defect flight inject neednt quaint sextet trivet muumuu window aseity
degust floret inkpot nidget rabbet shiest truant ormolu winnow astray
deject fluent inmost nitwit rabbit shrift tryout Pushtu yarrow augury
delict foment insect nobbut racist shyest Tshirt reseau yellow aumbry
dement forest insert nocent racket signet tucket roucou adieux aviary
demist forget insist nonfat ragout silent tuffet saddhu afflux avidly
depart forgot insult nougat Rajput sinnet tumult teledu banjax aweary
depict forint intact nought ramjet sippet turbit Telugu bijoux babbly
deport format intent nudist rapist slight turbot Vishnu bollix bailey
desalt forrit intuit nugget rattat slyest turret moshav carfax bakery
desert fought invent nutant recant sobeit twilit anyhow caudex baldly
desist freest invert object recast socket typist barrow cervix barely
despot fright invest oblast recent soffit tyrant bashaw climax barfly
detect frowst irrupt oboist redact sonant umlaut bellow coccyx barley
detent fylfot jacket obtect redhot sonnet unbent bestow commix barney
detest gablet jennet obtest reedit sorbet unbitt billow convex barony
devest gadget Jesuit obvert refect sought unbolt borrow cortex basely
devout gainst joblot occult regent soviet ungirt bowsaw cowpox bawdry
dicast galiot junket ocelot reglet spigot unjust bowwow diplex bawley
digest galoot jurist octant regret spinet unknit burrow dogfox beachy
diglot gambit kainit oecist reheat spirit unknot byblow duplex beauty
diktat gannet kaputt offent reject splent unmeet byelaw earwax belfry
dimwit garget kismet offset relent splint unrest callow efflux betony
dipnet garnet kitcat oilnut relict spoilt unroot cashew fornix betray
direct garret klepht omelet reluct sprent unseat curfew frutex bewray
divert garrot knight oncost remint sprint unwept curlew hallux bieldy
divest gasket labret optant rennet sprout upbeat erenow hatbox bigamy
docent gerent lament orgeat repast spruit upcast eschew haybox binary
docket getout lancet orient repeat squint uplift escrow icebox biopsy
domett gibbet lappet outact repent squirt upmost fallow imbrex bitchy
dopant giglet lariat outfit report strait uproot farrow influx blanky
dought giglot latent outlet reseat street upshot fellow larynx bleary
dreamt gimlet latest output resect strict urgent fogbow lummox blenny
dryrot gobbet lavolt outsat resent strout utmost follow matrix blimey
dugout goblet layout outset resist strunt vacant furrow meninx bloody
dulcet gocart learnt outsit resort Stuart varlet gewgaw muskox bloomy
duplet godwit legist outwit result stylet Vedist goslow outfox blowsy
dynast goglet levant packet retest sublet velvet guffaw pollex blowzy
eaglet gokart limpet pallet retort submit verist hallow prefix blurry
effect gorget linnet pandit revert subset verset harrow premix bodily
effort grivet locket papist revest summit vervet hawhaw pretax boldly
egoist gullet locust parent revolt sunhat vibist haymow prolix bolshy
eldest gurnet loggat parget rident sunlit violet Hebrew reflex booksy
elicit gusset loment parrot rigout sunset volant heehaw reflux bosomy
eluant haffet loquat patent rillet tablet volost hollow scolex botany
eluent haffit loriot peanut robust tacket vorant inflow seafox botchy
encyst hagbut loupit pedant rochet talbot wallet jigsaw smilax botfly
engirt hamlet lucent peewit rocket talent walnut kowtow spadix bouncy
englut harlot lyrist pellet rodent tanist waught mallow sphinx bounty
enlist haslet maggot pelmet roquet Taoist wayout marrow storax bowery
enrapt height magnet penult rotgut tappet weight matlow styrax brainy
enroot helmet mahout permit runlet tappit whilst meadow suffix brandy
errant hepcat mallet picket russet target whisht mellow surtax brassy
escort hereat Maoist piglet sabbat taught wicket mildew syntax brawly
esprit heriot Marist pignut sachet teapot widget minnow syrinx brawny
except hermit market piolet sadist teaset willet moocow thorax breezy
exempt hexact marmot piquet saidst tenant wisent morrow unisex briary
exeunt hobbit mascot placet sallet tercet withit narrow vertex bricky
exhort hogget mayest plaint samlet terret wombat nephew volvox briery
expect honest merest planet savant territ worrit outlaw vortex briony
expert hornet midget pliant sawpit theist wright pawpaw abbacy brolly
export hotpot midgut plight sawset thirst yaourt pillow acidly bronzy
exsect humect millet pocket sayest threat yclept pitsaw acuity broody
exsert impact minuet poppet schist thrift yogurt powwow aerily browny
extant impart misfit posset script throat zealot redraw affray brumby
extent import mishit potent sculpt thrust acajou reflow agency brushy
extort impost modest preset seamat thwart amadou review airily bryony
eyalet incept molest priest secant ticket Basutu ripsaw airway bubbly
eyelet incest moment privet secret tidbit bateau sallow angary bulimy
faggot incult monist probit sejant tinpot bureau seacow anyway bunchy
fanjet indent moppet profit select tipcat cachou seamew apathy burbly

busboy
busily
byplay
cagily
calmly
calory
canary
canopy
carboy
carney
catchy
causey
cavity
cecity
celery
chaffy
chalky
chancy
chanty
chappy
chatty
cheeky
cheery
cheesy
cherry
cherty
chesty
chilly
chippy
chirpy
chitty
chivvy
chokey
choosy
choppy
chubby
chuffy
chummy
chunky
cicely
claggy
clammy
classy
clayey
clergy
cliffy
clingy
cliquy
cloddy
cloggy
cloudy
clumpy
clumsy
codify
coldly
colony
comedy
comely
comity
comply
conchy
convey
convoy
coolly
coonty
corody
cosily
costly
county
cowboy
crabby
crafty
craggy
cranky
cranny
crappy
crawly
creaky
creamy

creepy
crikey
crimpy
crispy
croaky
croppy
croupy
cruddy
crumby
crummy
crusty
cuddly
curacy
curtly
curtsy
cutely
daftly
dainty
damply
dankly
darkey
darkly
datary
dayfly
deadly
deafly
dearly
deejay
deeply
defray
deftly
denary
deploy
deputy
descry
dewily
dickey
digamy
dimity
dimply
dingey
dinghy
dipody
direly
dismay
donkey
doubly
doughy
dourly
doyley
dozily
drably
drafty
draggy
dreamy
dreary
dreggy
dressy
drifty
drippy
drolly
droopy
dropsy
drosky
drossy
drowsy
dryfly
dually
dukery
dumbly
dupery
earthy
easily
eatery
edgily
eerily
effigy
eighty
embody

emboly
empery
employ
energy
enmity
entity
equity
estray
eulogy
eutaxy
evenly
evilly
exequy
expiry
extasy
fainly
fairly
fakery
family
faulty
fealty
featly
feckly
feebly
feisty
felony
fiddly
filthy
finely
finery
firmly
fixity
flabby
flaggy
flappy
flashy
flatly
fleecy
fleshy
fleury
flimsy
flinty
flirty
floaty
floozy
floppy
flossy
floury
fluffy
flukey
flunky
flurry
flyway
folksy
fondly
forsay
foully
freaky
freely
frenzy
friary
Friday
frilly
fringy
frisky
frizzy
froggy
frosty
frothy
frowsy
frowzy
fruity
frumpy
gadfly
gaiety
gainly
galaxy
galley
gamely

gamily
gangly
gantry
gasify
gently
gentry
gharry
ghosty
giggly
gladly
glairy
glassy
gleamy
gleety
glibly
gloomy
glossy
glumly
glumpy
gnarly
goggly
goodly
googly
gooney
goramy
gorily
gowany
grabby
grainy
Grammy
granny
grassy
greasy
greedy
greeny
greyly
grimly
grippy
grisly
gritty
groggy
groovy
grotty
growly
grubby
grumly
grumpy
guilty
gulley
gunshy
hackly
hardly
hazily
hearty
heathy
hereby
heresy
heyday
hickey
highly
hockey
holily
homely
homily
hominy
hookey
hooray
horary
horsey
hourly
housey
hugely
humbly
humify
hungry
hurley
hurray
idiocy
infamy

injury
intray
jalopy
jarvey
jaunty
jersey
jiggly
jingly
jitney
jockey
johnny
jouncy
jumbly
jungly
justly
keenly
kersey
keyway
kidney
kindly
kingly
knaggy
knobby
knotty
lackey
ladify
ladyfy
lamely
lankly
lastly
lately
laxity
layday
lazily
lealty
leanly
leeway
legacy
lemony
lenity
levity
lewdly
likely
limply
linhay
linney
linsey
litany
lively
livery
lonely
lordly
loudly
lovely
lowboy
lowery
lowkey
lunacy
lushly
luxury
maguey
mainly
malady
manday
marbly
margay
marshy
maundy
mayday
mayfly
mazily
meanly
measly
medley
meekly
meetly
melody
memory
merely

mickey
midday
midway
mighty
milady
mildly
minify
misery
mislay
mizzly
modify
moiety
Monday
monkey
monody
mornay
mostly
motley
motory
mouldy
mouthy
mulley
murphy
murrey
mutely
mutiny
namely
Nazify
nearby
nearly
neatly
nebuly
nicely
nicety
nidify
nighty
nimbly
ninety
nobody
nonary
nosily
notary
notify
nubbly
nudely
nudity
numbly
occamy
occupy
oddity
offkey
oneway
oogamy
oogeny
oology
openly
orally
orfray
ornery
orrery
osprey
ossify
outcry
outlay
ovally
overly
pacify
paeony
palely
paltry
panary
pantry
papacy
papery
parity
parlay
parley
parody
partly

pastry
patchy
payday
peachy
pearly
peavey
pebbly
peltry
penury
pertly
phoney
phooey
pigsty
pimply
pinery
piracy
pitchy
plaguy
plashy
plebby
plenty
ploidy
plotty
plucky
plummy
plumpy
plushy
poetry
policy
polity
polony
poorly
popery
popply
portly
potboy
pouchy
prepay
pretty
pricey
primly
priory
prissy
puddly
pulley
punchy
punily
purely
purify
purity
purply
purvey
quaggy
qualmy
quarry
queasy
queazy
quinsy
quirky
racily
raguly
ramify
rankly
raptly
rarefy
rarely
rarity
rashly
ratify
really
realty
remedy
replay
revery
rheumy
richly
rickey
rifely
ripely

ripply
Romany
ropery
rosary
rosery
rosily
rosiny
rotary
rouncy
rubbly
rubefy
rubify
rudely
rumbly
runway
safely
safety
sagely
salary
salify
sanely
sanify
sanity
sashay
satiny
savory
sawfly
sawney
saxony
scabby
scanty
scarry
scatty
screwy
scummy
scurfy
scurry
scurvy
seaway
seemly
senary
sentry
severy
sexily
shabby
shaggy
shammy
shandy
shanny
shanty
sheeny
shelly
shelty
sherry
shifty
shimmy
shindy
shinny
shinty
shirty
shoaly
shoddy
shoppy
shorty
sickly
simony
simply
sinewy
singly
skeely
skerry
skiddy
skilly
skimpy
skinny
skivvy
skyway
slaggy
slangy

slavey
sleazy
sleepy
sleety
slimly
slinky
slippy
sloppy
sloshy
slowly
sludgy
sluicy
slummy
slurry
slushy
smarmy
smarty
smeary
smelly
smirky
smithy
smoggy
smudgy
smugly
smutty
snaggy
snappy
snarly
snazzy
sneaky
sneezy
sniffy
snippy
snobby
snoopy
snooty
snotty
snouty
snubby
snuffy
snugly
sodomy
softly
solely
sorely
sourly
sparry
speedy
sphery
spiffy
spoffy
spongy
spooky
spoony
sporty
spotty
spryly
spunky
spurry
stably
stagey
stalky
starry
steady
steamy
steely
sticky
stilly
stingy
stithy
stocky
stodgy
storey
stormy
strawy
stripy
stubby
stuffy
stumpy

sturdy
subtly
subway
sudary
sugary
sultry
Sunday
sundry
sunray
supply
surely
surety
surrey
survey
swaddy
swampy
swanky
sweaty
sweeny
swimmy
swirly
swishy
syrupy
syzygy
talcky
tamely
tangly
tartly
tautly
tawdry
tawery
teapoy
teensy
tepefy
termly
tetany
tetchy
theory
thingy
thinly
thirty
thorny
tickey
tickly
tiddly
tidily
timely
tingly
tinily
tinkly
tomboy
toothy
tootsy
touchy
towery
trappy
trashy
treaty
trebly
trendy
tressy
tricky
trilby
trimly
triply
trolly
trophy
trouty
trusty
tumefy
turkey
twangy
tweedy
tweeny
twenty
twiggy
twirly
twisty
twoply

two-way typify ubiety uglify uglily unduly uneasy unholy unruly
untidy unwary uppity vagary vainly valley vanity vastly vaulty
venery verify verily verity vestry vilely vilify vinery vintry
vivify volley votary wafery waggly wambly warcry warily warmly
watery wavery wavily waxily waylay weakly weekly weirdy whacky
wheezy wherry wheyey whimsy whinny whippy whirly whisky whitey
wholly widely wieldy wifely wiggly wildly wilily wincey winery
winsey wintry wirily wisely wobbly woodsy woolly worthy woundy
wrathy yarely yearly yeasty zanily zincky zonary blintz chintz
ersatz kibitz krantz quartz

7 letter words

abaddon abalone abandon abashed abattis abaxial Abbasid abdomen Abelian abetted abetter abettor abeyant abiding abigail ability abiotic abjurer ablator abolish abomasa aborter abought aboulia abrader abreact abreast abridge abroach abscess abscise abscond absence absinth absolve abstain abubble abusive abutted abutter abysmal abyssal academe academy Acadian acantha acarian accidie acclaim account accrete accrual accurst accusal accused accuser acequia acerbic acerola acerose acetate acetify acetone acetous Achaean

Achaian Achates achieve acicula acidify acidity acinous ackemma acolyte aconite acouchy acquest acquire acrasin acreage acridly acrobat acrogen acronym acroter acrylic actinia actinic actinon actress actuary actuate acutely acyclic adamant Adamite adapter adaptor adaxial addable addenda addible address adducer adenine adenoid adenoma adeptly adherer adhibit adipose adjoint adjourn adjudge adjunct admiral admirer adnexal adopter adrenal adulate adultly advance adverse advised adviser advisor aeolian aeonian aerator

aerobic aerosol afeared affable affably affaire affined afflict affront African against agamous ageless agelong aggress agilely agility agitate agitato agnatic agnomen agonise agonist agraffe agrapha aground aiblins aileron ailment aimless aircrew airdrop airfare airflow airglow airhole airless airlift airline airlock airmail airmiss airport airpost airship airsick airwave ajutage akvavit alameda alanine alation albumen albumin alcaide alcalde alcayde alcazar alchemy alcohol Alcoran alembic alertly aleuron alewife

alfalfa alforja algebra alginic alidade alienly aliform aliment alimony aliquot alkalis alkanet Alkoran alleged allegro allelic allergy allheal allonge allover allseed allstar alltime alluvia almanac almirah almoner almonry almsman alodial alodium aloetic aloofly alphorn already alright alsoran althaea althorn alumina alumnae alumnus alunite alveoli alyssum amalgam amanita amarant amateur amative amatory amazing ambages ambatch ambient amboina ambones amboyna ambsace amender amenity amentia amentum Amerind Amharic

amiable amiably amildar ammeter ammonal ammonia amnesia amnesic amnesty amoebae amoebas amoebic amongst amorist amorous amphora amplify ampoule ampulla amputee amtrack amusive amylase amyloid amylose anaemia anaemic anagoge anagogy anagram analogy analyse analyst Ananias anarchy anatase anatomy anchovy anchusa ancient ancones ancress andante andiron android anemone aneroid aneurin angelic angelus Angevin anginal angioma Anglian anglice angling Anglist angrily anguine anguish angular aniline anility animate animism

animist anionic aniseed annates annatta annatto annelid annicut annuity annular annulet annulus anodise anodyne anoesis anoetic anomaly anosmia anosmic another antacid antbear antefix antenna anthill anthrax antigen antilog antique antlion antonym anurous anxiety anxious anybody anymore anyroad anytime anyways anywise apagoge apanage apatite apetaly aphasia aphasic aphelia apheses aphesis aphetic aphides aphonia aphonic aphotic aphylly apishly aplasia aplenty apocope apodous apogamy apogean apology apolune apostil

apostle apothem apparat apparel appease applaud applied applier appoint apprise approve apraxia apricot apropos apsidal apsides apteryx aptness aquaria aquatic aquavit aqueous aquifer aquiver Arabian arabise Arabist Aramaic araneid Arapaho arbiter arbutus arcaded arcadia arcanum archaic archery archive archway arctoid arcuate arcweld ardency arduous areally areaway areolae areolar areolas aridity arietta aristae aristas armband armfuls armhole armiger armless armlike armoire Armoric armoury armrest armsful arousal

arraign arrange arrayer arrears arrival arriver arsenal arsenic article artisan artiste artless artwork ascarid ascaris ascesis ascetic ascidia ascites ascitic ascribe asepsis aseptic asexual ashamed ashtray Asiatic asinine askance askesis asocial asperse asphalt aspirer aspirin asquint assagai assault assayer assegai assizes assuage assured assurer astable astatic asteria astound astride asunder ataraxy atavism atavist atelier atheism atheist athirst athlete athwart atingle atomise atomism atomist atresia atrophy

attaboy attache attaint attempt attract attrite auction audible audient auditor augment augural aurally aureate aurelia aureola aureole auricle aurochs aurorae auroral auroras auspice austere austral autarky autobus autocar autocue autopsy auxesis auxetic avarice avenger average averred Avestan Avestic aviator avidity avionic avocado awarder aweless awesome awfully awkward awnless axially axillae axillar axolotl Azilean azimuth azurine azurite azygous Baalism babassu babbitt babbler babyish babysit baccara baccate

bacchic
bacilli
backing
backlog
backsaw
backset
baddish
badmash
badness
baffler
bagasse
baggage
baggily
bagging
bagpipe
Bahadur
Bahaism
Bahaist
Bahaite
bailiff
baklava
balance
balcony
balding
baldish
baldric
baleful
ballade
ballast
ballboy
balloon
balmily
baloney
bambini
bambino
banally
bananas
bandage
bandana
bandbox
bandeau
bandore
bandsaw
baneful
banjoes
banking
banksia
banning
bannock
banquet
banshee
banteng
banting
baptise
baptism
baptist
barbate
barbell
barbule
bargain
barilla
barline
barmaid
baronet
baroque
barrack
barrage
barrier
barring
barroom
barytes
barytic
bascule
baseman
basenji
bashful
basidia
basilar
basinet
bassist
bassoon
bastard
basting
bastion
bateaux
bathing
bathtub
batiste
batsman
battels
battery
batting
Bauhaus
bauxite
bawcock
bawdily
bayonet
bazooka
beading
beamish
beanbag
bearded
bearing
bearish
beastly
beatify
beating
beatnik
because
becloud
bedding
bedevil
bedfast
bedight
bedizen
bedouin
bedpost
bedrock
bedroll
bedroom
bedside
bedsock
bedsore
bedtime
beechen
beehive
beeline
beeswax
beggary
begging
begonia
begorra
begrime
beguile
beguine
behaver
behoove
beignet
bejewel
beknown
belated
belcher
beldame
Belgian
believe
bellboy
bellhop
belljar
bellman
bellows
beloved
Beltane
belting
belying
bencher
beneath
benefic
benefit
Benelux
Bengali
benison
benthic
benthos
benzene
benzine
benzoic
benzoin
benzole
benzoyl
bepaint
bequest
bereave
bergylt
berhyme
berline
berried
berserk
beseech
beshrew
besides
besiege
besmear
bespeak
bespoke
bestead
bestial
bestrew
betaken
bethink
betimes
betoken
betroth
betting
between
betwixt
bewitch
bezique
bheesty
bheetie
Biafran
biassed
biaxial
bibbery
bibbing
bibcock
bibelot
biblist
bicycle
bidding
biennia
bifilar
bifocal
bigener
biggest
biggish
bighead
bighorn
bigname
bigness
bigoted
bigotry
bigtime
bilboes
biliary
bilimbi
bilious
billing
billion
billowy
bilobar
bilobed
biltong
bimanal
bindery
binding
biology
biomass
bionics
biotite
bipedal
biplane
bipolar
birchen
birddog
birdman
biretta
biriani
biscuit
bismuth
bistort
bistred
bittern
bitters
bitting
bittock
bitumen
bivalve
bivouac
bizarre
blabbed
blabber
blacken
blackly
bladder
blandly
blanket
blankly
blarney
blasted
blaster
blatant
blather
blatter
bleakly
bleater
bleeder
bleeper
blemish
blender
blesbok
blessed
blether
blewits
blighty
blinder
blindly
blinker
blintze
blister
blither
bloated
bloater
blocker
blooded
bloomer
blossom
blotchy
blotted
blotter
blouson
blowdry
blowfly
blowgun
blowout
blowzed
blubber
blucher
blueing
bluffer
bluffly
blunder
blunger
bluntly
blurred
blusher
bluster
boarder
boarish
boaster
boating
boatman
bobbery
bobbing
bobbish
bobeche
bobsled
bobstay
bobtail
bodeful
bogbean
boggler
bogyman
bohemia
boiling
boletus
bolivar
bollard
bologna
boloney
bolshie
bolster
bombard
bombast
bonanza
bondage
bondman
bonedry
boneset
bonfire
bongoes
bonkers
bonnily
boobook
bookend
bookful
booking
bookish
booklet
bookman
booksie
Boolean
boomlet
boorish
booster
bootleg
boozeup
boozily
bopping
boracic
borazon
bordure
boredom
borings
bornite
borough
borscht
borstal
bortsch
boscage
boskage
bossism
Boswell
botanic
botargo
botcher
bottega
bottled
bottony
botulin
bouchee
boudoir
bouilli
boulder
boulter
bouncer
bounden
bounder
bouquet
bourbon
bourdon
bourree
bowhead
bowlder
bowlful
bowline
bowling
bowshot
boxcalf
boxhaul
boxkite
boxlike
boxroom
boxseat
boxwood
boycott
boyhood
brabble
bracing
bracken
bracket
bradawl
bragged
bragger
Brahman
Brahmin
braille
bramble
brambly
branchy
brander
brannew
bransle
brantle
brantub
brashly
brassie
brattle
braunch
bravado
bravely
bravery
bravura
brawler
brazier
breaded
breadth
breaker
breakin
breakup
breathe
breathy
breccia
breeder
brevier
brevity
brewage
brewery
bribery
brickie
brickle
bricole
bridoon
briefly
brigade
brigand
brimful
brimmed
brimmer
brinded
brindle
bringer
brinjal
brioche
briquet
brisken
brisket
briskly
bristle
bristly
British
brittle
brittly
britzka
broaden
broadly
brocade
brocket
broider
broiler
brokage
broking
bromate
bromide
bromine
bromism
bronchi
broncho
brooder
brothel
brother
brought
brownie
browser
brucine
brucite
bruhaha
bruiser
brumous
brusher
brusque
brutish
bruxism
Brython
bubonic
buccina
buckeye
buckler
buckram
bucksaw
bucolic
budding
buffalo
buffoon
bugaboo
bugbane
bugbear
bugeyed
bugging
bugloss
builded
builder
buildup
builtin
builtup
buirdly
bulbous
bulimia
bulkily
bullace
bullary
bullate
bullbat
bulldog
bullion
bullish
bullock
bullpen
bulrush
bulwark
bumbler
bumboat
bummalo
bumming
bumpily
bumpkin
bungler
bunraku
bunting
buoyage
buoyant
burbler
burdock
bureaus
bureaux
burette
burgage
burgeon
burgess
burghal
burgher
burglar
Burmese
burning
burnish
burnous
bursary
burster
burthen
burweed
bushido
bushman
bushtit
busking
bussing
bustard
bustler
butcher
buttend
buttery
buttock
buttons
buttony
butyric
buyable
buzzard
buzzsaw
byebyes
bygones
Byronic
bywoner
cabaret
cabbage
cabbagy
cabbala
cabinet
cabling
caboose
cabrank
cacanny
cachexy
cacique
cackler
cacodyl
cacoepy
cacumen
cadaver
caddice
caddish
cadence
cadency
cadenza
Cadmean
cadmium
caducei
caesium
caesura
cagoule
cahoots
caimans
caisson
caitiff
cajoler
calamus
calando
calcify
calcine
calcite
calcium
calculi
caldera
caldron
calends
calibre
calices
caliche
calicle
calipee
caliper
callant
callbox
callboy
calling
callous
calomel
caloric
calorie
calotte
caloyer
calpack
caltrap
caltrop
calumet
calumny
calvary
calyces
calycle
calypso
calyxes
camaron
cambial
cambist
cambium
cambrel
cambric
camelot
camelry
cameral
camorra
campbed
camphor
camping
campion
camwood
canakin
canasta
candela
candent
candied
candour
canikin
cannery
cannily
canning
cannula
canonic
canonry
Canopic
cantata
cantate
canteen
canthus
cantina
canting
cantrip
canvass
canzone
canzoni
capable
capably
capelin
caperer

capital
capitol
caporal
capping
caprice
caprine
caproic
Capsian
capsize
capstan
capsule
captain
caption
captive
capture
capuche
caracal
caracul
caramel
caravan
caravel
caraway
carbide
carbine
carcase
carcass
cardiac
cardoon
careful
caribou
carinae
carinal
carinas
carioca
cariole
carious
carking
carline
Carlism
Carlist
carload
carmine
carnage
caroche
carotid
carotin
carouse
carping
carport
carrack
carrier
carrion
carroty
carryon
carsick
cartage
cartful
cartoon
carving
cascade
cascara
caseous
caserne
cashier
cassata
cassava
cassino
cassock
castile
casting
castled
castoff
casuals
casuist
Catalan
catalos
catalpa
catarrh
catawba
catbird
catboat
catcall
catcher
catchup
catechu
catenae
catenas
cateran
caterer
catfish
Cathari
Cathars
cathead
cathode
cathood
catlike
catling
catmint
catseye
catspaw
catsuit
cattalo
cattery
cattily
catwalk
caudate
caulker
caustic
cautery
caution
cavally
cavalry
caveman
cavetti
cavetto
caviare
cayenne
caymans
cedilla
ceilidh
ceiling
celadon
celesta
celeste
cellist
cellule
Celsius
cembalo
cenacle
censure
centaur
centavo
centime
centner
central
centred
centric
centrum
century
cepheid
ceramic
cerebra
ceresin
certain
certify
cerumen
cervine
cession
cesspit
cestode
cestoid
Chablis
chaffer
chagrin
chalaza
Chaldee
chalice
challis
chalone
chamber
chamfer
chamois
champac
champak
chancel
chancre
changer
channel
chanson
chanter
chantry
chaotic
chapati
chaplet
chapman
chapped
chappie
chapter
charade
charger
charily
chariot
charism
charity
charley
charlie
charmer
charnel
charpoy
charqui
charred
charter
chassis
chasten
chateau
chatted
chattel
chatter
cheapen
cheaply
cheater
checker
checkup
cheddar
cheerer
cheerio
cheetah
chelate
chemise
chemism
chemist
chequer
cherish
cheroot
chervil
chessel
chested
cheviot
chevron
Chianti
chiasma
chibouk
chicane
Chicano
chicken
chicory
chidden
chiefly
chiffon
chigger
chignon
childer
childly
chiliad
chillum
chimera
chimere
chimney
chindit
Chinese
Chinook
chintzy
chinwag
chipped
chipper
chirrup
chitter
chlamys
chloral
chloric
chocice
Choctaw
cholera
choline
chooser
choosey
chopine
chopped
chopper
chorale
chordal
chorine
chorion
choroid
chortle
chowder
chrisom
christy
chromic
chronic
chuckle
chuddah
chuddar
chuffed
chugged
chukker
chummed
chunnel
chunter
chupati
churchy
chutney
chymous
ciboria
cichlid
cidaris
ciliary
ciliate
cimices
cindery
cineast
cineole
cingula
cipolin
Circean
circler
circlet
circuit
circusy
cirrose
cirrous
cistern
citable
citadel
cithara
cithern
citizen
citrate
citrine
cittern
civilly
civvies
clabber
clacker
cladode
claimer
clamant
clamber
clammed
clamour
clanger
clapped
clapper
clarify
clarion
clarity
clarkia
classes
classic
classis
clastic
clatter
clausal
clavate
clavier
claypan
cleaner
cleanly
cleanse
cleanup
clearly
cleaver
clement
clerisy
clerkly
clicker
climate
climber
clinker
clipped
clipper
clippie
cliquey
clivers
cloacae
cloacal
clobber
clocker
clogged
clogger
closely
closeup
closure
clothes
clotted
cloture
clubbed
clubman
clumber
Cluniac
clupeid
cluster
clutter
clypeal
clypeus
clyster
coacher
coagula
coaltit
coaming
coarsen
coastal
coaster
coating
coaxial
cobbler
cocaine
coccoid
cochlea
cockade
cockeye
cockily
cockney
cockpit
cockshy
coconut
cocotte
codable
coddler
codeine
codfish
codices
codicil
codling
coeliac
coequal
coexist
coffers
cogency
cogging
cognate
cognise
cohabit
coherer
coinage
coinbox
coition
coldish
coletit
colicky
colitis
collage
collard
collate
collect
colleen
college
collide
collier
collins
colloid
collude
colobus
cologne
colonel
colonic
colossi
colours
coloury
coltish
combine
combout
combust
comedic
cometic
comfort
comfrey
comical
comitia
command
commend
comment
commode
commons
commove
commune
commute
compact
company
compare
compart
compass
compeer
compend
compere
compete
compile
complex
complin
complot
compony
comport
compose
compost
compote
compute
comrade
Comtian
Comtism
Comtist
conacre
conatus
concave
conceal
concede
conceit
concent
concept
concern
concert
conchae
conchie
concise
concoct
concord
concuss
condemn
condign
condole
condone
conduce
conduct
conduit
condyle
confect
confess
confide
confine
confirm
conflux
conform
confuse
confute
congeal
congest
conical
conidia
conifer
coniine
conjoin
conjure
conkers
connate
connect
conning
connive
connote
conquer
consent
consign
consist
console
consort
consult
consume
contact
contain
contemn
contend
content
contest
context
contort
contour
control
contuse
convect
convene
convent
convert
convict
convoke
cookery
cooking
cookout
coolant
coolish
cooncan
coontie
copaiba
copaiva
copepod
copilot
copious
coppery
coppice
copular
copycat
copyist
coquito
coracle
coranto
corbeil
cordage
cordate
cordial
cordite
cordoba
corella
corkage
corking
cornage
corncob
corneal
cornett
cornfed
cornice
cornily
Cornish
cornist
cornual
cornuto
corolla
coronae
coronal
coronas
coroner
coronet
corpora
correct
corrida
corrode
corrody
corrupt
corsage
corsair
corslet
cortege
cortile
corvina
corvine
corydon
cosmism
cosmist
cossack
costard
costate
costean
costing
costive
costrel
costume
coterie
cotidal
cottage
cottier
cottony
Coueism
couldst
couloir
coulomb
coulter
council
counsel
counter
country
coupler
couplet
courage
courier
courlan
courser
courtly
couthie
couture
couvade
couvert
coverup
cowbane
cowbell
cowbird
cowfish
cowhage
cowhand
cowheel
cowherd
cowhide
cowlick
cowling
cowpoke
cowshed
cowslip
coxcomb
coyness
cozener
crabbed
cracked
cracker
crackle
crackly
crackup
cragged
crammed
crammer
crampet
crampit
crampon
cranage
cranial
cranium
crankle
crannog
crappie
crassly
craunch
craving
crawler
crazily
creamer
creator
credent
creedal
creeper
cremate
cremona
crenate
cresset
crested
crevice
cribbed
cribble
cricket
cricoid
crimine
crimper
crimple
crimson
cringer
cringle
crinite
crinkle

crinkly
crinoid
criollo
cripple
crisper
crisply
cristae
critter
croaker
crochet
crocket
Croesus
crofter
crooked
crooner
cropped
cropper
croquet
croquis
crosier
crossly
crouton
crowbar
crowdie
crowned
crowner
crownet
crowtoe
crozier
crucial
crucian
crucify
crudely
crudity
cruelly
cruelty
cruiser
cruller
crumble
crumbly
crumpet
crumple
crunchy
crupper
crusade
crusado
crusher
crustal
crusted
crybaby
cryogen
cryptal
cryptic
crystal
csardas
ctenoid
cubbing
cubhood
cubical
cubicle
cubital
cuckold
cudbear
cudweed
cuirass
cuisine
cuittle
culices
cullion
culotte
culprit
cultism
cultist
culture
culvert
cumquat
cumshaw
cumulus
cuneate

cunette
cunning
cupcake
cupmoss
cupping
cuprite
cuprous
cupsful
cupular
curable
curacao
curacoa
curator
curcuma
cureall
curette
curiosa
curious
curling
currach
curragh
currant
current
currier
currish
cursive
cursory
curtail
curtain
curtana
curtsey
curvate
cushion
cuspate
custard
custody
customs
cutaway
cutback
cuticle
cutlass
cutlery
cutline
cutrate
cutting
cutworm
cuvette
cyanide
cyanine
cyanite
cyathus
cyclist
cycloid
cyclone
cyclops
cymbalo
cynical
cypress
Cyprian
Cypriot
cypsela
cystine
cystoid
czardas
czardom
czarina
czarism
czarist
dabbing
dabbler
dacoity
Dadaism
Dadaist
dallier
damming
damnify
damning
damosel
damozel

dampish
dandify
Danelaw
dangler
danseur
Dantean
dapsone
darbies
dariole
darkish
darling
darning
darshan
dashiki
dashing
dashpot
dastard
dasyure
datable
datival
dauphin
dawdler
dawning
daybook
daylong
dayroom
daystar
daytime
daywork
dazedly
dazzler
deadend
deadeye
deadpan
deafaid
dealing
deanery
deathly
debacle
debater
debauch
debouch
Debrett
debrief
decadal
decagon
decanal
decapod
decease
deceive
decency
deciare
decibel
decided
decider
decidua
decimal
decking
declaim
declare
declass
decline
decoder
decorum
decrier
decrypt
decuman
decuple
deepfry
deepsea
default
defence
defiant
deficit
defiler
definer
deflate
deflect
defocus

deforce
defraud
defrock
defrost
defunct
degauss
degrade
dehisce
deicide
deictic
deiform
deistic
delaine
delator
delayer
delight
Delilah
delimit
deliver
delouse
Delphic
deltaic
deltoid
deluder
demerit
demesne
demigod
demirep
demoded
demonic
demotic
demount
denarii
denizen
densely
density
dentate
dentine
dentist
denture
deodand
deodara
deplane
deplete
deplore
deplume
deposal
deposit
deprave
depress
deprive
derange
derider
derrick
dervish
descant
descend
descent
deserve
despair
despise
despite
despoil
despond
dessert
destine
destiny
destroy
deterge
detinue
detract
detrain
detrude
deutzia
devalue
develop
deviant
deviate
devilry

devious
devisal
devisee
deviser
devisor
devolve
devoted
devotee
dewclaw
dewdrop
dewfall
dewpond
dextral
dextran
dextrin
diabase
diabolo
diadrom
diagram
dialect
dialled
dialyse
diamond
diarchy
diarise
diarist
dibasic
dibbing
dickens
dictate
diction
diddler
diehard
dietary
diffuse
digamma
digging
digital
dignify
dignity
digraph
digress
dilated
dilator
dilemma
diluent
dilutee
diluter
dilutor
dimeric
dimeter
dimmest
dimming
dimmish
dimness
dinette
dingily
dingoes
dinning
diocese
diopter
dioptre
diorama
diorism
diorite
dioxide
diploid
diploma
dipnoan
dipolar
dipping
diptera
diptych
direful
dirtily
disable
disavow
disband
disbark

discant
discard
discern
discerp
discoid
discord
discuss
disdain
disease
diseuse
disfame
disgust
dishorn
disjoin
dislike
dislimn
dismast
dismiss
disobey
dispark
dispart
display
disport
dispose
dispute
disrank
disrate
disrobe
disroot
disrupt
dissave
disseat
dissect
dissent
distaff
distain
distant
distend
distent
distich
distill
distort
disturb
ditcher
dithery
dittany
diurnal
diverge
diverse
divider
diviner
divisor
divorce
divulge
dizzard
dizzily
djibbah
docetic
dockage
dockise
doddard
doddery
dodgems
dodgery
doeskin
dogbane
dogcart
dogdays
dogeate
dogfish
doggery
dogging
doggish
doggone
dogrose
dogskin
dogstar
dogtrot
dogvane

dogwood
doleful
dollish
dolphin
doltish
domical
dominie
donator
donning
donnish
doodler
doomful
doorman
doormat
doorway
dorhawk
Dorking
dormant
dormice
dornick
dortour
dossier
dotting
doubler
doubles
doublet
doubter
doucely
douceur
doughty
dovecot
dovekie
dowager
dowdily
downbow
doyenne
dozenth
drabber
drabbet
drabble
drabler
drachma
draftee
drafter
dragged
draggle
dragnet
dragoon
drainer
drapery
drastic
dratted
draught
drawbar
drawing
drawler
drayage
drayman
dreamed
dreamer
dredger
dresser
dribble
driblet
driedup
drifter
driller
drinker
dripdry
dripped
drivein
driving
drizzle
drizzly
drogher
dromond
droplet
dropout
dropped

dropper
drosera
droshky
drought
drouthy
droving
drubbed
drudger
drugged
drugget
druidic
drumlin
drummed
drummer
drunken
drycell
drydock
dryeyed
dryness
drysalt
dryshod
dualise
dualism
dualist
duality
dubbing
dubiety
dubious
ducally
duchess
ducking
duckpin
ductile
ducting
dudgeon
duelled
dueller
dukedom
dulcify
dullard
dullish
dulness
dumpish
dunbird
dungeon
Dunkirk
dunnage
dunning
dunnock
duodena
duopoly
dupable
durable
durably
duramen
durance
durmast
duskily
dustbin
dustily
dustman
dustpan
duteous
dutiful
duumvir
dwarves
dweller
dwindle
dyarchy
dyewood
dynamic
dynasty
eagerly
earache
eardrop
eardrum
earflap
earhole
earldom

earlobe
earlock
earmark
earmuff
earnest
earplug
earring
earshot
earthen
earthly
easeful
eastern
easting
eatable
ebbtide
ebonise
ebonite
ebriate
ebriety
eccrine
ecdyses
ecdysis
echelon
echidna
echinus
echoism
eclipse
eclogue
ecology
economy
ecstasy
ectopic
edacity
edaphic
edictal
edifice
edition
educate
eductor
eelpout
eelworm
effects
effendi
effulge
egality
eggcosy
eggflip
egghead
egotise
egotism
egotist
egotrip
eidetic
eidolon
einkorn
eirenic
ejector
ekistic
elastic
elastin
elation
elderly
Eleatic
elector
electro
elegant
elegiac
elegise
elegist
element
elenchi
elevate
elevens
elfbolt
elfland
elflock
elision
elitism
elitist

ellipse
Elohism
Elohist
elusion
elusive
elusory
elution
eluvial
eluvium
elysian
Elysium
elytron
elytrum
Elzevir
emanate
embargo
embassy
emblaze
embolic
embolus
embosom
embowed
embowel
embower
embrace
embroil
embrown
embryon
emerald
emeriti
emersed
emetine
emicate
eminent
emirate
emitted
emitter
emotion
emotive
empanel
empathy
emperor
empiric
emplace
emplane
emporia
empower
empress
emprise
emptier
emptily
emption
empyema
emulate
emulous
enactor
enamour
enation
enchain
enchant
enchase
enclasp
enclave
enclose
encoder
encomia
Encraty
encrust
endarch
endemic
enderon
endless
endlong
endmost
endogen
endorse
endozoa
endways
endwise

enemata
energid
enfeoff
enfiled
enforce
enframe
engaged
English
engorge
engraft
engrail
engrain
engrave
engross
enhance
enlarge
enliven
ennoble
enounce
enplane
enprint
enquire
enquiry
enslave
ensnare
ensnarl
entasis
entente
enteral
enteric
enteron
enthral
enthuse
entitle
entomic
entotic
entozoa
entrain
entrant
entreat
entropy
entrust
entwine
entwist
envelop
envenom
envious
environ
enwheel
enwound
enzymic
eparchy
epatant
epaulet
epergne
ephebus
ephedra
epicarp
epicede
epicene
epicure
epidote
epigeal
epigean
epigene
epigone
epigoni
epigram
epigyny
epilate
episode
epistle
epitaph
epitaxy
epithem
epithet
epitome
epizoic
epizoon

epochal
eponymy
epoxide
epsilon
equable
equably
equally
equator
equerry
equinal
equinox
erasure
erectly
erector
erelong
eremite
erepsin
ergates
ergodic
ericoid
eristic
erlking
ermined
erodent
erosion
erosive
erotica
erotism
errancy
erratic
erratum
erudite
escapee
escaper
escheat
escolar
escribe
esotery
esparto
espouse
esquire
essayer
essence
essoyne
estrade
estreat
estuary
etaerio
etamine
etching
eternal
etesian
ethanol
etheric
ethical
ethiops
ethmoid
Etonian
euclase
eucrite
eugenic
euglena
eulogia
eupepsy
euphony
Euratom
eustasy
eutexia
evacuee
evangel
evanish
evasion
evasive
evening
evictor
evident
evolute
ewelamb
eweneck

exactly
exactor
examine
example
exarate
excerpt
excited
exciter
exciton
excitor
exclaim
exclave
exclude
excrete
excurse
excusal
execute
exedrae
exegete
exempla
exergue
exhaust
exhibit
exhumer
exigent
exocarp
exogamy
exordia
exotica
expanse
expense
expiate
explain
explant
explode
exploit
explore
exposal
exposed
exposer
exposit
expound
express
expulse
expunge
exscind
externe
extinct
extract
extreme
extrude
exudate
exurban
exurbia
exuviae
exuvial
eyeball
eyebath
eyebolt
eyebrow
eyedrop
eyehole
eyelash
eyeless
eyelike
eyeshot
eyesore
eyespot
eyewash
eyewink
Faberge
fabliau
fabular
faceoff
faceted
faction
factory
factual
facture

faculae
faculty
faddish
faddism
faddist
fadedly
fadeout
fagging
fagotto
faience
failing
failure
faintly
fairing
fairish
fairway
Falange
falbala
falcate
falcula
fallacy
fallguy
falling
falloff
fallout
falsely
falsies
falsify
falsity
famulus
fanatic
fancier
fancily
fanclub
fanfare
fanfold
fanmail
fanning
fantail
fantasm
fantast
fantasy
fantods
faraday
faradic
faraway
farceur
farcing
fargone
farming
farmost
Faroese
farrago
farrier
farruca
farther
fascial
fascine
Fascism
Fascist
fashion
fastday
fatally
fateful
fathead
fatigue
fatling
fatness
fattest
fatting
fattish
fatuity
fatuous
faucial
faunist
fauvism
fauvist
fearful
feaster

feather
feature
febrile
fedayee
federal
feeding
feedlot
feeling
feigner
felonry
felsite
felspar
felting
felucca
felwort
feminal
femoral
fencing
fenfire
fenland
feoffee
feoffer
feoffor
fermata
ferment
fermion
fermium
fernery
fernowl
ferrate
ferrety
ferrite
ferrous
ferrugo
ferrule
fertile
fervent
fervour
festive
festoon
fetidly
fetlock
fetters
feudist
fewness
feyness
fiancee
fibbing
fibroid
fibroin
fibroma
fibrous
fibster
fibulae
fibular
fibulas
fictile
fiction
fictive
fiddler
fideism
fideist
fidgets
fidgety
fiefdom
fielder
fierily
fifteen
fifthly
fifties
figging
fighter
figleaf
figment
figtree
figural
figured
figwort
filacer

filaria
filasse
filbert
filemot
filiate
filibeg
filings
filling
filmdom
filmset
fimbria
finagle
finally
finance
finback
finding
finesse
finical
finicky
finikin
finings
finning
Finnish
firearm
firebox
firebug
firedog
firefly
fireman
firenew
firstly
firtree
fishery
fisheye
fishily
fishing
fishnet
fishway
fissile
fission
fissure
fistful
fistula
fitchet
fitchew
fitment
fitness
fittest
fitting
fixable
fixedly
fixings
fixture
flaccid
flagday
flagged
flagman
flamfew
flaming
flaneur
flanker
flannel
flapped
flapper
flareup
flasher
flatcap
flatcar
flatlet
flatout
flatten
flatter
flattop
flaught
flaunty
flavine
flavour
fleabag
fleapit

flecker
fleeced
fleecer
fleeing
fleetly
Fleming
Flemish
fleshed
flesher
fleshly
fletton
fleuret
fleuron
flexile
flexion
flexure
flicker
flighty
flipped
flipper
flitted
flitter
flivver
floater
floccus
flogged
floorer
floosie
floozie
flopped
floreat
florist
floruit
flotage
flotsam
flounce
flowage
flowery
flubbed
fluence
fluency
fluidal
fluidic
fluidly
flummox
flunkey
fluster
fluting
flutist
flutter
fluvial
fluxion
flyable
flyaway
flyback
flybane
flybelt
flyblow
flyboat
flybook
flyhalf
flyleaf
flyover
flypast
flyting
flytrap
fobbing
focused
fogbank
foggage
foggily
fogging
foghorn
foglamp
fogydom
fogyish
fogyism
folding
foldout

foliage
foliate
foliole
foliose
folkway
follies
fondant
fondler
foolery
foolish
footage
footboy
footing
footman
footpad
footrot
footsie
footway
fopling
foppery
foppish
forager
foramen
forayer
forbade
forbear
forbode
forbore
forceps
fordone
forearm
foreign
foreleg
foreman
forepaw
foreran
forerun
foresaw
foresay
foresee
foretop
forever
forfeit
forfend
forgave
forgery
forging
forgive
forgoer
forgone
forkful
forlorn
formant
formate
formula
forsake
forsook
forties
fortify
Fortran
fortune
forward
forwent
forworn
fossick
fossula
fouette
foulard
foumart
founder
foundry
fourale
fourgon
foveate
foveola
fowling
foxhole
foxhunt
foxtail

foxtrot
fracted
fraenum
fragile
frailly
frailty
Fraktur
frameup
frankly
frantic
frapped
fratery
fraught
frazzle
freaked
freckle
freckly
freebie
freedom
freeman
freesia
freeway
freezer
freight
Frenchy
frenula
frescos
freshen
fresher
freshet
freshly
fretful
fretsaw
fretted
friable
friarly
fribble
frigate
frijole
fripper
friseur
Frisian
frisker
frisket
frisson
fritted
fritter
frizzle
frizzly
frogeye
frogged
frogman
fronded
frontal
fronton
frosted
froward
frowsty
fructed
fruited
fruiter
frustum
fuchsia
fuddler
Fuehrer
fuelled
fueller
fugally
fugging
fuguist
fulcrum
fulgent
fulgour
fullage
fullout
fulmine
fulness
fulsome
fulvous
fumbler
funeral
funfair
fungoid
fungous
funicle
funnies
funnily
funning
furbish
furcate
furcula
furioso
furious
furlong
furmety
furmity
furnace
furnish
furrier
furring
furrowy
further
furtive
fuscous
fusible
fussily
fusspot
fustian
fustily
futhark
futhorc
futhork
futtock
fuzzily
gabbing
gabbler
gabelle
gabfest
gabnash
gadding
gadgety
gadroon
gadwall
gagging
gagster
gahnite
gainful
gainsay
Galahad
galanga
galatea
galeate
galenic
galilee
galipot
gallant
gallate
galleon
gallery
gallfly
gallice
galling
galliot
gallium
gallnut
galloon
gallows
galumph
gambade
gambado
gambier
gambler
gamboge
gambrel
gamebag
gamelan
gametic
ganglia
gangrel
gangway
gantlet
garbage
garbler
garboil
gardant
garfish
garland
garment
garnish
garotte
garpike
gascoal
gaseous
gasfire
gasmask
gasring
gassing
gastric
gateaux
gateleg
gateway
gathers
gatling
gaudery
gaudily
Gaulish
gauntly
gauntry
gavotte
gawkily
gayness
gazelle
gazette
gearbox
gearing
geckoes
geebung
Gehenna
gelatin
gelding
gelidly
gelling
gemmate
gemmery
gemming
gemmule
gemsbok
general
generic
geneses
genesis
genetic
genette
Genevan
genista
genitor
genizah
genning
Genoese
genteel
gentian
gentile
genuine
geodesy
geogony
geoidal
geology
Geordie
georgic
gerbera
germane
gestalt
gestapo
gestate
gesture
getaway
getting
gharial
ghastly
gherkin
ghettos
ghillie
ghostly
giantry
gibbous
giblets
giddily
gigging
giggler
gilbert
gilding
gillnet
giltcup
gimbals
gimmick
gingery
gingham
gingili
ginning
ginseng
giraffe
girasol
girdler
girlish
gittern
gizzard
glacial
glacier
gladded
gladden
gladder
glaikit
glamour
glaring
glassen
glasses
glazier
glazing
gleaner
gleeful
gleeman
glenoid
gliadin
glimmer
glimpse
glisten
glister
glitter
globoid
globose
globule
glorify
glossal
Glossic
glottal
glottis
glozing
glucose
glummer
gluteal
gluteus
glutted
glutton
glycine
glyphic
glyptal
glyptic
gnarled
gnathic
gnocchi
gnomish
gnostic
goahead
goatgod
goatish
gobbler
Gobelin
goddamn
goddess
godetia
godevil
godhead
godhood
godless
godlike
godling
godsend
godship
godward
goggler
goggles
goitred
goldbug
golfbag
golfing
goliard
Goliath
gombeen
gomeral
gomeril
gonadal
gondola
gonidia
goodbye
goodday
goodish
goodman
gooiest
gorcock
gorcrow
Gordian
gorilla
gorsedd
goshawk
gosling
gossipy
gossoon
gouache
goulash
gourami
gourmet
goutfly
grabbed
grabber
grabble
gracile
grackle
gradate
gradely
gradine
gradual
grafter
grained
grainer
gramary
grammar
grampus
granary
grandad
grandam
grandee
grandly
grandma
grandpa
granger
granita
granite
grannie
grantee
granter
grantor
granule
grapery
graphic
grapnel
grapple
grasper
gratify
grating
graunch
gravely
gravity
gravure
grazier
grazing
greaser
greaten
greatly
greaves
Grecian
grecise
Grecism
greenly
greenth
greisen
gremial
gremlin
grenade
greyhen
greyish
greylag
gribble
griddle
griffin
griffon
grifter
grilled
griller
grimace
grimmer
grinder
grinned
gripped
gripper
griskin
gristle
gristly
gritted
grizzle
grizzly
Grobian
grocery
grogram
Grolier
grommet
groover
grossly
grottos
grouchy
grouper
groupie
grouser
growler
grownup
grubbed
grubber
gruffly
grumble
grumbly
grummet
grumose
grumous
grunion
grunter
gruntle
grutten
gruyere
gryphon
grysbok
Gstring
guanaco
guanine
guarana
guarani
guarded
guardee
guayule
gubbins
gudgeon
Guelfic
guerdon
guereza
guesser
guichet
Guignol
guilder
guipure
guisard
gullery
gumboil
gumboot
gumdrop
gumming
gummite
gumshoe
gunboat
gunfire
gunlock
gunnera
gunnery
gunning
gunplay
gunroom
gunship
gunshot
gunwale
gurnard
gushing
gustily
gutless
gutsily
guttate
gutting
guzzler
gwyniad
gymnast
gymslip
gypping
habitat
habitue
hachure
hackbut
hackery
hacking
hackler
hackney
hacksaw
haddock
hafnium
hagfish
Haggada
haggard
haggish
haggler
hagweed
haircut
hairnet
hairpin
Halakah
halberd
halbert
halcyon
halfway
halfwit
halibut
halidom
hallali
hallway
halogen
halting
halvers
halyard
Hamburg
Hamitic
hamming
hammock
hamster
hamulus
handbag
handcar
handful
handgun
handily
handler
handoff
handout
handsaw
handsel
handset
hangdog
hanging
hangman
hangout
Hansard
hanuman
hapence
hapenny
hapless
haploid
haporth
happily
happing
harbour
hardhit
hardpan
hardset
hardtop
harelip
haricot
harijan
harmala
harmful
harmony
harness
harpist
harpoon
harrier
harshen
harshly
harslet
harvest
hasbeen
hashish
hassock
hastate
hastily
hatable
hatband
hatcher
hatchet
hateful
hatless
hatting
hauberk
haughty
haulage
haulier
haunted
haunter
hautboy
hauteur
havenot
hawkish
haycock
hayfork
hayloft
hayrick
hayseed
hayward
haywire
headily
heading
headman
headpin
headset
headway
healthy
hearing
hearken
hearsay
hearted
hearten
heathen
heather
heating
heavily
hebenon
Hebraic
heckler
hectare
hedonic
heedful
heeltap
heftily
heighho
heinous
heiress
helical
helices
helicon
hellbox
hellcat
Hellene
hellion
hellish
helluva
helotry
helpful
helping
hemiola
hemione
hemline
hemlock
hemming
henbane
hencoop
hennery
henpeck
henwife
heparin
hepatic
heptane
herbage
heretic
heritor
herniae
hernial
hernias
heroics
heroine
heroise
heroism
heronry
herring
herself
hessian
hetaera
hetaira
hexadic
hexagon
hexapla
hexapod
heyduck
hiccupy
hickory
hidalga
hidalgo
hideous
hideout
higgler
highboy

highhat
highman
highway
hilding
hillman
hillock
hilltop
himself
hindgut
hipbath
hipbone
hipness
hipping
hiproof
hipster
hirable
hircine
hirsute
hirudin
histone
history
hitcher
hitting
Hittite
hoarsen
hoatzin
Hobbian
Hobbism
Hobbist
hobbler
hobnail
hockday
hocused
hoecake
hoedown
hogback
hogfish
hoggery
hogging
hoggish
hogwash
hogweed
holdall
holding
holibut
holiday
holland
holmium
holmoak
holster
homager
homburg
Homeric
Homerid
hominid
homonym
honesty
honeyed
honours
hoodlum
hooklet
hopbind
hopeful
hophead
hoplite
hopping
hopsack
horizon
hormone
hornmad
horrent
horrify
horsily
hosanna
hosiery
hospice
hostage
hostess
hostile
hostler
hotfoot
hothead
hotness
hotshot
hottest
hottish
housing
howbeit
however
howling
huanaco
hueless
huffish
hugeous
hugging
hulking
humanly
humbles
humbuzz
humdrum
humeral
humerus
humidly
humidor
humming
hummock
humoral
hundred
hunkers
Hunnish
hunting
hurdler
hurdles
hurling
hurried
hurtful
husband
hushaby
huskily
husking
Hussite
hustler
hutment
hutting
hyaline
hyalite
hyaloid
hydatid
hydrant
hydrate
hydride
hydroid
hydrous
hygeian
hygiene
hymenia
hymnary
hymnist
hymnody
hyperon
hypnoid
hypogea
hypoxia
hypoxic
Iberian
iceberg
iceboat
icecold
icefall
icefloe
icefoot
icepack
icerink
iceshow
ichabod
iciness
icteric
icterus
ideally
identic
idiotic
idlesse
idolise
idyllic
igneous
igniter
ignoble
ignobly
ignorer
ikebana
ileitis
ilkaday
illbred
illegal
illicit
illness
imagery
imagine
imagism
imagist
imamate
imbiber
imbower
imbrute
imitate
immense
immerge
immerse
immoral
impaint
impanel
impasse
impaste
impasto
impeach
impearl
imperil
impetus
impiety
impinge
impious
implant
implead
implete
implode
implore
imposer
impound
impresa
impress
imprest
imprint
improve
impulse
inanely
inanity
inaptly
inboard
inbreed
inbuilt
incense
incipit
incised
incisor
inciter
incline
inclose
include
incomer
incrust
incubus
incudes
incurve
incused
indepth
indexer
indican
indices
indicia
inditer
indoors
indorse
indraft
indrawn
inducer
indulge
indusia
indwell
indwelt
ineptly
inertia
inertly
inexact
infancy
infanta
infante
infarct
infauna
inferno
infidel
infield
inflame
inflate
inflect
inflict
infract
infulae
ingenue
ingesta
ingoing
ingraft
ingrain
ingrate
ingress
ingroup
ingrown
inhabit
inhaler
inherit
inhibit
inhouse
inhuman
initial
injurer
inkhorn
inkling
inkwell
inlayer
innards
innerve
innings
inocula
inphase
inquest
inquire
inquiry
insculp
insecty
inshore
insider
insight
insigne
insipid
insofar
inspect
inspire
install
instant
instate
instead
insular
insulin
insured
insurer
inswing
integer
intense
interim
interne
intoner
intrant
intreat
introit
intrude
intrust
intwine
inutile
invader
invalid
inveigh
inverse
invitee
inviter
invoice
involve
inwards
inweave
inwoven
ipomoea
Iranian
irately
irideal
iridise
iridium
Irishry
irksome
ironing
ironist
ischial
ischium
Ishmael
Islamic
Ismaili
isobath
isochor
isogamy
isogeny
isogram
isohyet
isokont
isolate
isonomy
isotope
isotopy
isotron
Israeli
issuant
isthmus
itacism
Italian
Italiot
itemise
iterant
iterate
ivories
jabbing
jacamar
jacinth
jackass
jackdaw
jackpot
jacktar
Jacobin
jacobus
jaconet
jadedly
jadeite
jaggery
Jainism
jaloppy
jamming
Janeite
jangler
janitor
jannock
January
japonic
jargoon
jarring
jasmine
javelin
jawbone
jaybird
jaywalk
jazzily
jazzman
jealous
jejunum
jellaba
jellied
jemadar
jerkily
jetting
jewelry
jewfish
Jezebel
jibbing
jibboom
jibdoor
jigging
jimjams
jingler
jitters
jittery
jobbery
jobbing
jocular
jogging
jogtrot
joinder
joinery
joining
jointer
jointly
jollify
jollity
jonquil
jotting
journal
journey
jouster
joyance
joyless
joyride
jubilee
Judaean
Judaise
Judaism
Judaist
judoist
jugging
juggins
juggler
jugular
juicily
jujitsu
jukebox
jumbuck
jumpjet
jumpoff
juncoes
Jungian
juniper
Jupiter
jurally
juryman
jussive
justice
justify
jutting
kabbala
Kaddish
kainite
kalends
Kalmuck
kalpack
kampong
Kannada
Kantian
Karaite
karakul
karting
kathode
katydid
keelson
keeping
kenning
kenosis
kenotic
kentish
keramic
keratin
kermess
kerogen
kerygma
kestrel
ketchup
keyhole
keyless
keynote
keyring
keyword
khaddar
khamsin
khanate
khedive
kibbutz
kickoff
kidding
kiddish
kidskin
killick
killing
killjoy
kilobar
kiloton
kinchin
kindler
kindred
kinesis
kinetic
kinfolk
kingcup
kingdom
kinglet
kingpin
kinship
kinsman
Kirghiz
kissing
kitchen
kitschy
klipdas
knacker
knapped
knapper
knavery
knavish
kneader
kneecap
kneeler
kneepan
kneesup
knitted
knitter
knobbed
knobble
knobbly
knocker
knockon
knotted
knotter
knowall
knowhow
knowing
knuckle
knurled
kolkhoz
Koranic
koumiss
kremlin
krimmer
Krishna
krypton
kumquat
Kurdish
kursaal
kyanise
kyanite
labarum
labella
labiate
lacking
laconic
lacquer
lactate
lacteal
lactose
lacunae
lacunal
lacunar
lacunas
ladanum
ladybug
ladykin
laggard
lagging
laicise
laicism
lairage
lakelet
Lallans
Lamaism
Lamaist
lambast
lambent
lambert
lambkin
lamella
laminae
laminar
lamming
lampion
lampoon
lamprey
lancers
landing
languet
languid
languor
laniary
lankily
lanolin
lantana
lantern
lanyard
Laotian
lapilli
lapping
Laputan
lapwing
larceny
lardoon
largely
largess
largish
lasagna
lasagne
lashing
lashkar
lassoes
lasting
latakia
latchet
latency
lateral
latexes
lathery
lathing
latices
latrine
lattice
Latvian
laugher
launder
laundry
laurels
lavolta
lavrock
lawhand
lawless
lawlist
lawlord
lawsuit
laxness
layered
layette
lazaret
leading
leadoff
leafage
leafbud
leaflet
leaguer
leakage
leaning
learned
learner
leather
lechery
lectern
lection
lecture
leeward
leftism
leftist
legally
legatee
legator
legbail
legging
leghorn
legible
legibly
legiron
legless
legpull
legrest
legroom
legshow
legwork
leister
leisure
lemmata
lemming
lending
lengthy
lenient
lentigo
lentisk
lentoid
leonine
leopard
leotard
leprosy
leprous
lesbian
letdown
lethean
letters
letting

Lettish lettuce leucine leucite leucoma levator levelly leveret lexical lexicon liaison Liassic liberal liberty library librate licence license lichowl licitly licking lidless lieabed lifeful liftoff lighted lighten lighter lightly lignify lignite ligroin likable lilting limbate limbeck limbous liminal limited limiter limosis limpkin limulus linctus lindane lineage lineate lineman lineout lingual linkage linkboy linkman Linnean linocut linsang linseed lioncel lioness lionise lipdeep lipless lipping lipread liquate liquefy liqueur lissome listeth listing literal lithely lithium lithoid litotes littery liturgy livable livebox

liveoak llanero loading loaning loather loathly lobbing lobelia lobster lobular lobworm locally locater lockage lockjaw locknut lockout locular loculus lodging loftily logbook logging logical logline logwood Lollard Lombard lomenta longago longbow longday longhop longing longish looking lookout looksee loosely lopping lording lorette lorgnon loricae lorimer loriner losable lottery lotting loudish lounger lousily loutish louvred lovable lovably loverly lowborn lowbred lowbrow lowdown lowland lowlily lowness lowrise loyally loyalty lozenge lubbard lucarne lucency lucerne lucidly Lucifer luckily Luddite luggage lugging lughole

lugsail lugworm lullaby lumbago lumbang lumenal luminal lumpily lumpish lunatic luncher lunette lunular lupulin lurcher lurdane luridly lustful lustily lustral lustrum luteous lychnis lychowl lycopod lyddite lyingin lyingly lymphad lyncean lynchet lyrated lyrical macabre macadam macaque machair machete machine macrame macrami maculae macular maddest madding Madeira madness madonna madrona madrono madwort maestri maestro maffick mafiosi mafioso magenta maggoty magical magmata magnate magneto magnify mahaleb mahatma Mahdism Mahdist mahjong mahonia mahound mahseer maidish maidism mailbag mailbox mailing maillot mailman mailvan

maintop majesty makings malacia malaise malaria Malayan malefic malines malison mallard malleus malmsey maltase Maltese malting maltose mamelon mamilla mammary mammate mammock mammoth manacle manager manakin manatee manchet mandala mandate mandola mandora mandrel mandril mangily mangoes mangold manhole manhood manhour manhunt manihot manikin manilla manille maniple manitou manjack mankind manless manlike manmade manners manning mannish mannite mannose mansard mansion mansize manteau mantlet mantram mantrap manumit manward manweek Manxcat Manxman manyear mapping marabou Maratha Marathi marbled marbles marcher marconi maremma

margent marimba mariner marital markhor marking marline marlite marmite marplot marquee marquis Marrano married marring marrowy Marsala marshal martial Martian martini martlet martyry Marxian Marxism Marxist marybud mascara mashtub Masonic masonry Masorah masquer massage masseur massive mastaba masters mastery mastich mastiff mastoid matador matchet matelot matinal matinee matrass mattery matting mattins mattock mattoid matzoth maudlin maunder mauther mawkish mawworm maxilla maximal maximum maxwell mayoral maypole Maytime mayweed mazurka mazzard meadowy mealies meander meaning measles measure meatfly meatman Mechlin meconic

meddler mediacy mediant mediate medical medulla medusae medusan medusas meerkat meeting megaron megaton meiosis meiotic Meissen melange melanic melanin melilot melisma melodic melting memento memoirs mending menfolk menisci menorah menthol mention mercery merchet mercury mermaid merrily meseems mesonic message messiah Messias messily messtin mestiza mestizo metamer metayer metazoa methane metonym metopic metopon metrics metrist mettled Mexican mezuzah miasmal miasmic micelle microbe midland midline midmost midriff midship midweek Midwest midwife midyear mightst migrant migrate mildewy mileage milfoil miliary militia milking

milkleg milkman milksop milldam million milreis mimesis mimetic mimical mimicry mimulus minaret mincing mindful mineral minever miniate minibus minicab minicar minikin minimal minimum minimus miniver minorca minster mintage minuend minutes minutia Miocene miracle mirador mirkily miscall miscast miscopy misdate misdeal misdeed misdeem misdone miserly misfire misgave misgive mishear Mishnah misknow mislaid mislead mislike mismate misname misplay misread misrule missend missent missile missing mission missish missive misstep mistake mistful mistily mistime misting mistook mistral mitoses mitosis mitotic mitzvah mixedly mixedup

mixture Moabite mobbing mobbish mobster mockery modally modesty modicum modiste modular modulus mofette moidore moisten moistly moither molimen mollify mollusc molossi momenta monacal monadic monarch mondial moneyed moneyer mongrel moniker monitor monkery monkish monocle monocot monodic monomer monsoon monster montage montane montero monthly moocher moodily mooneye moonlit moonset moorage moorhen mooring Moorish moorlog mopping moraine morally morassy mordant mordent moreish morello morendo Moresco Morisco morning morocco moronic morphia mortice mortify mortise morulae morular morwong Moselle mosshag mottled mouflon moulder

mounter Mountie mourner mousaka mousing mousmee mouther movable mowburn mozetta mudbath muddily muddler mudfish mudflat mudlark mudpack muezzin muffler mugging muggins mugwort mugwump mulatto mullein mullion mullock multure mumbler mummery mummify mumming mumpish mundane mundify munnion munting muntjac muntjak muonium muraena murexes muriate murices murkily murrain murther muscled musette musical muskrat mustang mustard mutable mutably mutagen muttony muzzily muzzler myalgia myalgic myalism mycelia mycoses mycosis mycotic myeloid myeloma myiasis mylodon mynheer myogram myology myomata mystery mystify mythise mythist myxomas

nabbing
nacarat
nacelle
nacrous
nagging
Nahuatl
naiades
nailery
naively
naivete
naivety
nakedly
namable
nameday
nankeen
naphtha
napless
napping
narrate
narrows
narthex
narwhal
nasally
nascent
nastily
nattily
natural
naughty
nauplii
nautics
nautili
navarin
Naziism
nearest
nebbish
nebulae
nebular
nebulas
necklet
necktie
necrose
nectary
needful
needler
neglect
neglige
Negress
Negrito
negroid
neither
nelumbo
nemesia
nemesis
Neogaea
neolith
neology
neonate
neoteny
neozoic
nephric
Neptune
neritic
nervate
nervine
nervous
nervure
nesting
netball
netfish
netlike
netsuke
netting
network
neurine
neuroma
neurone
neuston
neutral
neutron
newborn
newcome
newlaid
newmown
newness
newsboy
newsman
nibbler
niblick
niceish
nictate
niggard
niggler
nightie
nightly
nigrify
Nilotic
nimiety
ninepin
niobium
nippers
nippily
nipping
nirvana
nitrate
nitride
nitrify
nitrile
nitrite
nitrous
niveous
Noachic
nobbler
noctuid
noctule
nocturn
nocuous
nodally
nodated
nodding
nodical
nodular
nogging
noisily
noisome
nomadic
nomarch
nombril
nominal
nominee
nonagon
noniron
nonplus
nonskid
nonslip
nonstop
nonsuch
nonsuit
nonuser
noology
noonday
nooning
norland
norther
norward
nosebag
nosegay
noserag
nostril
nostrum
notable
notably
notched
notedly
notelet
notepad
nothing
notitia
noumena
nourish
novella
novelle
novelty
nowhere
noxious
nuclear
nucleic
nuclein
nucleon
nucleus
nuclide
nullify
nullity
numbles
numeral
numeric
nummary
nunatak
nunhood
nunnery
nunnish
nunship
nuptial
nursery
nursing
nurture
nutcase
nutgall
nutlike
nutpine
nutting
nylghau
nymphal
nymphet
oakfern
oakgall
oakling
oaktree
oakwood
oarfish
oarless
oarlock
oarsman
oarweed
oatcake
oatmeal
obconic
obelise
obelisk
obesity
obitual
obligee
obligor
oblique
obloquy
obolary
obovate
obovoid
obscene
obscure
observe
obtrude
obverse
obviate
obvious
ocarina
occiput
occlude
oceanic
ocellar
ocellus
ochrous
octagon
octaval
octette
October
octopod
octopus
octuple
oculate
oculist
odalisk
oddball
oddment
oddness
odontic
odorant
odorous
odoured
odyssey
oedipal
oenomel
oersted
oestral
oestrum
oestrus
offbeat
offence
offhand
officer
offload
offpeak
offside
oghamic
ogreish
oilbath
oilbird
oilcake
oildrum
oilseed
oilskin
oilwell
oldster
oldtime
olefine
olivary
olivine
oloroso
Olympic
omental
omentum
omicron
ominous
omitted
omneity
omnibus
omnific
onanism
oneeyed
oneiric
oneness
onerous
oneself
oneshot
onestep
onetime
ongoing
onshore
onstage
onwards
onymous
oolitic
oomiack
oophyte
oosperm
oospore
opacity
opaline
openair
openend
opening
operand
operant
operate
operose
ophitic
opinion
opossum
oppidan
opposer
oppress
opsonic
opsonin
optical
optimal
optimum
opulent
opuntia
opuscle
oration
oratory
oratrix
orbital
orchard
orderer
orderly
ordinal
orectic
oregano
organic
organon
organum
organza
orifice
origami
orogeny
orology
orotund
Orphean
Orphism
orphrey
ortolan
osculum
osmosis
osmotic
osmunda
osselet
osseous
osseter
ossicle
ossific
ossuary
osteoid
ostiary
ostiole
ostraca
ostraka
ostrich
otolith
otology
ottoman
ouabain
ourself
outback
outcast
outcome
outcrop
outdone
outdoor
outface
outfall
outflow
outfoot
outgone
outgrew
outgrow
outhaul
outland
outlast
outlier
outline
outlive
outlook
outmost
outpace
outplay
outport
outpost
outrage
outrank
outride
outrode
outrush
outsell
outshot
outside
outsize
outsold
outsole
outstay
outtake
outtalk
outturn
outvote
outward
outwear
outwent
outwore
outwork
outworn
ovarian
ovation
overact
overage
overall
overarm
overate
overawe
overbid
overbuy
overdid
overdue
overeat
overfed
overfly
overlap
overlay
overlie
overman
overpay
overran
overrun
oversaw
oversea
oversee
overset
oversew
overtax
overtly
overtop
overuse
ovicide
oviduct
oviform
ovoidal
ovulate
oxalate
oxfence
oxidant
oxidase
oxidate
oxidise
Oxonian
oxyacid
oxytone
ozonise
pabulum
pachisi
pacific
package
packice
packing
packman
padding
paddler
paddock
padlock
padrone
padroni
paeonic
pageant
pageboy
paginal
pahlavi
pailful
painful
painter
pairoar
paisley
pajamas
paladin
palatal
palaver
paletot
palette
palfrey
palings
pallium
palmary
palmate
palmist
palmoil
palmyra
palpate
palsied
paludal
pampean
pampero
panacea
panache
pancake
Pandean
pandect
pandora
pandore
panicky
panicle
Panjabi
pannage
pannier
panning
panocha
panoply
panther
panties
pantile
papadam
papally
paperer
Paphian
papilla
papoose
pappose
paprika
papulae
papular
papyrus
parable
parader
parados
paradox
paragon
parapet
parasol
parboil
pardner
parerga
paresis
paretic
parfait
pargana
parkway
parlour
parlous
parodic
parolee
paronym
parotid
parpend
parquet
parsley
parsnip
partake
partial
parting
partita
partite
partlet
partner
partook
parvenu
parvise
paschal
passade
passado
passage
passant
passing
passion
passive
passkey
pastern
pasteup
pastime
pasture
patagia
patella
patency
pathway
patient
patrial
patriot
patroon
pattern
patting
paucity
Pauline
paunchy
paviour
payable
paydesk
payload
payment
payroll
paysage
peacock
peafowl
pearled
pearler
peartly
peasant
peascod
peasoup
pebrine
peccant
peccary
peckish
peddler
pedicab
pedicel
pedicle
pedlary
peerage
peeress
peevish
Pegasus
pegging
pelagic
pelican
pelisse
peloria
peloric
pelorus
peltate
pelting
pemican
penally
penalty
penance
pendant
pendent
pending
penguin
penname
pennant
pennate
pennies
pennill
pennine
penning
pensile
pension
pensive
pentane
pentode
pentose
peonage
peppery
peppill
pepping
peptalk
peptide
peptise
peptone
percale
percent
percept
percher
percine
percoid
percuss
perdure
perfect
perfidy
perform
perfume
perfuse
pergola
perhaps
periapt
peridot
perigee
perique
periwig
perjure
perjury
perkily
perlite
Permian
permute
perpend
perpent
perplex
Persian
persist
persona
pertain
perturb
pertuse
perusal
peruser
pervade
pervert
pessary
petasus
petiole
petrify
Petrine
petrous
pettily
petting
pettish

petunia
pfennig
phaeton
phalanx
phallic
phallus
phantom
pharaoh
pharynx
phasmid
phellem
philter
philtre
phlegmy
phoenix
phonate
phoneme
phonics
phonily
photism
phrasal
phratry
phrenic
phrensy
physics
piaffer
pianism
pianist
piastre
pibroch
picador
piccolo
piceous
pickaxe
pickeer
pickled
picotee
picquet
picrate
Pictish
picture
piddock
pidgeon
piebald
pieeyed
pierrot
pietism
pietist
piffler
piggery
pigging
piggish
pigiron
piglead
pigling
pigmean
pigment
pigskin
pigtail
pigwash
pigweed
pikelet
pikeman
pileate
pilgrim
pillage
pillbox
pillion
pillock
pillory
pillowy
pillule
pilsner
pilular
pimento
pimping
pinball
pincers
pincher

pinetum
pinfire
pinfish
pinfold
pinguid
pinhead
pinhole
pinkeye
pinking
pinkish
pinnace
pinnate
pinning
pinnule
pintado
pintail
pintuck
pinworm
pioneer
piously
pipeful
piperic
pipette
pipping
piquant
piragua
piranha
piratic
pirogue
piscary
piscina
piscine
pismire
pissoir
pistole
pitapat
pitched
pitcher
piteous
pitfall
pithead
pithhat
pithily
pitiful
pitpony
pitprop
pitting
pivotal
pivoter
placard
placate
placebo
placket
placoid
plafond
plaided
plainly
planish
planned
planner
plantar
planter
planula
planxty
plasmic
plasmid
plasmin
plaster
plastic
plastid
platane
plateau
platina
plating
platoon
platted
platter
plaudit
playact

playboy
playful
playing
playlet
playoff
playpen
pleader
pleased
plectra
pledgee
pledger
pledget
pledgor
plenary
plenish
pleurae
pleural
pleuron
pliable
pliably
pliancy
plicate
pliskie
plodded
plodder
plopped
plosion
plosive
plotted
plotter
plucker
plugged
plugger
plumage
plumate
plumber
plumbic
plumbob
plumery
plummet
plumose
plumper
plumply
plumule
plunder
plunger
plunker
plusage
plushly
pluvial
plywood
poacher
pochard
podagra
podding
podesta
poetess
poetics
poetise
pofaced
poinder
pointed
pointer
polacca
polacre
poleaxe
polecat
polemic
polenta
politic
pollack
pollard
pollock
pollute
poloist
polygon
polymer
polynia
polynya

polypod
polypus
pomatum
pomfret
pompano
pompous
pondage
poniard
pontage
pontiff
pontify
pontoon
poofter
poohbah
poorish
popadum
popcorn
popeyed
popover
poppied
popping
popular
porcine
porifer
porrect
portage
portend
portent
portico
portion
portray
poseuse
possess
postage
postbag
postbox
postboy
posteen
postern
postfix
posting
postman
posture
postwar
potable
potamic
potbank
potence
potency
pothead
potheen
potherb
pothole
pothook
potluck
potshot
pottage
pottery
potting
pouched
poulard
poulter
poultry
poundal
pounder
poussin
pouting
poverty
powdery
praetor
prairie
praiser
Prakrit
praline
prancer
prattle
pravity
preachy
prebend

precast
precede
precept
precise
precook
predate
predial
predict
predoom
preempt
preface
prefect
preform
preheat
prelacy
prelate
prelect
prelims
prelude
premier
premise
premiss
premium
prepack
prepaid
prepare
preplan
presage
present
preside
presoak
presser
pressup
presume
pretend
pretest
pretext
pretzel
prevail
prevent
preview
previse
priapic
pricker
pricket
prickle
prickly
primacy
primage
primary
primate
primely
primero
priming
primmed
primula
printer
prithee
privacy
private
privily
privity
proband
probang
probate
probity
problem
proceed
process
proctor
procure
prodded
prodder
prodigy
produce
product
profane
profess
proffer

profile
profuse
progeny
program
project
prolate
prolong
promise
promote
pronaoi
pronaos
pronate
pronely
pronged
pronoun
propane
propend
prophet
propine
propjet
propone
propose
propped
prorate
prosaic
prosify
prosily
prosody
prosper
protean
protect
protege
proteid
protein
protend
protest
proteus
protist
protium
proudly
proverb
provide
proviso
provoke
provost
prowess
prowler
proximo
prudent
prudery
prudish
pruning
prurigo
prussic
psalter
psychic
pteroic
pteryla
ptyalin
puberal
puberty
publish
puccoon
puckery
puckish
pudding
puddler
pudency
puerile
puffery
pugging
puggish
puggree
pugmill
pugnose
Pullman
pullout
pulpous
pulsate

pulvini
pumpkin
puncher
punchup
punctum
pungent
Punjabi
punning
punster
puparia
pupilar
pupping
puritan
purlieu
purloin
purport
purpose
purpura
purpure
pursuer
pursuit
purview
pushful
pushing
pushrod
pustule
putamen
putdown
putlock
putrefy
puttier
putting
puzzler
pyaemia
pyaemic
pycnite
pygmean
pygmoid
pyjamas
pyloric
pylorus
pyralid
pyralis
pyramid
pyretic
pyrexia
pyrexic
pyrites
pyritic
pyrosis
pyrrhic
Pythian
pyxides
pyxidia
quadrat
quadric
quaffer
quahaug
qualify
quality
quamash
quantic
quantum
quarrel
quartan
quarter
quartet
quartic
quassia
quavery
quayage
Quechua
queenly
queerly
queller
querist
quester
questor
quetsch

quetzal
queuing
quibble
quicken
quickie
quickly
quieten
quietly
quietus
quillet
quilter
quinary
quinate
quinine
quinone
quintal
quintan
quintet
quintic
quipped
quitted
quitter
quivery
quixote
quizzed
quizzer
quizzes
quondam
rabbity
rabbler
rabidly
raccoon
racemic
rackety
racquet
radiant
radiate
radical
radices
radicle
radulae
radular
raffish
ragbolt
ragdoll
raggedy
ragging
ragtime
ragweed
ragworm
ragwort
railcar
railing
railman
railway
raiment
rainbow
Rajpoot
rakeoff
rallier
ralline
Ramadan
rambler
ramekin
ramenta
ramming
rampage
rampant
rampart
rampion
ramsons
rancher
rancour
ranking
ransack
rapeoil
raphide
rapidly
rapping

rapport
rapture
rarebit
raschel
rasping
ratable
ratafia
ratatat
ratchet
rations
ratlike
ratling
rattail
ratteen
rattery
ratting
rattler
rattrap
raucous
raunchy
ravager
ravelin
ravined
ravings
ravioli
rawhide
rawness
rayless
reacher
reactor
readily
reading
readout
reagent
realgar
realign
realise
realism
realist
reality
reallot
realtor
rebirth
reboant
rebound
rebuild
rebuilt
rebuker
receipt
receive
recency
recital
reciter
reclaim
reclame
recline
recluse
recount
recover
recruit
rectify
rectory
rectrix
recurve
recycle
redcoat
reddest
reddish
redhead
redlegs
redneck
redness
redoubt
redound
redpoll
redraft
redress
redskin
reducer

redwing
redwood
reeding
reelect
reenact
reenter
reentry
referee
refined
refiner
reflate
reflect
refloat
refocus
refract
refrain
refresh
refugee
refusal
refuser
refutal
refuter
regalia
regally
regards
regatta
regency
regimen
reginal
regnant
regorge
regrant
regrate
regress
regrets
regroup
regular
regulus
reheard
rehouse
reissue
rejoice
relapse
related
relater
relator
relayed
release
reliant
relieve
relievo
relight
relique
remains
remarry
remblai
remiges
remnant
remodel
remorse
remould
remount
removal
removed
remover
reneger
renegue
renewal
renewer
rentier
reorder
repaint
repaper
repiner
repique
replace
replant
replete
replevy
replica
replier
reposal
reposit
repress
reprint
reprise
reproof
reprove
reptile
repulse
reputed
request
requiem
require
requite
reredos
rescale
rescind
rescuer
reseaux
reserve
reshape
residua
residue
resolve
resound
respect
respell
respelt
respire
respite
respond
respray
restart
restate
restful
restiff
restive
restock
restore
restyle
resurge
retable
retaken
rethink
retiary
reticle
retinae
retinal
retinas
retinol
retinue
retired
retouch
retrace
retract
retrain
retread
retreat
retrial
retsina
rettery
retting
returns
reunion
reunite
revalue
revelry
revenge
revenue
reverie
reverse
reversi
reviler
revisal
reviser
revisit
revival
reviver
revivor
revolve
revving
rewound
rewrite
rewrote
reynard
rhabdom
Rhaetic
rhamnus
rhatany
rhenium
rhiancy
rhizoid
rhizome
rhodium
rhodora
rhombic
rhombus
rhubarb
rhymist
ribband
ribbing
ribston
ribwork
ribwort
rickets
rickety
ricksha
ricotta
ridable
ridding
riddler
ridging
ridotto
riffler
rifling
rigging
righten
righter
rightly
rigidly
rilievo
rimming
ringent
ringing
ringlet
ringtaw
riotous
ripcord
ripieni
ripieno
riposte
ripping
ripplet
riptide
risible
risotto
rissole
rivalry
rivered
riveter
riviera
riviere
rivulet
roadbed
roadhog
roadman
roadway
roaring
roaster
robbery
robbing
rockery
rockier
rockily
rocking
rocklet
rockoil
rocktar
rodding
rodlike
rodsman
roebuck
roedeer
roguery
roguish
roister
rollick
rolling
rollmop
rolltop
romance
Romanic
Romansh
romaunt
Rommany
rondeau
rondure
rontgen
roofing
rooftop
rooinek
rookery
roomful
rooster
rootage
rootlet
ropable
ropeway
rorqual
roseate
rosebay
rosebud
rosecut
rosehip
rosella
roseola
rosered
rosette
rostral
rostrum
rotator
rotifer
rotting
rotunda
roughen
roughly
roulade
rouleau
rounded
roundel
rounder
roundly
roundup
rousing
rouster
routine
rowboat
rowdily
rowlock
royally
royalty
royster
rubadub
rubbers
rubbery
rubbing
rubbish
rubdown
rubella
rubeola
rubicon
rubious
ruching
ruction
ruddily
ruddock
ruderal
rudesby
ruffian
ruffler
ruinate
ruinous
rumbler
rummage
rumness
rumshop
runaway
rundale
rundlet
rundown
runless
running
rupture
rurally
russety
Russian
Russify
rustily
rustler
ruthful
rutting
ruttish
Sabaism
Sabaoth
Sabbath
saccade
saccate
saccule
sacculi
sackbut
sackful
sacking
sacring
sacrist
saddest
saddish
saddler
sadness
saffron
sagging
sagitta
saguaro
saidest
sailing
sainted
saintly
sakeret
Saktism
salable
salicet
salicin
salient
Salique
sallowy
salpinx
salsify
saltant
saltbox
saltcat
saltern
salting
saltire
saltish
saltpan
saluter
salvage
salvoes
sambuca
samisen
samovar
Samoyed
sampler
samurai
sanctum
Sanctus
sandbag
sandbar
sandbed
sandbox
sandboy
sanders
sandfly
sandlot
sandman
sandpit
sangria
sanicle
santour
sapajou
saphead
sapient
sapless
sapling
saponin
sapphic
sapping
saprobe
sapsago
sapwood
Saracen
sarangi
sarcasm
sarcode
sarcoid
sarcoma
sarcous
sardine
sardius
sarking
sashimi
sassaby
satanic
satchel
satiate
satiety
satinet
satiric
satisfy
satrapy
satsuma
satyral
satyric
satyrid
saucily
saunter
saurian
sauroid
sausage
savable
savanna
saveall
saveloy
savings
saviour
savoury
sawbill
sawbuck
sawdust
sawfish
sawgate
sawmill
sawnoff
sawwort
saxhorn
saxtuba
sayable
scabbed
scabble
scabies
scabrid
scaglia
scalade
scalado
scalder
scaldic
scalene
scallop
scalpel
scalper
scamper
scandal
scanned
scanner
scantly
scapple
scapula
scarfed
scarify
scarlet
scarper
scarred
scarves
scatted
scatter
scauper
scenery
scented
scepsis
sceptic
sceptre
schappe
schemer
scherzi
scherzo
schlepp
schlock
schmuck
schnook
scholar
scholia
sciarid
sciatic
science
scirrhi
scissel
scissor
scleral
scoffer
scolder
scollop
scomber
scooper
scooter
scopula
scoriae
scorify
scoring
scorner
scorper
Scorpio
scotice
Scotism
Scotist
scotoma
Scottie
scourer
scourge
scouter
scraggy
scranny
scraper
scrapie
scrappy
scratch
scrawly
scrawny
screech
screeve
screwed
screwer
scribal
scriber
scrieve
scrimpy
scrooge
scrouge
scrubby
scruffy
scrumpy
scrunch
scruple
scudded
scuffle
sculler
sculpin
scumble
scummed
scunner
scupper
scurril
scutage
scutate
scutter
scuttle
seabass
seabear
seabird
seablue
seaboot
seafish
seafood
seafowl
seagirt
seagull
seakale
sealane
sealant
sealegs
sealery
seamaid
seamark
seapink
seaport
searoom
seasick
seaside
seaslug
seatang
seating
seawall
seaward
seaware
seaweed
seawhip
seawife
seawolf
seceder
seclude
seconde
secondi
secondo
secrecy
secrete
sectary
sectile
section
secular
securer
sedilia
seducer
seeable
seedbed
seedily
seedlip
seeming
seepage
segment
seismal
seismic
seizing
seizure
selenic
selffed
selfish
sellout
seltzer
selvage
sematic
semilog
seminal
seminar
semiped
Semitic
senarii
senator
senatus
sendoff
senecio
senhora
senores
sensory
sensual
Senussi
seppuku
septate
septime
sequela
sequent
sequoia
Serbian
serfage
serfdom
seriate
sericin
seriema
seringa
serious
serpent
serpigo
serpula
serrate
serried
servant
servery
Servian
service
servile
serving
Servite
sessile
session
sestina
setback
setdown
setting
settler
settlor
setwall
seventh
seventy
several
sexfoil
sexless
Sextans
sextant
sextile
sferics
sfumato
shackle
shadily
shading
shadoof
shadowy
shaitan
shakeup
shakily
shallop
shallot
shallow
shamble

shammed
shammer
shampoo
shanked
shapely
sharpen
sharper
sharply
shaslik
shaster
shastra
shatter
Shavian
shaving
shearer
sheathe
sheaves
shebang
shebear
shebeen
shedder
sheerly
shellac
shelled
sheller
shelter
sheltie
shelved
shelves
Shemite
sherbet
shereef
sheriff
sherris
shicker
shifter
shikari
shilpit
shimmer
shindig
shingle
shingly
shinned
shinpad
shiplap
shipman
shipped
shippen
shipper
shippon
shipway
shirker
shittim
shivers
shivery
shocker
shoeing
shogged
shoofly
shooter
shopboy
shopman
shopped
shopper
shoring
shorten
shortie
shortly
shotgun
shotten
shouter
showbiz
showery
showily
showing
showman
showoff
shrieve
shrilly
shrinal
shrivel
shriven
shrubby
shucker
shudder
shuffle
shunned
shunner
shunter
shuteye
shutout
shutter
shuttle
shylock
shyness
shyster
sialoid
siamang
Siamese
sibling
sibship
sickbay
sickbed
sickish
sickpay
sidecar
sideway
siemens
sierran
sighted
sightly
sigmate
sigmoid
signary
signify
signior
signora
signore
signori
signory
Sikhism
silence
silenus
silesia
silicic
silicle
silicon
siliqua
silique
silkily
sillily
silvern
silvery
similar
similor
simitar
simpler
simplex
simular
sincere
singlet
sinkage
sinless
sinning
sinopia
sinsyne
sintery
sinuate
sinuous
sipping
sirgang
sirloin
sirocco
Sistine
sistrum
sitdown
sitfast
sithens
sitting
situate
Sivaism
Sivaite
sixaine
sixfold
sixteen
sixthly
sixties
Sixtine
sizable
sizably
sizzler
sjambok
skaldic
skating
skeeter
skegger
skellum
skelter
skepsis
sketchy
skiable
skidded
skidlid
skidpan
skiffle
skijump
skilful
skilift
skilled
skillet
skimmed
skimmer
skimmia
skinful
skinker
skinned
skinner
skipped
skipper
skippet
skirret
skirted
skirter
skitter
skittle
skolion
skulker
skyblue
skyborn
skyhigh
skyjack
skylark
skyline
skysail
skyward
slabbed
slabber
slacken
slacker
slackly
slagged
slammed
slander
slantly
slapped
slasher
slather
slating
slatted
slavery
slavish
Slavism
sledded
sleeken
sleekit
sleekly
sleeper
sleeved
sleight
slender
slicker
slickly
slidden
slimily
slimmer
slinger
slinker
slipped
slipper
slipway
slither
slobber
sloegin
slogged
slogger
slopped
sloshed
slotcar
slotted
slouchy
sloughy
Slovene
slowish
slubbed
slubber
slugged
slugger
slumber
slummed
slummer
slurred
slyness
smacker
smaragd
smarten
smartly
smasher
smashup
smatter
smeddum
smeller
smelter
smidgen
smidgin
smitten
smokeho
smokily
smoking
smoochy
smother
smuggle
smutted
snaffle
snagged
snakily
snapped
snapper
snarler
snarlup
snatchy
sneaker
sneerer
sneezer
snicker
sniffer
sniffle
snifter
snigger
sniggle
snipped
snipper
snippet
snooker
snooper
snoozer
snoozle
snorkel
snorter
snouted
snowcap
snowily
snowman
snubbed
snubber
snuffer
snuffle
snuggle
soakage
soaking
soapbox
soapily
soaring
sobbing
soberly
socager
soccage
society
sockeye
sofabed
softish
soggily
soignee
soilure
sojourn
sokeman
solanum
solaria
solatia
soldier
solicit
solidly
solidus
soliped
soloist
Solomon
soluble
solvate
solvent
somatic
someday
somehow
someone
someway
somitic
sonance
sonancy
songful
sonless
sonship
soonish
soother
soothly
sootily
sophism
sophist
soppily
sopping
soprani
soprano
sorbent
Sorbian
sorcery
sordini
sordino
sorghum
sorites
soroban
sororal
sorosis
sorrily
sotting
sottish
soubise
souffle
soulful
sounder
soundly
soupcon
sourish
soursop
soutane
souther
sowback
soybean
sozzled
spacial
spacing
spadger
spancel
spangle
spangly
spaniel
Spanish
spanker
spanned
spanner
sparely
sparger
sparing
sparkle
sparoid
sparred
sparrow
Spartan
spastic
spathic
spatial
spatted
spattee
spatter
spatula
spawner
speaker
special
species
specify
speckle
spectra
spectre
specula
speeder
speedup
speller
spelter
spencer
spender
sphenic
spheral
spheric
spicate
spicery
spicily
spicula
spicule
spidery
spieler
spignel
spikily
spiller
spinach
spindle
spindly
spindry
spinner
spinney
spinode
spinoff
spinose
spinous
spinule
spiraea
spirant
spireme
spirits
spitted
spitter
spittle
splashy
spleeny
splenic
splicer
splodge
splotch
splurge
spodium
spoiler
spondee
spondyl
sponger
spongin
sponson
sponsor
spoofer
spooney
spoorer
sporran
sporter
sporule
spotted
spotter
spousal
spouter
sprawly
sprayer
sprayey
spriggy
springe
springy
spryest
spumous
spunkie
spurner
spurred
spurrey
spurtle
sputnik
sputter
spyhole
squabby
squacco
squaddy
squails
squalid
squally
squalor
squamae
squarer
squashy
squatty
squeaky
squeeze
squelch
squiffy
squinch
squinny
squirmy
squishy
squitch
stabbed
stabber
stabile
stabler
stables
stacker
staddle
stadium
stagger
stagily
staging
staidly
stainer
staithe
stalely
stalked
stalker
stamina
stammel
stammer
stamper
standby
stander
standin
standup
staniel
stannic
stapler
starchy
stardom
starkly
starlet
starlit
starred
starter
startle
statant
stately
statice
statics
station
statism
statist
stative
statued
stature
statute
staunch
stealer
stealth
steamer
stearic
stearin
steekit
steepen
steeple
steeply
steerer
stellar
stemmed
stemple
stemson
stenchy
stencil
stentor
stepney
stepped
stepper
stepson
sterile
sterlet
sternal
sterned
sternly
sternum
steroid
stetson
stetted
steward
stewpan
stewpot
sthenic
stibine
sticker
stickit
stickle
stickup
stiffen
stiffly
stifler
stilted
Stilton
stimuli
stinger
stinker
stipend
stipple
stipule
stirpes
stirred
stirrer
stirrup
stocker
stoical
stomach
stomata
stonily
stonker
stopgap
stopoff
stopped
stopper
stopple
storage
storied
stouten
stoutly
stovies
stowage
straits
strange
stratum
stratus
strayer
streaky
stretch
stretta
stretto
strewth
striate
strider
stridor
strigil
striker
stringy
striped
striven
striver
strophe
stroppy
strudel
strumae
stubbed
stubble
stubbly
stuccos
stuckup
studded
student
studied
stuffer
stumble
stummed
stumper
stunned
stunner
stunted
stupefy
stutter
stygian
stylise
stylish
stylist
stylite
styloid
styptic
styrene
suasion
suasive
suavely
suavity
subacid
subadar

subaqua
subbing
subdean
subdual
subduct
subdued
subedit
suberic
suberin
subfusc
subhead
subject
subjoin
sublate
sublime
subplot
subside
subsidy
subsist
subsoil
subsume
subtend
subtile
suburbs
subvert
subzero
succade
succeed
success
succory
succour
succuba
succubi
succumb
sucking
suckler
sucrose
suction
sudaria
suffice
Suffolk
suffuse
suggest
suicide
suiting
sulcate
sulkily
sullage
sulphur
sultana
summand
summary
summery
summing
summons
sumpter
sunbath
sunbeam
sunbear
sunbird
sunburn
sundeck
sundial
sundisc
sundown
sunfish
sunlamp
sunless
sunnily
sunning
Sunnite
sunrise
sunroof
sunspot
sunstar
sunsuit
suntrap
sunward
sunwise
supping
support
suppose
supreme
supremo
surbase
surcoat
surface
surfeit
surfing
surfman
surgeon
surgery
surlily
surmise
surname
surpass
surplus
surreal
surtout
survive
suspect
suspend
suspire
sustain
sutural
sutured
swabbed
swabber
swaddle
swagged
swagger
swagman
Swahili
swallow
swanker
swanned
swapped
swapper
swarded
swarmer
swarthy
swasher
swatted
swatter
swearer
sweater
Swedish
sweeper
sweeten
sweetie
sweetly
swelter
swiftly
swigged
swiller
swimmer
swindle
swinery
swinger
swingle
swinish
swipple
swither
Switzer
swizzle
swobbed
swollen
swopped
swopper
swotted
syconia
sycosis
syenite
syllabi
sylphid
sylvine
sylvite
symptom
synapse
syncarp
syncope
synergy
synesis
syngamy
synodal
synodic
synonym
synovia
syringa
syringe
syrphid
systole
tabanid
tabaret
tabasco
tabbing
tabetic
tabinet
tableau
tabloid
taborer
tabular
tachism
tachist
tacitly
tacking
tackler
tactful
tactics
tactile
taction
tactual
tadpole
taeniae
taffeta
Tagalog
tagetes
tagging
tailend
tailing
takeoff
takings
talaria
talayot
talcose
talcous
talipes
talipot
talking
tallage
tallboy
tallish
tallith
tallowy
tallyho
taloned
tamable
tamarin
tamasha
tambour
Tammany
tamping
tampion
tanager
tanagra
tanbark
tandoor
tangelo
tangent
tanghin
tangram
tankage
tankard
tankcar
tankful
tannage
tannate
tannery
tanning
tannish
tanooze
tantara
tantivy
tantric
tantrum
tanyard
taperer
tapetal
tapetum
tapioca
tapping
taproom
taproot
tapsman
tapster
tarbush
tardily
tarnish
tarrier
tarring
tartare
tartish
tartlet
Tartufe
tastily
tatters
tattery
tattily
tatting
tattler
taunter
taurine
taxable
taxfree
taxicab
taxiing
taximan
taxless
taxying
teacake
teacher
teachin
teacosy
teagown
tealeaf
tearful
teargas
tearing
tearoom
tearose
teashop
teatime
teatray
technic
tectrix
tedding
tedious
teeming
teenage
tegmina
tegular
tektite
telamon
teleost
telergy
telling
telpher
Telstar
tempera
tempest
Templar
templet
tempter
tempura
tenable
tenably
tenancy
tendril
tenfold
tenoner
tenpins
tensely
tensile
tension
tensity
tensive
tentbed
tentfly
tenthly
tentpeg
tenuity
tenuous
tepidly
tequila
terbium
terebra
tergite
termini
termite
ternary
ternate
terpene
terrace
terrain
terrene
terrier
terrify
terrine
tersely
tertial
tertian
tessera
testacy
testate
testban
testbed
testfly
testify
testily
testoon
testudo
tetanic
tetanus
tetrode
textile
textual
texture
thalami
thallic
thallus
thalweg
thanage
thankee
thanker
theatre
thecate
themata
theorbo
theorem
therapy
thereat
thereby
therein
thereof
thereon
thereto
theriac
thermae
thermal
thermic
theurgy
thiamin
thicken
thicket
thickly
thieves
thigger
thiller
thimble
thinker
thinned
thinner
thirdly
thirsty
thistle
thistly
thither
Thomism
Thomist
thorite
thorium
thorned
thought
thready
thrifty
thriven
throaty
thrombi
throned
through
thrower
throwin
thrummy
thudded
thuggee
thulium
thummim
thumper
thunder
thymine
thyroid
thyrsus
thyself
Tibetan
ticking
tickler
tidally
tiddler
tiddley
tiderip
tideway
tidings
tieback
tiebeam
tiercel
tiercet
tiffany
tighten
tightly
tigress
tigrish
tilbury
tillage
timbale
timbrel
timelag
timeous
timidly
timothy
timpani
timpano
tinamou
tindery
tinfoil
tingler
tinhorn
tinnily
tinning
tintack
tinware
tipcart
tipping
tippler
tipsify
tipsily
tipster
titanic
tithing
titlark
titling
titmice
Titoism
Titoist
titrate
tittupy
titular
toaster
tobacco
toccata
toddler
toeclip
toehold
toeless
toenail
toggery
toilful
tollbar
tollman
toluene
tombola
tombolo
tomenta
tomfool
tompion
tonally
tonemic
tonerow
tonight
tonnage
tonneau
tonsure
tontine
toolbox
tooling
toothed
tootsie
topcoat
topfull
tophole
topiary
topical
topknot
topless
topmast
topmost
toponym
topping
topsail
topside
topsoil
torchon
torgoch
torment
tormina
tornado
torpedo
torpids
torrefy
torrent
torsade
torsion
tortile
tortrix
torture
torulae
Toryism
tosspot
totally
totemic
tottery
totting
touched
toucher
touchup
toughen
toughly
touraco
touring
tourism
tourist
tourney
towards
towboat
towered
towhead
towline
towmond
towmont
townish
townlet
towpath
towrope
toyshop
tracery
trachea
tracker
tractor
tradein
trading
traduce
traffic
tragedy
trailer
trainee
trainer
traipse
traitor
traject
tramcar
trammel
trample
tramway
tranche
trangam
transit
transom
tranter
trapeze
trapped
trapper
travail
travois
trawler
trayful
treacle
treacly
treader
treadle
treason
treater
treetop
trefoil
trehala
trekked
trekker
trellis
tremble
trembly
tremolo
trenail
trental
trepang
tressed
tressel
trestle
triable
triacid
triadic
tribade
triblet
tribune
tribute
triceps
tricker
trickle
tricksy
tricorn
trident
triduan
triduum
trifler
triform
trigamy
trigger
trilith
trilogy
trimmed
trimmer
trinary
trindle
tringle
trinity
trinket
trinkum
triolet
tripery
triplet
triplex
tripody
tripoli
tripped
tripper
trippet
tripple
trireme
trisect
trishaw
trismus
tritely
tritium
tritone
triumph
trivial
trivium
trochal
trochee
trochus
trodden
troller
trolley
trollop
trommel
trooper
trophic
tropics
tropism
trotted
trotter
trouble
trounce
trouper
trouser
truancy
trucial
trucker
truckle
trudgen
truffle
trumeau
trumpet
truncal
trundle
trusser
trustee
truster
trypsin
tryptic
trysail
tsardom
tsarina
tsarism

tsarist
Tsquare
tsunami
tuatara
tubbing
tubbish
tubular
tuckbox
Tuesday
tugboat
tugging
tuition
tulchan
tumbler
tumbrel
tumbril
tumidly
tumular
tumulus
tunable
tunably
tundish
tuneful
tunicle
tunning
turbary
turbine
turdine
turdoid
turfite
turfman
turgent
Turkish
turmoil
turnery
turning
turnipy
turnkey
turnout
turpeth
tushery
tussive
tussock
tussore
tutelar
tutenag
tutting
tutwork
twaddle
twaddly
twangle
twankay
tweeter
tweezer
twelfth
twelves
twibill
twiddle
twiddly
twigged
twilled
twinkle
twinkly
twinned
twister
twitchy
twitted
twitter
twofold
twoline
twoness
twosome
twostep
twotime
twotone
tychism
tylopod
tympana
tympani

tympano
tympany
Tynwald
typebar
typeset
typhoid
typhoon
typhous
typical
typonym
tyranny
tzigane
tzigany
uberous
udaller
ukelele
ukulele
ulcered
ululant
ululate
umbonal
umbones
umbrage
Umbrian
umpteen
unaptly
unarmed
unasked
unaware
unbated
unblest
unblock
unbosom
unbound
unbowed
unboxed
unbrace
unbuild
unbuilt
uncanny
unchain
uncinus
uncivil
unclasp
unclean
uncloak
unclose
uncouth
uncover
uncross
uncrown
unction
underdo
undergo
undoing
undress
undying
unearth
unequal
unfaith
unfitly
unfrock
unfroze
unfunny
unfussy
ungodly
unguard
unguent
ungulae
unhandy
unhappy
unheard
unhinge
unhitch
unhoped
unhorse
unhouse
unicity
unicorn

unideal
unifier
uniform
unitary
unitive
unjoint
unkempt
unknown
unladen
unlatch
unlearn
unleash
unlined
unloose
unlucky
unmanly
unmeant
unmixed
unmoral
unmoved
unnerve
unpaged
unquiet
unquote
unravel
unready
unright
unroost
unsaved
unscrew
unsexed
unshell
unsight
unsnarl
unsound
unstick
unstuck
unswear
unswore
unsworn
unteach
unthink
untried
untruly
untruss
untruth
untuned
untwine
untwist
untying
unusual
unweave
unwound
unwoven
upbraid
upfield
upgrade
upheave
upraise
upright
upriser
upsides
upsilon
upstage
upstair
upstart
upsurge
upsweep
upswept
upswing
upthrew
upthrow
uptight
uptrend
upwards
uraemia
Uralian
uralite
uranide

uranism
uranium
uranous
urethan
urethra
urgency
urinary
urodele
urology
useless
usually
usurper
utensil
uterine
utilise
utility
utopian
utopism
utopist
utricle
utterer
utterly
uveitis
uxorial
vacancy
vaccine
vacuity
vacuole
vacuous
vagally
vagrant
vaguely
vaguish
Vaishya
valance
valence
valency
valeric
valiant
validly
vallate
valonia
valuate
valvate
valvula
valvule
vamoose
vampire
vampish
vanadic
Vandyke
vanessa
vanilla
vantage
vanward
vapidly
vapours
vapoury
vaquero
variant
variate
varices
variety
variola
variole
various
varment
varmint
varnish
varsity
vascula
vastity
Vatican
vatting
Vaudois
vaulted
vaulter
vaunter
Vedanta

Veddoid
vedette
vegetal
vehicle
veiling
veining
veinlet
velamen
velaria
veliger
velours
veloute
velvety
venally
venatic
vendace
venefic
venerer
venison
ventage
ventail
ventral
venture
venturi
veranda
verbena
verbose
verdant
verdict
verdure
verglas
veriest
verismo
vermeil
vermian
vernier
verruca
versant
versify
versine
version
vertigo
vervain
vesicae
vesical
vesicle
vespers
vespine
vestige
vestral
vesture
veteran
vetiver
vetting
vexedly
vexilla
viaduct
viatica
vibrant
vibrate
vibrato
viceroy
vicinal
vicious
victory
victual
vidette
vidimus
viduity
viewing
vilayet
village
villain
villein
villose
villous
vinasse
vincula
vinegar

vintage
vintner
violate
violent
violist
violone
virelay
virgate
virgule
virtual
visaged
viscera
viscose
viscous
visible
visibly
visitor
visored
vistaed
vitally
vitamin
vitelli
vitiate
vitrify
vitrine
vitriol
vittate
vittles
vitular
vivaria
vividly
vivific
vixenly
vocable
vocalic
vocally
voguish
voivode
volante
volcano
voltage
voltaic
voluble
volubly
volumed
voluted
volutin
votable
vouchee
voucher
vowelly
voyager
vulgate
vulpine
vulture
wadable
wadding
waddler
waftage
wafture
wagerer
waggery
wagging
waggish
wagoner
wagtail
Wahabee
wailful
waisted
waister
waiting
wakeful
wakener
walking
walkout
walkway
wallaby
walleye
walling

Walloon
wallrue
waltzer
wanigan
wanness
wannish
wanting
waratah
warbler
warfare
wargame
warhead
warison
warlike
warlock
warlord
warmish
warning
warpath
warrant
warring
warrior
warship
warthog
wartime
washing
washout
washpot
washtub
waspish
wassail
wastage
wastrel
watcher
watered
waterer
wattage
Watteau
wattled
wattles
wavelet
waverer
waxbill
waxtree
waxwing
waxwork
waybill
waylaid
wayless
waymark
wayside
wayward
wayworn
weakish
wealden
wealthy
wearily
wearing
weasand
weather
webbing
webfoot
webster
webworm
wedding
wedging
wedlock
weekday
weekend
weevily
weigher
weighin
weighty
weirdie
weirdly
welcher
welcome
welfare
wellies

welloff
wellset
welsher
wencher
Wendish
wergild
werwolf
western
westing
wetback
wetness
wettest
wetting
wettish
whacker
whaling
whangee
wharves
whatnot
wheaten
wheedle
wheeled
wheeler
whereas
whereat
whereby
wherein
whereof
whereon
whereto
whether
whetted
whetter
wheyish
whicker
whidder
whiffle
whimper
whimsey
whinger
whipped
whipper
whippet
whipsaw
whirler
whirred
whisker
whiskey
whisper
whistle
whitely
whither
whiting
whitish
whitlow
Whitsun
whittle
whizkid
whizzed
whoever
whoopee
whooper
whopper
whorish
whorled
whoseso
wickiup
widgeon
widowed
widower
wielder
wigging
wiggler
wigless
wildcat
wilding
wildish
willies
willing

willowy
windage
windbag
windegg
windily
winding
windrow
Windsor
winesap
winglet
wingnut
winkers
winning
winnock
winsome
wintery
wireman
wiretap
wishful
wishing
wistful
withers
without
witless
witling
witloof
witness
wittily
witting
wizened
wobbler
wolfcub
wolfdog
wolfish
wolfram
wolvish
womanly
woodcut
woodman
woodpie
woolfat
woolled
woollen
wooloil
woolsey
woomera
woozily
wordage
wordily
wording
workbag
workbox
workday
working
workman
workout
worldly
wornout
worrier
worship
worsted
wottest
wouldbe
wouldst
wrangle
wrapped
wrapper
wreathe
wreathy
wrecker
wrestle
wriggle
wriggly
wringer
wrinkle
wrinkly
writeup
writhen
writing

written
wrongly
wrought
wrybill
wryneck
wryness
wychelm
xanthic
xanthin
xiphoid
Yahvist
Yahwist
yapping
yardage
yardang
yardarm
yardman
yashmak
yatagan
ycleped
yeggman
yellowy
yenning
yestern
yewtree
Yiddish
yielder
yipping
yoghurt
yolksac
Yorkist
younger
younker
yttrium
yulelog
zapping
zaptieh
zealous
zebrine
zebroid
zedoary
zemstvo
zeolite
zestful
zetetic
ziganka
zillion
zincify
zincing
zincite
zincked
Zingari
Zingaro
zinkify
zinking
Zionism
Zionist
zipcode
zipping
zithern
zoarium
Zoilism
Zoilist
zonated
zoogamy
zoogeny
zoogony
zooidal
zoology
zoonomy
zootaxy
zootomy
zygosis
zygotic
zymogen
zymosis
zymotic
zymurgy

Baalism
babassu
babbitt
babbler
babyish
babysit
baccara
baccate
bacchic
bacilli
backing
backlog
backsaw
backset
baddish
badmash
badness
baffler
bagasse
baggage
baggily
bagging
bagpipe
Bahadur
Bahaism
Bahaist
Bahaite
bailiff
baklava
balance
balcony
balding
baldish
baldric
baleful
ballade
ballast
ballboy
balloon
balmily
baloney
bambini
bambino
banally
bananas
bandage
bandana
bandbox
bandeau
bandore
bandsaw
baneful
banjoes
banking
banksia
banning
bannock
banquet
banshee
banteng
banting
baptise
baptism
baptist
barbate
barbell
barbule
bargain
barilla
barline
barmaid
baronet
baroque
barrack
barrage
barrier
barring
barroom
barytes

barytic
bascule
baseman
basenji
bashful
basidia
basilar
basinet
bassist
bassoon
bastard
basting
bastion
bateaux
bathing
bathtub
batiste
batsman
battels
battery
batting
Bauhaus
bauxite
bawcock
bawdily
bayonet
bazooka
cabaret
cabbage
cabbagy
cabbala
cabinet
cabling
caboose
cabrank
cacanny
cachexy
cacique
cackler
cacodyl
cacoepy
cacumen
cadaver
caddice
caddish
cadence
cadency
cadenza
Cadmean
cadmium
caducei
caesium
caesura
cagoule
cahoots
caimans
caisson
caitiff
cajoler
calamus
calando
calcify
calcine
calcite
calcium
calculi
caldera
caldron
calends
calibre
calices
caliche
calicle
calipee
caliper
callant
callbox
callboy
calling

callous
calomel
caloric
calorie
calotte
caloyer
calpack
caltrap
caltrop
calumet
calumny
calvary
calyces
calycle
calypso
calyxes
camaron
cambial
cambist
cambium
cambrel
cambric
camelot
camelry
cameral
camorra
campbed
camphor
camping
campion
camwood
canakin
canasta
candela
candent
candied
candour
canikin
cannery
cannily
canning
cannula
canonic
canonry
Canopic
cantata
cantate
canteen
canthus
cantina
canting
cantrip
canvass
canzone
canzoni
capable
capably
capelin
caperer
capital
capitol
caporal
capping
caprice
caprine
caproic
Capsian
capsize
capstan
capsule
captain
caption
captive
capture
capuche
caracal
caracul
caramel
caravan

caravel
caraway
carbide
carbine
carcase
carcass
cardiac
cardoon
careful
caribou
carinae
carinal
carinas
carioca
cariole
carious
carking
carline
Carlism
Carlist
carload
carmine
carnage
caroche
carotid
carotin
carouse
carping
carport
carrack
carrier
carrion
carroty
carryon
carsick
cartage
cartful
cartoon
carving
cascade
cascara
caseous
caserne
cashier
cassata
cassava
cassino
cassock
castile
casting
castled
castoff
casuals
casuist
Catalan
catalos
catalpa
catarrh
catawba
catbird
catboat
catcall
catcher
catchup
catechu
catenae
catenas
cateran
caterer
catfish
Cathari
Cathars
cathead
cathode
cathood
catlike
catling
catmint
catseye

catspaw
catsuit
cattalo
cattery
cattily
catwalk
caudate
caulker
caustic
cautery
caution
cavally
cavalry
caveman
cavetti
cavetto
caviare
cayenne
caymans
dabbing
dabbler
dacoity
Dadaism
Dadaist
dallier
damming
damnify
damning
damosel
damozel
dampish
dandify
Danelaw
dangler
danseur
Dantean
dapsone
darbies
dariole
darkish
darling
darning
darshan
dashiki
dashing
dashpot
dastard
dasyure
datable
datival
dauphin
dawdler
dawning
daybook
daylong
dayroom
daystar
daytime
daywork
dazedly
dazzler
eagerly
earache
eardrop
eardrum
earflap
earhole
earldom
earlobe
earlock
earmark
earmuff
earnest
earplug
earring
earshot
earthen
earthly
easeful

eastern
easting
eatable
Faberge
fabliau
fabular
faceoff
faceted
faction
factory
factual
facture
faculae
faculty
faddish
faddism
faddist
fadedly
fadeout
fagging
fagotto
faience
failing
failure
faintly
fairing
fairish
fairway
Falange
falbala
falcate
falcula
fallacy
fallguy
falling
falloff
fallout
falsely
falsies
falsify
falsity
famulus
fanatic
fancier
fancily
fanclub
fanfare
fanfold
fanmail
fanning
fantail
fantasm
fantast
fantasy
fantods
faraday
faradic
faraway
farceur
farcing
fargone
farming
farmost
Faroese
farrago
farrier
farruca
farther
fascial
fascine
Fascism
Fascist
fashion
fastday
fatally
fateful
fathead
fatigue
fatling

fatness
fattest
fatting
fattish
fatuity
fatuous
faucial
faunist
fauvism
fauvist
gabbing
gabbler
gabelle
gabfest
gabnash
gadding
gadgety
gadroon
gadwall
gagging
gagster
gahnite
gainful
gainsay
Galahad
galanga
galatea
galeate
galenic
galilee
galipot
gallant
gallate
galleon
gallery
gallfly
gallice
galling
galliot
gallium
gallnut
galloon
gallows
galumph
gambade
gambado
gambier
gambler
gamboge
gambrel
gamebag
gamelan
gametic
ganglia
gangrel
gangway
gantlet
garbage
garbler
garboil
gardant
garfish
garland
garment
garnish
garotte
garpike
gascoal
gaseous
gasfire
gasmask
gasring
gassing
gastric
gateaux
gateleg
gateway
gathers
gatling

gaudery
gaudily
Gaulish
gauntly
gauntry
gavotte
gawkily
gayness
gazelle
gazette
habitat
habitue
hachure
hackbut
hackery
hacking
hackler
hackney
hacksaw
haddock
hafnium
hagfish
Haggada
haggard
haggish
haggler
hagweed
haircut
hairnet
hairpin
Halakah
halberd
halbert
halcyon
halfway
halfwit
halibut
halidom
hallali
hallway
halogen
halting
halvers
halyard
Hamburg
Hamitic
hamming
hammock
hamster
hamulus
handbag
handcar
handful
handgun
handily
handler
handoff
handout
handsaw
handsel
handset
hangdog
hanging
hangman
hangout
Hansard
hanuman
hapence
hapenny
hapless
haploid
haporth
happily
happing
harbour
hardhit
hardpan
hardset
hardtop

harelip
haricot
harijan
harmala
harmful
harmony
harness
harpist
harpoon
harrier
harshen
harshly
harslet
harvest
hasbeen
hashish
hassock
hastate
hastily
hatable
hatband
hatcher
hatchet
hateful
hatless
hatting
hauberk
haughty
haulage
haulier
haunted
haunter
hautboy
hauteur
havenot
hawkish
haycock
hayfork
hayloft
hayrick
hayseed
hayward
haywire
jabbing
jacamar
jacinth
jackass
jackdaw
jackpot
jacktar
Jacobin
jacobus
jaconet
jadedly
jadeite
jaggery
Jainism
jaloppy
jamming
Janeite
jangler
janitor
jannock
January
japonic
jargoon
jarring
jasmine
javelin
jawbone
jaybird
jaywalk
jazzily
jazzman
kabbala
Kaddish
kainite
kalends
Kalmuck
kalpack
kampong
Kannada
Kantian
Karaite
karakul
karting
kathode
katydid
labarum
labella
labiate
lacking
laconic
lacquer
lactate
lacteal
lactose
lacunae
lacunal
lacunar
lacunas
ladanum
ladybug
ladykin
laggard
lagging
laicise
laicism
lairage
lakelet
Lallans
Lamaism
Lamaist
lambast
lambent
lambert
lambkin
lamella
laminae
laminar
lamming
lampion
lampoon
lamprey
lancers
landing
languet
languid
languor
laniary
lankily
lanolin
lantana
lantern
lanyard
Laotian
lapilli
lapping
Laputan
lapwing
larceny
lardoon
largely
largess
largish
lasagna
lasagne
lashing
lashkar
lassoes
lasting
latakia
latchet
latency
lateral
latexes
lathery
lathing
latices
latrine
lattice
Latvian
laugher
launder
laundry
laurels
lavolta
lavrock
lawhand
lawless
lawlist
lawlord
lawsuit
laxness
layered
layette
lazaret
macabre
macadam
macaque
machair
machete
machine
macrame
macrami
maculae
macular
maddest
madding
Madeira
madness
madonna
madrona
madrono
madwort
maestri
maestro
maffick
mafiosi
mafioso
magenta
maggoty
magical
magmata
magnate
magneto
magnify
mahaleb
mahatma
Mahdism
Mahdist
mahjong
mahonia
mahound
mahseer
maidish
maidism
mailbag
mailbox
mailing
maillot
mailman
mailvan
maintop
majesty
makings
malacia
malaise
malaria
Malayan
malefic
malines
malison
mallard
malleus
malmsey
maltase
Maltese
malting
maltose
mamelon
mamilla
mammary
mammate
mammock
mammoth
manacle
manager
manakin
manatee
manchet
mandala
mandate
mandola
mandora
mandrel
mandril
mangily
mangoes
mangold
manhole
manhood
manhour
manhunt
manihot
manikin
manilla
manille
maniple
manitou
manjack
mankind
manless
manlike
manmade
manners
manning
mannish
mannite
mannose
mansard
mansion
mansize
manteau
mantlet
mantram
mantrap
manumit
manward
manweek
Manxcat
Manxman
manyear
mapping
marabou
Maratha
Marathi
marbled
marbles
marcher
marconi
maremma
margent
marimba
mariner
marital
markhor
marking
marline
marlite
marmite
marplot
marquee
marquis
Marrano
married
marring
marrowy
Marsala
marshal
martial
Martian
martini
martlet
martyry
Marxian
Marxism
Marxist
marybud
mascara
mashtub
Masonic
masonry
Masorah
masquer
massage
masseur
massive
mastaba
masters
mastery
mastich
mastiff
mastoid
matador
matchet
matelot
matinal
matinee
matrass
mattery
matting
mattins
mattock
mattoid
matzoth
maudlin
maunder
mauther
mawkish
mawworm
maxilla
maximal
maximum
maxwell
mayoral
maypole
Maytime
mayweed
mazurka
mazzard
nabbing
nacarat
nacelle
nacrous
nagging
Nahuatl
naiades
nailery
naively
naivete
naivety
nakedly
namable
nameday
nankeen
naphtha
napless
napping
narrate
narrows
narthex
narwhal
nasally
nascent
nastily
nattily
natural
naughty
nauplii
nautics
nautili
navarin
Naziism
oakfern
oakgall
oakling
oaktree
oakwood
oarfish
oarless
oarlock
oarsman
oarweed
oatcake
oatmeal
pabulum
pachisi
pacific
package
packice
packing
packman
padding
paddler
paddock
padlock
padrone
padroni
paeonic
pageant
pageboy
paginal
pahlavi
pailful
painful
painter
pairoar
paisley
pajamas
paladin
palatal
palaver
paletot
palette
palfrey
palings
pallium
palmary
palmate
palmist
palmoil
palmyra
palpate
palsied
paludal
pampean
pampero
panacea
panache
pancake
Pandean
pandect
pandora
pandore
panicky
panicle
Panjabi
pannage
pannier
panning
panocha
panoply
panther
panties
pantile
papadam
papally
paperer
Paphian
papilla
papoose
pappose
paprika
papulae
papular
papyrus
parable
parader
parados
paradox
paragon
parapet
parasol
parboil
pardner
parerga
paresis
paretic
parfait
pargana
parkway
parlour
parlous
parodic
parolee
paronym
parotid
parpend
parquet
parsley
parsnip
partake
partial
parting
partita
partite
partlet
partner
partook
parvenu
parvise
paschal
passade
passado
passage
passant
passing
passion
passive
passkey
pastern
pasteup
pastime
pasture
patagia
patella
patency
pathway
patient
patrial
patriot
patroon
pattern
patting
paucity
Pauline
paunchy
paviour
payable
paydesk
payload
payment
payroll
paysage
rabbity
rabbler
rabidly
raccoon
racemic
rackety
racquet
radiant
radiate
radical
radices
radicle
radulae
radular
raffish
ragbolt
ragdoll
raggedy
ragging
ragtime
ragweed
ragworm
ragwort
railcar
railing
railman
railway
raiment
rainbow
Rajpoot
rakeoff
rallier
ralline
Ramadan
rambler
ramekin
ramenta
ramming
rampage
rampant
rampart
rampion
ramsons
rancher
rancour
ranking
ransack
rapeoil
raphide
rapidly
rapping
rapport
rapture
rarebit
raschel
rasping
ratable
ratafia
ratatat
ratchet
rations
ratlike
ratling
rattail
ratteen
rattery
ratting
rattler
rattrap
raucous
raunchy
ravager
ravelin
ravined
ravings
ravioli
rawhide
rawness
rayless
Sabaism
Sabaoth
Sabbath
saccade
saccate
saccule
sacculi
sackbut
sackful
sacking
sacring
sacrist
saddest
saddish
saddler
sadness
saffron
sagging
sagitta
saguaro
saidest
sailing
sainted
saintly
sakeret
Saktism
salable
salicet
salicin
salient
Salique
sallowy
salpinx
salsify
saltant
saltbox
saltcat
saltern
salting
saltire
saltish
saltpan
saluter
salvage
salvoes
sambuca
samisen
samovar
Samoyed
sampler
samurai
sanctum
Sanctus
sandbag
sandbar
sandbed
sandbox
sandboy
sanders
sandfly
sandlot
sandman
sandpit
sangria
sanicle
santour
sapajou
saphead
sapient
sapless
sapling
saponin
sapphic
sapping
saprobe
sapsago
sapwood

Saracen
sarangi
sarcasm
sarcode
sarcoid
sarcoma
sarcous
sardine
sardius
sarking
sashimi
sassaby
satanic
satchel
satiate
satiety
satinet
satiric
satisfy
satrapy
satsuma
satyral
satyric
satyrid
saucily
saunter
saurian
sauroid
sausage
savable
savanna
saveall
saveloy
savings
saviour
savoury
sawbill
sawbuck
sawdust
sawfish
sawgate
sawmill
sawnoff
sawwort
saxhorn
saxtuba
sayable
tabanid
tabaret
tabasco
tabbing
tabetic
tabinet
tableau
tabloid
taborer
tabular
tachism
tachist
tacitly
tacking
tackler
tactful
tactics
tactile
taction
tactual
tadpole
taeniae
taffeta
Tagalog
tagetes
tagging
tailend
tailing
takeoff
takings
talaria
talayot

talcose
talcous
talipes
talipot
talking
tallage
tallboy
tallish
tallith
tallowy
tallyho
taloned
tamable
tamarin
tamasha
tambour
Tammany
tamping
tampion
tanager
tanagra
tanbark
tandoor
tangelo
tangent
tanghin
tangram
tankage
tankard
tankcar
tankful
tannage
tannate
tannery
tanning
tannish
tanooze
tantara
tantivy
tantric
tantrum
tanyard
taperer
tapetal
tapetum
tapioca
tapping
taproom
taproot
tapsman
tapster
tarbush
tardily
tarnish
tarrier
tarring
tartare
tartish
tartlet
Tartufe
tastily
tatters
tattery
tattily
tatting
tattler
taunter
taurine
taxable
taxfree
taxicab
taxiing
taximan
taxless
taxying
vacancy
vaccine
vacuity
vacuole

vacuous
vagally
vagrant
vaguely
vaguish
Vaishya
valance
valence
valency
valeric
valiant
validly
vallate
valonia
valuate
valvate
valvula
valvule
vamoose
vampire
vampish
vanadic
Vandyke
vanessa
vanilla
vantage
vanward
vapidly
vapours
vapoury
vaquero
variant
variate
varices
variety
variola
variole
various
varment
varmint
varnish
varsity
vascula
vastity
Vatican
vatting
Vaudois
vaulted
vaulter
vaunter
wadable
wadding
waddler
waftage
wafture
wagerer
waggery
wagging
waggish
wagoner
wagtail
Wahabee
wailful
waisted
waister
waiting
wakeful
wakener
walking
walkout
walkway
wallaby
walleye
walling
Walloon
wallrue
waltzer
wanigan
wanness

wannish
wanting
waratah
warbler
warfare
wargame
warhead
warison
warlike
warlock
warlord
warmish
warning
warpath
warrant
warring
warrior
warship
warthog
wartime
washing
washout
washpot
washtub
waspish
wassail
wastage
wastrel
watcher
watered
waterer
wattage
Watteau
wattled
wattles
wavelet
waverer
waxbill
waxtree
waxwing
waxwork
waybill
waylaid
wayless
waymark
wayside
wayward
wayworn
xanthic
xanthin
Yahvist
Yahwist
yapping
yardage
yardang
yardarm
yardman
yashmak
yatagan
zapping
zaptieh
abaddon
abalone
abandon
abashed
abattis
abaxial
Abbasid
abdomen
Abelian
abetted
abetter
abettor
abeyant
abiding
abigail
ability
abiotic
abjurer

ablator
abolish
abomasa
aborter
abought
aboulia
abrader
abreact
abreast
abridge
abroach
abscess
abscise
abscond
absence
absinth
absolve
abstain
abubble
abusive
abutted
abutter
abysmal
abyssal
ebbtide
ebonise
ebonite
ebriate
ebriety
Iberian
obconic
obelise
obelisk
obesity
obitual
obligee
obligor
oblique
obloquy
obolary
obovate
obovoid
obscene
obscure
observe
obtrude
obverse
obviate
obvious
uberous
academe
academy
Acadian
acantha
acarian
accidie
acclaim
account
accrete
accrual
accurst
accusal
accused
accuser
acequia
acerbic
acerola
acerose
acetate
acetify
acetone
acetous
Achaean
Achaian
Achates
achieve
acicula
acidify
acidity

acinous
ackemma
acolyte
aconite
acouchy
acquest
acquire
acrasin
acreage
acridly
acrobat
acrogen
acronym
acroter
acrylic
actinia
actinic
actinon
actress
actuary
actuate
acutely
acyclic
eccrine
ecdyses
ecdysis
echelon
echidna
echinus
echoism
eclipse
eclogue
ecology
economy
ecstasy
ectopic
iceberg
iceboat
icecold
icefall
icefloe
icefoot
icepack
icerink
iceshow
ichabod
iciness
icteric
icterus
ocarina
occiput
occlude
oceanic
ocellar
ocellus
ochrous
octagon
octaval
octette
October
octopod
octopus
octuple
oculate
oculist
scabbed
scabble
scabies
scabrid
scaglia
scalade
scalado
scalder
scaldic
scalene
scallop
scalpel
scalper
scamper

scandal
scanned
scanner
scantly
scapple
scapula
scarfed
scarify
scarlet
scarper
scarred
scarves
scatted
scatter
scauper
scenery
scented
scepsis
sceptic
sceptre
schappe
schemer
scherzi
scherzo
schlepp
schlock
schmuck
schnook
scholar
scholia
sciarid
sciatic
science
scirrhi
scissel
scissor
scleral
scoffer
scolder
scollop
scomber
scooper
scooter
scopula
scoriae
scorify
scoring
scorner
scorper
Scorpio
scotice
Scotism
Scotist
scotoma
Scottie
scourer
scourge
scouter
scraggy
scranny
scraper
scrapie
scrappy
scratch
scrawly
scrawny
screech
screeve
screwed
screwer
scribal
scriber
scrieve
scrimpy
scrooge
scrouge
scrubby
scruffy
scrumpy

scrunch
scruple
scudded
scuffle
sculler
sculpin
scumble
scummed
scunner
scupper
scurril
scutage
scutate
scutter
scuttle
ycleped
adamant
Adamite
adapter
adaptor
adaxial
addable
addenda
addible
address
adducer
adenine
adenoid
adenoma
adeptly
adherer
adhibit
adipose
adjoint
adjourn
adjudge
adjunct
admiral
admirer
adnexal
adopter
adrenal
adulate
adultly
advance
adverse
advised
adviser
advisor
edacity
edaphic
edictal
edifice
edition
educate
eductor
ideally
identic
idiotic
idlesse
idolise
idyllic
odalisk
oddball
oddment
oddness
odontic
odorant
odorous
odoured
odyssey
udaller
aeolian
aeonian
aerator
aerobic
aerosol
beading
beamish

beanbag
bearded
bearing
bearish
beastly
beatify
beating
beatnik
because
becloud
bedding
bedevil
bedfast
bedight
bedizen
bedouin
bedpost
bedrock
bedroll
bedroom
bedside
bedsock
bedsore
bedtime
beechen
beehive
beeline
beeswax
beggary
begging
begonia
begorra
begrime
beguile
beguine
behaver
behoove
beignet
bejewel
beknown
belated
belcher
beldame
Belgian
believe
bellboy
bellhop
belljar
bellman
bellows
beloved
Beltane
belting
belying
bencher
beneath
benefic
benefit
Benelux
Bengali
benison
benthic
benthos
benzene
benzine
benzoic
benzoin
benzole
benzoyl
bepaint
bequest
bereave
bergylt
berhyme
berline
berried
berserk
beseech
beshrew

besides
besiege
besmear
bespeak
bespoke
bestead
bestial
bestrew
betaken
bethink
betimes
betoken
betroth
betting
between
betwixt
bewitch
bezique
cedilla
ceilidh
ceiling
celadon
celesta
celeste
cellist
cellule
Celsius
cembalo
cenacle
censure
centaur
centavo
centime
centner
central
centred
centric
centrum
century
cepheid
ceramic
cerebra
ceresin
certain
certify
cerumen
cervine
cession
cesspit
cestode
cestoid
deadend
deadeye
deadpan
deafaid
dealing
deanery
deathly
debacle
debater
debauch
debouch
Debrett
debrief
decadal
decagon
decanal
decapod
decease
deceive
decency
deciare
decibel
decided
decider
decidua
decimal
decking
declaim
declare
declass
decline
decoder
decorum
decrier
decrypt
decuman
decuple
deepfry
deepsea
default
defence
defiant
deficit
defiler
definer
deflate
deflect
defocus
deforce
defraud
defrock
defrost
defunct
degauss
degrade
dehisce
deicide
deictic
deiform
deistic
delaine
delator
delayer
delight
Delilah
delimit
deliver
delouse
Delphic
deltaic
deltoid
deluder
demerit
demesne
demigod
demirep
demoded
demonic
demotic
demount
denarii
denizen
densely
density
dentate
dentine
dentist
denture
deodand
deodara
deplane
deplete
deplore
deplume
deposal
deposit
deprave
depress
deprive
derange
derider
derrick
dervish
descant
descend
descent
deserve
despair
despise
despite
despoil
despond
dessert
destine
destiny
destroy
deterge
detinue
detract
detrain
detrude
deutzia
devalue
develop
deviant
deviate
devilry
devious
devisal
devisee
deviser
devisor
devolve
devoted
devotee
dewclaw
dewdrop
dewfall
dewpond
dextral
dextran
dextrin
eelpout
eelworm
fearful
feaster
feather
feature
febrile
fedayee
federal
feeding
feedlot
feeling
feigner
felonry
felsite
felspar
felting
felucca
felwort
feminal
femoral
fencing
fenfire
fenland
feoffee
feoffer
feoffor
fermata
ferment
fermion
fermium
fernery
fernowl
ferrate
ferrety
ferrite
ferrous
ferrugo
ferrule
fertile
fervent
fervour
festive
festoon
fetidly
fetlock
fetters
feudist
fewness
feyness
gearbox
gearing
geckoes
geebung
Gehenna
gelatin
gelding
gelidly
gelling
gemmate
gemmery
gemming
gemmule
gemsbok
general
generic
geneses
genesis
genetic
genette
Genevan
genista
genitor
genizah
genning
Genoese
genteel
gentian
gentile
genuine
geodesy
geogony
geoidal
geology
Geordie
georgic
gerbera
germane
gestalt
gestapo
gestate
gesture
getaway
getting
headily
heading
headman
headpin
headset
headway
healthy
hearing
hearken
hearsay
hearted
hearten
heathen
heather
heating
heavily
hebenon
Hebraic
heckler
hectare
hedonic
heedful
heeltap
heftily
heighho
heinous
heiress
helical
helices
helicon
hellbox
hellcat
Hellene
hellion
hellish
helluva
helotry
helpful
helping
hemiola
hemione
hemline
hemlock
hemming
henbane
hencoop
hennery
henpeck
henwife
heparin
hepatic
heptane
herbage
heretic
heritor
herniae
hernial
hernias
heroics
heroine
heroise
heroism
heronry
herring
herself
hessian
hetaera
hetaira
hexadic
hexagon
hexapla
hexapod
heyduck
jealous
jejunum
jellaba
jellied
jemadar
jerkily
jetting
jewelry
jewfish
Jezebel
keelson
keeping
kenning
kenosis
kenotic
kentish
keramic
keratin
kermess
kerogen
kerygma
kestrel
ketchup
keyhole
keyless
keynote
keyring
keyword
leading
leadoff
leafage
leafbud
leaflet
leaguer
leakage
leaning
learned
learner
leather
lechery
lectern
lection
lecture
leeward
leftism
leftist
legally
legatee
legator
legbail
legging
leghorn
legible
legibly
legiron
legless
legpull
legrest
legroom
legshow
legwork
leister
leisure
lemmata
lemming
lending
lengthy
lenient
lentigo
lentisk
lentoid
leonine
leopard
leotard
leprosy
leprous
lesbian
letdown
lethean
letters
letting
Lettish
lettuce
leucine
leucite
leucoma
levator
levelly
leveret
lexical
lexicon
meadowy
mealies
meander
meaning
measles
measure
meatfly
meatman
Mechlin
meconic
meddler
mediacy
mediant
mediate
medical
medulla
medusae
medusan
medusas
meerkat
meeting
megaron
megaton
meiosis
meiotic
Meissen
melange
melanic
melanin
melilot
melisma
melodic
melting
memento
memoirs
mending
menfolk
menisci
menorah
menthol
mention
mercery
merchet
mercury
mermaid
merrily
meseems
mesonic
message
messiah
Messias
messily
messtin
mestiza
mestizo
metamer
metayer
metazoa
methane
metonym
metopic
metopon
metrics
metrist
mettled
Mexican
mezuzah
nearest
nebbish
nebulae
nebular
nebulas
necklet
necktie
necrose
nectary
needful
needler
neglect
neglige
Negress
Negrito
negroid
neither
nelumbo
nemesia
nemesis
Neogaea
neolith
neology
neonate
neoteny
neozoic
nephric
Neptune
neritic
nervate
nervine
nervous
nervure
nesting
netball
netfish
netlike
netsuke
netting
network
neurine
neuroma
neurone
neuston
neutral
neutron
newborn
newcome
newlaid
newmown
newness
newsboy
newsman
oedipal
oenomel
oersted
oestral
oestrum
oestrus
peacock
peafowl
pearled
pearler
peartly
peasant
peascod
peasoup
pebrine
peccant
peccary
peckish
peddler
pedicab
pedicel
pedicle
pedlary
peerage
peeress
peevish
Pegasus
pegging
pelagic
pelican
pelisse
peloria
peloric
pelorus
peltate
pelting
pemican
penally
penalty
penance
pendant
pendent
pending
penguin
penname
pennant
pennate
pennies
pennill
pennine
penning
pensile
pension
pensive
pentane
pentode
pentose
peonage
peppery
peppill
pepping
peptalk
peptide
peptise
peptone
percale
percent
percept
percher
percine
percoid
percuss
perdure
perfect
perfidy
perform
perfume
perfuse
pergola
perhaps
periapt
peridot
perigee
perique
periwig
perjure
perjury
perkily
perlite
Permian
permute
perpend
perpent
perplex
Persian
persist
persona
pertain
perturb
pertuse
perusal
peruser
pervade
pervert
pessary
petasus
petiole
petrify
Petrine
petrous
pettily
petting
pettish
petunia
reacher
reactor
readily
reading
readout
reagent
realgar
realign
realise
realism
realist
reality
reallot
realtor
rebirth
reboant
rebound
rebuild
rebuilt
rebuker
receipt
receive
recency
recital
reciter
reclaim

reclame
recline
recluse
recount
recover
recruit
rectify
rectory
rectrix
recurve
recycle
redcoat
reddest
reddish
redhead
redlegs
redneck
redness
redoubt
redound
redpoll
redraft
redress
redskin
reducer
redwing
redwood
reeding
reelect
reenact
reenter
reentry
referee
refined
refiner
reflate
reflect
refloat
refocus
refract
refrain
refresh
refugee
refusal
refuser
refutal
refuter
regalia
regally
regards
regatta
regency
regimen
reginal
regnant
regorge
regrant
regrate
regress
regrets
regroup
regular
regulus
reheard
rehouse
reissue
rejoice
relapse
related
relater
relator
relayed
release
reliant
relieve
relievo
relight
relique
remains

remarry
remblai
remiges
remnant
remodel
remorse
remould
remount
removal
removed
remover
reneger
renegue
renewal
renewer
rentier
reorder
repaint
repaper
repiner
repique
replace
replant
replete
replevy
replica
replier
reposal
reposit
repress
reprint
reprise
reproof
reprove
reptile
repulse
reputed
request
requiem
require
requite
reredos
rescale
rescind
rescuer
reseaux
reserve
reshape
residua
residue
resolve
resound
respect
respell
respelt
respire
respite
respond
respray
restart
restate
restful
restiff
restive
restock
restore
restyle
resurge
retable
retaken
rethink
retiary
reticle
retinae
retinal
retinas
retinol
retinue
retired

retouch
retrace
retract
retrain
retread
retreat
retrial
retsina
rettery
retting
returns
reunion
reunite
revalue
revelry
revenge
revenue
reverie
reverse
reversi
reviler
revisal
reviser
revisit
revival
reviver
revivor
revolve
revving
rewound
rewrite
rewrote
reynard
seabass
seabear
seabird
seablue
seaboot
seafish
seafood
seafowl
seagirt
seagull
seakale
sealane
sealant
sealegs
sealery
seamaid
seamark
seapink
seaport
searoom
seasick
seaside
seaslug
seatang
seating
seawall
seaward
seaware
seaweed
seawhip
seawife
seawolf
seceder
seclude
seconde
secondi
secondo
secrecy
secrete
sectary
sectile
section
secular
securer
sedilia
seducer

seeable
seedbed
seedily
seedlip
seeming
seepage
segment
seismal
seismic
seizing
seizure
selenic
selffed
selfish
sellout
seltzer
selvage
sematic
semilog
seminal
seminar
semiped
Semitic
senarii
senator
senatus
sendoff
senecio
senhora
senores
sensory
sensual
Senussi
seppuku
septate
septime
sequela
sequent
sequoia
Serbian
serfage
serfdom
seriate
sericin
seriema
seringa
serious
serpent
serpigo
serpula
serrate
serried
servant
servery
Servian
service
servile
serving
Servite
sessile
session
sestina
setback
setdown
setting
settler
settlor
setwall
seventh
seventy
several
sexfoil
sexless
Sextans
sextant
sextile
teacake
teacher
teachin

teacosy
teagown
tealeaf
tearful
teargas
tearing
tearoom
tearose
teashop
teatime
teatray
technic
tectrix
tedding
tedious
teeming
teenage
tegmina
tegular
tektite
telamon
teleost
telergy
telling
telpher
Telstar
tempera
tempest
Templar
templet
tempter
tempura
tenable
tenably
tenancy
tendril
tenfold
tenoner
tenpins
tensely
tensile
tension
tensity
tensive
tentbed
tentfly
tenthly
tentpeg
tenuity
tenuous
tepidly
tequila
terbium
terebra
tergite
termini
termite
ternary
ternate
terpene
terrace
terrain
terrene
terrier
terrify
terrine
tersely
tertial
tertian
tessera
testacy
testate
testban
testbed
testfly
testify
testily
testoon
testudo

tetanic
tetanus
tetrode
textile
textual
texture
Vedanta
Veddoid
vedette
vegetal
vehicle
veiling
veining
veinlet
velamen
velaria
veliger
velours
veloute
velvety
venally
venatic
vendace
venefic
venerer
venison
ventage
ventail
ventral
venture
venturi
veranda
verbena
verbose
verdant
verdict
verdure
verglas
veriest
verismo
vermeil
vermian
vernier
verruca
versant
versify
versine
version
vertigo
vervain
vesicae
vesical
vesicle
vespers
vespine
vestige
vestral
vesture
veteran
vetiver
vetting
vexedly
vexilla
weakish
wealden
wealthy
wearily
wearing
weasand
weather
webbing
webfoot
webster
webworm
wedding
wedging
wedlock
weekday
weekend

weevily
weigher
weighin
weighty
weirdie
weirdly
welcher
welcome
welfare
wellies
welloff
wellset
welsher
wencher
Wendish
wergild
werwolf
western
westing
wetback
wetness
wettest
wetting
wettish
yeggman
yellowy
yenning
yestern
yewtree
zealous
zebrine
zebroid
zedoary
zemstvo
zeolite
zestful
zetetic
afeared
affable
affably
affaire
affined
afflict
affront
African
effects
effendi
effulge
offbeat
offence
offhand
officer
offload
offpeak
offside
pfennig
sferics
sfumato
against
agamous
ageless
agelong
aggress
agilely
agility
agitate
agitato
agnatic
agnomen
agonise
agonist
agraffe
agrapha
aground
egality
eggcosy
eggflip
egghead
egotise

egotism
egotist
egotrip
igneous
igniter
ignoble
ignobly
ignorer
oghamic
ogreish
bheesty
bheetie
Chablis
chaffer
chagrin
chalaza
Chaldee
chalice
challis
chalone
chamber
chamfer
chamois
champac
champak
chancel
chancre
changer
channel
chanson
chanter
chantry
chaotic
chapati
chaplet
chapman
chapped
chappie
chapter
charade
charger
charily
chariot
charism
charity
charley
charlie
charmer
charnel
charpoy
charqui
charred
charter
chassis
chasten
chateau
chatted
chattel
chatter
cheapen
cheaply
cheater
checker
checkup
cheddar
cheerer
cheerio
cheetah
chelate
chemise
chemism
chemist
chequer
cherish
cheroot
chervil
chessel
chested
cheviot

chevron
Chianti
chiasma
chibouk
chicane
Chicano
chicken
chicory
chidden
chiefly
chiffon
chigger
chignon
childer
childly
chiliad
chillum
chimera
chimere
chimney
chindit
Chinese
Chinook
chintzy
chinwag
chipped
chipper
chirrup
chitter
chlamys
chloral
chloric
chocice
Choctaw
cholera
choline
chooser
choosey
chopine
chopped
chopper
chorale
chordal
chorine
chorion
choroid
chortle
chowder
chrisom
christy
chromic
chronic
chuckle
chuddah
chuddar
chuffed
chugged
chukker
chummed
chunnel
chunter
chupati
churchy
chutney
chymous
gharial
ghastly
gherkin
ghettos
ghillie
ghostly
khaddar
khamsin
khanate
khedive
phaeton
phalanx
phallic
phallus

phantom pharaoh pharynx phasmid phellem philter philtre phlegmy phoenix phonate phoneme phonics phonily photism phrasal phratry phrenic phrensy physics rhabdom Rhaetic rhamnus rhatany rhenium rhiancy rhizoid rhizome rhodium rhodora rhombic rhombus rhubarb rhymist shackle shadily shading shadoof shadowy shaitan shakeup shakily shallop shallot shallow shamble shammed shammer shampoo shanked shapely sharpen sharper sharply shaslik shaster shastra shatter Shavian shaving shearer sheathe sheaves shebang shebear shebeen shedder sheerly shellac shelled sheller shelter sheltie shelved shelves Shemite sherbet shereef sheriff sherris

shicker shifter shikari shilpit shimmer shindig shingle shingly shinned shinpad shiplap shipman shipped shippen shipper shippon shipway shirker shittim shivers shivery shocker shoeing shogged shoofly shooter shopboy shopman shopped shopper shoring shorten shortie shortly shotgun shotten shouter showbiz showery showily showing showman showoff shrieve shrilly shrinal shrivel shriven shrubby shucker shudder shuffle shunned shunner shunter shuteye shutout shutter shuttle shylock shyness shyster thalami thallic thallus thalweg thanage thankee thanker theatre thecate themata theorbo theorem therapy thereat thereby therein thereof

thereon thereto theriac thermae thermal thermic theurgy thiamin thicken thicket thickly thieves thigger thiller thimble thinker thinned thinner thirdly thirsty thistle thistly thither Thomism Thomist thorite thorium thorned thought thready thrifty thriven throaty thrombi throned through thrower throwin thrummy thudded thuggee thulium thummim thumper thunder thymine thyroid thyrsus thyself whacker whaling whangee wharves whatnot wheaten wheedle wheeled wheeler whereas whereat whereby wherein whereof whereon whereto whether whetted whetter wheyish whicker whidder whiffle whimper whimsey whinger whipped whipper whippet whipsaw

whirler whirred whisker whiskey whisper whistle whitely whither whiting whitish whitlow Whitsun whittle whizkid whizzed whoever whoopee whooper whopper whorish whorled whoseso aiblins aileron ailment aimless aircrew airdrop airfare airflow airglow airhole airless airlift airline airlock airmail airmiss airport airpost airship airsick airwave Biafran biassed biaxial bibbery bibbing bibcock bibelot biblist bicycle bidding biennia bifilar bifocal bigener biggest biggish bighead bighorn bigname bigness bigoted bigotry bigtime bilboes biliary bilimbi bilious billing billion billowy bilobar bilobed biltong bimanal bindery binding

biology biomass bionics biotite bipedal biplane bipolar birchen birddog birdman biretta biriani biscuit bismuth bistort bistred bittern bitters bitting bittock bitumen bivalve bivouac bizarre ciboria cichlid cidaris ciliary ciliate cimices cindery cineast cineole cingula cipolin Circean circler circlet circuit circusy cirrose cirrous cistern citable citadel cithara cithern citizen citrate citrine cittern civilly civvies diabase diabolo diadrom diagram dialect dialled dialyse diamond diarchy diarise diarist dibasic dibbing dickens dictate diction diddler diehard dietary diffuse digamma digging digital dignify dignity digraph

digress dilated dilator dilemma diluent dilutee diluter dilutor dimeric dimeter dimmest dimming dimmish dimness dinette dingily dingoes dinning diocese diopter dioptre diorama diorism diorite dioxide diploid diploma dipnoan dipolar dipping diptera diptych direful dirtily disable disavow disband disbark discant discard discern discerp discoid discord discuss disdain disease diseuse disfame disgust dishorn disjoin dislike dislimn dismast dismiss disobey dispark dispart display disport dispose dispute disrank disrate disrobe disroot disrupt dissave disseat dissect dissent distaff distain distant distend distent distich distill

distort disturb ditcher dithery dittany diurnal diverge diverse divider diviner divisor divorce divulge dizzard dizzily eidetic eidolon einkorn eirenic fiancee fibbing fibroid fibroin fibroma fibrous fibster fibulae fibular fibulas fictile fiction fictive fiddler fideism fideist fidgets fidgety fiefdom fielder fierily fifteen fifthly fifties figging fighter figleaf figment figtree figural figured figwort filacer filaria filasse filbert filemot filiate filibeg filings filling filmdom filmset fimbria finagle finally finance finback finding finesse finical finicky finikin finings finning Finnish firearm firebox firebug firedog

firefly fireman firenew firstly firtree fishery fisheye fishily fishing fishnet fishway fissile fission fissure fistful fistula fitchet fitchew fitment fitness fittest fitting fixable fixedly fixings fixture giantry gibbous giblets giddily gigging giggler gilbert gilding gillnet giltcup gimbals gimmick gingery gingham gingili ginning ginseng giraffe girasol girdler girlish gittern gizzard hiccupy hickory hidalga hidalgo hideous hideout higgler highboy highhat highman highway hilding hillman hillock hilltop himself hindgut hipbath hipbone hipness hipping hiproof hipster hirable hircine hirsute hirudin histone history hitcher

hitting Hittite jibbing jibboom jibdoor jigging jimjams jingler jitters jittery kibbutz kickoff kidding kiddish kidskin killick killing killjoy kilobar kiloton kinchin kindler kindred kinesis kinetic kinfolk kingcup kingdom kinglet kingpin kinship kinsman Kirghiz kissing kitchen kitschy liaison Liassic liberal liberty library librate licence license lichowl licitly licking lidless lieabed lifeful liftoff lighted lighten lighter lightly lignify lignite ligroin likable lilting limbate limbeck limbous liminal limited limiter limosis limpkin limulus linctus lindane lineage lineate lineman lineout lingual linkage linkboy linkman

Linnean
linocut
linsang
linseed
lioncel
lioness
lionise
lipdeep
lipless
lipping
lipread
liquate
liquefy
liqueur
lissome
listeth
listing
literal
lithely
lithium
lithoid
litotes
littery
liturgy
livable
livebox
liveoak
miasmal
miasmic
micelle
microbe
midland
midline
midmost
midriff
midship
midweek
Midwest
midwife
midyear
mightst
migrant
migrate
mildewy
mileage
milfoil
miliary
militia
milking
milkleg
milkman
milksop
milldam
million
milreis
mimesis
mimetic
mimical
mimicry
mimulus
minaret
mincing
mindful
mineral
minever
miniate
minibus
minicab
minicar
minikin
minimal
minimum
minimus
miniver
minorca
minster
mintage
minuend
minutes
minutia
Miocene
miracle
mirador
mirkily
miscall
miscast
miscopy
misdate
misdeal
misdeed
misdeem
misdone
miserly
misfire
misgave
misgive
mishear
Mishnah
misknow
mislaid
mislead
mislike
mismate
misname
misplay
misread
misrule
missend
missent
missile
missing
mission
missish
missive
misstep
mistake
mistful
mistily
mistime
misting
mistook
mistral
mitoses
mitosis
mitotic
mitzvah
mixedly
mixedup
mixture
nibbler
niblick
niceish
nictate
niggard
niggler
nightie
nightly
nigrify
Nilotic
nimiety
ninepin
niobium
nippers
nippily
nipping
nirvana
nitrate
nitride
nitrify
nitrile
nitrite
nitrous
niveous
oilbath
oilbird
oilcake
oildrum
oilseed
oilskin
oilwell
piaffer
pianism
pianist
piastre
pibroch
picador
piccolo
piceous
pickaxe
pickeer
pickled
picotee
picquet
picrate
Pictish
picture
piddock
pidgeon
piebald
pieeyed
pierrot
pietism
pietist
piffler
piggery
pigging
piggish
pigiron
piglead
pigling
pigmean
pigment
pigskin
pigtail
pigwash
pigweed
pikelet
pikeman
pileate
pilgrim
pillage
pillbox
pillion
pillock
pillory
pillowy
pillule
pilsner
pilular
pimento
pimping
pinball
pincers
pincher
pinetum
pinfire
pinfish
pinfold
pinguid
pinhead
pinhole
pinkeye
pinking
pinkish
pinnace
pinnate
pinning
pinnule
pintado
pintail
pintuck
pinworm
pioneer
piously
pipeful
piperic
pipette
pipping
piquant
piragua
piranha
piratic
pirogue
piscary
piscina
piscine
pismire
pissoir
pistole
pitapat
pitched
pitcher
piteous
pitfall
pithead
pithhat
pithily
pitiful
pitpony
pitprop
pitting
pivotal
pivoter
ribband
ribbing
ribston
ribwork
ribwort
rickets
rickety
ricksha
ricotta
ridable
ridding
riddler
ridging
ridotto
riffler
rifling
rigging
righten
righter
rightly
rigidly
rilievo
rimming
ringent
ringing
ringlet
ringtaw
riotous
ripcord
ripieni
ripieno
riposte
ripping
ripplet
riptide
risible
risotto
rissole
rivalry
rivered
riveter
riviera
riviere
rivulet
sialoid
siamang
Siamese
sibling
sibship
sickbay
sickbed
sickish
sickpay
sidecar
sideway
siemens
sierran
sighted
sightly
sigmate
sigmoid
signary
signify
signior
signora
signore
signori
signory
Sikhism
silence
silenus
silesia
silicic
silicle
silicon
siliqua
silique
silkily
sillily
silvern
silvery
similar
similor
simitar
simpler
simplex
simular
sincere
singlet
sinkage
sinless
sinning
sinopia
sinsyne
sintery
sinuate
sinuous
sipping
sirgang
sirloin
sirocco
Sistine
sistrum
sitdown
sitfast
sithens
sitting
situate
Sivaism
Sivaite
sixaine
sixfold
sixteen
sixthly
sixties
Sixtine
sizable
sizably
sizzler
Tibetan
ticking
tickler
tidally
tiddler
tiddley
tiderip
tideway
tidings
tieback
tiebeam
tiercel
tiercet
tiffany
tighten
tightly
tigress
tigrish
tilbury
tillage
timbale
timbrel
timelag
timeous
timidly
timothy
timpani
timpano
tinamou
tindery
tinfoil
tingler
tinhorn
tinnily
tinning
tintack
tinware
tipcart
tipping
tippler
tipsify
tipsily
tipster
titanic
tithing
titlark
titling
titmice
Titoism
Titoist
titrate
tittupy
titular
viaduct
viatica
vibrant
vibrate
vibrato
viceroy
vicinal
vicious
victory
victual
vidette
vidimus
viduity
viewing
vilayet
village
villain
villein
villose
villous
vinasse
vincula
vinegar
vintage
vintner
violate
violent
violist
violone
virelay
virgate
virgule
virtual
visaged
viscera
viscose
viscous
visible
visibly
visitor
visored
vistaed
vitally
vitamin
vitelli
vitiate
vitrify
vitrine
vitriol
vittate
vittles
vitular
vivaria
vividly
vivific
vixenly
wickiup
widgeon
widowed
widower
wielder
wigging
wiggler
wigless
wildcat
wilding
wildish
willies
willing
willowy
windage
windbag
windegg
windily
winding
windrow
Windsor
winesap
winglet
wingnut
winkers
winning
winnock
winsome
wintery
wireman
wiretap
wishful
wishing
wistful
withers
without
witless
witling
witloof
witness
wittily
witting
wizened
xiphoid
Yiddish
yielder
yipping
ziganka
zillion
zincify
zincing
zincite
zincked
Zingari
Zingaro
zinkify
zinking
Zionism
Zionist
zipcode
zipping
zithern
ajutage
djibbah
ejector
sjambok
akvavit
ekistic
ikebana
skaldic
skating
skeeter
skegger
skellum
skelter
skepsis
sketchy
skiable
skidded
skidlid
skidpan
skiffle
skijump
skilful
skilift
skilled
skillet
skimmed
skimmer
skimmia
skinful
skinker
skinned
skinner
skipped
skipper
skippet
skirret
skirted
skirter
skitter
skittle
skolion
skulker
skyblue
skyborn
skyhigh
skyjack
skylark
skyline
skysail
skyward
ukelele
ukulele
alameda
alanine
alation
albumen
albumin
alcaide
alcalde
alcayde
alcazar
alchemy
alcohol
Alcoran
alembic
alertly
aleuron
alewife
alfalfa
alforja
algebra
alginic
alidade
alienly
aliform
aliment
alimony
aliquot
alkalis
alkanet
Alkoran
alleged
allegro
allelic
allergy
allheal
allonge
allover
allseed
allstar
alltime
alluvia
almanac
almirah
almoner
almonry
almsman
alodial
alodium
aloetic
aloofly
alphorn
already
alright
alsoran
althaea
althorn
alumina
alumnae
alumnus
alunite
alveoli
alyssum
blabbed
blabber
blacken
blackly
bladder
blandly
blanket
blankly
blarney
blasted
blaster
blatant
blather
blatter
bleakly
bleater
bleeder
bleeper
blemish
blender
blesbok
blessed
blether
blewits
blighty
blinder
blindly
blinker
blintze
blister
blither
bloated
bloater
blocker
blooded
bloomer
blossom
blotchy
blotted
blotter
blouson
blowdry
blowfly
blowgun
blowout

blowzed
blubber
blucher
blueing
bluffer
bluffly
blunder
blunger
bluntly
blurred
blusher
bluster
clabber
clacker
cladode
claimer
clamant
clamber
clammed
clamour
clanger
clapped
clapper
clarify
clarion
clarity
clarkia
classes
classic
classis
clastic
clatter
clausal
clavate
clavier
claypan
cleaner
cleanly
cleanse
cleanup
clearly
cleaver
clement
clerisy
clerkly
clicker
climate
climber
clinker
clipped
clipper
clippie
cliquey
clivers
cloacae
cloacal
clobber
clocker
clogged
clogger
closely
closeup
closure
clothes
clotted
cloture
clubbed
clubman
clumber
Cluniac
clupeid
cluster
clutter
clypeal
clypeus
clyster
elastic
elastin
elation
elderly
Eleatic
elector
electro
elegant
elegiac
elegise
elegist
element
elenchi
elevate
elevens
elfbolt
elfland
elflock
elision
elitism
elitist
ellipse
Elohism
Elohist
elusion
elusive
elusory
elution
eluvial
eluvium
elysian
Elysium
elytron
elytrum
Elzevir
flaccid
flagday
flagged
flagman
flamfew
flaming
flaneur
flanker
flannel
flapped
flapper
flareup
flasher
flatcap
flatcar
flatlet
flatout
flatten
flatter
flattop
flaught
flaunty
flavine
flavour
fleabag
fleapit
flecker
fleeced
fleecer
fleeing
fleetly
Fleming
Flemish
fleshed
flesher
fleshly
fletton
fleuret
fleuron
flexile
flexion
flexure
flicker
flighty
flipped
flipper
flitted
flitter
flivver
floater
floccus
flogged
floorer
floosie
floozie
flopped
floreat
florist
floruit
flotage
flotsam
flounce
flowage
flowery
flubbed
fluence
fluency
fluidal
fluidic
fluidly
flummox
flunkey
fluster
fluting
flutist
flutter
fluvial
fluxion
flyable
flyaway
flyback
flybane
flybelt
flyblow
flyboat
flybook
flyhalf
flyleaf
flyover
flypast
flyting
flytrap
glacial
glacier
gladded
gladden
gladder
glaikit
glamour
glaring
glassen
glasses
glazier
glazing
gleaner
gleeful
gleeman
glenoid
gliadin
glimmer
glimpse
glisten
glister
glitter
globoid
globose
globule
glorify
glossal
Glossic
glottal
glottis
glozing
glucose
glummer
gluteal
gluteus
glutted
glutton
glycine
glyphic
glyptal
glyptic
ileitis
ilkaday
illbred
illegal
illicit
illness
klipdas
llanero
oldster
oldtime
olefine
olivary
olivine
oloroso
Olympic
placard
placate
placebo
placket
placoid
plafond
plaided
plainly
planish
planned
planner
plantar
planter
planula
planxty
plasmic
plasmid
plasmin
plaster
plastic
plastid
platane
plateau
platina
plating
platoon
platted
platter
plaudit
playact
playboy
playful
playing
playlet
playoff
playpen
pleader
pleased
plectra
pledgee
pledger
pledget
pledgor
plenary
plenish
pleurae
pleural
pleuron
pliable
pliably
pliancy
plicate
pliskie
plodded
plodder
plopped
plosion
plosive
plotted
plotter
plucker
plugged
plugger
plumage
plumate
plumber
plumbic
plumbob
plumery
plummet
plumose
plumper
plumply
plumule
plunder
plunger
plunker
plusage
plushly
pluvial
plywood
slabbed
slabber
slacken
slacker
slackly
slagged
slammed
slander
slantly
slapped
slasher
slather
slating
slatted
slavery
slavish
Slavism
sledded
sleeken
sleekit
sleekly
sleeper
sleeved
sleight
slender
slicker
slickly
slidden
slimily
slimmer
slinger
slinker
slipped
slipper
slipway
slither
slobber
sloegin
slogged
slogger
slopped
sloshed
slotcar
slotted
slouchy
sloughy
Slovene
slowish
slubbed
slubber
slugged
slugger
slumber
slummed
slummer
slurred
slyness
ulcered
ululant
ululate
amalgam
amanita
amarant
amateur
amative
amatory
amazing
ambages
ambatch
ambient
amboina
ambones
amboyna
ambsace
amender
amenity
amentia
amentum
Amerind
Amharic
amiable
amiably
amildar
ammeter
ammonal
ammonia
amnesia
amnesic
amnesty
amoebae
amoebas
amoebic
amongst
amorist
amorous
amphora
amplify
ampoule
ampulla
amputee
amtrack
amusive
amylase
amyloid
amylose
emanate
embargo
embassy
emblaze
embolic
embolus
embosom
embowed
embowel
embower
embrace
embroil
embrown
embryon
emerald
emeriti
emersed
emetine
emicate
eminent
emirate
emitted
emitter
emotion
emotive
empanel
empathy
emperor
empiric
emplace
emplane
emporia
empower
empress
emprise
emptier
emptily
emption
empyema
emulate
emulous
imagery
imagine
imagism
imagist
imamate
imbiber
imbower
imbrute
imitate
immense
immerge
immerse
immoral
impaint
impanel
impasse
impaste
impasto
impeach
impearl
imperil
impetus
impiety
impinge
impious
implant
implead
implete
implode
implore
imposer
impound
impresa
impress
imprest
imprint
improve
impulse
omental
omentum
omicron
ominous
omitted
omneity
omnibus
omnific
smacker
smaragd
smarten
smartly
smasher
smashup
smatter
smeddum
smeller
smelter
smidgen
smidgin
smitten
smokeho
smokily
smoking
smoochy
smother
smuggle
smutted
umbonal
umbones
umbrage
Umbrian
umpteen
anaemia
anaemic
anagoge
anagogy
anagram
analogy
analyse
analyst
Ananias
anarchy
anatase
anatomy
anchovy
anchusa
ancient
ancones
ancress
andante
andiron
android
anemone
aneroid
aneurin
angelic
angelus
Angevin
anginal
angioma
Anglian
anglice
angling
Anglist
angrily
anguine
anguish
angular
aniline
anility
animate
animism
animist
anionic
aniseed
annates
annatta
annatto
annelid
annicut
annuity
annular
annulet
annulus
anodise
anodyne
anoesis
anoetic
anomaly
anosmia
anosmic
another
antacid
antbear
antefix
antenna
anthill
anthrax
antigen
antilog
antique
antlion
antonym
anurous
anxiety
anxious
anybody
anymore
anyroad
anytime
anyways
anywise
enactor
enamour
enation
enchain
enchant
enchase
enclasp
enclave
enclose
encoder
encomia
Encraty
encrust
endarch
endemic
enderon
endless
endlong
endmost
endogen
endorse
endozoa
endways
endwise
enemata
energid
enfeoff
enfiled
enforce
enframe
engaged
English
engorge
engraft
engrail
engrain
engrave
engross
enhance
enlarge
enliven
ennoble
enounce
enplane
enprint
enquire
enquiry
enslave
ensnare
ensnarl
entasis
entente
enteral
enteric
enteron
enthral
enthuse
entitle
entomic
entotic
entozoa
entrain
entrant
entreat
entropy
entrust
entwine
entwist
envelop
envenom
envious
environ
enwheel
enwound

enzymic
gnarled
gnathic
gnocchi
gnomish
gnostic
inanely
inanity
inaptly
inboard
inbreed
inbuilt
incense
incipit
incised
incisor
inciter
incline
inclose
include
incomer
incrust
incubus
incudes
incurve
incused
indepth
indexer
indican
indices
indicia
inditer
indoors
indorse
indraft
indrawn
inducer
indulge
indusia
indwell
indwelt
ineptly
inertia
inertly
inexact
infancy
infanta
infante
infarct
infauna
inferno
infidel
infield
inflame
inflate
inflect
inflict
infract
infulae
ingenue
ingesta
ingoing
ingraft
ingrain
ingrate
ingress
ingroup
ingrown
inhabit
inhaler
inherit
inhibit
inhouse
inhuman
initial
injurer
inkhorn
inkling
inkwell

inlayer
innards
innerve
innings
inocula
inphase
inquest
inquire
inquiry
insculp
insecty
inshore
insider
insight
insigne
insipid
insofar
inspect
inspire
install
instant
instate
instead
insular
insulin
insured
insurer
inswing
integer
intense
interim
interne
intoner
intrant
intreat
introit
intrude
intrust
intwine
inutile
invader
invalid
inveigh
inverse
invitee
inviter
invoice
involve
inwards
inweave
inwoven
knacker
knapped
knapper
knavery
knavish
kneader
kneecap
kneeler
kneepan
kneesup
knitted
knitter
knobbed
knobble
knobbly
knocker
knockon
knotted
knotter
knowall
knowhow
knowing
knuckle
knurled
onanism
oneeyed
oneiric
oneness

onerous
oneself
oneshot
onestep
onetime
ongoing
onshore
onstage
onwards
onymous
snaffle
snagged
snakily
snapped
snapper
snarler
snarlup
snatchy
sneaker
sneerer
sneezer
snicker
sniffer
sniffle
snifter
snigger
sniggle
snipped
snipper
snippet
snooker
snooper
snoozer
snoozle
snorkel
snorter
snouted
snowcap
snowily
snowman
snubbed
snubber
snuffer
snuffle
snuggle
unaptly
unarmed
unasked
unaware
unbated
unblest
unblock
unbosom
unbound
unbowed
unboxed
unbrace
unbuild
unbuilt
uncanny
unchain
uncinus
uncivil
unclasp
unclean
uncloak
unclose
uncouth
uncover
uncross
uncrown
unction
underdo
undergo
undoing
undress
undying
unearth
unequal

unfaith
unfitly
unfrock
unfroze
unfunny
unfussy
ungodly
unguard
unguent
ungulae
unhandy
unhappy
unheard
unhinge
unhitch
unhoped
unhorse
unhouse
unicity
unicorn
unideal
unifier
uniform
unitary
unitive
unjoint
unkempt
unknown
unladen
unlatch
unlearn
unleash
unlined
unloose
unlucky
unmanly
unmeant
unmixed
unmoral
unmoved
unnerve
unpaged
unquiet
unquote
unravel
unready
unright
unroost
unsaved
unscrew
unsexed
unshell
unsight
unsnarl
unsound
unstick
unstuck
unswear
unswore
unsworn
unteach
unthink
untried
untruly
untruss
untruth
untuned
untwine
untwist
untying
unusual
unweave
unwound
unwoven
boarder
boarish
boaster
boating
boatman

bobbery
bobbing
bobbish
bobeche
bobsled
bobstay
bobtail
bodeful
bogbean
boggler
bogyman
bohemia
boiling
boletus
bolivar
bollard
bologna
boloney
bolshie
bolster
bombard
bombast
bonanza
bondage
bondman
bonedry
boneset
bonfire
bongoes
bonkers
bonnily
boobook
bookend
bookful
booking
bookish
booklet
bookman
booksie
Boolean
boomlet
boorish
booster
bootleg
boozeup
boozily
bopping
boracic
borazon
bordure
boredom
borings
bornite
borough
borscht
borstal
bortsch
boscage
boskage
bossism
Boswell
botanic
botargo
botcher
bottega
bottled
bottony
botulin
bouchee
boudoir
bouilli
boulder
boulter
bouncer
bounden
bounder
bouquet
bourbon
bourdon

bourree
bowhead
bowlder
bowlful
bowline
bowling
bowshot
boxcalf
boxhaul
boxkite
boxlike
boxroom
boxseat
boxwood
boycott
boyhood
coacher
coagula
coaltit
coaming
coarsen
coastal
coaster
coating
coaxial
cobbler
cocaine
coccoid
cochlea
cockade
cockeye
cockily
cockney
cockpit
cockshy
coconut
cocotte
codable
coddler
codeine
codfish
codices
codicil
codling
coeliac
coequal
coexist
coffers
cogency
cogging
cognate
cognise
cohabit
coherer
coinage
coinbox
coition
coldish
coletit
colicky
colitis
collage
collard
collate
collect
colleen
college
collide
collier
collins
colloid
collude
colobus
cologne
colonel
colonic
colossi
colours
coloury

coltish
combine
combout
combust
comedic
cometic
comfort
comfrey
comical
comitia
command
commend
comment
commode
commons
commove
commune
commute
compact
company
compare
compart
compass
compeer
compend
compere
compete
compile
complex
complin
complot
compony
comport
compose
compost
compote
compute
comrade
Comtian
Comtism
Comtist
conacre
conatus
concave
conceal
concede
conceit
concent
concept
concern
concert
conchae
conchie
concise
concoct
concord
concuss
condemn
condign
condole
condone
conduce
conduct
conduit
condyle
confect
confess
confide
confine
confirm
conflux
conform
confuse
confute
congeal
congest
conical
conidia
conifer

coniine
conjoin
conjure
conkers
connate
connect
conning
connive
connote
conquer
consent
consign
consist
console
consort
consult
consume
contact
contain
contemn
contend
content
contest
context
contort
contour
control
contuse
convect
convene
convent
convert
convict
convoke
cookery
cooking
cookout
coolant
coolish
cooncan
coontie
copaiba
copaiva
copepod
copilot
copious
coppery
coppice
copular
copycat
copyist
coquito
coracle
coranto
corbeil
cordage
cordate
cordial
cordite
cordoba
corella
corkage
corking
cornage
corncob
corneal
cornett
cornfed
cornice
cornily
Cornish
cornist
cornual
cornuto
corolla
coronae
coronal
coronas
coroner

coronet
corpora
correct
corrida
corrode
corrody
corrupt
corsage
corsair
corslet
cortege
cortile
corvina
corvine
corydon
cosmism
cosmist
cossack
costard
costate
costean
costing
costive
costrel
costume
coterie
cotidal
cottage
cottier
cottony
Coueism
couldst
couloir
coulomb
coulter
council
counsel
counter
country
coupler
couplet
courage
courier
courlan
courser
courtly
couthie
couture
couvade
couvert
coverup
cowbane
cowbell
cowbird
cowfish
cowhage
cowhand
cowheel
cowherd
cowhide
cowlick
cowling
cowpoke
cowshed
cowslip
coxcomb
coyness
cozener
docetic
dockage
dockise
doddard
doddery
dodgems
dodgery
doeskin
dogbane
dogcart
dogdays

dogeate
dogfish
doggery
dogging
doggish
doggone
dogrose
dogskin
dogstar
dogtrot
dogvane
dogwood
doleful
dollish
dolphin
doltish
domical
dominie
donator
donning
donnish
doodler
doomful
doorman
doormat
doorway
dorhawk
Dorking
dormant
dormice
dornick
dortour
dossier
dotting
doubler
doubles
doublet
doubter
doucely
douceur
doughty
dovecot
dovekie
dowager
dowdily
downbow
doyenne
dozenth
fobbing
focused
fogbank
foggage
foggily
fogging
foghorn
foglamp
fogydom
fogyish
fogyism
folding
foldout
foliage
foliate
foliole
foliose
folkway
follies
fondant
fondler
foolery
foolish
footage
footboy
footing
footman
footpad
footrot
footsie
footway

fopling
foppery
foppish
forager
foramen
forayer
forbade
forbear
forbode
forbore
forceps
fordone
forearm
foreign
foreleg
foreman
forepaw
foreran
forerun
foresaw
foresay
foresee
foretop
forever
forfeit
forfend
forgave
forgery
forging
forgive
forgoer
forgone
forkful
forlorn
formant
formate
formula
forsake
forsook
forties
fortify
Fortran
fortune
forward
forwent
forworn
fossick
fossula
fouette
foulard
foumart
founder
foundry
fourale
fourgon
foveate
foveola
fowling
foxhole
foxhunt
foxtail
foxtrot
goahead
goatgod
goatish
gobbler
Gobelin
goddamn
goddess
godetia
godevil
godhead
godhood
godless
godlike
godling
godsend
godship
godward

goggler
goggles
goitred
goldbug
golfbag
golfing
goliard
Goliath
gombeen
gomeral
gomeril
gonadal
gondola
gonidia
goodbye
goodday
goodish
goodman
gooiest
gorcock
gorcrow
Gordian
gorilla
gorsedd
goshawk
gosling
gossipy
gossoon
gouache
goulash
gourami
gourmet
goutfly
hoarsen
hoatzin
Hobbian
Hobbism
Hobbist
hobbler
hobnail
hockday
hocused
hoecake
hoedown
hogback
hogfish
hoggery
hogging
hoggish
hogwash
hogweed
holdall
holding
holibut
holiday
holland
holmium
holmoak
holster
homager
homburg
Homeric
Homerid
hominid
homonym
honesty
honeyed
honours
hoodlum
hooklet
hopbind
hopeful
hophead
hoplite
hopping
hopsack
horizon
hormone
hornmad

horrent
horrify
horsily
hosanna
hosiery
hospice
hostage
hostess
hostile
hostler
hotfoot
hothead
hotness
hotshot
hottest
hottish
housing
howbeit
however
howling
jobbery
jobbing
jocular
jogging
jogtrot
joinder
joinery
joining
jointer
jointly
jollify
jollity
jonquil
jotting
journal
journey
jouster
joyance
joyless
joyride
kolkhoz
Koranic
koumiss
loading
loaning
loather
loathly
lobbing
lobelia
lobster
lobular
lobworm
locally
locater
lockage
lockjaw
locknut
lockout
locular
loculus
lodging
loftily
logbook
logging
logical
logline
logwood
Lollard
Lombard
lomenta
longago
longbow
longday
longhop
longing
longish
looking
lookout
looksee

loosely
lopping
lording
lorette
lorgnon
loricae
lorimer
loriner
losable
lottery
lotting
loudish
lounger
lousily
loutish
louvred
lovable
lovably
loverly
lowborn
lowbred
lowbrow
lowdown
lowland
lowlily
lowness
lowrise
loyally
loyalty
lozenge
Moabite
mobbing
mobbish
mobster
mockery
modally
modesty
modicum
modiste
modular
modulus
mofette
moidore
moisten
moistly
moither
molimen
mollify
mollusc
molossi
momenta
monacal
monadic
monarch
mondial
moneyed
moneyer
mongrel
moniker
monitor
monkery
monkish
monocle
monocot
monodic
monomer
monsoon
monster
montage
montane
montero
monthly
moocher
moodily
mooneye
moonlit
moonset
moorage
moorhen

mooring
Moorish
moorlog
mopping
moraine
morally
morassy
mordant
mordent
moreish
morello
morendo
Moresco
Morisco
morning
morocco
moronic
morphia
mortice
mortify
mortise
morulae
morular
morwong
Moselle
mosshag
mottled
mouflon
moulder
mounter
Mountie
mourner
mousaka
mousing
mousmee
mouther
movable
mowburn
mozetta
Noachic
nobbler
noctuid
noctule
nocturn
nocuous
nodally
nodated
nodding
nodical
nodular
nogging
noisily
noisome
nomadic
nomarch
nombril
nominal
nominee
nonagon
noniron
nonplus
nonskid
nonslip
nonstop
nonsuch
nonsuit
nonuser
noology
noonday
nooning
norland
norther
norward
nosebag
nosegay
noserag
nostril
nostrum
notable

notably
notched
notedly
notelet
notepad
nothing
notitia
noumena
nourish
novella
novelle
novelty
nowhere
noxious
oolitic
oomiack
oophyte
oosperm
oospore
poacher
pochard
podagra
podding
podesta
poetess
poetics
poetise
pofaced
poinder
pointed
pointer
polacca
polacre
poleaxe
polecat
polemic
polenta
politic
pollack
pollard
pollock
pollute
poloist
polygon
polymer
polynia
polynya
polypod
polypus
pomatum
pomfret
pompano
pompous
pondage
poniard
pontage
pontiff
pontify
pontoon
poofter
poohbah
poorish
popadum
popcorn
popeyed
popover
poppied
popping
popular
porcine
porifer
porrect
portage
portend
portent
portico
portion
portray
poseuse

possess
postage
postbag
postbox
postboy
posteen
postern
postfix
posting
postman
posture
postwar
potable
potamic
potbank
potence
potency
pothead
potheen
potherb
pothole
pothook
potluck
potshot
pottage
pottery
potting
pouched
poulard
poulter
poultry
poundal
pounder
poussin
pouting
poverty
powdery
roadbed
roadhog
roadman
roadway
roaring
roaster
robbery
robbing
rockery
rockier
rockily
rocking
rocklet
rockoil
rocktar
rodding
rodlike
rodsman
roebuck
roedeer
roguery
roguish
roister
rollick
rolling
rollmop
rolltop
romance
Romanic
Romansh
romaunt
Rommany
rondeau
rondure
rontgen
roofing
rooftop
rooinek
rookery
roomful
rooster
rootage

rootlet
ropable
ropeway
rorqual
roseate
rosebay
rosebud
rosecut
rosehip
rosella
roseola
rosered
rosette
rostral
rostrum
rotator
rotifer
rotting
rotunda
roughen
roughly
roulade
rouleau
rounded
roundel
rounder
roundly
roundup
rousing
rouster
routine
rowboat
rowdily
rowlock
royally
royalty
royster
soakage
soaking
soapbox
soapily
soaring
sobbing
soberly
socager
soccage
society
sockeye
sofabed
softish
soggily
soignee
soilure
sojourn
sokeman
solanum
solaria
solatia
soldier
solicit
solidly
solidus
soliped
soloist
Solomon
soluble
solvate
solvent
somatic
someday
somehow
someone
someway
somitic
sonance
sonancy
songful
sonless
sonship

soonish
soother
soothly
sootily
sophism
sophist
soppily
sopping
soprani
soprano
sorbent
Sorbian
sorcery
sordini
sordino
sorghum
sorites
soroban
sororal
sorosis
sorrily
sotting
sottish
soubise
souffle
soulful
sounder
soundly
soupcon
sourish
soursop
soutane
souther
sowback
soybean
sozzled
toaster
tobacco
toccata
toddler
toeclip
toehold
toeless
toenail
toggery
toilful
tollbar
tollman
toluene
tombola
tombolo
tomenta
tomfool
tompion
tonally
tonemic
tonerow
tonight
tonnage
tonneau
tonsure
tontine
toolbox
tooling
toothed
tootsie
topcoat
topfull
tophole
topiary
topical
topknot
topless
topmast
topmost
toponym
topping
topsail
topside
topsoil
torchon
torgoch
torment
tormina
tornado
torpedo
torpids
torrefy
torrent
torsade
torsion
tortile
tortrix
torture
torulae
Toryism
tosspot
totally
totemic
tottery
totting
touched
toucher
touchup
toughen
toughly
touraco
touring
tourism
tourist
tourney
towards
towboat
towered
towhead
towline
towmond
towmont
townish
townlet
towpath
towrope
toyshop
vocable
vocalic
vocally
voguish
voivode
volante
volcano
voltage
voltaic
voluble
volubly
volumed
voluted
volutin
votable
vouchee
voucher
vowelly
voyager
wobbler
wolfcub
wolfdog
wolfish
wolfram
wolvish
womanly
woodcut
woodman
woodpie
woolfat
woolled
woollen
wooloil
woolsey
woomera
woozily
wordage
wordily
wording
workbag
workbox
workday
working
workman
workout
worldly
wornout
worrier
worship
worsted
wottest
wouldbe
wouldst
yoghurt
yolksac
Yorkist
younger
younker
zoarium
Zoilism
Zoilist
zonated
zoogamy
zoogeny
zoogony
zooidal
zoology
zoonomy
zootaxy
zootomy
apagoge
apanage
apatite
apetaly
aphasia
aphasic
aphelia
apheses
aphesis
aphetic
aphides
aphonia
aphonic
aphotic
aphylly
apishly
aplasia
aplenty
apocope
apodous
apogamy
apogean
apology
apolune
apostil
apostle
apothem
apparat
apparel
appease
applaud
applied
applier
appoint
apprise
approve
apraxia
apricot
apropos
apsidal
apsides
apteryx
aptness
eparchy
epatant
epaulet
epergne
ephebus
ephedra
epicarp
epicede
epicene
epicure
epidote
epigeal
epigean
epigene
epigone
epigoni
epigram
epigyny
epilate
episode
epistle
epitaph
epitaxy
epithem
epithet
epitome
epizoic
epizoon
epochal
eponymy
epoxide
epsilon
ipomoea
opacity
opaline
openair
openend
opening
operand
operant
operate
operose
ophitic
opinion
opossum
oppidan
opposer
oppress
opsonic
opsonin
optical
optimal
optimum
opulent
opuntia
opuscle
spacial
spacing
spadger
spancel
spangle
spangly
spaniel
Spanish
spanker
spanned
spanner
sparely
sparger
sparing
sparkle
sparoid
sparred
sparrow
Spartan
spastic
spathic
spatial
spatted
spattee
spatter
spatula
spawner
speaker
special
species
specify
speckle
spectra
spectre
specula
speeder
speedup
speller
spelter
spencer
spender
sphenic
spheral
spheric
spicate
spicery
spicily
spicula
spicule
spidery
spieler
spignel
spikily
spiller
spinach
spindle
spindly
spindry
spinner
spinney
spinode
spinoff
spinose
spinous
spinule
spiraea
spirant
spireme
spirits
spitted
spitter
spittle
splashy
spleeny
splenic
splicer
splodge
splotch
splurge
spodium
spoiler
spondee
spondyl
sponger
spongin
sponson
sponsor
spoofer
spooney
spoorer
sporran
sporter
sporule
spotted
spotter
spousal
spouter
sprawly
sprayer
sprayey
spriggy
springe
springy
spryest
spumous
spunkie
spurner
spurred
spurrey
spurtle
sputnik
sputter
spyhole
upbraid
upfield
upgrade
upheave
upraise
upright
upriser
upsides
upsilon
upstage
upstair
upstart
upsurge
upsweep
upswept
upswing
upthrew
upthrow
uptight
uptrend
upwards
aquaria
aquatic
aquavit
aqueous
aquifer
aquiver
equable
equably
equally
equator
equerry
equinal
equinox
squabby
squacco
squaddy
squails
squalid
squally
squalor
squamae
squarer
squashy
squatty
squeaky
squeeze
squelch
squiffy
squinch
squinny
squirmy
squishy
squitch
Arabian
arabise
Arabist
Aramaic
araneid
Arapaho
arbiter
arbutus
arcaded
arcadia
arcanum
archaic
archery
archive
archway
arctoid
arcuate
arcweld
ardency
arduous
areally
areaway
areolae
areolar
areolas
aridity
arietta
aristae
aristas
armband
armfuls
armhole
armiger
armless
armlike
armoire
Armoric
armoury
armrest
armsful
arousal
arraign
arrange
arrayer
arrears
arrival
arriver
arsenal
arsenic
article
artisan
artiste
artless
artwork
brabble
bracing
bracken
bracket
bradawl
bragged
bragger
Brahman
Brahmin
braille
bramble
brambly
branchy
brander
brannew
bransle
brantle
brantub
brashly
brassie
brattle
braunch
bravado
bravely
bravery
bravura
brawler
brazier
breaded
breadth
breaker
breakin
breakup
breathe
breathy
breccia
breeder
brevier
brevity
brewage
brewery
bribery
brickie
brickle
bricole
bridoon
briefly
brigade
brigand
brimful
brimmed
brimmer
brinded
brindle
bringer
brinjal
brioche
briquet
brisken
brisket
briskly
bristle
bristly
British
brittle
brittly
britzka
broaden
broadly
brocade
brocket
broider
broiler
brokage
broking
bromate
bromide
bromine
bromism
bronchi
broncho
brooder
brothel
brother
brought
brownie
browser
brucine
brucite
bruhaha
bruiser
brumous
brusher
brusque
brutish
bruxism
Brython
crabbed
cracked
cracker
crackle
crackly
crackup
cragged
crammed
crammer
crampet
crampit
crampon
cranage
cranial
cranium
crankle
crannog
crappie
crassly
craunch
craving
crawler
crazily
creamer
creator
credent
creedal
creeper
cremate
cremona
crenate
cresset
crested
crevice
cribbed
cribble
cricket
cricoid
crimine
crimper
crimple
crimson
cringer
cringle
crinite
crinkle
crinkly
crinoid
criollo
cripple
crisper
crisply
cristae
critter
croaker
crochet
crocket
Croesus
crofter
crooked
crooner
cropped
cropper
croquet
croquis
crosier
crossly
crouton
crowbar
crowdie
crowned
crowner
crownet
crowtoe
crozier
crucial
crucian
crucify
crudely
crudity
cruelly
cruelty
cruiser
cruller
crumble
crumbly
crumpet
crumple
crunchy
crupper
crusade
crusado
crusher
crustal
crusted
crybaby
cryogen
cryptal
cryptic
crystal
drabber

drabbet
drabble
drabler
drachma
draftee
drafter
dragged
draggle
dragnet
dragoon
drainer
drapery
drastic
dratted
draught
drawbar
drawing
drawler
drayage
drayman
dreamed
dreamer
dredger
dresser
dribble
driblet
driedup
drifter
driller
drinker
dripdry
dripped
drivein
driving
drizzle
drizzly
drogher
dromond
droplet
dropout
dropped
dropper
drosera
droshky
drought
drouthy
droving
drubbed
drudger
drugged
drugget
druidic
drumlin
drummed
drummer
drunken
drycell
drydock
dryeyed
dryness
drysalt
dryshod
erasure
erectly
erector
erelong
eremite
erepsin
ergates
ergodic
ericoid
eristic
erlking
ermined
erodent
erosion
erosive
erotica
erotism
errancy
erratic
erratum
erudite
fracted
fraenum
fragile
frailly
frailty
Fraktur
frameup
frankly
frantic
frapped
fratery
fraught
frazzle
freaked
freckle
freckly
freebie
freedom
freeman
freesia
freeway
freezer
freight
Frenchy
frenula
frescos
freshen
fresher
freshet
freshly
fretful
fretsaw
fretted
friable
friarly
fribble
frigate
frijole
fripper
friseur
Frisian
frisker
frisket
frisson
fritted
fritter
frizzle
frizzly
frogeye
frogged
frogman
fronded
frontal
fronton
frosted
froward
frowsty
fructed
fruited
fruiter
frustum
grabbed
grabber
grabble
gracile
grackle
gradate
gradely
gradine
gradual
grafter
grained
grainer
gramary
grammar
grampus
granary
grandad
grandam
grandee
grandly
grandma
grandpa
granger
granita
granite
grannie
grantee
granter
grantor
granule
grapery
graphic
grapnel
grapple
grasper
gratify
grating
graunch
gravely
gravity
gravure
grazier
grazing
greaser
greaten
greatly
greaves
Grecian
grecise
Grecism
greenly
greenth
greisen
gremial
gremlin
grenade
greyhen
greyish
greylag
gribble
griddle
griffin
griffon
grifter
grilled
griller
grimace
grimmer
grinder
grinned
gripped
gripper
griskin
gristle
gristly
gritted
grizzle
grizzly
Grobian
grocery
grogram
Grolier
grommet
groover
grossly
grottos
grouchy
grouper
groupie
grouser
growler
grownup
grubbed
grubber
gruffly
grumble
grumbly
grummet
grumose
grumous
grunion
grunter
gruntle
grutten
gruyere
gryphon
grysbok
Iranian
irately
irideal
iridise
iridium
Irishry
irksome
ironing
ironist
kremlin
krimmer
Krishna
krypton
oration
oratory
oratrix
orbital
orchard
orderer
orderly
ordinal
orectic
oregano
organic
organon
organum
organza
orifice
origami
orogeny
orology
orotund
Orphean
Orphism
orphrey
ortolan
praetor
prairie
praiser
Prakrit
praline
prancer
prattle
pravity
preachy
prebend
precast
precede
precept
precise
precook
predate
predial
predict
predoom
preempt
preface
prefect
preform
preheat
prelacy
prelate
prelect
prelims
prelude
premier
premise
premiss
premium
prepack
prepaid
prepare
preplan
presage
present
preside
presoak
presser
pressup
presume
pretend
pretest
pretext
pretzel
prevail
prevent
preview
previse
priapic
pricker
pricket
prickle
prickly
primacy
primage
primary
primate
primely
primero
priming
primmed
primula
printer
prithee
privacy
private
privily
privity
proband
probang
probate
probity
problem
proceed
process
proctor
procure
prodded
prodder
prodigy
produce
product
profane
profess
proffer
profile
profuse
progeny
program
project
prolate
prolong
promise
promote
pronaoi
pronaos
pronate
pronely
pronged
pronoun
propane
propend
prophet
propine
propjet
propone
propose
propped
prorate
prosaic
prosify
prosily
prosody
prosper
protean
protect
protege
proteid
protein
protend
protest
proteus
protist
protium
proudly
proverb
provide
proviso
provoke
provost
prowess
prowler
proximo
prudent
prudery
prudish
pruning
prurigo
prussic
tracery
trachea
tracker
tractor
tradein
trading
traduce
traffic
tragedy
trailer
trainee
trainer
traipse
traitor
traject
tramcar
trammel
trample
tramway
tranche
trangam
transit
transom
tranter
trapeze
trapped
trapper
travail
travois
trawler
trayful
treacle
treacly
treader
treadle
treason
treater
treetop
trefoil
trehala
trekked
trekker
trellis
tremble
trembly
tremolo
trenail
trental
trepang
tressed
tressel
trestle
triable
triacid
triadic
tribade
triblet
tribune
tribute
triceps
tricker
trickle
tricksy
tricorn
trident
triduan
triduum
trifler
triform
trigamy
trigger
trilith
trilogy
trimmed
trimmer
trinary
trindle
tringle
trinity
trinket
trinkum
triolet
tripery
triplet
triplex
tripody
tripoli
tripped
tripper
trippet
tripple
trireme
trisect
trishaw
trismus
tritely
tritium
tritone
triumph
trivial
trivium
trochal
trochee
trochus
trodden
troller
trolley
trollop
trommel
trooper
trophic
tropics
tropism
trotted
trotter
trouble
trounce
trouper
trouser
truancy
trucial
trucker
truckle
trudgen
truffle
trumeau
trumpet
truncal
trundle
trusser
trustee
truster
trypsin
tryptic
trysail
uraemia
Uralian
uralite
uranide
uranism
uranium
uranous
urethan
urethra
urgency
urinary
urodele
urology
wrangle
wrapped
wrapper
wreathe
wreathy
wrecker
wrestle
wriggle
wriggly
wringer
wrinkle
wrinkly
writeup
writhen
writing
written
wrongly
wrought
wrybill
wryneck
wryness
ascarid
ascaris
ascesis
ascetic
ascidia
ascites
ascitic
ascribe
asepsis
aseptic
asexual
ashamed
ashtray
Asiatic
asinine
askance
askesis
asocial
asperse
asphalt
aspirer
aspirin
asquint
assagai
assault
assayer
assegai
assizes
assuage
assured
assurer
astable
astatic
asteria
astound
astride
asunder
csardas
escapee
escaper
escheat
escolar
escribe
esotery
esparto
espouse
esquire
essayer
essence
essoyne
estrade
estreat
estuary
Gstring
ischial
ischium
Ishmael
Islamic
Ismaili
isobath
isochor
isogamy
isogeny
isogram
isohyet
isokont
isolate
isonomy
isotope
isotopy
isotron
Israeli
issuant
isthmus
osculum
osmosis
osmotic
osmunda
osselet
osseous
osseter
ossicle
ossific
ossuary
osteoid
ostiary
ostiole
ostraca
ostraka
ostrich
psalter
psychic
tsardom
tsarina
tsarism
tsarist
Tsquare
tsunami
useless
usually
usurper
ataraxy
atavism
atavist
atelier
atheism
atheist
athirst
athlete
athwart
atingle
atomise

atomism
atomist
atresia
atrophy
attaboy
attache
attaint
attempt
attract
attrite
ctenoid
etaerio
etamine
etching
eternal
etesian
ethanol
etheric
ethical
ethiops
ethmoid
Etonian
itacism
Italian
Italiot
itemise
iterant
iterate
otolith
otology
ottoman
pteroic
pteryla
ptyalin
stabbed
stabber
stabile
stabler
stables
stacker
staddle
stadium
stagger
stagily
staging
staidly
stainer
staithe
stalely
stalked
stalker
stamina
stammel
stammer
stamper
standby
stander
standin
standup
staniel
stannic
stapler
starchy
stardom
starkly
starlet
starlit
starred
starter
startle
statant
stately
statice
statics
station
statism
statist
stative
statued
stature
statute
staunch
stealer
stealth
steamer
stearic
stearin
steekit
steepen
steeple
steeply
steerer
stellar
stemmed
stemple
stemson
stenchy
stencil
stentor
stepney
stepped
stepper
stepson
sterile
sterlet
sternal
sterned
sternly
sternum
steroid
stetson
stetted
steward
stewpan
stewpot
sthenic
stibine
sticker
stickit
stickle
stickup
stiffen
stiffly
stifler
stilted
Stilton
stimuli
stinger
stinker
stipend
stipple
stipule
stirpes
stirred
stirrer
stirrup
stocker
stoical
stomach
stomata
stonily
stonker
stopgap
stopoff
stopped
stopper
stopple
storage
storied
stouten
stoutly
stovies
stowage
straits
strange
stratum
stratus
strayer
streaky
stretch
stretta
stretto
strewth
striate
strider
stridor
strigil
striker
stringy
striped
striven
striver
strophe
stroppy
strudel
strumae
stubbed
stubble
stubbly
stuccos
stuckup
studded
student
studied
stuffer
stumble
stummed
stumper
stunned
stunner
stunted
stupefy
stutter
stygian
stylise
stylish
stylist
stylite
styloid
styptic
styrene
utensil
uterine
utilise
utility
utopian
utopism
utopist
utricle
utterer
utterly
yttrium
auction
audible
audient
auditor
augment
augural
aurally
aureate
aurelia
aureola
aureole
auricle
aurochs
aurorae
auroral
auroras
auspice
austere
austral
autarky
autobus
autocar
autocue
autopsy
auxesis
auxetic
bubonic
buccina
buckeye
buckler
buckram
bucksaw
bucolic
budding
buffalo
buffoon
bugaboo
bugbane
bugbear
bugeyed
bugging
bugloss
builded
builder
buildup
builtin
builtup
buirdly
bulbous
bulimia
bulkily
bullace
bullary
bullate
bullbat
bulldog
bullion
bullish
bullock
bullpen
bulrush
bulwark
bumbler
bumboat
bummalo
bumming
bumpily
bumpkin
bungler
bunraku
bunting
buoyage
buoyant
burbler
burdock
bureaus
bureaux
burette
burgage
burgeon
burgess
burghal
burgher
burglar
Burmese
burning
burnish
burnous
bursary
burster
burthen
burweed
bushido
bushman
bushtit
busking
bussing
bustard
bustler
butcher
buttend
buttery
buttock
buttons
buttony
butyric
buyable
buzzard
buzzsaw
cubbing
cubhood
cubical
cubicle
cubital
cuckold
cudbear
cudweed
cuirass
cuisine
cuittle
culices
cullion
culotte
culprit
cultism
cultist
culture
culvert
cumquat
cumshaw
cumulus
cuneate
cunette
cunning
cupcake
cupmoss
cupping
cuprite
cuprous
cupsful
cupular
curable
curacao
curacoa
curator
curcuma
cureall
curette
curiosa
curious
curling
currach
curragh
currant
current
currier
currish
cursive
cursory
curtail
curtain
curtana
curtsey
curvate
cushion
cuspate
custard
custody
customs
cutaway
cutback
cuticle
cutlass
cutlery
cutline
cutrate
cutting
cutworm
cuvette
dualise
dualism
dualist
duality
dubbing
dubiety
dubious
ducally
duchess
ducking
duckpin
ductile
ducting
dudgeon
duelled
dueller
dukedom
dulcify
dullard
dullish
dulness
dumpish
dunbird
dungeon
Dunkirk
dunnage
dunning
dunnock
duodena
duopoly
dupable
durable
durably
duramen
durance
durmast
duskily
dustbin
dustily
dustman
dustpan
duteous
dutiful
duumvir
euclase
eucrite
eugenic
euglena
eulogia
eupepsy
euphony
Euratom
eustasy
eutexia
fuchsia
fuddler
Fuehrer
fuelled
fueller
fugally
fugging
fuguist
fulcrum
fulgent
fulgour
fullage
fullout
fulmine
fulness
fulsome
fulvous
fumbler
funeral
funfair
fungoid
fungous
funicle
funnies
funnily
funning
furbish
furcate
furcula
furioso
furious
furlong
furmety
furmity
furnace
furnish
furrier
furring
furrowy
further
furtive
fuscous
fusible
fussily
fusspot
fustian
fustily
futhark
futhorc
futhork
futtock
fuzzily
guanaco
guanine
guarana
guarani
guarded
guardee
guayule
gubbins
gudgeon
Guelfic
guerdon
guereza
guesser
guichet
Guignol
guilder
guipure
guisard
gullery
gumboil
gumboot
gumdrop
gumming
gummite
gumshoe
gunboat
gunfire
gunlock
gunnera
gunnery
gunning
gunplay
gunroom
gunship
gunshot
gunwale
gurnard
gushing
gustily
gutless
gutsily
guttate
gutting
guzzler
huanaco
hueless
huffish
hugeous
hugging
hulking
humanly
humbles
humbuzz
humdrum
humeral
humerus
humidly
humidor
humming
hummock
humoral
hundred
hunkers
Hunnish
hunting
hurdler
hurdles
hurling
hurried
hurtful
husband
hushaby
huskily
husking
Hussite
hustler
hutment
hutting
jubilee
Judaean
Judaise
Judaism
Judaist
judoist
jugging
juggins
juggler
jugular
juicily
jujitsu
jukebox
jumbuck
jumpjet
jumpoff
juncoes
Jungian
juniper
Jupiter
jurally
juryman
jussive
justice
justify
jutting
kumquat
Kurdish
kursaal
lubbard
lucarne
lucency
lucerne
lucidly
Lucifer
luckily
Luddite
luggage
lugging
lughole
lugsail
lugworm
lullaby
lumbago
lumbang
lumenal
luminal
lumpily
lumpish
lunatic
luncher
lunette
lunular
lupulin
lurcher
lurdane
luridly
lustful
lustily
lustral
lustrum
luteous
mudbath
muddily
muddler
mudfish
mudflat
mudlark
mudpack
muezzin
muffler
mugging
muggins
mugwort
mugwump
mulatto
mullein
mullion
mullock
multure
mumbler
mummery
mummify
mumming
mumpish
mundane
mundify
munnion
munting
muntjac
muntjak
muonium
muraena
murexes
muriate
murices
murkily
murrain
murther
muscled
musette
musical
muskrat
mustang
mustard
mutable
mutably
mutagen
muttony
muzzily
muzzler
nuclear
nucleic
nuclein
nucleon
nucleus
nuclide
nullify
nullity
numbles
numeral
numeric
nummary
nunatak
nunhood
nunnery
nunnish
nunship
nuptial
nursery
nursing
nurture
nutcase
nutgall
nutlike
nutpine

nutting
ouabain
ourself
outback
outcast
outcome
outcrop
outdone
outdoor
outface
outfall
outflow
outfoot
outgone
outgrew
outgrow
outhaul
outland
outlast
outlier
outline
outlive
outlook
outmost
outpace
outplay
outport
outpost
outrage
outrank
outride
outrode
outrush
outsell
outshot
outside
outsize
outsold
outsole
outstay
outtake
outtalk
outturn
outvote
outward
outwear
outwent
outwore
outwork
outworn
puberal
puberty
publish
puccoon
puckery
puckish
pudding
puddler
pudency
puerile
puffery
pugging
puggish
puggree
pugmill
pugnose
Pullman
pullout
pulpous
pulsate
pulvini
pumpkin
puncher
punchup
punctum
pungent
Punjabi
punning
punster

puparia
pupilar
pupping
puritan
purlieu
purloin
purport
purpose
purpura
purpure
pursuer
pursuit
purview
pushful
pushing
pushrod
pustule
putamen
putdown
putlock
putrefy
puttier
putting
puzzler
quadrat
quadric
quaffer
quahaug
qualify
quality
quamash
quantic
quantum
quarrel
quartan
quarter
quartet
quartic
quassia
quavery
quayage
Quechua
queenly
queerly
queller
querist
quester
questor
quetsch
quetzal
queuing
quibble
quicken
quickie
quickly
quieten
quietly
quietus
quillet
quilter
quinary
quinate
quinine
quinone
quintal
quintan
quintet
quintic
quipped
quitted
quitter
quivery
quixote
quizzed
quizzer
quizzes
quondam
rubadub
rubbers

rubbery
rubbing
rubbish
rubdown
rubella
rubeola
rubicon
rubious
ruching
ruction
ruddily
ruddock
ruderal
rudesby
ruffian
ruffler
ruinate
ruinous
rumbler
rummage
rumness
rumshop
runaway
rundale
rundlet
rundown
runless
running
rupture
rurally
russety
Russian
Russify
rustily
rustler
ruthful
rutting
ruttish
suasion
suasive
suavely
suavity
subacid
subadar
subaqua
subbing
subdean
subdual
subduct
subdued
subedit
suberic
suberin
subfusc
subhead
subject
subjoin
sublate
sublime
subplot
subside
subsidy
subsist
subsoil
subsume
subtend
subtile
suburbs
subvert
subzero
succade
succeed
success
succory
succour
succuba
succubi
succumb
sucking

suckler
sucrose
suction
sudaria
suffice
Suffolk
suffuse
suggest
suicide
suiting
sulcate
sulkily
sullage
sulphur
sultana
summand
summary
summery
summing
summons
sumpter
sunbath
sunbeam
sunbear
sunbird
sunburn
sundeck
sundial
sundisc
sundown
sunfish
sunlamp
sunless
sunnily
sunning
Sunnite
sunrise
sunroof
sunspot
sunstar
sunsuit
suntrap
sunward
sunwise
supping
support
suppose
supreme
supremo
surbase
surcoat
surface
surfeit
surfing
surfman
surgeon
surgery
surlily
surmise
surname
surpass
surplus
surreal
surtout
survive
suspect
suspend
suspire
sustain
sutural
sutured
tuatara
tubbing
tubbish
tubular
tuckbox
Tuesday
tugboat
tugging

tuition
tulchan
tumbler
tumbrel
tumbril
tumidly
tumular
tumulus
tunable
tunably
tundish
tuneful
tunicle
tunning
turbary
turbine
turdine
turdoid
turfite
turfman
turgent
Turkish
turmoil
turnery
turning
turnipy
turnkey
turnout
turpeth
tushery
tussive
tussock
tussore
tutelar
tutenag
tutting
tutwork
vulgate
vulpine
vulture
yulelog
avarice
avenger
average
averred
Avestan
Avestic
aviator
avidity
avionic
avocado
evacuee
evangel
evanish
evasion
evasive
evening
evictor
evident
evolute
ivories
ovarian
ovation
overact
overage
overall
overarm
overate
overawe
overbid
overbuy
overdid
overdue
overeat
overfed
overfly
overlap
overlay
overlie

overman
overpay
overran
overrun
oversaw
oversea
oversee
overset
oversew
overtax
overtly
overtop
overuse
ovicide
oviduct
oviform
ovoidal
ovulate
uveitis
awarder
aweless
awesome
awfully
awkward
awnless
dwarves
dweller
dwindle
ewelamb
eweneck
gwyniad
swabbed
swabber
swaddle
swagged
swagger
swagman
Swahili
swallow
swanker
swanned
swapped
swapper
swarded
swarmer
swarthy
swasher
swatted
swatter
swearer
sweater
Swedish
sweeper
sweeten
sweetie
sweetly
swelter
swiftly
swigged
swiller
swimmer
swindle
swinery
swinger
swingle
swinish
swipple
swither
Switzer
swizzle
swobbed
swollen
swopped
swopper
swotted
twaddle
twaddly
twangle
twankay

tweeter
tweezer
twelfth
twelves
twibill
twiddle
twiddly
twigged
twilled
twinkle
twinkly
twinned
twister
twitchy
twitted
twitter
twofold
twoline
twoness
twosome
twostep
twotime
twotone
axially
axillae
axillar
axolotl
exactly
exactor
examine
example
exarate
excerpt
excited
exciter
exciton
excitor
exclaim
exclave
exclude
excrete
excurse
excusal
execute
exedrae
exegete
exempla
exergue
exhaust
exhibit
exhumer
exigent
exocarp
exogamy
exordia
exotica
expanse
expense
expiate
explain
explant
explode
exploit
explore
exposal
exposed
exposer
exposit
expound
express
expulse
expunge
exscind
externe
extinct
extract
extreme
extrude
exudate

exurban
exurbia
exuviae
exuvial
oxalate
oxfence
oxidant
oxidase
oxidate
oxidise
Oxonian
oxyacid
oxytone
uxorial
byebyes
bygones
Byronic
bywoner
cyanide
cyanine
cyanite
cyathus
cyclist
cycloid
cyclone
cyclops
cymbalo
cynical
cypress
Cyprian
Cypriot
cypsela
cystine
cystoid
dyarchy
dyewood
dynamic
dynasty
eyeball
eyebath
eyebolt
eyebrow
eyedrop
eyehole
eyelash
eyeless
eyelike
eyeshot
eyesore
eyespot
eyewash
eyewink
gymnast
gymslip
gypping
hyaline
hyalite
hyaloid
hydatid
hydrant
hydrate
hydride
hydroid
hydrous
hygeian
hygiene
hymenia
hymnary
hymnist
hymnody
hyperon
hypnoid
hypogea
hypoxia
hypoxic
kyanise
kyanite
lychnis
lychowl

lycopod
lyddite
lyingin
lyingly
lymphad
lyncean
lynchet
lyrated
lyrical
myalgia
myalgic
myalism
mycelia
mycoses
mycosis
mycotic
myeloid
myeloma
myiasis
mylodon
mynheer
myogram
myology
myomata
mystery
mystify
mythise
mythist
myxomas
nylghau
nymphal
nymphet
pyaemia
pyaemic
pycnite
pygmean
pygmoid
pyjamas
pyloric
pylorus
pyralid
pyralis
pyramid
pyretic
pyrexia
pyrexic
pyrites
pyritic
pyrosis
pyrrhic
Pythian
pyxides
pyxidia
syconia
sycosis
syenite
syllabi
sylphid
sylvine
sylvite
symptom
synapse
syncarp
syncope
synergy
synesis
syngamy
synodal
synodic
synonym
synovia
syringa
syringe
syrphid
systole
tychism
tylopod
tympana
tympani

tympano
tympany
Tynwald
typebar
typeset
typhoid
typhoon
typhous
typical
typonym
tyranny
wychelm
zygosis
zygotic
zymogen
zymosis
zymotic
zymurgy
Azilean
azimuth
azurine
azurite
azygous
czardas
czardom
czarina
czarism
czarist
ozonise
tzigane
tzigany

---

abaddon
abalone
abandon
abashed
abattis
abaxial
academe
academy
Acadian
acantha
acarian
adamant
Adamite
adapter
adaptor
adaxial
against
agamous
alameda
alanine
alation
amalgam
amanita
amarant
amateur
amative
amatory
amazing
anaemia
anaemic
anagoge
anagogy
anagram
analogy
analyse
analyst
Ananias
anarchy
anatase
anatomy
apagoge
apanage
apatite
Arabian
arabise
Arabist
Aramaic

araneid
Arapaho
ataraxy
atavism
atavist
avarice
awarder
Baalism
beading
beamish
beanbag
bearded
bearing
bearish
beastly
beatify
beating
beatnik
Biafran
biassed
biaxial
blabbed
blabber
blacken
blackly
bladder
blandly
blanket
blankly
blarney
blasted
blaster
blatant
blather
blatter
boarder
boarish
boaster
boating
boatman
brabble
bracing
bracken
bracket
bradawl
bragged
bragger
Brahman
Brahmin
braille
bramble
brambly
branchy
brander
brannew
bransle
brantle
brantub
brashly
brassie
brattle
braunch
bravado
bravely
bravery
bravura
brawler
brazier
Chablis
chaffer
chagrin
chalaza
Chaldee
chalice
challis
chalone
chamber
chamfer
chamois

champac
champak
chancel
chancre
changer
channel
chanson
chanter
chantry
chaotic
chapati
chaplet
chapman
chapped
chappie
chapter
charade
charger
charily
chariot
charism
charity
charley
charlie
charmer
charnel
charpoy
charqui
charred
charter
chassis
chasten
chateau
chatted
chattel
chatter
clabber
clacker
cladode
claimer
clamant
clamber
clammed
clamour
clanger
clapped
clapper
clarify
clarion
clarity
clarkia
classes
classic
classis
clastic
clatter
clausal
clavate
clavier
claypan
coacher
coagula
coaltit
coaming
coarsen
coastal
coaster
coating
coaxial
crabbed
cracked
cracker
crackle
crackly
crackup
cragged
crammed
crammer
crampet

crampit
crampon
cranage
cranial
cranium
crankle
crannog
crappie
crassly
craunch
craving
crawler
crazily
csardas
cyanide
cyanine
cyanite
cyathus
czardas
czardom
czarina
czarism
czarist
deadend
deadeye
deadpan
deafaid
dealing
deanery
deathly
diabase
diabolo
diadrom
diagram
dialect
dialled
dialyse
diamond
diarchy
diarise
diarist
drabber
drabbet
drabble
drabler
drachma
draftee
drafter
dragged
draggle
dragnet
dragoon
drainer
drapery
drastic
dratted
draught
drawbar
drawing
drawler
drayage
drayman
dualise
dualism
dualist
duality
dwarves
dyarchy
edacity
edaphic
egality
elastic
elastin
elation
emanate
enactor
enamour
enation
eparchy

epatant
epaulet
erasure
etaerio
etamine
evacuee
evangel
evanish
evasion
evasive
exactly
exactor
examine
example
exarate
fearful
feaster
feather
feature
fiancee
flaccid
flagday
flagged
flagman
flamfew
flaming
flaneur
flanker
flannel
flapped
flapper
flareup
flasher
flatcap
flatcar
flatlet
flatout
flatten
flatter
flattop
flaught
flaunty
flavine
flavour
fracted
fraenum
fragile
frailly
frailty
Fraktur
frameup
frankly
frantic
frapped
fratery
fraught
frazzle
gearbox
gearing
gharial
ghastly
giantry
glacial
glacier
gladded
gladden
gladder
glaikit
glamour
glaring
glassen
glasses
glazier
glazing
gnarled
gnathic
goahead
goatgod
goatish

grabbed
grabber
grabble
gracile
grackle
gradate
gradely
gradine
gradual
grafter
grained
grainer
gramary
grammar
grampus
granary
grandad
grandam
grandee
grandly
grandma
grandpa
granger
granita
granite
grannie
grantee
granter
grantor
granule
grapery
graphic
grapnel
grapple
grasper
gratify
grating
graunch
gravely
gravity
gravure
grazier
grazing
guanaco
guanine
guarana
guarani
guarded
guardee
guayule
headily
heading
headman
headpin
headset
headway
healthy
hearing
hearken
hearsay
hearted
hearten
heathen
heather
heating
heavily
hoarsen
hoatzin
huanaco
hyaline
hyalite
hyaloid
imagery
imagine
imagism
imagist
imamate
inanely
inanity

inaptly
Iranian
irately
itacism
Italian
Italiot
jealous
khaddar
khamsin
khanate
knacker
knapped
knapper
knavery
knavish
kyanise
kyanite
leading
leadoff
leafage
leafbud
leaflet
leaguer
leakage
leaning
learned
learner
leather
liaison
Liassic
llanero
loading
loaning
loather
loathly
meadowy
mealies
meander
meaning
measles
measure
meatfly
meatman
miasmal
miasmic
Moabite
myalgia
myalgic
myalism
nearest
Noachic
ocarina
odalisk
onanism
opacity
opaline
oration
oratory
oratrix
ouabain
ovarian
ovation
oxalate
peacock
peafowl
pearled
pearler
peartly
peasant
peascod
peasoup
phaeton
phalanx
phallic
phallus
phantom
pharaoh
pharynx
phasmid

piaffer
pianism
pianist
piastre
placard
placate
placebo
placket
placoid
plafond
plaided
plainly
planish
planned
planner
plantar
planter
planula
planxty
plasmic
plasmid
plasmin
plaster
plastic
plastid
platane
plateau
platina
plating
platoon
platted
platter
plaudit
playact
playboy
playful
playing
playlet
playoff
playpen
poacher
praetor
prairie
praiser
Prakrit
praline
prancer
prattle
pravity
psalter
pyaemia
pyaemic
quadrat
quadric
quaffer
quahaug
qualify
quality
quamash
quantic
quantum
quarrel
quartan
quarter
quartet
quartic
quassia
quavery
quayage
reacher
reactor
readily
reading
readout
reagent
realgar
realign
realise
realism

realist
reality
reallot
realtor
rhabdom
Rhaetic
rhamnus
rhatany
roadbed
roadhog
roadman
roadway
roaring
roaster
scabbed
scabble
scabies
scabrid
scaglia
scalade
scalado
scalder
scaldic
scalene
scallop
scalpel
scalper
scamper
scandal
scanned
scanner
scantly
scapple
scapula
scarfed
scarify
scarlet
scarper
scarred
scarves
scatted
scatter
scauper
seabass
seabear
seabird
seablue
seaboot
seafish
seafood
seafowl
seagirt
seagull
seakale
sealane
sealant
sealegs
sealery
seamaid
seamark
seapink
seaport
searoom
seasick
seaside
seaslug
seatang
seating
seawall
seaward
seaware
seaweed
seawhip
seawife
seawolf
shackle
shadily
shading
shadoof

shadowy shaitan shakeup shakily shallop shallot shallow shamble shammed shammer shampoo shanked shapely sharpen sharper sharply shaslik shaster shastra shatter Shavian shaving sialoid siamang Siamese sjambok skaldic skating slabbed slabber slacken slacker slackly slagged slammed slander slantly slapped slasher slather slating slatted slavery slavish Slavism smacker smaragd smarten smartly smasher smashup smatter snaffle snagged snakily snapped snapper snarler snarlup snatchy soakage soaking soapbox soapily soaring spacial spacing spadger spancel spangle spangly spaniel Spanish spanker spanned spanner sparely sparger sparing

sparkle sparoid sparred sparrow Spartan spastic spathic spatial spatted spattee spatter spatula spawner stabbed stabber stabile stabler stables stacker staddle stadium stagger stagily staging staidly stainer staithe stalely stalked stalker stamina stammel stammer stamper standby stander standin standup staniel stannic stapler starchy stardom starkly starlet starlit starred starter startle statant stately statice statics station statism statist stative statued stature statute staunch suasion suasive suavely suavity swabbed swabber swaddle swagged swagger swagman Swahili swallow swanker swanned swapped swapper swarded swarmer

swarthy swasher swatted swatter teacake teacher teachin teacosy teagown tealeaf tearful teargas tearing tearoom tearose teashop teatime teatray thalami thallic thallus thalweg thanage thankee thanker toaster tracery trachea tracker tractor tradein trading traduce traffic tragedy trailer trainee trainer traipse traitor traject tramcar trammel trample tramway tranche trangam transit transom tranter trapeze trapped trapper travail travois trawler trayful tsardom tsarina tsarism tsarist tuatara twaddle twaddly twangle twankay udaller unaptly unarmed unasked unaware uraemia Uralian uralite uranide uranism uranium uranous viaduct

viatica weakish wealden wealthy wearily wearing weasand weather whacker whaling whangee wharves whatnot wrangle wrapped wrapper zealous zoarium Abbasid aiblins albumen albumin ambages ambatch ambient amboina ambones amboyna ambsace arbiter arbutus babassu babbitt babbler babyish babysit bibbery bibbing bibcock bibelot biblist bobbery bobbing bobbish bobeche bobsled bobstay bobtail bubonic cabaret cabbage cabbagy cabbala cabinet cabling caboose cabrank ciboria cobbler cubbing cubhood cubical cubicle cubital dabbing dabbler debacle debater debauch debouch Debrett debrief dibasic dibbing dubbing dubiety dubious ebbtide embargo

embassy emblaze embolic embolus embosom embowed embowel embower embrace embroil embrown embryon Faberge fabliau fabular febrile fibbing fibroid fibroin fibroma fibrous fibster fibulae fibular fibulas fobbing gabbing gabbler gabelle gabfest gabnash gibbous giblets gobbler Gobelin gubbins habitat habitue hebenon Hebraic Hobbian Hobbism Hobbist hobbler hobnail imbiber imbower imbrute inboard inbreed inbuilt jabbing jibbing jibboom jibdoor jobbery jobbing jubilee kabbala kibbutz labarum labella labiate liberal liberty library librate lobbing lobelia lobster lobular lobworm lubbard mobbing mobbish mobster nabbing nebbish nebulae

nebular nebulas nibbler niblick nobbler orbital pabulum pebrine pibroch puberal puberty publish rabbity rabbler rabidly rebirth reboant rebound rebuild rebuilt rebuker ribband ribbing ribston ribwork ribwort robbery robbing rubadub rubbers rubbery rubbing rubbish rubdown rubella rubeola rubicon rubious Sabaism Sabaoth Sabbath sibling sibship sobbing soberly subacid subadar subaqua subbing subdean subdual subduct subdued subedit suberic suberin subfusc subhead subject subjoin sublate sublime subplot subside subsidy subsist subsoil subsume subtend subtile suburbs subvert subzero tabanid tabaret tabasco tabbing tabetic tabinet

tableau tabloid taborer tabular Tibetan tobacco tubbing tubbish tubular umbonal umbones umbrage Umbrian unbated unblest unblock unbosom unbound unbowed unboxed unbrace unbuild unbuilt upbraid vibrant vibrate vibrato webbing webfoot webster webworm wobbler zebrine zebroid accidie acclaim account accrete accrual accurst accusal accused accuser alcaide alcalde alcayde alcazar alchemy alcohol Alcoran anchovy anchusa ancient ancones ancress arcaded arcadia arcanum archaic archery archive archway arctoid arcuate arcweld ascarid ascaris ascesis ascetic ascidia ascites ascitic ascribe auction baccara baccate bacchic bacilli backing

backlog backsaw backset because becloud bicycle buccina buckeye buckler buckram bucksaw bucolic cacanny cachexy cacique cackler cacodyl cacoepy cacumen cichlid cocaine coccoid cochlea cockade cockeye cockily cockney cockpit cockshy coconut cocotte cuckold cyclist cycloid cyclone cyclops dacoity decadal decagon decanal decapod decease deceive decency deciare decibel decided decider decidua decimal decking declaim declare declass decline decoder decorum decrier decrypt decuman decuple dickens dictate diction docetic dockage dockise ducally duchess ducking duckpin ductile ducting eccrine enchain enchant enchase enclasp enclave

enclose encoder encomia Encraty encrust escapee escaper escheat escolar escribe etching euclase eucrite excerpt excited exciter exciton excitor exclaim exclave exclude excrete excurse excusal faceoff faceted faction factory factual facture faculae faculty fictile fiction fictive focused fuchsia geckoes hachure hackbut hackery hacking hackler hackney hacksaw heckler hectare hiccupy hickory hockday hocused incense incipit incised incisor inciter incline inclose include incomer incrust incubus incudes incurve incused ischial ischium jacamar jacinth jackass jackdaw jackpot jacktar Jacobin jacobus jaconet jocular kickoff lacking

laconic
lacquer
lactate
lacteal
lactose
lacunae
lacunal
lacunar
lacunas
lechery
lectern
lection
lecture
licence
license
lichowl
licitly
licking
locally
locater
lockage
lockjaw
locknut
lockout
locular
loculus
lucarne
lucency
lucerne
lucidly
Lucifer
luckily
lychnis
lychowl
lycopod
macabre
macadam
macaque
machair
machete
machine
macrame
macrami
maculae
macular
Mechlin
meconic
micelle
microbe
mockery
mycelia
mycoses
mycosis
mycotic
nacarat
nacelle
nacrous
necklet
necktie
necrose
nectary
niceish
nictate
noctuid
noctule
nocturn
nocuous
nuclear
nucleic
nuclein
nucleon
nucleus
nuclide
obconic
occiput
occlude
orchard
osculum
pachisi

pacific
package
packice
packing
packman
peccant
peccary
peckish
picador
piccolo
piceous
pickaxe
pickeer
pickled
picotee
picquet
picrate
Pictish
picture
pochard
puccoon
puckery
puckish
pycnite
raccoon
racemic
rackety
racquet
receipt
receive
recency
recital
reciter
reclaim
reclame
recline
recluse
recount
recover
recruit
rectify
rectory
rectrix
recurve
recycle
rickets
rickety
ricksha
ricotta
rockery
rockier
rockily
rocking
rocklet
rockoil
rocktar
ruching
ruction
saccade
saccate
saccule
sacculi
sackbut
sackful
sacking
sacring
sacrist
seceder
seclude
seconde
secondi
secondo
secrecy
secrete
sectary
sectile
section
secular
securer

sickbay
sickbed
sickish
sickpay
socager
soccage
society
sockeye
succade
succeed
success
succory
succour
succuba
succubi
succumb
sucking
suckler
sucrose
suction
syconia
sycosis
tachism
tachist
tacitly
tacking
tackler
tactful
tactics
tactile
taction
tactual
technic
tectrix
ticking
tickler
toccata
tuckbox
tychism
ulcered
uncanny
unchain
uncinus
uncivil
unclasp
unclean
uncloak
unclose
uncouth
uncover
uncross
uncrown
unction
vacancy
vaccine
vacuity
vacuole
vacuous
viceroy
vicinal
vicious
victory
victual
vocable
vocalic
vocally
wickiup
wychelm
abdomen
addable
addenda
addible
address
adducer
andante
andiron
android
ardency
arduous

audible
audient
auditor
baddish
badmash
badness
bedding
bedevil
bedfast
bedight
bedizen
bedouin
bedpost
bedrock
bedroll
bedroom
bedside
bedsock
bedsore
bedtime
bidding
bodeful
budding
cadaver
caddice
caddish
cadence
cadency
cadenza
Cadmean
cadmium
caducei
cedilla
cidaris
codable
coddler
codeine
codfish
codices
codicil
codling
cudbear
cudweed
Dadaism
Dadaist
diddler
doddard
doddery
dodgems
dodgery
dudgeon
ecdyses
ecdysis
eidetic
eidolon
elderly
endarch
endemic
enderon
endless
endlong
endmost
endogen
endorse
endozoa
endways
endwise
faddish
faddism
faddist
fadedly
fadeout
fedayee
federal
fiddler
fideism
fideist
fidgets
fidgety

fuddler
gadding
gadgety
gadroon
gadwall
giddily
goddamn
goddess
godetia
godevil
godhead
godhood
godless
godlike
godling
godsend
godship
godward
gudgeon
haddock
hedonic
hidalga
hidalgo
hideous
hideout
hydatid
hydrant
hydrate
hydride
hydroid
hydrous
indepth
indexer
indican
indices
indicia
inditer
indoors
indorse
indraft
indrawn
inducer
indulge
indusia
indwell
indwelt
jadedly
jadeite
Judaean
Judaise
Judaism
Judaist
judoist
Kaddish
kidding
kiddish
kidskin
ladanum
ladybug
ladykin
lidless
lodging
Luddite
lyddite
maddest
madding
Madeira
madness
madonna
madrona
madrono
madwort
meddler
mediacy
mediant
mediate
medical
medulla
medusae

medusan
medusas
midland
midline
midmost
midriff
midship
midweek
Midwest
midwife
midyear
modally
modesty
modicum
modiste
modular
modulus
mudbath
muddily
muddler
mudfish
mudflat
mudlark
mudpack
nodally
nodated
nodding
nodical
nodular
oddball
oddment
oddness
oedipal
oldster
oldtime
orderer
orderly
ordinal
padding
paddler
paddock
padlock
padrone
padroni
peddler
pedicab
pedicel
pedicle
pedlary
piddock
pidgeon
podagra
podding
podesta
pudding
puddler
pudency
radiant
radiate
radical
radices
radicle
radulae
radular
redcoat
reddest
reddish
redhead
redlegs
redneck
redness
redoubt
redound
redpoll
redraft
redress
redskin
reducer
redwing

redwood
ridable
ridding
riddler
ridging
ridotto
rodding
rodlike
rodsman
ruddily
ruddock
ruderal
rudesby
saddest
saddish
saddler
sadness
sedilia
seducer
sidecar
sideway
sudaria
tadpole
tedding
tedious
tidally
tiddler
tiddley
tiderip
tideway
tidings
toddler
underdo
undergo
undoing
undress
undying
Vedanta
Veddoid
vedette
vidette
vidimus
viduity
wadable
wadding
waddler
wedding
wedging
wedlock
widgeon
widowed
widower
Yiddish
zedoary
Abelian
abetted
abetter
abettor
abeyant
acequia
acerbic
acerola
acerose
acetate
acetify
acetone
acetous
adenine
adenoid
adenoma
adeptly
afeared
ageless
agelong
alembic
alertly
aleuron
alewife
amender

amenity
amentia
amentum
Amerind
anemone
aneroid
aneurin
apetaly
areally
areaway
areolae
areolar
areolas
asepsis
aseptic
asexual
atelier
avenger
average
averred
Avestan
Avestic
aweless
awesome
beechen
beehive
beeline
beeswax
bheesty
bheetie
biennia
bleakly
bleater
bleeder
bleeper
blemish
blender
blesbok
blessed
blether
blewits
breaded
breadth
breaker
breakin
breakup
breathe
breathy
breccia
breeder
brevier
brevity
brewage
brewery
byebyes
caesium
caesura
cheapen
cheaply
cheater
checker
checkup
cheddar
cheerer
cheerio
cheetah
chelate
chemise
chemism
chemist
chequer
cherish
cheroot
chervil
chessel
chested
cheviot
chevron
cleaner

cleanly
cleanse
cleanup
clearly
cleaver
clement
clerisy
clerkly
coeliac
coequal
coexist
creamer
creator
credent
creedal
creeper
cremate
cremona
crenate
cresset
crested
crevice
ctenoid
deepfry
deepsea
diehard
dietary
doeskin
dreamed
dreamer
dredger
dresser
duelled
dueller
dweller
dyewood
ejector
Eleatic
elector
electro
elegant
elegiac
elegise
elegist
element
elenchi
elevate
elevens
emerald
emeriti
emersed
emetine
enemata
energid
epergne
erectly
erector
erelong
eremite
erepsin
eternal
etesian
evening
ewelamb
eweneck
execute
exedrae
exegete
exempla
exergue
eyeball
eyebath
eyebolt
eyebrow
eyedrop
eyehole
eyelash
eyeless
eyelike

eyeshot
eyesore
eyespot
eyewash
eyewink
feeding
feedlot
feeling
fiefdom
fielder
fierily
fleabag
fleapit
flecker
fleeced
fleecer
fleeing
fleetly
Fleming
Flemish
fleshed
flesher
fleshly
fletton
fleuret
fleuron
flexile
flexion
flexure
freaked
freckle
freckly
freebie
freedom
freeman
freesia
freeway
freezer
freight
Frenchy
frenula
frescos
freshen
fresher
freshet
freshly
fretful
fretsaw
fretted
Fuehrer
fuelled
fueller
geebung
gherkin
ghettos
gleaner
gleeful
gleeman
glenoid
greaser
greaten
greatly
greaves
Grecian
grecise
Grecism
greenly
greenth
greisen
gremial
gremlin
grenade
greyhen
greyish
greylag
Guelfic
guerdon
guereza
guesser
heedful
heeltap
hoecake
hoedown
hueless
Iberian
iceberg
iceboat
icecold
icefall
icefloe
icefoot
icepack
icerink
iceshow
ideally
identic
ikebana
ileitis
ineptly
inertia
inertly
inexact
itemise
iterant
iterate
keelson
keeping
khedive
kneader
kneecap
kneeler
kneepan
kneesup
kremlin
leeward
lieabed
maestri
maestro
meerkat
meeting
muezzin
myeloid
myeloma
needful
needler
obelise
obelisk
obesity
oceanic
ocellar
ocellus
olefine
omental
omentum
oneeyed
oneiric
oneness
onerous
oneself
oneshot
onestep
onetime
openair
openend
opening
operand
operant
operate
operose
orectic
oregano
overact
overage
overall
overarm
overate
overawe
overbid
overbuy
overdid
overdue
overeat
overfed
overfly
overlap
overlay
overlie
overman
overpay
overran
overrun
oversaw
oversea
oversee
overset
oversew
overtax
overtly
overtop
overuse
paeonic
peerage
peeress
peevish
pfennig
phellem
piebald
pieeyed
pierrot
pietism
pietist
pleader
pleased
plectra
pledgee
pledger
pledget
pledgor
plenary
plenish
pleurae
pleural
pleuron
poetess
poetics
poetise
preachy
prebend
precast
precede
precept
precise
precook
predate
predial
predict
predoom
preempt
preface
prefect
preform
preheat
prelacy
prelate
prelect
prelims
prelude
premier
premise
premiss
premium
prepack
prepaid
prepare
preplan
presage
present
preside
presoak
presser
pressup
presume
pretend
pretest
pretext
pretzel
prevail
prevent
preview
previse
pteroic
pteryla
puerile
Quechua
queenly
queerly
queller
querist
quester
questor
quetsch
quetzal
queuing
reeding
reelect
reenact
reenter
reentry
rhenium
roebuck
roedeer
scenery
scented
scepsis
sceptic
sceptre
seeable
seedbed
seedily
seedlip
seeming
seepage
sferics
shearer
sheathe
sheaves
shebang
shebear
shebeen
shedder
sheerly
shellac
shelled
sheller
shelter
sheltie
shelved
shelves
Shemite
sherbet
shereef
sheriff
sherris
siemens
sierran
skeeter
skegger
skellum
skelter
skepsis
sketchy
sledded
sleeken
sleekit
sleekly
sleeper
sleeved
sleight
slender
smeddum
smeller
smelter
sneaker
sneerer
sneezer
speaker
special
species
specify
speckle
spectra
spectre
specula
speeder
speedup
speller
spelter
spencer
spender
stealer
stealth
steamer
stearic
stearin
steekit
steepen
steeple
steeply
steerer
stellar
stemmed
stemple
stemson
stenchy
stencil
stentor
stepney
stepped
stepper
stepson
sterile
sterlet
sternal
sterned
sternly
sternum
steroid
stetson
stetted
steward
stewpan
stewpot
swearer
sweater
Swedish
sweeper
sweeten
sweetie
sweetly
swelter
syenite
taeniae
teeming
teenage
theatre
thecate
themata
theorbo
theorem
therapy
thereat
thereby
therein
thereof
thereon
thereto
theriac
thermae
thermal
thermic
theurgy
tieback
tiebeam
tiercel
tiercet
toeclip
toehold
toeless
toenail
treacle
treacly
treader
treadle
treason
treater
treetop
trefoil
trehala
trekked
trekker
trellis
tremble
trembly
tremolo
trenail
trental
trepang
tressed
tressel
trestle
Tuesday
tweeter
tweezer
twelfth
twelves
uberous
ukelele
unearth
unequal
urethan
urethra
useless
utensil
uterine
uveitis
viewing
weekday
weekend
weevily
wheaten
wheedle
wheeled
wheeler
whereas
whereat
whereby
wherein
whereof
whereon
whereto
whether
whetted
whetter
wheyish
wielder
wreathe
wreathy
wrecker
wrestle
yielder
affable
affably
affaire
affined
afflict
affront
alfalfa
alforja
awfully
baffler
bifilar
bifocal
buffalo
buffoon
coffers
default
defence
defiant
deficit
defiler
definer
deflate
deflect
defocus
deforce
defraud
defrock
defrost
defunct
diffuse
effects
effendi
effulge
elfbolt
elfland
elflock
enfeoff
enfiled
enforce
enframe
fifteen
fifthly
fifties
hafnium
heftily
huffish
infancy
infanta
infante
infarct
infauna
inferno
infidel
infield
inflame
inflate
inflect
inflict
infract
infulae
leftism
leftist
lifeful
liftoff
loftily
maffick
mafiosi
mafioso
mofette
muffler
offbeat
offence
offhand
officer
offload
offpeak
offside
oxfence
piffler
pofaced
puffery
raffish
referee
refined
refiner
reflate
reflect
refloat
refocus
refract
refrain
refresh
refugee
refusal
refuser
refutal
refuter
riffler
rifling
ruffian
ruffler
saffron
sofabed
softish
suffice
Suffolk
suffuse
taffeta
tiffany
unfaith
unfitly
unfrock
unfroze
unfunny
unfussy
upfield
waftage
wafture
aggress
algebra
alginic
angelic
angelus
Angevin
anginal
angioma
Anglian
anglice
angling
Anglist
angrily
anguine
anguish
angular
augment
augural
bagasse
baggage
baggily
bagging
bagpipe
beggary
begging
begonia
begorra
begrime
beguile
beguine
bigener
biggest
biggish
bighead
bighorn
bigname
bigness
bigoted
bigotry
bigtime
bogbean
boggler
bogyman
bugaboo
bugbane
bugbear
bugeyed
bugging
bugloss
bygones
cagoule
cogency
cogging
cognate
cognise
degauss
degrade
digamma
digging
digital
dignify
dignity
digraph
digress
dogbane
dogcart
dogdays
dogeate
dogfish
doggery
dogging
doggish
doggone
dogrose
dogskin
dogstar
dogtrot
dogvane
dogwood
eagerly
eggcosy
eggflip
egghead
engaged
English
engorge
engraft
engrail
engrain
engrave
engross
ergates
ergodic
eugenic
euglena
fagging
fagotto
figging
fighter
figleaf
figment
figtree
figural
figured
figwort
fogbank
foggage
foggily
fogging
foghorn
foglamp
fogydom
fogyish
fogyism
fugally
fugging
fuguist
gagging
gagster
gigging
giggler
goggler
goggles

hagfish
Haggada
haggard
haggish
haggler
hagweed
higgler
highboy
highhat
highman
highway
hogback
hogfish
hoggery
hogging
hoggish
hogwash
hogweed
hugeous
hugging
hygeian
hygiene
ingenue
ingesta
ingoing
ingraft
ingrain
ingrate
ingress
ingroup
ingrown
jaggery
jigging
jogging
jogtrot
jugging
juggins
juggler
jugular
laggard
lagging
legally
legatee
legator
legbail
legging
leghorn
legible
legibly
legiron
legless
legpull
legrest
legroom
legshow
legwork
lighted
lighten
lighter
lightly
lignify
lignite
ligroin
logbook
logging
logical
logline
logwood
luggage
lugging
lughole
lugsail
lugworm
magenta
maggoty
magical
magmata
magnate
magneto
magnify
megaron
megaton
mightst
migrant
migrate
mugging
muggins
mugwort
mugwump
nagging
neglect
neglige
Negress
Negrito
negroid
niggard
niggler
nightie
nightly
nigrify
nogging
ongoing
organic
organon
organum
organza
pageant
pageboy
paginal
Pegasus
pegging
piggery
pigging
piggish
pigiron
piglead
pigling
pigmean
pigment
pigskin
pigtail
pigwash
pigweed
pugging
puggish
puggree
pugmill
pugnose
pygmean
pygmoid
ragbolt
ragdoll
raggedy
ragging
ragtime
ragweed
ragworm
ragwort
regalia
regally
regards
regatta
regency
regimen
reginal
regnant
regorge
regrant
regrate
regress
regrets
regroup
regular
regulus
rigging
righten
righter
rightly
rigidly
roguery
roguish
sagging
sagitta
saguaro
segment
sighted
sightly
sigmate
sigmoid
signary
signify
signior
signora
signore
signori
signory
soggily
suggest
Tagalog
tagetes
tagging
tegmina
tegular
tighten
tightly
tigress
tigrish
toggery
tugboat
tugging
ungodly
unguard
unguent
ungulae
upgrade
urgency
vagally
vagrant
vaguely
vaguish
vegetal
voguish
wagerer
waggery
wagging
waggish
wagoner
wagtail
wigging
wiggler
wigless
yeggman
yoghurt
ziganka
zygosis
zygotic
Achaean
Achaian
Achates
achieve
adherer
adhibit
Amharic
aphasia
aphasic
aphelia
apheses
aphesis
aphetic
aphides
aphonia
aphonic
aphotic
aphylly
ashamed
ashtray
atheism
atheist
athirst
athlete
athwart
Bahadur
Bahaism
Bahaist
Bahaite
behaver
behoove
bohemia
cahoots
cohabit
coherer
dehisce
echelon
echidna
echinus
echoism
enhance
ephebus
ephedra
ethanol
etheric
ethical
ethiops
ethmoid
exhaust
exhibit
exhumer
gahnite
Gehenna
ichabod
inhabit
inhaler
inherit
inhibit
inhouse
inhuman
Ishmael
mahaleb
mahatma
Mahdism
Mahdist
mahjong
mahonia
mahound
mahseer
Nahuatl
ochrous
oghamic
ophitic
pahlavi
reheard
rehouse
schappe
schemer
scherzi
scherzo
schlepp
schlock
schmuck
schnook
scholar
scholia
sphenic
spheral
spheric
sthenic
unhandy
unhappy
unheard
unhinge
unhitch
unhoped
unhorse
unhouse
upheave
vehicle
Wahabee
Yahvist
Yahwist
abiding
abigail
ability
abiotic
acicula
acidify
acidity
acinous
adipose
agilely
agility
agitate
agitato
alidade
alienly
aliform
aliment
alimony
aliquot
amiable
amiably
amildar
aniline
anility
animate
animism
animist
anionic
aniseed
apishly
aridity
arietta
aristae
aristas
Asiatic
asinine
atingle
aviator
avidity
avionic
axially
axillae
axillar
Azilean
azimuth
bailiff
beignet
blighty
blinder
blindly
blinker
blintze
blister
blither
boiling
bribery
brickie
brickle
bricole
bridoon
briefly
brigade
brigand
brimful
brimmed
brimmer
brinded
brindle
bringer
brinjal
brioche
briquet
brisken
brisket
briskly
bristle
bristly
British
brittle
brittly
britzka
builded
builder
buildup
builtin
builtup
buirdly
caimans
caisson
caitiff
ceilidh
ceiling
Chianti
chiasma
chibouk
chicane
Chicano
chicken
chicory
chidden
chiefly
chiffon
chigger
chignon
childer
childly
chiliad
chillum
chimera
chimere
chimney
chindit
Chinese
Chinook
chintzy
chinwag
chipped
chipper
chirrup
chitter
clicker
climate
climber
clinker
clipped
clipper
clippie
cliquey
clivers
coinage
coinbox
coition
cribbed
cribble
cricket
cricoid
crimine
crimper
crimple
crimson
cringer
cringle
crinite
crinkle
crinkly
crinoid
criollo
cripple
crisper
crisply
cristae
critter
cuirass
cuisine
cuittle
deicide
deictic
deiform
deistic
djibbah
dribble
driblet
driedup
drifter
driller
drinker
dripdry
dripped
drivein
driving
drizzle
drizzly
dwindle
edictal
edifice
edition
ekistic
elision
elitism
elitist
emicate
eminent
emirate
emitted
emitter
epicarp
epicede
epicene
epicure
epidote
epigeal
epigean
epigene
epigone
epigoni
epigram
epigyny
epilate
episode
epistle
epitaph
epitaxy
epithem
epithet
epitome
epizoic
epizoon
ericoid
eristic
evictor
evident
exigent
faience
failing
failure
faintly
fairing
fairish
fairway
feigner
flicker
flighty
flipped
flipper
flitted
flitter
flivver
friable
friarly
fribble
frigate
frijole
fripper
friseur
Frisian
frisker
frisket
frisson
fritted
fritter
frizzle
frizzly
gainful
gainsay
ghillie
gliadin
glimmer
glimpse
glisten
glister
glitter
goitred
gribble
griddle
griffin
griffon
grifter
grilled
griller
grimace
grimmer
grinder
grinned
gripped
gripper
griskin
gristle
gristly
gritted
grizzle
grizzly
guichet
Guignol
guilder
guipure
guisard
haircut
hairnet
hairpin
heighho
heinous
heiress
iciness
idiotic
imitate
initial
irideal
iridise
iridium
Irishry
Jainism
joinder
joinery
joining
jointer
jointly
juicily
kainite
klipdas
knitted
knitter
krimmer
Krishna
laicise
laicism
lairage
leister
leisure
lyingin
lyingly
maidish
maidism
mailbag
mailbox
mailing
maillot
mailman
mailvan
maintop
meiosis
meiotic
Meissen
moidore
moisten
moistly
moither
myiasis
naiades
nailery
naively
naivete
naivety
neither
noisily
noisome
obitual
olivary
olivine
omicron
ominous
omitted
opinion
orifice
origami
ovicide
oviduct
oviform
oxidant
oxidase
oxidate
oxidise
pailful
painful
painter
pairoar
paisley
philter
philtre
pliable
pliably
pliancy
plicate
pliskie
poinder
pointed
pointer
priapic
pricker
pricket
prickle
prickly
primacy
primage
primary
primate
primely
primero
priming
primmed
primula
printer
prithee
privacy
private
privily
privity
quibble
quicken
quickie
quickly
quieten
quietly

quietus
quillet
quilter
quinary
quinate
quinine
quinone
quintal
quintan
quintet
quintic
quipped
quitted
quitter
quivery
quixote
quizzed
quizzer
quizzes
railcar
railing
railman
railway
raiment
rainbow
reissue
rhiancy
rhizoid
rhizome
roister
ruinate
ruinous
saidest
sailing
sainted
saintly
sciarid
sciatic
science
scirrhi
scissel
scissor
seismal
seismic
seizing
seizure
shicker
shifter
shikari
shilpit
shimmer
shindig
shingle
shingly
shinned
shinpad
shiplap
shipman
shipped
shippen
shipper
shippon
shipway
shirker
shittim
shivers
shivery
skiable
skidded
skidlid
skidpan
skiffle
skijump
skilful
skilift
skilled
skillet
skimmed
skimmer

skimmia
skinful
skinker
skinned
skinner
skipped
skipper
skippet
skirret
skirted
skirter
skitter
skittle
slicker
slickly
slidden
slimily
slimmer
slinger
slinker
slipped
slipper
slipway
slither
smidgen
smidgin
smitten
snicker
sniffer
sniffle
snifter
snigger
sniggle
snipped
snipper
snippet
soignee
soilure
spicate
spicery
spicily
spicula
spicule
spidery
spieler
spignel
spikily
spiller
spinach
spindle
spindly
spindry
spinner
spinney
spinode
spinoff
spinose
spinous
spinule
spiraea
spirant
spireme
spirits
spitted
spitter
spittle
stibine
sticker
stickit
stickle
stickup
stiffen
stiffly
stifler
stilted
Stilton
stimuli
stinger
stinker

stipend
stipple
stipule
stirpes
stirred
stirrer
stirrup
suicide
suiting
swiftly
swigged
swiller
swimmer
swindle
swinery
swinger
swingle
swinish
swipple
swither
Switzer
swizzle
tailend
tailing
thiamin
thicken
thicket
thickly
thieves
thigger
thiller
thimble
thinker
thinned
thinner
thirdly
thirsty
thistle
thistly
thither
toilful
triable
triacid
triadic
tribade
triblet
tribune
tribute
triceps
tricker
trickle
tricksy
tricorn
trident
triduan
triduum
trifler
triform
trigamy
trigger
trilith
trilogy
trimmed
trimmer
trinary
trindle
tringle
trinity
trinket
trinkum
triolet
tripery
triplet
triplex
tripody
tripoli
tripped
tripper
trippet

tripple
trireme
trisect
trishaw
trismus
tritely
tritium
tritone
triumph
trivial
trivium
tuition
twibill
twiddle
twiddly
twigged
twilled
twinkle
twinkly
twinned
twister
twitchy
twitted
twitter
tzigane
tzigany
unicity
unicorn
unideal
unifier
uniform
unitary
unitive
urinary
utilise
utility
Vaishya
veiling
veining
veinlet
voivode
wailful
waisted
waister
waiting
weigher
weighin
weighty
weirdie
weirdly
whicker
whidder
whiffle
whimper
whimsey
whinger
whipped
whipper
whippet
whipsaw
whirler
whirred
whisker
whiskey
whisper
whistle
whitely
whither
whiting
whitish
whitlow
Whitsun
whittle
whizkid
whizzed
wriggle
wriggly
wringer
wrinkle

wrinkly
writeup
writhen
writing
written
Zoilism
Zoilist
abjurer
adjoint
adjourn
adjudge
adjunct
bejewel
cajoler
injurer
jejunum
jujitsu
majesty
pajamas
pyjamas
Rajpoot
rejoice
sojourn
unjoint
ackemma
alkalis
alkanet
Alkoran
askance
askesis
awkward
baklava
beknown
dukedom
ilkaday
inkhorn
inkling
inkwell
irksome
jukebox
lakelet
likable
makings
nakedly
oakfern
oakgall
oakling
oaktree
oakwood
pikelet
pikeman
rakeoff
sakeret
Saktism
Sikhism
sokeman
takeoff
takings
tektite
unkempt
unknown
wakeful
wakener
ablator
aileron
ailment
alleged
allegro
allelic
allergy
allheal
allonge
allover
allseed
allstar
alltime
alluvia
aplasia
aplenty

balance
balcony
balding
baldish
baldric
baleful
ballade
ballast
ballboy
balloon
balmily
baloney
belated
belcher
beldame
Belgian
believe
bellboy
bellhop
belljar
bellman
bellows
beloved
Beltane
belting
belying
bilboes
biliary
bilimbi
bilious
billing
billion
billowy
bilobar
bilobed
biltong
boletus
bolivar
bollard
bologna
boloney
bolshie
bolster
bulbous
bulimia
bulkily
bullace
bullary
bullate
bullbat
bulldog
bullion
bullish
bullock
bullpen
bulrush
bulwark
calamus
calando
calcify
calcine
calcite
calcium
calculi
caldera
caldron
calends
calibre
calices
caliche
calicle
calipee
caliper
callant
callbox
callboy
calling
callous
calomel

caloric
calorie
calotte
caloyer
calpack
caltrap
caltrop
calumet
calumny
calvary
calyces
calycle
calypso
calyxes
celadon
celesta
celeste
cellist
cellule
Celsius
chlamys
chloral
chloric
ciliary
ciliate
coldish
coletit
colicky
colitis
collage
collard
collate
collect
colleen
college
collide
collier
collins
colloid
collude
colobus
cologne
colonel
colonic
colossi
colours
coloury
coltish
culices
cullion
culotte
culprit
cultism
cultist
culture
culvert
dallier
delaine
delator
delayer
delight
Delilah
delimit
deliver
delouse
Delphic
deltaic
deltoid
deluder
dilated
dilator
dilemma
diluent
dilutee
diluter
dilutor
doleful
dollish
dolphin

doltish
dulcify
dullard
dullish
dulness
eclipse
eclogue
eelpout
eelworm
ellipse
enlarge
enliven
erlking
eulogia
Falange
falbala
falcate
falcula
fallacy
fallguy
falling
falloff
fallout
falsely
falsies
falsify
falsity
felonry
felsite
felspar
felting
felucca
felwort
filacer
filaria
filasse
filbert
filemot
filiate
filibeg
filings
filling
filmdom
filmset
folding
foldout
foliage
foliate
foliole
foliose
folkway
follies
fulcrum
fulgent
fulgour
fullage
fullout
fulmine
fulness
fulsome
fulvous
Galahad
galanga
galatea
galeate
galenic
galilee
galipot
gallant
gallate
galleon
gallery
gallfly
gallice
galling
galliot
gallium
gallnut
galloon

gallows
galumph
gelatin
gelding
gelidly
gelling
gilbert
gilding
gillnet
giltcup
goldbug
golfbag
golfing
goliard
Goliath
gullery
Halakah
halberd
halbert
halcyon
halfway
halfwit
halibut
halidom
hallali
hallway
halogen
halting
halvers
halyard
helical
helices
helicon
hellbox
hellcat
Hellene
hellion
hellish
helluva
helotry
helpful
helping
hilding
hillman
hillock
hilltop
holdall
holding
holibut
holiday
holland
holmium
holmoak
holster
hulking
idlesse
illbred
illegal
illicit
illness
inlayer
Islamic
jaloppy
jellaba
jellied
jollify
jollity
kalends
Kalmuck
kalpack
killick
killing
killjoy
kilobar
kiloton
kolkhoz
Lallans
lilting
Lollard

lullaby
malacia
malaise
malaria
Malayan
malefic
malines
malison
mallard
malleus
malmsey
maltase
Maltese
malting
maltose
melange
melanic
melanin
melilot
melisma
melodic
melting
mildewy
mileage
milfoil
miliary
militia
milking
milkleg
milkman
milksop
milldam
million
milreis
molimen
mollify
mollusc
molossi
mulatto
mullein
mullion
mullock
multure
mylodon
nelumbo
Nilotic
nullify
nullity
nylghau
obligee
obligor
oblique
obloquy
oilbath
oilbird
oilcake
oildrum
oilseed
oilskin
oilwell
oolitic
paladin
palatal
palaver
paletot
palette
palfrey
palings
pallium
palmary
palmate
palmist
palmoil
palmyra
palpate
palsied
paludal
pelagic
pelican
pelisse
peloria
peloric
pelorus
peltate
pelting
phlegmy
pileate
pilgrim
pillage
pillbox
pillion
pillock
pillory
pillowy
pillule
pilsner
pilular
polacca
polacre
poleaxe
polecat
polemic
polenta
politic
pollack
pollard
pollock
pollute
poloist
polygon
polymer
polynia
polynya
polypod
polypus
Pullman
pullout
pulpous
pulsate
pulvini
pyloric
pylorus
rallier
ralline
relapse
related
relater
relator
relayed
release
reliant
relieve
relievo
relight
relique
rilievo
rollick
rolling
rollmop
rolltop
salable
salicet
salicin
salient
Salique
sallowy
salpinx
salsify
saltant
saltbox
saltcat
saltern
salting
saltire
saltish
saltpan
saluter
salvage
salvoes
scleral
selenic
selffed
selfish
sellout
seltzer
selvage
silence
silenus
silesia
silicic
silicle
silicon
siliqua
silique
silkily
sillily
silvern
silvery
solanum
solaria
solatia
soldier
solicit
solidly
solidus
soliped
soloist
Solomon
soluble
solvate
solvent
splashy
spleeny
splenic
splicer
splodge
splotch
splurge
sulcate
sulkily
sullage
sulphur
sultana
syllabi
sylphid
sylvine
sylvite
talaria
talayot
talcose
talcous
talipes
talipot
talking
tallage
tallboy
tallish
tallith
tallowy
tallyho
taloned
telamon
teleost
telergy
telling
telpher
Telstar
tilbury
tillage
tollbar
tollman
toluene
tulchan
tylopod
unladen
unlatch
unlearn
unleash
unlined
unloose
unlucky
valance
valence
valency
valeric
valiant
validly
vallate
valonia
valuate
valvate
valvula
valvule
velamen
velaria
veliger
velours
veloute
velvety
vilayet
village
villain
villein
villose
villous
volante
volcano
voltage
voltaic
voluble
volubly
volumed
voluted
volutin
vulgate
vulpine
vulture
walking
walkout
walkway
wallaby
walleye
walling
Walloon
wallrue
waltzer
welcher
welcome
welfare
wellies
welloff
wellset
welsher
wildcat
wilding
wildish
willies
willing
willowy
wolfcub
wolfdog
wolfish
wolfram
wolvish
ycleped
yellowy
yolksac
yulelog
zillion
admiral
admirer
aimless
almanac
almirah
almoner
almonry
almsman
ammeter
ammonal
ammonia
armband
armfuls
armhole
armiger
armless
armlike
armoire
Armoric
armoury
armrest
armsful
bambini
bambino
bimanal
bombard
bombast
bumbler
bumboat
bummalo
bumming
bumpily
bumpkin
camaron
cambial
cambist
cambium
cambrel
cambric
camelot
camelry
cameral
camorra
campbed
camphor
camping
campion
camwood
cembalo
cimices
combine
combout
combust
comedic
cometic
comfort
comfrey
comical
comitia
command
commend
comment
commode
commons
commove
commune
commute
compact
company
compare
compart
compass
compeer
compend
compere
compete
compile
complex
complin
complot
compony
comport
compose
compost
compote
compute
comrade
Comtian
Comtism
Comtist
cumquat
cumshaw
cumulus
cymbalo
damming
damnify
damning
damosel
damozel
dampish
demerit
demesne
demigod
demirep
demoded
demonic
demotic
demount
dimeric
dimeter
dimmest
dimming
dimmish
dimness
domical
dominie
dumpish
ermined
famulus
feminal
femoral
fimbria
fumbler
gambade
gambado
gambier
gambler
gamboge
gambrel
gamebag
gamelan
gametic
gemmate
gemmery
gemming
gemmule
gemsbok
gimbals
gimmick
gombeen
gomeral
gomeril
gumboil
gumboot
gumdrop
gumming
gummite
gumshoe
gymnast
gymslip
Hamburg
Hamitic
hamming
hammock
hamster
hamulus
hemiola
hemione
hemline
hemlock
hemming
himself
homager
homburg
Homeric
Homerid
hominid
homonym
humanly
humbles
humbuzz
humdrum
humeral
humerus
humidly
humidor
humming
hummock
humoral
hymenia
hymnary
hymnist
hymnody
immense
immerge
immerse
immoral
Ismaili
jamming
jemadar
jimjams
jumbuck
jumpjet
jumpoff
kampong
kumquat
Lamaism
Lamaist
lambast
lambent
lambert
lambkin
lamella
laminae
laminar
lamming
lampion
lampoon
lamprey
lemmata
lemming
limbate
limbeck
limbous
liminal
limited
limiter
limosis
limpkin
limulus
Lombard
lomenta
lumbago
lumbang
lumenal
luminal
lumpily
lumpish
lymphad
mamelon
mamilla
mammary
mammate
mammock
mammoth
memento
memoirs
mimesis
mimetic
mimical
mimicry
mimulus
momenta
mumbler
mummery
mummify
mumming
mumpish
namable
nameday
nemesia
nemesis
nimiety
nomadic
nomarch
nombril
nominal
nominee
numbles
numeral
numeric
nummary
nymphal
nymphet
oomiack
osmosis
osmotic
osmunda
pampean
pampero
pemican
pimento
pimping
pomatum
pomfret
pompano
pompous
pumpkin
Ramadan
rambler
ramekin
ramenta
ramming
rampage
rampant
rampart
rampion
ramsons
remains
remarry
remblai
remiges
remnant
remodel
remorse
remould
remount
removal
removed
remover
rimming
romance
Romanic
Romansh
romaunt
Rommany
rumbler
rummage
rumness
rumshop
sambuca
samisen
samovar
Samoyed
sampler
samurai
sematic
semilog
seminal
seminar
semiped
Semitic
similar
similor
simitar
simpler
simplex
simular
somatic
someday
somehow
someone
someway
somitic
summand
summary
summery
summing
summons
sumpter
symptom
tamable
tamarin
tamasha
tambour
Tammany
tamping
tampion
tempera
tempest
Templar
templet
tempter
tempura
timbale
timbrel
timelag
timeous
timidly
timothy
timpani
timpano
tombola
tombolo
tomenta
tomfool
tompion
tumbler
tumbrel
tumbril
tumidly
tumular
tumulus
tympana
tympani
tympano
tympany
unmanly
unmeant
unmixed
unmoral
unmoved
vamoose
vampire
vampish
womanly
zemstvo
zymogen
zymosis
zymotic
zymurgy
adnexal
agnatic
agnomen
amnesia
amnesic
amnesty
annates
annatta
annatto
annelid
annicut

annuity
annular
annulet
annulus
awnless
banally
bananas
bandage
bandana
bandbox
bandeau
bandore
bandsaw
baneful
banjoes
banking
banksia
banning
bannock
banquet
banshee
banteng
banting
bencher
beneath
benefic
benefit
Benelux
Bengali
benison
benthic
benthos
benzene
benzine
benzoic
benzoin
benzole
benzoyl
bindery
binding
bonanza
bondage
bondman
bonedry
boneset
bonfire
bongoes
bonkers
bonnily
bungler
bunraku
bunting
canakin
canasta
candela
candent
candied
candour
canikin
cannery
cannily
canning
cannula
canonic
canonry
Canopic
cantata
cantate
canteen
canthus
cantina
canting
cantrip
canvass
canzone
canzoni
cenacle
censure
centaur
centavo
centime
centner
central
centred
centric
centrum
century
cindery
cineast
cineole
cingula
conacre
conatus
concave
conceal
concede
conceit
concent
concept
concern
concert
conchae
conchie
concise
concoct
concord
concuss
condemn
condign
condole
condone
conduce
conduct
conduit
condyle
confect
confess
confide
confine
confirm
conflux
conform
confuse
confute
congeal
congest
conical
conidia
conifer
coniine
conjoin
conjure
conkers
connate
connect
conning
connive
connote
conquer
consent
consign
consist
console
consort
consult
consume
contact
contain
contemn
contend
content
contest
context
contort
contour
control
contuse
convect
convene
convent
convert
convict
convoke
cuneate
cunette
cunning
cynical
dandify
Danelaw
dangler
danseur
Dantean
denarii
denizen
densely
density
dentate
dentine
dentist
denture
dinette
dingily
dingoes
dinning
donator
donning
donnish
dunbird
dungeon
Dunkirk
dunnage
dunning
dunnock
dynamic
dynasty
einkorn
ennoble
fanatic
fancier
fancily
fanclub
fanfare
fanfold
fanmail
fanning
fantail
fantasm
fantast
fantasy
fantods
fencing
fenfire
fenland
finagle
finally
finance
finback
finding
finesse
finical
finicky
finikin
finings
finning
Finnish
fondant
fondler
funeral
funfair
fungoid
fungous
funicle
funnies
funnily
funning
ganglia
gangrel
gangway
gantlet
general
generic
geneses
genesis
genetic
genette
Genevan
genista
genitor
genizah
genning
Genoese
genteel
gentian
gentile
genuine
gingery
gingham
gingili
ginning
ginseng
gonadal
gondola
gonidia
gunboat
gunfire
gunlock
gunnera
gunnery
gunning
gunplay
gunroom
gunship
gunshot
gunwale
handbag
handcar
handful
handgun
handily
handler
handoff
handout
handsaw
handsel
handset
hangdog
hanging
hangman
hangout
Hansard
hanuman
henbane
hencoop
hennery
henpeck
henwife
hindgut
honesty
honeyed
honours
hundred
hunkers
Hunnish
hunting
igneous
igniter
ignoble
ignobly
ignorer
innards
innerve
innings
Janeite
jangler
janitor
jannock
January
jingler
jonquil
juncoes
Jungian
juniper
Kannada
Kantian
kenning
kenosis
kenotic
kentish
kinchin
kindler
kindred
kinesis
kinetic
kinfolk
kingcup
kingdom
kinglet
kingpin
kinship
kinsman
lancers
landing
languet
languid
languor
laniary
lankily
lanolin
lantana
lantern
lanyard
lending
lengthy
lenient
lentigo
lentisk
lentoid
linctus
lindane
lineage
lineate
lineman
lineout
lingual
linkage
linkboy
linkman
Linnean
linocut
linsang
linseed
longago
longbow
longday
longhop
longing
longish
lunatic
luncher
lunette
lunular
lyncean
lynchet
manacle
manager
manakin
manatee
manchet
mandala
mandate
mandola
mandora
mandrel
mandril
mangily
mangoes
mangold
manhole
manhood
manhour
manhunt
manihot
manikin
manilla
manille
maniple
manitou
manjack
mankind
manless
manlike
manmade
manners
manning
mannish
mannite
mannose
mansard
mansion
mansize
manteau
mantlet
mantram
mantrap
manumit
manward
manweek
Manxcat
Manxman
manyear
mending
menfolk
menisci
menorah
menthol
mention
minaret
mincing
mindful
mineral
minever
miniate
minibus
minicab
minicar
minikin
minimal
minimum
minimus
miniver
minorca
minster
mintage
minuend
minutes
minutia
monacal
monadic
monarch
mondial
moneyed
moneyer
mongrel
moniker
monitor
monkery
monkish
monocle
monocot
monodic
monomer
monsoon
monster
montage
montane
montero
monthly
mundane
mundify
munnion
munting
muntjac
muntjak
mynheer
nankeen
ninepin
nonagon
noniron
nonplus
nonskid
nonslip
nonstop
nonsuch
nonsuit
nonuser
nunatak
nunhood
nunnery
nunnish
nunship
oenomel
omneity
omnibus
omnific
panacea
panache
pancake
Pandean
pandect
pandora
pandore
panicky
panicle
Panjabi
pannage
pannier
panning
panocha
panoply
panther
panties
pantile
penally
penalty
penance
pendant
pendent
pending
penguin
penname
pennant
pennate
pennies
pennill
pennine
penning
pensile
pension
pensive
pentane
pentode
pentose
pinball
pincers
pincher
pinetum
pinfire
pinfish
pinfold
pinguid
pinhead
pinhole
pinkeye
pinking
pinkish
pinnace
pinnate
pinning
pinnule
pintado
pintail
pintuck
pinworm
pondage
poniard
pontage
pontiff
pontify
pontoon
puncher
punchup
punctum
pungent
Punjabi
punning
punster
rancher
rancour
ranking
ransack
reneger
renegue
renewal
renewer
rentier
ringent
ringing
ringlet
ringtaw
rondeau
rondure
rontgen
runaway
rundale
rundlet
rundown
runless
running
sanctum
Sanctus
sandbag
sandbar
sandbed
sandbox
sandboy
sanders
sandfly
sandlot
sandman
sandpit
sangria
sanicle
santour
senarii
senator
senatus
sendoff
senecio
senhora
senores
sensory
sensual
Senussi
sincere
singlet
sinkage
sinless
sinning
sinopia
sinsyne
sintery
sinuate
sinuous
sonance
sonancy
songful
sonless
sonship
sunbath
sunbeam
sunbear
sunbird
sunburn
sundeck
sundial
sundisc
sundown
sunfish
sunlamp
sunless
sunnily
sunning
Sunnite
sunrise
sunroof
sunspot
sunstar
sunsuit
suntrap
sunward
sunwise
synapse
syncarp
syncope
synergy
synesis
syngamy
synodal
synodic
synonym
synovia
tanager
tanagra
tanbark
tandoor
tangelo
tangent
tanghin
tangram
tankage
tankard
tankcar
tankful
tannage
tannate
tannery
tanning
tannish
tanooze
tantara
tantivy
tantric
tantrum
tanyard
tenable
tenably
tenancy
tendril
tenfold
tenoner
tenpins
tensely
tensile
tension
tensity
tensive
tentbed
tentfly
tenthly
tentpeg
tenuity

tenuous
tinamou
tindery
tinfoil
tingler
tinhorn
tinnily
tinning
tintack
tinware
tonally
tonemic
tonerow
tonight
tonnage
tonneau
tonsure
tontine
tunable
tunably
tundish
tuneful
tunicle
tunning
Tynwald
unnerve
vanadic
Vandyke
vanessa
vanilla
vantage
vanward
venally
venatic
vendace
venefic
venerer
venison
ventage
ventail
ventral
venture
venturi
vinasse
vincula
vinegar
vintage
vintner
wanigan
wanness
wannish
wanting
wencher
Wendish
windage
windbag
windegg
windily
winding
windrow
Windsor
winesap
winglet
wingnut
winkers
winning
winnock
winsome
wintery
xanthic
xanthin
yenning
zincify
zincing
zincite
zincked
Zingari
Zingaro
zinkify

zinking
zonated
abolish
abomasa
aborter
abought
aboulia
acolyte
aconite
acouchy
adopter
aeolian
aeonian
agonise
agonist
alodial
alodium
aloetic
aloofly
amoebae
amoebas
amoebic
amongst
amorist
amorous
anodise
anodyne
anoesis
anoetic
anomaly
anosmia
anosmic
another
apocope
apodous
apogamy
apogean
apology
apolune
apostil
apostle
apothem
arousal
asocial
atomise
atomism
atomist
avocado
axolotl
biology
biomass
bionics
biotite
bloated
bloater
blocker
blooded
bloomer
blossom
blotchy
blotted
blotter
blouson
blowdry
blowfly
blowgun
blowout
blowzed
boobook
bookend
bookful
booking
bookish
booklet
bookman
booksie
Boolean
boomlet
boorish

booster
bootleg
boozeup
boozily
broaden
broadly
brocade
brocket
broider
broiler
brokage
broking
bromate
bromide
bromine
bromism
bronchi
broncho
brooder
brothel
brother
brought
brownie
browser
buoyage
buoyant
chocice
Choctaw
cholera
choline
chooser
choosey
chopine
chopped
chopper
chorale
chordal
chorine
chorion
choroid
chortle
chowder
cloacae
cloacal
clobber
clocker
clogged
clogger
closely
closeup
closure
clothes
clotted
cloture
cookery
cooking
cookout
coolant
coolish
cooncan
coontie
croaker
crochet
crocket
Croesus
crofter
crooked
crooner
cropped
cropper
croquet
croquis
crosier
crossly
crouton
crowbar
crowdie
crowned
crowner

crownet
crowtoe
crozier
deodand
deodara
diocese
diopter
dioptre
diorama
diorism
diorite
dioxide
doodler
doomful
doorman
doormat
doorway
drogher
dromond
droplet
dropout
dropped
dropper
drosera
droshky
drought
drouthy
droving
duodena
duopoly
ebonise
ebonite
ecology
economy
egotise
egotism
egotist
egotrip
Elohism
Elohist
emotion
emotive
enounce
epochal
eponymy
epoxide
erodent
erosion
erosive
erotica
erotism
esotery
Etonian
evolute
exocarp
exogamy
exordia
exotica
feoffee
feoffer
feoffor
floater
floccus
flogged
floorer
floosie
floozie
flopped
floreat
florist
floruit
flotage
flotsam
flounce
flowage
flowery
foolery
foolish
footage

footboy
footing
footman
footpad
footrot
footsie
footway
frogeye
frogged
frogman
fronded
frontal
fronton
frosted
froward
frowsty
geodesy
geogony
geoidal
geology
Geordie
georgic
ghostly
globoid
globose
globule
glorify
glossal
Glossic
glottal
glottis
glozing
gnocchi
gnomish
gnostic
goodbye
goodday
goodish
goodman
gooiest
Grobian
grocery
grogram
Grolier
grommet
groover
grossly
grottos
grouchy
grouper
groupie
grouser
growler
grownup
hoodlum
hooklet
idolise
inocula
ipomoea
ironing
ironist
isobath
isochor
isogamy
isogeny
isogram
isohyet
isokont
isolate
isonomy
isotope
isotopy
isotron
ivories
knobbed
knobble
knobbly
knocker
knockon

knotted
knotter
knowall
knowhow
knowing
Laotian
leonine
leopard
leotard
lioncel
lioness
lionise
looking
lookout
looksee
loosely
Miocene
moocher
moodily
mooneye
moonlit
moonset
moorage
moorhen
mooring
Moorish
moorlog
muonium
myogram
myology
myomata
Neogaea
neolith
neology
neonate
neoteny
neozoic
niobium
noology
noonday
nooning
obolary
obovate
obovoid
odontic
odorant
odorous
odoured
oloroso
opossum
orogeny
orology
orotund
otolith
otology
ovoidal
Oxonian
ozonise
peonage
phoenix
phonate
phoneme
phonics
phonily
photism
pioneer
piously
plodded
plodder
plopped
plosion
plosive
plotted
plotter
poofter
poohbah
poorish
proband
probang

probate
probity
problem
proceed
process
proctor
procure
prodded
prodder
prodigy
produce
product
profane
profess
proffer
profile
profuse
progeny
program
project
prolate
prolong
promise
promote
pronaoi
pronaos
pronate
pronely
pronged
pronoun
propane
propend
prophet
propine
propjet
propone
propose
propped
prorate
prosaic
prosify
prosily
prosody
prosper
protean
protect
protege
proteid
protein
protend
protest
proteus
protist
protium
proudly
proverb
provide
proviso
provoke
provost
prowess
prowler
proximo
quondam
reorder
rhodium
rhodora
rhombic
rhombus
riotous
roofing
rooftop
rooinek
rookery
roomful
rooster
rootage
rootlet
scoffer

scolder
scollop
scomber
scooper
scooter
scopula
scoriae
scorify
scoring
scorner
scorper
Scorpio
scotice
Scotism
Scotist
scotoma
Scottie
scourer
scourge
scouter
shocker
shoeing
shogged
shoofly
shooter
shopboy
shopman
shopped
shopper
shoring
shorten
shortie
shortly
shotgun
shotten
shouter
showbiz
showery
showily
showing
showman
showoff
skolion
slobber
sloegin
slogged
slogger
slopped
sloshed
slotcar
slotted
slouchy
sloughy
Slovene
slowish
smokeho
smokily
smoking
smoochy
smother
snooker
snooper
snoozer
snoozle
snorkel
snorter
snouted
snowcap
snowily
snowman
soonish
soother
soothly
sootily
spodium
spoiler
spondee
spondyl
sponger

spongin
sponson
sponsor
spoofer
spooney
spoorer
sporran
sporter
sporule
spotted
spotter
spousal
spouter
stocker
stoical
stomach
stomata
stonily
stonker
stopgap
stopoff
stopped
stopper
stopple
storage
storied
stouten
stoutly
stovies
stowage
swobbed
swollen
swopped
swopper
swotted
Thomism
Thomist
thorite
thorium
thorned
thought
toolbox
tooling
toothed
tootsie
trochal
trochee
trochus
trodden
troller
trolley
trollop
trommel
trooper
trophic
tropics
tropism
trotted
trotter
trouble
trounce
trouper
trouser
twofold
twoline
twoness
twosome
twostep
twotime
twotone
urodele
urology
utopian
utopism
utopist
uxorial
violate
violent
violist

violone
whoever
whoopee
whooper
whopper
whorish
whorled
whoseso
woodcut
woodman
woodpie
woolfat
woolled
woollen
wooloil
woolsey
woomera
woozily
wrongly
wrought
zeolite
Zionism
Zionist
zoogamy
zoogeny
zoogony
zooidal
zoology
zoonomy
zootaxy
zootomy
alphorn
amphora
amplify
ampoule
ampulla
amputee
apparat
apparel
appease
applaud
applied
applier
appoint
apprise
approve
asperse
asphalt
aspirer
aspirin
baptise
baptism
baptist
bepaint
bipedal
biplane
bipolar
bopping
capable
capably
capelin
caperer
capital
capitol
caporal
capping
caprice
caprine
caproic
Capsian
capsize
capstan
capsule
captain
caption
captive
capture
capuche
cepheid

cipolin
copaiba
copaiva
copepod
copilot
copious
coppery
coppice
copular
copycat
copyist
cupcake
cupmoss
cupping
cuprite
cuprous
cupsful
cupular
cypress
Cyprian
Cypriot
cypsela
dapsone
deplane
deplete
deplore
deplume
deposal
deposit
deprave
depress
deprive
diploid
diploma
dipnoan
dipolar
dipping
diptera
diptych
dupable
empanel
empathy
emperor
empiric
emplace
emplane
emporia
empower
empress
emprise
emptier
emptily
emption
empyema
enplane
enprint
esparto
espouse
eupepsy
euphony
expanse
expense
expiate
explain
explant
explode
exploit
explore
exposal
exposed
exposer
exposit
expound
express
expulse
expunge
fopling
foppery
foppish

gypping
hapence
hapenny
hapless
haploid
haporth
happily
happing
heparin
hepatic
heptane
hipbath
hipbone
hipness
hipping
hiproof
hipster
hopbind
hopeful
hophead
hoplite
hopping
hopsack
hyperon
hypnoid
hypogea
hypoxia
hypoxic
impaint
impanel
impasse
impaste
impasto
impeach
impearl
imperil
impetus
impiety
impinge
impious
implant
implead
implete
implode
implore
imposer
impound
impresa
impress
imprest
imprint
improve
impulse
inphase
japonic
Jupiter
lapilli
lapping
Laputan
lapwing
leprosy
leprous
lipdeep
lipless
lipping
lipread
lopping
lupulin
mapping
mopping
naphtha
napless
napping
nephric
Neptune
nippers
nippily
nipping
nuptial

oophyte
oppidan
opposer
oppress
Orphean
Orphism
orphrey
papadam
papally
paperer
Paphian
papilla
papoose
pappose
paprika
papulae
papular
papyrus
peppery
peppill
pepping
peptalk
peptide
peptise
peptone
pipeful
piperic
pipette
pipping
popadum
popcorn
popeyed
popover
poppied
popping
popular
puparia
pupilar
pupping
rapeoil
raphide
rapidly
rapping
rapport
rapture
repaint
repaper
repiner
repique
replace
replant
replete
replevy
replica
replier
reposal
reposit
repress
reprint
reprise
reproof
reprove
reptile
repulse
reputed
ripcord
ripieni
ripieno
riposte
ripping
ripplet
riptide
ropable
ropeway
rupture
sapajou
saphead
sapient
sapless

sapling
saponin
sapphic
sapping
saprobe
sapsago
sapwood
seppuku
septate
septime
sipping
sophism
sophist
soppily
sopping
soprani
soprano
supping
support
suppose
supreme
supremo
taperer
tapetal
tapetum
tapioca
tapping
taproom
taproot
tapsman
tapster
tepidly
tipcart
tipping
tippler
tipsify
tipsily
tipster
topcoat
topfull
tophole
topiary
topical
topknot
topless
topmast
topmost
toponym
topping
topsail
topside
topsoil
typebar
typeset
typhoid
typhoon
typhous
typical
typonym
umpteen
unpaged
vapidly
vapours
vapoury
xiphoid
yapping
yipping
zapping
zaptieh
zipcode
zipping
acquest
acquire
asquint
bequest
coquito
enquire
enquiry
esquire

inquest
inquire
inquiry
liquate
liquefy
liqueur
piquant
request
requiem
require
requite
sequela
sequent
sequoia
tequila
Tsquare
unquiet
unquote
vaquero
abrader
abreact
abreast
abridge
abroach
acrasin
acreage
acridly
acrobat
acrogen
acronym
acroter
acrylic
adrenal
aerator
aerobic
aerosol
African
agraffe
agrapha
aground
aircrew
airdrop
airfare
airflow
airglow
airhole
airless
airlift
airline
airlock
airmail
airmiss
airport
airpost
airship
airsick
airwave
already
alright
apraxia
apricot
apropos
arraign
arrange
arrayer
arrears
arrival
arriver
atresia
atrophy
aurally
aureate
aurelia
aureola
aureole
auricle
aurochs
aurorae
auroral

auroras
barbate
barbell
barbule
bargain
barilla
barline
barmaid
baronet
baroque
barrack
barrage
barrier
barring
barroom
barytes
barytic
bereave
bergylt
berhyme
berline
berried
berserk
birchen
birddog
birdman
biretta
biriani
boracic
borazon
bordure
boredom
borings
bornite
borough
borscht
borstal
bortsch
burbler
burdock
bureaus
bureaux
burette
burgage
burgeon
burgess
burghal
burgher
burglar
Burmese
burning
burnish
burnous
bursary
burster
burthen
burweed
Byronic
caracal
caracul
caramel
caravan
caravel
caraway
carbide
carbine
carcase
carcass
cardiac
cardoon
careful
caribou
carinae
carinal
carinas
carioca
cariole
carious
carking

carline
Carlism
Carlist
carload
carmine
carnage
caroche
carotid
carotin
carouse
carping
carport
carrack
carrier
carrion
carroty
carryon
carsick
cartage
cartful
cartoon
carving
ceramic
cerebra
ceresin
certain
certify
cerumen
cervine
chrisom
christy
chromic
chronic
Circean
circler
circlet
circuit
circusy
cirrose
cirrous
coracle
coranto
corbeil
cordage
cordate
cordial
cordite
cordoba
corella
corkage
corking
cornage
corncob
corneal
cornett
cornfed
cornice
cornily
Cornish
cornist
cornual
cornuto
corolla
coronae
coronal
coronas
coroner
coronet
corpora
correct
corrida
corrode
corrody
corrupt
corsage
corsair
corslet
cortege
cortile

corvina
corvine
corydon
curable
curacao
curacoa
curator
curcuma
cureall
curette
curiosa
curious
curling
currach
curragh
currant
current
currier
currish
cursive
cursory
curtail
curtain
curtana
curtsey
curvate
darbies
dariole
darkish
darling
darning
darshan
derange
derider
derrick
dervish
direful
dirtily
dorhawk
Dorking
dormant
dormice
dornick
dortour
durable
durably
duramen
durance
durmast
earache
eardrop
eardrum
earflap
earhole
earldom
earlobe
earlock
earmark
earmuff
earnest
earplug
earring
earshot
earthen
earthly
ebriate
ebriety
eirenic
errancy
erratic
erratum
Euratom
faraday
faradic
faraway
farceur
farcing
fargone
farming

farmost
Faroese
farrago
farrier
farruca
farther
fermata
ferment
fermion
fermium
fernery
fernowl
ferrate
ferrety
ferrite
ferrous
ferrugo
ferrule
fertile
fervent
fervour
firearm
firebox
firebug
firedog
firefly
fireman
firenew
firstly
firtree
forager
foramen
forayer
forbade
forbear
forbode
forbore
forceps
fordone
forearm
foreign
foreleg
foreman
forepaw
foreran
forerun
foresaw
foresay
foresee
foretop
forever
forfeit
forfend
forgave
forgery
forging
forgive
forgoer
forgone
forkful
forlorn
formant
formate
formula
forsake
forsook
forties
fortify
Fortran
fortune
forward
forwent
forworn
furbish
furcate
furcula
furioso
furious
furlong
furmety
furmity
furnace
furnish
furrier
furring
furrowy
further
furtive
garbage
garbler
garboil
gardant
garfish
garland
garment
garnish
garotte
garpike
gerbera
germane
giraffe
girasol
girdler
girlish
gorcock
gorcrow
Gordian
gorilla
gorsedd
gurnard
harbour
hardhit
hardpan
hardset
hardtop
harelip
haricot
harijan
harmala
harmful
harmony
harness
harpist
harpoon
harrier
harshen
harshly
harslet
harvest
herbage
heretic
heritor
herniae
hernial
hernias
heroics
heroine
heroise
heroism
heronry
herring
herself
hirable
hircine
hirsute
hirudin
horizon
hormone
hornmad
horrent
horrify
horsily
hurdler
hurdles
hurling
hurried
hurtful
Israeli
jargoon
jarring
jerkily
jurally
juryman
Karaite
karakul
karting
keramic
keratin
kermess
kerogen
kerygma
Kirghiz
Koranic
Kurdish
kursaal
larceny
lardoon
largely
largess
largish
lording
lorette
lorgnon
loricae
lorimer
loriner
lurcher
lurdane
luridly
lyrated
lyrical
marabou
Maratha
Marathi
marbled
marbles
marcher
marconi
maremma
margent
marimba
mariner
marital
markhor
marking
marline
marlite
marmite
marplot
marquee
marquis
Marrano
married
marring
marrowy
Marsala
marshal
martial
Martian
martini
martlet
martyry
Marxian
Marxism
Marxist
marybud
mercery
merchet
mercury
mermaid
merrily
miracle
mirador
mirkily
moraine
morally
morassy
mordant
mordent
moreish
morello
morendo
Moresco
Morisco
morning
morocco
moronic
morphia
mortice
mortify
mortise
morulae
morular
morwong
muraena
murexes
muriate
murices
murkily
murrain
murther
narrate
narrows
narthex
narwhal
neritic
nervate
nervine
nervous
nervure
nirvana
norland
norther
norward
nursery
nursing
nurture
oarfish
oarless
oarlock
oarsman
oarweed
oersted
ogreish
ourself
parable
parader
parados
paradox
paragon
parapet
parasol
parboil
pardner
parerga
paresis
paretic
parfait
pargana
parkway
parlour
parlous
parodic
parolee
paronym
parotid
parpend
parquet
parsley
parsnip
partake
partial
parting
partita
partite
partlet
partner
partook
parvenu
parvise
percale
percent
percept
percher
percine
percoid
percuss
perdure
perfect
perfidy
perform
perfume
perfuse
pergola
perhaps
periapt
peridot
perigee
perique
periwig
perjure
perjury
perkily
perlite
Permian
permute
perpend
perpent
perplex
Persian
persist
persona
pertain
perturb
pertuse
perusal
peruser
pervade
pervert
phrasal
phratry
phrenic
phrensy
piragua
piranha
piratic
pirogue
porcine
porifer
porrect
portage
portend
portent
portico
portion
portray
puritan
purlieu
purloin
purport
purpose
purpura
purpure
pursuer
pursuit
purview
pyralid
pyralis
pyramid
pyretic
pyrexia
pyrexic
pyrites
pyritic
pyrosis
pyrrhic
rarebit
reredos
rorqual
rurally
Saracen
sarangi
sarcasm
sarcode
sarcoid
sarcoma
sarcous
sardine
sardius
sarking
scraggy
scranny
scraper
scrapie
scrappy
scratch
scrawly
scrawny
screech
screeve
screwed
screwer
scribal
scriber
scrieve
scrimpy
scrooge
scrouge
scrubby
scruffy
scrumpy
scrunch
scruple
Serbian
serfage
serfdom
seriate
sericin
seriema
seringa
serious
serpent
serpigo
serpula
serrate
serried
servant
servery
Servian
service
servile
serving
Servite
shrieve
shrilly
shrinal
shrivel
shriven
shrubby
sirgang
sirloin
sirocco
sorbent
Sorbian
sorcery
sordini
sordino
sorghum
sorites
soroban
sororal
sorosis
sorrily
sprawly
sprayer
sprayey
spriggy
springe
springy
spryest
straits
strange
stratum
stratus
strayer
streaky
stretch
stretta
stretto
strewth
striate
strider
stridor
strigil
striker
stringy
striped
striven
striver
strophe
stroppy
strudel
strumae
surbase
surcoat
surface
surfeit
surfing
surfman
surgeon
surgery
surlily
surmise
surname
surpass
surplus
surreal
surtout
survive
syringa
syringe
syrphid
tarbush
tardily
tarnish
tarrier
tarring
tartare
tartish
tartlet
Tartufe
terbium
terebra
tergite
termini
termite
ternary
ternate
terpene
terrace
terrain
terrene
terrier
terrify
terrine
tersely
tertial
tertian
thready
thrifty
thriven
throaty
thrombi
throned
through
thrower
throwin
thrummy
torchon
torgoch
torment
tormina
tornado
torpedo
torpids
torrefy
torrent
torsade
torsion
tortile
tortrix
torture
torulae
Toryism
turbary
turbine
turdine
turdoid
turfite
turfman
turgent
Turkish
turmoil
turnery
turning
turnipy
turnkey
turnout
turpeth
tyranny
unravel
unready
unright
unroost
upraise
upright
upriser
utricle
variant
variate
varices
variety
variola
variole
various
varment
varmint
varnish
varsity
veranda
verbena
verbose
verdant
verdict
verdure
verglas
veriest
verismo
vermeil
vermian
vernier
verruca
versant
versify
versine
version
vertigo
vervain
virelay
virgate
virgule
virtual
waratah
warbler
warfare
wargame
warhead
warison
warlike
warlock
warlord
warmish
warning
warpath
warrant
warring
warrior
warship
warthog
wartime
wergild
werwolf
wireman
wiretap
wordage
wordily
wording
workbag
workbox
workday
working
workman
workout
worldly
wornout
worrier
worship
worsted
yardage
yardang
yardarm
yardman
Yorkist
abscess
abscise
abscond
absence
absinth
absolve
abstain
alsoran
apsidal
apsides
arsenal
arsenic
assagai
assault
assayer
assegai
assizes
assuage
assured
assurer
auspice
austere
austral
bascule
baseman
basenji
bashful
basidia
basilar
basinet
bassist
bassoon
bastard
basting
bastion
beseech
beshrew
besides

besiege
besmear
bespeak
bespoke
bestead
bestial
bestrew
biscuit
bismuth
bistort
bistred
boscage
boskage
bossism
Boswell
bushido
bushman
bushtit
busking
bussing
bustard
bustler
cascade
cascara
caseous
caserne
cashier
cassata
cassava
cassino
cassock
castile
casting
castled
castoff
casuals
casuist
cession
cesspit
cestode
cestoid
cistern
cosmism
cosmist
cossack
costard
costate
costean
costing
costive
costrel
costume
cushion
cuspate
custard
custody
customs
cystine
cystoid
dashiki
dashing
dashpot
dastard
dasyure
descant
descend
descent
deserve
despair
despise
despite
despoil
despond
dessert
destine
destiny
destroy
disable
disavow
disband
disbark
discant
discard
discern
discerp
discoid
discord
discuss
disdain
disease
diseuse
disfame
disgust
dishorn
disjoin
dislike
dislimn
dismast
dismiss
disobey
dispark
dispart
display
disport
dispose
dispute
disrank
disrate
disrobe
disroot
disrupt
dissave
disseat
dissect
dissent
distaff
distain
distant
distend
distent
distich
distill
distort
disturb
dossier
duskily
dustbin
dustily
dustman
dustpan
easeful
eastern
easting
ecstasy
enslave
ensnare
ensnarl
epsilon
essayer
essence
essoyne
eustasy
exscind
fascial
fascine
Fascism
Fascist
fashion
fastday
festive
festoon
fishery
fisheye
fishily
fishing
fishnet
fishway
fissile
fission
fissure
fistful
fistula
fossick
fossula
fuscous
fusible
fussily
fusspot
fustian
fustily
gascoal
gaseous
gasfire
gasmask
gasring
gassing
gastric
gestalt
gestapo
gestate
gesture
goshawk
gosling
gossipy
gossoon
gushing
gustily
hasbeen
hashish
hassock
hastate
hastily
hessian
histone
history
hosanna
hosiery
hospice
hostage
hostess
hostile
hostler
husband
hushaby
huskily
husking
Hussite
hustler
insculp
insecty
inshore
insider
insight
insigne
insipid
insofar
inspect
inspire
install
instant
instate
instead
insular
insulin
insured
insurer
inswing
issuant
jasmine
jussive
justice
justify
kestrel
kissing
lasagna
lasagne
lashing
lashkar
lassoes
lasting
lesbian
lissome
listeth
listing
losable
lustful
lustily
lustral
lustrum
mascara
mashtub
Masonic
masonry
Masorah
masquer
massage
masseur
massive
mastaba
masters
mastery
mastich
mastiff
mastoid
meseems
mesonic
message
messiah
Messias
messily
messtin
mestiza
mestizo
miscall
miscast
miscopy
misdate
misdeal
misdeed
misdeem
misdone
miserly
misfire
misgave
misgive
mishear
Mishnah
misknow
mislaid
mislead
mislike
mismate
misname
misplay
misread
misrule
missend
missent
missile
missing
mission
missish
missive
misstep
mistake
mistful
mistily
mistime
misting
mistook
mistral
Moselle
mosshag
muscled
musette
musical
muskrat
mustang
mustard
mystery
mystify
nasally
nascent
nastily
nesting
nosebag
nosegay
noserag
nostril
nostrum
obscene
obscure
observe
oestral
oestrum
oestrus
onshore
onstage
oosperm
oospore
opsonic
opsonin
osselet
osseous
osseter
ossicle
ossific
ossuary
paschal
passade
passado
passage
passant
passing
passion
passive
passkey
pastern
pasteup
pastime
pasture
pessary
piscary
piscina
piscine
pismire
pissoir
pistole
poseuse
possess
postage
postbag
postbox
postboy
posteen
postern
postfix
posting
postman
posture
postwar
pushful
pushing
pushrod
pustule
raschel
rasping
rescale
rescind
rescuer
reseaux
reserve
reshape
residua
residue
resolve
resound
respect
respell
respelt
respire
respite
respond
respray
restart
restate
restful
restiff
restive
restock
restore
restyle
resurge
risible
risotto
rissole
roseate
rosebay
rosebud
rosecut
rosehip
rosella
roseola
rosered
rosette
rostral
rostrum
russety
Russian
Russify
rustily
rustler
sashimi
sassaby
sessile
session
sestina
Sistine
sistrum
suspect
suspend
suspire
sustain
systole
tastily
tessera
testacy
testate
testban
testbed
testfly
testify
testily
testoon
testudo
tosspot
tushery
tussive
tussock
tussore
unsaved
unscrew
unsexed
unshell
unsight
unsnarl
unsound
unstick
unstuck
unswear
unswore
unsworn
upsides
upsilon
upstage
upstair
upstart
upsurge
upsweep
upswept
upswing
vascula
vastity
vesicae
vesical
vesicle
vespers
vespine
vestige
vestral
vesture
visaged
viscera
viscose
viscous
visible
visibly
visitor
visored
vistaed
washing
washout
washpot
washtub
waspish
wassail
wastage
wastrel
western
westing
wishful
wishing
wistful
yashmak
yestern
zestful
actinia
actinic
actinon
actress
actuary
actuate
althaea
althorn
amtrack
antacid
antbear
antefix
antenna
anthill
anthrax
antigen
antilog
antique
antlion
antonym
apteryx
aptness
article
artisan
artiste
artless
artwork
astable
astatic
asteria
astound
astride
attaboy
attache
attaint
attempt
attract
attrite
autarky
autobus
autocar
autocue
autopsy
bateaux
bathing
bathtub
batiste
batsman
battels
battery
batting
betaken
bethink
betimes
betoken
betroth
betting
between
betwixt
bittern
bitters
bitting
bittock
bitumen
botanic
botargo
botcher
bottega
bottled
bottony
botulin
butcher
buttend
buttery
buttock
buttons
buttony
butyric
Catalan
catalos
catalpa
catarrh
catawba
catbird
catboat
catcall
catcher
catchup
catechu
catenae
catenas
cateran
caterer
catfish
Cathari
Cathars
cathead
cathode
cathood
catlike
catling
catmint
catseye
catspaw
catsuit
cattalo
cattery
cattily
catwalk
citable
citadel
cithara
cithern
citizen
citrate
citrine
cittern
coterie
cotidal
cottage
cottier
cottony
cutaway
cutback
cuticle
cutlass
cutlery
cutline
cutrate
cutting
cutworm
datable
datival
deterge
detinue
detract
detrain
detrude
ditcher
dithery
dittany
dotting
duteous
dutiful
eatable
ectopic
entasis
entente
enteral
enteric
enteron
enthral
enthuse
entitle
entomic
entotic
entozoa
entrain
entrant
entreat
entropy
entrust
entwine
entwist
estrade
estreat
estuary
eutexia
externe
extinct
extract
extreme
extrude
fatally
fateful
fathead
fatigue
fatling
fatness
fattest
fatting
fattish
fatuity
fatuous
fetidly
fetlock
fetters
fitchet
fitchew
fitment
fitness
fittest
fitting
futhark
futhorc

futhork
futtock
gateaux
gateleg
gateway
gathers
gatling
getaway
getting
gittern
Gstring
gutless
gutsily
guttate
gutting
hatable
hatband
hatcher
hatchet
hateful
hatless
hatting
hetaera
hetaira
hitcher
hitting
Hittite
hotfoot
hothead
hotness
hotshot
hottest
hottish
hutment
hutting
icteric
icterus
integer
intense
interim
interne
intoner
intrant
intreat
introit
intrude
intrust
intwine
isthmus
jetting
jitters
jittery
jotting
jutting
kathode
katydid
ketchup
kitchen
kitschy
latakia
latchet
latency
lateral
latexes
lathery
lathing
latices
latrine
lattice
Latvian
letdown
lethean
letters
letting
Lettish
lettuce
literal
lithely
lithium
lithoid
litotes
littery
liturgy
lottery
lotting
luteous
matador
matchet
matelot
matinal
matinee
matrass
mattery
matting
mattins
mattock
mattoid
matzoth
metamer
metayer
metazoa
methane
metonym
metopic
metopon
metrics
metrist
mettled
mitoses
mitosis
mitotic
mitzvah
mottled
mutable
mutably
mutagen
muttony
mythise
mythist
nattily
natural
netball
netfish
netlike
netsuke
netting
network
nitrate
nitride
nitrify
nitrile
nitrite
nitrous
notable
notably
notched
notedly
notelet
notepad
nothing
notitia
nutcase
nutgall
nutlike
nutpine
nutting
oatcake
oatmeal
obtrude
octagon
octaval
octette
October
octopod
octopus
octuple
optical
optimal
optimum
ortolan
osteoid
ostiary
ostiole
ostraca
ostraka
ostrich
ottoman
outback
outcast
outcome
outcrop
outdone
outdoor
outface
outfall
outflow
outfoot
outgone
outgrew
outgrow
outhaul
outland
outlast
outlier
outline
outlive
outlook
outmost
outpace
outplay
outport
outpost
outrage
outrank
outride
outrode
outrush
outsell
outshot
outside
outsize
outsold
outsole
outstay
outtake
outtalk
outturn
outvote
outward
outwear
outwent
outwore
outwork
outworn
patagia
patella
patency
pathway
patient
patrial
patriot
patroon
pattern
patting
petasus
petiole
petrify
Petrine
petrous
pettily
petting
pettish
petunia
pitapat
pitched
pitcher
piteous
pitfall
pithead
pithhat
pithily
pitiful
pitpony
pitprop
pitting
potable
potamic
potbank
potence
potency
pothead
potheen
potherb
pothole
pothook
potluck
potshot
pottage
pottery
potting
putamen
putdown
putlock
putrefy
puttier
putting
Pythian
ratable
ratafia
ratatat
ratchet
rations
ratlike
ratling
rattail
ratteen
rattery
ratting
rattler
rattrap
retable
retaken
rethink
retiary
reticle
retinae
retinal
retinas
retinol
retinue
retired
retouch
retrace
retract
retrain
retread
retreat
retrial
retsina
rettery
retting
returns
rotator
rotifer
rotting
rotunda
ruthful
rutting
ruttish
satanic
satchel
satiate
satiety
satinet
satiric
satisfy
satrapy
satsuma
satyral
satyric
satyrid
setback
setdown
setting
settler
settlor
setwall
sitdown
sitfast
sithens
sitting
situate
sotting
sottish
sutural
sutured
tatters
tattery
tattily
tatting
tattler
tetanic
tetanus
tetrode
titanic
tithing
titlark
titling
titmice
Titoism
Titoist
titrate
tittupy
titular
totally
totemic
tottery
totting
tutelar
tutenag
tutting
tutwork
unteach
unthink
untried
untruly
untruss
untruth
untuned
untwine
untwist
untying
upthrew
upthrow
uptight
uptrend
utterer
utterly
Vatican
vatting
veteran
vetiver
vetting
vitally
vitamin
vitelli
vitiate
vitrify
vitrine
vitriol
vittate
vittles
vitular
votable
watcher
watered
waterer
wattage
Watteau
wattled
wattles
wetback
wetness
wettest
wetting
wettish
withers
without
witless
witling
witloof
witness
wittily
witting
wottest
yatagan
yttrium
zetetic
zithern
abubble
abusive
abutted
abutter
acutely
adulate
adultly
ajutage
alumina
alumnae
alumnus
alunite
amusive
anurous
aquaria
aquatic
aquavit
aqueous
aquifer
aquiver
asunder
azurine
azurite
Bauhaus
bauxite
blubber
blucher
blueing
bluffer
bluffly
blunder
blunger
bluntly
blurred
blusher
bluster
bouchee
boudoir
bouilli
boulder
boulter
bouncer
bounden
bounder
bouquet
bourbon
bourdon
bourree
brucine
brucite
bruhaha
bruiser
brumous
brusher
brusque
brutish
bruxism
caudate
caulker
caustic
cautery
caution
chuckle
chuddah
chuddar
chuffed
chugged
chukker
chummed
chunnel
chunter
chupati
churchy
chutney
clubbed
clubman
clumber
Cluniac
clupeid
cluster
clutter
Coueism
couldst
couloir
coulomb
coulter
council
counsel
counter
country
coupler
couplet
courage
courier
courlan
courser
courtly
couthie
couture
couvade
couvert
crucial
crucian
crucify
crudely
crudity
cruelly
cruelty
cruiser
cruller
crumble
crumbly
crumpet
crumple
crunchy
crupper
crusade
crusado
crusher
crustal
crusted
dauphin
deutzia
diurnal
doubler
doubles
doublet
doubter
doucely
douceur
doughty
drubbed
drudger
drugged
drugget
druidic
drumlin
drummed
drummer
drunken
duumvir
educate
eductor
elusion
elusive
elusory
elution
eluvial
eluvium
emulate
emulous
equable
equably
equally
equator
equerry
equinal
equinox
erudite
exudate
exurban
exurbia
exuviae
exuvial
faucial
faunist
fauvism
fauvist
feudist
flubbed
fluence
fluency
fluidal
fluidic
fluidly
flummox
flunkey
fluster
fluting
flutist
flutter
fluvial
fluxion
fouette
foulard
foumart
founder
foundry
fourale
fourgon
fructed
fruited
fruiter
frustum
gaudery
gaudily
Gaulish
gauntly
gauntry
glucose
glummer
gluteal
gluteus
glutted
glutton
gouache
goulash
gourami
gourmet
goutfly
grubbed
grubber
gruffly
grumble
grumbly
grummet
grumose
grumous
grunion
grunter
gruntle
grutten
gruyere
hauberk
haughty
haulage
haulier
haunted
haunter
hautboy
hauteur
housing
inutile
journal
journey
jouster
knuckle
knurled
koumiss
laugher
launder
laundry
laurels
leucine
leucite
leucoma
loudish
lounger
lousily
loutish
louvred
maudlin
maunder
mauther
mouflon
moulder
mounter
Mountie
mourner
mousaka
mousing
mousmee
mouther
naughty
nauplii
nautics
nautili
neurine
neuroma
neurone
neuston
neutral
neutron
noumena
nourish
oculate
oculist
opulent
opuntia
opuscle
ovulate
paucity
Pauline
paunchy
plucker
plugged
plugger
plumage
plumate
plumber
plumbic
plumbob

plumery
plummet
plumose
plumper
plumply
plumule
plunder
plunger
plunker
plusage
plushly
pluvial
pouched
poulard
poulter
poultry
poundal
pounder
poussin
pouting
prudent
prudery
prudish
pruning
prurigo
prussic
raucous
raunchy
reunion
reunite
rhubarb
roughen
roughly
roulade
rouleau
rounded
roundel
rounder
roundly
roundup
rousing
rouster
routine
saucily
saunter
saurian
sauroid
sausage
scudded
scuffle
sculler
sculpin
scumble
scummed
scunner
scupper
scurril
scutage
scutate
scutter
scuttle
sfumato
shucker
shudder
shuffle
shunned
shunner
shunter
shuteye
shutout
shutter
shuttle
skulker
slubbed
slubber
slugged
slugger
slumber
slummed
slummer
slurred
smuggle
smutted
snubbed
snubber
snuffer
snuffle
snuggle
soubise
souffle
soulful
sounder
soundly
soupcon
sourish
soursop
soutane
souther
spumous
spunkie
spurner
spurred
spurrey
spurtle
sputnik
sputter
squabby
squacco
squaddy
squails
squalid
squally
squalor
squamae
squarer
squashy
squatty
squeaky
squeeze
squelch
squiffy
squinch
squinny
squirmy
squishy
squitch
stubbed
stubble
stubbly
stuccos
stuckup
studded
student
studied
stuffer
stumble
stummed
stumper
stunned
stunner
stunted
stupefy
stutter
taunter
taurine
thudded
thuggee
thulium
thummim
thumper
thunder
touched
toucher
touchup
toughen
toughly
touraco
touring
tourism
tourist
tourney
truancy
trucial
trucker
truckle
trudgen
truffle
trumeau
trumpet
truncal
trundle
trusser
trustee
truster
tsunami
ukulele
ululant
ululate
unusual
usually
usurper
Vaudois
vaulted
vaulter
vaunter
vouchee
voucher
wouldbe
wouldst
younger
younker
advance
adverse
advised
adviser
advisor
akvavit
alveoli
bivalve
bivouac
cavally
cavalry
caveman
cavetti
cavetto
caviare
civilly
civvies
coverup
cuvette
devalue
develop
deviant
deviate
devilry
devious
devisal
devisee
deviser
devisor
devolve
devoted
devotee
diverge
diverse
divider
diviner
divisor
divorce
divulge
dovecot
dovekie
envelop
envenom
envious
environ
foveate
foveola
gavotte
havenot
invader
invalid
inveigh
inverse
invitee
inviter
invoice
involve
javelin
lavolta
lavrock
levator
levelly
leveret
livable
livebox
liveoak
lovable
lovably
loverly
movable
navarin
niveous
novella
novelle
novelty
obverse
obviate
obvious
paviour
pivotal
pivoter
poverty
ravager
ravelin
ravined
ravings
ravioli
revalue
revelry
revenge
revenue
reverie
reverse
reversi
reviler
revisal
reviser
revisit
revival
reviver
revivor
revolve
revving
rivalry
rivered
riveter
riviera
riviere
rivulet
savable
savanna
saveall
saveloy
savings
saviour
savoury
seventh
seventy
several
Sivaism
Sivaite
vivaria
vividly
vivific
wavelet
waverer
bawcock
bawdily
bewitch
bowhead
bowlder
bowlful
bowline
bowling
bowshot
bywoner
cowbane
cowbell
cowbird
cowfish
cowhage
cowhand
cowheel
cowherd
cowhide
cowlick
cowling
cowpoke
cowshed
cowslip
dawdler
dawning
dewclaw
dewdrop
dewfall
dewpond
dowager
dowdily
downbow
enwheel
enwound
fewness
fowling
gawkily
hawkish
howbeit
however
howling
inwards
inweave
inwoven
jawbone
jewelry
jewfish
lawhand
lawless
lawlist
lawlord
lawsuit
lowborn
lowbred
lowbrow
lowdown
lowland
lowlily
lowness
lowrise
mawkish
mawworm
mowburn
newborn
newcome
newlaid
newmown
newness
newsboy
newsman
nowhere
onwards
powdery
rawhide
rawness
rewound
rewrite
rewrote
rowboat
rowdily
rowlock
sawbill
sawbuck
sawdust
sawfish
sawgate
sawmill
sawnoff
sawwort
sowback
towards
towboat
towered
towhead
towline
towmond
towmont
townish
townlet
towpath
towrope
unweave
unwound
unwoven
upwards
vowelly
yewtree
anxiety
anxious
auxesis
auxetic
boxcalf
boxhaul
boxkite
boxlike
boxroom
boxseat
boxwood
coxcomb
dextral
dextran
dextrin
fixable
fixedly
fixings
fixture
foxhole
foxhunt
foxtail
foxtrot
hexadic
hexagon
hexapla
hexapod
laxness
lexical
lexicon
maxilla
maximal
maximum
maxwell
Mexican
mixedly
mixedup
mixture
myxomas
noxious
pyxides
pyxidia
saxhorn
saxtuba
sexfoil
sexless
Sextans
sextant
sextile
sixaine
sixfold
sixteen
sixthly
sixties
Sixtine
taxable
taxfree
taxicab
taxiing
taximan
taxless
taxying
textile
textual
texture
vexedly
vexilla
vixenly
waxbill
waxtree
waxwing
waxwork
abysmal
abyssal
acyclic
alyssum
amylase
amyloid
amylose
anybody
anymore
anyroad
anytime
anyways
anywise
azygous
bayonet
boycott
boyhood
Brython
buyable
cayenne
caymans
chymous
clypeal
clypeus
clyster
coyness
crybaby
cryogen
cryptal
cryptic
crystal
daybook
daylong
dayroom
daystar
daytime
daywork
doyenne
drycell
drydock
dryeyed
dryness
drysalt
dryshod
elysian
Elysium
elytron
elytrum
feyness
flyable
flyaway
flyback
flybane
flybelt
flyblow
flyboat
flybook
flyhalf
flyleaf
flyover
flypast
flyting
flytrap
gayness
glycine
glyphic
glyptal
glyptic
gryphon
grysbok
gwyniad
haycock
hayfork
hayloft
hayrick
hayseed
hayward
haywire
heyduck
idyllic
jaybird
jaywalk
joyance
joyless
joyride
keyhole
keyless
keynote
keyring
keyword
krypton
layered
layette
loyally
loyalty
mayoral
maypole
Maytime
mayweed
odyssey
Olympic
onymous
oxyacid
oxytone
payable
paydesk
payload
payment
payroll
paysage
physics
plywood
psychic
ptyalin
rayless
reynard
rhymist
royally
royalty
royster
sayable
shylock
shyness
shyster
skyblue
skyborn
skyhigh
skyjack
skylark
skyline
skysail
skyward
slyness
soybean
spyhole
stygian
stylise
stylish
stylist
stylite
styloid
styptic
styrene
thymine
thyroid
thyrsus
thyself
toyshop
trypsin
tryptic
trysail
voyager
waybill
waylaid
wayless
waymark
wayside
wayward
wayworn
wrybill
wryneck
wryness
bazooka
bezique
bizarre
buzzard
buzzsaw
cozener
dazedly
dazzler
dizzard
dizzily
dozenth
Elzevir
enzymic
fuzzily
gazelle
gazette
gizzard
guzzler
jazzily
jazzman
Jezebel
lazaret
lozenge
mazurka
mazzard
mezuzah
mozetta
muzzily
muzzler
Naziism
puzzler
sizable
sizably
sizzler
sozzled
wizened

Abbasid
ablator
abrader
Achaean
Achaian
Achates
acrasin
addable
advance
aerator
afeared
affable
affably
affaire
agnatic

agraffe
agrapha
akvavit
alcaide
alcalde
alcayde
alcazar
alfalfa
alkalis
alkanet
almanac
ambages
ambatch
Amharic
amiable
amiably
andante
annates
annatta
annatto
antacid
aphasia
aphasic
aplasia
apparat
apparel
apraxia
aquaria
aquatic
aquavit
arcaded
arcadia
arcanum
areally
areaway
arraign
arrange
arrayer
ascarid
ascaris
ashamed
Asiatic
askance
assagai
assault
assayer
astable
astatic
attaboy
attache
attaint
aurally
autarky
aviator
axially
babassu
bagasse
Bahadur
Bahaism
Bahaist
Bahaite
balance
banally
bananas
because
behaver
belated
bepaint
betaken
bimanal
bivalve
bizarre
bleakly
bleater
bloated
bloater
bonanza
boracic
borazon

botanic
botargo
breaded
breadth
breaker
breakin
breakup
breathe
breathy
broaden
broadly
bugaboo
buyable
cabaret
cacanny
cadaver
calamus
calando
camaron
canakin
canasta
capable
capably
caracal
caracul
caramel
caravan
caravel
caraway
Catalan
catalos
catalpa
catarrh
catawba
cavally
cavalry
celadon
cenacle
ceramic
cheapen
cheaply
cheater
Chianti
chiasma
chlamys
cidaris
citable
citadel
cleaner
cleanly
cleanse
cleanup
clearly
cleaver
cloacae
cloacal
cocaine
codable
cohabit
conacre
conatus
copaiba
copaiva
coracle
coranto
creamer
creator
croaker
curable
curacao
curacoa
curator
cutaway
Dadaism
Dadaist
datable
debacle
debater
debauch

decadal
decagon
decanal
decapod
default
degauss
delaine
delator
delayer
denarii
derange
devalue
dibasic
digamma
dilated
dilator
disable
disavow
donator
dowager
dreamed
dreamer
ducally
dupable
durable
durably
duramen
durance
dynamic
dynasty
earache
eatable
Eleatic
embargo
embassy
empanel
empathy
endarch
engaged
enhance
enlarge
entasis
equable
equably
equally
equator
ergates
errancy
erratic
erratum
escapee
escaper
esparto
essayer
ethanol
Euratom
exhaust
expanse
Falange
fanatic
faraday
faradic
faraway
fatally
fedayee
filacer
filaria
filasse
finagle
finally
finance
fixable
fleabag
fleapit
floater
flyable
flyaway
forager
foramen

forayer
freaked
friable
friarly
fugally
Galahad
galanga
galatea
gelatin
getaway
giraffe
girasol
gleaner
gliadin
gonadal
gouache
greaser
greaten
greatly
greaves
Halakah
hatable
heparin
hepatic
hetaera
hetaira
hexadic
hexagon
hexapla
hexapod
hidalga
hidalgo
hirable
homager
hosanna
humanly
hydatid
ichabod
ideally
ilkaday
impaint
impanel
impasse
impaste
impasto
infancy
infanta
infante
infarct
infauna
inhabit
inhaler
inlayer
innards
invader
invalid
inwards
Islamic
Ismaili
Israeli
jacamar
jemadar
joyance
Judaean
Judaise
Judaism
Judaist
jurally
Karaite
karakul
keramic
keratin
kneader
Koranic
labarum
ladanum
Lamaism
Lamaist
lasagna

lasagne
latakia
lazaret
legally
legatee
legator
levator
lieabed
likable
livable
locally
locater
losable
lovable
lovably
loyally
loyalty
lucarne
lunatic
lyrated
macabre
macadam
macaque
mahaleb
mahatma
malacia
malaise
malaria
Malayan
manacle
manager
manakin
manatee
marabou
Maratha
Marathi
matador
megaron
megaton
melange
melanic
melanin
metamer
metayer
metazoa
minaret
miracle
mirador
modally
monacal
monadic
monarch
moraine
morally
morassy
movable
mulatto
muraena
mutable
mutably
mutagen
myiasis
nacarat
naiades
namable
nasally
navarin
nodally
nodated
nomadic
nomarch
nonagon
notable
notably
nunatak
oceanic
octagon
octaval
oghamic

onwards
organic
organon
organum
organza
oxyacid
pajamas
paladin
palatal
palaver
panacea
panache
papadam
papally
parable
parader
parados
paradox
paragon
parapet
parasol
patagia
payable
Pegasus
pelagic
penally
penalty
penance
petasus
phrasal
phratry
picador
piragua
piranha
piratic
pitapat
pleader
pleased
pliable
pliably
pliancy
podagra
pofaced
polacca
polacre
pomatum
popadum
potable
potamic
preachy
priapic
ptyalin
puparia
putamen
pyjamas
pyralid
pyralis
pyramid
Ramadan
ratable
ratafia
ratatat
ravager
regalia
regally
regards
regatta
relapse
related
relater
relator
relayed
remains
remarry
repaint
repaper
retable
retaken
revalue

rhiancy
ridable
rivalry
romance
Romanic
Romansh
romaunt
ropable
rotator
royally
royalty
rubadub
runaway
rurally
Sabaism
Sabaoth
salable
sapajou
Saracen
sarangi
satanic
savable
savanna
sayable
schappe
sciarid
sciatic
scraggy
scranny
scraper
scrapie
scrappy
scratch
scrawly
scrawny
seeable
sematic
senarii
senator
senatus
shearer
sheathe
sheaves
Sivaism
Sivaite
sixaine
sizable
sizably
skiable
sneaker
socager
sofabed
solanum
solaria
solatia
somatic
sonance
sonancy
speaker
splashy
sprawly
sprayer
sprayey
squabby
squacco
squaddy
squails
squalid
squally
squalor
squamae
squarer
squashy
squatty
stealer
stealth
steamer
stearic
stearin

straits
strange
stratum
stratus
strayer
subacid
subadar
subaqua
sudaria
swearer
sweater
synapse
tabanid
tabaret
tabasco
Tagalog
talaria
talayot
tamable
tamarin
tamasha
tanager
tanagra
taxable
telamon
tenable
tenably
tenancy
tetanic
tetanus
theatre
thiamin
tidally
tinamou
titanic
tobacco
tonally
totally
towards
treacle
treacly
treader
treadle
treason
treater
triable
triacid
triadic
truancy
tunable
tunably
tyranny
unbated
uncanny
unearth
unfaith
unhandy
unhappy
unladen
unlatch
unmanly
unpaged
unravel
unsaved
upraise
upwards
usually
vacancy
vagally
valance
vanadic
Vedanta
velamen
velaria
venally
venatic
veranda
vilayet
vinasse

visaged
vitally
vitamin
vivaria
vocable
vocalic
vocally
volante
votable
voyager
wadable
Wahabee
waratah
wheaten
womanly
wreathe
wreathy
yatagan
ziganka
zonated
abubble
antbear
anybody
Arabian
arabise
Arabist
armband
babbitt
babbler
bambini
bambino
barbate
barbell
barbule
bibbery
bibbing
bilboes
blabbed
blabber
blubber
bobbery
bobbing
bobbish
bogbean
bombard
bombast
boobook
brabble
bribery
bugbane
bugbear
bulbous
bumbler
bumboat
burbler
byebyes
cabbage
cabbagy
cabbala
cambial
cambist
cambium
cambrel
cambric
carbide
carbine
catbird
catboat
cembalo
Chablis
chibouk
clabber
clobber
clubbed
clubman
cobbler
combine
combout
combust

corbeil
cowbane
cowbell
cowbird
crabbed
cribbed
cribble
crybaby
cubbing
cudbear
cutback
cymbalo
dabbing
dabbler
darbies
daybook
diabase
diabolo
dibbing
disband
disbark
djibbah
dogbane
doubler
doubles
doublet
doubter
drabber
drabbet
drabble
drabler
dribble
driblet
drubbed
dubbing
dunbird
elfbolt
eyeball
eyebath
eyebolt
eyebrow
falbala
fibbing
filbert
fimbria
finback
flubbed
flyback
flybane
flybelt
flyblow
flyboat
flybook
fobbing
fogbank
forbade
forbear
forbode
forbore
fribble
fumbler
furbish
gabbing
gabbler
gambade
gambado
gambier
gambler
gamboge
gambrel
garbage
garbler
garboil
geebung
gerbera
gibbous
gilbert
gimbals
globoid

globose
globule
gobbler
gombeen
grabbed
grabber
grabble
gribble
Grobian
grubbed
grubber
gubbins
gumboil
gumboot
gunboat
halberd
halbert
Hamburg
harbour
hasbeen
hatband
hauberk
henbane
herbage
hipbath
hipbone
Hobbian
Hobbism
Hobbist
hobbler
hogback
homburg
hopbind
howbeit
humbles
humbuzz
husband
iceberg
iceboat
ikebana
illbred
isobath
jabbing
jawbone
jaybird
jibbing
jibboom
jobbery
jobbing
jumbuck
kabbala
kibbutz
knobbed
knobble
knobbly
lambast
lambent
lambert
lambkin
legbail
lesbian
limbate
limbeck
limbous
lobbing
logbook
Lombard
lowborn
lowbred
lowbrow
lubbard
lumbago
lumbang
marbled
marbles
Moabite
mobbing
mobbish
mowburn

mudbath
mumbler
nabbing
nebbish
netball
newborn
nibbler
niobium
nobbler
nombril
numbles
oddball
offbeat
oilbath
oilbird
ouabain
outback
parboil
piebald
pinball
potbank
prebend
proband
probang
probate
probity
problem
quibble
rabbity
rabbler
ragbolt
rambler
remblai
rhabdom
rhubarb
ribband
ribbing
robbery
robbing
roebuck
rowboat
rubbers
rubbery
rubbing
rubbish
rumbler
Sabbath
sambuca
sawbill
sawbuck
scabbed
scabble
scabies
scabrid
seabass
seabear
seabird
seablue
seaboot
Serbian
setback
shebang
shebear
shebeen
skyblue
skyborn
slabbed
slabber
slobber
slubbed
slubber
snubbed
snubber
sobbing
sorbent
Sorbian
soubise
sowback
soybean

stabbed
stabber
stabile
stabler
stables
stibine
stubbed
stubble
stubbly
subbing
sunbath
sunbeam
sunbear
sunbird
sunburn
surbase
swabbed
swabber
swobbed
tabbing
tambour
tanbark
tarbush
terbium
tieback
tiebeam
tilbury
timbale
timbrel
tombola
tombolo
towboat
tribade
triblet
tribune
tribute
tubbing
tubbish
tugboat
tumbler
tumbrel
tumbril
turbary
turbine
twibill
verbena
verbose
warbler
waxbill
waybill
webbing
wetback
wobbler
wrybill
abscess
abscise
abscond
acicula
acyclic
aircrew
apocope
asocial
avocado
baccara
baccate
bacchic
balcony
bascule
bawcock
beechen
belcher
bencher
bibcock
birchen
biscuit
blacken
blackly
blocker
blucher

boscage
botcher
bouchee
boxcalf
boycott
bracing
bracken
bracket
breccia
brickie
brickle
bricole
brocade
brocket
brucine
brucite
buccina
butcher
calcify
calcine
calcite
calcium
calculi
carcase
carcass
cascade
cascara
catcall
catcher
catchup
checker
checkup
chicane
Chicano
chicken
chicory
chocice
Choctaw
chuckle
Circean
circler
circlet
circuit
circusy
clacker
clicker
clocker
coacher
coccoid
concave
conceal
concede
conceit
concent
concept
concern
concert
conchae
conchie
concise
concoct
concord
concuss
coxcomb
cracked
cracker
crackle
crackly
crackup
cricket
cricoid
crochet
crocket
crucial
crucian
crucify
cupcake
curcuma
deicide

deictic
descant
descend
descent
dewclaw
diocese
discant
discard
discern
discerp
discoid
discord
discuss
ditcher
dogcart
doucely
douceur
drachma
drycell
dulcify
edacity
edictal
educate
eductor
eggcosy
ejector
elector
electro
emicate
enactor
epicarp
epicede
epicene
epicure
epochal
erectly
erector
ericoid
evacuee
evictor
exactly
exactor
execute
exocarp
exscind
falcate
falcula
fancier
fancily
fanclub
farceur
farcing
fascial
fascine
Fascism
Fascist
faucial
fencing
fitchet
fitchew
flaccid
flecker
flicker
floccus
forceps
fracted
freckle
freckly
fructed
fulcrum
furcate
furcula
fuscous
gascoal
glacial
glacier
glucose
glycine
gnocchi

gorcock
gorcrow
gracile
grackle
Grecian
grecise
Grecism
grocery
guichet
halcyon
hatcher
hatchet
haycock
hencoop
hiccupy
hircine
hitcher
hoecake
icecold
inocula
insculp
isochor
itacism
juicily
juncoes
ketchup
kinchin
kitchen
knacker
knocker
knockon
knuckle
laicise
laicism
lancers
larceny
latchet
leucine
leucite
leucoma
linctus
luncher
lurcher
lyncean
lynchet
manchet
marcher
marconi
mascara
matchet
mercery
merchet
mercury
mincing
Miocene
miscall
miscast
miscopy
moocher
muscled
nascent
newcome
Noachic
notched
nutcase
oatcake
obscene
obscure
oilcake
omicron
opacity
orectic
outcast
outcome
outcrop
ovicide
pancake
paschal
paucity

peacock
peccant
peccary
percale
percent
percept
percher
percine
percoid
percuss
piccolo
pincers
pincher
piscary
piscina
piscine
pitched
pitcher
placard
placate
placebo
placket
placoid
plectra
plicate
plucker
poacher
popcorn
porcine
pouched
precast
precede
precept
precise
precook
pricker
pricket
prickle
prickly
proceed
process
proctor
procure
psychic
puccoon
puncher
punchup
punctum
Quechua
quicken
quickie
quickly
raccoon
rancher
rancour
raschel
ratchet
raucous
reacher
reactor
redcoat
rescale
rescind
rescuer
ripcord
saccade
saccate
saccule
sacculi
sanctum
Sanctus
sarcasm
sarcode
sarcoid
sarcoma
sarcous
satchel
saucily
shackle

shicker
shocker
shucker
sincere
slacken
slacker
slackly
slicker
slickly
smacker
snicker
soccage
sorcery
spacial
spacing
special
species
specify
speckle
spectra
spectre
specula
spicate
spicery
spicily
spicula
spicule
stacker
sticker
stickit
stickle
stickup
stocker
stuccos
stuckup
succade
succeed
success
succory
succour
succuba
succubi
succumb
suicide
sulcate
surcoat
syncarp
syncope
talcose
talcous
teacake
teacher
teachin
teacosy
thecate
thicken
thicket
thickly
tipcart
toccata
toeclip
topcoat
torchon
touched
toucher
touchup
tracery
trachea
tracker
tractor
triceps
tricker
trickle
tricksy
tricorn
trochal
trochee
trochus
trucial

trucker
truckle
tulchan
unicity
unicorn
unscrew
vaccine
vascula
vincula
viscera
viscose
viscous
volcano
vouchee
voucher
watcher
welcher
welcome
wencher
whacker
whicker
wrecker
zincify
zincing
zincite
zincked
zipcode
abaddon
abiding
academe
academy
Acadian
acidify
acidity
airdrop
alidade
alodial
alodium
anodise
anodyne
apodous
aridity
avidity
baddish
balding
baldish
baldric
bandage
bandana
bandbox
bandeau
bandore
bandsaw
bawdily
beading
bedding
beldame
bidding
bindery
binding
birddog
birdman
bladder
bondage
bondman
bordure
boudoir
bradawl
bridoon
budding
burdock
caddice
caddish
caldera
caldron
candela
candent
candied
candour
cardiac
cardoon
caudate
cheddar
chidden
chuddah
chuddar
cindery
cladode
coddler
coldish
condemn
condign
condole
condone
conduce
conduct
conduit
condyle
cordage
cordate
cordial
cordite
cordoba
credent
crudely
crudity
dandify
dawdler
deadend
deadeye
deadpan
deodand
deodara
dewdrop
diadrom
diddler
disdain
doddard
doddery
dogdays
doodler
dowdily
dredger
drudger
drydock
duodena
eardrop
eardrum
epidote
erodent
erudite
evident
exedrae
exudate
eyedrop
faddish
faddism
faddist
feeding
feedlot
feudist
fiddler
finding
folding
foldout
fondant
fondler
fordone
fuddler
gadding
gardant
gaudery
gaudily
gelding
geodesy
giddily
gilding
girdler
gladded
gladden
gladder
goddamn
goddess
goldbug
gondola
goodbye
goodday
goodish
goodman
Gordian
gradate
gradely
gradine
gradual
griddle
gumdrop
haddock
handbag
handcar
handful
handgun
handily
handler
handoff
handout
handsaw
handsel
handset
hardhit
hardpan
hardset
hardtop
headily
heading
headman
headpin
headset
headway
heedful
heyduck
hilding
hindgut
hoedown
holdall
holding
hoodlum
humdrum
hundred
hurdler
hurdles
irideal
iridise
iridium
jibdoor
Kaddish
khaddar
khedive
kidding
kiddish
kindler
kindred
Kurdish
landing
lardoon
leading
leadoff
lending
letdown
lindane
lipdeep
loading
lording
loudish
lowdown
Luddite
lurdane
lyddite
maddest
madding
Mahdism
Mahdist
maidish
maidism
mandala
mandate
mandola
mandora
mandrel
mandril
maudlin
meadowy
meddler
mending
mildewy
mindful
misdate
misdeal
misdeed
misdeem
misdone
moidore
mondial
moodily
mordant
mordent
muddily
muddler
mundane
mundify
needful
needler
nodding
oildrum
outdone
outdoor
oviduct
oxidant
oxidase
oxidate
oxidise
padding
paddler
paddock
Pandean
pandect
pandora
pandore
pardner
paydesk
peddler
pendant
pendent
pending
perdure
piddock
pledgee
pledger
pledget
pledgor
plodded
plodder
podding
pondage
powdery
predate
predial
predict
predoom
prodded
prodder
prodigy
produce
product
prudent
prudery
prudish
pudding
puddler
putdown
quadrat
quadric
ragdoll
readily
reading
readout
reddest
reddish
reeding
rhodium
rhodora
ridding
riddler
roadbed
roadhog
roadman
roadway
rodding
roedeer
rondeau
rondure
rowdily
rubdown
ruddily
ruddock
rundale
rundlet
rundown
saddest
saddish
saddler
saidest
sandbag
sandbar
sandbed
sandbox
sandboy
sanders
sandfly
sandlot
sandman
sandpit
sardine
sardius
sawdust
scudded
seedbed
seedily
seedlip
sendoff
setdown
shadily
shading
shadoof
shadowy
shedder
shudder
sitdown
skidded
skidlid
skidpan
sledded
slidden
smeddum
smidgen
smidgin
soldier
sordini
sordino
spadger
spidery
spodium
staddle
stadium
studded
student
studied
subdean
subdual
subduct
subdued
sundeck
sundial
sundisc
sundown
swaddle
Swedish
tandoor
tardily
tedding
tendril
thudded
tiddler
tiddley
tindery
toddler
tradein
trading
traduce
trident
triduan
triduum
trodden
trudgen
tundish
turdine
turdoid
twaddle
twaddly
twiddle
twiddly
unideal
urodele
Vandyke
Vaudois
Veddoid
vendace
verdant
verdict
verdure
viaduct
wadding
waddler
wedding
Wendish
whidder
wildcat
wilding
wildish
windage
windbag
windegg
windily
winding
windrow
Windsor
woodcut
woodman
woodpie
wordage
wordily
wording
yardage
yardang
yardarm
yardman
Yiddish
abreact
abreast
absence
ackemma
acreage
addenda
adherer
adnexal
adrenal
adverse
aileron
algebra
alienly
alleged
allegro
allelic
allergy
aloetic
already
alveoli
ammeter
amnesia
amnesic
amnesty
amoebae
amoebas
amoebic
anaemia
anaemic
angelic
angelus
Angevin
annelid
anoesis
anoetic
antefix
antenna
aphelia
apheses
aphesis
aphetic
aplenty
appease
apteryx
aqueous
ardency
arietta
arrears
arsenal
arsenic
ascesis
ascetic
askesis
asperse
assegai
asteria
atheism
atheist
atresia
attempt
aureate
aurelia
aureola
aureole
auxesis
auxetic
baleful
baneful
baseman
basenji
bateaux
bedevil
bejewel
beneath
benefic
benefit
Benelux
bereave
beseech
bheesty
bheetie
bibelot
bigener
bipedal
biretta
bleeder
bleeper
blueing
bobeche
bodeful
bohemia
boletus
bonedry
boneset
boredom
breeder
briefly
bugeyed
bureaus
bureaux
burette
cadence
cadency
cadenza
calends
camelot
camelry
cameral
capelin
caperer
careful
caseous
caserne
catechu
catenae
catenas
cateran
caterer
caveman
cavetti
cavetto
cayenne
celesta
celeste
cerebra
ceresin
cheerer
cheerio
cheetah
chiefly
cineast
cineole
codeine
cogency
coherer
coletit
comedic
cometic
copepod
corella
coterie
Coueism
coverup
cozener
creedal
creeper
Croesus
cruelly
cruelty
cuneate
cunette
cureall
curette
cuvette
Danelaw
dazedly
decease
deceive
decency
defence
demerit
demesne
deserve
deterge
develop
dilemma
dimeric
dimeter
dinette
direful
disease
diseuse
diverge
diverse
docetic
dogeate
doleful
dovecot
dovekie
doyenne
dozenth
driedup
dryeyed
dukedom
duteous
eagerly
easeful
echelon
effects
effendi
eidetic
eirenic
elderly
Elzevir
emperor
endemic
enderon
enfeoff
entente
enteral
enteric
enteron
envelop
envenom
ephebus
ephedra
equerry
essence
etaerio
etheric
eugenic
eupepsy
eutexia
excerpt
expense
externe
Faberge
faceoff
faceted
fadedly
fadeout
faience
fateful
federal
fideism
fideist
filemot
finesse
firearm
firebox
firebug
firedog
firefly
fireman
firenew
fixedly
fleeced
fleecer
fleeing
fleetly
fluence
fluency
forearm
foreign
foreleg

foreman
forepaw
foreran
forerun
foresaw
foresay
foresee
foretop
forever
fouette
foveate
foveola
fraenum
freebie
freedom
freeman
freesia
freeway
freezer
funeral
gabelle
galeate
galenic
gamebag
gamelan
gametic
gaseous
gateaux
gateleg
gateway
gazelle
gazette
Gehenna
general
generic
geneses
genesis
genetic
genette
Genevan
gleeful
gleeman
Gobelin
godetia
godevil
gomeral
gomeril
greenly
greenth
hapence
hapenny
harelip
hateful
havenot
hebenon
heretic
hideous
hideout
Homeric
Homerid
honesty
honeyed
hopeful
however
hugeous
humeral
humerus
hygeian
hymenia
hyperon
icteric
icterus
idlesse
igneous
illegal
immense
immerge
immerse
impeach
impearl
imperil
impetus
incense
indepth
indexer
inferno
ingenue
ingesta
inherit
innerve
insecty
integer
intense
interim
interne
inveigh
inverse
inweave
jadedly
jadeite
Janeite
javelin
jewelry
Jezebel
jukebox
kalends
kinesis
kinetic
kneecap
kneeler
kneepan
kneesup
labella
lakelet
lamella
latency
lateral
latexes
layered
layette
levelly
leveret
liberal
liberty
licence
license
lifeful
lineage
lineate
lineman
lineout
literal
livebox
liveoak
lobelia
lomenta
lorette
loverly
lozenge
lucency
lucerne
lumenal
lunette
luteous
Madeira
magenta
majesty
malefic
mamelon
maremma
matelot
memento
meseems
micelle
mileage
mimesis
mimetic
mineral
minever
miserly
mixedly
mixedup
modesty
mofette
momenta
moneyed
moneyer
moreish
morello
morendo
Moresco
Moselle
mozetta
murexes
musette
mycelia
nacelle
nakedly
nameday
nemesia
nemesis
niceish
ninepin
niveous
nosebag
nosegay
noserag
notedly
notelet
notepad
novella
novelle
novelty
numeral
numeric
observe
obverse
octette
offence
ogreish
omneity
oneeyed
orderer
orderly
osselet
osseous
osseter
osteoid
oxfence
pageant
pageboy
paletot
palette
paperer
parerga
paresis
paretic
patella
patency
phaeton
phlegmy
phoenix
phrenic
phrensy
piceous
pieeyed
pikelet
pikeman
pileate
pimento
pinetum
pipeful
piperic
pipette
piteous
podesta
poleaxe
polecat
polemic
polenta
popeyed
poseuse
potence
potency
poverty
praetor
preempt
puberal
puberty
pudency
pyaemia
pyaemic
pyretic
pyrexia
pyrexic
queenly
queerly
quieten
quietly
quietus
racemic
rakeoff
ramekin
ramenta
rapeoil
rarebit
ravelin
receipt
receive
recency
referee
regency
reheard
release
reneger
renegue
renewal
renewer
reredos
reseaux
reserve
revelry
revenge
revenue
reverie
reverse
reversi
Rhaetic
rivered
riveter
ropeway
roseate
rosebay
rosebud
rosecut
rosehip
rosella
roseola
rosered
rosette
rubella
rubeola
ruderal
rudesby
sakeret
saveall
saveloy
schemer
scherzi
scherzo
science
scleral
screech
screeve
screwed
screwer
seceder
selenic
senecio
seventh
seventy
several
sheerly
shoeing
sidecar
sideway
silence
silenus
silesia
skeeter
sleeken
sleekit
sleekly
sleeper
sleeved
sloegin
sneerer
sneezer
soberly
sokeman
someday
somehow
someone
someway
speeder
speedup
sphenic
spheral
spheric
spieler
spleeny
splenic
squeaky
squeeze
squelch
steekit
steepen
steeple
steeply
steerer
sthenic
streaky
stretch
stretta
stretto
strewth
subedit
suberic
suberin
sweeper
sweeten
sweetie
sweetly
synergy
synesis
tabetic
tagetes
takeoff
taperer
tapetal
tapetum
teleost
telergy
terebra
thieves
thready
Tibetan
tiderip
tideway
timelag
timeous
tomenta
tonemic
tonerow
totemic
towered
treetop
tuneful
tutelar
tutenag
tweeter
tweezer
typebar
typeset
ulcered
underdo
undergo
unheard
unkempt
unlearn
unleash
unmeant
unnerve
unready
unsexed
unteach
unweave
upheave
uraemia
urgency
utterer
utterly
valence
valency
valeric
vanessa
vedette
vegetal
venefic
venerer
veteran
vexedly
viceroy
vidette
vinegar
virelay
vitelli
vixenly
vowelly
wagerer
wakeful
wakener
watered
waterer
wavelet
waverer
wheedle
wheeled
wheeler
whoever
winesap
wireman
wiretap
wizened
ycleped
yulelog
zetetic
airfare
airflow
aliform
armfuls
baffler
bedfast
Biafran
bluffer
bluffly
bonfire
buffalo
buffoon
catfish
chaffer
chiffon
chuffed
codfish
coffers
comfort
comfrey
confect
confess
confide
confine
confirm
conflux
conform
confuse
confute
cowfish
crofter
deafaid
deiform
dewfall
diffuse
disfame
dogfish
draftee
drafter
drifter
earflap
edifice
eggflip
fanfare
fanfold
fenfire
feoffee
feoffer
feoffor
fiefdom
forfeit
forfend
funfair
gabfest
garfish
gasfire
golfbag
golfing
grafter
griffin
griffon
grifter
gruffly
gunfire
hagfish
halfway
halfwit
hayfork
hogfish
hotfoot
huffish
icefall
icefloe
icefoot
jewfish
kinfolk
leafage
leafbud
leaflet
maffick
menfolk
milfoil
misfire
mouflon
mudfish
mudflat
muffler
netfish
oakfern
oarfish
olefine
orifice
outface
outfall
outflow
outfoot
oviform
palfrey
parfait
peafowl
perfect
perfidy
perform
perfume
perfuse
piaffer
piffler
pinfire
pinfish
pinfold
pitfall
plafond
pomfret
poofter
preface
prefect
preform
profane
profess
proffer
profile
profuse
puffery
quaffer
raffish
riffler
roofing
rooftop
ruffian
ruffler
saffron
sawfish
scoffer
scuffle
seafish
seafood
seafowl
selffed
selfish
serfage
serfdom
sexfoil
shifter
shuffle
sitfast
sixfold
skiffle
snaffle
sniffer
sniffle
snifter
snuffer
snuffle
souffle
stiffen
stiffly
stifler
stuffer
subfusc
suffice
Suffolk
suffuse
sunfish
surface
surfeit
surfing
surfman
swiftly
taffeta
taxfree
tenfold
tiffany
tinfoil
tomfool
topfull
traffic
trefoil
trifler
triform
truffle
turfite
turfman
twofold
unifier
uniform
warfare
webfoot
welfare
whiffle
wolfcub
wolfdog
wolfish
wolfram
abigail
airglow
anagoge
anagogy
anagram
apagoge
apogamy
apogean
azygous
baggage
baggily
bagging
bargain
beggary
begging
beignet
Belgian
Bengali
bergylt
biggest
biggish
blighty
boggler
bongoes
bragged
bragger
brigade
brigand
bugging
bungler
burgage
burgeon
burgess
burghal
burgher
burglar
chagrin
chigger
chignon
chugged
cingula
clogged
clogger
coagula
cogging
congeal
congest
cragged
dangler
diagram
digging
dingily
dingoes
disgust
dodgems
dodgery
doggery
dogging
doggish
doggone
doughty

dragged
draggle
dragnet
dragoon
drogher
drugged
drugget
dudgeon
dungeon
elegant
elegiac
elegise
elegist
epigeal
epigean
epigene
epigone
epigoni
epigram
epigyny
exegete
exigent
exogamy
fagging
fargone
feigner
fidgets
fidgety
figging
flagday
flagged
flagman
flighty
flogged
foggage
foggily
fogging
forgave
forgery
forging
forgive
forgoer
forgone
fragile
frigate
frogeye
frogged
frogman
fugging
fulgent
fulgour
fungoid
fungous
gadgety
gagging
ganglia
gangrel
gangway
geogony
gigging
giggler
gingery
gingham
gingili
goggler
goggles
grogram
gudgeon
Guignol
Haggada
haggard
haggish
haggler
hangdog
hanging
hangman
hangout
haughty
heighho

higgler
hoggery
hogging
hoggish
hugging
imagery
imagine
imagism
imagist
isogamy
isogeny
isogram
jaggery
jangler
jargoon
jigging
jingler
jogging
jugging
juggins
juggler
Jungian
kingcup
kingdom
kinglet
kingpin
Kirghiz
laggard
lagging
languet
languid
languor
largely
largess
largish
laugher
leaguer
legging
lengthy
lingual
lodging
logging
longago
longbow
longday
longhop
longing
longish
lorgnon
luggage
lugging
maggoty
mangily
mangoes
mangold
margent
misgave
misgive
mongrel
mugging
muggins
myogram
nagging
naughty
Neogaea
niggard
niggler
nogging
nutgall
nylghau
oakgall
oregano
origami
orogeny
outgone
outgrew
outgrow
pargana
pegging

penguin
pergola
pidgeon
piggery
pigging
piggish
pilgrim
pinguid
plugged
plugger
progeny
program
pugging
puggish
puggree
pungent
raggedy
ragging
reagent
ridging
rigging
ringent
ringing
ringlet
ringtaw
roughen
roughly
sagging
sangria
sawgate
scaglia
seagirt
seagull
shogged
singlet
sirgang
skegger
slagged
slogged
slogger
slugged
slugger
smuggle
snagged
snigger
sniggle
snuggle
soggily
soignee
songful
sorghum
spignel
stagger
stagily
staging
stygian
suggest
surgeon
surgery
swagged
swagger
swagman
swigged
syngamy
tagging
tangelo
tangent
tanghin
tangram
teagown
tergite
thigger
thuggee
tingler
toggery
torgoch
toughen
toughly
tragedy

trigamy
trigger
tugging
turgent
twigged
tzigane
tzigany
verglas
virgate
virgule
vulgate
waggery
wagging
waggish
wargame
wedging
weigher
weighin
weighty
wergild
widgeon
wigging
wiggler
winglet
wingnut
wriggle
wriggly
yeggman
Zingari
Zingaro
zoogamy
zoogeny
zoogony
airhole
alchemy
allheal
alphorn
althaea
althorn
amphora
anchovy
anchusa
anthill
anthrax
archaic
archery
archive
archway
armhole
asphalt
bashful
bathing
bathtub
Bauhaus
beehive
berhyme
beshrew
bethink
bighead
bighorn
bowhead
boxhaul
boyhood
Brahman
Brahmin
bruhaha
bushido
bushman
bushtit
cachexy
cashier
Cathari
Cathars
cathead
cathode
cathood
cepheid
cichlid
cithara

cithern
cochlea
cowhage
cowhand
cowheel
cowherd
cowhide
cubhood
cushion
dashiki
dashing
dashpot
diehard
dishorn
dithery
dorhawk
duchess
earhole
egghead
Elohism
Elohist
enchain
enchant
enchase
enthral
enthuse
enwheel
escheat
etching
euphony
eyehole
fashion
fathead
fighter
fishery
fisheye
fishily
fishing
fishnet
fishway
flyhalf
foghorn
foxhole
foxhunt
fuchsia
Fuehrer
futhark
futhorc
futhork
gathers
goahead
godhead
godhood
goshawk
gushing
hachure
hashish
highboy
highhat
highman
highway
hophead
hothead
hushaby
inkhorn
inphase
inshore
ischial
ischium
isohyet
isthmus
kathode
keyhole
lashing
lashkar
lathery
lathing
lawhand
lechery

leghorn
lethean
lichowl
lighted
lighten
lighter
lightly
lithely
lithium
lithoid
lughole
lychnis
lychowl
machair
machete
machine
manhole
manhood
manhour
manhunt
mashtub
Mechlin
methane
mightst
mishear
Mishnah
mynheer
mythise
mythist
naphtha
nephric
nightie
nightly
nothing
nowhere
nunhood
offhand
onshore
oophyte
orchard
Orphean
Orphism
orphrey
outhaul
pachisi
Paphian
pathway
perhaps
pinhead
pinhole
pithead
pithhat
pithily
pochard
poohbah
pothead
potheen
potherb
pothole
pothook
preheat
pushful
pushing
pushrod
Pythian
quahaug
raphide
rawhide
redhead
reshape
rethink
righten
righter
rightly
ruching
ruthful
saphead
sashimi
saxhorn

senhora
sighted
sightly
Sikhism
sithens
skyhigh
sophism
sophist
spyhole
subhead
Swahili
tachism
tachist
technic
tighten
tightly
tinhorn
tithing
toehold
tophole
towhead
trehala
tushery
tychism
typhoid
typhoon
typhous
unchain
unshell
unthink
upthrew
upthrow
warhead
washing
washout
washpot
washtub
wishful
wishing
withers
without
wychelm
xiphoid
yashmak
yoghurt
zithern
abridge
absinth
accidie
achieve
acridly
actinia
actinic
actinon
addible
adhibit
admiral
admirer
advised
adviser
advisor
affined
African
against
alginic
almirah
alright
ambient
ancient
andiron
anginal
angioma
annicut
antigen
antilog
antique
anxiety
anxious
aphides

apricot
apsidal
apsides
aquifer
aquiver
arbiter
armiger
arrival
arriver
article
artisan
artiste
ascidia
ascites
ascitic
aspirer
aspirin
assizes
athirst
audible
audient
auditor
auricle
bacilli
barilla
basidia
basilar
basinet
batiste
bedight
bedizen
believe
benison
besides
besiege
betimes
bewitch
bezique
bifilar
biliary
bilimbi
bilious
biriani
bolivar
borings
bouilli
braille
broider
broiler
bruiser
bulimia
cabinet
cacique
calibre
calices
caliche
calicle
calipee
caliper
canikin
capital
capitol
caribou
carinae
carinal
carinas
carioca
cariole
carious
caviare
cedilla
chrisom
christy
ciliary
ciliate
cimices
citizen
civilly
claimer

codices
codicil
colicky
colitis
comical
comitia
conical
conidia
conifer
coniine
copilot
copious
cotidal
cruiser
cubical
cubicle
cubital
culices
curiosa
curious
cuticle
cynical
dariole
datival
deciare
decibel
decided
decider
decidua
decimal
defiant
deficit
defiler
definer
dehisce
delight
Delilah
delimit
deliver
demigod
demirep
denizen
derider
detinue
deviant
deviate
devilry
devious
devisal
devisee
deviser
devisor
digital
divider
diviner
divisor
domical
dominie
drainer
druidic
dubiety
dubious
dutiful
ebriate
ebriety
echidna
echinus
eclipse
ellipse
empiric
enfiled
enliven
entitle
envious
environ
epsilon
equinal
equinox
ermined

ethical impious Mexican plaided satisfy tidings subject jacktar sinkage
ethiops incipit miliary plainly savings timidly subjoin jerkily smokeho
excited incised militia politic saviour tonight traject kickoff smokily
exciter incisor mimical poniard scribal topiary backing kolkhoz smoking
exciton inciter mimicry porifer scriber topical backlog lacking snakily
excitor indican miniate prairie scrieve trailer backsaw lankily soakage
exhibit indices minibus praiser scrimpy trainee backset leakage soaking
expiate indicia minicab pupilar sedilia trainer banking licking sockeye
extinct inditer minicar puritan semilog traipse banksia linkage spikily
fatigue infidel minikin pyrites seminal traitor bonkers linkboy sucking
feminal infield minimal pyritic seminar tumidly bookend linkman suckler
fetidly inhibit minimum pyxides semiped tunicle bookful lockage sulkily
filiate innings minimus pyxidia Semitic typical booking lockjaw tacking
filibeg insider miniver rabidly seriate uncinus bookish locknut tackler
filings insight modicum radiant sericin uncivil booklet lockout talking
finical insigne modiste radiate seriema unfitly bookman looking tankage
finicky insipid molimen radical seringa unhinge booksie lookout tankard
finikin invitee moniker radices serious unhitch boskage looksee tankcar
finings inviter monitor radicle shaitan unlined boxkite luckily tankful
fixings jacinth Morisco rapidly shrieve unmixed brokage mankind ticking
fluidal janitor muriate rations shrilly unright broking markhor tickler
fluidic jubilee murices ravined shrinal unsight buckeye marking topknot
fluidly jujitsu musical ravings shrivel upfield buckler mawkish trekked
foliage juniper Naziism ravioli shriven upright buckram milking trekker
foliate Jupiter neritic rebirth silicic upriser bucksaw milkleg tuckbox
foliole labiate nimiety recital silicle upsides bulkily milkman Turkish
foliose laminae nodical reciter silicon upsilon busking milksop walking
frailly laminar nominal refined siliqua uptight cackler mirkily walkout
frailty laniary nominee refiner silique utricle carking misknow walkway
freight lapilli noniron regimen similar uveitis chukker mockery weakish
fruited latices notitia reginal similor valiant cockade monkery weekday
fruiter legible noxious reliant simitar validly cockeye monkish weekend
funicle legibly obligee relieve sleight vanilla cockily murkily wickiup
furioso legiron obligor relievo society vapidly cockney muskrat winkers
furious lenient oblique relight solicit variant cockpit nankeen workbag
fusible lexical obviate relique solidly variate cockshy necklet workbox
galilee lexicon obvious remiges solidus varices conkers necktie workday
galipot liaison occiput repiner soliped variety cookery package working
gelidly licitly oedipal repique somitic variola cooking packice workman
genista liminal officer residua sorites variole cookout packing workout
genitor limited omnibus residue splicer various corkage packman yolksac
genizah limiter omnific retiary spoiler Vatican corking parkway Yorkist
geoidal logical oneiric reticle spriggy vehicle cuckold peckish zinkify
glaikit loricae oolitic retinae springe veliger darkish perkily zinking
goliard lorimer oomiack retinal springy venison decking pickaxe abalone
Goliath loriner ophitic retinas squiffy veriest dickens pickeer Abelian
gonidia lucidly oppidan retinol squinch verismo dockage pickled ability
gooiest Lucifer optical retinue squinny vesicae dockise pinkeye abolish
gorilla luminal optimal retired squirmy vesical Dorking pinking acclaim
grained luridly optimum reviler squishy vesicle ducking pinkish acolyte
grainer lyrical orbital revisal squitch vetiver duckpin Prakrit adulate
greisen mafiosi ordinal reviser staidly vexilla Dunkirk puckery adultly
habitat mafioso ossicle revisit stainer vicinal duskily puckish aeolian
habitue magical ossific revival staithe vicious einkorn rackety afflict
halibut makings ostiary reviver stoical vidimus erlking ranking ageless
halidom malines ostiole revivor striate visible folkway rickets agelong
Hamitic malison ovoidal rigidly strider visibly forkful rickety agilely
haricot mamilla pacific rilievo stridor visitor Fraktur ricksha agility
harijan manihot paginal ripieni strigil vitiate gawkily rockery aiblins
helical manikin palings ripieno striker vividly geckoes rockier aimless
helices manilla panicky risible stringy vivific hackbut rockily airless
helicon manille panicle riviera striped wanigan hackery rocking airlift
hemiola maniple papilla riviere striven warison hacking rocklet airline
hemione manitou patient rooinek striver zooidal hackler rockoil airlock
heritor marimba paviour rotifer syringa banjoes hackney rocktar amalgam
holibut mariner pedicab rubicon syringe conjoin hacksaw rookery amildar
holiday marital pedicel rubious tabinet conjure hawkish sackbut amplify
hominid matinal pedicle sagitta tacitly disjoin heckler sackful amylase
horizon matinee pelican salicet takings frijole hickory sacking amyloid
hosiery maxilla pelisse salicin talipes jimjams hockday sarking amylose
humidly maximal pemican salient talipot mahjong hooklet seakale analogy
humidor maximum periapt Salique tapioca manjack hulking shakeup analyse
hygiene mediacy peridot samisen taxicab Panjabi hunkers shakily analyst
igniter mediant perigee sanicle taxiing perjure huskily shikari Anglian
ileitis mediate perique sapient taximan perjury husking sickbay anglice
illicit medical periwig satiate tedious project isokont sickbed angling
imbiber melilot petiole satiety tepidly Punjabi jackass sickish Anglist
impiety melisma pigiron satinet thrifty skijump jackdaw sickpay aniline
impinge menisci pitiful satiric thriven skyjack jackpot silkily anility

antlion
apology
apolune
applaud
applied
applier
armless
armlike
artless
atelier
athlete
aweless
awnless
axillae
axillar
axolotl
Azilean
Baalism
bailiff
baklava
ballade
ballast
ballboy
balloon
barline
becloud
beeline
bellboy
bellhop
belljar
bellman
bellows
berline
biblist
billing
billion
billowy
biology
biplane
boiling
bollard
Boolean
boulder
boulter
bowlder
bowlful
bowline
bowling
boxlike
bugloss
builded
builder
buildup
builtin
builtup
bullace
bullary
bullate
bullbat
bulldog
bullion
bullish
bullock
bullpen
cabling
callant
callbox
callboy
calling
callous
carline
Carlism
Carlist
carload
catlike
catling
caulker
ceilidh
ceiling
cellist
cellule
chalaza
Chaldee
chalice
challis
chalone
chelate
childer
childly
chiliad
chillum
cholera
choline
coaltit
codling
coeliac
collage
collard
collate
collect
colleen
college
collide
collier
collins
colloid
collude
coolant
coolish
couldst
couloir
coulomb
coulter
cowlick
cowling
cruller
cullion
curling
cutlass
cutlery
cutline
cyclist
cycloid
cyclone
cyclops
dallier
darling
daylong
dealing
declaim
declare
declass
decline
deflate
deflect
deplane
deplete
deplore
deplume
dialect
dialled
dialyse
diploid
diploma
dislike
dislimn
dollish
driller
dualise
dualism
dualist
duality
duelled
dueller
dullard
dullish
dweller
earldom
earlobe
earlock
ecology
egality
elfland
elflock
emblaze
emplace
emplane
emulate
emulous
enclasp
enclave
enclose
endless
endlong
English
enplane
enslave
epilate
erelong
euclase
euglena
evolute
ewelamb
exclaim
exclave
exclude
explain
explant
explode
exploit
explore
eyelash
eyeless
eyelike
fabliau
failing
failure
fallacy
fallguy
falling
falloff
fallout
fatling
feeling
fenland
fetlock
fielder
figleaf
filling
flyleaf
foglamp
follies
foolery
foolish
fopling
forlorn
foulard
fowling
fuelled
fueller
fullage
fullout
furlong
gallant
gallate
galleon
gallery
gallfly
gallice
galling
galliot
gallium
gallnut
galloon
gallows
garland
gatling
Gaulish
gelling
geology
ghillie
giblets
gillnet
girlish
godless
godlike
godling
gosling
goulash
grilled
griller
Grolier
Guelfic
guilder
gullery
gunlock
gutless
hallali
hallway
hapless
haploid
hatless
haulage
haulier
hayloft
healthy
heeltap
hellbox
hellcat
Hellene
hellion
hellish
helluva
hemline
hemlock
hillman
hillock
hilltop
holland
hoplite
howling
hueless
hurling
hyaline
hyalite
hyaloid
idolise
idyllic
implant
implead
implete
implode
implore
incline
inclose
include
inflame
inflate
inflect
inflict
inkling
isolate
Italian
Italiot
jealous
jellaba
jellied
jollify
jollity
joyless
keelson
keyless
killick
killing
killjoy
Lallans
lawless
lawlist
lawlord
legless
lidless
lipless
logline
Lollard
lowland
lowlily
lullaby
mailbag
mailbox
mailing
maillot
mailman
mailvan
mallard
malleus
manless
manlike
marline
marlite
mealies
midland
midline
milldam
million
mislaid
mislead
mislike
mollify
mollusc
moulder
mudlark
mullein
mullion
mullock
myalgia
myalgic
myalism
myeloid
myeloma
myology
nailery
napless
neglect
neglige
neolith
neology
netlike
newlaid
niblick
noology
norland
nuclear
nucleic
nuclein
nucleon
nucleus
nuclide
nullify
nullity
nutlike
oakling
oarless
oarlock
obelise
obelisk
obolary
occlude
ocellar
ocellus
oculate
oculist
odalisk
offload
opaline
opulent
orology
otolith
otology
outland
outlast
outlier
outline
outlive
outlook
ovulate
oxalate
padlock
pahlavi
pailful
pallium
parlour
parlous
Pauline
payload
pedlary
perlite
phalanx
phallic
phallus
phellem
philter
philtre
piglead
pigling
pillage
pillbox
pillion
pillock
pillory
pillowy
pillule
pollack
pollard
pollock
pollute
potluck
poulard
poulter
poultry
praline
prelacy
prelate
prelect
prelims
prelude
prolate
prolong
psalter
publish
Pullman
pullout
purlieu
purloin
putlock
qualify
quality
queller
quillet
quilter
railcar
railing
railman
railway
rallier
ralline
ratlike
ratling
rayless
realgar
realign
realise
realism
realist
reality
reallot
realtor
reclaim
reclame
recline
recluse
redlegs
reelect
reflate
reflect
refloat
replace
replant
replete
replevy
replica
replier
rifling
rodlike
rollick
rolling
rollmop
rolltop
roulade
rouleau
rowlock
runless
sailing
sallowy
sapless
sapling
scalade
scalado
scalder
scaldic
scalene
scallop
scalpel
scalper
schlepp
schlock
scolder
scollop
sculler
sculpin
sealane
sealant
sealegs
sealery
seclude
sellout
sexless
shallop
shallot
shallow
shellac
shelled
sheller
shelter
sheltie
shelved
shelves
shilpit
shylock
sialoid
sibling
sillily
sinless
sirloin
skaldic
skellum
skelter
skilful
skilift
skilled
skillet
skolion
skulker
skylark
skyline
smeller
smelter
soilure
sonless
soulful
speller
spelter
spiller
stalely
stalked
stalker
stellar
stilted
Stilton
stylise
stylish
stylist
stylite
styloid
sublate
sublime
sullage
sunlamp
sunless
surlily
swallow
swelter
swiller
swollen
syllabi
tableau
tabloid
tailend
tailing
tallage
tallboy
tallish
tallith
tallowy
tallyho
taxless
tealeaf
telling
thalami
thallic
thallus
thalweg
thiller
thulium
tillage
titlark
titling
toeless
toilful
tollbar
tollman
toolbox
tooling
topless
towline
trellis
trilith
trilogy
troller
trolley
trollop
twelfth
twelves
twilled
twoline
udaller
ukelele
ukulele
ululant
ululate
unblest
unblock
unclasp
unclean
uncloak
unclose
Uralian
uralite
urology
useless
utilise
utility
vallate
vaulted
vaulter
veiling
village
villain
villein
villose
villous
violate
violent
violist
violone
wailful
wallaby
walleye
walling
Walloon
wallrue
warlike
warlock
warlord
waylaid
wayless
wealden
wealthy
wedlock
wellies
welloff
wellset
whaling
wielder
wigless
willies
willing
willowy
witless
witling
witloof
woolfat
woolled
woollen
wooloil
woolsey
worldly
wouldbe
wouldst
yellowy
yielder
zealous
zeolite
zillion
Zoilism
Zoilist
zoology
abomasa
adamant
Adamite
agamous
ailment
airmail
airmiss
alameda
alembic
aliment
alimony
alumina
alumnae
alumnus
anemone

animate
animism
animist
anomaly
anymore
Aramaic
atomise
atomism
atomist
augment
azimuth
badmash
balmily
barmaid
beamish
besmear
biomass
bismuth
blemish
boomlet
bramble
brambly
brimful
brimmed
brimmer
bromate
bromide
bromine
bromism
brumous
bummalo
bumming
Burmese
Cadmean
cadmium
caimans
carmine
catmint
caymans
chamber
chamfer
chamois
champac
champak
chemise
chemism
chemist
chimera
chimere
chimney
chummed
chymous
clamant
clamber
clammed
clamour
clement
climate
climber
clumber
coaming
command
commend
comment
commode
commons
commove
commune
commute
cosmism
cosmist
crammed
crammer
crampet
crampit
crampon
cremate
cremona
crimine
crimper
crimple
crimson
crumble
crumbly
crumpet
crumple
cupmoss
damming
diamond
dimmest
dimming
dimmish
dismast
dismiss
doomful
dormant
dormice
dromond
drumlin
drummed
drummer
durmast
duumvir
earmark
earmuff
element
enamour
endmost
enemata
eremite
etamine
ethmoid
examine
example
exempla
fanmail
farming
farmost
fermata
ferment
fermion
fermium
figment
filmdom
filmset
fitment
flamfew
flaming
Fleming
Flemish
flummox
formant
formate
formula
foumart
frameup
fulmine
furmety
furmity
garment
gasmask
gemmate
gemmery
gemming
gemmule
germane
gimmick
glamour
glimmer
glimpse
glummer
gnomish
gramary
grammar
grampus
gremial
gremlin
grimace
grimmer
grommet
grumble
grumbly
grummet
grumose
grumous
gumming
gummite
hamming
hammock
harmala
harmful
harmony
hemming
holmium
holmoak
hormone
humming
hummock
hutment
imamate
ipomoea
Ishmael
itemise
jamming
jasmine
Kalmuck
kermess
khamsin
koumiss
kremlin
krimmer
lamming
lemmata
lemming
magmata
malmsey
mammary
mammate
mammock
mammoth
manmade
marmite
mermaid
midmost
mismate
mummery
mummify
mumming
myomata
newmown
noumena
nummary
oatmeal
oddment
Olympic
onymous
outmost
palmary
palmate
palmist
palmoil
palmyra
payment
Permian
permute
pigmean
pigment
pismire
plumage
plumate
plumber
plumbic
plumbob
plumery
plummet
plumose
plumper
plumply
plumule
premier
premise
premiss
premium
primacy
primage
primary
primate
primely
primero
priming
primmed
primula
promise
promote
pugmill
pygmean
pygmoid
quamash
raiment
ramming
rhamnus
rhombic
rhombus
rhymist
rimming
Rommany
roomful
rummage
sawmill
scamper
schmuck
scomber
scumble
scummed
seamaid
seamark
seeming
segment
sfumato
shamble
shammed
shammer
shampoo
Shemite
shimmer
siamang
Siamese
siemens
sigmate
sigmoid
sjambok
skimmed
skimmer
skimmia
slammed
slimily
slimmer
slumber
slummed
slummer
spumous
stamina
stammel
stammer
stamper
stemmed
stemple
stemson
stimuli
stomach
stomata
stumble
stummed
stumper
summand
summary
summery
summing
summons
surmise
swimmer
Tammany
teeming
tegmina
termini
termite
themata
thimble
Thomism
Thomist
thummim
thumper
thymine
titmice
topmast
topmost
torment
tormina
towmond
towmont
tramcar
trammel
trample
tramway
tremble
trembly
tremolo
trimmed
trimmer
trommel
trumeau
trumpet
turmoil
varment
varmint
vermeil
vermian
warmish
waymark
whimper
whimsey
woomera
abandon
acantha
acinous
aconite
adenine
adenoid
adenoma
aeonian
agonise
agonist
alanine
alunite
amanita
amender
amenity
amentia
amentum
amongst
Ananias
apanage
aptness
araneid
asinine
asunder
atingle
avenger
badness
banning
bannock
beanbag
beknown
biennia
bigname
bigness
bionics
blandly
blanket
blankly
blender
blinder
blindly
blinker
blintze
blunder
blunger
bluntly
bonnily
bornite
bouncer
bounden
bounder
branchy
brander
brannew
bransle
brantle
brantub
brinded
brindle
bringer
brinjal
bronchi
broncho
burning
burnish
burnous
cannery
cannily
canning
cannula
carnage
chancel
chancre
changer
channel
chanson
chanter
chantry
chindit
Chinese
Chinook
chintzy
chinwag
chunnel
chunter
clanger
clinker
Cluniac
cognate
cognise
coinage
coinbox
connate
connect
conning
connive
connote
cooncan
coontie
cornage
corncob
corneal
cornett
cornfed
cornice
cornily
Cornish
cornist
cornual
cornuto
council
counsel
counter
country
coyness
cranage
cranial
cranium
crankle
crannog
crenate
cringer
cringle
crinite
crinkle
crinkly
crinoid
crunchy
ctenoid
cunning
cyanide
cyanine
cyanite
damnify
damning
darning
dawning
deanery
dignify
dignity
dimness
dinning
dipnoan
donning
donnish
dornick
downbow
drinker
drunken
dryness
dulness
dunnage
dunning
dunnock
dwindle
earnest
ebonise
ebonite
economy
elenchi
emanate
eminent
ensnare
ensnarl
eponymy
Etonian
evangel
evanish
evening
eweneck
faintly
fanning
fatness
faunist
fernery
fernowl
fewness
feyness
fiancee
finning
Finnish
fitness
flaneur
flanker
flannel
flunkey
founder
foundry
frankly
frantic
Frenchy
frenula
fronded
frontal
fronton
fulness
funnies
funnily
funning
furnace
furnish
gabnash
gahnite
gainful
gainsay
garnish
gauntly
gauntry
gayness
genning
giantry
ginning
glenoid
granary
grandad
grandam
grandee
grandly
grandma
grandpa
granger
granita
granite
grannie
grantee
granter
grantor
granule
grenade
grinder
grinned
grunion
grunter
gruntle
guanaco
guanine
gunnera
gunnery
gunning
gurnard
gwyniad
gymnast
hafnium
harness
haunted
haunter
heinous
hennery
herniae
hernial
hernias
hipness
hobnail
hornmad
hotness
huanaco
Hunnish
hymnary
hymnist
hymnody
hypnoid
iciness
identic
illness
inanely
inanity
Iranian
ironing
ironist
isonomy
Jainism
jannock
joinder
joinery
joining
jointer
jointly
kainite
Kannada
kenning
keynote
khanate
kyanise
kyanite
launder
laundry
laxness
leaning
leonine
lignify
lignite
Linnean
lioncel
lioness
lionise
llanero
loaning
lounger
lowness
lyingin
lyingly
madness
magnate
magneto
magnify
maintop
manners
manning
mannish
mannite
mannose
maunder
meander
meaning
misname
mooneye
moonlit
moonset
morning
mounter
Mountie
munnion
muonium
neonate
newness
noonday
nooning
nunnery
nunnish
oddness
odontic
omental
omentum
ominous
onanism
oneness
openair
openend
opening
opinion
opuntia
Oxonian
ozonise
painful
painter
pannage
pannier
panning
paunchy

penname
pennant
pennate
pennies
pennill
pennine
penning
peonage
pfennig
phantom
phonate
phoneme
phonics
phonily
pianism
pianist
pinnace
pinnate
pinning
pinnule
pioneer
planish
planned
planner
plantar
planter
planula
planxty
plenary
plenish
plunder
plunger
plunker
poinder
pointed
pointer
poundal
pounder
prancer
printer
pronaoi
pronaos
pronate
pronely
pronged
pronoun
pruning
pugnose
punning
pycnite
quantic
quantum
quinary
quinate
quinine
quinone
quintal
quintan
quintet
quintic
quondam
rainbow
raunchy
rawness
redneck
redness
reenact
reenter
reentry
regnant
remnant
reunion
reunite
reynard
rhenium
rounded
roundel
rounder
roundly
roundup
ruinate
ruinous
rumness
running
sadness
sainted
saintly
saunter
sawnoff
scandal
scanned
scanner
scantly
scenery
scented
schnook
scunner
shanked
shindig
shingle
shingly
shinned
shinpad
shunned
shunner
shunter
shyness
signary
signify
signior
signora
signore
signori
signory
sinning
skinful
skinker
skinned
skinner
slander
slantly
slender
slinger
slinker
slyness
soonish
sounder
soundly
spancel
spangle
spangly
spaniel
Spanish
spanker
spanned
spanner
spencer
spender
spinach
spindle
spindly
spindry
spinner
spinney
spinode
spinoff
spinose
spinous
spinule
spondee
spondyl
sponger
spongin
sponson
sponsor
spunkie
standby
stander
standin
standup
staniel
stannic
stenchy
stencil
stentor
stinger
stinker
stonily
stonker
stunned
stunner
stunted
sunnily
sunning
Sunnite
surname
swanker
swanned
swindle
swinery
swinger
swingle
swinish
syenite
taeniae
tannage
tannate
tannery
tanning
tannish
tarnish
taunter
teenage
ternary
ternate
thanage
thankee
thanker
thinker
thinned
thinner
thunder
tinnily
tinning
toenail
tonnage
tonneau
tornado
townish
townlet
tranche
trangam
transit
transom
tranter
trenail
trental
trinary
trindle
tringle
trinity
trinket
trinkum
truncal
trundle
tsunami
tunning
turnery
turning
turnipy
turnkey
turnout
twangle
twankay
twinkle
twinkly
twinned
twoness
unknown
unsnarl
uranide
uranism
uranium
uranous
urinary
utensil
varnish
vaunter
veining
veinlet
vernier
wanness
wannish
warning
wetness
whangee
whinger
winning
winnock
witness
wornout
wrangle
wringer
wrinkle
wrinkly
wrongly
wryneck
wryness
yenning
younger
younker
Zionism
Zionist
zoonomy
abdomen
abiotic
abroach
absolve
account
acrobat
acrogen
acronym
acroter
adjoint
adjourn
aerobic
aerosol
agnomen
aground
alcohol
Alcoran
alforja
Alkoran
allonge
allover
almoner
almonry
aloofly
alsoran
amboina
ambones
amboyna
ammonal
ammonia
ampoule
ancones
anionic
antonym
aphonia
aphonic
aphotic
appoint
apropos
areolae
areolar
areolas
armoire
Armoric
armoury
astound
atrophy
aurochs
aurorae
auroral
auroras
autobus
autocar
autocue
autopsy
avionic
baloney
baronet
baroque
bayonet
bazooka
bedouin
begonia
begorra
behoove
beloved
betoken
bifocal
bigoted
bigotry
bilobar
bilobed
bipolar
bivouac
blooded
bloomer
bologna
boloney
borough
brioche
brooder
bubonic
bucolic
bygones
Byronic
bywoner
caboose
cacodyl
cacoepy
cagoule
cahoots
cajoler
calomel
caloric
calorie
calotte
caloyer
camorra
canonic
canonry
Canopic
caporal
caroche
carotid
carotin
carouse
chaotic
chloral
chloric
chooser
choosey
chromic
chronic
ciboria
cipolin
coconut
cocotte
colobus
cologne
colonel
colonic
colossi
colours
coloury
corolla
coronae
coronal
coronas
coroner
coronet
criollo
crooked
crooner
cryogen
culotte
dacoity
damosel
damozel
debouch
decoder
decorum
defocus
deforce
delouse
demoded
demonic
demotic
demount
deposal
deposit
devolve
devoted
devotee
dipolar
disobey
divorce
echoism
eclogue
ectopic
eidolon
embolic
embolus
embosom
embowed
embowel
embower
emporia
empower
encoder
encomia
endogen
endorse
endozoa
enforce
engorge
ennoble
entomic
entotic
entozoa
enwound
ergodic
escolar
espouse
essoyne
eulogia
exposal
exposed
exposer
exposit
expound
fagotto
Faroese
felonry
femoral
floorer
floosie
floozie
flyover
garotte
gavotte
Genoese
groover
halogen
haporth
hedonic
helotry
heroics
heroine
heroise
heroism
heronry
homonym
honours
humoral
hypogea
hypoxia
hypoxic
idiotic
ignoble
ignobly
ignorer
imbower
immoral
imposer
impound
inboard
incomer
indoors
indorse
ingoing
inhouse
insofar
intoner
invoice
involve
inwoven
Jacobin
jacobus
jaconet
jaloppy
japonic
judoist
kenosis
kenotic
kerogen
kilobar
kiloton
laconic
lanolin
lavolta
limosis
linocut
litotes
lycopod
madonna
mahonia
mahound
Masonic
masonry
Masorah
mayoral
meconic
meiosis
meiotic
melodic
memoirs
menorah
mesonic
metonym
metopic
metopon
minorca
mitoses
mitosis
mitotic
molossi
monocle
monocot
monodic
monomer
morocco
moronic
mycoses
mycosis
mycotic
mylodon
myxomas
Nilotic
obconic
obloquy
October
octopod
octopus
oenomel
ongoing
opposer
opsonic
opsonin
ortolan
osmosis
osmotic
ottoman
paeonic
panocha
panoply
papoose
parodic
parolee
paronym
parotid
peloria
peloric
pelorus
picotee
pirogue
pivotal
pivoter
poloist
popover
pyloric
pylorus
pyrosis
reboant
rebound
recount
recover
redoubt
redound
refocus
regorge
rehouse
rejoice
remodel
remorse
remould
remount
removal
removed
remover
reposal
reposit
resolve
resound
retouch
revolve
rewound
ricotta
ridotto
riposte
risotto
samovar
Samoyed
saponin
savoury
scholar
scholia
scooper
scooter
scrooge
scrouge
seconde
secondi
secondo
senores
shoofly
shooter
sinopia
sirocco
smoochy
snooker
snooper
snoozer
snoozle
sojourn
soloist
Solomon
soroban
sororal
sorosis
splodge
splotch
spoofer
spooney
spoorer
strophe
stroppy
syconia
sycosis
synodal
synodic
synonym
synovia
taborer
taloned
tanooze
tenoner
theorbo
theorem
throaty
thrombi
throned
through
thrower
throwin
timothy
Titoism
Titoist
toponym
triolet
trooper
tylopod
typonym
umbonal
umbones
unbosom
unbound
unbowed
unboxed
uncouth
uncover
undoing
ungodly
unhoped
unhorse
unhouse
unjoint
unloose
unmoral
unmoved
unroost
unsound
unwound
unwoven
valonia
vamoose
vapours
vapoury

velours
veloute
visored
wagoner
whoopee
whooper
widowed
widower
zedoary
zygosis
zygotic
zymogen
zymosis
zymotic
adapter
adaptor
adeptly
adipose
adopter
airport
airpost
Arapaho
asepsis
aseptic
auspice
bagpipe
bedpost
bespeak
bespoke
bopping
bumpily
bumpkin
calpack
campbed
camphor
camping
campion
capping
carping
carport
chapati
chaplet
chapman
chapped
chappie
chapter
chipped
chipper
chopine
chopped
chopper
chupati
clapped
clapper
clipped
clipper
clippie
clupeid
clypeal
clypeus
compact
company
compare
compart
compass
compeer
compend
compere
compete
compile
complex
complin
complot
compony
comport
compose
compost
compote
compute

coppery
coppice
corpora
coupler
couplet
cowpoke
crappie
cripple
cropped
cropper
crupper
cryptal
cryptic
culprit
cupping
cuspate
dampish
dauphin
deepfry
deepsea
Delphic
despair
despise
despite
despoil
despond
dewpond
diopter
dioptre
dipping
dispark
dispart
display
disport
dispose
dispute
dolphin
drapery
dripdry
dripped
droplet
dropout
dropped
dropper
dumpish
duopoly
earplug
edaphic
eelpout
erepsin
flapped
flapper
flipped
flipper
flopped
flypast
foppery
foppish
frapped
fripper
garpike
glyphic
glyptal
glyptic
grapery
graphic
grapnel
grapple
gripped
gripper
gryphon
guipure
gunplay
gypping
happily
happing
harpist
harpoon
helpful

helping
henpeck
hipping
hopping
hospice
icepack
inaptly
ineptly
inspect
inspire
jumpjet
jumpoff
kalpack
kampong
keeping
klipdas
knapped
knapper
krypton
lampion
lampoon
lamprey
lapping
legpull
leopard
limpkin
lipping
lopping
lumpily
lumpish
lymphad
mapping
marplot
maypole
misplay
mopping
morphia
mudpack
mumpish
napping
nauplii
nippers
nippily
nipping
nonplus
nutpine
nymphal
nymphet
offpeak
oosperm
oospore
outpace
outplay
outport
outpost
palpate
pampean
pampero
pappose
parpend
peppery
peppill
pepping
perpend
perpent
perplex
pimping
pipping
pitpony
pitprop
plopped
pompano
pompous
poppied
popping
prepack
prepaid
prepare
preplan

propane
propend
prophet
propine
propjet
propone
propose
propped
pulpous
pumpkin
pupping
purport
purpose
purpura
purpure
quipped
Rajpoot
rampage
rampant
rampart
rampion
rapping
rapport
rasping
redpoll
respect
respell
respelt
respire
respite
respond
respray
ripping
ripplet
salpinx
sampler
sapphic
sapping
scapple
scapula
scepsis
sceptic
sceptre
scopula
scupper
seapink
seaport
seepage
seppuku
serpent
serpigo
serpula
shapely
shiplap
shipman
shipped
shippen
shipper
shippon
shipway
shopboy
shopman
shopped
shopper
simpler
simplex
sipping
skepsis
skipped
skipper
skippet
slapped
slipped
slipper
slipway
slopped
snapped
snapper
snipped

snipper
snippet
soapbox
soapily
soppily
sopping
soupcon
stapler
stepney
stepped
stepper
stepson
stipend
stipple
stipule
stopgap
stopoff
stopped
stopper
stopple
stupefy
styptic
subplot
sulphur
sumpter
supping
support
suppose
surpass
surplus
suspect
suspend
suspire
swapped
swapper
swipple
swopped
swopper
sylphid
symptom
syrphid
tadpole
tamping
tampion
tapping
telpher
tempera
tempest
Templar
templet
tempter
tempura
tenpïns
terpene
timpani
timpano
tipping
tippler
tompion
topping
torpedo
torpids
towpath
trapeze
trapped
trapper
trepang
tripery
triplet
triplex
tripody
tripoli
tripped
tripper
trippet
tripple
trophic
tropics
tropism

trypsin
tryptic
turpeth
tympana
tympani
tympano
tympany
unaptly
utopian
utopism
utopist
vampire
vampish
vespers
vespine
vulpine
warpath
waspish
whipped
whipper
whippet
whipsaw
whopper
wrapped
wrapper
yapping
yipping
zapping
zipping
acequia
aliquot
banquet
bouquet
briquet
chequer
cliquey
coequal
conquer
croquet
croquis
cumquat
jonquil
kumquat
lacquer
marquee
marquis
masquer
parquet
picquet
racquet
rorqual
unequal
aborter
acarian
accrete
accrual
acerbic
acerola
acerose
actress
address
affront
aggress
alertly
amarant
Amerind
amorist
amorous
amtrack
anarchy
ancress
android
aneroid
angrily
anurous
anyroad
apprise
approve
armrest

ascribe
astride
ataraxy
attract
attrite
avarice
average
averred
awarder
azurine
azurite
barrack
barrage
barrier
barring
barroom
bearded
bearing
bearish
bedrock
bedroll
bedroom
begrime
berried
betroth
blarney
blurred
boarder
boarish
boorish
bourbon
bourdon
bourree
boxroom
buirdly
bulrush
bunraku
cabrank
caprice
caprine
caproic
carrack
carrier
carrion
carroty
carryon
charade
charger
charily
chariot
charism
charity
charley
charlie
charmer
charnel
charpoy
charqui
charred
charter
cherish
cheroot
chervil
chirrup
chorale
chordal
chorine
chorion
choroid
chortle
churchy
cirrose
cirrous
citrate
citrine
clarify
clarion
clarity
clarkia

clerisy
clerkly
coarsen
comrade
correct
corrida
corrode
corrody
corrupt
courage
courier
courlan
courser
courtly
csardas
cuirass
cuprite
cuprous
currach
curragh
currant
current
currier
currish
cutrate
cypress
Cyprian
Cypriot
czardas
czardom
czarina
czarism
czarist
dayroom
Debrett
debrief
decrier
decrypt
defraud
defrock
defrost
degrade
deprave
depress
deprive
derrick
detract
detrain
detrude
diarchy
diarise
diarist
digraph
digress
diorama
diorism
diorite
disrank
disrate
disrobe
disroot
disrupt
diurnal
dogrose
doorman
doormat
doorway
dwarves
dyarchy
earring
eccrine
embrace
embroil
embrown
embryon
emerald
emeriti
emersed
emirate

empress
emprise
Encraty
encrust
energid
enframe
engraft
engrail
engrain
engrave
engross
enprint
entrain
entrant
entreat
entropy
entrust
eparchy
epergne
escribe
estrade
estreat
eternal
eucrite
exarate
excrete
exergue
exordia
express
extract
extreme
extrude
exurban
exurbia
fairing
fairish
fairway
farrago
farrier
farruca
fearful
febrile
ferrate
ferrety
ferrite
ferrous
ferrugo
ferrule
fibroid
fibroin
fibroma
fibrous
fierily
flareup
floreat
florist
floruit
fourale
fourgon
furrier
furring
furrowy
gadroon
gasring
gearbox
gearing
Geordie
georgic
gharial
gherkin
glaring
glorify
gnarled
gourami
gourmet
Gstring
guarana
guarani
guarded

guardee
guerdon
guereza
gunroom
haircut
hairnet
hairpin
harrier
hayrick
hearing
hearken
hearsay
hearted
hearten
Hebraic
heiress
herring
hiproof
hoarsen
horrent
horrify
hurried
hydrant
hydrate
hydride
hydroid
hydrous
Iberian
icerink
imbrute
impresa
impress
imprest
imprint
improve
inbreed
incrust
indraft
indrawn
inertia
inertly
infract
ingraft
ingrain
ingrate
ingress
ingroup
ingrown
intrant
intreat
introit
intrude
intrust
iterant
iterate
ivories
jarring
journal
journey
joyride
keyring
knurled
lairage
latrine
laurels
lavrock
learned
learner
legrest
legroom
leprosy
leprous
library
librate
ligroin
lipread
lowrise
macrame
macrami
madrona
madrono
Marrano
married
marring
marrowy
matrass
meerkat
merrily
metrics
metrist
microbe
midriff
migrant
migrate
milreis
misread
misrule
moorage
moorhen
mooring
Moorish
moorlog
mourner
murrain
nacrous
narrate
narrows
nearest
necrose
Negress
Negrito
negroid
neurine
neuroma
neurone
nigrify
nitrate
nitride
nitrify
nitrile
nitrite
nitrous
nourish
obtrude
ocarina
ochrous
odorant
odorous
oloroso
onerous
operand
operant
operate
operose
oppress
ostraca
ostraka
ostrich
outrage
outrank
outride
outrode
outrush
ovarian
overact
overage
overall
overarm
overate
overawe
overbid
overbuy
overdid
overdue
overeat
overfed
overfly
overlap
overlay
overlie
overman
overpay
overran
overrun
oversaw
oversea
oversee
overset
oversew
overtax
overtly
overtop
overuse
padrone
padroni
pairoar
paprika
patrial
patriot
patroon
payroll
pearled
pearler
peartly
pebrine
peerage
peeress
petrify
Petrine
petrous
pharaoh
pharynx
pibroch
picrate
pierrot
poorish
porrect
prorate
prurigo
pteroic
pteryla
puerile
putrefy
pyrrhic
quarrel
quartan
quarter
quartet
quartic
querist
recruit
redraft
redress
refract
refrain
refresh
regrant
regrate
regress
regrets
regroup
reorder
repress
reprint
reprise
reproof
reprove
retrace
retract
retrain
retread
retreat
retrial
rewrite
rewrote
roaring
sacring
sacrist
saprobe
satrapy
saurian
sauroid
scarfed
scarify
scarlet
scarper
scarred
scarves
scirrhi
scoriae
scorify
scoring
scorner
scorper
Scorpio
scurril
searoom
secrecy
secrete
serrate
serried
sferics
sharpen
sharper
sharply
sherbet
shereef
sheriff
sherris
shirker
shoring
shorten
shortie
shortly
sierran
skirret
skirted
skirter
slurred
smaragd
smarten
smartly
snarler
snarlup
snorkel
snorter
soaring
soprani
soprano
sorrily
sourish
soursop
sparely
sparger
sparing
sparkle
sparoid
sparred
sparrow
Spartan
spiraea
spirant
spireme
spirits
sporran
sporter
sporule
spurner
spurred
spurrey
spurtle
starchy
stardom
starkly
starlet
starlit
starred
starter
startle
sterile
sterlet
sternal
sterned
sternly
sternum
steroid
stirpes
stirred
stirrer
stirrup
storage
storied
styrene
sucrose
sunrise
sunroof
supreme
supremo
surreal
swarded
swarmer
swarthy
taproom
taproot
tarrier
tarring
taurine
tearful
teargas
tearing
tearoom
tearose
terrace
terrain
terrene
terrier
terrify
terrine
tetrode
therapy
thereat
thereby
therein
thereof
thereon
thereto
theriac
thermae
thermal
thermic
thirdly
thirsty
thorite
thorium
thorned
thyroid
thyrsus
tiercel
tiercet
tigress
tigrish
titrate
torrefy
torrent
touraco
touring
tourism
tourist
tourney
towrope
trireme
tsardom
tsarina
tsarism
tsarist
uberous
umbrage
Umbrian
unarmed
unbrace
uncross
uncrown
undress
unfrock
unfroze
untried
untruly
untruss
untruth
upbraid
upgrade
uptrend
usurper
uterine
uxorial
vagrant
verruca
vibrant
vibrate
vibrato
vitrify
vitrine
vitriol
warrant
warring
warrior
wearily
wearing
weirdie
weirdly
wharves
whereas
whereat
whereby
wherein
whereof
whereon
whereto
whirler
whirred
whorish
whorled
worrier
yttrium
zebrine
zebroid
zoarium
abashed
abusive
abysmal
abyssal
airship
airsick
allseed
allstar
almsman
alyssum
ambsace
amusive
aniseed
anosmia
anosmic
apishly
apostil
apostle
aristae
aristas
armsful
Avestan
Avestic
awesome
banshee
bassist
bassoon
batsman
beastly
bedside
bedsock
bedsore
beeswax
berserk
biassed
blasted
blaster
blesbok
blessed
blister
blossom
blusher
bluster
boaster
bobsled
bobstay
bolshie
bolster
booster
borscht
borstal
bossism
bowshot
boxseat
brashly
brassie
brisken
brisket
briskly
bristle
bristly
brusher
brusque
bursary
burster
bussing
caesium
caesura
caisson
Capsian
capsize
capstan
capsule
carsick
cassata
cassava
cassino
cassock
catseye
catspaw
catsuit
caustic
Celsius
censure
cession
cesspit
chassis
chasten
chessel
chested
classes
classic
classis
clastic
closely
closeup
closure
cluster
clyster
coastal
coaster
consent
consign
consist
console
consort
consult
consume
corsage
corsair
corslet
cossack
cowshed
cowslip
crassly
cresset
crested
crisper
crisply
cristae
crosier
crossly
crusade
crusado
crusher
crustal
crusted
crystal
cuisine
cumshaw
cupsful
cursive
cursory
cypsela
danseur
dapsone
darshan
daystar
deistic
densely
density
dessert
dissave
disseat
dissect
dissent
doeskin
dogskin
dogstar
dossier
drastic
dresser
drosera
droshky
drysalt
dryshod
earshot
ekistic
elastic
elastin
elision
elusion
elusive
elusory
elysian
Elysium
episode
epistle
erasure
eristic
erosion
erosive
etesian
evasion
evasive
eyeshot
eyesore
eyespot
falsely
falsies
falsify
falsity
feaster
felsite
felspar
fibster
firstly
fissile
fission
fissure
flasher
fleshed
flesher
fleshly
fluster
forsake
forsook
fossick
fossula
frescos
freshen
fresher
freshet
freshly
friseur
Frisian
frisker
frisket
frisson
frosted
frustum
fulsome
fussily
fusspot
gagster
gassing
gemsbok
ghastly
ghostly
ginseng
glassen
glasses
glisten
glister
glossal
Glossic
gnostic
godsend
godship
gorsedd
gossipy
gossoon
grasper
griskin
gristle
gristly
grossly
grysbok
guesser
guisard
gumshoe
gunship
gunshot
gutsily
gymslip
hamster
Hansard
harshen
harshly
harslet
hassock
hayseed
herself
hessian
himself
hipster
hirsute
holster
hopsack
horsily
hotshot
housing
Hussite
iceshow

Irishry
irksome
jouster
jussive
kidskin
kinship
kinsman
kissing
kitschy
Krishna
kursaal
lassoes
lawsuit
legshow
leister
leisure
Liassic
linsang
linseed
lissome
lobster
loosely
lousily
lugsail
maestri
maestro
mahseer
mansard
mansion
mansize
Marsala
marshal
massage
masseur
massive
measles
measure
Meissen
message
messiah
Messias
messily
messtin
miasmal
miasmic
midship
minster
missend
missent
missile
missing
mission
missish
missive
misstep
mobster
moisten
moistly
monsoon
monster
mosshag
mousaka
mousing
mousmee
netsuke
neuston
newsboy
newsman
noisily
noisome
nonskid
nonslip
nonstop
nonsuch
nonsuit
nunship
nursery
nursing
oarsman

obesity
odyssey
oersted
offside
oilseed
oilskin
oldster
oneself
oneshot
onestep
opossum
opuscle
ourself
outsell
outshot
outside
outsize
outsold
outsole
outstay
paisley
palsied
parsley
parsnip
passade
passado
passage
passant
passing
passion
passive
passkey
paysage
peasant
peascod
peasoup
pensile
pension
pensive
Persian
persist
persona
pessary
phasmid
physics
piastre
pigskin
pilsner
pissoir
plasmic
plasmid
plasmin
plaster
plastic
plastid
pliskie
plosion
plosive
plusage
plushly
possess
potshot
poussin
presage
present
preside
presoak
presser
pressup
presume
prosaic
prosify
prosily
prosody
prosper
prussic
pulsate
punster
pursuer

pursuit
quassia
quester
questor
ramsons
ransack
redskin
reissue
retsina
ribston
rissole
roaster
rodsman
roister
rooster
rousing
rouster
royster
rumshop
russety
Russian
Russify
salsify
sapsago
sassaby
satsuma
sausage
scissel
scissor
seasick
seaside
seaslug
seismal
seismic
sensory
sensual
sessile
session
shaslik
shaster
shastra
shyster
sibship
sinsyne
skysail
slasher
sloshed
smasher
smashup
sonship
spastic
suasion
suasive
subside
subsidy
subsist
subsoil
subsume
sunspot
sunstar
sunsuit
swasher
tapsman
tapster
teashop
Telstar
tensely
tensile
tension
tensity
tensive
tersely
tessera
thistle
thistly
thyself
tipsify
tipsily
tipster

toaster
tonsure
topsail
topside
topsoil
torsade
torsion
tosspot
toyshop
tressed
tressel
trestle
trisect
trishaw
trismus
trusser
trustee
truster
trysail
Tuesday
tussive
tussock
tussore
twister
twosome
twostep
unasked
unusual
Vaishya
varsity
versant
versify
versine
version
waisted
waister
warship
wassail
wayside
weasand
webster
welsher
whisker
whiskey
whisper
whistle
whoseso
winsome
worship
worsted
wrestle
zemstvo
abattis
abetted
abetter
abettor
abstain
abutted
abutter
acetate
acetify
acetone
acetous
acutely
agitate
agitato
ajutage
alation
alltime
amateur
amative
amatory
anatase
anatomy
another
anytime
apatite
apetaly
apothem

arctoid
ashtray
auction
austere
austral
banteng
banting
baptise
baptism
baptist
bastard
basting
bastion
battels
battery
batting
beatify
beating
beatnik
bedtime
Beltane
belting
benthic
benthos
bestead
bestial
bestrew
betting
bigtime
biltong
biotite
bistort
bistred
bittern
bitters
bitting
bittock
blatant
blather
blatter
blether
blither
blotchy
blotted
blotter
boating
boatman
bobtail
bootleg
bortsch
bottega
bottled
bottony
brattle
British
brittle
brittly
britzka
brothel
brother
brutish
Brython
bunting
burthen
bustard
bustler
buttend
buttery
buttock
buttons
buttony
caitiff
caltrap
caltrop
cantata
cantate
canteen
canthus
cantina

canting
cantrip
captain
caption
captive
capture
cartage
cartful
cartoon
castile
casting
castled
castoff
cattalo
cattery
cattily
cautery
caution
centaur
centavo
centime
centner
central
centred
centric
centrum
century
certain
certify
cestode
cestoid
chateau
chatted
chattel
chatter
chitter
chutney
cistern
cittern
clatter
clothes
clotted
cloture
clutter
coating
coition
coltish
Comtian
Comtism
Comtist
contact
contain
contemn
contend
content
contest
context
contort
contour
control
contuse
cortege
cortile
costard
costate
costean
costing
costive
costrel
costume
cottage
cottier
cottony
couthie
couture
critter
cuittle
cultism
cultist

culture
curtail
curtain
curtana
curtsey
custard
custody
customs
cutting
cyathus
cystine
cystoid
Dantean
dastard
daytime
deathly
deltaic
deltoid
dentate
dentine
dentist
denture
destine
destiny
destroy
deutzia
dextral
dextran
dextrin
dictate
diction
dietary
diptera
diptych
dirtily
distaff
distain
distant
distend
distent
distich
distill
distort
disturb
dittany
dogtrot
doltish
dortour
dotting
dratted
ductile
ducting
dustbin
dustily
dustman
dustpan
earthen
earthly
eastern
easting
ebbtide
ecstasy
edition
egotise
egotism
egotist
egotrip
elation
elitism
elitist
elution
elytron
elytrum
emetine
emitted
emitter
emotion
emotive
emptier

emptily
emption
enation
epatant
epitaph
epitaxy
epithem
epithet
epitome
erotica
erotism
esotery
eustasy
exotica
faction
factory
factual
facture
fantail
fantasm
fantast
fantasy
fantods
farther
fastday
fattest
fatting
fattish
feather
feature
felting
fertile
festive
festoon
fetters
fictile
fiction
fictive
fifteen
fifthly
fifties
figtree
firtree
fistful
fistula
fittest
fitting
fixture
flatcap
flatcar
flatlet
flatout
flatten
flatter
flattop
fletton
flitted
flitter
flotage
flotsam
fluting
flutist
flutter
flyting
flytrap
footage
footboy
footing
footman
footpad
footrot
footsie
footway
forties
fortify
Fortran
fortune
foxtail
foxtrot

fratery
fretful
fretsaw
fretted
fritted
fritter
further
furtive
fustian
fustily
futtock
gantlet
gastric
genteel
gentian
gentile
gestalt
gestapo
gestate
gesture
getting
ghettos
giltcup
gittern
glitter
glottal
glottis
gluteal
gluteus
glutted
glutton
gnathic
goatgod
goatish
goitred
goutfly
gratify
grating
gritted
grottos
grutten
gustily
guttate
gutting
halting
hastate
hastily
hatting
hautboy
hauteur
heathen
heather
heating
hectare
heftily
heptane
histone
history
hitting
Hittite
hoatzin
hostage
hostess
hostile
hostler
hottest
hottish
hunting
hurtful
hustler
hutting
imitate
initial
install
instant
instate
instead
inutile
irately

isotope
isotopy
isotron
jetting
jitters
jittery
jogtrot
jotting
justice
justify
jutting
Kantian
karting
kentish
kestrel
knitted
knitter
knotted
knotter
lactate
lacteal
lactose
lantana
lantern
Laotian
lasting
lattice
leather
lectern
lection
lecture
leftism
leftist
lentigo
lentisk
lentoid
leotard
letters
letting
Lettish
lettuce
liftoff
lilting
listeth
listing
littery
loather
loathly
loftily
lottery
lotting
loutish
lustful
lustily
lustral
lustrum
maltase
Maltese
malting
maltose
manteau
mantlet
mantram
mantrap
martial
Martian
martini
martlet
martyry
mastaba
masters
mastery
mastich
mastiff
mastoid
mattery
matting
mattins
mattock

mattoid
mauther
Maytime
meatfly
meatman
meeting
melting
menthol
mention
mestiza
mestizo
mettled
mintage
mistake
mistful
mistily
mistime
misting
mistook
mistral
mixture
moither
montage
montane
montero
monthly
mortice
mortify
mortise
mottled
mouther
multure
munting
muntjac
muntjak
murther
mustang
mustard
muttony
mystery
mystify
narthex
nastily
nattily
nautics
nautili
nectary
neither
neoteny
Neptune
nesting
netting
neutral
neutron
nictate
noctuid
noctule
nocturn
norther
nostril
nostrum
nuptial
nurture
nutting
oaktree
obitual
oestral
oestrum
oestrus
oldtime
omitted
onetime
onstage
oration
oratory
oratrix
orotund
outtake
outtalk

outturn
ovation
oxytone
panther
panties
pantile
partake
partial
parting
partita
partite
partlet
partner
partook
pastern
pasteup
pastime
pasture
pattern
patting
peltate
pelting
pentane
pentode
pentose
peptalk
peptide
peptise
peptone
pertain
perturb
pertuse
pettily
petting
pettish
photism
Pictish
picture
pietism
pietist
pigtail
pintado
pintail
pintuck
pistole
pitting
platane
plateau
platina
plating
platoon
platted
platter
plotted
plotter
poetess
poetics
poetise
pontage
pontiff
pontify
pontoon
portage
portend
portent
portico
portion
portray
postage
postbag
postbox
postboy
posteen
postern
postfix
posting
postman
posture
postwar

pottage
pottery
potting
pouting
prattle
pretend
pretest
pretext
pretzel
prithee
protean
protect
protege
proteid
protein
protend
protest
proteus
protist
protium
pustule
puttier
putting
quetsch
quetzal
quitted
quitter
ragtime
rapture
rattail
ratteen
rattery
ratting
rattler
rattrap
rectify
rectory
rectrix
rentier
reptile
restart
restate
restful
restiff
restive
restock
restore
restyle
rettery
retting
rhatany
riotous
riptide
rontgen
rootage
rootlet
rostral
rostrum
rotting
routine
ruction
rupture
rustily
rustler
rutting
ruttish
Saktism
saltant
saltbox
saltcat
saltern
salting
saltire
saltish
saltpan
santour
saxtuba
scatted
scatter

scotice
Scotism
Scotist
scotoma
Scottie
scutage
scutate
scutter
scuttle
seatang
seating
sectary
sectile
section
seltzer
septate
septime
sestina
setting
settler
settlor
Sextans
sextant
sextile
shatter
shittim
shotgun
shotten
shuteye
shutout
shutter
shuttle
sintery
Sistine
sistrum
sitting
sixteen
sixthly
sixties
Sixtine
skating
sketchy
skitter
skittle
slather
slating
slatted
slither
slotcar
slotted
smatter
smitten
smother
smutted
snatchy
softish
soother
soothly
sootily
sotting
sottish
soutane
souther
spathic
spatial
spatted
spattee
spatter
spatula
spitted
spitter
spittle
spotted
spotter
sputnik
sputter
statant
stately
statice

statics
station
statism
statist
stative
statued
stature
statute
stetson
stetted
stutter
subtend
subtile
suction
suiting
sultana
suntrap
surtout
sustain
swatted
swatter
swither
Switzer
swotted
systole
tactful
tactics
tactile
taction
tactual
tantara
tantivy
tantric
tantrum
tartare
tartish
tartlet
Tartufe
tastily
tatters
tattery
tattily
tatting
tattler
teatime
teatray
tectrix
tektite
tentbed
tentfly
tenthly
tentpeg
tertial
tertian
testacy
testate
testban
testbed
testfly
testify
testily
testoon
testudo
textile
textual
texture
thither
tintack
tittupy
tontine
toothed
tootsie
tortile
tortrix
torture
tottery
totting
tritely
tritium

tritone
trotted
trotter
tuatara
tuition
tutting
twitchy
twitted
twitter
twotime
twotone
umpteen
unction
unitary
unitive
unstick
unstuck
upstage
upstair
upstart
urethan
urethra
vantage
vastity
vatting
ventage
ventail
ventral
venture
venturi
vertigo
vestige
vestral
vesture
vetting
viatica
victory
victual
vintage
vintner
virtual
vistaed
vittate
vittles
voltage
voltaic
vulture
waftage
wafture
wagtail
waiting
waltzer
wanting
warthog
wartime
wastage
wastrel
wattage
Watteau
wattled
wattles
waxtree
weather
western
westing
wettest
wetting
wettish
whatnot
whether
whetted
whetter
whitely
whither
whiting
whitish
whitlow
Whitsun
whittle

wintery
wistful
wittily
witting
wottest
writeup
writhen
writing
written
xanthic
xanthin
yestern
yewtree
zaptieh
zestful
zootaxy
zootomy
abjurer
abought
aboulia
accurst
accusal
accused
accuser
acouchy
acquest
acquire
actuary
actuate
adducer
adjudge
adjunct
albumen
albumin
aleuron
alluvia
ampulla
amputee
aneurin
anguine
anguish
angular
annuity
annular
annulet
annulus
arbutus
arcuate
arduous
arousal
asquint
assuage
assured
assurer
augural
awfully
beguile
beguine
bequest
bitumen
blouson
botulin
braunch
brought
cacumen
caducei
calumet
calumny
capuche
casuals
casuist
cerumen
clausal
copular
coquito
craunch
crouton
cumulus
cupular

decuman
decuple
defunct
deluder
diluent
dilutee
diluter
dilutor
divulge
draught
drought
drouthy
effulge
enounce
enquire
enquiry
epaulet
esquire
estuary
excurse
excusal
exhumer
expulse
expunge
fabular
faculae
faculty
famulus
fatuity
fatuous
felucca
fibulae
fibular
fibulas
figural
figured
flaught
flaunty
fleuret
fleuron
flounce
focused
fraught
fuguist
galumph
genuine
graunch
grouchy
grouper
groupie
grouser
hamulus
hanuman
hirudin
hocused
impulse
inbuilt
incubus
incudes
incurve
incused
inducer
indulge
indusia
infulae
inhuman
injurer
inquest
inquire
inquiry
insular
insulin
insured
insurer
issuant
January
jejunum
jocular
jugular

lacunae
lacunal
lacunar
lacunas
Laputan
limulus
liquate
liquefy
liqueur
liturgy
lobular
locular
loculus
lunular
lupulin
maculae
macular
manumit
mazurka
medulla
medusae
medusan
medusas
mezuzah
mimulus
minuend
minutes
minutia
modular
modulus
morulae
morular
Nahuatl
natural
nebulae
nebular
nebulas
nelumbo
nocuous
nodular
nonuser
octuple
odoured
osculum
osmunda
ossuary
pabulum
paludal
papulae
papular
perusal
peruser
petunia
pilular
piously
piquant
plaudit
pleurae
pleural
pleuron
popular
proudly
queuing
radulae
radular
rebuild
rebuilt
rebuker
recurve
reducer
refugee
refusal
refuser
refutal
refuter
regular
regulus
repulse
reputed

request
requiem
require
requite
resurge
returns
rivulet
roguery
roguish
rotunda
saguaro
saluter
samurai
scauper
scourer
scourge
scouter
scrubby
scruffy
scrumpy
scrunch
scruple
secular
securer
seducer
Senussi
sequela
sequent
sequoia
shouter
shrubby
simular
sinuate
sinuous
situate
slouchy
sloughy
snouted
soluble
splurge
spousal
spouter
staunch
stouten
stoutly
strudel
strumae
suburbs
sutural
sutured
tabular
tegular
tenuity
tenuous
tequila
theurgy
thought
thrummy
titular
toluene
torulae
triumph
trouble
trounce
trouper
trouser
Tsquare
tubular
tumular
tumulus
unbuild
unbuilt
unfunny
unfussy
unguard
unguent
ungulae
unlucky
unquiet

unquote
untuned
upsurge
vacuity
vacuole
vacuous
vaguely
vaguish
valuate
vaquero
viduity
vitular
voguish
voluble
volubly
volumed
voluted
volutin
wrought
zymurgy
atavism
atavist
bravado
bravely
bravery
bravura
brevier
brevity
calvary
canvass
carving
cervine
cheviot
chevron
civvies
clavate
clavier
clivers
convect
convene
convent
convert
convict
convoke
corvina
corvine
couvade
couvert
craving
crevice
culvert
curvate
dervish
dogvane
drivein
driving
droving
elevate
elevens
eluvial
eluvium
exuviae
exuvial
fauvism
fauvist
fervent
fervour
flavine
flavour
flivver
fluvial
fulvous
gravely
gravity
gravure
halvers
harvest
heavily
knavery

knavish
Latvian
louvred
naively
naivete
naivety
nervate
nervine
nervous
nervure
nirvana
obovate
obovoid
olivary
olivine
outvote
parvenu
parvise
peevish
pervade
pervert
pluvial
pravity
prevail
prevent
preview
previse
privacy
private
privily
privity
proverb
provide
proviso
provoke
provost
pulvini
purview
quavery
quivery
revving
salvage
salvoes
selvage
servant
servery
Servian
service
servile
serving
Servite
Shavian
shaving
shivers
shivery
silvern
silvery
slavery
slavish
Slavism
Slovene
solvate
solvent
stovies
suavely
suavity
subvert
survive
sylvine
sylvite
travail
travois
trivial
trivium
valvate
valvula
valvule
velvety
vervain

voivode
weevily
wolvish
Yahvist
airwave
alewife
anyways
anywise
arcweld
artwork
athwart
awkward
between
betwixt
blewits
blowdry
blowfly
blowgun
blowout
blowzed
Boswell
boxwood
brawler
brewage
brewery
brownie
browser
bulwark
burweed
camwood
catwalk
chowder
crawler
crowbar
crowdie
crowned
crowner
crownet
crowtoe
cudweed
cutworm
daywork
dogwood
drawbar
drawing
drawler
dyewood
eelworm
endways
endwise
entwine
entwist
eyewash
eyewink
felwort
figwort
flowage
flowery
forward
forwent
forworn
froward
frowsty
gadwall
godward
growler
grownup
gunwale
hagweed
hayward
haywire
henwife
hogwash
hogweed
indwell
indwelt
inkwell
inswing
intwine

jaywalk
keyword
knowall
knowhow
knowing
lapwing
leeward
legwork
lobworm
logwood
lugworm
madwort
manward
manweek
mawworm
maxwell
mayweed
midweek
Midwest
midwife
morwong
mugwort
mugwump
narwhal
network
norward
oakwood
oarweed
oilwell
outward
outwear
outwent
outwore
outwork
outworn
pigwash
pigweed
pinworm
plywood
prowess
prowler
ragweed
ragworm
ragwort
redwing
redwood
ribwork
ribwort
sapwood
sawwort
seawall
seaward
seaware
seaweed
seawhip
seawife
seawolf
setwall
showbiz
showery
showily
showing
showman
showoff
skyward
slowish
snowcap
snowily
snowman
spawner
steward
stewpan
stewpot
stowage
sunward
sunwise
tinware
trawler
tutwork

Tynwald
unaware
unswear
unswore
unsworn
untwine
untwist
upsweep
upswept
upswing
vanward
viewing
waxwing
waxwork
wayward
wayworn
webworm
werwolf
Yahwist
abaxial
adaxial
asexual
bauxite
biaxial
bruxism
coaxial
coexist
dioxide
epoxide
flexile
flexion
flexure
fluxion
inexact
Manxcat
Manxman
Marxian
Marxism
Marxist
proximo
quixote
abeyant
acrylic
aphylly
babyish
babysit
barytes
barytic
belying
bicycle
bogyman
buoyage
buoyant
butyric
calyces
calycle
calypso
calyxes
claypan
copycat
copyist
corydon
dasyure
drayage
drayman
ecdyses
ecdysis
empyema
enzymic
fogydom
fogyish
fogyism
greyhen
greyish
greylag
gruyere
guayule
halyard
juryman

katydid
kerygma
ladybug
ladykin
lanyard
manyear
marybud
midyear
papyrus
playact
playboy
playful
playing
playlet
playoff
playpen
polygon
polymer
polynia
polynya
polypod
polypus
quayage
recycle
satyral
satyric
satyrid
spryest
tanyard
taxying
Toryism
trayful
undying
untying
wheyish
amazing
benzene
benzine
benzoic
benzoin
benzole
benzoyl
boozeup
boozily
brazier
buzzard
buzzsaw
canzone
canzoni
crazily
crozier
dazzler
dizzard
dizzily
drizzle
drizzly
epizoic
epizoon
frazzle
frizzle
frizzly
fuzzily
gizzard
glazier
glazing
glozing
grazier
grazing
grizzle
grizzly
guzzler
jazzily
jazzman
matzoth
mazzard
mitzvah
muezzin
muzzily
muzzler

neozoic
puzzler
quizzed
quizzer
quizzes
rhizoid
rhizome
seizing
seizure
sizzler
sozzled
subzero
swizzle
whizkid
whizzed
woozily

---

abeyant
abigail
abomasa
abreact
abreast
abroach
abstain
acclaim
acetate
acreage
actuary
actuate
adamant
adulate
agitate
agitato
airfare
airmail
airwave
ajutage
alidade
already
althaea
amarant
ambsace
amtrack
amylase
anatase
animate
anomaly
anyways
apanage
apetaly
apogamy
appease
applaud
Aramaic
Arapaho
archaic
arcuate
armband
arrears
asphalt
assuage
ataraxy
athwart
attract
aureate
average
avocado
awkward
baccara
baccate
badmash
baggage
baklava
ballade
ballast
bandage
bandana
barbate
bargain

barmaid
barrack
barrage
bastard
bateaux
Bauhaus
bedfast
beggary
beldame
Beltane
beneath
Bengali
bereave
bigname
biliary
biomass
biplane
biriani
blatant
bobtail
bollard
bombard
bombast
bondage
boscage
boskage
boxcalf
boxhaul
bradawl
bravado
brewage
brigade
brigand
brocade
brokage
bromate
bruhaha
buffalo
bugbane
bullace
bullary
bullate
bulwark
bummalo
bunraku
buoyage
buoyant
bureaus
bureaux
burgage
bursary
bustard
buzzard
cabbage
cabbagy
cabbala
cabrank
caimans
callant
calpack
calvary
cantata
cantate
canvass
captain
carcase
carcass
carnage
carrack
cartage
cascade
cascara
cassata
cassava
casuals
catcall
Cathari
Cathars
cattalo
catwalk
caudate
caviare
caymans
cembalo
centaur
centavo
certain
chalaza
chapati
charade
chelate
chicane
Chicano
chorale
chupati
ciliary
ciliate
cineast
cithara
citrate
clamant
clavate
climate
cockade
cognate
coinage
collage
collard
collate
command
compact
company
compare
compart
compass
comrade
concave
connate
contact
contain
coolant
cordage
cordate
corkage
cornage
corsage
corsair
cossack
costard
costate
cottage
courage
couvade
cowbane
cowhage
cowhand
cranage
cremate
crenate
crusade
crusado
crybaby
cuirass
cuneate
cupcake
cureall
currach
curragh
currant
curtail
curtain
curtana
curvate
cuspate
custard
cutback
cutlass
cutrate
cymbalo
dastard
deafaid
decease
deciare
declaim
declare
declass
defiant
deflate
defraud
degrade
deltaic
dentate
deodand
deodara
deplane
deprave
descant
despair
detract
detrain
deviant
deviate
dewfall
diabase
dictate
diehard
dietary
digraph
diorama
disband
disbark
discant
discard
disdain
disease
disfame
dismast
dispark
dispart
disrank
disrate
dissave
distaff
distain
distant
dittany
dizzard
dockage
doddard
dogbane
dogcart
dogdays
dogeate
dogvane
dorhawk
dormant
drayage
drysalt
dullard
dunnage
durmast
earmark
ebriate
ecstasy
educate
elegant
elevate
elfland
emanate
emblaze
embrace
emerald
emicate
emirate
emplace
emplane
emulate
enchain
enchant
enchase
enclasp
enclave
Encraty
endways
enemata
enframe
engraft
engrail
engrain
engrave
enplane
enslave
ensnare
ensnarl
entrain
entrant
epatant
epicarp
epilate
epitaph
epitaxy
estrade
estuary
euclase
eustasy
ewelamb
exarate
exclaim
exclave
exocarp
exogamy
expiate
explain
explant
extract
exudate
eyeball
eyebath
eyelash
eyewash
falbala
falcate
fallacy
fanfare
fanmail
fantail
fantasm
fantast
fantasy
farrago
fenland
fermata
ferrate
filiate
finback
firearm
flotage
flowage
flyback
flybane
flyhalf
flypast
fogbank
foggage
foglamp
foliage
foliate
fondant
footage
forbade
forearm
forgave
formant
formate
forsake
forward
foulard
foumart
fourale
foveate
foxtail
frigate
froward
fullage
funfair
furcate
furnace
futhark
gabnash
gadwall
galeate
gallant
gallate
gambade
gambado
garbage
gardant
garland
gasmask
gateaux
gemmate
germane
gestalt
gestapo
gestate
gimbals
gizzard
goddamn
godward
goliard
Goliath
goshawk
goulash
gourami
gradate
gramary
granary
grenade
grimace
guanaco
guarana
guarani
guisard
gunwale
gurnard
guttate
gymnast
Haggada
haggard
hallali
halyard
Hansard
harmala
hastate
hatband
haulage
hayward
Hebraic
hectare
henbane
heptane
herbage
hipbath
hobnail
hoecake
hogback
hogwash
holdall
holland
hopsack
hostage
huanaco
husband
hushaby
hydrant
hydrate
hymnary
icefall
icepack
ikebana
imamate
imitate
impeach
impearl
implant
inboard
indraft
indrawn
inexact
inflame
inflate
infract
ingraft
ingrain
ingrate
inphase
install
instant
instate
intrant
inweave
Ishmael
isobath
isogamy
isolate
issuant
iterant
iterate
jackass
January
jaywalk
jellaba
jimjams
kabbala
kalpack
Kannada
khanate
knowall
kursaal
labiate
lactate
laggard
lairage
Lallans
lambast
laniary
lantana
lanyard
lawhand
leafage
leakage
leeward
legbail
lemmata
leopard
leotard
library
librate
limbate
lindane
lineage
lineate
linkage
linsang
liquate
lockage
Lollard
Lombard
longago
lowland
lubbard
luggage
lugsail
lullaby
lumbago
lumbang
lurdane
machair
macrame
macrami
magmata
magnate
mallard
maltase
mammary
mammate
mandala
mandate
manjack
manmade
mansard
manward
Marrano
Marsala
mascara
massage
mastaba
matrass
mazzard
mediacy
mediant
mediate
mermaid
message
methane
midland
migrant
migrate
mileage
miliary
miniate
mintage
miscall
miscast
misdate
misgave
mislaid
mismate
misname
mistake
montage
montane
moorage
mordant
mousaka
mudbath
mudlark
mudpack
mundane
muriate
murrain
mustang
mustard
myomata
Nahuatl
narrate
nectary
Neogaea
neonate
nervate
netball
newlaid
nictate
niggard
nirvana
nitrate
norland
norward
nummary
nutcase
nutgall
oakgall
oatcake
obolary
obovate
obviate
oculate
oddball
odorant
offhand
oilbath
oilcake
olivary
onstage
oomiack
openair
operand
operant
operate
orchard
oregano
origami
ossuary
ostiary
ostraca
ostraka
ouabain
outback
outcast
outface
outfall
outhaul
outland
outlast
outpace
outrage
outrank
outtake
outtalk
outward
overact
overage
overall
overarm
overate
overawe
ovulate
oxalate
oxidant
oxidase
oxidate
package
pageant
pahlavi
palmary
palmate
palpate
pancake
Panjabi
pannage
parfait
pargana
partake
passade
passado
passage
passant
paysage
peasant
peccant
peccary
pedlary
peerage
peltate
pendant
penname
pennant
pennate
pentane
peonage
peptalk
percale
perhaps
periapt
pertain
pervade
pessary
phalanx
pharaoh
phonate
pickaxe
picrate
piebald
pigtail
pigwash
pileate
pillage
pinball
pinnace
pinnate
pintado
pintail
piquant
piscary
pitfall
placard
placate
platane
playact
plenary
plicate
plumage
plumate
plusage
pochard
poleaxe
pollack
pollard
pompano
pondage
poniard
pontage
portage
postage
potbank
pottage
poulard
precast
predate
preface
prelacy
prelate
prepack
prepaid
prepare
presage
prevail
primacy
primage
primary
primate
privacy
private
proband
probang
probate
profane
prolate
pronaoi
pronaos
pronate
propane
prorate
prosaic
pulsate
Punjabi
quahaug
quamash
quayage
quinary
quinate

radiant
radiate
rampage
rampant
rampart
ransack
rattail
reboant
reclaim
reclame
redraft
reenact
reflate
refract
refrain
regnant
regrant
regrate
reheard
release
reliant
remnant
replace
replant
rescale
reseaux
reshape
restart
restate
retiary
retrace
retract
retrain
reynard
rhatany
rhubarb
ribband
Rommany
rootage
roseate
roulade
ruinate
rummage
rundale
Sabbath
saccade
saccate
saguaro
saltant
salvage
sapsago
sarcasm
sassaby
satiate
satrapy
sausage
saveall
sawgate
scalade
scalado
scutage
scutate
seabass
seakale
sealane
sealant
seamaid
seamark
seatang
seawall
seaward
seaware
sectary
seepage
selvage
septate
serfage
seriate
serrate
servant
setback
setwall
Sextans
sextant
sfumato
shebang
shikari
siamang
sigmate
signary
sinkage
sinuate
sirgang
sitfast
situate
skyjack
skylark
skysail
skyward
smaragd
soakage
soccage
solvate
soprani
soprano
soutane
sowback
spicate
spinach
spiraea
spirant
squeaky
statant
steward
stomach
stomata
storage
stowage
streaky
striate
sublate
succade
sulcate
sullage
sultana
summand
summary
sunbath
sunlamp
sunward
surbase
surface
surname
surpass
sustain
syllabi
syncarp
syngamy
tallage
Tammany
tanbark
tankage
tankard
tannage
tannate
tantara
tanyard
tartare
teacake
teenage
ternary
ternate
terrace
terrain
testacy
testate
thalami
thanage
thecate
themata
therapy
thready
throaty
tieback
tiffany
tillage
timbale
timpani
timpano
tintack
tinware
tipcart
titlark
titrate
toccata
toenail
tonnage
topiary
topmast
topsail
tornado
torsade
touraco
towpath
travail
trehala
trenail
trepang
tribade
trigamy
trinary
trysail
Tsquare
tsunami
tuatara
turbary
tympana
tympani
tympano
tympany
Tynwald
tzigane
tzigany
ululant
ululate
umbrage
unaware
unbrace
unchain
unclasp
unguard
unheard
unitary
unlearn
unleash
unmeant
unready
unsnarl
unteach
unweave
upbraid
upgrade
upheave
upstage
upstair
upstart
urinary
vagrant
valiant
vallate
valuate
valvate
vantage
vanward
variant
variate
vendace
ventage
ventail
verdant
versant
vervain
vibrant
vibrate
vibrato
village
villain
vintage
violate
virgate
vistaed
vitiate
vittate
volcano
voltage
voltaic
vulgate
waftage
wagtail
wallaby
warfare
wargame
warpath
warrant
wassail
wastage
wattage
waylaid
waymark
wayward
weasand
welfare
wetback
windage
wordage
yardage
yardang
yardarm
zedoary
Zingari
Zingaro
zoogamy
zootaxy
abubble
acerbic
acrobat
addable
addible
adhibit
aerobic
affable
affably
alembic
algebra
amiable
amiably
amoebae
amoebas
amoebic
astable
attaboy
audible
autobus
ballboy
bandbox
beanbag
bellboy
bilobar
bilobed
blabbed
blabber
blesbok
blubber
bourbon
brabble
bramble
brambly
bugaboo
bullbat
buyable
calibre
callbox
callboy
campbed
capable
capably
caribou
cerebra
chamber
citable
clabber
clamber
climber
clobber
clubbed
clumber
codable
cohabit
coinbox
colobus
crabbed
cribbed
cribble
crowbar
crumble
crumbly
curable
datable
decibel
disable
disobey
djibbah
downbow
drabber
drabbet
drabble
drawbar
dribble
drubbed
dupable
durable
durably
dustbin
eatable
ennoble
ephebus
equable
equably
exhibit
exurban
exurbia
filibeg
firebox
firebug
fixable
fleabag
flubbed
flyable
footboy
freebie
friable
fribble
fusible
gamebag
gearbox
gemsbok
goldbug
golfbag
goodbye
grabbed
grabber
grabble
gribble
grubbed
grubber
grumble
grumbly
grysbok
hackbut
halibut
handbag
hatable
hautboy
hellbox
highboy
hirable
holibut
ichabod
ignoble
ignobly
imbiber
incubus
inhabit
inhibit
Jacobin
jacobus
Jezebel
jukebox
kilobar
knobbed
knobble
knobbly
ladybug
leafbud
legible
legibly
lieabed
likable
linkboy
livable
livebox
longbow
losable
lovable
lovably
macabre
mailbag
mailbox
marabou
marybud
minibus
movable
mutable
mutably
namable
newsboy
nosebag
notable
notably
October
omnibus
overbid
overbuy
pageboy
parable
payable
pillbox
playboy
pliable
pliably
plumber
plumbic
plumbob
poohbah
postbag
postbox
postboy
potable
quibble
rainbow
rarebit
ratable
retable
rhombic
rhombus
ridable
risible
roadbed
ropable
rosebay
rosebud
sackbut
salable
saltbox
sandbag
sandbar
sandbed
sandbox
sandboy
savable
sayable
scabbed
scabble
scomber
scribal
scriber
scrubby
scumble
seeable
seedbed
shamble
sherbet
shopboy
showbiz
shrubby
sickbay
sickbed
sizable
sizably
sjambok
skiable
slabbed
slabber
slobber
slubbed
slubber
slumber
snubbed
snubber
soapbox
sofabed
soluble
soroban
squabby
stabbed
stabber
stubbed
stubble
stubbly
stumble
swabbed
swabber
swobbed
tallboy
tamable
taxable
tenable
tenably
tentbed
terebra
testban
testbed
thimble
tollbar
toolbox
tremble
trembly
triable
trouble
tuckbox
tunable
tunably
typebar
visible
visibly
vocable
voluble
volubly
votable
wadable
Wahabee
windbag
workbag
workbox
acouchy
adducer
African
anarchy
annicut
antacid
apricot
article
attache
auricle
aurochs
autocar
autocue
bicycle
bifocal
blotchy
bobeche
boracic
borscht
bouncer
branchy
breccia
brioche
bronchi
broncho
caducei
calices
caliche
calicle
calyces
calycle
capuche
caracal
caracul
caroche
catechu
cenacle
chancel
chancre
churchy
cimices
cloacae
cloacal
codices
codicil
colicky
comical
conacre
conical
cooncan
copycat
coracle
corncob
council
crunchy
cubical
cubicle
culices
curacao
curacoa
cuticle
cynical
debacle
deficit
defocus
diarchy
domical
dovecot
dyarchy
earache
effects
elenchi
eparchy
ethical
felucca
fiancee
filacer
finical
finicky
flaccid
flatcap
flatcar
fleeced
fleecer
floccus
Frenchy
frescos
funicle
giltcup
gnocchi
gouache
grouchy
haircut
handcar
haricot
helical
helices
helicon
hellcat
illicit
indican
indices
indicia
inducer
insecty
kingcup
kitschy
kneecap
latices
lexical
lexicon
linocut
lioncel
logical
loricae
lyrical
magical
malacia
manacle
Manxcat
medical
Mexican
mimical
mimicry
minicab
minicar
miracle
modicum
monacal
monocle
monocot
morocco
murices
musical
nodical
officer
optical
opuscle
ossicle
oxyacid
panacea
panache
panicky
panicle
panocha
paunchy
peascod

pedicab	abaddon	decadal	khaddar	serfdom	worldly	bowhead	cookery	enwheel
pedicel	abandon	decided	kingdom	shedder	wouldbe	boxseat	coppery	epicede
pedicle	abrader	decider	klipdas	shindig	wouldst	bravely	corbeil	epicene
pelican	abridge	decidua	kneader	shudder	yielder	bravery	corneal	epigeal
pemican	accidie	decoder	launder	skaldic	zooidal	brewery	cornett	epigean
pofaced	acridly	deluder	laundry	skidded	abscess	bribery	correct	epigene
polacca	adjudge	demoded	longday	slander	academe	buckeye	cortege	erodent
polacre	amender	derider	lucidly	sledded	academy	bugbear	costean	escheat
polecat	amildar	divider	luridly	slender	accrete	burgeon	couvert	esotery
prancer	aphides	driedup	macadam	slidden	Achaean	burgess	cowbell	estreat
preachy	apsidal	dripdry	matador	smeddum	achieve	Burmese	cowheel	euglena
radical	apsides	druidic	maunder	solidly	acquest	burweed	cowherd	evident
radices	arcaded	dukedom	meander	solidus	actress	buttend	coyness	eweneck
radicle	arcadia	dwindle	melodic	someday	acutely	buttery	credent	excrete
railcar	ascidia	earldom	milldam	sounder	address	cachexy	crudely	exegete
raunchy	asunder	echidna	mirador	soundly	ageless	cacoepy	cudbear	exigent
recycle	awarder	encoder	mixedly	speeder	aggress	Cadmean	cudweed	express
reducer	Bahadur	ephedra	mixedup	speedup	agilely	caldera	culvert	extreme
refocus	basidia	ergodic	monadic	spender	ailment	candela	current	eyeless
reticle	bearded	exordia	monodic	spindle	aimless	candent	cutlery	falsely
rosecut	besides	fadedly	moulder	spindly	airless	cannery	cypress	farceur
rubicon	bipedal	faraday	mylodon	spindry	alameda	canteen	cypsela	Faroese
salicet	birddog	faradic	naiades	splodge	alchemy	cathead	danseur	fathead
salicin	bladder	fastday	nakedly	spondee	aliment	catseye	Dantean	fatness
saltcat	blandly	fetidly	nameday	spondyl	allheal	cattery	deadend	fattest
sanicle	bleeder	fiefdom	nomadic	squaddy	allseed	cautery	deadeye	ferment
Saracen	blender	fielder	noonday	staddle	amateur	cepheid	deanery	fernery
seducer	blinder	filmdom	notedly	staidly	ambient	chateau	Debrett	ferrety
senecio	blindly	firedog	oppidan	standby	ancient	chimera	deflect	fervent
sericin	blooded	fixedly	overdid	stander	ancress	chimere	densely	fetters
sidecar	blowdry	flagday	overdue	standin	aniseed	Chinese	deplete	fewness
silicic	blunder	fluidal	ovoidal	standup	antbear	cholera	depress	feyness
silicle	boarder	fluidic	paladin	stardom	anxiety	cindery	descend	fidgets
silicon	bonedry	fluidly	paludal	strider	apogean	Circean	descent	fidgety
sirocco	boredom	fogydom	papadam	stridor	aptness	cistern	dessert	fifteen
sketchy	boulder	founder	parader	strudel	araneid	cithern	dialect	figleaf
slotcar	bounden	foundry	parados	studded	archery	cittern	dickens	figment
slouchy	bounder	freedom	paradox	subadar	arcweld	clement	digress	filbert
smoochy	bourdon	fronded	parodic	subedit	armless	clivers	diluent	fishery
snatchy	bowlder	gelidly	peridot	swaddle	armrest	closely	dimmest	fisheye
snowcap	brander	geoidal	picador	swarded	artless	closeup	dimness	fitment
solicit	breaded	Geordie	plaided	swindle	athlete	clupeid	diocese	fitness
soupcon	breadth	gladded	plaudit	synodal	audient	clypeal	diptera	fittest
spancel	breeder	gladden	pleader	synodic	augment	clypeus	discern	flaneur
spencer	brinded	gladder	plodded	tepidly	austere	cockeye	discerp	flareup
splicer	brindle	gliadin	plodder	thirdly	aweless	coffers	disseat	floreat
squacco	broaden	gonadal	plunder	thudded	awnless	collect	dissect	flowery
starchy	broadly	gonidia	poinder	thunder	Azilean	colleen	dissent	flybelt
stenchy	broider	goodday	popadum	timidly	badness	college	distend	flyleaf
stencil	brooder	grandad	poundal	treader	bandeau	commend	distent	foolery
stoical	builded	grandam	pounder	treadle	banteng	comment	dithery	foppery
stuccos	builder	grandee	prodded	triadic	barbell	compeer	doddery	forbear
subacid	buildup	grandly	prodder	trindle	battels	compend	dodgems	forceps
tankcar	buirdly	grandma	proudly	trodden	battery	compere	dodgery	forfeit
taxicab	bulldog	grandpa	pyxides	trundle	believe	compete	doggery	forfend
tiercel	cacodyl	griddle	pyxidia	tsardom	benzene	conceal	doucely	forgery
tiercet	celadon	grinder	quondam	Tuesday	bequest	concede	douceur	forwent
tobacco	Chaldee	guarded	rabidly	tumidly	berserk	conceit	drapery	frameup
topical	cheddar	guardee	Ramadan	twaddle	beseech	concent	drivein	fratery
tramcar	chidden	guerdon	rapidly	twaddly	besiege	concept	drosera	friseur
tranche	childer	guilder	remodel	twiddle	besmear	concern	drycell	frogeye
treacle	childly	halidom	reorder	twiddly	bespeak	concert	dryness	fulgent
treacly	chindit	hangdog	reredos	ungodly	bestead	condemn	dubiety	fulness
triacid	chordal	hexadic	residua	unladen	between	confect	duchess	furmety
truncal	chowder	hirudin	residue	upsides	bibbery	confess	dudgeon	gabfest
tunicle	chuddah	hockday	rhabdom	validly	biggest	congeal	dulness	gadgety
twitchy	chuddar	holiday	rigidly	vanadic	bighead	congest	dungeon	galleon
typical	citadel	humidly	rounded	vapidly	bigness	conkers	duodena	gallery
unlucky	comedic	humidor	roundel	vexedly	bindery	connect	earnest	garment
utricle	conidia	ilkaday	rounder	vividly	bittern	consent	eastern	gathers
varices	corydon	incudes	roundly	wealden	bitters	contemn	ebriety	gaudery
Vatican	cotidal	infidel	roundup	weekday	bobbery	contend	egghead	gayness
vehicle	couldst	insider	rubadub	weirdie	bogbean	content	element	gemmery
vesicae	creedal	invader	scalder	weirdly	bonkers	contest	elevens	Genoese
vesical	crowdie	jackdaw	scaldic	wheedle	bookend	context	eminent	genteel
vesicle	csardas	jadedly	scandal	whidder	Boolean	convect	empress	geodesy
wildcat	czardas	jemadar	scolder	wielder	boozeup	convene	empyema	gerbera
wolfcub	czardom	joinder	scudded	wolfdog	Boswell	convent	endless	giblets
woodcut	dazedly	katydid	seceder	workday	bottega	convert	entreat	gilbert

gingery instead minuend peeress raiment shapely tensely wetness gruffly
ginseng intreat Miocene pendent ratteen shebear terpene wettest Guelfic
gittern irately misdeal peppery rattery shebeen terrene whereas handful
gluteal irideal misdeed percent rawness shereef tersely whereat harmful
gluteus isogeny misdeem percept rayless shivers tessera whereby hateful
goahead Israeli mishear perfect reagent shivery thereat wherein heedful
goddess jaggery mislead perpend reddest showery thereby whereof helpful
godhead jitters misread perpent redhead shrieve therein whereon hopeful
godless jittery missend pervert redlegs shuteye thereof whereto hurtful
godsend jobbery missent phoneme redneck shyness thereon whitely insofar
gombeen joinery mockery pickeer redness Siamese thereto whoseso lifeful
gooiest joyless monkery pidgeon redress siemens thyself widgeon Lucifer
gorsedd Judaean montero piggery reelect silvern tiebeam wigless lustful
gradely kermess mooneye piglead reflect silvery tigress windegg malefic
grapery keyless mordent pigmean refresh sincere tindery winkers meatfly
gravely knavery mullein pigment regress sinless toeless wintery mindful
grocery lacteal mummery pigweed regrets sintery toggery withers mistful
gruyere lambent muraena pincers relieve sithens toluene witless needful
gudgeon lambert mynheer pinhead relievo sixteen tonneau witness omnific
guereza lancers mystery pinkeye replete slavery topless woomera ossific
gullery lantern nailery pioneer replevy Slovene torment wottest overfed
gunnera larceny naively pithead repress slyness torpedo writeup overfly
gunnery largely naivete placebo request smokeho torrefy wryneck pacific
gutless largess naivety plateau respect society torrent wryness pailful
hackery lathery nankeen plumery respell sockeye tottery wychelm painful
hagweed laurels napless poetess respelt solvent towhead yestern piaffer
halberd lawless nascent porrect retread sonless tracery zithern pipeful
halbert laxness nearest portend retreat sorbent tradein zoogeny pitiful
halvers lechery neglect portent rettery sorcery tragedy agraffe playful
hapless lectern Negress possess rickets soybean traject aloofly porifer
harness legless neoteny posteen rickety sparely trapeze antefix postfix
harvest legrest newness postern rilievo spicery triceps aquifer proffer
hasbeen lenient nimiety pothead ringent spidery trident armsful pushful
hatless lethean nippers potheen ripieni spireme tripery baleful quaffer
hauberk letters noumena potherb ripieno spleeny trireme baneful ratafia
hauteur lidless nowhere pottery riviera spryest trisect bashful restful
hayseed limbeck nuclear powdery riviere squeeze tritely benefic roomful
heiress Linnean nucleic prebend robbery stalely trumeau benefit rotifer
Hellene linseed nuclein precede rockery stately turgent blowfly ruthful
hennery lioness nucleon precept roedeer stipend turnery bluffer sackful
henpeck lipdeep nucleus prefect roguery student turpeth bluffly sandfly
herself lipless nunnery preheat rondeau stupefy tushery bodeful scarfed
hetaera lipread nursery prelect rookery styrene twoness bookful scoffer
himself liquefy oakfern present rouleau suavely ukelele bowlful scruffy
hipness liqueur oarless pretend rubbers subdean ukulele briefly scuffle
hoggery listeth oarweed pretest rubbery subhead umpteen brimful selffed
hogweed lithely oatmeal pretext rumness subject unblest careful shoofly
hophead littery obscene prevent runless subtend unclean cartful shuffle
horrent llanero oddment primely russety subvert undress chaffer skiffle
hosiery loosely oddness primero saddest subzero unguent chamfer skilful
hostess lottery offbeat proceed sadness succeed unideal chiefly skinful
hothead lowness offpeak process saidest success unshell chiffon snaffle
hotness lyncean oilseed profess salient suggest unswear chuffed sniffer
hottest machete oilwell progeny saltern summery upfield conifer sniffle
howbeit maddest oneness project sanders sunbeam upsweep cornfed snuffer
hueless madness oneself pronely saphead sunbear upswept cupsful snuffle
hunkers magneto oosperm propend sapient sundeck uptrend deepfry songful
hutment mahseer openend protean sapless sunless urodele direful souffle
hygiene malleus oppress protect satiety supreme useless doleful soulful
iceberg Maltese opulent protege scalene supremo vaguely doomful spoofer
iciness manless orogeny proteid scenery surfeit vaquero dutiful squiffy
illness manners Orphean protein schlepp surgeon variety easeful stiffen
imagery manteau ourself protend screech surgery varment fateful stiffly
impiety manweek outsell protest screeve surreal velvety fearful stuffer
implead manyear outwear proteus scrieve suspect verbena feoffee tactful
implete margent outwent proverb seabear suspend veriest feoffer tankful
impresa masseur overeat prowess sealegs swinery vermeil feoffor tearful
impress masters pampean prudent sealery tableau vespers firefly tentfly
imprest mastery pampero prudery seaweed taffeta villein fistful testfly
inanely mattery Pandean puckery secrecy tailend violent flamfew thrifty
inbreed maxwell pandect puffery secrete tangelo viscera forkful toilful
indwell mayweed parpend pungent segment tangent waggery fretful traffic
indwelt mercery parvenu putrefy sequela tannery walleye gainful trayful
infield meseems pastern pygmean sequent tatters wanness gallfly truffle
inflect midweek pasteup quavery seriema tattery warhead giraffe tuneful
ingress Midwest patient quivery serpent taxless Watteau gleeful twelfth
inkwell midyear pattern rackety servery tealeaf wayless goutfly venefic
inquest mildewy paydesk raggedy sexless tempera weekend griffin vivific
inspect milreis payment ragweed shakeup tempest western griffon wailful

wakeful
whiffle
wishful
wistful
woolfat
zestful
abought
acrogen
alleged
allegro
alright
amalgam
ambages
amongst
antigen
armiger
assagai
assegai
atingle
avenger
bedight
blowgun
blunger
bologna
bragged
bragger
bringer
brought
changer
charger
chigger
chugged
clanger
clogged
clogger
cologne
cragged
cringer
cringle
cryogen
decagon
delight
demigod
dowager
dragged
draggle
draught
dredger
drought
drudger
drugged
drugget
eclogue
endogen
energid
engaged
epergne
eulogia
evangel
exergue
fallguy
fatigue
finagle
flagged
flaught
flogged
forager
fourgon
fraught
freight
frogged
georgic
goatgod
granger
halogen
handgun
hexagon
hindgut
homager

hypogea
illegal
insight
insigne
integer
kerogen
kerygma
lasagna
lasagne
lounger
lyingin
lyingly
manager
mutagen
myalgia
myalgic
nonagon
nosegay
obligee
obligor
octagon
paragon
patagia
pelagic
perigee
phlegmy
piragua
pirogue
pledgee
pledger
pledget
pledgor
plugged
plugger
plunger
podagra
polygon
pronged
ravager
realgar
refugee
relight
remiges
reneger
renegue
rontgen
scraggy
shingle
shingly
shogged
shotgun
skegger
slagged
sleight
slinger
sloegin
slogged
slogger
sloughy
slugged
slugger
smidgen
smidgin
smuggle
snagged
snigger
sniggle
snuggle
socager
spadger
spangle
spangly
sparger
sponger
spongin
spriggy
stagger
stinger
stopgap

strigil
swagged
swagger
swigged
swinger
swingle
tanager
tanagra
teargas
thigger
thought
thuggee
tonight
trangam
trigger
tringle
trudgen
twangle
twigged
unpaged
unright
unsight
upright
uptight
veliger
vinegar
visaged
voyager
wanigan
whangee
whinger
wrangle
wriggle
wriggly
wringer
wrongly
wrought
yatagan
younger
zymogen
abashed
airship
alcohol
another
apishly
apothem
bacchic
banshee
beechen
belcher
bellhop
bencher
benthic
benthos
birchen
blather
blether
blighty
blither
blucher
blusher
bolshie
botcher
bouchee
bowshot
brashly
brothel
brother
brusher
Brython
burghal
burgher
burthen
butcher
camphor
canthus
catcher
catchup
clothes

coacher
conchae
conchie
couthie
cowshed
crochet
crusher
cumshaw
cyathus
darshan
dauphin
deathly
Delphic
ditcher
dolphin
doughty
drachma
drogher
droshky
dryshod
earshot
earthen
earthly
edaphic
epithem
epithet
epochal
eyeshot
farther
feather
fifthly
fitchet
fitchew
flasher
fleshed
flesher
fleshly
flighty
freshen
fresher
freshet
freshly
further
Galahad
gingham
glyphic
gnathic
godship
graphic
greyhen
gryphon
guichet
gumshoe
gunship
gunshot
hardhit
harshen
harshly
hatcher
hatchet
haughty
heathen
heather
heighho
highhat
hitcher
hotshot
iceshow
Irishry
isochor
ketchup
kinchin
kinship
Kirghiz
kitchen
knowhow
kolkhoz
Krishna
latchet

laugher
leather
legshow
loather
loathly
longhop
luncher
lurcher
lymphad
lynchet
manchet
manihot
marcher
markhor
marshal
matchet
mauther
menthol
merchet
midship
moither
monthly
moocher
moorhen
morphia
mosshag
mouther
murther
narthex
narwhal
naughty
neither
Noachic
norther
notched
nunship
nylghau
nymphal
nymphet
oneshot
outshot
panther
paschal
percher
pincher
pitched
pitcher
pithhat
plushly
poacher
potshot
pouched
prithee
prophet
psychic
puncher
punchup
pyrrhic
Quechua
rancher
raschel
ratchet
reacher
roadhog
rosehip
roughen
roughly
rumshop
sapphic
satchel
seawhip
sibship
sixthly
slasher
slather
slither
sloshed
smasher
smashup

smother
somehow
sonship
soother
soothly
sorghum
souther
spathic
sulphur
swasher
swither
sylphid
syrphid
tanghin
teacher
teachin
teashop
telpher
tenthly
thither
toothed
torchon
touched
toucher
touchup
toughen
toughly
toyshop
trachea
trishaw
trochal
trochee
trochus
trophic
tulchan
urethan
urethra
Vaishya
vouchee
voucher
warship
warthog
watcher
weather
weigher
weighin
weighty
welcher
welsher
wencher
whether
whither
worship
writhen
xanthic
xanthin
abaxial
Abelian
abiding
ability
abolish
abscise
abusive
Acadian
acarian
acetify
Achaian
acidify
acidity
aconite
acquire
Adamite
adaxial
adenine
adjoint
aeolian
aeonian
affaire
afflict

agility
agonise
agonist
aiblins
airlift
airline
airmiss
airsick
alanine
alation
alcaide
alewife
alltime
alodial
alodium
alumina
alunite
amanita
amative
amazing
amboina
amenity
Amerind
amorist
amplify
amusive
Ananias
Anglian
anglice
angling
Anglist
angrily
anguine
anguish
aniline
anility
animism
animist
annuity
anodise
anthill
antlion
anytime
anywise
apatite
applied
applier
appoint
apprise
Arabian
arabise
Arabist
archive
aridity
armlike
armoire
arraign
ascribe
asinine
asocial
asquint
astride
atavism
atavist
atelier
atheism
atheist
atomise
atomism
atomist
attaint
attrite
auction
auspice
avarice
avidity
azurine
azurite
Baalism

babbitt
babyish
backing
baddish
baggily
bagging
bagpipe
Bahaism
Bahaist
Bahaite
bailiff
balding
baldish
balmily
bambini
bambino
banking
banning
banting
baptise
baptism
baptist
barline
barrier
barring
bassist
basting
bastion
bathing
batting
bauxite
bawdily
beading
beamish
bearing
bearish
beatify
beating
bedding
bedside
bedtime
beehive
beeline
begging
begrime
beguile
beguine
Belgian
belting
belying
benzine
bepaint
berline
berried
bestial
bethink
betting
betwixt
biaxial
bibbing
biblist
bidding
biggish
bigtime
billing
billion
binding
bionics
biotite
bitting
blemish
blewits
blueing
boarish
boating
bobbing
bobbish
boiling
bonfire

bonnily
booking
bookish
boorish
boozily
bopping
bornite
bossism
bowline
bowling
boxkite
boxlike
bracing
brazier
brevier
brevity
British
broking
bromide
bromine
bromism
brucine
brucite
brutish
bruxism
buccina
budding
bugging
bulkily
bullion
bullish
bumming
bumpily
bunting
burning
burnish
bushido
busking
bussing
cabling
caddice
caddish
cadmium
caesium
caitiff
calcify
calcine
calcite
calcium
calling
cambial
cambist
cambium
camping
campion
candied
cannily
canning
cantina
canting
capping
caprice
caprine
Capsian
capsize
caption
captive
carbide
carbine
cardiac
carking
carline
Carlism
Carlist
carmine
carping
carrier
carrion
carsick

carving cashier cassino castile casting casuist catbird catfish catlike catling catmint cattily caution ceilidh ceiling cellist Celsius centime certify cervine cession chalice charily chariot charism charity chemise chemism chemist cherish cheviot chiliad chocice choline chopine chorine chorion citrine civvies clarify clarion clarity clavier clerisy Cluniac coaming coating coaxial cocaine cockily codeine codfish codling coeliac coexist cogging cognise coition coldish collide collier collins coltish combine compile Comtian Comtism Comtist concise condign confide confine confirm coniine conning connive consign consist convict

cooking coolish copaiba copaiva coppice copyist coquito cordial cordite corking cornice cornily Cornish cornist corrida cortile corvina corvine cosmism cosmist costing costive cottier Coueism courier cowbird cowfish cowhide cowlick cowling cranial cranium craving crazily crevice crimine crinite crosier crozier crucial crucian crucify crudity cubbing cuisine cullion cultism cultist cunning cupping cuprite curling currier currish cursive cushion cutline cutting cyanide cyanine cyanite cyclist Cyprian Cypriot cystine czarina czarism czarist dabbing dacoity Dadaism Dadaist dallier damming damnify damning dampish dandify darbies

darkish darling darning dashiki dashing dawning daytime dealing debrief deceive decking decline decrier deicide delaine density dentine dentist deprive derrick dervish despise despite destine destiny diarise diarist dibbing diction digging dignify dignity dimming dimmish dingily dinning diorism diorite dioxide dipping dirtily dislike dislimn dismiss distich distill dizzily dockise dogfish dogging doggish dollish doltish donning donnish Dorking dormice dornick dossier dotting dowdily drawing driving droving dualise dualism dualist duality dubbing ducking ductile ducting dulcify dullish dumpish dunbird Dunkirk dunning duskily

dustily earring easting ebbtide ebonise ebonite eccrine echoism edacity edifice edition egality egotise egotism egotist elation elegiac elegise elegist elision elitism elitist Elohism Elohist elusion elusive elution eluvial eluvium elysian Elysium emeriti emetine emotion emotive emprise emptier emptily emption enation endwise English enprint enquire enquiry entwine entwist epoxide eremite erlking erosion erosive erotica erotism erudite escribe esquire etamine etching etesian Etonian eucrite evanish evasion evasive evening examine exotica exscind exuviae exuvial eyelike eyewink fabliau faction faddish faddism faddist fagging

failing fairing fairish falling falsies falsify falsity fancier fancily fanning farcing farming farrier fascial fascine Fascism Fascist fashion fatling fatting fattish fatuity faucial faunist fauvism fauvist febrile feeding feeling felsite felting fencing fenfire fermion fermium ferrite fertile festive feudist fibbing fictile fiction fictive fideism fideist fierily fifties figging filling finding finning Finnish fishily fishing fissile fission fitting flaming flavine fleeing Fleming Flemish flexile flexion florist fluting flutist fluvial fluxion flyting fobbing foggily fogging fogyish fogyism folding follies foolish footing

fopling foppish foreign forging forgive forties fortify fossick fowling fragile Frisian fugging fuguist fulmine funnies funnily funning furbish furmity furnish furrier furring furtive fussily fustian fustily fuzzily gabbing gadding gagging gahnite gallice galling galliot gallium gambier garfish garnish garpike gasfire gasring gassing gatling gaudily Gaulish gawkily gearing gelding gelling gemming genning gentian gentile genuine getting gharial giddily gigging gilding gimmick gingili ginning girlish glacial glacier glaring glazier glazing glorify glozing glycine gnomish goatish godlike godling golfing goodish Gordian gosling

gossipy gracile gradine granita granite gratify grating gravity grazier grazing Grecian grecise Grecism gremial greyish Grobian Grolier grunion Gstring guanine gubbins gumming gummite gunfire gunning gushing gustily gutsily gutting gwyniad gypping hacking hafnium hagfish haggish halting hamming handily hanging happily happing harpist harrier hashish hastily hatting haulier hawkish hayrick haywire headily heading hearing heating heavily heftily hellion hellish helping hemline hemming henwife herniae hernial hernias heroics heroine heroise heroism herring hessian hetaira hilding hipping hircine hitting Hittite Hobbian Hobbism

Hobbist hogfish hogging hoggish holding holmium hopbind hoplite hopping horrify horsily hospice hostile hottish housing howling huffish hugging hulking humming Hunnish hunting hurling hurried huskily husking Hussite hutting hyaline hyalite hydride hygeian hymnist Iberian icerink idolise imagine imagism imagist impaint imprint inanity inbuilt incline inflict ingoing initial inkling inquire inquiry inspire inswing intwine inutile inveigh invoice Iranian iridise iridium ironing ironist ischial ischium Ismaili itacism Italian Italiot itemise ivories jabbing jadeite Jainism jamming Janeite jarring jasmine jaybird jazzily jellied

jerkily jetting jewfish jibbing jigging jobbing jogging joining jollify jollity jotting joyride Judaise Judaism Judaist judoist jugging juggins juicily Jungian jussive justice justify jutting Kaddish kainite Kantian Karaite karting keeping kenning kentish keyring khedive kidding kiddish killick killing kissing knavish knowing koumiss Kurdish kyanise kyanite lacking lagging laicise laicism Lamaism Lamaist lamming lampion landing lankily Laotian lapping lapwing largish lashing lasting lathing latrine lattice Latvian lawlist leading leaning lection leftism leftist legging lemming lending lentigo lentisk leonine lesbian letting

Lettish	melting	netfish	Paphian	poetics	rasping	running	sickish	stonily
leucine	memoirs	netlike	paprika	poetise	ratlike	Russian	signify	storied
leucite	mending	netting	partial	poloist	ratling	Russify	signior	stovies
licking	mention	neurine	parting	pontiff	ratting	rustily	Sikhism	straits
lignify	merrily	niblick	partita	pontify	rawhide	rutting	silkily	studied
lignite	messiah	niceish	partite	poorish	readily	ruttish	sillily	stygian
lilting	Messias	nigrify	parvise	poppied	reading	Sabaism	sinning	stylise
lionise	messily	niobium	passing	popping	realign	sacking	sipping	stylish
lipping	mestiza	nippily	passion	porcine	realise	sacring	Sistine	stylist
listing	mestizo	nipping	passive	portico	realism	sacrist	sitting	stylite
lithium	metrics	nitride	pastime	portion	realist	saddish	Sivaism	suasion
loading	metrist	nitrify	patrial	posting	reality	sagging	Sivaite	suasive
loaning	midline	nitrile	patriot	potting	rebuild	sailing	sixaine	suavity
lobbing	midriff	nitrite	patting	pouting	rebuilt	Saktism	sixties	subbing
lodging	midwife	nodding	paucity	praline	receipt	salpinx	Sixtine	sublime
loftily	milking	nogging	Pauline	pravity	receive	salsify	skating	subside
logging	million	noisily	pebrine	precise	recline	salting	skilift	subsidy
logline	mincing	nooning	peckish	predial	rectify	saltire	skolion	subsist
longing	mirkily	nothing	peevish	predict	reddish	saltish	skyhigh	subtile
longish	misfire	nourish	pegging	prelims	redwing	sapling	skyline	sucking
looking	misgive	nuclide	pelting	premier	reeding	sapping	slating	suction
lopping	mislike	nullify	pending	premise	rejoice	sardine	slavish	suffice
lording	missile	nullity	pennies	premiss	remains	sardius	Slavism	suicide
lotting	missing	nunnish	pennill	premium	rentier	sarking	slimily	suiting
loudish	mission	nuptial	pennine	preside	repaint	sashimi	slowish	sulkily
lousily	missish	nursing	penning	preview	replica	saucily	smokily	summing
loutish	missive	nutlike	pensile	previse	replier	saurian	smoking	sunbird
lowlily	mistily	nutpine	pension	priming	reprint	sawbill	snakily	sundial
lowrise	mistime	nutting	pensive	privily	reprise	sawfish	snowily	sundisc
luckily	misting	oakling	peppill	privity	reptile	sawmill	soaking	sunfish
Luddite	Moabite	oarfish	pepping	probity	requiem	scabies	soapily	sunnily
lugging	mobbing	obelise	peptide	prodigy	require	scarify	soaring	sunning
lumpily	mobbish	obelisk	peptise	profile	requite	scoriae	sobbing	Sunnite
lumpish	mollify	obesity	percine	promise	rescind	scorify	softish	sunrise
lustily	mondial	ocarina	perfidy	propine	respire	scoring	soggily	sunwise
lyddite	monkish	oculist	perkily	prosify	respite	scotice	soldier	supping
machine	moodily	odalisk	perlite	prosily	restiff	Scotism	soloist	surfing
madding	mooring	offside	Permian	protist	restive	Scotist	soonish	surlily
Madeira	Moorish	ogreish	Persian	protium	rethink	seabird	sootily	surmise
maffick	mopping	oilbird	persist	provide	retrial	seafish	sophism	survive
magnify	moraine	oldtime	petrify	proviso	retsina	seagirt	sophist	suspire
Mahdism	moreish	olefine	Petrine	proximo	retting	seapink	soppily	Swahili
Mahdist	morning	olivine	pettily	prudish	reunion	seasick	sopping	Swedish
maidish	mortice	omneity	petting	pruning	reunite	seaside	Sorbian	swinish
maidism	mortify	onanism	pettish	prurigo	revving	seating	sordini	syenite
mailing	mortise	onetime	phonics	publish	rewrite	seawife	sordino	sylvine
malaise	mousing	ongoing	phonily	puckish	rhenium	sectile	sorrily	sylvite
malting	muddily	opacity	photism	pudding	rhodium	section	sotting	tabbing
mangily	mudfish	opaline	physics	puerile	rhymist	seedily	sottish	tachism
mankind	mugging	opening	pianism	pugging	ribbing	seeming	soubise	tachist
manlike	muggins	opinion	pianist	puggish	ridding	seizing	sourish	tacking
manning	mullion	oration	Pictish	pugmill	ridging	selfish	spacial	tactics
mannish	mummify	orifice	pietism	pulvini	rifling	septime	spacing	tactile
mannite	mumming	Orphism	pietist	punning	rigging	Serbian	spaniel	taction
mansion	mumpish	ostrich	pigging	pupping	rimming	serpigo	Spanish	taeniae
mansize	mundify	otolith	piggish	purlieu	ringing	serried	sparing	tagging
mapping	munnion	outlier	pigling	purview	ripping	Servian	spatial	tailing
marking	munting	outline	pillion	pushing	riptide	service	special	talking
marline	muonium	outlive	pimping	puttier	roaring	servile	species	tallish
marlite	murkily	outride	pinfire	putting	robbing	serving	specify	tallith
marmite	muzzily	outside	pinfish	pycnite	rockier	Servite	spicily	tamping
married	myalism	outsize	pinking	Pythian	rockily	sessile	spikily	tampion
marring	mystify	ovarian	pinkish	qualify	rocking	session	spirits	tanning
martial	mythise	ovation	pinning	quality	rodding	sestina	spodium	tannish
Martian	mythist	ovicide	pipping	querist	rodlike	setting	squails	tantivy
martini	nabbing	oxidise	piscina	queuing	roguish	sextile	stabile	tapping
Marxian	nagging	Oxonian	piscine	quinine	rollick	sferics	stadium	tardily
Marxism	napping	ozonise	pismire	rabbity	rolling	shadily	stagily	tarnish
Marxist	nastily	pachisi	pithily	raffish	roofing	shading	staging	tarrier
massive	nattily	packice	pitting	ragging	rotting	shakily	stamina	tarring
mastich	nautics	packing	planish	ragtime	rousing	Shavian	staniel	tartish
mastiff	nautili	padding	platina	railing	routine	shaving	statice	tastily
matting	Naziism	pallium	plating	rallier	rowdily	Shemite	statics	tattily
mattins	nebbish	palmist	playing	ralline	rubbing	sheriff	station	tatting
mawkish	neglige	palsied	plenish	ramming	rubbish	shoeing	statism	taurine
Maytime	Negrito	pannier	plosion	rampion	ruching	shoring	statist	taxiing
mealies	neolith	panning	plosive	ranking	ruction	showily	stative	taxying
meaning	nervine	panties	pluvial	raphide	ruddily	showing	sterile	tearing
meeting	nesting	pantile	podding	rapping	ruffian	sibling	stibine	teatime

tedding
teeming
tegmina
tektite
telling
tenpins
tensile
tension
tensity
tensive
tenuity
tequila
terbium
tergite
termini
termite
terrier
terrify
terrine
tertial
tertian
testify
testily
textile
theriac
Thomism
Thomist
thorite
thorium
thulium
thymine
ticking
tigrish
tinnily
tinning
tipping
tipsify
tipsily
tithing
titling
titmice
Titoism
Titoist
tompion
tontine
tooling
topping
topside
tormina
torpids
torsion
tortile
Toryism
totting
touring
tourism
tourist
towline
townish
trading
trilith
trinity
tritium
trivial
trivium
tropics
tropism
trucial
tsarina
tsarism
tsarist
tubbing
tubbish
tugging
tuition
tundish
tunning
turbine
turdine

turfite
Turkish
turning
turnipy
tussive
tutting
twibill
twoline
twotime
tychism
Umbrian
unbuild
unbuilt
unction
undoing
undying
unfaith
unicity
unifier
unitive
unjoint
unquiet
unstick
unthink
untried
untwine
untwist
untying
upraise
upswing
Uralian
uralite
uranide
uranism
uranium
uterine
utilise
utility
utopian
utopism
utopist
uxorial
vaccine
vacuity
vaguish
vampire
vampish
varmint
varnish
varsity
vastity
vatting
veiling
veining
verdict
vermian
vernier
versify
versine
version
vertigo
vespine
vestige
vetting
viatica
viduity
viewing
violist
vitrify
vitrine
vitriol
voguish
vulpine
wadding
wagging
waggish
waiting
walking
walling

wannish
wanting
warlike
warmish
warning
warring
warrior
wartime
washing
waspish
waxbill
waxwing
waybill
wayside
weakish
wearily
wearing
webbing
wedding
wedging
weevily
wellies
Wendish
wergild
westing
wetting
wettish
whaling
wheyish
whiting
whitish
whorish
wickiup
wigging
wilding
wildish
willies
willing
windily
winding
winning
wishing
witling
wittily
witting
wolfish
wolvish
woozily
wordily
wording
working
worrier
writing
wrybill
Yahvist
Yahwist
yapping
yenning
Yiddish
yipping
Yorkist
yttrium
zapping
zaptieh
zebrine
zeolite
zillion
zincify
zincing
zincite
zinkify
zinking
Zionism
Zionist
zipping
zoarium
Zoilism
Zoilist
belljar

brinjal
harijan
jumpjet
killjoy
lockjaw
muntjac
muntjak
propjet
sapajou
betaken
betoken
blacken
blackly
blanket
blankly
bleakly
blinker
blocker
bracken
bracket
breaker
breakin
breakup
brickie
brickle
brisken
brisket
briskly
brocket
bumpkin
canakin
canikin
caulker
checker
checkup
chicken
chuckle
chukker
clacker
clarkia
clerkly
clicker
clinker
clocker
cracked
cracker
crackle
crackly
crackup
crankle
cricket
crinkle
crinkly
croaker
crocket
crooked
doeskin
dogskin
dovekie
drinker
drunken
finikin
flanker
flecker
flicker
flunkey
frankly
freaked
freckle
freckly
frisker
frisket
gherkin
glaikit
grackle
griskin
Halakah
hearken
karakul

kidskin
knacker
knocker
knockon
knuckle
ladykin
lambkin
lashkar
latakia
limpkin
manakin
manikin
meerkat
minikin
moniker
nonskid
oilskin
passkey
pigskin
placket
pliskie
plucker
plunker
pricker
pricket
prickle
prickly
pumpkin
quicken
quickie
quickly
ramekin
rebuker
redskin
retaken
shackle
shanked
shicker
shirker
shocker
shucker
skinker
skulker
slacken
slacker
slackly
sleeken
sleekit
sleekly
slicker
slickly
slinker
smacker
sneaker
snicker
snooker
snorkel
spanker
sparkle
speaker
speckle
spunkie
stacker
stalked
stalker
starkly
steekit
sticker
stickit
stickle
stickup
stinker
stocker
stonker
striker
stuckup
swanker
thankee
thanker

thicken
thicket
thickly
thinker
tracker
trekked
trekker
tricker
trickle
tricksy
trinket
trinkum
trucker
truckle
turnkey
twankay
twinkle
twinkly
unasked
whacker
whicker
whisker
whiskey
whizkid
wrecker
wrinkle
wrinkly
younker
zincked
aboulia
absolve
acrylic
acyclic
airflow
airglow
alcalde
alfalfa
alkalis
allelic
ampulla
angelic
angelus
angular
annelid
annular
annulet
annulus
antilog
aphelia
aphylly
areally
areolae
areolar
areolas
aurally
aurelia
awfully
axially
axillae
axillar
babbler
bacilli
backlog
baffler
banally
barilla
basilar
Benelux
bibelot
bifilar
bipolar
bivalve
bobsled
boggler
booklet
boomlet
bootleg
bottled
botulin

bouilli
braille
brawler
broiler
buckler
bucolic
bumbler
bungler
burbler
burglar
bustler
cackler
cajoler
camelot
camelry
capelin
castled
Catalan
catalos
catalpa
cavally
cavalry
cedilla
Chablis
challis
chaplet
charley
charlie
chillum
cichlid
cipolin
circler
circlet
civilly
cobbler
cochlea
coddler
complex
complin
complot
conflux
copilot
copular
corella
corolla
corslet
coupler
couplet
courlan
cowslip
crawler
criollo
cruelly
cruelty
cruller
cumulus
cupular
dabbler
Danelaw
dangler
dawdler
dazzler
defiler
Delilah
devalue
develop
devilry
devolve
dewclaw
dialled
diddler
dipolar
display
divulge
doodler
doubler
doubles
doublet
drabler

drawler
driblet
driller
droplet
drumlin
ducally
duelled
dueller
dweller
earflap
earplug
echelon
effulge
eggflip
eidolon
embolic
embolus
enfiled
envelop
epaulet
epsilon
equally
escolar
expulse
fabular
faculae
faculty
famulus
fanclub
fatally
feedlot
fibulae
fibular
fibulas
fiddler
finally
flatlet
flyblow
fondler
foreleg
frailly
frailty
fuddler
fuelled
fueller
fugally
fumbler
gabbler
gabelle
galilee
gambler
gamelan
ganglia
gantlet
garbler
gateleg
gazelle
ghillie
giggler
girdler
gnarled
gobbler
Gobelin
goggler
goggles
gorilla
gremlin
greylag
grilled
griller
growler
gunplay
guzzler
gymslip
hackler
haggler
hamulus
handler
harelip

harslet
heckler
hidalga
hidalgo
higgler
hobbler
hoodlum
hooklet
hostler
humbles
hurdler
hurdles
hustler
icefloe
ideally
idyllic
impulse
indulge
infulae
inhaler
insular
insulin
invalid
involve
jangler
javelin
jewelry
jingler
jocular
jubilee
juggler
jugular
jurally
kindler
kinglet
kneeler
knurled
kremlin
labella
lakelet
lamella
lanolin
lapilli
lavolta
leaflet
legally
levelly
limulus
lobelia
lobular
locally
locular
loculus
loyally
loyalty
lunular
lupulin
maculae
macular
mahaleb
maillot
mamelon
mamilla
manilla
manille
mantlet
marbled
marbles
marplot
martlet
matelot
maudlin
maxilla
measles
Mechlin
meddler
medulla
melilot
mettled

micelle
milkleg
mimulus
misplay
modally
modular
modulus
moonlit
moorlog
morally
morello
morulae
morular
Moselle
mottled
mouflon
muddler
mudflat
muffler
mumbler
muscled
muzzler
mycelia
nacelle
nasally
nauplii
nebulae
nebular
nebulas
necklet
needler
nibbler
niggler
nobbler
nodally
nodular
nonplus
nonslip
notelet
novella
novelle
novelty
numbles
ocellar
ocellus
ortolan
osculum
osselet
outflow
outplay
overlap
overlay
overlie
pabulum
paddler
paisley
papally
papilla
papulae
papular
parolee
parsley
partlet
patella
pearled
pearler
peddler
penally
penalty
perplex
phallic
phallus
phellem
pickled
piffler
pikelet
pilular
playlet
popular
preplan
problem
prowler
ptyalin
puddler
pupilar
puzzler
pyralid
pyralis
queller
quillet
rabbler
radulae
radular
rambler
rattler
ravelin
reallot
regalia
regally
regular
regulus
remblai
repulse
resolve
revalue
revelry
reviler
revolve
riddler
riffler
ringlet
ripplet
rivalry
rivulet
rocklet
rootlet
rosella
royally
royalty
rubella
ruffler
rumbler
rundlet
rurally
rustler
saddler
sampler
sandlot
saveloy
scaglia
scallop
scarlet
scholar
scholia
scollop
sculler
seablue
seaslug
secular
sedilia
seedlip
semilog
settler
settlor
shallop
shallot
shallow
shaslik
shellac
shelled
sheller
shiplap
shrilly
similar
similor
simpler
simplex
simular
singlet
sizzler
skellum
skidlid
skilled
skillet
skyblue
smeller
snarler
snarlup
sozzled
speller
spieler
spiller
spoiler
squalid
squally
squalor
squelch
stabler
stables
stapler
starlet
starlit
stealer
stealth
stellar
sterlet
stifler
subplot
suckler
surplus
swallow
swiller
swollen
tabular
tackler
Tagalog
tartlet
tattler
tegular
Templar
templet
thallic
thallus
thiller
tickler
tidally
tiddler
tiddley
timelag
tingler
tippler
titular
toddler
toeclip
tonally
torulae
totally
townlet
trailer
trawler
trellis
triblet
trifler
triolet
triplet
triplex
troller
trolley
trollop
tubular
tumbler
tumular
tumulus
tutelar
twilled
udaller
ungulae
upsilon
usually
vagally
vanilla
veinlet
venally
verglas
vexilla
virelay
vitally
vitelli
vittles
vitular
vocalic
vocally
vowelly
waddler
warbler
wattled
wattles
wavelet
wheeled
wheeler
whirler
whitlow
whorled
wiggler
winglet
wobbler
woolled
woollen
yulelog
abdomen
abysmal
ackemma
agnomen
albumen
albumin
almsman
anaemia
anaemic
anosmia
anosmic
ashamed
attempt
baseman
batsman
bellman
betimes
bilimbi
birdman
bitumen
bloomer
boatman
bogyman
bohemia
bondman
bookman
Brahman
Brahmin
brimmed
brimmer
bulimia
bushman
cacumen
calamus
calomel
calumet
calumny
caramel
caveman
ceramic
cerumen
chapman
charmer
chlamys
chromic
chummed
claimer
clammed
clubman
crammed
crammer
creamer
decimal
decuman
delimit
digamma
dilemma
doorman
doormat
drayman
dreamed
dreamer
drummed
drummer
duramen
dustman
dynamic
encomia
endemic
entomic
enzymic
exhumer
filemot
fireman
flagman
flummox
footman
foramen
foreman
freeman
frogman
galumph
gleeman
glimmer
glummer
goodman
gourmet
grammar
grimmer
grommet
grummet
hangman
hanuman
headman
highman
hillman
hornmad
incomer
inhuman
Islamic
isthmus
jacamar
jazzman
juryman
keramic
kinsman
krimmer
lineman
linkman
lorimer
mailman
manumit
Manxman
maremma
marimba
maximal
maximum
meatman
metamer
miasmal
miasmic
milkman
minimal
minimum
minimus
molimen
monomer
mousmee
myxomas
nelumbo
newsman
oarsman
oenomel
oghamic
optimal
optimum
ottoman
overman
packman
pajamas
phasmid
pikeman
plasmic
plasmid
plasmin
plummet
polemic
polymer
postman
potamic
preempt
primmed
Pullman
putamen
pyaemia
pyaemic
pyjamas
pyramid
racemic
railman
regimen
roadman
rodsman
rollmop
sandman
schemer
scrimpy
scrumpy
scummed
seismal
seismic
shammed
shammer
shimmer
shipman
shopman
showman
skimmed
skimmer
skimmia
slammed
slimmer
slummed
slummer
snowman
sokeman
Solomon
squamae
stammel
stammer
steamer
stemmed
strumae
stummed
surfman
swagman
swarmer
swimmer
tapsman
taximan
telamon
thermae
thermal
thermic
thiamin
thrombi
thrummy
thummim
tinamou
tollman
tonemic
totemic
trammel
trimmed
trimmer
trismus
triumph
trommel
turfman
unarmed
unkempt
uraemia
velamen
vidimus
vitamin
volumed
wireman
woodman
workman
yardman
yashmak
yeggman
absence
absinth
acronym
actinia
actinic
actinon
addenda
adjunct
adrenal
advance
affined
against
alginic
alienly
alkanet
allonge
almanac
almoner
almonry
alumnae
alumnus
ambones
ammonal
ammonia
ancones
andante
anginal
anionic
antenna
antonym
aphonia
aphonic
aplenty
arcanum
ardency
arrange
arsenal
arsenic
askance
avionic
balance
baloney
bananas
baronet
basenji
basinet
bayonet
beatnik
begonia
beignet
biennia
bigener
bimanal
blarney
boloney
bonanza
borings
botanic
brannew
braunch
brownie
bubonic
bygones
Byronic
bywoner
cabinet
cacanny
cadence
cadency
cadenza
calando
calends
canonic
canonry
carinae
carinal
carinas
catenae
catenas
cayenne
centner
channel
charnel
Chianti
chignon
chimney
chronic
chunnel
chutney
cleaner
cleanly
cleanse
cleanup
cockney
coconut
cogency
colonel
colonic
coranto
coronae
coronal
coronas
coroner
coronet
cozener
crannog
craunch
crooner
crowned
crowner
crownet
decanal
decency
defence
definer
defunct
demonic
derange
detinue
diurnal
diviner
dominie
doyenne
dozenth
dragnet
drainer
durance
echinus
effendi
eirenic
empanel
enhance
enounce
entente
envenom
equinal
equinox
ermined
errancy
essence
eternal
ethanol
eugenic
expanse
expense
expunge
extinct
faience
Falange
feigner
felonry
feminal
filings
finance
finings
firenew
fishnet
fixings
flannel
flaunty
flounce
fluence
fluency
fraenum
galanga
galenic
gallnut
Gehenna
gillnet
gleaner
grained
grainer
grannie
grapnel
graunch
greenly
greenth
grinned
grownup
Guignol
hackney
hairnet
hapence
hapenny
havenot
hebenon
hedonic
heronry
hominid
homonym
hosanna
humanly
hymenia
immense
impanel
impinge
incense
infancy
infanta
infante
ingenue
innings
intense
intoner
jacinth
jaconet
japonic
jejunum
journal
journey

joyance
kalends
Koranic
laconic
lacunae
lacunal
lacunar
lacunas
ladanum
laminae
laminar
latency
learned
learner
licence
license
liminal
locknut
lomenta
lorgnon
loriner
lozenge
lucency
lumenal
luminal
lychnis
madonna
magenta
mahonia
makings
malines
mariner
Masonic
masonry
matinal
matinee
meconic
melange
melanic
melanin
memento
mesonic
metonym
Mishnah
misknow
momenta
morendo
moronic
mourner
nominal
nominee
obconic
oceanic
offence
opsonic
opsonin
ordinal
organic
organon
organum
organza
osmunda
oxfence
paeonic
paginal
palings
pardner
paronym
parsnip
partner
patency
penance
petunia
pfennig
phoenix
phrenic
phrensy
pilsner
pimento
piranha
plainly
planned
planner
pliancy
polenta
polynia
polynya
potence
potency
pudency
queenly
ramenta
ravined
ravings
recency
refined
refiner
regency
reginal
repiner
retinae
retinal
retinas
retinol
retinue
revenge
revenue
rhamnus
rhiancy
romance
Romanic
Romansh
rooinek
rotunda
saponin
sarangi
satanic
satinet
savanna
savings
scanned
scanner
science
scorner
scranny
scrunch
scunner
seconde
secondi
secondo
selenic
seminal
seminar
seringa
seventh
seventy
shinned
shrinal
shunned
shunner
silence
silenus
skinned
skinner
soignee
solanum
sonance
sonancy
spanned
spanner
spawner
sphenic
spignel
spinner
spinney
splenic
spooney
springe
springy
spurner
sputnik
squinch
squinny
stainer
stannic
staunch
stepney
sternal
sterned
sternly
sternum
sthenic
strange
stringy
stunned
stunner
swanned
syconia
synonym
syringa
syringe
tabanid
tabinet
takings
taloned
technic
tenancy
tenoner
tetanic
tetanus
thinned
thinner
thorned
throned
tidings
titanic
tomenta
topknot
toponym
tourney
trainee
trainer
trounce
truancy
tutenag
twinned
typonym
tyranny
umbonal
umbones
uncanny
uncinus
unfunny
unhandy
unhinge
unlined
unmanly
untuned
urgency
vacancy
valance
valence
valency
valonia
Vedanta
veranda
vicinal
vintner
vixenly
volante
wagoner
wakener
whatnot
wingnut
wizened
womanly
ziganka
abalone
abscond
acerola
acerose
acetone
acetous
acinous
adenoid
adenoma
adipose
affront
agamous
agelong
airhole
airlock
airport
airpost
aliform
alimony
alphorn
althorn
alveoli
amatory
amorous
amphora
amyloid
amylose
anagoge
anagogy
analogy
anatomy
anchovy
android
anemone
aneroid
angioma
anurous
anxious
anybody
anymore
anyroad
apagoge
apocope
apodous
apology
approve
aqueous
arctoid
arduous
armhole
artwork
aureola
aureole
awesome
axolotl
azygous
balcony
balloon
bandore
banjoes
bannock
barroom
bassoon
bawcock
bazooka
becloud
bedpost
bedrock
bedroll
bedroom
bedsock
bedsore
behoove
beknown
bellows
benzoic
benzoin
benzole
benzoyl
bespoke
betroth
bibcock
bighorn
bilboes
bilious
billowy
biltong
biology
bistort
bittock
blowout
bongoes
boobook
bottony
boudoir
boxroom
boxwood
boycott
boyhood
bricole
bridoon
brumous
buffoon
bugloss
bulbous
bullock
bumboat
burdock
burnous
buttock
buttons
buttony
caboose
cahoots
callous
camwood
candour
canzone
canzoni
caproic
cardoon
carioca
cariole
carious
carload
carport
carroty
cartoon
caseous
cassock
castoff
catboat
cathode
cathood
cestode
cestoid
chalone
chamois
cheroot
chibouk
chicory
Chinook
choroid
chymous
cineole
cirrose
cirrous
cladode
clamour
coccoid
colloid
combout
comfort
commode
commons
commove
compony
comport
compose
compost
compote
concoct
concord
condole
condone
conform
conjoin
connote
console
consort
contort
contour
convoke
cookout
copious
cordoba
corpora
corrode
corrody
cottony
couloir
coulomb
cowpoke
coxcomb
cremona
cricoid
crinoid
ctenoid
cubhood
cuckold
cupmoss
cuprous
curiosa
curious
cursory
custody
customs
cutworm
cycloid
cyclone
cyclops
cystoid
dapsone
dariole
daybook
daylong
dayroom
daywork
defrock
defrost
deiform
deltoid
deplore
despoil
despond
devious
dewpond
diabolo
diamond
dingoes
diploid
diploma
dipnoan
discoid
discord
dishorn
disjoin
disport
dispose
disrobe
disroot
distort
doggone
dogrose
dogwood
dortour
dragoon
dromond
dropout
drydock
dubious
dunnock
duopoly
duteous
dyewood
earhole
earlobe
earlock
ecology
economy
eelpout
eelworm
eggcosy
einkorn
elfbolt
elflock
elusory
embroil
embrown
emulous
enamour
enclose
endlong
endmost
enfeoff
engross
entropy
envious
epidote
epigone
epigoni
episode
epitome
epizoic
epizoon
erelong
ericoid
ethiops
ethmoid
euphony
explode
exploit
explore
eyebolt
eyehole
eyesore
faceoff
factory
fadeout
falloff
fallout
fanfold
fantods
fargone
farmost
fatuous
felwort
fernowl
ferrous
fervour
festoon
fetlock
fibroid
fibroin
fibroma
fibrous
figwort
flatout
flavour
flyboat
flybook
foghorn
foldout
foliole
foliose
forbode
forbore
fordone
forgoer
forgone
forlorn
forsook
forworn
foveola
foxhole
frijole
fulgour
fullout
fulsome
fulvous
fungoid
fungous
furioso
furious
furlong
furrowy
fuscous
futhorc
futhork
futtock
gadroon
galloon
gallows
gamboge
garboil
gascoal
gaseous
geckoes
geogony
geology
gibbous
glamour
glenoid
globoid
globose
glucose
godhood
gondola
gorcock
gossoon
grumose
grumous
gumboil
gumboot
gunboat
gunlock
gunroom
haddock
hammock
handoff
handout
hangout
haploid
harbour
harmony
harpoon
hassock
haycock
hayfork
hayloft
heinous
hemiola
hemione
hemlock
hencoop
hickory
hideous
hideout
hillock
hipbone
hiproof
histone
history
hoedown
holmoak
hormone
hotfoot
hugeous
hummock
hyaloid
hydroid
hydrous
hymnody
hypnoid
iceboat
icecold
icefoot
igneous
impious
implode
implore
improve
inclose
indoors
ingroup
ingrown
inkhorn
inshore
introit
ipomoea
irksome
isokont
isonomy
isotope
isotopy
jannock
jargoon
jawbone
jealous
jibboom
jibdoor
jumpoff
juncoes
kampong
kathode
keyhole
keynote
keyword
kickoff
kinfolk
lactose
lampoon
lardoon
lassoes
lavrock
lawlord
leadoff
leghorn
legroom
legwork
lentoid
leprosy
leprous
letdown
leucoma
lichowl
liftoff
ligroin
limbous
lineout
lissome
lithoid
liveoak
lobworm
lockout
logbook
logwood
lookout
lowborn
lowdown
lughole
lugworm
luteous
lychowl

madrona
madrono
madwort
mafiosi
mafioso
maggoty
mahjong
maltose
mammock
mammoth
mandola
mandora
mangoes
mangold
manhole
manhood
manhour
mannose
marconi
marrowy
mastoid
mattock
mattoid
matzoth
mawworm
maypole
meadowy
menfolk
microbe
midmost
milfoil
miscopy
misdone
mistook
moidore
monsoon
morwong
mugwort
mullock
muttony
myeloid
myeloma
myology
nacrous
narrows
necrose
negroid
neology
neozoic
nervous
network
neuroma
neurone
newborn
newcome
newmown
nitrous
niveous
nocuous
noisome
noology
noxious
nunhood
oakwood
oarlock
obovoid
obvious
ochrous
odorous
offload
oloroso
ominous
onerous
onshore
onymous
oospore
operose
oratory
orology

osseous
osteoid
ostiole
otology
outcome
outdone
outdoor
outfoot
outgone
outlook
outmost
outport
outpost
outrode
outsold
outsole
outvote
outwore
outwork
outworn
oviform
oxytone
paddock
padlock
padrone
padroni
pairoar
palmoil
pandora
pandore
papoose
pappose
parboil
parlour
parlous
partook
patroon
paviour
payload
payroll
peacock
peafowl
peasoup
pentode
pentose
peptone
percoid
perform
pergola
persona
petiole
petrous
pibroch
piccolo
piceous
piddock
pillock
pillory
pillowy
pinfold
pinhole
pinworm
pissoir
pistole
piteous
pitpony
placoid
plafond
platoon
playoff
plumose
plywood
pollock
pompous
pontoon
popcorn
pothole
pothook
precook

predoom
preform
presoak
prolong
promote
pronoun
propone
propose
prosody
provoke
provost
pteroic
puccoon
pugnose
pullout
pulpous
purloin
purport
purpose
putdown
putlock
pygmoid
quinone
quixote
raccoon
ragbolt
ragdoll
ragworm
ragwort
Rajpoot
rakeoff
ramsons
rancour
rapeoil
rapport
rations
raucous
ravioli
readout
rectory
redcoat
redpoll
redwood
refloat
regroup
reproof
reprove
respond
restock
restore
rewrote
rhizoid
rhizome
rhodora
ribwork
ribwort
riotous
ripcord
rissole
rockoil
roseola
rowboat
rowlock
rubdown
rubeola
rubious
ruddock
ruinous
rundown
Sabaoth
sallowy
salvoes
santour
saprobe
sapwood
sarcode
sarcoid
sarcoma
sarcous

sauroid
saviour
sawnoff
sawwort
saxhorn
schlock
schnook
scotoma
scrooge
seaboot
seafood
seafowl
seaport
searoom
seawolf
sellout
sendoff
senhora
sensory
sequoia
serious
setdown
sexfoil
shadoof
shadowy
showoff
shutout
shylock
sialoid
sigmoid
signora
signore
signori
signory
sinuous
sirloin
sitdown
sixfold
skyborn
someone
sparoid
spinode
spinoff
spinose
spinous
spumous
spyhole
steroid
stopoff
styloid
subjoin
subsoil
succory
succour
sucrose
Suffolk
summons
sundown
sunroof
support
suppose
surcoat
surtout
syncope
systole
tabloid
tadpole
takeoff
talcose
talcous
tallowy
tambour
tandoor
tanooze
tapioca
taproom
taproot
teacosy
teagown

tearoom
tearose
tedious
teleost
tenfold
tenuous
testoon
tetrode
thyroid
timeous
tinfoil
tinhorn
toehold
tombola
tombolo
tomfool
topcoat
tophole
topmost
topsoil
torgoch
towboat
towmond
towmont
towrope
travois
trefoil
tremolo
tricorn
triform
trilogy
tripody
tripoli
tritone
tugboat
turdoid
turmoil
turnout
tussock
tussore
tutwork
twofold
twosome
twotone
typhoid
typhoon
typhous
uberous
unblock
uncloak
unclose
uncross
uncrown
unfrock
unfroze
unicorn
uniform
unknown
unloose
unquote
unroost
unswore
unsworn
uranous
urology
vacuole
vacuous
vamoose
variola
variole
various
Vaudois
Veddoid
verbose
vicious
victory
villose
villous
violone

viscose
viscous
voivode
walkout
Walloon
warlock
warlord
washout
waxwork
wayworn
webfoot
webworm
wedlock
welcome
welloff
werwolf
willowy
winnock
winsome
without
witloof
wooloil
workout
wornout
xiphoid
yellowy
zealous
zebroid
zipcode
zoogony
zoology
zoonomy
zootomy
agrapha
apropos
atrophy
autopsy
bleeper
bullpen
calipee
caliper
calypso
Canopic
catspaw
cesspit
champac
champak
chapped
chappie
charpoy
cheapen
cheaply
chipped
chipper
chopped
chopper
clapped
clapper
claypan
clipped
clipper
clippie
cockpit
copepod
crampet
crampit
crampon
crappie
creeper
crimper
crimple
cripple
crisper
crisply
cropped
cropper
crumpet
crumple
crupper

dashpot
deadpan
decapod
decuple
dripped
dropped
dropper
duckpin
dustpan
eclipse
ectopic
ellipse
escapee
escaper
eupepsy
example
exempla
eyespot
felspar
flapped
flapper
fleapit
flipped
flipper
flopped
footpad
forepaw
frapped
fripper
fusspot
galipot
glimpse
grampus
grapple
grasper
gripped
gripper
grouper
groupie
hairpin
hardpan
headpin
hexapla
hexapod
incipit
indepth
insipid
jackpot
jaloppy
juniper
kingpin
knapped
knapper
kneepan
lycopod
maniple
metopic
metopon
ninepin
notepad
occiput
octopod
octopus
octuple
oedipal
Olympic
overpay
panoply
parapet
pitapat
playpen
plopped
plumper
plumply
polypod
polypus
priapic
propped
prosper

quipped
relapse
repaper
saltpan
sandpit
scalpel
scalper
scamper
scapple
scarper
scauper
schappe
scooper
scorper
Scorpio
scraper
scrapie
scrappy
scruple
sculpin
scupper
semiped
shampoo
sharpen
sharper
sharply
shilpit
shinpad
shipped
shippen
shipper
shippon
shopped
shopper
sickpay
sinopia
skidpan
skipped
skipper
skippet
slapped
sleeper
slipped
slipper
slopped
snapped
snapper
snipped
snipper
snippet
snooper
soliped
stamper
steepen
steeple
steeply
stemple
stepped
stepper
stewpan
stewpot
stipple
stirpes
stopped
stopper
stopple
striped
strophe
stroppy
stumper
sunspot
swapped
swapper
sweeper
swipple
swopped
swopper
synapse
talipes

talipot
tentpeg
thumper
tosspot
traipse
trample
trapped
trapper
tripped
tripper
trippet
tripple
trooper
trouper
trumpet
tylopod
unhappy
unhoped
usurper
washpot
whimper
whipped
whipper
whippet
whisper
whoopee
whooper
whopper
woodpie
wrapped
wrapper
ycleped
antique
baroque
bezique
brusque
cacique
charqui
macaque
oblique
obloquy
perique
relique
repique
Salique
siliqua
silique
subaqua
abjurer
accurst
adherer
admiral
admirer
adverse
afeared
aileron
aircrew
airdrop
Alcoran
aleuron
alforja
Alkoran
allergy
almirah
alsoran
Amharic
anagram
andiron
aneurin
anthrax
apparat
apparel
apteryx
aquaria
Armoric
ascarid
ascaris
ashtray
asperse

aspirer
aspirin
assured
assurer
asteria
athirst
augural
aurorae
auroral
auroras
austral
autarky
averred
baldric
begorra
beshrew
bestrew
Biafran
bistred
bizarre
blurred
botargo
bourree
buckram
butyric
cabaret
caldron
caloric
calorie
caltrap
caltrop
camaron
cambrel
cambric
cameral
camorra
cantrip
caperer
caporal
caserne
catarrh
cateran
caterer
central
centred
centric
centrum
chagrin
charred
cheerer
cheerio
chevron
chirrup
chloral
chloric
ciboria
cidaris
clearly
coherer
comfrey
control
costrel
coterie
coverup
culprit
decorum
deforce
demerit
demirep
denarii
deserve
destroy
deterge
dewdrop
dextral
dextran
dextrin
diadrom
diagram

dimeric
diverge
diverse
divorce
dogtrot
eagerly
eardrop
eardrum
egotrip
elderly
elytron
elytrum
embargo
emperor
empiric
emporia
endarch
enderon
endorse
enforce
engorge
enlarge
enteral
enteric
enteron
enthral
environ
epigram
equerry
esparto
etaerio
etheric
excerpt
excurse
exedrae
externe
eyebrow
eyedrop
Faberge
federal
femoral
figtree
figural
figured
filaria
fimbria
firtree
fleuret
fleuron
floorer
flytrap
footrot
foreran
forerun
Fortran
foxtrot
friarly
Fuehrer
fulcrum
funeral
gambrel
gangrel
gastric
general
generic
goitred
gomeral
gomeril
gorcrow
grogram
gumdrop
haporth
heparin
Homeric
Homerid
humdrum
humeral
humerus
humoral

hundred
hyperon
icteric
icterus
ignorer
illbred
immerge
immerse
immoral
imperil
incurve
indorse
infarct
inferno
inherit
injurer
innards
innerve
insured
insurer
interim
interne
inverse
inwards
isogram
isotron
jogtrot
kestrel
kindred
labarum
lamprey
lateral
layered
lazaret
legiron
leveret
liberal
liberty
literal
liturgy
louvred
loverly
lowbred
lowbrow
lucarne
lucerne
lustral
lustrum
malaria
mandrel
mandril
mantram
mantrap
Masorah
mayoral
mazurka
megaron
menorah
minaret
mineral
minorca
miserly
mistral
monarch
mongrel
muskrat
myogram
nacarat
natural
navarin
nephric
neutral
neutron
nomarch
nombril
noniron
noserag
nostril
nostrum

numeral
numeric
oaktree
observe
obverse
odoured
oestral
oestrum
oestrus
oildrum
omicron
oneiric
onwards
oratrix
orderer
orderly
orphrey
outcrop
outgrew
outgrow
overran
overrun
palfrey
paperer
papyrus
parerga
peloria
peloric
pelorus
pierrot
pigiron
pilgrim
piperic
pitprop
pleurae
pleural
pleuron
pomfret
portray
poverty
prairie
Prakrit
program
puberal
puberty
puggree
puparia
pushrod
pyloric
pylorus
quadrat
quadric
quarrel
queerly
rattrap
rebirth
rectrix
recurve
referee
regards
regorge
remarry
remorse
reserve
respray
resurge
retired
returns
reverie
reverse
reversi
rivered
rosered
rostral
rostrum
ruderal
saffron
sakeret
samurai

sangria
satiric
satyral
satyric
satyrid
scabrid
scarred
scherzi
scherzo
sciarid
scirrhi
scleral
scourer
scourge
scurril
securer
senarii
senores
several
shearer
sheerly
sherris
sierran
sistrum
skirret
slurred
sneerer
soberly
solaria
sororal
sparred
sparrow
spheral
spheric
splurge
spoorer
sporran
spurred
spurrey
squarer
squirmy
starred
stearic
stearin
steerer
stirred
stirrer
stirrup
suberic
suberin
suburbs
sudaria
suntrap
sutural
sutured
swearer
synergy
tabaret
taborer
talaria
tamarin
tangram
tantric
tantrum
taperer
taxfree
teatray
tectrix
telergy
tendril
theorbo
theorem
theurgy
tiderip
timbrel
tonerow
tortrix
towards
towered

tumbrel
tumbril
ulcered
underdo
undergo
unearth
unhorse
unmoral
unnerve
unscrew
upsurge
upthrew
upthrow
upwards
utterer
utterly
valeric
velaria
venerer
ventral
vestral
veteran
viceroy
visored
vivaria
wagerer
wallrue
wastrel
watered
waterer
waverer
waxtree
whirred
windrow
wolfram
yewtree
zymurgy
Abbasid
abyssal
accusal
accused
accuser
acrasin
advised
adviser
advisor
aerosol
alyssum
amnesia
amnesic
amnesty
anoesis
aphasia
aphasic
apheses
aphesis
aplasia
arousal
artisan
artiste
ascesis
asepsis
askesis
atresia
auxesis
babassu
babysit
backsaw
backset
bagasse
bandsaw
banksia
batiste
benison
bheesty
biassed
blessed
blossom
blouson

boneset
booksie
bortsch
bransle
brassie
browser
bruiser
bucksaw
buzzsaw
caisson
canasta
celesta
celeste
ceresin
chanson
chassis
chessel
chiasma
chooser
choosey
chrisom
christy
classes
classic
classis
clausal
coarsen
cockshy
colossi
counsel
courser
crassly
cresset
crimson
Croesus
crossly
cruiser
curtsey
damosel
deepsea
dehisce
demesne
deposal
deposit
devisal
devisee
deviser
devisor
dibasic
divisor
dresser
dynasty
ecdyses
ecdysis
embassy
embosom
emersed
entasis
erepsin
excusal
exposal
exposed
exposer
exposit
filasse
filmset
finesse
floosie
flotsam
focused
footsie
foresaw
foresay
foresee
freesia
fretsaw
frisson
frowsty
fuchsia

gainsay
geneses
genesis
genista
girasol
glassen
glasses
glossal
Glossic
greaser
greisen
grossly
grouser
guesser
hacksaw
handsaw
handsel
handset
hardset
headset
hearsay
hoarsen
hocused
honesty
idlesse
impasse
impaste
impasto
imposer
incised
incisor
incused
indusia
ingesta
keelson
kenosis
khamsin
kinesis
kneesup
liaison
Liassic
limosis
looksee
majesty
malison
malmsey
medusae
medusan
medusas
meiosis
Meissen
melisma
menisci
milksop
mimesis
mitoses
mitosis
modesty
modiste
molossi
moonset
morassy
Moresco
Morisco
mycoses
mycosis
myiasis
nemesia
nemesis
nonuser
odyssey
opossum
opposer
osmosis
oversaw
oversea
oversee
overset
oversew

parasol
paresis
Pegasus
pelisse
perusal
peruser
petasus
phrasal
piously
pleased
podesta
poussin
praiser
presser
pressup
prussic
pyrosis
quassia
quetsch
refusal
refuser
reissue
reposal
reposit
revisal
reviser
revisit
ricksha
riposte
rudesby
samisen
satisfy
scepsis
scissel
scissor
Senussi
silesia
skepsis
sorosis
soursop
splashy
sponson
sponsor
spousal
squashy
squishy
stemson
stepson
stetson
sycosis
synesis
tabasco
tamasha
thirsty
thyrsus
tootsie
transit
transom
treason
tressed
tressel
trouser
trusser
trypsin
typeset
unbosom
unfussy
upriser
utensil
vanessa
venison
verismo
vinasse
warison
wellset
whimsey
whipsaw
Whitsun
Windsor

winesap boaster cubital fletton holster monster punster senator stretto
woolsey bobstay cuittle flitted hydatid mounter puritan senatus stunted
yolksac boletus culotte flitter identic Mountie pyretic shaitan stutter
zygosis bolster cunette floater idiotic mozetta pyrites shaster styptic
zymosis booster curator fluster igniter mulatto pyritic shastra sumpter
abattis borstal curette flutter ileitis musette quantic shatter sunstar
abetted boulter cuvette foretop impetus mycotic quantum sheathe swarthy
abetter brantle daystar fouette inaptly naphtha quartan shelter swatted
abettor brantub debater fracted inciter necktie quarter sheltie swatter
abiotic brattle deictic Fraktur inditer neritic quartet shifter sweater
ablator breathe deistic frantic ineptly neuston quartic shittim sweeten
aborter breathy delator fretted inertia nightie quester shooter sweetie
abutted bristle demotic fritted inertly nightly questor shorten sweetly
abutter bristly devoted fritter invitee Nilotic quieten shortie swelter
acantha brittle devotee frontal inviter nodated quietly shortly swiftly
Achates brittly digital fronton jacktar nonstop quietus shotten swotted
acroter builtin dilated frosted janitor notitia quilter shouter symptom
adapter builtup dilator fructed jointer nunatak quintal shunter tabetic
adaptor burette dilutee fruited jointly octette quintan shutter tacitly
adeptly burster diluter fruiter jouster odontic quintet shuttle tagetes
adopter bushtit dilutor frustum jujitsu oersted quintic shyster tapetal
adultly calotte dimeter gagster Jupiter oldster quitted sighted tapetum
aerator capital dinette galatea kenotic omental quitter sightly tapster
agnatic capitol diopter gametic keratin omentum ratatat simitar taunter
alertly capstan dioptre garotte kiloton omitted reactor skeeter Telstar
allstar carotid docetic gauntly kinetic onestep realtor skelter tempter
aloetic carotin dogstar gauntry knitted oolitic recital skirted theatre
ambatch caustic donator gavotte knitter ophitic reciter skirter thistle
amentia cavetti doubter gazette knotted opuntia reenter skitter thistly
amentum cavetto draftee gelatin knotter orbital reentry skittle Tibetan
ammeter chanter drafter genetic krypton orectic refutal slantly tighten
amputee chantry drastic genette Laputan osmotic refuter slatted tightly
annates chaotic dratted genitor layette osseter regatta slotted timothy
annatta chapter drifter ghastly legatee outstay related smarten tipster
annatto charter drouthy ghettos legator overtax relater smartly toaster
anoetic chasten edictal ghostly leister overtly relator smatter tractor
aphetic chatted eductor giantry lengthy overtop reputed smelter traitor
aphotic chattel eidetic glisten levator painter Rhaetic smitten tranter
apostil chatter ejector glister licitly palatal ribston smutted treater
apostle cheater ekistic glitter lighted paletot ricotta snifter treetop
aquatic cheetah elastic glottal lighten palette ridotto snorter trental
arbiter chested elastin glottis lighter paretic righten snouted trestle
arbutus chintzy Eleatic glutted lightly parotid righter solatia trotted
arietta chitter elector glutton limited peartly rightly somatic trotter
aristae Choctaw electro glyptal limiter phaeton ringtaw somitic trustee
aristas chortle emitted glyptic linctus phantom risotto sorites truster
ascetic chunter emitter gnostic litotes philter riveter Spartan tryptic
ascites clastic empathy godetia lobster philtre roaster spastic tweeter
ascitic clatter enactor grafter locater phratry rocktar spatted twister
aseptic clotted entitle grantee lorette piastre roister spattee twitted
Asiatic cluster entotic granter lunatic picotee rolltop spatter twitter
astatic clutter epistle grantor lunette pinetum rooftop spectra twostep
auditor clyster equator greaten lyrated pipette rooster spectre unaptly
auxetic coaltit erectly greatly maestri piratic rosette spelter unbated
Avestan coastal erector grifter maestro pivotal rotator spitted unfitly
Avestic coaster ergates gristle mahatma pivoter rouster spitter unhitch
aviator cocotte eristic gristly maintop plantar royster spittle unlatch
barytes coletit erratic gritted manatee planter sagitta splotch uveitis
barytic colitis erratum grottos manitou plaster sainted sporter vaulted
bathtub cometic Euratom grunter Maratha plastic saintly spotted vaulter
beastly comitia evictor gruntle Marathi plastid saluter spotter vaunter
belated conatus exactly grutten marital platted sanctum spouter vedette
bewitch coontie exactor habitat mashtub platter Sanctus spurtle vegetal
bheetie coulter excited habitue megaton plectra saunter sputter venatic
bigoted counter exciter Hamitic meiotic plotted scantly squatty vidette
bigotry country exciton hamster messtin plotter scatted squitch visitor
biretta courtly excitor hardtop mightst pointed scatter staithe voluted
blasted creator faceted haunted militia pointer scented starter volutin
blaster crested fagotto haunter mimetic politic sceptic startle waisted
blatter cristae faintly healthy minster pomatum sceptre stentor waister
bleater critter fanatic hearted minutes poofter sciatic stetted waratah
blintze crofter feaster hearten minutia poulter scooter stilted washtub
blister crouton fibster heeltap misstep poultry Scottie Stilton wealthy
bloated crowtoe fighter helotry mitotic praetor scouter stouten webster
bloater crustal firstly hepatic mobster prattle scratch stoutly wheaten
blotted crusted flatten heretic mofette printer scutter stratum whetted
blotter cryptal flatter heritor moisten proctor scuttle stratus whetter
bluntly cryptic flattop hilltop moistly psalter sematic stretch whistle
bluster crystal fleetly hipster monitor punctum Semitic stretta whittle

wiretap
worsted
wreathe
wreathy
wrestle
written
zemstvo
zetetic
zonated
zygotic
zymotic
account
accrual
acequia
acicula
adjourn
aground
aliquot
ampoule
anchusa
apolune
armfuls
armoury
asexual
assault
astound
azimuth
banquet
barbule
bascule
because
bedouin
biscuit
bismuth
bivouac
bordure
borough
bouquet
bravura
briquet
bulrush
caesura
cagoule
calculi
cannula
capsule
capture
carouse
catsuit
cellule
censure
century
chequer
cingula
circuit
circusy
cliquey
closure
cloture
coagula
coequal
collude
colours
coloury
combust
commune
commute
compute
concuss
conduce
conduct
conduit
confuse
confute
conjure
conquer
consult
consume
contuse

cornual
cornuto
corrupt
costume
couture
croquet
croquis
culture
cumquat
curcuma
dasyure
debauch
debouch
default
degauss
delouse
demount
denture
deplume
detrude
diffuse
discuss
diseuse
disgust
dispute
disrupt
disturb
earmuff
encrust
enthuse
entrust
enwound
epicure
erasure
espouse
evacuee
evolute
exclude
execute
exhaust
expound
extrude
factual
facture
failure
falcula
farruca
feature
ferrugo
ferrule
fissure
fistula
fixture
flexure
floruit
formula
fortune
fossula
foxhunt
frenula
furcula
geebung
gemmule
gesture
globule
gradual
granule
gravure
guayule
guipure
hachure
Hamburg
helluva
heyduck
hiccupy
hirsute
homburg
honours
humbuzz

imbrute
impound
include
incrust
infauna
inhouse
inocula
insculp
intrude
intrust
jonquil
jumbuck
Kalmuck
kibbutz
kumquat
lacquer
languet
languid
languor
lawsuit
leaguer
lecture
legpull
leisure
lettuce
lingual
mahound
manhunt
marquee
marquis
masquer
measure
mercury
misrule
mixture
mollusc
mowburn
mugwump
multure
Neptune
nervure
netsuke
noctuid
noctule
nocturn
nonsuch
nonsuit
nurture
obitual
obscure
obtrude
occlude
orotund
outrush
outturn
overuse
oviduct
parquet
pasture
penguin
percuss
perdure
perfume
perfuse
perjure
perjury
permute
perturb
pertuse
picquet
picture
pillule
pinguid
pinnule
pintuck
planula
plumule
pollute
poseuse

posture
potluck
prelude
presume
primula
procure
produce
product
profuse
purpura
purpure
pursuer
pursuit
pustule
racquet
rapture
rebound
recluse
recount
recruit
redoubt
redound
rehouse
remould
remount
rescuer
resound
retouch
rewound
roebuck
romaunt
rondure
rorqual
rupture
saccule
sacculi
sambuca
satsuma
savoury
sawbuck
sawdust
saxtuba
scapula
schmuck
scopula
scrouge
seagull
seclude
seizure
sensual
seppuku
serpula
skijump
soilure
sojourn
spatula
specula
spicula
spicule
spinule
sporule
statued
stature
statute
stimuli
stipule
subdual
subduct
subdued
subfusc
subsume
succuba
succubi
succumb
suffuse
sunburn
sunsuit
tactual
tarbush

Tartufe
tempura
testudo
textual
texture
through
tilbury
tittupy
tonsure
topfull
torture
traduce
tribune
tribute
triduan
triduum
unbound
uncouth
unequal
unhouse
unsound
unstuck
untruly
untruss
untruth
unusual
unwound
valvula
valvule
vapours
vapoury
vascula
velours
veloute
venture
venturi
verdure
verruca
vesture
viaduct
victual
vincula
virgule
virtual
vulture
wafture
yoghurt
akvavit
allover
alluvia
Angevin
aquavit
aquiver
arrival
arriver
bedevil
behaver
beloved
bolivar
cadaver
caravan
caravel
chervil
cleaver
datival
deliver
disavow
duumvir
dwarves
Elzevir
enliven
flivver
flyover
forever
Genevan
godevil
greaves
groover
however

inwoven
mailvan
minever
miniver
mitzvah
octaval
palaver
popover
recover
removal
removed
remover
revival
reviver
revivor
samovar
scarves
sheaves
shelved
shelves
shrivel
shriven
sleeved
striven
striver
synovia
thieves
thriven
twelves
uncivil
uncover
unmoved
unravel
unsaved
unwoven
vetiver
wharves
whoever
archway
areaway
beeswax
bejewel
caraway
catawba
chinwag
cutaway
doorway
embowed
embowel
embower
empower
fairway
faraway
fishway
flyaway
folkway
footway
freeway
gangway
gateway
getaway
halfway
halfwit
hallway
headway
highway
imbower
parkway
pathway
periwig
postwar
railway
renewal
renewer
roadway
ropeway
runaway
scrawly
scrawny

screwed
screwer
shipway
sideway
slipway
someway
sprawly
strewth
thalweg
thrower
throwin
tideway
tramway
unbowed
walkway
widowed
widower
adnexal
apraxia
calyxes
eutexia
hypoxia
hypoxic
indexer
latexes
murexes
planxty
pyrexia
pyrexic
unboxed
unmixed
unsexed
acolyte
alcayde
amboyna
analyse
analyst
anodyne
arrayer
assayer
bergylt
berhyme
bugeyed
byebyes
caloyer
carryon
condyle
decrypt
delayer
dialyse
diptych
dryeyed
embryon
epigyny
eponymy
essayer
essoyne
fedayee
forayer
halcyon
honeyed
inlayer
isohyet
Malayan
martyry
metayer
moneyed
moneyer
oneeyed
oophyte
palmyra
pharynx
pieeyed
popeyed
pteryla
relayed
restyle
Samoyed
sinsyne

sprayer
sprayey
strayer
talayot
tallyho
Vandyke
vilayet
alcazar
assizes
bedizen
blowzed
borazon
britzka
citizen
damozel
denizen
deutzia
drizzle
drizzly
endozoa
entozoa
floozie
frazzle
freezer
frizzle
frizzly
genizah
grizzle
grizzly
hoatzin
horizon
metazoa
mezuzah
muezzin
pretzel
quetzal
quizzed
quizzer
quizzes
seltzer
sneezer
snoozer
snoozle
Switzer
swizzle
tweezer
waltzer
whizzed

---

abaxial
Abelian
abysmal
abyssal
Acadian
acarian
accrual
accusal
Achaean
Achaian
acrobat
adaxial
admiral
adnexal
adrenal
aeolian
aeonian
African
alcazar
Alcoran
Alkoran
allheal
allstar
almanac
almirah
almsman
alodial
alsoran
alumnae
amalgam

amildar
ammonal
amoebae
amoebas
anagram
Ananias
anginal
Anglian
angular
annular
antbear
anthrax
anyroad
apogean
apparat
apsidal
Arabian
archway
areaway
areolae
areolar
areolas
aristae
aristas
arousal
arrival
arsenal
artisan
asexual
ashtray
asocial
assagai
assegai
augural
aurorae
auroral
auroras
austral
autocar
Avestan
axillae
axillar
Azilean
backsaw
bananas
bandeau
bandsaw
baseman
basilar
batsman
beanbag
beeswax
Belgian
belljar
bellman
besmear
bespeak
bestead
bestial
Biafran
biaxial
bifilar
bifocal
bighead
bilobar
bimanal
bipedal
bipolar
birdman
bivouac
boatman
bobstay
bogbean
bogyman
bolivar
bondman
bookman
Boolean
borstal

bowhead
boxseat
Brahman
brinjal
buckram
bucksaw
bugbear
bullbat
bumboat
burghal
burglar
bushman
buzzsaw
Cadmean
caltrap
cambial
cameral
capital
caporal
Capsian
capstan
caracal
caravan
caraway
cardiac
carinae
carinal
carinas
carload
Catalan
catboat
catenae
catenas
cateran
cathead
catspaw
caveman
central
champac
champak
chapman
chateau
cheddar
cheetah
chiliad
chinwag
chloral
Choctaw
chordal
chuddah
chuddar
Circean
clausal
claypan
cloacae
cloacal
clubman
Cluniac
clypeal
coastal
coaxial
coeliac
coequal
comical
Comtian
conceal
conchae
congeal
conical
cooncan
copular
copycat
cordial
corneal
cornual
coronae
coronal
coronas
costean
cotidal
courlan
cranial
creedal
cristae
crowbar
crucial
crucian
crustal
cryptal
crystal
csardas
cubical
cubital
cudbear
cumquat
cumshaw
cupular
curacao
cutaway
cynical
Cyprian
czardas
Danelaw
Dantean
darshan
datival
daystar
deadpan
decadal
decanal
decimal
decuman
Delilah
deposal
devisal
dewclaw
dextral
dextran
diagram
digital
dipnoan
dipolar
display
disseat
diurnal
djibbah
dogstar
domical
doorman
doormat
doorway
drawbar
drayman
dustman
dustpan
earflap
edictal
egghead
elegiac
eluvial
elysian
enteral
enthral
entreat
epigeal
epigean
epigram
epochal
equinal
escheat
escolar
estreat
eternal
etesian
ethical
Etonian
excusal
exedrae
exposal
exurban
exuviae
exuvial
fabliau
fabular
factual
faculae
fairway
faraday
faraway
fascial
fastday
fathead
faucial
federal
felspar
feminal
femoral
fibulae
fibular
fibulas
figleaf
figural
finical
fireman
fishway
flagday
flagman
flatcap
flatcar
fleabag
floreat
flotsam
fluidal
fluvial
flyaway
flyboat
flyleaf
flytrap
folkway
footman
footpad
footway
forbear
foreman
forepaw
foreran
foresaw
foresay
Fortran
freeman
freeway
fretsaw
Frisian
frogman
frontal
funeral
fustian
gainsay
Galahad
gamebag
gamelan
gangway
gascoal
gateway
general
Genevan
genizah
gentian
geoidal
getaway
gharial
gingham
glacial
gleeman
glossal
glottal
gluteal
glyptal
goahead
godhead
golfbag
gomeral
gonadal
goodday
goodman
Gordian
gradual
grammar
grandad
grandam
Grecian
gremial
greylag
Grobian
grogram
gunboat
gunplay
gwyniad
habitat
hacksaw
Halakah
halfway
hallway
handbag
handcar
handsaw
hangman
hanuman
hardpan
harijan
headman
headway
hearsay
heeltap
helical
hellcat
herniae
hernial
hernias
hessian
highhat
highman
highway
hillman
Hobbian
hockday
holiday
holmoak
hophead
hornmad
hothead
humeral
humoral
hygeian
Iberian
iceboat
ilkaday
illegal
immoral
implead
indican
infulae
inhuman
initial
insofar
instead
insular
intreat
Iranian
irideal
ischial
isogram
Italian
jacamar
jackdaw
jacktar
jazzman
jemadar
jocular
journal
Judaean
jugular
Jungian
juryman
Kantian
khaddar
kilobar
kinsman
klipdas
kneecap
kneepan
kumquat
kursaal
lacteal
lacunae
lacunal
lacunar
lacunas
laminae
laminar
Laotian
Laputan
lashkar
lateral
Latvian
lesbian
lethean
lexical
liberal
liminal
lineman
lingual
linkman
Linnean
lipread
literal
liveoak
lobular
lockjaw
locular
logical
longday
loricae
lumenal
luminal
lunular
lustral
lymphad
lyncean
lyrical
macadam
maculae
macular
magical
mailbag
mailman
mailvan
Malayan
manteau
mantram
mantrap
Manxcat
Manxman
manyear
marital
marshal
martial
Martian
Marxian
Masorah
matinal
maximal
mayoral
meatman
medical
medusae
medusan
medusas
meerkat
menorah
messiah
Messias
Mexican
mezuzah
miasmal
midyear
milkman
milldam
mimical
mineral
minicab
minicar
minimal
misdeal
mishear
Mishnah
mislead
misplay
misread
mistral
mitzvah
modular
monacal
mondial
morulae
morular
mosshag
mudflat
muntjac
muntjak
musical
muskrat
myogram
myxomas
nacarat
nameday
narwhal
natural
nebulae
nebular
nebulas
neutral
newsman
nodical
nodular
nominal
noonday
nosebag
nosegay
noserag
notepad
nuclear
numeral
nunatak
nuptial
nylghau
nymphal
oarsman
oatmeal
obitual
ocellar
octaval
oedipal
oestral
offbeat
offload
offpeak
omental
oppidan
optical
optimal
orbital
ordinal
Orphean
ortolan
ottoman
outplay
outstay
outwear
ovarian
overeat
overlap
overlay
overman
overpay
overran
oversaw
overtax
ovoidal
Oxonian
packman
paginal
pairoar
pajamas
palatal
paludal
pampean
Pandean
papadam
Paphian
papulae
papular
parkway
partial
paschal
pathway
patrial
payload
pedicab
pelican
pemican
Permian
Persian
perusal
phrasal
piglead
pigmean
pikeman
pilular
pinhead
pitapat
pithead
pithhat
pivotal
plantar
plateau
pleurae
pleural
pluvial
polecat
poohbah
popular
portray
postbag
postman
postwar
pothead
poundal
predial
preheat
preplan
presoak
program
protean
puberal
Pullman
pupilar
puritan
pygmean
pyjamas
Pythian
quadrat
quartan
quetzal
quintal
quintan
quondam
radical
radulae
radular
railcar
railman
railway
Ramadan
ratatat
rattrap
realgar
recital
redcoat
redhead
refloat
refusal
refutal
reginal
regular
remblai
removal
renewal
reposal
respray
retinae
retinal
retinas
retread
retreat
retrial
revisal
revival
ringtaw
roadman
roadway
rocktar
rodsman
rondeau
ropeway
rorqual
rosebay
rostral
rouleau
rowboat
ruderal
ruffian
runaway
Russian
saltcat
saltpan
samovar
samurai
sandbag
sandbar
sandman
saphead
satyral
saurian
scandal
scholar
scleral
scoriae
scribal
seabear
secular
seismal
seminal
seminar
sensual
Serbian
Servian
several
shaitan
Shavian
shebear
shellac
shinpad
shiplap
shipman
shipway
shopman
showman
shrinal
sickbay
sickpay
sidecar
sideway
sierran
similar
simitar
simular
skidpan
slipway
slotcar
snowcap
snowman
sokeman
someday
someway
Sorbian
soroban
sororal
soybean
spacial
Spartan
spatial
special
spheral
sporran
spousal
squamae
stellar
sternal
stewpan
stoical
stopgap
strumae
stygian
subadar
subdean
subdual
subhead
sunbeam
sunbear
sundial
sunstar
suntrap
surcoat
surfman
surreal
sutural
swagman
synodal
tableau
tabular
tactual
taeniae
tangram
tankcar
tapetal
tapsman
taxicab
taximan
tealeaf
teargas
teatray
tegular
Telstar
Templar
tertial
tertian
testban
textual
thereat
theriac

thermae
thermal
Tibetan
tideway
tiebeam
timelag
titular
tollbar
tollman
tonneau
topcoat
topical
torulae
towboat
towhead
tramcar
tramway
trangam
trental
triduan
trishaw
trivial
trochal
trucial
trumeau
truncal
tubular
Tuesday
tugboat
tulchan
tumular
turfman
tutelar
tutenag
twankay
typebar
typical
umbonal
Umbrian
unclean
uncloak
unequal
ungulae
unideal
unmoral
unswear
unusual
Uralian
urethan
utopian
uxorial
Vatican
vegetal
ventral
verglas
vermian
vesicae
vesical
vestral
veteran
vicinal
victual
vinegar
virelay
virtual
vitular
walkway
wanigan
waratah
warhead
Watteau
weekday
whereas
whereat
whipsaw
wildcat
windbag
winesap
wireman

wiretap
wolfram
woodman
woolfat
workbag
workday
workman
yardman
yashmak
yatagan
yeggman
yolksac
zooidal
ascribe
bilimbi
catawba
copaiba
cordoba
crybaby
disrobe
earlobe
escribe
hushaby
jellaba
lullaby
marimba
mastaba
microbe
nelumbo
Panjabi
placebo
Punjabi
redoubt
rudesby
saprobe
sassaby
saxtuba
scrubby
shrubby
squabby
standby
suburbs
succuba
succubi
syllabi
theorbo
thereby
thrombi
wallaby
whereby
wouldbe
abreact
abroach
absence
adjunct
advance
afflict
airlock
airsick
ambatch
ambsace
amtrack
anglice
ardency
askance
attract
auspice
avarice
balance
bannock
barrack
bawcock
bedrock
bedsock
beseech
bewitch
bibcock
bionics
bittock

bortsch
braunch
bullace
bullock
burdock
buttock
caddice
cadence
cadency
calpack
caprice
carioca
carrack
carsick
cassock
chalice
chocice
cogency
collect
compact
concoct
conduce
conduct
confect
connect
contact
convect
convict
coppice
cornice
correct
cossack
cowlick
craunch
crevice
currach
cutback
debauch
debouch
decency
defence
deflect
deforce
defrock
defunct
dehisce
derrick
detract
dialect
diptych
dissect
distich
divorce
dormice
dornick
drydock
dunnock
durance
earlock
edifice
elflock
embrace
emplace
endarch
enforce
enhance
enounce
erotica
errancy
essence
eweneck
exotica
extinct
extract
faience
fallacy
farruca
felucca
fetlock

finance
finback
flounce
fluence
fluency
flyback
fossick
furnace
futtock
gallice
gimmick
gorcock
graunch
grimace
guanaco
gunlock
haddock
hammock
hapence
hassock
haycock
hayrick
hemlock
henpeck
heroics
heyduck
hillock
hogback
hopsack
hospice
huanaco
hummock
icepack
impeach
inexact
infancy
infarct
inflect
inflict
infract
inspect
invoice
jannock
joyance
jumbuck
justice
Kalmuck
kalpack
killick
latency
lattice
lavrock
lettuce
licence
limbeck
lucency
maffick
mammock
manjack
mastich
mattock
mediacy
menisci
metrics
minorca
monarch
Moresco
Morisco
morocco
mortice
mudpack
mullock
nautics
neglect
niblick
nomarch
nonsuch
oarlock
offence

oomiack
orifice
ostraca
ostrich
outback
outface
outpace
overact
oviduct
oxfence
packice
paddock
padlock
pandect
patency
peacock
penance
perfect
phonics
physics
pibroch
piddock
pillock
pinnace
pintuck
playact
pliancy
poetics
polacca
pollack
pollock
porrect
portico
potence
potency
potluck
predict
preface
prefect
prelacy
prelect
prepack
primacy
privacy
produce
product
project
protect
pudency
putlock
quetsch
ransack
recency
redneck
reelect
reenact
reflect
refract
regency
rejoice
replace
replica
respect
restock
retouch
retrace
retract
rhiancy
roebuck
rollick
romance
rowlock
ruddock
sambuca
sawbuck
schlock
schmuck
science
scotice

scratch
screech
scrunch
seasick
secrecy
service
setback
sferics
shylock
silence
sirocco
skyjack
sonance
sonancy
sowback
spinach
splotch
squacco
squelch
squinch
squitch
statice
statics
staunch
stomach
stretch
subduct
subject
suffice
sundeck
surface
suspect
tabasco
tactics
tapioca
tenancy
terrace
testacy
tieback
tintack
titmice
tobacco
torgoch
touraco
traduce
traject
trisect
tropics
trounce
truancy
tussock
unblock
unbrace
unfrock
unhitch
unlatch
unstick
unstuck
unteach
urgency
vacancy
valance
valence
valency
vendace
verdict
verruca
viaduct
viatica
warlock
wedlock
wetback
winnock
wryneck
addenda
alameda
alcaide
alcalde
alcayde

alidade
already
anybody
astride
avocado
ballade
bedside
bravado
brigade
brocade
bromide
bushido
calando
calends
carbide
cascade
cathode
ceilidh
cestode
charade
cladode
cockade
collide
collude
commode
comrade
concede
confide
corrida
corrode
corrody
couvade
cowhide
crusade
crusado
custody
cyanide
degrade
deicide
detrude
dioxide
ebbtide
effendi
epicede
episode
epoxide
estrade
exclude
explode
extrude
fantods
forbade
forbode
gambade
gambado
gorsedd
grenade
Haggada
hydride
hymnody
implode
include
innards
intrude
inwards
joyride
kalends
Kannada
kathode
manmade
morendo
nitride
nuclide
obtrude
occlude
offside
onwards
osmunda
outride

outrode
outside
ovicide
passade
passado
pentode
peptide
perfidy
pervade
pintado
precede
prelude
preside
prosody
provide
raggedy
raphide
rawhide
regards
riptide
rotunda
roulade
saccade
sarcode
scalade
scalado
seaside
seclude
seconde
secondi
secondo
spinode
squaddy
subside
subsidy
succade
suicide
testudo
tetrode
thready
topside
tornado
torpedo
torpids
torsade
towards
tragedy
tribade
tripody
underdo
unhandy
unready
upgrade
upwards
uranide
veranda
voivode
wayside
zipcode
abashed
abdomen
abetted
abetter
abjurer
aborter
abrader
abutted
abutter
accused
accuser
Achates
acrogen
acroter
adapter
adducer
adherer
admirer
adopter
advised

adviser
afeared
affined
agnomen
aircrew
albumen
alkanet
alleged
allover
allseed
almoner
althaea
ambages
ambones
amender
ammeter
amputee
ancones
aniseed
annates
annulet
another
antigen
apheses
aphides
apothem
apparel
applied
applier
apsides
aquifer
aquiver
arbiter
arcaded
armiger
arrayer
arriver
ascites
ashamed
aspirer
assayer
assizes
assured
assurer
asunder
atelier
avenger
averred
awarder
babbler
backset
baffler
baloney
banjoes
banquet
banshee
baronet
barrier
barytes
basinet
bayonet
bearded
bedizen
beechen
behaver
beignet
bejewel
belated
belcher
beloved
bencher
berried
beshrew
besides
bestrew
betaken
betimes
betoken
between

biassed
bigener
bigoted
bilboes
bilobed
birchen
bistred
bitumen
blabbed
blabber
blacken
bladder
blanket
blarney
blasted
blaster
blather
blatter
bleater
bleeder
bleeper
blender
blessed
blether
blinder
blinker
blister
blither
bloated
bloater
blocker
blooded
bloomer
blotted
blotter
blowzed
blubber
blucher
bluffer
blunder
blunger
blurred
blusher
bluster
boarder
boaster
bobsled
boggler
boloney
bolster
boneset
bongoes
booklet
boomlet
booster
bootleg
botcher
bottled
bouchee
boulder
boulter
bouncer
bounden
bounder
bouquet
bourree
bowlder
bracken
bracket
bragged
bragger
brander
brannew
brawler
brazier
breaded
breaker
breeder
brevier
brimmed
brimmer
brinded
bringer
briquet
brisken
brisket
broaden
brocket
broider
broiler
brooder
brothel
brother
browser
bruiser
brusher
buckler
bugeyed
builded
builder
bullpen
bumbler
bungler
burbler
burgher
burster
burthen
burweed
bustler
butcher
byebyes
bygones
bywoner
cabaret
cabinet
cackler
cacumen
cadaver
caducei
cajoler
calices
calipee
caliper
calomel
caloyer
calumet
calyces
calyxes
cambrel
campbed
candied
canteen
caperer
caramel
caravel
carrier
cashier
castled
catcher
caterer
caulker
centner
centred
cerumen
chaffer
Chaldee
chamber
chamfer
chancel
changer
channel
chanter
chaplet
chapped
chapter
charger
charley
charmer
charnel
charred
charter
chasten
chatted
chattel
chatter
cheapen
cheater
checker
cheerer
chequer
chessel
chested
chicken
chidden
chigger
childer
chimney
chipped
chipper
chitter
chooser
choosey
chopped
chopper
chowder
chuffed
chugged
chukker
chummed
chunnel
chunter
chutney
cimices
circler
circlet
citadel
citizen
civvies
clabber
clacker
claimer
clamber
clammed
clanger
clapped
clapper
classes
clatter
clavier
cleaner
cleaver
clicker
climber
clinker
clipped
clipper
cliquey
clobber
clocker
clogged
clogger
clothes
clotted
clubbed
clumber
cluster
clutter
clyster
coacher
coarsen
coaster
cobbler
cochlea
cockney
coddler
codices
coherer
colleen
collier
colonel
comfrey
compeer
complex
conifer
conquer
cornfed
coroner
coronet
corslet
costrel
cottier
coulter
counsel
counter
coupler
couplet
courier
courser
cowheel
cowshed
cozener
crabbed
cracked
cracker
cragged
crammed
crammer
crampet
crawler
creamer
creeper
cresset
crested
cribbed
cricket
crimper
cringer
crisper
critter
croaker
crochet
crocket
crofter
crooked
crooner
cropped
cropper
croquet
crosier
crowned
crowner
crownet
crozier
cruiser
cruller
crumpet
crupper
crusher
crusted
cryogen
cudweed
culices
currier
curtsey
dabbler
dallier
damosel
damozel
dangler
darbies
dawdler
dazzler
debater
debrief
decibel
decided
decider
decoder
decrier
deepsea
defiler
definer
delayer
deliver
deluder
demirep
demoded
denizen
derider
devisee
deviser
devoted
devotee
dialled
diddler
dilated
dilutee
diluter
dimeter
dingoes
diopter
disobey
ditcher
divider
diviner
doodler
dossier
doubler
doubles
doublet
doubter
dowager
drabber
drabbet
drabler
draftee
drafter
dragged
dragnet
drainer
dratted
drawler
dreamed
dreamer
dredger
dresser
driblet
drifter
driller
drinker
dripped
drogher
droplet
dropped
dropper
drubbed
drudger
drugged
drugget
drummed
drummer
drunken
dryeyed
duelled
dueller
duramen
dwarves
dweller
earthen
ecdyses
embowed
embowel
embower
emersed
emitted
emitter
empanel
empower
emptier
encoder
endogen
enfiled
engaged
enliven
enwheel
epaulet
epithem
epithet
ergates
ermined
escapee
escaper
essayer
evacuee
evangel
excited
exciter
exhumer
exposed
exposer
faceted
falsies
fancier
farrier
farther
feaster
feather
fedayee
feigner
feoffee
feoffer
fiancee
fibster
fiddler
fielder
fifteen
fifties
fighter
figtree
figured
filacer
filibeg
filmset
firenew
firtree
fishnet
fitchet
fitchew
flagged
flamfew
flanker
flannel
flapped
flapper
flasher
flatlet
flatten
flatter
flecker
fleeced
fleecer
fleshed
flesher
fleuret
flicker
flipped
flipper
flitted
flitter
flivver
floater
flogged
floorer
flopped
flubbed
flunkey
fluster
flutter
flyover
focused
follies
fondler
forager
foramen
forayer
foreleg
foresee
forever
forgoer
forties
founder
fracted
frapped
freaked
freezer
freshen
fresher
freshet
fretted
fripper
frisker
frisket
fritted
fritter
frogged
fronded
frosted
fructed
fruited
fruiter
fuddler
Fuehrer
fuelled
fueller
fumbler
funnies
furrier
further
gabbler
gagster
galatea
galilee
gambier
gambler
gambrel
gangrel
gantlet
garbler
gateleg
geckoes
geneses
genteel
giggler
gillnet
girdler
glacier
gladded
gladden
gladder
glassen
glasses
glazier
gleaner
glimmer
glisten
glister
glitter
glummer
glutted
gnarled
gobbler
goggler
goggles
goitred
gombeen
gourmet
grabbed
grabber
grafter
grained
grainer
grandee
granger
grantee
granter
grapnel
grasper
grazier
greaser
greaten
greaves
greisen
greyhen
grifter
grilled
griller
grimmer
grinder
grinned
gripped
gripper
gritted
Grolier
grommet
groover
grouper
grouser
growler
grubbed
grubber
grummet
grunter
grutten
guarded
guardee
guesser
guichet
guilder
guzzler
hackler
hackney
haggler
hagweed
hairnet
halogen
hamster
handler
handsel
handset
hardset
harrier
harshen
harslet
hasbeen
hatcher
hatchet
haulier
haunted
haunter
hayseed
headset
hearken
hearted
hearten
heathen
heather
heckler
helices
higgler
hipster
hitcher
hoarsen
hobbler
hocused
hogweed
holster
homager
honeyed
hooklet
hostler
however
humbles
hundred
hurdler
hurdles
hurried
hustler
hypogea
igniter
ignorer
illbred
imbiber
imbower
impanel
imposer
inbreed
incised
inciter
incomer
incudes
incused
indexer
indices
inditer
inducer
infidel
inhaler
injurer
inlayer
insider
insured
insurer
integer
intoner
invader
invitee
inviter
inwoven
ipomoea
Ishmael
isohyet
ivories
jaconet
jangler
jellied
Jezebel
jingler
joinder
jointer
journey
jouster
jubilee
juggler
jumpjet
juncoes
juniper
Jupiter
kerogen
kestrel
kindler
kindred
kinglet
kitchen
knacker
knapped
knapper
kneader
kneeler
knitted
knitter
knobbed

knocker
knotted
knotter
knurled
krimmer
lacquer
lakelet
lamprey
languet
lassoes
latchet
latexes
latices
laugher
launder
layered
lazaret
leaflet
leaguer
learned
learner
leather
legatee
leister
leveret
lieabed
lighted
lighten
lighter
limited
limiter
linseed
lioncel
lipdeep
litotes
loather
lobster
locater
looksee
lorimer
loriner
lounger
louvred
lowbred
Lucifer
luncher
lurcher
lynchet
lyrated
mahaleb
mahseer
malines
malmsey
manager
manatee
manchet
mandrel
mangoes
mantlet
manweek
marbled
marbles
marcher
mariner
marquee
married
martlet
masquer
matchet
matinee
maunder
mauther
mayweed
mealies
meander
measles
meddler
Meissen
merchet
metamer
metayer
mettled
midweek
milkleg
minaret
minever
miniver
minster
minutes
misdeed
misdeem
misstep
mitoses
mobster
moisten
moither
molimen
moneyed
moneyer
mongrel
moniker
monomer
monster
moocher
moonset
moorhen
mottled
moulder
mounter
mourner
mousmee
mouther
muddler
muffler
mumbler
murexes
murices
murther
muscled
mutagen
muzzler
mycoses
mynheer
naiades
nankeen
narthex
necklet
needler
neither
Neogaea
nibbler
niggler
nobbler
nodated
nominee
nonuser
norther
notched
notelet
numbles
nymphet
oaktree
oarweed
obligee
October
odoured
odyssey
oenomel
oersted
officer
oilseed
oldster
omitted
oneeyed
onestep
opposer
orderer
orphrey
osselet
osseter
outgrew
outlier
overfed
oversea
oversee
overset
oversew
paddler
painter
paisley
palaver
palfrey
palsied
panacea
pannier
panther
panties
paperer
parader
parapet
pardner
parolee
parquet
parsley
partlet
partner
passkey
pearled
pearler
peddler
pedicel
pennies
percher
perigee
perplex
peruser
phellem
philter
piaffer
pickeer
pickled
picotee
picquet
pieeyed
piffler
pigweed
pikelet
pilsner
pincher
pioneer
pitched
pitcher
pivoter
placket
plaided
planned
planner
planter
plaster
platted
platter
playlet
playpen
pleader
pleased
pledgee
pledger
pledget
plodded
plodder
plopped
plotted
plotter
plucker
plugged
plugger
plumber
plummet
plumper
plunder
plunger
plunker
poacher
pofaced
poinder
pointed
pointer
polymer
pomfret
poofter
popeyed
popover
poppied
porifer
posteen
potheen
pouched
poulter
pounder
praiser
prancer
premier
presser
pretzel
preview
pricker
pricket
primmed
printer
prithee
problem
proceed
prodded
prodder
proffer
pronged
prophet
propjet
propped
prosper
prowler
psalter
puddler
puggree
puncher
punster
purlieu
pursuer
purview
putamen
puttier
puzzler
pyrites
pyxides
quaffer
quarrel
quarter
quartet
queller
quester
quicken
quieten
quillet
quilter
quintet
quipped
quitted
quitter
quizzed
quizzer
quizzes
rabbler
racquet
radices
ragweed
rallier
rambler
rancher
raschel
ratchet
ratteen
rattler
ravager
ravined
reacher
rebuker
reciter
recover
reducer
reenter
referee
refined
refiner
refugee
refuser
refuter
regimen
related
relater
relayed
remiges
remodel
removed
remover
reneger
renewer
rentier
reorder
repaper
repiner
replier
reputed
requiem
rescuer
retaken
retired
reviler
reviser
reviver
riddler
riffler
righten
righter
ringlet
ripplet
rivered
riveter
rivulet
roadbed
roaster
rockier
rocklet
roedeer
roister
rontgen
rooinek
rooster
rootlet
rosered
rotifer
roughen
rounded
roundel
rounder
rouster
royster
ruffler
rumbler
rundlet
rustler
saddler
sainted
sakeret
salicet
saluter
salvoes
samisen
Samoyed
sampler
sandbed
Saracen
satchel
satinet
saunter
scabbed
scabies
scalder
scalpel
scalper
scamper
scanned
scanner
scarfed
scarlet
scarper
scarred
scarves
scatted
scatter
scauper
scented
schemer
scissel
scoffer
scolder
scomber
scooper
scooter
scorner
scorper
scourer
scouter
scraper
screwed
screwer
scriber
scudded
sculler
scummed
scunner
scupper
scutter
seaweed
seceder
securer
seducer
seedbed
selffed
seltzer
semiped
senores
serried
settler
shammed
shammer
shanked
sharpen
sharper
shaster
shatter
shearer
sheaves
shebeen
shedder
shelled
sheller
shelter
shelved
shelves
sherbet
shereef
shicker
shifter
shimmer
shinned
shipped
shippen
shipper
shirker
shocker
shogged
shooter
shopped
shopper
shorten
shotten
shouter
shrivel
shriven
shucker
shudder
shunned
shunner
shunter
shutter
shyster
sickbed
sighted
simpler
simplex
singlet
sixteen
sixties
sizzler
skeeter
skegger
skelter
skidded
skilled
skillet
skimmed
skimmer
skinker
skinned
skinner
skipped
skipper
skippet
skirret
skirted
skirter
skitter
skulker
slabbed
slabber
slacken
slacker
slagged
slammed
slander
slapped
slasher
slather
slatted
sledded
sleeken
sleeper
sleeved
slender
slicker
slidden
slimmer
slinger
slinker
slipped
slipper
slither
slobber
slogged
slogger
slopped
sloshed
slotted
slubbed
slubber
slugged
slugger
slumber
slummed
slummer
slurred
smacker
smarten
smasher
smatter
smeller
smelter
smidgen
smitten
smother
smutted
snagged
snapped
snapper
snarler
sneaker
sneerer
sneezer
snicker
sniffer
snifter
snigger
snipped
snipper
snippet
snooker
snooper
snoozer
snorkel
snorter
snouted
snubbed
snubber
snuffer
socager
sofabed
soignee
soldier
soliped
soother
sorites
sounder
souther
sozzled
spadger
spancel
spaniel
spanker
spanned
spanner
sparger
sparred
spatted
spattee
spatter
spawner
speaker
species
speeder
speller
spelter
spencer
spender
spieler
spignel
spiller
spinner
spinney
spiraea
spitted
spitter
splicer
spoiler
spondee
sponger
spoofer
spooney
spoorer
sporter
spotted
spotter
spouter
sprayer
sprayey
spurner
spurred
spurrey
sputter
squarer
stabbed
stabber
stabler
stables
stacker
stagger
stainer
stalked
stalker
stammel
stammer
stamper
stander
staniel
stapler
starlet
starred
starter
statued
stealer
steamer
steepen
steerer
stemmed
stepney
stepped
stepper
sterlet
sterned
stetted
sticker
stiffen
stifler
stilted
stinger
stinker
stirpes
stirred
stirrer
stocker
stonker
stopped
stopper
storied
stouten
stovies
strayer
strider
striker
striped
striven
striver
strudel
stubbed
studded
studied
stuffer
stummed
stumper
stunned
stunner
stunted

stutter
subdued
succeed
suckler
sumpter
sutured
swabbed
swabber
swagged
swagger
swanker
swanned
swapped
swapper
swarded
swarmer
swasher
swatted
swatter
swearer
sweater
sweeper
sweeten
swelter
swigged
swiller
swimmer
swinger
swither
Switzer
swobbed
swollen
swopped
swopper
swotted
tabaret
tabinet
taborer
tackler
tagetes
talipes
taloned
tanager
taperer
tapster
tarrier
tartlet
tattler
taunter
taxfree
teacher
telpher
templet
tempter
tenoner
tentbed
tentpeg
terrier
testbed
thalweg
thankee
thanker
theorem
thicken
thicket
thieves
thigger
thiller
thinker
thinned
thinner
thither
thorned
thriven
throned
thrower
thudded
thuggee
thumper
thunder
tickler
tiddler
tiddley
tiercel
tiercet
tighten
timbrel
tingler
tippler
tipster
toaster
toddler
toothed
touched
toucher
toughen
tourney
towered
townlet
trachea
tracker
trailer
trainee
trainer
trammel
tranter
trapped
trapper
trawler
treader
treater
trekked
trekker
tressed
tressel
triblet
tricker
trifler
trigger
trimmed
trimmer
trinket
triolet
triplet
triplex
tripped
tripper
trippet
trochee
trodden
troller
trolley
trommel
trooper
trotted
trotter
trouper
trouser
trucker
trudgen
trumpet
trusser
trustee
truster
tumbler
tumbrel
turnkey
tweeter
tweezer
twelves
twigged
twilled
twinned
twister
twitted
twitter
twostep
typeset
udaller
ulcered
umbones
umpteen
unarmed
unasked
unbated
unbowed
unboxed
uncover
unhoped
unifier
unladen
unlined
unmixed
unmoved
unpaged
unquiet
unravel
unsaved
unscrew
unsexed
untried
untuned
unwoven
upriser
upsides
upsweep
upthrew
usurper
utterer
varices
vaulted
vaulter
vaunter
veinlet
velamen
veliger
venerer
vernier
vetiver
vilayet
vintner
visaged
visored
vistaed
vittles
volumed
voluted
vouchee
voucher
voyager
waddler
wagerer
wagoner
Wahabee
waisted
waister
wakener
waltzer
warbler
wastrel
watcher
watered
waterer
wattled
wattles
wavelet
waverer
waxtree
wealden
weather
webster
weigher
welcher
wellies
wellset
welsher
wencher
whacker
whangee
wharves
wheaten
wheeled
wheeler
whether
whetted
whetter
whicker
whidder
whimper
whimsey
whinger
whipped
whipper
whippet
whirler
whirred
whisker
whiskey
whisper
whither
whizzed
whoever
whoopee
whooper
whopper
whorled
widowed
widower
wielder
wiggler
willies
winglet
wizened
wobbler
woolled
woollen
woolsey
worrier
worsted
wrapped
wrapper
wrecker
wringer
writhen
written
ycleped
yewtree
yielder
younger
younker
zaptieh
zincked
zonated
zymogen
acetify
acidify
agraffe
airlift
alewife
alfalfa
amplify
bailiff
beatify
caitiff
calcify
castoff
certify
clarify
crucify
damnify
dandify
dignify
distaff
dulcify
earmuff
enfeoff
engraft
faceoff
falloff
falsify
fortify
giraffe
glorify
gratify
handoff
hayloft
henwife
horrify
indraft
ingraft
jollify
jumpoff
justify
kickoff
leadoff
liftoff
lignify
liquefy
magnify
mastiff
midriff
midwife
mollify
mortify
mummify
mundify
mystify
nigrify
nitrify
nullify
petrify
playoff
pontiff
pontify
prosify
putrefy
qualify
rakeoff
rectify
redraft
restiff
Russify
salsify
satisfy
sawnoff
scarify
scorify
scruffy
seawife
sendoff
sheriff
showoff
signify
skilift
specify
spinoff
squiffy
stopoff
stupefy
takeoff
Tartufe
terrify
testify
tipsify
torrefy
versify
vitrify
welloff
zincify
zinkify
abridge
acreage
adjudge
ajutage
allergy
allonge
anagoge
anagogy
analogy
apagoge
apanage
apology
arraign
arrange
assuage
average
baggage
bandage
barrage
besiege
biology
bondage
borings
borough
boscage
boskage
botargo
bottega
brewage
brokage
buoyage
burgage
cabbage
cabbagy
carnage
cartage
coinage
collage
college
condign
consign
cordage
corkage
cornage
corsage
cortege
cottage
courage
cowhage
cranage
curragh
derange
deterge
diverge
divulge
dockage
drayage
dunnage
ecology
effulge
embargo
engorge
enlarge
expunge
Faberge
Falange
farrago
ferrugo
filings
finings
fixings
flotage
flowage
foggage
foliage
footage
foreign
fullage
galanga
gamboge
garbage
geology
haulage
herbage
hidalga
hidalgo
hostage
immerge
impinge
indulge
innings
inveigh
lairage
leafage
leakage
lentigo
lineage
linkage
liturgy
lockage
longago
lozenge
luggage
lumbago
makings
massage
melange
message
mileage
mintage
montage
moorage
myology
neglige
neology
noology
onstage
orology
otology
outrage
overage
package
palings
pannage
parerga
passage
paysage
peerage
peonage
pillage
plumage
plusage
pondage
pontage
portage
postage
pottage
presage
primage
prodigy
protege
prurigo
quayage
rampage
ravings
realign
redlegs
regorge
resurge
revenge
rootage
rummage
salvage
sapsago
sarangi
sausage
savings
scourge
scraggy
scrooge
scrouge
scutage
sealegs
seepage
selvage
serfage
seringa
serpigo
sinkage
skyhigh
smaragd
soakage
soccage
splodge
splurge
spriggy
springe
springy
storage
stowage
strange
stringy
sullage
synergy
syringa
syringe
takings
tallage
tankage
tannage
teenage
telergy
thanage
theurgy
through
tidings
tillage
tonnage
trilogy
umbrage
undergo
unhinge
upstage
upsurge
urology
vantage
ventage
vertigo
vestige
village
vintage
voltage
waftage
wastage
wattage
windage
windegg
wordage
yardage
zoology
zymurgy
abought
acantha
acouchy
agrapha
alright
anarchy
Arapaho
atrophy
attache
aurochs
bedight
blotchy
bobeche
borscht
branchy
breathe
breathy
brioche
bronchi
broncho
brought
bruhaha
caliche
capuche
caroche
catechu
churchy
cockshy
crunchy
delight
diarchy
draught
drought
drouthy
dyarchy
earache
elenchi
empathy
eparchy
flaught
fraught
freight
Frenchy
gnocchi
gouache
grouchy
healthy
heighho
insight
kitschy
lengthy
Maratha
Marathi
naphtha
panache
panocha
paunchy
piranha
preachy
raunchy
relight
ricksha
scirrhi
sheathe
sketchy
sleight
slouchy
sloughy
smokeho
smoochy
snatchy
splashy
squashy
squishy
staithe
starchy
stenchy
strophe
swarthy
tallyho
tamasha
thought
timothy
tonight
tranche
twitchy
unright
unsight
upright
uptight
wealthy
wreathe
wreathy
wrought
abattis
Abbasid
abigail
abiotic
aboulia
abstain

accidie
acclaim
acequia
acerbic
acrasin
acrylic
actinia
actinic
acyclic
adenoid
adhibit
aerobic
agnatic
airmail
airship
akvavit
albumin
alembic
alginic
alkalis
allelic
alluvia
aloetic
amentia
Amharic
ammonia
amnesia
amnesic
amoebic
amyloid
anaemia
anaemic
android
aneroid
aneurin
angelic
Angevin
anionic
annelid
anoesis
anoetic
anosmia
anosmic
antacid
antefix
aphasia
aphasic
aphelia
aphesis
aphetic
aphonia
aphonic
aphotic
aplasia
apostil
apraxia
aquaria
aquatic
aquavit
Aramaic
araneid
arcadia
archaic
arctoid
Armoric
arsenic
ascarid
ascaris
ascesis
ascetic
ascidia
ascitic
asepsis
aseptic
Asiatic
askesis
aspirin
astatic
asteria
atresia
aurelia
auxesis
auxetic
Avestic
avionic
babysit
bacchic
baldric
banksia
bargain
barmaid
barytic
basidia
beatnik
bedevil
bedouin
begonia
benefic
benefit
benthic
benzoic
benzoin
bheetie
biennia
biscuit
bobtail
bohemia
bolshie
booksie
boracic
botanic
botulin
boudoir
Brahmin
brassie
breakin
breccia
brickie
brownie
bubonic
bucolic
builtin
bulimia
bumpkin
bushtit
butyric
Byronic
caloric
calorie
cambric
canakin
canikin
canonic
Canopic
cantrip
capelin
caproic
captain
carotid
carotin
catsuit
caustic
centric
cepheid
ceramic
ceresin
certain
cesspit
cestoid
Chablis
chagrin
challis
chamois
chaotic
chappie
charlie
chassis
cheerio
chervil
chindit
chloric
choroid
chromic
chronic
ciboria
cichlid
cidaris
cipolin
circuit
clarkia
classic
classis
clastic
clippie
clupeid
coaltit
coccoid
cockpit
codicil
cohabit
coletit
colitis
colloid
colonic
comedic
cometic
comitia
complin
conceit
conchie
conduit
conidia
conjoin
contain
coontie
corbeil
corsair
coterie
couloir
council
couthie
cowslip
crampit
crappie
cricoid
crinoid
croquis
crowdie
cryptic
ctenoid
culprit
curtail
curtain
cycloid
cystoid
dauphin
deafaid
declaim
deficit
deictic
deistic
delimit
Delphic
deltaic
deltoid
demerit
demonic
demotic
denarii
deposit
despair
despoil
detrain
deutzia
dextrin
dibasic
dimeric
diploid
discoid
disdain
disjoin
distain
docetic
doeskin
dogskin
dolphin
dominie
dovekie
drastic
drivein
druidic
drumlin
duckpin
dustbin
duumvir
dynamic
ecdysis
ectopic
edaphic
eggflip
egotrip
eidetic
eirenic
ekistic
elastic
elastin
Eleatic
Elzevir
embolic
embroil
empiric
emporia
enchain
encomia
endemic
energid
engrail
engrain
entasis
enteric
entomic
entotic
entrain
enzymic
epizoic
erepsin
ergodic
ericoid
eristic
erratic
etaerio
etheric
ethmoid
eugenic
eulogia
eutexia
exclaim
exhibit
exordia
explain
exploit
exposit
exurbia
fanatic
fanmail
fantail
faradic
fibroid
fibroin
filaria
fimbria
finikin
flaccid
fleapit
floosie
floozie
floruit
fluidic
footsie
forfeit
foxtail
frantic
freebie
freesia
fuchsia
funfair
fungoid
galenic
gametic
ganglia
garboil
gastric
gelatin
generic
genesis
genetic
Geordie
georgic
gherkin
ghillie
glaikit
glenoid
gliadin
globoid
Glossic
glottis
glyphic
glyptic
gnathic
gnostic
Gobelin
godetia
godevil
godship
gomeril
gonidia
grannie
graphic
gremlin
griffin
griskin
groupie
Guelfic
gumboil
gunship
gymslip
hairpin
halfwit
Hamitic
haploid
hardhit
harelip
headpin
Hebraic
hedonic
heparin
hepatic
heretic
hexadic
hirudin
hoatzin
hobnail
Homeric
Homerid
hominid
howbeit
hyaloid
hydatid
hydroid
hymenia
hypnoid
hypoxia
hypoxic
icteric
identic
idiotic
idyllic
ileitis
illicit
imperil
incipit
indicia
indusia
inertia
ingrain
inhabit
inherit
inhibit
insipid
insulin
interim
introit
invalid
Islamic
Jacobin
japonic
javelin
jonquil
katydid
kenosis
kenotic
keramic
keratin
khamsin
kidskin
kinchin
kinesis
kinetic
kingpin
kinship
Kirghiz
Koranic
kremlin
laconic
ladykin
lambkin
languid
lanolin
latakia
lawsuit
legbail
lentoid
Liassic
ligroin
limosis
limpkin
lithoid
lobelia
lugsail
lunatic
lupulin
lychnis
lyingin
machair
mahonia
malacia
malaria
malefic
manakin
mandril
manikin
manumit
marquis
Masonic
mastoid
mattoid
maudlin
Mechlin
meconic
meiosis
meiotic
melanic
melanin
melodic
mermaid
mesonic
messtin
metopic
miasmic
midship
milfoil
militia
milreis
mimesis
mimetic
minikin
minutia
mislaid
mitosis
mitotic
monadic
monodic
moonlit
moronic
morphia
Mountie
muezzin
mullein
murrain
myalgia
myalgic
mycelia
mycosis
mycotic
myeloid
myiasis
nauplii
navarin
necktie
negroid
nemesia
nemesis
neozoic
nephric
neritic
newlaid
nightie
Nilotic
ninepin
Noachic
noctuid
nomadic
nombril
nonskid
nonslip
nonsuit
nostril
notitia
nucleic
nuclein
numeric
nunship
obconic
obovoid
oceanic
odontic
oghamic
oilskin
Olympic
omnific
oneiric
oolitic
openair
ophitic
opsonic
opsonin
opuntia
oratrix
orectic
organic
osmosis
osmotic
ossific
osteoid
ouabain
overbid
overdid
overlie
oxyacid
pacific
paeonic
paladin
palmoil
parboil
paresis
paretic
parfait
parodic
parotid
parsnip
patagia
pelagic
peloria
peloric
penguin
percoid
periwig
pertain
petunia
pfennig
phallic
phasmid
phoenix
phrenic
pigskin
pigtail
pilgrim
pinguid
pintail
piperic
piratic
pissoir
placoid
plasmic
plasmid
plasmin
plastic
plastid
plaudit
pliskie
plumbic
polemic
politic
polynia
postfix
potamic
poussin
prairie
Prakrit
prepaid
prevail
priapic
prosaic
proteid
protein
prussic
psychic
pteroic
ptyalin
pumpkin
puparia
purloin
pursuit
pyaemia
pyaemic
pygmoid
pyloric
pyralid
pyralis
pyramid
pyretic
pyrexia
pyrexic
pyritic
pyrosis
pyrrhic
pyxidia
quadric
quantic
quartic
quassia
quickie
quintic
racemic
ramekin
rapeoil
rarebit
ratafia
rattail
ravelin
reclaim
recruit
rectrix
redskin
refrain
regalia
reposit
retrain
reverie
revisit
Rhaetic
rhizoid
rhombic
rockoil
Romanic
rosehip
salicin
sandpit
sangria
saponin
sapphic
sarcoid
satanic
satiric
satyric
satyrid
sauroid
scabrid
scaglia
scaldic
scepsis
sceptic
scholia
sciarid
sciatic
Scorpio
Scottie
scrapie
sculpin
scurril
seamaid
seawhip
sedilia
seedlip
seismic
selenic
sematic
Semitic
senarii
senecio
sequoia
sericin
sexfoil
shaslik
sheltie
sherris
shilpit
shindig
shittim
shortie
showbiz

sialoid
sibship
sigmoid
silesia
silicic
sinopia
sirloin
skaldic
skepsis
skidlid
skimmia
skysail
sleekit
sloegin
smidgin
solaria
solatia
solicit
somatic
somitic
sonship
sorosis
sparoid
spastic
spathic
sphenic
spheric
splenic
spongin
spunkie
sputnik
squalid
standin
stannic
starlit
stearic
stearin
steekit
stencil
steroid
sthenic
stickit
strigil
styloid
styptic
subacid
subedit
suberic
suberin
subjoin
subsoil
sudaria
sunsuit
surfeit
sustain
sweetie
syconia
sycosis
sylphid
synesis
synodic
synovia
syrphid
tabanid
tabetic
tabloid
talaria
tamarin
tanghin
tantric
teachin
technic
tectrix
tendril
terrain
tetanic
thallic
therein
thermic
thiamin
throwin
thummim
thyroid
tiderip
tinfoil
titanic
toeclip
toenail
tonemic
tootsie
topsail
topsoil
tortrix
totemic
tradein
traffic
transit
travail
travois
trefoil
trellis
trenail
triacid
triadic
trophic
trypsin
tryptic
trysail
tumbril
turdoid
turmoil
typhoid
unchain
uncivil
upbraid
upstair
uraemia
utensil
uveitis
valeric
valonia
vanadic
Vaudois
Veddoid
velaria
venatic
venefic
ventail
vermeil
vervain
villain
villein
vitamin
vivaria
vivific
vocalic
voltaic
volutin
wagtail
warship
wassail
waylaid
weighin
weirdie
wherein
whizkid
woodpie
wooloil
worship
xanthic
xanthin
xiphoid
zebroid
zetetic
zygosis
zygotic
zymosis
zymotic
alforja
basenji
armlike
autarky
bazooka
bespoke
boxlike
britzka
bunraku
catlike
colicky
convoke
cowpoke
cupcake
dashiki
dislike
droshky
eyelike
finicky
forsake
garpike
godlike
hoecake
manlike
mazurka
mislike
mistake
mousaka
netlike
netsuke
nutlike
oatcake
oilcake
ostraka
outtake
pancake
panicky
paprika
partake
provoke
ratlike
rodlike
seppuku
squeaky
streaky
teacake
unlucky
Vandyke
warlike
ziganka
abubble
acerola
acicula
acridly
acutely
addable
addible
adeptly
adultly
affable
affably
agilely
airhole
alertly
alienly
aloofly
alveoli
amiable
amiably
ampoule
ampulla
angrily
anomaly
anthill
apetaly
aphylly
apishly
apostle
arcweld
areally
armfuls
armhole
article
asphalt
assault
astable
atingle
audible
aurally
aureola
aureole
auricle
awfully
axially
bacilli
baggily
balmily
banally
barbell
barbule
barilla
bascule
battels
bawdily
beastly
bedroll
beguile
Bengali
benzole
bergylt
bicycle
blackly
blandly
blankly
bleakly
blindly
blowfly
bluffly
bluntly
bonnily
boozily
Boswell
bouilli
boxcalf
brabble
braille
bramble
brambly
bransle
brantle
brashly
brattle
bravely
brickle
bricole
briefly
brindle
briskly
bristle
bristly
brittle
brittly
broadly
buffalo
buirdly
bulkily
bummalo
bumpily
buyable
cabbala
cagoule
calculi
calicle
calycle
candela
cannily
cannula
capable
capably
capsule
cariole
castile
casuals
catcall
cattalo
cattily
catwalk
cavally
cedilla
cellule
cembalo
cenacle
charily
cheaply
chiefly
childly
chorale
chortle
chuckle
cineole
cingula
citable
civilly
cleanly
clearly
clerkly
closely
coagula
cockily
codable
compile
condole
condyle
console
consult
coracle
corella
cornily
corolla
cortile
courtly
cowbell
crackle
crackly
crankle
crassly
crazily
cribble
crimple
cringle
crinkle
crinkly
criollo
cripple
crisply
crossly
crudely
cruelly
crumble
crumbly
crumple
cubicle
cuckold
cuittle
curable
cureall
cuticle
cymbalo
cypsela
dariole
datable
dazedly
deathly
debacle
decuple
default
densely
dewfall
diabolo
dingily
dirtily
disable
distill
dizzily
doucely
dowdily
drabble
draggle
dribble
drizzle
drizzly
drycell
drysalt
ducally
ductile
duopoly
dupable
durable
durably
duskily
dustily
dwindle
eagerly
earhole
earthly
eatable
elderly
elfbolt
emerald
emptily
ennoble
entitle
epistle
equable
equably
equally
erectly
exactly
example
exempla
eyeball
eyebolt
eyehole
fadedly
faintly
falbala
falcula
falsely
fancily
fanfold
fatally
febrile
ferrule
fertile
fetidly
fictile
fierily
fifthly
finagle
finally
firefly
firstly
fishily
fissile
fistula
fixable
fixedly
fleetly
fleshly
flexile
fluidly
flyable
flybelt
flyhalf
foggily
foliole
formula
fossula
fourale
foveola
foxhole
fragile
frailly
frankly
frazzle
freckle
freckly
frenula
freshly
friable
friarly
fribble
frijole
frizzle
frizzly
fugally
funicle
funnily
furcula
fusible
fussily
fustily
fuzzily
gabelle
gadwall
gallfly
gaudily
gauntly
gawkily
gazelle
gelidly
gemmule
gentile
gestalt
ghastly
ghostly
giddily
gimbals
gingili
globule
gondola
gorilla
goutfly
grabble
gracile
grackle
gradely
grandly
granule
grapple
gravely
greatly
greenly
gribble
griddle
gristle
gristly
grizzle
grizzly
grossly
gruffly
grumble
grumbly
gruntle
guayule
gunwale
gustily
gutsily
hallali
handily
happily
harmala
harshly
hastily
hatable
headily
heavily
heftily
hemiola
herself
hexapla
himself
hirable
holdall
horsily
hostile
humanly
humidly
huskily
icecold
icefall
ideally
ignoble
ignobly
inanely
inaptly
inbuilt
indwell
indwelt
ineptly
inertly
infield
inkwell
inocula
insculp
install
inutile
irately
Ismaili
Israeli
jadedly
jaywalk
jazzily
jerkily
jointly
juicily
jurally
kabbala
keyhole
kinfolk
knobble
knobbly
knowall
knuckle
labella
lamella
lankily
lapilli
largely
laurels
legally
legible
legibly
legpull
levelly
licitly
lightly
likable
lithely
livable
loathly
locally
loftily
loosely
losable
lousily
lovable
lovably
loverly
lowlily
loyally
lucidly
luckily
lughole
lumpily
luridly
lustily
lyingly
mamilla
manacle
mandala
mandola
mangily
mangold
manhole
manilla
manille
maniple
Marsala
maxilla
maxwell
maypole
meatfly
medulla
menfolk
merrily
messily
micelle
miracle
mirkily
miscall
miserly
misrule
missile
mistily
mixedly
modally
moistly
monocle
monthly
moodily
morally
morello
Moselle
movable
muddily
murkily
mutable
mutably
muzzily
nacelle
naively
nakedly
namable
nasally
nastily
nattily
nautili
netball
nightly
nippily
nitrile
noctule
nodally
noisily
notable
notably
notedly
novella
novelle
nutgall
oakgall
octuple
oddball
oilwell
oneself
opuscle
orderly
ossicle
ostiole
ourself
outfall
outsell

outsold
outsole
outtalk
overall
overfly
overtly
panicle
panoply
pantile
papally
papilla
parable
patella
payable
payroll
peartly
pedicle
penally
pennill
pensile
peppill
peptalk
percale
pergola
perkily
petiole
pettily
phonily
piccolo
piebald
pillule
pinball
pinfold
pinhole
pinnule
piously
pistole
pitfall
pithily
plainly
planula
pliable
pliably
plumply
plumule
plushly
potable
pothole
prattle
prickle
prickly
primely
primula
privily
profile
pronely
prosily
proudly
pteryla
puerile
pugmill
pustule
queenly
queerly
quibble
quickly
quietly
rabidly
radicle
ragbolt
ragdoll
rapidly
ratable
ravioli
readily
rebuild
rebuilt
recycle
redpoll

regally
remould
reptile
rescale
respell
respelt
restyle
retable
reticle
ridable
rightly
rigidly
risible
rissole
rockily
ropable
rosella
roseola
roughly
roundly
rowdily
royally
rubella
rubeola
ruddily
rundale
rurally
rustily
saccule
sacculi
saintly
salable
sandfly
sanicle
saucily
savable
saveall
sawbill
sawmill
sayable
scabble
scantly
scapple
scapula
scopula
scrawly
scruple
scuffle
scumble
scuttle
seagull
seakale
seawall
seawolf
sectile
seeable
seedily
sequela
serpula
servile
sessile
setwall
sextile
shackle
shadily
shakily
shamble
shapely
sharply
sheerly
shingle
shingly
shoofly
shortly
showily
shrilly
shuffle
shuttle
sightly

silicle
silkily
sillily
sixfold
sixthly
sizable
sizably
skiable
skiffle
skittle
slackly
slantly
sleekly
slickly
slimily
smartly
smokily
smuggle
snaffle
snakily
sniffle
sniggle
snoozle
snowily
snuffle
snuggle
soapily
soberly
soggily
solidly
soluble
soothly
sootily
soppily
sorrily
souffle
soundly
spangle
spangly
sparely
sparkle
spatula
speckle
specula
spicily
spicula
spicule
spikily
spindle
spindly
spinule
spittle
sporule
sprawly
spurtle
spyhole
squails
squally
stabile
staddle
stagily
staidly
stalely
starkly
startle
stately
steeple
steeply
stemple
sterile
sternly
stickle
stiffly
stimuli
stipple
stipule
stonily
stopple
stoutly

stubble
stubbly
stumble
suavely
subtile
Suffolk
sulkily
sunnily
surlily
swaddle
Swahili
sweetly
swiftly
swindle
swingle
swipple
swizzle
systole
tacitly
tactile
tadpole
tamable
tangelo
tardily
tastily
tattily
taxable
tenable
tenably
tenfold
tensely
tensile
tentfly
tenthly
tepidly
tequila
tersely
testfly
testily
textile
thickly
thimble
thirdly
thistle
thistly
thyself
tidally
tightly
timbale
timidly
tinnily
tipsily
toehold
tombola
tombolo
tonally
topfull
tophole
tortile
totally
toughly
trample
treacle
treacly
treadle
trehala
tremble
trembly
tremolo
trestle
triable
trickle
trindle
tringle
tripoli
tripple
tritely
trouble
truckle

truffle
trundle
tumidly
tunable
tunably
tunicle
twaddle
twaddly
twangle
twibill
twiddle
twiddly
twinkle
twinkly
twofold
Tynwald
ukelele
ukulele
unaptly
unbuild
unbuilt
unfitly
ungodly
unmanly
unshell
untruly
upfield
urodele
usually
utricle
utterly
vacuole
vagally
vaguely
validly
valvula
valvule
vanilla
vapidly
variola
variole
vascula
vehicle
venally
vesicle
vexedly
vexilla
vincula
virgule
visible
visibly
vitally
vitelli
vividly
vixenly
vocable
vocally
voluble
volubly
votable
vowelly
wadable
waxbill
waybill
wearily
weevily
weirdly
wergild
werwolf
wheedle
whiffle
whistle
whitely
whittle
windily
wittily
womanly
woozily
wordily

worldly
wrangle
wrestle
wriggle
wriggly
wrinkle
wrinkly
wrongly
wrybill
wychelm
academe
academy
ackemma
adenoma
alchemy
alltime
anatomy
angioma
anytime
apogamy
awesome
bedtime
begrime
beldame
berhyme
bigname
bigtime
centime
chiasma
condemn
consume
contemn
costume
coulomb
coxcomb
curcuma
customs
daytime
deplume
digamma
dilemma
diorama
diploma
disfame
dislimn
dodgems
drachma
economy
empyema
enframe
epitome
eponymy
ewelamb
exogamy
extreme
fibroma
foglamp
fulsome
goddamn
gourami
grandma
inflame
irksome
isogamy
isonomy
jimjams
kerygma
leucoma
lissome
macrame
macrami
mahatma
maremma
Maytime
melisma
meseems
misname
mistime
mugwump

myeloma
neuroma
newcome
noisome
oldtime
onetime
origami
outcome
pastime
penname
perfume
phlegmy
phoneme
prelims
presume
proximo
ragtime
reclame
rhizome
sarcoma
sashimi
satsuma
scotoma
septime
seriema
skijump
spireme
squirmy
sublime
subsume
succumb
sunlamp
supreme
supremo
surname
syngamy
teatime
thalami
thrummy
trigamy
trireme
tsunami
twosome
twotime
verismo
wargame
wartime
welcome
winsome
zoogamy
zoonomy
zootomy
abalone
abeyant
abiding
abscond
account
acetone
adamant
adenine
adjoint
affront
agelong
aground
aiblins
ailment
airline
alanine
aliment
alimony
alumina
amarant
amazing
ambient
amboina
amboyna
Amerind
ancient
anemone

angling
anguine
aniline
anodyne
antenna
apolune
appoint
armband
asinine
asquint
astound
attaint
audient
augment
azurine
backing
bagging
balcony
balding
bambini
bambino
bandana
banking
banning
banteng
banting
barline
barring
basting
bathing
batting
beading
bearing
beating
bedding
beeline
begging
beguine
Beltane
belting
belying
benzene
benzine
bepaint
berline
bethink
betting
bibbing
bidding
billing
biltong
binding
biplane
biriani
bitting
blatant
blueing
boating
bobbing
boiling
bologna
bookend
booking
bopping
bottony
bowline
bowling
bracing
brigand
broking
bromine
brucine
buccina
budding
bugbane
bugging
bumming
bunting
buoyant

burning
busking
bussing
buttend
buttons
buttony
cabling
cabrank
cacanny
caimans
calcine
callant
calling
calumny
camping
candent
canning
cantina
canting
canzone
canzoni
capping
caprine
carbine
carking
carline
carmine
carping
carving
caserne
cassino
casting
catling
catmint
cayenne
caymans
ceiling
cervine
chalone
chicane
Chicano
choline
chopine
chorine
citrine
clamant
clement
coaming
coating
cocaine
codeine
codling
cogging
collins
cologne
combine
command
commend
comment
commons
commune
company
compend
compony
concent
condone
confine
coniine
conning
consent
contend
content
convene
convent
cooking
coolant
corking
corvina
corvine

costing
cottony
cowbane
cowhand
cowling
craving
credent
cremona
crimine
cubbing
cuisine
cunning
cupping
curling
currant
current
curtana
cutline
cutting
cyanine
cyclone
cystine
czarina
dabbing
damming
damning
dapsone
darling
darning
dashing
dawning
daylong
deadend
dealing
decking
decline
defiant
delaine
demesne
demount
dentine
deodand
deplane
descant
descend
descent
despond
destine
destiny
deviant
dewpond
diamond
dibbing
dickens
digging
diluent
dimming
dinning
dipping
disband
discant
disrank
dissent
distant
distend
distent
dittany
dogbane
dogging
doggone
dogvane
donning
Dorking
dormant
dotting
doyenne
drawing
driving
dromond

droving
dubbing
ducking
ducting
dunning
duodena
earring
easting
eccrine
echidna
elegant
element
elevens
elfland
emetine
eminent
emplane
enchant
endlong
enplane
enprint
entrant
entwine
enwound
epatant
epergne
epicene
epigene
epigone
epigoni
epigyny
erelong
erlking
erodent
essoyne
etamine
etching
euglena
euphony
evening
evident
examine
exigent
explant
expound
exscind
externe
eyewink
fagging
failing
fairing
falling
fanning
farcing
fargone
farming
fascine
fatling
fatting
feeding
feeling
felting
fencing
fenland
ferment
fervent
fibbing
figging
figment
filling
finding
finning
fishing
fitment
fitting
flaming
flavine
fleeing
Fleming

fluting
flybane
flyting
fobbing
fogbank
fogging
folding
fondant
footing
fopling
fordone
forfend
forging
forgone
formant
fortune
forwent
fowling
foxhunt
fugging
fulgent
fulmine
funning
furlong
furring
gabbing
gadding
gagging
gallant
galling
gardant
garland
garment
gasring
gassing
gatling
gearing
geebung
Gehenna
gelding
gelling
gemming
genning
genuine
geogony
germane
getting
gigging
gilding
ginning
ginseng
glaring
glazing
glozing
glycine
godling
godsend
golfing
gosling
gradine
grating
grazing
Gstring
guanine
guarana
guarani
gubbins
gumming
gunning
gushing
gutting
gypping
hacking
halting
hamming
hanging
hapenny
happing
harmony

hatband
hatting
heading
hearing
heating
Hellene
helping
hemione
hemline
hemming
henbane
heptane
heroine
herring
hilding
hipbone
hipping
hircine
histone
hitting
hogging
holding
holland
hopbind
hopping
hormone
horrent
hosanna
housing
howling
hugging
hulking
humming
hunting
hurling
husband
husking
hutment
hutting
hyaline
hydrant
hygiene
icerink
ikebana
imagine
impaint
implant
impound
imprint
incline
infauna
inferno
ingoing
inkling
insigne
instant
inswing
interne
intrant
intwine
ironing
isogeny
isokont
issuant
iterant
jabbing
jamming
jarring
jasmine
jawbone
jetting
jibbing
jigging
jobbing
jogging
joining
jotting
jugging
juggins

jutting
kampong
karting
keeping
kenning
keyring
kidding
killing
kissing
knowing
Krishna
lacking
lagging
Lallans
lambent
lamming
landing
lantana
lapping
lapwing
larceny
lasagna
lasagne
lashing
lasting
lathing
latrine
lawhand
leading
leaning
legging
lemming
lending
lenient
leonine
letting
leucine
licking
lilting
lindane
linsang
lipping
listing
loading
loaning
lobbing
lodging
logging
logline
longing
looking
lopping
lording
lotting
lowland
lucarne
lucerne
lugging
lumbang
lurdane
machine
madding
madonna
madrona
madrono
mahjong
mahound
mailing
malting
manhunt
mankind
manning
mapping
marconi
margent
marking
marline
Marrano
marring

martini
matting
mattins
meaning
mediant
meeting
melting
mending
methane
midland
midline
migrant
milking
mincing
minuend
Miocene
misdone
missend
missent
missing
misting
mobbing
montane
mooring
mopping
moraine
mordant
mordent
morning
morwong
mousing
mugging
muggins
mumming
mundane
munting
muraena
mustang
muttony
nabbing
nagging
napping
nascent
neoteny
Neptune
nervine
nesting
netting
neurine
neurone
nipping
nirvana
nodding
nogging
nooning
norland
nothing
noumena
nursing
nutpine
nutting
oakling
obscene
ocarina
oddment
odorant
offhand
olefine
olivine
ongoing
opaline
openend
opening
operand
operant
opulent
oregano
orogeny
orotund

outdone
outgone
outland
outline
outrank
outwent
oxidant
oxytone
packing
padding
padrone
padroni
pageant
panning
pargana
parpend
parting
parvenu
passant
passing
patient
patting
Pauline
payment
peasant
pebrine
peccant
pegging
pelting
pendant
pendent
pending
pennant
pennine
penning
pentane
pepping
peptone
percent
percine
perpend
perpent
persona
Petrine
petting
phalanx
pharynx
pigging
pigling
pigment
pimping
pinking
pinning
pipping
piquant
piscina
piscine
pitpony
pitting
plafond
platane
platina
plating
playing
podding
pompano
popping
porcine
portend
portent
posting
potbank
potting
pouting
praline
prebend
present
pretend
prevent

priming
proband
probang
profane
progeny
prolong
propane
propend
propine
propone
protend
prudent
pruning
pudding
pugging
pulvini
pungent
punning
pupping
pushing
putting
queuing
quinine
quinone
radiant
ragging
railing
raiment
ralline
ramming
rampant
ramsons
ranking
rapping
rasping
rations
ratling
ratting
reading
reagent
reboant
rebound
recline
recount
redound
redwing
reeding
regnant
regrant
reliant
remains
remnant
remount
repaint
replant
reprint
rescind
resound
respond
rethink
retsina
retting
returns
revving
rewound
rhatany
ribband
ribbing
ridding
ridging
rifling
rigging
rimming
ringent
ringing
ripieni
ripieno
ripping
roaring

robbing
rocking
rodding
rolling
romaunt
Rommany
roofing
rotting
rousing
routine
rubbing
ruching
running
rutting
sacking
sacring
sagging
sailing
salient
salpinx
saltant
salting
sapient
sapling
sapping
sardine
sarking
savanna
scalene
scoring
scranny
scrawny
sealane
sealant
seapink
seatang
seating
seeming
segment
seizing
sequent
serpent
servant
serving
sestina
setting
Sextans
sextant
shading
shaving
shebang
shoeing
shoring
showing
siamang
sibling
siemens
sinning
sinsyne
sipping
sirgang
Sistine
sithens
sitting
sixaine
Sixtine
skating
skyline
slating
Slovene
smoking
soaking
soaring
sobbing
solvent
someone
sopping
soprani
soprano

sorbent
sordini
sordino
sotting
soutane
spacing
sparing
spirant
spleeny
squinny
staging
stamina
statant
stibine
stipend
student
styrene
subbing
subtend
sucking
suiting
sultana
summand
summing
summons
sunning
supping
surfing
suspend
sylvine
tabbing
tacking
tagging
tailend
tailing
talking
Tammany
tamping
tangent
tanning
tapping
tarring
tatting
taurine
taxiing
taxying
tearing
tedding
teeming
tegmina
telling
tenpins
termini
terpene
terrene
terrine
thymine
ticking
tiffany
timpani
timpano
tinning
tipping
tithing
titling
toluene
tontine
tooling
topping
torment
tormina
torrent
totting
touring
towline
towmond
towmont
trading
trepang
tribune
trident
tritone
tsarina
tubbing
tugging
tunning
turbine
turdine
turgent
turning
tutting
twoline
twotone
tympana
tympani
tympano
tympany
tyranny
tzigane
tzigany
ululant
unbound
uncanny
undoing
undying
unfunny
unguent
unjoint
unmeant
unsound
unthink
untwine
untying
unwound
upswing
uptrend
uterine
vaccine
vagrant
valiant
variant
varment
varmint
vatting
veiling
veining
verbena
verdant
versant
versine
vespine
vetting
vibrant
viewing
violent
violone
vitrine
volcano
vulpine
wadding
wagging
waiting
walking
walling
wanting
warning
warrant
warring
washing
waxwing
wearing
weasand
webbing
wedding
wedging
weekend
westing
wetting
whaling
whiting
wigging
wilding
willing
winding
winning
wishing
witling
witting
wording
working
writing
yapping
yardang
yenning
yipping
zapping
zebrine
zincing
zinking
zipping
zoogeny
zoogony
abaddon
abandon
abettor
ablator
actinon
adaptor
advisor
aerator
aerosol
aileron
airdrop
airflow
airglow
alation
alcohol
aleuron
aliquot
andiron
antilog
antlion
apricot
apropos
attaboy
auction
auditor
aviator
backlog
ballboy
balloon
bandbox
barroom
bassoon
bastion
bedroom
bellboy
bellhop
benison
benthos
bibelot
billion
birddog
blesbok
blossom
blouson
boobook
borazon
boredom
bourbon
bourdon
bowshot
boxroom
boxwood
boyhood
bridoon
Brython
buffoon
bugaboo
bulldog
bullion
burgeon
caisson
caldron
callbox
callboy
caltrop
camaron
camelot
camphor
campion
camwood
capitol
caption
cardoon
caribou
carrion
carryon
cartoon
catalos
cathood
caution
celadon
cession
chanson
chariot
charpoy
cheroot
cheviot
chevron
chiffon
chignon
Chinook
chorion
chrisom
clarion
coinbox
coition
complot
control
copepod
copilot
corncob
corydon
crampon
crannog
creator
crimson
crouton
crowtoe
cubhood
cullion
curacoa
curator
cushion
Cypriot
czardom
dashpot
daybook
dayroom
decagon
decapod
delator
demigod
destroy
develop
devisor
dewdrop
diadrom
diction
dilator
dilutor
disavow
disroot
divisor
dogtrot
dogwood
donator
dovecot
downbow
dragoon
dryshod
dudgeon
dukedom
dungeon
dyewood
eardrop
earldom
earshot
echelon
edition
eductor
eidolon
ejector
elation
elector
elision
elusion
elution
elytron
embosom
embryon
emotion
emperor
emption
enactor
enation
enderon
endozoa
enteron
entozoa
envelop
envenom
environ
epizoon
epsilon
equator
equinox
erector
erosion
ethanol
Euratom
evasion
evictor
exactor
exciton
excitor
eyebrow
eyedrop
eyeshot
eyespot
faction
fashion
feedlot
feoffor
fermion
festoon
fiction
fiefdom
filemot
filmdom
firebox
firedog
fission
flattop
fletton
fleuron
flexion
flummox
fluxion
flyblow
flybook
fogydom
footboy
footrot
foretop
forsook
fourgon
foxtrot
freedom
frescos
frisson
fronton
fusspot
gadroon
galipot
galleon
galliot
galloon
gearbox
gemsbok
genitor
ghettos
girasol
glutton
goatgod
godhood
gorcrow
gossoon
grantor
griffon
grottos
grunion
gryphon
grysbok
gudgeon
guerdon
Guignol
gumboot
gumdrop
gumshoe
gunroom
gunshot
halcyon
halidom
hangdog
hardtop
haricot
harpoon
hautboy
havenot
hebenon
helicon
hellbox
hellion
hencoop
heritor
hexagon
hexapod
highboy
hilltop
hiproof
horizon
hotfoot
hotshot
humidor
hyperon
icefloe
icefoot
iceshow
ichabod
incisor
isochor
isotron
Italiot
jackpot
janitor
jargoon
jibboom
jibdoor
jogtrot
jukebox
keelson
killjoy
kiloton
kingdom
knockon
knowhow
kolkhoz
krypton
lampion
lampoon
languor
lardoon
lection
legator
legiron
legroom
legshow
levator
lexicon
liaison
linkboy
livebox
logbook
logwood
longbow
longhop
lorgnon
lowbrow
lycopod
mailbox
maillot
maintop
malison
mamelon
manhood
manihot
manitou
mansion
marabou
markhor
marplot
matador
matelot
megaron
megaton
melilot
menthol
mention
metazoa
metopon
milksop
million
mirador
misknow
mission
mistook
monitor
monocot
monsoon
moorlog
mouflon
mullion
munnion
mylodon
neuston
neutron
newsboy
nonagon
noniron
nonstop
nucleon
nunhood
oakwood
obligor
octagon
octopod
omicron
oneshot
opinion
oration
organon
outcrop
outdoor
outflow
outfoot
outgrow
outlook
outshot
ovation
overtop
pageboy
paletot
parados
paradox
paragon
parasol
partook
passion
patriot
patroon
peascod
pension
peridot
phaeton
phantom
pharaoh
picador
pidgeon
pierrot
pigiron
pillbox
pillion
pitprop
platoon
playboy
pledgor
pleuron
plosion
plumbob
plywood
polygon
polypod
pontoon
portion
postbox
postboy
pothook
potshot
praetor
precook
predoom
proctor
pronaoi
pronaos
puccoon
pushrod
questor
raccoon
rainbow
Rajpoot
rampion
reactor
reallot
realtor
redwood
relator
reproof
reredos
retinol
reunion
revivor
rhabdom
ribston
roadhog
rollmop
rolltop
rooftop
rotator
rubicon
ruction
rumshop
saffron
saltbox
sandbox
sandboy
sandlot
sapajou
sapwood
saveloy
scallop
schnook
scissor
scollop
seaboot
seafood
searoom
section
semilog
senator
serfdom
session
settlor
shadoof
shallop
shallot
shallow
shampoo
shippon
shopboy
signior
silicon
similor
sjambok
skolion
soapbox
Solomon
somehow
soupcon
soursop
sparrow
sponson
sponsor
squalor
stardom
station
stemson
stentor
stepson
stetson
stewpot
Stilton
stridor
stuccos
suasion
subplot
suction
sunroof
sunspot
surgeon
swallow
symptom
taction
Tagalog
talayot
talipot
tallboy
tampion
tandoor
taproom
taproot
tearoom
teashop
telamon
tension
testoon
thereof
thereon
tinamou
tomfool

tompion
tonerow
toolbox
topknot
torchon
torsion
tosspot
toyshop
tractor
traitor
transom
treason
treetop
trollop
tsardom
tuckbox
tuition
tylopod
typhoon
unbosom
unction
upsilon
upthrow
venison
version
viceroy
visitor
vitriol
Walloon
warison
warrior
warthog
washpot
webfoot
whatnot
whereof
whereon
whitlow
widgeon
windrow
Windsor
witloof
wolfdog
workbox
yulelog
zillion
apocope
attempt
bagpipe
cacoepy
catalpa
concept
corrupt
cyclops
decrypt
digraph
disrupt
entropy
epitaph
ethiops
excerpt
forceps
galumph
gestapo
gossipy
grandpa
hiccupy
isotope
isotopy
jaloppy
miscopy
percept
perhaps
periapt
precept
preempt
receipt
reshape
satrapy
schappe
schlepp
scrappy
scrimpy
scrumpy
stroppy
syncope
therapy
tittupy
towrope
triceps
triumph
turnipy
unhappy
unkempt
upswept
acquire
actuary
adjourn
affaire
airfare
airport
algebra
aliform
allegro
almonry
alphorn
althorn
amatory
amphora
anymore
archery
armoire
armoury
arrears
artwork
athwart
austere
awkward
baccara
bandore
bastard
battery
bedsore
beggary
begorra
berserk
bibbery
bighorn
bigotry
biliary
bindery
bistort
bittern
bitters
bizarre
blowdry
bobbery
bollard
bombard
bonedry
bonfire
bonkers
bordure
bravery
bravura
brewery
bribery
bullary
bulwark
bursary
bustard
buttery
buzzard
caesura
caldera
calibre
calvary
camelry
camorra
cannery
canonry
capture
carport
cascara
catarrh
catbird
Cathari
Cathars
cattery
cautery
cavalry
caviare
censure
century
cerebra
chancre
chantry
chicory
chimera
chimere
cholera
ciliary
cindery
cistern
cithara
cithern
cittern
clivers
closure
cloture
coffers
collard
colours
coloury
comfort
compare
compart
compere
comport
conacre
concern
concert
concord
confirm
conform
conjure
conkers
consort
contort
convert
cookery
coppery
corpora
costard
country
couture
couvert
cowbird
cowherd
culture
culvert
cursory
custard
cutlery
cutworm
dastard
dasyure
daywork
deanery
deciare
declare
deepfry
deiform
denture
deodara
deplore
dessert
devilry
diehard
dietary
dioptre
diptera
disbark
discard
discern
discerp
discord
dishorn
dispark
dispart
disport
distort
disturb
dithery
dizzard
doddard
doddery
dodgery
dogcart
doggery
drapery
dripdry
drosera
dullard
dunbird
Dunkirk
earmark
eastern
eelworm
einkorn
electro
elusory
enquire
enquiry
ensnare
ensnarl
ephedra
epicarp
epicure
equerry
erasure
esotery
esquire
estuary
exocarp
explore
eyesore
factory
facture
failure
fanfare
feature
felonry
felwort
fenfire
fernery
fetters
figwort
filbert
firearm
fishery
fissure
fixture
flexure
flowery
foghorn
foolery
foppery
forbore
forearm
forgery
forlorn
forward
forworn
foulard
foumart
foundry
fratery
froward
futhark
futhorc
futhork
gallery
gasfire
gathers
gaudery
gauntry
gemmery
gerbera
gesture
giantry
gilbert
gingery
gittern
gizzard
godward
goliard
gramary
granary
grapery
gravure
grocery
gruyere
guipure
guisard
gullery
gunfire
gunnera
gunnery
gurnard
hachure
hackery
haggard
halberd
halbert
halvers
halyard
Hamburg
Hansard
hauberk
hayfork
hayward
haywire
hectare
helotry
hennery
heronry
hetaera
hetaira
hickory
history
hoggery
homburg
honours
hosiery
hunkers
hymnary
iceberg
imagery
impearl
implore
inboard
indoors
inkhorn
inquire
inquiry
inshore
inspire
Irishry
jaggery
January
jaybird
jewelry
jitters
jittery
jobbery
joinery
keyword
knavery
laggard
lambert
lancers
laniary
lantern
lanyard
lathery
laundry
lawlord
lechery
lectern
lecture
leeward
leghorn
legwork
leisure
leopard
leotard
letters
library
littery
llanero
lobworm
Lollard
Lombard
lottery
lowborn
lubbard
lugworm
macabre
Madeira
madwort
maestri
maestro
mallard
mammary
mandora
manners
mansard
manward
martyry
mascara
masonry
masters
mastery
mattery
mawworm
mazzard
measure
memoirs
mercery
mercury
miliary
mimicry
misfire
mixture
mockery
moidore
monkery
montero
mowburn
mudlark
mugwort
multure
mummery
mustard
mystery
nailery
nectary
nervure
network
newborn
niggard
nippers
nocturn
norward
nowhere
nummary
nunnery
nursery
nurture
oakfern
obolary
obscure
oilbird
olivary
onshore
oosperm
oospore
oratory
orchard
ossuary
ostiary
outport
outturn
outward
outwore
outwork
outworn
overarm
oviform
palmary
palmyra
pampero
pandora
pandore
pastern
pasture
pattern
peccary
pedlary
peppery
perdure
perform
perjure
perjury
perturb
pervert
pessary
philtre
phratry
piastre
picture
piggery
pillory
pincers
pinfire
pinworm
piscary
pismire
placard
plectra
plenary
plumery
pochard
podagra
polacre
pollard
poniard
popcorn
postern
posture
potherb
pottery
poulard
poultry
powdery
preform
prepare
primary
primero
procure
proverb
prudery
puckery
puffery
purport
purpura
purpure
quavery
quinary
quivery
ragworm
ragwort
rampart
rapport
rapture
rattery
rectory
reentry
reheard
remarry
require
respire
restart
restore
retiary
rettery
revelry
reynard
rhodora
rhubarb
ribwork
ribwort
ripcord
rivalry
riviera
riviere
robbery
rockery
roguery
rondure
rookery
rubbers
rubbery
rupture
saguaro
saltern
saltire
sanders
savoury
sawwort
saxhorn
scenery
sceptre
seabird
seagirt
sealery
seamark
seaport
seaward
seaware
sectary
seizure
senhora
sensory
servery
shastra
shikari
shivers
shivery
showery
signary
signora
signore
signori
signory
silvern
silvery
sincere
sintery
skyborn
skylark
skyward
slavery
soilure
sojourn
sorcery
spectra
spectre
spicery
spidery
spindry
stature
steward
subvert
subzero
succory
summary
summery
sunbird
sunburn
sunward
support
surgery
suspire
swinery
syncarp
tanagra
tanbark
tankard
tannery
tantara
tanyard
tartare
tatters
tattery
tempera
tempura
terebra
ternary
tessera
texture
theatre
tilbury
tindery
tinhorn
tinware
tipcart
titlark
toggery
tonsure
topiary
torture
tottery
tracery
tricorn
triform
trinary
tripery
Tsquare
tuatara
turbary
turnery
tushery
tussore
tutwork
unaware
unguard
unheard
unicorn
uniform
unitary
unlearn
unsnarl
unswore
unsworn
upstart
urethra
urinary
vampire
vanward

vapours
vapoury
vaquero
velours
venture
venturi
verdure
vespers
vesture
victory
viscera
vulture
wafture
waggery
warfare
warlord
waxwork
waymark
wayward
wayworn
webworm
welfare
western
winkers
wintery
withers
woomera
yardarm
yestern
yoghurt
zedoary
Zingari
Zingaro
zithern
abolish
abomasa
abreast
abscess
abscise
accurst
acerose
acquest
actress
address
adipose
adverse
against
ageless
aggress
agonise
agonist
aimless
airless
airmiss
airpost
amongst
amorist
amylase
amylose
analyse
analyst
anatase
anchusa
ancress
Anglist
anguish
animism
animist
anodise
anywise
appease
apprise
aptness
arabise
Arabist
armless
armrest
artless
asperse
atavism
atavist
atheism
atheist
athirst
atomise
atomism
atomist
autopsy
aweless
awnless
Baalism
babassu
babyish
baddish
badmash
badness
bagasse
Bahaism
Bahaist
baldish
ballast
baptise
baptism
baptist
bassist
beamish
bearish
because
bedfast
bedpost
bequest
biblist
biggest
biggish
bigness
biomass
blemish
boarish
bobbish
bombast
bookish
boorish
bossism
British
bromism
brutish
bruxism
bugloss
bullish
bulrush
burgess
Burmese
burnish
caboose
caddish
calypso
cambist
canvass
carcase
carcass
Carlism
Carlist
carouse
casuist
catfish
cellist
charism
chemise
chemism
chemist
cherish
Chinese
cineast
circusy
cirrose
cleanse
clerisy
codfish
coexist
cognise
coldish
colossi
coltish
combust
compass
compose
compost
Comtism
Comtist
concise
concuss
confess
confuse
congest
consist
contest
contuse
coolish
copyist
Cornish
cornist
cosmism
cosmist
Coueism
couldst
cowfish
coyness
cuirass
cultism
cultist
cupmoss
curiosa
currish
cutlass
cyclist
cypress
czarism
czarist
Dadaism
Dadaist
dampish
darkish
decease
declass
defrost
degauss
delouse
dentist
depress
dervish
despise
diabase
dialyse
diarise
diarist
diffuse
digress
dimmest
dimmish
dimness
diocese
diorism
discuss
disease
diseuse
disgust
dismast
dismiss
dispose
diverse
dockise
dogfish
doggish
dogrose
dollish
doltish
donnish
dryness
dualise
dualism
dualist
duchess
dullish
dulness
dumpish
durmast
earnest
ebonise
echoism
eclipse
ecstasy
eggcosy
egotise
egotism
egotist
elegise
elegist
elitism
elitist
ellipse
Elohism
Elohist
embassy
empress
emprise
enchase
enclasp
enclose
encrust
endless
endmost
endorse
endwise
English
engross
enthuse
entrust
entwist
erotism
espouse
euclase
eupepsy
eustasy
evanish
excurse
exhaust
expanse
expense
express
expulse
eyelash
eyeless
eyewash
faddish
faddism
faddist
fairish
fantasm
fantast
fantasy
farmost
Faroese
Fascism
Fascist
fatness
fattest
fattish
faunist
fauvism
fauvist
feudist
fewness
feyness
fideism
fideist
filasse
finesse
Finnish
fitness
fittest
Flemish
florist
flutist
flypast
fogyish
fogyism
foliose
foolish
foppish
fuguist
fulness
furbish
furioso
furnish
gabfest
gabnash
garfish
garnish
gasmask
Gaulish
gayness
Genoese
geodesy
girlish
glimpse
globose
glucose
gnomish
goatish
goddess
godless
goodish
gooiest
goulash
grecise
Grecism
greyish
grumose
gutless
gymnast
hagfish
haggish
hapless
harness
harpist
harvest
hashish
hatless
hawkish
heiress
hellish
heroise
heroism
hipness
Hobbism
Hobbist
hogfish
hoggish
hogwash
hostess
hotness
hottest
hottish
hueless
huffish
Hunnish
hymnist
iciness
idlesse
idolise
illness
imagism
imagist
immense
immerse
impasse
impresa
impress
imprest
impulse
incense
inclose
incrust
indorse
ingress
inhouse
inphase
inquest
intense
intrust
inverse
iridise
ironist
itacism
itemise
jackass
Jainism
jewfish
joyless
Judaise
Judaism
Judaist
judoist
jujitsu
Kaddish
kentish
kermess
keyless
kiddish
knavish
koumiss
Kurdish
kyanise
lactose
laicise
laicism
Lamaism
Lamaist
lambast
largess
largish
lawless
lawlist
laxness
leftism
leftist
legless
legrest
lentisk
leprosy
Lettish
license
lidless
lioness
lionise
lipless
longish
loudish
loutish
lowness
lowrise
lumpish
maddest
madness
mafiosi
mafioso
Mahdism
Mahdist
maidish
maidism
malaise
maltase
Maltese
maltose
manless
mannish
mannose
Marxism
Marxist
matrass
mawkish
metrist
midmost
Midwest
mightst
miscast
missish
mobbish
mollusc
molossi
monkish
Moorish
morassy
moreish
mortise
mudfish
mumpish
myalism
mythise
mythist
napless
Naziism
nearest
nebbish
necrose
Negress
netfish
newness
niceish
nourish
nunnish
nutcase
oarfish
oarless
obelise
obelisk
obverse
oculist
odalisk
oddness
ogreish
oloroso
onanism
oneness
operose
oppress
Orphism
outcast
outlast
outmost
outpost
outrush
overuse
oxidase
oxidise
ozonise
pachisi
palmist
papoose
pappose
parvise
paydesk
peckish
peeress
peevish
pelisse
pentose
peptise
percuss
perfuse
persist
pertuse
pettish
photism
phrensy
pianism
pianist
Pictish
pietism
pietist
piggish
pigwash
pinfish
pinkish
planish
plenish
plumose
poetess
poetise
poloist
poorish
poseuse
possess
precast
precise
premise
premiss
pretest
previse
process
profess
profuse
promise
propose
protest
protist
proviso
provost
prowess
prudish
publish
puckish
puggish
pugnose
purpose
quamash
querist
raffish
rawness
rayless
realise
realism
realist
recluse
reddest
reddish
redness
redress
refresh
regress
rehouse
relapse
release
remorse
repress
reprise
repulse
request
reverse
reversi
rhymist
roguish
Romansh
rubbish
rumness
runless
ruttish
Sabaism
sacrist
saddest
saddish
sadness
saidest
Saktism
saltish
sapless
sarcasm
sawdust
sawfish
Scotism
Scotist
seabass
seafish
selfish
Senussi
sexless
shyness
Siamese
sickish
Sikhism
sinless
sitfast
Sivaism
slavish
Slavism
slowish
slyness
softish
soloist
sonless
soonish
sophism
sophist
sottish
soubise
sourish
Spanish
spinose
spryest
statism
statist
stylise
stylish
stylist
subfusc
subsist
success
sucrose
suffuse
suggest
sundisc
sunfish
sunless
sunrise
sunwise
suppose
surbase
surmise
surpass
Swedish
swinish
synapse
tachism
tachist
talcose
tallish
tannish
tarbush
tarnish
tartish
taxless
teacosy
tearose
teleost
tempest
Thomism
Thomist
tigress
tigrish
Titoism
Titoist

toeless
topless
topmast
topmost
Toryism
tourism
tourist
townish
traipse
tricksy
tropism
tsarism
tsarist
tubbish
tundish
Turkish
twoness
tychism
unblest
unclasp
unclose
uncross
undress
unfussy
unhorse
unhouse
unleash
unloose
unroost
untruss
untwist
upraise
uranism
useless
utilise
utopism
utopist
vaguish
vamoose
vampish
vanessa
varnish
verbose
veriest
villose
vinasse
violist
viscose
voguish
waggish
wanness
wannish
warmish
waspish
wayless
weakish
Wendish
wetness
wettest
wettish
wheyish
whitish
whorish
whoseso
wigless
wildish
witless
witness
wolfish
wolvish
wottest
wouldst
wryness
Yahvist
Yahwist
Yiddish
Yorkist
Zionism
Zionist

Zoilism
Zoilist
ability
absinth
accrete
acetate
acidity
acolyte
aconite
actuate
Adamite
adulate
agility
agitate
agitato
alunite
amanita
amenity
amnesty
andante
anility
animate
annatta
annatto
annuity
anxiety
apatite
aplenty
arcuate
aridity
arietta
artiste
athlete
attrite
aureate
avidity
axolotl
azimuth
azurite
babbitt
baccate
Bahaite
barbate
batiste
bauxite
beneath
betroth
bheesty
biotite
biretta
bismuth
blewits
blighty
bornite
boxkite
boycott
breadth
brevity
bromate
brucite
bullate
burette
cahoots
calcite
calotte
canasta
cantata
cantate
carroty
cassata
caudate
cavetti
cavetto
celesta
celeste
chapati
charity
chelate
Chianti

christy
chupati
ciliate
citrate
clarity
clavate
climate
cocotte
cognate
collate
commute
compete
compote
compute
confute
connate
connote
coquito
coranto
cordate
cordite
cornett
cornuto
costate
cremate
crenate
crinite
crudity
cruelty
culotte
cuneate
cunette
cuprite
curette
curvate
cuspate
cutrate
cuvette
cyanite
dacoity
Debrett
deflate
density
dentate
deplete
despite
deviate
dictate
dignity
dinette
diorite
dispute
disrate
dogeate
doughty
dozenth
duality
dubiety
dynasty
ebonite
ebriate
ebriety
edacity
educate
effects
egality
elevate
emanate
emeriti
emicate
emirate
emulate
Encraty
enemata
entente
epidote
epilate
eremite
erudite

esparto
eucrite
evolute
exarate
excrete
execute
exegete
expiate
exudate
eyebath
faculty
fagotto
falcate
falsity
fatuity
felsite
fermata
ferrate
ferrety
ferrite
fidgets
fidgety
filiate
flaunty
flighty
foliate
formate
fouette
foveate
frailty
frigate
frowsty
furcate
furmety
furmity
gadgety
gahnite
galeate
gallate
garotte
gavotte
gazette
gemmate
genette
genista
gestate
giblets
Goliath
gradate
granita
granite
gravity
greenth
gummite
guttate
haporth
hastate
haughty
hipbath
hirsute
Hittite
honesty
hoplite
Hussite
hyalite
hydrate
imamate
imbrute
imitate
impaste
impasto
impiety
implete
inanity
indepth
infanta
infante
inflate
ingesta

ingrate
insecty
instate
isobath
isolate
iterate
jacinth
jadeite
Janeite
jollity
kainite
Karaite
keynote
khanate
kibbutz
kyanite
labiate
lactate
lavolta
layette
lemmata
leucite
liberty
librate
lignite
limbate
lineate
liquate
listeth
lomenta
lorette
loyalty
Luddite
lunette
lyddite
machete
magenta
maggoty
magmata
magnate
magneto
majesty
mammate
mammoth
mandate
mannite
marlite
marmite
matzoth
mediate
memento
migrate
miniate
misdate
mismate
Moabite
modesty
modiste
mofette
momenta
mozetta
mudbath
mulatto
muriate
musette
myomata
Nahuatl
naivete
naivety
narrate
naughty
Negrito
neolith
neonate
nervate
nictate
nimiety
nitrate
nitrite

novelty
nullity
obesity
obovate
obviate
octette
oculate
oilbath
omneity
oophyte
opacity
operate
otolith
outvote
overate
ovulate
oxalate
oxidate
palette
palmate
palpate
partita
partite
paucity
peltate
penalty
pennate
perlite
permute
phonate
picrate
pileate
pimento
pinnate
pipette
placate
planxty
plicate
plumate
podesta
polenta
pollute
poverty
pravity
predate
prelate
primate
private
privity
probate
probity
prolate
promote
pronate
prorate
puberty
pulsate
pycnite
quality
quinate
quixote
rabbity
rackety
radiate
ramenta
reality
rebirth
reflate
regatta
regrate
regrets
replete
requite
respite
restate
reunite
rewrite
rewrote
rickets

rickety
ricotta
ridotto
riposte
risotto
roseate
rosette
royalty
ruinate
russety
Sabaoth
Sabbath
saccate
sagitta
satiate
satiety
sawgate
scutate
secrete
septate
seriate
serrate
Servite
seventh
seventy
sfumato
Shemite
sigmate
sinuate
situate
Sivaite
society
solvate
spicate
spirits
squatty
statute
stealth
stomata
straits
stretta
stretto
strewth
striate
stylite
suavity
sublate
sulcate
sunbath
Sunnite
syenite
sylvite
taffeta
tallith
tannate
tektite
tensity
tenuity
tergite
termite
ternate
testate
thecate
themata
thereto
thirsty
thorite
thrifty
throaty
titrate
toccata
tomenta
towpath
tribute
trilith
trinity
turfite
turpeth
twelfth

ululate
uncouth
unearth
unfaith
unicity
unquote
untruth
uralite
utility
vacuity
vallate
valuate
valvate
variate
variety
varsity
vastity
Vedanta
vedette
veloute
velvety
vibrate
vibrato
vidette
viduity
violate
virgate
vitiate
vittate
volante
vulgate
warpath
weighty
whereto
zeolite
zincite
acetous
acinous
agamous
alodium
alumnus
alyssum
amateur
amentum
amorous
angelus
annicut
annulus
antique
anurous
anxious
apodous
applaud
aqueous
arbutus
arcanum
arduous
armsful
autobus
autocue
azygous
Bahadur
baleful
baneful
baroque
bashful
bateaux
bathtub
Bauhaus
becloud
Benelux
bezique
bilious
blowgun
blowout
bodeful
boletus
bookful
boozeup

bowlful
boxhaul
brantub
breakup
brimful
brumous
brusque
buildup
builtup
bulbous
bureaus
bureaux
burnous
cacique
cadmium
caesium
calamus
calcium
callous
cambium
candour
canthus
caracul
careful
carious
cartful
caseous
catchup
Celsius
centaur
centrum
charqui
checkup
chibouk
chillum
chirrup
chymous
cirrous
clamour
cleanup
closeup
clypeus
coconut
colobus
combout
conatus
conflux
contour
cookout
copious
coverup
crackup
cranium
Croesus
cumulus
cuprous
cupsful
curious
cyathus
danseur
decidua
decorum
defocus
defraud
detinue
devalue
devious
direful
doleful
doomful
dortour
douceur
driedup
dropout
dubious
duteous
dutiful
eardrum
earplug

easeful
echinus
eclogue
eelpout
eluvium
Elysium
elytrum
embolus
emulous
enamour
envious
ephebus
erratum
exergue
fadeout
fallguy
fallout
famulus
fanclub
farceur
fateful
fatigue
fatuous
fearful
fermium
ferrous
fervour
fibrous
firebug
fistful
flaneur
flareup
flatout
flavour
floccus
foldout
forerun
forkful
fraenum
Fraktur
frameup
fretful
friseur
frustum
fulcrum
fulgour
fullout
fulvous
fungous
furious
fuscous
gainful
gallium
gallnut
gaseous
gateaux
gibbous
giltcup
glamour
gleeful
gluteus
goldbug
grampus
grownup
grumous
habitue
hackbut
hafnium
haircut
halibut
hamulus
handful
handgun
handout
hangout
harbour
harmful
hateful
hauteur

heedful
heinous
helpful
hideous
hideout
hindgut
holibut
holmium
hoodlum
hopeful
hugeous
humdrum
humerus
hurtful
hydrous
icterus
igneous
impetus
impious
incubus
ingenue
ingroup
iridium
ischium
isthmus
jacobus
jealous
jejunum
karakul
ketchup
kingcup
kneesup
labarum
ladanum
ladybug
leafbud
leprous
lifeful
limbous
limulus
linctus
lineout
linocut
liqueur
lithium
locknut
lockout
loculus
lookout
lustful
lustrum
luteous
macaque
malleus
manhour
marybud
mashtub
masseur
maximum
mimulus
mindful
minibus
minimum
minimus
mistful
mixedup
modicum
modulus
muonium
nacrous
needful
nervous
niobium
nitrous
niveous
nocuous
nonplus
nostrum
noxious

nucleus
oblique
obloquy
obvious
occiput
ocellus
ochrous
octopus
odorous
oestrum
oestrus
oildrum
omentum
ominous
omnibus
onerous
onymous
opossum
optimum
organum
osculum
osseous
outhaul
overbuy
overdue
overrun
pabulum
pailful
painful
pallium
papyrus
parlour
parlous
pasteup
paviour
peasoup
Pegasus
pelorus
perique
petasus
petrous
phallus
piceous
pinetum
pipeful
piragua
pirogue
piteous
pitiful
playful
polypus
pomatum
pompous
popadum
premium
pressup
pronoun
proteus
protium
pullout
pulpous
punchup
punctum
pushful
pylorus
quahaug
quantum
Quechua
quietus
rancour
raucous
readout
refocus
regroup
regulus
reissue
relique
renegue
repique

reseaux
residua
residue
restful
retinue
revalue
revenue
rhamnus
rhenium
rhodium
rhombus
riotous
roomful
rosebud
rosecut
rostrum
roundup
rubadub
rubious
ruinous
ruthful
sackbut
sackful
Salique
sanctum
Sanctus
santour
sarcous
sardius
saviour
seablue
seaslug
sellout
senatus
serious
shakeup
shotgun
shutout
silenus
siliqua
silique
sinuous
sistrum
skellum
skilful
skinful
skyblue
smashup
smeddum
snarlup
solanum
solidus
songful
sorghum
soulful
speedup
spinous
spodium
spumous
stadium
standup
sternum
stickup
stirrup
stratum
stratus
stuckup
subaqua
succour
sulphur
surplus
surtout
tactful
talcous
tambour
tankful
tantrum
tapetum
tearful

tedious
tenuous
terbium
tetanus
thallus
thorium
thulium
thyrsus
timeous
toilful
touchup
trayful
triduum
trinkum
trismus
tritium
trivium
trochus
tumulus
tuneful
turnout
typhous
uberous
uncinus
uranium
uranous
vacuous
various
vicious
vidimus
villous
viscous
wailful
wakeful
walkout
wallrue
washout
washtub
Whitsun
wickiup
wingnut
wishful
wistful
without
wolfcub
woodcut
workout
wornout
writeup
yttrium
zealous
zestful
zoarium
absolve
abusive
achieve
airwave
amative
amusive
anchovy
approve
archive
baklava
beehive
behoove
believe
bereave
bivalve
captive
cassava
centavo
commove
concave
connive
copaiva
costive
cursive
deceive
deprave

deprive
deserve
devolve
dissave
elusive
emotive
enclave
engrave
enslave
erosive
evasive
exclave
festive
fictive
forgave
forgive
furtive
helluva
improve
incurve
innerve
involve
inweave
jussive
khedive
massive
misgave
misgive
missive
observe
outlive
pahlavi
passive
pensive
plosive
receive
recurve
relieve
relievo
replevy
reprove
reserve
resolve
restive
revolve
rilievo
screeve
scrieve
shrieve
stative
suasive
survive
tantivy
tensive
tussive
unitive
unnerve
unweave
upheave
zemstvo
beknown
bellows
billowy
bradawl
dorhawk
embrown
fernowl
furrowy
gallows
goshawk
hoedown
indrawn
ingrown
letdown
lichowl
lowdown
lychowl
marrowy
meadowy

mildewy
narrows
newmown
overawe
peafowl
pillowy
putdown
rubdown
rundown
sallowy
seafowl
setdown
shadowy
sitdown
sundown
tallowy
teagown
uncrown
unknown
willowy
yellowy
ataraxy
betwixt
cachexy
context
epitaxy
pickaxe
poleaxe
pretext
zootaxy
acronym
antonym
anyways
apteryx
benzoyl
buckeye
cacodyl
catseye
chlamys
cockeye
deadeye
dogdays
endways
fisheye
frogeye
goodbye
homonym
metonym
mooneye
paronym
pinkeye
polynya
shuteye
sockeye
spondyl
synonym
toponym
typonym
Vaishya
walleye
blintze
bonanza
cadenza
capsize
chalaza
chintzy
emblaze
guereza
humbuzz
mansize
mestiza
mestizo
organza
outsize
scherzi
scherzo
squeeze
tanooze
trapeze

unfroze

abomasa
aboulia
acantha
acequia
acerola
acicula
ackemma
actinia
addenda
adenoma
agrapha
alameda
alfalfa
alforja
algebra
alluvia
althaea
alumina
amanita
amboina
amboyna
amentia
ammonia
amnesia
amphora
ampulla
anaemia
anchusa
angioma
annatta
anosmia
antenna
aphasia
aphelia
aphonia
aplasia
apraxia
aquaria
arcadia
arietta
ascidia
asteria
atresia
aurelia
aureola
baccara
baklava
bandana
banksia
barilla
basidia
bazooka
begonia
begorra
biennia
biretta
bohemia
bologna
bonanza
bottega
bravura
breccia
britzka
bruhaha
buccina
bulimia
cabbala
cadenza
caesura
caldera
camorra
canasta
candela
cannula
cantata
cantina
carioca

cascara
cassata
cassava
catalpa
catawba
cedilla
celesta
cerebra
chalaza
chiasma
chimera
cholera
ciboria
cingula
cithara
clarkia
coagula
cochlea
comitia
conidia
copaiba
copaiva
cordoba
corella
corolla
corpora
corrida
corvina
cremona
curacoa
curcuma
curiosa
curtana
cypsela
czarina
decidua
deepsea
deodara
deutzia
digamma
dilemma
diorama
diploma
diptera
drachma
drosera
duodena
echidna
emporia
empyema
encomia
endozoa
enemata
entozoa
ephedra
erotica
euglena
eulogia
eutexia
exempla
exordia
exotica
exurbia
falbala
falcula
farruca
felucca
fermata
fibroma
filaria
fimbria
fistula
formula
fossula
foveola
freesia
frenula
fuchsia
furcula

galanga
galatea
ganglia
Gehenna
genista
gerbera
godetia
gondola
gonidia
gorilla
grandma
grandpa
granita
guarana
guereza
gunnera
Haggada
harmala
helluva
hemiola
hetaera
hetaira
hexapla
hidalga
hosanna
hymenia
hypogea
hypoxia
ikebana
impresa
indicia
indusia
inertia
infanta
infauna
ingesta
inocula
ipomoea
jellaba
kabbala
Kannada
kerygma
Krishna
labella
lamella
lantana
lasagna
latakia
lavolta
lemmata
leucoma
lobelia
lomenta
Madeira
madonna
madrona
magenta
magmata
mahatma
mahonia
malacia
malaria
mamilla
mandala
mandola
mandora
manilla
Maratha
maremma
marimba
Marsala
mascara
mastaba
maxilla
mazurka
medulla
melisma
mestiza
metazoa

militia
minorca
minutia
momenta
morphia
mousaka
mozetta
muraena
myalgia
mycelia
myeloma
myomata
naphtha
nemesia
Neogaea
neuroma
nirvana
notitia
noumena
novella
ocarina
opuntia
organza
osmunda
ostraca
ostraka
oversea
palmyra
panacea
pandora
panocha
papilla
paprika
parerga
pargana
partita
patagia
patella
peloria
pergola
persona
petunia
piragua
piranha
piscina
planula
platina
plectra
podagra
podesta
polacca
polenta
polynia
polynya
primula
pteryla
puparia
purpura
pyaemia
pyrexia
pyxidia
quassia
Quechua
ramenta
ratafia
regalia
regatta
replica
residua
retsina
rhodora
ricksha
ricotta
riviera
rosella
roseola
rotunda
rubella
rubeola

sagitta
sambuca
sangria
sarcoma
satsuma
savanna
saxtuba
scaglia
scapula
scholia
scopula
scotoma
sedilia
senhora
sequela
sequoia
seriema
seringa
serpula
sestina
shastra
signora
silesia
siliqua
sinopia
skimmia
solaria
solatia
spatula
spectra
specula
spicula
spiraea
stamina
stomata
stretta
subaqua
succuba
sudaria
sultana
syconia
synovia
syringa
taffeta
talaria
tamasha
tanagra
tantara
tapioca
tegmina
tempera
tempura
tequila
terebra
tessera
themata
toccata
tombola
tomenta
tormina
trachea
trehala
tsarina
tuatara
tympana
uraemia
urethra
Vaishya
valonia
valvula
vanessa
vanilla
variola
vascula
Vedanta
velaria
veranda
verbena
verruca

vexilla
viatica
vincula
viscera
vivaria
woomera
ziganka
bathtub
brantub
corncob
coulomb
coxcomb
disturb
ewelamb
fanclub
mahaleb
mashtub
minicab
pedicab
perturb
plumbob
potherb
proverb
rhubarb
rubadub
succumb
taxicab
washtub
wolfcub
abiotic
acerbic
acrylic
actinic
acyclic
aerobic
agnatic
alembic
alginic
allelic
almanac
aloetic
Amharic
amnesic
amoebic
anaemic
angelic
anionic
anoetic
anosmic
aphasic
aphetic
aphonic
aphotic
aquatic
Aramaic
archaic
Armoric
arsenic
ascetic
ascitic
aseptic
Asiatic
astatic
auxetic
Avestic
avionic
bacchic
baldric
barytic
benefic
benthic
benzoic
bivouac
boracic
botanic
bubonic
bucolic
butyric
Byronic

caloric
cambric
canonic
Canopic
caproic
cardiac
caustic
centric
ceramic
champac
chaotic
chloric
chromic
chronic
classic
clastic
Cluniac
coeliac
colonic
comedic
cometic
cryptic
deictic
deistic
Delphic
deltaic
demonic
demotic
dibasic
dimeric
docetic
drastic
druidic
dynamic
ectopic
edaphic
eidetic
eirenic
ekistic
elastic
Eleatic
elegiac
embolic
empiric
endemic
enteric
entomic
entotic
enzymic
epizoic
ergodic
eristic
erratic
etheric
eugenic
fanatic
faradic
fluidic
frantic
futhorc
galenic
gametic
gastric
generic
genetic
georgic
Glossic
glyphic
glyptic
gnathic
gnostic
graphic
Guelfic
Hamitic
Hebraic
hedonic
hepatic
heretic
hexadic

Homeric
hypoxic
icteric
identic
idiotic
idyllic
Islamic
japonic
kenotic
keramic
kinetic
Koranic
laconic
Liassic
lunatic
malefic
Masonic
meconic
meiotic
melanic
melodic
mesonic
metopic
miasmic
mimetic
mitotic
mollusc
monadic
monodic
moronic
muntjac
myalgic
mycotic
neozoic
nephric
neritic
Nilotic
Noachic
nomadic
nucleic
numeric
obconic
oceanic
odontic
oghamic
Olympic
omnific
oneiric
oolitic
ophitic
opsonic
orectic
organic
osmotic
ossific
pacific
paeonic
paretic
parodic
pelagic
peloric
phallic
phrenic
piperic
piratic
plasmic
plastic
plumbic
polemic
politic
potamic
priapic
prosaic
prussic
psychic
pteroic
pyaemic
pyloric
pyretic

pyrexic
pyritic
pyrrhic
quadric
quantic
quartic
quintic
racemic
Rhaetic
rhombic
Romanic
sapphic
satanic
satiric
satyric
scaldic
sceptic
sciatic
seismic
selenic
sematic
Semitic
shellac
silicic
skaldic
somatic
somitic
spastic
spathic
sphenic
spheric
splenic
stannic
stearic
sthenic
styptic
suberic
subfusc
sundisc
synodic
tabetic
tantric
technic
tetanic
thallic
theriac
thermic
titanic
tonemic
totemic
traffic
triadic
trophic
tryptic
valeric
vanadic
venatic
venefic
vivific
vocalic
voltaic
xanthic
yolksac
zetetic
zygotic
zymotic
abashed
Abbasid
abetted
abscond
abutted
accused
adenoid
advised
afeared
affined
aground
alleged
allseed

Amerind
amyloid
android
aneroid
aniseed
annelid
antacid
anyroad
applaud
applied
araneid
arcaded
arctoid
arcweld
armband
ascarid
ashamed
assured
astound
averred
awkward
barmaid
bastard
bearded
becloud
belated
beloved
berried
bestead
biassed
bighead
bigoted
bilobed
bistred
blabbed
blasted
blessed
bloated
blooded
blotted
blowzed
blurred
bobsled
bollard
bombard
bookend
bottled
bowhead
boxwood
boyhood
bragged
breaded
brigand
brimmed
brinded
bugeyed
builded
burweed
bustard
buttend
buzzard
campbed
camwood
candied
carload
carotid
castled
catbird
cathead
cathood
centred
cepheid
cestoid
chapped
charred
chatted
chested
chiliad
chipped

chopped
choroid
chuffed
chugged
chummed
cichlid
clammed
clapped
clipped
clogged
clotted
clubbed
clupeid
coccoid
collard
colloid
command
commend
compend
concord
contend
copepod
cornfed
costard
cowbird
cowhand
cowherd
cowshed
crabbed
cracked
cragged
crammed
crested
cribbed
cricoid
crinoid
crooked
cropped
crowned
crusted
ctenoid
cubhood
cuckold
cudweed
custard
cycloid
cystoid
dastard
deadend
deafaid
decapod
decided
defraud
deltoid
demigod
demoded
deodand
descend
despond
devoted
dewpond
dialled
diamond
diehard
dilated
diploid
disband
discard
discoid
discord
distend
dizzard
doddard
dogwood
dragged
dratted
dreamed
dripped
dromond

dropped
drubbed
drugged
drummed
dryeyed
dryshod
duelled
dullard
dunbird
dyewood
egghead
elfland
embowed
emerald
emersed
emitted
energid
enfiled
engaged
enwound
ericoid
ermined
ethmoid
excited
exposed
expound
exscind
faceted
fanfold
fathead
fenland
fibroid
figured
flaccid
flagged
flapped
fleeced
fleshed
flipped
flitted
flogged
flopped
flubbed
focused
footpad
forfend
forward
foulard
fracted
frapped
freaked
fretted
fritted
frogged
fronded
frosted
froward
fructed
fruited
fuelled
fungoid
Galahad
garland
gizzard
gladded
glenoid
globoid
glutted
gnarled
goahead
goatgod
godhead
godhood
godsend
godward
goitred
goliard
gorsedd
grabbed
grained
grandad
grilled
grinned
gripped
gritted
grubbed
guarded
guisard
gurnard
gwyniad
haggard
hagweed
halberd
halyard
Hansard
haploid
hatband
haunted
hayseed
hayward
hearted
hexapod
hocused
hogweed
holland
Homerid
hominid
honeyed
hopbind
hophead
hornmad
hothead
hundred
hurried
husband
hyaloid
hydatid
hydroid
hypnoid
icecold
ichabod
illbred
implead
impound
inboard
inbreed
incised
incused
infield
insipid
instead
insured
invalid
jaybird
jellied
katydid
keyword
kindred
knapped
knitted
knobbed
knotted
knurled
laggard
languid
lanyard
lawhand
lawlord
layered
leafbud
learned
leeward
lentoid
leopard
leotard
lieabed
lighted
limited
linseed
lipread
lithoid
logwood
Lollard
Lombard
louvred
lowbred
lowland
lubbard
lycopod
lymphad
lyrated
mahound
mallard
mangold
manhood
mankind
mansard
manward
marbled
married
marybud
mastoid
mattoid
mayweed
mazzard
mermaid
mettled
midland
minuend
misdeed
mislaid
mislead
misread
missend
moneyed
mottled
muscled
mustard
myeloid
negroid
newlaid
niggard
noctuid
nodated
nonskid
norland
norward
notched
notepad
nunhood
oakwood
oarweed
obovoid
octopod
odoured
oersted
offhand
offload
oilbird
oilseed
omitted
oneeyed
openend
operand
orchard
orotund
osteoid
outland
outsold
outward
overbid
overdid
overfed
oxyacid
palsied
parotid
parpend
payload
pearled
peascod
percoid
perpend
phasmid
pickled
piebald
pieeyed
piglead
pigweed
pinfold
pinguid
pinhead
pitched
pithead
placard
placoid
plafond
plaided
planned
plasmid
plastid
platted
pleased
plodded
plopped
plotted
plugged
plywood
pochard
pofaced
pointed
pollard
polypod
poniard
popeyed
poppied
portend
pothead
pouched
poulard
prebend
prepaid
pretend
primmed
proband
proceed
prodded
pronged
propend
propped
proteid
protend
pushrod
pygmoid
pyralid
pyramid
quipped
quitted
quizzed
ragweed
ravined
rebound
rebuild
redhead
redound
redwood
refined
reheard
related
relayed
remould
removed
reputed
rescind
resound
respond
retired
retread
rewound
reynard
rhizoid
ribband
ripcord
rivered
roadbed
rosebud
rosered
rounded
sainted
Samoyed
sandbed
saphead
sapwood
sarcoid
satyrid
sauroid
scabbed
scabrid
scanned
scarfed
scarred
scatted
scented
sciarid
screwed
scudded
scummed
seabird
seafood
seamaid
seaward
seaweed
seedbed
selffed
semiped
serried
shammed
shanked
shelled
shelved
shinned
shinpad
shipped
shogged
shopped
shunned
sialoid
sickbed
sighted
sigmoid
sixfold
skidded
skidlid
skilled
skimmed
skinned
skipped
skirted
skyward
slabbed
slagged
slammed
slapped
slatted
sledded
sleeved
slipped
slogged
slopped
sloshed
slotted
slubbed
slugged
slummed
slurred
smaragd
smutted
snagged
snapped
snipped
snouted
snubbed
sofabed
soliped
sozzled
spanned
sparoid
sparred
spatted
spitted
spotted
spurred
squalid
stabbed
stalked
starred
statued
stemmed
stepped
sterned
steroid
stetted
steward
stilted
stipend
stirred
stopped
storied
striped
stubbed
studded
studied
stummed
stunned
stunted
styloid
subacid
subdued
subhead
subtend
succeed
summand
sunbird
sunward
suspend
sutured
swabbed
swagged
swanned
swapped
swarded
swatted
swigged
swobbed
swopped
swotted
sylphid
syrphid
tabanid
tabloid
tailend
taloned
tankard
tanyard
tenfold
tentbed
testbed
thinned
thorned
throned
thudded
thyroid
toehold
toothed
touched
towered
towhead
towmond
trapped
trekked
tressed
triacid
trimmed
tripped
trotted
turdoid
twigged
twilled
twinned
twitted
twofold
tylopod
Tynwald
typhoid
ulcered
unarmed
unasked
unbated
unbound
unbowed
unboxed
unbuild
unguard
unheard
unhoped
unlined
unmixed
unmoved
unpaged
unsaved
unsexed
unsound
untried
untuned
unwound
upbraid
upfield
uptrend
vanward
vaulted
Veddoid
visaged
visored
vistaed
volumed
voluted
waisted
warhead
warlord
watered
wattled
waylaid
wayward
weasand
weekend
wergild
wheeled
whetted
whipped
whirred
whizkid
whizzed
whorled
widowed
wizened
woolled
worsted
wrapped
xiphoid
ycleped
zebroid
zincked
zonated
abalone
abridge
abscise
absence
absolve
abubble
abusive
academe
accidie
accrete
acerose
acetate
acetone
achieve
acolyte
aconite
acquire
acreage
actuate
Adamite
addable
addible
adenine
adipose
adjudge
adulate
advance
adverse
affable
affaire
agitate
agonise
agraffe
airfare
airhole
airline
airwave
ajutage
alanine
alcaide
alcalde
alcayde
alewife
alidade
allonge
alltime
alumnae
alunite
amative
ambsace
amiable
amoebae
ampoule
amputee
amusive
amylase
amylose
anagoge
analyse
anatase
andante
anemone
anglice
anguine
aniline
animate
anodise
anodyne
antique
anymore
anytime
anywise
apagoge
apanage
apatite
apocope
apolune
apostle
appease
apprise
approve
arabise
archive
arcuate
areolae
aristae
armhole
armlike
armoire
arrange
article
artiste
ascribe
asinine
askance
asperse
assuage
astable
astride
athlete
atingle
atomise
attache
attrite
audible
aureate
aureole
auricle
aurorae
auspice
austere
autocue
avarice
average
awesome
axillae
azurine
azurite
baccate
bagasse
baggage
bagpipe
Bahaite
balance
ballade
bandage
bandore
banshee
baptise
barbate
barbule
barline
baroque
barrage
bascule
batiste
bauxite
because
bedside
bedsore
bedtime
beehive
beeline
begrime
beguile
beguine
behoove
beldame
believe
Beltane
benzene
benzine
benzole
bereave
berhyme
berline
besiege
bespoke
bezique

bheetie capsule cologne cripple dilutee enforce fanfare furcate hectare
bicycle captive combine cristae dinette enframe fargone furnace Hellene
bigname capture commode crowdie diocese engorge Faroese furtive hemione
bigtime capuche commove crowtoe dioptre engrave fascine fusible hemline
biotite carbide commune crumble diorite enhance fatigue gabelle henbane
biplane carbine commute crumple dioxide enlarge feature gahnite henwife
bivalve carcase compare crusade disable ennoble febrile galeate heptane
bizarre carinae compere cubicle disease enounce fedayee galilee herbage
blintze cariole compete cuisine diseuse enplane felsite gallate herniae
bobeche carline compile cuittle disfame enquire fenfire gallice heroine
bolshie carmine compose culotte dislike enslave feoffee gambade heroise
bondage carnage compote culture dispose ensnare ferrate gamboge hipbone
bonfire caroche compute cuneate dispute entente ferrite garbage hirable
booksie carouse comrade cunette disrate enthuse ferrule garotte hircine
bordure cartage conacre cupcake disrobe entitle fertile garpike hirsute
bornite cascade concave cuprite dissave entwine festive gasfire histone
boscage caserne concede curable diverge epergne fiancee gavotte Hittite
boskage castile conchae curette diverse epicede fibulae gazelle hoecake
bouchee catenae conchie cursive divorce epicene fictile gazette hoplite
bourree cathode concise curvate divulge epicure fictive gemmate hormone
bowline catlike condole cuspate dockage epidote figtree gemmule hospice
boxkite catseye condone cuticle dockise epigene filasse genette hostage
boxlike caudate conduce cutline dogbane epigone filiate Genoese hostile
brabble caviare condyle cutrate dogeate epilate finagle gentile Hussite
braille cayenne confide cuvette doggone episode finance genuine hyaline
bramble celeste confine cyanide dogrose epistle finesse Geordie hyalite
bransle cellule confuse cyanine dogvane epitome firtree germane hydrate
brantle cenacle confute cyanite dominie epoxide fisheye gestate hydride
brassie censure coniine cyclone dormice equable fissile gesture hygiene
brattle centime conjure cystine dovekie erasure fissure ghillie icefloe
breathe cervine connate dapsone doyenne eremite fixable giraffe idlesse
brewage cestode connive dariole drabble erosive fixture glimpse idolise
brickie Chaldee connote dasyure draftee erudite flavine globose ignoble
brickle chalice console datable draggle escapee flexile globule imagine
bricole chalone consume daytime drayage escribe flexure glucose imamate
brigade chancre contuse deadeye dribble espouse floosie glycine imbrute
brindle chappie convene debacle drizzle esquire floozie godlike imitate
brioche charade convoke decease dualise essence flotage goodbye immense
bristle charlie coontie deceive ductile essoyne flounce gouache immerge
brittle chelate coppice deciare dunnage estrade flowage grabble immerse
brocade chemise coracle declare dupable etamine fluence gracile impasse
brokage chicane cordage decline durable euclase flyable grackle impaste
bromate chimere cordate decuple durance eucrite flybane gradate impinge
bromide Chinese cordite defence dwindle evacuee foggage gradine implete
bromine chocice corkage deflate earache evasive foliage grandee implode
brownie choline cornage deforce earhole evolute foliate granite implore
brucine chopine cornice degrade earlobe examine foliole grannie improve
brucite chorale coronae dehisce eatable example foliose grantee impulse
brusque chorine corrode deicide ebbtide exarate footage granule incense
buckeye chortle corsage delaine ebonise exclave footsie grapple incline
bugbane chuckle cortege delouse ebonite exclude forbade gravure inclose
bullace ciliate cortile demesne ebriate excrete forbode grecise include
bullate cineole corvine dentate eccrine excurse forbore grenade incurve
buoyage cirrose costate dentine eclipse execute fordone gribble indorse
burette citable costive denture eclogue exedrae foresee griddle indulge
burgage citrate costume deplane edifice exegete forgave grimace infante
Burmese citrine coterie deplete educate exergue forgive gristle inflame
buyable cladode cottage deplore effulge expanse forgone grizzle inflate
cabbage clavate courage deplume egotise expense formate groupie infulae
caboose cleanse couthie deprave elegise expiate forsake grumble ingenue
cacique climate couture deprive elevate explode fortune grumose ingrate
caddice clippie couvade derange ellipse explore fouette gruntle inhouse
cadence cloacae cowbane deserve elusive expulse fourale gruyere innerve
cagoule closure cowhage despise emanate expunge foveate guanine inphase
calcine cloture cowhide despite emblaze externe foxhole guardee inquire
calcite cocaine cowpoke destine embrace extreme fragile guayule inshore
calibre cockade crackle deterge emetine extrude frazzle guipure insigne
caliche cockeye cranage detinue emicate exudate freckle gummite inspire
calicle cocotte crankle detrude emirate exuviae freebie gumshoe instate
calipee codable crappie devalue emotive eyehole friable gunfire intense
calorie codeine cremate deviate emplace eyelike fribble gunwale interne
calotte cognate crenate devisee emplane eyesore frigate guttate intrude
calycle cognise crevice devolve emprise Faberge frijole habitue intwine
cantate coinage cribble devotee emulate facture frizzle hachure inutile
canzone collage crimine diabase enchase faculae frogeye hapence inverse
capable collate crimple dialyse enclave faience fullage hastate invitee
caprice college cringle diarise enclose failure fulmine hatable invoice
caprine collide crinite dictate endorse Falange fulsome haulage involve
capsize collude crinkle diffuse endwise falcate funicle haywire inweave

iridise	macabre	multure	outline	perigee	probate	respire	seablue	speckle
irksome	macaque	mundane	outlive	perique	procure	respite	seakale	spectre
isolate	machete	muriate	outpace	perjure	produce	restate	sealane	spicate
isotope	machine	musette	outrage	perlite	profane	restive	seaside	spicule
itemise	macrame	mutable	outride	permute	profile	restore	seaware	spindle
iterate	maculae	mythise	outrode	pertuse	profuse	restyle	seawife	spinode
jadeite	magnate	nacelle	outside	pervade	prolate	resurge	seclude	spinose
Janeite	malaise	naivete	outsize	petiole	promise	retable	seconde	spinule
jasmine	maltase	namable	outsole	Petrine	promote	reticle	secrete	spireme
jawbone	Maltese	narrate	outtake	philtre	pronate	retinae	sectile	spittle
joyance	maltose	nebulae	outvote	phonate	propane	retinue	seeable	splodge
joyride	mammate	necktie	outwore	phoneme	propine	retrace	seepage	splurge
jubilee	manacle	necrose	overage	piastre	propone	reunite	seizure	spondee
Judaise	manatee	neglige	overate	pickaxe	propose	revalue	selvage	sporule
jussive	mandate	neonate	overawe	picotee	prorate	revenge	septate	springe
justice	manhole	Neptune	overdue	picrate	protege	revenue	septime	spunkie
kainite	manille	nervate	overlie	picture	provide	reverie	serfage	spurtle
Karaite	maniple	nervine	oversee	pileate	provoke	reverse	seriate	spyhole
kathode	manlike	nervure	overuse	pillage	puerile	revolve	serrate	squamae
keyhole	manmade	netlike	ovicide	pillule	puggree	rewrite	service	squeeze
keynote	mannite	netsuke	ovulate	pinfire	pugnose	rewrote	servile	stabile
khanate	mannose	neurine	oxalate	pinhole	pulsate	rhizome	Servite	staddle
khedive	mansize	neurone	oxfence	pinkeye	purpose	ridable	sessile	staithe
knobble	marline	newcome	oxidase	pinnace	purpure	riposte	sextile	startle
knuckle	marlite	nictate	oxidate	pinnate	pustule	riptide	shackle	statice
kyanise	marmite	nightie	oxidise	pinnule	pycnite	risible	shamble	stative
kyanite	marquee	nitrate	oxytone	pipette	quayage	rissole	sheathe	stature
labiate	massage	nitride	ozonise	pirogue	quibble	riviere	sheltie	statute
lactate	massive	nitrile	package	piscine	quickie	rodlike	Shemite	steeple
lactose	matinee	nitrite	packice	pismire	quinate	romance	shingle	stemple
lacunae	maypole	noctule	padrone	pistole	quinine	rondure	shortie	sterile
laicise	Maytime	noisome	palette	placate	quinone	rootage	shrieve	stibine
lairage	measure	nominee	palmate	platane	quixote	ropable	shuffle	stickle
laminae	mediate	notable	palpate	pledgee	radiate	roseate	shuteye	stipple
lasagne	medusae	novelle	panache	pleurae	radicle	rosette	shuttle	stipule
latrine	melange	nowhere	pancake	pliable	radulae	roulade	Siamese	stopple
lattice	message	nuclide	pandore	plicate	ragtime	routine	sigmate	storage
layette	methane	nurture	panicle	pliskie	ralline	ruinate	signore	stowage
leafage	micelle	nutcase	pannage	plosive	rampage	rummage	silence	strange
leakage	microbe	nutlike	pantile	plumage	raphide	rundale	silicle	striate
lecture	midline	nutpine	papoose	plumate	rapture	rupture	silique	strophe
legatee	midwife	oaktree	pappose	plumose	ratable	saccade	sincere	strumae
legible	migrate	oatcake	papulae	plumule	ratlike	saccate	sinkage	stubble
leisure	mileage	obelise	parable	plusage	rawhide	saccule	sinsyne	stumble
leonine	miniate	obligee	parolee	poetise	realise	salable	sinuate	stylise
lettuce	mintage	oblique	partake	polacre	receive	Salique	Sistine	stylite
leucine	Miocene	obovate	partite	poleaxe	reclame	saltire	situate	styrene
leucite	miracle	obscene	parvise	pollute	recline	salvage	Sivaite	suasive
librate	misdate	obscure	passade	pondage	recluse	sanicle	sixaine	sublate
licence	misdone	observe	passage	pontage	recurve	saprobe	Sixtine	sublime
license	misfire	obtrude	passive	porcine	recycle	sarcode	sizable	subside
lignite	misgave	obverse	pastime	portage	referee	sardine	skiable	subsume
likable	misgive	obviate	pasture	poseuse	reflate	satiate	skiffle	subtile
limbate	mislike	occlude	Pauline	postage	refugee	sausage	skittle	succade
lindane	mismate	octette	payable	posture	regorge	savable	skyblue	sucrose
lineage	misname	octuple	paysage	potable	regrate	sawgate	skyline	suffice
lineate	misrule	oculate	pebrine	potence	rehouse	sayable	Slovene	suffuse
linkage	missile	offence	pedicle	pothole	reissue	scabble	smuggle	suicide
lionise	missive	offside	peerage	pottage	rejoice	scalade	snaffle	sulcate
liquate	mistake	oilcake	pelisse	prairie	relapse	scalene	sniffle	sullage
lissome	mistime	oldtime	peltate	praline	release	scapple	sniggle	Sunnite
livable	mixture	olefine	penance	prattle	relieve	sceptre	snoozle	sunrise
lockage	Moabite	olivine	penname	precede	relique	schappe	snuffle	sunwise
logline	modiste	onetime	pennate	precise	remorse	science	snuggle	suppose
looksee	mofette	onshore	pennine	predate	renegue	scoriae	soakage	supreme
lorette	moidore	onstage	pensile	preface	repique	scotice	soccage	surbase
loricae	monocle	oophyte	pensive	prelate	replace	Scottie	sockeye	surface
losable	montage	oospore	pentane	prelude	replete	scourge	soignee	surmise
lovable	montane	opaline	pentode	premise	reprise	scrapie	soilure	surname
lowrise	mooneye	operate	pentose	prepare	reprove	screeve	soluble	survive
lozenge	moorage	operose	peonage	presage	reptile	scrieve	solvate	suspire
lucarne	moraine	opuscle	peptide	preside	repulse	scrooge	someone	swaddle
lucerne	mortice	orifice	peptise	presume	require	scrouge	sonance	sweetie
Luddite	mortise	ossicle	peptone	previse	requite	scruple	soubise	swindle
luggage	morulae	ostiole	percale	prickle	rescale	scuffle	souffle	swingle
lughole	Moselle	outcome	percine	primage	reserve	scumble	soutane	swipple
lunette	Mountie	outdone	perdure	primate	reshape	scutage	spangle	swizzle
lurdane	mousmee	outface	perfume	prithee	residue	scutate	sparkle	syenite
lyddite	movable	outgone	perfuse	private	resolve	scuttle	spattee	sylvine

sylvite tribune vendace debrief bobbing fagging halting lobbing plating
synapse tribute ventage distaff boiling failing Hamburg lodging playing
syncope trickle venture earmuff booking fairing hamming logging podding
syringe trindle verbose enfeoff bootleg falling handbag longing popping
systole tringle verdure faceoff bopping fanning hangdog looking postbag
tactile tripple versine falloff bowling farcing hanging lopping posting
tadpole trireme vesicae figleaf bracing farming happing lording potting
taeniae tritone vesicle flyhalf broking fatling hatting lotting pouting
talcose trochee vespine flyleaf budding fatting heading lugging priming
tallage trouble vestige handoff bugging feeding hearing lumbang probang
tamable trounce vesture herself bulldog feeling heating madding prolong
tankage truckle vibrate himself bumming felting helping mahjong pruning
tannage truffle vidette hiproof bunting fencing hemming mailbag pudding
tannate trundle village jumpoff burning fibbing herring mailing pugging
tanooze trustee villose kickoff busking figging hilding malting punning
tartare Tsquare vinasse leadoff bussing filibeg hipping manning pupping
Tartufe tunable vintage liftoff cabling filling hitting mapping pushing
taurine tunicle violate mastiff calling finding hogging marking putting
taxable turbine violone midriff camping finning holding marring quahaug
taxfree turdine virgate oneself canning firebug homburg matting queuing
teacake turfite virgule ourself canting firedog hopping meaning ragging
tearose tussive viscose playoff capping fishing housing meeting railing
teatime tussore visible pontiff carking fitting howling melting ramming
teenage twaddle vitiate rakeoff carping flaming hugging mending ranking
tektite twangle vitrine reproof carving fleabag hulking milking rapping
tenable twiddle vittate restiff casting fleeing humming milkleg rasping
tensile twinkle vocable sawnoff catling Fleming hunting mincing ratling
tensive twoline voivode seawolf ceiling fluting hurling missing ratting
tergite twosome volante sendoff chinwag flyting husking misting reading
termite twotime voltage shadoof coaming fobbing hutting mobbing redwing
ternate twotone voluble shereef coating fogging iceberg mooring reeding
terpene tzigane votable sheriff codling folding ingoing moorlog retting
terrace ukelele vouchee showoff cogging footing inkling mopping revving
terrene ukulele vulgate spinoff conning fopling inswing morning ribbing
terrine ululate vulpine stopoff cooking foreleg ironing morwong ridding
testate umbrage vulture sunroof corking forging jabbing mosshag ridging
tetrode unaware wadable takeoff costing fowling jamming mousing rifling
textile unbrace waftage tealeaf cowling fugging jarring mugging rigging
texture unclose wafture thereof crannog funning jetting mumming rimming
thanage unfroze Wahabee thyself craving furlong jibbing munting ringing
thankee ungulae walleye welloff cubbing furring jigging mustang ripping
theatre unhinge wallrue werwolf cunning gabbing jobbing nabbing roadhog
thecate unhorse warfare whereof cupping gadding jogging nagging roaring
thermae unhouse wargame witloof curling gagging joining napping robbing
thimble unitive warlike abiding cutting galling jotting nesting rocking
thistle unloose wartime agelong dabbing gamebag jugging netting rodding
thorite unnerve wastage amazing damming gasring jutting nipping rolling
thuggee unquote wattage angling damning gassing kampong nodding roofing
thymine unswore waxtree antilog darling gateleg karting nogging rotting
tillage untwine wayside backing darning gatling keeping nooning rousing
timbale unweave weirdie backlog dashing gearing kenning nosebag rubbing
tinware upgrade welcome bagging dawning geebung keyring noserag ruching
titmice upheave welfare balding daylong gelding kidding nothing running
titrate upraise whangee banking dealing gelling killing nursing rutting
toluene upstage wheedle banning decking gemming kissing nutting sacking
tonnage upsurge whiffle banteng dibbing genning knowing oakling sacring
tonsure uralite whistle banting digging getting lacking ongoing sagging
tontine uranide whittle barring dimming gigging ladybug opening sailing
tootsie urodele whoopee basting dinning gilding lagging packing salting
tophole uterine windage bathing dipping ginning lamming padding sandbag
topside utilise winsome batting dogging ginseng landing panning sapling
torsade utricle woodpie beading donning glaring lapping parting sapping
tortile vaccine wordage beanbag Dorking glazing lapwing passing sarking
torture vacuole wouldbe bearing dotting glozing lashing patting scoring
torulae valance wrangle beating drawing godling lasting pegging seaslug
towline valence wreathe bedding driving goldbug lathing pelting seatang
towrope vallate wrestle begging droving golfbag leading pending seating
traduce valuate wriggle belting dubbing golfing leaning penning seeming
trainee valvate wrinkle belying ducking gosling legging pepping seizing
traipse valvule yardage betting ducting grating lemming periwig semilog
trample vamoose yewtree bibbing dunning grazing lending petting serving
tranche vampire zebrine bidding earplug greylag letting pfennig setting
trapeze Vandyke zeolite billing earring Gstring licking pigging shading
treacle vantage zincite biltong easting gumming lilting pigling shaving
treadle variate zipcode binding endlong gunning linsang pimping shebang
tremble variole bailiff birddog erelong gushing lipping pinking shindig
trestle vedette boxcalf bitting erlking gutting listing pinning shoeing
triable vehicle caitiff blueing etching gypping loading pipping shoring
tribade veloute castoff boating evening hacking loaning pitting showing

siamang
sibling
sinning
sipping
sirgang
sitting
skating
slating
smoking
soaking
soaring
sobbing
sopping
sotting
spacing
sparing
staging
subbing
sucking
suiting
summing
sunning
supping
surfing
tabbing
tacking
Tagalog
tagging
tailing
talking
tamping
tanning
tapping
tarring
tatting
taxiing
taxying
tearing
tedding
teeming
telling
tentpeg
thalweg
ticking
timelag
tinning
tipping
tithing
titling
tooling
topping
totting
touring
trading
trepang
tubbing
tugging
tunning
turning
tutenag
tutting
undoing
undying
untying
upswing
vatting
veiling
veining
vetting
viewing
wadding
wagging
waiting
walking
walling
wanting
warning
warring
warthog
washing
waxwing
wearing
webbing
wedding
wedging
westing
wetting
whaling
whiting
wigging
wilding
willing
windbag
windegg
winding
winning
wishing
witling
witting
wolfdog
wording
workbag
working
writing
yapping
yardang
yenning
yipping
yulelog
zapping
zincing
zinking
zipping
abolish
abroach
absinth
almirah
ambatch
anguish
azimuth
babyish
baddish
badmash
baldish
beamish
bearish
beneath
beseech
betroth
bewitch
biggish
bismuth
blemish
boarish
bobbish
bookish
boorish
borough
bortsch
braunch
breadth
British
brutish
bullish
bulrush
burnish
caddish
catarrh
catfish
ceilidh
cheetah
cherish
chuddah
codfish
coldish
coltish
coolish
Cornish
cowfish
craunch
currach
curragh
currish
dampish
darkish
debauch
debouch
Delilah
dervish
digraph
dimmish
diptych
distich
djibbah
dogfish
doggish
dollish
doltish
donnish
dozenth
dullish
dumpish
endarch
English
epitaph
evanish
eyebath
eyelash
eyewash
faddish
fairish
fattish
Finnish
Flemish
fogyish
foolish
foppish
furbish
furnish
gabnash
galumph
garfish
garnish
Gaulish
genizah
girlish
gnomish
goatish
Goliath
goodish
goulash
graunch
greenth
greyish
hagfish
haggish
Halakah
haporth
hashish
hawkish
hellish
hipbath
hogfish
hoggish
hogwash
hottish
huffish
Hunnish
impeach
indepth
inveigh
isobath
jacinth
jewfish
Kaddish
kentish
kiddish
knavish
Kurdish
largish
Lettish
listeth
longish
loudish
loutish
lumpish
maidish
mammoth
mannish
Masorah
mastich
matzoth
mawkish
menorah
messiah
mezuzah
Mishnah
missish
mitzvah
mobbish
monarch
monkish
Moorish
moreish
mudbath
mudfish
mumpish
nebbish
neolith
netfish
niceish
nomarch
nonsuch
nourish
nunnish
oarfish
ogreish
oilbath
ostrich
otolith
outrush
peckish
peevish
pettish
pharaoh
pibroch
Pictish
piggish
pigwash
pinfish
pinkish
planish
plenish
poohbah
poorish
prudish
publish
puckish
puggish
quamash
quetsch
raffish
rebirth
reddish
refresh
retouch
roguish
Romansh
rubbish
ruttish
Sabaoth
Sabbath
saddish
saltish
sawfish
scratch
screech
scrunch
seafish
selfish
seventh
sickish
skyhigh
slavish
slowish
softish
soonish
sottish
sourish
Spanish
spinach
splotch
squelch
squinch
squitch
staunch
stealth
stomach
stretch
strewth
stylish
sunbath
sunfish
Swedish
swinish
tallish
tallith
tannish
tarbush
tarnish
tartish
through
tigrish
torgoch
townish
towpath
trilith
triumph
tubbish
tundish
Turkish
turpeth
twelfth
uncouth
unearth
unfaith
unhitch
unlatch
unleash
unteach
untruth
vaguish
vampish
varnish
voguish
waggish
wannish
waratah
warmish
warpath
waspish
weakish
Wendish
wettish
wheyish
whitish
whorish
wildish
wolfish
wolvish
Yiddish
zaptieh
alveoli
assagai
assegai
bacilli
bambini
basenji
Bengali
bilimbi
biriani
bouilli
bronchi
caducei
calculi
canzoni
Cathari
cavetti
chapati
charqui
Chianti
chupati
colossi
dashiki
denarii
effendi
elenchi
emeriti
epigoni
gingili
gnocchi
gourami
guarani
hallali
Ismaili
Israeli
lapilli
macrami
maestri
mafiosi
Marathi
marconi
martini
menisci
molossi
nauplii
nautili
origami
pachisi
padroni
pahlavi
Panjabi
pronaoi
pulvini
Punjabi
ravioli
remblai
reversi
ripieni
sacculi
samurai
sarangi
sashimi
scherzi
scirrhi
secondi
senarii
Senussi
shikari
signori
soprani
sordini
stimuli
succubi
Swahili
syllabi
termini
thalami
thrombi
timpani
tripoli
tsunami
tympani
venturi
vitelli
Zingari
airlock
airsick
amtrack
artwork
bannock
barrack
bawcock
beatnik
bedrock
bedsock
berserk
bespeak
bethink
bibcock
bittock
blesbok
boobook
bullock
bulwark
burdock
buttock
cabrank
calpack
carrack
carsick
cassock
catwalk
champak
chibouk
Chinook
cossack
cowlick
cutback
daybook
daywork
defrock
derrick
disbark
dispark
disrank
dorhawk
dornick
drydock
Dunkirk
dunnock
earlock
earmark
elflock
eweneck
eyewink
fetlock
finback
flyback
flybook
fogbank
forsook
fossick
futhark
futhork
futtock
gasmask
gemsbok
gimmick
gorcock
goshawk
grysbok
gunlock
haddock
hammock
hassock
hauberk
haycock
hayfork
hayrick
hemlock
henpeck
heyduck
hillock
hogback
holmoak
hopsack
hummock
icepack
icerink
jannock
jaywalk
jumbuck
Kalmuck
kalpack
killick
kinfolk
lavrock
legwork
lentisk
limbeck
liveoak
logbook
maffick
mammock
manjack
manweek
mattock
menfolk
midweek
mistook
mudlark
mudpack
mullock
muntjak
network
niblick
nunatak
oarlock
obelisk
odalisk
offpeak
oomiack
outback
outlook
outrank
outtalk
outwork
paddock
padlock
partook
paydesk
peacock
peptalk
piddock
pillock
pintuck
pollack
pollock
potbank
pothook
potluck
precook
prepack
presoak
putlock
ransack
redneck
restock
rethink
ribwork
roebuck
rollick
rooinek
rowlock
ruddock
sawbuck
schlock
schmuck
schnook
seamark
seapink
seasick
setback
shaslik
shylock
sjambok
skyjack
skylark
sowback
sputnik
Suffolk
sundeck
tanbark
tieback
tintack
titlark
tussock
tutwork
unblock
uncloak
unfrock
unstick
unstuck
unthink
warlock
waxwork
waymark
wedlock
wetback
winnock
wryneck
yashmak
abaxial
abigail
abysmal
abyssal
accrual
accusal
adaxial
admiral
adnexal
adrenal
aerosol
airmail
alcohol
allheal
alodial
ammonal
anginal
anthill
apostil
apparel
apsidal
armsful
arousal
arrival
arsenal
asexual
asocial
augural
auroral
austral
axolotl
baleful
baneful
barbell
bashful
bedevil
bedroll
bejewel
benzoyl
bestial
biaxial
bifocal
bimanal
bipedal
bobtail
bodeful
bookful
borstal

Boswell
bowlful
boxhaul
bradawl
brimful
brinjal
brothel
burghal
cacodyl
calomel
cambial
cambrel
cameral
capital
capitol
caporal
caracal
caracul
caramel
caravel
careful
carinal
cartful
catcall
central
chancel
channel
charnel
chattel
chervil
chessel
chloral
chordal
chunnel
citadel
clausal
cloacal
clypeal
coastal
coaxial
codicil
coequal
colonel
comical
conceal
congeal
conical
control
corbeil
cordial
corneal
cornual
coronal
costrel
cotidal
council
counsel
cowbell
cowheel
cranial
creedal
crucial
crustal
cryptal
crystal
cubical
cubital
cupsful
cureall
curtail
cynical
damosel
damozel
datival
decadal
decanal
decibel
decimal
deposal
despoil
devisal
dewfall
dextral
digital
direful
distill
diurnal
doleful
domical
doomful
drycell
dutiful
easeful
edictal
eluvial
embowel
embroil
empanel
engrail
ensnarl
enteral
enthral
enwheel
epigeal
epochal
equinal
eternal
ethanol
ethical
evangel
excusal
exposal
exuvial
eyeball
factual
fanmail
fantail
fascial
fateful
faucial
fearful
federal
feminal
femoral
fernowl
figural
finical
fistful
flannel
fluidal
fluvial
forkful
foxtail
fretful
frontal
funeral
gadwall
gainful
gambrel
gangrel
garboil
gascoal
general
genteel
geoidal
gharial
girasol
glacial
gleeful
glossal
glottal
gluteal
glyptal
godevil
gomeral
gomeril
gonadal
gradual
grapnel
gremial
Guignol
gumboil
handful
handsel
harmful
hateful
heedful
helical
helpful
hernial
hobnail
holdall
hopeful
humeral
humoral
hurtful
icefall
illegal
immoral
impanel
impearl
imperil
indwell
infidel
initial
inkwell
install
irideal
ischial
Ishmael
Jezebel
jonquil
journal
karakul
kestrel
knowall
kursaal
lacteal
lacunal
lateral
legbail
legpull
lexical
liberal
lichowl
lifeful
liminal
lingual
lioncel
literal
logical
lugsail
lumenal
luminal
lustful
lustral
lychowl
lyrical
magical
mandrel
mandril
marital
marshal
martial
matinal
maximal
maxwell
mayoral
medical
menthol
miasmal
milfoil
mimical
mindful
mineral
minimal
miscall
misdeal
mistful
mistral
monacal
mondial
mongrel
musical
Nahuatl
narwhal
natural
needful
netball
neutral
nodical
nombril
nominal
nostril
numeral
nuptial
nutgall
nymphal
oakgall
oatmeal
obitual
octaval
oddball
oedipal
oenomel
oestral
oilwell
omental
optical
optimal
orbital
ordinal
outfall
outhaul
outsell
overall
ovoidal
paginal
pailful
painful
palatal
palmoil
paludal
parasol
parboil
partial
paschal
patrial
payroll
peafowl
pedicel
pennill
peppill
perusal
phrasal
pigtail
pinball
pintail
pipeful
pitfall
pitiful
pivotal
playful
pleural
pluvial
poundal
predial
pretzel
prevail
puberal
pugmill
pushful
quarrel
quetzal
quintal
radical
ragdoll
rapeoil
raschel
rattail
recital
redpoll
refusal
refutal
reginal
remodel
removal
renewal
reposal
respell
restful
retinal
retinol
retrial
revisal
revival
rockoil
roomful
rorqual
rostral
roundel
ruderal
ruthful
sackful
satchel
satyral
saveall
sawbill
sawmill
scalpel
scandal
scissel
scleral
scribal
scurril
seafowl
seagull
seawall
seismal
seminal
sensual
setwall
several
sexfoil
shrinal
shrivel
skilful
skinful
skysail
snorkel
songful
sororal
soulful
spacial
spancel
spaniel
spatial
special
spheral
spignel
spondyl
spousal
stammel
staniel
stencil
sternal
stoical
strigil
strudel
subdual
subsoil
sundial
surreal
sutural
synodal
tactful
tactual
tankful
tapetal
tearful
tendril
tertial
textual
thermal
tiercel
timbrel
tinfoil
toenail
toilful
tomfool
topfull
topical
topsail
topsoil
trammel
travail
trayful
trefoil
trenail
trental
tressel
trivial
trochal
trommel
trucial
truncal
trysail
tumbrel
tumbril
tuneful
turmoil
twibill
typical
umbonal
uncivil
unequal
unideal
unmoral
unravel
unshell
unsnarl
unusual
utensil
uxorial
vegetal
ventail
ventral
vermeil
vesical
vestral
vicinal
victual
virtual
vitriol
wagtail
wailful
wakeful
wassail
wastrel
waxbill
waybill
wishful
wistful
wooloil
wrybill
zestful
zooidal
acclaim
acronym
aliform
alodium
alyssum
amalgam
amentum
anagram
animism
antonym
apothem
arcanum
atavism
atheism
atomism
Baalism
Bahaism
baptism
barroom
bedroom
blossom
boredom
bossism
boxroom
bromism
bruxism
buckram
cadmium
caesium
calcium
cambium
Carlism
centrum
charism
chemism
chillum
chrisom
Comtism
confirm
conform
cosmism
Coueism
cranium
cultism
cutworm
czardom
czarism
Dadaism
dayroom
declaim
decorum
deiform
diadrom
diagram
diorism
dualism
dukedom
eardrum
earldom
echoism
eelworm
egotism
elitism
Elohism
eluvium
Elysium
elytrum
embosom
envenom
epigram
epithem
erotism
erratum
Euratom
exclaim
faddism
fantasm
Fascism
fauvism
fermium
fideism
fiefdom
filmdom
firearm
flotsam
fogydom
fogyism
forearm
fraenum
freedom
frustum
fulcrum
gallium
gingham
grandam
Grecism
grogram
gunroom
hafnium
halidom
heroism
Hobbism
holmium
homonym
hoodlum
humdrum
imagism
interim
iridium
ischium
isogram
itacism
Jainism
jejunum
jibboom
Judaism
kingdom
labarum
ladanum
laicism
Lamaism
leftism
legroom
lithium
lobworm
lugworm
lustrum
macadam
Mahdism
maidism
mantram
Marxism
mawworm
maximum
metonym
milldam
minimum
misdeem
modicum
muonium
myalism
myogram
Naziism
niobium
nostrum
oestrum
oildrum
omentum
onanism
oosperm
opossum
optimum
organum
Orphism
osculum
overarm
oviform
pabulum
pallium
papadam
paronym
perform
phantom
phellem
photism
pianism
pietism
pilgrim
pinetum
pinworm
pomatum
popadum
predoom
preform
premium
problem
program
protium
punctum
quantum
quondam
ragworm
realism
reclaim
requiem
rhabdom
rhenium
rhodium
rostrum
Sabaism
Saktism
sanctum
sarcasm
Scotism
searoom
serfdom
shittim
Sikhism
sistrum
Sivaism
skellum
Slavism
smeddum
solanum
sophism
sorghum
spodium
stadium
stardom
statism
sternum
stratum
sunbeam
symptom
synonym
tachism
tangram
tantrum
tapetum
taproom
tearoom
terbium
theorem
Thomism
thorium
thulium
thummim
tiebeam
Titoism
toponym
Toryism
tourism
trangam
transom
triduum
triform
trinkum
tritium
trivium
tropism
tsardom
tsarism
tychism
typonym

unbosom
uniform
uranism
uranium
utopism
webworm
wolfram
wychelm
yardarm
yttrium
Zionism
zoarium
Zoilism
abaddon
abandon
abdomen
Abelian
abstain
Acadian
acarian
Achaean
Achaian
acrasin
acrogen
actinon
adjourn
aeolian
aeonian
African
agnomen
aileron
alation
albumen
albumin
Alcoran
aleuron
Alkoran
almsman
alphorn
alsoran
althorn
andiron
aneurin
Angevin
Anglian
antigen
antlion
apogean
Arabian
arraign
artisan
aspirin
auction
Avestan
Azilean
balloon
bargain
baseman
bassoon
bastion
batsman
bedizen
bedouin
beechen
beknown
Belgian
bellman
benison
benzoin
betaken
betoken
between
Biafran
bighorn
billion
birchen
birdman
bittern
bitumen
blacken
blouson
blowgun
boatman
bogbean
bogyman
bondman
bookman
Boolean
borazon
botulin
bounden
bourbon
bourdon
bracken
Brahman
Brahmin
breakin
bridoon
brisken
broaden
Brython
buffoon
builtin
bullion
bullpen
bumpkin
burgeon
burthen
bushman
cacumen
Cadmean
caisson
caldron
camaron
campion
canakin
canikin
canteen
capelin
Capsian
capstan
captain
caption
caravan
cardoon
carotin
carrion
carryon
cartoon
Catalan
cateran
caution
caveman
celadon
ceresin
certain
cerumen
cession
chagrin
chanson
chapman
chasten
cheapen
chevron
chicken
chidden
chiffon
chignon
chorion
cipolin
Circean
cistern
cithern
citizen
cittern
clarion
claypan
clubman
coarsen
coition
colleen
complin
Comtian
concern
condemn
condign
conjoin
consign
contain
contemn
cooncan
corydon
costean
courlan
crampon
crimson
crouton
crucian
cryogen
cullion
curtain
cushion
Cyprian
Dantean
darshan
dauphin
deadpan
decagon
decuman
denizen
detrain
dextran
dextrin
diction
dipnoan
discern
disdain
dishorn
disjoin
dislimn
distain
doeskin
dogskin
dolphin
doorman
dragoon
drayman
drivein
drumlin
drunken
duckpin
dudgeon
dungeon
duramen
dustbin
dustman
dustpan
earthen
eastern
echelon
edition
eidolon
einkorn
elastin
elation
elision
elusion
elution
elysian
elytron
embrown
embryon
emotion
emption
enation
enchain
enderon
endogen
engrain
enliven
enteron
entrain
environ
epigean
epizoon
epsilon
erepsin
erosion
etesian
Etonian
evasion
exciton
explain
exurban
faction
fashion
fermion
festoon
fibroin
fiction
fifteen
finikin
fireman
fission
flagman
flatten
fletton
fleuron
flexion
fluxion
foghorn
footman
foramen
foreign
foreman
foreran
forerun
forlorn
Fortran
forworn
fourgon
freeman
freshen
Frisian
frisson
frogman
fronton
fustian
gadroon
galleon
galloon
gamelan
gelatin
Genevan
gentian
gherkin
gittern
gladden
glassen
gleeman
gliadin
glisten
glutton
Gobelin
goddamn
gombeen
goodman
Gordian
gossoon
greaten
Grecian
greisen
gremlin
greyhen
griffin
griffon
griskin
Grobian
grunion
grutten
gryphon
gudgeon
guerdon
hairpin
halcyon
halogen
handgun
hangman
hanuman
hardpan
harijan
harpoon
harshen
hasbeen
headman
headpin
hearken
hearten
heathen
hebenon
helicon
hellion
heparin
hessian
hexagon
highman
hillman
hirudin
hoarsen
hoatzin
Hobbian
hoedown
horizon
hygeian
hyperon
Iberian
indican
indrawn
ingrain
ingrown
inhuman
inkhorn
insulin
inwoven
Iranian
isotron
Italian
Jacobin
jargoon
javelin
jazzman
Judaean
Jungian
juryman
Kantian
keelson
keratin
kerogen
khamsin
kidskin
kiloton
kinchin
kingpin
kinsman
kitchen
kneepan
knockon
kremlin
krypton
ladykin
lambkin
lampion
lampoon
lanolin
lantern
Laotian
Laputan
lardoon
Latvian
lectern
lection
leghorn
legiron
lesbian
letdown
lethean
lexicon
liaison
lighten
ligroin
limpkin
lineman
linkman
Linnean
lorgnon
lowborn
lowdown
lupulin
lyingin
lyncean
mailman
mailvan
Malayan
malison
mamelon
manakin
manikin
mansion
Manxman
Martian
Marxian
maudlin
meatman
Mechlin
medusan
megaron
megaton
Meissen
melanin
mention
messtin
metopon
Mexican
milkman
million
minikin
mission
moisten
molimen
monsoon
moorhen
mouflon
mowburn
muezzin
mullein
mullion
munnion
murrain
mutagen
mylodon
nankeen
navarin
neuston
neutron
newborn
newmown
newsman
ninepin
nocturn
nonagon
noniron
nuclein
nucleon
oakfern
oarsman
octagon
oilskin
omicron
opinion
oppidan
opsonin
oration
organon
Orphean
ortolan
ottoman
ouabain
outturn
outworn
ovarian
ovation
overman
overran
overrun
Oxonian
packman
paladin
pampean
Pandean
Paphian
paragon
passion
pastern
patroon
pattern
pelican
pemican
penguin
pension
Permian
Persian
pertain
phaeton
pidgeon
pigiron
pigmean
pigskin
pikeman
pillion
plasmin
platoon
playpen
pleuron
plosion
polygon
pontoon
popcorn
portion
posteen
postern
postman
potheen
poussin
preplan
pronoun
protean
protein
ptyalin
puccoon
Pullman
pumpkin
puritan
purloin
putamen
putdown
pygmean
Pythian
quartan
quicken
quieten
quintan
raccoon
railman
Ramadan
ramekin
rampion
ratteen
ravelin
realign
redskin
refrain
regimen
retaken
retrain
reunion
ribston
righten
roadman
rodsman
rontgen
roughen
rubdown
rubicon
ruction
ruffian
rundown
Russian
saffron
salicin
saltern
saltpan
samisen
sandman
saponin
Saracen
saurian
saxhorn
sculpin
section
Serbian
sericin
Servian
session
setdown
shaitan
sharpen
Shavian
shebeen
shipman
shippen
shippon
shopman
shorten
shotgun
shotten
showman
shriven
sierran
silicon
silvern
sirloin
sitdown
sixteen
skidpan
skolion
skyborn
slacken
sleeken
slidden
sloegin
smarten
smidgen
smidgin
smitten
snowman
sojourn
sokeman
Solomon
Sorbian
soroban
soupcon
soybean
Spartan
spongin
sponson
sporran
standin
station
stearin
steepen
stemson
stepson
stetson
stewpan
stiffen
Stilton
stouten
striven
stygian
suasion
subdean
suberin
subjoin
suction
sunburn
sundown
surfman
surgeon
sustain
swagman
sweeten
swollen
taction
tamarin
tampion
tanghin
tapsman
taximan
teachin
teagown
telamon
tension
terrain
tertian
testban
testoon
therein
thereon
thiamin
thicken
thriven
throwin
Tibetan
tighten
tinhorn
tollman
tompion
torchon
torsion
toughen
tradein
treason
tricorn
triduan
trodden
trudgen
trypsin
tuition
tulchan
turfman
typhoon
Umbrian
umpteen
unchain
unclean
uncrown
unction
unicorn
unknown
unladen
unlearn

unsworn
unwoven
upsilon
Uralian
urethan
utopian
Vatican
velamen
venison
vermian
version
vervain
veteran
villain
villein
vitamin
volutin
Walloon
wanigan
warison
wayworn
wealden
weighin
western
wheaten
wherein
whereon
Whitsun
widgeon
wireman
woodman
woollen
workman
writhen
written
xanthin
yardman
yatagan
yeggman
yestern
zillion
zithern
zymogen
agitato
allegro
annatto
Arapaho
avocado
bambino
botargo
bravado
broncho
buffalo
bugaboo
bummalo
bushido
calando
calypso
cassino
cattalo
cavetto
cembalo
centavo
cheerio
Chicano
coquito
coranto
cornuto
criollo
crusado
curacao
cymbalo
diabolo
electro
embargo
esparto
etaerio
fagotto
farrago
ferrugo
furioso
gambado
gestapo
guanaco
heighho
hidalgo
huanaco
impasto
inferno
lentigo
llanero
longago
lumbago
madrono
maestro
mafioso
magneto
Marrano
memento
mestizo
montero
morello
morendo
Moresco
Morisco
morocco
mulatto
Negrito
nelumbo
oloroso
oregano
pampero
passado
piccolo
pimento
pintado
placebo
pompano
portico
primero
proviso
proximo
prurigo
relievo
ridotto
rilievo
ripieno
risotto
saguaro
sapsago
scalado
scherzo
Scorpio
secondo
senecio
serpigo
sfumato
shampoo
sirocco
smokeho
soprano
sordino
squacco
stretto
subzero
supremo
tabasco
tallyho
tangelo
testudo
theorbo
thereto
timpano
tobacco
tombolo
tornado
torpedo
touraco
tremolo
tympano
underdo
undergo
vaquero
verismo
vertigo
vibrato
volcano
whereto
whoseso
zemstvo
Zingaro
airdrop
airship
bellhop
boozeup
breakup
buildup
builtup
caltrap
caltrop
cantrip
catchup
checkup
chirrup
cleanup
closeup
coverup
cowslip
crackup
demirep
develop
dewdrop
discerp
driedup
eardrop
earflap
eggflip
egotrip
enclasp
envelop
epicarp
exocarp
eyedrop
flareup
flatcap
flattop
flytrap
foglamp
foretop
frameup
giltcup
godship
grownup
gumdrop
gunship
gymslip
hardtop
harelip
heeltap
hencoop
hilltop
ingroup
insculp
ketchup
kingcup
kinship
kneecap
kneesup
lipdeep
longhop
maintop
mantrap
midship
milksop
misstep
mixedup
mugwump
nonslip
nonstop
nunship
onestep
outcrop
overlap
overtop
parsnip
pasteup
peasoup
pitprop
pressup
punchup
rattrap
regroup
rollmop
rolltop
rooftop
rosehip
roundup
rumshop
scallop
schlepp
scollop
seawhip
seedlip
shakeup
shallop
shiplap
sibship
skijump
smashup
snarlup
snowcap
sonship
soursop
speedup
standup
stickup
stirrup
stopgap
stuckup
sunlamp
suntrap
syncarp
teashop
tiderip
toeclip
touchup
toyshop
treetop
trollop
twostep
unclasp
upsweep
warship
wickiup
winesap
wiretap
worship
writeup
abetter
abettor
abjurer
ablator
aborter
abrader
abutter
accuser
acroter
adapter
adaptor
adducer
adherer
admirer
adopter
adviser
advisor
aerator
alcazar
allover
allstar
almoner
amateur
amender
amildar
ammeter
angular
annular
another
antbear
applier
aquifer
aquiver
arbiter
areolar
armiger
arrayer
arriver
aspirer
assayer
assurer
asunder
atelier
auditor
autocar
avenger
aviator
awarder
axillar
babbler
baffler
Bahadur
barrier
basilar
behaver
belcher
belljar
bencher
besmear
bifilar
bigener
bilobar
bipolar
blabber
bladder
blaster
blather
blatter
bleater
bleeder
bleeper
blender
blether
blinder
blinker
blister
blither
bloater
blocker
bloomer
blotter
blubber
blucher
bluffer
blunder
blunger
blusher
bluster
boarder
boaster
boggler
bolivar
bolster
booster
botcher
boudoir
boulder
boulter
bouncer
bounder
bowlder
bragger
brander
brawler
brazier
breaker
breeder
brevier
brimmer
bringer
broider
broiler
brooder
brother
browser
bruiser
brusher
buckler
bugbear
builder
bumbler
bungler
burbler
burgher
burglar
burster
bustler
butcher
bywoner
cackler
cadaver
cajoler
caliper
caloyer
camphor
candour
caperer
carrier
cashier
catcher
caterer
caulker
centaur
centner
chaffer
chamber
chamfer
changer
chanter
chapter
charger
charmer
charter
chatter
cheater
checker
cheddar
cheerer
chequer
chigger
childer
chipper
chitter
chooser
chopper
chowder
chuddar
chukker
chunter
circler
clabber
clacker
claimer
clamber
clamour
clanger
clapper
clatter
clavier
cleaner
cleaver
clicker
climber
clinker
clipper
clobber
clocker
clogger
clumber
cluster
clutter
clyster
coacher
coaster
cobbler
coddler
coherer
collier
compeer
conifer
conquer
contour
copular
coroner
corsair
cottier
couloir
coulter
counter
coupler
courier
courser
cozener
cracker
crammer
crawler
creamer
creator
creeper
crimper
cringer
crisper
critter
croaker
crofter
crooner
cropper
crosier
crowbar
crowner
crozier
cruiser
cruller
crupper
crusher
cudbear
cupular
curator
currier
dabbler
dallier
dangler
danseur
dawdler
daystar
dazzler
debater
decider
decoder
decrier
defiler
definer
delator
delayer
deliver
deluder
derider
despair
deviser
devisor
diddler
dilator
diluter
dilutor
dimeter
diopter
dipolar
ditcher
divider
diviner
divisor
dogstar
donator
doodler
dortour
dossier
doubler
doubter
douceur
dowager
drabber
drabler
drafter
drainer
drawbar
drawler
dreamer
dredger
dresser
drifter
driller
drinker
drogher
dropper
drudger
drummer
dueller
duumvir
dweller
eductor
ejector
elector
Elzevir
embower
emitter
emperor
empower
emptier
enactor
enamour
encoder
equator
erector
escaper
escolar
essayer
evictor
exactor
exciter
excitor
exhumer
exposer
fabular
fancier
farceur
farrier
farther
feaster
feather
feigner
felspar
feoffer
feoffor
fervour
fibster
fibular
fiddler
fielder
fighter
filacer
flaneur
flanker
flapper
flasher
flatcar
flatter
flavour
flecker
fleecer
flesher
flicker
flipper
flitter
flivver
floater
floorer
fluster
flutter
flyover
fondler
forager
forayer
forbear
forever
forgoer
founder
Fraktur
freezer
fresher
fripper
friseur
frisker
fritter
fruiter
fuddler
Fuehrer
fueller
fulgour
fumbler
funfair
furrier
further
gabbler
gagster
gambier
gambler
garbler
genitor
giggler
girdler
glacier
gladder
glamour
glazier
gleaner
glimmer
glister
glitter
glummer
gobbler
goggler
grabber
grafter
grainer
grammar
granger
granter
grantor
grasper
grazier
greaser
grifter
griller

grimmer
grinder
gripper
Grolier
groover
grouper
grouser
growler
grubber
grunter
guesser
guilder
guzzler
hackler
haggler
hamster
handcar
handler
harbour
harrier
hatcher
haulier
haunter
hauteur
heather
heckler
heritor
higgler
hipster
hitcher
hobbler
holster
homager
hostler
however
humidor
hurdler
hustler
igniter
ignorer
imbiber
imbower
imposer
incisor
inciter
incomer
indexer
inditer
inducer
inhaler
injurer
inlayer
insider
insofar
insular
insurer
integer
intoner
invader
inviter
isochor
jacamar
jacktar
jangler
janitor
jemadar
jibdoor
jingler
jocular
joinder
jointer
jouster
juggler
jugular
juniper
Jupiter
khaddar
kilobar
kindler

knacker
knapper
kneader
kneeler
knitter
knocker
knotter
krimmer
lacquer
lacunar
laminar
languor
lashkar
laugher
launder
leaguer
learner
leather
legator
leister
levator
lighter
limiter
liqueur
loather
lobster
lobular
locater
locular
lorimer
loriner
lounger
Lucifer
luncher
lunular
lurcher
machair
macular
mahseer
manager
manhour
manyear
marcher
mariner
markhor
masquer
masseur
matador
maunder
mauther
meander
meddler
metamer
metayer
midyear
minever
minicar
miniver
minster
mirador
mishear
mobster
modular
moither
moneyer
moniker
monitor
monomer
monster
moocher
morular
moulder
mounter
mourner
mouther
muddler
muffler
mumbler
murther

muzzler
mynheer
nebular
needler
neither
nibbler
niggler
nobbler
nodular
nonuser
norther
nuclear
obligor
ocellar
October
officer
oldster
openair
opposer
orderer
osseter
outdoor
outlier
outwear
paddler
painter
pairoar
palaver
pannier
panther
paperer
papular
parader
pardner
parlour
partner
paviour
pearler
peddler
percher
peruser
philter
piaffer
picador
pickeer
piffler
pilsner
pilular
pincher
pioneer
pissoir
pitcher
pivoter
planner
plantar
planter
plaster
platter
pleader
pledger
pledgor
plodder
plotter
plucker
plugger
plumber
plumper
plunder
plunger
plunker
poacher
poinder
pointer
polymer
poofter
popover
popular
porifer
postwar

poulter
pounder
praetor
praiser
prancer
premier
presser
pricker
printer
proctor
prodder
proffer
prosper
prowler
psalter
puddler
puncher
punster
pupilar
pursuer
puttier
puzzler
quaffer
quarter
queller
quester
questor
quilter
quitter
quizzer
rabbler
radular
railcar
rallier
rambler
rancher
rancour
rattler
ravager
reacher
reactor
realgar
realtor
rebuker
reciter
recover
reducer
reenter
refiner
refuser
refuter
regular
relater
relator
remover
reneger
renewer
rentier
reorder
repaper
repiner
replier
rescuer
reviler
reviser
reviver
revivor
riddler
riffler
righter
riveter
roaster
rockier
rocktar
roedeer
roister
rooster
rotator
rotifer

rounder
rouster
royster
ruffler
rumbler
rustler
saddler
saluter
samovar
sampler
sandbar
santour
saunter
saviour
scalder
scalper
scamper
scanner
scarper
scatter
scauper
schemer
scholar
scissor
scoffer
scolder
scomber
scooper
scooter
scorner
scorper
scourer
scouter
scraper
screwer
scriber
sculler
scunner
scupper
scutter
seabear
seceder
secular
securer
seducer
seltzer
seminar
senator
settler
settlor
shammer
sharper
shaster
shatter
shearer
shebear
shedder
sheller
shelter
shicker
shifter
shimmer
shipper
shirker
shocker
shooter
shopper
shouter
shucker
shudder
shunner
shunter
shutter
shyster
sidecar
signior
similar
similor
simitar

simpler
simular
sizzler
skeeter
skegger
skelter
skimmer
skinker
skinner
skipper
skirter
skitter
skulker
slabber
slacker
slander
slasher
slather
sleeper
slender
slicker
slimmer
slinger
slinker
slipper
slither
slobber
slogger
slotcar
slubber
slugger
slumber
slummer
smacker
smasher
smatter
smeller
smelter
smother
snapper
snarler
sneaker
sneerer
sneezer
snicker
sniffer
snifter
snigger
snipper
snooker
snooper
snoozer
snorter
snubber
snuffer
socager
soldier
soother
sounder
souther
spadger
spanker
spanner
sparger
spatter
spawner
speaker
speeder
speller
spelter
spencer
spender
spieler
spiller
spinner
spitter
splicer
spoiler
sponger

sponsor
spoofer
spoorer
sporter
spotter
spouter
sprayer
spurner
sputter
squalor
squarer
stabber
stabler
stacker
stagger
stainer
stalker
stammer
stamper
stander
stapler
starter
stealer
steamer
steerer
stellar
stentor
stepper
sticker
stifler
stinger
stinker
stirrer
stocker
stonker
stopper
strayer
strider
stridor
striker
striver
stuffer
stumper
stunner
stutter
subadar
succour
suckler
sulphur
sumpter
sunbear
sunstar
swabber
swagger
swanker
swapper
swarmer
swasher
swatter
swearer
sweater
sweeper
swelter
swiller
swimmer
swinger
swither
Switzer
swopper
taborer
tabular
tackler
tambour
tanager
tandoor
tankcar
taperer
tapster
tarrier

tattler
taunter
teacher
tegular
telpher
Telstar
Templar
tempter
tenoner
terrier
thanker
thigger
thiller
thinker
thinner
thither
thrower
thumper
thunder
tickler
tiddler
tingler
tippler
tipster
titular
toaster
toddler
tollbar
toucher
tracker
tractor
trailer
trainer
traitor
tramcar
tranter
trapper
trawler
treader
treater
trekker
tricker
trifler
trigger
trimmer
tripper
troller
trooper
trotter
trouper
trouser
trucker
trusser
truster
tubular
tumbler
tumular
tutelar
tweeter
tweezer
twister
twitter
typebar
udaller
uncover
unifier
unswear
upriser
upstair
usurper
utterer
vaulter
vaunter
veliger
venerer
vernier
vetiver
vinegar
vintner

visitor
vitular
voucher
voyager
waddler
wagerer
wagoner
waister
wakener
waltzer
warbler
warrior
watcher
waterer
waverer
weather
webster
weigher
welcher
welsher
wencher
whacker
wheeler
whether
whetter
whicker
whidder
whimper
whinger
whipper
whirler
whisker
whisper
whither
whoever
whooper
whopper
widower
wielder
wiggler
Windsor
wobbler
worrier
wrapper
wrecker
wringer
yielder
younger
younker
abattis
abscess
acetous
Achates
acinous
actress
address
agamous
ageless
aggress
aiblins
aimless
airless
airmiss
alkalis
alumnus
ambages
ambones
amoebas
amorous
Ananias
ancones
ancress
angelus
annates
annulus
anoesis
anurous
anxious
anyways

apheses
aphesis
aphides
apodous
apropos
apsides
aptness
aqueous
arbutus
arduous
areolas
aristas
armfuls
armless
arrears
artless
ascaris
ascesis
ascites
asepsis
askesis
assizes
aurochs
auroras
autobus
auxesis
aweless
awnless
azygous
badness
bananas
banjoes
barytes
battels
Bauhaus
bellows
benthos
besides
betimes
bigness
bilboes
bilious
biomass
bionics
bitters
blewits
boletus
bongoes
bonkers
borings
brumous
bugloss
bulbous
bureaus
burgess
burnous
buttons
byebyes
bygones
cahoots
caimans
calamus
calends
calices
callous
calyces
calyxes
canthus
canvass
carcass
carinas
carious
caseous
casuals
catalos
catenas
Cathars
caymans
Celsius
Chablis
challis
chamois
chassis
chlamys
chymous
cidaris
cimices
cirrous
civvies
classes
classis
clivers
clothes
clypeus
codices
coffers
colitis
collins
colobus
colours
commons
compass
conatus
concuss
confess
conkers
copious
coronas
coyness
Croesus
croquis
csardas
cuirass
culices
cumulus
cupmoss
cuprous
curious
customs
cutlass
cyathus
cyclops
cypress
czardas
darbies
declass
defocus
degauss
depress
devious
dickens
digress
dimness
dingoes
discuss
dismiss
dodgems
dogdays
doubles
dryness
dubious
duchess
dulness
duteous
dwarves
ecdyses
ecdysis
echinus
effects
elevens
embolus
empress
emulous
endless
endways
engross
entasis
envious
ephebus
ergates
ethiops
express
eyeless
falsies
famulus
fantods
fatness
fatuous
ferrous
fetters
fewness
feyness
fibrous
fibulas
fidgets
fifties
filings
finings
fitness
fixings
floccus
follies
forceps
forties
frescos
fulness
fulvous
fungous
funnies
furious
fuscous
gallows
gaseous
gathers
gayness
geckoes
geneses
genesis
ghettos
gibbous
giblets
gimbals
glasses
glottis
gluteus
goddess
godless
goggles
grampus
greaves
grottos
grumous
gubbins
gutless
halvers
hamulus
hapless
harness
hatless
heinous
heiress
helices
hernias
heroics
hideous
hipness
honours
hostess
hotness
hueless
hugeous
humbles
humerus
hunkers
hurdles
hydrous
iciness
icterus
igneous
ileitis
illness
impetus
impious
impress
incubus
incudes
indices
indoors
ingress
innards
innings
inwards
isthmus
ivories
jackass
jacobus
jealous
jimjams
jitters
joyless
juggins
juncoes
kalends
kenosis
kermess
keyless
kinesis
klipdas
koumiss
lacunas
Lallans
lancers
largess
lassoes
latexes
latices
laurels
lawless
laxness
legless
leprous
letters
lidless
limbous
limosis
limulus
linctus
lioness
lipless
litotes
loculus
lowness
luteous
lychnis
madness
makings
malines
malleus
mangoes
manless
manners
marbles
marquis
masters
matrass
mattins
mealies
measles
medusas
meiosis
memoirs
meseems
Messias
metrics
milreis
mimesis
mimulus
minibus
minimus
minutes
mitoses
mitosis
modulus
muggins
murexes
murices
mycoses
mycosis
myiasis
myxomas
nacrous
naiades
napless
narrows
nautics
nebulas
Negress
nemesis
nervous
newness
nippers
nitrous
niveous
nocuous
nonplus
noxious
nucleus
numbles
oarless
obvious
ocellus
ochrous
octopus
oddness
odorous
oestrus
ominous
omnibus
oneness
onerous
onwards
onymous
oppress
osmosis
osseous
pajamas
palings
panties
papyrus
parados
paresis
parlous
peeress
Pegasus
pelorus
pennies
percuss
perhaps
petasus
petrous
phallus
phonics
physics
piceous
pincers
piteous
poetess
poetics
polypus
pompous
possess
prelims
premiss
process
profess
pronaos
proteus
prowess
pulpous
pyjamas
pylorus
pyralis
pyrites
pyrosis
pyxides
quietus
quizzes
radices
ramsons
rations
raucous
ravings
rawness
rayless
redlegs
redness
redress
refocus
regards
regress
regrets
regulus
remains
remiges
repress
reredos
retinas
returns
rhamnus
rhombus
rickets
riotous
rubbers
rubious
ruinous
rumness
runless
sadness
salvoes
Sanctus
sanders
sapless
sarcous
sardius
savings
scabies
scarves
scepsis
seabass
sealegs
senatus
senores
serious
sexless
Sextans
sferics
sheaves
shelves
sherris
shivers
shyness
siemens
silenus
sinless
sinuous
sithens
sixties
skepsis
slyness
solidus
sonless
sorites
sorosis
species
spinous
spirits
spumous
squails
stables
statics
stirpes
stovies
straits
stratus
stuccos
suburbs
success
summons
sunless
surpass
surplus
sycosis
synesis
tactics
tagetes
takings
talcous
talipes
tatters
taxless
teargas
tedious
tenpins
tenuous
tetanus
thallus
thieves
thyrsus
tidings
tigress
timeous
toeless
topless
torpids
towards
travois
trellis
triceps
trismus
trochus
tropics
tumulus
twelves
twoness
typhous
uberous
umbones
uncinus
uncross
undress
untruss
upsides
upwards
uranous
useless
uveitis
vacuous
vapours
varices
various
Vaudois
velours
verglas
vespers
vicious
vidimus
villous
viscous
vittles
wanness
wattles
wayless
wellies
wetness
wharves
whereas
wigless
willies
winkers
withers
witless
witness
wryness
zealous
zygosis
zymosis
abeyant
abought
abreact
abreast
account
accurst
acquest
acrobat
adamant
adhibit
adjoint
adjunct
afflict
affront
against
agonist
ailment
airlift
airport
airpost
akvavit
aliment
aliquot
alkanet
alright
amarant
ambient
amongst
amorist
analyst
ancient
Anglist
animist
annicut
annulet
apparat
appoint
apricot
aquavit
Arabist
armrest
asphalt
asquint
assault
atavist
atheist
athirst
athwart
atomist
attaint
attempt
attract
audient
augment
babbitt
babysit
backset
Bahaist
ballast
banquet
baptist
baronet
basinet
bassist
bayonet
bedfast
bedight
bedpost
beignet
benefit
bepaint
bequest
bergylt
betwixt
bibelot
biblist
biggest
biscuit
bistort
blanket
blatant
blowout
bombast
boneset
booklet
boomlet
borscht
bouquet
bowshot
boxseat
boycott
bracket
briquet
brisket
brocket
brought
bullbat
bumboat
buoyant
bushtit
cabaret
cabinet
callant
calumet
cambist
camelot
candent
Carlist
carport
casuist
catboat
catmint
catsuit
cellist
cesspit
chaplet
chariot
chemist
cheroot
cheviot
chindit
cineast
circlet
circuit
clamant
clement
coaltit
cockpit
coconut
coexist
cohabit
coletit
collect
combout
combust
comfort
comment
compact
compart
complot
comport
compost
Comtist
conceit
concent

concept
concert
concoct
conduct
conduit
confect
congest
connect
consent
consist
consort
consult
contact
content
contest
context
contort
convect
convent
convert
convict
cookout
coolant
copilot
copycat
copyist
cornett
cornist
coronet
correct
corrupt
corslet
cosmist
couldst
couplet
couvert
crampet
crampit
credent
cresset
cricket
crochet
crocket
croquet
crownet
crumpet
culprit
cultist
culvert
cumquat
currant
current
cyclist
Cypriot
czarist
Dadaist
dashpot
Debrett
decrypt
default
defiant
deficit
deflect
defrost
defunct
delight
delimit
demerit
demount
dentist
deposit
descant
descent
dessert
detract
deviant
dialect
diarist
diluent

dimmest
discant
disgust
dismast
dispart
disport
disroot
disrupt
disseat
dissect
dissent
distant
distent
distort
dogcart
dogtrot
doormat
dormant
doublet
dovecot
drabbet
dragnet
draught
driblet
droplet
dropout
drought
drugget
drysalt
dualist
durmast
earnest
earshot
eelpout
egotist
elegant
elegist
element
elfbolt
elitist
Elohist
eminent
enchant
encrust
endmost
engraft
enprint
entrant
entreat
entrust
entwist
epatant
epaulet
epithet
erodent
escheat
estreat
evident
excerpt
exhaust
exhibit
exigent
explant
exploit
exposit
extinct
extract
eyebolt
eyeshot
eyespot
faddist
fadeout
fallout
fantast
farmost
Fascist
fattest
faunist
fauvist

feedlot
felwort
ferment
fervent
feudist
fideist
figment
figwort
filbert
filemot
filmset
fishnet
fitchet
fitment
fittest
flatlet
flatout
flaught
fleapit
fleuret
floreat
florist
floruit
flutist
flybelt
flyboat
flypast
foldout
fondant
footrot
forfeit
formant
forwent
foumart
foxhunt
foxtrot
fraught
freight
freshet
frisket
fuguist
fulgent
fullout
fusspot
gabfest
galipot
gallant
galliot
gallnut
gantlet
gardant
garment
gestalt
gilbert
gillnet
glaikit
gooiest
gourmet
grommet
grummet
guichet
gumboot
gunboat
gunshot
gymnast
habitat
hackbut
haircut
hairnet
halbert
halfwit
halibut
handout
handset
hangout
hardhit
hardset
haricot
harpist

harslet
harvest
hatchet
havenot
hayloft
headset
hellcat
hideout
highhat
hindgut
Hobbist
holibut
hooklet
horrent
hotfoot
hotshot
hottest
howbeit
hutment
hydrant
hymnist
iceboat
icefoot
illicit
imagist
impaint
implant
imprest
imprint
inbuilt
incipit
incrust
indraft
indwelt
inexact
infarct
inflect
inflict
infract
ingraft
inhabit
inherit
inhibit
inquest
insight
inspect
instant
intrant
intreat
introit
intrust
ironist
isohyet
isokont
issuant
Italiot
iterant
jackpot
jaconet
jogtrot
Judaist
judoist
jumpjet
kinglet
kumquat
lakelet
Lamaist
lambast
lambent
lambert
languet
latchet
lawlist
lawsuit
lazaret
leaflet
leftist
legrest
lenient

leveret
lineout
linocut
locknut
lockout
lookout
lynchet
maddest
madwort
Mahdist
maillot
manchet
manhunt
manihot
mantlet
manumit
Manxcat
margent
marplot
martlet
Marxist
matchet
matelot
mediant
meerkat
melilot
merchet
metrist
midmost
Midwest
mightst
migrant
minaret
miscast
missent
monocot
moonlit
moonset
mordant
mordent
mudflat
mugwort
muskrat
mythist
nacarat
nascent
nearest
necklet
neglect
nonsuit
notelet
nymphet
occiput
oculist
oddment
odorant
offbeat
oneshot
operant
opulent
osselet
outcast
outfoot
outlast
outmost
outport
outpost
outshot
outwent
overact
overeat
overset
oviduct
oxidant
pageant
paletot
palmist
pandect
parapet

parfait
parquet
partlet
passant
patient
patriot
payment
peasant
peccant
pendant
pendent
pennant
percent
percept
perfect
periapt
peridot
perpent
persist
pervert
pianist
picquet
pierrot
pietist
pigment
pikelet
piquant
pitapat
pithhat
placket
plaudit
playact
playlet
pledget
plummet
polecat
poloist
pomfret
porrect
portent
potshot
Prakrit
precast
precept
predict
preempt
prefect
preheat
prelect
present
pretest
pretext
prevent
pricket
product
project
prophet
propjet
protect
protest
protist
provost
prudent
pullout
pungent
purport
pursuit
quadrat
quartet
querist
quillet
quintet
racquet
radiant
ragbolt
ragwort
raiment
Rajpoot
rampant

rampart
rapport
rarebit
ratatat
ratchet
readout
reagent
realist
reallot
reboant
rebuilt
receipt
recount
recruit
redcoat
reddest
redoubt
redraft
reelect
reenact
reflect
refloat
refract
regnant
regrant
reliant
relight
remnant
remount
repaint
replant
reposit
reprint
request
respect
respelt
restart
retract
retreat
revisit
rhymist
ribwort
ringent
ringlet
ripplet
rivulet
rocklet
romaunt
rootlet
rosecut
rowboat
rundlet
sackbut
sacrist
saddest
saidest
sakeret
salicet
salient
saltant
saltcat
sandlot
sandpit
sapient
satinet
sawdust
sawwort
scarlet
Scotist
seaboot
seagirt
sealant
seaport
segment
sellout
sequent
serpent
servant
sextant

shallot
sherbet
shilpit
shutout
singlet
sitfast
skilift
skillet
skippet
skirret
sleekit
sleight
snippet
solicit
soloist
solvent
sophist
sorbent
spirant
spryest
starlet
starlit
statant
statist
steekit
sterlet
stewpot
stickit
student
stylist
subduct
subedit
subject
subplot
subsist
subvert
suggest
sunspot
sunsuit
support
surcoat
surfeit
surtout
suspect
tabaret
tabinet
tachist
talayot
talipot
tangent
taproot
tartlet
teleost
tempest
templet
thereat
thicket
Thomist
thought
tiercet
tipcart
Titoist
tonight
topcoat
topknot
topmast
topmost
torment
torrent
tosspot
tourist
towboat
towmont
townlet
traject
transit
triblet
trident
trinket

triolet
triplet
trippet
trisect
trumpet
tsarist
tugboat
turgent
turnout
typeset
ululant
unblest
unbuilt
unguent
unjoint
unkempt
unmeant
unquiet
unright
unroost
unsight
untwist
upright
upstart
upswept
uptight
utopist
vagrant
valiant
variant
varment
varmint
veinlet
verdant
verdict
veriest
versant
viaduct
vibrant
vilayet
violent
violist
walkout
warrant
washout
washpot
wavelet
webfoot
wellset
wettest
whatnot
whereat
whippet
wildcat
winglet
wingnut
without
woodcut
woolfat
workout
wornout
wottest
wouldst
wrought
Yahvist
Yahwist
yoghurt
Yorkist
Zionist
Zoilist
babassu
bandeau
bunraku
caribou
catechu
chateau
fabliau
jujitsu
manitou

manteau
marabou
nylghau
parvenu
plateau
purlieu
rondeau
rouleau
sapajou
seppuku
tableau
tinamou
tonneau
trumeau
Watteau
aircrew
airflow
airglow
backsaw
bandsaw
beshrew
bestrew
brannew
bucksaw
buzzsaw
catspaw
Choctaw
cumshaw
Danelaw
dewclaw
disavow
downbow
eyebrow
firenew
fitchew
flamfew
flyblow
forepaw
foresaw
fretsaw
gorcrow
hacksaw
handsaw
iceshow
jackdaw
knowhow
legshow
lockjaw
longbow
lowbrow
misknow
outflow
outgrew
outgrow
oversaw
oversew
preview
purview
rainbow
ringtaw
shallow
somehow
sparrow
swallow
tonerow
trishaw
unscrew
upthrew
upthrow
whipsaw
whitlow
windrow
antefix
anthrax
apteryx
bandbox
bateaux
beeswax
Benelux

bureaux
callbox
coinbox
complex
conflux
equinox
firebox
flummox
gateaux
gearbox
hellbox
jukebox
livebox
mailbox
narthex
oratrix
overtax
paradox
perplex
phalanx
pharynx
phoenix
pillbox
postbox
postfix
rectrix
reseaux
salpinx
saltbox
sandbox
simplex
soapbox
tectrix
toolbox
tortrix
triplex
tuckbox
workbox
ability
academy
acetify
acidify
acidity
acouchy
acridly
actuary
acutely
adeptly
adultly
affably
agilely
agility
alchemy
alertly
alienly
alimony
allergy
almonry
aloofly
already
amatory
amenity
amiably
amnesty
amplify
anagogy
analogy
anarchy
anatomy
anchovy
angrily
anility
annuity
anomaly
anxiety
anybody
apetaly
aphylly
apishly

aplenty
apogamy
apology
archery
archway
ardency
areally
areaway
aridity
armoury
ashtray
ataraxy
atrophy
attaboy
aurally
autarky
autopsy
avidity
awfully
axially
baggily
balcony
ballboy
balmily
baloney
banally
battery
bawdily
beastly
beatify
beggary
bellboy
bheesty
bibbery
bigotry
biliary
billowy
bindery
biology
blackly
blandly
blankly
blarney
bleakly
blighty
blindly
blotchy
blowdry
blowfly
bluffly
bluntly
bobbery
bobstay
boloney
bonedry
bonnily
boozily
bottony
brambly
branchy
brashly
bravely
bravery
breathy
brevity
brewery
bribery
briefly
briskly
bristly
brittly
broadly
buirdly
bulkily
bullary
bumpily
bursary
buttery
buttony

cabbagy
cacanny
cachexy
cacoepy
cadency
calcify
callboy
calumny
calvary
camelry
cannery
cannily
canonry
capably
caraway
carroty
cattery
cattily
cautery
cavally
cavalry
century
certify
chantry
charily
charity
charley
charpoy
cheaply
chicory
chiefly
childly
chimney
chintzy
choosey
christy
churchy
chutney
ciliary
cindery
circusy
civilly
clarify
clarity
cleanly
clearly
clerisy
clerkly
cliquey
closely
cockily
cockney
cockshy
cogency
colicky
coloury
comfrey
company
compony
cookery
coppery
cornily
corrody
cottony
country
courtly
crackly
crassly
crazily
crinkly
crisply
crossly
crucify
crudely
crudity
cruelly
cruelty
crumbly
crunchy

crybaby
cursory
curtsey
custody
cutaway
cutlery
dacoity
damnify
dandify
dazedly
deanery
deathly
decency
deepfry
densely
density
destiny
destroy
devilry
diarchy
dietary
dignify
dignity
dingily
dirtily
disobey
display
dithery
dittany
dizzily
doddery
dodgery
doggery
doorway
doucely
doughty
dowdily
drapery
dripdry
drizzly
droshky
drouthy
duality
dubiety
ducally
dulcify
duopoly
durably
duskily
dustily
dyarchy
dynasty
eagerly
earthly
ebriety
ecology
economy
ecstasy
edacity
egality
eggcosy
elderly
elusory
embassy
empathy
emptily
Encraty
enquiry
entropy
eparchy
epigyny
epitaxy
eponymy
equably
equally
equerry
erectly
errancy
esotery

estuary
eupepsy
euphony
eustasy
exactly
exogamy
factory
faculty
fadedly
faintly
fairway
fallacy
fallguy
falsely
falsify
falsity
fancily
fantasy
faraday
faraway
fastday
fatally
fatuity
felonry
fernery
ferrety
fetidly
fidgety
fierily
fifthly
finally
finicky
firefly
firstly
fishery
fishily
fishway
fixedly
flagday
flaunty
fleetly
fleshly
flighty
flowery
fluency
fluidly
flunkey
flyaway
foggily
folkway
foolery
footboy
footway
foppery
foresay
forgery
fortify
foundry
frailly
frailty
frankly
fratery
freckly
freeway
Frenchy
freshly
friarly
frizzly
frowsty
fugally
funnily
furmety
furmity
furrowy
fussily
fustily
fuzzily
gadgety
gainsay

gallery
gallfly
gangway
gateway
gaudery
gaudily
gauntly
gauntry
gawkily
gelidly
gemmery
geodesy
geogony
geology
getaway
ghastly
ghostly
giantry
giddily
gingery
glorify
goodday
gossipy
goutfly
gradely
gramary
granary
grandly
grapery
gratify
gravely
gravity
greatly
greenly
gristly
grizzly
grocery
grossly
grouchy
gruffly
grumbly
gullery
gunnery
gunplay
gustily
gutsily
hackery
hackney
halfway
hallway
handily
hapenny
happily
harmony
harshly
hastily
haughty
hautboy
headily
headway
healthy
hearsay
heavily
heftily
helotry
hennery
heronry
hiccupy
hickory
highboy
highway
history
hockday
hoggery
holiday
honesty
horrify
horsily
hosiery

humanly
humidly
hushaby
huskily
hymnary
hymnody
ideally
ignobly
ilkaday
imagery
impiety
inanely
inanity
inaptly
ineptly
inertly
infancy
inquiry
insecty
irately
Irishry
isogamy
isogeny
isonomy
isotopy
jadedly
jaggery
jaloppy
January
jazzily
jerkily
jewelry
jittery
jobbery
joinery
jointly
jollify
jollity
journey
juicily
jurally
justify
killjoy
kitschy
knavery
knobbly
lamprey
laniary
lankily
larceny
largely
latency
lathery
laundry
lechery
legally
legibly
lengthy
leprosy
levelly
liberty
library
licitly
lightly
lignify
linkboy
liquefy
lithely
littery
liturgy
loathly
locally
loftily
longday
loosely
lottery
lousily
lovably
loverly

lowlily
loyally
loyalty
lucency
lucidly
luckily
lullaby
lumpily
luridly
lustily
lyingly
maggoty
magnify
majesty
malmsey
mammary
mangily
marrowy
martyry
masonry
mastery
mattery
meadowy
meatfly
mediacy
mercery
mercury
merrily
messily
mildewy
miliary
mimicry
mirkily
miscopy
miserly
misplay
mistily
mixedly
mockery
modally
modesty
moistly
mollify
monkery
monthly
moodily
morally
morassy
mortify
muddily
mummery
mummify
mundify
murkily
mutably
muttony
muzzily
myology
mystery
mystify
nailery
naively
naivety
nakedly
nameday
nasally
nastily
nattily
naughty
nectary
neology
neoteny
newsboy
nightly
nigrify
nimiety
nippily
nitrify
nodally

noisily noology noonday nosegay notably notedly novelty nullify nullity nummary nunnery nursery obesity obloquy obolary odyssey olivary omneity opacity oratory orderly orogeny orology orphrey ossuary ostiary otology outplay outstay overbuy overfly overlay overpay overtly pageboy paisley palfrey palmary panicky panoply papally parkway parsley passkey patency pathway paucity paunchy peartly peccary pedlary penally penalty peppery perfidy perjury perkily

pessary petrify pettily phlegmy phonily phratry phrensy piggery pillory pillowy piously piscary pithily pitpony plainly planxty playboy plenary pliably pliancy plumery plumply plushly pontify portray postboy potency pottery poultry poverty powdery pravity preachy prelacy prickly primacy primary primely privacy privily privity probity prodigy progeny pronely prosify prosily prosody proudly prudery puberty puckery pudency puffery putrefy qualify quality

quavery queenly queerly quickly quietly quinary quivery rabbity rabidly rackety raggedy railway rapidly rattery raunchy readily reality recency rectify rectory reentry regally regency remarry replevy respray retiary rettery revelry rhatany rhiancy rickety rightly rigidly rivalry roadway robbery rockery rockily roguery Rommany rookery ropeway rosebay roughly roundly rowdily royally royalty rubbery ruddily rudesby runaway rurally russety Russify rustily

saintly sallowy salsify sandboy sandfly sassaby satiety satisfy satrapy saucily saveloy savoury scantly scarify scenery scorify scraggy scranny scrappy scrawly scrawny scrimpy scrubby scruffy scrumpy sealery secrecy sectary seedily sensory servery seventy shadily shadowy shakily shapely sharply sheerly shingly shipway shivery shoofly shopboy shortly showery showily shrilly shrubby sickbay sickpay sideway sightly signary signify signory silkily sillily

silvery sintery sixthly sizably sketchy slackly slantly slavery sleekly slickly slimily slipway slouchy sloughy smartly smokily smoochy snakily snatchy snowily soapily soberly society soggily solidly someday someway sonancy soothly sootily soppily sorcery sorrily soundly spangly sparely specify spicery spicily spidery spikily spindly spindry spinney splashy spleeny spooney sprawly sprayey spriggy springy spurrey squabby squaddy squally squashy squatty

squeaky squiffy squinny squirmy squishy stagily staidly stalely standby starchy starkly stately steeply stenchy stepney sternly stiffly stonily stoutly streaky stringy stroppy stubbly stupefy suavely suavity subsidy succory sulkily summary summery sunnily surgery surlily swarthy sweetly swiftly swinery synergy syngamy tacitly tallboy tallowy Tammany tannery tantivy tardily tastily tattery tattily teacosy teatray telergy tenably tenancy tensely tensity

tentfly tenthly tenuity tepidly ternary terrify tersely testacy testfly testify testily therapy thereby theurgy thickly thirdly thirsty thistly thready thrifty throaty thrummy tidally tiddley tideway tiffany tightly tilbury timidly timothy tindery tinnily tipsify tipsily tittupy toggery tonally topiary torrefy totally tottery toughly tourney tracery tragedy tramway treacly trembly tricksy trigamy trilogy trinary trinity tripery tripody tritely trolley

truancy Tuesday tumidly tunably turbary turnery turnipy turnkey tushery twaddly twankay twiddly twinkly twitchy tympany tyranny tzigany unaptly uncanny unfitly unfunny unfussy ungodly unhandy unhappy unicity unitary unlucky unmanly unready untruly urgency urinary urology usually utility utterly vacancy vacuity vagally vaguely valency validly vapidly vapoury variety varsity vastity velvety venally versify vexedly viceroy victory viduity virelay visibly

vitally vitrify vividly vixenly vocally volubly vowelly waggery walkway wallaby wealthy wearily weekday weevily weighty weirdly whereby whimsey whiskey whitely willowy windily wintery wittily womanly woolsey woozily wordily workday worldly wreathy wriggly wrinkly wrongly yellowy zedoary zincify zinkify zoogamy zoogeny zoogony zoology zoonomy zootaxy zootomy zymurgy humbuzz kibbutz Kirghiz kolkhoz showbiz

8 letter words

aardvark aardwolf aasvogel abacuses abattoir Abbaside abbatial Abderite abdicate abducens abducent abductor abelmosk aberrant abetment abetting abeyance

abeyancy abhorred abhorrer abidance abjectly ablation ablative ablution abnegate abnormal abomasum abomasus aborally aborning abortion abortive abradant

abrasion abrasive abridger abrogate abruptly abscissa absentee absently absinthe absolute absolver absonant absorber absterge abstract abstrict abstruse

absurdly abundant abutilon abutment abuttals abutting academia academic acanthus acarpous Accadian accentor accepter acceptor accident accolade accoutre

accredit accuracy accurate accursed accustom aceldama acentric acerbate acerbity acervate acescent achenial achiever achiness achingly aciculae acicular

aciculas acidfast acidhead acidosis acierage acierate aconitic aconitum acosmism acoustic acquaint acrefoot acreinch acridine acridity acrimony acrolein

acrolith acrostic acrotism acrylate actiniae actinian actinias actinide actinism actinium activate actively activism activist activity actually actuator

acturial aculeate Adamical adamitic adaption adaptive addendum addition additive adducent adductor adenitis adenoids adequacy adequate adespota adherent

adhesion
adhesive
adiantum
adjacent
adjuster
adjustor
adjutage
adjutant
adjuvant
Adlerian
adlibbed
admitted
admonish
adnation
adoption
adoptive
adorable
adorably
adroitly
adularia
adulator
adultery
aduncate
aduncous
advanced
advisory
advocaat
advocacy
advocate
advowson
adynamia
adynamic
aegirine
aegrotat
aeration
aerially
aeriform
aerodyne
aerofoil
aerogram
aerolite
aerolith
aerology
aeronaut
aeronomy
aerostat
aesthete
aestival
affected
affecter
afferent
affiance
affinity
affirmer
afflatus
affluent
afforest
affright
affusion
aflutter
agaragar
agedness
agential
aggrieve
agiotage
agitator
agitprop
aglimmer
aglitter
agnation
agnostic
agonised
agraphia
agrarian
agrement
agrestic
agrimony
agrology
agronomy
aguishly
aigrette
aiguille
airborne
airbrake
airbrush
aircraft
Airedale
airfield
airframe
airiness
airliner
airscrew
airshaft
airspace
airspeed
airstrip
airtight
airwoman
Akkadian
alacrity
alarmist
albacore
Albanian
albinism
alburnum
alcahest
alchemic
aldehyde
alderman
Alderney
aleatory
alebench
alehouse
aleurone
alewives
alfresco
algicide
algidity
alginate
algology
Algonkin
algorism
alguazil
alienage
alienate
alienism
alienist
alizarin
alkahest
alkalies
alkalify
alkaline
alkaloid
allegory
alleluia
allergen
allergic
alleyway
alliance
allnight
allocate
allodial
allodium
allogamy
allopath
allotted
allottee
allround
allspice
allusion
allusive
alluvial
alluvion
alluvium
almagest
almanack
almighty
alogical
alopecia
alphabet
alpinism
alpinist
Alsatian
although
altitude
altruism
altruist
alumroot
alveolar
alveolus
amadavat
amaranth
amazedly
ambiance
ambience
ambition
ambivert
ambrosia
ambulant
ambulate
ambusher
amenable
amenably
American
amethyst
amiantus
amicable
amicably
amitosis
amitotic
ammoniac
ammonify
ammonite
ammonium
amnesiac
amniotic
amoebean
amoeboid
amorally
amoretti
amoretto
amortise
amperage
amphibia
amphipod
amphorae
amphoras
ampullae
amputate
amusedly
amygdala
anabases
anabasis
anabatic
anabolic
anaconda
anaerobe
anaglyph
anagogic
analcime
analcite
analecta
analects
analogic
analogue
analyser
analyses
analysis
analytic
anapaest
anaphase
anaphora
anarchic
anasarca
anathema
anatomic
ancestor
ancestry
anchoret
andesine
andesite
androgen
anecdote
anechoic
aneurism
aneurysm
angelica
Anglican
angstrom
anhedral
aniconic
animally
animator
anisette
ankerite
ankylose
annalist
annotate
announce
annually
annulate
annulled
anorexia
anorexic
anorthic
anourous
anserine
answerer
anteater
antecede
antedate
antefixa
antelope
antennae
antennal
antennas
antepost
anterior
anteroom
anthelia
anthemia
antheral
anthesis
anthozoa
antibody
antidote
antihero
antilogy
antimask
antimony
antinode
antinomy
antiphon
antipode
antipole
antipope
antisera
antitype
antlered
antrorse
anyplace
anything
anywhere
aoristic
apagogic
aperient
aperitif
aperture
aphasiac
aphelion
aphicide
aphorise
aphorism
aphorist
apiarian
apiarist
apically
aplastic
apocrine
apodoses
apodosis
apogamic
apograph
apologia
apologue
apomixis
apoplexy
apostasy
apostate
apothegm
appalled
appanage
apparent
appendix
appetent
appetite
applause
applepie
applique
apposite
appraise
approach
approval
apresski
apterous
aptitude
aquacade
aqualung
aquanaut
aquarist
aquarium
aquatint
aqueduct
aquiline
araceous
arachnid
Aramaean
Arapahoe
arapaima
arbalest
arbalist
arbitral
arboreal
arboreta
arborist
Arcadian
archaean
archaise
archaism
archaist
archduke
archival
archives
archness
Arcturus
arcuated
ardently
areolate
arethusa
argentic
argonaut
arguable
arguably
argufier
argument
Arianism
arillate
aristate
Armagnac
armament
armature
armchair
Armenian
Arminian
armorial
armoured
armourer
armyworm
aromatic
arpeggio
arquebus
arranger
arrantly
arrestee
arrester
arrestor
arrogant
arrogate
arsenate
arsenide
arsenite
arsonist
arsonous
artefact
arterial
artesian
artfully
articled
artifact
artifice
artistic
artistry
asbestic
asbestos
ascender
ascidian
ascidium
ascocarp
aseptate
asperges
asperity
asphodel
asphyxia
aspirant
aspirate
assassin
assemble
assembly
assenter
assentor
assertor
assessor
assiento
assignat
assignee
assignor
assonant
assonate
assorted
assuming
Assyrian
astatine
asterisk
asterism
asteroid
asthenia
asthenic
astonied
astonish
astragal
astutely
asyndeta
ataraxia
ataraxic
atheling
Athenian
atheroma
athletic
atlantes
Atlantic
atomiser
atremble
atrocity
atropine
attender
attested
attester
attestor
atticism
attitude
attorney
attrited
atwitter
atypical
aubretia
audacity
audience
audition
auditive
auditory
Augustan
augustly
aurelian
auricula
auriform
aurorean
auspices
autacoid
autarchy
autarkic
autistic
autobahn
autocade
autocrat
autodafe
autodyne
autogamy
autogiro
autogyro
autolyse
automata
automate
autonomy
autosome
autotomy
autotype
autumnal
autunite
avadavat
aventail
averment
averring
aversely
aversion
aversive
aviarist
aviation
aviatrix
avidness
avifauna
avionics
avowable
avowedly
avulsion
aweather
axiality
axillary
axiology
axletree
Ayrshire
babirusa
babouche
babushka
babyhood
baccarat
bacchant
bachelor
bacillar
bacillus
backache
backbite
backbone
backchat
backcomb
backdate
backdoor
backdrop
backfire
backhand
backlash
backless
backlist
backmost
backpack
backrest
backroom
backseat
backside
backspin
backstay
backveld
backward
backwash
backyard
Baconian
bacteria
Bactrian
badinage
badlands
bagpiper
baguette
bailable
bailment
bailsman
bakshish
balanced
balancer
baldhead
baldness
baldpate
balefire
Balinese
balkline
balladic
balladry
ballcock
balletic
ballista
ballonet
ballroom
ballyhoo
ballyrag
balmoral
balsamic
baluster
bambinos
banality
banausic
bandanna
bandeaux
banderol
banditry
banditti
bandsman
bangtail
banister
banjoist
bankable
bankbill
bankbook
banknote
bankroll
bankrupt
bannered
banneret
bannerol
banterer
bantling
banxring
barathea
barbaric
barbecue

barberry
barbette
barbican
barbital
bareback
barefoot
bareness
bargeman
baritone
barkless
barnacle
barndoor
barnyard
baronage
baroness
baronial
barouche
barracks
barranca
barranco
barrator
barratry
barrenly
barrette
barterer
bartizan
baryonic
barytone
basaltic
baseball
baseborn
baseless
baseline
basement
baseness
basicity
basidial
basidium
basilica
basilisk
basinful
basketry
bassinet
basswood
bastardy
bastille
Batavian
bateleur
bathetic
bathotic
bathrobe
bathroom
battalia
battleax
baudrons
bauxitic
Bavarian
bayadere
bayberry
bdellium
beadroll
beadsman
beadwork
beagling
beamends
beanpole
bearable
bearably
bearings
bearskin
beatific
beautify
bebopper
becalmed
bechamel
bechance
becoming
bedabble
bedazzle
bedeguar
bedimmed
bedmaker
bedplate
bedstead
bedstraw
bedtable
beebread
beechnut
beeeater
beefcake
beefwood
beeswing
beetling
beetroot
befallen
befitted
befogged
befriend
befuddle
begetter
beggarly
beginner
begirded
begotten
begrudge
beguiler
behemoth
beholden
beholder
bejabers
belabour
believer
belittle
bellbird
bellbuoy
bellcote
bellpull
bellpush
bellwort
bellyful
beltless
benedick
benedict
benefice
benignly
Benjamin
bentwood
benzoate
benzylic
bequeath
berberis
berceuse
bereaved
bergamot
beriberi
berliner
Bermudas
besieger
beslaver
besmirch
besotted
besought
bespoken
besprent
bestiary
bestowal
bestrewn
bestride
bestrode
betacism
betatron
bethesda
betrayal
betrayer
bevelled
beveller
beverage
bewigged
bewilder
bezonian
biannual
biassing
biathlon
bibation
biblical
bibulous
biconvex
bicuspid
biddable
biennial
biennium
bifacial
bifocals
bigamist
bigamous
bignonia
bilabial
bilberry
billfold
billhead
billhook
billiard
billyboy
billycan
bilobate
bimanous
bimbashi
binaural
bindweed
binnacle
binomial
bioassay
biocidal
biogenic
biograph
biometry
biomorph
bionomic
bioplasm
bioplast
bioscope
biparous
birdbath
birdcage
birdcall
birdlime
birdseed
birdseye
birthday
bisector
bisexual
bistable
bistoury
bitchily
bitingly
bitterly
bivalent
biweekly
biyearly
blabbing
blackboy
blackcap
blackfly
blacking
blackish
blackleg
blackout
blacktie
blacktop
bladdery
blahblah
blamable
blamably
blameful
blandish
blankety
blastema
blastoff
blastoid
blastula
blatancy
blazoner
blazonry
bleacher
bleakish
blearily
bleeding
Blenheim
blesbuck
blessing
blighter
blimpish
blindage
blinding
blinkers
blinking
blissful
blistery
blithely
blizzard
blockade
blockage
blockish
blondish
bloodily
bloodred
bloomers
bloomery
blooming
blossomy
blotting
blowball
blowfish
blowhard
blowhole
blowlamp
blowpipe
blubbery
bludgeon
bluebell
bluebird
bluechip
bluecoat
bluefish
blueness
bluenose
blueweed
blurrily
blurring
blushful
blustery
boarding
boastful
boatbill
boatdeck
boathook
boatload
bobbinet
bobbypin
bobbysox
bobolink
bobwheel
bobwhite
bodement
bodiless
Bodleian
bodyshop
bodywork
Boeotian
bogeyman
bohemian
boldface
boldness
bollworm
bolthole
boltrope
bombsite
bondmaid
bondmans
bondsman
bonefish
bonehead
boneless
bonemeal
boneyard
bonhomie
boniface
boniness
bonspiel
bontebok
bookcase
bookends
bookland
booklice
booklore
bookmark
bookpost
bookrest
bookwork
bookworm
bootjack
bootlace
bootlast
bootless
boottree
boracite
Bordeaux
bordello
borderer
borecole
borehole
boringly
borrower
bosseyed
botanise
botanist
botflies
botryoid
bottomry
botulism
botyrose
bouffant
boughten
bouillon
bouncily
bouncing
boundary
bourgeon
boursier
bourtree
boutique
bouzouki
bowfront
bowsprit
boxpleat
boyishly
bracelet
brachial
brachium
brackish
bracteal
bractlet
Bradshaw
braggart
bragging
braiding
brainish
brainpan
brakeman
brakevan
brancard
branched
brancher
branchia
brandied
brandish
brandnew
brassage
brassard
brassart
brassica
brassily
brattice
brattish
brazenly
brazenry
braziery
breakage
breaking
breakout
breasted
breather
breeches
breeding
breezily
bregmata
brethren
brettese
brettice
breveted
breviary
brewster
Briarean
bribable
brickbat
brickred
briefing
brighten
brightly
brimfull
brimless
brimming
brindled
briskish
brisling
britches
britzska
broacher
broadish
broadway
brocaded
brocatel
broccoli
brochure
broidery
brokenly
bromelia
bromidic
bronchia
bronchus
broodily
brookite
brooklet
brougham
brouhaha
browband
browbeat
browning
brownish
brunette
brushoff
brutally
bryology
bryozoan
bubaline
buckaroo
buckbean
buckhorn
buckling
buckshee
buckshot
buckskin
Buddhism
Buddhist
buddleia
budgeree
buhlwork
building
bulkhead
bullcalf
bulldoze
bulletin
bullfrog
bullhead
bullhorn
bullocky
bullring
bullseye
bullyboy
bullyoff
bullyrag
bummaree
buncombe
bundling
bunfight
bungalow
bunghole
bunkered
buntline
buoyancy
Burberry
burglary
burgonet
Burgundy
burletta
burnouse
burntout
burrower
bursitis
bushbaby
bushbuck
bushfire
bushveld
business
bustling
busybody
busyness
butchery
buttoner
buttress
butylene
butyrate
buzzword
Byronism
bystreet
cabalism
cabalist
caballed
cabinboy
cableway
cabochon
caboodle
cabotage
cabriole
cabstand
cachalot
cachepot
cachexia
cachucha
cacology
cacomixl
cactuses
cadastre
cadenced
caducean
caduceus
caducity
caducous
caesious
caesural
caffeine
cagebird
cageling
caginess
cajolery
cakewalk
calabash
caladium
calamary
calamine
calamint
calamite
calamity
calcanea
calcaria
calcific
calcitic
calcspar
calctuff
calculus
calendar
calender
calfskin
calidity
califate
calipash
calipers
callable
callgirl
calliope
calliper
calmness
calthrop
calvados
calycine
calycoid
calycule
calyptra
Cambrian
cameleer
camellia
camisade
camisado
camisole
camomile
campagna
campaign
campfire
camphene
camphine
campsite
camshaft
Canadian
canaille
canalise
canaster
cancrine
cancroid
candidly
canister
cannabin
cannabis
cannibal
cannikin
cannonry
cannulae
cannular
cannulas
canoeing
canoeist
canoness
canonise
canonist
canoodle
canorous
canthari
canticle
cantonal
cantoris
canzonet
capacity
capeline

capellet
capeskin
capitate
capitula
caponier
caponise
caprifig
capriole
capsicum
capstone
capsular
captious
capuchin
capybara
carabine
caracara
caracole
carapace
carbolic
carbonic
carbonyl
carboxyl
carburet
carcajou
carcanet
cardamom
cardamum
cardigan
cardinal
carefree
careless
careworn
carillon
carinate
carnally
carnauba
carnival
Carolean
Caroline
carolled
carotene
carousal
carousel
carouser
carriage
carriole
carryall
carryout
cartload
cartouch
caruncle
caryatid
Casanova
cascabel
casebook
casemate
casement
casework
cashbook
cashmere
cassette
castaway
castiron
castrate
castrati
castrato
casually
casualty
catacomb
catalase
cataloes
catalyse
catalyst
catamite
catapult
cataract
catchall
catchfly
catching

catechol
category
catenary
catenate
cateress
catering
cathedra
catheter
cathexes
cathexis
cathodal
cathodic
catholic
cationic
catsfoot
catstail
cattleya
caudally
caudated
caudexes
caudices
caudillo
cauldron
causally
causerie
causeway
cautious
cavalier
cavatina
caverned
cavesson
cavicorn
cavilled
caviller
celeriac
celerity
celibacy
celibate
cellarer
cellaret
cellular
cemetery
cenotaph
Cenozoic
centaury
centring
centrism
centrist
centroid
centuple
cephalic
ceramics
ceramist
cerastes
ceratoid
cercaria
cerebral
cerebrum
cerement
ceremony
cernuous
cerulean
cerusite
cervelat
cervical
cervices
cesspool
cetacean
chaconne
chainsaw
chairman
chalazae
Chaldaic
Chaldean
chaldron
chalkpit
chambers
chambray
champers

champion
chancery
chandler
chapatti
chapbook
chapelry
chaperon
chapiter
chaplain
chapping
charcoal
charisma
charlady
charlock
charming
charring
Chartism
Chartist
chasseur
chastely
chastise
chastity
chasuble
chateaux
chattily
chatting
chaunter
chauntry
cheapish
checkers
checkout
cheekily
cheerful
cheerily
cheering
Chellean
chemical
chemurgy
chenille
chequers
Cherokee
cherubic
cherubim
chessman
chestnut
Cheyenne
chiasmus
chiastic
chickpea
chiefdom
childbed
childish
children
chiliasm
chiliast
chimaera
chimeric
Chinaman
chinchin
chinless
chipmuck
chipmunk
chipping
chirpily
chirrupy
chitchat
chivalry
chlorate
chloride
chlorine
chlorite
chlorous
choicely
choirboy
choleric
chondrus
chopchop
chopping
chopsuey

choragic
choragus
chorally
chordate
choregic
choregus
choriamb
chorioid
chowchow
christen
christie
Christly
chromate
chromite
chromium
chthonic
chugging
chummily
chumming
chupatti
chupatty
churchly
churinga
churlish
churning
chutzpah
ciborium
cicatrix
cicerone
ciceroni
cicisbei
cicisbeo
cidevant
ciliated
cinchona
cincture
cineaste
cinerary
cingulum
cinnabar
cinnamic
cinnamon
cinquain
Circaean
circuity
circular
cirriped
cislunar
citation
citified
cityfied
civilian
civilise
civility
cladding
claimant
clambake
clammily
clamming
clanging
clangour
clannish
clanship
clansman
clapping
claptrap
claqueur
clarence
clarinet
classics
classify
clavicle
clawback
claymore
cleancut
cleaning
cleanser
clearcut
clearing

clearway
cleavage
cleavers
clematis
clemency
clerical
clerihew
clerkdom
clerkess
cleverly
climatic
clincher
clinical
clinking
clipclop
clippers
clipping
cliquish
cliquism
cloddish
clodpole
clodpoll
clogging
cloister
clopclop
closeset
closeted
clothier
clothing
clotting
cloudily
cloudlet
clownery
clownish
clubbing
clubfoot
clubhaul
clubland
clueless
clumsily
clupeoid
clustery
clypeate
coachdog
coachman
coaction
coactive
coagulum
coaldust
coalesce
coalfish
coalhole
coalmine
coalsack
coarsely
coatrack
coatroom
coauthor
cobaltic
cobblers
cobwebby
coccyges
cochleae
cochlear
cockatoo
cockboat
cockcrow
cockerel
cockeyed
cockloft
cockshut
cocksure
cocktail
codifier
codpiece
codriver
coelomic
coenobia
coenzyme

coercion
coercive
cofactor
cogently
cogitate
cognomen
cognosce
cognovit
cogwheel
coherent
cohesion
cohesive
coiffeur
coiffure
coincide
coistrel
cokernut
colander
coldness
coleseed
coleslaw
colewort
coliform
coliseum
collagen
collapse
collared
collator
colleger
colliery
collogue
colloquy
collyria
colonial
colonise
colonist
colophon
colossal
colossus
coloured
colubrid
columnal
columnar
columned
comatose
combings
comeback
comedian
comedist
comedown
cometary
commando
commence
commerce
commoner
commoney
commonly
communal
commuter
compages
compiler
complain
compleat
complete
complice
complier
compline
composed
composer
compound
compress
comprise
computer
conation
conative
concasse
conceder
conceive
concerti

concerto
concetti
concetto
conchate
conchoid
conclave
conclude
concrete
condense
condylar
conferee
conferva
confetti
confider
confiner
confines
conflate
conflict
confound
confrere
confront
congener
conglobe
congress
congreve
conidial
conidium
coniform
conjoint
conjugal
conjunct
conjurer
conjuror
conniver
conoidal
conquest
conserve
consider
consoler
consomme
conspire
constant
construe
consular
consumer
contagia
contango
contempt
contents
contessa
continua
continue
continuo
contline
contorno
contract
contrail
contrary
contrast
contrate
contrite
contrive
conurbia
convener
convenor
converge
converse
convexly
conveyer
conveyor
convince
convolve
convulse
cookbook
coolabah
coolibah
coolness
coonskin
cooption

cooptive
coplanar
copperas
copulate
copybook
copyedit
copyhold
coquetry
coquette
coracoid
cordless
cordovan
corduroy
cordwain
cordwood
corelate
corkwing
corkwood
cornball
corneous
cornetcy
cornetti
cornetto
corniced
corniche
cornicle
cornific
cornpone
coronach
coronary
coronoid
corporal
corridor
corrival
corselet
corseted
corsetry
cortical
cortices
corundum
corvette
Corybant
coryphee
cosecant
cosiness
cosmetic
cosmical
costmary
costplus
costpush
costumer
cotenant
cothurni
cotillon
cotquean
Cotswold
cottager
cottagey
couchant
couching
couldest
coulisse
coumarin
countess
coupling
courante
coursing
courtesy
courtier
couscous
cousinly
covalent
covenant
coverage
coverall
covering
coverlet
covertly
covetous

cowardly
cowberry
cowgrass
coworker
coxalgia
coxswain
cozenage
crabbing
crackers
cracking
crackjaw
cracknel
crackpot
cradling
craftily
cragsman
cramfull
cramming
cramoisy
cranefly
craniate
crankily
crankpin
crannied
crashing
crashpad
cratches
cravenly
crawfish
crayfish
creakily
creamery
creatine
creation
creative
creatrix
creature
credence
credenza
credible
credibly
credited
creditor
creeping
crenated
crenelle
creosote
crepitus
crescent
crescive
cretonne
crevasse
cribbage
cribbing
criminal
crispate
cristate
criteria
critical
critique
croakily
Croatian
croceate
crockery
crocoite
crofting
cromlech
cromorna
cromorne
cropping
crossbar
crossbow
crosscut
crossing
crosslet
crossply
crosstie
crossway
crotched
crotchet
croupier
croupous
crowbill
crowfoot
cruciate
crucible
crucifer
crucifix
crueller
crumhorn
crummock
crusader
crustily
cruzeiro
cryogeny
cryolite
cryostat
cryotron
cubature
cubiform
cuboidal
cucumber
cucurbit
culdesac
culicine
culinary
culottes
culpable
culpably
cultivar
cultural
cultured
culverin
Cumbrian
cumbrous
cumulate
cumulous
cupboard
cupelled
cupidity
cupreous
cupulate
curarine
curarise
curassow
curative
curculio
cureless
curlicue
currency
curricle
cursedly
curtains
curtness
curveted
cushiony
Cushitic
cuspidor
cussedly
cussword
customer
cuteness
cutprice
cutpurse
cutwater
cyanogen
cyanoses
cyanosis
cyanotic
cyclamen
cycleway
cyclical
cyclonic
cyclopes
cyclosis
cylinder
cymatium
cynicism
cynosure
Cypriote
cypselae
Cyrenaic
Cyrillic
cysteine
cystitis
cytidine
cytology
cytosine
czaritza
dabchick
dactylar
dactylic
daemonic
daffodil
daftness
dahabieh
daimonic
daintily
daiquiri
dairying
dairyman
dalesman
dalmatic
damassin
damnable
damnably
dampness
dancette
dancetty
dandruff
dandyish
dandyism
danegeld
dankness
danseuse
daringly
darkling
darkness
darkroom
darksome
dartrous
dastardy
dateless
dateline
daughter
daybreak
daydream
daylight
deadbeat
deadener
deadfall
deadhead
deadline
deadlock
deadness
deadwood
deaerate
deafmute
deafness
dealfish
deanship
dearness
deathbed
deathcap
deathray
debagged
debarred
debility
debonair
debugged
debutant
decadent
decagram
decanter
deceased
decedent
deceiver
December
decemvir
decennia
decently
decigram
decimate
decipher
decision
decisive
deckhand
declarer
declasse
declutch
decolour
decorate
decorous
decouple
decrease
decrepit
decretal
decurion
dedicate
deedless
deemster
deeplaid
deepness
deerskin
defector
defender
deferent
deferral
deferred
deferrer
defiance
defilade
definite
deflower
deforest
deformed
defrayal
deftness
degrease
deionise
dejected
delation
delegacy
delegate
deletion
delibate
delicacy
delicate
delirium
delivery
Delphian
delusion
delusive
delusory
demagogy
demander
demarche
demented
dementia
demerara
demersal
demijohn
demitted
demiurge
demobbed
democrat
demolish
demoness
demoniac
demonian
demonise
demonism
demotion
demurely
demurred
demurrer
denarius
denature
denazify
dendrite
dendroid
denehole
deniable
denounce
dentalia
dentated
denticle
departed
depicter
depictor
depilate
deponent
deportee
depraved
deprival
deprived
depurate
deputise
deration
derelict
derision
derisive
derisory
derivate
derogate
derriere
describe
deserter
designer
desirous
desolate
despatch
despiser
despotic
destrier
destruct
detached
detailed
detainee
detainer
detector
deterred
deterrer
dethrone
detonate
detoxify
detrital
detritus
deucedly
deuteron
deviance
deviancy
deviator
deviling
devilish
devilism
devilkin
devilled
deviltry
Devonian
devotion
devourer
devoutly
dewberry
dewiness
dewpoint
dewyeyed
dextrine
dextrose
dextrous
diabasic
diabetes
diabetic
diabolic
diaconal
diagnose
diagonal
diagraph
diallage
dialling
dialogic
dialogue
dialyser
dialyses
dialysis
dialytic
diamante
diameter
dianthus
diapason
diapause
diaphone
diarchal
diarchic
diarrhea
diaspora
diaspore
diastase
diastema
diastole
diatomic
diatonic
diatribe
dicacity
dichasia
dichroic
dicrotic
dictator
dicyclic
didactic
didapper
didymium
didymous
dieldrin
diereses
dieresis
diestock
dietetic
diffract
diffuser
digamist
digamous
digester
diggings
digitate
digitise
dihedral
dihybrid
dilatant
dilation
dilative
dilatory
diligent
dilution
diluvial
diluvian
diluvium
dimerism
dimerous
diminish
dimmable
dinerout
dingdong
dinornis
dinosaur
diocesan
dioecism
diopside
dioptase
dioptric
dioramic
dioritic
diphenyl
diplogen
diploidy
diplomat
diplopia
dipnoous
dipstick
dipteral
dipteran
directly
director
dirigism
diriment
disabuse
disagree
disallow
disarray
disaster
disbench
disbound
disburse
disciple
disclaim
disclose
discount
discover
discreet
discrete
discrown
diseased
disendow
disfrock
disgorge
disgrace
disguise
dishevel
disinter
disjoint
disjunct
dislodge
disloyal
dismally
dismount
disorder
dispatch
dispense
disperse
dispirit
displace
displant
displode
displume
disposal
disposer
dispread
disprize
disproof
disprove
disquiet
disseise
disserve
dissever
dissolve
dissuade
distally
distance
distaste
distinct
distract
distrain
distrait
distress
district
distrust
disunion
disunite
disunity
disusage
disvalue
ditheism
ditheist
ditherer
dittybag
dittybox
diuresis
diuretic
divagate
divalent
divebomb
dividend
dividivi
dividual
divinely
divinise
divinity
division
divisive
divorcee
djellaba
Docetism
Docetist
docilely
docility
dockland
dockside
dockyard
doctoral
doctrine
document
doddered
dodderer
dogberry
dogeared
dogfaced
dogfight
doggedly
doggerel
doghouse
dogmatic
dogooder
dogsbody
dogshore
dogtired
dogtooth
dogwatch
dogwhelk
doldrums
dolerite
dolesome
dolomite
doloroso
dolorous
domestic
domicile
dominant
dominate
domineer
dominion
dominoes
donation
Donatism
Donatist
donative
donatory
donought
doomsday
doomsman
doomster
doorbell
doorcase
doorknob
doornail
doorpost
doorsill
doorstep
doorstop
dooryard
dopiness
dormancy
dormouse

dorsally
dotation
dotingly
dotterel
douanier
doubloon
doubtful
doughboy
doughnut
doumpalm
dourness
dovecote
dovetail
dowdyish
dowelled
downbeat
downcast
downcome
downfall
downhaul
downhill
downland
downmost
downpipe
downpour
downtime
downtown
downturn
downward
downwind
doxology
doziness
drabbler
drabness
dracaena
drachmae
drachmai
drachmas
draconic
dragging
dragline
dragoman
dragomen
dragonet
dragsman
dragster
drainage
dramatic
drammock
dramshop
draughts
draughty
drawable
drawback
drawtube
drawwell
dreadful
dreamful
dreamily
dreaming
drearily
drencher
dressage
dressing
dribbler
dribblet
driftage
driftice
driftway
drilling
drinking
dripfeed
dripping
drivable
driveway
drollery
drophead
dropkick
dropleaf
dropping
dropshot
dropwort
droughty
drownded
drowsily
drubbing
drudgery
drugging
druggist
druidess
druidism
drumfire
drumhead
drumming
drummock
drumroll
drunkard
drupelet
dryclean
drynurse
dryplate
drypoint
drystone
duchesse
duckbill
duckhawk
duckling
duckpond
duckweed
ductless
duelling
duellist
duettist
Dukhobor
dulciana
dulcimer
Dulcinea
dullness
dumbbell
dumbhead
dumbness
dumbshow
dumfound
dumpling
dundiver
dungaree
dungcart
dunghill
duodenal
duodenum
duologue
durables
duration
durative
durukuli
dustbowl
dustcart
dustcoat
dustless
dustlike
dustshot
Dutchman
dutiable
dutyfree
dutypaid
dwarfish
dwarfism
dwelling
dybbukim
dyestuff
dynamics
dynamism
dynamist
dynamite
dynastic
dynatron
dysgenic
dyslexia
dyslexic
dyspnoea
dystopia
eagleowl
earmuffs
earnings
earphone
earpiece
earthnut
easement
easiness
easterly
eastmost
eastward
ebriated
ecclesia
echinate
echinoid
echogram
echoless
eclectic
ecliptic
eclosion
ecologic
economic
ecstatic
ectoderm
ectozoon
edacious
edentate
edgeless
edgeways
edgewise
edginess
editress
educable
educated
educator
educible
eduction
eelgrass
eeriness
effector
efferent
efficacy
effluent
effluvia
effusion
effusive
eftsoons
egestion
egestive
eggplant
eggshell
egoistic
egomania
Egyptian
eighteen
eighthly
eighties
ejection
ejective
ekistics
elatedly
eldorado
eldritch
election
elective
electret
electric
electron
electrum
elegance
elegancy
elenchus
elenctic
elephant
elevated
elevator
eleventh
elfarrow
elflocks
eligible
eligibly
elkhound
ellipses
ellipsis
elliptic
elongate
eloquent
emaciate
embalmer
embattle
embedded
embezzle
embitter
emblazon
embolden
embolism
embosser
embracer
embussed
emceeing
emendate
emergent
emeritus
emersion
emetical
emigrant
emigrate
eminence
eminency
emissary
emission
emissive
emitting
Emmental
empathic
empeople
emphases
emphasis
emphatic
employee
employer
empoison
emporium
empurple
empyreal
empyrean
emulator
emulgent
emulsify
emulsion
emulsive
emulsoid
enaction
enactive
enarched
encaenia
enceinte
encipher
encircle
enclitic
enclothe
encomion
encomium
encrinal
encrinic
encroach
encumber
encyclic
endamage
endanger
endemism
endermic
endocarp
endoderm
endogamy
endogeny
endorsee
endorser
endostea
endozoic
endozoon
endpaper
energise
enervate
enfeeble
enfetter
enfilade
enforcer
enforest
engaging
engender
engineer
enginery
engirdle
engramma
engraver
enkindle
enlarger
enneagon
enormity
enormous
enquirer
enricher
enrolled
ensample
ensconce
ensemble
ensheath
enshrine
enshroud
ensiform
ensigncy
ensilage
enslaver
ensphere
enswathe
entailer
entangle
entellus
enterate
enthalpy
enthrall
enthrone
entirely
entirety
entoderm
entoptic
entozoic
entozoon
entracte
entrails
entrance
entreaty
entrench
entrepot
entresol
enuresis
enuretic
envelope
enviable
enviably
environs
envisage
envision
enzootic
eohippus
eolithic
ephemera
Ephesian
ephorate
epiblast
epically
epicalyx
epicotyl
epicycle
epidemic
epidural
epifauna
epigeous
epigraph
epilepsy
epilogue
epinasty
epiphany
epiphyte
episcope
episemon
episodal
episodic
epistler
epistyle
epitasis
epopoeia
epyllion
equalise
equality
equalled
equation
equinity
equipage
equipped
equitant
equities
equivoke
erasable
Erastian
erectile
erection
eremitic
erethism
erewhile
ergogram
ergotise
ergotism
erigeron
erodible
erogenic
erotical
errantly
errantry
eruption
eruptive
erythema
escalade
escalate
escallop
escalope
escapade
escapism
escapist
escargot
escarole
eschalot
eschewal
esculent
Eskimoan
esoteric
espalier
especial
espousal
espouser
espresso
Esquimau
essayist
Essenism
essonite
esterify
estimate
Estonian
estopped
estoppel
estovers
estrange
estuaril
esurient
etcetera
eternise
eternity
ethereal
etherial
etherise
etherism
etherist
ethicism
ethicist
Ethiopic
ethnarch
ethnical
ethology
ethylene
etiolate
Etrurian
Etruscan
eucalypt
eucritic
eugenics
eugenism
eugenist
eulachon
eulogise
eulogist
eulogium
euonymin
euonymus
eupatrid
eupepsia
eupeptic
euphonic
euphoria
euphoric
euphrasy
euphuism
euphuist
Eurasian
Eurocrat
European
europium
eustatic
eutectic
eutrophy
evacuant
evacuate
evadable
evaluate
evanesce
evection
evenfall
evenness
evensong
eventful
eventide
eventual
evermore
eversion
everyday
everyman
everyone
everyway
eviction
evidence
evildoer
evilness
evincive
evitable
evulsion
exacting
exaction
examinee
examiner
exanthem
excavate
excelled
exchange
excision
excitant
exciting
excluder
excursus
execrate
executor
exegesis
exegetic
exemplar
exemplum
exequies
exercise
exergual
exertion
exhalant
exhorter
exigence
exigency
exigible
exiguity
exiguous
eximious
existent
exlibris
exocrine
exogamic
exorcise
exorcism
exorcist
exordial
exordium
exospore
exoteric
expander
expedite
expelled
expellee
expertly
expiable
expiator
expirant
explicit
exploder
explorer
exponent
exporter
exposure
exserted
extender
extensor
exterior
external
extolled
extrados
extremes
extrorse
exultant
exuviate
eyeglass
eyeliner
eyepiece
eyerhyme
eyeshade
eyesight
eyestalk
eyetooth
eyewater
fabliaux
fabulist
fabulous
faceache
facecard
faceless
facelift
facepack
facetiae
facially

facilely
facility
factious
factotum
fadeaway
fadeless
fagoting
failsafe
faineant
faintish
fairlead
fairness
fairyism
faithful
falcated
falchion
falconer
falconet
falconry
falderal
fallback
fallfish
fallible
fallibly
falsetto
faltboat
familial
familiar
famously
fanciful
fancyman
fandance
fandango
fanfaron
fangless
fanlight
fantasia
faradaic
faradism
farcical
farewell
farflung
farinose
farmhand
farmland
farmyard
farouche
farriery
farthest
farthing
fascicle
fasciola
fasciole
Fascista
Fascisti
fashious
fastback
fastener
fastfood
fastness
fasttalk
fastuous
fatalism
fatalist
fatality
fatherly
fatigues
fatstock
fattener
faubourg
faultily
faunally
Faustian
fauteuil
favonian
favoured
favourer
fearless
fearsome
feasible
feasibly
feastday
feathery
featured
features
febrific
February
feckless
feculent
fedayeen
federate
feeblish
feedback
feedhead
feedpipe
feedtank
feldsher
feldspar
felicity
felinity
fellable
fellahin
fellness
fellowly
felsitic
feminine
feminise
feminism
feminist
feminity
fenberry
fencible
fenestra
feretory
fernshaw
ferocity
ferreter
ferriage
ferritic
ferryman
fervency
fervidly
festally
festival
fetching
feticide
feudally
feverfew
feverish
feverous
fewtrils
fibrilla
fibrosis
fibrotic
fiddling
fidelity
fiducial
fiendish
fiercely
fiftieth
fiftyish
fighting
figurant
figurine
filagree
filament
filariae
filarial
filature
filefish
filially
filiform
filigree
Filipina
Filipino
filmgoer
filmstar
filthily
filtrate
fimbriae
finalise
finalism
finalist
finality
finedraw
fineness
finespun
fingered
finisher
finitely
finitude
finnesko
firearms
fireback
fireball
firebird
fireboat
firebomb
firebrat
fireclay
firedamp
fireeyed
firehose
firelock
fireopal
fireplug
fireship
fireside
firetrap
fireweed
firewood
firework
firmness
firstaid
fiscally
fishable
fishball
fishbone
fishbowl
fishcake
fishfarm
fishglue
fishhawk
fishhook
fishless
fishmeal
fishpond
fishtail
fishwife
fissiped
fistiana
fistical
fistulae
fistular
fitfully
fivefold
fivestar
fixation
fixative
flabella
flagella
flagging
flagpole
flagrant
flagship
flambeau
flamenco
flamingo
flanerie
flapjack
flapping
flashgun
flashily
flashing
flatboat
flatfeet
flatfish
flatfoot
flathead
flatiron
flatling
flatmate
flatness
flatrace
flattery
flattest
flattish
flatware
flatways
flatwise
flatworm
flautist
flawless
flaxseed
fleabane
fleabite
fleawort
flection
fleeting
fleshfly
fleshpot
fletcher
flexible
flexibly
flexuose
flexuous
flexural
flickery
flimflam
flimsily
flincher
flinders
flintily
flipflap
flipflop
flippant
flipping
flipside
flitting
floatage
floating
floccose
floccule
flocculi
flockbed
flogging
floodlit
floodway
flooring
floppily
flopping
florally
floridly
florigen
flotilla
flounder
flourish
flowered
flowerer
floweret
flubbing
fluellin
fluently
fluepipe
fluidics
fluidify
fluidise
fluidity
flummery
fluoride
fluorine
fluorite
fluttery
flyblown
flypaper
flywheel
foamless
focalise
focusing
focussed
foetidly
fogbound
foldaway
foldboat
folderol
foliaged
folklore
folkmoot
folksong
folktale
follicle
follower
followon
followup
fomenter
fondling
fondness
fontanel
fontange
foodless
foolscap
football
footbath
footfall
footgear
foothill
foothold
footless
footling
footmark
footmuff
footnote
footpace
footpath
footpost
footrace
footrest
footrope
footrule
footslog
footsore
footstep
footwear
footwork
foramina
forborne
forcedly
forcefed
forceful
forcible
forcibly
fordable
fordoing
forebear
forebode
forecast
foredeck
foredoom
foreedge
forefeel
forefelt
forefoot
foregoer
foregone
forehand
forehead
foreknew
foreknow
forelady
foreland
forelock
foremast
foremost
forename
forenoon
forensic
forepart
forepast
forepeak
foreplay
foresaid
foresail
foreseen
foreshow
foreside
foreskin
forestal
forestay
forested
forester
forestry
foretell
foretime
foretold
forewarn
forewent
foreword
foreyard
forgiven
forgoing
forklift
formalin
formally
formerly
formless
formroom
formulae
formulas
formwork
fornices
forrader
forsaken
forsooth
forspeak
forspent
forswear
forswore
forsworn
fortieth
fortress
fortuity
fortyish
forwards
forzando
fosterer
fougasse
foulness
founding
fountain
fourball
foureyes
fourfold
fourleaf
fourpart
foursome
fourstar
fourteen
fourthly
foveolae
fowlpest
foxglove
foxhound
foxiness
foxshark
frabjous
fraction
fracture
fraenula
fragment
fragrant
framesaw
francium
Frankish
franklin
frapping
Fraulein
freakish
freakout
freeborn
freedman
freefall
freehand
freehold
freeload
freeness
freesoil
freewill
freezeup
freezing
fremitus
frenetic
frenulum
frenzied
frequent
frescoes
freshman
freshrun
fretting
fretwork
Freudian
fribbler
friction
friendly
Friesian
frighten
frigidly
frijoles
frillies
fringing
frippery
frisette
friskily
fritting
frocking
frogfish
frogging
frogspit
frondage
frondent
frondeur
frondose
frontage
frontier
frontlet
frostily
frosting
frothily
frottage
froufrou
fructify
fructose
frugally
fruitage
fruitbat
fruitery
fruitfly
fruitful
fruition
frumenty
frumpish
frustule
frutices
fuchsine
fuelling
fugacity
fugitive
fugleman
fullback
fullness
fullpage
fullsize
fulltime
fumarole
fumigant
fumigate
fumitory
function
funebral
funerary
funereal
fungible
funkhole
funnyman
furbelow
furcated
furculae
furcular
furfural
furfuran
furlough
furriery
furthest
furuncle
fuselage
fusiform
fusileer
fusilier
futilely
futility
futurism
futurist
futurity
gabbroic
gabbroid
gableend
gadabout
gadarene
gadgetry
Gadhelic
gadzooks
gainable
gainings
gainless
gainsaid
galactic
galangal
galbanum
galeated
Galenism
galenite
Galilean
galleass
galliard
Gallican
gallipot
galloper
Galloway
galluses
gallwasp
galvanic
gambados
gambeson
gambroon
gamebird
gamecock
gameness
gamesome
gamester
gaminess
gangland
gangling
ganglion
gangrene
gangster
ganister
gantline
gantlope
Ganymede
gaolbird
gapeworm
gapingly
garboard

gardener
gardenia
gardyloo
garefowl
garganey
gargoyle
garishly
garlicky
garotter
garreted
garrison
garrotte
gaselier
gasfired
gashouse
gaslight
gasmeter
gasolene
gasolier
gasoline
gastight
gastraea
gastrula
gasworks
gatefold
gatepost
gatherer
Gaullism
Gaullist
gauntlet
gavelock
gazogene
gazpacho
gearcase
gefuffle
gelastic
gelatine
gelation
gelidity
gematria
geminate
gemstone
gendarme
generate
generous
genetics
Genevese
genially
genitive
geniture
genocide
genotype
gentrice
geodesic
geodetic
geognosy
geologic
geomancy
geometer
geometry
geophagy
geophone
geophyte
geoponic
Georgian
geotaxis
geraniol
geranium
gerbille
Germanic
germcell
germfree
germinal
gerontic
gestagen
gestural
Ghanaian
ghastful
ghettoes

ghoulish
giantess
giantism
giftbook
gigantic
gillaroo
gilthead
gimcrack
gimmicky
gingerly
gingival
gipsydom
gipsyism
girasole
girlhood
giveaway
glabella
glabrous
glaciate
gladdest
gladding
gladhand
gladioli
gladness
gladsome
glancing
glanders
glandule
glassful
glassily
glassine
glaucoma
glaucous
glaziery
gleaning
gleesome
glibness
glissade
glittery
gloaming
globally
globular
globulin
gloomily
gloriole
glorious
glossary
glossily
glossina
glowworm
gloxinia
glucagon
glucinum
glummest
glumness
glutting
gluttony
glycerin
glycerol
glyceryl
glycogen
glyconic
glyptics
gnathite
gneissic
gnomonic
goadster
goalkick
goalline
goalpost
goatfish
goatherd
goatling
goatmoth
goatskin
Gobelins
godawful
godchild
Godspeed

godwards
gogetter
Goidelic
goingson
goitrous
Golconda
golddust
goldenly
goldfish
goldfoil
goldleaf
goldmine
goldrush
golfclub
golliwog
gonfalon
gonidial
gonidium
goodness
goodtime
goodwife
goodwill
goodyear
goofball
goosegog
gorgeous
gorgonia
gormless
gossamer
gossiper
gossipry
gossypol
gourmand
goutweed
goutwort
governor
gownsman
Graafian
grabbing
grabbler
graceful
gracioso
gracious
gradient
graduand
graduate
Graecise
Graecism
graffiti
graffito
graining
gralloch
gramarye
gramatom
gramercy
grandame
granddad
grandeur
grandson
granitic
granular
grapheme
graphics
graphite
grasping
grateful
gratuity
gravamen
gravelly
graviton
grayling
greasily
greedily
greegree
greenery
greenfly
greening
greenish
greenlet

greeting
greffier
greyfish
greyness
gridiron
grievous
grillage
grimacer
grimmest
grimness
grimoire
grindery
grinning
gripping
gripsack
Griselda
griseous
grisette
grisgris
grissini
gritting
grizzled
groggily
grogshop
gromwell
groogroo
grosbeak
groschen
grottoes
grounder
grouping
grouting
growling
grubbily
grubbing
grudging
gruesome
grumbler
grumpily
gruntled
guacharo
guaiacum
guaranty
guardant
guardian
Guelphic
guerilla
guernsey
guidable
guidance
guidedog
guideway
guileful
guiltily
Gujarati
gulfweed
gullable
gullible
gulosity
gummosis
gumption
gunfight
gunflint
gunlayer
gunmetal
gunpoint
gunsmith
gunstock
gusseted
guttural
gymkhana
gymnasia
gynandry
gynocrat
gynoecia
gypseous
gypsydom
gypsyism
gyration

gyratory
gyrostat
habanera
habitant
habitual
habitude
hacienda
hadronic
haematic
haematin
Haggadah
hairgrip
hairless
hairlike
hairline
hairworm
Halachah
halation
haleness
halfback
halfbeak
halfboot
halfbred
halflife
halfmast
halfmoon
halfnote
halfpint
halfsole
halfterm
halftime
halftone
haliotis
halliard
hallmark
hallowed
halluces
halteres
hamartia
hamululi
handball
handbell
handbill
handbook
handcart
handclap
handcuff
handfast
handgrip
handheld
handhold
handicap
handless
handline
handling
handlist
handloom
handmade
handmaid
handmill
handpick
handrail
handsewn
handsome
handwork
handyman
hangable
hangeron
hangnail
hangover
haploidy
harakiri
harangue
harasser
hardback
hardbake
hardcase
hardcore
hardener

hardhack
hardhead
hardline
hardness
hardship
hardtack
hardware
hardwood
harebell
haresear
harikari
harlotry
harmless
harmonic
harpseal
harridan
harrumph
haruspex
hasheesh
hastener
hastings
hatchery
hatching
hatchway
hateable
hatstand
haulyard
haunting
hausfrau
havelock
havildar
havocked
Hawaiian
hawfinch
hawkeyed
hawklike
hawkmoth
hawkweed
hawthorn
hayfield
haymaker
haystack
hazelnut
haziness
headache
headachy
headband
headfast
headgear
headlamp
headland
headless
headline
headlock
headlong
headmost
headnote
headrace
headrest
headroom
headsail
headsman
headwind
headword
headwork
heartily
heatedly
heathery
heathhen
heavenly
hebdomad
hebetate
hebetude
hebraise
Hebraism
Hebraist
hecatomb
hedgehog
hedgehop

hedgepig
hedgerow
hedonics
hedonism
hedonist
heedless
heelball
heelless
Hegelian
hegemony
heighten
heirless
heirloom
heirship
heliacal
helicoid
heliosis
heliport
Helladic
hellbent
Hellenic
hellfire
hellhole
helmeted
helminth
helmsman
helotism
helpless
helpmate
helpmeet
henchman
henequen
henparty
henroost
hepatica
hepatise
heptagon
heraldic
heraldry
herbaria
herbless
Hercules
herdbook
herdsman
herdwick
hereaway
heredity
Hereford
hereunto
hereupon
herewith
heritage
hermetic
hernshaw
heroical
herpetic
Hertzian
hesitant
hesitate
Hesperus
hetaerae
hetairai
hexagram
hexapody
hexylene
hibernal
hibiscus
hiccough
hickwall
hideaway
hidrosis
hidrotic
hidyhole
hielaman
hierarch
hieratic
highball
highborn
highbred

highbrow
higherup
highjack
highland
highlows
highmost
highness
highrise
highroad
hightail
hightest
hijacker
hilarity
hillfort
hillocky
hillside
himation
hinderer
hindlegs
hindmost
hinduise
Hinduism
hipflask
hipsters
hireable
hireling
hirrient
Hispanic
histogen
historic
hitherto
hoarding
hoarsely
hobbitry
hobbyist
hocktide
hocusing
hocussed
Hogmanay
hogsback
hogshead
holdback
holdfast
holdover
holidays
holiness
holistic
hollands
hollowly
Holocene
hologram
holozoic
holstein
homebody
homeborn
homebred
homebrew
homefelt
homeland
homeless
homelike
homemade
homesick
homespun
hometown
homeward
homework
homicide
hominoid
homodont
homogamy
homogeny
homology
homonymy
homuncle
honestly
honeybee
honeydew
honeypot

honorary
honourer
hoodwink
hoofbeat
hookworm
hooligan
hoosegow
hopeless
Horatian
hormonal
hornbeam
hornbill
hornbook
hornfels
hornless
hornpipe
hornrims
horntail
hornworm
hornwort
horologe
horology
horrible
horribly
horridly
horrific
horsebox
horsecar
horsefly
horseman
hosepipe
hospital
hostelry
hotchpot
hotelier
hothouse
hotplate
hotpress
hourlong
houseboy
housedog
housefly
houseful
houseman
housetop
hoverfly
howitzer
huckster
hugeness
huggable
Huguenot
hulahula
humanely
humanise
humanism
humanist
humanity
humanoid
humidify
humidity
humility
hummocky
humorist
humorous
humoured
humpback
humuncle
hungrily
huntress
huntsman
hurtless
hushhush
hustings
hyacinth
hydatoid
hydranth
hydrogen
hydromel
hydropic
hydropsy
hydroski
hydroxyl
hygienic
hymenial
hymenium
hymnbook
hyoscine
hypnoses
hypnosis
hypnotic
hypobole
hypoderm
hypogeal
hypogean
hypogene
hypogeum
hypogyny
hypothec
hysteria
hysteric
ianthine
Ibsenism
iceblink
icebound
icecream
icefield
iceplant
iceskate
icewater
iceyacht
ichorous
idealess
idealise
idealism
idealist
ideality
ideation
identify
identity
ideogram
ideology
idiolect
idiotism
idleness
idocrase
idolater
idolatry
idoliser
idyllist
ignition
ignitron
ignominy
ignorant
illation
illative
illfated
illiquid
illtimed
illtreat
illumine
illusage
illusion
illusive
illusory
Illyrian
ilmenite
imaginal
imagines
imbecile
imitable
imitator
immanent
immature
immersed
imminent
immingle
immobile
immodest
immolate
immortal
immunise
immunity
impacted
impanate
imparity
impelled
impeller
imperial
imperium
impetigo
impishly
impledge
implicit
impolder
impolicy
impolite
imponent
importer
imposing
imposter
impostor
impotent
imprimis
imprison
improper
improver
impudent
impugner
impunity
impurely
impurity
inaction
inactive
inasmuch
inceptor
inchmeal
inchoate
inchworm
incident
incision
incisive
incitant
incivism
included
incoming
increase
increate
incubate
incurred
indagate
indebted
indecent
Indiaman
indicant
indicate
indicium
indigene
indigent
indirect
indocile
indolent
inductee
inductor
indulger
induline
indurate
indusium
industry
inedible
inedited
inequity
inerrant
inertial
inexpert
infamise
infamous
infantry
infector
inferior
infernal
inferred
infilter
infinite
infinity
infirmly
inflamer
inflated
inflator
inflatus
inflexed
inflight
influent
informal
informed
informer
infrared
infringe
infusion
ingather
ingrowth
inguinal
inhalant
inherent
inhesion
inhumane
inimical
iniquity
initiate
injector
inkiness
inkstand
inlander
innately
innocent
innovate
innuendo
inoculum
inositol
inquirer
insanely
insanity
inscient
inscribe
inscroll
insecure
inserted
insignia
insolate
insolent
insomnia
insomuch
insphere
inspired
inspirer
inspirit
instable
instance
instancy
instinct
instruct
insulant
insulate
insulter
insurant
intaglio
intarsia
integral
intended
intently
interact
interbed
intercom
intercut
interest
interior
intermit
intermix
internal
internee
Interpol
interred
interrex
intersex
intertie
interval
interwar
inthrall
intimacy
intimate
intimism
intitule
intonate
intrados
intrench
intrepid
intrigue
intromit
introrse
intruder
intubate
inundate
inurbane
invasion
invasive
invected
inveigle
inventor
inverted
inverter
investor
inviable
inviting
invocate
involute
inwardly
iodinate
iodoform
iotacism
irenical
irenicon
Irishism
Irishman
ironbark
ironclad
irongray
irongrey
ironical
ironside
ironware
ironwood
ironwork
Iroquois
irrigate
irritant
irritate
isabella
isagogic
ischemia
ischemic
Islamise
Islamism
Islamite
islander
isobaric
isocheim
isocracy
isodicon
isogamic
isogloss
isogonal
isogonic
isolable
isolator
isomeric
isometry
isomorph
isophote
isopleth
isoprene
isoptera
isospory
isostasy
isothere
isotherm
isotonic
isotopic
isotropy
issuable
issuance
isthmian
Italiote
iterance
ivorynut
jabberer
jackaroo
jackboot
jackeroo
jackstay
Jacobean
Jacobite
jacquard
jaggedly
jailbird
jalousie
jamboree
janizary
Japanese
japanned
japhetic
japonica
jaundice
jauntily
Javanese
jealousy
Jehovist
jejunely
jeopardy
jeremiad
Jeremiah
jeroboam
jerrican
jerrycan
jesuitic
jesuitry
jetblack
jetplane
jettison
jewelled
jeweller
jiggered
jingoish
jingoism
jingoist
jipijapa
jiujitsu
jobation
jocosely
jocosity
jocundly
jodhpurs
joinable
jointure
jokingly
jolthead
Jonathan
jongleur
jovially
joyfully
joyously
joystick
jubilant
jubilate
Judaical
Judaiser
judgment
judicial
jugglery
Jugoslav
jugulate
julienne
jumpedup
jumpseat
jumpsuit
junction
juncture
junkshop
junkyard
Jurassic
juristic
justness
juvenile
Kaffiyeh
kailyard
kakemono
kalaazar
kamikaze
Kanarese
kangaroo
Kashmiri
katakana
kedgeree
keelhaul
keelless
keenness
keepsake
keeshond
kefuffle
keratose
kerchief
kerosene
kerosine
keyboard
keystone
khedival
Khmerian
khuskhus
kibitzer
kickback
kickshaw
kidglove
killdeer
kilogram
kilowatt
kindless
kindling
kindness
kinesics
kinetics
kingbird
kingbolt
kingcrab
kingfish
kinghood
kinglike
kingship
kingsize
kinkajou
kinsfolk
kissable
kisscurl
klephtic
klondike
klystron
knackery
knapping
knapsack
knapweed
kneedeep
kneehigh
kneehole
kneejerk
knickers
knightly
knitting
knitwear
knocking
knockout
knothole
knotting
knotwork
knowable
Kohinoor
kohlrabi
kolinsky
komitaji
Komsomol
korfball
kourbash
kreutzer
kromesky
krumhorn
kurtosis
kyphosis
kyphotic
labdanum
labelled
labellum
labially
lability
labourer
labrador
laburnum
lacerate
lacewing
lacework
lackaday
laconian
laconism
lacrimal
lacrosse
lacrymal
lacunary
lacunate
lacunose
ladybird
ladyfern
ladyhood
ladylike
ladylove
ladyship
laically
lakeland
lallygag
lamasery
lambaste
lambency
lamblike
lambskin
lamellae
lamellar
lameness
lamented
laminate
lamppost
lancelet
landarmy
landcrab
landfall
landform
landgirl
landlady
landless
landline
landlord
landmark
landmass
landmine
landrail
landslip
landsman
langlauf
Langshan

language
languish
lankness
lanneret
lanthorn
lapboard
lapelled
lapicide
lapidary
lapidate
lapidify
larboard
larcener
largesse
larkspur
larrikin
larynges
larynxes
lashings
latchkey
lateness
latently
laterite
Latinate
latinise
Latinism
Latinist
latinity
latitant
latitude
latterly
latticed
laudable
laudably
laudanum
laudator
laughing
laughter
launcher
laureate
lavalava
lavation
lavatory
lavender
laverock
lavishly
lawcourt
lawfully
lawgiver
lawmaker
lawyerly
laxative
layabout
layshaft
laystall
laywoman
Lazarist
laziness
lazulite
lazurite
leadenly
leadless
leadsman
leadwork
leafless
leaflike
leanness
leapfrog
learning
leathern
leathery
leavings
lecithin
lecturer
leeboard
lefthand
leftover
leftward
legalese
legalise
legalism
legalist
legality
legatine
legation
legbreak
legendry
legerity
leggings
legguard
legioned
leisured
lemonade
lemurine
lemuroid
lengthen
lenience
leniency
Leninism
Leninist
Leninite
lenitive
lensless
lenticel
lenticle
lepidote
leporine
lethally
lethargy
lettered
leucitic
levanter
levelled
leveller
leverage
leviable
levigate
levirate
levitate
levulose
lewdness
lewisite
libation
libatory
libeccio
libelled
libellee
libeller
liberate
libretti
libretto
licensed
licensee
licenser
lichened
lichenin
lichgate
licorice
liegeman
lifebelt
lifeboat
lifebuoy
lifeless
lifelike
lifeline
lifelong
lifesize
lifetime
lifework
liftable
ligament
ligation
ligature
lighting
lightish
ligneous
lignitic
ligulate
likeable
likeness
likewise
limbless
limekiln
limerick
limetwig
limewash
limitary
limonite
limpidly
limpness
linchpin
lineally
linearly
linesman
lingerer
lingerie
linguist
liniment
Linnaean
linoleum
linstock
lintseed
lipogram
lipomata
lipsalve
lipstick
liquidly
liripoop
listener
listless
literacy
literary
literate
literati
litharge
litigant
litigate
littlego
littling
littoral
liturgic
liveable
liveborn
livelily
livelong
liveried
liverish
livewire
lividity
lixivium
loadline
loadstar
loanable
loanword
loathful
loathing
lobation
lobbyist
lobeline
loblolly
lobotomy
lobulate
localise
localism
locality
locative
lockable
lockfast
lockknit
lockstep
locofoco
locomote
loculate
locution
locutory
lodestar
lodgings
lodgment
lodicule
logician
logistic
logogram
logotype
loiterer
Lollardy
lollipop
lollypop
lomentum
Londoner
loneness
lonesome
longboat
longeron
longeval
longhair
longhand
longhorn
longness
longship
longsome
longstop
longterm
longtime
longueur
longwall
longwave
longways
longwise
lookeron
loonybin
loophole
loosebox
loosener
lopeared
lopgrass
lopsided
lordless
lordling
lordosis
lordotic
lordship
loricate
lorikeet
lothario
loudness
louvered
lovebird
loveknot
loveless
lovelily
lovelock
lovelorn
lovenest
loveseat
lovesick
lovesome
lovesong
lovingly
lowering
lowgrade
lowlevel
lowlying
loyalist
lubberly
lubrical
lucidity
luckless
luculent
Lucullan
lukewarm
lumberer
luminant
luminary
luminist
luminous
lumpfish
lunarian
lunation
luncheon
lungfish
lungwort
lunulate
luscious
lushness
lustrate
lustrine
lustring
lustrous
lutanist
lutecium
lutenist
lutetium
Lutheran
luxation
lychgate
lykewake
lymphoid
lymphoma
lynchpin
lynxeyed
lyophile
lyrebird
lyricism
lyricist
lysosome
lysozyme
macaroni
macaroon
macerate
machismo
mackerel
mackinaw
maculate
madapple
madhouse
madrigal
madwoman
Maecenas
maenadic
maestoso
magazine
magdalen
magician
magicked
magister
magmatic
magnesia
magnetic
magneton
magnific
magnolia
maharaja
maharani
mahjongg
mahogany
Mahratta
Mahratti
maidenly
maidhood
maieutic
mailable
mailboat
mailcart
mainland
mainline
mainmast
mainsail
mainstay
maintain
mainyard
maiolica
majestic
majolica
majority
makebate
makefast
makimono
Malagasy
malamute
malapert
malaprop
malarial
malarian
malarkey
maledict
malefern
malemute
maleness
maligner
malignly
malinger
malodour
maltreat
maltster
malvasia
Mameluke
mamillae
mamillar
mancando
manciple
Mandaean
mandamus
mandarin
mandator
mandible
Mandingo
mandolin
mandorla
mandrake
mandrill
maneater
manfully
mangabey
manganic
mangonel
mangrove
maniacal
Manichee
manicure
manifest
manifold
maniform
mannered
mannerly
mannikin
mannitol
manorial
manpower
mansized
mantelet
mantilla
mantissa
mantling
manually
manubria
manurial
maquette
marabout
marasmic
marasmus
marathon
marauder
maravedi
marbling
marchesa
marchese
marginal
margrave
marigold
marinade
marinate
maritage
maritime
marjoram
markdown
markedly
marketer
marksman
marmoset
marocain
maroquin
marquess
marquise
marriage
marrieds
marrying
marshman
martagon
martello
martenot
martinet
marzipan
mascaron
Masorete
Masoreth
massacre
masseter
masseuse
massicot
massless
masterly
masthead
mastitis
mastodon
matamata
matchbox
matelote
material
materiel
maternal
matgrass
matiness
matrices
matrixes
matronal
matronly
mattress
maturate
maturely
maturity
maverick
maxillae
maximise
mayapple
mayoress
Mayqueen
mazarine
Mazdaism
mazement
maziness
meagrely
mealtime
mealworm
mealybug
meanness
meantime
measured
meatball
meatsafe
mechanic
meconium
medalled
medallic
medially
mediator
medicate
medicine
medieval
mediocre
meditate
medusoid
meekness
meetness
megalith
megapode
megawatt
melamine
melanism
melanite
melinite
mellowly
melodeon
melodise
melodist
membered
membrane
mementos
memorial
memorise
memsahib
menarche
mendable
menhaden
menially
meninges
meniscus
menology
menstrua
mensural
menswear
mentally
mephitic
mephitis
merchant
merciful
mercuric
mergence
meridian
meringue
meristem
meristic
merosome
mescalin
Mesdames
meshwork
mesially
mesmeric
mesocarp
mesoderm
mesotron
Mesozoic
mesquite
messmate
messuage
metalled
metallic
metamere
metaphor
metayage
metazoan
metazoon
meteoric
methanol
methinks
methodic
methylic
methysis
metonymy
metrical
mezereon
miasmata
miasmous
micellar
microbar
microbic
microdot
micrurgy
midbrain
middling
midfield
midlands
midnight

midpoint
midships
midwives
mightest
mightily
migraine
migrator
mildness
milepost
Milesian
militant
military
militate
milkmaid
milkweed
milkwort
millhand
milliard
milliary
millibar
millieme
milliner
millpond
millrace
Miltonic
mimester
mimicked
mimicker
minacity
minatory
mindless
minimise
minister
ministry
Minoress
Minorite
minority
Minotaur
minstrel
mintmark
minutely
minutiae
mirepoix
mirthful
misalign
misapply
misbegot
miscarry
miscegen
mischief
miscible
miscount
misdealt
misdoing
misdoubt
miserere
misgiven
misguide
misheard
mishmash
Mishnaic
misjudge
mismatch
misnomer
misogamy
misogyny
misology
misplace
misprint
misprise
misprize
misquote
misshape
missilry
misspell
misspelt
misspend
misspent
misstate
mistaken
misthink
mistreat
mistress
mistrial
mistrust
misusage
miswrite
Mithraic
mitigant
mitigate
mittened
mittimus
mitzvoth
mnemonic
mobilise
mobility
mobocrat
moccasin
modalism
modalist
modality
modelled
modeller
moderate
moderato
modernly
modestly
modifier
modishly
modulate
Moharram
moisture
molality
molarity
molasses
molecule
molehill
moleskin
molester
Molinism
Molinist
molossus
molybdic
momently
momentum
monachal
monadism
monandry
monarchy
monastic
monaural
monaxial
monazite
mondaine
monetary
monetise
moneybag
moneybox
Mongolic
mongoose
monicker
monistic
monition
monitive
monitory
monkfish
MonKhmer
monkhood
monkseal
monkship
monoacid
monocrat
monocyte
monodist
monogamy
monogeny
monoglot
monogony
monogram
monogyny
monolith
monomial
monopode
monopoly
monorail
monotint
monotone
monotony
monotype
monoxide
monsieur
monteith
monument
moonbeam
mooncalf
moonface
moonfish
moonless
moonrise
moonsail
moonshee
moonshot
moonwort
moorcock
moorfowl
moorings
moorland
mopishly
moquette
morainic
moralise
moralism
moralist
morality
moratory
Moravian
morbidly
morbific
mordancy
moreover
moresque
moribund
mornings
morosely
morosity
morpheme
morphine
mortally
mortgage
mortmain
mortuary
moshavim
mosquito
mossback
mothball
motherly
motility
motional
motivate
motivity
motorail
motorcar
motorial
motoring
motorise
motorist
motorium
motorman
motormen
motorway
mottling
moufflon
moulding
mountain
mounting
mournful
mourning
mouseear
moussaka
mouthful
moveable
moveless
movement
movingly
mowburnt
muchness
mucilage
muckluck
muckrake
muckworm
mucosity
mucrones
mudguard
mudstone
Muharram
mulberry
muleteer
mulishly
mulloway
multeity
multifid
multiped
multiple
multiply
muniment
munition
murderer
muriatic
murmurer
murrelet
murrhine
muscadel
muscatel
muscling
muscular
mushroom
musicale
musician
musingly
muskdeer
muskduck
musketry
muskrose
musktree
muslined
musquash
mustache
mutation
mutchkin
muteness
muticous
mutilate
mutineer
mutinous
mutterer
mutually
mycelial
mycelium
mycetoma
mycology
myelinic
myelitis
mylonite
myoblast
myogenic
myograph
myositic
myositis
myosotis
myriapod
myriopod
myrmidon
mystical
mystique
mythical
myxomata
nacreous
nailfile
nainsook
nameable
namedrop
nameless
namepart
namesake
nametape
nanogram
naphthol
napiform
napoleon
narceine
narcissi
narcoses
narcosis
narcotic
narghile
narrator
narrowly
nasalise
nasality
nascence
nascency
natality
natation
natatory
nathless
national
natively
nativism
nativist
nativity
naturism
naturist
naumachy
nauplius
nauseant
nauseate
nauseous
nautical
nautilus
navigate
Nazarene
Nazarite
Nazirite
neaptide
Nearctic
nearness
neatherd
neatness
nebulise
nebulium
nebulous
neckband
necklace
neckline
necropsy
necrosis
necrotic
nectared
needfire
needless
needment
negation
negative
negatory
negatron
negligee
Negrillo
negroism
nematode
nematoid
nenuphar
NeoLatin
neomycin
neonatal
neophyte
neoplasm
neoprene
neotenic
neoteric
Nepalese
nepenthe
nephrite
nepotism
nescient
nestling
neurally
neuritic
neuritis
neuronal
neuronic
neuroses
neurosis
neurotic
neutrino
newblown
newcomer
newfound
newlywed
newscast
newsheet
newspeak
newsreel
newsroom
nextdoor
niceness
nickelic
nicknack
nickname
nicotian
nicotine
nielloed
niggling
nightcap
nighthag
nightjar
nightowl
nihilism
nihilist
nihility
nimbused
ninefold
ninepins
nineteen
nineties
nitrogen
Noachian
nobelium
nobility
nobleman
noblesse
nocturne
nodalise
nodality
nodation
nodosity
nodulose
nodulous
noisette
nomadise
nomadism
nominate
nomistic
nomogram
nomology
nonclaim
nondairy
nonesuch
nonevent
nonhuman
nonjuror
nonlegal
nonmetal
nonmoral
nonparty
nonrigid
nonsense
nonstick
nonunion
nonusage
nonwhite
noontide
noontime
normalcy
normally
Norseman
northern
northing
Northman
noseband
nosecone
nosedive
nosepipe
nosering
nosiness
nosology
notarial
notation
notching
notebook
notecase
noteless
notional
notornis
noumenal
noumenon
nouvelle
novation
novelise
novelist
November
novercal
nowadays
nubiform
nubility
nubilous
nucellus
nuclease
nucleate
nucleole
nucleoli
nuclidic
nudeness
nugatory
nuisance
nullness
numberer
numbfish
numbness
numeracy
numerary
numerate
numerous
numinous
numskull
nuptials
nursling
nurturer
nutarian
nutation
nutbrown
nuthatch
nuthouse
nutrient
nutshell
nymphean
oafishly
oakapple
oakegger
oatgrass
obduracy
obdurate
obedient
obeisant
obituary
objector
oblation
oblatory
obligate
obliging
oblivion
observer
obsidian
obsolete
obstacle
obstruct
obtainer
obtected
obturate
obtusely
obtusity
occasion
occident
occluded
occlusal
occultly
occupant
occupier
occurred
ocellate
ochreous
octarchy
octaroon
octonary
octoroon
ocularly
oddments
odiously
odograph
odometer
odontoid
Odyssean
oecology
oeillade
oenology
oenophil
oestrone
oestrous
offbreak
offdrive
offender
offering
official
offprint
offshoot
offshore
offsider
offstage
ofttimes
ohmmeter
oilcloth
oilfield
oilfired
oiliness
oilstone
ointment
oiticica
okeydoke
oldtimer
oldworld
oleander
oleaster
olibanum
oligarch
oligomer
oliphant
olympiad
Olympian
omadhaum
omelette
omission
omitting
ommateum

omnivore
omophagy
omoplate
omphalic
omphalos
onceover
oncidium
oncology
oncoming
onehorse
onepiece
onesided
onetrack
onlooker
ontogeny
ontology
onychite
oogamous
oogonial
oogonium
oologist
ooziness
opaquely
openable
opencast
openeyed
openness
openplan
openwork
operable
operatic
operator
opercula
operetta
ophidian
oppilate
opponent
opposite
oppugner
opsimath
optative
optician
optimise
optimism
optimist
optional
opulence
opuscula
opuscule
oracular
orangery
Orangism
oratorio
oratress
Orcadian
orchilla
ordainer
ordinand
ordinary
ordinate
ordnance
oreology
organdie
organise
organism
organist
orgasmic
orgastic
orgulous
oriental
oriented
origanum
original
ornament
ornately
ornithic
orogenic
orpiment
orthicon

orthodox
orthoepy
oscinine
osculant
osculate
Ossianic
osteitis
ostinato
ostracod
ostracon
ostrakon
otiosely
otiosity
otoscope
ottavino
outboard
outbound
outbrave
outbreak
outburst
outcaste
outclass
outdated
outdoors
outdrawn
outfield
outflank
outgoing
outgrown
outguess
outHerod
outhouse
outlawry
outlying
outmatch
outmoded
outpoint
outrange
outreach
outreign
outrider
outright
outrival
outshine
outshone
outsider
outsight
outsmart
outspend
outspent
outstare
outstrip
outvalue
outvying
outwards
outwatch
outweigh
outworks
ovalness
ovariole
ovaritis
ovenbird
ovenware
overalls
overarch
overbear
overbook
overbore
overbusy
overcall
overcame
overcast
overcoat
overcome
overcrop
overdone
overdose
overdraw
overdrew

overfall
overfeed
overfill
overfish
overflew
overflow
overfold
overfond
overgrew
overgrow
overhand
overhang
overhaul
overhead
overhear
overheat
overhung
overjump
overkill
overlaid
overlain
overland
overleaf
overleap
overload
overlong
overlook
overlord
overmuch
overnice
overpaid
overpass
overpast
overplay
overplus
overrate
override
overripe
overrode
overrule
oversail
overseas
overseen
overseer
oversell
oversewn
overshoe
overshot
overside
oversize
overslip
oversold
oversoul
overstay
overstep
overtake
overtask
overtime
overtone
overtook
overture
overturn
overview
overwear
overwind
overwork
overworn
oviposit
owlishly
oxidiser
oximeter
oxpecker
oxtongue
oxymoron
oxytocin
ozoniser
pachalic
pacifier
pacifism

pacifist
padishah
paduasoy
paganise
paganish
paganism
paginate
pagurian
painless
paintbox
palatial
palatine
paleface
paleness
palestra
palinode
palisade
palliate
pallidly
pallmall
palmette
palmetto
palmiped
palmitin
palomino
palpable
palpably
palterer
paludism
pamperer
pamphlet
pancreas
pandanus
pandemic
pandowdy
panelled
pangolin
panicked
panmixia
pannikin
panorama
panpipes
pansophy
pantheon
pantofle
pantsuit
papalise
papalism
papalist
paperboy
papillae
papillar
papillon
papistic
papistry
pappadom
papulose
papulous
parabola
paradigm
paradise
paraffin
paragoge
parakeet
parallax
parallel
paralyse
paramour
paranoia
paranoid
paraquat
parasang
parasite
paravane
parcener
parclose
pardoner
parental
parergon

pargeter
parhelia
parhelic
parietal
parkland
parlance
parlando
Parmesan
parodist
paroquet
paroxysm
parrotry
Parsiism
parsonic
partaken
parterre
Parthian
partible
particle
partisan
partizan
partsong
parttime
pashalic
pashalik
passable
passably
passbook
passerby
passible
Passover
passport
password
pastiche
pastille
pastoral
pastrami
pastries
pastural
patagium
patchily
patellae
patellar
patentee
patently
patentor
paternal
pathetic
pathless
pathogen
patience
patronal
pattypan
patulous
pavement
pavilion
pawnshop
payphone
paysheet
peaceful
peacocky
peagreen
peardrop
pearlies
pearling
pearlite
pearmain
peasecod
peccable
peccancy
pectines
pectoral
peculate
peculiar
pedagogy
pedalier
pedalled
pedantic
pedantry

pederast
pedestal
pedicled
pedicure
pedigree
pediment
pedipalp
pedology
peduncle
peekaboo
peelings
peephole
peepshow
peerless
Pegasean
pegboard
peignoir
Pekinese
Pelagian
Pelasgic
pelerine
pellagra
pellicle
pellmell
pellucid
pelorism
pembroke
pemmican
penalise
penchant
pendency
pendicle
pendular
pendulum
penitent
penknife
penology
penstock
pentacle
pentagon
pentroof
penumbra
peperino
perceive
perfecto
perforce
perfumer
perianth
pericarp
pericope
periderm
peridium
peridote
perigean
perigyny
perilled
perilous
perilune
perineal
perineum
periodic
periotic
peripety
periplus
perisher
perjurer
perlitic
permeate
peroneal
perorate
peroxide
personae
personal
perspire
persuade
pertness
Peruvian
perverse
pervious

petaline
petalled
petalody
petaloid
petalous
petechia
petiolar
petioled
petition
petrolic
petronel
petrosal
pettifog
petulant
petuntse
phalange
phantasm
phantasy
pharisee
pharmacy
phaseout
pheasant
phenolic
phenylic
Philomel
phlegmon
phonemic
phonetic
phormium
phosgene
phosphor
photogen
photopia
photopic
photopsy
phrasing
phreatic
Phrygian
phthalic
phthisic
phthisis
phyletic
phyllary
phyllode
phylloid
phyllome
physical
physicky
physique
piacular
pianiste
piassava
picaroon
picayune
pickerel
picketer
pickings
picklock
picnicky
pictures
piddling
piecrust
piedmont
piercing
piffling
pigswill
pilaster
pilchard
pileated
pilewort
pilferer
piliform
pillager
pillwort
pilosity
pilotage
pilsener
pimiento
pinafore

pinaster
pincenez
pinchers
Pindaric
pinecone
pinewood
pinkness
pinmoney
pinnacle
pinnated
pinniped
pinnular
pinochle
pinpoint
pinprick
pintable
pintsize
pinwheel
pipeclay
pipefish
pipeline
piperack
piperine
piquancy
pirarucu
piscator
piscinae
pishogue
pisiform
pisolite
pitiable
pitiably
pitiless
pittance
pitviper
pivotman
pixieish
pixiness
pizzeria
placable
placably
placeman
placenta
placidly
plagiary
plaguily
plaiding
plaister
planchet
plangent
planking
plankton
planning
plantain
planulae
planular
plastery
plastics
plastron
plateaux
plateful
platelet
platform
platinic
platinum
platonic
platting
platypus
plaudits
playable
playback
playbill
playbook
playgirl
playgoer
playmate
playroom
playsuit
playtime

pleading
pleasant
pleasing
pleasure
plebeian
plectrum
pleinair
pleonasm
plethora
pleurisy
pliantly
plighted
plimsoll
Pliocene
plodding
plopping
plotting
plougher
pluckily
plugging
plumaged
plumbago
plumbate
plumbing
plumbism
plumelet
plumiped
plumpish
plumular
plurally
plussage
plutonic
pluvious
pochette
pockmark
podagral
podagric
podiatry
poetical
poignant
pointing
poisoner
polarise
polarity
polemics
polemise
polemist
polestar
polisher
politely
politick
politico
politics
pollices
pollinia
pollinic
polliwog
pollster
polluter
pollywog
polonium
poltfoot
poltroon
polygala
polygamy
polygene
polygeny
polyglot
polygyny
polymath
polypary
polypide
polypite
polypody
polypoid
polypous
polyseme
polysemy
polysomy
polyzoan
polyzoic
polyzoon
pomander
pomology
ponderer
pondweed
pontifex
ponytail
poohpooh
poorness
popinjay
popishly
poppadum
populace
populate
populism
populist
populous
poristic
porkling
porosity
porphyry
porpoise
porridge
portable
portfire
porthole
porticos
portiere
portrait
portress
position
positive
positron
posology
possible
possibly
postcard
postcode
postdate
postfree
posthorn
postiche
postlude
postmark
postmill
postobit
postpaid
postpone
postural
posturer
potassic
potation
potbelly
potbound
potently
potholer
pothouse
potlatch
potplant
potroast
potsherd
potstill
potstone
potterer
poultice
poundage
pounding
pourable
powdered
powerful
practice
practise
praecipe
praedial
prandial
prankful
prankish
pratique
prattler
preacher
preamble
precinct
precious
preclude
predator
predella
preelect
preexist
pregnant
prehuman
prejudge
prelatic
prelease
premiere
premolar
premorse
prenatal
prentice
preparer
prepense
preprint
presager
prescind
presence
preserve
presidio
pressbox
pressing
pressman
pressure
prestige
presumer
pretence
prettify
prettily
previous
priapism
prideful
priedieu
priestly
priggery
priggish
priggism
primally
Primates
primeval
primming
primness
primrose
princely
princess
printing
printout
priorate
prioress
priority
prismoid
prisoner
prissily
pristine
probable
probably
proceeds
proclaim
procurer
prodding
prodigal
prodrome
producer
proemial
profaner
profiler
profound
progress
prohibit
prolamin
prolapse
prolific
prolixly
prologue
prolonge
promisee
promiser
promisor
promoter
prompter
promptly
promulge
pronator
proofing
propense
properly
property
prophase
prophecy
prophesy
propolis
proposal
proposer
propound
propping
propylic
prorogue
prosaism
prosaist
prosodic
prospect
prostate
prostyle
protasis
protatic
protease
protegee
protista
protocol
protonic
protozoa
protract
protrude
provable
provably
provided
provider
province
provisor
proximal
prudence
pruinose
prunella
prunelle
prunello
prurient
pruritic
pruritus
Prussian
pryingly
psalmist
psalmody
psaltery
psilosis
psychics
psychism
psychist
pteropod
pterylae
ptomaine
ptyalism
pubertal
publican
publicly
puffball
puffbird
puggaree
pugilism
pugilist
pugnosed
puissant
pullback
pullover
pulmonic
pulpiter
pulpwood
pulsator
pulvilli
pulvinus
pumproom
puncheon
punctate
punctual
puncture
punditry
pungency
puniness
punisher
punition
punitive
punitory
puparial
puparium
pupation
pupilage
pupilary
pupillar
puppetry
puppydog
puppydom
puppyfat
puppyish
purblind
purchase
purebred
pureness
purfling
purifier
puristic
purplish
purpuric
purpurin
pursenet
purslane
pursuant
purulent
purveyor
pushball
pushbike
pushcart
pushover
pushpull
pussycat
pustular
putative
putridly
pyelitis
pygidial
pygidium
pygmaean
pyogenic
pyrenoid
pyrexial
pyridine
pyriform
pyroxene
pyrrhoea
pyrrhous
pythonic
pyxidium
quackery
quackish
quadrant
quadrate
quadriga
quadroon
quaestor
quagmire
quaintly
Quakerly
qualmish
quandary
quandong
quantify
quantise
quantity
quarrier
quartern
quarters
quartile
quatrain
quayside
queasily
Quechuan
queendom
queening
queenlet
queerish
quencher
quenelle
question
queueing
quibbler
quickset
quiddity
quidnunc
quietism
quietist
quietude
quillpen
quilting
quincunx
quintain
quipping
quirkily
quisling
quitrent
quitting
quixotic
quixotry
quizzing
quotable
quotient
rabbinic
rabbiter
rabbitry
rabidity
racecard
racegoer
racemate
racemise
racemose
rachides
rachitic
rachitis
racially
raciness
rackrent
radially
radiance
radiancy
radiator
radicant
radicate
raftsman
raggedly
railhead
raillery
railroad
rainbird
raincoat
raindrop
rainfall
rainwash
rainwear
rakehell
rakishly
rallying
rallyist
rambling
rambutan
ramentum
ramequin
rampancy
ranarian
ranarium
ranchero
ranchman
randomly
rankness
ransomer
rapacity
rapecake
rapeseed
rapidity
rapparee
raptness
raptures
rarefied
rareness
rascally
rashness
rasorial
rataplan
rateable
ratguard
ratifier
rational
ratsbane
ratstail
rattling
ravelled
ravenous
ravisher
rawboned
reabsorb
reactant
reaction
reactive
readable
readably
readjust
reaffirm
reagency
realness
realtime
reappear
rearlamp
rearmice
rearmost
rearview
rearward
reascend
reasoner
reassert
reassess
reassign
reassure
reawaken
rebelled
rebeller
rebellow
rebuttal
rebutted
rebutter
recapped
receiver
recently
receptor
recharge
recision
reckless
reckoner
recommit
reconvey
recorder
recourse
recovery
recreant
recreate
rectoral
recurred
recusant
redactor
redblind
redbrick
redeemer
redefine
redeless
redeploy
redesign
redfaced
redirect
redistil
redolent
redouble
redshank
redshift
redshirt
redstart
redwater
reedbird
reedling
reedmace
reedpipe
reedstop
reedwren
reefknot
reembark
reemerge
reemploy
reexport
referent
referral
referred
refinery
refitted
reflexed
refluent
reforest
reformed
reformer
regalism
regality
regelate
regicide
regiment
regional
register
registry
regolith
regrater
regrowth
regulate
rehandle
rehearse
rehoboam
reignite
reimpose
reindeer
reinless
reinsert
reinsman
reinsure
reinvest
rejecter
rejigger
rejoicer
rekindle
relation
relative
relaxant
releasee
releaser
releasor

relegate
relevant
reliable
reliably
reliance
reliever
religion
relocate
relucent
relumine
remanent
remedial
remember
reminder
remissly
remittal
remitted
remittee
remitter
remotely
renderer
renegade
renegado
reneguer
reniform
renitent
renounce
renovate
renowned
rentable
renumber
reoccupy
reorient
repairer
repartee
repealer
repeater
repelled
repeller
repenter
repeople
repetend
replacer
replevin
reporter
repotted
repousse
reprieve
reprisal
reproach
reproval
republic
requital
requiter
rerearch
rerecord
reremice
rereward
rescript
research
resemble
reserved
resetter
resettle
resident
residual
residuum
resigned
resinate
resinify
resinoid
resinous
resister
resistor
resolute
resonant
resonate
resorcin
resorter

resource
respects
response
respring
resprung
restcure
restless
restorer
restrain
restrict
resupine
resurvey
retailer
retainer
retarded
retarder
retiarii
reticent
reticule
retiform
retinula
retiring
retorted
retrench
retrieve
retroact
retrorse
reusable
revanche
revealer
reveille
revelled
reveller
revenant
revenger
reverend
reverent
reversal
reverser
reverter
revetted
reviewal
reviewer
reviling
revision
revisory
revivify
revolter
revolute
revolver
rewaking
rewarder
Rhaetian
rhapsode
rhapsody
rheology
rheostat
rhetoric
rhinitis
Rhinodon
rhizopod
rhomboid
rhonchal
rhonchus
rhyolite
rhythmic
ribaldry
ribbonry
ribgrass
ribosome
ricebird
ricercar
richness
rickrack
rickshaw
ricochet
riddance
rideable
ridgeway

ridicule
Riesling
rifeness
riffraff
rifleman
rigadoon
rightful
rightist
rigidify
rigidity
rigorism
rigorist
rigorous
rimbrake
rimester
ringbark
ringbolt
ringbone
ringdove
ringmain
ringneck
ringroad
ringside
ringtail
ringwall
ringworm
rinsings
riparian
ripeness
ritually
rivalled
rivelled
riverain
riverbed
riverine
riverman
riverway
roadbook
roadless
roadside
roadsign
roadster
roasting
roborant
robustly
rocaille
rockbird
rockcake
rockcork
rockdove
rocketry
rockfall
rockfish
rockhewn
rocklike
rockling
rockrose
rocksalt
rockweed
rockwood
rockwork
roentgen
rogation
rogatory
rollcall
rollneck
rolypoly
romancer
Romanian
romanise
Romanism
Romanist
Romansch
romantic
rondeaux
roodbeam
roodloft
roofless
roofrack

rooftree
roommate
roothold
rootless
ropeable
ropewalk
ropeyarn
ropiness
rosarian
rosebowl
rosebush
rosefish
roseleaf
rosemary
roseolar
rosepink
roseroot
rosetree
rosewood
rosiness
rostrate
rosulate
Rotarian
rotation
rotative
rotatory
rotenone
rottenly
rotundly
roturier
roughage
roughdry
roughhew
roughish
rouleaus
rouleaux
roulette
roundarm
rounders
roundish
roundtop
rowdyish
rowdyism
royalism
royalist
rubbishy
rubicund
rubidium
rubrical
rubytail
rucksack
rudeness
rudiment
ruefully
ruggedly
rugosely
rugosity
rugulose
ruinable
ruleless
Rumanian
Rumansch
ruminant
ruminate
rummager
runabout
runagate
runcible
runnerup
ruralise
ruralism
ruralist
rurality
rushhour
rushlike
rustical
rustless
rutabaga
ruthless

rutilant
ryegrass
ryotwari
sabbatic
sabotage
saboteur
saccadic
saccular
sacculus
sackcoat
sackless
sackrace
sacraria
sacredly
sacristy
saddlery
Sadducee
sadistic
safeness
saffrony
safranin
sagacity
sagamore
sageness
saginate
sagittal
sailable
sailboat
sailfish
sailless
sailorly
sailyard
sainfoin
saintdom
salacity
salariat
salaried
saleable
saleroom
Salesian
salesman
salience
saliency
salinity
salivary
salivate
Salopian
saltbush
saltless
saltlick
saltmine
saltness
saltwort
salutary
salvable
salvific
samarium
sameness
samizdat
Samoyede
samphire
sampling
sanative
sanatory
sanctify
sanction
sanctity
sandarac
sandbank
sandbath
sandflea
sandshoe
sandwich
sandworm
sandwort
sandyish
saneness
sangaree
Sangrail

Sangreal
sanguine
sanitary
sanitate
sanitise
sannyasi
sanserif
Sanskrit
santonin
sapgreen
sapidity
sapience
saponify
saponite
saporous
sapphics
sapphire
sapphism
saraband
sarcenet
sardelle
sardonic
sardonyx
sargasso
sarsenet
sashcord
Sassanid
satanism
satanist
sateless
satiable
satiably
satirise
satirist
saturant
saturate
Saturday
saturnic
saucebox
saucepan
saunders
sauouari
sauropod
Sauterne
savagely
savagery
savannah
savorous
Savoyard
sawbones
sawedged
sawedoff
sawframe
sawhorse
sawtooth
saxatile
Saxondom
Saxonism
Saxonist
sayonara
scabbard
scabious
scabrous
scaffold
scalable
scalawag
scalepan
scallion
scammony
scampish
scandent
Scandian
scandium
scanning
scansion
scanties
scantily
scaphoid
scapulae

scapular
scapulas
scarcely
scarcity
scarfpin
scarious
scarless
scarring
scathing
scattily
scatting
scavenge
scenario
scenical
sceptred
schedule
schemata
scheming
schiedam
schiller
schizoid
schmaltz
schnapps
scholium
schooner
sciagram
sciatica
scilicet
scimitar
sciolism
sciolist
scirocco
scirrhus
scissile
scission
scissors
sciurine
sciuroid
sclereid
sclerite
scleroma
sclerose
sclerous
scolding
scolices
scombrid
scoopful
scoopnet
scopulae
scopulas
scorcher
scornful
scorpion
scotfree
scotopic
Scotsman
scottice
Scottish
scourger
scouting
scrabble
scragend
scragged
scramble
scrammed
scrannel
scraping
scrapped
scrapper
scratchy
scrawler
screamer
screechy
screener
screever
screwtop
scribble
scribbly
scrofula

scrounge
scrubbed
scrubber
scrutiny
scudding
scullery
scullion
sculptor
scumming
scurrile
scurvily
scutcher
scutella
seaboard
seaborne
seachest
seacoast
seacraft
seadrome
seafarer
seafloor
seafront
seagoing
seagreen
seaholly
seahorse
sealable
sealevel
sealskin
sealyham
seamanly
seamless
seamount
seamouse
seamster
seaonion
seapiece
seaplane
seapurse
seaquake
searcher
seascape
seashell
seashore
seasnail
seasnake
seasonal
seasoner
seatbelt
seatrout
seawards
seawater
seawrack
sebesten
secluded
seconder
secondly
secretin
secretly
secretor
sectoral
securely
security
sedately
sedation
sedative
sederunt
sediment
sedition
sedulity
sedulous
seedcake
seedcase
seedcoat
seedcorn
seedfish
seedleaf
seedless
seedling

seedlobe
seedplot
seedsman
seedtime
segreant
seicento
seigneur
seignior
seignory
seizable
seladang
selcouth
selectee
selector
selenate
selenide
selenite
selenium
selfborn
selfheal
selfhelp
selfhood
selfless
selflove
selfmade
selfmate
selfness
selfpity
selfrule
selfsame
selfsown
selfwill
selvedge
semantic
semester
semibull
semidome
seminary
seminude
semiotic
Semitise
Semitism
Semitist
semitone
semolina
semplice
sempster
senarius
senility
sennight
senorita
senseful
sensible
sensibly
sensoria
sensuous
sentence
sentient
sentinel
sentrygo
sepaloid
sepalous
separate
Sephardi
septette
septfoil
septimal
septuple
sequelae
sequence
seraglio
seraphic
seraphim
serenade
serenata
serenely
serenity
serfhood
sergeant
serially
seriatim
sericite
serjeant
serology
serosity
serotine
serpulae
serranid
serrated
servient
servitor
sesamoid
sesterce
setscrew
severely
severity
sewellel
sewerage
sewergas
sewerrat
sexiness
sexology
sextette
sextuple
sexually
sforzato
shabbily
shabrack
Shabuoth
shadbush
shaddock
shadower
shafting
shagbark
shaggily
shagreen
shagroon
shakable
shakeout
Shaktism
shaleoil
shalloon
shallows
shambles
shameful
shamming
shamrock
shanghai
shantung
shapable
shareout
sharpish
sharpset
shashlik
sheading
shealing
shedding
shedevil
sheepdip
sheepdog
sheepish
sheepked
sheeppen
sheeprun
sheeting
sheikdom
Shekinah
shelduck
shelfful
shelving
Shemitic
shepherd
Sheraton
sherlock
Shetland
shielder
shieling
shiftily
shiftkey
shigella
shikaree
shilling
shimmery
shinbone
shingler
shingles
shinning
shipload
shipmate
shipment
shipping
shipworm
shipyard
shiralee
shirring
shirting
shivaree
shocking
shoddily
shoebill
shoehorn
shoelace
shoeless
shoetree
shofroth
shogging
shooting
shootout
shopbell
shopgirl
shopping
shoptalk
shopworn
shortage
shortarm
shortcut
shortday
shortish
shothole
shoulder
shouldst
showbill
showboat
showcard
showcase
showdown
showgirl
showroom
shrapnel
shredded
shredder
shrewdly
shrewish
shrieval
shrimper
shrinker
shrugged
shrunken
shuddery
shuffler
shunning
shutdown
shutting
Siberian
sibilant
sibilate
Sicilian
sickener
sickerly
sickflag
sicklist
sickness
sickroom
sidearms
sideband
sidedish
sidedoor
sidedrum
sidehead
sidekick
sideline
sideling
sidelong
sidenote
sidereal
siderite
sideroad
sideshow
sideslip
sidesman
sidestep
sideview
sidewalk
sideward
sideways
sidewind
sidewise
siftings
sigmatic
signally
signpost
silencer
silently
silicane
silicate
silicide
silicify
silicone
silkworm
sillabub
silphium
Silurian
siluroid
silvatic
silverly
similise
simoniac
simonist
simplify
simplism
simulant
simulate
Sinaitic
sinapism
sinciput
sinecure
sinfonia
sinfully
singable
singeing
singsong
singular
sinicise
sinister
sinkable
sinkhole
sinology
sinophil
sinusoid
siphonal
siphonet
siphonic
sirenian
siriasis
sirvente
sisterly
sitarist
sithence
sitology
situated
sitzbath
sixpence
sixpenny
sixtieth
sizeable
sizzling
skeletal
skeleton
skerrick
sketcher
skewback
skewbald
skewness
skiagram
skidding
skilless
skilling
skimmilk
skimming
skimpily
skindeep
skinfood
skinhead
skinless
skinning
skipjack
skipping
skirmish
skirting
skislope
skittish
skittles
skullcap
skylight
skypilot
skyscape
skywards
slabbing
slagging
slagheap
slamming
slangily
slapbang
slapdash
slapjack
slapping
slashing
slattern
Slavonic
sleazily
sledding
sleepily
sleeping
slideway
slightly
slimmest
slimming
slimmish
slimness
slinkily
slipcase
slipform
slipknot
slipover
slippage
slippery
slipping
slipring
sliproad
slipshod
slipslop
slithery
slitting
slobbery
slobbish
slobland
sloeeyed
slogging
sloppail
sloppily
slopping
slopshop
slopwork
slothful
slotting
sloucher
slovenly
slovenry
slowdown
slowness
slowpoke
slowworm
slubbing
slugabed
sluggard
slugging
sluggish
slumbery
slumming
slurring
sluttish
slyboots
smallage
smallfry
smallish
smallpox
smaltite
smarmily
smartish
smashing
smelling
smeltery
smithers
smithery
smocking
smokable
smoothen
smoothie
smoothly
smothery
smoulder
smudgily
smuggler
smugness
smuttily
snackbar
snagging
snakepit
snapbrim
snaplink
snappily
snapping
snappish
snapshot
snatcher
snazzily
sneakily
sneakish
sneeshan
sniffily
sniffler
sniffles
sniggler
snippety
snipping
snipsnap
snitcher
snobbery
snobbish
snobbism
snogging
snootily
snowball
snowbird
snowboot
snowdrop
snowfall
snowless
snowlike
snowline
snowshoe
snubbing
snuffbox
snuffers
snuffler
snuffles
snuggery
snugness
soakaway
soapbark
soapdish
soapless
soaproot
soapsuds
soapwort
soberise
sobriety
sobstory
sobstuff
socalled
sociable
sociably
socially
societal
Socinian
Socratic
sodalite
sodality
sodomite
softball
softboil
softener
softhead
softness
softshoe
softsoap
software
softwood
soilless
soilpipe
solander
solanine
solarise
solarism
solarist
solarium
solation
solatium
solderer
soldiery
solecism
solecist
solemnly
soleness
solenoid
solfaist
solfeggi
solidary
solidify
solidity
solitary
solitude
solleret
solstice
solution
solvable
solvency
somatism
sombrely
sombrero
sombrous
somebody
somedeal
somedele
sometime
someways
somewhat
somewhen
somnific
sonatina
songbird
songbook
songless
songster
sonobuoy
sonority
sonorous
soothing
soothsay
sorcerer
sordidly
sorehead
soreness
sorochen
sororate
sorority
sorption
sorptive
sorrower
sortable
soterial
souchong
soulless
soundbow
soundbox
sounding
sourdine
sourness
sourpuss
soutache
southern
southing
southpaw
Southron
souvenir
sovranty
sowbread
spacebar
spaceman
spacious
spadeful
spadices
spadille
spadones
spaewife
spagyric
spalpeen
spandrel
spandril
Spaniard
spanking
spanning
spanroof
sparable
sparbuoy
spardeck
sparkgap
sparkish
sparkler
sparklet
sparling
sparring
sparsely
sparsity
spathose
spatting
spatular
spavined
speaking
spearman
speciate
specific
specimen
specious
spectral
spectrum
specular
speculum
speedily
speedway
spelling
spermary

sphagnum
sphenoid
spherics
spheroid
spherule
sphingid
sphygmus
spicated
spiccato
spicebox
spicknel
spiculae
spicular
spiculum
spiffing
spikelet
spillage
spillway
spinifex
spinning
spinster
spiracle
spirally
spirilla
spirited
spiritus
spiteful
spitfire
spitting
spittoon
spivvery
splasher
splatter
splendid
splenial
splenius
splinter
splitter
splotchy
splutter
spoffish
spoilage
spoliate
spondaic
spongily
sponsion
spontoon
spookily
spookish
spoonfed
spoonful
spoonily
sporadic
sporozoa
sportful
sportily
sporting
sportive
sporular
spotless
spottily
spotting
spousage
spraints
sprawler
spraygun
spreader
sprigged
springal
springer
sprinkle
sprinter
sprocket
sprucely
spryness
spunkily
spurgear
spurious
spurling
spurrier
spurring
spyglass
squabble
squadron
squaller
squamate
squamose
squamous
squamule
squander
squarely
squarish
squarson
squasher
squatted
squatter
squawker
squawman
squeaker
squealer
squeedge
squeegee
squeezer
squelchy
squibbed
squidded
squiggle
squiggly
squilgee
squinter
squireen
squirely
squirrel
squirter
stabbing
stabling
stablish
staccato
staffage
staggard
staggers
staghorn
stagnant
stagnate
stairrod
stairway
stakenet
stallage
stallfed
stalling
stallion
stalwart
staminal
stampede
stancher
stanchly
standard
standing
standish
standoff
stanhope
stannary
stannate
stannite
stannous
stanzaic
stapelia
stardust
starfish
stargaze
starkers
starless
starlike
starling
starrily
starring
starting
startler
starwort
stasimon
statable
statedly
statical
statuary
statured
staylace
staysail
steadily
steading
stealing
stealthy
steamily
stearate
stearine
steatite
stedfast
steenbok
steening
steepish
steepled
steerage
steering
steinbok
stellate
stellify
stellion
stemless
stemmata
stemming
stenosed
stenosis
stenotic
stepping
stepwise
sterigma
sterling
sternite
sternson
sternway
stetting
stibnite
stickful
stickily
stickjaw
stickler
stiffish
stigmata
stilbene
stilbite
stiletto
stillage
stimulus
stingily
stingray
stinkard
stinking
stinkpot
stipites
stippler
stipular
stirring
stitcher
stoccado
stoccata
stockade
stockcar
stockily
stocking
stockish
stockist
stockman
stockpot
stodgily
stoicism
stolidly
stomachy
stomatal
stomatic
stonefly
stopcock
stopover
stoppage
stopping
storable
storeman
storeyed
stormily
stoutish
stowaway
strabism
straddle
straggle
straggly
straight
strained
strainer
straiten
straitly
stramash
stranded
stranger
strangle
strapoil
strapped
strapper
strategy
stratify
stravaig
streaked
streaker
streamer
streeted
strength
strepent
Strepyan
stretchy
stricken
strickle
strictly
stridden
strident
strigose
striking
stringed
stringer
stripped
stripper
strobila
strobile
strobili
stroller
stromata
strongly
strontia
strophic
stropped
strucken
struggle
strummed
strummer
strumose
strumous
strumpet
strutted
strutter
stubbing
stubborn
stubnail
stuccoes
studbook
studding
studfarm
studious
studwork
stuffily
stuffing
stultify
stumbler
stumming
stumpily
stunning
stunsail
stuntman
stupidly
stuprate
sturdied
sturdily
sturgeon
stylised
subacute
subagent
subahdar
subbasal
subclass
suberect
suberise
suberose
suberous
subfloor
subframe
subgenus
subgroup
subhuman
subimago
subjoint
sublease
sublunar
submerge
submerse
suborder
suborner
suboxide
subphyla
subpoena
subprior
subserve
subshrub
subsolar
subsonic
substage
subtitle
subtlety
subtonic
subtopia
subtotal
subtract
subulate
suburban
suburbia
subvocal
succinct
succinic
succinum
succubae
succubus
suchlike
suckling
Sudanese
sudarium
sudatory
suddenly
sufferer
suffrage
suicidal
suitable
suitably
suitcase
suitings
sukiyaki
sullenly
sulphate
sulphide
sulphite
sulphone
sultrily
Sumerian
summerly
summitry
summoner
sunbaked
sunbathe
sunblind
sunburnt
sunburst
sundance
sunderer
sundress
sundried
sundries
sundrops
sunlight
sunproof
sunshade
sunshine
sunshiny
sunstone
sunwards
superadd
superate
superbly
superego
superior
superman
supernal
supertax
supinate
supinely
supplant
supplely
supplial
supplier
supplies
supposal
supposed
suppress
surcease
surefire
sureness
surfacer
surfbird
surfboat
surfduck
surffish
surgical
suricate
surmisal
surmiser
surmount
surplice
surprise
surround
surroyal
surveyor
survival
survivor
suspense
susurrus
suzerain
swabbing
swagging
swainish
swanherd
swanking
swanlike
swanmark
swanneck
swannery
swanning
swanshot
swanskin
swansong
swapping
swastika
swatting
swayback
swearing
sweeping
sweepnet
sweeting
sweetish
sweetpea
sweetsop
swelling
swiftlet
swigging
swimming
swimsuit
swindler
swinging
switchel
swobbing
swopping
swotting
sybarite
sycamine
sycamore
sycomore
syconium
syenitic
syllabic
syllable
syllabub
syllabus
sylphide
sylphine
sylphish
sylvatic
symbiont
symbolic
symmetry
sympathy
symphile
symphony
sympodia
symposia
synapsis
synaptic
synastry
syncline
syncopal
syncytia
syndesis
syndetic
syndical
syndrome
synergic
synergid
syngamic
synonymy
synopses
synopsis
synoptic
synovial
syntagma
syntonic
syphilis
syringes
syrinxes
systemic
systolic
syzygial
taberdar
tableaux
tablecut
tableful
tablemat
tabletop
tabouret
tabulate
tachisme
tachiste
taciturn
tackling
tackroom
tactical
tactless
taenioid
tafferel
taffrail
tagalong
Tahitian
tailback
tailcoat
tailgate
tailings
tailless
tailpipe
tailrace
tailspin
tainture
takeaway
takehome
takeover
takingly
talapoin
talented
talesman
talisman
tallness
tallyman
Talmudic
tamandua
tamanoir
tamarack
tamarind
tamarisk
tamboura
tameable
tameless
tameness
Tamilian
tamperer
tandoori
tangency
tangible
tangibly
tangoist
tanistry
tannable
tantalic
tantalum
tantalus
Tantrism
tantrist
tapdance
tapedeck
tapeless
tapelike
tapeline
tapestry
tapeworm
taphouse
tapwater
tarboosh
tarlatan
Tarpeian
tarragon
tartaric
tartness
tartrate
Tartuffe
taskwork
tasselly
tastebud
tasteful
tattered
tattooer
tautness
tautomer
tautonym
taverner
tawdrily

taxation
taxingly
taxonomy
taxpayer
teaboard
teabread
teabreak
teacaddy
teachest
teaching
teacloth
teahouse
teammate
teamster
teamwork
teaparty
tearaway
teardrop
tearduct
tearless
teaspoon
teatable
teatowel
technics
tectonic
teenager
teething
teetotal
teetotum
tegmenta
tegument
telecast
telecine
telefilm
telegony
telegram
telemark
telepath
teleport
telethon
teleview
televise
tellable
telltale
telluric
temerity
tempered
temperer
template
temporal
tempting
tenacity
tenacula
tenaille
tenantry
tendence
tendency
tenderly
Tenebrae
tenement
tenesmus
tenonsaw
tenorite
tenotomy
tenpence
tenpenny
tensible
tentacle
tenurial
teocalli
tepidity
teraphim
teratoma
terebene
terebrae
terminal
terminer
terminus
termless
termtime
terraced
terrapin
terraria
terrazzo
terrible
terribly
terrific
tertiary
tesserae
tesseral
testable
testator
testatum
testtube
tetanise
tetchily
tetradic
tetragon
tetrapla
tetrapod
tetrarch
Teutonic
textbook
texthand
textuary
textural
textured
thalamic
thalamus
thallium
thalloid
thallous
Thanatos
thanedom
thankful
thankyou
thatcher
thearchy
theistic
thematic
theocrat
theodicy
theogony
theology
theorise
theorist
therefor
thereout
thermion
thermite
thesauri
thespian
thetical
theurgic
thiamine
thickety
thickish
thickset
thievery
thievish
thingamy
thinking
thinness
thinnest
thinning
thinnish
thirlage
thirster
thirteen
thisness
tholepin
thoraces
thoracic
thoraxes
thorough
thoughts
thousand
thraldom
thrasher
thrawart
threader
threaten
threeply
threeway
threnode
threnody
thresher
thridace
thriller
thriving
throated
throbbed
thrombin
thrombus
throstle
throttle
thrummed
thruster
thudding
thuggery
thuggism
thumbpot
thumping
thundery
thurible
thurifer
Thursday
thusness
thwacker
thwarter
thwartly
thyroxin
thyrsoid
ticklish
tickseed
ticktack
ticktock
tidegate
tideland
tideless
tidelock
tidemark
tidemill
tidewave
tidiness
tiebreak
tigereye
tigerish
tightwad
tilefish
tillable
tiltyard
timbered
timeball
timebomb
timefuse
timeless
timework
timeworn
timidity
timorous
timously
tincture
tingeing
tininess
tinkerer
tinnitus
tinplate
tinselly
tinsmith
tinstone
tintless
tipstaff
tireless
tiresome
titanate
titaness
titanism
titanite
titanium
tithable
titivate
titmouse
tittuped
tittuppy
toadfish
toadflax
toadyish
toadyism
toboggan
tocology
toepiece
toeplate
together
toiletry
toilette
toilsome
toilworn
tokenism
tokology
tolbooth
tolerant
tolerate
tollcall
tolldish
tollgate
tomahawk
tomalley
tombless
tomentum
tommybar
tommygun
tommyrot
tomnoddy
tomogram
tomorrow
tonality
tonedeaf
toneless
tonepoem
tonguing
tonicity
toolroom
toolshed
toothful
toothily
toothing
topdress
topheavy
toplevel
topliner
toplofty
topnotch
topology
toponymy
topstone
torchere
toreador
toreutic
tornadic
toroidal
torpidly
torquate
torridly
tortilla
tortious
tortoise
tortuous
torturer
totalise
totality
totalled
totemism
totemist
totterer
touchily
touching
toughish
touristy
tournure
tovarish
towardly
towelled
townhall
township
townsman
toxaemia
toxaemic
toxicant
toxicity
trabeate
tracheae
tracheal
tracheid
trachoma
trachyte
trackage
tracking
trackman
trackway
tractate
traction
tractive
tradeoff
traditor
traducer
tragical
tragopan
trailnet
training
tramline
trammels
trampler
tramroad
tranquil
transact
transect
transept
transfer
transfix
tranship
transire
transmit
transude
trapball
trapdoor
trapezia
trappean
trapping
Trappist
traprock
trashery
trashily
traumata
traverse
travesty
trawlnet
treacher
treadler
treasure
treasury
treatise
trecento
treefern
treefrog
treeless
treenail
trekking
trembler
trembles
trencher
trendily
trephine
trespass
tressure
trevally
trialist
triangle
triarchy
Triassic
triaxial
tribally
tribasic
tribrach
tribunal
trichina
trichite
trichoid
trichome
trichord
trickery
trickily
trickish
tricorne
tricycle
triennia
trifling
trifocal
triforia
triglyph
trigonal
trigraph
trilling
trillion
trillium
trilobed
trimaran
trimeric
trimeter
trimming
trimness
trioxide
tripeman
triplane
triploid
tripodal
trippery
tripping
triptych
tripwire
triskele
trisomic
tristful
tristich
tritical
triumvir
triunity
trochaic
trochili
trochlea
trochoid
troilite
trollopy
trombone
trophied
tropical
trotting
trottoir
troupial
trousers
troutlet
trouvere
truantry
truckage
trucking
truckler
trueblue
trueborn
truebred
truelove
trueness
truistic
trumeaux
trumpery
truncate
trunnion
trussing
trustful
trustily
truthful
tryingly
tsarevna
tsaritsa
tsaritza
tubeless
tubercle
tuberose
tuberous
tubiform
tubulate
tuckahoe
tuckshop
tumbling
tumidity
tumorous
tuneable
tuneless
tungsten
tungstic
tunicate
Tunisian
tuppence
tuppenny
Turanian
turbaned
turbidly
turbinal
turbofan
turbojet
Turcoman
turgidly
Turkoman
turmeric
turnable
turnback
turncoat
turncock
turndown
turnings
turnover
turnpike
turnskin
turnsole
turnspit
turreted
turtling
tussocky
tutelage
tutelary
tutorage
tutoress
tutorial
twaddler
tweezers
twelvemo
twenties
twiddler
twilight
twinborn
twinkler
twinling
twinning
twinship
twitcher
twittery
twitting
twoedged
twofaced
twopence
twopenny
twopiece
twosided
twotimer
Tychonic
tympanic
tympanum
typecast
typeface
typehigh
typhonic
typifier
typology
tyrannic
Tyrolean
tyrosine
Tyrrhene
ubiquity
udometer
ugliness
uintaite
ulcerate
ulcerous
ulterior
ultimacy
ultimata
ultimate
ultraism
ultraist
umbonate
umbrella
umbrette
umpirage
umptieth
unabated
unaneled
unawares
unbacked
unbarred
unbeaten
unbelief
unbiased
unbidden
unbolted
unbottle
unbridle
unbroken
unbuckle
unburden
unburied
unbutton
uncalled
uncandid
uncapped
uncaused
unchancy
unchaste
unchurch
uncially
unciform
uncinate
unclench
unclinch
unclothe
uncoined
uncommon
uncouple
uncreate
unctuous
underact
underage
underarm
underbid
undercut
underdid
underdog
underfur
underlap
underlay
underlet
underlie
underlip
underman

underpin
underrun
undersea
underset
undertow
underway
undraped
undreamt
undulant
undulate
unearned
uneasily
unedited
unending
unerring
unevenly
unfading
unfairly
unfasten
unfetter
unfilial
unfitted
unforced
unformed
unfreeze
unfrozen
unfunded
ungainly
unglazed
ungotten
ungulate
unhinged
unhoused
uniaxial
unicycle
unifilar
unionise
unionism
unionist
unipolar
uniquely
unisonal
unitedly
univalve
universe
univocal
unjustly
unkennel
unkindly
unkingly
unlawful
unleaded
unlearnt
unlikely
unlimber
unlinked
unlisted
unloader
unloosen
unlovely
unmanned
unmarked
unmeetly
unmuffle
unmuzzle
unopened
unpaired
unpegged
unperson
unpinned
unplaced
unreason
unriddle
unrigged
unroofed
unsaddle
unsealed
unseated
unseeded

unseeing
unseemly
unsettle
unshaped
unsocial
unsought
unsprung
unstable
unstably
unstated
unsteady
unstring
unstrung
unstuffy
unsuited
unsunned
unswathe
untangle
untapped
untaught
untented
untether
unthread
unthrift
unthrone
untidily
untimely
untitled
untoward
unvalued
unversed
unvoiced
unwanted
unwarily
unwashed
unweaned
unwieldy
unwisdom
unwisely
unwished
unwonted
unwordly
unworthy
unzipped
upheaval
upholder
uplander
uplifter
uppercut
uppishly
uprising
uprooter
upsetter
upsprang
upspring
upsprung
upstairs
upstream
upstroke
upthrown
upthrust
upwardly
uralitic
urbanely
urbanise
urbanism
urbanist
urbanite
urbanity
urethane
urgently
urochord
urostyle
Ursuline
urticant
urticate
usefully
usufruct
usurious

utiliser
uvularly
uvulitis
uxorious
vacantly
vacation
vaccinal
vaccinia
vacuolar
vagabond
vagility
vagrancy
vainness
valanced
valerate
valerian
Valhalla
valiance
valiancy
validate
validity
valorise
valorous
valuable
valuably
valuator
valvulae
valvular
vambrace
vampiric
vamplate
vanadate
vanadium
vanadous
Vandalic
vaneless
vanguard
vanillin
vanisher
vanquish
vapidity
vaporise
vaporous
vapourer
varactor
variable
variably
variance
varicose
variedly
varietal
variform
variolar
variorum
varletry
vascular
vasculum
vasiform
vastness
vaulting
vauntful
vavasory
vavasour
Vedantic
vegetate
vegetive
vehement
veilless
velamina
velarium
velleity
velocity
velskoen
venality
venation
vendetta
vendible
veneerer
venerate

venereal
Venetian
vengeful
venially
venomous
venosity
venously
ventless
venturer
Venusian
veracity
verandah
veratrin
veratrum
verbally
verbatim
verbiage
verboten
verdancy
verderer
verderor
verditer
verdured
verecund
vergence
verifier
veristic
verjuice
vermouth
vernally
vernicle
veronica
verrucae
versicle
vertebra
vertexes
vertical
vertices
verticil
vesicant
vesicate
vesperal
vespiary
vestiary
vestment
vesturer
vesuvian
vexation
vexillum
viameter
viaticum
vibrancy
vibrator
vibrissa
viburnum
vicarage
vicarate
vicarial
vicinage
vicinity
victoria
victress
victuals
Viennese
Vietcong
Vietminh
viewable
viewless
vigilant
vigneron
vignette
vigorous
vileness
vilifier
vilipend
villadom
villager
villainy
villatic

vincible
vinculum
vinegary
vineyard
vinosity
vinously
vintager
violable
violably
violator
violence
viperine
viperish
viperous
virement
virginal
Virginia
viricide
viridian
viridity
virilism
virility
virology
virtuosa
virtuosi
virtuoso
virtuous
virulent
viscacha
visceral
viscidly
viscount
Visigoth
visional
visitant
visually
vitalise
vitalism
vitalist
vitality
vitellin
vitellus
vitiable
vitiator
vitiligo
vitreous
vituline
vivacity
vivarium
vivifier
vivisect
vixenish
vizarded
vizcacha
vocalise
vocalism
vocalist
vocality
vocation
vocative
voicebox
voiceful
voidable
voidance
voidness
volatile
volcanic
volcanos
volitant
volition
volitive
volplane
voltaism
volution
volvulus
vomerine
vomitive
vomitory
voracity

vortexes
vortical
vortices
votaress
votarist
voteless
voussoir
vowelise
vowelled
voyageur
vulcanic
vulgarly
waesucks
waggoner
wagonage
wagonlit
Wahabism
Wahabite
wainscot
waitress
wakeless
wakening
wakerife
waleknot
Walhalla
walkable
walkaway
walkover
Walkyrie
wallaroo
walleyed
wallfern
wallgame
wallknot
walloper
wallower
wanderer
wanderoo
wantonly
warcloud
wardance
wardenry
wardress
wardrobe
wardroom
wardship
warhorse
wariness
warmness
warpaint
warplane
warragal
warranty
warrener
warrigal
wartweed
wartwort
warweary
warwhoop
washable
washbowl
washroom
wastable
wasteful
watchdog
watchful
watchkey
watchman
waterage
waterbed
waterbus
watergas
waterice
watering
waterish
waterlog
waterloo
waterman
waterski

waterway
watthour
waveband
waveform
waveless
waviness
waxberry
waxcloth
waxiness
waxlight
waxworks
wayfarer
waygoing
weakfish
weakling
weakness
weanling
weaponry
wearable
weariful
weaselly
Wedgwood
weedless
weeklong
weeviled
weevilly
weldable
weldment
welladay
wellaway
wellborn
wellbred
welldeck
wellhead
wellknit
wellnigh
wellread
Wellsian
wellworn
Welshman
weregild
werewolf
Wesleyan
westerly
westward
wetlands
wetnurse
wettable
whacking
whapping
wharfage
whatever
whatness
wheatear
wheedler
wheelman
wheezily
whenever
wherever
whetting
wheyface
whidding
whiffler
Whiggery
Whiggish
Whiggism
whimbrel
whimwham
whinchat
whinsill
whipcord
whiplash
whiplike
whipping
whipworm
whirring
whiskers
whiskery
whispery

whistler
whiteboy
whitecap
whitefly
whitehot
whitener
whiteout
whitetie
whittret
whizbang
whizzing
whizzkid
whodunit
wholehog
whomever
whooping
whopping
whoredom
whoreson
wickedly
wideeyed
wideness
wifehood
wifeless
wifelike
wigmaker
wildeyed
wildfire
wildfowl
wildlife
wildness
wildwood
wilfully
wiliness
williwaw
windburn
windcone
windfall
windgall
windlass
windless
windmill
windowed
windpipe
windrose
windsail
windsock
windward
winepalm
wineshop
wineskin
wingbeat
wingcase
wingless
wingspan
winnable
winnings
winnower
winterly
wintrily
wiredraw
wirehair
wireless
wirework
wireworm
wirewove
wiriness
wiseacre
wiseness
wishbone
wishwash
wistaria
wisteria
witchelm
witchery
witchety
witching
withdraw
withdrew

withheld
withhold
wizardly
wizardry
woefully
wolffish
wolfpack
wolfskin
womanise
womanish
wondrous
wontedly
woodbind
woodbine
woodchat
woodcock
woodenly
woodland
woodlark
woodlice
woodnote
woodpile
woodpulp
woodruff
woodshed
woodsman
woodwind
woodwool
woodwork
woodworm
wooldyed
woolfell
woollens
woolpack
woolsack
woolshed
woolskin
woolwork
wordbook
wordless
wordplay
workable
workaday
workfolk
workings
workless
workmate
workroom
workshop
wormcast
wormgear
wormhole
wormlike
wormseed
wormwood
worthful
worthily
wouldest
woundily
wrackful
wrangler
wrappage
wrapping
wrathful
wrathily
wreathen
wreckage
wrestler
wrestpin
wretched
wriggler
wristlet
wristpin
writable
writeoff
writings
wrongful
wrongous
wrymouth
xanthate
xanthein
xanthene
xanthine
xanthium
xanthoma
Xantippe
xenogamy
xenolith
xylocarp
xylology
xylonite
yachting
Yankeefy
yarmulka
yataghan
yeanling
yearbook
yearling
yearlong
yearning
yeastily
yellowly
yeomanly
yeomanry
yestreen
yielding
yodelled
yodeller
yoghourt
yokemate
youngest
youngish
yourself
youthful
Yugoslav
yuletide
zabaione
zamindar
zaniness
zarzuela
zealotry
zecchini
zecchino
zemindar
zenithal
zeolitic
zeppelin
zibeline
ziggurat
zinckify
zincking
zirconia
zodiacal
zoetrope
zoiatria
zombiism
zonation
zoogenic
zoolater
zoolatry
zoomancy
zoometry
zoomorph
zoonosis
zoophily
zoophyte
zoospore
zucchini
zugzwang
zwieback
zygaenid
zymology

---

aardvark
aardwolf
aasvogel
babirusa
babouche
babushka
babyhood
baccarat
bacchant
bachelor
bacillar
bacillus
backache
backbite
backbone
backchat
backcomb
backdate
backdoor
backdrop
backfire
backhand
backlash
backless
backlist
backmost
backpack
backrest
backroom
backseat
backside
backspin
backstay
backveld
backward
backwash
backyard
Baconian
bacteria
Bactrian
badinage
badlands
bagpiper
baguette
bailable
bailment
bailsman
bakshish
balanced
balancer
baldhead
baldness
baldpate
balefire
Balinese
balkline
balladic
balladry
ballcock
balletic
ballista
ballonet
ballroom
ballyhoo
ballyrag
balmoral
balsamic
baluster
bambinos
banality
banausic
bandanna
bandeaux
banderol
banditry
banditti
bandsman
bangtail
banister
banjoist
bankable
bankbill
bankbook
banknote
bankroll
bankrupt
bannered
banneret
bannerol
banterer
bantling
banxring
barathea
barbaric
barbecue
barberry
barbette
barbican
barbital
bareback
barefoot
bareness
bargeman
baritone
barkless
barnacle
barndoor
barnyard
baronage
baroness
baronial
barouche
barracks
barranca
barranco
barrator
barratry
barrenly
barrette
barterer
bartizan
baryonic
barytone
basaltic
baseball
baseborn
baseless
baseline
basement
baseness
basicity
basidial
basidium
basilica
basilisk
basinful
basketry
bassinet
basswood
bastardy
bastille
Batavian
bateleur
bathetic
bathotic
bathrobe
bathroom
battalia
battleax
baudrons
bauxitic
Bavarian
bayadere
bayberry
cabalism
cabalist
caballed
cabinboy
cableway
cabochon
caboodle
cabotage
cabriole
cabstand
cachalot
cachepot
cachexia
cachucha
cacology
cacomixl
cactuses
cadastre
cadenced
caducean
caduceus
caducity
caducous
caesious
caesural
caffeine
cagebird
cageling
caginess
cajolery
cakewalk
calabash
caladium
calamary
calamine
calamint
calamite
calamity
calcanea
calcaria
calcific
calcitic
calcspar
calctuff
calculus
calendar
calender
calfskin
calidity
califate
calipash
calipers
callable
callgirl
calliope
calliper
calmness
calthrop
calvados
calycine
calycoid
calycule
calyptra
Cambrian
cameleer
camellia
camisade
camisado
camisole
camomile
campagna
campaign
campfire
camphene
camphine
campsite
camshaft
Canadian
canaille
canalise
canaster
cancrine
cancroid
candidly
canister
cannabin
cannabis
cannibal
cannikin
cannonry
cannulae
cannular
cannulas
canoeing
canoeist
canoness
canonise
canonist
canoodle
canorous
canthari
canticle
cantonal
cantoris
canzonet
capacity
capeline
capellet
capeskin
capitate
capitula
caponier
caponise
caprifig
capriole
capsicum
capstone
capsular
captious
capuchin
capybara
carabine
caracara
caracole
carapace
carbolic
carbonic
carbonyl
carboxyl
carburet
carcajou
carcanet
cardamom
cardamum
cardigan
cardinal
carefree
careless
careworn
carillon
carinate
carnally
carnauba
carnival
Carolean
Caroline
carolled
carotene
carousal
carousel
carouser
carriage
carriole
carryall
carryout
cartload
cartouch
caruncle
caryatid
Casanova
cascabel
casebook
casemate
casement
casework
cashbook
cashmere
cassette
castaway
castiron
castrate
castrati
castrato
casually
casualty
catacomb
catalase
cataloes
catalyse
catalyst
catamite
catapult
cataract
catchall
catchfly
catching
catechol
category
catenary
catenate
cateress
catering
cathedra
catheter
cathexes
cathexis
cathodal
cathodic
catholic
cationic
catsfoot
catstail
cattleya
caudally
caudated
caudexes
caudices
caudillo
cauldron
causally
causerie
causeway
cautious
cavalier
cavatina
caverned
cavesson
cavicorn
cavilled
caviller
dabchick
dactylar
dactylic
daemonic
daffodil
daftness
dahabieh
daimonic
daintily
daiquiri
dairying
dairyman
dalesman
dalmatic
damassin
damnable
damnably
dampness
dancette
dancetty
dandruff
dandyish
dandyism
danegeld
dankness
danseuse
daringly
darkling
darkness
darkroom
darksome
dartrous
dastardy
dateless
dateline
daughter
daybreak
daydream
daylight
eagleowl
earmuffs
earnings
earphone
earpiece
earthnut
easement
easiness
easterly
eastmost
eastward
fabliaux
fabulist
fabulous
faceache
facecard
faceless
facelift
facepack
facetiae
facially
facilely
facility
factious
factotum
fadeaway
fadeless
fagoting
failsafe
faineant
faintish
fairlead
fairness
fairyism
faithful
falcated
falchion
falconer
falconet
falconry
falderal
fallback
fallfish
fallible
fallibly
falsetto
faltboat
familial
familiar
famously
fanciful
fancyman
fandance
fandango
fanfaron
fangless
fanlight
fantasia
faradaic
faradism
farcical
farewell
farflung
farinose
farmhand
farmland

farmyard
farouche
farriery
farthest
farthing
fascicle
fasciola
fasciole
Fascista
Fascisti
fashious
fastback
fastener
fastfood
fastness
fasttalk
fastuous
fatalism
fatalist
fatality
fatherly
fatigues
fatstock
fattener
faubourg
faultily
faunally
Faustian
fauteuil
favonian
favoured
favourer
gabbroic
gabbroid
gableend
gadabout
gadarene
gadgetry
Gadhelic
gadzooks
gainable
gainings
gainless
gainsaid
galactic
galangal
galbanum
galeated
Galenism
galenite
Galilean
galleass
galliard
Gallican
gallipot
galloper
Galloway
galluses
gallwasp
galvanic
gambados
gambeson
gambroon
gamebird
gamecock
gameness
gamesome
gamester
gaminess
gangland
gangling
ganglion
gangrene
gangster
ganister
gantline
gantlope
Ganymede
gaolbird

gapeworm
gapingly
garboard
gardener
gardenia
gardyloo
garefowl
garganey
gargoyle
garishly
garlicky
garotter
garreted
garrison
garrotte
gaselier
gasfired
gashouse
gaslight
gasmeter
gasolene
gasolier
gasoline
gastight
gastraea
gastrula
gasworks
gatefold
gatepost
gatherer
Gaullism
Gaullist
gauntlet
gavelock
gazogene
gazpacho
habanera
habitant
habitual
habitude
hacienda
hadronic
haematic
haematin
Haggadah
hairgrip
hairless
hairlike
hairline
hairworm
Halachah
halation
haleness
halfback
halfbeak
halfboot
halfbred
halflife
halfmast
halfmoon
halfnote
halfpint
halfsole
halfterm
halftime
halftone
haliotis
halliard
hallmark
hallowed
halluces
halteres
hamartia
hamululi
handball
handbell
handbill
handbook
handcart

handclap
handcuff
handfast
handgrip
handheld
handhold
handicap
handless
handline
handling
handlist
handloom
handmade
handmaid
handmill
handpick
handrail
handsewn
handsome
handwork
handyman
hangable
hangeron
hangnail
hangover
haploidy
harakiri
harangue
harasser
hardback
hardbake
hardcase
hardcore
hardener
hardhack
hardhead
hardline
hardness
hardship
hardtack
hardware
hardwood
harebell
haresear
harikari
harlotry
harmless
harmonic
harpseal
harridan
harrumph
haruspex
hasheesh
hastener
hastings
hatchery
hatching
hatchway
hateable
hatstand
haulyard
haunting
hausfrau
havelock
havildar
havocked
Hawaiian
hawfinch
hawkeyed
hawklike
hawkmoth
hawkweed
hawthorn
hayfield
haymaker
haystack
hazelnut
haziness
ianthine

jabberer
jackaroo
jackboot
jackeroo
jackstay
Jacobean
Jacobite
jacquard
jaggedly
jailbird
jalousie
jamboree
janizary
Japanese
japanned
japhetic
japonica
jaundice
jauntily
Javanese
Kaffiyeh
kailyard
kakemono
kalaazar
kamikaze
Kanarese
kangaroo
Kashmiri
katakana
labdanum
labelled
labellum
labially
lability
labourer
labrador
laburnum
lacerate
lacewing
lacework
lackaday
laconian
laconism
lacrimal
lacrosse
lacrymal
lacunary
lacunate
lacunose
ladybird
ladyfern
ladyhood
ladylike
ladylove
ladyship
laically
lakeland
lallygag
lamasery
lambaste
lambency
lamblike
lambskin
lamellae
lamellar
lameness
lamented
laminate
lamppost
lancelet
landarmy
landcrab
landfall
landform
landgirl
landlady
landless
landline
landlord

landmark
landmass
landmine
landrail
landslip
landsman
langlauf
Langshan
language
languish
lankness
lanneret
lanthorn
lapboard
lapelled
lapicide
lapidary
lapidate
lapidify
larboard
larcener
largesse
larkspur
larrikin
larynges
larynxes
lashings
latchkey
lateness
latently
laterite
Latinate
latinise
Latinism
Latinist
latinity
latitant
latitude
latterly
latticed
laudable
laudably
laudanum
laudator
laughing
laughter
launcher
laureate
lavalava
lavation
lavatory
lavender
laverock
lavishly
lawcourt
lawfully
lawgiver
lawmaker
lawyerly
laxative
layabout
layshaft
laystall
laywoman
Lazarist
laziness
lazulite
lazurite
macaroni
macaroon
macerate
machismo
mackerel
mackinaw
maculate
madapple
madhouse
madrigal
madwoman

Maecenas
maenadic
maestoso
magazine
magdalen
magician
magicked
magister
magmatic
magnesia
magnetic
magneton
magnific
magnolia
maharaja
maharani
mahjongg
mahogany
Mahratta
Mahratti
maidenly
maidhood
maieutic
mailable
mailboat
mailcart
mainland
mainline
mainmast
mainsail
mainstay
maintain
mainyard
maiolica
majestic
majolica
majority
makebate
makefast
makimono
Malagasy
malamute
malapert
malaprop
malarial
malarian
malarkey
maledict
malefern
malemute
maleness
maligner
malignly
malinger
malodour
maltreat
maltster
malvasia
Mameluke
mamillae
mamillar
mancando
manciple
Mandaean
mandamus
mandarin
mandator
mandible
Mandingo
mandolin
mandorla
mandrake
mandrill
maneater
manfully
mangabey
manganic
mangonel
mangrove

maniacal
Manichee
manicure
manifest
manifold
maniform
mannered
mannerly
mannikin
mannitol
manorial
manpower
mansized
mantelet
mantilla
mantissa
mantling
manually
manubria
manurial
maquette
marabout
marasmic
marasmus
marathon
marauder
maravedi
marbling
marchesa
marchese
marginal
margrave
marigold
marinade
marinate
maritage
maritime
marjoram
markdown
markedly
marketer
marksman
marmoset
marocain
maroquin
marquess
marquise
marriage
marrieds
marrying
marshman
martagon
martello
martenot
martinet
marzipan
mascaron
Masorete
Masoreth
massacre
masseter
masseuse
massicot
massless
masterly
masthead
mastitis
mastodon
matamata
matchbox
matelote
material
materiel
maternal
matgrass
matiness
matrices
matrixes
matronal

matronly
mattress
maturate
maturely
maturity
maverick
maxillae
maximise
mayapple
mayoress
Mayqueen
mazarine
Mazdaism
mazement
maziness
nacreous
nailfile
nainsook
nameable
namedrop
nameless
namepart
namesake
nametape
nanogram
naphthol
napiform
napoleon
narceine
narcissi
narcoses
narcosis
narcotic
narghile
narrator
narrowly
nasalise
nasality
nascence
nascency
natality
natation
natatory
nathless
national
natively
nativism
nativist
nativity
naturism
naturist
naumachy
nauplius
nauseant
nauseate
nauseous
nautical
nautilus
navigate
Nazarene
Nazarite
Nazirite
oafishly
oakapple
oakegger
oatgrass
pachalic
pacifier
pacifism
pacifist
padishah
paduasoy
paganise
paganish
paganism
paginate
pagurian
painless
paintbox

palatial
palatine
paleface
paleness
palestra
palinode
palisade
palliate
pallidly
pallmall
palmette
palmetto
palmiped
palmitin
palomino
palpable
palpably
palterer
paludism
pamperer
pamphlet
pancreas
pandanus
pandemic
pandowdy
panelled
pangolin
panicked
panmixia
pannikin
panorama
panpipes
pansophy
pantheon
pantofle
pantsuit
papalise
papalism
papalist
paperboy
papillae
papillar
papillon
papistic
papistry
pappadom
papulose
papulous
parabola
paradigm
paradise
paraffin
paragoge
parakeet
parallax
parallel
paralyse
paramour
paranoia
paranoid
paraquat
parasang
parasite
paravane
parcener
parclose
pardoner
parental
parergon
pargeter
parhelia
parhelic
parietal
parkland
parlance
parlando
Parmesan
parodist
paroquet
paroxysm
parrotry
Parsiism
parsonic
partaken
parterre
Parthian
partible
particle
partisan
partizan
partsong
parttime
pashalic
pashalik
passable
passably
passbook
passerby
passible
Passover
passport
password
pastiche
pastille
pastoral
pastrami
pastries
pastural
patagium
patchily
patellae
patellar
patentee
patently
patentor
paternal
pathetic
pathless
pathogen
patience
patronal
pattypan
patulous
pavement
pavilion
pawnshop
payphone
paysheet
rabbinic
rabbiter
rabbitry
rabidity
racecard
racegoer
racemate
racemise
racemose
rachides
rachitic
rachitis
racially
raciness
rackrent
radially
radiance
radiancy
radiator
radicant
radicate
raftsman
raggedly
railhead
raillery
railroad
rainbird
raincoat
raindrop
rainfall
rainwash
rainwear
rakehell
rakishly
rallying
rallyist
rambling
rambutan
ramentum
ramequin
rampancy
ranarian
ranarium
ranchero
ranchman
randomly
rankness
ransomer
rapacity
rapecake
rapeseed
rapidity
rapparee
raptness
raptures
rarefied
rareness
rascally
rashness
rasorial
rataplan
rateable
ratguard
ratifier
rational
ratsbane
ratstail
rattling
ravelled
ravenous
ravisher
rawboned
sabbatic
sabotage
saboteur
saccadic
saccular
sacculus
sackcoat
sackless
sackrace
sacraria
sacredly
sacristy
saddlery
Sadducee
sadistic
safeness
saffrony
safranin
sagacity
sagamore
sageness
saginate
sagittal
sailable
sailboat
sailfish
sailless
sailorly
sailyard
sainfoin
saintdom
salacity
salariat
salaried
saleable
saleroom
Salesian
salesman
salience
saliency
salinity
salivary
salivate
Salopian
saltbush
saltless
saltlick
saltmine
saltness
saltwort
salutary
salvable
salvific
samarium
sameness
samizdat
Samoyede
samphire
sampling
sanative
sanatory
sanctify
sanction
sanctity
sandarac
sandbank
sandbath
sandflea
sandshoe
sandwich
sandworm
sandwort
sandyish
saneness
sangaree
Sangrail
Sangreal
sanguine
sanitary
sanitate
sanitise
sannyasi
sanserif
Sanskrit
santonin
sapgreen
sapidity
sapience
saponify
saponite
saporous
sapphics
sapphire
sapphism
saraband
sarcenet
sardelle
sardonic
sardonyx
sargasso
sarsenet
sashcord
Sassanid
satanism
satanist
sateless
satiable
satiably
satirise
satirist
saturant
saturate
Saturday
saturnic
saucebox
saucepan
saunders
sauouari
sauropod
Sauterne
savagely
savagery
savannah
savorous
Savoyard
sawbones
sawedged
sawedoff
sawframe
sawhorse
sawtooth
saxatile
Saxondom
Saxonism
Saxonist
sayonara
taberdar
tableaux
tablecut
tableful
tablemat
tabletop
tabouret
tabulate
tachisme
tachiste
taciturn
tackling
tackroom
tactical
tactless
taenioid
tafferel
taffrail
tagalong
Tahitian
tailback
tailcoat
tailgate
tailings
tailless
tailpipe
tailrace
tailspin
tainture
takeaway
takehome
takeover
takingly
talapoin
talented
talesman
talisman
tallness
tallyman
Talmudic
tamandua
tamanoir
tamarack
tamarind
tamarisk
tamboura
tameable
tameless
tameness
Tamilian
tamperer
tandoori
tangency
tangible
tangibly
tangoist
tanistry
tannable
tantalic
tantalum
tantalus
Tantrism
tantrist
tapdance
tapedeck
tapeless
tapelike
tapeline
tapestry
tapeworm
taphouse
tapwater
tarboosh
tarlatan
Tarpeian
tarragon
tartaric
tartness
tartrate
Tartuffe
taskwork
tasselly
tastebud
tasteful
tattered
tattooer
tautness
tautomer
tautonym
taverner
tawdrily
taxation
taxingly
taxonomy
taxpayer
vacantly
vacation
vaccinal
vaccinia
vacuolar
vagabond
vagility
vagrancy
vainness
valanced
valerate
valerian
Valhalla
valiance
valiancy
validate
validity
valorise
valorous
valuable
valuably
valuator
valvulae
valvular
vambrace
vampiric
vamplate
vanadate
vanadium
vanadous
Vandalic
vaneless
vanguard
vanillin
vanisher
vanquish
vapidity
vaporise
vaporous
vapourer
varactor
variable
variably
variance
varicose
variedly
varietal
variform
variolar
variorum
varletry
vascular
vasculum
vasiform
vastness
vaulting
vauntful
vavasory
vavasour
waesucks
waggoner
wagonage
wagonlit
Wahabism
Wahabite
wainscot
waitress
wakeless
wakening
wakerife
waleknot
Walhalla
walkable
walkaway
walkover
Walkyrie
wallaroo
walleyed
wallfern
wallgame
wallknot
walloper
wallower
wanderer
wanderoo
wantonly
warcloud
wardance
wardenry
wardress
wardrobe
wardroom
wardship
warhorse
wariness
warmness
warpaint
warplane
warragal
warranty
warrener
warrigal
wartweed
wartwort
warweary
warwhoop
washable
washbowl
washroom
wastable
wasteful
watchdog
watchful
watchkey
watchman
waterage
waterbed
waterbus
watergas
waterice
watering
waterish
waterlog
waterloo
waterman
waterski
waterway
watthour
waveband
waveform
waveless
waviness
waxberry
waxcloth
waxiness
waxlight
waxworks
wayfarer
waygoing
xanthate
xanthein
xanthene
xanthine
xanthium
xanthoma
Xantippe
yachting
Yankeefy
yarmulka
yataghan
zabaione
zamindar
zaniness
zarzuela
abacuses
abattoir
Abbaside
abbatial
Abderite
abdicate
abducens
abducent
abductor
abelmosk
aberrant
abetment
abetting
abeyance
abeyancy
abhorred
abhorrer
abidance
abjectly
ablation
ablative
ablution
abnegate
abnormal
abomasum
abomasus
aborally
aborning
abortion
abortive
abradant
abrasion
abrasive
abridger
abrogate
abruptly
abscissa
absentee
absently
absinthe
absolute
absolver
absonant
absorber
absterge
abstract
abstrict

abstruse acrylate scarring sculptor idocrase believer cervical delegate
absurdly actiniae scathing scumming idolater belittle cervices deletion
abundant actinian scattily scurrile idolatry bellbird cesspool delibate
abutilon actinias scatting scurvily idoliser bellbuoy cetacean delicacy
abutment actinide scavenge scutcher idyllist bellcote deadbeat delicate
abuttals actinism scenario scutella oddments bellpull deadener delirium
abutting actinium scenical Adamical odiously bellpush deadfall delivery
ebriated activate sceptred adamitic odograph bellwort deadhead Delphian
Ibsenism actively schedule adaption odometer bellyful deadline delusion
obduracy activism schemata adaptive odontoid beltless deadlock delusive
obdurate activist scheming addendum Odyssean benedick deadness delusory
obedient activity schiedam addition udometer benedict deadwood demagogy
obeisant actually schiller additive aegirine benefice deaerate demander
obituary actuator schizoid adducent aegrotat benignly deafmute demarche
objector acturial schmaltz adductor aeration Benjamin deafness demented
oblation aculeate schnapps adenitis aerially bentwood dealfish dementia
oblatory ecclesia scholium adenoids aeriform benzoate deanship demerara
obligate echinate schooner adequacy aerodyne benzylic dearness demersal
obliging echinoid sciagram adequate aerofoil bequeath deathbed demijohn
oblivion echogram sciatica adespota aerogram berberis deathcap demitted
observer echoless scilicet adherent aerolite berceuse deathray demiurge
obsidian eclectic scimitar adhesion aerolith bereaved debagged demobbed
obsolete ecliptic sciolism adhesive aerology bergamot debarred democrat
obstacle eclosion sciolist adiantum aeronaut beriberi debility demolish
obstruct ecologic scirocco adjacent aeronomy berliner debonair demoness
obtainer economic scirrhus adjuster aerostat Bermudas debugged demoniac
obtected ecstatic scissile adjustor aesthete besieger debutant demonian
obturate ectoderm scission adjutage aestival beslaver decadent demonise
obtusely ectozoon scissors adjutant beadroll besmirch decagram demonism
obtusity iceblink sciurine adjuvant beadsman besotted decanter demotion
ubiquity icebound sciuroid Adlerian beadwork besought deceased demurely
academia icecream sclereid adlibbed beagling bespoken decedent demurred
academic icefield sclerite admitted beamends besprent deceiver demurrer
acanthus iceplant scleroma admonish beanpole bestiary December denarius
acarpous iceskate sclerose adnation bearable bestowal decemvir denature
Accadian icewater sclerous adoption bearably bestrewn decennia denazify
accentor iceyacht scolding adoptive bearings bestride decently dendrite
accepter ichorous scolices adorable bearskin bestrode decigram dendroid
acceptor occasion scombrid adorably beatific betacism decimate denehole
accident occident scoopful adroitly beautify betatron decipher deniable
accolade occluded scoopnet adularia bebopper bethesda decision denounce
accoutre occlusal scopulae adulator becalmed betrayal decisive dentalia
accredit occultly scopulas adultery bechamel betrayer deckhand dentated
accuracy occupant scorcher aduncate bechance bevelled declarer denticle
accurate occupier scornful aduncous becoming beveller declasse departed
accursed occurred scorpion advanced bedabble beverage declutch depicter
accustom ocellate scotfree advisory bedazzle bewigged decolour depictor
aceldama ochreous scotopic advocaat bedeguar bewilder decorate depilate
acentric octarchy Scotsman advocacy bedimmed bezonian decorous deponent
acerbate octaroon scottice advocate bedmaker celeriac decouple deportee
acerbity octonary Scottish advowson bedplate celerity decrease depraved
acervate octoroon scourger adynamia bedstead celibacy decrepit deprival
acescent ocularly scouting adynamic bedstraw celibate decretal deprived
achenial scabbard scrabble bdellium bedtable cellarer decurion depurate
achiever scabious scragend edacious beebread cellaret dedicate deputise
achiness scabrous scragged edentate beechnut cellular deedless deration
achingly scaffold scramble edgeless beeeater cemetery deemster derelict
aciculae scalable scrammed edgeways beefcake cenotaph deeplaid derision
acicular scalawag scrannel edgewise beefwood Cenozoic deepness derisive
aciculas scalepan scraping edginess beeswing centaury deerskin derisory
acidfast scallion scrapped editress beetling centring defector derivate
acidhead scammony scrapper educable beetroot centrism defender derogate
acidosis scampish scratchy educated befallen centrist deferent derriere
acierage scandent scrawler educator befitted centroid deferral describe
acierate Scandian screamer educible befogged centuple deferred deserter
aconitic scandium screechy eduction befriend cephalic deferrer designer
aconitum scanning screener idealess befuddle ceramics defiance desirous
acosmism scansion screever idealise begetter ceramist defilade desolate
acoustic scanties screwtop idealism beggarly cerastes definite despatch
acquaint scantily scribble idealist beginner ceratoid deflower despiser
acrefoot scaphoid scribbly ideality begirded cercaria deforest despotic
acreinch scapulae scrofula ideation begotten cerebral deformed destrier
acridine scapular scrounge identify begrudge cerebrum defrayal destruct
acridity scapulas scrubbed identity beguiler cerement deftness detached
acrimony scarcely scrubber ideogram behemoth ceremony degrease detailed
acrolein scarcity scrutiny ideology beholden cernuous deionise detainee
acrolith scarfpin scudding idiolect beholder cerulean dejected detainer
acrostic scarious scullery idiotism bejabers cerusite delation detector
acrotism scarless scullion idleness belabour cervelat delegacy deterred

deterrer
dethrone
detonate
detoxify
detrital
detritus
deucedly
deuteron
deviance
deviancy
deviator
deviling
devilish
devilism
devilkin
devilled
deviltry
Devonian
devotion
devourer
devoutly
dewberry
dewiness
dewpoint
dewyeyed
dextrine
dextrose
dextrous
eelgrass
eeriness
fearless
fearsome
feasible
feasibly
feastday
feathery
featured
features
febrific
February
feckless
feculent
fedayeen
federate
feeblish
feedback
feedhead
feedpipe
feedtank
feldsher
feldspar
felicity
felinity
fellable
fellahin
fellness
fellowly
felsitic
feminine
feminise
feminism
feminist
feminity
fenberry
fencible
fenestra
feretory
fernshaw
ferocity
ferreter
ferriage
ferritic
ferryman
fervency
fervidly
festally
festival
fetching
feticide
feudally
feverfew
feverish
feverous
fewtrils
gearcase
gefuffle
gelastic
gelatine
gelation
gelidity
gematria
geminate
gemstone
gendarme
generate
generous
genetics
Genevese
genially
genitive
geniture
genocide
genotype
gentrice
geodesic
geodetic
geognosy
geologic
geomancy
geometer
geometry
geophagy
geophone
geophyte
geoponic
Georgian
geotaxis
geraniol
geranium
gerbille
Germanic
germcell
germfree
germinal
gerontic
gestagen
gestural
headache
headachy
headband
headfast
headgear
headlamp
headland
headless
headline
headlock
headlong
headmost
headnote
headrace
headrest
headroom
headsail
headsman
headwind
headword
headwork
heartily
heatedly
heathery
heathhen
heavenly
hebdomad
hebetate
hebetude
hebraise
Hebraism
Hebraist
hecatomb
hedgehog
hedgehop
hedgepig
hedgerow
hedonics
hedonism
hedonist
heedless
heelball
heelless
Hegelian
hegemony
heighten
heirless
heirloom
heirship
heliacal
helicoid
heliosis
heliport
Helladic
hellbent
Hellenic
hellfire
hellhole
helmeted
helminth
helmsman
helotism
helpless
helpmate
helpmeet
henchman
henequen
henparty
henroost
hepatica
hepatise
heptagon
heraldic
heraldry
herbaria
herbless
Hercules
herdbook
herdsman
herdwick
hereaway
heredity
Hereford
hereunto
hereupon
herewith
heritage
hermetic
hernshaw
heroical
herpetic
Hertzian
hesitant
hesitate
Hesperus
hetaerae
hetairai
hexagram
hexapody
hexylene
jealousy
Jehovist
jejunely
jeopardy
jeremiad
Jeremiah
jeroboam
jerrican
jerrycan
jesuitic
jesuitry
jetblack
jetplane
jettison
jewelled
jeweller
kedgeree
keelhaul
keelless
keenness
keepsake
keeshond
kefuffle
keratose
kerchief
kerosene
kerosine
keyboard
keystone
leadenly
leadless
leadsman
leadwork
leafless
leaflike
leanness
leapfrog
learning
leathern
leathery
leavings
lecithin
lecturer
leeboard
lefthand
leftover
leftward
legalese
legalise
legalism
legalist
legality
legatine
legation
legbreak
legendry
legerity
leggings
legguard
legioned
leisured
lemonade
lemurine
lemuroid
lengthen
lenience
leniency
Leninism
Leninist
Leninite
lenitive
lensless
lenticel
lenticle
lepidote
leporine
lethally
lethargy
lettered
leucitic
levanter
levelled
leveller
leverage
leviable
levigate
levirate
levitate
levulose
lewdness
lewisite
meagrely
mealtime
mealworm
mealybug
meanness
meantime
measured
meatball
meatsafe
mechanic
meconium
medalled
medallic
medially
mediator
medicate
medicine
medieval
mediocre
meditate
medusoid
meekness
meetness
megalith
megapode
megawatt
melamine
melanism
melanite
melinite
mellowly
melodeon
melodise
melodist
membered
membrane
mementos
memorial
memorise
memsahib
menarche
mendable
menhaden
menially
meninges
meniscus
menology
menstrua
mensural
menswear
mentally
mephitic
mephitis
merchant
merciful
mercuric
mergence
meridian
meringue
meristem
meristic
merosome
mescalin
mesdames
meshwork
mesially
mesmeric
mesocarp
mesoderm
mesotron
Mesozoic
mesquite
messmate
messuage
metalled
metallic
metamere
metaphor
metayage
metazoan
metazoon
meteoric
methanol
methinks
methodic
methylic
methysis
metonymy
metrical
mezereon
neaptide
Nearctic
nearness
neatherd
neatness
nebulise
nebulium
nebulous
neckband
necklace
neckline
necropsy
necrosis
necrotic
nectared
needfire
needless
needment
negation
negative
negatory
negatron
negligee
Negrillo
negroism
nematode
nematoid
nenuphar
NeoLatin
neomycin
neonatal
neophyte
neoplasm
neoprene
neotenic
neoteric
Nepalese
nepenthe
nephrite
nepotism
nescient
nestling
neurally
neuritic
neuritis
neuronal
neuronic
neuroses
neurosis
neurotic
neutrino
newblown
newcomer
newfound
newlywed
newscast
newsheet
newspeak
newsreel
newsroom
nextdoor
oecology
oeillade
oenology
oenophil
oestrone
oestrous
peaceful
peacocky
peagreen
peardrop
pearlies
pearling
pearlite
pearmain
peasecod
peccable
peccancy
pectines
pectoral
peculate
peculiar
pedagogy
pedalier
pedalled
pedantic
pedantry
pederast
pedestal
pedicled
pedicure
pedigree
pediment
pedipalp
pedology
peduncle
peekaboo
peelings
peephole
peepshow
peerless
Pegasean
pegboard
peignoir
Pekinese
Pelagian
Pelasgic
pelerine
pellagra
pellicle
pellmell
pellucid
pelorism
pembroke
pemmican
penalise
penchant
pendency
pendicle
pendular
pendulum
penitent
penknife
penology
penstock
pentacle
pentagon
pentroof
penumbra
peperino
perceive
perfecto
perforce
perfumer
perianth
pericarp
pericope
periderm
peridium
peridote
perigean
perigyny
perilled
perilous
perilune
perineal
perineum
periodic
periotic
peripety
periplus
perisher
perjurer
perlitic
permeate
peroneal
perorate
peroxide
personae
personal
perspire
persuade
pertness
Peruvian
perverse
pervious
petaline
petalled
petalody
petaloid
petalous
petechia
petiolar
petioled
petition
petrolic
petronel
petrosal
pettifog
petulant
petuntse
reabsorb
reactant
reaction
reactive
readable
readably
readjust
reaffirm
reagency
realness
realtime
reappear
rearlamp
rearmice
rearmost
rearview
rearward
reascend
reasoner
reassert
reassess
reassign
reassure
reawaken
rebelled
rebeller
rebellow
rebuttal
rebutted
rebutter
recapped
receiver
recently
receptor
recharge
recision
reckless
reckoner
recommit
reconvey
recorder
recourse
recovery

recreant
recreate
rectoral
recurred
recusant
redactor
redblind
redbrick
redeemer
redefine
redeless
redeploy
redesign
redfaced
redirect
redistil
redolent
redouble
redshank
redshift
redshirt
redstart
redwater
reedbird
reedling
reedmace
reedpipe
reedstop
reedwren
reefknot
reembark
reemerge
reemploy
reexport
referent
referral
referred
refinery
refitted
reflexed
refluent
reforest
reformed
reformer
regalism
regality
regelate
regicide
regiment
regional
register
registry
regolith
regrater
regrowth
regulate
rehandle
rehearse
rehoboam
reignite
reimpose
reindeer
reinless
reinsert
reinsman
reinsure
reinvest
rejecter
rejigger
rejoicer
rekindle
relation
relative
relaxant
releasee
releaser
releasor
relegate
relevant

reliable
reliably
reliance
reliever
religion
relocate
relucent
relumine
remanent
remedial
remember
reminder
remissly
remittal
remitted
remittee
remitter
remotely
renderer
renegade
renegado
reneguer
reniform
renitent
renounce
renovate
renowned
rentable
renumber
reoccupy
reorient
repairer
repartee
repealer
repeater
repelled
repeller
repenter
repeople
repetend
replacer
replevin
reporter
repotted
repousse
reprieve
reprisal
reproach
reproval
republic
requital
requiter
rerearch
rerecord
reremice
rereward
rescript
research
resemble
reserved
resetter
resettle
resident
residual
residuum
resigned
resinate
resinify
resinoid
resinous
resister
resistor
resolute
resonant
resonate
resorcin
resorter
resource
respects

response
respring
resprung
restcure
restless
restorer
restrain
restrict
resupine
resurvey
retailer
retainer
retarded
retarder
retiarii
reticent
reticule
retiform
retinula
retiring
retorted
retrench
retrieve
retroact
retrorse
reusable
revanche
revealer
reveille
revelled
reveller
revenant
revenger
reverend
reverent
reversal
reverser
reverter
revetted
reviewal
reviewer
reviling
revision
revisory
revivify
revolter
revolute
revolver
rewaking
rewarder
seaboard
seaborne
seachest
seacoast
seacraft
seadrome
seafarer
seafloor
seafront
seagoing
seagreen
seaholly
seahorse
sealable
sealevel
sealskin
sealyham
seamanly
seamless
seamount
seamouse
seamster
seaonion
seapiece
seaplane
seapurse
seaquake
searcher
seascape

seashell
seashore
seasnail
seasnake
seasonal
seasoner
seatbelt
seatrout
seawards
seawater
seawrack
sebesten
secluded
seconder
secondly
secretin
secretly
secretor
sectoral
securely
security
sedately
sedation
sedative
sederunt
sediment
sedition
sedulity
sedulous
seedcake
seedcase
seedcoat
seedcorn
seedfish
seedleaf
seedless
seedling
seedlobe
seedplot
seedsman
seedtime
segreant
seicento
seigneur
seignior
seignory
seizable
seladang
selcouth
selectee
selector
selenate
selenide
selenite
selenium
selfborn
selfheal
selfhelp
selfhood
selfless
selflove
selfmade
selfmate
selfness
selfpity
selfrule
selfsame
selfsown
selfwill
selvedge
semantic
semester
semibull
semidome
seminary
seminude
semiotic
Semitise
Semitism

Semitist
semitone
semolina
semplice
sempster
senarius
senility
sennight
senorita
senseful
sensible
sensibly
sensoria
sensuous
sentence
sentient
sentinel
sentrygo
sepaloid
sepalous
separate
Sephardi
septette
septfoil
septimal
septuple
sequelae
sequence
seraglio
seraphic
seraphim
serenade
serenata
serenely
serenity
serfhood
sergeant
serially
seriatim
sericite
serjeant
serology
serosity
serotine
serpulae
serranid
serrated
servient
servitor
sesamoid
sesterce
setscrew
severely
severity
sewellel
sewerage
sewergas
sewerrat
sexiness
sexology
sextette
sextuple
sexually
teaboard
teabread
teabreak
teacaddy
teachest
teaching
teacloth
teahouse
teammate
teamster
teamwork
teaparty
tearaway
teardrop
tearduct
tearless

teaspoon
teatable
teatowel
technics
tectonic
teenager
teething
teetotal
teetotum
tegmenta
tegument
telecast
telecine
telefilm
telegony
telegram
telemark
telepath
teleport
telethon
teleview
televise
tellable
telltale
telluric
temerity
tempered
temperer
template
temporal
tempting
tenacity
tenacula
tenaille
tenantry
tendence
tendency
tenderly
Tenebrae
tenement
tenesmus
tenonsaw
tenorite
tenotomy
tenpence
tenpenny
tensible
tentacle
tenurial
teocalli
tepidity
teraphim
teratoma
terebene
terebrae
terminal
terminer
terminus
termless
termtime
terraced
terrapin
terraria
terrazzo
terrible
terribly
terrific
tertiary
tesserae
tesseral
testable
testator
testatum
testtube
tetanise
tetchily
tetradic
tetragon
tetrapla

tetrapod
tetrarch
Teutonic
textbook
texthand
textuary
textural
textured
Vedantic
vegetate
vegetive
vehement
veilless
velamina
velarium
velleity
velocity
velskoen
venality
venation
vendetta
vendible
veneerer
venerate
venereal
Venetian
vengeful
venially
venomous
venosity
venously
ventless
venturer
Venusian
veracity
verandah
veratrin
veratrum
verbally
verbatim
verbiage
verboten
verdancy
verderer
verderor
verditer
verdured
verecund
vergence
verifier
veristic
verjuice
vermouth
vernally
vernicle
veronica
verrucae
versicle
vertebra
vertexes
vertical
vertices
verticil
vesicant
vesicate
vesperal
vespiary
vestiary
vestment
vesturer
vesuvian
vexation
vexillum
weakfish
weakling
weakness
weanling
weaponry
wearable

weariful
weaselly
Wedgwood
weedless
weeklong
weeviled
weevilly
weldable
weldment
welladay
wellaway
wellborn
wellbred
welldeck
wellhead
wellknit
wellnigh
wellread
Wellsian
wellworn
Welshman
weregild
werewolf
Wesleyan
westerly
westward
wetlands
wetnurse
wettable
xenogamy
xenolith
yeanling
yearbook
yearling
yearlong
yearning
yeastily
yellowly
yeomanly
yeomanry
yestreen
zealotry
zecchini
zecchino
zemindar
zenithal
zeolitic
zeppelin
affected
affecter
afferent
affiance
affinity
affirmer
afflatus
affluent
afforest
affright
affusion
aflutter
effector
efferent
efficacy
effluent
effluvia
effusion
effusive
eftsoons
offbreak
offdrive
offender
offering
official
offprint
offshoot
offshore
offsider
offstage
ofttimes

sforzato
agaragar
agedness
agential
aggrieve
agiotage
agitator
agitprop
aglimmer
aglitter
agnation
agnostic
agonised
agraphia
agrarian
agrement
agrestic
agrimony
agrology
agronomy
aguishly
egestion
egestive
eggplant
eggshell
egoistic
egomania
Egyptian
ignition
ignitron
ignominy
ignorant
ugliness
chaconne
chainsaw
chairman
chalazae
Chaldaic
Chaldean
chaldron
chalkpit
chambers
chambray
champers
champion
chancery
chandler
chapatti
chapbook
chapelry
chaperon
chapiter
chaplain
chapping
charcoal
charisma
charlady
charlock
charming
charring
Chartism
Chartist
chasseur
chastely
chastise
chastity
chasuble
chateaux
chattily
chatting
chaunter
chauntry
cheapish
checkers
checkout
cheekily
cheerful
cheerily
cheering

Chellean
chemical
chemurgy
chenille
chequers
Cherokee
cherubic
cherubim
chessman
chestnut
Cheyenne
chiasmus
chiastic
chickpea
chiefdom
childbed
childish
children
chiliasm
chiliast
chimaera
chimeric
Chinaman
chinchin
chinless
chipmuck
chipmunk
chipping
chirpily
chirrupy
chitchat
chivalry
chlorate
chloride
chlorine
chlorite
chlorous
choicely
choirboy
choleric
chondrus
chopchop
chopping
chopsuey
choragic
choragus
chorally
chordate
choregic
choregus
choriamb
chorioid
chowchow
christen
christie
Christly
chromate
chromite
chromium
chthonic
chugging
chummily
chumming
chupatti
chupatty
churchly
churinga
churlish
churning
chutzpah
Ghanaian
ghastful
ghettoes
ghoulish
khedival
Khmerian
khuskhus
ohmmeter
phalange

phantasm
phantasy
pharisee
pharmacy
phaseout
pheasant
phenolic
phenylic
Philomel
phlegmon
phonemic
phonetic
phormium
phosgene
phosphor
photogen
photopia
photopic
photopsy
phrasing
phreatic
Phrygian
phthalic
phthisic
phthisis
phyletic
phyllary
phyllode
phylloid
phyllome
physical
physicky
physique
Rhaetian
rhapsode
rhapsody
rheology
rheostat
rhetoric
rhinitis
Rhinodon
rhizopod
rhomboid
rhonchal
rhonchus
rhyolite
rhythmic
shabbily
shabrack
Shabuoth
shadbush
shaddock
shadower
shafting
shagbark
shaggily
shagreen
shagroon
shakable
shakeout
Shaktism
shaleoil
shalloon
shallows
shambles
shameful
shamming
shamrock
shanghai
shantung
shapable
shareout
sharpish
sharpset
shashlik
sheading
shealing
shedding
shedevil

sheepdip
sheepdog
sheepish
sheepked
sheeppen
sheeprun
sheeting
sheikdom
Shekinah
shelduck
shelfful
shelving
Shemitic
shepherd
Sheraton
sherlock
Shetland
shielder
shieling
shiftily
shiftkey
shigella
shikaree
shilling
shimmery
shinbone
shingler
shingles
shinning
shipload
shipmate
shipment
shipping
shipworm
shipyard
shiralee
shirring
shirting
shivaree
shocking
shoddily
shoebill
shoehorn
shoelace
shoeless
shoetree
shofroth
shogging
shooting
shootout
shopbell
shopgirl
shopping
shoptalk
shopworn
shortage
shortarm
shortcut
shortday
shortish
shothole
shoulder
shouldst
showbill
showboat
showcard
showcase
showdown
showgirl
showroom
shrapnel
shredded
shredder
shrewdly
shrewish
shrieval
shrimper
shrinker
shrugged

shrunken
shuddery
shuffler
shunning
shutdown
shutting
thalamic
thalamus
thallium
thalloid
thallous
Thanatos
thanedom
thankful
thankyou
thatcher
thearchy
theistic
thematic
theocrat
theodicy
theogony
theology
theorise
theorist
therefor
thereout
thermion
thermite
thesauri
thespian
thetical
theurgic
thiamine
thickety
thickish
thickset
thievery
thievish
thingamy
thinking
thinness
thinnest
thinning
thinnish
thirlage
thirster
thirteen
thisness
tholepin
thoraces
thoracic
thoraxes
thorough
thoughts
thousand
thraldom
thrasher
thrawart
threader
threaten
threeply
threeway
threnode
threnody
thresher
thridace
thriller
thriving
throated
throbbed
thrombin
thrombus
throstle
throttle
thrummed
thruster
thudding
thuggery

thuggism
thumbpot
thumping
thundery
thurible
thurifer
Thursday
thusness
thwacker
thwarter
thwartly
thyroxin
thyrsoid
whacking
whapping
wharfage
whatever
whatness
wheatear
wheedler
wheelman
wheezily
whenever
wherever
whetting
wheyface
whidding
whiffler
Whiggery
Whiggish
Whiggism
whimbrel
whimwham
whinchat
whinsill
whipcord
whiplash
whiplike
whipping
whipworm
whirring
whiskers
whiskery
whispery
whistler
whiteboy
whitecap
whitefly
whitehot
whitener
whiteout
whitetie
whittret
whizbang
whizzing
whizzkid
whodunit
wholehog
whomever
whooping
whopping
whoredom
whoreson
aigrette
aiguille
airborne
airbrake
airbrush
aircraft
Airedale
airfield
airframe
airiness
airliner
airscrew
airshaft
airspace
airspeed
airstrip

airtight
airwoman
biannual
biassing
biathlon
bibation
biblical
bibulous
biconvex
bicuspid
biddable
biennial
biennium
bifacial
bifocals
bigamist
bigamous
bignonia
bilabial
bilberry
billfold
billhead
billhook
billiard
billyboy
billycan
bilobate
bimanous
bimbashi
binaural
bindweed
binnacle
binomial
bioassay
biocidal
biogenic
biograph
biometry
biomorph
bionomic
bioplasm
bioplast
bioscope
biparous
birdbath
birdcage
birdcall
birdlime
birdseed
birdseye
birthday
bisector
bisexual
bistable
bistoury
bitchily
bitingly
bitterly
bivalent
biweekly
biyearly
ciborium
cicatrix
cicerone
ciceroni
cicisbei
cicisbeo
cidevant
ciliated
cinchona
cincture
cineaste
cinerary
cingulum
cinnabar
cinnamic
cinnamon
cinquain
Circaean

circuity
circular
cirriped
cislunar
citation
citified
cityfied
civilian
civilise
civility
diabasic
diabetes
diabetic
diabolic
diaconal
diagnose
diagonal
diagraph
diallage
dialling
dialogic
dialogue
dialyser
dialyses
dialysis
dialytic
diamante
diameter
dianthus
diapason
diapause
diaphone
diarchal
diarchic
diarrhea
diaspora
diaspore
diastase
diastema
diastole
diatomic
diatonic
diatribe
dicacity
dichasia
dichroic
dicrotic
dictator
dicyclic
didactic
didapper
didymium
didymous
dieldrin
diereses
dieresis
diestock
dietetic
diffract
diffuser
digamist
digamous
digester
diggings
digitate
digitise
dihedral
dihybrid
dilatant
dilation
dilative
dilatory
diligent
dilution
diluvial
diluvian
diluvium
dimerism
dimerous

diminish
dimmable
dinerout
dingdong
dinornis
dinosaur
diocesan
dioecism
diopside
dioptase
dioptric
dioramic
dioritic
diphenyl
diplogen
diploidy
diplomat
diplopia
dipnoous
dipstick
dipteral
dipteran
directly
director
dirigism
diriment
disabuse
disagree
disallow
disarray
disaster
disbench
disbound
disburse
disciple
disclaim
disclose
discount
discover
discreet
discrete
discrown
diseased
disendow
disfrock
disgorge
disgrace
disguise
dishevel
disinter
disjoint
disjunct
dislodge
disloyal
dismally
dismount
disorder
dispatch
dispense
disperse
dispirit
displace
displant
displode
displume
disposal
disposer
dispread
disprize
disproof
disprove
disquiet
disseise
disserve
dissever
dissolve
dissuade
distally
distance
distaste
distinct
distract
distrain
distrait
distress
district
distrust
disunion
disunite
disunity
disusage
disvalue
ditheism
ditheist
ditherer
dittybag
dittybox
diuresis
diuretic
divagate
divalent
divebomb
dividend
dividivi
dividual
divinely
divinise
divinity
division
divisive
divorcee
eighteen
eighthly
eighties
fibrilla
fibrosis
fibrotic
fiddling
fidelity
fiducial
fiendish
fiercely
fiftieth
fiftyish
fighting
figurant
figurine
filagree
filament
filariae
filarial
filature
filefish
filially
filiform
filigree
Filipina
Filipino
filmgoer
filmstar
filthily
filtrate
fimbriae
finalise
finalism
finalist
finality
finedraw
fineness
finespun
fingered
finisher
finitely
finitude
finnesko
firearms
fireback
fireball
firebird
fireboat
firebomb
firebrat
fireclay
firedamp
fireeyed
firehose
firelock
fireopal
fireplug
fireship
fireside
firetrap
fireweed
firewood
firework
firmness
firstaid
fiscally
fishable
fishball
fishbone
fishbowl
fishcake
fishfarm
fishglue
fishhawk
fishhook
fishless
fishmeal
fishpond
fishtail
fishwife
fissiped
fistiana
fistical
fistulae
fistular
fitfully
fivefold
fivestar
fixation
fixative
giantess
giantism
giftbook
gigantic
gillaroo
gilthead
gimcrack
gimmicky
gingerly
gingival
gipsydom
gipsyism
girasole
girlhood
giveaway
hibernal
hibiscus
hiccough
hickwall
hideaway
hidrosis
hidrotic
hidyhole
hielaman
hierarch
hieratic
highball
highborn
highbred
highbrow
higherup
highjack
highland
highlows
highmost
highness
highrise
highroad
hightail
hightest
hijacker
hilarity
hillfort
hillocky
hillside
himation
hinderer
hindlegs
hindmost
hinduise
Hinduism
hipflask
hipsters
hireable
hireling
hirrient
Hispanic
histogen
historic
hitherto
jiggered
jingoish
jingoism
jingoist
jipijapa
jiujitsu
kibitzer
kickback
kickshaw
kidglove
killdeer
kilogram
kilowatt
kindless
kindling
kindness
kinesics
kinetics
kingbird
kingbolt
kingcrab
kingfish
kinghood
kinglike
kingship
kingsize
kinkajou
kinsfolk
kissable
kisscurl
libation
libatory
libeccio
libelled
libellee
libeller
liberate
libretti
libretto
licensed
licensee
licenser
lichened
lichenin
lichgate
licorice
liegeman
lifebelt
lifeboat
lifebuoy
lifeless
lifelike
lifeline
lifelong
lifesize
lifetime
lifework
liftable
ligament
ligation
ligature
lighting
lightish
ligneous
lignitic
ligulate
likeable
likeness
likewise
limbless
limekiln
limerick
limetwig
limewash
limitary
limonite
limpidly
limpness
linchpin
lineally
linearly
linesman
lingerer
lingerie
linguist
liniment
Linnaean
linoleum
linstock
lintseed
lipogram
lipomata
lipsalve
lipstick
liquidly
liripoop
listener
listless
literacy
literary
literate
literati
litharge
litigant
litigate
littlego
littling
littoral
liturgic
liveable
liveborn
livelily
livelong
liveried
liverish
livewire
lividity
lixivium
miasmata
miasmous
micellar
microbar
microbic
microdot
micrurgy
midbrain
middling
midfield
midlands
midnight
midpoint
midships
midwives
mightest
mightily
migraine
migrator
mildness
milepost
Milesian
militant
military
militate
milkmaid
milkweed
milkwort
millhand
milliard
milliary
millibar
millieme
milliner
millpond
millrace
Miltonic
mimester
mimicked
mimicker
minacity
minatory
mindless
minimise
minister
ministry
Minoress
Minorite
minority
Minotaur
minstrel
mintmark
minutely
minutiae
mirepoix
mirthful
misalign
misapply
misbegot
miscarry
miscegen
mischief
miscible
miscount
misdealt
misdoing
misdoubt
miserere
misgiven
misguide
misheard
mishmash
Mishnaic
misjudge
mismatch
misnomer
misogamy
misogyny
misology
misplace
misprint
misprise
misprize
misquote
misshape
missilry
misspell
misspelt
misspend
misspent
misstate
mistaken
misthink
mistreat
mistress
mistrial
mistrust
misusage
miswrite
Mithraic
mitigant
mitigate
mittened
mittimus
mitzvoth
niceness
nickelic
nicknack
nickname
nicotian
nicotine
nielloed
niggling
nightcap
nighthag
nightjar
nightowl
nihilism
nihilist
nihility
nimbused
ninefold
ninepins
nineteen
nineties
nitrogen
oilcloth
oilfield
oilfired
oiliness
oilstone
ointment
oiticica
piacular
pianiste
piassava
picaroon
picayune
pickerel
picketer
pickings
picklock
picnicky
pictures
piddling
piecrust
piedmont
piercing
piffling
pigswill
pilaster
pilchard
pileated
pilewort
pilferer
piliform
pillager
pillwort
pilosity
pilotage
pilsener
pimiento
pinafore
pinaster
pincenez
pinchers
Pindaric
pinecone
pinewood
pinkness
pinmoney
pinnacle
pinnated
pinniped
pinnular
pinochle
pinpoint
pinprick
pintable
pintsize
pinwheel
pipeclay
pipefish
pipeline
piperack
piperine
piquancy
pirarucu
piscator
piscinae
pishogue
pisiform
pisolite
pitiable
pitiably
pitiless
pittance
pitviper
pivotman
pixieish
pixiness
pizzeria
ribaldry
ribbonry
ribgrass
ribosome
ricebird
ricercar
richness
rickrack
rickshaw
ricochet
riddance
rideable
ridgeway
ridicule
Riesling
rifeness
riffraff
rifleman
rigadoon
rightful
rightist
rigidify
rigidity
rigorism
rigorist
rigorous
rimbrake
rimester
ringbark
ringbolt
ringbone
ringdove
ringmain
ringneck
ringroad
ringside
ringtail
ringwall
ringworm
rinsings
riparian
ripeness
ritually
rivalled
rivelled
riverain
riverbed
riverine
riverman
riverway

Siberian
sibilant
sibilate
Sicilian
sickener
sickerly
sickflag
sicklist
sickness
sickroom
sidearms
sideband
sidedish
sidedoor
sidedrum
sidehead
sidekick
sideline
sideling
sidelong
sidenote
sidereal
siderite
sideroad
sideshow
sideslip
sidesman
sidestep
sideview
sidewalk
sideward
sideways
sidewind
sidewise
siftings
sigmatic
signally
signpost
silencer
silently
silicane
silicate
silicide
silicify
silicone
silkworm
sillabub
silphium
Silurian
siluroid
silvatic
silverly
similise
simoniac
simonist
simplify
simplism
simulant
simulate
Sinaitic
sinapism
sinciput
sinecure
sinfonia
sinfully
singable
singeing
singsong
singular
sinicise
sinister
sinkable
sinkhole
sinology
sinophil
sinusoid
siphonal
siphonet
siphonic
sirenian
siriasis
sirvente
sisterly
sitarist
sithence
sitology
situated
sitzbath
sixpence
sixpenny
sixtieth
sizeable
sizzling
ticklish
tickseed
ticktack
ticktock
tidegate
tideland
tideless
tidelock
tidemark
tidemill
tidewave
tidiness
tiebreak
tigereye
tigerish
tightwad
tilefish
tillable
tiltyard
timbered
timeball
timebomb
timefuse
timeless
timework
timeworn
timidity
timorous
timously
tincture
tingeing
tininess
tinkerer
tinnitus
tinplate
tinselly
tinsmith
tinstone
tintless
tipstaff
tireless
tiresome
titanate
titaness
titanism
titanite
titanium
tithable
titivate
titmouse
tittuped
tittuppy
uintaite
viameter
viaticum
vibrancy
vibrator
vibrissa
viburnum
vicarage
vicarate
vicarial
vicinage
vicinity
victoria
victress
victuals
Viennese
Vietcong
Vietminh
viewable
viewless
vigilant
vigneron
vignette
vigorous
vileness
vilifier
vilipend
villadom
villager
villainy
villatic
vincible
vinculum
vinegary
vineyard
vinosity
vinously
vintager
violable
violably
violator
violence
viperine
viperish
viperous
virement
virginal
Virginia
viricide
viridian
viridity
virilism
virility
virology
virtuosa
virtuosi
virtuoso
virtuous
virulent
viscacha
visceral
viscidly
viscount
Visigoth
visional
visitant
visually
vitalise
vitalism
vitalist
vitality
vitellin
vitellus
vitiable
vitiator
vitiligo
vitreous
vituline
vivacity
vivarium
vivifier
vivisect
vixenish
vizarded
vizcacha
wickedly
wideeyed
wideness
wifehood
wifeless
wifelike
wigmaker
wildeyed
wildfire
wildfowl
wildlife
wildness
wildwood
wilfully
wiliness
williwaw
windburn
windcone
windfall
windgall
windlass
windless
windmill
windowed
windpipe
windrose
windsail
windsock
windward
winepalm
wineshop
wineskin
wingbeat
wingcase
wingless
wingspan
winnable
winnings
winnower
winterly
wintrily
wiredraw
wirehair
wireless
wirework
wireworm
wirewove
wiriness
wiseacre
wiseness
wishbone
wishwash
wistaria
wisteria
witchelm
witchery
witchety
witching
withdraw
withdrew
withheld
withhold
wizardly
wizardry
yielding
zibeline
ziggurat
zinckify
zincking
zirconia
djellaba
ejection
ejective
Akkadian
ekistics
okeydoke
skeletal
skeleton
skerrick
sketcher
skewback
skewbald
skewness
skiagram
skidding
skilless
skilling
skimmilk
skimming
skimpily
skindeep
skinfood
skinhead
skinless
skinning
skipjack
skipping
skirmish
skirting
skislope
skittish
skittles
skullcap
skylight
skypilot
skyscape
skywards
alacrity
alarmist
albacore
Albanian
albinism
alburnum
alcahest
alchemic
aldehyde
alderman
Alderney
aleatory
alebench
alehouse
aleurone
alewives
alfresco
algicide
algidity
alginate
algology
Algonkin
algorism
alguazil
alienage
alienate
alienism
alienist
alizarin
alkahest
alkalies
alkalify
alkaline
alkaloid
allegory
alleluia
allergen
allergic
alleyway
alliance
allnight
allocate
allodial
allodium
allogamy
allopath
allotted
allottee
allround
allspice
allusion
allusive
alluvial
alluvion
alluvium
almagest
almanack
almighty
alogical
alopecia
alphabet
alpinism
alpinist
Alsatian
although
altitude
altruism
altruist
alumroot
alveolar
alveolus
blabbing
blackboy
blackcap
blackfly
blacking
blackish
blackleg
blackout
blacktie
blacktop
bladdery
blahblah
blamable
blamably
blameful
blandish
blankety
blastema
blastoff
blastoid
blastula
blatancy
blazoner
blazonry
bleacher
bleakish
blearily
bleeding
Blenheim
blesbuck
blessing
blighter
blimpish
blindage
blinding
blinkers
blinking
blissful
blistery
blithely
blizzard
blockade
blockage
blockish
blondish
bloodily
bloodred
bloomers
bloomery
blooming
blossomy
blotting
blowball
blowfish
blowhard
blowhole
blowlamp
blowpipe
blubbery
bludgeon
bluebell
bluebird
bluechip
bluecoat
bluefish
blueness
bluenose
blueweed
blurrily
blurring
blushful
blustery
cladding
claimant
clambake
clammily
clamming
clanging
clangour
clannish
clanship
clansman
clapping
claptrap
claqueur
clarence
clarinet
classics
classify
clavicle
clawback
claymore
cleancut
cleaning
cleanser
clearcut
clearing
clearway
cleavage
cleavers
clematis
clemency
clerical
clerihew
clerkdom
clerkess
cleverly
climatic
clincher
clinical
clinking
clipclop
clippers
clipping
cliquish
cliquism
cloddish
clodpole
clodpoll
clogging
cloister
clopclop
closeset
closeted
clothier
clothing
clotting
cloudily
cloudlet
clownery
clownish
clubbing
clubfoot
clubhaul
clubland
clueless
clumsily
clupeoid
clustery
clypeate
elatedly
eldorado
eldritch
election
elective
electret
electric
electron
electrum
elegance
elegancy
elenchus
elenctic
elephant
elevated
elevator
eleventh
elfarrow
elflocks
eligible
eligibly
elkhound
ellipses
ellipsis
elliptic
elongate
eloquent
flabella
flagella
flagging
flagpole
flagrant
flagship
flambeau
flamenco
flamingo
flanerie
flapjack
flapping
flashgun
flashily
flashing
flatboat
flatfeet
flatfish
flatfoot
flathead
flatiron
flatling
flatmate
flatness
flatrace
flattery
flattest
flattish
flatware
flatways
flatwise
flatworm
flautist
flawless
flaxseed
fleabane
fleabite
fleawort
flection
fleeting
fleshfly
fleshpot
fletcher
flexible
flexibly
flexuose
flexuous
flexural
flickery
flimflam
flimsily
flincher
flinders
flintily
flipflap
flipflop
flippant

flipping
flipside
flitting
floatage
floating
floccose
floccule
flocculi
flockbed
flogging
floodlit
floodway
flooring
floppily
flopping
florally
floridly
florigen
flotilla
flounder
flourish
flowered
flowerer
floweret
flubbing
fluellin
fluently
fluepipe
fluidics
fluidify
fluidise
fluidity
flummery
fluoride
fluorine
fluorite
fluttery
flyblown
flypaper
flywheel
glabella
glabrous
glaciate
gladdest
gladding
gladhand
gladioli
gladness
gladsome
glancing
glanders
glandule
glassful
glassily
glassine
glaucoma
glaucous
glaziery
gleaning
gleesome
glibness
glissade
glittery
gloaming
globally
globular
globulin
gloomily
gloriole
glorious
glossary
glossily
glossina
glowworm
gloxinia
glucagon
glucinum
glummest
glumness

glutting
gluttony
glycerin
glycerol
glyceryl
glycogen
glyconic
glyptics
illation
illative
illfated
illiquid
illtimed
illtreat
illumine
illusage
illusion
illusive
illusory
Illyrian
ilmenite
klephtic
klondike
klystron
oldtimer
oldworld
oleander
oleaster
olibanum
oligarch
oligomer
oliphant
olympiad
Olympian
placable
placably
placeman
placenta
placidly
plagiary
plaguily
plaiding
plaister
planchet
plangent
planking
plankton
planning
plantain
planulae
planular
plastery
plastics
plastron
plateaux
plateful
platelet
platform
platinic
platinum
platonic
platting
platypus
plaudits
playable
playback
playbill
playbook
playgirl
playgoer
playmate
playroom
playsuit
playtime
pleading
pleasant
pleasing
pleasure
plebeian

plectrum
pleinair
pleonasm
plethora
pleurisy
pliantly
plighted
plimsoll
Pliocene
plodding
plopping
plotting
plougher
pluckily
plugging
plumaged
plumbago
plumbate
plumbing
plumbism
plumelet
plumiped
plumpish
plumular
plurally
plussage
plutonic
pluvious
slabbing
slagging
slagheap
slamming
slangily
slapbang
slapdash
slapjack
slapping
slashing
slattern
Slavonic
sleazily
sledding
sleepily
sleeping
slideway
slightly
slimmest
slimming
slimmish
slimness
slinkily
slipcase
slipform
slipknot
slipover
slippage
slippery
slipping
slipring
sliproad
slipshod
slipslop
slithery
slitting
slobbery
slobbish
slobland
sloeeyed
slogging
sloppail
sloppily
slopping
slopshop
slopwork
slothful
slotting
sloucher
slovenly
slovenry

slowdown
slowness
slowpoke
slowworm
slubbing
slugabed
sluggard
slugging
sluggish
slumbery
slumming
slurring
sluttish
slyboots
ulcerate
ulcerous
ulterior
ultimacy
ultimata
ultimate
ultraism
ultraist
amadavat
amaranth
amazedly
ambiance
ambience
ambition
ambivert
ambrosia
ambulant
ambulate
ambusher
amenable
amenably
American
amethyst
amiantus
amicable
amicably
amitosis
amitotic
ammoniac
ammonify
ammonite
ammonium
amnesiac
amniotic
amoebean
amoeboid
amorally
amoretti
amoretto
amortise
amperage
amphibia
amphipod
amphorae
amphoras
ampullae
amputate
amusedly
amygdala
emaciate
embalmer
embattle
embedded
embezzle
embitter
emblazon
embolden
embolism
embosser
embracer
embussed
emceeing
emendate
emergent
emeritus

emersion
emetical
emigrant
emigrate
eminence
eminency
emissary
emission
emissive
emitting
Emmental
empathic
empeople
emphases
emphasis
emphatic
employee
employer
empoison
emporium
empurple
empyreal
empyrean
emulator
emulgent
emulsify
emulsion
emulsive
emulsoid
imaginal
imagines
imbecile
imitable
imitator
immanent
immature
immersed
imminent
immingle
immobile
immodest
immolate
immortal
immunise
immunity
impacted
impanate
imparity
impelled
impeller
imperial
imperium
impetigo
impishly
impledge
implicit
impolder
impolicy
impolite
imponent
importer
imposing
imposter
impostor
impotent
imprimis
imprison
improper
improver
impudent
impugner
impunity
impurely
impurity
omadhaum
omelette
omission
omitting
ommateum

omnivore
omophagy
omoplate
omphalic
omphalos
smallage
smallfry
smallish
smallpox
smaltite
smarmily
smartish
smashing
smelling
smeltery
smithers
smithery
smocking
smokable
smoothen
smoothie
smoothly
smothery
smoulder
smudgily
smuggler
smugness
smuttily
umbonate
umbrella
umbrette
umpirage
umptieth
anabases
anabasis
anabatic
anabolic
anaconda
anaerobe
anaglyph
anagogic
analcime
analcite
analecta
analects
analogic
analogue
analyser
analyses
analysis
analytic
anapaest
anaphase
anaphora
anarchic
anasarca
anathema
anatomic
ancestor
ancestry
anchoret
andesine
andesite
androgen
anecdote
anechoic
aneurism
aneurysm
angelica
Anglican
angstrom
anhedral
aniconic
animally
animator
anisette
ankerite
ankylose
annalist

annotate
announce
annually
annulate
annulled
anorexia
anorexic
anorthic
anourous
anserine
answerer
anteater
antecede
antedate
antefixa
antelope
antennae
antennal
antennas
antepost
anterior
anteroom
anthelia
anthemia
antheral
anthesis
anthozoa
antibody
antidote
antihero
antilogy
antimask
antimony
antinode
antinomy
antiphon
antipode
antipole
antipope
antisera
antitype
antlered
antrorse
anyplace
anything
anywhere
enaction
enactive
enarched
encaenia
enceinte
encipher
encircle
enclitic
enclothe
encomion
encomium
encrinal
encrinic
encroach
encumber
encyclic
endamage
endanger
endemism
endermic
endocarp
endoderm
endogamy
endogeny
endorsee
endorser
endostea
endozoic
endozoon
endpaper
energise
enervate
enfeeble

enfetter
enfilade
enforcer
enforest
engaging
engender
engineer
enginery
engirdle
engramma
engraver
enkindle
enlarger
enneagon
enormity
enormous
enquirer
enricher
enrolled
ensample
ensconce
ensemble
ensheath
enshrine
enshroud
ensiform
ensigncy
ensilage
enslaver
ensphere
enswathe
entailer
entangle
entellus
enterate
enthalpy
enthrall
enthrone
entirely
entirety
entoderm
entoptic
entozoic
entozoon
entracte
entrails
entrance
entreaty
entrench
entrepot
entresol
enuresis
enuretic
envelope
enviable
enviably
environs
envisage
envision
enzootic
gnathite
gneissic
gnomonic
inaction
inactive
inasmuch
inceptor
inchmeal
inchoate
inchworm
incident
incision
incisive
incitant
incivism
included
incoming
increase
increate

incubate
incurred
indagate
indebted
indecent
Indiaman
indicant
indicate
indicium
indigene
indigent
indirect
indocile
indolent
inductee
inductor
indulger
induline
indurate
indusium
industry
inedible
inedited
inequity
inerrant
inertial
inexpert
infamise
infamous
infantry
infector
inferior
infernal
inferred
infilter
infinite
infinity
infirmly
inflamer
inflated
inflator
inflatus
inflexed
inflight
influent
informal
informed
informer
infrared
infringe
infusion
ingather
ingrowth
inguinal
inhalant
inherent
inhesion
inhumane
inimical
iniquity
initiate
injector
inkiness
inkstand
inlander
innately
innocent
innovate
innuendo
inoculum
inositol
inquirer
insanely
insanity
inscient
inscribe
inscroll
insecure
inserted

insignia
insolate
insolent
insomnia
insomuch
insphere
inspired
inspirer
inspirit
instable
instance
instancy
instinct
instruct
insulant
insulate
insulter
insurant
intaglio
intarsia
integral
intended
intently
interact
interbed
intercom
intercut
interest
interior
intermit
intermix
internal
internee
Interpol
interred
interrex
intersex
intertie
interval
interwar
inthrall
intimacy
intimate
intimism
intitule
intonate
intrados
intrench
intrepid
intrigue
intromit
introrse
intruder
intubate
inundate
inurbane
invasion
invasive
invected
inveigle
inventor
inverted
inverter
investor
inviable
inviting
invocate
involute
inwardly
knackery
knapping
knapsack
knapweed
kneedeep
kneehigh
kneehole
kneejerk
knickers
knightly

knitting
knitwear
knocking
knockout
knothole
knotting
knotwork
knowable
mnemonic
onceover
oncidium
oncology
oncoming
onehorse
onepiece
onesided
onetrack
onlooker
ontogeny
ontology
onychite
snackbar
snagging
snakepit
snapbrim
snaplink
snappily
snapping
snappish
snapshot
snatcher
snazzily
sneakily
sneakish
sneeshan
sniffily
sniffler
sniffles
sniggler
snippety
snipping
snipsnap
snitcher
snobbery
snobbish
snobbism
snogging
snootily
snowball
snowbird
snowboot
snowdrop
snowfall
snowless
snowlike
snowline
snowshoe
snubbing
snuffbox
snuffers
snuffler
snuffles
snuggery
snugness
unabated
unaneled
unawares
unbacked
unbarred
unbeaten
unbelief
unbiased
unbidden
unbolted
unbottle
unbridle
unbroken
unbuckle
unburden

unburied
unbutton
uncalled
uncandid
uncapped
uncaused
unchancy
unchaste
unchurch
uncially
unciform
uncinate
unclench
unclinch
unclothe
uncoined
uncommon
uncouple
uncreate
unctuous
underact
underage
underarm
underbid
undercut
underdid
underdog
underfur
underlap
underlay
underlet
underlie
underlip
underman
underpin
underrun
undersea
underset
undertow
underway
undraped
undreamt
undulant
undulate
unearned
uneasily
unedited
unending
unerring
unevenly
unfading
unfairly
unfasten
unfetter
unfilial
unfitted
unforced
unformed
unfreeze
unfrozen
unfunded
ungainly
unglazed
ungotten
ungulate
unhinged
unhoused
uniaxial
unicycle
unifilar
unionise
unionism
unionist
unipolar
uniquely
unisonal
unitedly
univalve
universe

univocal
unjustly
unkennel
unkindly
unkingly
unlawful
unleaded
unlearnt
unlikely
unlimber
unlinked
unlisted
unloader
unloosen
unlovely
unmanned
unmarked
unmeetly
unmuffle
unmuzzle
unopened
unpaired
unpegged
unperson
unpinned
unplaced
unreason
unriddle
unrigged
unroofed
unsaddle
unsealed
unseated
unseeded
unseeing
unseemly
unsettle
unshaped
unsocial
unsought
unsprung
unstable
unstably
unstated
unsteady
unstring
unstrung
unstuffy
unsuited
unsunned
unswathe
untangle
untapped
untaught
untented
untether
unthread
unthrift
unthrone
untidily
untimely
untitled
untoward
unvalued
unversed
unvoiced
unwanted
unwarily
unwashed
unweaned
unwieldy
unwisdom
unwisely
unwished
unwonted
unwordly
unworthy
unzipped
aoristic

boarding
boastful
boatbill
boatdeck
boathook
boatload
bobbinet
bobbypin
bobbysox
bobolink
bobwheel
bobwhite
bodement
bodiless
Bodleian
bodyshop
bodywork
Boeotian
bogeyman
bohemian
boldface
boldness
bollworm
bolthole
boltrope
bombsite
bondmaid
bondmans
bondsman
bonefish
bonehead
boneless
bonemeal
boneyard
bonhomie
boniface
boniness
bonspiel
bontebok
bookcase
bookends
bookland
booklice
booklore
bookmark
bookpost
bookrest
bookwork
bookworm
bootjack
bootlace
bootlast
bootless
boottree
boracite
Bordeaux
bordello
borderer
borecole
borehole
boringly
borrower
bosseyed
botanise
botanist
botflies
botryoid
bottomry
botulism
botyrose
bouffant
boughten
bouillon
bouncily
bouncing
boundary
bourgeon
boursier
bourtree

boutique
bouzouki
bowfront
bowsprit
boxpleat
boyishly
coachdog
coachman
coaction
coactive
coagulum
coaldust
coalesce
coalfish
coalhole
coalmine
coalsack
coarsely
coatrack
coatroom
coauthor
cobaltic
cobblers
cobwebby
coccyges
cochleae
cochlear
cockatoo
cockboat
cockcrow
cockerel
cockeyed
cockloft
cockshut
cocksure
cocktail
codifier
codpiece
codriver
coelomic
coenobia
coenzyme
coercion
coercive
cofactor
cogently
cogitate
cognomen
cognosce
cognovit
cogwheel
coherent
cohesion
cohesive
coiffeur
coiffure
coincide
coistrel
cokernut
colander
coldness
coleseed
coleslaw
colewort
coliform
coliseum
collagen
collapse
collared
collator
colleger
colliery
collogue
colloquy
collyria
colonial
colonise
colonist
colophon

colossal
colossus
coloured
colubrid
columnal
columnar
columned
comatose
combings
comeback
comedian
comedist
comedown
cometary
commando
commence
commerce
commoner
commoney
commonly
communal
commuter
compages
compiler
complain
compleat
complete
complice
complier
compline
composed
composer
compound
compress
comprise
computer
conation
conative
concasse
conceder
conceive
concerti
concerto
concetti
concetto
conchate
conchoid
conclave
conclude
concrete
condense
condylar
conferee
conferva
confetti
confider
confiner
confines
conflate
conflict
confound
confrere
confront
congener
conglobe
congress
congreve
conidial
conidium
coniform
conjoint
conjugal
conjunct
conjurer
conjuror
conniver
conoidal
conquest
conserve

consider
consoler
consomme
conspire
constant
construe
consular
consumer
contagia
contango
contempt
contents
contessa
continua
continue
continuo
contline
contorno
contract
contrail
contrary
contrast
contrate
contrite
contrive
conurbia
convener
convenor
converge
converse
convexly
conveyer
conveyor
convince
convolve
convulse
cookbook
coolabah
coolibah
coolness
coonskin
cooption
cooptive
coplanar
copperas
copulate
copybook
copyedit
copyhold
coquetry
coquette
coracoid
cordless
cordovan
corduroy
cordwain
cordwood
corelate
corkwing
corkwood
cornball
corneous
cornetcy
cornetti
cornetto
corniced
corniche
cornicle
cornific
cornpone
coronach
coronary
coronoid
corporal
corridor
corrival
corselet
corseted
corsetry

cortical
cortices
corundum
corvette
Corybant
coryphee
cosecant
cosiness
cosmetic
cosmical
costmary
costplus
costpush
costumer
cotenant
cothurni
cotillon
cotquean
Cotswold
cottager
cottagey
couchant
couching
couldest
coulisse
coumarin
countess
coupling
courante
coursing
courtesy
courtier
couscous
cousinly
covalent
covenant
coverage
coverall
covering
coverlet
covertly
covetous
cowardly
cowberry
cowgrass
coworker
coxalgia
coxswain
cozenage
Docetism
Docetist
docilely
docility
dockland
dockside
dockyard
doctoral
doctrine
document
doddered
dodderer
dogberry
dogeared
dogfaced
dogfight
doggedly
doggerel
doghouse
dogmatic
dogooder
dogsbody
dogshore
dogtired
dogtooth
dogwatch
dogwhelk
doldrums
dolerite
dolesome

dolomite
doloroso
dolorous
domestic
domicile
dominant
dominate
domineer
dominion
dominoes
donation
Donatism
Donatist
donative
donatory
donought
doomsday
doomsman
doomster
doorbell
doorcase
doorknob
doornail
doorpost
doorsill
doorstep
doorstop
dooryard
dopiness
dormancy
dormouse
dorsally
dotation
dotingly
dotterel
douanier
doubloon
doubtful
doughboy
doughnut
doumpalm
dourness
dovecote
dovetail
dowdyish
dowelled
downbeat
downcast
downcome
downfall
downhaul
downhill
downland
downmost
downpipe
downpour
downtime
downtown
downturn
downward
downwind
doxology
doziness
eohippus
eolithic
foamless
focalise
focusing
focussed
foetidly
fogbound
foldaway
foldboat
folderol
foliaged
folklore
folkmoot
folksong
folktale

follicle
follower
followon
followup
fomenter
fondling
fondness
fontanel
fontange
foodless
foolscap
football
footbath
footfall
footgear
foothill
foothold
footless
footling
footmark
footmuff
footnote
footpace
footpath
footpost
footrace
footrest
footrope
footrule
footslog
footsore
footstep
footwear
footwork
foramina
forborne
forcedly
forcefed
forceful
forcible
forcibly
fordable
fordoing
forebear
forebode
forecast
foredeck
foredoom
foreedge
forefeel
forefelt
forefoot
foregoer
foregone
forehand
forehead
foreknew
foreknow
forelady
foreland
forelock
foremast
foremost
forename
forenoon
forensic
forepart
forepast
forepeak
foreplay
foresaid
foresail
foreseen
foreshow
foreside
foreskin
forestal
forestay
forested

forester
forestry
foretell
foretime
foretold
forewarn
forewent
foreword
foreyard
forgiven
forgoing
forklift
formalin
formally
formerly
formless
formroom
formulae
formulas
formwork
fornices
forrader
forsaken
forsooth
forspeak
forspent
forswear
forswore
forsworn
fortieth
fortress
fortuity
fortyish
forwards
forzando
fosterer
fougasse
foulness
founding
fountain
fourball
foureyes
fourfold
fourleaf
fourpart
foursome
fourstar
fourteen
fourthly
foveolae
fowlpest
foxglove
foxhound
foxiness
foxshark
goadster
goalkick
goalline
goalpost
goatfish
goatherd
goatling
goatmoth
goatskin
Gobelins
godawful
godchild
Godspeed
godwards
gogetter
Goidelic
goingson
goitrous
Golconda
golddust
goldenly
goldfish
goldfoil
goldleaf

goldmine
goldrush
golfclub
golliwog
gonfalon
gonidial
gonidium
goodness
goodtime
goodwife
goodwill
goodyear
goofball
goosegog
gorgeous
gorgonia
gormless
gossamer
gossiper
gossipry
gossypol
gourmand
goutweed
goutwort
governor
gownsman
hoarding
hoarsely
hobbitry
hobbyist
hocktide
hocusing
hocussed
Hogmanay
hogsback
hogshead
holdback
holdfast
holdover
holidays
holiness
holistic
hollands
hollowly
Holocene
hologram
holozoic
holstein
homebody
homeborn
homebred
homebrew
homefelt
homeland
homeless
homelike
homemade
homesick
homespun
hometown
homeward
homework
homicide
hominoid
homodont
homogamy
homogeny
homology
homonymy
homuncle
honestly
honeybee
honeydew
honeypot
honorary
honourer
hoodwink
hoofbeat
hookworm

hooligan
hoosegow
hopeless
Horatian
hormonal
hornbeam
hornbill
hornbook
hornfels
hornless
hornpipe
hornrims
horntail
hornworm
hornwort
horologe
horology
horrible
horribly
horridly
horrific
horsebox
horsecar
horsefly
horseman
hosepipe
hospital
hostelry
hotchpot
hotelier
hothouse
hotplate
hotpress
hourlong
houseboy
housedog
housefly
houseful
houseman
housetop
hoverfly
howitzer
iodinate
iodoform
iotacism
jobation
jocosely
jocosity
jocundly
jodhpurs
joinable
jointure
jokingly
jolthead
Jonathan
jongleur
jovially
joyfully
joyously
joystick
Kohinoor
kohlrabi
kolinsky
komitaji
Komsomol
korfball
kourbash
loadline
loadstar
loanable
loanword
loathful
loathing
lobation
lobbyist
lobeline
loblolly
lobotomy
lobulate

localise
localism
locality
locative
lockable
lockfast
lockknit
lockstep
locofoco
locomote
loculate
locution
locutory
lodestar
lodgings
lodgment
lodicule
logician
logistic
logogram
logotype
loiterer
Lollardy
lollipop
lollypop
lomentum
Londoner
loneness
lonesome
longboat
longeron
longeval
longhair
longhand
longhorn
longness
longship
longsome
longstop
longterm
longtime
longueur
longwall
longwave
longways
longwise
lookeron
loonybin
loophole
loosebox
loosener
lopeared
lopgrass
lopsided
lordless
lordling
lordosis
lordotic
lordship
loricate
lorikeet
lothario
loudness
louvered
lovebird
loveknot
loveless
lovelily
lovelock
lovelorn
lovenest
loveseat
lovesick
lovesome
lovesong
lovingly
lowering
lowgrade
lowlevel

lowlying
loyalist
mobilise
mobility
mobocrat
moccasin
modalism
modalist
modality
modelled
modeller
moderate
moderato
modernly
modestly
modifier
modishly
modulate
Moharram
moisture
molality
molarity
molasses
molecule
molehill
moleskin
molester
Molinism
Molinist
molossus
molybdic
momently
momentum
monachal
monadism
monandry
monarchy
monastic
monaural
monaxial
monazite
mondaine
monetary
monetise
moneybag
moneybox
Mongolic
mongoose
monicker
monistic
monition
monitive
monitory
monkfish
MonKhmer
monkhood
monkseal
monkship
monoacid
monocrat
monocyte
monodist
monogamy
monogeny
monoglot
monogony
monogram
monogyny
monolith
monomial
monopode
monopoly
monorail
monotint
monotone
monotony
monotype
monoxide
monsieur
monteith
monument
moonbeam
mooncalf
moonface
moonfish
moonless
moonrise
moonsail
moonshee
moonshot
moonwort
moorcock
moorfowl
moorings
moorland
mopishly
moquette
morainic
moralise
moralism
moralist
morality
moratory
Moravian
morbidly
morbific
mordancy
moreover
moresque
moribund
mornings
morosely
morosity
morpheme
morphine
mortally
mortgage
mortmain
mortuary
moshavim
mosquito
mossback
mothball
motherly
motility
motional
motivate
motivity
motorail
motorcar
motorial
motoring
motorise
motorist
motorium
motorman
motormen
motorway
mottling
moufflon
moulding
mountain
mounting
mournful
mourning
mouseear
moussaka
mouthful
moveable
moveless
movement
movingly
mowburnt
Noachian
nobelium
nobility
nobleman
noblesse
nocturne
nodalise
nodality
nodation
nodosity
nodulose
nodulous
noisette
nomadise
nomadism
nominate
nomistic
nomogram
nomology
nonclaim
nondairy
nonesuch
nonevent
nonhuman
nonjuror
nonlegal
nonmetal
nonmoral
nonparty
nonrigid
nonsense
nonstick
nonunion
nonusage
nonwhite
noontide
noontime
normalcy
normally
Norseman
northern
northing
Northman
noseband
nosecone
nosedive
nosepipe
nosering
nosiness
nosology
notarial
notation
notching
notebook
notecase
noteless
notional
notornis
noumenal
noumenon
nouvelle
novation
novelise
novelist
November
novercal
nowadays
oogamous
oogonial
oogonium
oologist
ooziness
pochette
pockmark
podagral
podagric
podiatry
poetical
poignant
pointing
poisoner
polarise
polarity
polemics
polemise
polemist
polestar
polisher
politely
politick
politico
politics
pollices
pollinia
pollinic
polliwog
pollster
polluter
pollywog
polonium
poltfoot
poltroon
polygala
polygamy
polygene
polygeny
polyglot
polygyny
polymath
polypary
polypide
polypite
polypody
polypoid
polypous
polyseme
polysemy
polysomy
polyzoan
polyzoic
polyzoon
pomander
pomology
ponderer
pondweed
pontifex
ponytail
poohpooh
poorness
popinjay
popishly
poppadum
populace
populate
populism
populist
populous
poristic
porkling
porosity
porphyry
porpoise
porridge
portable
portfire
porthole
porticos
portiere
portrait
portress
position
positive
positron
posology
possible
possibly
postcard
postcode
postdate
postfree
posthorn
postiche
postlude
postmark
postmill
postobit
postpaid
postpone
postural
posturer
potassic
potation
potbelly
potbound
potently
potholer
pothouse
potlatch
potplant
potroast
potsherd
potstill
potstone
potterer
poultice
poundage
pounding
pourable
powdered
powerful
roadbook
roadless
roadside
roadsign
roadster
roasting
roborant
robustly
rocaille
rockbird
rockcake
rockcork
rockdove
rocketry
rockfall
rockfish
rockhewn
rocklike
rockling
rockrose
rocksalt
rockweed
rockwood
rockwork
roentgen
rogation
rogatory
rollcall
rollneck
rolypoly
romancer
Romanian
romanise
Romanism
Romanist
Romansch
romantic
rondeaux
roodbeam
roodloft
roofless
roofrack
rooftree
roommate
roothold
rootless
ropeable
ropewalk
ropeyarn
ropiness
rosarian
rosebowl
rosebush
rosefish
roseleaf
rosemary
roseolar
rosepink
roseroot
rosetree
rosewood
rosiness
rostrate
rosulate
Rotarian
rotation
rotative
rotatory
rotenone
rottenly
rotundly
roturier
roughage
roughdry
roughhew
roughish
rouleaus
rouleaux
roulette
roundarm
rounders
roundish
roundtop
rowdyish
rowdyism
royalism
royalist
soakaway
soapbark
soapdish
soapless
soaproot
soapsuds
soapwort
soberise
sobriety
sobstory
sobstuff
socalled
sociable
sociably
socially
societal
Socinian
Socratic
sodalite
sodality
sodomite
softball
softboil
softener
softhead
softness
softshoe
softsoap
software
softwood
soilless
soilpipe
solander
solanine
solarise
solarism
solarist
solarium
solation
solatium
solderer
soldiery
solecism
solecist
solemnly
soleness
solenoid
solfaist
solfeggi
solidary
solidify
solidity
solitary
solitude
solleret
solstice
solution
solvable
solvency
somatism
sombrely
sombrero
sombrous
somebody
somedeal
somedele
sometime
someways
somewhat
somewhen
somnific
sonatina
songbird
songbook
songless
songster
sonobuoy
sonority
sonorous
soothing
soothsay
sorcerer
sordidly
sorehead
soreness
sorochen
sororate
sorority
sorption
sorptive
sorrower
sortable
soterial
souchong
soulless
soundbow
soundbox
sounding
sourdine
sourness
sourpuss
soutache
southern
southing
southpaw
Southron
souvenir
sovranty
sowbread
toadfish
toadflax
toadyish
toadyism
toboggan
tocology
toepiece
toeplate
together
toiletry
toilette
toilsome
toilworn
tokenism
tokology
tolbooth
tolerant
tolerate
tollcall
tolldish
tollgate
tomahawk
tomalley
tombless
tomentum
tommybar
tommygun
tommyrot
tomnoddy
tomogram
tomorrow
tonality
tonedeaf
toneless
tonepoem
tonguing
tonicity
toolroom
toolshed
toothful
toothily
toothing
topdress
topheavy
toplevel
topliner
toplofty
topnotch
topology
toponymy
topstone
torchere
toreador
toreutic
tornadic
toroidal
torpidly
torquate
torridly
tortilla
tortious
tortoise
tortuous
torturer
totalise
totality
totalled
totemism
totemist
totterer
touchily
touching
toughish
touristy
tournure
tovarish
towardly
towelled
townhall
township
townsman
toxaemia
toxaemic
toxicant
toxicity
vocalise
vocalism
vocalist
vocality
vocation
vocative
voicebox
voiceful

voidable
voidance
voidness
volatile
volcanic
volcanos
volitant
volition
volitive
volplane
voltaism
volution
volvulus
vomerine
vomitive
vomitory
voracity
vortexes
vortical
vortices
votaress
votarist
voteless
voussoir
vowelise
vowelled
voyageur
woefully
wolffish
wolfpack
wolfskin
womanise
womanish
wondrous
wontedly
woodbind
woodbine
woodchat
woodcock
woodenly
woodland
woodlark
woodlice
woodnote
woodpile
woodpulp
woodruff
woodshed
woodsman
woodwind
woodwool
woodwork
woodworm
wooldyed
woolfell
woollens
woolpack
woolsack
woolshed
woolskin
woolwork
wordbook
wordless
wordplay
workable
workaday
workfolk
workings
workless
workmate
workroom
workshop
wormcast
wormgear
wormhole
wormlike
wormseed
wormwood
worthful
worthily
wouldest
woundily
yodelled
yodeller
yoghourt
yokemate
youngest
youngish
yourself
youthful
zodiacal
zoetrope
zoiatria
zombiism
zonation
zoogenic
zoolater
zoolatry
zoomancy
zoometry
zoomorph
zoonosis
zoophily
zoophyte
zoospore
apagogic
aperient
aperitif
aperture
aphasiac
aphelion
aphicide
aphorise
aphorism
aphorist
apiarian
apiarist
apically
aplastic
apocrine
apodoses
apodosis
apogamic
apograph
apologia
apologue
apomixis
apoplexy
apostasy
apostate
apothegm
appalled
appanage
apparent
appendix
appetent
appetite
applause
applepie
applique
apposite
appraise
approach
approval
apresski
apterous
aptitude
ephemera
Ephesian
ephorate
epiblast
epically
epicalyx
epicotyl
epicycle
epidemic
epidural
epifauna
epigeous
epigraph
epilepsy
epilogue
epinasty
epiphany
epiphyte
episcope
episemon
episodal
episodic
epistler
epistyle
epitasis
epopoeia
epyllion
opaquely
openable
opencast
openeyed
openness
openplan
openwork
operable
operatic
operator
opercula
operetta
ophidian
oppilate
opponent
opposite
oppugner
opsimath
optative
optician
optimise
optimism
optimist
optional
opulence
opuscula
opuscule
spacebar
spaceman
spacious
spadeful
spadices
spadille
spadones
spaewife
spagyric
spalpeen
spandrel
spandril
Spaniard
spanking
spanning
spanroof
sparable
sparbuoy
spardeck
sparkgap
sparkish
sparkler
sparklet
sparling
sparring
sparsely
sparsity
spathose
spatting
spatular
spavined
speaking
spearman
speciate
specific
specimen
specious
spectral
spectrum
specular
speculum
speedily
speedway
spelling
spermary
sphagnum
sphenoid
spherics
spheroid
spherule
sphingid
sphygmus
spicated
spiccato
spicebox
spicknel
spiculae
spicular
spiculum
spiffing
spikelet
spillage
spillway
spinifex
spinning
spinster
spiracle
spirally
spirilla
spirited
spiritus
spiteful
spitfire
spitting
spittoon
spivvery
splasher
splatter
splendid
splenial
splenius
splinter
splitter
splotchy
splutter
spoffish
spoilage
spoliate
spondaic
spongily
sponsion
spontoon
spookily
spookish
spoonfed
spoonful
spoonily
sporadic
sporozoa
sportful
sportily
sporting
sportive
sporular
spotless
spottily
spotting
spousage
spraints
sprawler
spraygun
spreader
sprigged
springal
springer
sprinkle
sprinter
sprocket
sprucely
spryness
spunkily
spurgear
spurious
spurling
spurrier
spurring
spyglass
upheaval
upholder
uplander
uplifter
uppercut
uppishly
uprising
uprooter
upsetter
upsprang
upspring
upsprung
upstairs
upstream
upstroke
upthrown
upthrust
upwardly
aquacade
aqualung
aquanaut
aquarist
aquarium
aquatint
aqueduct
aquiline
equalise
equality
equalled
equation
equinity
equipage
equipped
equitant
equities
equivoke
squabble
squadron
squaller
squamate
squamose
squamous
squamule
squander
squarely
squarish
squarson
squasher
squatted
squatter
squawker
squawman
squeaker
squealer
squeedge
squeegee
squeezer
squelchy
squibbed
squidded
squiggle
squiggly
squilgee
squinter
squireen
squirely
squirrel
squirter
araceous
arachnid
Aramaean
Arapahoe
arapaima
arbalest
arbalist
arbitral
arboreal
arboreta
arborist
Arcadian
archaean
archaise
archaism
archaist
archduke
archival
archives
archness
Arcturus
arcuated
ardently
areolate
arethusa
argentic
argonaut
arguable
arguably
argufier
argument
Arianism
arillate
aristate
Armagnac
armament
armature
armchair
Armenian
Arminian
armorial
armoured
armourer
armyworm
aromatic
arpeggio
arquebus
arranger
arrantly
arrestee
arrester
arrestor
arrogant
arrogate
arsenate
arsenide
arsenite
arsonist
arsonous
artefact
arterial
artesian
artfully
articled
artifact
artifice
artistic
artistry
bracelet
brachial
brachium
brackish
bracteal
bractlet
Bradshaw
braggart
bragging
braiding
brainish
brainpan
brakeman
brakevan
brancard
branched
brancher
branchia
brandied
brandish
brandnew
brassage
brassard
brassart
brassica
brassily
brattice
brattish
brazenly
brazenry
braziery
breakage
breaking
breakout
breasted
breather
breeches
breeding
breezily
bregmata
brethren
brettese
brettice
breveted
breviary
brewster
Briarean
bribable
brickbat
brickred
briefing
brighten
brightly
brimfull
brimless
brimming
brindled
briskish
brisling
britches
britzska
broacher
broadish
broadway
brocaded
brocatel
broccoli
brochure
broidery
brokenly
bromelia
bromidic
bronchia
bronchus
broodily
brookite
brooklet
brougham
brouhaha
browband
browbeat
browning
brownish
brunette
brushoff
brutally
bryology
bryozoan
crabbing
crackers
cracking
crackjaw
cracknel
crackpot
cradling
craftily
cragsman
cramfull
cramming
cramoisy
cranefly
craniate
crankily
crankpin
crannied
crashing
crashpad
cratches
cravenly
crawfish
crayfish
creakily
creamery
creatine
creation
creative
creatrix
creature
credence
credenza
credible
credibly
credited
creditor
creeping
crenated
crenelle
creosote
crepitus
crescent
crescive
cretonne
crevasse
cribbage
cribbing
criminal
crispate
cristate
criteria
critical
critique
croakily
Croatian
croceate
crockery
crocoite
crofting
cromlech
cromorna
cromorne
cropping
crossbar
crossbow
crosscut
crossing
crosslet
crossply
crosstie
crossway
crotched
crotchet
croupier
croupous
crowbill
crowfoot
cruciate
crucible
crucifer

crucifix
crueller
crumhorn
crummock
crusader
crustily
cruzeiro
cryogeny
cryolite
cryostat
cryotron
drabbler
drabness
dracaena
drachmae
drachmai
drachmas
draconic
dragging
dragline
dragoman
dragomen
dragonet
dragsman
dragster
drainage
dramatic
drammock
dramshop
draughts
draughty
drawable
drawback
drawtube
drawwell
dreadful
dreamful
dreamily
dreaming
drearily
drencher
dressage
dressing
dribbler
dribblet
driftage
driftice
driftway
drilling
drinking
dripfeed
dripping
drivable
driveway
drollery
drophead
dropkick
dropleaf
dropping
dropshot
dropwort
droughty
drownded
drowsily
drubbing
drudgery
drugging
druggist
druidess
druidism
drumfire
drumhead
drumming
drummock
drumroll
drunkard
drupelet
dryclean
drynurse
dryplate
drypoint
drystone
erasable
Erastian
erectile
erection
eremitic
erethism
erewhile
ergogram
ergotise
ergotism
erigeron
erodible
erogenic
erotical
errantly
errantry
eruption
eruptive
erythema
frabjous
fraction
fracture
fraenula
fragment
fragrant
framesaw
francium
Frankish
franklin
frapping
Fraulein
freakish
freakout
freeborn
freedman
freefall
freehand
freehold
freeload
freeness
freesoil
freewill
freezeup
freezing
fremitus
frenetic
frenulum
frenzied
frequent
frescoes
freshman
freshrun
fretting
fretwork
Freudian
fribbler
friction
friendly
Friesian
frighten
frigidly
frijoles
frillies
fringing
frippery
frisette
friskily
fritting
frocking
frogfish
frogging
frogspit
frondage
frondent
frondeur
frondose
frontage
frontier
frontlet
frostily
frosting
frothily
frottage
froufrou
fructify
fructose
frugally
fruitage
fruitbat
fruitery
fruitfly
fruitful
fruition
frumenty
frumpish
frustule
frutices
Graafian
grabbing
grabbler
graceful
gracioso
gracious
gradient
graduand
graduate
Graecise
Graecism
graffiti
graffito
graining
gralloch
gramarye
gramatom
gramercy
grandame
granddad
grandeur
grandson
granitic
granular
grapheme
graphics
graphite
grasping
grateful
gratuity
gravamen
gravelly
graviton
grayling
greasily
greedily
greegree
greenery
greenfly
greening
greenish
greenlet
greeting
greffier
greyfish
greyness
gridiron
grievous
grillage
grimacer
grimmest
grimness
grimoire
grindery
grinning
gripping
gripsack
Griselda
griseous
grisette
grisgris
grissini
gritting
grizzled
groggily
grogshop
gromwell
groogroo
grosbeak
groschen
grottoes
grounder
grouping
grouting
growling
grubbily
grubbing
grudging
gruesome
grumbler
grumpily
gruntled
irenical
irenicon
Irishism
Irishman
ironbark
ironclad
irongray
irongrey
ironical
ironside
ironware
ironwood
ironwork
Iroquois
irrigate
irritant
irritate
kreutzer
kromesky
krumhorn
oracular
orangery
Orangism
oratorio
oratress
Orcadian
orchilla
ordainer
ordinand
ordinary
ordinate
ordnance
oreology
organdie
organise
organism
organist
orgasmic
orgastic
orgulous
oriental
oriented
origanum
original
ornament
ornately
ornithic
orogenic
orpiment
orthicon
orthodox
orthoepy
practice
practise
praecipe
praedial
prandial
prankful
prankish
pratique
prattler
preacher
preamble
precinct
precious
preclude
predator
predella
preelect
preexist
pregnant
prehuman
prejudge
prelatic
prelease
premiere
premolar
premorse
prenatal
prentice
preparer
prepense
preprint
presager
prescind
presence
preserve
presidio
pressbox
pressing
pressman
pressure
prestige
presumer
pretence
prettify
prettily
previous
priapism
prideful
priedieu
priestly
priggery
priggish
priggism
primally
Primates
primeval
primming
primness
primrose
princely
princess
printing
printout
priorate
prioress
priority
prismoid
prisoner
prissily
pristine
probable
probably
proceeds
proclaim
procurer
prodding
prodigal
prodrome
producer
proemial
profaner
profiler
profound
progress
prohibit
prolamin
prolapse
prolific
prolixly
prologue
prolonge
promisee
promiser
promisor
promoter
prompter
promptly
promulge
pronator
proofing
propense
properly
property
prophase
prophecy
prophesy
propolis
proposal
proposer
propound
propping
propylic
prorogue
prosaism
prosaist
prosodic
prospect
prostate
prostyle
protasis
protatic
protease
protegee
protista
protocol
protonic
protozoa
protract
protrude
provable
provably
provided
provider
province
provisor
proximal
prudence
pruinose
prunella
prunelle
prunello
prurient
pruritic
pruritus
Prussian
pryingly
trabeate
tracheae
tracheal
tracheid
trachoma
trachyte
trackage
tracking
trackman
trackway
tractate
traction
tractive
tradeoff
traditor
traducer
tragical
tragopan
trailnet
training
tramline
trammels
trampler
tramroad
tranquil
transact
transect
transept
transfer
transfix
tranship
transire
transmit
transude
trapball
trapdoor
trapezia
trappean
trapping
Trappist
traprock
trashery
trashily
traumata
traverse
travesty
trawlnet
treacher
treadler
treasure
treasury
treatise
trecento
treefern
treefrog
treeless
treenail
trekking
trembler
trembles
trencher
trendily
trephine
trespass
tressure
trevally
trialist
triangle
triarchy
Triassic
triaxial
tribally
tribasic
tribrach
tribunal
trichina
trichite
trichoid
trichome
trichord
trickery
trickily
trickish
tricorne
tricycle
triennia
trifling
trifocal
triforia
triglyph
trigonal
trigraph
trilling
trillion
trillium
trilobed
trimaran
trimeric
trimeter
trimming
trimness
trioxide
tripeman
triplane
triploid
tripodal
trippery
tripping
triptych
tripwire
triskele
trisomic
tristful
tristich
tritical
triumvir
triunity
trochaic
trochili
trochlea
trochoid
troilite
trollopy
trombone
trophied
tropical
trotting
trottoir
troupial
trousers
troutlet
trouvere
truantry
truckage
trucking
truckler
trueblue
trueborn
truebred
truelove
trueness
truistic
trumeaux
trumpery
truncate
trunnion
trussing
trustful
trustily
truthful
tryingly
uralitic
urbanely
urbanise
urbanism
urbanist
urbanite
urbanity
urethane
urgently
urochord
urostyle
Ursuline
urticant
urticate
wrackful
wrangler
wrappage
wrapping
wrathful
wrathily
wreathen
wreckage

wrestler
wrestpin
wretched
wriggler
wristlet
wristpin
writable
writeoff
writings
wrongful
wrongous
wrymouth
asbestic
asbestos
ascender
ascidian
ascidium
ascocarp
aseptate
asperges
asperity
asphodel
asphyxia
aspirant
aspirate
assassin
assemble
assembly
assenter
assentor
assertor
assessor
assiento
assignat
assignee
assignor
assonant
assonate
assorted
assuming
Assyrian
astatine
asterisk
asterism
asteroid
asthenia
asthenic
astonied
astonish
astragal
astutely
asyndeta
escalade
escalate
escallop
escalope
escapade
escapism
escapist
escargot
escarole
eschalot
eschewal
esculent
Eskimoan
esoteric
espalier
especial
espousal
espouser
espresso
Esquimau
essayist
Essenism
essonite
esterify
estimate
Estonian
estopped
estoppel
estovers
estrange
estuaril
esurient
isabella
isagogic
ischemia
ischemic
Islamise
Islamism
Islamite
islander
isobaric
isocheim
isocracy
isodicon
isogamic
isogloss
isogonal
isogonic
isolable
isolator
isomeric
isometry
isomorph
isophote
isopleth
isoprene
isoptera
isospory
isostasy
isothere
isotherm
isotonic
isotopic
isotropy
issuable
issuance
isthmian
oscinine
osculant
osculate
Ossianic
osteitis
ostinato
ostracod
ostracon
ostrakon
psalmist
psalmody
psaltery
psilosis
psychics
psychism
psychist
tsarevna
tsaritsa
tsaritza
usefully
usufruct
usurious
ataraxia
ataraxic
atheling
Athenian
atheroma
athletic
atlantes
Atlantic
atomiser
atremble
atrocity
atropine
attender
attested
attester
attestor
atticism
attitude
attorney
attrited
atwitter
atypical
etcetera
eternise
eternity
ethereal
etherial
etherise
etherism
etherist
ethicism
ethicist
Ethiopic
ethnarch
ethnical
ethology
ethylene
etiolate
Etrurian
Etruscan
Italiote
iterance
otiosely
otiosity
otoscope
ottavino
pteropod
pterylae
ptomaine
ptyalism
stabbing
stabling
stablish
staccato
staffage
staggard
staggers
staghorn
stagnant
stagnate
stairrod
stairway
stakenet
stallage
stallfed
stalling
stallion
stalwart
staminal
stampede
stancher
stanchly
standard
standing
standish
standoff
stanhope
stannary
stannate
stannite
stannous
stanzaic
stapelia
stardust
starfish
stargaze
starkers
starless
starlike
starling
starrily
starring
starting
startler
starwort
stasimon
statable
statedly
statical
statuary
statured
staylace
staysail
steadily
steading
stealing
stealthy
steamily
stearate
stearine
steatite
stedfast
steenbok
steening
steepish
steepled
steerage
steering
steinbok
stellate
stellify
stellion
stemless
stemmata
stemming
stenosed
stenosis
stenotic
stepping
stepwise
sterigma
sterling
sternite
sternson
sternway
stetting
stibnite
stickful
stickily
stickjaw
stickler
stiffish
stigmata
stilbene
stilbite
stiletto
stillage
stimulus
stingily
stingray
stinkard
stinking
stinkpot
stipites
stippler
stipular
stirring
stitcher
stoccado
stoccata
stockade
stockcar
stockily
stocking
stockish
stockist
stockman
stockpot
stodgily
stoicism
stolidly
stomachy
stomatal
stomatic
stonefly
stopcock
stopover
stoppage
stopping
storable
storeman
storeyed
stormily
stoutish
stowaway
strabism
straddle
straggle
straggly
straight
strained
strainer
straiten
straitly
stramash
stranded
stranger
strangle
strapoil
strapped
strapper
strategy
stratify
stravaig
streaked
streaker
streamer
streeted
strength
strepent
Strepyan
stretchy
stricken
strickle
strictly
stridden
strident
strigose
striking
stringed
stringer
stripped
stripper
strobila
strobile
strobili
stroller
stromata
strongly
strontia
strophic
stropped
strucken
struggle
strummed
strummer
strumose
strumous
strumpet
strutted
strutter
stubbing
stubborn
stubnail
stuccoes
studbook
studding
studfarm
studious
studwork
stuffily
stuffing
stultify
stumbler
stumming
stumpily
stunning
stunsail
stuntman
stupidly
stuprate
sturdied
sturdily
sturgeon
stylised
utiliser
aubretia
audacity
audience
audition
auditive
auditory
Augustan
augustly
aurelian
auricula
auriform
aurorean
auspices
autacoid
autarchy
autarkic
autistic
autobahn
autocade
autocrat
autodafe
autodyne
autogamy
autogiro
autogyro
autolyse
automata
automate
autonomy
autosome
autotomy
autotype
autumnal
autunite
bubaline
buckaroo
buckbean
buckhorn
buckling
buckshee
buckshot
buckskin
Buddhism
Buddhist
buddleia
budgeree
buhlwork
building
bulkhead
bullcalf
bulldoze
bulletin
bullfrog
bullhead
bullhorn
bullocky
bullring
bullseye
bullyboy
bullyoff
bullyrag
bummaree
buncombe
bundling
bunfight
bungalow
bunghole
bunkered
buntline
buoyancy
Burberry
burglary
burgonet
Burgundy
burletta
burnouse
burntout
burrower
bursitis
bushbaby
bushbuck
bushfire
bushveld
business
bustling
busybody
busyness
butchery
buttoner
buttress
butylene
butyrate
buzzword
cubature
cubiform
cuboidal
cucumber
cucurbit
culdesac
culicine
culinary
culottes
culpable
culpably
cultivar
cultural
cultured
culverin
Cumbrian
cumbrous
cumulate
cumulous
cupboard
cupelled
cupidity
cupreous
cupulate
curarine
curarise
curassow
curative
curculio
cureless
curlicue
currency
curricle
cursedly
curtains
curtness
curveted
cushiony
Cushitic
cuspidor
cussedly
cussword
customer
cuteness
cutprice
cutpurse
cutwater
duchesse
duckbill
duckhawk
duckling
duckpond
duckweed
ductless
duelling
duellist
duettist
Dukhobor
dulciana
dulcimer
Dulcinea
dullness
dumbbell
dumbhead
dumbness
dumbshow
dumfound
dumpling
dundiver
dungaree
dungcart
dunghill
duodenal
duodenum
duologue
durables
duration
durative
durukuli
dustbowl
dustcart
dustcoat
dustless
dustlike
dustshot
Dutchman
dutiable
dutyfree
dutypaid
eucalypt
eucritic
eugenics
eugenism
eugenist
eulachon
eulogise
eulogist
eulogium
euonymin
euonymus
eupatrid
eupepsia
eupeptic
euphonic
euphoria
euphoric
euphrasy
euphuism
euphuist
Eurasian
Eurocrat
European
europium
eustatic
eutectic
eutrophy
fuchsine
fuelling
fugacity
fugitive
fugleman
fullback
fullness
fullpage
fullsize
fulltime
fumarole
fumigant
fumigate
fumitory
function
funebral

funerary
funereal
fungible
funkhole
funnyman
furbelow
furcated
furculae
furcular
furfural
furfuran
furlough
furriery
furthest
furuncle
fuselage
fusiform
fusileer
fusilier
futilely
futility
futurism
futurist
futurity
guacharo
guaiacum
guaranty
guardant
guardian
Guelphic
guerilla
guernsey
guidable
guidance
guidedog
guideway
guileful
guiltily
Gujarati
gulfweed
gullable
gullible
gulosity
gummosis
gumption
gunfight
gunflint
gunlayer
gunmetal
gunpoint
gunsmith
gunstock
gusseted
guttural
huckster
hugeness
huggable
Huguenot
hulahula
humanely
humanise
humanism
humanist
humanity
humanoid
humidify
humidity
humility
hummocky
humorist
humorous
humoured
humpback
humuncle
hungrily
huntress
huntsman
hurtless
hushhush
hustings
jubilant
jubilate
Judaical
Judaiser
judgment
judicial
jugglery
Jugoslav
jugulate
julienne
jumpedup
jumpseat
jumpsuit
junction
juncture
junkshop
junkyard
Jurassic
juristic
justness
juvenile
kurtosis
lubberly
lubrical
lucidity
luckless
luculent
Lucullan
lukewarm
lumberer
luminant
luminary
luminist
luminous
lumpfish
lunarian
lunation
luncheon
lungfish
lungwort
lunulate
luscious
lushness
lustrate
lustrine
lustring
lustrous
lutanist
lutecium
lutenist
lutetium
Lutheran
luxation
muchness
mucilage
muckluck
muckrake
muckworm
mucosity
mucrones
mudguard
mudstone
Muharram
mulberry
muleteer
mulishly
mulloway
multeity
multifid
multiped
multiple
multiply
muniment
munition
murderer
muriatic
murmurer
murrelet
murrhine
muscadel
muscatel
muscling
muscular
mushroom
musicale
musician
musingly
muskdeer
muskduck
musketry
muskrose
musktree
muslined
musquash
mustache
mutation
mutchkin
muteness
muticous
mutilate
mutineer
mutinous
mutterer
mutually
nubiform
nubility
nubilous
nucellus
nuclease
nucleate
nucleole
nucleoli
nuclidic
nudeness
nugatory
nuisance
nullness
numberer
numbfish
numbness
numeracy
numerary
numerate
numerous
numinous
numskull
nuptials
nursling
nurturer
nutarian
nutation
nutbrown
nuthatch
nuthouse
nutrient
nutshell
outboard
outbound
outbrave
outbreak
outburst
outcaste
outclass
outdated
outdoors
outdrawn
outfield
outflank
outgoing
outgrown
outguess
outHerod
outhouse
outlawry
outlying
outmatch
outmoded
outpoint
outrange
outreach
outreign
outrider
outright
outrival
outshine
outshone
outsider
outsight
outsmart
outspend
outspent
outstare
outstrip
outvalue
outvying
outwards
outwatch
outweigh
outworks
pubertal
publican
publicly
puffball
puffbird
puggaree
pugilism
pugilist
pugnosed
puissant
pullback
pullover
pulmonic
pulpiter
pulpwood
pulsator
pulvilli
pulvinus
pumproom
puncheon
punctate
punctual
puncture
punditry
pungency
puniness
punisher
punition
punitive
punitory
puparial
puparium
pupation
pupilage
pupilary
pupillar
puppetry
puppydog
puppydom
puppyfat
puppyish
purblind
purchase
purebred
pureness
purfling
purifier
puristic
purplish
purpuric
purpurin
pursenet
purslane
pursuant
purulent
purveyor
pushball
pushbike
pushcart
pushover
pushpull
pussycat
pustular
putative
putridly
quackery
quackish
quadrant
quadrate
quadriga
quadroon
quaestor
quagmire
quaintly
Quakerly
qualmish
quandary
quandong
quantify
quantise
quantity
quarrier
quartern
quarters
quartile
quatrain
quayside
queasily
Quechuan
queendom
queening
queenlet
queerish
quencher
quenelle
question
queueing
quibbler
quickset
quiddity
quidnunc
quietism
quietist
quietude
quillpen
quilting
quincunx
quintain
quipping
quirkily
quisling
quitrent
quitting
quixotic
quixotry
quizzing
quotable
quotient
rubbishy
rubicund
rubidium
rubrical
rubytail
rucksack
rudeness
rudiment
ruefully
ruggedly
rugosely
rugosity
rugulose
ruinable
ruleless
Rumanian
Rumansch
ruminant
ruminate
rummager
runabout
runagate
runcible
runnerup
ruralise
ruralism
ruralist
rurality
rushhour
rushlike
rustical
rustless
rutabaga
ruthless
rutilant
subacute
subagent
subahdar
subbasal
subclass
suberect
suberise
suberose
suberous
subfloor
subframe
subgenus
subgroup
subhuman
subimago
subjoint
sublease
sublunar
submerge
submerse
suborder
suborner
suboxide
subphyla
subpoena
subprior
subserve
subshrub
subsolar
subsonic
substage
subtitle
subtlety
subtonic
subtopia
subtotal
subtract
subulate
suburban
suburbia
subvocal
succinct
succinic
succinum
succubae
succubus
suchlike
suckling
Sudanese
sudarium
sudatory
suddenly
sufferer
suffrage
suicidal
suitable
suitably
suitcase
suitings
sukiyaki
sullenly
sulphate
sulphide
sulphite
sulphone
sultrily
Sumerian
summerly
summitry
summoner
sunbaked
sunbathe
sunblind
sunburnt
sunburst
sundance
sunderer
sundress
sundried
sundries
sundrops
sunlight
sunproof
sunshade
sunshine
sunshiny
sunstone
sunwards
superadd
superate
superbly
superego
superior
superman
supernal
supertax
supinate
supinely
supplant
supplely
supplial
supplier
supplies
supposal
supposed
suppress
surcease
surefire
sureness
surfacer
surfbird
surfboat
surfduck
surffish
surgical
suricate
surmisal
surmiser
surmount
surplice
surprise
surround
surroyal
surveyor
survival
survivor
suspense
susurrus
suzerain
tubeless
tubercle
tuberose
tuberous
tubiform
tubulate
tuckahoe
tuckshop
tumbling
tumidity
tumorous
tuneable
tuneless
tungsten
tungstic
tunicate
Tunisian
tuppence
tuppenny
Turanian
turbaned
turbidly
turbinal
turbofan
turbojet
Turcoman
turgidly
Turkoman
turmeric
turnable
turnback
turncoat
turncock
turndown
turnings
turnover
turnpike
turnskin
turnsole
turnspit
turreted
turtling
tussocky
tutelage
tutelary
tutorage
tutoress
tutorial
vulcanic
vulgarly
Yugoslav
yuletide
zucchini
zugzwang
avadavat
aventail
averment
averring
aversely
aversion
aversive
aviarist
aviation
aviatrix
avidness
avifauna
avionics
avowable
avowedly
avulsion
evacuant
evacuate
evadable
evaluate
evanesce
evection
evenfall
evenness
evensong
eventful
eventide
eventual
evermore
eversion
everyday
everyman
everyone
everyway
eviction
evidence
evildoer

evilness
evincive
evitable
evulsion
ivorynut
ovalness
ovariole
ovaritis
ovenbird
ovenware
overalls
overarch
overbear
overbook
overbore
overbusy
overcall
overcame
overcast
overcoat
overcome
overcrop
overdone
overdose
overdraw
overdrew
overfall
overfeed
overfill
overfish
overflew
overflow
overfold
overfond
overgrew
overgrow
overhand
overhang
overhaul
overhead
overhear
overheat
overhung
overjump
overkill
overlaid
overlain
overland
overleaf
overleap
overload
overlong
overlook
overlord
overmuch
overnice
overpaid
overpass
overpast
overplay
overplus
overrate
override
overripe
overrode
overrule
oversail
overseas
overseen
overseer
oversell
oversewn
overshoe
overshot
overside
oversize
overslip
oversold
oversoul
overstay
overstep
overtake
overtask
overtime
overtone
overtook
overture
overturn
overview
overwear
overwind
overwork
overworn
oviposit
uvularly
uvulitis
aweather
dwarfish
dwarfism
dwelling
owlishly
swabbing
swagging
swainish
swanherd
swanking
swanlike
swanmark
swanneck
swannery
swanning
swanshot
swanskin
swansong
swapping
swastika
swatting
swayback
swearing
sweeping
sweepnet
sweeting
sweetish
sweetpea
sweetsop
swelling
swiftlet
swigging
swimming
swimsuit
swindler
swinging
switchel
swobbing
swopping
swotting
twaddler
tweezers
twelvemo
twenties
twiddler
twilight
twinborn
twinkler
twinling
twinning
twinship
twitcher
twittery
twitting
twoedged
twofaced
twopence
twopenny
twopiece
twosided
twotimer
zwieback
axiality
axillary
axiology
axletree
exacting
exaction
examinee
examiner
exanthem
excavate
excelled
exchange
excision
excitant
exciting
excluder
excursus
execrate
executor
exegesis
exegetic
exemplar
exemplum
exequies
exercise
exergual
exertion
exhalant
exhorter
exigence
exigency
exigible
exiguity
exiguous
eximious
existent
exlibris
exocrine
exogamic
exorcise
exorcism
exorcist
exordial
exordium
exospore
exoteric
expander
expedite
expelled
expellee
expertly
expiable
expiator
expirant
explicit
exploder
explorer
exponent
exporter
exposure
exserted
extender
extensor
exterior
external
extolled
extrados
extremes
extrorse
exultant
exuviate
oxidiser
oximeter
oxpecker
oxtongue
oxymoron
oxytocin
uxorious
Ayrshire
Byronism
bystreet
cyanogen
cyanoses
cyanosis
cyanotic
cyclamen
cycleway
cyclical
cyclonic
cyclopes
cyclosis
cylinder
cymatium
cynicism
cynosure
Cypriote
cypselae
Cyrenaic
Cyrillic
cysteine
cystitis
cytidine
cytology
cytosine
dybbukim
dyestuff
dynamics
dynamism
dynamist
dynamite
dynastic
dynatron
dysgenic
dyslexia
dyslexic
dyspnoea
dystopia
eyeglass
eyeliner
eyepiece
eyerhyme
eyeshade
eyesight
eyestalk
eyetooth
eyewater
gymkhana
gymnasia
gynandry
gynocrat
gynoecia
gypseous
gypsydom
gypsyism
gyration
gyratory
gyrostat
hyacinth
hydatoid
hydranth
hydrogen
hydromel
hydropic
hydropsy
hydroski
hydroxyl
hygienic
hymenial
hymenium
hymnbook
hyoscine
hypnoses
hypnosis
hypnotic
hypobole
hypoderm
hypogeal
hypogean
hypogene
hypogeum
hypogyny
hypothec
hysteria
hysteric
kyphosis
kyphotic
lychgate
lykewake
lymphoid
lymphoma
lynchpin
lynxeyed
lyophile
lyrebird
lyricism
lyricist
lysosome
lysozyme
mycelial
mycelium
mycetoma
mycology
myelinic
myelitis
mylonite
myoblast
myogenic
myograph
myositic
myositis
myosotis
myriapod
myriopod
myrmidon
mystical
mystique
mythical
myxomata
nymphean
pyelitis
pygidial
pygidium
pygmaean
pyogenic
pyrenoid
pyrexial
pyridine
pyriform
pyroxene
pyrrhoea
pyrrhous
pythonic
pyxidium
ryegrass
ryotwari
sybarite
sycamine
sycamore
sycomore
syconium
syenitic
syllabic
syllable
syllabub
syllabus
sylphide
sylphine
sylphish
sylvatic
symbiont
symbolic
symmetry
sympathy
symphile
symphony
sympodia
symposia
synapsis
synaptic
synastry
syncline
syncopal
syncytia
syndesis
syndetic
syndical
syndrome
synergic
synergid
syngamic
synonymy
synopses
synopsis
synoptic
synovial
syntagma
syntonic
syphilis
syringes
syrinxes
systemic
systolic
syzygial
Tychonic
tympanic
tympanum
typecast
typeface
typehigh
typhonic
typifier
typology
tyrannic
Tyrolean
tyrosine
Tyrrhene
xylocarp
xylology
xylonite
zygaenid
zymology
czaritza
ozoniser
———
abacuses
abattoir
academia
academic
acanthus
acarpous
Adamical
adamitic
adaption
adaptive
agaragar
alacrity
alarmist
amadavat
amaranth
amazedly
anabases
anabasis
anabatic
anabolic
anaconda
anaerobe
anaglyph
anagogic
analcime
analcite
analecta
analects
analogic
analogue
analyser
analyses
analysis
analytic
anapaest
anaphase
anaphora
anarchic
anasarca
anathema
anatomic
apagogic
araceous
arachnid
Aramaean
Arapahoe
arapaima
ataraxia
ataraxic
avadavat
beadroll
beadsman
beadwork
beagling
beamends
beanpole
bearable
bearably
bearings
bearskin
beatific
beautify
biannual
biassing
biathlon
blabbing
blackboy
blackcap
blackfly
blacking
blackish
blackleg
blackout
blacktie
blacktop
bladdery
blahblah
blamable
blamably
blameful
blandish
blankety
blastema
blastoff
blastoid
blastula
blatancy
blazoner
blazonry
boarding
boastful
boatbill
boatdeck
boathook
boatload
bracelet
brachial
brachium
brackish
bracteal
bractlet
Bradshaw
braggart
bragging
braiding
brainish
brainpan
brakeman
brakevan
brancard
branched
brancher
branchia
brandied
brandish
brandnew
brassage
brassard
brassart
brassica
brassily
brattice
brattish
brazenly
brazenry
braziery
chaconne
chainsaw
chairman
chalazae
Chaldaic
Chaldean
chaldron
chalkpit
chambers
chambray
champers
champion
chancery
chandler
chapatti
chapbook
chapelry
chaperon
chapiter
chaplain
chapping
charcoal
charisma
charlady
charlock
charming
charring
Chartism
Chartist
chasseur
chastely
chastise
chastity
chasuble
chateaux
chattily
chatting
chaunter
chauntry
cladding
claimant
clambake
clammily
clamming
clanging
clangour
clannish
clanship
clansman
clapping
claptrap
claqueur
clarence
clarinet
classics
classify
clavicle
clawback
claymore
coachdog
coachman
coaction
coactive
coagulum

coaldust
coalesce
coalfish
coalhole
coalmine
coalsack
coarsely
coatrack
coatroom
coauthor
crabbing
crackers
cracking
crackjaw
cracknel
crackpot
cradling
craftily
cragsman
cramfull
cramming
cramoisy
cranefly
craniate
crankily
crankpin
crannied
crashing
crashpad
cratches
cravenly
crawfish
crayfish
cyanogen
cyanoses
cyanosis
cyanotic
czaritza
deadbeat
deadener
deadfall
deadhead
deadline
deadlock
deadness
deadwood
deaerate
deafmute
deafness
dealfish
deanship
dearness
deathbed
deathcap
deathray
diabasic
diabetes
diabetic
diabolic
diaconal
diagnose
diagonal
diagraph
diallage
dialling
dialogic
dialogue
dialyser
dialyses
dialysis
dialytic
diamante
diameter
dianthus
diapason
diapause
diaphone
diarchal
diarchic
diarrhea
diaspora
diaspore
diastase
diastema
diastole
diatomic
diatonic
diatribe
drabbler
drabness
dracaena
drachmae
drachmai
drachmas
draconic
dragging
dragline
dragoman
dragomen
dragonet
dragsman
dragster
drainage
dramatic
drammock
dramshop
draughts
draughty
drawable
drawback
drawtube
drawwell
dwarfish
dwarfism
edacious
elatedly
emaciate
enaction
enactive
enarched
erasable
Erastian
evacuant
evacuate
evadable
evaluate
evanesce
exacting
exaction
examinee
examiner
exanthem
fearless
fearsome
feasible
feasibly
feastday
feathery
featured
features
flabella
flagella
flagging
flagpole
flagrant
flagship
flambeau
flamenco
flamingo
flanerie
flapjack
flapping
flashgun
flashily
flashing
flatboat
flatfeet
flatfish
flatfoot
flathead
flatiron
flatling
flatmate
flatness
flatrace
flattery
flattest
flattish
flatware
flatways
flatwise
flatworm
flautist
flawless
flaxseed
foamless
frabjous
fraction
fracture
fraenula
fragment
fragrant
framesaw
francium
Frankish
franklin
frapping
Fraulein
gearcase
Ghanaian
ghastful
giantess
giantism
glabella
glabrous
glaciate
gladdest
gladding
gladhand
gladioli
gladness
gladsome
glancing
glanders
glandule
glassful
glassily
glassine
glaucoma
glaucous
glaziery
gnathite
goadster
goalkick
goalline
goalpost
goatfish
goatherd
goatling
goatmoth
goatskin
Graafian
grabbing
grabbler
graceful
gracioso
gracious
gradient
graduand
graduate
Graecise
Graecism
graffiti
graffito
graining
gralloch
gramarye
gramatom
gramercy
grandame
granddad
grandeur
grandson
granitic
granular
grapheme
graphics
graphite
grasping
grateful
gratuity
gravamen
gravelly
graviton
grayling
guacharo
guaiacum
guaranty
guardant
guardian
headache
headachy
headband
headfast
headgear
headlamp
headland
headless
headline
headlock
headlong
headmost
headnote
headrace
headrest
headroom
headsail
headsman
headwind
headword
headwork
heartily
heatedly
heathery
heathhen
heavenly
hoarding
hoarsely
hyacinth
imaginal
imagines
inaction
inactive
inasmuch
isabella
isagogic
Italiote
jealousy
knackery
knapping
knapsack
knapweed
leadenly
leadless
leadsman
leadwork
leafless
leaflike
leanness
leapfrog
learning
leathern
leathery
leavings
loadline
loadstar
loanable
loanword
loathful
loathing
meagrely
mealtime
mealworm
mealybug
meanness
meantime
measured
meatball
meatsafe
miasmata
miasmous
neaptide
Nearctic
nearness
neatherd
neatness
Noachian
omadhaum
opaquely
oracular
orangery
Orangism
oratorio
oratress
ovalness
ovariole
ovaritis
peaceful
peacocky
peagreen
peardrop
pearlies
pearling
pearlite
pearmain
peasecod
phalange
phantasm
phantasy
pharisee
pharmacy
phaseout
piacular
pianiste
piassava
placable
placably
placeman
placenta
placidly
plagiary
plaguily
plaiding
plaister
planchet
plangent
planking
plankton
planning
plantain
planulae
planular
plastery
plastics
plastron
plateaux
plateful
platelet
platform
platinic
platinum
platonic
platting
platypus
plaudits
playable
playback
playbill
playbook
playgirl
playgoer
playmate
playroom
playsuit
playtime
practice
practise
praecipe
praedial
prandial
prankful
prankish
pratique
prattler
psalmist
psalmody
psaltery
quackery
quackish
quadrant
quadrate
quadriga
quadroon
quaestor
quagmire
quaintly
Quakerly
qualmish
quandary
quandong
quantify
quantise
quantity
quarrier
quartern
quarters
quartile
quatrain
quayside
reabsorb
reactant
reaction
reactive
readable
readably
readjust
reaffirm
reagency
realness
realtime
reappear
rearlamp
rearmice
rearmost
rearview
rearward
reascend
reasoner
reassert
reassess
reassign
reassure
reawaken
Rhaetian
rhapsode
rhapsody
roadbook
roadless
roadside
roadsign
roadster
roasting
scabbard
scabious
scabrous
scaffold
scalable
scalawag
scalepan
scallion
scammony
scampish
scandent
Scandian
scandium
scanning
scansion
scanties
scantily
scaphoid
scapulae
scapular
scapulas
scarcely
scarcity
scarfpin
scarious
scarless
scarring
scathing
scattily
scatting
scavenge
seaboard
seaborne
seachest
seacoast
seacraft
seadrome
seafarer
seafloor
seafront
seagoing
seagreen
seaholly
seahorse
sealable
sealevel
sealskin
sealyham
seamanly
seamless
seamount
seamouse
seamster
seaonion
seapiece
seaplane
seapurse
seaquake
searcher
seascape
seashell
seashore
seasnail
seasnake
seasonal
seasoner
seatbelt
seatrout
seawards
seawater
seawrack
shabbily
shabrack
Shabuoth
shadbush
shaddock
shadower
shafting
shagbark
shaggily
shagreen
shagroon
shakable
shakeout
Shaktism
shaleoil
shalloon
shallows
shambles
shameful
shamming
shamrock
shanghai
shantung
shapable
shareout
sharpish
sharpset
shashlik
slabbing
slagging
slagheap
slamming
slangily
slapbang
slapdash
slapjack
slapping
slashing
slattern
Slavonic
smallage
smallfry
smallish
smallpox
smaltite
smarmily
smartish
smashing
snackbar
snagging
snakepit
snapbrim
snaplink
snappily
snapping
snappish
snapshot
snatcher
snazzily
soakaway
soapbark
soapdish
soapless
soaproot
soapsuds
soapwort
spacebar
spaceman
spacious
spadeful
spadices
spadille
spadones
spaewife
spagyric
spalpeen
spandrel
spandril
Spaniard
spanking
spanning
spanroof
sparable
sparbuoy
spardeck
sparkgap
sparkish
sparkler
sparklet

sparling teabread tsarevna cabochon libretto suboxide ancestry cockboat
sparring teabreak tsaritsa caboodle lobation subphyla anchoret cockcrow
sparsely teacaddy tsaritza cabotage lobbyist subpoena Arcadian cockerel
sparsity teachest twaddler cabriole lobeline subprior archaean cockeyed
spathose teaching unabated cabstand loblolly subserve archaise cockloft
spatting teacloth unaneled ciborium lobotomy subshrub archaism cockshut
spatular teahouse unawares cobaltic lobulate subsolar archaist cocksure
spavined teammate uralitic cobblers lubberly subsonic archduke cocktail
stabbing teamster viameter cobwebby lubrical substage archival cucumber
stabling teamwork viaticum cubature mobilise subtitle archives cucurbit
stablish teaparty weakfish cubiform mobility subtlety archness cyclamen
staccato tearaway weakling cuboidal mobocrat subtonic Arcturus cycleway
staffage teardrop weakness dabchick nebulise subtopia arcuated cyclical
staggard tearduct weanling debagged nebulium subtotal ascender cyclonic
staggers tearless weaponry debarred nebulous subtract ascidian cyclopes
staghorn teaspoon wearable debility nobelium subulate ascidium cyclosis
stagnant teatable weariful debonair nobility suburban ascocarp dactylar
stagnate teatowel weaselly debugged nobleman suburbia baccarat dactylic
stairrod thalamic whacking debutant noblesse subvocal bacchant decadent
stairway thalamus whapping dybbukim nubiform sybarite bachelor decagram
stakenet thallium wharfage embalmer nubility taberdar bacillar decanter
stallage thalloid whatever embattle nubilous tableaux bacillus deceased
stallfed thallous whatness embedded pubertal tablecut backache decedent
stalling Thanatos wrackful embezzle publican tableful backbite deceiver
stallion thanedom wrangler embitter publicly tablemat backbone December
stalwart thankful wrappage emblazon rabbinic tabletop backchat decemvir
staminal thankyou wrapping embolden rabbiter tabouret backcomb decennia
stampede thatcher wrathful embolism rabbitry tabulate backdate decently
stancher toadfish wrathily embosser rabidity toboggan backdoor decigram
stanchly toadflax yeanling embracer rebelled tubeless backdrop decimate
standard toadyish yearbook embussed rebeller tubercle backfire decipher
standing toadyism yearling fabliaux rebellow tuberose backhand decision
standish trabeate yearlong fabulist rebuttal tuberous backlash decisive
standoff tracheae yearning fabulous rebutted tubiform backless deckhand
stanhope tracheal yeastily febrific rebutter tubulate backlist declarer
stannary tracheid zealotry February ribaldry umbonate backmost declasse
stannate trachoma Abbaside fibrilla ribbonry umbrella backpack declutch
stannite trachyte abbatial fibrosis ribgrass umbrette backrest decolour
stannous trackage albacore fibrotic ribosome unbacked backroom decorate
stanzaic tracking Albanian gabbroic roborant unbarred backseat decorous
stapelia trackman albinism gabbroid robustly unbeaten backside decouple
stardust trackway alburnum gableend rubbishy unbelief backspin decrease
starfish tractate ambiance Gobelins rubicund unbiased backstay decrepit
stargaze traction ambience habanera rubidium unbidden backveld decretal
starkers tractive ambition habitant rubrical unbolted backward decurion
starless tradeoff ambivert habitual rubytail unbottle backwash dicacity
starlike traditor ambrosia habitude sabbatic unbridle backyard dichasia
starling traducer ambulant hebdomad sabotage unbroken Baconian dichroic
starrily tragical ambulate hebetate saboteur unbuckle bacteria dicrotic
starring tragopan ambusher hebetude sebesten unburden Bactrian dictator
starting trailnet arbalest hebraise Siberian unburied becalmed dicyclic
startler training arbalist Hebraism sibilant unbutton bechamel Docetism
starwort tramline arbitral Hebraist sibilate urbanely bechance Docetist
stasimon trammels arboreal hibernal soberise urbanise becoming docilely
statable trampler arboreta hibiscus sobriety urbanism biconvex docility
statedly tramroad arborist hobbitry sobstory urbanist bicuspid dockland
statical tranquil asbestic hobbyist sobstuff urbanite buckaroo dockside
statuary transact asbestos imbecile subacute urbanity buckbean dockyard
statured transect aubretia jabberer subagent vibrancy buckhorn doctoral
staylace transept babirusa jobation subahdar vibrator buckling doctrine
staysail transfer babouche jubilant subbasal vibrissa buckshee document
swabbing transfix babushka jubilate subclass viburnum buckshot duchesse
swagging tranship babyhood kibitzer suberect zabaione buckskin duckbill
swainish transire bebopper labdanum suberise zibeline cachalot duckhawk
swanherd transmit bibation labelled suberose Accadian cachepot duckling
swanking transude biblical labellum suberous accentor cachexia duckpond
swanlike trapball bibulous labially subfloor accepter cachucha duckweed
swanmark trapdoor bobbinet lability subframe acceptor cacology ductless
swanneck trapezia bobbypin labourer subgenus accident cacomixl ecclesia
swannery trappean bobbysox labrador subgroup accolade cactuses emceeing
swanning trapping bobolink laburnum subhuman accoutre cicatrix encaenia
swanshot Trappist bobwheel libation subimago accredit cicerone enceinte
swanskin traprock bobwhite libatory subjoint accuracy ciceroni encipher
swansong trashery bubaline libeccio sublease accurate cicisbei encircle
swapping trashily cabalism libelled sublunar accursed cicisbeo enclitic
swastika traumata cabalist libellee submerge accustom coccyges enclothe
swatting traverse caballed libeller submerse alcahest cochleae encomion
swayback travesty cabinboy liberate suborder alchemic cochlear encomium
teaboard trawlnet cableway libretti suborner ancestor cockatoo encrinal

encrinic
encroach
encumber
encyclic
escalade
escalate
escallop
escalope
escapade
escapism
escapist
escargot
escarole
eschalot
eschewal
esculent
etcetera
eucalypt
eucritic
excavate
excelled
exchange
excision
excitant
exciting
excluder
excursus
faceache
facecard
faceless
facelift
facepack
facetiae
facially
facilely
facility
factious
factotum
feckless
feculent
focalise
focusing
focussed
fuchsine
hacienda
hecatomb
hiccough
hickwall
hocktide
hocusing
hocussed
huckster
inceptor
inchmeal
inchoate
inchworm
incident
incision
incisive
incitant
incivism
included
incoming
increase
increate
incubate
incurred
ischemia
ischemic
jackaroo
jackboot
jackeroo
jackstay
Jacobean
Jacobite
jacquard
jocosely
jocosity
jocundly
kickback
kickshaw
lacerate
lacewing
lacework
lackaday
laconian
laconism
lacrimal
lacrosse
lacrymal
lacunary
lacunate
lacunose
lecithin
lecturer
licensed
licensee
licenser
lichened
lichenin
lichgate
licorice
localise
localism
locality
locative
lockable
lockfast
lockknit
lockstep
locofoco
locomote
loculate
locution
locutory
lucidity
luckless
luculent
Lucullan
lychgate
macaroni
macaroon
macerate
machismo
mackerel
mackinaw
maculate
mechanic
meconium
micellar
microbar
microbic
microdot
micrurgy
moccasin
muchness
mucilage
muckluck
muckrake
muckworm
mucosity
mucrones
mycelial
mycelium
mycetoma
mycology
nacreous
neckband
necklace
neckline
necropsy
necrosis
necrotic
nectared
niceness
nickelic
nicknack
nickname
nicotian
nicotine
nocturne
nucellus
nuclease
nucleate
nucleole
nucleoli
nuclidic
occasion
occident
occluded
occlusal
occultly
occupant
occupier
occurred
oecology
onceover
oncidium
oncology
oncoming
Orcadian
orchilla
oscinine
osculant
osculate
pachalic
pacifier
pacifism
pacifist
peccable
peccancy
pectines
pectoral
peculate
peculiar
picaroon
picayune
pickerel
picketer
pickings
picklock
picnicky
pictures
pochette
pockmark
racecard
racegoer
racemate
racemise
racemose
rachides
rachitic
rachitis
racially
raciness
rackrent
recapped
receiver
recently
receptor
recharge
recision
reckless
reckoner
recommit
reconvey
recorder
recourse
recovery
recreant
recreate
rectoral
recurred
recusant
ricebird
ricercar
richness
rickrack
rickshaw
ricochet
rocaille
rockbird
rockcake
rockcork
rockdove
rocketry
rockfall
rockfish
rockhewn
rocklike
rockling
rockrose
rocksalt
rockweed
rockwood
rockwork
rucksack
saccadic
saccular
sacculus
sackcoat
sackless
sackrace
sacraria
sacredly
sacristy
secluded
seconder
secondly
secretin
secretly
secretor
sectoral
securely
security
Sicilian
sickener
sickerly
sickflag
sicklist
sickness
sickroom
socalled
sociable
sociably
socially
societal
Socinian
Socratic
succinct
succinic
succinum
succubae
succubus
suchlike
suckling
sycamine
sycamore
sycomore
syconium
tachisme
tachiste
taciturn
tackling
tackroom
tactical
tactless
technics
tectonic
ticklish
tickseed
ticktack
ticktock
tocology
tuckahoe
tuckshop
Tychonic
ulcerate
ulcerous
uncalled
uncandid
uncapped
uncaused
unchancy
unchaste
unchurch
uncially
unciform
uncinate
unclench
unclinch
unclothe
uncoined
uncommon
uncouple
uncreate
unctuous
vacantly
vacation
vaccinal
vaccinia
vacuolar
vicarage
vicarate
vicarial
vicinage
vicinity
victoria
victress
victuals
vocalise
vocalism
vocalist
vocality
vocation
vocative
wickedly
yachting
zecchini
zecchino
zucchini
Abderite
abdicate
abducens
abducent
abductor
addendum
addition
additive
adducent
adductor
aldehyde
alderman
Alderney
andesine
andesite
androgen
ardently
audacity
audience
audition
auditive
auditory
badinage
badlands
bedabble
bedazzle
bedeguar
bedimmed
bedmaker
bedplate
bedstead
bedstraw
bedtable
biddable
bodement
bodiless
Bodleian
bodyshop
bodywork
Buddhism
Buddhist
buddleia
budgeree
cadastre
cadenced
caducean
caduceus
caducity
caducous
cidevant
codifier
codpiece
codriver
dedicate
didactic
didapper
didymium
didymous
doddered
dodderer
eldorado
eldritch
endamage
endanger
endemism
endermic
endocarp
endoderm
endogamy
endogeny
endorsee
endorser
endostea
endozoic
endozoon
endpaper
fadeaway
fadeless
fedayeen
federate
fiddling
fidelity
fiducial
gadabout
gadarene
gadgetry
Gadhelic
gadzooks
godawful
godchild
Godspeed
godwards
hadronic
hedgehog
hedgehop
hedgepig
hedgerow
hedonics
hedonism
hedonist
hideaway
hidrosis
hidrotic
hidyhole
hydatoid
hydranth
hydrogen
hydromel
hydropic
hydropsy
hydroski
hydroxyl
indagate
indebted
indecent
Indiaman
indicant
indicate
indicium
indigene
indigent
indirect
indocile
indolent
inductee
inductor
indulger
induline
indurate
indusium
industry
iodinate
iodoform
jodhpurs
Judaical
Judaiser
judgment
judicial
kedgeree
kidglove
ladybird
ladyfern
ladyhood
ladylike
ladylove
ladyship
lodestar
lodgings
lodgment
lodicule
madapple
madhouse
madrigal
madwoman
medalled
medallic
medially
mediator
medicate
medicine
medieval
mediocre
meditate
medusoid
midbrain
middling
midfield
midlands
midnight
midpoint
midships
midwives
modalism
modalist
modality
modelled
modeller
moderate
moderato
modernly
modestly
modifier
modishly
modulate
mudguard
mudstone
nodalise
nodality
nodation
nodosity
nodulose
nodulous
nudeness
obduracy
obdurate
oddments
oldtimer
oldworld
ordainer
ordinand
ordinary
ordinate
ordnance
padishah
paduasoy
pedagogy
pedalier
pedalled
pedantic
pedantry
pederast
pedestal
pedicled
pedicure
pedigree
pediment
pedipalp
pedology
peduncle
piddling
podagral
podagric
podiatry
radially
radiance
radiancy
radiator
radicant
radicate
redactor
redblind
redbrick
redeemer
redefine
redeless
redeploy
redesign
redfaced
redirect
redistil
redolent
redouble
redshank
redshift
redshirt
redstart
redwater
riddance
rideable
ridgeway
ridicule
rudeness
rudiment
saddlery
Sadducee
sadistic
sedately
sedation
sedative
sederunt
sediment
sedition
sedulity
sedulous
sidearms
sideband
sidedish
sidedoor
sidedrum
sidehead
sidekick

sideline
sideling
sidelong
sidenote
sidereal
siderite
sideroad
sideshow
sideslip
sidesman
sidestep
sideview
sidewalk
sideward
sideways
sidewind
sidewise
sodalite
sodality
sodomite
Sudanese
sudarium
sudatory
suddenly
tidegate
tideland
tideless
tidelock
tidemark
tidemill
tidewave
tidiness
underact
underage
underarm
underbid
undercut
underdid
underdog
underfur
underlap
underlay
underlet
underlie
underlip
underman
underpin
underrun
undersea
underset
undertow
underway
undraped
undreamt
undulant
undulate
Vedantic
Wedgwood
wideeyed
wideness
yodelled
yodeller
zodiacal
abelmosk
aberrant
abetment
abetting
abeyance
abeyancy
aceldama
acentric
acerbate
acerbity
acervate
acescent
adenitis
adenoids
adequacy
adequate
adespota
agedness
agential
aleatory
alebench
alehouse
aleurone
alewives
amenable
amenably
American
amethyst
anecdote
anechoic
aneurism
aneurysm
aperient
aperitif
aperture
areolate
arethusa
aseptate
aventail
averment
averring
aversely
aversion
aversive
aweather
bdellium
beebread
beechnut
beeeater
beefcake
beefwood
beeswing
beetling
beetroot
biennial
biennium
bleacher
bleakish
blearily
bleeding
Blenheim
blesbuck
blessing
Boeotian
breakage
breaking
breakout
breasted
breather
breeches
breeding
breezily
bregmata
brethren
brettese
brettice
breveted
breviary
brewster
caesious
caesural
cheapish
checkers
checkout
cheekily
cheerful
cheerily
cheering
Chellean
chemical
chemurgy
chenille
chequers
Cherokee
cherubic
cherubim
chessman
chestnut
Cheyenne
cleancut
cleaning
cleanser
clearcut
clearing
clearway
cleavage
cleavers
clematis
clemency
clerical
clerihew
clerkdom
clerkess
cleverly
coelomic
coenobia
coenzyme
coercion
coercive
creakily
creamery
creatine
creation
creative
creatrix
creature
credence
credenza
credible
credibly
credited
creditor
creeping
crenated
crenelle
creosote
crepitus
crescent
crescive
cretonne
crevasse
daemonic
deedless
deemster
deeplaid
deepness
deerskin
dieldrin
diereses
dieresis
diestock
dietetic
djellaba
dreadful
dreamful
dreamily
dreaming
drearily
drencher
dressage
dressing
duelling
duellist
duettist
dwelling
dyestuff
edentate
egestion
egestive
ejection
ejective
election
elective
electret
electric
electron
electrum
elegance
elegancy
elenchus
elenctic
elephant
elevated
elevator
eleventh
emendate
emergent
emeritus
emersion
emetical
energise
enervate
erectile
erection
eremitic
erethism
erewhile
eternise
eternity
evection
evenfall
evenness
evensong
eventful
eventide
eventual
evermore
eversion
everyday
everyman
everyone
everyway
execrate
executor
exegesis
exegetic
exemplar
exemplum
exequies
exercise
exergual
exertion
eyeglass
eyeliner
eyepiece
eyerhyme
eyeshade
eyesight
eyestalk
eyetooth
eyewater
feeblish
feedback
feedhead
feedpipe
feedtank
fiendish
fiercely
fleabane
fleabite
fleawort
flection
fleeting
fleshfly
fleshpot
fletcher
flexible
flexibly
flexuose
flexuous
flexural
foetidly
freakish
freakout
freeborn
freedman
freefall
freehand
freehold
freeload
freeness
freesoil
freewill
freezeup
freezing
fremitus
frenetic
frenulum
frenzied
frequent
frescoes
freshman
freshrun
fretting
fretwork
Freudian
fuelling
ghettoes
gleaning
gleesome
gneissic
greasily
greedily
greegree
greenery
greenfly
greening
greenish
greenlet
greeting
greffier
greyfish
greyness
Guelphic
guerilla
guernsey
haematic
haematin
heedless
heelball
heelless
hielaman
hierarch
hieratic
iceblink
icebound
icecream
icefield
iceplant
iceskate
icewater
iceyacht
idealess
idealise
idealism
idealist
ideality
ideation
identify
identity
ideogram
ideology
inedible
inedited
inequity
inerrant
inertial
inexpert
irenical
irenicon
iterance
keelhaul
keelless
keenness
keepsake
keeshond
khedival
klephtic
kneedeep
kneehigh
kneehole
kneejerk
kreutzer
leeboard
liegeman
Maecenas
maenadic
maestoso
meekness
meetness
mnemonic
myelinic
myelitis
needfire
needless
needment
nielloed
obedient
obeisant
ocellate
okeydoke
oleander
oleaster
omelette
onehorse
onepiece
onesided
onetrack
openable
opencast
openeyed
openness
openplan
openwork
operable
operatic
operator
opercula
operetta
oreology
ovenbird
ovenware
overalls
overarch
overbear
overbook
overbore
overbusy
overcall
overcame
overcast
overcoat
overcome
overcrop
overdone
overdose
overdraw
overdrew
overfall
overfeed
overfill
overfish
overflew
overflow
overfold
overfond
overgrew
overgrow
overhand
overhang
overhaul
overhead
overhear
overheat
overhung
overjump
overkill
overlaid
overlain
overland
overleaf
overleap
overload
overlong
overlook
overlord
overmuch
overnice
overpaid
overpass
overpast
overplay
overplus
overrate
override
overripe
overrode
overrule
oversail
overseas
overseen
overseer
oversell
oversewn
overshoe
overshot
overside
oversize
overslip
oversold
oversoul
overstay
overstep
overtake
overtask
overtime
overtone
overtook
overture
overturn
overview
overwear
overwind
overwork
overworn
peekaboo
peelings
peephole
peepshow
peerless
pheasant
phenolic
phenylic
piecrust
piedmont
piercing
pleading
pleasant
pleasing
pleasure
plebeian
plectrum
pleinair
pleonasm
plethora
pleurisy
poetical
preacher
preamble
precinct
precious
preclude
predator
predella
preelect
preexist
pregnant
prehuman
prejudge
prelatic
prelease
premiere
premolar
premorse
prenatal
prentice
preparer
prepense
preprint
presager
prescind
presence
preserve
presidio
pressbox
pressing
pressman
pressure
prestige
presumer
pretence
prettify
prettily
previous
pteropod
pterylae
pyelitis
queasily
Quechuan
queendom
queening
queenlet
queerish
quencher
quenelle
question
queueing
reedbird
reedling
reedmace
reedpipe
reedstop
reedwren
reefknot
reembark
reemerge
reemploy
reexport
rheology
rheostat
rhetoric
Riesling
roentgen
ruefully
ryegrass
scenario
scenical
sceptred
seedcake
seedcase
seedcoat
seedcorn
seedfish
seedleaf
seedless
seedling
seedlobe
seedplot
seedsman

seedtime
sheading
shealing
shedding
shedevil
sheepdip
sheepdog
sheepish
sheepked
sheeppen
sheeprun
sheeting
sheikdom
Shekinah
shelduck
shelfful
shelving
Shemitic
shepherd
Sheraton
sherlock
Shetland
skeletal
skeleton
skerrick
sketcher
skewback
skewbald
skewness
sleazily
sledding
sleepily
sleeping
smelling
smeltery
sneakily
sneakish
sneeshan
speaking
spearman
speciate
specific
specimen
specious
spectral
spectrum
specular
speculum
speedily
speedway
spelling
spermary
steadily
steading
stealing
stealthy
steamily
stearate
stearine
steatite
stedfast
steenbok
steening
steepish
steepled
steerage
steering
steinbok
stellate
stellify
stellion
stemless
stemmata
stemming
stenosed
stenosis
stenotic
stepping
stepwise

sterigma
sterling
sternite
sternson
sternway
stetting
swearing
sweeping
sweepnet
sweeting
sweetish
sweetpea
sweetsop
swelling
syenitic
taenioid
teenager
teething
teetotal
teetotum
thearchy
theistic
thematic
theocrat
theodicy
theogony
theology
theorise
theorist
therefor
thereout
thermion
thermite
thesauri
thespian
thetical
theurgic
tiebreak
toepiece
toeplate
treacher
treadler
treasure
treasury
treatise
trecento
treefern
treefrog
treeless
treenail
trekking
trembler
trembles
trencher
trendily
trephine
trespass
tressure
trevally
tweezers
twelvemo
twenties
unearned
uneasily
unedited
unending
unerring
unevenly
urethane
usefully
Viennese
Vietcong
Vietminh
viewable
viewless
waesucks
weedless
weeklong
weeviled

weevilly
wheatear
wheedler
wheelman
wheezily
whenever
wherever
whetting
wheyface
woefully
wreathen
wreckage
wrestler
wrestpin
wretched
yielding
zoetrope
affected
affecter
afferent
affiance
affinity
affirmer
afflatus
affluent
afforest
affright
affusion
alfresco
befallen
befitted
befogged
befriend
befuddle
bifacial
bifocals
caffeine
cofactor
daffodil
daftness
defector
defender
deferent
deferral
deferred
deferrer
defiance
defilade
definite
deflower
deforest
deformed
defrayal
deftness
diffract
diffuser
effector
efferent
efficacy
effluent
effluvia
effusion
effusive
elfarrow
elflocks
enfeeble
enfetter
enfilade
enforcer
enforest
fiftieth
fiftyish
gefuffle
giftbook
infamise
infamous
infantry
infector
inferior

infernal
inferred
infilter
infinite
infinity
infirmly
inflamer
inflated
inflator
inflatus
inflexed
inflight
influent
informal
informed
informer
infrared
infringe
infusion
Kaffiyeh
kefuffle
lefthand
leftover
leftward
lifebelt
lifeboat
lifebuoy
lifeless
lifelike
lifeline
lifelong
lifesize
lifetime
lifework
liftable
oafishly
offbreak
offdrive
offender
offering
official
offprint
offshoot
offshore
offsider
offstage
piffling
puffball
puffbird
raftsman
referent
referral
referred
refinery
refitted
reflexed
refluent
reforest
reformed
reformer
rifeness
riffraff
rifleman
safeness
saffrony
safranin
siftings
softball
softboil
softener
softhead
softness
softshoe
softsoap
software
softwood
sufferer
suffrage
tafferel

taffrail
unfading
unfairly
unfasten
unfetter
unfilial
unfitted
unforced
unformed
unfreeze
unfrozen
unfunded
wifehood
wifeless
wifelike
aegirine
aegrotat
aggrieve
aigrette
aiguille
algicide
algidity
alginate
algology
Algonkin
algorism
alguazil
angelica
Anglican
angstrom
argentic
argonaut
arguable
arguably
argufier
argument
Augustan
augustly
bagpiper
baguette
begetter
beggarly
beginner
begirded
begotten
begrudge
beguiler
bigamist
bigamous
bignonia
bogeyman
cagebird
cageling
caginess
cogently
cogitate
cognomen
cognosce
cognovit
cogwheel
degrease
digamist
digamous
digester
diggings
digitate
digitise
dogberry
dogeared
dogfaced
dogfight
doggedly
doggerel
doghouse
dogmatic
dogooder
dogsbody
dogshore
dogtired

dogtooth
dogwatch
dogwhelk
eagleowl
edgeless
edgeways
edgewise
edginess
eggplant
eggshell
eighteen
eighthly
eighties
engaging
engender
engineer
enginery
engirdle
engramma
engraver
ergogram
ergotise
ergotism
eugenics
eugenism
eugenist
fagoting
fighting
figurant
figurine
fogbound
fugacity
fugitive
fugleman
gigantic
gogetter
Haggadah
Hegelian
hegemony
highball
highborn
highbred
highbrow
higherup
highjack
highland
highlows
highmost
highness
highrise
highroad
hightail
hightest
Hogmanay
hogsback
hogshead
hugeness
huggable
Huguenot
hygienic
ingather
ingrowth
inguinal
jaggedly
jiggered
jugglery
Jugoslav
jugulate
legalese
legalise
legalism
legalist
legality
legatine
legation
legbreak
legendry
legerity
leggings

legguard
legioned
ligament
ligation
ligature
lighting
lightish
ligneous
lignitic
ligulate
logician
logistic
logogram
logotype
magazine
magdalen
magician
magicked
magister
magmatic
magnesia
magnetic
magneton
magnific
magnolia
megalith
megapode
megawatt
mightest
mightily
migraine
migrator
negation
negative
negatory
negatron
negligee
Negrillo
negroism
niggling
nightcap
nighthag
nightjar
nightowl
nugatory
oogamous
oogonial
oogonium
organdie
organise
organism
organist
orgasmic
orgastic
orgulous
paganise
paganish
paganism
paginate
pagurian
Pegasean
pegboard
pigswill
puggaree
pugilism
pugilist
pugnosed
pygidial
pygidium
pygmaean
raggedly
regalism
regality
regelate
regicide
regiment
regional
register
registry

regolith
regrater
regrowth
regulate
rigadoon
rightful
rightist
rigidify
rigidity
rigorism
rigorist
rigorous
rogation
rogatory
ruggedly
rugosely
rugosity
rugulose
sagacity
sagamore
sageness
saginate
sagittal
segreant
sigmatic
signally
signpost
tagalong
tegmenta
tegument
tigereye
tigerish
tightwad
together
ungainly
unglazed
ungotten
ungulate
urgently
vagabond
vagility
vagrancy
vegetate
vegetive
vigilant
vigneron
vignette
vigorous
waggoner
wagonage
wagonlit
wigmaker
yoghourt
Yugoslav
ziggurat
zugzwang
zygaenid
abhorred
abhorrer
achenial
achiever
achiness
achingly
adherent
adhesion
adhesive
anhedral
aphasiac
aphelion
aphicide
aphorise
aphorism
aphorist
atheling
Athenian
atheroma
athletic
behemoth
beholden

beholder
bohemian
buhlwork
coherent
cohesion
cohesive
dahabieh
dihedral
dihybrid
echinate
echinoid
echogram
echoless
eohippus
ephemera
Ephesian
ephorate
ethereal
etherial
etherise
etherism
etherist
ethicism
ethicist
Ethiopic
ethnarch
ethnical
ethology
ethylene
exhalant
exhorter
ichorous
inhalant
inherent
inhesion
inhumane
Jehovist
Kohinoor
kohlrabi
maharaja
maharani
mahjongg
mahogany
Mahratta
Mahratti
Moharram
Muharram
nihilism
nihilist
nihility
ochreous
ophidian
rehandle
rehearse
rehoboam
schedule
schemata
scheming
schiedam
schiller
schizoid
schmaltz
schnapps
scholium
schooner
sphagnum
sphenoid
spherics
spheroid
spherule
sphingid
sphygmus
Tahitian
unhinged
unhoused
upheaval
upholder
vehement
Wahabism
Wahabite
abidance
aciculae
acicular
aciculas
acidfast
acidhead
acidosis
acierage
acierate
adiantum
agiotage
agitator
agitprop
alienage
alienate
alienism
alienist
alizarin
amiantus
amicable
amicably
amitosis
amitotic
aniconic
animally
animator
anisette
apiarian
apiarist
apically
Arianism
arillate
aristate
aviarist
aviation
aviatrix
avidness
avifauna
avionics
axiality
axillary
axiology
bailable
bailment
bailsman
blighter
blimpish
blindage
blinding
blinkers
blinking
blissful
blistery
blithely
blizzard
Briarean
bribable
brickbat
brickred
briefing
brighten
brightly
brimfull
brimless
brimming
brindled
briskish
brisling
britches
britzska
building
chiasmus
chiastic
chickpea
chiefdom
childbed
childish
children
chiliasm
chiliast
chimaera
chimeric
Chinaman
chinchin
chinless
chipmuck
chipmunk
chipping
chirpily
chirrupy
chitchat
chivalry
climatic
clincher
clinical
clinking
clipclop
clippers
clipping
cliquish
cliquism
coiffeur
coiffure
coincide
coistrel
cribbage
cribbing
criminal
crispate
cristate
criteria
critical
critique
daimonic
daintily
daiquiri
dairying
dairyman
deionise
dribbler
dribblet
driftage
driftice
driftway
drilling
drinking
dripfeed
dripping
drivable
driveway
editress
ekistics
eligible
eligibly
emigrant
emigrate
eminence
eminency
emissary
emission
emissive
emitting
epiblast
epically
epicalyx
epicotyl
epicycle
epidemic
epidural
epifauna
epigeous
epigraph
epilepsy
epilogue
epinasty
epiphany
epiphyte
episcope
episemon
episodal
episodic
epistler
epistyle
epitasis
erigeron
etiolate
eviction
evidence
evildoer
evilness
evincive
evitable
exigence
exigency
exigible
exiguity
exiguous
eximious
existent
failsafe
faineant
faintish
fairlead
fairness
fairyism
faithful
flickery
flimflam
flimsily
flincher
flinders
flintily
flipflap
flipflop
flippant
flipping
flipside
flitting
fribbler
friction
friendly
Friesian
frighten
frigidly
frijoles
frillies
fringing
frippery
frisette
friskily
fritting
gainable
gainings
gainless
gainsaid
glibness
glissade
glittery
Goidelic
goingson
goitrous
gridiron
grievous
grillage
grimacer
grimmest
grimness
grimoire
grindery
grinning
gripping
gripsack
Griselda
griseous
grisette
grisgris
grissini
gritting
grizzled
guidable
guidance
guidedog
guideway
guileful
guiltily
hairgrip
hairless
hairlike
hairline
hairworm
heighten
heirless
heirloom
heirship
idiolect
idiotism
imitable
imitator
inimical
iniquity
initiate
Irishism
Irishman
jailbird
joinable
jointure
kailyard
knickers
knightly
knitting
knitwear
laically
leisured
loiterer
maidenly
maidhood
maieutic
mailable
mailboat
mailcart
mainland
mainline
mainmast
mainsail
mainstay
maintain
mainyard
maiolica
moisture
nailfile
nainsook
noisette
nuisance
obituary
odiously
oeillade
olibanum
oligarch
oligomer
oliphant
omission
omitting
oriental
oriented
origanum
original
otiosely
otiosity
oviposit
oxidiser
oximeter
painless
paintbox
peignoir
Philomel
pliantly
plighted
plimsoll
Pliocene
poignant
pointing
poisoner
priapism
prideful
priedieu
priestly
priggery
priggish
priggism
primally
Primates
primeval
primming
primness
primrose
princely
princess
printing
printout
priorate
prioress
priority
prismoid
prisoner
prissily
pristine
psilosis
puissant
quibbler
quickset
quiddity
quidnunc
quietism
quietist
quietude
quillpen
quilting
quincunx
quintain
quipping
quirkily
quisling
quitrent
quitting
quixotic
quixotry
quizzing
railhead
raillery
railroad
rainbird
raincoat
raindrop
rainfall
rainwash
rainwear
reignite
reimpose
reindeer
reinless
reinsert
reinsman
reinsure
reinvest
rhinitis
Rhinodon
rhizopod
ruinable
sailable
sailboat
sailfish
sailless
sailorly
sailyard
sainfoin
saintdom
sciagram
sciatica
scilicet
scimitar
sciolism
sciolist
scirocco
scirrhus
scissile
scission
scissors
sciurine
sciuroid
seicento
seigneur
seignior
seignory
seizable
shielder
shieling
shiftily
shiftkey
shigella
shikaree
shilling
shimmery
shinbone
shingler
shingles
shinning
shipload
shipmate
shipment
shipping
shipworm
shipyard
shiralee
shirring
shirting
shivaree
skiagram
skidding
skilless
skilling
skimmilk
skimming
skimpily
skindeep
skinfood
skinhead
skinless
skinning
skipjack
skipping
skirmish
skirting
skislope
skittish
skittles
slideway
slightly
slimmest
slimming
slimmish
slimness
slinkily
slipcase
slipform
slipknot
slipover
slippage
slippery
slipping
slipring
sliproad
slipshod
slipslop
slithery
slitting
smithers
smithery
sniffily
sniffler
sniffles
sniggler
snippety
snipping
snipsnap
snitcher
soilless
soilpipe
spicated
spiccato
spicebox
spicknel
spiculae
spicular
spiculum
spiffing
spikelet
spillage
spillway
spinifex
spinning
spinster
spiracle
spirally
spirilla
spirited
spiritus
spiteful
spitfire
spitting
spittoon
spivvery
stibnite
stickful
stickily
stickjaw
stickler
stiffish
stigmata
stilbene
stilbite
stiletto
stillage
stimulus
stingily
stingray
stinkard
stinking
stinkpot
stipites
stippler
stipular
stirring
stitcher
suicidal
suitable
suitably
suitcase
suitings
swiftlet
swigging
swimming
swimsuit
swindler
swinging
switchel
tailback
tailcoat
tailgate
tailings
tailless
tailpipe
tailrace

tailspin
tainture
thiamine
thickety
thickish
thickset
thievery
thievish
thingamy
thinking
thinness
thinnest
thinning
thinnish
thirlage
thirster
thirteen
thisness
toiletry
toilette
toilsome
toilworn
trialist
triangle
triarchy
Triassic
triaxial
tribally
tribasic
tribrach
tribunal
trichina
trichite
trichoid
trichome
trichord
trickery
trickily
trickish
tricorne
tricycle
triennia
trifling
trifocal
triforia
triglyph
trigonal
trigraph
trilling
trillion
trillium
trilobed
trimaran
trimeric
trimeter
trimming
trimness
trioxide
tripeman
triplane
triploid
tripodal
trippery
tripping
triptych
tripwire
triskele
trisomic
tristful
tristich
tritical
triumvir
triunity
twiddler
twilight
twinborn
twinkler
twinling
twinning

twinship
twitcher
twittery
twitting
ubiquity
uniaxial
unicycle
unifilar
unionise
unionism
unionist
unipolar
uniquely
unisonal
unitedly
univalve
universe
univocal
utiliser
vainness
veilless
voicebox
voiceful
voidable
voidance
voidness
wainscot
waitress
whidding
whiffler
Whiggery
Whiggish
Whiggism
whimbrel
whimwham
whinchat
whinsill
whipcord
whiplash
whiplike
whipping
whipworm
whirring
whiskers
whiskery
whispery
whistler
whiteboy
whitecap
whitefly
whitehot
whitener
whiteout
whitetie
whittret
whizbang
whizzing
whizzkid
wriggler
wristlet
wristpin
writable
writeoff
writings
zoiatria
zwieback
abjectly
adjacent
adjuster
adjustor
adjutage
adjutant
adjuvant
bejabers
cajolery
dejected
Gujarati
hijacker
injector

jejunely
majestic
majolica
majority
objector
rejecter
rejigger
rejoicer
unjustly
Akkadian
alkahest
alkalies
alkalify
alkaline
alkaloid
ankerite
ankylose
bakshish
cakewalk
cokernut
Dukhobor
elkhound
enkindle
Eskimoan
inkiness
inkstand
jokingly
kakemono
lakeland
likeable
likeness
likewise
lukewarm
lykewake
makebate
makefast
makimono
oakapple
oakegger
Pekinese
rakehell
rakishly
rekindle
sukiyaki
takeaway
takehome
takeover
takingly
tokenism
tokology
unkennel
unkindly
unkingly
wakeless
wakening
wakerife
yokemate
ablation
ablative
ablution
Adlerian
adlibbed
aflutter
aglimmer
aglitter
allegory
alleluia
allergen
allergic
alleyway
alliance
allnight
allocate
allodial
allodium
allogamy
allopath
allotted
allottee

allround
allspice
allusion
allusive
alluvial
alluvion
alluvium
aplastic
atlantes
Atlantic
axletree
balanced
balancer
baldhead
baldness
baldpate
balefire
Balinese
balkline
balladic
balladry
ballcock
balletic
ballista
ballonet
ballroom
ballyhoo
ballyrag
balmoral
balsamic
baluster
belabour
believer
belittle
bellbird
bellbuoy
bellcote
bellpull
bellpush
bellwort
bellyful
beltless
bilabial
bilberry
billfold
billhead
billhook
billiard
billyboy
billycan
bilobate
boldface
boldness
bollworm
bolthole
boltrope
bulkhead
bullcalf
bulldoze
bulletin
bullfrog
bullhead
bullhorn
bullocky
bullring
bullseye
bullyboy
bullyoff
bullyrag
calabash
caladium
calamary
calamine
calamint
calamite
calamity
calcanea
calcaria
calcific

calcitic
calcspar
calctuff
calculus
calendar
calender
calfskin
calidity
califate
calipash
calipers
callable
callgirl
calliope
calliper
calmness
calthrop
calvados
calycine
calycoid
calycule
calyptra
celeriac
celerity
celibacy
celibate
cellarer
cellaret
cellular
chlorate
chloride
chlorine
chlorite
chlorous
ciliated
colander
coldness
coleseed
coleslaw
colewort
coliform
coliseum
collagen
collapse
collared
collator
colleger
colliery
collogue
colloquy
collyria
colonial
colonise
colonist
colophon
colossal
colossus
coloured
colubrid
columnal
columnar
columned
culdesac
culicine
culinary
culottes
culpable
culpably
cultivar
cultural
cultured
culverin
cylinder
dalesman
dalmatic
delation
delegacy
delegate
deletion

delibate
delicacy
delicate
delirium
delivery
Delphian
delusion
delusive
delusory
dilatant
dilation
dilative
dilatory
diligent
dilution
diluvial
diluvian
diluvium
doldrums
dolerite
dolesome
dolomite
doloroso
dolorous
dulciana
dulcimer
Dulcinea
dullness
eclectic
ecliptic
eclosion
eelgrass
ellipses
ellipsis
elliptic
enlarger
eolithic
eulachon
eulogise
eulogist
eulogium
exlibris
falcated
falchion
falconer
falconet
falconry
falderal
fallback
fallfish
fallible
fallibly
falsetto
faltboat
feldsher
feldspar
felicity
felinity
fellable
fellahin
fellness
fellowly
felsitic
filagree
filament
filariae
filarial
filature
filefish
filially
filiform
filigree
Filipina
Filipino
filmgoer
filmstar
filthily
filtrate
foldaway

foldboat
folderol
foliaged
folklore
folkmoot
folksong
folktale
follicle
follower
followon
followup
fullback
fullness
fullpage
fullsize
fulltime
galactic
galangal
galbanum
galeated
Galenism
galenite
Galilean
galleass
galliard
Gallican
gallipot
galloper
Galloway
galluses
gallwasp
galvanic
gelastic
gelatine
gelation
gelidity
gillaroo
gilthead
Golconda
golddust
goldenly
goldfish
goldfoil
goldleaf
goldmine
goldrush
golfclub
golliwog
gulfweed
gullable
gullible
gulosity
Halachah
halation
haleness
halfback
halfbeak
halfboot
halfbred
halflife
halfmast
halfmoon
halfnote
halfpint
halfsole
halfterm
halftime
halftone
haliotis
halliard
hallmark
hallowed
halluces
halteres
heliacal
helicoid
heliosis
heliport
Helladic

hellbent
Hellenic
hellfire
hellhole
helmeted
helminth
helmsman
helotism
helpless
helpmate
helpmeet
hilarity
hillfort
hillocky
hillside
holdback
holdfast
holdover
holidays
holiness
holistic
hollands
hollowly
Holocene
hologram
holozoic
holstein
hulahula
idleness
illation
illative
illfated
illiquid
illtimed
illtreat
illumine
illusage
illusion
illusive
illusory
Illyrian
inlander
Islamise
Islamism
Islamite
islander
jalousie
jolthead
julienne
kalaazar
killdeer
kilogram
kilowatt
kolinsky
lallygag
Lollardy
lollipop
lollypop
Malagasy
malamute
malapert
malaprop
malarial
malarian
malarkey
maledict
malefern
malemute
maleness
maligner
malignly
malinger
malodour
maltreat
maltster
malvasia
melamine
melanism
melanite

melinite
mellowly
melodeon
melodise
melodist
mildness
milepost
Milesian
militant
military
militate
milkmaid
milkweed
milkwort
millhand
milliard
milliary
millibar
millieme
milliner
millpond
millrace
Miltonic
molality
molarity
molasses
molecule
molehill
moleskin
molester
Molinism
Molinist
molossus
molybdic
mulberry
muleteer
mulishly
mulloway
multeity
multifid
multiped
multiple
multiply
mylonite
nullness
oblation
oblatory
obligate
obliging
oblivion
oilcloth
oilfield
oilfired
oiliness
oilstone
onlooker
oologist
owlishly
palatial
palatine
paleface
paleness
palestra
palinode
palisade
palliate
pallidly
pallmall
palmette
palmetto
palmiped
palmitin
palomino
palpable
palpably
palterer
paludism
Pelagian
Pelasgic

pelerine
pellagra
pellicle
pellmell
pellucid
pelorism
phlegmon
pilaster
pilchard
pileated
pilewort
pilferer
piliform
pillager
pillwort
pilosity
pilotage
pilsener
polarise
polarity
polemics
polemise
polemist
polestar
polisher
politely
politick
politico
politics
pollices
pollinia
pollinic
polliwog
pollster
polluter
pollywog
polonium
poltfoot
poltroon
polygala
polygamy
polygene
polygeny
polyglot
polygyny
polymath
polypary
polypide
polypite
polypody
polypoid
polypous
polyseme
polysemy
polysomy
polyzoan
polyzoic
polyzoon
pullback
pullover
pulmonic
pulpiter
pulpwood
pulsator
pulvilli
pulvinus
rallying
rallyist
relation
relative
relaxant
releasee
releaser
releasor
relegate
relevant
reliable
reliably
reliance

reliever
religion
relocate
relucent
relumine
rollcall
rollneck
rolypoly
ruleless
salacity
salariat
salaried
saleable
saleroom
Salesian
salesman
salience
saliency
salinity
salivary
salivate
Salopian
saltbush
saltless
saltlick
saltmine
saltness
saltwort
salutary
salvable
salvific
sclereid
sclerite
scleroma
sclerose
sclerous
seladang
selcouth
selectee
selector
selenate
selenide
selenite
selenium
selfborn
selfheal
selfhelp
selfhood
selfless
selflove
selfmade
selfmate
selfness
selfpity
selfrule
selfsame
selfsown
selfwill
selvedge
silencer
silently
silicane
silicate
silicide
silicify
silicone
silkworm
sillabub
silphium
Silurian
siluroid
silvatic
silverly
solander
solanine
solarise
solarism
solarist
solarium

solation
solatium
solderer
soldiery
solecism
solecist
solemnly
soleness
solenoid
solfaist
solfeggi
solidary
solidify
solidity
solitary
solitude
solleret
solstice
solution
solvable
solvency
splasher
splatter
splendid
splenial
splenius
splinter
splitter
splotchy
splutter
sullenly
sulphate
sulphide
sulphite
sulphone
sultrily
syllabic
syllable
syllabub
syllabus
sylphide
sylphine
sylphish
sylvatic
talapoin
talented
talesman
talisman
tallness
tallyman
Talmudic
telecast
telecine
telefilm
telegony
telegram
telemark
telepath
teleport
telethon
teleview
televise
tellable
telltale
telluric
tilefish
tillable
tiltyard
tolbooth
tolerant
tolerate
tollcall
tolldish
tollgate
ugliness
unlawful
unleaded
unlearnt
unlikely

unlimber
unlinked
unlisted
unloader
unloosen
unlovely
uplander
uplifter
valanced
valerate
valerian
Valhalla
valiance
valiancy
validate
validity
valorise
valorous
valuable
valuably
valuator
valvulae
valvular
velamina
velarium
velleity
velocity
velskoen
vileness
vilifier
vilipend
villadom
villager
villainy
villatic
volatile
volcanic
volcanos
volitant
volition
volitive
volplane
voltaism
volution
volvulus
vulcanic
vulgarly
waleknot
Walhalla
walkable
walkaway
walkover
Walkyrie
wallaroo
walleyed
wallfern
wallgame
wallknot
walloper
wallower
weldable
weldment
welladay
wellaway
wellborn
wellbred
welldeck
wellhead
wellknit
wellnigh
wellread
Wellsian
wellworn
Welshman
wildeyed
wildfire
wildfowl
wildlife
wildness

wildwood
wilfully
wiliness
williwaw
wolffish
wolfpack
wolfskin
xylocarp
xylology
xylonite
yellowly
yuletide
admitted
admonish
almagest
almanack
almighty
ammoniac
ammonify
ammonite
ammonium
Armagnac
armament
armature
armchair
Armenian
Arminian
armorial
armoured
armourer
armyworm
bambinos
bimanous
bimbashi
bombsite
bummaree
Cambrian
cameleer
camellia
camisade
camisado
camisole
camomile
campagna
campaign
campfire
camphene
camphine
campsite
camshaft
cemetery
comatose
combings
comeback
comedian
comedist
comedown
cometary
commando
commence
commerce
commoner
commoney
commonly
communal
commuter
compages
compiler
complain
compleat
complete
complice
complier
compline
composed
composer
compound
compress
comprise

computer
Cumbrian
cumbrous
cumulate
cumulous
cymatium
damassin
damnable
damnably
dampness
demagogy
demander
demarche
demented
dementia
demerara
demersal
demijohn
demitted
demiurge
demobbed
democrat
demolish
demoness
demoniac
demonian
demonise
demonism
demotion
demurely
demurred
demurrer
dimerism
dimerous
diminish
dimmable
domestic
domicile
dominant
dominate
domineer
dominion
dominoes
dumbbell
dumbhead
dumbness
dumbshow
dumfound
dumpling
Emmental
familial
familiar
famously
feminine
feminise
feminism
feminist
feminity
fimbriae
fomenter
fumarole
fumigant
fumigate
fumitory
gambados
gambeson
gambroon
gamebird
gamecock
gameness
gamesome
gamester
gaminess
gematria
geminate
gemstone
gimcrack
gimmicky
gummosis

gumption
gymkhana
gymnasia
hamartia
hamululi
himation
homebody
homeborn
homebred
homebrew
homefelt
homeland
homeless
homelike
homemade
homesick
homespun
hometown
homeward
homework
homicide
hominoid
homodont
homogamy
homogeny
homology
homonymy
homuncle
humanely
humanise
humanism
humanist
humanity
humanoid
humidify
humidity
humility
hummocky
humorist
humorous
humoured
humpback
humuncle
hymenial
hymenium
hymnbook
ilmenite
immanent
immature
immersed
imminent
immingle
immobile
immodest
immolate
immortal
immunise
immunity
jamboree
jumpedup
jumpseat
jumpsuit
kamikaze
Khmerian
komitaji
Komsomol
lamasery
lambaste
lambency
lamblike
lambskin
lamellae
lamellar
lameness
lamented
laminate
lamppost
lemonade
lemurine

lemuroid
limbless
limekiln
limerick
limetwig
limewash
limitary
limonite
limpidly
limpness
lomentum
lumberer
luminant
luminary
luminist
luminous
lumpfish
lymphoid
lymphoma
Mameluke
mamillae
mamillar
membered
membrane
mementos
memorial
memorise
memsahib
mimester
mimicked
mimicker
momently
momentum
nameable
namedrop
nameless
namepart
namesake
nametape
nematode
nematoid
nimbused
nomadise
nomadism
nominate
nomistic
nomogram
nomology
numberer
numbfish
numbness
numeracy
numerary
numerate
numerous
numinous
numskull
nymphean
ohmmeter
ommateum
pamperer
pamphlet
pembroke
pemmican
pimiento
pomander
pomology
pumproom
rambling
rambutan
ramentum
ramequin
rampancy
remanent
remedial
remember
reminder
remissly
remittal

remitted
remittee
remitter
remotely
rimbrake
rimester
romancer
Romanian
romanise
Romanism
Romanist
Romansch
romantic
Rumanian
Rumansch
ruminant
ruminate
rummager
samarium
sameness
samizdat
Samoyede
samphire
sampling
semantic
semester
semibull
semidome
seminary
seminude
semiotic
Semitise
Semitism
Semitist
semitone
semolina
semplice
sempster
similise
simoniac
simonist
simplify
simplism
simulant
simulate
somatism
sombrely
sombrero
sombrous
somebody
somedeal
somedele
sometime
someways
somewhat
somewhen
somnific
Sumerian
summerly
summitry
summoner
symbiont
symbolic
symmetry
sympathy
symphile
symphony
sympodia
symposia
tamandua
tamanoir
tamarack
tamarind
tamarisk
tamboura
tameable
tameless
tameness
Tamilian

tamperer
temerity
tempered
temperer
template
temporal
tempting
timbered
timeball
timebomb
timefuse
timeless
timework
timeworn
timidity
timorous
timously
tomahawk
tomalley
tombless
tomentum
tommybar
tommygun
tommyrot
tomnoddy
tomogram
tomorrow
tumbling
tumidity
tumorous
tympanic
tympanum
unmanned
unmarked
unmeetly
unmuffle
unmuzzle
vambrace
vampiric
vamplate
vomerine
vomitive
vomitory
womanise
womanish
zamindar
zemindar
zombiism
zymology
abnegate
abnormal
adnation
agnation
agnostic
amnesiac
amniotic
annalist
annotate
announce
annually
annulate
annulled
banality
banausic
bandanna
bandeaux
banderol
banditry
banditti
bandsman
bangtail
banister
banjoist
bankable
bankbill
bankbook
banknote
bankroll
bankrupt

bannered
banneret
bannerol
banterer
bantling
banxring
benedick
benedict
benefice
benignly
Benjamin
bentwood
benzoate
benzylic
binaural
bindweed
binnacle
binomial
bondmaid
bondmans
bondsman
bonefish
bonehead
boneless
bonemeal
boneyard
bonhomie
boniface
boniness
bonspiel
bontebok
buncombe
bundling
bunfight
bungalow
bunghole
bunkered
buntline
Canadian
canaille
canalise
canaster
cancrine
cancroid
candidly
canister
cannabin
cannabis
cannibal
cannikin
cannonry
cannulae
cannular
cannulas
canoeing
canoeist
canoness
canonise
canonist
canoodle
canorous
canthari
canticle
cantonal
cantoris
canzonet
cenotaph
Cenozoic
centaury
centring
centrism
centrist
centroid
centuple
cinchona
cincture
cineaste
cinerary
cingulum

cinnabar
cinnamic
cinnamon
cinquain
conation
conative
concasse
conceder
conceive
concerti
concerto
concetti
concetto
conchate
conchoid
conclave
conclude
concrete
condense
condylar
conferee
conferva
confetti
confider
confiner
confines
conflate
conflict
confound
confrere
confront
congener
conglobe
congress
congreve
conidial
conidium
coniform
conjoint
conjugal
conjunct
conjurer
conjuror
conniver
conoidal
conquest
conserve
consider
consoler
consomme
conspire
constant
construe
consular
consumer
contagia
contango
contempt
contents
contessa
continua
continue
continuo
contline
contorno
contract
contrail
contrary
contrast
contrate
contrite
contrive
conurbia
convener
convenor
converge
converse
convexly
conveyer

conveyor
convince
convolve
convulse
cynicism
cynosure
dancette
dancetty
dandruff
dandyish
dandyism
danegeld
dankness
danseuse
denarius
denature
denazify
dendrite
dendroid
denehole
deniable
denounce
dentalia
dentated
denticle
dinerout
dingdong
dinornis
dinosaur
donation
Donatism
Donatist
donative
donatory
donought
dundiver
dungaree
dungcart
dunghill
dynamics
dynamism
dynamist
dynamite
dynastic
dynatron
enneagon
fanciful
fancyman
fandance
fandango
fanfaron
fangless
fanlight
fantasia
fenberry
fencible
fenestra
finalise
finalism
finalist
finality
finedraw
fineness
finespun
fingered
finisher
finitely
finitude
finnesko
fondling
fondness
fontanel
fontange
function
funebral
funerary
funereal
fungible
funkhole

funnyman
gangland
gangling
ganglion
gangrene
gangster
ganister
gantline
gantlope
Ganymede
gendarme
generate
generous
genetics
Genevese
genially
genitive
geniture
genocide
genotype
gentrice
gingerly
gingival
gonfalon
gonidial
gonidium
gunfight
gunflint
gunlayer
gunmetal
gunpoint
gunsmith
gunstock
gynandry
gynocrat
gynoecia
handball
handbell
handbill
handbook
handcart
handclap
handcuff
handfast
handgrip
handheld
handhold
handicap
handless
handline
handling
handlist
handloom
handmade
handmaid
handmill
handpick
handrail
handsewn
handsome
handwork
handyman
hangable
hangeron
hangnail
hangover
henchman
henequen
henparty
henroost
hinderer
hindlegs
hindmost
hinduise
Hinduism
honestly
honeybee
honeydew
honeypot

honorary
honourer
hungrily
huntress
huntsman
ianthine
ignition
ignitron
ignominy
ignorant
innately
innocent
innovate
innuendo
janizary
jingoish
jingoism
jingoist
Jonathan
jongleur
junction
juncture
junkshop
junkyard
Kanarese
kangaroo
kindless
kindling
kindness
kinesics
kinetics
kingbird
kingbolt
kingcrab
kingfish
kinghood
kinglike
kingship
kingsize
kinkajou
kinsfolk
lancelet
landarmy
landcrab
landfall
landform
landgirl
landlady
landless
landline
landlord
landmark
landmass
landmine
landrail
landslip
landsman
langlauf
Langshan
language
languish
lankness
lanneret
lanthorn
lengthen
lenience
leniency
Leninism
Leninist
Leninite
lenitive
lensless
lenticel
lenticle
linchpin
lineally
linearly
linesman
lingerer

lingerie
linguist
liniment
Linnaean
linoleum
linstock
lintseed
Londoner
loneness
lonesome
longboat
longeron
longeval
longhair
longhand
longhorn
longness
longship
longsome
longstop
longterm
longtime
longueur
longwall
longwave
longways
longwise
lunarian
lunation
luncheon
lungfish
lungwort
lunulate
lynchpin
lynxeyed
mancando
manciple
Mandaean
mandamus
mandarin
mandator
mandible
Mandingo
mandolin
mandorla
mandrake
mandrill
maneater
manfully
mangabey
manganic
mangonel
mangrove
maniacal
Manichee
manicure
manifest
manifold
maniform
mannered
mannerly
mannikin
mannitol
manorial
manpower
mansized
mantelet
mantilla
mantissa
mantling
manually
manubria
manurial
menarche
mendable
menhaden
menially
meninges
meniscus
menology
menstrua
mensural
menswear
mentally
minacity
minatory
mindless
minimise
minister
ministry
Minoress
Minorite
minority
Minotaur
minstrel
mintmark
minutely
minutiae
monachal
monadism
monandry
monarchy
monastic
monaural
monaxial
monazite
mondaine
monetary
monetise
moneybag
moneybox
Mongolic
mongoose
monicker
monistic
monition
monitive
monitory
monkfish
MonKhmer
monkhood
monkseal
monkship
monoacid
monocrat
monocyte
monodist
monogamy
monogeny
monoglot
monogony
monogram
monogyny
monolith
monomial
monopode
monopoly
monorail
monotint
monotone
monotony
monotype
monoxide
monsieur
monteith
monument
muniment
munition
nanogram
nenuphar
ninefold
ninepins
nineteen
nineties
nonclaim
nondairy
nonesuch
nonevent
nonhuman
nonjuror
nonlegal
nonmetal
nonmoral
nonparty
nonrigid
nonsense
nonstick
nonunion
nonusage
nonwhite
oenology
oenophil
ointment
omnivore
ornament
ornately
ornithic
pancreas
pandanus
pandemic
pandowdy
panelled
pangolin
panicked
panmixia
pannikin
panorama
panpipes
pansophy
pantheon
pantofle
pantsuit
penalise
penchant
pendency
pendicle
pendular
pendulum
penitent
penknife
penology
penstock
pentacle
pentagon
pentroof
penumbra
pinafore
pinaster
pincenez
pinchers
Pindaric
pinecone
pinewood
pinkness
pinmoney
pinnacle
pinnated
pinniped
pinnular
pinochle
pinpoint
pinprick
pintable
pintsize
pinwheel
ponderer
pondweed
pontifex
ponytail
puncheon
punctate
punctual
puncture
punditry
pungency
puniness
punisher
punition
punitive
punitory
ranarian
ranarium
ranchero
ranchman
randomly
rankness
ransomer
renderer
renegade
renegado
reneguer
reniform
renitent
renounce
renovate
renowned
rentable
renumber
ringbark
ringbolt
ringbone
ringdove
ringmain
ringneck
ringroad
ringside
ringtail
ringwall
ringworm
rinsings
rondeaux
runabout
runagate
runcible
runnerup
sanative
sanatory
sanctify
sanction
sanctity
sandarac
sandbank
sandbath
sandflea
sandshoe
sandwich
sandworm
sandwort
sandyish
saneness
sangaree
Sangrail
Sangreal
sanguine
sanitary
sanitate
sanitise
sannyasi
sanserif
Sanskrit
santonin
senarius
senility
sennight
senorita
senseful
sensible
sensibly
sensoria
sensuous
sentence
sentient
sentinel
sentrygo
Sinaitic
sinapism
sinciput
sinecure
sinfonia
sinfully
singable
singeing
singsong
singular
sinicise
sinister
sinkable
sinkhole
sinology
sinophil
sinusoid
sonatina
songbird
songbook
songless
songster
sonobuoy
sonority
sonorous
sunbaked
sunbathe
sunblind
sunburnt
sunburst
sundance
sunderer
sundress
sundried
sundries
sundrops
sunlight
sunproof
sunshade
sunshine
sunshiny
sunstone
sunwards
synapsis
synaptic
synastry
syncline
syncopal
syncytia
syndesis
syndetic
syndical
syndrome
synergic
synergid
syngamic
synonymy
synopses
synopsis
synoptic
synovial
syntagma
syntonic
tandoori
tangency
tangible
tangibly
tangoist
tanistry
tannable
tantalic
tantalum
tantalus
Tantrism
tantrist
tenacity
tenacula
tenaille
tenantry
tendence
tendency
tenderly
Tenebrae
tenement
tenesmus
tenonsaw
tenorite
tenotomy
tenpence
tenpenny
tensible
tentacle
tenurial
tincture
tingeing
tininess
tinkerer
tinnitus
tinplate
tinselly
tinsmith
tinstone
tintless
tonality
tonedeaf
toneless
tonepoem
tonguing
tonicity
tuneable
tuneless
tungsten
tungstic
tunicate
Tunisian
uintaite
vanadate
vanadium
vanadous
Vandalic
vaneless
vanguard
vanillin
vanisher
vanquish
venality
venation
vendetta
vendible
veneerer
venerate
venereal
Venetian
vengeful
venially
venomous
venosity
venously
ventless
venturer
Venusian
vincible
vinculum
vinegary
vineyard
vinosity
vinously
vintager
wanderer
wanderoo
wantonly
windburn
windcone
windfall
windgall
windlass
windless
windmill
windowed
windpipe
windrose
windsail
windsock
windward
winepalm
wineshop
wineskin
wingbeat
wingcase
wingless
wingspan
winnable
winnings
winnower
winterly
wintrily
wondrous
wontedly
xanthate
xanthein
xanthene
xanthine
xanthium
xanthoma
Xantippe
xenogamy
xenolith
Yankeefy
zaniness
zenithal
zinckify
zincking
zonation
abomasum
abomasus
aborally
aborning
abortion
abortive
aconitic
aconitum
acosmism
acoustic
adoption
adoptive
adorable
adorably
agonised
alogical
alopecia
amoebean
amoeboid
amorally
amoretti
amoretto
amortise
anorexia
anorexic
anorthic
anourous
apocrine
apodoses
apodosis
apogamic
apograph
apologia
apologue
apomixis
apoplexy
apostasy
apostate
apothegm
aromatic
atomiser
avowable
avowedly
bioassay
biocidal
biogenic
biograph
biometry
biomorph
bionomic
bioplasm
bioplast
bioscope
blockade
blockage
blockish
blondish
bloodily
bloodred
bloomers
bloomery
blooming
blossomy
blotting
blowball
blowfish
blowhard
blowhole
blowlamp
blowpipe
bookcase
bookends
bookland
booklice
booklore
bookmark
bookpost
bookrest
bookwork
bookworm
bootjack
bootlace
bootlast
bootless
boottree
broacher
broadish
broadway
brocaded
brocatel
broccoli
brochure
broidery
brokenly
bromelia
bromidic
bronchia
bronchus
broodily
brookite
brooklet
brougham
brouhaha
browband
browbeat
browning
brownish
buoyancy
choicely
choirboy
choleric
chondrus
chopchop
chopping
chopsuey
choragic
choragus
chorally
chordate
choregic
choregus
choriamb
chorioid
chowchow
cloddish

clodpole
clodpoll
clogging
cloister
clopclop
closeset
closeted
clothier
clothing
clotting
cloudily
cloudlet
clownery
clownish
cookbook
coolabah
coolibah
coolness
coonskin
cooption
cooptive
croakily
Croatian
croceate
crockery
crocoite
crofting
cromlech
cromorna
cromorne
cropping
crossbar
crossbow
crosscut
crossing
crosslet
crossply
crosstie
crossway
crotched
crotchet
croupier
croupous
crowbill
crowfoot
diocesan
dioecism
diopside
dioptase
dioptric
dioramic
dioritic
doomsday
doomsman
doomster
doorbell
doorcase
doorknob
doornail
doorpost
doorsill
doorstep
doorstop
dooryard
drollery
drophead
dropkick
dropleaf
dropping
dropshot
dropwort
droughty
drownded
drowsily
duodenal
duodenum
duologue
ecologic
economic
egoistic
egomania
elongate
eloquent
enormity
enormous
epopoeia
erodible
erogenic
erotical
esoteric
euonymin
euonymus
exocrine
exogamic
exorcise
exorcism
exorcist
exordial
exordium
exospore
exoteric
floatage
floating
floccose
floccule
flocculi
flockbed
flogging
floodlit
floodway
flooring
floppily
flopping
florally
floridly
florigen
flotilla
flounder
flourish
flowered
flowerer
floweret
foodless
foolscap
football
footbath
footfall
footgear
foothill
foothold
footless
footling
footmark
footmuff
footnote
footpace
footpath
footpost
footrace
footrest
footrope
footrule
footslog
footsore
footstep
footwear
footwork
frocking
frogfish
frogging
frogspit
frondage
frondent
frondeur
frondose
frontage
frontier
frontlet
frostily
frosting
frothily
frottage
froufrou
gaolbird
geodesic
geodetic
geognosy
geologic
geomancy
geometer
geometry
geophagy
geophone
geophyte
geoponic
Georgian
geotaxis
ghoulish
gloaming
globally
globular
globulin
gloomily
gloriole
glorious
glossary
glossily
glossina
glowworm
gloxinia
gnomonic
goodness
goodtime
goodwife
goodwill
goodyear
goofball
goosegog
groggily
grogshop
gromwell
groogroo
grosbeak
groschen
grottoes
grounder
grouping
grouting
growling
hoodwink
hoofbeat
hookworm
hooligan
hoosegow
hyoscine
idocrase
idolater
idolatry
idoliser
inoculum
inositol
ironbark
ironclad
irongray
irongrey
ironical
ironside
ironware
ironwood
ironwork
Iroquois
isobaric
isocheim
isocracy
isodicon
isogamic
isogloss
isogonal
isogonic
isolable
isolator
isomeric
isometry
isomorph
isophote
isopleth
isoprene
isoptera
isospory
isostasy
isothere
isotherm
isotonic
isotopic
isotropy
ivorynut
jeopardy
klondike
knocking
knockout
knothole
knotting
knotwork
knowable
kromesky
lookeron
loonybin
loophole
loosebox
loosener
lyophile
moonbeam
mooncalf
moonface
moonfish
moonless
moonrise
moonsail
moonshee
moonshot
moonwort
moorcock
moorfowl
moorings
moorland
myoblast
myogenic
myograph
myositic
myositis
myosotis
NeoLatin
neomycin
neonatal
neophyte
neoplasm
neoprene
neotenic
neoteric
noontide
noontime
odograph
odometer
odontoid
omophagy
omoplate
orogenic
otoscope
ozoniser
phonemic
phonetic
phormium
phosgene
phosphor
photogen
photopia
photopic
photopsy
plodding
plopping
plotting
plougher
poohpooh
poorness
probable
probably
proceeds
proclaim
procurer
prodding
prodigal
prodrome
producer
proemial
profaner
profiler
profound
progress
prohibit
prolamin
prolapse
prolific
prolixly
prologue
prolonge
promisee
promiser
promisor
promoter
prompter
promptly
promulge
pronator
proofing
propense
properly
property
prophase
prophecy
prophesy
propolis
proposal
proposer
propound
propping
propylic
prorogue
prosaism
prosaist
prosodic
prospect
prostate
prostyle
protasis
protatic
protease
protegee
protista
protocol
protonic
protozoa
protract
protrude
provable
provably
provided
provider
province
provisor
proximal
ptomaine
pyogenic
quotable
quotient
reoccupy
reorient
rhomboid
rhonchal
rhonchus
roodbeam
roodloft
roofless
roofrack
rooftree
roommate
roothold
rootless
ryotwari
scolding
scolices
scombrid
scoopful
scoopnet
scopulae
scopulas
scorcher
scornful
scorpion
scotfree
scotopic
Scotsman
scottice
Scottish
scourger
scouting
sforzato
shocking
shoddily
shoebill
shoehorn
shoelace
shoeless
shoetree
shofroth
shogging
shooting
shootout
shopbell
shopgirl
shopping
shoptalk
shopworn
shortage
shortarm
shortcut
shortday
shortish
shothole
shoulder
shouldst
showbill
showboat
showcard
showcase
showdown
showgirl
showroom
slobbery
slobbish
slobland
sloeeyed
slogging
sloppail
sloppily
slopping
slopshop
slopwork
slothful
slotting
slouching
slovenly
slovenry
slowdown
slowness
slowpoke
slowworm
smocking
smokable
smoothen
smoothie
smoothly
smothery
smoulder
snobbery
snobbish
snobbism
snogging
snootily
snowball
snowbird
snowboot
snowdrop
snowfall
snowless
snowlike
snowline
snowshoe
soothing
soothsay
spoffish
spoilage
spoliate
spondaic
spongily
sponsion
spontoon
spookily
spookish
spoonfed
spoonful
spoonily
sporadic
sporozoa
sportful
sportily
sporting
sportive
sporular
spotless
spottily
spotting
spousage
stoccado
stoccata
stockade
stockcar
stockily
stocking
stockish
stockist
stockman
stockpot
stodgily
stoicism
stolidly
stomachy
stomatal
stomatic
stonefly
stopcock
stopover
stoppage
stopping
storable
storeman
storeyed
stormily
stoutish
stowaway
swobbing
swopping
swotting
teocalli
tholepin
thoraces
thoracic
thoraxes
thorough
thoughts
thousand
toolroom
toolshed
toothful
toothily
toothing
trochaic
trochili
trochlea
trochoid
troilite
trollopy
trombone
trophied
tropical
trotting
trottoir
troupial
trousers
troutlet
trouvere
twoedged
twofaced
twopence
twopenny
twopiece
twosided
twotimer
udometer
unopened
urochord
urostyle
uxorious
violable
violably
violator
violence
whodunit
wholehog
whomever
whooping
whopping
whoredom
whoreson
woodbind
woodbine
woodchat
woodcock
woodenly
woodland
woodlark
woodlice
woodnote
woodpile
woodpulp
woodruff
woodshed
woodsman
woodwind
woodwool
woodwork
woodworm
wooldyed
woolfell
woollens
woolpack
woolsack
woolshed
woolskin
woolwork
wrongful
wrongous
yeomanly

yeomanry
zeolitic
zoogenic
zoolater
zoolatry
zoomancy
zoometry
zoomorph
zoonosis
zoophily
zoophyte
zoospore
alphabet
alpinism
alpinist
amperage
amphibia
amphipod
amphorae
amphoras
ampullae
amputate
appalled
appanage
apparent
appendix
appetent
appetite
applause
applepie
applique
apposite
appraise
approach
approval
arpeggio
asperges
asperity
asphodel
asphyxia
aspirant
aspirate
biparous
capacity
capeline
capellet
capeskin
capitate
capitula
caponier
caponise
caprifig
capriole
capsicum
capstone
capsular
captious
capuchin
capybara
cephalic
coplanar
copperas
copulate
copybook
copyedit
copyhold
cupboard
cupelled
cupidity
cupreous
cupulate
Cypriote
cypselae
departed
depicter
depictor
depilate
deponent
deportee
depraved
deprival
deprived
depurate
deputise
diphenyl
diplogen
diploidy
diplomat
diplopia
dipnoous
dipstick
dipteral
dipteran
dopiness
empathic
empeople
emphases
emphasis
emphatic
employee
employer
empoison
emporium
empurple
empyreal
empyrean
espalier
especial
espousal
espouser
espresso
eupatrid
eupepsia
eupeptic
euphonic
euphoria
euphoric
euphrasy
euphuism
euphuist
expander
expedite
expelled
expellee
expertly
expiable
expiator
expirant
explicit
exploder
explorer
exponent
exporter
exposure
gapeworm
gapingly
gipsydom
gipsyism
gypseous
gypsydom
gypsyism
haploidy
hepatica
hepatise
heptagon
hipflask
hipsters
hopeless
hypnoses
hypnosis
hypnotic
hypobole
hypoderm
hypogeal
hypogean
hypogene
hypogeum
hypogyny
hypothec
impacted
impanate
imparity
impelled
impeller
imperial
imperium
impetigo
impishly
impledge
implicit
impolder
impolicy
impolite
imponent
importer
imposing
imposter
impostor
impotent
imprimis
imprison
improper
improver
impudent
impugner
impunity
impurely
impurity
Japanese
japanned
japhetic
japonica
jipijapa
kyphosis
kyphotic
lapboard
lapelled
lapicide
lapidary
lapidate
lapidify
lepidote
leporine
lipogram
lipomata
lipsalve
lipstick
lopeared
lopgrass
lopsided
mephitic
mephitis
mopishly
naphthol
napiform
napoleon
Nepalese
nepenthe
nephrite
nepotism
nuptials
omphalic
omphalos
oppilate
opponent
opposite
oppugner
orpiment
oxpecker
papalise
papalism
papalist
paperboy
papillae
papillar
papillon
papistic
papistry
pappadom
papulose
papulous
peperino
pipeclay
pipefish
pipeline
piperack
piperine
popinjay
popishly
poppadum
populace
populate
populism
populist
populous
puparial
puparium
pupation
pupilage
pupilary
pupillar
puppetry
puppydog
puppydom
puppyfat
puppyish
rapacity
rapecake
rapeseed
rapidity
rapparee
raptness
raptures
repairer
repartee
repealer
repeater
repelled
repeller
repenter
repeople
repetend
replacer
replevin
reporter
repotted
repousse
reprieve
reprisal
reproach
reproval
republic
riparian
ripeness
ropeable
ropewalk
ropeyarn
ropiness
sapgreen
sapidity
sapience
saponify
saponite
saporous
sapphics
sapphire
sapphism
sepaloid
sepalous
separate
Sephardi
septette
septfoil
septimal
septuple
siphonal
siphonet
siphonic
superadd
superate
superbly
superego
superior
superman
supernal
supertax
supinate
supinely
supplant
supplely
supplial
supplier
supplies
supposal
supposed
suppress
syphilis
tapdance
tapedeck
tapeless
tapelike
tapeline
tapestry
tapeworm
taphouse
tapwater
tepidity
tipstaff
topdress
topheavy
toplevel
topliner
toplofty
topnotch
topology
toponymy
topstone
tuppence
tuppenny
typecast
typeface
typehigh
typhonic
typifier
typology
umpirage
umptieth
unpaired
unpegged
unperson
unpinned
unplaced
uppercut
uppishly
vapidity
vaporise
vaporous
vapourer
viperine
viperish
viperous
zeppelin
acquaint
arquebus
bequeath
coquetry
coquette
enquirer
Esquimau
inquirer
liquidly
maquette
moquette
piquancy
requital
requiter
sequelae
sequence
aardvark
aardwolf
abradant
abrasion
abrasive
abridger
abrogate
abruptly
acrefoot
acreinch
acridine
acridity
acrimony
acrolein
acrolith
acrostic
acrotism
acrylate
adroitly
aeration
aerially
aeriform
aerodyne
aerofoil
aerogram
aerolite
aerolith
aerology
aeronaut
aeronomy
aerostat
agraphia
agrarian
agrement
agrestic
agrimony
agrology
agronomy
airborne
airbrake
airbrush
aircraft
Airedale
airfield
airframe
airiness
airliner
airscrew
airshaft
airspace
airspeed
airstrip
airtight
airwoman
aoristic
apresski
arranger
arrantly
arrestee
arrester
arrestor
arrogant
arrogate
atremble
atrocity
atropine
aurelian
auricula
auriform
aurorean
Ayrshire
barathea
barbaric
barbecue
barberry
barbette
barbican
barbital
bareback
barefoot
bareness
bargeman
baritone
barkless
barnacle
barndoor
barnyard
baronage
baroness
baronial
barouche
barracks
barranca
barranco
barrator
barratry
barrenly
barrette
barterer
bartizan
baryonic
barytone
berberis
berceuse
bereaved
bergamot
beriberi
berliner
Bermudas
birdbath
birdcage
birdcall
birdlime
birdseed
birdseye
birthday
boracite
Bordeaux
bordello
borderer
borecole
borehole
boringly
borrower
Burberry
burglary
burgonet
Burgundy
burletta
burnouse
burntout
burrower
bursitis
Byronism
carabine
caracara
caracole
carapace
carbolic
carbonic
carbonyl
carboxyl
carburet
carcajou
carcanet
cardamom
cardamum
cardigan
cardinal
carefree
careless
careworn
carillon
carinate
carnally
carnauba
carnival
Carolean
Caroline
carolled
carotene
carousal
carousel
carouser
carriage
carriole
carryall
carryout
cartload
cartouch
caruncle
caryatid
ceramics
ceramist
cerastes
ceratoid
cercaria
cerebral
cerebrum
cerement
ceremony
cernuous
cerulean
cerusite
cervelat
cervical
cervices
christen
christie
Christly
chromate
chromite
chromium
Circaean
circuity
circular
cirriped
coracoid
cordless
cordovan
corduroy
cordwain
cordwood
corelate
corkwing
corkwood
cornball
corneous
cornetcy
cornetti
cornetto
corniced
corniche
cornicle
cornific
cornpone
coronach
coronary
coronoid
corporal
corridor
corrival
corselet
corseted
corsetry
cortical
cortices
corundum
corvette
Corybant
coryphee
curarine
curarise
curassow

curative
curculio
cureless
curlicue
currency
curricle
cursedly
curtains
curtness
curveted
Cyrenaic
Cyrillic
daringly
darkling
darkness
darkroom
darksome
dartrous
deration
derelict
derision
derisive
derisory
derivate
derogate
derriere
directly
director
dirigism
diriment
dormancy
dormouse
dorsally
durables
duration
durative
durukuli
earmuffs
earnings
earphone
earpiece
earthnut
ebriated
eeriness
enricher
enrolled
errantly
errantry
Etrurian
Etruscan
Eurasian
Eurocrat
European
europium
faradaic
faradism
farcical
farewell
farflung
farinose
farmhand
farmland
farmyard
farouche
farriery
farthest
farthing
feretory
fernshaw
ferocity
ferreter
ferriage
ferritic
ferryman
fervency
fervidly
firearms
fireback
fireball
firebird
fireboat
firebomb
firebrat
fireclay
firedamp
fireeyed
firehose
firelock
fireopal
fireplug
fireship
fireside
firetrap
fireweed
firewood
firework
firmness
firstaid
foramina
forborne
forcedly
forcefed
forceful
forcible
forcibly
fordable
fordoing
forebear
forebode
forecast
foredeck
foredoom
foreedge
forefeel
forefelt
forefoot
foregoer
foregone
forehand
forehead
foreknew
foreknow
forelady
foreland
forelock
foremast
foremost
forename
forenoon
forensic
forepart
forepast
forepeak
foreplay
foresaid
foresail
foreseen
foreshow
foreside
foreskin
forestal
forestay
forested
forester
forestry
foretell
foretime
foretold
forewarn
forewent
foreword
foreyard
forgiven
forgoing
forklift
formalin
formally
formerly
formless
formroom
formulae
formulas
formwork
fornices
forrader
forsaken
forsooth
forspeak
forspent
forswear
forswore
forsworn
fortieth
fortress
fortuity
fortyish
forwards
forzando
furbelow
furcated
furculae
furcular
furfural
furfuran
furlough
furriery
furthest
furuncle
garboard
gardener
gardenia
gardyloo
garefowl
garganey
gargoyle
garishly
garlicky
garotter
garreted
garrison
garrotte
geraniol
geranium
gerbille
Germanic
germcell
germfree
germinal
gerontic
girasole
girlhood
gorgeous
gorgonia
gormless
gyration
gyratory
gyrostat
harakiri
harangue
harasser
hardback
hardbake
hardcase
hardcore
hardener
hardhack
hardhead
hardline
hardness
hardship
hardtack
hardware
hardwood
harebell
haresear
harikari
harlotry
harmless
harmonic
harpseal
harridan
harrumph
haruspex
heraldic
heraldry
herbaria
herbless
Hercules
herdbook
herdsman
herdwick
hereaway
heredity
Hereford
hereunto
hereupon
herewith
heritage
hermetic
hernshaw
heroical
herpetic
Hertzian
hireable
hireling
hirrient
Horatian
hormonal
hornbeam
hornbill
hornbook
hornfels
hornless
hornpipe
hornrims
horntail
hornworm
hornwort
horologe
horology
horrible
horribly
horridly
horrific
horsebox
horsecar
horsefly
horseman
hurtless
irrigate
irritant
irritate
jeremiad
Jeremiah
jeroboam
jerrican
jerrycan
Jurassic
juristic
keratose
kerchief
kerosene
kerosine
korfball
kurtosis
larboard
larcener
largesse
larkspur
larrikin
larynges
larynxes
liripoop
lordless
lordling
lordosis
lordotic
lordship
loricate
lorikeet
lyrebird
lyricism
lyricist
marabout
marasmic
marasmus
marathon
marauder
maravedi
marbling
marchesa
marchese
marginal
margrave
marigold
marinade
marinate
maritage
maritime
marjoram
markdown
markedly
marketer
marksman
marmoset
marocain
maroquin
marquess
marquise
marriage
marrieds
marrying
marshman
martagon
martello
martenot
martinet
marzipan
merchant
merciful
mercuric
mergence
meridian
meringue
meristem
meristic
merosome
mirepoix
mirthful
morainic
moralise
moralism
moralist
morality
moratory
Moravian
morbidly
morbific
mordancy
moreover
moresque
moribund
mornings
morosely
morosity
morpheme
morphine
mortally
mortgage
mortmain
mortuary
murderer
muriatic
murmurer
murrelet
murrhine
myriapod
myriopod
myrmidon
narceine
narcissi
narcoses
narcosis
narcotic
narghile
narrator
narrowly
normalcy
normally
Norseman
northern
northing
Northman
nursling
nurturer
parabola
paradigm
paradise
paraffin
paragoge
parakeet
parallax
parallel
paralyse
paramour
paranoia
paranoid
paraquat
parasang
parasite
paravane
parcener
parclose
pardoner
parental
parergon
pargeter
parhelia
parhelic
parietal
parkland
parlance
parlando
Parmesan
parodist
paroquet
paroxysm
parrotry
Parsiism
parsonic
partaken
parterre
Parthian
partible
particle
partisan
partizan
partsong
parttime
perceive
perfecto
perforce
perfumer
perianth
pericarp
pericope
periderm
peridium
peridote
perigean
perigyny
perilled
perilous
perilune
perineal
perineum
periodic
periotic
peripety
periplus
perisher
perjurer
perlitic
permeate
peroneal
perorate
peroxide
personae
personal
perspire
persuade
pertness
Peruvian
perverse
pervious
phrasing
phreatic
Phrygian
pirarucu
poristic
porkling
porosity
porphyry
porpoise
porridge
portable
portfire
porthole
porticos
portiere
portrait
portress
purblind
purchase
purebred
pureness
purfling
purifier
puristic
purplish
purpuric
purpurin
pursenet
purslane
pursuant
purulent
purveyor
pyrenoid
pyrexial
pyridine
pyriform
pyroxene
pyrrhoea
pyrrhous
rarefied
rareness
rerearch
rerecord
reremice
rereward
ruralise
ruralism
ruralist
rurality
saraband
sarcenet
sardelle
sardonic
sardonyx
sargasso
sarsenet
scrabble
scragend
scragged
scramble
scrammed
scrannel
scraping
scrapped
scrapper
scratchy
scrawler
screamer
screechy
screener
screever
screwtop
scribble
scribbly
scrofula
scrounge
scrubbed
scrubber
scrutiny
seraglio
seraphic
seraphim
serenade
serenata
serenely
serenity
serfhood
sergeant
serially
seriatim
sericite
serjeant
serology
serosity
serotine
serpulae
serranid
serrated
servient
servitor
shrapnel
shredded
shredder
shrewdly
shrewish
shrieval
shrimper
shrinker
shrugged
shrunken
sirenian
siriasis
sirvente
sorcerer
sordidly
sorehead
soreness
sorochen
sororate
sorority
sorption
sorptive
sorrower
sortable
spraints
sprawler
spraygun
spreader
sprigged
springal
springer
sprinkle
sprinter
sprocket
sprucely
spryness
strabism

straddle
straggle
straggly
straight
strained
strainer
straiten
straitly
stramash
stranded
stranger
strangle
strapoil
strapped
strapper
strategy
stratify
stravaig
streaked
streaker
streamer
streeted
strength
strepent
Strepyan
stretchy
stricken
strickle
strictly
stridden
strident
strigose
striking
stringed
stringer
stripped
stripper
strobila
strobile
strobili
stroller
stromata
strongly
strontia
strophic
stropped
strucken
struggle
strummed
strummer
strumose
strumous
strumpet
strutted
strutter
surcease
surefire
sureness
surfacer
surfbird
surfboat
surfduck
surffish
surgical
suricate
surmisal
surmiser
surmount
surplice
surprise
surround
surroyal
surveyor
survival
survivor
syringes
syrinxes
tarboosh
tarlatan

Tarpeian
tarragon
tartaric
tartness
tartrate
Tartuffe
teraphim
teratoma
terebene
terebrae
terminal
terminer
terminus
termless
termtime
terraced
terrapin
terraria
terrazzo
terrible
terribly
terrific
tertiary
thraldom
thrasher
thrawart
threader
threaten
threeply
threeway
threnode
threnody
thresher
thridace
thriller
thriving
throated
throbbed
thrombin
thrombus
throstle
throttle
thrummed
thruster
tireless
tiresome
torchere
toreador
toreutic
tornadic
toroidal
torpidly
torquate
torridly
tortilla
tortious
tortoise
tortuous
torturer
Turanian
turbaned
turbidly
turbinal
turbofan
turbojet
Turcoman
turgidly
Turkoman
turmeric
turnable
turnback
turncoat
turncock
turndown
turnings
turnover
turnpike
turnskin
turnsole

turnspit
turreted
turtling
tyrannic
Tyrolean
tyrosine
Tyrrhene
unreason
unriddle
unrigged
unroofed
uprising
uprooter
varactor
variable
variably
variance
varicose
variedly
varietal
variform
variolar
variorum
varletry
veracity
verandah
veratrin
veratrum
verbally
verbatim
verbiage
verboten
verdancy
verderer
verderor
verditer
verdured
verecund
vergence
verifier
veristic
verjuice
vermouth
vernally
vernicle
veronica
verrucae
versicle
vertebra
vertexes
vertical
vertices
verticil
virement
virginal
Virginia
viricide
viridian
viridity
virilism
virility
virology
virtuosa
virtuosi
virtuoso
virtuous
virulent
voracity
vortexes
vortical
vortices
warcloud
wardance
wardenry
wardress
wardrobe
wardroom
wardship
warhorse

wariness
warmness
warpaint
warplane
warragal
warranty
warrener
warrigal
wartweed
wartwort
warweary
warwhoop
weregild
werewolf
wiredraw
wirehair
wireless
wirework
wireworm
wirewove
wiriness
wordbook
wordless
wordplay
workable
workaday
workfolk
workings
workless
workmate
workroom
workshop
wormcast
wormgear
wormhole
wormlike
wormseed
wormwood
worthful
worthily
yarmulka
zarzuela
zirconia
aasvogel
abscissa
absentee
absently
absinthe
absolute
absolver
absonant
absorber
absterge
abstract
abstrict
abstruse
absurdly
aesthete
aestival
Alsatian
anserine
answerer
arsenate
arsenide
arsenite
arsonist
arsonous
assassin
assemble
assembly
assenter
assentor
assertor
assessor
assiento
assignat
assignee
assignor
assonant

assonate
assorted
assuming
Assyrian
auspices
basaltic
baseball
baseborn
baseless
baseline
basement
baseness
basicity
basidial
basidium
basilica
basilisk
basinful
basketry
bassinet
basswood
bastardy
bastille
besieger
beslaver
besmirch
besotted
besought
bespoken
besprent
bestiary
bestowal
bestrewn
bestride
bestrode
bisector
bisexual
bistable
bistoury
bosseyed
bushbaby
bushbuck
bushfire
bushveld
business
bustling
busybody
busyness
bystreet
Casanova
cascabel
casebook
casemate
casement
casework
cashbook
cashmere
cassette
castaway
castiron
castrate
castrati
castrato
casually
casualty
cesspool
cislunar
cosecant
cosiness
cosmetic
cosmical
costmary
costplus
costpush
costumer
cushiony
Cushitic
cuspidor
cussedly

cussword
customer
cysteine
cystitis
dastardy
describe
deserter
designer
desirous
desolate
despatch
despiser
despotic
destrier
destruct
disabuse
disagree
disallow
disarray
disaster
disbench
disbound
disburse
disciple
disclaim
disclose
discount
discover
discreet
discrete
discrown
diseased
disendow
disfrock
disgorge
disgrace
disguise
dishevel
disinter
disjoint
disjunct
dislodge
disloyal
dismally
dismount
disorder
dispatch
dispense
disperse
dispirit
displace
displant
displode
displume
disposal
disposer
dispread
disprize
disproof
disprove
disquiet
disseise
disserve
dissever
dissolve
dissuade
distally
distance
distaste
distinct
distract
distrain
distrait
distress
district
distrust
disunion
disunite
disunity

disusage
disvalue
dustbowl
dustcart
dustcoat
dustless
dustlike
dustshot
dysgenic
dyslexia
dyslexic
dyspnoea
dystopia
easement
easiness
easterly
eastmost
eastward
ecstatic
ensample
ensconce
ensemble
ensheath
enshrine
enshroud
ensiform
ensigncy
ensilage
enslaver
ensphere
enswathe
essayist
Essenism
essonite
eustatic
exserted
fascicle
fasciola
fasciole
Fascista
Fascisti
fashious
fastback
fastener
fastfood
fastness
fasttalk
fastuous
festally
festival
fiscally
fishable
fishball
fishbone
fishbowl
fishcake
fishfarm
fishglue
fishhawk
fishhook
fishless
fishmeal
fishpond
fishtail
fishwife
fissiped
fistiana
fistical
fistulae
fistular
fosterer
fuselage
fusiform
fusileer
fusilier
gaselier
gasfired
gashouse
gaslight

gasmeter
gasolene
gasolier
gasoline
gastight
gastraea
gastrula
gasworks
gestagen
gestural
gossamer
gossiper
gossipry
gossypol
gusseted
hasheesh
hastener
hastings
hesitant
hesitate
Hesperus
Hispanic
histogen
historic
hosepipe
hospital
hostelry
hushhush
hustings
hysteria
hysteric
Ibsenism
insanely
insanity
inscient
inscribe
inscroll
insecure
inserted
insignia
insolate
insolent
insomnia
insomuch
insphere
inspired
inspirer
inspirit
instable
instance
instancy
instinct
instruct
insulant
insulate
insulter
insurant
issuable
issuance
jesuitic
jesuitry
justness
Kashmiri
kissable
kisscurl
lashings
listener
listless
luscious
lushness
lustrate
lustrine
lustring
lustrous
lysosome
lysozyme
mascaron
Masorete
Masoreth

massacre
masseter
masseuse
massicot
massless
masterly
masthead
mastitis
mastodon
mescalin
mesdames
meshwork
mesially
mesmeric
mesocarp
mesoderm
mesotron
Mesozoic
mesquite
messmate
messuage
misalign
misapply
misbegot
miscarry
miscegen
mischief
miscible
miscount
misdealt
misdoing
misdoubt
miserere
misgiven
misguide
misheard
mishmash
Mishnaic
misjudge
mismatch
misnomer
misogamy
misogyny
misology
misplace
misprint
misprise
misprize
misquote
misshape
missilry
misspell
misspelt
misspend
misspent
misstate
mistaken
misthink
mistreat
mistress
mistrial
mistrust
misusage
miswrite
moshavim
mosquito
mossback
muscadel
muscatel
muscling
muscular
mushroom
musicale
musician
musingly
muskdeer
muskduck
musketry
muskrose
musktree
muslined
musquash
mustache
mystical
mystique
nasalise
nasality
nascence
nascency
nescient
nestling
noseband
nosecone
nosedive
nosepipe
nosering
nosiness
nosology
observer
obsidian
obsolete
obstacle
obstruct
oestrone
oestrous
opsimath
Ossianic
pashalic
pashalik
passable
passably
passbook
passerby
passible
Passover
passport
password
pastiche
pastille
pastoral
pastrami
pastries
pastural
piscator
piscinae
pishogue
pisiform
pisolite
position
positive
positron
posology
possible
possibly
postcard
postcode
postdate
postfree
posthorn
postiche
postlude
postmark
postmill
postobit
postpaid
postpone
postural
posturer
pushball
pushbike
pushcart
pushover
pushpull
pussycat
pustular
rascally
rashness
rasorial
rescript
research
resemble
reserved
resetter
resettle
resident
residual
residuum
resigned
resinate
resinify
resinoid
resinous
resister
resistor
resolute
resonant
resonate
resorcin
resorter
resource
respects
response
respring
resprung
restcure
restless
restorer
restrain
restrict
resupine
resurvey
rosarian
rosebowl
rosebush
rosefish
roseleaf
rosemary
roseolar
rosepink
roseroot
rosetree
rosewood
rosiness
rostrate
rosulate
rushhour
rushlike
rustical
rustless
sashcord
Sassanid
sesamoid
sesterce
sisterly
suspense
susurrus
systemic
systolic
taskwork
tasselly
tastebud
tasteful
tesserae
tesseral
testable
testator
testatum
testtube
tussocky
unsaddle
unsealed
unseated
unseeded
unseeing
unseemly
unsettle
unshaped
unsocial
unsought
unsprung
unstable
unstably
unstated
unsteady
unstring
unstrung
unstuffy
unsuited
unsunned
unswathe
upsetter
upsprang
upspring
upsprung
upstairs
upstream
upstroke
Ursuline
vascular
vasculum
vasiform
vastness
vesicant
vesicate
vesperal
vespiary
vestiary
vestment
vesturer
vesuvian
viscacha
visceral
viscidly
viscount
Visigoth
visional
visitant
visually
washable
washbowl
washroom
wastable
wasteful
Wesleyan
westerly
westward
wiseacre
wiseness
wishbone
wishwash
wistaria
wisteria
yestreen
actiniae
actinian
actinias
actinide
actinism
actinium
activate
actively
activism
activist
activity
actually
actuator
acturial
although
altitude
altruism
altruist
anteater
antecede
antedate
antefixa
antelope
antennae
antennal
antennas
antepost
anterior
anteroom
anthelia
anthemia
antheral
anthesis
anthozoa
antibody
antidote
antihero
antilogy
antimask
antimony
antinode
antinomy
antiphon
antipode
antipole
antipope
antisera
antitype
antlered
antrorse
apterous
aptitude
artefact
arterial
artesian
artfully
articled
artifact
artifice
artistic
artistry
astatine
asterisk
asterism
asteroid
asthenia
asthenic
astonied
astonish
astragal
astutely
attender
attested
attester
attestor
atticism
attitude
attorney
attrited
autacoid
autarchy
autarkic
autistic
autobahn
autocade
autocrat
autodafe
autodyne
autogamy
autogiro
autogyro
autolyse
automata
automate
autonomy
autosome
autotomy
autotype
autumnal
autunite
Batavian
bateleur
bathetic
bathotic
bathrobe
bathroom
battalia
battleax
betacism
betatron
bethesda
betrayal
betrayer
bitchily
bitingly
bitterly
botanise
botanist
botflies
botryoid
bottomry
botulism
botyrose
butchery
buttoner
buttress
butylene
butyrate
catacomb
catalase
cataloes
catalyse
catalyst
catamite
catapult
cataract
catchall
catchfly
catching
catechol
category
catenary
catenate
cateress
catering
cathedra
catheter
cathexes
cathexis
cathodal
cathodic
catholic
cationic
catsfoot
catstail
cattleya
cetacean
chthonic
citation
citified
cityfied
cotenant
cothurni
cotillon
cotquean
Cotswold
cottager
cottagey
cuteness
cutprice
cutpurse
cutwater
cytidine
cytology
cytosine
dateless
dateline
detached
detailed
detainee
detainer
detector
deterred
deterrer
dethrone
detonate
detoxify
detrital
detritus
ditheism
ditheist
ditherer
dittybag
dittybox
dotation
dotingly
dotterel
Dutchman
dutiable
dutyfree
dutypaid
ectoderm
ectozoon
eftsoons
entailer
entangle
entellus
enterate
enthalpy
enthrall
enthrone
entirely
entirety
entoderm
entoptic
entozoic
entozoon
entracte
entrails
entrance
entreaty
entrench
entrepot
entresol
esterify
estimate
Estonian
estopped
estoppel
estovers
estrange
estuaril
eutectic
eutrophy
extender
extensor
exterior
external
extolled
extrados
extremes
extrorse
fatalism
fatalist
fatality
fatherly
fatigues
fatstock
fattener
fetching
feticide
fitfully
futilely
futility
futurism
futurist
futurity
gatefold
gatepost
gatherer
guttural
hatchery
hatching
hatchway
hateable
hatstand
hetaerae
hetairai
hitherto
hotchpot
hotelier
hothouse
hotplate
hotpress
intaglio
intarsia
integral
intended
intently
interact
interbed
intercom
intercut
interest
interior
intermit
intermix
internal
internee
Interpol
interred
interrex
intersex
intertie
interval
interwar
inthrall
intimacy
intimate
intimism
intitule
intonate
intrados
intrench
intrepid
intrigue
intromit
introrse
intruder
intubate
iotacism
isthmian
jetblack
jetplane
jettison
katakana
latchkey
lateness
latently
laterite
Latinate
latinise
Latinism
Latinist
latinity
latitant
latitude
latterly
latticed
lethally
lethargy
lettered
literacy
literary
literate
literati
litharge
litigant
litigate

littlego
littling
littoral
liturgic
lothario
lutanist
lutecium
lutenist
lutetium
Lutheran
matamata
matchbox
matelote
material
materiel
maternal
matgrass
matiness
matrices
matrixes
matronal
matronly
mattress
maturate
maturely
maturity
metalled
metallic
metamere
metaphor
metayage
metazoan
metazoon
meteoric
methanol
methinks
methodic
methylic
methysis
metonymy
metrical
Mithraic
mitigant
mitigate
mittened
mittimus
mitzvoth
mothball
motherly
motility
motional
motivate
motivity
motorail
motorcar
motorial
motoring
motorise
motorist
motorium
motorman
motormen
motorway
mottling
mutation
mutchkin
muteness
muticous
mutilate
mutineer
mutinous
mutterer
mutually
mythical
natality
natation
natatory
nathless
national
natively
nativism
nativist
nativity
naturism
naturist
nitrogen
notarial
notation
notching
notebook
notecase
noteless
notional
notornis
nutarian
nutation
nutbrown
nuthatch
nuthouse
nutrient
nutshell
oatgrass
obtainer
obtected
obturate
obtusely
obtusity
octarchy
octaroon
octonary
octoroon
ofttimes
oiticica
ontogeny
ontology
optative
optician
optimise
optimism
optimist
optional
orthicon
orthodox
orthoepy
osteitis
ostinato
ostracod
ostracon
ostrakon
ottavino
outboard
outbound
outbrave
outbreak
outburst
outcaste
outclass
outdated
outdoors
outdrawn
outfield
outflank
outgoing
outgrown
outguess
outHerod
outhouse
outlawry
outlying
outmatch
outmoded
outpoint
outrange
outreach
outreign
outrider
outright
outrival
outshine
outshone
outsider
outsight
outsmart
outspend
outspent
outstare
outstrip
outvalue
outvying
outwards
outwatch
outweigh
outworks
oxtongue
patagium
patchily
patellae
patellar
patentee
patently
patentor
paternal
pathetic
pathless
pathogen
patience
patronal
pattypan
patulous
petaline
petalled
petalody
petaloid
petalous
petechia
petiolar
petioled
petition
petrolic
petronel
petrosal
pettifog
petulant
petuntse
phthalic
phthisic
phthisis
pitiable
pitiably
pitiless
pittance
pitviper
potassic
potation
potbelly
potbound
potently
potholer
pothouse
potlatch
potplant
potroast
potsherd
potstill
potstone
potterer
putative
putridly
pythonic
rataplan
rateable
ratguard
ratifier
rational
ratsbane
ratstail
rattling
retailer
retainer
retarded
retarder
retiarii
reticent
reticule
retiform
retinula
retiring
retorted
retrench
retrieve
retroact
retrorse
ritually
Rotarian
rotation
rotative
rotatory
rotenone
rottenly
rotundly
roturier
rutabaga
ruthless
rutilant
satanism
satanist
sateless
satiable
satiably
satirise
satirist
saturant
saturate
Saturday
saturnic
setscrew
sitarist
sithence
sitology
situated
sitzbath
soterial
tattered
tattooer
tetanise
tetchily
tetradic
tetragon
tetrapla
tetrapod
tetrarch
titanate
titaness
titanism
titanite
titanium
tithable
titivate
titmouse
tittuped
tittuppy
totalise
totality
totalled
totemism
totemist
totterer
tutelage
tutelary
tutorage
tutoress
tutorial
ulterior
ultimacy
ultimata
ultimate
ultraism
ultraist
untangle
untapped
untaught
untented
untether
unthread
unthrift
unthrone
untidily
untimely
untitled
untoward
upthrown
upthrust
urticant
urticate
vitalise
vitalism
vitalist
vitality
vitellin
vitellus
vitiable
vitiator
vitiligo
vitreous
vituline
votaress
votarist
voteless
watchdog
watchful
watchkey
watchman
waterage
waterbed
waterbus
watergas
waterice
watering
waterish
waterlog
waterloo
waterman
waterski
waterway
watthour
wetlands
wetnurse
wettable
witchelm
witchery
witchety
witching
withdraw
withdrew
withheld
withhold
yataghan
abundant
abutilon
abutment
abuttals
abutting
aculeate
adularia
adulator
adultery
aduncate
aduncous
aguishly
alumroot
amusedly
aquacade
aqualung
aquanaut
aquarist
aquarium
aquatint
aqueduct
aquiline
avulsion
baudrons
bauxitic
blubbery
bludgeon
bluebell
bluebird
bluechip
bluecoat
bluefish
blueness
bluenose
blueweed
blurrily
blurring
blushful
blustery
bouffant
boughten
bouillon
bouncily
bouncing
boundary
bourgeon
boursier
bourtree
boutique
bouzouki
brunette
brushoff
brutally
caudally
caudated
caudexes
caudices
caudillo
cauldron
causally
causerie
causeway
cautious
chugging
chummily
chumming
chupatti
chupatty
churchly
churinga
churlish
churning
chutzpah
clubbing
clubfoot
clubhaul
clubland
clueless
clumsily
clupeoid
clustery
couchant
couching
couldest
coulisse
coumarin
countess
coupling
courante
coursing
courtesy
courtier
couscous
cousinly
cruciate
crucible
crucifer
crucifix
crueller
crumhorn
crummock
crusader
crustily
cruzeiro
daughter
deucedly
deuteron
diuresis
diuretic
douanier
doubloon
doubtful
doughboy
doughnut
doumpalm
dourness
drubbing
drudgery
drugging
druggist
druidess
druidism
drumfire
drumhead
drumming
drummock
drumroll
drunkard
drupelet
educable
educated
educator
educible
eduction
emulator
emulgent
emulsify
emulsion
emulsive
emulsoid
enuresis
enuretic
equalise
equality
equalled
equation
equinity
equipage
equipped
equitant
equities
equivoke
eruption
eruptive
esurient
evulsion
exultant
exuviate
faubourg
faultily
faunally
Faustian
fauteuil
feudally
flubbing
fluellin
fluently
fluepipe
fluidics
fluidify
fluidise
fluidity
flummery
fluoride
fluorine
fluorite
fluttery
fougasse
foulness
founding
fountain
fourball
foureyes
fourfold
fourleaf
fourpart
foursome
fourstar
fourteen
fourthly
fructify
fructose
frugally
fruitage
fruitbat
fruitery
fruitfly
fruitful
fruition
frumenty
frumpish
frustule
frutices
Gaullism
Gaullist
gauntlet
glucagon
glucinum
glummest
glumness
glutting
gluttony
gourmand
goutweed
goutwort
grubbily
grubbing
grudging
gruesome
grumbler
grumpily
gruntled
haulyard
haunting
hausfrau
hourlong
houseboy
housedog
housefly
houseful
houseman
housetop
inundate
inurbane
jaundice
jauntily
jiujitsu
khuskhus
kourbash
krumhorn
laudable
laudably
laudanum
laudator
laughing
laughter
launcher
laureate
leucitic
loudness
louvered
moufflon
moulding
mountain
mounting

mournful
mourning
mouseear
moussaka
mouthful
naumachy
nauplius
nauseant
nauseate
nauseous
nautical
nautilus
neurally
neuritic
neuritis
neuronal
neuronic
neuroses
neurosis
neurotic
neutrino
noumenal
noumenon
nouvelle
ocularly
opulence
opuscula
opuscule
pluckily
plugging
plumaged
plumbago
plumbate
plumbing
plumbism
plumelet
plumiped
plumpish
plumular
plurally
plussage
plutonic
pluvious
poultice
poundage
pounding
pourable
prudence
pruinose
prunella
prunelle
prunello
prurient
pruritic
pruritus
Prussian
reusable
roughage
roughdry
roughhew
roughish
rouleaus
rouleaux
roulette
roundarm
rounders
roundish
roundtop
saucebox
saucepan
saunders
sauouari
sauropod
Sauterne
scudding
scullery
scullion
sculptor
scumming
scurrile
scurvily
scutcher
scutella
shuddery
shuffler
shunning
shutdown
shutting
skullcap
slubbing
slugabed
sluggard
slugging
sluggish
slumbery
slumming
slurring
sluttish
smudgily
smuggler
smugness
smuttily
snubbing
snuffbox
snuffers
snuffler
snuffles
snuggery
snugness
souchong
soulless
soundbow
soundbox
sounding
sourdine
sourness
sourpuss
soutache
southern
southing
southpaw
Southron
souvenir
spunkily
spurgear
spurious
spurling
spurrier
spurring
squabble
squadron
squaller
squamate
squamose
squamous
squamule
squander
squarely
squarish
squarson
squasher
squatted
squatter
squawker
squawman
squeaker
squealer
squeedge
squeegee
squeezer
squelchy
squibbed
squidded
squiggle
squiggly
squilgee
squinter
squireen
squirely
squirrel
squirter
stubbing
stubborn
stubnail
stuccoes
studbook
studding
studfarm
studious
studwork
stuffily
stuffing
stultify
stumbler
stumming
stumpily
stunning
stunsail
stuntman
stupidly
stuprate
sturdied
sturdily
sturgeon
tautness
tautomer
tautonym
Teutonic
thudding
thuggery
thuggism
thumbpot
thumping
thundery
thurible
thurifer
Thursday
thusness
touchily
touching
toughish
touristy
tournure
truantry
truckage
trucking
truckler
trueblue
trueborn
truebred
truelove
trueness
truistic
trumeaux
trumpery
truncate
trunnion
trussing
trustful
trustily
truthful
usufruct
usurious
uvularly
uvulitis
vaulting
vauntful
voussoir
wouldest
woundily
youngest
youngish
yourself
youthful
advanced
advisory
advocaat
advocacy
advocate
advowson
alveolar
alveolus
Bavarian
bevelled
beveller
beverage
bivalent
cavalier
cavatina
caverned
cavesson
cavicorn
cavilled
caviller
civilian
civilise
civility
covalent
covenant
coverage
coverall
covering
coverlet
covertly
covetous
deviance
deviancy
deviator
deviling
devilish
devilism
devilkin
devilled
deviltry
Devonian
devotion
devourer
devoutly
divagate
divalent
divebomb
dividend
dividivi
dividual
divinely
divinise
divinity
division
divisive
divorcee
dovecote
dovetail
envelope
enviable
enviably
environs
envisage
envision
favonian
favoured
favourer
feverfew
feverish
feverous
fivefold
fivestar
foveolae
gavelock
giveaway
governor
havelock
havildar
havocked
hoverfly
invasion
invasive
invected
inveigle
inventor
inverted
inverter
investor
inviable
inviting
invocate
involute
Javanese
jovially
juvenile
lavalava
lavation
lavatory
lavender
laverock
lavishly
levanter
levelled
leveller
leverage
leviable
levigate
levirate
levitate
levulose
liveable
liveborn
livelily
livelong
liveried
liverish
livewire
lividity
lovebird
loveknot
loveless
lovelily
lovelock
lovelorn
lovenest
loveseat
lovesick
lovesome
lovesong
lovingly
maverick
moveable
moveless
movement
movingly
navigate
novation
novelise
novelist
November
novercal
pavement
pavilion
pivotman
ravelled
ravenous
ravisher
revanche
revealer
reveille
revelled
reveller
revenant
revenger
reverend
reverent
reversal
reverser
reverter
revetted
reviewal
reviewer
reviling
revision
revisory
revivify
revolter
revolute
revolver
rivalled
rivelled
riverain
riverbed
riverine
riverman
riverway
savagely
savagery
savannah
savorous
Savoyard
severely
severity
sovranty
taverner
tovarish
unvalued
unversed
unvoiced
vavasory
vavasour
vivacity
vivarium
vivifier
vivisect
waveband
waveform
waveless
waviness
atwitter
bewigged
bewilder
biweekly
bowfront
bowsprit
cowardly
cowberry
cowgrass
coworker
dewberry
dewiness
dewpoint
dewyeyed
dowdyish
dowelled
downbeat
downcast
downcome
downfall
downhaul
downhill
downland
downmost
downpipe
downpour
downtime
downtown
downturn
downward
downwind
fewtrils
fowlpest
gownsman
Hawaiian
hawfinch
hawkeyed
hawklike
hawkmoth
hawkweed
hawthorn
howitzer
inwardly
jewelled
jeweller
lawcourt
lawfully
lawgiver
lawmaker
lawyerly
lewdness
lewisite
lowering
lowgrade
lowlevel
lowlying
mowburnt
newblown
newcomer
newfound
newlywed
newscast
newsheet
newspeak
newsreel
newsroom
nowadays
pawnshop
powdered
powerful
rawboned
rewaking
rewarder
rowdyish
rowdyism
sawbones
sawedged
sawedoff
sawframe
sawhorse
sawtooth
sewellel
sewerage
sewergas
sewerrat
sowbread
tawdrily
thwacker
thwarter
thwartly
towardly
towelled
townhall
township
townsman
unwanted
unwarily
unwashed
unweaned
unwieldy
unwisdom
unwisely
unwished
unwonted
unwordly
unworthy
upwardly
vowelise
vowelled
boxpleat
coxalgia
coxswain
dextrine
dextrose
dextrous
doxology
fixation
fixative
foxglove
foxhound
foxiness
foxshark
hexagram
hexapody
hexylene
laxative
lixivium
luxation
maxillae
maximise
myxomata
nextdoor
pixieish
pixiness
pyxidium
saxatile
Saxondom
Saxonism
Saxonist
sexiness
sexology
sextette
sextuple
sexually
sixpence
sixpenny
sixtieth
taxation
taxingly
taxonomy
taxpayer
textbook
texthand
textuary
textural
textured
toxaemia
toxaemic
toxicant
toxicity
vexation
vexillum
vixenish
waxberry
waxcloth
waxiness
waxlight
waxworks
adynamia
adynamic
amygdala
anyplace
anything
anywhere
asyndeta
atypical
bayadere
bayberry
biyearly
boyishly
bryology
bryozoan
clypeate
cryogeny
cryolite
cryostat
cryotron
daybreak
daydream
daylight
dryclean
drynurse
dryplate
drypoint
drystone
Egyptian
epyllion
erythema
flyblown

flypaper
flywheel
glycerin
glycerol
glyceryl
glycogen
glyconic
glyptics
hayfield
haymaker
haystack
idyllist
joyfully
joyously
joystick
keyboard
keystone
klystron
layabout
layshaft
laystall
laywoman
loyalist
mayapple
mayoress
Mayqueen
Odyssean
olympiad
Olympian
onychite
oxymoron
oxytocin
payphone
paysheet
phyletic
phyllary
phyllode
phylloid
phyllome
physical
physicky
physique
pryingly
psychics
psychism
psychist
ptyalism
rhyolite
rhythmic
royalism
royalist
sayonara
skylight
skypilot
skyscape
skywards
slyboots
spyglass
stylised
thyroxin
thyrsoid
tryingly
voyageur
wayfarer
waygoing
wrymouth
bezonian
buzzword
cozenage
doziness
enzootic
gazogene
gazpacho
hazelnut
haziness
Lazarist
laziness
lazulite
lazurite
mazarine
Mazdaism
mazement
maziness
mezereon
Nazarene
Nazarite
Nazirite
ooziness
pizzeria
sizeable
sizzling
suzerain
syzygial
unzipped
vizarded
vizcacha
wizardly
wizardry

————

Abbaside
abbatial
ablation
ablative
abradant
abrasion
abrasive
Accadian
adiantum
adjacent
adnation
advanced
aeration
agnation
agraphia
agrarian
Akkadian
albacore
Albanian
alcahest
aleatory
alkahest
alkalies
alkalify
alkaline
alkaloid
almagest
almanack
Alsatian
amiantus
annalist
aphasiac
apiarian
apiarist
aplastic
appalled
appanage
apparent
aquacade
aqualung
aquanaut
aquarist
aquarium
aquatint
arbalest
arbalist
Arcadian
Arianism
Armagnac
armament
armature
arranger
arrantly
assassin
astatine
atlantes
Atlantic
audacity
autacoid
autarchy
autarkic
aviarist
aviation
aviatrix
aweather
axiality
balanced
balancer
banality
banausic
barathea
basaltic
Batavian
Bavarian
bayadere
becalmed
bedabble
bedazzle
befallen
bejabers
belabour
betacism
betatron
bibation
bifacial
bigamist
bigamous
bilabial
bimanous
binaural
bioassay
biparous
bivalent
bleacher
bleakish
blearily
boracite
botanise
botanist
breakage
breaking
breakout
breasted
breather
Briarean
broacher
broadish
broadway
bubaline
cabalism
cabalist
caballed
cadastre
calabash
caladium
calamary
calamine
calamint
calamite
calamity
Canadian
canaille
canalise
canaster
capacity
carabine
caracara
caracole
carapace
Casanova
catacomb
catalase
cataloes
catalyse
catalyst
catamite
catapult
cataract
cavalier
cavatina
ceramics
ceramist
cerastes
ceratoid
cetacean
cheapish
chiasmus
chiastic
cicatrix
citation
cleancut
cleaning
cleanser
clearcut
clearing
clearway
cleavage
cleavers
cobaltic
cofactor
colander
comatose
conation
conative
coracoid
covalent
cowardly
coxalgia
creakily
creamery
creatine
creation
creative
creatrix
creature
croakily
Croatian
cubature
curarine
curarise
curassow
curative
cymatium
dahabieh
damassin
debagged
debarred
decadent
decagram
decanter
delation
demagogy
demander
demarche
denarius
denature
denazify
departed
deration
detached
detailed
detainee
detainer
dicacity
didactic
didapper
digamist
digamous
dilatant
dilation
dilative
dilatory
disabuse
disagree
disallow
disarray
disaster
divagate
divalent
donation
Donatism
Donatist
donative
donatory
dotation
douanier
dreadful
dreamful
dreamily
dreaming
drearily
durables
duration
durative
dynamics
dynamism
dynamist
dynamite
dynastic
dynatron
elfarrow
embalmer
embattle
empathic
encaenia
endamage
endanger
engaging
enlarger
ensample
entailer
entangle
equalise
equality
equalled
equation
errantly
errantry
escalade
escalate
escallop
escalope
escapade
escapism
escapist
escargot
escarole
espalier
essayist
eucalypt
eulachon
eupatrid
Eurasian
excavate
exhalant
expander
faradaic
faradism
fatalism
fatalist
fatality
fedayeen
filagree
filament
filariae
filarial
filature
finalise
finalism
finalist
finality
fixation
fixative
fleabane
fleabite
fleawort
floatage
floating
focalise
foramina
freakish
freakout
fugacity
fumarole
gadabout
gadarene
galactic
galangal
gelastic
gelatine
gelation
gematria
geraniol
geranium
gigantic
girasole
gleaning
gloaming
godawful
Graafian
greasily
Gujarati
gynandry
gyration
gyratory
habanera
Halachah
halation
hamartia
harakiri
harangue
harasser
Hawaiian
hecatomb
hepatica
hepatise
heraldic
heraldry
hetaerae
hetairai
hexagram
hexapody
hijacker
hilarity
himation
Horatian
hulahula
humanely
humanise
humanism
humanist
humanity
humanoid
hydatoid
idealess
idealise
idealism
idealist
ideality
ideation
illation
illative
immanent
immature
impacted
impanate
imparity
indagate
infamise
infamous
infantry
ingather
inhalant
inlander
innately
insanely
insanity
intaglio
intarsia
invasion
invasive
inwardly
iotacism
Islamise
Islamism
Islamite
islander
Japanese
japanned
Javanese
jobation
Jonathan
Judaical
Judaiser
Jurassic
kalaazar
Kanarese
katakana
keratose
lamasery
lavalava
lavation
lavatory
laxative
layabout
Lazarist
legalese
legalise
legalism
legalist
legality
legatine
legation
levanter
libation
libatory
ligament
ligation
ligature
lobation
localise
localism
locality
locative
loyalist
lunarian
lunation
lutanist
luxation
macaroni
macaroon
madapple
magazine
maharaja
maharani
Malagasy
malamute
malapert
malaprop
malarial
malarian
malarkey
marabout
marasmic
marasmus
marathon
marauder
maravedi
matamata
mayapple
mazarine
medalled
medallic
megalith
megapode
megawatt
melamine
melanism
melanite
menarche
metalled
metallic
metamere
metaphor
metayage
metazoan
metazoon
minacity
minatory
misalign
misapply
modalism
modalist
modality
Moharram
molality
molarity
molasses
monachal
monadism
monandry
monarchy
monastic
monaural
monaxial
monazite
morainic
moralise
moralism
moralist
morality
moratory
Moravian
Muharram
mutation
nasalise
nasality
natality
natation
natatory
Nazarene
Nazarite
negation
negative
negatory
negatron
nematode
nematoid
Nepalese
nodalise
nodality
nodation
nomadise
nomadism
notarial
notation
novation
nowadays
nugatory
nutarian
nutation
oakapple
oblation
oblatory
obtainer
occasion
octarchy
octaroon
oleander
oleaster
ommateum
oogamous
optative

Orcadian
ordainer
organdie
organise
organism
organist
orgasmic
orgastic
ornament
ornately
ottavino
paganise
paganish
paganism
palatial
palatine
papalise
papalism
papalist
parabola
paradigm
paradise
paraffin
paragoge
parakeet
parallax
parallel
paralyse
paramour
paranoia
paranoid
paraquat
parasang
parasite
paravane
patagium
pedagogy
pedalier
pedalled
pedantic
pedantry
Pegasean
Pelagian
Pelasgic
penalise
petaline
petalled
petalody
petaloid
petalous
pheasant
phrasing
picaroon
picayune
pilaster
pinafore
pinaster
pirarucu
pleading
pleasant
pleasing
pleasure
pliantly
podagral
podagric
polarise
polarity
pomander
potassic
potation
preacher
preamble
priapism
ptyalism
puparial
puparium
pupation
putative
queasily

ranarian
ranarium
rapacity
rataplan
recapped
redactor
regalism
regality
rehandle
relation
relative
relaxant
remanent
repairer
repartee
retailer
retainer
retarded
retarder
revanche
rewaking
rewarder
ribaldry
rigadoon
riparian
rivalled
rocaille
rogation
rogatory
romancer
Romanian
romanise
Romanism
Romanist
Romansch
romantic
rosarian
Rotarian
rotation
rotative
rotatory
royalism
royalist
Rumanian
Rumansch
runabout
runagate
ruralise
ruralism
ruralist
rurality
rutabaga
sagacity
sagamore
salacity
salariat
salaried
samarium
sanative
sanatory
saraband
satanism
satanist
savagely
savagery
savannah
saxatile
sciagram
sciatica
scrabble
scragend
scragged
scramble
scrammed
scrannel
scraping
scrapped
scrapper
scratchy

scrawler
sedately
sedation
sedative
seladang
semantic
senarius
sepaloid
sepalous
separate
seraglio
seraphic
seraphim
sesamoid
sheading
shealing
shrapnel
Sinaitic
sinapism
sitarist
skiagram
sleazily
sneakily
sneakish
socalled
sodalite
sodality
solander
solanine
solarise
solarism
solarist
solarium
solation
solatium
somatism
sonatina
speaking
spearman
sphagnum
splasher
splatter
spraints
sprawler
spraygun
squabble
squadron
squaller
squamate
squamose
squamous
squamule
squander
squarely
squarish
squarson
squasher
squatted
squatter
squawker
squawman
steadily
steading
stealing
stealthy
steamily
stearate
stearine
steatite
strabism
straddle
straggle
straggly
straight
strained
strainer
straiten
straitly
stramash

stranded
stranger
strangle
strapoil
strapped
strapper
strategy
stratify
stravaig
subacute
subagent
subahdar
Sudanese
sudarium
sudatory
swearing
sybarite
sycamine
sycamore
synapsis
synaptic
synastry
tagalong
talapoin
tamandua
tamanoir
tamarack
tamarind
tamarisk
taxation
tenacity
tenacula
tenaille
tenantry
teraphim
teratoma
tetanise
thearchy
thiamine
thraldom
thrasher
thrawart
thwacker
thwarter
thwartly
titanate
titaness
titanism
titanite
titanium
tomahawk
tomalley
tonality
totalise
totality
totalled
tovarish
towardly
toxaemia
toxaemic
treacher
treadler
treasure
treasury
treatise
trialist
triangle
triarchy
Triassic
triaxial
truantry
Turanian
tyrannic
unbacked
unbarred
uncalled
uncandid
uncapped
uncaused

unearned
uneasily
unfading
unfairly
unfasten
ungainly
uniaxial
unlawful
unmanned
unmarked
unpaired
unsaddle
untangle
untapped
untaught
unvalued
unwanted
unwarily
unwashed
uplander
upwardly
urbanely
urbanise
urbanism
urbanist
urbanite
urbanity
vacantly
vacation
vagabond
valanced
vanadate
vanadium
vanadous
varactor
vavasory
vavasour
Vedantic
velamina
velarium
venality
venation
veracity
verandah
veratrin
veratrum
vexation
vicarage
vicarate
vicarial
vitalise
vitalism
vitalist
vitality
vivacity
vivarium
vizarded
vocalise
vocalism
vocalist
vocality
vocation
vocative
volatile
voracity
votaress
votarist
voyageur
Wahabism
Wahabite
wheatear
wizardly
wizardry
womanise
womanish
wreathen
yataghan
zabaione
zoiatria

zonation
zygaenid
airborne
airbrake
airbrush
alebench
anabases
anabasis
anabatic
anabolic
bambinos
barbaric
barbecue
barberry
barbette
barbican
barbital
bayberry
beebread
berberis
bilberry
bimbashi
blabbing
blubbery
bobbinet
bobbypin
bobbysox
bombsite
bribable
Burberry
Cambrian
carbolic
carbonic
carbonyl
carboxyl
carburet
clubbing
clubfoot
clubhaul
clubland
cobblers
combings
cowberry
crabbing
cribbage
cribbing
Cumbrian
cumbrous
cupboard
daybreak
dewberry
diabasic
diabetes
diabetic
diabolic
disbench
disbound
disburse
dogberry
doubloon
doubtful
drabbler
drabness
dribbler
dribblet
drubbing
dumbbell
dumbhead
dumbness
dumbshow
dybbukim
epiblast
faubourg
feeblish
fenberry
fimbriae
flabella
flubbing
flyblown

fogbound
forborne
frabjous
fribbler
furbelow
gabbroic
gabbroid
galbanum
gambados
gambeson
gambroon
garboard
gerbille
glabella
glabrous
glibness
globally
globular
globulin
grabbing
grabbler
grubbily
grubbing
herbaria
herbless
hobbitry
hobbyist
iceblink
icebound
isabella
isobaric
jabberer
jamboree
jetblack
keyboard
lambaste
lambency
lamblike
lambskin
lapboard
larboard
leeboard
legbreak
limbless
lobbyist
lubberly
lumberer
marbling
membered
membrane
midbrain
misbegot
morbidly
morbific
mowburnt
mulberry
myoblast
newblown
nimbused
numberer
numbfish
numbness
nutbrown
offbreak
olibanum
outboard
outbound
outbrave
outbreak
outburst
pegboard
pembroke
plebeian
potbelly
potbound
probable
probably
purblind
quibbler

rabbinic
rabbiter
rabbitry
rambling
rambutan
rawboned
reabsorb
redblind
redbrick
ribbonry
rimbrake
rubbishy
sabbatic
sawbones
scabbard
scabious
scabrous
seaboard
seaborne
shabbily
shabrack
Shabuoth
slabbing
slobbery
slobbish
slobland
slubbing
slyboots
snobbery
snobbish
snobbism
snubbing
sombrely
sombrero
sombrous
sowbread
stabbing
stabling
stablish
stibnite
stubbing
stubborn
stubnail
subbasal
sunbaked
sunbathe
sunblind
sunburnt
sunburst
swabbing
swobbing
symbiont
symbolic
tamboura
tarboosh
teaboard
teabread
teabreak
tiebreak
timbered
tolbooth
tombless
trabeate
tribally
tribasic
tribrach
tribunal
tumbling
turbaned
turbidly
turbinal
turbofan
turbojet
unabated
vambrace
verbally
verbatim
verbiage
verboten

waxberry
zombiism
abacuses
abscissa
aciculae
acicular
aciculas
aircraft
alacrity
amicable
amicably
anaconda
anecdote
anechoic
aniconic
apically
apocrine
araceous
arachnid
armchair
baccarat
bacchant
beechnut
berceuse
biocidal
bitchily
blackboy
blackcap
blackfly
blacking
blackish
blackleg
blackout
blacktie
blacktop
blockade
blockage
blockish
bracelet
brachial
brachium
brackish
bracteal
bractlet
brickbat
brickred
brocaded
brocatel
broccoli
brochure
buncombe
butchery
calcanea
calcaria
calcific
calcitic
calcspar
calctuff
calculus
cancrine
cancroid
carcajou
carcanet
cascabel
catchall
catchfly
catching
cercaria
chaconne
checkers
checkout
chickpea
cinchona
cincture
Circaean
circuity
circular
coachdog
coachman
coaction
coactive
coccyges
concasse
conceder
conceive
concerti
concerto
concetti
concetto
conchate
conchoid
conclave
conclude
concrete
couchant
couching
crackers
cracking
crackjaw
cracknel
crackpot
croceate
crockery
crocoite
cruciate
crucible
crucifer
crucifix
curculio
dabchick
dancette
dancetty
describe
deucedly
diaconal
diocesan
disciple
disclaim
disclose
discount
discover
discreet
discrete
discrown
dracaena
drachmae
drachmai
drachmas
draconic
dryclean
dulciana
dulcimer
Dulcinea
Dutchman
edacious
educable
educated
educator
educible
eduction
ejection
ejective
election
elective
electret
electric
electron
electrum
emaciate
enaction
enactive
ensconce
epically
epicalyx
epicotyl
epicycle
erectile
erection
evacuant
evacuate
evection
eviction
exacting
exaction
execrate
executor
exocrine
falcated
falchion
falconer
falconet
falconry
fanciful
fancyman
farcical
fascicle
fasciola
fasciole
Fascista
Fascisti
fencible
fetching
fiscally
flection
flickery
floccose
floccule
flocculi
flockbed
forcedly
forcefed
forceful
forcible
forcibly
fraction
fracture
friction
frocking
fructify
fructose
function
furcated
furculae
furcular
gimcrack
glaciate
glucagon
glucinum
glycerin
glycerol
glyceryl
glycogen
glyconic
godchild
Golconda
graceful
gracioso
gracious
guacharo
hatchery
hatching
hatchway
henchman
Hercules
hiccough
hotchpot
hyacinth
icecream
idocrase
inaction
inactive
inoculum
inscient
inscribe
inscroll
isocheim
isocracy
junction
juncture
kerchief
knackery
knickers
knocking
knockout
laically
lancelet
larcener
latchkey
lawcourt
leucitic
linchpin
luncheon
luscious
lynchpin
Maecenas
mancando
manciple
marchesa
marchese
mascaron
matchbox
merchant
merciful
mercuric
mescalin
miscarry
miscegen
mischief
miscible
miscount
moccasin
muscadel
muscatel
muscling
muscular
mutchkin
narceine
narcissi
narcoses
narcosis
narcotic
nascence
nascency
nescient
newcomer
Noachian
nonclaim
notching
oilcloth
onychite
oracular
outcaste
outclass
pancreas
parcener
parclose
patchily
peaceful
peacocky
peccable
peccancy
penchant
perceive
piacular
piecrust
pilchard
pincenez
pinchers
piscator
piscinae
placable
placably
placeman
placenta
placidly
plectrum
pluckily
practice
practise
precinct
precious
preclude
proceeds
proclaim
procurer
psychics
psychism
psychist
puncheon
punctate
punctual
puncture
purchase
quackery
quackish
Quechuan
quickset
ranchero
ranchman
rascally
reactant
reaction
reactive
reoccupy
rescript
runcible
saccadic
saccular
sacculus
sanctify
sanction
sanctity
sarcenet
saucebox
saucepan
seachest
seacoast
seacraft
seicento
selcouth
shocking
sinciput
smocking
snackbar
sorcerer
souchong
spacebar
spaceman
spacious
speciate
specific
specimen
specious
spectral
spectrum
specular
speculum
spicated
spiccato
spicebox
spicknel
spiculae
spicular
spiculum
staccato
stickful
stickily
stickjaw
stickler
stoccado
stoccata
stockade
stockcar
stockily
stocking
stockish
stockist
stockman
stockpot
stuccoes
subclass
succinct
succinic
succinum
succubae
succubus
suicidal
surcease
syncline
syncopal
syncytia
teacaddy
teachest
teaching
teacloth
teocalli
tetchily
thickety
thickish
thickset
tincture
torchere
touchily
touching
tracheae
tracheal
tracheid
trachoma
trachyte
trackage
tracking
trackman
trackway
tractate
traction
tractive
trecento
trichina
trichite
trichoid
trichome
trichord
trickery
trickily
trickish
tricorne
tricycle
trochaic
trochili
trochlea
trochoid
truckage
trucking
truckler
Turcoman
unicycle
urochord
vaccinal
vaccinia
vascular
vasculum
vincible
vinculum
viscacha
visceral
viscidly
viscount
vizcacha
voicebox
voiceful
volcanic
volcanos
vulcanic
warcloud
watchdog
watchful
watchkey
watchman
waxcloth
whacking
witchelm
witchery
witchety
witching
wrackful
wreckage
zecchini
zecchino
zinckify
zincking
zirconia
zucchini
aardvark
aardwolf
abidance
academia
academic
acidfast
acidhead
acidosis
agedness
amadavat
apodoses
apodosis
avadavat
avidness
baldhead
baldness
baldpate
bandanna
bandeaux
banderol
banditry
banditti
bandsman
baudrons
beadroll
beadsman
beadwork
biddable
bindweed
birdbath
birdcage
birdcall
birdlime
birdseed
birdseye
bladdery
bludgeon
boldface
boldness
bondmaid
bondmans
bondsman
Bordeaux
bordello
borderer
Bradshaw
Buddhism
Buddhist
buddleia
bundling
candidly
cardamom
cardamum
cardigan
cardinal
caudally
caudated
caudexes
caudices
caudillo
cladding
cloddish
clodpole
clodpoll
coldness
condense
condylar
cordless
cordovan
corduroy
cordwain
cordwood
cradling
credence
credenza
credible
credibly
credited
creditor
culdesac
dandruff
dandyish
dandyism
daydream
deadbeat
deadener
deadfall
deadhead
deadline
deadlock
deadness
deadwood
deedless
dendrite
dendroid
doddered
dodderer
doldrums
dowdyish
drudgery
dundiver
duodenal
duodenum
epidemic
epidural
erodible
evadable
evidence
falderal
fandance
fandango
feedback
feedhead
feedpipe
feedtank
feldsher
feldspar
feudally
fiddling
foldaway
foldboat
folderol
fondling
fondness
foodless
fordable
fordoing
gardener
gardenia
gardyloo
gendarme
geodesic
geodetic
gladdest
gladding
gladhand
gladioli
gladness
gladsome
goadster

Goidelic
golddust
goldenly
goldfish
goldfoil
goldleaf
goldmine
goldrush
goodness
goodtime
goodwife
goodwill
goodyear
gradient
graduand
graduate
gridiron
grudging
guidable
guidance
guidedog
guideway
handball
handbell
handbill
handbook
handcart
handclap
handcuff
handfast
handgrip
handheld
handhold
handicap
handless
handline
handling
handlist
handloom
handmade
handmaid
handmill
handpick
handrail
handsewn
handsome
handwork
handyman
hardback
hardbake
hardcase
hardcore
hardener
hardhack
hardhead
hardline
hardness
hardship
hardtack
hardware
hardwood
headache
headachy
headband
headfast
headgear
headlamp
headland
headless
headline
headlock
headlong
headmost
headnote
headrace
headrest
headroom
headsail
headsman
headwind
headword
headwork
hebdomad
heedless
herdbook
herdsman
herdwick
hinderer
hindlegs
hindmost
hinduise
Hinduism
holdback
holdfast
holdover
hoodwink
inedible
inedited
isodicon
khedival
kindless
kindling
kindness
labdanum
landarmy
landcrab
landfall
landform
landgirl
landlady
landless
landline
landlord
landmark
landmass
landmine
landrail
landslip
landsman
laudable
laudably
laudanum
laudator
leadenly
leadless
leadsman
leadwork
lewdness
loadline
loadstar
Londoner
lordless
lordling
lordosis
lordotic
lordship
loudness
magdalen
maidenly
maidhood
Mandaean
mandamus
mandarin
mandator
mandible
Mandingo
mandolin
mandorla
mandrake
mandrill
Mazdaism
mendable
mesdames
middling
mildness
mindless
misdealt
misdoing
misdoubt
mondaine
mordancy
murderer
needfire
needless
needment
nondairy
obedient
offdrive
omadhaum
outdated
outdoors
outdrawn
oxidiser
pandanus
pandemic
pandowdy
pardoner
pendency
pendicle
pendular
pendulum
piddling
piedmont
Pindaric
plodding
ponderer
pondweed
powdered
predator
predella
prideful
prodding
prodigal
prodrome
producer
prudence
punditry
quadrant
quadrate
quadriga
quadroon
quiddity
quidnunc
randomly
readable
readably
readjust
reedbird
reedling
reedmace
reedpipe
reedstop
reedwren
renderer
riddance
roadbook
roadless
roadside
roadsign
roadster
rondeaux
roodbeam
roodloft
rowdyish
rowdyism
saddlery
Sadducee
sandarac
sandbank
sandbath
sandflea
sandshoe
sandwich
sandworm
sandwort
sandyish
sardelle
sardonic
sardonyx
scudding
seadrome
seedcake
seedcase
seedcoat
seedcorn
seedfish
seedleaf
seedless
seedling
seedlobe
seedplot
seedsman
seedtime
shadbush
shaddock
shadower
shedding
shedevil
shoddily
shuddery
skidding
sledding
slideway
smudgily
solderer
soldiery
sordidly
spadeful
spadices
spadille
spadones
stedfast
stodgily
studbook
studding
studfarm
studious
studwork
suddenly
sundance
sunderer
sundress
sundried
sundries
sundrops
syndesis
syndetic
syndical
syndrome
tandoori
tapdance
tawdrily
tendence
tendency
tenderly
thudding
toadfish
toadflax
toadyish
toadyism
topdress
tradeoff
traditor
traducer
twaddler
twiddler
unedited
Vandalic
vendetta
vendible
verdancy
verderer
verderor
verditer
verdured
voidable
voidance
voidness
wanderer
wanderoo
wardance
wardenry
wardress
wardrobe
wardroom
wardship
weedless
weldable
weldment
whidding
whodunit
wildeyed
wildfire
wildfowl
wildlife
wildness
wildwood
windburn
windcone
windfall
windgall
windlass
windless
windmill
windowed
windpipe
windrose
windsail
windsock
windward
wondrous
woodbind
woodbine
woodchat
woodcock
woodenly
woodland
woodlark
woodlice
woodnote
woodpile
woodpulp
woodruff
woodshed
woodsman
woodwind
woodwool
woodwork
woodworm
wordbook
wordless
wordplay
Abderite
abjectly
abnegate
absentee
absently
accentor
accepter
acceptor
achenial
acierage
acierate
acrefoot
acreinch
addendum
adherent
adhesion
adhesive
Adlerian
affected
affecter
afferent
agrement
agrestic
Airedale
aldehyde
alderman
Alderney
alienage
alienate
alienism
alienist
allegory
alleluia
allergen
allergic
alleyway
alveolar
alveolus
amnesiac
amoebean
amoeboid
amperage
anaerobe
ancestor
ancestry
andesine
andesite
angelica
anhedral
ankerite
anserine
anteater
antecede
antedate
antefixa
antelope
antennae
antennal
antennas
antepost
anterior
anteroom
aphelion
appendix
appetent
appetite
apresski
apterous
aqueduct
ardently
argentic
Armenian
arpeggio
arrestee
arrester
arrestor
arsenate
arsenide
arsenite
artefact
arterial
artesian
asbestic
asbestos
ascender
asperges
asperity
assemble
assembly
assenter
assentor
assertor
assessor
asterisk
asterism
asteroid
atheling
Athenian
atheroma
atremble
attender
attested
attester
attestor
aurelian
axletree
balefire
bareback
barefoot
bareness
baseball
baseborn
baseless
baseline
basement
baseness
bateleur
bedeguar
beeeater
begetter
behemoth
benedick
benedict
benefice
bereaved
bevelled
beveller
beverage
bisector
bisexual
biweekly
biyearly
bleeding
bluebell
bluebird
bluechip
bluecoat
bluefish
blueness
bluenose
blueweed
bodement
bogeyman
bohemian
bonefish
bonehead
boneless
bonemeal
boneyard
borecole
borehole
breeches
breeding
breezily
briefing
cadenced
cagebird
cageling
cakewalk
calendar
calender
cameleer
camellia
capeline
capellet
capeskin
carefree
careless
careworn
casebook
casemate
casement
casework
catechol
category
catenary
catenate
cateress
catering
caverned
cavesson
celeriac
celerity
cemetery
cerebral
cerebrum
cerement
ceremony
cheekily
cheerful
cheerily
cheering
chiefdom
cicerone
ciceroni
cidevant
cineaste
cinerary
clueless
cogently
coherent
cohesion
cohesive
cokernut
coleseed
coleslaw
colewort
comeback
comedian
comedist
comedown
cometary
corelate
cosecant
cotenant
covenant
coverage
coverall
covering
coverlet
covertly
covetous
cozenage
creeping
crueller
cupelled
cureless
cuteness
Cyrenaic
dalesman
danegeld
dateless
dateline
deaerate
deceased
decedent
deceiver
December
decemvir
decennia
decently
defector
defender
deferent
deferral
deferred
deferrer
dejected
delegacy
delegate
deletion
demented
dementia
demerara
demersal
denehole
derelict
deserter
detector
deterred

deterrer
digester
dihedral
dimerism
dimerous
dinerout
dioecism
directly
director
diseased
disendow
divebomb
Docetism
Docetist
dogeared
dolerite
dolesome
domestic
dovecote
dovetail
dowelled
easement
eclectic
edgeless
edgeways
edgewise
effector
efferent
embedded
embezzle
emceeing
Emmental
empeople
enceinte
endemism
endermic
enfeeble
enfetter
engender
enneagon
ensemble
entellus
enterate
envelope
ephemera
Ephesian
especial
Essenism
esterify
etcetera
ethereal
etherial
etherise
etherism
etherist
eugenics
eugenism
eugenist
eupepsia
eupeptic
eutectic
excelled
expedite
expelled
expellee
expertly
exserted
extender
extensor
exterior
external
faceache
facecard
faceless
facelift
facepack
facetiae
fadeaway
fadeless
farewell
federate
fenestra
feretory
feverfew
feverish
feverous
fidelity
filefish
finedraw
fineness
finespun
firearms
fireback
fireball
firebird
fireboat
firebomb
firebrat
fireclay
firedamp
fireeyed
firehose
firelock
fireopal
fireplug
fireship
fireside
firetrap
fireweed
firewood
firework
fivefold
fivestar
fleeting
fluellin
fluently
fluepipe
fomenter
forebear
forebode
forecast
foredeck
foredoom
foreedge
forefeel
forefelt
forefoot
foregoer
foregone
forehand
forehead
foreknew
foreknow
forelady
foreland
forelock
foremast
foremost
forename
forenoon
forensic
forepart
forepast
forepeak
foreplay
foresaid
foresail
foreseen
foreshow
foreside
foreskin
forestal
forestay
forested
forester
forestry
foretell
foretime
foretold
forewarn
forewent
foreword
foreyard
foveolae
fraenula
freeborn
freedman
freefall
freehand
freehold
freeload
freeness
freesoil
freewill
freezeup
freezing
friendly
Friesian
funebral
funerary
funereal
fuselage
galeated
Galenism
galenite
gamebird
gamecock
gameness
gamesome
gamester
gapeworm
garefowl
gaselier
gatefold
gatepost
gavelock
generate
generous
genetics
Genevese
giveaway
gleesome
Gobelins
gogetter
governor
Graecise
Graecism
greedily
greegree
greenery
greenfly
greening
greenish
greenlet
greeting
grievous
gruesome
haleness
harebell
haresear
hateable
havelock
hazelnut
hebetate
hebetude
Hegelian
hegemony
henequen
hereaway
heredity
Hereford
hereunto
hereupon
herewith
hibernal
hideaway
hireable
hireling
homebody
homeborn
homebred
homebrew
homefelt
homeland
homeless
homelike
homemade
homesick
homespun
hometown
homeward
homework
honestly
honeybee
honeydew
honeypot
hopeless
hosepipe
hotelier
hoverfly
hugeness
hymenial
hymenium
Ibsenism
idleness
ilmenite
imbecile
immersed
impelled
impeller
imperial
imperium
impetigo
inceptor
indebted
indecent
infector
inferior
infernal
inferred
inherent
inhesion
injector
insecure
inserted
integral
intended
intently
interact
interbed
intercom
intercut
interest
interior
intermit
intermix
internal
internee
Interpol
interred
interrex
intersex
intertie
interval
interwar
invected
inveigle
inventor
inverted
inverter
investor
jeremiad
Jeremiah
jewelled
jeweller
juvenile
kakemono
Khmerian
kinesics
kinetics
kneedeep
kneehigh
kneehole
kneejerk
labelled
labellum
lacerate
lacewing
lacework
lakeland
lamellae
lamellar
lameness
lamented
lapelled
lateness
latently
laterite
lavender
laverock
legendry
legerity
levelled
leveller
leverage
libeccio
libelled
libellee
libeller
liberate
licensed
licensee
licenser
lifebelt
lifeboat
lifebuoy
lifeless
lifelike
lifeline
lifelong
lifesize
lifetime
lifework
likeable
likeness
likewise
limekiln
limerick
limetwig
limewash
lineally
linearly
linesman
literacy
literary
literate
literati
liveable
liveborn
livelily
livelong
liveried
liverish
livewire
lobeline
lodestar
lomentum
loneness
lonesome
lopeared
lovebird
loveknot
loveless
lovelily
lovelock
lovelorn
lovenest
loveseat
lovesick
lovesome
lovesong
lowering
lukewarm
lutecium
lutenist
lutetium
lykewake
lyrebird
macerate
maieutic
majestic
makebate
makefast
maledict
malefern
malemute
maleness
Mameluke
maneater
matelote
material
materiel
maternal
maverick
mazement
mementos
meteoric
mezereon
micellar
milepost
Milesian
mimester
mirepoix
miserere
modelled
modeller
moderate
moderato
modernly
modestly
molecule
molehill
moleskin
molester
momently
momentum
monetary
monetise
moneybag
moneybox
moreover
moresque
moveable
moveless
movement
muleteer
muteness
mycelial
mycelium
mycetoma
nameable
namedrop
nameless
namepart
namesake
nametape
nepenthe
niceness
ninefold
ninepins
nineteen
nineties
nobelium
nonesuch
nonevent
noseband
nosecone
nosedive
nosepipe
nosering
notebook
notecase
noteless
novelise
novelist
November
novercal
nucellus
nudeness
numeracy
numerary
numerate
numerous
oakegger
objector
observer
obtected
offender
offering
onceover
oriental
oriented
osteitis
oxpecker
paleface
paleness
palestra
panelled
paperboy
parental
parergon
patellae
patellar
patentee
patently
patentor
paternal
pavement
pederast
pedestal
pelerine
peperino
petechia
phlegmon
phreatic
pileated
pilewort
pinecone
pinewood
pipeclay
pipefish
pipeline
piperack
piperine
polemics
polemise
polemist
polestar
potently
powerful
praecipe
praedial
preelect
preexist
priedieu
priestly
proemial
pubertal
purebred
pureness
pyrenoid
pyrexial
quaestor
queendom
queening
queenlet
queerish
quietism
quietist
quietude
racecard
racegoer
racemate
racemise
racemose
rakehell
ramentum
ramequin
rapecake
rapeseed
rarefied
rareness
rateable
ravelled
ravenous
rebelled
rebeller
rebellow
receiver
recently
receptor
redeemer
redefine
redeless
redeploy
redesign
referent
referral
referred
regelate
rehearse
rejecter
releasee
releaser
releasor
relegate
relevant
remedial
remember
renegade
renegado
reneguer
repealer
repeater
repelled
repeller
repenter
repeople
repetend
rerearch
rerecord
reremice
rereward
research
resemble
reserved
resetter
resettle
revealer
reveille
revelled
reveller
revenant
revenger
reverend
reverent
reversal
reverser
reverter
revetted
Rhaetian
ricebird

ricercar
rideable
rifeness
rimester
ripeness
rivelled
riverain
riverbed
riverine
riverman
riverway
ropeable
ropewalk
ropeyarn
rosebowl
rosebush
rosefish
roseleaf
rosemary
roseolar
rosepink
roseroot
rosetree
rosewood
rotenone
rudeness
ruleless
safeness
sageness
saleable
saleroom
Salesian
salesman
sameness
saneness
sateless
sawedged
sawedoff
schedule
schemata
scheming
sclereid
sclerite
scleroma
sclerose
sclerous
screamer
screechy
screener
screever
screwtop
sebesten
sederunt
selectee
selector
selenate
selenide
selenite
selenium
semester
serenade
serenata
serenely
serenity
severely
severity
sewellel
sewerage
sewergas
sewerrat
sheepdip
sheepdog
sheepish
sheepked
sheeppen
sheeprun
sheeting
shielder
shieling
shoebill
shoehorn
shoelace
shoeless
shoetree
shredded
shredder
shrewdly
shrewish
Siberian
sidearms
sideband
sidedish
sidedoor
sidedrum
sidehead
sidekick
sideline
sideling
sidelong
sidenote
sidereal
siderite
sideroad
sideshow
sideslip
sidesman
sidestep
sideview
sidewalk
sideward
sideways
sidewind
sidewise
silencer
silently
sinecure
sirenian
sizeable
sleepily
sleeping
sloeeyed
sneeshan
soberise
solecism
solecist
solemnly
soleness
solenoid
somebody
somedeal
somedele
sometime
someways
somewhat
somewhen
sorehead
soreness
soterial
spaewife
speedily
speedway
sphenoid
spherics
spheroid
spherule
splendid
splenial
splenius
spreader
squeaker
squealer
squeedge
squeegee
squeezer
squelchy
steenbok
steening
steepish
steepled
steerage
steering
streaked
streaker
streamer
streeted
strength
strepent
Strepyan
stretchy
suberect
suberise
suberose
suberous
Sumerian
superadd
superate
superbly
superego
superior
superman
supernal
supertax
surefire
sureness
suzerain
sweeping
sweepnet
sweeting
sweetish
sweetpea
sweetsop
synergic
synergid
taberdar
takeaway
takehome
takeover
talented
talesman
tameable
tameless
tameness
tapedeck
tapeless
tapelike
tapeline
tapestry
tapeworm
taverner
telecast
telecine
telefilm
telegony
telegram
telemark
telepath
teleport
telethon
teleview
televise
temerity
Tenebrae
tenement
tenesmus
terebene
terebrae
thievery
thievish
threader
threaten
threeply
threeway
threnode
threnody
thresher
tidegate
tideland
tideless
tidelock
tidemark
tidemill
tidewave
tigereye
tigerish
tilefish
timeball
timebomb
timefuse
timeless
timework
timeworn
tireless
tiresome
together
tokenism
tolerant
tolerate
tomentum
tonedeaf
toneless
tonepoem
toreador
toreutic
totemism
totemist
towelled
treefern
treefrog
treeless
treenail
triennia
trueblue
trueborn
truebred
truelove
trueness
tubeless
tubercle
tuberose
tuberous
tuneable
tuneless
tutelage
tutelary
tweezers
twoedged
typecast
typeface
typehigh
ulcerate
ulcerous
ulterior
unbeaten
unbelief
underact
underage
underarm
underbid
undercut
underdid
underdog
underfur
underlap
underlay
underlet
underlie
underlip
underman
underpin
underrun
undersea
underset
undertow
underway
unfetter
unkennel
unleaded
unlearnt
unmeetly
unpegged
unperson
unreason
unsealed
unseated
unseeded
unseeing
unseemly
unsettle
untented
untether
unversed
unweaned
upheaval
uppercut
upsetter
urgently
valerate
valerian
vaneless
vegetate
vegetive
vehement
veneerer
venerate
venereal
Venetian
verecund
vileness
vinegary
vineyard
viperine
viperish
viperous
virement
vitellin
vitellus
vixenish
vomerine
voteless
vowelise
vowelled
wakeless
wakening
wakerife
waleknot
waterage
waterbed
waterbus
watergas
waterice
watering
waterish
waterlog
waterloo
waterman
waterski
waterway
waveband
waveform
waveless
weregild
werewolf
wheedler
wheelman
wheezily
wideeyed
wideness
wifehood
wifeless
wifelike
winepalm
wineshop
wineskin
wiredraw
wirehair
wireless
wirework
wireworm
wirewove
wiseacre
wiseness
yodelled
yodeller
yokemate
yuletide
zibeline
zwieback
airfield
airframe
artfully
avifauna
beefcake
beefwood
botflies
bouffant
bowfront
bunfight
caffeine
calfskin
coiffeur
coiffure
conferee
conferva
confetti
confider
confiner
confines
conflate
conflict
confound
confrere
confront
craftily
crofting
daffodil
deafmute
deafness
diffract
diffuser
disfrock
dogfaced
dogfight
driftage
driftice
driftway
dumfound
epifauna
fanfaron
farflung
fitfully
furfural
furfuran
gasfired
golfclub
gonfalon
goofball
graffiti
graffito
greffier
gulfweed
gunfight
gunflint
halfback
halfbeak
halfboot
halfbred
halflife
halfmast
halfmoon
halfnote
halfpint
halfsole
halfterm
halftime
halftone
hawfinch
hayfield
hipflask
hoofbeat
icefield
illfated
joyfully
Kaffiyeh
korfball
lawfully
leafless
leaflike
manfully
midfield
moufflon
newfound
oilfield
oilfired
outfield
outflank
perfecto
perforce
perfumer
piffling
pilferer
profaner
profiler
profound
puffball
puffbird
purfling
reaffirm
redfaced
reefknot
riffraff
roofless
roofrack
rooftree
ruefully
saffrony
sawframe
scaffold
seafarer
seafloor
seafront
selfborn
selfheal
selfhelp
selfhood
selfless
selflove
selfmade
selfmate
selfness
selfpity
selfrule
selfsame
selfsown
selfwill
serfhood
shafting
shiftily
shiftkey
shofroth
shuffler
sinfonia
sinfully
sniffily
sniffler
sniffles
snuffbox
snuffers
snuffler
snuffles
solfaist
solfeggi
spiffing
spoffish
staffage
stiffish
stuffily
stuffing
subfloor
subframe
sufferer
suffrage
surfacer
surfbird
surfboat
surfduck
surffish
swiftlet
tafferel
taffrail
trifling
trifocal
triforia
twofaced
unifilar
usefully
usufruct
wayfarer
whiffler
wilfully
woefully
wolffish
wolfpack
wolfskin
alogical
amygdala
anaglyph
anagogic
apagogic
apogamic
apograph
bangtail
bargeman
beagling
beggarly
bergamot
biogenic
biograph
blighter
boughten
braggart
bragging
bregmata
brighten
brightly
budgeree
bungalow
bunghole
burglary
burgonet
Burgundy
chugging
cingulum
clogging
coagulum
congener
conglobe
congress
congreve
cowgrass
cragsman
daughter
diagnose
diagonal
diagraph
diggings
dingdong
disgorge
disgrace
disguise
doggedly
doggerel
doughboy

doughnut
dragging
dragline
dragoman
dragomen
dragonet
dragsman
dragster
drugging
druggist
dungaree
dungcart
dunghill
dysgenic
eelgrass
elegance
elegancy
eligible
eligibly
emigrant
emigrate
epigeous
epigraph
erigeron
erogenic
exegesis
exegetic
exigence
exigency
exigible
exiguity
exiguous
exogamic
eyeglass
fangless
fingered
flagella
flagging
flagpole
flagrant
flagship
flogging
forgiven
forgoing
fougasse
foxglove
fragment
fragrant
frighten
frigidly
frogfish
frogging
frogspit
frugally
fungible
gadgetry
gangland
gangling
ganglion
gangrene
gangster
garganey
gargoyle
geognosy
gingerly
gingival
gorgeous
gorgonia
groggily
grogshop
Haggadah
hangable
hangeron
hangnail
hangover
hedgehog
hedgehop
hedgepig
hedgerow

heighten
huggable
hungrily
imaginal
imagines
isagogic
isogamic
isogloss
isogonal
isogonic
jaggedly
jiggered
jingoish
jingoism
jingoist
jongleur
judgment
jugglery
kangaroo
kedgeree
kidglove
kingbird
kingbolt
kingcrab
kingfish
kinghood
kinglike
kingship
kingsize
knightly
langlauf
Langshan
language
languish
largesse
laughing
laughter
lawgiver
leggings
legguard
lengthen
liegeman
lingerer
lingerie
linguist
lodgings
lodgment
longboat
longeron
longeval
longhair
longhand
longhorn
longness
longship
longsome
longstop
longterm
longtime
longueur
longwall
longwave
longways
longwise
lopgrass
lowgrade
lungfish
lungwort
mangabey
manganic
mangonel
mangrove
marginal
margrave
matgrass
meagrely
mergence
misgiven
misguide

Mongolic
mongoose
mudguard
myogenic
myograph
narghile
niggling
oatgrass
odograph
oligarch
oligomer
origanum
original
orogenic
outgoing
outgrown
outguess
pangolin
pargeter
peagreen
peignoir
plagiary
plaguily
plighted
plugging
poignant
pregnant
priggery
priggish
priggism
progress
puggaree
pungency
pyogenic
quagmire
raggedly
ratguard
reagency
reignite
ribgrass
ridgeway
ringbark
ringbolt
ringbone
ringdove
ringmain
ringneck
ringroad
ringside
ringtail
ringwall
ringworm
roughage
roughdry
roughhew
roughish
ruggedly
ryegrass
sangaree
Sangrail
Sangreal
sanguine
sapgreen
sargasso
seagoing
seagreen
seigneur
seignior
seignory
sergeant
shagbark
shaggily
shagreen
shagroon
shigella
shogging
singable
singeing
singsong

singular
slagging
slagheap
slightly
slogging
slugabed
sluggard
slugging
sluggish
smuggler
smugness
snagging
sniggler
snogging
snuggery
snugness
songbird
songbook
songless
songster
spagyric
spyglass
staggard
staggers
staghorn
stagnant
stagnate
stigmata
subgenus
subgroup
surgical
swagging
swigging
syngamic
tangency
tangible
tangibly
tangoist
thuggery
thuggism
tingeing
tonguing
toughish
tragical
tragopan
triglyph
trigonal
trigraph
tungsten
tungstic
turgidly
vanguard
vengeful
vergence
virginal
Virginia
vulgarly
waggoner
waygoing
Wedgwood
Whiggery
Whiggish
Whiggism
wingbeat
wingcase
wingless
wingspan
wriggler
ziggurat
zoogenic
alchemic
alehouse
alphabet
although
amphibia
amphipod
amphorae
amphoras
anchoret

anthelia
anthemia
antheral
anthesis
anthozoa
archaean
archaise
archaism
archaist
archduke
archival
archives
archness
asphodel
asphyxia
asthenia
asthenic
bachelor
bathetic
bathotic
bathrobe
bathroom
bechamel
bechance
bethesda
blahblah
bonhomie
bushbaby
bushbuck
bushfire
bushveld
cachalot
cachepot
cachexia
cachucha
cashbook
cashmere
cathedra
catheter
cathexes
cathexis
cathodal
cathodic
catholic
cephalic
chthonic
cochleae
cochlear
cothurni
cushiony
Cushitic
dethrone
dichasia
dichroic
diphenyl
dishevel
ditheism
ditheist
ditherer
doghouse
duchesse
Dukhobor
eighteen
eighthly
eighties
elkhound
emphases
emphasis
emphatic
ensheath
enshrine
enshroud
enthalpy
enthrall
enthrone
eschalot
eschewal
euphonic
euphoria

euphoric
euphrasy
euphuism
euphuist
exchange
fashious
fatherly
fighting
fishable
fishball
fishbone
fishbowl
fishcake
fishfarm
fishglue
fishhawk
fishhook
fishless
fishmeal
fishpond
fishtail
fishwife
foxhound
fuchsine
Gadhelic
gashouse
gatherer
hasheesh
highball
highborn
highbred
highbrow
higherup
highjack
highland
highlows
highmost
highness
highrise
highroad
hightail
hightest
hitherto
hothouse
hushhush
inchmeal
inchoate
inchworm
inthrall
ischemia
ischemic
isthmian
japhetic
jodhpurs
Kashmiri
kyphosis
kyphotic
lashings
lethally
lethargy
lichened
lichenin
lichgate
lighting
lightish
litharge
lothario
lushness
Lutheran
lychgate
machismo
madhouse
mechanic
menhaden
mephitic
mephitis
meshwork
methanol
methinks

methodic
methylic
methysis
mightest
mightily
misheard
mishmash
Mishnaic
Mithraic
moshavim
mothball
motherly
muchness
mushroom
mythical
naphthol
nathless
nephrite
nightcap
nighthag
nightjar
nightowl
nonhuman
nuthatch
nuthouse
omphalic
omphalos
onehorse
orchilla
orthicon
orthodox
orthoepy
outHerod
outhouse
pachalic
parhelia
parhelic
pashalic
pashalik
pathetic
pathless
pathogen
phthalic
phthisic
phthisis
pishogue
pochette
poohpooh
potholer
pothouse
prehuman
prohibit
pushball
pushbike
pushcart
pushover
pushpull
pythonic
rachides
rachitic
rachitis
rashness
recharge
richness
rightful
rightist
rushhour
rushlike
ruthless
sashcord
sawhorse
seaholly
seahorse
Sephardi
siphonal
siphonet
siphonic
sithence
subhuman

suchlike
syphilis
tachisme
tachiste
taphouse
teahouse
technics
tightwad
tithable
topheavy
Tychonic
typhonic
unchancy
unchaste
unchurch
unshaped
unthread
unthrift
unthrone
upthrown
upthrust
Valhalla
Walhalla
warhorse
washable
washbowl
washroom
wishbone
wishwash
withdraw
withdrew
withheld
withhold
yachting
yoghourt
abdicate
abridger
absinthe
accident
achiever
achiness
achingly
acridine
acridity
acrimony
actiniae
actinian
actinias
actinide
actinism
actinium
activate
actively
activism
activist
activity
addition
additive
adlibbed
admitted
advisory
aegirine
aerially
aeriform
affiance
affinity
affirmer
aglimmer
aglitter
agrimony
aguishly
airiness
albinism
algicide
algidity
alginate
alliance
almighty
alpinism

alpinist
altitude
ambiance
ambience
ambition
ambivert
amniotic
antibody
antidote
antihero
antilogy
antimask
antimony
antinode
antinomy
antiphon
antipode
antipole
antipope
antisera
antitype
aoristic
aphicide
aptitude
aquiline
arbitral
Arminian
articled
artifact
artifice
artistic
artistry
ascidian
ascidium
aspirant
aspirate
assiento
assignat
assignee
assignor
atticism
attitude
atwitter
audience
audition
auditive
auditory
auricula
auriform
autistic
babirusa
bacillar
bacillus
badinage
Balinese
banister
baritone
basicity
basidial
basidium
basilica
basilisk
basinful
bedimmed
befitted
beginner
begirded
believer
belittle
benignly
beriberi
besieger
bewigged
bewilder
bitingly
bodiless
boniface
boniness
boringly
bouillon
boyishly
braiding
brainish
brainpan
broidery
business
cabinboy
caginess
calidity
califate
calipash
calipers
camisade
camisado
camisole
canister
capitate
capitula
carillon
carinate
cationic
cavicorn
cavilled
caviller
celibacy
celibate
chainsaw
chairman
choicely
choirboy
christen
christie
Christly
cicisbei
cicisbeo
ciliated
citified
civilian
civilise
civility
claimant
cloister
codifier
cogitate
coliform
coliseum
conidial
conidium
coniform
cosiness
cotillon
cubiform
culicine
culinary
cupidity
cylinder
cynicism
Cyrillic
cytidine
daringly
debility
decigram
decimate
decipher
decision
decisive
dedicate
defiance
defilade
definite
delibate
delicacy
delicate
delirium
delivery
demijohn
demitted
demiurge
deniable
depicter
depictor
depilate
derision
derisive
derisory
derivate
designer
desirous
deviance
deviancy
deviator
deviling
devilish
devilism
devilkin
devilled
deviltry
dewiness
digitate
digitise
diligent
diminish
dirigism
diriment
disinter
dividend
dividivi
dividual
divinely
divinise
divinity
division
divisive
docilely
docility
domicile
dominant
dominate
domineer
dominion
dominoes
dopiness
dotingly
doziness
drainage
druidess
druidism
dutiable
easiness
ebriated
echinate
echinoid
ecliptic
edginess
eeriness
efficacy
egoistic
ellipses
ellipsis
elliptic
embitter
encipher
encircle
enfilade
engineer
enginery
engirdle
enkindle
enricher
ensiform
ensigncy
ensilage
entirely
entirety
enviable
enviably
environs
envisage
envision
eohippus
eolithic
equinity
equipage
equipped
equitant
equities
equivoke
Eskimoan
estimate
ethicism
ethicist
Ethiopic
excision
excitant
exciting
exlibris
expiable
expiator
expirant
facially
facilely
facility
familial
familiar
farinose
fatigues
felicity
felinity
feminine
feminise
feminism
feminist
feminity
feticide
filially
filiform
filigree
Filipina
Filipino
finisher
finitely
finitude
fluidics
fluidify
fluidise
fluidity
foliaged
foxiness
fruitage
fruitbat
fruitery
fruitfly
fruitful
fruition
fugitive
fumigant
fumigate
fumitory
fusiform
fusileer
fusilier
futilely
futility
Galilean
gaminess
ganister
gapingly
garishly
gelidity
geminate
genially
genitive
geniture
gneissic
gonidial
gonidium
graining
guaiacum
habitant
habitual
habitude
hacienda
haliotis
harikari
havildar
haziness
heliacal
helicoid
heliosis
heliport
heritage
hesitant
hesitate
hibiscus
holidays
holiness
holistic
homicide
hominoid
howitzer
humidify
humidity
humility
hygienic
ignition
ignitron
illiquid
imminent
immingle
impishly
incident
incision
incisive
incitant
incivism
Indiaman
indicant
indicate
indicium
indigene
indigent
indirect
infilter
infinite
infinity
infirmly
inkiness
insignia
intimacy
intimate
intimism
intitule
inviable
inviting
iodinate
irrigate
irritant
irritate
janizary
jipijapa
jokingly
jovially
jubilant
jubilate
judicial
julienne
juristic
kamikaze
kibitzer
Kohinoor
kolinsky
komitaji
labially
lability
laminate
lapicide
lapidary
lapidate
lapidify
Latinate
latinise
Latinism
Latinist
latinity
latitant
latitude
lavishly
laziness
lecithin
legioned
lenience
leniency
Leninism
Leninist
Leninite
lenitive
lepidote
leviable
levigate
levirate
levitate
lewisite
limitary
liniment
liripoop
litigant
litigate
lividity
lixivium
lodicule
logician
logistic
loricate
lorikeet
lovingly
lucidity
luminant
luminary
luminist
luminous
lyricism
lyricist
magician
magicked
magister
makimono
maligner
malignly
malinger
mamillae
mamillar
maniacal
Manichee
manicure
manifest
manifold
maniform
marigold
marinade
marinate
maritage
maritime
matiness
maxillae
maximise
maziness
medially
mediator
medicate
medicine
medieval
mediocre
meditate
melinite
menially
meninges
meniscus
meridian
meringue
meristem
meristic
mesially
militant
military
militate
mimicked
mimicker
minimise
minister
ministry
mitigant
mitigate
mobilise
mobility
modifier
modishly
Molinism
Molinist
monicker
monistic
monition
monitive
monitory
mopishly
moribund
motility
motional
motivate
motivity
movingly
mucilage
mulishly
muniment
munition
muriatic
musicale
musician
musingly
muticous
mutilate
mutineer
mutinous
myriapod
myriopod
napiform
national
natively
nativism
nativist
nativity
navigate
Nazirite
nihilism
nihilist
nihility
nobility
nominate
nomistic
nosiness
notional
nubiform
nubility
nubilous
numinous
oafishly
obeisant
obligate
obliging
oblivion
obsidian
occident
official
oiliness
oiticica
omnivore
oncidium
ooziness
ophidian
oppilate
opsimath
optician
optimise
optimism
optimist
optional
ordinand
ordinary
ordinate
ornithic
orpiment
oscinine
Ossianic
ostinato
owlishly
pacifier
pacifism
pacifist
padishah
paginate
palinode
palisade
panicked
papillae
papillar
papillon
papistic
papistry
parietal
patience
pavilion
pedicled
pedicure
pedigree
pediment
pedipalp
Pekinese
penitent
perianth
pericarp
pericope
periderm
peridium
peridote
perigean
perigyny
perilled
perilous
perilune
perineal
perineum
periodic
periotic
peripety
periplus
perisher
petiolar
petioled
petition
piliform
pimiento
pisiform
pitiable
pitiably
pitiless
pixieish
pixiness
plaiding
plaister
pleinair
podiatry
polisher
politely

politick
politico
politics
popinjay
popishly
poristic
position
positive
positron
pruinose
pryingly
pugilism
pugilist
puniness
punisher
punition
punitive
punitory
pupilage
pupilary
pupillar
purifier
puristic
pygidial
pygidium
pyridine
pyriform
pyxidium
quaintly
rabidity
racially
raciness
radially
radiance
radiancy
radiator
radicant
radicate
rakishly
rapidity
ratifier
rational
ravisher
recision
redirect
redistil
refinery
refitted
regicide
regiment
regional
register
registry
rejigger
rekindle
reliable
reliably
reliance
reliever
religion
reminder
remissly
remittal
remitted
remittee
remitter
reniform
renitent
resident
residual
residuum
resigned
resinate
resinify
resinoid
resinous
resister
resistor
retiarii
reticent
reticule
retiform
retinula
retiring
reviewal
reviewer
reviling
revision
revisory
revivify
ridicule
rigidify
rigidity
ropiness
rosiness
rubicund
rubidium
rudiment
ruminant
ruminate
rutilant
sadistic
saginate
sagittal
salience
saliency
salinity
salivary
salivate
samizdat
sanitary
sanitate
sanitise
sapidity
sapience
satiable
satiably
satirise
satirist
schiedam
schiller
schizoid
scribble
scribbly
sediment
sedition
semibull
semidome
seminary
seminude
semiotic
Semitise
Semitism
Semitist
semitone
senility
serially
seriatim
sericite
sexiness
sheikdom
shrieval
shrimper
shrinker
sibilant
sibilate
Sicilian
silicane
silicate
silicide
silicify
silicone
similise
sinicise
sinister
siriasis
sociable
sociably
socially
societal
Socinian
solidary
solidify
solidity
solitary
solitude
sphingid
splinter
splitter
spoilage
sprigged
springal
springer
sprinkle
sprinter
squibbed
squidded
squiggle
squiggly
squilgee
squinter
squireen
squirely
squirrel
squirter
stairrod
stairway
steinbok
stoicism
stricken
strickle
strictly
stridden
strident
strigose
striking
stringed
stringer
stripped
stripper
subimago
sukiyaki
supinate
supinely
suricate
swainish
syringes
syrinxes
taciturn
Tahitian
takingly
talisman
Tamilian
tanistry
taxingly
tepidity
theistic
thridace
thriller
thriving
tidiness
timidity
tininess
titivate
tonicity
toxicant
toxicity
trailnet
training
troilite
truistic
tryingly
tubiform
tumidity
tunicate
Tunisian
typifier
ugliness
ultimacy
ultimata
ultimate
umpirage
unbiased
unbidden
uncially
unciform
uncinate
unfilial
unfitted
unhinged
unkindly
unkingly
unlikely
unlimber
unlinked
unlisted
unpinned
unriddle
unrigged
untidily
untimely
untitled
unwieldy
unwisdom
unwisely
unwished
unzipped
uplifter
uppishly
uprising
urticant
urticate
vagility
valiance
valiancy
validate
validity
vanillin
vanisher
vapidity
variable
variably
variance
varicose
variedly
varietal
variform
variolar
variorum
vasiform
venially
verifier
veristic
vesicant
vesicate
vexillum
vicinage
vicinity
vigilant
vilifier
vilipend
viricide
viridian
viridity
virilism
virility
Visigoth
visional
visitant
vitiable
vitiator
vitiligo
vivifier
vivisect
volitant
volition
volitive
vomitive
vomitory
wariness
waviness
waxiness
wiliness
wiriness
zamindar
zaniness
zemindar
zenithal
zodiacal
banjoist
Benjamin
conjoint
conjugal
conjunct
conjurer
conjuror
disjoint
disjunct
frijoles
jiujitsu
mahjongg
marjoram
misjudge
nonjuror
perjurer
prejudge
serjeant
subjoint
verjuice
backache
backbite
backbone
backchat
backcomb
backdate
backdoor
backdrop
backfire
backhand
backlash
backless
backlist
backmost
backpack
backrest
backroom
backseat
backside
backspin
backstay
backveld
backward
backwash
backyard
balkline
bankable
bankbill
bankbook
banknote
bankroll
bankrupt
barkless
basketry
bookcase
bookends
bookland
booklice
booklore
bookmark
bookpost
bookrest
bookwork
bookworm
brakeman
brakevan
brokenly
buckaroo
buckbean
buckhorn
buckling
buckshee
buckshot
buckskin
bulkhead
bunkered
cockatoo
cockboat
cockcrow
cockerel
cockeyed
cockloft
cockshut
cocksure
cocktail
cookbook
corkwing
corkwood
dankness
darkling
darkness
darkroom
darksome
deckhand
dockland
dockside
dockyard
duckbill
duckhawk
duckling
duckpond
duckweed
feckless
folklore
folkmoot
folksong
folktale
forklift
funkhole
gymkhana
hawkeyed
hawklike
hawkmoth
hawkweed
hickwall
hocktide
hookworm
huckster
jackaroo
jackboot
jackeroo
jackstay
junkshop
junkyard
kickback
kickshaw
kinkajou
lackaday
lankness
larkspur
lockable
lockfast
lockknit
lockstep
lookeron
luckless
mackerel
mackinaw
markdown
markedly
marketer
marksman
meekness
milkmaid
milkweed
milkwort
monkfish
MonKhmer
monkhood
monkseal
monkship
muckluck
muckrake
muckworm
muskdeer
muskduck
musketry
muskrose
musktree
neckband
necklace
neckline
nickelic
nicknack
nickname
parkland
peekaboo
penknife
pickerel
picketer
pickings
picklock
pinkness
pockmark
porkling
Quakerly
rackrent
rankness
reckless
reckoner
rickrack
rickshaw
rockbird
rockcake
rockcork
rockdove
rocketry
rockfall
rockfish
rockhewn
rocklike
rockling
rockrose
rocksalt
rockweed
rockwood
rockwork
rucksack
sackcoat
sackless
sackrace
shakable
shakeout
Shaktism
Shekinah
shikaree
sickener
sickerly
sickflag
sicklist
sickness
sickroom
silkworm
sinkable
sinkhole
smokable
snakepit
soakaway
spikelet
stakenet
suckling
tackling
tackroom
taskwork
ticklish
tickseed
ticktack
ticktock
tinkerer
trekking
tuckahoe
tuckshop
Turkoman
walkable
walkaway
walkover
Walkyrie
weakfish
weakling
weakness
weeklong
wickedly
workable
workaday
workfolk
workings
workless
workmate
workroom
workshop
Yankeefy
abelmosk
aceldama
aculeate
adularia
adulator
adultery
afflatus
affluent
airliner
analcime
analcite
analecta
analects
analogic
analogue
analyser
analyses
analysis
analytic
Anglican
antlered
apologia
apologue
applause
applepie
applique
arillate
athletic
avulsion
axillary
badlands
bailable
bailment
bailsman
balladic
balladry
ballcock
balletic
ballista
ballonet
ballroom
ballyhoo
ballyrag
bdellium
bellbird
bellbuoy
bellcote
bellpull
bellpush
bellwort
bellyful
berliner

beslaver
biblical
billfold
billhead
billhook
billiard
billyboy
billycan
Bodleian
bollworm
buhlwork
building
bullcalf
bulldoze
bulletin
bullfrog
bullhead
bullhorn
bullocky
bullring
bullseye
bullyboy
bullyoff
bullyrag
burletta
cableway
callable
callgirl
calliope
calliper
cauldron
cellarer
cellaret
cellular
chalazae
Chaldaic
Chaldean
chaldron
chalkpit
Chellean
childbed
childish
children
chiliasm
chiliast
choleric
cislunar
coaldust
coalesce
coalfish
coalhole
coalmine
coalsack
coelomic
collagen
collapse
collared
collator
colleger
colliery
collogue
colloquy
collyria
coolabah
coolibah
coolness
coplanar
couldest
coulisse
curlicue
cyclamen
cycleway
cyclical
cyclonic
cyclopes
cyclosis
daylight
dealfish
declarer

declasse
declutch
deflower
diallage
dialling
dialogic
dialogue
dialyser
dialyses
dialysis
dialytic
dieldrin
diplogen
diploidy
diplomat
diplopia
dislodge
disloyal
djellaba
drilling
drollery
duelling
duellist
dullness
duologue
dwelling
dyslexia
dyslexic
eagleowl
ecclesia
ecologic
effluent
effluvia
elflocks
emblazon
employee
employer
emulator
emulgent
emulsify
emulsion
emulsive
emulsoid
enclitic
enclothe
enslaver
epilepsy
epilogue
epyllion
evaluate
evildoer
evilness
evulsion
excluder
explicit
exploder
explorer
exultant
eyeliner
fabliaux
failsafe
fallback
fallfish
fallible
fallibly
fanlight
faultily
fellable
fellahin
fellness
fellowly
follicle
follower
followon
followup
foolscap
foulness
fowlpest
frillies

fuelling
fugleman
fullback
fullness
fullpage
fullsize
fulltime
furlough
gableend
galleass
galliard
Gallican
gallipot
galloper
Galloway
galluses
gallwasp
gaolbird
garlicky
gaslight
Gaullism
Gaullist
geologic
gillaroo
girlhood
goalkick
goalline
goalpost
golliwog
gralloch
grillage
Guelphic
guileful
guiltily
gullable
gullible
gunlayer
halliard
hallmark
hallowed
halluces
haploidy
harlotry
haulyard
heelball
heelless
Helladic
hellbent
Hellenic
hellfire
hellhole
hielaman
hillfort
hillocky
hillside
hollands
hollowly
hooligan
idolater
idolatry
idoliser
idyllist
impledge
implicit
included
inflamer
inflated
inflator
inflatus
inflexed
inflight
influent
isolable
isolator
Italiote
jailbird
jealousy
kailyard
keelhaul

keelless
killdeer
kohlrabi
lallygag
loblolly
Lollardy
lollipop
lollypop
lowlevel
lowlying
mailable
mailboat
mailcart
mealtime
mealworm
mealybug
mellowly
midlands
millhand
milliard
milliary
millibar
millieme
milliner
millpond
millrace
moulding
mulloway
muslined
myelinic
myelitis
nailfile
negligee
NeoLatin
newlywed
nielloed
nobleman
noblesse
nonlegal
nuclease
nucleate
nucleole
nucleoli
nuclidic
nullness
occluded
occlusal
ocellate
ocularly
oeillade
omelette
opulence
outlawry
outlying
ovalness
palliate
pallidly
pallmall
parlance
parlando
peelings
pellagra
pellicle
pellmell
pellucid
perlitic
phalange
Philomel
phyletic
phyllary
phyllode
phylloid
phyllome
pillager
pillwort
pollices
pollinia
pollinic
polliwog

pollster
polluter
pollywog
potlatch
poultice
prelatic
prelease
prolamin
prolapse
prolific
prolixly
prologue
prolonge
psalmist
psalmody
psaltery
psilosis
publican
publicly
pullback
pullover
pyelitis
qualmish
quillpen
quilting
railhead
raillery
railroad
rallying
rallyist
realness
realtime
reflexed
refluent
replacer
replevin
rifleman
rollcall
rollneck
rouleaus
rouleaux
roulette
sailable
sailboat
sailfish
sailless
sailorly
sailyard
scalable
scalawag
scalepan
scallion
scilicet
scolding
scolices
scullery
scullion
sculptor
sealable
sealevel
sealskin
sealyham
secluded
shaleoil
shalloon
shallows
shelduck
shelfful
shelving
shilling
sillabub
skeletal
skeleton
skilless
skilling
skullcap
skylight
smallage
smallfry

smallish
smallpox
smaltite
smelling
smeltery
soilless
soilpipe
solleret
soulless
spalpeen
spelling
spillage
spillway
spoliate
stallage
stallfed
stalling
stallion
stalwart
stellate
stellify
stellion
stilbene
stilbite
stiletto
stillage
stolidly
stultify
stylised
sublease
sublunar
sullenly
sunlight
swelling
syllabic
syllable
syllabub
syllabus
tableaux
tablecut
tableful
tablemat
tabletop
tailback
tailcoat
tailgate
tailings
tailless
tailpipe
tailrace
tailspin
tallness
tallyman
tarlatan
tellable
telltale
telluric
thalamic
thalamus
thallium
thalloid
thallous
tholepin
tillable
toiletry
toilette
toilsome
toilworn
tollcall
tolldish
tollgate
toolroom
toolshed
toplevel
topliner
toplofty
trilling
trillion
trillium

trilobed
trollopy
twelvemo
twilight
unclench
unclinch
unclothe
unglazed
unplaced
uralitic
utiliser
uvularly
uvulitis
varletry
vaulting
veilless
velleity
villadom
villager
villainy
villatic
violable
violably
violator
violence
wallaroo
walleyed
wallfern
wallgame
wallknot
walloper
wallower
waxlight
welladay
wellaway
wellborn
wellbred
welldeck
wellhead
wellknit
wellnigh
wellread
Wellsian
wellworn
Wesleyan
wetlands
wholehog
williwaw
wooldyed
woolfell
woollens
woolpack
woolsack
woolshed
woolskin
woolwork
wouldest
yellowly
yielding
zealotry
zeolitic
zoolater
zoolatry
abomasum
abomasus
Adamical
adamitic
alumroot
animally
animator
apomixis
Aramaean
aromatic
atomiser
balmoral
beamends
bedmaker
Bermudas
besmirch

biometry
biomorph
blamable
blamably
blameful
blimpish
brimfull
brimless
brimming
bromelia
bromidic
bummaree
calmness
chambers
chambray
champers
champion
chemical
chemurgy
chimaera
chimeric
chummily
chumming
clambake
clammily
clamming
clematis
clemency
climatic
clumsily
commando
commence
commerce
commoner
commoney
commonly
communal
commuter
cosmetic
cosmical
coumarin
cramfull
cramming
cramoisy
criminal
cromlech
cromorna
cromorne
crumhorn
crummock
daemonic
daimonic
dalmatic
deemster
diamante
diameter
dimmable
dismally
dismount
dogmatic
doomsday
doomsman
doomster
dormancy
dormouse
doumpalm
dramatic
drammock
dramshop
drumfire
drumhead
drumming
drummock
drumroll
earmuffs
egomania
eremitic
examinee
examiner

exemplar
exemplum
eximious
farmhand
farmland
farmyard
filmgoer
filmstar
firmness
flambeau
flamenco
flamingo
flimflam
flimsily
flummery
foamless
formalin
formally
formerly
formless
formroom
formulae
formulas
formwork
framesaw
fremitus
frumenty
frumpish
gasmeter
geomancy
geometer
geometry
Germanic
germcell
germfree
germinal
gimmicky
glummest
glumness
gnomonic
gormless
gramarye
gramatom
gramercy
grimacer
grimmest
grimness
grimoire
gromwell
grumbler
grumpily
gummosis
gunmetal
haematic
haematin
harmless
harmonic
haymaker
helmeted
helminth
helmsman
hermetic
Hogmanay
hormonal
hummocky
inimical
isomeric
isometry
isomorph
kromesky
krumhorn
lawmaker
magmatic
marmoset
mesmeric
mismatch
mnemonic
murmurer
myrmidon
naumachy
neomycin
nonmetal
nonmoral
normalcy
normally
noumenal
noumenon
oddments
odometer
ohmmeter
olympiad
Olympian
outmatch
outmoded
oximeter
oxymoron
palmette
palmetto
palmiped
palmitin
panmixia
Parmesan
pemmican
permeate
pinmoney
plimsoll
plumaged
plumbago
plumbate
plumbing
plumbism
plumelet
plumiped
plumpish
plumular
premiere
premolar
premorse
primally
Primates
primeval
primming
primness
primrose
promisee
promiser
promisor
promoter
prompter
promptly
promulge
ptomaine
pulmonic
pygmaean
reembark
reemerge
reemploy
reimpose
rhomboid
roommate
rummager
scammony
scampish
schmaltz
scimitar
scombrid
scumming
seamanly
seamless
seamount
seamouse
seamster
shambles
shameful
shamming
shamrock
Shemitic
shimmery
sigmatic
skimmilk
skimming
skimpily
slamming
slimmest
slimming
slimmish
slimness
slumbery
slumming
staminal
stampede
stemless
stemmata
stemming
stimulus
stomachy
stomatal
stomatic
stumbler
stumming
stumpily
submerge
submerse
summerly
summitry
summoner
surmisal
surmiser
surmount
swimming
swimsuit
symmetry
Talmudic
teammate
teamster
teamwork
tegmenta
terminal
terminer
terminus
termless
termtime
thematic
thumbpot
thumping
titmouse
tommybar
tommygun
tommyrot
tramline
trammels
trampler
tramroad
trembler
trembles
trimaran
trimeric
trimeter
trimming
trimness
trombone
trumeaux
trumpery
turmeric
udometer
vermouth
viameter
warmness
whimbrel
whimwham
whomever
wigmaker
wormcast
wormgear
wormhole
wormlike
wormseed
wormwood
wrymouth
yarmulka
yeomanly
yeomanry
zoomancy
zoometry
zoomorph
abundant
acanthus
acentric
aconitic
aconitum
adenitis
adenoids
aduncate
aduncous
adynamia
adynamic
agential
agonised
allnight
amenable
amenably
asyndeta
aventail
bannered
banneret
bannerol
barnacle
barndoor
barnyard
beanpole
biannual
biennial
biennium
bignonia
binnacle
bionomic
blandish
blankety
Blenheim
blindage
blinding
blinkers
blinking
blondish
bouncily
bouncing
boundary
brancard
branched
brancher
branchia
brandied
brandish
brandnew
brindled
bronchia
bronchus
brunette
burnouse
burntout
cannabin
cannabis
cannibal
cannikin
cannonry
cannulae
cannular
cannulas
carnally
carnauba
carnival
cernuous
chancery
chandler
chenille
Chinaman
chinchin
chinless
chondrus
cinnabar
cinnamic
cinnamon
clanging
clangour
clannish
clanship
clansman
clincher
clinical
clinking
coenobia
coenzyme
cognomen
cognosce
cognovit
coincide
conniver
coonskin
cornball
corneous
cornetcy
cornetti
cornetto
corniced
corniche
cornicle
cornific
cornpone
countess
cranefly
craniate
crankily
crankpin
crannied
crenated
crenelle
cyanogen
cyanoses
cyanosis
cyanotic
daintily
damnable
damnably
deanship
dianthus
dipnoous
downbeat
downcast
downcome
downfall
downhaul
downhill
downland
downmost
downpipe
downpour
downtime
downtown
downturn
downward
downwind
drencher
drinking
drunkard
drynurse
earnings
economic
edentate
elenchus
elenctic
elongate
emendate
eminence
eminency
epinasty
ethnarch
ethnical
euonymin
euonymus
evanesce
evenfall
evenness
evensong
eventful
eventide
eventual
evincive
exanthem
faineant
faintish
faunally
fernshaw
fiendish
finnesko
flanerie
flincher
flinders
flintily
fornices
founding
fountain
francium
Frankish
franklin
frenetic
frenulum
frenzied
fringing
frondage
frondent
frondeur
frondose
frontage
frontier
frontlet
funnyman
gainable
gainings
gainless
gainsaid
gauntlet
Ghanaian
giantess
giantism
glancing
glanders
glandule
goingson
gownsman
grandame
granddad
grandeur
grandson
granitic
granular
grindery
grinning
gruntled
gymnasia
haunting
hernshaw
hornbeam
hornbill
hornbook
hornfels
hornless
hornpipe
hornrims
horntail
hornworm
hornwort
hymnbook
hypnoses
hypnosis
hypnotic
identify
identity
inundate
irenical
irenicon
ironbark
ironclad
irongray
irongrey
ironical
ironside
ironware
ironwood
ironwork
jaundice
jauntily
joinable
jointure
keenness
klondike
lanneret
launcher
leanness
ligneous
lignitic
Linnaean
loanable
loanword
loonybin
maenadic
magnesia
magnetic
magneton
magnific
magnolia
mainland
mainline
mainmast
mainsail
mainstay
maintain
mainyard
mannered
mannerly
mannikin
mannitol
meanness
meantime
midnight
misnomer
moonbeam
mooncalf
moonface
moonfish
moonless
moonrise
moonsail
moonshee
moonshot
moonwort
mornings
mountain
mounting
nainsook
neonatal
noontide
noontime
odontoid
openable
opencast
openeyed
openness
openplan
openwork
orangery
Orangism
ordnance
ovenbird
ovenware
ozoniser
painless
paintbox
pannikin
pawnshop
phantasm
phantasy
phenolic
phenylic
phonemic
phonetic
pianiste
picnicky
pinnacle
pinnated
pinniped
pinnular
planchet
plangent
planking
plankton
planning
plantain
planulae
planular
pointing
poundage
pounding
prandial
prankful
prankish
prenatal
prentice
princely
princess
printing
printout
pronator
prunella
prunelle
prunello
pugnosed
quandary
quandong
quantify
quantise
quantity
quencher
quenelle
quincunx
quintain
rainbird
raincoat
raindrop
rainfall
rainwash
rainwear
reindeer
reinless
reinsert
reinsman
reinsure
reinvest
rhinitis
Rhinodon
rhonchal
rhonchus
roentgen
roundarm
rounders
roundish
roundtop
ruinable
runnerup
sainfoin
saintdom
sannyasi
saunders

scandent
Scandian
scandium
scanning
scansion
scanties
scantily
scenario
scenical
schnapps
sennight
shanghai
shantung
shinbone
shingler
shingles
shinning
shunning
signally
signpost
skindeep
skinfood
skinhead
skinless
skinning
slangily
slinkily
somnific
soundbow
soundbox
sounding
spandrel
spandril
Spaniard
spanking
spanning
spanroof
spinifex
spinning
spinster
spondaic
spongily
sponsion
spontoon
spunkily
stancher
stanchly
standard
standing
standish
standoff
stanhope
stannary
stannate
stannite
stannous
stanzaic
stenosed
stenosis
stenotic
stingily
stingray
stinkard
stinking
stinkpot
stonefly
stunning
stunsail
stuntman
swanherd
swanking
swanlike
swanmark
swanneck
swannery
swanning
swanshot
swanskin
swansong
swindler
swinging
syenitic
taenioid
tainture
tannable
teenager
Thanatos
thanedom
thankful
thankyou
thingamy
thinking
thinness
thinnest
thinning
thinnish
thundery
tinnitus
tomnoddy
topnotch
tornadic
townhall
township
townsman
tranquil
transact
transect
transept
transfer
transfix
tranship
transire
transmit
transude
trencher
trendily
truncate
trunnion
turnable
turnback
turncoat
turncock
turndown
turnings
turnover
turnpike
turnskin
turnsole
turnspit
twenties
twinborn
twinkler
twinling
twinning
twinship
unaneled
unending
vainness
vauntful
vernally
vernicle
Viennese
vigneron
vignette
wainscot
weanling
wetnurse
whenever
whinchat
whinsill
winnable
winnings
winnower
woundily
wrangler
wrongful
wrongous
yeanling
youngest
youngish
zoonosis
abhorred
abhorrer
abnormal
abrogate
absolute
absolver
absonant
absorber
accolade
accoutre
acrolein
acrolith
acrostic
acrotism
admonish
adroitly
advocaat
advocacy
advocate
advowson
aerodyne
aerofoil
aerogram
aerolite
aerolith
aerology
aeronaut
aeronomy
aerostat
afforest
agiotage
agnostic
agrology
agronomy
algology
Algonkin
algorism
allocate
allodial
allodium
allogamy
allopath
allotted
allottee
ammoniac
ammonify
ammonite
ammonium
annotate
announce
aphorise
aphorism
aphorist
apposite
arboreal
arboreta
arborist
areolate
argonaut
armorial
armoured
armourer
arrogant
arrogate
arsonist
arsonous
ascocarp
assonant
assonate
assorted
astonied
astonish
atrocity
atropine
attorney
aurorean
autobahn
autocade
autocrat
autodafe
autodyne
autogamy
autogiro
autogyro
autolyse
automata
automate
autonomy
autosome
autotomy
autotype
avionics
axiology
babouche
Baconian
baronage
baroness
baronial
barouche
bebopper
becoming
befogged
begotten
beholden
beholder
besotted
besought
bezonian
biconvex
bifocals
bilobate
binomial
bloodily
bloodred
bloomers
bloomery
blooming
bobolink
Boeotian
broodily
brookite
brooklet
bryology
bryozoan
Byronism
cabochon
caboodle
cabotage
cacology
cacomixl
cajolery
camomile
canoeing
canoeist
canoness
canonise
canonist
canoodle
canorous
caponier
caponise
Carolean
Caroline
carolled
carotene
carousal
carousel
carouser
cenotaph
Cenozoic
chlorate
chloride
chlorine
chlorite
chlorous
chromate
chromite
chromium
ciborium
colonial
colonise
colonist
colophon
colossal
colossus
coloured
conoidal
coronach
coronary
coronoid
coworker
creosote
cryogeny
cryolite
cryostat
cryotron
cuboidal
culottes
cynosure
cytology
cytosine
debonair
decolour
decorate
decorous
decouple
deforest
deformed
deionise
demobbed
democrat
demolish
demoness
demoniac
demonian
demonise
demonism
demotion
denounce
deponent
deportee
derogate
desolate
detonate
detoxify
Devonian
devotion
devourer
devoutly
dinornis
dinosaur
disorder
divorcee
dogooder
dolomite
doloroso
dolorous
donought
doxology
echogram
echoless
eclosion
ectoderm
ectozoon
eldorado
embolden
embolism
embosser
empoison
emporium
encomion
encomium
endocarp
endoderm
endogamy
endogeny
endorsee
endorser
endostea
endozoic
endozoon
enforcer
enforest
enrolled
entoderm
entoptic
entozoic
entozoon
enzootic
ephorate
ergogram
ergotise
ergotism
espousal
espouser
essonite
Estonian
estopped
estoppel
estovers
ethology
etiolate
eulogise
eulogist
eulogium
Eurocrat
European
europium
exhorter
exponent
exporter
exposure
extolled
fagoting
famously
farouche
favonian
favoured
favourer
ferocity
floodlit
floodway
flooring
fluoride
fluorine
fluorite
garotter
gasolene
gasolier
gasoline
gazogene
genocide
genotype
gerontic
gloomily
groogroo
gulosity
gynocrat
gynoecia
gyrostat
havocked
hedonics
hedonism
hedonist
helotism
heroical
Holocene
hologram
holozoic
homodont
homogamy
homogeny
homology
homonymy
honorary
honourer
horologe
horology
humorist
humorous
humoured
hypobole
hypoderm
hypogeal
hypogean
hypogene
hypogeum
hypogyny
hypothec
ichorous
ideogram
ideology
idiolect
idiotism
ignominy
ignorant
immobile
immodest
immolate
immortal
impolder
impolicy
impolite
imponent
importer
imposing
imposter
impostor
impotent
incoming
indocile
indolent
informal
informed
informer
innocent
innovate
insolate
insolent
insomnia
insomuch
intonate
invocate
involute
iodoform
Jacobean
Jacobite
jalousie
japonica
Jehovist
jeroboam
jocosely
jocosity
joyously
Jugoslav
kerosene
kerosine
kilogram
kilowatt
labourer
laconian
laconism
lemonade
leporine
licorice
limonite
linoleum
lipogram
lipomata
lobotomy
locofoco
locomote
logogram
logotype
lysosome
lysozyme
mahogany
maiolica
majolica
majority
malodour
manorial
marocain
maroquin
Masorete
Masoreth
mayoress
meconium
melodeon
melodise
melodist
memorial
memorise
menology
merosome
mesocarp
mesoderm
mesotron
Mesozoic
metonymy
Minoress
Minorite
minority
Minotaur
misogamy
misogyny
misology
mobocrat
molossus
monoacid
monocrat
monocyte
monodist
monogamy
monogeny
monoglot
monogony
monogram
monogyny
monolith
monomial
monopode
monopoly
monorail
monotint
monotone
monotony
monotype
monoxide
morosely
morosity
motorail
motorcar
motorial
motoring
motorise
motorist
motorium
motorman
motormen
motorway
mucosity
mycology
mylonite
myxomata
nanogram
napoleon
nepotism
nicotian
nicotine
nodosity

nomogram
nomology
nosology
notornis
obsolete
octonary
octoroon
odiously
oecology
oenology
oenophil
oncology
oncoming
onlooker
ontogeny
ontology
oogonial
oogonium
oologist
opponent
opposite
oreology
otiosely
otiosity
oxtongue
palomino
panorama
parodist
paroquet
paroxysm
pedology
pelorism
penology
peroneal
perorate
peroxide
pilosity
pilotage
pinochle
pisolite
pivotman
pleonasm
Pliocene
polonium
pomology
porosity
posology
priorate
prioress
priority
proofing
pyroxene
rasorial
recommit
reconvey
recorder
recourse
recovery
redolent
redouble
reforest
reformed
reformer
regolith
rehoboam
rejoicer
relocate
remotely
renounce
renovate
renowned
reporter
repotted
repousse
resolute
resonant
resonate
resorcin
resorter
resource
retorted
revolter
revolute
revolver
rheology
rheostat
rhyolite
ribosome
ricochet
rigorism
rigorist
rigorous
roborant
rugosely
rugosity
sabotage
saboteur
Salopian
Samoyede
saponify
saponite
saporous
sauouari
savorous
Savoyard
Saxondom
Saxonism
Saxonist
sayonara
scholium
schooner
sciolism
sciolist
scoopful
scoopnet
scrofula
scrounge
seaonion
seconder
secondly
semolina
senorita
serology
serosity
serotine
sexology
shooting
shootout
simoniac
simonist
sinology
sinophil
sitology
smoothen
smoothie
smoothly
snootily
sodomite
sonobuoy
sonority
sonorous
sorochen
sororate
sorority
splotchy
spookily
spookish
spoonfed
spoonful
spoonily
sprocket
strobila
strobile
strobili
stroller
stromata
strongly
strontia
strophic
stropped
suborder
suborner
suboxide
sycomore
syconium
synonymy
synopses
synopsis
synoptic
synovial
tabouret
taxonomy
tenonsaw
tenorite
tenotomy
theocrat
theodicy
theogony
theology
theorise
theorist
throated
throbbed
thrombin
thrombus
throstle
throttle
timorous
timously
toboggan
tocology
tokology
tomogram
tomorrow
topology
toponymy
toroidal
trioxide
tumorous
tutorage
tutoress
tutorial
typology
Tyrolean
tyrosine
umbonate
unbolted
unbottle
uncoined
uncommon
uncouple
unforced
unformed
ungotten
unhoused
unionise
unionism
unionist
unloader
unloosen
unlovely
unroofed
unsocial
unsought
untoward
unvoiced
unwonted
unwordly
unworthy
upholder
uprooter
valorise
valorous
vaporise
vaporous
vapourer
velocity
venomous
venosity
venously
veronica
vigorous
vinosity
vinously
virology
wagonage
wagonlit
whooping
xenogamy
xenolith
xylocarp
xylology
xylonite
Yugoslav
zymology
adaption
adaptive
adoption
adoptive
alopecia
anapaest
anaphase
anaphora
anyplace
apoplexy
Arapahoe
arapaima
aseptate
atypical
auspices
bagpiper
bedplate
bespoken
besprent
bioplasm
bioplast
boxpleat
campagna
campaign
campfire
camphene
camphine
campsite
chapatti
chapbook
chapelry
chaperon
chapiter
chaplain
chapping
chipmuck
chipmunk
chipping
chopchop
chopping
chopsuey
chupatti
chupatty
clapping
claptrap
clipclop
clippers
clipping
clopclop
clupeoid
clypeate
codpiece
compages
compiler
complain
compleat
complete
complice
complier
compline
composed
composer
compound
compress
comprise
computer
cooption
cooptive
copperas
corporal
coupling
crepitus
cropping
culpable
culpably
cuspidor
cutprice
cutpurse
dampness
deeplaid
deepness
Delphian
despatch
despiser
despotic
dewpoint
diapason
diapause
diaphone
diopside
dioptase
dioptric
dispatch
dispense
disperse
dispirit
displace
displant
displode
displume
disposal
disposer
dispread
disprize
disproof
disprove
dripfeed
dripping
drophead
dropkick
dropleaf
dropping
dropshot
dropwort
drupelet
dryplate
drypoint
dumpling
dyspnoea
earphone
earpiece
eggplant
Egyptian
elephant
endpaper
ensphere
epiphany
epiphyte
epopoeia
eruption
eruptive
eyepiece
flapjack
flapping
flipflap
flipflop
flippant
flipping
flipside
floppily
flopping
flypaper
frapping
frippery
gazpacho
geophagy
geophone
geophyte
geoponic
glyptics
grapheme
graphics
graphite
gripping
gripsack
gumption
gunpoint
harpseal
helpless
helpmate
helpmeet
henparty
herpetic
Hesperus
Hispanic
hospital
hotplate
hotpress
humpback
iceplant
insphere
inspired
inspirer
inspirit
isophote
isopleth
isoprene
isoptera
jeopardy
jetplane
jumpedup
jumpseat
jumpsuit
keepsake
klephtic
knapping
knapsack
knapweed
lamppost
leapfrog
limpidly
limpness
loophole
lumpfish
lymphoid
lymphoma
lyophile
manpower
midpoint
misplace
misprint
misprise
misprize
morpheme
morphine
nauplius
neaptide
neophyte
neoplasm
neoprene
nonparty
nymphean
offprint
oliphant
omophagy
omoplate
onepiece
outpoint
oviposit
palpable
palpably
pamperer
pamphlet
panpipes
pappadom
payphone
peephole
peepshow
pinpoint
pinprick
plopping
poppadum
porphyry
porpoise
potplant
preparer
prepense
preprint
propense
properly
property
prophase
prophecy
prophesy
propolis
proposal
proposer
propound
propping
propylic
pulpiter
pulpwood
pumproom
puppetry
puppydog
puppydom
puppyfat
puppyish
purplish
purpuric
purpurin
quipping
rampancy
rapparee
reappear
respects
response
respring
resprung
rhapsode
rhapsody
samphire
sampling
sapphics
sapphire
sapphism
scaphoid
scapulae
scapular
scapulas
sceptred
scopulae
scopulas
seapiece
seaplane
seapurse
semplice
sempster
serpulae
shapable
shepherd
shipload
shipmate
shipment
shipping
shipworm
shipyard
shopbell
shopgirl
shopping
shoptalk
shopworn
silphium
simplify
simplism
sixpence
sixpenny
skipjack
skipping
skypilot
slapbang
slapdash
slapjack
slapping
slipcase
slipform
slipknot
slipover
slippage
slippery
slipping
slipring
sliproad
slipshod
slipslop
sloppail
sloppily
slopping
slopshop
slopwork
snapbrim
snaplink
snappily
snapping
snappish
snapshot
snippety
snipping
snipsnap
soapbark
soapdish
soapless
soaproot
soapsuds
soapwort
sorption
sorptive
stapelia
stepping
stepwise
stipites
stippler
stipular
stopcock
stopover
stoppage
stopping
stupidly
stuprate
subphyla
subpoena
subprior
sulphate
sulphide
sulphite
sulphone
sunproof
supplant
supplely
supplial
supplier
supplies
supposal
supposed
suppress
surplice
surprise

suspense
swapping
swopping
sylphide
sylphine
sylphish
sympathy
symphile
symphony
sympodia
symposia
tamperer
Tarpeian
taxpayer
teaparty
tempered
temperer
template
temporal
tempting
tenpence
tenpenny
tinplate
toepiece
toeplate
torpidly
trapball
trapdoor
trapezia
trappean
trapping
Trappist
traprock
trephine
tripeman
triplane
triploid
tripodal
trippery
tripping
triptych
tripwire
trophied
tropical
tuppence
tuppenny
twopence
twopenny
twopiece
tympanic
tympanum
unipolar
unopened
unsprung
upsprang
upspring
upsprung
vampiric
vamplate
vesperal
vespiary
volplane
warpaint
warplane
weaponry
whapping
whipcord
whiplash
whiplike
whipping
whipworm
whopping
wrappage
wrapping
zeppelin
zoophily
zoophyte
adequacy
adequate
chequers
cinquain
claqueur
cliquish
cliquism
conquest
cotquean
daiquiri
disquiet
eloquent
exequies
frequent
inequity
iniquity
Iroquois
jacquard
marquess
marquise
Mayqueen
mesquite
misquote
mosquito
musquash
opaquely
seaquake
torquate
ubiquity
uniquely
vanquish
aberrant
aborally
aborning
abortion
abortive
acarpous
accredit
acerbate
acerbity
acervate
adorable
adorably
aegrotat
affright
agaragar
aggrieve
aigrette
alarmist
alfresco
allround
altruism
altruist
amaranth
ambrosia
American
amorally
amoretti
amoretto
amortise
anarchic
androgen
anorexia
anorexic
anorthic
antrorse
aperient
aperitif
aperture
appraise
approach
approval
astragal
ataraxia
ataraxic
attrited
aubretia
averment
averring
aversely
aversion
aversive
barracks
barranca
barranco
barrator
barratry
barrenly
barrette
bearable
bearably
bearings
bearskin
befriend
begrudge
betrayal
betrayer
blurrily
blurring
boarding
borrower
botryoid
bourgeon
boursier
bourtree
burrower
cabriole
caprifig
capriole
carriage
carriole
carryall
carryout
charcoal
charisma
charlady
charlock
charming
charring
Chartism
Chartist
Cherokee
cherubic
cherubim
chirpily
chirrupy
choragic
choragus
chorally
chordate
choregic
choregus
choriamb
chorioid
churchly
churinga
churlish
churning
cirriped
clarence
clarinet
clerical
clerihew
clerkdom
clerkess
coarsely
codriver
coercion
coercive
corridor
corrival
courante
coursing
courtesy
courtier
cupreous
currency
curricle
Cypriote
czaritza
dairying
dairyman
dearness
decrease
decrepit
decretal
deerskin
defrayal
degrease
depraved
deprival
deprived
derriere
detrital
detritus
diarchal
diarchic
diarrhea
dicrotic
diereses
dieresis
dioramic
dioritic
diuresis
diuretic
doorbell
doorcase
doorknob
doornail
doorpost
doorsill
doorstep
doorstop
dooryard
dourness
dwarfish
dwarfism
eldritch
embracer
emergent
emeritus
emersion
enarched
encrinal
encrinic
encroach
energise
enervate
engramma
engraver
enormity
enormous
entracte
entrails
entrance
entreaty
entrench
entrepot
entresol
enuresis
enuretic
espresso
estrange
esurient
eternise
eternity
eucritic
eutrophy
evermore
eversion
everyday
everyman
everyone
everyway
exercise
exergual
exertion
exorcise
exorcism
exorcist
exordial
exordium
extrados
extremes
extrorse
eyerhyme
fairlead
fairness
fairyism
farriery
fearless
fearsome
febrific
February
ferreter
ferriage
ferritic
ferryman
fibrilla
fibrosis
fibrotic
fiercely
florally
floridly
florigen
forrader
fourball
foureyes
fourfold
fourleaf
fourpart
foursome
fourstar
fourteen
fourthly
furriery
garreted
garrison
garrotte
gearcase
Georgian
gloriole
glorious
gourmand
guaranty
guardant
guardian
guerilla
guernsey
hadronic
hairgrip
hairless
hairlike
hairline
hairworm
harridan
harrumph
heartily
hebraise
Hebraism
Hebraist
heirless
heirloom
heirship
henroost
hidrosis
hidrotic
hierarch
hieratic
hirrient
hoarding
hoarsely
horrible
horribly
horridly
horrific
hourlong
hydranth
hydrogen
hydromel
hydropic
hydropsy
hydroski
hydroxyl
imprimis
imprison
improper
improver
increase
increate
inerrant
inertial
infrared
infringe
ingrowth
intrados
intrench
intrepid
intrigue
intromit
introrse
intruder
inurbane
iterance
ivorynut
jerrican
jerrycan
kourbash
labrador
lacrimal
lacrosse
lacrymal
larrikin
laureate
learning
libretti
libretto
lubrical
madrigal
Mahratta
Mahratti
marriage
marrieds
marrying
matrices
matrixes
matronal
matronly
metrical
microbar
microbic
microdot
micrurgy
migraine
migrator
moorcock
moorfowl
moorings
moorland
mournful
mourning
mucrones
murrelet
murrhine
nacreous
narrator
narrowly
Nearctic
nearness
necropsy
necrosis
necrotic
Negrillo
negroism
neurally
neuritic
neuritis
neuronal
neuronic
neuroses
neurosis
neurotic
nitrogen
nonrigid
nutrient
ochreous
operable
operatic
operator
opercula
operetta
ostracod
ostracon
ostrakon
outrange
outreach
outreign
outrider
outright
outrival
ovariole
ovaritis
overalls
overarch
overbear
overbook
overbore
overbusy
overcall
overcame
overcast
overcoat
overcome
overcrop
overdone
overdose
overdraw
overdrew
overfall
overfeed
overfill
overfish
overflew
overflow
overfold
overfond
overgrew
overgrow
overhand
overhang
overhaul
overhead
overhear
overheat
overhung
overjump
overkill
overlaid
overlain
overland
overleaf
overleap
overload
overlong
overlook
overlord
overmuch
overnice
overpaid
overpass
overpast
overplay
overplus
overrate
override
overripe
overrode
overrule
oversail
overseas
overseen
overseer
oversell
oversewn
overshoe
overshot
overside
oversize
overslip
oversold
oversoul
overstay
overstep
overtake
overtask
overtime
overtone
overtook
overture
overturn
overview
overwear
overwind
overwork
overworn
parrotry
patronal
peardrop
pearlies
pearling
pearlite
pearmain
peerless
petrolic
petronel
petrosal
pharisee
pharmacy
phormium
piercing
plurally
poorness
porridge
potroast
pourable
prorogue
prurient
pruritic
pruritus
pteropod
pterylae
putridly
pyrrhoea
pyrrhous
quarrier
quartern
quarters
quartile
quirkily
rearlamp
rearmice
rearmost
rearview
rearward
recreant
recreate
regrater
regrowth
reorient
reprieve
reprisal
reproach
reproval
retrench
retrieve

retroact
retrorse
rubrical
sacraria
sacredly
sacristy
safranin
sauropod
scarcely
scarcity
scarfpin
scarious
scarless
scarring
scirocco
scirrhus
scorcher
scornful
scorpion
scurrile
scurvily
searcher
secretin
secretly
secretor
segreant
serranid
serrated
sforzato
shareout
sharpish
sharpset
Sheraton
sherlock
shiralee
shirring
shirting
shortage
shortarm
shortcut
shortday
shortish
skerrick
skirmish
skirting
slurring
smarmily
smartish
sobriety
Socratic
sorrower
sourdine
sourness
sourpuss
sovranty
sparable
sparbuoy
spardeck
sparkgap
sparkish
sparkler
sparklet
sparling
sparring
sparsely
sparsity
spermary
spiracle
spirally
spirilla
spirited
spiritus
sporadic
sporozoa
sportful
sportily
sporting
sportive
sporular
spurgear
spurious
spurling
spurrier
spurring
stardust
starfish
stargaze
starkers
starless
starlike
starling
starrily
starring
starting
startler
starwort
sterigma
sterling
sternite
sternson
sternway
stirring
storable
storeman
storeyed
stormily
sturdied
sturdily
sturgeon
surround
surroyal
tarragon
tearaway
teardrop
tearduct
tearless
terraced
terrapin
terraria
terrazzo
terrible
terribly
terrific
tetradic
tetragon
tetrapla
tetrapod
tetrarch
therefor
thereout
thermion
thermite
thirlage
thirster
thirteen
thoraces
thoracic
thoraxes
thorough
thurible
thurifer
Thursday
thyroxin
thyrsoid
torridly
touristy
tournure
tsarevna
tsaritsa
tsaritza
turreted
Tyrrhene
ultraism
ultraist
umbrella
umbrette
unbridle
unbroken
uncreate
undraped
undreamt
unerring
unfreeze
unfrozen
usurious
uxorious
vagrancy
verrucae
vibrancy
vibrator
vibrissa
vitreous
warragal
warranty
warrener
warrigal
wearable
weariful
wharfage
wherever
whirring
whoredom
whoreson
yearbook
yearling
yearlong
yearning
yourself
acescent
acosmism
adespota
airscrew
airshaft
airspace
airspeed
airstrip
allspice
amusedly
anasarca
angstrom
anisette
apostasy
apostate
aristate
Ayrshire
bakshish
balsamic
bassinet
basswood
bedstead
bedstraw
beeswing
biassing
bioscope
blastema
blastoff
blastoid
blastula
blesbuck
blessing
blissful
blistery
blossomy
blushful
blustery
boastful
bonspiel
bosseyed
bowsprit
brassage
brassard
brassart
brassica
brassily
briskish
brisling
brushoff
bursitis
cabstand
caesious
caesural
camshaft
capsicum
capstone
capsular
cassette
catsfoot
catstail
causally
causerie
causeway
cesspool
chasseur
chastely
chastise
chastity
chasuble
chessman
chestnut
classics
classify
closeset
closeted
clustery
coistrel
conserve
consider
consoler
consomme
conspire
constant
construe
consular
consumer
corselet
corseted
corsetry
Cotswold
couscous
cousinly
coxswain
crashing
crashpad
crescent
crescive
crispate
cristate
crossbar
crossbow
crosscut
crossing
crosslet
crossply
crosstie
crossway
crusader
crustily
cursedly
cussedly
cussword
cypselae
danseuse
diaspora
diaspore
diastase
diastema
diastole
diestock
dipstick
disseise
disserve
dissever
dissolve
dissuade
dogsbody
dogshore
dorsally
dressage
dressing
drystone
dyestuff
eftsoons
egestion
egestive
eggshell
ekistics
emissary
emission
emissive
episcope
episemon
episodal
episodic
epistler
epistyle
erasable
Erastian
existent
exospore
eyeshade
eyesight
eyestalk
falsetto
fatstock
Faustian
feasible
feasibly
feastday
felsitic
firstaid
fissiped
flashgun
flashily
flashing
fleshfly
fleshpot
forsaken
forsooth
forspeak
forspent
forswear
forswore
forsworn
foxshark
frescoes
freshman
freshrun
frisette
friskily
frostily
frosting
frustule
gemstone
ghastful
gipsydom
gipsyism
glassful
glassily
glassine
glissade
glossary
glossily
glossina
Godspeed
goosegog
gossamer
gossiper
gossipry
gossypol
grasping
Griselda
griseous
grisette
grisgris
grissini
grosbeak
groschen
gunsmith
gunstock
gusseted
gypseous
gypsydom
gypsyism
hatstand
hausfrau
haystack
hipsters
hogsback
hogshead
holstein
hoosegow
horsebox
horsecar
horsefly
horseman
houseboy
housedog
housefly
houseful
houseman
housetop
hyoscine
iceskate
inasmuch
inkstand
inositol
Irishism
Irishman
isospory
isostasy
joystick
keeshond
keystone
khuskhus
kinsfolk
kissable
kisscurl
klystron
Komsomol
layshaft
laystall
leisured
lensless
linstock
lipsalve
lipstick
loosebox
loosener
lopsided
maestoso
mansized
marshman
massacre
masseter
masseuse
massicot
massless
measured
memsahib
menstrua
mensural
menswear
messmate
messuage
miasmata
miasmous
midships
minstrel
misshape
missilry
misspell
misspelt
misspend
misspent
misstate
moisture
monsieur
mossback
mouseear
moussaka
mudstone
myositic
myositis
myosotis
nauseant
nauseate
nauseous
newscast
newsheet
newspeak
newsreel
newsroom
noisette
nonsense
nonstick
Norseman
nuisance
numskull
nursling
nutshell
Odyssean
offshoot
offshore
offsider
offstage
oilstone
omission
onesided
opuscula
opuscule
otoscope
outshine
outshone
outsider
outsight
outsmart
outspend
outspent
outstare
outstrip
pansophy
Parsiism
parsonic
passable
passably
passbook
passerby
passible
Passover
passport
password
paysheet
peasecod
penstock
personae
personal
perspire
persuade
phaseout
phosgene
phosphor
physical
physicky
physique
piassava
pigswill
pilsener
plastery
plastics
plastron
plussage
poisoner
possible
possibly
potsherd
potstill
potstone
presager
prescind
presence
preserve
presidio
pressbox
pressing
pressman
pressure
prestige
presumer
prismoid
prisoner
prissily
pristine
prosaism
prosaist
prosodic
prospect
prostate
prostyle
Prussian
puissant
pulsator
pursenet
purslane
pursuant
pussycat
question
quisling
ransomer
ratsbane
ratstail
reascend
reasoner
reassert
reassess
reassign
reassure
redshank
redshift
redshirt
redstart
reusable
Riesling
rinsings
roasting
sanserif
Sanskrit
sarsenet
Sassanid
scissile
scission
scissors
seascape
seashell
seashore
seasnail
seasnake
seasonal
seasoner
senseful
sensible
sensibly
sensoria
sensuous
setscrew
shashlik
skislope
skyscape
slashing
smashing
sobstory
sobstuff
solstice

stasimon
subserve
subshrub
subsolar
subsonic
substage
sunshade
sunshine
sunshiny
sunstone
swastika
tasselly
teaspoon
tensible
tesserae
tesseral
thesauri
thespian
thisness
thusness
tinselly
tinsmith
tinstone
tipstaff
topstone
trashery
trashily
trespass
tressure
triskele
trisomic
tristful
tristich
trussing
trustful
trustily
tussocky
twosided
unisonal
urostyle
velskoen
versicle
voussoir
waesucks
weaselly
Welshman
whiskers
whiskery
whispery
whistler
wrestler
wrestpin
wristlet
wristpin
yeastily
zoospore
abattoir
abetment
abetting
absterge
abstract
abstrict
abstruse
abutilon
abutment
abuttals
abutting
aesthete
aestival
agitator
agitprop
airtight
amethyst
amitosis
amitotic
anathema
anatomic
anything
apothegm
Arcturus
arethusa
bacteria
Bactrian
banterer
bantling
barterer
bartizan
bastardy
bastille
battalia
battleax
beatific
bedtable
beetling
beetroot
beltless
bentwood
bestiary
bestowal
bestrewn
bestride
bestrode
biathlon
birthday
bistable
bistoury
bitterly
blatancy
blithely
blotting
boatbill
boatdeck
boathook
boatload
bolthole
boltrope
bontebok
bootjack
bootlace
bootlast
bootless
boottree
bottomry
boutique
brattice
brattish
brethren
brettese
brettice
britches
britzska
brutally
buntline
bustling
buttoner
buttress
bystreet
cactuses
calthrop
canthari
canticle
cantonal
cantoris
captious
cartload
cartouch
castaway
castiron
castrate
castrati
castrato
cattleya
cautious
centaury
centring
centrism
centrist
centroid
centuple
chateaux
chattily
chatting
chitchat
chutzpah
clothier
clothing
clotting
coatrack
coatroom
contagia
contango
contempt
contents
contessa
continua
continue
continuo
contline
contorno
contract
contrail
contrary
contrast
contrate
contrite
contrive
cortical
cortices
costmary
costplus
costpush
costumer
cottager
cottagey
cratches
cretonne
criteria
critical
critique
crotched
crotchet
cultivar
cultural
cultured
curtains
curtness
customer
cysteine
cystitis
dactylar
dactylic
daftness
dartrous
dastardy
deathbed
deathcap
deathray
deftness
dentalia
dentated
denticle
destrier
destruct
deuteron
dextrine
dextrose
dextrous
diatomic
diatonic
diatribe
dictator
dietetic
dipteral
dipteran
distally
distance
distaste
distinct
distract
distrain
distrait
distress
district
distrust
dittybag
dittybox
doctoral
doctrine
dogtired
dogtooth
dotterel
ductless
duettist
dustbowl
dustcart
dustcoat
dustless
dustlike
dustshot
dystopia
earthnut
easterly
eastmost
eastward
ecstatic
editress
elatedly
emetical
emitting
epitasis
erethism
erotical
erythema
esoteric
eustatic
evitable
exoteric
eyetooth
factious
factotum
faithful
faltboat
fantasia
farthest
farthing
fastback
fastener
fastfood
fastness
fasttalk
fastuous
fattener
fauteuil
feathery
featured
features
festally
festival
fewtrils
fiftieth
fiftyish
filthily
filtrate
fistiana
fistical
fistulae
fistular
flatboat
flatfeet
flatfish
flatfoot
flathead
flatiron
flatling
flatmate
flatness
flatrace
flattery
flattest
flattish
flatware
flatways
flatwise
flatworm
fletcher
flitting
flotilla
fluttery
foetidly
fontanel
fontange
football
footbath
footfall
footgear
foothill
foothold
footless
footling
footmark
footmuff
footnote
footpace
footpath
footpost
footrace
footrest
footrope
footrule
footslog
footsore
footstep
footwear
footwork
fortieth
fortress
fortuity
fortyish
fosterer
fretting
fretwork
fritting
frothily
frottage
frutices
furthest
gantline
gantlope
gastight
gastraea
gastrula
gentrice
geotaxis
gestagen
gestural
ghettoes
giftbook
gilthead
glittery
glutting
gluttony
gnathite
goatfish
goatherd
goatling
goatmoth
goatskin
goitrous
goutweed
goutwort
grateful
gratuity
gritting
grottoes
guttural
halteres
hastener
hastings
hawthorn
heatedly
heathery
heathhen
heptagon
Hertzian
histogen
historic
hostelry
huntress
huntsman
hurtless
hustings
hysteria
hysteric
ianthine
illtimed
illtreat
imitable
imitator
initiate
instable
instance
instancy
instinct
instruct
isothere
isotherm
isotonic
isotopic
isotropy
jettison
jolthead
justness
knitting
knitwear
knothole
knotting
knotwork
kurtosis
lanthorn
latterly
latticed
leathern
leathery
lecturer
lefthand
leftover
leftward
lenticel
lenticle
lettered
liftable
lintseed
listener
listless
littlego
littling
littoral
loathful
loathing
loiterer
lustrate
lustrine
lustring
lustrous
maltreat
maltster
mantelet
mantilla
mantissa
mantling
martagon
martello
martenot
martinet
masterly
masthead
mastitis
mastodon
mattress
meatball
meatsafe
meetness
mentally
Miltonic
mintmark
mirthful
mistaken
misthink
mistreat
mistress
mistrial
mistrust
mittened
mittimus
monteith
mortally
mortgage
mortmain
mortuary
mottling
mouthful
multeity
multifid
multiped
multiple
multiply
mustache
mutterer
mystical
mystique
nautical
nautilus
neatherd
neatness
nectared
neotenic
neoteric
nestling
neutrino
nextdoor
nocturne
northern
northing
Northman
nuptials
nurturer
obituary
obstacle
obstruct
oestrone
oestrous
ofttimes
ointment
oldtimer
omitting
onetrack
oratorio
oratress
oxytocin
palterer
pantheon
pantofle
pantsuit
partaken
parterre
Parthian
partible
particle
partisan
partizan
partsong
parttime
pastiche
pastille
pastoral
pastrami
pastries
pastural
pattypan
pectines
pectoral
pentacle
pentagon
pentroof
pertness
pettifog
photogen
photopia
photopic
photopsy
pictures
pintable
pintsize
pittance
plateaux
plateful
platelet
platform
platinic
platinum
platonic
platting
platypus
plethora
plotting
plutonic
poetical
poltfoot
poltroon
pontifex
portable
portfire
porthole
porticos
portiere
portrait
portress
postcard
postcode
postdate
postfree
posthorn
postiche
postlude
postmark
postmill
postobit
postpaid
postpone
postural
posturer
potterer
pratique
prattler
pretence
prettify
prettily
protasis
protatic
protease
protegee
protista
protocol
protonic
protozoa
protract
protrude
pustular
quatrain
quitrent
quitting
quotable

quotient
raftsman
raptness
raptures
rattling
rectoral
rentable
restcure
restless
restorer
restrain
restrict
rhetoric
rhythmic
roothold
rootless
rostrate
rottenly
rustical
rustless
ryotwari
saltbush
saltless
saltlick
saltmine
saltness
saltwort
santonin
Sauterne
sawtooth
scathing
scattily
scatting
scotfree
scotopic
Scotsman
scottice
Scottish
scutcher
scutella
seatbelt
seatrout
sectoral
sentence
sentient
sentinel
sentrygo
septette
septfoil
septimal
septuple
sesterce
sextette
sextuple
Shetland
shothole
shutdown
shutting
siftings
sisterly
sixtieth
sketcher
skittish
skittles
slattern
slithery
slitting
slothful
slotting
sluttish
smithers
smithery
smothery
smuttily
snatcher
snitcher
softball
softboil
softener
softhead
softness
softshoe
softsoap
software
softwood
soothing
soothsay
sortable
soutache
southern
southing
southpaw
Southron
spathose
spatting
spatular
spiteful
spitfire
spitting
spittoon
spotless
spottily
spotting
statable
statedly
statical
statuary
statured
stetting
stitcher
subtitle
subtlety
subtonic
subtopia
subtotal
subtract
suitable
suitably
suitcase
suitings
sultrily
swatting
switchel
swotting
syntagma
syntonic
systemic
systolic
tactical
tactless
tantalic
tantalum
tantalus
Tantrism
tantrist
tartaric
tartness
tartrate
Tartuffe
tastebud
tasteful
tattered
tattooer
tautness
tautomer
tautonym
teatable
teatowel
tectonic
teething
teetotal
teetotum
tentacle
tertiary
testable
testator
testatum
testtube
Teutonic
textbook
texthand
textuary
textural
textured
thatcher
thetical
tiltyard
tintless
tittuped
tittuppy
toothful
toothily
toothing
tortilla
tortious
tortoise
tortuous
torturer
totterer
tritical
trotting
trottoir
truthful
turtling
twitcher
twittery
twitting
twotimer
uintaite
umptieth
unctuous
unitedly
unstable
unstably
unstated
unsteady
unstring
unstrung
unstuffy
upstairs
upstream
upstroke
urethane
vastness
ventless
venturer
vertebra
vertexes
vertical
vertices
verticil
vestiary
vestment
vesturer
viaticum
victoria
victress
victuals
Vietcong
Vietminh
vintager
virtuosa
virtuosi
virtuoso
virtuous
voltaism
vortexes
vortical
vortices
waitress
wantonly
wartweed
wartwort
wastable
wasteful
watthour
westerly
westward
wettable
whatever
whatness
whetting
whiteboy
whitecap
whitefly
whitehot
whitener
whiteout
whitetie
whittret
winterly
wintrily
wistaria
wisteria
wontedly
worthful
worthily
wrathful
wrathily
wretched
writable
writeoff
writings
xanthate
xanthein
xanthene
xanthine
xanthium
xanthoma
Xantippe
yestreen
youthful
zoetrope
abducens
abducent
abductor
ablution
abruptly
absurdly
accuracy
accurate
accursed
accustom
acoustic
acquaint
actually
actuator
acturial
adducent
adductor
adjuster
adjustor
adjutage
adjutant
adjuvant
affusion
aflutter
aiguille
alburnum
aleurone
alguazil
allusion
allusive
alluvial
alluvion
alluvium
ambulant
ambulate
ambusher
ampullae
amputate
aneurism
aneurysm
annually
annulate
annulled
anourous
arcuated
arguable
arguably
argufier
argument
arquebus
assuming
astutely
Augustan
augustly
autumnal
autunite
babushka
baguette
baluster
beautify
befuddle
beguiler
bequeath
bibulous
bicuspid
botulism
brougham
brouhaha
caducean
caduceus
caducity
caducous
capuchin
caruncle
casually
casualty
cerulean
cerusite
chaunter
chauntry
cloudily
cloudlet
coauthor
colubrid
columnal
columnar
columned
conurbia
copulate
coquetry
coquette
corundum
croupier
croupous
cucumber
cucurbit
cumulate
cumulous
cupulate
debugged
debutant
decurion
delusion
delusive
delusory
demurely
demurred
demurrer
depurate
deputise
dilution
diluvial
diluvian
diluvium
disunion
disunite
disunity
disusage
document
draughts
draughty
droughty
durukuli
effusion
effusive
embussed
empurple
encumber
enquirer
esculent
Esquimau
estuaril
Etrurian
Etruscan
excursus
fabulist
fabulous
feculent
fiducial
figurant
figurine
flautist
flounder
flourish
focusing
focussed
Fraulein
Freudian
froufrou
furuncle
futurism
futurist
futurity
gefuffle
ghoulish
glaucoma
glaucous
grounder
grouping
grouting
hamululi
haruspex
hocusing
hocussed
homuncle
Huguenot
humuncle
illumine
illusage
illusion
illusive
illusory
immunise
immunity
impudent
impugner
impunity
impurely
impurity
incubate
incurred
inductee
inductor
indulger
induline
indurate
indusium
industry
infusion
inguinal
inhumane
innuendo
inquirer
insulant
insulate
insulter
insurant
intubate
issuable
issuance
jejunely
jesuitic
jesuitry
jocundly
jugulate
kefuffle
kreutzer
laburnum
lacunary
lacunate
lacunose
lazulite
lazurite
lemurine
lemuroid
levulose
ligulate
liquidly
liturgic
lobulate
loculate
locution
locutory
luculent
Lucullan
lunulate
maculate
manually
manubria
manurial
maquette
maturate
maturely
maturity
medusoid
minutely
minutiae
misusage
modulate
monument
moquette
mutually
naturism
naturist
nebulise
nebulium
nebulous
nenuphar
nodulose
nodulous
nonunion
nonusage
obduracy
obdurate
obturate
obtusely
obtusity
occultly
occupant
occupier
occurred
oppugner
orgulous
osculant
osculate
paduasoy
pagurian
paludism
papulose
papulous
patulous
peculate
peculiar
peduncle
penumbra
Peruvian
petulant
petuntse
piquancy
plaudits
pleurisy
plougher
populace
populate
populism
populist
populous
purulent
queueing
rebuttal
rebutted
rebutter
recurred
recusant
regulate
relucent
relumine
renumber
republic
requital
requiter
resupine
resurvey
ritually
robustly
rosulate
rotundly
roturier
rugulose
salutary
saturant
saturate
Saturday
saturnic
sciurine
sciuroid
scourger
scouting
scrubbed
scrubber
scrutiny
securely
security
sedulity
sedulous
sequelae
sequence
sexually
shoulder
shouldst
shrugged
shrunken
Silurian
siluroid
simulant
simulate
sinusoid
situated
slouched
smoulder
solution
splutter
spousage
sprucely
stoutish
strucken
struggle
strummed
strummer
strumose
strumous
strumpet
strutted
strutter
subulate
suburban
suburbia
susurrus
tabulate

tegument
tenurial
theurgic
thoughts
thousand
thrummed
thruster
traumata
triumvir
triunity
troupial
trousers
troutlet
trouvere
tubulate
unbuckle
unburden
unburied
unbutton
undulant
undulate
unfunded
ungulate
unjustly
unmuffle
unmuzzle
unsuited
unsunned
Ursuline
vacuolar
valuable
valuably
valuator
Venusian
vesuvian
viburnum
virulent
visually
vituline
volution
aasvogel
breveted
breviary
calvados
cervelat
cervical
cervices
chivalry
clavicle
cleverly
convener
convenor
converge
converse
convexly
conveyer
conveyor
convince
convolve
convulse
corvette
cravenly
crevasse
culverin
curveted
disvalue
drivable
driveway
elevated
elevator
eleventh
exuviate
fervency
fervidly
galvanic
gravamen
gravelly
graviton
heavenly
leavings
louvered
malvasia
nouvelle
outvalue
outvying
perverse
pervious
pitviper
pluvious
previous
provable
provably
provided
provider
province
provisor
pulvilli
pulvinus
purveyor
salvable
salvific
scavenge
selvedge
servient
servitor
shivaree
silvatic
silverly
sirvente
Slavonic
slovenly
slovenry
solvable
solvency
souvenir
spavined
spivvery
subvocal
surveyor
survival
survivor
sylvatic
traverse
travesty
trevally
unevenly
univalve
universe
univocal
valvulae
valvular
volvulus
weeviled
weevilly
airwoman
alewives
answerer
anywhere
avowable
avowedly
blowball
blowfish
blowhard
blowhole
blowlamp
blowpipe
bobwheel
bobwhite
brewster
browband
browbeat
browning
brownish
chowchow
clawback
clownery
clownish
cobwebby
cogwheel
crawfish
crowbill
crowfoot
cutwater
dogwatch
dogwhelk
drawable
drawback
drawtube
drawwell
drownded
drowsily
enswathe
erewhile
eyewater
flawless
flowered
flowerer
floweret
flywheel
forwards
gasworks
glowworm
godwards
growling
icewater
knowable
laywoman
madwoman
midwives
miswrite
nonwhite
oldworld
outwards
outwatch
outweigh
outworks
pinwheel
reawaken
redwater
seawards
seawater
seawrack
showbill
showboat
showcard
showcase
showdown
showgirl
showroom
skewback
skewbald
skewness
skywards
slowdown
slowness
slowpoke
slowworm
snowball
snowbird
snowboot
snowdrop
snowfall
snowless
snowlike
snowline
snowshoe
stowaway
sunwards
tapwater
trawlnet
unawares
unswathe
viewable
viewless
warweary
warwhoop
waxworks
banxring
bauxitic
flaxseed
flexible
flexibly
flexuose
flexuous
flexural
gloxinia
inexpert
lynxeyed
proximal
quixotic
quixotry
reexport
abeyance
abeyancy
acrylate
ankylose
armyworm
Assyrian
babyhood
baryonic
barytone
bodyshop
bodywork
botyrose
buoyancy
busybody
busyness
butylene
butyrate
calycine
calycoid
calycule
calyptra
capybara
caryatid
Cheyenne
cityfied
claymore
copybook
copyedit
copyhold
Corybant
coryphee
crayfish
dewyeyed
dicyclic
didymium
didymous
dihybrid
dutyfree
dutypaid
empyreal
empyrean
encyclic
ethylene
Ganymede
grayling
greyfish
greyness
hexylene
hidyhole
iceyacht
Illyrian
ladybird
ladyfern
ladyhood
ladylike
ladylove
ladyship
larynges
larynxes
lawyerly
molybdic
okeydoke
Phrygian
playable
playback
playbill
playbook
playgirl
playgoer
playmate
playroom
playsuit
playtime
polygala
polygamy
polygene
polygeny
polyglot
polygyny
polymath
polypary
polypide
polypite
polypody
polypoid
polypous
polyseme
polysemy
polysomy
polyzoan
polyzoic
polyzoon
ponytail
quayside
rolypoly
rubytail
sphygmus
spryness
staylace
staysail
swayback
syzygial
wheyface
alizarin
amazedly
benzoate
benzylic
blazoner
blazonry
blizzard
bouzouki
brazenly
brazenry
braziery
buzzword
canzonet
cruzeiro
forzando
gadzooks
glaziery
grizzled
marzipan
mitzvoth
pizzeria
quizzing
rhizopod
seizable
sitzbath
sizzling
snazzily
whizbang
whizzing
whizzkid
zarzuela
zugzwang

---

abeyance
abeyancy
abidance
abomasum
abomasus
aborally
acquaint
actually
actuator
adorable
adorably
adularia
adulator
adynamia
adynamic
aerially
affiance
afflatus
agaragar
agitator
alguazil
alizarin
alliance
alphabet
amadavat
amaranth
ambiance
amenable
amenably
amicable
amicably
amorally
anabases
anabasis
anabatic
anapaest
anasarca
animally
animator
annually
anteater
apically
apogamic
applause
appraise
Aramaean
Arapahoe
arapaima
archaean
archaise
archaism
archaist
arcuated
arguable
arguably
aromatic
astragal
ataraxia
ataraxic
avadavat
avifauna
avowable
baccarat
backache
badlands
bailable
balladic
balladry
balsamic
bandanna
bankable
barbaric
barnacle
barracks
barranca
barranco
barrator
barratry
bastardy
battalia
bearable
bearably
bechamel
bechance
bedmaker
bedtable
beeeater
beggarly
Benjamin
bereaved
bergamot
beslaver
betrayal
betrayer
biddable
bimbashi
binnacle
bistable
biyearly
blamable
blamably
blatancy
bribable
brocaded
brocatel
brutally
buckaroo
bummaree
bungalow
buoyancy
cachalot
calcanea
calcaria
callable
calvados
campagna
campaign
cannabin
cannabis
carcajou
carcanet
cardamom
cardamum
carnally
carnauba
caryatid
cascabel
castaway
casually
casualty
caudally
caudated
causally
cellarer
cellaret
centaury
cephalic
cercaria
chalazae
chapatti
chimaera
Chinaman
chivalry
choragic
choragus
chorally
chupatti
chupatty
ciliated
cineaste
cinnabar
cinnamic
cinnamon
Circaean
clematis
climatic
cockatoo
collagen
collapse
collared
collator
commando
compages
concasse
contagia
contango
coolabah
coplanar
cottager
cottagey
coumarin
courante
crenated
crevasse
crusader
culpable
culpably
curtains
cutwater
cyclamen
dalmatic
damnable
damnably
dastardy
deceased
declarer
declasse
defiance
defrayal
deniable
dentalia
dentated
depraved
despatch
deviance
deviancy
deviator
diabasic
diamante
diapason
diapause
dichasia
dictator
dimmable
dioramic
diseased
dismally
dispatch
distally
distance
distaste
disvalue
dogeared
dogfaced
dogmatic
dogwatch
dormancy
dorsally
dracaena
dramatic
drawable
drivable
dungaree
dutiable
ebriated
ecstatic
educable
educated
educator
egomania
elegance
elegancy
elevated
elevator
emblazon
embracer
emphases
emphasis
emphatic
emulator
endpaper
engramma
engraver
enneagon

enslaver
enswathe
enthalpy
entracte
entrails
entrance
enviable
enviably
epically
epicalyx
epifauna
epinasty
epitasis
erasable
eschalot
estrange
estuaril
ethnarch
eustatic
evadable
evitable
exchange
exogamic
expiable
expiator
extrados
eyewater
faceache
facially
fadeaway
falcated
fandance
fandango
fanfaron
fantasia
faunally
fellable
fellahin
festally
feudally
filially
firearms
fiscally
fishable
florally
flypaper
foldaway
foliaged
fontanel
fontange
fordable
formalin
formally
forrader
forsaken
forwards
forzando
fougasse
frugally
furcated
gainable
galbanum
galeated
galvanic
gambados
garganey
gazpacho
gendarme
genially
geomancy
geotaxis
Germanic
gestagen
Ghanaian
gillaroo
giveaway
globally
glucagon
godwards
gonfalon
gossamer
gramarye
gramatom
gravamen
grimacer
guaiacum
guaranty
guidable
guidance
gullable
gunlayer
gymnasia
haematic
haematin
Haggadah
hangable
hateable
haymaker
headache
headachy
hebraise
Hebraism
Hebraist
heliacal
Helladic
henparty
heptagon
herbaria
hereaway
hideaway
hielaman
hierarch
hieratic
hireable
Hispanic
Hogmanay
hollands
huggable
hydranth
icewater
iceyacht
idolater
idolatry
illfated
imitable
imitator
Indiaman
inflamer
inflated
inflator
inflatus
infrared
instable
instance
instancy
intrados
inviable
isobaric
isogamic
isolable
isolator
issuable
issuance
iterance
jackaroo
jeopardy
joinable
jovially
kalaazar
kangaroo
kinkajou
kissable
knowable
labdanum
labially
labrador
lackaday
laically
lambaste
landarmy
laudable
laudably
laudanum
laudator
lawmaker
lethally
lethargy
leviable
liftable
likeable
lineally
linearly
Linnaean
lipsalve
litharge
liveable
loanable
lockable
Lollardy
lopeared
lothario
maenadic
magdalen
magmatic
Mahratta
Mahratti
mailable
malvasia
mancando
Mandaean
mandamus
mandarin
mandator
maneater
mangabey
manganic
maniacal
manually
martagon
mascaron
massacre
Mazdaism
mechanic
medially
mediator
memsahib
mendable
menhaden
menially
mentally
mescalin
mesdames
mesially
methanol
midlands
migraine
migrator
miscarry
mismatch
mistaken
moccasin
mondaine
monoacid
mordancy
mortally
moshavim
moveable
muriatic
muscadel
muscatel
mustache
mutually
myriapod
nameable
narrator
naumachy
nectared
NeoLatin
neonatal
neurally
nondairy
nonparty
normalcy
normally
nuisance
nuthatch
obstacle
ocularly
olibanum
oligarch
omphalic
omphalos
openable
operable
operatic
operator
ordnance
origanum
Ossianic
ostracod
ostracon
ostrakon
outcaste
outdated
outlawry
outmatch
outrange
outvalue
outwards
outwatch
overalls
overarch
pachalic
paduasoy
palpable
palpably
pandanus
pappadom
parlance
parlando
partaken
pashalic
pashalik
passable
passably
peccable
peccancy
peekaboo
pellagra
pentacle
pentagon
perianth
phalange
phreatic
phthalic
pileated
pillager
Pindaric
pinnacle
pinnated
pintable
piquancy
piscator
pitiable
pitiably
pittance
placable
placably
playable
plumaged
plurally
podiatry
poppadum
portable
potlatch
pourable
predator
prelatic
prenatal
preparer
presager
primally
Primates
probable
probably
profaner
prolamin
prolapse
pronator
prosaism
prosaist
protasis
protatic
provable
provably
ptomaine
puggaree
pulsator
pygmaean
quotable
racially
radially
radiance
radiancy
radiator
rampancy
rapparee
rascally
rateable
readable
readably
reawaken
recharge
redfaced
redwater
regrater
rehearse
releasee
releaser
releasor
reliable
reliably
reliance
rentable
repealer
repeater
replacer
rerearch
research
retiarii
reusable
revealer
riddance
rideable
ritually
ropeable
ruinable
rummager
sabbatic
saccadic
sacraria
safranin
sailable
saleable
salvable
sandarac
sangaree
sargasso
Sassanid
satiable
satiably
scalable
scalawag
scenario
schmaltz
schnapps
screamer
seafarer
sealable
seamanly
seawards
seawater
seizable
Sephardi
serially
seriatim
serranid
serrated
sexually
shakable
shapable
Sheraton
shikaree
shiralee
shivaree
sidearms
sigmatic
signally
sillabub
silvatic
singable
sinkable
siriasis
situated
sizeable
skywards
slugabed
smokable
soakaway
sociable
sociably
socially
Socratic
solfaist
solvable
sortable
soutache
sovranty
sparable
spicated
spiracle
spirally
sporadic
spreader
squeaker
squealer
statable
stomachy
stomatal
stomatic
storable
stowaway
streaked
streaker
streamer
subbasal
suitable
suitably
sunbaked
sunbathe
sundance
sunwards
surfacer
syllabic
syllable
syllabub
syllabus
sylvatic
sympathy
syngamic
syntagma
takeaway
tameable
tannable
tantalic
tantalum
tantalus
tapdance
tapwater
tarlatan
tarragon
tartaric
taxpayer
teacaddy
teaparty
tearaway
teatable
teenager
tellable
tentacle
teocalli
terraced
terrapin
terraria
terrazzo
testable
testator
testatum
tetradic
tetragon
tetrapla
tetrapod
tetrarch
thalamic
thalamus
Thanatos
thematic
thesauri
thoraces
thoracic
thoraxes
threader
threaten
throated
tillable
tithable
toreador
tornadic
trevally
tribally
tribasic
trimaran
tuckahoe
tuneable
turbaned
turnable
twofaced
tympanic
tympanum
uintaite
ultraism
ultraist
unabated
unawares
unbeaten
unbiased
unchancy
unchaste
uncially
undraped
unglazed
univalve
unleaded
unlearnt
unloader
unplaced
unreason
unsealed
unseated
unshaped
unstable
unstably
unstated
unswathe
unweaned
upheaval
upstairs
uvularly
vagrancy
Valhalla
valiance
valiancy
valuable
valuably
valuator
Vandalic
variable
variably
variance
venially
verbally
verbatim
verdancy
vernally
vibrancy
vibrator
viewable
villadom
villager
villainy
villatic
vintager
violable
violably
violator
viscacha
visually
vitiable
vitiator
vizcacha
voidable
voidance
volcanic
volcanos
voltaism
vulcanic
vulgarly
Walhalla
walkable
walkaway
wallaroo
wardance
warpaint
warragal
warranty
washable
wastable
wayfarer
wearable
weldable
welladay
wellaway
wetlands
wettable
wigmaker
winnable
wiseacre
wistaria
workable
workaday
writable
yeomanly
yeomanry
zodiacal
zoolater
zoolatry
zoomancy
acerbate
acerbity
adlibbed
amoebean
amoeboid

antibody
autobahn
backbite
backbone
bankbill
bankbook
bareback
baseball
baseborn
bedabble
bejabers
belabour
bellbird
bellbuoy
beriberi
bilabial
bilobate
birdbath
blabbing
blahblah
blesbuck
blowball
blubbery
bluebell
bluebird
boatbill
browband
browbeat
buckbean
bushbaby
bushbuck
busybody
cagebird
calabash
capybara
carabine
casebook
cashbook
celibacy
celibate
cerebral
cerebrum
chambers
chambray
chapbook
clambake
clawback
clubbing
cockboat
colubrid
comeback
cookbook
copybook
cornball
Corybant
crabbing
cribbage
cribbing
crowbill
dahabieh
deadbeat
delibate
demobbed
dihybrid
disabuse
divebomb
dogsbody
doorbell
downbeat
drabbler
drawback
dribbler
dribblet
drubbing
duckbill
dumbbell
durables
dustbowl
exlibris

fallback
faltboat
fastback
feedback
fireback
fireball
firebird
fireboat
firebomb
firebrat
fishball
fishbone
fishbowl
flambeau
flatboat
fleabane
fleabite
flubbing
foldboat
football
footbath
forebear
forebode
fourball
freeborn
fribbler
fullback
funebral
gadabout
gamebird
gaolbird
giftbook
goofball
grabbing
grabbler
grosbeak
grubbily
grubbing
grumbler
halfback
halfbeak
halfboot
halfbred
handball
handbell
handbill
handbook
hardback
hardbake
harebell
headband
heelball
hellbent
herdbook
highball
highborn
highbred
highbrow
hogsback
holdback
homebody
homeborn
homebred
homebrew
hoofbeat
hornbeam
hornbill
hornbook
humpback
hymnbook
hypobole
immobile
incubate
indebted
intubate
inurbane
ironbark
jackboot
Jacobean

Jacobite
jailbird
jeroboam
kickback
kingbird
kingbolt
korfball
kourbash
ladybird
layabout
lifebelt
lifeboat
lifebuoy
liveborn
longboat
lovebird
lyrebird
mailboat
makebate
manubria
marabout
meatball
molybdic
moonbeam
moribund
mossback
mothball
neckband
noseband
notebook
ovenbird
overbear
overbook
overbore
overbusy
parabola
passbook
playback
playbill
playbook
plumbago
plumbate
plumbing
plumbism
puffball
puffbird
pullback
purebred
pushball
pushbike
quibbler
rainbird
ratsbane
reedbird
reembark
rehoboam
republic
rhomboid
ricebird
ringbark
ringbolt
ringbone
roadbook
rockbird
roodbeam
rosebowl
rosebush
runabout
rutabaga
sailboat
saltbush
sandbank
sandbath
saraband
scabbard
scombrid
scrabble
scribble
scribbly

scrubbed
scrubber
seatbelt
selfborn
semibull
shabbily
shadbush
shagbark
shambles
shinbone
shoebill
shopbell
showbill
showboat
sideband
sitzbath
skewback
skewbald
slabbing
slapbang
slobbery
slobbish
slubbing
slumbery
snapbrim
snobbery
snobbish
snobbism
snowball
snowbird
snowboot
snubbing
soapbark
softball
softboil
somebody
songbird
songbook
sonobuoy
sparbuoy
squabble
squibbed
stabbing
stilbene
stilbite
strabism
strobila
strobile
strobili
stubbing
stubborn
studbook
stumbler
surfbird
surfboat
swabbing
swayback
swobbing
tailback
Tenebrae
terebene
terebrae
textbook
throbbed
thumbpot
timeball
timebomb
trapball
trembler
trembles
trombone
trueblue
trueborn
truebred
turnback
twinborn
vagabond
Wahabism
Wahabite

washbowl
waveband
wellborn
wellbred
whimbrel
whizbang
windburn
wingbeat
wishbone
woodbind
woodbine
wordbook
yearbook
zwieback
abdicate
abducens
abducent
abductor
abjectly
acescent
adducent
adductor
adjacent
aduncate
aduncous
advocaat
advocacy
advocate
affected
affecter
airscrew
albacore
algicide
allocate
analcime
analcite
anarchic
antecede
aphicide
aquacade
articled
ascocarp
atrocity
atticism
audacity
auricula
autacoid
autocade
autocrat
backchat
backcomb
ballcock
basicity
beefcake
bellcote
betacism
bifacial
bifocals
bioscope
birdcage
birdcall
bisector
bleacher
bluechip
bluecoat
bookcase
boracite
borecole
bouncily
bouncing
brancard
branched
brancher
branchia
breeches
britches
broacher
broccoli
bronchia

bronchus
bullcalf
cabochon
caducean
caduceus
caducity
caducous
calycine
calycoid
calycule
capacity
capuchin
caracara
caracole
catacomb
catechol
cavicorn
cetacean
chancery
charcoal
chinchin
chitchat
choicely
chopchop
chowchow
churchly
clincher
clipclop
clopclop
cockcrow
coercion
coercive
cofactor
coincide
coracoid
cosecant
couscous
cratches
crescent
crescive
crotched
crotchet
culicine
cynicism
dedicate
defector
dejected
delicacy
delicate
democrat
depicter
depictor
detached
detector
diarchal
diarchic
dicacity
dicyclic
didactic
dioecism
directly
director
domicile
doorcase
dovecote
downcast
downcome
drencher
dungcart
dustcart
dustcoat
eclectic
effector
efficacy
elenchus
elenctic
enarched
encyclic
endocarp

enricher
episcope
especial
ethicism
ethicist
eulachon
Eurocrat
eutectic
evincive
exercise
exorcise
exorcism
exorcist
facecard
felicity
ferocity
feticide
fiducial
fiercely
fireclay
fishcake
fletcher
flincher
floccose
floccule
flocculi
forecast
francium
frescoes
fugacity
galactic
gamecock
gearcase
genocide
germcell
glancing
glaucoma
glaucous
golfclub
Graecise
Graecism
groschen
gynocrat
Halachah
handcart
handclap
handcuff
hardcase
hardcore
havocked
helicoid
hijacker
Holocene
homicide
hyoscine
imbecile
impacted
indecent
indicant
indicate
indicium
indocile
inductee
inductor
infector
injector
innocent
insecure
invected
invocate
iotacism
ironclad
judicial
kingcrab
kisscurl
landcrab
lapicide
launcher
libeccio

lodicule
logician
loricate
lutecium
lyricism
lyricist
magician
magicked
mailcart
Manichee
manicure
marocain
medicate
medicine
mesocarp
mimicked
mimicker
minacity
mobocrat
molecule
monachal
monicker
monocrat
monocyte
mooncalf
moorcock
musicale
musician
muticous
Nearctic
newscast
nosecone
notecase
objector
obtected
official
oiticica
opencast
opercula
optician
opuscula
opuscule
otoscope
overcall
overcame
overcast
overcoat
overcome
overcrop
oxpecker
panicked
pedicled
pedicure
pericarp
pericope
petechia
piercing
pinecone
pinochle
pipeclay
planchet
Pliocene
postcard
postcode
praecipe
preacher
prescind
princely
princess
pushcart
quencher
quincunx
racecard
radicant
radicate
raincoat
rapacity
rapecake
reascend

redactor
regicide
rejecter
relocate
relucent
reoccupy
rerecord
restcure
reticent
reticule
rhonchal
rhonchus
ricochet
ridicule
rockcake
rockcork
rollcall
rubicund
sackcoat
sagacity
salacity
sashcord
scarcely
scarcity
scorcher
scutcher
searcher
seascape
seedcake
seedcase
seedcoat
seedcorn
selectee
selector
sericite
setscrew
showcard
showcase
silicane
silicate
silicide
silicify
silicone
sinecure
sinicise
sketcher
skyscape
slipcase
sloucher
snatcher
snitcher
solecism
solecist
sorochen
spiccato
sprocket
sprucely
staccato
stancher
stanchly
stitcher
stoccado
stoccata
stoicism
stopcock
stricken
strickle
strictly
strucken
stuccoes
subacute
suitcase
suricate
switchel
tailcoat
telecast
telecine
tenacity
tenacula
thatcher
theocrat
thwacker
tollcall
tonicity
toxicant
toxicity
treacher
trencher
truncate
tunicate
turncoat
turncock
twitcher
typecast
unbacked
unbuckle
unsocial
urticant
urticate
varactor
varicose
velocity
veracity
verecund
vesicant
vesicate
Vietcong
viricide
vivacity
voracity
whinchat
whipcord
windcone
wingcase
woodchat
woodcock
wormcast
wretched
xylocarp
abradant
abridger
abundant
Accadian
accident
aceldama
acridine
acridity
aerodyne
Airedale
Akkadian
algidity
allodial
allodium
amygdala
anecdote
anhedral
antedate
antidote
aqueduct
Arcadian
archduke
ascidian
ascidium
asyndeta
autodafe
autodyne
backdate
backdoor
backdrop
barndoor
basidial
basidium
bayadere
befuddle
benedick
benedict
bladdery
blandish
bleeding
blindage
blinding
blondish
bloodily
bloodred
boarding
boatdeck
boundary
braiding
brandied
brandish
brandnew
breeding
brindled
broadish
broadway
broidery
broodily
building
bulldoze
caladium
calidity
Canadian
cauldron
Chaldaic
Chaldean
chaldron
chandler
childbed
childish
children
chondrus
chordate
cladding
cloddish
cloudily
cloudlet
coaldust
comedian
comedist
comedown
conidial
conidium
couldest
cupidity
cytidine
decadent
decedent
dieldrin
dihedral
dingdong
dividend
dividivi
dividual
dreadful
druidess
druidism
ectoderm
embedded
emendate
endoderm
entoderm
evildoer
exordial
exordium
expedite
faradaic
faradism
fiendish
finedraw
firedamp
flinders
floodlit
floodway
fluidics
fluidify
fluidise
fluidity
foredeck
foredoom
founding
freedman
Freudian
frondage
frondent
frondeur
frondose
gelidity
gladdest
gladding
glanders
glandule
golddust
gonidial
gonidium
grandame
granddad
grandeur
grandson
greedily
grindery
guardant
guardian
heredity
hoarding
holidays
homodont
humidify
humidity
hypoderm
immodest
impudent
incident
inundate
jaundice
killdeer
klondike
kneedeep
lapidary
lapidate
lapidify
lepidote
lividity
lucidity
maledict
malodour
markdown
melodeon
melodise
melodist
meridian
mesoderm
monadism
monodist
moulding
muskdeer
muskduck
namedrop
nextdoor
nomadise
nomadism
nosedive
nowadays
obsidian
occident
okeydoke
oncidium
ophidian
Orcadian
overdone
overdose
overdraw
overdrew
paludism
paradigm
paradise
parodist
peardrop
periderm
peridium
peridote
plaiding
plaudits
pleading
plodding
postdate
poundage
pounding
praedial
prandial
priedieu
prodding
pygidial
pygidium
pyridine
pyxidium
quandary
quandong
quiddity
rabidity
raindrop
rapidity
reindeer
remedial
resident
residual
residuum
rigadoon
rigidify
rigidity
ringdove
rockdove
roundarm
rounders
roundish
roundtop
rubidium
sapidity
saunders
sawedged
sawedoff
scandent
Scandian
scandium
schedule
scolding
scudding
seladang
semidome
shaddock
sheading
shedding
shelduck
shoddily
showdown
shredded
shredder
shuddery
shutdown
sidedish
sidedoor
sidedrum
skidding
skindeep
slapdash
sledding
slowdown
snowdrop
soapdish
solidary
solidify
solidity
somedeal
somedele
soundbow
soundbox
sounding
sourdine
spandrel
spandril
spardeck
speedily
speedway
spondaic
squadron
squidded
standard
standing
standish
standoff
stardust
steadily
steading
straddle
stridden
strident
studding
sturdied
sturdily
surfduck
swindler
tapedeck
teardrop
tearduct
tepidity
theodicy
thridace
thudding
thundery
timidity
tolldish
tonedeaf
trapdoor
treadler
trendily
tumidity
turndown
twaddler
twiddler
twoedged
unbidden
unending
unfading
unriddle
unsaddle
untidily
validate
validity
vanadate
vanadium
vanadous
vapidity
viridian
viridity
welldeck
wheedler
whidding
wiredraw
withdraw
withdrew
wooldyed
wouldest
woundily
yielding
absterge
academia
academic
accredit
achiever
aculeate
aigrette
alchemic
alebench
alfresco
alopecia
amazedly
ambience
amoretti
amoretto
amusedly
analecta
analects
anisette
anorexia
anorexic
answerer
anthelia
anthemia
antheral
anthesis
antlered
applepie
araceous
arquebus
assiento
asthenia
asthenic
athletic
aubretia
audience
avowedly
bachelor
bacteria
baguette
balletic
bandeaux
banderol
bannered
banneret
bannerol
banterer
barbecue
barberry
barbette
bargeman
barrenly
barrette
barterer
basketry
bathetic
bayberry
beamends
believer
bequeath
berberis
berceuse
besieger
bethesda
bilberry
biogenic
biometry
bitterly
biweekly
blameful
Bodleian
bontebok
bookends
Bordeaux
bordello
borderer
bosseyed
bracelet
brakeman
brakevan
brazenly
brazenry
breveted
brokenly
bromelia
brunette
budgeree
bulletin
bunkered
Burberry
burletta
cableway
cachepot
cachexia
caffeine
canoeing
canoeist
cassette
cathedra
catheter
cathexes
cathexis
caudexes
causerie
causeway
cervelat
chapelry
chaperon
chateaux
Cheyenne
chimeric
choleric
choregic
choregus
clarence
clemency
cleverly
closeset
closeted
clupeoid
clypeate
coalesce
cobwebby
cockerel
cockeyed
colleger
commence
commerce
conceder
conceive
concerti
concerto
concetti
concetto
condense
conferee
conferva
confetti
congener
conserve
contempt
contents
contessa
convener
convenor
converge
converse
convexly
conveyer
conveyor
copperas
copyedit
coquetry
coquette
corneous
cornetcy
cornetti
cornetto
corselet
corseted
corsetry
corvette
cosmetic
cowberry
cranefly
cravenly
credence
credenza
crenelle

criteria
croceate
cruzeiro
culdesac
culverin
cupreous
currency
cursedly
curveted
cussedly
cycleway
cypselae
cysteine
dancette
dancetty
danseuse
deadener
decrease
decrepit
decretal
degrease
deucedly
deuteron
dewberry
dewyeyed
diabetes
diabetic
diameter
diereses
dieresis
dietetic
diocesan
diphenyl
dipteral
dipteran
disbench
dishevel
dispense
disperse
disseise
disserve
dissever
ditheism
ditheist
ditherer
diuresis
diuretic
doddered
dodderer
dogberry
doggedly
doggerel
dotterel
driveway
drupelet
duchesse
duodenal
duodenum
dysgenic
dyslexia
dyslexic
eagleowl
easterly
ecclesia
elatedly
eleventh
emceeing
eminence
eminency
encaenia
enfeeble
ensheath
entreaty
entrench
entrepot
entresol
enuresis
enuretic
epidemic
epigeous
epilepsy
episemon
erigeron
erogenic
eschewal
esoteric
espresso
evanesce
evidence
exegesis
exegetic
exigence
exigency
exoteric
extremes
faineant
falderal
falsetto
fastener
fatherly
fattener
fauteuil
fenberry
ferreter
fervency
fingered
finnesko
fireeyed
flabella
flagella
flamenco
flanerie
flowered
flowerer
floweret
folderol
forcedly
forcefed
forceful
foreedge
formerly
fosterer
foureyes
framesaw
frenetic
frisette
frumenty
fugleman
furbelow
gableend
gadgetry
Gadhelic
galleass
gambeson
gardener
gardenia
garreted
gasmeter
gatherer
geodesic
geodetic
geometer
geometry
gingerly
glabella
glycerin
glycerol
glyceryl
Goidelic
goldenly
goosegog
gorgeous
graceful
gramercy
grateful
gravelly
Griselda
griseous
grisette
guidedog
guideway
guileful
gunmetal
gusseted
gynoecia
gypseous
hacienda
halteres
hangeron
hardener
hasheesh
hastener
hawkeyed
heatedly
heavenly
hedgehog
hedgehop
hedgepig
hedgerow
Hellenic
helmeted
hermetic
herpetic
Hesperus
hetaerae
higherup
hinderer
hitherto
hoosegow
horsebox
horsecar
horsefly
horseman
hostelry
houseboy
housedog
housefly
houseful
houseman
housetop
Huguenot
hygienic
hysteria
hysteric
impledge
increase
increate
inflexed
innuendo
intrench
intrepid
isabella
ischemia
ischemic
isomeric
isometry
jabberer
jackeroo
jaggedly
japhetic
jiggered
julienne
jumpedup
kedgeree
kromesky
lambency
lancelet
lanneret
larcener
largesse
latterly
laureate
lawyerly
leadenly
lenience
leniency
lettered
libretti
libretto
lichened
lichenin
liegeman
ligneous
lingerer
lingerie
listener
loiterer
longeron
longeval
lookeron
loosebox
loosener
louvered
lowlevel
lubberly
lumberer
Lutheran
lynxeyed
mackerel
Maecenas
magnesia
magnetic
magneton
maidenly
mannered
mannerly
mantelet
maquette
markedly
marketer
martello
martenot
masseter
masseuse
masterly
medieval
membered
mergence
mesmeric
misbegot
miscegen
misdealt
misheard
mittened
monteith
moquette
motherly
mouseear
mulberry
multeity
murderer
murrelet
musketry
mutterer
myogenic
nacreous
narceine
nascence
nascency
nauseant
nauseate
nauseous
neotenic
neoteric
nickelic
nobleman
noblesse
noisette
nonlegal
nonmetal
nonsense
Norseman
noumenal
noumenon
nouvelle
nuclease
nucleate
nucleole
nucleoli
numberer
ochreous
oddments
odometer
ohmmeter
omelette
openeyed
operetta
opulence
orogenic
outHerod
outreach
outreign
outweigh
oximeter
palmette
palmetto
palterer
pamperer
pandemic
parcener
pargeter
parhelia
parhelic
parietal
Parmesan
parterre
passerby
pathetic
patience
peaceful
peasecod
pendency
perceive
perfecto
permeate
perverse
phaseout
phonemic
phonetic
phyletic
pickerel
picketer
pilferer
pilsener
pimiento
pincenez
pixieish
pizzeria
placeman
placenta
plateaux
plateful
platelet
plebeian
plumelet
pochette
ponderer
potbelly
potterer
powdered
predella
prelease
prepense
presence
preserve
pretence
prideful
primeval
proceeds
propense
properly
property
protease
protegee
prudence
prunella
prunelle
prunello
pungency
puppetry
pursenet
purveyor
pyogenic
Quakerly
quenelle
queueing
raggedly
reagency
recreant
recreate
redeemer
reemerge
reflexed
reliever
renderer
replevin
respects
retrench
reviewal
reviewer
ridgeway
rifleman
rocketry
rondeaux
rottenly
rouleaus
rouleaux
roulette
ruggedly
runnerup
sacredly
salience
saliency
sanserif
sapience
sarcenet
sardelle
sarsenet
saucebox
saucepan
Sauterne
scalepan
scavenge
schiedam
screechy
screener
screever
scutella
sealevel
secretin
secretly
secretor
segreant
seicento
selvedge
senseful
sentence
septette
sequelae
sequence
sergeant
serjeant
sesterce
sextette
shakeout
shaleoil
shameful
shareout
shedevil
shigella
shrieval
sickener
sickerly
silverly
singeing
sirvente
sisterly
sithence
sixpence
sixpenny
skeletal
skeleton
slideway
sloeeyed
slovenly
slovenry
snakepit
societal
softener
solderer
solfeggi
solleret
solvency
sorcerer
souvenir
spacebar
spaceman
spadeful
spicebox
spikelet
spiteful
squeedge
squeegee
squeezer
stakenet
stapelia
statedly
stiletto
stonefly
storeman
storeyed
streeted
subgenus
sublease
submerge
submerse
subserve
suddenly
sufferer
sullenly
summerly
sunderer
surcease
surveyor
suspense
symmetry
syndesis
syndetic
systemic
tableaux
tablecut
tableful
tablemat
tabletop
tafferel
tamperer
tangency
Tarpeian
tasselly
tastebud
tasteful
tattered
tegmenta
tempered
temperer
tendence
tendency
tenderly
tenpence
tenpenny
tesserae
tesseral
thanedom
therefor
thereout
tholepin
threeply
threeway
timbered
tingeing
tinkerer
tinselly
toiletry
toilette
topheavy
toplevel
totterer
toxaemia
toxaemic
trabeate
tradeoff
trapezia
traverse
travesty
trecento
trimeric
trimeter
tripeman
trumeaux
tsarevna
tuppence
tuppenny
turmeric
turreted
twopence
twopenny
udometer
umbrella
umbrette
unaneled
unclench
uncreate
undreamt
unevenly
unfreeze
unitedly
universe
unmeetly
unopened
unseeded
unseeing
unseemly
unsteady
unwieldy
variedly
varietal
varletry
velleity
vendetta
veneerer
vengeful
verderer
verderor
vergence
vertebra
vertexes
vesperal
viameter
vigneron
vignette
violence
visceral
vitreous
voicebox
voiceful
vortexes
walleyed
wanderer
wanderoo
wardenry
warrener
warweary

wasteful dripfeed overfeed uplifter engaging nomogram squiggly Blenheim
waxberry drumfire overfill variform ensigncy oakegger staggard blighter
weaselly dutyfree overfish vasiform ergogram obligate staggers blithely
Wesleyan dwarfish overflew verifier eulogise obliging stargaze blowhard
westerly dwarfism overflow vilifier eulogist ontogeny stingily blowhole
whatever ensiform overfold vivifier eulogium oologist stingray blushful
whenever evenfall overfond wallfern exergual oppugner stodgily boathook
wherever fallfish pacifier waveform fatigues orangery straggle bobwheel
whiteboy fastfood pacifism weakfish filagree Orangism straggly bobwhite
whitecap filefish pacifist wharfage filigree overgrew strigose bolthole
whitefly filiform paleface wheyface filmgoer overgrow struggle bonehead
whitehot fishfarm paraffin whiffler fishglue paragoge sturgeon borehole
whitener fivefold piliform wildfire flagging patagium subagent boughten
whiteout flatfeet pinafore wildfowl flogging pedagogy swagging brachial
whitetie flatfish pipefish windfall footgear pedigree swigging brachium
wholehog flatfoot pisiform wolffish foregoer Pelagian swinging brethren
whomever flimflam platform woolfell foregone perigean syzygial brighten
whoredom flipflap poltfoot workfolk fringing perigyny tailgate brightly
whoreson flipflop portfire abnegate frogging phlegmon telegony brochure
wickedly footfall postfree abrogate fumigant phosgene telegram brouhaha
wideeyed forefeel proofing aerogram fumigate Phrygian theogony brushoff
wildeyed forefelt purifier allegory gazogene plangent thingamy buckhorn
winterly forefoot pyriform allogamy Georgian playgirl thoughts Buddhism
wisteria fourfold rainfall almagest goingson playgoer thuggery Buddhist
wontedly freefall rarefied almighty greegree plougher thuggism bulkhead
woodenly frogfish ratifier Armagnac grisgris plugging tidegate bullhead
writeoff froufrou reaffirm arpeggio groggily podagral toboggan bullhorn
Yankeefy fusiform redefine arrogant groogroo podagric tollgate bunghole
zeppelin garefowl reniform arrogate grudging polygala tomogram butchery
zoogenic gatefold retiform assignat hairgrip polygamy unpegged calthrop
zoometry gefuffle rockfall assignee handgrip polygene unrigged camphene
zygaenid germfree rockfish assignor headgear polygeny vinegary camphine
acidfast goatfish rosefish autogamy hexagram polyglot Visigoth camshaft
acrefoot goldfish sailfish autogiro hologram polygyny voyageur canthari
aeriform goldfoil sainfoin autogyro homogamy priggery wallgame catchall
aerofoil Graafian sandflea bedeguar homogeny priggish weregild catchfly
antefixa graffiti scaffold befogged hypogeal priggism Whiggery catching
argufier graffito scarfpin benignly hypogean racegoer Whiggish cinchona
artefact greffier scotfree bewigged hypogene rejigger Whiggism clothier
artifact greyfish scrofula bludgeon hypogeum relegate windgall clothing
artifice handfast seedfish bourgeon hypogyny religion wormgear clubhaul
auriform hausfrau septfoil braggart ideogram renegade wrangler coachdog
backfire headfast shelfful bragging impugner renegado wriggler coachman
balefire hellfire shuffler brougham indagate reneguer wrongful coalhole
barefoot Hereford sickflag callgirl indigene resigned wrongous cogwheel
benefice hillfort skinfood category indigent runagate xenogamy conchate
billfold holdfast slipform chugging insignia savagely yataghan conchoid
blowfish homefelt sniffily clanging intaglio savagery youngest copyhold
bluefish hornfels sniffler clangour integral sciagram youngish couchant
boldface iodoform sniffles clogging irongray scragend acidhead couching
bonefish kefuffle snowfall cryogeny irongrey scragged aesthete crashing
boniface kingfish snuffbox danegeld irrigate seraglio airshaft crashpad
bouffant kinsfolk snuffers debagged kilogram shaggily alcahest crumhorn
briefing ladyfern snuffler debugged landgirl shanghai aldehyde dabchick
brimfull landfall snuffles decagram levigate shingler alkahest daughter
bullfrog landform spiffing decigram lichgate shingles amethyst deadhead
bushfire leapfrog spitfire delegacy lipogram shogging anaphase deathbed
califate lockfast spoffish delegate litigant shopgirl anaphora deathcap
campfire locofoco staffage demagogy litigate showgirl anathema deathray
carefree lumpfish starfish derogate logogram shrugged anechoic deckhand
catsfoot lungfish stedfast designer lychgate skiagram antihero Delphian
chiefdom makefast stiffish diligent mahogany slagging anything denehole
citified malefern studfarm dirigism Malagasy slangily anywhere diaphone
cityfied manifest stuffily disagree maligner slogging apothegm dogshore
clubfoot manifold stuffing divagate malignly sluggard arachnid dogwhelk
coalfish maniform surefire dragging marigold slugging arethusa doughboy
codifier modifier surffish draughts misogamy sluggish armchair doughnut
coiffeur monkfish telefilm draughty misogyny smudgily Ayrshire downhaul
coiffure moonface tilefish droughty mitigant smuggler babyhood downhill
coliform moonfish timefuse drudgery mitigate snagging bacchant drachmae
coniform moorfowl toadfish drugging monogamy sniggler backhand drachmai
cramfull moufflon toadflax druggist monogeny snogging bakshish drachmas
crawfish nailfile treefern echogram monoglot snuggery baldhead drophead
crayfish napiform treefrog elongate monogony sphagnum beechnut drumhead
crowfoot needfire tubiform emergent monogram sphygmus biathlon duckhawk
cubiform ninefold typeface emulgent monogyny spongily billhead dumbhead
deadfall nubiform typifier endogamy mortgage sprigged billhook dunghill
dealfish numbfish unciform endogeny nanogram spurgear birthday Dutchman
downfall overfall unmuffle energise navigate squiggle bitchily earphone

earthnut
eggshell
elephant
ensphere
epiphany
epiphyte
erethism
erewhile
erythema
eyerhyme
eyeshade
faithful
falchion
farmhand
farthest
farthing
feathery
feedhead
fetching
filthily
firehose
fishhawk
fishhook
flashgun
flashily
flashing
flathead
fleshfly
fleshpot
flywheel
foothill
foothold
forehand
forehead
foxshark
freehand
freehold
freshman
freshrun
frighten
frothily
funkhole
furthest
geophagy
geophone
geophyte
gilthead
girlhood
gladhand
gnathite
goatherd
godchild
grapheme
graphics
graphite
guacharo
gymkhana
handheld
handhold
hardhack
hardhead
hatchery
hatching
hatchway
hawthorn
heathery
heathhen
heighten
hellhole
henchman
hidyhole
hogshead
hotchpot
hulahula
hushhush
ianthine
insphere
Irishism
Irishman
isocheim
isophote
isothere
isotherm
jolthead
keelhaul
keeshond
kerchief
kinghood
klephtic
kneehigh
kneehole
knightly
knothole
krumhorn
ladyhood
lanthorn
latchkey
laughing
laughter
layshaft
leathern
leathery
lefthand
linchpin
loathful
loathing
longhair
longhand
longhorn
loophole
luncheon
lymphoid
lymphoma
lynchpin
lyophile
maidhood
marchesa
marchese
marshman
masthead
matchbox
merchant
midships
millhand
mirthful
mischief
misshape
misthink
molehill
MonKhmer
monkhood
morpheme
morphine
mouthful
murrhine
mutchkin
narghile
neatherd
neophyte
newsheet
Noachian
nonwhite
northern
northing
Northman
notching
nutshell
nymphean
offshoot
offshore
oliphant
omadhaum
omophagy
onychite
outshine
outshone
overhand
overhang
overhaul
overhead
overhear
overheat
overhung
pamphlet
pantheon
Parthian
patchily
payphone
paysheet
peephole
penchant
pilchard
pinchers
pinwheel
plethora
plighted
porphyry
porthole
posthorn
potsherd
prophase
prophecy
prophesy
psychics
psychism
psychist
puncheon
purchase
pyrrhoea
pyrrhous
Quechuan
railhead
rakehell
ranchero
ranchman
redshank
redshift
redshirt
rhythmic
rockhewn
roothold
roughage
roughdry
roughhew
roughish
rushhour
samphire
sapphics
sapphire
sapphism
scaphoid
scathing
seachest
seashell
seashore
selfheal
selfhelp
selfhood
serfhood
shashlik
shepherd
shoehorn
shothole
sidehead
silphium
sinkhole
skinhead
slagheap
slashing
slightly
slithery
slothful
smashing
smithers
smithery
smothery
softhead
soothing
soothsay
sorehead
souchong
southern
southing
southpaw
Southron
spathose
staghorn
stanhope
subahdar
subphyla
subshrub
sulphate
sulphide
sulphite
sulphone
sunshade
sunshine
sunshiny
swanherd
sylphide
sylphine
sylphish
symphile
symphony
takehome
teachest
teaching
teething
tetchily
texthand
tomahawk
toothful
toothily
toothing
torchere
touchily
touching
toughish
townhall
tracheae
tracheal
tracheid
trachoma
trachyte
trashery
trashily
trephine
trichina
trichite
trichoid
trichome
trichord
trochaic
trochili
trochlea
trochoid
trophied
truthful
typehigh
Tyrrhene
urethane
urochord
warwhoop
watchdog
watchful
watchkey
watchman
watthour
wellhead
Welshman
wifehood
wirehair
witchelm
witchery
witchety
witching
withheld
withhold
wormhole
worthful
worthily
wrathful
wrathily
xanthate
xanthein
xanthene
xanthine
xanthium
xanthoma
youthful
zecchini
zecchino
zoophily
zoophyte
zucchini
abscissa
abutilon
aconitic
aconitum
acreinch
Adamical
adamitic
adenitis
adroitly
aestival
affright
aggrieve
agonised
aiguille
airfield
airliner
airtight
alewives
allnight
alogical
American
amphibia
amphipod
Anglican
aperient
aperitif
apomixis
applique
archival
archives
atomiser
attrited
atypical
auspices
bagpiper
ballista
bambinos
banditry
banditti
barbican
barbital
bartizan
bassinet
bastille
bauxitic
bearings
beatific
befriend
beguiler
berliner
besmirch
bestiary
biblical
billiard
biocidal
bobbinet
boutique
braziery
breviary
bromidic
bunfight
bursitis
cabriole
caesious
calcific
calcitic
calliope
calliper
canaille
candidly
cannibal
cannikin
canticle
caprifig
capriole
capsicum
captious
cardigan
cardinal
carnival
carriage
carriole
castiron
caudices
caudillo
cautious
cervical
cervices
chapiter
charisma
chemical
chenille
chiliasm
chiliast
choriamb
chorioid
churinga
cirriped
clarinet
clavicle
clerical
clerihew
clinical
codpiece
codriver
colliery
combings
compiler
confider
confiner
confines
conniver
conoidal
consider
continua
continue
continuo
convince
coolibah
corniced
corniche
cornicle
cornific
corridor
corrival
cortical
cortices
cosmical
coulisse
cousinly
craniate
credible
credibly
credited
creditor
crepitus
criminal
critical
critique
cruciate
crucible
crucifer
crucifix
cuboidal
cultivar
curlicue
curricle
cushiony
Cushitic
cuspidor
cyclical
Cypriote
cystitis
czaritza
daylight
deceiver
denticle
deprival
deprived
derriere
despiser
detailed
detainee
detainer
detrital
detritus
diggings
dioritic
disciple
dispirit
distinct
dogfight
dogtired
dulciana
dulcimer
Dulcinea
dundiver
earnings
earpiece
edacious
educible
eldritch
eligible
eligibly
emaciate
emeritus
emetical
empoison
enceinte
enclitic
encrinal
encrinic
enquirer
entailer
eremitic
erodible
erotical
Esquimau
esurient
ethnical
eucritic
examinee
examiner
exigible
eximious
explicit
exuviate
eyeliner
eyepiece
eyesight
fabliaux
factious
fallible
fallibly
fanciful
fanlight
farcical
farriery
fascicle
fasciola
fasciole
Fascista
Fascisti
fashious
feasible
feasibly
febrific
felsitic
fencible
ferriage
ferritic
fervidly
festival
fibrilla
fiftieth
fissiped
fistiana
fistical
flamingo
flatiron
flexible
flexibly
floridly
florigen
flotilla
foetidly
follicle
forcible
forcibly
forgiven
fornices
fortieth
fremitus
frigidly
frutices
fungible
furriery
gainings
galliard
Gallican
gallipot
garlicky
garrison
gasfired
gaslight
gastight
gerbille
germinal
gimmicky
gingival
glaciate
gladioli
glaziery
gloriole
glorious
gloxinia
glucinum
golliwog
gossiper
gossipry
gracioso
gracious
gradient
granitic
graviton
gridiron
guerilla
gullible
gunfight
halliard
handicap
harridan
hastings
Hawaiian
hawfinch
hayfield
helminth

heroical
hetairai
hirrient
hobbitry
hooligan
horrible
horribly
horridly
horrific
hospital
hustings
hyacinth
icefield
idoliser
illtimed
imaginal
imagines
implicit
imprimis
imprison
inedible
inedited
inflight
infringe
inguinal
inimical
initiate
inositol
inquirer
inscient
inspired
inspirer
inspirit
instinct
intrigue
inveigle
irenical
irenicon
ironical
isodicon
Italiote
jerrican
jesuitic
jesuitry
jettison
jiujitsu
Judaical
Judaiser
Kaffiyeh
khedival
lacrimal
larrikin
lashings
latticed
lawgiver
leavings
leggings
lenticel
lenticle
leucitic
lignitic
limpidly
liquidly
lodgings
lollipop
lopsided
lubrical
luscious
machismo
mackinaw
madrigal
magnific
manciple
mandible
Mandingo
mannikin
mannitol
mansized
mantilla

mantissa
marginal
marriage
marrieds
martinet
marzipan
massicot
mastitis
matrices
matrixes
mephitic
mephitis
merciful
methinks
metrical
midfield
midnight
midwives
milliard
milliary
millibar
millieme
milliner
miscible
misgiven
missilry
mittimus
monsieur
moorings
morainic
morbidly
morbific
mornings
multifid
multiped
multiple
multiply
muslined
myelinic
myelitis
myositic
myositis
myrmidon
mystical
mystique
mythical
narcissi
nautical
nautilus
negligee
Negrillo
nescient
neuritic
neuritis
nonrigid
nuclidic
nuptials
nutrient
obedient
obtainer
offsider
ofttimes
oilfield
oilfired
oldtimer
onepiece
onesided
orchilla
ordainer
original
orthicon
osteitis
outfield
outrider
outright
outrival
outsider
outsight
ovariole

ovaritis
oxidiser
ozoniser
palliate
pallidly
palmiped
palmitin
panmixia
pannikin
panpipes
Parsiism
partible
particle
partisan
partizan
passible
pastiche
pastille
pectines
peelings
pellicle
pemmican
pendicle
perlitic
pervious
pettifog
pharisee
phthisic
phthisis
physical
physicky
physique
pianiste
pickings
picnicky
pinniped
piscinae
pitviper
placidly
plagiary
platinic
platinum
plumiped
pluvious
poetical
pollices
pollinia
pollinic
polliwog
pontifex
porridge
porticos
portiere
possible
possibly
postiche
pratique
precinct
precious
premiere
presidio
previous
prodigal
profiler
prohibit
prolific
prolixly
promisee
promiser
promisor
protista
provided
provider
province
provisor
proximal
prurient
pruritic
pruritus

publican
publicly
pulpiter
pulvilli
pulvinus
punditry
putridly
pyelitis
quotient
rabbinic
rabbiter
rabbitry
rachides
rachitic
rachitis
receiver
rejoicer
reorient
repairer
reprieve
reprisal
requital
requiter
retailer
retainer
retrieve
reveille
rhinitis
rinsings
rocaille
rubbishy
rubrical
runcible
rustical
sacristy
salvific
scabious
scarious
scenical
scilicet
scimitar
scolices
seapiece
sennight
sensible
sensibly
sentient
sentinel
septimal
servient
servitor
Shekinah
Shemitic
siftings
Sinaitic
sinciput
sixtieth
skylight
skypilot
sobriety
soldiery
somnific
sordidly
spacious
spadices
spadille
Spaniard
spavined
speciate
specific
specimen
specious
spinifex
spirilla
spirited
spiritus
spoliate
spraints
spurious

staminal
stasimon
statical
sterigma
stipites
stolidly
straight
strained
strainer
straiten
straitly
studious
stupidly
stylised
subtitle
succinct
succinic
succinum
suicidal
suitings
summitry
sunlight
surgical
surmisal
surmiser
survival
survivor
syenitic
symbiont
syndical
syphilis
tachisme
tachiste
tactical
taenioid
tailings
tangible
tangibly
tenaille
tensible
terminal
terminer
terminus
terrible
terribly
terrific
tertiary
thetical
thurible
thurifer
tinnitus
toepiece
topliner
toroidal
torpidly
torridly
tortilla
tortious
touristy
traditor
tragical
tritical
tropical
tsaritsa
tsaritza
turbidly
turbinal
turgidly
turnings
twilight
twopiece
twosided
twotimer
umptieth
unbridle
unclinch
uncoined
unedited
unfairly

ungainly
unifilar
unpaired
unsuited
unvoiced
uralitic
usurious
utiliser
uvulitis
uxorious
vaccinal
vaccinia
vampiric
vendible
verbiage
verditer
vernicle
versicle
vertical
vertices
verticil
vespiary
vestiary
viaticum
vibrissa
vincible
virginal
Virginia
viscidly
vortical
vortices
warrigal
waxlight
weariful
weeviled
weevilly
williwaw
winnings
workings
writings
Xantippe
zabaione
zeolitic
zombiism
bootjack
demijohn
flapjack
frabjous
highjack
jipijapa
kneejerk
overjump
readjust
skipjack
slapjack
blackboy
blackcap
blackfly
blacking
blackish
blackleg
blackout
blacktie
blacktop
blankety
bleakish
blinkers
blinking
blockade
blockage
blockish
brackish
breakage
breaking
breakout
brickbat
brickred
briskish
brookite

brooklet
chalkpit
checkers
checkout
cheekily
chickpea
clerkdom
clerkess
clinking
crackers
cracking
crackjaw
cracknel
crackpot
crankily
crankpin
creakily
croakily
crockery
doorknob
drinking
dropkick
drunkard
durukuli
flickery
flockbed
foreknew
foreknow
Frankish
franklin
freakish
freakout
friskily
frocking
goalkick
harakiri
harikari
iceskate
kamikaze
katakana
khuskhus
knackery
knickers
knocking
knockout
limekiln
lockknit
lorikeet
loveknot
numskull
overkill
parakeet
planking
plankton
pluckily
prankful
prankish
quackery
quackish
quickset
quirkily
reefknot
rewaking
Sanskrit
sheikdom
shocking
sidekick
slinkily
slipknot
smocking
snackbar
sneakily
sneakish
spanking
sparkgap
sparkish
sparkler
sparklet
speaking

spicknel
spookily
spookish
spunkily
starkers
stickful
stickily
stickjaw
stickler
stinkard
stinking
stinkpot
stockade
stockcar
stockily
stocking
stockish
stockist
stockman
stockpot
striking
swanking
thankful
thankyou
thickety
thickish
thickset
thinking
trackage
tracking
trackman
trackway
trekking
trickery
trickily
trickish
triskele
truckage
trucking
truckler
twinkler
unlikely
velskoen
waleknot
wallknot
wellknit
whacking
whiskers
whiskery
wrackful
wreckage
zinckify
zincking
absolute
absolver
accolade
acrolein
acrolith
acrylate
aerolite
aerolith
aerology
agrology
algology
alkalies
alkalify
alkaline
alkaloid
alleluia
ambulant
ambulate
ampullae
anaglyph
angelica
ankylose
annalist
annulate
annulled
antelope

antilogy
anyplace
aphelion
apoplexy
appalled
aqualung
aquiline
arbalest
arbalist
areolate
arillate
atheling
aurelian
autolyse
axiality
axillary
axiology
bacillar
bacillus
backlash
backless
backlist
balkline
banality
bantling
barkless
basaltic
baseless
baseline
basilica
basilisk
bateleur
battleax
bdellium
beagling
becalmed
bedplate
beetling
befallen
beholden
beholder
beltless
bevelled
beveller
bewilder
bibulous
bioplasm
bioplast
birdlime
bivalent
blowlamp
boatload
bobolink
bodiless
boneless
bookland
booklice
booklore
bootlace
bootlast
bootless
botflies
botulism
bouillon
boxpleat
brimless
brisling
bryology
bubaline
buckling
buddleia
bundling
buntline
burglary
bustling
butylene
cabalism
cabalist
caballed
cacology
cageling
cajolery
cameleer
camellia
canalise
capeline
capellet
careless
carillon
Carolean
Caroline
carolled
cartload
catalase
cataloes
catalyse
catalyst
cattleya
cavalier
cavilled
caviller
cerulean
chaplain
charlady
charlock
Chellean
chinless
churlish
civilian
civilise
civility
clubland
clueless
cobaltic
cobblers
cochleae
cochlear
cockloft
complain
compleat
complete
complice
complier
compline
conclave
conclude
conflate
conflict
conglobe
contline
copulate
cordless
corelate
cotillon
coupling
covalent
coxalgia
cradling
cromlech
crueller
cryolite
cumulate
cumulous
cupelled
cupulate
cureless
Cyrillic
cytology
darkling
dateless
dateline
deadline
deadlock
debility
decolour
deedless
deeplaid
defilade
demolish
depilate
derelict
desolate
deviling
devilish
devilism
devilkin
devilled
deviltry
diallage
dialling
disallow
disclaim
disclose
displace
displant
displode
displume
divalent
djellaba
docilely
docility
dockland
doubloon
dowelled
downland
doxology
dragline
drilling
drollery
dropleaf
dryclean
dryplate
duckling
ductless
duelling
duellist
dumpling
dustless
dustlike
dwelling
echoless
edgeless
eggplant
embalmer
embolden
embolism
enfilade
enrolled
ensilage
entellus
envelope
epiblast
epyllion
equalise
equality
equalled
escalade
escalate
escallop
escalope
esculent
espalier
ethology
ethylene
etiolate
eucalypt
excelled
exhalant
expelled
expellee
extolled
eyeglass
fabulist
fabulous
faceless
facelift
facilely
facility
fadeless
fairlead
familial
familiar
fangless
farflung
farmland
fatalism
fatalist
fatality
fearless
feckless
feculent
feeblish
fiddling
fidelity
finalise
finalism
finalist
finality
firelock
fishless
flatling
flawless
fluellin
flyblown
foamless
focalise
folklore
fondling
foodless
footless
footling
forelady
foreland
forelock
forklift
formless
fourleaf
foxglove
Fraulein
freeload
frillies
fuelling
fuselage
fusileer
fusilier
futilely
futility
gainless
Galilean
gangland
gangling
ganglion
gantline
gantlope
gaselier
gasolene
gasolier
gasoline
Gaullism
Gaullist
gavelock
ghoulish
goalline
goatling
Gobelins
goldleaf
gormless
gralloch
grayling
grillage
growling
gunflint
hairless
hairlike
hairline
halflife
hamululi
handless
handline
handling
handlist
handloom
hardline
harmless
havelock
havildar
hawklike
hazelnut
headlamp
headland
headless
headline
headlock
headlong
heedless
heelless
Hegelian
heirless
heirloom
helpless
heraldic
heraldry
herbless
hexylene
highland
highlows
hindlegs
hipflask
hireling
homeland
homeless
homelike
homology
hopeless
hornless
horologe
horology
hotelier
hotplate
hourlong
humility
hurtless
iceblink
iceplant
idealess
idealise
idealism
idealist
ideality
ideology
idiolect
idyllist
immolate
impelled
impeller
impolder
impolicy
impolite
indolent
indulger
induline
infilter
inhalant
insolate
insolent
insulant
insulate
insulter
involute
isogloss
isopleth
jetblack
jetplane
jewelled
jeweller
jongleur
jubilant
jubilate
jugglery
jugulate
keelless
kidglove
kindless
kindling
kinglike
labelled
labellum
lability
ladylike
ladylove
lakeland
lamblike
lamellae
lamellar
landlady
landless
landline
landlord
langlauf
lapelled
lavalava
lazulite
leadless
leafless
leaflike
legalese
legalise
legalism
legalist
legality
lensless
levelled
leveller
levulose
libelled
libellee
libeller
lifeless
lifelike
lifeline
lifelong
ligulate
limbless
linoleum
listless
littlego
littling
livelily
livelong
loadline
lobeline
lobulate
localise
localism
locality
loculate
lordless
lordling
loveless
lovelily
lovelock
lovelorn
loyalist
luckless
luculent
Lucullan
lunulate
maculate
mainland
mainline
maiolica
majolica
Mameluke
mamillae
mamillar
mantling
marbling
massless
matelote
maxillae
medalled
medallic
megalith
menology
metalled
metallic
micellar
middling
mindless
misalign
misology
misplace
mobilise
mobility
modalism
modalist
modality
modelled
modeller
modulate
molality
monolith
moonless
moorland
moralise
moralism
moralist
morality
motility
mottling
moveless
mucilage
muckluck
muscling
mutilate
mycelial
mycelium
mycology
myoblast
nameless
napoleon
nasalise
nasality
natality
nathless
nauplius
nebulise
nebulium
nebulous
necklace
neckline
needless
neoplasm
Nepalese
nestling
newblown
nielloed
niggling
nihilism
nihilist
nihility
nobelium
nobility
nodalise
nodality
nodulose
nodulous
nomology
nonclaim
nosology
noteless
novelise
novelist
nubility
nubilous
nucellus
nursling
obsolete
occultly
ocellate
oecology
oeillade
oenology
oilcloth
omoplate
oncology
ontology
oppilate
oreology
orgulous
osculant
osculate
outclass
outflank
overlaid
overlain
overland
overleaf
overleap
overload
overlong
overlook
overlord
painless
panelled
papalise
papalism
papalist
papillae
papillar
papillon
papulose
papulous
parallax
parallel
paralyse
parclose
parkland
patellae
patellar
pathless
patulous
pavilion
pearlies
pearling
pearlite
peculate
peculiar
pedalier
pedalled
pedology
peerless
penalise
penology
perilled
perilous
perilune
petaline
petalled
petalody
petaloid
petalous
petulant
phyllary
phyllode
phylloid
phyllome
picklock
piddling
piffling
pipeline
pisolite

pitiless
pomology
populace
populate
populism
populist
populous
porkling
posology
postlude
potplant
preclude
preelect
proclaim
ptyalism
pugilism
pugilist
pupilage
pupilary
pupillar
purblind
purfling
purplish
purslane
purulent
quillpen
quisling
raillery
rambling
rattling
ravelled
rearlamp
rebelled
rebeller
rebellow
reckless
redblind
redeless
redolent
reedling
regalism
regality
regelate
regolith
regulate
reinless
repelled
repeller
resolute
restless
revelled
reveller
reviling
revolter
revolute
revolver
rheology
rhyolite
ribaldry
Riesling
rivalled
rivelled
roadless
rocklike
rockling
roodloft
roofless
rootless
roseleaf
rosulate
royalism
royalist
rugulose
ruleless
ruralise
ruralism
ruralist
rurality
rushlike

rustless
ruthless
rutilant
sackless
saddlery
sailless
saltless
saltlick
sampling
sateless
scallion
scarless
schiller
scholium
sciolism
sciolist
scullery
scullion
seafloor
seamless
seaplane
sedulity
sedulous
seedleaf
seedless
seedling
seedlobe
selfless
selflove
semolina
semplice
senility
sepaloid
sepalous
serology
sewellel
sexology
shalloon
shallows
shealing
sherlock
Shetland
shielder
shieling
shilling
shipload
shoelace
shoeless
shoulder
shouldst
sibilant
sibilate
Sicilian
sicklist
sideline
sideling
sidelong
similise
simplify
simplism
simulant
simulate
sinology
sitology
sizzling
skilless
skilling
skinless
skislope
skullcap
slobland
smallage
smallfry
smallish
smallpox
smelling
smoulder
snaplink
snowless

snowlike
snowline
soapless
socalled
sodalite
sodality
soilless
songless
soulless
sparling
spelling
spillage
spillway
spoilage
spotless
spurling
spyglass
squaller
squelchy
squilgee
stabling
stablish
stallage
stallfed
stalling
stallion
starless
starlike
starling
staylace
stealing
stealthy
stellate
stellify
stellion
stemless
sterling
stillage
stroller
subclass
subfloor
subtlety
subulate
suchlike
suckling
sunblind
supplant
supplely
supplial
supplier
supplies
surplice
swanlike
swelling
syncline
tabulate
tackling
tactless
tagalong
tailless
tameless
Tamilian
tapeless
tapelike
tapeline
teacloth
tearless
template
termless
thallium
thalloid
thallous
theology
thirlage
thraldom
thriller
ticklish
tideland
tideless

tidelock
timeless
tinplate
tintless
tireless
tocology
toeplate
tokology
tomalley
tombless
tonality
toneless
topology
totalise
totality
totalled
towelled
trailnet
tramline
trawlnet
treeless
trialist
trifling
triglyph
trilling
trillion
trillium
triplane
triploid
troilite
trollopy
truelove
tubeless
tubulate
tumbling
tuneless
turtling
tutelage
tutelary
twinling
typology
Tyrolean
unbelief
unbolted
uncalled
undulant
undulate
unfilial
ungulate
unvalued
upholder
Ursuline
vagility
vamplate
vaneless
vanillin
veilless
venality
ventless
vexillum
viewless
vigilant
virilism
virility
virology
virulent
vitalise
vitalism
vitalist
vitality
vitellin
vitellus
vitiligo
vituline
vocalise
vocalism
vocalist
vocality
volplane

voteless
vowelise
vowelled
wakeless
warcloud
warplane
waveless
waxcloth
weakling
weanling
weedless
weeklong
wheelman
whiplash
whiplike
wifeless
wifelike
wildlife
windlass
windless
wingless
wireless
woodland
woodlark
woodlice
woollens
wordless
workless
wormlike
xenolith
xylology
yeanling
yearling
yearlong
yodelled
yodeller
zibeline
zymology
abelmosk
abetment
abutment
acosmism
acrimony
aglimmer
agrement
agrimony
alarmist
antimask
antimony
argument
armament
assemble
assembly
assuming
atremble
automata
automate
autumnal
averment
backmost
bailment
basement
becoming
bedimmed
behemoth
bigamist
bigamous
binomial
bloomers
bloomery
blooming
bodement
bohemian
bondmaid
bondmans
bonemeal
bookmark
bregmata
brimming

cacomixl
calamary
calamine
calamint
calamite
calamity
camomile
casemate
casement
cashmere
catamite
ceramics
ceramist
cerement
ceremony
charming
chipmuck
chipmunk
chromate
chromite
chromium
chummily
chumming
claimant
clammily
clamming
claymore
coalmine
columnal
columnar
columned
costmary
cramming
creamery
crummock
cucumber
deafmute
December
decemvir
decimate
didymium
didymous
digamist
digamous
diriment
document
dolomite
downmost
drammock
dreamful
dreamily
dreaming
drumming
drummock
dynamics
dynamism
dynamist
dynamite
easement
eastmost
encomion
encomium
encumber
endamage
endemism
enormity
enormous
ensample
ensemble
ephemera
Eskimoan
estimate
evermore
filament
fishmeal
flatmate
flummery
folkmoot
footmark

footmuff
foramina
foremast
foremost
fragment
Ganymede
gloaming
gloomily
glummest
goatmoth
goldmine
gourmand
grimmest
gunsmith
halfmast
halfmoon
hallmark
handmade
handmaid
handmill
hawkmoth
headmost
hegemony
helpmate
helpmeet
highmost
hindmost
homemade
ignominy
illumine
inasmuch
inchmeal
incoming
infamise
infamous
inhumane
insomnia
insomuch
intimacy
intimate
intimism
Islamise
Islamism
Islamite
isthmian
jeremiad
Jeremiah
judgment
kakemono
Kashmiri
landmark
landmass
landmine
ligament
liniment
lipomata
locomote
lodgment
mainmast
makimono
malamute
malemute
matamata
maximise
mazement
melamine
messmate
metamere
miasmata
miasmous
milkmaid
minimise
mintmark
mishmash
monomial
monument
mortmain
movement
muniment

myxomata
needment
November
ointment
oncoming
oogamous
opsimath
optimise
optimism
optimist
ornament
orpiment
outsmart
overmuch
pallmall
palomino
paramour
pavement
pearmain
pediment
pellmell
penumbra
pharmacy
phormium
piedmont
playmate
pockmark
polemics
polemise
polemist
polymath
postmark
postmill
preamble
primming
prismoid
proemial
psalmist
psalmody
quagmire
qualmish
racemate
racemise
racemose
rearmice
rearmost
recommit
reedmace
regiment
relumine
remember
renumber
reremice
resemble
ringmain
roommate
rosemary
rudiment
sagamore
saltmine
scammony
schemata
scheming
scramble
scrammed
scumming
sediment
selfmade
selfmate
sesamoid
shamming
shimmery
shipmate
shipment
shrimper
skimmilk
skimming
skirmish
slamming

slimmest
slimming
slimmish
slumming
smarmily
sodomite
solemnly
spermary
squamate
squamose
squamous
squamule
steamily
stemmata
stemming
stigmata
stormily
stramash
stromata
strummed
strummer
strumose
strumous
strumpet
stumming
subimago
swanmark
swimming
sycamine
sycamore
sycomore
teammate
tegument
telemark
tenement
thermion
thermite
thiamine
thrombin
thrombus
thrummed
tidemark
tidemill
tinsmith
totemism
totemist
trammels
traumata
trimming
triumvir
ultimacy
ultimata
ultimate
uncommon
unlimber
untimely
vehement
velamina
venomous
vestment
Vietminh
virement
weldment
windmill
workmate
yokemate
aborning
absentee
absently
absinthe
absonant
accentor
achenial
achiness
achingly
actiniae
actinian
actinias
actinide
actinism
actinium
addendum
adiantum
admonish
advanced
aeronaut
aeronomy
affinity
agedness
agronomy
airiness
Albanian
albinism
alginate
Algonkin
alienage
alienate
alienism
alienist
almanack
alpinism
alpinist
amiantus
ammoniac
ammonify
ammonite
ammonium
antennae
antennal
antennas
antinode
antinomy
appanage
appendix
aquanaut
archness
ardently
argentic
argonaut
Arianism
Armenian
Arminian
arranger
arrantly
arsenate
arsenide
arsenite
arsonist
arsonous
ascender
assenter
assentor
assonant
assonate
astonied
astonish
Athenian
atlantes
Atlantic
attender
autonomy
autunite
avidness
avionics
Baconian
badinage
balanced
balancer
baldness
Balinese
banknote
bareness
baronage
baroness
baronial
baseness
basinful
beginner
bezonian
biannual
biconvex
biennial
biennium
bimanous
bitingly
blueness
bluenose
boldness
boniness
boringly
botanise
botanist
brainish
brainpan
browning
brownish
business
busyness
Byronism
cabinboy
cadenced
caginess
calendar
calender
calmness
canoness
canonise
canonist
caponier
caponise
carinate
caruncle
Casanova
catenary
catenate
chainsaw
chaunter
chauntry
churning
clannish
cleancut
cleaning
cleanser
clownery
clownish
cogently
colander
coldness
colonial
colonise
colonist
coolness
coronach
coronary
coronoid
corundum
cosiness
cotenant
covenant
cozenage
crannied
culinary
curtness
cuteness
cylinder
Cyrenaic
daftness
dampness
dankness
daringly
darkness
deadness
deafness
dearness
debonair
decanter
decennia
decently
deepness
defender
definite
deftness
deionise
demander
demented
dementia
demoness
demoniac
demonian
demonise
demonism
deponent
detonate
Devonian
dewiness
diagnose
diminish
disendow
disinter
disunion
disunite
disunity
divinely
divinise
divinity
dominant
dominate
domineer
dominion
dominoes
doornail
dopiness
dotingly
douanier
dourness
doziness
drabness
drainage
drownded
dullness
dumbness
dyspnoea
easiness
echinate
echinoid
edginess
eeriness
Emmental
endanger
engender
engineer
enginery
enkindle
entangle
equinity
errantly
errantry
Essenism
essonite
Estonian
eternise
eternity
eugenics
eugenism
eugenist
evenness
evilness
expander
exponent
extender
extensor
fairness
farinose
fastness
favonian
felinity
fellness
feminine
feminise
feminism
feminist
feminity
fineness
firmness
flatness
flounder
fluently
fomenter
fondness
footnote
forename
forenoon
forensic
foulness
foxiness
fraenula
freeness
friendly
fullness
furuncle
galangal
Galenism
galenite
gameness
gaminess
gapingly
geminate
geognosy
geraniol
geranium
gerontic
gigantic
gladness
gleaning
glibness
glumness
goodness
graining
greenery
greenfly
greening
greenish
greenlet
greyness
grimness
grinning
grounder
guernsey
gynandry
habanera
haleness
halfnote
hangnail
harangue
hardness
haziness
headnote
hedonics
hedonism
hedonist
highness
holiness
hominoid
homonymy
homuncle
hugeness
humanely
humanise
humanism
humanist
humanity
humanoid
humuncle
hymenial
hymenium
Ibsenism
idleness
ilmenite
immanent
imminent
immingle
immunise
immunity
impanate
imponent
impunity
infantry
infinite
infinity
inkiness
inlander
insanely
insanity
intended
intently
intonate
inventor
iodinate
islander
Japanese
japanned
japonica
Javanese
jejunely
jocundly
jokingly
justness
juvenile
keenness
kindness
Kohinoor
kolinsky
laconian
laconism
lacunary
lacunate
lacunose
lameness
lamented
laminate
lankness
larynges
larynxes
lateness
latently
Latinate
latinise
Latinism
Latinist
latinity
lavender
laziness
leanness
learning
legendry
lemonade
Leninism
Leninist
Leninite
levanter
lewdness
licensed
licensee
licenser
likeness
limonite
limpness
lomentum
loneness
longness
loudness
lovenest
lovingly
luminant
luminary
luminist
luminous
lushness
lutanist
lutenist
maleness
malinger
marinade
marinate
matiness
maziness
meanness
meconium
meekness
meetness
melanism
melanite
melinite
mementos
meninges
meringue
metonymy
mildness
Mishnaic
Molinism
Molinist
momently
momentum
monandry
mournful
mourning
movingly
muchness
musingly
muteness
mutineer
mutinous
mylonite
nearness
neatness
nepenthe
niceness
nicknack
nickname
nominate
nonunion
nosiness
nudeness
nullness
numbness
numinous
octonary
offender
oiliness
oleander
oogonial
oogonium
ooziness
openness
opponent
ordinand
ordinary
ordinate
organdie
organise
organism
organist
oriental
oriented
oscinine
ostinato
ovalness
overnice
oxtongue
paganise
paganish
paganism
paginate
paleness
palinode
paranoia
paranoid
parental
patentee
patently
patentor
pedantic
pedantry
peduncle
peignoir
Pekinese
penknife
perineal
perineum
peroneal
pertness
petuntse
pinkness
pixiness
planning
pleinair
pleonasm
pliantly
poignant
polonium
pomander
poorness
popinjay
potently
pregnant
primness
pruinose
pryingly
puniness
pureness
pyrenoid
quaintly
queendom
queening
queenlet
quidnunc
raciness
ramentum
rankness
raptness
rareness
rashness
ravenous
realness
recently
reconvey
refinery
rehandle
reignite
rekindle
remanent
reminder
repenter
resinate
resinify
resinoid
resinous
resonant
resonate
retinula
revanche
revenant
revenger
richness
rifeness
ringneck
ripeness
rollneck
romancer
Romanian
romanise
Romanism

Romanist
Romansch
romantic
ropiness
rosiness
rotenone
rotundly
rudeness
Rumanian
Rumansch
ruminant
ruminate
safeness
sageness
saginate
salinity
saltness
sameness
saneness
saponify
saponite
satanism
satanist
savannah
Saxondom
Saxonism
Saxonist
sayonara
scanning
scornful
scrannel
seaonion
seasnail
seasnake
seconder
secondly
seigneur
seignior
seignory
selenate
selenide
selenite
selenium
selfness
semantic
seminary
seminude
serenade
serenata
serenely
serenity
sexiness
shinning
shrinker
shrunken
shunning
sickness
sidenote
silencer
silently
simoniac
simonist
sirenian
skewness
skinning
slimness
slowness
smugness
snugness
Socinian
softness
solander
solanine
soleness
solenoid
soreness
sourness
spanning
sphenoid
sphingid
spinning
splendid
splenial
splenius
splinter
spoonfed
spoonful
spoonily
springal
springer
sprinkle
sprinter
spryness
squander
squinter
stagnant
stagnate
stannary
stannate
stannite
stannous
steenbok
steening
steinbok
sternite
sternson
sternway
stibnite
stranded
stranger
strangle
strength
stringed
stringer
strongly
strontia
stubnail
stunning
Sudanese
supinate
supinely
sureness
swainish
swanneck
swannery
swanning
syconium
synonymy
syringes
syrinxes
takingly
talented
tallness
tamandua
tamanoir
tameness
tartness
tautness
taxingly
taxonomy
technics
tenantry
tenonsaw
tetanise
thinness
thinnest
thinning
thinnish
thisness
threnode
threnody
thusness
tidiness
tininess
titanate
titaness
titanism
titanite
titanium
tokenism
tomentum
toponymy
tournure
training
treenail
triangle
triennia
trimness
triunity
truantry
trueness
trunnion
tryingly
Turanian
twinning
tyrannic
ugliness
umbonate
uncandid
uncinate
unfunded
unhinged
unionise
unionism
unionist
unkennel
unkindly
unkingly
unlinked
unmanned
unpinned
unsunned
untangle
untented
unwanted
unwonted
uplander
urbanely
urbanise
urbanism
urbanist
urbanite
urbanity
urgently
vacantly
vainness
valanced
vastness
Vedantic
verandah
veronica
vicinage
vicinity
Viennese
vileness
vixenish
voidness
wagonage
wagonlit
wakening
wariness
warmness
waviness
waxiness
weakness
wellnigh
whatness
wideness
wildness
wiliness
wiriness
wiseness
womanise
womanish
woodnote
xylonite
yearning
zamindar
zaniness
zemindar
aasvogel
acidosis
adenoids
aegrotat
airborne
airwoman
alehouse
allround
although
alveolar
alveolus
ambrosia
amitosis
amitotic
amniotic
amphorae
amphoras
anabolic
anaconda
anagogic
analogic
analogue
anatomic
anchoret
androgen
aniconic
anthozoa
antrorse
apagogic
apodoses
apodosis
apologia
apologue
approach
approval
asphodel
ballonet
balmoral
banjoist
baryonic
bathotic
benzoate
bespoken
bestowal
bignonia
biomorph
bionomic
bistoury
blazoner
blazonry
bonhomie
borrower
bottomry
bouzouki
bullocky
buncombe
burgonet
burnouse
burrower
buttoner
caboodle
cannonry
canoodle
cantonal
cantoris
canzonet
carbolic
carbonic
carbonyl
carboxyl
cartouch
cathodal
cathodic
catholic
cationic
chaconne
Cherokee
chthonic
coelomic
coenobia
cognomen
cognosce
cognovit
collogue
colloquy
commoner
commoney
commonly
composed
composer
compound
confound
conjoint
consoler
consomme
contorno
convolve
cordovan
corporal
cramoisy
cretonne
crocoite
cromorna
cromorne
cupboard
customer
cyanogen
cyanoses
cyanosis
cyanotic
cyclonic
cyclopes
cyclosis
daemonic
daffodil
daimonic
deflower
despotic
dewpoint
diabolic
diaconal
diagonal
dialogic
dialogue
diatomic
diatonic
dicrotic
diplogen
diploidy
diplomat
diplopia
dipnoous
disbound
discount
discover
disgorge
disjoint
dislodge
disloyal
dismount
disposal
disposer
dissolve
doctoral
doghouse
dogooder
dogtooth
dormouse
draconic
dragoman
dragomen
dragonet
drypoint
Dukhobor
dumfound
duologue
dystopia
ecologic
economic
eftsoons
elflocks
elkhound
empeople
employee
employer
enclothe
encroach
ensconce
enzootic
epicotyl
epilogue
episodal
episodic
epopoeia
Ethiopic
euphonic
euphoria
euphoric
eutrophy
exploder
explorer
extrorse
eyetooth
factotum
falconer
falconet
falconry
faubourg
fellowly
fibrosis
fibrotic
fireopal
fogbound
follower
followon
followup
forborne
fordoing
forgoing
forsooth
foveolae
foxhound
frijoles
furlough
gadzooks
galloper
Galloway
garboard
gargoyle
garrotte
gashouse
gasworks
geologic
geoponic
glycogen
glyconic
gnomonic
Golconda
gorgonia
grimoire
gummosis
gunpoint
hadronic
haliotis
hallowed
hangover
haploidy
harlotry
harmonic
hebdomad
heliosis
henroost
hiccough
hidrosis
hidrotic
hillocky
histogen
historic
holdover
hollowly
hormonal
hothouse
hummocky
hydrogen
hydromel
hydropic
hydropsy
hydroski
hydroxyl
hypnoses
hypnosis
hypnotic
icebound
improper
improver
inchoate
ingrowth
intromit
introrse
isagogic
isogonal
isogonic
isomorph
isotonic
isotopic
jamboree
jealousy
jingoish
jingoism
jingoist
keyboard
Komsomol
kurtosis
kyphosis
kyphotic
lacrosse
lapboard
larboard
lawcourt
laywoman
leeboard
leftover
legioned
littoral
loblolly
Londoner
lordosis
lordotic
madhouse
madwoman
magnolia
mahjongg
mandolin
mandorla
mangonel
manpower
marjoram
marmoset
mastodon
matronal
matronly
mediocre
mellowly
meteoric
methodic
microbar
microbic
microdot
midpoint
Miltonic
miscount
misdoing
misdoubt
misnomer
mnemonic
Mongolic
mongoose
moreover
motional
mucrones
mulloway
myosotis
myriopod
narcoses
narcosis
narcotic
narrowly
national
necropsy
necrosis
necrotic
negroism
neuronal
neuronic
neuroses
neurosis
neurotic
newcomer
newfound
nitrogen
nonmoral
notional
nuthouse
oldworld
oligomer
onceover
onehorse
onlooker
optional
oratorio
orthodox
orthoepy
outboard
outbound
outdoors
outgoing
outhouse
outmoded
outpoint
outworks
oviposit
oxymoron
oxytocin
pandowdy
pangolin
pansophy
pantofle
pardoner
parrotry
parsonic
Passover
pastoral
pathogen
patronal
peacocky
pectoral
pegboard
perforce
periodic
periotic
personae
personal
petiolar
petioled
petrolic
petronel
petrosal
phenolic
Philomel
photogen
photopia
photopic

photopsy
pinmoney
pinpoint
pishogue
platonic
plutonic
poisoner
porpoise
postobit
potbound
potholer
pothouse
potroast
premolar
premorse
prisoner
profound
prologue
prolonge
promoter
propolis
proposal
proposer
propound
prorogue
prosodic
protocol
protonic
protozoa
psilosis
pteropod
pugnosed
pullover
pulmonic
pushover
pythonic
quixotic
quixotry
randomly
ransomer
rational
rawboned
reasoner
reckoner
rectoral
regional
regrowth
repeople
reproach
reproval
response
restorer
retroact
retrorse
rhetoric
Rhinodon
rhizopod
ribbonry
roseolar
sailorly
santonin
sardonic
sardonyx
sauropod
sawbones
sawhorse
sawtooth
schooner
scirocco
scotopic
seaboard
seaborne
seacoast
seagoing
seaholly
seahorse
seamount
seamouse
seasonal
seasoner
sectoral
selcouth
semiotic
sensoria
shadower
sinfonia
siphonal
siphonet
siphonic
Slavonic
slipover
slyboots
sorrower
spadones
sporozoa
stenosed
stenosis
stenotic
stopover
subjoint
subpoena
subsolar
subsonic
subtonic
subtopia
subtotal
subvocal
summoner
supposal
supposed
surmount
surround
surroyal
symbolic
sympodia
symposia
syncopal
syntonic
systolic
takeover
tamboura
tandoori
tangoist
taphouse
tarboosh
tattooer
tautomer
tautonym
teaboard
teahouse
teatowel
tectonic
teetotal
teetotum
temporal
Teutonic
thorough
thyroxin
titmouse
tolbooth
tomnoddy
toplofty
topnotch
tortoise
tragopan
tricorne
trifocal
triforia
trigonal
trilobed
tripodal
trisomic
turbofan
turbojet
Turcoman
Turkoman
turnover
tussocky
Tychonic
typhonic
unbroken
unclothe
unfrozen
unipolar
unisonal
univocal
unloosen
unroofed
uprooter
vacuolar
variolar
variorum
verboten
vermouth
victoria
viscount
visional
waggoner
walkover
walloper
wallower
wantonly
warhorse
waxworks
waygoing
weaponry
windowed
winnower
wrymouth
yellowly
yoghourt
zealotry
zirconia
zoomorph
zoonosis
abruptly
acarpous
accepter
acceptor
adespota
agitprop
agraphia
airspace
airspeed
allopath
allspice
antepost
antiphon
antipode
antipole
antipope
atropine
backpack
baldpate
beanpole
bebopper
bellpull
bellpush
blimpish
blowpipe
bonspiel
bookpost
bowsprit
calipash
calipers
calyptra
carapace
catapult
cesspool
champers
champion
chapping
cheapish
chipping
chirpily
chopping
clapping
clippers
clipping
clodpole
clodpoll
colophon
conspire
cornpone
coryphee
costplus
costpush
creeping
crispate
cropping
croupier
croupous
decipher
diaspora
diaspore
didapper
doorpost
doumpalm
downpipe
downpour
dripping
dropping
duckpond
dutypaid
ecliptic
ellipses
ellipsis
elliptic
encipher
entoptic
eohippus
equipage
equipped
escapade
escapism
escapist
estopped
estoppel
eupepsia
eupeptic
European
europium
exemplar
exemplum
exospore
facepack
feedpipe
Filipina
Filipino
fireplug
fishpond
flagpole
flapping
flippant
flipping
floppily
flopping
fluepipe
footpace
footpath
footpost
forepart
forepast
forepeak
foreplay
forspeak
forspent
fourpart
fowlpest
frapping
frippery
frumpish
fullpage
gatepost
goalpost
Godspeed
grasping
gripping
grouping
grumpily
Guelphic
halfpint
handpick
heliport
hexapody
hornpipe
hosepipe
inceptor
inexpert
isospory
jodhpurs
knapping
lamppost
liripoop
madapple
malapert
malaprop
mayapple
megapode
metaphor
milepost
millpond
mirepoix
misapply
misspell
misspelt
misspend
misspent
monopode
monopoly
namepart
nenuphar
newspeak
ninepins
nosepipe
oakapple
occupant
occupier
oenophil
olympiad
Olympian
openplan
outspend
outspent
overpaid
overpass
overpast
overplay
overplus
passport
pedipalp
peripety
periplus
perspire
phosphor
plopping
plumpish
polypary
polypide
polypite
polypody
polypoid
polypous
poohpooh
postpaid
postpone
priapism
prompter
promptly
propping
prospect
pushpull
quipping
rataplan
reappear
recapped
receptor
redeploy
reedpipe
reemploy
reexport
reimpose
resupine
rolypoly
rosepink
Salopian
scampish
scoopful
scoopnet
scorpion
scraping
scrapped
scrapper
sculptor
seedplot
selfpity
seraphic
seraphim
sharpish
sharpset
sheepdip
sheepdog
sheepish
sheepked
sheeppen
sheeprun
shipping
shopping
shrapnel
signpost
sinapism
sinophil
skimpily
skipping
slapping
sleepily
sleeping
slippage
slippery
slipping
sloppail
sloppily
slopping
slowpoke
snappily
snapping
snappish
snippety
snipping
soilpipe
sourpuss
spalpeen
stampede
steepish
steepled
stepping
stippler
stoppage
stopping
strapoil
strapped
strapper
strepent
Strepyan
stripped
stripper
strophic
stropped
stumpily
swapping
sweeping
sweepnet
swopping
synapsis
synaptic
synopses
synopsis
synoptic
tailpipe
talapoin
teaspoon
telepath
teleport
teraphim
thespian
thumping
tonepoem
trampler
trappean
trapping
Trappist
trespass
trippery
tripping
troupial
trumpery
turnpike
uncapped
untapped
unzipped
vilipend
whapping
whipping
whispery
whooping
whopping
windpipe
winepalm
wolfpack
woodpile
woodpulp
woolpack
wordplay
wrappage
wrapping
zoospore
henequen
illiquid
maroquin
paraquat
paroquet
ramequin
tranquil
Abderite
aberrant
abhorred
abhorrer
abnormal
absorber
abstract
abstrict
abstruse
absurdly
accuracy
accurate
accursed
acierage
acierate
acturial
adherent
Adlerian
aegirine
afferent
affirmer
afforest
agrarian
airbrake
airbrush
aircraft
airframe
alacrity
alburnum
alderman
Alderney
aleurone
algorism
allergen
allergic
alumroot
amperage
anaerobe
aneurism
aneurysm
ankerite
anourous
anserine
anterior
anteroom
aphorise
aphorism
aphorist
apiarian
apiarist
apocrine
apograph
apparent
apterous
aquarist
aquarium
arboreal
arboreta
arborist
armorial
arterial
asperges
asperity
aspirant
aspirate
assertor
assorted
Assyrian
asterisk
asterism
asteroid
atheroma
attorney
aurorean
autarchy
autarkic
averring
aviarist
babirusa
backrest
backroom
Bactrian
ballroom
bankroll
bankrupt
banxring
bathrobe
bathroom
baudrons
Bavarian
beadroll
beebread
beetroot
begirded
besprent
bestrewn
bestride
bestrode
beverage
biograph
biparous
blearily
blurrily
blurring
boltrope
bookrest
botyrose
bowfront
Briarean

bullring
buttress
butyrate
bystreet
Cambrian
cancrine
cancroid
canorous
castrate
castrati
castrato
cataract
cateress
catering
caverned
celeriac
celerity
centring
centrism
centrist
centroid
chairman
charring
cheerful
cheerily
cheering
chirrupy
chlorate
chloride
chlorine
chlorite
chlorous
choirboy
ciborium
cicerone
ciceroni
cinerary
clearcut
clearing
clearway
coatrack
coatroom
coherent
cokernut
compress
comprise
concrete
confrere
confront
congress
congreve
contract
contrail
contrary
contrast
contrate
contrite
contrive
conurbia
coverage
coverall
covering
coverlet
covertly
cowardly
cowgrass
coworker
cucurbit
Cumbrian
cumbrous
curarine
curarise
cutprice
dandruff
darkroom
dartrous
daybreak
daydream
deaerate

debarred
decorate
decorous
decurion
deferent
deferral
deferred
deferrer
deforest
deformed
delirium
demarche
demerara
demersal
demurely
demurred
demurrer
denarius
dendrite
dendroid
departed
deportee
depurate
describe
deserter
desirous
destrier
destruct
deterred
deterrer
dethrone
dextrine
dextrose
dextrous
diagraph
diarrhea
diatribe
dichroic
diffract
dimerism
dimerous
dinerout
dinornis
disarray
discreet
discrete
discrown
disfrock
disgrace
disorder
dispread
disprize
disproof
disprove
distract
distrain
distrait
distress
district
distrust
divorcee
doctrine
doldrums
dolerite
doloroso
dolorous
drearily
drumroll
editress
eelgrass
efferent
eldorado
elfarrow
emigrant
emigrate
emporium
empurple
empyreal
empyrean

encircle
endermic
endorsee
endorser
enforcer
enforest
engirdle
enlarger
enshrine
enshroud
enterate
enthrall
enthrone
entirely
entirety
environs
ephorate
epigraph
escargot
escarole
esterify
ethereal
etherial
etherise
etherism
etherist
Etrurian
euphrasy
excursus
execrate
exhorter
exocrine
expertly
expirant
exporter
exserted
exterior
external
federate
feverfew
feverish
feverous
fewtrils
figurant
figurine
filariae
filarial
filtrate
fimbriae
flagrant
flatrace
flooring
flourish
fluoride
fluorine
fluorite
footrace
footrest
footrope
footrule
formroom
fortress
fragrant
fumarole
funerary
funereal
futurism
futurist
futurity
gabbroic
gabbroid
gadarene
gambroon
gangrene
gastraea
gastrula
generate
generous
gentrice

gimcrack
glabrous
goitrous
goldrush
governor
Gujarati
hamartia
handrail
headrace
headrest
headroom
hibernal
highrise
highroad
hilarity
honorary
hornrims
hotpress
hoverfly
humorist
humorous
hungrily
huntress
icecream
ichorous
idocrase
ignorant
illtreat
Illyrian
immersed
immortal
imparity
imperial
imperium
importer
impurely
impurity
incurred
indirect
indurate
inerrant
inferior
infernal
inferred
infirmly
informal
informed
informer
inherent
inscribe
inscroll
inserted
instruct
insurant
intarsia
interact
interbed
intercom
intercut
interest
interior
intermit
intermix
internal
internee
Interpol
interred
interrex
intersex
intertie
interval
interwar
inthrall
inverted
inverter
inwardly
isocracy
isoprene
isotropy

Kanarese
Khmerian
kohlrabi
laburnum
lacerate
landrail
laterite
laverock
Lazarist
lazurite
legbreak
legerity
lemurine
lemuroid
leporine
leverage
levirate
liberate
licorice
limerick
literacy
literary
literate
literati
liturgic
liveried
liverish
lopgrass
lowering
lowgrade
lunarian
lustrate
lustrine
lustring
lustrous
macaroni
macaroon
macerate
maharaja
maharani
majority
malarial
malarian
malarkey
maltreat
mandrake
mandrill
mangrove
manorial
manurial
margrave
Masorete
Masoreth
material
materiel
maternal
matgrass
mattress
maturate
maturely
maturity
maverick
mayoress
mazarine
meagrely
membrane
memorial
memorise
menarche
mezereon
midbrain
millrace
Minoress
Minorite
minority
miserere
misprint
misprise
misprize

mistreat
mistress
mistrial
mistrust
miswrite
Mithraic
moderate
moderato
modernly
Moharram
molarity
monarchy
monorail
moonrise
motorail
motorcar
motorial
motoring
motorise
motorist
motorium
motorman
motormen
motorway
muckrake
Muharram
mushroom
muskrose
myograph
naturism
naturist
Nazarene
Nazarite
Nazirite
neoprene
nephrite
neutrino
newsreel
newsroom
nosering
notarial
notornis
novercal
numeracy
numerary
numerate
numerous
nutarian
nutbrown
oatgrass
obduracy
obdurate
observer
obstruct
obturate
occurred
octarchy
octaroon
octoroon
odograph
oestrone
oestrous
offbreak
offdrive
offering
offprint
onetrack
oratress
outbrave
outbreak
outdrawn
outgrown
overrate
override
overripe
overrode
overrule
paguria
pancreas

panorama
paperboy
parergon
pastrami
pastries
paternal
peagreen
pederast
pelerine
pelorism
pembroke
pentroof
peperino
perorate
picaroon
piecrust
pinprick
piperack
piperine
pirarucu
playroom
pleurisy
polarise
polarity
poltroon
portrait
portress
powerful
preprint
primrose
priorate
prioress
priority
prodrome
progress
protract
protrude
pubertal
pumproom
puparial
puparium
quadrant
quadrate
quadriga
quadroon
quarrier
quatrain
queerish
quitrent
rackrent
railroad
ranarian
ranarium
rasorial
recorder
recurred
redbrick
redirect
referent
referral
referred
reforest
reformed
reformer
repartee
reporter
rescript
reserved
resorcin
resorter
respring
resprung
restrain
restrict
resurvey
retarded
retarder
retiring
retorted

reverend
reverent
reversal
reverser
reverter
rewarder
ribgrass
ricercar
rickrack
riffraff
rigorism
rigorist
rigorous
rimbrake
ringroad
riparian
riverain
riverbed
riverine
riverman
riverway
roborant
rockrose
roofrack
rosarian
roseroot
rostrate
Rotarian
roturier
ryegrass
sackrace
saffrony
salariat
salaried
saleroom
samarium
Sangrail
Sangreal
sapgreen
saporous
satirise
satirist
saturant
saturate
Saturday
saturnic
savorous
sawframe
scabrous
scarring
scirrhus
sciurine
sciuroid
sclereid
sclerite
scleroma
sclerose
sclerous
scourger
scurrile
seacraft
seadrome
seafront
seagreen
seatrout
seawrack
securely
security
sederunt
selfrule
senarius
senorita
sentrygo
separate
severely
severity
sewerage
sewergas
sewerrat

shabrack
shagreen
shagroon
shamrock
shirring
shofroth
showroom
Siberian
sickroom
sidereal
siderite
sideroad
Silurian
siluroid
sitarist
skerrick
slipring
sliproad
slurring
soaproot
soberise
solarise
solarism
solarist
solarium
sombrely
sombrero
sombrous
sonority
sonorous
sororate
sorority
soterial
sowbread
spanroof
sparring
spearman
spherics
spheroid
spherule
spurrier
spurring
squarely
squarish
squarson
squireen
squirely
squirrel
squirter
stairrod
stairway
starrily
starring
stearate
stearine
steerage
steering
stirring
stuprate
suberect
suberise
suberose
suberous
subframe
subgroup
suborder
suborner
subprior
subtract
suburban
suburbia
sudarium
suffrage
sultrily
Sumerian
sundress
sundried
sundries
sundrops

sunproof
superadd
superate
superbly
superego
superior
superman
supernal
supertax
suppress
surprise
susurrus
suzerain
swearing
sybarite
syndrome
synergic
synergid
taberdar
tackroom
taffrail
tailrace
tamarack
tamarind
tamarisk
Tantrism
Tantrist
tartrate
taverner
tawdrily
teabread
teabreak
temerity
tenorite
tenurial
thearchy
theorise
theorist
theurgic
thwarter
thwartly
tiebreak
tigereye
tigerish
timorous
tolerant
tolerate
tomorrow
toolroom
topdress
tovarish
towardly
tramroad
traprock
triarchy
tribrach
trigraph
tubercle
tuberose
tuberous
tumorous
tutorage
tutoress
tutorial
ulcerate
ulcerous
ulterior
umpirage
unbarred
unburden
unburied
underact
underage
underarm
underbid
undercut
underdid
underdog
underfur

underlap
underlay
underlet
underlie
underlip
underman
underpin
underrun
undersea
underset
undertow
underway
unearned
unerring
unforced
unformed
unmarked
unperson
unsprung
unstring
unstrung
unthread
unthrift
unthrone
unversed
unwarily
unwordly
unworthy
uppercut
upsprang
upspring
upsprung
upstream
upstroke
upthrown
upthrust
upwardly
usufruct
valerate
valerian
valorise
valorous
vambrace
vaporise
vaporous
velarium
venerate
venereal
viburnum
vicarage
vicarate
vicarial
victress
vigorous
viperine
viperish
viperous
vivarium
vizarded
vomerine
votaress
votarist
waitress
wakerife
wardress
wardrobe
wardroom
washroom
waterage
waterbed
waterbus
watergas
waterice
watering
waterish
waterlog
waterloo
waterman
waterski

waterway
wellread
whirring
windrose
wintrily
wizardly
wizardry
wondrous
woodruff
workroom
yestreen
zoetrope
Abbaside
abrasion
abrasive
accustom
acoustic
acrostic
adhesion
adhesive
adjuster
adjustor
advisory
aerostat
affusion
agnostic
agrestic
aguishly
allusion
allusive
ambusher
amnesiac
ancestor
ancestry
andesine
andesite
antisera
aoristic
aphasiac
aplastic
apposite
apresski
arrestee
arrester
arrestor
artesian
artistic
artistry
asbestic
asbestos
assassin
assessor
attested
attester
attestor
Augustan
augustly
autistic
autosome
aversely
aversion
aversive
avulsion
babushka
backseat
backside
backspin
backstay
bailsman
baluster
bandsman
banister
beadsman
bearskin
biassing
bicuspid
bioassay
birdseed
birdseye

blessing
blissful
blossomy
bodyshop
bombsite
bondsman
boursier
boyishly
Bradshaw
brassage
brassard
brassart
brassica
brassily
breasted
brewster
buckshee
buckshot
buckskin
bullseye
cadastre
calcspar
calfskin
camisade
camisado
camisole
campsite
canaster
canister
capeskin
cavesson
cerastes
cerusite
chasseur
chessman
chiasmus
chiastic
chopsuey
christen
christie
Christly
cicisbei
cicisbeo
clanship
clansman
classics
classify
cloister
clumsily
coalsack
coarsely
cockshut
cocksure
cohesion
cohesive
coleseed
coleslaw
coliseum
colossal
colossus
coonskin
coursing
cragsman
creosote
crossbar
crossbow
crosscut
crossing
crosslet
crossply
crosstie
crossway
cryostat
curassow
cynosure
cytosine
dalesman
damassin
darksome

deanship
decision
decisive
deemster
deerskin
delusion
delusive
delusory
derision
derisive
derisory
digester
dinosaur
diopside
disaster
disusage
division
divisive
dockside
dolesome
domestic
doomsday
doomsman
doomster
doorsill
doorstep
doorstop
dragsman
dragster
dramshop
dressage
dressing
dropshot
drowsily
dumbshow
dustshot
dynastic
eclosion
effusion
effusive
egoistic
embosser
embussed
emersion
emissary
emission
emissive
emulsify
emulsion
emulsive
emulsoid
endostea
envisage
envision
Ephesian
Etruscan
Eurasian
evensong
eversion
evulsion
excision
exposure
failsafe
fearsome
feldsher
feldspar
fenestra
fernshaw
filmstar
finespun
finisher
fireship
fireside
fivestar
flagship
flaxseed
flimsily
flipside
focusing

focussed
folksong
foolscap
footslog
footsore
footstep
foresaid
foresail
foreseen
foreshow
foreside
foreskin
forestal
forestay
forested
forester
forestry
foursome
fourstar
freesoil
Friesian
frogspit
fuchsine
fullsize
gainsaid
gamesome
gamester
gangster
ganister
garishly
gelastic
girasole
gladsome
glassful
glassily
glassine
gleesome
glissade
glossary
glossily
glossina
gneissic
goadster
goatskin
gownsman
greasily
gripsack
grissini
grogshop
gruesome
gulosity
gyrostat
halfsole
handsewn
handsome
harasser
hardship
haresear
harpseal
haruspex
headsail
headsman
heirship
helmsman
herdsman
hernshaw
hibiscus
hillside
hoarsely
hocusing
hocussed
holistic
homesick
homespun
honestly
huckster
huntsman
illusage
illusion

illusive
illusory
impishly
imposing
imposter
impostor
incision
incisive
indusium
industry
infusion
inhesion
invasion
invasive
investor
ironside
jackstay
jocosely
jocosity
Jugoslav
jumpseat
jumpsuit
junkshop
Jurassic
juristic
keepsake
kerosene
kerosine
kickshaw
kinesics
kingship
kingsize
knapsack
ladyship
lamasery
lambskin
landslip
landsman
Langshan
larkspur
lavishly
leadsman
lewisite
lifesize
linesman
lintseed
loadstar
lockstep
lodestar
logistic
lonesome
longship
longsome
longstop
lordship
loveseat
lovesick
lovesome
lovesong
lysosome
magister
mainsail
mainstay
majestic
maltster
marasmic
marasmus
marksman
meatsafe
medusoid
meniscus
meristem
meristic
merosome
Milesian
mimester
minister
ministry
misusage

modestly
modishly
molasses
moleskin
molester
molossus
monastic
monistic
monkseal
monkship
moonsail
moonshee
moonshot
mopishly
moresque
morosely
morosity
moussaka
mucosity
mulishly
nainsook
namesake
nodosity
nomistic
nonesuch
nonusage
oafishly
obeisant
obtusely
obtusity
occasion
Odyssean
oleaster
omission
opposite
orgasmic
orgastic
otiosely
otiosity
oversail
overseas
overseen
overseer
oversell
oversewn
overshoe
overshot
overside
oversize
overslip
oversold
oversoul
overstay
overstep
owlishly
padishah
palestra
palisade
pantsuit
papistic
papistry
parasang
parasite
partsong
pawnshop
pedestal
peepshow
Pegasean
Pelasgic
perisher
pheasant
phrasing
piassava
pilaster
pilosity
pinaster
pintsize
plaister
playsuit
pleasant
pleasing
pleasure
plimsoll
plussage
polestar
polisher
pollster
polyseme
polysemy
polysomy
popishly
poristic
porosity
potassic
pressbox
pressing
pressman
pressure
priestly
prissily
Prussian
puissant
punisher
puristic
quaestor
quayside
queasily
raftsman
rakishly
rapeseed
ravisher
reabsorb
reassert
reassess
reassign
reassure
recision
recusant
redesign
redistil
reedstop
register
registry
reinsert
reinsman
reinsure
remissly
resister
resistor
revision
revisory
rhapsode
rhapsody
rheostat
ribosome
rickshaw
rimester
ringside
roadside
roadsign
roadster
robustly
rocksalt
rucksack
rugosely
rugosity
sadistic
Salesian
salesman
sandshoe
scansion
scissile
scission
scissors
Scotsman
sealskin
seamster
sebesten
seedsman
selfsame
selfsown
semester
sempster
serosity
sideshow
sideslip
sidesman
sidestep
singsong
sinister
sinusoid
slipshod
slipslop
slopshop
snapshot
sneeshan
snipsnap
snowshoe
soapsuds
softshoe
softsoap
songster
sparsely
sparsity
spinster
splasher
sponsion
spousage
squasher
staysail
stunsail
swanshot
swanskin
swansong
swimsuit
synastry
tailspin
talesman
talisman
tanistry
tapestry
teamster
tenesmus
theistic
thirster
thousand
thrasher
thresher
throstle
thruster
Thursday
thyrsoid
tickseed
tiresome
toilsome
toolshed
township
townsman
transact
transect
transept
transfer
transfix
tranship
transire
transmit
transude
treasure
treasury
tressure
Triassic
trousers
truistic
trussing
tuckshop
tungsten
tungstic
Tunisian
turnskin
turnsole
turnspit
twinship
tyrosine
uneasily
unfasten
unjustly
unlisted
unwashed
unwisdom
unwisely
unwished
uppishly
uprising
vanisher
vavasory
vavasour
venosity
Venusian
veristic
vinosity
vivisect
voussoir
wainscot
wardship
Wellsian
whinsill
windsail
windsock
wineshop
wineskin
wingspan
wolfskin
woodshed
woodsman
woolsack
woolshed
woolskin
workshop
wormseed
yourself
Yugoslav
abattoir
abbatial
abetting
ablation
ablative
ablution
abortion
abortive
abuttals
abutting
acanthus
acentric
acrotism
adaption
adaptive
addition
additive
adjutage
adjutant
admitted
adnation
adoption
adoptive
adultery
aeration
aflutter
agential
agiotage
aglitter
agnation
airstrip
aleatory
allotted
allottee
Alsatian
altitude
ambition
amortise
amputate
angstrom
annotate
anorthic
antitype
aperture
apostasy
apostate
appetent
appetite
aptitude
aquatint
arbitral
aristate
armature
aseptate
astatine
astutely
attitude
atwitter
audition
auditive
auditory
autotomy
autotype
aventail
aviation
aviatrix
aweather
axletree
bangtail
barathea
baritone
barytone
beautify
bedstead
bedstraw
befitted
begetter
begotten
belittle
besotted
betatron
bibation
blastema
blastoff
blastoid
blastula
blistery
blotting
blustery
boastful
Boeotian
boottree
bourtree
bracteal
bractlet
brattice
brattish
breather
brettese
brettice
burntout
cabotage
cabstand
calctuff
capitate
capitula
capstone
carotene
catstail
cavatina
cemetery
cenotaph
ceratoid
Chartism
Chartist
chastely
chastise
chastity
chattily
chatting
chestnut
cicatrix
cincture
citation
claptrap
clotting
clustery
coaction
coactive
coauthor
cocktail
cogitate
coistrel
comatose
cometary
conation
conative
constant
construe
cooption
cooptive
countess
courtesy
courtier
covetous
craftily
creatine
creation
creative
creatrix
creature
cristate
Croatian
crofting
crustily
cryotron
cubature
culottes
curative
cymatium
daintily
debutant
delation
deletion
demitted
demotion
denature
deputise
deration
devotion
dianthus
diastase
diastema
diastole
diestock
digitate
digitise
dilatant
dilation
dilative
dilatory
dilution
dioptase
dioptric
dipstick
Docetism
Docetist
donation
Donatism
Donatist
donative
donatory
dotation
doubtful
dovetail
downtime
downtown
downturn
drawtube
driftage
driftice
driftway
drystone
duettist
duration
durative
dyestuff
dynatron
edentate
eduction
egestion
egestive
Egyptian
eighteen
eighthly
eighties
ejection
ejective
ekistics
election
elective
electret
electric
electron
electrum
embattle
embitter
emitting
empathic
enaction
enactive
enfetter
eolithic
epistler
epistyle
equation
equitant
equities
Erastian
erectile
erection
ergotise
ergotism
eruption
eruptive
etcetera
eupatrid
evection
eventful
eventide
eventual
eviction
exacting
exaction
exanthem
excitant
exciting
exertion
existent
exultant
eyestalk
facetiae
fagoting
faintish
fasttalk
fatstock
faultily
Faustian
feastday
feedtank
feretory
fighting
filature
finitely
finitude
firetrap
firstaid
fishtail
fixation
fixative
flattery
flattest
flattish
flautist
flection
fleeting
flintily
flitting
floatage
floating
fluttery
folktale
foretell
foretime
foretold
fountain
fourteen
fourthly
fraction
fracture
fretting
friction
fritting
frontage
frontier
frontlet
frostily
frosting
frottage
fructify
fructose
fruitage
fruitbat
fruitery
fruitfly
fruitful
fruition
frustule
fugitive
fulltime
fumitory
function
garotter
gauntlet
gelatine
gelation
gematria
gemstone
genetics
genitive
geniture
genotype
ghastful
ghettoes
giantess
giantism
glittery
glutting
gluttony
glyptics
gogetter
goodtime
greeting
gritting
grottoes
grouting
gruntled
guiltily
gumption
gunstock
gyration

gyratory
habitant
habitual
habitude
halation
halfterm
halftime
halftone
hardtack
hatstand
haunting
haystack
heartily
hebetate
hebetude
hecatomb
helotism
hepatica
hepatise
heritage
hesitant
hesitate
hightail
hightest
himation
hipsters
hocktide
holstein
hometown
Horatian
horntail
howitzer
hydatoid
hypothec
ideation
identify
identity
idiotism
ignition
ignitron
illation
illative
immature
impetigo
impotent
inaction
inactive
incitant
inertial
ingather
inkstand
innately
intitule
inviting
irritant
irritate
isoptera
isostasy
jauntily
jobation
jointure
Jonathan
joystick
junction
juncture
keratose
keystone
kibitzer
kinetics
klystron
knitting
knotting
komitaji
kreutzer
latitant
latitude
lavation
lavatory
laxative
laystall
lecithin
legatine
legation
lengthen
lenitive
levitate
libation
libatory
lifetime
ligation
ligature
lighting
lightish
limetwig
limitary
linstock
lipstick
lobation
lobotomy
locative
locution
locutory
logotype
longterm
longtime
lunation
lutetium
luxation
maestoso
maintain
marathon
maritage
maritime
mealtime
meantime
meditate
menstrua
mesotron
mightest
mightily
militant
military
militate
minatory
Minotaur
minstrel
minutely
minutiae
misstate
moisture
monetary
monetise
monition
monitive
monitory
monotint
monotone
monotony
monotype
moratory
mountain
mounting
mudstone
muleteer
munition
musktree
mutation
mycetoma
nametape
naphthol
natation
natatory
neaptide
negation
negative
negatory
negatron
nematode
nematoid
nepotism
nicotian
nicotine
nightcap
nighthag
nightjar
nightowl
nineteen
nineties
nodation
nonstick
noontide
noontime
notation
novation
nugatory
nutation
oblation
oblatory
odontoid
offstage
oilstone
omitting
ommateum
optative
ornately
ornithic
outstare
outstrip
overtake
overtask
overtime
overtone
overtook
overture
overturn
paintbox
palatial
palatine
parttime
penitent
penstock
petition
phantasm
phantasy
pilotage
pivotman
plantain
plastery
plastics
plastron
platting
playtime
plectrum
plotting
pointing
politely
politick
politico
politics
ponytail
position
positive
positron
potation
potstill
potstone
poultice
practice
practise
prattler
prentice
prestige
prettify
prettily
printing
printout
pristine
prostate
prostyle
psaltery
punctate
punctual
puncture
punition
punitive
punitory
pupation
putative
quantify
quantise
quantity
quartern
quarters
quartile
question
quietism
quietist
quietude
quilting
quintain
quitting
ratstail
reactant
reaction
reactive
realtime
rebuttal
rebutted
rebutter
redstart
refitted
relation
relative
remittal
remitted
remittee
remitter
remotely
renitent
repetend
repotted
resetter
resettle
revetted
Rhaetian
rightful
rightist
ringtail
roasting
roentgen
rogation
rogatory
rooftree
rosetree
rotation
rotative
rotatory
rubytail
sabotage
saboteur
sagittal
saintdom
salutary
sanative
sanatory
sanctify
sanction
sanctity
sanitary
sanitate
sanitise
saxatile
scanties
scantily
scattily
scatting
sceptred
sciatica
scottice
Scottish
scouting
scratchy
scrutiny
sedately
sedation
sedative
sedition
seedtime
Semitise
Semitism
Semitist
semitone
serotine
shafting
Shaktism
shantung
sheeting
shiftily
shiftkey
shirting
shoetree
shooting
shootout
shoptalk
shortage
shortarm
shortcut
shortday
shortish
shutting
skirting
skittish
skittles
slattern
slitting
slotting
sluttish
smaltite
smartish
smeltery
smoothen
smoothie
smoothly
smuttily
snootily
sobstory
sobstuff
solation
solatium
solitary
solitude
solstice
solution
somatism
sometime
sonatina
sorption
sorptive
spatting
spectral
spectrum
spitting
spittoon
splatter
splitter
splotchy
splutter
spontoon
sportful
sportily
sporting
sportive
spottily
spotting
squatted
squatter
starting
startler
steatite
stetting
stoutish
strategy
stratify
stretchy
strutted
strutter
stultify
stuntman
substage
sudatory
sunstone
swastika
swatting
sweeting
sweetish
sweetpea
sweetsop
swiftlet
swotting
taciturn
Tahitian
tainture
taxation
telethon
telltale
tempting
tenotomy
teratoma
termtime
testtube
thirteen
throttle
ticktack
ticktock
tightwad
tincture
tinstone
tipstaff
together
topstone
tractate
traction
tractive
treatise
triptych
tristful
tristich
trotting
trottoir
troutlet
trustful
trustily
twenties
twittery
twitting
unbottle
unbutton
unfetter
unfitted
ungotten
unsettle
untether
untitled
upsetter
urostyle
vacation
vaulting
vauntful
vegetate
vegetive
venation
Venetian
veratrin
veratrum
vexation
visitant
vocation
vocative
volatile
volitant
volition
volitive
volution
vomitive
vomitory
wheatear
whetting
whistler
whittret
wreathen
wrestler
wrestpin
wristlet
wristpin
yachting
yeastily
yuletide
zenithal
zoiatria
zonation
abacuses
accoutre
aciculae
acicular
aciculas
adequacy
adequate
affluent
altruism
altruist
announce
Arcturus
armoured
armourer
artfully
babouche
banausic
barouche
begrudge
Bermudas
besought
binaural
Burgundy
cachucha
cactuses
caesural
calculus
cannulae
cannular
cannulas
capsular
carburet
carousal
carousel
carouser
cellular
centuple
cernuous
chasuble
chemurgy
chequers
cherubic
cherubim
cingulum
cinquain
circuity
circular
cislunar
claqueur
cliquish
cliquism
coagulum
coloured
communal
commuter
computer
conjugal
conjunct
conjurer
conjuror
conquest
consular
consumer
convulse
corduroy
costumer
cothurni
cotquean
cultural
cultured
curculio
cutpurse
daiquiri
declutch
decouple
demiurge
denounce
devourer
devoutly
diffuser
disburse
disguise
disjunct
disquiet
dissuade
donought
drynurse
dybbukim
earmuffs
effluent
effluvia
eloquent
epidural
espousal
espouser
euphuism
euphuist
evacuant
evacuate
evaluate
excluder
executor
exequies
exiguity
exiguous
famously
farouche
fastuous
favoured
favourer
featured
features
February
fistulae
fistular
fitfully
flexuose
flexuous
flexural
formulae
formulas
fortuity
frenulum
frequent
furculae
furcular
furfural
furfuran
galluses
gestural
globular
globulin

graduand
graduate
granular
gratuity
guttural
halluces
harrumph
Hercules
hereunto
hereupon
hinduise
Hinduism
honourer
humoured
included
inequity
influent
iniquity
inoculum
intruder
Iroquois
jacquard
jalousie
joyfully
joyously
labourer
language
languish
lawfully
lecturer
legguard
leisured
linguist
longueur
maieutic
manfully
marauder
marquess
marquise
Mayqueen
measured
mensural
mercuric
mesquite
messuage
micrurgy
misguide
misjudge
misquote
monaural
mortuary
mosquito
mowburnt
mudguard
murmurer
muscular
musquash
nimbused
nocturne
nonhuman
nonjuror
nurturer
obituary
occluded
occlusal
odiously
opaquely
oracular
outburst
outguess
pastural
pellucid
pendular
pendulum
perfumer
perjurer
persuade
piacular
pictures
pinnular
plaguily
planulae
planular
plumular
polluter
postural
posturer
prehuman
prejudge
presumer
procurer
producer
promulge
purpuric
purpurin
pursuant
pustular
rambutan
raptures
ratguard
recourse
redouble
refluent
renounce
repousse
resource
ruefully
saccular
sacculus
Sadducee
sanguine
sauouari
scapulae
scapular
scapulas
scopulae
scopulas
scrounge
seapurse
seaquake
secluded
sensuous
septuple
serpulae
sextuple
Shabuoth
sinfully
singular
spatular
specular
speculum
spiculae
spicular
spiculum
sporular
statuary
statured
stimulus
stipular
subhuman
sublunar
succubae
succubus
sunburnt
sunburst
tabouret
Talmudic
Tartuffe
telluric
textuary
textural
textured
timously
tittuped
tittuppy
tonguing
toreutic
torquate
tortuous
torturer
traducer
tribunal
ubiquity
uncaused
unchurch
uncouple
unctuous
unhoused
uniquely
unsought
unstuffy
untaught
usefully
valvulae
valvular
vanguard
vanquish
vapourer
vascular
vasculum
venously
venturer
verdured
verjuice
verrucae
vesturer
victuals
vinculum
vinously
virtuosa
virtuosi
virtuoso
virtuous
volvulus
waesucks
wetnurse
whodunit
wilfully
woefully
yarmulka
zarzuela
ziggurat
aardvark
acervate
activate
actively
activism
activist
activity
adjuvant
alluvial
alluvion
alluvium
ambivert
backveld
Batavian
bushveld
cidevant
cleavage
cleavers
delivery
derivate
diluvial
diluvian
diluvium
enervate
equivoke
estovers
excavate
Genevese
grievous
incivism
innovate
Jehovist
lixivium
maravedi
mitzvoth
Moravian
motivate
motivity
natively
nativism
nativist
nativity
nonevent
oblivion
omnivore
ottavino
overview
paravane
Peruvian
rearview
recovery
reinvest
relevant
renovate
revivify
salivary
salivate
scurvily
shelving
sideview
spivvery
stravaig
synovial
teleview
televise
thievery
thievish
thriving
titivate
trouvere
twelvemo
unlovely
vesuvian
aardwolf
advowson
armyworm
backward
backwash
basswood
beadwork
beefwood
beeswing
bellwort
bentwood
bindweed
blueweed
bodywork
bollworm
bookwork
bookworm
buhlwork
buzzword
cakewalk
careworn
casework
colewort
cordwain
cordwood
corkwing
corkwood
Cotswold
coxswain
cussword
deadwood
downward
downwind
drawwell
dropwort
duckweed
eastward
edgeways
edgewise
farewell
fireweed
firewood
firework
fishwife
flatware
flatways
flatwise
flatworm
fleawort
footwear
footwork
forewarn
forewent
foreword
formwork
forswear
forswore
forsworn
freewill
fretwork
gallwasp
gapeworm
glowworm
godawful
goodwife
goodwill
goutweed
goutwort
gromwell
gulfweed
hairworm
handwork
hardware
hardwood
hawkweed
headwind
headword
headwork
herdwick
herewith
hickwall
homeward
homework
hoodwink
hookworm
hornworm
hornwort
inchworm
ironware
ironwood
ironwork
kilowatt
knapweed
knitwear
knotwork
lacewing
lacework
leadwork
leftward
lifework
likewise
limewash
livewire
loanword
longwall
longwave
longways
longwise
lukewarm
lungwort
lykewake
mealworm
megawatt
menswear
meshwork
milkweed
milkwort
moonwort
muckworm
openwork
ovenware
overwear
overwind
overwork
overworn
password
pigswill
pilewort
pillwort
pinewood
pondweed
pulpwood
rainwash
rainwear
rearward
reedwren
renowned
rereward
ringwall
ringworm
rockweed
rockwood
rockwork
ropewalk
rosewood
ryotwari
saltwort
sandwich
sandworm
sandwort
scrawler
screwtop
selfwill
shipworm
shopworn
shrewdly
shrewish
sidewalk
sideward
sideways
sidewind
sidewise
silkworm
slopwork
slowworm
soapwort
software
softwood
someways
somewhat
somewhen
spaewife
sprawler
squawker
squawman
stalwart
starwort
stepwise
studwork
tapeworm
taskwork
teamwork
thrawart
tidewave
timework
timeworn
toilworn
tripwire
unlawful
untoward
wartweed
wartwort
Wedgwood
wellworn
werewolf
westward
whimwham
whipworm
wildwood
windward
wirework
wireworm
wirewove
wishwash
woodwind
woodwool
woodwork
woodworm
woolwork
wormwood
zugzwang
bisexual
detoxify
monaxial
monoxide
paroxysm
peroxide
preexist
pyrexial
pyroxene
relaxant
suboxide
triaxial
trioxide
uniaxial
alleyway
analyser
analyses
analysis
analytic
asphyxia
backyard
ballyhoo
ballyrag
barnyard
bellyful
benzylic
billyboy
billycan
bobbypin
bobbysox
bogeyman
boneyard
botryoid
bullyboy
bullyoff
bullyrag
carryall
carryout
coccyges
collyria
condylar
dactylar
dactylic
dairying
dairyman
dandyish
dandyism
dialyser
dialyses
dialysis
dialytic
dittybag
dittybox
dockyard
dooryard
dowdyish
epicycle
essayist
euonymin
euonymus
everyday
everyman
everyone
everyway
fairyism
fancyman
farmyard
fedayeen
ferryman
fiftyish
foreyard
fortyish
funnyman
gardyloo
gipsydom
gipsyism
goodyear
gossypol
gypsydom
gypsyism
handyman
haulyard
hobbyist
honeybee
honeydew
honeypot
ivorynut
jerrycan
junkyard
kailyard
lacrymal
lallygag
lobbyist
lollypop
loonybin
lowlying
mainyard
marrying
mealybug
metayage
methylic
methysis
moneybag
moneybox
neomycin
newlywed
outlying
outvying
pattypan
phenylic
picayune
platypus
pollywog
propylic
pterylae
puppydog
puppydom
puppyfat
puppyish
pussycat
rallying
rallyist
ropeyarn
rowdyish
rowdyism
sailyard
Samoyede
sandyish
sannyasi
Savoyard
sealyham
shipyard
spagyric
spraygun
sukiyaki
syncytia
tallyman
tiltyard
toadyish
toadyism
tommybar
tommygun
tommyrot
tricycle
unicycle
vineyard

Walkyrie
bedazzle
blizzard
breezily
britzska
bryozoan
Cenozoic
chutzpah
coenzyme
denazify
ectozoon
embezzle
endozoic
endozoon
entozoic
entozoon
freezeup
freezing
frenzied
grizzled
Hertzian
holozoic
janizary
lysozyme
magazine
Mesozoic
metazoan
metazoon
monazite
polyzoan
polyzoic
polyzoon
quizzing
samizdat
schizoid
sforzato
sleazily
snazzily
stanzaic
tweezers
unmuzzle
wheezily
whizzing
whizzkid

---

aardvark
abdicate
aberrant
abnegate
abradant
abrogate
absonant
abstract
abundant
abuttals
accolade
accuracy
accurate
aceldama
acerbate
acervate
acidfast
acierage
acierate
acrylate
activate
aculeate
adequacy
adequate
adjutage
adjutant
adjuvant
aduncate
advocaat
advocacy
advocate
aeronaut
agiotage
airbrake
aircraft
Airedale
airframe
airshaft
airspace
alginate
alienage
alienate
allocate
allogamy
allopath
almanack
ambulant
ambulate
amperage
amputate
amygdala
anaphase
annotate
annulate
antedate
antimask
anyplace
apograph
apostasy
apostate
appanage
approach
aquacade
aquanaut
areolate
argonaut
arillate
aristate
armchair
arrogant
arrogate
arsenate
artefact
artifact
ascocarp
aseptate
aspirant
aspirate
assonant
assonate
autobahn
autocade
autodafe
autogamy
automata
automate
aventail
axillary
bacchant
backdate
backhand
backlash
backpack
backward
backwash
backyard
badinage
baldpate
bandeaux
bangtail
bareback
barnyard
baronage
baseball
bedplate
beefcake
benzoate
bequeath
bestiary
beverage
bifocals
billiard
bilobate
biograph
bioplasm
bioplast
birdbath
birdcage
birdcall
blindage
blizzard
blockade
blockage
blowball
blowhard
blowlamp
boldface
bondmaid
bondmans
boneyard
boniface
bookcase
bookland
bookmark
bootjack
bootlace
bootlast
Bordeaux
bouffant
boundary
braggart
brancard
brassage
brassard
brassart
breakage
bregmata
breviary
brouhaha
browband
bullcalf
burglary
bushbaby
butyrate
cabotage
cabstand
cakewalk
calabash
calamary
califate
calipash
camisade
camisado
camshaft
canthari
capitate
capybara
caracara
carapace
carinate
carriage
carryall
casemate
castrate
castrati
castrato
catalase
cataract
catchall
catenary
catenate
catstail
celibacy
celibate
cenotaph
Chaldaic
chaplain
charlady
chateaux
chiliasm
chiliast
chlorate
chordate
choriamb
chromate
cidevant
cinerary
cinquain
claimant
clambake
clawback
cleavage
clubhaul
clubland
clypeate
coalsack
coatrack
cocktail
cogitate
comeback
cometary
complain
conchate
conclave
conflate
constant
contract
contrail
contrary
contrast
contrate
copulate
cordwain
corelate
cornball
coronach
coronary
Corybant
cosecant
costmary
cotenant
couchant
covenant
coverage
coverall
cowgrass
coxswain
cozenage
craniate
cribbage
crispate
cristate
croceate
cruciate
culinary
cumulate
cupboard
cupulate
Cyrenaic
deadfall
deaerate
debonair
debutant
decimate
deckhand
decorate
decrease
dedicate
deeplaid
defilade
degrease
delegacy
delegate
delibate
delicacy
delicate
demerara
depilate
depurate
derivate
derogate
desolate
detonate
diagraph
diallage
diastase
diffract
digitate
dilatant
dinosaur
dioptase
disclaim
disgrace
displace
displant
dissuade
distract
distrain
distrait
disusage
divagate
djellaba
dockland
dockyard
dominant
dominate
doorcase
doornail
dooryard
doumpalm
dovetail
downcast
downfall
downhaul
downland
downward
drainage
drawback
dressage
driftage
drunkard
dryplate
duckhawk
dulciana
dungcart
dustcart
dutypaid
eastward
echinate
edentate
edgeways
eelgrass
efficacy
eggplant
eldorado
elephant
elongate
emaciate
emendate
emigrant
emigrate
emissary
encroach
endamage
endocarp
endogamy
enervate
enfilade
ensheath
ensilage
enterate
enthrall
entreaty
envisage
ephorate
epiblast
epigraph
epiphany
equipage
equitant
escalade
escalate
escapade
estimate
etiolate
euphrasy
evacuant
evacuate
evaluate
evenfall
excavate
excitant
execrate
exhalant
expirant
exultant
exuviate
eyeglass
eyeshade
eyestalk
fabliaux
facecard
facepack
failsafe
faineant
fallback
faradaic
farmhand
farmland
farmyard
fastback
fasttalk
February
federate
feedback
feedtank
ferriage
figurant
filtrate
fireback
fireball
firedamp
firstaid
fishball
fishcake
fishfarm
fishhawk
fishtail
fistiana
flagrant
flapjack
flatmate
flatrace
flatware
flatways
fleabane
flippant
floatage
folktale
football
footbath
footfall
footmark
footpace
footpath
footrace
forecast
forehand
forelady
foreland
foremast
forename
forepart
forepast
foresaid
foresail
forewarn
foreyard
fountain
fourball
fourpart
foxshark
fragrant
freefall
freehand
frondage
frontage
frottage
fruitage
fullback
fullpage
fumigant
fumigate
funerary
fuselage
gainsaid
galleass
galliard
gallwasp
gangland
garboard
gastraea
gearcase
geminate
generate
geophagy
gimcrack
glaciate
gladhand
glissade
glossary
goofball
gourmand
graduand
graduate
grandame
grillage
gripsack
guacharo
guardant
Gujarati
gymkhana
habitant
halfback
halfmast
halliard
hallmark
handball
handcart
handfast
handmade
handmaid
handrail
hangnail
hardback
hardbake
hardcase
hardhack
hardtack
hardware
harikari
hatstand
haulyard
haystack
headband
headfast
headlamp
headland
headrace
headsail
hebetate
heelball
helpmate
heritage
hesitant
hesitate
hickwall
highball
highjack
highland
hightail
hipflask
hogsback
holdback
holdfast
holidays
homeland
homemade
homeward
homogamy
honorary
horntail
hotplate
humpback
iceplant
iceskate
idocrase
ignorant
illusage
immolate
impanate
inchoate
incitant
increase
increate
incubate
indagate
indicant
indicate
indurate
inerrant
inhalant
inhumane
initiate
inkstand
innovate
insolate
insulant
insulate
insurant
interact
inthrall
intimacy
intimate
intonate
intubate
inundate
inurbane
invocate
iodinate
ironbark
ironware
irrigate
irritant
irritate
isocracy
isostasy
jacquard
janizary
jetblack
jetplane
jipijapa
jubilant
jubilate
jugulate
junkyard
kailyard
kamikaze
katakana
keelhaul
keepsake
keyboard
kickback
kilowatt
knapsack
kohlrabi
komitaji

korfball
kourbash
lacerate
lacunary
lacunate
lakeland
laminate
landfall
landlady
landmark
landmass
landrail
langlauf
language
lapboard
lapidary
lapidate
larboard
Latinate
latitant
laureate
lavalava
layshaft
laystall
leeboard
lefthand
leftward
legguard
lemonade
leverage
levigate
levirate
levitate
liberate
lichgate
ligulate
limewash
limitary
lipomata
literacy
literary
literate
literati
litigant
litigate
lobulate
lockfast
loculate
longhair
longhand
longwall
longwave
longways
lopgrass
loricate
lowgrade
lukewarm
luminant
luminary
lunulate
lustrate
lychgate
lykewake
macerate
maculate
maharaja
maharani
mahogany
mailcart
mainland
mainmast
mainsail
maintain
mainyard
makebate
makefast
Malagasy
mandrake
margrave
marinade
marinate
maritage
marocain
marriage
matamata
matgrass
maturate
meatball
meatsafe
medicate
meditate
megawatt
membrane
merchant
mesocarp
messmate
messuage
metayage
miasmata
midbrain
militant
military
militate
milkmaid
millhand
milliard
milliary
millrace
Minotaur
mintmark
misdealt
misheard
mishmash
Mishnaic
misogamy
misplace
misshape
misstate
misusage
Mithraic
mitigant
mitigate
moderate
moderato
modulate
monetary
monogamy
monorail
mooncalf
moonface
moonsail
moorland
mortgage
mortmain
mortuary
mossback
mothball
motivate
motorail
mountain
moussaka
mucilage
muckrake
mudguard
musicale
musquash
mutilate
myoblast
myograph
myxomata
namepart
namesake
nametape
nauseant
nauseate
navigate
neckband
necklace
neoplasm
newscast
nicknack
nickname
nominate
nonclaim
nonusage
noseband
notecase
nowadays
nuclease
nucleate
numeracy
numerary
numerate
nuptials
oatgrass
obduracy
obdurate
obeisant
obituary
obligate
obturate
occupant
ocellate
octonary
odograph
oeillade
offstage
oliphant
omadhaum
omophagy
omoplate
onetrack
opencast
oppilate
opsimath
ordinand
ordinary
ordinate
osculant
osculate
ostinato
outboard
outbrave
outclass
outdrawn
outflank
outreach
outsmart
outstare
ovenware
overcall
overcame
overcast
overfall
overhand
overhang
overhaul
overlaid
overlain
overland
overpaid
overpass
overpast
overrate
oversail
overtake
overtask
paginate
paleface
palisade
palliate
pallmall
panorama
parasang
paravane
parkland
pastrami
pearmain
peculate
pederast
pedipalp
pegboard
penchant
pericarp
permeate
perorate
persuade
petulant
phantasm
phantasy
pharmacy
pheasant
phyllary
piassava
pilchard
pilotage
piperack
plagiary
plantain
plateaux
playback
playmate
pleasant
pleinair
pleonasm
plumbago
plumbate
plussage
pockmark
poignant
polygala
polygamy
polymath
polypary
ponytail
populace
populate
portrait
postcard
postdate
postmark
postpaid
potplant
potroast
poundage
pregnant
prelease
priorate
proclaim
prophase
prostate
protease
protract
puffball
puissant
pullback
punctate
pupilage
pupilary
purchase
purslane
pursuant
pushball
pushcart
quadrant
quadrate
quandary
quatrain
quintain
racecard
racemate
radicant
radicate
rainfall
rainwash
rapecake
ratguard
ratsbane
ratstail
reactant
rearlamp
rearward
recreant
recreate
recusant
redshank
redstart
reedmace
reembark
regelate
regulate
relaxant
relegate
relevant
relocate
renegade
renegado
renovate
reproach
rereward
resinate
resonant
resonate
restrain
retroact
revenant
ribgrass
rickrack
riffraff
rimbrake
ringbark
ringmain
ringtail
ringwall
riverain
roborant
rockcake
rockfall
rocksalt
rollcall
rondeaux
roofrack
roommate
ropewalk
ropeyarn
rosemary
rostrate
rosulate
roughage
rouleaus
rouleaux
roundarm
rubytail
rucksack
ruminant
ruminate
runagate
rutabaga
rutilant
ryegrass
ryotwari
sabotage
sackrace
saginate
sailyard
salivary
salivate
salutary
sandbank
sandbath
Sangrail
sanitary
sanitate
sannyasi
saraband
saturant
saturate
sauouari
Savoyard
sawframe
sayonara
scabbard
schemata
seaboard
seacoast
seacraft
seaplane
seaquake
seascape
seasnail
seasnake
seawrack
seedcake
seedcase
segreant
seladang
selenate
selfmade
selfmate
selfsame
seminary
separate
serenade
serenata
sergeant
serjeant
sewerage
sforzato
shabrack
shagbark
Shetland
shipmate
shipyard
shoelace
shoptalk
shortage
shortarm
showcard
showcase
sibilant
sibilate
sideband
sidewalk
sideward
sideways
silicane
silicate
simulant
simulate
sitzbath
skewback
skewbald
skipjack
skyscape
slapbang
slapdash
slapjack
slipcase
slippage
slobland
sloppail
sluggard
smallage
snowball
snowfall
soapbark
softball
software
solidary
solitary
someways
sororate
Spaniard
speciate
spermary
spiccato
spillage
spoilage
spoliate
spondaic
spousage
spyglass
squamate
staccato
staffage
staggard
stagnant
stagnate
stallage
stalwart
standard
stannary
stannate
stanzaic
stargaze
statuary
staylace
staysail
stearate
stedfast
steerage
stellate
stemmata
stigmata
stillage
stinkard
stoccado
stoccata
stockade
stoppage
stramash
stravaig
stromata
stubnail
studfarm
stunsail
stuprate
subclass
subframe
subimago
sublease
substage
subtract
subulate
suffrage
suitcase
sukiyaki
sulphate
sunshade
superadd
superate
supinate
supplant
surcease
suricate
suzerain
swanmark
swayback
tableaux
tabulate
taffrail
tailback
tailgate
tailrace
tamarack
tartrate
teaboard
teammate
telecast
telemark
telepath
telltale
template
tertiary
texthand
textuary
thingamy
thirlage
thousand
thrawart
thridace
ticktack
tidegate
tideland
tidemark
tidewave
tiltyard
timeball
tinplate
tipstaff
titanate
titivate
toeplate
tolerant
tolerate
tollcall
tollgate
tomahawk
topheavy
torquate
townhall
toxicant
trabeate
trackage
tractate
transact
trapball
traumata
treenail
trespass
tribrach
trigraph
triplane
trochaic
truckage
trumeaux
truncate
tubulate
tunicate
turnback
tutelage
tutelary
tutorage
typecast
typeface
ulcerate
ultimacy
ultimata
ultimate
umbonate
umpirage
uncinate
uncreate
underact
underage
underarm
undreamt
undulant
undulate
ungulate
unsteady
untoward
upsprang
urethane
urticant
urticate
valerate
validate
vambrace
vamplate
vanadate
vanguard

vegetate
venerate
verbiage
vesicant
vesicate
vespiary
vestiary
vicarage
vicarate
vicinage
victuals
vigilant
vinegary
vineyard
visitant
volitant
volplane
wagonage
wallgame
warplane
warweary
waterage
waveband
westward
wharfage
wheyface
whiplash
whizbang
windfall
windgall
windlass
windsail
windward
winepalm
wingcase
wirehair
wishwash
wolfpack
woodland
woodlark
woolpack
woolsack
workmate
wormcast
wrappage
wreckage
xanthate
xenogamy
xylocarp
yokemate
zugzwang
zwieback
absorber
adlibbed
adorable
adorably
alphabet
amenable
amenably
amicable
amicably
amphibia
arguable
arguably
arquebus
assemble
assembly
atremble
avowable
bailable
bankable
bearable
bearably
bedabble
bedtable
biddable
billyboy
bistable
blackboy

blamable
blamably
bontebok
bribable
brickbat
bullyboy
cabinboy
callable
cannabin
cannabis
cannibal
cascabel
chasuble
cherubic
cherubim
childbed
choirboy
cicisbei
cicisbeo
cinnabar
cobwebby
coenobia
conurbia
coolabah
coolibah
credible
credibly
crossbar
crossbow
crucible
cucumber
cucurbit
culpable
culpably
damnable
damnably
deathbed
December
demobbed
deniable
dimmable
dittybag
dittybox
doughboy
drawable
drivable
Dukhobor
dutiable
educable
educible
eligible
eligibly
encumber
enfeeble
ensemble
enviable
enviably
erasable
erodible
evadable
evitable
exigible
expiable
fallible
fallibly
feasible
feasibly
fellable
fencible
fishable
flexible
flexibly
flockbed
forcible
forcibly
fordable
fruitbat
fungible
gainable

guidable
gullable
gullible
hangable
hateable
hireable
honeybee
horrible
horribly
horsebox
houseboy
huggable
imitable
inedible
instable
interbed
inviable
isolable
issuable
joinable
kissable
knowable
laudable
laudably
leviable
liftable
likeable
liveable
loanable
lockable
loonybin
loosebox
mailable
mandible
mangabey
matchbox
mealybug
mendable
microbar
microbic
millibar
miscible
moneybag
moneybox
moveable
nameable
November
openable
operable
paintbox
palpable
palpably
paperboy
partible
passable
passably
passible
peccable
peekaboo
penumbra
pintable
pitiable
pitiably
placable
placably
playable
portable
possible
possibly
postobit
pourable
preamble
pressbox
probable
probably
prohibit
provable
provably
quotable

rateable
readable
readably
redouble
reliable
reliably
remember
rentable
renumber
resemble
reusable
rideable
riverbed
ropeable
ruinable
runcible
sailable
saleable
salvable
satiable
satiably
saucebox
scalable
scrabble
scramble
scribble
scribbly
scrubbed
scrubber
sealable
seizable
sensible
sensibly
shakable
shapable
sillabub
singable
sinkable
sizeable
slugabed
smokable
snackbar
snuffbox
sociable
sociably
solvable
sortable
soundbow
soundbox
spacebar
sparable
spicebox
squabble
squibbed
statable
steenbok
steinbok
storable
suburban
suburbia
succubae
succubus
suitable
suitably
superbly
syllabic
syllable
syllabub
syllabus
tameable
tangible
tangibly
tannable
tastebud
teatable
tellable
tensible
terrible
terribly

testable
throbbed
thrombin
thrombus
thurible
tillable
tithable
tommybar
trilobed
tuneable
turnable
underbid
unlimber
unstable
unstably
valuable
valuably
variable
variably
vendible
vertebra
viewable
vincible
violable
violably
vitiable
voicebox
voidable
walkable
washable
wastable
waterbed
waterbus
wearable
weldable
wettable
whiteboy
winnable
workable
writable
Adamical
advanced
alogical
alopecia
American
analecta
analects
Anglican
atypical
auspices
autarchy
babouche
backache
balanced
balancer
barbecue
barbican
barnacle
barouche
barracks
biblical
billycan
binnacle
blackcap
bullocky
cachucha
cadenced
canticle
capsicum
caruncle
caudices
cervical
cervices
chemical
clavicle
cleancut
clearcut
clerical
clinical

corniced
corniche
cornicle
cortical
cortices
cosmical
critical
crosscut
curlicue
curricle
cyclical
deathcap
demarche
denticle
divorcee
dogfaced
elflocks
embracer
emetical
encircle
enforcer
entracte
epicycle
erotical
ethnical
Etruscan
explicit
faceache
farcical
farouche
fascicle
fistical
follicle
foolscap
fornices
frutices
furuncle
Gallican
garlicky
gazpacho
gimmicky
grimacer
guaiacum
gynoecia
halluces
handicap
headache
headachy
heliacal
heroical
hibiscus
hillocky
homuncle
horsecar
hummocky
humuncle
iceyacht
implicit
inimical
intercom
intercut
irenical
irenicon
ironical
isodicon
jerrican
jerrycan
Judaical
latticed
lenticel
lenticle
libeccio
lubrical
maniacal
massacre
massicot
matrices
mediocre
menarche

meniscus
metrical
monarchy
monoacid
motorcar
mustache
mystical
mythical
naumachy
nautical
neomycin
nightcap
novercal
obstacle
octarchy
orthicon
ostracod
ostracon
oxytocin
particle
pastiche
peacocky
peasecod
peduncle
pellicle
pellucid
pemmican
pendicle
pentacle
perfecto
physical
physicky
picnicky
pinnacle
poetical
pollices
porticos
postiche
producer
protocol
publican
publicly
pussycat
redfaced
rejoicer
replacer
resorcin
respects
revanche
ricercar
romancer
rubrical
rustical
Sadducee
scenical
scilicet
scirocco
scolices
scratchy
screechy
shortcut
silencer
skullcap
soutache
spadices
spiracle
splotchy
squelchy
statical
stockcar
stomachy
stretchy
subvocal
surfacer
surgical
syndical
tablecut
tactical
tentacle

terraced
thearchy
thetical
thoraces
thoracic
traducer
tragical
triarchy
tricycle
trifocal
tritical
tropical
tubercle
tussocky
twofaced
undercut
unforced
unicycle
univocal
unplaced
unvoiced
uppercut
valanced
vernicle
verrucae
versicle
vertical
vertices
verticil
viaticum
viscacha
vizcacha
vortical
vortices
waesucks
wainscot
whitecap
wiseacre
zodiacal
absurdly
accredit
addendum
amazedly
amusedly
appendix
ascender
asphodel
attender
avowedly
balladic
balladry
befuddle
begirded
begrudge
beholden
beholder
Bermudas
bewilder
biocidal
birthday
brocaded
bromidic
caboodle
calendar
calender
calvados
candidly
canoodle
cathedra
cathodal
cathodic
chiefdom
clerkdom
coachdog
colander
conceder
confider
conoidal
consider

copyedit
corridor
corundum
cowardly
crusader
cuboidal
cursedly
cuspidor
cussedly
cylinder
daffodil
defender
demander
deucedly
disendow
dislodge
disorder
doggedly
dogooder
doomsday
drownded
elatedly
embedded
embolden
engender
engirdle
enkindle
episodal
episodic
everyday
excluder
expander
exploder
extender
extrados
feastday
fervidly
floridly
flounder
foetidly
forcedly
foreedge
forrader
friendly
frigidly
gambados
gipsydom
granddad
grounder
guidedog
gynandry
gypsydom
Haggadah
harridan
havildar
heatedly
Helladic
heraldic
heraldry
honeydew
horridly
housedog
impledge
impolder
included
inlander
intended
intrados
intruder
inwardly
islander
jaggedly
jocundly
jumpedup
labrador
lackaday
lavender
legendry
limpidly
liquidly
lopsided
maenadic
marauder
markedly
mastodon
menhaden
methodic
microdot
misjudge
molybdic
monandry
morbidly
muscadel
myrmidon
nuclidic
occluded
offender
offsider
oleander
onesided
organdie
orthodox
outmoded
outrider
outsider
pallidly
pappadom
periodic
placidly
pomander
poppadum
porridge
prejudge
presidio
prosodic
provided
provider
puppydog
puppydom
putridly
queendom
rachides
raggedly
recorder
rehandle
rekindle
reminder
retarded
retarder
rewarder
Rhinodon
ribaldry
rotundly
roughdry
ruggedly
saccadic
sacredly
saintdom
samizdat
Saturday
Saxondom
schiedam
secluded
seconder
secondly
selvedge
sheepdip
sheepdog
sheikdom
shielder
shortday
shoulder
shouldst
shredded
shredder
shrewdly
smoulder
solander
sordidly
splendid
sporadic
spreader
squander
squeedge
squidded
statedly
stolidly
straddle
stranded
stridden
stupidly
subahdar
suborder
suicidal
sympodia
taberdar
Talmudic
tamandua
teacaddy
tetradic
thanedom
thraldom
threader
Thursday
tomnoddy
toreador
tornadic
toroidal
torpidly
torridly
towardly
tripodal
turbidly
turgidly
twosided
unbidden
unbridle
unburden
uncandid
underdid
underdog
unfunded
unitedly
unkindly
unleaded
unloader
unriddle
unsaddle
unseeded
unwisdom
unwordly
upholder
uplander
upwardly
variedly
verandah
villadom
viscidly
vizarded
watchdog
welladay
whoredom
wickedly
wizardly
wizardry
wontedly
workaday
zamindar
zemindar
abducens
abducent
abetment
abutment
accident
acescent
achiness
acidhead
acrolein
actively
adducent
adherent
adjacent
adultery
aesthete
afferent
affluent
afforest
agedness
aggrieve
agrement
airfield
airiness
airspeed
alcahest
alkahest
almagest
ambivert
amoebean
anapaest
anathema
antecede
antihero
antisera
anywhere
aperient
apoplexy
apothegm
apparent
appetent
Aramaean
arbalest
arboreal
arboreta
archaean
archness
argument
armament
astutely
asyndeta
aurorean
averment
aversely
avidness
backless
backrest
backseat
backveld
bailment
baldhead
baldness
Balinese
bareness
barkless
baroness
baseless
basement
baseness
bateleur
battleax
bayadere
bedstead
beebread
befriend
bejabers
beltless
beriberi
besprent
bestrewn
billhead
bindweed
birdseed
birdseye
bivalent
bladdery
blankety
blastema
Blenheim
blinkers
blistery
blithely
bloomers
bloomery
blubbery
bludgeon
bluebell
blueness
blueweed
blustery
boatdeck
bobwheel
bodement
bodiless
boldness
bonehead
boneless
bonemeal
boniness
bookrest
bootless
bourgeon
boxpleat
bracteal
braziery
brettese
Briarean
brimless
broidery
browbeat
buckbean
buddleia
bulkhead
bullhead
bullseye
bushveld
business
busyness
butchery
buttress
butylene
bystreet
caducean
caduceus
caginess
cajolery
calipers
calmness
cameleer
camphene
canoness
careless
Carolean
carotene
casement
cashmere
cateress
cattleya
cemetery
cerement
cerulean
cetacean
Chaldean
chambers
champers
chancery
chasseur
chastely
checkers
Chellean
chequers
chimaera
chinless
choicely
Circaean
claqueur
cleavers
clerkess
clippers
clownery
clueless
clustery
coarsely
cobblers
cochleae
cochlear
codpiece
cogwheel
coherent
coiffeur
coldness
coleseed
coliseum
colliery
compleat
complete
compress
concrete
confrere
congress
congreve
conquest
coolness
cordless
cosiness
cotquean
couldest
countess
courtesy
covalent
crackers
creamery
crescent
crockery
cromlech
cryogeny
cureless
curtness
cuteness
daftness
dampness
danegeld
dankness
darkness
dateless
daybreak
daydream
deadbeat
deadhead
deadness
deafness
dearness
decadent
decedent
deedless
deepness
deferent
deforest
deftness
delivery
demoness
demurely
deponent
derriere
dewiness
diastema
diligent
diriment
discreet
discrete
dispread
distress
divalent
dividend
divinely
docilely
document
dogwhelk
domineer
doorbell
dopiness
dourness
downbeat
doziness
drabness
dracaena
drawwell
dripfeed
drollery
drophead
dropleaf
drudgery
druidess
drumhead
dryclean
duckweed
ductless
dullness
dumbbell
dumbhead
dumbness
dustless
earpiece
easement
easiness
echoless
ectoderm
edgeless
edginess
editress
eeriness
efferent
effluent
eggshell
eighteen
eloquent
emergent
empyreal
empyrean
emulgent
endoderm
endogeny
enforest
engineer
enginery
ensphere
entirely
entirety
entoderm
ephemera
epopoeia
erythema
esculent
estovers
esurient
etcetera
ethereal
ethylene
European
evenness
evilness
existent
exponent
eyepiece
faceless
facilely
fadeless
fairlead
fairness
fangless
farewell
farriery
farthest
fastness
fearless
feathery
feckless
feculent
fedayeen
feedhead
fellness
fiercely
fiftieth
filament
fineness
finitely
fireweed
firmness
fishless
fishmeal
flambeau
flatfeet
flathead
flatness
flattery
flattest
flawless
flaxseed
flickery
flinders
flummery
fluttery
flywheel
foamless
fondness
foodless
footgear
footless
footrest
footwear
forebear
foredeck
forefeel
forefelt
forehead
forepeak
foreseen
foretell
forewent
formless
forspeak
forspent
forswear
fortieth
fortress
foulness
fourleaf
fourteen
fowlpest
foxiness
fragment
Fraulein
freeness
freezeup
frequent
frippery
frondent
frondeur
fruitery
fullness
funereal
furriery
furthest
fusileer
futilely
gableend
gadarene
gainless
Galilean
gameness
gaminess
gangrene
Ganymede
gasolene

gazogene
Genevese
germcell
giantess
gilthead
gladdest
gladness
glanders
glaziery
glibness
glittery
glummest
glumness
goatherd
Godspeed
goldleaf
goodness
goodyear
gormless
goutweed
gradient
grandeur
grapheme
greenery
greyness
grimmest
grimness
grindery
gromwell
grosbeak
gulfweed
habanera
hairless
haleness
halfbeak
halfterm
handbell
handheld
handless
handsewn
hardhead
hardness
harebell
haresear
harmless
harpseal
hasheesh
hatchery
hawkweed
hayfield
haziness
headgear
headless
headrest
heathery
heedless
heelless
heirless
hellbent
helpless
helpmeet
herbless
hexylene
highness
hightest
hindlegs
hipsters
hirrient
hoarsely
hogshead
holiness
Holocene
holstein
homefelt
homeless
homogeny
hoofbeat
hopeless
hornbeam

hornfels
hornless
hotpress
hugeness
humanely
huntress
hurtless
hypoderm
hypogeal
hypogean
hypogene
hypogeum
icecream
icefield
idealess
idiolect
idleness
illtreat
immanent
imminent
immodest
imponent
impotent
impudent
impurely
inchmeal
incident
indecent
indigene
indigent
indirect
indolent
inexpert
influent
inherent
inkiness
innately
innocent
insanely
inscient
insolent
insphere
interest
isocheim
isopleth
isoprene
isoptera
isothere
isotherm
Jacobean
Japanese
Javanese
jejunely
jocosely
jolthead
jongleur
judgment
jugglery
jumpseat
justness
Kanarese
keelless
keenness
kerosene
killdeer
kindless
kindness
knackery
knapweed
kneedeep
kneejerk
knickers
knitwear
ladyfern
lamasery
lameness
landless
lankness
lateness

laziness
leadless
leafless
leanness
leathern
leathery
legalese
legbreak
lensless
lewdness
lifebelt
lifeless
ligament
likeness
limbless
limpness
liniment
Linnaean
linoleum
lintseed
listless
littlego
lodgment
loneness
longness
longterm
longueur
lordless
lorikeet
loudness
loveless
lovenest
loveseat
luckless
luculent
luncheon
lushness
malapert
malefern
maleness
maltreat
Mandaean
manifest
maravedi
marchesa
marchese
marquess
marrieds
Masorete
Masoreth
massless
masthead
matiness
mattress
maturely
mayoress
Mayqueen
mazement
maziness
meagrely
meanness
meekness
meetness
melodeon
menswear
mesoderm
metamere
mezereon
midfield
mightest
mildness
milkweed
millieme
mindless
Minoress
minutely
miserere
misspell
misspelt

misspend
misspent
mistreat
mistress
monkseal
monogeny
monsieur
monument
moonbeam
moonless
morosely
morpheme
mouseear
moveless
movement
muchness
muleteer
muniment
muskdeer
muteness
mutineer
nameless
napoleon
nathless
natively
Nazarene
nearness
neatherd
neatness
needless
needment
neoprene
Nepalese
nescient
newsheet
newspeak
newsreel
niceness
nineteen
nonevent
northern
nosiness
noteless
nudeness
nullness
numbness
nutrient
nutshell
nymphean
obedient
obsolete
obtusely
occident
Odyssean
offbreak
oilfield
oiliness
ointment
ommateum
onepiece
ontogeny
ooziness
opaquely
openness
opponent
orangery
oratress
ornament
ornately
orpiment
orthoepy
otiosely
outbreak
outfield
outguess
outspend
outspent
ovalness
overbear

overfeed
overhead
overhear
overheat
overleaf
overleap
overseas
overseen
overseer
oversell
oversewn
overwear
painless
paleness
pancreas
pantheon
parakeet
pathless
pavement
paysheet
peagreen
pediment
peerless
Pegasean
Pekinese
pellmell
penitent
periderm
perigean
perineal
perineum
peripety
peroneal
pertness
phosgene
pinchers
pinkness
pinwheel
pitiless
pixiness
plangent
plastery
Pliocene
politely
polygene
polygeny
polyseme
polysemy
pondweed
poorness
portiere
portress
potsherd
preelect
premiere
priggery
primness
princely
princess
prioress
proceeds
progress
prophecy
prophesy
prospect
prurient
psaltery
puncheon
puniness
pureness
purulent
pygmaean
pyroxene
quackery
quartern
quarters
quitrent
quotient
raciness

rackrent
railhead
raillery
rainwear
rakehell
ranchero
rankness
rapeseed
raptness
rareness
rashness
realness
reappear
reascend
reassert
reassess
reckless
recovery
redeless
redirect
redolent
referent
refinery
refluent
reforest
regiment
reindeer
reinless
reinsert
reinvest
relucent
remanent
remotely
renitent
reorient
repetend
reprieve
resident
restless
reticent
retrieve
reverend
reverent
richness
rifeness
ringneck
ripeness
roadless
rockhewn
rockweed
rollneck
roodbeam
roofless
rootless
ropiness
roseleaf
rosiness
rounders
rudeness
rudiment
rugosely
ruleless
rustless
ruthless
saboteur
sackless
saddlery
safeness
sageness
sailless
saltless
saltness
sameness
Samoyede
saneness
Sangreal
sapgreen
sateless
saunders

savagely
savagery
scandent
scarcely
scarless
sclereid
scragend
scullery
seachest
seagreen
seamless
seapiece
seashell
seatbelt
securely
sedately
sediment
seedleaf
seedless
seigneur
selfheal
selfhelp
selfless
selfness
sentient
serenely
servient
severely
sexiness
shagreen
shepherd
shimmery
shipment
shoeless
shopbell
shuddery
sickness
sidehead
sidereal
sixtieth
skewness
skilless
skindeep
skinhead
skinless
slagheap
slattern
slimmest
slimness
slippery
slithery
slobbery
slowness
slumbery
smeltery
smithers
smithery
smothery
smugness
snippety
snobbery
snowless
snuffers
snuggery
snugness
soapless
sobriety
softhead
softness
soilless
soldiery
soleness
sombrely
sombrero
somedeal
somedele
songless
sorehead
soreness

soulless
sourness
southern
sowbread
spalpeen
spardeck
sparsely
spivvery
spotless
sprucely
spryness
spurgear
squarely
squireen
squirely
staggers
stampede
starkers
starless
stemless
stilbene
strategy
strepent
strident
sturgeon
subagent
suberect
subpoena
subtlety
Sudanese
sundress
superego
supinely
supplely
suppress
sureness
swanherd
swanneck
swannery
tactless
tailless
tallness
tameless
tameness
tapedeck
tapeless
tartness
tautness
teabread
teabreak
teachest
tearless
tegument
tenement
terebene
termless
thickety
thievery
thinness
thinnest
thirteen
thisness
thuggery
thundery
thusness
tickseed
tideless
tidiness
tiebreak
tigereye
timeless
tininess
tintless
tireless
titaness
toepiece
tombless
tonedeaf
toneless

topdress
torchere
tracheae
tracheal
tracheid
trammels
transect
transept
trappean
trashery
treefern
treeless
trickery
trimness
trippery
triskele
trousers
trouvere
trueness
trumpery
tubeless
tuneless
tutoress
tweezers
twelvemo
twittery
twopiece
Tyrolean
Tyrrhene
ugliness
umptieth
unfreeze
uniquely
unlikely
unlovely
unthread
untimely
unwisely
upstream
urbanely
vainness
vaneless
vastness
vehement
veilless
venereal
ventless
vestment
victress
Viennese
viewless
vileness
vilipend
virement
virulent
vivisect
voidness
votaress
voteless
voyageur
waitress
wakeless
wallfern
wardress
wariness
warmness
wartweed
waveless
waviness
waxiness
weakness
weedless
weldment
welldeck
wellhead
wellread
whatness
wheatear
Whiggery
whiskers
whiskery
whispery
wideness
wifeless
wildness
wiliness
windless
wingbeat
wingless
wireless
wiriness
wiseness
witchelm
witchery
witchety
withheld
woolfell
woollens
wordless
workless
wormgear
wormseed
wouldest
xanthein
xanthene
Yankeefy
yestreen
youngest
yourself
zaniness
zarzuela
basinful
beatific
bellyful
blackfly
blameful
blissful
blushful
boastful
calcific
caprifig
catchfly
cheerful
cornific
cranefly
crucifer
crucifix
doubtful
dreadful
dreamful
earmuffs
eventful
faithful
fanciful
febrific
feverfew
fleshfly
forcefed
forceful
fruitfly
fruitful
gefuffle
ghastful
glassful
godawful
graceful
grateful
greenfly
guileful
horrific
horsefly
housefly
houseful
hoverfly
kefuffle
loathful
magnific
merciful
mirthful
morbific
mournful
mouthful
multifid
pantofle
paraffin
peaceful
pettifog
plateful
pontifex
powerful
prankful
prideful
prolific
puppyfat
rightful
salvific
scoopful
scornful
senseful
shameful
shelfful
slothful
smallfry
somnific
spadeful
specific
spinifex
spiteful
spoonfed
spoonful
sportful
stallfed
stickful
stonefly
tableful
Tartuffe
tasteful
terrific
thankful
therefor
thurifer
toothful
toplofty
transfer
transfix
tristful
trustful
truthful
turbofan
underfur
unlawful
unmuffle
unroofed
unstuffy
vauntful
vengeful
voiceful
wasteful
watchful
weariful
whitefly
worthful
wrackful
wrathful
wrongful
youthful
aasvogel
abridger
achingly
affright
agaragar
airtight
allergen
allergic
allnight
anagogic
analogic
analogue
androgen
apagogic
apologia
apologue
arpeggio
arranger
asperges
astragal
befogged
besieger
besought
bewigged
bitingly
boringly
bunfight
campagna
cardigan
choragic
choragus
choregic
choregus
coccyges
collagen
colleger
collogue
compages
conjugal
contagia
cottager
cottagey
coxalgia
cyanogen
daringly
daylight
debagged
debugged
dialogic
dialogue
diplogen
dogfight
donought
dotingly
duologue
ecologic
endanger
enlarger
enneagon
entangle
epilogue
escargot
eyesight
fanlight
flashgun
florigen
foliaged
galangal
gapingly
gaslight
gastight
geologic
gestagen
glucagon
glycogen
goosegog
gunfight
harangue
heptagon
histogen
hooligan
hoosegow
hydrogen
immingle
indulger
inflight
intrigue
inveigle
isagogic
jokingly
lallygag
larynges
liturgic
lovingly
madrigal
malinger
martagon
meninges
meringue
midnight
misbegot
miscegen
movingly
musingly
negligee
nitrogen
nonlegal
nonrigid
oakegger
outright
outsight
oxtongue
parergon
pathogen
Pelasgic
pellagra
pentagon
photogen
pillager
pishogue
plumaged
presager
prodigal
prologue
prorogue
protegee
pryingly
rejigger
revenger
roentgen
rummager
sawedged
scourger
scragged
sennight
sewergas
shrugged
skylight
solfeggi
sparkgap
sphingid
spraygun
sprigged
springal
springer
squeegee
squiggle
squiggly
squilgee
sterigma
straggle
straggly
straight
stranger
strangle
strength
stringed
stringer
strongly
struggle
sunlight
synergic
synergid
syntagma
syringes
takingly
tarragon
taxingly
teenager
tetragon
theurgic
toboggan
tommygun
triangle
tryingly
twilight
twoedged
unhinged
unkingly
unpegged
unrigged
unsought
untangle
untaught
villager
vintager
warragal
warrigal
watergas
waxlight
acanthus
agraphia
aguishly
almighty
ambusher
anarchic
anorthic
antiphon
Arapahoe
aweather
babushka
backchat
ballyhoo
barathea
bleacher
bluechip
bodyshop
boyishly
Bradshaw
branched
brancher
branchia
breather
breeches
britches
broacher
bronchia
bronchus
brougham
buckshee
buckshot
cabochon
capuchin
catechol
chinchin
chitchat
chopchop
chowchow
churchly
clanship
clerihew
clincher
coauthor
cockshut
colophon
coryphee
cratches
crotched
crotchet
deanship
decipher
detached
dianthus
diarchal
diarchic
diarrhea
dramshop
draughts
draughty
drencher
dropshot
droughty
dumbshow
dustshot
eighthly
elenchus
empathic
enarched
encipher
enricher
eolithic
eulachon
exanthem
feldsher
fellahin
fernshaw
finisher
fireship
flagship
fletcher
flincher
foreshow
fourthly
garishly
grogshop
groschen
Guelphic
Halachah
hardship
heathhen
hedgehog
hedgehop
heirship
hernshaw
hypothec
impishly
ingather
Jonathan
junkshop
khuskhus
kickshaw
kingship
ladyship
Langshan
launcher
lavishly
lecithin
lengthen
longship
lordship
Manichee
marathon
memsahib
metaphor
modishly
monachal
monkship
moonshee
moonshot
mopishly
mulishly
naphthol
nenuphar
nighthag
oafishly
oenophil
ornithic
overshoe
overshot
owlishly
padishah
pawnshop
peepshow
perisher
petechia
phosphor
pinochle
planchet
plougher
polisher
popishly
preacher
punisher
quencher
rakishly
ravisher
rhonchal
rhonchus
rickshaw
ricochet
roughhew
sandshoe
scirrhus
scorcher
scutcher
sealyham
searcher
seraphic
seraphim
shanghai
sideshow
sinophil
sketcher
slipshod
slopshop
sloucher
smoothen
smoothie
smoothly
snapshot
snatcher
sneeshan
snitcher
snowshoe
softshoe
somewhat
somewhen
sorochen
splasher
squasher
stancher
stanchly
stitcher
strophic
swanshot
switchel
telethon
teraphim
thatcher
thoughts
thrasher
thresher
together
toolshed
township
tranship
treacher
trencher
tuckahoe
tuckshop
twinship
twitcher
untether
unwashed
unwished
uppishly
vanisher
wardship
whimwham
whinchat
whitehot
wholehog
wineshop
woodchat
woodshed
woolshed

workshop
wreathen
wretched
yataghan
zenithal
Abbaside
abbatial
Abderite
abetting
ablation
ablative
ablution
aborning
abortion
abortive
abrasion
abrasive
abstrict
abutting
Accadian
acerbity
achenial
acosmism
acquaint
acridine
acridity
acrolith
acrotism
actiniae
actinian
actinias
actinide
actinism
actinium
activism
activist
activity
acturial
adaption
adaptive
addition
additive
adenoids
adhesion
adhesive
Adlerian
admonish
adnation
adoption
adoptive
aegirine
aeration
aerolite
aerolith
affinity
affusion
agential
agnation
agrarian
Akkadian
alacrity
alarmist
Albanian
albinism
algicide
algidity
algorism
alienism
alienist
alkalies
alkalify
alkaline
allodial
allodium
allspice
allusion
allusive
alluvial
alluvion
alluvium
alpinism
alpinist
Alsatian
altruism
altruist
ambition
ammoniac
ammonify
ammonite
ammonium
amnesiac
amortise
analcime
analcite
andesine
andesite
aneurism
angelica
ankerite
annalist
anserine
antefixa
anterior
anything
aphasiac
aphelion
aphicide
aphorise
aphorism
aphorist
apiarian
apiarist
apocrine
appetite
apposite
appraise
aquarist
aquarium
aquatint
aquiline
arapaima
arbalist
arborist
Arcadian
archaise
archaism
archaist
argufier
Arianism
Armenian
Arminian
armorial
arsenide
arsenite
arsonist
arterial
artesian
artifice
ascidian
ascidium
asperity
assuming
Assyrian
astatine
asterisk
asterism
astonied
astonish
atheling
Athenian
atrocity
atropine
atticism
audacity
audition
auditive
aurelian
autogiro
autunite
averring
aversion
aversive
aviarist
aviation
avionics
avulsion
axiality
Ayrshire
backbite
backfire
backlist
backside
Baconian
Bactrian
bakshish
balefire
balkline
banality
banjoist
bankbill
bantling
banxring
baronial
baseline
basicity
basidial
basidium
basilica
basilisk
Batavian
Bavarian
bdellium
beagling
beautify
becoming
beeswing
beetling
bellbird
benedick
benedict
benefice
bestride
betacism
bezonian
biassing
bibation
biennial
biennium
bifacial
bigamist
bilabial
binomial
birdlime
bitchily
blabbing
blacking
blackish
blandish
bleakish
blearily
bleeding
blessing
blimpish
blinding
blinking
blockish
blondish
bloodily
blooming
blotting
blowfish
blowpipe
bluebird
bluefish
blurrily
blurring
boarding
boatbill
bobolink
bobwhite
Bodleian
Boeotian
bohemian
bombsite
bonefish
bonspiel
booklice
boracite
botanise
botanist
botflies
botulism
bouncily
bouncing
boursier
brachial
brachium
brackish
bragging
braiding
brainish
brandied
brandish
brassica
brassily
brattice
brattish
breaking
breeding
breezily
brettice
briefing
brimming
briskish
brisling
broadish
broodily
brookite
browning
brownish
bubaline
buckling
Buddhism
Buddhist
building
bullring
bundling
buntline
bushfire
bustling
Byronism
cabalism
cabalist
cacomixl
caducity
caffeine
cagebird
cageling
caladium
calamine
calamint
calamite
calamity
calidity
callgirl
calycine
Cambrian
camomile
campaign
campfire
camphine
campsite
Canadian
canalise
cancrine
canoeing
canoeist
canonise
canonist
capacity
capeline
caponier
caponise
carabine
Caroline
catamite
catching
catering
cavalier
cavatina
celeriac
celerity
centring
centrism
centrist
ceramics
ceramist
cerusite
champion
chapping
charming
charring
Chartism
Chartist
chastise
chastity
chattily
chatting
cheapish
cheekily
cheerily
cheering
childish
chipping
chirpily
chloride
chlorine
chlorite
chopping
chromite
chromium
chugging
chummily
chumming
churlish
churning
ciborium
circuity
citation
citified
cityfied
civilian
civilise
civility
cladding
clammily
clamming
clanging
clannish
clapping
classics
classify
cleaning
clearing
clinking
clipping
cliquish
cliquism
cloddish
clogging
clothier
clothing
clotting
cloudily
clownish
clubbing
clumsily
coaction
coactive
coalfish
coalmine
codifier
coercion
coercive
cohesion
cohesive
coincide
colonial
colonise
colonist
comedian
comedist
complice
complier
compline
comprise
conation
conative
conceive
conflict
conidial
conidium
conjoint
conspire
contline
contrite
contrive
cooption
cooptive
corkwing
couching
coupling
coursing
courtier
covering
crabbing
cracking
cradling
craftily
cramming
cramoisy
crankily
crannied
crashing
crawfish
crayfish
creakily
creatine
creation
creative
creeping
crescive
cribbing
croakily
Croatian
crocoite
crofting
cropping
crossing
croupier
crowbill
crustily
cruzeiro
cryolite
culicine
Cumbrian
cupidity
curarine
curarise
curative
curtains
cutprice
cymatium
cynicism
cysteine
cytidine
cytosine
dabchick
dahabieh
daintily
daiquiri
dairying
dandyish
dandyism
darkling
dateline
deadline
dealfish
debility
decision
decisive
decurion
definite
deionise
delation
deletion
delirium
Delphian
delusion
delusive
demolish
demoniac
demonian
demonise
demonism
demotion
denarius
denazify
dendrite
deputise
deration
derelict
derision
derisive
describe
destrier
detoxify
deviling
devilish
devilism
Devonian
devotion
dewpoint
dextrine
dialling
diatribe
dicacity
didymium
digamist
digitise
dilation
dilative
dilution
diluvial
diluvian
diluvium
dimerism
diminish
dioecism
diopside
diploidy
dipstick
dirigism
disguise
disjoint
disprize
disquiet
disseise
district
disunion
disunite
disunity
ditheism
ditheist
dividivi
divinise
divinity
division
divisive
Docetism
Docetist
docility
dockside
doctrine
dolerite
dolomite
domicile
dominion
donation
Donatism
Donatist
donative
doorsill
dotation
douanier
dowdyish
downhill
downpipe
downtime
downwind
dragging
dragline
dreamily
dreaming
drearily
dressing
driftice
drilling
drinking
dripping
dropkick
dropping
drowsily
drubbing
drugging
druggist
druidism
drumfire
drumming
drypoint
duckbill
duckling
duelling
duellist
duettist
dumpling
dunghill
duration
durative
dustlike
dwarfish
dwarfism
dwelling
dynamics
dynamism
dynamist
dynamite
eclosion
edgewise
eduction
effusion
effusive
egestion
egestive
Egyptian
eighties
ejection
ejective
ekistics
election
elective
embolism

emceeing
emersion
emission
emissive
emitting
emporium
emulsify
emulsion
emulsive
enaction
enactive
encomion
encomium
endemism
energise
engaging
enormity
enshrine
entrails
envision
Ephesian
epyllion
equalise
equality
equation
equinity
equities
Erastian
erectile
erection
erethism
erewhile
ergotise
ergotism
eruption
eruptive
escapism
escapist
espalier
especial
essayist
Essenism
essonite
esterify
Estonian
eternise
eternity
etherial
etherise
etherism
etherist
ethicism
ethicist
Etrurian
eugenics
eugenism
eugenist
eulogise
eulogist
eulogium
euphuism
euphuist
Eurasian
europium
evection
eventide
eversion
eviction
evincive
evulsion
exacting
exaction
excision
exciting
exequies
exercise
exertion
exiguity
exocrine
exorcise
exorcism
exorcist
exordial
exordium
expedite
exterior
fabulist
facelift
facetiae
facility
fagoting
faintish
fairyism
falchion
fallfish
familial
familiar
faradism
farthing
fatalism
fatalist
fatality
faultily
Faustian
favonian
feeblish
feedpipe
felicity
felinity
feminine
feminise
feminism
feminist
feminity
ferocity
fetching
feticide
feverish
fewtrils
fiddling
fidelity
fiducial
fiendish
fiftyish
fighting
figurine
filariae
filarial
filefish
Filipina
Filipino
filthily
fimbriae
finalise
finalism
finalist
finality
firebird
fireside
fishwife
fixation
fixative
flagging
flapping
flashily
flashing
flatfish
flatling
flattish
flatwise
flautist
fleabite
flection
fleeting
flimsily
flintily
flipping
flipside
flitting
floating
flogging
flooring
floppily
flopping
flourish
flubbing
fluepipe
fluidics
fluidify
fluidise
fluidity
fluoride
fluorine
fluorite
focalise
focusing
fondling
foothill
footling
foramina
fordoing
foreside
foretime
forgoing
forklift
fortuity
fortyish
founding
fraction
francium
Frankish
frapping
freakish
freewill
freezing
frenzied
fretting
Freudian
friction
Friesian
frillies
fringing
friskily
fritting
frocking
frogfish
frogging
frontier
frostily
frosting
frothily
fructify
fruition
frumpish
fuchsine
fuelling
fugacity
fugitive
fullsize
fulltime
function
fusilier
futility
futurism
futurist
futurity
Galenism
galenite
gamebird
gangling
ganglion
gantline
gaolbird
gaselier
gasolier
gasoline
Gaullism
Gaullist
gelatine
gelation
gelidity
genetics
genitive
genocide
gentrice
Georgian
geraniol
geranium
Ghanaian
ghoulish
giantism
gipsyism
gladding
glancing
glassily
glassine
gleaning
gloaming
gloomily
glossily
glossina
glutting
glyptics
gnathite
goalkick
goalline
goatfish
goatling
Gobelins
godchild
goldfish
goldmine
gonidial
gonidium
goodtime
goodwife
goodwill
Graafian
grabbing
Graecise
Graecism
graffiti
graffito
graining
graphics
graphite
grasping
gratuity
grayling
greasily
greedily
greening
greenish
greeting
greffier
greyfish
grimoire
grinning
gripping
grissini
gritting
groggily
grouping
grouting
growling
grubbily
grubbing
grudging
grumpily
guardian
guiltily
gulosity
gumption
gunflint
gunpoint
gunsmith
gypsyism
gyration
hairlike
hairline
halation
halflife
halfpint
halftime
handbill
handline
handling
handlist
handmill
handpick
haploidy
harakiri
hardline
hatching
haunting
Hawaiian
hawklike
headline
headwind
heartily
hebraise
Hebraism
Hebraist
hedonics
hedonism
hedonist
Hegelian
hellfire
helotism
hepatica
hepatise
herdwick
heredity
herewith
Hertzian
highrise
hilarity
hillside
himation
hinduise
Hinduism
hireling
hoarding
hobbyist
hocktide
hocusing
homelike
homesick
homicide
hoodwink
Horatian
hornbill
hornpipe
hornrims
hosepipe
hotelier
humanise
humanism
humanist
humanity
humidify
humidity
humility
humorist
hungrily
hymenial
hymenium
hyoscine
ianthine
Ibsenism
iceblink
idealise
idealism
idealist
ideality
ideation
identify
identity
idiotism
idyllist
ignition
ignominy
illation
illative
illumine
illusion
illusive
Illyrian
ilmenite
imbecile
immobile
immunise
immunity
imparity
imperial
imperium
impetigo
impolicy
impolite
imposing
impunity
impurity
inaction
inactive
incision
incisive
incivism
incoming
indicium
indocile
induline
indusium
inequity
inertial
infamise
inferior
infinite
infinity
infusion
inhesion
iniquity
insanity
inscribe
interior
intimism
invasion
invasive
inviting
iotacism
Irishism
ironside
Islamise
Islamism
Islamite
isthmian
Jacobite
jailbird
japonica
jaundice
jauntily
Jehovist
jeremiad
Jeremiah
jingoish
jingoism
jingoist
jobation
jocosity
joystick
judicial
junction
juvenile
Kashmiri
kerchief
kerosine
Khmerian
kindling
kinesics
kinetics
kingbird
kingfish
kinglike
kingsize
klondike
knapping
kneehigh
knitting
knocking
knotting
lability
lacewing
laconian
laconism
ladybird
ladylike
lamblike
landgirl
landline
landmine
languish
lapicide
lapidify
laterite
latinise
Latinism
Latinist
latinity
laughing
lavation
laxative
Lazarist
lazulite
lazurite
leaflike
learning
legalise
legalism
legalist
legality
legatine
legation
legerity
lemurine
Leninism
Leninist
Leninite
lenitive
leporine
lewisite
libation
licorice
lifelike
lifeline
lifesize
lifetime
ligation
lighting
lightish
likewise
limekiln
limerick
limonite
linguist
lipstick
littling
livelily
liveried
liverish
livewire
lividity
lixivium
loadline
loathing
lobation
lobbyist
lobeline
localise
localism
locality
locative
locution
logician
longtime
longwise
lordling
lovebird
lovelily
lovesick
lowering
lowlying
loyalist
lucidity
luminist
lumpfish
lunarian
lunation
lungfish
lustrine
lustring
lutanist
lutecium
lutenist
lutetium
luxation
lyophile
lyrebird
lyricism
lyricist
magazine
magician
mainline
maiolica
majolica
majority
malarial
malarian
maledict
mandrill
manorial
mantling
manurial
marbling
maritime
marquise
marrying
material
materiel
maturity
maverick
maximise
mazarine
Mazdaism
mealtime
meantime
meconium
medicine
megalith
melamine
melanism
melanite
melinite
melodise
melodist
memorial
memorise
meridian
mesquite
middling
midpoint
midships
mightily
migraine

Milesian
minacity
minimise
Minorite
minority
minutiae
misalign
mischief
misdoing
misguide
misprint
misprise
misprize
misthink
mistrial
miswrite
mobilise
mobility
modalism
modalist
modality
modifier
molality
molarity
molehill
Molinism
Molinist
monadism
monaxial
monazite
mondaine
monetise
monition
monitive
monkfish
monodist
monolith
monomial
monotint
monoxide
monteith
moonfish
moonrise
moralise
moralism
moralist
morality
Moravian
morosity
morphine
mosquito
motility
motivity
motorial
motoring
motorise
motorist
motorium
mottling
moulding
mounting
mourning
mucosity
multeity
munition
murrhine
muscling
musician
mutation
mycelial
mycelium
mylonite
nailfile
narceine
narghile
nasalise
nasality
natality
natation
nativism
nativist
nativity
naturism
naturist
nauplius
Nazarite
Nazirite
neaptide
nebulise
nebulium
neckline
needfire
negation
negative
negroism
nephrite
nepotism
nestling
neutrino
nicotian
nicotine
niggling
nihilism
nihilist
nihility
ninepins
nineties
Noachian
nobelium
nobility
nodalise
nodality
nodation
nodosity
nomadise
nomadism
nondairy
nonstick
nonunion
nonwhite
noontide
noontime
northing
nosedive
nosepipe
nosering
notarial
notation
notching
novation
novelise
novelist
nubility
numbfish
nursling
nutarian
nutation
oblation
obliging
oblivion
obsidian
obtusity
occasion
occupier
offdrive
offering
official
offprint
oiticica
olympiad
Olympian
omission
omitting
oncidium
oncoming
onychite
oogonial
oogonium
oologist
ophidian
opposite
optative
optician
optimise
optimism
optimist
Orangism
Orcadian
organise
organism
organist
oscinine
otiosity
ottavino
outgoing
outlying
outpoint
outreign
outshine
outvying
outweigh
ovenbird
overfill
overfish
overkill
overnice
override
overripe
overside
oversize
overtime
overview
overwind
pacifier
pacifism
pacifist
paganise
paganish
paganism
pagurian
palatial
palatine
palomino
paludism
papalise
papalism
papalist
paradigm
paradise
parasite
parodist
Parsiism
Parthian
parttime
pastries
patagium
patchily
pavilion
pearlies
pearling
pearlite
peculiar
pedalier
Pelagian
pelerine
pelorism
penalise
penknife
peperino
perceive
peridium
peroxide
perspire
Peruvian
petaline
petition
phormium
phrasing
Phrygian
piddling
piercing
piffling
pigswill
pilosity
pinpoint
pinprick
pintsize
pipefish
pipeline
piperine
pisolite
pixieish
plaguily
plaiding
planking
planning
plastics
platting
plaudits
playbill
playgirl
playtime
pleading
pleasing
plebeian
pleurisy
plodding
plopping
plotting
pluckily
plugging
plumbing
plumbism
plumpish
pointing
polarise
polarity
polemics
polemise
polemist
politick
politico
politics
polonium
polypide
polypite
populism
populist
porkling
porosity
porpoise
portfire
position
positive
postmill
potation
potstill
poultice
pounding
practice
practise
praecipe
praedial
prandial
prankish
preexist
prentice
preprint
prescind
pressing
prestige
prettify
prettily
priapism
priedieu
priggish
priggism
primming
printing
priority
prissily
pristine
prodding
proemial
proofing
propping
prosaism
prosaist
Prussian
psalmist
psychics
psychism
psychist
ptomaine
ptyalism
puffbird
pugilism
pugilist
punition
punitive
puparial
puparium
pupation
puppyish
purblind
purfling
purifier
purplish
pushbike
putative
pygidial
pygidium
pyrexial
pyridine
pyxidium
quackish
quadriga
quagmire
qualmish
quantify
quantise
quantity
quarrier
quartile
quayside
queasily
queening
queerish
question
queueing
quiddity
quietism
quietist
quilting
quipping
quirkily
quisling
quitting
quizzing
rabidity
racemise
rainbird
rallying
rallyist
rambling
ranarian
ranarium
rapacity
rapidity
rarefied
rasorial
ratifier
rattling
reaction
reactive
reaffirm
realtime
rearmice
rearview
reassign
recision
redblind
redbrick
redefine
redesign
redshift
redshirt
reedbird
reedling
reedpipe
regalism
regality
regicide
regolith
reignite
relation
relative
religion
relumine
remedial
reremice
rescript
resinify
respring
restrict
resupine
retiring
reviling
revision
revivify
rewaking
Rhaetian
rhyolite
ricebird
Riesling
rightist
rigidify
rigidity
rigorism
rigorist
ringside
riparian
riverine
roadside
roadsign
roasting
rockbird
rockfish
rocklike
rockling
rogation
Romanian
romanise
Romanism
Romanist
rosarian
rosefish
rosepink
Rotarian
rotation
rotative
roturier
roughish
roundish
rowdyish
rowdyism
royalism
royalist
rubidium
rugosity
Rumanian
ruralise
ruralism
ruralist
rurality
rushlike
sagacity
sailfish
salacity
salariat
salaried
Salesian
salinity
Salopian
saltlick
saltmine
samarium
samphire
sampling
sanative
sanctify
sanction
sanctity
sandwich
sandyish
sanguine
sanitise
sapidity
saponify
saponite
sapphics
sapphire
sapphism
satanism
satanist
satirise
satirist
saxatile
Saxonism
Saxonist
scallion
scampish
Scandian
scandium
scanning
scansion
scanties
scantily
scarcity
scarring
scathing
scattily
scatting
scheming
scholium
sciatica
sciolism
sciolist
scissile
scission
sciurine
sclerite
scolding
scorpion
scottice
Scottish
scouting
scraping
scrutiny
scudding
scullion
scumming
scurrile
scurvily
seagoing
seaonion
security
sedation
sedative
sedition
sedulity
seedfish
seedling
seedtime
seignior
selenide
selenite
selenium
selfpity
selfwill
Semitise
Semitism
Semitist
semolina
semplice
senarius
senility
senorita
serenity
sericite
serosity
serotine
severity
shabbily
shafting
shaggily
Shaktism
shamming
sharpish
sheading
shealing
shedding
sheepish
sheeting
shelving
shieling
shiftily
shilling
shinning
shipping
shirring
shirting
shocking
shoddily
shoebill
shogging
shooting
shopgirl
shopping
shortish
showbill
showgirl
shrewish
shunning
shutting
Siberian
Sicilian
sicklist
sidedish
sidekick
sideline
sideling
siderite
sideview
sidewind
sidewise
silicide
silicify
silphium
Silurian
similise
simoniac
simonist
simplify
simplism
sinapism
singeing
sinicise
sirenian
sitarist
sizzling
skerrick

skidding
skilling
skimmilk
skimming
skimpily
skinning
skipping
skirmish
skirting
skittish
slabbing
slagging
slamming
slangily
slapping
slashing
sleazily
sledding
sleepily
sleeping
slimming
slimmish
slinkily
slipping
slipring
slitting
slobbish
slogging
sloppily
slopping
slotting
slubbing
slugging
sluggish
slumming
slurring
sluttish
smallish
smaltite
smarmily
smartish
smashing
smelling
smocking
smudgily
smuttily
snagging
snaplink
snappily
snapping
snappish
snazzily
sneakily
sneakish
sniffily
snipping
snobbish
snobbism
snogging
snootily
snowbird
snowlike
snowline
snubbing
soapdish
soberise
Socinian
sodalite
sodality
sodomite
soilpipe
solanine
solarise
solarism
solarist
solarium
solation
solatium
solecism
solecist
solfaist
solidify
solidity
solstice
solution
somatism
sometime
sonatina
songbird
sonority
soothing
sorority
sorption
sorptive
soterial
sounding
sourdine
southing
spaewife
spanking
spanning
sparkish
sparling
sparring
sparsity
spatting
speaking
speedily
spelling
spherics
spiffing
spinning
spitfire
spitting
splenial
splenius
spoffish
spongily
sponsion
spookily
spookish
spoonily
sportily
sporting
sportive
spottily
spotting
spunkily
spurling
spurrier
spurring
squarish
stabbing
stabling
stablish
stalling
stallion
standing
standish
stannite
starfish
starlike
starling
starrily
starring
starting
steadily
steading
stealing
steamily
stearine
steatite
steening
steepish
steering
stellify
stellion
stemming
stepping
stepwise
sterling
sternite
stetting
stibnite
stickily
stiffish
stilbite
stingily
stinking
stirring
stockily
stocking
stockish
stockist
stodgily
stoicism
stopping
stormily
stoutish
strabism
stratify
striking
strobila
strobile
strobili
stubbing
studding
stuffily
stuffing
stultify
stumming
stumpily
stunning
sturdied
sturdily
suberise
subjoint
suboxide
subprior
suchlike
suckling
sudarium
sulphide
sulphite
sultrily
Sumerian
sunblind
sundried
sundries
sunshine
sunshiny
superior
supplial
supplier
supplies
surefire
surfbird
surffish
surplice
surprise
swabbing
swagging
swainish
swanking
swanlike
swanning
swapping
swastika
swatting
swearing
sweeping
sweeting
sweetish
swelling
swigging
swimming
swinging
swobbing
swopping
swotting
sybarite
sycamine
syconium
sylphide
sylphine
sylphish
symphile
syncline
synovial
syzygial
tackling
Tahitian
tailpipe
tamarind
tamarisk
Tamilian
tangoist
Tantrism
Tantrist
tapelike
tapeline
Tarpeian
tawdrily
taxation
teaching
technics
teething
telecine
telefilm
teleview
televise
temerity
tempting
tenacity
tenorite
tenurial
tepidity
termtime
tetanise
tetchily
thallium
theodicy
theorise
theorist
thermion
thermite
thespian
thiamine
thickish
thievish
thinking
thinning
thinnish
thriving
thudding
thuggism
thumping
ticklish
tidemill
tigerish
tilefish
timidity
tingeing
tinsmith
titanism
titanite
titanium
toadfish
toadyish
toadyism
tokenism
tolldish
tonality
tonguing
tonicity
toothily
toothing
tortoise
totalise
totality
totemism
totemist
touchily
touching
toughish
tovarish
toxicity
tracking
traction
tractive
training
tramline
transire
trapping
Trappist
trashily
treatise
trekking
trendily
trephine
trialist
triaxial
trichina
trichite
trickily
trickish
trifling
trilling
trillion
trillium
trimming
trioxide
tripping
tripwire
tristich
triunity
trochili
troilite
trophied
trotting
troupial
trucking
trunnion
trussing
trustily
tumbling
tumidity
Tunisian
Turanian
turnpike
turtling
tutorial
twenties
twinling
twinning
twitting
typehigh
typifier
tyrosine
ubiquity
uintaite
ulterior
ultraism
ultraist
unbelief
unburied
uneasily
unending
unerring
unfading
unfilial
uniaxial
unionise
unionism
unionist
unseeing
unsocial
unstring
unthrift
untidily
unwarily
uprising
upspring
upstairs
urbanise
urbanism
urbanist
urbanite
urbanity
Ursuline
vacation
vagility
valerian
validity
valorise
vanadium
vanquish
vapidity
vaporise
vaulting
vegetive
velamina
velarium
velleity
velocity
venality
venation
Venetian
venosity
Venusian
veracity
verifier
verjuice
veronica
vesuvian
vexation
vicarial
vicinity
Vietminh
vilifier
villainy
vinosity
viperine
viperish
viricide
viridian
viridity
virilism
virility
vitalise
vitalism
vitalist
vitality
vitiligo
vituline
vivacity
vivarium
vivifier
vixenish
vocalise
vocalism
vocalist
vocality
vocation
vocative
volatile
volition
volitive
voltaism
volution
vomerine
vomitive
voracity
votarist
vowelise
Wahabism
Wahabite
wakening
wakerife
warpaint
waterice
watering
waterish
waygoing
weakfish
weakling
weanling
wellnigh
Wellsian
weregild
whacking
whapping
wheezily
whetting
whidding
Whiggish
Whiggism
whinsill
whiplike
whipping
whirring
whizzing
whooping
whopping
wifelike
wildfire
wildlife
windmill
windpipe
wintrily
witching
wolffish
womanise
womanish
woodbind
woodbine
woodlice
woodpile
woodwind
wormlike
worthily
woundily
wrapping
wrathily
xanthine
xanthium
xenolith
xylonite
yachting
yeanling
yearling
yearning
yeastily
yielding
youngish
yuletide
zecchini
zecchino
zibeline
zinckify
zincking
zombiism
zonation
zoophily
zucchini
carcajou
crackjaw
kinkajou
nightjar
popinjay
stickjaw
turbojet
Algonkin
autarkic
bearskin
bedmaker
bespoken
biweekly
buckskin
calfskin
cannikin
capeskin
Cherokee
coonskin
coworker
deerskin
devilkin
dybbukim
foreskin
forsaken
goatskin
havocked
haymaker
hijacker
lambskin
larrikin
latchkey
lawmaker
magicked
malarkey
mannikin
mimicked
mimicker
mistaken
moleskin
monicker
mutchkin
onlooker
ostrakon
oxpecker
panicked
pannikin
partaken
reawaken
sealskin
sheepked
shiftkey
shrinker
shrunken
sprinkle
sprocket
squawker
squeaker
streaked
streaker
stricken
strickle
strucken
sunbaked
swanskin
thwacker
turnskin
unbacked
unbroken
unbuckle
unlinked
unmarked
watchkey
whizzkid
wigmaker
wineskin
wolfskin
woolskin
aborally
abutilon
aciculae
acicular
aciculas
actually
aerially
aiguille
alveolar

alveolus
amorally
ampullae
anabolic
animally
annually
annulled
anthelia
apically
appalled
artfully
articled
bachelor
bacillar
bacillus
bastille
battalia
befallen
beguiler
benzylic
bevelled
beveller
biathlon
blackleg
blahblah
bordello
bouillon
bracelet
bractlet
brindled
bromelia
brooklet
brutally
bungalow
caballed
cachalot
calculus
camellia
canaille
cannulae
cannular
cannulas
capellet
capsular
carbolic
carillon
carnally
carolled
casually
casualty
catholic
caudally
caudillo
causally
cavilled
caviller
cellular
cephalic
cervelat
chandler
chapelry
chenille
chivalry
chorally
cingulum
circular
clipclop
clopclop
cloudlet
coagulum
coleslaw
compiler
condylar
consoler
consular
convolve
convulse
corselet
costplus
cotillon
coverlet
crenelle
crosslet
crueller
cupelled
curculio
cypselae
Cyrillic
dactylar
dactylic
dentalia
detailed
devilled
diabolic
dicyclic
disallow
dismally
dissolve
distally
disvalue
dorsally
dowelled
drabbler
dribbler
dribblet
drupelet
durables
encyclic
enrolled
entailer
entellus
enthalpy
epically
epicalyx
epistler
equalled
escallop
eschalot
excelled
exemplar
exemplum
expelled
expellee
extolled
facially
faunally
festally
feudally
fibrilla
filially
fireclay
fireplug
fiscally
fishglue
fistulae
fistular
fitfully
flabella
flagella
flimflam
flipflap
flipflop
floodlit
florally
flotilla
fluellin
footslog
foreplay
formalin
formally
formulae
formulas
foveolae
franklin
frenulum
fribbler
frijoles
frontlet
frugally
furbelow
furculae
furcular
Gadhelic
gardyloo
gauntlet
genially
gerbille
glabella
globally
globular
globulin
Goidelic
golfclub
gonfalon
grabbler
granular
gravelly
greenlet
Griselda
grizzled
grumbler
gruntled
guerilla
handclap
Hercules
hostelry
impelled
impeller
inoculum
intaglio
ironclad
isabella
jewelled
jeweller
jovially
joyfully
Jugoslav
labelled
labellum
labially
laically
lamellae
lamellar
lancelet
landslip
lapelled
lawfully
lethally
levelled
leveller
libelled
libellee
libeller
lineally
lipsalve
loblolly
Lucullan
magdalen
magnolia
mamillae
mamillar
mandolin
manfully
mantelet
mantilla
manually
martello
maxillae
medalled
medallic
medially
menially
mentally
mescalin
mesially
metalled
metallic
methylic
micellar
missilry
modelled
modeller
Mongolic
monoglot
mortally
moufflon
murrelet
muscular
mutually
nautilus
Negrillo
neurally
nickelic
normalcy
normally
nouvelle
nucellus
omphalic
omphalos
openplan
oracular
orchilla
outvalue
overalls
overflew
overflow
overplay
overplus
overslip
pachalic
pamphlet
panelled
pangolin
papillae
papillar
papillon
parallax
parallel
parhelia
parhelic
pashalic
pashalik
pastille
patellae
patellar
pedalled
pedicled
pendular
pendulum
perilled
periplus
petalled
petiolar
petioled
petrolic
phenolic
phenylic
phthalic
piacular
pinnular
pipeclay
planulae
planular
platelet
plumelet
plumular
plurally
polyglot
potbelly
potholer
prattler
predella
premolar
primally
profiler
promulge
propolis
propylic
prunella
prunelle
prunello
pterylae
pulvilli
pupillar
pustular
queenlet
quenelle
quibbler
racially
radially
rascally
rataplan
ravelled
rebelled
rebeller
rebellow
redeploy
reemploy
repealer
repelled
repeller
republic
retailer
revealer
reveille
revelled
reveller
ritually
rivalled
rivelled
rocaille
roseolar
ruefully
saccular
sacculus
sandflea
sardelle
scapulae
scapular
scapulas
schiller
schmaltz
scopulae
scopulas
scrawler
scutella
seaholly
seedplot
sequelae
seraglio
serially
serpulae
sewellel
sexually
shambles
shashlik
shigella
shingler
shingles
shiralee
shuffler
sickflag
sideslip
signally
sinfully
singular
skittles
skypilot
slipslop
smuggler
sniffler
sniffles
sniggler
snuffler
snuffles
socalled
socially
spadille
sparkler
sparklet
spatular
specular
speculum
spiculae
spicular
spiculum
spikelet
spirally
spirilla
sporular
sprawler
squaller
squealer
stapelia
startler
steepled
stickler
stimulus
stippler
stipular
stroller
stumbler
subsolar
swiftlet
swindler
symbolic
syphilis
systolic
tantalic
tantalum
tantalus
tasselly
tenaille
teocalli
thriller
tinselly
toadflax
tomalley
tortilla
totalled
towelled
trampler
treadler
trembler
trembles
trevally
tribally
trochlea
troutlet
truckler
trueblue
twaddler
twiddler
twinkler
umbrella
unaneled
uncalled
uncially
underlap
underlay
underlet
underlie
underlip
unifilar
unipolar
univalve
unsealed
untitled
unwieldy
usefully
vacuolar
Valhalla
valvulae
valvular
Vandalic
vanillin
variolar
vascular
vasculum
venially
verbally
vernally
vexillum
vinculum
visually
vitellin
vitellus
volvulus
vowelled
wagonlit
Walhalla
waterlog
waterloo
weaselly
weeviled
weevilly
wheedler
whiffler
whistler
wilfully
woefully
wordplay
wrangler
wrestler
wriggler
wristlet
yarmulka
yodelled
yodeller
Yugoslav
zeppelin
abnormal
academia
academic
adynamia
adynamic
affirmer
aglimmer
airwoman
alchemic
alderman
anatomic
anthemia
apogamic
bailsman
balsamic
bandsman
bargeman
beadsman
becalmed
bechamel
bedimmed
Benjamin
bergamot
bionomic
bogeyman
bondsman
bonhomie
bottomry
brakeman
buncombe
cardamom
cardamum
chairman
chessman
chiasmus
Chinaman
cinnamic
cinnamon
clansman
coachman
coelomic
cognomen
consomme
consumer
contempt
costumer
cragsman
customer
cyclamen
dairyman
dalesman
deformed
diatomic
dioramic
diplomat
doomsman
drachmae
drachmai
drachmas
dragoman
dragomen
dragsman
dulcimer
Dutchman
economic
embalmer
endermic
engramma
epidemic
episemon
Esquimau
euonymin
euonymus
everyman
exogamic
extremes
fancyman
ferryman
freedman
freshman
fugleman
funnyman
gossamer
gownsman
gravamen
handyman
harrumph
headsman
hebdomad
helmsman
henchman
herdsman
hielaman
horseman
houseman
huntsman
hydromel
illtimed
imprimis
Indiaman
infirmly
inflamer
informal
informed
informer
intermit
intermix
intromit
Irishman
ischemia
ischemic
isogamic
Komsomol
lacrimal
lacrymal
landsman
laywoman
leadsman
liegeman
linesman
madwoman

mandamus
marasmic
marasmus
marksman
marshman
mesdames
misnomer
mittimus
MonKhmer
motorman
motormen
newcomer
nobleman
nonhuman
Norseman
Northman
ofttimes
oldtimer
oligomer
orgasmic
pandemic
perfumer
Philomel
phlegmon
phonemic
pivotman
placeman
prehuman
pressman
presumer
prolamin
proximal
raftsman
ranchman
randomly
ransomer
recommit
redeemer
reformed
reformer
reinsman
rhythmic
rifleman
riverman
salesman
Scotsman
scrammed
screamer
seedsman
septimal
sidesman
spaceman
spearman
specimen
sphygmus
squawman
stasimon
stockman
storeman
streamer
strummed
strummer
stuntman
subhuman
superman
syngamic
systemic
tablemat
talesman
talisman
tallyman
tautomer
tenesmus
thalamic
thalamus
thrummed
townsman
toxaemia
toxaemic
trackman
transmit
tripeman
trisomic
Turcoman
Turkoman
twotimer
uncommon
underman
unformed
unseemly
watchman
waterman
Welshman
wheelman
woodsman
abeyance
abeyancy
abidance
acreinch
affiance
airliner
alburnum
Alderney
alebench
alliance
amaranth
ambiance
ambience
anaconda
aniconic
announce
antennae
antennal
antennas
arachnid
Armagnac
assiento
assignat
assignee
assignor
asthenia
asthenic
attorney
audience
autumnal
badlands
ballonet
bambinos
bandanna
barranca
barranco
barrenly
baryonic
bassinet
beamends
bearings
bechance
beechnut
beginner
benignly
berliner
bignonia
biogenic
blatancy
blazoner
blazonry
bobbinet
bookends
brandnew
brazenly
brazenry
brokenly
buoyancy
burgonet
Burgundy
buttoner
calcanea
cannonry
cantonal
canzonet
carbonic
carbonyl
carcanet
cardinal
cationic
caverned
chaconne
chestnut
Cheyenne
chthonic
churinga
cislunar
clarence
clarinet
clemency
cokernut
columnal
columnar
columned
combings
commando
commence
commoner
commoney
commonly
communal
condense
confiner
confines
congener
conjunct
contango
contents
continua
continue
continuo
convener
convenor
convince
coplanar
courante
cousinly
cracknel
cravenly
credence
credenza
cretonne
criminal
currency
cyclonic
daemonic
daimonic
deadener
decennia
defiance
denounce
designer
detainee
detainer
deviance
deviancy
diaconal
diagonal
diamante
diatonic
diggings
dinornis
diphenyl
disbench
disjunct
dispense
distance
distinct
doorknob
dormancy
doughnut
draconic
dragonet
Dulcinea
duodenal
duodenum
dysgenic
earnings
earthnut
egomania
elegance
elegancy
eleventh
eminence
eminency
encaenia
enceinte
encrinal
encrinic
ensconce
ensigncy
entrance
entrench
erogenic
estrange
euphonic
evidence
examinee
examiner
exchange
exigence
exigency
external
eyeliner
falconer
falconet
falconry
fandance
fandango
fastener
fattener
fervency
flamenco
flamingo
fontanel
fontange
foreknew
foreknow
forzando
frumenty
gainings
galbanum
galvanic
gardener
gardenia
garganey
geomancy
geoponic
Germanic
germinal
gloxinia
glucinum
glyconic
gnomonic
Golconda
goldenly
gorgonia
governor
guaranty
guidance
hacienda
hadronic
hardener
harmonic
hastener
hastings
hawfinch
hazelnut
heavenly
Hellenic
helminth
hereunto
hibernal
Hispanic
Hogmanay
hollands
hormonal
Huguenot
hustings
hyacinth
hydranth
hygienic
imaginal
imagines
impugner
infernal
infringe
inguinal
innuendo
insignia
insomnia
instance
instancy
instinct
internal
internee
intrench
isogonal
isogonic
isotonic
issuance
iterance
ivorynut
japanned
julienne
labdanum
laburnum
lambency
larcener
lashings
laudanum
leadenly
leavings
leggings
legioned
lenience
leniency
lichened
lichenin
listener
lockknit
lodgings
Londoner
loosener
loveknot
mackinaw
Maecenas
mahjongg
maidenly
maligner
malignly
mancando
Mandingo
manganic
mangonel
marginal
martenot
martinet
maternal
matronal
matronly
mechanic
mergence
methanol
methinks
midlands
milliner
Miltonic
mittened
mnemonic
modernly
moorings
morainic
mordancy
mornings
motional
mucrones
muslined
myelinic
myogenic
nascence
nascency
national
neotenic
neuronal
neuronic
nonsense
notional
notornis
noumenal
noumenon
nuisance
obtainer
oddments
olibanum
oppugner
optional
opulence
ordainer
ordnance
origanum
original
orogenic
Ossianic
outrange
pandanus
parcener
pardoner
parlance
parlando
parsonic
paternal
patience
patronal
peccancy
pectines
peelings
pendency
perianth
personae
personal
petronel
phalange
pickings
pilsener
pimiento
pincenez
pinmoney
piquancy
piscinae
pittance
placenta
platinic
platinum
platonic
plutonic
poisoner
pollinia
pollinic
precinct
prepense
presence
pretence
prisoner
profaner
prolonge
propense
protonic
province
prudence
pulmonic
pulvinus
pungency
pursenet
pyogenic
pythonic
rabbinic
radiance
radiancy
rampancy
rational
rawboned
reagency
reasoner
reckoner
reefknot
regional
reliance
renounce
renowned
resigned
response
retainer
retrench
ribbonry
riddance
rinsings
rottenly
safranin
salience
saliency
santonin
sapience
sarcenet
sardonic
sardonyx
sarsenet
Sassanid
saturnic
savannah
sawbones
scavenge
schooner
scoopnet
scrannel
screener
scrounge
seamanly
seasonal
seasoner
seicento
sentence
sentinel
sequence
serranid
Shekinah
shrapnel
sickener
siftings
sinfonia
siphonal
siphonet
siphonic
sirvente
sithence
sixpence
sixpenny
Slavonic
slipknot
slovenly
slovenry
snipsnap
softener
solemnly
solvency
souvenir
sovranty
spadones
spavined
sphagnum
spicknel
spraints
stakenet
staminal
strained
strainer
subgenus
sublunar
suborner
subsonic
subtonic
succinct
succinic
succinum
suddenly
suitings
sullenly
summoner
sundance
supernal
suspense
sweepnet
syntonic
tailings
tangency
tapdance
tautonym
taverner
tectonic
tegmenta
tendence
tendency
tenpence
tenpenny
terminal
terminer
terminus
Teutonic
topliner
trailnet
trawlnet
trecento
tribunal
triennia
trigonal
tuppence
tuppenny
turbaned
turbinal
turnings
twopence
twopenny
Tychonic
tympanic
tympanum
typhonic
tyrannic
unchancy
unclench
unclinch
uncoined
unearned
unevenly
ungainly
unisonal
unkennel
unmanned
unopened
unpinned
unsunned
unweaned
vaccinal
vaccinia
vagrancy
valiance
valiancy
variance

verdancy
vergence
vibrancy
viburnum
violence
virginal
Virginia
visional
voidance
volcanic
volcanos
vulcanic
waggoner
waleknot
wallknot
wantonly
wardance
wardenry
warranty
warrener
weaponry
wellknit
wetlands
whitener
whodunit
winnings
woodenly
workings
writings
yeomanly
yeomanry
zirconia
zoogenic
zoomancy
zygaenid
aardwolf
abattoir
abelmosk
acarpous
acrefoot
acrimony
adespota
aduncous
advisory
aeriform
aerofoil
aerology
aeronomy
agrimony
agrology
agronomy
albacore
aleatory
aleurone
algology
alkaloid
allegory
alumroot
amoeboid
anaerobe
anaphora
anecdote
anechoic
ankylose
anourous
antelope
antepost
anteroom
antibody
antidote
antilogy
antimony
antinode
antinomy
antipode
antipole
antipope
apterous
araceous
armyworm
arsonous
asteroid
atheroma
auditory
auriform
autacoid
autonomy
autosome
autotomy
axiology
babyhood
backbone
backcomb
backdoor
backmost
backroom
ballcock
ballroom
bankbook
banknote
bankroll
barefoot
baritone
barndoor
barytone
baseborn
basswood
bathrobe
bathroom
baudrons
beadroll
beadwork
beanpole
beefwood
beetroot
behemoth
belabour
bellcote
bellwort
bentwood
bestrode
bibulous
bigamous
billfold
billhook
bimanous
bioscope
biparous
blackout
blastoff
blastoid
blossomy
blowhole
bluecoat
bluenose
boathook
boatload
bodywork
bollworm
bolthole
boltrope
booklore
bookpost
bookwork
bookworm
borecole
borehole
botryoid
botyrose
bowfront
breakout
broccoli
brushoff
bryology
bryozoan
buckhorn
buhlwork
bulldoze
bullhorn
bullyoff
bunghole
burntout
busybody
buzzword
cabriole
cacology
caducous
caesious
calliope
calycoid
camisole
cancroid
canorous
capriole
capstone
captious
caracole
careworn
carriole
carryout
cartload
Casanova
casebook
casework
cashbook
catacomb
cataloes
category
catsfoot
cautious
cavicorn
Cenozoic
centroid
ceratoid
ceremony
cernuous
cesspool
chapbook
charcoal
charlock
checkout
chlorous
chorioid
cicerone
ciceroni
cinchona
clangour
claymore
clodpole
clodpoll
clubfoot
clupeoid
coalhole
coatroom
cockboat
cockloft
colewort
coliform
comatose
comedown
conchoid
confront
conglobe
coniform
cookbook
copybook
copyhold
coracoid
cordwood
corkwood
corneous
cornpone
coronoid
Cotswold
couscous
covetous
creosote
croupous
crowfoot
crumhorn
crummock
cubiform
cumbrous
cumulous
cupreous
cushiony
cussword
Cypriote
cytology
darkroom
darksome
dartrous
deadlock
deadwood
decolour
decorous
delusory
demagogy
demijohn
dendroid
denehole
derisory
desirous
dethrone
dextrose
dextrous
diagnose
diaphone
diaspora
diaspore
diastole
dichroic
didymous
diestock
digamous
dilatory
dimerous
dinerout
dingdong
dipnoous
disclose
discrown
disfrock
displode
disproof
disprove
divebomb
dogsbody
dogshore
dogtooth
dolesome
doloroso
dolorous
dominoes
donatory
doorpost
doubloon
dovecote
downcome
downmost
downpour
downtown
doxology
drammock
dropwort
drummock
drumroll
drystone
duckpond
dustbowl
dustcoat
dyspnoea
eagleowl
earphone
eastmost
echinoid
ectozoon
edacious
eftsoons
emulsoid
endozoic
endozoon
enormous
enshroud
ensiform
enthrone
entozoic
entozoon
envelope
environs
epigeous
episcope
equivoke
escalope
escarole
Eskimoan
ethology
evensong
evermore
everyone
evildoer
exiguous
eximious
exospore
eyetooth
fabulous
factious
faltboat
farinose
fasciola
fasciole
fashious
fastfood
fastuous
fatstock
fearsome
feretory
feverous
filiform
filmgoer
fireboat
firebomb
firehose
firelock
firewood
firework
fishbone
fishbowl
fishhook
fishpond
fivefold
flagpole
flatboat
flatfoot
flatworm
fleawort
flexuose
flexuous
floccose
flyblown
foldboat
folklore
folkmoot
folksong
foothold
footnote
footpost
footrope
footsore
footwork
forebode
foredoom
forefoot
foregoer
foregone
forelock
foremost
forenoon
foretold
foreword
formroom
formwork
forsooth
forswore
forsworn
fourfold
foursome
foxglove
frabjous
freakout
freeborn
freehold
freeload
freesoil
frescoes
fretwork
frondose
fructose
fumarole
fumitory
funkhole
fusiform
gabbroic
gabbroid
gadabout
gadzooks
gambroon
gamecock
gamesome
gantlope
gapeworm
garefowl
gatefold
gatepost
gavelock
gemstone
generous
geognosy
geophone
ghettoes
giftbook
girasole
girlhood
glabrous
gladioli
gladsome
glaucoma
glaucous
gleesome
gloriole
glorious
glowworm
gluttony
goalpost
goatmoth
goitrous
goldfoil
gorgeous
goutwort
gracioso
gracious
gralloch
grievous
griseous
grottoes
gruesome
gunstock
gypseous
gyratory
hairworm
halfboot
halfmoon
halfnote
halfsole
halftone
handbook
handhold
handloom
handsome
handwork
hardcore
hardwood
havelock
hawkmoth
hawthorn
headlock
headlong
headmost
headnote
headroom
headword
headwork
hecatomb
hegemony
heirloom
helicoid
heliport
hellhole
henroost
herdbook
Hereford
hexapody
hidyhole
highborn
highlows
highmost
highroad
hillfort
hindmost
holozoic
homebody
homeborn
hometown
homework
hominoid
homodont
homology
hookworm
hornbook
hornworm
hornwort
horologe
horology
hourlong
humanoid
humorous
hydatoid
hymnbook
hypobole
ichorous
ideology
illusory
inchworm
infamous
inscroll
iodoform
ironwood
ironwork
Iroquois
isogloss
isophote
isospory
isotropy
Italiote
jackboot
jeroboam
kakemono
keeshond
keratose
keystone
kidglove
kingbolt
kinghood
kinsfolk
kneehole
knockout
knothole
knotwork
Kohinoor
krumhorn
lacework
lacunose
ladyhood
ladylove
lamppost
landform
landlord
lanthorn
lavatory
laverock
layabout
leadwork
lemuroid
lepidote
levulose
libatory
lifeboat
lifelong
lifework
ligneous
linstock
liripoop
liveborn
livelong
loanword
lobotomy
locofoco
locomote
locutory
lonesome
longboat
longhorn
longsome
loophole
lovelock
lovelorn
lovesome
lovesong
luminous
lungwort
luscious
lustrous
lymphoid
lymphoma
lysosome
macaroni
macaroon
maestoso
maidhood
mailboat
makimono
malodour
mangrove
manifold
maniform
marabout
marigold
markdown
matelote
mealworm
medusoid
megapode
menology
merosome
meshwork
Mesozoic
metazoan
metazoon
miasmous
milepost
milkwort
millpond

minatory
mirepoix
misology
misquote
mitzvoth
mongoose
monitory
monkhood
monogony
monopode
monopoly
monotone
monotony
moonwort
moorcock
moorfowl
moratory
muckworm
mudstone
mushroom
muskrose
muticous
mutinous
mycetoma
mycology
nacreous
nainsook
napiform
natatory
nauseous
nebulous
negatory
nematode
nematoid
newblown
newsroom
nextdoor
nielloed
nightowl
ninefold
nodulose
nodulous
nomology
nosecone
nosology
notebook
nubiform
nubilous
nucleole
nucleoli
nugatory
numerous
numinous
nutbrown
oblatory
ochreous
octaroon
octoroon
odontoid
oecology
oenology
oestrone
oestrous
offshoot
offshore
oilcloth
oilstone
okeydoke
omnivore
oncology
ontology
oogamous
openwork
oreology
orgulous
otoscope
outdoors
outgrown
outshone

ovariole
overbook
overbore
overcoat
overcome
overdone
overdose
overfold
overfond
overload
overlong
overlook
overlord
overrode
oversold
oversoul
overtone
overtook
overwork
overworn
palinode
papulose
papulous
parabola
paragoge
paramour
paranoia
paranoid
parclose
partsong
passbook
passport
password
patulous
payphone
pedagogy
pedology
peephole
peignoir
pembroke
penology
penstock
pentroof
pericope
peridote
perilous
pervious
petalody
petaloid
petalous
phaseout
phyllode
phylloid
phyllome
picaroon
picklock
piedmont
pilewort
piliform
pillwort
pinafore
pinecone
pinewood
pisiform
platform
playbook
playgoer
playroom
plethora
plimsoll
pluvious
poltfoot
poltroon
polypody
polypoid
polypous
polysomy
polyzoan
polyzoic

polyzoon
pomology
poohpooh
populous
porthole
posology
postcode
posthorn
postpone
potstone
precious
previous
primrose
printout
prismoid
prodrome
pruinose
psalmody
pulpwood
pumproom
punitory
pyrenoid
pyriform
pyrrhoea
pyrrhous
quadroon
quandong
racegoer
racemose
railroad
raincoat
ravenous
reabsorb
rearmost
reexport
rehoboam
reimpose
reniform
rerecord
resinoid
resinous
retiform
revisory
rhapsode
rhapsody
rheology
rhomboid
ribosome
rigadoon
rigorous
ringbolt
ringbone
ringdove
ringroad
ringworm
roadbook
rockcork
rockdove
rockrose
rockwood
rockwork
rogatory
rolypoly
roodloft
roothold
rosebowl
roseroot
rosewood
rotatory
rotenone
rugulose
runabout
rushhour
sackcoat
saffrony
sagamore
sailboat
sainfoin
saleroom

saltwort
sanatory
sandworm
sandwort
saporous
sashcord
savorous
sawedoff
sawtooth
scabious
scabrous
scaffold
scammony
scaphoid
scarious
schizoid
scissors
sciuroid
scleroma
sclerose
sclerous
seadrome
seafloor
seafront
seashore
seatrout
sedulous
seedcoat
seedcorn
seedlobe
seignory
selfborn
selfhood
selflove
selfsown
semidome
semitone
sensuous
sepaloid
sepalous
septfoil
serfhood
serology
sesamoid
sexology
Shabuoth
shaddock
shagroon
shakeout
shaleoil
shalloon
shallows
shamrock
shareout
sherlock
shinbone
shipload
shipworm
shoehorn
shofroth
shootout
shopworn
shothole
showboat
showdown
showroom
shutdown
sickroom
sidedoor
sidelong
sidenote
sideroad
signpost
silicone
silkworm
siluroid
singsong
sinkhole
sinology

sinusoid
sitology
skinfood
skislope
slipform
sliproad
slopwork
slowdown
slowpoke
slowworm
slyboots
snowboot
soaproot
soapwort
sobstory
softboil
softsoap
softwood
solenoid
sombrous
somebody
songbook
sonorous
souchong
spacious
spanroof
spathose
specious
sphenoid
spheroid
spittoon
spontoon
spurious
squamose
squamous
staghorn
standoff
stanhope
stannous
starwort
stopcock
strapoil
strigose
strumose
strumous
stubborn
stuccoes
studbook
studious
studwork
suberose
suberous
subfloor
subgroup
sudatory
sulphone
sundrops
sunproof
sunstone
surfboat
swansong
sycamore
sycomore
symbiont
symphony
syndrome
tackroom
taenioid
tagalong
tailcoat
takehome
talapoin
tamanoir
tandoori
tapeworm
tarboosh
taskwork
tattooer
taxonomy

teacloth
teamwork
teaspoon
telegony
teleport
tenotomy
teratoma
textbook
thalloid
thallous
theogony
theology
thereout
threnode
threnody
thyrsoid
ticktock
tidelock
timebomb
timework
timeworn
timorous
tinstone
tiresome
tocology
toilsome
toilworn
tokology
tolbooth
tonepoem
toolroom
topology
topstone
tortious
tortuous
trachoma
tradeoff
tramroad
trapdoor
traprock
trichoid
trichome
trichord
triploid
trochoid
trollopy
trombone
trottoir
trueborn
truelove
tuberose
tuberous
tubiform
tumorous
turncoat
turncock
turndown
turnsole
twinborn
typology
ulcerous
unciform
unctuous
unthrone
upstroke
upthrown
urochord
usurious
uxorious
vagabond
valorous
vanadous
vaporous
varicose
variform
vasiform
vavasory
vavasour
velskoen

venomous
Vietcong
vigorous
viperous
virology
virtuosa
virtuosi
virtuoso
virtuous
Visigoth
vitreous
vomitory
voussoir
warcloud
wardrobe
wardroom
wartwort
warwhoop
washbowl
washroom
watthour
waveform
waxcloth
Wedgwood
weeklong
wellborn
wellworn
werewolf
whipcord
whipworm
whiteout
wifehood
wildfowl
wildwood
windcone
windrose
windsock
wirework
wireworm
wirewove
wishbone
withhold
wondrous
woodcock
woodnote
woodwool
woodwork
woodworm
woolwork
wordbook
workfolk
workroom
wormhole
wormwood
writeoff
wrongous
xanthoma
xylology
yearbook
yearlong
zabaione
zoetrope
zoospore
zymology
amphipod
applepie
backspin
bagpiper
bebopper
bicuspid
bobbypin
brainpan
cachepot
calcspar
calliper
centuple
chalkpit
chickpea
chutzpah

cirriped
collapse
crackpot
crankpin
crashpad
crossply
cyclopes
decouple
decrepit
didapper
diplopia
disciple
dystopia
empeople
empurple
endpaper
ensample
entrepot
eohippus
epilepsy
equipped
estopped
estoppel
Ethiopic
eutrophy
feldspar
finespun
fireopal
fissiped
fleshpot
flypaper
frogspit
gallipot
galloper
gossiper
gossipry
gossypol
haruspex
hedgepig
hereupon
homespun
honeypot
hotchpot
hydropic
hydropsy
improper
Interpol
intrepid
isotopic
larkspur
linchpin
lollipop
lollypop
lynchpin
madapple
manciple
marzipan
mayapple
misapply
multiped
multiple
multiply
myriapod
myriopod
necropsy
oakapple
palmiped
panpipes
pansophy
pattypan
photopia
photopic
photopsy
pinniped
pitviper
platypus
plumiped
prolapse
pteropod

quillpen
recapped
repeople
rhizopod
saucepan
sauropod
scalepan
scarfpin
schnapps
scotopic
scrapped
scrapper
septuple
sextuple
sheeppen
shrimper
sinciput
smallpox
snakepit
southpaw
stinkpot
stockpot
strapped
strapper
stripped
stripper
stropped
strumpet
subtopia
sweetpea
syncopal
tailspin
terrapin
tetrapla
tetrapod
tholepin
threeply
thumbpot
tittuped
tittuppy
tragopan
turnspit
uncapped
uncouple
underpin
undraped
unshaped
untapped
unzipped
walloper
wingspan
wrestpin
wristpin
Xantippe
applique
boutique
colloquy
critique
moresque
mystique
physique
pratique
abhorred
abhorrer
absterge
acentric
adularia
aerogram
agitprop
airborne
airscrew
airstrip
alizarin
amphorae
amphoras
anasarca
anchoret
angstrom
anhedral
answerer
antheral
antlered
antrorse
arbitral
Arcturus
armoured
armourer
autocrat
aviatrix
axletree
baccarat
backdrop
bacteria
ballyrag
balmoral
banderol
bannered
banneret
bannerol
banterer
barbaric
barberry
barterer
bastardy
bayberry
bedstraw
beggarly
berberis
besmirch
betatron
bilberry
binaural
biomorph
bitterly
biyearly
bloodred
boottree
borderer
bourtree
bowsprit
brethren
brickred
buckaroo
budgeree
bullfrog
bullyrag
bummaree
bunkered
Burberry
caesural
calcaria
calthrop
cantoris
carburet
carefree
castiron
cauldron
causerie
cellarer
cellaret
cercaria
cerebral
cerebrum
chaldron
chambray
chaperon
chemurgy
children
chimeric
choleric
chondrus
cicatrix
claptrap
cleverly
cockcrow
cockerel
coistrel
collared
collyria
coloured
colubrid
commerce
concerti
concerto
conferee
conferva
conjurer
conjuror
conserve
construe
contorno
converge
converse
copperas
corduroy
corporal
cothurni
coumarin
cowberry
creatrix
criteria
cromorna
cromorne
cryotron
cultural
cultured
culverin
cutpurse
dastardy
deathray
debarred
decagram
decigram
declarer
deferral
deferred
deferrer
demiurge
democrat
demurred
demurrer
deterred
deterrer
deuteron
devourer
dewberry
dieldrin
dihedral
dihybrid
dioptric
dipteral
dipteran
disagree
disarray
disburse
disgorge
disperse
dispirit
disserve
ditherer
doctoral
doddered
dodderer
dogberry
dogeared
doggerel
dogtired
dotterel
drynurse
dungaree
dutyfree
dynatron
easterly
echogram
electret
electric
electron
electrum
elfarrow
enquirer
epidural
ergogram
erigeron
esoteric
estuaril
ethnarch
eupatrid
euphoria
euphoric
Eurocrat
exlibris
exoteric
explorer
extrorse
falderal
fanfaron
fatherly
favoured
favourer
featured
features
fenberry
filagree
filigree
finedraw
fingered
firearms
firebrat
firetrap
flanerie
flatiron
flexural
flowered
flowerer
floweret
folderol
forborne
formerly
forwards
fosterer
freshrun
froufrou
funebral
furfural
furfuran
gasfired
gasworks
gatherer
gematria
gendarme
germfree
gestural
gillaroo
gingerly
glycerin
glycerol
glyceryl
godwards
gramarye
gramercy
greegree
gridiron
grisgris
groogroo
guttural
gynocrat
hairgrip
halfbred
halteres
handgrip
hangeron
hausfrau
hedgerow
henparty
herbaria
Hesperus
hetaerae
hetairai
hexagram
hierarch
highbred
highbrow
higherup
hinderer
historic
hitherto
hologram
homebred
homebrew
honourer
humoured
hysteria
hysteric
ideogram
ignitron
incurred
inferred
infrared
inquirer
inspired
inspirer
inspirit
integral
interred
interrex
introrse
irongray
irongrey
isobaric
isomeric
isomorph
jabberer
jackaroo
jackeroo
jamboree
jeopardy
jiggered
kangaroo
kedgeree
kilogram
kingcrab
klystron
labourer
landarmy
landcrab
lanneret
latterly
lawyerly
leapfrog
lecturer
leisured
lethargy
lettered
linearly
lingerer
lingerie
lipogram
litharge
littoral
logogram
loiterer
Lollardy
longeron
lookeron
lopeared
lothario
louvered
lubberly
lumberer
Lutheran
mackerel
malaprop
mandarin
mandorla
mannered
mannerly
manubria
marjoram
mascaron
masterly
measured
membered
menstrua
mensural
mercuric
mesmeric
mesotron
meteoric
micrurgy
minstrel
miscarry
mobocrat
Moharram
monaural
monocrat
monogram
motherly
mowburnt
Muharram
mulberry
murderer
murmurer
musktree
mutterer
namedrop
nanogram
nectared
negatron
neoteric
nocturne
nomogram
nonjuror
nonmoral
nonparty
numberer
nurturer
occurred
ocularly
oilfired
oldworld
oligarch
onehorse
oratorio
outburst
outHerod
outstrip
outwards
outworks
overarch
overcrop
overdraw
overdrew
overgrew
overgrow
oxymoron
palterer
pamperer
parterre
passerby
pastoral
pastural
peardrop
pectoral
pedigree
perforce
perjurer
perverse
pickerel
pictures
pilferer
Pindaric
pizzeria
plastron
plectrum
podagral
podagric
ponderer
positron
postfree
postural
posturer
potterer
powdered
premorse
preparer
preserve
procurer
properly
property
puggaree
purebred
purpuric
purpurin
Quakerly
raindrop
rapparee
raptures
recharge
recourse
rectoral
recurred
reedwren
reemerge
referral
referred
rehearse
renderer
repairer
rerearch
research
resource
restorer
retiarii
retrorse
rhetoric
rooftree
rosetree
runnerup
sacraria
sailorly
sandarac
sangaree
sanserif
Sanskrit
Sauterne
sawhorse
scenario
sceptred
sciagram
scombrid
scotfree
seaborne
seafarer
seahorse
seapurse
seawards
sectoral
sensoria
Sephardi
sesterce
setscrew
sewerrat
sheeprun
shikaree
shivaree
shoetree
sickerly
sidearms
sidedrum
silverly
sisterly
skiagram
skywards
snapbrim
snowdrop
solderer
solleret
sorcerer
Southron
spagyric
spandrel
spandril
spectral
spectrum
squadron
squirrel
stairrod
statured
stingray
submerge
submerse
subserve
subshrub
sufferer
summerly
sunburnt
sunburst
sunderer
sunwards
susurrus
tabouret
tafferel
tamperer
tartaric
tattered
teaparty
teardrop
telegram
telluric
tempered
temperer
temporal
tenderly
Tenebrae
terebrae
terraria
tesserae
tesseral
tetrarch
textural
textured
theocrat
timbered
tinkerer
tommyrot
tomogram
tomorrow
torturer
totterer
traverse
treefrog
tricorne
triforia
trimaran
trimeric
truebred
turmeric
unawares
unbarred
unchurch
underrun
unfairly
universe
unlearnt
unpaired
uvularly
vampiric
vapourer
variorum
veneerer
venturer
veratrin

veratrum
verderer
verderor
verdured
vesperal
vesturer
victoria
vigneron
visceral
vulgarly
Walkyrie
wallaroo
wanderer
wanderoo
warhorse
waxberry
waxworks
wayfarer
wellbred
westerly
wetnurse
whimbrel
whittret
winterly
wiredraw
wistaria
wisteria
withdraw
withdrew
ziggurat
zoiatria
zoomorph
abacuses
abomasum
abomasus
abscissa
accursed
acidosis
advowson
agonised
alfresco
ambrosia
amitosis
anabases
anabasis
analyser
analyses
analysis
anthesis
apodoses
apodosis
apresski
assassin
assessor
atomiser
ballista
banausic
bethesda
bimbashi
bioassay
bobbysox
britzska
cactuses
carousal
carousel
carouser
cavesson
chainsaw
charisma
cineaste
cleanser
closeset
coalesce
cognosce
colossal
colossus
composed
composer
concasse
contessa
coulisse
crevasse
culdesac
curassow
cyanoses
cyanosis
cyclosis
damassin
deceased
declasse
demersal
despiser
diabasic
dialyser
dialyses
dialysis
diapason
dichasia
diereses
dieresis
diffuser
diocesan
diseased
disposal
disposer
distaste
diuresis
duchesse
ecclesia
ellipses
ellipsis
embosser
embussed
emphases
emphasis
empoison
endorsee
endorser
entresol
enuresis
epinasty
epitasis
espousal
espouser
espresso
eupepsia
evanesce
excursus
exegesis
extensor
famously
fantasia
Fascista
Fascisti
fibrosis
finnesko
focussed
forensic
fougasse
framesaw
galluses
gambeson
garrison
geodesic
gneissic
goingson
grandson
guernsey
gummosis
gymnasia
harasser
heliosis
hidrosis
hocussed
hydroski
hypnoses
hypnosis
idoliser
immersed
imprison
intarsia
intersex
jalousie
jettison
joyously
Judaiser
Jurassic
kolinsky
kromesky
kurtosis
kyphosis
lacrosse
lambaste
largesse
licensed
licensee
licenser
lordosis
machismo
magnesia
malvasia
mantissa
marmoset
methysis
moccasin
molasses
molossus
narcissi
narcoses
narcosis
necrosis
neuroses
neurosis
nimbused
noblesse
occlusal
odiously
outcaste
oviposit
oxidiser
ozoniser
paduasoy
Parmesan
partisan
petrosal
pharisee
phthisic
phthisis
pianiste
potassic
promisee
promiser
promisor
proposal
proposer
protasis
protista
provisor
psilosis
pugnosed
quickset
releasee
releaser
releasor
remissly
repousse
reprisal
reversal
reverser
Romansch
rubbishy
Rumansch
sacristy
sargasso
sharpset
siriasis
soothsay
squarson
stenosed
stenosis
sternson
stylised
subbasal
supposal
supposed
surmisal
surmiser
sweetsop
symposia
synapsis
syndesis
synopses
synopsis
tachisme
tachiste
tenonsaw
thickset
timously
touristy
travesty
Triassic
tribasic
unbiased
uncaused
unchaste
undersea
underset
unhoused
unloosen
unperson
unreason
unversed
utiliser
venously
vibrissa
vinously
waterski
whoreson
zoonosis
abductor
abjectly
abruptly
absentee
absently
absinthe
accentor
accepter
acceptor
accoutre
accustom
aconitic
aconitum
acoustic
acrostic
actuator
adamitic
adductor
adenitis
adiantum
adjuster
adjustor
admitted
adroitly
adulator
aegrotat
aerostat
affected
affecter
afflatus
aflutter
agitator
aglitter
agnostic
agrestic
aigrette
allotted
allottee
amiantus
amitotic
amniotic
amoretti
amoretto
anabatic
analytic
ancestor
ancestry
animator
anisette
anteater
aoristic
aperitif
aplastic
arcuated
ardently
argentic
aromatic
arrantly
arrestee
arrester
arrestor
artistic
artistry
asbestic
asbestos
assenter
assentor
assertor
assorted
athletic
atlantes
Atlantic
attested
attester
attestor
attrited
atwitter
aubretia
Augustan
augustly
autistic
backstay
baguette
balletic
baluster
banditry
banditti
banister
barbette
barbital
barrator
barratry
barrette
basaltic
basketry
bathetic
bathotic
bauxitic
beeeater
befitted
begetter
begotten
belittle
besotted
biometry
bisector
blacktie
blacktop
blighter
boughten
breasted
breveted
brewster
brighten
brightly
brocatel
brunette
bulletin
burletta
bursitis
cadastre
calcitic
calyptra
canaster
canister
caryatid
cassette
catheter
caudated
cerastes
chapatti
chapiter
chaunter
chauntry
chiastic
christen
christie
Christly
chupatti
chupatty
ciliated
clematis
climatic
cloister
closeted
cobaltic
cockatoo
cofactor
cogently
collator
commuter
computer
concetti
concetto
confetti
coquetry
coquette
cornetcy
cornetti
cornetto
corseted
corsetry
corvette
cosmetic
covertly
credited
creditor
crenated
crepitus
crosstie
cryostat
culottes
curveted
Cushitic
cutwater
cyanotic
cystitis
czaritza
dalmatic
dancette
dancetty
daughter
decanter
decently
declutch
decretal
deemster
defector
dejected
demented
dementia
demitted
dentated
departed
depicter
depictor
deportee
deserter
despatch
despotic
detector
detrital
detritus
deviator
deviltry
devoutly
diabetes
diabetic
dialytic
diameter
dicrotic
dictator
didactic
dietetic
digester
dioritic
directly
director
disaster
disinter
dispatch
diuretic
dogmatic
dogwatch
domestic
doomster
doorstep
doorstop
dragster
dramatic
dynastic
ebriated
eclectic
ecliptic
ecstatic
educated
educator
effector
egoistic
eldritch
elenctic
elevated
elevator
elliptic
embattle
embitter
emeritus
Emmental
emphatic
emulator
enclitic
enclothe
endostea
enfetter
enswathe
entoptic
enuretic
enzootic
epicotyl
eremitic
errantly
errantry
eucritic
eupeptic
eustatic
eutectic
executor
exegetic
exhorter
expertly
expiator
exporter
exserted
eyewater
factotum
falcated
falsetto
felsitic
fenestra
ferreter
ferritic
fibrotic
filmstar
fivestar
fluently
fomenter
footstep
forestal
forestay
forested
forester
forestry
fourstar
fremitus
frenetic
frighten
frisette
furcated
gadgetry
galactic
galeated
gamester
gangster
ganister
garotter
garreted
garrotte
gasmeter
gelastic
geodetic
geometer
geometry
gerontic
gigantic
goadster
gogetter
gramatom
granitic
graviton
grisette
gunmetal
gusseted
gyrostat
haematic
haematin
haliotis
hamartia
harlotry
heighten
helmeted
hermetic
herpetic
hidrotic
hieratic
hobbitry
holistic
honestly
hospital
housetop
huckster
hypnotic
icewater
idolater
idolatry
illfated
imitator
immortal
impacted
importer
imposter
impostor
inceptor
indebted

inductee
inductor
industry
inedited
infantry
infector
infilter
inflated
inflator
inflatus
injector
inositol
inserted
insulter
intently
intertie
invected
inventor
inverted
inverter
investor
isolator
isometry
jackstay
japhetic
jesuitic
jesuitry
jiujitsu
juristic
klephtic
knightly
kyphotic
lamented
latently
laudator
laughter
leucitic
levanter
libretti
libretto
lignitic
loadstar
lockstep
lodestar
logistic
lomentum
longstop
lordotic
magister
magmatic
magnetic
magneton
Mahratta
Mahratti
maieutic
mainstay
majestic
maltster
mandator
maneater
mannitol
maquette
marketer
masseter
mastitis
mediator
mementos
mephitic
mephitis
meristem
meristic
migrator
mimester
minister
ministry
mismatch
modestly
molester
momently
momentum
monastic
monistic
moquette
muriatic
muscatel
musketry
myelitis
myositic
myositis
myosotis
narcotic
narrator
Nearctic
necrotic
NeoLatin
neonatal
nepenthe
neuritic
neuritis
neurotic
noisette
nomistic
nonmetal
nuthatch
objector
obtected
occultly
odometer
ohmmeter
oleaster
omelette
operatic
operator
operetta
orgastic
oriental
oriented
osteitis
outdated
outmatch
outwatch
ovaritis
overstay
overstep
oximeter
palestra
palmette
palmetto
palmitin
papistic
papistry
parental
pargeter
parietal
parrotry
patentee
patently
patentor
pathetic
pedantic
pedantry
pedestal
periotic
perlitic
petuntse
phonetic
phreatic
phyletic
picketer
pilaster
pileated
pinaster
pinnated
piscator
plaister
plankton
pliantly
plighted
pochette
podiatry
polestar
pollster
polluter
poristic
potently
potlatch
predator
prelatic
prenatal
priestly
Primates
promoter
prompter
promptly
pronator
protatic
pruritic
pruritus
pubertal
pulpiter
pulsator
punditry
puppetry
puristic
pyelitis
quaestor
quaintly
quixotic
quixotry
rabbiter
rabbitry
rachitic
rachitis
radiator
rambutan
ramentum
rebuttal
rebutted
rebutter
recently
receptor
redactor
redistil
redwater
reedstop
refitted
register
registry
regrater
rejecter
remittal
remitted
remittee
remitter
repartee
repeater
repenter
reporter
repotted
requital
requiter
resetter
resettle
resister
resistor
resorter
retorted
reverter
revetted
revolter
rheostat
rhinitis
rimester
roadster
robustly
rocketry
romantic
roulette
roundtop
sabbatic
sadistic
sagittal
scimitar
screwtop
sculptor
seamster
seawater
sebesten
secretin
secretly
secretor
selectee
selector
semantic
semester
semiotic
sempster
septette
seriatim
serrated
servitor
sextette
Shemitic
Sheraton
sidestep
sigmatic
silently
silvatic
Sinaitic
sinister
situated
skeletal
skeleton
slightly
societal
Socratic
songster
spicated
spinster
spirited
spiritus
splatter
splinter
splitter
splutter
sprinter
squatted
squatter
squinter
squirter
stealthy
stenotic
stiletto
stipites
stomatal
stomatic
straiten
straitly
streeted
strictly
strontia
strutted
strutter
subtitle
subtotal
summitry
sunbathe
supertax
syenitic
sylvatic
symmetry
sympathy
synaptic
synastry
syncytia
syndetic
synoptic
tabletop
talented
tanistry
tapestry
tapwater
tarlatan
teamster
teetotal
teetotum
tenantry
testator
testatum
Thanatos
theistic
thematic
thirster
threaten
throated
throstle
throttle
thruster
thwarter
thwartly
tinnitus
toiletry
toilette
tomentum
topnotch
toreutic
traditor
trimeter
truantry
truistic
tsaritsa
tsaritza
tungsten
tungstic
turreted
udometer
umbrette
unabated
unbeaten
unbolted
unbottle
unbutton
unclothe
undertow
unedited
unfasten
unfetter
unfitted
ungotten
unjustly
unlisted
unmeetly
unseated
unsettle
unstated
unsuited
unswathe
untented
unwanted
unwonted
unworthy
uplifter
uprooter
upsetter
uralitic
urgently
uvulitis
vacantly
valuator
varactor
varietal
varletry
Vedantic
vendetta
verbatim
verboten
verditer
veristic
viameter
vibrator
vignette
villatic
violator
vitiator
whitetie
zealotry
zeolitic
zoolater
zoolatry
zoometry
absolute
abstruse
airbrush
alehouse
alleluia
allround
although
altitude
aperture
applause
aptitude
aqualung
aqueduct
archduke
arethusa
armature
attitude
auricula
avifauna
babirusa
bankrupt
bedeguar
bellbuoy
bellpull
bellpush
berceuse
biannual
bisexual
bistoury
blastula
blesbuck
bouzouki
brimfull
brochure
burnouse
bushbuck
calctuff
calycule
capitula
carnauba
cartouch
catapult
centaury
chipmuck
chipmunk
chirrupy
chopsuey
cincture
coaldust
cocksure
coiffure
compound
conclude
confound
costpush
cramfull
creature
cubature
cynosure
dandruff
danseuse
deafmute
denature
destruct
diapause
disabuse
disbound
discount
dismount
displume
distrust
dividual
doghouse
doldrums
dormouse
downturn
drawtube
dumfound
durukuli
dyestuff
elkhound
epifauna
eventual
exergual
exposure
farflung
fatigues
faubourg
fauteuil
filature
finitude
floccule
flocculi
fogbound
footmuff
footrule
foxhound
fracture
fraenula
frustule
furlough
gashouse
gastrula
geniture
glandule
golddust
goldrush
habitual
habitude
hamululi
handcuff
hebetude
henequen
hiccough
hothouse
hulahula
hushhush
icebound
illiquid
immature
inasmuch
insecure
insomuch
instruct
intitule
involute
jealousy
jodhpurs
jointure
jumpsuit
juncture
kisscurl
latitude
lawcourt
lifebuoy
ligature
lodicule
madhouse
malamute
malemute
Mameluke
manicure
maroquin
masseuse
miscount
misdoubt
mistrust
moisture
molecule
moribund
muckluck
muskduck
newfound
nonesuch
numskull
nuthouse
obstruct
opercula
opuscula
opuscule
outbound
outhouse
overbusy
overhung
overjump
overmuch
overrule
overture
overturn
pantsuit
paraquat
paroquet
pedicure
perilune
picayune
piecrust
pirarucu
playsuit
pleasure
postlude
potbound
pothouse
preclude
pressure
profound
propound
protrude
punctual
puncture
pushpull
Quechuan
quidnunc
quietude
quincunx
ramequin
readjust
reassure
reinsure
reneguer
reoccupy
residual
residuum
resolute
resprung
restcure
reticule
retinula
revolute
ridicule
rosebush
rubicund
saltbush
schedule
scrofula
seamount
seamouse
sederunt
selcouth
selfrule
semibull
seminude
shadbush

shantung
shelduck
sinecure
soapsuds
sobstuff
solitude
sonobuoy
sourpuss
sparbuoy
spherule
squamule
stardust
subacute
surfduck
surmount
surround
swimsuit
taciturn
tainture
tamboura
taphouse
teahouse
tearduct
tenacula
testtube
thesauri
thorough
timefuse
tincture
titmouse
tournure
tranquil
transude
treasure
treasury
tressure
unsprung
unstrung
unvalued
upsprung
upthrust
usufruct
verecund
vermouth
viscount
windburn
woodpulp
woodruff
wrymouth
yoghourt
absolver
achiever
aestival
alewives
amadavat
approval
archival
archives
avadavat
believer
bereaved
beslaver
biconvex
brakevan
carnival
codriver
cognovit
conniver
cordovan
corrival
cultivar
deceiver
decemvir
depraved
deprival
deprived
discover
dishevel
dissever
dundiver
effluvia
engraver
enslaver
festival
forgiven
gingival
hangover
holdover
improver
interval
khedival
lawgiver
leftover
longeval
lowlevel
medieval
midwives
misgiven
moreover
moshavim
observer
onceover
outrival
Passover
primeval
pullover
pushover
receiver
reconvey
reliever
replevin
reproval
reserved
resurvey
revolver
screever
sealevel
shedevil
shrieval
slipover
stopover
survival
survivor
takeover
toplevel
triumvir
tsarevna
turnover
upheaval
walkover
whatever
whenever
wherever
whomever
alleyway
bestowal
borrower
broadway
burrower
cableway
castaway
causeway
clearway
crossway
cycleway
deflower
driftway
driveway
eschewal
everyway
fadeaway
fellowly
floodway
foldaway
follower
followon
followup
Galloway
giveaway
golliwog
guideway
hallowed
hatchway
hereaway
hideaway
hollowly
ingrowth
interwar
limetwig
manpower
mellowly
motorway
mulloway
narrowly
newlywed
outlawry
pandowdy
polliwog
pollywog
regrowth
reviewal
reviewer
ridgeway
riverway
scalawag
shadower
slideway
soakaway
sorrower
speedway
spillway
stairway
sternway
stowaway
takeaway
tearaway
teatowel
threeway
tightwad
trackway
underway
walkaway
wallower
waterway
wellaway
williwaw
windowed
winnower
yellowly
anorexia
anorexic
apomixis
asphyxia
ataraxia
ataraxic
cachexia
carboxyl
cathexes
cathexis
caudexes
convexly
dyslexia
dyslexic
geotaxis
hydroxyl
inflexed
larynxes
matrixes
panmixia
prolixly
reflexed
syrinxes
thoraxes
thyroxin
vertexes
vortexes
aerodyne
aldehyde
amethyst
anaglyph
aneurysm
antitype
autodyne
autogyro
autolyse
autotype
betrayal
betrayer
bosseyed
catalyse
catalyst
cockeyed
coenzyme
conveyer
conveyor
defrayal
dewyeyed
disloyal
employee
employer
epiphyte
epistyle
eucalypt
eyerhyme
fireeyed
foureyes
gargoyle
genotype
geophyte
gunlayer
hawkeyed
homonymy
hypogyny
Kaffiyeh
logotype
lynxeyed
lysozyme
metonymy
misogyny
monocyte
monogyny
monotype
neophyte
openeyed
paralyse
paroxysm
perigyny
polygyny
porphyry
prostyle
purveyor
sentrygo
sloeeyed
storeyed
Strepyan
subphyla
surroyal
surveyor
synonymy
taxpayer
thankyou
toponymy
trachyte
triglyph
triptych
urostyle
walleyed
Wesleyan
wideeyed
wildeyed
wooldyed
zoophyte
alguazil
anthozoa
bartizan
bedazzle
chalazae
embezzle
emblazon
howitzer
kalaazar
kibitzer
kreutzer
mansized
partizan
protozoa
sporozoa
squeezer
terrazzo
trapezia
unfrozen
unglazed
unmuzzle

---

abbatial
abnormal
Accadian
achenial
aciculae
acicular
aciculas
acidhead
actiniae
actinian
actinias
acturial
Adamical
Adlerian
advocaat
aegrotat
aerogram
aerostat
aestival
agaragar
agential
agrarian
airwoman
Akkadian
Albanian
alderman
alleyway
allodial
alluvial
alogical
Alsatian
alveolar
amadavat
American
ammoniac
amnesiac
amoebean
amphorae
amphoras
ampullae
Anglican
anhedral
antennae
antennal
antennas
antheral
aphasiac
apiarian
approval
Aramaean
arbitral
arboreal
Arcadian
archaean
archival
Armagnac
Armenian
Arminian
armorial
arterial
artesian
ascidian
assignat
Assyrian
astragal
Athenian
atypical
Augustan
aurelian
aurorean
autocrat
autumnal
avadavat
baccarat
bacillar
backchat
backseat
backstay
Baconian
Bactrian
bailsman
baldhead
ballyrag
balmoral
bandsman
barbican
barbital
bargeman
baronial
bartizan
basidial
Batavian
battleax
Bavarian
beadsman
bedeguar
bedstead
bedstraw
beebread
Bermudas
bestowal
betrayal
bezonian
biannual
biblical
biennial
bifacial
bilabial
billhead
billycan
binaural
binomial
bioassay
biocidal
birthday
bisexual
blackcap
blahblah
bluecoat
boatload
Bodleian
Boeotian
bogeyman
bohemian
bondsman
bonehead
bonemeal
boxpleat
brachial
bracteal
Bradshaw
brainpan
brakeman
brakevan
Briarean
brickbat
broadway
brougham
browbeat
bryozoan
buckbean
bulkhead
bullhead
bullyrag
cableway
caducean
caesural
calcspar
calendar
Cambrian
Canadian
cannibal
cannulae
cannular
cannulas
cantonal
capsular
cardigan
cardinal
carnival
Carolean
carousal
cartload
castaway
cathodal
causeway
celeriac
cellular
cerebral
cerulean
cervelat
cervical
cetacean
chainsaw
chairman
chalazae
Chaldean
chambray
charcoal
Chellean
chemical
chessman
Chinaman
chitchat
chutzpah
cinnabar
Circaean
circular
cislunar
civilian
clansman
claptrap
clearway
clerical
clinical
coachman
cochleae
cochlear
cockboat
coleslaw
colonial
colossal
columnal
columnar
comedian
communal
compleat
condylar
conidial
conjugal
conoidal
consular
coolabah
coolibah
coplanar
copperas
cordovan
corporal
corrival
cortical
cosmical
cotquean
crackjaw
cragsman
crashpad
criminal
critical
Croatian
crossbar
crossway
cryostat
cuboidal
culdesac
cultivar
cultural
Cumbrian
cycleway
cyclical
cypselae
dactylar
dairyman
dalesman
daybreak
daydream
deadbeat
deadhead
deathcap
deathray
decagram
decigram
decretal
deferral
defrayal
Delphian
demersal
democrat
demoniac
demonian
deprival
detrital
Devonian
diaconal
diagonal
diarchal
dihedral
diluvial
diluvian
diocesan
diplomat
dipteral
dipteran
disarray
disloyal
disposal
dispread
dittybag
dividual
doctoral
doomsday
doomsman
downbeat
drachmae
drachmai
drachmas
dragoman
dragsman
driftway
driveway
drophead
dropleaf
drumhead
dryclean
dumbhead
duodenal
dustcoat
Dutchman
echogram
Egyptian

emetical
Emmental
empyreal
empyrean
encrinal
Ephesian
epidural
episodal
Erastian
ergogram
erotical
eschewal
Eskimoan
especial
espousal
Esquimau
Estonian
ethereal
etherial
ethnical
Etrurian
Etruscan
Eurasian
Eurocrat
European
eventual
everyday
everyman
everyway
exemplar
exergual
exordial
external
facetiae
fadeaway
fairlead
falderal
faltboat
familial
familiar
fancyman
farcical
Faustian
favonian
feastday
feedhead
feldspar
fernshaw
ferryman
festival
fiducial
filariae
filarial
filmstar
fimbriae
finedraw
fireboat
firebrat
fireclay
fireopal
firetrap
fishmeal
fistical
fistulae
fistular
fivestar
flambeau
flatboat
flathead
flexural
flimflam
flipflap
floodway
foldaway
foldboat
foolscap
footgear
footwear
forebear

forehead
forepeak
foreplay
forestal
forestay
formulae
formulas
forspeak
forswear
fourleaf
fourstar
foveolae
framesaw
freedman
freeload
freshman
Freudian
Friesian
fruitbat
fugleman
funebral
funereal
funnyman
furculae
furcular
furfural
furfuran
galangal
Galilean
Gallican
Galloway
Georgian
germinal
gestural
Ghanaian
gilthead
gingival
giveaway
globular
goldleaf
gonidial
goodyear
gownsman
Graafian
granddad
granular
grosbeak
guardian
guideway
gunmetal
guttural
gynocrat
gyrostat
habitual
Haggadah
Halachah
halfbeak
handclap
handicap
handyman
hardhead
haresear
harpseal
harridan
hatchway
hausfrau
havildar
Hawaiian
headgear
headsman
hebdomad
Hegelian
heliacal
helmsman
henchman
herdsman
hereaway
hernshaw
heroical

Hertzian
hetaerae
hetairai
hexagram
hibernal
hideaway
hielaman
highroad
Hogmanay
hogshead
hologram
hoofbeat
hooligan
Horatian
hormonal
hornbeam
horsecar
horseman
hospital
houseman
huntsman
hymenial
hypogeal
hypogean
icecream
ideogram
illtreat
Illyrian
imaginal
immortal
imperial
inchmeal
Indiaman
inertial
infernal
informal
inguinal
inimical
integral
internal
interval
interwar
irenical
Irishman
ironclad
irongray
ironical
isogonal
isthmian
jackstay
Jacobean
jeremiad
Jeremiah
jeroboam
jerrican
jerrycan
jolthead
Jonathan
Judaical
judicial
Jugoslav
jumpseat
kalaazar
khedival
Khmerian
kickshaw
kilogram
kingcrab
knitwear
lackaday
laconian
lacrimal
lacrymal
lallygag
lamellae
lamellar
landcrab
landsman
Langshan

laywoman
leadsman
legbreak
liegeman
lifeboat
linesman
Linnaean
lipogram
littoral
loadstar
lodestar
logician
logogram
longboat
longeval
loveseat
lubrical
Lucullan
lunarian
Lutheran
mackinaw
madrigal
madwoman
Maecenas
magician
mailboat
mainstay
malarial
malarian
maltreat
mamillae
mamillar
Mandaean
maniacal
manorial
manurial
marginal
marjoram
marksman
marshman
marzipan
masthead
material
maternal
matronal
maxillae
medieval
memorial
mensural
menswear
meridian
metazoan
metrical
micellar
microbar
Milesian
millibar
minutiae
mistreat
mistrial
mobocrat
Moharram
monachal
monaural
monaxial
moneybag
monkseal
monocrat
monogram
monomial
moonbeam
Moravian
motional
motorcar
motorial
motorman
motorway
mouseear
Muharram

mulloway
muscular
musician
mycelial
mystical
mythical
nanogram
national
nautical
nenuphar
neonatal
neuronal
newspeak
nicotian
nightcap
nighthag
nightjar
Noachian
nobleman
nomogram
nonhuman
nonlegal
nonmetal
nonmoral
Norseman
Northman
notarial
notional
noumenal
novercal
nutarian
nymphean
obsidian
occlusal
Odyssean
offbreak
official
olympiad
Olympian
oogonial
openplan
ophidian
optician
optional
oracular
Orcadian
oriental
original
outbreak
outrival
overbear
overcoat
overdraw
overhead
overhear
overheat
overleaf
overleap
overload
overplay
overseas
overstay
overwear
padishah
pagurian
palatial
pancreas
papillae
papillar
parallax
paraquat
parental
parietal
Parmesan
Parthian
partisan
partizan
pastoral
pastural

patellae
patellar
paternal
patronal
pattypan
pectoral
peculiar
pedestal
Pegasean
Pelagian
pemmican
pendular
perigean
perineal
peroneal
personae
personal
Peruvian
petiolar
petrosal
Phrygian
physical
piacular
pinnular
pipeclay
piscinae
pivotman
placeman
planulae
planular
plebeian
plumular
podagral
poetical
polestar
polyzoan
popinjay
postural
praedial
prandial
prehuman
premolar
prenatal
pressman
primeval
prodigal
proemial
proposal
proximal
Prussian
pterylae
pubertal
publican
punctual
puparial
pupillar
puppyfat
pussycat
pustular
pygidial
pygmaean
pyrexial
Quechuan
raftsman
railhead
railroad
raincoat
rainwear
rambutan
ranarian
ranchman
rasorial
rataplan
rational
reappear
rebuttal
rectoral
referral
regional

rehoboam
reinsman
remedial
remittal
reprisal
reproval
requital
residual
reversal
reviewal
Rhaetian
rheostat
rhonchal
ricercar
rickshaw
ridgeway
rifleman
ringroad
riparian
riverman
riverway
Romanian
roodbeam
rosarian
roseleaf
roseolar
Rotarian
rubrical
Rumanian
rustical
saccular
sackcoat
sagittal
sailboat
salariat
Salesian
salesman
Salopian
samizdat
sandarac
Sangreal
Saturday
saucepan
savannah
scalawag
scalepan
Scandian
scapulae
scapular
scapulas
scenical
schiedam
sciagram
scimitar
scopulae
scopulas
Scotsman
sealyham
seasonal
sectoral
seedcoat
seedleaf
seedsman
selfheal
septimal
sequelae
serpulae
sewergas
sewerrat
shanghai
Shekinah
shipload
shortday
showboat
shrieval
Siberian
Sicilian
sickflag
sidehead

sidereal
sideroad
sidesman
Silurian
simoniac
singular
siphonal
sirenian
skeletal
skiagram
skinhead
skullcap
slagheap
slideway
sliproad
snackbar
sneeshan
snipsnap
soakaway
societal
Socinian
softhead
softsoap
somedeal
somewhat
soothsay
sorehead
soterial
southpaw
sowbread
spacebar
spaceman
sparkgap
spatular
spearman
spectral
specular
speedway
spiculae
spicular
spillway
splenial
sporular
springal
spurgear
squawman
stairway
staminal
statical
sternway
stickjaw
stingray
stipular
stockcar
stockman
stomatal
storeman
stowaway
Strepyan
stuntman
subahdar
subbasal
subhuman
sublunar
subsolar
subtotal
suburban
subvocal
succubae
suicidal
Sumerian
superman
supernal
supertax
supplial
supposal
surfboat
surgical
surmisal

surroyal
survival
syncopal
syndical
synovial
syzygial
taberdar
tablemat
tactical
Tahitian
tailcoat
takeaway
talesman
talisman
tallyman
Tamilian
tarlatan
Tarpeian
teabread
teabreak
tearaway
teetotal
telegram
temporal
Tenebrae
tenonsaw
tenurial
terebrae
terminal
tesserae
tesseral
textural
theocrat
thespian
thetical
threeway
Thursday
tiebreak
tightwad
toadflax
toboggan
tommybar
tomogram
tonedeaf
toroidal
townsman
tracheae
tracheal
trackman
trackway
tragical
tragopan
tramroad
trappean
triaxial
tribunal
trifocal
trigonal
trimaran
tripeman
tripodal
tritical
tropical
troupial
Tunisian
Turanian
turbinal
turbofan
Turcoman
Turkoman
turncoat
tutorial
Tyrolean
underlap
underlay
underman
underway
unfilial
uniaxial

unifilar
unipolar
unisonal
univocal
unsocial
unthread
upheaval
upstream
vaccinal
vacuolar
valerian
valvulae
valvular
varietal
variolar
vascular
venereal
Venetian
Venusian
verandah
verrucae
vertical
vesperal
vesuvian
vicarial
virginal
viridian
visceral
visional
vortical
walkaway
warragal
warrigal
watchman
watergas
waterman
waterway
welladay
wellaway
wellhead
wellread
Wellsian
Welshman
Wesleyan
wheatear
wheelman
whimwham
whinchat
whitecap
williwaw
wingbeat
wingspan
wiredraw
withdraw
woodchat
woodsman
wordplay
workaday
wormgear
yataghan
Yugoslav
zamindar
zemindar
zenithal
ziggurat
zodiacal
anaerobe
bathrobe
buncombe
bushbaby
carnauba
cobwebby
conglobe
describe
diatribe
djellaba
drawtube
inscribe
kohlrabi

misdoubt
passerby
seedlobe
testtube
wardrobe
abeyance
abeyancy
abidance
abstract
abstrict
accuracy
acreinch
adequacy
advocacy
affiance
airspace
alebench
alfresco
alliance
allspice
almanack
ambiance
ambience
anasarca
angelica
announce
anyplace
approach
aqueduct
artefact
artifact
artifice
audience
avionics
backpack
ballcock
bareback
barranca
barranco
basilica
bechance
benedick
benedict
benefice
besmirch
blatancy
blesbuck
boatdeck
boldface
boniface
booklice
bootjack
bootlace
brassica
brattice
brettice
buoyancy
bushbuck
carapace
cartouch
cataract
celibacy
ceramics
charlock
chipmuck
clarence
classics
clawback
clemency
coalesce
coalsack
coatrack
codpiece
cognosce
comeback
commence
commerce
complice
conflict

conjunct
contract
convince
cornetcy
coronach
credence
cromlech
crummock
currency
cutprice
dabchick
deadlock
declutch
defiance
delegacy
delicacy
denounce
derelict
despatch
destruct
deviance
deviancy
diestock
diffract
dipstick
disbench
disfrock
disgrace
disjunct
dispatch
displace
distance
distinct
distract
district
dogwatch
dormancy
drammock
drawback
driftice
dropkick
drummock
dynamics
earpiece
efficacy
ekistics
eldritch
elegance
elegancy
eminence
eminency
encroach
ensconce
ensigncy
entrance
entrench
ethnarch
eugenics
evanesce
evidence
exigence
exigency
eyepiece
facepack
fallback
fandance
fastback
fatstock
feedback
fervency
fireback
firelock
flamenco
flapjack
flatrace
fluidics
footpace
footrace
foredeck

forelock
fullback
gamecock
gavelock
genetics
gentrice
geomancy
gimcrack
glyptics
goalkick
gralloch
gramercy
graphics
gripsack
guidance
gunstock
halfback
handpick
hardback
hardhack
hardtack
havelock
hawfinch
haystack
headlock
headrace
hedonics
hepatica
herdwick
hierarch
highjack
hogsback
holdback
homesick
humpback
idiolect
impolicy
inasmuch
indirect
insomuch
instance
instancy
instinct
instruct
interact
intimacy
intrench
isocracy
issuance
iterance
japonica
jaundice
jetblack
joystick
kickback
kinesics
kinetics
knapsack
lambency
laverock
lenience
leniency
licorice
limerick
linstock
lipstick
literacy
locofoco
lovelock
lovesick
maiolica
majolica
maledict
maverick
mergence
millrace
mismatch
misplace
moonface

moorcock
mordancy
mossback
muckluck
muskduck
nascence
nascency
necklace
nicknack
nonesuch
nonstick
normalcy
nuisance
numeracy
nuthatch
obduracy
obstruct
oiticica
oligarch
onepiece
onetrack
opulence
ordnance
outmatch
outreach
outwatch
overarch
overmuch
overnice
paleface
parlance
patience
peccancy
pendency
penstock
perforce
pharmacy
picklock
pinprick
piperack
piquancy
pirarucu
pittance
plastics
playback
polemics
politick
politico
politics
populace
potlatch
poultice
practice
precinct
preelect
prentice
presence
pretence
prophecy
prospect
protract
province
prudence
psychics
pullback
pungency
radiance
radiancy
rampancy
reagency
rearmice
redbrick
redirect
reedmace
reliance
renounce
reproach
rerearch
reremice

research
resource
restrict
retrench
retroact
rickrack
riddance
ringneck
rollneck
Romansch
roofrack
rucksack
Rumansch
sackrace
salience
saliency
saltlick
sandwich
sapience
sapphics
sciatica
scirocco
scottice
seapiece
seawrack
semplice
sentence
sequence
sesterce
shabrack
shaddock
shamrock
shelduck
sherlock
shoelace
sidekick
sithence
sixpence
skerrick
skewback
skipjack
slapjack
solstice
solvency
spardeck
spherics
staylace
stopcock
suberect
subtract
succinct
sundance
surfduck
surplice
swanneck
swayback
tailback
tailrace
tamarack
tangency
tapdance
tapedeck
tearduct
technics
tendence
tendency
tenpence
tetrarch
theodicy
thridace
ticktack
ticktock
tidelock
toepiece
topnotch
transact
transect
traprock
tribrach

triptych
tristich
tuppence
turnback
turncock
twopence
twopiece
typeface
ultimacy
unchancy
unchurch
unclench
unclinch
underact
usufruct
vagrancy
valiance
valiancy
vambrace
variance
verdancy
vergence
verjuice
veronica
vibrancy
violence
vivisect
voidance
wardance
waterice
welldeck
wheyface
windsock
wolfpack
woodcock
woodlice
woolpack
woolsack
zoomancy
zwieback
Abbaside
accolade
actinide
adenoids
aldehyde
algicide
altitude
anaconda
antecede
antibody
antinode
antipode
aphicide
aptitude
aquacade
arsenide
attitude
autocade
backside
badlands
bastardy
beamends
bestride
bestrode
bethesda
blockade
bookends
Burgundy
busybody
camisade
camisado
charlady
chloride
coincide
commando
conclude
dastardy
defilade
diopside

diploidy
displode
dissuade
dockside
dogsbody
eldorado
enfilade
escalade
escapade
eventide
eyeshade
feticide
finitude
fireside
flipside
fluoride
forebode
forelady
foreside
forwards
forzando
Ganymede
genocide
glissade
godwards
Golconda
Griselda
habitude
hacienda
handmade
haploidy
hebetude
hexapody
hillside
hocktide
hollands
homebody
homemade
homicide
innuendo
ironside
jeopardy
landlady
lapicide
latitude
lemonade
Lollardy
lowgrade
mancando
maravedi
marinade
marrieds
megapode
midlands
misguide
monopode
monoxide
neaptide
nematode
noontide
oeillade
outwards
override
overrode
overside
palinode
palisade
pandowdy
parlando
peroxide
persuade
petalody
phyllode
polypide
polypody
postcode
postlude
preclude
proceeds
protrude
psalmody
quayside
quietude
regicide
renegade
renegado
rhapsode
rhapsody
ringside
roadside
Samoyede
seawards
selenide
selfmade
seminude
Sephardi
serenade
silicide
skywards
soapsuds
solitude
somebody
stampede
stoccado
stockade
suboxide
sulphide
sunshade
sunwards
superadd
sylphide
teacaddy
threnode
threnody
tomnoddy
transude
trioxide
unsteady
unwieldy
viricide
wetlands
yuletide
aasvogel
abacuses
abhorred
abhorrer
abridger
absentee
absolver
absorber
accepter
accursed
achiever
adjuster
adlibbed
admitted
advanced
affected
affecter
affirmer
aflutter
aglimmer
aglitter
agonised
airliner
airscrew
airspeed
Alderney
alewives
alkalies
allergen
allotted
allottee
alphabet
ambusher
anabases
analyser
analyses
anchoret
androgen
annulled
answerer
anteater
antlered
apodoses
appalled
archives
arcuated
argufier
armoured
armourer
arranger
arrestee
arrester
articled
ascender
asperges
asphodel
assenter
assignee
assorted
astonied
atlantes
atomiser
attender
attested
attester
attorney
attrited
atwitter
auspices
aweather
axletree
bagpiper
balanced
balancer
ballonet
baluster
banister
bannered
banneret
banterer
barathea
barterer
bassinet
bebopper
becalmed
bechamel
bedimmed
bedmaker
beeeater
befallen
befitted
befogged
begetter
beginner
begirded
begotten
beguiler
beholden
beholder
believer
bereaved
berliner
besieger
beslaver
besotted
bespoken
betrayer
bevelled
beveller
bewigged
bewilder
biconvex
bindweed
birdseed
blackleg
blazoner
bleacher
blighter
bloodred
blueweed
bobbinet
bobwheel
bonspiel
boottree
borderer
borrower
bosseyed
botflies
boughten
boursier
bourtree
bracelet
bractlet
branched
brancher
brandied
brandnew
breasted
breather
breeches
brethren
breveted
brewster
brickred
brighten
brindled
britches
broacher
brocaded
brocatel
brooklet
buckshee
budgeree
bummaree
bunkered
burgonet
burrower
buttoner
bystreet
caballed
cactuses
cadenced
calcanea
calender
calliper
cameleer
canaster
canister
canzonet
capellet
caponier
carburet
carcanet
carefree
carolled
carousel
carouser
cascabel
cataloes
catheter
cathexes
caudated
caudexes
caudices
cavalier
caverned
cavilled
caviller
cellarer
cellaret
cerastes
cervices
chandler
chapiter
chaunter
Cherokee
chickpea
childbed
children
chopsuey
christen
cicisbei
cicisbeo
ciliated
cirriped
citified
cityfied
clarinet
cleanser
clerihew
clincher
cloister
closeset
closeted
clothier
cloudlet
coccyges
cockerel
cockeyed
codifier
codriver
cognomen
cogwheel
coistrel
colander
coleseed
collagen
collared
colleger
coloured
columned
commoner
commoney
commuter
compages
compiler
complier
composed
composer
computer
conceder
conferee
confider
confiner
confines
congener
conjurer
conniver
consider
consoler
consumer
convener
conveyer
corniced
corselet
corseted
cortices
coryphee
costumer
cottager
cottagey
courtier
coverlet
coworker
cracknel
crannied
cratches
credited
crenated
crosslet
crotched
crotchet
croupier
crucifer
crueller
crusader
cucumber
culottes
cultured
cupelled
curveted
customer
cutwater
cyanogen
cyanoses
cyclamen
cyclopes
cylinder
dahabieh
daughter
deadener
deathbed
debagged
debarred
debugged
decanter
deceased
deceiver
December
decipher
declarer
deemster
defender
deferred
deferrer
deflower
deformed
dejected
demander
demented
demitted
demobbed
demurred
demurrer
dentated
departed
depicter
deportee
depraved
deprived
deserter
designer
despiser
destrier
detached
detailed
detainee
detainer
deterred
deterrer
devilled
devourer
dewyeyed
diabetes
dialyser
dialyses
diameter
diarrhea
didapper
diereses
diffuser
digester
diplogen
disagree
disaster
discover
discreet
diseased
dishevel
disinter
disorder
disposer
disquiet
dissever
ditherer
divorcee
doddered
dodderer
dogeared
dogfaced
doggerel
dogooder
dogtired
domineer
dominoes
doomster
doorstep
dotterel
douanier
dowelled
drabbler
dragomen
dragonet
dragster
drencher
dribbler
dribblet
dripfeed
drownded
drupelet
duckweed
dulcimer
Dulcinea
dundiver
dungaree
durables
dutyfree
dyspnoea
ebriated
educated
eighteen
eighties
electret
elevated
ellipses
embalmer
embedded
embitter
embolden
embosser
embracer
embussed
emphases
employee
employer
enarched
encipher
encumber
endanger
endorsee
endorser
endostea
endpaper
enfetter
enforcer
engender
engineer
engraver
enlarger
enquirer
enricher
enrolled
enslaver
entailer
epistler
equalled
equipped
equities
espalier
espouser
estopped
estoppel
evildoer
examinee
examiner
exanthem
excelled
excluder
exequies
exhorter
expander
expelled
expellee
exploder
explorer
exporter
exserted
extender
extolled
extremes
eyeliner
eyewater
falcated
falconer
falconet
fastener
fatigues
fattener
favoured
favourer
featured
features
fedayeen
feldsher
ferreter
feverfew
filagree
filigree
filmgoer
fingered
finisher
fireeyed
fireweed
fissiped
flatfeet
flaxseed
fletcher
flincher
flockbed
florigen
flounder
flowered
flowerer
floweret
flypaper
flywheel
focussed
foliaged
follower
fomenter
fontanel
footstep
forcefed
forefeel
foregoer
foreknew
foreseen
forested
forester
forgiven
fornices
forrader
forsaken
fosterer
foureyes
fourteen
frenzied
frescoes
fribbler
frighten

frijoles
frillies
frontier
frontlet
frutices
furcated
fusileer
fusilier
galeated
galloper
galluses
gamester
gangster
ganister
gardener
garganey
garotter
garreted
gaselier
gasfired
gasmeter
gasolier
gastraea
gatherer
gauntlet
geometer
germfree
gestagen
ghettoes
glycogen
goadster
Godspeed
gogetter
gossamer
gossiper
goutweed
grabbler
gravamen
greegree
greenlet
greffier
grimacer
grizzled
groschen
grottoes
grounder
grumbler
gruntled
guernsey
gulfweed
gunlayer
gusseted
halfbred
hallowed
halluces
halteres
hangover
harasser
hardener
haruspex
hastener
havocked
hawkeyed
hawkweed
haymaker
heathhen
heighten
helmeted
helpmeet
henequen
Hercules
highbred
hijacker
hinderer
histogen
hocussed
holdover
homebred
homebrew
honeybee
honeydew
honourer
hotelier
howitzer
huckster
humoured
hydrogen
hydromel
hypnoses
hypothec
icewater
idolater
idoliser
illfated
illtimed
imagines
immersed
impacted
impelled
impeller
impolder
importer
imposter
improper
improver
impugner
included
incurred
indebted
inductee
indulger
inedited
inferred
infilter
inflamer
inflated
inflexed
informed
informer
infrared
ingather
inlander
inquirer
inserted
inspired
inspirer
insulter
intended
interbed
internee
interred
interrex
intersex
intruder
invected
inverted
inverter
irongrey
islander
jabberer
jamboree
japanned
jewelled
jeweller
jiggered
Judaiser
Kaffiyeh
kedgeree
kerchief
kibitzer
killdeer
knapweed
kneedeep
kreutzer
labelled
labourer
lamented
lancelet
lanneret
lapelled
larcener
larynges
larynxes
latchkey
latticed
laughter
launcher
lavender
lawgiver
lawmaker
lecturer
leftover
legioned
leisured
lengthen
lenticel
lettered
levanter
levelled
leveller
libelled
libellee
libeller
licensed
licensee
licenser
lichened
lingerer
lintseed
listener
liveried
lockstep
loiterer
Londoner
loosener
lopeared
lopsided
lorikeet
louvered
lowlevel
lumberer
lynxeyed
mackerel
magdalen
magicked
magister
malarkey
maligner
malinger
maltster
maneater
mangabey
mangonel
Manichee
mannered
manpower
mansized
mantelet
marauder
marketer
marmoset
martinet
masseter
materiel
matrices
matrixes
Mayqueen
measured
medalled
membered
menhaden
meninges
meristem
mesdames
metalled
midwives
milkweed
milliner
mimester
mimicked
mimicker
minister
minstrel
miscegen
mischief
misgiven
misnomer
mistaken
mittened
modelled
modeller
modifier
molasses
molester
monicker
MonKhmer
moonshee
moreover
motormen
mucrones
muleteer
multiped
murderer
murmurer
murrelet
muscadel
muscatel
muskdeer
musktree
muslined
mutineer
mutterer
narcoses
nectared
negligee
neuroses
newcomer
newlywed
newsheet
newsreel
nielloed
nimbused
nineteen
nineties
nitrogen
November
numberer
nurturer
oakegger
observer
obtainer
obtected
occluded
occupier
occurred
odometer
offender
offsider
ofttimes
ohmmeter
oilfired
oldtimer
oleander
oleaster
oligomer
onceover
onesided
onlooker
openeyed
oppugner
ordainer
oriented
outdated
outmoded
outrider
outsider
overdrew
overfeed
overflew
overgrew
overseen
overseer
overstep
overview
oxidiser
oximeter
oxpecker
ozoniser
pacifier
palmiped
palterer
pamperer
pamphlet
panelled
panicked
panpipes
parakeet
parallel
parcener
pardoner
pargeter
paroquet
partaken
Passover
pastries
patentee
pathogen
paysheet
peagreen
pearlies
pectines
pedalier
pedalled
pedicled
pedigree
perfumer
perilled
perisher
perjurer
petalled
petioled
petronel
pharisee
Philomel
photogen
pickerel
picketer
pictures
pilaster
pileated
pilferer
pillager
pilsener
pinaster
pincenez
pinmoney
pinnated
pinniped
pinwheel
pitviper
plaister
planchet
platelet
playgoer
plighted
plougher
plumaged
plumelet
plumiped
poisoner
polisher
pollices
pollster
polluter
pomander
ponderer
pondweed
pontifex
postfree
posturer
potholer
potterer
powdered
prattler
preacher
preparer
presager
presumer
priedieu
Primates
prisoner
procurer
producer
profaner
profiler
promisee
promiser
promoter
prompter
proposer
protegee
provided
provider
puggaree
pugnosed
pullover
pulpiter
punisher
purebred
purifier
pursenet
pushover
pyrrhoea
quarrier
queenlet
quencher
quibbler
quickset
quillpen
rabbiter
racegoer
rachides
ransomer
rapeseed
rapparee
raptures
rarefied
ratifier
ravelled
ravisher
rawboned
rearview
reasoner
reawaken
rebelled
rebeller
rebutted
rebutter
recapped
receiver
reckoner
reconvey
recorder
recurred
redeemer
redfaced
redwater
reedwren
referred
refitted
reflexed
reformed
reformer
register
regrater
reindeer
rejecter
rejigger
rejoicer
releasee
releaser
reliever
remember
reminder
remitted
remittee
remitter
renderer
reneguer
renowned
renumber
repairer
repartee
repealer
repeater
repelled
repeller
repenter
replacer
reporter
repotted
requiter
reserved
resetter
resigned
resister
resorter
restorer
resurvey
retailer
retainer
retarded
retarder
retorted
revealer
revelled
reveller
revenger
reverser
reverter
revetted
reviewer
revolter
revolver
rewarder
ricochet
rimester
rivalled
rivelled
riverbed
roadster
rockweed
roentgen
romancer
rooftree
rosetree
roturier
roughhew
rummager
Sadducee
salaried
sandflea
sangaree
sapgreen
sarcenet
sarsenet
sawbones
sawedged
scanties
sceptred
schiller
schooner
scilicet
scolices
scoopnet
scorcher
scotfree
scourger
scragged
scrammed
scrannel
scrapped
scrapper
scrawler
screamer
screener
screever
scrubbed
scrubber
scutcher
seafarer
seagreen
sealevel
seamster
searcher
seasoner
seawater
sebesten
secluded
seconder
selectee
semester
sempster
sentinel
serrated
setscrew
sewellel
shadower
shagreen
shambles
sharpset
sheepked
sheeppen
shielder
shiftkey
shikaree
shingler
shingles
shiralee
shivaree
shoetree
shoulder
shrapnel
shredded
shredder
shrimper
shrinker
shrugged
shrunken
shuffler
sickener
sidestep
sideview
silencer
sinister
siphonet
situated
sketcher
skindeep
skittles
slipover
sloeeyed
sloucher
slugabed
smoothen
smoulder
smuggler
snatcher
sniffler
sniffles
sniggler
snitcher

snuffler
snuffles
socalled
softener
solander
solderer
solleret
somewhen
songster
sorcerer
sorochen
sorrower
spadices
spadones
spalpeen
spandrel
sparkler
sparklet
spavined
specimen
spicated
spicknel
spikelet
spinifex
spinster
spirited
splasher
splatter
splinter
splitter
splutter
spoonfed
sprawler
spreader
sprigged
springer
sprinter
sprocket
spurrier
squaller
squander
squasher
squatted
squatter
squawker
squeaker
squealer
squeegee
squeezer
squibbed
squidded
squilgee
squinter
squireen
squirrel
squirter
stakenet
stallfed
stancher
startler
statured
steepled
stenosed
stickler
stipites
stippler
stitcher
stopover
storeyed
strained
strainer
straiten
stranded
stranger
strapped
strapper
streaked
streaker
streamer
streeted
stricken
stridden
stringed
stringer
stripped
stripper
stroller
stropped
strucken
strummed
strummer
strumpet
strutted
strutter
stuccoes
stumbler
sturdied
stylised
suborder
suborner
sufferer
summoner
sunbaked
sunderer
sundried
sundries
supplier
supplies
supposed
surfacer
surmiser
sweepnet
sweetpea
swiftlet
swindler
switchel
synopses
syringes
syrinxes
tabouret
tafferel
takeover
talented
tamperer
tapwater
tattered
tattooer
tautomer
taverner
taxpayer
teamster
teatowel
teenager
teleview
tempered
temperer
terminer
terraced
textured
thatcher
thickset
thirster
thirteen
thoraces
thoraxes
thrasher
threader
threaten
thresher
thriller
throated
throbbed
thrummed
thruster
thurifer
thwacker
thwarter
tickseed
timbered
tinkerer
tittuped
together
tomalley
tonepoem
toolshed
toplevel
topliner
torturer
totalled
totterer
towelled
traducer
trailnet
trampler
transfer
trawlnet
treacher
treadler
trembler
trembles
trencher
trilobed
trimeter
trochlea
trophied
troutlet
truckler
truebred
tungsten
turbaned
turbojet
turnover
turreted
twaddler
twenties
twiddler
twinkler
twitcher
twoedged
twofaced
twosided
twotimer
typifier
udometer
unabated
unaneled
unawares
unbacked
unbarred
unbeaten
unbelief
unbiased
unbidden
unbolted
unbroken
unburden
unburied
uncalled
uncapped
uncaused
uncoined
underlet
undersea
underset
undraped
unearned
unedited
unfasten
unfetter
unfitted
unforced
unformed
unfrozen
unfunded
unglazed
ungotten
unhinged
unhoused
unkennel
unleaded
unlimber
unlinked
unlisted
unloader
unloosen
unmanned
unmarked
unopened
unpaired
unpegged
unpinned
unplaced
unrigged
unroofed
unsealed
unseated
unseeded
unshaped
unstated
unsuited
unsunned
untapped
untented
untether
untitled
unvalued
unversed
unvoiced
unwanted
unwashed
unweaned
unwished
unwonted
unzipped
upholder
uplander
uplifter
uprooter
upsetter
utiliser
valanced
vanisher
vapourer
velskoen
veneerer
venturer
verboten
verderer
verditer
verdured
verifier
vertexes
vertices
vesturer
viameter
vilifier
villager
vintager
vivifier
vizarded
vortexes
vortices
vowelled
waggoner
walkover
walleyed
walloper
wallower
wanderer
warrener
wartweed
watchkey
waterbed
wayfarer
weeviled
wellbred
whatever
wheedler
whenever
wherever
whiffler
whimbrel
whistler
whitener
whittret
whomever
wideeyed
wigmaker
wildeyed
windowed
winnower
withdrew
woodshed
wooldyed
woolshed
wormseed
wrangler
wreathen
wrestler
wretched
wriggler
wristlet
yestreen
yodelled
yodeller
zoolater
aircraft
airshaft
alkalify
ammonify
autodafe
beautify
blastoff
brushoff
bullyoff
calctuff
camshaft
classify
cockloft
dandruff
denazify
detoxify
dyestuff
earmuffs
emulsify
esterify
facelift
failsafe
fishwife
fluidify
footmuff
forklift
fructify
goodwife
halflife
handcuff
humidify
identify
lapidify
layshaft
meatsafe
penknife
prettify
quantify
redshift
resinify
revivify
riffraff
rigidify
roodloft
sanctify
saponify
sawedoff
seacraft
silicify
simplify
sobstuff
solidify
spaewife
standoff
stellify
stratify
stultify
Tartuffe
tipstaff
tradeoff
unstuffy
unthrift
wakerife
wildlife
woodruff
writeoff
Yankeefy
zinckify
absterge
acierage
adjutage
aerology
agiotage
agrology
algology
alienage
although
amperage
antilogy
apothegm
appanage
axiology
badinage
baronage
bearings
begrudge
beverage
birdcage
blindage
blockage
brassage
breakage
bryology
cabotage
cacology
campaign
carriage
chemurgy
churinga
cleavage
combings
contango
converge
coverage
cozenage
cribbage
cytology
demagogy
demiurge
diallage
diggings
disgorge
dislodge
disusage
doxology
drainage
dressage
driftage
earnings
endamage
ensilage
envisage
equipage
estrange
ethology
exchange
fandango
ferriage
flamingo
floatage
fontange
foreedge
frondage
frontage
frottage
fruitage
fullpage
furlough
fuselage
gainings
geophagy
grillage
hastings
heritage
hiccough
hindlegs
homology
horologe
horology
hustings
ideology
illusage
impetigo
impledge
infringe
kneehigh
language
lashings
leavings
leggings
lethargy
leverage
litharge
littlego
lodgings
mahjongg
Mandingo
maritage
marriage
menology
messuage
metayage
micrurgy
misalign
misjudge
misology
misusage
moorings
mornings
mortgage
mucilage
mycology
nomology
nonusage
nosology
oecology
oenology
offstage
omophagy
oncology
ontology
oreology
outrange
outreign
outweigh
paradigm
paragoge
pedagogy
pedology
peelings
penology
phalange
pickings
pilotage
plumbago
plussage
pomology
porridge
posology
poundage
prejudge
prestige
prolonge
promulge
pupilage
quadriga
reassign
recharge
redesign
reemerge
rheology
rinsings
roadsign
roughage
rutabaga
sabotage
scavenge
scrounge
selvedge
sentrygo
serology
sewerage
sexology
shortage
siftings
sinology
sitology
slippage
smallage
solfeggi
spillage
spoilage
spousage
squeedge
staffage
stallage
steerage
stillage
stoppage
strategy
subimago
submerge
substage
suffrage
suitings
superego
tailings
theology
thirlage
thorough
tocology
tokology
topology
trackage
truckage
turnings
tutelage
tutorage
typehigh
typology
umpirage
underage
verbiage
vicarage
vicinage
virology
vitiligo
wagonage
waterage
wellnigh
wharfage
winnings
workings
wrappage
wreckage
writings

xylology
zymology
absinthe
affright
airtight
allnight
autarchy
autobahn
babouche
backache
barouche
besought
bimbashi
brouhaha
bunfight
cachucha
corniche
daylight
demarche
demijohn
dogfight
donought
enclothe
enswathe
eutrophy
eyesight
faceache
fanlight
farouche
gaslight
gastight
gazpacho
gunfight
headache
headachy
iceyacht
inflight
menarche
midnight
monarchy
mustache
naumachy
nepenthe
octarchy
outright
outsight
pansophy
pastiche
postiche
revanche
rubbishy
scratchy
screechy
sennight
skylight
soutache
splotchy
squelchy
stealthy
stomachy
straight
stretchy
sunbathe
sunlight
sympathy
thearchy
triarchy
twilight
unclothe
unsought
unswathe
untaught
unworthy
viscacha
vizcacha
waxlight
abattoir
academia
academic
accredit
acentric
acidosis
aconitic
acoustic
acrolein
acrostic
adamitic
adenitis
adularia
adynamia
adynamic
aerofoil
agnostic
agraphia
agrestic
airstrip
alchemic
Algonkin
alguazil
alizarin
alkaloid
alleluia
allergic
alopecia
ambrosia
amitosis
amitotic
amniotic
amoeboid
amphibia
anabasis
anabatic
anabolic
anagogic
analogic
analysis
analytic
anarchic
anatomic
anechoic
aniconic
anorexia
anorexic
anorthic
anthelia
anthemia
anthesis
aoristic
apagogic
aperitif
aplastic
apodosis
apogamic
apologia
apomixis
appendix
applepie
arachnid
argentic
armchair
aromatic
arpeggio
artistic
asbestic
asphyxia
assassin
asteroid
asthenia
asthenic
ataraxia
ataraxic
athletic
Atlantic
aubretia
autacoid
autarkic
autistic
aventail
aviatrix
backspin
bacteria
balladic
balletic
balsamic
banausic
bangtail
barbaric
baryonic
basaltic
bathetic
bathotic
battalia
bauxitic
bearskin
beatific
Benjamin
benzylic
berberis
bicuspid
bignonia
biogenic
bionomic
blacktie
blastoid
Blenheim
bluechip
bobbypin
bondmaid
bonhomie
botryoid
bowsprit
branchia
bromelia
bromidic
bronchia
buckskin
buddleia
bulletin
bursitis
cachexia
calcaria
calcific
calcitic
calfskin
calycoid
camellia
cancroid
cannabin
cannabis
cannikin
cantoris
capeskin
caprifig
capuchin
carbolic
carbonic
caryatid
cathexis
cathodic
catholic
cationic
catstail
causerie
Cenozoic
centroid
cephalic
ceratoid
cercaria
Chaldaic
chalkpit
chaplain
cherubic
cherubim
chiastic
chimeric
chinchin
choleric
choragic
choregic
chorioid
christie
chthonic
cicatrix
cinnamic
cinquain
clanship
clematis
climatic
clupeoid
cobaltic
cocktail
coelomic
coenobia
cognovit
collyria
colubrid
complain
conchoid
contagia
contrail
conurbia
coonskin
copyedit
coracoid
cordwain
cornific
coronoid
cosmetic
coumarin
coxalgia
coxswain
crankpin
creatrix
criteria
crosstie
crucifix
cucurbit
culverin
curculio
Cushitic
cyanosis
cyanotic
cyclonic
cyclosis
Cyrenaic
Cyrillic
cystitis
dactylic
daemonic
daffodil
daimonic
dalmatic
damassin
deanship
debonair
decemvir
decennia
decrepit
deeplaid
deerskin
dementia
dendroid
dentalia
despotic
devilkin
diabasic
diabetic
diabolic
dialogic
dialysis
dialytic
diarchic
diatomic
diatonic
dichasia
dichroic
dicrotic
dicyclic
didactic
dieldrin
dieresis
dietetic
dihybrid
dinornis
dioptric
dioramic
dioritic
diplopia
disclaim
dispirit
distrain
distrait
diuresis
diuretic
dogmatic
domestic
doornail
dovetail
draconic
dramatic
dutypaid
dybbukim
dynastic
dysgenic
dyslexia
dyslexic
dystopia
ecclesia
echinoid
eclectic
ecliptic
ecologic
economic
ecstatic
effluvia
egoistic
egomania
electric
elenctic
ellipsis
elliptic
empathic
emphasis
emphatic
emulsoid
encaenia
enclitic
encrinic
encyclic
endermic
endozoic
entoptic
entozoic
enuresis
enuretic
enzootic
eolithic
epidemic
episodic
epitasis
epopoeia
eremitic
erogenic
esoteric
estuaril
Ethiopic
eucritic
euonymin
eupatrid
eupepsia
eupeptic
euphonic
euphoria
euphoric
eustatic
eutectic
exegesis
exegetic
exlibris
exogamic
exoteric
explicit
fantasia
faradaic
fauteuil
febrific
fellahin
felsitic
ferritic
fibrosis
fibrotic
fireship
firstaid
fishtail
flagship
flanerie
floodlit
fluellin
forensic
foresaid
foresail
foreskin
formalin
fountain
franklin
Fraulein
freesoil
frenetic
frogspit
gabbroic
gabbroid
Gadhelic
gainsaid
galactic
galvanic
gardenia
gelastic
gematria
geodesic
geodetic
geologic
geoponic
geotaxis
Germanic
gerontic
gigantic
globulin
gloxinia
glycerin
glyconic
gneissic
gnomonic
goatskin
Goidelic
goldfoil
gorgonia
granitic
grisgris
Guelphic
gummosis
gymnasia
gynoecia
hadronic
haematic
haematin
hairgrip
haliotis
hamartia
handgrip
handmaid
handrail
hangnail
hardship
harmonic
headsail
hedgepig
heirship
helicoid
heliosis
Helladic
Hellenic
heraldic
herbaria
hermetic
herpetic
hidrosis
hidrotic
hieratic
hightail
Hispanic
historic
holistic
holozoic
holstein
hominoid
horntail
horrific
humanoid
hydatoid
hydropic
hygienic
hypnosis
hypnotic
hysteria
hysteric
illiquid
implicit
imprimis
insignia
insomnia
inspirit
intaglio
intarsia
intermit
intermix
intertie
intrepid
intromit
Iroquois
isagogic
ischemia
ischemic
isobaric
isocheim
isogamic
isogonic
isomeric
isotonic
isotopic
jalousie
japhetic
jesuitic
jumpsuit
Jurassic
juristic
kingship
klephtic
kurtosis
kyphosis
kyphotic
ladyship
lambskin
landrail
landslip
larrikin
lecithin
lemuroid
leucitic
libeccio
lichenin
lignitic
limetwig
linchpin
lingerie
liturgic
lockknit
logistic
longhair
longship
loonybin
lordosis
lordotic
lordship
lothario
lymphoid
lynchpin
maenadic
magmatic
magnesia
magnetic
magnific
magnolia
maieutic
mainsail
maintain
majestic
malvasia
mandarin
mandolin
manganic
mannikin
manubria
marasmic
marocain
maroquin
mastitis
mechanic
medallic
medusoid
memsahib
mephitic
mephitis
mercuric
meristic
mescalin
mesmeric
Mesozoic
metallic
meteoric
methodic
methylic
methysis
microbic
midbrain
milkmaid
Miltonic
mirepoix
Mishnaic
Mithraic
mnemonic
moccasin
moleskin
molybdic
monastic
Mongolic
monistic
monkship
monoacid
monorail
moonsail
morainic
morbific
mortmain
moshavim
motorail
mountain
multifid
muriatic
mutchkin
myelinic
myelitis
myogenic

myositic
myositis
myosotis
narcosis
narcotic
Nearctic
necrosis
necrotic
nematoid
NeoLatin
neomycin
neotenic
neoteric
neuritic
neuritis
neuronic
neurosis
neurotic
nickelic
nomistic
nonclaim
nonrigid
notornis
nuclidic
odontoid
oenophil
omphalic
operatic
oratorio
organdie
orgasmic
orgastic
ornithic
orogenic
Ossianic
osteitis
outstrip
ovaritis
overlaid
overlain
overpaid
oversail
overslip
oviposit
oxytocin
pachalic
palmitin
pandemic
pangolin
panmixia
pannikin
pantsuit
papistic
paraffin
paranoia
paranoid
parhelia
parhelic
parsonic
pashalic
pashalik
pathetic
pearmain
pedantic
peignoir
Pelasgic
pellucid
periodic
periotic
perlitic
petaloid
petechia
petrolic
phenolic
phenylic
phonemic
phonetic
photopia
photopic
phreatic
phthalic
phthisic
phthisis
phyletic
phylloid
Pindaric
pizzeria
plantain
platinic
platonic
playsuit
pleinair
plutonic
podagric
pollinia
pollinic
polypoid
polyzoic
ponytail
poristic
portrait
postobit
postpaid
potassic
prelatic
presidio
prismoid
proclaim
prohibit
prolamin
prolific
propolis
propylic
prosodic
protasis
protatic
protonic
pruritic
psilosis
pulmonic
puristic
purpuric
purpurin
pyelitis
pyogenic
pyrenoid
pythonic
quatrain
quintain
quixotic
rabbinic
rachitic
rachitis
ramequin
ratstail
recommit
redistil
replevin
republic
resinoid
resorcin
restrain
retiarii
rhetoric
rhinitis
rhomboid
rhythmic
ringmain
ringtail
riverain
romantic
rubytail
sabbatic
saccadic
sacraria
sadistic
safranin
sainfoin
salvific
Sangrail
sanserif
Sanskrit
santonin
sardonic
Sassanid
saturnic
scaphoid
scarfpin
scenario
schizoid
sciuroid
sclereid
scombrid
scotopic
sealskin
seasnail
secretin
semantic
semiotic
sensoria
sepaloid
septfoil
seraglio
seraphic
seraphim
seriatim
serranid
sesamoid
shaleoil
shashlik
shedevil
sheepdip
Shemitic
sideslip
sigmatic
siluroid
silvatic
Sinaitic
sinfonia
sinophil
sinusoid
siphonic
siriasis
Slavonic
sloppail
smoothie
snakepit
snapbrim
Socratic
softboil
solenoid
somnific
souvenir
spagyric
spandril
specific
sphenoid
spheroid
sphingid
splendid
spondaic
sporadic
stanzaic
stapelia
staysail
stenosis
stenotic
stomatic
strapoil
stravaig
strontia
strophic
stubnail
stunsail
subsonic
subtonic
subtopia
suburbia
succinic
suzerain
swanskin
swimsuit
syenitic
syllabic
sylvatic
symbolic
sympodia
symposia
synapsis
synaptic
syncytia
syndesis
syndetic
synergic
synergid
syngamic
synopsis
synoptic
syntonic
syphilis
systemic
systolic
taenioid
taffrail
tailspin
talapoin
Talmudic
tamanoir
tantalic
tartaric
tectonic
telluric
teraphim
terrapin
terraria
terrific
tetradic
Teutonic
thalamic
thalloid
theistic
thematic
theurgic
tholepin
thoracic
thrombin
thyroxin
thyrsoid
toreutic
tornadic
township
toxaemia
toxaemic
tracheid
tranquil
transfix
tranship
transmit
trapezia
treenail
Triassic
tribasic
trichoid
triennia
triforia
trimeric
triploid
trisomic
triumvir
trochaic
trochoid
trottoir
truistic
tungstic
turmeric
turnskin
turnspit
twinship
Tychonic
tympanic
typhonic
tyrannic
uncandid
underbid
underdid
underlie
underlip
underpin
uralitic
uvulitis
vaccinia
vampiric
Vandalic
vanillin
Vedantic
veratrin
verbatim
veristic
verticil
victoria
villatic
Virginia
vitellin
volcanic
voussoir
vulcanic
wagonlit
Walkyrie
wardship
wellknit
whitetie
whizzkid
whodunit
windsail
wineskin
wirehair
wistaria
wisteria
wolfskin
woolskin
wrestpin
wristpin
xanthein
zeolitic
zeppelin
zirconia
zoiatria
zoogenic
zoonosis
zygaenid
komitaji
maharaja
airbrake
apresski
archduke
babushka
barracks
beefcake
bouzouki
britzska
bullocky
clambake
dustlike
elflocks
equivoke
finnesko
fishcake
gadzooks
garlicky
gasworks
gimmicky
hairlike
hardbake
hawklike
hillocky
homelike
hummocky
hydroski
keepsake
kinglike
klondike
kolinsky
kromesky
ladylike
lamblike
leaflike
lifelike
lykewake
Mameluke
mandrake
methinks
moussaka
muckrake
namesake
okeydoke
outworks
overtake
peacocky
pembroke
physicky
picnicky
pushbike
rapecake
rimbrake
rockcake
rocklike
rushlike
seaquake
seasnake
seedcake
slowpoke
snowlike
starlike
suchlike
sukiyaki
swanlike
swastika
tapelike
turnpike
tussocky
upstroke
waesucks
waterski
waxworks
whiplike
wifelike
wormlike
yarmulka
aardwolf
abjectly
aborally
abruptly
absently
absurdly
abuttals
achingly
actively
actually
adorable
adorably
adroitly
aerially
aguishly
aiguille
Airedale
airfield
amazedly
amenable
amenably
amicable
amicably
amorally
amusedly
amygdala
animally
annually
antipole
apically
ardently
arguable
arguably
arrantly
artfully
assemble
assembly
astutely
atremble
augustly
auricula
aversely
avowable
avowedly
backveld
bailable
bankable
bankbill
bankroll
barnacle
barrenly
baseball
bastille
beadroll
beanpole
bearable
bearably
bedabble
bedazzle
bedtable
befuddle
beggarly
belittle
bellpull
benignly
biddable
bifocals
billfold
binnacle
birdcall
bistable
bitchily
bitingly
bitterly
biweekly
biyearly
blackfly
blamable
blamably
blastula
blearily
blithely
bloodily
blowball
blowhole
bluebell
blurrily
boatbill
bolthole
bordello
borecole
borehole
boringly
bouncily
boyishly
brassily
brazenly
breezily
bribable
brightly
brimfull
broccoli
brokenly
broodily
brutally
bullcalf
bunghole
bushveld
caboodle
cabriole
cakewalk
callable
calycule
camisole
camomile
canaille
candidly
canoodle
canticle
capitula
capriole
caracole
carnally
carriole
carryall
caruncle
casually
catapult
catchall
catchfly
caudally
caudillo
causally
centuple
chastely
chasuble
chattily
cheekily
cheerily
chenille
chirpily
choicely
chorally
Christly
chummily
churchly
clammily
clavicle
cleverly
clodpole
clodpoll
cloudily
clumsily
coalhole
coarsely
cogently
commonly
convexly
copyhold
cornball
cornicle
Cotswold
cousinly
coverall
covertly
cowardly
craftily
cramfull
cranefly
crankily
cravenly
creakily
credible
credibly
crenelle
croakily
crossply
crowbill
crucible
crustily
culpable
culpably
curricle
cursedly

cussedly
daintily
damnable
damnably
danegeld
daringly
deadfall
decently
decouple
demurely
denehole
deniable
denticle
deucedly
devoutly
diastole
dimmable
directly
disciple
dismally
distally
divinely
docilely
doggedly
dogwhelk
domicile
doorbell
doorsill
dorsally
dotingly
doumpalm
downfall
downhill
drawable
drawwell
dreamily
drearily
drivable
drowsily
drumroll
duckbill
dumbbell
dunghill
durukuli
dutiable
easterly
educable
educible
eggshell
eighthly
elatedly
eligible
eligibly
embattle
embezzle
empeople
empurple
encircle
enfeeble
engirdle
enkindle
ensample
ensemble
entangle
enthrall
entirely
entrails
enviable
enviably
epically
epicycle
epistyle
erasable
erectile
erewhile
erodible
errantly
escarole
evadable
evenfall
evitable
exigible
expertly
expiable
eyestalk
facially
facilely
fallible
fallibly
famously
farewell
fascicle
fasciola
fasciole
fasttalk
fatherly
faultily
faunally
feasible
feasibly
fellable
fellowly
fencible
fervidly
festally
feudally
fewtrils
fibrilla
fiercely
filially
filthily
finitely
fireball
fiscally
fishable
fishball
fitfully
fivefold
flabella
flagella
flagpole
flashily
fleshfly
flexible
flexibly
flimsily
flintily
floccule
flocculi
floppily
florally
floridly
flotilla
fluently
foetidly
folktale
follicle
football
footfall
foothill
foothold
footrule
forcedly
forcible
forcibly
fordable
forefelt
foretell
foretold
formally
formerly
fourball
fourfold
fourthly
fraenula
freefall
freehold
freewill
friendly
frigidly
friskily
frostily
frothily
frugally
fruitfly
frustule
fumarole
fungible
funkhole
furuncle
futilely
gainable
gapingly
gargoyle
garishly
gastrula
gatefold
gefuffle
genially
gerbille
germcell
gingerly
girasole
glabella
gladioli
glandule
glassily
globally
gloomily
gloriole
glossily
godchild
goldenly
goodwill
goofball
gravelly
greasily
greedily
greenfly
groggily
gromwell
grubbily
grumpily
guerilla
guidable
guiltily
gullable
gullible
halfsole
hamululi
handball
handbell
handbill
handheld
handhold
handmill
hangable
harebell
hateable
hayfield
heartily
heatedly
heavenly
heelball
hellhole
hickwall
hidyhole
highball
hireable
hoarsely
hollowly
homefelt
homuncle
honestly
hornbill
hornfels
horrible
horribly
horridly
horsefly
housefly
hoverfly
huggable
hulahula
humanely
humuncle
hungrily
hypobole
icefield
imbecile
imitable
immingle
immobile
impishly
impurely
indocile
inedible
infirmly
innately
insanely
inscroll
instable
intently
inthrall
intitule
inveigle
inviable
inwardly
isabella
isolable
issuable
jaggedly
jauntily
jejunely
jocosely
jocundly
joinable
jokingly
jovially
joyfully
joyously
juvenile
kefuffle
kingbolt
kinsfolk
kissable
kneehole
knightly
knothole
knowable
korfball
labially
laically
landfall
latently
latterly
laudable
laudably
lavishly
lawfully
lawyerly
laystall
leadenly
lenticle
lethally
leviable
lifebelt
liftable
likeable
limekiln
limpidly
lineally
linearly
liquidly
liveable
livelily
loanable
loblolly
lockable
lodicule
longwall
loophole
lovelily
lovingly
lubberly
lyophile
madapple
maidenly
mailable
malignly
manciple
mandible
mandorla
mandrill
manfully
manifold
mannerly
mantilla
manually
marigold
markedly
martello
masterly
matronly
maturely
mayapple
meagrely
meatball
medially
mellowly
mendable
menially
mentally
mesially
midfield
mightily
minutely
misapply
miscible
misdealt
misspell
misspelt
modernly
modestly
modishly
molecule
molehill
momently
monopoly
mooncalf
mopishly
morbidly
morosely
mortally
mothball
motherly
moveable
movingly
mulishly
multiple
multiply
musicale
musingly
mutually
nailfile
nameable
narghile
narrowly
natively
Negrillo
neurally
ninefold
normally
nouvelle
nucleole
nucleoli
numskull
nuptials
nutshell
oafishly
oakapple
obstacle
obtusely
occultly
ocularly
odiously
oilfield
oldworld
opaquely
openable
operable
opercula
opuscula
opuscule
orchilla
ornately
otiosely
outfield
ovariole
overalls
overcall
overfall
overfill
overfold
overkill
overrule
oversell
oversold
owlishly
pallidly
pallmall
palpable
palpably
pantofle
parabola
partible
particle
passable
passably
passible
pastille
patchily
patently
peccable
pedipalp
peduncle
peephole
pellicle
pellmell
pendicle
pentacle
pigswill
pinnacle
pinochle
pintable
pitiable
pitiably
placable
placably
placidly
plaguily
playable
playbill
pliantly
plimsoll
pluckily
plurally
politely
polygala
popishly
portable
porthole
possible
possibly
postmill
potbelly
potently
potstill
pourable
preamble
predella
prettily
priestly
primally
princely
prissily
probable
probably
prolixly
promptly
properly
prostyle
provable
provably
prunella
prunelle
prunello
pryingly
publicly
puffball
pulvilli
pushball
pushpull
putridly
quaintly
Quakerly
quartile
queasily
quenelle
quirkily
quotable
racially
radially
raggedly
rainfall
rakehell
rakishly
randomly
rascally
rateable
readable
readably
recently
redouble
rehandle
rekindle
reliable
reliably
remissly
remotely
rentable
repeople
resemble
resettle
reticule
retinula
reusable
reveille
rideable
ridicule
ringbolt
ringwall
ritually
robustly
rocaille
rockfall
rocksalt
rollcall
rolypoly
roothold
ropeable
ropewalk
rottenly
rotundly
ruefully
ruggedly
rugosely
ruinable
runcible
sacredly
sailable
sailorly
saleable
salvable
sardelle
satiable
satiably
savagely
saxatile
scaffold
scalable
scantily
scarcely
scattily
schedule
scissile
scrabble
scramble
scribble
scribbly
scrofula
scurrile
scurvily
scutella
seaholly
sealable
seamanly
seashell
seatbelt
secondly
secretly
securely
sedately
seizable
selfhelp
selfrule
selfwill
semibull
sensible
sensibly
septuple
serenely
serially
severely
sextuple
sexually
shabbily
shaggily
shakable
shapable
shiftily
shigella
shoddily
shoebill
shopbell
shoptalk
shothole
showbill
shrewdly
sickerly
sidewalk
signally
silently
silverly
sinfully
singable
sinkable
sinkhole
sisterly
sizeable
skewbald
skimmilk

skimpily
slangily
sleazily
sleepily
slightly
slinkily
sloppily
slovenly
smarmily
smokable
smoothly
smudgily
smuttily
snappily
snazzily
sneakily
sniffily
snootily
snowball
snowfall
sociable
sociably
socially
softball
solemnly
solvable
sombrely
somedele
sordidly
sortable
spadille
sparable
sparsely
speedily
spherule
spiracle
spirally
spirilla
spongily
spookily
spoonily
sportily
spottily
sprinkle
sprucely
spunkily
squabble
squamule
squarely
squiggle
squiggly
squirely
stanchly
starrily
statable
statedly
steadily
steamily
stickily
stingily
stockily
stodgily
stolidly
stonefly
storable
stormily
straddle
straggle
straggly
straitly
strangle
strickle
strictly
strobila
strobile
strobili
strongly
struggle
stuffily
stumpily
stupidly
sturdily
subphyla
subtitle
suddenly
suitable
suitably
sullenly
sultrily
summerly
superbly
supinely
supplely
syllable
symphile
takingly
tameable
tangible
tangibly
tannable
tasselly
tawdrily
taxingly
teatable
telefilm
tellable
telltale
tenacula
tenaille
tenderly
tensible
tentacle
teocalli
terrible
terribly
testable
tetchily
tetrapla
threeply
throstle
throttle
thurible
thwartly
tidemill
tillable
timeball
timously
tinselly
tithable
tollcall
toothily
torpidly
torridly
tortilla
touchily
towardly
townhall
trammels
trapball
trashily
trendily
trevally
triangle
tribally
trickily
tricycle
triskele
trochili
trustily
tryingly
tubercle
tuneable
turbidly
turgidly
turnable
turnsole
umbrella
unbottle
unbridle
unbuckle
uncially
uncouple
uneasily
unevenly
unfairly
ungainly
unicycle
uniquely
unitedly
unjustly
unkindly
unkingly
unlikely
unlovely
unmeetly
unmuffle
unmuzzle
unriddle
unsaddle
unseemly
unsettle
unstable
unstably
untangle
untidily
untimely
unwarily
unwisely
unwordly
uppishly
upwardly
urbanely
urgently
urostyle
usefully
uvularly
vacantly
Valhalla
valuable
valuably
variable
variably
variedly
vendible
venially
venously
verbally
vernally
vernicle
versicle
victuals
viewable
vincible
vinously
violable
violably
viscidly
visually
vitiable
voidable
volatile
vulgarly
Walhalla
walkable
wantonly
washable
wastable
wearable
weaselly
weevilly
weldable
weregild
werewolf
westerly
wettable
wheezily
whinsill
whitefly
wickedly
wilfully
windfall
windgall
windmill
winepalm
winnable
winterly
wintrily
witchelm
withheld
withhold
wizardly
woefully
wontedly
woodenly
woodpile
woodpulp
woolfell
workable
workfolk
wormhole
worthily
woundily
wrathily
writable
yeastily
yellowly
yeomanly
yourself
zarzuela
zoophily
aceldama
aeronomy
agronomy
airframe
allogamy
analcime
anathema
antinomy
arapaima
atheroma
autogamy
autonomy
autosome
autotomy
backcomb
birdlime
blastema
blossomy
blowlamp
catacomb
charisma
choriamb
coenzyme
consomme
darksome
diastema
displume
divebomb
doldrums
dolesome
downcome
downtime
endogamy
engramma
erythema
eyerhyme
fearsome
firearms
firebomb
firedamp
forename
foretime
foursome
fulltime
gamesome
gendarme
gladsome
glaucoma
gleesome
goodtime
grandame
grapheme
gruesome
halftime
handsome
headlamp
hecatomb
homogamy
homonymy
hornrims
landarmy
lifetime
lobotomy
lonesome
longsome
longtime
lovesome
lymphoma
lysosome
lysozyme
machismo
maritime
mealtime
meantime
merosome
metonymy
millieme
misogamy
monogamy
morpheme
mycetoma
nickname
noontime
overcame
overcome
overjump
overtime
panorama
parttime
pastrami
phyllome
playtime
polygamy
polyseme
polysemy
polysomy
prodrome
realtime
rearlamp
ribosome
sawframe
scleroma
seadrome
seedtime
selfsame
semidome
sidearms
sometime
sterigma
subframe
syndrome
synonymy
syntagma
tachisme
takehome
taxonomy
tenotomy
teratoma
termtime
thingamy
timebomb
tiresome
toilsome
toponymy
trachoma
trichome
twelvemo
undreamt
wallgame
xanthoma
xenogamy
abducens
abducent
aberrant
abetment
abetting
aborning
abradant
absonant
abundant
abutment
abutting
accident
acescent
acquaint
acridine
acrimony
adducent
adherent
adjacent
adjutant
adjuvant
aegirine
aerodyne
afferent
affluent
agrement
agrimony
airborne
aleurone
alkaline
allround
ambulant
andesine
anserine
antimony
anything
aperient
apocrine
apparent
appetent
aqualung
aquatint
aquiline
argument
armament
arrogant
aspirant
assonant
assuming
astatine
atheling
atropine
autodyne
averment
averring
avifauna
bacchant
backbone
backhand
bailment
balkline
bandanna
bantling
banxring
baritone
barytone
baseline
basement
baudrons
beagling
becoming
beeswing
beetling
befriend
besprent
biassing
bivalent
blabbing
blacking
bleeding
blessing
blinding
blinking
blooming
blotting
blurring
boarding
bobolink
bodement
bondmans
bookland
bouffant
bouncing
bowfront
bragging
braiding
breaking
breeding
briefing
brimming
brisling
browband
browning
bubaline
buckling
building
bullring
bundling
buntline
bustling
butylene
cabstand
caffeine
cageling
calamine
calamint
calycine
campagna
camphene
camphine
cancrine
canoeing
capeline
capstone
carabine
Caroline
carotene
casement
catching
catering
cavatina
centring
cerement
ceremony
chaconne
chapping
charming
charring
chatting
cheering
Cheyenne
chipmunk
chipping
chlorine
chopping
chugging
chumming
churning
cicerone
ciceroni
cidevant
cinchona
cladding
claimant
clamming
clanging
clapping
cleaning
clearing
clinking
clipping
clogging
clothing
clotting
clubbing
clubland
coalmine
coherent
compline
compound
confound
confront
conjoint
constant
contline
contorno
corkwing
cornpone
Corybant
cosecant
cotenant
cothurni
couchant
couching
coupling
coursing
covalent
covenant
covering
crabbing
cracking
cradling
cramming
crashing
creatine
creeping
crescent
cretonne
cribbing
crofting
cromorna
cromorne
cropping
crossing
cryogeny
culicine
curarine
curtains
cushiony
cysteine
cytidine
cytosine
dairying
darkling
dateline
deadline
debutant
decadent
decedent
deckhand
deferent
deponent
dethrone
deviling
dewpoint
dextrine
dialling
diaphone
dilatant
diligent
dingdong

diriment feedtank glossina indicant medicine ornament pregnant rosepink
disbound feminine glutting indigene melamine orpiment preprint rotenone
discount fetching gluttony indigent membrane oscinine prescind rubicund
disjoint fiddling goalline indolent merchant osculant pressing rudiment
dismount fighting goatling induline middling ottavino primming ruminant
displant figurant Gobelins inerrant midpoint outbound printing rutilant
divalent figurine goldmine influent migraine outflank pristine saffrony
dividend filament gourmand inhalant militant outgoing prodding saltmine
dockland Filipina grabbing inherent millhand outlying profound sampling
doctrine Filipino gradient inhumane millpond outpoint proofing sandbank
document fishbone graduand inkstand miscount outshine propound sanguine
dominant fishpond graining innocent misdoing outshone propping saraband
downland fistiana grasping inscient misogyny outspend prurient saturant
downwind flagging grayling insolent misprint outspent ptomaine Sauterne
dracaena flagrant greening insulant misspend outvying puissant scammony
dragging flapping greeting insurant misspent overdone purblind scandent
dragline flashing grinning inurbane misthink overfond purfling scanning
dreaming flatling gripping inviting mitigant overhand purslane scarring
dressing fleabane grissini irritant mondaine overhang pursuant scathing
drilling fleeting gritting isoprene monogeny overhung purulent scatting
drinking flippant grouping jetplane monogony overland pyridine scheming
dripping flipping grouting jubilant monogyny overlong pyroxene sciurine
dropping flitting growling judgment monotint overtone quadrant scolding
drubbing floating grubbing julienne monotone overwind quandong scouting
drugging flogging grudging kakemono monotony palatine queening scragend
drumming flooring guardant katakana monument palomino queueing scraping
drypoint flopping gunflint keeshond moorland parasang quidnunc scrutiny
drystone flubbing gunpoint kerosene moribund paravane quilting scudding
duckling fluorine gymkhana kerosine morphine parkland quincunx scumming
duckpond focusing habitant keystone motoring partsong quipping seaborne
duelling fogbound hairline kindling mottling pavement quisling seafront
dulciana folksong halfpint knapping moulding payphone quitrent seagoing
dumfound fondling halftone knitting mounting pearling quitting seamount
dumpling footling handline knocking mourning pediment quizzing seaplane
dwelling foramina handling knotting movement pelerine quotient sederunt
earphone forborne hardline lacewing mowburnt penchant rackrent sediment
easement fordoing hatching lakeland mudstone penitent radicant seedling
efferent foregone hatstand landline muniment peperino rallying segreant
effluent forehand haunting landmine murrhine perigyny rambling seladang
eftsoons foreland headband latitant muscling perilune ratsbane semitone
eggplant forewent headland laughing narceine petaline rattling semolina
elephant forgoing headline learning nauseant petulant reactant sentient
elkhound forspent headlong lefthand Nazarene pheasant reascend sergeant
eloquent founding headwind legatine neckband phosgene recreant serjeant
emceeing foxhound hegemony lemurine neckline phrasing recusant serotine
emergent fragment hellbent leporine needment picayune redblind servient
emigrant fragrant hesitant lifeline neoprene piddling redefine shafting
emitting frapping hexylene lifelong nescient piedmont redolent shamming
emulgent freehand highland ligament nestling piercing redshank shantung
endogeny freezing hireling lighting neutrino piffling reedling sheading
engaging frequent hirrient liniment newfound pinecone referent shealing
enshrine fretting hoarding litigant nicotine pinpoint refluent shedding
enthrone fringing hocusing littling niggling pipeline regiment sheeting
environs fritting Holocene livelong ninepins piperine relaxant shelving
epifauna frocking homeland loadline nocturne plaiding relevant Shetland
epiphany frogging homodont loathing nonevent plangent relucent shieling
equitant frondent homogeny lobeline northing planking relumine shilling
esculent frosting hoodwink lodgment noseband planning remanent shinbone
esurient fuchsine hourlong longhand nosecone platting renitent shinning
ethylene fuelling hyoscine lordling nosering pleading reorient shipment
evacuant fumigant hypogene lovesong notching pleasant repetend shipping
evensong gableend hypogyny lowering nursling pleasing resident shirring
everyone gadarene ianthine lowlying nutrient Pliocene resonant shirting
exacting gangland iceblink luculent obedient plodding respring shocking
excitant gangling icebound luminant obeisant plopping resprung shogging
exciting gangrene iceplant lustrine obliging plotting resupine shooting
exhalant gantline ignominy lustring occident plugging reticent shopping
existent gasolene ignorant macaroni occupant plumbing retiring shunning
exocrine gasoline illumine magazine oestrone poignant revenant shutting
expirant gazogene immanent maharani offering pointing reverend sibilant
exponent gelatine imminent mahogany offprint polygene reverent sideband
exultant gemstone imponent mainland oilstone polygeny reviling sideline
fagoting geophone imposing mainline ointment polygyny rewaking sideling
faineant gladding impotent makimono oliphant porkling Riesling sidelong
farflung gladhand impudent mantling omitting postpone ringbone sidewind
farmhand glancing incident marbling oncoming potbound riverine silicane
farmland glassine incitant marrying ontogeny potplant roasting silicone
farthing gleaning incoming mazarine opponent potstone roborant simulant
feculent gloaming indecent mazement ordinand pounding rockling singeing

singsong
sixpenny
sizzling
skidding
skilling
skimming
skinning
skipping
skirting
slabbing
slagging
slamming
slapbang
slapping
slashing
sledding
sleeping
slimming
slipping
slipring
slitting
slobland
slogging
slopping
slotting
slubbing
slugging
slumming
slurring
smashing
smelling
smocking
snagging
snaplink
snapping
snipping
snogging
snowline
snubbing
solanine
sonatina
soothing
souchong
sounding
sourdine
southing
spanking
spanning
sparling
sparring
spatting
speaking
spelling
spiffing
spinning
spitting
sporting
spotting
spurling
spurring
stabbing
stabling
stagnant
stalling
standing
starling
starring
starting
steading
stealing
stearine
steening
steering
stemming
stepping
sterling
stetting
stilbene
stinking

stirring
stocking
stopping
strepent
strident
striking
stubbing
studding
stuffing
stumming
stunning
subagent
subjoint
subpoena
suckling
sulphone
sunblind
sunburnt
sunshine
sunshiny
sunstone
supplant
surmount
surround
swabbing
swagging
swanking
swanning
swansong
swapping
swatting
swearing
sweeping
sweeting
swelling
swigging
swimming
swinging
swobbing
swopping
swotting
sycamine
sylphine
symbiont
symphony
syncline
tackling
tagalong
tamarind
tapeline
teaching
teething
tegument
telecine
telegony
tempting
tenement
tenpenny
terebene
texthand
theogony
thiamine
thinking
thinning
thousand
thriving
thudding
thumping
tideland
tingeing
tinstone
tolerant
tonguing
toothing
topstone
touching
toxicant
tracking
training

tramline
trapping
trekking
trephine
trichina
tricorne
trifling
trilling
trimming
triplane
tripping
trombone
trotting
trucking
trussing
tsarevna
tumbling
tuppenny
turtling
twinling
twinning
twitting
twopenny
tyrosine
Tyrrhene
undulant
unending
unerring
unfading
unlearnt
unseeing
unsprung
unstring
unstrung
unthrone
uprising
upsprang
upspring
upsprung
urethane
Ursuline
urticant
vagabond
vaulting
vehement
velamina
verecund
vesicant
vestment
Vietcong
Vietminh
vigilant
vilipend
villainy
viperine
virement
virulent
viscount
visitant
vituline
volitant
volplane
vomerine
wakening
warpaint
warplane
watering
waveband
waygoing
weakling
weanling
weeklong
weldment
whacking
whapping
whetting
whidding
whipping
whirring

whizbang
whizzing
whooping
whopping
windcone
wishbone
witching
woodbind
woodbine
woodland
woodwind
woollens
wrapping
xanthene
xanthine
yachting
yeanling
yearling
yearlong
yearning
yielding
zabaione
zecchini
zecchino
zibeline
zincking
zucchini
zugzwang
abductor
ablation
ablution
abortion
abrasion
abutilon
accentor
acceptor
accustom
acrefoot
actuator
adaption
addition
adductor
adhesion
adjustor
adnation
adoption
adulator
advowson
aeration
affusion
agitator
agitprop
agnation
allusion
alluvion
alumroot
ambition
amphipod
ancestor
angstrom
animator
anterior
anteroom
anthozoa
antiphon
aphelion
Arapahoe
arrestor
asbestos
assentor
assertor
assessor
assignor
attestor
audition
aversion
aviation
avulsion
babyhood

bachelor
backdoor
backdrop
backroom
ballroom
ballyhoo
bambinos
banderol
bankbook
bannerol
barefoot
barndoor
barrator
basswood
bathroom
beefwood
beetroot
bellbuoy
bentwood
bergamot
betatron
biathlon
bibation
billhook
billyboy
bisector
blackboy
blacktop
bludgeon
boathook
bobbysox
bodyshop
bontebok
bouillon
bourgeon
buckaroo
buckshot
bullfrog
bullyboy
bungalow
cabinboy
cabochon
cachalot
cachepot
calthrop
calvados
carcajou
cardamom
carillon
casebook
cashbook
castiron
catechol
catsfoot
cauldron
cavesson
cesspool
chaldron
champion
chapbook
chaperon
chiefdom
choirboy
chopchop
chowchow
cinnamon
citation
clerkdom
clipclop
clopclop
clubfoot
coachdog
coaction
coatroom
coauthor
cockatoo
cockcrow
coercion
cofactor

cohesion
collator
colophon
conation
conjuror
convenor
conveyor
cookbook
cooption
copybook
corduroy
cordwood
corkwood
corridor
cotillon
crackpot
creation
creditor
crossbow
crowfoot
cryotron
curassow
cuspidor
darkroom
deadwood
decision
decurion
defector
delation
deletion
delusion
demotion
depictor
deration
derision
detector
deuteron
deviator
devotion
diapason
dictator
dilation
dilution
director
disallow
disendow
disproof
disunion
dittybox
division
dominion
donation
doorknob
doorstop
dotation
doubloon
doughboy
dramshop
dropshot
Dukhobor
dumbshow
duration
dustshot
dynatron
eclosion
ectozoon
educator
eduction
effector
effusion
egestion
ejection
election
electron
elevator
elfarrow
emblazon
emersion
emission

empoison
emulator
emulsion
enaction
encomion
endozoon
enneagon
entozoon
entrepot
entresol
envision
episemon
epyllion
equation
erection
erigeron
eruption
escallop
escargot
eschalot
eulachon
evection
eversion
eviction
evulsion
exaction
excision
executor
exertion
expiator
extensor
exterior
extrados
falchion
fanfaron
fastfood
firewood
fishhook
fixation
flatfoot
flatiron
flection
fleshpot
flipflop
folderol
folkmoot
followon
footslog
foredoom
forefoot
foreknow
forenoon
foreshow
formroom
fraction
friction
froufrou
fruition
function
furbelow
gallipot
gambados
gambeson
gambroon
ganglion
gardyloo
garrison
gelation
geraniol
giftbook
gillaroo
gipsydom
girlhood
glucagon
glycerol
goingson
golliwog
gonfalon
goosegog

gossypol
governor
gramatom
grandson
graviton
gridiron
grogshop
groogroo
guidedog
gumption
gypsydom
gyration
halation
halfboot
halfmoon
handbook
handloom
hangeron
hardwood
headroom
hedgehog
hedgehop
hedgerow
heirloom
heptagon
herdbook
hereupon
highbrow
himation
honeypot
hoosegow
hornbook
horsebox
hotchpot
houseboy
housedog
housetop
Huguenot
hymnbook
ideation
ignition
ignitron
illation
illusion
imitator
impostor
imprison
inaction
inceptor
incision
inductor
infector
inferior
inflator
infusion
inhesion
injector
inositol
intercom
interior
Interpol
intrados
invasion
inventor
investor
irenicon
ironwood
isodicon
isolator
jackaroo
jackboot
jackeroo
jettison
jobation
junction
junkshop
kangaroo
kinghood
kinkajou

klystron
Kohinoor
Komsomol
labrador
ladyhood
laudator
lavation
leapfrog
legation
libation
lifebuoy
ligation
liripoop
lobation
locution
lollipop
lollypop
longeron
longstop
lookeron
loosebox
loveknot
lunation
luncheon
luxation
macaroon
magneton
maidhood
malaprop
mandator
mannitol
marathon
martagon
martenot
mascaron
massicot
mastodon
matchbox
mediator
melodeon
mementos
mesotron
metaphor
metazoon
methanol
mezereon
microdot
migrator
misbegot
moneybox
monition
monkhood
monoglot
moonshot
moufflon
munition
mushroom
mutation
myriapod
myriopod
myrmidon
nainsook
namedrop
naphthol
napoleon
narrator
natation
negation
negatron
newsroom
nextdoor
nodation
nonjuror
nonunion
notation
notebook
noumenon
novation
nutation
objector
oblation
oblivion
occasion
octaroon
octoroon
offshoot
omission
omphalos
operator
orthicon
orthodox
ostracod
ostracon
ostrakon
outHerod
overbook
overcrop
overflow
overgrow
overlook
overshoe
overshot
overtook
oxymoron
paduasoy
paintbox
pantheon
paperboy
papillon
pappadom
parergon
passbook
patentor
pavilion
pawnshop
peardrop
peasecod
peekaboo
peepshow
pentagon
pentroof
petition
pettifog
phlegmon
phosphor
picaroon
pinewood
piscator
plankton
plastron
playbook
playroom
polliwog
pollywog
poltfoot
poltroon
polyglot
polyzoon
poohpooh
porticos
position
positron
potation
predator
pressbox
promisor
pronator
protocol
protozoa
provisor
pteropod
pulpwood
pulsator
pumproom
puncheon
punition
pupation
puppydog
puppydom
purveyor
quadroon
quaestor
queendom
question
radiator
raindrop
reaction
rebellow
receptor
recision
redactor
redeploy
reedstop
reefknot
reemploy
relation
releasor
religion
resistor
revision
Rhinodon
rhizopod
rigadoon
roadbook
rockwood
rogation
roseroot
rosewood
rotation
roundtop
saintdom
saleroom
sanction
sandshoe
saucebox
sauropod
Saxondom
scallion
scansion
scission
scorpion
screwtop
scullion
sculptor
seafloor
seaonion
secretor
sedation
sedition
seedplot
seignior
selector
selfhood
serfhood
servitor
shagroon
shalloon
sheepdog
sheikdom
Sheraton
showroom
sickroom
sidedoor
sideshow
skeleton
skinfood
skypilot
slipknot
slipshod
slipslop
slopshop
smallpox
snapshot
snowboot
snowdrop
snowshoe
snuffbox
soaproot
softshoe
softwood
solation
solution
songbook
sonobuoy
sorption
soundbow
soundbox
Southron
spanroof
sparbuoy
spicebox
spittoon
sponsion
spontoon
sporozoa
squadron
squarson
stairrod
stallion
stasimon
steenbok
steinbok
stellion
sternson
stinkpot
stockpot
studbook
sturgeon
subfloor
subprior
sunproof
superior
surveyor
survivor
swanshot
sweetsop
tabletop
tackroom
tarragon
taxation
teardrop
teaspoon
telethon
testator
tetragon
tetrapod
textbook
Thanatos
thanedom
thankyou
therefor
thermion
thraldom
thumbpot
tommyrot
tomorrow
toolroom
toreador
traction
traditor
trapdoor
treefrog
trillion
trunnion
tuckahoe
tuckshop
ulterior
unbutton
uncommon
underdog
undertow
unperson
unreason
unwisdom
vacation
valuator
varactor
venation
verderor
vexation
vibrator
vigneron
villadom
violator
vitiator
vocation
voicebox
volcanos
volition
volution
wainscot
waleknot
wallaroo
wallknot
wanderoo
wardroom
warwhoop
washroom
watchdog
waterlog
waterloo
Wedgwood
whiteboy
whitehot
wholehog
whoredom
whoreson
wifehood
wildwood
wineshop
woodwool
wordbook
workroom
workshop
wormwood
yearbook
zonation
anaglyph
antelope
antipope
antitype
apograph
autotype
bankrupt
biograph
biomorph
bioscope
blowpipe
boltrope
calliope
cenotaph
chirrupy
contempt
diagraph
downpipe
enthalpy
envelope
epigraph
episcope
escalope
eucalypt
feedpipe
fluepipe
footrope
gantlope
genotype
harrumph
hornpipe
hosepipe
isomorph
isotropy
jipijapa
logotype
midships
misshape
monotype
myograph
nametape
nosepipe
odograph
orthoepy
otoscope
overripe
pericope
praecipe
reedpipe
reoccupy
rescript
schnapps
seascape
skislope
skyscape
soilpipe
stanhope
sundrops
tailpipe
tittuppy
transept
triglyph
trigraph
trollopy
windpipe
Xantippe
zoetrope
zoomorph
aardvark
accoutre
adultery
advisory
aeriform
albacore
aleatory
allegory
ambivert
anaphora
ancestry
antihero
antisera
anywhere
aperture
armature
armyworm
artistry
ascocarp
auditory
auriform
autogiro
autogyro
axillary
Ayrshire
backfire
backward
backyard
balefire
balladry
banditry
barberry
barnyard
barratry
baseborn
basketry
bayadere
bayberry
beadwork
bejabers
bellbird
bellwort
beriberi
bestiary
bilberry
billiard
biometry
bistoury
bladdery
blazonry
blinkers
blistery
blizzard
bloomers
bloomery
blowhard
blubbery
bluebird
blustery
bodywork
bollworm
boneyard
booklore
bookmark
bookwork
bookworm
bottomry
boundary
braggart
brancard
brassard
brassart
brazenry
braziery
breviary
brochure
broidery
buckhorn
buhlwork
bullhorn
Burberry
burglary
bushfire
butchery
buzzword
cadastre
cagebird
cajolery
calamary
calipers
callgirl
calyptra
campfire
cannonry
canthari
capybara
caracara
careworn
casework
cashmere
category
catenary
cathedra
cavicorn
cemetery
centaury
chambers
champers
chancery
chapelry
chauntry
checkers
chequers
chimaera
chivalry
cincture
cinerary
claymore
cleavers
clippers
clownery
clustery
cobblers
cocksure
coiffure
colewort
coliform
colliery
cometary
confrere
coniform
conspire
contrary
coquetry
coronary
corsetry
costmary
cowberry
crackers
creamery
creature
crockery
crumhorn
cruzeiro
cubature
cubiform
culinary
cupboard
cussword
cynosure
daiquiri
delivery
delusory
demerara
denature
derisory
derriere
deviltry
dewberry
diaspora
diaspore
dilatory
dockyard
dogberry
dogshore
donatory
dooryard
downturn
downward
drollery
dropwort
drudgery
drumfire
drunkard
dungcart
dustcart
eastward
ectoderm
emissary
endocarp
endoderm
enginery
ensiform
ensphere
entoderm
ephemera
errantry
estovers
etcetera
evermore
exospore
exposure
facecard
falconry
farmyard
farriery
faubourg
feathery
February
fenberry
fenestra
feretory
filature
filiform
firebird
firework
fishfarm

flattery
flatware
flatworm
fleawort
flickery
flinders
flummery
fluttery
folklore
footmark
footsore
footwork
forepart
forestry
forewarn
foreword
foreyard
formwork
forswore
forsworn
fourpart
foxshark
fracture
freeborn
fretwork
frippery
fruitery
fumitory
funerary
furriery
fusiform
gadgetry
galliard
gamebird
gaolbird
gapeworm
garboard
geniture
geometry
glanders
glaziery
glittery
glossary
glowworm
goatherd
gossipry
goutwort
greenery
grimoire
grindery
guacharo
gynandry
gyratory
habanera
hairworm
halfterm
halliard
hallmark
handcart
handwork
harakiri
hardcore
hardware
harikari
harlotry
hatchery
haulyard
hawthorn
headword
headwork
heathery
heliport
hellfire
heraldry
Hereford
highborn
hillfort
hipsters
hobbitry
homeborn
homeward
homework
honorary
hookworm
hornworm
hornwort
hostelry
hypoderm
idolatry
illusory
immature
inchworm
industry
inexpert
infantry
insecure
insphere
iodoform
ironbark
ironware
ironwork
isometry
isoptera
isospory
isothere
isotherm
jacquard
jailbird
janizary
jesuitry
jodhpurs
jointure
jugglery
juncture
junkyard
kailyard
Kashmiri
keyboard
kingbird
kisscurl
knackery
kneejerk
knickers
knotwork
krumhorn
lacework
lacunary
ladybird
ladyfern
lamasery
landform
landgirl
landlord
landmark
lanthorn
lapboard
lapidary
larboard
lavatory
lawcourt
leadwork
leathern
leathery
leeboard
leftward
legendry
legguard
libatory
lifework
ligature
limitary
literary
liveborn
livewire
loanword
locutory
longhorn
longterm
lovebird
lovelorn
lukewarm
luminary
lungwort
lyrebird
mailcart
mainyard
malapert
malefern
manicure
maniform
massacre
mealworm
mediocre
meshwork
mesocarp
mesoderm
metamere
military
milkwort
milliard
milliary
minatory
ministry
mintmark
miscarry
miserere
misheard
missilry
moisture
monandry
monetary
monitory
moonwort
moratory
mortuary
muckworm
mudguard
mulberry
musketry
namepart
napiform
natatory
neatherd
needfire
negatory
nondairy
northern
nubiform
nugatory
numerary
obituary
oblatory
octonary
offshore
omnivore
openwork
orangery
ordinary
outboard
outdoors
outlawry
outsmart
outstare
ovenbird
ovenware
overbore
overlord
overture
overturn
overwork
overworn
palestra
papistry
parrotry
parterre
passport
password
pedantry
pedicure
pegboard
pellagra
penumbra
pericarp
periderm
perspire
phyllary
pilchard
pilewort
piliform
pillwort
pinafore
pinchers
pisiform
plagiary
plastery
platform
playgirl
pleasure
plethora
pockmark
podiatry
polypary
porphyry
portfire
portiere
postcard
posthorn
postmark
potsherd
premiere
pressure
priggery
psaltery
puffbird
puncture
punditry
punitory
pupilary
puppetry
pushcart
pyriform
quackery
quagmire
quandary
quartern
quarters
quixotry
rabbitry
racecard
raillery
rainbird
ranchero
ratguard
reabsorb
reaffirm
rearward
reassert
reassure
recovery
redshirt
redstart
reedbird
reembark
reexport
refinery
registry
reinsert
reinsure
reniform
rerecord
rereward
restcure
retiform
revisory
ribaldry
ribbonry
ricebird
ringbark
ringworm
rockbird
rockcork
rocketry
rockwork
rogatory
ropeyarn
rosemary
rotatory
roughdry
roundarm
rounders
ryotwari
saddlery
sagamore
sailyard
salivary
saltwort
salutary
samphire
sanatory
sandworm
sandwort
sanitary
sapphire
sashcord
saunders
sauouari
savagery
Savoyard
sayonara
scabbard
scissors
scullery
seaboard
seashore
seedcorn
seignory
selfborn
seminary
shagbark
shepherd
shimmery
shipworm
shipyard
shoehorn
shopgirl
shopworn
shortarm
showcard
showgirl
shuddery
sideward
silkworm
sinecure
slattern
slipform
slippery
slithery
slobbery
slopwork
slovenry
slowworm
sluggard
slumbery
smallfry
smeltery
smithers
smithery
smothery
snobbery
snowbird
snuffers
snuggery
soapbark
soapwort
sobstory
software
soldiery
solidary
solitary
sombrero
songbird
southern
Spaniard
spermary
spitfire
spivvery
staggard
staggers
staghorn
stalwart
standard
stannary
starkers
starwort
statuary
stinkard
stubborn
studfarm
studwork
sudatory
summitry
surefire
surfbird
swanherd
swanmark
swannery
sycamore
sycomore
symmetry
synastry
taciturn
tainture
tamboura
tandoori
tanistry
tapestry
tapeworm
taskwork
teaboard
teamwork
telemark
teleport
tenantry
tertiary
textuary
thesauri
thievery
thrawart
thuggery
thundery
tidemark
tiltyard
timework
timeworn
tincture
toiletry
toilworn
torchere
tournure
transire
trashery
treasure
treasury
treefern
tressure
trichord
trickery
trippery
tripwire
trousers
trouvere
truantry
trueborn
trumpery
tubiform
tutelary
tweezers
twinborn
twittery
unciform
underarm
untoward
upstairs
urochord
vanguard
variform
varletry
vasiform
vavasory
vertebra
vespiary
vestiary
vinegary
vineyard
vomitory
wallfern
wardenry
wartwort
warweary
waveform
waxberry
weaponry
wellborn
wellworn
westward
Whiggery
whipcord
whipworm
whiskers
whiskery
whispery
wildfire
windburn
windward
wirework
wireworm
wiseacre
witchery
wizardry
woodlark
woodwork
woodworm
woolwork
xylocarp
yeomanry
yoghourt
zealotry
zoolatry
zoometry
zoospore
abelmosk
abscissa
abstruse
achiness
acidfast
acosmism
acrotism
actinism
activism
activist
admonish
afforest
agedness
airbrush
airiness
alarmist
albinism
alcahest
alehouse
algorism
alienism
alienist
alkahest
almagest
alpinism
alpinist
altruism
altruist
amethyst
amortise
anapaest
anaphase
aneurism
aneurysm
ankylose
annalist
antepost
antimask
antrorse
aphorise
aphorism
aphorist
apiarist
apostasy
applause
appraise
aquarist
arbalest
arbalist
arborist
archaise
archaism
archaist
archness
arethusa
Arianism
arsonist
asterisk
asterism
astonish
atticism
autolyse
aviarist
avidness
babirusa
backlash
backless
backlist
backmost
backrest
backwash
bakshish
baldness
Balinese
banjoist
bareness
barkless
baroness
baseless
baseness
basilisk
bellpush
beltless
berceuse
betacism
bigamist
bioplasm
bioplast
blackish
blandish
bleakish
blimpish
blockish
blondish
blowfish
bluefish
blueness
bluenose
bodiless
boldness
bonefish
boneless

boniness
bookcase
bookpost
bookrest
bootlast
bootless
botanise
botanist
botulism
botyrose
brackish
brainish
brandish
brattish
brettese
brimless
briskish
broadish
brownish
Buddhism
Buddhist
burnouse
business
busyness
buttress
Byronism
cabalism
cabalist
caginess
calabash
calipash
calmness
canalise
canoeist
canoness
canonise
canonist
caponise
careless
catalase
catalyse
catalyst
cateress
centrism
centrist
ceramist
Chartism
Chartist
chastise
cheapish
childish
chiliasm
chiliast
chinless
churlish
civilise
clannish
clerkess
cliquish
cliquism
cloddish
clownish
clueless
coaldust
coalfish
coldness
collapse
colonise
colonist
comatose
comedist
compress
comprise
concasse
condense
congress
conquest
contessa
contrast
converse
convulse
coolness
cordless
cosiness
costpush
couldest
coulisse
countess
courtesy
cowgrass
cramoisy
crawfish
crayfish
crevasse
curarise
cureless
curtness
cuteness
cutpurse
cynicism
daftness
dampness
dandyish
dandyism
dankness
danseuse
darkness
dateless
deadness
deafness
dealfish
dearness
declasse
decrease
deedless
deepness
deforest
deftness
degrease
deionise
demolish
demoness
demonise
demonism
deputise
devilish
devilism
dewiness
dextrose
diagnose
diapause
diastase
digamist
digitise
dimerism
diminish
dioecism
dioptase
dirigism
disabuse
disburse
disclose
disguise
dispense
disperse
disseise
distress
distrust
ditheism
ditheist
divinise
Docetism
Docetist
doghouse
doloroso
Donatism
Donatist
doorcase
doorpost
dopiness
dormouse
dourness
dowdyish
downcast
downmost
doziness
drabness
druggist
druidess
druidism
drynurse
duchesse
ductless
duellist
duettist
dullness
dumbness
dustless
dwarfish
dwarfism
dynamism
dynamist
easiness
eastmost
echoless
edgeless
edgewise
edginess
editress
eelgrass
eeriness
embolism
endemism
energise
enforest
epiblast
epilepsy
equalise
erethism
ergotise
ergotism
escapism
escapist
espresso
essayist
Essenism
eternise
etherise
etherism
etherist
ethicism
ethicist
eugenism
eugenist
eulogise
eulogist
euphrasy
euphuism
euphuist
evenness
evilness
exercise
exorcise
exorcism
exorcist
extrorse
eyeglass
fabulist
faceless
fadeless
faintish
fairness
fairyism
fallfish
fangless
faradism
farinose
farthest
fastness
fatalism
fatalist
fearless
feckless
feeblish
fellness
feminise
feminism
feminist
feverish
fiendish
fiftyish
filefish
finalise
finalism
finalist
fineness
firehose
firmness
fishless
flatfish
flatness
flattest
flattish
flatwise
flautist
flawless
flexuose
floccose
flourish
fluidise
foamless
focalise
fondness
foodless
footless
footpost
footrest
forecast
foremast
foremost
forepast
formless
fortress
fortyish
fougasse
foulness
fowlpest
foxiness
Frankish
freakish
freeness
frogfish
frondose
fructose
frumpish
fullness
furthest
futurism
futurist
gainless
Galenism
galleass
gallwasp
gameness
gaminess
gashouse
gatepost
Gaullism
Gaullist
gearcase
Genevese
geognosy
ghoulish
giantess
giantism
gipsyism
gladdest
gladness
glibness
glummest
glumness
goalpost
goatfish
golddust
goldfish
goldrush
goodness
gormless
gracioso
Graecise
Graecism
greenish
greyfish
greyness
grimmest
grimness
gypsyism
hairless
haleness
halfmast
handfast
handless
handlist
hardcase
hardness
harmless
hasheesh
haziness
headfast
headless
headmost
headrest
hebraise
Hebraism
Hebraist
hedonism
hedonist
heedless
heelless
heirless
helotism
helpless
henroost
hepatise
herbless
highmost
highness
highrise
hightest
hindmost
hinduise
Hinduism
hipflask
hobbyist
holdfast
holiness
homeless
hopeless
hornless
hothouse
hotpress
hugeness
humanise
humanism
humanist
humorist
huntress
hurtless
hushhush
hydropsy
Ibsenism
idealess
idealise
idealism
idealist
idiotism
idleness
idocrase
idyllist
immodest
immunise
incivism
increase
infamise
inkiness
interest
intimism
introrse
iotacism
Irishism
Islamise
Islamism
isogloss
isostasy
Japanese
Javanese
jealousy
Jehovist
jingoish
jingoism
jingoist
jiujitsu
justness
Kanarese
keelless
keenness
keratose
kindless
kindness
kingfish
kourbash
laconism
lacrosse
lacunose
lameness
lamppost
landless
landmass
languish
lankness
largesse
lateness
latinise
Latinism
Latinist
Lazarist
laziness
leadless
leafless
leanness
legalese
legalise
legalism
legalist
Leninism
Leninist
lensless
levulose
lewdness
lifeless
lightish
likeness
likewise
limbless
limewash
limpness
linguist
listless
liverish
lobbyist
localise
localism
lockfast
loneness
longness
longwise
lopgrass
lordless
loudness
loveless
lovenest
loyalist
luckless
luminist
lumpfish
lungfish
lushness
lutanist
lutenist
lyricism
lyricist
madhouse
maestoso
mainmast
makefast
Malagasy
maleness
manifest
mantissa
marchesa
marchese
marquess
marquise
masseuse
massless
matgrass
matiness
mattress
maximise
mayoress
Mazdaism
maziness
meanness
meekness
meetness
melanism
melodise
melodist
memorise
mightest
mildness
milepost
mindless
minimise
Minoress
mishmash
misprise
mistress
mistrust
mobilise
modalism
modalist
Molinism
Molinist
monadism
monetise
mongoose
monkfish
monodist
moonfish
moonless
moonrise
moralise
moralism
moralist
motorise
motorist
moveless
muchness
muskrose
musquash
muteness
myoblast
nameless
narcissi
nasalise
nathless
nativism
nativist
naturism
naturist
nearness
neatness
nebulise
necropsy
needless
negroism
neoplasm
Nepalese
nepotism
newscast
niceness
nihilism
nihilist
noblesse
nodalise
nodulose
nomadise
nomadism
nonsense
nosiness
notecase
noteless
novelise
novelist
nuclease
nudeness
nullness
numbfish
numbness
nuthouse
oatgrass
oiliness
onehorse
oologist
ooziness
opencast
openness
optimise
optimism
optimist
Orangism
oratress
organise
organism
organist
outburst
outclass
outguess
outhouse
ovalness
overbusy
overcast
overdose
overfish
overpass
overpast
overtask
pacifism
pacifist
paganise
paganish
paganism
painless
paleness
paludism
papalise
papalism
papalist
papulose
paradise
paralyse

parclose
parodist
paroxysm
Parsiism
pathless
pederast
peerless
Pekinese
pelorism
penalise
pertness
perverse
petuntse
phantasm
phantasy
photopsy
piecrust
pinkness
pipefish
pitiless
pixieish
pixiness
pleonasm
pleurisy
plumbism
plumpish
polarise
polemise
polemist
poorness
populism
populist
porpoise
portress
pothouse
potroast
practise
prankish
preexist
prelease
premorse
prepense
priapism
priggish
priggism
primness
primrose
princess
prioress
progress
prolapse
propense
prophase
prophesy
prosaism
prosaist
protease
pruinose
psalmist
psychism
psychist
ptyalism
pugilism
pugilist
puniness
puppyish
purchase
pureness
purplish
quackish
qualmish
quantise
queerish
quietism
quietist
racemise
racemose
raciness
rainwash
rallyist
rankness
raptness
rareness
rashness
readjust
realness
rearmost
reassess
reckless
recourse
redeless
reforest
regalism
rehearse
reimpose
reinless
reinvest
repousse
response
restless
retrorse
ribgrass
richness
rifeness
rightist
rigorism
rigorist
ripeness
roadless
rockfish
rockrose
romanise
Romanism
Romanist
roofless
rootless
ropiness
rosebush
rosefish
rosiness
roughish
roundish
rowdyish
rowdyism
royalism
royalist
rudeness
rugulose
ruleless
ruralise
ruralism
ruralist
rustless
ruthless
ryegrass
sackless
safeness
sageness
sailfish
sailless
saltbush
saltless
saltness
sameness
sandyish
saneness
sanitise
sannyasi
sapphism
sargasso
satanism
satanist
sateless
satirise
satirist
sawhorse
Saxonism
Saxonist
scampish
scarless
sciolism
sciolist
sclerose
Scottish
seachest
seacoast
seahorse
seamless
seamouse
seapurse
seedcase
seedfish
seedless
selfless
selfness
Semitise
Semitism
Semitist
sexiness
shadbush
Shaktism
sharpish
sheepish
shoeless
shortish
shouldst
showcase
shrewish
sicklist
sickness
sidedish
sidewise
signpost
similise
simonist
simplism
sinapism
sinicise
sitarist
skewness
skilless
skinless
skirmish
skittish
slapdash
slimmest
slimmish
slimness
slipcase
slobbish
slowness
sluggish
sluttish
smallish
smartish
smugness
snappish
sneakish
snobbish
snobbism
snowless
snugness
soapdish
soapless
soberise
softness
soilless
solarise
solarism
solarist
solecism
solecist
soleness
solfaist
somatism
songless
soreness
soulless
sourness
sourpuss
sparkish
spathose
spoffish
spookish
spotless
spryness
spyglass
squamose
squarish
stablish
standish
stardust
starfish
starless
stedfast
steepish
stemless
stepwise
stiffish
stockish
stockist
stoicism
stoutish
strabism
stramash
strigose
strumose
subclass
suberise
suberose
sublease
submerse
Sudanese
suitcase
sunburst
sundress
suppress
surcease
sureness
surffish
surprise
suspense
swainish
sweetish
sylphish
tactless
tailless
tallness
tamarisk
tameless
tameness
tangoist
Tantrism
Tantrist
tapeless
taphouse
tarboosh
tartness
tautness
teachest
teahouse
tearless
telecast
televise
termless
tetanise
theorise
theorist
thickish
thievish
thinness
thinnest
thinnish
thisness
thuggism
thusness
ticklish
tideless
tidiness
tigerish
tilefish
timefuse
timeless
tininess
tintless
tireless
titaness
titanism
titmouse
toadfish
toadyish
toadyism
tokenism
tolldish
tombless
toneless
topdress
tortoise
totalise
totemism
totemist
toughish
tovarish
Trappist
traverse
treatise
treeless
trespass
trialist
trickish
trimness
trueness
tsaritsa
tubeless
tuberose
tuneless
tutoress
typecast
ugliness
ultraism
ultraist
unionise
unionism
unionist
universe
upthrust
urbanise
urbanism
urbanist
vainness
valorise
vaneless
vanquish
vaporise
varicose
vastness
veilless
ventless
vibrissa
victress
Viennese
viewless
vileness
viperish
virilism
virtuosa
virtuosi
virtuoso
vitalise
vitalism
vitalist
vixenish
vocalise
vocalism
vocalist
voidness
voltaism
votaress
votarist
voteless
vowelise
Wahabism
waitress
wakeless
wardress
warhorse
wariness
warmness
waterish
waveless
waviness
waxiness
weakfish
weakness
weedless
wetnurse
whatness
Whiggish
Whiggism
whiplash
wideness
wifeless
wildness
wiliness
windlass
windless
windrose
wingcase
wingless
wireless
wiriness
wiseness
wishwash
wolffish
womanise
womanish
wordless
workless
wormcast
wouldest
youngest
youngish
zaniness
zombiism
Abderite
abdicate
abnegate
abrogate
absolute
accurate
acerbate
acerbity
acervate
acierate
acridity
acrolith
acrylate
activate
activity
aculeate
adequate
adespota
aduncate
advocate
aerolite
aerolith
aesthete
affinity
aigrette
alacrity
algidity
alginate
alienate
allocate
allopath
almighty
amaranth
ambulate
ammonite
amoretti
amoretto
amputate
analcite
analecta
analects
andesite
anecdote
anisette
ankerite
annotate
annulate
antedate
antidote
apostate
appetite
apposite
arboreta
areolate
arillate
aristate
arrogate
arsenate
arsenite
aseptate
asperity
aspirate
assiento
assonate
asyndeta
atrocity
audacity
automata
automate
autunite
axiality
backbite
backdate
baguette
baldpate
ballista
banality
banditti
banknote
barbette
barrette
basicity
bedplate
behemoth
bellcote
benzoate
bequeath
bilobate
birdbath
blankety
bobwhite
bombsite
boracite
bregmata
brookite
brunette
burletta
butyrate
caducity
calamite
calamity
calidity
califate
campsite
capacity
capitate
carinate
casemate
cassette
castrate
castrati
castrato
casualty
catamite
catenate
celerity
celibate
cerusite
chapatti
chastity
chlorate
chlorite
chordate
chromate
chromite
chupatti
chupatty
cineaste
circuity
civility
clypeate
cogitate
complete
concerti
concerto
concetti
concetto
conchate
concrete
confetti
conflate
contents
contrate
contrite
copulate
coquette
corelate
cornetti
cornetto
corvette
courante
craniate
creosote
crispate
cristate
croceate
crocoite
cruciate
cryolite
cumulate
cupidity
cupulate
Cypriote
dancette
dancetty
deaerate
deafmute
debility
decimate
decorate
dedicate
definite
delegate
delibate
delicate
dendrite
depilate
depurate
derivate
derogate
desolate
detonate
diamante
dicacity
digitate
discrete
distaste
disunite

disunity
divagate
divinity
docility
dogtooth
dolerite
dolomite
dominate
dovecote
draughts
draughty
droughty
dryplate
dynamite
echinate
edentate
eleventh
elongate
emaciate
emendate
emigrate
enceinte
enervate
enormity
ensheath
enterate
entirety
entracte
entreaty
ephorate
epinasty
epiphyte
equality
equinity
escalate
essonite
estimate
eternity
etiolate
evacuate
evaluate
excavate
execrate
exiguity
expedite
exuviate
eyetooth
facility
falsetto
Fascista
Fascisti
fatality
federate
felicity
felinity
feminity
ferocity
fidelity
fiftieth
filtrate
finality
flatmate
fleabite
fluidity
fluorite
footbath
footnote
footpath
forsooth
fortieth
fortuity
frisette
frumenty
fugacity
fumigate
futility
futurity
galenite
garrotte

gelidity
geminate
generate
geophyte
glaciate
gnathite
goatmoth
graduate
graffiti
graffito
graphite
gratuity
grisette
guaranty
Gujarati
gulosity
gunsmith
halfnote
hawkmoth
headnote
hebetate
helminth
helpmate
henparty
heredity
hereunto
herewith
hesitate
hilarity
hitherto
hotplate
humanity
humidity
humility
hyacinth
hydranth
iceskate
ideality
identity
ilmenite
immolate
immunity
impanate
imparity
impolite
impunity
impurity
inchoate
increate
incubate
indagate
indicate
indurate
inequity
infinite
infinity
ingrowth
iniquity
initiate
innovate
insanity
insolate
insulate
intimate
intonate
intubate
inundate
invocate
involute
iodinate
irrigate
irritate
Islamite
isophote
isopleth
Italiote
Jacobite
jocosity
jubilate

jugulate
kilowatt
lability
lacerate
lacunate
lambaste
laminate
lapidate
laterite
Latinate
latinity
laureate
lazulite
lazurite
legality
legerity
Leninite
lepidote
levigate
levirate
levitate
lewisite
liberate
libretti
libretto
lichgate
ligulate
limonite
lipomata
literate
literati
litigate
lividity
lobulate
locality
locomote
loculate
loricate
lucidity
lunulate
lustrate
lychgate
macerate
maculate
Mahratta
Mahratti
majority
makebate
malamute
malemute
maquette
marinate
Masorete
Masoreth
matamata
matelote
maturate
maturity
medicate
meditate
megalith
megawatt
melanite
melinite
mesquite
messmate
miasmata
militate
minacity
Minorite
minority
misquote
misstate
miswrite
mitigate
mitzvoth
mobility
modality
moderate

moderato
modulate
molality
molarity
monazite
monocyte
monolith
monteith
moquette
morality
morosity
mosquito
motility
motivate
motivity
mucosity
multeity
mutilate
mylonite
myxomata
nasality
natality
nativity
nauseate
navigate
Nazarite
Nazirite
neophyte
nephrite
nihility
nobility
nodality
nodosity
noisette
nominate
nonparty
nonwhite
nubility
nucleate
numerate
obdurate
obligate
obsolete
obturate
obtusity
ocellate
oddments
oilcloth
omelette
omoplate
onychite
operetta
oppilate
opposite
opsimath
ordinate
osculate
ostinato
otiosity
outcaste
overrate
paginate
palliate
palmette
palmetto
parasite
pearlite
peculate
perfecto
perianth
peridote
peripety
permeate
perorate
pianiste
pilosity
pimiento
pisolite
placenta

plaudits
playmate
plumbate
pochette
polarity
polymath
polypite
populate
porosity
postdate
priorate
priority
property
prostate
protista
punctate
quadrate
quantity
quiddity
rabidity
racemate
radicate
rapacity
rapidity
recreate
regality
regelate
regolith
regrowth
regulate
reignite
relegate
relocate
renovate
resinate
resolute
resonate
respects
revolute
rhyolite
rigidity
roommate
rostrate
rosulate
roulette
rugosity
ruminate
runagate
rurality
sacristy
sagacity
saginate
salacity
salinity
salivate
sanctity
sandbath
sanitate
sapidity
saponite
saturate
sawtooth
scarcity
schemata
schmaltz
sclerite
security
sedulity
seicento
selcouth
selenate
selenite
selfmate
selfpity
senility
senorita
separate
septette
serenata

serenity
sericite
serosity
severity
sextette
sforzato
Shabuoth
shipmate
shofroth
sibilate
sidenote
siderite
silicate
simulate
sirvente
sitzbath
sixtieth
slyboots
smaltite
snippety
sobriety
sodalite
sodality
sodomite
solidity
sonority
sororate
sorority
sovranty
sparsity
speciate
spiccato
spoliate
spraints
squamate
staccato
stagnate
stannate
stannite
stearate
steatite
stellate
stemmata
sternite
stibnite
stigmata
stilbite
stiletto
stoccata
strength
stromata
stuprate
subacute
subtlety
subulate
sulphate
sulphite
superate
supinate
suricate
sybarite
tabulate
tachiste
tailgate
tartrate
teacloth
teammate
teaparty
tegmenta
telepath
temerity
template
tenacity
tenorite
tepidity
thermite
thickety
thoughts
tidegate

timidity
tinplate
tinsmith
titanate
titanite
titivate
toeplate
toilette
tolbooth
tolerate
tollgate
tonality
tonicity
toplofty
torquate
totality
touristy
toxicity
trabeate
trachyte
tractate
traumata
travesty
trecento
trichite
triunity
troilite
truncate
tubulate
tumidity
tunicate
ubiquity
uintaite
ulcerate
ultimata
ultimate
umbonate
umbrette
umptieth
unchaste
uncinate
uncreate
undulate
ungulate
urbanite
urbanity
urticate
vagility
valerate
validate
validity
vamplate
vanadate
vapidity
vegetate
velleity
velocity
venality
vendetta
venerate
venosity
veracity
vermouth
vesicate
vicarate
vicinity
vignette
vinosity
viridity
virility
Visigoth
vitality
vivacity
vocality
voracity
Wahabite
warranty
waxcloth
witchety

woodnote
workmate
wrymouth
xanthate
xenolith
xylonite
yokemate
zoophyte
abomasum
abomasus
acanthus
acarpous
aconitum
actinium
addendum
adiantum
aduncous
aeronaut
afflatus
alburnum
allodium
alluvium
alveolus
amiantus
ammonium
analogue
anourous
apologue
applique
apterous
aquanaut
aquarium
araceous
Arcturus
argonaut
arquebus
arsonous
ascidium
bacillus
bandeaux
barbecue
basidium
basinful
bateleur
bdellium
beechnut
belabour
bellyful
bibulous
biennium
bigamous
bimanous
biparous
blackout
blameful
blissful
blushful
boastful
Bordeaux
boutique
brachium
breakout
bronchus
burntout
caduceus
caducous
caesious
caladium
calculus
canorous
capsicum
captious
cardamum
carryout
cautious
cerebrum
cernuous
chasseur
chateaux

checkout
cheerful
chestnut
chiasmus
chlorous
chondrus
choragus
choregus
chromium
ciborium
cingulum
clangour
claqueur
cleancut
clearcut
clubhaul
coagulum
cockshut
coiffeur
cokernut
coliseum
collogue
colloquy
colossus
conidium
construe
continua
continue
continuo
corneous
corundum
costplus
couscous
covetous
crepitus
critique
crosscut
croupous
cumbrous
cumulous
cupreous
curlicue
cymatium
dartrous
decolour
decorous
delirium
denarius
desirous
detritus
dextrous
dialogue
dianthus
didymium
didymous
digamous
diluvium
dimerous
dinerout
dinosaur
dipnoous
disvalue
dolorous
doubtful
doughnut
downhaul
downpour
dreadful
dreamful
duodenum
duologue
earthnut
edacious
electrum
elenchus
emeritus
emporium
encomium
enormous

enshroud
entellus
eohippus
epigeous
epilogue
eulogium
euonymus
europium
eventful
excursus
exemplum
exiguous
eximious
exordium
fabliaux
fabulous
factious
factotum
faithful
fanciful
fashious
fastuous
feverous
finespun
fireplug
fishglue
flashgun
flexuous
followup
forceful
frabjous
francium
freakout
freezeup
fremitus
frenulum
freshrun
frondeur
fruitful
gadabout
galbanum
generous
geranium
ghastful
glabrous
glassful
glaucous
glorious
glucinum
godawful
goitrous
golfclub
gonidium
gorgeous
graceful
gracious
grandeur
grateful
grievous
griseous
guaiacum
guileful
gypseous
harangue
hazelnut
Hesperus
hibiscus
higherup
homespun
houseful
humorous
hymenium
hypogeum
ichorous
imperium
indicium
indusium
infamous
inflatus

inoculum
intercut
intrigue
ivorynut
jongleur
jumpedup
keelhaul
khuskhus
knockout
labdanum
labellum
laburnum
langlauf
larkspur
laudanum
layabout
ligneous
linoleum
lixivium
loathful
lomentum
longueur
luminous
luscious
lustrous
lutecium
lutetium
malodour
mandamus
marabout
marasmus
mealybug
meconium
meniscus
menstrua
merciful
meringue
miasmous
Minotaur
mirthful
mittimus
molossus
momentum
monsieur
moresque
motorium
mournful
mouthful
muticous
mutinous
mycelium
mystique
nacreous
nauplius
nauseous
nautilus
nebulium
nebulous
nobelium
nodulous
nubilous
nucellus
numerous
numinous
ochreous
oestrous
olibanum
omadhaum
ommateum
oncidium
oogamous
oogonium
orgulous
origanum
outvalue
overhaul
overplus
oversoul
oxtongue

pandanus
papulous
paramour
patagium
patulous
peaceful
pendulum
peridium
perilous
perineum
periplus
pervious
petalous
phaseout
phormium
physique
pishogue
plateaux
plateful
platinum
platypus
plectrum
pluvious
polonium
polypous
poppadum
populous
powerful
prankful
pratique
precious
previous
prideful
printout
prologue
prorogue
pruritus
pulvinus
puparium
pygidium
pyrrhous
pyxidium
ramentum
ranarium
ravenous
residuum
resinous
rhonchus
rightful
rigorous
rondeaux
rouleaus
rouleaux
rubidium
runabout
runnerup
rushhour
saboteur
sacculus
samarium
saporous
savorous
scabious
scabrous
scandium
scarious
scholium
scirrhus
sclerous
scoopful
scornful
seatrout
sedulous
seigneur
selenium
senarius
senseful
sensuous
sepalous

shakeout
shameful
shareout
sheeprun
shelfful
shootout
shortcut
sidedrum
sillabub
silphium
sinciput
slothful
solarium
solatium
sombrous
sonorous
spacious
spadeful
specious
spectrum
speculum
sphagnum
sphygmus
spiculum
spiritus
spiteful
splenius
spoonful
sportful
spraygun
spurious
squamous
stannous
stickful
stimulus
strumous
studious
suberous
subgenus
subgroup
subshrub
succinum
succubus
sudarium
susurrus
syconium
syllabub
syllabus
tableaux
tablecut
tableful
tamandua
tantalum
tantalus
tastebud
tasteful
teetotum
tenesmus
terminus
testatum
thalamus
thallium
thallous
thankful
thereout
thrombus
timorous
tinnitus
titanium
tomentum
tommygun
toothful
tortious
tortuous
trillium
tristful
trueblue
trumeaux
trustful

truthful
tuberous
tumorous
tympanum
ulcerous
unctuous
undercut
underfur
underrun
unlawful
uppercut
usurious
uxorious
valorous
vanadium
vanadous
vaporous
variorum
vasculum
vauntful
vavasour
velarium
vengeful
venomous
veratrum
vexillum
viaticum
viburnum
vigorous
vinculum
viperous
virtuous
vitellus
vitreous
vivarium
voiceful
volvulus
voyageur
warcloud
wasteful
watchful
waterbus
watthour
weariful
whiteout
wondrous
worthful
wrackful
wrathful
wrongful
wrongous
xanthium
youthful
ablative
abortive
abrasive
adaptive
additive
adhesive
adoptive
aggrieve
allusive
auditive
aversive
Casanova
coactive
coercive
cohesive
conative
conceive
conclave
conferva
congreve
conserve
contrive
convolve
cooptive
creative
crescive

curative
decisive
delusive
derisive
dilative
disprove
disserve
dissolve
dividivi
divisive
donative
durative
effusive
egestive
ejective
elective
emissive
emulsive
enactive
eruptive
evincive
fixative
foxglove
fugitive
genitive
illative
illusive
inactive
incisive
invasive
kidglove
ladylove
lavalava
laxative
lenitive
lipsalve
locative
longwave
mangrove
margrave
monitive
negative
nosedive
offdrive
optative
outbrave
perceive
piassava
positive
preserve
punitive
putative
reactive
relative
reprieve
retrieve
ringdove
rockdove
rotative
sanative
sedative
selflove
sorptive
sportive
subserve
tidewave
topheavy
tractive
truelove
univalve
vegetive
vocative
volitive
vomitive
wirewove
bestrewn
comedown
discrown
downtown

duckhawk
dustbowl
eagleowl
fishbowl
fishhawk
flyblown
garefowl
handsewn
highlows
hometown
markdown
moorfowl
newblown
nightowl
nutbrown
outdrawn
outgrown
oversewn
rockhewn
rosebowl
selfsown
shallows
showdown
shutdown
slowdown
tomahawk
turndown
upthrown
washbowl
wildfowl
antefixa
apoplexy
cacomixl
birdseye
bullseye
carbonyl
carboxyl
cattleya
diphenyl
edgeways
epicalyx
epicotyl
flatways
glyceryl
gramarye
holidays
hydroxyl
longways
nowadays
sardonyx
sideways
someways
tautonym
tigereye
bulldoze
credenza
czaritza
disprize
fullsize
kamikaze
kingsize
lifesize
misprize
oversize
pintsize
stargaze
terrazzo
tsaritza
unfreeze

---

abscissa
academia
aceldama
adespota
adularia
adynamia
agraphia
alleluia
alopecia

ambrosia
amphibia
amygdala
anaconda
analecta
anaphora
anasarca
anathema
angelica
anorexia
antefixa
anthelia
anthemia
anthozoa
antisera
apologia
arapaima
arboreta
arethusa
asphyxia
asthenia
asyndeta
ataraxia
atheroma
aubretia
auricula
automata
avifauna
babirusa
babushka
bacteria
ballista
bandanna
barathea
barranca
basilica
battalia
bethesda
bignonia
blastema
blastula
branchia
brassica
bregmata
britzska
bromelia
bronchia
brouhaha
buddleia
burletta
cachexia
cachucha
calcanea
calcaria
calyptra
camellia
campagna
capitula
capybara
caracara
carnauba
Casanova
cathedra
cattleya
cavatina
cercaria
charisma
chickpea
chimaera
churinga
cinchona
coenobia
collyria
conferva
contagia
contessa
continua
conurbia
coxalgia

credenza
criteria
cromorna
czaritza
decennia
dementia
demerara
dentalia
diarrhea
diaspora
diastema
dichasia
diplopia
djellaba
dracaena
dulciana
Dulcinea
dyslexia
dyspnoea
dystopia
ecclesia
effluvia
egomania
encaenia
endostea
engramma
ephemera
epifauna
epopoeia
erythema
etcetera
eupepsia
euphoria
fantasia
fasciola
Fascista
fenestra
fibrilla
Filipina
fistiana
flabella
flagella
flotilla
foramina
fraenula
gardenia
gastraea
gastrula
gematria
glabella
glaucoma
glossina
gloxinia
Golconda
gorgonia
Griselda
guerilla
gymkhana
gymnasia
gynoecia
habanera
hacienda
hamartia
hepatica
herbaria
hulahula
hysteria
insignia
insomnia
intarsia
isabella
ischemia
isoptera
japonica
jipijapa
katakana
lavalava
lipomata
lymphoma

magnesia
magnolia
maharaja
Mahratta
maiolica
majolica
malvasia
mandorla
mantilla
mantissa
manubria
marchesa
matamata
menstrua
miasmata
moussaka
mycetoma
myxomata
oiticica
opercula
operetta
opuscula
orchilla
palestra
panmixia
panorama
parabola
paranoia
parhelia
pellagra
penumbra
petechia
photopia
piassava
pizzeria
placenta
plethora
pollinia
polygala
predella
protista
protozoa
prunella
pyrrhoea
quadriga
retinula
rutabaga
sacraria
sandflea
sayonara
schemata
sciatica
scleroma
scrofula
scutella
semolina
senorita
sensoria
serenata
shigella
sinfonia
sonatina
spirilla
sporozoa
stapelia
stemmata
sterigma
stigmata
stoccata
strobila
stromata
strontia
subphyla
subpoena
subtopia
suburbia
swastika
sweetpea
sympodia

symposia
syncytia
syntagma
tamandua
tamboura
tegmenta
tenacula
teratoma
terraria
tetrapla
tortilla
toxaemia
trachoma
trapezia
traumata
trichina
triennia
triforia
trochlea
tsarevna
tsaritsa
tsaritza
ultimata
umbrella
undersea
vaccinia
Valhalla
velamina
vendetta
veronica
vertebra
vibrissa
victoria
Virginia
virtuosa
viscacha
vizcacha
Walhalla
wistaria
wisteria
xanthoma
yarmulka
zarzuela
zirconia
zoiatria
backcomb
catacomb
choriamb
divebomb
doorknob
firebomb
golfclub
hecatomb
kingcrab
landcrab
memsahib
reabsorb
sillabub
subshrub
syllabub
timebomb
academic
acentric
aconitic
acoustic
acrostic
adamitic
adynamic
agnostic
agrestic
alchemic
allergic
amitotic
ammoniac
amnesiac
amniotic
anabatic
anabolic
anagogic

analogic
analytic
anarchic
anatomic
anechoic
aniconic
anorexic
anorthic
aoristic
apagogic
aphasiac
aplastic
apogamic
argentic
Armagnac
aromatic
artistic
asbestic
asthenic
ataraxic
athletic
Atlantic
autarkic
autistic
balladic
balletic
balsamic
banausic
barbaric
baryonic
basaltic
bathetic
bathotic
bauxitic
beatific
benzylic
biogenic
bionomic
bromidic
calcific
calcitic
carbolic
carbonic
cathodic
catholic
cationic
celeriac
Cenozoic
cephalic
Chaldaic
cherubic
chiastic
chimeric
choleric
choragic
choregic
chthonic
cinnamic
climatic
cobaltic
coelomic
cornific
cosmetic
culdesac
Cushitic
cyanotic
cyclonic
Cyrenaic
Cyrillic
dactylic
daemonic
daimonic
dalmatic
demoniac
despotic
diabasic
diabetic
diabolic
dialogic

dialytic
diarchic
diatomic
diatonic
dichroic
dicrotic
dicyclic
didactic
dietetic
dioptric
dioramic
dioritic
diuretic
dogmatic
domestic
draconic
dramatic
dynastic
dysgenic
dyslexic
eclectic
ecliptic
ecologic
economic
ecstatic
egoistic
electric
elenctic
elliptic
empathic
emphatic
enclitic
encrinic
encyclic
endermic
endozoic
entoptic
entozoic
enuretic
enzootic
eolithic
epidemic
episodic
eremitic
erogenic
esoteric
Ethiopic
eucritic
eupeptic
euphonic
euphoric
eustatic
eutectic
exegetic
exogamic
exoteric
faradaic
febrific
felsitic
ferritic
fibrotic
forensic
frenetic
gabbroic
Gadhelic
galactic
galvanic
gelastic
geodesic
geodetic
geologic
geoponic
Germanic
gerontic
gigantic
glyconic
gneissic
gnomonic
Goidelic

granitic
Guelphic
hadronic
haematic
harmonic
Helladic
Hellenic
heraldic
hermetic
herpetic
hidrotic
hieratic
Hispanic
historic
holistic
holozoic
horrific
hydropic
hygienic
hypnotic
hypothec
hysteric
isagogic
ischemic
isobaric
isogamic
isogonic
isomeric
isotonic
isotopic
japhetic
jesuitic
Jurassic
juristic
klephtic
kyphotic
leucitic
lignitic
liturgic
logistic
lordotic
maenadic
magmatic
magnetic
magnific
maieutic
majestic
manganic
marasmic
mechanic
medallic
mephitic
mercuric
meristic
mesmeric
Mesozoic
metallic
meteoric
methodic
methylic
microbic
Miltonic
Mishnaic
Mithraic
mnemonic
molybdic
monastic
Mongolic
monistic
morainic
morbific
muriatic
myelinic
myogenic
myositic
narcotic
Nearctic
necrotic
neotenic

neoteric
neuritic
neuronic
neurotic
nickelic
nomistic
nuclidic
omphalic
operatic
orgasmic
orgastic
ornithic
orogenic
Ossianic
pachalic
pandemic
papistic
parhelic
parsonic
pashalic
pathetic
pedantic
Pelasgic
periodic
periotic
perlitic
petrolic
phenolic
phenylic
phonemic
phonetic
photopic
phreatic
phthalic
phthisic
phyletic
Pindaric
platinic
platonic
plutonic
podagric
pollinic
polyzoic
poristic
potassic
prelatic
prolific
propylic
prosodic
protatic
protonic
pruritic
pulmonic
puristic
purpuric
pyogenic
pythonic
quidnunc
quixotic
rabbinic
rachitic
republic
rhetoric
rhythmic
romantic
sabbatic
saccadic
sadistic
salvific
sandarac
sardonic
saturnic
scotopic
semantic
semiotic
seraphic
Shemitic
sigmatic
silvatic

simoniac
Sinaitic
siphonic
Slavonic
Socratic
somnific
spagyric
specific
spondaic
sporadic
stanzaic
stenotic
stomatic
strophic
subsonic
subtonic
succinic
syenitic
syllabic
sylvatic
symbolic
synaptic
syndetic
synergic
syngamic
synoptic
syntonic
systemic
systolic
Talmudic
tantalic
tartaric
tectonic
telluric
terrific
tetradic
Teutonic
thalamic
theistic
thematic
theurgic
thoracic
toreutic
tornadic
toxaemic
Triassic
tribasic
trimeric
trisomic
trochaic
truistic
tungstic
turmeric
Tychonic
tympanic
typhonic
tyrannic
uralitic
vampiric
Vandalic
Vedantic
veristic
villatic
volcanic
vulcanic
zeolitic
zoogenic
abhorred
accursed
acidhead
adlibbed
admitted
advanced
affected
agonised
airfield
airspeed
alkaloid
allotted
allround
amoeboid
amphipod
annulled
antlered
appalled
arachnid
arcuated
armoured
articled
assorted
asteroid
astonied
attested
attrited
autacoid
babyhood
backhand
backveld
backward
backyard
balanced
baldhead
bannered
barnyard
basswood
becalmed
bedimmed
bedstead
beebread
beefwood
befitted
befogged
befriend
begirded
bellbird
bentwood
bereaved
besotted
bevelled
bewigged
bicuspid
billfold
billhead
billiard
bindweed
birdseed
blastoid
blizzard
bloodred
blowhard
bluebird
blueweed
boatload
bondmaid
bonehead
boneyard
bookland
bosseyed
botryoid
brancard
branched
brandied
brassard
breasted
breveted
brickred
brindled
brocaded
browband
bulkhead
bullhead
bunkered
bushveld
buzzword
caballed
cabstand
cadenced
cagebird
calycoid
cancroid
carolled
cartload
caryatid
caudated
caverned
cavilled
centroid
ceratoid
childbed
chorioid
ciliated
cirriped
citified
cityfied
closeted
clubland
clupeoid
cockeyed
coleseed
collared
coloured
colubrid
columned
composed
compound
conchoid
confound
copyhold
coracoid
cordwood
corkwood
corniced
coronoid
corseted
Cotswold
crannied
crashpad
credited
crenated
crotched
cultured
cupboard
cupelled
curveted
cussword
danegeld
deadhead
deadwood
deathbed
debagged
debarred
debugged
deceased
deckhand
deeplaid
deferred
deformed
dejected
demented
demitted
demobbed
demurred
dendroid
dentated
departed
depraved
deprived
detached
detailed
deterred
devilled
dewyeyed
dihybrid
disbound
diseased
dispread
dividend
dockland
dockyard
doddered
dogeared
dogfaced
dogtired
dooryard
dowelled
downland
downward
downwind
dripfeed
drophead
drownded
drumhead
drunkard
duckpond
duckweed
dumbhead
dumfound
dutypaid
eastward
ebriated
echinoid
educated
elevated
elkhound
embedded
embussed
emulsoid
enarched
enrolled
enshroud
equalled
equipped
estopped
eupatrid
excelled
expelled
exserted
extolled
facecard
fairlead
falcated
farmhand
farmland
farmyard
fastfood
favoured
featured
feedhead
fingered
firebird
fireeyed
fireweed
firewood
firstaid
fishpond
fissiped
fivefold
flathead
flaxseed
flockbed
flowered
focussed
fogbound
foliaged
foothold
forcefed
forehand
forehead
foreland
foresaid
forested
foretold
foreword
foreyard
fourfold
foxhound
freehand
freehold
freeload
frenzied
furcated
gabbroid
gableend
gainsaid
galeated
galliard
gamebird
gangland
gaolbird
garboard
garreted
gasfired
gatefold
gilthead
girlhood
gladhand
goatherd
godchild
Godspeed
gourmand
goutweed
graduand
granddad
grizzled
gruntled
gulfweed
gusseted
halfbred
halliard
hallowed
handheld
handhold
handmaid
hardhead
hardwood
hatstand
haulyard
havocked
hawkeyed
hawkweed
hayfield
headband
headland
headwind
headword
hebdomad
helicoid
helmeted
Hereford
highbred
highland
highroad
hocussed
hogshead
homebred
homeland
homeward
hominoid
humanoid
humoured
hydatoid
icebound
icefield
illfated
illiquid
illtimed
immersed
impacted
impelled
included
incurred
indebted
inedited
inferred
inflated
inflexed
informed
infrared
inkstand
inserted
inspired
intended
interbed
interred
intrepid
invected
inverted
ironclad
ironwood
jacquard
jailbird
japanned
jeremiad
jewelled
jiggered
jolthead
junkyard
kailyard
keeshond
keyboard
kingbird
kinghood
knapweed
labelled
ladybird
ladyhood
lakeland
lamented
landlord
lapboard
lapelled
larboard
latticed
leeboard
lefthand
leftward
legguard
legioned
leisured
lemuroid
lettered
levelled
libelled
licensed
lichened
lintseed
liveried
loanword
longhand
lopeared
lopsided
louvered
lovebird
lymphoid
lynxeyed
lyrebird
magicked
maidhood
mainland
mainyard
manifold
mannered
mansized
marigold
masthead
measured
medalled
medusoid
membered
metalled
midfield
milkmaid
milkweed
millhand
milliard
millpond
mimicked
misheard
misspend
mittened
modelled
monkhood
monoacid
moorland
moribund
mudguard
multifid
multiped
muslined
myriapod
myriopod
neatherd
neckband
nectared
nematoid
newfound
newlywed
nielloed
nimbused
ninefold
nonrigid
noseband
obtected
occluded
occurred
odontoid
oilfield
oilfired
oldworld
olympiad
onesided
openeyed
ordinand
oriented
ostracod
outboard
outbound
outdated
outfield
outHerod
outmoded
outspend
ovenbird
overfeed
overfold
overfond
overhand
overhead
overlaid
overland
overload
overlord
overpaid
oversold
overwind
palmiped
panelled
panicked
paranoid
parkland
password
peasecod
pedalled
pedicled
pegboard
pellucid
perilled
petalled
petaloid
petioled
phylloid
pilchard
pileated
pinewood
pinnated
pinniped
plighted
plumaged
plumiped
polypoid
pondweed
postcard
postpaid
potbound
potsherd
powdered
prescind
prismoid
profound
propound
provided
pteropod
puffbird
pugnosed
pulpwood
purblind
purebred
pyrenoid
racecard
railhead
railroad
rainbird
rapeseed
rarefied
ratguard
ravelled
rawboned
rearward
reascend
rebelled
rebutted
recapped
recurred
redblind
redfaced
reedbird
referred
refitted
reflexed
reformed
remitted
renowned
repelled
repetend
repotted
rerecord
rereward
reserved
resigned
resinoid
retarded
retorted
revelled
reverend
revetted
rhizopod
rhomboid
ricebird
ringroad
rivalled
rivelled
riverbed
rockbird
rockweed
rockwood
roothold
rosewood
rubicund
sailyard
salaried
saraband
sashcord

Sassanid storeyed unedited wormseed amperage autotype boottree causerie
sauropod strained unfitted wormwood amphorae autunite boracite celibate
Savoyard stranded unforced wretched ampullae aversive borecole centuple
sawedged strapped unformed yodelled amputate avowable borehole cerusite
scabbard streaked unfunded zygaenid anaerobe axletree botanise chaconne
scaffold streeted unglazed Abbaside analcime Ayrshire botyrose chalazae
scaphoid stringed unhinged Abderite analcite babouche bourtree chastise
sceptred stripped unhoused abdicate analogue backache boutique chasuble
schizoid stropped unleaded abeyance anaphase backbite brassage chenille
sciuroid strummed unlinked abidance andesine backbone brattice Cherokee
sclereid strutted unlisted ablative andesite backdate breakage Cheyenne
scombrid sturdied unmanned abnegate anecdote backfire brettese chlorate
scragend stylised unmarked abortive anisette backside brettice chloride
scragged sunbaked unopened abrasive ankerite badinage bribable chlorine
scrammed sunblind unpaired abrogate ankylose baguette brochure chlorite
scrapped sundried unpegged absentee annotate bailable brookite chordate
scrubbed superadd unpinned absinthe announce baldpate brunette christie
seaboard supposed unplaced absolute annulate balefire bubaline chromate
secluded surfbird unrigged absterge anserine Balinese buckshee chromite
selfhood surround unroofed abstruse antecede balkline budgeree cicerone
sepaloid swanherd unsealed accolade antedate bankable bulldoze cincture
serfhood synergid unseated accoutre antelope banknote bullseye cineaste
serranid taenioid unseeded accurate antennae barbecue bummaree civilise
serrated talented unshaped acerbate antidote barbette buncombe clambake
sesamoid tamarind unstated acervate antinode baritone bunghole clarence
sheepked tastebud unsuited aciculae antipode barnacle buntline clavicle
shepherd tattered unsunned acierage antipole baronage burnouse claymore
Shetland teaboard untapped acierate antipope barouche bushfire cleavage
shipload teabread untented acridine antitype barrette butylene clodpole
shipyard tempered unthread acrylate antrorse barytone butyrate clypeate
showcard terraced untitled actiniae anyplace baseline caboodle coactive
shredded tetrapod untoward actinide anywhere bastille cabotage coalesce
shrugged texthand unvalued activate aperture bathrobe cabriole coalhole
sideband textured unversed aculeate aphicide bayadere cadastre coalmine
sidehead thalloid unvoiced adaptive aphorise beanpole caffeine cochleae
sideroad thousand unwanted additive apocrine bearable calamine cocksure
sideward throated unwashed adequate apologue bechance calamite codpiece
sidewind throbbed unweaned adhesive apostate bedabble califate coenzyme
siluroid thrummed unwished adjutage appanage bedazzle callable coercive
sinusoid thyrsoid unwonted adoptive appetite bedplate calliope cogitate
situated tickseed unzipped adorable applause bedtable calycine cognosce
skewbald tideland urochord aduncate applepie beefcake calycule cohesive
skinfood tightwad vagabond advocate applique befuddle camisade coiffure
skinhead tiltyard valanced aegirine apposite begrudge camisole coincide
sliproad timbered vanguard aerodyne appraise belittle camomile collapse
slipshod tittuped verdured aerolite aptitude bellcote campfire collogue
slobland toolshed verecund aesthete aquacade benefice camphene colonise
sloeeyed totalled vilipend affiance aquiline benzoate camphine comatose
slugabed towelled vineyard aggrieve Arapahoe berceuse campsite commence
sluggard tracheid vizarded agiotage archaise bestride canaille commerce
snowbird tramroad vowelled aigrette archduke bestrode canalise complete
socalled trichoid walleyed aiguille areolate beverage cancrine complice
softhead trichord warcloud airborne arguable biddable cannulae compline
softwood trilobed wartweed airbrake arillate bilobate canonise comprise
solenoid triploid waterbed Airedale aristate binnacle canoodle conative
songbird trochoid waveband airframe armature bioscope canticle concasse
sorehead trophied Wedgwood airspace arrestee birdcage capeline conceive
sowbread truebred weeviled albacore arrogate birdlime capitate conchate
Spaniard turbaned wellbred aldehyde arsenate birdseye caponise conclave
spavined turreted wellhead alehouse arsenide bistable capriole conclude
sphenoid twoedged wellread aleurone arsenite blacktie capstone concrete
spheroid twofaced weregild algicide artifice blamable carabine condense
sphingid twosided westward alginate aseptate blindage caracole conferee
spicated unabated whipcord alienage aspirate blockade carapace conflate
spirited unaneled whizzkid alienate assemble blockage carefree confrere
splendid unbacked wideeyed alkaline assignee blowhole carinate conglobe
spoonfed unbarred wifehood alliance assonate blowpipe Caroline congreve
sprigged unbiased wildeyed allocate astatine bluenose carotene conserve
squatted unbolted wildwood allottee atremble bobwhite carriage consomme
squibbed unburied windowed allspice atropine boldface carriole conspire
squidded uncalled windward allusive attitude bolthole caruncle construe
staggard uncandid withheld altitude audience boltrope casemate continue
stairrod uncapped withhold ambiance auditive bombsite cashmere contline
stallfed uncaused woodbind ambience autocade bonhomie cassette contrate
standard uncoined woodland ambulate autodafe boniface castrate contrite
statured underbid woodshed amenable autodyne bookcase catalase contrive
steepled underdid woodwind amicable autolyse booklice catalyse converge
stenosed undraped wooldyed ammonite automate booklore catamite converse
stinkard unearned woolshed amortise autosome bootlace catenate convince

convolve
convulse
cooptive
copulate
coquette
corelate
corniche
cornicle
cornpone
corvette
coryphee
coulisse
courante
coverage
cozenage
craniate
creatine
creative
creature
credence
credible
crenelle
creosote
crescive
cretonne
crevasse
cribbage
crispate
cristate
critique
croceate
crocoite
cromorne
crosstie
cruciate
crucible
cryolite
cubature
culicine
culpable
cumulate
cupulate
curarine
curarise
curative
curlicue
curricle
cutprice
cutpurse
cynosure
Cypriote
cypselae
cysteine
cytidine
cytosine
damnable
dancette
danseuse
darksome
dateline
deadline
deaerate
deafmute
decimate
decisive
declasse
decorate
decouple
decrease
dedicate
defiance
defilade
definite
degrease
deionise
delegate
delibate
delicate
delusive
demarche
demiurge
demonise
denature
dendrite
denehole
deniable
denounce
denticle
depilate
deportee
depurate
deputise
derisive
derivate
derogate
derriere
describe
desolate
detainee
dethrone
detonate
deviance
dextrine
dextrose
diagnose
diallage
dialogue
diamante
diapause
diaphone
diaspore
diastase
diastole
diatribe
digitate
digitise
dilative
dimmable
diopside
dioptase
disabuse
disagree
disburse
disciple
disclose
discrete
disgorge
disgrace
disguise
dislodge
dispense
disperse
displace
displode
displume
disprize
disprove
disseise
disserve
dissolve
dissuade
distance
distaste
disunite
disusage
disvalue
divagate
divinise
divisive
divorcee
dockside
doctrine
doghouse
dogshore
dolerite
dolesome
dolomite
domicile
dominate
donative
doorcase
dormouse
dovecote
downcome
downpipe
downtime
drachmae
dragline
drainage
drawable
drawtube
dressage
driftage
driftice
drivable
drumfire
drynurse
dryplate
drystone
duchesse
dungaree
duologue
durative
dustlike
dutiable
dutyfree
dynamite
earphone
earpiece
echinate
edentate
edgewise
educable
educible
effusive
egestive
ejective
elective
elegance
eligible
elongate
emaciate
embattle
embezzle
emendate
emigrate
eminence
emissive
empeople
employee
empurple
emulsive
enactive
enceinte
encircle
enclothe
endamage
endorsee
energise
enervate
enfeeble
enfilade
engirdle
enkindle
ensample
ensconce
ensemble
enshrine
ensilage
ensphere
enswathe
entangle
enterate
enthrone
entracte
entrance
envelope
enviable
envisage
ephorate
epicycle
epilogue
epiphyte
episcope
epistyle
equalise
equipage
equivoke
erasable
erectile
erewhile
ergotise
erodible
eruptive
escalade
escalate
escalope
escapade
escarole
essonite
estimate
estrange
eternise
etherise
ethylene
etiolate
eulogise
evacuate
evadable
evaluate
evanesce
eventide
evermore
everyone
evidence
evincive
evitable
examinee
excavate
exchange
execrate
exercise
exigence
exigible
exocrine
exorcise
exospore
expedite
expellee
expiable
exposure
extrorse
exuviate
eyepiece
eyerhyme
eyeshade
faceache
facetiae
failsafe
fallible
fandance
farinose
farouche
fascicle
fasciole
fearsome
feasible
federate
feedpipe
fellable
feminine
feminise
fencible
ferriage
feticide
figurine
filagree
filariae
filature
filigree
filtrate
fimbriae
finalise
finitude
firehose
fireside
fishable
fishbone
fishcake
fishglue
fishwife
fistulae
fixative
flagpole
flanerie
flatmate
flatrace
flatware
flatwise
fleabane
fleabite
flexible
flexuose
flipside
floatage
floccose
floccule
fluepipe
fluidise
fluoride
fluorine
fluorite
focalise
folklore
folktale
follicle
fontange
footnote
footpace
footrace
footrope
footrule
footsore
forborne
forcible
fordable
forebode
foreedge
foregone
forename
foreside
foretime
formulae
forswore
fougasse
foursome
foveolae
foxglove
fracture
frisette
frondage
frondose
frontage
frottage
fructose
fruitage
frustule
fuchsine
fugitive
fullpage
fullsize
fulltime
fumarole
fumigate
fungible
funkhole
furculae
furuncle
fuselage
gadarene
gainable
galenite
gamesome
gangrene
gantline
gantlope
Ganymede
gargoyle
garrotte
gashouse
gasolene
gasoline
gazogene
gearcase
gefuffle
gelatine
geminate
gemstone
gendarme
generate
Genevese
genitive
geniture
genocide
genotype
gentrice
geophone
geophyte
gerbille
germfree
girasole
glaciate
gladsome
glandule
glassine
gleesome
glissade
gloriole
gnathite
goalline
goldmine
goodtime
goodwife
graduate
Graecise
gramarye
grandame
grapheme
graphite
greegree
grillage
grimoire
grisette
gruesome
guidable
guidance
gullable
gullible
habitude
hairlike
hairline
halflife
halfnote
halfsole
halftime
halftone
handline
handmade
handsome
hangable
harangue
hardbake
hardcase
hardcore
hardline
hardware
hateable
hawklike
headache
headline
headnote
headrace
hebetate
hebetude
hebraise
hellfire
hellhole
helpmate
hepatise
heritage
hesitate
hetaerae
hexylene
hidyhole
highrise
hillside
hinduise
hireable
hocktide
Holocene
homelike
homemade
homicide
homuncle
honeybee
hornpipe
horologe
horrible
hosepipe
hothouse
hotplate
huggable
humanise
humuncle
hyoscine
hypobole
hypogene
ianthine
iceskate
idealise
idocrase
illative
illumine
illusage
illusive
ilmenite
imbecile
imitable
immature
immingle
immobile
immolate
immunise
impanate
impledge
impolite
inactive
inchoate
incisive
increase
increate
incubate
indagate
indicate
indigene
indocile
inductee
induline
indurate
inedible
infamise
infinite
infringe
inhumane
initiate
innovate
inscribe
insecure
insolate
insphere
instable
instance
insulate
internee
intertie
intimate
intitule
intonate
intrigue
introrse
intubate
inundate
inurbane
invasive
inveigle
inviable
invocate
involute
iodinate
ironside
ironware
irrigate
irritate
Islamise
Islamite
isolable
isophote
isoprene
isothere
issuable
issuance
Italiote
iterance
Jacobite
jalousie
jamboree
Japanese
jaundice
Javanese
jetplane
joinable
jointure
jubilate
jugulate
julienne
juncture
juvenile
kamikaze
Kanarese
kedgeree
keepsake
kefuffle
keratose
kerosene
kerosine
keystone
kidglove
kinglike
kingsize
kissable
klondike
kneehole
knothole
knowable
lacerate
lacrosse
lacunate
lacunose
ladylike
ladylove
lambaste
lamblike

lamellae
laminate
landline
landmine
language
lapicide
lapidate
largesse
laterite
Latinate
latinise
latitude
laudable
laureate
laxative
lazulite
lazurite
leaflike
legalese
legalise
legatine
lemonade
lemurine
lenience
Leninite
lenitive
lenticle
lepidote
leporine
leverage
leviable
levigate
levirate
levitate
levulose
lewisite
libellee
liberate
licensee
lichgate
licorice
lifelike
lifeline
lifesize
lifetime
liftable
ligature
ligulate
likeable
likewise
limonite
lingerie
lipsalve
literate
litharge
litigate
liveable
livewire
loadline
loanable
lobeline
lobulate
localise
locative
lockable
locomote
loculate
lodicule
logotype
lonesome
longsome
longtime
longwave
longwise
loophole
loricate
lovesome
lowgrade
lunulate
lustrate
lustrine
lychgate
lykewake
lyophile
lysosome
lysozyme
macerate
maculate
madapple
madhouse
magazine
mailable
mainline
makebate
malamute
malemute
Mameluke
mamillae
manciple
mandible
mandrake
mangrove
Manichee
manicure
maquette
marchese
margrave
marinade
marinate
maritage
maritime
marquise
marriage
Masorete
massacre
masseuse
matelote
maturate
maxillae
maximise
mayapple
mazarine
mealtime
meantime
meatsafe
medicate
medicine
mediocre
meditate
megapode
melamine
melanite
melinite
melodise
membrane
memorise
menarche
mendable
mergence
meringue
merosome
mesquite
messmate
messuage
metamere
metayage
migraine
militate
millieme
millrace
minimise
Minorite
minutiae
miscible
miserere
misguide
misjudge
misplace
misprise
misprize
misquote
misshape
misstate
misusage
miswrite
mitigate
mobilise
moderate
modulate
moisture
molecule
monazite
mondaine
monetise
mongoose
monitive
monocyte
monopode
monotone
monotype
monoxide
moonface
moonrise
moonshee
moquette
moralise
moresque
morpheme
morphine
mortgage
motivate
motorise
moveable
mucilage
muckrake
mudstone
multiple
murrhine
musicale
muskrose
musktree
mustache
mutilate
mylonite
mystique
nailfile
nameable
namesake
nametape
narceine
narghile
nasalise
nascence
nauseate
navigate
Nazarene
Nazarite
Nazirite
neaptide
nebulise
necklace
neckline
needfire
negative
negligee
nematode
neophyte
neoprene
Nepalese
nepenthe
nephrite
nickname
nicotine
noblesse
nocturne
nodalise
nodulose
noisette
nomadise
nominate
nonsense
nonusage
nonwhite
noontide
noontime
nosecone
nosedive
nosepipe
notecase
nouvelle
novelise
nuclease
nucleate
nucleole
nuisance
numerate
nuthouse
oakapple
obdurate
obligate
obsolete
obstacle
obturate
ocellate
oeillade
oestrone
offdrive
offshore
offstage
oilstone
okeydoke
omelette
omnivore
omoplate
onehorse
onepiece
onychite
openable
operable
oppilate
opposite
optative
optimise
opulence
opuscule
ordinate
ordnance
organdie
organise
oscinine
osculate
otoscope
outbrave
outcaste
outhouse
outrange
outshine
outshone
outstare
outvalue
ovariole
ovenware
overbore
overcame
overcome
overdone
overdose
overnice
overrate
override
overripe
overrode
overrule
overshoe
overside
oversize
overtake
overtime
overtone
overture
oxtongue
paganise
paginate
palatine
paleface
palinode
palisade
palliate
palmette
palpable
pantofle
papalise
papillae
papulose
paradise
paragoge
paralyse
parasite
paravane
parclose
parlance
parterre
partible
particle
parttime
passable
passible
pastiche
pastille
patellae
patentee
patience
payphone
pearlite
peccable
peculate
pedicure
pedigree
peduncle
peephole
Pekinese
pelerine
pellicle
pembroke
penalise
pendicle
penknife
pentacle
perceive
perforce
pericope
peridote
perilune
permeate
perorate
peroxide
personae
perspire
persuade
perverse
petaline
petuntse
phalange
pharisee
phosgene
phyllode
phyllome
physique
pianiste
picayune
pilotage
pinafore
pinecone
pinnacle
pinochle
pintable
pintsize
pipeline
piperine
piscinae
pishogue
pisolite
pitiable
pittance
placable
planulae
playable
playmate
playtime
pleasure
Pliocene
plumbate
plussage
pochette
polarise
polemise
polygene
polypide
polypite
polyseme
populace
populate
porpoise
porridge
portable
portfire
porthole
portiere
positive
possible
postcode
postdate
postfree
postiche
postlude
postpone
pothouse
potstone
poultice
poundage
pourable
practice
practise
praecipe
pratique
preamble
preclude
prejudge
prelease
premiere
premorse
prentice
prepense
presence
preserve
pressure
prestige
pretence
primrose
priorate
pristine
probable
prodrome
prolapse
prologue
prolonge
promisee
promulge
propense
prophase
prorogue
prostate
prostyle
protease
protegee
protrude
provable
province
prudence
pruinose
prunelle
pterylae
ptomaine
puggaree
punctate
puncture
punitive
pupilage
purchase
purslane
pushbike
putative
pyridine
pyroxene
quadrate
quagmire
quantise
quartile
quayside
quenelle
quietude
quotable
racemate
racemise
racemose
radiance
radicate
rapecake
rapparee
rateable
ratsbane
reactive
readable
realtime
rearmice
reassure
recharge
recourse
recreate
redefine
redouble
reedmace
reedpipe
reemerge
regelate
regicide
regulate
rehandle
rehearse
reignite
reimpose
reinsure
rekindle
relative
releasee
relegate
reliable
reliance
relocate
relumine
remittee
renegade
renounce
renovate
rentable
repartee
repeople
repousse
reprieve
reremice
resemble
resettle
resinate
resolute
resonate
resource
response
restcure
resupine
reticule
retrieve
retrorse
reusable
revanche
reveille
revolute
rhapsode
rhyolite
ribosome
riddance
rideable
ridicule
rimbrake
ringbone
ringdove
ringside
riverine
roadside
rocaille
rockcake
rockdove
rocklike
rockrose
romanise
rooftree
roommate
ropeable
rosetree
rostrate
rosulate
rotative
rotenone
roughage
roulette
rugulose
ruinable
ruminate
runagate
runcible
ruralise
rushlike
sabotage
sackrace
Sadducee
sagamore
saginate
sailable
saleable
salience
salivate
saltmine
salvable
Samoyede
samphire
sanative
sandshoe
sangaree
sanguine
sanitate
sanitise
sapience
saponite
sapphire
sardelle
satiable
satirise
saturate
Sauterne
sawframe
sawhorse
saxatile
scalable

scapulae
scavenge
schedule
scissile
sciurine
sclerite
sclerose
scopulae
scotfree
scottice
scrabble
scramble
scribble
scrounge
scurrile
seaborne
seadrome
seahorse
sealable
seamouse
seapiece
seaplane
seapurse
seaquake
seascape
seashore
seasnake
sedative
seedcake
seedcase
seedlobe
seedtime
seizable
selectee
selenate
selenide
selenite
selflove
selfmade
selfmate
selfrule
selfsame
selvedge
semidome
seminude
Semitise
semitone
semplice
sensible
sentence
separate
septette
septuple
sequelae
sequence
serenade
sericite
serotine
serpulae
sesterce
sewerage
sextette
sextuple
shakable
shapable
shikaree
shinbone
shipmate
shiralee
shivaree
shoelace
shoetree
shortage
shothole
showcase
sibilate
sideline
sidenote
siderite

sidewise
silicane
silicate
silicide
silicone
similise
simulate
sinecure
singable
sinicise
sinkable
sinkhole
sirvente
sithence
sixpence
sizeable
skislope
skyscape
slipcase
slippage
slowpoke
smallage
smaltite
smokable
smoothie
snowlike
snowline
snowshoe
soberise
sociable
sodalite
sodomite
softshoe
software
soilpipe
solanine
solarise
solitude
solstice
solvable
somedele
sometime
sororate
sorptive
sortable
sourdine
soutache
spadille
spaewife
sparable
spathose
speciate
spherule
spiculae
spillage
spiracle
spitfire
spoilage
spoliate
sportive
spousage
sprinkle
squabble
squamate
squamose
squamule
squeedge
squeegee
squiggle
squilgee
staffage
stagnate
stallage
stampede
stanhope
stannate
stannite
stargaze
starlike

statable
staylace
stearate
stearine
steatite
steerage
stellate
stepwise
sternite
stibnite
stilbene
stilbite
stillage
stockade
stoppage
storable
straddle
straggle
strangle
strickle
strigose
strobile
struggle
strumose
stuprate
subacute
suberise
suberose
subframe
sublease
submerge
submerse
suboxide
subserve
substage
subtitle
subulate
succubae
suchlike
Sudanese
suffrage
suitable
suitcase
sulphate
sulphide
sulphite
sulphone
sunbathe
sundance
sunshade
sunshine
sunstone
superate
supinate
surcease
surefire
suricate
surplice
surprise
suspense
swanlike
sybarite
sycamine
sycamore
sycomore
syllable
sylphide
sylphine
symphile
syncline
syndrome
tabulate
tachisme
tachiste
tailgate
tailpipe
tailrace
tainture
takehome

tameable
tangible
tannable
tapdance
tapelike
tapeline
taphouse
tartrate
Tartuffe
teahouse
teammate
teatable
telecine
televise
tellable
telltale
template
tenaille
tendence
Tenebrae
tenorite
tenpence
tensible
tentacle
terebene
terebrae
termtime
terrible
tesserae
testable
testtube
tetanise
theorise
thermite
thiamine
thirlage
threnode
thridace
throstle
throttle
thurible
tidegate
tidewave
tigereye
tillable
timefuse
tincture
tinplate
tinstone
tiresome
titanate
titanite
tithable
titivate
titmouse
toepiece
toeplate
toilette
toilsome
tolerate
tollgate
topstone
torchere
torquate
tortoise
totalise
tournure
trabeate
tracheae
trachyte
trackage
tractate
tractive
tramline
transire
transude
traverse
treasure
treatise

trephine
tressure
triangle
trichite
trichome
tricorne
tricycle
trioxide
triplane
tripwire
triskele
troilite
trombone
trouvere
truckage
trueblue
truelove
truncate
tubercle
tuberose
tubulate
tuckahoe
tuneable
tunicate
tuppence
turnable
turnpike
turnsole
tutelage
tutorage
twopence
twopiece
typeface
tyrosine
Tyrrhene
uintaite
ulcerate
ultimate
umbonate
umbrette
umpirage
unbottle
unbridle
unbuckle
unchaste
uncinate
unclothe
uncouple
uncreate
underage
underlie
undulate
unfreeze
ungulate
unicycle
unionise
univalve
universe
unmuffle
unmuzzle
unriddle
unsaddle
unsettle
unstable
unswathe
untangle
unthrone
upstroke
urbanise
urbanite
urethane
urostyle
Ursuline
urticate
valerate
valiance
validate
valorise
valuable

valvulae
vambrace
vamplate
vanadate
vaporise
variable
variance
varicose
vegetate
vegetive
vendible
venerate
verbiage
vergence
verjuice
vernicle
verrucae
versicle
vesicate
vicarage
vicarate
vicinage
Viennese
viewable
vignette
vincible
violable
violence
viperine
viricide
vitalise
vitiable
vituline
vocalise
vocative
voidable
voidance
volatile
volitive
volplane
vomerine
vomitive
vowelise
wagonage
Wahabite
wakerife
walkable
Walkyrie
wallgame
wardance
wardrobe
warhorse
warplane
washable
wastable
waterage
waterice
wearable
weldable
wetnurse
wettable
wharfage
wheyface
whiplike
whitetie
wifelike
wildfire
wildlife
windcone
windpipe
windrose
wingcase
winnable
wirewove
wiseacre
wishbone
womanise
woodbine
woodlice

woodnote
woodpile
workable
workmate
wormhole
wormlike
wrappage
wreckage
writable
xanthate
xanthene
xanthine
Xantippe
xylonite
yokemate
yuletide
zabaione
zibeline
zoetrope
zoophyte
zoospore
aardwolf
aperitif
blastoff
brushoff
bullcalf
bullyoff
calctuff
dandruff
disproof
dropleaf
dyestuff
footmuff
fourleaf
goldleaf
handcuff
kerchief
langlauf
mischief
mooncalf
overleaf
pentroof
riffraff
roseleaf
sanserif
sawedoff
seedleaf
sobstuff
spanroof
standoff
sunproof
tipstaff
tonedeaf
tradeoff
unbelief
werewolf
woodruff
writeoff
yourself
abetting
aborning
abutting
anything
aqualung
assuming
atheling
averring
ballyrag
bantling
banxring
beagling
becoming
beeswing
beetling
biassing
blabbing
blacking
blackleg
bleeding

blessing
blinding
blinking
blooming
blotting
blurring
boarding
bouncing
bragging
braiding
breaking
breeding
briefing
brimming
brisling
browning
buckling
building
bullfrog
bullring
bullyrag
bundling
bustling
cageling
canoeing
caprifig
catching
catering
centring
chapping
charming
charring
chatting
cheering
chipping
chopping
chugging
chumming
churning
cladding
clamming
clanging
clapping
cleaning
clearing
clinking
clipping
clogging
clothing
clotting
clubbing
coachdog
corkwing
couching
coupling
coursing
covering
crabbing
cracking
cradling
cramming
crashing
creeping
cribbing
crofting
cropping
crossing
dairying
darkling
deviling
dialling
dingdong
dittybag
dragging
dreaming
dressing
drilling
drinking
dripping

dropping
drubbing
drugging
drumming
duckling
duelling
dumpling
dwelling
emceeing
emitting
engaging
evensong
exacting
exciting
fagoting
farflung
farthing
faubourg
fetching
fiddling
fighting
fireplug
flagging
flapping
flashing
flatling
fleeting
flipping
flitting
floating
flogging
flooring
flopping
flubbing
focusing
folksong
fondling
footling
footslog
fordoing
forgoing
founding
frapping
freezing
fretting
fringing
fritting
frocking
frogging
frosting
fuelling
gangling
gladding
glancing
gleaning
gloaming
glutting
goatling
golliwog
goosegog
grabbing
graining
grasping
grayling
greening
greeting
grinning
gripping
gritting
grouping
grouting
growling
grubbing
grudging
guidedog
handling
hatching
haunting
headlong
hedgehog
hedgepig
hireling
hoarding
hocusing
hourlong
housedog
imposing
incoming
inviting
kindling
knapping
knitting
knocking
knotting
lacewing
lallygag
laughing
leapfrog
learning
lifelong
lighting
limetwig
littling
livelong
loathing
lordling
lovesong
lowering
lowlying
lustring
mahjongg
mantling
marbling
marrying
mealybug
middling
misdoing
moneybag
motoring
mottling
moulding
mounting
mourning
muscling
nestling
niggling
nighthag
northing
nosering
notching
nursling
obliging
offering
omitting
oncoming
outgoing
outlying
outvying
overhang
overhung
overlong
parasang
partsong
pearling
pettifog
phrasing
piddling
piercing
piffling
plaiding
planking
planning
platting
pleading
pleasing
plodding
plopping
plotting
plugging
plumbing
pointing
polliwog
pollywog
porkling
pounding
pressing
primming
printing
prodding
proofing
propping
puppydog
purfling
quandong
queening
queueing
quilting
quipping
quisling
quitting
quizzing
rallying
rambling
rattling
reedling
respring
resprung
retiring
reviling
rewaking
Riesling
roasting
rockling
sampling
scalawag
scanning
scarring
scathing
scatting
scheming
scolding
scouting
scraping
scudding
scumming
seagoing
seedling
seladang
shafting
shamming
shantung
sheading
shealing
shedding
sheepdog
sheeting
shelving
shieling
shilling
shinning
shipping
shirring
shirting
shocking
shogging
shooting
shopping
shunning
shutting
sickflag
sideling
sidelong
singeing
singsong
sizzling
skidding
skilling
skimming
skinning
skipping
skirting
slabbing
slagging
slamming
slapbang
slapping
slashing
sledding
sleeping
slimming
slipping
slipring
slitting
slogging
slopping
slotting
slubbing
slugging
slumming
slurring
smashing
smelling
smocking
snagging
snapping
snipping
snogging
snubbing
soothing
souchong
sounding
southing
spanking
spanning
sparling
sparring
spatting
speaking
spelling
spiffing
spinning
spitting
sporting
spotting
spurling
spurring
stabbing
stabling
stalling
standing
starling
starring
starting
steading
stealing
steening
steering
stemming
stepping
sterling
stetting
stinking
stirring
stocking
stopping
stravaig
striking
stubbing
studding
stuffing
stumming
stunning
suckling
swabbing
swagging
swanking
swanning
swansong
swapping
swatting
swearing
sweeping
sweeting
swelling
swigging
swimming
swinging
swobbing
swopping
swotting
tackling
tagalong
teaching
teething
tempting
thinking
thinning
thriving
thudding
thumping
tingeing
tonguing
toothing
touching
tracking
training
trapping
treefrog
trekking
trifling
trilling
trimming
tripping
trotting
trucking
trussing
tumbling
turtling
twinling
twinning
twitting
underdog
unending
unerring
unfading
unseeing
unsprung
unstring
unstrung
uprising
upsprang
upspring
upsprung
vaulting
Vietcong
wakening
watchdog
watering
waterlog
waygoing
weakling
weanling
weeklong
whacking
whapping
whetting
whidding
whipping
whirring
whizbang
whizzing
wholehog
whooping
whopping
witching
wrapping
yachting
yeanling
yearling
yearlong
yearning
yielding
zincking
zugzwang
acreinch
acrolith
admonish
aerolith
airbrush
alebench
allopath
although
amaranth
anaglyph
apograph
approach
astonish
backlash
backwash
bakshish
behemoth
bellpush
bequeath
besmirch
biograph
biomorph
birdbath
blackish
blahblah
blandish
bleakish
blimpish
blockish
blondish
blowfish
bluefish
bonefish
brackish
brainish
brandish
brattish
briskish
broadish
brownish
calabash
calipash
cartouch
cenotaph
cheapish
childish
churlish
chutzpah
clannish
cliquish
cloddish
clownish
coalfish
coolabah
coolibah
coronach
costpush
crawfish
crayfish
cromlech
dahabieh
dandyish
dealfish
declutch
demolish
despatch
devilish
diagraph
diminish
disbench
dispatch
dogtooth
dogwatch
dowdyish
dwarfish
eldritch
eleventh
encroach
ensheath
entrench
epigraph
ethnarch
eyetooth
faintish
fallfish
feeblish
feverish
fiendish
fiftieth
fiftyish
filefish
flatfish
flattish
flourish
footbath
footpath
forsooth
fortieth
fortyish
Frankish
freakish
frogfish
frumpish
furlough
ghoulish
goatfish
goatmoth
goldfish
goldrush
gralloch
greenish
greyfish
gunsmith
Haggadah
Halachah
harrumph
hasheesh
hawfinch
hawkmoth
helminth
herewith
hiccough
hierarch
hushhush
hyacinth
hydranth
inasmuch
ingrowth
insomuch
intrench
isomorph
isopleth
Jeremiah
jingoish
Kaffiyeh
kingfish
kneehigh
kourbash
languish
lightish
limewash
liverish
lumpfish
lungfish
Masoreth
megalith
mishmash
mismatch
mitzvoth
monkfish
monolith
monteith
moonfish
musquash
myograph
nonesuch
numbfish
nuthatch
odograph
oilcloth
oligarch
opsimath
outmatch
outreach
outwatch
outweigh
overarch
overfish
overmuch
padishah
paganish
perianth
pipefish
pixieish
plumpish
polymath
poohpooh
potlatch
prankish
priggish
puppyish
purplish
quackish
qualmish
queerish
rainwash
regolith
regrowth
reproach
rerearch
research
retrench
rockfish
Romansch
rosebush
rosefish
roughish
roundish
rowdyish
Rumansch
sailfish
saltbush
sandbath
sandwich
sandyish
savannah
sawtooth
scampish
Scottish
seedfish
selcouth
Shabuoth
shadbush
sharpish
sheepish
Shekinah
shofroth
shortish
shrewish
sidedish
sitzbath
sixtieth
skirmish
skittish
slapdash
slimmish
slobbish
sluggish

sluttish
smallish
smartish
snappish
sneakish
snobbish
soapdish
sparkish
spoffish
spookish
squarish
stablish
standish
starfish
steepish
stiffish
stockish
stoutish
stramash
strength
surffish
swainish
sweetish
sylphish
tarboosh
teacloth
telepath
tetrarch
thickish
thievish
thinnish
thorough
ticklish
tigerish
tilefish
tinsmith
toadfish
toadyish
tolbooth
tolldish
topnotch
toughish
tovarish
tribrach
trickish
triglyph
trigraph
triptych
tristich
typehigh
umptieth
unchurch
unclench
unclinch
vanquish
verandah
vermouth
Vietminh
viperish
Visigoth
vixenish
waterish
waxcloth
weakfish
wellnigh
Whiggish
whiplash
wishwash
wolffish
womanish
wrymouth
xenolith
youngish
zoomorph
amoretti
apresski
banditti
beriberi
bimbashi
bouzouki
broccoli
canthari
castrati
chapatti
chupatti
ciceroni
cicisbei
concerti
concetti
confetti
cornetti
cothurni
daiquiri
dividivi
drachmai
durukuli
Fascisti
flocculi
gladioli
graffiti
grissini
Gujarati
hamululi
harakiri
harikari
hetairai
hydroski
Kashmiri
kohlrabi
komitaji
libretti
literati
macaroni
maharani
Mahratti
maravedi
narcissi
nucleoli
pastrami
pulvilli
retiarii
ryotwari
sannyasi
sauouari
Sephardi
shanghai
solfeggi
strobili
sukiyaki
tandoori
teocalli
thesauri
trochili
virtuosi
waterski
zecchini
zucchini
aardvark
abelmosk
almanack
antimask
asterisk
backpack
ballcock
bankbook
bareback
basilisk
beadwork
benedick
billhook
blesbuck
boatdeck
boathook
bobolink
bodywork
bontebok
bookmark
bookwork
bootjack
buhlwork
bushbuck
cakewalk
casebook
casework
cashbook
chapbook
charlock
chipmuck
chipmunk
clawback
coalsack
coatrack
comeback
cookbook
copybook
crummock
dabchick
daybreak
deadlock
diestock
dipstick
disfrock
dogwhelk
drammock
drawback
dropkick
drummock
duckhawk
eyestalk
facepack
fallback
fastback
fasttalk
fatstock
feedback
feedtank
fireback
firelock
firework
fishhawk
fishhook
flapjack
footmark
footwork
foredeck
forelock
forepeak
formwork
forspeak
foxshark
fretwork
fullback
gamecock
gavelock
giftbook
gimcrack
goalkick
gripsack
grosbeak
gunstock
halfback
halfbeak
hallmark
handbook
handpick
handwork
hardback
hardhack
hardtack
havelock
haystack
headlock
headwork
herdbook
herdwick
highjack
hipflask
hogsback
holdback
homesick
homework
hoodwink
hornbook
humpback
hymnbook
iceblink
ironbark
ironwork
jetblack
joystick
kickback
kinsfolk
knapsack
kneejerk
knotwork
lacework
landmark
laverock
leadwork
legbreak
lifework
limerick
linstock
lipstick
lovelock
lovesick
maverick
meshwork
mintmark
misthink
moorcock
mossback
muckluck
muskduck
nainsook
newspeak
nicknack
nonstick
notebook
offbreak
onetrack
openwork
outbreak
outflank
overbook
overlook
overtask
overtook
overwork
pashalik
passbook
penstock
picklock
pinprick
piperack
playback
playbook
pockmark
politick
postmark
pullback
redbrick
redshank
reembark
rickrack
ringbark
ringneck
roadbook
rockcork
rockwork
rollneck
roofrack
ropewalk
rosepink
rucksack
saltlick
sandbank
seawrack
shabrack
shaddock
shagbark
shamrock
shashlik
shelduck
sherlock
shoptalk
sidekick
sidewalk
skerrick
skewback
skimmilk
skipjack
slapjack
slopwork
snaplink
soapbark
songbook
spardeck
steenbok
steinbok
stopcock
studbook
studwork
surfduck
swanmark
swanneck
swayback
tailback
tamarack
tamarisk
tapedeck
taskwork
teabreak
teamwork
telemark
textbook
ticktack
ticktock
tidelock
tidemark
tiebreak
timework
tomahawk
traprock
turnback
turncock
welldeck
windsock
wirework
wolfpack
woodcock
woodlark
woodwork
woolpack
woolsack
woolwork
wordbook
workfolk
yearbook
zwieback
aasvogel
abbatial
abnormal
achenial
acturial
Adamical
aerofoil
aestival
agential
alguazil
allodial
alluvial
alogical
anhedral
antennal
antheral
approval
arbitral
arboreal
archival
armorial
arterial
asphodel
astragal
atypical
autumnal
aventail
balmoral
banderol
bangtail
bankbill
bankroll
bannerol
barbital
baronial
baseball
basidial
basinful
beadroll
bechamel
bellpull
bellyful
bestowal
betrayal
biannual
biblical
biennial
bifacial
bilabial
binaural
binomial
biocidal
birdcall
bisexual
blameful
blissful
blowball
bluebell
blushful
boastful
boatbill
bobwheel
bonemeal
bonspiel
brachial
bracteal
brimfull
brocatel
cacomixl
caesural
callgirl
cannibal
cantonal
carbonyl
carboxyl
cardinal
carnival
carousal
carousel
carryall
cascabel
catchall
catechol
cathodal
catstail
cerebral
cervical
cesspool
charcoal
cheerful
chemical
clerical
clinical
clodpoll
clubhaul
cockerel
cocktail
cogwheel
coistrel
colonial
colossal
columnal
communal
conidial
conjugal
conoidal
contrail
cornball
corporal
corrival
cortical
cosmical
coverall
cracknel
cramfull
criminal
critical
crowbill
cuboidal
cultural
cyclical
daffodil
deadfall
decretal
deferral
defrayal
demersal
deprival
detrital
diaconal
diagonal
diarchal
dihedral
diluvial
diphenyl
dipteral
dishevel
disloyal
disposal
dividual
doctoral
doggerel
doorbell
doornail
doorsill
dotterel
doubtful
dovetail
downfall
downhaul
downhill
drawwell
dreadful
dreamful
drumroll
duckbill
dumbbell
dunghill
duodenal
dustbowl
eagleowl
eggshell
emetical
Emmental
empyreal
encrinal
enthrall
entresol
epicotyl
epidural
episodal
erotical
eschewal
especial
espousal
estoppel
estuaril
ethereal
etherial
ethnical
evenfall
eventful
eventual
exergual
exordial
external
faithful
falderal
familial
fanciful
farcical
farewell
fauteuil
festival
fiducial
filarial
fireball
fireopal
fishball
fishbowl
fishmeal
fishtail
fistical
flexural
flywheel
folderol
fontanel
football
footfall
foothill
forceful
forefeel
foresail
forestal
foretell
fourball
freefall
freesoil
freewill
fruitful
funebral
funereal
furfural
galangal
garefowl
geraniol
germcell
germinal
gestural
ghastful
gingival
glassful
glycerol
glyceryl
godawful
goldfoil
gonidial
goodwill
goofball
gossypol
graceful
grateful
gromwell
guileful
gunmetal
guttural
habitual
handball
handbell
handbill
handmill
handrail

hangnail
harebell
harpseal
headsail
heelball
heliacal
heroical
hibernal
hickwall
highball
hightail
hormonal
hornbill
horntail
hospital
houseful
hydromel
hydroxyl
hymenial
hypogeal
imaginal
immortal
imperial
inchmeal
inertial
infernal
informal
inguinal
inimical
inositol
inscroll
integral
internal
Interpol
interval
inthrall
irenical
ironical
isogonal
Judaical
judicial
keelhaul
khedival
kisscurl
Komsomol
korfball
lacrimal
lacrymal
landfall
landgirl
landrail
laystall
lenticel
littoral
loathful
longeval
longwall
lowlevel
lubrical
mackerel
madrigal
mainsail
malarial
mandrill
mangonel
maniacal
mannitol
manorial
manurial
marginal
material
materiel
maternal
matronal
meatball
medieval
memorial
mensural
merciful

methanol
metrical
minstrel
mirthful
misspell
mistrial
molehill
monachal
monaural
monaxial
monkseal
monomial
monorail
moonsail
moorfowl
mothball
motional
motorail
motorial
mournful
mouthful
muscadel
muscatel
mycelial
mystical
mythical
naphthol
national
nautical
neonatal
neuronal
newsreel
nightowl
nonlegal
nonmetal
nonmoral
notarial
notional
noumenal
novercal
numskull
nutshell
occlusal
oenophil
official
oogonial
optional
oriental
original
outrival
overcall
overfall
overfill
overhaul
overkill
oversail
oversell
oversoul
palatial
pallmall
parallel
parental
parietal
pastoral
pastural
paternal
patronal
peaceful
pectoral
pedestal
pellmell
perineal
peroneal
personal
petronel
petrosal
Philomel
physical
pickerel

pigswill
pinwheel
plateful
playbill
playgirl
plimsoll
podagral
poetical
ponytail
postmill
postural
potstill
powerful
praedial
prandial
prankful
prenatal
prideful
primeval
prodigal
proemial
proposal
protocol
proximal
pubertal
puffball
punctual
puparial
pushball
pushpull
pygidial
pyrexial
rainfall
rakehell
rasorial
rational
ratstail
rebuttal
rectoral
redistil
referral
regional
remedial
remittal
reprisal
reproval
requital
residual
reversal
reviewal
rhonchal
rightful
ringtail
ringwall
rockfall
rollcall
rosebowl
rubrical
rubytail
rustical
sagittal
Sangrail
Sangreal
scenical
scoopful
scornful
scrannel
sealevel
seashell
seasnail
seasonal
sectoral
selfheal
selfwill
semibull
senseful
sentinel
septfoil
septimal

sewellel
shaleoil
shameful
shedevil
shelfful
shoebill
shopbell
shopgirl
showbill
showgirl
shrapnel
shrieval
sidereal
sinophil
siphonal
skeletal
sloppail
slothful
snowball
snowfall
societal
softball
softboil
somedeal
soterial
spadeful
spandrel
spandril
spectral
spicknel
spiteful
splenial
spoonful
sportful
springal
squirrel
staminal
statical
staysail
stickful
stomatal
strapoil
stubnail
stunsail
subbasal
subtotal
subvocal
suicidal
supernal
supplial
supposal
surgical
surmisal
surroyal
survival
switchel
syncopal
syndical
synovial
syzygial
tableful
tactical
tafferel
taffrail
tasteful
teatowel
teetotal
temporal
tenurial
terminal
tesseral
textural
thankful
thetical
tidemill
timeball
tollcall
toothful
toplevel

toroidal
townhall
tracheal
tragical
tranquil
trapball
treenail
triaxial
tribunal
trifocal
trigonal
tripodal
tristful
tritical
tropical
troupial
trustful
truthful
turbinal
tutorial
unfilial
uniaxial
unisonal
univocal
unkennel
unlawful
unsocial
upheaval
vaccinal
varietal
vauntful
venereal
vengeful
vertical
verticil
vesperal
vicarial
virginal
visceral
visional
voiceful
vortical
warragal
warrigal
washbowl
wasteful
watchful
weariful
whimbrel
whinsill
wildfowl
windfall
windgall
windmill
windsail
woodwool
woolfell
worthful
wrackful
wrathful
wrongful
youthful
zenithal
zodiacal
abomasum
accustom
aconitum
acosmism
acrotism
actinism
actinium
activism
addendum
adiantum
aeriform
aerogram
albinism
alburnum
algorism

alienism
allodium
alluvium
alpinism
altruism
ammonium
aneurism
aneurysm
angstrom
anteroom
aphorism
apothegm
aquarium
archaism
Arianism
armyworm
ascidium
asterism
atticism
auriform
backroom
ballroom
basidium
bathroom
bdellium
betacism
biennium
bioplasm
Blenheim
bollworm
bookworm
botulism
brachium
brougham
Buddhism
Byronism
cabalism
caladium
capsicum
cardamom
cardamum
centrism
cerebrum
Chartism
cherubim
chiefdom
chiliasm
chromium
ciborium
cingulum
clerkdom
cliquism
coagulum
coatroom
coliform
coliseum
conidium
coniform
corundum
cubiform
cymatium
cynicism
dandyism
darkroom
daydream
decagram
decigram
delirium
demonism
devilism
didymium
diluvium
dimerism
dioecism
dirigism
disclaim
ditheism
Docetism
Donatism

doumpalm
druidism
duodenum
dwarfism
dybbukim
dynamism
echogram
ectoderm
electrum
embolism
emporium
encomium
endemism
endoderm
ensiform
entoderm
erethism
ergogram
ergotism
escapism
Essenism
etherism
ethicism
eugenism
eulogium
euphuism
europium
exanthem
exemplum
exorcism
exordium
factotum
fairyism
faradism
fatalism
feminism
filiform
finalism
fishfarm
flatworm
flimflam
foredoom
formroom
francium
frenulum
fusiform
futurism
galbanum
Galenism
gapeworm
Gaullism
geranium
giantism
gipsydom
gipsyism
glowworm
glucinum
gonidium
Graecism
gramatom
guaiacum
gypsydom
gypsyism
hairworm
halfterm
handloom
headroom
Hebraism
hedonism
heirloom
helotism
hexagram
Hinduism
hologram
hookworm
hornbeam
hornworm
humanism
hymenium

hypoderm
hypogeum
Ibsenism
icecream
idealism
ideogram
idiotism
imperium
inchworm
incivism
indicium
indusium
inoculum
intercom
intimism
iodoform
iotacism
Irishism
Islamism
isocheim
isotherm
jeroboam
jingoism
kilogram
labdanum
labellum
laburnum
laconism
landform
Latinism
laudanum
legalism
Leninism
linoleum
lipogram
lixivium
localism
logogram
lomentum
longterm
lukewarm
lutecium
lutetium
lyricism
maniform
marjoram
Mazdaism
mealworm
meconium
melanism
meristem
mesoderm
modalism
Moharram
Molinism
momentum
monadism
monogram
moonbeam
moralism
moshavim
motorium
muckworm
Muharram
mushroom
mycelium
nanogram
napiform
nativism
naturism
nebulium
negroism
neoplasm
nepotism
newsroom
nihilism
nobelium
nomadism
nomogram

nonclaim
nubiform
olibanum
omadhaum
ommateum
oncidium
oogonium
optimism
Orangism
organism
origanum
pacifism
paganism
paludism
papalism
pappadom
paradigm
paroxysm
Parsiism
patagium
pelorism
pendulum
periderm
peridium
perineum
phantasm
phormium
piliform
pisiform
platform
platinum
playroom
plectrum
pleonasm
plumbism
polonium
poppadum
populism
priapism
priggism
proclaim
prosaism
psychism
ptyalism
pugilism
pumproom
puparium
puppydom
pygidium
pyriform
pyxidium
queendom
quietism
ramentum
ranarium
reaffirm
regalism
rehoboam
reniform
residuum
retiform
rigorism
ringworm
Romanism
roodbeam
roundarm
rowdyism
royalism
rubidium
ruralism
saintdom
saleroom
samarium
sandworm
sapphism
satanism
Saxondom
Saxonism
scandium
schiedam
scholium
sciagram
sciolism
sealyham
selenium
Semitism
seraphim
seriatim
Shaktism
sheikdom
shipworm
shortarm
showroom
sickroom
sidedrum
silkworm
silphium
simplism
sinapism
skiagram
slipform
slowworm
snapbrim
snobbism
solarism
solarium
solatium
solecism
somatism
spectrum
speculum
sphagnum
spiculum
stoicism
strabism
studfarm
succinum
sudarium
syconium
tackroom
tantalum
Tantrism
tapeworm
tautonym
teetotum
telefilm
telegram
teraphim
testatum
thallium
thanedom
thraldom
thuggism
titanism
titanium
toadyism
tokenism
tomentum
tomogram
tonepoem
toolroom
totemism
trillium
tubiform
tympanum
ultraism
unciform
underarm
unionism
unwisdom
upstream
urbanism
vanadium
variform
variorum
vasculum
vasiform
velarium
veratrum
verbatim
vexillum
viaticum
viburnum
villadom
vinculum
virilism
vitalism
vivarium
vocalism
voltaism
Wahabism
wardroom
washroom
waveform
Whiggism
whimwham
whipworm
whoredom
winepalm
wireworm
witchelm
woodworm
workroom
xanthium
zombiism
ablation
ablution
abortion
abrasion
abutilon
Accadian
acrolein
actinian
adaption
addition
adhesion
Adlerian
adnation
adoption
advowson
aeration
affusion
agnation
agrarian
airwoman
Akkadian
Albanian
alderman
Algonkin
alizarin
allergen
allusion
alluvion
Alsatian
ambition
American
amoebean
androgen
Anglican
antiphon
aphelion
apiarian
Aramaean
Arcadian
archaean
Armenian
Arminian
artesian
ascidian
assassin
Assyrian
Athenian
audition
Augustan
aurelian
aurorean
autobahn
aversion
aviation
avulsion
backspin
Baconian
Bactrian
bailsman
bandsman
barbican
bargeman
bartizan
baseborn
Batavian
Bavarian
beadsman
bearskin
befallen
begotten
beholden
Benjamin
bespoken
bestrewn
betatron
bezonian
biathlon
bibation
billycan
bludgeon
bobbypin
Bodleian
Boeotian
bogeyman
bohemian
bondsman
boughten
bouillon
bourgeon
brainpan
brakeman
brakevan
brethren
Briarean
brighten
bryozoan
buckbean
buckhorn
buckskin
bulletin
bullhorn
cabochon
caducean
calfskin
Cambrian
campaign
Canadian
cannabin
cannikin
capeskin
capuchin
cardigan
careworn
carillon
Carolean
castiron
cauldron
cavesson
cavicorn
cerulean
cetacean
chairman
Chaldean
chaldron
champion
chaperon
chaplain
Chellean
chessman
children
Chinaman
chinchin
christen
cinnamon
cinquain
Circaean
citation
civilian
clansman
coachman
coaction
coercion
cognomen
cohesion
collagen
colophon
comedian
comedown
complain
conation
coonskin
cooption
cordovan
cordwain
cotillon
cotquean
coumarin
coxswain
cragsman
crankpin
creation
Croatian
crumhorn
cryotron
culverin
Cumbrian
cyanogen
cyclamen
dairyman
dalesman
damassin
decision
decurion
deerskin
delation
deletion
Delphian
delusion
demijohn
demonian
demotion
deration
derision
deuteron
devilkin
Devonian
devotion
diapason
dieldrin
dilation
dilution
diluvian
diocesan
diplogen
dipteran
discrown
distrain
disunion
division
dominion
donation
doomsman
dotation
doubloon
downtown
downturn
dragoman
dragomen
dragsman
dryclean
duration
Dutchman
dynatron
eclosion
ectozoon
eduction
effusion
egestion
Egyptian
eighteen
ejection
election
electron
emblazon
embolden
emersion
emission
empoison
empyrean
emulsion
enaction
encomion
endozoon
enneagon
entozoon
envision
Ephesian
episemon
epyllion
equation
Erastian
erection
erigeron
eruption
Eskimoan
Estonian
Etrurian
Etruscan
eulachon
euonymin
Eurasian
European
evection
eversion
everyman
eviction
evulsion
exaction
excision
exertion
falchion
fancyman
fanfaron
Faustian
favonian
fedayeen
fellahin
ferryman
finespun
fixation
flashgun
flatiron
flection
florigen
fluellin
flyblown
followon
forenoon
foreseen
foreskin
forewarn
forgiven
formalin
forsaken
forsworn
fountain
fourteen
fraction
franklin
Fraulein
freeborn
freedman
freshman
freshrun
Freudian
friction
Friesian
frighten
fruition
fugleman
function
funnyman
furfuran
Galilean
Gallican
gambeson
gambroon
ganglion
garrison
gelation
Georgian
gestagen
Ghanaian
globulin
glucagon
glycerin
glycogen
goatskin
goingson
gonfalon
gownsman
Graafian
grandson
gravamen
graviton
gridiron
groschen
guardian
gumption
gyration
haematin
halation
halfmoon
handsewn
handyman
hangeron
harridan
Hawaiian
hawthorn
headsman
heathhen
Hegelian
heighten
helmsman
henchman
henequen
heptagon
herdsman
hereupon
Hertzian
hielaman
highborn
himation
histogen
holstein
homeborn
homespun
hometown
hooligan
Horatian
horseman
houseman
huntsman
hydrogen
hypogean
ideation
ignition
ignitron
illation
illusion
Illyrian
imprison
inaction
incision
Indiaman
infusion
inhesion
invasion
irenicon
Irishman
isodicon
isthmian
Jacobean
jerrican
jerrycan
jettison
jobation
Jonathan
junction
Khmerian
klystron
krumhorn
laconian
ladyfern
lambskin
landsman
Langshan
lanthorn
larrikin
lavation
laywoman
leadsman
leathern
lecithin
legation
lengthen
libation
lichenin
liegeman
ligation
limekiln
linchpin
linesman
Linnaean
liveborn
lobation
locution
logician
longeron
longhorn
lookeron
loonybin
lovelorn
Lucullan
lunarian
lunation
luncheon
Lutheran
luxation
lynchpin
macaroon
madwoman
magdalen
magician
magneton
maintain
malarian
malefern
Mandaean
mandarin
mandolin
mannikin
marathon
markdown
marksman
marocain
maroquin

marshman
martagon
marzipan
mascaron
mastodon
Mayqueen
melodeon
menhaden
meridian
mescalin
mesotron
metazoan
metazoon
mezereon
midbrain
Milesian
misalign
miscegen
misgiven
mistaken
moccasin
moleskin
monition
Moravian
mortmain
motorman
motormen
moufflon
mountain
munition
musician
mutation
mutchkin
myrmidon
napoleon
natation
negation
negatron
NeoLatin
neomycin
newblown
nicotian
nineteen
nitrogen
Noachian
nobleman
nodation
nonhuman
nonunion
Norseman
northern
Northman
notation
noumenon
novation
nutarian
nutation
nutbrown
nymphean
oblation
oblivion
obsidian
occasion
octaroon
octoroon
Odyssean
Olympian
omission
openplan
ophidian
optician
Orcadian
orthicon
ostracon
ostrakon
outdrawn
outgrown
outreign
overlain
overseen
oversewn
overturn
overworn
oxymoron
oxytocin
pagurian
palmitin
pangolin
pannikin
pantheon
papillon
paraffin
parergon
Parmesan
partaken
Parthian
partisan
partizan
pathogen
pattypan
pavilion
peagreen
pearmain
Pegasean
Pelagian
pemmican
pentagon
perigean
Peruvian
petition
phlegmon
photogen
Phrygian
picaroon
pivotman
placeman
plankton
plantain
plastron
plebeian
poltroon
polyzoan
polyzoon
position
positron
posthorn
potation
prehuman
pressman
prolamin
Prussian
publican
puncheon
punition
pupation
purpurin
pygmaean
quadroon
quartern
quatrain
Quechuan
question
quillpen
quintain
raftsman
rambutan
ramequin
ranarian
ranchman
rataplan
reaction
reassign
reawaken
recision
redesign
reedwren
reinsman
relation
religion
replevin
resorcin
restrain
revision
Rhaetian
Rhinodon
rifleman
rigadoon
ringmain
riparian
riverain
riverman
roadsign
rockhewn
roentgen
rogation
Romanian
ropeyarn
rosarian
Rotarian
rotation
Rumanian
safranin
sainfoin
Salesian
salesman
Salopian
sanction
santonin
sapgreen
saucepan
scalepan
scallion
Scandian
scansion
scarfpin
scission
scorpion
Scotsman
scullion
seagreen
sealskin
seaonion
sebesten
secretin
sedation
sedition
seedcorn
seedsman
selfborn
selfsown
shagreen
shagroon
shalloon
sheeppen
sheeprun
Sheraton
shoehorn
shopworn
showdown
shrunken
shutdown
Siberian
Sicilian
sidesman
Silurian
sirenian
skeleton
slattern
slowdown
smoothen
sneeshan
Socinian
solation
solution
somewhen
sorochen
sorption
southern
Southron
spaceman
spalpeen
spearman
specimen
spittoon
sponsion
spontoon
spraygun
squadron
squarson
squawman
squireen
staghorn
stallion
stasimon
stellion
sternson
stockman
storeman
straiten
Strepyan
stricken
stridden
strucken
stubborn
stuntman
sturgeon
subhuman
suburban
Sumerian
superman
suzerain
swanskin
taciturn
Tahitian
tailspin
talapoin
talesman
talisman
tallyman
Tamilian
tarlatan
Tarpeian
tarragon
taxation
teaspoon
telethon
terrapin
tetragon
thermion
thespian
thirteen
tholepin
threaten
thrombin
thyroxin
timeworn
toboggan
toilworn
tommygun
townsman
trackman
traction
tragopan
trappean
treefern
trillion
trimaran
tripeman
trueborn
trunnion
tungsten
Tunisian
Turanian
turbofan
Turcoman
Turkoman
turndown
turnskin
twinborn
Tyrolean
unbeaten
unbidden
unbroken
unburden
unbutton
uncommon
underman
underpin
underrun
unfasten
unfrozen
ungotten
unloosen
unperson
unreason
upthrown
vacation
valerian
vanillin
velskoen
venation
Venetian
Venusian
veratrin
verboten
vesuvian
vexation
vigneron
viridian
vitellin
vocation
volition
volution
wallfern
watchman
waterman
wellborn
Wellsian
wellworn
Welshman
Wesleyan
wheelman
whoreson
windburn
wineskin
wingspan
wolfskin
woodsman
woolskin
wreathen
wrestpin
wristpin
xanthein
yataghan
yestreen
zeppelin
zonation
alfresco
amoretto
antihero
arpeggio
assiento
autogiro
autogyro
ballyhoo
barranco
bordello
buckaroo
camisado
castrato
caudillo
cicisbeo
cockatoo
commando
concerto
concetto
contango
continuo
contorno
cornetto
cruzeiro
curculio
doloroso
eldorado
espresso
falsetto
fandango
Filipino
finnesko
flamenco
flamingo
forzando
gardyloo
gazpacho
gillaroo
gracioso
graffito
groogroo
guacharo
hereunto
hitherto
impetigo
innuendo
intaglio
jackaroo
jackeroo
kakemono
kangaroo
libeccio
libretto
littlego
locofoco
lothario
machismo
maestoso
makimono
mancando
Mandingo
martello
moderato
mosquito
Negrillo
neutrino
oratorio
ostinato
ottavino
palmetto
palomino
parlando
peekaboo
peperino
perfecto
pimiento
plumbago
politico
presidio
prunello
ranchero
renegado
sargasso
scenario
scirocco
seicento
sentrygo
seraglio
sforzato
sombrero
spiccato
staccato
stiletto
stoccado
subimago
superego
terrazzo
trecento
twelvemo
virtuoso
vitiligo
wallaroo
wanderoo
waterloo
zecchino
agitprop
airstrip
ascocarp
backdrop
blackcap
blacktop
blowlamp
bluechip
bodyshop
calthrop
chopchop
clanship
claptrap
clipclop
clopclop
deanship
deathcap
doorstep
doorstop
dramshop
endocarp
escallop
firedamp
fireship
firetrap
flagship
flipflap
flipflop
followup
foolscap
footstep
freezeup
gallwasp
grogshop
hairgrip
handclap
handgrip
handicap
hardship
headlamp
hedgehop
heirship
higherup
housetop
jumpedup
junkshop
kingship
kneedeep
ladyship
landslip
liripoop
lockstep
lollipop
lollypop
longship
longstop
lordship
malaprop
mesocarp
monkship
namedrop
nightcap
outstrip
overcrop
overjump
overleap
overslip
overstep
pawnshop
peardrop
pedipalp
pericarp
raindrop
rearlamp
reedstop
roundtop
runnerup
screwtop
selfhelp
sheepdip
sideslip
sidestep
skindeep
skullcap
slagheap
slipslop
slopshop
snipsnap
snowdrop
softsoap
sparkgap
subgroup
sweetsop
tabletop
teardrop
township
tranship
tuckshop
twinship
underlap
underlip
wardship
warwhoop
whitecap
wineshop
woodpulp
workshop
xylocarp
abattoir
abductor
abhorrer
abridger
absolver
absorber
accentor
accepter
acceptor
achiever
acicular
actuator
adductor
adjuster
adjustor
adulator
affecter
affirmer
aflutter
agaragar
agitator
aglimmer
aglitter
airliner
alveolar
ambusher
analyser
ancestor
animator
answerer
anteater
anterior
argufier
armchair
armourer
arranger
arrester
arrestor
ascender
assenter
assentor
assertor

assessor
assignor
atomiser
attender
attester
attestor
atwitter
aweather
bachelor
bacillar
backdoor
bagpiper
balancer
baluster
banister
banterer
barndoor
barrator
barterer
bateleur
bebopper
bedeguar
bedmaker
beeeater
begetter
beginner
beguiler
beholder
belabour
believer
berliner
besieger
beslaver
betrayer
beveller
bewilder
bisector
blazoner
bleacher
blighter
borderer
borrower
boursier
brancher
breather
brewster
broacher
burrower
buttoner
calcspar
calendar
calender
calliper
cameleer
canaster
canister
cannular
caponier
capsular
carouser
catheter
cavalier
caviller
cellarer
cellular
chandler
chapiter
chasseur
chaunter
cinnabar
circular
cislunar
clangour
claqueur
cleanser
clincher
cloister
clothier
coauthor
cochlear
codifier
codriver
cofactor
coiffeur
colander
collator
colleger
columnar
commoner
commuter
compiler
complier
composer
computer
conceder
condylar
confider
confiner
congener
conjurer
conjuror
conniver
consider
consoler
consular
consumer
convener
convenor
conveyer
conveyor
coplanar
corridor
costumer
cottager
courtier
coworker
creditor
crossbar
croupier
crucifer
crueller
crusader
cucumber
cultivar
cuspidor
customer
cutwater
cylinder
dactylar
daughter
deadener
debonair
decanter
deceiver
December
decemvir
decipher
declarer
decolour
deemster
defector
defender
deferrer
deflower
demander
demurrer
depicter
depictor
deserter
designer
despiser
destrier
detainer
detector
deterrer
deviator
devourer
dialyser
diameter
dictator
didapper
diffuser
digester
dinosaur
director
disaster
discover
disinter
disorder
disposer
dissever
ditherer
dodderer
dogooder
domineer
doomster
douanier
downpour
drabbler
dragster
drencher
dribbler
Dukhobor
dulcimer
dundiver
educator
effector
elevator
embalmer
embitter
embosser
embracer
employer
emulator
encipher
encumber
endanger
endorser
endpaper
enfetter
enforcer
engender
engineer
engraver
enlarger
enquirer
enricher
enslaver
entailer
epistler
espalier
espouser
evildoer
examiner
excluder
executor
exemplar
exhorter
expander
expiator
exploder
explorer
exporter
extender
extensor
exterior
eyeliner
eyewater
falconer
familiar
fastener
fattener
favourer
feldsher
feldspar
ferreter
filmgoer
filmstar
finisher
fistular
fivestar
fletcher
flincher
flounder
flowerer
flypaper
follower
fomenter
footgear
footwear
forebear
foregoer
forester
forrader
forswear
fosterer
fourstar
fribbler
frondeur
frontier
furcular
fusileer
fusilier
galloper
gamester
gangster
ganister
gardener
garotter
gaselier
gasmeter
gasolier
gatherer
geometer
globular
goadster
gogetter
goodyear
gossamer
gossiper
governor
grabbler
grandeur
granular
greffier
grimacer
grounder
grumbler
gunlayer
hangover
harasser
hardener
haresear
hastener
havildar
haymaker
headgear
hijacker
hinderer
holdover
honourer
horsecar
hotelier
howitzer
huckster
icewater
idolater
idoliser
imitator
impeller
impolder
importer
imposter
impostor
improper
improver
impugner
inceptor
inductor
indulger
infector
inferior
infilter
inflamer
inflator
informer
ingather
injector
inlander
inquirer
inspirer
insulter
interior
interwar
intruder
inventor
inverter
investor
islander
isolator
jabberer
jeweller
jongleur
Judaiser
kalaazar
kibitzer
killdeer
knitwear
Kohinoor
kreutzer
labourer
labrador
lamellar
larcener
larkspur
laudator
laughter
launcher
lavender
lawgiver
lawmaker
lecturer
leftover
levanter
leveller
libeller
licenser
lingerer
listener
loadstar
lodestar
loiterer
Londoner
longhair
longueur
loosener
lumberer
magister
maligner
malinger
malodour
maltster
mamillar
mandator
maneater
manpower
marauder
marketer
masseter
mediator
menswear
metaphor
micellar
microbar
migrator
millibar
milliner
mimester
mimicker
minister
Minotaur
misnomer
modeller
modifier
molester
monicker
MonKhmer
monsieur
moreover
motorcar
mouseear
muleteer
murderer
murmurer
muscular
muskdeer
mutineer
mutterer
narrator
nenuphar
newcomer
nextdoor
nightjar
nonjuror
November
numberer
nurturer
oakegger
objector
observer
obtainer
occupier
odometer
offender
offsider
ohmmeter
oldtimer
oleander
oleaster
oligomer
onceover
onlooker
operator
oppugner
oracular
ordainer
outrider
outsider
overbear
overhear
overseer
overwear
oxidiser
oximeter
oxpecker
ozoniser
pacifier
palterer
pamperer
papillar
paramour
parcener
pardoner
pargeter
Passover
patellar
patentor
peculiar
pedalier
peignoir
pendular
perfumer
perisher
perjurer
petiolar
phosphor
piacular
picketer
pilaster
pilferer
pillager
pilsener
pinaster
pinnular
piscator
pitviper
plaister
planular
playgoer
pleinair
plougher
plumular
poisoner
polestar
polisher
pollster
polluter
pomander
ponderer
posturer
potholer
potterer
prattler
preacher
predator
premolar
preparer
presager
presumer
prisoner
procurer
producer
profaner
profiler
promiser
promisor
promoter
prompter
pronator
proposer
provider
provisor
pullover
pulpiter
pulsator
punisher
pupillar
purifier
purveyor
pushover
pustular
quaestor
quarrier
quencher
quibbler
rabbiter
racegoer
radiator
rainwear
ransomer
ratifier
ravisher
reappear
reasoner
rebeller
rebutter
receiver
receptor
reckoner
recorder
redactor
redeemer
redwater
reformer
register
regrater
reindeer
rejecter
rejigger
rejoicer
releaser
releasor
reliever
remember
reminder
remitter
renderer
reneguer
renumber
repairer
repealer
repeater
repeller
repenter
replacer
reporter
requiter
resetter
resister
resistor
resorter
restorer
retailer
retainer
retarder
revealer
reveller
revenger
reverser
reverter
reviewer
revolter
revolver
rewarder
ricercar
rimester
roadster
romancer
roseolar
roturier
rummager
rushhour
saboteur
saccular
scapular
schiller
schooner
scimitar
scorcher
scourger
scrapper
scrawler
screamer
screener
screever
scrubber
sculptor
scutcher
seafarer
seafloor
seamster
searcher
seasoner
seawater
seconder
secretor
seigneur
seignior
selector
semester
sempster
servitor

shadower
shielder
shingler
shoulder
shredder
shrimper
shrinker
shuffler
sickener
sidedoor
silencer
singular
sinister
sketcher
slipover
sloucher
smoulder
smuggler
snackbar
snatcher
sniffler
sniggler
snitcher
snuffler
softener
solander
solderer
songster
sorcerer
sorrower
souvenir
spacebar
sparkler
spatular
specular
spicular
spinster
splasher
splatter
splinter
splitter
splutter
sporular
sprawler
spreader
springer
sprinter
spurgear
spurrier
squaller
squander
squasher
squatter
squawker
squeaker
squealer
squeezer
squinter
squirter
stancher
startler
stickler
stippler
stipular
stitcher
stockcar
stopover
strainer
stranger
strapper
streaker
streamer
stringer
stripper
stroller
strummer
strutter
stumbler
subahdar
subfloor
sublunar
suborder
suborner
subprior
subsolar
sufferer
summoner
sunderer
superior
supplier
surfacer
surmiser
surveyor
survivor
swindler
taberdar
takeover
tamanoir
tamperer
tapwater
tattooer
tautomer
taverner
taxpayer
teamster
teenager
temperer
terminer
testator
thatcher
therefor
thirster
thrasher
threader
thresher
thriller
thruster
thurifer
thwacker
thwarter
tinkerer
together
tommybar
topliner
toreador
torturer
totterer
traditor
traducer
trampler
transfer
trapdoor
treacher
treadler
trembler
trencher
trimeter
triumvir
trottoir
truckler
turnover
twaddler
twiddler
twinkler
twitcher
twotimer
typifier
udometer
ulterior
underfur
unfetter
unifilar
unipolar
unlimber
unloader
untether
upholder
uplander
uplifter
uprooter
upsetter
utiliser
vacuolar
valuator
valvular
vanisher
vapourer
varactor
variolar
vascular
vavasour
veneerer
venturer
verderer
verderor
verditer
verifier
vesturer
viameter
vibrator
vilifier
villager
vintager
violator
vitiator
vivifier
voussoir
voyageur
waggoner
walkover
walloper
wallower
wanderer
warrener
watthour
wayfarer
whatever
wheatear
wheedler
whenever
wherever
whiffler
whistler
whitener
whomever
wigmaker
winnower
wirehair
wormgear
wrangler
wrestler
wriggler
yodeller
zamindar
zemindar
zoolater
abacuses
abducens
abomasus
abuttals
acanthus
acarpous
achiness
aciculas
acidosis
actinias
adenitis
adenoids
aduncous
afflatus
agedness
airiness
alewives
alkalies
alveolus
amiantus
amitosis
amphoras
anabases
anabasis
analects
analyses
analysis
anourous
antennas
anthesis
apodoses
apodosis
apomixis
apterous
araceous
archives
archness
Arcturus
arquebus
arsonous
asbestos
asperges
atlantes
auspices
avidness
avionics
bacillus
backless
badlands
baldness
bambinos
bareness
barkless
baroness
barracks
baseless
baseness
baudrons
beamends
bearings
bejabers
beltless
berberis
Bermudas
bibulous
bifocals
bigamous
bimanous
biparous
blinkers
bloomers
blueness
bodiless
boldness
bondmans
boneless
boniness
bookends
bootless
botflies
breeches
brimless
britches
bronchus
bursitis
business
busyness
buttress
cactuses
caduceus
caducous
caesious
caginess
calculus
calipers
calmness
calvados
cannabis
cannulas
canoness
canorous
cantoris
captious
careless
cataloes
cateress
cathexes
cathexis
caudexes
caudices
cautious
ceramics
cerastes
cernuous
cervices
chambers
champers
checkers
chequers
chiasmus
chinless
chlorous
chondrus
choragus
choregus
classics
cleavers
clematis
clerkess
clippers
clueless
cobblers
coccyges
coldness
colossus
combings
compages
compress
confines
congress
contents
coolness
copperas
cordless
corneous
cortices
cosiness
costplus
countess
couscous
covetous
cowgrass
crackers
cratches
crepitus
croupous
culottes
cumbrous
cumulous
cupreous
cureless
curtains
curtness
cuteness
cyanoses
cyanosis
cyclopes
cyclosis
cystitis
daftness
dampness
dankness
darkness
dartrous
dateless
deadness
deafness
dearness
decorous
deedless
deepness
deftness
demoness
denarius
desirous
detritus
dewiness
dextrous
diabetes
dialyses
dialysis
dianthus
didymous
diereses
dieresis
digamous
diggings
dimerous
dinornis
dipnoous
distress
diuresis
doldrums
dolorous
dominoes
dopiness
dourness
doziness
drabness
drachmas
draughts
druidess
ductless
dullness
dumbness
durables
dustless
dynamics
earmuffs
earnings
easiness
echoless
edacious
edgeless
edgeways
edginess
editress
eelgrass
eeriness
eftsoons
eighties
ekistics
elenchus
elflocks
ellipses
ellipsis
emeritus
emphases
emphasis
enormous
entellus
entrails
enuresis
environs
eohippus
epigeous
epitasis
equities
estovers
eugenics
euonymus
evenness
evilness
excursus
exegesis
exequies
exiguous
eximious
exlibris
extrados
extremes
eyeglass
fabulous
faceless
factious
fadeless
fairness
fangless
fashious
fastness
fastuous
fatigues
fearless
features
feckless
fellness
feverous
fewtrils
fibrosis
fineness
firearms
firmness
fishless
flatness
flatways
flawless
flexuous
flinders
fluidics
foamless
fondness
foodless
footless
formless
formulas
fornices
fortress
forwards
foulness
foureyes
foxiness
frabjous
freeness
fremitus
frescoes
frijoles
frillies
frutices
fullness
gadzooks
gainings
gainless
galleass
galluses
gambados
gameness
gaminess
gasworks
generous
genetics
geotaxis
ghettoes
giantess
glabrous
gladness
glanders
glaucous
glibness
glorious
glumness
glyptics
Gobelins
godwards
goitrous
goodness
gorgeous
gormless
gracious
graphics
greyness
grievous
grimness
griseous
grisgris
grottoes
gummosis
gypseous
hairless
haleness
haliotis
halluces
halteres
handless
hardness
harmless
hastings
haziness
headless
hedonics
heedless
heelless
heirless
heliosis
helpless
herbless
Hercules
Hesperus
hibiscus
hidrosis
highlows
highness
hindlegs
hipsters
holidays
holiness
hollands
homeless
hopeless
hornfels
hornless
hornrims
hotpress
hugeness
humorous
huntress
hurtless
hustings
hypnoses
hypnosis
ichorous
idealess
idleness
imagines
imprimis
infamous
inflatus
inkiness
intrados
Iroquois
isogloss
jodhpurs
justness
keelless
keenness
khuskhus
kindless
kindness
kinesics
kinetics
knickers
kurtosis
kyphosis
lameness
landless
landmass
lankness

larynges
larynxes
lashings
lateness
laziness
leadless
leafless
leanness
leavings
leggings
lensless
lewdness
lifeless
ligneous
likeness
limbless
limpness
listless
lodgings
loneness
longness
longways
lopgrass
lordless
lordosis
loudness
loveless
luckless
luminous
luscious
lushness
lustrous
Maecenas
maleness
mandamus
marasmus
marquess
marrieds
massless
mastitis
matgrass
matiness
matrices
matrixes
mattress
mayoress
maziness
meanness
meekness
meetness
mementos
meninges
meniscus
mephitis
Mesdames
methinks
methysis
miasmous
midlands
midships
midwives
mildness
mindless
Minoress
mistress
mittimus
molasses
molossus
moonless
moorings
mornings
moveless
muchness
mucrones
muteness
muticous
mutinous
myelitis
myositis
myosotis
nacreous
nameless
narcoses
narcosis
nathless
nauplius
nauseous
nautilus
nearness
neatness
nebulous
necrosis
needless
neuritis
neuroses
neurosis
niceness
ninepins
nineties
nodulous
nosiness
noteless
notornis
nowadays
nubilous
nucellus
nudeness
nullness
numbness
numerous
numinous
nuptials
oatgrass
ochreous
oddments
oestrous
ofttimes
oiliness
omphalos
oogamous
ooziness
openness
oratress
orgulous
osteitis
outclass
outdoors
outguess
outwards
outworks
ovalness
ovaritis
overalls
overpass
overplus
overseas
painless
paleness
pancreas
pandanus
panpipes
papulous
pastries
pathless
patulous
pearlies
pectines
peelings
peerless
perilous
periplus
pertness
pervious
petalous
phthisis
pickings
pictures
pinchers
pinkness
pitiless
pixiness
plastics
platypus
plaudits
pluvious
polemics
politics
pollices
polypous
poorness
populous
porticos
portress
precious
previous
Primates
primness
princess
prioress
proceeds
progress
propolis
protasis
pruritus
psilosis
psychics
pulvinus
puniness
pureness
pyelitis
pyrrhous
quarters
rachides
rachitis
raciness
rankness
raptness
raptures
rareness
rashness
ravenous
realness
reassess
reckless
redeless
reinless
resinous
respects
restless
rhinitis
rhonchus
ribgrass
richness
rifeness
rigorous
rinsings
ripeness
roadless
roofless
rootless
ropiness
rosiness
rouleaus
rounders
rudeness
ruleless
rustless
ruthless
ryegrass
sacculus
sackless
safeness
sageness
sailless
saltless
saltness
sameness
saneness
saporous
sapphics
sateless
saunders
savorous
sawbones
scabious
scabrous
scanties
scapulas
scarious
scarless
schnapps
scirrhus
scissors
sclerous
scolices
scopulas
seamless
seawards
sedulous
seedless
selfless
selfness
senarius
sensuous
sepalous
sewergas
sexiness
shallows
shambles
shingles
shoeless
sickness
sidearms
sideways
siftings
siriasis
skewness
skilless
skinless
skittles
skywards
slimness
slowness
slyboots
smithers
smugness
sniffles
snowless
snuffers
snuffles
snugness
soapless
soapsuds
softness
soilless
soleness
sombrous
someways
songless
sonorous
soreness
soulless
sourness
sourpuss
spacious
spadices
spadones
specious
spherics
sphygmus
spiritus
splenius
spotless
spraints
spryness
spurious
spyglass
squamous
staggers
stannous
starkers
starless
stemless
stenosis
stimulus
stipites
strumous
stuccoes
studious
subclass
suberous
subgenus
succubus
suitings
sundress
sundries
sundrops
sunwards
supplies
suppress
sureness
susurrus
syllabus
synapsis
syndesis
synopses
synopsis
syphilis
syringes
syrinxes
tactless
tailings
tailless
tallness
tameless
tameness
tantalus
tapeless
tartness
tautness
tearless
technics
tenesmus
terminus
termless
thalamus
thallous
Thanatos
thinness
thisness
thoraces
thoraxes
thoughts
thrombus
thusness
tideless
tidiness
timeless
timorous
tininess
tinnitus
tintless
tireless
titaness
tombless
toneless
topdress
tortious
tortuous
trammels
treeless
trembles
trespass
trimness
trousers
trueness
tubeless
tuberous
tumorous
tuneless
turnings
tutoress
tweezers
twenties
ugliness
ulcerous
unawares
unctuous
upstairs
usurious
uvulitis
uxorious
vainness
valorous
vanadous
vaneless
vaporous
vastness
veilless
venomous
ventless
vertexes
vertices
victress
victuals
viewless
vigorous
vileness
viperous
virtuous
vitellus
vitreous
voidness
volcanos
volvulus
vortexes
vortices
votaress
voteless
waesucks
waitress
wakeless
wardress
wariness
warmness
waterbus
watergas
waveless
waviness
waxiness
waxworks
weakness
weedless
wetlands
whatness
whiskers
wideness
wifeless
wildness
wiliness
windlass
windless
wingless
winnings
wireless
wiriness
wiseness
wondrous
woollens
wordless
workings
workless
writings
wrongous
zaniness
zoonosis
abducent
aberrant
abetment
abradant
absonant
abstract
abstrict
abundant
abutment
accident
accredit
acescent
acidfast
acquaint
acrefoot
activist
adducent
adherent
adjacent
adjutant
adjuvant
advocaat
aegrotat
aeronaut
aerostat
afferent
affluent
afforest
affright
agrement
aircraft
airshaft
airtight
alarmist
alcahest
alienist
alkahest
allnight
almagest
alphabet
alpinist
altruist
alumroot
amadavat
ambivert
ambulant
amethyst
anapaest
anchoret
annalist
antepost
aperient
aphorist
apiarist
apparent
appetent
aquanaut
aquarist
aquatint
aqueduct
arbalest
arbalist
arborist
archaist
argonaut
argument
armament
arrogant
arsonist
artefact
artifact
aspirant
assignat
assonant
autocrat
avadavat
averment
aviarist
baccarat
bacchant
backchat
backlist
backmost
backrest
backseat
bailment
ballonet
banjoist
bankrupt
banneret
barefoot
basement
bassinet
beechnut
beetroot
bellwort
benedict
bergamot
besought
besprent
bigamist
bioplast
bivalent
blackout
bluecoat
bobbinet
bodement
bookpost
bookrest
bootlast
botanist
bouffant
bowfront
bowsprit
boxpleat
bracelet
bractlet
braggart
brassart
breakout
brickbat
brooklet
browbeat
buckshot
Buddhist
bunfight
burgonet
burntout
bystreet
cabalist
cachalot
cachepot
calamint
camshaft
canoeist
canonist
canzonet
capellet
carburet
carcanet
carryout
casement
catalyst
catapult
cataract
catsfoot
cellaret
centrist
ceramist
cerement
cervelat
chalkpit
Chartist
checkout
chestnut
chiliast

chitchat
cidevant
claimant
clarinet
cleancut
clearcut
closeset
cloudlet
clubfoot
coaldust
cockboat
cockloft
cockshut
cognovit
coherent
cokernut
colewort
colonist
comedist
compleat
conflict
confront
conjoint
conjunct
conquest
constant
contempt
contract
contrast
copyedit
corselet
Corybant
cosecant
cotenant
couchant
couldest
covalent
covenant
coverlet
crackpot
crescent
crosscut
crosslet
crotchet
crowfoot
cryostat
cucurbit
daylight
deadbeat
debutant
decadent
decedent
decrepit
deferent
deforest
democrat
deponent
derelict
destruct
dewpoint
diffract
digamist
dilatant
diligent
dinerout
diplomat
diriment
discount
discreet
disjoint
disjunct
dismount
dispirit
displant
disquiet
distinct
distract
distrait
district
distrust
ditheist
divalent
Docetist
document
dogfight
dominant
Donatist
donought
doorpost
doughnut
downbeat
downcast
downmost
dragonet
dribblet
dropshot
dropwort
druggist
drupelet
drypoint
duellist
duettist
dungcart
dustcart
dustcoat
dustshot
dynamist
earthnut
easement
eastmost
efferent
effluent
eggplant
electret
elephant
eloquent
emergent
emigrant
emulgent
enforest
entrepot
epiblast
equitant
escapist
escargot
eschalot
esculent
essayist
esurient
etherist
ethicist
eucalypt
eugenist
eulogist
euphuist
Eurocrat
evacuant
excitant
exhalant
existent
exorcist
expirant
explicit
exponent
exultant
eyesight
fabulist
facelift
faineant
falconet
faltboat
fanlight
farthest
fatalist
feculent
feminist
figurant
filament
finalist
fireboat
firebrat
flagrant
flatboat
flatfeet
flatfoot
flattest
flautist
fleawort
fleshpot
flippant
floodlit
floweret
foldboat
folkmoot
footpost
footrest
forecast
forefelt
forefoot
foremast
foremost
forepart
forepast
forewent
forklift
forspent
fourpart
fowlpest
fragment
fragrant
freakout
frequent
frogspit
frondent
frontlet
fruitbat
fumigant
furthest
futurist
gadabout
gallipot
gaslight
gastight
gatepost
Gaullist
gauntlet
gladdest
glummest
goalpost
golddust
goutwort
gradient
greenlet
grimmest
guardant
gunfight
gunflint
gunpoint
gynocrat
gyrostat
habitant
halfboot
halfmast
halfpint
handcart
handfast
handlist
hazelnut
headfast
headmost
headrest
Hebraist
hedonist
heliport
hellbent
helpmeet
henroost
hesitant
highmost
hightest
hillfort
hindmost
hirrient
hobbyist
holdfast
homefelt
homodont
honeypot
hoofbeat
hornwort
hotchpot
Huguenot
humanist
humorist
iceplant
iceyacht
idealist
idiolect
idyllist
ignorant
illtreat
immanent
imminent
immodest
implicit
imponent
impotent
impudent
incident
incitant
indecent
indicant
indigent
indirect
indolent
inerrant
inexpert
inflight
influent
inhalant
inherent
innocent
inscient
insolent
inspirit
instinct
instruct
insulant
insurant
interact
intercut
interest
intermit
intromit
irritant
ivorynut
jackboot
Jehovist
jingoist
jubilant
judgment
jumpseat
jumpsuit
kilowatt
kingbolt
knockout
lamppost
lancelet
lanneret
Latinist
latitant
lawcourt
layabout
layshaft
Lazarist
legalist
Leninist
lifebelt
lifeboat
ligament
linguist
liniment
litigant
lobbyist
lockfast
lockknit
lodgment
longboat
lorikeet
loveknot
lovenest
loveseat
loyalist
luculent
luminant
luminist
lungwort
lutanist
lutenist
lyricist
mailboat
mailcart
mainmast
makefast
malapert
maledict
maltreat
manifest
mantelet
marabout
marmoset
martenot
martinet
massicot
mazement
megawatt
melodist
merchant
microdot
midnight
midpoint
mightest
milepost
militant
milkwort
misbegot
miscount
misdealt
misdoubt
misprint
misspelt
misspent
mistreat
mistrust
mitigant
mobocrat
modalist
Molinist
monocrat
monodist
monoglot
monotint
monument
moonshot
moonwort
moralist
motorist
movement
mowburnt
muniment
murrelet
myoblast
namepart
nativist
naturist
nauseant
needment
nescient
newscast
newsheet
nihilist
nonevent
novelist
nutrient
obedient
obeisant
obstruct
occident
occupant
offprint
offshoot
ointment
oliphant
oologist
opencast
opponent
optimist
organist
ornament
orpiment
osculant
outburst
outpoint
outright
outsight
outsmart
outspent
overcast
overcoat
overheat
overpast
overshot
oviposit
pacifist
pamphlet
pantsuit
papalist
parakeet
paraquat
parodist
paroquet
passport
pavement
paysheet
pederast
pediment
penchant
penitent
petulant
phaseout
pheasant
piecrust
piedmont
pilewort
pillwort
pinpoint
planchet
plangent
platelet
playsuit
pleasant
plumelet
poignant
polemist
poltfoot
polyglot
populist
portrait
postobit
potplant
potroast
precinct
preelect
preexist
pregnant
preprint
printout
prohibit
prosaist
prospect
protract
prurient
psalmist
psychist
pugilist
puissant
puppyfat
pursenet
pursuant
purulent
pushcart
pussycat
quadrant
queenlet
quickset
quietist
quitrent
quotient
rackrent
radicant
raincoat
rallyist
reactant
readjust
rearmost
reassert
recommit
recreant
recusant
redirect
redolent
redshift
redshirt
redstart
reefknot
reexport
referent
refluent
reforest
regiment
reinsert
reinvest
relaxant
relevant
relucent
remanent
renitent
reorient
rescript
resident
resonant
restrict
reticent
retroact
revenant
reverent
rheostat
ricochet
rightist
rigorist
ringbolt
roborant
rocksalt
Romanist
roodloft
roseroot
royalist
rudiment
ruminant
runabout
ruralist
rutilant
sackcoat
sailboat
salariat
saltwort
samizdat
sandwort
Sanskrit
sarcenet
sarsenet
satanist
satirist
saturant
Saxonist
scandent
scilicet
sciolist
scoopnet
seachest
seacoast
seacraft
seafront
seamount
seatbelt
seatrout
sederunt
sediment
seedcoat
seedplot
segreant
Semitist
sennight
sentient
sergeant
serjeant
servient
sewerrat
shakeout
shareout
sharpset
shipment
shootout
shortcut
shouldst
showboat
sibilant
sicklist
signpost
simonist
simulant
sinciput
siphonet
sitarist
skylight
skypilot
slimmest
slipknot
snakepit
snapshot
snowboot
soaproot
soapwort
solarist
solecist
solfaist
solleret
somewhat
sparklet
spikelet
sprocket
stagnant
stakenet
stalwart
stardust
starwort
stedfast
stinkpot
stockist
stockpot
straight
strepent

strident
strumpet
subagent
suberect
subjoint
subtract
succinct
sunburnt
sunburst
sunlight
supplant
surfboat
surmount
swanshot
sweepnet
swiftlet
swimsuit
symbiont
tablecut
tablemat
tabouret
tailcoat
tangoist
Tantrist
teachest
tearduct
tegument
telecast
teleport
tenement
theocrat
theorist
thereout
thickset
thinnest
thrawart
thumbpot
tolerant
tommyrot
totemist
toxicant
trailnet
transact
transect
transept
transmit
Trappist
trawlnet
trialist
troutlet
turbojet
turncoat
turnspit
twilight
typecast
ultraist
underact
undercut
underlet
underset
undreamt
undulant
unionist
unlearnt
unsought
untaught
unthrift
uppercut
upthrust
urbanist
urticant
usufruct
vehement
vesicant
vestment
vigilant
virement
virulent
viscount

visitant
vitalist
vivisect
vocalist
volitant
votarist
wagonlit
wainscot
waleknot
wallknot
warpaint
wartwort
waxlight
weldment
wellknit
whinchat
whitehot
whiteout
whittret
whodunit
wingbeat
woodchat
wormcast
wouldest
wristlet
yoghourt
youngest
ziggurat
carcajou
Esquimau
flambeau
froufrou
hausfrau
jiujitsu
kinkajou
pirarucu
priedieu
thankyou
Jugoslav
Yugoslav
airscrew
bedstraw
Bradshaw
brandnew
bungalow
chainsaw
chowchow
clerihew
cockcrow
coleslaw
crackjaw
crossbow
curassow
disallow
disendow
dumbshow
elfarrow
fernshaw
feverfew
finedraw
foreknew
foreknow
foreshow
framesaw
furbelow
hedgerow
hernshaw
highbrow
homebrew
honeydew
hoosegow
kickshaw
mackinaw
overdraw
overdrew
overflew
overflow
overgrew
overgrow

overview
peepshow
rearview
rebellow
rickshaw
roughhew
setscrew
sideshow
sideview
soundbow
southpaw
stickjaw
teleview
tenonsaw
tomorrow
undertow
williwaw
wiredraw
withdraw
withdrew
appendix
aviatrix
bandeaux
battleax
biconvex
bobbysox
Bordeaux
chateaux
cicatrix
creatrix
crucifix
dittybox
epicalyx
fabliaux
haruspex
horsebox
intermix
interrex
intersex
loosebox
matchbox
mirepoix
moneybox
orthodox
paintbox
parallax
plateaux
pontifex
pressbox
quincunx
rondeaux
rouleaux
sardonyx
saucebox
smallpox
snuffbox
soundbox
spicebox
spinifex
supertax
tableaux
toadflax
transfix
trumeaux
voicebox
abeyancy
abjectly
aborally
abruptly
absently
absurdly
accuracy
acerbity
achingly
acridity
acrimony
actively
activity
actually

adequacy
adorably
adroitly
adultery
advisory
advocacy
aerially
aerology
aeronomy
affinity
agrimony
agrology
agronomy
aguishly
alacrity
Alderney
aleatory
algidity
algology
alkalify
allegory
alleyway
allogamy
almighty
amazedly
amenably
amicably
ammonify
amorally
amusedly
ancestry
animally
annually
antibody
antilogy
antimony
antinomy
apically
apoplexy
apostasy
ardently
arguably
arrantly
artfully
artistry
asperity
assembly
astutely
atrocity
attorney
audacity
auditory
augustly
autarchy
autogamy
autonomy
autotomy
aversely
avowedly
axiality
axillary
axiology
backstay
balladry
banality
banditry
barberry
barratry
barrenly
basicity
basketry
bastardy
bayberry
bearably
beautify
beggarly
bellbuoy
benignly
bestiary

bilberry
billyboy
bioassay
biometry
birthday
bistoury
bitchily
bitingly
bitterly
biweekly
biyearly
blackboy
blackfly
bladdery
blamably
blankety
blatancy
blazonry
blearily
blistery
blithely
bloodily
bloomery
blossomy
blubbery
blurrily
blustery
boringly
bottomry
bouncily
boundary
boyishly
brassily
brazenly
brazenry
braziery
breezily
breviary
brightly
broadway
broidery
brokenly
broodily
brutally
bryology
bullocky
bullyboy
buoyancy
Burberry
burglary
Burgundy
bushbaby
busybody
butchery
cabinboy
cableway
cacology
caducity
cajolery
calamary
calamity
calidity
candidly
cannonry
capacity
carnally
castaway
casually
casualty
catchfly
category
catenary
caudally
causally
causeway
celerity
celibacy
cemetery
centaury

ceremony
chambray
chancery
chapelry
charlady
chastely
chastity
chattily
chauntry
cheekily
cheerily
chemurgy
chirpily
chirrupy
chivalry
choicely
choirboy
chopsuey
chorally
Christly
chummily
chupatty
churchly
cinerary
circuity
civility
clammily
classify
clearway
clemency
cleverly
cloudily
clownery
clumsily
clustery
coarsely
cobwebby
cogently
colliery
colloquy
cometary
commoney
commonly
contrary
convexly
coquetry
corduroy
cornetcy
coronary
corsetry
costmary
cottagey
courtesy
cousinly
covertly
cowardly
cowberry
craftily
cramoisy
cranefly
crankily
cravenly
creakily
creamery
credibly
croakily
crockery
crossply
crossway
crustily
cryogeny
culinary
culpably
cupidity
currency
cursedly
cushiony
cussedly
cycleway

cytology
daintily
damnably
dancetty
daringly
dastardy
deathray
debility
decently
delegacy
delicacy
delivery
delusory
demagogy
demurely
denazify
derisory
detoxify
deucedly
deviancy
deviltry
devoutly
dewberry
dicacity
dilatory
diploidy
directly
disarray
dismally
distally
disunity
divinely
divinity
docilely
docility
dogberry
doggedly
dogsbody
donatory
doomsday
dormancy
dorsally
dotingly
doughboy
doxology
draughty
dreamily
drearily
driftway
driveway
drollery
droughty
drowsily
drudgery
easterly
efficacy
eighthly
elatedly
elegancy
eligibly
eminency
emissary
emulsify
endogamy
endogeny
enginery
enormity
ensigncy
enthalpy
entirely
entirety
entreaty
enviably
epically
epilepsy
epinasty
epiphany
equality
equinity

errantly
errantry
esterify
eternity
ethology
euphrasy
eutrophy
everyday
everyway
exigency
exiguity
expertly
facially
facilely
facility
fadeaway
falconry
fallibly
famously
farriery
fatality
fatherly
faultily
faunally
feasibly
feastday
feathery
February
felicity
felinity
fellowly
feminity
fenberry
feretory
ferocity
fervency
fervidly
festally
feudally
fidelity
fiercely
filially
filthily
finality
finitely
fireclay
fiscally
fitfully
flashily
flattery
fleshfly
flexibly
flickery
flimsily
flintily
floodway
floppily
florally
floridly
fluently
fluidify
fluidity
flummery
fluttery
foetidly
foldaway
forcedly
forcibly
forelady
foreplay
forestay
forestry
formally
formerly
fortuity
fourthly
friendly
frigidly
frippery

friskily
frostily
frothily
fructify
frugally
fruitery
fruitfly
frumenty
fugacity
fumitory
funerary
furriery
futilely
futility
futurity
gadgetry
Galloway
gapingly
garganey
garishly
garlicky
gelidity
genially
geognosy
geomancy
geometry
geophagy
gimmicky
gingerly
giveaway
glassily
glaziery
glittery
globally
gloomily
glossary
glossily
gluttony
goldenly
gossipry
gramercy
gratuity
gravelly
greasily
greedily
greenery
greenfly
grindery
groggily
grubbily
grumpily
guaranty
guernsey
guideway
guiltily
gulosity
gynandry
gyratory
haploidy
harlotry
hatchery
hatchway
headachy
heartily
heatedly
heathery
heavenly
hegemony
henparty
heraldry
hereaway
heredity
hexapody
hideaway
hilarity
hillocky
hoarsely
hobbitry
Hogmanay
hollowly
homebody
homogamy
homogeny
homology
homonymy
honestly
honorary
horology
horribly
horridly
horsefly
hostelry
houseboy
housefly
hoverfly
humanely
humanity
humidify
humidity
humility
hummocky
hungrily
hydropsy
hypogyny
ideality
identify
identity
ideology
idolatry
ignominy
illusory
immunity
imparity
impishly
impolicy
impunity
impurely
impurity
industry
inequity
infantry
infinity
infirmly
iniquity
innately
insanely
insanity
instancy
intently
intimacy
inwardly
irongray
irongrey
isocracy
isometry
isospory
isostasy
isotropy
jackstay
jaggedly
janizary
jauntily
jealousy
jejunely
jeopardy
jesuitry
jocosely
jocosity
jocundly
jokingly
jovially
joyfully
joyously
jugglery
knackery
knightly
kolinsky
kromesky
labially
lability
lackaday
lacunary
laically
lamasery
lambency
landarmy
landlady
lapidary
lapidify
latchkey
latently
latinity
latterly
laudably
lavatory
lavishly
lawfully
lawyerly
leadenly
leathery
legality
legendry
legerity
leniency
lethally
lethargy
libatory
lifebuoy
limitary
limpidly
lineally
linearly
liquidly
literacy
literary
livelily
lividity
loblolly
lobotomy
locality
locutory
Lollardy
lovelily
lovingly
lubberly
lucidity
luminary
mahogany
maidenly
mainstay
majority
Malagasy
malarkey
malignly
manfully
mangabey
mannerly
manually
markedly
masterly
matronly
maturely
maturity
meagrely
medially
mellowly
menially
menology
mentally
mesially
metonymy
micrurgy
mightily
military
milliary
minacity
minatory
ministry
minority
minutely
misapply
miscarry
misogamy
misogyny
misology
missilry
mobility
modality
modernly
modestly
modishly
molality
molarity
momently
monandry
monarchy
monetary
monitory
monogamy
monogeny
monogony
monogyny
monopoly
monotony
mopishly
morality
moratory
morbidly
mordancy
morosely
morosity
mortally
mortuary
motherly
motility
motivity
motorway
movingly
mucosity
mulberry
mulishly
mulloway
multeity
multiply
musingly
musketry
mutually
mycology
narrowly
nasality
nascency
natality
natatory
natively
nativity
naumachy
necropsy
negatory
neurally
nihility
nobility
nodality
nodosity
nomology
nondairy
nonparty
normalcy
normally
nosology
nubility
nugatory
numeracy
numerary
oafishly
obduracy
obituary
oblatory
obtusely
obtusity
occultly
octarchy
octonary
ocularly
odiously
oecology
oenology
omophagy
oncology
ontogeny
ontology
opaquely
orangery
ordinary
oreology
ornately
orthoepy
otiosely
otiosity
outlawry
overbusy
overplay
overstay
owlishly
paduasoy
pallidly
palpably
pandowdy
pansophy
paperboy
papistry
parrotry
passably
passerby
patchily
patently
peacocky
peccancy
pedagogy
pedantry
pedology
pendency
penology
perigyny
peripety
petalody
phantasy
pharmacy
photopsy
phyllary
physicky
picnicky
pilosity
pinmoney
pipeclay
piquancy
pitiably
placably
placidly
plagiary
plaguily
plastery
pleurisy
pliantly
pluckily
plurally
podiatry
polarity
politely
polygamy
polygeny
polygyny
polypary
polypody
polysemy
polysomy
pomology
popinjay
popishly
porosity
porphyry
posology
possibly
potbelly
potently
prettify
prettily
priestly
priggery
primally
princely
priority
prissily
probably
prolixly
promptly
properly
property
prophecy
prophesy
provably
pryingly
psalmody
psaltery
publicly
punditry
pungency
punitory
pupilary
puppetry
putridly
quackery
quaintly
Quakerly
quandary
quantify
quantity
queasily
quiddity
quirkily
quixotry
rabbitry
rabidity
racially
radially
radiancy
raggedly
raillery
rakishly
rampancy
randomly
rapacity
rapidity
rascally
readably
reagency
recently
reconvey
recovery
redeploy
reemploy
refinery
regality
registry
reliably
remissly
remotely
reoccupy
resinify
resurvey
revisory
revivify
rhapsody
rheology
ribaldry
ribbonry
ridgeway
rigidify
rigidity
ritually
riverway
robustly
rocketry
rogatory
rolypoly
rosemary
rotatory
rottenly
rotundly
roughdry
rubbishy
ruefully
ruggedly
rugosely
rugosity
rurality
sacredly
sacristy
saddlery
saffrony
sagacity
sailorly
salacity
saliency
salinity
salivary
salutary
sanatory
sanctify
sanctity
sanitary
sapidity
saponify
satiably
Saturday
savagely
savagery
scammony
scantily
scarcely
scarcity
scattily
scratchy
screechy
scribbly
scrutiny
scullery
scurvily
seaholly
seamanly
secondly
secretly
securely
security
sedately
sedulity
seignory
selfpity
seminary
senility
sensibly
serenely
serenity
serially
serology
serosity
severely
severity
sexology
sexually
shabbily
shaggily
shiftily
shiftkey
shimmery
shoddily
shortday
shrewdly
shuddery
sickerly
signally
silently
silicify
silverly
simplify
sinfully
sinology
sisterly
sitology
sixpenny
skimpily
slangily
sleazily
sleepily
slideway
slightly
slinkily
slippery
slithery
slobbery
sloppily
slovenly
slovenry
slumbery
smallfry
smarmily
smeltery
smithery
smoothly
smothery
smudgily
smuttily
snappily
snazzily
sneakily
sniffily
snippety
snobbery
snootily
snuggery
soakaway
sobriety
sobstory
sociably
socially
sodality
soldiery
solemnly
solidary
solidify
solidity
solitary
solvency
sombrely
somebody
sonobuoy
sonority
soothsay
sordidly
sorority
sovranty
sparbuoy
sparsely
sparsity
speedily
speedway
spermary
spillway
spirally
spivvery
splotchy
spongily
spookily

spoonily
sportily
spottily
sprucely
spunkily
squarely
squelchy
squiggly
squirely
stairway
stanchly
stannary
starrily
statedly
statuary
steadily
stealthy
steamily
stellify
sternway
stickily
stingily
stingray
stockily
stodgily
stolidly
stomachy
stonefly
stormily
stowaway
straggly
straitly
strategy
stratify
stretchy
strictly
strongly
stuffily
stultify
stumpily
stupidly
sturdily
subtlety
sudatory
suddenly
suitably
sullenly
sultrily
summerly
summitry
sunshiny
superbly
supinely
supplely
swannery
symmetry
sympathy
symphony
synastry
synonymy
takeaway
takingly
tangency
tangibly
tanistry
tapestry
tasselly
tawdrily
taxingly
taxonomy
teacaddy
teaparty
tearaway
telegony
temerity
tenacity
tenantry
tendency
tenderly
tenotomy
tenpenny
tepidity
terribly
tertiary
tetchily
textuary
thearchy
theodicy
theogony
theology
thickety
thievery
thingamy
threeply
threeway
threnody
thuggery
thundery
Thursday
thwartly
timidity
timously
tinselly
tittuppy
tocology
toiletry
tokology
tomalley
tomnoddy
tonality
tonicity
toothily
topheavy
toplofty
topology
toponymy
torpidly
torridly
totality
touchily
touristy
towardly
toxicity
trackway
trashery
trashily
travesty
treasury
trendily
trevally
triarchy
tribally
trickery
trickily
trippery
triunity
trollopy
truantry
trumpery
trustily
tryingly
tumidity
tuppenny
turbidly
turgidly
tussocky
tutelary
twittery
twopenny
typology
ubiquity
ultimacy
unchancy
uncially
underlay
underway
uneasily
unevenly
unfairly
ungainly
uniquely
unitedly
unjustly
unkindly
unkingly
unlikely
unlovely
unmeetly
unseemly
unstably
unsteady
unstuffy
untidily
untimely
unwarily
unwieldy
unwisely
unwordly
unworthy
uppishly
upwardly
urbanely
urbanity
urgently
usefully
uvularly
vacantly
vagility
vagrancy
valiancy
validity
valuably
vapidity
variably
variedly
varletry
vavasory
velleity
velocity
venality
venially
venosity
venously
veracity
verbally
verdancy
vernally
vespiary
vestiary
vibrancy
vicinity
villainy
vinegary
vinosity
vinously
violably
viridity
virility
virology
viscidly
visually
vitality
vivacity
vocality
vomitory
voracity
vulgarly
walkaway
wantonly
wardenry
warranty
warweary
watchkey
waterway
waxberry
weaponry
weaselly
weevilly
welladay
wellaway
westerly
wheezily
Whiggery
whiskery
whispery
whiteboy
whitefly
wickedly
wilfully
winterly
wintrily
witchery
witchety
wizardly
wizardry
woefully
wontedly
woodenly
wordplay
workaday
worthily
woundily
wrathily
xenogamy
xylology
Yankeefy
yeastily
yellowly
yeomanly
yeomanry
zealotry
zinckify
zoolatry
zoomancy
zoometry
zoophily
zymology
pincenez
schmaltz

9 letter words

abandoned
abandonee
abandoner
abasement
abashment
abatement
abdicable
abdicator
abdominal
abduction
aberrance
aberrancy
abhorrent
abhorring
abidingly
abjection
ablatival
ablutions
abnegator
abnormity
abolisher
abolition
abominate
aborigine
abounding
aboutface
aboutturn
abradable
abrogator
abruption
abscissae
abscissas
absconder
abseiling
absorbent
absorbing
abstainer
abstinent
absurdism
absurdist
absurdity
abundance
abusively
abysmally
academism
acariasis
accentual
acceptant
acceptive
accessary
accession
accessory
accidence
accipiter
acclaimer
acclimate
acclivity
accompany
accordant
according
accordion
accretion
accretive
accusable
acellular
acescence
acetabula
acetamide
acetifier
acetylate
acetylcoA
acetylene
Acheulean
Acheulian
aciculate
acidifier
acidophil
acidulate
acidulent
acidulous
aciniform
aconitine
acoustics
acquiesce
acquittal
acquitted
acrobatic
acropetal
acropolis
acroteria
actinozoa
activator
actualise
actuality
actuarial
actuation
acuminate
adamantly
adaptable
addiction
addictive
addressee
addresser
addressor
adducible
adduction
adductive
ademption
adenoidal
adenomata
adenosine
adeptness
adherence
adiabatic
adipocere
adiposity
adjacency
adjoining
adjunctly
adjutancy
adlibbing
admeasure
adminicle
admirable
admirably
admiralty
admission
admissive
admitting
admixture
admonitor
adnominal
adoptable
adoration
adoringly
adornment
adrenalin
adsorbate
adsorbent
adulation
adulatory
adulterer
adulthood
adultness
adumbrate
advantage
advection
advective
Adventism
Adventist
adventive
adventure
adverbial
adversary
adversely
adversity
advertent
advertise
advisable
advisably
advisedly
advocator
aepyornis
aerialist
aeriality
aerobatic
aerobiont
aerodrome
aerograph
aerolitic
aerometer
aerometry
aerophyte
aeroplane
aerospace
aesthesia
aesthesis
aesthetic
aestivate
aetiology
affecting
affection
affective
affianced
affidavit
affiliate
affirmant
affixture
afflation
affluence
affricate
aflatoxin
aforesaid
Afrikaans
Afrikaner
aftercare
afterclap
afterglow
afterlife
aftermath
aftermost
afternoon
aftertime
afterword
agapemone
aggravate
aggregate
aggressor
aggrieved
agistment
agitation
agitative
agnatical
agonising
agonistic
agreeable
agreeably
agreement
agriology
agrologic
agronomic
ahistoric
ailanthus
aimlessly
aircooled
airjacket
airminded
airstream
airworthy
airyfairy
aitchbone
alabaster
albatross
albescent
albinotic
alchemise
alchemist
alcoholic
aldehydic
aleatoric
Alemannic
alertness
algarroba
algebraic
Algonkian
Algonquin
algorithm
alicyclic
alienable
alienator
alignment
alinement
aliphatic
aliveness
alkaloses
alkalosis
allantois
allegedly
allegiant
allegoric
allemande
alleviate
alligator
allocable
allograph
allomorph

allopathy
allophone
alloplasm
allotment
allotrope
allotropy
allotting
allowable
allowably
allowance
allowedly
almandine
almsgiver
almshouse
aloneness
alongside
aloofness
alpargata
alpenhorn
alterable
altercate
alternant
alternate
altimeter
altricial
aluminate
aluminise
aluminium
aluminous
alveolate
amaryllis
amassment
amauroses
amaurosis
amaurotic
amazement
amazingly
amazonian
ambergris
ambiguity
ambiguous
ambitious
amblyopia
amblyopic
ambrosial
ambulacra
ambulance
ambuscade
amendable
amendment
americium
Amerindic
amianthus
amidships
aminoacid
amoebaean
amoralism
amorality
amorously
amorphism
amorphous
amourette
ampersand
amphibian
amphibole
amphigory
amphioxus
ampleness
amplifier
amplitude
amputator
amusement
amusingly
amygdalin
amyloidal
amylopsin
anabioses
anabiosis
anabiotic
anabolism
anabranch
anacruses
anacrusis
anaerobic
analeptic
analgesia
analgesic
analogise
analogist
analogous
analysand
anamnesis
anandrous
anaphoric
anaptyxis
anarchism
anarchist
anatomise
anatomist
ancestral
anchorage
anchoress
anchorite
anchorman
anchylose
anciently
ancientry
ancillary
andantino
andesitic
androecia
androgyne
androgyny
anecdotal
anecdotic
anemogram
angelfish
angelical
angiology
angiomata
angleiron
anglesite
angleworm
anglicise
anglicism
Anglicist
anglophil
angriness
anguished
angularly
anhydride
anhydrite
anhydrous
animalise
animalism
animalist
animality
animation
animatism
animistic
animosity
anklebone
ankylosis
ankylotic
annectent
annelidan
annotator
announcer
annoyance
annuitant
annularly
annulated
annulling
annulment
anomalous
anomalure
anonymity
anonymous
anopheles
anorectic
anorthite
anovulant
anoxaemia
anschluss
antarctic
antefixal
antenatal
antennary
antennule
anthelion
anthemion
anthocyan
anthology
anthozoan
anthracic
anthropic
anticline
anticodon
antidotal
antigenic
antiknock
antimonic
antinodal
antinomic
antinovel
antipasto
antipathy
antiphony
antipodal
antipodes
antiquary
antiquate
antiquity
antiserum
antitoxic
antitoxin
antitrade
antitrust
antivenin
antiviral
anxiously
apartheid
apartment
apartness
apathetic
aperiodic
aperitive
apetalous
aphereses
apheresis
aphyllous
apiculate
apishness
aplanatic
apocrypha
apodictic
apogamous
apologise
apologist
apomictic
apophyses
apophysis
apostolic
apothecia
appalling
Appaloosa
apparatus
apparitor
appealing
appellant
appellate
appendage
appendant
appertain
appetence
appetency
appetiser
applauder
applejack
appliance
applicant
appointee
apportion
appraisal
appraiser
apprehend
appressed
approbate
aquaplane
aquarelle
aqueously
aquilegia
arabesque
arabicise
arachnoid
aragonite
araneidal
araneidan
araucaria
arbitrage
arbitrary
arbitrate
arbitress
arboreous
arboretum
archangel
archducal
archduchy
archenemy
archetype
archfiend
architect
archivist
archivolt
arcuately
arduously
Areopagus
argentine
argentite
argentous
argillite
argumenta
Arguseyed
argybargy
armadillo
armigeral
armillary
armistice
Armorican
aromatise
arrearage
arrestant
arresting
arriviste
arrogance
arrowhead
arrowroot
arrowwood
arrowworm
arsenical
arsenious
artemisia
arteriole
arteritis
arthritic
arthritis
arthropod
arthrosis
Arthurian
artichoke
articular
artificer
artillery
artlessly
arytenoid
asafetida
asbestine
asbestous
ascendant
ascendent
ascension
ascensive
ascertain
ascetical
asclepiad
ascospore
asepalous
asexually
ashamedly
Ashkenazi
ashlaring
asininity
askewness
asparagus
aspartate
aspectual
aspersion
asphaltic
asphaltum
aspirator
assailant
assaulter
assayable
assembler
assertion
assertive
assiduity
assiduous
assistant
associate
assonance
assuasive
assumable
assumably
assumpsit
assurance
assuredly
assurgent
asthmatic
astraddle
astrakhan
astrocyte
astrodome
astrolabe
astrology
astronaut
astronomy
asymmetry
asymptote
asyndetic
asyndeton
atacamite
ataractic
atavistic
atheistic
athematic
Athenaeum
athletics
Atlantean
atmometer
atomicity
atomistic
atonalism
atonality
atonement
atonicity
atrocious
attainder
attempter
attendant
attention
attentive
attenuate
attractor
attribute
attrition
aubergine
aubrietia
auctorial
audacious
audiology
auditable
auditoria
augmented
augmenter
augmentor
auricular
auspicate
austenite
austerely
austerity
autarchic
autarkist
authentic
authoress
authorial
authorise
authority
autoclave
autocracy
autocross
autocycle
autograft
autograph
autolysis
autolytic
automatic
automaton
autonomic
autopilot
autoroute
autosomal
autotelic
autotroph
auxiliary
available
availably
avalanche
aventaile
averagely
avertible
avizandum
avocation
avoidable
avoidably
avoidance
avuncular
awakening
awardable
awareness
awesomely
awestruck
awfulness
awkwardly
axiomatic
Axminster
Aylesbury
azeotrope
azimuthal
babacoote
Babbittry
babirussa
baboonish
bacchanal
bacchante
bacillary
backbiter
backboard
backcloth
backcross
backpedal
backsight
backslang
backslide
backspace
backstage
backsword
backtrack
backwards
backwater
backwoods
bacterial
bacterise
bacterium
bacteroid
badminton
bagatelle
bagginess
bailiwick
bainmarie
bakehouse
baksheesh
balaclava
balalaika
balconied
baldachin
baldaquin
baldfaced
balefully
balkanise
balladeer
balladist
ballerina
ballistae
ballistic
ballpoint
balminess
baltimore
bamboozle
banderole
bandicoot
bandoleer
bandolero
bandolier
bandoline
bandstand
bandwagon
bandwidth
baneberry
banefully
banjulele
bannister
banqueter
banquette
Bantustan
baptismal
baptistry
barathrum
Barbadian
barbarian
barbarise
barbarism
barbarity
barbarous
barbitone
barcarole
barefaced
bargainer
bargepole
barkeeper
barleymow
barmbrack
Barmecide
barnacled
barnstorm
barograph
barometer
barometry
baronetcy
barracker
barracoon
barracuda
barrelful

barrelled
barricade
barricado
barrister
bartender
bashfully
basically
basilican
basipetal
basketful
basrelief
bastardly
bastinade
bastinado
bastioned
bathhouse
batholite
batholith
Bathonian
bathybius
battalion
battening
battiness
battleaxe
battlecry
bawdiness
bayoneted
beachhead
beachwear
beadledom
beamingly
beanfeast
beanstalk
bearberry
beardless
beastings
beatitude
beauteous
beautiful
beccafico
bedfellow
bedjacket
bedlamite
bedraggle
bedridden
bedsettee
bedsitter
bedspread
bedspring
beechfern
beechmast
beefeater
beefiness
beefsteak
beekeeper
beemaster
beeorchis
beestings
befitting
befogging
begetting
beginning
behaviour
bejabbers
belatedly
beleaguer
belemnite
bellglass
bellicose
bellpunch
bellyache
bellyband
bellyflop
belvedere
bemusedly
beneficed
bengaline
benighted
benignant
benignity
bentonite
benzidine
benzoline
berberine
bergamask
berkelium
berserker
beryllium
besetment
besetting
beslobber
besotting
bespangle
bespatter
bestially
bestirred
bethought
betrothal
betrothed
bevelling
biblicism
biblicist
bicameral
bicipital
biconcave
bicyclist
bifarious
bifoliate
bifurcate
bigeneric
bigheaded
bilabiate
bilateral
bilgekeel
bilharzia
bilingual
biliously
bilirubin
biliteral
billabong
billboard
billiards
billionth
billycock
billygoat
bimonthly
binocular
binominal
binturong
biogenous
biography
biologist
biometric
bionomics
biorhythm
biosphere
bipartite
bipinnate
birchbark
birdbrain
birdsfoot
birdsnest
birdtable
birdwatch
birthmark
birthrate
birthwort
bisection
bishopric
bismillah
bitterish
bivalence
bivalency
bivariant
bivariate
bizarrely
blackball
blackbird
blackbuck
blackcoat
blackcock
blackdamp
blackface
Blackfeet
blackfish
blackflag
Blackfoot
blackgame
blackhead
blackjack
blacklead
blacklist
blackmail
blackness
blackwash
blaeberry
blameable
blameably
blameless
blandness
blankness
blaspheme
blasphemy
blasthole
blastment
blastulae
blastular
blatantly
blazingly
bleachery
bleakness
bleareyed
blessedly
blindfold
blindness
blinkered
blockader
blockhead
blockship
bloodbath
bloodless
bloodlust
bloodroot
bloodshed
bloodshot
bloodworm
bloodwort
blotchily
blowtorch
bluebeard
blueberry
blueblack
bluegrass
bluepoint
blueprint
bluestone
bluffness
blunderer
bluntness
blushless
blusterer
Boanerges
boardfoot
boardroom
boardwalk
boathouse
boatswain
boattrain
bobsleigh
bobtailed
bodyguard
boldfaced
bolection
boliviano
bolometer
bolometry
Bolshevik
bombardon
bombasine
bombastic
bombazine
bombhappy
bombilate
bombinate
bombproof
bombshell
bombsight
bondslave
bondstone
bondwoman
bonechina
bonhomous
bonniness
boobytrap
bookishly
booklouse
bookmaker
bookplate
bookshelf
bookstall
bookstand
bookstore
boomerang
boomslang
boondocks
boorishly
bootblack
bordereau
borrowing
boskiness
bossiness
botanical
bottlefed
bottleful
boulevard
boundless
bounteous
bountiful
bouquetin
bourgeois
bowerbird
bowlegged
bowstring
bowwindow
boxgirder
boxoffice
boycotter
boyfriend
brachiate
brachyura
bracteate
bracteole
Brahmanic
Brahminee
Brahminic
braincase
brainless
brainwash
brainwave
brakeless
brakeshoe
brakesman
brambling
branchiae
branchial
branchlet
brandling
brandreth
brashness
brasserie
brassiere
bratwurst
brazilnut
breadline
breadtree
breakable
breakaway
breakdown
breakeven
breakfast
breakneck
breastpin
breathily
breathing
brecciate
breeching
breezeway
bregmatic
bretasche
Bretwalda
breveting
brevetted
briarroot
briarwood
bricabrac
brickwork
brickyard
bridecake
bridesman
bridewell
bridleway
briefcase
briefless
briefness
brierroot
brierwood
brigadier
brigandry
brightish
brilliant
brimstone
bringdown
briquette
briskness
bristling
Britannia
Britannic
Briticise
Briticism
Britisher
brittlely
broadcast
broadleaf
broadloom
broadness
broadside
broadtail
broadways
broadwise
brochette
broiderer
brokerage
bromeliad
bronchial
broomcorn
broomrape
brotherly
brownness
brummagem
brushfire
brushwood
brushwork
brusquely
brutalise
brutalism
brutality
brutishly
bryophyte
Brythonic
buccaneer
buckboard
bucketful
buckhound
buckshish
buckthorn
bucktooth
buckwheat
budgetary
buffaloes
buffeting
bughunter
buhrstone
bulbously
Bulgarian
bulginess
bulkiness
bulldozer
bullfight
bullfinch
bullishly
bulltrout
bullybeef
bullytree
bumblebee
bumbledon
bumpiness
bumptious
bundobust
bunkhouse
buoyantly
burdenous
burlesque
burliness
burnedout
burningly
burnisher
burrstone
bursarial
bushcraft
bushelful
bushiness
bushwhack
butadiene
butcherer
butcherly
butterbur
buttercup
butterfat
butterfly
butterine
butternut
buttinsky
buttygang
buxomness
byproduct
bystander
Byzantine
caballero
caballine
caballing
cabbalism
cabbalist
cablegram
cablelaid
cabriolet
cachectic
cacholong
caciquism
cacodemon
cacodylic
cacoethes
cacophony
cacuminal
cadastral
cadaveric
caddisfly
cadential
cadetship
caecilian
Caenozoic
caerulean
Caesarean
Caesarian
Caesarism
Caesarist
cafeteria
cageyness
cailleach
Cainozoic
cairngorm
calaboose
calabrese
calamanco
calandria
calcaneal
calcaneum
calcarate
calcicole
calcifuge
calculate
calculous
caldarium
calendric
calendula
calenture
calibrate
calicular
caliology
caliphate
callipers
callosity
callously
calmative
calorific
Calvinism
Calvinist
calycinal
camarilla
Cambodian
camelback
camelhair
Camembert
cameraman
camorrist
campanile
campanili
campanula
campchair
campcraft
campfever
camphoric
campstool
canalboat
cancelled
cancerous
candidacy
candidate
Candlemas
candlenut
candytuft
canebrake
canescent
canesugar
canetrash
canicular
cankerous
cannelure
canniness
cannonade
cannoneer
cannonier
cannulate
canonical
cantabile
cantaloup
cantharid
cantharis
cantharus
cantilena
Cantonese
cantorial
canvasser
capacious

capacitor
caparison
capillary
capitally
capitular
capitulum
capriccio
Capricorn
capsulate
capsulise
captaincy
captivate
captivity
carambola
carbamate
carbamide
carbonado
carbonate
carbonise
carbuncle
carburise
carcinoma
cardboard
cardsharp
careerism
careerist
carefully
caretaker
carfuffle
Caribbean
Carmelite
carnality
carnation
carnelian
carnitine
carnivore
carolling
carpenter
carpentry
carpetbag
carpeting
carpingly
carpology
carrageen
carrefour
carronade
carryover
Cartesian
carthorse
cartilage
cartogram
cartology
cartouche
cartridge
cartulary
cartwheel
caryopses
caryopsis
caseation
Cassandra
cassareep
cassaripe
cassation
casserole
cassimere
cassoulet
cassowary
Castalian
castanets
castellan
castigate
Castilian
Castroism
casuarina
casuistic
casuistry
catabolic
cataclasm
cataclysm
catalepsy
catalexes
catalexis
catalogue
catalyser
catalyses
catalysis
catalytic
catamaran
catamount
cataplasm
cataplexy
catarhine
catarrhal
catatonia
catatonic
catchable
catchment
catchpole
catchpoll
catchword
catechise
catechism
catechist
caterwaul
Catharism
Catharist
catharses
catharsis
cathartic
cathectic
cathedral
catoptric
cattaloes
cattiness
cattleman
Caucasian
causality
causation
causative
causeless
cauterise
cavalcade
cavendish
cavernous
cavilling
ceanothus
ceasefire
ceaseless
cedarwood
celandine
celebrant
celebrate
celebrity
celestial
cellarage
celluloid
cellulose
Celticism
cementite
censorial
centenary
centering
centigram
centipede
centrally
centreing
centurion
cephalous
cerastium
ceratodus
cerebella
cerebrate
cerecloth
cerograph
certainly
certainty
certified
certifier
certitude
cerussite
cessation
cetaceous
chachacha
chaetopod
chafferer
chaffinch
chaingang
chaingear
chainless
chainmail
chairlady
challenge
chameleon
chamomile
champagne
champaign
champerty
champleve
chanceful
chancroid
chancrous
chandlery
changeful
chanteuse
chantilly
chantress
chaparral
chaperone
chapleted
charabanc
character
chariness
charivari
charlatan
charlotte
charmeuse
charmless
Charolais
chartered
charterer
charwoman
chassepot
chastener
chastiser
chatelain
chatoyant
chatterer
chauffeur
cheapjack
cheapness
checkered
checklist
checkmate
checkrein
cheekbone
cheerless
chelation
chelicera
chelonian
chemistry
chemitype
chemurgic
cheongsam
chequered
cherimoya
chernozem
cherrypie
chevalier
chevelure
chibouque
chicanery
chickadee
chickaree
chickling
chickweed
chiefship
chieftain
chihuahua
chilblain
childhood
childless
childlike
chillness
chimaeric
Chinatown
chinaware
chinstrap
chipboard
chipolata
chiropody
chiselled
chiseller
chisquare
chitinous
chitlings
chivalric
chlamydes
chlorella
chloritic
chlorosis
chlorotic
chockfull
chocolate
chokedamp
choleraic
chondrite
chondrule
chophouse
choplogic
chopstick
chorister
chorology
Christian
Christmas
chromatic
chromatin
chronical
chronicle
chrysalid
chrysalis
chthonian
churching
churchman
cicatrice
cicatrise
cigarette
cigarillo
Cimmerian
cinematic
cineraria
cinereous
Cingalese
cipollino
circadian
circinate
circuitry
circulate
cirrhosis
cirripede
cisalpine
citizenly
citizenry
citystate
civically
civiliser
claimable
clamantly
clamorous
clamshell
clapboard
clarifier
clarionet
classable
classical
classless
classlist
classmate
classroom
clathrate
clatterer
claustral
clavation
claviform
cleanness
cleansing
clearance
clearcole
cleareyed
clearness
cleavable
clemently
clepsydra
clergyman
clergymen
clerkship
clientage
clientele
cliffhang
climactic
climbable
clinician
clinquant
clipboard
clitellum
cloakroom
clockwise
clockwork
cloisonne
cloistral
closedown
closeness
cloudland
cloudless
clubbable
clubhouse
coachwork
coadjutor
coadunate
coagulant
coagulate
coalfield
coalition
coalmouse
coarctate
coastline
coastward
coastwise
coattails
coaxially
coaxingly
cobaltite
cobaltous
Cobdenism
cobwebbed
cocainise
cocainism
coccidium
coccygeal
cochineal
cochleate
cockahoop
Cockaigne
cockatiel
cockfight
cockhorse
cockiness
cockneyfy
cockroach
cockscomb
cocksfoot
cocoonery
coecilian
coelomata
coelomate
coelostat
coemption
coenobite
coenobium
coenosarc
coequally
coercible
coercibly
coeternal
coffeecup
coffeepot
cofferdam
coffinite
cogitable
cognately
cognation
cognisant
cognition
cognitive
coheiress
coherence
coherency
coiffeuse
coinsurer
colcannon
colchicum
colcothar
coldshort
colemouse
collagist
collation
colleague
collected
collector
collegial
collegian
collegium
colligate
collimate
collinear
collision
collocate
collodion
colloidal
colloquia
collotype
collusion
collusive
collyrium
colocynth
colonelcy
coloniser
colonnade
colophony
colorific
colosseum
colostomy
colostrum
colourful
colouring
colourist
colourman
coltishly
coltsfoot
colubrine
columbary
Columbian
columbine
columbite
columbium
columella
columnist
combatant
combative
combinate
comedones
comfiture
comforter
comically
Cominform
Comintern
comitadji
commander
commandos
commendam
commensal
commenter
commingle
comminute
commissar
committal
committed
committee
commodity
commodore
commonage
commonlaw
commotion
communard
communion
communise
communism
communist
community
commutate
compactly
compactor
companion
compasses
compelled
compendia
competent
complaint
complexly
complexus
compliant
component
composite
composure
comprador
comprisal
comptroll
comradely
comradery
concavely
concavity
conceited
concentre
concerned
concerted
concierge
conciliar
concisely
concision
concocter
concoctor
concordat
concourse
concubine
concurred
condenser
condignly
condiment
condition
conducive
conductor
condyloid
condyloma
confabbed
conferral
conferred
conferrer
confervae
confessor
confidant
confident
confiding
configure
confirmed

confirmer
confirmor
confiteor
confluent
conformal
conformer
Confucian
confusion
congenial
congeries
congruent
congruity
congruous
conically
conjugate
connately
connation
connature
connected
connecter
connector
connexion
connivent
connubial
conqueror
conscious
conscribe
conscript
consensus
conserver
consignee
consignor
consonant
consortia
constable
constancy
constrain
constrict
construct
consulage
consulate
consulter
consultor
contactor
contadina
contadino
contagion
contagium
container
contemner
contender
contented
continent
continual
continuer
continuum
contralto
contrasty
contrived
contriver
contumacy
contumely
contusion
conundrum
convector
converter
convexity
convincer
convivial
convolute
convolved
cookhouse
cooperage
cooperant
cooperate
copacetic
copartner
copesmate
copestone
copiously
copolymer
coproduce
coprolite
coprology
copsewood
copyright
coralline
corallite
coralloid
corbeille
corbelled
corbicula
cordelier
cordially
cordiform
corduroys
coreopsis
coriander
corkscrew
cormorant
cornbrash
corncrake
cornelian
cornemuse
cornerboy
cornerman
cornetist
cornfield
cornflour
cornopean
cornsalad
cornstalk
cornstone
corollary
coroneted
corporate
corporeal
corposant
corpulent
corpuscle
corralled
corrasion
correctly
corrector
correlate
corrosion
corrosive
corrugate
corrupter
corruptly
corticate
corticoid
cortisone
coruscant
coruscate
Corybants
corydalis
corymbose
coryphaei
coseismal
coseismic
cosmogeny
cosmogony
cosmology
cosmonaut
cosmorama
costively
costumier
cotangent
cothurnus
cotillion
cotyledon
couchette
coumarone
countable
countdown
countless
countship
courgette
courtcard
courteous
courtesan
courtroom
courtship
courtyard
couturier
covalence
covalency
covariant
coverable
coverslip
coverture
covetable
cowardice
cowlstaff
coxcombry
crabbedly
crackdown
crackling
cracksman
craftsman
crampfish
cranberry
crankcase
cranreuch
crapulent
crapulous
crashdive
crashland
crassness
craziness
creatable
creatress
creatural
crediting
credulity
credulous
cremaster
cremation
crematory
crenation
crenature
crenelled
crenulate
crepitant
crepitate
crepuscle
crescendo
crestless
cretinism
cretinous
cricketer
criminate
criminous
crinoidal
crinoline
crippling
crispness
criterion
criticise
criticism
crocodile
croissant
CroMagnon
crookback
crookedly
crookneck
cropeared
croquette
crossable
crossbeam
crossbill
crossbred
crossette
crosseyed
crossfade
crossfire
crossfish
crosshead
crosslink
crossness
crossover
crossroad
crossruff
crosstalk
crossways
crosswind
crosswise
crossword
crotchety
croustade
crowberry
crownless
crowsfoot
crowsnest
crucially
cruciform
crudeness
cruellest
crushable
crustacea
cryogenic
cryoscope
cryoscopy
cryptical
cryptogam
cryptonym
cubbyhole
cubically
cuckoldry
cucullate
cudgelled
cullender
culminant
culminate
culsdesac
cultivate
cumbrance
cunctator
cuneiform
cunningly
cupbearer
cupelling
cuplichen
curbstone
curettage
curialism
curiosity
curiously
curliness
curlpaper
currently
curricula
currishly
currycomb
cursively
cursorial
cursorily
curstness
curtilage
curvature
curveting
curvetted
curviform
cuspidate
custodial
custodian
customary
customise
cutaneous
cuticular
cutinised
cutthroat
cuttysark
cyanamide
cyclamate
cycloidal
cyclopean
cyclopian
cyclopses
cyclorama
cyclotron
cylindric
cymbalist
cymbidium
cymbiform
cymophane
cynically
cyprinoid
cystocarp
cystolith
cystotomy
Cytherean
cytolysis
cytoplasm
cytotoxic
cytotoxin
czarevich
dachshund
Daedalean
Daedalian
dahabiyah
dairymaid
dalliance
dalmatian
daltonism
damascene
damnation
damnatory
damnedest
damningly
Damoclean
dancehall
dandelion
dandiacal
dangerous
Dantesque
daredevil
dartboard
Darwinian
Darwinism
Darwinist
dashboard
dashingly
dastardly
dauntless
davenport
dayschool
dayspring
deacidify
deaconess
deadalive
deadlight
deathblow
deathless
deathlike
deathmask
deathroll
debagging
debarment
debarring
debatable
debauched
debauchee
debaucher
debenture
debugging
debutante
decadence
decadency
decagonal
decalcify
decalitre
decalogue
decametre
decapodal
decapodan
decastere
decathlon
deceitful
decennary
decennial
decennium
deception
deceptive
decidable
decidedly
deciduate
deciduous
decilitre
decillion
decimally
decimator
decimetre
decistere
deckhouse
declaimer
declarant
declinate
declivity
declivous
decoction
decollate
decollete
decomplex
decompose
decongest
decontrol
decorator
decrement
decretive
decretory
decumbent
decussate
dedicator
deducible
deduction
deductive
deerberry
deerhound
defalcate
defaulter
defeatism
defeatist
defeature
defection
defective
defendant
defensive
deference
deferment
deferring
defiantly
deficient
definable
definably
deflation
deflector
deflexion
defoliant
defoliate
deformity
defroster
dehiscent
dehydrate
deinosaur
deistical
dejection
delftware
delicious
delineate
delirious
deliverer
deludable
demagogic
demagogue
demandant
demanding
demarcate
demeanour
demimonde
demission
demitasse
demitting
demiurgic
demobbing
democracy
demulcent
demurrage
demurring
demystify
dendritic
denigrate
denitrate
denitrify
denouncer
denseness
dentalium
dentation
dentiform
dentistry
dentition
denyingly
deodorant
deodorise
deoxidise
departure
depasture
dependant
dependent
depiction
depictive
depletion
depletive
deposable
depositor
depravity
deprecate
depredate
depressed
depressor
depthbomb
depthless
depurator
derivable
dermatoid
derringdo
derringer
descended
describer
desecrate
desertion
desiccant
desiccate
designate
designing
desirable
desirably
desolater
desolator
desperado
desperate
despoiler
despotism
destitute
destroyer
desuetude
desultory
detection
detective
detention
detergent
determent

determine
deterrent
deterring
detersion
detersive
dethroner
detonator
detractor
detriment
detrition
detrusion
deuterate
deuterium
devaluate
devastate
developer
deviation
devilfish
devilling
devilment
deviously
devisable
devitrify
devotedly
dewlapped
dexterity
dexterous
dextrally
dextrorse
dharmsala
diablerie
diabolise
diabolism
diabolist
diachrony
diachylom
diachylum
diaconate
diacritic
diactinic
diaereses
diaeresis
diagnoses
diagnosis
dialectal
dialectic
dialogise
dialogism
dialogist
diametral
diametric
diandrous
diaphragm
diaphysis
diarrhoea
diastasis
diastatic
diastolic
diathermy
diathesis
diathetic
diatomite
diatropic
dichasial
dichasium
dichogamy
dichotomy
dichroism
dichromat
dichromic
dickybird
diclinous
dicrotism
dictation
didactics
didelphic
didrachma
dieselise
diesinker
dietetics
dietician
dietitian
different
difficile
difficult
diffident
diffusely
diffusion
diffusive
digastric
digestion
digestive
digitalin
digitalis
digitally
digitated
dignified
dignitary
dilatable
dilatancy
diligence
dimension
dimidiate
dimissory
dimorphic
dimwitted
dinginess
diningcar
dinnerset
dinoceras
dinothere
dioecious
Dionysiac
Dionysian
dipcircle
dipeptide
diphthong
diplomacy
diplomate
dipswitch
dipterous
direction
directive
directory
directrix
direfully
dirigible
dirigisme
dirtiness
dirttrack
disaccord
disaffect
disaffirm
disannual
disappear
disarming
disavouch
disavowal
disbarred
disbelief
disbranch
disbudded
disburden
disbursal
discalced
discarder
discerner
discharge
discoidal
discolour
discomfit
discommon
discourse
discovert
discovery
discredit
disembark
disembody
disengage
disentail
disentomb
disesteem
disfavour
disfigure
disforest
disgracer
dishcloth
dishclout
dishfaced
dishonest
dishonour
dishwater
disinfect
disinfest
dislocate
dismantle
dismember
dismissal
disoblige
disorient
disparage
disparate
disparity
dispelled
dispenser
dispeople
dispersal
disperser
displease
disposure
dispraise
disputant
disregard
disrelish
disrepair
disrepute
dissector
disseisin
dissemble
dissenter
dissident
dissipate
dissocial
dissolute
dissonant
dissuader
distantly
distemper
distilled
distiller
distraint
disturbed
disturber
dithyramb
dittander
dittology
diurnally
divergent
diversely
diversify
diversion
diversity
diverting
dividable
divisible
divulsion
dixieland
dizygotic
dizziness
doctorate
doctorial
doctrinal
dodecagon
dogcollar
doggishly
doglegged
dogmatics
dogmatise
dogmatism
dogmatist
dogoodism
dogshores
dogstooth
dogviolet
dolefully
doleritic
dolomitic
doltishly
dominance
dominator
dominical
Dominican
donnishly
donothing
doodlebug
doorframe
doorplate
dopefiend
dorbeetle
dormition
dormitory
dosimeter
dosimetry
dosshouse
dottiness
doubleton
doubtable
doubtless
doughtily
Doukhobor
dowdiness
dowelling
dowerless
downfield
downgrade
downright
downriver
downstage
downthrow
downwards
draconian
draftsman
draghound
dragomans
dragoness
dragonfly
dragonish
drainpipe
dramatics
dramatise
dramatist
Dravidian
drawerful
drawnwork
drawplate
drawsheet
drayhorse
dreamboat
dreamland
dreamless
dreamlike
dresscoat
driftsail
driftweed
driftwood
drinkable
dripstone
drivelled
driveller
drollness
dromedary
dropscene
dropscone
dropsical
drugstore
druidical
drummajor
drumstick
drunkenly
dryasdust
drysalter
dualistic
dubiosity
dubiously
dubitable
duckboard
ductility
dulcamara
dulcitude
dumbfound
dumpiness
dungarees
duodecimo
duodenary
duplicate
duplicity
duralumin
duskiness
dustcover
dustiness
dustsheet
duteously
dutifully
dynamical
dynamiter
dyscrasia
dysentery
dysgenics
dyspepsia
dyspeptic
dysphagia
dysphagic
dysphonia
dysphoria
dysphoric
dysplasia
dyspnoeic
dystrophy
dziggetai
eagerness
ealdorman
earliness
earnestly
earthborn
earthling
earthstar
earthward
earthwork
earthworm
earwigged
easefully
eastbound
Eastender
easterner
eastwards
easygoing
eavesdrop
ebullient
eccentric
ecclesial
ecdysiast
echolalia
echovirus
eclampsia
eclamptic
ecologist
economics
economise
economist
ecosphere
ecossaise
ecosystem
ecritoire
ecstasise
ectoblast
ectogenic
ectomorph
ectophyte
ectoplasm
ecumenism
edelweiss
edibility
editorial
education
educative
Edwardian
effective
effectual
efficient
effluence
effluvial
effluvium
effluxion
effortful
effulgent
eggbeater
eglantine
egomaniac
egotistic
egregious
egression
eiderdown
eiderduck
eidograph
eightfold
eightieth
eightsome
eightyish
eirenicon
ejaculate
ejectment
elaborate
elastomer
elbowroom
eldership
electoral
electress
electrify
electrode
electuary
elegantly
elegiacal
elemental
elevation
elevenses
eliminate
ellipsoid
elocution
elongated
elopement
eloquence
elsewhere
elucidate
elusively
elutriate
emaciated
emanation
emanative
embarrass
embassage
embattled
embayment
embedding
embedment
embellish
embezzler
embraceor
embracery
embracive
embrangle
embrasure
embrittle
embrocate
embroglio
embroider
embryonal
embryonic
embryotic
embussing
emendable
emendator
emergence
emergency
eminently
Emmenthal
emolliate
emollient
emolument
emotional
emotively
emotivity
empathise
empennage
emphasise
emphysema
empirical
emplastic
emptiness
empyreuma
emulation
emulative
emulously
emunctory
enactment
enamelled
enameller
enamoured
encaustic
encephala
enchanter
enchilada
enchorial
enclosure
encomiast
encompass
encounter
encourage
encrimson
encrinite
endearing
endeavour
endlessly
endoblast
endocrine
endogamic
endogenic
endolymph
endomixis
endomorph
endophagy
endophyte
endoplasm
endoscope
endoscopy
endosperm
endospore
endosteal
endosteum
endowment
endurable
endurably
endurance
energetic
energiser
energumen
engarland
Englander
englutted
engraving
engrosser
enhearten
enigmatic
enjoyable

enjoyably
enjoyment
enlighten
enrapture
enrolling
enrolment
ensheathe
entelechy
enterable
enteritis
entertain
enthymeme
entoblast
entophyte
entourage
entrammel
entrapped
entrechat
entrecote
entremets
enucleate
enumerate
enunciate
enviously
enwrapped
enwreathe
enzymatic
epaenetic
epaulette
ephedrine
ephemeral
ephemerid
ephemeris
ephemeron
epicentre
epiclesis
epicurean
epicurism
epicyclic
epidermal
epidermic
epidermis
epidosite
epigraphy
epigynous
epilation
epileptic
epilogist
epinastic
epiphragm
epiphyses
epiphysis
epiphytal
epiphytic
epipolism
episcopal
epistaxis
epistemic
epistoler
epistolic
epithelia
epithesis
epithetic
epitomise
epitomist
epizootic
eponymous
equaliser
equalling
equipment
equipoise
equipping
equisetum
equitable
equitably
equivocal
equivoque
eradicate
erectness
eremitism
ergograph
ergometer
ergonomic
eristical
erogenous
eroticism
erratical
erroneous
errorless
erstwhile
eruciform
eruditely
erudition
erythrism
erythrite
escalator
escapable
escheator
escortage
esemplasy
esoterica
esoterism
esperance
Esperanto
espionage
esplanade
espousals
Esquimaux
essential
establish
estaminet
Esthonian
estimable
estimator
estoppage
estopping
estranger
estrapade
estuarian
estuarine
esurience
esuriency
eternally
etherical
ethically
Ethiopian
ethmoidal
ethnarchy
ethnicity
ethnology
ethylenic
etiquette
etymology
eucalypti
eucaryote
Eucharist
euchology
euclidean
eulogiser
eunuchism
eunuchoid
euphemise
euphemism
euphonise
euphonium
euphorbia
eurhythmy
eutectoid
euthenics
eutherian
eutrophic
evaginate
evangelic
evaporate
evasively
eventless
eventuate
everglade
evergreen
everybody
evidently
evincible
evocation
evocative
evocatory
evolution
evolutive
evolvable
ewenecked
exactable
exactment
exactness
examinant
exanimate
exanthema
exarchate
excavator
exceeding
excellent
excelling
excelsior
excentric
exceptant
excepting
exception
exceptive
excerptor
excessive
exchanger
exchequer
excipient
excisable
exciseman
excitable
excitancy
excitedly
exclosure
exclusion
exclusive
excoriate
excrement
excretion
excretive
excretory
exculpate
excurrent
excursion
excursive
excusable
excusably
execrable
execrably
executant
execution
executive
executory
executrix
exegetist
exemplary
exemplify
exemption
exequatur
exercises
exfoliate
exhauster
exhibitor
exilement
existence
exodermis
exogamous
exogenous
exonerate
exopodite
exorciser
exosmosis
exosmotic
exosphere
exostosis
exoticism
expansile
expansion
expansive
expatiate
expectant
expecting
expedient
expediter
expellent
expelling
expensive
expertise
expiation
expiatory
explainer
expletive
expletory
explicate
exploiter
explosion
explosive
expositor
expounder
expressly
expulsion
expulsive
expurgate
exquisite
exsertile
exsertion
exservice
exsiccate
exsuccous
extempore
extendant
extensile
extension
extensity
extensive
extenuate
externals
extirpate
extolling
extolment
extorsive
extortion
extortive
extractor
extradite
extravert
extremely
extremism
extremist
extremity
extricate
extrinsic
extrovert
extrusion
extrusive
exuberant
exuberate
exudation
exudative
exultance
exultancy
eyebright
eyeglance
eyeopener
eyeshadow
eyestrain
fabaceous
Fabianism
fabricant
fabricate
facecloth
facetious
facsimile
factional
factitive
factorage
factorial
factorise
factually
facundity
faddiness
faggoting
faintness
fairfaced
fairyhood
fairyland
fairylike
fairyring
fairytale
faithcure
faithless
Falangism
Falangist
falciform
faldstool
Falernian
fallalery
falsehood
falseness
falsifier
familyman
fanatical
fancyfree
fancywork
fandangle
fandangos
fanfarade
fantasied
fantasise
fantasist
fantastic
fantastry
farandole
farestage
farmhouse
farmstead
farseeing
fasciated
fascicled
fascicule
fasciculi
fascinate
Fascistic
fashioner
fastening
fastigium
fatefully
fatheaded
fatidical
fatigable
fattiness
fatuously
fatwitted
faultless
faunistic
faveolate
favourite
fawningly
fearfully
feathered
febricity
febrifuge
feculence
fecundate
fecundity
federally
feedstock
feedstuff
feelingly
feiseanna
felicific
fellowman
felonious
femineity
fenceless
fenestrae
fenestral
Fenianism
fenugreek
feoffment
ferocious
ferrotype
ferryboat
fertilely
fertilise
fertility
fervently
festinate
festively
festivity
festology
fetichism
fetichist
fetidness
fetishism
fetishist
feudalise
feudalism
feudalist
feudality
feudatory
fibreless
fibriform
fibrillar
fibrinoid
fibrinous
fibroline
fibromata
fictional
fideistic
fiduciary
fieldbook
fieldboot
fieldfare
fieldsman
fieldwork
fiendlike
fieriness
fifteenth
figurante
filaceous
filiation
filigreed
fillister
filminess
filmstrip
filoselle
filterbed
filtertip
filtrable
fimbriate
financial
financier
finedrawn
fingering
fingertip
finically
finicking
fioritura
fioriture
firealarm
fireblast
firebrand
firebreak
firebrick
firecrest
firedrake
firedrill
fireeater
fireguard
firehouse
fireirons
firelight
fireplace
firepower
fireproof
firestone
firewater
fireworks
firmament
firstborn
firstfoot
firsthand
firstling
firstrate
fisherman
fishiness
fishplate
fishslice
fishyback
fissility
fissipede
fistulous
fittingly
fivepence
fivepenny
fixedness
flabellum
flagellum
flageolet
flagrance
flagrancy
flagstaff
flagstick
flagstone
flakiness
flambeaus
flambeaux
flameless
flamingly
flamingos
flammable
flannelly
flarepath
flaringly
flashback
flashbulb
flashcube
flashover
flashtube
flatterer
flatulent
flavorous
flayflint
fleckless
fledgling
fleetness
fleshings
fleshless
fleshment
flightily
flintlock
flippancy
floatable
flocculus
floodgate
floodmark
floodtide
flophouse
floriated
floridean
floridity
floristic
floristry
floscular
flotation
flouncing
flowchart
flowerage
flowerbed

flowering	formality	frivolous	gallicise	gentleman	glomeruli	grapevine
flowerpot	formation	frockcoat	gallicism	genuflect	gloryhole	graphemic
flowingly	formative	frogmarch	gallingly	genuinely	glossator	graphical
flowsheet	formatted	frogspawn	gallinule	geobotany	glossitis	graphitic
flowstone	formicary	frolicked	gallivant	geodesist	glowingly	grappling
fluctuant	formicate	frontally	galliwasp	geography	glucoside	graspable
fluctuate	formulaic	frontless	gallmidge	geologise	glueyness	grassland
fluecured	formulary	frontline	gallonage	geologist	glutamate	graticule
fluoresce	formulate	frontpage	gallooned	geomancer	glutinous	gratitude
fluorosis	formulise	frontward	gallopade	geomantic	glyceride	gratulate
fluorspar	fornicate	frontways	Gallophil	geometric	glycerine	gravamina
flushness	forsythia	frontwise	galloping	geometrid	glycoside	graveless
fluxional	fortalice	frostbite	gallowses	geoponics	glyptodon	gravelled
flyfisher	forthwith	frostwork	gallstone	georgette	gnathonic	graveness
flyweight	fortifier	frowardly	galvanise	geosphere	gneissoid	graveyard
focussing	fortitude	fructuate	galvanism	geostatic	gneissose	gravidity
foeticide	fortnight	fructuous	galvanist	geotropic	goalmouth	gravitate
fogginess	fortunate	frugality	gambadoes	gerfalcon	gobetween	graywacke
foliation	fortyfive	fruitcake	gambolled	geriatric	goddamned	greasegun
folkdance	forwander	fruiterer	gammadion	germander	godfather	greataunt
folkmusic	forwarder	fruitless	gammoning	germanely	godliness	greatcoat
folkweave	forwardly	fruittree	ganderism	germanise	godmother	greatness
following	fossicker	frustrate	gangboard	Germanish	godparent	Greekless
foodchain	fossilise	fruticose	gangplank	Germanism	goffering	greenback
foodstuff	fossorial	fugacious	gannister	Germanist	gogglebox	greenbelt
foolhardy	fosterage	fulfilled	gaolbreak	germanium	goingover	greeneyed
foolishly	foulbrood	fulfiller	gardening	germicide	goldbrick	greengage
foolproof	foundling	fulgently	garderobe	germinate	goldcrest	greenhorn
footboard	foundress	fulgurant	garibaldi	germplasm	goldeneye	greenness
footcloth	fourflush	fulgurate	garmented	germproof	goldenrod	greenroom
footfault	fourpence	fulgurite	garnishee	gerundial	goldfever	greensand
footlight	fourpenny	fulgurous	garniture	gerundive	goldfield	greenweed
footloose	fourscore	fullblown	garreteer	gestalten	goldfinch	greenwood
footplate	fourwheel	fullcream	garrotter	gestation	goldsinny	gregarian
footpound	foxhunter	fulldress	garrulity	gestatory	goldsmith	gregarine
footprint	fractious	fullgrown	garrulous	getatable	golflinks	Gregorian
footstalk	fraenulum	fullscale	gasconade	geyserite	goliardic	grenadier
footstall	fragility	fulminant	gasfitter	ghostlike	gomphosis	grenadine
footstool	fragrance	fulminate	gasholder	ghostword	gondolier	greybeard
foppishly	fragrancy	fulminous	gasmantle	giantlike	gongorism	greyhound
foragecap	frailness	fulsomely	gasometer	gibberish	gonophore	greywacke
forasmuch	framework	fumarolic	gaspereau	gibbosity	goodnight	griefless
forbidden	franchise	fumigator	gastraeum	gibbously	goodwives	grievance
forcefeed	francolin	fundament	gastritis	giddiness	goosander	grillroom
forceland	frangible	funebrial	gastropod	gigahertz	goosefoot	grillwork
forceless	Franglais	fungicide	gastrulae	gigantism	goosegirl	grimalkin
forcemeat	frankness	fungiform	gatecrash	giltedged	gooseherd	griminess
forcepump	franticly	funicular	gatehouse	gimmickry	gooseneck	grisaille
foreboder	fraternal	funiculus	gathering	gingerade	gooseskin	gristmill
forebrain	freeboard	funkiness	gaucherie	gingerale	goosestep	gritstone
forecaddy	freehouse	funnelled	gaudiness	ginglymus	gorblimey	groomsman
foreclose	freelance	funniness	gaugeable	ginpalace	gorgonian	grosgrain
forecourt	freeliver	furbisher	gauleiter	girandole	gorgonise	grossness
forefront	Freemason	furcation	gauntness	girlishly	gospeller	grossular
foregoing	freerange	furiously	gauziness	Girondist	gossamery	grotesque
foreigner	freerider	furnisher	gavelkind	glabellae	Gothamite	grouchily
forejudge	freestone	furniture	gawkiness	glabellar	gothicise	groundage
foreknown	freestyle	furtherer	gazehound	glacially	Gothicism	groundash
forenamed	freewheel	furtively	gazetteer	gladiator	governess	groundhog
forereach	freewoman	fusillade	gearlever	gladiolus	graceless	grounding
foreshore	freezable	fusionist	gearshift	gladstone	gracility	groundivy
foreshown	freezedry	fussiness	gearwheel	glaireous	gradation	groundnut
foresight	freighter	fustigate	gelignite	glamorise	gradatory	groundsel
forespeak	frenchify	fustiness	gemmation	glamorous	Gradgrind	grovelled
forestage	Frenchman	fuzziness	gemmology	glandered	gradually	groveller
forestall	frequence	gabardine	gemutlich	glandular	graduator	grubscrew
foretaste	frequency	gaberdine	genealogy	glaringly	grandaddy	grubstake
foretoken	freshener	gabionade	generable	glassgall	grandaunt	gruelling
forewoman	freshness	gadgeteer	generalia	glassware	grandiose	gruffness
forfeiter	fretfully	Gaeltacht	generally	glasswork	grandness	grumbling
forgather	friarbird	gainfully	generator	glasswort	grandpapa	Grundyism
forgeable	fricassee	gainsayer	genetical	gleefully	grandsire	guacamole
forgetful	fricative	galactose	genialise	glengarry	grandslam	guarantee
forgiving	frigatoon	galantine	geniality	glissandi	granitoid	guarantor
forgotten	frightful	galenical	genitival	glissando	grantable	guardbook
forlornly	frigidity	galingale	genocidal	globefish	granulate	guardedly
formalise	fritterer	gallantly	genotypic	globosity	granulite	guardrail
formalism	frivolity	gallantry	genteelly	glomerate	granulose	guardring
formalist	frivolled	galleried	gentility	glomerule	grapeshot	guardroom

guardship
guardsman
guerrilla
guesswork
guestroom
guidebook
guideline
guidepost
guiderope
guildhall
guildship
guileless
guillemot
guilloche
guiltless
guitarist
gumminess
guncotton
gunpowder
gunrunner
gushingly
gustation
gustative
gustatory
gustiness
gutsiness
guttation
guttering
gymnasial
gymnasium
gymnastic
gynaeceum
gynocracy
gynoecium
gynophore
gyrfalcon
gyroplane
gyroscope
habergeon
habitable
habitably
habituate
hackamore
hackberry
hackneyed
haematite
haematoid
haematoma
haemostat
haggadist
haggardly
hagiarchy
hagiology
hagridden
hailstone
hailstorm
hairbrush
haircloth
hairgrass
hairiness
hairpiece
hairshirt
hairslide
hairspace
hairstyle
halfbaked
halfblood
halfbound
halfbreed
halfcaste
halfcrown
halfhardy
halflight
halfpence
halfpenny
halfprice
halfshell
halfstaff
halftitle
halftrack
halftruth
halieutic
halitosis
Halloween
Hallowmas
hallstand
Hallstatt
halophile
halophyte
halothane
haltingly
hamadryad
hamamelis
hamburger
hamfisted
hamhanded
hammerman
hammertoe
hamstring
hamstrung
handbrake
handcraft
handcuffs
handglass
handiness
handiwork
handlebar
handorgan
handpress
handsdown
handshake
handspike
handstand
handwheel
handywork
hangerson
hankering
Hanseatic
hanselled
haphazard
haplessly
haplology
happening
happiness
haranguer
harbinger
harbourer
hardboard
hardcover
hardihood
hardiment
hardiness
hardnosed
hardshell
haresfoot
harlequin
harmaline
harmattan
harmfully
harmonica
harmonics
harmonise
harmonist
harmonium
harmotome
harpooner
harquebus
Harrovian
harrowing
harshness
hartshorn
harvester
Hashemite
Hashimite
hastiness
hatchback
hatchling
hatchment
hatefully
haughtily
haustella
haustoria
haverings
haversack
havocking
hawksbill
hawsehole
hawsepipe
hazardous
headboard
headcloth
headdress
headfirst
headiness
headlight
headliner
headphone
headpiece
headscarf
headstall
headstock
headstone
headwater
healthful
healthily
heartache
heartbeat
heartburn
heartfelt
heartfree
hearthrug
heartland
heartless
heartsick
heartsore
heartwood
heathcock
heathenry
heaviness
heavyduty
Hebridean
hectogram
hedgingly
heedfully
heelpiece
heftiness
hegemonic
heinously
helically
heliogram
heliostat
heliotype
heliozoan
heliozoic
hellebore
hellenise
Hellenism
Hellenist
hellhound
hellishly
helpfully
Helvetian
hemicycle
hemistich
hemitrope
hemstitch
hendiadys
hepatitis
heptaglot
heptarchy
Heraclean
herbalist
herbarium
herbicide
herbivore
herborise
Herculean
Hercynian
hereabout
hereafter
heretical
hereunder
heritable
hermitage
herniated
herpetoid
hesitance
hesitancy
hesitator
Hesperian
hessonite
hetaerism
hetairism
heterodox
heteronym
heterosis
heuristic
hexachord
hexagonal
hexameter
hexaploid
hexastich
hexastyle
Hexateuch
hibernate
Hibernian
hiddenite
hidebound
hideously
hierarchy
hieratica
hierodule
hierogram
hierology
highchair
highclass
highflier
highflown
highflyer
highgrade
highgrown
highlands
highlevel
highlight
highspeed
hightoned
highwater
hilarious
hillbilly
Himalayan
Himyarite
hindbrain
hindrance
hindsight
hippocras
hircosity
hirsutism
hirundine
hispidity
histamine
histidine
histogeny
histogram
histology
historian
hitchhike
Hitlerism
Hitlerite
hoarfrost
hoarhound
hoariness
hoarstone
Hobbesian
hobgoblin
hobnailed
hobnobbed
hobnobber
hocussing
hodiernal
hodograph
hodometer
hoggishly
Holarctic
hollyhock
Hollywood
holocaust
holograph
holophote
holystone
homebound
homegrown
homemaker
homeopath
homestead
homewards
homicidal
homiletic
homogamic
homograft
homograph
homologue
homonymic
homophone
homophony
homoplasy
homopolar
homotaxis
homotonic
homousian
homuncule
homunculi
honeycomb
honeymoon
honkytonk
honoraria
honorific
hoofprint
hopefully
hopscotch
horehound
horniness
hornstone
hornwrack
horologer
horologic
horoscope
horoscopy
horseback
horsebean
horsehair
horsehide
horseless
horsemint
horseplay
horsepond
horseshoe
horsetail
horsewhip
horsiness
hortation
hortative
hortatory
hortensia
hosteller
hostilely
hostility
hotheaded
Hottentot
hourglass
houseboat
housebote
housecarl
housecoat
houseflag
household
housekeep
houseleek
houseless
houselled
housemaid
housemate
houseroom
housewife
housework
howsoever
hoydenish
hubristic
huckaback
huckstery
huffiness
hugeously
humankind
humanness
humblebee
humbugged
humdinger
humectant
humiliate
hunchback
hundredth
Hungarian
hunkydory
hurricane
hurriedly
hurtfully
husbandly
husbandry
huskiness
hybridise
hybridism
hybridity
hydathode
hydraemia
hydrangea
hydration
hydraulic
hydrazine
hydriodic
hydrocele
hydrofoil
hydrology
hydrolyse
hydrolyte
hydronium
hydrosome
hydroxide
hydrozoan
hydrozoon
hygienics
hygienist
hygrostat
hylozoism
hymnology
hypallage
hyperbola
hyperbole
hypergamy
hypericum
hyperopia
hyperopic
hypethral
hyphenate
hypnoidal
hypnology
hypnotise
hypnotism
hypnotist
hypoblast
hypocaust
hypocotyl
hypocrisy
hypocrite
hypogeous
hypomania
hypomanic
hyponasty
hypostyle
hypotaxis
hysterics
hysteroid
Icelander
Icelandic
iceskater
ichneumon
ichnology
ichthyoid
iconology
idealiser
idealless
identical
identikit
ideograph
ideologic
ideologue
idiograph
idiomatic
idiopathy
idioplasm
idiotical
ignescent
ignitable
ignitible
ignorable
ignoramus
ignorance
iguanodon
illboding
illegally
illegible
illegibly
illgotten
illiberal
illicitly
illjudged
illogical
illomened
illwisher
imageable
imageless
imaginary
imbalance
imbecilic
imbricate
imbroglio
imitation
imitative
immanence
immanency
immediacy
immediate
immensely
immensity
immersion
immigrant
immigrate
imminence
imminency
immixture
immodesty
immolator
immorally
immovable
immovably
immutable
immutably
impaction
impartial
impassion
impassive
impastoed
impatiens
impatient
impeccant

impedance
impelling
impendent
impending
imperator
imperfect
imperious
impetrate
impetuous
impiously
impleader
implement
impletion
implicate
impliedly
implosion
implosive
impluvium
impolitic
important
importune
impostume
imposture
impotence
impotency
impounder
imprecate
imprecise
impresari
improbity
impromptu
improvise
imprudent
impudence
impulsion
impulsive
impulsory
imputable
inability
inamorata
inanimate
inanition
inaptness
inaudible
inaudibly
inaugural
inbetween
inbreathe
incapable
incapably
incarnate
incaution
incensory
incentive
inception
inceptive
incessant
incidence
incipient
inclement
inclosure
inclusion
inclusive
incognito
incommode
incondite
incorrect
incorrupt
increaser
increment
incubator
inculcate
inculpate
incumbent
incunable
incurable
incurably
incurious
incurrent
incurring
incursion
incursive
incurvate
indagator
indecency
indecorum
indelible
indelibly
indemnify
indemnity
indention
indenture
Indianise
indicator
indiction
indigence
indignant
indignity
indigotin
indispose
IndoAryan
indolence
indraught
inducible
induction
inductive
indulgent
indweller
inebriant
inebriate
inebriety
ineffable
ineffably
inelastic
inelegant
ineptness
inequable
inerrable
inerrancy
inertness
inexactly
infantile
infantine
infatuate
infection
infective
inferable
inference
inferring
infertile
infielder
infilling
infirmary
infirmity
inflation
inflexion
inflictor
inflowing
influence
influenza
informant
infractor
infuriate
infuscate
infusible
infusoria
ingenious
ingenuity
ingenuous
ingestion
ingestive
inglenook
ingrained
ingrowing
inhalator
inharmony
inherence
inheritor
inhibitor
inhumanly
initially
initiator
injection
injurious
injustice
innermost
innervate
innholder
innkeeper
innocence
innocency
innocuity
innocuous
innovator
innoxious
innuendos
inoculate
inodorous
inorganic
inpatient
inpouring
inquiline
insatiate
insatiety
inscriber
insectary
insectile
insensate
insertion
inservice
insetting
inshallah
insidious
insincere
insinuate
insipidly
insistent
insolence
insoluble
insolubly
insolvent
insomniac
inspanned
inspector
instanter
instantly
instigate
instilled
institute
insularly
insulator
insurable
insurance
insurgent
integrand
integrant
integrate
integrity
intellect
intendant
intensely
intensify
intension
intensity
intensive
intention
interbred
intercede
intercept
intercity
intercrop
interdict
interface
interfere
interfile
interflow
interfuse
interject
interknit
interlace
interlard
interleaf
interline
interlink
interlock
interlope
interlude
interment
internode
interpage
interplay
interpose
interpret
interring
interrupt
intersect
intervein
intervene
interview
interwind
interwove
interzone
intestacy
intestate
intestine
intorsion
intricacy
intricate
intrigant
intriguer
intrinsic
introduce
introject
introvert
intrusion
intrusive
intuition
intuitive
intumesce
inunction
inurement
inutility
invalidly
invariant
invective
inveigler
invention
inventive
inventory
inverness
inversely
inversion
inversive
invertase
invidious
inviolacy
inviolate
invisible
invisibly
involucre
involuted
inwrought
ionisable
irascible
irascibly
irksomely
ironbound
ironmould
ironsides
ironsmith
ironstone
ironworks
Iroquoian
irradiant
irradiate
irreality
irregular
irrigable
irrigator
irritable
irritably
irruption
irruptive
isagogics
isallobar
ischaemia
ischaemic
ischiadic
ischiatic
isinglass
Islamitic
isobathic
isochrone
isoclinal
isoclinic
isocyclic
isogamete
isogamous
isogenous
isohyetal
isolation
isolative
isomerise
isomerism
isomerous
isometric
isoniazid
isooctane
isopodous
isosceles
isostatic
isotropic
Israelite
issueless
italicise
Italicism
itchiness
iteration
iterative
itineracy
itinerant
itinerary
itinerate
itsybitsy
ittybitty
jaborandi
jacaranda
jackknife
jackplane
jacksnipe
jackstraw
Jacobinic
jacquerie
jactation
jailbreak
jambalaya
jampacked
janissary
janitress
Jansenism
Jansenist
japanning
jargonise
jarringly
jaundiced
jaywalker
jazziness
jealously
jeeringly
jellyfish
jerkiness
jessamine
jesuitise
jesuitism
jetsetter
jetstream
jewellery
jewelweed
jitterbug
jobmaster
jockstrap
jocularly
jocundity
Johannine
jointress
jollyboat
Jordanian
josshouse
jossstick
journeyer
joviality
joylessly
jubilance
Judaistic
Judastree
judgement
judgeship
judgmatic
judiciary
judicious
juiceless
juiciness
jumpiness
Juneberry
juniorate
juniority
junkerdom
junkerism
junketing
Junoesque
juridical
jurywoman
justiciar
justifier
juvenilia
juxtapose
kaiserdom
kaiserism
kaolinise
kaolinite
karabiner
karyotype
katabasis
katabatic
katabolic
katharsis
keelivine
kennelled
kentledge
Keplerian
keratitis
keratosis
kerbstone
kerfuffle
Keynesian
khedivial
kibbutzim
kickstart
kiddingly
kidnapped
kidnapper
kilderkin
killifish
kilocycle
kilohertz
kilolitre
kilometre
kinematic
kingcraft
kingdomed
kingmaker
kingsized
kinkiness
kinswoman
kitchener
kittenish
kittiwake
klinostat
knavishly
kneadable
knifeedge
knightage
knockdown
knockknee
knotgrass
knowingly
knowledge
krummhorn
Kshatriya
kurrajong
kymograph
labelling
labialise
labialism
laborious
labourite
labyrinth
laccolith
lacerable
lacertian
lacertine
lachrymal
laciniate
lacrimose
lacrymose
lactation
ladysmock
laevulose
laggardly
lagniappe
lagomorph
lairdship
lallation
lambently
lamellate
lamellose
laminaria
laminated
lampblack
lamplight
lampooner
lampshade
lampshell
lancejack
lancewood
lancinate
landagent
landaulet
landdross
landdrost
landgrave
landloper
landowner
landscape
landslide
Langobard
langouste
languidly
lankiness
lanthanum
Laodicean
lapideous
Laplander
lapstrake
lapstreak
larcenist
larcenous
lardycake
largeness
larghetto
larvicide
laryngeal
lassitude

lastditch
lastingly
latecomer
laterally
latescent
lathering
latitancy
latterday
latticing
laudation
laudative
laudatory
laughable
laughably
launching
launderer
laundress
laurelled
lavaliere
lawgiving
lawlessly
lawnmower
lazaretto
lazybones
lazytongs
lazzarone
lazzaroni
leafgreen
leafmould
leafstalk
leakiness
learnable
learnedly
leasehold
leaselend
leastways
leastwise
leavening
lecherous
leeringly
leewardly
leftovers
leftwards
legendary
legerline
legginess
legionary
legislate
Leicester
leisurely
leitmotif
leitmotiv
lendlease
lengthily
leniently
lentiform
leptosome
lethality
lethargic
letterbox
lettering
leucaemia
leucocyte
leucotome
leucotomy
leukaemia
leukaemic
leukocyte
Levantine
levelling
levelness
leviathan
leviratic
levitator
Levitical
lexically
liability
libecchio
libellant

libelling
libellist
libellous
liberally
liberated
liberator
libertine
libidinal
librarian
libration
libratory
librettos
licensure
lichenous
lickerish
liegelord
lifeblood
lifecycle
lifeforce
lifeguard
lifesaver
lifesized
lifestyle
lifetable
lightfoot
lightless
lightness
lightning
lightship
lightsome
lightsout
lightwood
lightyear
lignaloes
ligniform
liltingly
lilywhite
Limburger
limejuice
limelight
limestone
limewater
limitable
limitedly
limitless
limnology
limonitic
limousine
limpidity
lineality
lineament
linearise
linearity
lineation
linenfold
lineolate
lingering
lingually
lingulate
lintelled
lintwhite
lioncelle
lionheart
lipreader
liquation
liquefier
liquidate
liquidise
liquidity
liquorice
liquorish
lispingly
lissomely
Listerism
literally
literatim
literator
literatus
litheness

lithesome
lithology
lithopone
lithotomy
litigable
litigious
litterbin
litterbug
liturgics
liturgist
liverwort
liveryman
livestock
lividness
lixiviate
loadstone
loafsugar
loanshark
loathsome
lobectomy
lobscouse
lobulated
locatable
locksmith
locomotor
lodestone
lodgement
lodgepole
loftiness
logaoedic
logarithm
logically
logistics
logogriph
logomachy
loincloth
Lombardic
Londonise
Londonism
longaeval
longchain
longcoats
longeared
longevity
longevous
longfaced
longhouse
longicorn
longingly
longitude
longlived
Longobard
longrange
longshore
lookalike
looseleaf
looseness
lophodont
loquacity
lorgnette
lotusland
loudmouth
louringly
lousewort
lousiness
loutishly
loveapple
lovechild
lovefeast
lovelight
lovematch
loverless
lovestory
lovetoken
lovingcup
lowercase
lowerdeck
lowermost
lowlander

lowliness
lowloader
lowminded
lownecked
loxodrome
lubricant
lubricate
lubricity
lubricous
lucidness
luciferin
luckiness
lucrative
lucubrate
ludicrous
luftwaffe
lumbering
lumberman
lumbrical
lumbricus
luminance
lumpiness
lumpishly
lunchtime
lunisolar
lunitidal
luridness
lustfully
lustihood
lustiness
luxuriant
luxuriate
luxurious
lyamhound
lymegrass
lymehound
lymphatic
lyophilic
lyophobic
lyrically
lysimeter
macaronic
Maccabean
macedoine
macerator
machinate
machinery
machinist
machmeter
macintosh
macrocosm
macrocyte
maddening
madeleine
madrepore
maelstrom
magdalene
Magianism
magically
magicking
magistery
magistral
magnalium
magnesian
magnesite
magnesium
magnetics
magnetise
magnetism
magnetist
magnetite
magnetron
magnifico
magnifier
magnitude
maharajah
maharanee
maharishi
mahlstick

Mahometan
maidenish
mailplane
mailtrain
mainbrace
mainliner
mainsheet
majordomo
majorette
majorship
majuscule
makeready
makeshift
malachite
maladroit
malanders
malarious
malathion
Malayalam
malformed
malicious
malignant
malignity
malleable
malleehen
mallemuck
malleolar
malleolus
malthouse
malvoisie
mamillary
mamillate
mammalian
mammalogy
mammiform
mammonish
mammonism
mammonist
mammonite
Mancunian
mandarine
mandatary
mandatory
mandoline
manducate
maneating
manganate
manganese
manganite
manganous
manginess
manhandle
manhattan
Manichean
manifesto
manipular
manliness
mannequin
mannerism
mannerist
manoeuvre
manometer
manorseat
mansarded
mansionry
manslayer
manticore
manubrium
Manxwoman
manyplies
manysided
manzanita
maquisard
marcasite
marcelled
marchpane
marchpast
marestail
margarine

margarite
marginate
marihuana
marijuana
maritally
marketday
marketing
marlstone
marmalade
marmoreal
marquetry
marrowfat
marshalcy
marshland
marshwort
marsupial
marsupium
martially
Martinmas
martyrdom
martyrise
marvelled
masculine
masochism
masochist
masonried
Masoretic
massagist
massiness
massively
masterdom
masterful
masterkey
masticate
matchless
matchlock
matchwood
maternity
mateyness
matriarch
matricide
matricula
matrimony
matronage
matronise
mattamore
matutinal
maulstick
maunderer
mausoleum
mawkishly
maxillary
maximally
maybeetle
mayflower
mayoralty
mayorship
mealiness
meandrine
meandrous
meaningly
meanwhile
meatiness
mechanics
mechanise
mechanism
mechanist
medallion
medallist
mediaeval
mediately
mediation
mediatise
mediative
mediatory
mediatrix
medicable
medically
medicinal

meditator
medullary
medullate
megacycle
megadeath
megahertz
megaphone
megaspore
mekometer
melanosis
melanotic
melaphyre
melatonin
meliorate
meliorism
meliorist
meliority
melismata
melocoton
melodious
melodrama
melomania
meltingly
meltwater
mementoes
memoirist
memorable
memorably
memoranda
memoriter
menadione
menagerie
mendacity
Mendelian
Mendelism
mendicant
mendicity
meningeal
Mennonite
menopause
Menshevik
menstrual
menstruum
mentalism
mentalist
mentality
mentation
mepacrine
mercaptan
mercenary
mercerise
merciless
mercurial
mercurous
merganser
meropidan
merriment
merriness
mescaline
mesentery
mesmerise
mesmerism
mesmerist
mesoblast
mesogloea
mesomorph
mesophyll
mesophyte
messenger
messianic
messieurs
messiness
metabolic
metalline
metalling
metallise
metalloid
metalwork
metameric

metaphase
metaplasm
meteorist
meteorite
meteoroid
methadone
metheglin
methodise
Methodism
Methodist
methought
methylate
methylene
metonymic
metricate
metrician
metricise
metricist
metrology
metronome
mezzanine
mezzotint
miasmatic
micaceous
micaslate
microbial
microchip
microcosm
microcyte
microfilm
microgram
microlite
microlith
micrology
micromesh
micropsia
micropyle
microsome
microtome
microtomy
microtone
microwave
micturate
middleman
midinette
midstream
midsummer
midwicket
midwifery
midwinter
migration
migratory
milestone
militancy
milkfever
milkfloat
milkiness
milkshake
milktooth
millboard
millenary
millennia
millepede
millepore
millerite
milligram
millinery
millionth
millipede
millivolt
millstone
millwheel
milometer
Miltonian
mimicking
minacious
mincemeat
mincingly
mindfully
minefield
minelayer
miniature
minimally
miniskirt
minuscule
minutegun
minuteman
mirkiness
mirthless
misadvise
misassign
misbecome
misbehave
misbelief
misbeseem
miscegene
miscegine
mischance
miscreant
miscreate
misdemean
misdirect
misemploy
miserable
miserably
misesteem
misfeasor
misgiving
misgovern
misguided
mishandle
mishanter
misinform
misleared
mismanage
misoneism
misoneist
mispickel
misreckon
misreport
misshapen
missioner
mistigris
mistiness
mistletoe
mistyeyed
Mithraism
Mithraist
mitigable
mitigator
mitraille
mixedness
mnemonics
mnemonist
mobocracy
mockingly
modelling
moderator
modernise
modernism
modernist
modernity
modillion
modulator
moistener
moistness
molecular
molluscan
mollymawk
molybdate
momentary
momentous
monachism
monarchal
monarchic
monastery
monatomic
Mondayish
monergism
moneybags
moneybill
moneywort
Mongolian
mongolism
Mongoloid
mongooses
mongrelly
monitress
monkeyish
monkeyism
monkeynut
monkshood
monobasic
monoceros
monochord
monocline
monocoque
monocracy
monocular
monodical
monodrama
monoecism
monogamic
monograph
monolatry
monologic
monologue
monomania
monomeric
monophagy
monoplane
monorhyme
monostich
monostyle
monotonic
monotreme
monotypic
monsignor
monsoonal
monstrous
Montanism
monthling
monticule
monzonite
moodiness
moonblind
moonlight
moonquake
moonraker
moonscape
moonshine
moonstone
moraceous
moraliser
moratoria
morbidity
mordacity
mordantly
Mormonism
morphemic
morrisman
mortality
mortgagee
mortgager
mortgagor
mortician
mosaicism
mosaicist
mosaicked
moschatel
mosquitos
mossagate
mossgrown
motheaten
motherwit
mothproof
motivator
motocross
motorable
motorbike
motorboat
motorcade
mouldable
mountable
mousehole
mousetrap
moustache
mouthpart
mouthwash
moviegoer
muckraker
mucksweat
mucronate
muddiness
muffineer
muffinman
mugginess
mullioned
multifoil
multiform
multilane
multipara
multiplex
multitude
mumchance
mummified
mundanely
mundungus
municipal
muniments
munitions
murderess
murderous
murkiness
murmurous
muscadine
muscarine
muscleman
muscovado
muscovite
musically
musichall
musketeer
muskiness
muskmelon
Mussulman
mustachio
musteline
mustiness
mutagenic
mutilator
mutualise
mutualism
mutualist
mutuality
muzziness
Mycenaean
mycologic
mycophagy
mydriasis
mydriatic
myelomata
myography
myologist
myriorama
myrmecoid
myrobalan
mystagogy
mysticism
mystifier
mythicise
mythicism
mythicist
mythology
myxoedema
Nahuatlan
nailbrush
nakedness
nameplate
nannygoat
naphthene
napthalic
narcissus
narcotine
narcotise
narcotism
narration
narrative
narratory
naseberry
nastiness
natheless
natrolite
nattiness
naturally
naughtily
naumachia
navelwort
navicular
navigable
navigator
neathouse
nebuliser
necessary
necessity
neckcloth
neckverse
necrology
necrophil
necrotise
nectarean
nectarial
nectarine
nectarous
needfully
neediness
needleful
nefarious
negligent
negotiant
negotiate
negritude
negroidal
Negroness
negrophil
neighbour
nemertean
nemertine
nemophila
neodymium
neolithic
neologian
neologise
neologism
neologist
neoteinia
neoteinic
neoterise
neoterism
neoterist
nepenthes
nephalism
nephalist
nepheline
nephelite
nephology
nephritic
nephritis
nephrosis
Neptunian
neptunium
nervation
nervature
nerveless
nerviness
nervously
nescience
Nestorian
netveined
netwinged
neuralgia
neuralgic
neuration
neuroglia
neurology
neuromata
neuropath
neutrally
nevermore
newlyweds
newmarket
newsagent
newsflash
newshound
newsiness
newspaper
newsprint
newsstand
Newtonian
niccolite
nickelise
nickelled
nickelous
nicotiana
nicotinic
nictation
nictitate
niggardly
nightbird
nightclub
nightfall
nightgown
nighthawk
nightlife
nightline
nightlong
nightmare
nightside
nighttime
nightwork
nigricant
nigritude
nigrosine
Nilometer
ninepence
ninepenny
ninetieth
Nipponese
nitpicker
nitratine
nitration
nobiliary
nobleness
noctiluca
nocturnal
nocuously
nodulated
noiseless
noisiness
noisomely
nominable
nominally
nominator
nomocracy
nomograph
nondriver
nonentity
nonillion
nonjuring
nonlinear
nonpareil
nonperson
nonprofit
nonsmoker
nonviable
normalise
normality
Normanise
Normanism
normative
northeast
northerly
northland
northmost
northward
northwest
Norwegian
nosebleed
noseflute
nosepiece
nostalgia
nostalgic
nostology
notabilia
notedness
notepaper
notionist
notochord
notoriety
notorious
nourisher
novelette
noviciate
novitiate
nowhither
noxiously
nucleated
nucleolus
nucleonic
nuisancer
nullifier
nullipara
nullipore
numbskull
numerable
numerator
numerical
nummulite
nuncupate
nurseling
nursemaid
nutriment
nutrition
nutritive
nuttiness
nutweevil
nymphalid
nystagmic
nystagmus
oakenshaw
oasthouse
obbligato
obconical
obcordate
obedience
obeisance
obeseness
obfuscate
objectify
objection
objective
objurgate
obligated
obliquely
obliquity
oblivious
obnoxious
obscenely
obscenity
obscurant
obscurely
obscurity
obsecrate

obsequent
obsequial
obsequies
observant
obsession
obsessive
obsolesce
obstetric
obstinacy
obstinate
obtention
obtrusion
obtrusive
obturator
obversely
obversion
obviation
obviously
occipital
occludent
occlusion
occlusive
occultism
occultist
occupancy
occurrent
occurring
ocellated
ochlocrat
octachord
octagonal
octahedra
octameter
octastyle
octennial
octillion
Octobrist
octopodes
octostyle
odalisque
oddfellow
oddjobber
oddjobman
odontalgy
odorously
odourless
oecologic
oecumenic
oenomancy
oenophile
oenophily
oesophagi
oestrogen
offcentre
offchance
offcolour
offensive
offertory
offhanded
officiant
officiate
officinal
officious
offscreen
offseason
offspring
offstreet
oilburner
oilcolour
oilpaints
okeydokey
oleaceous
olecranal
olecranon
oleograph
oleoresin
olfaction
olfactive
olfactory
oligaemia
oligarchy
Oligocene
oligopoly
olivenite
ombudsman
ominously
omissible
ommatidia
omophagia
omophagic
onanistic
oncogenic
oncologic
onehanded
onelegged
onerously
onionskin
onlicence
onomastic
onsetting
onslaught
ontogenic
ontologic
oogenesis
oogenetic
openended
openheart
operation
operative
opercular
operculum
operosely
operosity
ophiology
opinioned
opodeldoc
opponency
opportune
opposable
oppressor
oppugnant
opsimathy
optically
optometer
optometry
optophone
opulently
opusculum
orangeade
Orangeism
Orangeman
orangetip
orangutan
oratorial
oratorian
orbicular
orchestic
orchestra
orchidist
orderbook
orderform
orderless
ordinance
organelle
organiser
organstop
organzine
orgiastic
orientate
orificial
oriflamme
originate
orography
orologist
orphanage
Orpington
orrisroot
orthodoxy
orthoepic
oscillate
oscitancy
osmometer
ossicular
ossifrage
ostensive
osteoderm
osteogeny
osteology
osteopath
ostracise
ostracism
Ostrogoth
otherness
otherwise
otologist
oubliette
ourselves
outbacker
outermost
outfitter
outgiving
outgoings
outgrowth
outgunned
outlander
outnumber
outputted
outridden
outrigger
outskirts
outspoken
outspread
outwardly
outwitted
outworker
ovenready
overblown
overboard
overborne
overcheck
overcloud
overcrowd
overdraft
overdrawn
overdress
overdrive
overeaten
overeater
overexert
overflown
overglaze
overgraze
overgrown
overheard
overissue
overjoyed
overladen
overleapt
overlying
overmatch
overnight
overpitch
overpower
overprice
overprint
overproof
overreach
overreact
oversexed
overshoot
oversight
oversized
overskirt
oversleep
overslept
overspend
overspent
overspill
overstate
oversteer
overstock
overstuff
overtaken
overthrew
overthrow
overtness
overtones
overtrain
overtrick
overtrump
overvalue
overwatch
overweary
overweigh
overwhelm
overwound
overwrite
overwrote
oviductal
oviferous
oviparity
oviparous
ovulation
ovulatory
ownership
oxidation
oxygenate
oxygenise
oxygenous
oysterbed
oysterman
ozocerite
ozokerite
pacemaker
pachyderm
packaging
packdrill
packhorse
packtrain
paederast
pageantry
paillasse
paillette
painfully
painterly
paintwork
pairhorse
Pakistani
palaestra
palafitte
palankeen
palanquin
palatable
palatably
palillogy
Palladian
palladium
palladous
palletise
palliasse
pallidity
palmation
palmipede
palmistry
palmitate
palpation
palpebral
palpitant
palpitate
palsgrave
paludinal
palustral
panatella
panchayat
pancratic
panderess
panegyric
panelling
panellist
panhandle
panicking
panoplied
panoramic
pantalets
pantaloon
pantheism
pantheist
pantingly
pantomime
pantryman
pantyhose
paperback
paperclip
papergirl
paperthin
paperwork
papeterie
papillary
papillate
papilloma
papillose
papillote
parabasis
parabolic
parachute
Paraclete
paradisal
paragraph
paralalia
paralexia
paralysis
paralytic
paramatta
paramedic
parameter
paramorph
paramount
paranoiac
paranymph
parapeted
parapodia
parasitic
parataxis
parathion
parbuckle
parcelled
parcenary
parchment
paregoric
parentage
parfleche
parhelion
parleyvoo
parlously
parochial
parotitis
parquetry
parrakeet
parricide
Parseeism
parsimony
parsonage
partially
partition
partitive
partridge
pasodoble
passenger
passerine
passersby
passional
passivate
passively
passivity
pastedown
pasticcio
pastiness
pastorale
pastorate
pasturage
patchouli
patchouly
patchwork
patellate
paternity
pathogeny
pathology
patiently
patinated
patriarch
patrician
patricide
patrimony
patriotic
patristic
patrolled
patroller
patrolman
patrology
patronage
patroness
patronise
paulownia
pauperise
pauperism
Pavlovian
paymaster
paypacket
peaceable
peaceably
peacetime
peachblow
pearlitic
pearlwort
peasantry
peasouper
peccantly
pectinate
peculator
pecuniary
pedagogic
pedagogue
pedalling
pederasty
pedicular
pedigreed
pedometer
peepsight
peevishly
pegmatite
Pekingese
Pelasgian
pellagrin
pelletise
pellitory
pemphigus
pencilled
penciller
pendently
pendragon
pendulate
penduline
pendulous
peneplain
peneplane
penetrant
penetrate
penfriend
penholder
peninsula
penitence
penniless
pennywort
penpusher
pensioner
pensively
pentagram
pentangle
pentarchy
Pentecost
penthouse
penultima
penumbral
penurious
pepperbox
pepperpot
peptonise
percaline
perceiver
perchance
percheron
percolate
perdition
peregrine
perennate
perennial
perfectly
perfector
perfervid
perforate
performer
perfumery
perfumier
perfusion
perfusive
pergunnah
periclase
pericycle
peridotic
perihelia
perilling
perilymph
perimeter
perimorph
perinatal
periodate
peripatus
periphery
periplast
periscope
perishing
perisperm
peristome
peristyle
perkiness
permanent
permeable
permeance
permitted
permitter
permutate
perpetual
persecute
persevere
persimmon
personage
personate
personify
personnel
persuader
pertinent
pertussis
pervasion
pervasive
perverter
pessimism
pessimist
pesthouse
pesticide
pestilent
pestology
petaurist
petechiae

petechial
petersham
pethidine
petiolate
petiolule
petroleum
petrology
petticoat
pettiness
pettishly
pettitoes
petulance
petulancy
phagedena
phagocyte
phalanger
phalanges
phalanxes
phalarope
phantasma
pharaonic
pharisaic
pharyngal
pharynges
pharynxes
phellogen
phenacite
phenakite
phenology
phenomena
phenotype
pheromone
philander
philately
philippic
philogyny
philology
Philomela
phlebitis
phonation
phonatory
phonemics
phonetics
phonetise
phonetism
phonetist
phoniness
phonogram
phonolite
phonology
phosphate
phosphene
phosphide
phosphine
phosphite
photocell
photocopy
photogene
photophil
photopsia
phototype
phrenetic
phthalein
phycology
phyllopod
phylogeny
physician
physicist
physicked
phytogeny
phytology
phytotomy
phytotron
pianistic
pickaback
picketing
picnicked
picnicker
pictogram
pictorial
picturise
piecemeal
piecerate
piecework
pierrette
pietistic
piggishly
piggyback
piggybank
pigheaded
pikeperch
pikestaff
pilferage
pilgarlic
pillarbox
pilotfish
pimpernel
pinchbeck
pinchcock
pineapple
pinkiness
pinnately
pinnipede
pinnulate
pinstripe
pintailed
pintsized
pipedream
pipeorgan
pipestone
pipsqueak
piquantly
piratical
pirouette
piscatory
pisciform
pisolitic
pistachio
pistoleer
pistolled
pitchdark
pitchfork
pitchpipe
piteously
pithecoid
pithiness
pitifully
pituitary
pityingly
pivotable
pivotally
pixilated
pizzicati
pizzicato
placation
placatory
placeable
placecard
placekick
placeless
placement
placename
placentae
placental
placidity
plainness
plainsman
plainsong
plaintiff
plaintive
planarian
planation
planetary
planetoid
plangency
planisher
plantable
plantlike
planuloid
plasmatic
plasmodia
plastered
plasterer
platemark
platinise
platinoid
platinous
platitude
Platonise
Platonism
Platonist
plausible
plausibly
playfully
playgroup
playhouse
plaything
pleadable
pleadings
pleasance
Pleiocene
plenarily
plenitude
plenteous
plentiful
plethoric
pleuritic
plicately
plication
plicature
ploughboy
ploughman
plumbeous
plumbline
plumdamas
plumpness
plumulate
plumulose
plunderer
pluralise
pluralism
pluralist
plurality
plusfours
plushness
plutocrat
plutonian
Plutonism
Plutonist
plutonium
pneumatic
pneumonia
pneumonic
pocketful
podagrous
podginess
podzolise
poetaster
poeticise
poeticism
poignancy
poinciana
pointduty
pointedly
pointille
pointlace
pointless
pointsman
poisonous
pokeberry
pokerface
pokerwork
polariser
polemical
polevault
policeman
politburo
politesse
political
pollinate
pollinium
pollutant
pollution
polonaise
polyamide
polyandry
polybasic
polyester
polygamic
polygenic
polygonal
polygonum
polygraph
polyhedra
polymathy
polymeric
polymorph
polyonymy
polyphagy
polyphase
polyphone
polyphony
polyploid
polyptych
polysemic
polysomic
polythene
polytonal
polytypic
polyvinyl
polywater
polyzoary
pomaceous
pommelled
pompadour
pomposity
pompously
ponderous
pontoneer
pontonier
poorhouse
popliteal
poppycock
poppyhead
popularly
porbeagle
porcelain
porcupine
poriferal
poriferan
porphyria
porringer
portative
porterage
portfolio
porticoes
portolano
portrayal
portrayer
portreeve
portulaca
possessed
possessor
postentry
posterior
posterity
posthaste
posthorse
posthouse
posticous
postilion
postnasal
postnatal
postulant
postulate
potassium
potboiler
potentate
potential
potholing
pothunter
potpourri
poulterer
pouncebox
poundcake
pourboire
pourpoint
poussette
powerboat
powerdive
powerless
pozzolana
practical
practised
praenomen
pragmatic
praiseful
pranksome
prankster
pratingly
prayerful
prayerrug
preachify
preachily
preadamic
prebendal
precancel
precative
precatory
precedent
preceding
precentor
preceptor
precipice
precisely
precisian
precision
precocial
precocity
preconise
precursor
predacity
predation
predative
predatory
predicant
predicate
predictor
predigest
predikant
preemptor
preengage
preexilic
prefatory
preferred
prefigure
prefixion
pregnable
pregnancy
prejudice
prelatess
prelatise
prelature
prelector
prelusion
prelusive
prelusory
premature
premonish
premotion
prenotion
preoccupy
preordain
prepotent
prerecord
presbyope
presbyter
preschool
prescient
prescribe
prescript
preselect
presentee
presenter
presently
preserver
preshrink
preshrunk
president
presidial
presidium
pressgang
pressmark
pressroom
pressstud
presswork
prestress
pretender
preterist
preterite
pretermit
prettyish
prettyism
prevalent
preventer
prevision
priceless
prideless
priestess
primaeval
primality
primarily
primatial
primeness
primipara
primitive
primordia
princedom
princekin
princelet
principal
principia
principle
printable
printshop
priorship
prismatic
privateer
privately
privation
privative
privilege
probation
probative
probatory
proboscis
procedure
procerity
processed
processer
processor
proclitic
proconsul
procreant
procreate
procuracy
procuress
prodromal
prodromic
proenzyme
profanely
profanity
professed
professor
profilist
profiteer
profusely
profusion
progestin
prognoses
prognosis
programme
projector
prolamine
prolapsus
prolately
prolation
prolative
prolepses
prolepsis
proleptic
prolicide
prolixity
prologise
prolusion
prolusory
promenade
prominent
promising
promotion
promotive
promptbox
pronation
proneness
pronghorn
pronounce
proofread
propagate
propelled
propeller
properdin
prophetic
propionic
proponent
propriety
proptosis
propylaea
propylene
prorogate
prosaical
proscenia
proscribe
prosector
prosecute
proselyte
prosiness
prosodist
prostatic
prostrate
protamine
protector
proteinic
protester
protestor
prothesis
prothetic
prothorax
protonema
prototype
protozoal
protozoan
protozoic
protozoon
proveably
Provencal
provender
provident
providing
provision
provisory
provoking
provostry
proximate

proximity
prudently
prudishly
prurience
pruriency
psalmbook
psalmodic
psalteria
pseudonym
pseudopod
psoriasis
psoriatic
psychical
psychoses
psychosis
psychotic
ptarmigan
pterosaur
pterygium
pterygoid
Ptolemaic
pubescent
publicise
publicist
publicity
publisher
pudginess
puerility
puerperal
puffadder
puffiness
pugnacity
puissance
pullulate
pulmonary
pulmonate
pulpboard
pulpiness
pulpiteer
pulpstone
pulsatile
pulsation
pulsatory
pulseless
pulserate
pulverise
pulverous
pulvillus
pulvinate
pumiceous
pummelled
punchball
punchbowl
punchcard
punchline
punctilio
punctuate
pungently
punishing
pupillage
pupillary
puppeteer
puppyhood
purchaser
pureblood
purgation
purgative
purgatory
puritanic
purloiner
purposely
purposive
purpureal
purringly
purselike
pursiness
pursuable
pursuance
purulence
purulency
pushchair
pushiness
pushingly
pussyfoot
pustulate
pustulous
putridity
puzzolana
pycnidium
pyracanth
pyramidal
pyramidic
pyramidon
pyrethrum
pyridoxin
pyrogenic
pyrolater
pyrolatry
pyrolysis
pyrolytic
pyromancy
pyromania
pyrometer
pyrometry
pyroscope
pyroxylin
quadratic
quadrifid
quadrigae
quadrille
quadruman
quadruped
quadruple
quadruply
Quakerdom
Quakeress
Quakerish
Quakerism
quakiness
qualified
qualifier
quantical
quarenden
quarender
quarryman
quarterly
quartette
quartzite
quartzose
quebracho
queenhood
queenless
queenlike
queenpost
queenship
queerness
quercetum
querulous
quibbling
quickener
quicklime
quickness
quicksand
quickstep
quiescent
quietness
quillwort
quinoline
quintette
quintuple
quirister
quitclaim
quittance
quixotism
quizzical
quodlibet
quotation
quotidian
rabbinate
rabbinism
rabbinist
rabidness
racehorse
racetrack
racialism
racialist
racketeer
raconteur
radialply
radiantly
radiately
radiation
radiative
radically
radicular
radiocast
radiogram
radiology
raffinate
raffinose
raffishly
rafflesia
raincheck
raincloud
raingauge
raininess
rainmaker
rainproof
rainstorm
rainwater
rakehelly
rampantly
rancidity
rancorous
randiness
randomise
ranginess
ransacker
rantingly
ranunculi
rapacious
rapidfire
rapidness
raptorial
rapturous
rareeshow
rascaldom
rascalism
rascality
raspatory
raspberry
raspingly
ratepayer
rationale
rationing
raucously
raunchily
rauwolfia
ravelling
ravelment
ravishing
razorback
razorbill
razoredge
razorfish
reachable
reactance
readdress
readiness
readymade
realistic
reanimate
rearguard
rearhorse
rearlight
rearmouse
rearrange
rearwards
reasoning
rebaptise
rebelling
rebellion
rebidding
rebukable
rebutting
recalesce
recapping
recapture
recension
reception
receptive
recession
recessive
rechauffe
recherche
recipient
reckoning
reclinate
reclusion
reclusive
recognise
recoinage
recollect
recombine
recommend
recompose
reconcile
recondite
reconfirm
reconvene
reconvert
recording
recordist
recoverer
recreancy
recruital
recruiter
rectangle
rectifier
rectitude
rectorate
rectorial
rectrices
recumbent
recurrent
recurring
recursion
recursive
recusance
recusancy
redaction
redbreast
redevelop
redhanded
redheaded
redingote
redivivus
redletter
redolence
redoubted
redresser
reducible
reductant
reduction
reductive
redundant
reediness
reedorgan
reeducate
reefpoint
reenforce
reentrant
reexamine
refashion
refection
refectory
referable
reference
referenda
referring
refitment
refitting
reflation
reflector
reflexion
reflexive
refluence
reformism
reformist
refractor
refreshen
refresher
refuelled
refulgent
refurbish
refurnish
refusable
refutable
regardant
regardful
regicidal
regisseur
registrar
regretful
regretted
regularly
regulator
rehearsal
rehydrate
Reichstag
reimburse
reinforce
reinstate
reiterate
rejection
rejoicing
rejoinder
relevance
relevancy
reliantly
religiose
religious
reliquary
reliquiae
reluctant
reluctate
remainder
remanence
remeasure
remediate
remindful
reminisce
remission
remitment
remittent
remitting
remontant
removable
renascent
rencontre
rendition
renewable
renitency
renouncer
renovator
reparable
repayable
repayment
repechage
repellant
repellent
repelling
repentant
repertory
replenish
repletion
replicate
reportage
reposeful
repossess
repotting
reprehend
represent
repressor
reprieval
reprimand
reprobate
reprocess
reproduce
reptilian
republish
repudiate
repugnant
repulsion
repulsive
reputable
reputably
reputedly
requester
requisite
rerebrace
rerelease
reremouse
rerunning
resalable
resection
resentful
reserpine
reservist
reservoir
resetting
reshuffle
residence
residency
residuary
resilient
resistant
resistive
resitting
resoluble
resolvent
resonance
resonator
resorbent
resources
respecter
responder
restfully
restiform
restitute
restively
restraint
resultant
resultful
resumable
resurface
resurgent
resurrect
retaliate
retardant
retention
retentive
rethought
retiarius
reticence
reticency
reticular
reticulum
retinitis
retinulae
retinular
retortion
retoucher
retractor
retrieval
retriever
retrocede
retrodden
retroflex
retroject
retrousse
retrovert
revelator
revelling
reverence
reversely
reversion
revetment
revetting
revictual
revisable
revivable
revocable
revolting
revulsion
revulsive
rewarding
rewritten
rhapsodic
rheumatic
Rhineodon
rhinology
rhizocarp
rhizoidal
rhodamine
rhodolite
rhodonite
rhodopsin
rhonchial
rhymester
rhythmics
rhythmise
rhythmist
Ribbonism
ribosomal
ricepaper
riderless
ridgepole
ridgetile
ridiculer
riflebird
rightable
righteous
righthand
rightness
rightward
rigidness
rigmarole
ringfence
ringingly
ringshake
ringsnake
riotously
Ripuarian
riskiness
ritualise
ritualism
ritualist
rivalling
rivalrous
rivelling
riverbank
riverboat
riverhead
riverside
riverweed
roadblock
roadhouse
roadmetal
roadstead
roadworks
rocambole
rockbound

rockbrake
rockdrill
rocketeer
rockiness
rockplant
rocksnake
rodfisher
roguishly
roisterer
roodcloth
roofplate
roominess
rootstock
Roquefort
rosaceous
roseapple
roseately
rosenoble
rosewater
rosinweed
rostellum
rotatable
rotundity
roughcast
roughhewn
roughneck
roughness
roughshod
Roumanian
Roumansch
rounceval
roundelay
roundhead
roundness
roundsman
roundworm
rousement
routinely
routinism
routinist
rowantree
rowdiness
rubberise
rubellite
rubicelle
rubricate
rubrician
rudbeckia
ruddiness
ruddleman
rufescent
ruffianly
ruggedise
ruination
ruinously
rulership
ruminator
rumrunner
runcinate
rushlight
russeting
Russophil
rusticate
rusticity
rustiness
rustproof
ruthenium
ruthfully
sabadilla
sabbatise
sabbatism
Sabellian
saccharin
sacciform
sacculate
sackcloth
sacrament
sacrarium
sacrifice
sacrilege
sacristan
saddlebag
saddlebow
Sadducean
safeguard
safetypin
safflower
safranine
sagacious
sagebrush
sagegreen
sagittate
sailcloth
sailoring
sailorman
sailplane
sainthood
saintlike
saintling
saintship
salacious
salangane
saleratus
salesgirl
saleslady
salicetum
salicylic
saliently
sallowish
salmonoid
salpinges
saltation
saltatory
saltglaze
saltiness
saltmarsh
saltpetre
saltspoon
saltwater
saltworks
salubrity
salvation
Samaritan
Samoyedic
sanatoria
sanbenito
sanctuary
sandalled
sandarach
sandblast
sandblind
sandcrack
sandglass
sandiness
sandpaper
sandpiper
sandspout
sandstone
sandstorm
sandtable
sandyacht
sangfroid
Sanhedrim
Sanhedrin
sanitaria
santolina
santonica
sapanwood
sapheaded
sapiently
sapodilla
sappiness
sapraemia
sapraemic
Saracenic
sarcastic
sarcocarp
sarcomata
Sardinian
sargassos
Sarmation
sartorial
sartorius
sasquatch
sassafras
Sassanian
Sassenach
satanical
satellite
satiation
satinbird
satinette
satinspar
satinwood
satirical
saturable
saturator
Saturnian
saturnine
saturnism
sauceboat
sauceless
saucerful
sauciness
saunterer
sauropoda
Sauternes
savagedom
savourily
saxifrage
saxophone
scagliola
scaldfish
scalefern
scalefish
scaleleaf
scaleless
scalelike
scalemoss
scaliness
scallawag
scallywag
scalplock
scantling
scantness
scapegoat
scapolite
scapulary
scarecrow
scarehead
scarfring
scarfskin
scarfwise
scarifier
scatology
scatterer
scavenger
scenarist
scenedock
scentless
sceptical
scheelite
schematic
schilling
schistose
schistous
schlemiel
schlemihl
schlieren
schmaltzy
schnauzer
schnitzel
schnorkel
schnorrer
scholarly
scholiast
schoolbag
schoolboy
schooling
schoolman
sciaenoid
sciagraph
sciamachy
sciascopy
sciential
scientism
scientist
scintilla
scirrhous
scleritis
sclerosis
sclerotic
scolecite
scoliosis
scoliotic
scombroid
scorbutic
scorching
scorebook
scorecard
scoredraw
scorifier
scorpioid
Scotchman
Scoticise
scotomata
scoundrel
scraggily
scrambler
scramming
scrapbook
scrapheap
scrapiron
scrappily
scrapping
scrapyard
scratcher
scratches
screecher
screening
screwball
screwbolt
screwpile
screwpine
screwworm
scribbler
scrimmage
scrimpily
scrimshaw
scripture
scrivener
scrollsaw
scrounger
scrubbing
scruffily
scrumhalf
scrummage
scrutable
scrutator
sculpture
scuncheon
scutcheon
scutellar
scutellum
scutiform
seaanchor
seachange
seafaring
seagirdle
sealetter
seaminess
seanettle
searching
searingly
seasoning
seasquirt
seastrand
seatangle
seaurchin
seaworthy
sebaceous
secateurs
secernent
secession
seclusion
seclusive
secondary
secretage
secretary
secretion
secretive
secretory
sectarian
sectility
sectional
sectorial
secularly
securable
sedentary
sedgewren
seditious
seduction
seductive
seedeater
seediness
seedpearl
seedplant
seemingly
segmental
segregate
seigneury
seigniory
selachian
selection
selective
selectman
selenious
selenitic
selfabuse
selfaware
selfdoubt
selfdrive
selffaced
selfglory
selfimage
selfishly
selfmoved
selfpride
selftrust
Seljukian
semanteme
semantics
semaphore
semblable
semblably
semblance
semeiotic
semestral
semibreve
semicolon
semifinal
semifluid
semilunar
semimetal
seminally
semiology
semiotics
semiplume
semirigid
semisolid
semisweet
semitonic
semivowel
senescent
seneschal
senhorita
seniority
sensation
sensedata
senseless
sensitise
sensitive
sensorial
sensorium
sensually
sentenate
sentience
sentiency
sentiment
sentrybox
separable
separably
separates
separator
Sephardic
Sephardim
sepiolite
septation
September
septemvir
septenary
septennia
septicity
septuplet
sepulcher
sepulchre
sepulture
sequacity
sequester
sequestra
sequinned
serenader
sergeancy
serialise
serialism
serialist
seriality
seriately
sericeous
serigraph
serinette
seriously
serjeancy
serjeanty
sermonise
serotonin
serpentry
serranoid
serration
serrefile
serrulate
serviette
servilely
servility
servitude
sessional
sestertia
setaceous
setsquare
sevenfold
seventeen
seventhly
seventies
severable
severally
severalty
severance
sexennial
sexlessly
sexlinked
sextuplet
sexualise
sexuality
sforzando
sgraffiti
sgraffito
shadberry
shadeless
shadetree
shadiness
shakeable
shakedown
shakerism
shakiness
shallowly
shamanism
shamanist
shamateur
shambling
shambolic
shamefast
shameless
Shangrila
shantyman
shapeable
shapeless
sharecrop
sharkskin
sharpener
sharpeyed
sharpness
sharpshod
shaveling
shearling
sheatfish
sheathing
Shechinah
sheepcote
sheepfold
sheephook
sheeplice
sheepskin
sheeptick
sheepwalk
sheepwash
sheerhulk
sheerlegs
sheerness
sheetbend
sheikhdom
sheldduck
sheldrake
shelflife
shelfmark
shelfroom
shellback
shellbark
shellfire
shellfish
shellheap
shellwork
shemozzle
shewbread
shieldbug
shieldfem
shiftless
shillelah
shinguard
shininess
Shintoism
Shintoist
shipboard
shipcanal
shipfever
shipmoney
shipowner
shipshape
shipwreck
shirtless
shirttail
shockable
shockhead
shoeblack

shoemaker
shoeshine
shogunate
shootable
shopfloor
shopfront
shoreless
shoreline
shoreside
shoreward
shoreweed
shortcake
shortener
shortfall
shorthand
shorthorn
shortness
shortstop
shortterm
shortwave
shotproof
shottower
shouldest
shovelful
shovelhat
shovelled
shoveller
showiness
showpiece
showplace
shredding
shrewmice
shrinkage
shrubbery
shrugging
sibilance
sibilancy
sibylline
siccative
sickening
sickishly
sickleave
sideboard
sideburns
sidedness
sideissue
sidelight
sideritic
siderosis
sideswipe
sidetable
sidetrack
sidewards
sidewheel
sightless
sightseer
sigillary
sigillate
sigmoidal
signalbox
signalise
signalled
signaller
signalman
signatory
signature
signboard
significs
signorial
signorina
siliceous
silicious
silicosis
silicotic
siliquose
silkgland
silkiness
silliness
siltation

siltstone
silverfir
similarly
simpatico
simpleton
simplices
simulacra
simulacre
simulator
simulcast
sincerely
sincerity
sinewless
singalong
singleton
singspiel
Sinhalese
sinistral
sinlessly
sinologue
sinophile
sinuately
sinuation
sinuosity
sinuously
sinusitis
siphonage
siphuncle
Sisyphean
situation
sitzkrieg
sixfooter
sixteenmo
sixteenth
skedaddle
skeesicks
sketchily
sketchmap
skewwhiff
skiagraph
skiamachy
skiascopy
skijoring
skilfully
skindiver
skinflick
skinflint
skingraft
skintight
skirtings
skirtless
skydiving
skyjacker
skyrocket
slabsided
slabstone
slackness
slakeless
slanderer
slantways
slantwise
slaphappy
slapstick
slateclub
slategrey
slaughter
slaveship
slavishly
Slavonian
Slavophil
sleekness
sleepless
sleevenut
slenderly
slickness
sliderule
slightish
sliminess
slingback

slingshot
slinkweed
slipcoach
slipcover
slivovitz
slopbasin
slopewise
slothbear
Slovakian
Slovenian
slowcoach
slowmatch
sluiceway
slumberer
slumbrous
slushfund
smackeroo
smallarms
smallness
smalltime
smartness
smartweed
smatterer
smileless
smilingly
smokeball
smokebomb
smokebush
smokejack
smokeless
smoketree
smokiness
smoothish
smuggling
snailfish
snakebird
snakebite
snakelike
snakeroot
snakeskin
snakeweed
snakewood
snakiness
snaredrum
sniggerer
snipefish
snivelled
sniveller
snowberry
snowblind
snowblink
snowbound
snowbroth
snowdrift
snowfield
snowflake
snowgoose
snowguard
snowiness
snowplant
snowscape
snowstorm
snowwhite
snubnosed
soapberry
soapiness
soapstone
soapworks
sobbingly
soberness
sobriquet
sobsister
socialise
socialism
socialist
socialite
sociality
sociogram
sociology

sociopath
sodabread
sodawater
softgoods
softpedal
softshell
sogginess
soidisant
sojourner
solacious
soldierly
solemnise
solemnity
soleplate
solfatara
solfeggio
solferino
solicitor
solidness
soliloquy
solipsism
solipsist
solitaire
solmisate
Solomonic
Solutrean
Solutrian
solvation
something
sometimes
somewhere
somewhile
sommelier
somnolent
songcycle
songfully
songsmith
sonneteer
sonnetise
sonometer
sooterkin
soothfast
sootiness
sophister
sophistic
sophistry
sophomore
soporific
soppiness
sopranino
sopranist
sorbapple
Sorbonist
sorceress
sorcerous
soritical
sorriness
sorrowful
sortilege
sortition
sostenuto
sottishly
soubrette
Soudanese
soulfully
soundfilm
soundhole
soundings
soundless
soundness
soundpost
soundwave
soupplate
soupspoon
sourdough
souteneur
Southdown
southeast
southerly

southland
southmost
southward
southwest
souwester
sovereign
sovietise
sovietism
spaceband
spaceless
spaceport
spaceship
spacesuit
spacetime
spadefoot
spadework
spaghetti
spagyrist
spareness
spareribs
sparingly
sparkcoil
sparkless
sparkplug
spasmodic
spatially
spatulate
speakable
speakeasy
spearfish
spearhead
spearmint
spearside
spearwort
specially
specialty
specifier
speckless
spectacle
spectator
speculate
speechful
speechify
speedball
speedboat
speedster
speedwell
spellbind
spellican
spendable
spermatic
spermatid
sphagnous
spherical
spherular
sphincter
sphygmoid
spicebush
spiciness
spiculate
spiderman
spiderweb
spikenard
spikiness
spillikin
spindling
spindrier
spindrift
spineless
spininess
spinnaker
spinneret
spinosity
Spinozism
Spinozist
spinulose
spinulous
spiracula
spirality

spiralled
spirillum
spiritism
spiritist
spiritoso
spiritous
spiritual
spirituel
spirogyra
splashily
splayfoot
spleenful
splendent
splendour
splenetic
splenitis
spleuchan
splintery
splitting
spluttery
spodumene
spoilsman
spokesman
spokewise
spoliator
spongebag
spongeous
spoonbeak
spoonbill
spoonfeed
spoonmeat
sporangia
sporocarp
sporocyst
sporogeny
sportsman
sporulate
spotcheck
spotlight
spouthole
spoutless
sprigging
sprightly
sprigtail
springald
springbok
springily
springing
springlet
sprinkler
spritsail
spurwheel
sputterer
squabbler
squalidly
squamosal
squarrose
squashily
squatness
squatting
squeakily
squeamish
squelcher
squibbing
squidding
squinancy
squirarch
squiredom
squirelet
stabilise
stability
stableboy
stableman
stackable
stackroom
stackyard
stagedoor
stagehand
staggerer

staghound
staginess
Stagirite
stagnancy
stagparty
staidness
stainable
stainless
staircase
stairfoot
stairhead
stairwell
stakeboat
stalactic
stalemate
staleness
Stalinism
Stalinist
stalkeyed
stalkless
stallfeed
stalworth
staminate
stammerer
stampduty
stampmill
stampnote
stanchion
standpipe
stapedial
starapple
starboard
starchily
stardrift
stargazer
stargrass
starkness
starlight
starshell
starstone
startling
statehood
stateless
statement
stateroom
stateside
statesman
statewide
stational
stationer
statistic
statocyst
statolith
statuette
statutory
stauncher
staunchly
staymaker
steadfast
steamboat
steampipe
steamship
steatitic
steelclad
steelhead
steelwork
steelyard
steenkirk
steepness
steersman
stegosaur
stellated
stenotype
stenotypy
stepchild
stepdance
steradian
stercoral
sterilise

sterility
sternmost
sternness
sternpost
sternward
steroidal
stevedore
stickwork
stiffener
stiffness
stigmatic
stilettos
stillborn
stillhunt
stillness
stillroom
stiltedly
stimulant
stimulate
stingaree
stingless
stinkball
stinkbomb
stinkhorn
stinktrap
stinkweed
stinkwood
stintless
stipitate
stippling
stipulate
stirabout
stitchery
stockbook
stockdove
stockfish
stockinet
stocklist
stockpile
stockroom
stockwhip
stockyard
stoically
stokehold
stokehole
stolidity
stolonate
stomachal
stomacher
stomachic
stonechat
stonecoal
stonecold
stonecrop
stonedead
stonedeaf
stonefish
stoneless
stonewall
stoneware
stonework
stonewort
stoniness
stoolball
stoplight
stoppress
stopwatch
storeroom
storeship
storiated
stormbelt
stormbird
stormcock
stormcone
stormless
stormsail
storybook
storyline
stoutness
stovepipe
straggler
strangely
strangler
strangles
straphang
strapless
strappado
strapping
strapwork
strapwort
stratagem
strategic
strawworm
streakily
streaking
streamlet
streetcar
strenuous
stressful
stretcher
strewment
striation
striature
stricture
stridence
stridency
stringent
stripling
stripping
strobilae
strobilus
stromatic
strongarm
strongbox
strongish
strongyle
strontium
stropping
strouding
structure
struggler
strumitis
strumming
strutting
strychnic
studhorse
studiedly
stupefier
stupidity
stuporous
stutterer
stylebook
styliform
stylishly
stylistic
stylobate
suability
suasively
subaerial
subagency
subalpine
subaltern
subarctic
subastral
subatomic
subbranch
subcaudal
subcostal
subdeacon
subdivide
subduable
subduedly
subeditor
subereous
subfamily
subgenera
subjacent
subjugate
sublation
sublethal
sublimate
sublimely
sublimity
sublunary
submarine
submaster
submental
submitted
subnormal
subocular
subphylum
subregion
subrogate
subscribe
subscript
subsellia
subsidise
substance
substrata
substrate
subtenant
subtilise
subtopian
subverter
succeeder
succentor
successor
succinate
succotash
succourer
succulent
succursal
suctorial
suctorian
sudatoria
sudorific
suffering
suffocate
suffragan
suffusion
sugarbeet
sugarcane
sugarloaf
sugarplum
suggester
sulcation
sulkiness
sulphonic
sulphuret
sulphuric
sultanate
sultaness
summarily
summarise
summarist
summation
summative
summingup
sumptuary
sumptuous
sunbather
sunbonnet
sunburned
sundowner
sunflower
sunhelmet
sunlounge
sunniness
sunspurge
sunstroke
sunstruck
suntanned
superable
supercool
superfine
superfuse
superheat
supernova
superpose
supersede
superstar
supervene
supervise
supinator
suppliant
supporter
supposing
suppurate
supremacy
supremely
surcharge
surcingle
surculose
surfacing
surfboard
surfeiter
surficial
surgeoncy
surliness
surmullet
surpliced
surprisal
surrender
surrogate
surveying
suspender
suspensor
suspicion
sustainer
susurrant
sutteeism
suturally
swaddling
swaggerer
swangoose
swansdown
swarajist
swartness
swearword
sweatband
sweatshop
sweepback
sweetcorn
sweetener
sweetmeal
sweetmeat
sweetness
sweetshop
sweettalk
swellfish
sweptback
swiftness
swimmable
swimmeret
swineherd
swingeing
swinishly
switchman
swivelled
swordcane
swordfish
swordknot
swordlike
swordplay
swordsman
swordtail
sybaritic
sycophant
syllabary
syllabise
syllabism
syllabled
syllepses
syllepsis
sylleptic
syllogise
syllogism
sylphlike
sylvanite
symbiosis
symbiotic
symbolics
symbolise
symbolism
symbolist
symbology
symmetric
symphonic
symphysis
sympodial
sympodium
symposiac
symposial
symposium
synagogal
synagogue
synchrony
synclinal
syncopate
syncretic
syncytial
syncytium
syndactyl
syndicate
synectics
syneresis
synergism
synergist
syngamous
synizesis
synodical
synoecete
synonymic
synoptist
synovitis
syntactic
syntheses
synthesis
synthetic
syphilise
syphiloid
syringeal
systaltic
tablature
tableland
tableleaf
tabletalk
tableware
tabularly
tabulator
tacamahac
tachylite
tachylyte
tacitness
tackiness
tactfully
tactician
tactility
tactitian
tactually
taeniasis
tahsildar
tailboard
taillight
tailoress
tailoring
tailpiece
taintless
taioseach
talismans
talkathon
talkative
tallowish
tallyshop
Talmudist
tambourin
tamponade
tangerine
tanliquor
tanpickle
tantalate
tantalise
tantalite
tapdancer
tarantara
tarantass
tarantism
tarantula
taraxacum
tardiness
Targumist
tarpaulin
tarragona
Tartarean
Tartarian
tartishly
Tartufian
Tartufism
taskforce
Tasmanian
tasselled
tasteless
tastiness
tattiness
tattooist
tautology
tawniness
taxidermy
taximeter
taxonomic
taxpaying
teachable
teachably
teacupful
teakettle
tearfully
teasingly
technical
technique
tectonics
tectorial
tectrices
tediously
tegmental
tegmentum
tegularly
teknonymy
telamones
telegenic
telegraph
telemeter
telemetry
teleology
telepathy
telephone
telephony
telephoto
telescope
telescopy
televisor
tellingly
tellurate
tellurian
telluride
tellurite
tellurium
tellurous
telophase
temperate
temporary
temporise
temptable
temptress
tenacious
tenaculum
tenderise
tendinous
tenebrist
tenebrous
tenseness
tensility
tensional
tentacled
tentation
tentative
tenthrate
tentmaker
tenuously
tepidness
teratogen
terebinth
terebrant
termagant
terminate
terminism
terminist
termitary
ternately
terramara
terramare
terrarium
territory
terrorise
terrorism
terrorist
terseness
tervalent
tessitura
testament
testation
testatrix
testdrive
testifier
testimony
testiness
tetradite
tetragram
tetralogy
tetrapody
tetrarchy
teutonise
Teutonism
Teutonist
textually
thalassic
thaneship
thankless
thatching
theandric
theatrics
theocracy
theocrasy
theogonic
theologic
theologue
theomachy
theomania
theophany
theoretic
theoriser
theosophy
therapist
Theravada
therefore
therefrom
thereinto
thereunto
thereupon
therewith
thermally
thermidor
thesaurus
theurgist

thickener
thicketed
thickhead
thickknee
thickness
thighbone
thighboot
thingness
thingummy
thinkable
thinktank
thirdhand
thirdrate
thirdsman
thirstily
thirtieth
thitherto
Thomistic
thornback
thornbill
thornbush
thornless
thorntree
thoughted
thralldom
thrashing
threefold
threesome
threnodic
threshold
thriftily
thrilling
throatily
throbbing
thrombose
throttler
throughly
throwaway
throwback
throwster
thrumming
thumbhole
thumbmark
thumbnail
thumbtack
thunderer
Thyestean
thylacine
thyratron
thyristor
thyroxine
tidegauge
tidewater
tiedyeing
tigerlily
tigermoth
tigerseye
tigerwood
tightener
tightness
tightrope
tightwire
tilestone
timbering
timberman
timelapse
timelimit
timeously
timepiece
timesheet
timetable
timidness
timocracy
timpanist
tinderbox
tinniness
tinopener
tinselled
tipsiness
tipstaves
tiredness
tirewoman
titillate
titledeed
titlepage
titration
tittivate
tittlebat
tittuping
tittupped
titularly
toadeater
toadstone
toadstool
toastrack
Tocharian
tolerable
tolerably
tolerance
tollbooth
tollhouse
tombstone
tomentose
tomentous
tonguelet
tonguetie
tonically
tonometer
tonsillar
tonsorial
toolhouse
toothache
toothcomb
toothless
toothpick
toothsome
toothwort
tophamper
topiarian
topiarist
topically
toponymal
toponymic
torchrace
torchsong
toreutics
tormentil
tormentor
torpidity
torridity
torsional
tortrices
tortricid
torturous
totaliser
totalling
totempole
touchable
touchdown
touchhole
touchline
touchmark
touchtype
touchwood
toughness
touristic
tournedos
tourneyer
towelling
townhouse
townscape
townsfolk
toxically
toxophily
trabeated
trabecula
traceable
traceably
traceless
traceried
tracheary
tracheate
trachytic
trackless
tracksuit
tractable
tractably
trademark
tradename
tradesman
tradition
traducian
tragedian
trainable
trainband
trainload
traitress
tramlines
transcend
transenna
transform
transfuse
transient
translate
transmute
transonic
transpire
transport
transpose
transship
transumpt
transvest
trapezial
trapezium
trapezoid
trappings
trattoria
trattorie
traumatic
travelled
traveller
traversal
traverser
traycloth
treachery
treadmill
treasurer
treatable
treatment
trebuchet
trebucket
treillage
trematode
tremolant
tremolite
tremulant
tremulous
trenchant
trepanned
trepidant
trialogue
triatomic
tribadism
tribalism
tribesman
tribology
tribunate
tributary
trichinae
trichomic
trichroic
trickless
tricksily
trickster
triclinia
triclinic
tricolour
tridactyl
tridymite
triennial
triennium
trierarch
trifacial
trifocals
trifolium
triforium
trigamist
trigamous
trihedral
trihybrid
trilinear
trilithon
trilobate
trilobite
trimerous
trimester
trimetric
trimmings
trinketer
trinketry
trinomial
triploidy
triptyque
triquetra
trisagion
trisector
triteness
tritheism
tritheist
triturate
triumphal
triumviri
trivalent
trivially
triweekly
trochilus
trochleae
trochlear
troopship
tropology
troublous
trousered
trousseau
troutfarm
troutling
trowelled
troweller
truceless
truculent
truepenny
trumpedup
trumpeter
truncated
truncheon
trunkcall
trunkfish
trunkroad
trussbeam
trustdeed
trustless
truthless
trysquare
tsarevich
tubbiness
tubercule
tubularly
tuckerbag
tufaceous
tuitional
tuliproot
tuliptree
tulipwood
tumblebug
tumescent
tumidness
tunefully
tungstate
tunicated
tunnelled
tunnelnet
turbidity
turbinate
turboprop
turbulent
Turcomans
turgently
turgidity
Turkomans
turnabout
turnround
turnstile
turnstone
turntable
turpitude
turquoise
tutorship
twayblade
twelfthly
twentieth
twentyone
twiceborn
twicelaid
twicetold
twinkling
twistable
twitchily
twitterer
twofisted
twohanded
twosuiter
tympanist
typemetal
typewrite
typhlitis
typhoidal
typically
tyrannise
tyrannous
uintahite
Uitlander
Ukrainian
uliginous
ultimatum
ultrahigh
ululation
umbellate
umbellule
umberbird
umbilical
umbilicus
umpteenth
unabashed
unadopted
unadorned
unadvised
unalloyed
unaltered
unanimity
unanimous
unaptness
unashamed
unbalance
unbeknown
unbending
unberufen
unbiassed
unblessed
unblinded
unbounded
unbraided
unbridled
uncannily
unceasing
uncertain
uncharted
unchecked
uncinated
uncivilly
uncleanly
unclothed
unclouded
unconcern
uncounted
uncouthly
uncovered
uncreated
uncropped
uncrossed
uncrowned
undamaged
undaunted
undecagon
undeceive
undecided
undecimal
undefined
underbody
underbred
underclay
undercoat
underdone
underfelt
underfoot
undergird
undergone
undergrad
underhand
underhung
underlaid
underlain
underline
underling
undermine
undermost
underpaid
underpart
underpass
underplay
underplot
underrate
underripe
underseal
underseas
undersell
undershot
underside
undersign
undersold
undersong
underspin
undertake
undertint
undertone
undertook
undervest
underwear
underwent
underwing
underwood
undivided
undoubted
undreamed
undulated
undutiful
unearthly
uneatable
unequally
unethical
unfailing
unfeeling
unfeigned
unfitness
unfitting
unfledged
unfleshed
unfleshly
unfounded
ungallant
unguarded
unhappily
unharness
unhealthy
unheeding
unhelpful
unhurried
unicolour
unicuspid
unifiable
uniformly
uniparous
uniplanar
uniserial
unisexual
unisonant
unisonous
unitarian
unitively
univalent
universal
unknitted
unknowing
unlearned
unlimited
unluckily
unmatched
unmeaning
unmindful
unmusical
unnamable
unnatural
unpegging
unpeopled
unplugged
unplumbed
unpointed
unpopular
unreality
unreserve
unruffled
unsavoury
unsayable
unscathed
unselfish
unsettled
unshackle
unsheathe
unsighted
unsightly
unskilful
unskilled
unsmiling
unsoundly
unsparing
unspotted
unstopped
unstudied
unsuccess
unsullied
untenable
unthought
unthrifty
untimeous
untouched
untrodden
untrussed
untutored
unusually
unwearied
unweeting
unwelcome
unwilling
unwinking
unwitting

unwomanly
unwrapped
unwritten
unwrought
unzipping
Upanishad
upbraider
upcountry
upholster
uplifting
uppercase
uppermost
uprightly
upsetting
uraninite
uranology
urceolate
uropygium
urticaria
uselessly
usherette
usualness
usucapion
utricular
utterable
utterance
utterless
uttermost
utterness
uvarovite
uxoricide
vaccinate
vacillant
vacillate
vacuolate
vacuously
vademecum
vagarious
vagueness
vainglory
Vaishnava
valentine
valiantly
validness
vallation
vallecula
valuables
valuation
valueless
valveless
vampirism
vandalise
vandalism
vapidness
vaporable
vaporific
vaporiser
vapouring
vapourish
Varangian
variation
varicella
variegate
variolate
variolite
varioloid
variolous
variously
varnisher
vasectomy
vasomotor
vassalage
vastitude
vaticinal
vectorial
Vedantist
veeringly
vegetable
vegetably
vehemence
vehicular
veinstone
velodrome
velveteen
vendition
veneering
venerable
venerably
venerator
venereous
vengeance
veniality
ventiduct
ventifact
ventilate
ventrally
ventricle
venturous
veracious
verandaed
veratrine
verbalise
verbalism
verbalist
verbicide
verbosely
verbosity
verdantly
verdigris
veridical
veritable
veritably
vermicide
vermicule
vermiform
vermifuge
vermilion
verminate
verminous
vernalise
vernation
verrucose
verrucous
versatile
versifier
versiform
versional
vertebrae
vertebral
vesicular
vestibule
vestigial
vestigium
vestiture
vestryman
vetchling
vexatious
vexillary
viability
vibracula
vibraharp
vibratile
vibration
vibrative
vibratory
vibrissae
vicariate
vicarious
vicennial
viceregal
vicereine
viceroyal
vicesimal
viciously
victimise
Victorian
victorine
videlicet
videotape
viewpoint
vigesimal
vigilance
vigilante
vignetter
villagery
villanage
villenage
villiform
villosity
vimineous
vinaceous
vindicate
violation
violative
violently
violinist
virescent
Virgilian
virginals
virginity
virgulate
viricidal
virtually
virtuosic
virtuosos
virulence
virulency
viscerate
viscidity
viscosity
viscounty
viscously
visionary
visionist
visitable
visitress
visualise
vitellary
vitelline
vitiation
vitiosity
vitriform
vitriolic
Vitruvian
vivacious
viverrine
vivianite
vividness
vizierate
vizierial
vocabular
vocaliser
vocalness
voiceless
voiceover
volauvent
volcanism
volcanoes
volkslied
volteface
voltinism
voltmeter
volumeter
voluntary
volunteer
vomitoria
voodooism
voodooist
voracious
vorticism
vorticist
vorticity
vorticose
vouchsafe
vowelless
voyeurism
vulcanian
vulcanise
vulcanism
vulcanist
vulcanite
vulgarian
vulgarise
vulgarism
vulgarity
vulnerary
vulpinism
vulpinite
vulturine
vulturish
vulturous
wackiness
waggishly
waggonage
Wagnerian
Wagnerite
wagonette
wagonroof
wailingly
waistband
waistbelt
waistcoat
waistline
wakefully
wakerobin
Waldenses
waldgrave
walkabout
wallboard
wallcress
wallfruit
walloping
wallpaper
wallplate
wallydrag
Walpurgis
wandering
wapentake
warblefly
warbonnet
warehouse
warmonger
warningly
warrantee
warranter
warrantor
wartcress
washbasin
washboard
washcloth
washedout
washerman
washhouse
washiness
washstand
waspishly
wassailer
wasteland
wasteness
wastepipe
watchable
watchcase
watchfire
watchword
waterbath
waterbuck
waterbutt
watercart
watercool
waterfall
waterflea
waterfowl
watergate
waterhole
waterleaf
waterless
waterlily
waterline
watermark
watermill
waterpipe
watershed
waterside
waterweed
waterworn
wattmeter
wavefront
waveguide
wavellite
wayfaring
waywardly
wayzgoose
weakkneed
wealthily
weariless
weariness
wearisome
weathered
weatherly
webfooted
wedgewise
Wednesday
weediness
weeknight
weevilled
wehrmacht
weighable
weighbeam
weightily
weighting
weirdness
welcoming
welfarism
wellbeing
wellfound
wellknown
welltimed
werwolves
westbound
westering
westerner
westwards
whaleback
whaleboat
whalebone
whalehead
wheatmeal
wheedling
wheelbase
wheelless
wheelwork
wherefore
wherefrom
whereinto
whereunto
whereupon
wherewith
wherryman
whetstone
wheyfaced
whichever
whimperer
whimsical
whinstone
whipperin
whipround
whipsnake
whipstock
whirligig
whirlpool
whirlwind
whiskered
whisperer
whistling
whitebait
whitebass
whitebeam
whiteface
whitefish
Whitehall
whitehead
whiteness
whitening
whitewash
whitewing
whitewood
whizzbang
whodunnit
wholemeal
wholeness
wholesale
wholesome
whosoever
wideawake
widowbird
widowhood
widthways
widthwise
wieldable
willemite
willingly
willowish
willpower
windblown
windbound
windbreak
windchest
windhover
windiness
windowbox
windproof
windswept
windwards
wineberry
wineglass
winepress
winestone
winevault
wingchair
winningly
winsomely
winterise
wiredrawn
wiregauze
wirephoto
wisecrack
wishfully
wistfully
witchetty
witchhunt
witchmeal
withdrawn
withering
witherite
withstand
withstood
witlessly
witticism
wittiness
wittingly
woebegone
wolfhound
wolfishly
wolframic
wolfsbane
wolverene
wolverine
womanhood
womaniser
womankind
womanlike
womenfolk
womenkind
wonderful
woodblock
woodchuck
woodcraft
woodiness
woodlouse
woodnymph
woodwaxen
wooziness
Worcester
wordiness
wordsmith
workbench
workhorse
workhouse
workmanly
workpiece
worktable
workwoman
worldling
worldwide
wormeaten
wormwheel
worriedly
worriment
worrisome
worrywart
worthless
woundless
woundwort
wrathless
wrestling
wristband
wristdrop
wristshot
wrongdoer
wrongness
wulfenite
wyandotte
wychhazel
Wyclifite
wyliecoat
Xanthippe
xenograft
xenophile
xenophobe
xeromorph
xerophile
xerophily
xerophyte
xparticle
xylograph
xylophone
yachtclub
yachtsman
Yankeedom
Yankeeism
yardstick
yawningly
yearround
yellowdog
yellowish
yesterday
Yiddisher
yodelling
yohimbine
Yorkshire
youngling
youngness
youngster
ytterbium
zamindary
zapateado
zealously
zebrawood
zeitgeist
zemindary
zestfully
zeugmatic
zibelline

zigzagged
zincotype
zinkenite
zirconium
zoiatrics
zoogenous
zoography
zoologist
zoophagan
zoophobia
zoophytic
zootechny
zootomist
zucchetto
Zwinglian
zygomatic
zygospore
zymogenic

---

babacoote
Babbittry
babirussa
baboonish
bacchanal
bacchante
bacillary
backbiter
backboard
backcloth
backcross
backpedal
backsight
backslang
backslide
backspace
backstage
backsword
backtrack
backwards
backwater
backwoods
bacterial
bacterise
bacterium
bacteroid
badminton
bagatelle
bagginess
bailiwick
bainmarie
bakehouse
baksheesh
balaclava
balalaika
balconied
baldachin
baldaquin
baldfaced
balefully
balkanise
balladeer
balladist
ballerina
ballistae
ballistic
ballpoint
balminess
baltimore
bamboozle
banderole
bandicoot
bandoleer
bandolero
bandolier
bandoline
bandstand
bandwagon
bandwidth
baneberry
banefully
banjulele
bannister
banqueter
banquette
Bantustan
baptismal
baptistry
barathrum
Barbadian
barbarian
barbarise
barbarism
barbarity
barbarous
barbitone
barcarole
barefaced
bargainer
bargepole
barkeeper
barleymow
barmbrack
Barmecide
barnacled
barnstorm
barograph
barometer
barometry
baronetcy
barracker
barracoon
barracuda
barrelful
barrelled
barricade
barricado
barrister
bartender
bashfully
basically
basilican
basipetal
basketful
basrelief
bastardly
bastinade
bastinado
bastioned
bathhouse
batholite
batholith
Bathonian
bathybius
battalion
battening
battiness
battleaxe
battlecry
bawdiness
bayoneted
caballero
caballine
caballing
cabbalism
cabbalist
cablegram
cablelaid
cabriolet
cachectic
cacholong
caciquism
cacodemon
cacodylic
cacoethes
cacophony
cacuminal
cadastral
cadaveric
caddisfly
cadential
cadetship
caecilian
Caenozoic
caerulean
Caesarean
Caesarian
Caesarism
Caesarist
cafeteria
cageyness
cailleach
Cainozoic
cairngorm
calaboose
calabrese
calamanco
calandria
calcaneal
calcaneum
calcarate
calcicole
calcifuge
calculate
calculous
caldarium
calendric
calendula
calenture
calibrate
calicular
caliology
caliphate
callipers
callosity
callously
calmative
calorific
Calvinism
Calvinist
calycinal
camarilla
Cambodian
camelback
camelhair
Camembert
cameraman
camorrist
campanile
campanili
campanula
campchair
campcraft
campfever
camphoric
campstool
canalboat
cancelled
cancerous
candidacy
candidate
Candlemas
candlenut
candytuft
canebrake
canescent
canesugar
canetrash
canicular
cankerous
cannelure
canniness
cannonade
cannoneer
cannonier
cannulate
canonical
cantabile
cantaloup
cantharid
cantharis
cantharus
cantilena
Cantonese
cantorial
canvasser
capacious
capacitor
caparison
capillary
capitally
capitular
capitulum
capriccio
Capricorn
capsulate
capsulise
captaincy
captivate
captivity
carambola
carbamate
carbamide
carbonado
carbonate
carbonise
carbuncle
carburise
carcinoma
cardboard
cardsharp
careerism
careerist
carefully
caretaker
carfuffle
Caribbean
Carmelite
carnality
carnation
carnelian
carnitine
carnivore
carolling
carpenter
carpentry
carpetbag
carpeting
carpingly
carpology
carrageen
carrefour
carronade
carryover
Cartesian
carthorse
cartilage
cartogram
cartology
cartouche
cartridge
cartulary
cartwheel
caryopses
caryopsis
caseation
Cassandra
cassareep
cassaripe
cassation
casserole
cassimere
cassoulet
cassowary
Castalian
castanets
castellan
castigate
Castilian
Castroism
casuarina
casuistic
casuistry
catabolic
cataclasm
cataclysm
catalepsy
catalexes
catalexis
catalogue
catalyser
catalyses
catalysis
catalytic
catamaran
catamount
cataplasm
cataplexy
catarhine
catarrhal
catatonia
catatonic
catchable
catchment
catchpole
catchpoll
catchword
catechise
catechism
catechist
caterwaul
Catharism
Catharist
catharses
catharsis
cathartic
cathectic
cathedral
catoptric
cattaloes
cattiness
cattleman
Caucasian
causality
causation
causative
causeless
cauterise
cavalcade
cavendish
cavernous
cavilling
dachshund
Daedalean
Daedalian
dahabiyah
dairymaid
dalliance
dalmatian
daltonism
damascene
damnation
damnatory
damnedest
damningly
Damoclean
dancehall
dandelion
dandiacal
dangerous
Dantesque
daredevil
dartboard
Darwinian
Darwinism
Darwinist
dashboard
dashingly
dastardly
dauntless
davenport
dayschool
dayspring
eagerness
ealdorman
earliness
earnestly
earthborn
earthling
earthstar
earthward
earthwork
earthworm
earwigged
easefully
eastbound
Eastender
easterner
eastwards
easygoing
eavesdrop
fabaceous
Fabianism
fabricant
fabricate
facecloth
facetious
facsimile
factional
factitive
factorage
factorial
factorise
factually
facundity
faddiness
faggoting
faintness
fairfaced
fairyhood
fairyland
fairylike
fairyring
fairytale
faithcure
faithless
Falangism
Falangist
falciform
faldstool
Falernian
fallalery
falsehood
falseness
falsifier
familyman
fanatical
fancyfree
fancywork
fandangle
fandangos
fanfarade
fantasied
fantasise
fantasist
fantastic
fantastry
farandole
farestage
farmhouse
farmstead
farseeing
fasciated
fascicled
fascicule
fasciculi
fascinate
Fascistic
fashioner
fastening
fastigium
fatefully
fatheaded
fatidical
fatigable
fattiness
fatuously
fatwitted
faultless
faunistic
faveolate
favourite
fawningly
gabardine
gaberdine
gabionade
gadgeteer
Gaeltacht
gainfully
gainsayer
galactose
galantine
galenical
galingale
gallantly
gallantry
galleried
gallicise
gallicism
gallingly
gallinule
gallivant
galliwasp
gallmidge
gallonage
gallooned
gallopade
Gallophil
galloping
gallowses
gallstone
galvanise
galvanism
galvanist
gambadoes
gambolled
gammadion
gammoning
ganderism
gangboard
gangplank
gannister
gaolbreak
gardening
garderobe
garibaldi
garmented
garnishee
garniture
garreteer
garrotter
garrulity
garrulous
gasconade
gasfitter
gasholder
gasmantle
gasometer
gaspereau
gastraeum
gastritis
gastropod
gastrulae
gatecrash

gatehouse
gathering
gaucherie
gaudiness
gaugeable
gauleiter
gauntness
gauziness
gavelkind
gawkiness
gazehound
gazetteer
habergeon
habitable
habitably
habituate
hackamore
hackberry
hackneyed
haematite
haematoid
haematoma
haemostat
haggadist
haggardly
hagiarchy
hagiology
hagridden
hailstone
hailstorm
hairbrush
haircloth
hairgrass
hairiness
hairpiece
hairshirt
hairslide
hairspace
hairstyle
halfbaked
halfblood
halfbound
halfbreed
halfcaste
halfcrown
halfhardy
halflight
halfpence
halfpenny
halfprice
halfshell
halfstaff
halftitle
halftrack
halftruth
halieutic
halitosis
Halloween
Hallowmas
hallstand
Hallstatt
halophile
halophyte
halothane
haltingly
hamadryad
hamamelis
hamburger
hamfisted
hamhanded
hammerman
hammertoe
hamstring
hamstrung
handbrake
handcraft
handcuffs
handglass
handiness
handiwork
handlebar
handorgan
handpress
handsdown
handshake
handspike
handstand
handwheel
handywork
hangerson
hankering
Hanseatic
hanselled
haphazard
haplessly
haplology
happening
happiness
haranguer
harbinger
harbourer
hardboard
hardcover
hardihood
hardiment
hardiness
hardnosed
hardshell
haresfoot
harlequin
harmaline
harmattan
harmfully
harmonica
harmonics
harmonise
harmonist
harmonium
harmotome
harpooner
harquebus
Harrovian
harrowing
harshness
hartshorn
harvester
Hashemite
Hashimite
hastiness
hatchback
hatchling
hatchment
hatefully
haughtily
haustella
haustoria
haverings
haversack
havocking
hawksbill
hawsehole
hawsepipe
hazardous
jaborandi
jacaranda
jackknife
jackplane
jacksnipe
jackstraw
Jacobinic
jacquerie
jactation
jailbreak
jambalaya
jampacked
janissary
janitress
Jansenism
Jansenist
japanning
jargonise
jarringly
jaundiced
jaywalker
jazziness
kaiserdom
kaiserism
kaolinise
kaolinite
karabiner
karyotype
katabasis
katabatic
katabolic
katharsis
labelling
labialise
labialism
laborious
labourite
labyrinth
laccolith
lacerable
lacertian
lacertine
lachrymal
laciniate
lacrimose
lacrymose
lactation
ladysmock
laevulose
laggardly
lagniappe
lagomorph
lairdship
lallation
lambently
lamellate
lamellose
laminaria
laminated
lampblack
lamplight
lampooner
lampshade
lampshell
lancejack
lancewood
lancinate
landagent
landaulet
landdross
landdrost
landgrave
landloper
landowner
landscape
landslide
Langobard
langouste
languidly
lankiness
lanthanum
Laodicean
lapideous
Laplander
lapstrake
lapstreak
larcenist
larcenous
lardycake
largeness
larghetto
larvicide
laryngeal
lassitude
lastditch
lastingly
latecomer
laterally
latescent
lathering
latitancy
latterday
latticing
laudation
laudative
laudatory
laughable
laughably
launching
launderer
laundress
laurelled
lavaliere
lawgiving
lawlessly
lawnmower
lazaretto
lazybones
lazytongs
lazzarone
lazzaroni
macaronic
Maccabean
macedoine
macerator
machinate
machinery
machinist
machmeter
macintosh
macrocosm
macrocyte
maddening
madeleine
madrepore
maelstrom
magdalene
Magianism
magically
magicking
magistery
magistral
magnalium
magnesian
magnesite
magnesium
magnetics
magnetise
magnetism
magnetist
magnetite
magnetron
magnifico
magnifier
magnitude
maharajah
maharanee
maharishi
mahlstick
Mahometan
maidenish
mailplane
mailtrain
mainbrace
mainliner
mainsheet
majordomo
majorette
majorship
majuscule
makeready
makeshift
malachite
maladroit
malanders
malarious
malathion
Malayalam
malformed
malicious
malignant
malignity
malleable
malleehen
mallemuck
malleolar
malleolus
malthouse
malvoisie
mamillary
mamillate
mammalian
mammalogy
mammiform
mammonish
mammonism
mammonist
mammonite
Mancunian
mandarine
mandatary
mandatory
mandoline
manducate
maneating
manganate
manganese
manganite
manganous
manginess
manhandle
manhattan
Manichean
manifesto
manipular
manliness
mannequin
mannerism
mannerist
manoeuvre
manometer
manorseat
mansarded
mansionry
manslayer
manticore
manubrium
Manxwoman
manyplies
manysided
manzanita
maquisard
marcasite
marcelled
marchpane
marchpast
marestail
margarine
margarite
marginate
marihuana
marijuana
maritally
marketday
marketing
marlstone
marmalade
marmoreal
marquetry
marrowfat
marshalcy
marshland
marshwort
marsupial
marsupium
martially
Martinmas
martyrdom
martyrise
marvelled
masculine
masochism
masochist
masonried
Masoretic
massagist
massiness
massively
masterdom
masterful
masterkey
masticate
matchless
matchlock
matchwood
maternity
mateyness
matriarch
matricide
matricula
matrimony
matronage
matronise
mattamore
matutinal
maulstick
maunderer
mausoleum
mawkishly
maxillary
maximally
maybeetle
mayflower
mayoralty
mayorship
Nahuatlan
nailbrush
nakedness
nameplate
nannygoat
naphthene
napthalic
narcissus
narcotine
narcotise
narcotism
narration
narrative
narratory
naseberry
nastiness
natheless
natrolite
nattiness
naturally
naughtily
naumachia
navelwort
navicular
navigable
navigator
oakenshaw
oasthouse
pacemaker
pachyderm
packaging
packdrill
packhorse
packtrain
paederast
pageantry
paillasse
paillette
painfully
painterly
paintwork
pairhorse
Pakistani
palaestra
palafitte
palankeen
palanquin
palatable
palatably
palillogy
Palladian
palladium
palladous
palletise
palliasse
pallidity
palmation
palmipede
palmistry
palmitate
palpation
palpebral
palpitant
palpitate
palsgrave
paludinal
palustral
panatella
panchayat
pancratic
panderess
panegyric
panelling
panellist
panhandle
panicking
panoplied
panoramic
pantalets
pantaloon
pantheism
pantheist
pantingly
pantomime
pantryman
pantyhose
paperback
paperclip
papergirl
paperthin
paperwork
papeterie
papillary
papillate
papilloma
papillose
papillote
parabasis
parabolic
parachute
Paraclete
paradisal
paragraph
paralalia
paralexia
paralysis
paralytic
paramatta
paramedic
parameter
paramorph
paramount
paranoiac
paranymph
parapeted

parapodia
parasitic
parataxis
parathion
parbuckle
parcelled
parcenary
parchment
paregoric
parentage
parfleche
parhelion
parleyvoo
parlously
parochial
parotitis
parquetry
parrakeet
parricide
Parseeism
parsimony
parsonage
partially
partition
partitive
partridge
pasodoble
passenger
passerine
passersby
passional
passivate
passively
passivity
pastedown
pasticcio
pastiness
pastorale
pastorate
pasturage
patchouli
patchouly
patchwork
patellate
paternity
pathogeny
pathology
patiently
patinated
patriarch
patrician
patricide
patrimony
patriotic
patristic
patrolled
patroller
patrolman
patrology
patronage
patroness
patronise
paulownia
pauperise
pauperism
Pavlovian
paymaster
paypacket
rabbinate
rabbinism
rabbinist
rabidness
racehorse
racetrack
racialism
racialist
racketeer
raconteur
radialply
radiantly
radiately
radiation
radiative
radically
radicular
radiocast
radiogram
radiology
raffinate
raffinose
raffishly
rafflesia
raincheck
raincloud
raingauge
raininess
rainmaker
rainproof
rainstorm
rainwater
rakehelly
rampantly
rancidity
rancorous
randiness
randomise
ranginess
ransacker
rantingly
ranunculi
rapacious
rapidfire
rapidness
raptorial
rapturous
rareeshow
rascaldom
rascalism
rascality
raspatory
raspberry
raspingly
ratepayer
rationale
rationing
raucously
raunchily
rauwolfia
ravelling
ravelment
ravishing
razorback
razorbill
razoredge
razorfish
sabadilla
sabbatise
sabbatism
Sabellian
saccharin
sacciform
sacculate
sackcloth
sacrament
sacrarium
sacrifice
sacrilege
sacristan
saddlebag
saddlebow
Sadducean
safeguard
safetypin
safflower
safranine
sagacious
sagebrush
sagegreen
sagittate
sailcloth
sailoring
sailorman
sailplane
sainthood
saintlike
saintling
saintship
salacious
salangane
saleratus
salesgirl
saleslady
salicetum
salicylic
saliently
sallowish
salmonoid
salpinges
saltation
saltatory
saltglaze
saltiness
saltmarsh
saltpetre
saltspoon
saltwater
saltworks
salubrity
salvation
Samaritan
Samoyedic
sanatoria
sanbenito
sanctuary
sandalled
sandarach
sandblast
sandblind
sandcrack
sandglass
sandiness
sandpaper
sandpiper
sandspout
sandstone
sandstorm
sandtable
sandyacht
sangfroid
Sanhedrim
Sanhedrin
sanitaria
santolina
santonica
sapanwood
sapheaded
sapiently
sapodilla
sappiness
sapraemia
sapraemic
Saracenic
sarcastic
sarcocarp
sarcomata
Sardinian
sargassos
Sarmation
sartorial
sartorius
sasquatch
sassafras
Sassanian
Sassenach
satanical
satellite
satiation
satinbird
satinette
satinspar
satinwood
satirical
saturable
saturator
Saturnian
saturnine
saturnism
sauceboat
sauceless
saucerful
sauciness
saunterer
sauropoda
Sauternes
savagedom
savourily
saxifrage
saxophone
tablature
tableland
tableleaf
tabletalk
tableware
tabularly
tabulator
tacamahac
tachylite
tachylyte
tacitness
tackiness
tactfully
tactician
tactility
tactitian
tactually
taeniasis
tahsildar
tailboard
taillight
tailoress
tailoring
tailpiece
taintless
taioseach
talismans
talkathon
talkative
tallowish
tallyshop
Talmudist
tambourin
tamponade
tangerine
tanliquor
tanpickle
tantalate
tantalise
tantalite
tapdancer
tarantara
tarantass
tarantism
tarantula
taraxacum
tardiness
Targumist
tarpaulin
tarragona
Tartarean
Tartarian
tartishly
Tartufian
Tartufism
taskforce
Tasmanian
tasselled
tasteless
tastiness
tattiness
tattooist
tautology
tawniness
taxidermy
taximeter
taxonomic
taxpaying
vaccinate
vacillant
vacillate
vacuolate
vacuously
vademecum
vagarious
vagueness
vainglory
Vaishnava
valentine
valiantly
validness
vallation
vallecula
valuables
valuation
valueless
valveless
vampirism
vandalise
vandalism
vapidness
vaporable
vaporific
vaporiser
vapouring
vapourish
Varangian
variation
varicella
variegate
variolate
variolite
varioloid
variolous
variously
varnisher
vasectomy
vasomotor
vassalage
vastitude
vaticinal
wackiness
waggishly
waggonage
Wagnerian
Wagnerite
wagonette
wagonroof
wailingly
waistband
waistbelt
waistcoat
waistline
wakefully
wakerobin
Waldenses
waldgrave
walkabout
wallboard
wallcress
wallfruit
walloping
wallpaper
wallplate
wallydrag
Walpurgis
wandering
wapentake
warblefly
warbonnet
warehouse
warmonger
warningly
warrantee
warranter
warrantor
wartcress
washbasin
washboard
washcloth
washedout
washerman
washhouse
washiness
washstand
waspishly
wassailer
wasteland
wasteness
wastepipe
watchable
watchcase
watchfire
watchword
waterbath
waterbuck
waterbutt
watercart
watercool
waterfall
waterflea
waterfowl
watergate
waterhole
waterleaf
waterless
waterlily
waterline
watermark
watermill
waterpipe
watershed
waterside
waterweed
waterworn
wattmeter
wavefront
waveguide
wavellite
wayfaring
waywardly
wayzgoose
Xanthippe
yachtclub
yachtsman
Yankeedom
Yankeeism
yardstick
yawningly
zamindary
zapateado
abandoned
abandonee
abandoner
abasement
abashment
abatement
abdicable
abdicator
abdominal
abduction
aberrance
aberrancy
abhorrent
abhorring
abidingly
abjection
ablatival
ablutions
abnegator
abnormity
abolisher
abolition
abominate
aborigine
abounding
aboutface
aboutturn
abradable
abrogator
abruption
abscissae
abscissas
absconder
abseiling
absorbent
absorbing
abstainer
abstinent
absurdism
absurdist
absurdity
abundance
abusively
abysmally
ebullient
obbligato
obconical
obcordate
obedience
obeisance
obeseness
obfuscate
objectify
objection
objective
objurgate
obligated
obliquely
obliquity
oblivious
obnoxious
obscenely
obscenity
obscurant
obscurely
obscurity
obsecrate
obsequent
obsequial
obsequies
observant
obsession
obsessive
obsolesce
obstetric
obstinacy
obstinate
obtention
obtrusion
obtrusive
obturator
obversely
obversion
obviation
obviously
academism
acariasis
accentual
acceptant
acceptive
accessary
accession
accessory
accidence

accipiter
acclaimer
acclimate
acclivity
accompany
accordant
according
accordion
accretion
accretive
accusable
acellular
acescence
acetabula
acetamide
acetifier
acetylate
acetylcoA
acetylene
Acheulean
Acheulian
aciculate
acidifier
acidophil
acidulate
acidulent
acidulous
aciniform
aconitine
acoustics
acquiesce
acquittal
acquitted
acrobatic
acropetal
acropolis
acroteria
actinozoa
activator
actualise
actuality
actuarial
actuation
acuminate
eccentric
ecclesial
ecdysiast
echolalia
echovirus
eclampsia
eclamptic
ecologist
economics
economise
economist
ecosphere
ecossaise
ecosystem
ecritoire
ecstasise
ectoblast
ectogenic
ectomorph
ectophyte
ectoplasm
ecumenism
Icelander
Icelandic
iceskater
ichneumon
ichnology
ichthyoid
iconology
occipital
occludent
occlusion
occlusive
occultism
occultist
occupancy
occurrent
occurring
ocellated
ochlocrat
octachord
octagonal
octahedra
octameter
octastyle
octennial
octillion
Octobrist
octopodes
octostyle
scagliola
scaldfish
scalefern
scalefish
scaleleaf
scaleless
scalelike
scalemoss
scaliness
scallawag
scallywag
scalplock
scantling
scantness
scapegoat
scapolite
scapulary
scarecrow
scarehead
scarfring
scarfskin
scarfwise
scarifier
scatology
scatterer
scavenger
scenarist
scenedock
scentless
sceptical
scheelite
schematic
schilling
schistose
schistous
schlemiel
schlemihl
schlieren
schmaltzy
schnauzer
schnitzel
schnorkel
schnorrer
scholarly
scholiast
schoolbag
schoolboy
schooling
schoolman
sciaenoid
sciagraph
sciamachy
sciascopy
sciential
scientism
scientist
scintilla
scirrhous
scleritis
sclerosis
sclerotic
scolecite
scoliosis
scoliotic
scombroid
scorbutic
scorching
scorebook
scorecard
scoredraw
scorifier
scorpioid
Scotchman
Scoticise
scotomata
scoundrel
scraggily
scrambler
scramming
scrapbook
scrapheap
scrapiron
scrappily
scrapping
scrapyard
scratcher
scratches
screecher
screening
screwball
screwbolt
screwpile
screwpine
screwworm
scribbler
scrimmage
scrimpily
scrimshaw
scripture
scrivener
scrollsaw
scrounger
scrubbing
scruffily
scrumhalf
scrummage
scrutable
scrutator
sculpture
scuncheon
scutcheon
scutellar
scutellum
scutiform
adamantly
adaptable
addiction
addictive
addressee
addresser
addressor
adducible
adduction
adductive
ademption
adenoidal
adenomata
adenosine
adeptness
adherence
adiabatic
adipocere
adiposity
adjacency
adjoining
adjunctly
adjutancy
adlibbing
admeasure
adminicle
admirable
admirably
admiralty
admission
admissive
admitting
admixture
admonitor
adnominal
adoptable
adoration
adoringly
adornment
adrenalin
adsorbate
adsorbent
adulation
adulatory
adulterer
adulthood
adultness
adumbrate
advantage
advection
advective
Adventism
Adventist
adventive
adventure
adverbial
adversary
adversely
adversity
advertent
advertise
advisable
advisably
advisedly
advocator
edelweiss
edibility
editorial
education
educative
Edwardian
idealiser
idealless
identical
identikit
ideograph
ideologic
ideologue
idiograph
idiomatic
idiopathy
idioplasm
idiotical
odalisque
oddfellow
oddjobber
oddjobman
odontalgy
odorously
odourless
aepyornis
aerialist
aeriality
aerobatic
aerobiont
aerodrome
aerograph
aerolitic
aerometer
aerometry
aerophyte
aeroplane
aerospace
aesthesia
aesthesis
aesthetic
aestivate
aetiology
beachhead
beachwear
beadledom
beamingly
beanfeast
beanstalk
bearberry
beardless
beastings
beatitude
beauteous
beautiful
beccafico
bedfellow
bedjacket
bedlamite
bedraggle
bedridden
bedsettee
bedsitter
bedspread
bedspring
beechfern
beechmast
beefeater
beefiness
beefsteak
beekeeper
beemaster
beeorchis
beestings
befitting
befogging
begetting
beginning
behaviour
bejabbers
belatedly
beleaguer
belemnite
bellglass
bellicose
bellpunch
bellyache
bellyband
bellyflop
belvedere
bemusedly
beneficed
bengaline
benighted
benignant
benignity
bentonite
benzidine
benzoline
berberine
bergamask
berkelium
berserker
beryllium
besetment
besetting
beslobber
besotting
bespangle
bespatter
bestially
bestirred
bethought
betrothal
betrothed
bevelling
ceanothus
ceasefire
ceaseless
cedarwood
celandine
celebrant
celebrate
celebrity
celestial
cellarage
celluloid
cellulose
Celticism
cementite
censorial
centenary
centering
centigram
centipede
centrally
centreing
centurion
cephalous
cerastium
ceratodus
cerebella
cerebrate
cerecloth
cerograph
certainly
certainty
certified
certifier
certitude
cerussite
cessation
cetaceous
deacidify
deaconess
deadalive
deadlight
deathblow
deathless
deathlike
deathmask
deathroll
debagging
debarment
debarring
debatable
debauched
debauchee
debaucher
debenture
debugging
debutante
decadence
decadency
decagonal
decalcify
decalitre
decalogue
decametre
decapodal
decapodan
decastere
decathlon
deceitful
decennary
decennial
decennium
deception
deceptive
decidable
decidedly
deciduate
deciduous
decilitre
decillion
decimally
decimator
decimetre
decistere
deckhouse
declaimer
declarant
declinate
declivity
declivous
decoction
decollate
decollete
decomplex
decompose
decongest
decontrol
decorator
decrement
decretive
decretory
decumbent
decussate
dedicator
deducible
deduction
deductive
deerberry
deerhound
defalcate
defaulter
defeatism
defeatist
defeature
defection
defective
defendant
defensive
deference
deferment
deferring
defiantly
deficient
definable
definably
deflation
deflector
deflexion
defoliant
defoliate
deformity
defroster
dehiscent
dehydrate
deinosaur
deistical
dejection
delftware
delicious
delineate
delirious
deliverer
deludable
demagogic
demagogue
demandant
demanding
demarcate
demeanour
demimonde
demission
demitasse
demitting
demiurgic
demobbing
democracy
demulcent
demurrage
demurring
demystify
dendritic
denigrate
denitrate
denitrify
denouncer

denseness
dentalium
dentation
dentiform
dentistry
dentition
denyingly
deodorant
deodorise
deoxidise
departure
depasture
dependant
dependent
depiction
depictive
depletion
depletive
deposable
depositor
depravity
deprecate
depredate
depressed
depressor
depthbomb
depthless
depurator
derivable
dermatoid
derringdo
derringer
descended
describer
desecrate
desertion
desiccant
desiccate
designate
designing
desirable
desirably
desolater
desolator
desperado
desperate
despoiler
despotism
destitute
destroyer
desuetude
desultory
detection
detective
detention
detergent
determent
determine
deterrent
deterring
detersion
detersive
dethroner
detonator
detractor
detriment
detrition
detrusion
deuterate
deuterium
devaluate
devastate
developer
deviation
devilfish
devilling
devilment
deviously
devisable
devitrify
devotedly
dewlapped
dexterity
dexterous
dextrally
dextrorse
fearfully
feathered
febricity
febrifuge
feculence
fecundate
fecundity
federally
feedstock
feedstuff
feelingly
feiseanna
felicific
fellowman
felonious
femineity
fenceless
fenestrae
fenestral
Fenianism
fenugreek
feoffment
ferocious
ferrotype
ferryboat
fertilely
fertilise
fertility
fervently
festinate
festively
festivity
festology
fetichism
fetichist
fetidness
fetishism
fetishist
feudalise
feudalism
feudalist
feudality
feudatory
gearlever
gearshift
gearwheel
gelignite
gemmation
gemmology
gemutlich
genealogy
generable
generalia
generally
generator
genetical
genialise
geniality
genitival
genocidal
genotypic
genteelly
gentility
gentleman
genuflect
genuinely
geobotany
geodesist
geography
geologise
geologist
geomancer
geomantic
geometric
geometrid
geoponics
georgette
geosphere
geostatic
geotropic
gerfalcon
geriatric
germander
germanely
germanise
Germanish
Germanism
Germanist
germanium
germicide
germinate
germplasm
germproof
gerundial
gerundive
gestalten
gestation
gestatory
getatable
geyserite
headboard
headcloth
headdress
headfirst
headiness
headlight
headliner
headphone
headpiece
headscarf
headstall
headstock
headstone
headwater
healthful
healthily
heartache
heartbeat
heartburn
heartfelt
heartfree
hearthrug
heartland
heartless
heartsick
heartsore
heartwood
heathcock
heathenry
heaviness
heavyduty
Hebridean
hectogram
hedgingly
heedfully
heelpiece
heftiness
hegemonic
heinously
helically
heliogram
heliostat
heliotype
heliozoan
heliozoic
hellebore
hellenise
Hellenism
Hellenist
hellhound
hellishly
helpfully
Helvetian
hemicycle
hemistich
hemitrope
hemstitch
hendiadys
hepatitis
heptaglot
heptarchy
Heraclean
herbalist
herbarium
herbicide
herbivore
herborise
Herculean
Hercynian
hereabout
hereafter
heretical
hereunder
heritable
hermitage
herniated
herpetoid
hesitance
hesitancy
hesitator
Hesperian
hessonite
hetaerism
hetairism
heterodox
heteronym
heterosis
heuristic
hexachord
hexagonal
hexameter
hexaploid
hexastich
hexastyle
Hexateuch
jealously
jeeringly
jellyfish
jerkiness
jessamine
jesuitise
jesuitism
jetsetter
jetstream
jewellery
jewelweed
keelivine
kennelled
kentledge
Keplerian
keratitis
keratosis
kerbstone
kerfuffle
Keynesian
leafgreen
leafmould
leafstalk
leakiness
learnable
learnedly
leasehold
leaselend
leastways
leastwise
leavening
lecherous
leeringly
leewardly
leftovers
leftwards
legendary
legerline
legginess
legionary
legislate
Leicester
leisurely
leitmotif
leitmotiv
lendlease
lengthily
leniently
lentiform
leptosome
lethality
lethargic
letterbox
lettering
leucaemia
leucocyte
leucotome
leucotomy
leukaemia
leukaemic
leukocyte
Levantine
levelling
levelness
leviathan
leviratic
levitator
Levitical
lexically
mealiness
meandrine
meandrous
meaningly
meanwhile
meatiness
mechanics
mechanise
mechanism
mechanist
medallion
medallist
mediaeval
mediately
mediation
mediatise
mediative
mediatory
mediatrix
medicable
medically
medicinal
meditator
medullary
medullate
megacycle
megadeath
megahertz
megaphone
megaspore
mekometer
melanosis
melanotic
melaphyre
melatonin
meliorate
meliorism
meliorist
meliority
melismata
melocoton
melodious
melodrama
melomania
meltingly
meltwater
mementoes
memoirist
memorable
memorably
memoranda
memoriter
menadione
menagerie
mendacity
Mendelian
Mendelism
mendicant
mendicity
meningeal
Mennonite
menopause
Menshevik
menstrual
menstruum
mentalism
mentalist
mentality
mentation
mepacrine
mercaptan
mercenary
mercerise
merciless
mercurial
mercurous
merganser
meropidan
merriment
merriness
mescaline
mesentery
mesmerise
mesmerism
mesmerist
mesoblast
mesogloea
mesomorph
mesophyll
mesophyte
messenger
messianic
messieurs
messiness
metabolic
metalline
metalling
metallise
metalloid
metalwork
metameric
metaphase
metaplasm
meteorist
meteorite
meteoroid
methadone
metheglin
methodise
Methodism
Methodist
methought
methylate
methylene
metonymic
metricate
metrician
metricise
metricist
metrology
metronome
mezzanine
mezzotint
neathouse
nebuliser
necessary
necessity
neckcloth
neckverse
necrology
necrophil
necrotise
nectarean
nectarial
nectarine
nectarous
needfully
neediness
needleful
nefarious
negligent
negotiant
negotiate
negritude
negroidal
Negroness
negrophil
neighbour
nemertean
nemertine
nemophila
neodymium
neolithic
neologian
neologise
neologism
neologist
neoteinia
neoteinic
neoterise
neoterism
neoterist
nepenthes
nephalism
nephalist
nepheline
nephelite
nephology
nephritic
nephritis
nephrosis
Neptunian
neptunium
nervation
nervature
nerveless
nerviness
nervously
nescience
Nestorian
netveined
netwinged
neuralgia
neuralgic
neuration
neuroglia
neurology
neuromata
neuropath
neutrally
nevermore
newlyweds
newmarket
newsagent
newsflash
newshound
newsiness
newspaper
newsprint
newsstand
Newtonian
oecologic
oecumenic

oenomancy
oenophile
oenophily
oesophagi
oestrogen
peaceable
peaceably
peacetime
peachblow
pearlitic
pearlwort
peasantry
peasouper
peccantly
pectinate
peculator
pecuniary
pedagogic
pedagogue
pedalling
pederasty
pedicular
pedigreed
pedometer
peepsight
peevishly
pegmatite
Pekingese
Pelasgian
pellagrin
pelletise
pellitory
pemphigus
pencilled
penciller
pendently
pendragon
pendulate
penduline
pendulous
peneplain
peneplane
penetrant
penetrate
penfriend
penholder
peninsula
penitence
penniless
pennywort
penpusher
pensioner
pensively
pentagram
pentangle
pentarchy
Pentecost
penthouse
penultima
penumbral
penurious
pepperbox
pepperpot
peptonise
percaline
perceiver
perchance
percheron
percolate
perdition
peregrine
perennate
perennial
perfectly
perfector
perfervid
perforate
performer
perfumery
perfumier
perfusion
perfusive
pergunnah
periclase
pericycle
peridotic
perihelia
perilling
perilymph
perimeter
perimorph
perinatal
periodate
peripatus
periphery
periplast
periscope
perishing
perisperm
peristome
peristyle
perkiness
permanent
permeable
permeance
permitted
permitter
permutate
perpetual
persecute
persevere
persimmon
personage
personate
personify
personnel
persuader
pertinent
pertussis
pervasion
pervasive
perverter
pessimism
pessimist
pesthouse
pesticide
pestilent
pestology
petaurist
petechiae
petechial
petersham
pethidine
petiolate
petiolule
petroleum
petrology
petticoat
pettiness
pettishly
pettitoes
petulance
petulancy
reachable
reactance
readdress
readiness
readymade
realistic
reanimate
rearguard
rearhorse
rearlight
rearmouse
rearrange
rearwards
reasoning
rebaptise
rebelling
rebellion
rebidding
rebukable
rebutting
recalesce
recapping
recapture
recension
reception
receptive
recession
recessive
rechauffe
recherche
recipient
reckoning
reclinate
reclusion
reclusive
recognise
recoinage
recollect
recombine
recommend
recompose
reconcile
recondite
reconfirm
reconvene
reconvert
recording
recordist
recoverer
recreancy
recruital
recruiter
rectangle
rectifier
rectitude
rectorate
rectorial
rectrices
recumbent
recurrent
recurring
recursion
recursive
recusance
recusancy
redaction
redbreast
redevelop
redhanded
redheaded
redingote
redivivus
redletter
redolence
redoubted
redresser
reducible
reductant
reduction
reductive
redundant
reediness
reedorgan
reeducate
reefpoint
reenforce
reentrant
reexamine
refashion
refection
refectory
referable
reference
referenda
referring
refitment
refitting
reflation
reflector
reflexion
reflexive
refluence
reformism
reformist
refractor
refreshen
refresher
refuelled
refulgent
refurbish
refurnish
refusable
refutable
regardant
regardful
regicidal
regisseur
registrar
regretful
regretted
regularly
regulator
rehearsal
rehydrate
Reichstag
reimburse
reinforce
reinstate
reiterate
rejection
rejoicing
rejoinder
relevance
relevancy
reliantly
religiose
religious
reliquary
reliquiae
reluctant
reluctate
remainder
remanence
remeasure
remediate
remindful
reminisce
remission
remitment
remittent
remitting
remontant
removable
renascent
rencontre
rendition
renewable
renitency
renouncer
renovator
reparable
repayable
repayment
repechage
repellant
repellent
repelling
repentant
repertory
replenish
repletion
replicate
reportage
reposeful
repossess
repotting
reprehend
represent
repressor
reprieval
reprimand
reprobate
reprocess
reproduce
reptilian
republish
repudiate
repugnant
repulsion
repulsive
reputable
reputably
reputedly
requester
requisite
rerebrace
rerelease
reremouse
rerunning
resalable
resection
resentful
reserpine
reservist
reservoir
resetting
reshuffle
residence
residency
residuary
resilient
resistant
resistive
resitting
resoluble
resolvent
resonance
resonator
resorbent
resources
respecter
responder
restfully
restiform
restitute
restively
restraint
resultant
resultful
resumable
resurface
resurgent
resurrect
retaliate
retardant
retention
retentive
rethought
retiarius
reticence
reticency
reticular
reticulum
retinitis
retinulae
retinular
retortion
retoucher
retractor
retrieval
retriever
retrocede
retrodden
retroflex
retroject
retrousse
retrovert
revelator
revelling
reverence
reversely
reversion
revetment
revetting
revictual
revisable
revivable
revocable
revolting
revulsion
revulsive
rewarding
rewritten
seaanchor
seachange
seafaring
seagirdle
sealetter
seaminess
seanettle
searching
searingly
seasoning
seasquirt
seastrand
seatangle
seaurchin
seaworthy
sebaceous
secateurs
secernent
secession
seclusion
seclusive
secondary
secretage
secretary
secretion
secretive
secretory
sectarian
sectility
sectional
sectorial
secularly
securable
sedentary
sedgewren
seditious
seduction
seductive
seedeater
seediness
seedpearl
seedplant
seemingly
segmental
segregate
seigneury
seigniory
selachian
selection
selective
selectman
selenious
selenitic
selfabuse
selfaware
selfdoubt
selfdrive
selffaced
selfglory
selfimage
selfishly
selfmoved
selfpride
selftrust
Seljukian
semanteme
semantics
semaphore
semblable
semblably
semblance
semeiotic
semestral
semibreve
semicolon
semifinal
semifluid
semilunar
semimetal
seminally
semiology
semiotics
semiplume
semirigid
semisolid
semisweet
semitonic
semivowel
senescent
seneschal
senhorita
seniority
sensation
sensedata
senseless
sensitise
sensitive
sensorial
sensorium
sensually
sentenate
sentience
sentiency
sentiment
sentrybox
separable
separably
separates
separator
Sephardic
Sephardim
sepiolite
septation
September
septemvir
septenary
septennia
septicity
septuplet
sepulcher
sepulchre
sepulture
sequacity
sequester
sequestra
sequinned
serenader
sergeancy
serialise
serialism
serialist
seriality
seriately
sericeous
serigraph
serinette
seriously

serjeancy
serjeanty
sermonise
serotonin
serpentry
serranoid
serration
serrefile
serrulate
serviette
servilely
servility
servitude
sessional
sestertia
setaceous
setsquare
sevenfold
seventeen
seventhly
seventies
severable
severally
severalty
severance
sexennial
sexlessly
sexlinked
sextuplet
sexualise
sexuality
teachable
teachably
teacupful
teakettle
tearfully
teasingly
technical
technique
tectonics
tectorial
tectrices
tediously
tegmental
tegmentum
tegularly
teknonymy
telamones
telegenic
telegraph
telemeter
telemetry
teleology
telepathy
telephone
telephony
telephoto
telescope
telescopy
televisor
tellingly
tellurate
tellurian
telluride
tellurite
tellurium
tellurous
telophase
temperate
temporary
temporise
temptable
temptress
tenacious
tenaculum
tenderise
tendinous
tenebrist
tenebrous
tenseness
tensility
tensional
tentacled
tentation
tentative
tenthrate
tentmaker
tenuously
tepidness
teratogen
terebinth
terebrant
termagant
terminate
terminism
terminist
termitary
ternately
terramara
terramare
terrarium
territory
terrorise
terrorism
terrorist
terseness
tervalent
tessitura
testament
testation
testatrix
testdrive
testifier
testimony
testiness
tetradite
tetragram
tetralogy
tetrapody
tetrarchy
teutonise
Teutonism
Teutonist
textually
vectorial
Vedantist
veeringly
vegetable
vegetably
vehemence
vehicular
veinstone
velodrome
velveteen
vendition
veneering
venerable
venerably
venerator
venereous
vengeance
veniality
ventiduct
ventifact
ventilate
ventrally
ventricle
venturous
veracious
verandaed
veratrine
verbalise
verbalism
verbalist
verbicide
verbosely
verbosity
verdantly
verdigris
veridical
veritable
veritably
vermicide
vermicule
vermiform
vermifuge
vermilion
verminate
verminous
vernalise
vernation
verrucose
verrucous
versatile
versifier
versiform
versional
vertebrae
vertebral
vesicular
vestibule
vestigial
vestigium
vestiture
vestryman
vetchling
vexatious
vexillary
weakkneed
wealthily
weariless
weariness
wearisome
weathered
weatherly
webfooted
wedgewise
Wednesday
weediness
weeknight
weevilled
wehrmacht
weighable
weighbeam
weightily
weighting
weirdness
welcoming
welfarism
wellbeing
wellfound
wellknown
welltimed
werwolves
westbound
westering
westerner
westwards
xenograft
xenophile
xenophobe
xeromorph
xerophile
xerophily
xerophyte
yearround
yellowdog
yellowish
yesterday
zealously
zebrawood
zeitgeist
zemindary
zestfully
zeugmatic
affecting
affection
affective
affianced
affidavit
affiliate
affirmant
affixture
afflation
affluence
affricate
aflatoxin
aforesaid
Afrikaans
Afrikaner
aftercare
afterclap
afterglow
afterlife
aftermath
aftermost
afternoon
aftertime
afterword
effective
effectual
efficient
effluence
effluvial
effluvium
effluxion
effortful
effulgent
offcentre
offchance
offcolour
offensive
offertory
offhanded
officiant
officiate
officinal
officious
offscreen
offseason
offspring
offstreet
sforzando
agapemone
aggravate
aggregate
aggressor
aggrieved
agistment
agitation
agitative
agnatical
agonising
agonistic
agreeable
agreeably
agreement
agriology
agrologic
agronomic
eggbeater
eglantine
egomaniac
egotistic
egregious
egression
ignescent
ignitable
ignitible
ignorable
ignoramus
ignorance
iguanodon
sgraffiti
sgraffito
ahistoric
chachacha
chaetopod
chafferer
chaffinch
chaingang
chaingear
chainless
chainmail
chairlady
challenge
chameleon
chamomile
champagne
champaign
champerty
champleve
chanceful
chancroid
chancrous
chandlery
changeful
chanteuse
chantilly
chantress
chaparral
chaperone
chapleted
charabanc
character
chariness
charivari
charlatan
charlotte
charmeuse
charmless
Charolais
chartered
charterer
charwoman
chassepot
chastener
chastiser
chatelain
chatoyant
chatterer
chauffeur
cheapjack
cheapness
checkered
checklist
checkmate
checkrein
cheekbone
cheerless
chelation
chelicera
chelonian
chemistry
chemitype
chemurgic
cheongsam
chequered
cherimoya
chernozem
cherrypie
chevalier
chevelure
chibouque
chicanery
chickadee
chickaree
chickling
chickweed
chiefship
chieftain
chihuahua
chilblain
childhood
childless
childlike
chillness
chimaeric
Chinatown
chinaware
chinstrap
chipboard
chipolata
chiropody
chiselled
chiseller
chisquare
chitinous
chitlings
chivalric
chlamydes
chlorella
chloritic
chlorosis
chlorotic
chockfull
chocolate
chokedamp
choleraic
chondrite
chondrule
chophouse
choplogic
chopstick
chorister
chorology
Christian
Christmas
chromatic
chromatin
chronical
chronicle
chrysalid
chrysalis
chthonian
churching
churchman
dharmsala
ghostlike
ghostword
khedivial
phagedena
phagocyte
phalanger
phalanges
phalanxes
phalarope
phantasma
pharaonic
pharisaic
pharyngal
pharynges
pharynxes
phellogen
phenacite
phenakite
phenology
phenomena
phenotype
pheromone
philander
philately
philippic
philogyny
philology
Philomela
phlebitis
phonation
phonatory
phonemics
phonetics
phonetise
phonetism
phonetist
phoniness
phonogram
phonolite
phonology
phosphate
phosphene
phosphide
phosphine
phosphite
photocell
photocopy
photogene
photophil
photopsia
phototype
phrenetic
phthalein
phycology
phyllopod
phylogeny
physician
physicist
physicked
phytogeny
phytology
phytotomy
phytotron
rhapsodic
rheumatic
Rhineodon
rhinology
rhizocarp
rhizoidal
rhodamine
rhodolite
rhodonite
rhodopsin
rhonchial
rhymester
rhythmics
rhythmise
rhythmist
shadberry
shadeless
shadetree
shadiness
shakeable
shakedown
shakerism
shakiness
shallowly
shamanism
shamanist
shamateur
shambling
shambolic
shamefast
shameless
Shangrila
shantyman
shapeable
shapeless
sharecrop
sharkskin
sharpener
sharpeyed
sharpness
sharpshod
shaveling
shearling
sheatfish
sheathing
Shechinah
sheepcote
sheepfold
sheephook
sheeplice
sheepskin
sheeptick

sheepwalk
sheepwash
sheerhulk
sheerlegs
sheerness
sheetbend
sheikhdom
sheldduck
sheldrake
shelflife
shelfmark
shelfroom
shellback
shellbark
shellfire
shellfish
shellheap
shellwork
shemozzle
shewbread
shieldbug
shieldfem
shiftless
shillelah
shinguard
shininess
Shintoism
Shintoist
shipboard
shipcanal
shipfever
shipmoney
shipowner
shipshape
shipwreck
shirtless
shirttail
shockable
shockhead
shoeblack
shoemaker
shoeshine
shogunate
shootable
shopfloor
shopfront
shoreless
shoreline
shoreside
shoreward
shoreweed
shortcake
shortener
shortfall
shorthand
shorthorn
shortness
shortstop
shortterm
shortwave
shotproof
shottower
shouldest
shovelful
shovelhat
shovelled
shoveller
showiness
showpiece
showplace
shredding
shrewmice
shrinkage
shrubbery
shrugging
thalassic
thaneship
thankless
thatching
theandric
theatrics
theocracy
theocrasy
theogonic
theologic
theologue
theomachy
theomania
theophany
theoretic
theoriser
theosophy
therapist
Theravada
therefore
therefrom
thereinto
thereunto
thereupon
therewith
thermally
thermidor
thesaurus
theurgist
thickener
thicketed
thickhead
thickknee
thickness
thighbone
thighboot
thingness
thingummy
thinkable
thinktank
thirdhand
thirdrate
thirdsman
thirstily
thirtieth
thitherto
Thomistic
thornback
thornbill
thornbush
thornless
thorntree
thoughted
thralldom
thrashing
threefold
threesome
threnodic
threshold
thriftily
thrilling
throatily
throbbing
thrombose
throttler
throughly
throwaway
throwback
throwster
thrumming
thumbhole
thumbmark
thumbnail
thumbtack
thunderer
Thyestean
thylacine
thyratron
thyristor
thyroxine
whaleback
whaleboat
whalebone
whalehead
wheatmeal
wheedling
wheelbase
wheelless
wheelwork
wherefore
wherefrom
whereinto
whereunto
whereupon
wherewith
wherryman
whetstone
wheyfaced
whichever
whimperer
whimsical
whinstone
whipperin
whipround
whipsnake
whipstock
whirligig
whirlpool
whirlwind
whiskered
whisperer
whistling
whitebait
whitebass
whitebeam
whiteface
whitefish
Whitehall
whitehead
whiteness
whitening
whitewash
whitewing
whitewood
whizzbang
whodunnit
wholemeal
wholeness
wholesale
wholesome
whosoever
ailanthus
aimlessly
aircooled
airjacket
airminded
airstream
airworthy
airyfairy
aitchbone
biblicism
biblicist
bicameral
bicipital
biconcave
bicyclist
bifarious
bifoliate
bifurcate
bigeneric
bigheaded
bilabiate
bilateral
bilgekeel
bilharzia
bilingual
biliously
bilirubin
biliteral
billabong
billboard
billiards
billionth
billycock
billygoat
bimonthly
binocular
binominal
binturong
biogenous
biography
biologist
biometric
bionomics
biorhythm
biosphere
bipartite
bipinnate
birchbark
birdbrain
birdsfoot
birdsnest
birdtable
birdwatch
birthmark
birthrate
birthwort
bisection
bishopric
bismillah
bitterish
bivalence
bivalency
bivariant
bivariate
bizarrely
cicatrice
cicatrise
cigarette
cigarillo
Cimmerian
cinematic
cineraria
cinereous
Cingalese
cipollino
circadian
circinate
circuitry
circulate
cirrhosis
cirripede
cisalpine
citizenly
citizenry
citystate
civically
civiliser
diablerie
diabolise
diabolism
diabolist
diachrony
diachylom
diachylum
diaconate
diacritic
diactinic
diaereses
diaeresis
diagnoses
diagnosis
dialectal
dialectic
dialogise
dialogism
dialogist
diametral
diametric
diandrous
diaphragm
diaphysis
diarrhoea
diastasis
diastatic
diastolic
diathermy
diathesis
diathetic
diatomite
diatropic
dichasial
dichasium
dichogamy
dichotomy
dichroism
dichromat
dichromic
dickybird
diclinous
dicrotism
dictation
didactics
didelphic
didrachma
dieselise
diesinker
dietetics
dietician
dietitian
different
difficile
difficult
diffident
diffusely
diffusion
diffusive
digastric
digestion
digestive
digitalin
digitalis
digitally
digitated
dignified
dignitary
dilatable
dilatancy
diligence
dimension
dimidiate
dimissory
dimorphic
dimwitted
dinginess
diningcar
dinnerset
dinoceras
dinothere
dioecious
Dionysiac
Dionysian
dipcircle
dipeptide
diphthong
diplomacy
diplomate
dipswitch
dipterous
direction
directive
directory
directrix
direfully
dirigible
dirigisme
dirtiness
dirttrack
disaccord
disaffect
disaffirm
disannual
disappear
disarming
disavouch
disavowal
disbarred
disbelief
disbranch
disbudded
disburden
disbursal
discalced
discarder
discerner
discharge
discoidal
discolour
discomfit
discommon
discourse
discovert
discovery
discredit
disembark
disembody
disengage
disentail
disentomb
disesteem
disfavour
disfigure
disforest
disgracer
dishcloth
dishclout
dishfaced
dishonest
dishonour
dishwater
disinfect
disinfest
dislocate
dismantle
dismember
dismissal
disoblige
disorient
disparage
disparate
disparity
dispelled
dispenser
dispeople
dispersal
disperser
displease
disposure
dispraise
disputant
disregard
disrelish
disrepair
disrepute
dissector
disseisin
dissemble
dissenter
dissident
dissipate
dissocial
dissolute
dissonant
dissuader
distantly
distemper
distilled
distiller
distraint
disturbed
disturber
dithyramb
dittander
dittology
diurnally
divergent
diversely
diversify
diversion
diversity
diverting
dividable
divisible
divulsion
dixieland
dizygotic
dizziness
eiderdown
eiderduck
eidograph
eightfold
eightieth
eightsome
eightyish
eirenicon
fibreless
fibriform
fibrillar
fibrinoid
fibrinous
fibroline
fibromata
fictional
fideistic
fiduciary
fieldbook
fieldboot
fieldfare
fieldsman
fieldwork
fiendlike
fieriness
fifteenth
figurante
filaceous
filiation
filigreed
fillister
filminess
filmstrip
filoselle
filterbed
filtertip
filtrable
fimbriate
financial
financier
finedrawn
fingering
fingertip
finically
finicking
fioritura
fioriture
firealarm
fireblast
firebrand
firebreak
firebrick
firecrest
firedrake
firedrill
fireeater
fireguard
firehouse
fireirons
firelight
fireplace

firepower
fireproof
firestone
firewater
fireworks
firmament
firstborn
firstfoot
firsthand
firstling
firstrate
fisherman
fishiness
fishplate
fishslice
fishyback
fissility
fissipede
fistulous
fittingly
fivepence
fivepenny
fixedness
giantlike
gibberish
gibbosity
gibbously
giddiness
gigahertz
gigantism
giltedged
gimmickry
gingerade
gingerale
ginglymus
ginpalace
girandole
girlishly
Girondist
hibernate
Hibernian
hiddenite
hidebound
hideously
hierarchy
hieratica
hierodule
hierogram
hierology
highchair
highclass
highflier
highflown
highflyer
highgrade
highgrown
highlands
highlevel
highlight
highspeed
hightoned
highwater
hilarious
hillbilly
Himalayan
Himyarite
hindbrain
hindrance
hindsight
hippocras
hircosity
hirsutism
hirundine
hispidity
histamine
histidine
histogeny
histogram
histology
historian
hitchhike
Hitlerism
Hitlerite
jitterbug
kibbutzim
kickstart
kiddingly
kidnapped
kidnapper
kilderkin
killifish
kilocycle
kilohertz
kilolitre
kilometre
kinematic
kingcraft
kingdomed
kingmaker
kingsized
kinkiness
kinswoman
kitchener
kittenish
kittiwake
liability
libecchio
libellant
libelling
libellist
libellous
liberally
liberated
liberator
libertine
libidinal
librarian
libration
libratory
librettos
licensure
lichenous
lickerish
liegelord
lifeblood
lifecycle
lifeforce
lifeguard
lifesaver
lifesized
lifestyle
lifetable
lightfoot
lightless
lightness
lightning
lightship
lightsome
lightsout
lightwood
lightyear
lignaloes
ligniform
liltingly
lilywhite
Limburger
limejuice
limelight
limestone
limewater
limitable
limitedly
limitless
limnology
limonitic
limousine
limpidity
lineality
lineament
linearise
linearity
lineation
linenfold
lineolate
lingering
lingually
lingulate
lintelled
lintwhite
lioncelle
lionheart
lipreader
liquation
liquefier
liquidate
liquidise
liquidity
liquorice
liquorish
lispingly
lissomely
Listerism
literally
literatim
literator
literatus
litheness
lithesome
lithology
lithopone
lithotomy
litigable
litigious
litterbin
litterbug
liturgics
liturgist
liverwort
liveryman
livestock
lividness
lixiviate
miasmatic
micaceous
micaslate
microbial
microchip
microcosm
microcyte
microfilm
microgram
microlite
microlith
micrology
micromesh
micropsia
micropyle
microsome
microtome
microtomy
microtone
microwave
micturate
middleman
midinette
midstream
midsummer
midwicket
midwifery
midwinter
migration
migratory
milestone
militancy
milkfever
milkfloat
milkiness
milkshake
milktooth
millboard
millenary
millennia
millepede
millepore
millerite
milligram
millinery
millionth
millipede
millivolt
millstone
millwheel
milometer
Miltonian
mimicking
minacious
mincemeat
mincingly
mindfully
minefield
minelayer
miniature
minimally
miniskirt
minuscule
minutegun
minuteman
mirkiness
mirthless
misadvise
misassign
misbecome
misbehave
misbelief
misbeseem
miscegene
miscegine
mischance
miscreant
miscreate
misdemean
misdirect
misemploy
miserable
miserably
misesteem
misfeasor
misgiving
misgovern
misguided
mishandle
mishanter
misinform
misleared
mismanage
misoneism
misoneist
mispickel
misreckon
misreport
misshapen
missioner
mistigris
mistiness
mistletoe
mistyeyed
Mithraism
Mithraist
mitigable
mitigator
mitraille
mixedness
niccolite
nickelise
nickelled
nickelous
nicotiana
nicotinic
nictation
nictitate
niggardly
nightbird
nightclub
nightfall
nightgown
nighthawk
nightlife
nightline
nightlong
nightmare
nightside
nighttime
nightwork
nigricant
nigritude
nigrosine
Nilometer
ninepence
ninepenny
ninetieth
Nipponese
nitpicker
nitratine
nitration
oilburner
oilcolour
oilpaints
pianistic
pickaback
picketing
picnicked
picnicker
pictogram
pictorial
picturise
piecemeal
piecerate
piecework
pierrette
pietistic
piggishly
piggyback
piggybank
pigheaded
pikeperch
pikestaff
pilferage
pilgarlic
pillarbox
pilotfish
pimpernel
pinchbeck
pinchcock
pineapple
pinkiness
pinnately
pinnipede
pinnulate
pinstripe
pintailed
pintsized
pipedream
pipeorgan
pipestone
pipsqueak
piquantly
piratical
pirouette
piscatory
pisciform
pisolitic
pistachio
pistoleer
pistolled
pitchdark
pitchfork
pitchpipe
piteously
pithecoid
pithiness
pitifully
pituitary
pityingly
pivotable
pivotally
pixilated
pizzicati
pizzicato
Ribbonism
ribosomal
ricepaper
riderless
ridgepole
ridgetile
ridiculer
riflebird
rightable
righteous
righthand
rightness
rightward
rigidness
rigmarole
ringfence
ringingly
ringshake
ringsnake
riotously
Ripuarian
riskiness
ritualise
ritualism
ritualist
rivalling
rivalrous
rivelling
riverbank
riverboat
riverhead
riverside
riverweed
sibilance
sibilancy
sibylline
siccative
sickening
sickishly
sickleave
sideboard
sideburns
sidedness
sideissue
sidelight
sideritic
siderosis
sideswipe
sidetable
sidetrack
sidewards
sidewheel
sightless
sightseer
sigillary
sigillate
sigmoidal
signalbox
signalise
signalled
signaller
signalman
signatory
signature
signboard
significs
signorial
signorina
siliceous
silicious
silicosis
silicotic
siliquose
silkgland
silkiness
silliness
siltation
siltstone
silverfir
similarly
simpatico
simpleton
simplices
simulacra
simulacre
simulator
simulcast
sincerely
sincerity
sinewless
singalong
singleton
singspiel
Sinhalese
sinistral
sinlessly
sinologue
sinophile
sinuately
sinuation
sinuosity
sinuously
sinusitis
siphonage
siphuncle
Sisyphean
situation
sitzkrieg
sixfooter
sixteenmo
sixteenth
tidegauge
tidewater
tiedyeing
tigerlily
tigermoth
tigerseye
tigerwood
tightener
tightness
tightrope
tightwire
tilestone
timbering
timberman
timelapse
timelimit
timeously
timepiece
timesheet
timetable
timidness
timocracy
timpanist
tinderbox
tinniness
tinopener
tinselled
tipsiness
tipstaves
tiredness
tirewoman
titillate
titledeed
titlepage

titration
tittivate
tittlebat
tittuping
tittupped
titularly
uintahite
Uitlander
viability
vibracula
vibraharp
vibratile
vibration
vibrative
vibratory
vibrissae
vicariate
vicarious
vicennial
viceregal
vicereine
viceroyal
vicesimal
viciously
victimise
Victorian
victorine
videlicet
videotape
viewpoint
vigesimal
vigilance
vigilante
vignetter
villagery
villanage
villenage
villiform
villosity
vimineous
vinaceous
vindicate
violation
violative
violently
violinist
virescent
Virgilian
virginals
virginity
virgulate
viricidal
virtually
virtuosic
virtuosos
virulence
virulency
viscerate
viscidity
viscosity
viscounty
viscously
visionary
visionist
visitable
visitress
visualise
vitellary
vitelline
vitiation
vitiosity
vitriform
vitriolic
Vitruvian
vivacious
viverrine
vivianite
vividness
vizierate

vizierial
wideawake
widowbird
widowhood
widthways
widthwise
wieldable
willemite
willingly
willowish
willpower
windblown
windbound
windbreak
windchest
windhover
windiness
windowbox
windproof
windswept
windwards
wineberry
wineglass
winepress
winestone
winevault
wingchair
winningly
winsomely
winterise
wiredrawn
wiregauze
wirephoto
wisecrack
wishfully
wistfully
witchetty
witchhunt
witchmeal
withdrawn
withering
witherite
withstand
withstood
witlessly
witticism
wittiness
wittingly
Yiddisher
zibelline
zigzagged
zincotype
zinkenite
zirconium
ejaculate
ejectment
okeydokey
skedaddle
skeesicks
sketchily
sketchmap
skewwhiff
skiagraph
skiamachy
skiascopy
skijoring
skilfully
skindiver
skinflick
skinflint
skingraft
skintight
skirtings
skirtless
skydiving
skyjacker
skyrocket
Ukrainian
alabaster

albatross
albescent
albinotic
alchemise
alchemist
alcoholic
aldehydic
aleatoric
Alemannic
alertness
algarroba
algebraic
Algonkian
Algonquin
algorithm
alicyclic
alienable
alienator
alignment
alinement
aliphatic
aliveness
alkaloses
alkalosis
allantois
allegedly
allegiant
allegoric
allemande
alleviate
alligator
allocable
allograph
allomorph
allopathy
allophone
alloplasm
allotment
allotrope
allotropy
allotting
allowable
allowably
allowance
allowedly
almandine
almsgiver
almshouse
aloneness
alongside
aloofness
alpargata
alpenhorn
alterable
altercate
alternant
alternate
altimeter
altricial
aluminate
aluminise
aluminium
aluminous
alveolate
blackball
blackbird
blackbuck
blackcoat
blackcock
blackdamp
blackface
Blackfeet
blackfish
blackflag
Blackfoot
blackgame
blackhead
blackjack
blacklead

blacklist
blackmail
blackness
blackwash
blaeberry
blameable
blameably
blameless
blandness
blankness
blaspheme
blasphemy
blasthole
blastment
blastulae
blastular
blatantly
blazingly
bleachery
bleakness
bleareyed
blessedly
blindfold
blindness
blinkered
blockader
blockhead
blockship
bloodbath
bloodless
bloodlust
bloodroot
bloodshed
bloodshot
bloodworm
bloodwort
blotchily
blowtorch
bluebeard
blueberry
blueblack
bluegrass
bluepoint
blueprint
bluestone
bluffness
blunderer
bluntness
blushless
blusterer
claimable
clamantly
clamorous
clamshell
clapboard
clarifier
clarionet
classable
classical
classless
classlist
classmate
classroom
clathrate
clatterer
claustral
clavation
claviform
cleanness
cleansing
clearance
clearcole
cleareyed
clearness
cleavable
clemently
clepsydra
clergyman
clergymen

clerkship
clientage
clientele
cliffhang
climactic
climbable
clinician
clinquant
clipboard
clitellum
cloakroom
clockwise
clockwork
cloisonne
cloistral
closedown
closeness
cloudland
cloudless
clubbable
clubhouse
elaborate
elastomer
elbowroom
eldership
electoral
electress
electrify
electrode
electuary
elegantly
elegiacal
elemental
elevation
elevenses
eliminate
ellipsoid
elocution
elongated
elopement
eloquence
elsewhere
elucidate
elusively
elutriate
flabellum
flagellum
flageolet
flagrance
flagrancy
flagstaff
flagstick
flagstone
flakiness
flambeaus
flambeaux
flameless
flamingly
flamingos
flammable
flannelly
flarepath
flaringly
flashback
flashbulb
flashcube
flashover
flashtube
flatterer
flatulent
flavorous
flayflint
fleckless
fledgling
fleetness
fleshings
fleshless
fleshment
flightily

flintlock
flippancy
floatable
flocculus
floodgate
floodmark
floodtide
flophouse
floriated
floridean
floridity
floristic
floristry
floscular
flotation
flouncing
flowchart
flowerage
flowerbed
flowering
flowerpot
flowingly
flowsheet
flowstone
fluctuant
fluctuate
fluecured
fluoresce
fluorosis
fluorspar
flushness
fluxional
flyfisher
flyweight
glabellae
glabellar
glacially
gladiator
gladiolus
gladstone
glaireous
glamorise
glamorous
glandered
glandular
glaringly
glassgall
glassware
glasswork
glasswort
gleefully
glengarry
glissandi
glissando
globefish
globosity
glomerate
glomerule
glomeruli
gloryhole
glossator
glossitis
glowingly
glucoside
glueyness
glutamate
glutinous
glyceride
glycerine
glycoside
glyptodon
illboding
illegally
illegible
illegibly
illgotten
illiberal
illicitly
illjudged

illogical
illomened
illwisher
klinostat
oleaceous
olecranal
olecranon
oleograph
oleoresin
olfaction
olfactive
olfactory
oligaemia
oligarchy
Oligocene
oligopoly
olivenite
placation
placatory
placeable
placecard
placekick
placeless
placement
placename
placentae
placental
placidity
plainness
plainsman
plainsong
plaintiff
plaintive
planarian
planation
planetary
planetoid
plangency
planisher
plantable
plantlike
planuloid
plasmatic
plasmodia
plastered
plasterer
platemark
platinise
platinoid
platinous
platitude
Platonise
Platonism
Platonist
plausible
plausibly
playfully
playgroup
playhouse
plaything
pleadable
pleadings
pleasance
Pleiocene
plenarily
plenitude
plenteous
plentiful
plethoric
pleuritic
plicately
plication
plicature
ploughboy
ploughman
plumbeous
plumbline
plumdamas
plumpness

plumulate
plumulose
plunderer
pluralise
pluralism
pluralist
plurality
plusfours
plushness
plutocrat
plutonian
Plutonism
Plutonist
plutonium
slabsided
slabstone
slackness
slakeless
slanderer
slantways
slantwise
slaphappy
slapstick
slateclub
slategrey
slaughter
slaveship
slavishly
Slavonian
Slavophil
sleekness
sleepless
sleevenut
slenderly
slickness
sliderule
slightish
sliminess
slingback
slingshot
slinkweed
slipcoach
slipcover
slivovitz
slopbasin
slopewise
slothbear
Slovakian
Slovenian
slowcoach
slowmatch
sluiceway
slumberer
slumbrous
slushfund
uliginous
ultimatum
ultrahigh
ululation
amaryllis
amassment
amauroses
amaurosis
amaurotic
amazement
amazingly
amazonian
ambergris
ambiguity
ambiguous
ambitious
amblyopia
amblyopic
ambrosial
ambulacra
ambulance
ambuscade
amendable
amendment
americium
Amerindic
amianthus
amidships
aminoacid
amoebaean
amoralism
amorality
amorously
amorphism
amorphous
amourette
ampersand
amphibian
amphibole
amphigory
amphioxus
ampleness
amplifier
amplitude
amputator
amusement
amusingly
amygdalin
amyloidal
amylopsin
emaciated
emanation
emanative
embarrass
embassage
embattled
embayment
embedding
embedment
embellish
embezzler
embraceor
embracery
embracive
embrangle
embrasure
embrittle
embrocate
embroglio
embroider
embryonal
embryonic
embryotic
embussing
emendable
emendator
emergence
emergency
eminently
Emmenthal
emolliate
emollient
emolument
emotional
emotively
emotivity
empathise
empennage
emphasise
emphysema
empirical
emplastic
emptiness
empyreuma
emulation
emulative
emulously
emunctory
imageable
imageless
imaginary
imbalance
imbecilic
imbricate
imbroglio
imitation
imitative
immanence
immanency
immediacy
immediate
immensely
immensity
immersion
immigrant
immigrate
imminence
imminency
immixture
immodesty
immolator
immorally
immovable
immovably
immutable
immutably
impaction
impartial
impassion
impassive
impastoed
impatiens
impatient
impeccant
impedance
impelling
impendent
impending
imperator
imperfect
imperious
impetrate
impetuous
impiously
impleader
implement
impletion
implicate
impliedly
implosion
implosive
impluvium
impolitic
important
importune
impostume
imposture
impotence
impotency
impounder
imprecate
imprecise
impresari
improbity
impromptu
improvise
imprudent
impudence
impulsion
impulsive
impulsory
imputable
ombudsman
ominously
omissible
ommatidia
omophagia
omophagic
smackeroo
smallarms
smallness
smalltime
smartness
smartweed
smatterer
smileless
smilingly
smokeball
smokebomb
smokebush
smokejack
smokeless
smoketree
smokiness
smoothish
smuggling
umbellate
umbellule
umberbird
umbilical
umbilicus
umpteenth
anabioses
anabiosis
anabiotic
anabolism
anabranch
anacruses
anacrusis
anaerobic
analeptic
analgesia
analgesic
analogise
analogist
analogous
analysand
anamnesis
anandrous
anaphoric
anaptyxis
anarchism
anarchist
anatomise
anatomist
ancestral
anchorage
anchoress
anchorite
anchorman
anchylose
anciently
ancientry
ancillary
andantino
andesitic
androecia
androgyne
androgyny
anecdotal
anecdotic
anemogram
angelfish
angelical
angiology
angiomata
angleiron
anglesite
angleworm
anglicise
anglicism
Anglicist
anglophil
angriness
anguished
angularly
anhydride
anhydrite
anhydrous
animalise
animalism
animalist
animality
animation
animatism
animistic
animosity
anklebone
ankylosis
ankylotic
annectent
annelidan
annotator
announcer
annoyance
annuitant
annularly
annulated
annulling
annulment
anomalous
anomalure
anonymity
anonymous
anopheles
anorectic
anorthite
anovulant
anoxaemia
anschluss
antarctic
antefixal
antenatal
antennary
antennule
anthelion
anthemion
anthocyan
anthology
anthozoan
anthracic
anthropic
anticline
anticodon
antidotal
antigenic
antiknock
antimonic
antinodal
antinomic
antinovel
antipasto
antipathy
antiphony
antipodal
antipodes
antiquary
antiquate
antiquity
antiserum
antitoxic
antitoxin
antitrade
antitrust
antivenin
antiviral
anxiously
enactment
enamelled
enameller
enamoured
encaustic
encephala
enchanter
enchilada
enchorial
enclosure
encomiast
encompass
encounter
encourage
encrimson
encrinite
endearing
endeavour
endlessly
endoblast
endocrine
endogamic
endogenic
endolymph
endomixis
endomorph
endophagy
endophyte
endoplasm
endoscope
endoscopy
endosperm
endospore
endosteal
endosteum
endowment
endurable
endurably
endurance
energetic
energiser
energumen
engarland
Englander
englutted
engraving
engrosser
enhearten
enigmatic
enjoyable
enjoyably
enjoyment
enlighten
enrapture
enrolling
enrolment
ensheathe
entelechy
enterable
enteritis
entertain
enthymeme
entoblast
entophyte
entourage
entrammel
entrapped
entrechat
entrecote
entremets
enucleate
enumerate
enunciate
enviously
enwrapped
enwreathe
enzymatic
gnathonic
gneissoid
gneissose
inability
inamorata
inanimate
inanition
inaptness
inaudible
inaudibly
inaugural
inbetween
inbreathe
incapable
incapably
incarnate
incaution
incensory
incentive
inception
inceptive
incessant
incidence
incipient
inclement
inclosure
inclusion
inclusive
incognito
incommode
incondite
incorrect
incorrupt
increaser
increment
incubator
inculcate
inculpate
incumbent
incunable
incurable
incurably
incurious
incurrent
incurring
incursion
incursive
incurvate
indagator
indecency
indecorum
indelible
indelibly
indemnify
indemnity
indention
indenture
Indianise
indicator
indiction
indigence
indignant
indignity
indigotin
indispose
IndoAryan
indolence
indraught
inducible
induction
inductive
indulgent
indweller
inebriant
inebriate
inebriety
ineffable
ineffably
inelastic
inelegant
ineptness
inequable
inerrable
inerrancy
inertness
inexactly
infantile
infantine
infatuate
infection
infective
inferable
inference
inferring

infertile
infielder
infilling
infirmary
infirmity
inflation
inflexion
inflictor
inflowing
influence
influenza
informant
infractor
infuriate
infuscate
infusible
infusoria
ingenious
ingenuity
ingenuous
ingestion
ingestive
inglenook
ingrained
ingrowing
inhalator
inharmony
inherence
inheritor
inhibitor
inhumanly
initially
initiator
injection
injurious
injustice
innermost
innervate
innholder
innkeeper
innocence
innocency
innocuity
innocuous
innovator
innoxious
innuendos
inoculate
inodorous
inorganic
inpatient
inpouring
inquiline
insatiate
insatiety
inscriber
insectary
insectile
insensate
insertion
inservice
insetting
inshallah
insidious
insincere
insinuate
insipidly
insistent
insolence
insoluble
insolubly
insolvent
insomniac
inspanned
inspector
instanter
instantly
instigate
instilled
institute
insularly
insulator
insurable
insurance
insurgent
integrand
integrant
integrate
integrity
intellect
intendant
intensely
intensify
intension
intensity
intensive
intention
interbred
intercede
intercept
intercity
intercrop
interdict
interface
interfere
interfile
interflow
interfuse
interject
interknit
interlace
interlard
interleaf
interline
interlink
interlock
interlope
interlude
interment
internode
interpage
interplay
interpose
interpret
interring
interrupt
intersect
intervein
intervene
interview
interwind
interwove
interzone
intestacy
intestate
intestine
intorsion
intricacy
intricate
intrigant
intriguer
intrinsic
introduce
introject
introvert
intrusion
intrusive
intuition
intuitive
intumesce
inunction
inurement
inutility
invalidly
invariant
invective
inveigler
invention
inventive
inventory
inverness
inversely
inversion
inversive
invertase
invidious
inviolacy
inviolate
invisible
invisibly
involucre
involuted
inwrought
knavishly
kneadable
knifeedge
knightage
knockdown
knockknee
knotgrass
knowingly
knowledge
mnemonics
mnemonist
onanistic
oncogenic
oncologic
onehanded
onelegged
onerously
onionskin
onlicence
onomastic
onsetting
onslaught
ontogenic
ontologic
pneumatic
pneumonia
pneumonic
snailfish
snakebird
snakebite
snakelike
snakeroot
snakeskin
snakeweed
snakewood
snakiness
snaredrum
sniggerer
snipefish
snivelled
sniveller
snowberry
snowblind
snowblink
snowbound
snowbroth
snowdrift
snowfield
snowflake
snowgoose
snowguard
snowiness
snowplant
snowscape
snowstorm
snowwhite
snubnosed
unabashed
unadopted
unadorned
unadvised
unalloyed
unaltered
unanimity
unanimous
unaptness
unashamed
unbalance
unbeknown
unbending
unberufen
unbiassed
unblessed
unblinded
unbounded
unbraided
unbridled
uncannily
unceasing
uncertain
uncharted
unchecked
uncinated
uncivilly
uncleanly
unclothed
unclouded
unconcern
uncounted
uncouthly
uncovered
uncreated
uncropped
uncrossed
uncrowned
undamaged
undaunted
undecagon
undeceive
undecided
undecimal
undefined
underbody
underbred
underclay
undercoat
underdone
underfelt
underfoot
undergird
undergone
undergrad
underhand
underhung
underlaid
underlain
underline
underling
undermine
undermost
underpaid
underpart
underpass
underplay
underplot
underrate
underripe
underseal
underseas
undersell
undershot
underside
undersign
undersold
undersong
underspin
undertake
undertint
undertone
undertook
undervest
underwear
underwent
underwing
underwood
undivided
undoubted
undreamed
undulated
undutiful
unearthly
uneatable
unequally
unethical
unfailing
unfeeling
unfeigned
unfitness
unfitting
unfledged
unfleshed
unfleshly
unfounded
ungallant
unguarded
unhappily
unharness
unhealthy
unheeding
unhelpful
unhurried
unicolour
unicuspid
unifiable
uniformly
uniparous
uniplanar
uniserial
unisexual
unisonant
unisonous
unitarian
unitively
univalent
universal
unknitted
unknowing
unlearned
unlimited
unluckily
unmatched
unmeaning
unmindful
unmusical
unnamable
unnatural
unpegging
unpeopled
unplugged
unplumbed
unpointed
unpopular
unreality
unreserve
unruffled
unsavoury
unsayable
unscathed
unselfish
unsettled
unshackle
unsheathe
unsighted
unsightly
unskilful
unskilled
unsmiling
unsoundly
unsparing
unspotted
unstopped
unstudied
unsuccess
unsullied
untenable
unthought
unthrifty
untimeous
untouched
untrodden
untrussed
untutored
unusually
unwearied
unweeting
unwelcome
unwilling
unwinking
unwitting
unwomanly
unwrapped
unwritten
unwrought
unzipping
Boanerges
boardfoot
boardroom
boardwalk
boathouse
boatswain
boattrain
bobsleigh
bobtailed
bodyguard
boldfaced
bolection
boliviano
bolometer
bolometry
Bolshevik
bombardon
bombasine
bombastic
bombazine
bombhappy
bombilate
bombinate
bombproof
bombshell
bombsight
bondslave
bondstone
bondwoman
bonechina
bonhomous
bonniness
boobytrap
bookishly
booklouse
bookmaker
bookplate
bookshelf
bookstall
bookstand
bookstore
boomerang
boomslang
boondocks
boorishly
bootblack
bordereau
borrowing
boskiness
bossiness
botanical
bottlefed
bottleful
boulevard
boundless
bounteous
bountiful
bouquetin
bourgeois
bowerbird
bowlegged
bowstring
bowwindow
boxgirder
boxoffice
boycotter
boyfriend
coachwork
coadjutor
coadunate
coagulant
coagulate
coalfield
coalition
coalmouse
coarctate
coastline
coastward
coastwise
coattails
coaxially
coaxingly
cobaltite
cobaltous
Cobdenism
cobwebbed
cocainise
cocainism
coccidium
coccygeal
cochineal
cochleate
cockahoop
Cockaigne
cockatiel
cockfight
cockhorse
cockiness
cockneyfy
cockroach
cockscomb
cocksfoot
cocoonery
coecilian
coelomata
coelomate
coelostat
coemption
coenobite
coenobium
coenosarc
coequally
coercible
coercibly
coeternal
coffeecup
coffeepot
cofferdam
coffinite
cogitable
cognately
cognation
cognisant
cognition
cognitive
coheiress
coherence
coherency
coiffeuse
coinsurer
colcannon
colchicum
colcothar
coldshort
colemouse
collagist

collation
colleague
collected
collector
collegial
collegian
collegium
colligate
collimate
collinear
collision
collocate
collodion
colloidal
colloquia
collotype
collusion
collusive
collyrium
colocynth
colonelcy
coloniser
colonnade
colophony
colorific
colosseum
colostomy
colostrum
colourful
colouring
colourist
colourman
coltishly
coltsfoot
colubrine
columbary
Columbian
columbine
columbite
columbium
columella
columnist
combatant
combative
combinate
comedones
comfiture
comforter
comically
Cominform
Comintern
comitadji
commander
commandos
commendam
commensal
commenter
commingle
comminute
commissar
committal
committed
committee
commodity
commodore
commonage
commonlaw
commotion
communard
communion
communise
communism
communist
community
commutate
compactly
compactor
companion
compasses
compelled
compendia
competent
complaint
complexly
complexus
compliant
component
composite
composure
comprador
comprisal
comptroll
comradely
comradery
concavely
concavity
conceited
concentre
concerned
concerted
concierge
conciliar
concisely
concision
concocter
concoctor
concordat
concourse
concubine
concurred
condenser
condignly
condiment
condition
conducive
conductor
condyloid
condyloma
confabbed
conferral
conferred
conferrer
confervae
confessor
confidant
confident
confiding
configure
confirmed
confirmer
confirmor
confiteor
confluent
conformal
conformer
Confucian
confusion
congenial
congeries
congruent
congruity
congruous
conically
conjugate
connately
connation
connature
connected
connecter
connector
connexion
connivent
connubial
conqueror
conscious
conscribe
conscript
consensus
conserver
consignee
consignor
consonant
consortia
constable
constancy
constrain
constrict
construct
consulage
consulate
consulter
consultor
contactor
contadina
contadino
contagion
contagium
container
contemner
contender
contented
continent
continual
continuer
continuum
contralto
contrasty
contrived
contriver
contumacy
contumely
contusion
conundrum
convector
converter
convexity
convincer
convivial
convolute
convolved
cookhouse
cooperage
cooperant
cooperate
copacetic
copartner
copesmate
copestone
copiously
copolymer
coproduce
coprolite
coprology
copsewood
copyright
coralline
corallite
coralloid
corbeille
corbelled
corbicula
cordelier
cordially
cordiform
corduroys
coreopsis
coriander
corkscrew
cormorant
cornbrash
corncrake
cornelian
cornemuse
cornerboy
cornerman
cornetist
cornfield
cornflour
cornopean
cornsalad
cornstalk
cornstone
corollary
coroneted
corporate
corporeal
corposant
corpulent
corpuscle
corralled
corrasion
correctly
corrector
correlate
corrosion
corrosive
corrugate
corrupter
corruptly
corticate
corticoid
cortisone
coruscant
coruscate
Corybants
corydalis
corymbose
coryphaei
coseismal
coseismic
cosmogeny
cosmogony
cosmology
cosmonaut
cosmorama
costively
costumier
cotangent
cothurnus
cotillion
cotyledon
couchette
coumarone
countable
countdown
countless
countship
courgette
courtcard
courteous
courtesan
courtroom
courtship
courtyard
couturier
covalence
covalency
covariant
coverable
coverslip
coverture
covetable
cowardice
cowlstaff
coxcombry
doctorate
doctorial
doctrinal
dodecagon
dogcollar
doggishly
doglegged
dogmatics
dogmatise
dogmatism
dogmatist
dogoodism
dogshores
dogstooth
dogviolet
dolefully
doleritic
dolomitic
doltishly
dominance
dominator
dominical
Dominican
donnishly
donothing
doodlebug
doorframe
doorplate
dopefiend
dorbeetle
dormition
dormitory
dosimeter
dosimetry
dosshouse
dottiness
doubleton
doubtable
doubtless
doughtily
Doukhobor
dowdiness
dowelling
dowerless
downfield
downgrade
downright
downriver
downstage
downthrow
downwards
focussing
foeticide
fogginess
foliation
folkdance
folkmusic
folkweave
following
foodchain
foodstuff
foolhardy
foolishly
foolproof
footboard
footcloth
footfault
footlight
footloose
footplate
footpound
footprint
footstalk
footstall
footstool
foppishly
foragecap
forasmuch
forbidden
forcefeed
forceland
forceless
forcemeat
forcepump
foreboder
forebrain
forecaddy
foreclose
forecourt
forefront
foregoing
foreigner
forejudge
foreknown
forenamed
forereach
foreshore
foreshown
foresight
forespeak
forestage
forestall
foretaste
foretoken
forewoman
forfeiter
forgather
forgeable
forgetful
forgiving
forgotten
forlornly
formalise
formalism
formalist
formality
formation
formative
formatted
formicary
formicate
formulaic
formulary
formulate
formulise
fornicate
forsythia
fortalice
forthwith
fortifier
fortitude
fortnight
fortunate
fortyfive
forwander
forwarder
forwardly
fossicker
fossilise
fossorial
fosterage
foulbrood
foundling
foundress
fourflush
fourpence
fourpenny
fourscore
fourwheel
foxhunter
goalmouth
gobetween
goddamned
godfather
godliness
godmother
godparent
goffering
gogglebox
goingover
goldbrick
goldcrest
goldeneye
goldenrod
goldfever
goldfield
goldfinch
goldsinny
goldsmith
golflinks
goliardic
gomphosis
gondolier
gongorism
gonophore
goodnight
goodwives
goosander
goosefoot
goosegirl
gooseherd
gooseneck
gooseskin
goosestep
gorblimey
gorgonian
gorgonise
gospeller
gossamery
Gothamite
gothicise
Gothicism
governess
hoarfrost
hoarhound
hoariness
hoarstone
Hobbesian
hobgoblin
hobnailed
hobnobbed
hobnobber
hocussing
hodiernal
hodograph
hodometer
hoggishly
Holarctic
hollyhock
Hollywood
holocaust
holograph
holophote
holystone
homebound
homegrown
homemaker
homeopath
homestead
homewards
homicidal
homiletic
homogamic
homograft
homograph
homologue
homonymic
homophone
homophony
homoplasy
homopolar
homotaxis
homotonic
homousian
homuncule
homunculi
honeycomb
honeymoon
honkytonk
honoraria
honorific
hoofprint
hopefully
hopscotch
horehound
horniness
hornstone
hornwrack

horologer
horologic
horoscope
horoscopy
horseback
horsebean
horsehair
horsehide
horseless
horsemint
horseplay
horsepond
horseshoe
horsetail
horsewhip
horsiness
hortation
hortative
hortatory
hortensia
hosteller
hostilely
hostility
hotheaded
Hottentot
hourglass
houseboat
housebote
housecarl
housecoat
houseflag
household
housekeep
houseleek
houseless
houselled
housemaid
housemate
houseroom
housewife
housework
howsoever
hoydenish
ionisable
jobmaster
jockstrap
jocularly
jocundity
Johannine
jointress
jollyboat
Jordanian
josshouse
jossstick
journeyer
joviality
joylessly
loadstone
loafsugar
loanshark
loathsome
lobectomy
lobscouse
lobulated
locatable
locksmith
locomotor
lodestone
lodgement
lodgepole
loftiness
logaoedic
logarithm
logically
logistics
logogriph
logomachy
loincloth
Lombardic
Londonise
Londonism
longaeval
longchain
longcoats
longeared
longevity
longevous
longfaced
longhouse
longicorn
longingly
longitude
longlived
Longobard
longrange
longshore
lookalike
looseleaf
looseness
lophodont
loquacity
lorgnette
lotusland
loudmouth
louringly
lousewort
lousiness
loutishly
loveapple
lovechild
lovefeast
lovelight
lovematch
loverless
lovestory
lovetoken
lovingcup
lowercase
lowerdeck
lowermost
lowlander
lowliness
lowloader
lowminded
lownecked
loxodrome
mobocracy
mockingly
modelling
moderator
modernise
modernism
modernist
modernity
modillion
modulator
moistener
moistness
molecular
molluscan
mollymawk
molybdate
momentary
momentous
monachism
monarchal
monarchic
monastery
monatomic
Mondayish
monergism
moneybags
moneybill
moneywort
Mongolian
mongolism
Mongoloid
mongooses
mongrelly
monitress
monkeyish
monkeyism
monkeynut
monkshood
monobasic
monoceros
monochord
monocline
monocoque
monocracy
monocular
monodical
monodrama
monoecism
monogamic
monograph
monolatry
monologic
monologue
monomania
monomeric
monophagy
monoplane
monorhyme
monostich
monostyle
monotonic
monotreme
monotypic
monsignor
monsoonal
monstrous
Montanism
monthling
monticule
monzonite
moodiness
moonblind
moonlight
moonquake
moonraker
moonscape
moonshine
moonstone
moraceous
moraliser
moratoria
morbidity
mordacity
mordantly
Mormonism
morphemic
morrisman
mortality
mortgagee
mortgager
mortgagor
mortician
mosaicism
mosaicist
mosaicked
moschatel
mosquitos
mossagate
mossgrown
motheaten
motherwit
mothproof
motivator
motocross
motorable
motorbike
motorboat
motorcade
mouldable
mountable
mousehole
mousetrap
moustache
mouthpart
mouthwash
moviegoer
nobiliary
nobleness
noctiluca
nocturnal
nocuously
nodulated
noiseless
noisiness
noisomely
nominable
nominally
nominator
nomocracy
nomograph
nondriver
nonentity
nonillion
nonjuring
nonlinear
nonpareil
nonperson
nonprofit
nonsmoker
nonviable
normalise
normality
Normanise
Normanism
normative
northeast
northerly
northland
northmost
northward
northwest
Norwegian
nosebleed
noseflute
nosepiece
nostalgia
nostalgic
nostology
notabilia
notedness
notepaper
notionist
notochord
notoriety
notorious
nourisher
novelette
noviciate
novitiate
nowhither
noxiously
oogenesis
oogenetic
pocketful
podagrous
podginess
podzolise
poetaster
poeticise
poeticism
poignancy
poinciana
pointduty
pointedly
pointille
pointlace
pointless
pointsman
poisonous
pokeberry
pokerface
pokerwork
polariser
polemical
polevault
policeman
politburo
politesse
political
pollinate
pollinium
pollutant
pollution
polonaise
polyamide
polyandry
polybasic
polyester
polygamic
polygenic
polygonal
polygonum
polygraph
polyhedra
polymathy
polymeric
polymorph
polyonymy
polyphagy
polyphase
polyphone
polyphony
polyploid
polyptych
polysemic
polysomic
polythene
polytonal
polytypic
polyvinyl
polywater
polyzoary
pomaceous
pommelled
pompadour
pomposity
pompously
ponderous
pontoneer
pontonier
poorhouse
popliteal
poppycock
poppyhead
popularly
porbeagle
porcelain
porcupine
poriferal
poriferan
porphyria
porringer
portative
porterage
portfolio
porticoes
portolano
portrayal
portrayer
portreeve
portulaca
possessed
possessor
postentry
posterior
posterity
posthaste
posthorse
posthouse
posticous
postilion
postnasal
postnatal
postulant
postulate
potassium
potboiler
potentate
potential
potholing
pothunter
potpourri
poulterer
pouncebox
poundcake
pourboire
pourpoint
poussette
powerboat
powerdive
powerless
pozzolana
roadblock
roadhouse
roadmetal
roadstead
roadworks
rocambole
rockbound
rockbrake
rockdrill
rocketeer
rockiness
rockplant
rocksnake
rodfisher
roguishly
roisterer
roodcloth
roofplate
roominess
rootstock
Roquefort
rosaceous
roseapple
roseately
rosenoble
rosewater
rosinweed
rostellum
rotatable
rotundity
roughcast
roughhewn
roughneck
roughness
roughshod
Roumanian
Roumansch
rounceval
roundelay
roundhead
roundness
roundsman
roundworm
rousement
routinely
routinism
routinist
rowantree
rowdiness
soapberry
soapiness
soapstone
soapworks
sobbingly
soberness
sobriquet
sobsister
socialise
socialism
socialist
socialite
sociality
sociogram
sociology
sociopath
sodabread
sodawater
softgoods
softpedal
softshell
sogginess
soidisant
sojourner
solacious
soldierly
solemnise
solemnity
soleplate
solfatara
solfeggio
solferino
solicitor
solidness
soliloquy
solipsism
solipsist
solitaire
solmisate
Solomonic
Solutrean
Solutrian
solvation
something
sometimes
somewhere
somewhile
sommelier
somnolent
songcycle
songfully
songsmith
sonneteer
sonnetise
sonometer
sooterkin
soothfast
sootiness
sophister
sophistic
sophistry
sophomore
soporific
soppiness
sopranino
sopranist
sorbapple
Sorbonist
sorceress
sorcerous
soritical
sorriness
sorrowful
sortilege
sortition
sostenuto
sottishly
soubrette
Soudanese
soulfully
soundfilm
soundhole
soundings
soundless
soundness
soundpost

soundwave
soupplate
soupspoon
sourdough
souteneur
Southdown
southeast
southerly
southland
southmost
southward
southwest
souwester
sovereign
sovietise
sovietism
toadeater
toadstone
toadstool
toastrack
Tocharian
tolerable
tolerably
tolerance
tollbooth
tollhouse
tombstone
tomentose
tomentous
tonguelet
tonguetie
tonically
tonometer
tonsillar
tonsorial
toolhouse
toothache
toothcomb
toothless
toothpick
toothsome
toothwort
tophamper
topiarian
topiarist
topically
toponymal
toponymic
torchrace
torchsong
toreutics
tormentil
tormentor
torpidity
torridity
torsional
tortrices
tortricid
torturous
totaliser
totalling
totempole
touchable
touchdown
touchhole
touchline
touchmark
touchtype
touchwood
toughness
touristic
tournedos
tourneyer
towelling
townhouse
townscape
townsfolk
toxically
toxophily
vocabular
vocaliser
vocalness
voiceless
voiceover
volauvent
volcanism
volcanoes
volkslied
volteface
voltinism
voltmeter
volumeter
voluntary
volunteer
vomitoria
voodooism
voodooist
voracious
vorticism
vorticist
vorticity
vorticose
vouchsafe
vowelless
voyeurism
woebegone
wolfhound
wolfishly
wolframic
wolfsbane
wolverene
wolverine
womanhood
womaniser
womankind
womanlike
womenfolk
womenkind
wonderful
woodblock
woodchuck
woodcraft
woodiness
woodlouse
woodnymph
woodwaxen
wooziness
Worcester
wordiness
wordsmith
workbench
workhorse
workhouse
workmanly
workpiece
worktable
workwoman
worldling
worldwide
wormeaten
wormwheel
worriedly
worriment
worrisome
worrywart
worthless
woundless
woundwort
yodelling
yohimbine
Yorkshire
youngling
youngness
youngster
zoiatrics
zoogenous
zoography
zoologist
zoophagan
zoophobia
zoophytic
zootechny
zootomist
apartheid
apartment
apartness
apathetic
aperiodic
aperitive
apetalous
aphereses
apheresis
aphyllous
apiculate
apishness
aplanatic
apocrypha
apodictic
apogamous
apologise
apologist
apomictic
apophyses
apophysis
apostolic
apothecia
appalling
Appaloosa
apparatus
apparitor
appealing
appellant
appellate
appendage
appendant
appertain
appetence
appetency
appetiser
applauder
applejack
appliance
applicant
appointee
apportion
appraisal
appraiser
apprehend
appressed
approbate
epaenetic
epaulette
ephedrine
ephemeral
ephemerid
ephemeris
ephemeron
epicentre
epiclesis
epicurean
epicurism
epicyclic
epidermal
epidermic
epidermis
epidosite
epigraphy
epigynous
epilation
epileptic
epilogist
epinastic
epiphragm
epiphyses
epiphysis
epiphytal
epiphytic
epipolism
episcopal
epistaxis
epistemic
epistoler
epistolic
epithelia
epithesis
epithetic
epitomise
epitomist
epizootic
eponymous
openended
openheart
operation
operative
opercular
operculum
operosely
operosity
ophiology
opinioned
opodeldoc
opponency
opportune
opposable
oppressor
oppugnant
opsimathy
optically
optometer
optometry
optophone
opulently
opusculum
spaceband
spaceless
spaceport
spaceship
spacesuit
spacetime
spadefoot
spadework
spaghetti
spagyrist
spareness
spareribs
sparingly
sparkcoil
sparkless
sparkplug
spasmodic
spatially
spatulate
speakable
speakeasy
spearfish
spearhead
spearmint
spearside
spearwort
specially
specialty
specifier
speckless
spectacle
spectator
speculate
speechful
speechify
speedball
speedboat
speedster
speedwell
spellbind
spellican
spendable
spermatic
spermatid
sphagnous
spherical
spherular
sphincter
sphygmoid
spicebush
spiciness
spiculate
spiderman
spiderweb
spikenard
spikiness
spillikin
spindling
spindrier
spindrift
spineless
spininess
spinnaker
spinneret
spinosity
Spinozism
Spinozist
spinulose
spinulous
spiracula
spirality
spiralled
spirillum
spiritism
spiritist
spiritoso
spiritous
spiritual
spirituel
spirogyra
splashily
splayfoot
spleenful
splendent
splendour
splenetic
splenitis
spleuchan
splintery
splitting
spluttery
spodumene
spoilsman
spokesman
spokewise
spoliator
spongebag
spongeous
spoonbeak
spoonbill
spoonfeed
spoonmeat
sporangia
sporocarp
sporocyst
sporogeny
sportsman
sporulate
spotcheck
spotlight
spouthole
spoutless
sprigging
sprightly
sprigtail
springald
springbok
springily
springing
springlet
sprinkler
spritsail
spurwheel
sputterer
Upanishad
upbraider
upcountry
upholster
uplifting
uppercase
uppermost
uprightly
upsetting
xparticle
aquaplane
aquarelle
aqueously
aquilegia
equaliser
equalling
equipment
equipoise
equipping
equisetum
equitable
equitably
equivocal
equivoque
squabbler
squalidly
squamosal
squarrose
squashily
squatness
squatting
squeakily
squeamish
squelcher
squibbing
squidding
squinancy
squirarch
squiredom
squirelet
arabesque
arabicise
arachnoid
aragonite
araneidal
araneidan
araucaria
arbitrage
arbitrary
arbitrate
arbitress
arboreous
arboretum
archangel
archducal
archduchy
archenemy
archetype
archfiend
architect
archivist
archivolt
arcuately
arduously
Areopagus
argentine
argentite
argentous
argillite
argumenta
Arguseyed
argybargy
armadillo
armigeral
armillary
armistice
Armorican
aromatise
arrearage
arrestant
arresting
arriviste
arrogance
arrowhead
arrowroot
arrowwood
arrowworm
arsenical
arsenious
artemisia
arteriole
arteritis
arthritic
arthritis
arthropod
arthrosis
Arthurian
artichoke
articular
artificer
artillery
artlessly
arytenoid
brachiate
brachyura
bracteate
bracteole
Brahmanic
Brahminee
Brahminic
braincase
brainless
brainwash
brainwave
brakeless
brakeshoe
brakesman
brambling
branchiae
branchial
branchlet
brandling
brandreth
brashness
brasserie
brassiere
bratwurst
brazilnut
breadline
breadtree
breakable
breakaway
breakdown
breakeven
breakfast
breakneck
breastpin
breathily
breathing
brecciate
breeching
breezeway
bregmatic
bretasche
Bretwalda
breveting
brevetted
briarroot
briarwood
bricabrac
brickwork
brickyard
bridecake
bridesman
bridewell
bridleway

briefcase
briefless
briefness
brierroot
brierwood
brigadier
brigandry
brightish
brilliant
brimstone
bringdown
briquette
briskness
bristling
Britannia
Britannic
Briticise
Briticism
Britisher
brittlely
broadcast
broadleaf
broadloom
broadness
broadside
broadtail
broadways
broadwise
brochette
broiderer
brokerage
bromeliad
bronchial
broomcorn
broomrape
brotherly
brownness
brummagem
brushfire
brushwood
brushwork
brusquely
brutalise
brutalism
brutality
brutishly
bryophyte
Brythonic
crabbedly
crackdown
crackling
cracksman
craftsman
crampfish
cranberry
crankcase
cranreuch
crapulent
crapulous
crashdive
crashland
crassness
craziness
creatable
creatress
creatural
crediting
credulity
credulous
cremaster
cremation
crematory
crenation
crenature
crenelled
crenulate
crepitant
crepitate
crepuscle
crescendo
crestless
cretinism
cretinous
cricketer
criminate
criminous
crinoidal
crinoline
crippling
crispness
criterion
criticise
criticism
crocodile
croissant
CroMagnon
crookback
crookedly
crookneck
cropeared
croquette
crossable
crossbeam
crossbill
crossbred
crossette
crosseyed
crossfade
crossfire
crossfish
crosshead
crosslink
crossness
crossover
crossroad
crossruff
crosstalk
crossways
crosswind
crosswise
crossword
crotchety
croustade
crowberry
crownless
crowsfoot
crowsnest
crucially
cruciform
crudeness
cruellest
crushable
crustacea
cryogenic
cryoscope
cryoscopy
cryptical
cryptogam
cryptonym
draconian
draftsman
draghound
dragomans
dragoness
dragonfly
dragonish
drainpipe
dramatics
dramatise
dramatist
Dravidian
drawerful
drawnwork
drawplate
drawsheet
drayhorse
dreamboat
dreamland
dreamless
dreamlike
dresscoat
driftsail
driftweed
driftwood
drinkable
dripstone
drivelled
driveller
drollness
dromedary
dropscene
dropscone
dropsical
drugstore
druidical
drummajor
drumstick
drunkenly
dryasdust
drysalter
eradicate
erectness
eremitism
ergograph
ergometer
ergonomic
eristical
erogenous
eroticism
erratical
erroneous
errorless
erstwhile
eruciform
eruditely
erudition
erythrism
erythrite
fractious
fraenulum
fragility
fragrance
fragrancy
frailness
framework
franchise
francolin
frangible
Franglais
frankness
franticly
fraternal
freeboard
freehouse
freelance
freeliver
Freemason
freerange
freerider
freestone
freestyle
freewheel
freewoman
freezable
freezedry
freighter
frenchify
Frenchman
frequence
frequency
freshener
freshness
fretfully
friarbird
fricassee
fricative
frigatoon
frightful
frigidity
fritterer
frivolity
frivolled
frivolous
frockcoat
frogmarch
frogspawn
frolicked
frontally
frontless
frontline
frontpage
frontward
frontways
frontwise
frostbite
frostwork
frowardly
fructuate
fructuous
frugality
fruitcake
fruiterer
fruitless
fruittree
frustrate
fruticose
graceless
gracility
gradation
gradatory
Gradgrind
gradually
graduator
grandaddy
grandaunt
grandiose
grandness
grandpapa
grandsire
grandslam
granitoid
grantable
granulate
granulite
granulose
grapeshot
grapevine
graphemic
graphical
graphitic
grappling
graspable
grassland
graticule
gratitude
gratulate
gravamina
graveless
gravelled
graveness
graveyard
gravidity
gravitate
graywacke
greasegun
greataunt
greatcoat
greatness
Greekless
greenback
greenbelt
greeneyed
greengage
greenhorn
greenness
greenroom
greensand
greenweed
greenwood
gregarian
gregarine
Gregorian
grenadier
grenadine
greybeard
greyhound
greywacke
griefless
grievance
grillroom
grillwork
grimalkin
griminess
grisaille
gristmill
gritstone
groomsman
grosgrain
grossness
grossular
grotesque
grouchily
groundage
groundash
groundhog
grounding
groundivy
groundnut
groundsel
grovelled
groveller
grubscrew
grubstake
gruelling
gruffness
grumbling
Grundyism
irascible
irascibly
irksomely
ironbound
ironmould
ironsides
ironsmith
ironstone
ironworks
Iroquoian
irradiant
irradiate
irreality
irregular
irrigable
irrigator
irritable
irritably
irruption
irruptive
krummhorn
orangeade
Orangeism
Orangeman
orangetip
orangutan
oratorial
oratorian
orbicular
orchestic
orchestra
orchidist
orderbook
orderform
orderless
ordinance
organelle
organiser
organstop
organzine
orgiastic
orientate
orificial
oriflamme
originate
orography
orologist
orphanage
Orpington
orrisroot
orthodoxy
orthoepic
practical
practised
praenomen
pragmatic
praiseful
pranksome
prankster
pratingly
prayerful
prayerrug
preachify
preachily
preadamic
prebendal
precancel
precative
precatory
precedent
preceding
precentor
preceptor
precipice
precisely
precisian
precision
precocial
precocity
preconise
precursor
predacity
predation
predative
predatory
predicant
predicate
predictor
predigest
predikant
preemptor
preengage
preexilic
prefatory
preferred
prefigure
prefixion
pregnable
pregnancy
prejudice
prelatess
prelatise
prelature
prelector
prelusion
prelusive
prelusory
premature
premonish
premotion
prenotion
preoccupy
preordain
prepotent
prerecord
presbyope
presbyter
preschool
prescient
prescribe
prescript
preselect
presentee
presenter
presently
preserver
preshrink
preshrunk
president
presidial
presidium
pressgang
pressmark
pressroom
pressstud
presswork
prestress
pretender
preterist
preterite
pretermit
prettyish
prettyism
prevalent
preventer
prevision
priceless
prideless
priestess
primaeval
primality
primarily
primatial
primeness
primipara
primitive
primordia
princedom
princekin
princelet
principal
principia
principle
printable
printshop
priorship
prismatic
privateer
privately
privation
privative
privilege
probation
probative
probatory
proboscis
procedure
procerity
processed
processer
processor
proclitic
proconsul
procreant
procreate
procuracy
procuress
prodromal
prodromic
proenzyme
profanely
profanity
professed
professor
profilist
profiteer

profusely
profusion
progestin
prognoses
prognosis
programme
projector
prolamine
prolapsus
prolately
prolation
prolative
prolepses
prolepsis
proleptic
prolicide
prolixity
prologise
prolusion
prolusory
promenade
prominent
promising
promotion
promotive
promptbox
pronation
proneness
pronghorn
pronounce
proofread
propagate
propelled
propeller
properdin
prophetic
propionic
proponent
propriety
proptosis
propylaea
propylene
prorogate
prosaical
proscenia
proscribe
prosector
prosecute
proselyte
prosiness
prosodist
prostatic
prostrate
protamine
protector
proteinic
protester
protestor
prothesis
prothetic
prothorax
protonema
prototype
protozoal
protozoan
protozoic
protozoon
proveably
Provencal
provender
provident
providing
provision
provisory
provoking
provostry
proximate
proximity
prudently
prudishly
prurience
pruriency
trabeated
trabecula
traceable
traceably
traceless
traceried
tracheary
tracheate
trachytic
trackless
tracksuit
tractable
tractably
trademark
tradename
tradesman
tradition
traducian
tragedian
trainable
trainband
trainload
traitress
tramlines
transcend
transenna
transform
transfuse
transient
translate
transmute
transonic
transpire
transport
transpose
transship
transumpt
transvest
trapezial
trapezium
trapezoid
trappings
trattoria
trattorie
traumatic
travelled
traveller
traversal
traverser
traycloth
treachery
treadmill
treasurer
treatable
treatment
trebuchet
trebucket
treillage
trematode
tremolant
tremolite
tremulant
tremulous
trenchant
trepanned
trepidant
trialogue
triatomic
tribadism
tribalism
tribesman
tribology
tribunate
tributary
trichinae
trichomic
trichroic
trickless
tricksily
trickster
triclinia
triclinic
tricolour
tridactyl
tridymite
triennial
triennium
trierarch
trifacial
trifocals
trifolium
triforium
trigamist
trigamous
trihedral
trihybrid
trilinear
trilithon
trilobate
trilobite
trimerous
trimester
trimetric
trimmings
trinketer
trinketry
trinomial
triploidy
triptyque
triquetra
trisagion
trisector
triteness
tritheism
tritheist
triturate
triumphal
triumviri
trivalent
trivially
triweekly
trochilus
trochleae
trochlear
troopship
tropology
troublous
trousered
trousseau
troutfarm
troutling
trowelled
troweller
truceless
truculent
truepenny
trumpedup
trumpeter
truncated
truncheon
trunkcall
trunkfish
trunkroad
trussbeam
trustdeed
trustless
truthless
trysquare
uraninite
uranology
urceolate
uropygium
urticaria
wrathless
wrestling
wristband
wristdrop
wristshot
wrongdoer
wrongness
asafetida
asbestine
asbestous
ascendant
ascendent
ascension
ascensive
ascertain
ascetical
asclepiad
ascospore
asepalous
asexually
ashamedly
Ashkenazi
ashlaring
asininity
askewness
asparagus
aspartate
aspectual
aspersion
asphaltic
asphaltum
aspirator
assailant
assaulter
assayable
assembler
assertion
assertive
assiduity
assiduous
assistant
associate
assonance
assuasive
assumable
assumably
assumpsit
assurance
assuredly
assurgent
asthmatic
astraddle
astrakhan
astrocyte
astrodome
astrolabe
astrology
astronaut
astronomy
asymmetry
asymptote
asyndetic
asyndeton
escalator
escapable
escheator
escortage
esemplasy
esoterica
esoterism
esperance
Esperanto
espionage
esplanade
espousals
Esquimaux
essential
establish
estaminet
Esthonian
estimable
estimator
estoppage
estopping
estranger
estrapade
estuarian
estuarine
esurience
esuriency
isagogics
isallobar
ischaemia
ischaemic
ischiadic
ischiatic
isinglass
Islamitic
isobathic
isochrone
isoclinal
isoclinic
isocyclic
isogamete
isogamous
isogenous
isohyetal
isolation
isolative
isomerise
isomerism
isomerous
isometric
isoniazid
isooctane
isopodous
isosceles
isostatic
isotropic
Israelite
issueless
Kshatriya
oscillate
oscitancy
osmometer
ossicular
ossifrage
ostensive
osteoderm
osteogeny
osteology
osteopath
ostracise
ostracism
Ostrogoth
psalmbook
psalmodic
psalteria
pseudonym
pseudopod
psoriasis
psoriatic
psychical
psychoses
psychosis
psychotic
tsarevich
uselessly
usherette
usualness
usucapion
atacamite
ataractic
atavistic
atheistic
athematic
Athenaeum
athletics
Atlantean
atmometer
atomicity
atomistic
atonalism
atonality
atonement
atonicity
atrocious
attainder
attempter
attendant
attention
attentive
attenuate
attractor
attribute
attrition
eternally
etherical
ethically
Ethiopian
ethmoidal
ethnarchy
ethnicity
ethnology
ethylenic
etiquette
etymology
italicise
Italicism
itchiness
iteration
iterative
itineracy
itinerant
itinerary
itinerate
itsybitsy
ittybitty
otherness
otherwise
otologist
ptarmigan
pterosaur
pterygium
pterygoid
Ptolemaic
stabilise
stability
stableboy
stableman
stackable
stackroom
stackyard
stagedoor
stagehand
staggerer
staghound
staginess
Stagirite
stagnancy
stagparty
staidness
stainable
stainless
staircase
stairfoot
stairhead
stairwell
stakeboat
stalactic
stalemate
staleness
Stalinism
Stalinist
stalkeyed
stalkless
stallfeed
stalworth
staminate
stammerer
stampduty
stampmill
stampnote
stanchion
standpipe
stapedial
starapple
starboard
starchily
stardrift
stargazer
stargrass
starkness
starlight
starshell
starstone
startling
statehood
stateless
statement
stateroom
stateside
statesman
statewide
stational
stationer
statistic
statocyst
statolith
statuette
statutory
stauncher
staunchly
staymaker
steadfast
steamboat
steampipe
steamship
steatitic
steelclad
steelhead
steelwork
steelyard
steenkirk
steepness
steersman
stegosaur
stellated
stenotype
stenotypy
stepchild
stepdance
steradian
stercoral
sterilise
sterility
sternmost
sternness
sternpost
sternward
steroidal
stevedore
stickwork
stiffener
stiffness
stigmatic
stilettos
stillborn
stillhunt
stillness
stillroom
stiltedly
stimulant
stimulate
stingaree
stingless
stinkball
stinkbomb

stinkhorn
stinktrap
stinkweed
stinkwood
stintless
stipitate
stippling
stipulate
stirabout
stitchery
stockbook
stockdove
stockfish
stockinet
stocklist
stockpile
stockroom
stockwhip
stockyard
stoically
stokehold
stokehole
stolidity
stolonate
stomachal
stomacher
stomachic
stonechat
stonecoal
stonecold
stonecrop
stonedead
stonedeaf
stonefish
stoneless
stonewall
stoneware
stonework
stonewort
stoniness
stoolball
stoplight
stoppress
stopwatch
storeroom
storeship
storiated
stormbelt
stormbird
stormcock
stormcone
stormless
stormsail
storybook
storyline
stoutness
stovepipe
straggler
strangely
strangler
strangles
straphang
strapless
strappado
strapping
strapwork
strapwort
stratagem
strategic
strawworm
streakily
streaking
streamlet
streetcar
strenuous
stressful
stretcher
strewment
striation
striature
stricture
stridence
stridency
stringent
stripling
stripping
strobilae
strobilus
stromatic
strongarm
strongbox
strongish
strongyle
strontium
stropping
strouding
structure
struggler
strumitis
strumming
strutting
strychnic
studhorse
studiedly
stupefier
stupidity
stuporous
stutterer
stylebook
styliform
stylishly
stylistic
stylobate
utricular
utterable
utterance
utterless
uttermost
utterness
ytterbium
aubergine
aubrietia
auctorial
audacious
audiology
auditable
auditoria
augmented
augmenter
augmentor
auricular
auspicate
austenite
austerely
austerity
autarchic
autarkist
authentic
authoress
authorial
authorise
authority
autoclave
autocracy
autocross
autocycle
autograft
autograph
autolysis
autolytic
automatic
automaton
autonomic
autopilot
autoroute
autosomal
autotelic
autotroph
auxiliary
buccaneer
buckboard
bucketful
buckhound
buckshish
buckthorn
bucktooth
buckwheat
budgetary
buffaloes
buffeting
bughunter
buhrstone
bulbously
Bulgarian
bulginess
bulkiness
bulldozer
bullfight
bullfinch
bullishly
bulltrout
bullybeef
bullytree
bumblebee
bumbledon
bumpiness
bumptious
bundobust
bunkhouse
buoyantly
burdenous
burlesque
burliness
burnedout
burningly
burnisher
burrstone
bursarial
bushcraft
bushelful
bushiness
bushwhack
butadiene
butcherer
butcherly
butterbur
buttercup
butterfat
butterfly
butterine
butternut
buttinsky
buttygang
buxomness
cubbyhole
cubically
cuckoldry
cucullate
cudgelled
cullender
culminant
culminate
culsdesac
cultivate
cumbrance
cunctator
cuneiform
cunningly
cupbearer
cupelling
cuplichen
curbstone
curettage
curialism
curiosity
curiously
curliness
curlpaper
currently
curricula
currishly
currycomb
cursively
cursorial
cursorily
curstness
curtilage
curvature
curveting
curvetted
curviform
cuspidate
custodial
custodian
customary
customise
cutaneous
cuticular
cutinised
cutthroat
cuttysark
dualistic
dubiosity
dubiously
dubitable
duckboard
ductility
dulcamara
dulcitude
dumbfound
dumpiness
dungarees
duodecimo
duodenary
duplicate
duplicity
duralumin
duskiness
dustcover
dustiness
dustsheet
duteously
dutifully
eucalypti
eucaryote
Eucharist
euchology
euclidean
eulogiser
eunuchism
eunuchoid
euphemise
euphemism
euphonise
euphonium
euphorbia
eurhythmy
eutectoid
euthenics
eutherian
eutrophic
fugacious
fulfilled
fulfiller
fulgently
fulgurant
fulgurate
fulgurite
fulgurous
fullblown
fullcream
fulldress
fullgrown
fullscale
fulminant
fulminate
fulminous
fulsomely
fumarolic
fumigator
fundament
funebrial
fungicide
fungiform
funicular
funiculus
funkiness
funnelled
funniness
furbisher
furcation
furiously
furnisher
furniture
furtherer
furtively
fusillade
fusionist
fussiness
fustigate
fustiness
fuzziness
guacamole
guarantee
guarantor
guardbook
guardedly
guardrail
guardring
guardroom
guardship
guardsman
guerrilla
guesswork
guestroom
guidebook
guideline
guidepost
guiderope
guildhall
guildship
guileless
guillemot
guilloche
guiltless
guitarist
gumminess
guncotton
gunpowder
gunrunner
gushingly
gustation
gustative
gustatory
gustiness
gutsiness
guttation
guttering
hubristic
huckaback
huckstery
huffiness
hugeously
humankind
humanness
humblebee
humbugged
humdinger
humectant
humiliate
hunchback
hundredth
Hungarian
hunkydory
hurricane
hurriedly
hurtfully
husbandly
husbandry
huskiness
jubilance
Judaistic
Judastree
judgement
judgeship
judgmatic
judiciary
judicious
juiceless
juiciness
jumpiness
Juneberry
juniorate
juniority
junkerdom
junkerism
junketing
Junoesque
juridical
jurywoman
justiciar
justifier
juvenilia
juxtapose
kurrajong
lubricant
lubricate
lubricity
lubricous
lucidness
luciferin
luckiness
lucrative
lucubrate
ludicrous
luftwaffe
lumbering
lumberman
lumbrical
lumbricus
luminance
lumpiness
lumpishly
lunchtime
lunisolar
lunitidal
luridness
lustfully
lustihood
lustiness
luxuriant
luxuriate
luxurious
muckraker
mucksweat
mucronate
muddiness
muffineer
muffinman
mugginess
mullioned
multifoil
multiform
multilane
multipara
multiplex
multitude
mumchance
mummified
mundanely
mundungus
municipal
muniments
munitions
murderess
murderous
murkiness
murmurous
muscadine
muscarine
muscleman
muscovado
muscovite
musically
musichall
musketeer
muskiness
muskmelon
Mussulman
mustachio
musteline
mustiness
mutagenic
mutilator
mutualise
mutualism
mutualist
mutuality
muzziness
nucleated
nucleolus
nucleonic
nuisancer
nullifier
nullipara
nullipore
numbskull
numerable
numerator
numerical
nummulite
nuncupate
nurseling
nursemaid
nutriment
nutrition
nutritive
nuttiness
nutweevil
oubliette
ourselves
outbacker
outermost
outfitter
outgiving
outgoings
outgrowth
outgunned
outlander
outnumber
outputted
outridden
outrigger
outskirts
outspoken
outspread
outwardly
outwitted
outworker
pubescent
publicise
publicist
publicity
publisher
pudginess
puerility
puerperal
puffadder
puffiness
pugnacity
puissance
pullulate
pulmonary

pulmonate
pulpboard
pulpiness
pulpiteer
pulpstone
pulsatile
pulsation
pulsatory
pulseless
pulserate
pulverise
pulverous
pulvillus
pulvinate
pumiceous
pummelled
punchball
punchbowl
punchcard
punchline
punctilio
punctuate
pungently
punishing
pupillage
pupillary
puppeteer
puppyhood
purchaser
pureblood
purgation
purgative
purgatory
puritanic
purloiner
purposely
purposive
purpureal
purringly
purselike
pursiness
pursuable
pursuance
purulence
purulency
pushchair
pushiness
pushingly
pussyfoot
pustulate
pustulous
putridity
puzzolana
quadratic
quadrifid
quadrigae
quadrille
quadruman
quadruped
quadruple
quadruply
Quakerdom
Quakeress
Quakerish
Quakerism
quakiness
qualified
qualifier
quantical
quarenden
quarender
quarryman
quarterly
quartette
quartzite
quartzose
quebracho
queenhood
queenless
queenlike
queenpost
queenship
queerness
quercetum
querulous
quibbling
quickener
quicklime
quickness
quicksand
quickstep
quiescent
quietness
quillwort
quinoline
quintette
quintuple
quirister
quitclaim
quittance
quixotism
quizzical
quodlibet
quotation
quotidian
rubberise
rubellite
rubicelle
rubricate
rubrician
rudbeckia
ruddiness
ruddleman
rufescent
ruffianly
ruggedise
ruination
ruinously
rulership
ruminator
rumrunner
runcinate
rushlight
russeting
Russophil
rusticate
rusticity
rustiness
rustproof
ruthenium
ruthfully
suability
suasively
subaerial
subagency
subalpine
subaltern
subarctic
subastral
subatomic
subbranch
subcaudal
subcostal
subdeacon
subdivide
subduable
subduedly
subeditor
subereous
subfamily
subgenera
subjacent
subjugate
sublation
sublethal
sublimate
sublimely
sublimity
sublunary
submarine
submaster
submental
submitted
subnormal
subocular
subphylum
subregion
subrogate
subscribe
subscript
subsellia
subsidise
substance
substrata
substrate
subtenant
subtilise
subtopian
subverter
succeeder
succentor
successor
succinate
succotash
succourer
succulent
succursal
suctorial
suctorian
sudatoria
sudorific
suffering
suffocate
suffragan
suffusion
sugarbeet
sugarcane
sugarloaf
sugarplum
suggester
sulcation
sulkiness
sulphonic
sulphuret
sulphuric
sultanate
sultaness
summarily
summarise
summarist
summation
summative
summingup
sumptuary
sumptuous
sunbather
sunbonnet
sunburned
sundowner
sunflower
sunhelmet
sunlounge
sunniness
sunspurge
sunstroke
sunstruck
suntanned
superable
supercool
superfine
superfuse
superheat
supernova
superpose
supersede
superstar
supervene
supervise
supinator
suppliant
supporter
supposing
suppurate
supremacy
supremely
surcharge
surcingle
surculose
surfacing
surfboard
surfeiter
surficial
surgeoncy
surliness
surmullet
surpliced
surprisal
surrender
surrogate
surveying
suspender
suspensor
suspicion
sustainer
susurrant
sutteeism
suturally
tubbiness
tubercule
tubularly
tuckerbag
tufaceous
tuitional
tuliproot
tuliptree
tulipwood
tumblebug
tumescent
tumidness
tunefully
tungstate
tunicated
tunnelled
tunnelnet
turbidity
turbinate
turboprop
turbulent
Turcomans
turgently
turgidity
Turkomans
turnabout
turnround
turnstile
turnstone
turntable
turpitude
turquoise
tutorship
vulcanian
vulcanise
vulcanism
vulcanist
vulcanite
vulgarian
vulgarise
vulgarism
vulgarity
vulnerary
vulpinism
vulpinite
vulturine
vulturish
vulturous
wulfenite
zucchetto
available
availably
avalanche
aventaile
averagely
avertible
avizandum
avocation
avoidable
avoidably
avoidance
avuncular
evaginate
evangelic
evaporate
evasively
eventless
eventuate
everglade
evergreen
everybody
evidently
evincible
evocation
evocative
evocatory
evolution
evolutive
evolvable
ovenready
overblown
overboard
overborne
overcheck
overcloud
overcrowd
overdraft
overdrawn
overdress
overdrive
overeaten
overeater
overexert
overflown
overglaze
overgraze
overgrown
overheard
overissue
overjoyed
overladen
overleapt
overlying
overmatch
overnight
overpitch
overpower
overprice
overprint
overproof
overreach
overreact
oversexed
overshoot
oversight
oversized
overskirt
oversleep
overslept
overspend
overspent
overspill
overstate
oversteer
overstock
overstuff
overtaken
overthrew
overthrow
overtness
overtones
overtrain
overtrick
overtrump
overvalue
overwatch
overweary
overweigh
overwhelm
overwound
overwrite
overwrote
oviductal
oviferous
oviparity
oviparous
ovulation
ovulatory
uvarovite
awakening
awardable
awareness
awesomely
awestruck
awfulness
awkwardly
ewenecked
ownership
swaddling
swaggerer
swangoose
swansdown
swarajist
swartness
swearword
sweatband
sweatshop
sweepback
sweetcorn
sweetener
sweetmeal
sweetmeat
sweetness
sweetshop
sweettalk
swellfish
sweptback
swiftness
swimmable
swimmeret
swineherd
swingeing
swinishly
switchman
swivelled
swordcane
swordfish
swordknot
swordlike
swordplay
swordsman
swordtail
twayblade
twelfthly
twentieth
twentyone
twiceborn
twicelaid
twicetold
twinkling
twistable
twitchily
twitterer
twofisted
twohanded
twosuiter
Zwinglian
axiomatic
Axminster
exactable
exactment
exactness
examinant
exanimate
exanthema
exarchate
excavator
exceeding
excellent
excelling
excelsior
excentric
exceptant
excepting
exception
exceptive
excerptor
excessive
exchanger
exchequer
excipient
excisable
exciseman
excitable
excitancy
excitedly
exclosure
exclusion
exclusive
excoriate
excrement
excretion
excretive
excretory
exculpate
excurrent
excursion
excursive
excusable
excusably
execrable
execrably
executant
execution
executive
executory
executrix
exegetist
exemplary
exemplify
exemption
exequatur
exercises
exfoliate
exhauster
exhibitor
exilement
existence
exodermis
exogamous
exogenous
exonerate
exopodite
exorciser
exosmosis
exosmotic
exosphere
exostosis
exoticism
expansile
expansion
expansive
expatiate
expectant
expecting
expedient

expediter
expellent
expelling
expensive
expertise
expiation
expiatory
explainer
expletive
expletory
explicate
exploiter
explosion
explosive
expositor
expounder
expressly
expulsion
expulsive
expurgate
exquisite
exsertile
exsertion
exservice
exsiccate
exsuccous
extempore
extendant
extensile
extension
extensity
extensive
extenuate
externals
extirpate
extolling
extolment
extorsive
extortion
extortive
extractor
extradite
extravert
extremely
extremism
extremist
extremity
extricate
extrinsic
extrovert
extrusion
extrusive
exuberant
exuberate
exudation
exudative
exultance
exultancy
oxidation
oxygenate
oxygenise
oxygenous
uxoricide
Aylesbury
byproduct
bystander
Byzantine
cyanamide
cyclamate
cycloidal
cyclopean
cyclopian
cyclopses
cyclorama
cyclotron
cylindric
cymbalist
cymbidium
cymbiform
cymophane
cynically
cyprinoid
cystocarp
cystolith
cystotomy
Cytherean
cytolysis
cytoplasm
cytotoxic
cytotoxin
dynamical
dynamiter
dyscrasia
dysentery
dysgenics
dyspepsia
dyspeptic
dysphagia
dysphagic
dysphonia
dysphoria
dysphoric
dysplasia
dyspnoeic
dystrophy
eyebright
eyeglance
eyeopener
eyeshadow
eyestrain
gymnasial
gymnasium
gymnastic
gynaeceum
gynocracy
gynoecium
gynophore
gyrfalcon
gyroplane
gyroscope
hybridise
hybridism
hybridity
hydathode
hydraemia
hydrangea
hydration
hydraulic
hydrazine
hydriodic
hydrocele
hydrofoil
hydrology
hydrolyse
hydrolyte
hydronium
hydrosome
hydroxide
hydrozoan
hydrozoon
hygienics
hygienist
hygrostat
hylozoism
hymnology
hypallage
hyperbola
hyperbole
hypergamy
hypericum
hyperopia
hyperopic
hypethral
hyphenate
hypnoidal
hypnology
hypnotise
hypnotism
hypnotist
hypoblast
hypocaust
hypocotyl
hypocrisy
hypocrite
hypogeous
hypomania
hypomanic
hyponasty
hypostyle
hypotaxis
hysterics
hysteroid
kymograph
lyamhound
lymegrass
lymehound
lymphatic
lyophilic
lyophobic
lyrically
lysimeter
Mycenaean
mycologic
mycophagy
mydriasis
mydriatic
myelomata
myography
myologist
myriorama
myrmecoid
myrobalan
mystagogy
mysticism
mystifier
mythicise
mythicism
mythicist
mythology
myxoedema
nymphalid
nystagmic
nystagmus
oysterbed
oysterman
pycnidium
pyracanth
pyramidal
pyramidic
pyramidon
pyrethrum
pyridoxin
pyrogenic
pyrolater
pyrolatry
pyrolysis
pyrolytic
pyromancy
pyromania
pyrometer
pyrometry
pyroscope
pyroxylin
sybaritic
sycophant
syllabary
syllabise
syllabism
syllabled
syllepses
syllepsis
sylleptic
syllogise
syllogism
sylphlike
sylvanite
symbiosis
symbiotic
symbolics
symbolise
symbolism
symbolist
symbology
symmetric
symphonic
symphysis
sympodial
sympodium
symposiac
symposial
symposium
synagogal
synagogue
synchrony
synclinal
syncopate
syncretic
syncytial
syncytium
syndactyl
syndicate
synectics
syneresis
synergism
synergist
syngamous
synizesis
synodical
synoecete
synonymic
synoptist
synovitis
syntactic
syntheses
synthesis
synthetic
syphilise
syphiloid
syringeal
systaltic
tympanist
typemetal
typewrite
typhlitis
typhoidal
typically
tyrannise
tyrannous
wyandotte
wychhazel
Wyclifite
wyliecoat
xylograph
xylophone
zygomatic
zygospore
zymogenic
azeotrope
azimuthal
czarevich
dziggetai
ozocerite
ozokerite

---

abandoned
abandonee
abandoner
abasement
abashment
abatement
academism
acariasis
adamantly
adaptable
agapemone
alabaster
amaryllis
amassment
amauroses
amaurosis
amaurotic
amazement
amazingly
amazonian
anabioses
anabiosis
anabiotic
anabolism
anabranch
anacruses
anacrusis
anaerobic
analeptic
analgesia
analgesic
analogise
analogist
analogous
analysand
anamnesis
anandrous
anaphoric
anaptyxis
anarchism
anarchist
anatomise
anatomist
apartheid
apartment
apartness
apathetic
arabesque
arabicise
arachnoid
aragonite
araneidal
araneidan
araucaria
asafetida
atacamite
ataractic
atavistic
available
availably
avalanche
awakening
awardable
awareness
beachhead
beachwear
beadledom
beamingly
beanfeast
beanstalk
bearberry
beardless
beastings
beatitude
beauteous
beautiful
blackball
blackbird
blackbuck
blackcoat
blackcock
blackdamp
blackface
Blackfeet
blackfish
blackflag
Blackfoot
blackgame
blackhead
blackjack
blacklead
blacklist
blackmail
blackness
blackwash
blaeberry
blameable
blameably
blameless
blandness
blankness
blaspheme
blasphemy
blasthole
blastment
blastulae
blastular
blatantly
blazingly
Boanerges
boardfoot
boardroom
boardwalk
boathouse
boatswain
boattrain
brachiate
brachyura
bracteate
bracteole
Brahmanic
Brahminee
Brahminic
braincase
brainless
brainwash
brainwave
brakeless
brakeshoe
brakesman
brambling
branchiae
branchial
branchlet
brandling
brandreth
brashness
brasserie
brassiere
bratwurst
brazilnut
ceanothus
ceasefire
ceaseless
chachacha
chaetopod
chafferer
chaffinch
chaingang
chaingear
chainless
chainmail
chairlady
challenge
chameleon
chamomile
champagne
champaign
champerty
champleve
chanceful
chancroid
chancrous
chandlery
changeful
chanteuse
chantilly
chantress
chaparral
chaperone
chapleted
charabanc
character
chariness
charivari
charlatan
charlotte
charmeuse
charmless
Charolais
chartered
charterer
charwoman
chassepot
chastener
chastiser
chatelain
chatoyant
chatterer
chauffeur
claimable
clamantly
clamorous
clamshell
clapboard
clarifier
clarionet
classable
classical
classless
classlist
classmate
classroom
clathrate
clatterer
claustral
clavation
claviform
coachwork
coadjutor
coadunate
coagulant
coagulate
coalfield
coalition
coalmouse
coarctate
coastline
coastward
coastwise
coattails
coaxially
coaxingly
crabbedly
crackdown
crackling
cracksman
craftsman
crampfish
cranberry
crankcase
cranreuch
crapulent
crapulous
crashdive
crashland
crassness
craziness
cyanamide
czarevich
deacidify
deaconess
deadalive
deadlight
deathblow
deathless
deathlike
deathmask
deathroll

dharmsala
diablerie
diabolise
diabolism
diabolist
diachrony
diachylom
diachylum
diaconate
diacritic
diactinic
diaereses
diaeresis
diagnoses
diagnosis
dialectal
dialectic
dialogise
dialogism
dialogist
diametral
diametric
diandrous
diaphragm
diaphysis
diarrhoea
diastasis
diastatic
diastolic
diathermy
diathesis
diathetic
diatomite
diatropic
draconian
draftsman
draghound
dragomans
dragoness
dragonfly
dragonish
drainpipe
dramatics
dramatise
dramatist
Dravidian
drawerful
drawnwork
drawplate
drawsheet
drayhorse
dualistic
ejaculate
elaborate
elastomer
emaciated
emanation
emanative
enactment
enamelled
enameller
enamoured
epaenetic
epaulette
eradicate
evaginate
evangelic
evaporate
evasively
exactable
exactment
exactness
examinant
exanimate
exanthema
exarchate
fearfully
feathered
flabellum
flagellum
flageolet
flagrance
flagrancy
flagstaff
flagstick
flagstone
flakiness
flambeaus
flambeaux
flameless
flamingly
flamingos
flammable
flannelly
flarepath
flaringly
flashback
flashbulb
flashcube
flashover
flashtube
flatterer
flatulent
flavorous
flayflint
fractious
fraenulum
fragility
fragrance
fragrancy
frailness
framework
franchise
francolin
frangible
Franglais
frankness
franticly
fraternal
gearlever
gearshift
gearwheel
giantlike
glabellae
glabellar
glacially
gladiator
gladiolus
gladstone
glaireous
glamorise
glamorous
glandered
glandular
glaringly
glassgall
glassware
glasswork
glasswort
gnathonic
goalmouth
graceless
gracility
gradation
gradatory
Gradgrind
gradually
graduator
grandaddy
grandaunt
grandiose
grandness
grandpapa
grandsire
grandslam
granitoid
grantable
granulate
granulite
granulose
grapeshot
grapevine
graphemic
graphical
graphitic
grappling
graspable
grassland
graticule
gratitude
gratulate
gravamina
graveless
gravelled
graveness
graveyard
gravidity
gravitate
graywacke
guacamole
guarantee
guarantor
guardbook
guardedly
guardrail
guardring
guardroom
guardship
guardsman
headboard
headcloth
headdress
headfirst
headiness
headlight
headliner
headphone
headpiece
headscarf
headstall
headstock
headstone
headwater
healthful
healthily
heartache
heartbeat
heartburn
heartfelt
heartfree
hearthrug
heartland
heartless
heartsick
heartsore
heartwood
heathcock
heathenry
heaviness
heavyduty
hoarfrost
hoarhound
hoariness
hoarstone
imageable
imageless
imaginary
inability
inamorata
inanimate
inanition
inaptness
inaudible
inaudibly
inaugural
irascible
irascibly
isagogics
isallobar
italicise
Italicism
jealously
knavishly
leafgreen
leafmould
leafstalk
leakiness
learnable
learnedly
leasehold
leaselend
leastways
leastwise
leavening
liability
loadstone
loafsugar
loanshark
loathsome
lyamhound
mealiness
meandrine
meandrous
meaningly
meanwhile
meatiness
miasmatic
neathouse
odalisque
onanistic
orangeade
Orangeism
Orangeman
orangetip
orangutan
oratorial
oratorian
peaceable
peaceably
peacetime
peachblow
pearlitic
pearlwort
peasantry
peasouper
phagedena
phagocyte
phalanger
phalanges
phalanxes
phalarope
phantasma
pharaonic
pharisaic
pharyngal
pharynges
pharynxes
pianistic
placation
placatory
placeable
placecard
placekick
placeless
placement
placename
placentae
placental
placidity
plainness
plainsman
plainsong
plaintiff
plaintive
planarian
planation
planetary
planetoid
plangency
planisher
plantable
plantlike
planuloid
plasmatic
plasmodia
plastered
plasterer
platemark
platinise
platinoid
platinous
platitude
Platonise
Platonism
Platonist
plausible
plausibly
playfully
playgroup
playhouse
plaything
practical
practised
praenomen
pragmatic
praiseful
pranksome
prankster
pratingly
prayerful
prayerrug
psalmbook
psalmodic
psalteria
ptarmigan
quadratic
quadrifid
quadrigae
quadrille
quadruman
quadruped
quadruple
quadruply
Quakerdom
Quakeress
Quakerish
Quakerism
quakiness
qualified
qualifier
quantical
quarenden
quarender
quarryman
quarterly
quartette
quartzite
quartzose
reachable
reactance
readdress
readiness
readymade
realistic
reanimate
rearguard
rearhorse
rearlight
rearmouse
rearrange
rearwards
reasoning
rhapsodic
roadblock
roadhouse
roadmetal
roadstead
roadworks
scagliola
scaldfish
scalefern
scalefish
scaleleaf
scaleless
scalelike
scalemoss
scaliness
scallawag
scallywag
scalplock
scantling
scantness
scapegoat
scapolite
scapulary
scarecrow
scarehead
scarfring
scarfskin
scarfwise
scarifier
scatology
scatterer
scavenger
seaanchor
seachange
seafaring
seagirdle
sealetter
seaminess
seanettle
searching
searingly
seasoning
seasquirt
seastrand
seatangle
seaurchin
seaworthy
shadberry
shadeless
shadetree
shadiness
shakeable
shakedown
shakerism
shakiness
shallowly
shamanism
shamanist
shamateur
shambling
shambolic
shamefast
shameless
Shangrila
shantyman
shapeable
shapeless
sharecrop
sharkskin
sharpener
sharpeyed
sharpness
sharpshod
shaveling
slabsided
slabstone
slackness
slakeless
slanderer
slantways
slantwise
slaphappy
slapstick
slateclub
slategrey
slaughter
slaveship
slavishly
Slavonian
Slavophil
smackeroo
smallarms
smallness
smalltime
smartness
smartweed
smatterer
snailfish
snakebird
snakebite
snakelike
snakeroot
snakeskin
snakeweed
snakewood
snakiness
snaredrum
soapberry
soapiness
soapstone
soapworks
spaceband
spaceless
spaceport
spaceship
spacesuit
spacetime
spadefoot
spadework
spaghetti
spagyrist
spareness
spareribs
sparingly
sparkcoil
sparkless
sparkplug
spasmodic
spatially
spatulate
stabilise
stability
stableboy
stableman
stackable
stackroom
stackyard
stagedoor
stagehand
staggerer
staghound
staginess
Stagirite
stagnancy
stagparty
staidness
stainable
stainless
staircase
stairfoot
stairhead
stairwell
stakeboat
stalactic
stalemate
staleness
Stalinism
Stalinist
stalkeyed
stalkless
stallfeed

stalworth
staminate
stammerer
stampduty
stampmill
stampnote
stanchion
standpipe
stapedial
starapple
starboard
starchily
stardrift
stargazer
stargrass
starkness
starlight
starshell
starstone
startling
statehood
stateless
statement
stateroom
stateside
statesman
statewide
stational
stationer
statistic
statocyst
statolith
statuette
statutory
stauncher
staunchly
staymaker
suability
suasively
swaddling
swaggerer
swangoose
swansdown
swarajist
swartness
teachable
teachably
teacupful
teakettle
tearfully
teasingly
thalassic
thaneship
thankless
thatching
toadeater
toadstone
toadstool
toastrack
trabeated
trabecula
traceable
traceably
traceless
traceried
tracheary
tracheate
trachytic
trackless
tracksuit
tractable
tractably
trademark
tradename
tradesman
tradition
traducian
tragedian
trainable

trainband
trainload
traitress
tramlines
transcend
transenna
transform
transfuse
transient
translate
transmute
transonic
transpire
transport
transpose
transship
transumpt
transvest
trapezial
trapezium
trapezoid
trappings
trattoria
trattorie
traumatic
travelled
traveller
traversal
traverser
traycloth
tsarevich
twayblade
unabashed
unadopted
unadorned
unadvised
unalloyed
unaltered
unanimity
unanimous
unaptness
unashamed
Upanishad
uraninite
uranology
uvarovite
viability
weakkneed
wealthily
weariless
weariness
wearisome
weathered
weatherly
whaleback
whaleboat
whalebone
whalehead
wrathless
wyandotte
xparticle
yearround
zealously
albatross
albescent
albinotic
ambergris
ambiguity
ambiguous
ambitious
amblyopia
amblyopic
ambrosial
ambulacra
ambulance
ambuscade
arbitrage
arbitrary
arbitrate

arbitress
arboreous
arboretum
asbestine
asbestous
aubergine
aubrietia
babacoote
Babbittry
babirussa
baboonish
biblicism
biblicist
bobsleigh
bobtailed
caballero
caballine
caballing
cabbalism
cabbalist
cablegram
cablelaid
cabriolet
cobaltite
cobaltous
Cobdenism
cobwebbed
cubbyhole
cubically
debagging
debarment
debarring
debatable
debauched
debauchee
debaucher
debenture
debugging
debutante
dubiosity
dubiously
dubitable
elbowroom
embarrass
embassage
embattled
embayment
embedding
embedment
embellish
embezzler
embraceor
embracery
embracive
embrangle
embrasure
embrittle
embrocate
embroglio
embroider
embryonal
embryonic
embryotic
embussing
fabaceous
Fabianism
fabricant
fabricate
febricity
febrifuge
fibreless
fibriform
fibrillar
fibrinoid
fibrinous
fibroline
fibromata
gabardine
gaberdine

gabionade
gibberish
gibbosity
gibbously
gobetween
habergeon
habitable
habitably
habituate
Hebridean
hibernate
Hibernian
Hobbesian
hobgoblin
hobnailed
hobnobbed
hobnobber
hubristic
hybridise
hybridism
hybridity
imbalance
imbecilic
imbricate
imbroglio
inbetween
inbreathe
jaborandi
jobmaster
jubilance
kibbutzim
labelling
labialise
labialism
laborious
labourite
labyrinth
libecchio
libellant
libelling
libellist
libellous
liberally
liberated
liberator
libertine
libidinal
librarian
libration
libratory
librettos
lobectomy
lobscouse
lobulated
lubricant
lubricate
lubricity
lubricous
mobocracy
nebuliser
nobiliary
nobleness
obbligato
ombudsman
orbicular
oubliette
pubescent
publicise
publicist
publicity
publisher
rabbinate
rabbinism
rabbinist
rabidness
rebaptise
rebelling
rebellion
rebidding

rebukable
rebutting
Ribbonism
ribosomal
rubberise
rubellite
rubicelle
rubricate
rubrician
sabadilla
sabbatise
sabbatism
Sabellian
sebaceous
sibilance
sibilancy
sibylline
sobbingly
soberness
sobriquet
sobsister
subaerial
subagency
subalpine
subaltern
subarctic
subastral
subatomic
subbranch
subcaudal
subcostal
subdeacon
subdivide
subduable
subduedly
subeditor
subereous
subfamily
subgenera
subjacent
subjugate
sublation
sublethal
sublimate
sublimely
sublimity
sublunary
submarine
submaster
submental
submitted
subnormal
subocular
subphylum
subregion
subrogate
subscribe
subscript
subsellia
subsidise
substance
substrata
substrate
subtenant
subtilise
subtopian
subverter
sybaritic
tablature
tableland
tableleaf
tabletalk
tableware
tabularly
tabulator
tubbiness
tubercule
tubularly
umbellate

umbellule
umberbird
umbilical
umbilicus
unbalance
unbeknown
unbending
unberufen
unbiassed
unblessed
unblinded
unbounded
unbraided
unbridled
upbraider
vibracula
vibraharp
vibratile
vibration
vibrative
vibratory
vibrissae
webfooted
zebrawood
zibelline
accentual
acceptant
acceptive
accessary
accession
accessory
accidence
accipiter
acclaimer
acclimate
acclivity
accompany
accordant
according
accordion
accretion
accretive
accusable
alchemise
alchemist
alcoholic
ancestral
anchorage
anchoress
anchorite
anchorman
anchylose
anciently
ancientry
ancillary
archangel
archducal
archduchy
archenemy
archetype
archfiend
architect
archivist
archivolt
arcuately
ascendant
ascendent
ascension
ascensive
ascertain
ascetical
asclepiad
ascospore
auctorial
bacchanal
bacchante
bacillary
backbiter
backboard

backcloth
backcross
backpedal
backsight
backslang
backslide
backspace
backstage
backsword
backtrack
backwards
backwater
backwoods
bacterial
bacterise
bacterium
bacteroid
beccafico
bicameral
bicipital
biconcave
bicyclist
buccaneer
buckboard
bucketful
buckhound
buckshish
buckthorn
bucktooth
buckwheat
cachectic
cacholong
caciquism
cacodemon
cacodylic
cacoethes
cacophony
cacuminal
cicatrice
cicatrise
cocainise
cocainism
coccidium
coccygeal
cochineal
cochleate
cockahoop
Cockaigne
cockatiel
cockfight
cockhorse
cockiness
cockneyfy
cockroach
cockscomb
cocksfoot
cocoonery
cuckoldry
cucullate
cyclamate
cycloidal
cyclopean
cyclopian
cyclopses
cyclorama
cyclotron
dachshund
decadence
decadency
decagonal
decalcify
decalitre
decalogue
decametre
decapodal
decapodan
decastere
decathlon
deceitful

decennary
decennial
decennium
deception
deceptive
decidable
decidedly
deciduate
deciduous
decilitre
decillion
decimally
decimator
decimetre
decistere
deckhouse
declaimer
declarant
declinate
declivity
declivous
decoction
decollate
decollete
decomplex
decompose
decongest
decontrol
decorator
decrement
decretive
decretory
decumbent
decussate
dichasial
dichasium
dichogamy
dichotomy
dichroism
dichromat
dichromic
dickybird
diclinous
dicrotism
dictation
doctorate
doctorial
doctrinal
duckboard
ductility
eccentric
ecclesial
encaustic
encephala
enchanter
enchilada
enchorial
enclosure
encomiast
encompass
encounter
encourage
encrimson
encrinite
escalator
escapable
escheator
escortage
eucalypti
eucaryote
Eucharist
euchology
euclidean
excavator
exceeding
excellent
excelling
excelsior
excentric

exceptant
excepting
exception
exceptive
excerptor
excessive
exchanger
exchequer
excipient
excisable
exciseman
excitable
excitancy
excitedly
exclosure
exclusion
exclusive
excoriate
excrement
excretion
excretive
excretory
exculpate
excurrent
excursion
excursive
excusable
excusably
facecloth
facetious
facsimile
factional
factitive
factorage
factorial
factorise
factually
facundity
feculence
fecundate
fecundity
fictional
focussing
hackamore
hackberry
hackneyed
hectogram
hocussing
huckaback
huckstery
incapable
incapably
incarnate
incaution
incensory
incentive
inception
inceptive
incessant
incidence
incipient
inclement
inclosure
inclusion
inclusive
incognito
incommode
incondite
incorrect
incorrupt
increaser
increment
incubator
inculcate
inculpate
incumbent
incunable
incurable
incurably

incurious
incurrent
incurring
incursion
incursive
incurvate
ischaemia
ischaemic
ischiadic
ischiatic
itchiness
jacaranda
jackknife
jackplane
jacksnipe
jackstraw
Jacobinic
jacquerie
jactation
jockstrap
jocularly
jocundity
kickstart
laccolith
lacerable
lacertian
lacertine
lachrymal
laciniate
lacrimose
lacrymose
lactation
lecherous
licensure
lichenous
lickerish
locatable
locksmith
locomotor
lucidness
luciferin
luckiness
lucrative
lucubrate
macaronic
Maccabean
macedoine
macerator
machinate
machinery
machinist
machmeter
macintosh
macrocosm
macrocyte
mechanics
mechanise
mechanism
mechanist
micaceous
micaslate
microbial
microchip
microcosm
microcyte
microfilm
microgram
microlite
microlith
micrology
micromesh
micropsia
micropyle
microsome
microtome
microtomy
microtone
microwave
micturate

mockingly
muckraker
mucksweat
mucronate
Mycenaean
mycologic
mycophagy
necessary
necessity
neckcloth
neckverse
necrology
necrophil
necrotise
nectarean
nectarial
nectarine
nectarous
niccolite
nickelise
nickelled
nickelous
nicotiana
nicotinic
nictation
nictitate
noctiluca
nocturnal
nocuously
nucleated
nucleolus
nucleonic
obconical
obcordate
occipital
occludent
occlusion
occlusive
occultism
occultist
occupancy
occurrent
occurring
oecologic
oecumenic
oncogenic
oncologic
orchestic
orchestra
orchidist
oscillate
oscitancy
pacemaker
pachyderm
packaging
packdrill
packhorse
packtrain
peccantly
pectinate
peculator
pecuniary
pickaback
picketing
picnicked
picnicker
pictogram
pictorial
picturise
pocketful
pycnidium
racehorse
racetrack
racialism
racialist
racketeer
raconteur
recalesce
recapping

recapture
recension
reception
receptive
recession
recessive
rechauffe
recherche
recipient
reckoning
reclinate
reclusion
reclusive
recognise
recoinage
recollect
recombine
recommend
recompose
reconcile
recondite
reconfirm
reconvene
reconvert
recording
recordist
recoverer
recreancy
recruital
recruiter
rectangle
rectifier
rectitude
rectorate
rectorial
rectrices
recumbent
recurrent
recurring
recursion
recursive
recusance
recusancy
ricepaper
rocambole
rockbound
rockbrake
rockdrill
rocketeer
rockiness
rockplant
rocksnake
saccharin
sacciform
sacculate
sackcloth
sacrament
sacrarium
sacrifice
sacrilege
sacristan
secateurs
secernent
secession
seclusion
seclusive
secondary
secretage
secretary
secretion
secretive
secretory
sectarian
sectility
sectional
sectorial
secularly
securable
siccative

sickening
sickishly
sickleave
socialise
socialism
socialist
socialite
sociality
sociogram
sociology
sociopath
succeeder
succentor
successor
succinate
succotash
succourer
succulent
succursal
suctorial
suctorian
sycophant
tacamahac
tachylite
tachylyte
tacitness
tackiness
tactfully
tactician
tactility
tactitian
tactually
technical
technique
tectonics
tectorial
tectrices
Tocharian
tuckerbag
uncannily
unceasing
uncertain
uncharted
unchecked
uncinated
uncivilly
uncleanly
unclothed
unclouded
unconcern
uncounted
uncouthly
uncovered
uncreated
uncropped
uncrossed
uncrowned
upcountry
urceolate
vaccinate
vacillant
vacillate
vacuolate
vacuously
vectorial
vicariate
vicarious
vicennial
viceregal
vicereine
viceroyal
vicesimal
viciously
victimise
Victorian
victorine
vocabular
vocaliser
vocalness

wackiness
wychhazel
Wyclifite
yachtclub
yachtsman
zucchetto
abdicable
abdicator
abdominal
abduction
addiction
addictive
addressee
addresser
addressor
adducible
adduction
adductive
aldehydic
andantino
andesitic
androecia
androgyne
androgyny
arduously
audacious
audiology
auditable
auditoria
badminton
bedfellow
bedjacket
bedlamite
bedraggle
bedridden
bedsettee
bedsitter
bedspread
bedspring
bodyguard
budgetary
cadastral
cadaveric
caddisfly
cadential
cadetship
cedarwood
cudgelled
dedicator
deducible
deduction
deductive
didactics
didelphic
didrachma
dodecagon
ecdysiast
eiderdown
eiderduck
eidograph
eldership
endearing
endeavour
endlessly
endoblast
endocrine
endogamic
endogenic
endolymph
endomixis
endomorph
endophagy
endophyte
endoplasm
endoscope
endoscopy
endosperm
endospore
endosteal

endosteum
endowment
endurable
endurably
endurance
faddiness
federally
fideistic
fiduciary
gadgeteer
giddiness
goddamned
godfather
godliness
godmother
godparent
hedgingly
hiddenite
hidebound
hideously
hodiernal
hodograph
hodometer
hydathode
hydraemia
hydrangea
hydration
hydraulic
hydrazine
hydriodic
hydrocele
hydrofoil
hydrology
hydrolyse
hydrolyte
hydronium
hydrosome
hydroxide
hydrozoan
hydrozoon
indagator
indecency
indecorum
indelible
indelibly
indemnify
indemnity
indention
indenture
Indianise
indicator
indiction
indigence
indignant
indignity
indigotin
indispose
IndoAryan
indolence
indraught
inducible
induction
inductive
indulgent
indweller
Judaistic
Judastree
judgement
judgeship
judgmatic
judiciary
judicious
kiddingly
kidnapped
kidnapper
ladysmock
lodestone
lodgement
lodgepole
ludicrous
maddening
madeleine
madrepore
medallion
medallist
mediaeval
mediately
mediation
mediatise
mediative
mediatory
mediatrix
medicable
medically
medicinal
meditator
medullary
medullate
middleman
midinette
midstream
midsummer
midwicket
midwifery
midwinter
modelling
moderator
modernise
modernism
modernist
modernity
modillion
modulator
muddiness
mydriasis
mydriatic
nodulated
oddfellow
oddjobber
oddjobman
orderbook
orderform
orderless
ordinance
pedagogic
pedagogue
pedalling
pederasty
pedicular
pedigreed
pedometer
podagrous
podginess
podzolise
pudginess
radialply
radiantly
radiately
radiation
radiative
radically
radicular
radiocast
radiogram
radiology
redaction
redbreast
redevelop
redhanded
redheaded
redingote
redivivus
redletter
redolence
redoubted
redresser
reducible
reductant
reduction
reductive
redundant
riderless
ridgepole
ridgetile
ridiculer
rodfisher
rudbeckia
ruddiness
ruddleman
saddlebag
saddlebow
Sadducean
sedentary
sedgewren
seditious
seduction
seductive
sideboard
sideburns
sidedness
sideissue
sidelight
sideritic
siderosis
sideswipe
sidetable
sidetrack
sidewards
sidewheel
sodabread
sodawater
sudatoria
sudorific
tediously
tidegauge
tidewater
undamaged
undaunted
undecagon
undeceive
undecided
undecimal
undefined
underbody
underbred
underclay
undercoat
underdone
underfelt
underfoot
undergird
undergone
undergrad
underhand
underhung
underlaid
underlain
underline
underling
undermine
undermost
underpaid
underpart
underpass
underplay
underplot
underrate
underripe
underseal
underseas
undersell
undershot
underside
undersign
undersold
undersong
underspin
undertake
undertint
undertone
undertook
undervest
underwear
underwent
underwing
underwood
undivided
undoubted
undreamed
undulated
undutiful
vademecum
Vedantist
videlicet
videotape
wedgewise
Wednesday
wideawake
widowbird
widowhood
widthways
widthwise
Yiddisher
yodelling
aberrance
aberrancy
acellular
acescence
acetabula
acetamide
acetifier
acetylate
acetylcoA
acetylene
ademption
adenoidal
adenomata
adenosine
adeptness
aleatoric
Alemannic
alertness
amendable
amendment
americium
Amerindic
anecdotal
anecdotic
anemogram
aperiodic
aperitive
apetalous
Areopagus
asepalous
asexually
aventaile
averagely
avertible
awesomely
awestruck
azeotrope
beechfern
beechmast
beefeater
beefiness
beefsteak
beekeeper
beemaster
beeorchis
beestings
bleachery
bleakness
bleareyed
blessedly
breadline
breadtree
breakable
breakaway
breakdown
breakeven
breakfast
breakneck
breastpin
breathily
breathing
brecciate
breeching
breezeway
bregmatic
bretasche
Bretwalda
breveting
brevetted
caecilian
Caenozoic
caerulean
Caesarean
Caesarian
Caesarism
Caesarist
cheapjack
cheapness
checkered
checklist
checkmate
checkrein
cheekbone
cheerless
chelation
chelicera
chelonian
chemistry
chemitype
chemurgic
cheongsam
chequered
cherimoya
chernozem
cherrypie
chevalier
chevelure
cleanness
cleansing
clearance
clearcole
cleareyed
clearness
cleavable
clemently
clepsydra
clergyman
clergymen
clerkship
coecilian
coelomata
coelomate
coelostat
coemption
coenobite
coenobium
coenosarc
coequally
coercible
coercibly
coeternal
creatable
creatress
creatural
crediting
credulity
credulous
cremaster
cremation
crematory
crenation
crenature
crenelled
crenulate
crepitant
crepitate
crepuscle
crescendo
crestless
cretinism
cretinous
Daedalean
Daedalian
deerberry
deerhound
dieselise
diesinker
dietetics
dietician
dietitian
dreamboat
dreamland
dreamless
dreamlike
dresscoat
edelweiss
ejectment
electoral
electress
electrify
electrode
electuary
elegantly
elegiacal
elemental
elevation
elevenses
emendable
emendator
emergence
emergency
energetic
energiser
energumen
erectness
eremitism
esemplasy
eternally
eventless
eventuate
everglade
evergreen
everybody
ewenecked
execrable
execrably
executant
execution
executive
executory
executrix
exegetist
exemplary
exemplify
exemption
exequatur
exercises
eyebright
eyeglance
eyeopener
eyeshadow
eyestrain
feedstock
feedstuff
feelingly
fieldbook
fieldboot
fieldfare
fieldsman
fieldwork
fiendlike
fieriness
fleckless
fledgling
fleetness
fleshings
fleshless
fleshment
foeticide
freeboard
freehouse
freelance
freeliver
Freemason
freerange
freerider
freestone
freestyle
freewheel
freewoman
freezable
freezedry
freighter
frenchify
Frenchman
frequence
frequency
freshener
freshness
fretfully
Gaeltacht
gleefully
glengarry
gneissoid
gneissose
greasegun
greataunt
greatcoat
greatness
Greekless
greenback
greenbelt
greeneyed
greengage
greenhorn
greenness
greenroom
greensand
greenweed
greenwood
gregarian
gregarine
Gregorian
grenadier
grenadine
greybeard
greyhound
greywacke
guerrilla
guesswork
guestroom
haematite
haematoid
haematoma
haemostat
heedfully
heelpiece
hierarchy
hieratica
hierodule
hierogram
hierology
Icelander
Icelandic
iceskater
idealiser
idealless
identical
identikit

ideograph
ideologic
ideologue
inebriant
inebriate
inebriety
ineffable
ineffably
inelastic
inelegant
ineptness
inequable
inerrable
inerrancy
inertness
inexactly
iteration
iterative
jeeringly
keelivine
khedivial
kneadable
laevulose
leeringly
leewardly
liegelord
maelstrom
mnemonics
mnemonist
myelomata
needfully
neediness
needleful
obedience
obeisance
obeseness
ocellated
okeydokey
oleaceous
olecranal
olecranon
oleograph
oleoresin
onehanded
onelegged
onerously
openended
openheart
operation
operative
opercular
operculum
operosely
operosity
ovenready
overblown
overboard
overborne
overcheck
overcloud
overcrowd
overdraft
overdrawn
overdress
overdrive
overeaten
overeater
overexert
overflown
overglaze
overgraze
overgrown
overheard
overissue
overjoyed
overladen
overleapt
overlying
overmatch
overnight
overpitch
overpower
overprice
overprint
overproof
overreach
overreact
oversexed
overshoot
oversight
oversized
overskirt
oversleep
overslept
overspend
overspent
overspill
overstate
oversteer
overstock
overstuff
overtaken
overthrew
overthrow
overtness
overtones
overtrain
overtrick
overtrump
overvalue
overwatch
overweary
overweigh
overwhelm
overwound
overwrite
overwrote
paederast
peepsight
peevishly
phellogen
phenacite
phenakite
phenology
phenomena
phenotype
pheromone
piecemeal
piecerate
piecework
pierrette
pietistic
pleadable
pleadings
pleasance
Pleiocene
plenarily
plenitude
plenteous
plentiful
plethoric
pleuritic
pneumatic
pneumonia
pneumonic
poetaster
poeticise
poeticism
preachify
preachily
preadamic
prebendal
precancel
precative
precatory
precedent
preceding
precentor
preceptor
precipice
precisely
precisian
precision
precocial
precocity
preconise
precursor
predacity
predation
predative
predatory
predicant
predicate
predictor
predigest
predikant
preemptor
preengage
preexilic
prefatory
preferred
prefigure
prefixion
pregnable
pregnancy
prejudice
prelatess
prelatise
prelature
prelector
prelusion
prelusive
prelusory
premature
premonish
premotion
prenotion
preoccupy
preordain
prepotent
prerecord
presbyope
presbyter
preschool
prescient
prescribe
prescript
preselect
presentee
presenter
presently
preserver
preshrink
preshrunk
president
presidial
presidium
pressgang
pressmark
pressroom
pressstud
presswork
prestress
pretender
preterist
preterite
pretermit
prettyish
prettyism
prevalent
preventer
prevision
pseudonym
pseudopod
pterosaur
pterygium
pterygoid
puerility
puerperal
quebracho
queenhood
queenless
queenlike
queenpost
queenship
queerness
quercetum
querulous
reediness
reedorgan
reeducate
reefpoint
reenforce
reentrant
reexamine
rheumatic
scenarist
scenedock
scentless
sceptical
seedeater
seediness
seedpearl
seedplant
seemingly
shearling
sheatfish
sheathing
Shechinah
sheepcote
sheepfold
sheephook
sheeplice
sheepskin
sheeptick
sheepwalk
sheepwash
sheerhulk
sheerlegs
sheerness
sheetbend
sheikhdom
sheldduck
sheldrake
shelflife
shelfmark
shelfroom
shellback
shellbark
shellfire
shellfish
shellheap
shellwork
shemozzle
shewbread
skedaddle
skeesicks
sketchily
sketchmap
skewwhiff
sleekness
sleepless
sleevenut
slenderly
speakable
speakeasy
spearfish
spearhead
spearmint
spearside
spearwort
specially
specialty
specifier
speckless
spectacle
spectator
speculate
speechful
speechify
speedball
speedboat
speedster
speedwell
spellbind
spellican
spendable
spermatic
spermatid
steadfast
steamboat
steampipe
steamship
steatitic
steelclad
steelhead
steelwork
steelyard
steenkirk
steepness
steersman
stegosaur
stellated
stenotype
stenotypy
stepchild
stepdance
steradian
stercoral
sterilise
sterility
sternmost
sternness
sternpost
sternward
steroidal
stevedore
swearword
sweatband
sweatshop
sweepback
sweetcorn
sweetener
sweetmeal
sweetmeat
sweetness
sweetshop
sweettalk
swellfish
sweptback
taeniasis
theandric
theatrics
theocracy
theocrasy
theogonic
theologic
theologue
theomachy
theomania
theophany
theoretic
theoriser
theosophy
therapist
Theravada
therefore
therefrom
thereinto
thereunto
thereupon
therewith
thermally
thermidor
thesaurus
theurgist
tiedyeing
treachery
treadmill
treasurer
treatable
treatment
trebuchet
trebucket
treillage
trematode
tremolant
tremolite
tremulant
tremulous
trenchant
trepanned
trepidant
twelfthly
twentieth
twentyone
unearthly
uneatable
unequally
unethical
uselessly
veeringly
viewpoint
weediness
weeknight
weevilled
wheatmeal
wheedling
wheelbase
wheelless
wheelwork
wherefore
wherefrom
whereinto
whereunto
whereupon
wherewith
wherryman
whetstone
wheyfaced
wieldable
woebegone
wrestling
affecting
affection
affective
affianced
affidavit
affiliate
affirmant
affixture
afflation
affluence
affricate
awfulness
befitting
befogging
bifarious
bifoliate
bifurcate
buffaloes
buffeting
cafeteria
coffeecup
coffeepot
cofferdam
coffinite
defalcate
defaulter
defeatism
defeatist
defeature
defection
defective
defendant
defensive
deference
deferment
deferring
defiantly
deficient
definable
definably
deflation
deflector
deflexion
defoliant
defoliate
deformity
defroster
different
difficile
difficult
diffident
diffusely
diffusion
diffusive
effective
effectual
efficient
effluence
effluvial
effluvium
effluxion
effortful
effulgent
exfoliate
fifteenth
goffering
heftiness
huffiness
infantile
infantine
infatuate
infection
infective
inferable
inference
inferring
infertile
infielder
infilling
infirmary
infirmity
inflation
inflexion
inflictor
inflowing
influence
influenza
informant
infractor
infuriate
infuscate
infusible
infusoria
leftovers
leftwards
lifeblood
lifecycle
lifeforce
lifeguard
lifesaver
lifesized
lifestyle
lifetable
loftiness
luftwaffe
muffineer
muffinman
nefarious
obfuscate
offcentre

offchance
offcolour
offensive
offertory
offhanded
officiant
officiate
officinal
officious
offscreen
offseason
offspring
offstreet
olfaction
olfactive
olfactory
puffadder
puffiness
raffinate
raffinose
raffishly
rafflesia
refashion
refection
refectory
referable
reference
referenda
referring
refitment
refitting
reflation
reflector
reflexion
reflexive
refluence
reformism
reformist
refractor
refreshen
refresher
refuelled
refulgent
refurbish
refurnish
refusable
refutable
riflebird
rufescent
ruffianly
safeguard
safetypin
safflower
safranine
softgoods
softpedal
softshell
suffering
suffocate
suffragan
suffusion
tufaceous
unfailing
unfeeling
unfeigned
unfitness
unfitting
unfledged
unfleshed
unfleshly
unfounded
aggravate
aggregate
aggressor
aggrieved
algarroba
algebraic
Algonkian
Algonquin

algorithm
angelfish
angelical
angiology
angiomata
angleiron
anglesite
angleworm
anglicise
anglicism
Anglicist
anglophil
angriness
anguished
angularly
argentine
argentite
argentous
argillite
argumenta
Arguseyed
argybargy
augmented
augmenter
augmentor
bagatelle
bagginess
begetting
beginning
bigeneric
bigheaded
bughunter
cageyness
cigarette
cigarillo
cogitable
cognately
cognation
cognisant
cognition
cognitive
digastric
digestion
digestive
digitalin
digitalis
digitally
digitated
dignified
dignitary
dogcollar
doggishly
doglegged
dogmatics
dogmatise
dogmatism
dogmatist
dogoodism
dogshores
dogstooth
dogviolet
eagerness
eggbeater
eightfold
eightieth
eightsome
eightyish
engarland
Englander
englutted
engraving
engrosser
ergograph
ergometer
ergonomic
faggoting
figurante
fogginess
fugacious

gigahertz
gigantism
gogglebox
haggadist
haggardly
hagiarchy
hagiology
hagridden
hegemonic
highchair
highclass
highflier
highflown
highflyer
highgrade
highgrown
highlands
highlevel
highlight
highspeed
hightoned
highwater
hoggishly
hugeously
hygienics
hygienist
hygrostat
ingenious
ingenuity
ingenuous
ingestion
ingestive
inglenook
ingrained
ingrowing
laggardly
lagniappe
lagomorph
legendary
legerline
legginess
legionary
legislate
lightfoot
lightless
lightness
lightning
lightship
lightsome
lightsout
lightwood
lightyear
lignaloes
ligniform
logaoedic
logarithm
logically
logistics
logogriph
logomachy
magdalene
Magianism
magically
magicking
magistery
magistral
magnalium
magnesian
magnesite
magnesium
magnetics
magnetise
magnetism
magnetist
magnetite
magnetron
magnifico
magnifier
magnitude

megacycle
megadeath
megahertz
megaphone
megaspore
migration
migratory
mugginess
negligent
negotiant
negotiate
negritude
negroidal
Negroness
negrophil
niggardly
nightbird
nightclub
nightfall
nightgown
nighthawk
nightlife
nightline
nightlong
nightmare
nightside
nighttime
nightwork
nigricant
nigritude
nigrosine
oogenesis
oogenetic
organelle
organiser
organstop
organzine
orgiastic
pageantry
pegmatite
piggishly
piggyback
piggybank
pigheaded
pugnacity
regardant
regardful
regicidal
regisseur
registrar
regretful
regretted
regularly
regulator
rightable
righteous
righthand
rightness
rightward
rigidness
rigmarole
roguishly
ruggedise
sagacious
sagebrush
sagegreen
sagittate
segmental
segregate
sightless
sightseer
sigillary
sigillate
sigmoidal
signalbox
signalise
signalled
signaller
signalman

signatory
signature
signboard
significs
signorial
signorina
sogginess
sugarbeet
sugarcane
sugarloaf
sugarplum
suggester
tegmental
tegmentum
tegularly
tigerlily
tigermoth
tigerseye
tigerwood
tightener
tightness
tightrope
tightwire
ungallant
unguarded
vagarious
vagueness
vegetable
vegetably
vigesimal
vigilance
vigilante
vignetter
waggishly
waggonage
Wagnerian
Wagnerite
wagonette
wagonroof
zigzagged
zygomatic
zygospore
abhorrent
abhorring
Acheulean
Acheulian
adherence
anhydride
anhydrite
anhydrous
aphereses
apheresis
aphyllous
ashamedly
Ashkenazi
ashlaring
atheistic
athematic
Athenaeum
athletics
behaviour
buhrstone
coheiress
coherence
coherency
dahabiyah
dehiscent
dehydrate
echolalia
echovirus
enhearten
ephedrine
ephemeral
ephemerid
ephemeris
ephemeron
etherical
ethically
Ethiopian

ethmoidal
ethnarchy
ethnicity
ethnology
ethylenic
exhauster
exhibitor
ichneumon
ichnology
ichthyoid
inhalator
inharmony
inherence
inheritor
inhibitor
inhumanly
Johannine
Kshatriya
maharajah
maharanee
maharishi
mahlstick
Mahometan
Nahuatlan
ochlocrat
ophiology
otherness
otherwise
rehearsal
rehydrate
scheelite
schematic
schilling
schistose
schistous
schlemiel
schlemihl
schlieren
schmaltzy
schnauzer
schnitzel
schnorkel
schnorrer
scholarly
scholiast
schoolbag
schoolboy
schooling
schoolman
sphagnous
spherical
spherular
sphincter
sphygmoid
tahsildar
unhappily
unharness
unhealthy
unheeding
unhelpful
unhurried
upholster
usherette
vehemence
vehicular
wehrmacht
yohimbine
abidingly
aciculate
acidifier
acidophil
acidulate
acidulent
acidulous
aciniform
adiabatic
adipocere
adiposity
agistment

agitation
agitative
ahistoric
alicyclic
alienable
alienator
alignment
alinement
aliphatic
aliveness
amianthus
amidships
aminoacid
animalise
animalism
animalist
animality
animation
animatism
animistic
animosity
apiculate
apishness
asininity
avizandum
axiomatic
azimuthal
bailiwick
bainmarie
blindfold
blindness
blinkered
briarroot
briarwood
bricabrac
brickwork
brickyard
bridecake
bridesman
bridewell
bridleway
briefcase
briefless
briefness
brierroot
brierwood
brigadier
brigandry
brightish
brilliant
brimstone
bringdown
briquette
briskness
bristling
Britannia
Britannic
Briticise
Briticism
Britisher
brittlely
cailleach
Cainozoic
cairngorm
chibouque
chicanery
chickadee
chickaree
chickling
chickweed
chiefship
chieftain
chihuahua
chilblain
childhood
childless
childlike
chillness
chimaeric

Chinatown
chinaware
chinstrap
chipboard
chipolata
chiropody
chiselled
chiseller
chisquare
chitinous
chitlings
chivalric
clientage
clientele
cliffhang
climactic
climbable
clinician
clinquant
clipboard
clitellum
coiffeuse
coinsurer
cricketer
criminate
criminous
crinoidal
crinoline
crippling
crispness
criterion
criticise
criticism
dairymaid
deinosaur
deistical
driftsail
driftweed
driftwood
drinkable
dripstone
drivelled
driveller
dziggetai
edibility
editorial
eliminate
eminently
enigmatic
epicentre
epiclesis
epicurean
epicurism
epicyclic
epidermal
epidermic
epidermis
epidosite
epigraphy
epigynous
epilation
epileptic
epilogist
epinastic
epiphragm
epiphyses
epiphysis
epiphytal
epiphytic
epipolism
episcopal
epistaxis
epistemic
epistoler
epistolic
epithelia
epithesis
epithetic
epitomise
epitomist
epizootic
eristical
etiquette
evidently
evincible
exilement
existence
faintness
fairfaced
fairyhood
fairyland
fairylike
fairyring
fairytale
faithcure
faithless
feiseanna
flightily
flintlock
flippancy
friarbird
fricassee
fricative
frigatoon
frightful
frigidity
fritterer
frivolity
frivolled
frivolous
gainfully
gainsayer
glissandi
glissando
goingover
griefless
grievance
grillroom
grillwork
grimalkin
griminess
grisaille
gristmill
gritstone
guidebook
guideline
guidepost
guiderope
guildhall
guildship
guileless
guillemot
guilloche
guiltless
guitarist
hailstone
hailstorm
hairbrush
haircloth
hairgrass
hairiness
hairpiece
hairshirt
hairslide
hairspace
hairstyle
heinously
idiograph
idiomatic
idiopathy
idioplasm
idiotical
imitation
imitative
initially
initiator
isinglass
itineracy
itinerant
itinerary
itinerate
jailbreak
jointress
juiceless
juiciness
kaiserdom
kaiserism
klinostat
knifeedge
knightage
lairdship
Leicester
leisurely
leitmotif
leitmotiv
loincloth
maidenish
mailplane
mailtrain
mainbrace
mainliner
mainsheet
moistener
moistness
nailbrush
neighbour
noiseless
noisiness
noisomely
nuisancer
oligaemia
oligarchy
Oligocene
oligopoly
olivenite
ominously
omissible
onionskin
opinioned
orientate
orificial
oriflamme
originate
oviductal
oviferous
oviparity
oviparous
oxidation
paillasse
paillette
painfully
painterly
paintwork
pairhorse
philander
philately
philippic
philogyny
philology
Philomela
plicately
plication
plicature
poignancy
poinciana
pointduty
pointedly
pointille
pointlace
pointless
pointsman
poisonous
priceless
prideless
priestess
primaeval
primality
primarily
primatial
primeness
primipara
primitive
primordia
princedom
princekin
princelet
principal
principia
principle
printable
printshop
priorship
prismatic
privateer
privately
privation
privative
privilege
puissance
quibbling
quickener
quicklime
quickness
quicksand
quickstep
quiescent
quietness
quillwort
quinoline
quintette
quintuple
quirister
quitclaim
quittance
quixotism
quizzical
raincheck
raincloud
raingauge
raininess
rainmaker
rainproof
rainstorm
rainwater
Reichstag
reimburse
reinforce
reinstate
reiterate
Rhineodon
rhinology
rhizocarp
rhizoidal
roisterer
ruination
ruinously
sailcloth
sailoring
sailorman
sailplane
sainthood
saintlike
saintling
saintship
sciaenoid
sciagraph
sciamachy
sciascopy
sciential
scientism
scientist
scintilla
scirrhous
seigneury
seigniory
shieldbug
shieldfem
shiftless
shillelah
shinguard
shininess
Shintoism
Shintoist
shipboard
shipcanal
shipfever
shipmoney
shipowner
shipshape
shipwreck
shirtless
shirttail
skiagraph
skiamachy
skiascopy
skijoring
skilfully
skindiver
skinflick
skinflint
skingraft
skintight
skirtings
skirtless
slickness
sliderule
slightish
sliminess
slingback
slingshot
slinkweed
slipcoach
slipcover
slivovitz
smileless
smilingly
sniggerer
snipefish
snivelled
sniveller
soidisant
spicebush
spiciness
spiculate
spiderman
spiderweb
spikenard
spikiness
spillikin
spindling
spindrier
spindrift
spineless
spininess
spinnaker
spinneret
spinosity
Spinozism
Spinozist
spinulose
spinulous
spiracula
spirality
spiralled
spirillum
spiritism
spiritist
spiritoso
spiritous
spiritual
spirituel
spirogyra
stickwork
stiffener
stiffness
stigmatic
stilettos
stillborn
stillhunt
stillness
stillroom
stiltedly
stimulant
stimulate
stingaree
stingless
stinkball
stinkbomb
stinkhorn
stinktrap
stinkweed
stinkwood
stintless
stipitate
stippling
stipulate
stirabout
stitchery
swiftness
swimmable
swimmeret
swineherd
swingeing
swinishly
switchman
swivelled
tailboard
taillight
tailoress
tailoring
tailpiece
taintless
taioseach
thickener
thicketed
thickhead
thickknee
thickness
thighbone
thighboot
thingness
thingummy
thinkable
thinktank
thirdhand
thirdrate
thirdsman
thirstily
thirtieth
thitherto
trialogue
triatomic
tribadism
tribalism
tribesman
tribology
tribunate
tributary
trichinae
trichomic
trichroic
trickless
tricksily
trickster
triclinia
triclinic
tricolour
tridactyl
tridymite
triennial
triennium
trierarch
trifacial
trifocals
trifolium
triforium
trigamist
trigamous
trihedral
trihybrid
trilinear
trilithon
trilobate
trilobite
trimerous
trimester
trimetric
trimmings
trinketer
trinketry
trinomial
triploidy
triptyque
triquetra
trisagion
trisector
triteness
tritheism
tritheist
triturate
triumphal
triumviri
trivalent
trivially
triweekly
tuitional
twiceborn
twicelaid
twicetold
twinkling
twistable
twitchily
twitterer
uliginous
unicolour
unicuspid
unifiable
uniformly
uniparous
uniplanar
uniserial
unisexual
unisonant
unisonous
unitarian
unitively
univalent
universal
vainglory
Vaishnava
veinstone
voiceless
voiceover
wailingly
waistband
waistbelt
waistcoat
waistline
weighable
weighbeam
weightily
weighting
weirdness
whichever
whimperer
whimsical
whinstone
whipperin
whipround
whipsnake
whipstock
whirligig
whirlpool

whirlwind
whiskered
whisperer
whistling
whitebait
whitebass
whitebeam
whiteface
whitefish
Whitehall
whitehead
whiteness
whitening
whitewash
whitewing
whitewood
whizzbang
wristband
wristdrop
wristshot
zeitgeist
zoiatrics
Zwinglian
abjection
adjacency
adjoining
adjunctly
adjutancy
bejabbers
dejection
enjoyable
enjoyably
enjoyment
injection
injurious
injustice
majordomo
majorette
majorship
majuscule
objectify
objection
objective
objurgate
rejection
rejoicing
rejoinder
sojourner
alkaloses
alkalosis
anklebone
ankylosis
ankylotic
askewness
awkwardly
bakehouse
baksheesh
irksomely
makeready
makeshift
mekometer
nakedness
oakenshaw
Pakistani
Pekingese
pikeperch
pikestaff
pokeberry
pokerface
pokerwork
rakehelly
teknonymy
unknitted
unknowing
wakefully
wakerobin
ablatival
ablutions
adlibbing
aflatoxin
ailanthus
allantois
allegedly
allegiant
allegoric
allemande
alleviate
alligator
allocable
allograph
allomorph
allopathy
allophone
alloplasm
allotment
allotrope
allotropy
allotting
allowable
allowably
allowance
allowedly
aplanatic
Atlantean
Aylesbury
balaclava
balalaika
balconied
baldachin
baldaquin
baldfaced
balefully
balkanise
balladeer
balladist
ballerina
ballistae
ballistic
ballpoint
balminess
baltimore
belatedly
beleaguer
belemnite
bellglass
bellicose
bellpunch
bellyache
bellyband
bellyflop
belvedere
bilabiate
bilateral
bilgekeel
bilharzia
bilingual
biliously
bilirubin
biliteral
billabong
billboard
billiards
billionth
billycock
billygoat
boldfaced
bolection
boliviano
bolometer
bolometry
Bolshevik
bulbously
Bulgarian
bulginess
bulkiness
bulldozer
bullfight
bullfinch
bullishly
bulltrout
bullybeef
bullytree
calaboose
calabrese
calamanco
calandria
calcaneal
calcaneum
calcarate
calcicole
calcifuge
calculate
calculous
caldarium
calendric
calendula
calenture
calibrate
calicular
caliology
caliphate
callipers
callosity
callously
calmative
calorific
Calvinism
Calvinist
calycinal
celandine
celebrant
celebrate
celebrity
celestial
cellarage
celluloid
cellulose
Celticism
chlamydes
chlorella
chloritic
chlorosis
chlorotic
colcannon
colchicum
colcothar
coldshort
colemouse
collagist
collation
colleague
collected
collector
collegial
collegian
collegium
colligate
collimate
collinear
collision
collocate
collodion
colloidal
colloquia
collotype
collusion
collusive
collyrium
colocynth
colonelcy
coloniser
colonnade
colophony
colorific
colosseum
colostomy
colostrum
colourful
colouring
colourist
colourman
coltishly
coltsfoot
colubrine
columbary
Columbian
columbine
columbite
columbium
columella
columnist
cullender
culminant
culminate
culsdesac
cultivate
cylindric
dalliance
dalmatian
daltonism
delftware
delicious
delineate
delirious
deliverer
deludable
dilatable
dilatancy
diligence
dolefully
doleritic
dolomitic
doltishly
dulcamara
dulcitude
ealdorman
eclampsia
eclamptic
eglantine
ellipsoid
enlighten
eulogiser
Falangism
Falangist
falciform
faldstool
Falernian
fallalery
falsehood
falseness
falsifier
felicific
fellowman
felonious
filaceous
filiation
filigreed
fillister
filminess
filmstrip
filoselle
filterbed
filtertip
filtrable
foliation
folkdance
folkmusic
folkweave
following
fulfilled
fulfiller
fulgently
fulgurant
fulgurate
fulgurite
fulgurous
fullblown
fullcream
fulldress
fullgrown
fullscale
fulminant
fulminate
fulminous
fulsomely
galactose
galantine
galenical
galingale
gallantly
gallantry
galleried
gallicise
gallicism
gallingly
gallinule
gallivant
galliwasp
gallmidge
gallonage
gallooned
gallopade
Gallophil
galloping
gallowses
gallstone
galvanise
galvanism
galvanist
gelignite
giltedged
goldbrick
goldcrest
goldeneye
goldenrod
goldfever
goldfield
goldfinch
goldsinny
goldsmith
golflinks
goliardic
halfbaked
halfblood
halfbound
halfbreed
halfcaste
halfcrown
halfhardy
halflight
halfpence
halfpenny
halfprice
halfshell
halfstaff
halftitle
halftrack
halftruth
halieutic
halitosis
Halloween
Hallowmas
hallstand
Hallstatt
halophile
halophyte
halothane
haltingly
helically
heliogram
heliostat
heliotype
heliozoan
heliozoic
hellebore
hellenise
Hellenism
Hellenist
hellhound
hellishly
helpfully
Helvetian
hilarious
hillbilly
Holarctic
hollyhock
Hollywood
holocaust
holograph
holophote
holystone
hylozoism
illboding
illegally
illegible
illegibly
illgotten
illiberal
illicitly
illjudged
illogical
illomened
illwisher
Islamitic
jellyfish
jollyboat
kilderkin
killifish
kilocycle
kilohertz
kilolitre
kilometre
lallation
liltingly
lilywhite
malachite
maladroit
malanders
malarious
malathion
Malayalam
malformed
malicious
malignant
malignity
malleable
malleehen
mallemuck
malleolar
malleolus
malthouse
malvoisie
melanosis
melanotic
melaphyre
melatonin
meliorate
meliorism
meliorist
meliority
melismata
melocoton
melodious
melodrama
melomania
meltingly
meltwater
milestone
militancy
milkfever
milkfloat
milkiness
milkshake
milktooth
millboard
millenary
millennia
millepede
millepore
millerite
milligram
millinery
millionth
millipede
millivolt
millstone
millwheel
milometer
Miltonian
molecular
molluscan
mollymawk
molybdate
mullioned
multifoil
multiform
multilane
multipara
multiplex
multitude
Nilometer
nullifier
nullipara
nullipore
obligated
obliquely
obliquity
oblivious
oilburner
oilcolour
oilpaints
onlicence
palaestra
palafitte
palankeen
palanquin
palatable
palatably
palillogy
Palladian
palladium
palladous
palletise
palliasse
pallidity
palmation
palmipede
palmistry
palmitate
palpation
palpebral
palpitant
palpitate
palsgrave
paludinal
palustral
Pelasgian
pellagrin
pelletise
pellitory
phlebitis
pilferage
pilgarlic
pillarbox
pilotfish
polariser
polemical
polevault
policeman
politburo
politesse
political
pollinate

pollinium
pollutant
pollution
polonaise
polyamide
polyandry
polybasic
polyester
polygamic
polygenic
polygonal
polygonum
polygraph
polyhedra
polymathy
polymeric
polymorph
polyonymy
polyphagy
polyphase
polyphone
polyphony
polyploid
polyptych
polysemic
polysomic
polythene
polytonal
polytypic
polyvinyl
polywater
polyzoary
pullulate
pulmonary
pulmonate
pulpboard
pulpiness
pulpiteer
pulpstone
pulsatile
pulsation
pulsatory
pulseless
pulserate
pulverise
pulverous
pulvillus
pulvinate
relevance
relevancy
reliantly
religiose
religious
reliquary
reliquiae
reluctant
reluctate
rulership
salacious
salangane
saleratus
salesgirl
saleslady
salicetum
salicylic
saliently
sallowish
salmonoid
salpinges
saltation
saltatory
saltglaze
saltiness
saltmarsh
saltpetre
saltspoon
saltwater
saltworks
salubrity
salvation
scleritis
sclerosis
sclerotic
selachian
selection
selective
selectman
selenious
selenitic
selfabuse
selfaware
selfdoubt
selfdrive
selffaced
selfglory
selfimage
selfishly
selfmoved
selfpride
selftrust
Seljukian
siliceous
silicious
silicosis
silicotic
siliquose
silkgland
silkiness
silliness
siltation
siltstone
silverfir
solacious
soldierly
solemnise
solemnity
soleplate
solfatara
solfeggio
solferino
solicitor
solidness
soliloquy
solipsism
solipsist
solitaire
solmisate
Solomonic
Solutrean
Solutrian
solvation
splashily
splayfoot
spleenful
splendent
splendour
splenetic
splenitis
spleuchan
splintery
splitting
spluttery
sulcation
sulkiness
sulphonic
sulphuret
sulphuric
sultanate
sultaness
syllabary
syllabise
syllabism
syllabled
syllepses
syllepsis
sylleptic
syllogise
syllogism
sylphlike
sylvanite
talismans
talkathon
talkative
tallowish
tallyshop
Talmudist
telamones
telegenic
telegraph
telemeter
telemetry
teleology
telepathy
telephone
telephony
telephoto
telescope
telescopy
televisor
tellingly
tellurate
tellurian
telluride
tellurite
tellurium
tellurous
telophase
tilestone
tolerable
tolerably
tolerance
tollbooth
tollhouse
tuliproot
tuliptree
tulipwood
unlearned
unlimited
unluckily
uplifting
valentine
valiantly
validness
vallation
vallecula
valuables
valuation
valueless
valveless
velodrome
velveteen
villagery
villanage
villenage
villiform
villosity
volauvent
volcanism
volcanoes
volkslied
volteface
voltinism
voltmeter
volumeter
voluntary
volunteer
vulcanian
vulcanise
vulcanism
vulcanist
vulcanite
vulgarian
vulgarise
vulgarism
vulgarity
vulnerary
vulpinism
vulpinite
vulturine
vulturish
vulturous
Waldenses
waldgrave
walkabout
wallboard
wallcress
wallfruit
walloping
wallpaper
wallplate
wallydrag
Walpurgis
welcoming
welfarism
wellbeing
wellfound
wellknown
welltimed
willemite
willingly
willowish
willpower
wolfhound
wolfishly
wolframic
wolfsbane
wolverene
wolverine
wulfenite
wyliecoat
xylograph
xylophone
yellowdog
yellowish
admeasure
adminicle
admirable
admirably
admiralty
admission
admissive
admitting
admixture
admonitor
aimlessly
almandine
almsgiver
almshouse
armadillo
armigeral
armillary
armistice
Armorican
atmometer
Axminster
bamboozle
bemusedly
bimonthly
bombardon
bombasine
bombastic
bombazine
bombhappy
bombilate
bombinate
bombproof
bombshell
bombsight
bumblebee
bumbledon
bumpiness
bumptious
camarilla
Cambodian
camelback
camelhair
Camembert
cameraman
camorrist
campanile
campanili
campanula
campchair
campcraft
campfever
camphoric
campstool
cementite
Cimmerian
combatant
combative
combinate
comedones
comfiture
comforter
comically
Cominform
Comintern
comitadji
commander
commandos
commendam
commensal
commenter
commingle
comminute
commissar
committal
committed
committee
commodity
commodore
commonage
commonlaw
commotion
communard
communion
communise
communism
communist
community
commutate
compactly
compactor
companion
compasses
compelled
compendia
competent
complaint
complexly
complexus
compliant
component
composite
composure
comprador
comprisal
comptroll
comradely
comradery
cumbrance
cymbalist
cymbidium
cymbiform
cymophane
damascene
damnation
damnatory
damnedest
damningly
Damoclean
demagogic
demagogue
demandant
demanding
demarcate
demeanour
demimonde
demission
demitasse
demitting
demiurgic
demobbing
democracy
demulcent
demurrage
demurring
demystify
dimension
dimidiate
dimissory
dimorphic
dimwitted
dominance
dominator
dominical
Dominican
dumbfound
dumpiness
Emmenthal
familyman
femineity
fimbriate
fumarolic
fumigator
gambadoes
gambolled
gammadion
gammoning
gemmation
gemmology
gemutlich
gimmickry
gomphosis
gumminess
gymnasial
gymnasium
gymnastic
hamadryad
hamamelis
hamburger
hamfisted
hamhanded
hammerman
hammertoe
hamstring
hamstrung
hemicycle
hemistich
hemitrope
hemstitch
Himalayan
Himyarite
homebound
homegrown
homemaker
homeopath
homestead
homewards
homicidal
homiletic
homogamic
homograft
homograph
homologue
homonymic
homophone
homophony
homoplasy
homopolar
homotaxis
homotonic
homousian
homuncule
homunculi
humankind
humanness
humblebee
humbugged
humdinger
humectant
humiliate
hymnology
immanence
immanency
immediacy
immediate
immensely
immensity
immersion
immigrant
immigrate
imminence
imminency
immixture
immodesty
immolator
immorally
immovable
immovably
immutable
immutably
jambalaya
jampacked
jumpiness
kymograph
lambently
lamellate
lamellose
laminaria
laminated
lampblack
lamplight
lampooner
lampshade
lampshell
Limburger
limejuice
limelight
limestone
limewater
limitable
limitedly
limitless
limnology
limonitic
limousine
limpidity
Lombardic
lumbering
lumberman
lumbrical
lumbricus
luminance
lumpiness
lumpishly
lymegrass
lymehound
lymphatic
mamillary
mamillate
mammalian
mammalogy
mammiform
mammonish
mammonism
mammonist
mammonite
mementoes
memoirist
memorable
memorably

memoranda
memoriter
mimicking
momentary
momentous
mumchance
mummified
nameplate
nemertean
nemertine
nemophila
nominable
nominally
nominator
nomocracy
nomograph
numbskull
numerable
numerator
numerical
nummulite
nymphalid
ommatidia
osmometer
pemphigus
pimpernel
pomaceous
pommelled
pompadour
pomposity
pompously
pumiceous
pummelled
rampantly
remainder
remanence
remeasure
remediate
remindful
reminisce
remission
remitment
remittent
remitting
remontant
removable
ruminator
rumrunner
Samaritan
Samoyedic
semanteme
semantics
semaphore
semblable
semblably
semblance
semeiotic
semestral
semibreve
semicolon
semifinal
semifluid
semilunar
semimetal
seminally
semiology
semiotics
semiplume
semirigid
semisolid
semisweet
semitonic
semivowel
similarly
simpatico
simpleton
simplices
simulacra
simulacre

simulator
simulcast
something
sometimes
somewhere
somewhile
sommelier
somnolent
summarily
summarise
summarist
summation
summative
summingup
sumptuary
sumptuous
symbiosis
symbiotic
symbolics
symbolise
symbolism
symbolist
symbology
symmetric
symphonic
symphysis
sympodial
sympodium
symposiac
symposial
symposium
tambourin
tamponade
temperate
temporary
temporise
temptable
temptress
timbering
timberman
timelapse
timelimit
timeously
timepiece
timesheet
timetable
timidness
timocracy
timpanist
tombstone
tomentose
tomentous
tumblebug
tumescent
tumidness
tympanist
unmatched
unmeaning
unmindful
unmusical
vampirism
vimineous
vomitoria
womanhood
womaniser
womankind
womanlike
womenfolk
womenkind
zamindary
zemindary
zymogenic
abnegator
abnormity
adnominal
agnatical
annectent
annelidan
annotator

announcer
annoyance
annuitant
annularly
annulated
annulling
annulment
banderole
bandicoot
bandoleer
bandolero
bandolier
bandoline
bandstand
bandwagon
bandwidth
baneberry
banefully
banjulele
bannister
banqueter
banquette
Bantustan
beneficed
bengaline
benighted
benignant
benignity
bentonite
benzidine
benzoline
binocular
binominal
binturong
bondslave
bondstone
bondwoman
bonechina
bonhomous
bonniness
bundobust
bunkhouse
canalboat
cancelled
cancerous
candidacy
candidate
Candlemas
candlenut
candytuft
canebrake
canescent
canesugar
canetrash
canicular
cankerous
cannelure
canniness
cannonade
cannoneer
cannonier
cannulate
canonical
cantabile
cantaloup
cantharid
cantharis
cantharus
cantilena
Cantonese
cantorial
canvasser
censorial
centenary
centering
centigram
centipede
centrally
centreing

centurion
cinematic
cineraria
cinereous
Cingalese
concavely
concavity
conceited
concentre
concerned
concerted
concierge
conciliar
concisely
concision
concocter
concoctor
concordat
concourse
concubine
concurred
condenser
condignly
condiment
condition
conducive
conductor
condyloid
condyloma
confabbed
conferral
conferred
conferrer
confervae
confessor
confidant
confident
confiding
configure
confirmed
confirmer
confirmor
confiteor
confluent
conformal
conformer
Confucian
confusion
congenial
congeries
congruent
congruity
congruous
conically
conjugate
connately
connation
connature
connected
connecter
connector
connexion
connivent
connubial
conqueror
conscious
conscribe
conscript
consensus
conserver
consignee
consignor
consonant
consortia
constable
constancy
constrain
constrict
construct

consulage
consulate
consulter
consultor
contactor
contadina
contadino
contagion
contagium
container
contemner
contender
contented
continent
continual
continuer
continuum
contralto
contrasty
contrived
contriver
contumacy
contumely
contusion
conundrum
convector
converter
convexity
convincer
convivial
convolute
convolved
cunctator
cuneiform
cunningly
cynically
dancehall
dandelion
dandiacal
dangerous
Dantesque
dendritic
denigrate
denitrate
denitrify
denouncer
denseness
dentalium
dentation
dentiform
dentistry
dentition
denyingly
dinginess
diningcar
dinnerset
dinoceras
dinothere
donnishly
donothing
dungarees
dynamical
dynamiter
eunuchism
eunuchoid
fanatical
fancyfree
fancywork
fandangle
fandangos
fanfarade
fantasied
fantasise
fantasist
fantastic
fantastry
fenceless
fenestrae
fenestral

Fenianism
fenugreek
financial
financier
finedrawn
fingering
fingertip
finically
finicking
fundament
funebrial
fungicide
fungiform
funicular
funiculus
funkiness
funnelled
funniness
ganderism
gangboard
gangplank
gannister
genealogy
generable
generalia
generally
generator
genetical
genialise
geniality
genitival
genocidal
genotypic
genteelly
gentility
gentleman
genuflect
genuinely
gingerade
gingerale
ginglymus
ginpalace
gondolier
gongorism
gonophore
guncotton
gunpowder
gunrunner
gynaeceum
gynocracy
gynoecium
gynophore
handbrake
handcraft
handcuffs
handglass
handiness
handiwork
handlebar
handorgan
handpress
handsdown
handshake
handspike
handstand
handwheel
handywork
hangerson
hankering
Hanseatic
hanselled
hendiadys
hindbrain
hindrance
hindsight
honeycomb
honeymoon
honkytonk
honoraria

honorific
hunchback
hundredth
Hungarian
hunkydory
ignescent
ignitable
ignitible
ignorable
ignoramus
ignorance
innermost
innervate
innholder
innkeeper
innocence
innocency
innocuity
innocuous
innovator
innoxious
innuendos
ionisable
janissary
janitress
Jansenism
Jansenist
Juneberry
juniorate
juniority
junkerdom
junkerism
junketing
Junoesque
kennelled
kentledge
kinematic
kingcraft
kingdomed
kingmaker
kingsized
kinkiness
kinswoman
lancejack
lancewood
lancinate
landagent
landaulet
landdross
landdrost
landgrave
landloper
landowner
landscape
landslide
Langobard
langouste
languidly
lankiness
lanthanum
lendlease
lengthily
leniently
lentiform
lineality
lineament
linearise
linearity
lineation
linenfold
lineolate
lingering
lingually
lingulate
lintelled
lintwhite
Londonise
Londonism
longaeval

longchain
longcoats
longeared
longevity
longevous
longfaced
longhouse
longicorn
longingly
longitude
longlived
Longobard
longrange
longshore
lunchtime
lunisolar
lunitidal
Mancunian
mandarine
mandatary
mandatory
mandoline
manducate
maneating
manganate
manganese
manganite
manganous
manginess
manhandle
manhattan
Manichean
manifesto
manipular
manliness
mannequin
mannerism
mannerist
manoeuvre
manometer
manorseat
mansarded
mansionry
manslayer
manticore
manubrium
Manxwoman
manyplies
manysided
manzanita
menadione
menagerie
mendacity
Mendelian
Mendelism
mendicant
mendicity
meningeal
Mennonite
menopause
Menshevik
menstrual
menstruum
mentalism
mentalist
mentality
mentation
minacious
mincemeat
mincingly
mindfully
minefield
minelayer
miniature
minimally
miniskirt
minuscule
minutegun
minuteman

monachism
monarchal
monarchic
monastery
monatomic
Mondayish
monergism
moneybags
moneybill
moneywort
Mongolian
mongolism
Mongoloid
mongooses
mongrelly
monitress
monkeyish
monkeyism
monkeynut
monkshood
monobasic
monoceros
monochord
monocline
monocoque
monocracy
monocular
monodical
monodrama
monoecism
monogamic
monograph
monolatry
monologic
monologue
monomania
monomeric
monophagy
monoplane
monorhyme
monostich
monostyle
monotonic
monotreme
monotypic
monsignor
monsoonal
monstrous
Montanism
monthling
monticule
monzonite
mundanely
mundungus
municipal
muniments
munitions
nannygoat
ninepence
ninepenny
ninetieth
nondriver
nonentity
nonillion
nonjuring
nonlinear
nonpareil
nonperson
nonprofit
nonsmoker
nonviable
nuncupate
obnoxious
oenomancy
oenophile
oenophily
ownership
panatella
panchayat

pancratic
panderess
panegyric
panelling
panellist
panhandle
panicking
panoplied
panoramic
pantalets
pantaloon
pantheism
pantheist
pantingly
pantomime
pantryman
pantyhose
pencilled
penciller
pendently
pendragon
pendulate
penduline
pendulous
peneplain
peneplane
penetrant
penetrate
penfriend
penholder
peninsula
penitence
penniless
pennywort
penpusher
pensioner
pensively
pentagram
pentangle
pentarchy
Pentecost
penthouse
penultima
penumbral
penurious
pinchbeck
pinchcock
pineapple
pinkiness
pinnately
pinnipede
pinnulate
pinstripe
pintailed
pintsized
ponderous
pontoneer
pontonier
punchball
punchbowl
punchcard
punchline
punctilio
punctuate
pungently
punishing
rancidity
rancorous
randiness
randomise
ranginess
ransacker
rantingly
ranunculi
renascent
rencontre
rendition
renewable
renitency

renouncer
renovator
ringfence
ringingly
ringshake
ringsnake
runcinate
sanatoria
sanbenito
sanctuary
sandalled
sandarach
sandblast
sandblind
sandcrack
sandglass
sandiness
sandpaper
sandpiper
sandspout
sandstone
sandstorm
sandtable
sandyacht
sangfroid
Sanhedrim
Sanhedrin
sanitaria
santolina
santonica
senescent
seneschal
senhorita
seniority
sensation
sensedata
senseless
sensitise
sensitive
sensorial
sensorium
sensually
sentenate
sentience
sentiency
sentiment
sentrybox
sincerely
sincerity
sinewless
singalong
singleton
singspiel
Sinhalese
sinistral
sinlessly
sinologue
sinophile
sinuately
sinuation
sinuosity
sinuously
sinusitis
songcycle
songfully
songsmith
sonneteer
sonnetise
sonometer
sunbather
sunbonnet
sunburned
sundowner
sunflower
sunhelmet
sunlounge
sunniness
sunspurge
sunstroke

sunstruck
suntanned
synagogal
synagogue
synchrony
synclinal
syncopate
syncretic
syncytial
syncytium
syndactyl
syndicate
synectics
syneresis
synergism
synergist
syngamous
synizesis
synodical
synoecete
synonymic
synoptist
synovitis
syntactic
syntheses
synthesis
synthetic
tangerine
tanliquor
tanpickle
tantalate
tantalise
tantalite
tenacious
tenaculum
tenderise
tendinous
tenebrist
tenebrous
tenseness
tensility
tensional
tentacled
tentation
tentative
tenthrate
tentmaker
tenuously
tinderbox
tinniness
tinopener
tinselled
tonguelet
tonguetie
tonically
tonometer
tonsillar
tonsorial
tunefully
tungstate
tunicated
tunnelled
tunnelnet
uintahite
unnamable
unnatural
vandalise
vandalism
vendition
veneering
venerable
venerably
venerator
venereous
vengeance
veniality
ventiduct
ventifact
ventilate

ventrally
ventricle
venturous
vinaceous
vindicate
wandering
windblown
windbound
windbreak
windchest
windhover
windiness
windowbox
windproof
windswept
windwards
wineberry
wineglass
winepress
winestone
winevault
wingchair
winningly
winsomely
winterise
wonderful
Xanthippe
xenograft
xenophile
xenophobe
Yankeedom
Yankeeism
zincotype
zinkenite
abolisher
abolition
abominate
aborigine
abounding
aboutface
aboutturn
aconitine
acoustics
adoptable
adoration
adoringly
adornment
aforesaid
agonising
agonistic
aloneness
alongside
aloofness
amoebaean
amoralism
amorality
amorously
amorphism
amorphous
amourette
anomalous
anomalure
anonymity
anonymous
anopheles
anorectic
anorthite
anovulant
anoxaemia
apocrypha
apodictic
apogamous
apologise
apologist
apomictic
apophyses
apophysis
apostolic
apothecia

aromatise
atomicity
atomistic
atonalism
atonality
atonement
atonicity
avocation
avoidable
avoidably
avoidance
biogenous
biography
biologist
biometric
bionomics
biorhythm
biosphere
blockader
blockhead
blockship
bloodbath
bloodless
bloodlust
bloodroot
bloodshed
bloodshot
bloodworm
bloodwort
blotchily
blowtorch
boobytrap
bookishly
booklouse
bookmaker
bookplate
bookshelf
bookstall
bookstand
bookstore
boomerang
boomslang
boondocks
boorishly
bootblack
broadcast
broadleaf
broadloom
broadness
broadside
broadtail
broadways
broadwise
brochette
broiderer
brokerage
bromeliad
bronchial
broomcorn
broomrape
brotherly
brownness
buoyantly
chockfull
chocolate
chokedamp
choleraic
chondrite
chondrule
chophouse
choplogic
chopstick
chorister
chorology
cloakroom
clockwise
clockwork
cloisonne
cloistral

closedown
closeness
cloudland
cloudless
cookhouse
cooperage
cooperant
cooperate
crocodile
croissant
CroMagnon
crookback
crookedly
crookneck
cropeared
croquette
crossable
crossbeam
crossbill
crossbred
crossette
crosseyed
crossfade
crossfire
crossfish
crosshead
crosslink
crossness
crossover
crossroad
crossruff
crosstalk
crossways
crosswind
crosswise
crossword
crotchety
croustade
crowberry
crownless
crowsfoot
crowsnest
deodorant
deodorise
deoxidise
dioecious
Dionysiac
Dionysian
doodlebug
doorframe
doorplate
drollness
dromedary
dropscene
dropscone
dropsical
duodecimo
duodenary
ecologist
economics
economise
economist
ecosphere
ecossaise
ecosystem
egomaniac
egotistic
elocution
elongated
elopement
eloquence
emolliate
emollient
emolument
emotional
emotively
emotivity
eponymous
erogenous
eroticism
esoterica
esoterism
evocation
evocative
evocatory
evolution
evolutive
evolvable
exodermis
exogamous
exogenous
exonerate
exopodite
exorciser
exosmosis
exosmotic
exosphere
exostosis
exoticism
feoffment
fioritura
fioriture
floatable
flocculus
floodgate
floodmark
floodtide
flophouse
floriated
floridean
floridity
floristic
floristry
floscular
flotation
flouncing
flowchart
flowerage
flowerbed
flowering
flowerpot
flowingly
flowsheet
flowstone
foodchain
foodstuff
foolhardy
foolishly
foolproof
footboard
footcloth
footfault
footlight
footloose
footplate
footpound
footprint
footstalk
footstall
footstool
frockcoat
frogmarch
frogspawn
frolicked
frontally
frontless
frontline
frontpage
frontward
frontways
frontwise
frostbite
frostwork
frowardly
gaolbreak
geobotany
geodesist
geography
geologise
geologist
geomancer
geomantic
geometric
geometrid
geoponics
georgette
geosphere
geostatic
geotropic
ghostlike
ghostword
globefish
globosity
glomerate
glomerule
glomeruli
gloryhole
glossator
glossitis
glowingly
goodnight
goodwives
goosander
goosefoot
goosegirl
gooseherd
gooseneck
gooseskin
goosestep
groomsman
grosgrain
grossness
grossular
grotesque
grouchily
groundage
groundash
groundhog
grounding
groundivy
groundnut
groundsel
grovelled
groveller
hoofprint
iconology
inoculate
inodorous
inorganic
ironbound
ironmould
ironsides
ironsmith
ironstone
ironworks
Iroquoian
isobathic
isochrone
isoclinal
isoclinic
isocyclic
isogamete
isogamous
isogenous
isohyetal
isolation
isolative
isomerise
isomerism
isomerous
isometric
isoniazid
isooctane
isopodous
isosceles
isostatic
isotropic
kaolinise
kaolinite
knockdown
knockknee
knotgrass
knowingly
knowledge
Laodicean
lioncelle
lionheart
lookalike
looseleaf
looseness
lyophilic
lyophobic
moodiness
moonblind
moonlight
moonquake
moonraker
moonscape
moonshine
moonstone
myography
myologist
neodymium
neolithic
neologian
neologise
neologism
neologist
neoteinia
neoteinic
neoterise
neoterism
neoterist
odontalgy
odorously
odourless
omophagia
omophagic
onomastic
opodeldoc
orography
orologist
otologist
ozocerite
ozokerite
phonation
phonatory
phonemics
phonetics
phonetise
phonetism
phonetist
phoniness
phonogram
phonolite
phonology
phosphate
phosphene
phosphide
phosphine
phosphite
photocell
photocopy
photogene
photophil
photopsia
phototype
ploughboy
ploughman
poorhouse
probation
probative
probatory
proboscis
procedure
procerity
processed
processer
processor
proclitic
proconsul
procreant
procreate
procuracy
procuress
prodromal
prodromic
proenzyme
profanely
profanity
professed
professor
profilist
profiteer
profusely
profusion
progestin
prognoses
prognosis
programme
projector
prolamine
prolapsus
prolately
prolation
prolative
prolepses
prolepsis
proleptic
prolicide
prolixity
prologise
prolusion
prolusory
promenade
prominent
promising
promotion
promotive
promptbox
pronation
proneness
pronghorn
pronounce
proofread
propagate
propelled
propeller
properdin
prophetic
propionic
proponent
propriety
proptosis
propylaea
propylene
prorogate
prosaical
proscenia
proscribe
prosector
prosecute
proselyte
prosiness
prosodist
prostatic
prostrate
protamine
protector
proteinic
protester
protestor
prothesis
prothetic
prothorax
protonema
prototype
protozoal
protozoan
protozoic
protozoon
proveably
Provencal
provender
provident
providing
provision
provisory
provoking
provostry
proximate
proximity
psoriasis
psoriatic
Ptolemaic
quodlibet
quotation
quotidian
rhodamine
rhodolite
rhodonite
rhodopsin
rhonchial
riotously
roodcloth
roofplate
roominess
rootstock
scolecite
scoliosis
scoliotic
scombroid
scorbutic
scorching
scorebook
scorecard
scoredraw
scorifier
scorpioid
Scotchman
Scoticise
scotomata
scoundrel
sforzando
shockable
shockhead
shoeblack
shoemaker
shoeshine
shogunate
shootable
shopfloor
shopfront
shoreless
shoreline
shoreside
shoreward
shoreweed
shortcake
shortener
shortfall
shorthand
shorthorn
shortness
shortstop
shortterm
shortwave
shotproof
shottower
shouldest
shovelful
shovelhat
shovelled
shoveller
showiness
showpiece
showplace
slopbasin
slopewise
slothbear
Slovakian
Slovenian
slowcoach
slowmatch
smokeball
smokebomb
smokebush
smokejack
smokeless
smoketree
smokiness
smoothish
snowberry
snowblind
snowblink
snowbound
snowbroth
snowdrift
snowfield
snowflake
snowgoose
snowguard
snowiness
snowplant
snowscape
snowstorm
snowwhite
sooterkin
soothfast
sootiness
spodumene
spoilsman
spokesman
spokewise
spoliator
spongebag
spongeous
spoonbeak
spoonbill
spoonfeed
spoonmeat
sporangía
sporocarp
sporocyst
sporogeny
sportsman
sporulate
spotcheck
spotlight
spouthole
spoutless
stockbook
stockdove
stockfish
stockinet
stocklist
stockpile
stockroom
stockwhip
stockyard
stoically
stokehold
stokehole
stolidity
stolonate
stomachal
stomacher
stomachic
stonechat
stonecoal
stonecold
stonecrop
stonedead

stonedeaf
stonefish
stoneless
stonewall
stoneware
stonework
stonewort
stoniness
stoolball
stoplight
stoppress
stopwatch
storeroom
storeship
storiated
stormbelt
stormbird
stormcock
stormcone
stormless
stormsail
storybook
storyline
stoutness
stovepipe
swordcane
swordfish
swordknot
swordlike
swordplay
swordsman
swordtail
Thomistic
thornback
thornbill
thornbush
thornless
thorntree
thoughted
toolhouse
toothache
toothcomb
toothless
toothpick
toothsome
toothwort
trochilus
trochleae
trochlear
troopship
tropology
troublous
trousered
trousseau
troutfarm
troutling
trowelled
troweller
twofisted
twohanded
twosuiter
uropygium
uxoricide
violation
violative
violently
violinist
voodooism
voodooist
whodunnit
wholemeal
wholeness
wholesale
wholesome
whosoever
woodblock
woodchuck
woodcraft
woodiness
woodlouse
woodnymph
woodwaxen
wooziness
wrongdoer
wrongness
zoogenous
zoography
zoologist
zoophagan
zoophobia
zoophytic
zootechny
zootomist
aepyornis
alpargata
alpenhorn
ampersand
amphibian
amphibole
amphigory
amphioxus
ampleness
amplifier
amplitude
amputator
appalling
Appaloosa
apparatus
apparitor
appealing
appellant
appellate
appendage
appendant
appertain
appetence
appetency
appetiser
applauder
applejack
appliance
applicant
appointee
apportion
appraisal
appraiser
apprehend
appressed
approbate
asparagus
aspartate
aspectual
aspersion
asphaltic
asphaltum
aspirator
baptismal
baptistry
bipartite
bipinnate
byproduct
capacious
capacitor
caparison
capillary
capitally
capitular
capitulum
capriccio
Capricorn
capsulate
capsulise
captaincy
captivate
captivity
cephalous
cipollino
copacetic
copartner
copesmate
copestone
copiously
copolymer
coproduce
coprolite
coprology
copsewood
copyright
cupbearer
cupelling
cuplichen
cyprinoid
departure
depasture
dependant
dependent
depiction
depictive
depletion
depletive
deposable
depositor
depravity
deprecate
depredate
depressed
depressor
depthbomb
depthless
depurator
dipcircle
dipeptide
diphthong
diplomacy
diplomate
dipswitch
dipterous
dopefiend
duplicate
duplicity
empathise
empennage
emphasise
emphysema
empirical
emplastic
emptiness
empyreuma
esperance
Esperanto
espionage
esplanade
espousals
euphemise
euphemism
euphonise
euphonium
euphorbia
expansile
expansion
expansive
expatiate
expectant
expecting
expedient
expediter
expellent
expelling
expensive
expertise
expiation
expiatory
explainer
expletive
expletory
explicate
exploiter
explosion
explosive
expositor
expounder
expressly
expulsion
expulsive
expurgate
foppishly
haphazard
haplessly
haplology
happening
happiness
hepatitis
heptaglot
heptarchy
hippocras
hopefully
hopscotch
hypallage
hyperbola
hyperbole
hypergamy
hypericum
hyperopia
hyperopic
hypethral
hyphenate
hypnoidal
hypnology
hypnotise
hypnotism
hypnotist
hypoblast
hypocaust
hypocotyl
hypocrisy
hypocrite
hypogeous
hypomania
hypomanic
hyponasty
hypostyle
hypotaxis
impaction
impartial
impassion
impassive
impastoed
impatiens
impatient
impeccant
impedance
impelling
impendent
impending
imperator
imperfect
imperious
impetrate
impetuous
impiously
impleader
implement
impletion
implicate
impliedly
implosion
implosive
impluvium
impolitic
important
importune
impostume
imposture
impotence
impotency
impounder
imprecate
imprecise
impresari
improbity
impromptu
improvise
imprudent
impudence
impulsion
impulsive
impulsory
imputable
inpatient
inpouring
japanning
Keplerian
lapideous
Laplander
lapstrake
lapstreak
leptosome
lipreader
lophodont
mepacrine
naphthene
napthalic
nepenthes
nephalism
nephalist
nepheline
nephelite
nephology
nephritic
nephritis
nephrosis
Neptunian
neptunium
Nipponese
opponency
opportune
opposable
oppressor
oppugnant
orphanage
Orpington
paperback
paperclip
papergirl
paperthin
paperwork
papeterie
papillary
papillate
papilloma
papillose
papillote
pepperbox
pepperpot
peptonise
pipedream
pipeorgan
pipestone
pipsqueak
popliteal
poppycock
poppyhead
popularly
pupillage
pupillary
puppeteer
puppyhood
rapacious
rapidfire
rapidness
raptorial
rapturous
reparable
repayable
repayment
repechage
repellant
repellent
repelling
repentant
repertory
replenish
repletion
replicate
reportage
reposeful
repossess
repotting
reprehend
represent
repressor
reprieval
reprimand
reprobate
reprocess
reproduce
reptilian
republish
repudiate
repugnant
repulsion
repulsive
reputable
reputably
reputedly
Ripuarian
sapanwood
sapheaded
sapiently
sapodilla
sappiness
sapraemia
sapraemic
separable
separably
separates
separator
Sephardic
Sephardim
sepiolite
septation
September
septemvir
septenary
septennia
septicity
septuplet
sepulcher
sepulchre
sepulture
siphonage
siphuncle
sophister
sophistic
sophistry
sophomore
soporific
soppiness
sopranino
sopranist
superable
supercool
superfine
superfuse
superheat
supernova
superpose
supersede
superstar
supervene
supervise
supinator
suppliant
supporter
supposing
suppurate
supremacy
supremely
syphilise
syphiloid
tapdancer
tepidness
tipsiness
tipstaves
tophamper
topiarian
topiarist
topically
toponymal
toponymic
typemetal
typewrite
typhlitis
typhoidal
typically
umpteenth
unpegging
unpeopled
unplugged
unplumbed
unpointed
unpopular
uppercase
uppermost
vapidness
vaporable
vaporific
vaporiser
vapouring
vapourish
wapentake
zapateado
acquiesce
acquittal
acquitted
Esquimaux
exquisite
inquiline
liquation
liquefier
liquidate
liquidise
liquidity
liquorice
liquorish
loquacity
maquisard
piquantly
requester
requisite
Roquefort
sequacity
sequester
sequestra
sequinned
abradable
abrogator
abruption
acrobatic
acropetal
acropolis
acroteria
adrenalin
aerialist
aeriality
aerobatic
aerobiont
aerodrome
aerograph
aerolitic
aerometer
aerometry
aerophyte

aeroplane
aerospace
Afrikaans
Afrikaner
agreeable
agreeably
agreement
agriology
agrologic
agronomic
aircooled
airjacket
airminded
airstream
airworthy
airyfairy
arrearage
arrestant
arresting
arriviste
arrogance
arrowhead
arrowroot
arrowwood
arrowworm
atrocious
auricular
barathrum
Barbadian
barbarian
barbarise
barbarism
barbarity
barbarous
barbitone
barcarole
barefaced
bargainer
bargepole
barkeeper
barleymow
barmbrack
Barmecide
barnacled
barnstorm
barograph
barometer
barometry
baronetcy
barracker
barracoon
barracuda
barrelful
barrelled
barricade
barricado
barrister
bartender
berberine
bergamask
berkelium
berserker
beryllium
birchbark
birdbrain
birdsfoot
birdsnest
birdtable
birdwatch
birthmark
birthrate
birthwort
bordereau
borrowing
burdenous
burlesque
burliness
burnedout
burningly
burnisher
burrstone
bursarial
carambola
carbamate
carbamide
carbonado
carbonate
carbonise
carbuncle
carburise
carcinoma
cardboard
cardsharp
careerism
careerist
carefully
caretaker
carfuffle
Caribbean
Carmelite
carnality
carnation
carnelian
carnitine
carnivore
carolling
carpenter
carpentry
carpetbag
carpeting
carpingly
carpology
carrageen
carrefour
carronade
carryover
Cartesian
carthorse
cartilage
cartogram
cartology
cartouche
cartridge
cartulary
cartwheel
caryopses
caryopsis
cerastium
ceratodus
cerebella
cerebrate
cerecloth
cerograph
certainly
certainty
certified
certifier
certitude
cerussite
Christian
Christmas
chromatic
chromatin
chronical
chronicle
chrysalid
chrysalis
circadian
circinate
circuitry
circulate
cirrhosis
cirripede
coralline
corallite
coralloid
corbeille
corbelled
corbicula
cordelier
cordially
cordiform
corduroys
coreopsis
coriander
corkscrew
cormorant
cornbrash
corncrake
cornelian
cornemuse
cornerboy
cornerman
cornetist
cornfield
cornflour
cornopean
cornsalad
cornstalk
cornstone
corollary
coroneted
corporate
corporeal
corposant
corpulent
corpuscle
corralled
corrasion
correctly
corrector
correlate
corrosion
corrosive
corrugate
corrupter
corruptly
corticate
corticoid
cortisone
coruscant
coruscate
Corybants
corydalis
corymbose
coryphaei
curbstone
curettage
curialism
curiosity
curiously
curliness
curlpaper
currently
curricula
currishly
currycomb
cursively
cursorial
cursorily
curstness
curtilage
curvature
curveting
curvetted
curviform
daredevil
dartboard
Darwinian
Darwinism
Darwinist
derivable
dermatoid
derringdo
derringer
direction
directive
directory
directrix
direfully
dirigible
dirigisme
dirtiness
dirttrack
dorbeetle
dormition
dormitory
duralumin
earliness
earnestly
earthborn
earthling
earthstar
earthward
earthwork
earthworm
earwigged
ecritoire
egregious
egression
eirenicon
enrapture
enrolling
enrolment
erratical
erroneous
errorless
eurhythmy
farandole
farestage
farmhouse
farmstead
farseeing
ferocious
ferrotype
ferryboat
fertilely
fertilise
fertility
fervently
firealarm
fireblast
firebrand
firebreak
firebrick
firecrest
firedrake
firedrill
fireeater
fireguard
firehouse
fireirons
firelight
fireplace
firepower
fireproof
firestone
firewater
fireworks
firmament
firstborn
firstfoot
firsthand
firstling
firstrate
foragecap
forasmuch
forbidden
forcefeed
forceland
forceless
forcemeat
forcepump
foreboder
forebrain
forecaddy
foreclose
forecourt
forefront
foregoing
foreigner
forejudge
foreknown
forenamed
forereach
foreshore
foreshown
foresight
forespeak
forestage
forestall
foretaste
foretoken
forewoman
forfeiter
forgather
forgeable
forgetful
forgiving
forgotten
forlornly
formalise
formalism
formalist
formality
formation
formative
formatted
formicary
formicate
formulaic
formulary
formulate
formulise
fornicate
forsythia
fortalice
forthwith
fortifier
fortitude
fortnight
fortunate
fortyfive
forwander
forwarder
forwardly
furbisher
furcation
furiously
furnisher
furniture
furtherer
furtively
gardening
garderobe
garibaldi
garmented
garnishee
garniture
garreteer
garrotter
garrulity
garrulous
gerfalcon
geriatric
germander
germanely
germanise
Germanish
Germanism
Germanist
germanium
germicide
germinate
germplasm
germproof
gerundial
gerundive
girandole
girlishly
Girondist
gorblimey
gorgonian
gorgonise
gyrfalcon
gyroplane
gyroscope
haranguer
harbinger
harbourer
hardboard
hardcover
hardihood
hardiment
hardiness
hardnosed
hardshell
haresfoot
harlequin
harmaline
harmattan
harmfully
harmonica
harmonics
harmonise
harmonist
harmonium
harmotome
harpooner
harquebus
Harrovian
harrowing
harshness
hartshorn
harvester
Heraclean
herbalist
herbarium
herbicide
herbivore
herborise
Herculean
Hercynian
hereabout
hereafter
heretical
hereunder
heritable
hermitage
herniated
herpetoid
hircosity
hirsutism
hirundine
horehound
horniness
hornstone
hornwrack
horologer
horologic
horoscope
horoscopy
horseback
horsebean
horsehair
horsehide
horseless
horsemint
horseplay
horsepond
horseshoe
horsetail
horsewhip
horsiness
hortation
hortative
hortatory
hortensia
hurricane
hurriedly
hurtfully
irradiant
irradiate
irreality
irregular
irrigable
irrigator
irritable
irritably
irruption
irruptive
Israelite
jargonise
jarringly
jerkiness
Jordanian
juridical
jurywoman
karabiner
karyotype
keratitis
keratosis
kerbstone
kerfuffle
kurrajong
larcenist
larcenous
lardycake
largeness
larghetto
larvicide
laryngeal
lorgnette
luridness
lyrically
marcasite
marcelled
marchpane
marchpast
marestail
margarine
margarite
marginate
marihuana
marijuana
maritally
marketday
marketing
marlstone
marmalade
marmoreal
marquetry
marrowfat
marshalcy
marshland
marshwort
marsupial
marsupium
martially
Martinmas
martyrdom
martyrise
marvelled
mercaptan
mercenary
mercerise
merciless
mercurial
mercurous
merganser
meropidan
merriment
merriness

mirkiness
mirthless
moraceous
moraliser
moratoria
morbidity
mordacity
mordantly
Mormonism
morphemic
morrisman
mortality
mortgagee
mortgager
mortgagor
mortician
murderess
murderous
murkiness
murmurous
myriorama
myrmecoid
myrobalan
narcissus
narcotine
narcotise
narcotism
narration
narrative
narratory
nervation
nervature
nerveless
nerviness
nervously
normalise
normality
Normanise
Normanism
normative
northeast
northerly
northland
northmost
northward
northwest
Norwegian
nurseling
nursemaid
orrisroot
ourselves
parabasis
parabolic
parachute
Paraclete
paradisal
paragraph
paralalia
paralexia
paralysis
paralytic
paramatta
paramedic
parameter
paramorph
paramount
paranoiac
paranymph
parapeted
parapodia
parasitic
parataxis
parathion
parbuckle
parcelled
parcenary
parchment
paregoric
parentage
parfleche
parhelion
parleyvoo
parlously
parochial
parotitis
parquetry
parrakeet
parricide
Parseeism
parsimony
parsonage
partially
partition
partitive
partridge
percaline
perceiver
perchance
percheron
percolate
perdition
peregrine
perennate
perennial
perfectly
perfector
perfervid
perforate
performer
perfumery
perfumier
perfusion
perfusive
pergunnah
periclase
pericycle
peridotic
perihelia
perilling
perilymph
perimeter
perimorph
perinatal
periodate
peripatus
periphery
periplast
periscope
perishing
perisperm
peristome
peristyle
perkiness
permanent
permeable
permeance
permitted
permitter
permutate
perpetual
persecute
persevere
persimmon
personage
personate
personify
personnel
persuader
pertinent
pertussis
pervasion
pervasive
perverter
phrenetic
piratical
pirouette
porbeagle
porcelain
porcupine
poriferal
poriferan
porphyria
porringer
portative
porterage
portfolio
porticoes
portolano
portrayal
portrayer
portreeve
portulaca
purchaser
pureblood
purgation
purgative
purgatory
puritanic
purloiner
purposely
purposive
purpureal
purringly
purselike
pursiness
pursuable
pursuance
purulence
purulency
pyracanth
pyramidal
pyramidic
pyramidon
pyrethrum
pyridoxin
pyrogenic
pyrolater
pyrolatry
pyrolysis
pyrolytic
pyromancy
pyromania
pyrometer
pyrometry
pyroscope
pyroxylin
rareeshow
rerebrace
rerelease
reremouse
rerunning
Saracenic
sarcastic
sarcocarp
sarcomata
Sardinian
sargassos
Sarmation
sartorial
sartorius
scraggily
scrambler
scramming
scrapbook
scrapheap
scrapiron
scrappily
scrapping
scrapyard
scratcher
scratches
screecher
screening
screwball
screwbolt
screwpile
screwpine
screwworm
scribbler
scrimmage
scrimpily
scrimshaw
scripture
scrivener
scrollsaw
scrounger
scrubbing
scruffily
scrumhalf
scrummage
scrutable
scrutator
serenader
sergeancy
serialise
serialism
serialist
seriality
seriately
sericeous
serigraph
serinette
seriously
serjeancy
serjeanty
sermonise
serotonin
serpentry
serranoid
serration
serrefile
serrulate
serviette
servilely
servility
servitude
sgraffiti
sgraffito
shredding
shrewmice
shrinkage
shrubbery
shrugging
sorbapple
Sorbonist
sorceress
sorcerous
soritical
sorriness
sorrowful
sortilege
sortition
sprigging
sprightly
sprigtail
springald
springbok
springily
springing
springlet
sprinkler
spritsail
straggler
strangely
strangler
strangles
straphang
strapless
strappado
strapping
strapwork
strapwort
stratagem
strategic
strawworm
streakily
streaking
streamlet
streetcar
strenuous
stressful
stretcher
strewment
striation
striature
stricture
stridence
stridency
stringent
stripling
stripping
strobilae
strobilus
stromatic
strongarm
strongbox
strongish
strongyle
strontium
stropping
strouding
structure
struggler
strumitis
strumming
strutting
strychnic
surcharge
surcingle
surculose
surfacing
surfboard
surfeiter
surficial
surgeoncy
surliness
surmullet
surpliced
surprisal
surrender
surrogate
surveying
syringeal
tarantara
tarantass
tarantism
tarantula
taraxacum
tardiness
Targumist
tarpaulin
tarragona
Tartarean
Tartarian
tartishly
Tartufian
Tartufism
teratogen
terebinth
terebrant
termagant
terminate
terminism
terminist
termitary
ternately
terramara
terramare
terrarium
territory
terrorise
terrorism
terrorist
terseness
tervalent
thralldom
thrashing
threefold
threesome
threnodic
threshold
thriftily
thrilling
throatily
throbbing
thrombose
throttler
throughly
throwaway
throwback
throwster
thrumming
tiredness
tirewoman
torchrace
torchsong
toreutics
tormentil
tormentor
torpidity
torridity
torsional
tortrices
tortricid
torturous
turbidity
turbinate
turboprop
turbulent
Turcomans
turgently
turgidity
Turkomans
turnabout
turnround
turnstile
turnstone
turntable
turpitude
turquoise
tyrannise
tyrannous
Ukrainian
unreality
unreserve
unruffled
uprightly
utricular
Varangian
variation
varicella
variegate
variolate
variolite
varioloid
variolous
variously
varnisher
veracious
verandaed
veratrine
verbalise
verbalism
verbalist
verbicide
verbosely
verbosity
verdantly
verdigris
veridical
veritable
veritably
vermicide
vermicule
vermiform
vermifuge
vermilion
verminate
verminous
vernalise
vernation
verrucose
verrucous
versatile
versifier
versiform
versional
vertebrae
vertebral
virescent
Virgilian
virginals
virginity
virgulate
viricidal
virtually
virtuosic
virtuosos
virulence
virulency
voracious
vorticism
vorticist
vorticity
vorticose
warblefly
warbonnet
warehouse
warmonger
warningly
warrantee
warranter
warrantor
wartcress
werwolves
wiredrawn
wiregauze
wirephoto
Worcester
wordiness
wordsmith
workbench
workhorse
workhouse
workmanly
workpiece
worktable
workwoman
worldling
worldwide
wormeaten
wormwheel
worriedly
worriment
worrisome
worrywart
worthless
xeromorph
xerophile
xerophily
xerophyte
yardstick
Yorkshire
zirconium
abscissae
abscissas
absconder
abseiling
absorbent
absorbing
abstainer
abstinent
absurdism

absurdist
absurdity
adsorbate
adsorbent
aesthesia
aesthesis
aesthetic
aestivate
anschluss
arsenical
arsenious
assailant
assaulter
assayable
assembler
assertion
assertive
assiduity
assiduous
assistant
associate
assonance
assuasive
assumable
assumably
assumpsit
assurance
assuredly
assurgent
auspicate
austenite
austerely
austerity
bashfully
basically
basilican
basipetal
basketful
basrelief
bastardly
bastinade
bastinado
bastioned
besetment
besetting
beslobber
besotting
bespangle
bespatter
bestially
bestirred
bisection
bishopric
bismillah
boskiness
bossiness
bushcraft
bushelful
bushiness
bushwhack
bystander
caseation
Cassandra
cassareep
cassaripe
cassation
casserole
cassimere
cassoulet
cassowary
Castalian
castanets
castellan
castigate
Castilian
Castroism
casuarina
casuistic
casuistry
cessation
cisalpine
coseismal
coseismic
cosmogeny
cosmogony
cosmology
cosmonaut
cosmorama
costively
costumier
cuspidate
custodial
custodian
customary
customise
cystocarp
cystolith
cystotomy
dashboard
dashingly
dastardly
descended
describer
desecrate
desertion
desiccant
desiccate
designate
designing
desirable
desirably
desolater
desolator
desperado
desperate
despoiler
despotism
destitute
destroyer
desuetude
desultory
disaccord
disaffect
disaffirm
disannual
disappear
disarming
disavouch
disavowal
disbarred
disbelief
disbranch
disbudded
disburden
disbursal
discalced
discarder
discerner
discharge
discoidal
discolour
discomfit
discommon
discourse
discovert
discovery
discredit
disembark
disembody
disengage
disentail
disentomb
disesteem
disfavour
disfigure
disforest
disgracer
dishcloth
dishclout
dishfaced
dishonest
dishonour
dishwater
disinfect
disinfest
dislocate
dismantle
dismember
dismissal
disoblige
disorient
disparage
disparate
disparity
dispelled
dispenser
dispeople
dispersal
disperser
displease
disposure
dispraise
disputant
disregard
disrelish
disrepair
disrepute
dissector
disseisin
dissemble
dissenter
dissident
dissipate
dissocial
dissolute
dissonant
dissuader
distantly
distemper
distilled
distiller
distraint
disturbed
disturber
dosimeter
dosimetry
dosshouse
duskiness
dustcover
dustiness
dustsheet
dyscrasia
dysentery
dysgenics
dyspepsia
dyspeptic
dysphagia
dysphagic
dysphonia
dysphoria
dysphoric
dysplasia
dyspnoeic
dystrophy
easefully
eastbound
Eastender
easterner
eastwards
easygoing
ecstasise
elsewhere
ensheathe
erstwhile
essential
exsertile
exsertion
exservice
exsiccate
exsuccous
fasciated
fascicled
fascicule
fasciculi
fascinate
Fascistic
fashioner
fastening
fastigium
festinate
festively
festivity
festology
fisherman
fishiness
fishplate
fishslice
fishyback
fissility
fissipede
fistulous
fossicker
fossilise
fossorial
fosterage
fusillade
fusionist
fussiness
fustigate
fustiness
gasconade
gasfitter
gasholder
gasmantle
gasometer
gaspereau
gastraeum
gastritis
gastropod
gastrulae
gestalten
gestation
gestatory
gospeller
gossamery
gushingly
gustation
gustative
gustatory
gustiness
Hashemite
Hashimite
hastiness
hesitance
hesitancy
hesitator
Hesperian
hessonite
hispidity
histamine
histidine
histogeny
histogram
histology
historian
hosteller
hostilely
hostility
husbandly
husbandry
huskiness
hysterics
hysteroid
insatiate
insatiety
inscriber
insectary
insectile
insensate
insertion
inservice
insetting
inshallah
insidious
insincere
insinuate
insipidly
insistent
insolence
insoluble
insolubly
insolvent
insomniac
inspanned
inspector
instanter
instantly
instigate
instilled
institute
insularly
insulator
insurable
insurance
insurgent
issueless
itsybitsy
jessamine
jesuitise
jesuitism
josshouse
jossstick
justiciar
justifier
lassitude
lastditch
lastingly
lispingly
lissomely
Listerism
lustfully
lustihood
lustiness
lysimeter
masculine
masochism
masochist
masonried
Masoretic
massagist
massiness
massively
masterdom
masterful
masterkey
masticate
mescaline
mesentery
mesmerise
mesmerism
mesmerist
mesoblast
mesogloea
mesomorph
mesophyll
mesophyte
messenger
messianic
messieurs
messiness
misadvise
misassign
misbecome
misbehave
misbelief
misbeseem
miscegene
miscegine
mischance
miscreant
miscreate
misdemean
misdirect
misemploy
miserable
miserably
misesteem
misfeasor
misgiving
misgovern
misguided
mishandle
mishanter
misinform
misleared
mismanage
misoneism
misoneist
mispickel
misreckon
misreport
misshapen
missioner
mistigris
mistiness
mistletoe
mistyeyed
mosaicism
mosaicist
mosaicked
moschatel
mosquitos
mossagate
mossgrown
muscadine
muscarine
muscleman
muscovado
muscovite
musically
musichall
musketeer
muskiness
muskmelon
Mussulman
mustachio
musteline
mustiness
mystagogy
mysticism
mystifier
naseberry
nastiness
nescience
Nestorian
nosebleed
noseflute
nosepiece
nostalgia
nostalgic
nostology
nystagmic
nystagmus
oasthouse
obscenely
obscenity
obscurant
obscurely
obscurity
obsecrate
obsequent
obsequial
obsequies
observant
obsession
obsessive
obsolesce
obstetric
obstinacy
obstinate
oesophagi
oestrogen
onsetting
onslaught
opsimathy
ossicular
ossifrage
oysterbed
oysterman
pasodoble
passenger
passerine
passersby
passional
passivate
passively
passivity
pastedown
pasticcio
pastiness
pastorale
pastorate
pasturage
pessimism
pessimist
pesthouse
pesticide
pestilent
pestology
piscatory
pisciform
pisolitic
pistachio
pistoleer
pistolled
possessed
possessor
postentry
posterior
posterity
posthaste
posthorse
posthouse
posticous
postilion
postnasal
postnatal
postulant
postulate
pushchair
pushiness
pushingly
pussyfoot
pustulate
pustulous
rascaldom
rascalism
rascality
raspatory
raspberry
raspingly
resalable
resection
resentful
reserpine
reservist
reservoir
resetting
reshuffle
residence
residency
residuary
resilient

resistant
resistive
resitting
resoluble
resolvent
resonance
resonator
resorbent
resources
respecter
responder
restfully
restiform
restitute
restively
restraint
resultant
resultful
resumable
resurface
resurgent
resurrect
riskiness
rosaceous
roseapple
roseately
rosenoble
rosewater
rosinweed
rostellum
rushlight
russeting
Russophil
rusticate
rusticity
rustiness
rustproof
sasquatch
sassafras
Sassanian
Sassenach
sessional
sestertia
Sisyphean
sostenuto
suspender
suspensor
suspicion
sustainer
susurrant
systaltic
taskforce
Tasmanian
tasselled
tasteless
tastiness
tessitura
testament
testation
testatrix
testdrive
testifier
testimony
testiness
unsavoury
unsayable
unscathed
unselfish
unsettled
unshackle
unsheathe
unsighted
unsightly
unskilful
unskilled
unsmiling
unsoundly
unsparing
unspotted
unstopped
unstudied
unsuccess
unsullied
upsetting
vasectomy
vasomotor
vassalage
vastitude
vesicular
vestibule
vestigial
vestigium
vestiture
vestryman
viscerate
viscidity
viscosity
viscounty
viscously
visionary
visionist
visitable
visitress
visualise
washbasin
washboard
washcloth
washedout
washerman
washhouse
washiness
washstand
waspishly
wassailer
wasteland
wasteness
wastepipe
westbound
westering
westerner
westwards
wisecrack
wishfully
wistfully
yesterday
zestfully
actinozoa
activator
actualise
actuality
actuarial
actuation
aetiology
aftercare
afterclap
afterglow
afterlife
aftermath
aftermost
afternoon
aftertime
afterword
aitchbone
alterable
altercate
alternant
alternate
altimeter
altricial
antarctic
antefixal
antenatal
antennary
antennule
anthelion
anthemion
anthocyan
anthology
anthozoan
anthracic
anthropic
anticline
anticodon
antidotal
antigenic
antiknock
antimonic
antinodal
antinomic
antinovel
antipasto
antipathy
antiphony
antipodal
antipodes
antiquary
antiquate
antiquity
antiserum
antitoxic
antitoxin
antitrade
antitrust
antivenin
antiviral
artemisia
arteriole
arteritis
arthritic
arthritis
arthropod
arthrosis
Arthurian
artichoke
articular
artificer
artillery
artlessly
asthmatic
astraddle
astrakhan
astrocyte
astrodome
astrolabe
astrology
astronaut
astronomy
attainder
attempter
attendant
attention
attentive
attenuate
attractor
attribute
attrition
autarchic
autarkist
authentic
authoress
authorial
authorise
authority
autoclave
autocracy
autocross
autocycle
autograft
autograph
autolysis
autolytic
automatic
automaton
autonomic
autopilot
autoroute
autosomal
autotelic
autotroph
bathhouse
batholite
batholith
Bathonian
bathybius
battalion
battening
battiness
battleaxe
battlecry
bethought
betrothal
betrothed
bitterish
botanical
bottlefed
bottleful
butadiene
butcherer
butcherly
butterbur
buttercup
butterfat
butterfly
butterine
butternut
buttinsky
buttygang
catabolic
cataclasm
cataclysm
catalepsy
catalexes
catalexis
catalogue
catalyser
catalyses
catalysis
catalytic
catamaran
catamount
cataplasm
cataplexy
catarhine
catarrhal
catatonia
catatonic
catchable
catchment
catchpole
catchpoll
catchword
catechise
catechism
catechist
caterwaul
Catharism
Catharist
catharses
catharsis
cathartic
cathectic
cathedral
catoptric
cattaloes
cattiness
cattleman
cetaceous
chthonian
citizenly
citizenry
citystate
cotangent
cothurnus
cotillion
cotyledon
cutaneous
cuticular
cutinised
cutthroat
cuttysark
Cytherean
cytolysis
cytoplasm
cytotoxic
cytotoxin
detection
detective
detention
detergent
determent
determine
deterrent
deterring
detersion
detersive
dethroner
detonator
detractor
detriment
detrition
detrusion
dithyramb
dittander
dittology
dottiness
duteously
dutifully
ectoblast
ectogenic
ectomorph
ectophyte
ectoplasm
entelechy
enterable
enteritis
entertain
enthymeme
entoblast
entophyte
entourage
entrammel
entrapped
entrechat
entrecote
entremets
establish
estaminet
Esthonian
estimable
estimator
estoppage
estopping
estranger
estrapade
estuarian
estuarine
eutectoid
euthenics
eutherian
eutrophic
extempore
extendant
extensile
extension
extensity
extensive
extenuate
externals
extirpate
extolling
extolment
extorsive
extortion
extortive
extractor
extradite
extravert
extremely
extremism
extremist
extremity
extricate
extrinsic
extrovert
extrusion
extrusive
fatefully
fatheaded
fatidical
fatigable
fattiness
fatuously
fatwitted
fetichism
fetichist
fetidness
fetishism
fetishist
fittingly
gatecrash
gatehouse
gathering
getatable
Gothamite
gothicise
Gothicism
gutsiness
guttation
guttering
hatchback
hatchling
hatchment
hatefully
hetaerism
hetairism
heterodox
heteronym
heterosis
hitchhike
Hitlerism
Hitlerite
hotheaded
Hottentot
integrand
integrant
integrate
integrity
intellect
intendant
intensely
intensify
intension
intensity
intensive
intention
interbred
intercede
intercept
intercity
intercrop
interdict
interface
interfere
interfile
interflow
interfuse
interject
interknit
interlace
interlard
interleaf
interline
interlink
interlock
interlope
interlude
interment
internode
interpage
interplay
interpose
interpret
interring
interrupt
intersect
intervein
intervene
interview
interwind
interwove
interzone
intestacy
intestate
intestine
intorsion
intricacy
intricate
intrigant
intriguer
intrinsic
introduce
introject
introvert
intrusion
intrusive
intuition
intuitive
intumesce
ittybitty
jetsetter
jetstream
jitterbug
katabasis
katabatic
katabolic
katharsis
kitchener
kittenish
kittiwake
latecomer
laterally
latescent
lathering
latitancy
latterday
latticing
lethality
lethargic
letterbox
lettering
literally
literatim
literator
literatus
litheness
lithesome
lithology
lithopone
lithotomy
litigable
litigious
litterbin
litterbug
liturgics
liturgist
lotusland
matchless
matchlock
matchwood
maternity
mateyness
matriarch
matricide

matricula
matrimony
matronage
matronise
mattamore
matutinal
metabolic
metalline
metalling
metallise
metalloid
metalwork
metameric
metaphase
metaplasm
meteorist
meteorite
meteoroid
methadone
metheglin
methodise
Methodism
Methodist
methought
methylate
methylene
metonymic
metricate
metrician
metricise
metricist
metrology
metronome
Mithraism
Mithraist
mitigable
mitigator
mitraille
motheaten
motherwit
mothproof
motivator
motocross
motorable
motorbike
motorboat
motorcade
mutagenic
mutilator
mutualise
mutualism
mutualist
mutuality
mythicise
mythicism
mythicist
mythology
natheless
natrolite
nattiness
naturally
netveined
netwinged
nitpicker
nitratine
nitration
notabilia
notedness
notepaper
notionist
notochord
notoriety
notorious
nutriment
nutrition
nutritive
nuttiness
nutweevil
obtention
obtrusion
obtrusive
obturator
octachord
octagonal
octahedra
octameter
octastyle
octennial
octillion
Octobrist
octopodes
octostyle
ontogenic
ontologic
optically
optometer
optometry
optophone
orthodoxy
orthoepic
ostensive
osteoderm
osteogeny
osteology
osteopath
ostracise
ostracism
Ostrogoth
outbacker
outermost
outfitter
outgiving
outgoings
outgrowth
outgunned
outlander
outnumber
outputted
outridden
outrigger
outskirts
outspoken
outspread
outwardly
outwitted
outworker
patchouli
patchouly
patchwork
patellate
paternity
pathogeny
pathology
patiently
patinated
patriarch
patrician
patricide
patrimony
patriotic
patristic
patrolled
patroller
patrolman
patrology
patronage
patroness
patronise
petaurist
petechiae
petechial
petersham
pethidine
petiolate
petiolule
petroleum
petrology
petticoat
pettiness
pettishly
pettitoes
petulance
petulancy
phthalein
pitchdark
pitchfork
pitchpipe
piteously
pithecoid
pithiness
pitifully
pituitary
pityingly
potassium
potboiler
potentate
potential
potholing
pothunter
potpourri
putridity
ratepayer
rationale
rationing
retaliate
retardant
retention
retentive
rethought
retiarius
reticence
reticency
reticular
reticulum
retinitis
retinulae
retinular
retortion
retoucher
retractor
retrieval
retriever
retrocede
retrodden
retroflex
retroject
retrousse
retrovert
ritualise
ritualism
ritualist
rotatable
rotundity
ruthenium
ruthfully
satanical
satellite
satiation
satinbird
satinette
satinspar
satinwood
satirical
saturable
saturator
Saturnian
saturnine
saturnism
setaceous
setsquare
situation
sitzkrieg
sottishly
sutteeism
suturally
tattiness
tattooist
tetradite
tetragram
tetralogy
tetrapody
tetrarchy
titillate
titledeed
titlepage
titration
tittivate
tittlebat
tittuping
tittupped
titularly
totaliser
totalling
totempole
tutorship
Uitlander
ultimatum
ultrahigh
untenable
unthought
unthrifty
untimeous
untouched
untrodden
untrussed
untutored
urticaria
utterable
utterance
utterless
uttermost
utterness
vaticinal
vetchling
vitellary
vitelline
vitiation
vitiosity
vitriform
vitriolic
Vitruvian
watchable
watchcase
watchfire
watchword
waterbath
waterbuck
waterbutt
watercart
watercool
waterfall
waterflea
waterfowl
watergate
waterhole
waterleaf
waterless
waterlily
waterline
watermark
watermill
waterpipe
watershed
waterside
waterweed
waterworn
wattmeter
witchetty
witchhunt
witchmeal
withdrawn
withering
witherite
withstand
withstood
witlessly
witticism
wittiness
wittingly
ytterbium
abundance
abusively
acuminate
adulation
adulatory
adulterer
adulthood
adultness
adumbrate
aluminate
aluminise
aluminium
aluminous
amusement
amusingly
aquaplane
aquarelle
aqueously
aquilegia
avuncular
bluebeard
blueberry
blueblack
bluegrass
bluepoint
blueprint
bluestone
bluffness
blunderer
bluntness
blushless
blusterer
boulevard
boundless
bounteous
bountiful
bouquetin
bourgeois
brummagem
brushfire
brushwood
brushwork
brusquely
brutalise
brutalism
brutality
brutishly
Caucasian
causality
causation
causative
causeless
cauterise
churching
churchman
clubbable
clubhouse
couchette
coumarone
countable
countdown
countless
countship
courgette
courtcard
courteous
courtesan
courtroom
courtship
courtyard
couturier
crucially
cruciform
crudeness
cruellest
crushable
crustacea
dauntless
deuterate
deuterium
diurnally
doubleton
doubtable
doubtless
doughtily
Doukhobor
drugstore
druidical
drummajor
drumstick
drunkenly
ebullient
ecumenism
education
educative
elucidate
elusively
elutriate
emulation
emulative
emulously
emunctory
enucleate
enumerate
enunciate
equaliser
equalling
equipment
equipoise
equipping
equisetum
equitable
equitably
equivocal
equivoque
eruciform
eruditely
erudition
esurience
esuriency
exuberant
exuberate
exudation
exudative
exultance
exultancy
faultless
faunistic
feudalise
feudalism
feudalist
feudality
feudatory
fluctuant
fluctuate
fluecured
fluoresce
fluorosis
fluorspar
flushness
fluxional
foulbrood
foundling
foundress
fourflush
fourpence
fourpenny
fourscore
fourwheel
fructuate
fructuous
frugality
fruitcake
fruiterer
fruitless
fruittree
frustrate
fruticose
gaucherie
gaudiness
gaugeable
gauleiter
gauntness
gauziness
glucoside
glueyness
glutamate
glutinous
grubscrew
grubstake
gruelling
gruffness
grumbling
Grundyism
haughtily
haustella
haustoria
heuristic
hourglass
houseboat
housebote
housecarl
housecoat
houseflag
household
housekeep
houseleek
houseless
houselled
housemaid
housemate
houseroom
housewife
housework
iguanodon
inunction
inurement
inutility
jaundiced
journeyer
krummhorn
laudation
laudative
laudatory
laughable
laughably
launching
launderer
laundress
laurelled
leucaemia
leucocyte
leucotome
leucotomy
leukaemia
leukaemic
leukocyte
loudmouth
louringly
lousewort
lousiness
loutishly
maulstick
maunderer
mausoleum
mouldable
mountable
mousehole
mousetrap
moustache
mouthpart
mouthwash
naughtily

naumachia
neuralgia
neuralgic
neuration
neuroglia
neurology
neuromata
neuropath
neutrally
nourisher
opulently
opusculum
ovulation
ovulatory
paulownia
pauperise
pauperism
plumbeous
plumbline
plumdamas
plumpness
plumulate
plumulose
plunderer
pluralise
pluralism
pluralist
plurality
plusfours
plushness
plutocrat
plutonian
Plutonism
Plutonist
plutonium
poulterer
pouncebox
poundcake
pourboire
pourpoint
poussette
prudently
prudishly
prurience
pruriency
raucously
raunchily
rauwolfia
roughcast
roughhewn
roughneck
roughness
roughshod
Roumanian
Roumansch
rounceval
roundelay
roundhead
roundness
roundsman
roundworm
rousement
routinely
routinism
routinist
sauceboat
sauceless
saucerful
sauciness
saunterer
sauropoda
Sauternes
sculpture
scuncheon
scutcheon
scutellar
scutellum
scutiform
sluiceway
slumberer
slumbrous
slushfund
smuggling
snubnosed
soubrette
Soudanese
soulfully
soundfilm
soundhole
soundings
soundless
soundness
soundpost
soundwave
soupplate
soupspoon
sourdough
souteneur
Southdown
southeast
southerly
southland
southmost
southward
southwest
souwester
spurwheel
sputterer
squabbler
squalidly
squamosal
squarrose
squashily
squatness
squatting
squeakily
squeamish
squelcher
squibbing
squidding
squinancy
squirarch
squiredom
squirelet
studhorse
studiedly
stupefier
stupidity
stuporous
stutterer
tautology
teutonise
Teutonism
Teutonist
thumbhole
thumbmark
thumbnail
thumbtack
thunderer
touchable
touchdown
touchhole
touchline
touchmark
touchtype
touchwood
toughness
touristic
tournedos
tourneyer
truceless
truculent
truepenny
trumpedup
trumpeter
truncated
truncheon
trunkcall
trunkfish
trunkroad
trussbeam
trustdeed
trustless
truthless
ululation
unusually
usualness
usucapion
vouchsafe
woundless
woundwort
youngling
youngness
youngster
zeugmatic
advantage
advection
advective
Adventism
Adventist
adventive
adventure
adverbial
adversary
adversely
adversity
advertent
advertise
advisable
advisably
advisedly
advocator
alveolate
bevelling
bivalence
bivalency
bivariant
bivariate
cavalcade
cavendish
cavernous
cavilling
civically
civiliser
covalence
covalency
covariant
coverable
coverslip
coverture
covetable
davenport
devaluate
devastate
developer
deviation
devilfish
devilling
devilment
deviously
devisable
devitrify
devotedly
divergent
diversely
diversify
diversion
diversity
diverting
dividable
divisible
divulsion
eavesdrop
enviously
faveolate
favourite
fivepence
fivepenny
gavelkind
governess
haverings
haversack
havocking
invalidly
invariant
invective
inveigler
invention
inventive
inventory
inverness
inversely
inversion
inversive
invertase
invidious
inviolacy
inviolate
invisible
invisibly
involucre
involuted
joviality
juvenilia
lavaliere
Levantine
levelling
levelness
leviathan
leviratic
levitator
Levitical
liverwort
liveryman
livestock
lividness
loveapple
lovechild
lovefeast
lovelight
lovematch
loverless
lovestory
lovetoken
lovingcup
moviegoer
navelwort
navicular
navigable
navigator
nevermore
novelette
noviciate
novitiate
obversely
obversion
obviation
obviously
Pavlovian
pivotable
pivotally
ravelling
ravelment
ravishing
revelator
revelling
reverence
reversely
reversion
revetment
revetting
revictual
revisable
revivable
revocable
revolting
revulsion
revulsive
rivalling
rivalrous
rivelling
riverbank
riverboat
riverhead
riverside
riverweed
savagedom
savourily
sevenfold
seventeen
seventhly
seventies
severable
severally
severalty
severance
sovereign
sovietise
sovietism
vivacious
viverrine
vivianite
vividness
wavefront
waveguide
wavellite
bawdiness
bowerbird
bowlegged
bowstring
bowwindow
cowardice
cowlstaff
dewlapped
dowdiness
dowelling
dowerless
downfield
downgrade
downright
downriver
downstage
downthrow
downwards
Edwardian
enwrapped
enwreathe
fawningly
gawkiness
hawksbill
hawsehole
hawsepipe
howsoever
inwrought
jewellery
jewelweed
lawgiving
lawlessly
lawnmower
lowercase
lowerdeck
lowermost
lowlander
lowliness
lowloader
lowminded
lownecked
mawkishly
newlyweds
newmarket
newsagent
newsflash
newshound
newsiness
newspaper
newsprint
newsstand
Newtonian
nowhither
powerboat
powerdive
powerless
rewarding
rewritten
rowantree
rowdiness
tawniness
towelling
townhouse
townscape
townsfolk
unwearied
unweeting
unwelcome
unwilling
unwinking
unwitting
unwomanly
unwrapped
unwritten
unwrought
vowelless
yawningly
anxiously
auxiliary
boxgirder
boxoffice
buxomness
coxcombry
dexterity
dexterous
dextrally
dextrorse
dixieland
fixedness
foxhunter
hexachord
hexagonal
hexameter
hexaploid
hexastich
hexastyle
Hexateuch
juxtapose
lexically
lixiviate
loxodrome
luxuriant
luxuriate
luxurious
maxillary
maximally
mixedness
myxoedema
noxiously
pixilated
saxifrage
saxophone
sexennial
sexlessly
sexlinked
sextuplet
sexualise
sexuality
sixfooter
sixteenmo
sixteenth
taxidermy
taximeter
taxonomic
taxpaying
textually
toxically
toxophily
vexatious
vexillary
abysmally
amygdalin
amyloidal
amylopsin
arytenoid
asymmetry
asymptote
asyndetic
asyndeton
bayoneted
boycotter
boyfriend
bryophyte
Brythonic
cryogenic
cryoscope
cryoscopy
cryptical
cryptogam
cryptonym
dayschool
dayspring
dryasdust
drysalter
erythrism
erythrite
etymology
flyfisher
flyweight
geyserite
glyceride
glycerine
glycoside
glyptodon
hoydenish
jaywalker
joylessly
Keynesian
maybeetle
mayflower
mayoralty
mayorship
oxygenate
oxygenise
oxygenous
paymaster
paypacket
phycology
phyllopod
phylogeny
physician
physicist
physicked
phytogeny
phytology
phytotomy
phytotron
psychical
psychoses
psychosis
psychotic
rhymester
rhythmics
rhythmise
rhythmist
skydiving
skyjacker
skyrocket
stylebook
styliform
stylishly
stylistic
stylobate
Thyestean
thylacine
thyratron
thyristor

thyroxine
trysquare
voyeurism
wayfaring
waywardly
wayzgoose
bizarrely
Byzantine
dizygotic
dizziness
enzymatic
fuzziness
gazehound
gazetteer
hazardous
jazziness
lazaretto
lazybones
lazytongs
lazzarone
lazzaroni
mezzanine
mezzotint
muzziness
pizzicati
pizzicato
pozzolana
puzzolana
razorback
razorbill
razoredge
razorfish
unzipping
vizierate
vizierial

---

ablatival
abradable
adiabatic
adjacency
advantage
aflatoxin
agnatical
ailanthus
albatross
aleatoric
algarroba
alkaloses
alkalosis
allantois
almandine
alpargata
amianthus
andantino
antarctic
aplanatic
appalling
Appaloosa
apparatus
apparitor
aquaplane
aquarelle
armadillo
ashamedly
asparagus
aspartate
assailant
assaulter
assayable
Atlantean
attainder
audacious
autarchic
autarkist
babacoote
bagatelle
balaclava
balalaika
barathrum
behaviour
bejabbers
belatedly
bicameral
bifarious
bilabiate
bilateral
bipartite
bivalence
bivalency
bivariant
bivariate
bizarrely
bleachery
bleakness
bleareyed
botanical
breadline
breadtree
breakable
breakaway
breakdown
breakeven
breakfast
breakneck
breastpin
breathily
breathing
briarroot
briarwood
broadcast
broadleaf
broadloom
broadness
broadside
broadtail
broadways
broadwise
butadiene
Byzantine
caballero
caballine
caballing
cadastral
cadaveric
calaboose
calabrese
calamanco
calandria
camarilla
canalboat
capacious
capacitor
caparison
carambola
catabolic
cataclasm
cataclysm
catalepsy
catalexes
catalexis
catalogue
catalyser
catalyses
catalysis
catalytic
catamaran
catamount
cataplasm
cataplexy
catarhine
catarrhal
catatonia
catatonic
cavalcade
cedarwood
celandine
cerastium
ceratodus
cetaceous
cheapjack
cheapness
chlamydes
cicatrice
cicatrise
cigarette
cigarillo
cisalpine
cleanness
cleansing
clearance
clearcole
cleareyed
clearness
cleavable
cloakroom
cobaltite
cobaltous
cocainise
cocainism
copacetic
copartner
coralline
corallite
coralloid
cotangent
covalence
covalency
covariant
cowardice
creatable
creatress
creatural
cutaneous
dahabiyah
damascene
debagging
debarment
debarring
debatable
debauched
debauchee
debaucher
decadence
decadency
decagonal
decalcify
decalitre
decalogue
decametre
decapodal
decapodan
decastere
decathlon
defalcate
defaulter
demagogic
demagogue
demandant
demanding
demarcate
departure
depasture
devaluate
devastate
didactics
digastric
dilatable
dilatancy
disaccord
disaffect
disaffirm
disannual
disappear
disarming
disavouch
disavowal
dreamboat
dreamland
dreamless
dreamlike
dryasdust
duralumin
dynamical
dynamiter
eclampsia
eclamptic
Edwardian
eglantine
embarrass
embassage
embattled
embayment
empathise
encaustic
engarland
enrapture
equaliser
equalling
erratical
escalator
escapable
establish
estaminet
eucalypti
eucaryote
excavator
exhauster
expansile
expansion
expansive
expatiate
fabaceous
Falangism
Falangist
fanatical
farandole
filaceous
financial
financier
floatable
foragecap
forasmuch
friarbird
fugacious
fumarolic
gabardine
galactose
galantine
getatable
gigahertz
gigantism
girandole
greasegun
greataunt
greatcoat
greatness
gynaeceum
hamadryad
hamamelis
haranguer
hazardous
hepatitis
Heraclean
hetaerism
hetairism
hexachord
hexagonal
hexameter
hexaploid
hexastich
hexastyle
Hexateuch
hilarious
Himalayan
Holarctic
humankind
humanness
hydathode
hypallage
idealiser
idealless
iguanodon
imbalance
immanence
immanency
impaction
impartial
impassion
impassive
impastoed
impatiens
impatient
incapable
incapably
incarnate
incaution
indagator
infantile
infantine
infatuate
inhalator
inharmony
inpatient
insatiate
insatiety
invalidly
invariant
irradiant
irradiate
Islamitic
Israelite
jacaranda
japanning
Johannine
Judaistic
Judastree
karabiner
katabasis
katabatic
katabolic
keratitis
keratosis
kneadable
Kshatriya
lavaliere
lazaretto
Levantine
locatable
logaoedic
logarithm
macaronic
maharajah
maharanee
maharishi
malachite
maladroit
malanders
malarious
malathion
Malayalam
medallion
medallist
megacycle
megadeath
megahertz
megaphone
megaspore
melanosis
melanotic
melaphyre
melatonin
menadione
menagerie
mepacrine
metabolic
metalline
metalling
metallise
metalloid
metalwork
metameric
metaphase
metaplasm
micaceous
micaslate
minacious
misadvise
misassign
monachism
monarchal
monarchic
monastery
monatomic
moraceous
moraliser
moratoria
mosaicism
mosaicist
mosaicked
mutagenic
nefarious
notabilia
octachord
octagonal
octahedra
octameter
octastyle
oleaceous
olfaction
olfactive
olfactory
ommatidia
organelle
organiser
organstop
organzine
palaestra
palafitte
palankeen
palanquin
palatable
palatably
panatella
parabasis
parabolic
parachute
Paraclete
paradisal
paragraph
paralalia
paralexia
paralysis
paralytic
paramatta
paramedic
parameter
paramorph
paramount
paranoiac
paranymph
parapeted
parapodia
parasitic
parataxis
parathion
pedagogic
pedagogue
pedalling
Pelasgian
petaurist
piratical
pleadable
pleadings
pleasance
podagrous
polariser
pomaceous
potassium
preachify
preachily
preadamic
pyracanth
pyramidal
pyramidic
pyramidon
rapacious
rebaptise
recalesce
recapping
recapture
redaction
refashion
regardant
regardful
remainder
remanence
renascent
reparable
repayable
repayment
resalable
retaliate
retardant
rewarding
rivalling
rivalrous
rocambole
rosaceous
rotatable
rowantree
sabadilla
sagacious
salacious
salangane
Samaritan
sanatoria
sapanwood
Saracenic
satanical
savagedom
sciaenoid
sciagraph
sciamachy
sciascopy
scraggily
scrambler
scramming
scrapbook
scrapheap
scrapiron
scrappily
scrapping
scrapyard
scratcher
scratches
seaanchor
sebaceous
secateurs
selachian
semanteme
semantics
semaphore
separable
separably
separates
separator
setaceous
sgraffiti
sgraffito
shearling
sheatfish
sheathing
skiagraph

ski**a**machy
ski**a**scopy
sod**a**bread
sod**a**water
sol**a**cious
spe**a**kable
spe**a**keasy
spe**a**rfish
spe**a**rhead
spe**a**rmint
spe**a**rside
spe**a**rwort
sph**a**gnous
spl**a**shily
spl**a**yfoot
squ**a**bbler
squ**a**lidly
squ**a**mosal
squ**a**rrose
squ**a**shily
squ**a**tness
squ**a**tting
ste**a**dfast
ste**a**mboat
ste**a**mpipe
ste**a**mship
ste**a**titic
str**a**ggler
str**a**ngely
str**a**ngler
str**a**ngles
str**a**phang
str**a**pless
str**a**ppado
str**a**pping
str**a**pwork
str**a**pwort
str**a**tagem
str**a**tegic
str**a**wworm
sub**a**erial
sub**a**gency
sub**a**lpine
sub**a**ltern
sub**a**rctic
sub**a**stral
sub**a**tomic
sud**a**toria
sug**a**rbeet
sug**a**rcane
sug**a**rloaf
sug**a**rplum
swe**a**rword
swe**a**tband
swe**a**tshop
syb**a**ritic
syn**a**gogal
syn**a**gogue
tac**a**mahac
tar**a**ntara
tar**a**ntass
tar**a**ntism
tar**a**ntula
tar**a**xacum
tel**a**mones
ten**a**cious
ten**a**culum
ter**a**togen
the**a**ndric
the**a**trics
thr**a**lldom
thr**a**shing
tot**a**liser
tot**a**lling
tre**a**chery
tre**a**dmill
tre**a**surer
tre**a**table
tre**a**tment

tri**a**logue
tri**a**tomic
tuf**a**ceous
tyr**a**nnise
tyr**a**nnous
Ukr**a**inian
unb**a**lance
unc**a**nnily
und**a**maged
und**a**unted
une**a**rthly
une**a**table
unf**a**iling
ung**a**llant
unh**a**ppily
unh**a**rness
unm**a**tched
unn**a**mable
unn**a**tural
uns**a**voury
uns**a**yable
usu**a**lness
vag**a**rious
Var**a**ngian
Ved**a**ntist
ver**a**cious
ver**a**ndaed
ver**a**trine
vex**a**tious
vic**a**riate
vic**a**rious
vin**a**ceous
viv**a**cious
voc**a**bular
voc**a**liser
voc**a**lness
vol**a**uvent
vor**a**cious
whe**a**tmeal
wom**a**nhood
wom**a**niser
wom**a**nkind
wom**a**nlike
zap**a**teado
zoi**a**trics
ala**b**aster
ana**b**ioses
ana**b**iosis
ana**b**iotic
ana**b**olism
ana**b**ranch
ara**b**esque
ara**b**icise
Bab**b**ittry
bam**b**oozle
Bar**b**adian
bar**b**arian
bar**b**arise
bar**b**arism
bar**b**arity
bar**b**arous
bar**b**itone
ber**b**erine
bom**b**ardon
bom**b**asine
bom**b**astic
bom**b**azine
bom**b**happy
bom**b**ilate
bom**b**inate
bom**b**proof
bom**b**shell
bom**b**sight
boo**b**ytrap
bul**b**ously
bum**b**lebee
bum**b**ledon
cab**b**alism
cab**b**alist

Cam**b**odian
car**b**amate
car**b**amide
car**b**onado
car**b**onate
car**b**onise
car**b**uncle
car**b**urise
chi**b**ouque
clu**b**bable
clu**b**house
com**b**atant
com**b**ative
com**b**inate
cor**b**eille
cor**b**elled
cor**b**icula
cra**b**bedly
cub**b**yhole
cum**b**rance
cup**b**earer
cur**b**stone
cym**b**alist
cym**b**idium
cym**b**iform
dia**b**lerie
dia**b**olise
dia**b**olism
dia**b**olist
dis**b**arred
dis**b**elief
dis**b**ranch
dis**b**udded
dis**b**urden
dis**b**ursal
dor**b**eetle
dou**b**leton
dou**b**table
dou**b**tless
dum**b**found
edi**b**ility
egg**b**eater
ela**b**orate
exu**b**erant
exu**b**erate
eye**b**right
fim**b**riate
fla**b**ellum
for**b**idden
fur**b**isher
gam**b**adoes
gam**b**olled
geo**b**otany
gib**b**erish
gib**b**osity
gib**b**ously
gla**b**ellae
gla**b**ellar
glo**b**efish
glo**b**osity
gor**b**limey
gru**b**screw
gru**b**stake
ham**b**urger
har**b**inger
har**b**ourer
her**b**alist
her**b**arium
her**b**icide
her**b**ivore
her**b**orise
Hob**b**esian
hum**b**lebee
hum**b**ugged
hus**b**andly
hus**b**andry
ill**b**oding
ina**b**ility
ine**b**riant

ine**b**riate
ine**b**riety
iso**b**athic
jam**b**alaya
ker**b**stone
kib**b**utzim
lam**b**ently
lia**b**ility
Lim**b**urger
Lom**b**ardic
lum**b**ering
lum**b**erman
lum**b**rical
lum**b**ricus
may**b**eetle
mis**b**ecome
mis**b**ehave
mis**b**elief
mis**b**eseem
mor**b**idity
num**b**skull
oil**b**urner
out**b**acker
par**b**uckle
por**b**eagle
pot**b**oiler
pre**b**endal
pro**b**ation
pro**b**ative
pro**b**atory
pro**b**oscis
que**b**racho
qui**b**bling
rab**b**inate
rab**b**inism
rab**b**inist
red**b**reast
Rib**b**onism
rub**b**erise
rud**b**eckia
sab**b**atise
sab**b**atism
san**b**enito
sem**b**lable
sem**b**lably
sem**b**lance
sla**b**sided
sla**b**stone
snu**b**nosed
sob**b**ingly
sor**b**apple
Sor**b**onist
sou**b**rette
sta**b**ilise
sta**b**ility
sta**b**leboy
sta**b**leman
sua**b**ility
sub**b**ranch
sun**b**ather
sun**b**onnet
sun**b**urned
sym**b**iosis
sym**b**iotic
sym**b**olics
sym**b**olise
sym**b**olism
sym**b**olist
sym**b**ology
tam**b**ourin
tim**b**ering
tim**b**erman
tom**b**stone
tra**b**eated
tra**b**ecula
tre**b**uchet
tre**b**ucket
tri**b**adism
tri**b**alism

tri**b**esman
tri**b**ology
tri**b**unate
tri**b**utary
tub**b**iness
tum**b**lebug
tur**b**idity
tur**b**inate
tur**b**oprop
tur**b**ulent
una**b**ashed
ver**b**alise
ver**b**alism
ver**b**alist
ver**b**icide
ver**b**osely
ver**b**osity
via**b**ility
war**b**lefly
war**b**onnet
woe**b**egone
abs**c**issae
abs**c**issas
abs**c**onder
aci**c**ulate
air**c**ooled
ait**c**hbone
ali**c**yclic
ana**c**ruses
ana**c**rusis
ane**c**dotal
ane**c**dotic
ans**c**hluss
api**c**ulate
apo**c**rypha
ara**c**hnoid
ata**c**amite
avo**c**ation
bac**c**hanal
bac**c**hante
bal**c**onied
bar**c**arole
bea**c**hhead
bea**c**hwear
bec**c**afico
bee**c**hfern
bee**c**hmast
bir**c**hbark
bla**c**kball
bla**c**kbird
bla**c**kbuck
bla**c**kcoat
bla**c**kcock
bla**c**kdamp
bla**c**kface
Bla**c**kfeet
bla**c**kfish
bla**c**kflag
Bla**c**kfoot
bla**c**kgame
bla**c**khead
bla**c**kjack
bla**c**klead
bla**c**klist
bla**c**kmail
bla**c**kness
bla**c**kwash
blo**c**kader
blo**c**khead
blo**c**kship
boy**c**otter
bra**c**hiate
bra**c**hyura
bra**c**teate
bra**c**teole
bre**c**ciate
bri**c**abrac
bri**c**kwork
bri**c**kyard

bro**c**hette
buc**c**aneer
but**c**herer
but**c**herly
cae**c**ilian
cal**c**aneal
cal**c**aneum
cal**c**arate
cal**c**icole
cal**c**ifuge
cal**c**ulate
cal**c**ulous
can**c**elled
can**c**erous
car**c**inoma
cat**c**hable
cat**c**hment
cat**c**hpole
cat**c**hpoll
cat**c**hword
Cau**c**asian
cha**c**hacha
che**c**kered
che**c**klist
che**c**kmate
che**c**krein
chi**c**anery
chi**c**kadee
chi**c**karee
chi**c**kling
chi**c**kweed
cho**c**kfull
cho**c**olate
cir**c**adian
cir**c**inate
cir**c**uitry
cir**c**ulate
clo**c**kwise
clo**c**kwork
coa**c**hwork
coc**c**idium
coc**c**ygeal
coe**c**ilian
col**c**annon
col**c**hicum
col**c**othar
con**c**avely
con**c**avity
con**c**eited
con**c**entre
con**c**erned
con**c**erted
con**c**ierge
con**c**iliar
con**c**isely
con**c**ision
con**c**octer
con**c**octor
con**c**ordat
con**c**ourse
con**c**ubine
con**c**urred
cou**c**hette
cox**c**ombry
cra**c**kdown
cra**c**kling
cra**c**ksman
cri**c**keter
cro**c**odile
cru**c**ially
cru**c**iform
cun**c**tator
dan**c**ehall
dea**c**idify
dea**c**oness
des**c**ended
des**c**riber
dia**c**hrony
dia**c**hylom

dia**c**hylum
dia**c**onate
dia**c**ritic
dia**c**tinic
dip**c**ircle
dis**c**alced
dis**c**arder
dis**c**erner
dis**c**harge
dis**c**oidal
dis**c**olour
dis**c**omfit
dis**c**ommon
dis**c**ourse
dis**c**overt
dis**c**overy
dis**c**redit
dog**c**ollar
dra**c**onian
dul**c**amara
dul**c**itude
dys**c**rasia
edu**c**ation
edu**c**ative
eja**c**ulate
eje**c**tment
ele**c**toral
ele**c**tress
ele**c**trify
ele**c**trode
ele**c**tuary
elo**c**ution
elu**c**idate
ema**c**iated
ena**c**tment
enu**c**leate
epi**c**entre
epi**c**lesis
epi**c**urean
epi**c**urism
epi**c**yclic
ere**c**tness
eru**c**iform
evo**c**ation
evo**c**ative
evo**c**atory
exa**c**table
exa**c**tment
exa**c**tness
exe**c**rable
exe**c**rably
exe**c**utant
exe**c**ution
exe**c**utive
exe**c**utory
exe**c**utrix
fal**c**iform
fan**c**yfree
fan**c**ywork
fas**c**iated
fas**c**icled
fas**c**icule
fas**c**iculi
fas**c**inate
Fas**c**istic
fen**c**eless
fle**c**kless
flo**c**culus
flu**c**tuant
flu**c**tuate
for**c**efeed
for**c**eland
for**c**eless
for**c**emeat
for**c**epump
fra**c**tious
fri**c**assee
fri**c**ative
fro**c**kcoat

fructuate
fructuous
furcation
gasconade
gaucherie
glacially
glucoside
glyceride
glycerine
glycoside
graceless
gracility
guacamole
guncotton
hatchback
hatchling
hatchment
Herculean
Hercynian
hircosity
hitchhike
hunchback
inoculate
inscriber
isochrone
isoclinal
isoclinic
isocyclic
juiceless
juiciness
kitchener
knockdown
knockknee
laccolith
lancejack
lancewood
lancinate
larcenist
larcenous
Leicester
leucaemia
leucocyte
leucotome
leucotomy
lunchtime
Maccabean
Mancunian
marcasite
marcelled
marchpane
marchpast
masculine
matchless
matchlock
matchwood
mercaptan
mercenary
mercerise
merciless
mercurial
mercurous
mescaline
mincemeat
mincingly
miscegene
miscegine
mischance
miscreant
miscreate
moschatel
mumchance
muscadine
muscarine
muscleman
muscovado
muscovite
narcissus
narcotine
narcotise

narcotism
nescience
niccolite
nuncupate
obscenely
obscenity
obscurant
obscurely
obscurity
offcentre
offchance
offcolour
oilcolour
olecranal
olecranon
ozocerite
panchayat
pancratic
parcelled
parcenary
parchment
patchouli
patchouly
patchwork
peaceable
peaceably
peacetime
peachblow
peccantly
pencilled
penciller
percaline
perceiver
perchance
percheron
percolate
phycology
piecemeal
piecerate
piecework
pinchbeck
pinchcock
piscatory
pisciform
pitchdark
pitchfork
pitchpipe
placation
placatory
placeable
placecard
placekick
placeless
placement
placename
placentae
placental
placidity
plicately
plication
plicature
porcelain
porcupine
practical
practised
precancel
precative
precatory
precedent
preceding
precentor
preceptor
precipice
precisely
precisian
precision
precocial
precocity
preconise

precursor
priceless
procedure
procerity
processed
processer
processor
proclitic
proconsul
procreant
procreate
procuracy
procuress
psychical
psychoses
psychosis
psychotic
punchball
punchbowl
punchcard
punchline
punctilio
punctuate
purchaser
quickener
quicklime
quickness
quicksand
quickstep
rancidity
rancorous
rascaldom
rascalism
rascality
raucously
reachable
reactance
Reichstag
rencontre
runcinate
saccharin
sacciform
sacculate
sanctuary
sarcastic
sarcocarp
sarcomata
sauceboat
sauceless
saucerful
sauciness
seachange
Shechinah
shockable
shockhead
siccative
sincerely
sincerity
slackness
slickness
smackeroo
sorceress
sorcerous
spaceband
spaceless
spaceport
spaceship
spacesuit
spacetime
specially
specialty
specifier
speckless
spectacle
spectator
speculate
spicebush
spiciness
spiculate

stackable
stackroom
stackyard
stickwork
stockbook
stockdove
stockfish
stockinet
stocklist
stockpile
stockroom
stockwhip
stockyard
subcaudal
subcostal
succeeder
succentor
successor
succinate
succotash
succourer
succulent
succursal
sulcation
surcharge
surcingle
surculose
synchrony
synclinal
syncopate
syncretic
syncytial
syncytium
teachable
teachably
teacupful
thickener
thicketed
thickhead
thickknee
thickness
torchrace
torchsong
touchable
touchdown
touchhole
touchline
touchmark
touchtype
touchwood
traceable
traceably
traceless
traceried
tracheary
tracheate
trachytic
trackless
tracksuit
tractable
tractably
trichinae
trichomic
trichroic
trickless
tricksily
trickster
triclinia
triclinic
tricolour
trochilus
trochleae
trochlear
truceless
truculent
Turcomans
twiceborn
twicelaid
twicetold

unicolour
unicuspid
unscathed
usucapion
vaccinate
vetchling
viscerate
viscidity
viscosity
viscounty
viscously
voiceless
voiceover
volcanism
volcanoes
vouchsafe
vulcanian
vulcanise
vulcanism
vulcanist
vulcanite
watchable
watchcase
watchfire
watchword
welcoming
whichever
witchetty
witchhunt
witchmeal
Worcester
zincotype
zirconium
zucchetto
abidingly
academism
acidifier
acidophil
acidulate
acidulent
acidulous
amidships
apodictic
baldachin
baldaquin
baldfaced
banderole
bandicoot
bandoleer
bandolero
bandolier
bandoline
bandstand
bandwagon
bandwidth
bawdiness
beadledom
birdbrain
birdsfoot
birdsnest
birdtable
birdwatch
boldfaced
bondslave
bondstone
bondwoman
bordereau
bridecake
bridesman
bridewell
bridleway
bundobust
burdenous
caddisfly
caldarium
candidacy
candidate
Candlemas
candlenut

candytuft
cardboard
cardsharp
coadjutor
coadunate
Cobdenism
coldshort
condenser
condignly
condiment
condition
conducive
conductor
condyloid
condyloma
cordelier
cordially
cordiform
corduroys
crediting
credulity
credulous
crudeness
Daedalean
Daedalian
dandelion
dandiacal
deadalive
deadlight
dendritic
deodorant
deodorise
doodlebug
dowdiness
duodecimo
duodenary
ealdorman
epidermal
epidermic
epidermis
epidosite
eradicate
eruditely
erudition
evidently
exodermis
exudation
exudative
faddiness
faldstool
fandangle
fandangos
feedstock
feedstuff
feudalise
feudalism
feudalist
feudality
feudatory
fledgling
foodchain
foodstuff
fundament
ganderism
gardening
garderobe
gaudiness
geodesist
giddiness
gladiator
gladiolus
gladstone
goddamned
goldbrick
goldcrest
goldeneye
goldenrod
goldfever
goldfield

goldfinch
goldsinny
goldsmith
gondolier
goodnight
goodwives
gradation
gradatory
Gradgrind
gradually
graduator
guidebook
guideline
guidepost
guiderope
handbrake
handcraft
handcuffs
handglass
handiness
handiwork
handlebar
handorgan
handpress
handsdown
handshake
handspike
handstand
handwheel
handywork
hardboard
hardcover
hardihood
hardiment
hardiness
hardnosed
hardshell
headboard
headcloth
headdress
headfirst
headiness
headlight
headliner
headphone
headpiece
headscarf
headstall
headstock
headstone
headwater
heedfully
hendiadys
hiddenite
hindbrain
hindrance
hindsight
hoydenish
humdinger
hundredth
inodorous
Jordanian
khedivial
kiddingly
kilderkin
landagent
landaulet
landdross
landdrost
landgrave
landloper
landowner
landscape
landslide
Laodicean
lardycake
laudation
laudative
laudatory

lendlease
loadstone
Londonise
Londonism
loudmouth
maddening
magdalene
maidenish
mandarine
mandatary
mandatory
mandoline
manducate
mendacity
Mendelian
Mendelism
mendicant
mendicity
middleman
mindfully
misdemean
misdirect
Mondayish
moodiness
mordacity
mordantly
muddiness
mundanely
mundungus
murderess
murderous
needfully
neediness
needleful
neodymium
nondriver
obedience
opodeldoc
oviductal
oxidation
paederast
panderess
pendently
pendragon
pendulate
penduline
pendulous
perdition
ponderous
predacity
predation
predative
predatory
predicant
predicate
predictor
predigest
predikant
prideless
prodromal
prodromic
prudently
prudishly
quadratic
quadrifid
quadrigae
quadrille
quadruman
quadruped
quadruple
quadruply
quodlibet
randiness
randomise
readdress
readiness
readymade
reediness
reedorgan

reeducate
rendition
rhodamine
rhodolite
rhodonite
rhodopsin
roadblock
roadhouse
roadmetal
roadstead
roadworks
roodcloth
rowdiness
ruddiness
ruddleman
saddlebag
saddlebow
Sadducean
sandalled
sandarach
sandblast
sandblind
sandcrack
sandglass
sandiness
sandpaper
sandpiper
sandspout
sandstone
sandstorm
sandtable
sandyacht
Sardinian
seedeater
seediness
seedpearl
seedplant
shadberry
shadeless
shadetree
shadiness
skedaddle
skydiving
sliderule
soidisant
soldierly
Soudanese
spadefoot
spadework
spiderman
spiderweb
spodumene
studhorse
studiedly
subdeacon
subdivide
subduable
subduedly
sundowner
swaddling
syndactyl
syndicate
tapdancer
tardiness
tenderise
tendinous
tiedyeing
tinderbox
toadeater
toadstone
toadstool
trademark
tradename
tradesman
tradition
traducian
tridactyl
tridymite
unadopted

unadorned
unadvised
vandalise
vandalism
vendition
verdantly
verdigris
vindicate
voodooism
voodooist
Waldenses
waldgrave
wandering
weediness
whodunnit
windblown
windbound
windbreak
windchest
windhover
windiness
windowbox
windproof
windswept
windwards
wonderful
woodblock
woodchuck
woodcraft
woodiness
woodlouse
woodnymph
woodwaxen
wordiness
wordsmith
yardstick
Yiddisher
abjection
abnegator
abseiling
accentual
acceptant
acceptive
accessary
accession
accessory
Acheulean
Acheulian
adherence
admeasure
adrenalin
advection
advective
Adventism
Adventist
adventive
adventure
adverbial
adversary
adversely
adversity
advertent
advertise
affecting
affection
affective
aftercare
afterclap
afterglow
afterlife
aftermath
aftermost
afternoon
aftertime
afterword
agreeable
agreeably
agreement
albescent

aldehydic
algebraic
alienable
alienator
allegedly
allegiant
allegoric
allemande
alleviate
alpenhorn
alterable
altercate
alternant
alternate
alveolate
ambergris
amoebaean
ampersand
anaerobic
ancestral
andesitic
angelfish
angelical
annectent
annelidan
antefixal
antenatal
antennary
antennule
aphereses
apheresis
appealing
appellant
appellate
appendage
appendant
appertain
appetence
appetency
appetiser
aqueously
argentine
argentite
argentous
arrearage
arrestant
arresting
arsenical
arsenious
artemisia
arteriole
arteritis
asbestine
asbestous
ascendant
ascendent
ascension
ascensive
ascertain
ascetical
askewness
aspectual
aspersion
assembler
assertion
assertive
atheistic
athematic
Athenaeum
attempter
attendant
attention
attentive
attenuate
aubergine
Aylesbury
bakehouse
balefully
baneberry

banefully
barefaced
begetting
beleaguer
belemnite
beneficed
besetment
besetting
bevelling
bigeneric
bisection
blaeberry
bluebeard
blueberry
blueblack
bluegrass
bluepoint
blueprint
bluestone
bolection
bonechina
bowerbird
breeching
breezeway
briefcase
briefless
briefness
brierroot
brierwood
cadential
cadetship
cafeteria
cageyness
calendric
calendula
calenture
camelback
camelhair
Camembert
cameraman
canebrake
canescent
canesugar
canetrash
careerism
careerist
carefully
caretaker
caseation
catechise
catechism
catechist
caterwaul
cavendish
cavernous
celebrant
celebrate
celebrity
celestial
cementite
cerebella
cerebrate
cerecloth
chaetopod
cheekbone
cheerless
chiefship
chieftain
cinematic
cineraria
cinereous
clientage
clientele
coheiress
coherence
coherency
colemouse
comedones
copesmate

copestone
coreopsis
coseismal
coseismic
coverable
coverslip
coverture
covetable
cruellest
cuneiform
cupelling
curettage
daredevil
davenport
debenture
deceitful
decennary
decennial
decennium
deception
deceptive
defeatism
defeatist
defeature
defection
defective
defendant
defensive
deference
deferment
deferring
dejection
demeanour
dependant
dependent
desecrate
desertion
detection
detective
detention
detergent
determent
determine
deterrent
deterring
detersion
detersive
developer
diaereses
diaeresis
didelphic
digestion
digestive
dimension
dioecious
dipeptide
direction
directive
directory
directrix
direfully
disembark
disembody
disengage
disentail
disentomb
disesteem
divergent
diversely
diversify
diversion
diversity
diverting
dodecagon
dolefully
doleritic
dopefiend
dowelling
dowerless

duteously
dysentery
eagerness
easefully
eavesdrop
eccentric
effective
effectual
egregious
egression
eiderdown
eiderduck
eirenicon
eldership
elsewhere
embedding
embedment
embellish
embezzler
Emmenthal
empennage
encephala
endearing
endeavour
enhearten
entelechy
enterable
enteritis
entertain
epaenetic
ephedrine
ephemeral
ephemerid
ephemeris
ephemeron
esperance
Esperanto
essential
etherical
eutectoid
exceeding
excellent
excelling
excelsior
excentric
exceptant
excepting
exception
exceptive
excerptor
excessive
expectant
expecting
expedient
expediter
expellent
expelling
expensive
expertise
exsertile
exsertion
exservice
extempore
extendant
extensile
extension
extensity
extensive
extenuate
externals
facecloth
facetious
Falernian
farestage
fatefully
faveolate
federally
fenestrae
fenestral

fideistic
finedrawn
firealarm
fireblast
firebrand
firebreak
firebrick
firecrest
firedrake
firedrill
fireeater
fireguard
firehouse
fireirons
firelight
fireplace
firepower
fireproof
firestone
firewater
fireworks
fivepence
fivepenny
fixedness
fleetness
fluecured
foreboder
forebrain
forecaddy
foreclose
forecourt
forefront
foregoing
foreigner
forejudge
foreknown
forenamed
forereach
foreshore
foreshown
foresight
forespeak
forestage
forestall
foretaste
foretoken
forewoman
fraenulum
freeboard
freehouse
freelance
freeliver
Freemason
freerange
freerider
freestone
freestyle
freewheel
freewoman
freezable
freezedry
funebrial
gaberdine
galenical
gatecrash
gatehouse
gavelkind
gazehound
gazetteer
genealogy
generable
generalia
generally
generator
genetical
gleefully
glueyness
gobetween
governess
Greekless
greenback
greenbelt
greeneyed
greengage
greenhorn
greenness
greenroom
greensand
greenweed
greenwood
griefless
grievance
gruelling
habergeon
haresfoot
hatefully
haverings
haversack
hegemonic
hereabout
hereafter
heretical
hereunder
heterodox
heteronym
heterosis
hibernate
Hibernian
hidebound
hideously
homebound
homegrown
homemaker
homeopath
homestead
homewards
honeycomb
honeymoon
hopefully
horehound
hugeously
humectant
hyperbola
hyperbole
hypergamy
hypericum
hyperopia
hyperopic
hypethral
ignescent
illegally
illegible
illegibly
imbecilic
immediacy
immediate
immensely
immensity
immersion
impeccant
impedance
impelling
impendent
impending
imperator
imperfect
imperious
impetrate
impetuous
inbetween
incensory
incentive
inception
inceptive
incessant
indecency
indecorum
indelible
indelibly
indemnify
indemnity
indention
indenture
infection
infective
inferable
inference
inferring
infertile
ingenious
ingenuity
ingenuous
ingestion
ingestive
inherence
inheritor
injection
innermost
innervate
insectary
insectile
insensate
insertion
inservice
insetting
integrand
integrant
integrate
integrity
intellect
intendant
intensely
intensify
intension
intensity
intensive
intention
interbred
intercede
intercept
intercity
intercrop
interdict
interface
interfere
interfile
interflow
interfuse
interject
interknit
interlace
interlard
interleaf
interline
interlink
interlock
interlope
interlude
interment
internode
interpage
interplay
interpose
interpret
interring
interrupt
intersect
intervein
intervene
interview
interwind
interwove
interzone
intestacy
intestate
intestine
invective
inveigler
invention
inventive
inventory
inverness
inversely
inversion
inversive
invertase
irreality
irregular
jewellery
jewelweed
Juneberry
juvenilia
kinematic
labelling
lacerable
lacertian
lacertine
lamellate
lamellose
latecomer
laterally
latescent
legendary
legerline
levelling
levelness
libecchio
libellant
libelling
libellist
libellous
liberally
liberated
liberator
libertine
licensure
lifeblood
lifecycle
lifeforce
lifeguard
lifesaver
lifesized
lifestyle
lifetable
limejuice
limelight
limestone
limewater
lineality
lineament
linearise
linearity
lineation
linenfold
lineolate
literally
literatim
literator
literatus
liverwort
liveryman
livestock
lobectomy
lodestone
loveapple
lovechild
lovefeast
lovelight
lovematch
loverless
lovestory
lovetoken
lowercase
lowerdeck
lowermost
lymegrass
lymehound
macedoine
macerator
madeleine
makeready
makeshift
maneating
marestail
maternity
mateyness
mementoes
mesentery
meteorist
meteorite
meteoroid
milestone
minefield
minelayer
misemploy
miserable
miserably
misesteem
mixedness
modelling
moderator
modernise
modernism
modernist
modernity
molecular
momentary
momentous
monergism
moneybags
moneybill
moneywort
Mycenaean
nakedness
nameplate
naseberry
navelwort
necessary
necessity
nemertean
nemertine
nepenthes
nevermore
ninepence
ninepenny
ninetieth
nonentity
nosebleed
noseflute
nosepiece
notedness
notepaper
novelette
numerable
numerator
numerical
oakenshaw
objectify
objection
objective
obsecrate
obsequent
obsequial
obsequies
observant
obsession
obsessive
obtention
obversely
obversion
octennial
offensive
offertory
onsetting
oogenesis
oogenetic
orderbook
orderform
orderless
orientate
ostensive
osteoderm
osteogeny
osteology
osteopath
otherness
otherwise
outermost
ownership
pacemaker
pageantry
panegyric
panelling
panellist
paperback
paperclip
papergirl
paperthin
paperwork
papeterie
paregoric
parentage
patellate
paternity
pederasty
peneplain
peneplane
penetrant
penetrate
peregrine
perennate
perennial
petechiae
petechial
petersham
phlebitis
phrenetic
pikeperch
pikestaff
pineapple
pipedream
pipeorgan
pipestone
piteously
pokeberry
pokerface
pokerwork
polemical
polevault
potentate
potential
powerboat
powerdive
powerless
praenomen
preemptor
preengage
preexilic
priestess
proenzyme
pubescent
pureblood
pyrethrum
queenhood
queenless
queenlike
queenpost
queenship
queerness
quiescent
quietness
racehorse
racetrack
rakehelly
rareeshow
ratepayer
ravelling
ravelment
rebelling
rebellion
recension
reception
receptive
recession
recessive
redevelop
refection
refectory
referable
reference
referenda
referring
rehearsal
rejection
relevance
relevancy
remeasure
remediate
renewable
repechage
repellant
repellent
repelling
repentant
repertory
rerebrace
rerelease
reremouse
resection
resentful
reserpine
reservist
reservoir
resetting
retention
retentive
revelator
revelling
reverence
reversely
reversion
revetment
revetting
ricepaper
riderless
rivelling
riverbank
riverboat
riverhead
riverside
riverweed
roseapple
roseately
rosenoble
rosewater
rubellite
rufescent
rulership
Sabellian
safeguard
safetypin
sagebrush
sagegreen
saleratus
salesgirl
saleslady
satellite
scheelite
schematic
sciential
scientism
scientist
scleritis

sclerosis
sclerotic
screecher
screening
screwball
screwbolt
screwpile
screwpine
screwworm
secernent
secession
sedentary
selection
selective
selectman
selenious
selenitic
semeiotic
semestral
senescent
seneschal
serenader
sevenfold
seventeen
seventhly
seventies
severable
severally
severalty
severance
sexennial
sheepcote
sheepfold
sheephook
sheeplice
sheepskin
sheeptick
sheepwalk
sheepwash
sheerhulk
sheerlegs
sheerness
sheetbend
shieldbug
shieldfem
shoeblack
shoemaker
shoeshine
shredding
shrewmice
sideboard
sideburns
sidedness
sideissue
sidelight
sideritic
siderosis
sideswipe
sidetable
sidetrack
sidewards
sidewheel
sinewless
skeesicks
sleekness
sleepless
sleevenut
soberness
solemnise
solemnity
soleplate
something
sometimes
somewhere
somewhile
sovereign
speechful
speechify
speedball
speedboat
speedster
speedwell
spherical
spherular
spleenful
splendent
splendour
splenetic
splenitis
spleuchan
squeakily
squeamish
squelcher
steelclad
steelhead
steelwork
steelyard
steenkirk
steepness
steersman
streakily
streaking
streamlet
streetcar
strenuous
stressful
stretcher
strewment
subeditor
subereous
superable
supercool
superfine
superfuse
superheat
supernova
superpose
supersede
superstar
supervene
supervise
sweepback
sweetcorn
sweetener
sweetmeal
sweetmeat
sweetness
sweetshop
sweettalk
synectics
syneresis
synergism
synergist
telegenic
telegraph
telemeter
telemetry
teleology
telepathy
telephone
telephony
telephoto
telescope
telescopy
televisor
tenebrist
tenebrous
terebinth
terebrant
threefold
threesome
threnodic
threshold
Thyestean
tidegauge
tidewater
tigerlily
tigermoth
tigerseye
tigerwood
tilestone
timelapse
timelimit
timeously
timepiece
timesheet
timetable
tiredness
tirewoman
tolerable
tolerably
tolerance
tomentose
tomentous
toreutics
totempole
towelling
triennial
triennium
trierarch
truepenny
tubercule
tumescent
tunefully
typemetal
typewrite
umbellate
umbellule
umberbird
unbeknown
unbending
unberufen
unceasing
uncertain
undecagon
undeceive
undecided
undecimal
undefined
underbody
underbred
underclay
undercoat
underdone
underfelt
underfoot
undergird
undergone
undergrad
underhand
underhung
underlaid
underlain
underline
underling
undermine
undermost
underpaid
underpart
underpass
underplay
underplot
underrate
underripe
underseal
underseas
undersell
undershot
underside
undersign
undersold
undersong
underspin
undertake
undertint
undertone
undertook
undervest
underwear
underwent
underwing
underwood
unfeeling
unfeigned
unhealthy
unheeding
unhelpful
unlearned
unmeaning
unpegging
unpeopled
unreality
unreserve
unselfish
unsettled
untenable
unwearied
unweeting
unwelcome
uppercase
uppermost
upsetting
urceolate
usherette
utterable
utterance
utterless
uttermost
utterness
vademecum
valentine
vasectomy
vegetable
vegetably
vehemence
veneering
venerable
venerably
venerator
venereous
vicennial
viceregal
vicereine
viceroyal
vicesimal
videlicet
videotape
vigesimal
virescent
vitellary
vitelline
viverrine
vowelless
voyeurism
wakefully
wakerobin
wapentake
warehouse
waterbath
waterbuck
waterbutt
watercart
watercool
waterfall
waterflea
waterfowl
watergate
waterhole
waterleaf
waterless
waterlily
waterline
watermark
watermill
waterpipe
watershed
waterside
waterweed
waterworn
wavefront
waveguide
wavellite
wheedling
wheelbase
wheelless
wheelwork
wideawake
wineberry
wineglass
winepress
winestone
winevault
wiredrawn
wiregauze
wirephoto
wisecrack
womenfolk
womenkind
yodelling
ytterbium
zibelline
asafetida
bedfellow
beefeater
beefiness
beefsteak
bluffness
boyfriend
buffaloes
buffeting
carfuffle
chafferer
chaffinch
cliffhang
coffeecup
coffeepot
cofferdam
coffinite
coiffeuse
comfiture
comforter
confabbed
conferral
conferred
conferrer
confervae
confessor
confidant
confident
confiding
configure
confirmed
confirmer
confirmor
confiteor
confluent
conformal
conformer
Confucian
confusion
craftsman
delftware
different
difficile
difficult
diffident
diffusely
diffusion
diffusive
disfavour
disfigure
disforest
draftsman
driftsail
driftweed
driftwood
fanfarade
feoffment
flyfisher
forfeiter
fulfilled
fulfiller
gasfitter
gerfalcon
godfather
goffering
golflinks
gruffness
gyrfalcon
halfbaked
halfblood
halfbound
halfbreed
halfcaste
halfcrown
halfhardy
halflight
halfpence
halfpenny
halfprice
halfshell
halfstaff
halftitle
halftrack
halftruth
hamfisted
hoofprint
huffiness
ineffable
ineffably
kerfuffle
knifeedge
leafgreen
leafmould
leafstalk
loafsugar
malformed
mayflower
misfeasor
muffineer
muffinman
oddfellow
orificial
oriflamme
outfitter
oviferous
parfleche
penfriend
perfectly
perfector
perfervid
perforate
performer
perfumery
perfumier
perfusion
perfusive
pilferage
prefatory
preferred
prefigure
prefixion
profanely
profanity
professed
professor
profilist
profiteer
profusely
profusion
puffadder
puffiness
raffinate
raffinose
raffishly
rafflesia
reefpoint
rodfisher
roofplate
ruffianly
safflower
seafaring
selfabuse
selfaware
selfdoubt
selfdrive
selffaced
selfglory
selfimage
selfishly
selfmoved
selfpride
selftrust
shiftless
sixfooter
solfatara
solfeggio
solferino
stiffener
stiffness
subfamily
suffering
suffocate
suffragan
suffusion
sunflower
surfacing
surfboard
surfeiter
surficial
swiftness
trifacial
trifocals
trifolium
triforium
twofisted
unifiable
uniformly
wayfaring
webfooted
welfarism
wolfhound
wolfishly
wolframic
wolfsbane
wulfenite
alignment
amygdalin
apogamous
aragonite
bagginess
bargainer
bargepole
bengaline
bergamask
bilgekeel
biogenous
biography
boxgirder
bregmatic
brigadier
brigandry
brightish
budgetary
Bulgarian
bulginess
Cingalese
coagulant
coagulate
congenial
congeries
congruent
congruity

congruous
cudgelled
dangerous
diagnoses
diagnosis
dinginess
disgracer
doggishly
doughtily
draghound
dragomans
dragoness
dragonfly
dragonish
drugstore
dungarees
dysgenics
dziggetai
elegantly
elegiacal
enigmatic
epigraphy
epigynous
erogenous
evaginate
exegetist
exogamous
exogenous
eyeglance
faggoting
fingering
fingertip
flagellum
flageolet
flagrance
flagrancy
flagstaff
flagstick
flagstone
flightily
fogginess
forgather
forgeable
forgetful
forgiving
forgotten
fragility
fragrance
fragrancy
frigatoon
frightful
frigidity
frogmarch
frogspawn
frugality
fulgently
fulgurant
fulgurate
fulgurite
fulgurous
fungicide
fungiform
gadgeteer
gangboard
gangplank
gaugeable
geography
gingerade
gingerale
ginglymus
gogglebox
gongorism
gorgonian
gorgonise
gregarian
gregarine
Gregorian
haggadist
haggardly
hangerson
haughtily
hedgingly
hobgoblin
hoggishly
Hungarian
illgotten
imageable
imageless
imaginary
isagogics
isogamete
isogamous
isogenous
jargonise
judgement
judgeship
judgmatic
kingcraft
kingdomed
kingmaker
kingsized
knightage
laggardly
Langobard
langouste
languidly
largeness
larghetto
laughable
laughably
lawgiving
legginess
lengthily
liegelord
lingering
lingually
lingulate
lodgement
lodgepole
longaeval
longchain
longcoats
longeared
longevity
longevous
longfaced
longhouse
longicorn
longingly
longitude
longlived
Longobard
longrange
longshore
lorgnette
manganate
manganese
manganite
manganous
manginess
margarine
margarite
marginate
merganser
misgiving
misgovern
misguided
Mongolian
mongolism
Mongoloid
mongooses
mongrelly
mugginess
myography
naughtily
neighbour
niggardly
oligaemia
oligarchy
Oligocene
oligopoly
originate
orography
outgiving
outgoings
outgrowth
outgunned
oxygenate
oxygenise
oxygenous
pergunnah
phagedena
phagocyte
piggishly
piggyback
piggybank
pilgarlic
podginess
poignancy
pragmatic
pregnable
pregnancy
progestin
prognoses
prognosis
programme
pudginess
pungently
purgation
purgative
purgatory
ranginess
ridgepole
ridgetile
ringfence
ringingly
ringshake
ringsnake
roughcast
roughhewn
roughneck
roughness
roughshod
ruggedise
sangfroid
sargassos
scagliola
seagirdle
sedgewren
seigneury
seigniory
sergeancy
shogunate
singalong
singleton
singspiel
slightish
smuggling
sniggerer
sogginess
songcycle
songfully
songsmith
spaghetti
spagyrist
stagedoor
stagehand
staggerer
staghound
staginess
Stagirite
stagnancy
stagparty
stegosaur
stigmatic
subgenera
suggester
surgeoncy
swaggerer
syngamous
tangerine
Targumist
thighbone
thighboot
tonguelet
tonguetie
toughness
tragedian
trigamist
trigamous
tungstate
turgently
turgidity
uliginous
vengeance
Virgilian
virginals
virginity
virgulate
vulgarian
vulgarise
vulgarism
vulgarity
waggishly
waggonage
wedgewise
weighable
weighbeam
weightily
weighting
wingchair
zeugmatic
zoogenous
zoography
alchemise
alchemist
amphibian
amphibole
amphigory
amphioxus
anchorage
anchoress
anchorite
anchorman
anchylose
anthelion
anthemion
anthocyan
anthology
anthozoan
anthracic
anthropic
archangel
archducal
archduchy
archenemy
archetype
archfiend
architect
archivist
archivolt
arthritic
arthritis
arthropod
arthrosis
Arthurian
asphaltic
asphaltum
asthmatic
authentic
authoress
authorial
authorise
authority
bashfully
bathhouse
batholite
batholith
Bathonian
bathybius
bethought
bigheaded
bilharzia
bishopric
bonhomous
Brahmanic
Brahminee
Brahminic
bughunter
bushcraft
bushelful
bushiness
bushwhack
cachectic
cacholong
Catharism
Catharist
catharses
catharsis
cathartic
cathectic
cathedral
cephalous
chihuahua
chthonian
cochineal
cochleate
cothurnus
Cytherean
dachshund
dashboard
dashingly
dethroner
dichasial
dichasium
dichogamy
dichotomy
dichroism
dichromat
dichromic
diphthong
dishcloth
dishclout
dishfaced
dishonest
dishonour
dishwater
dithyramb
eightfold
eightieth
eightsome
eightyish
emphasise
emphysema
enchanter
enchilada
enchorial
ensheathe
enthymeme
escheator
Esthonian
Eucharist
euchology
euphemise
euphemism
euphonise
euphonium
euphorbia
eurhythmy
euthenics
eutherian
exchanger
exchequer
fashioner
fatheaded
fisherman
fishiness
fishplate
fishslice
fishyback
foxhunter
gasholder
gathering
Gothamite
gothicise
Gothicism
gushingly
hamhanded
haphazard
Hashemite
Hashimite
highchair
highclass
highflier
highflown
highflyer
highgrade
highgrown
highlands
highlevel
highlight
highspeed
hightoned
highwater
hotheaded
hyphenate
innholder
inshallah
ischaemia
ischaemic
ischiadic
ischiatic
isohyetal
itchiness
katharsis
lachrymal
lathering
lecherous
lethality
lethargic
lichenous
lightfoot
lightless
lightness
lightning
lightship
lightsome
lightsout
lightwood
lightyear
litheness
lithesome
lithology
lithopone
lithotomy
lophodont
machinate
machinery
machinist
machmeter
manhandle
manhattan
mechanics
mechanise
mechanism
mechanist
methadone
metheglin
methodise
Methodism
Methodist
methought
methylate
methylene
mishandle
mishanter
Mithraism
Mithraist
motheaten
motherwit
mothproof
mythicise
mythicism
mythicist
mythology
naphthene
natheless
nephalism
nephalist
nepheline
nephelite
nephology
nephritic
nephritis
nephrosis
nightbird
nightclub
nightfall
nightgown
nighthawk
nightlife
nightline
nightlong
nightmare
nightside
nighttime
nightwork
nowhither
offhanded
onehanded
orchestic
orchestra
orchidist
orphanage
orthodoxy
orthoepic
pachyderm
panhandle
parhelion
pathogeny
pathology
penholder
pethidine
phthalein
pigheaded
pithecoid
pithiness
potholing
pothunter
pushchair
pushiness
pushingly
rechauffe
recherche
redhanded
redheaded
reshuffle
rethought
rightable
righteous
righthand
rightness
rightward
rushlight
ruthenium
ruthfully
Sanhedrim
Sanhedrin
sapheaded
senhorita
Sephardic
Sephardim
sightless

sightseer
Sinhalese
siphonage
siphuncle
sophister
sophistic
sophistry
sophomore
sunhelmet
syphilise
syphiloid
tachylite
tachylyte
technical
technique
tightener
tightness
tightrope
tightwire
Tocharian
tophamper
trihedral
trihybrid
twohanded
typhlitis
typhoidal
uncharted
unchecked
unshackle
unsheathe
unthought
unthrifty
washbasin
washboard
washcloth
washedout
washerman
washhouse
washiness
washstand
wishfully
withdrawn
withering
witherite
withstand
withstood
wychhazel
yachtclub
yachtsman
abdicable
abdicator
accidence
accipiter
actinozoa
activator
addiction
addictive
adlibbing
adminicle
admirable
admirably
admiralty
admission
admissive
admitting
admixture
advisable
advisably
advisedly
aerialist
aeriality
aetiology
affianced
affidavit
affiliate
affirmant
affixture
Afrikaans
Afrikaner
agriology
albinotic
alligator
altimeter
ambiguity
ambiguous
ambitious
anciently
ancientry
ancillary
angiology
angiomata
anticline
anticodon
antidotal
antigenic
antiknock
antimonic
antinodal
antinomic
antinovel
antipasto
antipathy
antiphony
antipodal
antipodes
antiquary
antiquate
antiquity
antiserum
antitoxic
antitoxin
antitrade
antitrust
antivenin
antiviral
anxiously
aquilegia
arbitrage
arbitrary
arbitrate
arbitress
argillite
armigeral
armillary
armistice
arriviste
artichoke
articular
artificer
artillery
aspirator
assiduity
assiduous
assistant
audiology
auditable
auditoria
auricular
auxiliary
available
availably
avoidable
avoidably
avoidance
Axminster
babirussa
bacillary
basically
basilican
basipetal
befitting
beginning
benighted
benignant
benignity
bicipital
bilingual
biliously
bilirubin
biliteral
bipinnate
boliviano
braincase
brainless
brainwash
brainwave
broiderer
caciquism
calibrate
calicular
caliology
caliphate
canicular
capillary
capitally
capitular
capitulum
Caribbean
cavilling
chaingang
chaingear
chainless
chainmail
chairlady
Christian
Christmas
citizenly
citizenry
civically
civiliser
claimable
cloisonne
cloistral
cogitable
comically
Cominform
Comintern
comitadji
conically
copiously
coriander
cotillion
croissant
cubically
curialism
curiosity
curiously
cuticular
cutinised
cylindric
cynically
decidable
decidedly
deciduate
deciduous
decilitre
decillion
decimally
decimator
decimetre
decistere
dedicator
defiantly
deficient
definable
definably
dehiscent
delicious
delineate
delirious
deliverer
demimonde
demission
demitasse
demitting
demiurgic
denigrate
denitrate
denitrify
depiction
depictive
derivable
desiccant
desiccate
designate
designing
desirable
desirably
deviation
devilfish
devilling
devilment
deviously
devisable
devitrify
digitalin
digitalis
digitally
digitated
diligence
dimidiate
dimissory
diningcar
dirigible
dirigisme
disinfect
disinfest
dividable
divisible
dixieland
dominance
dominator
dominical
Dominican
dosimeter
dosimetry
drainpipe
druidical
dubiosity
dubiously
dubitable
dutifully
ecritoire
efficient
ellipsoid
empirical
enlighten
enviously
equipment
equipoise
equipping
equisetum
equitable
equitably
equivocal
equivoque
espionage
estimable
estimator
ethically
Ethiopian
excipient
excisable
exciseman
excitable
excitancy
excitedly
exhibitor
expiation
expiatory
exsiccate
extirpate
Fabianism
familyman
fatidical
fatigable
felicific
femineity
Fenianism
fetichism
fetichist
fetidness
fetishism
fetishist
filiation
filigreed
finically
finicking
foliation
frailness
freighter
fruitcake
fruiterer
fruitless
fruittree
fumigator
funicular
funiculus
furiously
fusillade
fusionist
gabionade
galingale
garibaldi
gelignite
genialise
geniality
genitival
geriatric
glaireous
gneissoid
gneissose
goliardic
habitable
habitably
habituate
hagiarchy
hagiology
halieutic
halitosis
helically
heliogram
heliostat
heliotype
heliozoan
heliozoic
hemicycle
hemistich
hemitrope
heritable
hesitance
hesitancy
hesitator
hodiernal
homicidal
homiletic
humiliate
hygienics
hygienist
ignitable
ignitible
illiberal
illicitly
immigrant
immigrate
imminence
imminency
immixture
impiously
incidence
incipient
Indianise
indicator
indiction
indigence
indignant
indignity
indigotin
indispose
infielder
infilling
infirmary
infirmity
inhibitor
insidious
insincere
insinuate
insipidly
insistent
invidious
inviolacy
inviolate
invisible
invisibly
ionisable
irrigable
irrigator
irritable
irritably
janissary
janitress
joviality
jubilance
judiciary
judicious
juniorate
juniority
juridical
labialise
labialism
laciniate
laminaria
laminated
lapideous
latitancy
legionary
legislate
leniently
leviathan
leviratic
levitator
Levitical
lexically
libidinal
limitable
limitedly
limitless
litigable
litigious
lividness
lixiviate
logically
logistics
lovingcup
lucidness
luciferin
ludicrous
luminance
lunisolar
lunitidal
luridness
lyrically
lysimeter
macintosh
Magianism
magically
magicking
magistery
magistral
malicious
malignant
malignity
mamillary
mamillate
Manichean
manifesto
manipular
marihuana
marijuana
maritally
maxillary
maximally
mediaeval
mediately
mediation
mediatise
mediative
mediatory
mediatrix
medicable
medically
medicinal
meditator
meliorate
meliorism
meliorist
meliority
melismata
meningeal
midinette
militancy
mimicking
miniature
minimally
miniskirt
misinform
mitigable
mitigator
modillion
monitress
motivator
moviegoer
municipal
muniments
munitions
musically
musichall
mutilator
myriorama
navicular
navigable
navigator
nobiliary
nominable
nominally
nominator
nonillion
notionist
noviciate
novitiate
noxiously
obeisance
obligated
obliquely
obliquity
oblivious
obviation
obviously
occipital
octillion
officiant
officiate
officinal
officious
onlicence
ophiology
opsimathy
optically
orbicular
ordinance
orgiastic
Orpington
orrisroot

oscillate
oscitancy
ossicular
ossifrage
Pakistani
palillogy
panicking
papillary
papillate
papilloma
papillose
papillote
patiently
patinated
pedicular
pedigreed
Pekingese
peninsula
penitence
periclase
pericycle
peridotic
perihelia
perilling
perilymph
perimeter
perimorph
perinatal
periodate
peripatus
periphery
periplast
periscope
perishing
perisperm
peristome
peristyle
petiolate
petiolule
pitifully
pixilated
plainness
plainsman
plainsong
plaintiff
plaintive
Pleiocene
policeman
politburo
politesse
political
poriferal
poriferan
praiseful
pumiceous
punishing
pupillage
pupillary
puritanic
pyridoxin
rabidness
racialism
racialist
radialply
radiantly
radiately
radiation
radiative
radically
radicular
radiocast
radiogram
radiology
rapidfire
rapidness
rationale
rationing
ravishing
rebidding

recipient
redingote
redivivus
refitment
refitting
regicidal
regisseur
registrar
reliantly
religiose
religious
reliquary
reliquiae
remindful
reminisce
remission
remitment
remittent
remitting
renitency
residence
residency
residuary
resilient
resistant
resistive
resitting
retiarius
reticence
reticency
reticular
reticulum
retinitis
retinulae
retinular
revictual
revisable
revivable
ridiculer
rigidness
rosinweed
rubicelle
ruminator
sagittate
salicetum
salicylic
saliently
sanitaria
sapiently
satiation
satinbird
satinette
satinspar
satinwood
satirical
saxifrage
schilling
schistose
schistous
scribbler
scrimmage
scrimpily
scrimshaw
scripture
scrivener
seditious
semibreve
semicolon
semifinal
semifluid
semilunar
semimetal
seminally
semiology
semiotics
semiplume
semirigid
semisolid
semisweet

semitonic
semivowel
seniority
sepiolite
serialise
serialism
serialist
seriality
seriately
sericeous
serigraph
serinette
seriously
sheikhdom
shrinkage
sibilance
sibilancy
sigillary
sigillate
siliceous
silicious
silicosis
silicotic
siliquose
similarly
sinistral
sluiceway
snailfish
socialise
socialism
socialist
socialite
sociality
sociogram
sociology
sociopath
solicitor
solidness
soliloquy
solipsism
solipsist
solitaire
soritical
sovietise
sovietism
sphincter
splintery
splitting
spoilsman
sprigging
sprightly
sprigtail
springald
springbok
springily
springing
springlet
sprinkler
spritsail
squibbing
squidding
squinancy
squirarch
squiredom
squirelet
staidness
stainable
stainless
staircase
stairfoot
stairhead
stairwell
stoically
striation
striature
stricture
stridence
stridency
stringent

stripling
stripping
supinator
synizesis
syringeal
tacitness
talismans
taxidermy
taximeter
tediously
tepidness
thriftily
thrilling
timidness
titillate
tonically
topiarian
topiarist
topically
toxically
trainable
trainband
trainload
traitress
treillage
tuliproot
tuliptree
tulipwood
tumidness
tunicated
typically
ultimatum
umbilical
umbilicus
unbiassed
uncinated
uncivilly
undivided
unfitness
unfitting
unlimited
unmindful
unsighted
unsightly
untimeous
unwilling
unwinking
unwitting
unzipping
uplifting
uprightly
urticaria
utricular
vacillant
vacillate
valiantly
validness
vapidness
variation
varicella
variegate
variolate
variolite
varioloid
variolous
variously
vaticinal
vehicular
veniality
veridical
veritable
veritably
vesicular
vexillary
viciously
vigilance
vigilante
vimineous
viricidal

visionary
visionist
visitable
visitress
vitiation
vitiosity
vivianite
vividness
vizierate
vizierial
vomitoria
wyliecoat
yohimbine
zamindary
zemindary
airjacket
banjulele
bedjacket
conjugate
illjudged
nonjuring
oddjobber
oddjobman
prejudice
projector
Seljukian
serjeancy
serjeanty
skijoring
skyjacker
subjacent
subjugate
Ashkenazi
awakening
backbiter
backboard
backcloth
backcross
backpedal
backsight
backslang
backslide
backspace
backstage
backsword
backtrack
backwards
backwater
backwoods
balkanise
barkeeper
basketful
beekeeper
berkelium
bookishly
booklouse
bookmaker
bookplate
bookshelf
bookstall
bookstand
bookstore
boskiness
brakeless
brakeshoe
brakesman
brokerage
buckboard
bucketful
buckhound
buckshish
buckthorn
bucktooth
buckwheat
bulkiness
bunkhouse
cankerous
chokedamp
cockahoop

Cockaigne
cockatiel
cockfight
cockhorse
cockiness
cockneyfy
cockroach
cockscomb
cocksfoot
cookhouse
corkscrew
cuckoldry
deckhouse
dickybird
Doukhobor
duckboard
duskiness
flakiness
folkdance
folkmusic
folkweave
funkiness
gawkiness
hackamore
hackberry
hackneyed
hankering
hawksbill
honkytonk
huckaback
huckstery
hunkydory
huskiness
innkeeper
jackknife
jackplane
jacksnipe
jackstraw
jerkiness
jockstrap
junkerdom
junkerism
junketing
kickstart
kinkiness
lankiness
leakiness
leukaemia
leukaemic
leukocyte
lickerish
locksmith
lookalike
luckiness
marketday
marketing
mawkishly
milkfever
milkfloat
milkiness
milkshake
milktooth
mirkiness
mockingly
monkeyish
monkeyism
monkeynut
monkshood
muckraker
mucksweat
murkiness
musketeer
muskiness
muskmelon
neckcloth
neckverse
nickelise
nickelled
nickelous

ozokerite
packaging
packdrill
packhorse
packtrain
perkiness
pickaback
picketing
pinkiness
pocketful
Quakerdom
Quakeress
Quakerish
Quakerism
quakiness
racketeer
reckoning
riskiness
rockbound
rockbrake
rockdrill
rocketeer
rockiness
rockplant
rocksnake
sackcloth
shakeable
shakedown
shakerism
shakiness
sickening
sickishly
sickleave
silkgland
silkiness
slakeless
smokeball
smokebomb
smokebush
smokejack
smokeless
smoketree
smokiness
snakebird
snakebite
snakelike
snakeroot
snakeskin
snakeweed
snakewood
snakiness
spikenard
spikiness
spokesman
spokewise
stakeboat
stokehold
stokehole
sulkiness
tackiness
talkathon
talkative
taskforce
teakettle
tuckerbag
Turkomans
unskilful
unskilled
volkslied
wackiness
walkabout
weakkneed
weeknight
workbench
workhorse
workhouse
workmanly
workpiece
worktable

workwoman
Yankeedom
Yankeeism
Yorkshire
zinkenite
abolisher
abolition
acclaimer
acclimate
acclivity
acellular
adulation
adulatory
adulterer
adulthood
adultness
afflation
affluence
aimlessly
amblyopia
amblyopic
ampleness
amplifier
amplitude
amyloidal
amylopsin
analeptic
analgesia
analgesic
analogise
analogist
analogous
analysand
angleiron
anglesite
angleworm
anglicise
anglicism
Anglicist
anglophil
anklebone
apologise
apologist
applauder
applejack
appliance
applicant
artlessly
asclepiad
ashlaring
athletics
avalanche
bailiwick
balladeer
balladist
ballerina
ballistae
ballistic
ballpoint
barleymow
bedlamite
bellglass
bellicose
bellpunch
bellyache
bellyband
bellyflop
beslobber
biblicism
biblicist
billabong
billboard
billiards
billionth
billycock
billygoat
biologist
boulevard
bowlegged
brilliant
bulldozer
bullfight
bullfinch
bullishly
bulltrout
bullybeef
bullytree
burlesque
burliness
cablegram
cablelaid
cailleach
callipers
callosity
callously
cellarage
celluloid
cellulose
challenge
chelation
chelicera
chelonian
chilblain
childhood
childless
childlike
chillness
choleraic
coalfield
coalition
coalmouse
coelomata
coelomate
coelostat
collagist
collation
colleague
collected
collector
collegial
collegian
collegium
colligate
collimate
collinear
collision
collocate
collodion
colloidal
colloquia
collotype
collusion
collusive
collyrium
cowlstaff
cullender
cuplichen
curliness
curlpaper
cyclamate
cycloidal
cyclopean
cyclopian
cyclopses
cyclorama
cyclotron
dalliance
declaimer
declarant
declinate
declivity
declivous
deflation
deflector
deflexion
depletion
depletive
dewlapped
dialectal
dialectic
dialogise
dialogism
dialogist
diclinous
diplomacy
diplomate
dislocate
doglegged
drollness
dualistic
duplicate
duplicity
earliness
ebullient
ecclesial
ecologist
edelweiss
effluence
effluvial
effluvium
effluxion
emolliate
emollient
emolument
emplastic
emulation
emulative
emulously
enclosure
endlessly
Englander
englutted
epilation
epileptic
epilogist
esplanade
euclidean
evolution
evolutive
evolvable
exclosure
exclusion
exclusive
exilement
explainer
expletive
expletory
explicate
exploiter
explosion
explosive
exultance
exultancy
fallalery
faultless
feelingly
fellowman
fieldbook
fieldboot
fieldfare
fieldsman
fieldwork
fillister
following
foolhardy
foolishly
foolproof
forlornly
foulbrood
frolicked
fullblown
fullcream
fulldress
fullgrown
fullscale
Gaeltacht
gallantly
gallantry
galleried
gallicise
gallicism
gallingly
gallinule
gallivant
galliwasp
gallmidge
gallonage
gallooned
gallopade
Gallophil
galloping
gallowses
gallstone
gaolbreak
gauleiter
geologise
geologist
girlishly
goalmouth
godliness
grillroom
grillwork
guildhall
guildship
guileless
guillemot
guilloche
guiltless
hailstone
hailstorm
Halloween
Hallowmas
hallstand
Hallstatt
haplessly
haplology
harlequin
healthful
healthily
heelpiece
hellebore
hellenise
Hellenism
Hellenist
hellhound
hellishly
hillbilly
Hitlerism
Hitlerite
hollyhock
Hollywood
Icelander
Icelandic
impleader
implement
impletion
implicate
impliedly
implosion
implosive
impluvium
inclement
inclosure
inclusion
inclusive
inelastic
inelegant
inflation
inflexion
inflictor
inflowing
influence
influenza
inglenook
isallobar
isolation
isolative
italicise
Italicism
jailbreak
jealously
jellyfish
jollyboat
joylessly
kaolinise
kaolinite
keelivine
Keplerian
killifish
lallation
Laplander
lawlessly
lowlander
lowliness
lowloader
maelstrom
mahlstick
mailplane
mailtrain
malleable
malleehen
mallemuck
malleolar
malleolus
manliness
marlstone
maulstick
mealiness
millboard
millenary
millennia
millepede
millepore
millerite
milligram
millinery
millionth
millipede
millivolt
millstone
millwheel
misleared
molluscan
mollymawk
mouldable
mullioned
myelomata
myologist
nailbrush
negligent
neolithic
neologian
neologise
neologism
neologist
newlyweds
nobleness
nonlinear
nucleated
nucleolus
nucleonic
nullifier
nullipara
nullipore
obbligato
occludent
occlusion
occlusive
ocellated
ochlocrat
odalisque
onelegged
onslaught
opulently
orologist
otologist
oubliette
outlander
ovulation
ovulatory
paillasse
paillette
Palladian
palladium
palladous
palletise
palliasse
pallidity
parleyvoo
parlously
paulownia
Pavlovian
pellagrin
pelletise
pellitory
phalanger
phalanges
phalanxes
phalarope
phellogen
philander
philately
philippic
philogyny
philology
Philomela
phyllopod
phylogeny
pillarbox
pollinate
pollinium
pollutant
pollution
popliteal
poulterer
prelatess
prelatise
prelature
prelector
prelusion
prelusive
prelusory
prolamine
prolapsus
prolately
prolation
prolative
prolepses
prolepsis
proleptic
prolicide
prolixity
prologise
prolusion
prolusory
psalmbook
psalmodic
psalteria
Ptolemaic
publicise
publicist
publicity
publisher
pullulate
purloiner
qualified
qualifier
quillwort
realistic
reclinate
reclusion
reclusive
redletter
reflation
reflector
reflexion
reflexive
refluence
replenish
repletion
replicate
riflebird
sailcloth
sailoring
sailorman
sailplane
sallowish
scaldfish
scalefern
scalefish
scaleleaf
scaleless
scalelike
scalemoss
scaliness
scallawag
scallywag
scalplock
schlemiel
schlemihl
schlieren
scolecite
scoliosis
scoliotic
sculpture
sealetter
seclusion
seclusive
sexlessly
sexlinked
shallowly
sheldduck
sheldrake
shelflife
shelfmark
shelfroom
shellback
shellbark
shellfire
shellfish
shellheap
shellwork
shillelah
silliness
sinlessly
skilfully
smallarms
smallness
smalltime
smileless
smilingly
soulfully
spellbind
spellican
spillikin
spoliator
stalactic
stalemate
staleness
Stalinism
Stalinist
stalkeyed
stalkless
stallfeed
stalworth
stellated
stilettos
stillborn
stillhunt
stillness
stillroom
stiltedly
stolidity

stolonate
stylebook
styliform
stylishly
stylistic
stylobate
sublation
sublethal
sublimate
sublimely
sublimity
sublunary
sunlounge
surliness
swellfish
syllabary
syllabise
syllabism
syllabled
syllepses
syllepsis
sylleptic
syllogise
syllogism
tablature
tableland
tableleaf
tabletalk
tableware
tailboard
taillight
tailoress
tailoring
tailpiece
tallowish
tallyshop
tanliquor
tellingly
tellurate
tellurian
telluride
tellurite
tellurium
tellurous
thalassic
thylacine
titledeed
titlepage
tollbooth
tollhouse
toolhouse
trilinear
trilithon
trilobate
trilobite
twelfthly
Uitlander
ululation
unalloyed
unaltered
unblessed
unblinded
uncleanly
unclothed
unclouded
unfledged
unfleshed
unfleshly
unplugged
unplumbed
uselessly
vallation
vallecula
villagery
villanage
villenage
villiform
villosity
violation
violative
violently
violinist
wailingly
wallboard
wallcress
wallfruit
walloping
wallpaper
wallplate
wallydrag
wealthily
wellbeing
wellfound
wellknown
welltimed
whaleback
whaleboat
whalebone
whalehead
wholemeal
wholeness
wholesale
wholesome
wieldable
willemite
willingly
willowish
willpower
witlessly
worldling
worldwide
Wyclifite
yellowdog
yellowish
zealously
zoologist
abominate
acuminate
adamantly
ademption
adumbrate
airminded
Alemannic
aluminate
aluminise
aluminium
aluminous
anamnesis
anemogram
animalise
animalism
animalist
animality
animation
animatism
animistic
animosity
anomalous
anomalure
apomictic
aromatise
asymmetry
asymptote
atomicity
atomistic
augmented
augmenter
augmentor
azimuthal
badminton
balminess
barmbrack
Barmecide
beamingly
beemaster
biometric
bismillah
blameable
blameably
blameless
boomerang
boomslang
brambling
brimstone
bromeliad
brummagem
calmative
Carmelite
chameleon
chamomile
champagne
champaign
champerty
champleve
chemistry
chemitype
chemurgic
chimaeric
Cimmerian
clamantly
clamorous
clamshell
clemently
climactic
climbable
coemption
commander
commandos
commendam
commensal
commenter
commingle
comminute
commissar
committal
committed
committee
commodity
commodore
commonage
commonlaw
commotion
communard
communion
communise
communism
communist
community
commutate
cormorant
cosmogeny
cosmogony
cosmology
cosmonaut
cosmorama
coumarone
crampfish
cremaster
cremation
crematory
criminate
criminous
CroMagnon
culminant
culminate
dalmatian
dermatoid
diametral
diametric
dismantle
dismember
dismissal
dogmatics
dogmatise
dogmatism
dogmatist
dormition
dormitory
dramatics
dramatise
dramatist
dromedary
drummajor
drumstick
ecumenism
egomaniac
elemental
eliminate
enamelled
enameller
enamoured
enumerate
eremitism
esemplasy
ethmoidal
etymology
examinant
exemplary
exemplify
exemption
farmhouse
farmstead
filminess
filmstrip
firmament
flambeaus
flambeaux
flameless
flamingly
flamingos
flammable
formalise
formalism
formalist
formality
formation
formative
formatted
formicary
formicate
formulaic
formulary
formulate
formulise
framework
fulminant
fulminate
fulminous
gammadion
gammoning
garmented
gasmantle
gemmation
gemmology
geomancer
geomantic
geometric
geometrid
germander
germanely
germanise
Germanish
Germanism
Germanist
germanium
germicide
germinate
germplasm
germproof
gimmickry
glamorise
glamorous
glomerate
glomerule
glomeruli
godmother
grimalkin
griminess
grumbling
gumminess
haematite
haematoid
haematoma
haemostat
hammerman
hammertoe
harmaline
harmattan
harmfully
harmonica
harmonics
harmonise
harmonist
harmonium
harmotome
hermitage
inamorata
isomerise
isomerism
isomerous
isometric
jobmaster
krummhorn
lowminded
lyamhound
mammalian
mammalogy
mammiform
mammonish
mammonism
mammonist
mammonite
marmalade
marmoreal
mesmerise
mesmerism
mesmerist
mismanage
mnemonics
mnemonist
Mormonism
mummified
murmurous
myrmecoid
naumachia
newmarket
normalise
normality
Normanise
Normanism
normative
nummulite
onomastic
palmation
palmipede
palmistry
palmitate
paymaster
pegmatite
permanent
permeable
permeance
permitted
permitter
permutate
plumbeous
plumbline
plumdamas
plumpness
plumulate
plumulose
pommelled
premature
premonish
premotion
primaeval
primality
primarily
primatial
primeness
primipara
primitive
primordia
promenade
prominent
promising
promotion
promotive
promptbox
pulmonary
pulmonate
pummelled
reimburse
rhymester
rigmarole
roominess
Roumanian
Roumansch
salmonoid
Sarmation
schmaltzy
scombroid
seaminess
seemingly
segmental
sermonise
shamanism
shamanist
shamateur
shambling
shambolic
shamefast
shameless
shemozzle
sigmoidal
sliminess
slumberer
slumbrous
solmisate
sommelier
staminate
stammerer
stampduty
stampmill
stampnote
stimulant
stimulate
stomachal
stomacher
stomachic
submarine
submaster
submental
submitted
summarily
summarise
summarist
summation
summative
summingup
surmullet
swimmable
swimmeret
symmetric
Talmudist
Tasmanian
tegmental
tegmentum
termagant
terminate
terminism
terminist
termitary
Thomistic
thumbhole
thumbmark
thumbnail
thumbtack
tormentil
tormentor
tramlines
trematode
tremolant
tremolite
tremulant
tremulous
trimerous
trimester
trimetric
trimmings
trumpedup
trumpeter
unsmiling
vermicide
vermicule
vermiform
vermifuge
vermilion
verminate
verminous
warmonger
whimperer
whimsical
wormeaten
wormwheel
abandoned
abandonee
abandoner
abundance
aciniform
aconitine
adenoidal
adenomata
adenosine
agonising
agonistic
alinement
aloneness
alongside
amendable
amendment
aminoacid
anandrous
anonymity
anonymous
araneidal
araneidan
asininity
asyndetic
asyndeton
atonalism
atonality
atonement
atonicity
aventaile
avuncular
bainmarie
bannister
barnacled
barnstorm
beanfeast
beanstalk
bionomics
blandness
blankness
blindfold
blindness
blinkered
blunderer
bluntness
Boanerges
bonniness
boondocks

boundless
bounteous
bountiful
branchiae
branchial
branchlet
brandling
brandreth
bringdown
bronchial
burnedout
burningly
burnisher
Caenozoic
Cainozoic
cannelure
canniness
cannonade
cannoneer
cannonier
cannulate
carnality
carnation
carnelian
carnitine
carnivore
ceanothus
chanceful
chancroid
chancrous
chandlery
changeful
chanteuse
chantilly
chantress
Chinatown
chinaware
chinstrap
chondrite
chondrule
clinician
clinquant
coenobite
coenobium
coenosarc
cognately
cognation
cognisant
cognition
cognitive
coinsurer
connately
connation
connature
connected
connecter
connector
connexion
connivent
connubial
cornbrash
corncrake
cornelian
cornemuse
cornerboy
cornerman
cornetist
cornfield
cornflour
cornopean
cornsalad
cornstalk
cornstone
countable
countdown
countless
countship
cranberry
crankcase
cranreuch
crenation
crenature
crenelled
crenulate
crinoidal
crinoline
cunningly
cyanamide
damnation
damnatory
damnedest
damningly
dauntless
deinosaur
diandrous
dignified
dignitary
dinnerset
Dionysiac
Dionysian
donnishly
downfield
downgrade
downright
downriver
downstage
downthrow
downwards
drinkable
drunkenly
earnestly
economics
economise
economist
elongated
emanation
emanative
emendable
emendator
eminently
emunctory
enunciate
epinastic
eponymous
ethnarchy
ethnicity
ethnology
evangelic
eventless
eventuate
evincible
ewenecked
exanimate
exanthema
exonerate
faintness
faunistic
fawningly
fiendlike
flannelly
flintlock
fornicate
foundling
foundress
franchise
francolin
frangible
Franglais
frankness
franticly
frenchify
Frenchman
frontally
frontless
frontline
frontpage
frontward
frontways
frontwise
funnelled
funniness
furnisher
furniture
gainfully
gainsayer
gannister
garnishee
garniture
gauntness
giantlike
glandered
glandular
glengarry
goingover
grandaddy
grandaunt
grandiose
grandness
grandpapa
grandsire
grandslam
granitoid
grantable
granulate
granulite
granulose
grenadier
grenadine
Grundyism
gymnasial
gymnasium
gymnastic
heinously
herniated
hobnailed
hobnobbed
hobnobber
horniness
hornstone
hornwrack
hymnology
hypnoidal
hypnology
hypnotise
hypnotism
hypnotist
ichneumon
ichnology
iconology
identical
identikit
inanimate
inanition
inunction
ironbound
ironmould
ironsides
ironsmith
ironstone
ironworks
isinglass
isoniazid
itineracy
itinerant
itinerary
itinerate
jaundiced
jointress
kennelled
Keynesian
kidnapped
kidnapper
klinostat
lagniappe
launching
launderer
laundress
lawnmower
lignaloes
ligniform
limnology
lioncelle
lionheart
loanshark
loincloth
lownecked
magnalium
magnesian
magnesite
magnesium
magnetics
magnetise
magnetism
magnetist
magnetite
magnetron
magnifico
magnifier
magnitude
mainbrace
mainliner
mainsheet
mannequin
mannerism
mannerist
maunderer
meandrine
meandrous
meaningly
meanwhile
Mennonite
moonblind
moonlight
moonquake
moonraker
moonscape
moonshine
moonstone
mountable
nannygoat
odontalgy
ominously
onanistic
openended
openheart
opinioned
orangeade
Orangeism
Orangeman
orangetip
orangutan
outnumber
ovenready
painfully
painterly
paintwork
penniless
pennywort
phantasma
phenacite
phenakite
phenology
phenomena
phenotype
phonation
phonatory
phonemics
phonetics
phonetise
phonetism
phonetist
phoniness
phonogram
phonolite
phonology
pianistic
picnicked
picnicker
pinnately
pinnipede
pinnulate
planarian
planation
planetary
planetoid
plangency
planisher
plantable
plantlike
planuloid
plenarily
plenitude
plenteous
plentiful
plunderer
poinciana
pointduty
pointedly
pointille
pointlace
pointless
pointsman
pouncebox
poundcake
pranksome
prankster
prenotion
princedom
princekin
princelet
principal
principia
principle
printable
printshop
pronation
proneness
pronghorn
pronounce
pugnacity
pycnidium
quantical
quinoline
quintette
quintuple
raincheck
raincloud
raingauge
raininess
rainmaker
rainproof
rainstorm
rainwater
raunchily
reanimate
reenforce
reentrant
reinforce
reinstate
Rhineodon
rhinology
rhonchial
rounceval
roundelay
roundhead
roundness
roundsman
roundworm
ruination
ruinously
sainthood
saintlike
saintling
saintship
saunterer
scantling
scantness
scenarist
scenedock
scentless
schnauzer
schnitzel
schnorkel
schnorrer
scintilla
scuncheon
seanettle
Shangrila
shantyman
shinguard
shininess
Shintoism
Shintoist
signalbox
signalise
signalled
signaller
signalman
signatory
signature
signboard
significs
signorial
signorina
skindiver
skinflick
skinflint
skingraft
skintight
slanderer
slantways
slantwise
slenderly
slingback
slingshot
slinkweed
somnolent
sonneteer
sonnetise
soundfilm
soundhole
soundings
soundless
soundness
soundpost
soundwave
spendable
spindling
spindrier
spindrift
spineless
spininess
spinnaker
spinneret
spinosity
Spinozism
Spinozist
spinulose
spinulous
spongebag
spongeous
stanchion
standpipe
stenotype
stenotypy
stingaree
stingless
stinkball
stinkbomb
stinkhorn
stinktrap
stinkweed
stinkwood
stintless
stonechat
stonecoal
stonecold
stonecrop
stonedead
stonedeaf
stonefish
stoneless
stonewall
stoneware
stonework
stonewort
stoniness
subnormal
sunniness
swangoose
swansdown
swineherd
swingeing
swinishly
taeniasis
taintless
tawniness
teknonymy
ternately
thaneship
thankless
thingness
thingummy
thinkable
thinktank
thunderer
tinniness
townhouse
townscape
townsfolk
transcend
transenna
transform
transfuse
transient
translate
transmute
transonic
transpire
transport
transpose
transship
transumpt
transvest
trenchant
trinketer
trinketry
trinomial
truncated
truncheon
trunkcall
trunkfish
trunkroad
tunnelled
tunnelnet
turnabout
turnround
turnstile
turnstone
turntable
twentieth
twentyone
twinkling
unanimity
unanimous
unknitted
unknowing
Upanishad
uraninite
uranology
vainglory
varnisher
veinstone

vernalise
vernation
vignetter
vulnerary
Wagnerian
Wagnerite
warningly
Wednesday
whinstone
winningly
woundless
woundwort
wrongdoer
wrongness
wyandotte
yawningly
youngling
youngness
youngster
Zwinglian
abdominal
abhorrent
abhorring
abnormity
abrogator
absorbent
absorbing
accompany
accordant
according
accordion
acrobatic
acropetal
acropolis
acroteria
adjoining
admonitor
adnominal
adsorbate
adsorbent
advocator
aerobatic
aerobiont
aerodrome
aerograph
aerolitic
aerometer
aerometry
aerophyte
aeroplane
aerospace
agrologic
agronomic
alcoholic
Algonkian
Algonquin
algorithm
allocable
allograph
allomorph
allopathy
allophone
alloplasm
allotment
allotrope
allotropy
allotting
allowable
allowably
allowance
allowedly
aloofness
annotator
announcer
annoyance
appointee
apportion
arboreous
arboretum
Areopagus
Armorican
arrogance
arrowhead
arrowroot
arrowwood
arrowworm
ascospore
associate
assonance
atmometer
atrocious
autoclave
autocracy
autocross
autocycle
autograft
autograph
autolysis
autolytic
automatic
automaton
autonomic
autopilot
autoroute
autosomal
autotelic
autotroph
axiomatic
azeotrope
baboonish
barograph
barometer
barometry
baronetcy
bayoneted
beeorchis
befogging
besotting
biconcave
bifoliate
bimonthly
binocular
binominal
bloodbath
bloodless
bloodlust
bloodroot
bloodshed
bloodshot
bloodworm
bloodwort
bolometer
bolometry
boxoffice
broomcorn
broomrape
bryophyte
buxomness
cacodemon
cacodylic
cacoethes
cacophony
calorific
camorrist
canonical
carolling
catoptric
cerograph
cheongsam
chlorella
chloritic
chlorosis
chlorotic
chromatic
chromatin
chronical
chronicle
cipollino
cocoonery
colocynth
colonelcy
coloniser
colonnade
colophony
colorific
colosseum
colostomy
colostrum
colourful
colouring
colourist
colourman
copolymer
corollary
coroneted
crookback
crookedly
crookneck
cryogenic
cryoscope
cryoscopy
cymophane
cytolysis
cytoplasm
cytotoxic
cytotoxin
Damoclean
decoction
decollate
decollete
decomplex
decompose
decongest
decontrol
decorator
defoliant
defoliate
deformity
demobbing
democracy
denouncer
deposable
depositor
desolater
desolator
detonator
devotedly
dimorphic
dinoceras
dinothere
disoblige
disorient
dogoodism
dolomitic
donothing
echolalia
echovirus
ectoblast
ectogenic
ectomorph
ectophyte
ectoplasm
effortful
eidograph
elbowroom
encomiast
encompass
encounter
encourage
endoblast
endocrine
endogamic
endogenic
endolymph
endomixis
endomorph
endophagy
endophyte
endoplasm
endoscope
endoscopy
endosperm
endospore
endosteal
endosteum
endowment
enjoyable
enjoyably
enjoyment
enrolling
enrolment
entoblast
entophyte
entourage
ergograph
ergometer
ergonomic
erroneous
errorless
escortage
espousals
estoppage
estopping
eulogiser
excoriate
exfoliate
expositor
expounder
extolling
extolment
extorsive
extortion
extortive
eyeopener
favourite
felonious
ferocious
filoselle
floodgate
floodmark
floodtide
fluoresce
fluorosis
fluorspar
gasometer
genocidal
genotypic
Girondist
gonophore
groomsman
gynocracy
gynoecium
gynophore
gyroplane
gyroscope
halophile
halophyte
halothane
havocking
hodograph
hodometer
holocaust
holograph
holophote
homogamic
homograft
homograph
homologue
homonymic
homophone
homophony
homoplasy
homopolar
homotaxis
homotonic
homousian
honoraria
honorific
horologer
horologic
horoscope
horoscopy
hylozoism
hypoblast
hypocaust
hypocotyl
hypocrisy
hypocrite
hypogeous
hypomania
hypomanic
hyponasty
hypostyle
hypotaxis
ideograph
ideologic
ideologue
idiograph
idiomatic
idiopathy
idioplasm
idiotical
ignorable
ignoramus
ignorance
illogical
illomened
immodesty
immolator
immorally
immovable
immovably
impolitic
important
importune
impostume
imposture
impotence
impotency
impounder
incognito
incommode
incondite
incorrect
incorrupt
IndoAryan
indolence
informant
innocence
innocency
innocuity
innocuous
innovator
innoxious
inpouring
insolence
insoluble
insolubly
insolvent
insomniac
intorsion
involucre
involuted
isooctane
jaborandi
Jacobinic
Junoesque
kilocycle
kilohertz
kilolitre
kilometre
kymograph
laborious
labourite
lagomorph
limonitic
limousine
locomotor
logogriph
logomachy
loxodrome
Mahometan
majordomo
majorette
majorship
manoeuvre
manometer
manorseat
masochism
masochist
masonried
Masoretic
mayoralty
mayorship
mekometer
melocoton
melodious
melodrama
melomania
memoirist
memorable
memorably
memoranda
memoriter
menopause
meropidan
mesoblast
mesogloea
mesomorph
mesophyll
mesophyte
metonymic
milometer
misoneism
misoneist
mobocracy
monobasic
monoceros
monochord
monocline
monocoque
monocracy
monocular
monodical
monodrama
monoecism
monogamic
monograph
monolatry
monologic
monologue
monomania
monomeric
monophagy
monoplane
monorhyme
monostich
monostyle
monotonic
monotreme
monotypic
motocross
motorable
motorbike
motorboat
motorcade
mycologic
mycophagy
myrobalan
myxoedema
negotiant
negotiate
nemophila
nicotiana
nicotinic
Nilometer
nomocracy
nomograph
notochord
notoriety
notorious
obconical
obcordate
obnoxious
obsolesce
Octobrist
octopodes
octostyle
oecologic
oenomancy
oenophile
oenophily
oesophagi
oleograph
oleoresin
oncogenic
oncologic
onionskin
ontogenic
ontologic
opponency
opportune
opposable
optometer
optometry
optophone
osmometer
panoplied
panoramic
parochial
parotitis
pasodoble
pedometer
pilotfish
pirouette
pisolitic
pivotable
pivotally
polonaise
preoccupy
preordain
priorship
proofread
pyrogenic
pyrolater
pyrolatry
pyrolysis
pyrolytic
pyromancy
pyromania
pyrometer
pyrometry
pyroscope
pyroxylin
raconteur
razorback
razorbill
razoredge
razorfish
recognise
recoinage
recollect
recombine
recommend
recompose
reconcile
recondite
reconfirm
reconvene
reconvert
recording
recordist
recoverer

redolence
redoubted
reformism
reformist
rejoicing
rejoinder
remontant
removable
renouncer
renovator
reportage
reposeful
repossess
repotting
resoluble
resolvent
resonance
resonator
resorbent
resources
retortion
retoucher
revocable
revolting
ribosomal
Samoyedic
sapodilla
savourily
saxophone
scholarly
scholiast
schoolbag
schoolboy
schooling
schoolman
scrollsaw
scrounger
secondary
serotonin
shootable
sinologue
sinophile
smoothish
sojourner
Solomonic
sonometer
soporific
spoonbeak
spoonbill
spoonfeed
spoonmeat
stoolball
strobilae
strobilus
stromatic
strongarm
strongbox
strongish
strongyle
strontium
stropping
strouding
subocular
sudorific
sycophant
synodical
synoecete
synonymic
synoptist
synovitis
taioseach
taxonomic
telophase
theocracy
theocrasy
theogonic
theologic
theologue
theomachy
theomania
theophany
theoretic
theoriser
theosophy
throatily
throbbing
thrombose
throttler
throughly
throwaway
throwback
throwster
timocracy
tinopener
tonometer
toponymal
toponymic
toxophily
troopship
tutorship
unbounded
unconcern
uncounted
uncouthly
uncovered
undoubted
unfounded
unpointed
unpopular
unsoundly
untouched
unwomanly
upcountry
upholster
vaporable
vaporific
vaporiser
vapouring
vapourish
vasomotor
velodrome
wagonette
wagonroof
widowbird
widowhood
xenograft
xenophile
xenophobe
xeromorph
xerophile
xerophily
xerophyte
xylograph
xylophone
zygomatic
zygospore
zymogenic
adaptable
adeptness
adipocere
adiposity
adoptable
agapemone
aliphatic
anaphoric
anaptyxis
anopheles
apophyses
apophysis
asepalous
auspicate
bespangle
bespatter
bumpiness
bumptious
campanile
campanili
campanula
campchair
campcraft
campfever
camphoric
campstool
carpenter
carpentry
carpetbag
carpeting
carpingly
carpology
chaparral
chaperone
chapleted
chipboard
chipolata
chophouse
choplogic
chopstick
clapboard
clepsydra
clipboard
compactly
compactor
companion
compasses
compelled
compendia
competent
complaint
complexly
complexus
compliant
component
composite
composure
comprador
comprisal
comptroll
cooperage
cooperant
cooperate
corporate
corporeal
corposant
corpulent
corpuscle
crapulent
crapulous
crepitant
crepitate
crepuscle
crippling
cropeared
cryptical
cryptogam
cryptonym
cuspidate
desperado
desperate
despoiler
despotism
diaphragm
diaphysis
disparage
disparate
disparity
dispelled
dispenser
dispeople
dispersal
disperser
displease
disposure
dispraise
disputant
dripstone
dropscene
dropscone
dropsical
dumpiness
dyspepsia
dyspeptic
dysphagia
dysphagic
dysphonia
dysphoria
dysphoric
dysplasia
dyspnoeic
elopement
epiphragm
epiphyses
epiphysis
epiphytal
epiphytic
epipolism
evaporate
exopodite
flippancy
flophouse
foppishly
gaspereau
geoponics
ginpalace
glyptodon
godparent
gomphosis
gospeller
grapeshot
grapevine
graphemic
graphical
graphitic
grappling
gunpowder
happening
happiness
harpooner
helpfully
herpetoid
Hesperian
hippocras
hispidity
inaptness
ineptness
inspanned
inspector
isopodous
jampacked
jumpiness
lampblack
lamplight
lampooner
lampshade
lampshell
limpidity
lispingly
lumpiness
lumpishly
lymphatic
lyophilic
lyophobic
mispickel
morphemic
Nipponese
nitpicker
nonpareil
nonperson
nonprofit
nymphalid
oilpaints
omophagia
omophagic
outputted
oviparity
oviparous
palpation
palpebral
palpitant
palpitate
pauperise
pauperism
paypacket
peepsight
pemphigus
penpusher
pepperbox
pepperpot
perpetual
pimpernel
pompadour
pomposity
pompously
poppycock
poppyhead
porphyria
potpourri
prepotent
propagate
propelled
propeller
properdin
prophetic
propionic
proponent
propriety
proptosis
propylaea
propylene
pulpboard
pulpiness
pulpiteer
pulpstone
puppeteer
puppyhood
purposely
purposive
purpureal
rampantly
raspatory
raspberry
raspingly
respecter
responder
rhapsodic
salpinges
sappiness
scapegoat
scapolite
scapulary
sceptical
serpentry
shapeable
shapeless
shipboard
shipcanal
shipfever
shipmoney
shipowner
shipshape
shipwreck
shopfloor
shopfront
simpatico
simpleton
simplices
slaphappy
slapstick
slipcoach
slipcover
slopbasin
slopewise
snipefish
soapberry
soapiness
soapstone
soapworks
soppiness
soupplate
soupspoon
stapedial
stepchild
stepdance
stipitate
stippling
stipulate
stoplight
stoppress
stopwatch
stupefier
stupidity
stuporous
subphylum
sulphonic
sulphuret
sulphuric
sumptuary
sumptuous
suppliant
supporter
supposing
suppurate
surpliced
surprisal
suspender
suspensor
suspicion
sweptback
sylphlike
symphonic
symphysis
sympodial
sympodium
symposiac
symposial
symposium
tamponade
tanpickle
tarpaulin
taxpaying
temperate
temporary
temporise
temptable
temptress
timpanist
torpidity
trapezial
trapezium
trapezoid
trappings
trepanned
trepidant
triploidy
triptyque
tropology
turpitude
tympanist
unaptness
uniparous
uniplanar
unsparing
unspotted
uropygium
vampirism
vulpinism
vulpinite
Walpurgis
waspishly
whipperin
whipround
whipsnake
whipstock
zoophagan
zoophobia
zoophytic
banqueter
banquette
bouquetin
briquette
chequered
coequally
conqueror
croquette
eloquence
etiquette
exequatur
frequence
frequency
harquebus
inequable
Iroquoian
jacquerie
marquetry
mosquitos
parquetry
sasquatch
triquetra
turquoise
unequally
aberrance
aberrancy
aborigine
acariasis
accretion
accretive
addressee
addresser
addressor
adoration
adoringly
adornment
affricate
aforesaid
aggravate
aggregate
aggressor
aggrieved
alertness
altricial
amaryllis
ambrosial
americium
Amerindic
amoralism
amorality
amorously
amorphism
amorphous
anarchism
anarchist
androecia
androgyne
androgyny
angriness
anorectic
anorthite
apartheid
apartment
apartness
aperiodic
aperitive
appraisal
appraiser
apprehend
appressed
approbate
astraddle
astrakhan
astrocyte
astrodome
astrolabe
astrology
astronaut

astronomy
ataractic
attractor
attribute
attrition
aubrietia
averagely
avertible
awardable
awareness
barracker
barracoon
barracuda
barrelful
barrelled
barricade
barricado
barrister
basrelief
bearberry
beardless
bedraggle
bedridden
betrothal
betrothed
biorhythm
boardfoot
boardroom
boardwalk
boorishly
borrowing
bourgeois
buhrstone
burrstone
byproduct
cabriolet
caerulean
cairngorm
capriccio
Capricorn
carrageen
carrefour
carronade
carryover
charabanc
character
chariness
charivari
charlatan
charlotte
charmeuse
charmless
Charolais
chartered
charterer
charwoman
cherimoya
chernozem
cherrypie
chiropody
chorister
chorology
churching
churchman
cirrhosis
cirripede
clarifier
clarionet
clergyman
clergymen
clerkship
coarctate
coercible
coercibly
comradely
comradery
coproduce
coprolite
coprology
corralled
corrasion
correctly
corrector
correlate
corrosion
corrosive
corrugate
corrupter
corruptly
courgette
courtcard
courteous
courtesan
courtroom
courtship
courtyard
currently
curricula
currishly
currycomb
cyprinoid
czarevich
dairymaid
decrement
decretive
decretory
deerberry
deerhound
defroster
depravity
deprecate
depredate
depressed
depressor
derringdo
derringer
detractor
detriment
detrition
detrusion
dharmsala
diarrhoea
dicrotism
didrachma
disregard
disrelish
disrepair
disrepute
diurnally
doorframe
doorplate
embraceor
embracery
embracive
embrangle
embrasure
embrittle
embrocate
embroglio
embroider
embryonal
embryonic
embryotic
emergence
emergency
encrimson
encrinite
energetic
energiser
energumen
engraving
engrosser
entrammel
entrapped
entrechat
entrecote
entremets
enwrapped
enwreathe
estranger
estrapade
esurience
esuriency
eternally
eutrophic
everglade
evergreen
everybody
exarchate
excrement
excretion
excretive
excretory
exercises
exorciser
expressly
extractor
extradite
extravert
extremely
extremism
extremist
extremity
extricate
extrinsic
extrovert
extrusion
extrusive
fabricant
fabricate
fairfaced
fairyhood
fairyland
fairylike
fairyring
fairytale
fearfully
febricity
febrifuge
ferrotype
ferryboat
fibreless
fibriform
fibrillar
fibrinoid
fibrinous
fibroline
fibromata
fieriness
fioritura
fioriture
flarepath
flaringly
floriated
floridean
floridity
floristic
floristry
fourflush
fourpence
fourpenny
fourscore
fourwheel
garreteer
garrotter
garrulity
garrulous
gearlever
gearshift
gearwheel
georgette
glaringly
gloryhole
guarantee
guarantor
guardbook
guardedly
guardrail
guardring
guardroom
guardship
guardsman
guerrilla
gunrunner
hagridden
hairbrush
haircloth
hairgrass
hairiness
hairpiece
hairshirt
hairslide
hairspace
hairstyle
Harrovian
harrowing
heartache
heartbeat
heartburn
heartfelt
heartfree
hearthrug
heartland
heartless
heartsick
heartsore
heartwood
Hebridean
heuristic
hierarchy
hieratica
hierodule
hierogram
hierology
hoarfrost
hoarhound
hoariness
hoarstone
hourglass
hubristic
hurricane
hurriedly
hybridise
hybridism
hybridity
hydraemia
hydrangea
hydration
hydraulic
hydrazine
hydriodic
hydrocele
hydrofoil
hydrology
hydrolyse
hydrolyte
hydronium
hydrosome
hydroxide
hydrozoan
hydrozoon
hygrostat
imbricate
imbroglio
imprecate
imprecise
impresari
improbity
impromptu
improvise
imprudent
inbreathe
increaser
increment
indraught
inerrable
inerrancy
inertness
infractor
ingrained
ingrowing
inorganic
intricacy
intricate
intrigant
intriguer
intrinsic
introduce
introject
introvert
intrusion
intrusive
inurement
inwrought
iteration
iterative
jarringly
jeeringly
journeyer
kurrajong
lacrimose
lacrymose
lairdship
laurelled
learnable
learnedly
leeringly
librarian
libration
libratory
librettos
lipreader
louringly
lubricant
lubricate
lubricity
lubricous
lucrative
macrocosm
macrocyte
madrepore
marrowfat
matriarch
matricide
matricula
matrimony
matronage
matronise
merriment
merriness
metricate
metrician
metricise
metricist
metrology
metronome
microbial
microchip
microcosm
microcyte
microfilm
microgram
microlite
microlith
micrology
micromesh
micropsia
micropyle
microsome
microtome
microtomy
microtone
microwave
migration
migratory
misreckon
misreport
mitraille
morrisman
mucronate
mydriasis
mydriatic
narration
narrative
narratory
natrolite
necrology
necrophil
necrotise
negritude
negroidal
Negroness
negrophil
neuralgia
neuralgic
neuration
neuroglia
neurology
neuromata
neuropath
nigricant
nigritude
nigrosine
nitratine
nitration
nourisher
nutriment
nutrition
nutritive
obtrusion
obtrusive
odorously
onerously
operation
operative
opercular
operculum
operosely
operosity
oppressor
ostracise
ostracism
Ostrogoth
outridden
outrigger
overblown
overboard
overborne
overcheck
overcloud
overcrowd
overdraft
overdrawn
overdress
overdrive
overeaten
overeater
overexert
overflown
overglaze
overgraze
overgrown
overheard
overissue
overjoyed
overladen
overleapt
overlying
overmatch
overnight
overpitch
overpower
overprice
overprint
overproof
overreach
overreact
oversexed
overshoot
oversight
oversized
overskirt
oversleep
overslept
overspend
overspent
overspill
overstate
oversteer
overstock
overstuff
overtaken
overthrew
overthrow
overtness
overtones
overtrain
overtrick
overtrump
overvalue
overwatch
overweary
overweigh
overwhelm
overwound
overwrite
overwrote
pairhorse
parrakeet
parricide
patriarch
patrician
patricide
patrimony
patriotic
patristic
patrolled
patroller
patrolman
patrology
patronage
patroness
patronise
pearlitic
pearlwort
petroleum
petrology
pharaonic
pharisaic
pharyngal
pharynges
pharynxes
pheromone
pierrette
pluralise
pluralism
pluralist
plurality
poorhouse
porringer
pourboire
pourpoint
prerecord
prorogate
prurience
pruriency
psoriasis
psoriatic
ptarmigan
pterosaur
pterygium
pterygoid
puerility

puerperal
purringly
putridity
quarenden
quarender
quarryman
quarterly
quartette
quartzite
quartzose
quercetum
querulous
quirister
rearguard
rearhorse
rearlight
rearmouse
rearrange
rearwards
recreancy
recruital
recruiter
redresser
refractor
refreshen
refresher
regretful
regretted
reprehend
represent
repressor
reprieval
reprimand
reprobate
reprocess
reproduce
retractor
retrieval
retriever
retrocede
retrodden
retroflex
retroject
retrousse
retrovert
rewritten
rubricate
rubrician
rumrunner
sacrament
sacrarium
sacrifice
sacrilege
sacristan
safranine
sapraemia
sapraemic
sauropoda
scarecrow
scarehead
scarfring
scarfskin
scarfwise
scarifier
scirrhous
scorbutic
scorching
scorebook
scorecard
scoredraw
scorifier
scorpioid
searching
searingly
secretage
secretary
secretion
secretive
secretory
segregate
serranoid
serration
serrefile
serrulate
sforzando
sharecrop
sharkskin
sharpener
sharpeyed
sharpness
sharpshod
shirtless
shirttail
shoreless
shoreline
shoreside
shoreward
shoreweed
shortcake
shortener
shortfall
shorthand
shorthorn
shortness
shortstop
shortterm
shortwave
skirtings
skirtless
skyrocket
smartness
smartweed
snaredrum
sobriquet
sopranino
sopranist
sorriness
sorrowful
sourdough
spareness
spareribs
sparingly
sparkcoil
sparkless
sparkplug
spermatic
spermatid
spiracula
spirality
spiralled
spirillum
spiritism
spiritist
spiritoso
spiritous
spiritual
spirituel
spirogyra
sporangia
sporocarp
sporocyst
sporogeny
sportsman
sporulate
spurwheel
starapple
starboard
starchily
stardrift
stargazer
stargrass
starkness
starlight
starshell
starstone
startling
steradian
stercoral
sterilise
sterility
sternmost
sternness
sternpost
sternward
steroidal
stirabout
storeroom
storeship
storiated
stormbelt
stormbird
stormcock
stormcone
stormless
stormsail
storybook
storyline
subregion
subrogate
supremacy
supremely
surrender
surrogate
swarajist
swartness
swordcane
swordfish
swordknot
swordlike
swordplay
swordsman
swordtail
tarragona
tearfully
terramara
terramare
terrarium
territory
terrorise
terrorism
terrorist
tetradite
tetragram
tetralogy
tetrapody
tetrarchy
therapist
Theravada
therefore
therefrom
thereinto
thereunto
thereupon
therewith
thermally
thermidor
thirdhand
thirdrate
thirdsman
thirstily
thirtieth
thornback
thornbill
thornbush
thornless
thorntree
thyratron
thyristor
thyroxine
titration
torridity
touristic
tournedos
tourneyer
tsarevich
ultrahigh
unbraided
unbridled
uncreated
uncropped
uncrossed
uncrowned
undreamed
untrodden
untrussed
unwrapped
unwritten
unwrought
upbraider
uvarovite
uxoricide
veeringly
verrucose
verrucous
vibracula
vibraharp
vibratile
vibration
vibrative
vibratory
vibrissae
vitriform
vitriolic
Vitruvian
warrantee
warranter
warrantor
weariless
weariness
wearisome
wehrmacht
weirdness
wherefore
wherefrom
whereinto
whereunto
whereupon
wherewith
wherryman
whirligig
whirlpool
whirlwind
worriedly
worriment
worrisome
worrywart
xparticle
yearround
zebrawood
abasement
abashment
abusively
abysmally
acescence
agistment
ahistoric
airstream
almsgiver
almshouse
amassment
amusement
amusingly
apishness
apostolic
awesomely
awestruck
baksheesh
beastings
bedsettee
bedsitter
bedspread
bedspring
beestings
berserker
biosphere
blaspheme
blasphemy
blasthole
blastment
blastulae
blastular
blessedly
blushless
blusterer
bobsleigh
Bolshevik
bossiness
bowstring
brashness
brasserie
brassiere
briskness
bristling
brushfire
brushwood
brushwork
brusquely
bursarial
caesarean
caesarian
Caesarism
Caesarist
capsulate
capsulise
Cassandra
cassareep
cassaripe
cassation
casserole
cassimere
cassoulet
cassowary
causality
causation
causative
causeless
ceasefire
ceaseless
censorial
cessation
chassepot
chastener
chastiser
chiselled
chiseller
chisquare
classable
classical
classless
classlist
classmate
classroom
closedown
closeness
coastline
coastward
coastwise
conscious
conscribe
conscript
consensus
conserver
consignee
consignor
consonant
consortia
constable
constancy
constrain
constrict
construct
consulage
consulate
consulter
consultor
copsewood
crashdive
crashland
crassness
crescendo
crestless
crispness
crossable
crossbeam
crossbill
crossbred
crossette
crosseyed
crossfade
crossfire
crossfish
crosshead
crosslink
crossness
crossover
crossroad
crossruff
crosstalk
crossways
crosswind
crosswise
crossword
crushable
crustacea
culsdesac
cursively
cursorial
cursorily
curstness
dayschool
dayspring
deistical
denseness
diastasis
diastatic
diastolic
dieselise
diesinker
dipswitch
dissector
disseisin
dissemble
dissenter
dissident
dissipate
dissocial
dissolute
dissonant
dissuader
dogshores
dogstooth
dosshouse
dresscoat
drysalter
ecosphere
ecossaise
ecosystem
elastomer
elusively
episcopal
epistaxis
epistemic
epistoler
epistolic
eristical
evasively
existence
exosmosis
exosmotic
exosphere
exostosis
eyeshadow
eyestrain
facsimile
falsehood
falseness
falsifier
farseeing
feiseanna
firstborn
firstfoot
firsthand
firstling
firstrate
fissility
fissipede
flashback
flashbulb
flashcube
flashover
flashtube
fleshings
fleshless
fleshment
floscular
flushness
forsythia
fossicker
fossilise
fossorial
freshener
freshness
frostbite
frostwork
frustrate
fulsomely
fussiness
geosphere
geostatic
geyserite
ghostlike
ghostword
glassgall
glassware
glasswork
glasswort
glissandi
glissando
glossator
glossitis
goosander
goosefoot
goosegirl
gooseherd
gooseneck
gooseskin
goosestep
gossamery
graspable
grassland
grisaille
gristmill
grosgrain
grossness
grossular
guesswork
guestroom
gutsiness
hamstring
hamstrung
Hanseatic
hanselled
harshness
haustella
haustoria
hawsehole
hawsepipe
hemstitch
hessonite
hirsutism
hopscotch
horseback
horsebean

horsehair
horsehide
horseless
horsemint
horseplay
horsepond
horseshoe
horsetail
horsewhip
horsiness
houseboat
housebote
housecarl
housecoat
houseflag
household
housekeep
houseleek
houseless
houselled
housemaid
housemate
houseroom
housewife
housework
howsoever
iceskater
irascible
irascibly
irksomely
isosceles
isostatic
Jansenism
Jansenist
jessamine
jetsetter
jetstream
josshouse
jossstick
kaiserdom
kaiserism
kinswoman
lapstrake
lapstreak
lassitude
leasehold
leaselend
leastways
leastwise
leisurely
lissomely
lobscouse
looseleaf
looseness
lousewort
lousiness
mansarded
mansionry
manslayer
marshalcy
marshland
marshwort
marsupial
marsupium
massagist
massiness
massively
mausoleum
Menshevik
menstrual
menstruum
messenger
messianic
messieurs
messiness
miasmatic
midstream
midsummer
misshapen
missioner
moistener
moistness
monsignor
monsoonal
monstrous
mossagate
mossgrown
mousehole
mousetrap
moustache
Mussulman
newsagent
newsflash
newshound
newsiness
newspaper
newsprint
newsstand
noiseless
noisiness
noisomely
nonsmoker
nuisancer
nurseling
nursemaid
obeseness
offscreen
offseason
offspring
offstreet
omissible
opusculum
ourselves
outskirts
outspoken
outspread
palsgrave
Parseeism
parsimony
parsonage
passenger
passerine
passersby
passional
passivate
passively
passivity
peasantry
peasouper
pensioner
pensively
persecute
persevere
persimmon
personage
personate
personify
personnel
persuader
pessimism
pessimist
phosphate
phosphene
phosphide
phosphine
phosphite
physician
physicist
physicked
pinstripe
pipsqueak
plasmatic
plasmodia
plastered
plasterer
plusfours
plushness
poisonous
possessed
possessor
poussette
presbyope
presbyter
preschool
prescient
prescribe
prescript
preselect
presentee
presenter
presently
preserver
preshrink
preshrunk
president
presidial
presidium
pressgang
pressmark
pressroom
pressstud
presswork
prestress
prismatic
prosaical
proscenia
proscribe
prosector
prosecute
proselyte
prosiness
prosodist
prostatic
prostrate
puissance
pulsatile
pulsation
pulsatory
pulseless
pulserate
purselike
pursiness
pursuable
pursuance
pussyfoot
ransacker
reasoning
roisterer
rousement
russeting
Russophil
sassafras
Sassanian
Sassenach
seasoning
seasquirt
seastrand
sensation
sensedata
senseless
sensitise
sensitive
sensorial
sensorium
sensually
sessional
setsquare
slushfund
sobsister
spasmodic
suasively
subscribe
subscript
subsellia
subsidise
substance
substrata
substrate
sunspurge
sunstroke
sunstruck
tahsildar
tasselled
teasingly
tenseness
tensility
tensional
terseness
tessitura
thesaurus
tinselled
tipsiness
tipstaves
toastrack
tonsillar
tonsorial
torsional
trisagion
trisector
trussbeam
trustdeed
trustless
trysquare
twistable
twosuiter
unashamed
uniserial
unisexual
unisonant
unisonous
unusually
Vaishnava
vassalage
versatile
versifier
versiform
versional
waistband
waistbelt
waistcoat
waistline
wassailer
whiskered
whisperer
whistling
whosoever
winsomely
wrestling
wristband
wristdrop
wristshot
abatement
abstainer
abstinent
acetabula
acetamide
acetifier
acetylate
acetylcoA
acetylene
aesthesia
aesthesis
aesthetic
aestivate
agitation
agitative
anatomise
anatomist
apathetic
apetalous
apothecia
arytenoid
auctorial
austenite
austerely
austerity
bacterial
bacterise
bacterium
bacteroid
baltimore
Bantustan
baptismal
baptistry
bartender
bastardly
bastinade
bastinado
bastioned
battalion
battening
battiness
battleaxe
battlecry
beatitude
bentonite
bestially
bestirred
binturong
birthmark
birthrate
birthwort
bitterish
blatantly
blotchily
boathouse
boatswain
boattrain
bobtailed
bootblack
bottlefed
bottleful
bratwurst
bretasche
Bretwalda
Britannia
Britannic
Briticise
Briticism
Britisher
brittlely
brotherly
brutalise
brutalism
brutality
brutishly
Brythonic
butterbur
buttercup
butterfat
butterfly
butterine
butternut
buttinsky
buttygang
bystander
cantabile
cantaloup
cantharid
cantharis
cantharus
cantilena
Cantonese
cantorial
captaincy
captivate
captivity
Cartesian
carthorse
cartilage
cartogram
cartology
cartouche
cartridge
cartulary
cartwheel
Castalian
castanets
castellan
castigate
Castilian
Castroism
cattaloes
cattiness
cattleman
cauterise
Celticism
centenary
centering
centigram
centipede
centrally
centreing
centurion
certainly
certainty
certified
certifier
certitude
chatelain
chatoyant
chatterer
chitinous
chitlings
clathrate
clatterer
clitellum
coattails
coeternal
coltishly
coltsfoot
contactor
contadina
contadino
contagion
contagium
container
contemner
contender
contented
continent
continual
continuer
continuum
contralto
contrasty
contrived
contriver
contumacy
contumely
contusion
corticate
corticoid
cortisone
costively
costumier
couturier
cretinism
cretinous
criterion
criticise
criticism
crotchety
cultivate
curtilage
custodial
custodian
customary
customise
cutthroat
cuttysark
cystocarp
cystolith
cystotomy
daltonism
Dantesque
dartboard
dastardly
deathblow
deathless
deathlike
deathmask
deathroll
dentalium
dentation
dentiform
dentistry
dentition
depthbomb
depthless
destitute
destroyer
deuterate
deuterium
dexterity
dexterous
dextrally
dextrorse
diathermy
diathesis
diathetic
diatomite
diatropic
dictation
dietetics
dietician
dietitian
dipterous
dirtiness
dirttrack
distantly
distemper
distilled
distiller
distraint
disturbed
disturber
dittander
dittology
doctorate
doctorial
doctrinal
doltishly
dottiness
ductility
dustcover
dustiness
dustsheet
dystrophy
earthborn
earthling
earthstar
earthward
earthwork
earthworm
eastbound
Eastender
easterner
eastwards
ecstasise
editorial
egotistic
elutriate
emotional
emotively
emotivity
emptiness
epithelia
epithesis
epithetic
epitomise
epitomist
eroticism

erstwhile
erythrism
erythrite
esoterica
esoterism
exoticism
factional
factitive
factorage
factorial
factorise
factually
faithcure
faithless
fantasied
fantasise
fantasist
fantastic
fantastry
fastening
fastigium
fattiness
feathered
fertilely
fertilise
fertility
festinate
festively
festivity
festology
fictional
fifteenth
filterbed
filtertip
filtrable
fistulous
fittingly
flatterer
flatulent
flotation
foeticide
footboard
footcloth
footfault
footlight
footloose
footplate
footpound
footprint
footstalk
footstall
footstool
fortalice
forthwith
fortifier
fortitude
fortnight
fortunate
fortyfive
fosterage
fraternal
fretfully
fritterer
fruticose
furtherer
furtively
fustigate
fustiness
gastraeum
gastritis
gastropod
gastrulae
genteelly
gentility
gentleman
geotropic
gestalten
gestation
gestatory
giltedged
glutamate
glutinous
gnathonic
graticule
gratitude
gratulate
gritstone
grotesque
guitarist
gustation
gustative
gustatory
gustiness
guttation
guttering
haltingly
hartshorn
hastiness
heathcock
heathenry
hectogram
heftiness
heptaglot
heptarchy
histamine
histidine
histogeny
histogram
histology
historian
hortation
hortative
hortatory
hortensia
hosteller
hostilely
hostility
Hottentot
hurtfully
hysterics
hysteroid
ichthyoid
imitation
imitative
initially
initiator
instanter
instantly
instigate
instilled
institute
inutility
isotropic
jactation
jitterbug
justiciar
justifier
juxtapose
kentledge
kittenish
kittiwake
knotgrass
lactation
lanthanum
lastditch
lastingly
latterday
latticing
leftovers
leftwards
leitmotif
leitmotiv
lentiform
leptosome
letterbox
lettering
liltingly
lintelled
lintwhite
Listerism
litterbin
litterbug
loathsome
loftiness
loutishly
luftwaffe
lustfully
lustihood
lustiness
malthouse
manticore
martially
Martinmas
martyrdom
martyrise
masterdom
masterful
masterkey
masticate
mattamore
meatiness
meltingly
meltwater
mentalism
mentalist
mentality
mentation
micturate
Miltonian
mirthless
mistigris
mistiness
mistletoe
mistyeyed
Montanism
monthling
monticule
mortality
mortgagee
mortgager
mortgagor
mortician
mouthpart
mouthwash
multifoil
multiform
multilane
multipara
multiplex
multitude
mustachio
musteline
mustiness
mystagogy
mysticism
mystifier
napthalic
nastiness
nattiness
neathouse
nectarean
nectarial
nectarine
nectarous
neoteinia
neoteinic
neoterise
neoterism
neoterist
Neptunian
neptunium
Nestorian
neutrally
Newtonian
nictation
nictitate
noctiluca
nocturnal
northeast
northerly
northland
northmost
northward
northwest
nostalgia
nostalgic
nostology
nuttiness
nystagmic
nystagmus
oasthouse
obstetric
obstinacy
obstinate
oestrogen
oratorial
oratorian
oysterbed
oysterman
pantalets
pantaloon
pantheism
pantheist
pantingly
pantomime
pantryman
pantyhose
partially
partition
partitive
partridge
pastedown
pasticcio
pastiness
pastorale
pastorate
pasturage
pectinate
pentagram
pentangle
pentarchy
Pentecost
penthouse
peptonise
pertinent
pertussis
pesthouse
pesticide
pestilent
pestology
petticoat
pettiness
pettishly
pettitoes
photocell
photocopy
photogene
photophil
photopsia
phototype
phytogeny
phytology
phytotomy
phytotron
pictogram
pictorial
picturise
pietistic
pintailed
pintsized
pistachio
pistoleer
pistolled
platemark
platinise
platinoid
platinous
platitude
Platonise
Platonism
Platonist
plethoric
plutocrat
plutonian
Plutonism
Plutonist
plutonium
poetaster
poeticise
poeticism
pontoneer
pontonier
portative
porterage
portfolio
porticoes
portolano
portrayal
portrayer
portreeve
portulaca
postentry
posterior
posterity
posthaste
posthorse
posthouse
posticous
postilion
postnasal
postnatal
postulant
postulate
pratingly
pretender
preterist
preterite
pretermit
prettyish
prettyism
protamine
protector
proteinic
protester
protestor
prothesis
prothetic
prothorax
protonema
prototype
protozoal
protozoan
protozoic
protozoon
pustulate
pustulous
quitclaim
quittance
quotation
quotidian
rantingly
raptorial
rapturous
rectangle
rectifier
rectitude
rectorate
rectorial
rectrices
reiterate
reptilian
restfully
restiform
restitute
restively
restraint
rhythmics
rhythmise
rhythmist
riotously
rootstock
rostellum
routinely
routinism
routinist
rusticate
rusticity
rustiness
rustproof
saltation
saltatory
saltglaze
saltiness
saltmarsh
saltpetre
saltspoon
saltwater
saltworks
santolina
santonica
sartorial
sartorius
Sauternes
scatology
scatterer
Scotchman
Scoticise
scotomata
scutcheon
scutellar
scutellum
scutiform
seatangle
sectarian
sectility
sectional
sectorial
sentenate
sentience
sentiency
sentiment
sentrybox
septation
September
septemvir
septenary
septennia
septicity
septuplet
sestertia
sextuplet
shotproof
shottower
siltation
siltstone
sixteenmo
sixteenth
sketchily
sketchmap
slateclub
slategrey
slothbear
smatterer
softgoods
softpedal
softshell
sooterkin
soothfast
sootiness
sortilege
sortition
sostenuto
sottishly
souteneur
Southdown
southeast
southerly
southland
southmost
southward
southwest
spatially
spatulate
spotcheck
spotlight
sputterer
statehood
stateless
statement
stateroom
stateside
statesman
statewide
stational
stationer
statistic
statocyst
statolith
statuette
statutory
stitchery
stutterer
subtenant
subtilise
subtopian
suctorial
suctorian
sultanate
sultaness
suntanned
sustainer
sutteeism
switchman
syntactic
syntheses
synthesis
synthetic
systaltic
tactfully
tactician
tactility
tactitian
tactually
tantalate
tantalise
tantalite
Tartarean
Tartarian
tartishly
Tartufian
Tartufism
tasteless
tastiness
tattiness
tattooist
tautology
tectonics
tectorial
tectrices
tentacled
tentation
tentative
tenthrate
tentmaker
testament
testation
testatrix
testdrive
testifier
testimony
testiness
teutonise
Teutonism

Teutonist
textually
thatching
thitherto
tittivate
tittlebat
tittuping
tittupped
toothache
toothcomb
toothless
toothpick
toothsome
toothwort
tortrices
tortricid
torturous
trattoria
trattorie
triteness
tritheism
tritheist
triturate
truthless
tuitional
twitchily
twitterer
uintahite
umpteenth
unethical
unitarian
unitively
unstopped
unstudied
vastitude
vectorial
ventiduct
ventifact
ventilate
ventrally
ventricle
venturous
vertebrae
vertebral
vestibule
vestigial
vestigium
vestiture
vestryman
victimise
Victorian
victorine
virtually
virtuosic
virtuosos
volteface
voltinism
voltmeter
vorticism
vorticist
vorticity
vorticose
vulturine
vulturish
vulturous
wartcress
wasteland
wasteness
wastepipe
wattmeter
weathered
weatherly
westbound
westering
westerner
westwards
whetstone
whitebait
whitebass

whitebeam
whiteface
whitefish
Whitehall
whitehead
whiteness
whitening
whitewash
whitewing
whitewood
widthways
widthwise
winterise
wistfully
witticism
wittiness
wittingly
worthless
wrathless
Xanthippe
yesterday
zeitgeist
zestfully
zootechny
zootomist
abduction
ablutions
abounding
aboutface
aboutturn
abruption
absurdism
absurdist
absurdity
accusable
acoustics
acquiesce
acquittal
acquitted
actualise
actuality
actuarial
actuation
adducible
adduction
adductive
adjunctly
adjutancy
amauroses
amaurosis
amaurotic
ambulacra
ambulance
ambuscade
amourette
amputator
anguished
angularly
annuitant
annularly
annulated
annulling
annulment
araucaria
arcuately
arduously
argumenta
Arguseyed
assuasive
assumable
assumably
assumpsit
assurance
assuredly
assurgent
awfulness
beauteous
beautiful
bemusedly

bifurcate
cacuminal
casuarina
casuistic
casuistry
cerussite
chauffeur
claustral
cloudland
cloudless
colubrine
columbary
Columbian
columbine
columbite
columbium
columella
columnist
conundrum
coruscant
coruscate
croustade
cucullate
debugging
debutante
decumbent
decussate
deducible
deduction
deductive
deludable
demulcent
demurrage
demurring
depurator
desuetude
desultory
divulsion
effulgent
embussing
endurable
endurably
endurance
epaulette
Esquimaux
estuarian
estuarine
eunuchism
eunuchoid
exculpate
excurrent
excursion
excursive
excusable
excusably
expulsion
expulsive
expurgate
exquisite
exsuccous
facundity
fatuously
feculence
fecundate
fecundity
fenugreek
fiduciary
figurante
flouncing
focussing
gemutlich
genuflect
genuinely
gerundial
gerundive
grouchily
groundage
groundash
groundhog

grounding
groundivy
groundnut
groundsel
hirundine
hocussing
homuncule
homunculi
immutable
immutably
impudence
impulsion
impulsive
impulsory
imputable
inaudible
inaudibly
inaugural
incubator
inculcate
inculpate
incumbent
incunable
incurable
incurably
incurious
incurrent
incurring
incursion
incursive
incurvate
inducible
induction
inductive
indulgent
infuriate
infuscate
infusible
infusoria
inhumanly
injurious
injustice
innuendos
inquiline
insularly
insulator
insurable
insurance
insurgent
intuition
intuitive
intumesce
irruption
irruptive
issueless
jesuitise
jesuitism
jocularly
jocundity
liquation
liquefier
liquidate
liquidise
liquidity
liquorice
liquorish
liturgics
liturgist
lobulated
loquacity
lotusland
lucubrate
luxuriant
luxuriate
luxurious
majuscule
manubrium
maquisard
matutinal

medullary
medullate
minuscule
minutegun
minuteman
modulator
mutualise
mutualism
mutualist
mutuality
Nahuatlan
naturally
nebuliser
nocuously
nodulated
obfuscate
objurgate
obturator
occultism
occultist
occupancy
occurrent
occurring
odourless
oecumenic
ombudsman
oppugnant
paludinal
palustral
peculator
pecuniary
penultima
penumbral
penurious
petulance
petulancy
piquantly
pituitary
plausible
plausibly
pleuritic
ploughboy
ploughman
pneumatic
pneumonia
pneumonic
popularly
pseudonym
pseudopod
purulence
purulency
ranunculi
rebukable
rebutting
recumbent
recurrent
recurring
recursion
recursive
recusance
recusancy
reducible
reductant
reduction
reductive
redundant
refuelled
refulgent
refurbish
refurnish
refusable
refutable
regularly
regulator
reluctant
reluctate
republish
repudiate
repugnant

repulsion
repulsive
reputable
reputably
reputedly
requester
requisite
rerunning
resultant
resultful
resumable
resurface
resurgent
resurrect
revulsion
revulsive
rheumatic
Ripuarian
ritualise
ritualism
ritualist
roguishly
Roquefort
rotundity
salubrity
saturable
saturator
Saturnian
saturnine
saturnism
scoundrel
scrubbing
scruffily
scrumhalf
scrummage
scrutable
scrutator
seaurchin
secularly
securable
seduction
seductive
sepulcher
sepulchre
sepulture
sequacity
sequester
sequestra
sequinned
sexualise
sexuality
shouldest
shrubbery
shrugging
simulacra
simulacre
simulator
simulcast
sinuately
sinuation
sinuosity
sinuously
sinusitis
situation
slaughter
Solutrean
Solutrian
spluttery
spouthole
spoutless
stauncher
staunchly
stoutness
structure
struggler
strumitis
strumming
strutting
susurrant

suturally
tabularly
tabulator
tegularly
tenuously
theurgist
thoughted
thrumming
titularly
traumatic
triumphal
triumviri
troublous
trousered
trousseau
troutfarm
troutling
tubularly
undulated
undutiful
unguarded
unhurried
unluckily
unmusical
unruffled
unsuccess
unsullied
untutored
vacuolate
vacuously
vagueness
valuables
valuation
valueless
virulence
virulency
visualise
volumeter
voluntary
volunteer
aliveness
anovulant
atavistic
belvedere
breveting
brevetted
Calvinism
Calvinist
canvasser
chevalier
chevelure
chivalric
clavation
claviform
convector
converter
convexity
convincer
convivial
convolute
convolved
curvature
curveting
curvetted
curviform
dogviolet
Dravidian
drivelled
driveller
elevation
elevenses
fervently
flavorous
frivolity
frivolled
frivolous
galvanise
galvanism
galvanist

gravamina
graveless
gravelled
graveness
graveyard
gravidity
gravitate
grovelled
groveller
harvester
heaviness
heavyduty
Helvetian
knavishly
laevulose
larvicide
leavening
malvoisie
marvelled
nervation
nervature
nerveless
nerviness
nervously
netveined
nonviable
olivenite
peevishly
pervasion
pervasive
perverter
prevalent
preventer
prevision
privateer
privately
privation
privative
privilege
proveably
Provencal
provender
provident
providing
provision
provisory
provoking
provostry
pulverise
pulverous
pulvillus
pulvinate
salvation
scavenger
serviette
servilely
servility
servitude
shaveling
shovelful
shovelhat
shovelled
shoveller
silverfir
slaveship
slavishly
Slavonian
Slavophil
slivovitz
Slovakian
Slovenian
snivelled
sniveller
solvation
stevedore
stovepipe
subverter
surveying
swivelled
sylvanite
tervalent
travelled
traveller
traversal
traverser
trivalent
trivially
univalent
universal
valveless
velveteen
weevilled
wolverene
wolverine
airworthy
awkwardly
blowtorch
bowwindow
brownness
cobwebbed
crowberry
crownless
crowsfoot
crowsnest
Darwinian
Darwinism
Darwinist
dimwitted
drawerful
drawnwork
drawplate
drawsheet
earwigged
fatwitted
flowchart
flowerage
flowerbed
flowering
flowerpot
flowingly
flowsheet
flowstone
flyweight
forwander
forwarder
forwardly
frowardly
glowingly
illwisher
indweller
jaywalker
knowingly
knowledge
leewardly
midwicket
midwifery
midwinter
netwinged
Norwegian
nutweevil
outwardly
outwitted
outworker
rauwolfia
seaworthy
shewbread
showiness
showpiece
showplace
skewwhiff
slowcoach
slowmatch
snowberry
snowblind
snowblink
snowbound
snowbroth
snowdrift
snowfield
snowflake
snowgoose
snowguard
snowiness
snowplant
snowscape
snowstorm
snowwhite
souwester
triweekly
trowelled
troweller
viewpoint
waywardly
werwolves
anoxaemia
asexually
coaxially
coaxingly
deoxidise
fluxional
inexactly
Manxwoman
proximate
proximity
quixotism
reexamine
aepyornis
airyfairy
anhydride
anhydrite
anhydrous
ankylosis
ankylotic
aphyllous
argybargy
beryllium
bicyclist
bodyguard
buoyantly
calycinal
caryopses
caryopsis
chrysalid
chrysalis
citystate
copyright
Corybants
corydalis
corymbose
coryphaei
cotyledon
dehydrate
demystify
denyingly
dizygotic
drayhorse
easygoing
ecdysiast
empyreuma
enzymatic
ethylenic
flayflint
graywacke
greybeard
greyhound
greywacke
Himyarite
holystone
itsybitsy
ittybitty
jurywoman
karyotype
labyrinth
ladysmock
laryngeal
lazybones
lazytongs
lilywhite
manyplies
manysided
molybdate
okeydokey
pityingly
playfully
playgroup
playhouse
plaything
polyamide
polyandry
polybasic
polyester
polygamic
polygenic
polygonal
polygonum
polygraph
polyhedra
polymathy
polymeric
polymorph
polyonymy
polyphagy
polyphase
polyphone
polyphony
polyploid
polyptych
polysemic
polysomic
polythene
polytonal
polytypic
polyvinyl
polywater
polyzoary
prayerful
prayerrug
rehydrate
sibylline
Sisyphean
sphygmoid
staymaker
strychnic
traycloth
twayblade
wheyfaced
amazement
amazingly
amazonian
avizandum
benzidine
benzoline
blazingly
brazilnut
craziness
dizziness
epizootic
fuzziness
gauziness
jazziness
lazzarone
lazzaroni
manzanita
mezzanine
mezzotint
monzonite
muzziness
pizzicati
pizzicato
podzolise
pozzolana
puzzolana
quizzical
rhizocarp
rhizoidal
sitzkrieg
wayzgoose
whizzbang
wooziness
zigzagged

---

abstainer
acclaimer
acetabula
acetamide
actualise
actuality
actuarial
actuation
adamantly
admeasure
adoration
adulation
adulatory
aerialist
aeriality
affianced
afflation
aggravate
agitation
agitative
airjacket
alabaster
Alemannic
amoralism
amorality
animalise
animalism
animalist
animality
animation
animatism
anomalous
anomalure
anoxaemia
apetalous
apogamous
appealing
applauder
appraisal
appraiser
archangel
arcuately
aromatise
arrearage
asepalous
ashlaring
asphaltic
asphaltum
assuasive
astraddle
astrakhan
atacamite
ataractic
atonalism
atonality
attractor
avalanche
averagely
avizandum
avocation
awkwardly
baldachin
baldaquin
balkanise
balladeer
balladist
Barbadian
barbarian
barbarise
barbarism
barbarity
barbarous
barcarole
bargainer
barnacled
barracker
barracoon
barracuda
bastardly
battalion
beccafico
bedjacket
bedlamite
bedraggle
beemaster
beleaguer
bengaline
bergamask
bespangle
bespatter
bilharzia
billabong
blatantly
bobtailed
bombardon
bombasine
bombastic
bombazine
bretasche
bricabrac
brigadier
brigandry
Britannia
Britannic
brutalise
brutalism
brutality
buccaneer
buffaloes
Bulgarian
buoyantly
bursarial
bystander
cabbalism
cabbalist
Caesarean
Caesarian
Caesarism
Caesarist
calcaneal
calcaneum
calcarate
caldarium
calmative
campanile
campanili
campanula
cantabile
cantaloup
canvasser
captaincy
carbamate
carbamide
carnality
carnation
carrageen
caseation
Cassandra
cassareep
cassaripe
cassation
Castalian
castanets
casuarina
Catharism
Catharist
catharses
catharsis
cathartic
cattaloes
Caucasian
causality
causation
causative
cellarage
cephalous
certainly
certainty
cessation
chaparral
charabanc
character
chelation
chevalier
chicanery
chimaeric
Chinatown
chinaware
chivalric
Cingalese
circadian
clamantly
clavation
climactic
cockahoop
Cockaigne
cockatiel
cognately
cognation
colcannon
collagist
collation
combatant
combative
commander
commandos
compactly
compactor
companion
compasses
comradely
comradery
concavely
concavity
confabbed
connately
connation
connature
contactor
contadina
contadino
contagion
contagium
container
coriander
corralled
corrasion
coumarone
cremaster
cremation
crematory
crenation
crenature
CroMagnon
curialism
curvature
cyanamide
cyclamate
cymbalist
Daedalean
Daedalian
dalmatian
damnation
damnatory
dastardly
deadalive
declaimer
declarant
defeatism
defeatist
defeature
defiantly

deflation
demeanour
dentalium
dentation
depravity
dermatoid
detractor
deviation
dewlapped
dichasial
dichasium
dictation
didrachma
disbarred
discalced
discarder
disfavour
dismantle
disparage
disparate
disparity
distantly
dittander
dogmatics
dogmatise
dogmatism
dogmatist
dramatics
dramatise
dramatist
drysalter
dulcamara
dungarees
ecstasise
education
educative
egomaniac
elegantly
elevation
emanation
emanative
embraceor
embracery
embracive
embrangle
embrasure
emphasise
emplastic
emulation
emulative
enchanter
endearing
endeavour
Englander
engraving
enhearten
entrammel
entrapped
enwrapped
epilation
epinastic
esplanade
estranger
estrapade
estuarian
estuarine
ethnarchy
Eucharist
evocation
evocative
evocatory
exchanger
exogamous
expiation
expiatory
explainer
extractor
extradite
extravert
exudation
exudative
Fabianism
fallalery
fandangle
fandangos
fanfarade
fantasied
fantasise
fantasist
fantastic
fantastry
Fenianism
feudalise
feudalism
feudalist
feudality
feudatory
filiation
firealarm
firmament
flotation
foliation
forgather
formalise
formalism
formalist
formality
formation
formative
formatted
fortalice
forwander
forwarder
forwardly
fricassee
fricative
frigatoon
frowardly
frugality
fundament
furcation
gallantly
gallantry
galvanise
galvanism
galvanist
gambadoes
gammadion
gasmantle
gemmation
genealogy
genialise
geniality
geomancer
geomantic
gerfalcon
geriatric
germander
germanely
germanise
Germanish
Germanism
Germanist
germanium
gestalten
gestation
gestatory
ginpalace
glutamate
goddamned
godfather
godparent
goliardic
goosander
gossamery
Gothamite
gradation
gradatory
gravamina
gregarian
gregarine
grenadier
grenadine
grimalkin
grisaille
guacamole
guarantee
guarantor
guitarist
gustation
gustative
gustatory
guttation
gymnasial
gymnasium
gymnastic
gyrfalcon
hackamore
haematite
haematoid
haematoma
haggadist
haggardly
hagiarchy
hamhanded
haphazard
harmaline
harmattan
heptaglot
heptarchy
herbalist
herbarium
hereabout
hereafter
hierarchy
hieratica
Himyarite
histamine
hobnailed
hortation
hortative
hortatory
huckaback
Hungarian
husbandly
husbandry
hydraemia
hydrangea
hydration
hydraulic
hydrazine
Icelander
Icelandic
imitation
imitative
Indianise
IndoAryan
indraught
inelastic
inexactly
inflation
infractor
ingrained
inshallah
inspanned
instanter
instantly
irreality
ischaemia
ischaemic
isobathic
isogamete
isogamous
isolation
isolative
iteration
iterative
jactation
jambalaya
jampacked
jaywalker
jessamine
jobmaster
Jordanian
joviality
juxtapose
katharsis
kidnapped
kidnapper
kurrajong
labialise
labialism
lactation
laggardly
lallation
landagent
landaulet
Laplander
laudation
laudative
laudatory
lazzarone
lazzaroni
leewardly
lethality
lethargic
leucaemia
leukaemia
leukaemic
leviathan
librarian
libration
libratory
lignaloes
lineality
lineament
linearise
linearity
lineation
liquation
Lombardic
longaeval
lookalike
loquacity
loveapple
lowlander
lucrative
Maccabean
magdalene
Magianism
magnalium
mammalian
mammalogy
mandarine
mandatary
mandatory
maneating
manganate
manganese
manganite
manganous
manhandle
manhattan
mansarded
manzanita
marcasite
margarine
margarite
marmalade
massagist
mattamore
mechanics
mechanise
mechanism
mechanist
mediaeval
mediately
mediation
mediatise
mediative
mediatory
mediatrix
mendacity
mentalism
mentalist
mentality
mentation
mercaptan
merganser
mescaline
methadone
mezzanine
migration
migratory
miniature
mishandle
mishanter
mismanage
mitraille
Mondayish
Montanism
mordacity
mordantly
mortality
mossagate
mundanely
muscadine
muscarine
mustachio
mutualise
mutualism
mutualist
mutuality
mystagogy
Nahuatlan
narration
narrative
narratory
naumachia
nectarean
nectarial
nectarine
nectarous
nephalism
nephalist
nervation
nervature
neuralgia
neuralgic
neuration
newmarket
newsagent
nictation
niggardly
nitratine
nitration
nonpareil
normalise
normality
Normanise
Normanism
normative
nostalgia
nostalgic
nuisancer
nystagmic
nystagmus
obviation
offhanded
oilpaints
oligaemia
oligarchy
onehanded
onomastic
onslaught
operation
operative
orgiastic
orphanage
ostracise
ostracism
outbacker
outlander
outwardly
oviparity
oviparous
ovulation
ovulatory
oxidation
packaging
pageantry
Palladian
palladium
palladous
palmation
palpation
panhandle
pantalets
pantaloon
parrakeet
paymaster
paypacket
peasantry
peccantly
pegmatite
pellagrin
pentagram
pentangle
pentarchy
percaline
permanent
pervasion
pervasive
phalanger
phalanges
phalanxes
phalarope
pharaonic
phenacite
phenakite
philander
philately
phonation
phonatory
phthalein
pickaback
pilgarlic
pillarbox
pineapple
pinnately
pintailed
piquantly
piscatory
pistachio
placation
placatory
planarian
planation
plenarily
plicately
plication
plicature
pluralise
pluralism
pluralist
plurality
poetaster
polyamide
polyandry
pompadour
portative
precancel
precative
precatory
predacity
predation
predative
predatory
prefatory
prelatess
prelatise
prelature
premature
prevalent
primaeval
primality
primarily
primatial
privateer
privately
privation
privative
probation
probative
probatory
profanely
profanity
prolamine
prolapsus
prolately
prolation
prolative
pronation
propagate
prosaical
protamine
puffadder
pugnacity
pulsatile
pulsation
pulsatory
purgation
purgative
purgatory
quotation
racialism
racialist
radialply
radiantly
radiately
radiation
radiative
rampantly
ransacker
rascaldom
rascalism
rascality
raspatory
rechauffe
rectangle
redhanded
reexamine
reflation
refractor
rehearsal
reliantly
remeasure
retiarius
retractor
rhodamine
rigmarole
Ripuarian
ritualise
ritualism
ritualist
roseapple
roseately
Roumanian
Roumansch
ruination
sabbatise
sabbatism
sacrament

sacrarium
safranine
saltation
saltatory
salvation
sandalled
sandarach
sapraemia
sapraemic
sarcastic
sargassos
Sarmation
sassafras
Sassanian
satiation
scenarist
schmaltzy
schnauzer
seafaring
seatangle
sectarian
selfabuse
selfaware
sensation
Sephardic
Sephardim
septation
sequacity
serialise
serialism
serialist
seriality
seriately
serranoid
serration
sexualise
sexuality
shamanism
shamanist
shamateur
siccative
signalbox
signalise
signalled
signaller
signalman
signatory
signature
siltation
simpatico
singalong
Sinhalese
sinuately
sinuation
situation
skedaddle
skyjacker
Slovakian
socialise
socialism
socialist
socialite
sociality
solfatara
solvation
sopranino
sopranist
sorbapple
Soudanese
spiracula
spirality
spiralled
sporangia
squeakily
squeamish
stalactic
starapple
steradian
stirabout
stomachal
stomacher
stomachic
streakily
streaking
streamlet
striation
striature
subcaudal
subfamily
subjacent
sublation
submarine
submaster
sulcation
sultanate
sultaness
summarily
summarise
summarist
summation
summative
sunbather
suntanned
surfacing
sustainer
swarajist
syllabary
syllabise
syllabism
syllabled
sylvanite
syndactyl
syngamous
syntactic
systaltic
tablature
talkathon
talkative
tantalate
tantalise
tantalite
tapdancer
tarpaulin
tarragona
Tartarean
Tartarian
Tasmanian
taxpaying
tentacled
tentation
tentative
termagant
ternately
terramara
terramare
terrarium
tervalent
testament
testation
testatrix
tetradite
tetragram
tetralogy
tetrapody
tetrarchy
thalassic
therapist
Theravada
thesaurus
throatily
thylacine
thyratron
timpanist
titration
Tocharian
tophamper
topiarian
topiarist
trematode
trepanned
tribadism
tribalism
tridactyl
trifacial
trigamist
trigamous
trisagion
trivalent
turnabout
twohanded
tympanist
uintahite
Uitlander
ultrahigh
ululation
unabashed
unbiassed
unbraided
unceasing
uncharted
unguarded
unhealthy
uniparous
unitarian
univalent
unlearned
unmeaning
unreality
unscathed
unshackle
unsparing
unwearied
unwrapped
upbraider
usucapion
valiantly
vallation
valuables
valuation
vandalise
vandalism
variation
vassalage
veniality
verbalise
verbalism
verbalist
verdantly
vernalise
vernation
versatile
vibracula
vibraharp
vibratile
vibration
vibrative
vibratory
villagery
villanage
violation
violative
visualise
vitiation
vivianite
volcanism
volcanoes
vulcanian
vulcanise
vulcanism
vulcanist
vulcanite
vulgarian
vulgarise
vulgarism
vulgarity
walkabout
warrantee
warranter
warrantor
wassailer
wayfaring
waywardly
welfarism
wideawake
zebrawood
zigzagged
acrobatic
adiabatic
adlibbing
adumbrate
aerobatic
aerobiont
algebraic
amoebaean
argybargy
backbiter
backboard
baneberry
barmbrack
bearberry
bejabbers
bilabiate
billboard
birdbrain
blaeberry
bluebeard
blueberry
blueblack
bootblack
brambling
buckboard
calaboose
calabrese
calibrate
canebrake
cardboard
Caribbean
catabolic
celebrant
celebrate
celebrity
cerebella
cerebrate
chilblain
chipboard
clapboard
climbable
clipboard
clubbable
colubrine
cornbrash
Corybants
crabbedly
cranberry
crowberry
dahabiyah
dartboard
dashboard
deerberry
demobbing
disoblige
duckboard
eastbound
ectoblast
endoblast
entoblast
establish
exhibitor
fireblast
firebrand
firebreak
firebrick
flambeaus
flambeaux
footboard
foreboder
forebrain
foulbrood
freeboard
fullblown
funebrial
gangboard
gaolbreak
garibaldi
goldbrick
greybeard
grumbling
hackberry
hairbrush
halfbaked
halfblood
halfbound
halfbreed
handbrake
hardboard
headboard
hidebound
hillbilly
hindbrain
homebound
hypoblast
illiberal
incubator
inhibitor
ironbound
itsybitsy
ittybitty
Jacobinic
jailbreak
Juneberry
karabiner
katabasis
katabatic
katabolic
lampblack
lazybones
lifeblood
lucubrate
mainbrace
manubrium
mesoblast
metabolic
millboard
molybdate
monobasic
moonblind
myrobalan
nailbrush
naseberry
nosebleed
notabilia
Octobrist
overblown
overboard
overborne
parabasis
parabolic
phlebitis
plumbeous
plumbline
pokeberry
polybasic
pourboire
presbyope
presbyter
pulpboard
pureblood
quibbling
raspberry
reimburse
republish
rerebrace
roadblock
rockbound
rockbrake
sagebrush
salubrity
sandblast
sandblind
scombroid
scorbutic
scribbler
scrubbing
semibreve
shadberry
shambling
shambolic
shewbread
shipboard
shoeblack
shrubbery
sideboard
sideburns
signboard
slopbasin
slumberer
slumbrous
snowberry
snowblind
snowblink
snowbound
snowbroth
soapberry
sodabread
squabbler
squibbing
starboard
strobilae
strobilus
surfboard
tailboard
tenebrist
tenebrous
terebinth
terebrant
throbbing
thumbhole
thumbmark
thumbnail
thumbtack
tollbooth
troublous
twayblade
vocabular
wallboard
washbasin
washboard
wellbeing
westbound
windblown
windbound
windbreak
wineberry
woodblock
workbench
abdicable
abdicator
abduction
abjection
acescence
addiction
addictive
adducible
adduction
adductive
adjacency
advection
advective
advocator
affecting
affection
affective
allocable
anarchism
anarchist
annectent
anticline
anticodon
araucaria
artichoke
articular
aspectual
associate
atrocious
audacious
auricular
autoclave
autocracy
autocross
autocycle
avuncular
babacoote
backcloth
backcross
balaclava
basically
bicyclist
binocular
bisection
bleachery
blotchily
bolection
bonechina
branchiae
branchial
branchlet
brecciate
breeching
bronchial
bushcraft
calicular
calycinal
campchair
campcraft
canicular
capacious
capacitor
cataclasm
cataclysm
catechise
catechism
catechist
cerecloth
cetaceous
chanceful
chancroid
chancrous
churching
churchman
civically
coarctate
coercible
coercibly
colocynth
comically
conically
conscious
conscribe
conscript
copacetic
corncrake
crescendo
crotchety
cubically
cuticular
cynically
Damoclean
dayschool
decoction
dedicator
deducible
deduction
deductive

defection
defective
deficient
dejection
delicious
democracy
depiction
depictive
desecrate
desiccant
desiccate
detection
detective
didactics
dinoceras
dioecious
direction
directive
directory
directrix
disaccord
dishcloth
dishclout
dodecagon
dustcover
effective
effectual
efficient
emunctory
endocrine
enunciate
episcopal
ethically
eunuchism
eunuchoid
eutectoid
evincible
exarchate
exercises
exorciser
expectant
expecting
exsiccate
exsuccous
fabaceous
facecloth
felicific
ferocious
fetichism
fetichist
fiduciary
filaceous
finically
finicking
firecrest
flocculus
floscular
flowchart
fluecured
foodchain
footcloth
forecaddy
foreclose
forecourt
franchise
francolin
frenchify
Frenchman
fugacious
fullcream
funicular
funiculus
galactose
gatecrash
genocidal
goldcrest
grouchily
gynocracy
haircloth
halfcaste
halfcrown
handcraft
handcuffs
hardcover
havocking
headcloth
helically
hemicycle
Heraclean
hexachord
highchair
highclass
holocaust
homicidal
hopscotch
humectant
hypocaust
hypocotyl
hypocrisy
hypocrite
illicitly
imbecilic
impaction
impeccant
indecency
indecorum
indicator
indiction
inducible
induction
inductive
infection
infective
injection
innocence
innocency
innocuity
innocuous
insectary
insectile
inunction
invective
irascible
irascibly
isooctane
isosceles
judiciary
judicious
kilocycle
kingcraft
latecomer
launching
lexically
libecchio
lifecycle
lioncelle
lobectomy
lobscouse
logically
loincloth
longchain
longcoats
lovechild
ludicrous
lyrically
magically
magicking
malachite
malicious
Manichean
masochism
masochist
medicable
medically
medicinal
megacycle
melocoton
mepacrine
micaceous
mimicking
minacious
mobocracy
molecular
monachism
monoceros
monochord
monocline
monocoque
monocracy
monocular
moraceous
motocross
municipal
musically
musichall
navicular
neckcloth
nomocracy
notochord
noviciate
objectify
objection
objective
obsecrate
octachord
officiant
officiate
officinal
officious
offscreen
oleaceous
olfaction
olfactive
olfactory
onlicence
opercular
operculum
optically
opusculum
orbicular
ossicular
overcheck
overcloud
overcrowd
panicking
parachute
Paraclete
parochial
pedicular
periclase
pericycle
petechiae
petechial
poinciana
policeman
pomaceous
pouncebox
preachify
preachily
preoccupy
preschool
prescient
prescribe
prescript
princedom
princekin
princelet
principal
principia
principle
proscenia
proscribe
pumiceous
pushchair
pyracanth
quercetum
quitclaim
radically
radicular
raincheck
raincloud
rapacious
raunchily
redaction
reducible
reductant
reduction
reductive
refection
refectory
regicidal
rejection
reluctant
reluctate
repechage
resection
reticence
reticency
reticular
reticulum
revictual
revocable
rhonchial
ridiculer
roodcloth
rosaceous
rounceval
rubicelle
sackcloth
sagacious
sailcloth
salacious
salicetum
salicylic
sandcrack
Saracenic
scorching
Scotchman
scuncheon
scutcheon
searching
sebaceous
seduction
seductive
selachian
selection
selective
selectman
semicolon
sericeous
setaceous
shipcanal
siliceous
silicious
silicosis
silicotic
sketchily
sketchmap
slipcoach
slipcover
slowcoach
sluiceway
solacious
solicitor
songcycle
speechful
speechify
spotcheck
stanchion
starchily
stepchild
stercoral
stitchery
stoically
stricture
structure
strychnic
subocular
subscribe
subscript
switchman
synectics
tenacious
tenaculum
thatching
theocracy
theocrasy
timocracy
tonically
topically
toxically
traycloth
treachery
trenchant
truncated
truncheon
tufaceous
tunicated
twitchily
typically
undecagon
undeceive
undecided
undecimal
unluckily
unsuccess
urticaria
utricular
varicella
vasectomy
vaticinal
vehicular
veracious
vesicular
vinaceous
viricidal
vivacious
voracious
wallcress
wartcress
washcloth
windchest
wingchair
wisecrack
woodchuck
woodcraft
abandoned
abandonee
abandoner
abradable
abundance
accidence
aerodrome
affidavit
amendable
amendment
amygdalin
anandrous
anecdotal
anecdotic
anhydride
anhydrite
anhydrous
antidotal
archducal
archduchy
armadillo
assiduity
assiduous
asyndetic
asyndeton
avoidable
avoidably
avoidance
awardable
beardless
blandness
blindfold
blindness
bloodbath
bloodless
bloodlust
bloodroot
bloodshed
bloodshot
bloodworm
bloodwort
blunderer
boardfoot
boardroom
boardwalk
boondocks
boundless
brandling
brandreth
breadline
breadtree
broadcast
broadleaf
broadloom
broadness
broadside
broadtail
broadways
broadwise
broiderer
bulldozer
butadiene
cacodemon
cacodylic
chandlery
childhood
childless
childlike
chondrite
chondrule
cloudland
cloudless
comedones
corydalis
culsdesac
daredevil
decadence
decadency
decidable
decidedly
deciduate
deciduous
dehydrate
deludable
diandrous
dimidiate
dividable
druidical
embedding
embedment
emendable
emendator
ephedrine
expedient
expediter
fatidical
fetidness
fieldbook
fieldboot
fieldfare
fieldsman
fieldwork
fiendlike
finedrawn
firedrake
firedrill
fixedness
floodgate
floodmark
floodtide
folkdance
foundling
foundress
fulldress
glandered
glandular
grandaddy
grandaunt
grandiose
grandness
grandpapa
grandsire
grandslam
Grundyism
guardbook
guardedly
guardrail
guardring
guardroom
guardship
guardsman
guildhall
guildship
hamadryad
headdress
immediacy
immediate
immodesty
impedance
impudence
inaudible
inaudibly
incidence
insidious
invidious
irradiant
irradiate
jaundiced
juridical
kingdomed
kneadable
lairdship
landdross
landdrost
lapideous
lastditch
launderer
laundress
libidinal
lividness
loxodrome
lucidness
luridness
macedoine
maladroit
maunderer
meandrine
meandrous
megadeath
melodious
melodrama
menadione
misadvise
mixedness
monodical
monodrama
mouldable
nakedness
notedness
okeydokey
ombudsman
overdraft
overdrawn
overdress
overdrive
packdrill
paludinal

paradisal
pasodoble
peridotic
pipedream
pleadable
pleadings
plumdamas
plunderer
poundcake
preadamic
pseudonym
pseudopod
pyridoxin
rabidness
rapidfire
rapidness
readdress
rebidding
rehydrate
remediate
repudiate
residence
residency
residuary
rigidness
rockdrill
roundelay
roundhead
roundness
roundsman
roundworm
sabadilla
sapodilla
scaldfish
selfdoubt
selfdrive
sheldduck
sheldrake
shredding
sidedness
skindiver
slanderer
slenderly
snowdrift
solidness
soundfilm
soundhole
soundings
soundless
soundness
soundpost
soundwave
sourdough
speedball
speedboat
speedster
speedwell
spendable
spindling
spindrier
spindrift
squidding
staidness
standpipe
stardrift
steadfast
stepdance
stridence
stridency
subeditor
swaddling
swordcane
swordfish
swordknot
swordlike
swordplay
swordsman
swordtail
synodical
taxidermy
tepidness
testdrive
thirdhand
thirdrate
thirdsman
thunderer
timidness
tiredness
treadmill
tumidness
validness
vapidness
velodrome
veridical
vividness
weirdness
wheedling
wieldable
wiredrawn
withdrawn
worldling
worldwide
woundless
woundwort
wyandotte
abasement
abatement
academism
accretion
accretive
addressee
addresser
addressor
aforesaid
agapemone
aggregate
aggressor
agreeable
agreeably
agreement
aimlessly
alchemise
alchemist
alinement
aliveness
aloneness
amazement
ampleness
amusement
analeptic
anciently
ancientry
angleiron
anglesite
angleworm
anklebone
anorectic
anthelion
anthemion
applejack
apprehend
appressed
arabesque
araneidal
araneidan
archenemy
archetype
artlessly
arytenoid
asafetida
asclepiad
Ashkenazi
athletics
atonement
augmented
augmenter
augmentor
austenite
austerely
austerity
authentic
awakening
awareness
bacterial
bacterise
bacterium
bacteroid
ballerina
banderole
bargepole
barkeeper
barleymow
Barmecide
barrelful
barrelled
bartender
basketful
basrelief
battening
bedfellow
bedsettee
beefeater
beekeeper
belvedere
berberine
berkelium
berserker
bigheaded
bilgekeel
biogenous
biometric
bitterish
blameable
blameably
blameless
Boanerges
boomerang
bordereau
boulevard
bowlegged
brakeless
brakeshoe
brakesman
breveting
brevetted
bridecake
bridesman
bridewell
brokerage
bromeliad
bucketful
budgetary
buffeting
burdenous
burlesque
burnedout
bushelful
butterbur
buttercup
butterfat
butterfly
butterine
butternut
cablegram
cablelaid
cachectic
cacoethes
cancelled
cancerous
cankerous
cannelure
careerism
careerist
Carmelite
carnelian
carpenter
carpentry
carpetbag
carpeting
carrefour
Cartesian
casserole
castellan
cathectic
cathedral
causeless
cauterise
ceasefire
ceaseless
centenary
centering
chameleon
chaperone
chatelain
chevelure
chiselled
chiseller
chokedamp
choleraic
Cimmerian
clemently
clitellum
closedown
closeness
Cobdenism
cobwebbed
coeternal
coffeecup
coffeepot
cofferdam
colleague
collected
collector
collegial
collegian
collegium
commendam
commensal
commenter
compelled
compendia
competent
conceited
concentre
concerned
concerted
condenser
conferral
conferred
conferrer
confervae
confessor
congenial
congeries
connected
connecter
connector
connexion
consensus
conserver
contemner
contender
contented
convector
converter
convexity
cooperage
cooperant
cooperate
copsewood
corbeille
corbelled
cordelier
cornelian
cornemuse
cornerboy
cornerman
cornetist
correctly
corrector
correlate
crenelled
criterion
cropeared
crudeness
cudgelled
cullender
cupbearer
currently
curveting
curvetted
Cytherean
czarevich
damnedest
dancehall
dandelion
dangerous
Dantesque
decrement
decretive
decretory
deflector
deflexion
denseness
depletion
depletive
deprecate
depredate
depressed
depressor
descended
desperado
desperate
desuetude
deuterate
deuterium
dexterity
dexterous
dialectal
dialectic
diametral
diametric
dieselise
dietetics
different
dinnerset
dipterous
disbelief
discerner
dismember
dispelled
dispenser
dispeople
dispersal
disperser
disregard
disrelish
disrepair
disrepute
dissector
disseisin
dissemble
dissenter
distemper
dixieland
doglegged
dorbeetle
drawerful
drivelled
driveller
dromedary
duodecimo
duodenary
dysgenics
dyspepsia
dyspeptic
earnestly
Eastender
easterner
ecclesial
ecumenism
eggbeater
elemental
elevenses
elopement
eminently
enamelled
enameller
endlessly
ensheathe
entrechat
entrecote
entremets
enumerate
enwreathe
epicentre
epidermal
epidermic
epidermis
epileptic
erogenous
escheator
esoterica
esoterism
euphemise
euphemism
euthenics
eutherian
evidently
ewenecked
exceeding
exchequer
excrement
excretion
excretive
excretory
exegetist
exilement
exodermis
exogenous
exonerate
expletive
expletory
expressly
extremely
extremism
extremist
extremity
exuberant
exuberate
falsehood
falseness
farseeing
fastening
fatheaded
feiseanna
fenceless
fervently
fibreless
fifteenth
filterbed
filtertip
fingering
fingertip
fireeater
fisherman
flabellum
flagellum
flageolet
flameless
flarepath
flowerage
flowerbed
flowering
flowerpot
flyweight
forcefeed
forceland
forceless
forcemeat
forcepump
forfeiter
forgeable
forgetful
fosterage
framework
fraternal
fulgently
funnelled
gadgeteer
galleried
ganderism
gardening
garderobe
garmented
garreteer
gaspereau
gathering
gaugeable
gauleiter
genteelly
geodesist
geometric
geometrid
geyserite
gibberish
giltedged
gingerade
gingerale
glabellae
glabellar
globefish
glomerate
glomerule
glomeruli
glyceride
glycerine
goffering
goldeneye
goldenrod
goosefoot
goosegirl
gooseherd
gooseneck
gooseskin
goosestep
gospeller
graceless
grapeshot
grapevine
graveless
gravelled
graveness
graveyard
grotesque
grovelled
groveller
guidebook
guideline
guidepost
guiderope
guileless
guttering
gynaeceum
gynoecium
halieutic
hammerman
hammertoe
hangerson
hankering
Hanseatic
hanselled
haplessly

happening
harlequin
harvester
Hashemite
hawsehole
hawsepipe
hellebore
hellenise
Hellenism
Hellenist
Helvetian
herpetoid
Hesperian
hetaerism
hiddenite
Hitlerism
Hitlerite
Hobbesian
hodiernal
horseback
horsebean
horsehair
horsehide
horseless
horsemint
horseplay
horsepond
horseshoe
horsetail
horsewhip
hortensia
hosteller
hotheaded
Hottentot
houseboat
housebote
housecarl
housecoat
houseflag
household
housekeep
houseleek
houseless
houselled
housemaid
housemate
houseroom
housewife
housework
hoydenish
hygienics
hygienist
hyphenate
hysterics
hysteroid
ichneumon
imageable
imageless
impleader
implement
impletion
imprecate
imprecise
impresari
inbreathe
inclement
increaser
increment
indweller
inelegant
infielder
inflexion
inglenook
innkeeper
innuendos
inspector
inurement
isogenous
isomerise
isomerism
isomerous
isometric
Israelite
issueless
itineracy
itinerant
itinerary
itinerate
Jansenism
Jansenist
jetsetter
jitterbug
joylessly
judgement
judgeship
juiceless
junkerdom
junkerism
junketing
Junoesque
kaiserdom
kaiserism
kennelled
Keplerian
Keynesian
kilderkin
kittenish
knifeedge
lambently
lancejack
lancewood
larcenist
larcenous
largeness
lathering
latterday
laurelled
lawlessly
leasehold
leaselend
leavening
lecherous
Leicester
leniently
letterbox
lettering
librettos
lichenous
lickerish
liegelord
lingering
lintelled
lipreader
liquefier
Listerism
litheness
lithesome
litterbin
litterbug
lodgement
lodgepole
longeared
longevity
longevous
looseleaf
looseness
lousewort
lownecked
lumbering
lumberman
maddening
madrepore
magnesian
magnesite
magnesium
magnetics
magnetise
magnetism
magnetist
magnetite
magnetron
maidenish
malleable
malleehen
mallemuck
malleolar
malleolus
mannequin
mannerism
mannerist
manoeuvre
marcelled
marketday
marketing
marvelled
masterdom
masterful
masterkey
maybeetle
Mendelian
Mendelism
mercenary
mercerise
mesmerise
mesmerism
mesmerist
messenger
metheglin
millenary
millennia
millepede
millepore
millerite
mincemeat
misbecome
misbehave
misbelief
misbeseem
miscegene
miscegine
misdemean
misfeasor
misleared
misreckon
misreport
monkeyish
monkeyism
monkeynut
monoecism
motheaten
motherwit
mousehole
mousetrap
moviegoer
murderess
murderous
musketeer
musteline
myrmecoid
myxoedema
natheless
neoteinia
neoteinic
neoterise
neoterism
neoterist
nepheline
nephelite
nerveless
netveined
nickelise
nickelled
nickelous
nobleness
noiseless
nonperson
Norwegian
nucleated
nucleolus
nucleonic
nurseling
nursemaid
nutweevil
obeseness
obscenely
obscenity
obstetric
oddfellow
offcentre
offseason
olivenite
onelegged
openended
opodeldoc
oppressor
opulently
orchestic
orchestra
ourselves
overeaten
overeater
overexert
oviferous
oxygenate
oxygenise
oxygenous
oysterbed
oysterman
ozocerite
ozokerite
paederast
palaestra
palletise
palpebral
panderess
parcelled
parcenary
parhelion
parleyvoo
Parseeism
passenger
passerine
passersby
pastedown
patiently
pauperise
pauperism
peaceable
peaceably
peacetime
pelletise
pendently
Pentecost
pepperbox
pepperpot
perceiver
perfectly
perfector
perfervid
permeable
permeance
perpetual
persecute
persevere
perverter
phagedena
phonemics
phonetics
phonetise
phonetism
phonetist
picketing
piecemeal
piecerate
piecework
pigheaded
pilferage
pimpernel
pithecoid
placeable
placecard
placekick
placeless
placement
placename
placentae
placental
planetary
planetoid
platemark
pocketful
polyester
pommelled
ponderous
porbeagle
porcelain
porterage
possessed
possessor
postentry
posterior
posterity
prayerful
prayerrug
prebendal
precedent
preceding
precentor
preceptor
preferred
prelector
prerecord
preselect
presentee
presenter
presently
preserver
pretender
preterist
preterite
pretermit
preventer
priceless
prideless
primeness
procedure
procerity
processed
processer
processor
professed
professor
progestin
projector
prolepses
prolepsis
proleptic
promenade
proneness
propelled
propeller
properdin
prosector
prosecute
proselyte
protector
proteinic
protester
protestor
proveably
Provencal
provender
prudently
Ptolemaic
pulseless
pulserate
pulverise
pulverous
pummelled
pungently
puppeteer
purselike
Quakerdom
Quakeress
Quakerish
Quakerism
quarenden
quarender
racketeer
rareeshow
recherche
recreancy
redheaded
redletter
redresser
reflector
reflexion
reflexive
refreshen
refresher
refuelled
regretful
regretted
reiterate
replenish
repletion
reprehend
represent
repressor
requester
respecter
Rhineodon
rhymester
ridgepole
ridgetile
riflebird
rocketeer
Roquefort
rostellum
rousement
rubberise
rudbeckia
ruggedise
russeting
ruthenium
saliently
sanbenito
Sanhedrim
Sanhedrin
sapheaded
sapiently
Sassenach
sauceboat
sauceless
saucerful
Sauternes
scalefern
scalefish
scaleleaf
scaleless
scalelike
scalemoss
scapegoat
scarecrow
scarehead
scavenger
scenedock
scheelite
schlemiel
schlemihl
sciaenoid
scolecite
scorebook
scorecard
scoredraw
screecher
screening
scutellar
scutellum
sealetter
seanettle
secretage
secretary
secretion
secretive
secretory
sedgewren
seedeater
segmental
segregate
sensedata
senseless
sentenate
September
septemvir
septenary
septennia
sequester
sequestra
sergeancy
serjeancy
serjeanty
serpentry
serrefile
sestertia
sexlessly
shadeless
shadetree
shakeable
shakedown
shakerism
shamefast
shameless
shapeable
shapeless
sharecrop
shaveling
shoreless
shoreline
shoreside
shoreward
shoreweed
shovelful
shovelhat
shovelled
shoveller
sickening
silverfir
sincerely
sincerity
sinlessly
sixteenmo
sixteenth
slakeless
slateclub
slategrey
slaveship
sliderule
slopewise
Slovenian
smileless
smokeball
smokebomb
smokebush
smokejack
smokeless
smoketree
snakebird
snakebite
snakelike
snakeroot
snakeskin
snakeweed

snakewood
snaredrum
snipefish
snivelled
sniveller
solfeggio
solferino
sommelier
sonneteer
sonnetise
sooterkin
sorceress
sorcerous
sostenuto
souteneur
souwester
sovietise
sovietism
spaceband
spaceless
spaceport
spaceship
spacesuit
spacetime
spadefoot
spadework
spareness
spareribs
spicebush
spiderman
spiderweb
spikenard
spineless
spleenful
spokesman
spokewise
stagedoor
stagehand
stakeboat
stalemate
staleness
stapedial
statehood
stateless
statement
stateroom
stateside
statesman
statewide
stevedore
stilettos
stokehold
stokehole
stonechat
stonecoal
stonecold
stonecrop
stonedead
stonedeaf
stonefish
stoneless
stonewall
stoneware
stonework
stonewort
storeroom
storeship
stovepipe
streetcar
stupefier
stylebook
subaerial
subdeacon
subgenera
sublethal
submental
subregion
subsellia
subtenant
subverter
succeeder
succentor
successor
suffering
suggester
sunhelmet
supremacy
supremely
surfeiter
surgeoncy
surrender
surveying
suspender
suspensor
sutteeism
swineherd
swivelled
syllepses
syllepsis
sylleptic
symmetric
synoecete
tableland
tableleaf
tabletalk
tableware
tangerine
tasselled
tasteless
teakettle
tegmental
tegmentum
temperate
tenderise
tenseness
terseness
thaneship
therefore
therefrom
thereinto
thereunto
thereupon
therewith
threefold
threesome
timbering
timberman
tinderbox
tinselled
titledeed
titlepage
toadeater
tormentil
tormentor
trabeated
trabecula
traceable
traceably
traceless
traceried
trademark
tradename
tradesman
tragedian
trapezial
trapezium
trapezoid
travelled
traveller
traversal
traverser
tribesman
trihedral
trimerous
trimester
trimetric
trisector
triteness
triweekly
trowelled
troweller
truceless
tsarevich
tuckerbag
tunnelled
tunnelnet
turgently
twiceborn
twicelaid
twicetold
umpteenth
unblessed
unchecked
uncleanly
uncreated
undreamed
unfeeling
unfledged
unfleshed
unfleshly
unheeding
uniserial
unisexual
universal
unsheathe
unweeting
uselessly
vagueness
vallecula
valueless
valveless
variegate
velveteen
veneering
vengeance
vertebrae
vertebral
vignetter
villenage
violently
viscerate
vizierate
vizierial
voiceless
voiceover
volteface
vulnerary
Wagnerian
Wagnerite
Waldenses
wandering
washedout
washerman
wasteland
wasteness
wastepipe
wedgewise
Wednesday
westering
westerner
whaleback
whaleboat
whalebone
whalehead
wherefore
wherefrom
whereinto
whereunto
whereupon
wherewith
whitebait
whitebass
whitebeam
whiteface
whitefish
Whitehall
whitehead
whiteness
whitening
whitewash
whitewing
whitewood
wholemeal
wholeness
wholesale
wholesome
willemite
winterise
withering
witherite
witlessly
woebegone
wolverene
wolverine
wonderful
Worcester
wormeaten
wulfenite
wyliecoat
Yankeedom
Yankeeism
yesterday
zinkenite
zoogenous
zootechny
airyfairy
aloofness
antefixal
archfiend
artificer
baldfaced
balefully
banefully
barefaced
bashfully
beanfeast
beneficed
bluffness
boldfaced
boxoffice
briefcase
briefless
briefness
bullfight
bullfinch
campfever
carefully
chafferer
chaffinch
chauffeur
chiefship
chieftain
cliffhang
coalfield
cockfight
coiffeuse
cornfield
cornflour
direfully
disaffect
disaffirm
dishfaced
dolefully
doorframe
dopefiend
downfield
dumbfound
dutifully
easefully
fairfaced
fatefully
fearfully
feoffment
flayflint
footfault
forefront
fourflush
fretfully
gainfully
genuflect
gleefully
goldfever
goldfield
goldfinch
griefless
gruffness
harmfully
hatefully
headfirst
heedfully
helpfully
highflier
highflown
highflyer
hoarfrost
hopefully
hurtfully
ineffable
ineffably
lifeforce
longfaced
lovefeast
luciferin
lustfully
manifesto
milkfever
milkfloat
mindfully
minefield
needfully
newsflash
noseflute
ossifrage
overflown
painfully
palafitte
pitifully
playfully
plusfours
poriferal
poriferan
portfolio
proofread
reenforce
reinforce
restfully
ringfence
ruthfully
sangfroid
saxifrage
scarfring
scarfskin
scarfwise
scruffily
selffaced
semifinal
semifluid
sgraffiti
sgraffito
shelflife
shelfmark
shelfroom
shipfever
shopfloor
shopfront
skilfully
skinflick
skinflint
snowfield
snowflake
songfully
soulfully
stiffener
stiffness
tactfully
taskforce
tearfully
thriftily
tunefully
twelfthly
undefined
unruffled
uplifting
wakefully
wallfruit
wavefront
wellfound
wheyfaced
wishfully
wistfully
zestfully
abnegator
abrogator
aerograph
allegedly
allegiant
allegoric
alligator
allograph
almsgiver
alongside
ambiguity
ambiguous
analgesia
analgesic
antigenic
armigeral
arrogance
autograft
autograph
barograph
befogging
bellglass
benighted
benignant
benignity
bluegrass
bodyguard
bourgeois
bringdown
cerograph
changeful
clergyman
clergymen
courgette
cryogenic
debagging
debugging
decagonal
demagogic
demagogue
denigrate
designate
designing
diligence
dirigible
dirigisme
dizygotic
downgrade
dziggetai
easygoing
ectogenic
egregious
eidograph
elongated
emergence
emergency
endogamic
endogenic
energetic
energiser
energumen
enlighten
ergograph
eulogiser
evangelic
everglade
evergreen
fatigable
fenugreek
filigreed
fireguard
fledgling
foragecap
foregoing
frangible
Franglais
freighter
fullgrown
fumigator
gelignite
georgette
glengarry
goingover
Gradgrind
grosgrain
hairgrass
handglass
hexagonal
highgrade
highgrown
hodograph
holograph
homegrown
homogamic
homograft
homograph
hourglass
hypogeous
ideograph
idiograph
illegally
illegible
illegibly
illogical
immigrant
immigrate
inaugural
incognito
indagator
indigence
indignant
indignity
indigotin
inorganic
integrand
integrant
integrate
integrity
irregular
irrigable
irrigator
isinglass
knotgrass
kymograph
landgrave
leafgreen
lifeguard
litigable
litigious
logogriph
lymegrass
malignant
malignity
menagerie
mesogloea
mitigable
mitigator
monogamic
monograph
mortgagee
mortgager
mortgagor

mossgrown
mutagenic
navigable
navigator
nomograph
obligated
octagonal
oleograph
oncogenic
ontogenic
oppugnant
orangeade
Orangeism
Orangeman
orangetip
orangutan
overglaze
overgraze
overgrown
palsgrave
panegyric
paragraph
paregoric
pedagogic
pedagogue
pedigreed
peregrine
plangency
playgroup
ploughboy
ploughman
podagrous
polygamic
polygenic
polygonal
polygonum
polygraph
pronghorn
pyrogenic
raingauge
rearguard
recognise
religiose
religious
repugnant
safeguard
sagegreen
saltglaze
sandglass
savagedom
sciagraph
scraggily
selfglory
serigraph
Shangrila
shinguard
shrugging
silkgland
skiagraph
skingraft
slaughter
slingback
slingshot
smuggling
sniggerer
snowgoose
snowguard
softgoods
sphagnous
sphygmoid
spongebag
spongeous
sprigging
sprightly
sprigtail
staggerer
stargazer
stargrass
stingaree
stingless
straggler
struggler
subagency
swaggerer
swangoose
swingeing
synagogal
synagogue
telegenic
telegraph
theogonic
thingness
thingummy
thoughted
tidegauge
unpegging
unsighted
unsightly
uprightly
vainglory
waldgrave
waveguide
wayzgoose
wineglass
wiregauze
wrongdoer
wrongness
xenograft
xylograph
youngling
youngness
youngster
zeitgeist
Zwinglian
zymogenic
abashment
aesthesia
aesthesis
aesthetic
aitchbone
alcoholic
aldehydic
aliphatic
almshouse
anaphoric
anopheles
anschluss
apathetic
apishness
apophyses
apophysis
apothecia
arachnoid
bacchanal
bacchante
bakehouse
baksheesh
bathhouse
beachhead
beachwear
beechfern
beechmast
biorhythm
birchbark
birthmark
birthrate
birthwort
blushless
boathouse
Bolshevik
bombhappy
brachiate
brachyura
brashness
brightish
brochette
brotherly
brushfire
brushwood
brushwork
Brythonic
buckhound
bunkhouse
butcherer
butcherly
camphoric
cantharid
cantharis
cantharus
carthorse
catchable
catchment
catchpole
catchpoll
catchword
chachacha
chophouse
cirrhosis
clathrate
clubhouse
coachwork
cockhorse
colchicum
cookhouse
couchette
crashdive
crashland
crushable
cutthroat
deathblow
deathless
deathlike
deathmask
deathroll
deckhouse
deerhound
depthbomb
depthless
diachrony
diachylom
diachylum
diaphragm
diaphysis
diathermy
diathesis
diathetic
discharge
dogshores
dosshouse
doughtily
Doukhobor
draghound
drayhorse
dysphagia
dysphagic
dysphonia
dysphoria
dysphoric
earthborn
earthling
earthstar
earthward
earthwork
earthworm
epiphragm
epiphyses
epiphysis
epiphytal
epiphytic
epithelia
epithesis
epithetic
erythrism
erythrite
eyeshadow
faithcure
faithless
farmhouse
feathered
firehouse
flashback
flashbulb
flashcube
flashover
flashtube
fleshings
fleshless
fleshment
flightily
flophouse
flushness
foolhardy
forthwith
freehouse
freshener
freshness
frightful
furtherer
gatehouse
gaucherie
gazehound
gigahertz
gnathonic
gomphosis
graphemic
graphical
graphitic
greyhound
halfhardy
harshness
hatchback
hatchling
hatchment
haughtily
heathcock
heathenry
hellhound
hitchhike
hoarhound
horehound
hunchback
ichthyoid
isochrone
josshouse
kilohertz
kitchener
knightage
lanthanum
larghetto
laughable
laughably
lionheart
loathsome
longhouse
lunchtime
lyamhound
lymehound
lymphatic
lyophilic
lyophobic
malthouse
marchpane
marchpast
marihuana
marshalcy
marshland
marshwort
matchless
matchlock
matchwood
megahertz
Menshevik
mirthless
mischance
misshapen
monthling
morphemic
moschatel
mouthpart
mouthwash
mumchance
napthalic
naughtily
neathouse
neighbour
newshound
northeast
northerly
northland
northmost
northward
northwest
nymphalid
oasthouse
octahedra
offchance
omophagia
omophagic
openheart
overheard
packhorse
pairhorse
panchayat
pantheism
pantheist
parchment
patchouli
patchouly
patchwork
peachblow
pemphigus
penthouse
perchance
percheron
perihelia
pesthouse
pinchbeck
pinchcock
pitchdark
pitchfork
pitchpipe
playhouse
plethoric
plushness
polyhedra
poorhouse
porphyria
posthaste
posthorse
posthouse
preshrink
preshrunk
prophetic
prothesis
prothetic
prothorax
psychical
psychoses
psychosis
psychotic
punchball
punchbowl
punchcard
punchline
purchaser
racehorse
rakehelly
reachable
rearhorse
Reichstag
rhythmics
rhythmise
rhythmist
roadhouse
roughcast
roughhewn
roughneck
roughness
roughshod
saccharin
seachange
Shechinah
slaphappy
slightish
slothbear
slushfund
soothfast
Southdown
southeast
southerly
southland
southmost
southward
southwest
spaghetti
staghound
studhorse
subphylum
sulphonic
sulphuret
sulphuric
surcharge
sylphlike
symphonic
symphysis
synchrony
syntheses
synthesis
synthetic
teachable
teachably
tenthrate
thighbone
thighboot
thitherto
tollhouse
toolhouse
toothache
toothcomb
toothless
toothpick
toothsome
toothwort
torchrace
torchsong
touchable
touchdown
touchhole
touchline
touchmark
touchtype
touchwood
toughness
townhouse
tracheary
tracheate
trachytic
trichinae
trichomic
trichroic
tritheism
tritheist
trochilus
trochleae
trochlear
truthless
unashamed
unethical
Vaishnava
vetchling
vouchsafe
warehouse
washhouse
watchable
watchcase
watchfire
watchword
weathered
weatherly
weighable
weighbeam
weightily
weighting
whichever
widthways
widthwise
windhover
witchetty
witchhunt
witchmeal
wolfhound
workhorse
workhouse
worthless
wrathless
wychhazel
Xanthippe
zoophagan
zoophobia
zoophytic
zucchetto
abidingly
abolisher
abolition
abominate
aborigine
abscissae
abscissas
abseiling
abstinent
abusively
acariasis
acclimate
acclivity
acetifier
acidifier
aciniform
aconitine
acquiesce
acquittal
acquitted
acuminate
adjoining
adoringly
aestivate
affricate
aggrieved
agonising
agonistic
airminded
altricial
aluminate
aluminise
aluminium
aluminous
amazingly
americium
Amerindic
amphibian
amphibole
amphigory
amphioxus
amplifier
amplitude
amusingly
anabioses
anabiosis
anabiotic
anglicise
anglicism
Anglicist
angriness
anguished

animistic
annuitant
aperiodic
aperitive
apodictic
apomictic
appliance
applicant
appointee
arabicise
architect
archivist
archivolt
asininity
assailant
atavistic
atheistic
atomicity
atomistic
atonicity
attainder
attribute
attrition
aubrietia
auspicate
Babbittry
badminton
bagginess
bailiwick
ballistae
ballistic
balminess
baltimore
bandicoot
bannister
baptismal
baptistry
barbitone
barricade
barricado
barrister
bastinade
bastinado
bastioned
battiness
bawdiness
beamingly
beatitude
bedridden
bedsitter
beefiness
bellicose
benzidine
bestially
bestirred
biblicism
biblicist
billiards
billionth
bismillah
blazingly
bombilate
bombinate
bonniness
bookishly
boorishly
boskiness
bossiness
bowwindow
boxgirder
brazilnut
Briticise
Briticism
Britisher
brutishly
bulginess
bulkiness
bullishly
bumpiness
burliness
burningly
burnisher
bushiness
buttinsky
cabriolet
caddisfly
caecilian
calcicole
calcifuge
callipers
Calvinism
Calvinist
candidacy
candidate
canniness
cantilena
capriccio
Capricorn
captivate
captivity
carcinoma
carnitine
carnivore
carpingly
cartilage
cassimere
castigate
Castilian
casuistic
casuistry
cattiness
Celticism
centigram
centipede
certified
certifier
certitude
chariness
charivari
chelicera
chemistry
chemitype
cherimoya
chitinous
chorister
circinate
cirripede
clarifier
clarionet
claviform
clinician
coalition
coaxially
coaxingly
cocainise
cocainism
coccidium
cochineal
cockiness
coecilian
coffinite
cognisant
cognition
cognitive
coheiress
colligate
collimate
collinear
collision
coltishly
combinate
comfiture
commingle
comminute
commissar
committal
committed
committee
concierge
conciliar
concisely
concision
condignly
condiment
condition
confidant
confident
confiding
configure
confirmed
confirmer
confirmor
confiteor
connivent
consignee
consignor
continent
continual
continuer
continuum
convincer
convivial
corbicula
cordially
cordiform
corticate
corticoid
cortisone
coseismal
coseismic
costively
craziness
crediting
crepitant
crepitate
cretinism
cretinous
criminate
criminous
criticise
criticism
crucially
cruciform
culminant
culminate
cultivate
cuneiform
cunningly
cuplichen
curliness
curricula
currishly
cursively
curtilage
curviform
cuspidate
cymbidium
cymbiform
cyprinoid
dalliance
damningly
dandiacal
Darwinian
Darwinism
Darwinist
dashingly
deacidify
deceitful
declinate
declivity
declivous
dentiform
dentistry
dentition
denyingly
deoxidise
derringdo
derringer
destitute
detriment
detrition
diclinous
diesinker
dietician
dietitian
difficile
difficult
diffident
dignified
dignitary
dimwitted
dinginess
dipcircle
dirtiness
disfigure
dismissal
dissident
dissipate
distilled
distiller
dizziness
doggishly
dogviolet
doltishly
donnishly
dormition
dormitory
dottiness
dowdiness
Dravidian
dualistic
ductility
dulcitude
dumpiness
duplicate
duplicity
duskiness
dustiness
earliness
earwigged
edibility
egotistic
elegiacal
eliminate
elucidate
elusively
emaciated
embrittle
emotional
emotively
emotivity
emptiness
enchilada
encrimson
encrinite
eradicate
eremitism
eroticism
eruciform
eruditely
erudition
Esquimaux
esurience
esuriency
ethnicity
euclidean
evaginate
evasively
examinant
exanimate
exoticism
explicate
exquisite
extricate
extrinsic
fabricant
fabricate
facsimile
factional
factitive
faddiness
falciform
falsifier
fasciated
fascicled
fascicule
fasciculi
fascinate
Fascistic
fashioner
fastigium
fattiness
fatwitted
faunistic
fawningly
febricity
febrifuge
feelingly
fertilely
fertilise
fertility
festinate
festively
festivity
fibriform
fibrillar
fibrinoid
fibrinous
fictional
fideistic
fieriness
fillister
filminess
fioritura
fioriture
fireirons
fishiness
fissility
fissipede
fittingly
flakiness
flamingly
flamingos
flaringly
floriated
floridean
floridity
floristic
floristry
flowingly
fluxional
flyfisher
foeticide
fogginess
foolishly
foppishly
forbidden
foreigner
forgiving
formicary
formicate
fornicate
fortifier
fortitude
fossicker
fossilise
fragility
frigidity
frolicked
fruticose
fulfilled
fulfiller
fulminant
fulminate
fulminous
fungicide
fungiform
funkiness
funniness
furbisher
furnisher
furniture
furtively
fussiness
fustigate
fustiness
fuzziness
gallicise
gallicism
gallingly
gallinule
gallivant
galliwasp
gannister
garnishee
garniture
gasfitter
gaudiness
gauziness
gawkiness
gentility
genuinely
germicide
germinate
giddiness
gimmickry
girlishly
glacially
gladiator
gladiolus
glaringly
glowingly
glutinous
godliness
gothicise
Gothicism
gracility
granitoid
graticule
gratitude
gravidity
gravitate
griminess
gumminess
gushingly
gustiness
gutsiness
hagridden
hairiness
haltingly
hamfisted
handiness
handiwork
happiness
harbinger
hardihood
hardiment
hardiness
Hashimite
hastiness
headiness
heaviness
Hebridean
hedgingly
heftiness
hellishly
hendiadys
herbicide
herbivore
hermitage
herniated
hetairism
heuristic
hispidity
histidine
hoariness
hoggishly
horniness
horsiness
hostilely
hostility
hubristic
huffiness
humdinger
hurricane
hurriedly
huskiness
hybridise
hybridism
hybridity
hydriodic
illwisher
imaginary
imbricate
implicate
impliedly
inability
inanimate
inanition
inflictor
initially
initiator
inquiline
instigate
instilled
institute
intricacy
intricate
intrigant
intriguer
intrinsic
intuition
intuitive
inutility
inveigler
ischiadic
ischiatic
isoniazid
italicise
Italicism
itchiness
jarringly
jazziness
jeeringly
jerkiness
jesuitise
jesuitism
Judaistic
juiciness
jumpiness
justiciar
justifier
kaolinise
kaolinite
keelivine
khedivial
kiddingly
killifish
kinkiness
kittiwake
knavishly
knowingly
lacrimose
lagniappe
lancinate
lankiness
Laodicean
larvicide
lassitude
lastingly
latticing
lawgiving
leakiness

leeringly
legginess
lentiform
liability
ligniform
liltingly
limpidity
liquidate
liquidise
liquidity
lispingly
loftiness
longicorn
longingly
longitude
louringly
lousiness
loutishly
lowliness
lowminded
lubricant
lubricate
lubricity
lubricous
luckiness
lumpiness
lumpishly
lustihood
lustiness
machinate
machinery
machinist
magnifico
magnifier
magnitude
mammiform
manginess
manliness
mansionry
manticore
maquisard
marginate
martially
Martinmas
massiness
massively
masticate
matriarch
matricide
matricula
matrimony
mawkishly
mealiness
meaningly
meatiness
meltingly
memoirist
mendicant
mendicity
merciless
merriment
merriness
messianic
messieurs
messiness
metricate
metrician
metricise
metricist
midwicket
midwifery
midwinter
milkiness
milligram
millinery
millionth
millipede
millivolt
mincingly
mirkiness
misdirect
misgiving
mispickel
missioner
mistigris
mistiness
mockingly
monsignor
monticule
moodiness
morbidity
morrisman
mortician
mosaicism
mosaicist
mosaicked
muddiness
muffineer
muffinman
mugginess
mullioned
multifoil
multiform
multilane
multipara
multiplex
multitude
mummified
murkiness
muskiness
mustiness
muzziness
mydriasis
mydriatic
mysticism
mystifier
mythicise
mythicism
mythicist
narcissus
nastiness
nattiness
neediness
negligent
negritude
neolithic
nerviness
nescience
netwinged
newsiness
nictitate
nigricant
nigritude
nitpicker
noctiluca
noisiness
nonlinear
nonviable
nourisher
nowhither
nullifier
nullipara
nullipore
nutriment
nutrition
nutritive
nuttiness
obbligato
obedience
obstinacy
obstinate
odalisque
onanistic
opinioned
orchidist
orificial
originate
oubliette
outfitter
outgiving
outridden
outrigger
outwitted
overissue
palliasse
pallidity
palmipede
palmistry
palmitate
palpitant
palpitate
pantingly
parricide
parsimony
partially
partition
partitive
passional
passivate
passively
passivity
pasticcio
pastiness
patriarch
patrician
patricide
patrimony
patriotic
patristic
pectinate
peevishly
pellitory
pencilled
penciller
penniless
pensioner
pensively
perdition
perkiness
permitted
permitter
persimmon
pertinent
pessimism
pessimist
pesticide
pestilent
pethidine
petticoat
pettiness
pettishly
pettitoes
pharisaic
philippic
phoniness
physician
physicist
physicked
pianistic
picnicked
picnicker
pietistic
piggishly
pinkiness
pinnipede
pisciform
pithiness
pituitary
pityingly
pizzicati
pizzicato
placidity
planisher
platinise
platinoid
platinous
platitude
plenitude
podginess
poeticise
poeticism
pollinate
pollinium
popliteal
porringer
porticoes
posticous
postilion
pratingly
precipice
precisely
precisian
precision
predicant
predicate
predictor
predigest
predikant
prefigure
prefixion
president
presidial
presidium
prevision
primipara
primitive
privilege
profilist
profiteer
prolicide
prolixity
prominent
promising
propionic
prosiness
provident
providing
provision
provisory
proximate
proximity
prudishly
prurience
pruriency
psoriasis
psoriatic
publicise
publicist
publicity
publisher
pudginess
puerility
puffiness
pulpiness
pulpiteer
pulvillus
pulvinate
purringly
pursiness
pushiness
pushingly
putridity
pycnidium
quakiness
qualified
qualifier
quirister
quotidian
rabbinate
rabbinism
rabbinist
raffinate
raffinose
raffishly
raininess
rancidity
randiness
ranginess
rantingly
raspingly
readiness
realistic
reanimate
reclinate
recoinage
rectifier
rectitude
reediness
rejoicing
rejoinder
remainder
rendition
replicate
reprieval
reprimand
reptilian
requisite
restiform
restitute
restively
retrieval
retriever
rewritten
ringingly
riskiness
rockiness
rodfisher
roguishly
roominess
routinely
routinism
routinist
rowdiness
rubricate
rubrician
ruddiness
ruffianly
runcinate
rusticate
rusticity
rustiness
sacciform
sacrifice
sacrilege
sacristan
salpinges
saltiness
sandiness
sappiness
Sardinian
sauciness
scaliness
scarifier
schlieren
schnitzel
scoliosis
scoliotic
scorifier
Scoticise
scutiform
seagirdle
seaminess
searingly
sectility
sectional
seediness
seemingly
selfimage
selfishly
semeiotic
sensitise
sensitive
sentience
sentiency
sentiment
septicity
sequinned
serviette
servilely
servility
servitude
sessional
sexlinked
shadiness
shakiness
shininess
showiness
sickishly
sideissue
significs
silkiness
silliness
skydiving
slavishly
sliminess
smilingly
smokiness
snakiness
snowiness
soapiness
sobbingly
sobriquet
sobsister
sogginess
soidisant
soldierly
solmisate
sootiness
sophister
sophistic
sophistry
soppiness
sorriness
sortilege
sortition
sottishly
sparingly
spatially
specially
specialty
specifier
spiciness
spikiness
spininess
spirillum
spiritism
spiritist
spiritoso
spiritous
spiritual
spirituel
spoliator
stabilise
stability
staginess
Stagirite
Stalinism
Stalinist
staminate
stational
stationer
statistic
sterilise
sterility
stipitate
stolidity
stoniness
storiated
studiedly
stupidity
styliform
stylishly
stylistic
suability
suasively
subdivide
sublimate
sublimely
sublimity
submitted
subsidise
subtilise
succinate
sulkiness
summingup
sunniness
surcingle
surficial
surliness
suspicion
swinishly
symbiosis
symbiotic
syndicate
syphilise
syphiloid
tackiness
tactician
tactility
tactitian
taeniasis
tahsildar
tanliquor
tanpickle
tardiness
tartishly
tastiness
tattiness
tawniness
teasingly
tellingly
tendinous
tensility
tensional
terminate
terminism
terminist
termitary
territory
tessitura
testifier
testimony
testiness
Thomistic
thyristor
tinniness
tipsiness
tittivate
tonsillar
torpidity
torridity
torsional
touristic
tradition
trepidant
trilinear
trilithon
trivially
tubbiness
tuitional
turbidity
turbinate
turgidity
turpitude
twofisted
Ukrainian
uliginous
unanimity
unanimous
unblinded
unbridled
unfailing
unfeigned

unifiable
unitively
unknitted
unpointed
unskilful
unskilled
unsmiling
unwritten
Upanishad
uraninite
uxoricide
vaccinate
vampirism
varnisher
vastitude
veeringly
vendition
ventiduct
ventifact
ventilate
verbicide
verdigris
vermicide
vermicule
vermiform
vermifuge
vermilion
verminate
verminous
versifier
versiform
versional
vestibule
vestigial
vestigium
vestiture
viability
vibrissae
victimise
villiform
vindicate
violinist
Virgilian
virginals
virginity
viscidity
vitriform
vitriolic
voltinism
vorticism
vorticist
vorticity
vorticose
vulpinism
vulpinite
wackiness
waggishly
wailingly
warningly
washiness
waspishly
weariless
weariness
wearisome
weediness
weevilled
willingly
windiness
winningly
witticism
wittiness
wittingly
wolfishly
woodiness
wooziness
wordiness
worriedly
worriment
worrisome

Wyclifite
yawningly
Yiddisher
coadjutor
forejudge
limejuice
marijuana
overjoyed
Afrikaans
Afrikaner
antiknock
blackball
blackbird
blackbuck
blackcoat
blackcock
blackdamp
blackface
Blackfeet
blackfish
blackflag
Blackfoot
blackgame
blackhead
blackjack
blacklead
blacklist
blackmail
blackness
blackwash
blankness
bleakness
blinkered
blockader
blockhead
blockship
breakable
breakaway
breakdown
breakeven
breakfast
breakneck
brickwork
brickyard
briskness
checkered
checklist
checkmate
checkrein
cheekbone
chickadee
chickaree
chickling
chickweed
chockfull
clerkship
cloakroom
clockwise
clockwork
crackdown
crackling
cracksman
crankcase
cricketer
crookback
crookedly
crookneck
drinkable
drunkenly
fleckless
foreknown
frankness
frockcoat
Greekless
iceskater
jackknife
knockdown
knockknee
outskirts

pranksome
prankster
quickener
quicklime
quickness
quicksand
quickstep
rebukable
sharkskin
sheikhdom
shockable
shockhead
sitzkrieg
slackness
sleekness
slickness
slinkweed
smackeroo
sparkcoil
sparkless
sparkplug
speakable
speakeasy
speckless
stackable
stackroom
stackyard
stalkeyed
stalkless
starkness
stickwork
stinkball
stinkbomb
stinkhorn
stinktrap
stinkweed
stinkwood
stockbook
stockdove
stockfish
stockinet
stocklist
stockpile
stockroom
stockwhip
stockyard
thankless
thickener
thicketed
thickhead
thickknee
thickness
thinkable
thinktank
trackless
tracksuit
trickless
tricksily
trickster
trinketer
trinketry
trunkcall
trunkfish
trunkroad
twinkling
unbeknown
weakkneed
wellknown
whiskered
acellular
aerolitic
affiliate
agrologic
alkaloses
alkalosis
ambulacra
ambulance
ancillary
angelfish

angelical
angularly
ankylosis
ankylotic
annelidan
annularly
annulated
annulling
annulment
aphyllous
appalling
Appaloosa
appellant
appellate
aquilegia
argillite
armillary
artillery
autolysis
autolytic
auxiliary
available
availably
awfulness
bacillary
balalaika
basilican
battleaxe
battlecry
beadledom
beryllium
bevelling
bifoliate
bivalence
bivalency
bobsleigh
booklouse
bottlefed
bottleful
bridleway
brilliant
bumblebee
bumbledon
caballero
caballine
caballing
cailleach
camelback
camelhair
canalboat
Candlemas
candlenut
capillary
carolling
catalepsy
catalexes
catalexis
catalogue
catalyser
catalyses
catalysis
catalytic
cattleman
cavalcade
cavilling
challenge
chapleted
charlatan
charlotte
chillness
chitlings
choplogic
cipollino
cisalpine
civiliser
cobaltite
cobaltous
cochleate
complaint

complexly
complexus
compliant
confluent
copolymer
coralline
corallite
coralloid
corollary
cotillion
cotyledon
covalence
covalency
cruellest
cucullate
cupelling
cytolysis
deadlight
decalcify
decalitre
decalogue
decilitre
decillion
decollate
decollete
defalcate
defoliant
defoliate
demulcent
desolater
desolator
desultory
devaluate
developer
devilfish
devilling
devilment
diablerie
didelphic
displease
divulsion
doodlebug
doubleton
dowelling
drollness
duralumin
dysplasia
ebullient
echolalia
effulgent
embellish
emolliate
emollient
endolymph
enrolling
enrolment
entelechy
enucleate
epaulette
epiclesis
equaliser
equalling
escalator
ethylenic
eucalypti
excellent
excelling
excelsior
exculpate
exfoliate
expellent
expelling
expulsion
expulsive
extolling
extolment
eyeglance
familyman
feculence

firelight
footlight
footloose
frailness
freelance
freeliver
fusillade
gavelkind
gearlever
gentleman
ginglymus
gogglebox
golflinks
gorblimey
grillroom
grillwork
gruelling
guillemot
guilloche
halflight
handlebar
headlight
headliner
highlands
highlevel
highlight
Himalayan
homiletic
homologue
horologer
horologic
humblebee
humiliate
hypallage
idealiser
idealless
ideologic
ideologue
imbalance
immolator
impelling
impolitic
impulsion
impulsive
impulsory
inculcate
inculpate
indelible
indelibly
indolence
indulgent
infilling
inhalator
insolence
insoluble
insolubly
insolvent
insularly
insulator
intellect
invalidly
involucre
involuted
isallobar
isoclinal
isoclinic
jewellery
jewelweed
jocularly
jubilance
kentledge
kilolitre
knowledge
labelling
lamellate
lamellose
lamplight
landloper
lavaliere

lendlease
levelling
levelness
libellant
libelling
libellist
libellous
limelight
lobulated
longlived
lovelight
madeleine
mainliner
mamillary
mamillate
manslayer
maxillary
mayflower
medallion
medallist
medullary
medullate
metalline
metalling
metallise
metalloid
metalwork
middleman
minelayer
mistletoe
modelling
modillion
modulator
monolatry
monologic
monologue
moonlight
moraliser
muscleman
mutilator
mycologic
navelwort
nebuliser
needleful
nobiliary
nodulated
nonillion
novelette
obsolesce
occultism
occultist
ocellated
octillion
oecologic
oncologic
ontologic
oriflamme
oscillate
overladen
overleapt
overlying
paillasse
paillette
palillogy
panelling
panellist
papillary
papillate
papilloma
papillose
papillote
paralalia
paralexia
paralysis
paralytic
parfleche
patellate
pearlitic
pearlwort

peculator
pedalling
penultima
perilling
perilymph
petulance
petulancy
phellogen
phyllopod
pisolitic
pixilated
popularly
proclitic
pupillage
pupillary
purulence
purulency
pyrolater
pyrolatry
pyrolysis
pyrolytic
quillwort
quodlibet
rafflesia
ravelling
ravelment
rearlight
rebelling
rebellion
recalesce
recollect
redolence
refulgent
regularly
regulator
repellant
repellent
repelling
repulsion
repulsive
rerelease
resalable
resilient
resoluble
resolvent
resultant
resultful
retaliate
revelator
revelling
revolting
revulsion
revulsive
rivalling
rivalrous
rivelling
rubellite
ruddleman
rushlight
Sabellian
saddlebag
saddlebow
safflower
satellite
scagliola
scallawag
scallywag
schilling
scholarly
scholiast
scrollsaw
secularly
semblable
semblably
semblance
semilunar
sepulcher
sepulchre
sepulture
shallowly
shellback
shellbark
shellfire
shellfish
shellheap
shellwork
shieldbug
shieldfem
shillelah
shouldest
sibilance
sibilancy
sibylline
sickleave
sidelight
sigillary
sigillate
similarly
simpleton
simplices
simulacra
simulacre
simulator
simulcast
singleton
sinologue
smallarms
smallness
smalltime
snailfish
soliloquy
spellbind
spellican
spillikin
spoilsman
spotlight
squalidly
squelcher
stableboy
stableman
stallfeed
starlight
steelclad
steelhead
steelwork
steelyard
stellated
stillborn
stillhunt
stillness
stillroom
stoolball
stoplight
subalpine
subaltern
sunflower
suppliant
surpliced
swellfish
synclinal
tabularly
tabulator
taillight
tegularly
theologic
theologue
thralldom
thrilling
timelapse
timelimit
titillate
tittlebat
titularly
totaliser
totalling
towelling
tramlines
treillage
trialogue
triclinia
triclinic
triploidy
tubularly
tumblebug
typhlitis
umbellate
umbellule
umbilical
umbilicus
unalloyed
unbalance
undulated
ungallant
unhelpful
uniplanar
unselfish
unsullied
unwelcome
unwilling
upholster
usualness
vacillant
vacillate
vexillary
videlicet
vigilance
vigilante
virulence
virulency
vitellary
vitelline
vocaliser
vocalness
vowelless
warblefly
wavellite
wheelbase
wheelless
wheelwork
whirligig
whirlpool
whirlwind
woodlouse
yodelling
zibelline
abdominal
abysmally
accompany
adnominal
aerometer
aerometry
allemande
allomorph
altimeter
antimonic
argumenta
artemisia
ashamedly
assembler
assumable
assumably
assumpsit
asthmatic
asymmetry
athematic
atmometer
attempter
automatic
automaton
axiomatic
bainmarie
barometer
barometry
belemnite
bicameral
binominal
bolometer
bolometry
bookmaker
Brahmanic
Brahminee
Brahminic
bregmatic
broomcorn
broomrape
brummagem
buxomness
cacuminal
calamanco
Camembert
carambola
catamaran
catamount
charmeuse
charmless
chlamydes
chromatic
chromatin
cinematic
claimable
coalmouse
colemouse
columbary
Columbian
columbine
columbite
columbium
columella
columnist
corymbose
decametre
decimally
decimator
decimetre
decomplex
decompose
decumbent
demimonde
dharmsala
disembark
disembody
dolomitic
dosimeter
dosimetry
dreamboat
dreamland
dreamless
dreamlike
drummajor
dynamical
dynamiter
eclampsia
eclamptic
ectomorph
encomiast
encompass
endomixis
endomorph
enigmatic
enzymatic
ephemeral
ephemerid
ephemeris
ephemeron
ergometer
estaminet
estimable
estimator
exosmosis
exosmotic
extempore
flammable
folkmusic
Freemason
frogmarch
gallmidge
gasometer
goalmouth
groomsman
hamamelis
hegemonic
hexameter
hodometer
homemaker
hypomania
hypomanic
idiomatic
illomened
incommode
incumbent
indemnify
indemnity
inhumanly
insomniac
intumesce
ironmould
Islamitic
judgmatic
kilometre
kinematic
kingmaker
krummhorn
lagomorph
lawnmower
leafmould
leitmotif
leitmotiv
locomotor
logomachy
loudmouth
lovematch
lysimeter
machmeter
Mahometan
manometer
maximally
mekometer
melomania
mesomorph
metameric
miasmatic
milometer
minimally
misemploy
monomania
monomeric
muniments
muskmelon
Nilometer
nonsmoker
octameter
oecumenic
oenomancy
opsimathy
optometer
optometry
osmometer
overmatch
pacemaker
paramatta
paramedic
parameter
paramorph
paramount
pedometer
penumbral
perimeter
perimorph
plasmatic
plasmodia
pneumatic
pneumonia
pneumonic
polemical
polymathy
polymeric
polymorph
pragmatic
preemptor
prismatic
psalmbook
psalmodic
ptarmigan
pyramidal
pyramidic
pyramidon
pyromancy
pyromania
pyrometer
pyrometry
rainmaker
rearmouse
recombine
recommend
recompose
recumbent
reremouse
resumable
rheumatic
roadmetal
rocambole
saltmarsh
schematic
sciamachy
scrambler
scramming
scrimmage
scrimpily
scrimshaw
scrumhalf
scrummage
selfmoved
semimetal
shipmoney
shoemaker
skiamachy
slowmatch
solemnise
solemnity
Solomonic
sonometer
spasmodic
spermatic
spermatid
squamosal
stammerer
staymaker
steamboat
steampipe
steamship
stigmatic
stormbelt
stormbird
stormcock
stormcone
stormless
stormsail
stromatic
strumitis
strumming
swimmable
swimmeret
tacamahac
taximeter
telamones
telemeter
telemetry
tentmaker
theomachy
theomania
thermally
thermidor
thrombose
thrumming
tonometer
totempole
traumatic
trimmings
triumphal
triumviri
typemetal
ultimatum
undamaged
unlimited
unnamable
untimeous
unwomanly
vademecum
vasomotor
vehemence
voltmeter
volumeter
wattmeter
wehrmacht
workmanly
xeromorph
yohimbine
zeugmatic
zygomatic
abounding
accentual
actinozoa
adjunctly
adminicle
admonitor
adornment
adrenalin
advantage
Adventism
Adventist
adventive
adventure
agronomic
ailanthus
albinotic
Algonkian
Algonquin
alienable
alienator
alignment
allantois
almandine
alpenhorn
amianthus
anamnesis
andantino
antenatal
antennary
antennule
antinodal
antinomic
antinovel
aplanatic
appendage
appendant
argentine
argentite
argentous
arsenical
arsenious
ascendant
ascendent
ascension
ascensive
assonance
Athenaeum
Atlantean
attendant
attention
attentive
attenuate
autonomic
Axminster

baronetcy
bayoneted
beginning
biconcave
bigeneric
bilingual
bimonthly
bipinnate
botanical
braincase
brainless
brainwash
brainwave
brownness
Byzantine
cadential
cairngorm
calandria
calendric
calendula
calenture
canonical
cavendish
celandine
cementite
chaingang
chaingear
chainless
chainmail
cheongsam
chernozem
chronical
chronicle
cleanness
cleansing
clientage
clientele
cockneyfy
colonelcy
coloniser
colonnade
Cominform
Comintern
conundrum
coroneted
cotangent
crownless
cutaneous
cutinised
cylindric
davenport
debenture
decennary
decennial
decennium
decongest
decontrol
defendant
defensive
definable
definably
delineate
demandant
demanding
dependant
dependent
detention
detonator
diagnoses
diagnosis
dimension
diningcar
disannual
disengage
disentail
disentomb
disinfect
disinfest
diurnally
dominance
dominator
dominical
Dominican
drainpipe
drawnwork
dysentery
dyspnoeic
eccentric
eglantine
eirenicon
Emmenthal
empennage
epaenetic
ergonomic
erroneous
essential
eternally
excentric
expansile
expansion
expansive
expensive
extendant
extensile
extension
extensity
extensive
extenuate
facundity
Falangism
Falangist
farandole
fecundate
fecundity
felonious
femineity
financial
financier
flannelly
flouncing
forenamed
fortnight
fraenulum
galantine
galenical
galingale
gerundial
gerundive
gigantism
girandole
Girondist
goodnight
greenback
greenbelt
greeneyed
greengage
greenhorn
greenness
greenroom
greensand
greenweed
greenwood
groundage
groundash
groundhog
grounding
groundivy
groundnut
groundsel
hackneyed
haranguer
hardnosed
hirundine
homonymic
homuncule
homunculi
humankind
humanness
hyponasty
iguanodon
immanence
immanency
immensely
immensity
imminence
imminency
impendent
impending
incensory
incentive
incondite
incunable
indention
indenture
infantile
infantine
ingenious
ingenuity
ingenuous
insensate
insincere
insinuate
intendant
intensely
intensify
intension
intensity
intensive
intention
invention
inventive
inventory
japanning
jocundity
Johannine
journeyer
juvenilia
laciniate
laminaria
laminated
laryngeal
learnable
learnedly
legendary
Levantine
licensure
limonitic
linenfold
lorgnette
lovingcup
luminance
macintosh
malanders
masonried
melanosis
melanotic
mementoes
meningeal
mesentery
metonymic
midinette
misinform
misoneism
misoneist
momentary
momentous
Mycenaean
nepenthes
nominable
nominally
nominator
nonentity
oakenshaw
obconical
obtention
octennial
offensive
onionskin
oogenesis
oogenetic
opponency
ordinance
organelle
organiser
organstop
organzine
orientate
Orpington
ostensive
overnight
palankeen
palanquin
paranoiac
paranymph
parentage
patinated
pecuniary
Pekingese
peninsula
perennate
perennial
perinatal
phrenetic
plainness
plainsman
plainsong
plaintiff
plaintive
poignancy
polonaise
postnasal
postnatal
potentate
potential
praenomen
preengage
pregnable
pregnancy
proenzyme
prognoses
prognosis
queenhood
queenless
queenlike
queenpost
queenship
raconteur
ranunculi
recension
reconcile
recondite
reconfirm
reconvene
reconvert
redingote
redundant
remanence
remindful
reminisce
remontant
repentant
rerunning
resentful
resonance
resonator
retention
retentive
retinitis
retinulae
retinular
rosenoble
rosinweed
rotundity
rowantree
ruminator
salangane
sapanwood
satanical
satinbird
satinette
satinspar
satinwood
sciential
scientism
scientist
scoundrel
seaanchor
secondary
sedentary
seigneury
seigniory
selenious
selenitic
semanteme
semantics
seminally
serenader
serinette
sevenfold
seventeen
seventhly
seventies
sexennial
shrinkage
snubnosed
sphincter
spinnaker
spinneret
splendent
splendour
splenetic
splenitis
splintery
spoonbeak
spoonbill
spoonfeed
spoonmeat
springald
springbok
springily
springing
springlet
sprinkler
squinancy
stagnancy
stainable
stainless
stauncher
staunchly
steenkirk
sternmost
sternness
sternpost
sternward
strangely
strangler
strangles
strenuous
stringent
strongarm
strongbox
strongish
strongyle
strontium
supinator
synonymic
syringeal
tarantara
tarantass
tarantism
tarantula
taxonomic
technical
technique
theandric
thornback
thornbill
thornbush
thornless
thorntree
threnodic
tomentose
tomentous
toponymal
toponymic
tournedos
tourneyer
trainable
trainband
trainload
triennial
triennium
tyrannise
tyrannous
unbending
uncannily
uncinated
unconcern
unmindful
untenable
unwinking
valentine
Varangian
Vedantist
verandaed
vicennial
vimineous
voluntary
volunteer
wagonette
wagonroof
wapentake
weeknight
womanhood
womaniser
womankind
womanlike
womenfolk
womenkind
woodnymph
zamindary
zemindary
absconder
acidophil
adenoidal
adenomata
adenosine
adipocere
adiposity
aepyornis
aetiology
agriology
aircooled
airworthy
alveolate
amazonian
ambrosial
aminoacid
amorously
amyloidal
amylopsin
anabolism
analogise
analogist
analogous
anatomise
anatomist
anchorage
anchoress
anchorite
anchorman
androecia
androgyne
androgyny
anemogram
angiology
angiomata
anglophil
animosity
anthocyan
anthology
anthozoan
anxiously
apologise
apologist
approbate
aqueously
aragonite
arduously
astrocyte
astrodome
astrolabe
astrology
astronaut
astronomy
auctorial
audiology
authoress
authorial
authorise
authority
awesomely
baboonish
balconied
bamboozle
bandoleer
bandolero
bandolier
bandoline
batholite
batholith
Bathonian
bentonite
benzoline
beslobber
bethought
betrothal
betrothed
biliously
biologist
bionomics
bishopric
bonhomous
borrowing
boycotter
bulbously
bundobust
byproduct
cacholong
Caenozoic
Cainozoic
caliology
callosity
callously
Cambodian
cannonade
cannoneer
cannonier
Cantonese
cantorial
carbonado
carbonate
carbonise
carpology
carronade
cartogram
cartology
cartouche
caryopses
caryopsis
cassoulet
cassowary
ceanothus

censorial
chamomile
Charolais
chatoyant
chelonian
chibouque
chipolata
chiropody
chocolate
chorology
chthonian
clamorous
cocoonery
coelomata
coelomate
coelostat
coenobite
coenobium
coenosarc
colcothar
collocate
collodion
colloidal
colloquia
collotype
comforter
commodity
commodore
commonage
commonlaw
commotion
component
composite
composure
concocter
concoctor
concordat
concourse
conformal
conformer
consonant
consortia
convolute
convolved
copiously
coproduce
coprolite
coprology
coreopsis
cormorant
cornopean
corporate
corporeal
corposant
corrosion
corrosive
cosmogeny
cosmogony
cosmology
cosmonaut
cosmorama
coxcombry
crinoidal
crinoline
crocodile
cuckoldry
curiosity
curiously
cursorial
cursorily
custodial
custodian
customary
customise
cycloidal
cyclopean
cyclopian
cyclopses
cyclorama
cyclotron
cystocarp
cystolith
cystotomy
daltonism
deaconess
defroster
deinosaur
deodorant
deodorise
despoiler
despotism
deviously
diabolise
diabolism
diabolist
diaconate
dialogise
dialogism
dialogist
diatomite
dichogamy
dichotomy
dicrotism
diplomacy
diplomate
discoidal
discolour
discomfit
discommon
discourse
discovert
discovery
disforest
dishonest
dishonour
dislocate
disposure
dissocial
dissolute
dissonant
dittology
doctorate
doctorial
dogcollar
dogoodism
draconian
dragomans
dragoness
dragonfly
dragonish
dubiosity
dubiously
duteously
ealdorman
ecologist
economics
economise
economist
editorial
elaborate
embrocate
embroglio
embroider
emulously
enamoured
enchorial
enclosure
engrosser
enviously
epidosite
epilogist
epipolism
epitomise
epitomist
epizootic
espionage
Esthonian
Ethiopian
ethmoidal
ethnology
etymology
euchology
euphonise
euphonium
euphorbia
eutrophic
evaporate
exclosure
exopodite
exploiter
explosion
explosive
extrovert
factorage
factorial
factorise
faggoting
fatuously
faveolate
fellowman
ferrotype
festology
fibroline
fibromata
flavorous
following
forgotten
forlornly
fossorial
frivolity
frivolled
frivolous
fulsomely
furiously
fusionist
gabionade
gallonage
gallooned
gallopade
Gallophil
galloping
gallowses
gambolled
gammoning
garrotter
gasconade
gasholder
gemmology
geobotany
geologise
geologist
geoponics
gibbosity
gibbously
glamorise
glamorous
globosity
glucoside
glycoside
godmother
gondolier
gongorism
gorgonian
gorgonise
Gregorian
guncotton
gunpowder
haemostat
hagiology
Halloween
Hallowmas
handorgan
haplology
harbourer
harmonica
harmonics
harmonise
harmonist
harmonium
harmotome
harpooner
Harrovian
harrowing
hectogram
heinously
heliogram
heliostat
heliotype
heliozoan
heliozoic
herborise
hessonite
hideously
hierodule
hierogram
hierology
hippocras
hircosity
histogeny
histogram
histology
historian
hobgoblin
hobnobbed
hobnobber
homeopath
howsoever
hugeously
hydrocele
hydrofoil
hydrology
hydrolyse
hydrolyte
hydronium
hydrosome
hydroxide
hydrozoan
hydrozoon
hygrostat
hymnology
hypnoidal
hypnology
hypnotise
hypnotism
hypnotist
ichnology
iconology
illboding
illgotten
imbroglio
impiously
implosion
implosive
improbity
impromptu
improvise
inamorata
inclosure
inflowing
ingrowing
innholder
inodorous
introduce
introject
introvert
inviolacy
inviolate
inwrought
irksomely
isagogics
isopodous
jargonise
jealously
juniorate
juniority
karyotype
klinostat
laccolith
lampooner
landowner
Langobard
langouste
leftovers
legionary
leptosome
leucocyte
leucotome
leucotomy
leukocyte
limnology
lineolate
liquorice
liquorish
lissomely
lithology
lithopone
lithotomy
logaoedic
Londonise
Londonism
Longobard
lophodont
lowloader
macrocosm
macrocyte
malformed
malvoisie
mammonish
mammonism
mammonist
mammonite
mandoline
marmoreal
marrowfat
matronage
matronise
mausoleum
meliorate
meliorism
meliorist
meliority
Mennonite
meteorist
meteorite
meteoroid
methodise
Methodism
Methodist
methought
metrology
metronome
mezzotint
microbial
microchip
microcosm
microcyte
microfilm
microgram
microlite
microlith
micrology
micromesh
micropsia
micropyle
microsome
microtome
microtomy
microtone
microwave
Miltonian
misgovern
mnemonics
mnemonist
Mongolian
mongolism
Mongoloid
mongooses
monsoonal
monzonite
Mormonism
mucronate
muscovado
muscovite
myelomata
myologist
myriorama
mythology
narcotine
narcotise
narcotism
natrolite
necrology
necrophil
necrotise
negroidal
Negroness
negrophil
neologian
neologise
neologism
neologist
nephology
nervously
Nestorian
neuroglia
neurology
neuromata
neuropath
Newtonian
niccolite
nigrosine
Nipponese
nocuously
noisomely
nostology
notionist
noxiously
obviously
ochlocrat
oddjobber
oddjobman
odorously
offcolour
oilcolour
Oligocene
oligopoly
ominously
onerously
operosely
operosity
ophiology
oratorial
oratorian
orologist
orthodoxy
orthoepic
osteoderm
osteogeny
osteology
osteopath
Ostrogoth
otologist
outgoings
outworker
pantomime
parlously
parsonage
pastorale
pastorate
pathogeny
pathology
patrolled
patroller
patrolman
patrology
patronage
patroness
patronise
paulownia
Pavlovian
peasouper
penholder
peptonise
percolate
perforate
performer
periodate
personage
personate
personify
personnel
pestology
petiolate
petiolule
petroleum
petrology
phagocyte
phenology
phenomena
phenotype
pheromone
philogyny
philology
Philomela
phonogram
phonolite
phonology
photocell
photocopy
photogene
photophil
photopsia
phototype
phycology
phylogeny
phytogeny
phytology
phytotomy
phytotron
pictogram
pictorial
pipeorgan
pistoleer
pistolled
piteously
Platonise
Platonism
Platonist
Pleiocene
plutocrat
plutonian
Plutonism
Plutonist
plutonium
podzolise
poisonous
polyonymy
pomposity
pompously
pontoneer
pontonier
portolano
potboiler
potholing
potpourri
pozzolana
precocial
precocity
preconise
premonish
premotion
prenotion
prepotent

primordia
proboscis
proconsul
prologise
promotion
promotive
pronounce
proponent
prorogate
prosodist
protonema
prototype
protozoal
protozoan
protozoic
protozoon
provoking
provostry
pterosaur
pulmonary
pulmonate
purloiner
purposely
purposive
puzzolana
quinoline
quixotism
radiocast
radiogram
radiology
rancorous
randomise
raptorial
rationale
rationing
raucously
rauwolfia
reasoning
reckoning
rectorate
rectorial
reedorgan
rencontre
reprobate
reprocess
reproduce
responder
rethought
retrocede
retrodden
retroflex
retroject
retrousse
retrovert
rhinology
rhizocarp
rhizoidal
rhodolite
rhodonite
rhodopsin
Ribbonism
riotously
ruinously
Russophil
sailoring
sailorman
sallowish
salmonoid
santolina
santonica
sarcocarp
sarcomata
sartorial
sartorius
sauropoda
scapolite
scatology
schnorkel
schnorrer
schoolbag
schoolboy
schooling
schoolman
scotomata
seasoning
seaworthy
sectorial
semiology
semiotics
senhorita
seniority
sensorial
sensorium
sepiolite
seriously
sermonise
shemozzle
shipowner
sigmoidal
signorial
signorina
sinuosity
sinuously
siphonage
sixfooter
skijoring
skyrocket
Slavonian
Slavophil
slivovitz
sociogram
sociology
sociopath
somnolent
sophomore
Sorbonist
sorrowful
spinosity
Spinozism
Spinozist
spirogyra
sporocarp
sporocyst
sporogeny
statocyst
statolith
stegosaur
stenotype
stenotypy
steroidal
stolonate
stuporous
stylobate
subcostal
subnormal
subrogate
subtopian
succotash
succourer
suctorial
suctorian
suffocate
sunbonnet
sundowner
sunlounge
supporter
supposing
surrogate
syllogise
syllogism
symbolics
symbolise
symbolism
symbolist
symbology
sympodial
sympodium
symposiac
symposial
symposium
syncopate
tailoress
tailoring
tallowish
tambourin
tamponade
tattooist
tautology
tectonics
tectorial
tediously
teknonymy
teleology
temporary
temporise
tenuously
terrorise
terrorism
terrorist
teutonise
Teutonism
Teutonist
thyroxine
timeously
tonsorial
tremolant
tremolite
tribology
tricolour
trifocals
trifolium
triforium
trilobate
trilobite
trinomial
tropology
turboprop
Turcomans
Turkomans
typhoidal
unadopted
unadorned
unclothed
unclouded
uncropped
uncrossed
uncrowned
unicolour
uniformly
unisonant
unisonous
unknowing
unpeopled
unspotted
unstopped
unthought
untrodden
unwrought
uranology
urceolate
uvarovite
vacuolate
vacuously
variolate
variolite
varioloid
variolous
variously
vectorial
verbosely
verbosity
viciously
Victorian
victorine
videotape
villosity
viscosity
viscounty
viscously
visionary
visionist
vitiosity
voodooism
voodooist
waggonage
walloping
warbonnet
warmonger
webfooted
welcoming
werwolves
whosoever
willowish
windowbox
winsomely
yellowdog
yellowish
zealously
zincotype
zirconium
zoologist
zootomist
abruption
acceptant
acceptive
accipiter
acropetal
acropolis
ademption
aerophyte
aeroplane
allopathy
allophone
alloplasm
amorphism
amorphous
antipasto
antipathy
antiphony
antipodal
antipodes
aquaplane
Areopagus
asymptote
autopilot
backpedal
ballpoint
basipetal
bedspread
bedspring
bellpunch
bicipital
biosphere
blaspheme
blasphemy
bluepoint
blueprint
bombproof
bookplate
bryophyte
cacophony
caliphate
cataplasm
cataplexy
catoptric
champagne
champaign
champerty
champleve
cheapjack
cheapness
coemption
colophony
coryphaei
crampfish
crippling
crispness
curlpaper
cymophane
cytoplasm
dayspring
decapodal
decapodan
deception
deceptive
dipeptide
disappear
doorplate
drawplate
ecosphere
ectophyte
ectoplasm
ellipsoid
encephala
endophagy
endophyte
endoplasm
enrapture
entophyte
equipment
equipoise
equipping
escapable
esemplasy
estoppage
estopping
exceptant
excepting
exception
exceptive
excipient
exemplary
exemplify
exemption
exosphere
eyeopener
fireplace
firepower
fireproof
fishplate
fivepence
fivepenny
flippancy
foolproof
footplate
footpound
footprint
fourpence
fourpenny
gangplank
geosphere
germplasm
germproof
gonophore
grappling
graspable
gynophore
gyroplane
hairpiece
halfpence
halfpenny
halfprice
halophile
halophyte
handpress
headphone
headpiece
heelpiece
hexaploid
holophote
homophone
homophony
homoplasy
homopolar
hoofprint
idiopathy
idioplasm
incapable
incapably
inception
inceptive
incipient
insipidly
irruption
irruptive
jackplane
mailplane
manipular
manyplies
megaphone
melaphyre
menopause
meropidan
mesophyll
mesophyte
metaphase
metaplasm
monophagy
monoplane
mothproof
mycophagy
nameplate
nemophila
newspaper
newsprint
ninepence
ninepenny
nosepiece
notepaper
occipital
occupancy
octopodes
oenophile
oenophily
oesophagi
offspring
optophone
outspoken
outspread
overpitch
overpower
overprice
overprint
overproof
panoplied
parapeted
parapodia
peneplain
peneplane
peripatus
periphery
periplast
phosphate
phosphene
phosphide
phosphine
phosphite
pikeperch
plumpness
polyphagy
polyphase
polyphone
polyphony
polyploid
polyptych
pourpoint
promptbox
puerperal
rainproof
ratepayer
rebaptise
recapping
recapture
reception
receptive
recipient
reefpoint
ricepaper
rockplant
roofplate
rustproof
sailplane
saltpetre
sandpaper
sandpiper
saxophone
scalplock
scorpioid
scrapbook
scrapheap
scrapiron
scrappily
scrapping
scrapyard
scripture
sculpture
seedpearl
seedplant
selfpride
semaphore
semiplume
sharpener
sharpeyed
sharpness
sharpshod
sheepcote
sheepfold
sheephook
sheeplice
sheepskin
sheeptick
sheepwalk
sheepwash
shotproof
showpiece
showplace
sinophile
Sisyphean
sleepless
snowplant
softpedal
soleplate
solipsism
solipsist
soupplate
stagparty
stampduty
stampmill
stampnote
steepness
stippling
stoppress
straphang
strapless
strappado
strapping
strapwork
strapwort
stripling
stripping
stropping
sunspurge
sweepback
sycophant
synoptist
tailpiece
telepathy
telephone
telephony
telephoto
telophase
theophany
timepiece

tinopener
toxophily
trappings
troopship
truepenny
trumpedup
trumpeter
tuliproot
tuliptree
tulipwood
unhappily
unpopular
unzipping
viewpoint
wallpaper
wallplate
whimperer
whipperin
whisperer
willpower
windproof
winepress
wirephoto
workpiece
xenophile
xenophobe
xerophile
xerophily
xerophyte
xylophone
antiquary
antiquate
antiquity
brusquely
caciquism
chisquare
clinquant
moonquake
obliquely
obliquity
obsequent
obsequial
obsequies
pipsqueak
reliquary
reliquiae
seasquirt
setsquare
siliquose
trysquare
aberrance
aberrancy
abhorrent
abhorring
abnormity
absorbent
absorbing
absurdism
absurdist
absurdity
accordant
according
accordion
adherence
admirable
admirably
admiralty
adsorbate
adsorbent
adverbial
adversary
adversely
adversity
advertent
advertise
affirmant
aftercare
afterclap
afterglow
afterlife
aftermath
aftermost
afternoon
aftertime
afterword
algarroba
algorithm
alpargata
alterable
altercate
alternant
alternate
amauroses
amaurosis
amaurotic
ambergris
amourette
ampersand
anabranch
anacruses
anacrusis
anaerobic
antarctic
anthracic
anthropic
aphereses
apheresis
apocrypha
apparatus
apparitor
appertain
apportion
aquarelle
arboreous
arboretum
Armorican
arteriole
arteritis
arthritic
arthritis
arthropod
arthrosis
ascertain
asparagus
aspartate
aspersion
aspirator
assertion
assertive
assurance
assuredly
assurgent
aubergine
autarchic
autarkist
autoroute
babirussa
beeorchis
bifarious
bifurcate
bilirubin
biography
bipartite
bivariant
bivariate
bizarrely
bleareyed
bowerbird
boyfriend
briarroot
briarwood
brierroot
brierwood
calorific
camarilla
cameraman
camorrist
caparison
cartridge
Castroism
catarhine
catarrhal
caterwaul
cavernous
cedarwood
centrally
centreing
chairlady
cheerless
cherrypie
chlorella
chloritic
chlorosis
chlorotic
cigarette
cigarillo
cineraria
cinereous
clearance
clearcole
cleareyed
clearness
cockroach
coherence
coherency
colorific
comprador
comprisal
congruent
congruity
congruous
contralto
contrasty
contrived
contriver
copartner
copyright
covariant
coverable
coverslip
coverture
cowardice
cranreuch
cumbrance
debarment
debarring
decorator
deference
deferment
deferring
deformity
delirious
demarcate
demurrage
demurring
dendritic
departure
depurator
describer
desertion
desirable
desirably
destroyer
detergent
determent
determine
deterrent
deterring
detersion
detersive
dethroner
dextrally
dextrorse
diacritic
diaereses
diaeresis
diarrhoea
diatropic
dichroism
dichromat
dichromic
dimorphic
disarming
disbranch
discredit
disgracer
disorient
dispraise
distraint
divergent
diversely
diversify
diversion
diversity
diverting
doctrinal
doleritic
dowerless
downright
downriver
dyscrasia
dystrophy
eagerness
Edwardian
effortful
eiderdown
eiderduck
eldership
elutriate
embarrass
empirical
empyreumâ
endurable
endurably
endurance
engarland
enterable
enteritis
entertain
epigraphy
errorless
escortage
esperance
Esperanto
etherical
eucaryote
excerptor
excoriate
excurrent
excursion
excursive
execrable
execrably
expertise
expurgate
exsertile
exsertion
exservice
externals
extirpate
extorsive
extortion
extortive
eyebright
Falernian
federally
figurante
filtrable
fimbriate
flagrance
flagrancy
fluoresce
fluorosis
fluorspar
forereach
fragrance
fragrancy
freerange
freerider
friarbird
fumarolic
gabardine
gaberdine
gastraeum
gastritis
gastropod
gastrulae
generable
generalia
generally
generator
geography
geotropic
glaireous
governess
guerrilla
habergeon
haverings
haversack
hazardous
heterodox
heteronym
heterosis
hibernate
Hibernian
hilarious
hindrance
Holarctic
honoraria
honorific
hundredth
hyperbola
hyperbole
hypergamy
hypericum
hyperopia
hyperopic
ignorable
ignoramus
ignorance
immersion
immorally
impartial
imperator
imperfect
imperious
important
importune
incarnate
incorrect
incorrupt
incurable
incurably
incurious
incurrent
incurring
incursion
incursive
incurvate
inebriant
inebriate
inebriety
inerrable
inerrancy
inferable
inference
inferring
infertile
infirmary
infirmity
informant
infuriate
inharmony
inherence
inheritor
injurious
innermost
innervate
inscriber
insertion
inservice
insurable
insurance
insurgent
interbred
intercede
intercept
intercity
intercrop
interdict
interface
interfere
interfile
interflow
interfuse
interject
interknit
interlace
interlard
interleaf
interline
interlink
interlock
interlope
interlude
interment
internode
interpage
interplay
interpose
interpret
interring
interrupt
intersect
intervein
intervene
interview
interwind
interwove
interzone
intorsion
invariant
inverness
inversely
inversion
inversive
invertase
isotropic
jaborandi
jacaranda
laborious
labyrinth
lacerable
lacertian
lacertine
lachrymal
laterally
lazaretto
legerline
leviratic
liberally
liberated
liberator
libertine
literally
literatim
literator
literatus
liturgics
liturgist
liverwort
liveryman
logarithm
longrange
loverless
lowercase
lowerdeck
lowermost
lumbrical
lumbricus
luxuriant
luxuriate
luxurious
macaronic
macerator
maharajah
maharanee
maharishi
majordomo
majorette
majorship
makeready
malarious
manorseat
Masoretic
maternity
mayoralty
mayorship
memorable
memorably
memoranda
memoriter
miscreant
miscreate
miserable
miserably
Mithraism
Mithraist
moderator
modernise
modernism
modernist
modernity
monarchal
monarchic
monergism
mongrelly
monorhyme
moonraker
motorable
motorbike
motorboat
motorcade
muckraker
myography
naturally
nefarious
nemertean
nemertine
nephritic
nephritis
nephrosis
neutrally
nevermore
nondriver
nonprofit
notoriety
notorious
numerable
numerator
numerical
obcordate
objurgate
observant
obturator
obversely
obversion
occurrent
occurring
odourless
oestrogen
offertory
olecranal

olecranon
oleoresin
opportune
orderbook
orderform
orderless
orography
otherness
otherwise
outermost
outgrowth
ovenready
overreach
overreact
ownership
pancratic
panoramic
pantryman
paperback
paperclip
papergirl
paperthin
paperwork
partridge
paternity
pederasty
pendragon
penfriend
penurious
petersham
pierrette
pleuritic
pokerface
pokerwork
polariser
portrayal
portrayer
portreeve
powerboat
powerdive
powerless
preordain
priorship
procreant
procreate
prodromal
prodromic
programme
propriety
quadratic
quadrifid
quadrigae
quadrille
quadruman
quadruped
quadruple
quadruply
quarryman
quebracho
queerness
razorback
razorbill
razoredge
razorfish
rearrange
recording
recordist
rectrices
recurrent
recurring
recursion
recursive
redbreast
referable
reference
referenda
referring
reformism
reformist
refurbish
refurnish
regardant
regardful
reparable
repertory
reportage
reserpine
reservist
reservoir
resorbent
restraint
resurface
resurgent
resurrect
retardant
retortion
reverence
reversely
reversion
rewarding
riderless
riverbank
riverboat
riverhead
riverside
riverweed
rulership
saleratus
Samaritan
satirical
saturable
saturator
Saturnian
saturnine
saturnism
scirrhous
scleritis
sclerosis
sclerotic
seaurchin
secernent
securable
semirigid
sentrybox
separable
separably
separates
separator
severable
severally
severalty
severance
shearling
sheerhulk
sheerlegs
sheerness
sideritic
siderosis
soberness
soporific
soubrette
sovereign
spearfish
spearhead
spearmint
spearside
spearwort
spherical
spherular
squarrose
squirarch
squiredom
squirelet
staircase
stairfoot
stairhead
stairwell
steersman
subarctic
subbranch
subereous
sudorific
suffragan
sugarbeet
sugarcane
sugarloaf
sugarplum
superable
supercool
superfine
superfuse
superheat
supernova
superpose
supersede
superstar
supervene
supervise
surprisal
susurrant
suturally
swearword
sybaritic
syncretic
syneresis
synergism
synergist
tectrices
theoretic
theoriser
theurgist
tigerlily
tigermoth
tigerseye
tigerwood
tolerable
tolerably
tolerance
tortrices
tortricid
trierarch
tubercule
turnround
tutorship
umberbird
unberufen
uncertain
underbody
underbred
underclay
undercoat
underdone
underfelt
underfoot
undergird
undergone
undergrad
underhand
underhung
underlaid
underlain
underline
underling
undermine
undermost
underpaid
underpart
underpass
underplay
underplot
underrate
underripe
underseal
underseas
undersell
undershot
underside
undersign
undersold
undersong
underspin
undertake
undertint
undertone
undertook
undervest
underwear
underwent
underwing
underwood
unearthly
unharness
unhurried
unthrifty
uppercase
uppermost
usherette
utterable
utterance
utterless
uttermost
utterness
vagarious
vaporable
vaporific
vaporiser
venerable
venerably
venerator
venereous
ventrally
ventricle
vestryman
vicariate
vicarious
viceregal
vicereine
viceroyal
viverrine
wakerobin
waterbath
waterbuck
waterbutt
watercart
watercool
waterfall
waterflea
waterfowl
watergate
waterhole
waterleaf
waterless
waterlily
waterline
watermark
watermill
waterpipe
watershed
waterside
waterweed
waterworn
wherryman
whipround
wolframic
yearround
ytterbium
zoography
accessary
accession
accessory
accusable
acoustics
admission
admissive
advisable
advisably
advisedly
aerospace
albescent
amassment
ambuscade
amidships
ancestral
andesitic
antiserum
Arguseyed
armistice
arrestant
arresting
asbestine
asbestous
ascospore
assistant
autosomal
Aylesbury
backsight
backslang
backslide
backspace
backstage
backsword
bandstand
barnstorm
beanstalk
beefsteak
bemusedly
birdsfoot
birdsnest
blessedly
bluestone
boatswain
bombshell
bombsight
bondslave
bondstone
bookshelf
bookstall
bookstand
bookstore
boomslang
brasserie
brassiere
breastpin
brimstone
buckshish
buhrstone
burrstone
cadastral
campstool
canescent
canesugar
cardsharp
celestial
cerastium
cerussite
chassepot
chinstrap
chopstick
Christian
Christmas
chrysalid
chrysalis
citystate
clamshell
classable
classical
classless
classlist
classmate
classroom
claustral
clepsydra
cloisonne
cloistral
cockscomb
cocksfoot
coinsurer
coldshort
colosseum
colostomy
colostrum
coltsfoot
copesmate
copestone
corkscrew
cornsalad
cornstalk
cornstone
coruscant
coruscate
cowlstaff
crassness
croissant
crossable
crossbeam
crossbill
crossbred
crossette
crosseyed
crossfade
crossfire
crossfish
crosshead
crosslink
crossness
crossover
crossroad
crossruff
crosstalk
crossways
crosswind
crosswise
crossword
croustade
crowsfoot
crowsnest
cryoscope
cryoscopy
curbstone
dachshund
damascene
decastere
decistere
decussate
dehiscent
demission
demystify
depasture
deposable
depositor
devastate
devisable
digastric
digestion
digestive
dimissory
disesteem
divisible
downstage
drawsheet
dresscoat
dripstone
dropscene
dropscone
dropsical
drugstore
drumstick
dryasdust
dustsheet
eavesdrop
ecdysiast
ecossaise
egression
embassage
embussing
endoscope
endoscopy
endosperm
endospore
endosteal
endosteum
equisetum
excessive
excisable
exciseman
excusable
excusably
expositor
faldstool
farestage
farmstead
feedstock
feedstuff
fenestrae
fenestral
fetishism
fetishist
filmstrip
filoselle
firestone
fishslice
flagstaff
flagstick
flagstone
flowsheet
flowstone
focussing
foodstuff
footstalk
footstall
footstool
forasmuch
foreshore
foreshown
foresight
forespeak
forestage
forestall
fourscore
freestone
freestyle
frogspawn
fullscale
gainsayer
gallstone
gearshift
gladstone
glassgall
glassware
glasswork
glasswort
glissandi
glissando
glossator
glossitis
gneissoid
gneissose
goldsinny
goldsmith
grassland
greasegun
gritstone
grossness
grossular
grubscrew
grubstake
guesswork
gyroscope
hailstone
hailstorm
hairshirt
hairslide
hairspace

hairstyle
halfshell
halfstaff
hallstand
Hallstatt
handsdown
handshake
handspike
handstand
hardshell
haresfoot
hartshorn
hawksbill
headscarf
headstall
headstock
headstone
hemistich
hexastich
hexastyle
highspeed
hindsight
hoarstone
hocussing
holystone
homestead
hornstone
horoscope
horoscopy
huckstery
hypostyle
ignescent
impassion
impassive
impastoed
impostume
imposture
incessant
indispose
infuscate
infusible
infusoria
ingestion
ingestive
injustice
insistent
intestacy
intestate
intestine
invisible
invisibly
ionisable
ironsides
ironsmith
ironstone
jacksnipe
jackstraw
janissary
jockstrap
jossstick
Judastree
kerbstone
kickstart
kingsized
ladysmock
lampshade
lampshell
landscape
landslide
latescent
leafstalk
legislate
lifesaver
lifesized
lifestyle
limestone
livestock
loadstone
loafsugar
loanshark
locksmith
lodestone
logistics
longshore
lotusland
lovestory
lunisolar
maelstrom
magistery
magistral
mahlstick
mainsheet
majuscule
makeshift
manysided
marestail
marlstone
maulstick
megaspore
melismata
micaslate
milestone
milkshake
millstone
miniskirt
minuscule
misassign
misesteem
monastery
monkshood
monostich
monostyle
moonscape
moonshine
moonstone
mucksweat
necessary
necessity
newsstand
numbskull
obeisance
obfuscate
obsession
obsessive
octastyle
octostyle
omissible
opposable
orrisroot
oversexed
overshoot
oversight
oversized
overskirt
oversleep
overslept
overspend
overspent
overspill
overstate
oversteer
overstock
overstuff
Pakistani
palustral
parasitic
peepsight
Pelasgian
periscope
perishing
perisperm
peristome
peristyle
pikestaff
pintsized
pipestone
plausible
plausibly
pleasance
polysemic
polysomic
potassium
poussette
praiseful
pressgang
pressmark
pressroom
pressstud
presswork
priestess
pubescent
puissance
pulpstone
punishing
pyroscope
quiescent
rainstorm
ravishing
recession
recessive
recusance
recusancy
refashion
refusable
regisseur
registrar
reinstate
remission
renascent
reposeful
repossess
resistant
resistive
revisable
rhapsodic
ribosomal
ringshake
ringsnake
roadstead
rocksnake
rootstock
rufescent
salesgirl
saleslady
saltspoon
sandspout
sandstone
sandstorm
schistose
schistous
sciascopy
secession
semestral
semisolid
semisweet
senescent
seneschal
shipshape
shoeshine
sideswipe
siltstone
singspiel
sinistral
sinusitis
skeesicks
skiascopy
slabsided
slabstone
slapstick
snowscape
snowstorm
soapstone
softshell
songsmith
soupspoon
splashily
squashily
starshell
starstone
stressful
subastral
swansdown
taioseach
talismans
telescope
telescopy
theosophy
thirstily
thrashing
threshold
Thyestean
tilestone
timesheet
toadstone
toadstool
tombstone
townscape
townsfolk
transcend
transenna
transform
transfuse
transient
translate
transmute
transonic
transpire
transport
transpose
transship
transumpt
transvest
treasurer
troursered
trousseau
trussbeam
tumescent
tungstate
turnstile
turnstone
unmusical
unreserve
veinstone
vicesimal
vigesimal
virescent
volkslied
washstand
whetstone
whimsical
whinstone
whipsnake
whipstock
windswept
winestone
withstand
withstood
wolfsbane
wordsmith
yardstick
Yorkshire
zygospore
ablatival
ablutions
aboutface
aboutturn
acroteria
adaptable
adeptness
adjutancy
admitting
adoptable
adulterer
adulthood
adultness
aflatoxin
agistment
agnatical
ahistoric
airstream
albatross
aleatoric
alertness
allotment
allotrope
allotropy
allotting
ambitious
amputator
anaptyxis
annotator
anorthite
antitoxic
antitoxin
antitrade
antitrust
apartheid
apartment
apartness
apostolic
appetence
appetency
appetiser
arbitrage
arbitrary
arbitrate
arbitress
ascetical
auditable
auditoria
autotelic
autotroph
aventaile
avertible
awestruck
azeotrope
backtrack
bagatelle
barathrum
beastings
beauteous
beautiful
beestings
befitting
begetting
belatedly
besetment
besetting
besotting
bilateral
biliteral
birdtable
blasthole
blastment
blastulae
blastular
blowtorch
bluntness
blusterer
boattrain
bounteous
bountiful
bowstring
bracteate
bracteole
breathily
breathing
bristling
brittlely
buckthorn
bucktooth
bulltrout
bumptious
cadetship
cafeteria
canetrash
capitally
capitular
capitulum
caretaker
catatonia
catatonic
ceratodus
chaetopod
chanteuse
chantilly
chantress
chartered
charterer
chastener
chastiser
chatterer
cicatrice
cicatrise
clatterer
coastline
coastward
coastwise
coattails
cogitable
comitadji
comptroll
constable
constancy
constrain
constrict
construct
countable
countdown
countless
countship
courtcard
courteous
courtesan
courtroom
courtship
courtyard
covetable
craftsman
creatable
creatress
creatural
crestless
crustacea
cryptical
cryptogam
cryptonym
cunctator
curettage
curstness
cytotoxic
cytotoxin
dauntless
debatable
debutante
decathlon
deistical
delftware
demitasse
demitting
denitrate
denitrify
devitrify
devotedly
diactinic
diastasis
diastatic
diastolic
digitalin
digitalis
digitally
digitated
dilatable
dilatancy
dinothere
diphthong
dirttrack
dogstooth
donothing
doubtable
doubtless
downthrow
draftsman
driftsail
driftweed
driftwood
dubitable
ecritoire
eightfold
eightieth
eightsome
eightyish
ejectment
elastomer
electoral
electress
electrify
electrode
electuary
embattled
empathise
enactment
epistaxis
epistemic
epistoler
epistolic
equitable
equitably
erectness
eristical
erratical
eventless
eventuate
exactable
exactment
exactness
exanthema
excitable
excitancy
excitedly
existence
exostosis
expatiate
exultance
exultancy
eyestrain
facetious
faintness
fanatical
faultless
firstborn
firstfoot
firsthand
firstling
firstrate
flatterer
fleetness
flintlock
floatable
fluctuant
fluctuate
foretaste
foretoken
fractious
franticly
fritterer
frontally
frontless
frontline
frontpage
frontward
frontways
frontwise

frostbite
frostwork
fructuate
fructuous
fruitcake
fruiterer
fruitless
fruittree
frustrate
Gaeltacht
gauntness
gazetteer
gemutlich
genetical
genitival
genotypic
geostatic
getatable
ghostlike
ghostword
giantlike
glyptodon
gobetween
grantable
greataunt
greatcoat
greatness
gristmill
guestroom
guiltless
habitable
habitably
habituate
halftitle
halftrack
halftruth
halitosis
halothane
hamstring
hamstrung
haustella
haustoria
healthful
healthily
heartache
heartbeat
heartburn
heartfelt
heartfree
hearthrug
heartland
heartless
heartsick
heartsore
heartwood
hemitrope
hemstitch
hepatitis
heretical
heritable
hesitance
hesitancy
hesitator
Hexateuch
hightoned
homotaxis
homotonic
hydathode
hypethral
hypotaxis
identical
identikit
idiotical
ignitable
ignitible
immutable
immutably
impatiens
impatient
impetrate
impetuous
impotence
impotency
imputable
inaptness
inbetween
ineptness
inertness
infatuate
inpatient
insatiate
insatiety
insetting
irritable
irritably
isostatic
janitress
jetstream
jointress
keratitis
keratosis
Kshatriya
lapstrake
lapstreak
latitancy
lazytongs
leastways
leastwise
lengthily
levitator
Levitical
lifetable
lightfoot
lightless
lightness
lightning
lightship
lightsome
lightsout
lightwood
lightyear
limitable
limitedly
limitless
locatable
lovetoken
lunitidal
mailtrain
malathion
maritally
matutinal
meditator
melatonin
menstrual
menstruum
midstream
militancy
milktooth
minutegun
minuteman
moistener
moistness
monatomic
monitress
monotonic
monotreme
monotypic
monstrous
moratoria
mountable
moustache
munitions
naphthene
negotiant
negotiate
nicotiana
nicotinic
nightbird
nightclub
nightfall
nightgown
nighthawk
nightlife
nightline
nightlong
nightmare
nightside
nighttime
nightwork
ninetieth
novitiate
odontalgy
offstreet
ommatidia
onsetting
oscitancy
overtaken
overthrew
overthrow
overtness
overtones
overtrain
overtrick
overtrump
packtrain
painterly
paintwork
palatable
palatably
panatella
papeterie
parataxis
parathion
parotitis
penetrant
penetrate
penitence
phantasma
pilotfish
pinstripe
piratical
pivotable
pivotally
plantable
plantlike
plastered
plasterer
plaything
plenteous
plentiful
pointduty
pointedly
pointille
pointlace
pointless
pointsman
politburo
politesse
political
polythene
polytonal
polytypic
poulterer
practical
practised
prestress
prettyish
prettyism
printable
printshop
proptosis
prostatic
prostrate
psalteria
punctilio
punctuate
puritanic
pyrethrum
quantical
quarterly
quartette
quartzite
quartzose
quietness
quintette
quintuple
quittance
racetrack
reactance
rebutting
reentrant
refitment
refitting
refutable
remitment
remittent
remitting
renitency
repotting
reputable
reputably
reputedly
resetting
resitting
revetment
revetting
rightable
righteous
righthand
rightness
rightward
roisterer
rotatable
safetypin
sagittate
sainthood
saintlike
saintling
saintship
sanatoria
sanctuary
sandtable
sanitaria
saunterer
scantling
scantness
scatterer
scentless
sceptical
scintilla
scratcher
scratches
scrutable
scrutator
seastrand
secateurs
seditious
selftrust
semitonic
serotonin
shantyman
sheatfish
sheathing
sheetbend
shiftless
Shintoism
Shintoist
shirtless
shirttail
shootable
shortcake
shortener
shortfall
shorthand
shorthorn
shortness
shortstop
shortterm
shortwave
shottower
sidetable
sidetrack
sightless
sightseer
skintight
skirtings
skirtless
slantways
slantwise
smartness
smartweed
smatterer
smoothish
solitaire
Solutrean
Solutrian
something
sometimes
soritical
spectacle
spectator
splitting
spluttery
sportsman
spouthole
spoutless
spritsail
sputterer
squatness
squatting
startling
steatitic
stiltedly
stintless
stoutness
stratagem
strategic
stretcher
strutting
stutterer
subatomic
substance
substrata
substrate
sudatoria
sumptuary
sumptuous
sunstroke
sunstruck
swartness
sweatband
sweatshop
sweetcorn
sweetener
sweetmeal
sweetmeat
sweetness
sweetshop
sweettalk
sweptback
swiftness
tacitness
taintless
temptable
temptress
teratogen
theatrics
thirtieth
throttler
tightener
tightness
tightrope
tightwire
timetable
tipstaves
toastrack
tractable
tractably
traitress
trattoria
trattorie
treatable
treatment
triatomic
triptyque
troutfarm
troutling
trustdeed
trustless
turntable
twentieth
twentyone
twistable
twitterer
unaltered
unaptness
undutiful
uneatable
unfitness
unfitting
unmatched
unnatural
unsettled
untutored
unwitting
upsetting
vegetable
vegetably
veratrine
veritable
veritably
vexatious
visitable
visitress
vomitoria
waistband
waistbelt
waistcoat
waistline
wealthily
welltimed
wheatmeal
whistling
worktable
wrestling
wristband
wristdrop
wristshot
xparticle
yachtclub
yachtsman
zapateado
zoiatrics
Acheulean
Acheulian
aciculate
acidulate
acidulent
acidulous
affluence
announcer
anovulant
apiculate
Arthurian
asexually
assaulter
azimuthal
banjulele
banqueter
banquette
Bantustan
binturong
bouquetin
briquette
bughunter
caerulean
calculate
calculous
cannulate
capsulate
capsulise
carbuncle
carburise
carfuffle
cartulary
celluloid
cellulose
centurion
chemurgic
chequered
chihuahua
circuitry
circulate
coadunate
coagulant
coagulate
coequally
collusion
collusive
colourful
colouring
colourist
colourman
communard
communion
communise
communism
communist
community
commutate
concubine
concurred
conducive
conductor
Confucian
confusion
conjugate
connubial
conqueror
consulage
consulate
consulter
consultor
contumacy
contumely
contusion
corduroys
corpulent
corpuscle
corrugate
corrupter
corruptly
costumier
cothurnus
couturier
crapulent
crapulous
credulity
credulous
crenulate
crepuscle
croquette
debauched
debauchee
debaucher
defaulter
demiurgic
denouncer
detrusion
diffusely
diffusion
diffusive
disbudded

disburden
disbursal
disputant
dissuader
disturbed
disturber
effluence
effluvial
effluvium
effluxion
ejaculate
elocution
eloquence
emolument
encaustic
encounter
encourage
englutted
entourage
epicurean
epicurism
espousals
etiquette
evolution
evolutive
exclusion
exclusive
executant
execution
executive
executory
executrix
exequatur
exhauster
expounder
extrusion
extrusive
factually
favourite
fistulous
flatulent
formulaic
formulary
formulate
formulise
fortunate
foxhunter
frequence
frequency
fulgurant
fulgurate
fulgurite
fulgurous
garrulity
garrulous
gradually
graduator
granulate
granulite
granulose
gratulate
gunrunner
hamburger
harquebus
Herculean
hereunder
hirsutism
homousian
humbugged
illjudged
impluvium
impounder
imprudent
incaution
inclusion
inclusive
inequable
influence
influenza
inoculate
inpouring
intrusion
intrusive
Iroquoian
jacquerie
kerfuffle
kibbutzim
labourite
laevulose
languidly
leisurely
Limburger
limousine
lingually
lingulate
Mancunian
manducate
marquetry
marsupial
marsupium
masculine
mercurial
mercurous
micturate
midsummer
misguided
molluscan
mosquitos
mundungus
murmurous
Mussulman
Neptunian
neptunium
nocturnal
nonjuring
nummulite
nuncupate
obscurant
obscurely
obscurity
obtrusion
obtrusive
occludent
occlusion
occlusive
oilburner
outgunned
outnumber
outputted
oviductal
parbuckle
parquetry
pasturage
pendulate
penduline
pendulous
penpusher
perfumery
perfumier
perfusion
perfusive
pergunnah
permutate
persuader
pertussis
petaurist
picturise
pinnulate
pirouette
planuloid
plumulate
plumulose
pollutant
pollution
porcupine
portulaca
postulant
postulate
pothunter
precursor
prejudice
prelusion
prelusive
prelusory
procuracy
procuress
profusely
profusion
prolusion
prolusory
pullulate
purpureal
pursuable
pursuance
pustulate
pustulous
querulous
rapturous
reclusion
reclusive
recruital
recruiter
redoubted
reeducate
refluence
renouncer
reshuffle
resources
retoucher
rumrunner
sacculate
Sadducean
sasquatch
savourily
scapulary
scrounger
seclusion
seclusive
Seljukian
sensually
septuplet
serrulate
sextuplet
shogunate
siphuncle
sojourner
spatulate
speculate
spiculate
spinulose
spinulous
spleuchan
spodumene
sporulate
statuette
statutory
stimulant
stimulate
stipulate
strouding
subduable
subduedly
subjugate
sublunary
succulent
succursal
suffusion
sunburned
suppurate
surculose
surmullet
tactually
Talmudist
Targumist
Tartufian
Tartufism
teacupful
tellurate
tellurian
telluride
tellurite
tellurium
tellurous
textually
throughly
tittuping
tittupped
tonguelet
tonguetie
toreutics
torturous
traducian
trebuchet
trebucket
tremulant
tremulous
tribunate
tributary
triquetra
triturate
truculent
turbulent
turquoise
twosuiter
unbounded
uncounted
uncouthly
undaunted
undoubted
unequally
unfounded
unicuspid
unplugged
unplumbed
unsoundly
unstudied
untouched
untrussed
unusually
upcountry
vapouring
vapourish
venturous
verrucose
verrucous
virgulate
virtually
virtuosic
virtuosos
Vitruvian
volauvent
voyeurism
vulturine
vulturish
vulturous
Walpurgis
whodunnit
activator
alleviate
antivenin
antiviral
arriviste
behaviour
boliviano
cadaveric
cleavable
deliverer
derivable
disavouch
disavowal
echovirus
equivocal
equivoque
evolvable
excavator
grievance
immovable
immovably
innovator
lixiviate
motivator
neckverse
oblivious
overvalue
polevault
polyvinyl
recoverer
redevelop
redivivus
relevance
relevancy
removable
renovator
revivable
scrivener
semivowel
sleevenut
synovitis
televisor
unadvised
uncivilly
uncovered
undivided
unsavoury
winevault
allowable
allowably
allowance
allowedly
arrowhead
arrowroot
arrowwood
arrowworm
askewness
backwards
backwater
backwoods
bandwagon
bandwidth
birdwatch
bondwoman
bratwurst
Bretwalda
buckwheat
bushwhack
cartwheel
charwoman
dipswitch
dishwater
downwards
eastwards
edelweiss
elbowroom
elsewhere
endowment
erstwhile
firewater
fireworks
folkweave
forewoman
fourwheel
freewheel
freewoman
gearwheel
goodwives
graywacke
greywacke
handwheel
headwater
highwater
homewards
hornwrack
ironworks
jurywoman
kinswoman
leftwards
lilywhite
limewater
lintwhite
luftwaffe
Manxwoman
meanwhile
meltwater
millwheel
overwatch
overweary
overweigh
overwhelm
overwound
overwrite
overwrote
polywater
rainwater
rearwards
renewable
roadworks
rosewater
saltwater
saltworks
screwball
screwbolt
screwpile
screwpine
screwworm
shipwreck
shrewmice
sidewards
sidewheel
sinewless
skewwhiff
snowwhite
soapworks
sodawater
somewhere
somewhile
spurwheel
stalworth
stopwatch
strawworm
strewment
throwaway
throwback
throwster
tidewater
tirewoman
typewrite
westwards
widowbird
widowhood
windwards
woodwaxen
workwoman
wormwheel
admixture
affixture
immixture
innoxious
obnoxious
preexilic
pyroxylin
taraxacum
acetylate
acetylcoA
acetylene
alicyclic
amaryllis
amblyopia
amblyopic
analysand
anchylose
annoyance
anonymity
anonymous
assayable
bathybius
bellyache
bellyband
bellyflop
billycock
billygoat
boobytrap
bullybeef
bullytree
buttygang
cageyness
candytuft
carryover
coccygeal
collyrium
condyloid
condyloma
cubbyhole
currycomb
cuttysark
dairymaid
dickybird
Dionysiac
Dionysian
dithyramb
ecosystem
embayment
embryonal
embryonic
embryotic
emphysema
enjoyable
enjoyably
enjoyment
enthymeme
epicyclic
epigynous
eponymous
eurhythmy
everybody
fairyhood
fairyland
fairylike
fairyring
fairytale
fancyfree
fancywork
ferryboat
fishyback
forsythia
fortyfive
gloryhole
glueyness
handywork
heavyduty
Hercynian
hollyhock
Hollywood
honeycomb
honeymoon
honkytonk
hunkydory
isocyclic
isohyetal
jellyfish
jollyboat
lacrymose
lardycake
Malayalam
martyrdom
martyrise
mateyness
methylate
methylene
mistyeyed
mollymawk
moneybags
moneybill
moneywort

nannygoat
neodymium
newlyweds
pachyderm
pantyhose
pennywort
pharyngal
pharynges
pharynxes
piggyback
piggybank
poppycock
poppyhead
propylaea
propylene
pterygium
pterygoid
puppyhood
pussyfoot
readymade
repayable
repayment
Samoyedic
sandyacht
spagyrist
splayfoot
storybook
storyline
syncytial
syncytium
tachylite
tachylyte
tallyshop
tiedyeing
tridymite
trihybrid
unsayable
uropygium
wallydrag
worrywart
breezeway
citizenly
citizenry
embezzler
freezable
freezedry
hylozoism
polyzoary
quizzical
sforzando
synizesis
whizzbang

---

abdicable
abdicator
aberrance
aberrancy
abnegator
abradable
abrogator
abundance
abysmally
acariasis
accusable
acrobatic
activator
adaptable
adiabatic
adjutancy
admirable
admirably
admiralty
adoptable
adrenalin
advisable
advisably
advocator
aerobatic
affidavit
Afrikaans
Afrikaner
agreeable
agreeably
airyfairy
alienable
alienator
aliphatic
allemande
alligator
allocable
allopathy
allowable
allowably
allowance
alterable
ambulacra
ambulance
amendable
aminoacid
amoebaean
amputator
amygdalin
anabranch
angularly
annotator
annoyance
annularly
annulated
antenatal
anthracic
antipasto
antipathy
aplanatic
apparatus
appliance
araucaria
Areopagus
argybargy
arrogance
asexually
asparagus
aspirator
assayable
assonance
assumable
assumably
assurance
asthmatic
athematic
Athenaeum
auditable
automatic
automaton
available
availably
aventaile
avoidable
avoidably
avoidance
awardable
axiomatic
bacchanal
bacchante
backwards
backwater
bainmarie
balalaika
baldfaced
bandwagon
barefaced
basically
beefeater
bellyache
bestially
bigheaded
billiards
biography
birdtable
birdwatch
blameable
blameably
blockader
boldfaced
bombhappy
bookmaker
Brahmanic
breakable
breakaway
bregmatic
Bretwalda
brummagem
calamanco
cameraman
cantharid
cantharis
cantharus
capitally
caretaker
catamaran
catchable
centrally
chachacha
champagne
champaign
charlatan
chickadee
chickaree
chihuahua
chromatic
chromatin
chrysalid
chrysalis
cinematic
cineraria
civically
claimable
classable
clearance
cleavable
climbable
clubbable
coattails
coaxially
coequally
cogitable
colleague
comically
comitadji
complaint
comprador
conically
constable
constancy
contralto
contrasty
cordially
cornsalad
Corybants
corydalis
countable
coverable
covetable
creatable
cropeared
crossable
crucially
crushable
crustacea
cubically
cumbrance
cunctator
cupbearer
curlpaper
cynically
dalliance
dandiacal
debatable
debutante
decidable
decimally
decimator
decorator
dedicator
definable
definably
deludable
demitasse
deposable
depurator
derivable
desirable
desirably
desolater
desolator
detonator
devisable
dextrally
diastasis
diastatic
digitalin
digitalis
digitally
digitated
dilatable
dilatancy
disbranch
discharge
disgracer
dishfaced
dishwater
dispraise
dissuader
distraint
diurnally
dividable
dodecagon
dominance
dominator
doubtable
downwards
drinkable
drummajor
dubitable
dyscrasia
dysphagia
dysphagic
dysplasia
eastwards
echolalia
ecossaise
eggbeater
elegiacal
elongated
emaciated
emendable
emendator
endogamic
endurable
endurably
endurance
enigmatic
enjoyable
enjoyably
ensheathe
enterable
enwreathe
enzymatic
epigraphy
epistaxis
equitable
equitably
escalator
escapable
escheator
esperance
Esperanto
estimable
estimator
eternally
ethically
evolvable
exactable
excavator
excisable
excitable
excitancy
excusable
excusably
execrable
execrably
exequatur
exultance
exultancy
eyeglance
eyeshadow
factually
fairfaced
fasciated
fatheaded
fatigable
federally
feiseanna
figurante
filtrable
finically
fireeater
firewater
flagrance
flagrancy
flammable
flippancy
floatable
floriated
folkdance
foolhardy
footfault
forecaddy
forenamed
foretaste
forgeable
fragrance
fragrancy
freelance
Freemason
freerange
freezable
frogmarch
frontally
fumigator
Gaeltacht
gainsayer
garibaldi
gastraeum
gaugeable
generable
generalia
generally
generator
geography
geostatic
getatable
glacially
gladiator
glengarry
glissandi
glissando
glossator
gradually
graduator
grandaddy
grandaunt
grantable
graspable
graywacke
greataunt
greywacke
grievance
habitable
habitably
halfbaked
halfcaste
halfhardy
Hanseatic
headwater
heartache
helically
hendiadys
heritable
herniated
hesitance
hesitancy
hesitator
highlands
highwater
Himalayan
hindrance
holocaust
homemaker
homewards
homogamic
homotaxis
honoraria
hotheaded
hypocaust
hypomania
hypomanic
hyponasty
hypotaxis
iceskater
idiomatic
idiopathy
ignitable
ignorable
ignoramus
ignorance
illegally
imageable
imbalance
immolator
immorally
immovable
immovably
immutable
immutably
impedance
imperator
impleader
imputable
inbreathe
incapable
incapably
increaser
incubator
incunable
incurable
incurably
indagator
indicator
ineffable
ineffably
inequable
inerrable
inerrancy
inferable
inhalator
inhumanly
initially
initiator
innovator
inorganic
insularly
insulator
insurable
insurance
ionisable
irrigable
irrigator
irritable
irritably
ischiadic
ischiatic
isoniazid
isostatic
jaborandi
jacaranda
jocularly
jubilance
judgmatic
katabasis
katabatic
kinematic
kingmaker
kneadable
lacerable
lagniappe
laminaria
laminated
lanthanum
laterally
latitancy
laughable
laughably
learnable
leftwards
leviratic
levitator
lexically
liberally
liberated
liberator
lifesaver
lifetable
limewater
limitable
lingually
lipreader
literally
literatim
literator
literatus
litigable
lobulated
locatable
logically
logomachy
longeared
longfaced
longrange
lovematch
lowloader
luftwaffe
luminance
lymphatic
lyrically
macerator
magically
maharajah
maharanee
Malayalam
malleable
manslayer
maritally
marshalcy
martially
matriarch
maximally
mayoralty
medicable
medically
meditator
melomania
meltwater
memorable

memorably
memoranda
menopause
messianic
miasmatic
militancy
minelayer
minimally
mischance
miserable
miserably
misfeasor
misleared
misshapen
Mithraism
Mithraist
mitigable
mitigator
moderator
modulator
monobasic
monogamic
monolatry
monomania
moonraker
mortgagee
mortgager
mortgagor
moschatel
motheaten
motivator
motorable
mouldable
mountable
moustache
muckraker
mumchance
musically
mutilator
Mycenaean
mydriasis
mydriatic
myography
myrobalan
napthalic
naturally
navigable
navigator
neutrally
newspaper
nodulated
nominable
nominally
nominator
nonviable
notepaper
nucleated
numerable
numerator
nymphalid
obeisance
obligated
obturator
occupancy
ocellated
odontalgy
oenomancy
offchance
offseason
olecranal
olecranon
omophagia
omophagic
opposable
opsimathy
optically
ordinance
oriflamme
orography
oscitancy
overeaten
overeater
overladen
overmatch
overtaken
overvalue
overwatch
pacemaker
paillasse
palatable
palatably
palliasse
panchayat
pancratic
panoramic
parabasis
paralalia
paramatta
parataxis
partially
patinated
patriarch
peaceable
peaceably
peculator
pederasty
pendragon
perchance
perinatal
peripatus
permeable
permeance
persuader
petulance
petulancy
phantasma
pigheaded
pivotable
pivotally
pixilated
placeable
plantable
plasmatic
pleadable
pleasance
plumdamas
pneumatic
poignancy
polevault
polonaise
polybasic
polygamic
polymathy
polywater
popularly
porbeagle
portrayal
portrayer
posthaste
postnasal
postnatal
pragmatic
preadamic
pregnable
pregnancy
printable
prismatic
programme
prostatic
proveably
psoriasis
psoriatic
puissance
purchaser
puritanic
pursuable
pursuance
pyracanth
pyrolater
pyrolatry
pyromancy
pyromania
quadratic
quebracho
quittance
radically
raingauge
rainmaker
rainwater
ratepayer
reachable
reactance
rearrange
rearwards
rebukable
recreancy
recusance
recusancy
redheaded
referable
refusable
refutable
regularly
regulator
relevance
relevancy
removable
renewable
renovator
reparable
repayable
reputable
reputably
resalable
resonance
resonator
restraint
resumable
revelator
revisable
revivable
revocable
rheumatic
ricepaper
rightable
rosewater
rotatable
ruffianly
ruminator
saccharin
saleratus
saltmarsh
saltwater
sandpaper
sandtable
sandyacht
sanitaria
sapheaded
sasquatch
saturable
saturator
scallawag
schematic
scholarly
sciamachy
scrutable
scrutator
seachange
secularly
securable
seedeater
selffaced
semblable
semblably
semblance
seminally
sensually
separable
separably
separates
separator
serenader
sergeancy
serjeancy
serjeanty
severable
severally
severalty
severance
sforzando
shakeable
shapeable
shipcanal
shockable
shoemaker
shootable
sibilance
sibilancy
sidetable
sidewards
similarly
simulacra
simulacre
simulator
skiamachy
slaphappy
slopbasin
slowmatch
smallarms
sodawater
solitaire
spatially
speakable
specially
specialty
spectacle
spectator
spendable
spermatic
spermatid
spinnaker
spoliator
squinancy
squirarch
stackable
stagnancy
stagparty
stainable
stargazer
staymaker
stellated
stepdance
stigmatic
stingaree
stoically
stopwatch
storiated
stratagem
stromatic
subbranch
subdeacon
subduable
substance
suffragan
superable
supinator
surcharge
suturally
swimmable
tabularly
tabulator
tacamahac
tactually
taeniasis
taraxacum
teachable
teachably
tegularly
telepathy
temptable
tentmaker
textually
theomachy
theomania
thermally
thinkable
throwaway
tidegauge
tidewater
timelapse
timetable
tipstaves
titularly
toadeater
tolerable
tolerably
tolerance
tonically
toothache
topically
touchable
toxically
trabeated
traceable
traceably
tractable
tractably
trainable
traumatic
treatable
trierarch
trivially
truncated
tubularly
tunicated
turntable
twistable
typically
ultimatum
unashamed
unbalance
uncinated
uncleanly
uncreated
undamaged
undecagon
undreamed
undulated
uneatable
unequally
unifiable
uniplanar
unnamable
unsayable
unsheathe
untenable
unusually
unwomanly
urticaria
utterable
utterance
vaporable
vegetable
vegetably
venerable
venerably
venerator
vengeance
ventrally
veritable
veritably
vigilance
vigilante
virtually
visitable
wallpaper
washbasin
watchable
wehrmacht
weighable
westwards
wheyfaced
wieldable
windwards
winevault
wiregauze
wolframic
woodwaxen
workmanly
worktable
wormeaten
wychhazel
zeugmatic
zoography
zoophagan
zygomatic
absorbent
absorbing
acetabula
adlibbing
adsorbate
adsorbent
adverbial
aitchbone
amphibian
amphibole
anklebone
approbate
assembler
attribute
Aylesbury
bathybius
bejabbers
bellyband
beslobber
billabong
birchbark
blackball
blackbird
blackbuck
bloodbath
bowerbird
bricabrac
bullybeef
bundobust
camelback
Camembert
canalboat
cantabile
carambola
Caribbean
charabanc
cheekbone
cobwebbed
coenobite
coenobium
columbary
Columbian
columbine
columbite
columbium
concubine
confabbed
connubial
corymbose
crookback
crossbeam
crossbill
crossbred
deathblow
decumbent
demobbing
depthbomb
dickybird
disembark
disembody
dreamboat
earthborn
everybody
ferryboat
fieldbook
fieldboot
firstborn
fishyback
flashback
flashbulb
friarbird
frostbite
greenback
greenbelt
guardbook
guidebook
hatchback
hawksbill
heartbeat
heartburn
hellebore
hereabout
hobgoblin
hobnobbed
hobnobber
horseback
horsebean
houseboat
housebote
huckaback
hunchback
hyperbola
hyperbole
improbity
incumbent
interbred
jollyboat
Langobard
Longobard
Maccabean
microbial
moneybags
moneybill
motorbike
motorboat
neighbour
nightbird
oddjobber
oddjobman
orderbook
palpebral
paperback
peachblow
penumbral
pickaback
piggyback
piggybank
pinchbeck
politburo
powerboat
psalmbook
punchball
punchbowl
razorback
razorbill
recombine
recumbent
redoubted
refurbish
reprobate
resorbent
riflebird
riverbank
riverboat
rocambole
satinbird
sauceboat

scorebook
scrambler
scrapbook
screwball
screwbolt
scribbler
scrubbing
selfabuse
sheetbend
shellback
shellbark
shrubbery
slingback
slothbear
smokeball
smokebomb
smokebush
snakebird
snakebite
spaceband
speedball
speedboat
spellbind
spicebush
spoonbeak
spoonbill
squabbler
squibbing
stakeboat
steamboat
stillborn
stinkball
stinkbomb
stirabout
stockbook
stoolball
stormbelt
stormbird
storybook
stylebook
stylobate
sugarbeet
sweatband
sweepback
sweptback
syllabary
syllabise
syllabism
syllabled
thighbone
thighboot
thornback
thornbill
thornbush
throbbing
thrombose
throwback
trainband
trihybrid
trilobate
trilobite
trussbeam
turnabout
twiceborn
umberbird
underbody
underbred
undoubted
valuables
vertebrae
vertebral
vestibule
waistband
waistbelt
walkabout
waterbath
waterbuck
waterbutt
weighbeam
whaleback
whaleboat
whalebone
wheelbase
whitebait
whitebass
whitebeam
whizzbang
widowbird
wolfsbane
wristband
yohimbine
ytterbium
adipocere
adjunctly
affricate
aftercare
afterclap
airjacket
albescent
alicyclic
altercate
altricial
ambuscade
americium
anglicise
anglicism
Anglicist
anorectic
antarctic
anthocyan
apodictic
apomictic
applicant
arabicise
astrocyte
ataractic
atomicity
atonicity
attractor
auspicate
autarchic
baldachin
bandicoot
Barmecide
barnacled
barracker
barracoon
barracuda
barricade
barricado
bedjacket
beeorchis
bellicose
biblicism
biblicist
biconcave
bifurcate
billycock
blackcoat
blackcock
braincase
bridecake
briefcase
Briticise
Briticism
broadcast
broomcorn
cachectic
calcicole
canescent
capriccio
Capricorn
cathectic
cavalcade
Celticism
character
chelicera
clearcole
climactic
clinician
cockscomb
collected
collector
collocate
compactly
compactor
concocter
concoctor
conducive
conductor
Confucian
connected
connecter
connector
contactor
convector
corbicula
corkscrew
correctly
corrector
corticate
corticoid
coruscant
coruscate
courtcard
crankcase
criticise
criticism
cryoscope
cryoscopy
cuplichen
curricula
currycomb
cystocarp
damascene
debauched
debauchee
debaucher
decalcify
defalcate
deflector
dehiscent
demarcate
demulcent
deprecate
desiccant
desiccate
detractor
dialectal
dialectic
didrachma
dietician
difficile
difficult
disaccord
dislocate
dissector
dissocial
dresscoat
dropscene
dropscone
duodecimo
duplicate
duplicity
embraceor
embracery
embracive
embrocate
endoscope
endoscopy
entrechat
entrecote
epicyclic
eradicate
eroticism
ethnicity
ewenecked
exoticism
explicate
exsiccate
exsuccous
extractor
extricate
fabricant
fabricate
faithcure
fascicled
fascicule
fasciculi
febricity
financial
financier
flashcube
flouncing
foeticide
formicary
formicate
fornicate
fossicker
fourscore
frockcoat
frolicked
fruitcake
fruticose
fullscale
fungicide
gallicise
gallicism
germicide
gimmickry
gothicise
Gothicism
graticule
greatcoat
grubscrew
gynaeceum
gynoecium
gyroscope
headscarf
heathcock
herbicide
hippocras
Holarctic
homuncule
homunculi
honeycomb
horoscope
horoscopy
housecarl
housecoat
hurricane
hydrocele
ignescent
imbricate
impeccant
implicate
imprecate
imprecise
inculcate
inexactly
inflictor
infractor
infuscate
insincere
inspector
intercede
intercept
intercity
intercrop
intricacy
intricate
isocyclic
italicise
Italicism
jampacked
justiciar
landscape
Laodicean
lardycake
larvicide
latescent
latticing
leucocyte
leukocyte
libecchio
longicorn
loquacity
lowercase
lownecked
lubricant
lubricate
lubricity
lubricous
macrocosm
macrocyte
majuscule
manducate
manticore
masticate
matricide
matricula
mendacity
mendicant
mendicity
metricate
metrician
metricise
metricist
microchip
microcosm
microcyte
midwicket
minuscule
misbecome
mispickel
misreckon
monarchal
monarchic
monoecism
monticule
moonscape
mordacity
mortician
mosaicism
mosaicist
mosaicked
motorcade
mustachio
myrmecoid
mysticism
mythicise
mythicism
mythicist
naumachia
nightclub
nigricant
nitpicker
obfuscate
ochlocrat
Oligocene
orificial
ostracise
ostracism
outbacker
oviductal
paperclip
parbuckle
parricide
pasticcio
patrician
patricide
paypacket
Pentecost
perfectly
perfector
periscope
persecute
pesticide
petticoat
phagocyte
phenacite
photocell
photocopy
physician
physicist
physicked
picnicked
picnicker
pinchcock
pistachio
pithecoid
pizzicati
pizzicato
placecard
Pleiocene
plutocrat
poeticise
poeticism
poppycock
porticoes
posticous
poundcake
precocial
precocity
predacity
predicant
predicate
predictor
prelector
preoccupy
prerecord
projector
prolicide
prosector
prosecute
protector
pubescent
publicise
publicist
publicity
pugnacity
punchcard
pyroscope
quiescent
radiocast
ransacker
ranunculi
reconcile
reeducate
reflector
refractor
rejoicing
renascent
replicate
reprocess
respecter
retoucher
retractor
retrocede
rhizocarp
roughcast
rubricate
rubrician
rudbeckia
rufescent
rusticate
rusticity
Sadducean
sarcocarp
scarecrow
sciascopy
scolecite
scorecard
Scoticise
scratcher
scratches
screecher
seaanchor
seaurchin
senescent
seneschal
septicity
sepulcher
sepulchre
sequacity
sharecrop
sheepcote
shortcake
simulcast
skiascopy
skyjacker
skyrocket
slateclub
snowscape
sparkcoil
sphincter
spiracula
spleuchan
sporocarp
sporocyst
squelcher
staircase
stalactic
statocyst
stauncher
staunchly
steelclad
stomachal
stomacher
stomachic
stonechat
stonecoal
stonecold
stonecrop
stormcock
stormcone
stretcher
subarctic
subjacent
suffocate
sugarcane
supercool
surfacing
surficial
suspicion
sweetcorn
swordcane
syndactyl
syndicate
synoecete
syntactic
tactician
tanpickle
telescope
telescopy
tentacled
thylacine
toothcomb
townscape
trabecula
traducian
transcend
trebuchet
trebucket
tridactyl
trifacial
trifocals
trisector
trunkcall
tubercule
tumescent
unchecked
unconcern

underclay
undercoat
unmatched
unshackle
unsuccess
untouched
unwelcome
uppercase
uxoricide
vallecula
verbicide
vermicide
vermicule
verrucose
verrucous
vibracula
vindicate
virescent
vorticism
vorticist
vorticity
vorticose
waistcoat
watchcase
watercart
watercool
witticism
wyliecoat
yachtclub
zootechny
abounding
absurdism
absurdist
absurdity
accordant
according
accordion
almandine
appendage
appendant
ascendant
ascendent
astraddle
astrodome
attendant
balladeer
balladist
Barbadian
bedridden
belvedere
benzidine
blackdamp
breakdown
brigadier
bringdown
burnedout
byproduct
calandria
calendric
calendula
Cambodian
candidacy
candidate
cathedral
cavendish
celandine
chokedamp
circadian
closedown
coccidium
collodion
commodity
commodore
comradely
comradery
confidant
confident
confiding
contadina
contadino
conundrum
coproduce
countdown
cowardice
crackdown
crashdive
crocodile
cuspidate
custodial
custodian
cylindric
cymbidium
damnedest
deacidify
defendant
demandant
demanding
deoxidise
dependant
dependent
depredate
diffident
disbudded
dissident
dogoodism
Dravidian
dromedary
dryasdust
eavesdrop
Edwardian
eiderdown
eiderduck
elucidate
embedding
euclidean
exceeding
exopodite
extendant
extradite
facundity
farandole
fecundate
fecundity
floridean
floridity
forbidden
frigidity
gabardine
gaberdine
gambadoes
gammadion
gerundial
gerundive
giltedged
girandole
Girondist
gravidity
grenadier
grenadine
groundage
groundash
groundhog
grounding
groundivy
groundnut
groundsel
haggadist
hagridden
handsdown
hazardous
heavyduty
Hebridean
hierodule
hirundine
hispidity
histidine
hunkydory
hybridise
hybridism
hybridity
illboding
illjudged
impendent
impending
imprudent
incondite
intendant
interdict
introduce
isopodous
jocundity
knockdown
legendary
limpidity
liquidate
liquidise
liquidity
lophodont
lowerdeck
majordomo
malanders
methadone
methodise
Methodism
Methodist
molybdate
morbidity
muscadine
myxoedema
obcordate
occludent
orchidist
orthodoxy
osteoderm
outridden
pachyderm
Palladian
palladium
palladous
pallidity
pastedown
periodate
pethidine
phagedena
pitchdark
placidity
pointduty
pompadour
powerdive
precedent
preceding
prejudice
preordain
president
presidial
presidium
procedure
prosodist
provident
providing
puffadder
putridity
pycnidium
quotidian
rancidity
rebidding
recondite
recording
recordist
redundant
regardant
regardful
remindful
reproduce
retardant
retrodden
rewarding
rotundity
ruggedise
Sanhedrim
Sanhedrin
scenedock
scoredraw
scoundrel
secondary
sensedata
shakedown
sheldduck
shieldbug
shieldfem
shouldest
shredding
skedaddle
snaredrum
Southdown
splendent
splendour
squidding
stagedoor
stampduty
stapedial
steradian
stevedore
stockdove
stolidity
stonedead
stonedeaf
strouding
stupidity
subsidise
swansdown
sympodial
sympodium
Talmudist
tetradite
theandric
titledeed
torpidity
torridity
touchdown
tragedian
trepidant
tribadism
trihedral
trustdeed
turbidity
turgidity
unbending
unbridled
underdone
unfledged
unheeding
unmindful
unstudied
untrodden
ventiduct
verandaed
viscidity
wallydrag
washedout
wristdrop
wrongdoer
zamindary
zemindary
accidence
acescence
acquiesce
acropetal
acroteria
adherence
adjacency
adulterer
advisedly
aerometer
aerometry
aesthesia
aesthesis
aesthetic
affluence
aggrieved
allegedly
allowedly
altimeter
amourette
analgesia
analgesic
anamnesis
androecia
anopheles
anoxaemia
antigenic
antiserum
antivenin
apathetic
aphereses
apheresis
apothecia
appetence
appetency
aquarelle
aquilegia
arboreous
arboretum
argumenta
Arguseyed
armigeral
ashamedly
assuredly
asymmetry
asyndetic
asyndeton
atmometer
aubrietia
autotelic
backpedal
bagatelle
baksheesh
baneberry
banqueter
banquette
barkeeper
barometer
barometry
baronetcy
basipetal
battleaxe
battlecry
bayoneted
beadledom
beanfeast
bearberry
beauteous
beekeeper
belatedly
bemusedly
bicameral
bigeneric
bilateral
biliteral
bivalence
bivalency
blaeberry
bleareyed
blessedly
blinkered
bluebeard
blueberry
blunderer
blusterer
bobsleigh
bolometer
bolometry
Bolshevik
bottlefed
bottleful
bounteous
bouquetin
bourgeois
bracteate
bracteole
brasserie
breakeven
breezeway
bridleway
briquette
brochette
broiderer
brotherly
bumblebee
bumbledon
butcherer
butcherly
cacodemon
cadaveric
cafeteria
cailleach
campfever
Candlemas
candlenut
catalepsy
catalexes
catalexis
cattleman
centreing
cerebella
cetaceous
chafferer
challenge
champerty
chanceful
changeful
chanteuse
chapleted
charmeuse
chartered
charterer
chassepot
chastener
chatterer
checkered
chequered
chimaeric
chlorella
cigarette
cinereous
citizenly
citizenry
clatterer
cleareyed
cochleate
cockneyfy
coffeecup
coffeepot
coherence
coherency
coiffeuse
colonelcy
columella
complexly
complexus
concierge
conqueror
copacetic
coroneted
cotyledon
couchette
courgette
courteous
courtesan
covalence
covalency
crabbedly
cranberry
cranreuch
crescendo
cricketer
crookedly
croquette
crossette
crosseyed
crowberry
cryogenic
culsdesac
cutaneous
daredevil
decadence
decadency
decametre
decidedly
decimetre
deerberry
deference
delineate
deliverer
devotedly
diablerie
diaereses
diaeresis
diathermy
diathesis
diathetic
diligence
dinoceras
discredit
displease
doodlebug
dorbeetle
dosimeter
dosimetry
doubleton
drunkenly
dziggetai
ectogenic
edelweiss
effluence
eloquence
emergence
emergency
empyreuma
endogenic
energetic
entelechy
enucleate
epaenetic
epaulette
ephemeral
ephemerid
ephemeris
ephemeron
epiclesis
epistemic
epithelia
epithesis
epithetic
equisetum
ergometer
erroneous
esurience
esuriency
ethylenic
etiquette
evangelic
exciseman
excitedly
existence
eyeopener
fabaceous
farseeing
feathered
feculence
femineity
fifteenth
filaceous

filoselle
fivepence
fivepenny
flambeaus
flambeaux
flannelly
flatterer
fluoresce
folkweave
foragecap
forereach
fourpence
fourpenny
freezedry
frequence
frequency
freshener
fritterer
fruiterer
furtherer
gasometer
gaucherie
gearlever
genteelly
gentleman
georgette
gigahertz
glaireous
glandered
gogglebox
goldfever
graphemic
greasegun
greeneyed
greybeard
guardedly
guillemot
hackberry
hackneyed
halfpence
halfpenny
hamamelis
handlebar
harquebus
haustella
heathenry
hexameter
Hexateuch
highlevel
hodometer
homiletic
howsoever
humblebee
hundredth
hurriedly
hydraemia
hypogeous
illiberal
illomened
immanence
immanency
imminence
imminency
immodesty
impliedly
impotence
impotency
impudence
incidence
indecency
indigence
indolence
inference
influence
influenza
inherence
innkeeper
innocence
innocency
insolence
intumesce
ischaemia
ischaemic
isohyetal
isosceles
jacquerie
journeyer
Juneberry
kentledge
kilohertz
kilometre
kitchener
knifeedge
knowledge
lapideous
larghetto
launderer
lazaretto
learnedly
lendlease
leucaemia
leukaemia
leukaemic
limitedly
lioncelle
lionheart
logaoedic
longaeval
lorgnette
lovefeast
luciferin
lysimeter
machmeter
madeleine
Mahometan
majorette
makeready
malleehen
manifesto
manometer
marquetry
Masoretic
maunderer
maybeetle
mediaeval
megadeath
megahertz
mekometer
menagerie
Menshevik
messieurs
metameric
micaceous
middleman
midinette
milkfever
milometer
minutegun
minuteman
miscreant
miscreate
misoneism
misoneist
mistletoe
mistyeyed
moistener
mongrelly
monoceros
monomeric
moraceous
morphemic
muniments
muscleman
muskmelon
mutagenic
naseberry
neckverse
needleful
nescience
Nilometer
ninepence
ninepenny
northeast
northerly
novelette
nutweevil
obedience
obsolesce
octahedra
octameter
oecumenic
oleaceous
oleoresin
oligaemia
oncogenic
onlicence
ontogenic
oogenesis
oogenetic
openheart
opponency
optometer
optometry
orangeade
Orangeism
Orangeman
orangetip
organelle
orthoepic
osmometer
oubliette
ovenready
overheard
overleapt
overreach
overreact
oversexed
overweary
overweigh
paillette
painterly
panatella
pantheism
pantheist
papeterie
paralexia
paramedic
parameter
parapeted
parfleche
parquetry
Parseeism
pedometer
penitence
percheron
perihelia
perimeter
phrenetic
pierrette
pikeperch
pirouette
plangency
plastered
plasterer
plenteous
plumbeous
plunderer
pointedly
pokeberry
policeman
politesse
polygenic
polyhedra
polymeric
polysemic
pomaceous
poriferal
poriferan
portreeve
poulterer
pouncebox
poussette
praiseful
primaeval
princedom
princekin
princelet
procreant
procreate
prophetic
proscenia
prothesis
prothetic
prurience
pruriency
psalteria
puerperal
pumiceous
purulence
purulency
pyrogenic
pyrometer
pyrometry
quarterly
quartette
quercetum
quickener
quintette
rafflesia
rakehelly
raspberry
razoredge
recalesce
recoverer
redbreast
redevelop
redolence
reference
referenda
refluence
remanence
renitency
reposeful
reprieval
reputedly
rerelease
residence
residency
reticence
reticency
retrieval
retriever
reverence
righteous
ringfence
roadmetal
roisterer
rosaceous
rounceval
roundelay
rubicelle
ruddleman
saddlebag
saddlebow
salicetum
saltpetre
Samoyedic
sapraemia
sapraemic
Saracenic
satinette
saunterer
savagedom
scatterer
schlieren
scrivener
sebaceous
secateurs
seedpearl
seigneury
semimetal
sentience
sentiency
sericeous
serinette
serviette
setaceous
shadberry
sharpener
sharpeyed
shillelah
shipfever
shortener
sickleave
siliceous
simpleton
singleton
sixteenmo
sixteenth
slanderer
sleevenut
slenderly
sluiceway
slumberer
smackeroo
smatterer
sniggerer
snowberry
soapberry
softpedal
soldierly
sonometer
soubrette
southeast
southerly
sovereign
spaghetti
speakeasy
spinneret
splenetic
spongebag
spongeous
sputterer
squiredom
squirelet
stableboy
stableman
staggerer
stalkeyed
stammerer
statuette
stiffener
stiltedly
strategic
stridence
stridency
studiedly
stutterer
subagency
subduedly
subereous
succeeder
sutteeism
swaggerer
sweetener
swimmeret
swingeing
syncretic
syneresis
synizesis
syntheses
synthesis
synthetic
taioseach
taxidermy
taximeter
telegenic
telemeter
telemetry
theoretic
thickener
thicketed
thitherto
thunderer
tiedyeing
tightener
tinopener
tittlebat
tonguelet
tonguetie
tonometer
tournedos
tourneyer
tracheary
tracheate
transenna
trinketer
trinketry
triquetra
tritheism
tritheist
triweekly
trousered
truepenny
trumpedup
trumpeter
tufaceous
tumblebug
twitterer
typemetal
umpteenth
unaltered
uncovered
undeceive
unreserve
untimeous
usherette
vademecum
varicella
vehemence
venereous
viceregal
vicereine
vimineous
vinaceous
virulence
virulency
voltmeter
volumeter
wagonette
warblefly
wattmeter
weathered
weatherly
wellbeing
whichever
whimperer
whipperin
whiskered
whisperer
whosoever
wineberry
witchetty
workbench
worriedly
Yankeedom
Yankeeism
zapateado
zeitgeist
zucchetto
zymogenic
aboutface
acetifier
acidifier
aciniform
amplifier
angelfish
beccafico
beechfern
bellyflop
birdsfoot
blackface
Blackfeet
blackfish
blackflag
Blackfoot
blindfold
boardfoot
boxoffice
breakfast
brushfire
calcifuge
carfuffle
carrefour
ceasefire
certified
certifier
chauffeur
chockfull
clarifier
claviform
cocksfoot
coltsfoot
Cominform
cordiform
crampfish
crossfade
crossfire
crossfish
crowsfoot
cruciform
cuneiform
curviform
cymbiform
dentiform
devilfish
dignified
disaffect
disaffirm
disinfect
disinfest
eightfold
eruciform
falciform
falsifier
fancyfree
febrifuge
fibriform
fieldfare
firstfoot
forcefeed
fortifier
fortyfive
fungiform
globefish
goosefoot
haresfoot
heartfelt
heartfree
hereafter
houseflag
hydrofoil
imperfect
interface
interfere
interfile
interflow
interfuse
jellyfish
justifier
kerfuffle
killifish
lentiform

lightfoot
ligniform
linenfold
liquefier
magnifico
magnifier
mammiform
microfilm
midwifery
misinform
multifoil
multiform
mummified
mystifier
nightfall
nullifier
orderform
pilotfish
pisciform
pitchfork
pokerface
pussyfoot
qualified
qualifier
rapidfire
razorfish
reconfirm
rectifier
reshuffle
restiform
resurface
retroflex
Roquefort
sacciform
sacrifice
sassafras
scaldfish
scalefern
scalefish
scarifier
scorifier
scruffily
scutiform
serrefile
sevenfold
sgraffiti
sgraffito
shamefast
sheatfish
sheepfold
shellfire
shellfish
shortfall
significs
slushfund
snailfish
snipefish
soothfast
soundfilm
spadefoot
spearfish
specifier
splayfoot
spoonfeed
stairfoot
stallfeed
steadfast
stockfish
stonefish
stupefier
styliform
superfine
superfuse
swellfish
swordfish
Tartufian
Tartufism
testifier
therefore
therefrom
threefold
townsfolk
transform
transfuse
troutfarm
trunkfish
underfelt
underfoot
unruffled
unselfish
ventifact
vermiform
vermifuge
versifier
versiform
villiform
vitriform
volteface
watchfire
waterfall
waterflea
waterfowl
wherefore
wherefrom
whiteface
whitefish
womenfolk
Wyclifite
aborigine
afterglow
aggregate
alpargata
ambergris
amphigory
analogise
analogist
analogous
androgyne
androgyny
anemogram
apologise
apologist
assurgent
aubergine
averagely
bedraggle
befogging
beleaguer
bilingual
billygoat
biologist
blackgame
bowlegged
buttygang
cablegram
cairngorm
carrageen
cartogram
castigate
centigram
chaingang
chaingear
cheongsam
coccygeal
collagist
collegial
collegian
collegium
colligate
condignly
configure
conjugate
consignee
consignor
contagion
contagium
corrugate
cosmogeny
cosmogony
cotangent
CroMagnon
debagging
debugging
decongest
detergent
dialogise
dialogism
dialogist
dichogamy
diningcar
disengage
disfigure
disregard
divergent
doglegged
earwigged
ecologist
effulgent
embroglio
epilogist
expurgate
Falangism
Falangist
fastigium
floodgate
foreigner
fustigate
galingale
geologise
geologist
glassgall
goosegirl
greengage
habergeon
haranguer
hectogram
heliogram
heptaglot
hierogram
histogeny
histogram
humbugged
hypergamy
imbroglio
indulgent
inelegant
instigate
insurgent
intrigant
intriguer
inveigler
isagogics
landagent
laryngeal
liturgics
liturgist
lovingcup
massagist
meningeal
metheglin
microgram
milligram
miscegene
miscegine
mistigris
monergism
monsignor
mossagate
moviegoer
myologist
mystagogy
nannygoat
negligent
neologian
neologise
neologism
neologist
neuroglia
newsagent
nightgown
Norwegian
nystagmic
nystagmus
obbligato
objurgate
onelegged
orologist
Orpington
osteogeny
Ostrogoth
otologist
outrigger
packaging
papergirl
pathogeny
Pekingese
Pelasgian
pellagrin
pentagram
philogyny
phonogram
photogene
phylogeny
phytogeny
pictogram
predigest
preengage
prefigure
pressgang
prologise
propagate
prorogate
pterygium
pterygoid
radiogram
redingote
refulgent
resurgent
salangane
salesgirl
scapegoat
scraggily
segregate
shrugging
slategrey
sociogram
solfeggio
spirogyra
sporogeny
sprigging
springald
springbok
springily
springing
springlet
straggler
strangely
strangler
strangles
stringent
strongarm
strongbox
strongish
strongyle
struggler
subjugate
subregion
subrogate
surrogate
syllogise
syllogism
synergism
synergist
syringeal
tarragona
termagant
tetragram
theurgist
throughly
trisagion
undergird
undergone
undergrad
unfeigned
unpegging
unplugged
uropygium
Varangian
variegate
verdigris
vestigial
vestigium
villagery
watergate
woebegone
zigzagged
zoologist
adulthood
aerophyte
allophone
alpenhorn
amidships
amorphism
amorphous
anarchism
anarchist
anorthite
antiphony
apartheid
apprehend
arrowhead
artichoke
barathrum
beachhead
benighted
biosphere
blackhead
blaspheme
blasphemy
blasthole
bleachery
blockhead
blotchily
bombshell
bonechina
bookshelf
branchiae
branchial
branchlet
breathily
breathing
breeching
bronchial
bryophyte
buckshish
buckthorn
buckwheat
bushwhack
cacophony
caliphate
camelhair
campchair
cardsharp
cartwheel
catarhine
catechise
catechism
catechist
childhood
churching
churchman
clamshell
cliffhang
cockahoop
coldshort
colophony
coryphaei
crosshead
crotchety
cubbyhole
cymophane
dachshund
dancehall
dayschool
decathlon
diarrhoea
dinothere
diphthong
donothing
downthrow
drawsheet
dustsheet
ecosphere
ectophyte
elsewhere
empathise
encephala
endophagy
endophyte
enlighten
entophyte
erstwhile
eunuchism
eunuchoid
exanthema
exarchate
exosphere
fairyhood
falsehood
fetichism
fetichist
fetishism
fetishist
firsthand
flowchart
flowsheet
foodchain
foreshore
foreshown
fourwheel
franchise
freewheel
freighter
frenchify
Frenchman
gearshift
gearwheel
geosphere
gloryhole
gonophore
gooseherd
greenhorn
grouchily
guildhall
gynophore
hairshirt
halfshell
halophile
halophyte
halothane
handshake
handwheel
hardihood
hardshell
hartshorn
hawsehole
headphone
healthful
healthily
hearthrug
hexachord
highchair
hitchhike
hollyhock
holophote
homophone
homophony
horsehair
horsehide
household
hydathode
hypethral
krummhorn
lampshade
lampshell
launching
leasehold
lengthily
lilywhite
lintwhite
loanshark
longchain
longshore
lovechild
lustihood
mainsheet
makeshift
malachite
malathion
Manichean
masochism
masochist
meanwhile
megaphone
melaphyre
mesophyll
mesophyte
metaphase
milkshake
millwheel
misbehave
monachism
monkshood
monochord
monophagy
monorhyme
moonshine
mousehole
musichall
mycophagy
naphthene
nemophila
nighthawk
notochord
octachord
oenophile
oenophily
oesophagi
optophone
overcheck
overshoot
overthrew
overthrow
overwhelm
pantyhose
parachute
parathion
parochial
periphery
perishing
petechiae
petechial
phosphate
phosphene
phosphide
phosphine
phosphite
plaything
ploughboy
ploughman
polyphagy
polyphase
polyphone

polyphony
polythene
poppyhead
preachify
preachily
preschool
pronghorn
punishing
puppyhood
pushchair
pyrethrum
queenhood
raincheck
raunchily
ravishing
refashion
repechage
reprehend
rhonchial
righthand
ringshake
riverhead
roughhewn
roundhead
sainthood
saxophone
scarehead
scirrhous
scorching
Scotchman
scrapheap
scrumhalf
scuncheon
scutcheon
searching
selachian
semaphore
sheathing
sheephook
sheerhulk
sheikhdom
shellheap
shipshape
shockhead
shoeshine
shorthand
shorthorn
sidewheel
sinophile
Sisyphean
sketchily
sketchmap
skewwhiff
slaughter
smoothish
snowwhite
softshell
something
somewhere
somewhile
soundhole
spearhead
speechful
speechify
splashily
spotcheck
spouthole
sprightly
spurwheel
squashily
stagehand
stairhead
stanchion
starchily
starshell
statehood
steelhead
stepchild
stillhunt
stinkhorn
stitchery
stokehold
stokehole
straphang
strychnic
superheat
swineherd
switchman
sycophant
telephone
telephony
telephoto
telophase
thatching
theophany
thickhead
thirdhand
thoughted
thrashing
threshold
thumbhole
timesheet
touchhole
toxophily
treachery
trenchant
truncheon
twitchily
uintahite
ultrahigh
underhand
underhung
unsighted
unsightly
uprightly
vibraharp
waterhole
wealthily
whalehead
Whitehall
whitehead
widowhood
windchest
wingchair
wirephoto
witchhunt
womanhood
woodchuck
wormwheel
xenophile
xenophobe
xerophile
xerophily
xerophyte
xylophone
Yorkshire
abdominal
ablatival
ablutions
abstainer
accipiter
acclaimer
adducible
adenoidal
adminicle
admonitor
adnominal
aerobiont
aerolitic
affiliate
agnatical
algorithm
allegiant
alleviate
almsgiver
ambitious
amyloidal
andesitic
angelical
angleiron
annelidan
antefixal
antiviral
apparitor
appetiser
appraisal
appraiser
araneidal
araneidan
archfiend
armadillo
Armorican
arriviste
arsenical
arsenious
artemisia
arteriole
arteritis
arthritic
arthritis
artificer
ascetical
associate
atrocious
audacious
autopilot
auxiliary
avertible
backbiter
backsight
bandwidth
bargainer
basilican
beastings
beautiful
beestings
behaviour
beneficed
bicipital
bifarious
bifoliate
bilabiate
binominal
bivariant
bivariate
bobtailed
boliviano
bombsight
botanical
bountiful
boyfriend
brachiate
Brahminee
Brahminic
brassiere
brecciate
brilliant
bullfight
bullfinch
bumptious
butadiene
cacuminal
calorific
calycinal
camarilla
canonical
capacious
capacitor
caparison
captaincy
cartridge
certainly
certainty
chaffinch
chantilly
chastiser
chitlings
chloritic
chronical
chronicle
cigarillo
circuitry
civiliser
classical
coalfield
Cockaigne
cockfight
coercible
coercibly
colchicum
colloidal
coloniser
colorific
compliant
comprisal
conceited
conscious
container
contrived
contriver
copyright
corbeille
cornfield
covariant
crinoidal
cryptical
cutinised
cycloidal
dahabiyah
deadlight
decalitre
decilitre
declaimer
deducible
deficient
defoliant
defoliate
deistical
delicious
delirious
dendritic
depositor
describer
despoiler
diacritic
diactinic
dimidiate
dioecious
dipswitch
dirigible
dirigisme
discoidal
disorient
disseisin
divisible
doctrinal
doleritic
dolomitic
dominical
Dominican
dopefiend
downfield
downright
downriver
dropsical
druidical
dynamical
dynamiter
ebullient
ecdysiast
echovirus
efficient
egregious
eightieth
eirenicon
elutriate
embroider
emolliate
emollient
empirical
encomiast
endomixis
energiser
enteritis
enunciate
equaliser
eristical
erratical
estaminet
etherical
ethmoidal
eulogiser
evincible
excipient
excoriate
exercises
exfoliate
exhibitor
exorciser
expatiate
expedient
expediter
explainer
exploiter
expositor
eyebright
facetious
fanatical
fatidical
felicific
felonious
ferocious
fiduciary
fimbriate
firelight
fleshings
flyweight
footlight
foresight
forfeiter
fortnight
fractious
frangible
franticly
freeliver
freerider
fugacious
galenical
gallmidge
gastritis
gauleiter
genetical
genitival
genocidal
glossitis
goldfield
goldfinch
goldsinny
golflinks
goodnight
goodwives
gorblimey
grandiose
graphical
graphitic
grisaille
guerrilla
hairpiece
halflight
halftitle
haverings
headfirst
headlight
headliner
headpiece
heelpiece
hemstitch
hepatitis
heretical
highlight
hilarious
hillbilly
hindsight
hobnailed
homicidal
honorific
humiliate
hypericum
hypnoidal
idealiser
identical
identikit
idiotical
ignitible
illegible
illegibly
illicitly
illogical
imbecilic
immediacy
immediate
impatiens
impatient
imperious
impolitic
inaudible
inaudibly
incipient
incurious
indelible
indelibly
inducible
inebriant
inebriate
inebriety
infuriate
infusible
ingenious
ingrained
inheritor
inhibitor
injurious
innoxious
inpatient
insatiate
insatiety
inscriber
insidious
insipidly
invalidly
invariant
invidious
invisible
invisibly
irascible
irascibly
ironsides
irradiant
irradiate
Islamitic
isoclinal
isoclinic
itsybitsy
ittybitty
Jacobinic
jaundiced
judiciary
judicious
juridical
juvenilia
karabiner
keratitis
kilolitre
kingsized
laborious
labyrinth
laciniate
lamplight
languidly
lastditch
lavaliere
Levitical
libidinal
lifesized
limelight
limonitic
litigious
lixiviate
logarithm
longlived
lovelight
lumbrical
lumbricus
lunitidal
luxuriant
luxuriate
luxurious
lyophilic
maharishi
mainliner
malarious
malicious
malvoisie
manysided
matutinal
medicinal
melodious
memoriter
menadione
meropidan
minacious
minefield
misguided
mitraille
monodical
moonlight
moraliser
mosquitos
municipal
munitions
nebuliser
nefarious
negotiant
negotiate
negroidal
neoteinia
neoteinic
nephritic
nephritis
netveined
nicotiana
nicotinic
ninetieth
nobiliary
nondriver
nosepiece
notabilia
notoriety
notorious
noviciate
novitiate
numerical
obconical
oblivious
obnoxious
occipital
officiant
officiate
officinal
officious
oilpaints
omissible
ommatidia

organiser
outgoings
outskirts
overnight
overpitch
oversight
oversized
palafitte
paludinal
paradisal
parasitic
parotitis
partridge
pearlitic
pecuniary
peepsight
pemphigus
penfriend
penurious
perceiver
phlebitis
pintailed
pintsized
piratical
pisolitic
plausible
plausibly
pleadings
plentiful
pleuritic
poinciana
pointille
polariser
polemical
political
polyvinyl
potboiler
practical
practised
preexilic
prescient
principal
principia
principle
proclitic
propriety
prosaical
proteinic
psychical
ptarmigan
punctilio
purloiner
pyramidal
pyramidic
pyramidon
quadrifid
quadrigae
quadrille
quantical
quizzical
quodlibet
rapacious
rearlight
recipient
recruital
recruiter
rectrices
redivivus
reducible
regicidal
religiose
religious
remediate
reminisce
repudiate
resilient
retaliate
retinitis
rhizoidal
rushlight
sabadilla
sagacious
salacious
Samaritan
sandpiper
sapodilla
satanical
satirical
scagliola
sceptical
scholiast
scintilla
scleritis
scorpioid
scrapiron
seditious
seigniory
selenious
selenitic
semifinal
semirigid
Shechinah
showpiece
sidelight
sideritic
sigmoidal
silicious
simplices
sinusitis
skeesicks
skindiver
skintight
skirtings
slabsided
snowfield
solacious
solicitor
sometimes
soporific
soritical
soundings
spellican
spherical
spillikin
splenitis
spotlight
squalidly
starlight
steatitic
steroidal
stockinet
stoplight
strobilae
strobilus
strumitis
subeditor
sudorific
suppliant
surfeiter
surpliced
surprisal
sustainer
sybaritic
synclinal
synodical
synovitis
taillight
tailpiece
technical
technique
tectrices
televisor
tenacious
terebinth
theoriser
thereinto
thermidor
thirtieth
timelimit
timepiece
tortrices
tortricid
totaliser
tramlines
transient
trappings
trichinae
triclinia
triclinic
trimmings
trochilus
twentieth
twosuiter
typhlitis
typhoidal
umbilical
umbilicus
unadvised
unbraided
uncivilly
undecided
undecimal
undefined
undivided
undutiful
unethical
unlimited
unmusical
unthrifty
upbraider
vagarious
vaporific
vaporiser
vaticinal
ventricle
veracious
veridical
vexatious
vicariate
vicarious
vicesimal
videlicet
vigesimal
viricidal
vivacious
vocaliser
voracious
wassailer
weeknight
welltimed
whereinto
whimsical
whirligig
womaniser
workpiece
Xanthippe
xparticle
applejack
blackjack
cheapjack
interject
introject
kurrajong
lancejack
retroject
smokejack
swarajist
Algonkian
astrakhan
autarkist
bilgekeel
finicking
gavelkind
havocking
housekeep
humankind
interknit
knockknee
magicking
mimicking
miniskirt
numbskull
overskirt
palankeen
panicking
parrakeet
phenakite
placekick
predikant
provoking
Seljukian
shrinkage
Slovakian
sprinkler
squeakily
steenkirk
streakily
streaking
swordknot
thickknee
unluckily
unwinking
womankind
womenkind
abseiling
acetylate
acetylcoA
acetylene
Acheulean
Acheulian
aciculate
acidulate
acidulent
acidulous
actualise
actuality
aerialist
aeriality
aeroplane
aetiology
afterlife
agriology
alloplasm
alveolate
amaryllis
amoralism
amorality
anabolism
anchylose
ancillary
angiology
animalise
animalism
animalist
animality
annulling
anomalous
anomalure
anovulant
anschluss
anthelion
anthology
anticline
apetalous
aphyllous
apiculate
appalling
appealing
appellant
appellate
aquaplane
argillite
armillary
artillery
asepalous
asphaltic
asphaltum
assailant
assaulter
astrolabe
astrology
atonalism
atonality
audiology
autoclave
bacillary
backcloth
backslang
backslide
balaclava
bandoleer
bandolero
bandolier
bandoline
banjulele
barrelful
barrelled
basrelief
batholite
batholith
battalion
beardless
bedfellow
bellglass
bengaline
benzoline
berkelium
beryllium
bevelling
bicyclist
bismillah
blacklead
blacklist
blameless
bloodless
bloodlust
blueblack
blushless
bombilate
bondslave
bookplate
boomslang
bootblack
boundless
brainless
brakeless
brambling
brandling
brazilnut
breadline
briefless
bristling
brittlely
broadleaf
broadloom
bromeliad
brutalise
brutalism
brutality
buffaloes
bushelful
caballero
caballine
caballing
cabbalism
cabbalist
cablelaid
cacholong
caecilian
caerulean
calculate
calculous
caliology
cancelled
cannelure
cannulate
cantaloup
cantilena
capillary
capsulate
capsulise
Carmelite
carnality
carnelian
carolling
carpology
cartilage
cartology
cartulary
Castalian
castellan
Castilian
cataclasm
cataclysm
cataplasm
cataplexy
cattaloes
causality
causeless
cavilling
ceaseless
celluloid
cellulose
cephalous
cerecloth
chainless
chairlady
chameleon
champleve
chandlery
charmless
Charolais
chatelain
checklist
cheerless
chevalier
chevelure
chickling
chilblain
childless
childlike
chipolata
chiselled
chiseller
chivalric
chocolate
chorology
Cingalese
cipollino
circulate
classless
classlist
clitellum
cloudland
cloudless
coagulant
coagulate
coastline
coecilian
compelled
conciliar
condyloid
condyloma
consulage
consulate
consulter
consultor
convolute
convolved
coprolite
coprology
coralline
corallite
coralloid
corbelled
cordelier
cornelian
cornflour
corollary
corpulent
corralled
correlate
cosmology
cotillion
countless
crackling
crapulent
crapulous
crashland
credulity
credulous
crenelled
crenulate
crestless
crinoline
crippling
crosslink
crownless
cruellest
cuckoldry
cucullate
cudgelled
cupelling
curialism
curtilage
cymbalist
cystolith
cytoplasm
Daedalean
Daedalian
Damoclean
dandelion
dauntless
deadalive
deathless
deathlike
decillion
decollate
decollete
defaulter
dentalium
depthless
devilling
diabolise
diabolism
diabolist
dieselise
disbelief
discalced
discolour
dishcloth
dishclout
disoblige
dispelled
disrelish
dissolute
distilled
distiller
dittology
dixieland
dogcollar
doorplate
doubtless
dowelling
dowerless
drawplate
dreamland
dreamless
dreamlike
drivelled
driveller
drysalter
ductility

earthling
ectoblast
ectoplasm
edibility
ejaculate
embellish
enamelled
enameller
enchilada
endoblast
endoplasm
engarland
enrolling
entoblast
epipolism
equalling
errorless
esemplasy
establish
ethnology
etymology
euchology
eventless
everglade
excellent
excelling
exemplary
exemplify
expellent
expelling
extolling
facecloth
fairyland
fairylike
faithless
fallalery
faultless
faveolate
fenceless
fertilely
fertilise
fertility
festology
feudalise
feudalism
feudalist
feudality
fibreless
fibrillar
fibroline
fiendlike
firealarm
fireblast
fireplace
firstling
fishplate
fishslice
fissility
fistulous
flabellum
flagellum
flameless
flatulent
flayflint
fleckless
fledgling
fleshless
flintlock
footcloth
footplate
forceland
forceless
foreclose
formalise
formalism
formalist
formality
formulaic
formulary
formulate
formulise
fortalice
fossilise
foundling
fourflush
fragility
Franglais
frivolity
frivolled
frivolous
frontless
frontline
frugality
fruitless
fulfilled
fulfiller
fullblown
funnelled
fusillade
gambolled
gangplank
garrulity
garrulous
gasholder
gemmology
gemutlich
genealogy
genialise
geniality
gentility
genuflect
gerfalcon
germplasm
gestalten
ghostlike
giantlike
ginpalace
glabellae
glabellar
gondolier
gospeller
graceless
gracility
granulate
granulite
granulose
grappling
grassland
gratulate
graveless
gravelled
Greekless
griefless
grimalkin
grovelled
groveller
gruelling
grumbling
guideline
guileless
guiltless
gyrfalcon
gyroplane
hagiology
haircloth
hairslide
halfblood
handglass
hanselled
haplology
harmaline
hatchling
headcloth
heartland
heartless
Heraclean
herbalist
Herculean
hexaploid
hierology
highclass
highflier
highflown
highflyer
histology
homoplasy
horseless
hosteller
hostilely
hostility
hourglass
houseleek
houseless
houselled
hydrology
hydrolyse
hydrolyte
hymnology
hypallage
hypnology
hypoblast
ichnology
iconology
idealless
idioplasm
imageless
impelling
inability
indweller
infielder
infilling
innholder
inoculate
inquiline
inshallah
instilled
intellect
interlace
interlard
interleaf
interline
interlink
interlock
interlope
interlude
inutility
inviolacy
inviolate
irreality
isinglass
Israelite
issueless
jackplane
jambalaya
jaywalker
jewellery
joviality
juiceless
kennelled
labelling
labialise
labialism
laccolith
laevulose
lamellate
lamellose
lampblack
landslide
laurelled
leaselend
legerline
legislate
lethality
levelling
liability
libellant
libelling
libellist
libellous
liegelord
lifeblood
lightless
lignaloes
limitless
limnology
lineality
lineolate
lingulate
lintelled
lithology
loincloth
lookalike
looseleaf
lotusland
loverless
magdalene
magnalium
mailplane
mamillary
mamillate
mammalian
mammalogy
mandoline
manyplies
marcelled
marmalade
marshland
marvelled
masculine
matchless
matchlock
mausoleum
maxillary
medallion
medallist
medullary
medullate
Mendelian
Mendelism
mentalism
mentalist
mentality
merciless
mescaline
mesoblast
mesogloea
metalline
metalling
metallise
metalloid
metaplasm
methylate
methylene
metrology
micaslate
microlite
microlith
micrology
milkfloat
mirthless
misbelief
modelling
modillion
Mongolian
mongolism
Mongoloid
monocline
monoplane
monthling
moonblind
mortality
multilane
Mussulman
musteline
mutualise
mutualism
mutualist
mutuality
mythology
nameplate
natheless
natrolite
neckcloth
necrology
nephalism
nephalist
nepheline
nephelite
nephology
nerveless
neuralgia
neuralgic
neurology
newsflash
niccolite
nickelise
nickelled
nickelous
nightlife
nightline
nightlong
noctiluca
noiseless
nonillion
normalise
normality
northland
nosebleed
noseflute
nostalgia
nostalgic
nostology
nummulite
nurseling
octillion
oddfellow
odourless
offcolour
oilcolour
ophiology
opodeldoc
orderless
oscillate
osteology
ourselves
overblown
overcloud
overflown
overglaze
oversleep
overslept
palillogy
panelling
panellist
panoplied
pantalets
pantaloon
papillary
papillate
papilloma
papillose
papillote
Paraclete
parcelled
parhelion
patellate
pathology
patrolled
patroller
patrolman
patrology
pedalling
pencilled
penciller
pendulate
penduline
pendulous
peneplain
peneplane
penholder
penniless
percaline
percolate
periclase
perilling
periplast
pestilent
pestology
petiolate
petiolule
petroleum
petrology
phenology
philology
phonolite
phonology
phthalein
phycology
phytology
pinnulate
pistoleer
pistolled
placeless
plantlike
planuloid
plumbline
plumulate
plumulose
pluralise
pluralism
pluralist
plurality
podzolise
pointlace
pointless
polyploid
pommelled
porcelain
portolano
portulaca
postilion
postulant
postulate
potholing
powerless
pozzolana
preselect
prevalent
priceless
prideless
primality
privilege
profilist
propelled
propeller
propylaea
propylene
proselyte
puerility
pullulate
pulseless
pulvillus
pummelled
punchline
pupillage
pupillary
pureblood
purselike
pustulate
pustulous
puzzolana
queenless
queenlike
querulous
quibbling
quicklime
quinoline
quitclaim
racialism
racialist
radialply
radiology
raincloud
rascaldom
rascalism
rascality
rauwolfia
ravelling
rebelling
rebellion
recollect
refuelled
repellant
repellent
repelling
reptilian
republish
revelling
rhinology
rhodolite
riderless
ritualise
ritualism
ritualist
rivalling
rivelling
roadblock
rockplant
roodcloth
roofplate
rostellum
rubellite
Sabellian
sacculate
sackcloth
sacrilege
sailcloth
sailplane
saintlike
saintling
saleslady
saltglaze
sandalled
sandblast
sandblind
sandglass
santolina
satellite
sauceless
scaleleaf
scaleless
scalelike
scalplock
scantling
scapolite
scapulary
scatology
scentless
scheelite
schilling
schmaltzy
schoolbag
schoolboy
schooling
schoolman
scrollsaw
scutellar
scutellum
sectility
seedplant
selfglory
semifluid
semiology

semiplume
senseless
sepiolite
serialise
serialism
serialist
seriality
serrulate
servilely
servility
sexualise
sexuality
shadeless
shambling
shameless
shapeless
shaveling
shearling
sheeplice
sheerlegs
shelflife
shiftless
shirtless
shoeblack
shopfloor
shoreless
shoreline
shovelful
shovelhat
shovelled
shoveller
showplace
sibylline
sightless
sigillary
sigillate
signalbox
signalise
signalled
signaller
signalman
silkgland
sinewless
singalong
Sinhalese
skinflick
skinflint
skirtless
slakeless
sleepless
smileless
smokeless
smuggling
snakelike
snivelled
sniveller
snowblind
snowblink
snowflake
snowplant
socialise
socialism
socialist
socialite
sociality
sociology
soleplate
sommelier
somnolent
sortilege
soundless
soupplate
southland
spaceless
sparkless
spatulate
speckless
speculate
spiculate
spindling
spineless
spinulose
spinulous
spirality
spiralled
spirillum
sporulate
spoutless
stabilise
stability
stainless
stalkless
startling
stateless
statolith
sterilise
sterility
stimulant
stimulate
stingless
stintless
stippling
stipulate
stocklist
stoneless
stormless
storyline
strapless
stripling
suability
subsellia
subtilise
succulent
sugarloaf
sunhelmet
surculose
surmullet
swaddling
swivelled
swordlike
sylphlike
symbolics
symbolise
symbolism
symbolist
symbology
syphilise
syphiloid
systaltic
tableland
tableleaf
tachylite
tachylyte
tactility
tahsildar
taintless
tantalate
tantalise
tantalite
tasselled
tasteless
tautology
teleology
tensility
tervalent
tetralogy
thankless
thornless
thralldom
thrilling
tigerlily
tinselled
titillate
tonsillar
toothless
totalling
touchline
towelling
traceless
trackless
trainload
translate
travelled
traveller
traycloth
treillage
tremolant
tremolite
tremulant
tremulous
tribalism
tribology
trickless
tricolour
trifolium
trivalent
trochleae
trochlear
tropology
troublous
troutling
trowelled
troweller
truceless
truculent
trustless
truthless
tunnelled
tunnelnet
turbulent
twayblade
twicelaid
twinkling
umbellate
umbellule
underlaid
underlain
underline
underling
unfailing
unfeeling
ungallant
unhealthy
unicolour
univalent
unreality
unskilful
unskilled
unsmiling
unsullied
unwilling
uranology
urceolate
utterless
vacillant
vacillate
vacuolate
vainglory
valueless
valveless
vandalise
vandalism
variolate
variolite
varioloid
variolous
vassalage
veniality
ventilate
verbalise
verbalism
verbalist
vermilion
vernalise
vetchling
vexillary
viability
Virgilian
virgulate
visualise
vitellary
vitelline
voiceless
volkslied
vowelless
waistline
wallplate
washcloth
wasteland
waterleaf
waterless
waterlily
waterline
wavellite
weariless
weevilled
werwolves
wheedling
wheelless
whistling
windblown
wineglass
womanlike
woodblock
worldling
worthless
woundless
wrathless
wrestling
yodelling
youngling
zibelline
Zwinglian
abasement
abashment
abatement
abnormity
academism
acclimate
acetamide
adenomata
adornment
affirmant
aftermath
aftermost
agapemone
agistment
agreement
alchemise
alchemist
alignment
alinement
allotment
amassment
amazement
amendment
amusement
anatomise
anatomist
angiomata
annulment
anonymity
anonymous
anthemion
apartment
apogamous
atacamite
atonement
awesomely
baltimore
bedlamite
beechmast
bergamask
besetment
bionomics
birthmark
blackmail
blastment
bonhomous
carbamate
carbamide
cassimere
catchment
chainmail
chamomile
checkmate
cherimoya
classmate
coelomata
coelomate
collimate
condiment
contemner
contumacy
contumely
copesmate
cornemuse
costumier
coxcombry
customary
customise
cyanamide
cyclamate
dairymaid
deathmask
debarment
decrement
deferment
deformity
determent
determine
detriment
devilment
diatomite
diplomacy
diplomate
disarming
discomfit
discommon
dismember
dissemble
distemper
dragomans
dulcamara
economics
economise
economist
ejectment
elopement
embayment
embedment
emolument
enactment
encrimson
endowment
enjoyment
enrolment
enthymeme
entrammel
entremets
epitomise
epitomist
eponymous
equipment
Esquimaux
euphemise
euphemism
exactment
exanimate
excrement
exilement
exogamous
extolment
extremely
extremism
extremist
extremity
facsimile
feoffment
fibromata
firmament
fleshment
floodmark
forasmuch
forcemeat
fulsomely
fundament
glutamate
goddamned
goldsmith
gossamery
Gothamite
gravamina
gristmill
guacamole
hackamore
hardiment
Hashemite
Hashimite
hatchment
histamine
honeymoon
horsemint
housemaid
housemate
implement
impromptu
inanimate
inclement
incommode
increment
infirmary
infirmity
informant
inharmony
innermost
interment
inurement
irksomely
ironsmith
isogamete
isogamous
jessamine
judgement
lacrimose
lacrymose
ladysmock
lineament
lissomely
locksmith
lodgement
lowermost
mallemuck
matrimony
mattamore
melismata
merriment
micromesh
midsummer
mincemeat
misdemean
mollymawk
myelomata
neodymium
neuromata
nevermore
nightmare
noisomely
northmost
nursemaid
nutriment
outermost
outnumber
pantomime
parchment
parsimony
patrimony
perfumery
perfumier
persimmon
pessimism
pessimist
phenomena
pheromone
Philomela
phonemics
piecemeal
placement
platemark
polyamide
pressmark
prolamine
protamine
proximate
proximity
Ptolemaic
randomise
ravelment
readymade
reanimate
recommend
reexamine
refitment
reformism
reformist
remitment
repayment
reprimand
revetment
rhodamine
rhythmics
rhythmise
rhythmist
rousement
sacrament
sarcomata
scalemoss
schlemiel
schlemihl
scotomata
scramming
scrimmage
scrummage
selfimage
sentiment
September
septemvir
shelfmark
shrewmice
songsmith
sophomore
southmost
spearmint
sphygmoid
spodumene
spoonmeat
squeamish
stalemate
stampmill
statement
sternmost
streamlet
strewment
strumming
subfamily
sublimate
sublimely
sublimity
supremacy
supremely
sweetmeal
sweetmeat
syngamous

talismans
Targumist
terramara
terramare
testament
testimony
thrumming
thumbmark
tigermoth
tophamper
touchmark
trademark
transmute
treadmill
treatment
tridymite
trigamist
trigamous
trinomial
Turcomans
Turkomans
unanimity
unanimous
undermine
undermost
unplumbed
uppermost
uttermost
victimise
watermark
watermill
welcoming
wheatmeal
wholemeal
willemite
winsomely
witchmeal
wordsmith
worriment
zootomist
abidingly
abominate
absconder
abstinent
acuminate
adamantly
adeptness
adjoining
adoringly
adultness
affianced
afternoon
airminded
Alemannic
alertness
aliveness
aloneness
aloofness
alternant
alternate
aluminate
aluminise
aluminium
aluminous
amazingly
amazonian
Amerindic
ampleness
amusingly
anciently
ancientry
angriness
announcer
antennary
antennule
antiknock
apartness
apishness
appointee
arachnoid
aragonite
archangel
archenemy
arytenoid
Ashkenazi
asininity
askewness
astronaut
astronomy
attainder
augmented
augmenter
augmentor
austenite
authentic
avalanche
avizandum
awakening
awareness
awfulness
baboonish
badminton
bagginess
balconied
balkanise
balminess
bartender
bastinade
bastinado
Bathonian
battening
battiness
bawdiness
beamingly
beefiness
beginning
belemnite
benignant
benignity
bentonite
bespangle
biogenous
bipinnate
birdsnest
blackness
blandness
blankness
blatantly
blazingly
bleakness
blindness
bluffness
bluntness
bombinate
bonniness
boskiness
bossiness
bowwindow
brashness
breakneck
briefness
brigandry
briskness
Britannia
Britannic
broadness
brownness
buccaneer
bughunter
bulginess
bulkiness
bumpiness
buoyantly
burdenous
burliness
burningly
bushiness
buttinsky
buxomness
bystander
cageyness
calcaneal
calcaneum
Calvinism
Calvinist
campanile
campanili
campanula
canniness
cannonade
cannoneer
cannonier
Cantonese
carbonado
carbonate
carbonise
carbuncle
carcinoma
carpenter
carpentry
carpingly
carronade
Cassandra
castanets
cattiness
cavernous
centenary
chariness
cheapness
chelonian
chicanery
chillness
chitinous
chthonian
circinate
clamantly
cleanness
clearness
clemently
closeness
coadunate
coaxingly
Cobdenism
cocainise
cocainism
cochineal
cockiness
cocoonery
coffinite
colcannon
collinear
colonnade
columnist
combinate
commander
commandos
commendam
commensal
commenter
commingle
comminute
commonage
commonlaw
communard
communion
communise
communism
communist
community
companion
compendia
component
concentre
condenser
congenial
consensus
consonant
contender
contented
continent
continual
continuer
continuum
convincer
coriander
cosmonaut
crassness
craziness
cretinism
cretinous
criminate
criminous
crispness
crookneck
crossness
crowsnest
crudeness
cullender
culminant
culminate
cunningly
curliness
currently
curstness
cyprinoid
daltonism
damningly
Darwinian
Darwinism
Darwinist
dashingly
deaconess
decennary
decennial
decennium
declinate
defiantly
demeanour
denouncer
denseness
denyingly
derringdo
derringer
descended
designate
designing
diaconate
diclinous
diesinker
dinginess
dirtiness
disannual
dishonest
dishonour
dismantle
dispenser
dissenter
dissonant
distantly
dittander
dizziness
dottiness
dowdiness
draconian
dragoness
dragonfly
dragonish
drollness
dumpiness
duodenary
duskiness
dustiness
dysgenics
eagerness
earliness
Eastender
ecumenism
egomaniac
elegantly
elemental
elevenses
eliminate
embrangle
eminently
empennage
emptiness
enchanter
encounter
encrinite
Englander
epicentre
epigynous
erectness
erogenous
espionage
esplanade
Esthonian
estranger
euphonise
euphonium
euthenics
evaginate
evidently
exactness
examinant
exchanger
exogenous
expounder
externals
extrinsic
Fabianism
faddiness
faintness
Falernian
falseness
fandangle
fandangos
fascinate
fastening
fattiness
fawningly
feelingly
Fenianism
fervently
festinate
fetidness
fibrinoid
fibrinous
fieriness
filminess
fishiness
fittingly
fixedness
flakiness
flamingly
flamingos
flaringly
fleetness
flowingly
flushness
fogginess
foreknown
fortunate
forwander
foxhunter
frailness
frankness
freshness
fulgently
fulminant
fulminate
fulminous
funkiness
funniness
fusionist
fussiness
fustiness
fuzziness
gabionade
gallantly
gallantry
gallingly
gallinule
gallonage
galvanise
galvanism
galvanist
gammoning
gardening
garmented
gasconade
gasmantle
gaudiness
gauntness
gauziness
gawkiness
gelignite
genuinely
geomancer
geomantic
geoponics
germander
germanely
germanise
Germanish
Germanism
Germanist
germanium
germinate
giddiness
glaringly
glowingly
glueyness
glutinous
godliness
goldeneye
goldenrod
goosander
gooseneck
gorgonian
gorgonise
governess
grandness
graveness
greatness
greenness
griminess
grossness
gruffness
guarantee
guarantor
gumminess
gunrunner
gushingly
gustiness
gutsiness
hairiness
haltingly
hamhanded
handiness
happening
happiness
harbinger
hardiness
harmonica
harmonics
harmonise
harmonist
harmonium
harshness
hastiness
headiness
heaviness
hedgingly
heftiness
hellenise
Hellenism
Hellenist
Hercynian
hereunder
hessonite
hibernate
Hibernian
hiddenite
hoariness
horniness
horsiness
hortensia
Hottentot
hoydenish
huffiness
humanness
humdinger
husbandly
husbandry
huskiness
hydrangea
hydronium
hygienics
hygienist
hyphenate
Icelander
Icelandic
imaginary
impounder
inaptness
incarnate
incognito
indemnify
indemnity
Indianise
indignant
indignity
ineptness
inertness
inglenook
innuendos
insomniac
inspanned
instanter
instantly
internode
intrinsic
inverness
isogenous
itchiness
jackknife
jacksnipe
Jansenism
Jansenist
japanning
jargonise
jarringly
jazziness
jeeringly
jerkiness
Johannine
Jordanian
juiciness
jumpiness
kaolinise
kaolinite
kiddingly
kinkiness
kittenish
knowingly
lambently
lancinate
lankiness
Laplander
larcenist
larcenous
largeness

lastingly
leakiness
leavening
leeringly
legginess
legionary
leniently
levelness
lichenous
lightness
lightning
liltingly
lispingly
litheness
lividness
loftiness
Londonise
Londonism
longingly
looseness
louringly
lousiness
lowlander
lowliness
lowminded
lucidness
luckiness
lumpiness
luridness
lustiness
machinate
machinery
machinist
maddening
Magianism
maidenish
malignant
malignity
mammonish
mammonism
mammonist
mammonite
Mancunian
manganate
manganese
manganite
manganous
manginess
manhandle
manliness
manzanita
marginate
Martinmas
massiness
maternity
mateyness
matronage
matronise
mealiness
meaningly
meatiness
mechanics
mechanise
mechanism
mechanist
meltingly
Mennonite
mercenary
merganser
merriness
messenger
messiness
metronome
mezzanine
midwinter
milkiness
millenary
millennia
millinery

Miltonian
mincingly
mirkiness
mishandle
mishanter
mismanage
mistiness
mixedness
mnemonics
mnemonist
mockingly
modernise
modernism
modernist
modernity
moistness
Montanism
monzonite
moodiness
mordantly
Mormonism
mucronate
muddiness
muffineer
muffinman
mugginess
mundanely
mundungus
murkiness
muskiness
mustiness
muzziness
nakedness
nastiness
nattiness
neediness
Negroness
Neptunian
neptunium
nerviness
netwinged
newsiness
Newtonian
Nipponese
nobleness
noisiness
nonlinear
Normanise
Normanism
notedness
notionist
nuisancer
nuttiness
obeseness
obscenely
obscenity
obstinacy
obstinate
octennial
offcentre
offhanded
olivenite
onehanded
openended
oppugnant
opulently
originate
orphanage
otherness
outgunned
outlander
overtness
oxygenate
oxygenise
oxygenous
pageantry
panhandle
pantingly
parcenary

parsonage
passenger
pastiness
paternity
patiently
patronage
patroness
patronise
peasantry
peccantly
pectinate
pendently
pentangle
peptonise
perennate
perennial
pergunnah
perkiness
permanent
personage
personate
personify
personnel
pertinent
pettiness
phalanger
phalanges
phalanxes
pharyngal
pharynges
pharynxes
philander
phoniness
pinkiness
piquantly
pithiness
pityingly
placename
placentae
placental
plainness
platinise
platinoid
platinous
Platonise
Platonism
Platonist
plumpness
plushness
plutonian
Plutonism
Plutonist
plutonium
podginess
poisonous
pollinate
pollinium
polyandry
polyonymy
pontoneer
pontonier
porringer
postentry
pothunter
pratingly
prebendal
precancel
precentor
preconise
premonish
presentee
presenter
presently
pretender
preventer
primeness
proconsul
profanely
profanity

promenade
prominent
proneness
proponent
prosiness
protonema
Provencal
provender
prudently
pudginess
puffiness
pulmonary
pulmonate
pulpiness
pulvinate
pungently
purringly
pursiness
pushiness
pushingly
quakiness
quarenden
quarender
queerness
quickness
quietness
rabbinate
rabbinism
rabbinist
rabidness
radiantly
raffinate
raffinose
raininess
rampantly
randiness
ranginess
rantingly
rapidness
raspingly
rationale
rationing
readiness
reasoning
reckoning
reclinate
recognise
recoinage
rectangle
redhanded
reediness
refurnish
rejoinder
reliantly
remainder
rencontre
renouncer
replenish
repugnant
rerunning
responder
rhodonite
Ribbonism
rightness
rigidness
ringingly
ringsnake
riskiness
rockiness
rocksnake
roominess
roughneck
roughness
Roumanian
Roumansch
roundness
routinely
routinism
routinist

rowdiness
ruddiness
rumrunner
runcinate
rustiness
ruthenium
safranine
saliently
salmonoid
salpinges
saltiness
sanbenito
sandiness
santonica
sapiently
sappiness
Sardinian
Sassanian
Sassenach
Saturnian
saturnine
saturnism
sauciness
scaliness
scantness
scavenger
sciaenoid
screening
scrounger
seaminess
searingly
seasoning
seatangle
secernent
seediness
seemingly
segmental
sentenate
septenary
septennia
sequinned
sermonise
serpentry
serranoid
sexennial
sexlinked
shadiness
shakiness
shamanism
shamanist
sharpness
sheerness
shininess
shogunate
shortness
showiness
sickening
sidedness
silkiness
silliness
siphonage
siphuncle
slackness
Slavonian
sleekness
slickness
sliminess
Slovenian
smallness
smartness
smilingly
smokiness
snakiness
snowiness
soapiness
sobbingly
soberness
sogginess
solemnise

solemnity
solidness
sootiness
soppiness
sopranino
sopranist
Sorbonist
sorriness
sostenuto
Soudanese
soundness
souteneur
spareness
sparingly
sphagnous
spiciness
spikenard
spikiness
spininess
spleenful
sporangia
squatness
staginess
staidness
staleness
Stalinism
Stalinist
staminate
stampnote
starkness
steepness
sternness
stiffness
stillness
stolonate
stoniness
stoutness
subgenera
sublunary
submental
subtenant
succentor
succinate
sulkiness
sultanate
sultaness
summingup
sunbonnet
sunniness
suntanned
supernova
surcingle
surliness
surrender
suspender
suspensor
swartness
sweetness
swiftness
sylvanite
tacitness
tackiness
tamponade
tapdancer
tardiness
Tasmanian
tastiness
tattiness
tawniness
teasingly
tectonics
tegmental
tegmentum
teknonymy
tellingly
tendinous
tenseness
tepidness
terminate

terminism
terminist
terseness
testiness
teutonise
Teutonism
Teutonist
thickness
thingness
thumbnail
tightness
timidness
timpanist
tinniness
tipsiness
tiredness
tormentil
tormentor
toughness
tradename
trepanned
tribunate
triennial
triennium
trilinear
triteness
tubbiness
tumidness
turbinate
turgently
twohanded
tympanist
tyrannise
tyrannous
Uitlander
Ukrainian
uliginous
unaptness
unbeknown
unblinded
unbounded
uncannily
uncounted
undaunted
unfitness
unfounded
unharness
unisonant
unisonous
unmeaning
unpointed
unsoundly
upcountry
uraninite
usualness
utterness
vaccinate
vagueness
Vaishnava
valiantly
validness
vapidness
veeringly
verdantly
verminate
verminous
vicennial
villanage
villenage
violently
violinist
virginals
virginity
visionary
visionist
vivianite
vividness
vocalness
volcanism

volcanoes
voltinism
vulcanian
vulcanise
vulcanism
vulcanist
vulcanite
vulpinism
vulpinite
wackiness
waggonage
wailingly
Waldenses
warbonnet
warmonger
warningly
warrantee
warranter
warrantor
washiness
wasteness
weakkneed
weariness
weediness
weirdness
wellknown
whipsnake
whiteness
whitening
whodunnit
wholeness
willingly
windiness
winningly
wittiness
wittingly
woodiness
wooziness
wordiness
wrongness
wulfenite
yawningly
youngness
zinkenite
zirconium
zoogenous
abandoned
abandonee
abandoner
acropolis
actinozoa
aflatoxin
agrologic
agronomic
ahistoric
aircooled
albinotic
alcoholic
aleatoric
alkaloses
alkalosis
allegoric
allomorph
almshouse
amauroses
amaurosis
amaurotic
amblyopia
amblyopic
amphioxus
anabioses
anabiosis
anabiotic
anaerobic
anaphoric
anecdotal
anecdotic
ankylosis
ankylotic
anthropic
anticodon
antidotal
antimonic
antinodal
antinomic
antinovel
antipodal
antipodes
antitoxic
antitoxin
aperiodic
apostolic
Appaloosa
arthropod
arthrosis
auditoria
autonomic
autoroute
autosomal
babacoote
backboard
backwoods
bakehouse
ballpoint
bamboozle
bastioned
bathhouse
billboard
billionth
blowtorch
bluepoint
boathouse
bondwoman
booklouse
boondocks
Brythonic
buckboard
buckhound
bucktooth
bulldozer
bunkhouse
cabriolet
calaboose
camphoric
cardboard
carryover
carthorse
Castroism
catabolic
catalogue
catamount
catatonia
catatonic
ceratodus
chaetopod
charlotte
charwoman
chernozem
chipboard
chlorosis
chlorotic
chophouse
choplogic
cirrhosis
clapboard
clarionet
clipboard
cloisonne
clubhouse
coalmouse
cockhorse
cockroach
colemouse
comedones
cookhouse
crossover
cryptogam
cryptonym
cytotoxic
cytotoxin
dartboard
dashboard
decagonal
decalogue
decapodal
decapodan
deckhouse
deerhound
demagogic
demagogue
demimonde
destroyer
dethroner
developer
dextrorse
diagnoses
diagnosis
diastolic
diatropic
dichroism
dichromat
dichromic
disavouch
disavowal
dispeople
dizygotic
dogshores
dogstooth
dogviolet
dosshouse
Doukhobor
draghound
drayhorse
duckboard
dumbfound
dustcover
dysphonia
dysphoria
dysphoric
dyspnoeic
dystrophy
eastbound
easygoing
ecritoire
ectomorph
elastomer
electoral
embryonal
embryonic
embryotic
emotional
endomorph
episcopal
epistoler
epistolic
epizootic
equipoise
equivocal
equivoque
ergonomic
exosmosis
exosmotic
exostosis
factional
farmhouse
fashioner
fictional
firehouse
firepower
fireworks
flageolet
flashover
flophouse
fluorosis
fluxional
footboard
footloose
footpound
foreboder
forecourt
foregoing
foretoken
forewoman
francolin
freeboard
freehouse
freewoman
fumarolic
gallooned
gangboard
gastropod
gatehouse
gazehound
geotropic
gladiolus
glyptodon
gnathonic
goalmouth
goingover
gomphosis
greyhound
guilloche
halfbound
halitosis
hardboard
hardcover
hardnosed
harpooner
haustoria
headboard
hegemonic
hellhound
heterodox
heteronym
heterosis
hexagonal
hidebound
hightoned
hoarhound
homebound
homologue
homopolar
homotonic
hopscotch
horehound
horologer
horologic
hydriodic
hylozoism
hyperopia
hyperopic
hypocotyl
ideologic
ideologue
iguanodon
indecorum
indigotin
infusoria
ironbound
ironmould
ironworks
Iroquoian
isallobar
isotropic
josshouse
jurywoman
katabolic
keratosis
kingdomed
kinswoman
lagomorph
lampooner
landloper
latecomer
lawnmower
lazybones
lazytongs
leafmould
leitmotif
leitmotiv
lifeforce
lobscouse
locomotor
longcoats
longhouse
loudmouth
lovetoken
lunisolar
lyamhound
lymehound
lyophobic
macaronic
macedoine
malleolar
malleolus
malthouse
mansionry
Manxwoman
mayflower
melanosis
melanotic
melatonin
melocoton
mesomorph
metabolic
milktooth
millboard
millionth
missioner
monatomic
mongooses
monocoque
monologic
monologue
monotonic
monsoonal
moratoria
mullioned
mycologic
neathouse
nephrosis
newshound
nonprofit
nonsmoker
nucleolus
nucleonic
oasthouse
octagonal
octopodes
oecologic
oestrogen
okeydokey
oncologic
ontologic
opinioned
outgrowth
outspoken
overboard
overborne
overjoyed
overpower
overtones
overwound
packhorse
pairhorse
parabolic
paramorph
paramount
paranoiac
parapodia
paregoric
pasodoble
passional
patchouli
patchouly
patriotic
pedagogic
pedagogue
pensioner
penthouse
peridotic
perimorph
pesthouse
pharaonic
phellogen
phyllopod
plasmodia
playhouse
plethoric
plusfours
pneumonia
pneumonic
polygonal
polygonum
polymorph
polysomic
polytonal
polyzoary
poorhouse
portfolio
posthorse
posthouse
pourboire
pourpoint
praenomen
prodromal
prodromic
prognoses
prognosis
propionic
proptosis
prothorax
psalmodic
pseudonym
pseudopod
psychoses
psychosis
psychotic
pulpboard
pyridoxin
racehorse
rearhorse
rearmouse
reefpoint
reenforce
reinforce
reremouse
rhapsodic
Rhineodon
ribosomal
roadhouse
roadworks
rockbound
rosenoble
safflower
saltworks
sanatoria
sclerosis
sclerotic
scoliosis
scoliotic
sectional
selfdoubt
selfmoved
semeiotic
semicolon
semisolid
semitonic
semivowel
serotonin
sessional
shallowly
shambolic
Shintoism
Shintoist
shipboard
shipmoney
shottower
sideboard
siderosis
signboard
silicosis
silicotic
sinologue
sixfooter
slipcoach
slipcover
slowcoach
snowbound
snowgoose
snubnosed
soapworks
softgoods
soliloquy
Solomonic
sourdough
spasmodic
squamosal
staghound
stalworth
starboard
stational
stationer
stercoral
studhorse
subatomic
sudatoria
sulphonic
sunflower
surfboard
surgeoncy
swangoose
symbiosis
symbiotic
symphonic
synagogal
synagogue
tailboard
taskforce
tattooist
taxonomic
telamones
tensional
teratogen
theogonic
theologic
theologue
theosophy
threnodic
tirewoman
tollbooth
tollhouse
toolhouse
torsional
townhouse
transonic
trattoria
trattorie
trialogue
triatomic
trichomic
triploidy
tuitional
turnround
turquoise
unalloyed
unsavoury
untutored
vasomotor
versional
viceroyal
viewpoint
virtuosic

virtuosos
vitriolic
voiceover
vomitoria
voodooism
voodooist
wakerobin
wallboard
warehouse
washboard
washhouse
wayzgoose
webfooted
wellfound
westbound
whipround
willpower
windbound
windhover
wolfhound
woodlouse
workhorse
workhouse
workwoman
wyandotte
xeromorph
yearround
zoophobia
accompany
acidophil
aerospace
amylopsin
analeptic
anglophil
asclepiad
ascospore
assumpsit
attempter
backspace
bargepole
bishopric
callipers
caryopses
caryopsis
catchpole
catchpoll
centipede
chiropody
cirripede
cisalpine
coreopsis
cornopean
corrupter
corruptly
cyclopean
cyclopian
cyclopses
davenport
decomplex
decompose
dewlapped
didelphic
dimorphic
disappear
disrepair
disrepute
dissipate
drainpipe
dyspepsia
dyspeptic
eclampsia
eclamptic
encompass
endosperm
endospore
entrapped
enwrapped
epileptic
equipping
estoppage
estopping
estrapade
Ethiopian
eutrophic
excerptor
exculpate
extempore
extirpate
fissipede
flarepath
forcepump
forespeak
frogspawn
frontpage
gallopade
Gallophil
galloping
grandpapa
guidepost
hairspace
handspike
hawsepipe
highspeed
homeopath
horseplay
horsepond
inculpate
indispose
interpage
interplay
interpose
interpret
juxtapose
kidnapped
kidnapper
lithopone
lodgepole
loveapple
madrepore
marchpane
marchpast
marsupial
marsupium
megaspore
mercaptan
micropsia
micropyle
millepede
millepore
millipede
misemploy
misreport
mouthpart
multipara
multiplex
necrophil
negrophil
neuropath
nullipara
nullipore
nuncupate
oligopoly
osteopath
overspend
overspent
overspill
palmipede
perisperm
philippic
photophil
photopsia
pineapple
pinnipede
pitchpipe
porcupine
preceptor
precipice
preemptor
primipara
prolapsus
prolepses
prolepsis
proleptic
queenpost
recapping
recompose
reserpine
rhodopsin
ridgepole
roseapple
Russophil
saltspoon
sandspout
sauropoda
scrappily
scrapping
screwpile
screwpine
scrimpily
septuplet
sextuplet
singspiel
Slavophil
sociopath
sorbapple
soundpost
soupspoon
spaceport
sparkplug
standpipe
starapple
steampipe
sternpost
stockpile
stovepipe
strappado
strapping
stripping
stropping
subalpine
subtopian
sugarplum
superpose
swordplay
syllepses
syllepsis
sylleptic
syncopate
teacupful
tetrapody
therapist
titlepage
tittuping
tittupped
toothpick
totempole
transpire
transport
transpose
triumphal
turboprop
unadopted
uncropped
underpaid
underpart
underpass
underplay
underplot
unhappily
unhelpful
unpeopled
unstopped
unwrapped
unzipping
usucapion
walloping
wastepipe
waterpipe
whirlpool
zygospore
Algonquin
baldaquin
colloquia
exchequer
harlequin
mannequin
palanquin
sobriquet
tanliquor
abhorrent
abhorring
actuarial
adumbrate
aepyornis
aerodrome
aerograph
airstream
airworthy
albatross
algarroba
algebraic
allograph
allotrope
allotropy
anandrous
anchorage
anchoress
anchorite
anchorman
anhydride
anhydrite
anhydrous
antitrade
antitrust
arbitrage
arbitrary
arbitrate
arbitress
arrearage
arrowroot
Arthurian
ashlaring
auctorial
austerely
austerity
authoress
authorial
authorise
authority
autocracy
autocross
autograft
autograph
autotroph
awestruck
awkwardly
azeotrope
backcross
backtrack
bacterial
bacterise
bacterium
bacteroid
ballerina
banderole
barbarian
barbarise
barbarism
barbarity
barbarous
barcarole
barmbrack
barograph
bastardly
bedspread
bedspring
berberine
berserker
bestirred
bilharzia
binturong
birdbrain
birthrate
bitterish
bizarrely
bloodroot
bluegrass
blueprint
Boanerges
boardroom
boattrain
bombardon
bombproof
boomerang
bordereau
bowstring
boxgirder
brandreth
briarroot
brierroot
brokerage
broomrape
Bulgarian
bulltrout
bursarial
bushcraft
butterbur
buttercup
butterfat
butterfly
butterine
butternut
caesarean
caesarian
Caesarism
Caesarist
calabrese
calcarate
caldarium
calibrate
camorrist
campcraft
cancerous
canebrake
canetrash
cankerous
cantorial
carburise
careerism
careerist
cassareep
cassaripe
casserole
casuarina
catarrhal
Catharism
Catharist
catharses
catharsis
cathartic
cauterise
celebrant
celebrate
celebrity
cellarage
censorial
centering
centurion
cerebrate
cerograph
chancroid
chancrous
chantress
chaparral
chaperone
checkrein
chemurgic
choleraic
chondrite
chondrule
cicatrice
cicatrise
Cimmerian
clamorous
classroom
clathrate
cloakroom
coeternal
cofferdam
coheiress
collyrium
colourful
colouring
colourist
colourman
colubrine
comforter
comptroll
concerned
concerted
concordat
concurred
conferral
conferred
conferrer
confervae
confirmed
confirmer
confirmor
conformal
conformer
congeries
conscribe
conscript
conserver
consortia
constrain
constrict
construct
converter
cooperage
cooperant
cooperate
corduroys
cormorant
cornbrash
corncrake
cornerboy
cornerman
corporate
corporeal
cosmorama
cothurnus
coumarone
courtroom
couturier
creatress
criterion
crossroad
crossruff
cursorial
cursorily
cutthroat
cyclorama
Cytherean
dangerous
dastardly
dayspring
deathroll
debarring
declarant
deferring
dehydrate
demiurgic
democracy
demurrage
demurring
denigrate
denitrate
denitrify
deodorant
deodorise
desecrate
desperado
desperate
deterrent
deterring
deuterate
deuterium
devitrify
dexterity
dexterous
diachrony
diandrous
diaphragm
different
dinnerset
dipcircle
dipterous
dirttrack
disbarred
disburden
disbursal
discarder
discerner
disforest
disparage
disparate
disparity
dispersal
disperser
disturbed
disturber
dithyramb
doctorate
doctorial
doorframe
downgrade
drawerful
dungarees
ealdorman
easterner
editorial
eidograph
elaborate
elbowroom
electress
electrify
electrode
embarrass
enchorial
encourage
endearing
endocrine
enhearten
entourage
enumerate
ephedrine
epicurean
epicurism
epidermal
epidermic
epidermis
epiphragm
ergograph
erythrism
erythrite
esoterica
esoterism
estuarian
estuarine
ethnarchy
Eucharist

euphorbia
eutherian
evaporate
evergreen
excurrent
exodermis
exonerate
exuberant
exuberate
eyestrain
factorage
factorial
factorise
fairyring
fanfarade
favourite
fenugreek
filigreed
filterbed
filtertip
finedrawn
fingering
fingertip
firebrand
firebreak
firebrick
firecrest
firedrake
firedrill
fireirons
fireproof
firstrate
fisherman
flavorous
flowerage
flowerbed
flowering
flowerpot
foolproof
footprint
forebrain
forefront
forlornly
forwarder
forwardly
fossorial
fosterage
foulbrood
foundress
fraternal
frowardly
frustrate
fulgurant
fulgurate
fulgurite
fulgurous
fullcream
fulldress
fullgrown
funebrial
galleried
ganderism
gaolbreak
garderobe
gaspereau
gatecrash
gathering
germproof
geyserite
gibberish
gingerade
gingerale
glamorise
glamorous
glomerate
glomerule
glomeruli
glyceride
glycerine
godparent
goffering
goldbrick
goldcrest
goliardic
gongorism
Gradgrind
greenroom
gregarian
gregarine
Gregorian
grillroom
grosgrain
guardrail
guardring
guardroom
guestroom
guiderope
guitarist
guttering
gynocracy
haggardly
hagiarchy
hairbrush
hairgrass
halfbreed
halfcrown
halfprice
halftrack
halftruth
hamadryad
hamburger
hammerman
hammertoe
hamstring
hamstrung
handbrake
handcraft
handorgan
handpress
hangerson
hankering
headdress
hemitrope
heptarchy
herbarium
herborise
Hesperian
hetaerism
hetairism
hierarchy
highgrade
highgrown
Himyarite
hindbrain
historian
Hitlerism
Hitlerite
hoarfrost
hodiernal
hodograph
holograph
homegrown
homograft
homograph
hoofprint
hornwrack
houseroom
Hungarian
hypocrisy
hypocrite
hysterics
hysteroid
ideograph
idiograph
immigrant
immigrate
impetrate
inamorata
incorrect
incorrupt
incurrent
incurring
IndoAryan
inferring
inodorous
inpouring
integrand
integrant
integrate
integrity
interring
interrupt
isochrone
isomerise
isomerism
isomerous
itineracy
itinerant
itinerary
itinerate
jailbreak
janitress
jetstream
jitterbug
jointress
juniorate
juniority
junkerdom
junkerism
kaiserdom
kaiserism
katharsis
Keplerian
kilderkin
kingcraft
knotgrass
Kshatriya
kymograph
labourite
laggardly
landdross
landdrost
landgrave
lapstrake
lapstreak
lathering
latterday
laundress
lazzarone
lazzaroni
leafgreen
lecherous
leewardly
leisurely
lethargic
letterbox
lettering
librarian
lickerish
Limburger
linearise
linearity
lingering
liquorice
liquorish
Listerism
litterbin
litterbug
logogriph
Lombardic
loxodrome
lucubrate
ludicrous
lumbering
lumberman
lymegrass
mailtrain
mainbrace
maladroit
malformed
mandarine
mannerism
mannerist
mansarded
manubrium
margarine
margarite
marmoreal
martyrdom
martyrise
masonried
masterdom
masterful
masterkey
meandrine
meandrous
meliorate
meliorism
meliorist
meliority
melodrama
memoirist
menstrual
menstruum
mepacrine
mercerise
mercurial
mercurous
mesmerise
mesmerism
mesmerist
meteorist
meteorite
meteoroid
micturate
midstream
millerite
misdirect
mobocracy
monitress
monocracy
monodrama
monograph
monotreme
monstrous
mossgrown
motherwit
mothproof
motocross
murderess
murderous
murmurous
muscarine
myriorama
nailbrush
nectarean
nectarial
nectarine
nectarous
neoterise
neoterism
neoterist
Nestorian
newmarket
newsprint
niggardly
nocturnal
nomocracy
nomograph
nonjuring
nonpareil
nonperson
obscurant
obscurely
obscurity
obsecrate
occurrent
occurring
Octobrist
offscreen
offspring
offstreet
oilburner
oleograph
oligarchy
oratorial
oratorian
orrisroot
ossifrage
outspread
outwardly
outworker
overcrowd
overdraft
overdrawn
overdress
overdrive
overgraze
overgrown
overprice
overprint
overproof
overtrain
overtrick
overtrump
overwrite
overwrote
oviferous
oviparity
oviparous
oysterbed
oysterman
ozocerite
ozokerite
packdrill
packtrain
paederast
palsgrave
panderess
paragraph
passerine
passersby
pastorale
pastorate
pasturage
pauperise
pauperism
pedigreed
penetrant
penetrate
pentarchy
pepperbox
pepperpot
peregrine
perfervid
perforate
performer
perverter
petaurist
phalarope
pictorial
picturise
piecerate
pilferage
pilgarlic
pillarbox
pimpernel
pinstripe
pipedream
pipeorgan
planarian
playgroup
plenarily
podagrous
polygraph
ponderous
porterage
posterior
posterity
prayerful
prayerrug
precursor
preferred
prescribe
prescript
preserver
preshrink
preshrunk
pressroom
prestress
preterist
preterite
pretermit
primarily
primordia
procerity
procuracy
procuress
proofread
properdin
proscribe
prostrate
pulserate
pulverise
pulverous
purpureal
Quakerdom
Quakeress
Quakerish
Quakerism
racetrack
rainproof
rancorous
raptorial
rapturous
readdress
recherche
rectorate
rectorial
recurrent
recurring
reedorgan
reentrant
referring
rehearsal
rehydrate
reiterate
rerebrace
resources
resurrect
retiarius
rigmarole
Ripuarian
rivalrous
rockbrake
rockdrill
rubberise
rustproof
sacrarium
sagebrush
sagegreen
sailoring
sailorman
salubrity
sandarach
sandcrack
sangfroid
sartorial
sartorius
saucerful
Sauternes
savourily
saxifrage
scarfring
scenarist
schnorkel
schnorrer
sciagraph
scombroid
seafaring
seagirdle
seastrand
seaworthy
sectarian
sectorial
selfdrive
selfpride
selftrust
semibreve
senhorita
seniority
sensorial
sensorium
Sephardic
Sephardim
serigraph
sestertia
shakerism
Shangrila
sheldrake
shelfroom
shewbread
shipwreck
shopfront
shotproof
sidetrack
signorial
signorina
silverfir
sincerely
sincerity
sitzkrieg
skiagraph
skijoring
skingraft
sliderule
slumbrous
snakeroot
snowbroth
snowdrift
sodabread
sojourner
solferino
Solutrean
Solutrian
sooterkin
sorceress
sorcerous
spagyrist
spareribs
spiderman
spiderweb
spindrier
spindrift
squarrose
stackroom
Stagirite
stardrift
stargrass
stateroom
stillroom
stockroom
stoppress
storeroom
stuporous
subaerial
submarine
subnormal
subscribe
subscript
substrata
substrate
subverter

succursal
suctorial
suctorian
suffering
summarily
summarise
summarist
sunburned
sunstroke
sunstruck
supporter
suppurate
susurrant
synchrony
tailoress
tailoring
tangerine
Tartarean
Tartarian
tectorial
telegraph
tellurate
tellurian
telluride
tellurite
tellurium
tellurous
temperate
temporary
temporise
temptress
tenderise
tenebrist
tenebrous
tenthrate
terebrant
terrarium
terrorise
terrorism
terrorist
testdrive
tetrarchy
theatrics
theocracy
theocrasy
thirdrate
tightrope
timbering
timberman
timocracy
tinderbox
toastrack
Tocharian
tonsorial
topiarian
topiarist
torchrace
torturous
traceried
traitress
traversal
traverser
trichroic
triforium
trimerous
triturate
trunkroad
tuckerbag
tuliproot
typewrite
unadorned
uncharted
underrate
underripe
unguarded
unhurried
uniformly
uniparous
uniserial
unitarian
universal
unlearned
unsparing
unwearied
vampirism
vapouring
vapourish
vectorial
velodrome
veneering
venturous
veratrine
Victorian
victorine
viscerate
visitress
viverrine
vizierate
vizierial
voyeurism
vulgarian
vulgarise
vulgarism
vulgarity
vulnerary
vulturine
vulturish
vulturous
Wagnerian
Wagnerite
wagonroof
waldgrave
wallcress
wallfruit
Walpurgis
wandering
wartcress
washerman
wavefront
wayfaring
waywardly
welfarism
westering
westerner
windbreak
windproof
winepress
winterise
wiredrawn
wisecrack
withdrawn
withering
witherite
wolverene
wolverine
wonderful
woodcraft
xenograft
xylograph
yesterday
zoiatrics
abolisher
abscissae
abscissas
accessary
accession
accessory
addressee
addresser
addressor
adenosine
adiposity
admeasure
admission
admissive
adversary
adversely
adversity
aforesaid
aggressor
agonising
agonistic
aimlessly
alabaster
alongside
ambrosial
ampersand
analysand
anglesite
anguished
animistic
animosity
appressed
arabesque
artlessly
ascension
ascensive
aspersion
assuasive
atavistic
atheistic
atomistic
Axminster
ballistae
ballistic
bannister
Bantustan
baptismal
baptistry
barrister
beemaster
blockship
bloodshed
bloodshot
bombasine
bombastic
bookishly
boorishly
brakeshoe
brakesman
bretasche
bridesman
Britisher
broadside
brutishly
bullishly
burlesque
burnisher
caddisfly
cadetship
callosity
canvasser
Cartesian
casuistic
casuistry
Caucasian
cerussite
chemistry
chiefship
chorister
cleansing
clerkship
coelostat
coenosarc
cognisant
collision
collusion
collusive
colosseum
coltishly
commissar
compasses
composite
composure
concisely
concision
confessor
confusion
contusion
corposant
corpuscle
corrasion
corrosion
corrosive
cortisone
coseismal
coseismic
countship
courtship
coverslip
cracksman
craftsman
cremaster
crepuscle
croissant
curiosity
currishly
cuttysark
Dantesque
decussate
defensive
defroster
deinosaur
demission
dentistry
depressed
depressor
detersion
detersive
detrusion
dharmsala
dichasial
dichasium
diffusely
diffusion
diffusive
dimension
dimissory
Dionysiac
Dionysian
dismissal
disposure
diversely
diversify
diversion
diversity
divulsion
doggishly
doltishly
donnishly
draftsman
driftsail
dualistic
dubiosity
earnestly
earthstar
ecclesial
ecosystem
ecstasise
egotistic
egression
eightsome
eldership
ellipsoid
embassage
embrasure
embussing
emphasise
emphysema
emplastic
encaustic
enclosure
endlessly
engrosser
epidosite
epinastic
espousals
excelsior
excessive
exclosure
exclusion
exclusive
excursion
excursive
exhauster
expansile
expansion
expansive
expensive
explosion
explosive
expressly
expulsion
expulsive
exquisite
extensile
extension
extensity
extensive
extorsive
extrusion
extrusive
fantasied
fantasise
fantasist
fantastic
fantastry
Fascistic
faunistic
fideistic
fieldsman
fillister
floristic
floristry
fluorspar
flyfisher
focussing
foolishly
foppishly
fricassee
furbisher
furnisher
gannister
garnishee
geodesist
gibbosity
girlishly
globosity
glucoside
glycoside
gneissoid
gneissose
gooseskin
goosestep
grandsire
grandslam
grapeshot
greensand
groomsman
grotesque
guardship
guardsman
guildship
gymnasial
gymnasium
gymnastic
haemostat
hamfisted
haplessly
harvester
haversack
heartsick
heartsore
heliostat
hellishly
heuristic
hircosity
Hobbesian
hocussing
hoggishly
homousian
horseshoe
hubristic
hydrosome
hygrostat
illwisher
immensely
immensity
immersion
impassion
impassive
implosion
implosive
impresari
impulsion
impulsive
impulsory
incensory
incessant
inclosure
inclusion
inclusive
incursion
incursive
inelastic
insensate
intensely
intensify
intension
intensity
intensive
intersect
intorsion
intrusion
intrusive
inversely
inversion
inversive
janissary
jobmaster
joylessly
Judaistic
judgeship
Junoesque
Keynesian
klinostat
knavishly
lairdship
lawlessly
Leicester
leptosome
licensure
lightship
lightsome
lightsout
limousine
lithesome
loathsome
loutishly
lumpishly
magnesian
magnesite
magnesium
majorship
manorseat
maquisard
marcasite
mawkishly
mayorship
microsome
misassign
misbeseem
molluscan
morrisman
narcissus
necessary
necessity
nightside
nigrosine
nourisher
oakenshaw
obsession
obsessive
obtrusion
obtrusive
obversely
obversion
occlusion
occlusive
odalisque
offensive
ombudsman
onanistic
onionskin
onomastic
operosely
operosity
oppressor
orchestic
orchestra
organstop
orgiastic
ostensive
overissue
ownership
palaestra
palmistry
patristic
paymaster
peevishly
peninsula
penpusher
perfusion
perfusive
pertussis
pervasion
pervasive
petersham
pettishly
pharisaic
pianistic
pietistic
piggishly
plainsman
plainsong
planisher
poetaster
pointsman
polyester
pomposity
possessed
possessor
potassium
pranksome
prankster
precisely
precisian
precision
prelusion
prelusive
prelusory
pressstud
prevision
printshop
priorship
proboscis
processed
processer
processor
professed
professor
profusely
profusion

progestin
prolusion
prolusory
promising
protester
protestor
provision
provisory
provostry
prudishly
pterosaur
publisher
purposely
purposive
queenship
quicksand
quickstep
quirister
raffishly
rareeshow
realistic
recension
recession
recessive
reclusion
reclusive
recursion
recursive
redresser
refreshen
refresher
regisseur
Reichstag
remeasure
remission
repossess
represent
repressor
repulsion
repulsive
requester
requisite
reversely
reversion
revulsion
revulsive
rhymester
riverside
rodfisher
roguishly
roughshod
roundsman
rulership
sacristan
saintship
sarcastic
sargassos
satinspar
scarfskin
scrimshaw
secession
seclusion
seclusive
selfishly
sequester
sequestra
sexlessly
sharkskin
sharpshod
sheepskin
shoreside
shortstop
sickishly
sideissue
sightseer
sinlessly
sinuosity
slaveship
slavishly
slingshot
snakeskin
sobsister
soidisant
solipsism
solipsist
solmisate
sophister
sophistic
sophistry
sottishly
souwester
spaceship
spacesuit
spearside
speedster
spinosity
spoilsman
spokesman
sportsman
spritsail
stateside
statesman
statistic
steamship
steersman
stegosaur
storeship
stormsail
stressful
stylishly
stylistic
subcostal
submaster
successor
suffusion
suggester
supersede
superstar
supposing
sweatshop
sweetshop
swinishly
swordsman
symposiac
symposial
symposium
tallyshop
tartishly
thalassic
thaneship
thirdsman
Thomistic
threesome
throwster
thyristor
tigerseye
toothsome
torchsong
touristic
tracksuit
tradesman
transship
tribesman
tricksily
trickster
trimester
troopship
trousseau
tutorship
twofisted
unabashed
unbiassed
unblessed
unceasing
uncrossed
underseal
underseas
undersell
undershot
underside
undersign
undersold
undersong
underspin
unfleshed
unfleshly
unicuspid
untrussed
Upanishad
upholster
uselessly
varnisher
verbosely
verbosity
vibrissae
villosity
viscosity
vitiosity
vouchsafe
waggishly
waspishly
watershed
waterside
wearisome
Wednesday
wholesale
wholesome
witlessly
wolfishly
Worcester
worrisome
wristshot
yachtsman
Yiddisher
youngster
abduction
abjection
abolition
aboutturn
abruption
accentual
acceptant
acceptive
accretion
accretive
aconitine
acoustics
acquittal
acquitted
actuation
addiction
addictive
adduction
adductive
ademption
admitting
admixture
adoration
adulation
adulatory
advantage
advection
advective
Adventism
Adventist
adventive
adventure
advertent
advertise
affecting
affection
affective
affixture
afflation
aftertime
agitation
agitative
ailanthus
allantois
allotting
amianthus
amplitude
ancestral
andantino
animation
animatism
annectent
annuitant
aperitive
appertain
apportion
archetype
architect
arcuately
argentine
argentite
argentous
armistice
aromatise
arrestant
arresting
asafetida
asbestine
asbestous
ascertain
aspartate
aspectual
assertion
assertive
assistant
asymptote
athletics
Atlantean
attention
attentive
attrition
avocation
azimuthal
Babbittry
backstage
bandstand
barbitone
barnstorm
basketful
beanstalk
beatitude
bedsettee
bedsitter
beefsteak
befitting
begetting
besetting
besotting
bespatter
betrothal
betrothed
bimonthly
biometric
bipartite
bisection
bluestone
bolection
bondstone
boobytrap
bookstall
bookstand
bookstore
boycotter
breadtree
breastpin
breveting
brevetted
brightish
brimstone
broadtail
bucketful
budgetary
buffeting
buhrstone
bullytree
burrstone
Byzantine
cacoethes
cadastral
cadential
calenture
calmative
campstool
candytuft
carnation
carnitine
carpetbag
carpeting
caseation
cassation
catoptric
causation
causative
ceanothus
celestial
cementite
cerastium
certitude
cessation
chelation
chemitype
chieftain
Chinatown
chinstrap
chopstick
Christian
Christmas
citystate
claustral
clavation
clientage
clientele
cloistral
coalition
coarctate
cobaltite
cobaltous
cockatiel
coemption
cognately
cognation
cognition
cognitive
colcothar
collation
collotype
colostomy
colostrum
combatant
combative
comfiture
Comintern
committal
committed
committee
commotion
commutate
competent
condition
confiteor
connately
connation
connature
copartner
copestone
cornetist
cornstalk
cornstone
coverture
cowlstaff
crediting
cremation
crematory
crenation
crenature
crepitant
crepitate
crosstalk
croustade
curbstone
curettage
curvature
curveting
curvetted
cyclotron
cystotomy
dalmatian
damnation
damnatory
debenture
decastere
deceitful
deception
deceptive
decistere
decoction
decontrol
decretive
decretory
deduction
deductive
defeatism
defeatist
defeature
defection
defective
deflation
dejection
demitting
demystify
dentation
dentition
departure
depasture
depiction
depictive
depletion
depletive
dermatoid
desertion
despotism
destitute
desuetude
desultory
detection
detective
detention
detrition
devastate
deviation
diametral
diametric
dichotomy
dicrotism
dictation
didactics
dietetics
dietitian
digastric
digestion
digestive
dignitary
dimwitted
dipeptide
direction
directive
directory
directrix
disentail
disentomb
disesteem
disputant
diverting
dogmatics
dogmatise
dogmatism
dogmatist
dormition
dormitory
doughtily
downstage
dramatics
dramatise
dramatist
dripstone
drugstore
drumstick
dulcitude
dysentery
eccentric
education
educative
effective
effectual
effortful
eglantine
elevation
elocution
emanation
emanative
embattled
embrittle
Emmenthal
emulation
emulative
emunctory
endosteal
endosteum
englutted
enrapture
entertain
epilation
eremitism
eruditely
erudition
escortage
essential
eurhythmy
eutectoid
evocation
evocative
evocatory
evolution
evolutive
excentric
exceptant
excepting
exception
exceptive
excretion
excretive
excretory
executant
execution
executive
executory
executrix
exegetist
exemption
expectant
expecting
expertise
expiation
expiatory
expletive
expletory
exsertile
exsertion

extortion
extortive
exudation
exudative
factitive
faggoting
fairytale
faldstool
farestage
farmstead
fatwitted
feedstock
feedstuff
fenestrae
fenestral
ferrotype
feudatory
filiation
filmstrip
fioritura
fioriture
firestone
flagstaff
flagstick
flagstone
flashtube
flightily
floodtide
flotation
flowstone
foliation
foodstuff
footstalk
footstall
footstool
forestage
forestall
forgather
forgetful
forgotten
formation
formative
formatted
forsythia
fortitude
freestone
freestyle
fricative
frigatoon
frightful
fruittree
furcation
furniture
gadgeteer
galactose
galantine
gallstone
garniture
garreteer
garrotter
gasfitter
gazetteer
gemmation
geobotany
geometric
geometrid
geriatric
gestation
gestatory
gigantism
gladstone
godfather
godmother
gradation
gradatory
granitoid
gratitude
gravitate
gritstone
grubstake
guncotton
gustation
gustative
gustatory
guttation
haematite
haematoid
haematoma
hailstone
hailstorm
hairstyle
halfstaff
hallstand
Hallstatt
handstand
harmattan
harmotome
haughtily
headstall
headstock
headstone
heliotype
Helvetian
hemistich
hermitage
herpetoid
hexastich
hexastyle
hieratica
hirsutism
hoarstone
holystone
homestead
honkytonk
hornstone
horsetail
hortation
hortative
hortatory
huckstery
humectant
hydration
hypnotise
hypnotism
hypnotist
hypostyle
illgotten
imitation
imitative
immixture
impaction
impartial
impastoed
impletion
important
importune
impostume
imposture
inanition
incaution
incentive
inception
inceptive
indention
indenture
indiction
induction
inductive
infantile
infantine
infection
infective
infertile
inflation
ingestion
ingestive
injection
injustice
insectary
insectile
insertion
insetting
insistent
institute
intention
intestacy
intestate
intestine
intuition
intuitive
inunction
invective
invention
inventive
inventory
invertase
ironstone
irruption
irruptive
isobathic
isolation
isolative
isometric
isooctane
iteration
iterative
jackstraw
jactation
jesuitise
jesuitism
jetsetter
jockstrap
josssstick
Judastree
junketing
karyotype
kerbstone
kibbutzim
kickstart
knightage
lacertian
lacertine
lactation
lallation
lassitude
laudation
laudative
laudatory
leafstalk
leucotome
leucotomy
Levantine
leviathan
libertine
libration
libratory
librettos
lifestyle
limestone
lineation
liquation
lithotomy
livestock
loadstone
lobectomy
lodestone
logistics
longitude
lovestory
lucrative
lunchtime
macintosh
maelstrom
magistery
magistral
magnetics
magnetise
magnetism
magnetist
magnetite
magnetron
magnitude
mahlstick
mandatary
mandatory
maneating
manhattan
marestail
marketday
marketing
marlstone
maulstick
mediately
mediation
mediatise
mediative
mediatory
mediatrix
mementoes
mentation
mesentery
mezzotint
microtome
microtomy
microtone
migration
migratory
milestone
millstone
miniature
misesteem
momentary
momentous
monastery
monostich
monostyle
moonstone
mousetrap
multitude
musketeer
Nahuatlan
narcotine
narcotise
narcotism
narration
narrative
narratory
naughtily
necrotise
negritude
nemertean
nemertine
neolithic
nepenthes
nervation
nervature
neuration
newsstand
nictation
nictitate
nighttime
nigritude
nitratine
nitration
nonentity
normative
nowhither
nutrition
nutritive
objectify
objection
objective
obstetric
obtention
obviation
occultism
occultist
octastyle
octostyle
offertory
olfaction
olfactive
olfactory
onsetting
operation
operative
opportune
orientate
outfitter
outputted
outwitted
overstate
oversteer
overstock
overstuff
ovulation
ovulatory
oxidation
Pakistani
palletise
palmation
palmitate
palpation
palpitant
palpitate
palustral
paperthin
parentage
partition
partitive
peacetime
pegmatite
pelletise
pellitory
penultima
perdition
peristome
peristyle
permitted
permitter
permutate
perpetual
pettitoes
phenotype
philately
phonation
phonatory
phonetics
phonetise
phonetism
phonetist
phototype
phytotomy
phytotron
picketing
pikestaff
pinnately
pipestone
piscatory
pituitary
placation
placatory
plaintiff
plaintive
planation
planetary
planetoid
platitude
plenitude
plicately
plication
plicature
pocketful
pollutant
pollution
polyptych
popliteal
portative
potentate
potential
precative
precatory
predation
predative
predatory
prefatory
prelatess
prelatise
prelature
premature
premotion
prenotion
prepotent
priestess
primatial
primitive
privateer
privately
privation
privative
probation
probative
probatory
profiteer
prolately
prolation
prolative
promotion
promotive
promptbox
pronation
prototype
pulpiteer
pulpstone
pulsatile
pulsation
pulsatory
puppeteer
purgation
purgative
purgatory
quixotism
quotation
racketeer
raconteur
radiately
radiation
radiative
rainstorm
raspatory
rebaptise
rebutting
recapture
reception
receptive
rectitude
redaction
redletter
reductant
reduction
reductive
refection
refectory
refitting
reflation
registrar
regretful
regretted
reinstate
rejection
reluctant
reluctate
remittent
remitting
remontant
rendition
repentant
repertory
repletion
reportage
repotting
resection
resentful
resetting
resistant
resistive
resitting
restitute
resultant
resultful
retention
retentive
retortion
revetting
revictual
revolting
rewritten
ridgetile
roadstead
rocketeer
rootstock
roseately
rowantree
ruination
russeting
sabbatise
sabbatism
sagittate
saltation
saltatory
salvation
sandstone
sandstorm
Sarmation
satiation
schistose
schistous
schnitzel
sciential
scientism
scientist
scripture
sculpture
sealetter
seanettle
secretage
secretary
secretion
secretive
secretory
sedentary
seduction
seductive
selection
selective
selectman
semanteme
semantics
semestral
semiotics
sensation
sensitise
sensitive
septation
sepulture
seriately
serration
servitude
seventeen
seventhly
seventies
shadetree
shamateur

sheeptick
shirttail
shortterm
siccative
signatory
signature
siltation
siltstone
simpatico
sinistral
sinuately
sinuation
situation
slabstone
slapstick
slightish
smalltime
smoketree
snowstorm
soapstone
solfatara
solvation
sonneteer
sonnetise
sortition
sovietise
sovietism
spacetime
spiritism
spiritist
spiritoso
spiritous
spiritual
spirituel
splintery
splitting
spluttery
sprigtail
squatting
starstone
statutory
stenotype
stenotypy
stilettos
stinktrap
stipitate
streetcar
striation
striature
stricture
strontium
structure
strutting
subaltern
subastral
sublation
sublethal
submitted
succotash
sulcation
summation
summative
sunbather
sweettalk
swordtail
symmetric
syncytial
syncytium
synectics
synoptist
tablature
tabletalk
tactitian
talkathon
talkative
tarantara
tarantass
tarantism
tarantula
teakettle
tentation
tentative
termitary
ternately
territory
tessitura
testation
testatrix
thinktank
thirstily
thorntree
thriftily
throatily
throttler
thumbtack
Thyestean
thyratron
tilestone
titration
toadstone
toadstool
tombstone
tomentose
tomentous
toreutics
touchtype
tradition
trematode
tributary
trilithon
trimetric
tuliptree
tungstate
turnstile
turnstone
turpitude
twelfthly
twicetold
ululation
uncertain
unclothed
uncouthly
undertake
undertint
undertone
undertook
unearthly
unfitting
unknitted
unscathed
unsettled
unspotted
unweeting
unwitting
unwritten
uplifting
upsetting
valentine
vallation
valuation
variation
vasectomy
vastitude
Vedantist
veinstone
velveteen
vendition
vernation
versatile
vestiture
vibratile
vibration
vibrative
vibratory
videotape
vignetter
violation
violative
vitiation
voluntary
volunteer
wapentake
washstand
weightily
weighting
whetstone
whinstone
whipstock
winestone
withstand
withstood
yardstick
zincotype
acellular
ambiguity
ambiguous
amorously
anacruses
anacrusis
antiquary
antiquate
antiquity
anxiously
applauder
aqueously
archducal
archduchy
arduously
articular
assiduity
assiduous
attenuate
auricular
avuncular
babirussa
balefully
banefully
bashfully
bellpunch
bethought
biliously
bilirubin
binocular
blastulae
blastular
bodyguard
bratwurst
brusquely
bulbously
caciquism
calicular
callously
canesugar
canicular
capitular
capitulum
carefully
cartouche
cassoulet
chibouque
chisquare
clinquant
coadjutor
coinsurer
concourse
confluent
congruent
congruity
congruous
copiously
creatural
curiously
cuticular
deciduate
deciduous
devaluate
deviously
direfully
discourse
dolefully
dubiously
duralumin
duteously
dutifully
easefully
electuary
emulously
enamoured
energumen
enviously
eventuate
extenuate
fatefully
fatuously
fearfully
fireguard
flocculus
floscular
fluctuant
fluctuate
fluecured
folkmusic
forejudge
fraenulum
fretfully
fructuate
fructuous
funicular
funiculus
furiously
gainfully
gastrulae
gibbously
glandular
gleefully
grossular
habituate
halieutic
handcuffs
harbourer
harmfully
hatefully
heedfully
heinously
helpfully
hideously
hopefully
hugeously
hurtfully
hydraulic
ichneumon
impetuous
impiously
inaugural
indraught
infatuate
ingenuity
ingenuous
innocuity
innocuous
insinuate
insoluble
insolubly
involucre
involuted
inwrought
irregular
jealously
landaulet
langouste
lifeguard
limejuice
loafsugar
lustfully
manipular
manoeuvre
marihuana
marijuana
methought
mindfully
molecular
monocular
moonquake
navicular
needfully
nervously
nocuously
noxiously
obliquely
obliquity
obsequent
obsequial
obsequies
obviously
odorously
ominously
onerously
onslaught
opercular
operculum
opusculum
orangutan
orbicular
ossicular
painfully
parlously
peasouper
pedicular
pipsqueak
piteously
pitifully
playfully
pompously
potpourri
pronounce
punctuate
quadruman
quadruped
quadruple
quadruply
quintuple
radicular
raucously
rearguard
rechauffe
reimburse
reliquary
reliquiae
residuary
resoluble
restfully
rethought
reticular
reticulum
retinulae
retinular
retrousse
ridiculer
riotously
ruinously
ruthfully
safeguard
sanctuary
schnauzer
scorbutic
seasquirt
semilunar
seriously
setsquare
shinguard
sideburns
siliquose
sinuously
skilfully
snowguard
songfully
soulfully
spherular
strenuous
subcaudal
subocular
succourer
sulphuret
sulphuric
sumptuary
sumptuous
sunlounge
sunspurge
tactfully
tambourin
tarpaulin
tearfully
tediously
tenaculum
tenuously
thereunto
thereupon
thesaurus
thingummy
timeously
transumpt
treasurer
trysquare
tunefully
unberufen
unclouded
unnatural
unpopular
unthought
unwrought
utricular
vacuously
variously
vehicular
vesicular
viciously
viscounty
viscously
vocabular
wakefully
waveguide
whereunto
whereupon
wishfully
wistfully
zealously
zestfully
abusively
acclivity
aestivate
aggravate
archivist
archivolt
boulevard
captivate
captivity
carnivore
charivari
concavely
concavity
connivent
convivial
costively
cultivate
cursively
czarevich
declivity
declivous
depravity
discovert
discovery
disfavour
effluvial
effluvium
elusively
emotively
emotivity
endeavour
engraving
evasively
exservice
extravert
extrovert
festively
festivity
forgiving
furtively
gallivant
grapevine
Harrovian
herbivore
impluvium
improvise
incurvate
innervate
inservice
insolvent
intervein
intervene
interview
introvert
keelivine
khedivial
lawgiving
leftovers
longevity
longevous
massively
millivolt
misadvise
misgiving
misgovern
muscovado
muscovite
observant
outgiving
passivate
passively
passivity
Pavlovian
pensively
persevere
reconvene
reconvert
reservist
reservoir
resolvent
restively
retrovert
skydiving
slivovitz
suasively
subdivide
supervene
supervise
Theravada
tittivate
transvest
triumviri
tsarevich
undervest
unitively
uvarovite
Vitruvian
volauvent
afterword
angleworm
arrowwood
arrowworm
backsword
bailiwick
beachwear
birthwort

blackwash
bloodworm
bloodwort
boardwalk
boatswain
borrowing
brainwash
brainwave
briarwood
brickwork
bridewell
brierwood
broadways
broadwise
brushwood
brushwork
cassowary
catchword
caterwaul
cedarwood
chickweed
chinaware
clockwise
clockwork
coachwork
coastward
coastwise
copsewood
crossways
crosswind
crosswise
crossword
delftware
drawnwork
driftweed
driftwood
earthward
earthwork
earthworm
fancywork
fellowman
fieldwork
following
forthwith
framework
frontward
frontways
frontwise
frostwork
galliwasp
gallowses
ghostword
glassware
glasswork
glasswort
gobetween
greenweed
greenwood
grillwork
guesswork
gunpowder
Halloween
Hallowmas
handiwork
handywork
harrowing
heartwood
Hollywood
horsewhip
housewife
housework
inbetween
inflowing
ingrowing
interwind
interwove
jewelweed
kittiwake
lancewood
landowner
leastways
leastwise
lightwood
liverwort
lousewort
marrowfat
marshwort
matchwood
metalwork
microwave
moneywort
mouthwash
mucksweat
navelwort
newlyweds
nightwork
northward
northwest
otherwise
paintwork
paperwork
patchwork
paulownia
pearlwort
pennywort
piecework
pokerwork
presswork
quillwort
rightward
riverweed
rosinweed
roundworm
sallowish
sapanwood
satinwood
scarfwise
screwworm
sedgewren
selfaware
semisweet
sheepwalk
sheepwash
shellwork
shipowner
shoreward
shoreweed
shortwave
sideswipe
slantways
slantwise
slinkweed
slopewise
smartweed
snakeweed
snakewood
sorrowful
soundwave
southward
southwest
spadework
spearwort
speedwell
spokewise
stairwell
statewide
steelwork
sternward
stickwork
stinkweed
stinkwood
stockwhip
stonewall
stoneware
stonework
stonewort
strapwork
strapwort
strawworm
sundowner
swearword
tableware
tallowish
therewith
tigerwood
tightwire
toothwort
touchwood
tulipwood
uncrowned
underwear
underwent
underwing
underwood
unknowing
watchword
waterweed
waterworn
wedgewise
wheelwork
wherewith
whirlwind
whitewash
whitewing
whitewood
wideawake
widthways
widthwise
willowish
windowbox
windswept
worldwide
worrywart
woundwort
yellowdog
yellowish
zebrawood
connexion
convexity
deflexion
effluxion
hydroxide
inflexion
overexert
prefixion
prolixity
reflexion
reflexive
thyroxine
unisexual
aldehydic
anaptyxis
apocrypha
apophyses
apophysis
autocycle
autolysis
autolytic
barleymow
biorhythm
brachyura
brickyard
cacodylic
catalyser
catalyses
catalysis
catalytic
chatoyant
cherrypie
chlamydes
clepsydra
clergyman
clergymen
colocynth
copolymer
courtyard
cytolysis
diachylom
diachylum
diaphysis
eightyish
endolymph
epiphyses
epiphysis
epiphytal
epiphytic
eucalypti
eucaryote
familyman
genotypic
ginglymus
graveyard
Grundyism
hemicycle
homonymic
ichthyoid
kilocycle
lachrymal
lifecycle
lightyear
liveryman
megacycle
metonymic
Mondayish
monkeyish
monkeyism
monkeynut
monotypic
overlying
panegyric
pantryman
paralysis
paralytic
paranymph
parleyvoo
pericycle
perilymph
polytypic
porphyria
presbyope
presbyter
prettyish
prettyism
pyrolysis
pyrolytic
pyroxylin
quarryman
safetypin
salicylic
scallywag
scrapyard
sentrybox
shantyman
songcycle
stackyard
steelyard
stockyard
subphylum
surveying
symphysis
synonymic
taxpaying
toponymal
toponymic
trachytic
triptyque
twentyone
vestryman
wherryman
woodnymph
zoophytic
anthozoan
bombazine
Caenozoic
Cainozoic
embezzler
haphazard
heliozoan
heliozoic
hydrazine
hydrozoan
hydrozoon
interzone
organzine
proenzyme
protozoal
protozoan
protozoic
protozoon
quartzite
quartzose
shemozzle
Spinozism
Spinozist
trapezial
trapezium
trapezoid

---

abominate
aboutface
acceptant
accessary
acclimate
accompany
accordant
acetylate
aciculate
acidulate
acuminate
adenomata
adsorbate
adumbrate
advantage
adversary
aerograph
aeroplane
aerospace
aestivate
affiliate
affirmant
affricate
aforesaid
Afrikaans
aftercare
aftermath
aggravate
aggregate
algebraic
allegiant
alleviate
allograph
alloplasm
alpargata
altercate
alternant
alternate
aluminate
alveolate
ambuscade
ampersand
analysand
anchorage
ancillary
angiomata
annuitant
anovulant
antennary
antiquary
antiquate
antitrade
apiculate
appellant
appellate
appendage
appendant
appertain
applejack
applicant
approbate
aquaplane
arbitrage
arbitrary
arbitrate
armillary
arrearage
arrestant
ascendant
ascertain
Ashkenazi
aspartate
assailant
assistant
associate
astrolabe
astronaut
attendant
attenuate
auspicate
autoclave
autocracy
autograft
autograph
auxiliary
bacillary
backboard
backslang
backspace
backstage
backtrack
balaclava
bandstand
barmbrack
barograph
barricade
barricado
bastinade
bastinado
battleaxe
beanfeast
beanstalk
beechmast
bellglass
bellyband
benignant
bergamask
biconcave
bifoliate
bifurcate
bilabiate
billboard
bipinnate
birchbark
birdbrain
birthmark
birthrate
bivariant
bivariate
blackball
blackdamp
blackface
blackgame
blackjack
blackmail
blackwash
bloodbath
bluebeard
blueblack
bluegrass
boardwalk
boatswain
boattrain
bodyguard
boliviano
bombilate
bombinate
bondslave
bookplate
bookstall
bookstand
boomerang
boomslang
bootblack
boulevard
brachiate
bracteate
braincase
brainwash
brainwave
breakfast
brecciate
brickyard
bridecake
briefcase
brilliant
broadcast
broadtail
broadways
brokerage
broomrape
buckboard
budgetary
bushcraft
bushwhack
buttygang
cablelaid
cailleach
calcarate
calculate
calibrate
caliphate
camelback
camelhair
campchair
campcraft
candidacy
candidate
canebrake
canetrash
cannonade
cannulate
capillary
capsulate
captivate
carbamate
carbonado
carbonate
cardboard
cardsharp
carronade
cartilage
cartulary
cassowary
castigate
cataclasm
cataplasm
caterwaul
cavalcade
celebrant
celebrate
cellarage
centenary
cerebrate
cerograph
chaingang
chainmail
chairlady
charabanc
charivari
Charolais
chatelain
chatoyant
cheapjack
checkmate

chieftain
chilblain
chinaware
chipboard
chipolata
chisquare
chocolate
chokedamp
choleraic
circinate
circulate
citystate
clapboard
classmate
clathrate
clientage
cliffhang
clinquant
clipboard
cloudland
coadunate
coagulant
coagulate
coarctate
coastward
cochleate
cockroach
coelomata
coelomate
coenosarc
cognisant
colligate
collimate
collocate
colonnade
columbary
combatant
combinate
commonage
communard
commutate
compliant
confidant
conjugate
consonant
constrain
consulage
consulate
contumacy
cooperage
cooperant
cooperate
copesmate
cormorant
cornbrash
corncrake
cornstalk
corollary
corporate
corposant
correlate
corrugate
corticate
coruscant
coruscate
coryphaei
cosmonaut
cosmorama
courtcard
courtyard
covariant
cowlstaff
crankcase
crashland
crenulate
crepitant
crepitate
criminate
croissant
crookback
crossfade
crosstalk
crossways
croustade
cucullate
culminant
culminate
cultivate
curettage
curtilage
cuspidate
customary
cuttysark
cyclamate
cyclorama
cymophane
cystocarp
cytoplasm
dairymaid
dancehall
dartboard
dashboard
deathmask
decennary
deciduate
declarant
declinate
decollate
decussate
defalcate
defendant
defoliant
defoliate
dehydrate
deinosaur
delftware
delineate
demandant
demarcate
democracy
demurrage
denigrate
denitrate
deodorant
dependant
deprecate
depredate
desecrate
desiccant
desiccate
designate
desperado
desperate
deuterate
devaluate
devastate
dharmsala
diaconate
diaphragm
dichogamy
dignitary
dimidiate
diplomacy
diplomate
dirttrack
disembark
disengage
disentail
dislocate
disparage
disparate
displease
disputant
disregard
disrepair
dissipate
dissonant
dithyramb
dixieland
doctorate
doorframe
doorplate
downgrade
downstage
dragomans
drawplate
dreamland
driftsail
dromedary
duckboard
dulcamara
duodenary
duplicate
earthward
ecdysiast
ectoblast
ectoplasm
eidograph
ejaculate
elaborate
electuary
eliminate
elucidate
elutriate
embarrass
embassage
embrocate
emolliate
empennage
encephala
enchilada
encomiast
encompass
encourage
endoblast
endophagy
endoplasm
engarland
entertain
entoblast
entourage
enucleate
enumerate
enunciate
epiphragm
eradicate
ergograph
escortage
esemplasy
espionage
esplanade
espousals
Esquimaux
estoppage
estrapade
evaginate
evaporate
eventuate
everglade
examinant
exanimate
exarchate
exceptant
excoriate
exculpate
executant
exemplary
exfoliate
exonerate
expatiate
expectant
explicate
expurgate
exsiccate
extendant
extenuate
externals
extirpate
extricate
exuberant
exuberate
eyestrain
fabricant
fabricate
factorage
fairyland
fairytale
fanfarade
farestage
fascinate
faveolate
fecundate
festinate
fibromata
fiduciary
fieldfare
fimbriate
finedrawn
firealarm
fireblast
firebrand
firedrake
fireguard
fireplace
firsthand
firstrate
fishplate
fishyback
flagstaff
flambeaus
flambeaux
flarepath
flashback
floodgate
floodmark
flowchart
flowerage
fluctuant
fluctuate
folkweave
foodchain
footboard
footplate
footstalk
footstall
forceland
forebrain
forereach
forestage
forestall
formicary
formicate
formulaic
formulary
formulate
fornicate
fortunate
fosterage
Franglais
freeboard
frogspawn
frontpage
frontward
frontways
fructuate
fruitcake
frustrate
fulgurant
fulgurate
fullscale
fulminant
fulminate
fusillade
fustigate
gabionade
galingale
gallivant
galliwasp
gallonage
gallopade
gangboard
gangplank
gasconade
gatecrash
geobotany
germinate
germplasm
gingerade
gingerale
ginpalace
glassgall
glassware
glomerate
glutamate
grandpapa
granulate
grassland
gratulate
graveyard
gravitate
greenback
greengage
greensand
greybeard
grosgrain
groundage
groundash
grubstake
guardrail
guildhall
gynocracy
gyroplane
habituate
hairgrass
hairspace
halfstaff
halftrack
hallstand
Hallstatt
halothane
handbrake
handcraft
handglass
handshake
handstand
haphazard
hardboard
hatchback
haversack
headboard
headscarf
headstall
heartland
hermitage
hibernate
highchair
highclass
highgrade
hindbrain
hodograph
holograph
homeopath
homograft
homograph
homoplasy
hornwrack
horseback
horsehair
horsetail
hourglass
housecarl
housemaid
housemate
huckaback
humectant
humiliate
hunchback
hurricane
hypallage
hypergamy
hyphenate
hypoblast
ideograph
idiograph
idioplasm
imaginary
imbricate
immediacy
immediate
immigrant
immigrate
impeccant
impetrate
implicate
important
imprecate
impresari
inamorata
inanimate
incarnate
incessant
inculcate
inculpate
incurvate
indignant
inebriant
inebriate
inelegant
infatuate
infirmary
informant
infuriate
infuscate
innervate
inoculate
insatiate
insectary
insensate
insinuate
instigate
integrand
integrant
integrate
intendant
interface
interlace
interlard
interpage
intestacy
intestate
intricacy
intricate
intrigant
invariant
invertase
inviolacy
inviolate
irradiant
irradiate
isinglass
isooctane
itineracy
itinerant
itinerary
itinerate
jackplane
jambalaya
janissary
judiciary
juniorate
kickstart
kingcraft
kittiwake
knightage
knotgrass
kymograph
laciniate
lamellate
lampblack
lampshade
lancejack
lancinate
landgrave
landscape
Langobard
lapstrake
lardycake
leafstalk
leastways
legendary
legionary
legislate
lendlease
libellant
lifeguard
lineolate
lingulate
lionheart
liquidate
lixiviate
loanshark
longchain
longcoats
Longobard
lotusland
lovefeast
lowercase
lubricant
lubricate
lucubrate
luxuriant
luxuriate
lymegrass
machinate
mailplane
mailtrain
mainbrace
makeready
malignant
mamillary
mamillate
mandatary
manducate
manganate
maquisard
marchpane
marchpast
marestail
marginate
marihuana
marijuana
marmalade
marshland
masticate
matronage
maxillary
medullary
medullate
megadeath
meliorate
melismata
melodrama
mendicant
mercenary
mesoblast
metaphase
metaplasm
methylate
metricate
micaslate
microwave
micturate
milkshake

millboard
millenary
misbehave
miscreant
miscreate
mismanage
mobocracy
mollymawk
molybdate
momentary
moneybags
monocracy
monodrama
monograph
monophagy
monoplane
moonquake
moonscape
mossagate
motorcade
mouthpart
mouthwash
mucronate
multilane
multipara
muscovado
musichall
mycophagy
myelomata
myriorama
nameplate
necessary
negotiant
negotiate
neuromata
neuropath
newsflash
newsstand
nicotiana
nictitate
nightfall
nighthawk
nightmare
nigricant
nobiliary
nomocracy
nomograph
northeast
northland
northward
noviciate
novitiate
nullipara
nuncupate
nursemaid
obbligato
obcordate
obfuscate
objurgate
obscurant
obsecrate
observant
obstinacy
obstinate
oesophagi
officiant
officiate
oleograph
openheart
oppugnant
orangeade
orientate
originate
orphanage
oscillate
ossifrage
osteopath
ovenready
overboard
overdraft
overdrawn
overglaze
overgraze
overheard
overleapt
overreach
overreact
overstate
overtrain
overweary
oxygenate
packtrain
paederast
Pakistani
palmitate
palpitant
palpitate
palsgrave
paperback
papillary
papillate
paragraph
parcenary
parentage
parsonage
passivate
pastorale
pastorate
pasturage
patellate
patronage
pectinate
pecuniary
pendulate
peneplain
peneplane
penetrant
penetrate
percolate
perennate
perforate
periclase
periodate
periplast
permutate
personage
personate
petiolate
pharisaic
phosphate
pickaback
piecerate
piggyback
piggybank
pikestaff
pilferage
pinnulate
pitchdark
pituitary
pizzicati
pizzicato
placecard
placename
planetary
platemark
plumulate
poinciana
pointlace
pokerface
pollinate
pollutant
polygraph
polyphagy
polyphase
polyzoary
porcelain
porterage
portolano
portulaca
postulant
postulate
potentate
poundcake
pozzolana
predicant
predicate
predikant
preengage
preordain
pressgang
pressmark
primipara
procreant
procreate
procuracy
promenade
propagate
propylaea
prorogate
prostrate
proximate
pterosaur
Ptolemaic
pullulate
pulmonary
pulmonate
pulpboard
pulserate
pulvinate
punchball
punchcard
punctuate
pupillage
pupillary
pushchair
pustulate
puzzolana
quicksand
quitclaim
rabbinate
racetrack
radiocast
raffinate
rationale
razorback
readymade
reanimate
rearguard
reclinate
recoinage
rectorate
redbreast
reductant
redundant
reeducate
reentrant
regardant
rehydrate
reinstate
reiterate
reliquary
reluctant
reluctate
remediate
remontant
repechage
repellant
repentant
replicate
reportage
reprimand
reprobate
repudiate
repugnant
rerebrace
rerelease
residuary
resistant
resultant
resurface
retaliate
retardant
rhizocarp
righthand
rightward
ringshake
ringsnake
riverbank
rockbrake
rockplant
rocksnake
roofplate
roughcast
rubricate
runcinate
rusticate
sacculate
safeguard
sagittate
sailplane
salangane
saleslady
saltglaze
sanctuary
sandarach
sandblast
sandcrack
sandglass
sarcocarp
sarcomata
Sassenach
saxifrage
scapulary
scholiast
sciagraph
scorecard
scotomata
scrapyard
screwball
scrimmage
scrumhalf
scrummage
seastrand
secondary
secretage
secretary
sedentary
seedpearl
seedplant
segregate
selfaware
selfimage
sensedata
sentenate
septenary
serigraph
serrulate
setsquare
shamefast
sheepwalk
sheepwash
sheldrake
shelfmark
shellback
shellbark
shinguard
shipboard
shipshape
shirttail
shoeblack
shogunate
shoreward
shortcake
shortfall
shorthand
shortwave
showplace
shrinkage
sickleave
sideboard
sidetrack
sigillary
sigillate
signboard
silkgland
simulcast
siphonage
skiagraph
skingraft
slantways
slingback
slipcoach
slowcoach
smokeball
smokejack
snowflake
snowguard
snowplant
snowscape
sociopath
soidisant
soleplate
solfatara
solmisate
soothfast
soundwave
soupplate
southeast
southland
southward
spaceband
spatulate
speakeasy
speculate
speedball
spiculate
spikenard
sporocarp
sporulate
sprigtail
springald
spritsail
stackyard
stagehand
staircase
stalemate
staminate
starboard
stargrass
steadfast
steelyard
stegosaur
sternward
stimulant
stimulate
stinkball
stipitate
stipulate
stockyard
stolonate
stonewall
stoneware
stoolball
stormsail
straphang
strappado
strongarm
stylobate
subjugate
sublimate
sublunary
subrogate
substrata
substrate
subtenant
succinate
succotash
suffocate
sugarcane
sultanate
sumptuary
suppliant
suppurate
supremacy
surfboard
surrogate
susurrant
sweatband
sweepback
sweettalk
sweptback
swordcane
swordtail
sycophant
syllabary
syncopate
syndicate
tableland
tabletalk
tableware
tailboard
taioseach
talismans
tamponade
tantalate
tarantara
tarantass
telegraph
tellurate
telophase
temperate
temporary
tenthrate
terebrant
termagant
terminate
termitary
terramara
terramare
theocracy
theocrasy
theophany
Theravada
thinktank
thirdhand
thirdrate
thornback
throwback
thumbmark
thumbnail
thumbtack
timocracy
titillate
titlepage
tittivate
toastrack
torchrace
touchmark
townscape
tracheary
tracheate
trademark
tradename
trainband
translate
treillage
tremolant
tremulant
trenchant
trepidant
tribunate
tributary
trifocals
trilobate
triturate
troutfarm
trunkcall
trysquare
tungstate
turbinate
Turcomans
Turkomans
twayblade
twicelaid
umbellate
uncertain
underhand
underlaid
underlain
underpaid
underpart
underpass
underrate
undertake
ungallant
unisonant
uppercase
urceolate
vaccinate
vacillant
vacillate
vacuolate
Vaishnava
variegate
variolate
vassalage
ventifact
ventilate
verandaed
verminate
vexillary
vibraharp
vicariate
videotape
villanage
villenage
vindicate
virginals
virgulate
viscerate
visionary
vitellary
vizierate
volteface
voluntary
vouchsafe
vulnerary
waggonage
waistband
waldgrave
wallboard
wallplate
wapentake
washboard
washstand
wasteland
watchcase
waterbath
watercart
waterfall
watergate
watermark
whaleback
wheelbase
whipsnake
whitebait
whitebass
whiteface
Whitehall
whitewash
whizzbang
wholesale
wideawake

widthways
wineglass
wingchair
wiredrawn
wisecrack
withdrawn
withstand
wolfsbane
woodcraft
worrywart
wristband
xenograft
xylograph
zamindary
zapateado
zemindary
abdicable
abradable
accusable
adaptable
adducible
admirable
admirably
adoptable
advisable
advisably
agreeable
agreeably
alienable
allocable
allowable
allowably
alterable
amendable
anaerobic
assayable
assumable
assumably
auditable
available
availably
avertible
avoidable
avoidably
awardable
beslobber
bilirubin
birdtable
blameable
blameably
breakable
bumblebee
butterbur
carpetbag
catchable
claimable
classable
cleavable
climbable
clubbable
cobwebbed
coercible
coercibly
cogitable
confabbed
constable
cornerboy
countable
coverable
covetable
coxcombry
creatable
crossable
crushable
debatable
decidable
deducible
definable
definably
deludable
deposable
derivable
describer
desirable
desirably
devisable
dilatable
dirigible
dismember
dissemble
disturbed
disturber
dividable
divisible
doodlebug
doubtable
Doukhobor
drinkable
dubitable
emendable
endurable
endurably
enjoyable
enjoyably
enterable
equitable
equitably
escapable
estimable
euphorbia
evincible
evolvable
exactable
excisable
excitable
excusable
excusably
execrable
execrably
fatigable
filterbed
filtrable
flammable
floatable
flowerbed
forgeable
frangible
freezable
gaugeable
generable
getatable
gogglebox
grantable
graspable
habitable
habitably
handlebar
harquebus
heritable
hobnobbed
hobnobber
humblebee
ignitable
ignitible
ignorable
illegible
illegibly
imageable
immovable
immovably
immutable
immutably
imputable
inaudible
inaudibly
incapable
incapably
incunable
incurable
incurably
indelible
indelibly
inducible
ineffable
ineffably
inequable
inerrable
inferable
infusible
inscriber
insoluble
insolubly
insurable
invisible
invisibly
ionisable
irascible
irascibly
irrigable
irritable
irritably
isallobar
jitterbug
kneadable
lacerable
laughable
laughably
learnable
letterbox
lifetable
limitable
litigable
litterbin
litterbug
locatable
lyophobic
malleable
medicable
memorable
memorably
miserable
miserably
mitigable
motorable
mouldable
mountable
navigable
nominable
nonviable
numerable
oddjobber
omissible
opposable
outnumber
oysterbed
palatable
palatably
pasodoble
peaceable
peaceably
pepperbox
permeable
pillarbox
pivotable
placeable
plantable
plausible
plausibly
pleadable
ploughboy
pouncebox
pregnable
printable
promptbox
proveably
pursuable
quodlibet
reachable
rebukable
reducible
referable
refusable
refutable
removable
renewable
reparable
repayable
reputable
reputably
resalable
resoluble
resumable
revisable
revivable
revocable
rightable
rosenoble
rotatable
saddlebag
saddlebow
sandtable
saturable
schoolbag
schoolboy
scrutable
securable
semblable
semblably
sentrybox
separable
separably
September
severable
shakeable
shapeable
shieldbug
shockable
shootable
sidetable
signalbox
speakable
spendable
spongebag
springbok
stableboy
stackable
stainable
strongbox
subduable
superable
swimmable
teachable
teachably
temptable
thinkable
timetable
tinderbox
tittlebat
tolerable
tolerably
touchable
traceable
traceably
tractable
tractably
trainable
treatable
tuckerbag
tumblebug
turntable
twistable
uneatable
unifiable
unnamable
unplumbed
unsayable
untenable
utterable
vaporable
vegetable
vegetably
venerable
venerably
veritable
veritably
visitable
wakerobin
watchable
weighable
wieldable
windowbox
worktable
zoophobia
acetylcoA
adminicle
affianced
agnatical
ambulacra
aminoacid
androecia
angelical
announcer
anthracic
apothecia
archducal
archduchy
Armorican
arsenical
artificer
ascetical
autocycle
avalanche
baldfaced
barefaced
basilican
battlecry
bellyache
beneficed
boldfaced
boondocks
botanical
bretasche
buttercup
canonical
capriccio
carbuncle
cartouche
chachacha
chronical
chronicle
classical
coffeecup
colchicum
convincer
corpuscle
crepuscle
crustacea
cryptical
dandiacal
deistical
denouncer
diningcar
dipcircle
discalced
disgracer
dishfaced
dominical
Dominican
dropsical
druidical
dynamical
eirenicon
elegiacal
empirical
entelechy
equivocal
eristical
erratical
etherical
ethnarchy
fairfaced
fanatical
fatidical
foragecap
franticly
Gaeltacht
galenical
genetical
geomancer
gerfalcon
graphical
graywacke
greywacke
guilloche
gyrfalcon
hagiarchy
heartache
hemicycle
heptarchy
heretical
hierarchy
hypericum
identical
idiotical
illogical
involucre
jaundiced
juridical
kilocycle
Levitical
lifecycle
logomachy
longfaced
lovingcup
lumbrical
lumbricus
megacycle
molluscan
monodical
moustache
nuisancer
numerical
obconical
oligarchy
parfleche
pasticcio
pentarchy
pericycle
piratical
polemical
political
practical
precancel
proboscis
prosaical
Provencal
psychical
quantical
quebracho
quizzical
recherche
rectrices
renouncer
resources
sandyacht
satanical
satirical
sceptical
sciamachy
selffaced
simplices
simulacra
simulacre
siphuncle
skeesicks
skiamachy
songcycle
soritical
spectacle
spellican
spherical
streetcar
subdeacon
surpliced
synodical
tapdancer
taraxacum
technical
tectrices
tetrarchy
theomachy
toothache
tortrices
tortricid
umbilical
umbilicus
unethical
unmusical
vademecum
ventricle
veridical
videlicet
wehrmacht
wheyfaced
whimsical
xparticle
absconder
adenoidal
advisedly
airminded
aldehydic
allegedly
allowedly
Amerindic
amyloidal
annelidan
anticodon
antinodal
antipodal
antipodes
aperiodic
applauder
araneidal
araneidan
ashamedly
assuredly
astraddle
attainder
avizandum
awkwardly
backpedal
bandwidth
bartender
bastardly
beadledom
bedridden
belatedly
bemusedly
bigheaded
blessedly
blockader
bombardon
bowwindow
boxgirder
brigandry
bumbledon
bystander
cartridge
Cassandra
ceratodus
chickadee
chlamydes
clepsydra

cofferdam
colloidal
comitadji
commander
commandos
commendam
compendia
comprador
concordat
contender
coriander
cotyledon
crabbedly
crinoidal
crookedly
cuckoldry
cullender
cycloidal
dastardly
decapodal
decapodan
decidedly
descended
devotedly
disbudded
disburden
discarder
discoidal
discredit
dissuader
dittander
Eastender
embroider
Englander
ethmoidal
excitedly
expounder
eyeshadow
fatheaded
forbidden
foreboder
forecaddy
forejudge
forwander
forwarder
forwardly
freerider
freezedry
frowardly
gallmidge
gasholder
genocidal
germander
glyptodon
goliardic
goosander
grandaddy
guardedly
gunpowder
haggardly
hagridden
hamhanded
hendiadys
hereunder
heterodox
homicidal
hotheaded
hundredth
hurriedly
husbandly
husbandry
hydriodic
hypnoidal
Icelander
Icelandic
iguanodon
impleader
impliedly
impounder

infielder
innholder
innuendos
insipidly
invalidly
ironsides
ischiadic
junkerdom
kaiserdom
kentledge
knifeedge
knowledge
laggardly
languidly
Laplander
latterday
learnedly
leewardly
limitedly
lipreader
logaoedic
Lombardic
lowlander
lowloader
lowminded
lunitidal
manhandle
mansarded
manysided
marketday
martyrdom
masterdom
meropidan
misguided
mishandle
negroidal
niggardly
octahedra
octopodes
offhanded
ommatidia
onehanded
openended
opodeldoc
outlander
outridden
outwardly
overladen
panhandle
paramedic
parapodia
partridge
penholder
persuader
philander
pigheaded
plasmodia
pointedly
polyandry
polyhedra
prebendal
pretender
primordia
princedom
properdin
provender
psalmodic
puffadder
pyramidal
pyramidic
pyramidon
Quakerdom
quarenden
quarender
rascaldom
razoredge
redhanded
redheaded
regicidal

rejoinder
remainder
reputedly
responder
retrodden
rhapsodic
Rhineodon
rhizoidal
Samoyedic
sapheaded
savagedom
seagirdle
Sephardic
Sephardim
serenader
sheikhdom
sigmoidal
skedaddle
slabsided
softpedal
spasmodic
squalidly
squiredom
steroidal
stiltedly
studiedly
subcaudal
subduedly
succeeder
surrender
suspender
tahsildar
thermidor
thralldom
threnodic
tournedos
trumpedup
twohanded
typhoidal
Uitlander
unblinded
unbounded
unbraided
unclouded
undecided
undivided
unfounded
unguarded
unsoundly
untrodden
upbraider
viricidal
waywardly
Wednesday
worriedly
Yankeedom
yellowdog
yesterday
abasement
abashment
abatement
abhorrent
absorbent
abstinent
abusively
acetylene
Acheulean
acidulent
adeptness
adipocere
adornment
adsorbent
adultness
adversely
advertent
agistment
agreement
airstream
albescent

alertness
alignment
alinement
aliveness
allotment
aloneness
aloofness
amassment
amazement
amendment
amoebaean
ampleness
amusement
anchoress
angriness
annectent
annulment
apartheid
apartment
apartness
apishness
apprehend
arbitress
archenemy
archfiend
architect
arcuately
arrowhead
artillery
ascendent
askewness
assurgent
Athenaeum
Atlantean
atonement
austerely
authoress
averagely
awareness
awesomely
awfulness
bagginess
baksheesh
balladeer
balminess
bandoleer
bandolero
banjulele
battiness
bawdiness
beachhead
beachwear
beardless
bedspread
beechfern
beefiness
beefsteak
bejabbers
belvedere
besetment
bilgekeel
biosphere
birdsnest
bizarrely
Blackfeet
blackhead
blacklead
blackness
blameless
blandness
blankness
blaspheme
blasphemy
blastment
bleachery
bleakness
blindness
blockhead
bloodless

bluffness
bluntness
blushless
bombshell
bonniness
bookshelf
bordereau
boskiness
bossiness
boundless
boyfriend
brainless
brakeless
brandreth
brashness
brassiere
breakneck
bridewell
briefless
briefness
briskness
brittlely
broadleaf
broadness
brownness
brusquely
buccaneer
buckwheat
bulginess
bulkiness
bullybeef
bumpiness
burliness
bushiness
butadiene
buxomness
caballero
caerulean
caesarean
cageyness
calabrese
calcaneal
calcaneum
callipers
Camembert
canescent
canniness
cannoneer
cantilena
Cantonese
Caribbean
carrageen
cartwheel
cassareep
cassimere
castanets
cataplexy
catchment
cattiness
causeless
ceaseless
centipede
chaingear
chainless
chameleon
champleve
chandlery
chantress
chariness
charmless
chauffeur
cheapness
checkrein
cheerless
chelicera
chicanery
chickweed
childless
chillness

Cingalese
cirripede
clamshell
classless
cleanness
clearness
clientele
closeness
cloudless
coalfield
coccygeal
cochineal
cockiness
cocoonery
cognately
coheiress
collinear
colosseum
Comintern
competent
component
comradely
comradery
concavely
concisely
condiment
confident
confiteor
confluent
congruent
connately
connivent
continent
contumely
cornfield
cornopean
corporeal
corpulent
cosmogeny
costively
cotangent
countless
crapulent
crassness
craziness
creatress
crestless
crispness
crookneck
crossbeam
crosshead
crossness
crotchety
crownless
crowsnest
crudeness
cruellest
curliness
cursively
curstness
cyclopean
Cytherean
Daedalean
damascene
damnedest
Damoclean
dauntless
deaconess
deathless
debarment
decastere
decistere
decollete
decongest
decrement
decumbent
deferment
deficient
dehiscent

demulcent
denseness
dependent
depthless
detergent
determent
deterrent
detriment
devilment
different
diffident
diffusely
dinginess
dinothere
dirtiness
disaffect
disappear
discovert
discovery
disesteem
disforest
dishonest
disinfect
disinfest
disorient
dissident
divergent
diversely
dizziness
dopefiend
dottiness
doubtless
dowdiness
dowerless
downfield
dragoness
drawsheet
dreamless
driftweed
drollness
dropscene
dumpiness
dungarees
duskiness
dustiness
dustsheet
dysentery
dyspnoeic
eagerness
earliness
ebullient
ecosphere
efficient
effulgent
eightieth
ejectment
electress
elopement
elsewhere
elusively
embayment
embedment
embraceor
embracery
emollient
emolument
emotively
emphysema
emptiness
enactment
endosperm
endosteal
endosteum
endowment
enjoyment
enrolment
enthymeme
entremets
epicurean

equipment
erectness
errorless
eruditely
euclidean
evasively
eventless
evergreen
exactment
exactness
exanthema
excellent
excipient
excrement
excurrent
exilement
exosphere
expedient
expellent
extolment
extravert
extremely
extrovert
faddiness
faintness
faithless
fallalery
falseness
farmstead
fattiness
faultless
fenceless
fenugreek
feoffment
fertilely
festively
fetidness
fibreless
fieriness
filigreed
filminess
firebreak
firecrest
firmament
fishiness
fissipede
fixedness
flakiness
flameless
flatulent
fleckless
fleetness
fleshless
fleshment
floridean
flowsheet
flushness
fogginess
forcefeed
forceless
forcemeat
forespeak
foundress
fourwheel
frailness
frankness
freewheel
freshness
frontless
fruitless
fullcream
fulldress
fulsomely
fundament
funkiness
funniness
furtively
fussiness
fustiness
fuzziness
gadgeteer
gaolbreak
garreteer
gaspereau
gastraeum
gaudiness
gauntness
gauziness
gawkiness
gazetteer
gearwheel
genuflect
genuinely
geosphere
germanely
giddiness
glueyness
gobetween
godliness
godparent
goldcrest
goldeneye
goldfield
gooseherd
gooseneck
gossamery
governess
graceless
grandness
graveless
graveness
greatness
Greekless
greenbelt
greenness
greenweed
griefless
griminess
grossness
gruffness
guileless
guiltless
gumminess
gustiness
gutsiness
gynaeceum
habergeon
hairiness
hairpiece
halfbreed
halfshell
Halloween
handiness
handpress
handwheel
happiness
hardiment
hardiness
hardshell
harshness
hastiness
hatchment
headdress
headiness
headpiece
heartbeat
heartfelt
heartless
heaviness
Hebridean
heelpiece
heftiness
Heraclean
Herculean
highspeed
histogeny
hoariness
homestead
horniness
horsebean
horseless
horsiness
hostilely
housekeep
houseleek
houseless
huckstery
huffiness
humanness
huskiness
hydrocele
idealless
ignescent
imageless
immensely
impatiens
impatient
impendent
imperfect
implement
imprudent
inaptness
inbetween
incipient
inclement
incorrect
increment
incumbent
incurrent
indulgent
inebriety
ineptness
inertness
inpatient
insatiety
insincere
insistent
insolvent
insurgent
intellect
intensely
intercede
intercept
interfere
interject
interleaf
interment
intersect
intervein
intervene
introject
introvert
inurement
inverness
inversely
irksomely
isogamete
issueless
itchiness
jailbreak
janitress
jazziness
jerkiness
jetstream
jewellery
jewelweed
jointress
judgement
juiceless
juiciness
jumpiness
kinkiness
lampshell
landagent
lankiness
Laodicean
lapstreak
largeness
laryngeal
latescent
laundress
lavaliere
leafgreen
leakiness
leaselend
leftovers
legginess
leisurely
levelness
lightless
lightness
lightyear
limitless
lineament
lissomely
litheness
lividness
lodgement
loftiness
looseleaf
looseness
lousiness
loverless
lowerdeck
lowliness
lucidness
luckiness
lumpiness
luridness
lustiness
Maccabean
machinery
magdalene
magistery
mainsheet
malanders
manganese
manginess
Manichean
manliness
manorseat
marmoreal
massiness
massively
matchless
mateyness
mausoleum
mealiness
meatiness
mediately
meningeal
merciless
merriment
merriness
mesentery
messiness
methylene
micromesh
midstream
midwifery
milkiness
millepede
millinery
millipede
millwheel
mincemeat
minefield
mirkiness
mirthless
misbeseem
miscegene
misdemean
misdirect
misesteem
misgovern
mistiness
mixedness
moistness
monastery
monitress
monotreme
moodiness
mucksweat
muddiness
muffineer
mugginess
mundanely
murderess
murkiness
musketeer
muskiness
mustiness
muzziness
Mycenaean
myxoedema
nakedness
naphthene
nastiness
natheless
nattiness
nectarean
neediness
negligent
Negroness
nemertean
nerveless
nerviness
newlyweds
newsagent
newsiness
ninetieth
Nipponese
nobleness
noiseless
noisiness
noisomely
nonlinear
nonpareil
northwest
nosebleed
nosepiece
notedness
notoriety
nutriment
nuttiness
obeseness
obliquely
obscenely
obscurely
obsequent
obversely
occludent
occurrent
odourless
offscreen
offstreet
Oligocene
operosely
orderless
osteoderm
osteogeny
otherness
outspread
overcheck
overdress
overexert
oversleep
overslept
overspend
overspent
oversteer
overtness
overwhelm
pachyderm
palankeen
palmipede
panderess
pantalets
Paraclete
parchment
parrakeet
passively
pastiness
pathogeny
patroness
pedigreed
Pekingese
penfriend
penniless
pensively
perfumery
periphery
perisperm
perkiness
permanent
persevere
pertinent
pestilent
petroleum
pettiness
phagedena
phenomena
philately
Philomela
phoniness
phosphene
photocell
photogene
phthalein
phylogeny
phytogeny
piecemeal
pinchbeck
pinkiness
pinnately
pinnipede
pipedream
pipsqueak
pistoleer
pithiness
placeless
placement
plainness
Pleiocene
plicately
plumpness
plushness
podginess
pointless
polythene
pontoneer
popliteal
poppyhead
portreeve
powerless
precedent
precisely
predigest
prelatess
prepotent
prescient
preselect
president
prestress
prevalent
priceless
prideless
priestess
primeness
privateer
privately
privilege
procuress
profanely
profiteer
profusely
prolately
prominent
proneness
proofread
proponent
propriety
propylene
prosiness
protonema
provident
pubescent
pudginess
puffiness
pulpiness
pulpiteer
pulseless
puppeteer
purposely
purpureal
pursiness
pushiness
Quakeress
quakiness
queenless
queerness
quickness
quiescent
quietness
rabidness
racketeer
raconteur
radiately
raincheck
raininess
randiness
ranginess
rapidness
ravelment
readdress
readiness
recipient
recollect
recommend
reconvene
reconvert
recumbent
recurrent
reediness
refitment
refulgent
regisseur
remitment
remittent
renascent
repayment
repellent
repossess
reprehend
represent
reprocess
resilient
resolvent
resorbent
restively
resurgent
resurrect
retrocede
retroject
retrovert
reversely
revetment
riderless
rightness
rigidness
riskiness
riverhead
riverweed

roadstead
rocketeer
rockiness
roominess
roseately
rosinweed
roughhewn
roughneck
roughness
roundhead
roundness
rousement
routinely
rowdiness
ruddiness
rufescent
rustiness
sacrament
sacrilege
Sadducean
sagegreen
saltiness
sandiness
sappiness
sauceless
sauciness
scalefern
scaleleaf
scaleless
scaliness
scantness
scarehead
scentless
scrapheap
scuncheon
scutcheon
seaminess
secernent
seediness
semanteme
semibreve
semisweet
senescent
senseless
sentiment
seriately
servilely
seventeen
shadeless
shadiness
shakiness
shamateur
shameless
shapeless
sharpness
sheerlegs
sheerness
sheetbend
shellheap
shewbread
shiftless
shininess
shipwreck
shirtless
shockhead
shoreless
shoreweed
shortness
shortterm
shouldest
showiness
showpiece
shrubbery
sidedness
sidewheel
sightless
sightseer
silkiness
silliness
sincerely
sinewless
Sinhalese
sinuately
Sisyphean
skirtless
slackness
slakeless
sleekness
sleepless
slickness
sliminess
slinkweed
slothbear
smallness
smartness
smartweed
smileless
smokeless
smokiness
snakeweed
snakiness
snowfield
snowiness
soapiness
soberness
sodabread
softshell
sogginess
solidness
Solutrean
somewhere
somnolent
sonneteer
sootiness
soppiness
sorceress
sorriness
sortilege
Soudanese
soundless
soundness
souteneur
southwest
spaceless
spareness
sparkless
spearhead
speckless
speedwell
spiciness
spikiness
spineless
spininess
splendent
splintery
spluttery
spodumene
spoonbeak
spoonfeed
spoonmeat
sporogeny
spotcheck
spoutless
spurwheel
squatness
staginess
staidness
stainless
stairhead
stairwell
staleness
stalkless
stallfeed
starkness
starshell
stateless
statement
steelhead
steepness
sternness
stiffness
stillness
stingless
stinkweed
stintless
stitchery
stonedead
stonedeaf
stoneless
stoniness
stoppress
stormbelt
stormless
stoutness
strangely
strapless
strewment
stringent
suasively
subaltern
subgenera
subjacent
sublimely
succulent
sugarbeet
sulkiness
sultaness
sunniness
superheat
supersede
supervene
supremely
surliness
swartness
sweetmeal
sweetmeat
sweetness
swiftness
swineherd
synoecete
syringeal
tableleaf
tacitness
tackiness
tailoress
tailpiece
taintless
tardiness
Tartarean
tasteless
tastiness
tattiness
tawniness
temptress
tenseness
tepidness
ternately
terseness
tervalent
testament
testiness
thankless
thickhead
thickness
thingness
thirtieth
thornless
Thyestean
tigerseye
tightness
timepiece
timesheet
timidness
tinniness
tipsiness
tiredness
titledeed
toothless
toughness
traceless
trackless
traitress
transcend
transient
transvest
treachery
treatment
trickless
trilinear
triteness
trivalent
trochleae
trochlear
trousseau
truceless
truculent
truncheon
trussbeam
trustdeed
trustless
truthless
tubbiness
tumescent
tumidness
turbulent
twentieth
unaptness
unconcern
underfelt
underseal
underseas
undersell
undervest
underwear
underwent
unfitness
unharness
unitively
univalent
unsuccess
usualness
utterless
utterness
vagueness
validness
valueless
valveless
vapidness
velveteen
verbosely
villagery
virescent
visitress
vividness
vocalness
voiceless
volauvent
volunteer
vowelless
wackiness
waistbelt
wallcress
wartcress
washiness
wasteness
waterleaf
waterless
waterweed
weakkneed
weariless
weariness
weediness
weighbeam
weirdness
whalehead
wheatmeal
wheelless
whitebeam
whitehead
whiteness
wholemeal
wholeness
windbreak
windchest
windiness
windswept
winepress
winsomely
witchmeal
wittiness
wolverene
woodiness
wooziness
wordiness
workpiece
wormwheel
worriment
worthless
woundless
wrathless
wrongness
youngness
barrelful
basketful
beautiful
bottlefed
bottleful
bountiful
bucketful
bushelful
butterfat
butterfly
caddisfly
calorific
carfuffle
chanceful
changeful
colorific
colourful
deceitful
discomfit
dragonfly
drawerful
effortful
felicific
forgetful
frightful
handcuffs
healthful
honorific
kerfuffle
luftwaffe
marrowfat
masterful
needleful
nonprofit
plentiful
pocketful
praiseful
prayerful
quadrifid
rauwolfia
rechauffe
regardful
regretful
remindful
reposeful
resentful
reshuffle
resultful
saucerful
shieldfem
shovelful
silverfir
soporific
sorrowful
speechful
spleenful
stressful
sudorific
teacupful
unberufen
undutiful
unhelpful
unmindful
unskilful
unthrifty
vaporific
warblefly
wonderful
abidingly
adoringly
agrologic
amazingly
amusingly
aquilegia
archangel
Areopagus
asparagus
backsight
bandwagon
beamingly
bedraggle
bespangle
bethought
blazingly
Boanerges
bombsight
bowlegged
brummagem
bullfight
burningly
canesugar
carpingly
catalogue
champagne
chemurgic
choplogic
coaxingly
Cockaigne
cockfight
colleague
commingle
copyright
cryptogam
cunningly
damningly
dashingly
deadlight
decalogue
demagogic
demagogue
demiurgic
denyingly
derringdo
derringer
dodecagon
doglegged
downright
dysphagia
dysphagic
earwigged
embrangle
estranger
exchanger
eyebright
fandangle
fandangos
fawningly
feelingly
firelight
fittingly
flamingly
flamingos
flaringly
flowingly
flyweight
footlight
foresight
fortnight
gallingly
giltedged
glaringly
glowingly
goodnight
greasegun
gushingly
halflight
haltingly
hamburger
handorgan
harbinger
headlight
hedgingly
highlight
hindsight
homologue
horologer
horologic
humbugged
humdinger
hydrangea
ideologic
ideologue
illjudged
indraught
inwrought
jarringly
jeeringly
kiddingly
knowingly
lamplight
lastingly
leeringly
lethargic
liltingly
Limburger
limelight
lispingly
loafsugar
longingly
louringly
lovelight
meaningly
meltingly
messenger
methought
mincingly
minutegun
mockingly
monologic
monologue
moonlight
mortgagee
mortgager
mortgagor
mundungus
mycologic
netwinged
neuralgia
neuralgic
nostalgia
nostalgic
oecologic
oestrogen
omophagia
omophagic
oncologic
onelegged
onslaught
ontologic
outrigger
overnight

oversight
pantingly
passenger
pedagogic
pedagogue
peepsight
pemphigus
pendragon
pentangle
phalanger
phalanges
pharyngal
pharynges
phellogen
pipeorgan
pityingly
porbeagle
porringer
pratingly
ptarmigan
purringly
pushingly
quadrigae
rantingly
raspingly
rearlight
rectangle
reedorgan
rethought
ringingly
rushlight
salpinges
scavenger
scrounger
searingly
seatangle
seemingly
semirigid
sidelight
sinologue
skintight
smilingly
sobbingly
solfeggio
sparingly
sporangia
spotlight
starlight
stoplight
stratagem
strategic
suffragan
summingup
surcingle
synagogal
synagogue
taillight
teasingly
tellingly
teratogen
theologic
theologue
trialogue
undamaged
undecagon
unfledged
unplugged
unthought
unwrought
veeringly
viceregal
wailingly
Walpurgis
warmonger
warningly
weeknight
whirligig
willingly
winningly
wittingly
yawningly
zigzagged
zoophagan
abolisher
acidophil
ailanthus
amianthus
anglophil
anguished
astrakhan
autarchic
azimuthal
baldachin
beeorchis
betrothal
betrothed
bimonthly
blockship
bloodshed
bloodshot
bookishly
boorishly
brakeshoe
Britisher
brutishly
bullishly
burnisher
cacoethes
cadetship
catarrhal
ceanothus
chiefship
chihuahua
clerkship
colcothar
coltishly
countship
courtship
cuplichen
currishly
debauched
debauchee
debaucher
didelphic
didrachma
dimorphic
doggishly
doltishly
donnishly
eldership
Emmenthal
entrechat
eurhythmy
eutrophic
flyfisher
foolishly
foppishly
forgather
forsythia
furbisher
furnisher
Gallophil
garnishee
girlishly
godfather
godmother
grapeshot
groundhog
guardship
guildship
hellishly
hoggishly
horseshoe
horsewhip
illwisher
isobathic
judgeship
knavishly
lairdship
leviathan
libecchio
lightship
loutishly
lumpishly
majorship
malleehen
mawkishly
mayorship
microchip
monarchal
monarchic
mustachio
naumachia
necrophil
negrophil
neolithic
nepenthes
nourisher
nowhither
oakenshaw
ownership
paperthin
peevishly
penpusher
petersham
pettishly
photophil
piggishly
pistachio
planisher
printshop
priorship
prudishly
publisher
queenship
raffishly
rareeshow
refreshen
refresher
retoucher
rodfisher
roguishly
roughshod
rulership
Russophil
saintship
scratcher
scratches
screecher
scrimshaw
seaanchor
seaurchin
selfishly
seneschal
sepulcher
sepulchre
seventhly
sharpshod
shovelhat
sickishly
slaveship
slavishly
Slavophil
slingshot
sottishly
spaceship
spleuchan
squelcher
stauncher
staunchly
steamship
stockwhip
stomachal
stomacher
stomachic
stonechat
storeship
stretcher
stylishly
sublethal
sunbather
sweatshop
sweetshop
swinishly
tacamahac
talkathon
tallyshop
tartishly
thaneship
throughly
transship
trebuchet
trilithon
triumphal
troopship
tutorship
twelfthly
unabashed
unclothed
uncouthly
undershot
unearthly
unfleshed
unfleshly
unmatched
unscathed
untouched
Upanishad
varnisher
waggishly
waspishly
watershed
wolfishly
wristshot
Yiddisher
zootechny
abduction
abhorring
abjection
abnormity
abolition
aborigine
abounding
abruption
abseiling
absorbing
absurdism
absurdist
absurdity
academism
acceptive
accession
acclivity
according
accordion
accretion
accretive
acetamide
acetifier
Acheulian
acidifier
aconitine
acoustics
actualise
actuality
actuarial
actuation
addiction
addictive
adduction
adductive
ademption
adenosine
adiposity
adjoining
adlibbing
admission
admissive
admitting
adoration
adulation
advection
advective
Adventism
Adventist
adventive
adverbial
adversity
advertise
aerialist
aeriality
affecting
affection
affective
afflation
afterlife
aftertime
agitation
agitative
agonising
airyfairy
alchemise
alchemist
Algonkian
allotting
almandine
alongside
altricial
aluminise
aluminium
amazonian
ambiguity
ambrosial
americium
amidships
amoralism
amorality
amorphism
amphibian
amplifier
anabolism
analogise
analogist
anarchism
anarchist
anatomise
anatomist
anchorite
andantino
angelfish
anglesite
anglicise
anglicism
Anglicist
anhydride
anhydrite
animalise
animalism
animalist
animality
animation
animatism
animosity
annulling
anonymity
anorthite
anthelion
anthemion
anticline
antiquity
aperitive
apologise
apologist
appalling
appealing
apportion
arabicise
aragonite
archivist
argentine
argentite
argillite
armistice
aromatise
arresting
Arthurian
asafetida
asbestine
ascension
ascensive
asclepiad
ashlaring
asininity
aspersion
assertion
assertive
assiduity
assuasive
atacamite
athletics
atomicity
atonalism
atonality
atonicity
attention
attentive
attrition
aubergine
auctorial
austenite
austerity
autarkist
authorial
authorise
authority
aventaile
avocation
awakening
baboonish
backslide
bacterial
bacterise
bacterium
bailiwick
balalaika
balconied
balkanise
balladist
ballerina
ballpoint
bandolier
bandoline
Barbadian
barbarian
barbarise
barbarism
barbarity
Barmecide
basrelief
batholite
batholith
Bathonian
bathybius
battalion
battening
beccafico
bedlamite
bedspring
befitting
befogging
begetting
beginning
belemnite
bengaline
benignity
bentonite
benzidine
benzoline
berberine
berkelium
beryllium
besetting
besotting
bevelling
biblicism
biblicist
bicyclist
biologist
bionomics
bipartite
bisection
bitterish
blackbird
blackfish
blacklist
blotchily
bluepoint
blueprint
bobsleigh
bolection
bombasine
bombazine
bonechina
borrowing
bowerbird
bowstring
boxoffice
brambling
branchiae
branchial
brandling
breadline
breathily
breathing
breeching
breveting
brigadier
brightish
bristling
Briticise
Briticism
broadside
broadwise
bromeliad
bronchial
brushfire
brutalise
brutalism
brutality
buckshish
buffeting
Bulgarian
bursarial
butterine
Byzantine
caballine
caballing
cabbalism
cabbalist
caciquism
cadential
caecilian
Caesarian
Caesarism
Caesarist
caldarium
callosity
calmative
Calvinism
Calvinist
Cambodian
camorrist
campanile

campanili
cannonier
cantabile
cantorial
capsulise
captivity
carbamide
carbonise
carburise
careerism
careerist
Carmelite
carnality
carnation
carnelian
carnitine
carolling
carpeting
Cartesian
caseation
cassaripe
cassation
Castalian
Castilian
Castroism
casuarina
catarhine
catechise
catechism
catechist
Catharism
Catharist
Caucasian
causality
causation
causative
cauterise
cavendish
cavilling
ceasefire
celandine
celebrity
celestial
Celticism
cementite
censorial
centering
centreing
centurion
cerastium
certified
certifier
cerussite
cessation
chamomile
champaign
checklist
chelation
chelonian
chevalier
chickling
childlike
chondrite
chopstick
Christian
chthonian
churching
cicatrice
cicatrise
Cimmerian
cipollino
circadian
cisalpine
clarifier
classlist
clavation
cleansing
clinician
clockwise
coalition
coastline
coastwise
coattails
cobaltite
Cobdenism
cocainise
cocainism
coccidium
cockatiel
coecilian
coemption
coenobite
coenobium
coffinite
cognation
cognition
cognitive
collagist
collation
collegial
collegian
collegium
collision
collodion
collusion
collusive
collyrium
colouring
colourist
colubrine
Columbian
columbine
columbite
columbium
columnist
combative
commodity
commotion
communion
communise
communism
communist
community
companion
complaint
composite
concavity
conciliar
concision
concubine
condition
conducive
confiding
Confucian
confusion
congenial
congeries
congruity
connation
connexion
connubial
conscribe
conscript
constrict
contadina
contadino
contagion
contagium
contusion
convexity
convivial
coprolite
coralline
corallite
cordelier
cornelian
cornetist
corrasion
corrosion
corrosive
costumier
cotillion
couturier
cowardice
crackling
crampfish
crashdive
crediting
credulity
cremation
crenation
cretinism
crinoline
crippling
criterion
criticise
criticism
crocodile
crossbill
crossfire
crossfish
crosslink
crosswind
crosswise
cupelling
curialism
curiosity
cursorial
cursorily
curveting
custodial
custodian
customise
cyanamide
cyclopian
cymbalist
cymbidium
cystolith
czarevich
Daedalian
dalmatian
daltonism
damnation
dandelion
Darwinian
Darwinism
Darwinist
dayspring
deacidify
deadalive
deathlike
debagging
debarring
debugging
decalcify
decennial
decennium
deception
deceptive
decillion
declivity
decoction
decretive
deduction
deductive
defeatism
defeatist
defection
defective
defensive
deferring
deflation
deflexion
deformity
dejection
demanding
demission
demitting
demobbing
demurring
demystify
denitrify
dentalium
dentation
dentition
deodorise
deoxidise
depiction
depictive
depletion
depletive
depravity
desertion
designing
despotism
detection
detective
detention
determine
deterring
detersion
detersive
detrition
detrusion
deuterium
deviation
devilfish
devilling
devitrify
dexterity
diabolise
diabolism
diabolist
dialogise
dialogism
dialogist
diatomite
dichasial
dichasium
dichroism
dickybird
dicrotism
dictation
didactics
dieselise
dietetics
dietician
dietitian
difficile
diffusion
diffusive
digestion
digestive
dignified
dimension
Dionysiac
Dionysian
dipeptide
direction
directive
disaffirm
disarming
disbelief
disoblige
disparity
dispraise
disrelish
dissocial
distraint
diversify
diversion
diversity
diverting
divulsion
doctorial
dogmatics
dogmatise
dogmatism
dogmatist
dogoodism
donothing
dormition
doughtily
dowelling
draconian
dragonish
drainpipe
dramatics
dramatise
dramatist
Dravidian
dreamlike
drumstick
dubiosity
ductility
duodecimo
duplicity
dysgenics
earthling
easygoing
ecclesial
ecologist
economics
economise
economist
ecossaise
ecritoire
ecstasise
ecumenism
edelweiss
edibility
editorial
education
educative
Edwardian
effective
effluvial
effluvium
effluxion
eglantine
egomaniac
egression
eightyish
electrify
elevation
elocution
emanation
emanative
embedding
embellish
embracive
embussing
emotivity
empathise
emphasise
emulation
emulative
enchorial
encrinite
endearing
endocrine
engraving
enrolling
ephedrine
epicurism
epidosite
epilation
epilogist
epipolism
epitomise
epitomist
equalling
equipoise
equipping
eremitism
eroticism
erstwhile
erudition
erythrism
erythrite
esoterica
esoterism
essential
establish
Esthonian
estopping
estuarian
estuarine
Ethiopian
ethnicity
Eucharist
eunuchism
euphemise
euphemism
euphonise
euphonium
euthenics
eutherian
evocation
evocative
evolution
evolutive
exceeding
excelling
excelsior
excepting
exception
exceptive
excessive
exclusion
exclusive
excretion
excretive
excursion
excursive
execution
executive
exegetist
exemplify
exemption
exopodite
exoticism
expansile
expansion
expansive
expecting
expelling
expensive
expertise
expiation
expletive
explosion
explosive
expulsion
expulsive
exquisite
exsertile
exsertion
exservice
extensile
extension
extensity
extensive
extolling
extorsive
extortion
extortive
extradite
extremism
extremist
extremity
extrusion
extrusive
exudation
exudative
Fabianism
facsimile
factitive
factorial
factorise
facundity
faggoting
fairylike
fairyring
Falangism
Falangist
Falernian
falsifier
fantasied
fantasise
fantasist
farseeing
fastening
fastigium
favourite
febricity
fecundity
femineity
Fenianism
fertilise
fertility
festivity
fetichism
fetichist
fetishism
fetishist
feudalise
feudalism
feudalist
feudality
fibroline
fiendlike
filiation
financial
financier
fingering
finicking
firebrick
firedrill
firstling
fishslice
fissility
flagstick
flayflint
fledgling
flightily
floodtide
floridity
flotation
flouncing
flowering
focussing
foeticide
foliation
following
footprint
foregoing
forgiving
formalise
formalism
formalist
formality
formation
formative
formulise
fortalice
forthwith
fortifier
fortyfive
fossilise
fossorial
foundling
fragility

franchise
frenchify
friarbird
fricative
frigidity
frivolity
frontline
frontwise
frostbite
frugality
fulgurite
funebrial
fungicide
furcation
fusionist
gabardine
gaberdine
galantine
galleried
gallicise
gallicism
galloping
galvanise
galvanism
galvanist
gammadion
gammoning
ganderism
gardening
garrulity
gathering
gavelkind
gearshift
gelignite
gemmation
gemutlich
genialise
geniality
gentility
geodesist
geologise
geologist
geoponics
germanise
Germanish
Germanism
Germanist
germanium
germicide
gerundial
gerundive
gestation
geyserite
ghostlike
giantlike
gibberish
gibbosity
gigantism
Girondist
glamorise
globefish
globosity
glucoside
glyceride
glycerine
glycoside
goffering
goldbrick
goldsmith
gondolier
gongorism
goosegirl
gorgonian
gorgonise
Gothamite
gothicise
Gothicism
gracility
gradation

Gradgrind
grandsire
granulite
grapevine
grappling
gravamina
gravidity
gregarian
gregarine
Gregorian
grenadier
grenadine
gristmill
grouchily
grounding
groundivy
gruelling
grumbling
Grundyism
guardring
guideline
guitarist
gustation
gustative
guttation
guttering
gymnasial
gymnasium
gynoecium
haematite
haggadist
hairshirt
hairslide
halfprice
halophile
hamstring
handspike
hankering
happening
harmaline
harmonica
harmonics
harmonise
harmonist
harmonium
Harrovian
harrowing
Hashemite
Hashimite
hatchling
haughtily
havocking
hawksbill
hawsepipe
healthily
heartsick
hellenise
Hellenism
Hellenist
Helvetian
hemistich
herbalist
herbarium
herbicide
herborise
Hercynian
Hesperian
hessonite
hetaerism
hetairism
hexastich
Hibernian
hiddenite
hieratica
highflier
Himyarite
hircosity
hirsutism
hirundine

hispidity
histamine
histidine
historian
hitchhike
Hitlerism
Hitlerite
Hobbesian
hocussing
homousian
hoofprint
horsehide
horsemint
hortation
hortative
hostility
housewife
hoydenish
humankind
Hungarian
hybridise
hybridism
hybridity
hydration
hydrazine
hydronium
hydroxide
hygienics
hygienist
hylozoism
hypnotise
hypnotism
hypnotist
hypocrisy
hypocrite
hysterics
illboding
imitation
imitative
immensity
immersion
impaction
impartial
impassion
impassive
impelling
impending
impletion
implosion
implosive
impluvium
imprecise
improbity
improvise
impulsion
impulsive
inability
inanition
incaution
incentive
inception
inceptive
inclusion
inclusive
incognito
incondite
incurring
incursion
incursive
indemnify
indemnity
indention
Indianise
indiction
indignity
induction
inductive
infantile
infantine

infection
infective
inferring
infertile
infilling
infirmity
inflation
inflexion
inflowing
ingenuity
ingestion
ingestive
ingrowing
injection
injustice
innocuity
inpouring
inquiline
insectile
insertion
inservice
insetting
insomniac
integrity
intensify
intension
intensity
intensive
intention
intercity
interdict
interfile
interline
interlink
interring
interview
interwind
intestine
intorsion
intrusion
intrusive
intuition
intuitive
inunction
inutility
invective
invention
inventive
inversion
inversive
ironsmith
Iroquoian
irreality
irruption
irruptive
isagogics
isolation
isolative
isomerise
isomerism
Israelite
italicise
Italicism
iteration
iterative
jackknife
jacksnipe
jactation
Jansenism
Jansenist
japanning
jargonise
jellyfish
jessamine
jesuitise
jesuitism
jocundity
Johannine
Jordanian

josstick
joviality
juniority
junkerism
junketing
justiciar
justifier
kaiserism
kaolinise
kaolinite
keelivine
Keplerian
Keynesian
khedivial
killifish
kittenish
Kshatriya
labelling
labialise
labialism
labourite
laccolith
lacertian
lacertine
lactation
lallation
landslide
larcenist
larvicide
lathering
latticing
laudation
laudative
launching
lawgiving
leastwise
leavening
legerline
lengthily
lethality
lettering
Levantine
levelling
liability
libelling
libellist
libertine
librarian
libration
lickerish
lightning
lilywhite
limejuice
limousine
limpidity
lineality
linearise
linearity
lineation
lingering
lintwhite
liquation
liquefier
liquidise
liquidity
liquorice
liquorish
Listerism
liturgics
liturgist
locksmith
logistics
logogriph
Londonise
Londonism
longevity
lookalike
loquacity
lovechild

lubricity
lucrative
lumbering
lunchtime
macedoine
machinist
maddening
madeleine
Magianism
magicking
magnalium
magnesian
magnesite
magnesium
magnetics
magnetise
magnetism
magnetist
magnetite
magnifico
magnifier
mahlstick
maidenish
makeshift
malachite
malathion
malignity
mammalian
mammonish
mammonism
mammonist
mammonite
Mancunian
mandarine
mandoline
maneating
manganite
mannerism
mannerist
manubrium
manyplies
manzanita
marcasite
margarine
margarite
marketing
marsupial
marsupium
martyrise
masculine
masochism
masochist
masonried
massagist
maternity
matricide
matronise
maulstick
meandrine
meanwhile
mechanics
mechanise
mechanism
mechanist
medallion
medallist
mediation
mediatise
mediative
meliorism
meliorist
meliority
memoirist
mendacity
Mendelian
Mendelism
mendicity
Mennonite
mentalism

mentalist
mentality
mentation
mepacrine
mercerise
mercurial
mescaline
mesmerise
mesmerism
mesmerist
metalline
metalling
metallise
meteorist
meteorite
methodise
Methodism
Methodist
metrician
metricise
metricist
mezzanine
mezzotint
microbial
microfilm
microlite
microlith
migration
millerite
Miltonian
mimicking
miniskirt
misadvise
misassign
misbelief
miscegine
misgiving
misoneism
misoneist
Mithraism
Mithraist
mnemonics
mnemonist
modelling
modernise
modernism
modernist
modernity
modillion
monachism
Mondayish
monergism
moneybill
Mongolian
mongolism
monkeyish
monkeyism
monocline
monoecism
monostich
Montanism
monthling
monzonite
moonblind
moonshine
morbidity
mordacity
Mormonism
mortality
mortician
mosaicism
mosaicist
motorbike
mummified
muscadine
muscarine
muscovite
musteline
mutualise

mutualism
mutualist
mutuality
myologist
mysticism
mystifier
mythicise
mythicism
mythicist
narcotine
narcotise
narcotism
narration
narrative
natrolite
naughtily
necessity
necrotise
nectarial
nectarine
nemertine
nemophila
neodymium
neologian
neologise
neologism
neologist
neoterise
neoterism
neoterist
nephalism
nephalist
nepheline
nephelite
Neptunian
neptunium
nervation
Nestorian
neuration
newsprint
Newtonian
niccolite
nickelise
nictation
nightbird
nightlife
nightline
nightside
nighttime
nigrosine
nitratine
nitration
nonentity
nonillion
nonjuring
normalise
normality
Normanise
Normanism
normative
Norwegian
notionist
nullifier
nummulite
nurseling
nutrition
nutritive
objectify
objection
objective
obliquity
obscenity
obscurity
obsequial
obsequies
obsession
obsessive
obtention
obtrusion
obtrusive
obversion
obviation
occlusion
occlusive
occultism
occultist
occurring
octennial
octillion
Octobrist
oenophile
oenophily
offensive
offspring
olfaction
olfactive
olivenite
onsetting
operation
operative
operosity
Orangeism
oratorial
oratorian
orchidist
organzine
orificial
orologist
ostensive
ostracise
ostracism
otherwise
otologist
outgiving
overdrive
overlying
overprice
overprint
overskirt
overspill
overtrick
overweigh
overwrite
oviparity
ovulation
oxidation
oxygenise
ozocerite
ozokerite
packaging
packdrill
Palladian
palladium
palletise
pallidity
palmation
palpation
panelling
panellist
panicking
panoplied
pantheism
pantheist
pantomime
papergirl
paranoiac
parathion
parhelion
parochial
parricide
Parseeism
partition
partitive
passerine
passivity
paternity
patrician
patricide
patronise
pauperise
pauperism
Pavlovian
peacetime
pedalling
pegmatite
Pelasgian
pelletise
penduline
penultima
peptonise
percaline
perdition
peregrine
perennial
perfumier
perfusion
perfusive
perilling
perishing
personify
pervasion
pervasive
pessimism
pessimist
pesticide
petaurist
petechiae
petechial
pethidine
phenacite
phenakite
phonation
phonemics
phonetics
phonetise
phonetism
phonetist
phonolite
phosphide
phosphine
phosphite
physician
physicist
picketing
pictorial
picturise
pilotfish
pinstripe
pitchpipe
placation
placekick
placidity
plaintiff
plaintive
planarian
planation
plantlike
platinise
Platonise
Platonism
Platonist
plaything
plenarily
plication
plumbline
pluralise
pluralism
pluralist
plurality
plutonian
Plutonism
Plutonist
plutonium
podzolise
poeticise
poeticism
pollinium
pollution
polonaise
polyamide
pomposity
pontonier
porcupine
portative
posterior
posterity
postilion
potassium
potential
potholing
pourboire
pourpoint
powerdive
preachify
preachily
precative
preceding
precipice
precisian
precision
precocial
precocity
preconise
predacity
predation
predative
prefixion
prejudice
prelatise
prelusion
prelusive
premonish
premotion
prenotion
prescribe
prescript
preshrink
presidial
presidium
preterist
preterite
prettyish
prettyism
prevision
primality
primarily
primatial
primitive
privation
privative
probation
probative
procerity
profanity
profilist
profusion
prolamine
prolation
prolative
prolicide
prolixity
prologise
prolusion
promising
promotion
promotive
pronation
proscribe
prosodist
protamine
providing
provision
provoking
proximity
pterygium
publicise
publicist
publicity
puerility
pugnacity
pulsatile
pulsation
pulverise
punchline
punishing
purgation
purgative
purposive
purselike
putridity
pycnidium
Quakerish
Quakerism
qualified
qualifier
quartzite
queenlike
quibbling
quicklime
quinoline
quixotism
quotation
quotidian
rabbinism
rabbinist
racialism
racialist
radiation
radiative
rancidity
randomise
rapidfire
raptorial
rascalism
rascality
rationing
raunchily
ravelling
ravishing
razorbill
razorfish
reasoning
rebaptise
rebelling
rebellion
rebidding
rebutting
recapping
recension
reception
receptive
recession
recessive
reckoning
reclusion
reclusive
recognise
recombine
reconcile
recondite
reconfirm
recording
recordist
rectifier
rectorial
recurring
recursion
recursive
redaction
reduction
reductive
reefpoint
reexamine
refashion
refection
referring
refitting
reflation
reflexion
reflexive
reformism
reformist
refurbish
refurnish
rejection
rejoicing
reliquiae
remission
remitting
rendition
repelling
replenish
repletion
repotting
reptilian
republish
repulsion
repulsive
requisite
rerunning
resection
reserpine
reservist
resetting
resistive
resitting
restraint
retention
retentive
retiarius
retortion
revelling
reversion
revetting
revolting
revulsion
revulsive
rewarding
rhodamine
rhodolite
rhodonite
rhonchial
rhythmics
rhythmise
rhythmist
Ribbonism
ridgetile
riflebird
Ripuarian
ritualise
ritualism
ritualist
rivalling
rivelling
riverside
rockdrill
rotundity
Roumanian
routinism
routinist
rubberise
rubellite
rubrician
ruggedise
ruination
russeting
rusticity
ruthenium
sabbatise
sabbatism
Sabellian
sacrarium
sacrifice
safranine
sailoring
saintlike
saintling
salesgirl
sallowish
saltation
salubrity
salvation
sanbenito
sandblind
santolina
santonica
Sardinian
Sarmation
sartorial
sartorius
Sassanian
satellite
satiation
satinbird
Saturnian
saturnine
saturnism
savourily
scaldfish
scalefish
scalelike
scantling
scapolite
scarfring
scarfwise
scarifier
scenarist
scheelite
schilling
schlemiel
schlemihl
schooling
sciential
scientism
scientist
scolecite
scorching
scorifier
Scoticise
scraggily
scramming
scrappily
scrapping
screening
screwpile
screwpine
scrimpily
scrubbing
scruffily
seafaring
searching
seasoning
seasquirt
secession
seclusion
seclusive
secretion
secretive
sectarian
sectility
sectorial
seduction
seductive
selachian
selection
selective
selfdrive
selfpride
Seljukian
semantics
semiotics
senhorita
seniority

sensation
sensitise
sensitive
sensorial
sensorium
sepiolite
septation
septicity
sequacity
serialise
serialism
serialist
seriality
sermonise
serration
serrefile
servility
seventies
sexennial
sexualise
sexuality
sgraffiti
sgraffito
shakerism
shamanism
shamanist
shambling
Shangrila
shaveling
shearling
sheatfish
sheathing
sheeplice
sheeptick
shelflife
shellfire
shellfish
Shintoism
Shintoist
shoeshine
shoreline
shoreside
shredding
shrewmice
shrugging
sibylline
siccative
sickening
sideswipe
signalise
significs
signorial
signorina
siltation
simpatico
sincerity
singspiel
sinophile
sinuation
sinuosity
situation
sitzkrieg
sketchily
skewwhiff
skijoring
skinflick
skinflint
skydiving
slantwise
slapstick
Slavonian
slightish
slivovitz
slopewise
Slovakian
Slovenian
smalltime
smoothish
smuggling
snailfish
snakebird
snakebite
snakelike
snipefish
snowblind
snowblink
snowdrift
snowwhite
socialise
socialism
socialist
socialite
sociality
solemnise
solemnity
solferino
solipsism
solipsist
solitaire
Solutrian
solvation
something
somewhile
sommelier
songsmith
sonnetise
sopranino
sopranist
Sorbonist
sortition
soundfilm
sovereign
sovietise
sovietism
spacetime
spagyrist
spareribs
spearfish
spearmint
spearside
specifier
speechify
spellbind
spindling
spindrier
spindrift
spinosity
Spinozism
Spinozist
spirality
spiritism
spiritist
splashily
splitting
spokewise
spoonbill
sprigging
springily
springing
squashily
squatting
squeakily
squeamish
squibbing
squidding
stabilise
stability
Stagirite
Stalinism
Stalinist
stampmill
stanchion
standpipe
stapedial
starchily
stardrift
startling
stateside
statewide
statolith
steampipe
steenkirk
stepchild
steradian
sterilise
sterility
stippling
stockfish
stocklist
stockpile
stolidity
stonefish
stormbird
storyline
stovepipe
strapping
streakily
streaking
striation
stripling
stripping
strongish
strontium
stropping
strouding
strumming
strutting
stupefier
stupidity
suability
subaerial
subalpine
subdivide
subfamily
sublation
sublimity
submarine
subregion
subscribe
subscript
subsidise
subtilise
subtopian
suctorial
suctorian
suffering
suffusion
sulcation
summarily
summarise
summarist
summation
summative
superfine
supervise
supposing
surfacing
surficial
surveying
suspicion
sutteeism
swaddling
swarajist
swellfish
swingeing
swordfish
swordlike
syllabise
syllabism
syllogise
syllogism
sylphlike
sylvanite
symbolics
symbolise
symbolism
symbolist
sympodial
sympodium
symposiac
symposial
symposium
syncytial
syncytium
synectics
synergism
synergist
synoptist
syphilise
tachylite
tactician
tactility
tactitian
tailoring
talkative
tallowish
Talmudist
tangerine
tantalise
tantalite
tarantism
Targumist
Tartarian
Tartufian
Tartufism
Tasmanian
tattooist
taxpaying
tectonics
tectorial
tellurian
telluride
tellurite
tellurium
temporise
tenderise
tenebrist
tensility
tentation
tentative
terminism
terminist
terrarium
terrorise
terrorism
terrorist
testation
testdrive
testifier
tetradite
teutonise
Teutonism
Teutonist
thatching
theatrics
therapist
therewith
theurgist
thirstily
thornbill
thrashing
thriftily
thrilling
throatily
throbbing
thrumming
thylacine
thyroxine
tiedyeing
tigerlily
tightwire
timbering
timpanist
titration
tittuping
Tocharian
tonsorial
toothpick
topiarian
topiarist
toreutics
torpidity
torridity
totalling
touchline
towelling
toxophily
traceried
tradition
traducian
tragedian
transpire
trapezial
trapezium
treadmill
tremolite
tribadism
tribalism
tricksily
tridymite
triennial
triennium
trifacial
trifolium
triforium
trigamist
trilobite
trinomial
triploidy
trisagion
tritheism
tritheist
triumviri
troutling
trunkfish
tsarevich
turbidity
turgidity
turnstile
turquoise
twinkling
twitchily
tympanist
typewrite
tyrannise
uintahite
Ukrainian
ultrahigh
ululation
umberbird
unanimity
unbending
uncannily
unceasing
undeceive
undergird
underline
underling
undermine
underripe
underside
undersign
undertint
underwing
unfailing
unfeeling
unfitting
unhappily
unheeding
unhurried
uniserial
unitarian
unknowing
unluckily
unmeaning
unpegging
unreality
unselfish
unsmiling
unsparing
unstudied
unsullied
unwearied
unweeting
unwilling
unwinking
unwitting
unzipping
uplifting
upsetting
uraninite
uropygium
usucapion
uvarovite
uxoricide
valentine
vallation
valuation
vampirism
vandalise
vandalism
vapouring
vapourish
Varangian
variation
variolite
vectorial
Vedantist
vendition
veneering
veniality
veratrine
verbalise
verbalism
verbalist
verbicide
verbosity
vermicide
vermilion
vernalise
vernation
versatile
versifier
vestigial
vestigium
vetchling
viability
vibratile
vibration
vibrative
vicennial
vicereine
victimise
Victorian
victorine
viewpoint
villosity
violation
violative
violinist
Virgilian
virginity
viscidity
viscosity
visionist
visualise
vitelline
vitiation
vitiosity
Vitruvian
viverrine
vivianite
vizierial
volcanism
volkslied
voltinism
voodooism
voodooist
vorticism
vorticist
vorticity
voyeurism
vulcanian
vulcanise
vulcanism
vulcanist
vulcanite
vulgarian
vulgarise
vulgarism
vulgarity
vulpinism
vulpinite
vulturine
vulturish
Wagnerian
Wagnerite
waistline
walloping
wandering
wastepipe
watchfire
waterlily
waterline
watermill
waterpipe
waterside
waveguide
wavellite
wayfaring
wealthily
wedgewise
weightily
weighting
welcoming
welfarism
wellbeing
westering
wheedling
wherewith
whirlwind
whistling
whitefish
whitening
whitewing
widowbird
widthwise
willemite
willowish
winterise
withering
witherite
witticism
wolverine
womankind
womanlike
womenkind
wordsmith
worldling
worldwide
wrestling
wulfenite
Wyclifite
xenophile
xerophile
xerophily
Yankeeism
yardstick
yellowish
yodelling
yohimbine
Yorkshire
youngling

ytterbium
zeitgeist
zibelline
zinkenite
zirconium
zoiatrics
zoologist
zootomist
Zwinglian
drummajor
maharajah
airjacket
barracker
bedjacket
berserker
bookmaker
caretaker
diesinker
ewenecked
foretoken
fossicker
frolicked
gimmickry
gooseskin
grimalkin
halfbaked
homemaker
identikit
jampacked
jaywalker
kilderkin
kingmaker
lovetoken
lownecked
masterkey
midwicket
mispickel
misreckon
moonraker
mosaicked
muckraker
newmarket
nitpicker
nonsmoker
okeydokey
onionskin
outbacker
outspoken
outworker
overtaken
pacemaker
parbuckle
paypacket
physicked
picnicked
picnicker
princekin
rainmaker
ransacker
rudbeckia
scarfskin
schnorkel
sexlinked
sharkskin
sheepskin
shoemaker
skyjacker
skyrocket
snakeskin
sooterkin
spillikin
spinnaker
staymaker
tanpickle
tentmaker
trebucket
triweekly
unchecked
unshackle
abysmally
acellular
acropolis
admiralty
adrenalin
afterclap
afterglow
aircooled
alcoholic
alicyclic
amaryllis
amygdalin
anopheles
apostolic
aquarelle
armadillo
articular
asexually
assembler
auricular
autopilot
autotelic
avuncular
bagatelle
balefully
banefully
barnacled
barrelled
bashfully
basically
bedfellow
bellyflop
bestially
binocular
bismillah
blackflag
blastulae
blastular
bobtailed
branchlet
Bretwalda
cabriolet
cacodylic
calicular
camarilla
cancelled
canicular
capitally
capitular
capitulum
carefully
cassoulet
castellan
catabolic
centrally
cerebella
chantilly
chiselled
chiseller
chlorella
chrysalid
chrysalis
cigarillo
civically
clitellum
coaxially
coequally
colonelcy
columella
comically
commonlaw
compelled
conically
contralto
corbeille
corbelled
cordially
cornsalad
corralled
corydalis
coverslip
crenelled
crucially
cubically
cudgelled
cuticular
cynically
deathblow
decathlon
decimally
decomplex
despoiler
dextrally
diachylom
diachylum
diastolic
digitalin
digitalis
digitally
direfully
dispelled
distilled
distiller
diurnally
dogcollar
dogviolet
dolefully
drivelled
driveller
dutifully
easefully
echolalia
embattled
embezzler
embroglio
enamelled
enameller
epicyclic
epistoler
epistolic
epithelia
eternally
ethically
evangelic
factually
fascicled
fatefully
fearfully
federally
fibrillar
filoselle
finically
flabellum
flagellum
flageolet
flannelly
flocculus
floscular
fraenulum
francolin
fretfully
frivolled
frontally
fulfilled
fulfiller
fumarolic
funicular
funiculus
funnelled
gainfully
gambolled
garibaldi
gastrulae
generalia
generally
genteelly
glabellae
glabellar
glacially
gladiolus
glandular
gleefully
gospeller
gradually
grandslam
gravelled
grisaille
grossular
grovelled
groveller
guerrilla
hamamelis
hanselled
harmfully
hatefully
haustella
heedfully
helically
helpfully
heptaglot
hillbilly
hobgoblin
hobnailed
homopolar
hopefully
horseplay
hosteller
houseflag
houselled
hurtfully
hydraulic
illegally
imbecilic
imbroglio
immorally
indweller
initially
inshallah
instilled
interflow
interplay
inveigler
irregular
isocyclic
isosceles
juvenilia
katabolic
kennelled
landaulet
laterally
laurelled
lexically
liberally
lingually
lintelled
lioncelle
literally
logically
lunisolar
lustfully
lyophilic
lyrically
magically
Malayalam
malleolar
malleolus
manipular
marcelled
maritally
marshalcy
martially
marvelled
maximally
mayoralty
medically
metabolic
metheglin
mindfully
minimally
misemploy
mitraille
molecular
mongrelly
monocular
multiplex
musically
muskmelon
myrobalan
Nahuatlan
napthalic
naturally
navicular
needfully
neuroglia
neutrally
nickelled
nightclub
nominally
notabilia
nucleolus
nymphalid
oddfellow
odontalgy
opercular
operculum
optically
opusculum
orbicular
organelle
ossicular
overvalue
painfully
panatella
paperclip
parabolic
paralalia
parcelled
partially
patrolled
patroller
peachblow
pedicular
pencilled
penciller
perihelia
pilgarlic
pintailed
pistolled
pitifully
pivotally
playfully
pointille
pommelled
portfolio
potboiler
preexilic
princelet
propelled
propeller
pulvillus
pummelled
punctilio
pyroxylin
quadrille
radically
radicular
rakehelly
redevelop
refuelled
restfully
reticular
reticulum
retinulae
retinular
retroflex
ridiculer
rostellum
roundelay
rubicelle
ruthfully
sabadilla
salicylic
sandalled
sapodilla
scintilla
scrambler
scribbler
scutellar
scutellum
semicolon
seminally
semisolid
sensually
septuplet
severally
severalty
sextuplet
shambolic
shillelah
shovelled
shoveller
signalled
signaller
skilfully
slateclub
snivelled
sniveller
songfully
soulfully
sparkplug
spatially
specially
specialty
spherular
spiralled
spirillum
springlet
sprinkler
squabbler
squirelet
steelclad
stoically
straggler
strangler
strangles
streamlet
strobilae
strobilus
struggler
subocular
subphylum
subsellia
sugarplum
surmullet
suturally
swivelled
swordplay
syllabled
tactfully
tactually
tarpaulin
tasselled
tearfully
tenaculum
tentacled
textually
thermally
throttler
tinselled
tonguelet
tonically
tonsillar
topically
toxically
travelled
traveller
trivially
trochilus
trowelled
troweller
tunefully
tunnelled
typically
unbridled
uncivilly
underclay
underplay
underplot
unequally
unpeopled
unpopular
unruffled
unsettled
unskilled
unusually
utricular
valuables
varicella
vehicular
ventrally
vesicular
virtually
vitriolic
vocabular
wakefully
wassailer
waterflea
weevilled
wishfully
wistfully
yachtclub
zestfully
acclaimer
agronomic
anchorman
anoxaemia
antinomic
autonomic
autosomal
baptismal
barleymow
bondwoman
brakesman
bridesman
cacodemon
cameraman
Candlemas
cattleman
charwoman
Christmas
churchman
clergyman
clergymen
colourman
confirmed
confirmer
confirmor
conformal
conformer
copolymer
cornerman
coseismal
coseismic
cracksman
craftsman
declaimer
dichromat
dichromic
discommon
draftsman
duralumin
ealdorman
elastomer
endogamic

endolymph
energumen
entrammel
epidermal
epidermic
epidermis
epistemic
ergonomic
exciseman
exodermis
familyman
fellowman
fieldsman
fisherman
forenamed
forewoman
freewoman
Frenchman
gentleman
ginglymus
gorblimey
graphemic
groomsman
guardsman
guillemot
Hallowmas
hammerman
homogamic
homonymic
hydraemia
ichneumon
ignoramus
ischaemia
ischaemic
jurywoman
kingdomed
kinswoman
lachrymal
latecomer
leucaemia
leukaemia
leukaemic
liveryman
lumberman
malformed
Manxwoman
Martinmas
metonymic
middleman
midsummer
minuteman
monatomic
monogamic
morphemic
morrisman
muffinman
muscleman
Mussulman
nystagmic
nystagmus
oddjobman
oligaemia
ombudsman
Orangeman
oriflamme
oysterman
panoramic
pantryman
paranymph
patrolman
performer
perilymph
persimmon
plainsman
ploughman
plumdamas
pointsman
policeman
polygamic
polysemic
polysomic
praenomen
preadamic
pretermit
prodromal
prodromic
programme
quadruman
quarryman
ribosomal
roundsman
ruddleman
sailorman
sapraemia
sapraemic
schoolman
Scotchman
selectman
shantyman
signalman
sketchmap
sometimes
spiderman
spoilsman
spokesman
sportsman
stableman
statesman
steersman
subatomic
subnormal
sunhelmet
switchman
swordsman
synonymic
taxonomic
thingummy
thirdsman
timberman
timelimit
tirewoman
toponymal
toponymic
tradesman
transumpt
triatomic
tribesman
trichomic
unashamed
undecimal
undreamed
uniformly
vestryman
vicesimal
vigesimal
washerman
welltimed
wherryman
wolframic
woodnymph
workwoman
yachtsman
abandoned
abandonee
abandoner
abdominal
aberrance
aberrancy
abstainer
abundance
accidence
acescence
adherence
adjacency
adjutancy
adnominal
aepyornis
affluence
Afrikaner
Alemannic
allemande
allowance
ambulance
anabranch
annoyance
antigenic
antimonic
antivenin
appetence
appetency
appliance
argumenta
arrogance
assonance
assurance
avoidance
bacchanal
bacchante
bargainer
bastioned
beastings
beestings
bellpunch
billionth
binominal
bivalence
bivalency
Brahmanic
Brahminee
Brahminic
brazilnut
Britannia
Britannic
Brythonic
bullfinch
butternut
cacuminal
calamanco
calycinal
candlenut
captaincy
catatonia
catatonic
certainly
certainty
chaffinch
challenge
chastener
chitlings
citizenly
citizenry
clarionet
clearance
cloisonne
coeternal
coherence
coherency
colcannon
colocynth
comedones
concerned
condignly
consignee
consignor
constancy
container
contemner
copartner
Corybants
cothurnus
covalence
covalency
crescendo
CroMagnon
cryogenic
cryptonym
cumbrance
dalliance
debutante
decadence
decadency
decagonal
deference
demimonde
dethroner
diactinic
dilatancy
diligence
disbranch
discerner
doctrinal
dominance
drunkenly
dysphonia
easterner
ectogenic
effluence
eloquence
embryonal
embryonic
emergence
emergency
emotional
endogenic
endurance
esperance
Esperanto
estaminet
esurience
esuriency
ethylenic
excitancy
existence
explainer
exultance
exultancy
eyeglance
eyeopener
factional
fashioner
feculence
feiseanna
fictional
fifteenth
figurante
fivepence
fivepenny
flagrance
flagrancy
fleshings
flippancy
fluxional
folkdance
foreigner
forlornly
fourpence
fourpenny
fragrance
fragrancy
fraternal
freelance
freerange
frequence
frequency
freshener
gallooned
glissandi
glissando
gnathonic
goddamned
goldfinch
goldsinny
golflinks
grievance
groundnut
gunrunner
halfpence
halfpenny
harpooner
haverings
headliner
heathenry
hegemonic
hesitance
hesitancy
heteronym
hexagonal
highlands
hightoned
hindrance
hodiernal
homotonic
hypomania
hypomanic
ignorance
illomened
imbalance
immanence
immanency
imminence
imminency
impedance
impotence
impotency
impudence
incidence
indecency
indigence
indolence
inerrancy
inference
influence
influenza
ingrained
inherence
inhumanly
innocence
innocency
inorganic
insolence
inspanned
insurance
interknit
isoclinal
isoclinic
jaborandi
jacaranda
Jacobinic
jubilance
karabiner
kitchener
knockknee
labyrinth
lampooner
landowner
lanthanum
latitancy
lazybones
lazytongs
libidinal
longrange
luminance
macaronic
maharanee
mainliner
mansionry
matutinal
medicinal
melatonin
melomania
memoranda
messianic
militancy
millennia
millionth
mischance
missioner
moistener
monkeynut
monomania
monotonic
monsignor
monsoonal
mullioned
mumchance
muniments
mutagenic
neoteinia
neoteinic
nescience
netveined
nicotinic
ninepence
ninepenny
nocturnal
nucleonic
obedience
obeisance
occupancy
octagonal
oecumenic
oenomancy
offchance
officinal
oilburner
oilpaints
olecranal
olecranon
oncogenic
onlicence
ontogenic
opinioned
opponency
ordinance
oscitancy
outgoings
outgunned
overtones
paludinal
passional
paulownia
penitence
pensioner
perchance
pergunnah
permeance
personnel
petulance
petulancy
pharaonic
pimpernel
plangency
pleadings
pleasance
pneumonia
pneumonic
poignancy
polygenic
polygonal
polygonum
polytonal
polyvinyl
pregnancy
pronounce
propionic
proscenia
proteinic
prurience
pruriency
pseudonym
puissance
puritanic
purloiner
pursuance
purulence
purulency
pyracanth
pyrogenic
pyromancy
pyromania
quickener
quittance
reactance
rearrange
recreancy
recusance
recusancy
redolence
reference
referenda
refluence
relevance
relevancy
remanence
renitency
residence
residency
resonance
reticence
reticency
reverence
ringfence
ruffianly
rumrunner
Saracenic
Sauternes
scrivener
seachange
sectional
semblance
semifinal
semilunar
semitonic
sentience
sentiency
septennia
sequinned
sergeancy
serjeancy
serjeanty
serotonin
sessional
severance
sforzando
sharpener
Shechinah
shipcanal
shipmoney
shipowner
shortener
sibilance
sibilancy
sixteenmo
sixteenth
skirtings
sleevenut
sojourner
Solomonic
soundings
squinancy
stagnancy
stational
stationer
stepdance
stiffener
stockinet
stridence
stridency
strychnic
subagency
subbranch
substance
sulphonic

sunbonnet
sunburned
sundowner
sunlounge
suntanned
surgeoncy
sustainer
sweetener
swordknot
symphonic
synclinal
telamones
telegenic
tensional
terebinth
theogonic
theomania
thereinto
thereunto
thickener
thickknee
tightener
tinopener
tolerance
torsional
tramlines
transenna
transonic
trappings
trepanned
trichinae
triclinia
triclinic
trimmings
truepenny
tuitional
tunnelnet
umpteenth
unadorned
unbalance
uncleanly
uncrowned
undefined
unfeigned
uniplanar
unlearned
unwomanly
utterance
vaticinal
vehemence
vengeance
versional
vigilance
vigilante
virulence
virulency
viscounty
warbonnet
westerner
whereinto
whereunto
whodunnit
workbench
workmanly
zymogenic
ablutions
accessory
acidulous
aciniform
adulatory
adulthood
aerobiont
aerodrome
aetiology
aftermost
afternoon
afterword
agapemone
agriology
aitchbone
albatross
algarroba
allantois
allophone
allotrope
allotropy
alpenhorn
aluminous
ambiguous
ambitious
amorphous
amphibole
amphigory
analogous
anandrous
anchylose
angiology
angleworm
anhydrous
anklebone
anomalous
anonymous
anthology
anthozoan
antiknock
antiphony
apetalous
aphyllous
apogamous
Appaloosa
arachnoid
arboreous
archivolt
argentous
arrowroot
arrowwood
arrowworm
arsenious
arteriole
artichoke
arytenoid
asbestous
ascospore
asepalous
assiduous
astrodome
astrology
astronomy
asymptote
atrocious
audacious
audiology
autocross
autotroph
azeotrope
babacoote
backcloth
backcross
backsword
backwoods
bacteroid
baltimore
banderole
bandicoot
barbarous
barbitone
barcarole
bargepole
barnstorm
barracoon
beauteous
behaviour
bellicose
bifarious
billabong
billycock
billygoat
binturong
biogenous
birdsfoot
birthwort
blackcoat
blackcock
Blackfoot
blasthole
blindfold
bloodroot
bloodworm
bloodwort
bluestone
boardfoot
boardroom
bombproof
bondstone
bonhomous
bookstore
bounteous
bourgeois
bracteole
breakdown
briarroot
briarwood
brickwork
brierroot
brierwood
brimstone
bringdown
broadloom
broomcorn
brushwood
brushwork
buckthorn
bucktooth
buffaloes
buhrstone
bulltrout
bumptious
burdenous
burnedout
burrstone
cacholong
cacophony
Caenozoic
Cainozoic
cairngorm
calaboose
calcicole
calculous
caliology
campstool
canalboat
cancerous
cankerous
cantaloup
capacious
Capricorn
carambola
carcinoma
carnivore
carpology
carrefour
cartology
casserole
catchpole
catchpoll
catchword
cattaloes
cavernous
cedarwood
celluloid
cellulose
cephalous
cerecloth
cetaceous
chancroid
chancrous
chaperone
cheekbone
cherimoya
childhood
Chinatown
chiropody
chitinous
chorology
cinereous
clamorous
classroom
claviform
clearcole
cloakroom
clockwork
closedown
coachwork
cobaltous
cockahoop
cockscomb
cocksfoot
coldshort
colophony
colostomy
coltsfoot
Cominform
commodore
comptroll
condyloid
condyloma
congruous
conscious
copestone
coprology
copsewood
coralloid
cordiform
corduroys
cornflour
cornstone
corticoid
cortisone
corymbose
cosmogony
cosmology
coumarone
countdown
courteous
courtroom
crackdown
crapulous
credulous
crematory
cretinous
criminous
crossroad
crossword
crowsfoot
cruciform
cryoscope
cryoscopy
cubbyhole
cuneiform
curbstone
currycomb
curviform
cutaneous
cutthroat
cymbiform
cyprinoid
cystotomy
damnatory
dangerous
davenport
dayschool
deathroll
deciduous
declivous
decompose
decretory
delicious
delirious
demeanour
dentiform
depthbomb
dermatoid
desultory
dexterous
diachrony
diandrous
diarrhoea
dichotomy
diclinous
dimissory
dioecious
diphthong
dipterous
directory
disaccord
discolour
disembody
disentomb
disfavour
dishcloth
dishclout
dishonour
dittology
dogstooth
dormitory
drawnwork
dreamboat
dresscoat
driftwood
dripstone
dropscone
drugstore
earthborn
earthwork
earthworm
egregious
eiderdown
eightfold
eightsome
elbowroom
electrode
ellipsoid
emunctory
endeavour
endoscope
endoscopy
endospore
entrecote
epigynous
eponymous
erogenous
erroneous
eruciform
ethnology
etymology
eucaryote
euchology
eunuchoid
eutectoid
everybody
evocatory
excretory
executory
exogamous
exogenous
expiatory
expletory
exsuccous
extempore
fabaceous
facecloth
facetious
fairyhood
falciform
faldstool
falsehood
fancywork
farandole
feedstock
felonious
ferocious
ferryboat
festology
feudatory
fibriform
fibrinoid
fibrinous
fieldbook
fieldboot
fieldwork
filaceous
fireirons
fireproof
firestone
firstborn
firstfoot
fistulous
flagstone
flavorous
flintlock
flowstone
foolproof
footcloth
footloose
footstool
foreclose
forefront
foreknown
foreshore
foreshown
foulbrood
fourscore
fractious
framework
freestone
frigatoon
frivolous
frockcoat
frostwork
fructuous
fruticose
fugacious
fulgurous
fullblown
fullgrown
fulminous
fungiform
galactose
gallstone
gambadoes
garderobe
garrulous
gemmology
genealogy
germproof
gestatory
ghostword
girandole
gladstone
glaireous
glamorous
glasswork
glasswort
gloryhole
glutinous
gneissoid
gneissose
gonophore
goosefoot
gradatory
grandiose
granitoid
granulose
greatcoat
greenhorn
greenroom
greenwood
grillroom
grillwork
gritstone
guacamole
guardbook
guardroom
guesswork
guestroom
guidebook
guidepost
guiderope
gustatory
gynophore
gyroscope
hackamore
haematoid
haematoma
hagiology
hailstone
hailstorm
haircloth
halfblood
halfcrown
handiwork
handsdown
handywork
haplology
hardihood
haresfoot
harmotome
hartshorn
hawsehole
hazardous
headcloth
headphone
headstock
headstone
heartsore
heartwood
heathcock
heliozoan
heliozoic
hellebore
hemitrope
herbivore
hereabout
herpetoid
hexachord
hexaploid
hierology
highflown
highgrown
hilarious
histology
hoarfrost
hoarstone
hollyhock
Hollywood
holophote
holystone
homegrown
homophone
homophony
honeycomb
honeymoon
honkytonk
hornstone
horoscope
horoscopy
horsepond
hortatory
houseboat
housebote
housecoat
household
houseroom

housework
hunkydory
hydathode
hydrofoil
hydrology
hydrosome
hydrozoan
hydrozoon
hymnology
hyperbola
hyperbole
hypnology
hypogeous
hysteroid
ichnology
ichthyoid
iconology
impastoed
imperious
impetuous
impulsory
incensory
incommode
incurious
indispose
ingenious
ingenuous
inglenook
inharmony
injurious
innermost
innocuous
innoxious
inodorous
insidious
interlock
interlope
internode
interpose
interwove
interzone
inventory
invidious
ironstone
isochrone
isogamous
isogenous
isomerous
isopodous
jollyboat
judicious
juxtapose
kerbstone
knockdown
krummhorn
kurrajong
laborious
lacrimose
lacrymose
ladysmock
laevulose
lamellose
lancewood
landdross
landdrost
lapideous
larcenous
laudatory
lazzarone
lazzaroni
leasehold
lecherous
lentiform
leptosome
leucotome
leucotomy
libellous
libratory
lichenous
liegelord
lifeblood
lightfoot
lightsome
lightsout
lightwood
lignaloes
ligniform
limestone
limnology
linenfold
lithesome
lithology
lithopone
lithotomy
litigious
liverwort
livestock
loadstone
loathsome
lobectomy
lodestone
lodgepole
loincloth
longevous
longicorn
longshore
lophodont
lousewort
lovestory
lowermost
loxodrome
lubricous
ludicrous
lustihood
luxurious
macintosh
macrocosm
madrepore
majordomo
maladroit
malarious
malicious
mammalogy
mammiform
mandatory
manganous
manticore
marlstone
marshwort
matchlock
matchwood
matrimony
mattamore
meandrous
mediatory
megaphone
megaspore
melodious
mementoes
menadione
mercurous
mesogloea
metalloid
metalwork
meteoroid
methadone
metrology
metronome
micaceous
microcosm
micrology
microsome
microtome
microtomy
microtone
migratory
milestone
milkfloat
milktooth
millepore
millivolt
millstone
minacious
misbecome
misinform
misreport
momentous
moneywort
Mongoloid
monkshood
monochord
monstrous
moonstone
moraceous
mossgrown
mothproof
motocross
motorboat
mousehole
moviegoer
multifoil
multiform
munitions
murderous
murmurous
myrmecoid
mystagogy
mythology
nannygoat
narratory
navelwort
neckcloth
necrology
nectarous
nefarious
neighbour
nephology
neurology
nevermore
nickelous
nightgown
nightlong
nightwork
northmost
nostology
notochord
notorious
nullipore
oblivious
obnoxious
octachord
offcolour
offertory
officious
oilcolour
oleaceous
olfactory
oligopoly
ophiology
optophone
orderbook
orderform
orrisroot
orthodoxy
osteology
Ostrogoth
outermost
overblown
overcloud
overcrowd
overflown
overgrown
overproof
overshoot
overstock
overwrote
oviferous
oviparous
ovulatory
oxygenous
paintwork
palillogy
palladous
pantaloon
pantyhose
paperwork
papilloma
papillose
papillote
parsimony
pastedown
patchwork
pathology
patrimony
patrology
pearlwort
pellitory
pendulous
pennywort
Pentecost
penurious
periscope
peristome
pestology
petrology
petticoat
pettitoes
phalarope
phenology
pheromone
philology
phonatory
phonology
photocopy
phycology
phytology
phytotomy
piecework
pinchcock
pipestone
piscatory
pisciform
pitchfork
pithecoid
placatory
plainsong
planetoid
planuloid
platinoid
platinous
playgroup
plenteous
plumbeous
plumulose
podagrous
poisonous
pokerwork
polyphone
polyphony
polyploid
pomaceous
pompadour
ponderous
poppycock
porticoes
posticous
powerboat
pranksome
precatory
predatory
prefatory
prelusory
prerecord
presbyope
preschool
pressroom
presswork
probatory
prolusory
pronghorn
protozoal
protozoan
protozoic
protozoon
provisory
psalmbook
pterygoid
pulpstone
pulsatory
pulverous
pumiceous
punchbowl
puppyhood
pureblood
purgatory
pussyfoot
pustulous
pyroscope
quartzose
queenhood
queenpost
querulous
quillwort
radiology
raffinose
raincloud
rainproof
rainstorm
rancorous
rapacious
rapturous
raspatory
recompose
redingote
refectory
religiose
religious
repertory
reservoir
restiform
rhinology
ridgepole
righteous
rigmarole
rivalrous
riverboat
roadblock
rocambole
roodcloth
rootstock
Roquefort
rosaceous
roundworm
rustproof
sacciform
sackcloth
sagacious
sailcloth
sainthood
salacious
salmonoid
saltatory
saltspoon
sandspout
sandstone
sandstorm
sangfroid
sapanwood
satinwood
sauceboat
sauropoda
saxophone
scagliola
scalemoss
scalplock
scapegoat
scatology
scenedock
schistose
schistous
sciaenoid
sciascopy
scirrhous
scombroid
scorebook
scorpioid
scrapbook
screwbolt
screwworm
scutiform
sebaceous
secretory
seditious
seigniory
selenious
selfglory
semaphore
semiology
sericeous
serranoid
setaceous
sevenfold
shakedown
sheepcote
sheepfold
sheephook
shelfroom
shellwork
shopfloor
shopfront
shorthorn
shotproof
signatory
siliceous
silicious
siliquose
siltstone
singalong
skiascopy
slabstone
slumbrous
smokebomb
snakeroot
snakewood
snowbroth
snowgoose
snowstorm
soapstone
sociology
softgoods
solacious
sophomore
sorcerous
soundhole
soundpost
soupspoon
Southdown
southmost
spaceport
spadefoot
spadework
sparkcoil
spearwort
speedboat
sphagnous
sphygmoid
spinulose
spinulous
spiritoso
spiritous
splayfoot
splendour
spongeous
spouthole
squarrose
stackroom
stagedoor
stairfoot
stakeboat
stampnote
starstone
statehood
stateroom
statutory
steamboat
steelwork
sternmost
sternpost
stevedore
stickwork
stillborn
stillroom
stinkbomb
stinkhorn
stinkwood
stirabout
stockbook
stockdove
stockroom
stokehold
stokehole
stonecoal
stonecold
stonework
stonewort
storeroom
stormcock
stormcone
storybook
strapwork
strapwort
strawworm
strenuous
stuporous
stylebook
styliform
subereous
sugarloaf
sumptuous
sunstroke
supercool
supernova
superpose
surculose
swangoose
swansdown
swearword
sweetcorn
symbology
synchrony
syngamous
syphiloid
tarragona
tautology
teleology
telephone
telephony
telephoto
telescope
telescopy
tellurous
tenacious
tendinous
tenebrous
territory
testimony
tetralogy
tetrapody
therefore
thighbone
thighboot
threefold
threesome

threshold
thrombose
thumbhole
tigermoth
tigerwood
tightrope
tilestone
toadstone
toadstool
tollbooth
tombstone
tomentose
tomentous
toothcomb
toothsome
toothwort
torchsong
torturous
totempole
touchdown
touchhole
touchwood
townsfolk
trainload
transform
transport
transpose
trapezoid
traycloth
trematode
tremulous
tribology
trichroic
tricolour
trigamous
trimerous
tropology
troublous
trunkroad
tufaceous
tuliproot
tulipwood
turnabout
turnstone
twentyone
twiceborn
twicetold
tyrannous
uliginous
unanimous
unbeknown
underbody
undercoat
underdone
underfoot
undergone
undermost
undersold
undersong
undertone
undertook
underwood
unicolour
uniparous
unisonous
untimeous
unwelcome
uppermost
uranology
uttermost
vagarious
vainglory
varioloid
variolous
vasectomy
veinstone
velodrome
venereous
venturous
veracious
vermiform
verminous
verrucose
verrucous
versiform
vexatious
vibratory
vicarious
villiform
vimineous
vinaceous
vitriform
vivacious
volcanoes
voracious
vorticose
vulturous
wagonroof
waistcoat
walkabout
washcloth
washedout
watchword
watercool
waterfowl
waterhole
waterworn
wavefront
wayzgoose
wearisome
wellknown
whaleboat
whalebone
wheelwork
wherefore
whetstone
whinstone
whipstock
whirlpool
whitewood
wholesome
widowhood
windblown
windproof
winestone
wirephoto
withstood
woebegone
womanhood
womenfolk
woodblock
worrisome
woundwort
wrongdoer
wyliecoat
xenophobe
xylophone
zebrawood
zoogenous
zygospore
amblyopia
amblyopic
anthropic
apocrypha
arthropod
barkeeper
beekeeper
biography
bombhappy
breastpin
catalepsy
chaetopod
chassepot
cherrypie
coffeepot
curlpaper
developer
dewlapped
diatropic
dispeople
distemper
dystrophy
entrapped
enwrapped
epigraphy
episcopal
eucalypti
flowerpot
fluorspar
gastropod
genotypic
geography
geotropic
hyperopia
hyperopic
impromptu
innkeeper
isotropic
kidnapped
kidnapper
lagniappe
landloper
loveapple
misshapen
monotypic
municipal
myography
newspaper
notepaper
orography
orthoepic
peasouper
pepperpot
philippic
phyllopod
pineapple
polytypic
principal
principia
principle
pseudopod
quadruped
quadruple
quadruply
quintuple
radialply
ricepaper
roseapple
safetypin
sandpaper
sandpiper
satinspar
slaphappy
sorbapple
starapple
theosophy
thereupon
timelapse
tittupped
tophamper
uncropped
underspin
unicuspid
unstopped
unwrapped
wallpaper
whereupon
Xanthippe
zoography
arabesque
burlesque
chibouque
Dantesque
equivoque
grotesque
Junoesque
monocoque
odalisque
soliloquy
technique
triptyque
acroteria
adulterer
ahistoric
aleatoric
allegoric
allomorph
ambergris
anaphoric
ancestral
anemogram
angleiron
angularly
annularly
antiserum
antiviral
araucaria
argybargy
armigeral
auditoria
backwards
bainmarie
baneberry
barathrum
bearberry
bestirred
bicameral
bigeneric
bilateral
biliteral
billiards
biometric
bishopric
blaeberry
blinkered
blowtorch
blueberry
blunderer
blusterer
boobytrap
brasserie
bratwurst
breadtree
bricabrac
broiderer
brotherly
bullytree
butcherer
butcherly
cablegram
cadastral
cadaveric
cafeteria
calandria
calendric
camphoric
cantharid
cantharis
cantharus
carthorse
cartogram
catamaran
cathedral
catoptric
centigram
chafferer
champerty
chaparral
chartered
charterer
chatterer
checkered
chequered
chickaree
chimaeric
chinstrap
chivalric
cineraria
clatterer
claustral
cloistral
cockhorse
coinsurer
colostrum
concierge
concourse
concurred
conferral
conferred
conferrer
conqueror
conundrum
corkscrew
cranberry
creatural
cropeared
crossbred
crowberry
cupbearer
cyclotron
cylindric
decontrol
deerberry
deliverer
dextrorse
diablerie
diametral
diametric
diathermy
digastric
dinoceras
directrix
disbarred
discharge
discourse
dogshores
downthrow
downwards
drayhorse
dysphoria
dysphoric
eastwards
eavesdrop
eccentric
echovirus
ectomorph
electoral
enamoured
endomorph
ephemeral
ephemerid
ephemeris
ephemeron
excentric
executrix
fancyfree
feathered
fenestrae
fenestral
filmstrip
fireworks
flatterer
fluecured
foolhardy
fritterer
frogmarch
fruiterer
fruittree
furtherer
gaucherie
geometric
geometrid
geriatric
gigahertz
glandered
glengarry
goldenrod
grubscrew
hackberry
halfhardy
harbourer
haustoria
headfirst
heartfree
hearthrug
hectogram
heliogram
hierogram
hippocras
histogram
homewards
honoraria
hypethral
illiberal
inaugural
indecorum
infusoria
insularly
interbred
intercrop
interpret
ironworks
isometric
jackstraw
jacquerie
jockstrap
jocularly
Judastree
Juneberry
kilohertz
lagomorph
laminaria
launderer
leftwards
lifeforce
longeared
luciferin
maelstrom
magistral
magnetron
matriarch
maunderer
mediatrix
megahertz
menagerie
mesomorph
metameric
microgram
milligram
misleared
mistigris
monoceros
monomeric
moratoria
mousetrap
naseberry
neckverse
northerly
obstetric
ochlocrat
outskirts
overborne
overthrew
overthrow
packhorse
painterly
pairhorse
palpebral
palustral
panegyric
papeterie
paramorph
paregoric
patriarch
pellagrin
pentagram
penumbral
percheron
perimorph
phonogram
phytotron
pictogram
pikeperch
plastered
plasterer
plethoric
plunderer
plutocrat
pokeberry
polymeric
polymorph
popularly
poriferal
poriferan
porphyria
posthorse
potpourri
poulterer
prayerrug
preferred
prothorax
psalteria
puerperal
pyrethrum
quarterly
racehorse
radiogram
raspberry
rearhorse
rearwards
recoverer
reenforce
registrar
regularly
reimburse
reinforce
roadworks
roisterer
rowantree
saccharin
saltmarsh
saltworks
sanatoria
Sanhedrim
Sanhedrin
sanitaria
sassafras
saunterer
scarecrow
scatterer
schlieren
schnorrer
scholarly
scoredraw
scoundrel
scrapiron
secularly
sedgewren
semestral
shadberry
shadetree
sharecrop
sideburns
sidewards
similarly
sinistral
slanderer
slategrey
slenderly
slumberer
smackeroo
smallarms
smatterer

smoketree
snaredrum
sniggerer
snowberry
soapberry
soapworks
sociogram
soldierly
southerly
spinneret
sputterer
squirarch
staggerer
stagparty
stalworth
stammerer
stercoral
stingaree
stinktrap
stonecrop
studhorse
stutterer
subastral
succourer
sudatoria
sulphuret
sulphuric
sunspurge
surcharge
swaggerer
swimmeret
symmetric
tabularly
tambourin
taskforce
taxidermy
tegularly
testatrix
tetragram
theandric
therefrom
thesaurus
thitherto
thorntree
thunderer
thyratron
titularly
trattoria
trattorie
treasurer
trierarch
trihedral
trihybrid
trimetric
trousered
tubularly
tuliptree
turboprop
twitterer
unaltered
uncovered
underbred
undergrad
unnatural
unreserve
untutored
urticaria
verdigris
vertebrae
vertebral
vomitoria
wallydrag
weathered
weatherly
westwards
wherefrom
whimperer
whipperin
whiskered
whisperer
windwards
wineberry
workhorse
wristdrop
xeromorph
abscissae
abscissas
acariasis
acquiesce
addressee
addresser
addressor
aesthesia
aesthesis
aggressor
aimlessly
alkaloses
alkalosis
amauroses
amaurosis
amorously
amylopsin
anabioses
anabiosis
anacruses
anacrusis
analgesia
analgesic
anamnesis
ankylosis
antipasto
anxiously
aphereses
apheresis
apophyses
apophysis
appetiser
appraisal
appraiser
appressed
aqueously
arduously
arriviste
artemisia
arthrosis
artlessly
assumpsit
autolysis
babirussa
biliously
bulbously
buttinsky
callously
canvasser
caparison
caryopses
caryopsis
catalyser
catalyses
catalysis
catharses
catharsis
chastiser
cheongsam
chlorosis
cirrhosis
civiliser
coloniser
commensal
commissar
compasses
comprisal
condenser
confessor
consensus
contrasty
copiously
coreopsis
courtesan
culsdesac
curiously
cutinised
cyclopses
cytolysis
demitasse
depressed
depressor
deviously
diaereses
diaeresis
diagnoses
diagnosis
diaphysis
diastasis
diathesis
dinnerset
dirigisme
disbursal
dismissal
dispenser
dispersal
disperser
disseisin
dubiously
duteously
dyscrasia
dyspepsia
dysplasia
eclampsia
elevenses
emulously
encrimson
endlessly
energiser
engrosser
enviously
epiclesis
epiphyses
epiphysis
epithesis
equaliser
eulogiser
exercises
exorciser
exosmosis
exostosis
expressly
extrinsic
fatuously
fluoresce
fluorosis
folkmusic
foretaste
Freemason
fricassee
furiously
gallowses
gibbously
gomphosis
groundsel
halfcaste
halitosis
hangerson
haplessly
hardnosed
heinously
heterosis
hideously
hortensia
hugeously
hyponasty
idealiser
immodesty
impiously
increaser
intrinsic
intumesce
jealously
joylessly
katabasis
katharsis
keratosis
langouste
lawlessly
maharishi
malvoisie
manifesto
melanosis
merganser
micropsia
misfeasor
mongooses
monobasic
moraliser
mydriasis
narcissus
nebuliser
nephrosis
nervously
nocuously
nonperson
noxiously
obsolesce
obviously
odorously
offseason
oleoresin
ominously
onerously
oogenesis
oppressor
organiser
overissue
paillasse
palliasse
parabasis
paradisal
paralysis
parlously
passersby
pederasty
pertussis
phantasma
photopsia
piteously
polariser
politesse
polybasic
pompously
possessed
possessor
posthaste
postnasal
practised
precursor
processed
processer
processor
proconsul
professed
professor
prognoses
prognosis
prolapsus
prolepses
prolepsis
proptosis
prothesis
psoriasis
psychoses
psychosis
purchaser
pyrolysis
rafflesia
raucously
recalesce
redresser
rehearsal
reminisce
repressor
retrousse
rhodopsin
riotously
Roumansch
ruinously
sargassos
sclerosis
scoliosis
scrollsaw
seriously
sexlessly
sideissue
siderosis
silicosis
sinlessly
sinuously
slopbasin
snubnosed
squamosal
successor
succursal
surprisal
suspensor
syllepses
syllepsis
symbiosis
symphysis
syneresis
synizesis
syntheses
synthesis
taeniasis
tediously
televisor
tenuously
thalassic
theoriser
timeously
totaliser
traversal
traverser
unadvised
unbiassed
unblessed
uncrossed
universal
untrussed
uselessly
vacuously
vaporiser
variously
vibrissae
viciously
virtuosic
virtuosos
viscously
vocaliser
Waldenses
washbasin
witlessly
womaniser
zealously
abdicator
abnegator
abrogator
accipiter
acquittal
acquitted
acrobatic
acropetal
activator
adamantly
adiabatic
adjunctly
admonitor
advocator
aerobatic
aerolitic
aerometer
aerometry
aesthetic
agonistic
airworthy
alabaster
albinotic
algorithm
alienator
aliphatic
alligator
allopathy
altimeter
amaurotic
amourette
amputator
anabiotic
analeptic
anciently
ancientry
andesitic
anecdotal
anecdotic
animistic
ankylotic
annotator
annulated
anorectic
antarctic
antenatal
antidotal
antipathy
apathetic
aplanatic
apodictic
apomictic
apparatus
apparitor
appointee
arboretum
arteritis
arthritic
arthritis
asphaltic
asphaltum
aspirator
assaulter
asthmatic
asymmetry
asyndetic
asyndeton
ataractic
atavistic
atheistic
athematic
atmometer
atomistic
attempter
attractor
aubrietia
augmented
augmenter
augmentor
authentic
autolytic
automatic
automaton
axiomatic
Axminster
Babbittry
backbiter
backwater
badminton
ballistae
ballistic
bannister
banqueter
banquette
Bantustan
baptistry
barometer
barometry
baronetcy
barrister
basipetal
bayoneted
bedsettee
bedsitter
beefeater
beemaster
benighted
bespatter
bicipital
biorhythm
birdwatch
blatantly
bolometer
bolometry
bombastic
bouquetin
boycotter
bregmatic
brevetted
briquette
brochette
bughunter
buoyantly
cachectic
capacitor
carpenter
carpentry
casuistic
casuistry
catalytic
cathartic
cathectic
chapleted
character
charlatan
charlotte
chemistry
chloritic
chlorotic
chorister
chromatic
chromatin
cigarette
cinematic
circuitry
clamantly
clemently
climactic
coadjutor
coelostat
collected
collector
comforter
commenter
committal
committed
committee
compactly
compactor
conceited
concentre
concerted
concocter
concoctor
conductor
connected
connecter
connector
consortia
consulter
consultor

contactor
contented
convector
converter
copacetic
coroneted
correctly
corrector
corrupter
corruptly
couchette
courgette
cremaster
cricketer
croquette
crossette
cunctator
currently
curvetted
decalitre
decametre
decilitre
decimator
decimetre
decorator
dedicator
defaulter
defiantly
deflector
defroster
dendritic
dentistry
depositor
depurator
desolater
desolator
detonator
detractor
diacritic
dialectal
dialectic
diastatic
diathetic
digitated
dimwitted
dipswitch
dishwater
dismantle
dissector
dissenter
distantly
dizygotic
doleritic
dolomitic
dominator
dorbeetle
dosimeter
dosimetry
doubleton
drysalter
dualistic
dynamiter
dyspeptic
dziggetai
earnestly
earthstar
eclamptic
ecosystem
eggbeater
egotistic
elegantly
elemental
elongated
emaciated
embrittle
embryotic
emendator
eminently
emplastic
encaustic
enchanter
encounter
energetic
englutted
enhearten
enigmatic
enlighten
ensheathe
enteritis
enwreathe
enzymatic
epaenetic
epaulette
epicentre
epileptic
epinastic
epiphytal
epiphytic
epithetic
epizootic
equisetum
ergometer
escalator
escheator
estimator
etiquette
evidently
excavator
excerptor
exequatur
exhauster
exhibitor
exosmotic
expediter
exploiter
expositor
extractor
fantastic
fantastry
fasciated
Fascistic
fatwitted
faunistic
fervently
fideistic
fillister
filtertip
fingertip
fireeater
firewater
floriated
floristic
floristry
forfeiter
forgotten
formatted
foxhunter
freighter
fulgently
fumigator
gallantly
gallantry
gannister
garmented
garrotter
gasfitter
gasmantle
gasometer
gastritis
gauleiter
generator
geomantic
georgette
geostatic
gestalten
gladiator
glossator
glossitis
goosestep
graduator
graphitic
guarantee
guarantor
guncotton
gymnastic
haemostat
halftitle
halieutic
hamfisted
hammertoe
Hanseatic
harmattan
harvester
headwater
heliostat
hemstitch
hepatitis
hereafter
herniated
hesitator
heuristic
hexameter
highwater
hodometer
Holarctic
homiletic
hopscotch
Hottentot
hubristic
hygrostat
hypocotyl
iceskater
idiomatic
idiopathy
illgotten
illicitly
immolator
imperator
impolitic
inbreathe
incubator
indagator
indicator
indigotin
inelastic
inexactly
inflictor
infractor
inhalator
inheritor
inhibitor
initiator
innovator
inspector
instanter
instantly
insulator
involuted
irrigator
ischiatic
Islamitic
isohyetal
isostatic
itsybitsy
ittybitty
jetsetter
jobmaster
Judaistic
judgmatic
katabatic
keratitis
kilolitre
kilometre
kinematic
klinostat
lambently
laminated
larghetto
lastditch
lazaretto
Leicester
leitmotif
leitmotiv
leniently
leviratic
levitator
liberated
liberator
librettos
limewater
limonitic
literatim
literator
literatus
lobulated
locomotor
logarithm
lorgnette
lovematch
lymphatic
lysimeter
macerator
machmeter
Mahometan
majorette
manhattan
manometer
marquetry
Masoretic
maybeetle
meditator
mekometer
melanotic
melocoton
meltwater
memoriter
mercaptan
miasmatic
midinette
midwinter
milometer
mishanter
mistletoe
mitigator
moderator
modulator
monolatry
mordantly
moschatel
mosquitos
motheaten
motivator
mutilator
mydriatic
navigator
nephritic
nephritis
Nilometer
nodulated
nominator
novelette
nucleated
numerator
obligated
obturator
occipital
ocellated
octameter
offcentre
onanistic
onomastic
oogenetic
opsimathy
optometer
optometry
opulently
orangetip
orangutan
orchestic
orchestra
organstop
orgiastic
Orpington
osmometer
oubliette
outfitter
outputted
outwitted
overeaten
overeater
overmatch
overpitch
overwatch
oviductal
pageantry
paillette
palaestra
palafitte
palmistry
pancratic
paralytic
paramatta
parameter
parapeted
parasitic
parotitis
parquetry
patiently
patinated
patriotic
patristic
paymaster
pearlitic
peasantry
peccantly
peculator
pedometer
pendently
perfectly
perfector
peridotic
perimeter
perinatal
peripatus
permitted
permitter
perverter
phlebitis
phrenetic
pianistic
pierrette
pietistic
piquantly
pirouette
pisolitic
pixilated
placentae
placental
plasmatic
pleuritic
pneumatic
poetaster
polyester
polymathy
polywater
postentry
postnatal
pothunter
poussette
pragmatic
prankster
precentor
preceptor
predictor
preemptor
prelector
presbyter
presentee
presenter
presently
pressstud
preventer
prismatic
proclitic
progestin
projector
proleptic
prophetic
prosector
prostatic
protector
protester
protestor
prothetic
provostry
prudently
psoriatic
psychotic
pungently
pyrolater
pyrolatry
pyrolytic
pyrometer
pyrometry
quadratic
quartette
quercetum
quickstep
quintette
quirister
radiantly
rainwater
rampantly
realistic
recruital
recruiter
redletter
redoubted
reflector
refractor
regretted
regulator
Reichstag
reliantly
rencontre
renovator
requester
resonator
respecter
retinitis
retractor
revelator
rewritten
rheumatic
rhymester
roadmetal
rosewater
ruminator
sacristan
saleratus
salicetum
saliently
saltpetre
saltwater
Samaritan
sapiently
sarcastic
sasquatch
satinette
saturator
schematic
schmaltzy
scleritis
sclerotic
scoliotic
scorbutic
scrutator
sealetter
seanettle
seaworthy
seedeater
segmental
selenitic
semeiotic
semimetal
separates
separator
sequester
sequestra
serinette
serpentry
serviette
sestertia
shortstop
sideritic
silicotic
simpleton
simulator
singleton
sinusitis
sixfooter
slaughter
slowmatch
sobsister
sodawater
solicitor
sonometer
sophister
sophistic
sophistry
soubrette
souwester
spaghetti
spectator
speedster
spermatic
spermatid
sphincter
splenetic
splenitis
spoliator
sprightly
stalactic
statistic
statuette
steatitic
stellated
stigmatic
stilettos
stopwatch
storiated
stromatic
strumitis
stylistic
subarctic
subcostal
subeditor
submaster
submental
submitted
subverter
succentor
suggester
superstar
supinator
supporter
surfeiter
sybaritic
sylleptic
symbiotic
syncretic
syndactyl
synovitis

syntactic
synthetic
systaltic
tabulator
taximeter
teakettle
tegmental
tegmentum
telemeter
telemetry
telepathy
theoretic
thicketed
Thomistic
thoughted
throwster
thyristor
tidewater
toadeater
tonguetie
tonometer
tormentil
tormentor
touristic
trabeated
trachytic
traumatic
trickster
tridactyl
trimester
trinketer
trinketry
triquetra
trisector
trumpeter
truncated
tunicated
turgently
twofisted
twosuiter
typemetal
typhlitis
ultimatum
unadopted
uncharted
uncinated
uncounted
uncreated
undaunted
undoubted
undulated
unhealthy
unknitted
unlimited
unpointed
unsheathe
unsighted
unsightly
unspotted
unwritten
upcountry
upholster
uprightly
usherette
valiantly
vasomotor
venerator
verdantly
vignetter
violently
voltmeter
volumeter
wagonette
warrantee
warranter
warrantor
wattmeter
webfooted
witchetty
Worcester
wormeaten
wyandotte
youngster
zeugmatic
zoophytic
zucchetto
zygomatic
abouttturn
accentual
acetabula
admeasure
admixture
adventure
affixture
Algonquin
almshouse
amplitude
anomalure
anschluss
antennule
antitrust
aspectual
attribute
autoroute
awestruck
Aylesbury
bakehouse
baldaquin
barracuda
bathhouse
beatitude
beleaguer
bilingual
blackbuck
bloodlust
boathouse
booklouse
brachyura
buckhound
bundobust
bunkhouse
byproduct
calcifuge
calendula
calenture
campanula
candytuft
cannelure
catamount
certitude
chanteuse
charmeuse
chevelure
chockfull
chondrule
chophouse
clubhouse
coalmouse
coiffeuse
colemouse
colloquia
comfiture
comminute
composure
configure
connature
construct
continual
continuer
continuum
convolute
cookhouse
coproduce
corbicula
cornemuse
coverture
cranreuch
crenature
crossruff
curricula
curvature
dachshund
debenture
deckhouse
deerhound
defeature
departure
depasture
destitute
desuetude
difficult
disannual
disavouch
disfigure
disposure
disrepute
dissolute
dosshouse
draghound
dryasdust
dulcitude
dumbfound
eastbound
effectual
eiderduck
embrasure
empyreuma
enclosure
enrapture
exchequer
exclosure
faithcure
farmhouse
fascicule
fasciculi
febrifuge
feedstuff
fioritura
fioriture
firehouse
flashbulb
flashcube
flashtube
flophouse
foodstuff
footfault
footpound
forasmuch
forcepump
forecourt
fortitude
fourflush
freehouse
furniture
gallinule
garniture
gatehouse
gazehound
glomerule
glomeruli
goalmouth
grandaunt
graticule
gratitude
greataunt
greyhound
hairbrush
halfbound
halftruth
hamstrung
haranguer
harlequin
heartburn
heavyduty
hellhound
Hexateuch
hidebound
hierodule
hoarhound
holocaust
homebound
homuncule
homunculi
horehound
hypocaust
immixture
importune
impostume
imposture
inclosure
incorrupt
indenture
institute
interfuse
interlude
interrupt
intriguer
introduce
ironbound
ironmould
josshouse
lassitude
leafmould
licensure
lobscouse
longhouse
longitude
loudmouth
lyamhound
lymehound
magnitude
majuscule
mallemuck
malthouse
mannequin
matricula
menopause
menstrual
menstruum
messieurs
miniature
minuscule
monticule
multitude
nailbrush
neathouse
negritude
nervature
newshound
nigritude
noctiluca
noseflute
numbskull
oasthouse
opportune
overstuff
overtrump
overwound
palanquin
parachute
paramount
patchouli
patchouly
peninsula
penthouse
perpetual
persecute
pesthouse
petiolule
platitude
playhouse
plenitude
plicature
plusfours
pointduty
polevault
politburo
poorhouse
posthouse
prefigure
prelature
premature
preoccupy
preshrunk
procedure
prosecute
raingauge
ranunculi
rearmouse
recapture
rectitude
remeasure
reproduce
reremouse
restitute
revictual
roadhouse
rockbound
sagebrush
scripture
sculpture
secateurs
seigneury
selfabuse
selfdoubt
selftrust
semifluid
semiplume
sepulture
servitude
sheerhulk
shelduck
signature
sliderule
slushfund
smokebush
snowbound
sobriquet
sostenuto
sourdough
spacesuit
spicebush
spiracula
spiritual
spirituel
staghound
stampduty
stillhunt
striature
stricture
structure
sunstruck
superfuse
tablature
tanliquor
tarantula
tessitura
thornbush
tidegauge
tollhouse
toolhouse
townhouse
trabecula
tracksuit
transfuse
transmute
tubercule
turnround
turpitude
umbellule
underhung
unisexual
unsavoury
vallecula
vastitude
ventiduct
vermicule
vermifuge
vestibule
vestiture
vibracula
wallfruit
warehouse
washhouse
waterbuck
waterbutt
wellfound
westbound
whipround
windbound
winevault
wiregauze
witchhunt
wolfhound
woodchuck
woodlouse
workhouse
yearround
ablatival
affidavit
aggrieved
almsgiver
antinovel
Bolshevik
breakeven
campfever
carryover
confervae
conserver
contrived
contriver
convolved
crossover
daredevil
downriver
dustcover
flashover
freeliver
gearlever
genitival
goingover
goldfever
goodwives
hardcover
highlevel
howsoever
lifesaver
longaeval
longlived
manoeuvre
mediaeval
Menshevik
milkfever
nondriver
nutweevil
ourselves
parleyvoo
perceiver
perfervid
preserver
primaeval
redivivus
reprieval
retrieval
retriever
rounceval
selfmoved
septemvir
shipfever
skindiver
slipcover
tipstaves
voiceover
werwolves
whichever
whosoever
windhover
breakaway
breezeway
bridleway
disavowal
firepower
lawnmower
mayflower
motherwit
outgrowth
overpower
safflower
scallawag
scallywag
semivowel
shallowly
shottower
sluiceway
spiderweb
sunflower
throwaway
willpower
aflatoxin
amphioxus
anaptyxis
antefixal
antitoxic
antitoxin
catalexes
catalexis
complexly
complexus
cytotoxic
cytotoxin
endomixis
epistaxis
homotaxis
hypotaxis
oversexed
paralexia
parataxis
phalanxes
pharynxes
pyridoxin
woodwaxen
aerophyte
androgyne
androgyny
anthocyan
archetype
Arguseyed
astrocyte
bleareyed
bryophyte
cataclysm
chemitype
cleareyed
cockneyfy
collotype
crosseyed
dahabiyah
destroyer
ectophyte
endophyte
entophyte
ferrotype
freestyle
gainsayer
greeneyed
hackneyed
hairstyle
halophyte
hamadryad
heliotype
hexastyle
highflyer
Himalayan

hydrolyse
hydrolyte
hypostyle
IndoAryan
journeyer
karyotype
leucocyte
leukocyte
lifestyle
macrocyte
manslayer
melaphyre
mesophyll
mesophyte
microcyte
micropyle
minelayer
mistyeyed
monorhyme
monostyle
octastyle
octostyle
overjoyed
panchayat
peristyle
phagocyte
phenotype
philogyny
phototype
polyonymy
polyptych
portrayal
portrayer
proenzyme
proselyte
prototype
ratepayer
sharpeyed
spirogyra
sporocyst
stalkeyed
statocyst
stenotype
stenotypy
strongyle
tachylyte
teknonymy
touchtype
tourneyer
unalloyed
viceroyal
xerophyte
zincotype
actinozoa
bamboozle
bilharzia
bulldozer
chernozem
isoniazid
kibbutzim
kingsized
lifesized
oversized
pintsized
schnauzer
schnitzel
shemozzle
stargazer
wychhazel

---

abdominal
ablatival
abscissae
abscissas
accentual
acellular
Acheulean
Acheulian
acquittal
acropetal
actuarial
adenoidal
adnominal
adverbial
afterclap
agnatical
airstream
Algonkian
altricial
amazonian
ambrosial
amoebaean
amphibian
amyloidal
ancestral
anchorman
anecdotal
anemogram
angelical
annelidan
antefixal
antenatal
anthocyan
anthozoan
antidotal
antinodal
antipodal
antiviral
appraisal
araneidal
araneidan
archducal
armigeral
Armorican
arrowhead
arsenical
Arthurian
articular
ascetical
asclepiad
aspectual
astrakhan
Atlantean
auctorial
auricular
authorial
autosomal
avuncular
azimuthal
bacchanal
backpedal
bacterial
ballistae
Bantustan
baptismal
Barbadian
barbarian
basilican
basipetal
Bathonian
beachhead
beachwear
bedspread
beefsteak
betrothal
bicameral
bicipital
bilateral
bilingual
biliteral
billygoat
binocular
binominal
bismillah
blackcoat
blackflag
blackhead
blacklead
blastulae
blastular
blockhead
bondwoman
boobytrap
bordereau
botanical
brakesman
branchiae
branchial
breakaway
breezeway
bricabrac
bridesman
bridleway
broadleaf
bromeliad
bronchial
buckwheat
Bulgarian
bursarial
butterfat
cablegram
cacuminal
cadastral
cadential
caecilian
caerulean
Caesarean
Caesarian
calcaneal
calicular
calycinal
Cambodian
cameraman
canalboat
Candlemas
canesugar
canicular
canonical
cantorial
capitular
Caribbean
carnelian
carpetbag
Cartesian
cartogram
Castalian
castellan
Castilian
catamaran
catarrhal
cathedral
cattleman
Caucasian
celestial
censorial
centigram
chaingear
chaparral
charlatan
charwoman
chelonian
cheongsam
chinstrap
Christian
Christmas
chronical
chthonian
churchman
Cimmerian
circadian
classical
claustral
clergyman
clinician
cloistral
coccygeal
cochineal
coecilian
coelostat
coeternal
cofferdam
colcothar
collegial
collegian
collinear
colloidal
colourman
Columbian
commendam
commensal
commissar
committal
commonlaw
comprisal
conciliar
concordat
conferral
confervae
conformal
Confucian
congenial
connubial
continual
convivial
cornelian
cornerman
cornopean
cornsalad
corporeal
coseismal
courtesan
cracksman
craftsman
creatural
crinoidal
crossbeam
crosshead
crossroad
cryptical
cryptogam
culsdesac
cursorial
custodial
custodian
cuticular
cutthroat
cycloidal
cyclopean
cyclopian
Cytherean
Daedalean
Daedalian
dahabiyah
dalmatian
Damoclean
dandiacal
Darwinian
decagonal
decapodal
decapodan
decennial
deistical
dialectal
diametral
dichasial
dichromat
dietician
dietitian
diningcar
dinoceras
Dionysiac
Dionysian
disannual
disappear
disavowal
disbursal
discoidal
dismissal
dispersal
dissocial
doctorial
doctrinal
dogcollar
dominical
Dominican
draconian
draftsman
Dravidian
dreamboat
dresscoat
dropsical
druidical
dynamical
dziggetai
ealdorman
earthstar
ecclesial
editorial
Edwardian
effectual
effluvial
egomaniac
electoral
elegiacal
elemental
embryonal
Emmenthal
emotional
empirical
enchorial
endosteal
entrechat
ephemeral
epicurean
epidermal
epiphytal
episcopal
equivocal
eristical
erratical
essential
Esthonian
estuarian
etherical
Ethiopian
ethmoidal
euclidean
eutherian
exciseman
factional
factorial
Falernian
familyman
fanatical
farmstead
fatidical
fellowman
fenestrae
fenestral
ferryboat
fibrillar
fictional
fieldsman
financial
firebreak
fisherman
floridean
floscular
fluorspar
fluxional
foragecap
forcemeat
forespeak
forewoman
fossorial
fraternal
freewoman
Frenchman
frockcoat
fullcream
funebrial
funicular
galenical
gaolbreak
gaspereau
gastrulae
genetical
genitival
genocidal
gentleman
gerundial
glabellae
glabellar
glandular
gorgonian
grandslam
graphical
greatcoat
gregarian
Gregorian
groomsman
grossular
guardsman
gymnasial
haemostat
Hallowmas
hamadryad
hammerman
handlebar
handorgan
harmattan
Harrovian
heartbeat
Hebridean
hectogram
heliogram
heliostat
heliozoan
Helvetian
Heraclean
Herculean
Hercynian
heretical
Hesperian
hexagonal
Hibernian
hierogram
Himalayan
hippocras
histogram
historian
Hobbesian
hodiernal
homestead
homicidal
homopolar
homousian
horsebean
horseplay
houseboat
housecoat
houseflag
Hungarian
hydrozoan
hygrostat
hypethral
hypnoidal
identical
idiotical
illiberal
illogical
impartial
inaugural
IndoAryan
inshallah
insomniac
interleaf
interplay
Iroquoian
irregular
isallobar
isoclinal
isohyetal
jackstraw
jailbreak
jetstream
jockstrap
jollyboat
Jordanian
juridical
jurywoman
justiciar
Keplerian
Keynesian
khedivial
kinswoman
klinostat
lacertian
lachrymal
Laodicean
lapstreak
laryngeal
latterday
leviathan
Levitical
libidinal
librarian
lightyear
liveryman
loafsugar
longaeval
looseleaf
lumberman
lumbrical
lunisolar
lunitidal
Maccabean
magistral
magnesian
maharajah
Mahometan
Malayalam
malleolar
mammalian
Mancunian
manhattan
Manichean
manipular
manorseat
Manxwoman
marketday
marmoreal
marrowfat
marsupial
Martinmas
matutinal
mediaeval
medicinal
Mendelian
meningeal
menstrual
mercaptan
mercurial
meropidan
metrician
microbial
microgram
middleman
midstream
milkfloat
milligram
Miltonian
mincemeat

minuteman
misdemean
molecular
molluscan
monarchal
Mongolian
monocular
monodical
monsoonal
morrisman
mortician
motorboat
mousetrap
mucksweat
muffinman
municipal
muscleman
Mussulman
Mycenaean
myrobalan
Nahuatlan
nannygoat
navicular
nectarean
nectarial
negroidal
nemertean
neologian
Neptunian
Nestorian
Newtonian
nocturnal
nonlinear
Norwegian
numerical
oakenshaw
obconical
obsequial
occipital
ochlocrat
octagonal
octennial
oddjobman
officinal
olecranal
ombudsman
opercular
Orangeman
orangutan
oratorial
oratorian
orbicular
orificial
ossicular
outspread
oviductal
oysterman
Palladian
palpebral
paludinal
palustral
panchayat
pantryman
paradisal
paranoiac
parochial
passional
patrician
patrolman
Pavlovian
pedicular
Pelasgian
pentagram
penumbral
perennial
pergunnah
perinatal
perpetual
petechiae
petechial
petersham
petticoat
pharyngal
phonogram
physician
pictogram
pictorial
piecemeal
pipedream
pipeorgan
pipsqueak
piratical
placentae
placental
plainsman
planarian
ploughman
plumdamas
plutocrat
plutonian
pointsman
polemical
policeman
political
polygonal
polytonal
popliteal
poppyhead
poriferal
poriferan
portrayal
postnasal
postnatal
potential
powerboat
practical
prebendal
precisian
precocial
presidial
primaeval
primatial
principal
prodromal
proofread
prosaical
prothorax
protozoal
protozoan
Provencal
psychical
ptarmigan
puerperal
purpureal
pyramidal
quadrigae
quadruman
quantical
quarryman
quizzical
quotidian
radicular
radiogram
raptorial
recruital
rectorial
reedorgan
regicidal
registrar
rehearsal
Reichstag
reliquiae
reprieval
reptilian
reticular
retinulae
retinular
retrieval
revictual
rhizoidal
rhonchial
ribosomal
Ripuarian
riverboat
riverhead
roadmetal
roadstead
Roumanian
rounceval
roundelay
roundhead
roundsman
rubrician
ruddleman
Sabellian
sacristan
saddlebag
Sadducean
sailorman
Samaritan
Sardinian
sartorial
sassafras
Sassanian
satanical
satinspar
satirical
Saturnian
sauceboat
scaleleaf
scallawag
scallywag
scapegoat
scarehead
sceptical
schoolbag
schoolman
sciential
scoredraw
Scotchman
scrapheap
scrimshaw
scrollsaw
scutellar
sectarian
sectional
sectorial
segmental
selachian
selectman
Seljukian
semestral
semifinal
semilunar
semimetal
seneschal
sensorial
sessional
sexennial
shantyman
Shechinah
shellheap
shewbread
shillelah
shipcanal
shockhead
shovelhat
sigmoidal
signalman
signorial
sinistral
Sisyphean
sketchmap
Slavonian
slothbear
Slovakian
Slovenian
sluiceway
sociogram
sodabread
softpedal
Solutrean
Solutrian
soritical
spearhead
speedboat
spellican
spherical
spherular
spiderman
spiritual
spleuchan
spoilsman
spokesman
spongebag
spoonbeak
spoonmeat
sportsman
squamosal
stableman
stairhead
stakeboat
stapedial
statesman
stational
steamboat
steelclad
steelhead
steersman
steradian
stercoral
steroidal
stinktrap
stomachal
stonechat
stonecoal
stonedead
stonedeaf
streetcar
strobilae
subaerial
subastral
subcaudal
subcostal
sublethal
submental
subnormal
subocular
subtopian
succursal
suctorial
suctorian
suffragan
sugarloaf
superheat
superstar
surficial
surprisal
sweetmeal
sweetmeat
switchman
swordplay
swordsman
sympodial
symposiac
symposial
synagogal
synclinal
syncytial
synodical
syringeal
tableleaf
tacamahac
tactician
tactitian
tahsildar
Tartarean
Tartarian
Tartufian
Tasmanian
technical
tectorial
tegmental
tellurian
tensional
tetragram
thickhead
thirdsman
throwaway
Thyestean
timberman
tirewoman
tittlebat
Tocharian
tonsillar
tonsorial
topiarian
toponymal
torsional
tradesman
traducian
tragedian
trainload
trapezial
traversal
tribesman
trichinae
triennial
trifacial
trihedral
trilinear
trinomial
triumphal
trochleae
trochlear
trousseau
trunkroad
trussbeam
tuckerbag
tuitional
typemetal
typhoidal
Ukrainian
umbilical
undecimal
underclay
undercoat
undergrad
underplay
underseal
underseas
underwear
unethical
uniplanar
uniserial
unisexual
unitarian
universal
unmusical
unnatural
unpopular
Upanishad
utricular
Varangian
vaticinal
vectorial
vehicular
veridical
versional
vertebrae
vertebral
vesicular
vestigial
vestryman
vibrissae
vicennial
viceregal
viceroyal
vicesimal
Victorian
vigesimal
Virgilian
viricidal
Vitruvian
vizierial
vocabular
vulcanian
vulgarian
Wagnerian
waistcoat
wallydrag
washerman
waterleaf
Wednesday
weighbeam
whaleboat
whalehead
wheatmeal
wherryman
whimsical
whitebeam
whitehead
wholemeal
windbreak
witchmeal
workwoman
wyliecoat
yachtsman
yesterday
zoophagan
Zwinglian
algarroba
astrolabe
conscribe
flashcube
flashtube
garderobe
passersby
prescribe
proscribe
selfdoubt
spareribs
subscribe
xenophobe
aberrance
aberrancy
aboutface
abundance
accidence
acescence
acoustics
acquiesce
adherence
adjacency
adjutancy
aerospace
affluence
allowance
ambulance
anabranch
annoyance
antiknock
appetence
appetency
applejack
appliance
architect
armistice
arrogance
assonance
assurance
athletics
autocracy
avoidance
awestruck
backspace
backtrack
bailiwick
barmbrack
baronetcy
beccafico
bellpunch
billycock
bionomics
birdwatch
bivalence
bivalency
blackbuck
blackcock
blackface
blackjack
blowtorch
blueblack
bootblack
boxoffice
breakneck
bullfinch
bushwhack
byproduct
cailleach
calamanco
camelback
candidacy
captaincy
chaffinch
cheapjack
chopstick
cicatrice
clearance
cockroach
coherence
coherency
colonelcy
constancy
constrict
construct
contumacy
coproduce
covalence
covalency
cowardice
cranreuch
crookback
crookneck
cumbrance
czarevich
dalliance
decadence
decadency
deference
democracy
didactics
dietetics
dilatancy
diligence
diplomacy
dipswitch
dirttrack
disaffect
disavouch
disbranch
disinfect
dogmatics
dominance
dramatics
drumstick
dysgenics
economics
effluence
eiderduck
eloquence
emergence
emergency

endurance
esoterica
esperance
esurience
esuriency
euthenics
excitancy
existence
exservice
exultance
exultancy
eyeglance
feculence
feedstock
firebrick
fireplace
fishslice
fishyback
fivepence
flagrance
flagrancy
flagstick
flashback
flintlock
flippancy
fluoresce
folkdance
forasmuch
forereach
fortalice
fourpence
fragrance
fragrancy
freelance
frequence
frequency
frogmarch
gemutlich
genuflect
geoponics
ginpalace
goldbrick
goldfinch
gooseneck
greenback
grievance
gynocracy
hairpiece
hairspace
halfpence
halfprice
halftrack
harmonica
harmonics
hatchback
haversack
headpiece
headstock
heartsick
heathcock
heelpiece
hemistich
hemstitch
hesitance
hesitancy
hexastich
Hexateuch
hieratica
hindrance
hollyhock
hopscotch
hornwrack
horseback
huckaback
hunchback
hygienics
hysterics
ignorance
imbalance
immanence
immanency
immediacy
imminence
imminency
impedance
imperfect
impotence
impotency
impudence
incidence
incorrect
indecency
indigence
indolence
inerrancy
inference
influence
inherence
injustice
innocence
innocency
inservice
insolence
insurance
intellect
interdict
interface
interject
interlace
interlock
intersect
intestacy
intricacy
introduce
introject
intumesce
inviolacy
isagogics
itineracy
jossstick
jubilance
ladysmock
lampblack
lancejack
lastditch
latitancy
lifeforce
limejuice
liquorice
liturgics
livestock
logistics
lovematch
lowerdeck
luminance
magnetics
magnifico
mahlstick
mainbrace
mallemuck
marshalcy
matchlock
matriarch
maulstick
mechanics
militancy
mischance
misdirect
mnemonics
mobocracy
monocracy
monostich
mumchance
nescience
ninepence
noctiluca
nomocracy
nosepiece
obedience
obeisance
obsolesce
obstinacy
occupancy
oenomancy
offchance
onlicence
opponency
ordinance
oscitancy
overcheck
overmatch
overpitch
overprice
overreach
overreact
overstock
overtrick
overwatch
paperback
patriarch
penitence
perchance
permeance
petulance
petulancy
phonemics
phonetics
pickaback
piggyback
pikeperch
pinchbeck
pinchcock
placekick
plangency
pleasance
poignancy
pointlace
pokerface
polyptych
poppycock
portulaca
precipice
pregnancy
prejudice
preselect
procuracy
pronounce
prurience
pruriency
puissance
pursuance
purulence
purulency
pyromancy
quittance
racetrack
raincheck
razorback
reactance
recalesce
recollect
recreancy
recusance
recusancy
redolence
reenforce
reference
refluence
reinforce
relevance
relevancy
remanence
reminisce
renitency
reproduce
rerebrace
residence
residency
resonance
resurface
resurrect
reticence
reticency
retroject
reverence
rhythmics
ringfence
roadblock
rootstock
roughneck
Roumansch
sacrifice
sandarach
sandcrack
santonica
sasquatch
Sassenach
scalplock
scenedock
semantics
semblance
semiotics
sentience
sentiency
sergeancy
serjeancy
severance
sheeplice
sheeptick
sheldduck
shellback
shipwreck
shoeblack
showpiece
showplace
shrewmice
sibilance
sibilancy
sidetrack
significs
simpatico
skinflick
slapstick
slingback
slipcoach
slowcoach
slowmatch
smokejack
spotcheck
squinancy
squirarch
stagnancy
stepdance
stopwatch
stormcock
stridence
stridency
subagency
subbranch
substance
sunstruck
supremacy
surgeoncy
sweepback
sweptback
symbolics
synectics
tailpiece
taioseach
taskforce
tectonics
theatrics
theocracy
thornback
throwback
thumbtack
timepiece
timocracy
toastrack
tolerance
toothpick
torchrace
toreutics
trierarch
tsarevich
unbalance
utterance
vehemence
vengeance
ventiduct
ventifact
vigilance
virulence
virulency
volteface
waterbuck
whaleback
whipstock
whiteface
wisecrack
woodblock
woodchuck
workbench
workpiece
yardstick
zoiatrics
acetamide
allemande
alongside
ambuscade
amplitude
anhydride
antitrade
asafetida
backslide
backwards
backwoods
Barmecide
barracuda
barricade
barricado
bastinade
bastinado
beatitude
billiards
Bretwalda
broadside
cannonade
carbamide
carbonado
carronade
cavalcade
centipede
certitude
chairlady
chiropody
cirripede
colonnade
crescendo
crossfade
croustade
cyanamide
demimonde
derringdo
desperado
desuetude
dipeptide
disembody
downgrade
downwards
dulcitude
eastwards
electrode
enchilada
esplanade
estrapade
everglade
everybody
fanfarade
fissipede
floodtide
foeticide
foolhardy
forecaddy
fortitude
fungicide
fusillade
gabionade
gallopade
garibaldi
gasconade
germicide
gingerade
glissandi
glissando
glucoside
glyceride
glycoside
grandaddy
gratitude
hairslide
halfhardy
herbicide
highgrade
highlands
homewards
horsehide
hydathode
hydroxide
incommode
intercede
interlude
internode
jaborandi
jacaranda
lampshade
landslide
larvicide
lassitude
leftwards
longitude
magnitude
makeready
marmalade
matricide
memoranda
millepede
millipede
motorcade
multitude
muscovado
negritude
newlyweds
nightside
nigritude
orangeade
ovenready
palmipede
parricide
patricide
pesticide
phosphide
pinnipede
platitude
plenitude
polyamide
prolicide
promenade
readymade
rearwards
rectitude
referenda
retrocede
riverside
saleslady
sauropoda
selfpride
servitude
sforzando
shoreside
sidewards
softgoods
spearside
stateside
statewide
strappado
subdivide
supersede
tamponade
telluride
tetrapody
Theravada
trematode
triploidy
turpitude
twayblade
underbody
underside
uxoricide
vastitude
verbicide
vermicide
waterside
waveguide
westwards
windwards
worldwide
zapateado
abandoned
abandonee
abandoner
abolisher
absconder
abstainer
accipiter
acclaimer
acetifier
acidifier
acquitted
addressee
addresser
adulterer
aerometer
affianced
Afrikaner
aggrieved
aircooled
airjacket
airminded
alabaster
alkaloses
almsgiver
altimeter
amauroses
amplifier
anabioses
anacruses
anguished
announcer
annulated
anopheles
antinovel
antipodes
aphereses
apophyses
appetiser
applauder
appointee
appraiser
appressed
archangel
Arguseyed
artificer

assaulter
assembler
atmometer
attainder
attempter
augmented
augmenter
Axminster
backbiter
backwater
balconied
baldfaced
balladeer
bandoleer
bandolier
bannister
banqueter
barefaced
bargainer
barkeeper
barnacled
barometer
barracker
barrelled
barrister
bartender
basrelief
bastioned
bayoneted
bedjacket
bedridden
bedsettee
bedsitter
beefeater
beekeeper
beemaster
beleaguer
beneficed
benighted
berserker
beslobber
bespatter
bestirred
betrothed
bigheaded
bilgekeel
Blackfeet
bleareyed
blinkered
blockader
bloodshed
blunderer
blusterer
Boanerges
bobtailed
boldfaced
bolometer
bookmaker
bottlefed
bowlegged
boxgirder
boycotter
Brahminee
branchlet
breadtree
breakeven
brevetted
brigadier
Britisher
broiderer
brummagem
buccaneer
buffaloes
bughunter
bulldozer
bullybeef
bullytree
bumblebee
burnisher
butcherer
bystander
cabriolet
cacoethes
campfever
cancelled
cannoneer
cannonier
canvasser
caretaker
carpenter
carrageen
carryover
cartwheel
caryopses
cassareep
cassoulet
catalexes
catalyser
catalyses
catharses
cattaloes
certified
certifier
chafferer
chapleted
character
chartered
charterer
chastener
chastiser
chatterer
checkered
chequered
chernozem
chevalier
chickadee
chickaree
chickweed
chiselled
chiseller
chlamydes
chorister
civiliser
clarifier
clarionet
clatterer
cleareyed
clergymen
cobwebbed
cockatiel
coinsurer
collected
coloniser
comedones
comforter
commander
commenter
committed
committee
compasses
compelled
conceited
concerned
concerted
concocter
concurred
condenser
confabbed
conferred
conferrer
confirmed
confirmer
conformer
congeries
connected
connecter
conserver
consignee
consulter
container
contemner
contender
contented
continuer
contrived
contriver
converter
convincer
convolved
copartner
copolymer
corbelled
cordelier
coriander
corkscrew
coroneted
corralled
corrupter
coryphaei
costumier
couturier
cremaster
crenelled
cricketer
cropeared
crossbred
crosseyed
crossover
crustacea
cudgelled
cullender
cupbearer
cuplichen
curlpaper
curvetted
cutinised
cyclopses
debauched
debauchee
debaucher
declaimer
decomplex
defaulter
defroster
deliverer
denouncer
depressed
derringer
descended
describer
desolater
despoiler
destroyer
dethroner
developer
dewlapped
diaereses
diagnoses
diarrhoea
diesinker
digitated
dignified
dimwitted
dinnerset
disbarred
disbelief
disbudded
disburden
discalced
discarder
discerner
disesteem
disgracer
dishfaced
dishwater
dismember
dispelled
dispenser
disperser
dissenter
dissuader
distemper
distilled
distiller
disturbed
disturber
dittander
doglegged
dogshores
dogviolet
dosimeter
downriver
drawsheet
driftweed
drivelled
driveller
drysalter
dungarees
dustcover
dustsheet
dynamiter
earwigged
Eastender
easterner
ecosystem
eggbeater
elastomer
elevenses
elongated
emaciated
embattled
embezzler
embroider
enamelled
enameller
enamoured
enchanter
encounter
energiser
energumen
Englander
englutted
engrosser
enhearten
enlighten
entrammel
entrapped
enwrapped
epiphyses
epistoler
equaliser
ergometer
estaminet
estranger
eulogiser
evergreen
ewenecked
exchanger
exchequer
exercises
exhauster
exorciser
expediter
explainer
exploiter
expounder
eyeopener
fairfaced
falsifier
fancyfree
fantasied
fasciated
fascicled
fashioner
fatheaded
fatwitted
feathered
fenugreek
filigreed
fillister
filterbed
financier
fireeater
firepower
firewater
flageolet
flashover
flatterer
floriated
flowerbed
flowsheet
fluecured
flyfisher
forbidden
forcefeed
foreboder
foreigner
forenamed
foretoken
forfeiter
forgather
forgotten
formatted
fortifier
forwander
forwarder
fossicker
fourwheel
foxhunter
freeliver
freerider
freewheel
freighter
freshener
fricassee
fritterer
frivolled
frolicked
fruiterer
fruittree
fulfilled
fulfiller
funnelled
furbisher
furnisher
furtherer
gadgeteer
gainsayer
galleried
gallooned
gallowses
gambadoes
gambolled
gannister
garmented
garnishee
garreteer
garrotter
gasfitter
gasholder
gasometer
gauleiter
gazetteer
gearlever
gearwheel
geomancer
germander
gestalten
giltedged
glandered
gobetween
goddamned
godfather
godmother
goingover
goldfever
gondolier
goodwives
goosander
goosestep
gorblimey
gospeller
gravelled
greeneyed
greenweed
grenadier
groundsel
grovelled
groveller
grubscrew
guarantee
gunpowder
gunrunner
hackneyed
hagridden
halfbaked
halfbreed
Halloween
hamburger
hamfisted
hamhanded
handwheel
hanselled
haranguer
harbinger
harbourer
hardcover
hardnosed
harpooner
harvester
headliner
headwater
heartfree
hereafter
hereunder
herniated
hexameter
highflier
highflyer
highlevel
highspeed
hightoned
highwater
hobnailed
hobnobbed
hobnobber
hodometer
homemaker
horologer
hosteller
hotheaded
housekeep
houseleek
houselled
howsoever
humblebee
humbugged
humdinger
hydrangea
Icelander
iceskater
idealiser
illgotten
illjudged
illomened
illwisher
impastoed
impleader
impounder
inbetween
increaser
indweller
infielder
ingrained
innholder
innkeeper
inscriber
inspanned
instanter
instilled
interbred
interpret
interview
intriguer
inveigler
involuted
ironsides
isosceles
jampacked
jaundiced
jaywalker
jetsetter
jewelweed
jobmaster
journeyer
Judastree
justifier
karabiner
kennelled
kidnapped
kidnapper
kingdomed
kingmaker
kingsized
kitchener
knockknee
laminated
lampooner
landaulet
landloper
landowner
Laplander
latecomer
launderer
laurelled
lawnmower
lazybones
leafgreen
Leicester
liberated
lifesaver
lifesized
lignaloes
Limburger
limewater
lintelled
lipreader
liquefier
lobulated
longeared
longfaced
longlived
lovetoken
lowlander
lowloader
lowminded
lownecked
lysimeter
machmeter
magnifier
maharanee
mainliner
mainsheet
malformed
malleehen
manometer
mansarded
manslayer
manyplies
manysided
marcelled
marvelled
masonried

masterkey
maunderer
mayflower
mekometer
meltwater
mementoes
memoriter
merganser
mesogloea
messenger
midsummer
midwicket
midwinter
milkfever
millwheel
milometer
minelayer
misbelief
misbeseem
misesteem
misguided
mishanter
misleared
mispickel
misshapen
missioner
mistyeyed
moistener
mongooses
moonraker
moraliser
mortgagee
mortgager
mosaicked
moschatel
motheaten
moviegoer
muckraker
muffineer
mullioned
multiplex
mummified
musketeer
mystifier
nebuliser
nepenthes
netveined
netwinged
newmarket
newspaper
nickelled
Nilometer
nitpicker
nodulated
nondriver
nonsmoker
nosebleed
notepaper
nourisher
nowhither
nucleated
nuisancer
nullifier
obligated
obsequies
ocellated
octameter
octopodes
oddjobber
oestrogen
offhanded
offscreen
offstreet
oilburner
okeydokey
onehanded
onelegged
openended
opinioned
optometer
organiser
osmometer
ourselves
outbacker
outfitter
outgunned
outlander
outnumber
outputted
outridden
outrigger
outspoken
outwitted
outworker
overeaten
overeater
overjoyed
overladen
overpower
oversexed
oversized
oversleep
oversteer
overtaken
overthrew
overtones
oysterbed
pacemaker
palankeen
panoplied
parameter
parapeted
parcelled
parrakeet
passenger
patinated
patrolled
patroller
paymaster
paypacket
peasouper
pedigreed
pedometer
pencilled
penciller
penholder
penpusher
pensioner
perceiver
performer
perfumier
perimeter
permitted
permitter
personnel
persuader
perverter
pettitoes
phalanger
phalanges
phalanxes
pharynges
pharynxes
phellogen
philander
physicked
picnicked
picnicker
pigheaded
pimpernel
pintailed
pintsized
pistoleer
pistolled
pixilated
planisher
plastered
plasterer
plunderer
poetaster
polariser
polyester
polywater
pommelled
pontoneer
pontonier
porringer
porticoes
portrayer
possessed
potboiler
pothunter
poulterer
practised
praenomen
prankster
precancel
preferred
presbyter
presentee
presenter
preserver
pretender
preventer
princelet
privateer
processed
processer
professed
profiteer
prognoses
prolepses
propelled
propeller
propylaea
protester
provender
psychoses
publisher
puffadder
pulpiteer
pummelled
puppeteer
purchaser
purloiner
pyrolater
pyrometer
quadruped
qualified
qualifier
quarenden
quarender
quickener
quickstep
quirister
quodlibet
racketeer
rainmaker
rainwater
ransacker
ratepayer
recoverer
recruiter
rectifier
rectrices
redhanded
redheaded
redletter
redoubted
redresser
refreshen
refresher
refuelled
regretted
rejoinder
remainder
renouncer
requester
resources
respecter
responder
retoucher
retriever
retrodden
retroflex
rewritten
rhymester
ricepaper
ridiculer
riverweed
rocketeer
rodfisher
roisterer
rosewater
rosinweed
rowantree
rumrunner
safflower
sagegreen
salpinges
saltwater
sandalled
sandpaper
sandpiper
sapheaded
saunterer
Sauternes
scarifier
scatterer
scavenger
schlemiel
schlieren
schnauzer
schnitzel
schnorkel
schnorrer
scorifier
scoundrel
scrambler
scratcher
scratches
screecher
scribbler
scrivener
scrounger
sealetter
sedgewren
seedeater
selffaced
selfmoved
semisweet
semivowel
separates
September
septuplet
sepulcher
sequester
sequinned
serenader
seventeen
seventies
sexlinked
sextuplet
shadetree
sharpener
sharpeyed
shieldfem
shipfever
shipmoney
shipowner
shoemaker
shoreweed
shortener
shottower
shovelled
shoveller
sidewheel
sightseer
signalled
signaller
simplices
singspiel
sitzkrieg
sixfooter
skindiver
skyjacker
skyrocket
slabsided
slanderer
slategrey
slaughter
slinkweed
slipcover
slumberer
smartweed
smatterer
smoketree
snakeweed
sniggerer
snivelled
sniveller
snubnosed
sobriquet
sobsister
sodawater
sojourner
sometimes
sommelier
sonneteer
sonometer
sophister
souwester
specifier
speedster
sphincter
spiderweb
spindrier
spinnaker
spinneret
spiralled
spirituel
spoonfeed
springlet
sprinkler
spurwheel
sputterer
squabbler
squelcher
squirelet
staggerer
stalkeyed
stallfeed
stammerer
stargazer
stationer
stauncher
staymaker
stellated
stiffener
stingaree
stinkweed
stockinet
stomacher
storiated
straggler
strangler
strangles
stratagem
streamlet
stretcher
struggler
stupefier
stutterer
submaster
submitted
subverter
succeeder
succourer
sugarbeet
suggester
sulphuret
sunbather
sunbonnet
sunburned
sundowner
sunflower
sunhelmet
suntanned
supporter
surfeiter
surmullet
surpliced
surrender
suspender
sustainer
swaggerer
sweetener
swimmeret
swivelled
syllabled
syllepses
syntheses
tapdancer
tasselled
taximeter
tectrices
telamones
telemeter
tentacled
tentmaker
teratogen
testifier
theoriser
thickener
thicketed
thickknee
thorntree
thoughted
throttler
throwster
thunderer
tidewater
tightener
timesheet
tinopener
tinselled
tipstaves
titledeed
tittupped
toadeater
tonguelet
tonometer
tophamper
tortrices
totaliser
tourneyer
trabeated
traceried
tramlines
travelled
traveller
traverser
treasurer
trebuchet
trebucket
trepanned
trickster
trimester
trinketer
trousered
trowelled
troweller
trumpeter
truncated
trustdeed
tuliptree
tunicated
tunnelled
tunnelnet
twitterer
twofisted
twohanded
twosuiter
Uitlander
unabashed
unadopted
unadorned
unadvised
unalloyed
unaltered
unashamed
unberufen
unbiassed
unblessed
unblinded
unbounded
unbraided
unbridled
uncharted
unchecked
uncinated
unclothed
unclouded
uncounted
uncovered
uncreated
uncropped
uncrossed
uncrowned
undamaged
undaunted
undecided
undefined
underbred
undivided
undoubted
undreamed
undulated
unfeigned
unfledged
unfleshed
unfounded
unguarded
unhurried
unknitted
unlearned
unlimited
unmatched
unpeopled
unplugged
unplumbed
unpointed
unruffled
unscathed
unsettled
unsighted
unskilled
unspotted
unstopped
unstudied
unsullied
untouched
untrodden
untrussed
untutored
unwearied
unwrapped
unwritten
upbraider
upholster
valuables
vaporiser
varnisher

velveteen
verandaed
versifier
videlicet
vignetter
vocaliser
voiceover
volcanoes
volkslied
voltmeter
volumeter
volunteer
Waldenses
wallpaper
warbonnet
warmonger
warrantee
warranter
wassailer
waterflea
watershed
waterweed
wattmeter
weakkneed
weathered
webfooted
weevilled
welltimed
werwolves
westerner
wheyfaced
whichever
whimperer
whiskered
whisperer
whosoever
willpower
windhover
womaniser
woodwaxen
Worcester
wormeaten
wormwheel
wrongdoer
wychhazel
Yiddisher
youngster
zigzagged
afterlife
autograft
bushcraft
campcraft
candytuft
cockneyfy
cowlstaff
crossruff
deacidify
decalcify
demystify
denitrify
devitrify
diversify
electrify
exemplify
feedstuff
flagstaff
foodstuff
frenchify
gearshift
halfstaff
handcraft
handcuffs
homograft
housewife
indemnify
intensify
jackknife
kingcraft
luftwaffe
makeshift
nightlife
objectify
overdraft
overstuff
personify
pikestaff
plaintiff
preachify
rechauffe
shelflife
skewwhiff
skingraft
snowdrift
speechify
spindrift
stardrift
vouchsafe
woodcraft
xenograft
advantage
aetiology
agriology
anchorage
angiology
anthology
appendage
arbitrage
argybargy
arrearage
astrology
audiology
backstage
beastings
beestings
bobsleigh
brokerage
calcifuge
caliology
carpology
cartilage
cartology
cartridge
cellarage
challenge
champaign
chitlings
chorology
clientage
commonage
concierge
consulage
cooperage
coprology
cosmology
curettage
curtilage
demurrage
diaphragm
discharge
disengage
disoblige
disparage
dittology
downstage
embassage
empennage
encourage
endophagy
entourage
epiphragm
escortage
espionage
estoppage
ethnology
etymology
euchology
factorage
farestage
febrifuge
festology
fleshings
flowerage
forejudge
forestage
fosterage
freerange
frontpage
gallmidge
gallonage
gemmology
genealogy
greengage
groundage
hagiology
haplology
haverings
hermitage
hierology
histology
hydrology
hymnology
hypallage
hypnology
ichnology
iconology
interpage
kentledge
knifeedge
knightage
knowledge
lazytongs
limnology
lithology
longrange
mammalogy
matronage
metrology
micrology
misassign
mismanage
moneybags
monophagy
mycophagy
mystagogy
mythology
necrology
nephology
neurology
nostology
odontalgy
oesophagi
ophiology
orphanage
ossifrage
osteology
outgoings
overweigh
palillogy
parentage
parsonage
partridge
pasturage
pathology
patrology
patronage
personage
pestology
petrology
phenology
philology
phonology
phycology
phytology
pilferage
pleadings
polyphagy
porterage
preengage
privilege
pupillage
radiology
raingauge
razoredge
rearrange
recoinage
repechage
reportage
rhinology
sacrilege
saxifrage
scatology
scrimmage
scrummage
seachange
secretage
selfimage
semiology
sheerlegs
shrinkage
siphonage
skirtings
sociology
sortilege
soundings
sourdough
sovereign
sunlounge
sunspurge
surcharge
symbology
tautology
teleology
tetralogy
tidegauge
titlepage
trappings
treillage
tribology
trimmings
tropology
ultrahigh
undersign
uranology
vassalage
vermifuge
villanage
villenage
waggonage
airworthy
algorithm
allopathy
antipathy
apocrypha
archduchy
avalanche
backsight
bellyache
bethought
biography
biorhythm
bombsight
bretasche
bullfight
cartouche
chachacha
cockfight
copyright
deadlight
downright
dystrophy
ensheathe
entelechy
enwreathe
epigraphy
ethnarchy
eyebright
firelight
flyweight
footlight
foresight
fortnight
Gaeltacht
geography
goodnight
guilloche
hagiarchy
halflight
headlight
heartache
heptarchy
hierarchy
highlight
hindsight
idiopathy
inbreathe
indraught
inwrought
lamplight
limelight
logarithm
logomachy
lovelight
maharishi
methought
moonlight
moustache
myography
oligarchy
onslaught
opsimathy
orography
overnight
oversight
parfleche
peepsight
pentarchy
polymathy
quebracho
rearlight
recherche
rethought
rushlight
sandyacht
schlemihl
sciamachy
seaworthy
sidelight
skiamachy
skintight
spotlight
starlight
stoplight
taillight
telepathy
tetrarchy
theomachy
theosophy
toothache
unhealthy
unsheathe
unthought
unwrought
weeknight
wehrmacht
zoography
acariasis
acidophil
acrobatic
acropolis
acroteria
adiabatic
adrenalin
aepyornis
aerobatic
aerolitic
aesthesia
aesthesis
aesthetic
affidavit
aflatoxin
aforesaid
agonistic
agrologic
agronomic
ahistoric
albinotic
alcoholic
aldehydic
aleatoric
Alemannic
algebraic
Algonquin
alicyclic
aliphatic
alkalosis
allantois
allegoric
amaryllis
amaurosis
amaurotic
ambergris
amblyopia
amblyopic
Amerindic
aminoacid
amygdalin
amylopsin
anabiosis
anabiotic
anacrusis
anaerobic
analeptic
analgesia
analgesic
anamnesis
anaphoric
anaptyxis
andesitic
androecia
anecdotic
anglophil
animistic
ankylosis
ankylotic
anorectic
anoxaemia
antarctic
anthracic
anthropic
antigenic
antimonic
antinomic
antitoxic
antitoxin
antivenin
apartheid
apathetic
aperiodic
apheresis
aplanatic
apodictic
apomictic
apophysis
apostolic
apothecia
appertain
aquilegia
arachnoid
araucaria
artemisia
arteritis
arthritic
arthritis
arthrosis
arytenoid
ascertain
asphaltic
assumpsit
asthmatic
asyndetic
ataractic
atavistic
atheistic
athematic
atomistic
aubrietia
auditoria
autarchic
authentic
autolysis
autolytic
automatic
autonomic
autotelic
axiomatic
bacteroid
bainmarie
baldachin
baldaquin
ballistic
beeorchis
bigeneric
bilharzia
bilirubin
biometric
birdbrain
bishopric
blackmail
blockship
boatswain
boattrain
Bolshevik
bombastic
bouquetin
bourgeois
Brahmanic
Brahminic
brasserie
breastpin
bregmatic
Britannia
Britannic
broadtail
Brythonic
cablelaid
cachectic
cacodylic
cadaveric
cadetship
Caenozoic
cafeteria
Cainozoic
calandria
calendric
calorific
camelhair
campchair
camphoric
cantharid
cantharis
capriccio
caryopsis
casuistic
catabolic
catalexis
catalysis
catalytic
catatonia
catatonic
catharsis
cathartic
cathectic
catoptric

celluloid
chainmail
chancroid
Charolais
chatelain
checkrein
chemurgic
cherrypie
chiefship
chieftain
chilblain
chimaeric
chivalric
chloritic
chlorosis
chlorotic
choleraic
choplogic
chromatic
chromatin
chrysalid
chrysalis
cinematic
cineraria
cirrhosis
clerkship
climactic
colloquia
colorific
compendia
condyloid
consortia
constrain
copacetic
coralloid
coreopsis
corticoid
corydalis
coseismic
countship
courtship
coverslip
cryogenic
cylindric
cyprinoid
cytolysis
cytotoxic
cytotoxin
dairymaid
daredevil
demagogic
demiurgic
dendritic
dermatoid
diablerie
diacritic
diactinic
diaeresis
diagnosis
dialectic
diametric
diaphysis
diastasis
diastatic
diastolic
diathesis
diathetic
diatropic
dichromic
didelphic
digastric
digitalin
digitalis
dimorphic
directrix
discomfit
discredit
disentail
disrepair
disseisin
dizygotic
doleritic
dolomitic
driftsail
dualistic
duralumin
dyscrasia
dyspepsia
dyspeptic
dysphagia
dysphagic
dysphonia
dysphoria
dysphoric
dysplasia
dyspnoeic
eccentric
echolalia
eclampsia
eclamptic
ectogenic
egotistic
eldership
ellipsoid
embroglio
embryonic
embryotic
emplastic
encaustic
endogamic
endogenic
endomixis
energetic
enigmatic
enteritis
entertain
enzymatic
epaenetic
ephemerid
ephemeris
epiclesis
epicyclic
epidermic
epidermis
epileptic
epinastic
epiphysis
epiphytic
epistaxis
epistemic
epistolic
epithelia
epithesis
epithetic
epizootic
ergonomic
ethylenic
eunuchoid
euphorbia
eutectoid
eutrophic
evangelic
excentric
executrix
exodermis
exosmosis
exosmotic
exostosis
extrinsic
eyestrain
fantastic
Fascistic
faunistic
felicific
fibrinoid
fideistic
filmstrip
filtertip
fingertip
floristic
fluorosis
folkmusic
foodchain
forebrain
formulaic
forsythia
francolin
Franglais
fumarolic
Gallophil
gastritis
gaucherie
generalia
genotypic
geomantic
geometric
geometrid
geostatic
geotropic
geriatric
glossitis
gnathonic
gneissoid
goliardic
gomphosis
gooseskin
granitoid
graphemic
graphitic
grimalkin
grosgrain
guardrail
guardship
guildship
gymnastic
haematoid
halieutic
halitosis
hamamelis
Hanseatic
harlequin
haustoria
hegemonic
heliozoic
hepatitis
herpetoid
heterosis
heuristic
hexaploid
highchair
hindbrain
hobgoblin
Holarctic
homiletic
homogamic
homonymic
homotaxis
homotonic
honoraria
honorific
horologic
horsehair
horsetail
horsewhip
hortensia
housemaid
hubristic
hydraemia
hydraulic
hydriodic
hydrofoil
hyperopia
hyperopic
hypomania
hypomanic
hypotaxis
hysteroid
Icelandic
ichthyoid
identikit
ideologic
idiomatic
imbecilic
imbroglio
impolitic
indigotin
inelastic
infusoria
inorganic
interknit
intervein
intrinsic
ischaemia
ischaemic
ischiadic
ischiatic
Islamitic
isobathic
isoclinic
isocyclic
isometric
isoniazid
isostatic
isotropic
Jacobinic
jacquerie
Judaistic
judgeship
judgmatic
juvenilia
katabasis
katabatic
katabolic
katharsis
keratitis
keratosis
kibbutzim
kilderkin
kinematic
lairdship
laminaria
leitmotif
leitmotiv
lethargic
leucaemia
leukaemia
leukaemic
leviratic
libecchio
lightship
limonitic
literatim
litterbin
logaoedic
Lombardic
longchain
luciferin
lymphatic
lyophilic
lyophobic
macaronic
mailtrain
majorship
maladroit
malvoisie
mannequin
marestail
Masoretic
mayorship
mediatrix
melanosis
melanotic
melatonin
melomania
menagerie
Menshevik
messianic
metabolic
metalloid
metameric
meteoroid
metheglin
metonymic
miasmatic
microchip
micropsia
millennia
mistigris
monarchic
monatomic
Mongoloid
monobasic
monogamic
monologic
monomania
monomeric
monotonic
monotypic
moratoria
morphemic
motherwit
multifoil
mustachio
mutagenic
mycologic
mydriasis
mydriatic
myrmecoid
napthalic
naumachia
necrophil
negrophil
neolithic
neoteinia
neoteinic
nephritic
nephritis
nephrosis
neuralgia
neuralgic
neuroglia
nicotinic
nonpareil
nonprofit
nostalgia
nostalgic
notabilia
nucleonic
nursemaid
nutweevil
nymphalid
nystagmic
obstetric
oecologic
oecumenic
oleoresin
oligaemia
ommatidia
omophagia
omophagic
onanistic
oncogenic
oncologic
onionskin
onomastic
ontogenic
ontologic
oogenesis
oogenetic
orangetip
orchestic
orgiastic
orthoepic
overtrain
ownership
packtrain
palanquin
pancratic
panegyric
panoramic
paperclip
paperthin
papeterie
parabasis
parabolic
paralalia
paralexia
paralysis
paralytic
paramedic
parapodia
parasitic
parataxis
paregoric
parotitis
pasticcio
patriotic
patristic
paulownia
pearlitic
pedagogic
pellagrin
peneplain
perfervid
peridotic
perihelia
pertussis
pharaonic
pharisaic
philippic
phlebitis
photophil
photopsia
phrenetic
phthalein
pianistic
pietistic
pilgarlic
pisolitic
pistachio
pithecoid
planetoid
planuloid
plasmatic
plasmodia
platinoid
plethoric
pleuritic
pneumatic
pneumonia
pneumonic
polybasic
polygamic
polygenic
polymeric
polyploid
polysemic
polysomic
polytypic
porcelain
porphyria
portfolio
pragmatic
preadamic
preexilic
preordain
pretermit
primordia
princekin
principia
priorship
prismatic
proboscis
proclitic
prodromic
progestin
prognosis
prolepsis
proleptic
properdin
prophetic
propionic
proptosis
proscenia
prostatic
proteinic
prothesis
prothetic
protozoic
psalmodic
psalteria
psoriasis
psoriatic
psychosis
psychotic
pterygoid
Ptolemaic
punctilio
puritanic
pushchair
pyramidic
pyridoxin
pyrogenic
pyrolysis
pyrolytic
pyromania
pyroxylin
quadratic
quadrifid
queenship
quitclaim
rafflesia
rauwolfia
realistic
reservoir
retinitis
rhapsodic
rheumatic
rhodopsin
rudbeckia
rulership
Russophil
saccharin
safetypin
saintship
salicylic
salmonoid
Samoyedic
sanatoria
sangfroid
Sanhedrim
Sanhedrin
sanitaria
sapraemia
sapraemic
Saracenic
sarcastic
scarfskin
schematic
sciaenoid
scleritis
sclerosis
sclerotic
scoliosis
scoliotic
scombroid
scorbutic
scorpioid
seaurchin
selenitic
semeiotic
semifluid
semirigid

semisolid
semitonic
Sephardic
Sephardim
septemvir
septennia
serotonin
serranoid
sestertia
shambolic
sharkskin
sheepskin
shirttail
sideritic
siderosis
silicosis
silicotic
silverfir
sinusitis
slaveship
Slavophil
slopbasin
snakeskin
solfeggio
Solomonic
sooterkin
sophistic
soporific
spaceship
spacesuit
sparkcoil
spasmodic
spermatic
spermatid
sphygmoid
spillikin
splenetic
splenitis
sporangia
sprigtail
spritsail
stalactic
statistic
steamship
steatitic
stigmatic
stockwhip
stomachic
storeship
stormsail
strategic
stromatic
strumitis
strychnic
stylistic
subarctic
subatomic
subsellia
sudatoria
sudorific
sulphonic
sulphuric
swordtail
sybaritic
syllepsis
sylleptic
symbiosis
symbiotic
symmetric
symphonic
symphysis
syncretic
syneresis
synizesis
synonymic
synovitis
syntactic
synthesis
synthetic
syphiloid
systaltic
taeniasis
tambourin
tarpaulin
taxonomic
telegenic
testatrix
thalassic
thaneship
theandric
theogonic
theologic
theomania
theoretic
Thomistic
threnodic
thumbnail
timelimit
tonguetie
toponymic
tormentil
tortricid
touristic
trachytic
tracksuit
transonic
transship
trapezoid
trattoria
trattorie
traumatic
triatomic
trichomic
trichroic
triclinia
triclinic
trihybrid
trimetric
troopship
tutorship
twicelaid
typhlitis
uncertain
underlaid
underlain
underpaid
underspin
unicuspid
urticaria
vaporific
varioloid
verdigris
virtuosic
vitriolic
vomitoria
wakerobin
wallfruit
Walpurgis
washbasin
whipperin
whirligig
whitebait
whodunnit
wingchair
wolframic
zeugmatic
zoophobia
zoophytic
zygomatic
zymogenic
comitadji
artichoke
balalaika
boondocks
bridecake
buttinsky
canebrake
childlike
corncrake
deathlike
dreamlike
fairylike
fiendlike
firedrake
fireworks
fruitcake
ghostlike
giantlike
golflinks
graywacke
greywacke
grubstake
handbrake
handshake
handspike
hitchhike
ironworks
kittiwake
lapstrake
lardycake
lookalike
milkshake
moonquake
motorbike
plantlike
poundcake
purselike
queenlike
ringshake
ringsnake
roadworks
rockbrake
rocksnake
saintlike
saltworks
scalelike
sheldrake
shortcake
skeesicks
snakelike
snowflake
soapworks
sunstroke
swordlike
sylphlike
undertake
wapentake
whipsnake
wideawake
womanlike
abdicable
abidingly
abradable
abusively
abysmally
accusable
acetabula
adamantly
adaptable
adducible
adjunctly
adminicle
admirable
admirably
adoptable
adoringly
adversely
advisable
advisably
advisedly
agreeable
agreeably
aimlessly
alienable
allegedly
allocable
allowable
allowably
allowedly
alterable
amazingly
amendable
amorously
amphibole
amusingly
anciently
angularly
annularly
antennule
anxiously
aquarelle
aqueously
archivolt
arcuately
arduously
armadillo
arteriole
artlessly
asexually
ashamedly
assayable
assumable
assumably
assuredly
astraddle
auditable
austerely
autocycle
available
availably
aventaile
averagely
avertible
avoidable
avoidably
awardable
awesomely
awkwardly
bagatelle
balefully
bamboozle
banderole
banefully
banjulele
barcarole
bargepole
bashfully
basically
bastardly
beamingly
beanstalk
bedraggle
belatedly
bemusedly
bespangle
bestially
biliously
bimonthly
birdtable
bizarrely
blackball
blameable
blameably
blasthole
blatantly
blazingly
blessedly
blindfold
blotchily
boardwalk
bombshell
bookishly
bookshelf
bookstall
boorishly
bracteole
breakable
breathily
bridewell
brittlely
brotherly
brusquely
brutishly
bulbously
bullishly
buoyantly
burningly
butcherly
butterfly
caddisfly
calcicole
calendula
callously
camarilla
campanile
campanili
campanula
cantabile
capitally
carambola
carbuncle
carefully
carfuffle
carpingly
casserole
catchable
catchpole
catchpoll
centrally
cerebella
certainly
chamomile
chantilly
chlorella
chockfull
chondrule
chronicle
cigarillo
citizenly
civically
claimable
clamantly
clamshell
classable
clearcole
cleavable
clemently
clientele
climbable
clubbable
coalfield
coattails
coaxially
coaxingly
coequally
coercible
coercibly
cogitable
cognately
coltishly
columella
comically
commingle
compactly
complexly
comptroll
comradely
concavely
concisely
condignly
conically
connately
constable
contumely
copiously
corbeille
corbicula
cordially
cornfield
cornstalk
corpuscle
correctly
corruptly
costively
countable
coverable
covetable
crabbedly
creatable
crepuscle
crocodile
crookedly
crossable
crossbill
crosstalk
crucially
crushable
cubbyhole
cubically
cunningly
curiously
currently
curricula
currishly
cursively
cursorily
cynically
damningly
dancehall
dashingly
dastardly
deathroll
debatable
decidable
decidedly
decimally
deducible
defiantly
definable
definably
deludable
denyingly
deposable
derivable
desirable
desirably
deviously
devisable
devotedly
dextrally
dharmsala
difficile
difficult
diffusely
digitally
dilatable
dipcircle
direfully
dirigible
dismantle
dispeople
dissemble
distantly
diurnally
diversely
dividable
divisible
doggishly
dolefully
doltishly
donnishly
dorbeetle
doubtable
doughtily
downfield
dragonfly
drinkable
drunkenly
dubiously
dubitable
duteously
dutifully
earnestly
easefully
eightfold
elegantly
elusively
embrangle
embrittle
emendable
eminently
emotively
emulously
encephala
endlessly
endurable
endurably
enjoyable
enjoyably
enterable
enviously
equitable
equitably
erstwhile
eruditely
escapable
espousals
estimable
eternally
ethically
evasively
evidently
evincible
evolvable
exactable
excisable
excitable
excitedly
excusable
excusably
execrable
execrably
expansile
expressly
exsertile
extensile
externals
extremely
facsimile
factually
fairytale
fandangle
farandole
fascicule
fasciculi
fatefully
fatigable
fatuously
fawningly
fearfully
federally
feelingly
fertilely
fervently
festively
filoselle
filtrable
finically
firedrill
fittingly
flamingly
flammable
flannelly

flaringly
flashbulb
flightily
floatable
flowingly
foolishly
footfault
footstalk
footstall
foppishly
forestall
forgeable
forlornly
forwardly
frangible
franticly
freestyle
freezable
fretfully
frontally
frowardly
fulgently
fullscale
fulsomely
furiously
furtively
gainfully
galingale
gallantly
gallingly
gallinule
gasmantle
gaugeable
generable
generally
genteelly
genuinely
germanely
getatable
gibbously
gingerale
girandole
girlishly
glacially
glaringly
glassgall
gleefully
glomerule
glomeruli
gloryhole
glowingly
goldfield
gradually
grantable
graspable
graticule
greenbelt
grisaille
gristmill
grouchily
guacamole
guardedly
guerrilla
guildhall
gushingly
habitable
habitably
haggardly
hairstyle
halfshell
halftitle
halophile
haltingly
haplessly
hardshell
harmfully
hatefully
haughtily
haustella
hawksbill
hawsehole
headstall
healthily
heartfelt
hedgingly
heedfully
heinously
helically
hellishly
helpfully
hemicycle
heritable
hexastyle
hideously
hierodule
hillbilly
hoggishly
homuncule
homunculi
hopefully
hostilely
household
hugeously
hurriedly
hurtfully
husbandly
hydrocele
hyperbola
hyperbole
hypostyle
ignitable
ignitible
ignorable
illegally
illegible
illegibly
illicitly
imageable
immensely
immorally
immovable
immovably
immutable
immutably
impiously
impliedly
imputable
inaudible
inaudibly
incapable
incapably
incunable
incurable
incurably
indelible
indelibly
inducible
ineffable
ineffably
inequable
inerrable
inexactly
infantile
inferable
infertile
infusible
inhumanly
initially
insectile
insipidly
insoluble
insolubly
instantly
insularly
insurable
intensely
interfile
invalidly
inversely
invisible
invisibly
ionisable
irascible
irascibly
irksomely
ironmould
irrigable
irritable
irritably
jarringly
jealously
jeeringly
jocularly
joylessly
kerfuffle
kiddingly
kilocycle
knavishly
kneadable
knowingly
lacerable
laggardly
lambently
lampshell
languidly
lastingly
laterally
laughable
laughably
lawlessly
leafmould
leafstalk
learnable
learnedly
leasehold
leeringly
leewardly
leisurely
lengthily
leniently
lexically
liberally
lifecycle
lifestyle
lifetable
liltingly
limitable
limitedly
linenfold
lingually
lioncelle
lispingly
lissomely
literally
litigable
locatable
lodgepole
logically
longingly
louringly
loutishly
loveapple
lovechild
lumpishly
lustfully
lyrically
magically
majuscule
malleable
manhandle
maritally
martially
massively
matricula
mawkishly
maximally
maybeetle
meaningly
meanwhile
mediately
medicable
medically
megacycle
meltingly
memorable
memorably
mesophyll
microfilm
micropyle
millivolt
mincingly
mindfully
minefield
minimally
minuscule
miserable
miserably
mishandle
mitigable
mitraille
mockingly
moneybill
mongrelly
monostyle
monticule
mordantly
motorable
mouldable
mountable
mousehole
mundanely
musically
musichall
naturally
naughtily
navigable
needfully
nemophila
nervously
neutrally
niggardly
nightfall
nocuously
noisomely
nominable
nominally
nonviable
northerly
noxiously
numbskull
numerable
obliquely
obscenely
obscurely
obversely
obviously
octastyle
octostyle
odorously
oenophile
oenophily
oligopoly
ominously
omissible
onerously
operosely
opposable
optically
opulently
organelle
outwardly
overspill
overwhelm
packdrill
painfully
painterly
palatable
palatably
panatella
panhandle
pantingly
parbuckle
parlously
partially
pasodoble
passively
pastorale
patchouli
patchouly
patiently
peaceable
peaceably
peccantly
peevishly
pendently
peninsula
pensively
pentangle
perfectly
pericycle
peristyle
permeable
petiolule
pettishly
philately
Philomela
photocell
piggishly
pineapple
pinnately
piquantly
piteously
pitifully
pityingly
pivotable
pivotally
placeable
plantable
plausible
plausibly
playfully
pleadable
plenarily
plicately
pointedly
pointille
polevault
pompously
popularly
porbeagle
pratingly
preachily
precisely
pregnable
presently
primarily
principle
printable
privately
profanely
profusely
prolately
proveably
prudently
prudishly
pulsatile
punchball
pungently
purposely
purringly
pursuable
pushingly
quadrille
quadruple
quadruply
quarterly
quintuple
radialply
radiantly
radiately
radically
raffishly
rakehelly
rampantly
rantingly
ranunculi
raspingly
rationale
raucously
raunchily
razorbill
reachable
rebukable
reconcile
rectangle
reducible
referable
refusable
refutable
regularly
reliantly
removable
renewable
reparable
repayable
reputable
reputably
reputedly
resalable
reshuffle
resoluble
restfully
restively
resumable
reversely
revisable
revivable
revocable
ridgepole
ridgetile
rightable
rigmarole
ringingly
riotously
rocambole
rockdrill
roguishly
roseapple
roseately
rosenoble
rotatable
routinely
rubicelle
ruffianly
ruinously
ruthfully
sabadilla
saliently
sandtable
sapiently
sapodilla
saturable
savourily
scagliola
scholarly
scintilla
scraggily
scrappily
screwball
screwbolt
screwpile
scrimpily
scruffily
scrumhalf
scrutable
seagirdle
seanettle
searingly
seatangle
secularly
securable
seemingly
selfishly
semblable
semblably
seminally
sensually
separable
separably
seriately
seriously
serrefile
servilely
sevenfold
seventhly
severable
severally
sexlessly
shakeable
shallowly
Shangrila
shapeable
sheepfold
sheepwalk
sheerhulk
shemozzle
shockable
shootable
shortfall
sickishly
sidetable
similarly
sincerely
sinlessly
sinophile
sinuately
sinuously
siphuncle
skedaddle
sketchily
skilfully
slavishly
slenderly
sliderule
smilingly
smokeball
snowfield
sobbingly
softshell
soldierly
somewhile
songcycle
songfully
sorbapple
sottishly
soulfully
soundfilm
soundhole
southerly
sparingly
spatially
speakable
specially
spectacle
speedball
speedwell
spendable
spiracula
splashily
spoonbill
spouthole
sprightly
springald

springily
squalidly
squashily
squeakily
stackable
stainable
stairwell
stampmill
starapple
starchily
starshell
staunchly
stepchild
stiltedly
stinkball
stockpile
stoically
stokehold
stokehole
stonecold
stonewall
stoolball
stormbelt
strangely
streakily
strongyle
studiedly
stylishly
suasively
subduable
subduedly
subfamily
sublimely
summarily
superable
supremely
surcingle
suturally
sweettalk
swimmable
swinishly
tabletalk
tabularly
tactfully
tactually
tanpickle
tarantula
tartishly
teachable
teachably
teakettle
tearfully
teasingly
tediously
tegularly
tellingly
temptable
tenuously
ternately
textually
thermally
thinkable
thirstily
thornbill
threefold
threshold
thriftily
throatily
throughly
thumbhole
tigerlily
timeously
timetable
titularly
tolerable
tolerably
tonically
topically
totempole

touchable
touchhole
townsfolk
toxically
toxophily
trabecula
traceable
traceably
tractable
tractably
trainable
treadmill
treatable
tricksily
trifocals
trivially
triweekly
trunkcall
tubercule
tubularly
tunefully
turgently
turnstile
turntable
twelfthly
twicetold
twistable
twitchily
typically
umbellule
uncannily
uncivilly
uncleanly
uncouthly
underfelt
undersell
undersold
unearthly
uneatable
unequally
unfleshly
unhappily
unifiable
uniformly
unitively
unluckily
unnamable
unsayable
unshackle
unsightly
unsoundly
untenable
unusually
unwomanly
uprightly
uselessly
utterable
vacuously
valiantly
vallecula
vaporable
varicella
variously
veeringly
vegetable
vegetably
venerable
venerably
ventrally
ventricle
verbosely
verdantly
veritable
veritably
vermicule
versatile
vestibule
vibracula
vibratile

viciously
violently
virginals
virtually
viscously
visitable
waggishly
wailingly
waistbelt
wakefully
warblefly
warningly
waspishly
watchable
waterfall
waterhole
waterlily
watermill
waywardly
wealthily
weatherly
weighable
weightily
Whitehall
wholesale
wieldable
willingly
winevault
winningly
winsomely
wishfully
wistfully
witlessly
wittingly
wolfishly
womenfolk
workmanly
worktable
worriedly
xenophile
xerophile
xerophily
xparticle
yawningly
zealously
zestfully
aerodrome
aftertime
archenemy
astrodome
astronomy
blackdamp
blackgame
blaspheme
blasphemy
carcinoma
chokedamp
cockscomb
colostomy
condyloma
cosmorama
currycomb
cyclorama
cystotomy
depthbomb
diathermy
dichogamy
dichotomy
didrachma
dirigisme
disentomb
dithyramb
doorframe
duodecimo
eightsome
emphysema
empyreuma
enthymeme
eurhythmy

exanthema
forcepump
haematoma
harmotome
honeycomb
hydrosome
hypergamy
impostume
leptosome
leucotome
leucotomy
lightsome
lithesome
lithotomy
loathsome
lobectomy
loxodrome
lunchtime
majordomo
melodrama
metronome
microsome
microtome
microtomy
misbecome
monodrama
monorhyme
monotreme
myriorama
myxoedema
nighttime
oriflamme
overtrump
pantomime
papilloma
peacetime
penultima
peristome
phantasma
phytotomy
placename
polyonymy
pranksome
proenzyme
programme
protonema
quicklime
semanteme
semiplume
sixteenmo
smallarms
smalltime
smokebomb
spacetime
stinkbomb
taxidermy
teknonymy
thingummy
threesome
toothcomb
toothsome
tradename
unwelcome
vasectomy
velodrome
wearisome
wholesome
worrisome
abasement
abashment
abatement
abhorrent
abhorring
ablutions
aborigine
abounding
abseiling
absorbent
absorbing

abstinent
acceptant
accompany
accordant
according
acetylene
acidulent
aconitine
adenosine
adjoining
adlibbing
admitting
adornment
adsorbent
advertent
aerobiont
aeroplane
affecting
affirmant
Afrikaans
agapemone
agistment
agonising
agreement
aitchbone
albescent
alignment
alinement
allegiant
allophone
allotment
allotting
almandine
alternant
amassment
amazement
amendment
ampersand
amusement
analysand
andantino
androgyne
androgyny
anklebone
annectent
annuitant
annulling
annulment
anovulant
anticline
antiphony
apartment
appalling
appealing
appellant
appendant
applicant
apprehend
aquaplane
archfiend
argentine
arrestant
arresting
asbestine
ascendant
ascendent
ashlaring
assailant
assistant
assurgent
atonement
attendant
aubergine
awakening
backslang
ballerina
ballpoint
bandoline
bandstand

barbitone
battening
bedspring
befitting
befogging
begetting
beginning
bellyband
bengaline
benignant
benzidine
benzoline
berberine
besetment
besetting
besotting
bevelling
billabong
binturong
bivariant
blastment
bluepoint
blueprint
bluestone
boliviano
bombasine
bombazine
bondstone
bonechina
bookstand
boomerang
boomslang
borrowing
bowstring
boyfriend
brambling
brandling
breadline
breathing
breeching
breveting
brilliant
brimstone
bristling
buckhound
buffeting
buhrstone
burrstone
butadiene
butterine
buttygang
Byzantine
caballine
caballing
cacholong
cacophony
canescent
cantilena
carnitine
carolling
carpeting
casuarina
catamount
catarhine
catchment
cavilling
celandine
celebrant
centering
centreing
chaingang
champagne
chaperone
charabanc
chatoyant
cheekbone
chickling
churching
cipollino

cisalpine
cleansing
cliffhang
clinquant
cloisonne
cloudland
coagulant
coastline
Cockaigne
cognisant
colophony
colouring
colubrine
columbine
combatant
competent
complaint
compliant
component
concubine
condiment
confidant
confident
confiding
confluent
congruent
connivent
consonant
contadina
contadino
continent
cooperant
copestone
coralline
cormorant
cornstone
corposant
corpulent
cortisone
coruscant
cosmogeny
cosmogony
cotangent
coumarone
covariant
crackling
crapulent
crashland
crediting
crepitant
crinoline
crippling
croissant
crosslink
crosswind
culminant
cupelling
curbstone
curveting
cymophane
dachshund
damascene
dayspring
debagging
debarment
debarring
debugging
declarant
decrement
decumbent
deerhound
defendant
deferment
deferring
deficient
defoliant
dehiscent
demandant
demanding

demitting
demobbing
demulcent
demurring
deodorant
dependant
dependent
desiccant
designing
detergent
determent
determine
deterrent
deterring
detriment
devilling
devilment
diachrony
different
diffident
diphthong
disarming
disorient
disputant
dissident
dissonant
distraint
divergent
diverting
dixieland
donothing
dopefiend
dowelling
draghound
dragomans
dreamland
dripstone
dropscene
dropscone
dumbfound
earthling
eastbound
easygoing
ebullient
efficient
effulgent
eglantine
ejectment
elopement
embayment
embedding
embedment
embussing
emollient
emolument
enactment
endearing
endocrine
endowment
engarland
engraving
enjoyment
enrolling
enrolment
ephedrine
equalling
equipment
equipping
estopping
estuarine
exactment
examinant
exceeding
excellent
excelling
exceptant
excepting
excipient
excrement
excurrent
executant
exilement
expectant
expecting
expedient
expellent
expelling
extendant
extolling
extolment
exuberant
fabricant
faggoting
fairyland
fairyring
farseeing
fastening
feiseanna
feoffment
fibroline
fingering
finicking
firebrand
fireirons
firestone
firmament
firsthand
firstling
fivepenny
flagstone
flatulent
flayflint
fledgling
fleshment
flouncing
flowering
flowstone
fluctuant
focussing
following
footpound
footprint
forceland
forefront
foregoing
forgiving
foundling
fourpenny
freestone
frontline
fulgurant
fulminant
fundament
gabardine
gaberdine
galantine
gallivant
galloping
gallstone
gammoning
gangplank
gardening
gathering
gavelkind
gazehound
geobotany
gladstone
glycerine
godparent
goffering
goldsinny
Gradgrind
grandaunt
grapevine
grappling
grassland
gravamina
greataunt
greensand
gregarine
grenadine
greyhound
gritstone
grounding
gruelling
grumbling
guardring
guideline
guttering
gyroplane
hailstone
halfbound
halfpenny
hallstand
halothane
hamstring
hamstrung
handstand
hankering
happening
hardiment
harmaline
harrowing
hatchling
hatchment
havocking
headphone
headstone
heartland
hellhound
hidebound
hirundine
histamine
histidine
histogeny
hoarhound
hoarstone
hocussing
holystone
homebound
homophone
homophony
honkytonk
hoofprint
horehound
hornstone
horsemint
horsepond
humankind
humectant
hurricane
hydrazine
ignescent
illboding
immigrant
impatiens
impatient
impeccant
impelling
impendent
impending
implement
important
importune
imprudent
incessant
incipient
inclement
increment
incumbent
incurrent
incurring
indignant
indulgent
inebriant
inelegant
infantine
inferring
infilling
inflowing
informant
ingrowing
inharmony
inpatient
inpouring
inquiline
insetting
insistent
insolvent
insurgent
integrand
integrant
intendant
interline
interlink
interment
interring
intervene
interwind
interzone
intestine
intrigant
inurement
invariant
ironbound
ironstone
irradiant
isochrone
isooctane
itinerant
jackplane
japanning
jessamine
Johannine
judgement
junketing
keelivine
kerbstone
kurrajong
labelling
lacertine
landagent
latescent
lathering
latticing
launching
lawgiving
lazzarone
lazzaroni
leaselend
leavening
legerline
lettering
Levantine
levelling
libellant
libelling
libertine
lightning
limestone
limousine
lineament
lingering
lithopone
loadstone
lodestone
lodgement
lophodont
lotusland
lubricant
lumbering
luxuriant
lyamhound
lymehound
macedoine
maddening
madeleine
magdalene
magicking
mailplane
malignant
mandarine
mandoline
maneating
marchpane
margarine
marihuana
marijuana
marketing
marlstone
marshland
masculine
matrimony
meandrine
megaphone
menadione
mendicant
mepacrine
merriment
mescaline
metalline
metalling
methadone
methylene
mezzanine
mezzotint
microtone
milestone
millstone
mimicking
miscegene
miscegine
miscreant
misgiving
modelling
monocline
monoplane
monthling
moonblind
moonshine
moonstone
multilane
munitions
muscadine
muscarine
musteline
naphthene
narcotine
nectarine
negligent
negotiant
nemertine
nepheline
newsagent
newshound
newsprint
newsstand
nicotiana
nightline
nightlong
nigricant
nigrosine
ninepenny
nitratine
nonjuring
northland
nurseling
nutriment
obscurant
obsequent
observant
occludent
occurrent
occurring
officiant
offspring
Oligocene
onsetting
opportune
oppugnant
optophone
organzine
osteogeny
outgiving
overborne
overlying
overprint
overspend
overspent
overwound
packaging
Pakistani
palpitant
panelling
panicking
paramount
parchment
parsimony
passerine
pathogeny
patrimony
pedalling
penduline
peneplane
penetrant
penfriend
percaline
peregrine
perilling
perishing
permanent
pertinent
pestilent
pethidine
phagedena
phenomena
pheromone
philogyny
phosphene
phosphine
photogene
phylogeny
phytogeny
picketing
piggybank
pipestone
placement
plainsong
plaything
Pleiocene
plumbline
poinciana
pollutant
polyphone
polyphony
polythene
porcupine
portolano
postulant
potholing
pourpoint
pozzolana
precedent
preceding
predicant
predikant
prepotent
prescient
preshrink
preshrunk
president
pressgang
prevalent
procreant
prolamine
prominent
promising
proponent
propylene
protamine
provident
providing
provoking
pubescent
pulpstone
punchline
punishing
puzzolana
quibbling
quicksand
quiescent
quinoline
rationing
ravelling
ravelment
ravishing
reasoning
rebelling
rebidding
rebutting
recapping
recipient
reckoning
recombine
recommend
reconvene
recording
recumbent
recurrent
recurring
reductant
redundant
reefpoint
reentrant
reexamine
referring
refitment
refitting
refulgent
regardant
rejoicing
reluctant
remitment
remittent
remitting
remontant
renascent
repayment
repellant
repellent
repelling
repentant
repotting
reprehend
represent
reprimand
repugnant
rerunning
reserpine
resetting
resilient
resistant
resitting
resolvent
resorbent
restraint
resultant
resurgent
retardant
revelling
revetment
revetting
revolting

rewarding
rhodamine
righthand
rivalling
rivelling
riverbank
rockbound
rockplant
rousement
rufescent
russeting
sacrament
safranine
sailoring
sailplane
saintling
salangane
sandblind
sandstone
santolina
saturnine
saxophone
scantling
scarfring
schilling
schooling
scorching
scramming
scrapping
screening
screwpine
scrubbing
seafaring
searching
seasoning
seastrand
secernent
seedplant
senescent
sentiment
shambling
shaveling
shearling
sheathing
sheetbend
shoeshine
shopfront
shoreline
shorthand
shredding
shrugging
sibylline
sickening
sideburns
signorina
silkgland
siltstone
singalong
skijoring
skinflint
skydiving
slabstone
slushfund
smuggling
snowblind
snowblink
snowbound
snowplant
soapstone
soidisant
solferino
something
somnolent
sopranino
southland
spaceband
spearmint
spellbind
spindling

splendent
splitting
spodumene
sporogeny
sprigging
springing
squatting
squibbing
squidding
stagehand
staghound
starstone
startling
statement
stillhunt
stimulant
stippling
stormcone
storyline
straphang
strapping
streaking
strewment
stringent
stripling
stripping
stropping
strouding
strumming
strutting
subalpine
subjacent
submarine
subtenant
succulent
suffering
sugarcane
superfine
supervene
suppliant
supposing
surfacing
surveying
susurrant
swaddling
sweatband
swingeing
swordcane
sycophant
synchrony
tableland
tailoring
talismans
tangerine
tarragona
taxpaying
telephone
telephony
terebrant
termagant
tervalent
testament
testimony
thatching
theophany
thighbone
thinktank
thirdhand
thrashing
thrilling
throbbing
thrumming
thylacine
thyroxine
tiedyeing
tilestone
timbering
tittuping
toadstone

tombstone
torchsong
totalling
touchline
towelling
trainband
transcend
transenna
transient
treatment
tremolant
tremulant
trenchant
trepidant
trivalent
troutling
truculent
truepenny
tumescent
turbulent
Turcomans
Turkomans
turnround
turnstone
twentyone
twinkling
unbending
unceasing
underdone
undergone
underhand
underhung
underline
underling
undermine
undersong
undertint
undertone
underwent
underwing
unfailing
unfeeling
unfitting
ungallant
unheeding
unisonant
univalent
unknowing
unmeaning
unpegging
unsmiling
unsparing
unweeting
unwilling
unwinking
unwitting
unzipping
uplifting
upsetting
vacillant
valentine
vapouring
veinstone
veneering
veratrine
vetchling
vicereine
victorine
viewpoint
virescent
vitelline
viverrine
volauvent
vulturine
waistband
waistline
walloping
wandering
washstand

wasteland
waterline
wavefront
wayfaring
weighting
welcoming
wellbeing
wellfound
westbound
westering
whalebone
wheedling
whetstone
whinstone
whipround
whirlwind
whistling
whitening
whitewing
whizzbang
windbound
winestone
witchhunt
withering
withstand
woebegone
wolfhound
wolfsbane
wolverene
wolverine
womankind
womenkind
worldling
worriment
wrestling
wristband
xylophone
yearround
yodelling
yohimbine
youngling
zibelline
zootechny
abdicator
abduction
abjection
abnegator
abolition
abrogator
abruption
accession
accordion
accretion
acetylcoA
actinozoa
activator
actuation
addiction
addressor
adduction
ademption
admission
admonitor
adoration
adulation
adulthood
advection
advocator
affection
afflation
afterglow
afternoon
aggressor
agitation
alienator
alligator
amputator
angleiron
animation

annotator
anthelion
anthemion
anticodon
apparitor
apportion
arrowroot
arrowwood
arthropod
ascension
aspersion
aspirator
assertion
asyndeton
attention
attractor
attrition
augmentor
automaton
autopilot
avocation
badminton
bandicoot
bandwagon
barleymow
barracoon
battalion
beadledom
bedfellow
bellyflop
birdsfoot
bisection
Blackfoot
bloodroot
bloodshot
boardfoot
boardroom
bolection
bombardon
bombproof
bowwindow
brakeshoe
briarroot
briarwood
brierroot
brierwood
broadloom
brushwood
bumbledon
cacodemon
campstool
capacitor
caparison
carnation
caseation
cassation
causation
cedarwood
centurion
cessation
chaetopod
chameleon
chassepot
chelation
childhood
classroom
clavation
cloakroom
coadjutor
coalition
cockahoop
cocksfoot
coemption
coffeepot
cognation
cognition
colcannon
collation
collector

collision
collodion
collusion
coltsfoot
commandos
commotion
communion
compactor
companion
comprador
concision
concoctor
condition
conductor
confessor
confirmor
confiteor
confusion
connation
connector
connexion
conqueror
consignor
consultor
contactor
contagion
contusion
convector
copsewood
cornerboy
corrasion
corrector
corrosion
cotillion
cotyledon
courtroom
cremation
crenation
criterion
CroMagnon
crowsfoot
cunctator
cyclotron
damnation
dandelion
dayschool
deathblow
decathlon
deception
decillion
decimator
decoction
decontrol
decorator
dedicator
deduction
defection
deflation
deflector
deflexion
dejection
demission
dentation
dentition
depiction
depletion
depositor
depressor
depurator
desertion
desolator
detection
detention
detersion
detonator
detractor
detrition
detrusion
deviation

diachylom
dictation
diffusion
digestion
dimension
direction
discommon
dissector
diversion
divulsion
dodecagon
dominator
dormition
doubleton
Doukhobor
downthrow
driftwood
drummajor
eavesdrop
education
effluxion
egression
eirenicon
elbowroom
elevation
elocution
emanation
embraceor
emendator
emulation
encrimson
ephemeron
epilation
erudition
escalator
escheator
estimator
evocation
evolution
excavator
excelsior
exception
excerptor
exclusion
excretion
excursion
execution
exemption
exhibitor
expansion
expiation
explosion
expositor
expulsion
exsertion
extension
extortion
extractor
extrusion
exudation
eyeshadow
fairyhood
faldstool
falsehood
fandangos
fieldbook
fieldboot
filiation
fireproof
firstfoot
flamingos
flotation
flowerpot
foliation
foolproof
footstool
formation
foulbrood
Freemason

frigatoon
fumigator
furcation
gammadion
gastropod
gemmation
generator
gerfalcon
germproof
gestation
gladiator
glossator
glyptodon
gogglebox
goldenrod
goosefoot
gradation
graduator
grapeshot
greenroom
greenwood
grillroom
groundhog
guarantor
guardbook
guardroom
guestroom
guidebook
guillemot
guncotton
gustation
guttation
gyrfalcon
habergeon
halfblood
hammertoe
hangerson
hardihood
haresfoot
heartwood
heptaglot
hesitator
heterodox
Hollywood
honeymoon
horseshoe
hortation
Hottentot
houseroom
hydration
hydrozoon
ichneumon
iguanodon
imitation
immersion
immolator
impaction
impassion
imperator
impletion
implosion
impulsion
inanition
incaution
inception
inclusion
incubator
incursion
indagator
indention
indicator
indiction
induction
infection
inflation
inflexion
inflictor
infractor
ingestion
inglenook
inhalator
inheritor
inhibitor
initiator
injection
innovator
innuendos
insertion
inspector
insulator
intension
intention
intercrop
interflow
intorsion
intrusion
intuition
inunction
invention
inversion
irrigator
irruption
isolation
iteration
jactation
junkerdom
kaiserdom
lactation
lallation
lancewood
laudation
letterbox
levitator
liberator
libration
librettos
lifeblood
lightfoot
lightwood
lineation
liquation
literator
locomotor
lustihood
macerator
maelstrom
magnetron
malathion
martyrdom
masterdom
matchwood
medallion
mediation
meditator
melocoton
mentation
migration
misemploy
misfeasor
misreckon
mistletoe
mitigator
moderator
modillion
modulator
monkshood
monoceros
monsignor
mortgagor
mosquitos
mothproof
motivator
muskmelon
mutilator
narration
navigator
nervation
neuration
nictation
nitration
nominator
nonillion
nonperson
numerator
nutrition
objection
obsession
obtention
obtrusion
obturator
obversion
obviation
occlusion
octillion
oddfellow
offseason
olecranon
olfaction
operation
opodeldoc
oppressor
orderbook
organstop
Orpington
orrisroot
overproof
overshoot
overthrow
ovulation
oxidation
palmation
palpation
pantaloon
parathion
parhelion
parleyvoo
partition
peachblow
peculator
pendragon
pepperbox
pepperpot
percheron
perdition
perfector
perfusion
persimmon
pervasion
phonation
phyllopod
phytotron
pillarbox
placation
planation
plication
ploughboy
pollution
possessor
posterior
postilion
pouncebox
precentor
preceptor
precision
precursor
predation
predictor
preemptor
prefixion
prelector
prelusion
premotion
prenotion
preschool
pressroom
prevision
princedom
printshop
privation
probation
processor
professor
profusion
projector
prolation
prolusion
promotion
promptbox
pronation
prosector
protector
protestor
protozoon
provision
psalmbook
pseudopod
pulsation
puppyhood
pureblood
purgation
pussyfoot
pyramidon
Quakerdom
queenhood
quotation
radiation
rainproof
rareeshow
rascaldom
rebellion
recension
reception
recession
reclusion
recursion
redaction
redevelop
reduction
refashion
refection
reflation
reflector
reflexion
refractor
regulator
rejection
remission
rendition
renovator
repletion
repressor
repulsion
resection
resonator
retention
retortion
retractor
revelator
reversion
revulsion
Rhineodon
roughshod
ruination
ruminator
rustproof
saddlebow
sainthood
saltation
saltspoon
salvation
sapanwood
sargassos
Sarmation
satiation
satinwood
saturator
savagedom
scarecrow
schoolboy
scorebook
scrapbook
scrapiron
scrutator
scuncheon
scutcheon
seaanchor
secession
seclusion
secretion
seduction
selection
semicolon
sensation
sentrybox
separator
septation
serration
sharecrop
sharpshod
sheephook
sheikhdom
shelfroom
shopfloor
shortstop
shotproof
signalbox
siltation
simpleton
simulator
singleton
sinuation
situation
slingshot
smackeroo
snakeroot
snakewood
solicitor
solvation
sortition
soupspoon
spadefoot
spectator
splayfoot
spoliator
springbok
squiredom
stableboy
stackroom
stagedoor
stairfoot
stanchion
statehood
stateroom
stilettos
stillroom
stinkwood
stockbook
stockroom
stonecrop
storeroom
storybook
striation
strongbox
stylebook
subdeacon
subeditor
sublation
subregion
succentor
successor
suffusion
sulcation
summation
supercool
supinator
suspensor
suspicion
sweatshop
sweetshop
swordknot
tabulator
talkathon
tallyshop
tanliquor
televisor
tentation
testation
therefrom
thereupon
thermidor
thighboot
thralldom
thyratron
thyristor
tigerwood
tinderbox
titration
toadstool
tormentor
touchwood
tournedos
tradition
trilithon
trisagion
trisector
truncheon
tuliproot
tulipwood
turboprop
ululation
undecagon
underfoot
underplot
undershot
undertook
underwood
usucapion
vallation
valuation
variation
vasomotor
vendition
venerator
vermilion
vernation
vibration
violation
virtuosos
vitiation
wagonroof
warrantor
watercool
wherefrom
whereupon
whirlpool
whitewood
widowhood
windowbox
windproof
withstood
womanhood
wristdrop
wristshot
Yankeedom
yellowdog
zebrawood
aerograph
allograph
allomorph
allotrope
allotropy
amidships
archetype
autograph
autotroph
azeotrope
barograph
bombhappy
broomrape
cassaripe
cerograph
chemitype
collotype
conscript
cryoscope
cryoscopy
drainpipe
ectomorph
eidograph
endolymph
endomorph
endoscope
endoscopy
ergograph
ferrotype
grandpapa
guiderope
gyroscope
hawsepipe
heliotype
hemitrope
hodograph
holograph
homograph
horoscope
horoscopy
ideograph
idiograph
incorrupt
intercept
interlope
interrupt
jacksnipe
karyotype
kymograph
lagniappe
lagomorph
landscape
logogriph
mesomorph
monograph
moonscape
nomograph
oleograph
overleapt
overslept
paragraph
paramorph
paranymph
perilymph
perimorph
periscope
phalarope
phenotype
photocopy
phototype
pinstripe
pitchpipe
polygraph
polymorph
preoccupy
presbyope
prescript
prototype
pyroscope
sciagraph
sciascopy
serigraph
shipshape
sideswipe
skiagraph
skiascopy
slaphappy

snowscape
standpipe
steampipe
stenotype
stenotypy
stovepipe
subscript
telegraph
telescope
telescopy
tightrope
touchtype
townscape
transumpt
underripe
videotape
wastepipe
waterpipe
windswept
woodnymph
Xanthippe
xeromorph
xylograph
zincotype
aboutturn
accessary
accessory
aciniform
adipocere
admeasure
admixture
adulatory
adventure
adversary
aerometry
affixture
aftercare
afterword
airyfairy
alpenhorn
ambulacra
amphigory
ancientry
ancillary
angleworm
anomalure
antennary
antiquary
arbitrary
armillary
arrowworm
artillery
ascospore
asymmetry
auxiliary
Aylesbury
Babbittry
bacillary
backboard
backsword
baltimore
bandolero
baneberry
baptistry
barnstorm
barometry
battlecry
bearberry
beechfern
bejabbers
belvedere
billboard
biosphere
birchbark
birthmark
birthwort
blackbird
blaeberry
bleachery
bloodworm
bloodwort
bluebeard
blueberry
bodyguard
bolometry
bookstore
boulevard
bowerbird
brachyura
brassiere
brickwork
brickyard
brigandry
broomcorn
brushfire
brushwork
buckboard
buckthorn
budgetary
caballero
cairngorm
calenture
callipers
Camembert
cannelure
capillary
Capricorn
cardboard
cardsharp
carnivore
carpentry
cartulary
Cassandra
cassimere
cassowary
casuistry
catchword
ceasefire
centenary
chandlery
charivari
chelicera
chemistry
chevelure
chicanery
chinaware
chipboard
chisquare
circuitry
citizenry
clapboard
claviform
clepsydra
clipboard
clockwork
coachwork
coastward
cocoonery
coenosarc
coldshort
columbary
comfiture
Cominform
Comintern
commodore
communard
composure
comradery
concentre
configure
connature
cordiform
corollary
courtcard
courtyard
coverture
coxcombry
cranberry
crematory
crenature
crossfire
crossword
crowberry
cruciform
cuckoldry
cuneiform
curvature
curviform
customary
cuttysark
cymbiform
cystocarp
damnatory
dartboard
dashboard
davenport
debenture
decalitre
decametre
decastere
decennary
decilitre
decimetre
decistere
decretory
deerberry
defeature
delftware
dentiform
dentistry
departure
depasture
desultory
dickybird
dignitary
dimissory
dinothere
directory
disaccord
disaffirm
discovert
discovery
disembark
disfigure
disposure
disregard
dormitory
dosimetry
drawnwork
dromedary
drugstore
duckboard
dulcamara
duodenary
dysentery
earthborn
earthward
earthwork
earthworm
ecosphere
ecritoire
electuary
elsewhere
embracery
embrasure
emunctory
enclosure
endosperm
endospore
enrapture
epicentre
eruciform
evocatory
exclosure
excretory
executory
exemplary
exosphere
expiatory
expletory
extempore
extravert
extrovert
faithcure
falciform
fallalery
fancywork
fantastry
feudatory
fibriform
fiduciary
fieldfare
fieldwork
fioritura
fioriture
firealarm
fireguard
firstborn
floodmark
floristry
flowchart
footboard
forecourt
foreshore
formicary
formulary
fourscore
framework
freeboard
freezedry
friarbird
frontward
frostwork
fungiform
furniture
gallantry
gangboard
garniture
geosphere
gestatory
ghostword
gimmickry
glassware
glasswork
glasswort
glengarry
gonophore
goosegirl
gooseherd
gossamery
gradatory
grandsire
graveyard
greenhorn
greybeard
grillwork
guesswork
gustatory
gynophore
hackamore
hackberry
hailstorm
hairshirt
handiwork
handywork
haphazard
hardboard
hartshorn
headboard
headscarf
heartburn
heartsore
heathenry
hellebore
herbivore
hexachord
hortatory
housecarl
housework
huckstery
hunkydory
husbandry
imaginary
immixture
imposture
impresari
impulsory
incensory
inclosure
indenture
infirmary
insectary
insincere
interfere
interlard
introvert
inventory
involucre
itinerary
janissary
jewellery
judiciary
Juneberry
kickstart
kilolitre
kilometre
krummhorn
Langobard
laudatory
lavaliere
leftovers
legendary
legionary
lentiform
libratory
licensure
liegelord
lifeguard
ligniform
lionheart
liverwort
loanshark
longicorn
Longobard
longshore
lousewort
lovestory
machinery
madrepore
magistery
malanders
mamillary
mammiform
mandatary
mandatory
manoeuvre
mansionry
manticore
maquisard
marquetry
marshwort
mattamore
maxillary
mediatory
medullary
megaspore
melaphyre
mercenary
mesentery
messieurs
metalwork
midwifery
migratory
millboard
millenary
millepore
millinery
miniature
miniskirt
misgovern
misinform
misreport
momentary
monastery
moneywort
monochord
monolatry
mouthpart
multiform
multipara
narratory
naseberry
navelwort
necessary
nervature
nevermore
nightbird
nightmare
nightwork
nobiliary
northward
notochord
nullipara
nullipore
octachord
octahedra
offcentre
offertory
olfactory
openheart
optometry
orchestra
orderform
osteoderm
overboard
overexert
overheard
overskirt
overweary
ovulatory
pachyderm
pageantry
paintwork
palaestra
palmistry
papergirl
paperwork
papillary
parcenary
parquetry
patchwork
pearlwort
peasantry
pecuniary
pellitory
pennywort
perfumery
periphery
perisperm
persevere
phonatory
piecework
piscatory
pisciform
pitchdark
pitchfork
pituitary
placatory
placecard
planetary
platemark
plicature
plusfours
pokeberry
pokerwork
politburo
polyandry
polyhedra
polyzoary
postentry
potpourri
pourboire
precatory
predatory
prefatory
prefigure
prelature
prelusory
premature
prerecord
pressmark
presswork
primipara
probatory
procedure
prolusory
pronghorn
provisory
provostry
pulmonary
pulpboard
pulsatory
punchcard
pupillary
purgatory
pyrolatry
pyrometry
quillwort
rainstorm
rapidfire
raspatory
raspberry
rearguard
recapture
reconfirm
reconvert
refectory
reliquary
remeasure
rencontre
repertory
residuary
restiform
retrovert
rhizocarp
riflebird
rightward
Roquefort
roundworm
sacciform
safeguard
salesgirl
saltatory
saltpetre
sanctuary
sandstorm
sarcocarp
satinbird
scalefern
scapulary
scorecard
scrapyard
screwworm
scripture
sculpture
scutiform
seasquirt
secateurs
secondary
secretary
secretory
sedentary
seedpearl

seigneury
seigniory
selfaware
selfglory
semaphore
septenary
sepulchre
sepulture
sequestra
serpentry
setsquare
shadberry
shelfmark
shellbark
shellfire
shellwork
shinguard
shipboard
shoreward
shorthorn
shortterm
shrubbery
sideboard
sigillary
signatory
signature
signboard
simulacra
simulacre
snakebird
snowberry
snowguard
snowstorm
soapberry
solfatara
solitaire
somewhere
sophistry
sophomore
southward
spaceport
spadework
spearwort
spikenard
spirogyra
splintery
spluttery
sporocarp
stackyard
starboard
statutory
steelwork
steelyard
steenkirk
sternward
stevedore
stickwork
stillborn
stinkhorn
stitchery
stockyard
stoneware
stonework
stonewort
stormbird
strapwork
strapwort
strawworm
striature
stricture
strongarm
structure
styliform
subaltern
subgenera
sublunary
sumptuary
surfboard
swearword
sweetcorn
swineherd
syllabary
tablature
tableware
tailboard
tarantara
telemetry
temporary
termitary
terramara
terramare
territory
tessitura
therefore
thumbmark
tightwire
toothwort
touchmark
tracheary
trademark
transform
transpire
transport
treachery
tributary
trinketry
triquetra
triumviri
troutfarm
trysquare
twiceborn
umberbird
unconcern
undergird
underpart
unsavoury
upcountry
vainglory
vermiform
versiform
vestiture
vexillary
vibraharp
vibratory
villagery
villiform
visionary
vitellary
vitriform
voluntary
vulnerary
wallboard
washboard
watchfire
watchword
watercart
watermark
waterworn
wheelwork
wherefore
widowbird
wineberry
worrywart
woundwort
Yorkshire
zamindary
zemindary
zygospore
absurdism
absurdist
academism
actualise
adeptness
adultness
Adventism
Adventist
advertise
aerialist
aftermost
albatross
alchemise
alchemist
alertness
aliveness
alloplasm
almshouse
aloneness
aloofness
aluminise
amoralism
amorphism
ampleness
anabolism
analogise
analogist
anarchism
anarchist
anatomise
anatomist
anchoress
anchylose
angelfish
anglicise
anglicism
Anglicist
angriness
animalise
animalism
animalist
animatism
anschluss
antitrust
apartness
apishness
apologise
apologist
Appaloosa
arabicise
arbitress
archivist
aromatise
askewness
atonalism
autarkist
authoress
authorise
autocross
awareness
awfulness
babirussa
baboonish
backcross
bacterise
bagginess
bakehouse
baksheesh
balkanise
balladist
balminess
barbarise
barbarism
bathhouse
battiness
bawdiness
beanfeast
beardless
beechmast
beefiness
bellglass
bellicose
bergamask
biblicism
biblicist
bicyclist
biologist
birdsnest
bitterish
blackfish
blacklist
blackness
blackwash
blameless
blandness
blankness
bleakness
blindness
bloodless
bloodlust
bluegrass
bluffness
bluntness
blushless
boathouse
bonniness
booklouse
boskiness
bossiness
boundless
braincase
brainless
brainwash
brakeless
brashness
bratwurst
breakfast
briefcase
briefless
briefness
brightish
briskness
Briticise
Briticism
broadcast
broadness
broadwise
brownness
brutalise
brutalism
buckshish
bulginess
bulkiness
bumpiness
bundobust
bunkhouse
burliness
bushiness
buxomness
cabbalism
cabbalist
caciquism
Caesarism
Caesarist
cageyness
calaboose
calabrese
Calvinism
Calvinist
camorrist
canetrash
canniness
Cantonese
capsulise
carbonise
carburise
careerism
careerist
carthorse
Castroism
cataclasm
cataclysm
catalepsy
cataplasm
catechise
catechism
catechist
Catharism
Catharist
cattiness
causeless
cauterise
cavendish
ceaseless
cellulose
Celticism
chainless
chanteuse
chantress
chariness
charmeuse
charmless
cheapness
checklist
cheerless
childless
chillness
chophouse
cicatrise
Cingalese
classless
classlist
cleanness
clearness
clockwise
closeness
cloudless
clubhouse
coalmouse
coastwise
Cobdenism
cocainise
cocainism
cockhorse
cockiness
coheiress
coiffeuse
colemouse
collagist
colourist
columnist
communise
communism
communist
concourse
cookhouse
cornbrash
cornemuse
cornetist
corymbose
countless
crampfish
crankcase
crassness
craziness
creatress
crestless
cretinism
crispness
criticise
criticism
crossfish
crossness
crosswise
crownless
crowsnest
crudeness
cruellest
curialism
curliness
curstness
customise
cymbalist
cytoplasm
daltonism
damnedest
Darwinism
Darwinist
dauntless
deaconess
deathless
deathmask
deckhouse
decompose
decongest
defeatism
defeatist
demitasse
denseness
deodorise
deoxidise
depthless
despotism
devilfish
dextrorse
diabolise
diabolism
diabolist
dialogise
dialogism
dialogist
dichroism
dicrotism
dieselise
dinginess
dirtiness
discourse
disforest
dishonest
disinfest
displease
dispraise
disrelish
dizziness
dogmatise
dogmatism
dogmatist
dogoodism
dosshouse
dottiness
doubtless
dowdiness
dowerless
dragoness
dragonish
dramatise
dramatist
drayhorse
dreamless
drollness
dryasdust
dumpiness
duskiness
dustiness
eagerness
earliness
ecdysiast
ecologist
economise
economist
ecossaise
ecstasise
ectoblast
ectoplasm
ecumenism
edelweiss
eightyish
electress
embarrass
embellish
empathise
emphasise
emptiness
encomiast
encompass
endoblast
endoplasm
entoblast
epicurism
epilogist
epipolism
epitomise
epitomist
equipoise
erectness
eremitism
eroticism
errorless
erythrism
esemplasy
esoterism
establish
Eucharist
eunuchism
euphemise
euphemism
euphonise
eventless
exactness
exegetist
exoticism
expertise
extremism
extremist
Fabianism
factorise
faddiness
faintness
faithless
Falangism
Falangist
falseness
fantasise
fantasist
farmhouse
fattiness
faultless
fenceless
Fenianism
fertilise
fetichism
fetichist
fetidness
fetishism
fetishist
feudalise
feudalism
feudalist
fibreless
fieriness
filminess
fireblast
firecrest
firehouse
fishiness
fixedness
flakiness
flameless
fleckless
fleetness
fleshless
flophouse
flushness
fogginess
footloose
forceless
foreclose
formalise
formalism
formalist
formulise
fossilise
foundress
fourflush
frailness

franchise
frankness
freehouse
freshness
frontless
frontwise
fruitless
fruticose
fulldress
funkiness
funniness
fusionist
fussiness
fustiness
fuzziness
galactose
gallicise
gallicism
galliwasp
galvanise
galvanism
galvanist
ganderism
gatecrash
gatehouse
gaudiness
gauntness
gauziness
gawkiness
genialise
geodesist
geologise
geologist
germanise
Germanish
Germanism
Germanist
germplasm
gibberish
giddiness
gigantism
Girondist
glamorise
globefish
glueyness
gneissose
godliness
goldcrest
gongorism
gorgonise
gothicise
Gothicism
governess
graceless
grandiose
grandness
granulose
graveless
graveness
greatness
Greekless
greenness
griefless
griminess
grossness
groundash
gruffness
Grundyism
guidepost
guileless
guiltless
guitarist
gumminess
gustiness
gutsiness
haggadist
hairbrush
hairgrass
hairiness
handglass
handiness
handpress
happiness
hardiness
harmonise
harmonist
harshness
hastiness
headdress
headfirst
headiness
heartless
heaviness
heftiness
hellenise
Hellenism
Hellenist
herbalist
herborise
hetaerism
hetairism
highclass
hirsutism
Hitlerism
hoarfrost
hoariness
holocaust
homoplasy
horniness
horseless
horsiness
hourglass
houseless
hoydenish
huffiness
humanness
huskiness
hybridise
hybridism
hydrolyse
hygienist
hylozoism
hypnotise
hypnotism
hypnotist
hypoblast
hypocaust
hypocrisy
idealless
idioplasm
imageless
imprecise
improvise
inaptness
Indianise
indispose
ineptness
inertness
innermost
interfuse
interpose
inverness
invertase
isinglass
isomerise
isomerism
issueless
italicise
Italicism
itchiness
itsybitsy
janitress
Jansenism
Jansenist
jargonise
jazziness
jellyfish
jerkiness
jesuitise
jesuitism
jointress
josshouse
juiceless
juiciness
jumpiness
junkerism
juxtapose
kaiserism
kaolinise
killifish
kinkiness
kittenish
knotgrass
labialise
labialism
lacrimose
lacrymose
laevulose
lamellose
landdross
landdrost
lankiness
larcenist
largeness
laundress
leakiness
leastwise
legginess
lendlease
levelness
libellist
lickerish
lightless
lightness
limitless
linearise
liquidise
liquorish
Listerism
litheness
liturgist
lividness
lobscouse
loftiness
Londonise
Londonism
longhouse
looseness
lousiness
lovefeast
loverless
lowercase
lowermost
lowliness
lucidness
luckiness
lumpiness
luridness
lustiness
lymegrass
machinist
macintosh
macrocosm
Magianism
magnetise
magnetism
magnetist
maidenish
malthouse
mammonish
mammonism
mammonist
manganese
manginess
manliness
mannerism
mannerist
marchpast
martyrise
masochism
masochist
massagist
massiness
matchless
mateyness
matronise
mealiness
meatiness
mechanise
mechanism
mechanist
medallist
mediatise
meliorism
meliorist
memoirist
Mendelism
menopause
mentalism
mentalist
mercerise
merciless
merriness
mesmerise
mesmerism
mesmerist
mesoblast
messiness
metallise
metaphase
metaplasm
meteorist
methodise
Methodism
Methodist
metricise
metricist
microcosm
micromesh
milkiness
mirkiness
mirthless
misadvise
misoneism
misoneist
mistiness
Mithraism
Mithraist
mixedness
mnemonist
modernise
modernism
modernist
moistness
monachism
Mondayish
monergism
mongolism
monitress
monkeyish
monkeyism
monoecism
Montanism
moodiness
Mormonism
mosaicism
mosaicist
motocross
mouthwash
muddiness
mugginess
murderess
murkiness
muskiness
mustiness
mutualise
mutualism
mutualist
muzziness
myologist
mysticism
mythicise
mythicism
mythicist
nailbrush
nakedness
narcotise
narcotism
nastiness
natheless
nattiness
neathouse
neckverse
necrotise
neediness
Negroness
neologise
neologism
neologist
neoterise
neoterism
neoterist
nephalism
nephalist
nerveless
nerviness
newsflash
newsiness
nickelise
Nipponese
nobleness
noiseless
noisiness
normalise
Normanise
Normanism
northeast
northmost
northwest
notedness
notionist
nuttiness
oasthouse
obeseness
occultism
occultist
Octobrist
odourless
Orangeism
orchidist
orderless
orologist
ostracise
ostracism
otherness
otherwise
otologist
outermost
overdress
overtness
oxygenise
packhorse
paederast
paillasse
pairhorse
palletise
palliasse
panderess
panellist
pantheism
pantheist
pantyhose
papillose
Parseeism
pastiness
patroness
patronise
pauperise
pauperism
Pekingese
pelletise
penniless
Pentecost
penthouse
peptonise
periclase
periplast
perkiness
pessimism
pessimist
pesthouse
petaurist
pettiness
phonetise
phonetism
phonetist
phoniness
physicist
picturise
pilotfish
pinkiness
pithiness
placeless
plainness
platinise
Platonise
Platonism
Platonist
playhouse
plumpness
plumulose
pluralise
pluralism
pluralist
plushness
Plutonism
Plutonist
podginess
podzolise
poeticise
poeticism
pointless
politesse
polonaise
polyphase
poorhouse
posthorse
posthouse
powerless
preconise
predigest
prelatess
prelatise
premonish
prestress
preterist
prettyish
prettyism
priceless
prideless
priestess
primeness
procuress
profilist
prologise
proneness
prosiness
prosodist
publicise
publicist
pudginess
puffiness
pulpiness
pulseless
pulverise
pursiness
pushiness
Quakeress
Quakerish
Quakerism
quakiness
quartzose
queenless
queenpost
queerness
quickness
quietness
quixotism
rabbinism
rabbinist
rabidness
racehorse
racialism
racialist
radiocast
raffinose
raininess
randiness
randomise
ranginess
rapidness
rascalism
razorfish
readdress
readiness
rearhorse
rearmouse
rebaptise
recognise
recompose
recordist
redbreast
reediness
reformism
reformist
refurbish
refurnish
reimburse
religiose
replenish
repossess
reprocess
republish
rerelease
reremouse
reservist
retrousse
rhythmise
rhythmist
Ribbonism
riderless
rightness
rigidness
riskiness
ritualise
ritualism
ritualist
roadhouse
rockiness
roominess
roughcast
roughness
roundness
routinism
routinist
rowdiness
rubberise
ruddiness
ruggedise
rustiness
sabbatise
sabbatism
sagebrush

sallowish
saltiness
saltmarsh
sandblast
sandglass
sandiness
sappiness
saturnism
sauceless
sauciness
scaldfish
scalefish
scaleless
scalemoss
scaliness
scantness
scarfwise
scenarist
scentless
schistose
scholiast
scientism
scientist
Scoticise
seaminess
seediness
selfabuse
selftrust
senseless
sensitise
serialise
serialism
serialist
sermonise
sexualise
shadeless
shadiness
shakerism
shakiness
shamanism
shamanist
shamefast
shameless
shapeless
sharpness
sheatfish
sheepwash
sheerness
shellfish
shiftless
shininess
Shintoism
Shintoist
shirtless
shoreless
shortness
shouldest
showiness
sidedness
sightless
signalise
siliquose
silkiness
silliness
simulcast
sinewless
Sinhalese
skirtless
slackness
slakeless
slantwise
sleekness
sleepless
slickness
slightish
sliminess
slopewise
smallness
smartness

smileless
smokebush
smokeless
smokiness
smoothish
snailfish
snakiness
snipefish
snowgoose
snowiness
soapiness
soberness
socialise
socialism
socialist
sogginess
solemnise
solidness
solipsism
solipsist
sonnetise
soothfast
sootiness
soppiness
sopranist
Sorbonist
sorceress
sorriness
Soudanese
soundless
soundness
soundpost
southeast
southmost
southwest
sovietise
sovietism
spaceless
spagyrist
spareness
sparkless
speakeasy
spearfish
speckless
spicebush
spiciness
spikiness
spineless
spininess
Spinozism
Spinozist
spinulose
spiritism
spiritist
spiritoso
spokewise
sporocyst
spoutless
squarrose
squatness
squeamish
stabilise
staginess
staidness
stainless
staircase
staleness
Stalinism
Stalinist
stalkless
stargrass
starkness
stateless
statocyst
steadfast
steepness
sterilise
sternmost
sternness

sternpost
stiffness
stillness
stingless
stintless
stockfish
stocklist
stonefish
stoneless
stoniness
stoppress
stormless
stoutness
strapless
strongish
studhorse
subsidise
subtilise
succotash
sulkiness
sultaness
summarise
summarist
sunniness
superfuse
superpose
supervise
surculose
surliness
sutteeism
swangoose
swarajist
swartness
sweetness
swellfish
swiftness
swordfish
syllabise
syllabism
syllogise
syllogism
symbolise
symbolism
symbolist
synergism
synergist
synoptist
syphilise
tacitness
tackiness
tailoress
taintless
tallowish
Talmudist
tantalise
tarantass
tarantism
tardiness
Targumist
Tartufism
tasteless
tastiness
tattiness
tattooist
tawniness
telophase
temporise
temptress
tenderise
tenebrist
tenseness
tepidness
terminism
terminist
terrorise
terrorism
terrorist
terseness
testiness

teutonise
Teutonism
Teutonist
thankless
theocrasy
therapist
theurgist
thickness
thingness
thornbush
thornless
thrombose
tightness
timelapse
timidness
timpanist
tinniness
tipsiness
tiredness
tollhouse
tomentose
toolhouse
toothless
topiarist
toughness
townhouse
traceless
trackless
traitress
transfuse
transpose
transvest
tribadism
tribalism
trickless
trigamist
triteness
tritheism
tritheist
truceless
trunkfish
trustless
truthless
tubbiness
tumidness
turquoise
tympanist
tyrannise
unaptness
undermost
underpass
undervest
unfitness
unharness
unselfish
unsuccess
uppercase
uppermost
usualness
utterless
uttermost
utterness
vagueness
validness
valueless
valveless
vampirism
vandalise
vandalism
vapidness
vapourish
Vedantist
verbalise
verbalism
verbalist
vernalise
verrucose
victimise
violinist

visionist
visitress
visualise
vividness
vocalness
voiceless
volcanism
voltinism
voodooism
voodooist
vorticism
vorticist
vorticose
vowelless
voyeurism
vulcanise
vulcanism
vulcanist
vulgarise
vulgarism
vulpinism
vulturish
wackiness
wallcress
warehouse
wartcress
washhouse
washiness
wasteness
watchcase
waterless
wayzgoose
weariless
weariness
wedgewise
weediness
weirdness
welfarism
wheelbase
wheelless
whitebass
whitefish
whiteness
whitewash
wholeness
widthwise
willowish
windchest
windiness
wineglass
winepress
winterise
witticism
wittiness
woodiness
woodlouse
wooziness
wordiness
workhorse
workhouse
worthless
woundless
wrathless
wrongness
Yankeeism
yellowish
youngness
zeitgeist
zoologist
zootomist
abnormity
abominate
absurdity
acclimate
acclivity
acetylate
aciculate
acidulate
actuality

acuminate
adenomata
adiposity
admiralty
adsorbate
adumbrate
adversity
aeriality
aerophyte
aestivate
affiliate
affricate
aftermath
aggravate
aggregate
alleviate
alpargata
altercate
alternate
aluminate
alveolate
ambiguity
amorality
amourette
anchorite
angiomata
anglesite
anhydrite
animality
animosity
anonymity
anorthite
antipasto
antiquate
antiquity
apiculate
appellate
approbate
aragonite
arbitrate
argentite
argillite
argumenta
arriviste
asininity
aspartate
assiduity
associate
astrocyte
asymptote
atacamite
atomicity
atonality
atonicity
attenuate
attribute
auspicate
austenite
austerity
authority
autoroute
babacoote
bacchante
backcloth
bandwidth
banquette
barbarity
batholite
batholith
bedlamite
belemnite
benignity
bentonite
bifoliate
bifurcate
bilabiate
billionth
bipartite
bipinnate

birthrate
bivariate
bloodbath
bombilate
bombinate
bookplate
brachiate
bracteate
brandreth
brecciate
briquette
brochette
brutality
bryophyte
bucktooth
calcarate
calculate
calibrate
caliphate
callosity
candidate
cannulate
capsulate
captivate
captivity
carbamate
carbonate
Carmelite
carnality
castanets
castigate
causality
celebrate
celebrity
cementite
cerebrate
cerecloth
certainty
cerussite
champerty
charlotte
checkmate
chipolata
chocolate
chondrite
cigarette
circinate
circulate
citystate
classmate
clathrate
coadunate
coagulate
coarctate
cobaltite
cochleate
coelomata
coelomate
coenobite
coffinite
colligate
collimate
collocate
colocynth
columbite
combinate
comminute
commodity
community
commutate
composite
concavity
congruity
conjugate
consulate
contralto
contrasty
convexity
convolute

cooperate
copesmate
coprolite
corallite
corporate
correlate
corrugate
corticate
coruscate
Corybants
couchette
courgette
credulity
crenulate
crepitate
criminate
croquette
crossette
crotchety
cucullate
culminate
cultivate
curiosity
cuspidate
cyclamate
cystolith
debutante
deciduate
declinate
declivity
decollate
decollete
decussate
defalcate
defoliate
deformity
dehydrate
delineate
demarcate
denigrate
denitrate
depravity
deprecate
depredate
desecrate
desiccate
designate
desperate
destitute
deuterate
devaluate
devastate
dexterity
diaconate
diatomite
dimidiate
diplomate
dishcloth
dislocate
disparate
disparity
disrepute
dissipate
dissolute
diversity
doctorate
dogstooth
doorplate
drawplate
dubiosity
ductility
duplicate
duplicity
ectophyte
edibility
eightieth
ejaculate
elaborate
eliminate
elucidate
elutriate
embrocate
emolliate
emotivity
encrinite
endophyte
entophyte
entrecote
entremets
enucleate
enumerate
enunciate
epaulette
epidosite
eradicate
erythrite
Esperanto
ethnicity
etiquette
eucalypti
eucaryote
evaginate
evaporate
eventuate
exanimate
exarchate
excoriate
exculpate
exfoliate
exonerate
exopodite
expatiate
explicate
expurgate
exquisite
exsiccate
extensity
extenuate
extirpate
extradite
extremity
extricate
exuberate
fabricate
facecloth
facundity
fascinate
faveolate
favourite
febricity
fecundate
fecundity
femineity
fertility
festinate
festivity
feudality
fibromata
fifteenth
figurante
fimbriate
firstrate
fishplate
fissility
flarepath
floodgate
floridity
fluctuate
footcloth
footplate
foretaste
formality
formicate
formulate
fornicate
forthwith
fortunate
fragility
frigidity
frivolity
frostbite
fructuate
frugality
frustrate
fulgurate
fulgurite
fulminate
fustigate
garrulity
gelignite
geniality
gentility
georgette
germinate
geyserite
gibbosity
gigahertz
globosity
glomerate
glutamate
goalmouth
goldsmith
Gothamite
gracility
granulate
granulite
gratulate
gravidity
gravitate
habituate
haematite
haircloth
halfcaste
halftruth
Hallstatt
halophyte
Hashemite
Hashimite
headcloth
heavyduty
hessonite
hibernate
hiddenite
Himyarite
hircosity
hispidity
Hitlerite
holophote
homeopath
hostility
housebote
housemate
humiliate
hundredth
hybridity
hydrolyte
hyphenate
hypocrite
hyponasty
imbricate
immediate
immensity
immigrate
immodesty
impetrate
implicate
imprecate
improbity
impromptu
inability
inamorata
inanimate
incarnate
incognito
incondite
inculcate
inculpate
incurvate
indemnity
indignity
inebriate
inebriety
infatuate
infirmity
infuriate
infuscate
ingenuity
innervate
innocuity
inoculate
insatiate
insatiety
insensate
insinuate
instigate
institute
integrate
integrity
intensity
intercity
intestate
intricate
inutility
inviolate
ironsmith
irradiate
irreality
isogamete
Israelite
itinerate
ittybitty
jocundity
joviality
juniorate
juniority
kaolinite
kilohertz
labourite
labyrinth
laccolith
laciniate
lamellate
lancinate
langouste
larghetto
lazaretto
legislate
lethality
leucocyte
leukocyte
liability
lilywhite
limpidity
lineality
linearity
lineolate
lingulate
lintwhite
liquidate
liquidity
lixiviate
locksmith
loincloth
longcoats
longevity
loquacity
lorgnette
loudmouth
lubricate
lubricity
lucubrate
luxuriate
machinate
macrocyte
magnesite
magnetite
majorette
malachite
malignity
mamillate
mammonite
manducate
manganate
manganite
manifesto
manzanita
marcasite
margarite
marginate
masticate
maternity
mayoralty
medullate
megadeath
megahertz
meliorate
meliority
melismata
mendacity
mendicity
Mennonite
mentality
mesophyte
meteorite
methylate
metricate
micaslate
microcyte
microlite
microlith
micturate
midinette
milktooth
millerite
millionth
miscreate
modernity
molybdate
monzonite
morbidity
mordacity
mortality
mossagate
mucronate
muniments
muscovite
mutuality
myelomata
nameplate
natrolite
necessity
neckcloth
negotiate
nephelite
neuromata
neuropath
niccolite
nictitate
ninetieth
nonentity
normality
noseflute
notoriety
novelette
noviciate
novitiate
nummulite
nuncupate
obbligato
obcordate
obfuscate
objurgate
obliquity
obscenity
obscurity
obsecrate
obstinate
officiate
oilpaints
olivenite
operosity
orientate
originate
oscillate
osteopath
Ostrogoth
oubliette
outgrowth
outskirts
overstate
overwrite
overwrote
oviparity
oxygenate
ozocerite
ozokerite
paillette
palafitte
pallidity
palmitate
palpitate
pantalets
papillate
papillote
parachute
Paraclete
paramatta
passivate
passivity
pastorate
patellate
paternity
pectinate
pederasty
pegmatite
pendulate
penetrate
percolate
perennate
perforate
periodate
permutate
persecute
personate
petiolate
phagocyte
phenacite
phenakite
phonolite
phosphate
phosphite
piecerate
pierrette
pinnulate
pirouette
pizzicati
pizzicato
placidity
plumulate
plurality
pointduty
pollinate
pomposity
posterity
posthaste
postulate
potentate
poussette
precocity
predacity
predicate
preterite
primality
procerity
procreate
profanity
prolixity
propagate
propriety
prorogate
prosecute
proselyte
prostrate
proximate
proximity
publicity
puerility
pugnacity
pullulate
pulmonate
pulserate
pulvinate
punctuate
pustulate
putridity
pyracanth
quartette
quartzite
quintette
rabbinate
raffinate
rancidity
rascality
reanimate
reclinate
recondite
rectorate
redingote
reeducate
rehydrate
reinstate
reiterate
reluctate
remediate
replicate
reprobate
repudiate
requisite
restitute
retaliate
rhodolite
rhodonite
roodcloth
roofplate
rotundity
rubellite
rubricate
runcinate
rusticate
rusticity
sacculate
sackcloth
sagittate
sailcloth
salubrity
sanbenito
sarcomata
satellite
satinette
scapolite
scheelite
scolecite
scotomata
sectility
segregate
senhorita
seniority
sensedata
sentenate
sepiolite
septicity
sequacity
seriality

serinette
serjeanty
serrulate
serviette
servility
severalty
sexuality
sgraffiti
sgraffito
sheepcote
shogunate
sigillate
sincerity
sinuosity
sixteenth
slivovitz
snakebite
snowbroth
snowwhite
socialite
sociality
sociopath
solemnity
soleplate
solmisate
songsmith
sostenuto
soubrette
soupplate
spaghetti
spatulate
specialty
speculate
spiculate
spinosity
spirality
sporulate
stability
Stagirite
stagparty
stalemate
stalworth
staminate
stampduty
stampnote
statolith
statuette
sterility
stimulate
stipitate
stipulate
stolidity
stolonate
stupidity
stylobate
suability
subjugate
sublimate
sublimity
subrogate
substrata
substrate
succinate
suffocate
sultanate
suppurate
surrogate
sylvanite
syncopate
syndicate
synoecete
tachylite
tachylyte
tactility
tantalate
tantalite
telephoto
tellurate
tellurite
temperate
tensility
tenthrate
terebinth
terminate
tetradite
thereinto
thereunto
therewith
thirdrate
thirtieth
thitherto
tigermoth
titillate
tittivate
tollbooth
torpidity
torridity
tracheate
translate
transmute
traycloth
tremolite
tribunate
tridymite
trilobate
trilobite
triturate
tungstate
turbidity
turbinate
turgidity
twentieth
typewrite
uintahite
umbellate
umpteenth
unanimity
underrate
unreality
unthrifty
uraninite
urceolate
usherette
uvarovite
vaccinate
vacillate
vacuolate
variegate
variolate
variolite
veniality
ventilate
verbosity
verminate
viability
vicariate
vigilante
villosity
vindicate
virginity
virgulate
viscerate
viscidity
viscosity
viscounty
vitiosity
vivianite
vizierate
vorticity
vulcanite
vulgarity
vulpinite
Wagnerite
wagonette
wallplate
washcloth
waterbath
waterbutt
watergate
wavellite
whereinto
whereunto
wherewith
willemite
wirephoto
witchetty
witherite
wordsmith
wulfenite
wyandotte
Wyclifite
xerophyte
zinkenite
zucchetto
acidulous
ailanthus
aluminium
aluminous
ambiguous
ambitious
americium
amianthus
amorphous
amphioxus
analogous
anandrous
anhydrous
anomalous
anonymous
antiserum
apetalous
aphyllous
apogamous
apparatus
arabesque
arboreous
arboretum
Areopagus
argentous
arsenious
asbestous
asepalous
asparagus
asphaltum
assiduous
astronaut
Athenaeum
atrocious
audacious
avizandum
bacterium
barathrum
barbarous
barrelful
basketful
bathybius
beauteous
beautiful
behaviour
berkelium
beryllium
bifarious
biogenous
bonhomous
bottleful
bounteous
bountiful
brazilnut
bucketful
bulltrout
bumptious
burdenous
burlesque
burnedout
bushelful
butterbur
buttercup
butternut
calcaneum
calculous
caldarium
cancerous
candlenut
cankerous
cantaloup
cantharus
capacious
capitulum
carrefour
catalogue
caterwaul
cavernous
ceanothus
cephalous
cerastium
ceratodus
cetaceous
chanceful
chancrous
changeful
chauffeur
chibouque
chihuahua
chitinous
cinereous
clamorous
clitellum
cobaltous
coccidium
coenobium
coffeecup
colchicum
colleague
collegium
collyrium
colosseum
colostrum
colourful
columbium
complexus
congruous
conscious
consensus
contagium
continuum
conundrum
cornflour
cosmonaut
cothurnus
courteous
crapulous
credulous
cretinous
criminous
cutaneous
cymbidium
dangerous
Dantesque
decalogue
deceitful
decennium
deciduous
declivous
deinosaur
delicious
delirious
demagogue
demeanour
dentalium
deuterium
dexterous
diachylum
diandrous
dichasium
diclinous
dioecious
dipterous
discolour
disfavour
dishclout
dishonour
doodlebug
drawerful
echovirus
effluvium
effortful
egregious
endeavour
endosteum
epigynous
eponymous
equisetum
equivoque
erogenous
erroneous
Esquimaux
euphonium
exequatur
exogamous
exogenous
exsuccous
fabaceous
facetious
fastigium
felonious
ferocious
fibrinous
filaceous
fistulous
flabellum
flagellum
flambeaus
flambeaux
flavorous
flocculus
forgetful
fractious
fraenulum
frightful
frivolous
fructuous
fugacious
fulgurous
fulminous
funiculus
garrulous
gastraeum
germanium
ginglymus
gladiolus
glaireous
glamorous
glutinous
greasegun
grotesque
groundnut
gymnasium
gynaeceum
gynoecium
harmonium
harquebus
hazardous
healthful
hearthrug
herbarium
hereabout
hilarious
homologue
hydronium
hypericum
hypogeous
ideologue
ignoramus
imperious
impetuous
impluvium
incurious
indecorum
ingenious
ingenuous
injurious
innocuous
innoxious
inodorous
insidious
invidious
isogamous
isogenous
isomerous
isopodous
jitterbug
judicious
Junoesque
laborious
lanthanum
lapideous
larcenous
lecherous
libellous
lichenous
lightsout
literatus
litigious
litterbug
longevous
lovingcup
lubricous
ludicrous
lumbricus
luxurious
magnalium
magnesium
malarious
malicious
malleolus
manganous
manubrium
marsupium
masterful
mausoleum
meandrous
melodious
menstruum
mercurous
micaceous
minacious
minutegun
momentous
monkeynut
monocoque
monologue
monstrous
moraceous
mundungus
murderous
murmurous
narcissus
nectarous
needleful
nefarious
neighbour
neodymium
neptunium
nickelous
nightclub
notorious
nucleolus
nystagmus
oblivious
obnoxious
odalisque
offcolour
officious
oilcolour
oleaceous
operculum
opusculum
overcloud
overissue
overvalue
oviferous
oviparous
oxygenous
palladium
palladous
pedagogue
pemphigus
pendulous
penurious
peripatus
petroleum
platinous
playgroup
plenteous
plentiful
plumbeous
plutonium
pocketful
podagrous
poisonous
pollinium
polygonum
pomaceous
pompadour
ponderous
posticous
potassium
praiseful
prayerful
prayerrug
presidium
pressstud
proconsul
prolapsus
pterosaur
pterygium
pulverous
pulvillus
pumiceous
pustulous
pycnidium
pyrethrum
quercetum
querulous
raconteur
raincloud
rancorous
rapacious
rapturous
redivivus
regardful
regisseur
regretful
religious
remindful
reposeful
resentful
resultful
retiarius
reticulum
righteous
rivalrous
rosaceous
rostellum
ruthenium
sacrarium
sagacious
salacious
saleratus
salicetum
sandspout
sartorius
saucerful

schistous
scirrhous
scutellum
sebaceous
seditious
selenious
sensorium
sericeous
setaceous
shamateur
shieldbug
shovelful
sideissue
siliceous
silicious
sinologue
slateclub
sleevenut
slumbrous
snaredrum
solacious
soliloquy
sorcerous
sorrowful
souteneur
sparkplug
speechful
sphagnous
spinulous
spirillum
spiritous
spleenful
splendour
spongeous
stegosaur
stirabout
strenuous
stressful
strobilus
strontium
stuporous
subereous
subphylum
sugarplum
summingup
sumptuous
sympodium
symposium
synagogue
syncytium
syngamous
taraxacum
teacupful
technique
tegmentum
tellurium
tellurous
tenacious
tenaculum
tendinous
tenebrous
terrarium
theologue
thesaurus
tomentous
torturous
trapezium
tremulous
trialogue
tricolour
triennium
trifolium
triforium
trigamous
trimerous
triptyque
trochilus
troublous
trumpedup

tufaceous
tumblebug
turnabout
tyrannous
uliginous
ultimatum
umbilicus
unanimous
undutiful
unhelpful
unicolour
uniparous
unisonous
unmindful
unskilful
untimeous
uropygium
vademecum
vagarious
variolous
venereous
venturous
veracious
verminous
verrucous
vestigium
vexatious
vicarious
vimineous
vinaceous
vivacious
voracious
vulturous
walkabout
washedout
wonderful
yachtclub
ytterbium
zirconium
zoogenous
acceptive
accretive
addictive
adductive
admissive
advective
adventive
affective
agitative
aperitive
ascensive
assertive
assuasive
attentive
autoclave
balaclava
biconcave
bondslave
brainwave
calmative
causative
champleve
cognitive
collusive
combative
conducive
corrosive
crashdive
deadalive
deceptive
decretive
deductive
defective
defensive
depictive
depletive
detective
detersive
diffusive

digestive
directive
educative
effective
emanative
embracive
emulative
evocative
evolutive
exceptive
excessive
exclusive
excretive
excursive
executive
expansive
expensive
expletive
explosive
expulsive
extensive
extorsive
extortive
extrusive
exudative
factitive
folkweave
formative
fortyfive
fricative
gerundive
groundivy
gustative
hortative
imitative
impassive
implosive
impulsive
incentive
inceptive
inclusive
incursive
inductive
infective
ingestive
intensive
interwove
intrusive
intuitive
invective
inventive
inversive
irruptive
isolative
iterative
landgrave
laudative
lucrative
mediative
microwave
misbehave
narrative
normative
nutritive
objective
obsessive
obtrusive
occlusive
offensive
olfactive
operative
ostensive
overdrive
palsgrave
partitive
perfusive
pervasive
plaintive
portative

portreeve
powerdive
precative
predative
prelusive
primitive
privative
probative
prolative
promotive
purgative
purposive
radiative
receptive
recessive
reclusive
recursive
reductive
reflexive
repulsive
resistive
retentive
revulsive
seclusive
secretive
seductive
selective
selfdrive
semibreve
sensitive
shortwave
siccative
sickleave
soundwave
stockdove
summative
supernova
talkative
tentative
testdrive
undeceive
unreserve
Vaishnava
vibrative
violative
waldgrave
breakdown
bringdown
Chinatown
closedown
countdown
crackdown
eiderdown
finedrawn
foreknown
foreshown
frogspawn
fullblown
fullgrown
halfcrown
handsdown
highflown
highgrown
homegrown
knockdown
mollymawk
mossgrown
nightgown
nighthawk
overblown
overcrowd
overdrawn
overflown
overgrown
pastedown
punchbowl
roughhewn
shakedown
Southdown

swansdown
touchdown
unbeknown
waterfowl
wellknown
windblown
wiredrawn
withdrawn
battleaxe
cataplexy
orthodoxy
broadways
cherimoya
corduroys
crossways
cryptonym
frontways
goldeneye
hendiadys
heteronym
hypocotyl
jambalaya
Kshatriya
leastways
polyvinyl
pseudonym
slantways
syndactyl
tigerseye
tridactyl
widthways
Ashkenazi
influenza
overglaze
overgraze
saltglaze
schmaltzy
wiregauze

---

acetabula
acetylcoA
acroteria
actinozoa
adenomata
aesthesia
algarroba
alpargata
amblyopia
ambulacra
analgesia
androecia
angiomata
anoxaemia
apocrypha
apothecia
Appaloosa
aquilegia
araucaria
argumenta
artemisia
asafetida
aubrietia
auditoria
babirussa
balaclava
balalaika
ballerina
barracuda
bilharzia
bonechina
brachyura
Bretwalda
Britannia
cafeteria
calandria
calendula
camarilla
campanula
cantilena

carambola
carcinoma
Cassandra
casuarina
catatonia
cerebella
chachacha
chelicera
cherimoya
chihuahua
chipolata
chlorella
cineraria
clepsydra
coelomata
colloquia
columella
compendia
condyloma
consortia
contadina
corbicula
cosmorama
crustacea
curricula
cyclorama
dharmsala
diarrhoea
didrachma
dulcamara
dyscrasia
dyspepsia
dysphagia
dysphonia
dysphoria
dysplasia
echolalia
eclampsia
emphysema
empyreuma
encephala
enchilada
epithelia
esoterica
euphorbia
exanthema
feiseanna
fibromata
fioritura
forsythia
generalia
grandpapa
gravamina
guerrilla
haematoma
harmonica
haustella
haustoria
hieratica
honoraria
hortensia
hydraemia
hydrangea
hyperbola
hyperopia
hypomania
inamorata
influenza
infusoria
ischaemia
jacaranda
jambalaya
juvenilia
Kshatriya
laminaria
leucaemia
leukaemia
manzanita
marihuana

marijuana
matricula
melismata
melodrama
melomania
memoranda
mesogloea
micropsia
millennia
monodrama
monomania
moratoria
multipara
myelomata
myriorama
myxoedema
naumachia
nemophila
neoteinia
neuralgia
neuroglia
neuromata
nicotiana
noctiluca
nostalgia
notabilia
nullipara
octahedra
oligaemia
ommatidia
omophagia
orchestra
palaestra
panatella
papilloma
paralalia
paralexia
paramatta
parapodia
paulownia
peninsula
penultima
perihelia
phagedena
phantasma
phenomena
Philomela
photopsia
plasmodia
pneumonia
poinciana
polyhedra
porphyria
portulaca
pozzolana
primipara
primordia
principia
propylaea
proscenia
protonema
psalteria
puzzolana
pyromania
rafflesia
rauwolfia
referenda
rudbeckia
sabadilla
sanatoria
sanitaria
santolina
santonica
sapodilla
sapraemia
sarcomata
sauropoda
scagliola
scintilla

scotomata
senhorita
sensedata
septennia
sequestra
sestertia
Shangrila
signorina
simulacra
solfatara
spiracula
spirogyra
sporangia
subgenera
subsellia
substrata
sudatoria
supernova
tarantara
tarantula
tarragona
terramara
tessitura
theomania
Theravada
trabecula
transenna
trattoria
triclinia
triquetra
urticaria
Vaishnava
vallecula
varicella
vibracula
vomitoria
waterflea
zoophobia
cockscomb
currycomb
depthbomb
disentomb
dithyramb
flashbulb
honeycomb
nightclub
slateclub
smokebomb
spiderweb
stinkbomb
toothcomb
yachtclub
acrobatic
adiabatic
aerobatic
aerolitic
aesthetic
agonistic
agrologic
agronomic
ahistoric
albinotic
alcoholic
aldehydic
aleatoric
Alemannic
algebraic
alicyclic
aliphatic
allegoric
amaurotic
amblyopic
Amerindic
anabiotic
anaerobic
analeptic
analgesic
anaphoric
andesitic

anecdotic
animistic
ankylotic
anorectic
antarctic
anthracic
anthropic
antigenic
antimonic
antinomic
antitoxic
apathetic
aperiodic
aplanatic
apodictic
apomictic
apostolic
arthritic
asphaltic
asthmatic
asyndetic
ataractic
atavistic
atheistic
athematic
atomistic
autarchic
authentic
autolytic
automatic
autonomic
autotelic
axiomatic
ballistic
bigeneric
biometric
bishopric
bombastic
Brahmanic
Brahminic
bregmatic
bricabrac
Britannic
Brythonic
cachectic
cacodylic
cadaveric
Caenozoic
Cainozoic
calendric
calorific
camphoric
casuistic
catabolic
catalytic
catatonic
cathartic
cathectic
catoptric
charabanc
chemurgic
chimaeric
chivalric
chloritic
chlorotic
choleraic
choplogic
chromatic
cinematic
climactic
coenosarc
colorific
copacetic
coseismic
cryogenic
culsdesac
cylindric
cytotoxic
demagogic

demiurgic
dendritic
diacritic
diactinic
dialectic
diametric
diastatic
diastolic
diathetic
diatropic
dichromic
didelphic
digastric
dimorphic
Dionysiac
dizygotic
doleritic
dolomitic
dualistic
dyspeptic
dysphagic
dysphoric
dyspnoeic
eccentric
eclamptic
ectogenic
egomaniac
egotistic
embryonic
embryotic
emplastic
encaustic
endogamic
endogenic
energetic
enigmatic
enzymatic
epaenetic
epicyclic
epidermic
epileptic
epinastic
epiphytic
epistemic
epistolic
epithetic
epizootic
ergonomic
ethylenic
eutrophic
evangelic
excentric
exosmotic
extrinsic
fantastic
Fascistic
faunistic
felicific
fideistic
floristic
folkmusic
formulaic
fumarolic
genotypic
geomantic
geometric
geostatic
geotropic
geriatric
gnathonic
goliardic
graphemic
graphitic
gymnastic
halieutic
Hanseatic
hegemonic
heliozoic
heuristic

Holarctic
homiletic
homogamic
homonymic
homotonic
honorific
horologic
hubristic
hydraulic
hydriodic
hyperopic
hypomanic
Icelandic
ideologic
idiomatic
imbecilic
impolitic
inelastic
inorganic
insomniac
intrinsic
ischaemic
ischiadic
ischiatic
Islamitic
isobathic
isoclinic
isocyclic
isometric
isostatic
isotropic
Jacobinic
Judaistic
judgmatic
katabatic
katabolic
kinematic
lethargic
leukaemic
leviratic
limonitic
logaoedic
Lombardic
lymphatic
lyophilic
lyophobic
macaronic
Masoretic
melanotic
messianic
metabolic
metameric
metonymic
miasmatic
monarchic
monatomic
monobasic
monogamic
monologic
monomeric
monotonic
monotypic
morphemic
mutagenic
mycologic
mydriatic
napthalic
neolithic
neoteinic
nephritic
neuralgic
nicotinic
nostalgic
nucleonic
nystagmic
obstetric
oecologic
oecumenic
omophagic

onanistic
oncogenic
oncologic
onomastic
ontogenic
ontologic
oogenetic
opodeldoc
orchestic
orgiastic
orthoepic
pancratic
panegyric
panoramic
parabolic
paralytic
paramedic
paranoiac
parasitic
paregoric
patriotic
patristic
pearlitic
pedagogic
peridotic
pharaonic
pharisaic
philippic
phrenetic
pianistic
pietistic
pilgarlic
pisolitic
plasmatic
plethoric
pleuritic
pneumatic
pneumonic
polybasic
polygamic
polygenic
polymeric
polysemic
polysomic
polytypic
pragmatic
preadamic
preexilic
prismatic
proclitic
prodromic
proleptic
prophetic
propionic
prostatic
proteinic
prothetic
protozoic
psalmodic
psoriatic
psychotic
Ptolemaic
puritanic
pyramidic
pyrogenic
pyrolytic
quadratic
realistic
rhapsodic
rheumatic
salicylic
Samoyedic
sapraemic
Saracenic
sarcastic
schematic
sclerotic
scoliotic
scorbutic

selenitic
semeiotic
semitonic
Sephardic
shambolic
sideritic
silicotic
Solomonic
sophistic
soporific
spasmodic
spermatic
splenetic
stalactic
statistic
steatitic
stigmatic
stomachic
strategic
stromatic
strychnic
stylistic
subarctic
subatomic
sudorific
sulphonic
sulphuric
sybaritic
sylleptic
symbiotic
symmetric
symphonic
symposiac
syncretic
synonymic
syntactic
synthetic
systaltic
tacamahac
taxonomic
telegenic
thalassic
theandric
theogonic
theologic
theoretic
Thomistic
threnodic
toponymic
touristic
trachytic
transonic
traumatic
triatomic
trichomic
trichroic
triclinic
trimetric
vaporific
virtuosic
vitriolic
wolframic
zeugmatic
zoophytic
zygomatic
zymogenic
abandoned
acquitted
adulthood
affianced
aforesaid
afterword
aggrieved
aircooled
airminded
aminoacid
ampersand
analysand
anguished

annulated
apartheid
apprehend
appressed
arachnoid
archfiend
Arguseyed
arrowhead
arrowwood
arthropod
arytenoid
asclepiad
augmented
backboard
backsword
bacteroid
balconied
baldfaced
bandstand
barefaced
barnacled
barrelled
bastioned
bayoneted
beachhead
bedspread
bellyband
beneficed
benighted
bestirred
betrothed
bigheaded
billboard
blackbird
blackhead
blacklead
bleareyed
blindfold
blinkered
blockhead
bloodshed
bluebeard
bobtailed
bodyguard
boldfaced
bookstand
bottlefed
boulevard
bowerbird
bowlegged
boyfriend
brevetted
briarwood
brickyard
brierwood
bromeliad
brushwood
buckboard
buckhound
cablelaid
cancelled
cantharid
cardboard
catchword
cedarwood
celluloid
certified
chaetopod
chancroid
chapleted
chartered
checkered
chequered
chickweed
childhood
chipboard
chiselled
chrysalid
clapboard

clearEyed
clipboard
cloudland
coalfield
coastward
cobwebbed
collected
committed
communard
compelled
conceited
concerned
concerted
concurred
condyloid
confabbed
conferred
confirmed
connected
contented
contrived
convolved
copsewood
coralloid
corbelled
cornfield
cornsalad
coroneted
corralled
corticoid
courtcard
courtyard
crashland
crenelled
cropeared
crossbred
crosseyed
crosshead
crossroad
crosswind
crossword
cudgelled
curvetted
cutinised
cyprinoid
dachshund
dairymaid
dartboard
dashboard
debauched
deerhound
depressed
dermatoid
descended
dewlapped
dickybird
digitated
dignified
dimwitted
disaccord
disbarred
disbudded
discalced
dishfaced
dispelled
disregard
distilled
disturbed
dixieland
doglegged
dopefiend
downfield
draghound
dreamland
driftweed
driftwood
drivelled
duckboard
dumbfound
earthward
earwigged
eastbound
eightfold
ellipsoid
elongated
emaciated
embattled
enamelled
enamoured
engarland
englutted
entrapped
enwrapped
ephemerid
eunuchoid
eutectoid
ewenecked
fairfaced
fairyhood
fairyland
falsehood
fantasied
farmstead
fasciated
fascicled
fatheaded
fatwitted
feathered
fibrinoid
filigreed
filterbed
firebrand
fireguard
firsthand
floriated
flowerbed
fluecured
footboard
footpound
forcefeed
forceland
forenamed
formatted
foulbrood
freeboard
friarbird
frivolled
frolicked
frontward
fulfilled
funnelled
galleried
gallooned
gambolled
gangboard
garmented
gastropod
gavelkind
gazehound
geometrid
ghostword
giltedged
glandered
gneissoid
goddamned
goldenrod
goldfield
gooseherd
Gradgrind
granitoid
grassland
gravelled
graveyard
greeneyed
greensand
greenweed
greenwood
greybeard
greyhound
grovelled
hackneyed
haematoid
halfbaked
halfblood
halfbound
halfbreed
hallstand
hamadryad
hamfisted
hamhanded
handstand
hanselled
haphazard
hardboard
hardihood
hardnosed
headboard
heartland
heartwood
hellhound
herniated
herpetoid
hexachord
hexaploid
hidebound
highspeed
hightoned
hoarhound
hobnailed
hobnobbed
Hollywood
homebound
homestead
horehound
horsepond
hotheaded
household
houselled
housemaid
humankind
humbugged
hysteroid
ichthyoid
illjudged
illomened
impastoed
ingrained
inspanned
instilled
integrand
interbred
interlard
interwind
involuted
ironbound
ironmould
isoniazid
jampacked
jaundiced
jewelweed
kennelled
kidnapped
kingdomed
kingsized
laminated
lancewood
Langobard
laurelled
leafmould
leasehold
leaselend
liberated
liegelord
lifeblood
lifeguard
lifesized
lightwood
linenfold
lintelled
lobulated
longeared
longfaced
longlived
Longobard
lotusland
lovechild
lowminded
lownecked
lustihood
lyamhound
lymehound
malformed
mansarded
manysided
maquisard
marcelled
marshland
marvelled
masonried
matchwood
metalloid
meteoroid
millboard
minefield
misguided
misleared
mistyeyed
Mongoloid
monkshood
monochord
moonblind
mosaicked
mullioned
mummified
myrmecoid
netveined
netwinged
newshound
newsstand
nickelled
nightbird
nodulated
northland
northward
nosebleed
notochord
nucleated
nursemaid
nymphalid
obligated
ocellated
octachord
offhanded
onehanded
onelegged
openended
opinioned
outgunned
outputted
outspread
outwitted
overboard
overcloud
overcrowd
overheard
overjoyed
oversexed
oversized
overspend
overwound
oysterbed
panoplied
parapeted
parcelled
patinated
patrolled
pedigreed
pencilled
penfriend
perfervid
permitted
phyllopod
physicked
picnicked
pigheaded
pintailed
pintsized
pistolled
pithecoid
pixilated
placecard
planetoid
planuloid
plastered
platinoid
polyploid
pommelled
poppyhead
possessed
practised
preferred
prerecord
pressstud
processed
professed
proofread
propelled
pseudopod
pterygoid
pulpboard
pummelled
punchcard
puppyhood
pureblood
quadrifid
quadruped
qualified
queenhood
quicksand
raincloud
rearguard
recommend
redhanded
redheaded
redoubted
refuelled
regretted
reprehend
reprimand
riflebird
righthand
rightward
riverhead
riverweed
roadstead
rockbound
rosinweed
roughshod
roundhead
safeguard
sainthood
salmonoid
sandalled
sandblind
sangfroid
sapanwood
sapheaded
satinbird
satinwood
scarehead
sciaenoid
scombroid
scorecard
scorpioid
scrapyard
seastrand
selffaced
selfmoved
semifluid
semirigid
semisolid
sequinned
serranoid
sevenfold
sexlinked
sharpeyed
sharpshod
sheepfold
sheetbend
shewbread
shinguard
shipboard
shockhead
shoreward
shoreweed
shorthand
shovelled
sideboard
signalled
signboard
silkgland
slabsided
slinkweed
slushfund
smartweed
snakebird
snakeweed
snakewood
snivelled
snowblind
snowbound
snowfield
snowguard
snubnosed
sodabread
southland
southward
spaceband
spearhead
spellbind
spermatid
sphygmoid
spikenard
spiralled
spoonfeed
springald
stackyard
stagehand
staghound
stairhead
stalkeyed
stallfeed
starboard
statehood
steelclad
steelhead
steelyard
stellated
stepchild
sternward
stinkweed
stinkwood
stockyard
stokehold
stonecold
stonedead
storiated
stormbird
submitted
sunburned
suntanned
surfboard
surpliced
swearword
sweatband
swineherd
swivelled
syllabled
syphiloid
tableland
tailboard
tasselled
tentacled
thicketed
thickhead
thirdhand
thoughted
threefold
threshold
tigerwood
tinselled
titledeed
tittupped
tortricid
touchwood
trabeated
traceried
trainband
trainload
transcend
trapezoid
travelled
trepanned
trihybrid
trousered
trowelled
truncated
trunkroad
trustdeed
tulipwood
tunicated
tunnelled
turnround
twicelaid
twicetold
twofisted
twohanded
umberbird
unabashed
unadopted
unadorned
unadvised
unalloyed
unaltered
unashamed
unbiassed
unblessed
unblinded
unbounded
unbraided
unbridled
uncharted
unchecked
uncinated
unclothed
unclouded
uncounted
uncovered
uncreated
uncropped
uncrossed
uncrowned
undamaged
undaunted
undecided
undefined
underbred
undergird
undergrad
underhand
underlaid
underpaid
undersold

underwood
undivided
undoubted
undreamed
undulated
unfeigned
unfledged
unfleshed
unfounded
unguarded
unhurried
unicuspid
unknitted
unlearned
unlimited
unmatched
unpeopled
unplugged
unplumbed
unpointed
unruffled
unscathed
unsettled
unsighted
unskilled
unspotted
unstopped
unstudied
unsullied
untouched
untrussed
untutored
unwearied
unwrapped
Upanishad
varioloid
verandaed
volkslied
waistband
wallboard
washboard
washstand
wasteland
watchword
watershed
waterweed
weakkneed
weathered
webfooted
weevilled
wellfound
welltimed
westbound
whalehead
wheyfaced
whipround
whirlwind
whiskered
whitehead
whitewood
widowbird
widowhood
windbound
withstand
withstood
wolfhound
womanhood
womankind
womenkind
wristband
yearround
zebrawood
zigzagged
abandonee
abdicable
aberrance
abominate
aborigine
aboutface
abradable
abscissae
abundance
acceptive
accidence
acclimate
accretive
accusable
acescence
acetamide
acetylate
acetylene
aciculate
acidulate
aconitine
acquiesce
actualise
acuminate
adaptable
addictive
addressee
adducible
adductive
adenosine
adherence
adipocere
admeasure
adminicle
admirable
admissive
admixture
adoptable
adsorbate
adumbrate
advantage
advective
adventive
adventure
advertise
advisable
aerodrome
aerophyte
aeroplane
aerospace
aestivate
affective
affiliate
affixture
affluence
affricate
aftercare
afterlife
aftertime
agapemone
aggravate
aggregate
agitative
agreeable
aitchbone
alchemise
alienable
allemande
alleviate
allocable
allophone
allotrope
allowable
allowance
almandine
almshouse
alongside
alterable
altercate
alternate
aluminate
aluminise
alveolate
ambulance
ambuscade
amendable
amourette
amphibole
amplitude
analogise
anatomise
anchorage
anchorite
anchylose
androgyne
anglesite
anglicise
anhydride
anhydrite
animalise
anklebone
annoyance
anomalure
anorthite
antennule
anticline
antiquate
antitrade
aperitive
apiculate
apologise
appellate
appendage
appetence
appliance
appointee
approbate
aquaplane
aquarelle
arabesque
arabicise
aragonite
arbitrage
arbitrate
archetype
argentine
argentite
argillite
armistice
aromatise
arrearage
arriviste
arrogance
arteriole
artichoke
asbestine
ascensive
ascospore
aspartate
assayable
assertive
associate
assonance
assuasive
assumable
assurance
astraddle
astrocyte
astrodome
astrolabe
asymptote
atacamite
attentive
attenuate
attribute
aubergine
auditable
auspicate
austenite
authorise
autoclave
autocycle
autoroute
available
avalanche
aventaile
avertible
avoidable
avoidance
awardable
azeotrope
babacoote
bacchante
backslide
backspace
backstage
bacterise
bagatelle
bainmarie
bakehouse
balkanise
ballistae
baltimore
bamboozle
banderole
bandoline
banjulele
banquette
barbarise
barbitone
barcarole
bargepole
Barmecide
barricade
bastinade
bathhouse
batholite
battleaxe
beatitude
bedlamite
bedraggle
bedsettee
belemnite
bellicose
bellyache
belvedere
bengaline
bentonite
benzidine
benzoline
berberine
bespangle
biconcave
bifoliate
bifurcate
bilabiate
biosphere
bipartite
bipinnate
birdtable
birthrate
bivalence
bivariate
blackface
blackgame
blameable
blaspheme
blasthole
blastulae
bluestone
boathouse
bombasine
bombazine
bombilate
bombinate
bondslave
bondstone
booklouse
bookplate
bookstore
boxoffice
brachiate
bracteate
bracteole
Brahminee
braincase
brainwave
brakeshoe
branchiae
brasserie
brassiere
breadline
breadtree
breakable
brecciate
bretasche
bridecake
briefcase
brimstone
briquette
Briticise
broadside
broadwise
brochette
brokerage
broomrape
brushfire
brutalise
bryophyte
buhrstone
bullytree
bumblebee
bunkhouse
burlesque
burrstone
butadiene
butterine
Byzantine
caballine
calaboose
calabrese
calcarate
calcicole
calcifuge
calculate
calenture
calibrate
caliphate
calmative
campanile
candidate
canebrake
cannelure
cannonade
cannulate
cantabile
Cantonese
capsulate
capsulise
captivate
carbamate
carbamide
carbonate
carbonise
carbuncle
carburise
carfuffle
Carmelite
carnitine
carnivore
carronade
carthorse
cartilage
cartouche
cartridge
cassaripe
casserole
cassimere
castigate
catalogue
catarhine
catchable
catchpole
catechise
causative
cauterise
cavalcade
ceasefire
celandine
celebrate
cellarage
cellulose
cementite
centipede
cerebrate
certitude
cerussite
challenge
chamomile
champagne
champleve
chanteuse
chaperone
charlotte
charmeuse
checkmate
cheekbone
chemitype
cherrypie
chevelure
chibouque
chickadee
chickaree
childlike
chinaware
chisquare
chocolate
chondrite
chondrule
chophouse
chronicle
cicatrice
cicatrise
cigarette
Cingalese
circinate
circulate
cirripede
cisalpine
citystate
claimable
classable
classmate
clathrate
clearance
clearcole
cleavable
clientage
clientele
climbable
clockwise
cloisonne
clubbable
clubhouse
coadunate
coagulate
coalmouse
coarctate
coastline
coastwise
cobaltite
cocainise
cochleate
Cockaigne
cockhorse
coelomate
coenobite
coercible
coffinite
cogitable
cognitive
coherence
coiffeuse
colemouse
colleague
colligate
collimate
collocate
collotype
collusive
colonnade
colubrine
columbine
columbite
combative
combinate
comfiture
commingle
comminute
committee
commodore
commonage
communise
commutate
composite
composure
concentre
concierge
concourse
concubine
conducive
confervae
configure
conjugate
connature
conscribe
consignee
constable
consulage
consulate
convolute
cookhouse
cooperage
cooperate
copesmate
copestone
coproduce
coprolite
coralline
corallite
corbeille
corncrake
cornemuse
cornstone
corporate
corpuscle
correlate
corrosive
corrugate
corticate
cortisone
coruscate
corymbose
couchette
coumarone
countable
courgette
covalence
coverable
coverture
covetable
cowardice
crankcase
crashdive
creatable
crenature
crenulate
crepitate
crepuscle
criminate

crinoline
criticise
crocodile
croquette
crossable
crossette
crossfade
crossfire
crosswise
croustade
crushable
cryoscope
cubbyhole
cucullate
culminate
cultivate
cumbrance
curbstone
curettage
curtilage
curvature
cuspidate
customise
cyanamide
cyclamate
cymophane
dalliance
damascene
Dantesque
deadalive
deathlike
debatable
debauchee
debenture
debutante
decadence
decalitre
decalogue
decametre
decastere
deceptive
decidable
deciduate
decilitre
decimetre
decistere
deckhouse
declinate
decollate
decollete
decompose
decretive
decussate
deducible
deductive
defalcate
defeature
defective
defensive
deference
definable
defoliate
dehydrate
delftware
delineate
deludable
demagogue
demarcate
demimonde
demitasse
demurrage
denigrate
denitrate
deodorise
deoxidise
departure
depasture
depictive
depletive
deposable
deprecate
depredate
derivable
desecrate
desiccate
designate
desirable
desperate
destitute
desuetude
detective
determine
detersive
deuterate
devaluate
devastate
devisable
dextrorse
diablerie
diabolise
diaconate
dialogise
diatomite
dieselise
difficile
diffusive
digestive
dilatable
diligence
dimidiate
dinothere
dipcircle
dipeptide
diplomate
directive
dirigible
dirigisme
discharge
discourse
disengage
disfigure
dislocate
dismantle
disoblige
disparage
disparate
dispeople
displease
disposure
dispraise
disrepute
dissemble
dissipate
dissolute
dividable
divisible
doctorate
dogmatise
dominance
doorframe
doorplate
dorbeetle
dosshouse
doubtable
downgrade
downstage
drainpipe
dramatise
drawplate
drayhorse
dreamlike
drinkable
dripstone
dropscene
dropscone
drugstore
dubitable
dulcitude
duplicate
economise
ecosphere
ecossaise
ecritoire
ecstasise
ectophyte
educative
effective
effluence
eglantine
eightsome
ejaculate
elaborate
electrode
eliminate
eloquence
elsewhere
elucidate
elutriate
emanative
embassage
embracive
embrangle
embrasure
embrittle
embrocate
emendable
emergence
emolliate
empathise
empennage
emphasise
emulative
enclosure
encourage
encrinite
endocrine
endophyte
endoscope
endospore
endurable
endurance
enjoyable
enrapture
ensheathe
enterable
enthymeme
entophyte
entourage
entrecote
enucleate
enumerate
enunciate
enwreathe
epaulette
ephedrine
epicentre
epidosite
epitomise
equipoise
equitable
equivoque
eradicate
erstwhile
erythrite
escapable
escortage
esperance
espionage
esplanade
estimable
estoppage
estrapade
estuarine
esurience
etiquette
eucaryote
euphemise
euphonise
evaginate
evaporate
eventuate
everglade
evincible
evocative
evolutive
evolvable
exactable
exanimate
exarchate
exceptive
excessive
excisable
excitable
exclosure
exclusive
excoriate
excretive
exculpate
excursive
excusable
execrable
executive
exfoliate
existence
exonerate
exopodite
exosphere
expansile
expansive
expatiate
expensive
expertise
expletive
explicate
explosive
expulsive
expurgate
exquisite
exsertile
exservice
exsiccate
extempore
extensile
extensive
extenuate
extirpate
extorsive
extortive
extradite
extricate
extrusive
exuberate
exudative
exultance
eyeglance
fabricate
facsimile
factitive
factorage
factorise
fairylike
fairytale
faithcure
fancyfree
fandangle
fanfarade
fantasise
farandole
farestage
farmhouse
fascicule
fascinate
fatigable
faveolate
favourite
febrifuge
feculence
fecundate
fenestrae
ferrotype
fertilise
festinate
feudalise
fibroline
fieldfare
fiendlike
figurante
filoselle
filtrable
fimbriate
fioriture
firedrake
firehouse
fireplace
firestone
firstrate
fishplate
fishslice
fissipede
fivepence
flagrance
flagstone
flammable
flashcube
flashtube
floatable
floodgate
floodtide
flophouse
flowerage
flowstone
fluctuate
fluoresce
foeticide
folkdance
folkweave
footloose
footplate
foreclose
forejudge
foreshore
forestage
foretaste
forgeable
formalise
formative
formicate
formulate
formulise
fornicate
fortalice
fortitude
fortunate
fortyfive
fossilise
fosterage
fourpence
fourscore
fragrance
franchise
frangible
freehouse
freelance
freerange
freestone
freestyle
freezable
frequence
fricassee
fricative
frontline
frontpage
frontwise
frostbite
fructuate
fruitcake
fruittree
frustrate
fruticose
fulgurate
fulgurite
fullscale
fulminate
fungicide
furniture
fusillade
fustigate
gabardine
gaberdine
gabionade
galactose
galantine
galingale
gallicise
gallinule
gallmidge
gallonage
gallopade
gallstone
galvanise
garderobe
garnishee
garniture
gasconade
gasmantle
gastrulae
gatehouse
gaucherie
gaugeable
gelignite
generable
genialise
geologise
georgette
geosphere
germanise
germicide
germinate
gerundive
getatable
geyserite
ghostlike
giantlike
gingerade
gingerale
ginpalace
girandole
glabellae
gladstone
glamorise
glassware
glomerate
glomerule
gloryhole
glucoside
glutamate
glyceride
glycerine
glycoside
gneissose
goldeneye
gonophore
gorgonise
Gothamite
gothicise
grandiose
grandsire
grantable
granulate
granulite
granulose
grapevine
graspable
graticule
gratitude
gratulate
gravitate
graywacke
greengage
gregarine
grenadine
greywacke
grievance
grisaille
gritstone
grotesque
groundage
grubstake
guacamole
guarantee
guideline
guiderope
guilloche
gustative
gynophore
gyroplane
gyroscope
habitable
habituate
hackamore
haematite
hailstone
hairpiece
hairslide
hairspace
hairstyle
halfcaste
halfpence
halfprice
halftitle
halophile
halophyte
halothane
hammertoe
handbrake
handshake
handspike
harmaline
harmonise
harmotome
Hashemite
Hashimite
hawsehole
hawsepipe
headphone
headpiece
headstone
heartache
heartfree
heartsore
heelpiece
heliotype
hellebore
hellenise
hemicycle
hemitrope
herbicide
herbivore
herborise
heritable
hermitage
hesitance
hessonite
hexastyle
hibernate
hiddenite
hierodule
highgrade
Himyarite
hindrance
hirundine
histamine
histidine

hitchhike
Hitlerite
hoarstone
holophote
holystone
homologue
homophone
homuncule
hornstone
horoscope
horsehide
horseshoe
hortative
housebote
housemate
housewife
humblebee
humiliate
hurricane
hybridise
hydathode
hydrazine
hydrocele
hydrolyse
hydrolyte
hydrosome
hydroxide
hypallage
hyperbole
hyphenate
hypnotise
hypocrite
hypostyle
ideologue
ignitable
ignitible
ignorable
ignorance
illegible
imageable
imbalance
imbricate
imitative
immanence
immediate
immigrate
imminence
immixture
immovable
immutable
impassive
impedance
impetrate
implicate
implosive
importune
impostume
imposture
impotence
imprecate
imprecise
improvise
impudence
impulsive
imputable
inanimate
inaudible
inbreathe
incapable
incarnate
incentive
inceptive
incidence
inclosure
inclusive
incommode
incondite
inculcate
inculpate
incunable
incurable
incursive
incurvate
indelible
indenture
Indianise
indigence
indispose
indolence
inducible
inductive
inebriate
ineffable
inequable
inerrable
infantile
infantine
infatuate
infective
inferable
inference
infertile
influence
infuriate
infuscate
infusible
ingestive
inherence
injustice
innervate
innocence
inoculate
inquiline
insatiate
insectile
insensate
inservice
insincere
insinuate
insolence
insoluble
instigate
institute
insurable
insurance
integrate
intensive
intercede
interface
interfere
interfile
interfuse
interlace
interline
interlope
interlude
internode
interpage
interpose
intervene
interwove
interzone
intestate
intestine
intricate
introduce
intrusive
intuitive
intumesce
invective
inventive
inversive
invertase
inviolate
invisible
involucre
ionisable
irascible
ironstone
irradiate
irrigable
irritable
irruptive
isochrone
isogamete
isolative
isomerise
isooctane
Israelite
italicise
iterative
itinerate
jackknife
jackplane
jacksnipe
jacquerie
jargonise
jessamine
jesuitise
Johannine
josshouse
jubilance
Judastree
juniorate
Junoesque
juxtapose
kaolinise
kaolinite
karyotype
keelivine
kentledge
kerbstone
kerfuffle
kilocycle
kilolitre
kilometre
kittiwake
kneadable
knifeedge
knightage
knockknee
knowledge
labialise
labourite
lacerable
lacertine
laciniate
lacrimose
lacrymose
laevulose
lagniappe
lamellate
lamellose
lampshade
lancinate
landgrave
landscape
landslide
langouste
lapstrake
lardycake
larvicide
lassitude
laudative
laughable
lavaliere
lazzarone
learnable
leastwise
legerline
legislate
lendlease
leptosome
leucocyte
leucotome
leukocyte
Levantine
libertine
licensure
lifecycle
lifeforce
lifestyle
lifetable
lightsome
lilywhite
limejuice
limestone
limitable
limousine
linearise
lineolate
lingulate
lintwhite
lioncelle
liquidate
liquidise
liquorice
lithesome
lithopone
litigable
lixiviate
loadstone
loathsome
lobscouse
locatable
lodestone
lodgepole
Londonise
longhouse
longitude
longrange
longshore
lookalike
lorgnette
loveapple
lowercase
loxodrome
lubricate
lucrative
lucubrate
luftwaffe
luminance
lunchtime
luxuriate
macedoine
machinate
macrocyte
madeleine
madrepore
magdalene
magnesite
magnetise
magnetite
magnitude
maharanee
mailplane
mainbrace
majorette
majuscule
malachite
malleable
malthouse
malvoisie
mamillate
mammonite
mandarine
mandoline
manducate
manganate
manganese
manganite
manhandle
manoeuvre
manticore
marcasite
marchpane
margarine
margarite
marginate
marlstone
marmalade
martyrise
masculine
masticate
matricide
matronage
matronise
mattamore
maybeetle
meandrine
meanwhile
mechanise
mediatise
mediative
medicable
medullate
megacycle
megaphone
megaspore
melaphyre
meliorate
memorable
menadione
menagerie
Mennonite
menopause
mepacrine
mercerise
mescaline
mesmerise
mesophyte
metalline
metallise
metaphase
meteorite
methadone
methodise
methylate
methylene
metricate
metricise
metronome
mezzanine
micaslate
microcyte
microlite
micropyle
microsome
microtome
microtone
microwave
micturate
midinette
milestone
milkshake
millepede
millepore
millerite
millipede
millstone
miniature
minuscule
misadvise
misbecome
misbehave
miscegene
miscegine
mischance
miscreate
miserable
mishandle
mismanage
mistletoe
mitigable
mitraille
modernise
molybdate
monocline
monocoque
monologue
monoplane
monorhyme
monostyle
monotreme
monticule
monzonite
moonquake
moonscape
moonshine
moonstone
mortgagee
mossagate
motorable
motorbike
motorcade
mouldable
mountable
mousehole
moustache
mucronate
multilane
multitude
mumchance
muscadine
muscarine
muscovite
musteline
mutualise
mythicise
nameplate
naphthene
narcotine
narcotise
narrative
natrolite
navigable
neathouse
neckverse
necrotise
nectarine
negotiate
negritude
nemertine
neologise
neoterise
nepheline
nephelite
nervature
nescience
nevermore
niccolite
nickelise
nictitate
nightlife
nightline
nightmare
nightside
nighttime
nigritude
nigrosine
ninepence
Nipponese
nitratine
nominable
nonviable
normalise
Normanise
normative
noseflute
nosepiece
novelette
noviciate
novitiate
nullipore
numerable
nummulite
nuncupate
nutritive
oasthouse
obcordate
obedience
obeisance
obfuscate
objective
objurgate
obsecrate
obsessive
obsolesce
obstinate
obtrusive
occlusive
octastyle
octostyle
odalisque
oenophile
offcentre
offchance
offensive
officiate
olfactive
Oligocene
olivenite
omissible
onlicence
operative
opportune
opposable
optophone
orangeade
ordinance
organelle
organzine
orientate
oriflamme
originate
orphanage
oscillate
ossifrage
ostensive
ostracise
otherwise
oubliette
overborne
overdrive
overglaze
overgraze
overissue
overprice
overstate
overvalue
overwrite
overwrote
oxygenate
oxygenise
ozocerite
ozokerite
packhorse
paillasse
paillette
pairhorse
palafitte
palatable
palletise
palliasse
palmipede
palmitate
palpitate
palsgrave
panhandle
pantomime
pantyhose
papeterie
papillate

papillose
papillote
parachute
Paraclete
parbuckle
parentage
parfleche
parricide
parsonage
partitive
partridge
pasodoble
passerine
passivate
pastorale
pastorate
pasturage
patellate
patricide
patronage
patronise
pauperise
peaceable
peacetime
pectinate
pedagogue
pegmatite
Pekingese
pelletise
pendulate
penduline
peneplane
penetrate
penitence
pentangle
penthouse
peptonise
percaline
perchance
percolate
peregrine
perennate
perforate
perfusive
periclase
pericycle
periodate
periscope
peristome
peristyle
permeable
permeance
permutate
persecute
persevere
personage
personate
pervasive
pesthouse
pesticide
petechiae
pethidine
petiolate
petiolule
petulance
phagocyte
phalarope
phenacite
phenakite
phenotype
pheromone
phonetise
phonolite
phosphate
phosphene
phosphide
phosphine
phosphite
photogene

phototype
picturise
piecerate
pierrette
pilferage
pineapple
pinnipede
pinnulate
pinstripe
pipestone
pirouette
pitchpipe
pivotable
placeable
placename
placentae
plaintive
plantable
plantlike
platinise
platitude
Platonise
plausible
playhouse
pleadable
pleasance
Pleiocene
plenitude
plicature
plumbline
plumulate
plumulose
pluralise
podzolise
poeticise
pointille
pointlace
pokerface
politesse
pollinate
polonaise
polyamide
polyphase
polyphone
polythene
poorhouse
porbeagle
porcupine
portative
porterage
portreeve
posthaste
posthorse
posthouse
postulate
potentate
poundcake
pourboire
poussette
powerdive
pranksome
precative
precipice
preconise
predative
predicate
preengage
prefigure
pregnable
prejudice
prelatise
prelature
prelusive
premature
presbyope
prescribe
presentee
preterite
primitive

principle
printable
privative
privilege
probative
procedure
procreate
proenzyme
programme
prolamine
prolative
prolicide
prologise
promenade
promotive
pronounce
propagate
propylene
prorogate
proscribe
prosecute
proselyte
prostrate
protamine
prototype
proximate
prurience
publicise
puissance
pullulate
pulmonate
pulpstone
pulsatile
pulserate
pulverise
pulvinate
punchline
punctuate
pupillage
purgative
purposive
purselike
pursuable
pursuance
purulence
pustulate
pyroscope
quadrigae
quadrille
quadruple
quartette
quartzite
quartzose
queenlike
quicklime
quinoline
quintette
quintuple
quittance
rabbinate
racehorse
radiative
raffinate
raffinose
raingauge
randomise
rapidfire
rationale
razoredge
reachable
reactance
readymade
reanimate
rearhorse
rearmouse
rearrange
rebaptise
rebukable
recalesce

recapture
receptive
recessive
rechauffe
recherche
reclinate
reclusive
recognise
recoinage
recombine
recompose
reconcile
recondite
reconvene
rectangle
rectitude
rectorate
recursive
recusance
redingote
redolence
reducible
reductive
reeducate
reenforce
reexamine
referable
reference
reflexive
refluence
refusable
refutable
rehydrate
reimburse
reinforce
reinstate
reiterate
relevance
religiose
reliquiae
reluctate
remanence
remeasure
remediate
reminisce
removable
rencontre
renewable
reparable
repayable
repechage
replicate
reportage
reprobate
reproduce
repudiate
repulsive
reputable
requisite
rerebrace
rerelease
reremouse
resalable
reserpine
reshuffle
residence
resistive
resoluble
resonance
restitute
resumable
resurface
retaliate
retentive
reticence
retinulae
retrocede
retrousse
reverence

revisable
revivable
revocable
revulsive
rhodamine
rhodolite
rhodonite
rhythmise
ridgepole
ridgetile
rightable
rigmarole
ringfence
ringshake
ringsnake
ritualise
riverside
roadhouse
rocambole
rockbrake
rocksnake
roofplate
roseapple
rosenoble
rotatable
rowantree
rubberise
rubellite
rubicelle
rubricate
ruggedise
runcinate
rusticate
sabbatise
sacculate
sacrifice
sacrilege
safranine
sagittate
sailplane
saintlike
salangane
saltglaze
saltpetre
sandstone
sandtable
satellite
satinette
saturable
saturnine
saxifrage
saxophone
scalelike
scapolite
scarfwise
scheelite
schistose
scolecite
Scoticise
screwpile
screwpine
scrimmage
scripture
scrummage
scrutable
sculpture
seachange
seagirdle
seanettle
seatangle
seclusive
secretage
secretive
securable
seductive
segregate
selective
selfabuse
selfaware

selfdrive
selfimage
selfpride
semanteme
semaphore
semblable
semblance
semibreve
semiplume
sensitise
sensitive
sentenate
sentience
separable
sepiolite
sepulchre
sepulture
serialise
serinette
sermonise
serrefile
serrulate
serviette
servitude
setsquare
severable
severance
sexualise
shadetree
shakeable
shapeable
sheepcote
sheeplice
sheldrake
shelflife
shellfire
shemozzle
shipshape
shockable
shoeshine
shogunate
shootable
shoreline
shoreside
shortcake
shortwave
showpiece
showplace
shrewmice
shrinkage
sibilance
sibylline
siccative
sickleave
sideissue
sideswipe
sidetable
sigillate
signalise
signature
siliquose
siltstone
simulacre
Sinhalese
sinologue
sinophile
siphonage
siphuncle
skedaddle
slabstone
slantwise
sliderule
slopewise
smalltime
smoketree
snakebite
snakelike
snowflake
snowgoose

snowscape
snowwhite
soapstone
socialise
socialite
solemnise
soleplate
solitaire
solmisate
somewhere
somewhile
songcycle
sonnetise
sophomore
sorbapple
sortilege
soubrette
Soudanese
soundhole
soundwave
soupplate
sovietise
spacetime
spatulate
speakable
spearside
spectacle
speculate
spendable
spiculate
spinulose
spodumene
spokewise
sporulate
spouthole
squarrose
stabilise
stackable
Stagirite
stainable
staircase
stalemate
staminate
stampnote
standpipe
starapple
starstone
stateside
statewide
statuette
steampipe
stenotype
stepdance
sterilise
stevedore
stimulate
stingaree
stipitate
stipulate
stockdove
stockpile
stokehole
stolonate
stoneware
stormcone
storyline
stovepipe
striature
stricture
stridence
strobilae
strongyle
structure
studhorse
stylobate
subalpine
subdivide
subduable
subjugate

sublimate
submarine
subrogate
subscribe
subsidise
substance
substrate
subtilise
succinate
suffocate
sugarcane
sultanate
summarise
summative
sunlounge
sunspurge
sunstroke
superable
superfine
superfuse
superpose
supersede
supervene
supervise
suppurate
surcharge
surcingle
surculose
surrogate
swangoose
swimmable
swordcane
swordlike
syllabise
syllogise
sylphlike
sylvanite
symbolise
synagogue
syncopate
syndicate
synoecete
syphilise
tablature
tableware
tachylite
tachylyte
tailpiece
talkative
tamponade
tangerine
tanpickle
tantalate
tantalise
tantalite
taskforce
teachable
teakettle
technique
telephone
telescope
tellurate
telluride
tellurite
telophase
temperate
temporise
temptable
tenderise
tentative
tenthrate
terminate
terramare
terrorise
testdrive
tetradite
teutonise
theologue
therefore
thickknee
thighbone
thinkable
thirdrate
thorntree
threesome
thrombose
thumbhole
thylacine
thyroxine
tidegauge
tigerseye
tightrope
tightwire
tilestone
timelapse
timepiece
timetable
titillate
titlepage
tittivate
toadstone
tolerable
tolerance
tollhouse
tombstone
tomentose
tonguetie
toolhouse
toothache
toothsome
torchrace
totempole
touchable
touchhole
touchline
touchtype
townhouse
townscape
traceable
tracheate
tractable
tradename
trainable
transfuse
translate
transmute
transpire
transpose
trattorie
treatable
treillage
trematode
tremolite
trialogue
tribunate
trichinae
tridymite
trilobate
trilobite
triptyque
triturate
trochleae
trysquare
tubercule
tuliptree
tungstate
turbinate
turnstile
turnstone
turntable
turpitude
turquoise
twayblade
twentyone
twistable
typewrite
tyrannise
uintahite
umbellate
umbellule
unbalance
undeceive
underdone
undergone
underline
undermine
underrate
underripe
underside
undertake
undertone
uneatable
unifiable
unnamable
unreserve
unsayable
unshackle
unsheathe
untenable
unwelcome
uppercase
uraninite
urceolate
usherette
utterable
utterance
uvarovite
uxoricide
vaccinate
vacillate
vacuolate
valentine
vandalise
vaporable
variegate
variolate
variolite
vassalage
vastitude
vegetable
vehemence
veinstone
velodrome
venerable
vengeance
ventilate
ventricle
veratrine
verbalise
verbicide
veritable
vermicide
vermicule
vermifuge
verminate
vernalise
verrucose
versatile
vertebrae
vestibule
vestiture
vibratile
vibrative
vibrissae
vicariate
vicereine
victimise
victorine
videotape
vigilance
vigilante
villanage
villenage
vindicate
violative
virgulate
virulence
viscerate
visitable
visualise
vitelline
viverrine
vivianite
vizierate
volteface
vorticose
vouchsafe
vulcanise
vulcanite
vulgarise
vulpinite
vulturine
waggonage
Wagnerite
wagonette
waistline
waldgrave
wallplate
wapentake
warehouse
warrantee
washhouse
wastepipe
watchable
watchcase
watchfire
watergate
waterhole
waterline
waterpipe
waterside
waveguide
wavellite
wayzgoose
wearisome
wedgewise
weighable
whalebone
wheelbase
wherefore
whetstone
whinstone
whipsnake
whiteface
wholesale
wholesome
wideawake
widthwise
wieldable
willemite
winestone
winterise
wiregauze
witherite
woebegone
wolfsbane
wolverene
wolverine
womanlike
woodlouse
workhorse
workhouse
workpiece
worktable
worldwide
worrisome
wulfenite
wyandotte
Wyclifite
Xanthippe
xenophile
xenophobe
xerophile
xerophyte
xparticle
xylophone
yohimbine
Yorkshire
zibelline
zincotype
zinkenite
zygospore
basrelief
bombproof
bookshelf
broadleaf
bullybeef
cowlstaff
crossruff
disbelief
feedstuff
fireproof
flagstaff
foodstuff
foolproof
germproof
halfstaff
headscarf
interleaf
leitmotif
looseleaf
misbelief
mothproof
overproof
overstuff
pikestaff
plaintiff
rainproof
rustproof
scaleleaf
scrumhalf
shotproof
skewwhiff
stonedeaf
sugarloaf
tableleaf
wagonroof
waterleaf
windproof
abhorring
abounding
abseiling
absorbing
according
adjoining
adlibbing
admitting
affecting
agonising
allotting
annulling
appalling
appealing
arresting
ashlaring
awakening
backslang
battening
bedspring
befitting
befogging
begetting
beginning
besetting
besotting
bevelling
billabong
binturong
blackflag
boomerang
boomslang
borrowing
bowstring
brambling
brandling
breathing
breeching
breveting
bristling
buffeting
buttygang
caballing
cacholong
carolling
carpetbag
carpeting
cavilling
centering
centreing
chaingang
chickling
churching
cleansing
cliffhang
colouring
confiding
crackling
crediting
crippling
cupelling
curveting
dayspring
debagging
debarring
debugging
deferring
demanding
demitting
demobbing
demurring
designing
deterring
devilling
diphthong
disarming
diverting
donothing
doodlebug
dowelling
earthling
easygoing
embedding
embussing
endearing
engraving
enrolling
equalling
equipping
estopping
exceeding
excelling
excepting
expecting
expelling
extolling
faggoting
fairyring
farseeing
fastening
fingering
finicking
firstling
fledgling
flouncing
flowering
focussing
following
foregoing
forgiving
foundling
galloping
gammoning
gardening
gathering
goffering
grappling
groundhog
grounding
gruelling
grumbling
guardring
guttering
hamstring
hamstrung
hankering
happening
harrowing
hatchling
havocking
hearthrug
hocussing
houseflag
illboding
impelling
impending
incurring
inferring
infilling
inflowing
ingrowing
inpouring
insetting
interring
japanning
jitterbug
junketing
kurrajong
labelling
lathering
latticing
launching
lawgiving
leavening
lettering
levelling
libelling
lightning
lingering
litterbug
lumbering
maddening
magicking
maneating
marketing
metalling
mimicking
misgiving
modelling
monthling
nightlong
nonjuring
nurseling
occurring
offspring
onsetting
outgiving
overlying
packaging
panelling
panicking
pedalling
perilling
perishing
picketing
plainsong
plaything
potholing
prayerrug
preceding
pressgang
promising
providing
provoking

punishing
quibbling
rationing
ravelling
ravishing
reasoning
rebelling
rebidding
rebutting
recapping
reckoning
recording
recurring
referring
refitting
Reichstag
rejoicing
remitting
repelling
repotting
rerunning
resetting
resitting
revelling
revetting
revolting
rewarding
rivalling
rivelling
russeting
saddlebag
sailoring
saintling
scallawag
scallywag
scantling
scarfring
schilling
schoolbag
schooling
scorching
scramming
scrapping
screening
scrubbing
seafaring
searching
seasoning
shambling
shaveling
shearling
sheathing
shieldbug
shredding
shrugging
sickening
singalong
sitzkrieg
skijoring
skydiving
smuggling
something
sparkplug
spindling
splitting
spongebag
sprigging
springing
squatting
squibbing
squidding
startling
stippling
straphang
strapping
streaking
stripling
stripping
stropping
strouding
strumming
strutting
suffering
supposing
surfacing
surveying
swaddling
swingeing
tailoring
taxpaying
thatching
thrashing
thrilling
throbbing
thrumming
tiedyeing
timbering
tittuping
torchsong
totalling
towelling
troutling
tuckerbag
tumblebug
twinkling
unbending
unceasing
underhung
underling
undersong
underwing
unfailing
unfeeling
unfitting
unheeding
unknowing
unmeaning
unpegging
unsmiling
unsparing
unweeting
unwilling
unwinking
unwitting
unzipping
uplifting
upsetting
vapouring
veneering
vetchling
walloping
wallydrag
wandering
wayfaring
weighting
welcoming
wellbeing
westering
wheedling
whirligig
whistling
whitening
whitewing
whizzbang
withering
worldling
wrestling
yellowdog
yodelling
youngling
aerograph
aftermath
allograph
allomorph
anabranch
angelfish
autograph
autotroph
baboonish
backcloth
baksheesh
bandwidth
barograph
batholith
bellpunch
billionth
birdwatch
bismillah
bitterish
blackfish
blackwash
bloodbath
blowtorch
bobsleigh
brainwash
brandreth
brightish
buckshish
bucktooth
bullfinch
cailleach
canetrash
cavendish
cerecloth
cerograph
chaffinch
cockroach
colocynth
cornbrash
crampfish
cranreuch
crossfish
cystolith
czarevich
dahabiyah
devilfish
dipswitch
disavouch
disbranch
dishcloth
disrelish
dogstooth
dragonish
ectomorph
eidograph
eightieth
eightyish
embellish
endolymph
endomorph
ergograph
establish
facecloth
fifteenth
flarepath
footcloth
forasmuch
forereach
forthwith
fourflush
frogmarch
gatecrash
gemutlich
Germanish
gibberish
globefish
goalmouth
goldfinch
goldsmith
groundash
hairbrush
haircloth
halftruth
headcloth
hemistich
hemstitch
hexastich
Hexateuch
hodograph
holograph
homeopath
homograph
hopscotch
hoydenish
hundredth
ideograph
idiograph
inshallah
ironsmith
jellyfish
killifish
kittenish
kymograph
labyrinth
laccolith
lagomorph
lastditch
lickerish
liquorish
locksmith
logogriph
loincloth
loudmouth
lovematch
macintosh
maharajah
maidenish
mammonish
matriarch
megadeath
mesomorph
microlith
micromesh
milktooth
millionth
Mondayish
monkeyish
monograph
monostich
mouthwash
nailbrush
neckcloth
neuropath
newsflash
ninetieth
nomograph
oleograph
osteopath
Ostrogoth
outgrowth
overmatch
overpitch
overreach
overwatch
overweigh
paragraph
paramorph
paranymph
patriarch
pergunnah
perilymph
perimorph
pikeperch
pilotfish
polygraph
polymorph
polyptych
premonish
prettyish
pyracanth
Quakerish
razorfish
refurbish
refurnish
replenish
republish
roodcloth
Roumansch
sackcloth
sagebrush
sailcloth
sallowish
saltmarsh
sandarach
sasquatch
Sassenach
scaldfish
scalefish
sciagraph
serigraph
sheatfish
Shechinah
sheepwash
shellfish
shillelah
sixteenth
skiagraph
slightish
slipcoach
slowcoach
slowmatch
smokebush
smoothish
snailfish
snipefish
snowbroth
sociopath
songsmith
sourdough
spearfish
spicebush
squeamish
squirarch
stalworth
statolith
stockfish
stonefish
stopwatch
strongish
subbranch
succotash
swellfish
swordfish
taioseach
tallowish
telegraph
terebinth
therewith
thirtieth
thornbush
tigermoth
tollbooth
traycloth
trierarch
trunkfish
tsarevich
twentieth
ultrahigh
umpteenth
unselfish
vapourish
vulturish
washcloth
waterbath
wherewith
whitefish
whitewash
willowish
woodnymph
wordsmith
workbench
xeromorph
xylograph
yellowish
Ashkenazi
campanili
charivari
comitadji
coryphaei
dziggetai
eucalypti
fasciculi
garibaldi
glissandi
glomeruli
homunculi
impresari
jaborandi
lazzaroni
maharishi
oesophagi
Pakistani
patchouli
pizzicati
potpourri
ranunculi
sgraffiti
spaghetti
triumviri
antiknock
applejack
awestruck
backtrack
bailiwick
barmbrack
beanstalk
beefsteak
bergamask
billycock
birchbark
birthmark
blackbuck
blackcock
blackjack
blueblack
boardwalk
Bolshevik
bootblack
breakneck
brickwork
brushwork
bushwhack
camelback
cheapjack
chopstick
clockwork
coachwork
cornstalk
crookback
crookneck
crosslink
crosstalk
cuttysark
deathmask
dirttrack
disembark
drawnwork
drumstick
earthwork
eiderduck
fancywork
feedstock
fenugreek
fieldbook
fieldwork
firebreak
firebrick
fishyback
flagstick
flashback
flintlock
floodmark
footstalk
forespeak
framework
frostwork
gangplank
gaolbreak
glasswork
goldbrick
gooseneck
greenback
grillwork
guardbook
guesswork
guidebook
halftrack
handiwork
handywork
hatchback
haversack
headstock
heartsick
heathcock
hollyhock
honkytonk
hornwrack
horseback
houseleek
housework
huckaback
hunchback
inglenook
interlink
interlock
jailbreak
jossstick
ladysmock
lampblack
lancejack
lapstreak
leafstalk
livestock
loanshark
lowerdeck
mahlstick
mallemuck
matchlock
maulstick
Menshevik
metalwork
mollymawk
nighthawk
nightwork
orderbook
overcheck
overstock
overtrick
paintwork
paperback
paperwork
patchwork
pickaback
piecework
piggyback
piggybank
pinchbeck
pinchcock
pipsqueak
pitchdark
pitchfork
placekick
platemark
pokerwork
poppycock
preshrink
preshrunk
pressmark
presswork
psalmbook
racetrack
raincheck
razorback

riverbank
roadblock
rootstock
roughneck
sandcrack
scalplock
scenedock
scorebook
scrapbook
sheephook
sheeptick
sheepwalk
sheerhulk
sheldduck
shelfmark
shellback
shellbark
shellwork
shipwreck
shoeblack
sidetrack
skinflick
slapstick
slingback
smokejack
snowblink
spadework
spoonbeak
spotcheck
springbok
steelwork
steenkirk
stickwork
stockbook
stonework
stormcock
storybook
strapwork
stylebook
sunstruck
sweepback
sweettalk
sweptback
tabletalk
thinktank
thornback
throwback
thumbmark
thumbtack
toastrack
toothpick
touchmark
townsfolk
trademark
undertook
waterbuck
watermark
whaleback
wheelwork
whipstock
windbreak
wisecrack
womenfolk
woodblock
woodchuck
yardstick
abdominal
ablatival
accentual
acidophil
acquittal
acropetal
actuarial
adenoidal
adnominal
adverbial
agnatical
altricial
ambrosial
amyloidal
ancestral
anecdotal
angelical
anglophil
antefixal
antenatal
antidotal
antinodal
antinovel
antipodal
antiviral
appraisal
araneidal
archangel
archducal
armigeral
arsenical
ascetical
aspectual
auctorial
authorial
autosomal
azimuthal
bacchanal
backpedal
bacterial
baptismal
barrelful
basipetal
basketful
beautiful
betrothal
bicameral
bicipital
bilateral
bilgekeel
bilingual
biliteral
binominal
blackball
blackmail
bombshell
bookstall
botanical
bottleful
bountiful
branchial
bridewell
broadtail
bronchial
bucketful
bursarial
bushelful
cacuminal
cadastral
cadential
calcaneal
calycinal
campstool
canonical
cantorial
cartwheel
catarrhal
catchpoll
caterwaul
cathedral
celestial
censorial
chainmail
chanceful
changeful
chaparral
chockfull
chronical
clamshell
classical
claustral
cloistral
coccygeal
cochineal
cockatiel
coeternal
collegial
colloidal
colourful
commensal
committal
comprisal
comptroll
conferral
conformal
congenial
connubial
continual
convivial
corporeal
coseismal
creatural
crinoidal
crossbill
cryptical
cursorial
custodial
cycloidal
dancehall
dandiacal
daredevil
dayschool
deathroll
decagonal
decapodal
deceitful
decennial
decontrol
deistical
dialectal
diametral
dichasial
disannual
disavowal
disbursal
discoidal
disentail
dismissal
dispersal
dissocial
doctorial
doctrinal
dominical
drawerful
driftsail
dropsical
druidical
dynamical
ecclesial
editorial
effectual
effluvial
effortful
electoral
elegiacal
elemental
embryonal
Emmenthal
emotional
empirical
enchorial
endosteal
entrammel
ephemeral
epidermal
epiphytal
episcopal
equivocal
eristical
erratical
essential
etherical
ethmoidal
factional
factorial
faldstool
fanatical
fatidical
fenestral
fictional
financial
firedrill
fluxional
footstall
footstool
forestall
forgetful
fossorial
fourwheel
fraternal
freewheel
frightful
funebrial
galenical
Gallophil
gearwheel
genetical
genitival
genocidal
gerundial
glassgall
goosegirl
graphical
gristmill
groundsel
guardrail
guildhall
gymnasial
halfshell
handwheel
hardshell
hawksbill
headstall
healthful
heretical
hexagonal
highlevel
hodiernal
homicidal
horsetail
housecarl
hydrofoil
hypethral
hypnoidal
hypocotyl
identical
idiotical
illiberal
illogical
impartial
inaugural
isoclinal
isohyetal
juridical
khedivial
lachrymal
lampshell
laryngeal
Levitical
libidinal
longaeval
lumbrical
lunitidal
magistral
marestail
marmoreal
marsupial
masterful
matutinal
mediaeval
medicinal
meningeal
menstrual
mercurial
mesophyll
microbial
millwheel
mispickel
monarchal
moneybill
monodical
monsoonal
moschatel
multifoil
municipal
musichall
necrophil
nectarial
needleful
negroidal
negrophil
nightfall
nocturnal
nonpareil
numbskull
numerical
nutweevil
obconical
obsequial
occipital
octagonal
octennial
officinal
olecranal
oratorial
orificial
overspill
oviductal
packdrill
palpebral
paludinal
palustral
papergirl
paradisal
parochial
passional
penumbral
perennial
perinatal
perpetual
personnel
petechial
pharyngal
photocell
photophil
pictorial
piecemeal
pimpernel
piratical
placental
plentiful
pocketful
polemical
political
polygonal
polytonal
polyvinyl
popliteal
poriferal
portrayal
postnasal
postnatal
potential
practical
praiseful
prayerful
prebendal
precancel
precocial
preschool
presidial
primaeval
primatial
principal
proconsul
prodromal
prosaical
protozoal
Provencal
psychical
puerperal
punchball
punchbowl
purpureal
pyramidal
quantical
quizzical
raptorial
razorbill
recruital
rectorial
regardful
regicidal
regretful
rehearsal
remindful
reposeful
reprieval
resentful
resultful
retrieval
revictual
rhizoidal
rhonchial
ribosomal
roadmetal
rockdrill
rounceval
Russophil
salesgirl
sartorial
satanical
satirical
saucerful
sceptical
schlemiel
schlemihl
schnitzel
schnorkel
sciential
scoundrel
screwball
sectional
sectorial
seedpearl
segmental
semestral
semifinal
semimetal
semivowel
seneschal
sensorial
sessional
sexennial
shipcanal
shirttail
shortfall
shovelful
sidewheel
sigmoidal
signorial
singspiel
sinistral
Slavophil
smokeball
softpedal
softshell
soritical
sorrowful
sparkcoil
speechful
speedball
speedwell
spherical
spiritual
spirituel
spleenful
spoonbill
sprigtail
spritsail
spurwheel
squamosal
stairwell
stampmill
stapedial
starshell
stational
stercoral
steroidal
stinkball
stomachal
stonecoal
stonewall
stoolball
stormsail
stressful
subaerial
subastral
subcaudal
subcostal
sublethal
submental
subnormal
succursal
suctorial
supercool
surficial
surprisal
sweetmeal
swordtail
sympodial
symposial
synagogal
synclinal
syncytial
syndactyl
synodical
syringeal
teacupful
technical
tectorial
tegmental
tensional
thornbill
thumbnail
toadstool
tonsorial
toponymal
tormentil
torsional
trapezial
traversal
treadmill
tridactyl
triennial
trifacial
trihedral
trinomial
triumphal
trunkcall
tuitional
typemetal
typhoidal
umbilical
undecimal
underseal
undersell

undutiful
unethical
unhelpful
uniserial
unisexual
universal
unmindful
unmusical
unnatural
unskilful
vaticinal
vectorial
veridical
versional
vertebral
vestigial
vicennial
viceregal
viceroyal
vicesimal
vigesimal
viricidal
vizierial
watercool
waterfall
waterfowl
watermill
wheatmeal
whimsical
whirlpool
Whitehall
wholemeal
witchmeal
wonderful
wormwheel
wychhazel
absurdism
academism
aciniform
Adventism
airstream
algorithm
alloplasm
aluminium
americium
amoralism
amorphism
anabolism
anarchism
anemogram
angleworm
anglicism
animalism
animatism
antiserum
arboretum
arrowworm
asphaltum
Athenaeum
atonalism
avizandum
bacterium
barathrum
barbarism
barnstorm
beadledom
berkelium
beryllium
biblicism
biorhythm
bloodworm
boardroom
Briticism
broadloom
brummagem
brutalism
cabbalism
cablegram
caciquism
Caesarism
cairngorm
calcaneum
caldarium
Calvinism
capitulum
careerism
cartogram
Castroism
cataclasm
cataclysm
cataplasm
catechism
Catharism
Celticism
centigram
cerastium
cheongsam
chernozem
classroom
claviform
clitellum
cloakroom
Cobdenism
cocainism
coccidium
coenobium
cofferdam
colchicum
collegium
collyrium
colosseum
colostrum
columbium
Cominform
commendam
communism
contagium
continuum
conundrum
cordiform
courtroom
cretinism
criticism
crossbeam
cruciform
cryptogam
cryptonym
cuneiform
curialism
curviform
cymbidium
cymbiform
cytoplasm
daltonism
Darwinism
decennium
defeatism
dentalium
dentiform
despotism
deuterium
diabolism
diachylom
diachylum
dialogism
diaphragm
dichasium
dichroism
dicrotism
disaffirm
disesteem
dogmatism
dogoodism
earthworm
ecosystem
ectoplasm
ecumenism
effluvium
elbowroom
endoplasm
endosperm
endosteum
epicurism
epiphragm
epipolism
equisetum
eremitism
eroticism
eruciform
erythrism
esoterism
eunuchism
euphemism
euphonium
exoticism
extremism
Fabianism
Falangism
falciform
fastigium
Fenianism
fetichism
fetishism
feudalism
fibriform
firealarm
flabellum
flagellum
formalism
fraenulum
fullcream
fungiform
gallicism
galvanism
ganderism
gastraeum
Germanism
germanium
germplasm
gigantism
gongorism
Gothicism
grandslam
greenroom
grillroom
Grundyism
guardroom
guestroom
gymnasium
gynaeceum
gynoecium
hailstorm
harmonium
hectogram
heliogram
Hellenism
herbarium
hetaerism
hetairism
heteronym
hierogram
hirsutism
histogram
Hitlerism
houseroom
hybridism
hydronium
hylozoism
hypericum
hypnotism
idioplasm
impluvium
indecorum
isomerism
Italicism
Jansenism
jesuitism
jetstream
junkerdom
junkerism
kaiserdom
kaiserism
kibbutzim
labialism
lanthanum
lentiform
ligniform
Listerism
literatim
logarithm
Londonism
macrocosm
maelstrom
Magianism
magnalium
magnesium
magnetism
Malayalam
mammiform
mammonism
mannerism
manubrium
marsupium
martyrdom
masochism
masterdom
mausoleum
mechanism
meliorism
Mendelism
menstruum
mentalism
mesmerism
metaplasm
Methodism
microcosm
microfilm
microgram
midstream
milligram
misbeseem
misesteem
misinform
misoneism
Mithraism
modernism
monachism
monergism
mongolism
monkeyism
monoecism
Montanism
Mormonism
mosaicism
multiform
mutualism
mysticism
mythicism
narcotism
neodymium
neologism
neoterism
nephalism
neptunium
Normanism
occultism
operculum
opusculum
Orangeism
orderform
osteoderm
ostracism
overwhelm
pachyderm
palladium
pantheism
Parseeism
pauperism
pentagram
perisperm
pessimism
petersham
petroleum
phonetism
phonogram
pictogram
pipedream
pisciform
Platonism
pluralism
Plutonism
plutonium
poeticism
pollinium
polygonum
potassium
presidium
pressroom
prettyism
princedom
pseudonym
pterygium
pycnidium
pyrethrum
Quakerdom
Quakerism
quercetum
quitclaim
quixotism
rabbinism
racialism
radiogram
rainstorm
rascaldom
rascalism
reconfirm
reformism
restiform
reticulum
Ribbonism
ritualism
rostellum
roundworm
routinism
ruthenium
sabbatism
sacciform
sacrarium
salicetum
sandstorm
Sanhedrim
saturnism
savagedom
scientism
screwworm
scutellum
scutiform
sensorium
Sephardim
serialism
shakerism
shamanism
sheikhdom
shelfroom
shieldfem
Shintoism
shortterm
snaredrum
snowstorm
socialism
sociogram
solipsism
soundfilm
sovietism
Spinozism
spirillum
spiritism
squiredom
stackroom
Stalinism
stateroom
stillroom
stockroom
storeroom
stratagem
strawworm
strongarm
strontium
styliform
subphylum
sugarplum
sutteeism
syllabism
syllogism
symbolism
sympodium
symposium
syncytium
synergism
tarantism
taraxacum
Tartufism
tegmentum
tellurium
tenaculum
terminism
terrarium
terrorism
tetragram
Teutonism
therefrom
thralldom
transform
trapezium
tribadism
tribalism
triennium
trifolium
triforium
tritheism
troutfarm
trussbeam
ultimatum
uropygium
vademecum
vampirism
vandalism
verbalism
vermiform
versiform
vestigium
villiform
vitriform
volcanism
voltinism
voodooism
vorticism
voyeurism
vulcanism
vulgarism
vulpinism
weighbeam
welfarism
wherefrom
whitebeam
witticism
Yankeedom
Yankeeism
ytterbium
zirconium
abduction
abjection
abolition
aboutturn
abruption
accession
accordion
accretion
Acheulean
Acheulian
actuation
addiction
adduction
ademption
admission
adoration
adrenalin
adulation
advection
affection
afflation
aflatoxin
afternoon
agitation
Algonkian
Algonquin
alpenhorn
amazonian
amoebaean
amphibian
amygdalin
amylopsin
anchorman
angleiron
animation
annelidan
anthelion
anthemion
anthocyan
anthozoan
anticodon
antitoxin
antivenin
appertain
apportion
araneidan
Armorican
Arthurian
ascension
ascertain
aspersion
assertion
astrakhan
asyndeton
Atlantean
attention
attrition
automaton
avocation
badminton
baldachin
baldaquin
bandwagon
Bantustan
Barbadian
barbarian
barracoon
basilican
Bathonian
battalion
bedridden
beechfern
bilirubin
birdbrain
bisection
boatswain
boattrain
bolection
bombardon
bondwoman
bouquetin
brakesman
breakdown

breakeven
breastpin
bridesman
bringdown
broomcorn
buckthorn
Bulgarian
bumbledon
cacodemon
caecilian
caerulean
Caesarean
Caesarian
Cambodian
cameraman
caparison
Capricorn
Caribbean
carnation
carnelian
carrageen
Cartesian
caseation
cassation
Castalian
castellan
Castilian
catamaran
cattleman
Caucasian
causation
centurion
cessation
chameleon
champaign
charlatan
charwoman
chatelain
checkrein
chelation
chelonian
chieftain
chilblain
Chinatown
Christian
chromatin
chthonian
churchman
Cimmerian
circadian
clavation
clergyman
clergymen
clinician
closedown
coalition
coecilian
coemption
cognation
cognition
colcannon
collation
collegian
collision
collodion
collusion
colourman
Columbian
Comintern
commotion
communion
companion
concision
condition
Confucian
confusion
connation
connexion
constrain
contagion
contusion
cornelian
cornerman
cornopean
corrasion
corrosion
cotillion
cotyledon
countdown
courtesan
crackdown
cracksman
craftsman
cremation
crenation
criterion
CroMagnon
cuplichen
custodian
cyclopean
cyclopian
cyclotron
Cytherean
cytotoxin
Daedalean
Daedalian
dalmatian
damnation
Damoclean
dandelion
Darwinian
decapodan
decathlon
deception
decillion
decoction
deduction
defection
deflation
deflexion
dejection
demission
dentation
dentition
depiction
depletion
desertion
detection
detention
detersion
detrition
detrusion
deviation
dictation
dietician
dietitian
diffusion
digestion
digitalin
dimension
Dionysian
direction
disburden
discommon
disseisin
diversion
divulsion
dodecagon
Dominican
dormition
doubleton
draconian
draftsman
Dravidian
duralumin
ealdorman
earthborn
education
Edwardian
effluxion
egression
eiderdown
eirenicon
elevation
elocution
emanation
emulation
encrimson
energumen
enhearten
enlighten
entertain
ephemeron
epicurean
epilation
erudition
Esthonian
estuarian
Ethiopian
euclidean
eutherian
evergreen
evocation
evolution
exception
exciseman
exclusion
excretion
excursion
execution
exemption
expansion
expiation
explosion
expulsion
exsertion
extension
extortion
extrusion
exudation
eyestrain
Falernian
familyman
fellowman
fieldsman
filiation
finedrawn
firstborn
fisherman
floridean
flotation
foliation
foodchain
forbidden
forebrain
foreknown
foreshown
foretoken
forewoman
forgotten
formation
francolin
Freemason
freewoman
Frenchman
frigatoon
frogspawn
fullblown
fullgrown
furcation
gammadion
gemmation
gentleman
gerfalcon
gestalten
gestation
glyptodon
gobetween
gooseskin
gorgonian
gradation
greasegun
greenhorn
gregarian
Gregorian
grimalkin
groomsman
grosgrain
guardsman
guncotton
gustation
guttation
gyrfalcon
habergeon
hagridden
halfcrown
Halloween
hammerman
handorgan
handsdown
hangerson
harlequin
harmattan
Harrovian
hartshorn
heartburn
Hebridean
heliozoan
Helvetian
Heraclean
Herculean
Hercynian
Hesperian
Hibernian
highflown
highgrown
Himalayan
hindbrain
historian
Hobbesian
hobgoblin
homegrown
homousian
honeymoon
horsebean
hortation
Hungarian
hydration
hydrozoan
hydrozoon
ichneumon
iguanodon
illgotten
imitation
immersion
impaction
impassion
impletion
implosion
impulsion
inanition
inbetween
incaution
inception
inclusion
incursion
indention
indiction
indigotin
IndoAryan
induction
infection
inflation
inflexion
ingestion
injection
insertion
intension
intention
intervein
intorsion
intrusion
intuition
inunction
invention
inversion
Iroquoian
irruption
isolation
iteration
jactation
Jordanian
jurywoman
Keplerian
Keynesian
kilderkin
kinswoman
knockdown
krummhorn
lacertian
lactation
lallation
Laodicean
laudation
leafgreen
leviathan
librarian
libration
lineation
liquation
litterbin
liveryman
longchain
longicorn
lovetoken
luciferin
lumberman
Maccabean
magnesian
magnetron
Mahometan
mailtrain
malathion
malleehen
mammalian
Mancunian
manhattan
Manichean
mannequin
Manxwoman
medallion
mediation
melatonin
melocoton
Mendelian
mentation
mercaptan
meropidan
metheglin
metrician
middleman
migration
Miltonian
minutegun
minuteman
misassign
misdemean
misgovern
misreckon
misshapen
modillion
molluscan
Mongolian
morrisman
mortician
mossgrown
motheaten
muffinman
muscleman
muskmelon
Mussulman
Mycenaean
myrobalan
Nahuatlan
narration
nectarean
nemertean
neologian
Neptunian
nervation
Nestorian
neuration
Newtonian
nictation
nightgown
nitration
nonillion
nonperson
Norwegian
nutrition
objection
obsession
obtention
obtrusion
obversion
obviation
occlusion
octillion
oddjobman
oestrogen
offscreen
offseason
olecranon
oleoresin
olfaction
ombudsman
onionskin
operation
Orangeman
orangutan
oratorian
Orpington
outridden
outspoken
overblown
overdrawn
overeaten
overflown
overgrown
overladen
overtaken
overtrain
ovulation
oxidation
oysterman
packtrain
palankeen
palanquin
Palladian
palmation
palpation
pantaloon
pantryman
paperthin
parathion
parhelion
partition
pastedown
patrician
patrolman
Pavlovian
Pelasgian
pellagrin
pendragon
peneplain
percheron
perdition
perfusion
persimmon
pervasion
phellogen
phonation
phthalein
physician
phytotron
pipeorgan
placation
plainsman
planarian
planation
plication
ploughman
plutonian
pointsman
policeman
pollution
porcelain
poriferan
postilion
praenomen
precisian
precision
predation
prefixion
prelusion
premotion
prenotion
preordain
prevision
princekin
privation
probation
profusion
progestin
prolation
prolusion
promotion
pronation
pronghorn
properdin
protozoan
protozoon
provision
ptarmigan
pulsation
purgation
pyramidon
pyridoxin
pyroxylin
quadruman
quarenden
quarryman
quotation
quotidian
radiation
rebellion
recension
reception
recession
reclusion
recursion
redaction
reduction
reedorgan
refashion
refection
reflation
reflexion
refreshen
rejection
remission
rendition
repletion

reptilian
repulsion
resection
retention
retortion
retrodden
reversion
revulsion
rewritten
Rhineodon
rhodopsin
Ripuarian
roughhewn
Roumanian
roundsman
rubrician
ruddleman
ruination
Sabellian
saccharin
sacristan
Sadducean
safetypin
sagegreen
sailorman
saltation
saltspoon
salvation
Samaritan
Sanhedrin
Sardinian
Sarmation
Sassanian
satiation
Saturnian
scalefern
scarfskin
schlieren
schoolman
Scotchman
scrapiron
scuncheon
scutcheon
seaurchin
secession
seclusion
secretion
sectarian
sedgewren
seduction
selachian
selection
selectman
Seljukian
semicolon
sensation
septation
serotonin
serration
seventeen
shakedown
shantyman
sharkskin
sheepskin
shorthorn
signalman
siltation
simpleton
singleton
sinuation
Sisyphean
situation
Slavonian
slopbasin
Slovakian
Slovenian
snakeskin
Solutrean
Solutrian
solvation
sooterkin
sortition
soupspoon
Southdown
sovereign
spellican
spiderman
spillikin
spleuchan
spoilsman
spokesman
sportsman
stableman
stanchion
statesman
steersman
steradian
stillborn
stinkhorn
striation
subaltern
subdeacon
sublation
subregion
subtopian
suctorian
suffragan
suffusion
sulcation
summation
suspicion
swansdown
sweetcorn
switchman
swordsman
tactician
tactitian
talkathon
tambourin
tarpaulin
Tartarean
Tartarian
Tartufian
Tasmanian
tellurian
tentation
teratogen
testation
thereupon
thirdsman
Thyestean
thyratron
timberman
tirewoman
titration
Tocharian
topiarian
touchdown
tradesman
tradition
traducian
tragedian
tribesman
trilithon
trisagion
truncheon
twiceborn
Ukrainian
ululation
unbeknown
unberufen
uncertain
unconcern
undecagon
underlain
undersign
underspin
unitarian
untrodden
unwritten
usucapion
vallation
valuation
Varangian
variation
velveteen
vendition
vermilion
vernation
vestryman
vibration
Victorian
violation
Virgilian
vitiation
Vitruvian
vulcanian
vulgarian
Wagnerian
wakerobin
washbasin
washerman
waterworn
wellknown
whereupon
wherryman
whipperin
windblown
wiredrawn
withdrawn
woodwaxen
workwoman
wormeaten
yachtsman
zoophagan
Zwinglian
andantino
antipasto
armadillo
bandolero
barricado
bastinado
beccafico
boliviano
caballero
calamanco
capriccio
carbonado
cigarillo
cipollino
contadino
contralto
crescendo
derringdo
desperado
duodecimo
embroglio
Esperanto
glissando
imbroglio
incognito
larghetto
lazaretto
libecchio
magnifico
majordomo
manifesto
muscovado
mustachio
obbligato
parleyvoo
pasticcio
pistachio
pizzicato
politburo
portfolio
portolano
punctilio
quebracho
sanbenito
sforzando
sgraffito
simpatico
sixteenmo
smackeroo
solfeggio
solferino
sopranino
sostenuto
spiritoso
strappado
telephoto
thereinto
thereunto
thitherto
whereinto
whereunto
wirephoto
zapateado
zucchetto
afterclap
bellyflop
blackdamp
blockship
boobytrap
buttercup
cadetship
cantaloup
cardsharp
cassareep
chiefship
chinstrap
chokedamp
clerkship
cockahoop
coffeecup
countship
courtship
coverslip
cystocarp
eavesdrop
eldership
filmstrip
filtertip
fingertip
foragecap
forcepump
galliwasp
goosestep
guardship
guildship
horsewhip
housekeep
intercrop
jockstrap
judgeship
lairdship
lightship
lovingcup
majorship
mayorship
microchip
mousetrap
orangetip
organstop
oversleep
overtrump
ownership
paperclip
playgroup
printshop
priorship
queenship
quickstep
redevelop
rhizocarp
rulership
saintship
sarcocarp
scrapheap
sharecrop
shellheap
shortstop
sketchmap
slaveship
spaceship
sporocarp
steamship
stinktrap
stockwhip
stonecrop
storeship
summingup
sweatshop
sweetshop
tallyshop
thaneship
transship
troopship
trumpedup
turboprop
tutorship
vibraharp
wristdrop
abandoner
abdicator
abnegator
abolisher
abrogator
absconder
abstainer
accipiter
acclaimer
acellular
acetifier
acidifier
activator
addresser
addressor
admonitor
adulterer
advocator
aerometer
Afrikaner
aggressor
alabaster
alienator
alligator
almsgiver
altimeter
amplifier
amputator
annotator
announcer
apparitor
appetiser
applauder
appraiser
articular
artificer
aspirator
assaulter
assembler
atmometer
attainder
attempter
attractor
augmenter
augmentor
auricular
avuncular
Axminster
backbiter
backwater
balladeer
bandoleer
bandolier
bannister
banqueter
bargainer
barkeeper
barometer
barracker
barrister
bartender
beachwear
bedsitter
beefeater
beekeeper
beemaster
behaviour
beleaguer
berserker
beslobber
bespatter
binocular
blastular
blockader
blunderer
blusterer
bolometer
bookmaker
boxgirder
boycotter
brigadier
Britisher
broiderer
buccaneer
bughunter
bulldozer
burnisher
butcherer
butterbur
bystander
calicular
camelhair
campchair
campfever
canesugar
canicular
cannoneer
cannonier
canvasser
capacitor
capitular
caretaker
carpenter
carrefour
carryover
catalyser
certifier
chafferer
chaingear
character
charterer
chastener
chastiser
chatterer
chauffeur
chevalier
chiseller
chorister
civiliser
clarifier
clatterer
coadjutor
coinsurer
colcothar
collector
collinear
coloniser
comforter
commander
commenter
commissar
compactor
comprador
conciliar
concocter
concoctor
condenser
conductor
conferrer
confessor
confirmer
confirmor
confiteor
conformer
connecter
connector
conqueror
conserver
consignor
consulter
consultor
contactor
container
contemner
contender
continuer
contriver
convector
converter
convincer
copartner
copolymer
cordelier
coriander
cornflour
corrector
corrupter
costumier
couturier
cremaster
cricketer
crossover
cullender
cunctator
cupbearer
curlpaper
cuticular
debaucher
decimator
declaimer
decorator
dedicator
defaulter
deflector
defroster
deinosaur
deliverer
demeanour
denouncer
depositor
depressor
depurator
derringer
describer
desolater
desolator
despoiler
destroyer
dethroner
detonator
detractor
developer
diesinker
diningcar
disappear
discarder
discerner
discolour
disfavour

disgracer
dishonour
dishwater
dismember
dispenser
disperser
disrepair
dissector
dissenter
dissuader
distemper
distiller
disturber
dittander
dogcollar
dominator
dosimeter
Doukhobor
downriver
driveller
drummajor
drysalter
dustcover
dynamiter
earthstar
Eastender
easterner
eggbeater
elastomer
embezzler
embraceor
embroider
emendator
enameller
enchanter
encounter
endeavour
energiser
Englander
engrosser
epistoler
equaliser
ergometer
escalator
escheator
estimator
estranger
eulogiser
excavator
excelsior
excerptor
exchanger
exchequer
exequatur
exhauster
exhibitor
exorciser
expediter
explainer
exploiter
expositor
expounder
extractor
eyeopener
falsifier
fashioner
fibrillar
fillister
financier
fireeater
firepower
firewater
flashover
flatterer
floscular
fluorspar
flyfisher
foreboder
foreigner
forfeiter
forgather
fortifier
forwander
forwarder
fossicker
foxhunter
freeliver
freerider
freighter
freshener
fritterer
fruiterer
fulfiller
fumigator
funicular
furbisher
furnisher
furtherer
gadgeteer
gainsayer
gannister
garreteer
garrotter
gasfitter
gasholder
gasometer
gauleiter
gazetteer
gearlever
generator
geomancer
germander
glabellar
gladiator
glandular
glossator
godfather
godmother
goingover
goldfever
gondolier
goosander
gospeller
graduator
grenadier
grossular
groveller
guarantor
gunpowder
gunrunner
hamburger
handlebar
haranguer
harbinger
harbourer
hardcover
harpooner
harvester
headliner
headwater
hereafter
hereunder
hesitator
hexameter
highchair
highflier
highflyer
highwater
hobnobber
hodometer
homemaker
homopolar
horologer
horsehair
hosteller
howsoever
humdinger
Icelander
iceskater
idealiser
illwisher
immolator
imperator
impleader
impounder
increaser
incubator
indagator
indicator
indweller
infielder
inflictor
infractor
inhalator
inheritor
inhibitor
initiator
innholder
innkeeper
innovator
inscriber
inspector
instanter
insulator
intriguer
inveigler
irregular
irrigator
isallobar
jaywalker
jetsetter
jobmaster
journeyer
justiciar
justifier
karabiner
kidnapper
kingmaker
kitchener
lampooner
landloper
landowner
Laplander
latecomer
launderer
lawnmower
Leicester
levitator
liberator
lifesaver
lightyear
Limburger
limewater
lipreader
liquefier
literator
loafsugar
locomotor
lowlander
lowloader
lunisolar
lysimeter
macerator
machmeter
magnifier
mainliner
malleolar
manipular
manometer
manslayer
maunderer
mayflower
meditator
mekometer
meltwater
memoriter
merganser
messenger
midsummer
midwinter
milkfever
milometer
minelayer
misfeasor
mishanter
missioner
mitigator
moderator
modulator
moistener
molecular
monocular
monsignor
moonraker
moraliser
mortgager
mortgagor
motivator
moviegoer
muckraker
muffineer
musketeer
mutilator
mystifier
navicular
navigator
nebuliser
neighbour
newspaper
Nilometer
nitpicker
nominator
nondriver
nonlinear
nonsmoker
notepaper
nourisher
nowhither
nuisancer
nullifier
numerator
obturator
octameter
oddjobber
offcolour
oilburner
oilcolour
opercular
oppressor
optometer
orbicular
organiser
osmometer
ossicular
outbacker
outfitter
outlander
outnumber
outrigger
outworker
overeater
overpower
oversteer
pacemaker
parameter
passenger
patroller
paymaster
peasouper
peculator
pedicular
pedometer
penciller
penholder
penpusher
pensioner
perceiver
perfector
performer
perfumier
perimeter
permitter
persuader
perverter
phalanger
philander
picnicker
pistoleer
planisher
plasterer
plunderer
poetaster
polariser
polyester
polywater
pompadour
pontoneer
pontonier
porringer
portrayer
possessor
posterior
potboiler
pothunter
poulterer
prankster
precentor
preceptor
precursor
predictor
preemptor
prelector
presbyter
presenter
preserver
pretender
preventer
privateer
processer
processor
professor
profiteer
projector
propeller
prosector
protector
protester
protestor
provender
pterosaur
publisher
puffadder
pulpiteer
puppeteer
purchaser
purloiner
pushchair
pyrolater
pyrometer
qualifier
quarender
quickener
quirister
racketeer
raconteur
radicular
rainmaker
rainwater
ransacker
ratepayer
recoverer
recruiter
rectifier
redletter
redresser
reflector
refractor
refresher
regisseur
registrar
regulator
rejoinder
remainder
renouncer
renovator
repressor
requester
reservoir
resonator
respecter
responder
reticular
retinular
retoucher
retractor
retriever
revelator
rhymester
ricepaper
ridiculer
rocketeer
rodfisher
roisterer
rosewater
ruminator
rumrunner
safflower
saltwater
sandpaper
sandpiper
satinspar
saturator
saunterer
scarifier
scatterer
scavenger
schnauzer
schnorrer
scorifier
scrambler
scratcher
screecher
scribbler
scrivener
scrounger
scrutator
scutellar
seaanchor
sealetter
seedeater
semilunar
separator
September
septemvir
sepulcher
sequester
serenader
shamateur
sharpener
shipfever
shipowner
shoemaker
shopfloor
shortener
shottower
shoveller
sightseer
signaller
silverfir
simulator
sixfooter
skindiver
skyjacker
slanderer
slaughter
slipcover
slothbear
slumberer
smatterer
sniggerer
sniveller
sobsister
sodawater
sojourner
solicitor
sommelier
sonneteer
sonometer
sophister
souteneur
souwester
specifier
spectator
speedster
spherular
sphincter
spindrier
spinnaker
splendour
spoliator
sprinkler
sputterer
squabbler
squelcher
stagedoor
staggerer
stammerer
stargazer
stationer
stauncher
staymaker
stegosaur
stiffener
stomacher
straggler
strangler
streetcar
stretcher
struggler
stupefier
stutterer
subeditor
submaster
subocular
subverter
succeeder
succentor
successor
succourer
suggester
sunbather
sundowner
sunflower
superstar
supinator
supporter
surfeiter
surrender
suspender
suspensor
sustainer
swaggerer
sweetener
tabulator
tahsildar
tanliquor
tapdancer
taximeter
telemeter
televisor
tentmaker
testifier
theoriser

thermidor aepyornis battiness ceratodus diaphysis felonious griminess
thickener aesthesis bawdiness cetaceous diastasis fenceless grossness
throttler Afrikaans beardless chainless diathesis ferocious gruffness
throwster ailanthus beastings chancrous diclinous fetidness guileless
thunderer albatross beauteous chantress didactics fibreless guiltless
thyristor alertness beefiness chariness dietetics fibrinous gumminess
tidewater aliveness beeorchis charmless digitalis fieriness gustiness
tightener alkaloses beestings Charolais dinginess filaceous gutsiness
tinopener alkalosis bejabbers cheapness dinoceras filminess hairgrass
toadeater allantois bellglass cheerless dioecious fireirons hairiness
tonometer aloneness bifarious childless dipterous fireworks halitosis
tonsillar aloofness billiards chillness dirtiness fishiness Hallowmas
tophamper aluminous biogenous chitinous dizziness fistulous hamamelis
tormentor amaryllis bionomics chitlings dogmatics fixedness handcuffs
totaliser amauroses blackness chlamydes dogshores flakiness handglass
tourneyer amaurosis blameless chlorosis dottiness flambeaus handiness
traveller ambergris blandness Christmas doubtless flameless handpress
traverser ambiguous blankness chrysalis dowdiness flamingos happiness
treasurer ambitious bleakness cinereous dowerless flavorous hardiness
trickster amianthus blindness cirrhosis downwards fleckless harmonics
tricolour amidships bloodless clamorous dragomans fleetness harquebus
trilinear amorphous bluegrass classless dragoness fleshings harshness
trimester amphioxus bluffness cleanness dramatics fleshless hastiness
trinketer ampleness bluntness clearness dreamless flocculus haverings
trisector anabioses blushless closeness drollness fluorosis hazardous
trochlear anabiosis Boanerges cloudless dumpiness flushness headdress
troweller anacruses bonhomous coattails dungarees fogginess headiness
trumpeter anacrusis bonniness cobaltous duskiness forceless heartless
twitterer analogous boondocks cockiness dustiness foundress heaviness
twosuiter anamnesis boskiness coheiress dysgenics fractious heftiness
Uitlander anandrous bossiness comedones eagerness frailness hendiadys
underwear anaptyxis boundless commandos earliness Franglais hepatitis
unicolour anchoress bounteous compasses eastwards frankness heterosis
uniplanar angriness bourgeois complexus echovirus freshness highclass
unpopular anhydrous brainless congeries economics frivolous highlands
upbraider ankylosis brakeless congruous edelweiss frontless hilarious
upholster anomalous brashness conscious egregious frontways hippocras
utricular anonymous briefless consensus electress fructuous hoariness
vaporiser anopheles briefness corduroys elevenses fruitless homewards
varnisher anschluss briskness coreopsis embarrass fugacious homotaxis
vasomotor antipodes broadness Corybants emptiness fulgurous horniness
vehicular apartness broadways corydalis encompass fulldress horseless
venerator apetalous brownness cothurnus endomixis fulminous horsiness
versifier aphereses buffaloes countless enteritis funiculus hourglass
vesicular apheresis bulginess courteous entremets funkiness houseless
vignetter aphyllous bulkiness crapulous ephemeris funniness huffiness
vocabular apishness bumpiness crassness epiclesis fussiness humanness
vocaliser apogamous bumptious craziness epidermis fustiness huskiness
voiceover apophyses burdenous creatress epigynous fuzziness hygienics
voltmeter apophysis burliness credulous epiphyses gallowses hypogeous
volumeter apparatus bushiness crestless epiphysis gambadoes hypotaxis
volunteer arbitress buxomness cretinous epistaxis garrulous hysterics
wallpaper arboreous cacoethes criminous epithesis gastritis idealless
warmonger Areopagus cageyness crispness eponymous gaudiness ignoramus
warranter argentous calculous crossness erectness gauntness imageless
warrantor arsenious callipers crossways erogenous gauziness impatiens
wassailer arteritis cancerous crownless erroneous gawkiness imperious
wattmeter arthritis Candlemas crudeness errorless geoponics impetuous
westerner arthrosis cankerous curliness espousals giddiness inaptness
whichever asbestous canniness curstness euthenics ginglymus incurious
whimperer asepalous cantharis cutaneous eventless gladiolus ineptness
whisperer askewness cantharus cyclopses exactness glaireous inertness
whosoever asparagus capacious cytolysis exercises glamorous ingenious
willpower assiduous caryopses dangerous exodermis glossitis ingenuous
windhover athletics caryopsis dauntless exogamous glueyness injurious
wingchair atrocious castanets deaconess exogenous glutinous innocuous
womaniser audacious catalexes deathless exosmosis godliness innoxious
Worcester authoress catalexis deciduous exostosis golflinks innuendos
wrongdoer autocross catalyses declivous exsuccous gomphosis inodorous
Yiddisher autolysis catalysis delicious externals goodwives insidious
youngster awareness catharses delirious fabaceous governess inverness
ablutions awfulness catharsis denseness facetious graceless invidious
abscissas backcross cattaloes depthless faddiness grandness ironsides
acariasis backwards cattiness dexterous faintness graveless ironworks
acidulous backwoods causeless diaereses faithless graveness isagogics
acoustics bagginess cavernous diaeresis falseness greatness isinglass
acropolis balminess ceanothus diagnoses fandangos Greekless isogamous
adeptness barbarous ceaseless diagnosis fattiness greenness isogenous
adultness bathybius cephalous diandrous faultless griefless isomerous

isopodous	meatiness	otherness	pulpiness	sebaceous	speckless	tenseness
isosceles	mechanics	ourselves	pulseless	secateurs	sphagnous	tepidness
issueless	melanosis	outgoings	pulverous	seditious	spiciness	terseness
itchiness	melodious	outskirts	pulvillus	seediness	spikiness	testiness
janitress	mementoes	overdress	pumiceous	selenious	spineless	thankless
jazziness	merciless	overtness	pursiness	semantics	spininess	theatrics
jerkiness	mercurous	overtones	pushiness	semiotics	spinulous	thesaurus
jointress	merriness	oviferous	pustulous	senseless	spiritous	thickness
judicious	messieurs	oviparous	pyrolysis	separates	splenitis	thingness
juiceless	messiness	oxygenous	Quakeress	sericeous	spongeous	thornless
juiciness	micaceous	palladous	quakiness	setaceous	spoutless	tightness
jumpiness	milkiness	panderess	queenless	seventies	squatness	timidness
katabasis	minacious	pantalets	queerness	shadeless	staginess	tinniness
katharsis	mirkiness	parabasis	querulous	shadiness	staidness	tipsiness
keratitis	mirthless	paralysis	quickness	shakiness	stainless	tipstaves
keratosis	mistigris	parataxis	quietness	shameless	staleness	tiredness
kinkiness	mistiness	parotitis	rabidness	shapeless	stalkless	tomentous
knotgrass	mixedness	pastiness	raininess	sharpness	stargrass	toothless
laborious	mnemonics	patroness	rancorous	sheerlegs	starkness	toreutics
landdross	moistness	pemphigus	randiness	sheerness	stateless	tortrices
lankiness	momentous	pendulous	ranginess	shiftless	steepness	torturous
lapideous	moneybags	penniless	rapacious	shininess	sternness	toughness
larcenous	mongooses	penurious	rapidness	shirtless	stiffness	tournedos
largeness	monitress	peripatus	rapturous	shoreless	stilettos	traceless
laundress	monoceros	perkiness	readdress	shortness	stillness	trackless
lazybones	monstrous	pertussis	readiness	showiness	stingless	traitress
lazytongs	moodiness	pettiness	rearwards	sideburns	stintless	tramlines
leakiness	moraceous	pettitoes	rectrices	sidedness	stoneless	trappings
leastways	mosquitos	phalanges	redivivus	siderosis	stoniness	tremulous
lecherous	motocross	phalanxes	reediness	sidewards	stoppress	trickless
leftovers	muddiness	pharynges	religious	sightless	stormless	trifocals
leftwards	mugginess	pharynxes	repossess	significs	stoutness	trigamous
legginess	mundungus	phlebitis	reprocess	siliceous	strangles	trimerous
levelness	muniments	phonemics	resources	silicious	strapless	trimmings
libellous	munitions	phonetics	retiarius	silicosis	strenuous	triteness
librettos	murderess	phoniness	retinitis	silkiness	strobilus	trochilus
lichenous	murderous	pinkiness	rhythmics	silliness	strumitis	troublous
lightless	murkiness	pithiness	riderless	simplices	stuporous	truceless
lightness	murmurous	placeless	righteous	sinewless	subereous	trustless
lignaloes	muskiness	plainness	rightness	sinusitis	sulkiness	truthless
limitless	mustiness	platinous	rigidness	skeesicks	sultaness	tubbiness
literatus	muzziness	pleadings	riskiness	skirtings	sumptuous	tufaceous
litheness	mydriasis	plenteous	rivalrous	skirtless	sunniness	tumidness
litigious	nakedness	plumbeous	roadworks	slackness	surliness	Turcomans
liturgics	narcissus	plumdamas	rockiness	slakeless	swartness	Turkomans
lividness	nastiness	plumpness	roominess	slantways	sweetness	typhlitis
loftiness	natheless	plusfours	rosaceous	sleekness	swiftness	tyrannous
logistics	nattiness	plushness	roughness	sleepless	syllepses	uliginous
longcoats	nectarous	podagrous	roundness	slickness	syllepsis	umbilicus
longevous	neediness	podginess	rowdiness	sliminess	symbiosis	unanimous
looseness	nefarious	pointless	ruddiness	slumbrous	symbolics	unaptness
lousiness	Negroness	poisonous	rustiness	smallarms	symphysis	underpass
loverless	nepenthes	pomaceous	sagacious	smallness	synectics	underseas
lowliness	nephritis	ponderous	salacious	smartness	syneresis	unfitness
lubricous	nephrosis	porticoes	saleratus	smileless	syngamous	unharness
lucidness	nerveless	posticous	salpinges	smokeless	synizesis	uniparous
luckiness	nerviness	powerless	saltiness	smokiness	synovitis	unisonous
ludicrous	newlyweds	prelatess	saltworks	snakiness	syntheses	unsuccess
lumbricus	newsiness	prestress	sandglass	snowiness	synthesis	untimeous
lumpiness	nickelous	priceless	sandiness	soapiness	tacitness	usualness
luridness	nobleness	prideless	sappiness	soapworks	tackiness	utterless
lustiness	noiseless	priestess	sargassos	soberness	taeniasis	utterness
luxurious	noisiness	primeness	sartorius	softgoods	tailoress	vagarious
lymegrass	notedness	proboscis	sassafras	sogginess	taintless	vagueness
magnetics	notorious	procuress	sauceless	solacious	talismans	validness
malanders	nucleolus	prognoses	sauciness	solidness	tarantass	valuables
malarious	nuttiness	prognosis	Sauternes	sometimes	tardiness	valueless
malicious	nystagmus	prolapsus	scaleless	sootiness	tasteless	valveless
malleolus	obeseness	prolepses	scalemoss	soppiness	tastiness	vapidness
manganous	oblivious	prolepsis	scaliness	sorceress	tattiness	variolous
manginess	obnoxious	proneness	scantness	sorcerous	tawniness	venereous
manliness	obsequies	proptosis	scentless	sorriness	tectonics	venturous
manyplies	octopodes	prosiness	schistous	soundings	tectrices	veracious
Martinmas	odourless	prothesis	scirrhous	soundless	telamones	verdigris
massiness	officious	psoriasis	scleritis	soundness	tellurous	verminous
matchless	oilpaints	psychoses	sclerosis	spaceless	temptress	verrucous
mateyness	oleaceous	psychosis	scoliosis	spareness	tenacious	vexatious
mealiness	oogenesis	pudginess	scratches	spareribs	tendinous	vicarious
meandrous	orderless	puffiness	seaminess	sparkless	tenebrous	vimineous

vinaceous
virginals
virtuosos
visitress
vivacious
vividness
vocalness
voiceless
volcanoes
voracious
vowelless
vulturous
wackiness
Waldenses
wallcress
Walpurgis
wartcress
washiness
wasteness
waterless
weariless
weariness
weediness
weirdness
werwolves
westwards
wheelless
whitebass
whiteness
wholeness
widthways
windiness
windwards
wineglass
winepress
wittiness
woodiness
wooziness
wordiness
worthless
woundless
wrathless
wrongness
youngness
zoiatrics
zoogenous
abasement
abashment
abatement
abhorrent
absorbent
abstinent
absurdist
acceptant
accordant
acidulent
adornment
adsorbent
Adventist
advertent
aerialist
aerobiont
affidavit
affirmant
aftermost
agistment
agreement
airjacket
albescent
alchemist
alignment
alinement
allegiant
allotment
alternant
amassment
amazement
amendment
amusement
analogist
anarchist
anatomist
Anglicist
animalist
annectent
annuitant
annulment
anovulant
antitrust
apartment
apologist
appellant
appendant
applicant
architect
archivist
archivolt
arrestant
arrowroot
ascendant
ascendent
assailant
assistant
assumpsit
assurgent
astronaut
atonement
attendant
autarkist
autograft
autopilot
backsight
balladist
ballpoint
bandicoot
beanfeast
bedjacket
beechmast
benignant
besetment
bethought
biblicist
bicyclist
billygoat
biologist
birdsfoot
birdsnest
birthwort
bivariant
blackcoat
Blackfeet
Blackfoot
blacklist
blastment
bloodlust
bloodroot
bloodshot
bloodwort
bluepoint
blueprint
boardfoot
bombsight
branchlet
bratwurst
brazilnut
breakfast
briarroot
brierroot
brilliant
broadcast
buckwheat
bullfight
bulltrout
bundobust
burnedout
bushcraft
butterfat
butternut
byproduct
cabbalist
cabriolet
Caesarist
Calvinist
Camembert
camorrist
campcraft
canalboat
candlenut
candytuft
canescent
careerist
cassoulet
catamount
catchment
catechist
Catharist
celebrant
chassepot
chatoyant
checklist
clarionet
classlist
clinquant
coagulant
cockfight
cocksfoot
coelostat
coffeepot
cognisant
coldshort
collagist
colourist
coltsfoot
columnist
combatant
communist
competent
complaint
compliant
component
concordat
condiment
confidant
confident
confluent
congruent
connivent
conscript
consonant
constrict
construct
continent
cooperant
copyright
cormorant
cornetist
corposant
corpulent
coruscant
cosmonaut
cotangent
covariant
crapulent
crepitant
croissant
crowsfoot
crowsnest
cruellest
culminant
cutthroat
cymbalist
damnedest
Darwinist
davenport
deadlight
debarment
declarant
decongest
decrement
decumbent
defeatist
defendant
deferment
deficient
defoliant
dehiscent
demandant
demulcent
deodorant
dependant
dependent
desiccant
detergent
determent
deterrent
detriment
devilment
diabolist
dialogist
dichromat
different
difficult
diffident
dinnerset
disaffect
discomfit
discovert
discredit
disforest
dishclout
dishonest
disinfect
disinfest
disorient
disputant
dissident
dissonant
distraint
divergent
dogmatist
dogviolet
downright
dramatist
drawsheet
dreamboat
dresscoat
dryasdust
dustsheet
ebullient
ecdysiast
ecologist
economist
ectoblast
efficient
effulgent
ejectment
elopement
embayment
embedment
emollient
emolument
enactment
encomiast
endoblast
endowment
enjoyment
enrolment
entoblast
entrechat
epilogist
epitomist
equipment
estaminet
Eucharist
exactment
examinant
excellent
exceptant
excipient
excrement
excurrent
executant
exegetist
exilement
expectant
expedient
expellent
extendant
extolment
extravert
extremist
extrovert
exuberant
eyebright
fabricant
Falangist
fantasist
feoffment
ferryboat
fetichist
fetishist
feudalist
fieldboot
fireblast
firecrest
firelight
firmament
firstfoot
flageolet
flatulent
flayflint
fleshment
flowchart
flowerpot
flowsheet
fluctuant
flyweight
footfault
footlight
footprint
forcemeat
forecourt
forefront
foresight
formalist
fortnight
frockcoat
fulgurant
fulminant
fundament
fusionist
Gaeltacht
gallivant
galvanist
gearshift
genuflect
geodesist
geologist
Germanist
Girondist
glasswort
godparent
goldcrest
goodnight
goosefoot
grandaunt
grapeshot
greataunt
greatcoat
greenbelt
groundnut
guidepost
guillemot
guitarist
haemostat
haggadist
hairshirt
halflight
Hallstatt
handcraft
hardiment
haresfoot
harmonist
hatchment
headfirst
headlight
heartbeat
heartfelt
heliostat
Hellenist
heptaglot
herbalist
hereabout
highlight
hindsight
hoarfrost
holocaust
homograft
hoofprint
horsemint
Hottentot
houseboat
housecoat
humectant
hygienist
hygrostat
hypnotist
hypoblast
hypocaust
identikit
ignescent
immigrant
impatient
impeccant
impendent
imperfect
implement
important
imprudent
incessant
incipient
inclement
incorrect
incorrupt
increment
incumbent
incurrent
indignant
indraught
indulgent
inebriant
inelegant
informant
innermost
inpatient
insistent
insolvent
insurgent
integrant
intellect
intendant
intercept
interdict
interject
interknit
interment
interpret
interrupt
intersect
intrigant
introject
introvert
inurement
invariant
inwrought
irradiant
itinerant
Jansenist
jollyboat
judgement
kickstart
kingcraft
klinostat
lamplight
landagent
landaulet
landdrost
larcenist
latescent
libellant
libellist
lightfoot
lightsout
limelight
lineament
lionheart
liturgist
liverwort
lodgement
lophodont
lousewort
lovefeast
lovelight
lowermost
lubricant
luxuriant
machinist
magnetist
mainsheet
makeshift
maladroit
malignant
mammonist
mannerist
manorseat
marchpast
marrowfat
marshwort
masochist
massagist
mechanist
medallist
meliorist
memoirist
mendicant
mentalist
merriment
mesmerist
mesoblast
meteorist
Methodist
methought
metricist
mezzotint
midwicket
milkfloat
millivolt
mincemeat
miniskirt
miscreant
misdirect
misoneist
misreport
Mithraist
mnemonist
modernist
moneywort
monkeynut
moonlight
mosaicist
motherwit
motorboat
mouthpart

mucksweat
mutualist
myologist
mythicist
nannygoat
navelwort
negligent
negotiant
neologist
neoterist
nephalist
newmarket
newsagent
newsprint
nigricant
nonprofit
northeast
northmost
northwest
notionist
nutriment
obscurant
obsequent
observant
occludent
occultist
occurrent
ochlocrat
Octobrist
officiant
offstreet
onslaught
openheart
oppugnant
orchidist
orologist
orrisroot
otologist
outermost
overdraft
overexert
overleapt
overnight
overprint
overreact
overshoot
oversight
overskirt
overslept
overspent
paederast
palpitant
panchayat
panellist
pantheist
paramount
parchment
parrakeet
paypacket
pearlwort
peepsight
penetrant
pennywort
Pentecost
pepperpot
periplast
permanent
pertinent
pessimist
pestilent
petaurist
petticoat
phonetist
physicist
placement
Platonist
pluralist
plutocrat
Plutonist

polevault
pollutant
postulant
pourpoint
powerboat
precedent
predicant
predigest
predikant
prepotent
prescient
prescript
preselect
president
preterist
pretermit
prevalent
princelet
procreant
profilist
prominent
proponent
prosodist
provident
pubescent
publicist
pussyfoot
queenpost
quiescent
quillwort
quodlibet
rabbinist
racialist
radiocast
ravelment
rearlight
recipient
recollect
reconvert
recordist
recumbent
recurrent
redbreast
reductant
redundant
reefpoint
reentrant
refitment
reformist
refulgent
regardant
reluctant
remitment
remittent
remontant
renascent
repayment
repellant
repellent
repentant
represent
repugnant
reservist
resilient
resistant
resolvent
resorbent
restraint
resultant
resurgent
resurrect
retardant
rethought
retroject
retrovert
revetment
rhythmist
ritualist
riverboat

rockplant
Roquefort
roughcast
rousement
routinist
rufescent
rushlight
sacrament
sandblast
sandspout
sandyacht
sauceboat
scapegoat
scenarist
scholiast
scientist
screwbolt
seasquirt
secernent
seedplant
selfdoubt
selftrust
semisweet
senescent
sentiment
septuplet
serialist
sextuplet
shamanist
shamefast
Shintoist
shopfront
shouldest
shovelhat
sidelight
simulcast
skinflint
skingraft
skintight
skyrocket
sleevenut
slingshot
snakeroot
snowdrift
snowplant
sobriquet
socialist
soidisant
solipsist
somnolent
soothfast
sopranist
Sorbonist
soundpost
southeast
southmost
southwest
spaceport
spacesuit
spadefoot
spagyrist
spearmint
spearwort
speedboat
spindrift
spinneret
Spinozist
spiritist
splayfoot
splendent
spoonmeat
sporocyst
spotlight
springlet
squirelet
stairfoot
stakeboat
Stalinist
stardrift

starlight
statement
statocyst
steadfast
steamboat
sternmost
sternpost
stillhunt
stimulant
stirabout
stockinet
stocklist
stonechat
stonewort
stoplight
stormbelt
strapwort
streamlet
strewment
stringent
subjacent
subscript
subtenant
succulent
sugarbeet
sulphuret
summarist
sunbonnet
sunhelmet
superheat
suppliant
surmullet
susurrant
swarajist
sweetmeat
swimmeret
swordknot
sycophant
symbolist
synergist
synoptist
taillight
Talmudist
Targumist
tattooist
tenebrist
terebrant
termagant
terminist
terrorist
tervalent
testament
Teutonist
therapist
theurgist
thighboot
timelimit
timesheet
timpanist
tittlebat
tonguelet
toothwort
topiarist
tracksuit
transient
transport
transumpt
transvest
treatment
trebuchet
trebucket
tremolant
tremulant
trenchant
trepidant
trigamist
tritheist
trivalent
truculent

tuliproot
tumescent
tunnelnet
turbulent
turnabout
tympanist
undercoat
underfelt
underfoot
undermost
underpart
underplot
undershot
undertint
undervest
underwent
ungallant
unisonant
univalent
unthought
unwrought
uppermost
uttermost
vacillant
Vedantist
ventiduct
ventifact
verbalist
videlicet
viewpoint
violinist
virescent
visionist
volauvent
voodooist
vorticist
vulcanist
waistbelt
waistcoat
walkabout
wallfruit
warbonnet
washedout
waterbutt
watercart
wavefront
weeknight
wehrmacht
whaleboat
whitebait
whodunnit
windchest
windswept
winevault
witchhunt
woodcraft
worriment
worrywart
woundwort
wristshot
wyliecoat
xenograft
zeitgeist
zoologist
zootomist
bordereau
gaspereau
impromptu
trousseau
leitmotiv
afterglow
barleymow
bedfellow
bowwindow
commonlaw
corkscrew
deathblow
downthrow
eyeshadow

grubscrew
interflow
interview
jackstraw
oakenshaw
oddfellow
overthrew
overthrow
peachblow
rareeshow
saddlebow
scarecrow
scoredraw
scrimshaw
scrollsaw
decomplex
directrix
Esquimaux
executrix
flambeaux
gogglebox
heterodox
letterbox
mediatrix
multiplex
pepperbox
pillarbox
pouncebox
promptbox
prothorax
retroflex
sentrybox
signalbox
strongbox
testatrix
tinderbox
windowbox
aberrancy
abidingly
abnormity
absurdity
abusively
abysmally
accessary
accessory
acclivity
accompany
actuality
adamantly
adiposity
adjacency
adjunctly
adjutancy
admirably
admiralty
adoringly
adulatory
adversary
adversely
adversity
advisably
advisedly
aeriality
aerometry
aetiology
agreeably
agriology
aimlessly
airworthy
airyfairy
allegedly
allopathy
allotropy
allowably
allowedly
amazingly
ambiguity
amorality
amorously

amphigory
amusingly
anciently
ancientry
ancillary
androgyny
angiology
angularly
animality
animosity
annularly
anonymity
antennary
anthology
antipathy
antiphony
antiquary
antiquity
anxiously
appetency
aqueously
arbitrary
archduchy
archenemy
arcuately
arduously
argybargy
armillary
artillery
artlessly
asexually
ashamedly
asininity
assiduity
assumably
assuredly
astrology
astronomy
asymmetry
atomicity
atonality
atonicity
audiology
austerely
austerity
authority
autocracy
auxiliary
availably
averagely
avoidably
awesomely
awkwardly
Aylesbury
Babbittry
bacillary
balefully
baneberry
banefully
baptistry
barbarity
barometry
baronetcy
bashfully
basically
bastardly
battlecry
beamingly
bearberry
belatedly
bemusedly
benignity
bestially
biliously
bimonthly
biography
bivalency
bizarrely
blaeberry

blameably
blasphemy
blatantly
blazingly
bleachery
blessedly
blotchily
blueberry
bolometry
bombhappy
bookishly
boorishly
breakaway
breathily
breezeway
bridleway
brigandry
brittlely
brotherly
brusquely
brutality
brutishly
budgetary
bulbously
bullishly
buoyantly
burningly
butcherly
butterfly
buttinsky
cacophony
caddisfly
caliology
callosity
callously
candidacy
capillary
capitally
captaincy
captivity
carefully
carnality
carpentry
carpingly
carpology
cartology
cartulary
cassowary
casuistry
catalepsy
cataplexy
causality
celebrity
centenary
centrally
certainly
certainty
chairlady
champerty
chandlery
chantilly
chemistry
chicanery
chiropody
chorology
circuitry
citizenly
citizenry
civically
clamantly
clemently
coaxially
coaxingly
cockneyfy
cocoonery
coequally
coercibly
cognately
coherency
colonelcy
colophony
colostomy
coltishly
columbary
comically
commodity
community
compactly
complexly
comradely
comradery
concavely
concavity
concisely
condignly
congruity
conically
connately
constancy
contrasty
contumacy
contumely
convexity
copiously
coprology
cordially
cornerboy
corollary
correctly
corruptly
cosmogeny
cosmogony
cosmology
costively
covalency
coxcombry
crabbedly
cranberry
credulity
crematory
crookedly
crotchety
crowberry
crucially
cryoscopy
cubically
cuckoldry
cunningly
curiosity
curiously
currently
currishly
cursively
cursorily
customary
cynically
cystotomy
damnatory
damningly
dashingly
dastardly
deacidify
decadency
decalcify
decennary
decidedly
decimally
declivity
decretory
deerberry
defiantly
definably
deformity
democracy
demystify
denitrify
dentistry
denyingly
depravity
desirably
desultory
deviously
devitrify
devotedly
dexterity
dextrally
diachrony
diathermy
dichogamy
dichotomy
diffusely
digitally
dignitary
dilatancy
dimissory
diplomacy
directory
direfully
discovery
disembody
disparity
distantly
dittology
diurnally
diversely
diversify
diversity
doggishly
dolefully
doltishly
donnishly
dormitory
dosimetry
doughtily
dragonfly
dromedary
drunkenly
dubiosity
dubiously
ductility
duodenary
duplicity
duteously
dutifully
dysentery
dystrophy
earnestly
easefully
edibility
electrify
electuary
elegantly
elusively
embracery
emergency
eminently
emotively
emotivity
emulously
emunctory
endlessly
endophagy
endoscopy
endurably
enjoyably
entelechy
enviously
epigraphy
equitably
eruditely
esemplasy
esuriency
eternally
ethically
ethnarchy
ethnicity
ethnology
etymology
euchology
eurhythmy
evasively
everybody
evidently
evocatory
excitancy
excitedly
excretory
excusably
execrably
executory
exemplary
exemplify
expiatory
expletory
expressly
extensity
extremely
extremity
exultancy
factually
facundity
fallalery
fantastry
fatefully
fatuously
fawningly
fearfully
febricity
fecundity
federally
feelingly
femineity
fertilely
fertility
fervently
festively
festivity
festology
feudality
feudatory
fiduciary
finically
fissility
fittingly
fivepenny
flagrancy
flamingly
flannelly
flaringly
flightily
flippancy
floridity
floristry
flowingly
foolhardy
foolishly
foppishly
forecaddy
forlornly
formality
formicary
formulary
forwardly
fourpenny
fragility
fragrancy
franticly
freezedry
frenchify
frequency
fretfully
frigidity
frivolity
frontally
frowardly
frugality
fulgently
fulsomely
furiously
furtively
gainfully
gallantly
gallantry
gallingly
garrulity
gemmology
genealogy
generally
geniality
genteelly
gentility
genuinely
geobotany
geography
germanely
gestatory
gibbosity
gibbously
gimmickry
girlishly
glacially
glaringly
gleefully
glengarry
globosity
glowingly
goldsinny
gorblimey
gossamery
gracility
gradatory
gradually
grandaddy
gravidity
grouchily
groundivy
guardedly
gushingly
gustatory
gynocracy
habitably
hackberry
haggardly
hagiarchy
hagiology
halfhardy
halfpenny
haltingly
haplessly
haplology
harmfully
hatefully
haughtily
healthily
heathenry
heavyduty
hedgingly
heedfully
heinously
helically
hellishly
helpfully
heptarchy
hesitancy
hideously
hierarchy
hierology
hillbilly
hircosity
hispidity
histogeny
histology
hoggishly
homophony
homoplasy
hopefully
horoscopy
horseplay
hortatory
hostilely
hostility
huckstery
hugeously
hunkydory
hurriedly
hurtfully
husbandly
husbandry
hybridity
hydrology
hymnology
hypergamy
hypnology
hypocrisy
hyponasty
ichnology
iconology
idiopathy
illegally
illegibly
illicitly
imaginary
immanency
immediacy
immensely
immensity
imminency
immodesty
immorally
immovably
immutably
impiously
impliedly
impotency
improbity
impulsory
inability
inaudibly
incapably
incensory
incurably
indecency
indelibly
indemnify
indemnity
indignity
inebriety
ineffably
inerrancy
inexactly
infirmary
infirmity
ingenuity
inharmony
inhumanly
initially
innocency
innocuity
insatiety
insectary
insipidly
insolubly
instantly
insularly
integrity
intensely
intensify
intensity
intercity
interplay
intestacy
intricacy
inutility
invalidly
inventory
inversely
inviolacy
invisibly
irascibly
irksomely
irreality
irritably
itineracy
itinerary
itsybitsy
ittybitty
janissary
jarringly
jealously
jeeringly
jewellery
jocularly
jocundity
joviality
joylessly
judiciary
Juneberry
juniority
kiddingly
knavishly
knowingly
laggardly
lambently
languidly
lastingly
laterally
latitancy
latterday
laudatory
laughably
lawlessly
learnedly
leeringly
leewardly
legendary
legionary
leisurely
lengthily
leniently
lethality
leucotomy
lexically
liability
liberally
libratory
liltingly
limitedly
limnology
limpidity
lineality
linearity
lingually
liquidity
lispingly
lissomely
literally
lithology
lithotomy
lobectomy
logically
logomachy
longevity
longingly
loquacity
louringly
loutishly
lovestory
lubricity
lumpishly
lustfully
lyrically
machinery
magically

magistery
makeready
malignity
mamillary
mammalogy
mandatary
mandatory
mansionry
maritally
marketday
marquetry
marshalcy
martially
massively
masterkey
maternity
matrimony
mawkishly
maxillary
maximally
mayoralty
meaningly
mediately
mediatory
medically
medullary
meliority
meltingly
memorably
mendacity
mendicity
mentality
mercenary
mesentery
metrology
micrology
microtomy
midwifery
migratory
militancy
millenary
millinery
mincingly
mindfully
minimally
misemploy
miserably
mobocracy
mockingly
modernity
momentary
monastery
mongrelly
monocracy
monolatry
monophagy
morbidity
mordacity
mordantly
mortality
mundanely
musically
mutuality
mycophagy
myography
mystagogy
mythology
narratory
naseberry
naturally
naughtily
necessary
necessity
necrology
needfully
nephology
nervously
neurology
neutrally
niggardly
ninepenny
nobiliary
nocuously
noisomely
nominally
nomocracy
nonentity
normality
northerly
nostology
notoriety
noxiously
objectify
obliquely
obliquity
obscenely
obscenity
obscurely
obscurity
obstinacy
obversely
obviously
occupancy
odontalgy
odorously
oenomancy
oenophily
offertory
okeydokey
olfactory
oligarchy
oligopoly
ominously
onerously
operosely
operosity
ophiology
opponency
opsimathy
optically
optometry
opulently
orography
orthodoxy
oscitancy
osteogeny
osteology
outwardly
ovenready
overweary
oviparity
ovulatory
pageantry
painfully
painterly
palatably
palillogy
pallidity
palmistry
pantingly
papillary
parcenary
parlously
parquetry
parsimony
partially
passersby
passively
passivity
patchouly
paternity
pathogeny
pathology
patiently
patrimony
patrology
peaceably
peasantry
peccantly
pecuniary
pederasty
peevishly
pellitory
pendently
pensively
pentarchy
perfectly
perfumery
periphery
personify
pestology
petrology
pettishly
petulancy
phenology
philately
philogyny
philology
phonatory
phonology
photocopy
phycology
phylogeny
phytogeny
phytology
phytotomy
piggishly
pinnately
piquantly
piscatory
piteously
pitifully
pituitary
pityingly
pivotally
placatory
placidity
planetary
plangency
plausibly
playfully
plenarily
plicately
ploughboy
plurality
poignancy
pointduty
pointedly
pokeberry
polyandry
polymathy
polyonymy
polyphagy
polyphony
polyzoary
pomposity
pompously
popularly
postentry
posterity
pratingly
preachify
preachily
precatory
precisely
precocity
predacity
predatory
prefatory
pregnancy
prelusory
preoccupy
presently
primality
primarily
privately
probatory
procerity
procuracy
profanely
profanity
profusely
prolately
prolixity
prolusory
propriety
proveably
provisory
provostry
proximity
prudently
prudishly
pruriency
publicity
puerility
pugnacity
pulmonary
pulsatory
pungently
pupillary
purgatory
purposely
purringly
purulency
pushingly
putridity
pyrolatry
pyromancy
pyrometry
quadruply
quarterly
radialply
radiantly
radiately
radically
radiology
raffishly
rakehelly
rampantly
rancidity
rantingly
rascality
raspatory
raspberry
raspingly
raucously
raunchily
recreancy
recusancy
refectory
regularly
relevancy
reliantly
reliquary
renitency
repertory
reputably
reputedly
residency
residuary
restfully
restively
reticency
reversely
rhinology
ringingly
riotously
roguishly
roseately
rotundity
roundelay
routinely
ruffianly
ruinously
rusticity
ruthfully
saleslady
saliently
saltatory
salubrity
sanctuary
sapiently
savourily
scapulary
scatology
schmaltzy
scholarly
schoolboy
sciamachy
sciascopy
scraggily
scrappily
scrimpily
scruffily
searingly
seaworthy
secondary
secretary
secretory
sectility
secularly
sedentary
seemingly
seigneury
seigniory
selfglory
selfishly
semblably
seminally
semiology
seniority
sensually
sentiency
separably
septenary
septicity
sequacity
sergeancy
seriality
seriately
seriously
serjeancy
serjeanty
serpentry
servilely
servility
seventhly
severally
severalty
sexlessly
sexuality
shadberry
shallowly
shipmoney
shrubbery
sibilancy
sickishly
sigillary
signatory
similarly
sincerely
sincerity
sinlessly
sinuately
sinuosity
sinuously
sketchily
skiamachy
skiascopy
skilfully
slaphappy
slategrey
slavishly
slenderly
sluiceway
smilingly
snowberry
soapberry
sobbingly
sociality
sociology
soldierly
solemnity
soliloquy
songfully
sophistry
sottishly
soulfully
southerly
sparingly
spatially
speakeasy
specially
specialty
speechify
spinosity
spirality
splashily
splintery
spluttery
sporogeny
sprightly
springily
squalidly
squashily
squeakily
squinancy
stability
stableboy
stagnancy
stagparty
stampduty
starchily
statutory
staunchly
stenotypy
sterility
stiltedly
stitchery
stoically
stolidity
strangely
streakily
stridency
studiedly
stupidity
stylishly
suability
suasively
subagency
subduedly
subfamily
sublimely
sublimity
sublunary
summarily
sumptuary
supremacy
supremely
surgeoncy
suturally
swinishly
swordplay
syllabary
symbology
synchrony
tabularly
tactfully
tactility
tactually
tartishly
tautology
taxidermy
teachably
tearfully
teasingly
tediously
tegularly
teknonymy
telemetry
teleology
telepathy
telephony
telescopy
tellingly
temporary
tensility
tenuously
termitary
ternately
territory
testimony
tetralogy
tetrapody
tetrarchy
textually
theocracy
theocrasy
theomachy
theophany
theosophy
thermally
thingummy
thirstily
thriftily
throatily
throughly
throwaway
tigerlily
timeously
timocracy
titularly
tolerably
tonically
topically
torpidity
torridity
toxically
toxophily
traceably
tracheary
tractably
treachery
tribology
tributary
tricksily
trinketry
triploidy
trivially
triweekly
tropology
truepenny
tubularly
tunefully
turbidity
turgently
turgidity
twelfthly
twitchily
typically
unanimity
uncannily
uncivilly
uncleanly
uncouthly
underbody
underclay
underplay
unearthly
unequally
unfleshly
unhappily
unhealthy

uniformly
unitively
unluckily
unreality
unsavoury
unsightly
unsoundly
unthrifty
unusually
unwomanly
upcountry
uprightly
uranology
uselessly
vacuously
vainglory
valiantly
variously
vasectomy
veeringly
vegetably
venerably
veniality
ventrally
verbosely
verbosity
verdantly
veritably
vexillary
viability
vibratory
viciously
villagery
villosity
violently
virginity
virtually
virulency
viscidity
viscosity
viscounty
viscously
visionary
vitellary
vitiosity
voluntary
vorticity
vulgarity
vulnerary
waggishly
wailingly
wakefully
warblefly
warningly
waspishly
waterlily
waywardly
wealthily
weatherly
Wednesday
weightily
willingly
wineberry
winningly
winsomely
wishfully
wistfully
witchetty
witlessly
wittingly
wolfishly
workmanly
worriedly
xerophily
yawningly
yesterday
zamindary
zealously
zemindary
zestfully
zoography
zootechny
gigahertz
kilohertz
megahertz
slivovitz

10 letter words

aardwolves
abacterial
abbreviate
abdication
abdominous
abducentes
aberdevine
aberrantly
aberration
abhorrence
abiogenist
abjectness
abjuration
ablebodied
abnegation
abnormally
abominable
abominably
abominator
aboriginal
abortively
aboveboard
Abrahamman
abrasively
abreaction
abridgment
abrogation
abruptness
abscission
absolutely
absolution
absolutism
absolutist
absolutory
absorbable
absorbance
absorbedly
absorbency
absorption
absorptive
abstemious
abstention
abstergent
abstersion
abstersive
abstinence
abstinency
abstracted
abstracter
abstractly
abstractor
abstrusely
abstrusity
absurdness
abundantly
academical
acarpelous
acatalepsy
accelerate
accentuate
acceptable
acceptably
acceptance
acceptedly
accessible
accessibly
accidental
accomplice
accomplish
accordance
accoucheur
accountant
accounting
accredited
accrescent
accumulate
accurately
accursedly
accusation
accusative
accusatory
accusingly
accustomed
acephalous
acervation
acetabular
acetabulum
achievable
achondrite
achromatic
acidimeter
acidimetry
acidophile
acoelomate
acotyledon
acoustical
acquirable
acquitting
acrobatics
acrogenous
acromegaly
acronychal
acrophobia
acroterion
acroterium
actinolite
actinozoan
actionable
actionably
activation
activeness
adamantine
adaptation
adaptively
additional
addlepated
adenectomy
adequately
adherently
adhesively
adhibition
adjacently
adjectival
adjudgment
adjudicate
adjunction
adjunctive
adjuration
adjuratory
adjustable
adjustment
administer
admiration
admiringly
admissible
admittable
admittance
admittedly
admonition
admonitive
admonitory
adolescent
adoptively
adrenaline
adrenergic
adroitness
adsorbable
adsorption
adsorptive
Adullamite
adulterant
adulterate
adulteress
adulterine
adulterous
adventurer
advertence
advertency
advertiser
advisement
advocation
advocatory
aeolotropy
aerenchyma
aerobatics
aerobiosis
aerobiotic
aeroengine
aerogramme
aerography
aerologist
aeronautic
aeronomist
aerophobia
aerostatic
aeruginous
aesthetics
aesthetism
Aethiopian
aetiologic
affability
affectedly
affectless
affeerment
afferently
affettuoso
affiliated
affirmable
affliction
afflictive
affluently
affordable
aficionado
Africander
Africanise
Africanism
Africanist
Afrikander
afterbirth
aftergrass
afterimage
afterlight
afterpains
aftershave
aftertaste
afterwards
agapanthus
agglutinin
aggrandise
aggression
aggressive
agitatedly
agrologist
agronomist
aircooling
aircushion
airmanship
alarmingly
Albigenses
albuminoid
albuminous
alchemical
alcoholise
alcoholism
alcyonaria
aldermanic
aldermanry
alexanders
algebraist
algolagnia
algolagnic
algologist
Algonquian
alienation
alightment
alimentary
alkalinity
allegation
allegiance
allegorise
allegorist
allegretto
allergenic
alleviator
alliaceous
alliterate
allocation
allocution
allogamous
allopathic
allophonic
allosteric
allotropic
alloverish
allpurpose
allrounder
allurement
allusively
almacanter
almondeyed
almsgiving
almucanter
alongshore
alpenstock
alphabetic
alphameric
altarpiece
altazimuth
alteration
alterative
alternance
alternator
altocumuli
altogether
altostrati
altruistic
amalgamate
amanuenses
amanuensis
amateurish
amateurism
ambassador
ambidexter
ambivalent
ambulacral
ambulacrum
ambulation
ambulatory
ambushment
ameliorate
amendatory
amercement
amerciable
Amerindian
amiability
ammoniacal
ammoniated
ammunition
amoebocyte
ampelopsis
amphibious
amphibrach
amphictyon
amphigouri
amphimacer
amphimixes
amphimixis
amphoteric
amputation
amygdaloid
amylaceous
anabaptism
anabaptist
anacolutha
anadromous
anaglyphic
anagogical
analogical
analphabet
analysable
analytical
anamorphic
anapaestic
anaplastic
anaptyctic
anarchical
anastigmat
anastomose
anastrophe
anatomical
anatropous
ancestress
anchoretic
anchoritic
anchorless
anchorring
anchylosis
anchylotic
ancipitous
Andalusian
andalusite
androecium
androgenic
anecdotage
anecdotist
anemograph
anemometer
anemometry
anemophily
aneurismal
aneurysmal
angiosperm
Anglistics
anglomania
anglophile
anglophobe
anglophone
AngloSaxon
angularity
angwantibo

animadvert
animalcula
animalcule
animatedly
anisotropy
annalistic
annexation
annihilate
annotation
annoyingly
annularity
annulation
annunciate
anointment
anonaceous
anopheline
answerable
answerably
antagonise
antagonism
antagonist
antebellum
antecedent
antecessor
antechapel
antemortem
antependia
antepenult
anteriorly
antheridia
anthracene
anthracite
anthracoid
anthropoid
antibiosis
antibiotic
Antichrist
anticipant
anticipate
anticlimax
anticlinal
antifreeze
antiheroic
antimasque
antimatter
antimonial
antimonite
antinomian
antipathic
antiphonal
antipodean
antiproton
antiquated
antiSemite
antisepsis
antiseptic
antisocial
antistatic
antitheism
antitheist
antitheses
antithesis
antithetic
antonymous
aphaereses
aphaeresis
aphoristic
aphrodisia
apiculture
aplacental
apocalypse
apocarpous
apochromat
apocryphal
apodeictic
apolaustic
apolitical
Apollinian
Apollonian
apologetic
apophthegm
apoplectic
aposematic
apostatise
apostolate
apostrophe
apothecary
apothecial
apothecium
apotheoses
apotheosis
apotropaic
apparelled
apparently
apparition
appealable
appearance
appeasable
appendices
appendixes
apperceive
appetising
appetitive
applicable
applicably
applicator
appointive
appositely
apposition
appositive
appreciate
apprentice
approvable
approvably
aquafortis
aquamarine
aquaplaner
aquiferous
aquilinity
aragonitic
araucarian
arbalester
arbalister
arbitrable
arbitrager
arbitrator
arboreally
arborvitae
archaistic
archbishop
archdeacon
archerfish
archetypal
architrave
archpriest
arenaceous
areolation
Areopagite
argumentum
aristocrat
arithmetic
Armageddon
armigerous
armorially
armourclad
armourless
arrestment
arrhythmia
arrhythmic
arrogantly
arrogation
arterially
arteriolar
artfulness
arthralgia
arthralgic
arthromere
articulate
artificial
artycrafty
arytaenoid
asafoetida
asbestosis
ascariasis
ascendable
ascendance
ascendancy
ascendence
ascendency
ascendible
asceticism
ascomycete
ascribable
ascription
asexuality
Ashkenazim
asparagine
aspergilla
asphyxiant
asphyxiate
aspidistra
aspiration
assafetida
assailable
assaultive
assemblage
assentient
assessable
assessment
asseverate
assibilate
assignable
assignment
assimilate
assistance
associable
assoilment
assortment
assumption
assumptive
asteriated
asteroidal
astigmatic
astragalus
astringent
astrologer
astrologic
astronomer
astronomic
astuteness
asymmetric
asymptotic
asynchrony
ateleiosis
Athanasian
atmosphere
atomically
attachable
attachment
attackable
attainable
attainment
attendance
attenuated
attenuator
attornment
attractant
attraction
attractive
attunement
atypically
auctioneer
audibility
audiometer
audiometry
audiophile
auditorial
auditorium
augustness
auriculate
auriferous
auscultate
auspicious
austenitic
Australian
autarkical
autecology
authorship
autochthon
autocratic
autodidact
autoerotic
autogamous
autogenous
autography
autoimmune
autologous
automation
automatise
automatism
automatist
automobile
automotive
autonomist
autonomous
autoplasty
autostrada
autostrade
autumnally
avantgarde
avaricious
aventurine
averseness
aversively
aviatrices
aviculture
avouchment
axiologist
azeotropic
babblement
babiroussa
Babylonian
babysitter
bacchantes
bacchantic
backbiting
backblocks
backgammon
background
backhanded
backhander
backsheesh
backslider
backstairs
backstitch
backstroke
backwardly
badderlock
bafflement
bafflingly
balbriggan
balderdash
baldheaded
ballflower
ballistics
ballooning
balloonist
balneology
balustrade
banderilla
bandmaster
banishment
bankruptcy
baptistery
barbellate
barbershop
barbituric
barcarolle
bardolatry
barebacked
barefooted
bareheaded
barelegged
bargeboard
barkentine
barleybree
barleybroo
barleycorn
Barmecidal
barometric
baronetage
barracouta
barramunda
barramundi
barratrous
barrelling
barrenness
barrenwort
barysphere
basketball
basketwork
bassethorn
bassoonist
bastardise
batfowling
batholitic
bathometer
bathymeter
bathymetry
bathyscaph
bathyscope
batrachian
battailous
battledore
battlement
battleship
bawdyhouse
beadleship
Beaujolais
beautician
beautifier
becomingly
bedchamber
bedclothes
bedevilled
Bedlington
bedraggled
beechdrops
beefburger
beekeeping
beforehand
beforetime
behindhand
bejewelled
Belgravian
believable
belladonna
belletrist
bellflower
bellringer
bellwether
bellyacher
bellydance
bellylaugh
belongings
bemedalled
bemusement
benedicite
Benedictus
benefactor
beneficent
beneficial
benevolent
benignancy
Benthamism
Benthamite
benzocaine
benzpyrene
bequeathal
beribboned
Berkeleian
besprinkle
bestialise
bestiality
bestirring
bestowment
bestridden
bestseller
betterment
bewitchery
biannually
biblically
bibliology
bibliopegy
bibliophil
bibliopole
bibliopoly
bibliotics
bibulously
bichromate
bicultural
bidonville
biennially
bigamously
bighearted
bigmouthed
bijouterie
bilgewater
biliverdin
billetdoux
billposter
bilocation
bimestrial
bimetallic
binaurally
binoculars
biochemist
biodegrade
biodynamic
bioecology
biogenesis
biogenetic
biographer
biographic
biological
biometrics
biomorphic
biophysics
bioscience
biparietal
bipartisan
bipetalous
bipolarity
birdspider
birdstrike
birthplace
birthright
birthstone
bisexually
bissextile
bisulphate
bisulphide
bisulphite
bitchiness
bitterling
bitterness
bitterroot
bitterwood
bituminise
bituminous
bivalvular
bivouacked
bizarrerie
blackamoor

blackberry
blackboard
blackfaced
blackguard
blackheart
Blackshirt
blacksmith
blackthorn
blackwater
bladdernut
blamefully
blancmange
blanketing
blanquette
blasphemer
blastemata
blastocyst
blastoderm
blastomere
blastopore
blazonment
bleachable
bleariness
blearyeyed
bleatingly
blepharism
blindingly
blissfully
blistering
blitheness
blithering
blithesome
blitzkrieg
blockboard
blockhouse
blockishly
bloodguilt
bloodhound
bloodiness
bloodmoney
bloodstain
bloodstock
bloodstone
blottesque
bluebonnet
bluebottle
bluecollar
bluejacket
bluepencil
blueribbon
bluethroat
bluetongue
bluishness
blurringly
blushingly
blusterous
boastfully
bobbinlace
bobbysocks
bobbysoxer
boisterous
bollweevil
bolometric
bolshevise
bolshevism
bolshevist
bombardier
bondholder
boneheaded
bonesetter
boneshaker
bookbinder
bookkeeper
bookmaking
bookmarker
bookseller
boondoggle
bootlegger
bootlessly
bootlicker
bootstraps
borborygmi
bordereaux
borderland
borderless
borderline
Boswellian
Boswellise
Boswellism
bothersome
botryoidal
bottlefeed
bottleneck
bottletree
bottomless
bottommost
bouncingly
bourbonism
bourbonist
bowdlerise
bowdlerism
boyishness
brachiator
brachiopod
brachylogy
brachyural
brachyuran
bradyseism
Brahmanism
Brahminism
brainchild
braininess
brainpower
brainstorm
brakeblock
brakelight
branchiate
brandyball
brandysnap
brantgoose
brassiness
bratticing
brawniness
brazenness
brazilwood
breadboard
breadcrumb
breadfruit
breadstick
breadstuff
breakables
breakpoint
breakwater
breastbone
breastwall
breastwork
breathable
breathless
breechless
breezeless
breeziness
brentgoose
bressummer
brevetting
brickfield
bricklayer
bridegroom
bridesmaid
bridgeable
bridgehead
bridgeless
bridgework
bridlepath
brigandage
brigandine
brigandism
brigantine
brightness
brightwork
brilliance
brilliancy
Britishism
broadcloth
broadsheet
broadsword
brocatelle
brokendown
brokenness
bromegrass
bronchiole
bronchitic
bronchitis
broodiness
broodingly
broomstick
browbeaten
brownshirt
brownstone
brusquerie
bryologist
bubblyjock
buccinator
Buchmanism
Buchmanite
bucketshop
Buddhistic
budgerigar
bufflehead
buffoonery
bullethead
bullheaded
bullroarer
bumblingly
bumpkinish
bunchgrass
bunglingly
burdensome
bureaucrat
burglarise
burramundi
bursarship
bushmaster
bushranger
bustlingly
butterball
butterbean
butterfish
buttermilk
butterwort
buttonball
buttonbush
buttondown
buttonhole
buttonhook
buttonless
buttonwood
byelection
byssaceous
byssinosis
cabalistic
cacciatore
cachinnate
cackhanded
cacodaemon
cacogenics
cacography
cacomistle
cadaverous
caddisworm
Caerphilly
caespitose
cajolement
cajolingly
calamander
calamitous
calcareous
calceolate
calciferol
calcsinter
calculable
calculably
calculator
Caledonian
calibrator
caliginous
callowness
calumniate
calumnious
calyciform
calyptrate
camelopard
camerlengo
camerlingo
camouflage
campaigner
campestral
camphorate
canaliculi
cancellate
cancelling
cancellous
candelabra
candescent
candidness
candlefish
candletree
candlewick
candlewood
candyfloss
cankerworm
cannelloni
cannonball
canonicals
canonicate
canonicity
canorously
cantaloupe
cantatrice
canterbury
cantilever
cantillate
cantonment
canvasback
canvaswork
canzonetta
caoutchouc
capability
capacitate
capacitive
capitalise
capitalism
capitalist
capitation
Capitoline
capitulary
capitulate
cappuccino
capricious
captiously
carabineer
carabinier
caramelise
caravaneer
caravanned
caravanner
carbonnade
carboxylic
carbuncled
carcinogen
carcinosis
cardialgia
cardiogram
cardiology
cardplayer
carelessly
caricature
carmagnole
carnallite
carnassial
carotenoid
carotinoid
carpellary
carpetweed
carphology
carragheen
carryingon
Carthusian
cartomancy
cartoonist
cartwright
caruncular
caryatides
cascarilla
caseharden
caseworker
cassolette
castration
casualness
catabolism
catafalque
catalectic
cataleptic
cataloguer
cataphract
catarrhine
catastasis
catburglar
catchpenny
catechesis
catechetic
catechiser
catechumen
categorise
catenation
catholicon
catholicos
catoptrics
cattlegrid
causticity
cautionary
cautiously
cavalierly
cavalryman
cavitation
celebrated
celebrator
cellophane
cellularly
cellulitis
cellulosic
censorious
censorship
censurable
centennial
centesimal
centigrade
centilitre
centillion
centimetre
centralise
centralism
centralist
centrality
centreback
centrefold
centrehalf
centricity
centrifuge
centromere
centrosome
cephalopod
cerebellum
ceremonial
cerography
certiorari
ceruminous
cessionary
chainsmoke
chairwoman
chalcedony
chalkboard
chalkstone
challenger
chalybeate
chamaeleon
chamberpot
champignon
chancellor
chandelier
changeable
changeably
changeless
changeling
changeover
channelise
channelled
chaparajos
chaparejos
chapfallen
chaplaincy
charactery
chargeable
chargehand
charioteer
charismata
charitable
charitably
Charleston
charmingly
chartreuse
chartulary
chasteness
chatelaine
chatoyance
chatterbox
chattiness
chaudfroid
chauffeuse
chauntress
chauvinism
chauvinist
cheapishly
cheapskate
checkpoint
cheekiness
cheerfully
cheeriness
cheesecake
cheesiness
chelicerae
chemically
chemisette
chemotaxis
chequebook
chersonese
chessboard
chevrotain
chickenpox
chiffchaff
chiffonier
childbirth
childermas
childishly
childproof
chiliastic
chilliness
chimerical
chimneypot
chimpanzee
chinagraph
chinchilla
chiromancy
chiselling
chivalrous

chlorinate
chloroform
choiceness
chokeberry
chondritic
choriambic
Christhood
Christlike
chromatics
chromatype
chromosome
chronicity
chronicler
chronogram
chronology
chrysolite
chrysotile
chubbiness
chuckerout
chuckwagon
churchgoer
churchyard
churlishly
cicatrices
Ciceronian
cicisbeism
cinchonine
Cinderella
cinecamera
cinerarium
cinquefoil
Circassian
circuitous
circularly
circulator
circumcise
circumflex
circumfuse
circumvent
cismontane
cispontine
Cistercian
citronella
clamminess
clangorous
clannishly
clarabella
Clarenceux
claspknife
classicise
classicism
classicist
classified
classifier
clavichord
clavicular
clawhammer
clearstory
clementine
clerestory
clerically
cleverness
clientship
clingstone
clinically
clinkstone
clinometer
clinometry
clodhopper
cloistered
closestool
closetplay
clothesbag
clothespeg
clothespin
cloudberry
cloudburst
cloudiness
clovehitch
cloverleaf
clownishly
clubfooted
clumsiness
Clydesdale
cnidoblast
coacervate
coachbuilt
coachhouse
coadjacent
coagulable
coalbunker
coalescent
coaptation
coarseness
coastguard
coastwards
coathanger
coatimundi
cochleated
cockalorum
cockatrice
cockchafer
cockneyish
cockneyism
cocksurely
codswallop
coelacanth
coenobitic
coenobytic
coequality
coercively
coetaneous
coeternity
coexistent
coffeemill
cogitation
cogitative
cognisable
cognisably
cognisance
cognominal
cohabitant
coherently
cohesively
coincident
colatitude
colchicine
coleoptera
coleoptile
coleorhiza
collarbeam
collarbone
collarette
collarless
collarstud
collatable
collateral
collection
collective
collegiate
collembola
collimator
collocutor
colloquial
colloquise
colloquist
colloquium
colonially
colonnaded
coloration
coloratura
colossally
colourable
colourably
colourfast
colourless
colportage
colporteur
columbaria
comanchero
combustion
combustive
comedienne
comehither
comeliness
comestible
comicality
comicopera
commandant
commandeer
commandery
commanding
commandoes
commentary
commentate
commercial
commissary
commission
commissure
commitment
committing
commixture
commodious
commonable
commonalty
commonness
commonroom
commonweal
communally
communique
commutable
commutator
compaction
comparable
comparably
comparator
comparison
compassion
compasssaw
compatible
compatibly
compatriot
compelling
compendium
compensate
competence
competency
competitor
complacent
complainer
complected
complement
completely
completion
completive
complexion
complexity
compliance
compliancy
complicacy
complicate
complicity
compliment
complotted
composedly
compositor
compotator
compounder
compradore
comprehend
compressed
compressor
compromise
compulsion
compulsive
compulsory
computable
computator
comstocker
concentric
conception
conceptive
conceptual
concerning
concertina
concertino
concession
concessive
concettism
conchoidal
conchology
conciliary
conciliate
concinnity
conclusion
conclusive
conclusory
concoction
concoctive
concordant
concretely
concretion
concretise
concretism
concretist
concurrent
concurring
concussion
concussive
condensate
condensery
condescend
condolence
conduction
conductive
confabbing
confection
conference
conferment
conferring
confervoid
confession
confidante
confidence
confirmand
confiscate
conflation
confluence
conformism
conformist
conformity
confounded
confusedly
congeneric
congenital
congestion
congestive
conglobate
congregant
congregate
congruence
congruency
coniferous
conjecture
conjointly
conjugally
connatural
connection
connective
conniption
connivance
conscience
consecrate
consectary
consensual
consequent
considered
consistent
consistory
consociate
consolable
consonance
consonancy
consortium
conspectus
conspiracy
conspirant
constantan
Constantia
constantly
constipate
constitute
constraint
constringe
consuetude
consulship
consultant
consulting
consultive
consumable
consumedly
consummate
contagious
contendent
contention
contestant
contextual
contexture
contiguity
contiguous
continence
contingent
continuant
continuate
continuity
continuous
contortion
contortive
contraband
contrabass
contractor
contradict
contraprop
contrarily
contravene
contribute
contritely
contrition
controlled
controller
controvert
convalesce
convection
convective
convenable
convenance
convenient
convention
conventual
convergent
conversant
conversely
conversion
conveyable
conveyance
conviction
convictive
convincing
convoluted
convulsant
convulsion
convulsive
coolheaded
coolingoff
cooperator
cooptation
cooptative
coordinate
coparcener
copartnery
Copernican
copesettic
copperhead
coproducer
coprolitic
copulation
copulative
copyholder
copyreader
copywriter
coquettish
coradicate
coralberry
coralsnake
corbelling
corbiculae
cordiality
cordierite
cordillera
cordwainer
corelation
corelative
coriaceous
Corinthian
corncockle
cornerwise
cornettist
cornflakes
cornflower
cornstarch
cornucopia
coromandel
coronation
corporally
corporator
corporeity
corpulence
corpulency
corpuscule
correction
corrective
correspond
corrigenda
corrigible
corrivalry
corroboree
corrugated
corrugator
corruption
corruptive
corsetiere
corticated
Corybantes
corybantic
coryphaeus
cosentient
cosmically
cosmogonic
cosmopolis
cosmoramic
costliness
cottoncake
cottonseed
cottontail
cottonweed
cottonwood
cottonwool
couchgrass
coulometry
councillor
councilman
counselled
counsellor
counteract

countryish
countryman
couplement
courageous
courthouse
cousinhood
cousinship
couturiere
couverture
covalently
covariance
covenanted
covenantee
covenanter
covenantor
covetingly
covetously
cowcatcher
coweringly
cowparsley
cowpuncher
crackajack
crackbrain
cradlesong
craftguild
craftiness
cragginess
cranesbill
craniology
crankiness
crankshaft
crapulence
craquelure
crassitude
cravenness
creaminess
creatinine
creatively
creativity
creaturely
credential
creditable
creditably
creepiness
crematoria
crenellate
crenulated
crepuscule
crescentic
cretaceous
crewelwork
cribriform
criminally
crinolette
crippledom
crispation
crispbread
crisscross
critically
crocoisite
crossbench
crossbones
crossbreed
crosscheck
crossgrain
crosshatch
crossindex
crosslight
crosspatch
crosspiece
crossrefer
crossroads
crosstrees
crowkeeper
crustacean
crustation
crustiness
cryogenics
cryoscopic
cryptogamy
cryptogram
cryptology
ctenophore
cuckoopint
cuckoospit
cucullated
cuddlesome
cudgelling
cuirassier
cultivable
cultivator
culturally
cumbersome
cumbrously
cummerbund
cumulation
cumulative
cumuliform
cunctation
cunctative
curability
curatorial
curmudgeon
curricular
curriculum
cursedness
curvaceous
curvacious
curvetting
cuspidated
cussedness
custommade
cuttlebone
cuttlefish
cuttystool
cybernetic
cyclically
cyclograph
cyclometer
cyclopedia
cyclopedic
cyclostome
cyclostyle
cylindered
cylindroid
cystoscope
cystoscopy
cytochrome
cytologist
czarevitch
daintiness
daisychain
damageable
damagingly
dampcourse
dampingoff
dapplegrey
datamation
daughterly
dauphiness
daydreamer
dazzlement
dazzlingly
deaconship
deactivate
deadliness
deadweight
deaeration
deathwatch
debasement
debatement
debauchery
debilitate
debonairly
debouchure
decadently
decagramme
decahedral
decahedron
decampment
decapitate
decapodous
deceivable
decelerate
Decembrist
decemviral
deceptible
decigramme
decimalise
decimalism
decimation
decisively
decivilise
declarable
declassify
declension
declinable
decolonise
decolorant
decolorise
decompound
decompress
decoration
decorative
decorously
decrescent
dedication
dedicative
dedicatory
deductible
deepfreeze
deepfrozen
deeprooted
deepseated
deerforest
deescalate
defacement
defalcator
defamation
defamatory
defeasance
defeasible
defeminise
defendable
defensible
defensibly
deferrable
deficiency
defilement
definement
definienda
definitely
definition
definitive
definitude
deflagrate
deflection
deflective
deflowerer
defoliator
deforciant
defrayable
defrayment
degeneracy
degenerate
degradable
degradedly
degressive
dehiscence
dehumanise
dehumidify
dejectedly
delaminate
delectable
delectably
delegation
deliberate
delicately
delightful
delimitate
delineator
delinquent
deliquesce
delocalise
delphinium
delphinoid
deltiology
delusional
delusively
demagogism
demandable
dementedly
demobilise
democratic
demography
demoiselle
demolition
demonetise
demoniacal
demonology
demoralise
demotivate
demureness
demurrable
denaturant
dendriform
dendrology
denegation
denigrator
denominate
denotation
denotative
denouement
densimeter
dentifrice
denudation
denunciate
deodoriser
deontology
deoxidiser
department
dependable
dependably
dependence
dependency
depilation
depilatory
deplorable
deplorably
deployment
depolarise
depopulate
deportment
depositary
deposition
depository
depravedly
depreciate
depredator
depressant
depression
depressive
deprivable
depuration
depurative
deputation
deracinate
derailleur
derailment
derestrict
deridingly
derisively
derivation
derivative
dermatitis
dermatogen
derogation
derogatory
desalinate
descendant
descendent
descension
descriptor
desecrater
desecrator
deservedly
deshabille
desiccator
desiderata
desiderate
designator
designedly
designment
desipience
desirously
desistance
desolately
desolation
desorption
despatcher
desperados
despicable
despicably
despisable
despiteful
despiteous
despondent
desquamate
destructor
detachable
detachedly
detachment
detainment
detectable
detergency
determined
deterrence
detestable
detestably
detonation
detonative
detoxicant
detoxicate
detraction
detractive
Devanagari
devilishly
devitalise
devocalise
devolution
devotement
devotional
devoutness
dextrality
dextrously
diabolical
diachronic
diagnostic
diagonally
diagraphic
dialysable
diapedesis
diapedetic
diaphanous
diarrhoeal
diarrhoeic
diastemata
diathermal
diathermic
diatropism
dichroitic
dichromate
dickcissel
Dickensian
dictatress
dictionary
didactical
didgeridoo
diecasting
dielectric
diesinking
difference
difficulty
diffidence
diffusible
digestible
digitalise
digitately
digitation
digitiform
digression
digressive
dilapidate
dilatation
dilatorily
dilemmatic
dilettante
dilettanti
diligently
dillydally
diluteness
diminished
diminuendo
diminution
diminutive
dimorphism
dimorphous
diningroom
dinnerless
diphtheria
diphtheric
diphyletic
diphyodont
diplodocus
diplomatic
dipsomania
directness
directoire
directress
disability
disappoint
disapprove
disarrange
disastrous
disbarring
disbelieve
disbudding
disburthen
discerning
discharger
discipline
disclaimer
disclosure
discobolus
discomfort
discommend
discommode
discompose
disconcert
disconfirm
disconnect
discontent
discophile
discordant
discounter
discourage
discourser
discoverer
discreetly
discrepant
discretely
discretion
discursive
discussant

discussion
discussive
discutient
disdainful
diseconomy
disembogue
disembosom
disembowel
disembroil
disenchant
disengaged
disenthral
disentitle
disentwine
disenviron
disfeature
disfurnish
disgruntle
disgustful
dishabille
disharmony
dishearten
dishonesty
dishwasher
disincline
disinherit
disjointed
dislikable
disloyally
disloyalty
dismalness
dismission
dismissive
disordered
disorderly
disownment
disparager
disparates
dispassion
dispatcher
dispelling
dispensary
dispersant
dispersion
dispersive
dispersoid
dispirited
dispiteous
disposable
dispossess
dispraiser
disputable
disputably
disqualify
disquieten
disquietly
disrespect
disruption
disruptive
dissatisfy
dissection
dissembler
dissension
dissertate
disservice
dissidence
dissilient
dissimilar
dissipated
dissociate
dissoluble
dissolvent
dissonance
dissonancy
dissuasion
dissuasive
distensile
distension
distention
distichous
distilland
distillate
distillery
distilling
distinctly
distortion
distracted
distrainer
distrainor
distraught
distressed
distribute
distringas
disulphate
disulphide
disutility
disyllabic
disyllable
ditriglyph
divagation
divaricate
divebomber
divergence
divergency
divestment
divination
divinatory
divineness
divisional
divisively
divulgence
doctorship
documental
doggedness
dogmatical
dogmatiser
dogstongue
dolomitise
dolorously
dominantly
domination
dominative
donkeywork
donnybrook
doorkeeper
dorsigrade
dosimetric
doublebass
doubleness
doublepark
doubletalk
doubletime
doubtfully
doubtingly
doughfaced
dovecolour
downfallen
downstairs
downstream
downstroke
downwardly
doxography
draconites
drafthorse
dragonhead
dragonnade
dragontree
dramatical
dramaturge
dramaturgy
drawbridge
drawingpin
drawlingly
drawstring
dreadfully
dreaminess
dreamworld
dreariness
dressiness
dressmaker
drivelling
driverless
droopingly
drophammer
drosophila
drowsihead
drowsiness
drudgingly
drupaceous
drysaltery
dubitation
dubitative
dumbledore
dumbstruck
dumbwaiter
dumfounder
dunderhead
dungbeetle
duniwassal
duodecimal
duodenitis
duplicator
durability
dustjacket
duumvirate
dwarfishly
dynamistic
dysenteric
dysgraphia
dysplastic
dysprosium
dystrophic
earthbound
earthiness
earthlight
earthquake
earthshine
earthwards
eartrumpet
earwigging
earwitness
easterling
Eastertide
ebullience
ebulliency
ebullition
ecchymosis
ecchymotic
ecclesiast
echinoderm
ecological
economical
economiser
ectodermal
ectodermic
ectogenous
ecumenical
eczematous
edentulous
edibleness
editorship
edulcorate
effaceable
effacement
effectuate
effeminacy
effeminate
effervesce
effeteness
efficacity
efficiency
effloresce
effortless
effrontery
effulgence
effusively
egocentric
egoistical
Egyptology
eigenvalue
eighteenmo
eighteenth
eisteddfod
elaborator
elasticise
elasticity
elatedness
elderberry
elecampane
electively
electorate
electrical
electronic
elementary
Eleusinian
elevenplus
eliminable
eliminator
elliptical
elongation
eloquently
elucidator
elutriator
emaciation
emancipate
emancipist
emarginate
emasculate
embalmment
embankment
embarkment
emblazoner
emblazonry
emblematic
emblements
embodiment
embolismic
embonpoint
embossment
embouchure
embowelled
embroidery
embryogeny
embryology
embryonate
emendation
emendatory
emeryboard
emerypaper
emerywheel
emigration
emigratory
emissivity
Emmentaler
emollition
empanelled
emparadise
empathetic
emphractic
empiricism
empiricist
employable
employment
emulsifier
enamelling
enamellist
enantiosis
encampment
encasement
encashment
encephalic
encephalon
enchanting
encourager
encroacher
encyclical
encystment
endearment
endemicity
endocrinal
endodermal
endodermis
endogamous
endogenous
endophytic
endopodite
endorsable
endoscopic
endosmosis
endosmotic
endothelia
endproduct
endstopped
enduringly
energetics
enervation
enervative
enfacement
engagement
engagingly
engineroom
Englishman
englutting
engrossing
engulfment
enharmonic
enigmatise
enigmatist
enjambment
enjoinment
enlacement
enlistment
enmeshment
enormously
enregister
enrichment
enrigiment
ensanguine
entailment
enterolith
enterotomy
enterprise
enthralled
enthusiasm
enthusiast
enticement
enticingly
entireness
entombment
entomology
entrancing
entrapment
enumerable
enumerator
enunciable
enunciator
enwrapping
enzymology
eosinophil
epeirogeny
epentheses
epenthesis
epenthetic
epexegeses
epexegesis
epexegetic
ephemerous
ephorality
epiblastic
epicentral
epicycloid
epideictic
epidemical
epidermoid
epigastric
epigenesis
epigenetic
epiglottal
epiglottic
epiglottis
epigrapher
epigraphic
epilimnion
epiphytism
episcopacy
episcopate
episematic
episodical
episternum
epistolary
epistrophe
epithelial
epithelium
equability
equanimity
equational
equatorial
equestrian
equilibria
equipotent
equitation
equivalent
equivocate
eradicable
eradicator
erectility
eremitical
erethismic
ergodicity
ergonomics
ergonomist
ergosterol
ericaceous
erotically
erotogenic
erotomania
erubescent
eructation
eruptively
erysipelas
escadrille
escalation
escallonia
escapement
escapology
escarpment
escharotic
escheatage
escritoire
Esculapian
escutcheon
espadrille
especially
essayistic
estimation
estimative
eternalise
eternalist
ethereally
ethicality
ethnically
ethnologic
ethologist
etiolation
eucalyptol
eucalyptus
eucaryotic
eudemonism
eudemonist
eudiometer
eudiometry
eugenicist
euhemerise
euhemerism

euhemerist
eulogistic
euphonious
euphuistic
eurhythmic
Eurodollar
Eurovision
eurypterid
euthanasia
evacuation
evacuative
evaluation
evaluative
evanescent
evangelise
evangelism
evangelist
evaporable
evaporator
evenhanded
eventually
everglades
everliving
everyplace
everything
everywhere
evidential
evilminded
eviscerate
evolvement
exactitude
exaggerate
exaltation
examinable
exasperate
excavation
excellence
excellency
excerption
excitation
excitative
excitatory
excitement
excitingly
excogitate
excrescent
excruciate
excusatory
execration
execrative
execratory
executable
exegetical
exenterate
exhalation
exhaustion
exhaustive
exhibition
exhibitory
exhilarant
exhilarate
exhumation
exobiology
exorbitant
exospheric
exoterical
exothermal
exothermic
exotically
expandable
expansible
expatriate
expectance
expectancy
expectedly
expedience
expediency
expedition
expendable
experience
experiment
expertness
expiration
expiratory
explicable
explicitly
exploitage
exploitive
exportable
exposition
expositive
expository
expressage
expression
expressive
expressway
exprobrate
expunction
expurgator
exsanguine
extemporal
extendedly
extendible
extensible
extenuator
exteriorly
externally
extinction
extinctive
extinguish
extirpator
extractant
extraction
extractive
extramural
extraneity
extraneous
extricable
exuberance
exulcerate
exultantly
exultation
exultingly
exurbanite
exuviation
eyeglasses
eyeservice
eyewitness
fabricator
fabulously
faceharden
facesaving
facileness
facilitate
factiously
factitious
factorship
factualism
factualist
factuality
fadelessly
Fahrenheit
faintheart
fairground
fairhaired
fairleader
fairminded
fairspoken
fairycycle
faithfully
fallacious
fallingoff
fallowness
familiarly
famishment
famousness
fanaticise
fanaticism
fancifully
fandangoes
fantastico
fantoccini
farcically
farfetched
farsighted
fasciation
fascicular
fasciculus
fascinator
fastidious
fastigiate
fatalistic
fatherhood
fatherland
fatherless
fatherlike
fathership
fathomable
fathomless
fatiguable
faultiness
favourable
favourably
fearlessly
fearnought
fearsomely
featherbed
feathering
febrifugal
fecklessly
federalise
federalism
federalist
federation
federative
feebleness
felicitate
felicitous
fellmonger
fellowship
felspathic
femaleness
feminality
femininely
femininity
fenestella
fenestrate
fertiliser
fervidness
fescennine
festoonery
fetchingly
fetterlock
feuilleton
feverishly
fianchetto
fibreboard
fibreglass
fibrillary
fibrillate
fibrillose
fibrinogen
fibrositis
fickleness
fictioneer
fictionist
fictitious
fiddleback
fiddlehead
fiddlewood
fiducially
fieldglass
fieldmouse
fieldpiece
fieldstone
fiendishly
fierceness
fiftyfifty
figuration
figurative
figurehead
filariasis
filibuster
filterable
filthiness
filtration
fimbriated
fingerbowl
fingerless
fingerling
fingermark
fingernail
fingerpost
finicality
finiteness
FinnoUgric
fireblight
fireescape
firepolicy
fireraiser
firescreen
firstclass
firstnight
fishcarver
fisherfolk
fishkettle
fishmonger
fisticuffs
fitfulness
fivefinger
fixedpoint
flabbiness
flabellate
flaccidity
flagellant
flagellate
flagitious
flagrantly
flagwaving
flamboyant
flameproof
flamingoes
flannelled
flapdoodle
flashboard
flashflood
flashiness
flashlight
flashpoint
flatfooted
flattering
flatulence
flatulency
flavescent
flavourful
flavouring
flawlessly
fleabitten
fleacircus
fleamarket
fledgeling
fleeringly
fleetingly
fleshiness
fleshwound
flexuously
flightdeck
flightless
flightpath
flimsiness
flintiness
flippantly
flirtation
floatation
floatboard
floatingly
floatplane
floatstone
flocculate
flocculent
floodlight
floodwater
floorboard
floorcloth
floppiness
florentine
florescent
floriation
floribunda
floridness
florilegia
floristics
flosculous
flowergirl
flowerless
fluffiness
flugelhorn
flunkeydom
flunkeyism
fluoridate
fluorinate
fluorotype
fluviatile
fluxionary
flycatcher
flyfishing
flyswatter
foamflower
foetidness
foliaceous
folklorist
folkmemory
folksiness
folksinger
follicular
fontanelle
footballer
footbridge
footcandle
footlights
footwarmer
foraminous
forbidding
forcefully
forcipated
foreboding
forecaster
forecastle
forecourse
forefather
forefinger
foregather
foreground
forehanded
foreignism
foreordain
forerunner
foreshadow
foresheets
foreteller
forfeiture
forgetting
forgivable
forgivably
formatting
formidable
formidably
formlessly
fornicator
fortepiano
forthright
fortissimi
fortissimo
fortuitism
fortuitist
fortuitous
fortyniner
forwarding
forwearied
fosterling
foudroyant
foundation
founderous
fourchette
fourfooted
fourhanded
Fourierism
fourinhand
fourleaved
fourposter
foursquare
fourstroke
fourteener
fourteenth
fowlplague
foxhunting
fractional
fragmental
fragrantly
framboesia
franchiser
Franciscan
Francophil
frangipane
frangipani
fraternise
fraternity
fratricide
fraudulent
fraxinella
freakiness
freakishly
freebooter
freedwoman
freehanded
freeholder
freelancer
freeliving
freeloader
freemartin
freesoiler
freespeech
freespoken
freightage
Frenchness
frenziedly
frequenter
frequently
freshwater
friability
fricandeau
fricasseed
frictional
friendless
friendlily
friendship
frigidness
frigorific
frilliness
fringeless
friskiness
fritillary
frivolling
frizziness
froghopper
frolicking
frolicsome
frontbench
frontwards
frostiness
frothiness
frowningly
fruitarian
fruitfully

frutescent
fuddyduddy
fugitively
fulfilling
fulfilment
fuliginous
fullbodied
fullbottom
fulllength
fumblingly
fumigation
functional
funereally
fungicidal
funnelling
furuncular
fusibility
fussbudget
fustanella
futureless
futuristic
futurology
fuzzywuzzy
gadolinite
gadolinium
gadrooning
gaillardia
gaingiving
galimatias
galleywest
galliambic
galloglass
Gallomania
Gallophile
Gallophobe
galvaniser
gambolling
gamekeeper
gametangia
ganglionic
gangrenous
gargantuan
garishness
garnierite
garnishing
gasconader
gaslighter
gaspereaux
gasteropod
gastrology
gastronome
gastronomy
gatekeeper
gatelegged
gaucheness
gaultheria
gauntleted
gelatinise
gelatinous
gemination
gemmaceous
generalise
generalist
generality
generation
generative
generatrix
generosity
generously
geneticist
genialness
geniculate
genteelism
gentilesse
gentlefolk
gentleness
geocentric
geochemist
geodetical
geognostic
geographer
geographic
geological
geometrise
geophysics
geoponical
geothermal
geothermic
geotropism
geriatrics
geriatrist
germicidal
germinally
gerundival
gesundheit
ghastfully
Ghibelline
Gilbertian
gingerbeer
gingersnap
gingivitis
girlfriend
glaciation
glaciology
gladhander
gladsomely
Glagolitic
glancingly
glasscloth
glassfibre
glasshouse
glassiness
glasspaper
glassworks
Glaswegian
glauberite
glauconite
glimmering
globularly
glomerular
glomerulus
gloominess
gloriously
glossarial
glossarist
glossiness
glossology
glottology
glumaceous
gluttonise
gluttonous
glycolyses
glycolysis
glycosuria
glycosuric
gnosticism
goalkeeper
goaltender
goatsbeard
goatsucker
gobemouche
gobstopper
Godfearing
goggleeyed
goldbeater
golddigger
goldenness
goldenseal
goldilocks
golfcourse
goloptious
goluptious
goniometer
goniometry
goodliness
goodlooker
goodygoody
gooseberry
gooseflesh
goosegrass
gorgeously
Gorgonzola
gormandise
gothically
governable
governance
governessy
government
gracefully
graciosity
graciously
gradualism
gradualist
graduation
gramicidin
gramineous
grammarian
gramophone
granadilla
grandchild
granddaddy
grandducal
grandmamma
grandniece
grandstand
granduncle
grangerise
grangerism
granophyre
granularly
granulator
granulitic
grapefruit
grapesugar
graphemics
graphitise
graphology
graptolite
graspingly
grasscloth
grassroots
grasssnake
gratefully
gratifying
gratuitous
gravestone
gravimeter
gravimetry
greasewood
greasiness
greatniece
greatuncle
GrecoRoman
greediness
greedyguts
greencloth
greenfinch
greenheart
greenhouse
greenshank
greenstick
greenstone
greenstuff
greensward
gregarious
grenadilla
gressorial
greyheaded
grievously
grindingly
grindstone
grisliness
grittiness
groceteria
grogginess
groundbait
groundless
groundling
groundmass
groundplan
groundrent
groundsman
groundwork
grovelling
growlingly
grubbiness
grudgingly
gruesomely
grumpiness
guardhouse
guesthouse
guestnight
guilefully
guillotine
guiltiness
gunfighter
gunrunning
gunslinger
gutturally
gymnastics
gymnosophy
gymnosperm
gynandrous
gynocratic
gypsophila
gyrational
gyrocopter
gyroscopic
habiliment
habilitate
habitation
habitually
hackbuteer
hackmatack
haematosis
haematuria
haemolysis
haemolytic
hagiolatry
hagiologic
hagioscope
hairraiser
hairspring
hairstreak
hairstroke
hakenkreuz
halberdier
halfcocked
halfdollar
halflength
halfnelson
halfvolley
halfwitted
halfyearly
halieutics
hallelujah
halogenate
halogenous
halophytic
hammerbeam
hammerhead
hammerless
hammerlock
hammerpond
hamshackle
handbarrow
handedness
handgallop
handicraft
handmaiden
handpicked
handselled
handsomely
handspring
handworked
hangglider
hankypanky
Hanoverian
Hansardise
hanselling
harassment
harbourage
hardbilled
hardbitten
hardboiled
hardfisted
hardhanded
hardheaded
harelipped
harmlessly
harmonical
harmonious
harmoniser
hartebeest
haruspices
harvestman
hauntingly
haustellum
haustorium
hawserlaid
headcheese
headhunter
headmaster
headphones
headspring
headsquare
headstream
headstrong
headwaiter
heartblock
heartblood
heartbreak
heartiness
heartsease
heartthrob
heartwhole
heathendom
heathenise
heathenish
heathenism
heatstroke
heavenborn
heavensent
heavenward
heavyarmed
hebdomadal
hebetation
Hebraistic
hectically
hectograph
hectolitre
hectometre
hedonistic
heedlessly
heliacally
helianthus
Heliconian
helicopter
heliograph
heliolater
heliolatry
heliometer
heliophyte
helioscope
heliotaxis
heliotrope
heliotropy
hellbender
helminthic
helplessly
hemicyclic
hemihedral
hemihedron
hemiplegia
hemiplegic
hemipteran
hemisphere
hempnettle
henceforth
hendecagon
henharrier
henhearted
henotheism
henotheist
heortology
heparinise
hepatology
heptachord
heptagonal
Heptameron
heptameter
heptarchic
Heptateuch
heptatonic
herbaceous
hereabouts
hereditary
heresiarch
hereticate
heretofore
hermetical
hermitcrab
heroically
heroicness
heroicomic
herrenvolk
Herrnhuter
hesitantly
hesitation
hesitative
heterodont
heterodoxy
heterodyne
heterogamy
heterogeny
heterogony
heterology
heteronomy
heterotaxy
heulandite
heuristics
hexahedral
hexahedron
hexamerous
hexametric
hibernacle
hierarchal
hierarchic
hierocracy
hieroglyph
hierograph
hierolatry
hierophant
highbinder
highflying
highhanded
highjacker
highlander
highminded
highoctane
highstrung
highwayman
Hindustani
hinterland
hippocampi
Hippocrene
hippodrome
hippogriff
hippogryph
hippomanes
hippophagy
hipsterism
hirudinean
histologic

histolysis
histolytic
historical
histrionic
hitchhiker
hithermost
hitherward
hoarseness
hobbyhorse
hobnobbing
hocuspocus
hodgepodge
hoitytoity
hokeypokey
holloweyed
hollowness
hollowware
holography
holohedral
holophrase
holophytic
holosteric
holusbolus
homebrewed
homecoming
homeliness
homemaking
homeopathy
homiletics
homocercal
homoeopath
homogamous
homogenise
homogenous
homologate
homologise
homologous
homonymous
homoousian
homophonic
homosexual
homozygote
homozygous
homunculus
honeyeater
honeyguide
honeysweet
honorarium
honourable
honourably
honourless
hookedness
hootenanny
hopelessly
horizontal
hormonally
hornblende
hornedness
hornrimmed
horologist
horoscopic
horrendous
horridness
horsecloth
horsecoper
horseflesh
horselaugh
horseleech
horsepower
horseshoer
horsewoman
hospitable
hospitably
hostelling
hotblooded
hotchpotch
hourcircle
houseagent
housebound
housecraft
houseguest
houselling
houseplant
houseproud
housetrain
housewives
hoverplane
hovertrain
hucklebone
hullabaloo
humaneness
humanistic
humanities
humbleness
humbuggery
humbugging
humidifier
humoresque
humoristic
humorously
humourless
humoursome
humpbacked
hungriness
hurdygurdy
hurlyburly
husbandage
husbandman
hyaloplasm
hybridiser
hydraulics
hydrically
hydrologic
hydrolysis
hydrolytic
hydromancy
hydrometer
hydrometry
hydropathy
hydrophane
hydrophily
hydrophone
hydrophyte
hydroplane
hydroscope
hydrotaxis
hygrograph
hygrometer
hygrometry
hygrophyte
hygroscope
hylotheism
hypabyssal
hypaethral
hypanthium
hyperaemia
hyperaemic
hyperbaric
hyperbaton
hyperbolae
hyperbolas
hyperbolic
hyperdulia
hypergolic
hypersonic
hyphenated
hypnagogic
hypnotiser
hypocorism
hypodermal
hypodermic
hypodermis
hypogynous
hypolimnia
hypophyses
hypophysis
hypostasis
hypostatic
hypotactic
hypotenuse
hypotheses
hypothesis
hypsometer
hypsometry
hysteresis
hysteretic
hysterical
iatrogenic
icebreaker
ichthyosis
iconoclasm
iconolater
iconolatry
iconomachy
iconometer
iconometry
iconoscope
idealistic
ideational
ideography
ideologist
idiopathic
idolatress
idolatrous
ignobility
ignorantly
ilangilang
illadvised
illatively
illaudable
illaudably
illegalise
illegality
illiteracy
illiterate
illnatured
illstarred
illuminant
illuminate
illuminati
illuminism
illuminist
illusional
illusively
illusorily
illustrate
imaginable
imaginably
imbecilely
imbecility
imbibition
immaculacy
immaculate
immaterial
immaturely
immaturity
immemorial
imminently
immiscible
immiscibly
immobilise
immobility
immoderacy
immoderate
immodestly
immolation
immoralist
immorality
immortally
immortelle
immoveable
immunology
immurement
impairment
impalement
impalpable
impalpably
impanation
impanelled
imparadise
impartible
impartment
impassable
impassably
impassible
impassibly
impatience
impeccable
impeccably
impeccancy
impediment
impendence
impendency
impenitent
imperative
imperially
imperilled
impersonal
impervious
impishness
implacable
implacably
implicitly
impolitely
importable
importance
importuner
imposingly
imposition
impossible
impossibly
imposthume
impotently
impoverish
impregnant
impregnate
impresario
impression
impressive
imprimatur
imprinting
improbable
improbably
improperly
improvable
improvably
improviser
imprudence
impudently
impudicity
impugnable
impugnment
impuissant
impureness
imputation
imputative
inaccuracy
inaccurate
inactivate
inactively
inactivity
inadequacy
inadequate
inappetent
inapposite
inaptitude
inartistic
inaugurate
inbreeding
incandesce
incantator
incapacity
incasement
incautious
incendiary
incessancy
incestuous
inchoately
inchoation
inchoative
incidental
incinerate
incipience
incipiency
incisively
incitation
incitement
incivility
inclemency
inclinable
includible
incogitant
incoherent
incomplete
inconstant
incrassate
incredible
incredibly
increscent
incubation
incubative
incubatory
inculcator
inculpable
incumbency
incunabula
incurrable
indagation
indecently
indecision
indecisive
indecorous
indefinite
indelicacy
indelicate
indexation
indication
indicative
indicatory
indictable
indictment
indigenous
indigested
indirectly
indiscreet
indiscrete
indisposed
indistinct
inditement
individual
indocility
indolently
Indonesian
inducement
inductance
indulgence
induration
indurative
industrial
ineducable
inefficacy
inelegance
ineligible
ineligibly
ineloquent
ineludible
ineptitude
inequality
inevitable
inevitably
inexistent
inexorable
inexorably
inexpertly
inexpiable
inexpiably
inexplicit
infallible
infallibly
infamously
infarction
infatuated
infeasible
infectious
infelicity
inferiorly
infernally
inferrable
infidelity
infighting
infiltrate
infinitely
infinitive
infinitude
inflatable
inflection
inflective
inflexible
inflexibly
infliction
inflictive
informally
infraction
infrahuman
infrasonic
infrequent
infusorial
infusorian
ingeminate
ingestible
inglorious
ingratiate
ingredient
ingression
inhabitant
inhalation
inharmonic
inherently
inheritrix
inhibition
inhibitory
inhumanely
inhumanity
inhumation
inimically
inimitable
inimitably
iniquitous
initialise
initialled
initiation
initiative
initiatory
injunction
injunctive
inkslinger
innateness
innerrably
innocently
innominate
innovation
innovative
innovatory
innuendoes
innumeracy
innumerate
innumerous
inoculable
inoculator
inoperable
inordinate
inosculate
inquietude
inquisitor

insaneness
insanitary
insatiable
insatiably
insecurely
insecurity
inseminate
insensible
insensibly
insentient
insightful
insinuator
insipidity
insistence
insistency
insobriety
insociable
insolation
insolently
insolvable
insolvency
insouciant
inspanning
inspection
inspective
inspirator
inspissate
instalment
instigator
instilling
institutor
instructor
instrument
insufflate
insularism
insularity
insulation
insurgence
insurgency
intactness
intangible
intangibly
integrable
integrally
integrator
integument
intendance
intendment
intenerate
intentness
interbreed
interceder
intercross
interested
interferer
interferon
intergrade
interiorly
interleave
interloper
interlunar
intermarry
intermezzi
intermezzo
internally
internment
internodal
internship
interphase
interplant
interplead
interposal
interposer
interregna
interspace
interstate
interstice
intertidal
intertrigo
intertwine
intertwist
interurban
intervener
intervenor
intervolve
interweave
interwound
interwoven
interzonal
intestinal
intimately
intimation
intimidate
intinction
intolerant
intonation
intoxicant
intoxicate
intramural
intraurban
intrepidly
intrigante
intriguant
introducer
introrsely
introspect
intubation
inundation
inundatory
inurbanity
invaginate
invalidate
invalidism
invalidity
invaluable
invaluably
invariable
invariably
invariance
inventress
inveracity
investment
inveteracy
inveterate
invigilate
invigorate
invincible
invincibly
inviolable
inviolably
invitation
invitatory
invitingly
invocation
invocatory
involucral
involucrum
involution
inwardness
iodination
ionisation
ionosphere
iridaceous
iridescent
iridosmine
Irishwoman
ironhanded
ironically
ironmaster
ironmonger
ironworker
irradiance
irradicate
irrational
irrelative
irrelevant
irreligion
irresolute
irreverent
irrigation
irritation
irritative
isentropic
Ishmaelite
isochronal
isodynamic
isogenetic
isoglossal
isolatable
isometrics
isomorphic
isoniazide
isopterous
isoseismal
isosporous
isothermal
italianate
italianise
Italianism
Italophile
itinerancy
jackanapes
jackassery
jackhammer
jackknives
jackrabbit
jacobinise
Jacobinism
Jacobitism
jaggedness
jaguarundi
janitorial
Janusfaced
Japanesque
jardiniere
jargonelle
jasperware
jauntiness
jawbreaker
jaywalking
Jehovistic
jejuneness
jeopardise
jerrybuilt
jesuitical
Jewishness
jimsonweed
jingoistic
jinricksha
jinrikisha
jobbernowl
jocoseness
jocularity
johnnycake
Johnsonese
johnsonian
jolterhead
journalese
journalise
journalism
journalist
journeyman
joyfulness
joyousness
jubilantly
jubilation
judgematic
judicatory
judicature
judicially
juggernaut
juristical
justiciary
juvenility
Kafkaesque
kaisership
Kantianism
karyoplasm
katabolism
kennelling
kenspeckle
keratinise
keratinous
kerchieves
kerseymere
kerygmatic
kettledrum
keyboarder
kibbutznik
kidnapping
kieselguhr
kilogramme
kimberlite
kindliness
kinematics
kineticist
kingfisher
kingliness
kinnikinic
knickknack
knifeboard
knighthood
knobkerrie
knockabout
knockkneed
knopkierie
knottiness
kookaburra
kriegspiel
Krishnaism
Krugerrand
Kuomintang
labiovelar
laboratory
laceration
lacerative
lachrymose
lacklustre
laconicism
lacrimator
lacrymator
lactescent
lacustrine
ladderback
ladychapel
ladyfinger
ladykiller
Lamarckian
Lamarckism
lambrequin
lamentable
lamentably
lamentedly
laminarian
lamination
Lammastide
lampoonery
lampoonist
lanceolate
landholder
landhunger
landingnet
landlocked
landlubber
landocracy
landowning
landscaper
languisher
languorous
lansquenet
lanternfly
lanthanide
lanuginose
lanuginous
laparotomy
lapidarian
lapidarist
lapidation
lardydardy
largescale
larvicidal
laryngitic
laryngitis
lascivious
laterality
latescence
latifundia
lattermost
laughingly
laundryman
lauraceous
laureation
laurelling
lavalliere
lavatorial
lavishment
lavishness
lawabiding
lawbreaker
lawfulness
lawntennis
lawrencium
Lawrentian
leadenness
leaderless
leadership
leafcutter
leafhopper
leafinsect
lebensraum
lectionary
lederhosen
ledgerbait
ledgerline
lefthanded
lefthander
legalistic
legateship
legibility
legislator
legitimacy
legitimate
legitimise
legitimism
legitimist
leguminous
Leibnizian
lemniscate
lemongrass
lengthways
lengthwise
lenticular
lentigines
leopardess
lepidolite
leprechaun
lesbianism
letterbomb
letterbook
lettercard
letterhead
letterless
leucocytic
leucoplast
leukocytic
levigation
levitation
lexicology
lexigraphy
liberalise
liberalism
liberalist
liberality
liberation
libidinous
librettist
licensable
licentiate
licentious
lieutenant
lifegiving
lifejacket
lifelessly
lifesaving
ligamental
lighterage
lighterman
lightfaced
lighthouse
lightingup
lightproof
likelihood
likeliness
likeminded
liliaceous
limaciform
limeburner
limitation
limitative
limitrophe
limpidness
linguiform
linguistic
lionhunter
Lipizzaner
lipography
lipomatous
Lippizaner
lipreading
lipservice
liquescent
liquidator
liquidiser
liquidness
lissomness
listlessly
literalise
literalism
literalist
literality
literarily
literation
literature
lithoglyph
lithograph
lithologic
lithophane
lithophyte
lithotrity
Lithuanian
litigation
litterlout
littleness
liturgical
livelihood
liveliness
livingroom
lobsterpot
lobulation
lockerroom
lockkeeper
lockstitch
locomotion
locomotive
locomotory
locustbean
loganberry
loganstone
loggerhead
logicality
logistical
logography
logorrhoea
logrolling

Lollardism
loneliness
lonesomely
longaevous
longhaired
longheaded
longlegged
longprimer
longshanks
longwinded
loosecover
lophophore
lopsidedly
loquacious
lordliness
lossleader
lotuseater
loudhailer
loungesuit
lovelessly
loveletter
loveliness
lovemaking
lovingness
lowerclass
lowpitched
lowprofile
loxodromic
lubricator
lubricious
luciferase
luciferous
lucifugous
lucubrator
luculently
lugubrious
lukewarmly
lumberjack
lumberroom
lumbersome
lumberyard
luminosity
luminously
lumpsucker
Lupercalia
lusciously
Lusitanian
lustration
lustreless
lustrously
lutestring
luxuriance
lycopodium
lymphocyte
lymphomata
lyophilise
Lysenkoism
macadamise
Maccabaean
macebearer
maceration
machinator
machinegun
mackintosh
macrophage
macrospore
maculation
maculature
madreporic
magistracy
magistrate
magnetiser
magnifical
magnificat
magnifying
Mahommedan
maidenhair
maidenhead
maidenhood
maidenlike
mainlander
mainspring
mainstream
maintainer
maisonette
majestical
majuscular
makeweight
malacoderm
malacology
maladapted
malapertly
malapropos
malcontent
malefactor
maleficent
malentendu
malevolent
malfeasant
malignance
malignancy
malingerer
malleebird
malleefowl
mallenders
malodorous
Malpighian
Malthusian
malvaceous
mamillated
manageable
manageably
management
manageress
managerial
manchineel
mandibular
mandragora
manfulness
mangosteen
maniacally
Manichaean
Manicheism
manicurist
manifestly
manifestos
manifoldly
manipulate
manoeuvrer
manoeuvres
manometric
manorhouse
manservant
mansuetude
manteltree
manumitted
manuscript
manzanilla
maquillage
maraschino
marcescent
Marcionite
marginalia
marginally
marginated
margravate
margravine
marguerite
Mariolater
Mariolatry
marionette
marketable
markethall
markettown
markswoman
marquisate
marrowbone
marrowless
marshalled
marshaller
marshalsea
marshiness
martensite
martialism
martingale
marvelling
marvellous
masquerade
Massoretic
mastectomy
masterhand
masterhood
masterless
mastermind
mastership
masterwork
masticable
masticator
matchboard
matchmaker
matchstick
materially
maternally
mathematic
matriarchy
matricidal
matronhood
matronship
matronymic
maturation
maturative
matureness
mavourneen
maxilliped
maximalist
mayblossom
mayonnaise
meadowland
meadowlark
meagreness
mealbeetle
meaningful
measliness
measurable
measurably
measuredly
mechanical
meddlesome
mediastina
mediatress
medicament
medicaster
medication
medicative
medievally
mediocrity
meditation
meditative
medullated
meerschaum
megalithic
megalosaur
megascopic
melancholy
Melanesian
melanistic
meliorator
melismatic
mellowness
meltingpot
membership
membranous
memorandum
menacingly
mendacious
mendicancy
meningioma
meningitis
menopausal
menstruate
menstruous
mensurable
mentorship
mercantile
mercifully
meridional
merrymaker
mesenteric
mesenteron
mesmeriser
Mesolithic
mesomerism
mesomorphy
mesophytic
mesoscaphe
mesosphere
mesothorax
messianism
metabolise
metabolism
metabolite
metacarpal
metacarpus
metacentre
metagalaxy
metalepsis
metallurgy
metamerism
metaphoric
metaphrase
metaphysic
metaplasia
metastable
metastases
metastasis
metastatic
metatarsal
metatarsus
metatheses
metathesis
metathetic
metathorax
metempiric
meteoritic
methodical
Methuselah
methylated
meticulous
metrically
metronomic
metronymic
metropolis
mettlesome
micaschist
Michaelmas
microbiota
microcline
microfarad
microfiche
micrograph
microlitic
micrometer
micrometry
microphone
microphyte
micropylar
microscope
microscopy
microseism
microspore
middleaged
middlebrow
middlemost
middlingly
midmorning
midshipman
mightiness
mignonette
migrainous
militantly
militarily
militarise
militarism
militarist
militiaman
millefiori
millennial
millennium
millesimal
millilitre
millimetre
millstream
millwright
mimeograph
mindedness
mindlessly
mineralise
mineralogy
minestrone
mineworker
minimalism
minimalist
ministrant
minstrelsy
mintmaster
minuscular
minutebook
minutehand
minuteness
miraculous
mirthfully
misaligned
misbelieve
miscellany
mischanter
mischmetal
misconduct
miscreance
misericord
misfortune
misgivings
mishitting
misjoinder
mismatched
mismeasure
misnomered
misogamist
misogynist
misogynous
misologist
misprision
missionary
missionise
mistakable
mistakenly
misthought
misventure
miswording
mithridate
mitigation
mitigative
mitigatory
mixedmedia
mixolydian
mizzenmast
mizzensail
mobocratic
mockheroic
moderately
moderation
moderatism
moderniser
modernness
modifiable
modishness
modulation
Mohammedan
moisturise
molendinar
molluscoid
molluscous
molybdenum
monandrous
monarchial
Monarchian
monarchism
monarchist
monetarily
monetarism
monetarist
moneymaker
moneytaker
mongrelise
mongrelism
moniliasis
moniliform
monistical
monitorial
monkeysuit
monocarpic
monochasia
monochrome
monoclinal
monoclinic
monocratic
monocyclic
monoecious
monogamist
monogamous
monogenism
monogynian
monogynous
monohybrid
monohydric
monolithic
monologise
monologist
monomaniac
monophonic
monopodial
monopodium
monopolise
monopolist
monorhymed
monotheism
monotheist
monotonous
monovalent
monsignori
monstrance
Montagnard
montbretia
monumental
moonflower
moonshiner
moonstruck
mopishness
moralistic
moratorium
morbidezza
morbidness
mordacious
morganatic
moroseness
morphemics
morphinism
morphogeny
morphology
morrispike
mosaically
mosaicking
mosasaurus
mosquitoes
mossbunker

motherhood
motherland
motherless
mothership
motherwort
motionless
motivation
motiveless
motorcycle
mouldboard
mouldiness
mountebank
mournfully
mousseline
moustached
moustachio
Mousterian
mouthorgan
mouthpiece
movability
movelessly
moviemaker
mozzarella
muciferous
mudskipper
mudslinger
muffinbell
Muhammadan
Muhammedan
muliebrity
mulishness
mulligrubs
multifaced
multiloquy
multimedia
multiphase
multiplier
multipolar
multistage
multivocal
mumbojumbo
munificent
muscularly
musicality
musicianly
musicology
musicpaper
musicstand
musicstool
muskmallow
Mussulmans
mutability
mutilation
mutinously
muttonhead
myasthenia
mycologist
mycoplasma
mycorrhiza
myocardium
myological
myopically
myrtaceous
mystagogic
mystagogue
mysterious
mystically
mythically
mythiciser
mythologer
mythologic
mythomania
mythopoeia
mythopoeic
myxomatous
myxomycete
nailpolish
nambypamby
namelessly
nanisation
nanosecond
naphthenic
narcissism
narcissist
narcolepsy
narrowness
nasturtium
natalitial
natatorial
natatorium
nationally
nationhood
nationless
nationwide
nativeborn
nativeness
nativistic
natterjack
naturalise
naturalism
naturalist
naturopath
nauseating
nauseously
nautically
navigation
Neapolitan
nebulosity
nebulously
necrolater
necrolatry
necromancy
necrophile
necrophily
necropolis
necroscopy
nectareous
needlebath
needlebook
needlecord
needlefish
needlessly
needlework
negatively
negativism
negativist
negativity
neglectful
negligence
negligible
negligibly
negotiable
negotiator
negrophile
negrophobe
nematocyst
neoclassic
neological
neoplastic
nepenthean
nephograph
nephoscope
nephralgia
nephridium
nephrology
nethermost
nettlerash
neurilemma
neurolemma
neuropathy
neuroplasm
neurotoxin
neutralise
neutralism
neutralist
neutrality
nevernever
newfangled
newsagency
newscaster
newsletter
newsmonger
newsreader
newsvendor
newsworthy
newswriter
nickelling
nicotinism
nidicolous
nidificate
nidifugous
nightdress
nightglass
nightlight
nightshade
nightshift
nightshirt
nightstick
nightwatch
nigrescent
nihilistic
nimbleness
nincompoop
nineteenth
nipplewort
nitpicking
nitrochalk
nitrogroup
noblewoman
nodulation
noisemaker
nominalism
nominalist
nominately
nomination
nominative
nomography
nomologist
nomothetic
nonaligned
nonchalant
noncontent
nondrinker
nonferrous
nonfiction
nonjoinder
nonlogical
nonnatural
nonnuclear
nonpayment
nonplaying
nonplussed
nonstarter
nonswimmer
nonviolent
noogenesis
northbound
northerner
northwards
nosography
nosologist
nosophobia
nostologic
notability
notarially
notchboard
noteworthy
noticeable
noticeably
notifiable
notionally
notonectal
nourishing
novaculite
novelistic
nubiferous
nuciferous
nucivorous
nucleation
nucleonics
nucleoside
nucleotide
nudibranch
nullanulla
numberless
numeration
numerology
numerosity
numerously
numismatic
nunciature
nuptiality
nurseryman
nutational
nutcracker
nutritious
nyctalopia
nyctalopic
nyctinasty
nympholept
oafishness
obdurately
obediently
obfuscated
obituarist
objectival
objectless
oblateness
obligation
obligatory
obligingly
obliterate
obnubilate
obsequious
observable
observably
observance
obstetrics
obstructor
obtainable
obtainment
obtruncate
obturation
obtuseness
occasional
occidental
occupation
occupative
occurrence
oceanarium
oceangoing
oceanology
ocellation
ochlocracy
octahedral
octahedron
octamerous
octandrian
octandrous
octodecimo
octonarian
octopodous
odiousness
odontalgia
odontology
oecologist
oecumenism
oedematose
oedematous
oenologist
oesophagus
officially
offlicence
offputting
offsetting
oftentimes
oldfangled
oldmaidish
oleaginous
oleiferous
oleography
oleraceous
oligarchic
oligoclase
oligopsony
olivaceous
ombrometer
ommatidium
omnigenous
omnipotent
omniscient
omnivorous
omophagous
oncogenous
oncologist
oneirology
onesidedly
ontologist
opalescent
opaqueness
openhanded
openhearth
openminded
operculate
operettist
ophicleide
ophiolater
ophiolatry
ophiologic
ophthalmia
ophthalmic
opinionist
opisometer
oppilation
opposeless
oppositely
opposition
oppression
oppressive
opprobrium
oppugnancy
optatively
optimalise
optimistic
optionally
oracularly
orangepeel
orangewood
oratorical
orchardist
orchardman
orchestics
orchestral
ordainment
ordinarily
ordination
ordonnance
Ordovician
oreography
oreologist
organicism
organicist
organismal
orientally
originally
originator
ornamental
ornateness
orneriness
orogenesis
orogenetic
orographic
orological
orotundity
orphanhood
orthoclase
orthodoxly
orthoepist
orthogenic
orthogonal
orthopedic
orthoptera
oscillator
oscitation
osculation
osculatory
osmeterium
osmiridium
ostensible
ostensibly
osteoblast
osteoclast
osteopathy
osteophyte
otherwhere
otherwhile
otherworld
otioseness
otterboard
ottershrew
outbalance
outbidding
outerspace
outfielder
outfitting
outgassing
outgeneral
outgunning
outlandish
outmeasure
outpatient
outpouring
outputting
outrageous
outrightly
outrunning
outsitting
outstation
outstretch
outswinger
outwitting
ovariotomy
overabound
overactive
overblouse
overbought
overburden
overcharge
overcommit
overcooked
overexcite
overexpose
overflight
overground
overgrowth
overhanded
overlander
overlapped
overlooker
overmanned
overmantel
overmaster
overnicety
overpraise
overrefine
overridden
overriding
overshadow
overslaugh
overspread
overstride
overstrung
oversubtle
oversupply

overthrown
overthrust
overtopped
overweight
overwinter
ovipositor
owlishness
oxidisable
oxygenator
oysterfarm
pacesetter
pacifiable
pacificate
pacificism
pacificist
packingbox
packsaddle
packthread
paddleboat
paddyfield
paddywagon
paddywhack
paedagogic
paederasty
paediatric
paedogogue
paedophile
pagination
painkiller
painlessly
paintbrush
Palaeocene
Palaeogene
palaeolith
palaeotype
Palaeozoic
palagonite
palatalise
palatinate
palimpsest
palindrome
palisander
palladious
pallbearer
palliation
palliative
palliatory
pallidness
palmaceous
palmatifid
palmbutter
palmerworm
PalmSunday
paltriness
palynology
Panamanian
pancratium
pancreatic
pancreatin
panegyrise
panegyrist
pangenesis
pangenetic
panhandler
paniculate
panjandrum
panopticon
pansophist
pantograph
pantomimic
pantrymaid
papaverine
papaverous
paperchase
paperknife
papermaker
papistical
papyrology
parabiosis
parabiotic
parabolise
paraboloid
paradisaic
paradisean
paradisiac
paradisian
paradoxure
paraffinic
paragnosis
paralipsis
paralogise
paralogism
paramecium
parametric
paramnesia
paranormal
paraphrase
paraphrast
paraplegia
paraplegic
parapodium
paraselene
parasitism
parasitoid
paratactic
paratroops
parcelling
pardonable
pardonably
parenchyma
parentally
parenteral
parenthood
parimutuel
parliament
Parnassian
paronymous
paroxysmal
paroxytone
parramatta
parricidal
parrotfish
parsonbird
parsonical
partiality
participle
particular
parturient
pasquinade
passageway
passionary
passionate
Passionist
pasteboard
pastellist
pasteurise
pasteurism
pastmaster
pastorally
pastorship
pastrycook
pasturable
pastyfaced
patchiness
patentable
paternally
pathetical
pathfinder
pathogenic
pathologic
patination
patisserie
patriality
patriarchy
patriciate
patricidal
patrilocal
patriotism
patristics
patrolling
patronymic
patulously
pawnbroker
peacefully
peacemaker
peacockery
peacockish
pearldiver
peashooter
pebbledash
peccadillo
pectinated
peculation
peculiarly
pedagogics
pedalorgan
pedalpoint
pederastic
pedestrian
pediculate
pediculous
pedicurist
pedimental
pedimented
pedologist
peduncular
peerlessly
pegmatitic
pejoration
pejorative
pellagrous
pellicular
pellucidly
pemphigoid
pemphigous
pencilling
pendentive
penetrable
penetrably
penetralia
penetrance
penetrator
penicillin
peninsular
penitently
penmanship
pennaceous
pennanular
pennillion
pennyroyal
pennyworth
penologist
penpushing
pensionary
pentachord
pentagonal
pentameter
pentastich
pentathlon
pentatomic
pentatonic
pentimento
pentstemon
peppercorn
peppermill
peppermint
pepperwort
percentage
percentile
perception
perceptive
perceptual
perchloric
percipient
percolator
percussion
percussive
perdurable
perdurably
peremptory
perfection
perfective
perfidious
perfoliate
perforator
performing
periclinal
pericyclic
peridermal
perigynous
perihelion
perilously
periodical
periosteal
periosteum
peripeteia
peripheral
peripteral
periscopic
perishable
perithecia
peritoneal
peritoneum
periwigged
periwinkle
perjurious
permafrost
permanence
permanency
permeation
permeative
permission
permissive
permitting
permutable
pernicious
pernickety
peroration
peroxidise
perpetrate
perpetuate
perpetuity
perplexity
perquisite
persecutor
persiflage
persistent
personable
personally
personalty
personator
persuasion
persuasive
pertinence
pertinency
perversely
perversion
perversity
perversive
pesticidal
pestilence
petiolated
petiteness
petitioner
petroglyph
petrolatum
petronella
petulantly
phagedaena
phagedenic
phagocytic
phalangeal
phallicism
phanerogam
phantasise
phantasmal
phantasmic
phantastic
phantastry
pharisaism
pharmacist
pharyngeal
pheasantry
phelloderm
phenacetin
phenocryst
phenomenal
phenomenon
phenotypic
pheromonal
philatelic
philippina
philippine
philistine
phillumeny
philologen
philopoena
philosophe
philosophy
phlebotomy
phlegmatic
phlogistic
phlogiston
phlogopite
Phoenician
phonematic
phonically
phonograph
phonolitic
phonologic
phonometer
phosphatic
phosphoric
phosphorus
photoflood
photogenic
photograph
photolitho
photolysis
photolytic
photometer
photometry
photonasty
photophily
photophore
photoprint
phototaxis
phototrope
phrasebook
phrenology
phthisical
phylactery
phyllotaxy
phylloxera
phylogenic
physically
physicking
physiocrat
physiology
phytogenic
phytophagy
phytotoxic
pianissimo
pianoforte
picaresque
picayunish
piccalilli
piccaninny
pichiciago
pickaninny
picketline
pickpocket
picnicking
picosecond
pictograph
pictorical
piecegoods
piercingly
piezometer
pigeonhole
pigeonpair
pigeonpost
pigeontoed
pigeonwing
pigmentary
pigsticker
piledriver
pilgarlick
pilgrimage
piliferous
pilliwinks
pillowcase
pillowlace
pillowslip
pilothouse
pilotlight
pilotwhale
pincerlike
pinchpenny
pincushion
pinebeauty
pinecarpet
pinfeather
pinnatifid
pinnulated
pinstriped
piperidine
piscifauna
pistillary
pistillate
pistolling
pistolshot
pistolwhip
pistonring
pitchblack
pitcherful
pitchstone
pitilessly
pityriasis
pixillated
placidness
plagiarise
plagiarism
plagiarist
plaguesome
plainchant
planchette
planetable
planetaria
plangently
planigraph
planimeter
planimetry
planktonic
planometer
plantation
plantlouse
plasmodesm
plasmodium
plasmogamy
plasmolyse
plasticise
plasticity
platelayer
playacting
playbyplay
playfellow
playground
playwright
pleadingly
pleasantly
pleasantry
pleasingly
plebiscite

plecoptera
pleochroic
pleonastic
plesiosaur
pliability
pliantness
ploddingly
ploughable
ploughland
pluckiness
plumassier
plunderage
plunderous
pluperfect
plutocracy
plutolatry
pneumatics
pocketable
pocketbook
pocketsize
pockmarked
podiatrist
poetically
pogonology
pogonotomy
poinsettia
pointblank
pokerfaced
polemicist
polemonium
politeness
politician
politicise
pollenosis
pollinator
polyandric
polyanthus
polyatamic
polychaete
polychrest
polychrome
polyclinic
polycyclic
polydactyl
polydipsia
polygamist
polygamous
polygenism
polygenist
polygenous
polygraphy
polygynous
polyhedral
polyhedric
polyhedron
polyhistor
polymathic
polymerise
polymerism
polymerous
Polynesian
polynomial
polyonymic
polyphasic
polyphonic
polyploidy
polysemous
polytheism
polytheist
polytocous
polyvalent
Pomeranian
pomiferous
pomologist
ponderable
pontifical
pontifices
popularise
popularity
population
populistic
populously
porismatic
pornocracy
porousness
porraceous
portamento
portcullis
portentous
portliness
Portuguese
positional
positively
positivism
positivist
positivity
possession
possessive
possessory
postbellum
postchaise
postexilic
posthumous
postillion
postliminy
postmaster
postmortem
postoffice
postpartum
postscript
postulator
potability
potamology
potbellied
potentiate
potentilla
pothunting
pouncetbox
pourparler
powderhorn
powderpuff
powerfully
powerhouse
pozzolanic
pozzuolana
practician
practising
praecocial
praemunire
praesidium
praetorial
praetorian
pragmatise
pragmatism
pragmatist
prairiedog
prancingly
pratincole
prayerbook
preachment
preadamite
prearrange
prebendary
precarious
precaution
precedence
precedency
preceptive
preceptory
precession
preciosity
preciously
precipitin
preclusion
preclusive
precocious
preconcert
precordial
precursory
predacious
predecease
predestine
predicable
prediction
predictive
predispose
prednisone
preeminent
preemption
preemptive
preexilian
prefecture
preferable
preferably
preference
preferment
preferring
prefixture
prefrontal
prefulgent
preglacial
pregnantly
prehensile
prehension
prehistory
prejudiced
prelatical
prelection
premarital
premaxilla
premedical
premonitor
prepackage
preparator
preparedly
prepayable
prepayment
prepensely
prepossess
prepotence
prepotency
presageful
presbyopia
presbyopic
presbytery
prescience
prescriber
presentday
presentive
presidency
presidiary
presignify
pressagent
pressingly
pressurise
presternum
presumable
presumably
presuppose
pretendant
pretendent
pretension
prettiness
prevailing
prevalence
prevenancy
prevenient
prevention
preventive
previously
pridefully
priesthood
priestling
priggishly
primevally
primiparae
primordial
primordium
princeling
princeship
principate
principial
principium
principled
prismoidal
prissiness
privileged
prizefight
procedural
proceeding
procession
proclaimer
proclivity
procreator
procrypsis
procryptic
proctorage
proctorial
proctorise
procumbent
procurable
procurance
procurator
prodigally
prodigious
producible
production
productive
profession
proficient
profitable
profitably
profitless
profligacy
profligate
profoundly
profundity
progenitor
proglottis
prognathic
prognostic
programmer
prohibiter
prohibitor
projectile
projection
projective
prolicidal
prolocutor
prologuise
prolongate
promenader
promethium
prominence
promissory
promontory
promptbook
promptness
promulgate
pronominal
pronounced
pronouncer
proofsheet
propagable
propaganda
propagator
propellant
propellent
propelling
propensity
properness
propertied
prophesier
prophetess
propionate
propitiate
propitious
proportion
propounder
propraetor
proprietor
propulsion
propulsive
propylaeum
prosaicism
proscenium
prosciutto
proscriber
prosecutor
prosilient
prosodical
prospector
prospectus
prosperity
prosperous
prosthesis
prosthetic
prostitute
prostomial
prostomium
protanopic
protection
protective
protectory
protectrix
proteiform
proteinous
protensive
proteolyse
protestant
prothallia
prothallus
protophyta
protophyte
protoplasm
protoplast
prototypal
prototypic
protracted
protractor
protreptic
protrusile
protrusion
protrusive
proudflesh
provenance
proverbial
providence
provincial
provisions
provitamin
provocator
proximally
prudential
pruriently
psalmodise
psalmodist
psalterium
psephology
pseudocarp
psilocybin
psittacine
psychiatry
psychicism
psychicist
psychology
psychopath
Ptolemaist
puberulent
pubescence
publishing
puerperium
puffpastry
pugilistic
pugnacious
puissantly
pulsatilla
pulsimeter
pulsometer
pulveriser
pulvinated
pummelling
punchboard
punchdrunk
punctation
punctually
punctuator
punctulate
punishable
punishment
punitively
pupilarity
pupiparous
purblindly
puristical
puritanise
puritanism
purposeful
purseproud
pursership
purseseine
pursuivant
purtenance
purulently
purveyance
pushbutton
putatively
putrescent
putrescine
putridness
puzzlement
pycnogonid
pycnometer
pycnostyle
pyknometer
pyracantha
pyretology
pyridoxine
pyrogallol
pyrogenous
pyrography
pyrolusite
pyromaniac
pyromantic
pyrometric
pyrophoric
pyrotechny
pyroxenite
Pyrrhonian
Pyrrhonism
Pyrrhonist
pyrrhotite
quadrangle
quadrantal
quadratics
quadrature
quadrennia
quadriceps
quadrireme
quadrivial
quadrivium
quadrumana
quadrumane
quadrumvir
quadruplet
quadruplex
quadrupole
quaintness
qualmishly
quantifier
quantitive
quarantine
quarrelled
quarreller

quarrender
quartation
quarterage
quarterday
quartering
quartzitic
quaternary
quaternate
quaternion
quaternity
quatorzain
quatrefoil
queasiness
quenchable
quenchless
quercitron
questioner
quickgrass
quickthorn
quiescence
quiescency
quinacrine
quintuplet
quirkiness
quixotical
quizmaster
rabbinical
rabblement
racecourse
Rachmanism
rackrenter
radicalise
radicalism
radication
radiogenic
radiograph
radiologic
radiometer
radiometry
radiopaque
radiophone
radioscopy
radiosonde
ragamuffin
raggedness
railroader
railwayman
rainmaking
rakishness
ramblingly
rampageous
ramshackle
rancidness
randomness
ranunculus
rapporteur
ratability
ratcatcher
rationally
rattlehead
rattlepate
rattletrap
ravenously
ravishment
razorblade
razorshell
razzmatazz
reactivate
reactively
reactivity
readership
reafforest
realisable
reallocate
reappraise
rearmament
reasonable
reasonably
reasonless
reassemble
reassembly
rebellious
rebuttable
recallable
receivable
recentness
receptacle
receptible
rechristen
recidivism
recidivist
recipiency
reciprocal
recitalist
recitation
recitative
recitativo
recklessly
recolonise
recommence
recompense
reconciler
reconsider
recordable
recoupment
recreantly
recreation
recreative
recrudesce
rectorship
recumbency
recuperate
recurrence
recyclable
redblooded
redcurrant
redecorate
redeemable
redemption
redemptive
redemptory
redescribe
rediscover
redolently
redundance
redundancy
reelection
reeligible
reentrance
referendum
refillable
refinement
reflection
reflective
reflexible
reformable
refraction
refractive
refractory
refreshing
refringent
refuelling
refulgence
refundable
refundment
refutation
regalement
regardless
regelation
regeneracy
regenerate
regentship
regimental
regionally
registered
registrant
regression
regressive
regretting
regularise
regularity
regulation
regulative
regulatory
reichsmark
reissuable
reiterance
rejectable
rejoicings
rejuvenate
rejuvenise
relational
relatively
relativise
relativism
relativist
relativity
relaxation
releasable
relegation
relentless
relevantly
relievable
relinquish
relishable
relocation
reluctance
reluctancy
remarkable
remarkably
remarriage
remediable
remedially
remediless
remissible
remissness
remittance
remodelled
remonetise
remorseful
remoteness
remunerate
renascence
rencounter
renderable
rendezvous
renovation
reorganise
repairable
reparation
reparative
repatriate
repealable
repeatable
repeatedly
repellance
repellancy
repellence
repellency
repentance
repertoire
repetiteur
repetition
repetitive
repopulate
reportable
reportedly
reposition
repository
repression
repressive
reprobance
reproducer
republican
repudiator
repugnance
repugnancy
repurchase
reputation
requiescat
reredorter
rescission
rescissory
researcher
resemblant
resentment
reservedly
reshipment
resignedly
resilience
resiliency
resistance
resistible
resistless
resolutely
resolution
resolutive
resolvable
resolvedly
resonantly
resorcinol
resorption
resorptive
resounding
respectful
respecting
respective
respirable
respirator
respondent
responsive
responsory
restaurant
restlessly
restorable
restrained
restrainer
resultless
resumption
resumptive
resupinate
resurgence
retainable
reticently
reticulate
retinacula
retirement
retiringly
retractile
retraction
retractive
retraining
retrochoir
retrograde
retrogress
retrorsely
retrospect
returnable
reunionism
reunionist
revalidate
revalorise
revanchism
revanchist
revealable
revealment
revelation
revelatory
revengeful
reverencer
reverently
reversible
revertible
reviewable
revilement
revisional
revitalise
revivalism
revivalist
revocation
revocatory
revolution
rewardable
rewardless
rhapsodise
rhapsodist
rheologist
rheotropic
rhetorical
rheumatics
rheumatism
rheumatoid
rhinestone
rhinoceros
rhinoscope
rhinoscopy
rhizogenic
rhizomorph
rhizophore
rhodophane
rhomboidal
rhomboidei
rhythmical
ribbonfish
ribbonworm
riboflavin
ricinoleic
rickettsia
ridgepiece
ridiculous
rightangle
rightfully
rightwards
rigorously
rinderpest
ringfinger
ringleader
ringmaster
ringnecked
ringtailed
ripplemark
riproaring
ripsnorter
risibility
ritardando
ritornelli
ritornello
riverhorse
roadrunner
roadworthy
robustious
robustness
rockabilly
rockbadger
rockbottom
rockgarden
rockhopper
rockpigeon
rockrabbit
rockribbed
rodfishing
roistering
roisterous
rollcollar
rollicking
rollingpin
Romanesque
Romanistic
rontgenise
roodscreen
roofgarden
rootedness
ropedancer
ropeladder
ropewalker
roquelaure
rosaniline
rosechafer
roseengine
roselipped
rosemallow
rotational
rotisserie
rottenness
rottweiler
roughhouse
roughrider
roundabout
roundhouse
rouseabout
roustabout
rovebeetle
rowanberry
rubberneck
rubiginous
rubrically
rubricator
rubythroat
rudderfish
rudderless
rudimental
ruefulness
ruffianism
ruggedness
ruminantly
rumination
ruminative
rumrunning
runnerbean
runthrough
rupicoline
rupicolous
Russianise
Russophile
Russophobe
rustically
ruthlessly
sabbatical
sabretache
sabretooth
saccharate
saccharide
saccharify
saccharine
saccharoid
saccharose
sacerdotal
sacredness
sacrificer
sacroiliac
sacrosanct
saddleback
saddlefast
saddletree
safeblower
safetybelt
sagination
sagittally
sailorless
salability
salamander
salesclerk
saleswoman
salicional
salicylate
salientian
saliferous
salivation
sallenders
sallowness
salmagundi
salmonella
salmonleap
salpingian

saltarello
saltcellar
saltigrade
salubrious
salutarily
salutation
salutatory
samarskite
sanatorium
sanctifier
sanctimony
sanctitude
sandalwood
sandbagger
sandcastle
sanderling
sandhopper
sandmartin
sanguinary
sanguinely
sanguinity
sanitarian
sanitarily
sanitarium
sanitation
Sanskritic
sapiential
sappanwood
sapphirine
saprogenic
saprophyte
sarcolemma
sarcophagi
sarcophagy
sarcoplasm
sargassoes
sarmentose
sarmentous
sarracenia
sashwindow
satanology
satellitic
satisfying
saturation
saturnalia
satyagraha
satyriasis
sauerkraut
savageness
savourless
sawtoothed
saxicoline
saxicolous
scabrously
scaffolder
scaleboard
scandalise
scandalous
scansorial
scantiness
scapegrace
scarabaeid
scarabaeus
scaramouch
scarceness
scaredycat
scarlatina
scatheless
scathingly
scattergun
scattering
scattiness
scavengery
scenically
scepticism
schematise
schematism
schemozzle
scherzando
schipperke
schismatic
schizocarp
schizogony
scholastic
schoolable
schoolbook
schooldays
schoolgirl
schoolmaam
schoolmarm
schoolmate
schoolroom
schooltime
schoolwork
sciagraphy
scientific
Scillonian
sciolistic
scleroderm
sclerotium
sclerotomy
scoffingly
scoreboard
scoresheet
scornfully
scorzonera
Scotswoman
Scotticise
Scotticism
scrapmetal
scratchily
scratchwig
screechowl
screenings
screenplay
screwplate
screwpress
scribbling
scrimmager
scrimshank
scriptoria
scriptural
scrofulous
scrollwork
scrupulous
scrutineer
scrutinise
sculptress
sculptural
sculptured
scurrility
scurrilous
scurviness
scutellate
scyphiform
scyphozoan
seaanemone
seabiscuit
seacaptain
sealingwax
seamanlike
seamanship
seamstress
searchable
searchless
seaserpent
seasonable
seasonably
seasonally
seborrhoea
secernment
secludedly
secondbest
secondhand
secondment
secondrate
secretaire
secularise
secularism
secularist
secularity
securement
secureness
securiform
sedateness
seducement
seductress
sedulously
seedpotato
seedvessel
seemliness
seersucker
seethrough
segmentary
seguidilla
seignorage
seignorial
seismicity
seismogram
seismology
selectness
selenodont
selenology
selfacting
selfaction
selfbinder
selfcolour
selfdeceit
selfdenial
selfesteem
selffeeder
selfglazed
selfguided
selflessly
selfloving
selfmotion
selfmurder
selfparody
selfpoised
selfpraise
selfprofit
selfraised
selfregard
selfrising
selfruling
selfseeker
selfstyled
selftaught
selfwilled
seltzogene
semeiology
semeiotics
semestrial
semiannual
semichorus
semicircle
semidivine
semidouble
semidrying
semifitted
semiliquid
semilunate
seminarian
seminarist
semination
semiopaque
semiotical
semiquaver
semiuncial
semiweekly
semiyearly
sempstress
senatorial
senescence
sensedatum
senseorgan
sensitiser
sensualise
sensualism
sensualist
sensuality
sensuously
sentential
sentiently
separately
separation
separatism
separatist
separative
separatory
septenarii
septennial
septennium
septically
septillion
Septuagint
sepulchral
sequacious
sequential
sequestrum
SerboCroat
sereneness
sergeantcy
serigraphy
seriocomic
serjeantcy
sermoniser
serologist
serotinous
serpentine
serradilla
serviceman
servomotor
sestertium
sestertius
setterwort
settlement
seventieth
severeness
sexagenary
Sexagesima
sexivalent
sexlimited
sexologist
sexpartite
sextillion
shabbiness
shadowless
shagginess
shamefaced
shamefully
shandrydan
shandygaff
shanghaier
shantytown
sharpnosed
sheabutter
shearwater
sheathbill
sheathless
sheepishly
sheeplouse
sheepshank
sheepshead
shellacked
shellmound
shellproof
shellshock
shenanigan
sherardise
sheriffdom
shibboleth
shieldless
shiftiness
shillelagh
shipbroker
shipfitter
shipmaster
shiprigged
shipwright
shirehorse
shirtfront
shirtwaist
shockingly
shockproof
shoddiness
shoebuckle
shoestring
shopkeeper
shoplifter
shopsoiled
shopwalker
shopwindow
shoreleave
shorewards
shortbread
shortcrust
shortdated
shortening
shortlived
shortrange
shouldered
shovelhead
shovelling
showerbath
showjumper
showwindow
shrewdness
shrewishly
shrewmouse
shrievalty
shrillness
shrinkable
shrinkwrap
shrivelled
shroudlaid
shroudless
Shrovetide
shuttering
sialagogic
sialagogue
sibilation
sicklebill
sickliness
sideboards
sideeffect
sideglance
siderolite
siderostat
sidesaddle
sidestreet
sidestroke
sidewinder
siegetrain
signalling
signwriter
silentness
silhouette
silkcotton
silkscreen
sillybilly
silverbath
silverfish
silverside
silverware
silverweed
similarity
similitude
simoniacal
simpleness
simplicity
simplifier
simplistic
simulacrum
simulation
simulative
simulatory
sincipital
sinecurism
sinecurist
sinfulness
Singhalese
singlefoot
singleness
singletree
singularly
sinisterly
sinistrous
sinologist
sinusoidal
sisterhood
sitophobia
sixshooter
skateboard
sketchable
sketchbook
skewbridge
skiagraphy
skibobbing
skijumping
skimpiness
skindiving
skinniness
skirmisher
skirtdance
skittishly
skrimshank
skyjacking
skyscraper
skywriting
slanderous
slanginess
slantingly
slatternly
slavetrade
slavocracy
Slavophile
Slavophobe
sleaziness
sleepiness
sleepyhead
sleeveless
sleevelink
sleighbell
slenderise
slidevalve
slightness
slipperily
slipstitch
slipstream
slitpocket
sloppiness
slothfully
slowfooted
slowmotion
slowwitted
sluggardly
sluggishly
sluicegate
slumberful
slumberous
sluttishly
smallscale
smallsword
smallwares
smaragdine
smaragdite
smartmoney
smattering
smelliness
smockfrock
smokedried
smokehouse
smokeplant

smokeproof
smokestack
smoothbore
smoothness
smorrebrod
smudginess
smuttiness
snafflebit
snailpaced
snailwheel
snakedance
snakestone
snapdragon
snappishly
sneakiness
sneakingly
sneakthief
sneeringly
sneezeweed
sneezewood
sneezewort
snickasnee
sniffiness
snivelling
snobbishly
snobocracy
snootiness
snowcapped
snowgrouse
snowmobile
snowplough
snubbingly
snuffiness
soapboiler
soapbubble
soapflakes
sobersided
sobersides
socialiser
societally
sociologic
sociometry
soddenness
softbilled
softboiled
softfinned
softheaded
softspoken
solacement
soldanella
solecistic
solemnness
solenoidal
solicitant
solicitous
solicitude
solidarism
solidarist
solidarity
solidstate
solifidian
solitarily
solstitial
solubilise
solubility
somatology
somatotype
sombreness
somersault
somniloquy
somnolence
somnolency
songstress
songthrush
songwriter
sonorously
soothingly
soothsayer
sophomoric
Sorbonnist
sordidness
sororicide
soubriquet
soullessly
soundboard
soundingly
soundproof
soundtrack
sourcebook
sousaphone
souterrain
southbound
southerner
southernly
southwards
sowthistle
spacecraft
spacewoman
spaciously
spadebeard
spadiceous
spagyrical
spallation
spankingly
sparseness
Spartacist
spasticity
spatchcock
spathulate
spatiality
speargrass
specialise
specialism
specialist
speciality
speciation
speciology
speciosity
speciously
spectacled
spectacles
spectrally
speculator
speechless
speediness
speedlimit
speleology
spellbound
Spencerian
Spenserian
spermaceti
spermicide
sperrylite
sphalerite
sphenodone
sphenogram
sphenoidal
sphericity
spheroidal
spherulite
spidercrab
spiderline
spiderwort
spiflicate
spillikins
spinescent
spiracular
spiraculum
spiralling
spiritedly
spiritless
spirituous
spirograph
spirometer
spirometry
spitchcock
spitefully
splanchnic
splashback
splashdown
spleenwort
splendidly
splintbone
splintcoal
splitlevel
splutterer
spodomancy
spoilsport
spokeshave
spoliation
spoliative
spoliatory
spongecake
spongewood
spongiform
sponginess
spongology
sponsorial
spookiness
spoondrift
spoonerism
sporangial
sporangium
sporophore
sporophyll
sporophyte
sportfully
sportiness
sportingly
sportively
sportswear
spotlessly
spottiness
sprightful
springhalt
springhead
springless
springlike
springtail
springtide
springtime
springwood
sprinkling
sprucebeer
spruceness
spumescent
spunkiness
spuriously
squalidity
squamation
squanderer
squareness
squaresail
squaretoed
squaretoes
squeezable
squeezebox
squeteague
squinteyed
squirarchy
squirearch
squirehood
squireling
squireship
stabiliser
stablemate
stableness
stadholder
staffnurse
stagbeetle
stagecoach
stagecraft
staggering
stagnantly
stagnation
stalactite
stalagmite
stalwartly
stanchless
stanchness
standpoint
standstill
staphyline
stargazing
starriness
starryeyed
starstream
starvation
starveling
statecraft
statically
stationary
stationery
statistics
statoscope
statuesque
statutable
statutably
staurolite
stavesacre
steadiness
steakhouse
stealthily
steamchest
steaminess
steamtight
steeliness
steelworks
stelliform
stenchtrap
stencilled
stenciller
stenograph
stentorian
stepfather
stephanite
stepladder
stepmother
stepparent
stepsister
stereobate
stereogram
stereopsis
stereotype
stereotypy
sterigmata
steriliser
sternwards
stertorous
stewardess
stickiness
stiffening
stiflebone
stiflingly
stigmatise
stigmatism
stigmatist
stilettoes
stillbirth
stillicide
stimulator
stinginess
stingingly
stinkingly
stinkstone
stipellate
stipulator
stirrupcup
stitchwort
stochastic
stockiness
stockpiler
stockproof
stockrider
stockstill
stodginess
stolidness
stomachful
stomatitis
stomatopod
stomodaeum
stoneblind
stoneborer
stonebrash
stonefruit
stonemason
stonesnipe
stopvolley
storehouse
storksbill
stormbound
stormcloud
storminess
stormproof
strabismal
strabismic
strabismus
strabotomy
straighten
straightly
strainedly
straitness
stramonium
strategist
strathspey
stratiform
stratocrat
strawberry
strawboard
streamless
streamline
streetdoor
streetward
strengthen
stressless
strictness
stridently
stridulant
stridulate
stridulous
strikingly
stringbean
stringency
stringendo
stringhalt
stringless
striptease
Stroganoff
stromatous
stronghold
strongroom
structural
structured
struthious
strychnine
strychnism
stubbiness
stubbornly
studiously
stuffiness
stumpiness
stunningly
stupendous
stupidness
sturdiness
stylistics
stylograph
stypticity
subacidity
subaquatic
subaqueous
subaverage
subcentral
subclavian
subcordate
subculture
subdeanery
subduction
subglacial
subheading
subjectify
subjection
subjective
subjugator
subkingdom
subletting
sublimable
subliminal
sublingual
submariner
submediant
submersion
submission
submissive
submitting
submontane
subnuclear
suborbital
subordinal
subreption
subroutine
subscriber
subsection
subsellium
subsequent
subshrubby
subsidence
subsidiary
subsistent
subspecies
substation
substitute
substratum
subtenancy
subterfuge
subtleness
subtrahend
subvention
subversion
subversive
succedanea
successful
succession
successive
succinctly
succulence
succulency
sudatorium
suddenness
sufferable
sufferably
sufferance
sufficient
suffragist
sugardaddy
sugarhouse
sugariness
sugarmaple
suggestion
suggestive
suicidally
sullenness
sulphonate
sulphurate
sulphurise
sulphurous
sultanship
sultriness
summerlike
summertime
summitless
summonable
sunderance
sunglasses

sunparlour
superacute
superaltar
superation
superbness
supercargo
superduper
supergiant
superhuman
superiorly
superlunar
supernally
supernovae
superorder
superpower
supersonic
superstore
supertonic
supervisor
supination
supineness
supperless
supplanter
supplejack
supplement
suppleness
suppletion
suppletive
suppletory
suppliance
supplicant
supplicate
supportive
supposable
supposably
supposedly
suppressor
suprarenal
surefooted
suretyship
surfactant
surgically
surmisable
surplusage
surprising
surrealism
surrealist
survivance
susceptive
suspenders
suspension
suspensive
suspensoid
suspensory
suspicious
sustaining
sustenance
sustention
sustentive
suzerainty
swaggering
swanmaiden
swanupping
swarmspore
swashplate
swaybacked
sweatgland
sweatiness
sweatshirt
sweepingly
sweepstake
sweetbread
sweetbriar
sweetbrier
sweetening
sweetheart
sweltering
swimmingly
swinefever
swingingly
swinglebar
switchback
switchover
swiveleyed
swivelling
swordcraft
sworddance
swordgrass
swordstick
sybaritism
sycophancy
syllabaria
syllogiser
symbolical
symboliser
symmetrise
sympathise
symphonion
symphonist
symphylous
symphyseal
symphysial
symposiast
synaeresis
synaloepha
synanthous
syncarpous
synchronal
synchronic
syncopated
syncopator
syncretise
syncretism
syncretist
syndicator
synecdoche
synecology
synergetic
syngenesis
synoecious
synonymist
synonymity
synonymous
synoptical
synostosis
syntagmata
synthesise
synthesist
synthetise
synthetist
syphilitic
systematic
systemless
tabernacle
tablecloth
tablelinen
tablespoon
tabularise
tabulation
tachometer
tachometry
tachymeter
tachymetry
taciturnly
tackdriver
tactically
tactlessly
tailorbird
tailormade
takingness
talebearer
talentless
taleteller
talismanic
Talmudical
tamability
tambourine
tangential
tanglement
tankengine
tantaliser
tantamount
taperecord
taperingly
tapestried
tapotement
taradiddle
tarantella
tarantelle
tardigrade
tarmacadam
Tartuffian
Tartuffism
taskmaster
tasselling
tastefully
tattletale
tauntingly
tauromachy
tautomeric
tautophony
tawdriness
taxability
taxidancer
taxidermal
taxidermic
taxonomist
teaplanter
tearjerker
tearlessly
teatrolley
technetium
technician
technicist
technocrat
technology
teenyweeny
teetotally
tegumental
telecamera
telecaster
telegraphy
telemetric
teleologic
teleostean
telepathic
telephoner
telephonic
telescopic
televiewer
television
televisual
tellership
telpherage
temperable
temperance
temperedly
temporally
temporalty
temporiser
temptation
temptingly
tenability
tenantable
tenantless
tenderfoot
tenderloin
tenderness
tendinitis
tendrillar
tendrilled
tenebrific
tenebrious
tenemental
tentacular
tenterhook
tepidarium
teratogeny
teratology
teratomata
termagancy
terminable
terminably
terminally
terminator
termitaria
terneplate
terracotta
terreplein
terrorless
tessellate
testaceous
testflight
tetchiness
tetrachord
tetragonal
tetrahedra
tetrameter
tetramorph
tetrapolis
tetrarchic
tetrastich
tetrastyle
tetterwort
textualist
texturally
thalecress
thankfully
theatrical
theistical
themselves
theocratic
theodicean
theodolite
theogonist
theologian
theologise
theologist
theophanic
theophoric
theopneust
theoretics
theosopher
thereabout
thereafter
thereanent
thereunder
thermionic
thermistor
thermogram
thermophil
thermopile
thermostat
theurgical
thickening
thievishly
thillhorse
thimbleful
thimblerig
thinkingly
thinkpiece
thirdclass
thirdparty
thirteenth
thirtyfold
thixotropy
thornapple
thorniness
thornproof
thoroughly
thoughtful
thousandth
threadbare
threadfish
threadmark
threadworm
threatener
threepence
threepenny
threepiece
threescore
threnodial
threnodist
thriftless
throatwort
thromboses
thrombosis
thrombotic
throneless
throughout
throughput
throughway
throwstick
thruppence
thumbprint
thumbscrew
thumbstall
thunderbox
thundering
thunderous
thwartship
thwartwise
tickertape
ticklishly
ticpolonga
tiddlywink
tidewaiter
tilthammer
timberhead
timberline
timbertoes
timberwolf
timberwork
timbrology
timekeeper
timelessly
timeliness
timesaving
timeserver
timocratic
timorously
tinctorial
tinselling
tirailleur
tirelessly
tiresomely
tiringroom
titanesque
titivation
tittupping
titubation
tobogganer
tocopherol
toffeenose
toilsomely
tolerantly
toleration
tollbridge
tomfoolery
tomography
tonelessly
tongueless
tonguetied
toothbrush
toothiness
toothpaste
toothshell
topazolite
topgallant
topicality
topography
topologist
topsyturvy
torchlight
toroidally
torpidness
torrential
torridness
tortellini
tortfeasor
tortiously
tortuosity
tortuously
totemistic
touchiness
touchingly
touchjudge
touchpaper
touchstone
tourbillon
tourmaline
tournament
tourniquet
towardness
toweringly
townswoman
toxication
toxicology
toxiphobia
trabeation
trabeculae
trabecular
tracheated
tracheitis
Tractarian
tractional
trafficked
trafficker
tragacanth
tragically
tragicomic
traitorous
trajection
trajectory
trammelled
tramontana
tramontane
trampoline
trancelike
tranquilly
transactor
transcribe
transcript
transducer
transeptal
transferee
transferor
transfuser
transgress
transience
transiency
transistor
transition
transitive
transitory
translator
translucid
translunar
transmuter
transplant
transposal
transposer
transshape
transvalue
transverse
trappiness
trashiness
traumatism
travelling
travelogue
travertine
trawlerman
treadboard
treadwheel

treasonous
trecentist
tremendous
tremolitic
trenchancy
trendiness
trepanning
trespasser
triacetate
triandrous
triangular
tribometer
tribrachic
trichiasis
trichinise
trichinous
trichology
trichotomy
trichroism
trichromat
trickiness
trickishly
triclinium
tricyclist
Tridentine
trierarchy
triflingly
trifoliate
trifurcate
trigeminal
triggerman
triglyphic
trigonally
trilateral
trilingual
triliteral
trillionth
trimonthly
trimorphic
trioecious
tripartite
triphammer
triphthong
triplicate
triplicity
triquetrae
triquetral
trisection
triskelion
triternate
triturable
triturator
triumphant
triumviral
trivialise
trivialism
triviality
trochanter
trochoidal
troctolite
troglodyte
trolleybus
trollopish
trombonist
tromometer
tropaeolum
trophology
tropically
tropologic
tropopause
tropophyte
Trotskyism
Trotskyist
Trotskyite
troubadour
trousseaux
trouvaille
trowelling
trucklebed
truculence
truculency
truncately
truncation
trundlebed
trustfully
trustiness
trustingly
truthfully
tryptophan
tsarevitch
tubercular
tuberculin
tuberosity
tubicolous
tuffaceous
tufthunter
tuitionary
tularaemia
tularaemic
tumbledown
tumblerful
tumbleweed
tumescence
tumultuary
tumultuous
tunelessly
tunnelling
turbidness
turbulence
turbulency
turgescent
turgidness
turkeycock
turnbuckle
turpentine
turtleback
turtledove
turtleneck
tutorially
twelvefold
twelvenote
twelvetone
twilighted
twowheeler
tympanites
tympanitic
tympanitis
typescript
typesetter
typewriter
typicality
typography
typologist
tyrannical
Tyrrhenian
ubiquitous
ulceration
ulcerative
ulotrichan
ulteriorly
ultimately
ultrabasic
ultrasonic
ultrasound
umbellifer
umbilicate
umbiliform
umbrageous
umbrellaed
umpireship
unabridged
unaccented
unaffected
unAmerican
unarguable
unassisted
unassuming
unattached
unattended
unavailing
unbalanced
unbearable
unbearably
unbeatable
unbeatably
unbecoming
unbeliever
unbesought
unbiblical
unbiddable
unblenched
unblinking
unblushing
unbonneted
unbrokenly
unbuttoned
unchanging
unchastity
uncloister
uncommonly
uncritical
unctuosity
unctuously
uncustomed
undefended
undeniable
undeniably
underbelly
underbrush
undercliff
undercover
undercroft
underdress
underfloor
underglaze
underlease
underlinen
underlying
underminer
underneath
underpants
underproof
underquote
underscore
undersense
undersexed
undershirt
undershoot
undershrub
undersized
underskirt
underslung
understand
understate
understeer
understock
understood
understudy
undertaken
undertaker
undertrick
undervalue
underwater
underworld
underwrite
underwrote
undeserved
undesigned
undesirous
undeterred
undigested
undulation
undulatory
uneasiness
uneconomic
unedifying
uneducated
unemphatic
unemployed
unendingly
unenviable
unequalled
unerringly
unevenness
uneventful
unexampled
unexcelled
unexpected
unexplored
unfadingly
unfairness
unfaithful
unfamiliar
unfathered
unfeminine
unfettered
unfilially
unfinished
unflagging
unforeseen
unfriended
unfriendly
ungenerous
ungraceful
ungracious
ungrateful
ungrounded
ungrudging
unguentary
unhallowed
unhandsome
unhistoric
unholiness
unhouseled
uniaxially
unicameral
unicyclist
uniformity
unilateral
unilingual
unilocular
unimproved
uninformed
uninitiate
unionistic
unipartite
uniqueness
university
univocally
unjustness
unkindness
unknowable
unlabelled
unlawfully
unlettered
unlikeness
unmannerly
unmeasured
unmeetness
unmerciful
unmorality
unmortised
unnameable
unnumbered
unoccupied
unofficial
unorthodox
unpleasant
unpleasing
unprepared
unprovoked
unravelled
unreadable
unredeemed
unreliable
unrelieved
unremarked
unrequited
unreserved
unresolved
unripeness
unrivalled
unruliness
unscalable
unschooled
unscramble
unscreened
unscripted
unseasoned
unselected
unsettling
unsociable
unsociably
unsocially
unsporting
unsteadily
unstrained
unstressed
unsuitable
unswerving
unthinking
untidiness
untowardly
untroubled
untruthful
unwariness
unwavering
unwieldily
unwontedly
unworkable
unworthily
unwrinkled
unyielding
upbraiding
upbringing
upholstery
upperclass
uppishness
uproarious
upstanding
upwardness
uranometry
urbanology
urethritis
urochordal
urticarial
urtication
usefulness
usquebaugh
ustulation
usucaption
usuriously
usurpation
utilisable
utopianism
uxoricidal
uxoriously
vaccinator
validation
valleculae
vallecular
valorously
valvulitis
vanadinite
vanquisher
vaporiform
vaporously
varicocele
varicosity
variegated
varietally
variolitic
variometer
vascularly
vasoactive
Vaticanism
Vaticanist
vaticinate
vaudeville
vectograph
vegetarian
vegetation
vegetative
vehemently
veldschoen
velitation
velocipede
velutinous
venational
veneration
vengefully
venialness
venomously
ventilator
ventricose
ventriculi
verandahed
verbaliser
verifiable
vermicelli
vermicidal
vermicular
vernacular
vernissage
versicular
vertebrate
vertically
vesication
vesicatory
vesiculate
vesperbell
vespertine
vestibular
vestibulum
vestpocket
veterinary
vibraculum
vibraphone
viceconsul
vicegerent
viceregent
victimiser
Victoriana
victorious
victualled
victualler
videophone
Vietnamese
viewfinder
viewlessly
vigilantly
vignettist
vigorously
villainage
villainess
villainous
villanelle
villeinage
vindicable
vindicator
vindictive
vinegarish
violaceous
viperiform
viperously
viraginous
virescence
virginally
virginhood
virologist
virtuality
virtueless
virtuosity
virtuously

virulently
viscerally
viscometer
viscountcy
visibility
Visigothic
visionally
visionless
visitation
visitorial
visualiser
vitalistic
vitaminise
vitiligate
vitrescent
vitriolise
vituperate
vivandiere
viviparity
viviparous
vivisector
viziership
vocabulary
vocational
vociferant
vociferate
vociferous
voiceprint
volatilise
volatility
volitional
volleyball
voltameter
volubility
volumetric
voluminous
voluptuary
voluptuous
vomitorium
vortically
vorticella
vorticular
voyageable
vulcaniser
vulnerable
vulnerably
waffleiron
waggonette
wagonvault
wainwright
waistcloth
Waldensian
wallflower
wallpepper
wampumpeag
wanderings
wanderlust
wanderplug
wantonness
wappenshaw
wardenship
warmingpan
wassailing
wastefully
wastepaper
watchfully
watchglass
watchguard
watchmaker
watchtower
waterborne
waterbrash
waterclock
watercraft
watercress
waterflood
waterfront
waterglass
wateriness

watermelon
waterpower
waterproof
waterskier
waterspout
watertight
waterwheel
waterworks
wattlebird
wavelength
waveringly
weakliness
weakminded
weaponless
wearifully
weatherbox
weathering
weatherman
weaverbird
weedkiller
weightless
weimaraner
wellheeled
wellington
wellspoken
wellspring
wellturned
wellwisher
Welshwoman
wentletrap
werewolves
Wertherian
Wertherism
westernise
westwardly
whaleshark
wharfinger
whatsoever
wheatstone
wheelchair
wheelhorse
wheelhouse
wheeziness
whensoever
whereabout
whipstitch
whirlybird
whiskified
whispering
whitebeard
whitefaced
whitesmith
whitethorn
WhitMonday
WhitSunday
wholesaler
whomsoever
whorehouse
wickedness
wickerwork
widespread
wildebeest
wilderment
wilderness
wildfowler
wilfulness
willowherb
willynilly
willywilly
winceyette
Winchester
windflower
windjammer
windowless
windowpane
windowseat
windowshop
windowsill
windscreen

windshield
windsleeve
winebibber
winebottle
winegrower
wingcollar
wingfooted
wingspread
wintertide
wintertime
wintriness
wiredrawer
wirehaired
wirepuller
wiretapper
wirewalker
wireworker
wishywashy
witchcraft
witchhazel
witchingly
withdrawal
withdrawer
withholder
witnessbox
wobbliness
woefulness
wolframite
womanishly
wonderland
wonderment
wonderwork
wondrously
wongawonga
wontedness
woodcarver
woodcutter
woodenhead
woodenness
woodlander
woodpecker
woodpigeon
woodturner
woodworker
woolgather
woolgrower
woolliness
woolsorter
wordlessly
workbasket
workingman
workpeople
worldclass
worldweary
worshipful
worshipped
worshipper
worthiness
worthwhile
wraparound
wrathfully
wrathiness
wretchedly
wristwatch
wrongdoing
wrongfully
wrongously
wunderkind
Wycliffite
Wykehamist
xenophobia
xerography
xerophytic
xiphosuran
xylography
xylophonic
yarborough
yardmaster
yearningly

yeastiness
yellowback
yellowbird
yellowness
yellowwood
yesteryear
yieldingly
ylangylang
yokefellow
youngberry
yourselves
youthfully
zabaglione
ZendAvesta
zigzagging
zincograph
zollverein
zoological
zoomorphic
zoophagous
zoophilous
zwitterion
zygodactyl
zygomorphy

---

aardwolves
babblement
babiroussa
Babylonian
babysitter
bacchantes
bacchantic
backbiting
backblocks
backgammon
background
backhanded
backhander
backsheesh
backslider
backstairs
backstitch
backstroke
backwardly
badderlock
bafflement
bafflingly
balbriggan
balderdash
baldheaded
ballflower
ballistics
ballooning
balloonist
balneology
balustrade
banderilla
bandmaster
banishment
bankruptcy
baptistery
barbellate
barbershop
barbituric
barcarolle
bardolatry
barebacked
barefooted
bareheaded
barelegged
bargeboard
barkentine
barleybree
barleybroo
barleycorn
Barmecidal
barometric
baronetage
barracouta

barramunda
barramundi
barratrous
barrelling
barrenness
barrenwort
barysphere
basketball
basketwork
bassethorn
bassoonist
bastardise
batfowling
batholitic
bathometer
bathymeter
bathymetry
bathyscaph
bathyscope
batrachian
battailous
battledore
battlement
battleship
bawdyhouse
cabalistic
cacciatore
cachinnate
cackhanded
cacodaemon
cacogenics
cacography
cacomistle
cadaverous
caddisworm
Caerphilly
caespitose
cajolement
cajolingly
calamander
calamitous
calcareous
calceolate
calciferol
calcsinter
calculable
calculably
calculator
Caledonian
calibrator
caliginous
callowness
calumniate
calumnious
calyciform
calyptrate
camelopard
camerlengo
camerlingo
camouflage
campaigner
campestral
camphorate
canaliculi
cancellate
cancelling
cancellous
candelabra
candescent
candidness
candlefish
candletree
candlewick
candlewood
candyfloss
cankerworm
cannelloni
cannonball
canonicals

canonicate
canonicity
canorously
cantaloupe
cantatrice
canterbury
cantilever
cantillate
cantonment
canvasback
canvaswork
canzonetta
caoutchouc
capability
capacitate
capacitive
capitalise
capitalism
capitalist
capitation
Capitoline
capitulary
capitulate
cappuccino
capricious
captiously
carabineer
carabinier
caramelise
caravaneer
caravanned
caravanner
carbonnade
carboxylic
carbuncled
carcinogen
carcinosis
cardialgia
cardiogram
cardiology
cardplayer
carelessly
caricature
carmagnole
carnallite
carnassial
carotenoid
carotinoid
carpellary
carpetweed
carphology
carragheen
carryingon
Carthusian
cartomancy
cartoonist
cartwright
caruncular
caryatides
cascarilla
caseharden
caseworker
cassolette
castration
casualness
catabolism
catafalque
catalectic
cataleptic
cataloguer
cataphract
catarrhine
catastasis
catburglar
catchpenny
catechesis
catechetic
catechiser
catechumen

categorise
catenation
catholicon
catholicos
catoptrics
cattlegrid
causticity
cautionary
cautiously
cavalierly
cavalryman
cavitation
daintiness
daisychain
damageable
damagingly
dampcourse
dampingoff
dapplegrey
datamation
daughterly
dauphiness
daydreamer
dazzlement
dazzlingly
earthbound
earthiness
earthlight
earthquake
earthshine
earthwards
eartrumpet
earwigging
earwitness
easterling
Eastertide
fabricator
fabulously
faceharden
facesaving
facileness
facilitate
factiously
factitious
factorship
factualism
factualist
factuality
fadelessly
Fahrenheit
faintheart
fairground
fairhaired
fairleader
fairminded
fairspoken
fairycycle
faithfully
fallacious
fallingoff
fallowness
familiarly
famishment
famousness
fanaticise
fanaticism
fancifully
fandangoes
fantastico
fantoccini
farcically
farfetched
farsighted
fasciation
fascicular
fasciculus
fascinator
fastidious
fastigiate
fatalistic
fatherhood
fatherland
fatherless
fatherlike
fathership
fathomable
fathomless
fatiguable
faultiness
favourable
favourably
gadolinite
gadolinium
gadrooning
gaillardia
gaingiving
galimatias
galleywest
galliambic
galloglass
Gallomania
Gallophile
Gallophobe
galvaniser
gambolling
gamekeeper
gametangia
ganglionic
gangrenous
gargantuan
garishness
garnierite
garnishing
gasconader
gaslighter
gaspereaux
gasteropod
gastrology
gastronome
gastronomy
gatekeeper
gatelegged
gaucheness
gaultheria
gauntleted
habiliment
habilitate
habitation
habitually
hackbuteer
hackmatack
haematosis
haematuria
haemolysis
haemolytic
hagiolatry
hagiologic
hagioscope
hairraiser
hairspring
hairstreak
hairstroke
hakenkreuz
halberdier
halfcocked
halfdollar
halflength
halfnelson
halfvolley
halfwitted
halfyearly
halieutics
hallelujah
halogenate
halogenous
halophytic
hammerbeam
hammerhead
hammerless
hammerlock
hammerpond
hamshackle
handbarrow
handedness
handgallop
handicraft
handmaiden
handpicked
handselled
handsomely
handspring
handworked
hangglider
hankypanky
Hanoverian
Hansardise
hanselling
harassment
harbourage
hardbilled
hardbitten
hardboiled
hardfisted
hardhanded
hardheaded
harelipped
harmlessly
harmonical
harmonious
harmoniser
hartebeest
haruspices
harvestman
hauntingly
haustellum
haustorium
hawserlaid
iatrogenic
jackanapes
jackassery
jackhammer
jackknives
jackrabbit
jacobinise
Jacobinism
Jacobitism
jaggedness
jaguarundi
janitorial
Janusfaced
Japanesque
jardiniere
jargonelle
jasperware
jauntiness
jawbreaker
jaywalking
Kafkaesque
kaisership
Kantianism
karyoplasm
katabolism
labiovelar
laboratory
laceration
lacerative
lachrymose
lacklustre
laconicism
lacrimator
lacrymator
lactescent
lacustrine
ladderback
ladychapel
ladyfinger
ladykiller
Lamarckian
Lamarckism
lambrequin
lamentable
lamentably
lamentedly
laminarian
lamination
Lammastide
lampoonery
lampoonist
lanceolate
landholder
landhunger
landingnet
landlocked
landlubber
landocracy
landowning
landscaper
languisher
languorous
lansquenet
lanternfly
lanthanide
lanuginose
lanuginous
laparotomy
lapidarian
lapidarist
lapidation
lardydardy
largescale
larvicidal
laryngitic
laryngitis
lascivious
laterality
latescence
latifundia
lattermost
laughingly
laundryman
lauraceous
laureation
laurelling
lavalliere
lavatorial
lavishment
lavishness
lawabiding
lawbreaker
lawfulness
lawntennis
lawrencium
Lawrentian
macadamise
Maccabaean
macebearer
maceration
machinator
machinegun
mackintosh
macrophage
macrospore
maculation
maculature
madreporic
magistracy
magistrate
magnetiser
magnifical
magnificat
magnifying
Mahommedan
maidenhair
maidenhead
maidenhood
maidenlike
mainlander
mainspring
mainstream
maintainer
maisonette
majestical
majuscular
makeweight
malacoderm
malacology
maladapted
malapertly
malapropos
malcontent
malefactor
maleficent
malentendu
malevolent
malfeasant
malignance
malignancy
malingerer
malleebird
malleefowl
mallenders
malodorous
Malpighian
Malthusian
malvaceous
mamillated
manageable
manageably
management
manageress
managerial
manchineel
mandibular
mandragora
manfulness
mangosteen
maniacally
Manichaean
Manicheism
manicurist
manifestly
manifestos
manifoldly
manipulate
manoeuvrer
manoeuvres
manometric
manorhouse
manservant
mansuetude
manteltree
manumitted
manuscript
manzanilla
maquillage
maraschino
marcescent
Marcionite
marginalia
marginally
marginated
margravate
margravine
marguerite
Mariolater
Mariolatry
marionette
marketable
markethall
markettown
markswoman
marquisate
marrowbone
marrowless
marshalled
marshaller
marshalsea
marshiness
martensite
martialism
martingale
marvelling
marvellous
masquerade
Massoretic
mastectomy
masterhand
masterhood
masterless
mastermind
mastership
masterwork
masticable
masticator
matchboard
matchmaker
matchstick
materially
maternally
mathematic
matriarchy
matricidal
matronhood
matronship
matronymic
maturation
maturative
matureness
mavourneen
maxilliped
maximalist
mayblossom
mayonnaise
nailpolish
nambypamby
namelessly
nanisation
nanosecond
naphthenic
narcissism
narcissist
narcolepsy
narrowness
nasturtium
natalitial
natatorial
natatorium
nationally
nationhood
nationless
nationwide
nativeborn
nativeness
nativistic
natterjack
naturalise
naturalism
naturalist
naturopath
nauseating
nauseously
nautically
navigation
oafishness
pacesetter
pacifiable
pacificate
pacificism
pacificist
packingbox
packsaddle
packthread
paddleboat
paddyfield

paddywagon
paddywhack
paedagogic
paederasty
paediatric
paedogogue
paedophile
pagination
painkiller
painlessly
paintbrush
Palaeocene
Palaeogene
palaeolith
palaeotype
Palaeozoic
palagonite
palatalise
palatinate
palimpsest
palindrome
palisander
palladious
pallbearer
palliation
palliative
palliatory
pallidness
palmaceous
palmatifid
palmbutter
palmerworm
PalmSunday
paltriness
palynology
Panamanian
pancratium
pancreatic
pancreatin
panegyrise
panegyrist
pangenesis
pangenetic
panhandler
paniculate
panjandrum
panopticon
pansophist
pantograph
pantomimic
pantrymaid
papaverine
papaverous
paperchase
paperknife
papermaker
papistical
papyrology
parabiosis
parabiotic
parabolise
paraboloid
paradisaic
paradisean
paradisiac
paradisian
paradoxure
paraffinic
paragnosis
paralipsis
paralogise
paralogism
paramecium
parametric
paramnesia
paranormal
paraphrase
paraphrast
paraplegia
paraplegic
parapodium
paraselene
parasitism
parasitoid
paratactic
paratroops
parcelling
pardonable
pardonably
parenchyma
parentally
parenteral
parenthood
parimutuel
parliament
Parnassian
paronymous
paroxysmal
paroxytone
parramatta
parricidal
parrotfish
parsonbird
parsonical
partiality
participle
particular
parturient
pasquinade
passageway
passionary
passionate
Passionist
pasteboard
pastellist
pasteurise
pasteurism
pastmaster
pastorally
pastorship
pastrycook
pasturable
pastyfaced
patchiness
patentable
paternally
pathetical
pathfinder
pathogenic
pathologic
patination
patisserie
patriality
patriarchy
patriciate
patricidal
patrilocal
patriotism
patristics
patrolling
patronymic
patulously
pawnbroker
rabbinical
rabblement
racecourse
Rachmanism
rackrenter
radicalise
radicalism
radication
radiogenic
radiograph
radiologic
radiometer
radiometry
radiopaque
radiophone
radioscopy
radiosonde
ragamuffin
raggedness
railroader
railwayman
rainmaking
rakishness
ramblingly
rampageous
ramshackle
rancidness
randomness
ranunculus
rapporteur
ratability
ratcatcher
rationally
rattlehead
rattlepate
rattletrap
ravenously
ravishment
razorblade
razorshell
razzmatazz
sabbatical
sabretache
sabretooth
saccharate
saccharide
saccharify
saccharine
saccharoid
saccharose
sacerdotal
sacredness
sacrificer
sacroiliac
sacrosanct
saddleback
saddlefast
saddletree
safeblower
safetybelt
sagination
sagittally
sailorless
salability
salamander
salesclerk
saleswoman
salicional
salicylate
salientian
saliferous
salivation
sallenders
sallowness
salmagundi
salmonella
salmonleap
salpingian
saltarello
saltcellar
saltigrade
salubrious
salutarily
salutation
salutatory
samarskite
sanatorium
sanctifier
sanctimony
sanctitude
sandalwood
sandbagger
sandcastle
sanderling
sandhopper
sandmartin
sanguinary
sanguinely
sanguinity
sanitarian
sanitarily
sanitarium
sanitation
Sanskritic
sapiential
sappanwood
sapphirine
saprogenic
saprophyte
sarcolemma
sarcophagi
sarcophagy
sarcoplasm
sargassoes
sarmentose
sarmentous
sarracenia
sashwindow
satanology
satellitic
satisfying
saturation
saturnalia
satyagraha
satyriasis
sauerkraut
savageness
savourless
sawtoothed
saxicoline
saxicolous
tabernacle
tablecloth
tablelinen
tablespoon
tabularise
tabulation
tachometer
tachometry
tachymeter
tachymetry
taciturnly
tackdriver
tactically
tactlessly
tailorbird
tailormade
takingness
talebearer
talentless
taleteller
talismanic
Talmudical
tamability
tambourine
tangential
tanglement
tankengine
tantaliser
tantamount
taperecord
taperingly
tapestried
tapotement
taradiddle
tarantella
tarantelle
tardigrade
tarmacadam
Tartuffian
Tartuffism
taskmaster
tasselling
tastefully
tattletale
tauntingly
tauromachy
tautomeric
tautophony
tawdriness
taxability
taxidancer
taxidermal
taxidermic
taxonomist
vaccinator
validation
valleculae
vallecular
valorously
valvulitis
vanadinite
vanquisher
vaporiform
vaporously
varicocele
varicosity
variegated
varietally
variolitic
variometer
vascularly
vasoactive
Vaticanism
Vaticanist
vaticinate
vaudeville
waffleiron
waggonette
wagonvault
wainwright
waistcloth
Waldensian
wallflower
wallpepper
wampumpeag
wanderings
wanderlust
wanderplug
wantonness
wappenshaw
wardenship
warmingpan
wassailing
wastefully
wastepaper
watchfully
watchglass
watchguard
watchmaker
watchtower
waterborne
waterbrash
waterclock
watercraft
watercress
waterflood
waterfront
waterglass
wateriness
watermelon
waterpower
waterproof
waterskier
waterspout
watertight
waterwheel
waterworks
wattlebird
wavelength
waveringly
yarborough
yardmaster
zabaglione
abacterial
abbreviate
abdication
abdominous
abducentes
aberdevine
aberrantly
aberration
abhorrence
abiogenist
abjectness
abjuration
ablebodied
abnegation
abnormally
abominable
abominably
abominator
aboriginal
abortively
aboveboard
Abrahamman
abrasively
abreaction
abridgment
abrogation
abruptness
abscission
absolutely
absolution
absolutism
absolutist
absolutory
absorbable
absorbance
absorbedly
absorbency
absorption
absorptive
abstemious
abstention
abstergent
abstersion
abstersive
abstinence
abstinency
abstracted
abstracter
abstractly
abstractor
abstrusely
abstrusity
absurdness
abundantly
ebullience
ebulliency
ebullition
obdurately
obediently
obfuscated
obituarist
objectival
objectless
oblateness
obligation
obligatory
obligingly
obliterate
obnubilate
obsequious
observable
observably
observance
obstetrics
obstructor
obtainable
obtainment

obtruncate
obturation
obtuseness
ubiquitous
academical
acarpelous
acatalepsy
accelerate
accentuate
acceptable
acceptably
acceptance
acceptedly
accessible
accessibly
accidental
accomplice
accomplish
accordance
accoucheur
accountant
accounting
accredited
accrescent
accumulate
accurately
accursedly
accusation
accusative
accusatory
accusingly
accustomed
acephalous
acervation
acetabular
acetabulum
achievable
achondrite
achromatic
acidimeter
acidimetry
acidophile
acoelomate
acotyledon
acoustical
acquirable
acquitting
acrobatics
acrogenous
acromegaly
acronychal
acrophobia
acroterion
acroterium
actinolite
actinozoan
actionable
actionably
activation
activeness
ecchymosis
ecchymotic
ecclesiast
echinoderm
ecological
economical
economiser
ectodermal
ectodermic
ectogenous
ecumenical
eczematous
icebreaker
ichthyosis
iconoclasm
iconolater
iconolatry
iconomachy
iconometer
iconometry
iconoscope
occasional
occidental
occupation
occupative
occurrence
oceanarium
oceangoing
oceanology
ocellation
ochlocracy
octahedral
octahedron
octamerous
octandrian
octandrous
octodecimo
octonarian
octopodous
scabrously
scaffolder
scaleboard
scandalise
scandalous
scansorial
scantiness
scapegrace
scarabaeid
scarabaeus
scaramouch
scarceness
scaredycat
scarlatina
scatheless
scathingly
scattergun
scattering
scattiness
scavengery
scenically
scepticism
schematise
schematism
schemozzle
scherzando
schipperke
schismatic
schizocarp
schizogony
scholastic
schoolable
schoolbook
schooldays
schoolgirl
schoolmaam
schoolmarm
schoolmate
schoolroom
schooltime
schoolwork
sciagraphy
scientific
Scillonian
sciolistic
scleroderm
sclerotium
sclerotomy
scoffingly
scoreboard
scoresheet
scornfully
scorzonera
Scotswoman
Scotticise
Scotticism
scrapmetal
scratchily
scratchwig
screechowl
screenings
screenplay
screwplate
screwpress
scribbling
scrimmager
scrimshank
scriptoria
scriptural
scrofulous
scrollwork
scrupulous
scrutineer
scrutinise
sculptress
sculptural
sculptured
scurrility
scurrilous
scurviness
scutellate
scyphiform
scyphozoan
adamantine
adaptation
adaptively
additional
addlepated
adenectomy
adequately
adherently
adhesively
adhibition
adjacently
adjectival
adjudgment
adjudicate
adjunction
adjunctive
adjuration
adjuratory
adjustable
adjustment
administer
admiration
admiringly
admissible
admittable
admittance
admittedly
admonition
admonitive
admonitory
adolescent
adoptively
adrenaline
adrenergic
adroitness
adsorbable
adsorption
adsorptive
Adullamite
adulterant
adulterate
adulteress
adulterine
adulterous
adventurer
advertence
advertency
advertiser
advisement
advocation
advocatory
edentulous
edibleness
editorship
edulcorate
idealistic
ideational
ideography
ideologist
idiopathic
idolatress
idolatrous
odiousness
odontalgia
odontology
aeolotropy
aerenchyma
aerobatics
aerobiosis
aerobiotic
aeroengine
aerogramme
aerography
aerologist
aeronautic
aeronomist
aerophobia
aerostatic
aeruginous
aesthetics
aesthetism
Aethiopian
aetiologic
beadleship
Beaujolais
beautician
beautifier
becomingly
bedchamber
bedclothes
bedevilled
Bedlington
bedraggled
beechdrops
beefburger
beekeeping
beforehand
beforetime
behindhand
bejewelled
Belgravian
believable
belladonna
belletrist
bellflower
bellringer
bellwether
bellyacher
bellydance
bellylaugh
belongings
bemedalled
bemusement
benedicite
Benedictus
benefactor
beneficent
beneficial
benevolent
benignancy
Benthamism
Benthamite
benzocaine
benzpyrene
bequeathal
beribboned
Berkeleian
besprinkle
bestialise
bestiality
bestirring
bestowment
bestridden
bestseller
betterment
bewitchery
celebrated
celebrator
cellophane
cellularly
cellulitis
cellulosic
censorious
censorship
censurable
centennial
centesimal
centigrade
centilitre
centillion
centimetre
centralise
centralism
centralist
centrality
centreback
centrefold
centrehalf
centricity
centrifuge
centromere
centrosome
cephalopod
cerebellum
ceremonial
cerography
certiorari
ceruminous
cessionary
deaconship
deactivate
deadliness
deadweight
deaeration
deathwatch
debasement
debatement
debauchery
debilitate
debonairly
debouchure
decadently
decagramme
decahedral
decahedron
decampment
decapitate
decapodous
deceivable
decelerate
Decembrist
decemviral
deceptible
decigramme
decimalise
decimalism
decimation
decisively
decivilise
declarable
declassify
declension
declinable
decolonise
decolorant
decolorise
decompound
decompress
decoration
decorative
decorously
decrescent
dedication
dedicative
dedicatory
deductible
deepfreeze
deepfrozen
deeprooted
deepseated
deerforest
deescalate
defacement
defalcator
defamation
defamatory
defeasance
defeasible
defeminise
defendable
defensible
defensibly
deferrable
deficiency
defilement
definement
definienda
definitely
definition
definitive
definitude
deflagrate
deflection
deflective
deflowerer
defoliator
deforciant
defrayable
defrayment
degeneracy
degenerate
degradable
degradedly
degressive
dehiscence
dehumanise
dehumidify
dejectedly
delaminate
delectable
delectably
delegation
deliberate
delicately
delightful
delimitate
delineator
delinquent
deliquesce
delocalise
delphinium
delphinoid
deltiology
delusional
delusively
demagogism
demandable
dementedly
demobilise
democratic
demography
demoiselle
demolition
demonetise
demoniacal
demonology
demoralise
demotivate
demureness
demurrable
denaturant
dendriform

dendrology
denegation
denigrator
denominate
denotation
denotative
denouement
densimeter
dentifrice
denudation
denunciate
deodoriser
deontology
deoxidiser
department
dependable
dependably
dependence
dependency
depilation
depilatory
deplorable
deplorably
deployment
depolarise
depopulate
deportment
depositary
deposition
depository
depravedly
depreciate
depredator
depressant
depression
depressive
deprivable
depuration
depurative
deputation
deracinate
derailleur
derailment
derestrict
deridingly
derisively
derivation
derivative
dermatitis
dermatogen
derogation
derogatory
desalinate
descendant
descendent
descension
descriptor
desecrater
desecrator
deservedly
deshabille
desiccator
desiderata
desiderate
designator
designedly
designment
desipience
desirously
desistance
desolately
desolation
desorption
despatcher
desperados
despicable
despicably
despisable
despiteful
despiteous
despondent
desquamate
destructor
detachable
detachedly
detachment
detainment
detectable
detergency
determined
deterrence
detestable
detestably
detonation
detonative
detoxicant
detoxicate
detraction
detractive
Devanagari
devilishly
devitalise
devocalise
devolution
devotement
devotional
devoutness
dextrality
dextrously
fearlessly
fearnought
fearsomely
featherbed
feathering
febrifugal
fecklessly
federalise
federalism
federalist
federation
federative
feebleness
felicitate
felicitous
fellmonger
fellowship
felspathic
femaleness
feminality
femininely
femininity
fenestella
fenestrate
fertiliser
fervidness
fescennine
festoonery
fetchingly
fetterlock
feuilleton
feverishly
gelatinise
gelatinous
gemination
gemmaceous
generalise
generalist
generality
generation
generative
generatrix
generosity
generously
geneticist
genialness
geniculate
genteelism
gentilesse
gentlefolk
gentleness
geocentric
geochemist
geodetical
geognostic
geographer
geographic
geological
geometrise
geophysics
geoponical
geothermal
geothermic
geotropism
geriatrics
geriatrist
germicidal
germinally
gerundival
gesundheit
headcheese
headhunter
headmaster
headphones
headspring
headsquare
headstream
headstrong
headwaiter
heartblock
heartblood
heartbreak
heartiness
heartsease
heartthrob
heartwhole
heathendom
heathenise
heathenish
heathenism
heatstroke
heavenborn
heavensent
heavenward
heavyarmed
hebdomadal
hebetation
Hebraistic
hectically
hectograph
hectolitre
hectometre
hedonistic
heedlessly
heliacally
helianthus
Heliconian
helicopter
heliograph
heliolater
heliolatry
heliometer
heliophyte
helioscope
heliotaxis
heliotrope
heliotropy
hellbender
helminthic
helplessly
hemicyclic
hemihedral
hemihedron
hemiplegia
hemiplegic
hemipteran
hemisphere
hempnettle
henceforth
hendecagon
henharrier
henhearted
henotheism
henotheist
heortology
heparinise
hepatology
heptachord
heptagonal
Heptameron
heptameter
heptarchic
Heptateuch
heptatonic
herbaceous
hereabouts
hereditary
heresiarch
hereticate
heretofore
hermetical
hermitcrab
heroically
heroicness
heroicomic
herrenvolk
Herrnhuter
hesitantly
hesitation
hesitative
heterodont
heterodoxy
heterodyne
heterogamy
heterogeny
heterogony
heterology
heteronomy
heterotaxy
heulandite
heuristics
hexahedral
hexahedron
hexamerous
hexametric
Jehovistic
jejuneness
jeopardise
jerrybuilt
jesuitical
Jewishness
kennelling
kenspeckle
keratinise
keratinous
kerchieves
kerseymere
kerygmatic
kettledrum
keyboarder
leadenness
leaderless
leadership
leafcutter
leafhopper
leafinsect
lebensraum
lectionary
lederhosen
ledgerbait
ledgerline
lefthanded
lefthander
legalistic
legateship
legibility
legislator
legitimacy
legitimate
legitimise
legitimism
legitimist
leguminous
Leibnizian
lemniscate
lemongrass
lengthways
lengthwise
lenticular
lentigines
leopardess
lepidolite
leprechaun
lesbianism
letterbomb
letterbook
lettercard
letterhead
letterless
leucocytic
leucoplast
leukocytic
levigation
levitation
lexicology
lexigraphy
meadowland
meadowlark
meagreness
mealbeetle
meaningful
measliness
measurable
measurably
measuredly
mechanical
meddlesome
mediastina
mediatress
medicament
medicaster
medication
medicative
medievally
mediocrity
meditation
meditative
medullated
meerschaum
megalithic
megalosaur
megascopic
melancholy
Melanesian
melanistic
meliorator
melismatic
mellowness
meltingpot
membership
membranous
memorandum
menacingly
mendacious
mendicancy
meningioma
meningitis
menopausal
menstruate
menstruous
mensurable
mentorship
mercantile
mercifully
meridional
merrymaker
mesenteric
mesenteron
mesmeriser
Mesolithic
mesomerism
mesomorphy
mesophytic
mesoscaphe
mesosphere
mesothorax
messianism
metabolise
metabolism
metabolite
metacarpal
metacarpus
metacentre
metagalaxy
metalepsis
metallurgy
metamerism
metaphoric
metaphrase
metaphysic
metaplasia
metastable
metastases
metastasis
metastatic
metatarsal
metatarsus
metatheses
metathesis
metathetic
metathorax
metempiric
meteoritic
methodical
Methuselah
methylated
meticulous
metrically
metronomic
metronymic
metropolis
mettlesome
Neapolitan
nebulosity
nebulously
necrolater
necrolatry
necromancy
necrophile
necrophily
necropolis
necroscopy
nectareous
needlebath
needlebook
needlecord
needlefish
needlessly
needlework
negatively
negativism
negativist
negativity
neglectful
negligence
negligible
negligibly
negotiable
negotiator
negrophile
negrophobe
nematocyst
neoclassic
neological
neoplastic

nepenthean
nephograph
nephoscope
nephralgia
nephridium
nephrology
nethermost
nettlerash
neurilemma
neurolemma
neuropathy
neuroplasm
neurotoxin
neutralise
neutralism
neutralist
neutrality
nevernever
newfangled
newsagency
newscaster
newsletter
newsmonger
newsreader
newsvendor
newsworthy
newswriter
oecologist
oecumenism
oedematose
oedematous
oenologist
oesophagus
peacefully
peacemaker
peacockery
peacockish
pearldiver
peashooter
pebbledash
peccadillo
pectinated
peculation
peculiarly
pedagogics
pedalorgan
pedalpoint
pederastic
pedestrian
pediculate
pediculous
pedicurist
pedimental
pedimented
pedologist
peduncular
peerlessly
pegmatitic
pejoration
pejorative
pellagrous
pellicular
pellucidly
pemphigoid
pemphigous
pencilling
pendentive
penetrable
penetrably
penetralia
penetrance
penetrator
penicillin
peninsular
penitently
penmanship
pennaceous
pennanular
pennillion
pennyroyal
pennyworth
penologist
penpushing
pensionary
pentachord
pentagonal
pentameter
pentastich
pentathlon
pentatomic
pentatonic
pentimento
pentstemon
peppercorn
peppermill
peppermint
pepperwort
percentage
percentile
perception
perceptive
perceptual
perchloric
percipient
percolator
percussion
percussive
perdurable
perdurably
peremptory
perfection
perfective
perfidious
perfoliate
perforator
performing
periclinal
pericyclic
peridermal
perigynous
perihelion
perilously
periodical
periosteal
periosteum
peripeteia
peripheral
peripteral
periscopic
perishable
perithecia
peritoneal
peritoneum
periwigged
periwinkle
perjurious
permafrost
permanence
permanency
permeation
permeative
permission
permissive
permitting
permutable
pernicious
pernickety
peroration
peroxidise
perpetrate
perpetuate
perpetuity
perplexity
perquisite
persecutor
persiflage
persistent
personable
personally
personalty
personator
persuasion
persuasive
pertinence
pertinency
perversely
perversion
perversity
perversive
pesticidal
pestilence
petiolated
petiteness
petitioner
petroglyph
petrolatum
petronella
petulantly
reactivate
reactively
reactivity
readership
reafforest
realisable
reallocate
reappraise
rearmament
reasonable
reasonably
reasonless
reassemble
reassembly
rebellious
rebuttable
recallable
receivable
recentness
receptacle
receptible
rechristen
recidivism
recidivist
recipiency
reciprocal
recitalist
recitation
recitative
recitativo
recklessly
recolonise
recommence
recompense
reconciler
reconsider
recordable
recoupment
recreantly
recreation
recreative
recrudesce
rectorship
recumbency
recuperate
recurrence
recyclable
redblooded
redcurrant
redecorate
redeemable
redemption
redemptive
redemptory
redescribe
rediscover
redolently
redundance
redundancy
reelection
reeligible
reentrance
referendum
refillable
refinement
reflection
reflective
reflexible
reformable
refraction
refractive
refractory
refreshing
refringent
refuelling
refulgence
refundable
refundment
refutation
regalement
regardless
regelation
regeneracy
regenerate
regentship
regimental
regionally
registered
registrant
regression
regressive
regretting
regularise
regularity
regulation
regulative
regulatory
reichsmark
reissuable
reiterance
rejectable
rejoicings
rejuvenate
rejuvenise
relational
relatively
relativise
relativism
relativist
relativity
relaxation
releasable
relegation
relentless
relevantly
relievable
relinquish
relishable
relocation
reluctance
reluctancy
remarkable
remarkably
remarriage
remediable
remedially
remediless
remissible
remissness
remittance
remodelled
remonetise
remorseful
remoteness
remunerate
renascence
rencounter
renderable
rendezvous
renovation
reorganise
repairable
reparation
reparative
repatriate
repealable
repeatable
repeatedly
repellance
repellancy
repellence
repellency
repentance
repertoire
repetiteur
repetition
repetitive
repopulate
reportable
reportedly
reposition
repository
repression
repressive
reprobance
reproducer
republican
repudiator
repugnance
repugnancy
repurchase
reputation
requiescat
reredorter
rescission
rescissory
researcher
resemblant
resentment
reservedly
reshipment
resignedly
resilience
resiliency
resistance
resistible
resistless
resolutely
resolution
resolutive
resolvable
resolvedly
resonantly
resorcinol
resorption
resorptive
resounding
respectful
respecting
respective
respirable
respirator
respondent
responsive
responsory
restaurant
restlessly
restorable
restrained
restrainer
resultless
resumption
resumptive
resupinate
resurgence
retainable
reticently
reticulate
retinacula
retirement
retiringly
retractile
retraction
retractive
retraining
retrochoir
retrograde
retrogress
retrorsely
retrospect
returnable
reunionism
reunionist
revalidate
revalorise
revanchism
revanchist
revealable
revealment
revelation
revelatory
revengeful
reverencer
reverently
reversible
revertible
reviewable
revilement
revisional
revitalise
revivalism
revivalist
revocation
revocatory
revolution
rewardable
rewardless
seaanemone
seabiscuit
seacaptain
sealingwax
seamanlike
seamanship
seamstress
searchable
searchless
seaserpent
seasonable
seasonably
seasonally
seborrhoea
secernment
secludedly
secondbest
secondhand
secondment
secondrate
secretaire
secularise
secularism
secularist
secularity
securement
secureness
securiform
sedateness
seducement
seductress
sedulously
seedpotato
seedvessel
seemliness
seersucker
seethrough
segmentary
seguidilla

seignorage
seignorial
seismicity
seismogram
seismology
selectness
selenodont
selenology
selfacting
selfaction
selfbinder
selfcolour
selfdeceit
selfdenial
selfesteem
selffeeder
selfglazed
selfguided
selflessly
selfloving
selfmotion
selfmurder
selfparody
selfpoised
selfpraise
selfprofit
selfraised
selfregard
selfrising
selfruling
selfseeker
selfstyled
selftaught
selfwilled
seltzogene
semeiology
semeiotics
semestrial
semiannual
semichorus
semicircle
semidivine
semidouble
semidrying
semifitted
semiliquid
semilunate
seminarian
seminarist
semination
semiopaque
semiotical
semiquaver
semiuncial
semiweekly
semiyearly
sempstress
senatorial
senescence
sensedatum
senseorgan
sensitiser
sensualise
sensualism
sensualist
sensuality
sensuously
sentential
sentiently
separately
separation
separatism
separatist
separative
separatory
septenarii
septennial
septennium
septically
septillion
Septuagint
sepulchral
sequacious
sequential
sequestrum
SerboCroat
sereneness
sergeantcy
serigraphy
seriocomic
serjeantcy
sermoniser
serologist
serotinous
serpentine
serradilla
serviceman
servomotor
sestertium
sestertius
setterwort
settlement
seventieth
severeness
sexagenary
Sexagesima
sexivalent
sexlimited
sexologist
sexpartite
sextillion
teaplanter
tearjerker
tearlessly
teatrolley
technetium
technician
technicist
technocrat
technology
teenyweeny
teetotally
tegumental
telecamera
telecaster
telegraphy
telemetric
teleologic
teleostean
telepathic
telephoner
telephonic
telescopic
televiewer
television
televisual
tellership
telpherage
temperable
temperance
temperedly
temporally
temporalty
temporiser
temptation
temptingly
tenability
tenantable
tenantless
tenderfoot
tenderloin
tenderness
tendinitis
tendrillar
tendrilled
tenebrific
tenebrious
tenemental
tentacular
tenterhook
tepidarium
teratogeny
teratology
teratomata
termagancy
terminable
terminably
terminally
terminator
termitaria
terneplate
terracotta
terreplein
terrorless
tessellate
testaceous
testflight
tetchiness
tetrachord
tetragonal
tetrahedra
tetrameter
tetramorph
tetrapolis
tetrarchic
tetrastich
tetrastyle
tetterwort
textualist
texturally
vectograph
vegetarian
vegetation
vegetative
vehemently
veldschoen
velitation
velocipede
velutinous
venational
veneration
vengefully
venialness
venomously
ventilator
ventricose
ventriculi
verandahed
verbaliser
verifiable
vermicelli
vermicidal
vermicular
vernacular
vernissage
versicular
vertebrate
vertically
vesication
vesicatory
vesiculate
vesperbell
vespertine
vestibular
vestibulum
vestpocket
veterinary
weakliness
weakminded
weaponless
wearifully
weatherbox
weathering
weatherman
weaverbird
weedkiller
weightless
weimaraner
wellheeled
wellington
wellspoken
wellspring
wellturned
wellwisher
Welshwoman
wentletrap
werewolves
Wertherian
Wertherism
westernise
westwardly
xenophobia
xerography
xerophytic
yearningly
yeastiness
yellowback
yellowbird
yellowness
yellowwood
yesteryear
ZendAvesta
affability
affectedly
affectless
affeerment
afferently
affettuoso
affiliated
affirmable
affliction
afflictive
affluently
affordable
aficionado
Africander
Africanise
Africanism
Africanist
Afrikander
afterbirth
aftergrass
afterimage
afterlight
afterpains
aftershave
aftertaste
afterwards
effaceable
effacement
effectuate
effeminacy
effeminate
effervesce
effeteness
efficacity
efficiency
effloresce
effortless
effrontery
effulgence
effusively
officially
offlicence
offputting
offsetting
oftentimes
agapanthus
agglutinin
aggrandise
aggression
aggressive
agitatedly
agrologist
agronomist
egocentric
egoistical
Egyptology
ignobility
ignorantly
chainsmoke
chairwoman
chalcedony
chalkboard
chalkstone
challenger
chalybeate
chamaeleon
chamberpot
champignon
chancellor
chandelier
changeable
changeably
changeless
changeling
changeover
channelise
channelled
chaparajos
chaparejos
chapfallen
chaplaincy
charactery
chargeable
chargehand
charioteer
charismata
charitable
charitably
Charleston
charmingly
chartreuse
chartulary
chasteness
chatelaine
chatoyance
chatterbox
chattiness
chaudfroid
chauffeuse
chauntress
chauvinism
chauvinist
cheapishly
cheapskate
checkpoint
cheekiness
cheerfully
cheeriness
cheesecake
cheesiness
chelicerae
chemically
chemisette
chemotaxis
chequebook
chersonese
chessboard
chevrotain
chickenpox
chiffchaff
chiffonier
childbirth
childermas
childishly
childproof
chiliastic
chilliness
chimerical
chimneypot
chimpanzee
chinagraph
chinchilla
chiromancy
chiselling
chivalrous
chlorinate
chloroform
choiceness
chokeberry
chondritic
choriambic
Christhood
Christlike
chromatics
chromatype
chromosome
chronicity
chronicler
chronogram
chronology
chrysolite
chrysotile
chubbiness
chuckerout
chuckwagon
churchgoer
churchyard
churlishly
ghastfully
Ghibelline
phagedaena
phagedenic
phagocytic
phalangeal
phallicism
phanerogam
phantasise
phantasmal
phantasmic
phantastic
phantastry
pharisaism
pharmacist
pharyngeal
pheasantry
phelloderm
phenacetin
phenocryst
phenomenal
phenomenon
phenotypic
pheromonal
philatelic
philippina
philippine
philistine
phillumeny
philologen
philopoena
philosophe
philosophy
phlebotomy
phlegmatic
phlogistic
phlogiston
phlogopite
Phoenician
phonematic
phonically
phonograph
phonolitic
phonologic
phonometer
phosphatic
phosphoric
phosphorus
photoflood
photogenic
photograph
photolitho
photolysis
photolytic

photometer
photometry
photonasty
photophily
photophore
photoprint
phototaxis
phototrope
phrasebook
phrenology
phthisical
phylactery
phyllotaxy
phylloxera
phylogenic
physically
physicking
physiocrat
physiology
phytogenic
phytophagy
phytotoxic
rhapsodise
rhapsodist
rheologist
rheotropic
rhetorical
rheumatics
rheumatism
rheumatoid
rhinestone
rhinoceros
rhinoscope
rhinoscopy
rhizogenic
rhizomorph
rhizophore
rhodophane
rhomboidal
rhomboidei
rhythmical
shabbiness
shadowless
shagginess
shamefaced
shamefully
shandrydan
shandygaff
shanghaier
shantytown
sharpnosed
sheabutter
shearwater
sheathbill
sheathless
sheepishly
sheeplouse
sheepshank
sheepshead
shellacked
shellmound
shellproof
shellshock
shenanigan
sherardise
sheriffdom
shibboleth
shieldless
shiftiness
shillelagh
shipbroker
shipfitter
shipmaster
shiprigged
shipwright
shirehorse
shirtfront
shirtwaist
shockingly
shockproof
shoddiness
shoebuckle
shoestring
shopkeeper
shoplifter
shopsoiled
shopwalker
shopwindow
shoreleave
shorewards
shortbread
shortcrust
shortdated
shortening
shortlived
shortrange
shouldered
shovelhead
shovelling
showerbath
showjumper
showwindow
shrewdness
shrewishly
shrewmouse
shrievalty
shrillness
shrinkable
shrinkwrap
shrivelled
shroudlaid
shroudless
Shrovetide
shuttering
thalecress
thankfully
theatrical
theistical
themselves
theocratic
theodicean
theodolite
theogonist
theologian
theologise
theologist
theophanic
theophoric
theopneust
theoretics
theosopher
thereabout
thereafter
thereanent
thereunder
thermionic
thermistor
thermogram
thermophil
thermopile
thermostat
theurgical
thickening
thievishly
thillhorse
thimbleful
thimblerig
thinkingly
thinkpiece
thirdclass
thirdparty
thirteenth
thirtyfold
thixotropy
thornapple
thorniness
thornproof
thoroughly
thoughtful
thousandth
threadbare
threadfish
threadmark
threadworm
threatener
threepence
threepenny
threepiece
threescore
threnodial
threnodist
thriftless
throatwort
thromboses
thrombosis
thrombotic
throneless
throughout
throughput
throughway
throwstick
thruppence
thumbprint
thumbscrew
thumbstall
thunderbox
thundering
thunderous
thwartship
thwartwise
whaleshark
wharfinger
whatsoever
wheatstone
wheelchair
wheelhorse
wheelhouse
wheeziness
whensoever
whereabout
whipstitch
whirlybird
whiskified
whispering
whitebeard
whitefaced
whitesmith
whitethorn
WhitMonday
WhitSunday
wholesaler
whomsoever
whorehouse
aircooling
aircushion
airmanship
biannually
biblically
bibliology
bibliopegy
bibliophil
bibliopole
bibliopoly
bibliotics
bibulously
bichromate
bicultural
bidonville
biennially
bigamously
bighearted
bigmouthed
bijouterie
bilgewater
biliverdin
billetdoux
billposter
bilocation
bimestrial
bimetallic
binaurally
binoculars
biochemist
biodegrade
biodynamic
bioecology
biogenesis
biogenetic
biographer
biographic
biological
biometrics
biomorphic
biophysics
bioscience
biparietal
bipartisan
bipetalous
bipolarity
birdspider
birdstrike
birthplace
birthright
birthstone
bisexually
bissextile
bisulphate
bisulphide
bisulphite
bitchiness
bitterling
bitterness
bitterroot
bitterwood
bituminise
bituminous
bivalvular
bivouacked
bizarrerie
cicatrices
Ciceronian
cicisbeism
cinchonine
Cinderella
cinecamera
cinerarium
cinquefoil
Circassian
circuitous
circularly
circulator
circumcise
circumflex
circumfuse
circumvent
cismontane
cispontine
Cistercian
citronella
diabolical
diachronic
diagnostic
diagonally
diagraphic
dialysable
diapedesis
diapedetic
diaphanous
diarrhoeal
diarrhoeic
diastemata
diathermal
diathermic
diatropism
dichroitic
dichromate
dickcissel
Dickensian
dictatress
dictionary
didactical
didgeridoo
diecasting
dielectric
diesinking
difference
difficulty
diffidence
diffusible
digestible
digitalise
digitately
digitation
digitiform
digression
digressive
dilapidate
dilatation
dilatorily
dilemmatic
dilettante
dilettanti
diligently
dillydally
diluteness
diminished
diminuendo
diminution
diminutive
dimorphism
dimorphous
diningroom
dinnerless
diphtheria
diphtheric
diphyletic
diphyodont
diplodocus
diplomatic
dipsomania
directness
directoire
directress
disability
disappoint
disapprove
disarrange
disastrous
disbarring
disbelieve
disbudding
disburthen
discerning
discharger
discipline
disclaimer
disclosure
discobolus
discomfort
discommend
discommode
discompose
disconcert
disconfirm
disconnect
discontent
discophile
discordant
discounter
discourage
discourser
discoverer
discreetly
discrepant
discretely
discretion
discursive
discussant
discussion
discussive
discutient
disdainful
diseconomy
disembogue
disembosom
disembowel
disembroil
disenchant
disengaged
disenthral
disentitle
disentwine
disenviron
disfeature
disfurnish
disgruntle
disgustful
dishabille
disharmony
dishearten
dishonesty
dishwasher
disincline
disinherit
disjointed
dislikable
disloyally
disloyalty
dismalness
dismission
dismissive
disordered
disorderly
disownment
disparager
disparates
dispassion
dispatcher
dispelling
dispensary
dispersant
dispersion
dispersive
dispersoid
dispirited
dispiteous
disposable
dispossess
dispraiser
disputable
disputably
disqualify
disquieten
disquietly
disrespect
disruption
disruptive
dissatisfy
dissection
dissembler
dissension
dissertate
disservice
dissidence
dissilient
dissimilar
dissipated
dissociate
dissoluble
dissolvent
dissonance
dissonancy
dissuasion
dissuasive

distensile
distension
distention
distichous
distilland
distillate
distillery
distilling
distinctly
distortion
distracted
distrainer
distrainor
distraught
distressed
distribute
distringas
disulphate
disulphide
disutility
disyllabic
disyllable
ditriglyph
divagation
divaricate
divebomber
divergence
divergency
divestment
divination
divinatory
divineness
divisional
divisively
divulgence
eigenvalue
eighteenmo
eighteenth
eisteddfod
fianchetto
fibreboard
fibreglass
fibrillary
fibrillate
fibrillose
fibrinogen
fibrositis
fickleness
fictioneer
fictionist
fictitious
fiddleback
fiddlehead
fiddlewood
fiducially
fieldglass
fieldmouse
fieldpiece
fieldstone
fiendishly
fierceness
fiftyfifty
figuration
figurative
figurehead
filariasis
filibuster
filterable
filthiness
filtration
fimbriated
fingerbowl
fingerless
fingerling
fingermark
fingernail
fingerpost
finicality
finiteness
FinnoUgric
fireblight
fireescape
firepolicy
fireraiser
firescreen
firstclass
firstnight
fishcarver
fisherfolk
fishkettle
fishmonger
fisticuffs
fitfulness
fivefinger
fixedpoint
Gilbertian
gingerbeer
gingersnap
gingivitis
girlfriend
hibernacle
hierarchal
hierarchic
hierocracy
hieroglyph
hierograph
hierolatry
hierophant
highbinder
highflying
highhanded
highjacker
highlander
highminded
highoctane
highstrung
highwayman
Hindustani
hinterland
hippocampi
Hippocrene
hippodrome
hippogriff
hippogryph
hippomanes
hippophagy
hipsterism
hirudinean
histologic
histolysis
histolytic
historical
histrionic
hitchhiker
hithermost
hitherward
jimsonweed
jingoistic
jinricksha
jinrikisha
kibbutznik
kidnapping
kieselguhr
kilogramme
kimberlite
kindliness
kinematics
kineticist
kingfisher
kingliness
kinnikinic
liberalise
liberalism
liberalist
liberality
liberation
libidinous
librettist
licensable
licentiate
licentious
lieutenant
lifegiving
lifejacket
lifelessly
lifesaving
ligamental
lighterage
lighterman
lightfaced
lighthouse
lightingup
lightproof
likelihood
likeliness
likeminded
liliaceous
limaciform
limeburner
limitation
limitative
limitrophe
limpidness
linguiform
linguistic
lionhunter
Lipizzaner
lipography
lipomatous
Lippizaner
lipreading
lipservice
liquescent
liquidator
liquidiser
liquidness
lissomness
listlessly
literalise
literalism
literalist
literality
literarily
literation
literature
lithoglyph
lithograph
lithologic
lithophane
lithophyte
lithotrity
Lithuanian
litigation
litterlout
littleness
liturgical
livelihood
liveliness
livingroom
micaschist
Michaelmas
microbiota
microcline
microfarad
microfiche
micrograph
microlitic
micrometer
micrometry
microphone
microphyte
micropylar
microscope
microscopy
microseism
microspore
middleaged
middlebrow
middlemost
middlingly
midmorning
midshipman
mightiness
mignonette
migrainous
militantly
militarily
militarise
militarism
militarist
militiaman
millefiori
millennial
millennium
millesimal
millilitre
millimetre
millstream
millwright
mimeograph
mindedness
mindlessly
mineralise
mineralogy
minestrone
mineworker
minimalism
minimalist
ministrant
minstrelsy
mintmaster
minuscular
minutebook
minutehand
minuteness
miraculous
mirthfully
misaligned
misbelieve
miscellany
mischanter
mischmetal
misconduct
miscreance
misericord
misfortune
misgivings
mishitting
misjoinder
mismatched
mismeasure
misnomered
misogamist
misogynist
misogynous
misologist
misprision
missionary
missionise
mistakable
mistakenly
misthought
misventure
miswording
mithridate
mitigation
mitigative
mitigatory
mixedmedia
mixolydian
mizzenmast
mizzensail
nickelling
nicotinism
nidicolous
nidificate
nidifugous
nightdress
nightglass
nightlight
nightshade
nightshift
nightshirt
nightstick
nightwatch
nigrescent
nihilistic
nimbleness
nincompoop
nineteenth
nipplewort
nitpicking
nitrochalk
nitrogroup
pianissimo
pianoforte
picaresque
picayunish
piccalilli
piccaninny
pichiciago
pickaninny
picketline
pickpocket
picnicking
picosecond
pictograph
pictorical
piecegoods
piercingly
piezometer
pigeonhole
pigeonpair
pigeonpost
pigeontoed
pigeonwing
pigmentary
pigsticker
piledriver
pilgarlick
pilgrimage
piliferous
pilliwinks
pillowcase
pillowlace
pillowslip
pilothouse
pilotlight
pilotwhale
pincerlike
pinchpenny
pincushion
pinebeauty
pinecarpet
pinfeather
pinnatifid
pinnulated
pinstriped
piperidine
piscifauna
pistillary
pistillate
pistolling
pistolshot
pistolwhip
pistonring
pitchblack
pitcherful
pitchstone
pitilessly
pityriasis
pixillated
ribbonfish
ribbonworm
riboflavin
ricinoleic
rickettsia
ridgepiece
ridiculous
rightangle
rightfully
rightwards
rigorously
rinderpest
ringfinger
ringleader
ringmaster
ringnecked
ringtailed
ripplemark
riproaring
ripsnorter
risibility
ritardando
ritornelli
ritornello
riverhorse
sialagogic
sialagogue
sibilation
sicklebill
sickliness
sideboards
sideeffect
sideglance
siderolite
siderostat
sidesaddle
sidestreet
sidestroke
sidewinder
siegetrain
signalling
signwriter
silentness
silhouette
silkcotton
silkscreen
sillybilly
silverbath
silverfish
silverside
silverware
silverweed
similarity
similitude
simoniacal
simpleness
simplicity
simplifier
simplistic
simulacrum
simulation
simulative
simulatory
sincipital
sinecurism
sinecurist
sinfulness
Singhalese
singlefoot
singleness
singletree
singularly
sinisterly
sinistrous
sinologist
sinusoidal
sisterhood
sitophobia
sixshooter
tickertape
ticklishly
ticpolonga

tiddlywink
tidewaiter
tilthammer
timberhead
timberline
timbertoes
timberwolf
timberwork
timbrology
timekeeper
timelessly
timeliness
timesaving
timeserver
timocratic
timorously
tinctorial
tinselling
tirailleur
tirelessly
tiresomely
tiringroom
titanesque
titivation
tittupping
titubation
vibraculum
vibraphone
viceconsul
vicegerent
viceregent
victimiser
Victoriana
victorious
victualled
victualler
videophone
Vietnamese
viewfinder
viewlessly
vigilantly
vignettist
vigorously
villainage
villainess
villainous
villanelle
villeinage
vindicable
vindicator
vindictive
vinegarish
violaceous
viperiform
viperously
viraginous
virescence
virginally
virginhood
virologist
virtuality
virtueless
virtuosity
virtuously
virulently
viscerally
viscometer
viscountcy
visibility
Visigothic
visionally
visionless
visitation
visitorial
visualiser
vitalistic
vitaminise
vitiligate
vitrescent
vitriolise
vituperate
vivandiere
viviparity
viviparous
vivisector
viziership
wickedness
wickerwork
widespread
wildebeest
wilderment
wilderness
wildfowler
wilfulness
willowherb
willynilly
willywilly
winceyette
Winchester
windflower
windjammer
windowless
windowpane
windowseat
windowshop
windowsill
windscreen
windshield
windsleeve
winebibber
winebottle
winegrower
wingcollar
wingfooted
wingspread
wintertide
wintertime
wintriness
wiredrawer
wirehaired
wirepuller
wiretapper
wirewalker
wireworker
wishywashy
witchcraft
witchhazel
witchingly
withdrawal
withdrawer
withholder
witnessbox
xiphosuran
yieldingly
zigzagging
zincograph
skateboard
sketchable
sketchbook
skewbridge
skiagraphy
skibobbing
skijumping
skimpiness
skindiving
skinniness
skirmisher
skirtdance
skittishly
skrimshank
skyjacking
skyscraper
skywriting
alarmingly
Albigenses
albuminoid
albuminous
alchemical
alcoholise
alcoholism
alcyonaria
aldermanic
aldermanry
alexanders
algebraist
algolagnia
algolagnic
algologist
Algonquian
alienation
alightment
alimentary
alkalinity
allegation
allegiance
allegorise
allegorist
allegretto
allergenic
alleviator
alliaceous
alliterate
allocation
allocution
allogamous
allopathic
allophonic
allosteric
allotropic
alloverish
allpurpose
allrounder
allurement
allusively
almacanter
almondeyed
almsgiving
almucanter
alongshore
alpenstock
alphabetic
alphameric
altarpiece
altazimuth
alteration
alterative
alternance
alternator
altocumuli
altogether
altostrati
altruistic
blackamoor
blackberry
blackboard
blackfaced
blackguard
blackheart
Blackshirt
blacksmith
blackthorn
blackwater
bladdernut
blamefully
blancmange
blanketing
blanquette
blasphemer
blastemata
blastocyst
blastoderm
blastomere
blastopore
blazonment
bleachable
bleariness
blearyeyed
bleatingly
blepharism
blindingly
blissfully
blistering
blitheness
blithering
blithesome
blitzkrieg
blockboard
blockhouse
blockishly
bloodguilt
bloodhound
bloodiness
bloodmoney
bloodstain
bloodstock
bloodstone
blottesque
bluebonnet
bluebottle
bluecollar
bluejacket
bluepencil
blueribbon
bluethroat
bluetongue
bluishness
blurringly
blushingly
blusterous
clamminess
clangorous
clannishly
clarabella
Clarenceux
claspknife
classicise
classicism
classicist
classified
classifier
clavichord
clavicular
clawhammer
clearstory
clementine
clerestory
clerically
cleverness
clientship
clingstone
clinically
clinkstone
clinometer
clinometry
clodhopper
cloistered
closestool
closetplay
clothesbag
clothespeg
clothespin
cloudberry
cloudburst
cloudiness
clovehitch
cloverleaf
clownishly
clubfooted
clumsiness
Clydesdale
elaborator
elasticise
elasticity
elatedness
elderberry
elecampane
electively
electorate
electrical
electronic
elementary
Eleusinian
elevenplus
eliminable
eliminator
elliptical
elongation
eloquently
elucidator
elutriator
flabbiness
flabellate
flaccidity
flagellant
flagellate
flagitious
flagrantly
flagwaving
flamboyant
flameproof
flamingoes
flannelled
flapdoodle
flashboard
flashflood
flashiness
flashlight
flashpoint
flatfooted
flattering
flatulence
flatulency
flavescent
flavourful
flavouring
flawlessly
fleabitten
fleacircus
fleamarket
fledgeling
fleeringly
fleetingly
fleshiness
fleshwound
flexuously
flightdeck
flightless
flightpath
flimsiness
flintiness
flippantly
flirtation
floatation
floatboard
floatingly
floatplane
floatstone
flocculate
flocculent
floodlight
floodwater
floorboard
floorcloth
floppiness
florentine
florescent
floriation
floribunda
floridness
florilegia
floristics
flosculous
flowergirl
flowerless
fluffiness
flugelhorn
flunkeydom
flunkeyism
fluoridate
fluorinate
fluorotype
fluviatile
fluxionary
flycatcher
flyfishing
flyswatter
glaciation
glaciology
gladhander
gladsomely
Glagolitic
glancingly
glasscloth
glassfibre
glasshouse
glassiness
glasspaper
glassworks
Glaswegian
glauberite
glauconite
glimmering
globularly
glomerular
glomerulus
gloominess
gloriously
glossarial
glossarist
glossiness
glossology
glottology
glumaceous
gluttonise
gluttonous
glycolyses
glycolysis
glycosuria
glycosuric
ilangilang
illadvised
illatively
illaudable
illaudably
illegalise
illegality
illiteracy
illiterate
illnatured
illstarred
illuminant
illuminate
illuminati
illuminism
illuminist
illusional
illusively
illusorily
illustrate
oldfangled
oldmaidish
oleaginous
oleiferous
oleography
oleraceous
oligarchic
oligoclase
oligopsony
olivaceous
placidness
plagiarise
plagiarism
plagiarist
plaguesome

plainchant
planchette
planetable
planetaria
plangently
planigraph
planimeter
planimetry
planktonic
planometer
plantation
plantlouse
plasmodesm
plasmodium
plasmogamy
plasmolyse
plasticise
plasticity
platelayer
playacting
playbyplay
playfellow
playground
playwright
pleadingly
pleasantly
pleasantry
pleasingly
plebiscite
plecoptera
pleochroic
pleonastic
plesiosaur
pliability
pliantness
ploddingly
ploughable
ploughland
pluckiness
plumassier
plunderage
plunderous
pluperfect
plutocracy
plutolatry
slanderous
slanginess
slantingly
slatternly
slavetrade
slavocracy
Slavophile
Slavophobe
sleaziness
sleepiness
sleepyhead
sleeveless
sleevelink
sleighbell
slenderise
slidevalve
slightness
slipperily
slipstitch
slipstream
slitpocket
sloppiness
slothfully
slowfooted
slowmotion
slowwitted
sluggardly
sluggishly
sluicegate
slumberful
slumberous
sluttishly
ulceration
ulcerative
ulotrichan
ulteriorly
ultimately
ultrabasic
ultrasonic
ultrasound
ylangylang
amalgamate
amanuenses
amanuensis
amateurish
amateurism
ambassador
ambidexter
ambivalent
ambulacral
ambulacrum
ambulation
ambulatory
ambushment
ameliorate
amendatory
amercement
amerciable
Amerindian
amiability
ammoniacal
ammoniated
ammunition
amoebocyte
ampelopsis
amphibious
amphibrach
amphictyon
amphigouri
amphimacer
amphimixes
amphimixis
amphoteric
amputation
amygdaloid
amylaceous
emaciation
emancipate
emancipist
emarginate
emasculate
embalmment
embankment
embarkment
emblazoner
emblazonry
emblematic
emblements
embodiment
embolismic
embonpoint
embossment
embouchure
embowelled
embroidery
embryogeny
embryology
embryonate
emendation
emendatory
emeryboard
emerypaper
emerywheel
emigration
emigratory
emissivity
Emmentaler
emollition
empanelled
emparadise
empathetic
emphractic
empiricism
empiricist
employable
employment
emulsifier
imaginable
imaginably
imbecilely
imbecility
imbibition
immaculacy
immaculate
immaterial
immaturely
immaturity
immemorial
imminently
immiscible
immiscibly
immobilise
immobility
immoderacy
immoderate
immodestly
immolation
immoralist
immorality
immortally
immortelle
immoveable
immunology
immurement
impairment
impalement
impalpable
impalpably
impanation
impanelled
imparadise
impartible
impartment
impassable
impassably
impassible
impassibly
impatience
impeccable
impeccably
impeccancy
impediment
impendence
impendency
impenitent
imperative
imperially
imperilled
impersonal
impervious
impishness
implacable
implacably
implicitly
impolitely
importable
importance
importuner
imposingly
imposition
impossible
impossibly
imposthume
impotently
impoverish
impregnant
impregnate
impresario
impression
impressive
imprimatur
imprinting
improbable
improbably
improperly
improvable
improvably
improviser
imprudence
impudently
impudicity
impugnable
impugnment
impuissant
impureness
imputation
imputative
ombrometer
ommatidium
omnigenous
omnipotent
omniscient
omnivorous
omophagous
smallscale
smallsword
smallwares
smaragdine
smaragdite
smartmoney
smattering
smelliness
smockfrock
smokedried
smokehouse
smokeplant
smokeproof
smokestack
smoothbore
smoothness
smorrebrod
smudginess
smuttiness
umbellifer
umbilicate
umbiliform
umbrageous
umbrellaed
umpireship
anabaptism
anabaptist
anacolutha
anadromous
anaglyphic
anagogical
analogical
analphabet
analysable
analytical
anamorphic
anapaestic
anaplastic
anaptyctic
anarchical
anastigmat
anastomose
anastrophe
anatomical
anatropous
ancestress
anchoretic
anchoritic
anchorless
anchorring
anchylosis
anchylotic
ancipitous
Andalusian
andalusite
androecium
androgenic
anecdotage
anecdotist
anemograph
anemometer
anemometry
anemophily
aneurismal
aneurysmal
angiosperm
Anglistics
anglomania
anglophile
anglophobe
anglophone
AngloSaxon
angularity
angwantibo
animadvert
animalcula
animalcule
animatedly
anisotropy
annalistic
annexation
annihilate
annotation
annoyingly
annularity
annulation
annunciate
anointment
anonaceous
anopheline
answerable
answerably
antagonise
antagonism
antagonist
antebellum
antecedent
antecessor
antechapel
antemortem
antependia
antepenult
anteriorly
antheridia
anthracene
anthracite
anthracoid
anthropoid
antibiosis
antibiotic
Antichrist
anticipant
anticipate
anticlimax
anticlinal
antifreeze
antiheroic
antimasque
antimatter
antimonial
antimonite
antinomian
antipathic
antiphonal
antipodean
antiproton
antiquated
antiSemite
antisepsis
antiseptic
antisocial
antistatic
antitheism
antitheist
antitheses
antithesis
antithetic
antonymous
cnidoblast
enamelling
enamellist
enantiosis
encampment
encasement
encashment
encephalic
encephalon
enchanting
encourager
encroacher
encyclical
encystment
endearment
endemicity
endocrinal
endodermal
endodermis
endogamous
endogenous
endophytic
endopodite
endorsable
endoscopic
endosmosis
endosmotic
endothelia
endproduct
endstopped
enduringly
energetics
enervation
enervative
enfacement
engagement
engagingly
engineroom
Englishman
englutting
engrossing
engulfment
enharmonic
enigmatise
enigmatist
enjambment
enjoinment
enlacement
enlistment
enmeshment
enormously
enregister
enrichment
enrigiment
ensanguine
entailment
enterolith
enterotomy
enterprise
enthralled
enthusiasm
enthusiast
enticement
enticingly
entireness
entombment
entomology
entrancing
entrapment
enumerable
enumerator
enunciable
enunciator
enwrapping
enzymology
gnosticism
inaccuracy

inaccurate
inactivate
inactively
inactivity
inadequacy
inadequate
inappetent
inapposite
inaptitude
inartistic
inaugurate
inbreeding
incandesce
incantator
incapacity
incasement
incautious
incendiary
incessancy
incestuous
inchoately
inchoation
inchoative
incidental
incinerate
incipience
incipiency
incisively
incitation
incitement
incivility
inclemency
inclinable
includible
incogitant
incoherent
incomplete
inconstant
incrassate
incredible
incredibly
increscent
incubation
incubative
incubatory
inculcator
inculpable
incumbency
incunabula
incurrable
indagation
indecently
indecision
indecisive
indecorous
indefinite
indelicacy
indelicate
indexation
indication
indicative
indicatory
indictable
indictment
indigenous
indigested
indirectly
indiscreet
indiscrete
indisposed
indistinct
inditement
individual
indocility
indolently
Indonesian
inducement
inductance
indulgence
induration
indurative
industrial
ineducable
inefficacy
inelegance
ineligible
ineligibly
ineloquent
ineludible
ineptitude
inequality
inevitable
inevitably
inexistent
inexorable
inexorably
inexpertly
inexpiable
inexpiably
inexplicit
infallible
infallibly
infamously
infarction
infatuated
infeasible
infectious
infelicity
inferiorly
infernally
inferrable
infidelity
infighting
infiltrate
infinitely
infinitive
infinitude
inflatable
inflection
inflective
inflexible
inflexibly
infliction
inflictive
informally
infraction
infrahuman
infrasonic
infrequent
infusorial
infusorian
ingeminate
ingestible
inglorious
ingratiate
ingredient
ingression
inhabitant
inhalation
inharmonic
inherently
inheritrix
inhibition
inhibitory
inhumanely
inhumanity
inhumation
inimically
inimitable
inimitably
iniquitous
initialise
initialled
initiation
initiative
initiatory
injunction
injunctive
inkslinger
innateness
innerrably
innocently
innominate
innovation
innovative
innovatory
innuendoes
innumeracy
innumerate
innumerous
inoculable
inoculator
inoperable
inordinate
inosculate
inquietude
inquisitor
insaneness
insanitary
insatiable
insatiably
insecurely
insecurity
inseminate
insensible
insensibly
insentient
insightful
insinuator
insipidity
insistence
insistency
insobriety
insociable
insolation
insolently
insolvable
insolvency
insouciant
inspanning
inspection
inspective
inspirator
inspissate
instalment
instigator
instilling
institutor
instructor
instrument
insufflate
insularism
insularity
insulation
insurgence
insurgency
intactness
intangible
intangibly
integrable
integrally
integrator
integument
intendance
intendment
intenerate
intentness
interbreed
interceder
intercross
interested
interferer
interferon
intergrade
interiorly
interleave
interloper
interlunar
intermarry
intermezzi
intermezzo
internally
internment
internodal
internship
interphase
interplant
interplead
interposal
interposer
interregna
interspace
interstate
interstice
intertidal
intertrigo
intertwine
intertwist
interurban
intervener
intervenor
intervolve
interweave
interwound
interwoven
interzonal
intestinal
intimately
intimation
intimidate
intinction
intolerant
intonation
intoxicant
intoxicate
intramural
intraurban
intrepidly
intrigante
intriguant
introducer
introrsely
introspect
intubation
inundation
inundatory
inurbanity
invaginate
invalidate
invalidism
invalidity
invaluable
invaluably
invariable
invariably
invariance
inventress
inveracity
investment
inveteracy
inveterate
invigilate
invigorate
invincible
invincibly
inviolable
inviolably
invitation
invitatory
invitingly
invocation
invocatory
involucral
involucrum
involution
inwardness
knickknack
knifeboard
knighthood
knobkerrie
knockabout
knockkneed
knopkierie
knottiness
oncogenous
oncologist
oneirology
onesidedly
ontologist
pneumatics
snafflebit
snailpaced
snailwheel
snakedance
snakestone
snapdragon
snappishly
sneakiness
sneakingly
sneakthief
sneeringly
sneezeweed
sneezewood
sneezewort
snickasnee
sniffiness
snivelling
snobbishly
snobocracy
snootiness
snowcapped
snowgrouse
snowmobile
snowplough
snubbingly
snuffiness
unabridged
unaccented
unaffected
unAmerican
unarguable
unassisted
unassuming
unattached
unattended
unavailing
unbalanced
unbearable
unbearably
unbeatable
unbeatably
unbecoming
unbeliever
unbesought
unbiblical
unbiddable
unblenched
unblinking
unblushing
unbonneted
unbrokenly
unbuttoned
unchanging
unchastity
uncloister
uncommonly
uncritical
unctuosity
unctuously
uncustomed
undefended
undeniable
undeniably
underbelly
underbrush
undercliff
undercover
undercroft
underdress
underfloor
underglaze
underlease
underlinen
underlying
underminer
underneath
underpants
underproof
underquote
underscore
undersense
undersexed
undershirt
undershoot
undershrub
undersized
underskirt
underslung
understand
understate
understeer
understock
understood
understudy
undertaken
undertaker
undertrick
undervalue
underwater
underworld
underwrite
underwrote
undeserved
undesigned
undesirous
undeterred
undigested
undulation
undulatory
uneasiness
uneconomic
unedifying
uneducated
unemphatic
unemployed
unendingly
unenviable
unequalled
unerringly
unevenness
uneventful
unexampled
unexcelled
unexpected
unexplored
unfadingly
unfairness
unfaithful
unfamiliar
unfathered
unfeminine
unfettered
unfilially
unfinished
unflagging
unforeseen
unfriended
unfriendly
ungenerous
ungraceful
ungracious
ungrateful
ungrounded
ungrudging

unguentary
unhallowed
unhandsome
unhistoric
unholiness
unhouseled
uniaxially
unicameral
unicyclist
uniformity
unilateral
unilingual
unilocular
unimproved
uninformed
uninitiate
unionistic
unipartite
uniqueness
university
univocally
unjustness
unkindness
unknowable
unlabelled
unlawfully
unlettered
unlikeness
unmannerly
unmeasured
unmeetness
unmerciful
unmorality
unmortised
unnameable
unnumbered
unoccupied
unofficial
unorthodox
unpleasant
unpleasing
unprepared
unprovoked
unravelled
unreadable
unredeemed
unreliable
unrelieved
unremarked
unrequited
unreserved
unresolved
unripeness
unrivalled
unruliness
unscalable
unschooled
unscramble
unscreened
unscripted
unseasoned
unselected
unsettling
unsociable
unsociably
unsocially
unsporting
unsteadily
unstrained
unstressed
unsuitable
unswerving
unthinking
untidiness
untowardly
untroubled
untruthful
unwariness
unwavering
unwieldily
unwontedly
unworkable
unworthily
unwrinkled
unyielding
boastfully
bobbinlace
bobbysocks
bobbysoxer
boisterous
bollweevil
bolometric
bolshevise
bolshevism
bolshevist
bombardier
bondholder
boneheaded
bonesetter
boneshaker
bookbinder
bookkeeper
bookmaking
bookmarker
bookseller
boondoggle
bootlegger
bootlessly
bootlicker
bootstraps
borborygmi
bordereaux
borderland
borderless
borderline
Boswellian
Boswellise
Boswellism
bothersome
botryoidal
bottlefeed
bottleneck
bottletree
bottomless
bottommost
bouncingly
bourbonism
bourbonist
bowdlerise
bowdlerism
boyishness
coacervate
coachbuilt
coachhouse
coadjacent
coagulable
coalbunker
coalescent
coaptation
coarseness
coastguard
coastwards
coathanger
coatimundi
cochleated
cockalorum
cockatrice
cockchafer
cockneyish
cockneyism
cocksurely
codswallop
coelacanth
coenobitic
coenobytic
coequality
coercively
coetaneous
coeternity
coexistent
coffeemill
cogitation
cogitative
cognisable
cognisably
cognisance
cognominal
cohabitant
coherently
cohesively
coincident
colatitude
colchicine
coleoptera
coleoptile
coleorhiza
collarbeam
collarbone
collarette
collarless
collarstud
collatable
collateral
collection
collective
collegiate
collembola
collimator
collocutor
colloquial
colloquise
colloquist
colloquium
colonially
colonnaded
coloration
coloratura
colossally
colourable
colourably
colourfast
colourless
colportage
colporteur
columbaria
comanchero
combustion
combustive
comedienne
comehither
comeliness
comestible
comicality
comicopera
commandant
commandeer
commandery
commanding
commandoes
commentary
commentate
commercial
commissary
commission
commissure
commitment
committing
commixture
commodious
commonable
commonalty
commonness
commonroom
commonweal
communally
communique
commutable
commutator
compaction
comparable
comparably
comparator
comparison
compassion
compasssaw
compatible
compatibly
compatriot
compelling
compendium
compensate
competence
competency
competitor
complacent
complainer
complected
complement
completely
completion
completive
complexion
complexity
compliance
compliancy
complicacy
complicate
complicity
compliment
complotted
composedly
compositor
compotator
compounder
compradore
comprehend
compressed
compressor
compromise
compulsion
compulsive
compulsory
computable
computator
comstocker
concentric
conception
conceptive
conceptual
concerning
concertina
concertino
concession
concessive
concettism
conchoidal
conchology
conciliary
conciliate
concinnity
conclusion
conclusive
conclusory
concoction
concoctive
concordant
concretely
concretion
concretise
concretism
concretist
concurrent
concurring
concussion
concussive
condensate
condensery
condescend
condolence
conduction
conductive
confabbing
confection
conference
conferment
conferring
confervoid
confession
confidante
confidence
confirmand
confiscate
conflation
confluence
conformism
conformist
conformity
confounded
confusedly
congeneric
congenital
congestion
congestive
conglobate
congregant
congregate
congruence
congruency
coniferous
conjecture
conjointly
conjugally
connatural
connection
connective
conniption
connivance
conscience
consecrate
consectary
consensual
consequent
considered
consistent
consistory
consociate
consolable
consonance
consonancy
consortium
conspectus
conspiracy
conspirant
constantan
Constantia
constantly
constipate
constitute
constraint
constringe
consuetude
consulship
consultant
consulting
consultive
consumable
consumedly
consummate
contagious
contendent
contention
contestant
contextual
contexture
contiguity
contiguous
continence
contingent
continuant
continuate
continuity
continuous
contortion
contortive
contraband
contrabass
contractor
contradict
contraprop
contrarily
contravene
contribute
contritely
contrition
controlled
controller
controvert
convalesce
convection
convective
convenable
convenance
convenient
convention
conventual
convergent
conversant
conversely
conversion
conveyable
conveyance
conviction
convictive
convincing
convoluted
convulsant
convulsion
convulsive
coolheaded
coolingoff
cooperator
cooptation
cooptative
coordinate
coparcener
copartnery
Copernican
copesettic
copperhead
coproducer
coprolitic
copulation
copulative
copyholder
copyreader
copywriter
coquettish
coradicate
coralberry
coralsnake
corbelling
corbiculae
cordiality
cordierite
cordillera
cordwainer
corelation
corelative
coriaceous
Corinthian
corncockle
cornerwise
cornettist
cornflakes

cornflower
cornstarch
cornucopia
coromandel
coronation
corporally
corporator
corporeity
corpulence
corpulency
corpuscule
correction
corrective
correspond
corrigenda
corrigible
corrivalry
corroboree
corrugated
corrugator
corruption
corruptive
corsetiere
corticated
Corybantes
corybantic
coryphaeus
cosentient
cosmically
cosmogonic
cosmopolis
cosmoramic
costliness
cottoncake
cottonseed
cottontail
cottonweed
cottonwood
cottonwool
couchgrass
coulometry
councillor
councilman
counselled
counsellor
counteract
countryish
countryman
couplement
courageous
courthouse
cousinhood
cousinship
couturiere
couverture
covalently
covariance
covenanted
covenantee
covenanter
covenantor
covetingly
covetously
cowcatcher
coweringly
cowparsley
cowpuncher
doctorship
documental
doggedness
dogmatical
dogmatiser
dogstongue
dolomitise
dolorously
dominantly
domination
dominative
donkeywork
donnybrook
doorkeeper
dorsigrade
dosimetric
doublebass
doubleness
doublepark
doubletalk
doubletime
doubtfully
doubtingly
doughfaced
dovecolour
downfallen
downstairs
downstream
downstroke
downwardly
doxography
eosinophil
foamflower
foetidness
foliaceous
folklorist
folkmemory
folksiness
folksinger
follicular
fontanelle
footballer
footbridge
footcandle
footlights
footwarmer
foraminous
forbidding
forcefully
forcipated
foreboding
forecaster
forecastle
forecourse
forefather
forefinger
foregather
foreground
forehanded
foreignism
foreordain
forerunner
foreshadow
foresheets
foreteller
forfeiture
forgetting
forgivable
forgivably
formatting
formidable
formidably
formlessly
fornicator
fortepiano
forthright
fortissimi
fortissimo
fortuitism
fortuitist
fortuitous
fortyniner
forwarding
forwearied
fosterling
foudroyant
foundation
founderous
fourchette
fourfooted
fourhanded
Fourierism
fourinhand
fourleaved
fourposter
foursquare
fourstroke
fourteener
fourteenth
fowlplague
foxhunting
goalkeeper
goaltender
goatsbeard
goatsucker
gobemouche
gobstopper
Godfearing
goggleeyed
goldbeater
golddigger
goldenness
goldenseal
goldilocks
golfcourse
goloptious
goluptious
goniometer
goniometry
goodliness
goodlooker
goodygoody
gooseberry
gooseflesh
goosegrass
gorgeously
Gorgonzola
gormandise
gothically
governable
governance
governessy
government
hoarseness
hobbyhorse
hobnobbing
hocuspocus
hodgepodge
hoitytoity
hokeypokey
holloweyed
hollowness
hollowware
holography
holohedral
holophrase
holophytic
holosteric
holusbolus
homebrewed
homecoming
homeliness
homemaking
homeopathy
homiletics
homocercal
homoeopath
homogamous
homogenise
homogenous
homologate
homologise
homologous
homonymous
homoousian
homophonic
homosexual
homozygote
homozygous
homunculus
honeyeater
honeyguide
honeysweet
honorarium
honourable
honourably
honourless
hookedness
hootenanny
hopelessly
horizontal
hormonally
hornblende
hornedness
hornrimmed
horologist
horoscopic
horrendous
horridness
horsecloth
horsecoper
horseflesh
horselaugh
horseleech
horsepower
horseshoer
horsewoman
hospitable
hospitably
hostelling
hotblooded
hotchpotch
hourcircle
houseagent
housebound
housecraft
houseguest
houselling
houseplant
houseproud
housetrain
housewives
hoverplane
hovertrain
iodination
ionisation
ionosphere
jobbernowl
jocoseness
jocularity
johnnycake
Johnsonese
johnsonian
jolterhead
journalese
journalise
journalism
journalist
journeyman
joyfulness
joyousness
kookaburra
lobsterpot
lobulation
lockerroom
lockkeeper
lockstitch
locomotion
locomotive
locomotory
locustbean
loganberry
loganstone
loggerhead
logicality
logistical
logography
logorrhoea
logrolling
Lollardism
loneliness
lonesomely
longaevous
longhaired
longheaded
longlegged
longprimer
longshanks
longwinded
loosecover
lophophore
lopsidedly
loquacious
lordliness
lossleader
lotuseater
loudhailer
loungesuit
lovelessly
loveletter
loveliness
lovemaking
lovingness
lowerclass
lowpitched
lowprofile
loxodromic
mobocratic
mockheroic
moderately
moderation
moderatism
moderniser
modernness
modifiable
modishness
modulation
Mohammedan
moisturise
molendinar
molluscoid
molluscous
molybdenum
monandrous
monarchial
Monarchian
monarchism
monarchist
monetarily
monetarism
monetarist
moneymaker
moneytaker
mongrelise
mongrelism
moniliasis
moniliform
monistical
monitorial
monkeysuit
monocarpic
monochasia
monochrome
monoclinal
monoclinic
monocratic
monocyclic
monoecious
monogamist
monogamous
monogenism
monogynian
monogynous
monohybrid
monohydric
monolithic
monologise
monologist
monomaniac
monophonic
monopodial
monopodium
monopolise
monopolist
monorhymed
monotheism
monotheist
monotonous
monovalent
monsignori
monstrance
Montagnard
montbretia
monumental
moonflower
moonshiner
moonstruck
mopishness
moralistic
moratorium
morbidezza
morbidness
mordacious
morganatic
moroseness
morphemics
morphinism
morphogeny
morphology
morrispike
mosaically
mosaicking
mosasaurus
mosquitoes
mossbunker
motherhood
motherland
motherless
mothership
motherwort
motionless
motivation
motiveless
motorcycle
mouldboard
mouldiness
mountebank
mournfully
mousseline
moustached
moustachio
Mousterian
mouthorgan
mouthpiece
movability
movelessly
moviemaker
mozzarella
noblewoman
nodulation
noisemaker
nominalism
nominalist
nominately
nomination
nominative
nomography
nomologist
nomothetic
nonaligned
nonchalant
noncontent
nondrinker
nonferrous
nonfiction
nonjoinder
nonlogical

nonnatural
nonnuclear
nonpayment
nonplaying
nonplussed
nonstarter
nonswimmer
nonviolent
noogenesis
northbound
northerner
northwards
nosography
nosologist
nosophobia
nostologic
notability
notarially
notchboard
noteworthy
noticeable
noticeably
notifiable
notionally
notonectal
nourishing
novaculite
novelistic
pocketable
pocketbook
pocketsize
pockmarked
podiatrist
poetically
pogonology
pogonotomy
poinsettia
pointblank
pokerfaced
polemicist
polemonium
politeness
politician
politicise
pollenosis
pollinator
polyandric
polyanthus
polyatamic
polychaete
polychrest
polychrome
polyclinic
polycyclic
polydactyl
polydipsia
polygamist
polygamous
polygenism
polygenist
polygenous
polygraphy
polygynous
polyhedral
polyhedric
polyhedron
polyhistor
polymathic
polymerise
polymerism
polymerous
Polynesian
polynomial
polyonymic
polyphasic
polyphonic
polyploidy
polysemous
polytheism
polytheist
polytocous
polyvalent
Pomeranian
pomiferous
pomologist
ponderable
pontifical
pontifices
popularise
popularity
population
populistic
populously
porismatic
pornocracy
porousness
porraceous
portamento
portcullis
portentous
portliness
Portuguese
positional
positively
positivism
positivist
positivity
possession
possessive
possessory
postbellum
postchaise
postexilic
posthumous
postillion
postliminy
postmaster
postmortem
postoffice
postpartum
postscript
postulator
potability
potamology
potbellied
potentiate
potentilla
pothunting
pouncetbox
pourparler
powderhorn
powderpuff
powerfully
powerhouse
pozzolanic
pozzuolana
roadrunner
roadworthy
robustious
robustness
rockabilly
rockbadger
rockbottom
rockgarden
rockhopper
rockpigeon
rockrabbit
rockribbed
rodfishing
roistering
roisterous
rollcollar
rollicking
rollingpin
Romanesque
Romanistic
rontgenise
roodscreen
roofgarden
rootedness
ropedancer
ropeladder
ropewalker
roquelaure
rosaniline
rosechafer
roseengine
roselipped
rosemallow
rotational
rotisserie
rottenness
rottweiler
roughhouse
roughrider
roundabout
roundhouse
rouseabout
roustabout
rovebeetle
rowanberry
soapboiler
soapbubble
soapflakes
sobersided
sobersides
socialiser
societally
sociologic
sociometry
soddenness
softbilled
softboiled
softfinned
softheaded
softspoken
solacement
soldanella
solecistic
solemnness
solenoidal
solicitant
solicitous
solicitude
solidarism
solidarist
solidarity
solidstate
solifidian
solitarily
solstitial
solubilise
solubility
somatology
somatotype
sombreness
somersault
somniloquy
somnolence
somnolency
songstress
songthrush
songwriter
sonorously
soothingly
soothsayer
sophomoric
Sorbonnist
sordidness
sororicide
soubriquet
soullessly
soundboard
soundingly
soundproof
soundtrack
sourcebook
sousaphone
souterrain
southbound
southerner
southernly
southwards
sowthistle
tobogganer
tocopherol
toffeenose
toilsomely
tolerantly
toleration
tollbridge
tomfoolery
tomography
tonelessly
tongueless
tonguetied
toothbrush
toothiness
toothpaste
toothshell
topazolite
topgallant
topicality
topography
topologist
topsyturvy
torchlight
toroidally
torpidness
torrential
torridness
tortellini
tortfeasor
tortiously
tortuosity
tortuously
totemistic
touchiness
touchingly
touchjudge
touchpaper
touchstone
tourbillon
tourmaline
tournament
tourniquet
towardness
toweringly
townswoman
toxication
toxicology
toxiphobia
vocabulary
vocational
vociferant
vociferate
vociferous
voiceprint
volatilise
volatility
volitional
volleyball
voltameter
volubility
volumetric
voluminous
voluptuary
voluptuous
vomitorium
vortically
vorticella
vorticular
voyageable
wobbliness
woefulness
wolframite
womanishly
wonderland
wonderment
wonderwork
wondrously
wongawonga
wontedness
woodcarver
woodcutter
woodenhead
woodenness
woodlander
woodpecker
woodpigeon
woodturner
woodworker
woolgather
woolgrower
woolliness
woolsorter
wordlessly
workbasket
workingman
workpeople
worldclass
worldweary
worshipful
worshipped
worshipper
worthiness
worthwhile
yokefellow
youngberry
yourselves
youthfully
zollverein
zoological
zoomorphic
zoophagous
zoophilous
aphaereses
aphaeresis
aphoristic
aphrodisia
apiculture
aplacental
apocalypse
apocarpous
apochromat
apocryphal
apodeictic
apolaustic
apolitical
Apollinian
Apollonian
apologetic
apophthegm
apoplectic
aposematic
apostatise
apostolate
apostrophe
apothecary
apothecial
apothecium
apotheoses
apotheosis
apotropaic
apparelled
apparently
apparition
appealable
appearance
appeasable
appendices
appendixes
apperceive
appetising
appetitive
applicable
applicably
applicator
appointive
appositely
apposition
appositive
appreciate
apprentice
approvable
approvably
epeirogeny
epentheses
epenthesis
epenthetic
epexegeses
epexegesis
epexegetic
ephemerous
ephorality
epiblastic
epicentral
epicycloid
epideictic
epidemical
epidermoid
epigastric
epigenesis
epigenetic
epiglottal
epiglottic
epiglottis
epigrapher
epigraphic
epilimnion
epiphytism
episcopacy
episcopate
episematic
episodical
episternum
epistolary
epistrophe
epithelial
epithelium
opalescent
opaqueness
openhanded
openhearth
openminded
operculate
operettist
ophicleide
ophiolater
ophiolatry
ophiologic
ophthalmia
ophthalmic
opinionist
opisometer
oppilation
opposeless
oppositely
opposition
oppression
oppressive
opprobrium
oppugnancy
optatively
optimalise
optimistic
optionally
spacecraft
spacewoman
spaciously
spadebeard
spadiceous
spagyrical
spallation

spankingly
sparseness
Spartacist
spasticity
spatchcock
spathulate
spatiality
speargrass
specialise
specialism
specialist
speciality
speciation
speciology
speciosity
speciously
spectacled
spectacles
spectrally
speculator
speechless
speediness
speedlimit
speleology
spellbound
Spencerian
Spenserian
spermaceti
spermicide
sperrylite
sphalerite
sphenodone
sphenogram
sphenoidal
sphericity
spheroidal
spherulite
spidercrab
spiderline
spiderwort
spiflicate
spillikins
spinescent
spiracular
spiraculum
spiralling
spiritedly
spiritless
spirituous
spirograph
spirometer
spirometry
spitchcock
spitefully
splanchnic
splashback
splashdown
spleenwort
splendidly
splintbone
splintcoal
splitlevel
splutterer
spodomancy
spoilsport
spokeshave
spoliation
spoliative
spoliatory
spongecake
spongewood
spongiform
sponginess
spongology
sponsorial
spookiness
spoondrift
spoonerism
sporangial
sporangium
sporophore
sporophyll
sporophyte
sportfully
sportiness
sportingly
sportively
sportswear
spotlessly
spottiness
sprightful
springhalt
springhead
springless
springlike
springtail
springtide
springtime
springwood
sprinkling
sprucebeer
spruceness
spumescent
spunkiness
spuriously
upbraiding
upbringing
upholstery
upperclass
uppishness
uproarious
upstanding
upwardness
aquafortis
aquamarine
aquaplaner
aquiferous
aquilinity
equability
equanimity
equational
equatorial
equestrian
equilibria
equipotent
equitation
equivalent
equivocate
squalidity
squamation
squanderer
squareness
squaresail
squaretoed
squaretoes
squeezable
squeezebox
squeteague
squinteyed
squirarchy
squirearch
squirehood
squireling
squireship
aragonitic
araucarian
arbalester
arbalister
arbitrable
arbitrager
arbitrator
arboreally
arborvitae
archaistic
archbishop
archdeacon
archerfish
archetypal
architrave
archpriest
arenaceous
areolation
Areopagite
argumentum
aristocrat
arithmetic
Armageddon
armigerous
armorially
armourclad
armourless
arrestment
arrhythmia
arrhythmic
arrogantly
arrogation
arterially
arteriolar
artfulness
arthralgia
arthralgic
arthromere
articulate
artificial
artycrafty
arytaenoid
brachiator
brachiopod
brachylogy
brachyural
brachyuran
bradyseism
Brahmanism
Brahminism
brainchild
braininess
brainpower
brainstorm
brakeblock
brakelight
branchiate
brandyball
brandysnap
brantgoose
brassiness
bratticing
brawniness
brazenness
brazilwood
breadboard
breadcrumb
breadfruit
breadstick
breadstuff
breakables
breakpoint
breakwater
breastbone
breastwall
breastwork
breathable
breathless
breechless
breezeless
breeziness
brentgoose
bressummer
brevetting
brickfield
bricklayer
bridegroom
bridesmaid
bridgeable
bridgehead
bridgeless
bridgework
bridlepath
brigandage
brigandine
brigandism
brigantine
brightness
brightwork
brilliance
brilliancy
Britishism
broadcloth
broadsheet
broadsword
brocatelle
brokendown
brokenness
bromegrass
bronchiole
bronchitic
bronchitis
broodiness
broodingly
broomstick
browbeaten
brownshirt
brownstone
brusquerie
bryologist
crackajack
crackbrain
cradlesong
craftguild
craftiness
cragginess
cranesbill
craniology
crankiness
crankshaft
crapulence
craquelure
crassitude
cravenness
creaminess
creatinine
creatively
creativity
creaturely
credential
creditable
creditably
creepiness
crematoria
crenellate
crenulated
crepuscule
crescentic
cretaceous
crewelwork
cribriform
criminally
crinolette
crippledom
crispation
crispbread
crisscross
critically
crocoisite
crossbench
crossbones
crossbreed
crosscheck
crossgrain
crosshatch
crossindex
crosslight
crosspatch
crosspiece
crossrefer
crossroads
crosstrees
crowkeeper
crustacean
crustation
crustiness
cryogenics
cryoscopic
cryptogamy
cryptogram
cryptology
draconites
drafthorse
dragonhead
dragonnade
dragontree
dramatical
dramaturge
dramaturgy
drawbridge
drawingpin
drawlingly
drawstring
dreadfully
dreaminess
dreamworld
dreariness
dressiness
dressmaker
drivelling
driverless
droopingly
drophammer
drosophila
drowsihead
drowsiness
drudgingly
drupaceous
drysaltery
eradicable
eradicator
erectility
eremitical
erethismic
ergodicity
ergonomics
ergonomist
ergosterol
ericaceous
erotically
erotogenic
erotomania
erubescent
eructation
eruptively
erysipelas
fractional
fragmental
fragrantly
framboesia
franchiser
Franciscan
Francophil
frangipane
frangipani
fraternise
fraternity
fratricide
fraudulent
fraxinella
freakiness
freakishly
freebooter
freedwoman
freehanded
freeholder
freelancer
freeliving
freeloader
freemartin
freesoiler
freespeech
freespoken
freightage
Frenchness
frenziedly
frequenter
frequently
freshwater
friability
fricandeau
fricasseed
frictional
friendless
friendlily
friendship
frigidness
frigorific
frilliness
fringeless
friskiness
fritillary
frivolling
frizziness
froghopper
frolicking
frolicsome
frontbench
frontwards
frostiness
frothiness
frowningly
fruitarian
fruitfully
frutescent
gracefully
graciosity
graciously
gradualism
gradualist
graduation
gramicidin
gramineous
grammarian
gramophone
granadilla
grandchild
granddaddy
grandducal
grandmamma
grandniece
grandstand
granduncle
grangerise
grangerism
granophyre
granularly
granulator
granulitic
grapefruit
grapesugar
graphemics
graphitise
graphology
graptolite
graspingly
grasscloth
grassroots
grasssnake
gratefully
gratifying
gratuitous
gravestone
gravimeter
gravimetry
greasewood
greasiness
greatniece
greatuncle
GrecoRoman

greediness
greedyguts
greencloth
greenfinch
greenheart
greenhouse
greenshank
greenstick
greenstone
greenstuff
greensward
gregarious
grenadilla
gressorial
greyheaded
grievously
grindingly
grindstone
grisliness
grittiness
groceteria
grogginess
groundbait
groundless
groundling
groundmass
groundplan
groundrent
groundsman
groundwork
grovelling
growlingly
grubbiness
grudgingly
gruesomely
grumpiness
iridaceous
iridescent
iridosmine
Irishwoman
ironhanded
ironically
ironmaster
ironmonger
ironworker
irradiance
irradicate
irrational
irrelative
irrelevant
irreligion
irresolute
irreverent
irrigation
irritation
irritative
kriegspiel
Krishnaism
Krugerrand
oracularly
orangepeel
orangewood
oratorical
orchardist
orchardman
orchestics
orchestral
ordainment
ordinarily
ordination
ordonnance
Ordovician
oreography
oreologist
organicism
organicist
organismal
orientally
originally
originator
ornamental
ornateness
orneriness
orogenesis
orogenetic
orographic
orological
orotundity
orphanhood
orthoclase
orthodoxly
orthoepist
orthogenic
orthogonal
orthopedic
orthoptera
practician
practising
praecocial
praemunire
praesidium
praetorial
praetorian
pragmatise
pragmatism
pragmatist
prairiedog
prancingly
pratincole
prayerbook
preachment
preadamite
prearrange
prebendary
precarious
precaution
precedence
precedency
preceptive
preceptory
precession
preciosity
preciously
precipitin
preclusion
preclusive
precocious
preconcert
precordial
precursory
predacious
predecease
predestine
predicable
prediction
predictive
predispose
prednisone
preeminent
preemption
preemptive
preexilian
prefecture
preferable
preferably
preference
preferment
preferring
prefixture
prefrontal
prefulgent
preglacial
pregnantly
prehensile
prehension
prehistory
prejudiced
prelatical
prelection
premarital
premaxilla
premedical
premonitor
prepackage
preparator
preparedly
prepayable
prepayment
prepensely
prepossess
prepotence
prepotency
presageful
presbyopia
presbyopic
presbytery
prescience
prescriber
presentday
presentive
presidency
presidiary
presignify
pressagent
pressingly
pressurise
presternum
presumable
presumably
presuppose
pretendant
pretendent
pretension
prettiness
prevailing
prevalence
prevenancy
prevenient
prevention
preventive
previously
pridefully
priesthood
priestling
priggishly
primevally
primiparae
primordial
primordium
princeling
princeship
principate
principial
principium
principled
prismoidal
prissiness
privileged
prizefight
procedural
proceeding
procession
proclaimer
proclivity
procreator
procrypsis
procryptic
proctorage
proctorial
proctorise
procumbent
procurable
procurance
procurator
prodigally
prodigious
producible
production
productive
profession
proficient
profitable
profitably
profitless
profligacy
profligate
profoundly
profundity
progenitor
proglottis
prognathic
prognostic
programmer
prohibiter
prohibitor
projectile
projection
projective
prolicidal
prolocutor
prologuise
prolongate
promenader
promethium
prominence
promissory
promontory
promptbook
promptness
promulgate
pronominal
pronounced
pronouncer
proofsheet
propagable
propaganda
propagator
propellant
propellent
propelling
propensity
properness
propertied
prophesier
prophetess
propionate
propitiate
propitious
proportion
propounder
propraetor
proprietor
propulsion
propulsive
propylaeum
prosaicism
proscenium
prosciutto
proscriber
prosecutor
prosilient
prosodical
prospector
prospectus
prosperity
prosperous
prosthesis
prosthetic
prostitute
prostomial
prostomium
protanopic
protection
protective
protectory
protectrix
proteiform
proteinous
protensive
proteolyse
protestant
prothallia
prothallus
protophyta
protophyte
protoplasm
protoplast
prototypal
prototypic
protracted
protractor
protreptic
protrusile
protrusion
protrusive
proudflesh
provenance
proverbial
providence
provincial
provisions
provitamin
provocator
proximally
prudential
pruriently
trabeation
trabeculae
trabecular
tracheated
tracheitis
Tractarian
tractional
trafficked
trafficker
tragacanth
tragically
tragicomic
traitorous
trajection
trajectory
trammelled
tramontana
tramontane
trampoline
trancelike
tranquilly
transactor
transcribe
transcript
transducer
transeptal
transferee
transferor
transfuser
transgress
transience
transiency
transistor
transition
transitive
transitory
translator
translucid
translunar
transmuter
transplant
transposal
transposer
transshape
transvalue
transverse
trappiness
trashiness
traumatism
travelling
travelogue
travertine
trawlerman
treadboard
treadwheel
treasonous
trecentist
tremendous
tremolitic
trenchancy
trendiness
trepanning
trespasser
triacetate
triandrous
triangular
tribometer
tribrachic
trichiasis
trichinise
trichinous
trichology
trichotomy
trichroism
trichromat
trickiness
trickishly
triclinium
tricyclist
Tridentine
trierarchy
triflingly
trifoliate
trifurcate
trigeminal
triggerman
triglyphic
trigonally
trilateral
trilingual
triliteral
trillionth
trimonthly
trimorphic
trioecious
tripartite
triphammer
triphthong
triplicate
triplicity
triquetrae
triquetral
trisection
triskelion
triternate
triturable
triturator
triumphant
triumviral
trivialise
trivialism
triviality
trochanter
trochoidal
troctolite
troglodyte
trolleybus
trollopish
trombonist
tromometer
tropaeolum
trophology
tropically
tropologic
tropopause
tropophyte
Trotskyism
Trotskyist

Trotskyite
troubadour
trousseaux
trouvaille
trowelling
trucklebed
truculence
truculency
truncately
truncation
trundlebed
trustfully
trustiness
trustingly
truthfully
tryptophan
uranometry
urbanology
urethritis
urochordal
urticarial
urtication
wraparound
wrathfully
wrathiness
wretchedly
wristwatch
wrongdoing
wrongfully
wrongously
asafoetida
asbestosis
ascariasis
ascendable
ascendance
ascendancy
ascendence
ascendency
ascendible
asceticism
ascomycete
ascribable
ascription
asexuality
Ashkenazim
asparagine
aspergilla
asphyxiant
asphyxiate
aspidistra
aspiration
assafetida
assailable
assaultive
assemblage
assentient
assessable
assessment
asseverate
assibilate
assignable
assignment
assimilate
assistance
associable
assoilment
assortment
assumption
assumptive
asteriated
asteroidal
astigmatic
astragalus
astringent
astrologer
astrologic
astronomer
astronomic
astuteness

asymmetric
asymptotic
asynchrony
escadrille
escalation
escallonia
escapement
escapology
escarpment
escharotic
escheatage
escritoire
Esculapian
escutcheon
espadrille
especially
essayistic
estimation
estimative
isentropic
Ishmaelite
isochronal
isodynamic
isogenetic
isoglossal
isolatable
isometrics
isomorphic
isoniazide
isopterous
isoseismal
isosporous
isothermal
oscillator
oscitation
osculation
osculatory
osmeterium
osmiridium
ostensible
ostensibly
osteoblast
osteoclast
osteopathy
osteophyte
psalmodise
psalmodist
psalterium
psephology
pseudocarp
psilocybin
psittacine
psychiatry
psychicism
psychicist
psychology
psychopath
tsarevitch
usefulness
usquebaugh
ustulation
usucaption
usuriously
usurpation
ateleiosis
Athanasian
atmosphere
atomically
attachable
attachment
attackable
attainable
attainment
attendance
attenuated
attenuator
attornment
attractant
attraction

attractive
attunement
atypically
ctenophore
eternalise
eternalist
ethereally
ethicality
ethnically
ethnologic
ethologist
etiolation
italianate
italianise
Italianism
Italophile
itinerancy
otherwhere
otherwhile
otherworld
otioseness
otterboard
ottershrew
Ptolemaist
stabiliser
stablemate
stableness
stadholder
staffnurse
stagbeetle
stagecoach
stagecraft
staggering
stagnantly
stagnation
stalactite
stalagmite
stalwartly
stanchless
stanchness
standpoint
standstill
staphyline
stargazing
starriness
starryeyed
starstream
starvation
starveling
statecraft
statically
stationary
stationery
statistics
statoscope
statuesque
statutable
statutably
staurolite
stavesacre
steadiness
steakhouse
stealthily
steamchest
steaminess
steamtight
steeliness
steelworks
stelliform
stenchtrap
stencilled
stenciller
stenograph
stentorian
stepfather
stephanite
stepladder
stepmother
stepparent

stepsister
stereobate
stereogram
stereopsis
stereotype
stereotypy
sterigmata
steriliser
sternwards
stertorous
stewardess
stickiness
stiffening
stiflebone
stiflingly
stigmatise
stigmatism
stigmatist
stilettoes
stillbirth
stillicide
stimulator
stinginess
stingingly
stinkingly
stinkstone
stipellate
stipulator
stirrupcup
stitchwort
stochastic
stockiness
stockpiler
stockproof
stockrider
stockstill
stodginess
stolidness
stomachful
stomatitis
stomatopod
stomodaeum
stoneblind
stoneborer
stonebrash
stonefruit
stonemason
stonesnipe
stopvolley
storehouse
storksbill
stormbound
stormcloud
storminess
stormproof
strabismal
strabismic
strabismus
strabotomy
straighten
straightly
strainedly
straitness
stramonium
strategist
strathspey
stratiform
stratocrat
strawberry
strawboard
streamless
streamline
streetdoor
streetward
strengthen
stressless
strictness
stridently
stridulant

stridulate
stridulous
strikingly
stringbean
stringency
stringendo
stringhalt
stringless
striptease
Stroganoff
stromatous
stronghold
strongroom
structural
structured
struthious
strychnine
strychnism
stubbiness
stubbornly
studiously
stuffiness
stumpiness
stunningly
stupendous
stupidness
sturdiness
stylistics
stylograph
stypticity
utilisable
utopianism
auctioneer
audibility
audiometer
audiometry
audiophile
auditorial
auditorium
augustness
auriculate
auriferous
auscultate
auspicious
austenitic
Australian
autarkical
autecology
authorship
autochthon
autocratic
autodidact
autoerotic
autogamous
autogenous
autography
autoimmune
autologous
automation
automatise
automatism
automatist
automobile
automotive
autonomist
autonomous
autoplasty
autostrada
autostrade
autumnally
bubblyjock
buccinator
Buchmanism
Buchmanite
bucketshop
Buddhistic
budgerigar
bufflehead
buffoonery

bullethead
bullheaded
bullroarer
bumblingly
bumpkinish
bunchgrass
bunglingly
burdensome
bureaucrat
burglarise
burramundi
bursarship
bushmaster
bushranger
bustlingly
butterball
butterbean
butterfish
buttermilk
butterwort
buttonball
buttonbush
buttondown
buttonhole
buttonhook
buttonless
buttonwood
cuckoopint
cuckoospit
cucullated
cuddlesome
cudgelling
cuirassier
cultivable
cultivator
culturally
cumbersome
cumbrously
cummerbund
cumulation
cumulative
cumuliform
cunctation
cunctative
curability
curatorial
curmudgeon
curricular
curriculum
cursedness
curvaceous
curvacious
curvetting
cuspidated
cussedness
custommade
cuttlebone
cuttlefish
cuttystool
dubitation
dubitative
dumbledore
dumbstruck
dumbwaiter
dumfounder
dunderhead
dungbeetle
duniwassal
duodecimal
duodenitis
duplicator
durability
dustjacket
duumvirate
eucalyptol
eucalyptus
eucaryotic
eudemonism
eudemonist

eudiometer
eudiometry
eugenicist
euhemerise
euhemerism
euhemerist
eulogistic
euphonious
euphuistic
eurhythmic
Eurodollar
Eurovision
eurypterid
euthanasia
fuddyduddy
fugitively
fulfilling
fulfilment
fuliginous
fullbodied
fullbottom
fulllength
fumblingly
fumigation
functional
funereally
fungicidal
funnelling
furuncular
fusibility
fussbudget
fustanella
futureless
futuristic
futurology
fuzzywuzzy
guardhouse
guesthouse
guestnight
guilefully
guillotine
guiltiness
gunfighter
gunrunning
gunslinger
gutturally
hucklebone
hullabaloo
humaneness
humanistic
humanities
humbleness
humbuggery
humbugging
humidifier
humoresque
humoristic
humorously
humourless
humoursome
humpbacked
hungriness
hurdygurdy
hurlyburly
husbandage
husbandman
jubilantly
jubilation
judgematic
judicatory
judicature
judicially
juggernaut
juristical
justiciary
juvenility
Kuomintang
lubricator
lubricious
luciferase
luciferous
lucifugous
lucubrator
luculently
lugubrious
lukewarmly
lumberjack
lumberroom
lumbersome
lumberyard
luminosity
luminously
lumpsucker
Lupercalia
lusciously
Lusitanian
lustration
lustreless
lustrously
lutestring
luxuriance
muciferous
mudskipper
mudslinger
muffinbell
Muhammadan
Muhammedan
muliebrity
mulishness
mulligrubs
multifaced
multiloquy
multimedia
multiphase
multiplier
multipolar
multistage
multivocal
mumbojumbo
munificent
muscularly
musicality
musicianly
musicology
musicpaper
musicstand
musicstool
muskmallow
Mussulmans
mutability
mutilation
mutinously
muttonhead
nubiferous
nuciferous
nucivorous
nucleation
nucleonics
nucleoside
nucleotide
nudibranch
nullanulla
numberless
numeration
numerology
numerosity
numerously
numismatic
nunciature
nuptiality
nurseryman
nutational
nutcracker
nutritious
outbalance
outbidding
outerspace
outfielder
outfitting
outgassing
outgeneral
outgunning
outlandish
outmeasure
outpatient
outpouring
outputting
outrageous
outrightly
outrunning
outsitting
outstation
outstretch
outswinger
outwitting
puberulent
pubescence
publishing
puerperium
puffpastry
pugilistic
pugnacious
puissantly
pulsatilla
pulsimeter
pulsometer
pulveriser
pulvinated
pummelling
punchboard
punchdrunk
punctation
punctually
punctuator
punctulate
punishable
punishment
punitively
pupilarity
pupiparous
purblindly
puristical
puritanise
puritanism
purposeful
purseproud
pursership
purseseine
pursuivant
purtenance
purulently
purveyance
pushbutton
putatively
putrescent
putrescine
putridness
puzzlement
quadrangle
quadrantal
quadratics
quadrature
quadrennia
quadriceps
quadrireme
quadrivial
quadrivium
quadrumana
quadrumane
quadrumvir
quadruplet
quadruplex
quadrupole
quaintness
qualmishly
quantifier
quantitive
quarantine
quarrelled
quarreller
quarrender
quartation
quarterage
quarterday
quartering
quartzitic
quaternary
quaternate
quaternion
quaternity
quatorzain
quatrefoil
queasiness
quenchable
quenchless
quercitron
questioner
quickgrass
quickthorn
quiescence
quiescency
quinacrine
quintuplet
quirkiness
quixotical
quizmaster
rubberneck
rubiginous
rubrically
rubricator
rubythroat
rudderfish
rudderless
rudimental
ruefulness
ruffianism
ruggedness
ruminantly
rumination
ruminative
rumrunning
runnerbean
runthrough
rupicoline
rupicolous
Russianise
Russophile
Russophobe
rustically
ruthlessly
subacidity
subaquatic
subaqueous
subaverage
subcentral
subclavian
subcordate
subculture
subdeanery
subduction
subglacial
subheading
subjectify
subjection
subjective
subjugator
subkingdom
subletting
sublimable
subliminal
sublingual
submariner
submediant
submersion
submission
submissive
submitting
submontane
subnuclear
suborbital
subordinal
subreption
subroutine
subscriber
subsection
subsellium
subsequent
subshrubby
subsidence
subsidiary
subsistent
subspecies
substation
substitute
substratum
subtenancy
subterfuge
subtleness
subtrahend
subvention
subversion
subversive
succedanea
successful
succession
successive
succinctly
succulence
succulency
sudatorium
suddenness
sufferable
sufferably
sufferance
sufficient
suffragist
sugardaddy
sugarhouse
sugariness
sugarmaple
suggestion
suggestive
suicidally
sullenness
sulphonate
sulphurate
sulphurise
sulphurous
sultanship
sultriness
summerlike
summertime
summitless
summonable
sunderance
sunglasses
sunparlour
superacute
superaltar
superation
superbness
supercargo
superduper
supergiant
superhuman
superiorly
superlunar
supernally
supernovae
superorder
superpower
supersonic
superstore
supertonic
supervisor
supination
supineness
supperless
supplanter
supplejack
supplement
suppleness
suppletion
suppletive
suppletory
suppliance
supplicant
supplicate
supportive
supposable
supposably
supposedly
suppressor
suprarenal
surefooted
suretyship
surfactant
surgically
surmisable
surplusage
surprising
surrealism
surrealist
survivance
susceptive
suspenders
suspension
suspensive
suspensoid
suspensory
suspicious
sustaining
sustenance
sustention
sustentive
suzerainty
tubercular
tuberculin
tuberosity
tubicolous
tuffaceous
tufthunter
tuitionary
tularaemia
tularaemic
tumbledown
tumblerful
tumbleweed
tumescence
tumultuary
tumultuous
tunelessly
tunnelling
turbidness
turbulence
turbulency
turgescent
turgidness
turkeycock
turnbuckle
turpentine
turtleback
turtledove
turtleneck
tutorially
vulcaniser
vulnerable
vulnerably
wunderkind
avantgarde
avaricious
aventurine
averseness
aversively

aviatrices
aviculture
avouchment
evacuation
evacuative
evaluation
evaluative
evanescent
evangelise
evangelism
evangelist
evaporable
evaporator
evenhanded
eventually
everglades
everliving
everyplace
everything
everywhere
evidential
evilminded
eviscerate
evolvement
ovariotomy
overabound
overactive
overblouse
overbought
overburden
overcharge
overcommit
overcooked
overexcite
overexpose
overflight
overground
overgrowth
overhanded
overlander
overlapped
overlooker
overmanned
overmantel
overmaster
overnicety
overpraise
overrefine
overridden
overriding
overshadow
overslaugh
overspread
overstride
overstrung
oversubtle
oversupply
overthrown
overthrust
overtopped
overweight
overwinter
ovipositor
dwarfishly
owlishness
swaggering
swanmaiden
swanupping
swarmspore
swashplate
swaybacked
sweatgland
sweatiness
sweatshirt
sweepingly
sweepstake
sweetbread
sweetbriar
sweetbrier
sweetening
sweetheart
sweltering
swimmingly
swinefever
swingingly
swinglebar
switchback
switchover
swiveleyed
swivelling
swordcraft
sworddance
swordgrass
swordstick
twelvefold
twelvenote
twelvetone
twilighted
twowheeler
zwitterion
axiologist
exactitude
exaggerate
exaltation
examinable
exasperate
excavation
excellence
excellency
excerption
excitation
excitative
excitatory
excitement
excitingly
excogitate
excrescent
excruciate
excusatory
execration
execrative
execratory
executable
exegetical
exenterate
exhalation
exhaustion
exhaustive
exhibition
exhibitory
exhilarant
exhilarate
exhumation
exobiology
exorbitant
exospheric
exoterical
exothermal
exothermic
exotically
expandable
expansible
expatriate
expectance
expectancy
expectedly
expedience
expediency
expedition
expendable
experience
experiment
expertness
expiration
expiratory
explicable
explicitly
exploitage
exploitive
exportable
exposition
expositive
expository
expressage
expression
expressive
expressway
exprobrate
expunction
expurgator
exsanguine
extemporal
extendedly
extendible
extensible
extenuator
exteriorly
externally
extinction
extinctive
extinguish
extirpator
extractant
extraction
extractive
extramural
extraneity
extraneous
extricable
exuberance
exulcerate
exultantly
exultation
exultingly
exurbanite
exuviation
oxidisable
oxygenator
uxoricidal
uxoriously
byelection
byssaceous
byssinosis
cybernetic
cyclically
cyclograph
cyclometer
cyclopedia
cyclopedic
cyclostome
cyclostyle
cylindered
cylindroid
cystoscope
cystoscopy
cytochrome
cytologist
dynamistic
dysenteric
dysgraphia
dysplastic
dysprosium
dystrophic
eyeglasses
eyeservice
eyewitness
gymnastics
gymnosophy
gymnosperm
gynandrous
gynocratic
gypsophila
gyrational
gyrocopter
gyroscopic
hyaloplasm
hybridiser
hydraulics
hydrically
hydrologic
hydrolysis
hydrolytic
hydromancy
hydrometer
hydrometry
hydropathy
hydrophane
hydrophily
hydrophone
hydrophyte
hydroplane
hydroscope
hydrotaxis
hygrograph
hygrometer
hygrometry
hygrophyte
hygroscope
hylotheism
hypabyssal
hypaethral
hypanthium
hyperaemia
hyperaemic
hyperbaric
hyperbaton
hyperbolae
hyperbolas
hyperbolic
hyperdulia
hypergolic
hypersonic
hyphenated
hypnagogic
hypnotiser
hypocorism
hypodermal
hypodermic
hypodermis
hypogynous
hypolimnia
hypophyses
hypophysis
hypostasis
hypostatic
hypotactic
hypotenuse
hypotheses
hypothesis
hypsometer
hypsometry
hysteresis
hysteretic
hysterical
lycopodium
lymphocyte
lymphomata
lyophilise
Lysenkoism
myasthenia
mycologist
mycoplasma
mycorrhiza
myocardium
myological
myopically
myrtaceous
mystagogic
mystagogue
mysterious
mystically
mythically
mythiciser
mythologer
mythologic
mythomania
mythopoeia
mythopoeic
myxomatous
myxomycete
nyctalopia
nyctalopic
nyctinasty
nympholept
oysterfarm
pycnogonid
pycnometer
pycnostyle
pyknometer
pyracantha
pyretology
pyridoxine
pyrogallol
pyrogenous
pyrography
pyrolusite
pyromaniac
pyromantic
pyrometric
pyrophoric
pyrotechny
pyroxenite
Pyrrhonian
Pyrrhonism
Pyrrhonist
pyrrhotite
sybaritism
sycophancy
syllabaria
syllogiser
symbolical
symboliser
symmetrise
sympathise
symphonion
symphonist
symphylous
symphyseal
symphysial
symposiast
synaeresis
synaloepha
synanthous
syncarpous
synchronal
synchronic
syncopated
syncopator
syncretise
syncretism
syncretist
syndicator
synecdoche
synecology
synergetic
syngenesis
synoecious
synonymist
synonymity
synonymous
synoptical
synostosis
syntagmata
synthesise
synthesist
synthetise
synthetist
syphilitic
systematic
systemless
tympanites
tympanitic
tympanitis
typescript
typesetter
typewriter
typicality
typography
typologist
tyrannical
Tyrrhenian
Wycliffite
Wykehamist
xylography
xylophonic
zygodactyl
zygomorphy
azeotropic
czarevitch

---

abacterial
academical
acarpelous
acatalepsy
adamantine
adaptation
adaptively
agapanthus
alarmingly
amalgamate
amanuenses
amanuensis
amateurish
amateurism
anabaptism
anabaptist
anacolutha
anadromous
anaglyphic
anagogical
analogical
analphabet
analysable
analytical
anamorphic
anapaestic
anaplastic
anaptyctic
anarchical
anastigmat
anastomose
anastrophe
anatomical
anatropous
aragonitic
araucarian
asafoetida
avantgarde
avaricious
beadleship
Beaujolais
beautician
beautifier
biannually
blackamoor
blackberry
blackboard
blackfaced
blackguard
blackheart
Blackshirt
blacksmith
blackthorn
blackwater
bladdernut
blamefully
blancmange
blanketing
blanquette
blasphemer
blastemata
blastocyst
blastoderm
blastomere

blastopore
blazonment
boastfully
brachiator
brachiopod
brachylogy
brachyural
brachyuran
bradyseism
Brahmanism
Brahminism
brainchild
braininess
brainpower
brainstorm
brakeblock
brakelight
branchiate
brandyball
brandysnap
brantgoose
brassiness
bratticing
brawniness
brazenness
brazilwood
chainsmoke
chairwoman
chalcedony
chalkboard
chalkstone
challenger
chalybeate
chamaeleon
chamberpot
champignon
chancellor
chandelier
changeable
changeably
changeless
changeling
changeover
channelise
channelled
chaparajos
chaparejos
chapfallen
chaplaincy
charactery
chargeable
chargehand
charioteer
charismata
charitable
charitably
Charleston
charmingly
chartreuse
chartulary
chasteness
chatelaine
chatoyance
chatterbox
chattiness
chaudfroid
chauffeuse
chauntress
chauvinism
chauvinist
clamminess
clangorous
clannishly
clarabella
Clarenceux
claspknife
classicise
classicism
classicist
classified
classifier
clavichord
clavicular
clawhammer
coacervate
coachbuilt
coachhouse
coadjacent
coagulable
coalbunker
coalescent
coaptation
coarseness
coastguard
coastwards
coathanger
coatimundi
crackajack
crackbrain
cradlesong
craftguild
craftiness
cragginess
cranesbill
craniology
crankiness
crankshaft
crapulence
craquelure
crassitude
cravenness
czarevitch
deaconship
deactivate
deadliness
deadweight
deaeration
deathwatch
diabolical
diachronic
diagnostic
diagonally
diagraphic
dialysable
diapedesis
diapedetic
diaphanous
diarrhoeal
diarrhoeic
diastemata
diathermal
diathermic
diatropism
draconites
drafthorse
dragonhead
dragonnade
dragontree
dramatical
dramaturge
dramaturgy
drawbridge
drawingpin
drawlingly
drawstring
dwarfishly
elaborator
elasticise
elasticity
elatedness
emaciation
emancipate
emancipist
emarginate
emasculate
enamelling
enamellist
enantiosis
eradicable
eradicator
evacuation
evacuative
evaluation
evaluative
evanescent
evangelise
evangelism
evangelist
evaporable
evaporator
exactitude
exaggerate
exaltation
examinable
exasperate
fearlessly
fearnought
fearsomely
featherbed
feathering
fianchetto
flabbiness
flabellate
flaccidity
flagellant
flagellate
flagitious
flagrantly
flagwaving
flamboyant
flameproof
flamingoes
flannelled
flapdoodle
flashboard
flashflood
flashiness
flashlight
flashpoint
flatfooted
flattering
flatulence
flatulency
flavescent
flavourful
flavouring
flawlessly
foamflower
fractional
fragmental
fragrantly
framboesia
franchiser
Franciscan
Francophil
frangipane
frangipani
fraternise
fraternity
fratricide
fraudulent
fraxinella
ghastfully
glaciation
glaciology
gladhander
gladsomely
Glagolitic
glancingly
glasscloth
glassfibre
glasshouse
glassiness
glasspaper
glassworks
Glaswegian
glauberite
glauconite
goalkeeper
goaltender
goatsbeard
goatsucker
gracefully
graciosity
graciously
gradualism
gradualist
graduation
gramicidin
gramineous
grammarian
gramophone
granadilla
grandchild
granddaddy
grandducal
grandmamma
grandniece
grandstand
granduncle
grangerise
grangerism
granophyre
granularly
granulator
granulitic
grapefruit
grapesugar
graphemics
graphitise
graphology
graptolite
graspingly
grasscloth
grassroots
grasssnake
gratefully
gratifying
gratuitous
gravestone
gravimeter
gravimetry
guardhouse
headcheese
headhunter
headmaster
headphones
headspring
headsquare
headstream
headstrong
headwaiter
heartblock
heartblood
heartbreak
heartiness
heartsease
heartthrob
heartwhole
heathendom
heathenise
heathenish
heathenism
heatstroke
heavenborn
heavensent
heavenward
heavyarmed
hoarseness
hyaloplasm
ilangilang
imaginable
imaginably
inaccuracy
inaccurate
inactivate
inactively
inactivity
inadequacy
inadequate
inappetent
inapposite
inaptitude
inartistic
inaugurate
italianate
italianise
Italianism
Italophile
leadenness
leaderless
leadership
leafcutter
leafhopper
leafinsect
meadowland
meadowlark
meagreness
mealbeetle
meaningful
measliness
measurable
measurably
measuredly
myasthenia
Neapolitan
opalescent
opaqueness
oracularly
orangepeel
orangewood
oratorical
ovariotomy
peacefully
peacemaker
peacockery
peacockish
pearldiver
peashooter
phagedaena
phagedenic
phagocytic
phalangeal
phallicism
phanerogam
phantasise
phantasmal
phantasmic
phantastic
phantastry
pharisaism
pharmacist
pharyngeal
pianissimo
pianoforte
placidness
plagiarise
plagiarism
plagiarist
plaguesome
plainchant
planchette
planetable
planetaria
plangently
planigraph
planimeter
planimetry
planktonic
planometer
plantation
plantlouse
plasmodesm
plasmodium
plasmogamy
plasmolyse
plasticise
plasticity
platelayer
playacting
playbyplay
playfellow
playground
playwright
practician
practising
praecocial
praemunire
praesidium
praetorial
praetorian
pragmatise
pragmatism
pragmatist
prairiedog
prancingly
pratincole
prayerbook
psalmodise
psalmodist
psalterium
quadrangle
quadrantal
quadratics
quadrature
quadrennia
quadriceps
quadrireme
quadrivial
quadrivium
quadrumana
quadrumane
quadrumvir
quadruplet
quadruplex
quadrupole
quaintness
qualmishly
quantifier
quantitive
quarantine
quarrelled
quarreller
quarrender
quartation
quarterage
quarterday
quartering
quartzitic
quaternary
quaternate
quaternion
quaternity
quatorzain
quatrefoil
reactivate
reactively
reactivity
readership
reafforest
realisable
reallocate
reappraise
rearmament
reasonable
reasonably
reasonless
reassemble
reassembly
rhapsodise
rhapsodist
roadrunner
roadworthy
scabrously

scaffolder
scaleboard
scandalise
scandalous
scansorial
scantiness
scapegrace
scarabaeid
scarabaeus
scaramouch
scarceness
scaredycat
scarlatina
scatheless
scathingly
scattergun
scattering
scattiness
scavengery
seaanemone
seabiscuit
seacaptain
sealingwax
seamanlike
seamanship
seamstress
searchable
searchless
seaserpent
seasonable
seasonably
seasonally
shabbiness
shadowless
shagginess
shamefaced
shamefully
shandrydan
shandygaff
shanghaier
shantytown
sharpnosed
sialagogic
sialagogue
skateboard
slanderous
slanginess
slantingly
slatternly
slavetrade
slavocracy
Slavophile
Slavophobe
smallscale
smallsword
smallwares
smaragdine
smaragdite
smartmoney
smattering
snafflebit
snailpaced
snailwheel
snakedance
snakestone
snapdragon
snappishly
soapboiler
soapbubble
soapflakes
spacecraft
spacewoman
spaciously
spadebeard
spadiceous
spagyrical
spallation
spankingly
sparseness
Spartacist
spasticity
spatchcock
spathulate
spatiality
stabiliser
stablemate
stableness
stadholder
staffnurse
stagbeetle
stagecoach
stagecraft
staggering
stagnantly
stagnation
stalactite
stalagmite
stalwartly
stanchless
stanchness
standpoint
standstill
staphyline
stargazing
starriness
starryeyed
starstream
starvation
starveling
statecraft
statically
stationary
stationery
statistics
statoscope
statuesque
statutable
statutably
staurolite
stavesacre
swaggering
swanmaiden
swanupping
swarmspore
swashplate
swaybacked
teaplanter
tearjerker
tearlessly
teatrolley
thalecress
thankfully
trabeation
trabeculae
trabecular
tracheated
tracheitis
Tractarian
tractional
trafficked
trafficker
tragacanth
tragically
tragicomic
traitorous
trajection
trajectory
trammelled
tramontana
tramontane
trampoline
trancelike
tranquilly
transactor
transcribe
transcript
transducer
transeptal
transferee
transferor
transfuser
transgress
transience
transiency
transistor
transition
transitive
transitory
translator
translucid
translunar
transmuter
transplant
transposal
transposer
transshape
transvalue
transverse
trappiness
trashiness
traumatism
travelling
travelogue
travertine
trawlerman
tsarevitch
unabridged
unaccented
unaffected
unAmerican
unarguable
unassisted
unassuming
unattached
unattended
unavailing
uranometry
weakliness
weakminded
weaponless
wearifully
weatherbox
weathering
weatherman
weaverbird
whaleshark
wharfinger
whatsoever
wraparound
wrathfully
wrathiness
yearningly
yeastiness
ylangylang
abbreviate
Albigenses
albuminoid
albuminous
ambassador
ambidexter
ambivalent
ambulacral
ambulacrum
ambulation
ambulatory
ambushment
arbalester
arbalister
arbitrable
arbitrager
arbitrator
arboreally
arborvitae
asbestosis
babblement
babiroussa
Babylonian
babysitter
biblically
bibliology
bibliopegy
bibliophil
bibliopole
bibliopoly
bibliotics
bibulously
bobbinlace
bobbysocks
bobbysoxer
bubblyjock
cabalistic
cybernetic
debasement
debatement
debauchery
debilitate
debonairly
debouchure
dubitation
dubitative
embalmment
embankment
embarkment
emblazoner
emblazonry
emblematic
emblements
embodiment
embolismic
embonpoint
embossment
embouchure
embowelled
embroidery
embryogeny
embryology
embryonate
fabricator
fabulously
febrifugal
fibreboard
fibreglass
fibrillary
fibrillate
fibrillose
fibrinogen
fibrositis
gobemouche
gobstopper
habiliment
habilitate
habitation
habitually
hebdomadal
hebetation
Hebraistic
hibernacle
hobbyhorse
hobnobbing
hybridiser
imbecilely
imbecility
imbibition
inbreeding
jobbernowl
jubilantly
jubilation
kibbutznik
labiovelar
laboratory
lebensraum
liberalise
liberalism
liberalist
liberality
liberation
libidinous
librettist
lobsterpot
lobulation
lubricator
lubricious
mobocratic
nebulosity
nebulously
noblewoman
nubiferous
ombrometer
pebbledash
puberulent
pubescence
publishing
rabbinical
rabblement
rebellious
rebuttable
ribbonfish
ribbonworm
riboflavin
robustious
robustness
rubberneck
rubiginous
rubrically
rubricator
rubythroat
sabbatical
sabretache
sabretooth
seborrhoea
sibilation
sobersided
sobersides
subacidity
subaquatic
subaqueous
subaverage
subcentral
subclavian
subcordate
subculture
subdeanery
subduction
subglacial
subheading
subjectify
subjection
subjective
subjugator
subkingdom
subletting
sublimable
subliminal
sublingual
submariner
submediant
submersion
submission
submissive
submitting
submontane
subnuclear
suborbital
subordinal
subreption
subroutine
subscriber
subsection
subsellium
subsequent
subshrubby
subsidence
subsidiary
subsistent
subspecies
substation
substitute
substratum
subtenancy
subterfuge
subtleness
subtrahend
subvention
subversion
subversive
sybaritism
tabernacle
tablecloth
tablelinen
tablespoon
tabularise
tabulation
tobogganer
tubercular
tuberculin
tuberosity
tubicolous
umbellifer
umbilicate
umbiliform
umbrageous
umbrellaed
unbalanced
unbearable
unbearably
unbeatable
unbeatably
unbecoming
unbeliever
unbesought
unbiblical
unbiddable
unblenched
unblinking
unblushing
unbonneted
unbrokenly
unbuttoned
upbraiding
upbringing
urbanology
vibraculum
vibraphone
wobbliness
zabaglione
accelerate
accentuate
acceptable
acceptably
acceptance
acceptedly
accessible
accessibly
accidental
accomplice
accomplish
accordance
accoucheur
accountant
accounting
accredited
accrescent
accumulate
accurately
accursedly
accusation
accusative
accusatory
accusingly
accustomed
alchemical
alcoholise
alcoholism
alcyonaria

ancestress
anchoretic
anchoritic
anchorless
anchorring
anchylosis
anchylotic
ancipitous
archaistic
archbishop
archdeacon
archerfish
archetypal
architrave
archpriest
ascariasis
ascendable
ascendance
ascendancy
ascendence
ascendency
ascendible
asceticism
ascomycete
ascribable
ascription
auctioneer
bacchantes
bacchantic
backbiting
backblocks
backgammon
background
backhanded
backhander
backsheesh
backslider
backstairs
backstitch
backstroke
backwardly
becomingly
bichromate
bicultural
buccinator
Buchmanism
Buchmanite
bucketshop
cacciatore
cachinnate
cackhanded
cacodaemon
cacogenics
cacography
cacomistle
cicatrices
Ciceronian
cicisbeism
cochleated
cockalorum
cockatrice
cockchafer
cockneyish
cockneyism
cocksurely
cuckoopint
cuckoospit
cucullated
cyclically
cyclograph
cyclometer
cyclopedia
cyclopedic
cyclostome
cyclostyle
decadently
decagramme
decahedral
decahedron
decampment
decapitate
decapodous
deceivable
decelerate
Decembrist
decemviral
deceptible
decigramme
decimalise
decimalism
decimation
decisively
decivilise
declarable
declassify
declension
declinable
decolonise
decolorant
decolorise
decompound
decompress
decoration
decorative
decorously
decrescent
dichroitic
dichromate
dickcissel
Dickensian
dictatress
dictionary
doctorship
documental
ecchymosis
ecchymotic
ecclesiast
encampment
encasement
encashment
encephalic
encephalon
enchanting
encourager
encroacher
encyclical
encystment
escadrille
escalation
escallonia
escapement
escapology
escarpment
escharotic
escheatage
escritoire
Esculapian
escutcheon
eucalyptol
eucalyptus
eucaryotic
excavation
excellence
excellency
excerption
excitation
excitative
excitatory
excitement
excitingly
excogitate
excrescent
excruciate
excusatory
faceharden
facesaving
facileness
facilitate
factiously
factitious
factorship
factualism
factualist
factuality
fecklessly
fickleness
fictioneer
fictionist
fictitious
hackbuteer
hackmatack
hectically
hectograph
hectolitre
hectometre
hocuspocus
hucklebone
incandesce
incantator
incapacity
incasement
incautious
incendiary
incessancy
incestuous
inchoately
inchoation
inchoative
incidental
incinerate
incipience
incipiency
incisively
incitation
incitement
incivility
inclemency
inclinable
includible
incogitant
incoherent
incomplete
inconstant
incrassate
incredible
incredibly
increscent
incubation
incubative
incubatory
inculcator
inculpable
incumbency
incunabula
incurrable
jackanapes
jackassery
jackhammer
jackknives
jackrabbit
jacobinise
Jacobinism
Jacobitism
jocoseness
jocularity
laceration
lacerative
lachrymose
lacklustre
laconicism
lacrimator
lacrymator
lactescent
lacustrine
lectionary
licensable
licentiate
licentious
lockerroom
lockkeeper
lockstitch
locomotion
locomotive
locomotory
locustbean
luciferase
luciferous
lucifugous
lucubrator
luculently
lycopodium
macadamise
Maccabaean
macebearer
maceration
machinator
machinegun
mackintosh
macrophage
macrospore
maculation
maculature
mechanical
micaschist
Michaelmas
microbiota
microcline
microfarad
microfiche
micrograph
microlitic
micrometer
micrometry
microphone
microphyte
micropylar
microscope
microscopy
microseism
microspore
mockheroic
muciferous
mycologist
mycoplasma
mycorrhiza
necrolater
necrolatry
necromancy
necrophile
necrophily
necropolis
necroscopy
nectareous
nickelling
nicotinism
nuciferous
nucivorous
nucleation
nucleonics
nucleoside
nucleotide
nyctalopia
nyctalopic
nyctinasty
occasional
occidental
occupation
occupative
occurrence
oecologist
oecumenism
oncogenous
oncologist
orchardist
orchardman
orchestics
orchestral
oscillator
oscitation
osculation
osculatory
pacesetter
pacifiable
pacificate
pacificism
pacificist
packingbox
packsaddle
packthread
peccadillo
pectinated
peculation
peculiarly
picaresque
picayunish
piccalilli
piccaninny
pichiciago
pickaninny
picketline
pickpocket
picnicking
picosecond
pictograph
pictorical
pocketable
pocketbook
pocketsize
pockmarked
pycnogonid
pycnometer
pycnostyle
racecourse
Rachmanism
rackrenter
recallable
receivable
recentness
receptacle
receptible
rechristen
recidivism
recidivist
recipiency
reciprocal
recitalist
recitation
recitative
recitativo
recklessly
recolonise
recommence
recompense
reconciler
reconsider
recordable
recoupment
recreantly
recreation
recreative
recrudesce
rectorship
recumbency
recuperate
recurrence
recyclable
ricinoleic
rickettsia
rockabilly
rockbadger
rockbottom
rockgarden
rockhopper
rockpigeon
rockrabbit
rockribbed
saccharate
saccharide
saccharify
saccharine
saccharoid
saccharose
sacerdotal
sacredness
sacrificer
sacroiliac
sacrosanct
secernment
secludedly
secondbest
secondhand
secondment
secondrate
secretaire
secularise
secularism
secularist
secularity
securement
secureness
securiform
sicklebill
sickliness
socialiser
societally
sociologic
sociometry
succedanea
successful
succession
successive
succinctly
succulence
succulency
sycophancy
tachometer
tachometry
tachymeter
tachymetry
taciturnly
tackdriver
tactically
tactlessly
technetium
technician
technicist
technocrat
technology
tickertape
ticklishly
ticpolonga
tocopherol
ulceration
ulcerative
unchanging
unchastity
uncloister
uncommonly
uncritical
unctuosity
unctuously
uncustomed
vaccinator
vectograph
viceconsul
vicegerent
viceregent
victimiser
Victoriana
victorious
victualled
victualler
vocabulary
vocational

vo**c**iferant
vo**c**iferate
vo**c**iferous
wi**c**kedness
wi**c**kerwork
Wy**c**liffite
ab**d**ication
ab**d**ominous
ab**d**ucentes
ad**d**itional
ad**d**lepated
al**d**ermanic
al**d**ermanry
An**d**alusian
an**d**alusite
an**d**roecium
an**d**rogenic
au**d**ibility
au**d**iometer
au**d**iometry
au**d**iophile
au**d**itorial
au**d**itorium
ba**d**derlock
be**d**chamber
be**d**clothes
be**d**evilled
Be**d**lington
be**d**raggled
bi**d**onville
Bu**d**dhistic
bu**d**gerigar
ca**d**averous
ca**d**disworm
co**d**swallop
cu**d**dlesome
cu**d**gelling
de**d**ication
de**d**icative
de**d**icatory
de**d**uctible
di**d**actical
di**d**geridoo
el**d**erberry
en**d**earment
en**d**emicity
en**d**ocrinal
en**d**odermal
en**d**odermis
en**d**ogamous
en**d**ogenous
en**d**ophytic
en**d**opodite
en**d**orsable
en**d**oscopic
en**d**osmosis
en**d**osmotic
en**d**othelia
en**d**product
en**d**stopped
en**d**uringly
eu**d**emonism
eu**d**emonist
eu**d**iometer
eu**d**iometry
fa**d**elessly
fe**d**eralise
fe**d**eralism
fe**d**eralist
fe**d**eration
fe**d**erative
fi**d**dleback
fi**d**dlehead
fi**d**dlewood
fi**d**ucially
fu**d**dyduddy
ga**d**olinite
ga**d**olinium
ga**d**rooning
Go**d**fearing
he**d**onistic
ho**d**gepodge
hy**d**raulics
hy**d**rically
hy**d**rologic
hy**d**rolysis
hy**d**rolytic
hy**d**romancy
hy**d**rometer
hy**d**rometry
hy**d**ropathy
hy**d**rophane
hy**d**rophily
hy**d**rophone
hy**d**rophyte
hy**d**roplane
hy**d**roscope
hy**d**rotaxis
in**d**agation
in**d**ecently
in**d**ecision
in**d**ecisive
in**d**ecorous
in**d**efinite
in**d**elicacy
in**d**elicate
in**d**exation
in**d**ication
in**d**icative
in**d**icatory
in**d**ictable
in**d**ictment
in**d**igenous
in**d**igested
in**d**irectly
in**d**iscreet
in**d**iscrete
in**d**isposed
in**d**istinct
in**d**itement
in**d**ividual
in**d**ocility
in**d**olently
In**d**onesian
in**d**ucement
in**d**uctance
in**d**ulgence
in**d**uration
in**d**urative
in**d**ustrial
io**d**ination
ju**d**gematic
ju**d**icatory
ju**d**icature
ju**d**icially
ki**d**napping
la**d**derback
la**d**ychapel
la**d**yfinger
la**d**ykiller
le**d**erhosen
le**d**gerbait
le**d**gerline
ma**d**reporic
me**d**dlesome
me**d**iastina
me**d**iatress
me**d**icament
me**d**icaster
me**d**ication
me**d**icative
me**d**ievally
me**d**iocrity
me**d**itation
me**d**itative
me**d**ullated
mi**d**dleaged
mi**d**dlebrow
mi**d**dlemost
mi**d**dlingly
mi**d**morning
mi**d**shipman
mo**d**erately
mo**d**eration
mo**d**eratism
mo**d**erniser
mo**d**ernness
mo**d**ifiable
mo**d**ishness
mo**d**ulation
mu**d**skipper
mu**d**slinger
ni**d**icolous
ni**d**ificate
ni**d**ifugous
no**d**ulation
nu**d**ibranch
ob**d**urately
oe**d**ematose
oe**d**ematous
ol**d**fangled
ol**d**maidish
or**d**ainment
or**d**inarily
or**d**ination
or**d**onnance
Or**d**ovician
pa**d**dleboat
pa**d**dyfield
pa**d**dywagon
pa**d**dywhack
pe**d**agogics
pe**d**alorgan
pe**d**alpoint
pe**d**erastic
pe**d**estrian
pe**d**iculate
pe**d**iculous
pe**d**icurist
pe**d**imental
pe**d**imented
pe**d**ologist
pe**d**uncular
po**d**iatrist
ra**d**icalise
ra**d**icalism
ra**d**ication
ra**d**iogenic
ra**d**iograph
ra**d**iologic
ra**d**iometer
ra**d**iometry
ra**d**iopaque
ra**d**iophone
ra**d**ioscopy
ra**d**iosonde
re**d**blooded
re**d**currant
re**d**ecorate
re**d**eemable
re**d**emption
re**d**emptive
re**d**emptory
re**d**escribe
re**d**iscover
re**d**olently
re**d**undance
re**d**undancy
ri**d**gepiece
ri**d**iculous
ro**d**fishing
ru**d**derfish
ru**d**derless
ru**d**imental
sa**d**dleback
sa**d**dlefast
sa**d**dletree
se**d**ateness
se**d**ucement
se**d**uctress
se**d**ulously
si**d**eboards
si**d**eeffect
si**d**eglance
si**d**erolite
si**d**erostat
si**d**esaddle
si**d**estreet
si**d**estroke
si**d**ewinder
so**d**denness
su**d**atorium
su**d**denness
ti**d**dlywink
ti**d**ewaiter
un**d**efended
un**d**eniable
un**d**eniably
un**d**erbelly
un**d**erbrush
un**d**ercliff
un**d**ercover
un**d**ercroft
un**d**erdress
un**d**erfloor
un**d**erglaze
un**d**erlease
un**d**erlinen
un**d**erlying
un**d**erminer
un**d**erneath
un**d**erpants
un**d**erproof
un**d**erquote
un**d**erscore
un**d**ersense
un**d**ersexed
un**d**ershirt
un**d**ershoot
un**d**ershrub
un**d**ersized
un**d**erskirt
un**d**erslung
un**d**erstand
un**d**erstate
un**d**ersteer
un**d**erstock
un**d**erstood
un**d**erstudy
un**d**ertaken
un**d**ertaker
un**d**ertrick
un**d**ervalue
un**d**erwater
un**d**erworld
un**d**erwrite
un**d**erwrote
un**d**eserved
un**d**esigned
un**d**esirous
un**d**eterred
un**d**igested
un**d**ulation
un**d**ulatory
vi**d**eophone
wi**d**espread
ab**e**rdevine
ab**e**rrantly
ab**e**rration
ac**e**phalous
ac**e**rvation
ac**e**tabular
ac**e**tabulum
ad**e**nectomy
ad**e**quately
al**e**xanders
am**e**liorate
am**e**ndatory
am**e**rcement
am**e**rciable
Am**e**rindian
an**e**cdotage
an**e**cdotist
an**e**mograph
an**e**mometer
an**e**mometry
an**e**mophily
an**e**urismal
an**e**urysmal
ar**e**naceous
ar**e**olation
Ar**e**opagite
as**e**xuality
at**e**leiosis
av**e**nturine
av**e**rseness
av**e**rsively
az**e**otropic
be**e**chdrops
be**e**fburger
be**e**keeping
bi**e**nnially
bl**e**achable
bl**e**ariness
bl**e**aryeyed
bl**e**atingly
bl**e**pharism
br**e**adboard
br**e**adcrumb
br**e**adfruit
br**e**adstick
br**e**adstuff
br**e**akables
br**e**akpoint
br**e**akwater
br**e**astbone
br**e**astwall
br**e**astwork
br**e**athable
br**e**athless
br**e**echless
br**e**ezeless
br**e**eziness
br**e**ntgoose
br**e**ssummer
br**e**vetting
by**e**lection
Ca**e**rphilly
ca**e**spitose
ch**e**apishly
ch**e**apskate
ch**e**ckpoint
ch**e**ekiness
ch**e**erfully
ch**e**eriness
ch**e**esecake
ch**e**esiness
ch**e**licerae
ch**e**mically
ch**e**misette
ch**e**motaxis
ch**e**quebook
ch**e**rsonese
ch**e**ssboard
ch**e**vrotain
cl**e**arstory
cl**e**mentine
cl**e**restory
cl**e**rically
cl**e**verness
co**e**lacanth
co**e**nobitic
co**e**nobytic
co**e**quality
co**e**rcively
co**e**taneous
co**e**ternity
co**e**xistent
cr**e**aminess
cr**e**atinine
cr**e**atively
cr**e**ativity
cr**e**aturely
cr**e**dential
cr**e**ditable
cr**e**ditably
cr**e**epiness
cr**e**matoria
cr**e**nellate
cr**e**nulated
cr**e**puscule
cr**e**scentic
cr**e**taceous
cr**e**welwork
ct**e**nophore
de**e**pfreeze
de**e**pfrozen
de**e**prooted
de**e**pseated
de**e**rforest
de**e**scalate
di**e**casting
di**e**lectric
di**e**sinking
dr**e**adfully
dr**e**aminess
dr**e**amworld
dr**e**ariness
dr**e**ssiness
dr**e**ssmaker
ed**e**ntulous
el**e**campane
el**e**ctively
el**e**ctorate
el**e**ctrical
el**e**ctronic
el**e**mentary
El**e**usinian
el**e**venplus
em**e**ndation
em**e**ndatory
em**e**ryboard
em**e**rypaper
em**e**rywheel
en**e**rgetics
en**e**rvation
en**e**rvative
ep**e**irogeny
ep**e**ntheses
ep**e**nthesis
ep**e**nthetic
ep**e**xegeses
ep**e**xegesis
ep**e**xegetic
er**e**ctility
er**e**mitical
er**e**thismic
et**e**rnalise
et**e**rnalist
ev**e**nhanded
ev**e**ntually
ev**e**rglades
ev**e**rliving
ev**e**ryplace
ev**e**rything
ev**e**rywhere
ex**e**cration
ex**e**crative
ex**e**cratory
ex**e**cutable
ex**e**getical
ex**e**nterate
ey**e**glasses
ey**e**service

eyewitness
feebleness
fieldglass
fieldmouse
fieldpiece
fieldstone
fiendishly
fierceness
fleabitten
fleacircus
fleamarket
fledgeling
fleeringly
fleetingly
fleshiness
fleshwound
flexuously
foetidness
freakiness
freakishly
freebooter
freedwoman
freehanded
freeholder
freelancer
freeliving
freeloader
freemartin
freesoiler
freespeech
freespoken
freightage
Frenchness
frenziedly
frequenter
frequently
freshwater
greasewood
greasiness
greatniece
greatuncle
GrecoRoman
greediness
greedyguts
greencloth
greenfinch
greenheart
greenhouse
greenshank
greenstick
greenstone
greenstuff
greensward
gregarious
grenadilla
gressorial
greyheaded
guesthouse
guestnight
haematosis
haematuria
haemolysis
haemolytic
heedlessly
hierarchal
hierarchic
hierocracy
hieroglyph
hierograph
hierolatry
hierophant
icebreaker
idealistic
ideational
ideography
ideologist
ineducable
inefficacy
inelegance
ineligible
ineligibly
ineloquent
ineludible
ineptitude
inequality
inevitable
inevitably
inexistent
inexorable
inexorably
inexpertly
inexpiable
inexpiably
inexplicit
isentropic
kieselguhr
lieutenant
meerschaum
needlebath
needlebook
needlecord
needlefish
needlessly
needlework
obediently
oceanarium
oceangoing
oceanology
ocellation
oleaginous
oleiferous
oleography
oleraceous
oneirology
onesidedly
openhanded
openhearth
openminded
operculate
operettist
oreography
oreologist
overabound
overactive
overblouse
overbought
overburden
overcharge
overcommit
overcooked
overexcite
overexpose
overflight
overground
overgrowth
overhanded
overlander
overlapped
overlooker
overmanned
overmantel
overmaster
overnicety
overpraise
overrefine
overridden
overriding
overshadow
overslaugh
overspread
overstride
overstrung
oversubtle
oversupply
overthrown
overthrust
overtopped
overweight
overwinter
paedagogic
paederasty
paediatric
paedogogue
paedophile
peerlessly
pheasantry
phelloderm
phenacetin
phenocryst
phenomenal
phenomenon
phenotypic
pheromonal
piecegoods
piercingly
piezometer
pleadingly
pleasantly
pleasantry
pleasingly
plebiscite
plecoptera
pleochroic
pleonastic
plesiosaur
pneumatics
poetically
preachment
preadamite
prearrange
prebendary
precarious
precaution
precedence
precedency
preceptive
preceptory
precession
preciosity
preciously
precipitin
preclusion
preclusive
precocious
preconcert
precordial
precursory
predacious
predecease
predestine
predicable
prediction
predictive
predispose
prednisone
preeminent
preemption
preemptive
preexilian
prefecture
preferable
preferably
preference
preferment
preferring
prefixture
prefrontal
prefulgent
preglacial
pregnantly
prehensile
prehension
prehistory
prejudiced
prelatical
prelection
premarital
premaxilla
premedical
premonitor
prepackage
preparator
preparedly
prepayable
prepayment
prepensely
prepossess
prepotence
prepotency
presageful
presbyopia
presbyopic
presbytery
prescience
prescriber
presentday
presentive
presidency
presidiary
presignify
pressagent
pressingly
pressurise
presternum
presumable
presumably
presuppose
pretendant
pretendent
pretension
prettiness
prevailing
prevalence
prevenancy
prevenient
prevention
preventive
previously
psephology
pseudocarp
puerperium
queasiness
quenchable
quenchless
quercitron
questioner
reelection
reeligible
reentrance
rheologist
rheotropic
rhetorical
rheumatics
rheumatism
rheumatoid
ruefulness
scenically
scepticism
seedpotato
seedvessel
seemliness
seersucker
seethrough
sheabutter
shearwater
sheathbill
sheathless
sheepishly
sheeplouse
sheepshank
sheepshead
shellacked
shellmound
shellproof
shellshock
shenanigan
sherardise
sheriffdom
siegetrain
sketchable
sketchbook
skewbridge
sleaziness
sleepiness
sleepyhead
sleeveless
sleevelink
sleighbell
slenderise
smelliness
sneakiness
sneakingly
sneakthief
sneeringly
sneezeweed
sneezewood
sneezewort
speargrass
specialise
specialism
specialist
speciality
speciation
speciology
speciosity
speciously
spectacled
spectacles
spectrally
speculator
speechless
speediness
speedlimit
speleology
spellbound
Spencerian
Spenserian
spermaceti
spermicide
sperrylite
steadiness
steakhouse
stealthily
steamchest
steaminess
steamtight
steeliness
steelworks
stelliform
stenchtrap
stencilled
stenciller
stenograph
stentorian
stepfather
stephanite
stepladder
stepmother
stepparent
stepsister
stereobate
stereogram
stereopsis
stereotype
stereotypy
sterigmata
steriliser
sternwards
stertorous
stewardess
sweatgland
sweatiness
sweatshirt
sweepingly
sweepstake
sweetbread
sweetbriar
sweetbrier
sweetening
sweetheart
sweltering
teenyweeny
teetotally
theatrical
theistical
themselves
theocratic
theodicean
theodolite
theogonist
theologian
theologise
theologist
theophanic
theophoric
theopneust
theoretics
theosopher
thereabout
thereafter
thereanent
thereunder
thermionic
thermistor
thermogram
thermophil
thermopile
thermostat
theurgical
treadboard
treadwheel
treasonous
trecentist
tremendous
tremolitic
trenchancy
trendiness
trepanning
trespasser
twelvefold
twelvenote
twelvetone
uneasiness
uneconomic
unedifying
uneducated
unemphatic
unemployed
unendingly
unenviable
unequalled
unerringly
unevenness
uneventful
unexampled
unexcelled
unexpected
unexplored
urethritis
usefulness
Vietnamese
viewfinder
viewlessly
weedkiller
wheatstone
wheelchair
wheelhorse
wheelhouse
wheeziness
whensoever
whereabout
woefulness
wretchedly
yieldingly

affability
affectedly
affectless
affeerment
afferently
affettuoso
affiliated
affirmable
affliction
afflictive
affluently
affordable
bafflement
bafflingly
beforehand
beforetime
bufflehead
buffoonery
coffeemill
defacement
defalcator
defamation
defamatory
defeasance
defeasible
defeminise
defendable
defensible
defensibly
deferrable
deficiency
defilement
definement
definienda
definitely
definition
definitive
definitude
deflagrate
deflection
deflective
deflowerer
defoliator
deforciant
defrayable
defrayment
difference
difficulty
diffidence
diffusible
effaceable
effacement
effectuate
effeminacy
effeminate
effervesce
effeteness
efficacity
efficiency
effloresce
effortless
effrontery
effulgence
effusively
enfacement
fiftyfifty
infallible
infallibly
infamously
infarction
infatuated
infeasible
infectious
infelicity
inferiorly
infernally
inferrable
infidelity
infighting
infiltrate
infinitely
infinitive
infinitude
inflatable
inflection
inflective
inflexible
inflexibly
infliction
inflictive
informally
infraction
infrahuman
infrasonic
infrequent
infusorial
infusorian
Kafkaesque
lefthanded
lefthander
lifegiving
lifejacket
lifelessly
lifesaving
muffinbell
oafishness
obfuscated
officially
offlicence
offputting
offsetting
puffpastry
referendum
refillable
refinement
reflection
reflective
reflexible
reformable
refraction
refractive
refractory
refreshing
refringent
refuelling
refulgence
refundable
refundment
refutation
ruffianism
safeblower
safetybelt
softbilled
softboiled
softfinned
softheaded
softspoken
sufferable
sufferably
sufferance
sufficient
suffragist
toffeenose
tuffaceous
tufthunter
unfadingly
unfairness
unfaithful
unfamiliar
unfathered
unfeminine
unfettered
unfilially
unfinished
unflagging
unforeseen
unfriended
unfriendly
waffleiron
agglutinin
aggrandise
aggression
aggressive
algebraist
algolagnia
algolagnic
algologist
Algonquian
angiosperm
Anglistics
anglomania
anglophile
anglophobe
anglophone
AngloSaxon
angularity
angwantibo
argumentum
augustness
bigamously
bighearted
bigmouthed
cogitation
cogitative
cognisable
cognisably
cognisance
cognominal
degeneracy
degenerate
degradable
degradedly
degressive
digestible
digitalise
digitately
digitation
digitiform
digression
digressive
doggedness
dogmatical
dogmatiser
dogstongue
eigenvalue
eighteenmo
eighteenth
engagement
engagingly
engineroom
Englishman
englutting
engrossing
engulfment
ergodicity
ergonomics
ergonomist
ergosterol
eugenicist
figuration
figurative
figurehead
fugitively
goggleeyed
hagiolatry
hagiologic
hagioscope
highbinder
highflying
highhanded
highjacker
highlander
highminded
highoctane
highstrung
highwayman
hygrograph
hygrometer
hygrometry
hygrophyte
hygroscope
ingeminate
ingestible
inglorious
ingratiate
ingredient
ingression
jaggedness
jaguarundi
juggernaut
legalistic
legateship
legibility
legislator
legitimacy
legitimate
legitimise
legitimism
legitimist
leguminous
ligamental
lighterage
lighterman
lightfaced
lighthouse
lightingup
lightproof
loganberry
loganstone
loggerhead
logicality
logistical
logography
logorrhoea
logrolling
lugubrious
magistracy
magistrate
magnetiser
magnifical
magnificat
magnifying
megalithic
megalosaur
megascopic
mightiness
mignonette
migrainous
negatively
negativism
negativist
negativity
neglectful
negligence
negligible
negligibly
negotiable
negotiator
negrophile
negrophobe
nightdress
nightglass
nightlight
nightshade
nightshift
nightshirt
nightstick
nightwatch
nigrescent
organicism
organicist
organismal
pagination
pegmatitic
pigeonhole
pigeonpair
pigeonpost
pigeontoed
pigeonwing
pigmentary
pigsticker
pogonology
pogonotomy
pugilistic
pugnacious
ragamuffin
raggedness
regalement
regardless
regelation
regeneracy
regenerate
regentship
regimental
regionally
registered
registrant
regression
regressive
regretting
regularise
regularity
regulation
regulative
regulatory
rightangle
rightfully
rightwards
rigorously
ruggedness
sagination
sagittally
segmentary
seguidilla
signalling
signwriter
sugardaddy
sugarhouse
sugariness
sugarmaple
suggestion
suggestive
tegumental
ungenerous
ungraceful
ungracious
ungrateful
ungrounded
ungrudging
unguentary
vegetarian
vegetation
vegetative
vigilantly
vignettist
vigorously
waggonette
wagonvault
zigzagging
zygodactyl
zygomorphy
abhorrence
achievable
achondrite
achromatic
adherently
adhesively
adhibition
aphaereses
aphaeresis
aphoristic
aphrodisia
Ashkenazim
Athanasian
behindhand
cohabitant
coherently
cohesively
dehiscence
dehumanise
dehumidify
echinoderm
enharmonic
ephemerous
ephorality
ethereally
ethicality
ethnically
ethnologic
ethologist
euhemerise
euhemerism
euhemerist
exhalation
exhaustion
exhaustive
exhibition
exhibitory
exhilarant
exhilarate
exhumation
Fahrenheit
ichthyosis
inhabitant
inhalation
inharmonic
inherently
inheritrix
inhibition
inhibitory
inhumanely
inhumanity
inhumation
Ishmaelite
Jehovistic
johnnycake
Johnsonese
johnsonian
Mahommedan
Mohammedan
Muhammadan
Muhammedan
nihilistic
ochlocracy
ophicleide
ophiolater
ophiolatry
ophiologic
ophthalmia
ophthalmic
otherwhere
otherwhile
otherworld
schematise
schematism
schemozzle
scherzando
schipperke
schismatic
schizocarp
schizogony
scholastic
schoolable
schoolbook
schooldays
schoolgirl
schoolmaam
schoolmarm
schoolmate
schoolroom
schooltime
schoolwork
sphalerite
sphenodone

sphenogram
sphenoidal
sphericity
spheroidal
spherulite
unhallowed
unhandsome
unhistoric
unholiness
unhouseled
upholstery
vehemently
abiogenist
acidimeter
acidimetry
acidophile
aficionado
agitatedly
alienation
alightment
alimentary
amiability
animadvert
animalcula
animalcule
animatedly
anisotropy
apiculture
aristocrat
arithmetic
aviatrices
aviculture
axiologist
blindingly
blissfully
blistering
blitheness
blithering
blithesome
blitzkrieg
boisterous
brickfield
bricklayer
bridegroom
bridesmaid
bridgeable
bridgehead
bridgeless
bridgework
bridlepath
brigandage
brigandine
brigandism
brigantine
brightness
brightwork
brilliance
brilliancy
Britishism
chickenpox
chiffchaff
chiffonier
childbirth
childermas
childishly
childproof
chiliastic
chilliness
chimerical
chimneypot
chimpanzee
chinagraph
chinchilla
chiromancy
chiselling
chivalrous
clientship
clingstone
clinically
clinkstone
clinometer
clinometry
cnidoblast
coincident
cribriform
criminally
crinolette
crippledom
crispation
crispbread
crisscross
critically
cuirassier
daintiness
daisychain
drivelling
driverless
edibleness
editorship
eliminable
eliminator
emigration
emigratory
emissivity
enigmatise
enigmatist
epiblastic
epicentral
epicycloid
epideictic
epidemical
epidermoid
epigastric
epigenesis
epigenetic
epiglottal
epiglottic
epiglottis
epigrapher
epigraphic
epilimnion
epiphytism
episcopacy
episcopate
episematic
episodical
episternum
epistolary
epistrophe
epithelial
epithelium
ericaceous
etiolation
evidential
evilminded
eviscerate
faintheart
fairground
fairhaired
fairleader
fairminded
fairspoken
fairycycle
faithfully
flightdeck
flightless
flightpath
flimsiness
flintiness
flippantly
flirtation
friability
fricandeau
fricasseed
frictional
friendless
friendlily
friendship
frigidness
frigorific
frilliness
fringeless
friskiness
fritillary
frivolling
frizziness
gaillardia
gaingiving
Ghibelline
glimmering
grievously
grindingly
grindstone
grisliness
grittiness
guilefully
guillotine
guiltiness
hairraiser
hairspring
hairstreak
hairstroke
hoitytoity
idiopathic
inimically
inimitable
inimitably
iniquitous
initialise
initialled
initiation
initiative
initiatory
iridaceous
iridescent
iridosmine
Irishwoman
itinerancy
kaisership
knickknack
knifeboard
knighthood
kriegspiel
Krishnaism
Leibnizian
maidenhair
maidenhead
maidenhood
maidenlike
mainlander
mainspring
mainstream
maintainer
maisonette
moisturise
nailpolish
noisemaker
obituarist
odiousness
oligarchic
oligoclase
oligopsony
olivaceous
opinionist
opisometer
orientally
originally
originator
otioseness
ovipositor
oxidisable
painkiller
painlessly
paintbrush
philatelic
philippina
philippine
philistine
phillumeny
philologen
philopoena
philosophe
philosophy
pliability
pliantness
poinsettia
pointblank
pridefully
priesthood
priestling
priggishly
primevally
primiparae
primordial
primordium
princeling
princeship
principate
principial
principium
principled
prismoidal
prissiness
privileged
prizefight
psilocybin
psittacine
puissantly
quickgrass
quickthorn
quiescence
quiescency
quinacrine
quintuplet
quirkiness
quixotical
quizmaster
railroader
railwayman
rainmaking
reichsmark
reissuable
reiterance
rhinestone
rhinoceros
rhinoscope
rhinoscopy
rhizogenic
rhizomorph
rhizophore
roistering
roisterous
sailorless
sciagraphy
scientific
Scillonian
sciolistic
seignorage
seignorial
seismicity
seismogram
seismology
shibboleth
shieldless
shiftiness
shillelagh
shipbroker
shipfitter
shipmaster
shiprigged
shipwright
shirehorse
shirtfront
shirtwaist
skiagraphy
skibobbing
skijumping
skimpiness
skindiving
skinniness
skirmisher
skirtdance
skittishly
slidevalve
slightness
slipperily
slipstitch
slipstream
slitpocket
snickasnee
sniffiness
snivelling
spidercrab
spiderline
spiderwort
spiflicate
spillikins
spinescent
spiracular
spiraculum
spiralling
spiritedly
spiritless
spirituous
spirograph
spirometer
spirometry
spitchcock
spitefully
stickiness
stiffening
stiflebone
stiflingly
stigmatise
stigmatism
stigmatist
stilettoes
stillbirth
stillicide
stimulator
stinginess
stingingly
stinkingly
stinkstone
stipellate
stipulator
stirrupcup
stitchwort
suicidally
swimmingly
swinefever
swingingly
swinglebar
switchback
switchover
swiveleyed
swivelling
tailorbird
tailormade
thickening
thievishly
thillhorse
thimbleful
thimblerig
thinkingly
thinkpiece
thirdclass
thirdparty
thirteenth
thirtyfold
thixotropy
toilsomely
triacetate
triandrous
triangular
tribometer
tribrachic
trichiasis
trichinise
trichinous
trichology
trichotomy
trichroism
trichromat
trickiness
trickishly
triclinium
tricyclist
Tridentine
trierarchy
triflingly
trifoliate
trifurcate
trigeminal
triggerman
triglyphic
trigonally
trilateral
trilingual
triliteral
trillionth
trimonthly
trimorphic
trioecious
tripartite
triphammer
triphthong
triplicate
triplicity
triquetrae
triquetral
trisection
triskelion
triternate
triturable
triturator
triumphant
triumviral
trivialise
trivialism
triviality
tuitionary
twilighted
ubiquitous
uniaxially
unicameral
unicyclist
uniformity
unilateral
unilingual
unilocular
unimproved
uninformed
uninitiate
unionistic
unipartite
uniqueness
university
univocally
utilisable
voiceprint
wainwright
waistcloth
weightless
weimaraner
whipstitch
whirlybird
whiskified
whispering
whitebeard
whitefaced
whitesmith
whitethorn
WhitMonday

WhitSunday
wristwatch
zwitterion
abjectness
abjuration
adjacently
adjectival
adjudgment
adjudicate
adjunction
adjunctive
adjuration
adjuratory
adjustable
adjustment
bejewelled
bijouterie
cajolement
cajolingly
dejectedly
enjambment
enjoinment
injunction
injunctive
jejuneness
majestical
majuscular
objectival
objectless
pejoration
pejorative
rejectable
rejoicings
rejuvenate
rejuvenise
unjustness
alkalinity
hakenkreuz
hokeypokey
inkslinger
likelihood
likeliness
likeminded
lukewarmly
makeweight
pokerfaced
pyknometer
rakishness
takingness
unkindness
unknowable
Wykehamist
yokefellow
ablebodied
allegation
allegiance
allegorise
allegorist
allegretto
allergenic
alleviator
alliaceous
alliterate
allocation
allocution
allogamous
allopathic
allophonic
allosteric
allotropic
alloverish
allpurpose
allrounder
allurement
allusively
aplacental
balbriggan
balderdash
baldheaded

ballflower
ballistics
ballooning
balloonist
balneology
balustrade
Belgravian
believable
belladonna
belletrist
bellflower
bellringer
bellwether
bellyacher
bellydance
bellylaugh
belongings
bilgewater
biliverdin
billetdoux
billposter
bilocation
bollweevil
bolometric
bolshevise
bolshevism
bolshevist
bullethead
bullheaded
bullroarer
calamander
calamitous
calcareous
calceolate
calciferol
calcsinter
calculable
calculably
calculator
Caledonian
calibrator
caliginous
callowness
calumniate
calumnious
calyciform
calyptrate
celebrated
celebrator
cellophane
cellularly
cellulitis
cellulosic
chlorinate
chloroform
colatitude
colchicine
coleoptera
coleoptile
coleorhiza
collarbeam
collarbone
collarette
collarless
collarstud
collatable
collateral
collection
collective
collegiate
collembola
collimator
collocutor
colloquial
colloquise
colloquist
colloquium
colonially
colonnaded

coloration
coloratura
colossally
colourable
colourably
colourfast
colourless
colportage
colporteur
columbaria
cultivable
cultivator
culturally
cylindered
cylindroid
delaminate
delectable
delectably
delegation
deliberate
delicately
delightful
delimitate
delineator
delinquent
deliquesce
delocalise
delphinium
delphinoid
deltiology
delusional
delusively
dilapidate
dilatation
dilatorily
dilemmatic
dilettante
dilettanti
diligently
dillydally
diluteness
dolomitise
dolorously
elliptical
enlacement
enlistment
eulogistic
fallacious
fallingoff
fallowness
felicitate
felicitous
fellmonger
fellowship
felspathic
filariasis
filibuster
filterable
filthiness
filtration
foliaceous
folklorist
folkmemory
folksiness
folksinger
follicular
fulfilling
fulfilment
fuliginous
fullbodied
fullbottom
fulllength
galimatias
galleywest
galliambic
galloglass
Gallomania
Gallophile
Gallophobe

galvaniser
gelatinise
gelatinous
Gilbertian
goldbeater
golddigger
goldenness
goldenseal
goldilocks
golfcourse
goloptious
goluptious
halberdier
halfcocked
halfdollar
halflength
halfnelson
halfvolley
halfwitted
halfyearly
halieutics
hallelujah
halogenate
halogenous
halophytic
heliacally
helianthus
Heliconian
helicopter
heliograph
heliolater
heliolatry
heliometer
heliophyte
helioscope
heliotaxis
heliotrope
heliotropy
hellbender
helminthic
helplessly
holloweyed
hollowness
hollowware
holography
holohedral
holophrase
holophytic
holosteric
holusbolus
hullabaloo
hylotheism
illadvised
illatively
illaudable
illaudably
illegalise
illegality
illiteracy
illiterate
illnatured
illstarred
illuminant
illuminate
illuminati
illuminism
illuminist
illusional
illusively
illusorily
illustrate
jolterhead
kilogramme
liliaceous
Lollardism
malacoderm
malacology
maladapted
malapertly

malapropos
malcontent
malefactor
maleficent
malentendu
malevolent
malfeasant
malignance
malignancy
malingerer
malleebird
malleefowl
mallenders
malodorous
Malpighian
Malthusian
malvaceous
melancholy
Melanesian
melanistic
meliorator
melismatic
mellowness
meltingpot
militantly
militarily
militarise
militarism
militarist
militiaman
millefiori
millennial
millennium
millesimal
millilitre
millimetre
millstream
millwright
molendinar
molluscoid
molluscous
molybdenum
muliebrity
mulishness
mulligrubs
multifaced
multiloquy
multimedia
multiphase
multiplier
multipolar
multistage
multivocal
nullanulla
oblateness
obligation
obligatory
obligingly
obliterate
owlishness
Palaeocene
Palaeogene
palaeolith
palaeotype
Palaeozoic
palagonite
palatalise
palatinate
palimpsest
palindrome
palisander
palladious
pallbearer
palliation
palliative
palliatory
pallidness
palmaceous
palmatifid

palmbutter
palmerworm
PalmSunday
paltriness
palynology
pellagrous
pellicular
pellucidly
phlebotomy
phlegmatic
phlogistic
phlogiston
phlogopite
piledriver
pilgarlick
pilgrimage
piliferous
pilliwinks
pillowcase
pillowlace
pillowslip
pilothouse
pilotlight
pilotwhale
polemicist
polemonium
politeness
politician
politicise
pollenosis
pollinator
polyandric
polyanthus
polyatamic
polychaete
polychrest
polychrome
polyclinic
polycyclic
polydactyl
polydipsia
polygamist
polygamous
polygenism
polygenist
polygenous
polygraphy
polygynous
polyhedral
polyhedric
polyhedron
polyhistor
polymathic
polymerise
polymerism
polymerous
Polynesian
polynomial
polyonymic
polyphasic
polyphonic
polyploidy
polysemous
polytheism
polytheist
polytocous
polyvalent
pulsatilla
pulsimeter
pulsometer
pulveriser
pulvinated
relational
relatively
relativise
relativism
relativist
relativity
relaxation

releasable
relegation
relentless
relevantly
relievable
relinquish
relishable
relocation
reluctance
reluctancy
rollcollar
rollicking
rollingpin
salability
salamander
salesclerk
saleswoman
salicional
salicylate
salientian
saliferous
salivation
sallenders
sallowness
salmagundi
salmonella
salmonleap
salpingian
saltarello
saltcellar
saltigrade
salubrious
salutarily
salutation
salutatory
scleroderm
sclerotium
sclerotomy
selectness
selenodont
selenology
selfacting
selfaction
selfbinder
selfcolour
selfdeceit
selfdenial
selfesteem
selffeeder
selfglazed
selfguided
selflessly
selfloving
selfmotion
selfmurder
selfparody
selfpoised
selfpraise
selfprofit
selfraised
selfregard
selfrising
selfruling
selfseeker
selfstyled
selftaught
selfwilled
seltzogene
silentness
silhouette
silkcotton
silkscreen
sillybilly
silverbath
silverfish
silverside
silverware
silverweed
solacement
soldanella
solecistic
solemnness
solenoidal
solicitant
solicitous
solicitude
solidarism
solidarist
solidarity
solidstate
solifidian
solitarily
solstitial
solubilise
solubility
splanchnic
splashback
splashdown
spleenwort
splendidly
splintbone
splintcoal
splitlevel
splutterer
sullenness
sulphonate
sulphurate
sulphurise
sulphurous
sultanship
sultriness
syllabaria
syllogiser
talebearer
talentless
taleteller
talismanic
Talmudical
telecamera
telecaster
telegraphy
telemetric
teleologic
teleostean
telepathic
telephoner
telephonic
telescopic
televiewer
television
televisual
tellership
telpherage
tilthammer
tolerantly
toleration
tollbridge
tularaemia
tularaemic
unlabelled
unlawfully
unlettered
unlikeness
validation
valleculae
vallecular
valorously
valvulitis
veldschoen
velitation
velocipede
velutinous
villainage
villainess
villainous
villanelle
villeinage
volatilise
volatility
volitional
volleyball
voltameter
volubility
volumetric
voluminous
voluptuary
voluptuous
vulcaniser
vulnerable
vulnerably
Waldensian
wallflower
wallpepper
wellheeled
wellington
wellspoken
wellspring
wellturned
wellwisher
Welshwoman
wildebeest
wilderment
wilderness
wildfowler
wilfulness
willowherb
willynilly
willywilly
wolframite
xylography
xylophonic
yellowback
yellowbird
yellowness
yellowwood
zollverein
administer
admiration
admiringly
admissible
admittable
admittance
admittedly
admonition
admonitive
admonitory
almacanter
almondeyed
almsgiving
almucanter
ammoniacal
ammoniated
ammunition
Armageddon
armigerous
armorially
armourclad
armourless
atmosphere
bemedalled
bemusement
bimestrial
bimetallic
bombardier
bumblingly
bumpkinish
camelopard
camerlengo
camerlingo
camouflage
campaigner
campestral
camphorate
comanchero
combustion
combustive
comedienne
comehither
comeliness
comestible
comicality
comicopera
commandant
commandeer
commandery
commanding
commandoes
commentary
commentate
commercial
commissary
commission
commissure
commitment
committing
commixture
commodious
commonable
commonalty
commonness
commonroom
commonweal
communally
communique
commutable
commutator
compaction
comparable
comparably
comparator
comparison
compassion
compasssaw
compatible
compatibly
compatriot
compelling
compendium
compensate
competence
competency
competitor
complacent
complainer
complected
complement
completely
completion
completive
complexion
complexity
compliance
compliancy
complicacy
complicate
complicity
compliment
complotted
composedly
compositor
compotator
compounder
compradore
comprehend
compressed
compressor
compromise
compulsion
compulsive
compulsory
computable
computator
comstocker
cumbersome
cumbrously
cummerbund
cumulation
cumulative
cumuliform
damageable
damagingly
dampcourse
dampingoff
demagogism
demandable
dementedly
demobilise
democratic
demography
demoiselle
demolition
demonetise
demoniacal
demonology
demoralise
demotivate
demureness
demurrable
diminished
diminuendo
diminution
diminutive
dimorphism
dimorphous
dominantly
domination
dominative
dumbledore
dumbstruck
dumbwaiter
dumfounder
Emmentaler
enmeshment
familiarly
famishment
famousness
femaleness
feminality
femininely
femininity
fimbriated
fumblingly
fumigation
gambolling
gamekeeper
gametangia
gemination
gemmaceous
gymnastics
gymnosophy
gymnosperm
hammerbeam
hammerhead
hammerless
hammerlock
hammerpond
hamshackle
hemicyclic
hemihedral
hemihedron
hemiplegia
hemiplegic
hemipteran
hemisphere
hempnettle
homebrewed
homecoming
homeliness
homemaking
homeopathy
homiletics
homocercal
homoeopath
homogamous
homogenise
homogenous
homologate
homologise
homologous
homonymous
homoousian
homophonic
homosexual
homozygote
homozygous
homunculus
humaneness
humanistic
humanities
humbleness
humbuggery
humbugging
humidifier
humoresque
humoristic
humorously
humourless
humoursome
humpbacked
immaculacy
immaculate
immaterial
immaturely
immaturity
immemorial
imminently
immiscible
immiscibly
immobilise
immobility
immoderacy
immoderate
immodestly
immolation
immoralist
immorality
immortally
immortelle
immoveable
immunology
immurement
jimsonweed
kimberlite
Lamarckian
Lamarckism
lambrequin
lamentable
lamentably
lamentedly
laminarian
lamination
Lammastide
lampoonery
lampoonist
lemniscate
lemongrass
limaciform
limeburner
limitation
limitative
limitrophe
limpidness
lumberjack
lumberroom
lumbersome
lumberyard
luminosity
luminously
lumpsucker
lymphocyte
lymphomata
mamillated
membership
membranous

memorandum
mimeograph
mumbojumbo
nambypamby
namelessly
nematocyst
nimbleness
nominalism
nominalist
nominately
nomination
nominative
nomography
nomologist
nomothetic
numberless
numeration
numerology
numerosity
numerously
numismatic
nympholept
ommatidium
osmeterium
osmiridium
pemphigoid
pemphigous
Pomeranian
pomiferous
pomologist
pummelling
ramblingly
rampageous
ramshackle
remarkable
remarkably
remarriage
remediable
remedially
remediless
remissible
remissness
remittance
remodelled
remonetise
remorseful
remoteness
remunerate
Romanesque
Romanistic
ruminantly
rumination
ruminative
rumrunning
samarskite
semeiology
semeiotics
semestrial
semiannual
semichorus
semicircle
semidivine
semidouble
semidrying
semifitted
semiliquid
semilunate
seminarian
seminarist
semination
semiopaque
semiotical
semiquaver
semiuncial
semiweekly
semiyearly
sempstress
similarity
similitude
simoniacal
simpleness
simplicity
simplifier
simplistic
simulacrum
simulation
simulative
simulatory
somatology
somatotype
sombreness
somersault
somniloquy
somnolence
somnolency
summerlike
summertime
summitless
summonable
symbolical
symboliser
symmetrise
sympathise
symphonion
symphonist
symphylous
symphyseal
symphysial
symposiast
tamability
tambourine
temperable
temperance
temperedly
temporally
temporalty
temporiser
temptation
temptingly
timberhead
timberline
timbertoes
timberwolf
timberwork
timbrology
timekeeper
timelessly
timeliness
timesaving
timeserver
timocratic
timorously
tomfoolery
tomography
tumbledown
tumblerful
tumbleweed
tumescence
tumultuary
tumultuous
tympanites
tympanitic
tympanitis
unmannerly
unmeasured
unmeetness
unmerciful
unmorality
unmortised
vomitorium
wampumpeag
womanishly
abnegation
abnormally
annalistic
annexation
annihilate
annotation
annoyingly
annularity
annulation
annunciate
banderilla
bandmaster
banishment
bankruptcy
benedicite
Benedictus
benefactor
beneficent
beneficial
benevolent
benignancy
Benthamism
Benthamite
benzocaine
benzpyrene
binaurally
binoculars
bondholder
boneheaded
bonesetter
boneshaker
bunchgrass
bunglingly
canaliculi
cancellate
cancelling
cancellous
candelabra
candescent
candidness
candlefish
candletree
candlewick
candlewood
candyfloss
cankerworm
cannelloni
cannonball
canonicals
canonicate
canonicity
canorously
cantaloupe
cantatrice
canterbury
cantilever
cantillate
cantonment
canvasback
canvaswork
canzonetta
censorious
censorship
censurable
centennial
centesimal
centigrade
centilitre
centillion
centimetre
centralise
centralism
centralist
centrality
centreback
centrefold
centrehalf
centricity
centrifuge
centromere
centrosome
cinchonine
Cinderella
cinecamera
cinerarium
cinquefoil
concentric
conception
conceptive
conceptual
concerning
concertina
concertino
concession
concessive
concettism
conchoidal
conchology
conciliary
conciliate
concinnity
conclusion
conclusive
conclusory
concoction
concoctive
concordant
concretely
concretion
concretise
concretism
concretist
concurrent
concurring
concussion
concussive
condensate
condensery
condescend
condolence
conduction
conductive
confabbing
confection
conference
conferment
conferring
confervoid
confession
confidante
confidence
confirmand
confiscate
conflation
confluence
conformism
conformist
conformity
confounded
confusedly
congeneric
congenital
congestion
congestive
conglobate
congregant
congregate
congruence
congruency
coniferous
conjecture
conjointly
conjugally
connatural
connection
connective
conniption
connivance
conscience
consecrate
consectary
consensual
consequent
considered
consistent
consistory
consociate
consolable
consonance
consonancy
consortium
conspectus
conspiracy
conspirant
constantan
Constantia
constantly
constipate
constitute
constraint
constringe
consuetude
consulship
consultant
consulting
consultive
consumable
consumedly
consummate
contagious
contendent
contention
contestant
contextual
contexture
contiguity
contiguous
continence
contingent
continuant
continuate
continuity
continuous
contortion
contortive
contraband
contrabass
contractor
contradict
contraprop
contrarily
contravene
contribute
contritely
contrition
controlled
controller
controvert
convalesce
convection
convective
convenable
convenance
convenient
convention
conventual
convergent
conversant
conversely
conversion
conveyable
conveyance
conviction
convictive
convincing
convoluted
convulsant
convulsion
convulsive
cunctation
cunctative
denaturant
dendriform
dendrology
denegation
denigrator
denominate
denotation
denotative
denouement
densimeter
dentifrice
denudation
denunciate
diningroom
dinnerless
donkeywork
donnybrook
dunderhead
dungbeetle
duniwassal
dynamistic
fanaticise
fanaticism
fancifully
fandangoes
fantastico
fantoccini
fenestella
fenestrate
fingerbowl
fingerless
fingerling
fingermark
fingernail
fingerpost
finicality
finiteness
FinnoUgric
fontanelle
functional
funereally
fungicidal
funnelling
ganglionic
gangrenous
generalise
generalist
generality
generation
generative
generatrix
generosity
generously
geneticist
genialness
geniculate
genteelism
gentilesse
gentlefolk
gentleness
gingerbeer
gingersnap
gingivitis
goniometer
goniometry
gunfighter
gunrunning
gunslinger
gynandrous
gynocratic
handbarrow
handedness
handgallop
handicraft
handmaiden
handpicked
handselled
handsomely
handspring
handworked
hangglider

hankypanky
Hanoverian
Hansardise
hanselling
henceforth
hendecagon
henharrier
henhearted
henotheism
henotheist
Hindustani
hinterland
honeyeater
honeyguide
honeysweet
honorarium
honourable
honourably
honourless
hungriness
ignobility
ignorantly
innateness
innerrably
innocently
innominate
innovation
innovative
innovatory
innuendoes
innumeracy
innumerate
innumerous
ionisation
ionosphere
janitorial
Janusfaced
jingoistic
jinricksha
jinrikisha
Kantianism
kennelling
kenspeckle
kindliness
kinematics
kineticist
kingfisher
kingliness
kinnikinic
lanceolate
landholder
landhunger
landingnet
landlocked
landlubber
landocracy
landowning
landscaper
languisher
languorous
lansquenet
lanternfly
lanthanide
lanuginose
lanuginous
lengthways
lengthwise
lenticular
lentigines
linguiform
linguistic
loneliness
lonesomely
longaevous
longhaired
longheaded
longlegged
longprimer
longshanks
longwinded
manageable
manageably
management
manageress
managerial
manchineel
mandibular
mandragora
manfulness
mangosteen
maniacally
Manichaean
Manicheism
manicurist
manifestly
manifestos
manifoldly
manipulate
manoeuvrer
manoeuvres
manometric
manorhouse
manservant
mansuetude
manteltree
manumitted
manuscript
manzanilla
menacingly
mendacious
mendicancy
meningioma
meningitis
menopausal
menstruate
menstruous
mensurable
mentorship
mindedness
mindlessly
mineralise
mineralogy
minestrone
mineworker
minimalism
minimalist
ministrant
minstrelsy
mintmaster
minuscular
minutebook
minutehand
minuteness
monandrous
monarchial
Monarchian
monarchism
monarchist
monetarily
monetarism
monetarist
moneymaker
moneytaker
mongrelise
mongrelism
moniliasis
moniliform
monistical
monitorial
monkeysuit
monocarpic
monochasia
monochrome
monoclinal
monoclinic
monocratic
monocyclic
monoecious
monogamist
monogamous
monogenism
monogynian
monogynous
monohybrid
monohydric
monolithic
monologise
monologist
monomaniac
monophonic
monopodial
monopodium
monopolise
monopolist
monorhymed
monotheism
monotheist
monotonous
monovalent
monsignori
monstrance
Montagnard
montbretia
monumental
munificent
nanisation
nanosecond
nincompoop
nineteenth
nonaligned
nonchalant
noncontent
nondrinker
nonferrous
nonfiction
nonjoinder
nonlogical
nonnatural
nonnuclear
nonpayment
nonplaying
nonplussed
nonstarter
nonswimmer
nonviolent
nunciature
obnubilate
oenologist
omnigenous
omnipotent
omniscient
omnivorous
ornamental
ornateness
orneriness
Panamanian
pancratium
pancreatic
pancreatin
panegyrise
panegyrist
pangenesis
pangenetic
panhandler
paniculate
panjandrum
panopticon
pansophist
pantograph
pantomimic
pantrymaid
pencilling
pendentive
penetrable
penetrably
penetralia
penetrance
penetrator
penicillin
peninsular
penitently
penmanship
pennaceous
pennanular
pennillion
pennyroyal
pennyworth
penologist
penpushing
pensionary
pentachord
pentagonal
pentameter
pentastich
pentathlon
pentatomic
pentatonic
pentimento
pentstemon
pincerlike
pinchpenny
pincushion
pinebeauty
pinecarpet
pinfeather
pinnatifid
pinnulated
pinstriped
ponderable
pontifical
pontifices
punchboard
punchdrunk
punctation
punctually
punctuator
punctulate
punishable
punishment
punitively
rancidness
randomness
ranunculus
renascence
rencounter
renderable
rendezvous
renovation
rinderpest
ringfinger
ringleader
ringmaster
ringnecked
ringtailed
rontgenise
runnerbean
runthrough
sanatorium
sanctifier
sanctimony
sanctitude
sandalwood
sandbagger
sandcastle
sanderling
sandhopper
sandmartin
sanguinary
sanguinely
sanguinity
sanitarian
sanitarily
sanitarium
sanitation
Sanskritic
senatorial
senescence
sensedatum
senseorgan
sensitiser
sensualise
sensualism
sensualist
sensuality
sensuously
sentential
sentiently
sincipital
sinecurism
sinecurist
sinfulness
Singhalese
singlefoot
singleness
singletree
singularly
sinisterly
sinistrous
sinologist
sinusoidal
songstress
songthrush
songwriter
sonorously
sunderance
sunglasses
sunparlour
synaeresis
synaloepha
synanthous
syncarpous
synchronal
synchronic
syncopated
syncopator
syncretise
syncretism
syncretist
syndicator
synecdoche
synecology
synergetic
syngenesis
synoecious
synonymist
synonymity
synonymous
synoptical
synostosis
syntagmata
synthesise
synthesist
synthetise
synthetist
tangential
tanglement
tankengine
tantaliser
tantamount
tenability
tenantable
tenantless
tenderfoot
tenderloin
tenderness
tendinitis
tendrillar
tendrilled
tenebrific
tenebrious
tenemental
tentacular
tenterhook
tinctorial
tinselling
tonelessly
tongueless
tonguetied
tunelessly
tunnelling
unnameable
unnumbered
vanadinite
vanquisher
venational
veneration
vengefully
venialness
venomously
ventilator
ventricose
ventriculi
vindicable
vindicator
vindictive
vinegarish
wanderings
wanderlust
wanderplug
wantonness
wentletrap
winceyette
Winchester
windflower
windjammer
windowless
windowpane
windowseat
windowshop
windowsill
windscreen
windshield
windsleeve
winebibber
winebottle
winegrower
wingcollar
wingfooted
wingspread
wintertide
wintertime
wintriness
wonderland
wonderment
wonderwork
wondrously
wongawonga
wontedness
wunderkind
xenophobia
ZendAvesta
zincograph
abominable
abominably
abominator
aboriginal
abortively
aboveboard
acoelomate
acotyledon
acoustical
adolescent
adoptively
aeolotropy
alongshore
amoebocyte
anointment
anonaceous
anopheline
apocalypse
apocarpous
apochromat
apocryphal
apodeictic

apolaustic
apolitical
Apollinian
Apollonian
apologetic
apophthegm
apoplectic
aposematic
apostatise
apostolate
apostrophe
apothecary
apothecial
apothecium
apotheoses
apotheosis
apotropaic
atomically
avouchment
biochemist
biodegrade
biodynamic
bioecology
biogenesis
biogenetic
biographer
biographic
biological
biometrics
biomorphic
biophysics
bioscience
blockboard
blockhouse
blockishly
bloodguilt
bloodhound
bloodiness
bloodmoney
bloodstain
bloodstock
bloodstone
blottesque
bookbinder
bookkeeper
bookmaking
bookmarker
bookseller
boondoggle
bootlegger
bootlessly
bootlicker
bootstraps
broadcloth
broadsheet
broadsword
brocatelle
brokendown
brokenness
bromegrass
bronchiole
bronchitic
bronchitis
broodiness
broodingly
broomstick
browbeaten
brownshirt
brownstone
caoutchouc
choiceness
chokeberry
chondritic
choriambic
clodhopper
cloistered
closestool
closetplay
clothesbag
clothespeg
clothespin
cloudberry
cloudburst
cloudiness
clovehitch
cloverleaf
clownishly
coolheaded
coolingoff
cooperator
cooptation
cooptative
coordinate
crocoisite
crossbench
crossbones
crossbreed
crosscheck
crossgrain
crosshatch
crossindex
crosslight
crosspatch
crosspiece
crossrefer
crossroads
crosstrees
crowkeeper
deodoriser
deontology
deoxidiser
doorkeeper
droopingly
drophammer
drosophila
drowsihead
drowsiness
duodecimal
duodenitis
ecological
economical
economiser
egocentric
egoistical
elongation
eloquently
emollition
enormously
erotically
erotogenic
erotomania
evolvement
exobiology
exorbitant
exospheric
exoterical
exothermal
exothermic
exotically
floatation
floatboard
floatingly
floatplane
floatstone
flocculate
flocculent
floodlight
floodwater
floorboard
floorcloth
floppiness
florentine
florescent
floriation
floribunda
floridness
florilegia
floristics
flosculous
flowergirl
flowerless
footballer
footbridge
footcandle
footlights
footwarmer
froghopper
frolicking
frolicsome
frontbench
frontwards
frostiness
frothiness
frowningly
geocentric
geochemist
geodetical
geognostic
geographer
geographic
geological
geometrise
geophysics
geoponical
geothermal
geothermic
geotropism
globularly
glomerular
glomerulus
gloominess
gloriously
glossarial
glossarist
glossiness
glossology
glottology
gnosticism
goodliness
goodlooker
goodygoody
gooseberry
gooseflesh
goosegrass
groceteria
grogginess
groundbait
groundless
groundling
groundmass
groundplan
groundrent
groundsman
groundwork
grovelling
growlingly
heortology
hookedness
hootenanny
iconoclasm
iconolater
iconolatry
iconomachy
iconometer
iconometry
iconoscope
idolatress
idolatrous
inoculable
inoculator
inoperable
inordinate
inosculate
ironhanded
ironically
ironmaster
ironmonger
ironworker
isochronal
isodynamic
isogenetic
isoglossal
isolatable
isometrics
isomorphic
isoniazide
isopterous
isoseismal
isosporous
isothermal
jeopardise
knobkerrie
knockabout
knockkneed
knopkierie
knottiness
kookaburra
Kuomintang
leopardess
lionhunter
loosecover
lyophilise
moonflower
moonshiner
moonstruck
myocardium
myological
myopically
neoclassic
neological
neoplastic
noogenesis
odontalgia
odontology
omophagous
orogenesis
orogenetic
orographic
orological
orotundity
Phoenician
phonematic
phonically
phonograph
phonolitic
phonologic
phonometer
phosphatic
phosphoric
phosphorus
photoflood
photogenic
photograph
photolitho
photolysis
photolytic
photometer
photometry
photonasty
photophily
photophore
photoprint
phototaxis
phototrope
ploddingly
ploughable
ploughland
procedural
proceeding
procession
proclaimer
proclivity
procreator
procrypsis
procryptic
proctorage
proctorial
proctorise
procumbent
procurable
procurance
procurator
prodigally
prodigious
producible
production
productive
profession
proficient
profitable
profitably
profitless
profligacy
profligate
profoundly
profundity
progenitor
proglottis
prognathic
prognostic
programmer
prohibiter
prohibitor
projectile
projection
projective
prolicidal
prolocutor
prologuise
prolongate
promenader
promethium
prominence
promissory
promontory
promptbook
promptness
promulgate
pronominal
pronounced
pronouncer
proofsheet
propagable
propaganda
propagator
propellant
propellent
propelling
propensity
properness
propertied
prophesier
prophetess
propionate
propitiate
propitious
proportion
propounder
propraetor
proprietor
propulsion
propulsive
propylaeum
prosaicism
proscenium
prosciutto
proscriber
prosecutor
prosilient
prosodical
prospector
prospectus
prosperity
prosperous
prosthesis
prosthetic
prostitute
prostomial
prostomium
protanopic
protection
protective
protectory
protectrix
proteiform
proteinous
protensive
proteolyse
protestant
prothallia
prothallus
protophyta
protophyte
protoplasm
protoplast
prototypal
prototypic
protracted
protractor
protreptic
protrusile
protrusion
protrusive
proudflesh
provenance
proverbial
providence
provincial
provisions
provitamin
provocator
proximally
Ptolemaist
reorganise
rhodophane
rhomboidal
rhomboidei
roodscreen
roofgarden
rootedness
scoffingly
scoreboard
scoresheet
scornfully
scorzonera
Scotswoman
Scotticise
Scotticism
shockingly
shockproof
shoddiness
shoebuckle
shoestring
shopkeeper
shoplifter
shopsoiled
shopwalker
shopwindow
shoreleave
shorewards
shortbread
shortcrust
shortdated
shortening
shortlived
shortrange
shouldered
shovelhead
shovelling
showerbath
showjumper
showwindow
sloppiness
slothfully

slowfooted
slowmotion
slowwitted
smockfrock
smokedried
smokehouse
smokeplant
smokeproof
smokestack
smoothbore
smoothness
smorrebrod
snobbishly
snobocracy
snootiness
snowcapped
snowgrouse
snowmobile
snowplough
soothingly
soothsayer
spodomancy
spoilsport
spokeshave
spoliation
spoliative
spoliatory
spongecake
spongewood
spongiform
sponginess
spongology
sponsorial
spookiness
spoondrift
spoonerism
sporangial
sporangium
sporophore
sporophyll
sporophyte
sportfully
sportiness
sportingly
sportively
sportswear
spotlessly
spottiness
stochastic
stockiness
stockpiler
stockproof
stockrider
stockstill
stodginess
stolidness
stomachful
stomatitis
stomatopod
stomodaeum
stoneblind
stoneborer
stonebrash
stonefruit
stonemason
stonesnipe
stopvolley
storehouse
storksbill
stormbound
stormcloud
storminess
stormproof
swordcraft
sworddance
swordgrass
swordstick
thornapple
thorniness
thornproof
thoroughly
thoughtful
thousandth
toothbrush
toothiness
toothpaste
toothshell
trochanter
trochoidal
troctolite
troglodyte
trolleybus
trollopish
trombonist
tromometer
tropaeolum
trophology
tropically
tropologic
tropopause
tropophyte
Trotskyism
Trotskyist
Trotskyite
troubadour
trousseaux
trouvaille
trowelling
twowheeler
ulotrichan
unoccupied
unofficial
unorthodox
urochordal
utopianism
uxoricidal
uxoriously
violaceous
wholesaler
whomsoever
whorehouse
woodcarver
woodcutter
woodenhead
woodenness
woodlander
woodpecker
woodpigeon
woodturner
woodworker
woolgather
woolgrower
woolliness
woolsorter
wrongdoing
wrongfully
wrongously
zoological
zoomorphic
zoophagous
zoophilous
alpenstock
alphabetic
alphameric
ampelopsis
amphibious
amphibrach
amphictyon
amphigouri
amphimacer
amphimixes
amphimixis
amphoteric
amputation
apparelled
apparently
apparition
appealable
appearance
appeasable
appendices
appendixes
apperceive
appetising
appetitive
applicable
applicably
applicator
appointive
appositely
apposition
appositive
appreciate
apprentice
approvable
approvably
asparagine
aspergilla
asphyxiant
asphyxiate
aspidistra
aspiration
baptistery
biparietal
bipartisan
bipetalous
bipolarity
capability
capacitate
capacitive
capitalise
capitalism
capitalist
capitation
Capitoline
capitulary
capitulate
cappuccino
capricious
captiously
cephalopod
coparcener
copartnery
Copernican
copesettic
copperhead
coproducer
coprolitic
copulation
copulative
copyholder
copyreader
copywriter
dapplegrey
department
dependable
dependably
dependence
dependency
depilation
depilatory
deplorable
deplorably
deployment
depolarise
depopulate
deportment
depositary
deposition
depository
depravedly
depreciate
depredator
depressant
depression
depressive
deprivable
depuration
depurative
deputation
diphtheria
diphtheric
diphyletic
diphyodont
diplodocus
diplomatic
dipsomania
duplicator
empanelled
emparadise
empathetic
emphractic
empiricism
empiricist
employable
employment
espadrille
especially
euphonious
euphuistic
expandable
expansible
expatriate
expectance
expectancy
expectedly
expedience
expediency
expedition
expendable
experience
experiment
expertness
expiration
expiratory
explicable
explicitly
exploitage
exploitive
exportable
exposition
expositive
expository
expressage
expression
expressive
expressway
exprobrate
expunction
expurgator
gypsophila
heparinise
hepatology
heptachord
heptagonal
Heptameron
heptameter
heptarchic
Heptateuch
heptatonic
hippocampi
Hippocrene
hippodrome
hippogriff
hippogryph
hippomanes
hippophagy
hipsterism
hopelessly
hypabyssal
hypaethral
hypanthium
hyperaemia
hyperaemic
hyperbaric
hyperbaton
hyperbolae
hyperbolas
hyperbolic
hyperdulia
hypergolic
hypersonic
hyphenated
hypnagogic
hypnotiser
hypocorism
hypodermal
hypodermic
hypodermis
hypogynous
hypolimnia
hypophyses
hypophysis
hypostasis
hypostatic
hypotactic
hypotenuse
hypotheses
hypothesis
hypsometer
hypsometry
impairment
impalement
impalpable
impalpably
impanation
impanelled
imparadise
impartible
impartment
impassable
impassably
impassible
impassibly
impatience
impeccable
impeccably
impeccancy
impediment
impendence
impendency
impenitent
imperative
imperially
imperilled
impersonal
impervious
impishness
implacable
implacably
implicitly
impolitely
importable
importance
importuner
imposingly
imposition
impossible
impossibly
imposthume
impotently
impoverish
impregnant
impregnate
impresario
impression
impressive
imprimatur
imprinting
improbable
improbably
improperly
improvable
improvably
improviser
imprudence
impudently
impudicity
impugnable
impugnment
impuissant
impureness
imputation
imputative
Japanesque
laparotomy
lapidarian
lapidarist
lapidation
lepidolite
leprechaun
Lipizzaner
lipography
lipomatous
Lippizaner
lipreading
lipservice
lophophore
lopsidedly
Lupercalia
mopishness
naphthenic
nepenthean
nephograph
nephoscope
nephralgia
nephridium
nephrology
nipplewort
nuptiality
oppilation
opposeless
oppositely
opposition
oppression
oppressive
opprobrium
oppugnancy
orphanhood
papaverine
papaverous
paperchase
paperknife
papermaker
papistical
papyrology
peppercorn
peppermill
peppermint
pepperwort
piperidine
popularise
popularity
population
populistic
populously
pupilarity
pupiparous
rapporteur
repairable
reparation
reparative
repatriate
repealable
repeatable
repeatedly
repellance
repellancy
repellence
repellency
repentance
repertoire
repetiteur
repetition

repetitive
repopulate
reportable
reportedly
reposition
repository
repression
repressive
reprobance
reproducer
republican
repudiator
repugnance
repugnancy
repurchase
reputation
ripplemark
riproaring
ripsnorter
ropedancer
ropeladder
ropewalker
rupicoline
rupicolous
sapiential
sappanwood
sapphirine
saprogenic
saprophyte
separately
separation
separatism
separatist
separative
separatory
septenarii
septennial
septennium
septically
septillion
Septuagint
sepulchral
sophomoric
superacute
superaltar
superation
superbness
supercargo
superduper
supergiant
superhuman
superiorly
superlunar
supernally
supernovae
superorder
superpower
supersonic
superstore
supertonic
supervisor
supination
supineness
supperless
supplanter
supplejack
supplement
suppleness
suppletion
suppletive
suppletory
suppliance
supplicant
supplicate
supportive
supposable
supposably
supposedly
suppressor
suprarenal
syphilitic
taperecord
taperingly
tapestried
tapotement
tepidarium
topazolite
topgallant
topicality
topography
topologist
topsyturvy
typescript
typesetter
typewriter
typicality
typography
typologist
umpireship
unpleasant
unpleasing
unprepared
unprovoked
upperclass
uppishness
vaporiform
vaporously
viperiform
viperously
wappenshaw
xiphosuran
acquirable
acquitting
bequeathal
coquettish
inquietude
inquisitor
liquescent
liquidator
liquidiser
liquidness
loquacious
maquillage
requiescat
roquelaure
sequacious
sequential
sequestrum
usquebaugh
aardwolves
Abrahamman
abrasively
abreaction
abridgment
abrogation
abruptness
acrobatics
acrogenous
acromegaly
acronychal
acrophobia
acroterion
acroterium
adrenaline
adrenergic
adroitness
aerenchyma
aerobatics
aerobiosis
aerobiotic
aeroengine
aerogramme
aerography
aerologist
aeronautic
aeronomist
aerophobia
aerostatic
aeruginous
Africander
Africanise
Africanism
Africanist
Afrikander
agrologist
agronomist
aircooling
aircushion
airmanship
arrestment
arrhythmia
arrhythmic
arrogantly
arrogation
auriculate
auriferous
barbellate
barbershop
barbituric
barcarolle
bardolatry
barebacked
barefooted
bareheaded
barelegged
bargeboard
barkentine
barleybree
barleybroo
barleycorn
Barmecidal
barometric
baronetage
barracouta
barramunda
barramundi
barratrous
barrelling
barrenness
barrenwort
barysphere
beribboned
Berkeleian
birdspider
birdstrike
birthplace
birthright
birthstone
borborygmi
bordereaux
borderland
borderless
borderline
burdensome
bureaucrat
burglarise
burramundi
bursarship
carabineer
carabinier
caramelise
caravaneer
caravanned
caravanner
carbonnade
carboxylic
carbuncled
carcinogen
carcinosis
cardialgia
cardiogram
cardiology
cardplayer
carelessly
caricature
carmagnole
carnallite
carnassial
carotenoid
carotinoid
carpellary
carpetweed
carphology
carragheen
carryingon
Carthusian
cartomancy
cartoonist
cartwright
caruncular
caryatides
cerebellum
ceremonial
cerography
certiorari
ceruminous
Christhood
Christlike
chromatics
chromatype
chromosome
chronicity
chronicler
chronogram
chronology
chrysolite
chrysotile
Circassian
circuitous
circularly
circulator
circumcise
circumflex
circumfuse
circumvent
coradicate
coralberry
coralsnake
corbelling
corbiculae
cordiality
cordierite
cordillera
cordwainer
corelation
corelative
coriaceous
Corinthian
corncockle
cornerwise
cornettist
cornflakes
cornflower
cornstarch
cornucopia
coromandel
coronation
corporally
corporator
corporeity
corpulence
corpulency
corpuscule
correction
corrective
correspond
corrigenda
corrigible
corrivalry
corroboree
corrugated
corrugator
corruption
corruptive
corsetiere
corticated
Corybantes
corybantic
coryphaeus
curability
curatorial
curmudgeon
curricular
curriculum
cursedness
curvaceous
curvacious
curvetting
deracinate
derailleur
derailment
derestrict
deridingly
derisively
derivation
derivative
dermatitis
dermatogen
derogation
derogatory
directness
directoire
directress
dorsigrade
durability
earthbound
earthiness
earthlight
earthquake
earthshine
earthwards
eartrumpet
earwigging
earwitness
enregister
enrichment
enrigiment
eurhythmic
Eurodollar
Eurovision
eurypterid
farcically
farfetched
farsighted
fertiliser
fervidness
fireblight
fireescape
firepolicy
fireraiser
firescreen
firstclass
firstnight
foraminous
forbidding
forcefully
forcipated
foreboding
forecaster
forecastle
forecourse
forefather
forefinger
foregather
foreground
forehanded
foreignism
foreordain
forerunner
foreshadow
foresheets
foreteller
forfeiture
forgetting
forgivable
forgivably
formatting
formidable
formidably
formlessly
fornicator
fortepiano
forthright
fortissimi
fortissimo
fortuitism
fortuitist
fortuitous
fortyniner
forwarding
forwearied
furuncular
gargantuan
garishness
garnierite
garnishing
geriatrics
geriatrist
germicidal
germinally
gerundival
girlfriend
gorgeously
Gorgonzola
gormandise
gyrational
gyrocopter
gyroscopic
harassment
harbourage
hardbilled
hardbitten
hardboiled
hardfisted
hardhanded
hardheaded
harelipped
harmlessly
harmonical
harmonious
harmoniser
hartebeest
haruspices
harvestman
herbaceous
hereabouts
hereditary
heresiarch
hereticate
heretofore
hermetical
hermitcrab
heroically
heroicness
heroicomic
herrenvolk
Herrnhuter
hirudinean
horizontal
hormonally
hornblende
hornedness
hornrimmed
horologist
horoscopic
horrendous
horridness
horsecloth
horsecoper
horseflesh
horselaugh
horseleech
horsepower
horseshoer

horsewoman
hurdygurdy
hurlyburly
irradiance
irradicate
irrational
irrelative
irrelevant
irreligion
irresolute
irreverent
irrigation
irritation
irritative
jardiniere
jargonelle
jerrybuilt
juristical
karyoplasm
keratinise
keratinous
kerchieves
kerseymere
kerygmatic
lardydardy
largescale
larvicidal
laryngitic
laryngitis
lordliness
maraschino
marcescent
Marcionite
marginalia
marginally
marginated
margravate
margravine
marguerite
Mariolater
Mariolatry
marionette
marketable
markethall
markettown
markswoman
marquisate
marrowbone
marrowless
marshalled
marshaller
marshalsea
marshiness
martensite
martialism
martingale
marvelling
marvellous
mercantile
mercifully
meridional
merrymaker
miraculous
mirthfully
moralistic
moratorium
morbidezza
morbidness
mordacious
morganatic
moroseness
morphemics
morphinism
morphogeny
morphology
morrispike
myrtaceous
narcissism
narcissist
narcolepsy
narrowness
northbound
northerner
northwards
nurseryman
parabiosis
parabiotic
parabolise
paraboloid
paradisaic
paradisean
paradisiac
paradisian
paradoxure
paraffinic
paragnosis
paralipsis
paralogise
paralogism
paramecium
parametric
paramnesia
paranormal
paraphrase
paraphrast
paraplegia
paraplegic
parapodium
paraselene
parasitism
parasitoid
paratactic
paratroops
parcelling
pardonable
pardonably
parenchyma
parentally
parenteral
parenthood
parimutuel
parliament
Parnassian
paronymous
paroxysmal
paroxytone
parramatta
parricidal
parrotfish
parsonbird
parsonical
partiality
participle
particular
parturient
percentage
percentile
perception
perceptive
perceptual
perchloric
percipient
percolator
percussion
percussive
perdurable
perdurably
peremptory
perfection
perfective
perfidious
perfoliate
perforator
performing
periclinal
pericyclic
peridermal
perigynous
perihelion
perilously
periodical
periosteal
periosteum
peripeteia
peripheral
peripteral
periscopic
perishable
perithecia
peritoneal
peritoneum
periwigged
periwinkle
perjurious
permafrost
permanence
permanency
permeation
permeative
permission
permissive
permitting
permutable
pernicious
pernickety
peroration
peroxidise
perpetrate
perpetuate
perpetuity
perplexity
perquisite
persecutor
persiflage
persistent
personable
personally
personalty
personator
persuasion
persuasive
pertinence
pertinency
perversely
perversion
perversity
perversive
phrasebook
phrenology
porismatic
pornocracy
porousness
porraceous
portamento
portcullis
portentous
portliness
Portuguese
purblindly
puristical
puritanise
puritanism
purposeful
purseproud
pursership
purseseine
pursuivant
purtenance
purulently
purveyance
pyracantha
pyretology
pyridoxine
pyrogallol
pyrogenous
pyrography
pyrolusite
pyromaniac
pyromantic
pyrometric
pyrophoric
pyrotechny
pyroxenite
Pyrrhonian
Pyrrhonism
Pyrrhonist
pyrrhotite
reredorter
sarcolemma
sarcophagi
sarcophagy
sarcoplasm
sargassoes
sarmentose
sarmentous
sarracenia
scrapmetal
scratchily
scratchwig
screechowl
screenings
screenplay
screwplate
screwpress
scribbling
scrimmager
scrimshank
scriptoria
scriptural
scrofulous
scrollwork
scrupulous
scrutineer
scrutinise
SerboCroat
sereneness
sergeantcy
serigraphy
seriocomic
serjeantcy
sermoniser
serologist
serotinous
serpentine
serradilla
serviceman
servomotor
shrewdness
shrewishly
shrewmouse
shrievalty
shrillness
shrinkable
shrinkwrap
shrivelled
shroudlaid
shroudless
Shrovetide
skrimshank
Sorbonnist
sordidness
sororicide
sprightful
springhalt
springhead
springless
springlike
springtail
springtide
springtime
springwood
sprinkling
sprucebeer
spruceness
strabismal
strabismic
strabismus
strabotomy
straighten
straightly
strainedly
straitness
stramonium
strategist
strathspey
stratiform
stratocrat
strawberry
strawboard
streamless
streamline
streetdoor
streetward
strengthen
stressless
strictness
stridently
stridulant
stridulate
stridulous
strikingly
stringbean
stringency
stringendo
stringhalt
stringless
striptease
Stroganoff
stromatous
stronghold
strongroom
structural
structured
struthious
strychnine
strychnism
surefooted
suretyship
surfactant
surgically
surmisable
surplusage
surprising
surrealism
surrealist
survivance
taradiddle
tarantella
tarantelle
tardigrade
tarmacadam
Tartuffian
Tartuffism
teratogeny
teratology
teratomata
termagancy
terminable
terminably
terminally
terminator
termitaria
terneplate
terracotta
terreplein
terrorless
threadbare
threadfish
threadmark
threadworm
threatener
threepence
threepenny
threepiece
threescore
threnodial
threnodist
thriftless
throatwort
thromboses
thrombosis
thrombotic
throneless
throughout
throughput
throughway
throwstick
thruppence
tirailleur
tirelessly
tiresomely
tiringroom
torchlight
toroidally
torpidness
torrential
torridness
tortellini
tortfeasor
tortiously
tortuosity
tortuously
turbidness
turbulence
turbulency
turgescent
turgidness
turkeycock
turnbuckle
turpentine
turtleback
turtledove
turtleneck
tyrannical
Tyrrhenian
unravelled
unreadable
unredeemed
unreliable
unrelieved
unremarked
unrequited
unreserved
unresolved
unripeness
unrivalled
unruliness
uproarious
varicocele
varicosity
variegated
varietally
variolitic
variometer
verandahed
verbaliser
verifiable
vermicelli
vermicidal
vermicular
vernacular
vernissage
versicular
vertebrate
vertically
viraginous
virescence
virginally
virginhood
virologist
virtuality
virtueless
virtuosity
virtuously

virulently
vortically
vorticella
vorticular
wardenship
warmingpan
werewolves
Wertherian
Wertherism
wiredrawer
wirehaired
wirepuller
wiretapper
wirewalker
wireworker
wordlessly
workbasket
workingman
workpeople
worldclass
worldweary
worshipful
worshipped
worshipper
worthiness
worthwhile
xerography
xerophytic
yarborough
yardmaster
abscission
absolutely
absolution
absolutism
absolutist
absolutory
absorbable
absorbance
absorbedly
absorbency
absorption
absorptive
abstemious
abstention
abstergent
abstersion
abstersive
abstinence
abstinency
abstracted
abstracter
abstractly
abstractor
abstrusely
abstrusity
absurdness
adsorbable
adsorption
adsorptive
aesthetics
aesthetism
answerable
answerably
assafetida
assailable
assaultive
assemblage
assentient
assessable
assessment
asseverate
assibilate
assignable
assignment
assimilate
assistance
associable
assoilment
assortment
assumption
assumptive
auscultate
auspicious
austenitic
Australian
basketball
basketwork
bassethorn
bassoonist
bastardise
besprinkle
bestialise
bestiality
bestirring
bestowment
bestridden
bestseller
bisexually
bissextile
bisulphate
bisulphide
bisulphite
Boswellian
Boswellise
Boswellism
bushmaster
bushranger
bustlingly
byssaceous
byssinosis
cascarilla
caseharden
caseworker
cassolette
castration
casualness
cessionary
cismontane
cispontine
Cistercian
cosentient
cosmically
cosmogonic
cosmopolis
cosmoramic
costliness
cuspidated
cussedness
custommade
cystoscope
cystoscopy
desalinate
descendant
descendent
descension
descriptor
desecrater
desecrator
deservedly
deshabille
desiccator
desiderata
desiderate
designator
designedly
designment
desipience
desirously
desistance
desolately
desolation
desorption
despatcher
desperados
despicable
despicably
despisable
despiteful
despiteous
despondent
desquamate
destructor
disability
disappoint
disapprove
disarrange
disastrous
disbarring
disbelieve
disbudding
disburthen
discerning
discharger
discipline
disclaimer
disclosure
discobolus
discomfort
discommend
discommode
discompose
disconcert
disconfirm
disconnect
discontent
discophile
discordant
discounter
discourage
discourser
discoverer
discreetly
discrepant
discretely
discretion
discursive
discussant
discussion
discussive
discutient
disdainful
diseconomy
disembogue
disembosom
disembowel
disembroil
disenchant
disengaged
disenthral
disentitle
disentwine
disenviron
disfeature
disfurnish
disgruntle
disgustful
dishabille
disharmony
dishearten
dishonesty
dishwasher
disincline
disinherit
disjointed
dislikable
disloyally
disloyalty
dismalness
dismission
dismissive
disordered
disorderly
disownment
disparager
disparates
dispassion
dispatcher
dispelling
dispensary
dispersant
dispersion
dispersive
dispersoid
dispirited
dispiteous
disposable
dispossess
dispraiser
disputable
disputably
disqualify
disquieten
disquietly
disrespect
disruption
disruptive
dissatisfy
dissection
dissembler
dissension
dissertate
disservice
dissidence
dissilient
dissimilar
dissipated
dissociate
dissoluble
dissolvent
dissonance
dissonancy
dissuasion
dissuasive
distensile
distension
distention
distichous
distilland
distillate
distillery
distilling
distinctly
distortion
distracted
distrainer
distrainor
distraught
distressed
distribute
distringas
disulphate
disulphide
disutility
disyllabic
disyllable
dosimetric
dustjacket
dysenteric
dysgraphia
dysplastic
dysprosium
dystrophic
easterling
Eastertide
eisteddfod
ensanguine
eosinophil
essayistic
exsanguine
fasciation
fascicular
fasciculus
fascinator
fastidious
fastigiate
fescennine
festoonery
fishcarver
fisherfolk
fishkettle
fishmonger
fisticuffs
fosterling
fusibility
fussbudget
fustanella
gasconader
gaslighter
gaspereaux
gasteropod
gastrology
gastronome
gastronomy
gesundheit
hesitantly
hesitation
hesitative
histologic
histolysis
histolytic
historical
histrionic
hospitable
hospitably
hostelling
husbandage
husbandman
hysteresis
hysteretic
hysterical
insaneness
insanitary
insatiable
insatiably
insecurely
insecurity
inseminate
insensible
insensibly
insentient
insightful
insinuator
insipidity
insistence
insistency
insobriety
insociable
insolation
insolently
insolvable
insolvency
insouciant
inspanning
inspection
inspective
inspirator
inspissate
instalment
instigator
instilling
institutor
instructor
instrument
insufflate
insularism
insularity
insulation
insurgence
insurgency
jasperware
jesuitical
justiciary
lascivious
lesbianism
lissomness
listlessly
lossleader
lusciously
Lusitanian
lustration
lustreless
lustrously
Lysenkoism
masquerade
Massoretic
mastectomy
masterhand
masterhood
masterless
mastermind
mastership
masterwork
masticable
masticator
mesenteric
mesenteron
mesmeriser
Mesolithic
mesomerism
mesomorphy
mesophytic
mesoscaphe
mesosphere
mesothorax
messianism
misaligned
misbelieve
miscellany
mischanter
mischmetal
misconduct
miscreance
misericord
misfortune
misgivings
mishitting
misjoinder
mismatched
mismeasure
misnomered
misogamist
misogynist
misogynous
misologist
misprision
missionary
missionise
mistakable
mistakenly
misthought
misventure
miswording
mosaically
mosaicking
mosasaurus
mosquitoes
mossbunker
muscularly
musicality
musicianly
musicology
musicpaper
musicstand
musicstool
muskmallow
Mussulmans
mystagogic
mystagogue
mysterious
mystically
nasturtium
nosography
nosologist
nosophobia

nostologic
obsequious
observable
observably
observance
obstetrics
obstructor
oesophagus
oysterfarm
pasquinade
passageway
passionary
passionate
Passionist
pasteboard
pastellist
pasteurise
pasteurism
pastmaster
pastorally
pastorship
pastrycook
pasturable
pastyfaced
pesticidal
pestilence
piscifauna
pistillary
pistillate
pistolling
pistolshot
pistolwhip
pistonring
positional
positively
positivism
positivist
positivity
possession
possessive
possessory
postbellum
postchaise
postexilic
posthumous
postillion
postliminy
postmaster
postmortem
postoffice
postpartum
postscript
postulator
pushbutton
rescission
rescissory
researcher
resemblant
resentment
reservedly
reshipment
resignedly
resilience
resiliency
resistance
resistible
resistless
resolutely
resolution
resolutive
resolvable
resolvedly
resonantly
resorcinol
resorption
resorptive
resounding
respectful
respecting
respective
respirable
respirator
respondent
responsive
responsory
restaurant
restlessly
restorable
restrained
restrainer
resultless
resumption
resumptive
resupinate
resurgence
risibility
rosaniline
rosechafer
roseengine
roselipped
rosemallow
Russianise
Russophile
Russophobe
rustically
sashwindow
sestertium
sestertius
sisterhood
susceptive
suspenders
suspension
suspensive
suspensoid
suspensory
suspicious
sustaining
sustenance
sustention
sustentive
systematic
systemless
taskmaster
tasselling
tastefully
tessellate
testaceous
testflight
unscalable
unschooled
unscramble
unscreened
unscripted
unseasoned
unselected
unsettling
unsociable
unsociably
unsocially
unsporting
unsteadily
unstrained
unstressed
unsuitable
unswerving
upstanding
vascularly
vasoactive
vesication
vesicatory
vesiculate
vesperbell
vespertine
vestibular
vestibulum
vestpocket
viscerally
viscometer
viscountcy
visibility
Visigothic
visionally
visionless
visitation
visitorial
visualiser
wassailing
wastefully
wastepaper
westernise
westwardly
wishywashy
yesteryear
actinolite
actinozoan
actionable
actionably
activation
activeness
Aethiopian
aetiologic
afterbirth
aftergrass
afterimage
afterlight
afterpains
aftershave
aftertaste
afterwards
altarpiece
altazimuth
alteration
alterative
alternance
alternator
altocumuli
altogether
altostrati
altruistic
antagonise
antagonism
antagonist
antebellum
antecedent
antecessor
antechapel
antemortem
antependia
antepenult
anteriorly
antheridia
anthracene
anthracite
anthracoid
anthropoid
antibiosis
antibiotic
Antichrist
anticipant
anticipate
anticlimax
anticlinal
antifreeze
antiheroic
antimasque
antimatter
antimonial
antimonite
antinomian
antipathic
antiphonal
antipodean
antiproton
antiquated
antiSemite
antisepsis
antiseptic
antisocial
antistatic
antitheism
antitheist
antitheses
antithesis
antithetic
antonymous
arterially
arteriolar
artfulness
arthralgia
arthralgic
arthromere
articulate
artificial
artycrafty
asteriated
asteroidal
astigmatic
astragalus
astringent
astrologer
astrologic
astronomer
astronomic
astuteness
attachable
attachment
attackable
attainable
attainment
attendance
attenuated
attenuator
attornment
attractant
attraction
attractive
attunement
autarkical
autecology
authorship
autochthon
autocratic
autodidact
autoerotic
autogamous
autogenous
autography
autoimmune
autologous
automation
automatise
automatism
automatist
automobile
automotive
autonomist
autonomous
autoplasty
autostrada
autostrade
autumnally
batfowling
batholitic
bathometer
bathymeter
bathymetry
bathyscaph
bathyscope
batrachian
battailous
battledore
battlement
battleship
betterment
bitchiness
bitterling
bitterness
bitterroot
bitterwood
bituminise
bituminous
bothersome
botryoidal
bottlefeed
bottleneck
bottletree
bottomless
bottommost
butterball
butterbean
butterfish
buttermilk
butterwort
buttonball
buttonbush
buttondown
buttonhole
buttonhook
buttonless
buttonwood
catabolism
catafalque
catalectic
cataleptic
cataloguer
cataphract
catarrhine
catastasis
catburglar
catchpenny
catechesis
catechetic
catechiser
catechumen
categorise
catenation
catholicon
catholicos
catoptrics
cattlegrid
citronella
cottoncake
cottonseed
cottontail
cottonweed
cottonwood
cottonwool
cuttlebone
cuttlefish
cuttystool
cytochrome
cytologist
datamation
detachable
detachedly
detachment
detainment
detectable
detergency
determined
deterrence
detestable
detestably
detonation
detonative
detoxicant
detoxicate
detraction
detractive
ditriglyph
ectodermal
ectodermic
ectogenous
entailment
enterolith
enterotomy
enterprise
enthralled
enthusiasm
enthusiast
enticement
enticingly
entireness
entombment
entomology
entrancing
entrapment
estimation
estimative
euthanasia
extemporal
extendedly
extendible
extensible
extenuator
exteriorly
externally
extinction
extinctive
extinguish
extirpator
extractant
extraction
extractive
extramural
extraneity
extraneous
extricable
fatalistic
fatherhood
fatherland
fatherless
fatherlike
fathership
fathomable
fathomless
fatiguable
fetchingly
fetterlock
fitfulness
futureless
futuristic
futurology
gatekeeper
gatelegged
gothically
gutturally
heterodont
heterodoxy
heterodyne
heterogamy
heterogeny
heterogony
heterology
heteronomy
heterotaxy
hitchhiker
hithermost
hitherward
hotblooded
hotchpotch
iatrogenic
intactness
intangible
intangibly
integrable
integrally
integrator
integument
intendance
intendment
intenerate
intentness
interbreed

interceder
intercross
interested
interferer
interferon
intergrade
interiorly
interleave
interloper
interlunar
intermarry
intermezzi
intermezzo
internally
internment
internodal
internship
interphase
interplant
interplead
interposal
interposer
interregna
interspace
interstate
interstice
intertidal
intertrigo
intertwine
intertwist
interurban
intervener
intervenor
intervolve
interweave
interwound
interwoven
interzonal
intestinal
intimately
intimation
intimidate
intinction
intolerant
intonation
intoxicant
intoxicate
intramural
intraurban
intrepidly
intrigante
intriguant
introducer
introrsely
introspect
intubation
katabolism
kettledrum
laterality
latescence
latifundia
lattermost
letterbomb
letterbook
lettercard
letterhead
letterless
literalise
literalism
literalist
literality
literarily
literation
literature
lithoglyph
lithograph
lithologic
lithophane
lithophyte
lithotrity
Lithuanian
litigation
litterlout
littleness
liturgical
lotuseater
lutestring
matchboard
matchmaker
matchstick
materially
maternally
mathematic
matriarchy
matricidal
matronhood
matronship
matronymic
maturation
maturative
matureness
metabolise
metabolism
metabolite
metacarpal
metacarpus
metacentre
metagalaxy
metalepsis
metallurgy
metamerism
metaphoric
metaphrase
metaphysic
metaplasia
metastable
metastases
metastasis
metastatic
metatarsal
metatarsus
metatheses
metathesis
metathetic
metathorax
metempiric
meteoritic
methodical
Methuselah
methylated
meticulous
metrically
metronomic
metronymic
metropolis
mettlesome
mithridate
mitigation
mitigative
mitigatory
motherhood
motherland
motherless
mothership
motherwort
motionless
motivation
motiveless
motorcycle
mutability
mutilation
mutinously
muttonhead
mythically
mythiciser
mythologer
mythologic
mythomania
mythopoeia
mythopoeic
natalitial
natatorial
natatorium
nationally
nationhood
nationless
nationwide
nativeborn
nativeness
nativistic
natterjack
naturalise
naturalism
naturalist
naturopath
nethermost
nettlerash
nitpicking
nitrochalk
nitrogroup
notability
notarially
notchboard
noteworthy
noticeable
noticeably
notifiable
notionally
notonectal
nutational
nutcracker
nutritious
obtainable
obtainment
obtruncate
obturation
obtuseness
octahedral
octahedron
octamerous
octandrian
octandrous
octodecimo
octonarian
octopodous
oftentimes
ontologist
optatively
optimalise
optimistic
optionally
orthoclase
orthodoxly
orthoepist
orthogenic
orthogonal
orthopedic
orthoptera
ostensible
ostensibly
osteoblast
osteoclast
osteopathy
osteophyte
otterboard
ottershrew
outbalance
outbidding
outerspace
outfielder
outfitting
outgassing
outgeneral
outgunning
outlandish
outmeasure
outpatient
outpouring
outputting
outrageous
outrightly
outrunning
outsitting
outstation
outstretch
outswinger
outwitting
patchiness
patentable
paternally
pathetical
pathfinder
pathogenic
pathologic
patination
patisserie
patriality
patriarchy
patriciate
patricidal
patrilocal
patriotism
patristics
patrolling
patronymic
patulously
petiolated
petiteness
petitioner
petroglyph
petrolatum
petronella
petulantly
phthisical
pitchblack
pitcherful
pitchstone
pitilessly
pityriasis
potability
potamology
potbellied
potentiate
potentilla
pothunting
putatively
putrescent
putrescine
putridness
ratability
ratcatcher
rationally
rattlehead
rattlepate
rattletrap
retainable
reticently
reticulate
retinacula
retirement
retiringly
retractile
retraction
retractive
retraining
retrochoir
retrograde
retrogress
retrorsely
retrospect
returnable
ritardando
ritornelli
ritornello
rotational
rotisserie
rottenness
rottweiler
ruthlessly
satanology
satellitic
satisfying
saturation
saturnalia
satyagraha
satyriasis
setterwort
settlement
sitophobia
tattletale
tetchiness
tetrachord
tetragonal
tetrahedra
tetrameter
tetramorph
tetrapolis
tetrarchic
tetrastich
tetrastyle
tetterwort
titanesque
titivation
tittupping
titubation
totemistic
tutorially
ulteriorly
ultimately
ultrabasic
ultrasonic
ultrasound
unthinking
untidiness
untowardly
untroubled
untruthful
urticarial
urtication
ustulation
Vaticanism
Vaticanist
vaticinate
veterinary
vitalistic
vitaminise
vitiligate
vitrescent
vitriolise
vituperate
watchfully
watchglass
watchguard
watchmaker
watchtower
waterborne
waterbrash
waterclock
watercraft
watercress
waterflood
waterfront
waterglass
wateriness
watermelon
waterpower
waterproof
waterskier
waterspout
watertight
waterwheel
waterworks
wattlebird
witchcraft
witchhazel
witchingly
withdrawal
withdrawer
withholder
witnessbox
abundantly
Adullamite
adulterant
adulterate
adulteress
adulterine
adulterous
aquafortis
aquamarine
aquaplaner
aquiferous
aquilinity
bluebonnet
bluebottle
bluecollar
bluejacket
bluepencil
blueribbon
bluethroat
bluetongue
bluishness
blurringly
blushingly
blusterous
bouncingly
bourbonism
bourbonist
brusquerie
causticity
cautionary
cautiously
chubbiness
chuckerout
chuckwagon
churchgoer
churchyard
churlishly
clubfooted
clumsiness
couchgrass
coulometry
councillor
councilman
counselled
counsellor
counteract
countryish
countryman
couplement
courageous
courthouse
cousinhood
cousinship
couturiere
couverture
crustacean
crustation
crustiness
daughterly
dauphiness
doublebass
doubleness
doublepark
doubletalk
doubletime
doubtfully
doubtingly
doughfaced
drudgingly
drupaceous
duumvirate
ebullience
ebulliency
ebullition

ecumenical
edulcorate
elucidator
elutriator
emulsifier
enumerable
enumerator
enunciable
enunciator
equability
equanimity
equational
equatorial
equestrian
equilibria
equipotent
equitation
equivalent
equivocate
erubescent
eructation
eruptively
exuberance
exulcerate
exultantly
exultation
exultingly
exurbanite
exuviation
faultiness
feuilleton
fluffiness
flugelhorn
flunkeydom
flunkeyism
fluoridate
fluorinate
fluorotype
fluviatile
fluxionary
foudroyant
foundation
founderous
fourchette
fourfooted
fourhanded
Fourierism
fourinhand
fourleaved
fourposter
foursquare
fourstroke
fourteener
fourteenth
fruitarian
fruitfully
frutescent
gaucheness
gaultheria
gauntleted
glumaceous
gluttonise
gluttonous
grubbiness
grudgingly
gruesomely
grumpiness
hauntingly
haustellum
haustorium
heulandite
heuristics
hourcircle
houseagent
housebound
housecraft
houseguest
houselling
houseplant

houseproud
housetrain
housewives
inundation
inundatory
inurbanity
jauntiness
journalese
journalise
journalism
journalist
journeyman
Krugerrand
laughingly
laundryman
lauraceous
laureation
laurelling
leucocytic
leucoplast
leukocytic
loudhailer
loungesuit
mouldboard
mouldiness
mountebank
mournfully
mousseline
moustached
moustachio
Mousterian
mouthorgan
mouthpiece
nauseating
nauseously
nautically
neurilemma
neurolemma
neuropathy
neuroplasm
neurotoxin
neutralise
neutralism
neutralist
neutrality
nourishing
pluckiness
plumassier
plunderage
plunderous
pluperfect
plutocracy
plutolatry
pouncetbox
pourparler
prudential
pruriently
reunionism
reunionist
roughhouse
roughrider
roundabout
roundhouse
rouseabout
roustabout
sauerkraut
sculptress
sculptural
sculptured
scurrility
scurrilous
scurviness
scutellate
shuttering
sluggardly
sluggishly
sluicegate
slumberful
slumberous

sluttishly
smudginess
smuttiness
snubbingly
snuffiness
soubriquet
soullessly
soundboard
soundingly
soundproof
soundtrack
sourcebook
sousaphone
souterrain
southbound
southerner
southernly
southwards
spumescent
spunkiness
spuriously
squalidity
squamation
squanderer
squareness
squaresail
squaretoed
squaretoes
squeezable
squeezebox
squeteague
squinteyed
squirarchy
squirearch
squirehood
squireling
squireship
stubbiness
stubbornly
studiously
stuffiness
stumpiness
stunningly
stupendous
stupidness
sturdiness
tauntingly
tauromachy
tautomeric
tautophony
thumbprint
thumbscrew
thumbstall
thunderbox
thundering
thunderous
touchiness
touchingly
touchjudge
touchpaper
touchstone
tourbillon
tourmaline
tournament
tourniquet
trucklebed
truculence
truculency
truncately
truncation
trundlebed
trustfully
trustiness
trustingly
truthfully
usucaption
usuriously
usurpation
vaudeville

youngberry
yourselves
youthfully
adventurer
advertence
advertency
advertiser
advisement
advocation
advocatory
bivalvular
bivouacked
cavalierly
cavalryman
cavitation
covalently
covariance
covenanted
covenantee
covenanter
covenantor
covetingly
covetously
Devanagari
devilishly
devitalise
devocalise
devolution
devotement
devotional
devoutness
divagation
divaricate
divebomber
divergence
divergency
divestment
divination
divinatory
divineness
divisional
divisively
divulgence
dovecolour
favourable
favourably
feverishly
fivefinger
governable
governance
governessy
government
hoverplane
hovertrain
invaginate
invalidate
invalidism
invalidity
invaluable
invaluably
invariable
invariably
invariance
inventress
inveracity
investment
inveteracy
inveterate
invigilate
invigorate
invincible
invincibly
inviolable
inviolably
invitation
invitatory
invitingly
invocation
invocatory

involucral
involucrum
involution
juvenility
lavalliere
lavatorial
lavishment
lavishness
levigation
levitation
livelihood
liveliness
livingroom
lovelessly
loveletter
loveliness
lovemaking
lovingness
mavourneen
movability
movelessly
moviemaker
navigation
nevernever
novaculite
novelistic
ravenously
ravishment
revalidate
revalorise
revanchism
revanchist
revealable
revealment
revelation
revelatory
revengeful
reverencer
reverently
reversible
revertible
reviewable
revilement
revisional
revitalise
revivalism
revivalist
revocation
revocatory
revolution
riverhorse
rovebeetle
savageness
savourless
seventieth
severeness
vivandiere
viviparity
viviparous
vivisector
wavelength
waveringly
bawdyhouse
bewitchery
bowdlerise
bowdlerism
cowcatcher
coweringly
cowparsley
cowpuncher
downfallen
downstairs
downstream
downstroke
downwardly
enwrapping
fowlplague
hawserlaid
inwardness

jawbreaker
Jewishness
lawabiding
lawbreaker
lawfulness
lawntennis
lawrencium
Lawrentian
lowerclass
lowpitched
lowprofile
newfangled
newsagency
newscaster
newsletter
newsmonger
newsreader
newsvendor
newsworthy
newswriter
pawnbroker
powderhorn
powderpuff
powerfully
powerhouse
rewardable
rewardless
rowanberry
sawtoothed
sowthistle
tawdriness
thwartship
thwartwise
towardness
toweringly
townswoman
unwariness
unwavering
unwieldily
unwontedly
unworkable
unworthily
unwrinkled
upwardness
dextrality
dextrously
doxography
fixedpoint
foxhunting
hexahedral
hexahedron
hexamerous
hexametric
lexicology
lexigraphy
loxodromic
luxuriance
maxilliped
maximalist
mixedmedia
mixolydian
myxomatous
myxomycete
pixillated
saxicoline
saxicolous
sexagenary
Sexagesima
sexivalent
sexlimited
sexologist
sexpartite
sextillion
sixshooter
taxability
taxidancer
taxidermal
taxidermic
taxonomist

textualist
texturally
toxication
toxicology
toxiphobia
amygdaloid
amylaceous
arytaenoid
asymmetric
asymptotic
asynchrony
atypically
boyishness
bryologist
Clydesdale
cryogenics
cryoscopic
cryptogamy
cryptogram
cryptology
daydreamer
drysaltery
Egyptology
erysipelas
flycatcher
flyfishing
flyswatter
glycolyses
glycolysis
glycosuria
glycosuric
jaywalking
joyfulness
joyousness
keyboarder
mayblossom
mayonnaise
oxygenator
phylactery
phyllotaxy
phylloxera
phylogenic
physically
physicking
physiocrat
physiology
phytogenic
phytophagy
phytotoxic
psychiatry
psychicism
psychicist
psychology
psychopath
rhythmical
scyphiform
scyphozoan
skyjacking
skyscraper
skywriting
stylistics
stylograph
stypticity
tryptophan
unyielding
voyageable
bizarrerie
dazzlement
dazzlingly
eczematous
enzymology
fuzzywuzzy
mizzenmast
mizzensail
mozzarella
pozzolanic
pozzuolana
puzzlement
razorblade
razorshell
razzmatazz
suzerainty
viziership

Abrahamman
abrasively
adjacently
affability
alkalinity
almacanter
altarpiece
altazimuth
ambassador
amiability
Andalusian
andalusite
annalistic
antagonise
antagonism
antagonist
aphaereses
aphaeresis
aplacental
apparelled
apparently
apparition
aquafortis
aquamarine
aquaplaner
arbalester
arbalister
Armageddon
ascariasis
asparagine
assafetida
assailable
assaultive
Athanasian
attachable
attachment
attackable
attainable
attainment
autarkical
aviatrices
bigamously
binaurally
biparietal
bipartisan
bivalvular
bizarrerie
bleachable
bleariness
blearyeyed
bleatingly
breadboard
breadcrumb
breadfruit
breadstick
breadstuff
breakables
breakpoint
breakwater
breastbone
breastwall
breastwork
breathable
breathless
broadcloth
broadsheet
broadsword
cabalistic
cadaverous
calamander
calamitous
canaliculi
capability
capacitate
capacitive
carabineer
carabinier
caramelise
caravaneer
caravanned
caravanner
catabolism
catafalque
catalectic
cataleptic
cataloguer
cataphract
catarrhine
catastasis
cavalierly
cavalryman
cheapishly
cheapskate
cicatrices
clearstory
cohabitant
colatitude
comanchero
coparcener
copartnery
coradicate
coralberry
coralsnake
covalently
covariance
creaminess
creatinine
creatively
creativity
creaturely
curability
curatorial
damageable
damagingly
datamation
debasement
debatement
debauchery
decadently
decagramme
decahedral
decahedron
decampment
decapitate
decapodous
defacement
defalcator
defamation
defamatory
delaminate
demagogism
demandable
denaturant
department
deracinate
derailleur
derailment
desalinate
detachable
detachedly
detachment
detainment
Devanagari
didactical
dilapidate
dilatation
dilatorily
disability
disappoint
disapprove
disarrange
disastrous
divagation
divaricate
dreadfully
dreaminess
dreamworld
dreariness
durability
dynamistic
effaceable
effacement
embalmment
embankment
embarkment
empanelled
emparadise
empathetic
encampment
encasement
encashment
enfacement
engagement
engagingly
enharmonic
enjambment
enlacement
ensanguine
entailment
equability
equanimity
equational
equatorial
escadrille
escalation
escallonia
escapement
escapology
escarpment
espadrille
essayistic
eucalyptol
eucalyptus
eucaryotic
excavation
exhalation
exhaustion
exhaustive
expandable
expansible
expatriate
exsanguine
fanaticise
fanaticism
fatalistic
femaleness
filariasis
fleabitten
fleacircus
fleamarket
floatation
floatboard
floatingly
floatplane
floatstone
foraminous
freakiness
freakishly
friability
gelatinise
gelatinous
greasewood
greasiness
greatniece
greatuncle
gynandrous
gyrational
harassment
heparinise
hepatology
hexahedral
hexahedron
hexamerous
hexametric
humaneness
humanistic
humanities
hypabyssal
hypaethral
hypanthium
idealistic
ideational
illadvised
illatively
illaudable
illaudably
immaculacy
immaculate
immaterial
immaturely
immaturity
impairment
impalement
impalpable
impalpably
impanation
impanelled
imparadise
impartible
impartment
impassable
impassably
impassible
impassibly
impatience
incandesce
incantator
incapacity
incasement
incautious
indagation
infallible
infallibly
infamously
infarction
infatuated
inhabitant
inhalation
inharmonic
innateness
insaneness
insanitary
insatiable
insatiably
intactness
intangible
intangibly
invaginate
invalidate
invalidism
invalidity
invaluable
invaluably
invariable
invariably
invariance
inwardness
irradiance
irradicate
irrational
Japanesque
katabolism
keratinise
keratinous
Lamarckian
Lamarckism
laparotomy
lavalliere
lavatorial
lawabiding
legalistic
legateship
ligamental
limaciform
loganberry
loganstone
macadamise
malacoderm
malacology
maladapted
malapertly
malapropos
manageable
manageably
management
manageress
managerial
maraschino
megalithic
megalosaur
megascopic
melancholy
Melanesian
melanistic
menacingly
metabolise
metabolism
metabolite
metacarpal
metacarpus
metacentre
metagalaxy
metalepsis
metallurgy
metamerism
metaphoric
metaphrase
metaphysic
metaplasia
metastable
metastases
metastasis
metastatic
metatarsal
metatarsus
metatheses
metathesis
metathetic
metathorax
micaschist
miraculous
misaligned
Mohammedan
monandrous
monarchial
Monarchian
monarchism
monarchist
moralistic
moratorium
mosaically
mosaicking
mosasaurus
movability
Muhammadan
Muhammedan
mutability
natalitial
natatorial
natatorium
negatively
negativism
negativist
negativity
nematocyst
nonaligned
notability
notarially
novaculite
nutational

oblateness
obtainable
obtainment
occasional
oceanarium
oceangoing
oceanology
octahedral
octahedron
octamerous
octandrian
octandrous
oleaginous
ommatidium
optatively
ordainment
organicism
organicist
organismal
ornamental
ornateness
Palaeocene
Palaeogene
palaeolith
palaeotype
Palaeozoic
palagonite
palatalise
palatinate
Panamanian
papaverine
papaverous
parabiosis
parabiotic
parabolise
paraboloid
paradisaic
paradisean
paradisiac
paradisian
paradoxure
paraffinic
paragnosis
paralipsis
paralogise
paralogism
paramecium
parametric
paramnesia
paranormal
paraphrase
paraphrast
paraplegia
paraplegic
parapodium
paraselene
parasitism
parasitoid
paratactic
paratroops
pedagogics
pedalorgan
pedalpoint
pheasantry
phrasebook
picaresque
picayunish
pleadingly
pleasantly
pleasantry
pleasingly
pliability
pliantness
potability
potamology
preachment
preadamite
prearrange
putatively
pyracantha
queasiness
ragamuffin
ratability
recallable
regalement
regardless
relational
relatively
relativise
relativism
relativist
relativity
relaxation
remarkable
remarkably
remarriage
renascence
repairable
reparation
reparative
repatriate
retainable
revalidate
revalorise
revanchism
revanchist
rewardable
rewardless
ritardando
Romanesque
Romanistic
rosaniline
rotational
rowanberry
salability
salamander
samarskite
sanatorium
satanology
savageness
sciagraphy
scrapmetal
scratchily
scratchwig
seaanemone
sedateness
senatorial
separately
separation
separatism
separatist
separative
separatory
sexagenary
Sexagesima
sheabutter
shearwater
sheathbill
sheathless
skiagraphy
sleaziness
sneakiness
sneakingly
sneakthief
solacement
somatology
somatotype
speargrass
sphalerite
splanchnic
splashback
splashdown
squalidity
squamation
squanderer
squareness
squaresail
squaretoed
squaretoes
steadiness
steakhouse
stealthily
steamchest
steaminess
steamtight
strabismal
strabismic
strabismus
strabotomy
straighten
straightly
strainedly
straitness
stramonium
strategist
strathspey
stratiform
stratocrat
strawberry
strawboard
subacidity
subaquatic
subaqueous
subaverage
sudatorium
sugardaddy
sugarhouse
sugariness
sugarmaple
sweatgland
sweatiness
sweatshirt
sybaritism
synaeresis
synaloepha
synanthous
tamability
taradiddle
tarantella
tarantelle
taxability
tenability
tenantable
tenantless
teratogeny
teratology
teratomata
theatrical
thwartship
thwartwise
tirailleur
titanesque
topazolite
towardness
treadboard
treadwheel
treasonous
triacetate
triandrous
triangular
tularaemia
tularaemic
tyrannical
unbalanced
uneasiness
unfadingly
unfairness
unfaithful
unfamiliar
unfathered
unhallowed
unhandsome
uniaxially
unlabelled
unlawfully
unmannerly
unnameable
unravelled
unwariness
unwavering
upwardness
urbanology
vanadinite
venational
verandahed
viraginous
vitalistic
vitaminise
vivandiere
vocabulary
vocational
volatilise
volatility
voyageable
wheatstone
womanishly
zabaglione
anabaptism
anabaptist
babblement
balbriggan
barbellate
barbershop
barbituric
bobbinlace
bobbysocks
bobbysoxer
bombardier
borborygmi
bubblyjock
bumblingly
carbonnade
carboxylic
carbuncled
catburglar
chubbiness
clubfooted
combustion
combustive
corbelling
corbiculae
cribriform
cumbersome
cumbrously
diabolical
disbarring
disbelieve
disbudding
disburthen
doublebass
doubleness
doublepark
doubletalk
doubletime
doubtfully
doubtingly
dumbledore
dumbstruck
dumbwaiter
edibleness
elaborator
epiblastic
erubescent
exobiology
exuberance
feebleness
fimbriated
flabbiness
flabellate
forbidding
fumblingly
gambolling
Ghibelline
Gilbertian
globularly
grubbiness
halberdier
harbourage
herbaceous
hobbyhorse
hotblooded
humbleness
humbuggery
humbugging
husbandage
husbandman
icebreaker
jawbreaker
jobbernowl
keyboarder
kibbutznik
kimberlite
knobkerrie
lambrequin
lawbreaker
Leibnizian
lesbianism
lumberjack
lumberroom
lumbersome
lumberyard
mayblossom
membership
membranous
misbelieve
morbidezza
morbidness
mumbojumbo
nambypamby
nimbleness
numberless
outbalance
outbidding
pebbledash
plebiscite
potbellied
prebendary
purblindly
rabbinical
rabblement
ramblingly
redblooded
ribbonfish
ribbonworm
rubberneck
sabbatical
scabrously
seabiscuit
SerboCroat
shabbiness
shibboleth
skibobbing
snobbishly
snobocracy
snubbingly
sombreness
Sorbonnist
soubriquet
stabiliser
stablemate
stableness
stubbiness
stubbornly
symbolical
symboliser
tambourine
timberhead
timberline
timbertoes
timberwolf
timberwork
timbrology
trabeation
trabeculae
trabecular
tribometer
tribrachic
tumbledown
tumblerful
tumbleweed
turbidness
turbulence
turbulency
unabridged
verbaliser
wobbliness
yarborough
abacterial
abscission
aficionado
aircooling
aircushion
anacolutha
anecdotage
anecdotist
apiculture
apocalypse
apocarpous
apochromat
apocryphal
auscultate
aviculture
bacchantes
bacchantic
barcarolle
bedchamber
bedclothes
beechdrops
biochemist
bitchiness
blackamoor
blackberry
blackboard
blackfaced
blackguard
blackheart
Blackshirt
blacksmith
blackthorn
blackwater
blockboard
blockhouse
blockishly
brachiator
brachiopod
brachylogy
brachyural
brachyuran
brickfield
bricklayer
brocatelle
buccinator
bunchgrass
cacciatore
calcareous
calceolate
calciferol
calcsinter
calculable
calculably
calculator
cancellate
cancelling
cancellous
carcinogen
carcinosis
cascarilla
catchpenny
checkpoint
chickenpox
chuckerout
chuckwagon
cinchonine
Circassian

circuitous
circularly
circulator
circumcise
circumflex
circumfuse
circumvent
coacervate
coachbuilt
coachhouse
colchicine
concentric
conception
conceptive
conceptual
concerning
concertina
concertino
concession
concessive
concettism
conchoidal
conchology
conciliary
conciliate
concinnity
conclusion
conclusive
conclusory
concoction
concoctive
concordant
concretely
concretion
concretise
concretism
concretist
concurrent
concurring
concussion
concussive
couchgrass
cowcatcher
crackajack
crackbrain
crocoisite
cunctation
cunctative
deaconship
deactivate
descendant
descendent
descension
descriptor
diachronic
diecasting
discerning
discharger
discipline
disclaimer
disclosure
discobolus
discomfort
discommend
discommode
discompose
disconcert
disconfirm
disconnect
discontent
discophile
discordant
discounter
discourage
discourser
discoverer
discreetly
discrepant
discretely
discretion
discursive
discussant
discussion
discussive
discutient
draconites
egocentric
elecampane
electively
electorate
electrical
electronic
elucidator
emaciation
epicentral
epicycloid
erectility
ericaceous
eructation
evacuation
evacuative
exactitude
execration
execrative
execratory
executable
fancifully
farcically
fasciation
fascicular
fasciculus
fascinator
fescennine
fetchingly
flaccidity
flocculate
flocculent
flycatcher
forcefully
forcipated
fractional
fricandeau
fricasseed
frictional
functional
gasconader
gaucheness
geocentric
geochemist
glaciation
glaciology
glycolyses
glycolysis
glycosuria
glycosuric
gracefully
graciosity
graciously
GrecoRoman
groceteria
henceforth
hitchhiker
hotchpotch
inaccuracy
inaccurate
inactivate
inactively
inactivity
inoculable
inoculator
isochronal
kerchieves
knickknack
knockabout
knockkneed
lanceolate
lascivious
leucocytic
leucoplast
lusciously
Maccabaean
malcontent
manchineel
marcescent
Marcionite
matchboard
matchmaker
matchstick
mercantile
mercifully
miscellany
mischanter
mischmetal
misconduct
miscreance
muscularly
myocardium
narcissism
narcissist
narcolepsy
neoclassic
nincompoop
nonchalant
noncontent
notchboard
nunciature
nutcracker
oracularly
pancratium
pancreatic
pancreatin
parcelling
patchiness
peacefully
peacemaker
peacockery
peacockish
peccadillo
pencilling
percentage
percentile
perception
perceptive
perceptual
perchloric
percipient
percolator
percussion
percussive
piccalilli
piccaninny
piecegoods
pincerlike
pinchpenny
pincushion
piscifauna
pitchblack
pitcherful
pitchstone
placidness
plecoptera
pluckiness
practician
practising
precarious
precaution
precedence
precedency
preceptive
preceptory
precession
preciosity
preciously
precipitin
preclusion
preclusive
precocious
preconcert
precordial
precursory
procedural
proceeding
procession
proclaimer
proclivity
procreator
procrypsis
procryptic
proctorage
proctorial
proctorise
procumbent
procurable
procurance
procurator
psychiatry
psychicism
psychicist
psychology
psychopath
punchboard
punchdrunk
punctation
punctually
punctuator
punctulate
quickgrass
quickthorn
rancidness
ratcatcher
reactivate
reactively
reactivity
redcurrant
reichsmark
rencounter
rescission
rescissory
saccharate
saccharide
saccharify
saccharine
saccharoid
saccharose
sanctifier
sanctimony
sanctitude
sarcolemma
sarcophagi
sarcophagy
sarcoplasm
seacaptain
shockingly
shockproof
sincipital
smockfrock
snickasnee
spacecraft
spacewoman
spaciously
specialise
specialism
specialist
speciality
speciation
speciology
speciosity
speciously
spectacled
spectacles
spectrally
speculator
stickiness
stochastic
stockiness
stockpiler
stockproof
stockrider
stockstill
subcentral
subclavian
subcordate
subculture
succedanea
successful
succession
successive
succinctly
succulence
succulency
suicidally
susceptive
syncarpous
synchronal
synchronic
syncopated
syncopator
syncretise
syncretism
syncretist
tetchiness
thickening
tinctorial
torchlight
touchiness
touchingly
touchjudge
touchpaper
touchstone
tracheated
tracheitis
Tractarian
tractional
trecentist
trichiasis
trichinise
trichinous
trichology
trichotomy
trichroism
trichromat
trickiness
trickishly
triclinium
tricyclist
trochanter
trochoidal
troctolite
trucklebed
truculence
truculency
unaccented
uneconomic
unicameral
unicyclist
unoccupied
unscalable
unschooled
unscramble
unscreened
unscripted
urochordal
usucaption
vaccinator
vascularly
viscerally
viscometer
viscountcy
voiceprint
vulcaniser
watchfully
watchglass
watchguard
watchmaker
watchtower
winceyette
Winchester
witchcraft
witchhazel
witchingly
zincograph
aardwolves
academical
acidimeter
acidimetry
acidophile
anadromous
apodeictic
badderlock
balderdash
baldheaded
banderilla
bandmaster
bardolatry
bawdyhouse
beadleship
biodegrade
biodynamic
birdspider
birdstrike
bladdernut
bondholder
bordereaux
borderland
borderless
borderline
bowdlerise
bowdlerism
bradyseism
bridegroom
bridesmaid
bridgeable
bridgehead
bridgeless
bridgework
bridlepath
Buddhistic
burdensome
caddisworm
candelabra
candescent
candidness
candlefish
candletree
candlewick
candlewood
candyfloss
cardialgia
cardiogram
cardiology
cardplayer
Cinderella
clodhopper
Clydesdale
cnidoblast
coadjacent
condensate
condensery
condescend
condolence
conduction
conductive
cordiality
cordierite
cordillera
cordwainer
cradlesong
credential
creditable
creditably
cuddlesome
daydreamer
deadliness
deadweight

dendriform
dendrology
deodoriser
disdainful
drudgingly
dunderhead
duodecimal
duodenitis
epideictic
epidemical
epidermoid
eradicable
eradicator
evidential
fandangoes
fiddleback
fiddlehead
fiddlewood
fledgeling
foudroyant
fuddyduddy
geodetical
gladhander
gladsomely
goldbeater
golddigger
goldenness
goldenseal
goldilocks
goodliness
goodlooker
goodygoody
gradualism
gradualist
graduation
grudgingly
handbarrow
handedness
handgallop
handicraft
handmaiden
handpicked
handselled
handsomely
handspring
handworked
hardbilled
hardbitten
hardboiled
hardfisted
hardhanded
hardheaded
headcheese
headhunter
headmaster
headphones
headspring
headsquare
headstream
headstrong
headwaiter
hebdomadal
heedlessly
hendecagon
Hindustani
hurdygurdy
inadequacy
inadequate
ineducable
iridaceous
iridescent
iridosmine
isodynamic
jardiniere
kindliness
ladderback
landholder
landhunger
landingnet
landlocked
landlubber
landocracy
landowning
landscaper
lardydardy
leadenness
leaderless
leadership
lordliness
loudhailer
maidenhair
maidenhead
maidenhood
maidenlike
mandibular
mandragora
meadowland
meadowlark
meddlesome
mendacious
mendicancy
middleaged
middlebrow
middlemost
middlingly
mindedness
mindlessly
mordacious
needlebath
needlebook
needlecord
needlefish
needlessly
needlework
nondrinker
obediently
oxidisable
paddleboat
paddyfield
paddywagon
paddywhack
paedagogic
paederasty
paediatric
paedogogue
paedophile
pardonable
pardonably
pendentive
perdurable
perdurably
ploddingly
ponderable
powderhorn
powderpuff
predacious
predecease
predestine
predicable
prediction
predictive
predispose
prednisone
pridefully
prodigally
prodigious
producible
production
productive
prudential
quadrangle
quadrantal
quadratics
quadrature
quadrennia
quadriceps
quadrireme
quadrivial
quadrivium
quadrumana
quadrumane
quadrumvir
quadruplet
quadruplex
quadrupole
randomness
readership
renderable
rendezvous
rhodophane
rinderpest
roadrunner
roadworthy
roodscreen
rudderfish
rudderless
saddleback
saddlefast
saddletree
sandalwood
sandbagger
sandcastle
sanderling
sandhopper
sandmartin
seedpotato
seedvessel
shadowless
shoddiness
slidevalve
smudginess
soddenness
soldanella
sordidness
spadebeard
spadiceous
spidercrab
spiderline
spiderwort
spodomancy
stadholder
stodginess
studiously
subdeanery
subduction
suddenness
sunderance
syndicator
tardigrade
tawdriness
tenderfoot
tenderloin
tenderness
tendinitis
tendrillar
tendrilled
tiddlywink
Tridentine
unedifying
uneducated
vaudeville
veldschoen
vindicable
vindicator
vindictive
Waldensian
wanderings
wanderlust
wanderplug
wardenship
weedkiller
wildebeest
wilderment
wilderness
wildfowler
windflower
windjammer
windowless
windowpane
windowseat
windowshop
windowsill
windscreen
windshield
windsleeve
wonderland
wonderment
wonderwork
wondrously
woodcarver
woodcutter
woodenhead
woodenness
woodlander
woodpecker
woodpigeon
woodturner
woodworker
wordlessly
wunderkind
yardmaster
ZendAvesta
abjectness
ablebodied
abnegation
abreaction
accelerate
accentuate
acceptable
acceptably
acceptance
acceptedly
accessible
accessibly
acoelomate
adherently
adhesively
adjectival
adrenaline
adrenergic
adventurer
advertence
advertency
advertiser
aerenchyma
affectedly
affectless
affeerment
afferently
affettuoso
afterbirth
aftergrass
afterimage
afterlight
afterpains
aftershave
aftertaste
afterwards
aldermanic
aldermanry
algebraist
alienation
allegation
allegiance
allegorise
allegorist
allegretto
allergenic
alleviator
alpenstock
alteration
alterative
alternance
alternator
amoebocyte
ampelopsis
ancestress
annexation
antebellum
antecedent
antecessor
antechapel
antemortem
antependia
antepenult
anteriorly
appealable
appearance
appeasable
appendices
appendixes
apperceive
appetising
appetitive
arrestment
arterially
arteriolar
asbestosis
ascendable
ascendance
ascendancy
ascendence
ascendency
ascendible
asceticism
aspergilla
assemblage
assentient
assessable
assessment
asseverate
asteriated
asteroidal
attendance
attenuated
attenuator
autecology
barebacked
barefooted
bareheaded
barelegged
bedevilled
bejewelled
bemedalled
benedicite
Benedictus
benefactor
beneficent
beneficial
benevolent
bimestrial
bimetallic
bioecology
bipetalous
bisexually
bluebonnet
bluebottle
bluecollar
bluejacket
bluepencil
blueribbon
bluethroat
bluetongue
boneheaded
bonesetter
boneshaker
breechless
breezeless
breeziness
bureaucrat
Caledonian
camelopard
camerlengo
camerlingo
carelessly
caseharden
caseworker
catechesis
catechetic
catechiser
catechumen
categorise
catenation
celebrated
celebrator
cerebellum
ceremonial
cheekiness
cheerfully
cheeriness
cheesecake
cheesiness
Ciceronian
cinecamera
cinerarium
clientship
coherently
cohesively
coleoptera
coleoptile
coleorhiza
comedienne
comehither
comeliness
comestible
Copernican
copesettic
corelation
corelative
cosentient
covenanted
covenantee
covenanter
covenantor
covetingly
covetously
coweringly
creepiness
cybernetic
deaeration
deceivable
decelerate
Decembrist
decemviral
deceptible
defeasance
defeasible
defeminise
defendable
defensible
defensibly
deferrable
degeneracy
degenerate
dejectedly
delectable
delectably
delegation
dementedly
denegation
dependable
dependably
dependence
dependency
derestrict
desecrater
desecrator
deservedly
detectable
detergency
determined
deterrence
detestable
detestably

digestible
dilemmatic
dilettante
dilettanti
directness
directoire
directress
diseconomy
disembogue
disembosom
disembowel
disembroil
disenchant
disengaged
disenthral
disentitle
disentwine
disenviron
divebomber
divergence
divergency
divestment
dovecolour
dysenteric
eczematous
effectuate
effeminacy
effeminate
effervesce
effeteness
eigenvalue
elderberry
Emmentaler
encephalic
encephalon
endearment
endemicity
enmeshment
enregister
enterolith
enterotomy
enterprise
ephemerous
equestrian
especially
ethereally
eudemonism
eudemonist
eugenicist
euhemerise
euhemerism
euhemerist
excellence
excellency
excerption
expectance
expectancy
expectedly
expedience
expediency
expedition
expendable
experience
experiment
expertness
extemporal
extendedly
extendible
extensible
extenuator
exteriorly
externally
faceharden
facesaving
fadelessly
federalise
federalism
federalist
federation
federative
fenestella
fenestrate
feverishly
fireblight
fireescape
firepolicy
fireraiser
firescreen
fivefinger
fixedpoint
fleeringly
fleetingly
foreboding
forecaster
forecastle
forecourse
forefather
forefinger
foregather
foreground
forehanded
foreignism
foreordain
forerunner
foreshadow
foresheets
foreteller
freebooter
freedwoman
freehanded
freeholder
freelancer
freeliving
freeloader
freemartin
freesoiler
freespeech
freespoken
friendless
friendlily
friendship
funereally
gamekeeper
gametangia
gatekeeper
gatelegged
generalise
generalist
generality
generation
generative
generatrix
generosity
generously
geneticist
gobemouche
governable
governance
governessy
government
greediness
greedyguts
greencloth
greenfinch
greenheart
greenhouse
greenshank
greenstick
greenstone
greenstuff
greensward
grievously
gruesomely
hakenkreuz
harelipped
hebetation
hereabouts
hereditary
heresiarch
hereticate
heretofore
heterodont
heterodoxy
heterodyne
heterogamy
heterogeny
heterogony
heterology
heteronomy
heterotaxy
hibernacle
hokeypokey
homebrewed
homecoming
homeliness
homemaking
homeopathy
honeyeater
honeyguide
honeysweet
hopelessly
hoverplane
hovertrain
hyperaemia
hyperaemic
hyperbaric
hyperbaton
hyperbolae
hyperbolas
hyperbolic
hyperdulia
hypergolic
hypersonic
illegalise
illegality
imbecilely
imbecility
immemorial
impeccable
impeccably
impeccancy
impediment
impendence
impendency
impenitent
imperative
imperially
imperilled
impersonal
impervious
incendiary
incessancy
incestuous
indecently
indecision
indecisive
indecorous
indefinite
indelicacy
indelicate
indexation
infeasible
infectious
infelicity
inferiorly
infernally
inferrable
ingeminate
ingestible
inherently
inheritrix
innerrably
insecurely
insecurity
inseminate
insensible
insensibly
insentient
integrable
integrally
integrator
integument
intendance
intendment
intenerate
intentness
interbreed
interceder
intercross
interested
interferer
interferon
intergrade
interiorly
interleave
interloper
interlunar
intermarry
intermezzi
intermezzo
internally
internment
internodal
internship
interphase
interplant
interplead
interposal
interposer
interregna
interspace
interstate
interstice
intertidal
intertrigo
intertwine
intertwist
interurban
intervener
intervenor
intervolve
interweave
interwound
interwoven
interzonal
intestinal
inventress
inveracity
investment
inveteracy
inveterate
irrelative
irrelevant
irreligion
irresolute
irreverent
juvenility
kinematics
kineticist
kriegspiel
laceration
lacerative
lamentable
lamentably
lamentedly
laterality
latescence
lebensraum
lederhosen
liberalise
liberalism
liberalist
liberality
liberation
licensable
licentiate
licentious
lifegiving
lifejacket
lifelessly
lifesaving
likelihood
likeliness
likeminded
limeburner
literalise
literalism
literalist
literality
literarily
literation
literature
livelihood
liveliness
loneliness
lonesomely
lovelessly
loveletter
loveliness
lovemaking
lowerclass
lukewarmly
Lupercalia
lutestring
Lysenkoism
macebearer
maceration
majestical
makeweight
malefactor
maleficent
malentendu
malevolent
materially
maternally
mesenteric
mesenteron
metempiric
meteoritic
mimeograph
mineralise
mineralogy
minestrone
mineworker
misericord
mixedmedia
moderately
moderation
moderatism
moderniser
modernness
molendinar
monetarily
monetarism
monetarist
moneymaker
moneytaker
movelessly
namelessly
nepenthean
nevernever
nineteenth
noteworthy
novelistic
numeration
numerology
numerosity
numerously
objectival
objectless
obsequious
observable
observably
observance
oedematose
oedematous
oftentimes
orientally
orneriness
osmeterium
ostensible
ostensibly
osteoblast
osteoclast
osteopathy
osteophyte
otherwhere
otherwhile
otherworld
otterboard
ottershrew
outerspace
pacesetter
panegyrise
panegyrist
paperchase
paperknife
papermaker
parenchyma
parentally
parenteral
parenthood
patentable
paternally
pederastic
pedestrian
penetrable
penetrably
penetralia
penetrance
penetrator
peremptory
phlebotomy
phlegmatic
Phoenician
phrenology
pigeonhole
pigeonpair
pigeonpost
pigeontoed
pigeonwing
piledriver
pinebeauty
pinecarpet
piperidine
pokerfaced
polemicist
polemonium
Pomeranian
potentiate
potentilla
powerfully
powerhouse
praecocial
praemunire
praesidium
praetorial
praetorian
preeminent
preemption
preemptive
preexilian
priesthood
priestling
puberulent
pubescence
pyretology
quiescence
quiescency
racecourse
ravenously
rebellious
receivable
recentness

receptacle
receptible
redecorate
redeemable
redemption
redemptive
redemptory
redescribe
referendum
regelation
regeneracy
regenerate
regentship
rejectable
releasable
relegation
relentless
relevantly
remediable
remedially
remediless
repealable
repeatable
repeatedly
repellance
repellancy
repellence
repellency
repentance
repertoire
repetiteur
repetition
repetitive
reredorter
researcher
resemblant
resentment
reservedly
revealable
revealment
revelation
revelatory
revengeful
reverencer
reverently
reversible
revertible
riverhorse
ropedancer
ropeladder
ropewalker
rosechafer
roseengine
roselipped
rosemallow
rovebeetle
sacerdotal
safeblower
safetybelt
salesclerk
saleswoman
satellitic
sauerkraut
schematise
schematism
schemozzle
scherzando
scientific
scleroderm
sclerotium
sclerotomy
screechowl
screenings
screenplay
screwplate
screwpress
secernment
selectness
selenodont
selenology
semeiology
semeiotics
semestrial
senescence
sereneness
seventieth
severeness
sheepishly
sheeplouse
sheepshank
sheepshead
shieldless
shoebuckle
shoestring
shrewdness
shrewishly
shrewmouse
sideboards
sideeffect
sideglance
siderolite
siderostat
sidesaddle
sidestreet
sidestroke
sidewinder
silentness
sinecurism
sinecurist
sleepiness
sleepyhead
sleeveless
sleevelink
sneeringly
sneezeweed
sneezewood
sneezewort
sobersided
sobersides
solecistic
solemnness
solenoidal
somersault
speechless
speediness
speedlimit
sphenodone
sphenogram
sphenoidal
sphericity
spheroidal
spherulite
spleenwort
splendidly
squeezable
squeezebox
squeteague
steeliness
steelworks
streamless
streamline
streetdoor
streetward
strengthen
stressless
superacute
superaltar
superation
superbness
supercargo
superduper
supergiant
superhuman
superiorly
superlunar
supernally
supernovae
superorder
superpower
supersonic
superstore
supertonic
supervisor
surefooted
suretyship
suzerainty
sweepingly
sweepstake
sweetbread
sweetbriar
sweetbrier
sweetening
sweetheart
synecdoche
synecology
synergetic
tabernacle
talebearer
talentless
taleteller
taperecord
taperingly
tapestried
telecamera
telecaster
telegraphy
telemetric
teleologic
teleostean
telepathic
telephoner
telephonic
telescopic
televiewer
television
televisual
tenebrific
tenebrious
tenemental
thievishly
threadbare
threadfish
threadmark
threadworm
threatener
threepence
threepenny
threepiece
threescore
threnodial
threnodist
tidewaiter
timekeeper
timelessly
timeliness
timesaving
timeserver
tirelessly
tiresomely
tolerantly
toleration
tonelessly
totemistic
toweringly
trierarchy
tubercular
tuberculin
tuberosity
tumescence
tunelessly
typescript
typesetter
typewriter
ulceration
ulcerative
ulteriorly
umbellifer
unbearable
unbearably
unbeatable
unbeatably
unbecoming
unbeliever
unbesought
undefended
undeniable
undeniably
underbelly
underbrush
undercliff
undercover
undercroft
underdress
underfloor
underglaze
underlease
underlinen
underlying
underminer
underneath
underpants
underproof
underquote
underscore
undersense
undersexed
undershirt
undershoot
undershrub
undersized
underskirt
underslung
understand
understate
understeer
understock
understood
understudy
undertaken
undertaker
undertrick
undervalue
underwater
underworld
underwrite
underwrote
undeserved
undesigned
undesirous
undeterred
unfeminine
unfettered
ungenerous
unlettered
unmeasured
unmeetness
unmerciful
unreadable
unredeemed
unreliable
unrelieved
unremarked
unrequited
unreserved
unresolved
unseasoned
unselected
unsettling
upperclass
vegetarian
vegetation
vegetative
vehemently
veneration
veterinary
viceconsul
vicegerent
viceregent
videophone
vinegarish
viperiform
viperously
virescence
waterborne
waterbrash
waterclock
watercraft
watercress
waterflood
waterfront
waterglass
wateriness
watermelon
waterpower
waterproof
waterskier
waterspout
watertight
waterwheel
waterworks
wavelength
waveringly
werewolves
wheelchair
wheelhorse
wheelhouse
wheeziness
widespread
winebibber
winebottle
winegrower
wiredrawer
wirehaired
wirepuller
wiretapper
wirewalker
wireworker
Wykehamist
yokefellow
artfulness
asafoetida
bafflement
bafflingly
batfowling
beefburger
bufflehead
buffoonery
chiffchaff
chiffonier
coffeemill
confabbing
confection
conference
conferment
conferring
confervoid
confession
confidante
confidence
confirmand
confiscate
conflation
confluence
conformism
conformist
conformity
confounded
confusedly
craftguild
craftiness
difference
difficulty
diffidence
diffusible
disfeature
disfurnish
drafthorse
dumfounder
farfetched
fitfulness
fluffiness
flyfishing
forfeiture
fulfilling
fulfilment
Godfearing
golfcourse
gunfighter
halfcocked
halfdollar
halflength
halfnelson
halfvolley
halfwitted
halfyearly
inefficacy
joyfulness
knifeboard
lawfulness
leafcutter
leafhopper
leafinsect
malfeasant
manfulness
misfortune
muffinbell
newfangled
nonferrous
nonfiction
oldfangled
outfielder
outfitting
perfection
perfective
perfidious
perfoliate
perforator
performing
pinfeather
prefecture
preferable
preferably
preference
preferment
preferring
prefixture
prefrontal
prefulgent
profession
proficient
profitable
profitably
profitless
profligacy
profligate
profoundly
profundity
puffpastry
reafforest
rodfishing
roofgarden
ruefulness
ruffianism
scaffolder
scoffingly
selfacting
selfaction
selfbinder
selfcolour
selfdeceit
selfdenial
selfesteem
selffeeder
selfglazed

sel**f**guided
sel**f**lessly
sel**f**loving
sel**f**motion
sel**f**murder
sel**f**parody
sel**f**poised
sel**f**praise
sel**f**profit
sel**f**raised
sel**f**regard
sel**f**rising
sel**f**ruling
sel**f**seeker
sel**f**styled
sel**f**taught
sel**f**willed
shi**f**tiness
sin**f**ulness
sna**f**flebit
sni**f**finess
snu**f**finess
spi**f**licate
sta**f**fnurse
sti**f**fening
sti**f**lebone
sti**f**lingly
stu**f**finess
suf**f**erable
suf**f**erably
suf**f**erance
suf**f**icient
suf**f**ragist
sur**f**actant
tof**f**eenose
tom**f**oolery
tra**f**ficked
tra**f**ficker
tri**f**lingly
tri**f**oliate
tri**f**urcate
tuf**f**aceous
una**f**fected
uni**f**ormity
uno**f**ficial
use**f**ulness
waf**f**leiron
wil**f**ulness
woe**f**ulness
wol**f**ramite
ali**g**htment
amy**g**daloid
ana**g**lyphic
ana**g**ogical
ara**g**onitic
bar**g**eboard
Bel**g**ravian
bil**g**ewater
bio**g**enesis
bio**g**enetic
bio**g**rapher
bio**g**raphic
bri**g**andage
bri**g**andine
bri**g**andism
bri**g**antine
bri**g**htness
bri**g**htwork
bud**g**erigar
bun**g**lingly
bur**g**larise
coa**g**ulable
con**g**eneric
con**g**enital
con**g**estion
con**g**estive
con**g**lobate
con**g**regant
con**g**regate
con**g**ruence
con**g**ruency
cra**g**giness
cud**g**elling
dau**g**hterly
dia**g**nostic
dia**g**onally
dia**g**raphic
did**g**eridoo
dis**g**runtle
dis**g**ustful
dog**g**edness
dou**g**hfaced
dra**g**onhead
dra**g**onnade
dra**g**ontree
dun**g**beetle
dys**g**raphia
emi**g**ration
emi**g**ratory
eni**g**matise
eni**g**matist
epi**g**astric
epi**g**enesis
epi**g**enetic
epi**g**lottal
epi**g**lottic
epi**g**lottis
epi**g**rapher
epi**g**raphic
exa**g**gerate
exe**g**etical
eye**g**lasses
fin**g**erbowl
fin**g**erless
fin**g**erling
fin**g**ermark
fin**g**ernail
fin**g**erpost
fla**g**ellant
fla**g**ellate
fla**g**itious
fla**g**rantly
fla**g**waving
fli**g**htdeck
fli**g**htless
fli**g**htpath
flu**g**elhorn
for**g**etting
for**g**ivable
for**g**ivably
fra**g**mental
fra**g**rantly
fri**g**idness
fri**g**orific
fro**g**hopper
fun**g**icidal
gan**g**lionic
gan**g**renous
gar**g**antuan
geo**g**nostic
geo**g**rapher
geo**g**raphic
gin**g**erbeer
gin**g**ersnap
gin**g**ivitis
Gla**g**olitic
gog**g**leeyed
gor**g**eously
Gor**g**onzola
gre**g**arious
gro**g**giness
han**g**glider
hod**g**epodge
hun**g**riness
ima**g**inable
ima**g**inably
iso**g**enetic
iso**g**lossal
jag**g**edness
jar**g**onelle
jin**g**oistic
jud**g**ematic
jug**g**ernaut
kin**g**fisher
kin**g**liness
kni**g**hthood
Kru**g**errand
lan**g**uisher
lan**g**uorous
lar**g**escale
lau**g**hingly
led**g**erbait
led**g**erline
len**g**thways
len**g**thwise
lin**g**uiform
lin**g**uistic
log**g**erhead
lon**g**aevous
lon**g**haired
lon**g**headed
lon**g**legged
lon**g**primer
lon**g**shanks
lon**g**winded
man**g**osteen
mar**g**inalia
mar**g**inally
mar**g**inated
mar**g**ravate
mar**g**ravine
mar**g**uerite
mea**g**reness
mis**g**ivings
mon**g**relise
mon**g**relism
mor**g**anatic
noo**g**enesis
oli**g**archic
oli**g**oclase
oli**g**opsony
ori**g**inally
ori**g**inator
oro**g**enesis
oro**g**enetic
oro**g**raphic
out**g**assing
out**g**eneral
out**g**unning
oxy**g**enator
pan**g**enesis
pan**g**enetic
pha**g**edaena
pha**g**edenic
pha**g**ocytic
pil**g**arlick
pil**g**rimage
pla**g**iarise
pla**g**iarism
pla**g**iarist
pla**g**uesome
pra**g**matise
pra**g**matism
pra**g**matist
pre**g**lacial
pre**g**nantly
pri**g**gishly
pro**g**enitor
pro**g**lottis
pro**g**nathic
pro**g**nostic
pro**g**rammer
rag**g**edness
rid**g**epiece
rin**g**finger
rin**g**leader
rin**g**master
rin**g**necked
rin**g**tailed
rou**g**hhouse
rou**g**hrider
rug**g**edness
san**g**uinary
san**g**uinely
san**g**uinity
sar**g**assoes
sei**g**norage
sei**g**norial
ser**g**eantcy
sha**g**giness
sie**g**etrain
Sin**g**halese
sin**g**lefoot
sin**g**leness
sin**g**letree
sin**g**ularly
sli**g**htness
slu**g**gardly
slu**g**gishly
son**g**stress
son**g**thrush
son**g**writer
spa**g**yrical
sta**g**beetle
sta**g**ecoach
sta**g**ecraft
sta**g**gering
sta**g**nantly
sta**g**nation
sti**g**matise
sti**g**matism
sti**g**matist
sub**g**lacial
sug**g**estion
sug**g**estive
sun**g**lasses
sur**g**ically
swa**g**gering
syn**g**enesis
tan**g**ential
tan**g**lement
ton**g**ueless
ton**g**uetied
top**g**allant
tra**g**acanth
tra**g**ically
tra**g**icomic
tri**g**eminal
tri**g**german
tri**g**lyphic
tri**g**onally
tro**g**lodyte
tur**g**escent
tur**g**idness
ven**g**efully
vir**g**inally
vir**g**inhood
wag**g**onette
wei**g**htless
win**g**collar
win**g**footed
win**g**spread
won**g**awonga
Aet**h**iopian
alc**h**emical
alp**h**abetic
alp**h**americ
amp**h**ibious
amp**h**ibrach
amp**h**ictyon
amp**h**igouri
amp**h**imacer
amp**h**imixes
amp**h**imixis
amp**h**oteric
anc**h**oretic
anc**h**oritic
anc**h**orless
anc**h**orring
anc**h**ylosis
anc**h**ylotic
ant**h**eridia
ant**h**racene
ant**h**racite
ant**h**racoid
ant**h**ropoid
arc**h**aistic
arc**h**bishop
arc**h**deacon
arc**h**erfish
arc**h**etypal
arc**h**itrave
arc**h**priest
arr**h**ythmia
arr**h**ythmic
art**h**ralgia
art**h**ralgic
art**h**romere
asp**h**yxiant
asp**h**yxiate
aut**h**orship
bat**h**olitic
bat**h**ometer
bat**h**ymeter
bat**h**ymetry
bat**h**yscaph
bat**h**yscope
bic**h**romate
big**h**earted
bot**h**ersome
Bra**h**manism
Bra**h**minism
Buc**h**manism
Buc**h**manite
bus**h**master
bus**h**ranger
cac**h**innate
cat**h**olicon
cat**h**olicos
cep**h**alopod
coc**h**leated
des**h**abille
dic**h**roitic
dic**h**romate
dip**h**theria
dip**h**theric
dip**h**yletic
dip**h**yodont
dis**h**abille
dis**h**armony
dis**h**earten
dis**h**onesty
dis**h**washer
ecc**h**ymosis
ecc**h**ymotic
eig**h**teenmo
eig**h**teenth
emp**h**ractic
enc**h**anting
ent**h**ralled
ent**h**usiasm
ent**h**usiast
esc**h**arotic
esc**h**eatage
eup**h**onious
eup**h**uistic
eur**h**ythmic
eut**h**anasia
fat**h**erhood
fat**h**erland
fat**h**erless
fat**h**erlike
fat**h**ership
fat**h**omable
fat**h**omless
fis**h**carver
fis**h**erfolk
fis**h**kettle
fis**h**monger
fox**h**unting
got**h**ically
hen**h**arrier
hen**h**earted
hig**h**binder
hig**h**flying
hig**h**handed
hig**h**jacker
hig**h**lander
hig**h**minded
hig**h**octane
hig**h**strung
hig**h**wayman
hit**h**ermost
hit**h**erward
hyp**h**enated
inc**h**oately
inc**h**oation
inc**h**oative
lac**h**rymose
lig**h**terage
lig**h**terman
lig**h**tfaced
lig**h**thouse
lig**h**tingup
lig**h**tproof
lit**h**oglyph
lit**h**ograph
lit**h**ologic
lit**h**ophane
lit**h**ophyte
lit**h**otrity
Lit**h**uanian
lop**h**ophore
mac**h**inator
mac**h**inegun
mat**h**ematic
mec**h**anical
met**h**odical
Met**h**uselah
met**h**ylated
Mic**h**aelmas
mig**h**tiness
mis**h**itting
mit**h**ridate
mot**h**erhood
mot**h**erland
mot**h**erless
mot**h**ership
mot**h**erwort
myt**h**ically
myt**h**iciser
myt**h**ologer
myt**h**ologic
myt**h**omania
myt**h**opoeia
myt**h**opoeic
nap**h**thenic
nep**h**ograph
nep**h**oscope
nep**h**ralgia
nep**h**ridium
nep**h**rology
net**h**ermost
nig**h**tdress
nig**h**tglass
nig**h**tlight
nig**h**tshade
nig**h**tshift
nig**h**tshirt
nig**h**tstick
nig**h**twatch
orc**h**ardist
orc**h**ardman
orc**h**estics

orchestral
orphanhood
orthoclase
orthodoxly
orthoepist
orthogenic
orthogonal
orthopedic
orthoptera
panhandler
pathetical
pathfinder
pathogenic
pathologic
phthisical
pichiciago
pothunting
prehensile
prehension
prehistory
prohibiter
prohibitor
pushbutton
Rachmanism
rechristen
reshipment
rightangle
rightfully
rightwards
ruthlessly
sashwindow
silhouette
sophomoric
subheading
syphilitic
tachometer
tachometry
tachymeter
tachymetry
technetium
technician
technicist
technocrat
technology
unchanging
unchastity
unthinking
wishywashy
withdrawal
withdrawer
withholder
xiphosuran
abdication
abridgment
accidental
achievable
actinolite
actinozoan
actionable
actionably
activation
activeness
additional
adhibition
administer
admiration
admiringly
admissible
admittable
admittance
admittedly
advisement
aetiologic
affiliated
affirmable
Africander
Africanise
Africanism
Africanist
Afrikander
Albigenses
alliaceous
alliterate
ambidexter
ambivalent
ancipitous
angiosperm
annihilate
anointment
antibiosis
antibiotic
Antichrist
anticipant
anticipate
anticlimax
anticlinal
antifreeze
antiheroic
antimasque
antimatter
antimonial
antimonite
antinomian
antipathic
antiphonal
antipodean
antiproton
antiquated
antiSemite
antisepsis
antiseptic
antisocial
antistatic
antitheism
antitheist
antitheses
antithesis
antithetic
aquiferous
aquilinity
arbitrable
arbitrager
arbitrator
armigerous
articulate
artificial
aspidistra
aspiration
assibilate
assignable
assignment
assimilate
assistance
astigmatic
audibility
audiometer
audiometry
audiophile
auditorial
auditorium
auriculate
auriferous
babiroussa
banishment
behindhand
believable
benignancy
beribboned
bewitchery
biliverdin
bluishness
boyishness
brainchild
braininess
brainpower
brainstorm
calibrator
caliginous
capitalise
capitalism
capitalist
capitation
Capitoline
capitulary
capitulate
caricature
cavitation
chainsmoke
chairwoman
choiceness
Christhood
Christlike
cicisbeism
cloistered
cogitation
cogitative
comicality
comicopera
coniferous
coriaceous
Corinthian
cylindered
cylindroid
debilitate
decigramme
decimalise
decimalism
decimation
decisively
decivilise
dedication
dedicative
dedicatory
deficiency
defilement
definement
definienda
definitely
definition
definitive
definitude
dehiscence
deliberate
delicately
delightful
delimitate
delineator
delinquent
deliquesce
denigrator
depilation
depilatory
deridingly
derisively
derivation
derivative
desiccator
desiderata
desiderate
designator
designedly
designment
desipience
desirously
desistance
devilishly
devitalise
digitalise
digitately
digitation
digitiform
diligently
diminished
diminuendo
diminution
diminutive
diningroom
disincline
disinherit
divination
divinatory
divineness
divisional
divisively
dominantly
domination
dominative
dosimetric
dubitation
dubitative
duniwassal
echinoderm
efficacity
efficiency
egoistical
elliptical
empiricism
empiricist
engineroom
enlistment
enrichment
enrigiment
enticement
enticingly
entireness
eosinophil
epeirogeny
equilibria
equipotent
equitation
equivalent
equivocate
estimation
estimative
ethicality
eudiometer
eudiometry
excitation
excitative
excitatory
excitement
excitingly
exhibition
exhibitory
exhilarant
exhilarate
expiration
expiratory
extinction
extinctive
extinguish
extirpator
facileness
facilitate
familiarly
famishment
fatiguable
felicitate
felicitous
feminality
femininely
femininity
feuilleton
filibuster
finicality
finiteness
foliaceous
freightage
fruitarian
fruitfully
fugitively
fuliginous
fumigation
fusibility
galimatias
garishness
gemination
genialness
geniculate
geriatrics
geriatrist
goniometer
goniometry
habiliment
habilitate
habitation
habitually
hagiolatry
hagiologic
hagioscope
halieutics
heliacally
helianthus
Heliconian
helicopter
heliograph
heliolater
heliolatry
heliometer
heliophyte
helioscope
heliotaxis
heliotrope
heliotropy
hemicyclic
hemihedral
hemihedron
hemiplegia
hemiplegic
hemipteran
hemisphere
hesitantly
hesitation
hesitative
homiletics
horizontal
humidifier
illiteracy
illiterate
imbibition
imminently
immiscible
immiscibly
impishness
incidental
incinerate
incipience
incipiency
incisively
incitation
incitement
incivility
indication
indicative
indicatory
indictable
indictment
indigenous
indigested
indirectly
indiscreet
indiscrete
indisposed
indistinct
inditement
individual
infidelity
infighting
infiltrate
infinitely
infinitive
infinitude
inhibition
inhibitory
insightful
insinuator
insipidity
insistence
insistency
intimately
intimation
intimidate
intinction
invigilate
invigorate
invincible
invincibly
inviolable
inviolably
invitation
invitatory
invitingly
iodination
ionisation
irrigation
irritation
irritative
janitorial
Jewishness
jubilantly
jubilation
judicatory
judicature
judicially
juristical
labiovelar
laminarian
lamination
lapidarian
lapidarist
lapidation
latifundia
lavishment
lavishness
legibility
legislator
legitimacy
legitimate
legitimise
legitimism
legitimist
lepidolite
levigation
levitation
lexicology
lexigraphy
libidinous
liliaceous
limitation
limitative
limitrophe
Lipizzaner
litigation
livingroom
logicality
logistical
lovingness
luciferase
luciferous
lucifugous
luminosity
luminously
Lusitanian
magistracy
magistrate
malignance
malignancy
malingerer
mamillated
maniacally
Manichaean
Manicheism
manicurist
manifestly

manifestos
manifoldly
manipulate
Mariolater
Mariolatry
marionette
maxilliped
maximalist
mediastina
mediatress
medicament
medicaster
medication
medicative
medievally
mediocrity
meditation
meditative
meliorator
melismatic
meningioma
meningitis
meridional
meticulous
militantly
militarily
militarise
militarism
militarist
militiaman
minimalism
minimalist
ministrant
mitigation
mitigative
mitigatory
modifiable
modishness
moniliasis
moniliform
monistical
monitorial
mopishness
motionless
motivation
motiveless
moviemaker
muciferous
muliebrity
mulishness
munificent
musicality
musicianly
musicology
musicpaper
musicstand
musicstool
mutilation
mutinously
nanisation
nationally
nationhood
nationless
nationwide
nativeborn
nativeness
nativistic
navigation
nidicolous
nidificate
nidifugous
nihilistic
nominalism
nominalist
nominately
nomination
nominative
noticeable
noticeably
notifiable
notionally
nubiferous
nuciferous
nucivorous
nudibranch
numismatic
oafishness
obligation
obligatory
obligingly
obliterate
occidental
officially
oleiferous
omnigenous
omnipotent
omniscient
omnivorous
oneirology
ophicleide
ophiolater
ophiolatry
ophiologic
oppilation
optimalise
optimistic
optionally
ordinarily
ordination
oscillator
oscitation
osmiridium
owlishness
pacifiable
pacificate
pacificism
pacificist
pagination
palimpsest
palindrome
palisander
paniculate
papistical
parimutuel
patination
patisserie
pediculate
pediculous
pedicurist
pedimental
pedimented
penicillin
peninsular
penitently
periclinal
pericyclic
peridermal
perigynous
perihelion
perilously
periodical
periosteal
periosteum
peripeteia
peripheral
peripteral
periscopic
perishable
perithecia
peritoneal
peritoneum
periwigged
periwinkle
petiolated
petiteness
petitioner
piliferous
pitilessly
pixillated
plainchant
podiatrist
politeness
politician
politicise
pomiferous
porismatic
positional
positively
positivism
positivist
positivity
prairiedog
pugilistic
punishable
punishment
punitively
pupilarity
pupiparous
puristical
puritanise
puritanism
pyridoxine
quaintness
radicalise
radicalism
radication
radiogenic
radiograph
radiologic
radiometer
radiometry
radiopaque
radiophone
radioscopy
radiosonde
rakishness
rationally
ravishment
recidivism
recidivist
recipiency
reciprocal
recitalist
recitation
recitative
recitativo
rediscover
refillable
refinement
regimental
regionally
registered
registrant
relievable
relinquish
relishable
remissible
remissness
remittance
resignedly
resilience
resiliency
resistance
resistible
resistless
reticently
reticulate
retinacula
retirement
retiringly
reviewable
revilement
revisional
revitalise
revivalism
revivalist
ricinoleic
ridiculous
risibility
rotisserie
rubiginous
rudimental
ruminantly
rumination
ruminative
rupicoline
rupicolous
sagination
sagittally
salicional
salicylate
salientian
saliferous
salivation
sanitarian
sanitarily
sanitarium
sanitation
sapiential
satisfying
saxicoline
saxicolous
schipperke
schismatic
schizocarp
schizogony
scribbling
scrimmager
scrimshank
scriptoria
scriptural
semiannual
semichorus
semicircle
semidivine
semidouble
semidrying
semifitted
semiliquid
semilunate
seminarian
seminarist
semination
semiopaque
semiotical
semiquaver
semiuncial
semiweekly
semiyearly
serigraphy
seriocomic
sexivalent
shrievalty
shrillness
shrinkable
shrinkwrap
shrivelled
sibilation
similarity
similitude
sinisterly
sinistrous
skrimshank
sleighbell
sluicegate
snailpaced
snailwheel
socialiser
societally
sociologic
sociometry
solicitant
solicitous
solicitude
solidarism
solidarist
solidarity
solidstate
solifidian
solitarily
splintbone
splintcoal
splitlevel
spoilsport
sprightful
springhalt
springhead
springless
springlike
springtail
springtide
springtime
springwood
sprinkling
squinteyed
squirarchy
squirearch
squirehood
squireling
squireship
strictness
stridently
stridulant
stridulate
stridulous
strikingly
stringbean
stringency
stringendo
stringhalt
stringless
striptease
supination
supineness
taciturnly
takingness
talismanic
taxidancer
taxidermal
taxidermic
tepidarium
theistical
thriftless
tiringroom
titivation
topicality
toxication
toxicology
toxiphobia
traitorous
tubicolous
typicality
ultimately
umbilicate
umbiliform
umpireship
unbiblical
unbiddable
undigested
unfilially
unfinished
unhistoric
unkindness
unlikeness
unripeness
unrivalled
untidiness
unwieldily
unyielding
uppishness
urticarial
urtication
validation
varicocele
varicosity
variegated
varietally
variolitic
variometer
Vaticanism
Vaticanist
vaticinate
velitation
venialness
verifiable
vesication
vesicatory
vesiculate
vigilantly
visibility
Visigothic
visionally
visionless
visitation
visitorial
vitiligate
viviparity
viviparous
vivisector
viziership
vociferant
vociferate
vociferous
volitional
vomitorium
conjecture
conjointly
conjugally
disjointed
misjoinder
nonjoinder
panjandrum
perjurious
prejudiced
projectile
projection
projective
serjeantcy
skijumping
skyjacking
subjectify
subjection
subjective
subjugator
trajection
trajectory
Ashkenazim
backbiting
backblocks
backgammon
background
backhanded
backhander
backsheesh
backslider
backstairs
backstitch
backstroke
backwardly
bankruptcy
barkentine
basketball
basketwork
beekeeping
Berkeleian
bookbinder
bookkeeper
bookmaking
bookmarker
bookseller
brakeblock
brakelight
brokendown
brokenness

bucketshop
cackhanded
cankerworm
chokeberry
cockalorum
cockatrice
cockchafer
cockneyish
cockneyism
cocksurely
cuckoopint
cuckoospit
dickcissel
Dickensian
donkeywork
fecklessly
fickleness
folklorist
folkmemory
folksiness
folksinger
hackbuteer
hackmatack
hankypanky
hookedness
hucklebone
jackanapes
jackassery
jackhammer
jackknives
jackrabbit
Kafkaesque
kookaburra
lacklustre
leukocytic
lockerroom
lockkeeper
lockstitch
mackintosh
marketable
markethall
markettown
markswoman
mockheroic
monkeysuit
muskmallow
nickelling
packingbox
packsaddle
packthread
pickaninny
picketline
pickpocket
pocketable
pocketbook
pocketsize
pockmarked
rackrenter
recklessly
rickettsia
rockabilly
rockbadger
rockbottom
rockgarden
rockhopper
rockpigeon
rockrabbit
rockribbed
sicklebill
sickliness
silkcotton
silkscreen
smokedried
smokehouse
smokeplant
smokeproof
smokestack
snakedance
snakestone
spokeshave
subkingdom
tackdriver
tankengine
taskmaster
tickertape
ticklishly
turkeycock
weakliness
weakminded
wickedness
wickerwork
workbasket
workingman
workpeople
addlepated
adolescent
Adullamite
adulterant
adulterate
adulteress
adulterine
adulterous
aeolotropy
affliction
afflictive
affluently
agglutinin
amalgamate
ameliorate
amylaceous
analogical
analphabet
analysable
analytical
Anglistics
anglomania
anglophile
anglophobe
anglophone
AngloSaxon
apolaustic
apolitical
Apollinian
Apollonian
apologetic
applicable
applicably
applicator
ateleiosis
ballflower
ballistics
ballooning
balloonist
barleybree
barleybroo
barleycorn
Bedlington
belladonna
belletrist
bellflower
bellringer
bellwether
bellyacher
bellydance
bellylaugh
biblically
bibliology
bibliopegy
bibliophil
bibliopole
bibliopoly
bibliotics
billetdoux
billposter
biological
bollweevil
brilliance
brilliancy
bullethead
bullheaded
bullroarer
byelection
callowness
cellophane
cellularly
cellulitis
cellulosic
chalcedony
chalkboard
chalkstone
challenger
chalybeate
chelicerae
childbirth
childermas
childishly
childproof
chiliastic
chilliness
coalbunker
coalescent
coelacanth
collarbeam
collarbone
collarette
collarless
collarstud
collatable
collateral
collection
collective
collegiate
collembola
collimator
collocutor
colloquial
colloquise
colloquist
colloquium
coolheaded
coolingoff
coulometry
cyclically
cyclograph
cyclometer
cyclopedia
cyclopedic
cyclostome
cyclostyle
declarable
declassify
declension
declinable
deflagrate
deflection
deflective
deflowerer
deplorable
deplorably
deployment
dialysable
dielectric
dillydally
diplodocus
diplomatic
dislikable
disloyally
disloyalty
duplicator
ebullience
ebulliency
ebullition
ecclesiast
ecological
edulcorate
effloresce
emblazoner
emblazonry
emblematic
emblements
emollition
employable
employment
emulsifier
Englishman
englutting
epilimnion
evaluation
evaluative
evilminded
evolvement
exaltation
explicable
explicitly
exploitage
exploitive
exulcerate
exultantly
exultation
exultingly
fallacious
fallingoff
fallowness
faultiness
fellmonger
fellowship
fieldglass
fieldmouse
fieldpiece
fieldstone
follicular
fowlplague
frilliness
frolicking
frolicsome
fullbodied
fullbottom
fulllength
gaillardia
galleywest
galliambic
galloglass
Gallomania
Gallophile
Gallophobe
gaslighter
gaultheria
geological
girlfriend
goalkeeper
goaltender
guilefully
guillotine
guiltiness
hallelujah
hellbender
heulandite
holloweyed
hollowness
hollowware
hullabaloo
hurlyburly
hyaloplasm
idolatress
idolatrous
implacable
implacably
implicitly
inclemency
inclinable
includible
inelegance
ineligible
ineligibly
ineloquent
ineludible
inflatable
inflection
inflective
inflexible
inflexibly
infliction
inflictive
inglorious
isolatable
italianate
italianise
Italianism
Italophile
Lollardism
malleebird
malleefowl
mallenders
mealbeetle
mellowness
millefiori
millennial
millennium
millesimal
millilitre
millimetre
millstream
millwright
molluscoid
molluscous
mouldboard
mouldiness
mulligrubs
myological
nailpolish
neglectful
negligence
negligible
negligibly
neological
noblewoman
nonlogical
nucleation
nucleonics
nucleoside
nucleotide
nullanulla
ocellation
ochlocracy
offlicence
opalescent
orological
outlandish
palladious
pallbearer
palliation
palliative
palliatory
pallidness
parliament
pellagrous
pellicular
pellucidly
phalangeal
phallicism
phelloderm
philatelic
philippina
philippine
philistine
phillumeny
philologen
philopoena
philosophe
philosophy
phylactery
phyllotaxy
phylloxera
phylogenic
pilliwinks
pillowcase
pillowlace
pillowslip
pollenosis
pollinator
prelatical
prelection
prolicidal
prolocutor
prologuise
prolongate
psalmodise
psalmodist
psalterium
psilocybin
Ptolemaist
publishing
qualmishly
railroader
railwayman
realisable
reallocate
reelection
reeligible
reflection
reflective
reflexible
rollcollar
rollicking
rollingpin
sailorless
sallenders
sallowness
scaleboard
Scillonian
sculptress
sculptural
sculptured
sealingwax
secludedly
sexlimited
shellacked
shellmound
shellproof
shellshock
shillelagh
sialagogic
sialagogue
sillybilly
smallscale
smallsword
smallwares
smelliness
soullessly
spallation
speleology
spellbound
spillikins
spoliation
spoliative
spoliatory
stalactite
stalagmite
stalwartly
stelliform
stilettoes
stillbirth
stillicide
stolidness
stylistics
stylograph
subletting
sublimable
subliminal
sublingual
sullenness
sweltering
syllabaria
syllogiser

tablecloth
tablelinen
tablespoon
tailorbird
tailormade
tellership
thalecress
thillhorse
toilsomely
tollbridge
trilateral
trilingual
triliteral
trillionth
trolleybus
trollopish
twelvefold
twelvenote
twelvetone
twilighted
unblenched
unblinking
unblushing
uncloister
unflagging
unilateral
unilingual
unilocular
unpleasant
unpleasing
utilisable
valleculae
vallecular
villainage
villainess
villainous
villanelle
villeinage
violaceous
volleyball
wallflower
wallpepper
wellheeled
wellington
wellspoken
wellspring
wellturned
wellwisher
whaleshark
wholesaler
willowherb
willynilly
willywilly
woolgather
woolgrower
woolliness
woolsorter
worldclass
worldweary
Wycliffite
yellowback
yellowbird
yellowness
yellowwood
yieldingly
zollverein
zoological
abominable
abominably
abominator
adamantine
airmanship
alimentary
anamorphic
anemograph
anemometer
anemometry
anemophily
animadvert
animalcula
animalcule
animatedly
asymmetric
asymptotic
atomically
Barmecidal
bigmouthed
biometrics
biomorphic
blamefully
bromegrass
carmagnole
chamaeleon
chamberpot
champignon
chemically
chemisette
chemotaxis
chimerical
chimneypot
chimpanzee
cismontane
clamminess
clementine
clumsiness
commandant
commandeer
commandery
commanding
commandoes
commentary
commentate
commercial
commissary
commission
commissure
commitment
committing
commixture
commodious
commonable
commonalty
commonness
commonroom
commonweal
communally
communique
commutable
commutator
cosmically
cosmogonic
cosmopolis
cosmoramic
crematoria
criminally
cummerbund
curmudgeon
dermatitis
dermatogen
dismalness
dismission
dismissive
dogmatical
dogmatiser
dramatical
dramaturge
dramaturgy
duumvirate
ecumenical
elementary
eliminable
eliminator
enamelling
enamellist
enumerable
enumerator
eremitical
examinable
flamboyant
flameproof
flamingoes
flimsiness
foamflower
formatting
formidable
formidably
formlessly
framboesia
gemmaceous
geometrise
germicidal
germinally
glimmering
glomerular
glomerulus
glumaceous
gormandise
gramicidin
gramineous
grammarian
gramophone
grumpiness
haematosis
haematuria
haemolysis
haemolytic
hammerbeam
hammerhead
hammerless
hammerlock
hammerpond
harmlessly
harmonical
harmonious
harmoniser
helminthic
hermetical
hermitcrab
hormonally
inimically
inimitable
inimitably
Ishmaelite
isometrics
isomorphic
Kuomintang
Lammastide
mesmeriser
midmorning
mismatched
mismeasure
oldmaidish
outmeasure
palmaceous
palmatifid
palmbutter
palmerworm
PalmSunday
pegmatitic
penmanship
permafrost
permanence
permanency
permeation
permeative
permission
permissive
permitting
permutable
pigmentary
plumassier
premarital
premaxilla
premedical
premonitor
primevally
primiparae
primordial
primordium
promenader
promethium
prominence
promissory
promontory
promptbook
promptness
promulgate
pummelling
rhomboidal
rhomboidei
salmagundi
salmonella
salmonleap
sarmentose
sarmentous
seamanlike
seamanship
seamstress
seemliness
segmentary
sermoniser
shamefaced
shamefully
skimpiness
slumberful
slumberous
spumescent
stimulator
stomachful
stomatitis
stomatopod
stomodaeum
stumpiness
submariner
submediant
submersion
submission
submissive
submitting
submontane
summerlike
summertime
summitless
summonable
surmisable
swimmingly
symmetrise
Talmudical
tarmacadam
termagancy
terminable
terminably
terminally
terminator
termitaria
themselves
thimbleful
thimblerig
thumbprint
thumbscrew
thumbstall
trammelled
tramontana
tramontane
trampoline
tremendous
tremolitic
trimonthly
trimorphic
trombonist
tromometer
unAmerican
unemphatic
unemployed
unimproved
vermicelli
vermicidal
vermicular
warmingpan
weimaraner
whomsoever
zoomorphic
abundantly
adenectomy
alongshore
amanuenses
amanuensis
amendatory
anonaceous
arenaceous
asynchrony
avantgarde
aventurine
balneology
biannually
biennially
blancmange
blanketing
blanquette
blindingly
boondoggle
bouncingly
branchiate
brandyball
brandysnap
brantgoose
brentgoose
bronchiole
bronchitic
bronchitis
cannelloni
cannonball
carnallite
carnassial
chancellor
chandelier
changeable
changeably
changeless
changeling
changeover
channelise
channelled
chinagraph
chinchilla
chondritic
clangorous
clannishly
clingstone
clinically
clinkstone
clinometer
clinometry
coenobitic
coenobytic
cognisable
cognisably
cognisance
cognominal
coincident
connatural
connection
connective
conniption
connivance
corncockle
cornerwise
cornettist
cornflakes
cornflower
cornstarch
cornucopia
councillor
councilman
counselled
counsellor
counteract
countryish
countryman
cranesbill
craniology
crankiness
crankshaft
crenellate
crenulated
crinolette
ctenophore
daintiness
deontology
dinnerless
donnybrook
downfallen
downstairs
downstream
downstroke
downwardly
economical
economiser
edentulous
elongation
emancipate
emancipist
emendation
emendatory
enantiosis
enunciable
enunciator
epentheses
epenthesis
epenthetic
ethnically
ethnologic
evanescent
evangelise
evangelism
evangelist
evenhanded
eventually
exenterate
faintheart
fianchetto
fiendishly
FinnoUgric
flannelled
flintiness
flunkeydom
flunkeyism
fornicator
foundation
founderous
franchiser
Franciscan
Francophil
frangipane
frangipani
Frenchness
frenziedly
fringeless
frontbench
frontwards
funnelling
gaingiving
garnierite
garnishing
gauntleted
glancingly
granadilla
grandchild
granddaddy
grandducal
grandmamma
grandniece
grandstand
granduncle

gra**n**gerise
gra**n**gerism
gra**n**ophyre
gra**n**ularly
gra**n**ulator
gra**n**ulitic
gre**n**adilla
gri**n**dingly
gri**n**dstone
gym**n**astics
gym**n**osophy
gym**n**osperm
hau**n**tingly
hob**n**obbing
hor**n**blende
hor**n**edness
hor**n**rimmed
hyp**n**agogic
hyp**n**otiser
ico**n**oclasm
ico**n**olater
ico**n**olatry
ico**n**omachy
ico**n**ometer
ico**n**ometry
ico**n**oscope
ila**n**gilang
ill**n**atured
inu**n**dation
inu**n**datory
iro**n**handed
iro**n**ically
iro**n**master
iro**n**monger
iro**n**worker
ise**n**tropic
iso**n**iazide
iti**n**erancy
jau**n**tiness
joh**n**nycake
Joh**n**sonese
joh**n**sonian
ken**n**elling
kid**n**apping
kin**n**ikinic
lau**n**dryman
law**n**tennis
lem**n**iscate
lio**n**hunter
lou**n**gesuit
mag**n**etiser
mag**n**ifical
mag**n**ificat
mag**n**ifying
mai**n**lander
mai**n**spring
mai**n**stream
mai**n**tainer
mea**n**ingful
mig**n**onette
mis**n**omered
moo**n**flower
moo**n**shiner
moo**n**struck
mou**n**tebank
non**n**atural
non**n**uclear
odo**n**talgia
odo**n**tology
ope**n**handed
ope**n**hearth
ope**n**minded
opi**n**ionist
ora**n**gepeel
ora**n**gewood
pai**n**killer
pai**n**lessly
pai**n**tbrush
Par**n**assian
paw**n**broker
pen**n**aceous
pen**n**anular
pen**n**illion
pen**n**yroyal
pen**n**yworth
per**n**icious
per**n**ickety
pha**n**erogam
pha**n**tasise
pha**n**tasmal
pha**n**tasmic
pha**n**tastic
pha**n**tastry
phe**n**acetin
phe**n**ocryst
phe**n**omenal
phe**n**omenon
phe**n**otypic
pho**n**ematic
pho**n**ically
pho**n**ograph
pho**n**olitic
pho**n**ologic
pho**n**ometer
pia**n**issimo
pia**n**oforte
pic**n**icking
pin**n**atifid
pin**n**ulated
pla**n**chette
pla**n**etable
pla**n**etaria
pla**n**gently
pla**n**igraph
pla**n**imeter
pla**n**imetry
pla**n**ktonic
pla**n**ometer
pla**n**tation
pla**n**tlouse
plu**n**derage
plu**n**derous
poi**n**settia
poi**n**tblank
por**n**ocracy
pou**n**cetbox
pra**n**cingly
pri**n**celing
pri**n**ceship
pri**n**cipate
pri**n**cipial
pri**n**cipium
pri**n**cipled
pro**n**ominal
pro**n**ounced
pro**n**ouncer
pug**n**acious
pyc**n**ogonid
pyc**n**ometer
pyc**n**ostyle
pyk**n**ometer
qua**n**tifier
qua**n**titive
que**n**chable
que**n**chless
qui**n**acrine
qui**n**tuplet
rai**n**making
ree**n**trance
reu**n**ionism
reu**n**ionist
rhi**n**estone
rhi**n**oceros
rhi**n**oscope
rhi**n**oscopy
rou**n**dabout
rou**n**dhouse
run**n**erbean
sca**n**dalise
sca**n**dalous
sca**n**sorial
sca**n**tiness
sce**n**ically
sha**n**drydan
sha**n**dygaff
sha**n**ghaier
sha**n**tytown
she**n**anigan
sig**n**alling
sig**n**writer
ski**n**diving
ski**n**niness
sla**n**derous
sla**n**giness
sla**n**tingly
sle**n**derise
som**n**iloquy
som**n**olence
som**n**olency
sou**n**dboard
sou**n**dingly
sou**n**dproof
sou**n**dtrack
spa**n**kingly
Spe**n**cerian
Spe**n**serian
spi**n**escent
spo**n**gecake
spo**n**gewood
spo**n**giform
spo**n**giness
spo**n**gology
spo**n**sorial
spu**n**kiness
sta**n**chless
sta**n**chness
sta**n**dpoint
sta**n**dstill
ste**n**chtrap
ste**n**cilled
ste**n**ciller
ste**n**ograph
ste**n**torian
sti**n**giness
sti**n**gingly
sti**n**kingly
sti**n**kstone
sto**n**eblind
sto**n**eborer
sto**n**ebrash
sto**n**efruit
sto**n**emason
sto**n**esnipe
stu**n**ningly
sub**n**uclear
swa**n**maiden
swa**n**upping
swi**n**efever
swi**n**gingly
swi**n**glebar
tau**n**tingly
tee**n**yweeny
ter**n**eplate
tha**n**kfully
thi**n**kingly
thi**n**kpiece
thu**n**derbox
thu**n**dering
thu**n**derous
tow**n**swoman
tra**n**celike
tra**n**quilly
tra**n**sactor
tra**n**scribe
tra**n**script
tra**n**sducer
tra**n**septal
tra**n**sferee
tra**n**sferor
tra**n**sfuser
tra**n**sgress
tra**n**sience
tra**n**siency
tra**n**sistor
tra**n**sition
tra**n**sitive
tra**n**sitory
tra**n**slator
tra**n**slucid
tra**n**slunar
tra**n**smuter
tra**n**splant
tra**n**sposal
tra**n**sposer
tra**n**sshape
tra**n**svalue
tra**n**sverse
tre**n**chancy
tre**n**diness
tru**n**cately
tru**n**cation
tru**n**dlebed
tun**n**elling
tur**n**buckle
une**n**dingly
une**n**viable
uni**n**formed
uni**n**itiate
unk**n**owable
ura**n**ometry
ver**n**acular
ver**n**issage
vig**n**ettist
vul**n**erable
vul**n**erably
wai**n**wright
whe**n**soever
wit**n**essbox
wro**n**gdoing
wro**n**gfully
wro**n**gously
yla**n**gylang
you**n**gberry
abd**o**minous
abh**o**rrence
abi**o**genist
abn**o**rmally
abr**o**gation
abs**o**lutely
abs**o**lution
abs**o**lutism
abs**o**lutist
abs**o**lutory
abs**o**rbable
abs**o**rbance
abs**o**rbedly
abs**o**rbency
abs**o**rption
abs**o**rptive
acc**o**mplice
acc**o**mplish
acc**o**rdance
acc**o**ucheur
acc**o**untant
acc**o**unting
ach**o**ndrite
acr**o**batics
acr**o**genous
acr**o**megaly
acr**o**nychal
acr**o**phobia
acr**o**terion
acr**o**terium
adm**o**nition
adm**o**nitive
adm**o**nitory
adr**o**itness
ads**o**rbable
ads**o**rption
ads**o**rptive
adv**o**cation
adv**o**catory
aer**o**batics
aer**o**biosis
aer**o**biotic
aer**o**engine
aer**o**gramme
aer**o**graphy
aer**o**logist
aer**o**nautic
aer**o**nomist
aer**o**phobia
aer**o**static
aff**o**rdable
agr**o**logist
agr**o**nomist
alc**o**holise
alc**o**holism
alg**o**lagnia
alg**o**lagnic
alg**o**logist
Alg**o**nquian
all**o**cation
all**o**cution
all**o**gamous
all**o**pathic
all**o**phonic
all**o**steric
all**o**tropic
all**o**verish
alm**o**ndeyed
alt**o**cumuli
alt**o**gether
alt**o**strati
amm**o**niacal
amm**o**niated
ann**o**tation
ann**o**yingly
ant**o**nymous
aph**o**ristic
app**o**intive
app**o**sitely
app**o**sition
app**o**sitive
arb**o**really
arb**o**rvitae
are**o**lation
Are**o**pagite
arm**o**rially
arm**o**urclad
arm**o**urless
arr**o**gantly
arr**o**gation
asc**o**mycete
ass**o**ciable
ass**o**ilment
ass**o**rtment
atm**o**sphere
att**o**rnment
aut**o**chthon
aut**o**cratic
aut**o**didact
aut**o**erotic
aut**o**gamous
aut**o**genous
aut**o**graphy
aut**o**immune
aut**o**logous
aut**o**mation
aut**o**matise
aut**o**matism
aut**o**matist
aut**o**mobile
aut**o**motive
aut**o**nomist
aut**o**nomous
aut**o**plasty
aut**o**strada
aut**o**strade
axi**o**logist
aze**o**tropic
bar**o**metric
bar**o**netage
bec**o**mingly
bef**o**rehand
bef**o**retime
bel**o**ngings
bid**o**nville
bij**o**uterie
bil**o**cation
bin**o**culars
bip**o**larity
biv**o**uacked
blo**o**dguilt
blo**o**dhound
blo**o**diness
blo**o**dmoney
blo**o**dstain
blo**o**dstock
blo**o**dstone
bol**o**metric
bro**o**diness
bro**o**dingly
bro**o**mstick
bry**o**logist
cac**o**daemon
cac**o**genics
cac**o**graphy
cac**o**mistle
caj**o**lement
caj**o**lingly
cam**o**uflage
can**o**nicals
can**o**nicate
can**o**nicity
can**o**rously
car**o**tenoid
car**o**tinoid
cat**o**ptrics
cer**o**graphy
chl**o**rinate
chl**o**roform
chr**o**matics
chr**o**matype
chr**o**mosome
chr**o**nicity
chr**o**nicler
chr**o**nogram
chr**o**nology
col**o**nially
col**o**nnaded
col**o**ration
col**o**ratura
col**o**ssally
col**o**urable
col**o**urably
col**o**urfast
col**o**urless
cor**o**mandel
cor**o**nation
cry**o**genics
cry**o**scopic
cyt**o**chrome
cyt**o**logist
deb**o**nairly
deb**o**uchure
dec**o**lonise
dec**o**lorant
dec**o**lorise
dec**o**mpound
dec**o**mpress
dec**o**ration
dec**o**rative
dec**o**rously

defoliator
deforciant
delocalise
demobilise
democratic
demography
demoiselle
demolition
demonetise
demoniacal
demonology
demoralise
demotivate
denominate
denotation
denotative
denouement
depolarise
depopulate
deportment
depositary
deposition
depository
derogation
derogatory
desolately
desolation
desorption
detonation
detonative
detoxicant
detoxicate
devocalise
devolution
devotement
devotional
devoutness
dimorphism
dimorphous
disordered
disorderly
disownment
dolomitise
dolorously
doxography
droopingly
ectodermal
ectodermic
ectogenous
effortless
embodiment
embolismic
embonpoint
embossment
embouchure
embowelled
encourager
endocrinal
endodermal
endodermis
endogamous
endogenous
endophytic
endopodite
endorsable
endoscopic
endosmosis
endosmotic
endothelia
enjoinment
entombment
entomology
ephorality
ergodicity
ergonomics
ergonomist
ergosterol
ethologist
etiolation
eulogistic
Eurodollar
Eurovision
excogitate
exportable
exposition
expositive
expository
famousness
favourable
favourably
floodlight
floodwater
floorboard
floorcloth
fluoridate
fluorinate
fluorotype
gadolinite
gadolinium
gloominess
goloptious
gynocratic
gyrocopter
gyroscopic
halogenate
halogenous
halophytic
Hanoverian
hedonistic
henotheism
henotheist
heroically
heroicness
heroicomic
holography
holohedral
holophrase
holophytic
holosteric
homocercal
homoeopath
homogamous
homogenise
homogenous
homologate
homologise
homologous
homonymous
homoousian
homophonic
homosexual
homozygote
homozygous
honorarium
honourable
honourably
honourless
horologist
horoscopic
humoresque
humoristic
humorously
humourless
humoursome
hylotheism
hypocorism
hypodermal
hypodermic
hypodermis
hypogynous
hypolimnia
hypophyses
hypophysis
hypostasis
hypostatic
hypotactic
hypotenuse
hypotheses
hypothesis
ideography
ideologist
idiopathic
ignobility
ignorantly
immobilise
immobility
immoderacy
immoderate
immodestly
immolation
immoralist
immorality
immortally
immortelle
immoveable
impolitely
importable
importance
importuner
imposingly
imposition
impossible
impossibly
imposthume
impotently
impoverish
incogitant
incoherent
incomplete
inconstant
indocility
indolently
Indonesian
informally
innocently
innominate
innovation
innovative
innovatory
insobriety
insociable
insolation
insolently
insolvable
insolvency
insouciant
intolerant
intonation
intoxicant
intoxicate
invocation
invocatory
involucral
involucrum
involution
ionosphere
jacobinise
Jacobinism
Jacobitism
Jehovistic
jocoseness
joyousness
kilogramme
laboratory
laconicism
lemongrass
lipography
lipomatous
locomotion
locomotive
locomotory
logography
logorrhoea
loxodromic
lycopodium
Mahommedan
malodorous
manoeuvrer
manoeuvres
manometric
manorhouse
mavourneen
mayonnaise
memorandum
menopausal
Mesolithic
mesomerism
mesomorphy
mesophytic
mesoscaphe
mesosphere
mesothorax
misogamist
misogynist
misogynous
misologist
mixolydian
mobocratic
monocarpic
monochasia
monochrome
monoclinal
monoclinic
monocratic
monocyclic
monoecious
monogamist
monogamous
monogenism
monogynian
monogynous
monohybrid
monohydric
monolithic
monologise
monologist
monomaniac
monophonic
monopodial
monopodium
monopolise
monopolist
monorhymed
monotheism
monotheist
monotonous
monovalent
moroseness
motorcycle
mycologist
mycoplasma
mycorrhiza
myxomatous
myxomycete
nanosecond
negotiable
negotiator
nicotinism
nomography
nomologist
nomothetic
nosography
nosologist
nosophobia
notonectal
octodecimo
octonarian
octopodous
odiousness
oecologist
oenologist
oesophagus
oleography
oncogenous
oncologist
ontologist
opposeless
oppositely
opposition
ordonnance
Ordovician
oreography
oreologist
otioseness
panopticon
paronymous
paroxysmal
paroxytone
pedologist
pejoration
pejorative
penologist
peroration
peroxidise
phlogistic
phlogiston
phlogopite
picosecond
pilothouse
pilotlight
pilotwhale
pleochroic
pleonastic
pogonology
pogonotomy
pomologist
porousness
proofsheet
pyrogallol
pyrogenous
pyrography
pyrolusite
pyromaniac
pyromantic
pyrometric
pyrophoric
pyrotechny
pyroxenite
razorblade
razorshell
recolonise
recommence
recompense
reconciler
reconsider
recordable
recoupment
redolently
reformable
rejoicings
relocation
remodelled
remonetise
remorseful
remoteness
renovation
repopulate
reportable
reportedly
reposition
repository
resolutely
resolution
resolutive
resolvable
resolvedly
resonantly
resorcinol
resorption
resorptive
resounding
revocation
revocatory
revolution
rheologist
rheotropic
riboflavin
rigorously
ritornelli
ritornello
savourless
scholastic
schoolable
schoolbook
schooldays
schoolgirl
schoolmaam
schoolmarm
schoolmate
schoolroom
schooltime
schoolwork
sciolistic
scrofulous
scrollwork
seborrhoea
secondbest
secondhand
secondment
secondrate
serologist
serotinous
sexologist
shroudlaid
shroudless
Shrovetide
simoniacal
sinologist
sitophobia
smoothbore
smoothness
snootiness
sonorously
sororicide
spookiness
spoondrift
spoonerism
Stroganoff
stromatous
stronghold
strongroom
suborbital
subordinal
sycophancy
synoecious
synonymist
synonymity
synonymous
synoptical
synostosis
tapotement
taxonomist
theocratic
theodicean
theodolite
theogonist
theologian
theologise
theologist
theophanic
theophoric
theopneust
theoretics
theosopher
throatwort
thromboses
thrombosis
thrombotic
throneless
throughout
throughput
throughway
throwstick
timocratic

timorously
tobogganer
tocopherol
tomography
topography
topologist
toroidally
trioecious
tutorially
typography
typologist
unbonneted
uncommonly
unforeseen
unholiness
unhouseled
unionistic
unmorality
unmortised
unsociable
unsociably
unsocially
untowardly
unwontedly
unworkable
unworthily
upholstery
uproarious
valorously
vaporiform
vaporously
vasoactive
velocipede
venomously
vigorously
virologist
wagonvault
xenophobia
xerography
xerophytic
xylography
xylophonic
zygodactyl
zygomorphy
acephalous
adaptation
adaptively
adoptively
agapanthus
allpurpose
anapaestic
anaplastic
anaptyctic
anopheline
apophthegm
apoplectic
atypically
auspicious
besprinkle
biophysics
blepharism
bumpkinish
campaigner
campestral
camphorate
cappuccino
carpellary
carpetweed
carphology
chaparajos
chaparejos
chapfallen
chaplaincy
cispontine
coaptation
colportage
colporteur
compaction
comparable
comparably
comparator
comparison
compassion
compasssaw
compatible
compatibly
compatriot
compelling
compendium
compensate
competence
competency
competitor
complacent
complainer
complected
complement
completely
completion
completive
complexion
complexity
compliance
compliancy
complicacy
complicate
complicity
compliment
complotted
composedly
compositor
compotator
compounder
compradore
comprehend
compressed
compressor
compromise
compulsion
compulsive
compulsory
computable
computator
cooperator
cooptation
cooptative
copperhead
corporally
corporator
corporeity
corpulence
corpulency
corpuscule
couplement
cowparsley
cowpuncher
crapulence
crepuscule
crippledom
cryptogamy
cryptogram
cryptology
cuspidated
dampcourse
dampingoff
dapplegrey
dauphiness
deepfreeze
deepfrozen
deeprooted
deepseated
delphinium
delphinoid
despatcher
desperados
despicable
despicably
despisable
despiteful
despiteous
despondent
diapedesis
diapedetic
diaphanous
disparager
disparates
dispassion
dispatcher
dispelling
dispensary
dispersant
dispersion
dispersive
dispersoid
dispirited
dispiteous
disposable
dispossess
dispraiser
disputable
disputably
drophammer
drupaceous
dysplastic
dysprosium
Egyptology
endproduct
epiphytism
eruptively
evaporable
evaporator
flapdoodle
flippantly
floppiness
gaspereaux
geophysics
geoponical
grapefruit
grapesugar
graphemics
graphitise
graphology
graptolite
helplessly
hempnettle
hippocampi
Hippocrene
hippodrome
hippogriff
hippogryph
hippomanes
hippophagy
hospitable
hospitably
humpbacked
inappetent
inapposite
inaptitude
ineptitude
inoperable
inspanning
inspection
inspective
inspirator
inspissate
isopterous
jasperware
jeopardise
knopkierie
lampoonery
lampoonist
leopardess
limpidness
Lippizaner
lowpitched
lowprofile
lumpsucker
lymphocyte
lymphomata
lyophilise
Malpighian
misprision
morphemics
morphinism
morphogeny
morphology
myopically
Neapolitan
neoplastic
nipplewort
nitpicking
nonpayment
nonplaying
nonplussed
nympholept
offputting
omophagous
outpatient
outpouring
outputting
ovipositor
pemphigoid
pemphigous
penpushing
peppercorn
peppermill
peppermint
pepperwort
perpetrate
perpetuate
perpetuity
perplexity
pluperfect
prepackage
preparator
preparedly
prepayable
prepayment
prepensely
prepossess
prepotence
prepotency
propagable
propaganda
propagator
propellant
propellent
propelling
propensity
properness
propertied
prophesier
prophetess
propionate
propitiate
propitious
proportion
propounder
propraetor
proprietor
propulsion
propulsive
propylaeum
psephology
purposeful
rampageous
rapporteur
reappraise
respectful
respecting
respective
respirable
respirator
respondent
responsive
responsory
rhapsodise
rhapsodist
ripplemark
salpingian
sappanwood
sapphirine
scapegrace
scepticism
scyphiform
scyphozoan
sempstress
serpentine
sexpartite
shipbroker
shipfitter
shipmaster
shiprigged
shipwright
shopkeeper
shoplifter
shopsoiled
shopwalker
shopwindow
simpleness
simplicity
simplifier
simplistic
slipperily
slipstitch
slipstream
sloppiness
snapdragon
snappishly
soapboiler
soapbubble
soapflakes
staphyline
stepfather
stephanite
stepladder
stepmother
stepparent
stepsister
stipellate
stipulator
stopvolley
stupendous
stupidness
stypticity
sulphonate
sulphurate
sulphurise
sulphurous
sunparlour
supperless
supplanter
supplejack
supplement
suppleness
suppletion
suppletive
suppletory
suppliance
supplicant
supplicate
supportive
supposable
supposably
supposedly
suppressor
surplusage
surprising
suspenders
suspension
suspensive
suspensoid
suspensory
suspicious
sympathise
symphonion
symphonist
symphylous
symphyseal
symphysial
symposiast
teaplanter
telpherage
temperable
temperance
temperedly
temporally
temporalty
temporiser
temptation
temptingly
ticpolonga
torpidness
trappiness
trepanning
tripartite
triphammer
triphthong
triplicate
triplicity
tropaeolum
trophology
tropically
tropologic
tropopause
tropophyte
tryptophan
turpentine
tympanites
tympanitic
tympanitis
unipartite
unsporting
utopianism
vesperbell
vespertine
wampumpeag
wappenshaw
weaponless
whipstitch
wraparound
zoophagous
zoophilous
adequately
chequebook
cinquefoil
coequality
craquelure
desquamate
disqualify
disquieten
disquietly
eloquently
frequenter
frequently
inequality
iniquitous
marquisate
masquerade
mosquitoes
opaqueness
pasquinade
perquisite
triquetrae
triquetral
ubiquitous
unequalled
uniqueness
vanquisher
abbreviate
aberdevine
aberrantly
aberration
aboriginal

abortively
acarpelous
accredited
accrescent
acervation
achromatic
aggrandise
aggression
aggressive
alarmingly
allrounder
altruistic
amercement
amerciable
Amerindian
anarchical
androecium
androgenic
aphrodisia
appreciate
apprentice
approvable
approvably
ascribable
ascription
astragalus
astringent
astrologer
astrologic
astronomer
astronomic
attractant
attraction
attractive
avaricious
averseness
aversively
barracouta
barramunda
barramundi
barratrous
barrelling
barrenness
barrenwort
batrachian
bedraggled
blurringly
botryoidal
bourbonism
bourbonist
burramundi
Caerphilly
capricious
carragheen
carryingon
charactery
chargeable
chargehand
charioteer
charismata
charitable
charitably
Charleston
charmingly
chartreuse
chartulary
chersonese
chiromancy
choriambic
churchgoer
churchyard
churlishly
citronella
clarabella
Clarenceux
clerestory
clerically
coarseness
coercively
coordinate
coproducer
coprolitic
correction
corrective
correspond
corrigenda
corrigible
corrivalry
corroboree
corrugated
corrugator
corruption
corruptive
courageous
courthouse
cuirassier
curricular
curriculum
czarevitch
decrescent
deerforest
defrayable
defrayment
degradable
degradedly
degressive
depravedly
depreciate
depredator
depressant
depression
depressive
deprivable
detraction
detractive
diarrhoeal
diarrhoeic
digression
digressive
disrespect
disruption
disruptive
ditriglyph
doorkeeper
dwarfishly
effrontery
emarginate
embroidery
embryogeny
embryology
embryonate
emeryboard
emerypaper
emerywheel
encroacher
energetics
enervation
enervative
engrossing
enormously
entrancing
entrapment
enwrapping
escritoire
eternalise
eternalist
everglades
everliving
everyplace
everything
everywhere
excrescent
excruciate
exorbitant
expressage
expression
expressive
expressway
exprobrate
extractant
extraction
extractive
extramural
extraneity
extraneous
extricable
exurbanite
fabricator
Fahrenheit
fairground
fairhaired
fairleader
fairminded
fairspoken
fairycycle
fearlessly
fearnought
fearsomely
febrifugal
fibreboard
fibreglass
fibrillary
fibrillate
fibrillose
fibrinogen
fibrositis
fierceness
flirtation
florentine
florescent
floriation
floribunda
floridness
florilegia
floristics
fourchette
fourfooted
fourhanded
Fourierism
fourinhand
fourleaved
fourposter
foursquare
fourstroke
fourteener
fourteenth
gadrooning
gloriously
guardhouse
gunrunning
hairraiser
hairspring
hairstreak
hairstroke
heartblock
heartblood
heartbreak
heartiness
heartsease
heartthrob
heartwhole
Hebraistic
heortology
herrenvolk
Herrnhuter
heuristics
hierarchal
hierarchic
hierocracy
hieroglyph
hierograph
hierolatry
hierophant
hoarseness
horrendous
horridness
hourcircle
hybridiser
hydraulics
hydrically
hydrologic
hydrolysis
hydrolytic
hydromancy
hydrometer
hydrometry
hydropathy
hydrophane
hydrophily
hydrophone
hydrophyte
hydroplane
hydroscope
hydrotaxis
hygrograph
hygrometer
hygrometry
hygrophyte
hygroscope
iatrogenic
impregnant
impregnate
impresario
impression
impressive
imprimatur
imprinting
improbable
improbably
improperly
improvable
improvably
improviser
imprudence
inartistic
inbreeding
incrassate
incredible
incredibly
increscent
infraction
infrahuman
infrasonic
infrequent
ingratiate
ingredient
ingression
inordinate
intramural
intraurban
intrepidly
intrigante
intriguant
introducer
introrsely
introspect
inurbanity
jerrybuilt
jinricksha
jinrikisha
journalese
journalise
journalism
journalist
journeyman
lacrimator
lacrymator
lauraceous
laureation
laurelling
lawrencium
Lawrentian
leprechaun
librettist
lipreading
logrolling
lubricator
lubricious
macrophage
macrospore
madreporic
marrowbone
marrowless
matriarchy
matricidal
matronhood
matronship
matronymic
meerschaum
merrymaker
metrically
metronomic
metronymic
metropolis
microbiota
microcline
microfarad
microfiche
micrograph
microlitic
micrometer
micrometry
microphone
microphyte
micropylar
microscope
microscopy
microseism
microspore
migrainous
morrispike
mournfully
narrowness
necrolater
necrolatry
necromancy
necrophile
necrophily
necropolis
necroscopy
negrophile
negrophobe
neurilemma
neurolemma
neuropathy
neuroplasm
neurotoxin
nigrescent
nitrochalk
nitrogroup
nourishing
nutritious
obtruncate
oleraceous
ombrometer
operculate
operettist
oppression
oppressive
opprobrium
outrageous
outrightly
outrunning
ovariotomy
overabound
overactive
overblouse
overbought
overburden
overcharge
overcommit
overcooked
overexcite
overexpose
overflight
overground
overgrowth
overhanded
overlander
overlapped
overlooker
overmanned
overmantel
overmaster
overnicety
overpraise
overrefine
overridden
overriding
overshadow
overslaugh
overspread
overstride
overstrung
oversubtle
oversupply
overthrown
overthrust
overtopped
overweight
overwinter
parramatta
parricidal
parrotfish
patriality
patriarchy
patriciate
patricidal
patrilocal
patriotism
patristics
patrolling
patronymic
pearldiver
peerlessly
petroglyph
petrolatum
petronella
pharisaism
pharmacist
pharyngeal
pheromonal
piercingly
porraceous
pourparler
pruriently
puerperium
putrescent
putrescine
putridness
Pyrrhonian
Pyrrhonism
Pyrrhonist
pyrrhotite
quarantine
quarrelled
quarreller
quarrender
quartation
quarterage
quarterday
quartering
quartzitic
quercitron
quirkiness
rearmament
recreantly
recreation
recreative
recrudesce
refraction
refractive
refractory
refreshing

refringent
regression
regressive
regretting
reorganise
repression
repressive
reprobance
reproducer
retractile
retraction
retractive
retraining
retrochoir
retrograde
retrogress
retrorsely
retrospect
riproaring
rubrically
rubricator
rumrunning
sabretache
sabretooth
sacredness
sacrificer
sacroiliac
sacrosanct
saprogenic
saprophyte
sarracenia
scarabaeid
scarabaeus
scaramouch
scarceness
scaredycat
scarlatina
scoreboard
scoresheet
scornfully
scorzonera
scurrility
scurrilous
scurviness
searchable
searchless
secretaire
seersucker
serradilla
sharpnosed
sherardise
sheriffdom
shirehorse
shirtfront
shirtwaist
shoreleave
shorewards
shortbread
shortcrust
shortdated
shortening
shortlived
shortrange
skirmisher
skirtdance
smaragdine
smaragdite
smartmoney
smorrebrod
sourcebook
sparseness
Spartacist
spermaceti
spermicide
sperrylite
spiracular
spiraculum
spiralling
spiritedly
spiritless
spirituous
spirograph
spirometer
spirometry
sporangial
sporangium
sporophore
sporophyll
sporophyte
sportfully
sportiness
sportingly
sportively
sportswear
spuriously
stargazing
starriness
starryeyed
starstream
starvation
starveling
stereobate
stereogram
stereopsis
stereotype
stereotypy
sterigmata
steriliser
sternwards
stertorous
stirrupcup
storehouse
storksbill
stormbound
stormcloud
storminess
stormproof
sturdiness
subreption
subroutine
suprarenal
surrealism
surrealist
swarmspore
swordcraft
sworddance
swordgrass
swordstick
tauromachy
tearjerker
tearlessly
terracotta
terreplein
terrorless
tetrachord
tetragonal
tetrahedra
tetrameter
tetramorph
tetrapolis
tetrarchic
tetrastich
tetrastyle
thereabout
thereafter
thereanent
thereunder
thermionic
thermistor
thermogram
thermophil
thermopile
thermostat
thirdclass
thirdparty
thirteenth
thirtyfold
thornapple
thorniness
thornproof
thoroughly
torrential
torridness
tourbillon
tourmaline
tournament
tourniquet
tsarevitch
Tyrrhenian
ultrabasic
ultrasonic
ultrasound
umbrageous
umbrellaed
unarguable
unbrokenly
uncritical
unerringly
unfriended
unfriendly
ungraceful
ungracious
ungrateful
ungrounded
ungrudging
unorthodox
unprepared
unprovoked
untroubled
untruthful
unwrinkled
upbraiding
upbringing
usuriously
usurpation
uxoricidal
uxoriously
vibraculum
vibraphone
vitrescent
vitriolise
wearifully
wharfinger
whereabout
whirlybird
whorehouse
yearningly
yourselves
almsgiving
anastigmat
anastomose
anastrophe
anisotropy
aposematic
apostatise
apostolate
apostrophe
aristocrat
bassethorn
bassoonist
bioscience
bissextile
blasphemer
blastemata
blastocyst
blastoderm
blastomere
blastopore
blissfully
blistering
blushingly
blusterous
boastfully
boisterous
bolshevise
bolshevism
bolshevist
brassiness
bressummer
brusquerie
bursarship
byssaceous
byssinosis
caespitose
cassolette
causticity
censorious
censorship
censurable
cessionary
chasteness
chessboard
chiselling
claspknife
classicise
classicism
classicist
classified
classifier
closestool
closetplay
coastguard
coastwards
codswallop
comstocker
conscience
consecrate
consectary
consensual
consequent
considered
consistent
consistory
consociate
consolable
consonance
consonancy
consortium
conspectus
conspiracy
conspirant
constantan
Constantia
constantly
constipate
constitute
constraint
constringe
consuetude
consulship
consultant
consulting
consultive
consumable
consumedly
consummate
corsetiere
cousinhood
cousinship
crassitude
crescentic
crispation
crispbread
crisscross
crossbench
crossbones
crossbreed
crosscheck
crossgrain
crosshatch
crossindex
crosslight
crosspatch
crosspiece
crossrefer
crossroads
crosstrees
crustacean
crustation
crustiness
cursedness
cussedness
daisychain
deescalate
densimeter
diastemata
diesinking
dipsomania
dissatisfy
dissection
dissembler
dissension
dissertate
disservice
dissidence
dissilient
dissimilar
dissipated
dissociate
dissoluble
dissolvent
dissonance
dissonancy
dissuasion
dissuasive
dogstongue
dorsigrade
dressiness
dressmaker
drosophila
drysaltery
elasticise
elasticity
emasculate
emissivity
endstopped
episcopacy
episcopate
episematic
episodical
episternum
epistolary
epistrophe
erysipelas
eviscerate
exasperate
exospheric
eyeservice
farsighted
felspathic
firstclass
firstnight
flashboard
flashflood
flashiness
flashlight
flashpoint
fleshiness
fleshwound
flosculous
flyswatter
freshwater
friskiness
frostiness
fussbudget
ghastfully
glasscloth
glassfibre
glasshouse
glassiness
glasspaper
glassworks
Glaswegian
glossarial
glossarist
glossiness
glossology
gnosticism
gobstopper
gooseberry
gooseflesh
goosegrass
graspingly
grasscloth
grassroots
grasssnake
gressorial
grisliness
guesthouse
guestnight
gunslinger
gypsophila
hamshackle
Hansardise
hanselling
haustellum
haustorium
hawserlaid
hipsterism
horsecloth
horsecoper
horseflesh
horselaugh
horseleech
horsepower
horseshoer
horsewoman
houseagent
housebound
housecraft
houseguest
houselling
houseplant
houseproud
housetrain
housewives
hypsometer
hypsometry
illstarred
inkslinger
inosculate
Irishwoman
isoseismal
isosporous
jimsonweed
kaisership
kenspeckle
kerseymere
kieselguhr
Krishnaism
lansquenet
lipservice
lissomness
lobsterpot
loosecover
lopsidedly
lossleader
maisonette
manservant
mansuetude
marshalled
marshaller
marshalsea
marshiness
Massoretic
measliness
measurable
measurably
measuredly
menstruate
menstruous
mensurable
messianism
midshipman

minstrelsy
missionary
missionise
moisturise
monsignori
monstrance
mossbunker
mousseline
moustached
moustachio
Mousterian
mudskipper
mudslinger
Mussulmans
myasthenia
nauseating
nauseously
newsagency
newscaster
newsletter
newsmonger
newsreader
newsvendor
newsworthy
newswriter
noisemaker
nonstarter
nonswimmer
nurseryman
offsetting
onesidedly
opisometer
outsitting
outstation
outstretch
outswinger
pansophist
parsonbird
parsonical
passageway
passionary
passionate
Passionist
peashooter
pensionary
persecutor
persiflage
persistent
personable
personally
personalty
personator
persuasion
persuasive
phosphatic
phosphoric
phosphorus
physically
physicking
physiocrat
physiology
pigsticker
pinstriped
plasmodesm
plasmodium
plasmogamy
plasmolyse
plasticise
plasticity
plesiosaur
possession
possessive
possessory
presageful
presbyopia
presbyopic
presbytery
prescience
prescriber
presentday
presentive
presidency
presidiary
presignify
pressagent
pressingly
pressurise
presternum
presumable
presumably
presuppose
prismoidal
prissiness
prosaicism
proscenium
prosciutto
proscriber
prosecutor
prosilient
prosodical
prospector
prospectus
prosperity
prosperous
prosthesis
prosthetic
prostitute
prostomial
prostomium
puissantly
pulsatilla
pulsimeter
pulsometer
purseproud
pursership
purseseine
pursuivant
questioner
ramshackle
reasonable
reasonably
reasonless
reassemble
reassembly
reissuable
ripsnorter
roistering
roisterous
rouseabout
roustabout
Russianise
Russophile
Russophobe
Sanskritic
seaserpent
seasonable
seasonably
seasonally
seismicity
seismogram
seismology
sensedatum
senseorgan
sensitiser
sensualise
sensualism
sensualist
sensuality
sensuously
sixshooter
skyscraper
solstitial
sousaphone
spasticity
subscriber
subsection
subsellium
subsequent
subshrubby
subsidence
subsidiary
subsistent
subspecies
substation
substitute
substratum
swashplate
tasselling
tessellate
tinselling
topsyturvy
trashiness
trespasser
trisection
triskelion
trustfully
trustiness
trustingly
unassisted
unassuming
versicular
waistcloth
wassailing
Welshwoman
whiskified
whispering
worshipful
worshipped
worshipper
wristwatch
yeastiness
abstemious
abstention
abstergent
abstersion
abstersive
abstinence
abstinency
abstracted
abstracter
abstractly
abstractor
abstrusely
abstrusity
acatalepsy
acetabular
acetabulum
acotyledon
aesthetics
aesthetism
agitatedly
amateurish
amateurism
anatomical
anatropous
apothecary
apothecial
apothecium
apotheoses
apotheosis
apotropaic
arithmetic
arytaenoid
auctioneer
austenitic
Australian
baptistery
bastardise
battailous
battledore
battlement
battleship
Benthamism
Benthamite
bestialise
bestiality
bestirring
bestowment
bestridden
bestseller
betterment
birthplace
birthright
birthstone
bitterling
bitterness
bitterroot
bitterwood
blitheness
blithering
blithesome
blitzkrieg
blottesque
bootlegger
bootlessly
bootlicker
bootstraps
bottlefeed
bottleneck
bottletree
bottomless
bottommost
bratticing
Britishism
bustlingly
butterball
butterbean
butterfish
buttermilk
butterwort
buttonball
buttonbush
buttondown
buttonhole
buttonhook
buttonless
buttonwood
cantaloupe
cantatrice
canterbury
cantilever
cantillate
cantonment
captiously
Carthusian
cartomancy
cartoonist
cartwright
castration
cattlegrid
cautionary
cautiously
centennial
centesimal
centigrade
centilitre
centillion
centimetre
centralise
centralism
centralist
centrality
centreback
centrefold
centrehalf
centricity
centrifuge
centromere
centrosome
certiorari
chatelaine
chatoyance
chatterbox
chattiness
Cistercian
clothesbag
clothespeg
clothespin
coathanger
coatimundi
coetaneous
coeternity
contagious
contendent
contention
contestant
contextual
contexture
contiguity
contiguous
continence
contingent
continuant
continuate
continuity
continuous
contortion
contortive
contraband
contrabass
contractor
contradict
contraprop
contrarily
contravene
contribute
contritely
contrition
controlled
controller
controvert
corticated
costliness
cottoncake
cottonseed
cottontail
cottonweed
cottonwood
cottonwool
couturiere
cretaceous
critically
cultivable
cultivator
culturally
custommade
cuttlebone
cuttlefish
cuttystool
cystoscope
cystoscopy
deathwatch
deltiology
dentifrice
destructor
dextrality
dextrously
diathermal
diathermic
diatropism
dictatress
dictionary
distensile
distension
distention
distichous
distilland
distillate
distillery
distilling
distinctly
distortion
distracted
distrainer
distrainor
distraught
distressed
distribute
distringas
doctorship
dustjacket
dystrophic
earthbound
earthiness
earthlight
earthquake
earthshine
earthwards
eartrumpet
easterling
Eastertide
editorship
eisteddfod
elatedness
elutriator
epithelial
epithelium
erethismic
erotically
erotogenic
erotomania
exoterical
exothermal
exothermic
exotically
factiously
factitious
factorship
factualism
factualist
factuality
faithfully
fantastico
fantoccini
fastidious
fastigiate
featherbed
feathering
fertiliser
festoonery
fetterlock
fictioneer
fictionist
fictitious
fiftyfifty
filterable
filthiness
filtration
fisticuffs
flatfooted
flattering
flatulence
flatulency
foetidness
fontanelle
footballer
footbridge
footcandle
footlights
footwarmer
fortepiano
forthright
fortissimi
fortissimo
fortuitism
fortuitist
fortuitous
fortyniner
fosterling
fraternise
fraternity
fratricide
fritillary
frothiness

frutescent
fustanella
gasteropod
gastrology
gastronome
gastronomy
genteelism
gentilesse
gentlefolk
gentleness
geothermal
geothermic
geotropism
glottology
gluttonise
gluttonous
goatsbeard
goatsucker
gratefully
gratifying
gratuitous
grittiness
gutturally
hartebeest
heathendom
heathenise
heathenish
heathenism
heatstroke
hectically
hectograph
hectolitre
hectometre
heptachord
heptagonal
Heptameron
heptameter
heptarchic
Heptateuch
heptatonic
hinterland
histologic
histolysis
histolytic
historical
histrionic
hoitytoity
hootenanny
hostelling
hysteresis
hysteretic
hysterical
ichthyosis
initialise
initialled
initiation
initiative
initiatory
instalment
instigator
instilling
institutor
instructor
instrument
isothermal
jolterhead
justiciary
Kantianism
kettledrum
knottiness
lactescent
lanternfly
lanthanide
lattermost
lectionary
lefthanded
lefthander
lenticular
lentigines
letterbomb
letterbook
lettercard
letterhead
letterless
listlessly
litterlout
littleness
lustration
lustreless
lustrously
Malthusian
manteltree
martensite
martialism
martingale
mastectomy
masterhand
masterhood
masterless
mastermind
mastership
masterwork
masticable
masticator
meltingpot
mentorship
mettlesome
mintmaster
mirthfully
mistakable
mistakenly
misthought
Montagnard
montbretia
mouthorgan
mouthpiece
multifaced
multiloquy
multimedia
multiphase
multiplier
multipolar
multistage
multivocal
muttonhead
myrtaceous
mystagogic
mystagogue
mysterious
mystically
nasturtium
natterjack
nautically
nectareous
nettlerash
neutralise
neutralism
neutralist
neutrality
northbound
northerner
northwards
nostologic
nuptiality
nyctalopia
nyctalopic
nyctinasty
obituarist
obstetrics
obstructor
ophthalmia
ophthalmic
oratorical
orotundity
oysterfarm
paltriness
pantograph
pantomimic
pantrymaid
partiality
participle
particular
parturient
pasteboard
pastellist
pasteurise
pasteurism
pastmaster
pastorally
pastorship
pastrycook
pasturable
pastyfaced
pectinated
pentachord
pentagonal
pentameter
pentastich
pentathlon
pentatomic
pentatonic
pentimento
pentstemon
pertinence
pertinency
pesticidal
pestilence
photoflood
photogenic
photograph
photolitho
photolysis
photolytic
photometer
photometry
photonasty
photophily
photophore
photoprint
phototaxis
phototrope
phytogenic
phytophagy
phytotoxic
pictograph
pictorical
pistillary
pistillate
pistolling
pistolshot
pistolwhip
pistonring
platelayer
plutocracy
plutolatry
poetically
pontifical
pontifices
portamento
portcullis
portentous
portliness
Portuguese
postbellum
postchaise
postexilic
posthumous
postillion
postliminy
postmaster
postmortem
postoffice
postpartum
postscript
postulator
pratincole
pretendant
pretendent
pretension
prettiness
protanopic
protection
protective
protectory
protectrix
proteiform
proteinous
protensive
proteolyse
protestant
prothallia
prothallus
protophyta
protophyte
protoplasm
protoplast
prototypal
prototypic
protracted
protractor
protreptic
protrusile
protrusion
protrusive
psittacine
purtenance
quaternary
quaternate
quaternion
quaternity
quatorzain
quatrefoil
rattlehead
rattlepate
rattletrap
rectorship
reiterance
restaurant
restlessly
restorable
restrained
restrainer
rhetorical
rhythmical
rontgenise
rootedness
rottenness
rottweiler
runthrough
rustically
saltarello
saltcellar
saltigrade
sawtoothed
scatheless
scathingly
scattergun
scattering
scattiness
Scotswoman
Scotticise
Scotticism
scutellate
seethrough
seltzogene
sentential
sentiently
septenarii
septennial
septennium
septically
septillion
Septuagint
sestertium
sestertius
setterwort
settlement
sextillion
shuttering
sisterhood
skateboard
sketchable
sketchbook
skittishly
slatternly
slitpocket
slothfully
sluttishly
smattering
smuttiness
softbilled
softboiled
softfinned
softheaded
softspoken
soothingly
soothsayer
souterrain
southbound
southerner
southernly
southwards
sowthistle
spatchcock
spathulate
spatiality
spitchcock
spitefully
spotlessly
spottiness
statecraft
statically
stationary
stationery
statistics
statoscope
statuesque
statutable
statutably
stitchwort
subtenancy
subterfuge
subtleness
subtrahend
sultanship
sultriness
sustaining
sustenance
sustention
sustentive
switchback
switchover
syntagmata
synthesise
synthesist
synthetise
synthetist
systematic
systemless
tactically
tactlessly
tantaliser
tantamount
Tartuffian
Tartuffism
tastefully
tattletale
tautomeric
tautophony
teatrolley
teetotally
tentacular
tenterhook
testaceous
testflight
tetterwort
textualist
texturally
tilthammer
tittupping
toothbrush
toothiness
toothpaste
toothshell
tortellini
tortfeasor
tortiously
tortuosity
tortuously
triternate
triturable
triturator
Trotskyism
Trotskyist
Trotskyite
truthfully
tufthunter
tuitionary
turtleback
turtledove
turtleneck
ulotrichan
unattached
unattended
unctuosity
unctuously
unsteadily
unstrained
unstressed
upstanding
urethritis
vectograph
ventilator
ventricose
ventriculi
vertebrate
vertically
vestibular
vestibulum
vestpocket
victimiser
Victoriana
victorious
victualled
victualler
Vietnamese
virtuality
virtueless
virtuosity
virtuously
voltameter
vortically
vorticella
vorticular
wantonness
wastefully
wastepaper
wattlebird
weatherbox
weathering
weatherman
wentletrap
Wertherian
Wertherism
westernise
westwardly
whatsoever
whitebeard
whitefaced
whitesmith
whitethorn
WhitMonday
WhitSunday
wintertide

wintertime
wintriness
wontedness
worthiness
worthwhile
wrathfully
wrathiness
wretchedly
yesteryear
youthfully
zwitterion
abducentes
abjuration
abruptness
absurdness
accumulate
accurately
accursedly
accusation
accusative
accusatory
accusingly
accustomed
acoustical
acquirable
acquitting
adjudgment
adjudicate
adjunction
adjunctive
adjuration
adjuratory
adjustable
adjustment
aeruginous
albuminoid
albuminous
allurement
allusively
almucanter
ambulacral
ambulacrum
ambulation
ambulatory
ambushment
ammunition
amputation
aneurismal
aneurysmal
angularity
annularity
annulation
annunciate
araucarian
argumentum
assumption
assumptive
astuteness
attunement
augustness
autumnally
avouchment
balustrade
Beaujolais
beautician
beautifier
bemusement
bequeathal
bibulously
bicultural
bisulphate
bisulphide
bisulphite
bituminise
bituminous
calumniate
calumnious
caoutchouc
caruncular
casualness
ceruminous
chaudfroid
chauffeuse
chauntress
chauvinism
chauvinist
cloudberry
cloudburst
cloudiness
columbaria
copulation
copulative
coquettish
cucullated
cumulation
cumulative
cumuliform
deductible
dehumanise
dehumidify
delusional
delusively
demureness
demurrable
denudation
denunciate
depuration
depurative
deputation
diluteness
disulphate
disulphide
disutility
divulgence
documental
effulgence
effusively
Eleusinian
enduringly
engulfment
Esculapian
escutcheon
excusatory
exhumation
expunction
expurgator
fabulously
fiducially
figuration
figurative
figurehead
fraudulent
furuncular
futureless
futuristic
futurology
gerundival
gesundheit
glauberite
glauconite
goluptious
groundbait
groundless
groundling
groundmass
groundplan
groundrent
groundsman
groundwork
haruspices
hirudinean
hocuspocus
holusbolus
homunculus
illuminant
illuminate
illuminati
illuminism
illuminist
illusional
illusively
illusorily
illustrate
immunology
immurement
impudently
impudicity
impugnable
impugnment
impuissant
impureness
imputation
imputative
inaugurate
incubation
incubative
incubatory
inculcator
inculpable
incumbency
incunabula
incurrable
inducement
inductance
indulgence
induration
indurative
industrial
infusorial
infusorian
inhumanely
inhumanity
inhumation
injunction
injunctive
innuendoes
innumeracy
innumerate
innumerous
inquietude
inquisitor
insufflate
insularism
insularity
insulation
insurgence
insurgency
intubation
jaguarundi
Janusfaced
jejuneness
jesuitical
jocularity
lacustrine
lanuginose
lanuginous
leguminous
lieutenant
liquescent
liquidator
liquidiser
liquidness
liturgical
lobulation
locustbean
loquacious
lotuseater
lucubrator
luculently
lugubrious
luxuriance
maculation
maculature
majuscular
manumitted
manuscript
maquillage
maturation
maturative
matureness
medullated
minuscular
minutebook
minutehand
minuteness
modulation
monumental
naturalise
naturalism
naturalist
naturopath
nebulosity
nebulously
nodulation
obdurately
obfuscated
obnubilate
obturation
obtuseness
occupation
occupative
occurrence
oecumenism
oppugnancy
osculation
osculatory
patulously
peculation
peculiarly
peduncular
petulantly
ploughable
ploughland
pneumatics
popularise
popularity
population
populistic
populously
proudflesh
pseudocarp
purulently
ranunculus
rebuttable
recumbency
recuperate
recurrence
redundance
redundancy
refuelling
refulgence
refundable
refundment
refutation
regularise
regularity
regulation
regulative
regulatory
rejuvenate
rejuvenise
reluctance
reluctancy
remunerate
republican
repudiator
repugnance
repugnancy
repurchase
reputation
requiescat
resultless
resumption
resumptive
resupinate
resurgence
returnable
rheumatics
rheumatism
rheumatoid
robustious
robustness
roquelaure
salubrious
salutarily
salutation
salutatory
saturation
saturnalia
scrupulous
scrutineer
scrutinise
secularise
secularism
secularist
secularity
securement
secureness
securiform
seducement
seductress
sedulously
seguidilla
sepulchral
sequacious
sequential
sequestrum
shouldered
simulacrum
simulation
simulative
simulatory
sinusoidal
solubilise
solubility
splutterer
sprucebeer
spruceness
staurolite
structural
structured
struthious
tabularise
tabulation
tegumental
theurgical
thoughtful
thousandth
thruppence
titubation
traumatism
triumphant
triumviral
troubadour
trousseaux
trouvaille
tumultuary
tumultuous
unbuttoned
uncustomed
undulation
undulatory
unguentary
unjustness
unnumbered
unruliness
unsuitable
usquebaugh
ustulation
velutinous
virulently
visualiser
vituperate
volubility
volumetric
voluminous
voluptuary
voluptuous
aboveboard
brevetting
canvasback
canvaswork
chevrotain
chivalrous
clavichord
clavicular
cleverness
clovehitch
cloverleaf
convalesce
convection
convective
convenable
convenance
convenient
convention
conventual
convergent
conversant
conversely
conversion
conveyable
conveyance
conviction
convictive
convincing
convoluted
convulsant
convulsion
convulsive
couverture
cravenness
curvaceous
curvacious
curvetting
drivelling
driverless
elevenplus
exuviation
fervidness
flavescent
flavourful
flavouring
fluviatile
frivolling
galvaniser
gravestone
gravimeter
gravimetry
grovelling
harvestman
heavenborn
heavensent
heavenward
heavyarmed
inevitable
inevitably
larvicidal
malvaceous
marvelling
marvellous
misventure
nonviolent
olivaceous
perversely
perversion
perversity
perversive
prevailing
prevalence
prevenancy
prevenient
prevention
preventive

previously
privileged
provenance
proverbial
providence
provincial
provisions
provitamin
provocator
pulveriser
pulvinated
purveyance
scavengery
serviceman
servomotor
shovelhead
shovelling
silverbath
silverfish
silverside
silverware
silverweed
slavetrade
slavocracy
Slavophile
Slavophobe
snivelling
stavesacre
subvention
subversion
subversive
survivance
swiveleyed
swivelling
travelling
travelogue
travertine
trivialise
trivialism
triviality
unavailing
unevenness
uneventful
university
univocally
valvulitis
weaverbird
angwantibo
answerable
answerably
Boswellian
Boswellise
Boswellism
brawniness
browbeaten
brownshirt
brownstone
clawhammer
clownishly
crewelwork
crowkeeper
drawbridge
drawingpin
drawlingly
drawstring
drowsihead
drowsiness
earwigging
earwitness
eyewitness
flawlessly
flowergirl
flowerless
forwarding
forwearied
frowningly
growlingly
jaywalking
miswording

outwitting
showerbath
showjumper
showwindow
skewbridge
skywriting
slowfooted
slowmotion
slowwitted
snowcapped
snowgrouse
snowmobile
snowplough
stewardess
trawlerman
trowelling
twowheeler
unswerving
viewfinder
viewlessly
alexanders
asexuality
coexistent
deoxidiser
epexegeses
epexegesis
epexegetic
flexuously
fluxionary
fraxinella
inexistent
inexorable
inexorably
inexpertly
inexpiable
inexpiably
inexplicit
proximally
quixotical
thixotropy
unexampled
unexcelled
unexpected
unexplored
alcyonaria
artycrafty
Babylonian
babysitter
barysphere
calyciform
calyptrate
caryatides
chrysolite
chrysotile
copyholder
copyreader
copywriter
Corybantes
corybantic
coryphaeus
disyllabic
disyllable
encyclical
encystment
enzymology
eurypterid
greyheaded
karyoplasm
kerygmatic
ladychapel
ladyfinger
ladykiller
laryngitic
laryngitis
molybdenum
palynology
papyrology
pityriasis
playacting

playbyplay
playfellow
playground
playwright
polyandric
polyanthus
polyatamic
polychaete
polychrest
polychrome
polyclinic
polycyclic
polydactyl
polydipsia
polygamist
polygamous
polygenism
polygenist
polygenous
polygraphy
polygynous
polyhedral
polyhedric
polyhedron
polyhistor
polymathic
polymerise
polymerism
polymerous
Polynesian
polynomial
polyonymic
polyphasic
polyphonic
polyploidy
polysemous
polytheism
polytheist
polytocous
polyvalent
prayerbook
recyclable
rubythroat
satyagraha
satyriasis
strychnine
strychnism
swaybacked
benzocaine
benzpyrene
blazonment
brazenness
brazilwood
canzonetta
dazzlement
dazzlingly
frizziness
fuzzywuzzy
manzanilla
mizzenmast
mizzensail
mozzarella
piezometer
pozzolanic
pozzuolana
prizefight
puzzlement
quizmaster
razzmatazz
rhizogenic
rhizomorph
rhizophore
zigzagging

---

abreaction
acatalepsy
acetabular
acetabulum
adamantine

agapanthus
aggrandise
agitatedly
airmanship
alexanders
alliaceous
alphabetic
alphameric
amylaceous
anabaptism
anabaptist
anapaestic
angwantibo
animadvert
animalcula
animalcule
animatedly
anonaceous
apocalypse
apocarpous
apolaustic
appealable
appearance
appeasable
archaistic
arenaceous
arytaenoid
astragalus
attractant
attraction
attractive
barcarolle
barracouta
barramunda
barramundi
barratrous
bastardise
batrachian
battailous
bedraggled
belladonna
bombardier
brigandage
brigandine
brigandism
brigantine
brocatelle
bureaucrat
burramundi
bursarship
byssaceous
calcareous
campaigner
cantaloupe
cantatrice
canvasback
canvaswork
carmagnole
carnallite
carnassial
carragheen
caryatides
cascarilla
casualness
cephalopod
chamaeleon
chaparajos
chaparejos
charactery
chinagraph
chivalrous
Circassian
clarabella
cockalorum
cockatrice
coelacanth
coetaneous
collarbeam
collarbone

collarette
collarless
collarstud
collatable
collateral
commandant
commandeer
commandery
commanding
commandoes
compaction
comparable
comparably
comparator
comparison
compassion
compasssaw
compatible
compatibly
compatriot
confabbing
connatural
contagious
convalesce
coriaceous
courageous
cowcatcher
cowparsley
crematoria
cretaceous
cuirassier
curvaceous
curvacious
declarable
declassify
defeasance
defeasible
deflagrate
defrayable
defrayment
degradable
degradedly
depravedly
dermatitis
dermatogen
deshabille
despatcher
detraction
detractive
dictatress
diecasting
disbarring
disdainful
dishabille
disharmony
dismalness
disparager
disparates
dispassion
dispatcher
dissatisfy
dogmatical
dogmatiser
dramatical
dramaturge
dramaturgy
drupaceous
drysaltery
elecampane
emblazoner
emblazonry
enchanting
endearment
entrancing
entrapment
enwrapping
epigastric
ericaceous
escharotic

euthanasia
extractant
extraction
extractive
extramural
extraneity
extraneous
fallacious
fandangoes
fantastico
flycatcher
foliaceous
fontanelle
formatting
forwarding
fricandeau
fricasseed
fustanella
galvaniser
gargantuan
gemmaceous
genialness
geriatrics
geriatrist
glumaceous
gormandise
granadilla
gregarious
grenadilla
gymnastics
haematosis
haematuria
Hansardise
Hebraistic
heliacally
helianthus
henharrier
heptachord
heptagonal
Heptameron
heptameter
heptarchic
Heptateuch
heptatonic
herbaceous
hereabouts
heulandite
hierarchal
hierarchic
hullabaloo
husbandage
husbandman
hydraulics
hypnagogic
idolatress
idolatrous
illnatured
implacable
implacably
incrassate
infeasible
inflatable
infraction
infrahuman
infrasonic
ingratiate
inspanning
instalment
intramural
intraurban
iridaceous
Ishmaelite
isolatable
jackanapes
jackassery
jaguarundi
jaywalking
jeopardise
Kafkaesque

kidnapping
kookaburra
Lammastide
lauraceous
leopardess
liliaceous
Lollardism
longaevous
loquacious
Maccabaean
malvaceous
maniacally
manzanilla
mechanical
mediastina
mediatress
mendacious
mercantile
Michaelmas
migrainous
mismatched
mistakable
mistakenly
Montagnard
mordacious
morganatic
mozzarella
myocardium
myrtaceous
mystagogic
mystagogue
nectareous
newfangled
newsagency
nonnatural
nonpayment
nullanulla
nyctalopia
nyctalopic
oldfangled
oldmaidish
oleraceous
oligarchic
olivaceous
orchardist
orchardman
orphanhood
outbalance
outgassing
outlandish
outpatient
outrageous
overabound
overactive
paedagogic
palladious
palmaceous
palmatifid
panhandler
panjandrum
Parnassian
parramatta
passageway
peccadillo
pegmatitic
pellagrous
penmanship
pennaceous
pennanular
pentachord
pentagonal
pentameter
pentastich
pentathlon
pentatomic
pentatonic
permafrost
permanence
permanency
phalangeal
phenacetin
philatelic
phylactery
piccalilli
piccaninny
pickaninny
pilgarlick
pinnatifid
playacting
plumassier
podiatrist
polyandric
polyanthus
polyatamic
porraceous
portamento
precarious
precaution
predacious
prelatical
premarital
premaxilla
prepackage
preparator
preparedly
prepayable
prepayment
presageful
prevailing
prevalence
propagable
propaganda
propagator
prosaicism
protanopic
pugnacious
pulsatilla
quarantine
quinacrine
rampageous
ratcatcher
refraction
refractive
refractory
releasable
repealable
repeatable
repeatedly
researcher
restaurant
retractile
retraction
retractive
retraining
revealable
revealment
rockabilly
sabbatical
salmagundi
saltarello
sandalwood
sappanwood
sargassoes
sarracenia
satyagraha
scarabaeid
scarabaeus
scaramouch
seacaptain
seamanlike
seamanship
selfacting
selfaction
semiannual
sequacious
serradilla
sexpartite
shenanigan
sherardise
sialagogic
sialagogue
signalling
skyjacking
smaragdine
smaragdite
socialiser
soldanella
sousaphone
spiracular
spiraculum
spiralling
sporangial
sporangium
stalactite
stalagmite
stewardess
stomachful
stomatitis
stomatopod
streamless
streamline
submariner
sultanship
sunparlour
suprarenal
surfactant
sustaining
syllabaria
sympathise
syncarpous
syntagmata
tantaliser
tantamount
tarmacadam
tentacular
termagancy
terracotta
testaceous
tetrachord
tetragonal
tetrahedra
tetrameter
tetramorph
tetrapolis
tetrarchic
tetrastich
tetrastyle
threadbare
threadfish
threadmark
threadworm
threatener
throatwort
topgallant
tragacanth
trepanning
trilateral
tripartite
tropaeolum
tuffaceous
tympanites
tympanitic
tympanitis
ultrabasic
ultrasonic
ultrasound
umbrageous
unavailing
unbearable
unbearably
unbeatable
unbeatably
unchanging
unchastity
unexampled
unflagging
ungraceful
ungracious
ungrateful
unicameral
unilateral
unipartite
unmeasured
unreadable
unscalable
unseasoned
upbraiding
uproarious
upstanding
usucaption
vasoactive
venialness
verbaliser
vernacular
vibraculum
vibraphone
villainage
villainess
villainous
villanelle
violaceous
visualiser
voltameter
vulcaniser
wassailing
weimaraner
wongawonga
wraparound
ZendAvesta
zigzagging
ablebodied
acrobatics
adhibition
aerobatics
aerobiosis
aerobiotic
affability
algebraist
amiability
amoebocyte
antebellum
antibiosis
antibiotic
archbishop
assibilate
audibility
backbiting
backblocks
barebacked
beefburger
beribboned
bluebonnet
bluebottle
bookbinder
bourbonism
bourbonist
browbeaten
calibrator
capability
carabineer
carabinier
catabolism
celebrated
celebrator
cerebellum
chamberpot
chubbiness
coalbunker
cohabitant
Corybantes
corybantic
curability
deliberate
demobilise
disability
divebomber
drawbridge
dungbeetle
durability
equability
exhibition
exhibitory
exorbitant
exurbanite
filibuster
fireblight
flabbiness
flamboyant
fleabitten
footballer
footbridge
foreboding
framboesia
freebooter
friability
fullbodied
fullbottom
fusibility
fussbudget
glauberite
goldbeater
grubbiness
hackbuteer
handbarrow
hardbilled
hardbitten
hardboiled
hellbender
highbinder
homebrewed
hornblende
humpbacked
hypabyssal
ignobility
imbibition
immobilise
immobility
incubation
incubative
incubatory
inhabitant
inhibition
inhibitory
insobriety
intubation
inurbanity
jacobinise
Jacobinism
Jacobitism
katabolism
lawabiding
legibility
limeburner
lucubrator
lugubrious
macebearer
mealbeetle
metabolise
metabolism
metabolite
molybdenum
montbretia
mossbunker
movability
mutability
notability
nudibranch
obnubilate
overblouse
overbought
overburden
pallbearer
palmbutter
parabiosis
parabiotic
parabolise
paraboloid
pawnbroker
phlebotomy
pinebeauty
playbyplay
pliability
postbellum
potability
presbyopia
presbyopic
presbytery
pushbutton
ratability
republican
rhomboidal
rhomboidei
risibility
rockbadger
rockbottom
rovebeetle
safeblower
salability
salubrious
sandbagger
scribbling
selfbinder
shabbiness
sheabutter
shibboleth
shipbroker
shoebuckle
sideboards
skewbridge
slumberful
slumberous
snobbishly
snubbingly
soapboiler
soapbubble
softbilled
softboiled
solubilise
solubility
stagbeetle
strabismal
strabismic
strabismus
strabotomy
stubbiness
stubbornly
swaybacked
talebearer
tamability
taxability
tenability
tenebrific
tenebrious
thimbleful
thimblerig
thumbprint
thumbscrew
thumbstall
titubation
tollbridge
tourbillon
trombonist
troubadour
turnbuckle
unbiblical
unlabelled
visibility
vocabulary
volubility
winebibber
winebottle
workbasket
abdication
abducentes

abjectness
adjacently
adjectival
advocation
advocatory
affectedly
affectless
Africander
Africanise
Africanism
Africanist
allocation
allocution
almacanter
almucanter
altocumuli
amercement
amerciable
anarchical
antecedent
antecessor
antechapel
Antichrist
anticipant
anticipate
anticlimax
anticlinal
aplacental
araucarian
articulate
artycrafty
associable
asynchrony
attachable
attachment
attackable
auriculate
autecology
autochthon
autocratic
avouchment
bilocation
binoculars
bioecology
bioscience
blancmange
bleachable
bluecollar
bouncingly
branchiate
breechless
bronchiole
bronchitic
bronchitis
calyciform
capacitate
capacitive
caricature
catechesis
catechetic
catechiser
catechumen
chalcedony
chancellor
chinchilla
choiceness
churchgoer
churchyard
cinecamera
cockchafer
coercively
coincident
comicality
comicopera
conscience
corncockle
councillor
councilman
crescentic
cytochrome
dampcourse
dedication
dedicative
dedicatory
deductible
deescalate
defacement
deficiency
dejectedly
delectable
delectably
delicately
delocalise
democratic
deracinate
desecrater
desecrator
desiccator
detachable
detachedly
detachment
detectable
devocalise
dickcissel
didactical
directness
directoire
directress
diseconomy
dovecolour
edulcorate
effaceable
effacement
effectuate
efficacity
efficiency
emancipate
emancipist
emasculate
encyclical
endocrinal
enfacement
enlacement
enrichment
enticement
enticingly
enunciable
enunciator
episcopacy
episcopate
especially
ethicality
eviscerate
expectance
expectancy
expectedly
exulcerate
felicitate
felicitous
fianchetto
fiducially
fierceness
finicality
fishcarver
flaccidity
fleacircus
flocculate
flocculent
flosculous
footcandle
forecaster
forecastle
forecourse
fourchette
franchiser
Franciscan
Francophil
Frenchness
geniculate
glancingly
glauconite
golfcourse
gynocratic
gyrocopter
halfcocked
headcheese
Heliconian
helicopter
hemicyclic
homecoming
homocercal
hourcircle
hypocorism
imbecilely
imbecility
immaculacy
immaculate
impeccable
impeccably
impeccancy
inaccuracy
inaccurate
indecently
indecision
indecisive
indecorous
indication
indicative
indicatory
indictable
indictment
indocility
inducement
inductance
infectious
innocently
inosculate
insecurely
insecurity
insociable
intactness
invocation
invocatory
judicatory
judicature
judicially
ladychapel
leafcutter
lexicology
limaciform
logicality
malacoderm
malacology
Manichaean
Manicheism
manicurist
medicament
medicaster
medication
medicative
menacingly
metacarpal
metacarpus
metacentre
meticulous
miraculous
mobocratic
monocarpic
monochasia
monochrome
monoclinal
monoclinic
monocratic
monocyclic
musicality
musicianly
musicology
musicpaper
musicstand
musicstool
newscaster
nidicolous
noticeable
noticeably
novaculite
objectival
objectless
officially
operculate
ophicleide
overcharge
overcommit
overcooked
paniculate
pediculate
pediculous
pedicurist
penicillin
periclinal
pericyclic
piercingly
pinecarpet
planchette
pleochroic
polychaete
polychrest
polychrome
polyclinic
polycyclic
portcullis
postchaise
pouncetbox
praecocial
prancingly
preachment
prescience
prescriber
princeling
princeship
principate
principial
principium
principled
proscenium
prosciutto
proscriber
pyracantha
quenchable
quenchless
quercitron
racecourse
radicalise
radicalism
radication
recyclable
redecorate
rejectable
relocation
reluctance
reluctancy
reticently
reticulate
revocation
revocatory
ridiculous
rollcollar
rosechafer
rupicoline
rupicolous
salicional
salicylate
saltcellar
sandcastle
saxicoline
saxicolous
scarceness
searchable
searchless
seducement
seductress
selectness
selfcolour
semichorus
semicircle
silkcotton
sinecurism
sinecurist
sketchable
sketchbook
skyscraper
sluicegate
snowcapped
solacement
solecistic
solicitant
solicitous
solicitude
sourcebook
spatchcock
speechless
Spencerian
spitchcock
sprucebeer
spruceness
stanchless
stanchness
stenchtrap
stencilled
stenciller
stitchwort
strictness
structural
structured
strychnine
strychnism
subacidity
subscriber
switchback
switchover
synecdoche
synecology
telecamera
telecaster
theocratic
timocratic
topicality
toxication
toxicology
trancelike
trenchancy
triacetate
truncately
truncation
tubicolous
typicality
unaccented
unbecoming
unexcelled
unoccupied
unsociable
unsociably
unsocially
urticarial
urtication
varicocele
varicosity
Vaticanism
Vaticanist
vaticinate
velocipede
vesication
vesicatory
vesiculate
viceconsul
wingcollar
woodcarver
woodcutter
wretchedly
aberdevine
abridgment
abundantly
accidental
adjudgment
adjudicate
ambidexter
amendatory
amygdaloid
anecdotage
anecdotist
archdeacon
aspidistra
autodidact
bemedalled
benedicite
Benedictus
bladdernut
blindingly
bloodguilt
bloodhound
bloodiness
bloodmoney
bloodstain
bloodstock
bloodstone
boondoggle
brandyball
brandysnap
breadboard
breadcrumb
breadfruit
breadstick
breadstuff
broadcloth
broadsheet
broadsword
broodiness
broodingly
cacodaemon
Caledonian
chandelier
chaudfroid
childbirth
childermas
childishly
childproof
chondritic
cloudberry
cloudburst
cloudiness
comedienne
coordinate
coradicate
decadently
denudation
deridingly
desiderata
desiderate
dreadfully
ectodermal
ectodermic
embodiment
emendation
emendatory
endodermal
endodermis
ergodicity
escadrille
espadrille
Eurodollar
expedience
expediency
expedition
fieldglass
fieldmouse

fieldpiece
fieldstone
fiendishly
fixedpoint
flapdoodle
floodlight
floodwater
foundation
founderous
fraudulent
freedwoman
golddigger
grandchild
granddaddy
grandducal
grandmamma
grandniece
grandstand
granduncle
greediness
greedyguts
grindingly
grindstone
guardhouse
halfdollar
hereditary
hirudinean
humidifier
hypodermal
hypodermic
hypodermis
illadvised
immoderacy
immoderate
immodestly
impediment
impudently
impudicity
incidental
infidelity
inordinate
inundation
inundatory
irradiance
irradicate
lapidarian
lapidarist
lapidation
laundryman
lepidolite
libidinous
loxodromic
macadamise
maladapted
malodorous
meridional
mixedmedia
mouldboard
mouldiness
occidental
octodecimo
paradisaic
paradisean
paradisiac
paradisian
paradoxure
peridermal
piledriver
pleadingly
ploddingly
plunderage
plunderous
polydactyl
polydipsia
preadamite
proudflesh
pseudocarp
pyridoxine
recidivism
recidivist
remediable
remedially
remediless
remodelled
repudiator
reredorter
ropedancer
roundabout
roundhouse
scandalise
scandalous
selfdeceit
selfdenial
semidivine
semidouble
semidrying
shandrydan
shandygaff
shoddiness
skindiving
slanderous
slenderise
snapdragon
solidarism
solidarist
solidarity
solidstate
soundboard
soundingly
soundproof
soundtrack
speediness
speedlimit
standpoint
standstill
steadiness
stridently
stridulant
stridulate
stridulous
sturdiness
swordcraft
sworddance
swordgrass
swordstick
tackdriver
taradiddle
taxidancer
taxidermal
taxidermic
tepidarium
theodicean
theodolite
thirdclass
thirdparty
thunderbox
thundering
thunderous
treadboard
treadwheel
trendiness
trundlebed
unbiddable
unendingly
unfadingly
unredeemed
untidiness
validation
vanadinite
wiredrawer
withdrawal
withdrawer
worldclass
worldweary
yieldingly
zygodactyl
abbreviate
aboveboard
abstemious
abstention
abstergent
abstersion
abstersive
academical
accredited
accrescent
achievable
addlepated
adenectomy
adolescent
aeroengine
affeerment
aggression
aggressive
alchemical
alimentary
amateurish
amateurism
answerable
answerably
antheridia
aphaereses
aphaeresis
apodeictic
aposematic
appreciate
apprentice
archerfish
archetypal
Ashkenazim
ateleiosis
austenitic
autoerotic
badderlock
balderdash
balneology
banderilla
barbellate
barbershop
bargeboard
barkentine
barleybree
barleybroo
barleycorn
Barmecidal
barrelling
barrenness
barrenwort
basketball
basketwork
bassethorn
beekeeping
believable
belletrist
bequeathal
Berkeleian
betterment
bighearted
bilgewater
billetdoux
biodegrade
biogenesis
biogenetic
biometrics
bissextile
bitterling
bitterness
bitterroot
bitterwood
blamefully
bordereaux
borderland
borderless
borderline
Boswellian
Boswellise
Boswellism
bothersome
brakeblock
brakelight
brazenness
brevetting
bridegroom
bridesmaid
brokendown
brokenness
bromegrass
bucketshop
budgerigar
bullethead
burdensome
butterball
butterbean
butterfish
buttermilk
butterwort
byelection
calceolate
campestral
cancellate
cancelling
cancellous
candelabra
candescent
cankerworm
cannelloni
canterbury
carpellary
carpetweed
centennial
centesimal
chatelaine
chimerical
chiselling
chokeberry
Cinderella
Cistercian
Clarenceux
clementine
clerestory
cleverness
closestool
closetplay
clovehitch
cloverleaf
Clydesdale
coacervate
coalescent
coeternity
coffeemill
collection
collective
collegiate
collembola
commentary
commentate
commercial
compelling
compendium
compensate
competence
competency
competitor
concentric
conception
conceptive
conceptual
concerning
concertina
concertino
concession
concessive
concettism
condensate
condensery
condescend
confection
conference
conferment
conferring
confervoid
confession
congeneric
congenital
congestion
congestive
conjecture
connection
connective
consecrate
consectary
consensual
consequent
contendent
contention
contestant
contextual
contexture
convection
convective
convenable
convenance
convenient
convention
conventual
convergent
conversant
conversely
conversion
conveyable
conveyance
cooperator
copperhead
coquettish
corbelling
cornerwise
cornettist
correction
corrective
correspond
corsetiere
couverture
cranesbill
cravenness
credential
crenellate
crewelwork
cudgelling
cumbersome
cummerbund
cursedness
curvetting
cussedness
czarevitch
declension
decrescent
deflection
deflective
degressive
depreciate
depredator
depressant
depression
depressive
descendant
descendent
descension
desperados
diapedesis
diapedetic
Dickensian
didgeridoo
dielectric
difference
digression
digressive
dinnerless
disbelieve
discerning
disfeature
dishearten
dispelling
dispensary
dispersant
dispersion
dispersive
dispersoid
disrespect
dissection
dissembler
dissension
dissertate
disservice
distensile
distension
distention
doggedness
donkeywork
drivelling
driverless
dunderhead
duodecimal
duodenitis
easterling
Eastertide
ecclesiast
ecumenical
egocentric
eisteddfod
elatedness
elementary
elevenplus
emblematic
emblements
enamelling
enamellist
enumerable
enumerator
epexegeses
epexegesis
epexegetic
epicentral
epideictic
epidemical
epidermoid
epigenesis
epigenetic
episematic
erubescent
escheatage
evanescent
evidential
excrescent
exegetical
exoterical
expressage
expression
expressive
expressway
exuberance
eyeservice
Fahrenheit
farfetched
fatherhood
fatherland
fatherless
fatherlike
fathership
fescennine
fetterlock
fibreboard
fibreglass
filterable
fingerbowl

fingerless
fingerling
fingermark
fingernail
fingerpost
fireescape
fisherfolk
flabellate
flagellant
flagellate
flameproof
flavescent
florentine
florescent
flowergirl
flowerless
flugelhorn
forcefully
forfeiture
forgetting
fortepiano
forwearied
fosterling
fraternise
fraternity
frutescent
funnelling
galleywest
gaspereaux
gasteropod
genteelism
geocentric
geodetical
geometrise
Ghibelline
Gilbertian
gingerbeer
gingersnap
glomerular
glomerulus
Godfearing
goldenness
goldenseal
gooseberry
gooseflesh
goosegrass
gorgeously
gracefully
grapefruit
grapesugar
gratefully
gravestone
groceteria
grovelling
guilefully
halberdier
halieutics
hallelujah
hammerbeam
hammerhead
hammerless
hammerlock
hammerpond
handedness
hanselling
hartebeest
harvestman
hawserlaid
heavenborn
heavensent
heavenward
henceforth
hendecagon
henhearted
hermetical
herrenvolk
hinterland
hithermost
hitherward
hodgepodge
homoeopath
hookedness
hootenanny
hornedness
horrendous
horsecloth
horsecoper
horseflesh
horselaugh
horseleech
horsepower
horseshoer
horsewoman
hostelling
houseagent
housebound
housecraft
houseguest
houselling
houseplant
houseproud
housetrain
housewives
hypaethral
hyphenated
hysteresis
hysteretic
hysterical
impregnant
impregnate
impresario
impression
impressive
inadequacy
inadequate
inbreeding
inclemency
incredible
incredibly
increscent
inelegance
inflection
inflective
inflexible
inflexibly
infrequent
ingredient
ingression
innuendoes
inoperable
inspection
inspective
intrepidly
iridescent
isogenetic
isometrics
isoseismal
itinerancy
jaggedness
jasperware
jobbernowl
jolterhead
judgematic
juggernaut
kaisership
kennelling
kerseymere
kieselguhr
kimberlite
knifeboard
Krugerrand
lactescent
ladderback
lanceolate
lanternfly
largescale
lattermost
laureation
laurelling
lawrencium
Lawrentian
leadenness
leaderless
leadership
ledgerbait
ledgerline
leprechaun
letterbomb
letterbook
lettercard
letterhead
letterless
librettist
lipreading
lipservice
liquescent
litterlout
lockerroom
loggerhead
loosecover
lumberjack
lumberroom
lumbersome
lumberyard
madreporic
magnetiser
maidenhair
maidenhead
maidenhood
maidenlike
malfeasant
malleebird
malleefowl
mallenders
manoeuvrer
manoeuvres
manservant
manteltree
marcescent
marketable
markethall
markettown
martensite
marvelling
marvellous
mastectomy
masterhand
masterhood
masterless
mastermind
mastership
masterwork
mathematic
medievally
membership
mesmeriser
millefiori
millennial
millennium
millesimal
mindedness
misbelieve
miscellany
mismeasure
misventure
mizzenmast
mizzensail
monkeysuit
monoecious
motherhood
motherland
motherless
mothership
motherwort
moviemaker
muliebrity
mysterious
natterjack
nauseating
nauseously
neglectful
nethermost
nickelling
nigrescent
noblewoman
noisemaker
nonferrous
noogenesis
nucleation
nucleonics
nucleoside
nucleotide
numberless
nurseryman
obstetrics
offsetting
opalescent
operettist
oppression
oppressive
orchestics
orchestral
orogenesis
orogenetic
outgeneral
outmeasure
overexcite
overexpose
oxygenator
oysterfarm
paederasty
Palaeocene
Palaeogene
palaeolith
palaeotype
Palaeozoic
palmerworm
pangenesis
pangenetic
parcelling
pasteboard
pastellist
pasteurise
pasteurism
pathetical
peacefully
peacemaker
pendentive
peppercorn
peppermill
peppermint
pepperwort
percentage
percentile
perception
perceptive
perceptual
perfection
perfective
permeation
permeative
perpetrate
perpetuate
perpetuity
persecutor
perversely
perversion
perversity
perversive
phagedaena
phagedenic
phanerogam
phonematic
picketline
piecegoods
pigmentary
pincerlike
pinfeather
planetable
planetaria
platelayer
pluperfect
pocketable
pocketbook
pocketsize
pollenosis
ponderable
portentous
possession
possessive
possessory
postexilic
potbellied
powderhorn
powderpuff
prayerbook
prebendary
precedence
precedency
preceptive
preceptory
precession
predecease
predestine
prefecture
preferable
preferably
preference
preferment
preferring
prehensile
prehension
prelection
premedical
prepensely
presentday
presentive
pretendant
pretendent
pretension
prevenancy
prevenient
prevention
preventive
pridefully
primevally
prizefight
procedural
proceeding
procession
profession
progenitor
projectile
projection
projective
promenader
promethium
propellant
propellent
propelling
propensity
properness
propertied
prosecutor
protection
protective
protectory
protectrix
proteiform
proteinous
protensive
proteolyse
protestant
provenance
proverbial
prudential
Ptolemaist
pulveriser
pummelling
purseproud
pursership
purseseine
purtenance
purveyance
putrescent
putrescine
quaternary
quaternate
quaternion
quaternity
raggedness
readership
recreantly
recreation
recreative
redeemable
reelection
reflection
reflective
reflexible
refreshing
refuelling
regression
regressive
regretting
reiterance
relievable
renderable
rendezvous
repression
repressive
respectful
respecting
respective
reviewable
rhinestone
rickettsia
ridgepiece
rinderpest
rootedness
roquelaure
roseengine
rottenness
rouseabout
rubberneck
rudderfish
rudderless
ruggedness
runnerbean
sabretache
sabretooth
sacredness
salientian
sallenders
sanderling
sapiential
sarmentose
sarmentous
scaleboard
scapegrace
scaredycat
scavengery
scoreboard
scoresheet
screechowl
screenings
screenplay
scutellate
seaserpent
secretaire
segmentary
selfesteem
sensedatum
senseorgan

sentential
septenarii
septennial
septennium
sequential
sequestrum
sergeantcy
serjeantcy
serpentine
sestertium
sestertius
setterwort
shamefaced
shamefully
shirehorse
shoreleave
shorewards
shovelhead
shovelling
showerbath
shrievalty
sideeffect
siegetrain
silverbath
silverfish
silverside
silverware
silverweed
sisterhood
skateboard
slavetrade
slidevalve
smokedried
smokehouse
smokeplant
smokeproof
smokestack
snakedance
snakestone
snivelling
societally
soddenness
souterrain
spacecraft
spacewoman
spadebeard
speleology
spidercrab
spiderline
spiderwort
spinescent
spitefully
spleenwort
spokeshave
spumescent
squeezable
squeezebox
stagecoach
stagecraft
statecraft
stavesacre
stereobate
stereogram
stereopsis
stereotype
stereotypy
stilettoes
stipellate
stoneblind
stoneborer
stonebrash
stonefruit
stonemason
stonesnipe
storehouse
streetdoor
streetward
stupendous
subcentral
subdeanery
subheading
subjectify
subjection
subjective
subletting
submediant
submersion
subreption
subsection
subsellium
subsequent
subtenancy
subterfuge
subvention
subversion
subversive
succedanea
successful
succession
successive
suddenness
sufferable
sufferably
sufferance
suggestion
suggestive
sullenness
summerlike
summertime
sunderance
supperless
surrealism
surrealist
susceptive
suspenders
suspension
suspensive
suspensoid
suspensory
sustenance
sustention
sustentive
swinefever
swiveleyed
swivelling
symmetrise
synaeresis
syngenesis
synoecious
systematic
systemless
tablecloth
tablelinen
tablespoon
tangential
tankengine
tasselling
tastefully
tellership
temperable
temperance
temperedly
tenderfoot
tenderloin
tenderness
tenterhook
terneplate
terreplein
tessellate
tetterwort
thalecress
thereabout
thereafter
thereanent
thereunder
threepence
threepenny
threepiece
threescore
tickertape
timberhead
timberline
timbertoes
timberwolf
timberwork
tinselling
toffeenose
torrential
tortellini
trabeation
trabeculae
trabecular
trajection
trajectory
travelling
travelogue
travertine
trecentist
tremendous
Tridentine
trigeminal
trioecious
trisection
triternate
trowelling
tsarevitch
tunnelling
turgescent
turkeycock
turpentine
umbrellaed
unAmerican
unblenched
unevenness
uneventful
unguentary
university
unmeetness
unpleasant
unpleasing
unprepared
unsteadily
unswerving
unwieldily
unyielding
usquebaugh
valleculae
vallecular
variegated
varietally
vaudeville
vengefully
vertebrate
vesperbell
vespertine
vignettist
villeinage
viscerally
vitrescent
viziership
voiceprint
volleyball
vulnerable
vulnerably
Waldensian
wanderings
wanderlust
wanderplug
wappenshaw
wardenship
wastefully
wastepaper
weaverbird
westernise
whaleshark
whereabout
whitebeard
whitefaced
whitesmith
whitethorn
wholesaler
whorehouse
wickedness
wickerwork
wildebeest
wilderment
wilderness
winceyette
wintertide
wintertime
witnessbox
wonderland
wonderment
wonderwork
wontedness
woodenhead
woodenness
wunderkind
yesteryear
antifreeze
aquafortis
aquiferous
artificial
assafetida
auriferous
ballflower
barefooted
bellflower
benefactor
beneficent
beneficial
catafalque
chapfallen
chauffeuse
chiffchaff
chiffonier
clubfooted
coniferous
cornflakes
cornflower
deepfreeze
deepfrozen
deerforest
downfallen
dwarfishly
fivefinger
flatfooted
fluffiness
foamflower
forefather
forefinger
fourfooted
girlfriend
hardfisted
highflying
indefinite
inefficacy
insufflate
kingfisher
ladyfinger
latifundia
luciferase
luciferous
lucifugous
malefactor
maleficent
manifestly
manifestos
manifoldly
modifiable
moonflower
muciferous
munificent
nidificate
nidifugous
notifiable
nubiferous
nuciferous
oleiferous
overflight
pacifiable
pacificate
pacificism
pacificist
paraffinic
pathfinder
piliferous
playfellow
pomiferous
proofsheet
reafforest
riboflavin
ringfinger
saliferous
scaffolder
scoffingly
scrofulous
selffeeder
semifitted
shipfitter
slowfooted
snafflebit
sniffiness
snuffiness
soapflakes
softfinned
solifidian
staffnurse
stepfather
stiffening
stuffiness
surefooted
testflight
thriftless
tortfeasor
trafficked
trafficker
unaffected
undefended
uninformed
unofficial
verifiable
viewfinder
vociferant
vociferate
vociferous
wallflower
wharfinger
wildfowler
windflower
wingfooted
yokefellow
abiogenist
abnegation
abrogation
acrogenous
aerogramme
aerography
aeruginous
Albigenses
allegation
allegiance
allegorise
allegorist
allegretto
allogamous
almsgiving
alongshore
altogether
amalgamate
antagonise
antagonism
antagonist
Armageddon
armigerous
arrogantly
arrogation
assignable
assignment
astigmatic
autogamous
autogenous
autography
backgammon
background
benignancy
bridgeable
bridgehead
bridgeless
bridgework
cacogenics
cacography
caliginous
categorise
cerography
changeable
changeably
changeless
changeling
changeover
chargeable
chargehand
clangorous
clingstone
cragginess
cryogenics
damageable
damagingly
decagramme
decigramme
delegation
delightful
demagogism
demography
denegation
denigrator
derogation
derogatory
designator
designedly
designment
diligently
divagation
doxography
drudgingly
ectogenous
elongation
emarginate
endogamous
endogenous
energetics
engagement
engagingly
enregister
enrigiment
eulogistic
evangelise
evangelism
evangelist
everglades
exaggerate
excogitate
fairground
fatiguable
fledgeling
foregather
foreground
frangipane
frangipani
freightage
fringeless
fuliginous
fumigation
gaingiving

grangerise
grangerism
grogginess
grudgingly
halogenate
halogenous
handgallop
hangglider
holography
homogamous
homogenise
homogenous
hypogynous
ideography
ilangilang
illegalise
illegality
impugnable
impugnment
inaugurate
incogitant
indagation
indigenous
indigested
infighting
insightful
integrable
integrally
integrator
integument
invaginate
invigilate
invigorate
irrigation
kerygmatic
kilogramme
kriegspiel
lanuginose
lanuginous
levigation
lexigraphy
lifegiving
lipography
litigation
logography
loungesuit
malignance
malignancy
manageable
manageably
management
manageress
managerial
metagalaxy
misogamist
misogynist
misogynous
mitigation
mitigative
mitigatory
monogamist
monogamous
monogenism
monogynian
monogynous
navigation
nomography
nosography
obligation
obligatory
obligingly
oleaginous
oleography
omnigenous
oncogenous
oppugnancy
orangepeel
orangewood
oreography
overground
overgrowth
palagonite
panegyrise
panegyrist
paragnosis
pedagogics
perigynous
phlegmatic
phlogistic
phlogiston
phlogopite
plangently
playground
ploughable
ploughland
polygamist
polygamous
polygenism
polygenist
polygenous
polygraphy
polygynous
priggishly
pyrogallol
pyrogenous
pyrography
relegation
reorganise
repugnance
repugnancy
resignedly
rockgarden
rontgenise
roofgarden
rubiginous
savageness
sciagraphy
selfglazed
selfguided
serigraphy
sexagenary
Sexagesima
shagginess
shanghaier
sideglance
skiagraphy
slanginess
sleighbell
sluggardly
sluggishly
smudginess
snowgrouse
spongecake
spongewood
spongiform
sponginess
spongology
sprightful
staggering
stargazing
stinginess
stingingly
stodginess
Stroganoff
swaggering
swingingly
swinglebar
telegraphy
theogonist
thoughtful
toboggancer
tomography
topography
triggerman
typography
unarguable
undigested
vicegerent
vinegarish
viraginous
Visigothic
voyageable
winegrower
woolgather
woolgrower
wrongdoing
wrongfully
wrongously
xerography
xylography
ylangylang
youngberry
zabaglione
Abrahamman
acephalous
aesthetics
aesthetism
alcoholise
alcoholism
alightment
annihilate
anopheline
antiheroic
apochromat
apophthegm
apothecary
apothecial
apothecium
apotheoses
apotheosis
arithmetic
bacchantes
bacchantic
backhanded
backhander
baldheaded
bareheaded
bedchamber
beechdrops
Benthamism
Benthamite
biochemist
biophysics
birthplace
birthright
birthstone
bitchiness
blepharism
blitheness
blithering
blithesome
blushingly
bolshevise
bolshevism
bolshevist
bondholder
boneheaded
brachiator
brachiopod
brachylogy
brachyural
brachyuran
brightness
brightwork
Buddhistic
bullheaded
bunchgrass
cackhanded
camphorate
carphology
Carthusian
caseharden
catchpenny
cinchonine
clawhammer
clodhopper
clothesbag
clothespeg
clothespin
coachbuilt
coachhouse
coathanger
colchicine
comehither
conchoidal
conchology
coolheaded
copyholder
couchgrass
daughterly
dauphiness
deathwatch
decahedral
decahedron
delphinium
delphinoid
diachronic
diaphanous
diathermal
diathermic
discharger
doughfaced
drophammer
earthbound
earthiness
earthlight
earthquake
earthshine
earthwards
epiphytism
epithelial
epithelium
erethismic
evenhanded
exothermal
exothermic
faceharden
fairhaired
faithfully
featherbed
feathering
fetchingly
filthiness
flashboard
flashflood
flashiness
flashlight
flashpoint
fleshiness
fleshwound
flightdeck
flightless
flightpath
forehanded
forthright
fourhanded
freehanded
freeholder
freshwater
froghopper
frothiness
gaucheness
geochemist
geophysics
geothermal
geothermic
gladhander
graphemics
graphitise
graphology
greyheaded
hamshackle
hardhanded
hardheaded
headhunter
heathendom
heathenise
heathenish
heathenism
hemihedral
hemihedron
hexahedral
hexahedron
highhanded
hitchhiker
holohedral
hotchpotch
ichthyosis
incoherent
Irishwoman
ironhanded
isochronal
isothermal
jackhammer
kerchieves
knighthood
Krishnaism
landholder
landhunger
lanthanide
laughingly
leafhopper
lefthanded
lefthander
lionhunter
longhaired
longheaded
loudhailer
lymphocyte
lymphomata
lyophilise
Malthusian
manchineel
marshalled
marshaller
marshalsea
marshiness
matchboard
matchmaker
matchstick
midshipman
mirthfully
mischanter
mischmetal
misthought
mockheroic
monohybrid
monohydric
morphemics
morphinism
morphogeny
morphology
mouthorgan
mouthpiece
nonchalant
northbound
northerner
northwards
notchboard
nympholept
octahedral
octahedron
omophagous
openhanded
openhearth
ophthalmia
ophthalmic
overhanded
patchiness
peashooter
pemphigoid
pemphigous
perchloric
perihelion
pinchpenny
pitchblack
pitcherful
pitchstone
polyhedral
polyhedric
polyhedron
polyhistor
posthumous
prophesier
prophetess
prothallia
prothallus
psephology
psychiatry
psychicism
psychicist
psychology
psychopath
punchboard
punchdrunk
Pyrrhonian
Pyrrhonism
Pyrrhonist
pyrrhotite
ramshackle
reichsmark
rhythmical
rockhopper
roughhouse
roughrider
runthrough
saccharate
saccharide
saccharify
saccharine
saccharoid
saccharose
sandhopper
sapphirine
scatheless
scathingly
scyphiform
scyphozoan
seethrough
Singhalese
sixshooter
slightness
slothfully
softheaded
soothingly
soothsayer
southbound
southerner
southernly
southwards
sowthistle
spathulate
stadholder
staphyline
stephanite
stochastic
subshrubby
sulphonate
sulphurate
sulphurise
sulphurous
swashplate
symphonion
symphonist
symphylous
symphyseal
symphysial
synchronal
synchronic
synthesise
synthesist
synthetise
synthetist
telpherage

tetchiness
tilthammer
toothbrush
toothiness
toothpaste
toothshell
torchlight
touchiness
touchingly
touchjudge
touchpaper
touchstone
tracheated
tracheitis
trashiness
trichiasis
trichinise
trichinous
trichology
trichotomy
trichroism
trichromat
triphammer
triphthong
trochanter
trochoidal
trophology
truthfully
tufthunter
twowheeler
Tyrrhenian
unschooled
urethritis
urochordal
watchfully
watchglass
watchguard
watchmaker
watchtower
weatherbox
weathering
weatherman
weightless
wellheeled
Welshwoman
Wertherian
Wertherism
Winchester
wirehaired
witchcraft
witchhazel
witchingly
withholder
worshipful
worshipped
worshipper
worthiness
worthwhile
wrathfully
wrathiness
Wykehamist
youthfully
zoophagous
zoophilous
abominable
abominably
abominator
aboriginal
abscission
abstinence
abstinency
acidimeter
acidimetry
acquirable
acquitting
adroitness
Aethiopian
affliction
afflictive
aficionado
ameliorate
Amerindian
amphibious
amphibrach
amphictyon
amphigouri
amphimacer
amphimixes
amphimixis
Anglistics
apolitical
applicable
applicably
applicator
appointive
architrave
ascribable
ascription
assailable
assoilment
astringent
atomically
attainable
attainment
atypically
auctioneer
auspicious
autoimmune
avaricious
ballistics
baptistery
barbituric
Bedlington
bestialise
bestiality
bestirring
biblically
bibliology
bibliopegy
bibliophil
bibliopole
bibliopoly
bibliotics
bobbinlace
brazilwood
Britishism
buccinator
byssinosis
cacciatore
cachinnate
caddisworm
calciferol
candidness
cantilever
cantillate
capricious
captiously
carcinogen
carcinosis
cardialgia
cardiogram
cardiology
cautionary
cautiously
centigrade
centilitre
centillion
centimetre
certiorari
cessionary
charioteer
charismata
charitable
charitably
chelicerae
chemically
chemisette
chiliastic
choriambic
clavichord
clavicular
clerically
clinically
coatimundi
coexistent
cognisable
cognisably
cognisance
collimator
commissary
commission
commissure
commitment
committing
commixture
conciliary
conciliate
concinnity
confidante
confidence
confirmand
confiscate
conniption
connivance
considered
consistent
consistory
contiguity
contiguous
continence
contingent
continuant
continuate
continuity
continuous
conviction
convictive
convincing
coolingoff
corbiculae
cordiality
cordierite
cordillera
corrigenda
corrigible
corrivalry
corticated
cosmically
cousinhood
cousinship
craniology
creditable
creditably
criminally
critically
cultivable
cultivator
curricular
curriculum
cuspidated
cyclically
dampingoff
deceivable
declinable
deltiology
demoiselle
densimeter
dentifrice
deoxidiser
deprivable
derailleur
derailment
despicable
despicably
despisable
despiteful
despiteous
detainment
dictionary
diesinking
difficulty
diffidence
discipline
dislikable
dismission
dismissive
dispirited
dispiteous
dissidence
dissilient
dissimilar
dissipated
distichous
distilland
distillate
distillery
distilling
distinctly
ditriglyph
dorsigrade
drawingpin
duplicator
earwigging
earwitness
eliminable
eliminator
elucidator
emaciation
Englishman
enjoinment
entailment
epilimnion
eradicable
eradicator
eremitical
erotically
erysipelas
escritoire
ethnically
examinable
exobiology
exotically
explicable
explicitly
extricable
exuviation
eyewitness
fabricator
factiously
factitious
fallingoff
fancifully
farcically
farsighted
fasciation
fascicular
fasciculus
fascinator
fastidious
fastigiate
febrifugal
fertiliser
fervidness
fibrillary
fibrillate
fibrillose
fibrinogen
fictioneer
fictionist
fictitious
fisticuffs
flagitious
flamingoes
floriation
floribunda
floridness
florilegia
floristics
fluviatile
fluxionary
flyfishing
foetidness
follicular
forbidding
forcipated
foreignism
forgivable
forgivably
formidable
formidably
fornicator
fortissimi
fortissimo
Fourierism
fourinhand
fraxinella
frigidness
fritillary
frolicking
frolicsome
fulfilling
fulfilment
fungicidal
galliambic
garnierite
garnishing
gaslighter
gentilesse
germicidal
germinally
gingivitis
glaciation
glaciology
gloriously
goldilocks
gothically
graciosity
graciously
gramicidin
gramineous
gratifying
gravimeter
gravimetry
gunfighter
handicraft
hectically
helminthic
hermitcrab
heroically
heroicness
heroicomic
heuristics
horridness
hospitable
hospitably
hybridiser
hydrically
imaginable
imaginably
impairment
implicitly
imprimatur
imprinting
impuissant
inclinable
ineligible
ineligibly
inevitable
inevitably
inexistent
infliction
inflictive
inimically
inimitable
inimitably
initialise
initialled
initiation
initiative
initiatory
inquietude
inquisitor
inspirator
inspissate
instigator
instilling
institutor
intrigante
intriguant
ironically
isoniazide
italianate
italianise
Italianism
jardiniere
jesuitical
jinricksha
jinrikisha
justiciary
Kantianism
kinnikinic
Kuomintang
lacrimator
landingnet
larvicidal
lascivious
leafinsect
lectionary
lemniscate
lenticular
lentigines
lesbianism
limpidness
Lippizaner
liquidator
liquidiser
liquidness
lopsidedly
lowpitched
lubricator
lubricious
lusciously
machinator
machinegun
mackintosh
magnifical
magnificat
magnifying
Malpighian
mandibular
maquillage
Marcionite
marginalia
marginally
marginated
martialism
martingale
masticable
masticator
matriarchy
matricidal
meaningful
meltingpot
mendicancy
mercifully
messianism
metrically
millilitre
millimetre
misgivings
mishitting
missionary
missionise
monsignori

morbidezza
morbidness
morrispike
mosaically
mosaicking
muffinbell
mulligrubs
multifaced
multiloquy
multimedia
multiphase
multiplier
multipolar
multistage
multivocal
myopically
mystically
mythically
mythiciser
narcissism
narcissist
nautically
negligence
negligible
negligibly
neurilemma
nitpicking
nonfiction
nonviolent
nourishing
nunciature
nuptiality
nutritious
nyctinasty
obediently
obtainable
obtainment
offlicence
onesidedly
opinionist
ordainment
originally
originator
outbidding
outfielder
outfitting
outrightly
outsitting
outwitting
ovariotomy
oxidisable
packingbox
paediatric
palliation
palliative
palliatory
pallidness
parliament
parricidal
partiality
participle
particular
passionary
passionate
Passionist
patriality
patriarchy
patriciate
patricidal
patrilocal
patriotism
patristics
pectinated
pellicular
pencilling
pennillion
pensionary
pentimento
percipient
perfidious
permission
permissive
permitting
pernicious
pernickety
persiflage
persistent
pertinence
pertinency
pesticidal
pestilence
pharisaism
philippina
philippine
philistine
phonically
phthisical
physically
physicking
physiocrat
physiology
pianissimo
pichiciago
picnicking
pilliwinks
piscifauna
pistillary
pistillate
placidness
plagiarise
plagiarism
plagiarist
planigraph
planimeter
planimetry
plebiscite
plesiosaur
poetically
pollinator
pontifical
pontifices
postillion
pratincole
preciosity
preciously
precipitin
predicable
prediction
predictive
predispose
prefixture
prehistory
presidency
presidiary
presignify
previously
primiparae
privileged
prodigally
prodigious
proficient
profitable
profitably
profitless
prohibiter
prohibitor
prolicidal
prominence
promissory
propionate
propitiate
propitious
prosilient
providence
provincial
provisions
provitamin
proximally
pruriently
publishing
pulsimeter
pulvinated
putridness
rabbinical
rancidness
realisable
receivable
reeligible
refringent
rejoicings
repairable
requiescat
rescission
rescissory
reshipment
respirable
respirator
retainable
reunionism
reunionist
rodfishing
rollicking
rollingpin
rubrically
rubricator
ruffianism
Russianise
rustically
sacrificer
salpingian
saltigrade
scenically
seabiscuit
sealingwax
seguidilla
semeiology
semeiotics
sensitiser
sentiently
septically
septillion
serviceman
sexlimited
sextillion
sheriffdom
sincipital
somniloquy
sordidness
spaciously
spadiceous
spatiality
specialise
specialism
specialist
speciality
speciation
speciology
speciosity
speciously
spiritedly
spiritless
spirituous
spoliation
spoliative
spoliatory
spuriously
stabiliser
statically
stationary
stationery
statistics
sterigmata
steriliser
stolidness
straighten
straightly
strainedly
straitness
studiously
stupidness
stylistics
subkingdom
sublimable
subliminal
sublingual
submission
submissive
submitting
subsidence
subsidiary
subsistent
succinctly
sufficient
suicidally
summitless
surgically
surmisable
survivance
suspicious
syndicator
syphilitic
tactically
tardigrade
tendinitis
terminable
terminably
terminally
terminator
termitaria
tirailleur
toroidally
torpidness
torridness
tortiously
tragically
tragicomic
trilingual
triliteral
trivialise
trivialism
triviality
tropically
tuitionary
turbidness
turgidness
twilighted
unblinking
uncritical
unedifying
unfairness
unfaithful
unfriended
unfriendly
unilingual
uninitiate
unsuitable
unthinking
unwrinkled
upbringing
usuriously
utilisable
utopianism
uxoricidal
uxoriously
vaccinator
ventilator
vermicelli
vermicidal
vermicular
vernissage
versicular
vertically
vestibular
vestibulum
victimiser
vindicable
vindicator
vindictive
virginally
virginhood
vitriolise
vortically
vorticella
vorticular
warmingpan
wearifully
wellington
workingman
Wycliffite
Beaujolais
bluejacket
coadjacent
dustjacket
highjacker
lifejacket
showjumper
tearjerker
windjammer
Afrikander
blackamoor
blackberry
blackboard
blackfaced
blackguard
blackheart
Blackshirt
blacksmith
blackthorn
blackwater
blanketing
blockboard
blockhouse
blockishly
bookkeeper
breakables
breakpoint
breakwater
brickfield
bricklayer
bumpkinish
chalkboard
chalkstone
checkpoint
cheekiness
chickenpox
chuckerout
chuckwagon
clinkstone
crackajack
crackbrain
crankiness
crankshaft
crowkeeper
doorkeeper
fishkettle
flunkeydom
flunkeyism
freakiness
freakishly
friskiness
gamekeeper
gatekeeper
goalkeeper
jackknives
knickknack
knobkerrie
knockabout
knockkneed
knopkierie
ladykiller
lockkeeper
mudskipper
painkiller
planktonic
pluckiness
quickgrass
quickthorn
quirkiness
Sanskritic
shockingly
shockproof
shopkeeper
smockfrock
sneakiness
sneakingly
sneakthief
snickasnee
spankingly
spookiness
spunkiness
steakhouse
stickiness
stinkingly
stinkstone
stockiness
stockpiler
stockproof
stockrider
stockstill
storksbill
strikingly
thankfully
thickening
thinkingly
thinkpiece
timekeeper
trickiness
trickishly
triskelion
trucklebed
unlikeness
weedkiller
whiskified
absolutely
absolution
absolutism
absolutist
absolutory
accelerate
acoelomate
Adullamite
aerologist
affiliated
agrologist
algolagnia
algolagnic
algologist
alkalinity
ambulacral
ambulacrum
ambulation
ambulatory
ampelopsis
anaglyphic
anaplastic
Andalusian
andalusite
angularity
annalistic
annularity
annulation
Apollinian
Apollonian
apoplectic
aquilinity
arbalester
arbalister
areolation
autologous
axiologist
babblement
Babylonian
bafflement
bafflingly

barelegged
battledore
battlement
battleship
beadleship
bedclothes
bibulously
bicultural
bipolarity
bisulphate
bisulphide
bisulphite
bivalvular
bootlegger
bootlessly
bootlicker
bottlefeed
bottleneck
bottletree
bowdlerise
bowdlerism
bridlepath
brilliance
brilliancy
bryologist
bubblyjock
bufflehead
bumblingly
bunglingly
burglarise
bustlingly
cabalistic
cajolement
cajolingly
camelopard
canaliculi
candlefish
candletree
candlewick
candlewood
carelessly
catalectic
cataleptic
cataloguer
cattlegrid
cavalierly
cavalryman
challenger
chaplaincy
Charleston
chilliness
churlishly
cochleated
comeliness
complacent
complainer
complected
complement
completely
completion
completive
complexion
complexity
compliance
compliancy
complicacy
complicate
complicity
compliment
complotted
conclusion
conclusive
conclusory
conflation
confluence
conglobate
copulation
copulative
coralberry
coralsnake
corelation
corelative
costliness
couplement
covalently
cradlesong
cucullated
cuddlesome
cumulation
cumulative
cumuliform
cuttlebone
cuttlefish
cytologist
dapplegrey
dazzlement
dazzlingly
deadliness
debilitate
decelerate
decolonise
decolorant
decolorise
defalcator
defilement
defoliator
demolition
depilation
depilatory
depolarise
desalinate
desolately
desolation
devilishly
devolution
disclaimer
disclosure
disulphate
disulphide
disyllabic
disyllable
divulgence
doublebass
doubleness
doublepark
doubletalk
doubletime
drawlingly
dumbledore
dysplastic
ebullience
ebulliency
ebullition
edibleness
effulgence
embalmment
embolismic
emollition
engulfment
epiblastic
epiglottal
epiglottic
epiglottis
equilibria
escalation
escallonia
Esculapian
ethologist
etiolation
eucalyptol
eucalyptus
everliving
excellence
excellency
exhalation
exhilarant
exhilarate
eyeglasses
fabulously
facileness
facilitate
fadelessly
fairleader
familiarly
fatalistic
fearlessly
fecklessly
feebleness
femaleness
feuilleton
fickleness
fiddleback
fiddlehead
fiddlewood
flawlessly
folklorist
footlights
formlessly
fourleaved
freelancer
freeliving
freeloader
frilliness
fulllength
fumblingly
gadolinite
gadolinium
gaillardia
ganglionic
gatelegged
gentlefolk
gentleness
goggleeyed
goodliness
goodlooker
grisliness
growlingly
guillotine
gunslinger
habiliment
habilitate
halflength
harelipped
harmlessly
heedlessly
helplessly
highlander
homeliness
homiletics
homologate
homologise
homologous
hopelessly
horologist
hotblooded
hucklebone
humbleness
hypolimnia
idealistic
ideologist
immolation
impalement
impalpable
impalpably
impolitely
inculcator
inculpable
indelicacy
indelicate
indolently
indulgence
infallible
infallibly
infelicity
infiltrate
inhalation
inkslinger
insolation
insolently
insolvable
insolvency
insularism
insularity
insulation
intolerant
invalidate
invalidism
invalidity
invaluable
invaluably
involucral
involucrum
involution
irrelative
irrelevant
irreligion
isoglossal
jocularity
jubilantly
jubilation
kettledrum
kindliness
kingliness
lacklustre
landlocked
landlubber
lavalliere
legalistic
lifelessly
likelihood
likeliness
listlessly
littleness
livelihood
liveliness
lobulation
loneliness
longlegged
lordliness
lossleader
lovelessly
loveletter
loveliness
luculently
maculation
maculature
mainlander
mamillated
maxilliped
mayblossom
measliness
meddlesome
medullated
megalithic
megalosaur
Mesolithic
metalepsis
metallurgy
mettlesome
middleaged
middlebrow
middlemost
middlingly
mindlessly
misaligned
misologist
mixolydian
modulation
moniliasis
moniliform
monolithic
monologise
monologist
moralistic
movelessly
mudslinger
mutilation
mycologist
namelessly
natalitial
nebulosity
nebulously
needlebath
needlebook
needlecord
needlefish
needlessly
needlework
neoclassic
neoplastic
nettlerash
newsletter
nihilistic
nimbleness
nipplewort
nodulation
nomologist
nonaligned
nonplaying
nonplussed
nosologist
novelistic
ocellation
oecologist
oenologist
oncologist
ontologist
oppilation
oreologist
oscillator
osculation
osculatory
overlander
overlapped
overlooker
paddleboat
painlessly
paralipsis
paralogise
paralogism
patulously
pearldiver
pebbledash
peculation
peculiarly
pedalorgan
pedalpoint
pedologist
peerlessly
penologist
perilously
perplexity
petulantly
phallicism
phelloderm
phillumeny
phyllotaxy
phylloxera
pitilessly
pixillated
pomologist
popularise
popularity
population
populistic
populously
portliness
postliminy
preclusion
preclusive
preglacial
proclaimer
proclivity
profligacy
profligate
proglottis
pugilistic
pupilarity
purblindly
purulently
puzzlement
pyrolusite
rabblement
ramblingly
rattlehead
rattlepate
rattletrap
reallocate
rebellious
recallable
recklessly
recolonise
redblooded
redolently
refillable
refulgence
regalement
regelation
regularise
regularity
regulation
regulative
regulatory
repellance
repellancy
repellence
repellency
resilience
resiliency
resolutely
resolution
resolutive
resolvable
resolvedly
restlessly
resultless
revalidate
revalorise
revelation
revelatory
revilement
revolution
rheologist
ringleader
ripplemark
ropeladder
roselipped
ruthlessly
saddleback
saddlefast
saddletree
satellitic
scarlatina
scholastic
Scillonian
sciolistic
scrollwork
secularise
secularism
secularist
secularity
sedulously
seemliness
selflessly
selfloving
semiliquid
semilunate
sepulchral
serologist
settlement
sexologist
shellacked
shellmound
shellproof

shellshock	timeliness	asymmetric	ephemerous	muskmallow	schematise
shieldless	tirelessly	automation	estimation	myxomatous	schematism
shillelagh	tonelessly	automatise	estimative	myxomycete	schemozzle
shoplifter	topologist	automatism	eudemonism	newsmonger	scrimmager
shouldered	trawlerman	automatist	eudemonist	octamerous	scrimshank
shrillness	triclinium	automobile	euhemerise	oecumenism	seismicity
sibilation	triflingly	automotive	euhemerism	oedematose	seismogram
sicklebill	triglyphic	autumnally	euhemerist	oedematous	seismology
sickliness	trillionth	bandmaster	evilminded	openminded	selfmotion
similarity	triplicate	barometric	exhumation	optimalise	selfmurder
similitude	triplicity	becomingly	extemporal	optimistic	shipmaster
simpleness	troglodyte	bigamously	fairminded	ornamental	skirmisher
simplicity	trolleybus	bituminise	fellmonger	overmanned	skrimshank
simplifier	trollopish	bituminous	fishmonger	overmantel	slowmotion
simplistic	tumbledown	bolometric	fleamarket	overmaster	snowmobile
simulacrum	tumblerful	bookmaking	folkmemory	palimpsest	solemnness
simulation	tumbleweed	bookmarker	foraminous	Panamanian	spermaceti
simulative	tumultuary	Brahmanism	fragmental	paramecium	spermicide
simulatory	tumultuous	Brahminism	freemartin	parametric	squamation
singlefoot	tunelessly	broomstick	galimatias	paramnesia	steamchest
singleness	turtleback	Buchmanism	glimmering	parimutuel	steaminess
singletree	turtledove	Buchmanite	gloominess	pastmaster	steamtight
sinologist	turtleneck	bushmaster	gobemouche	pedimental	stepmother
smallscale	typologist	cacomistle	grammarian	pedimented	stigmatise
smallsword	umbellifer	calamander	hackmatack	peremptory	stigmatism
smallwares	umbilicate	calamitous	handmaiden	pharmacist	stigmatist
smelliness	umbiliform	calumniate	headmaster	plasmodesm	stormbound
snailpaced	unbalanced	calumnious	hexamerous	plasmodium	stormcloud
snailwheel	unbeliever	caramelise	hexametric	plasmogamy	storminess
soullessly	undulation	ceremonial	highminded	plasmolyse	stormproof
spallation	undulatory	ceruminous	homemaking	pneumatics	stramonium
spellbound	unfilially	charmingly	illuminant	pockmarked	stromatous
sphalerite	unhallowed	chromatics	illuminate	polemicist	swanmaiden
spiflicate	unholiness	chromatype	illuminati	polemonium	swarmspore
spillikins	unreliable	chromosome	illuminism	polymathic	swimmingly
spoilsport	unrelieved	clamminess	illuminist	polymerise	taskmaster
spotlessly	unruliness	columbaria	immemorial	polymerism	tegumental
squalidity	unselected	coromandel	incomplete	polymerous	telemetric
stablemate	upholstery	creaminess	incumbency	postmaster	tenemental
stableness	ustulation	datamation	infamously	postmortem	thermionic
stealthily	viewlessly	decampment	ingeminate	potamology	thermistor
steeliness	vigilantly	Decembrist	inhumanely	praemunire	thermogram
steelworks	virologist	decemviral	inhumanity	pragmatise	thermophil
stelliform	virulently	decimalise	inhumation	pragmatism	thermopile
stepladder	vitalistic	decimalism	innominate	pragmatist	thermostat
stiflebone	vitiligate	decimation	innumeracy	preeminent	thromboses
stiflingly	waffleiron	decompound	innumerate	preemption	thrombosis
stillbirth	wattlebird	decompress	innumerous	preemptive	thrombotic
stillicide	wavelength	defamation	inseminate	prismoidal	totemistic
subclavian	weakliness	defamatory	intimately	psalmodise	tourmaline
subglacial	wentletrap	defeminise	intimation	psalmodist	trammelled
subtleness	wheelchair	dehumanise	intimidate	pyromaniac	traumatism
sunglasses	wheelhorse	dehumidify	ironmaster	pyromantic	triumphant
supplanter	wheelhouse	delaminate	ironmonger	pyrometric	triumviral
supplejack	whirlybird	delimitate	kinematics	qualmishly	ultimately
supplement	wobbliness	denominate	leguminous	quizmaster	uncommonly
suppleness	woodlander	dilemmatic	ligamental	Rachmanism	unfamiliar
suppletion	woolliness	disembogue	likeminded	ragamuffin	unfeminine
suppletive	wordlessly	disembosom	lipomatous	rainmaking	unnameable
suppletory	abdominous	disembowel	locomotion	razzmatazz	unnumbered
suppliance	accomplice	disembroil	locomotive	rearmament	unremarked
supplicant	accomplish	documental	locomotory	recommence	vehemently
supplicate	accumulate	dolomitise	lovemaking	recompense	venomously
surplusage	acromegaly	dosimetric	Mahommedan	recumbency	vitaminise
synaloepha	alarmingly	dreaminess	manometric	redemption	volumetric
tabularise	albuminoid	dreamworld	manumitted	redemptive	voluminous
tabulation	albuminous	dynamistic	maximalist	redemptory	weakminded
tactlessly	antemortem	eczematous	mesomerism	regimental	WhitMonday
tanglement	antimasque	effeminacy	mesomorphy	resemblant	yardmaster
tattletale	antimatter	effeminate	metamerism	resumption	zygomorphy
teaplanter	antimonial	encampment	metempiric	resumptive	accentuate
tearlessly	antimonite	endemicity	minimalism	rheumatics	achondrite
theologian	aquamarine	enigmatise	minimalist	rheumatism	acronychal
theologise	argumentum	enigmatist	mintmaster	rheumatoid	actinolite
theologist	ascomycete	enjambment	Mohammedan	ringmaster	actinozoan
thillhorse	assemblage	enormously	monomaniac	rosemallow	adjunction
ticklishly	assimilate	entombment	monumental	rudimental	adjunctive
tiddlywink	assumption	entomology	Muhammadan	salamander	administer
timelessly	assumptive	enzymology	Muhammedan	sandmartin	admonition

admonitive
admonitory
adrenaline
adrenergic
adventurer
aerenchyma
aeronautic
aeronomist
agronomist
Algonquian
alienation
almondeyed
alpenstock
ammoniacal
ammoniated
ammunition
annunciate
anointment
antinomian
antonymous
appendices
appendixes
ascendable
ascendance
ascendancy
ascendence
ascendency
ascendible
assentient
Athanasian
attendance
attenuated
attenuator
attunement
autonomist
autonomous
baronetage
behindhand
belongings
biannually
bidonville
biennially
brainchild
braininess
brainpower
brainstorm
brawniness
brownshirt
brownstone
canonicals
canonicate
canonicity
caruncular
catenation
chainsmoke
channelise
channelled
chauntress
chimneypot
chronicity
chronicler
chronogram
chronology
clannishly
clientship
clownishly
cockneyish
cockneyism
colonially
colonnaded
comanchero
Corinthian
coronation
cosentient
covenanted
covenantee
covenanter
covenantor
cylindered
cylindroid
debonairly
defendable
defensible
defensibly
definement
definienda
definitely
definition
definitive
definitude
degeneracy
degenerate
delineator
delinquent
demandable
dementedly
demonetise
demoniacal
demonology
denunciate
dependable
dependably
dependence
dependency
detonation
detonative
Devanagari
diagnostic
diminished
diminuendo
diminution
diminutive
diningroom
disenchant
disengaged
disenthral
disentitle
disentwine
disenviron
disincline
disinherit
divination
divinatory
divineness
dominantly
domination
dominative
dysenteric
echinoderm
eigenvalue
embankment
embonpoint
Emmentaler
empanelled
engineroom
ensanguine
eosinophil
equanimity
ergonomics
ergonomist
eternalise
eternalist
eugenicist
expandable
expansible
expendable
expunction
exsanguine
extendedly
extendible
extensible
extenuator
extinction
extinctive
extinguish
fearnought
feminality
femininely
femininity
flannelled
friendless
friendlily
friendship
frowningly
furuncular
gemination
geognostic
gerundival
gesundheit
greencloth
greenfinch
greenheart
greenhouse
greenshank
greenstick
greenstone
greenstuff
greensward
groundbait
groundless
groundling
groundmass
groundplan
groundrent
groundsman
groundwork
gynandrous
hakenkreuz
halfnelson
hedonistic
hempnettle
Herrnhuter
homonymous
homunculus
humaneness
humanistic
humanities
hypanthium
imminently
immunology
impanation
impanelled
impendence
impendency
impenitent
incandesce
incantator
incendiary
incinerate
inconstant
incunabula
Indonesian
infinitely
infinitive
infinitude
injunction
injunctive
insaneness
insanitary
insensible
insensibly
insentient
insinuator
intangible
intangibly
intendance
intendment
intenerate
intentness
intinction
intonation
inventress
invincible
invincibly
iodination
Japanesque
jejuneness
johnnycake
journalese
journalise
journalism
journalist
journeyman
juvenility
laconicism
lamentable
lamentably
lamentedly
laminarian
lamination
laryngitic
laryngitis
lebensraum
Leibnizian
lemongrass
licensable
licentiate
licentious
livingroom
loganberry
loganstone
lovingness
luminosity
luminously
Lysenkoism
malentendu
malingerer
mayonnaise
melancholy
Melanesian
melanistic
meningioma
meningitis
mesenteric
mesenteron
molendinar
monandrous
mournfully
mutinously
nepenthean
nominalism
nominalist
nominately
nomination
nominative
notonectal
oceanarium
oceangoing
oceanology
octandrian
octandrous
octonarian
oftentimes
ordinarily
ordination
ordonnance
organicism
organicist
organismal
orientally
ostensible
ostensibly
overnicety
pagination
palindrome
palynology
paranormal
parenchyma
parentally
parenteral
parenthood
paronymous
patentable
patination
peduncular
peninsular
Phoenician
phrenology
plainchant
pleonastic
pliantness
pogonology
pogonotomy
Polynesian
polynomial
potentiate
potentilla
prednisone
pregnantly
prognathic
prognostic
quaintness
ranunculus
ravenously
recentness
reconciler
reconsider
redundance
redundancy
refinement
refundable
refundment
regeneracy
regenerate
regentship
relentless
relinquish
remonetise
remunerate
repentance
resentment
resonantly
retinacula
revanchism
revanchist
revengeful
ricinoleic
ringnecked
ripsnorter
Romanesque
Romanistic
rosaniline
rowanberry
ruminantly
rumination
ruminative
sagination
satanology
scientific
scornfully
seaanemone
secondbest
secondhand
secondment
secondrate
seignorage
seignorial
selenodont
selenology
seminarian
seminarist
semination
sereneness
seventieth
shrinkable
shrinkwrap
silentness
simoniacal
skinniness
solenoidal
sphenodone
sphenogram
sphenoidal
splanchnic
splendidly
splintbone
splintcoal
spoondrift
spoonerism
springhalt
springhead
springless
springlike
springtail
springtide
springtime
springwood
sprinkling
squanderer
squinteyed
stagnantly
stagnation
sternwards
strengthen
stringbean
stringency
stringendo
stringhalt
stringless
stronghold
strongroom
stunningly
supination
supineness
synanthous
synonymist
synonymity
synonymous
takingness
talentless
tarantella
tarantelle
taxonomist
technetium
technician
technicist
technocrat
technology
tenantable
tenantless
thornapple
thorniness
thornproof
threnodial
threnodist
throneless
tiringroom
titanesque
tournament
tourniquet
triandrous
triangular
tyrannical
unbonneted
undeniable
undeniably
unfinished
ungenerous
unhandsome
unionistic
unkindness
unmannerly
unwontedly
urbanology
verandahed
Vietnamese
vivandiere
wagonvault
womanishly
yearningly
achromatic
acidophile
actionable
actionably

aeolotropy
aetiologic
aircooling
alcyonaria
allrounder
amphoteric
anacolutha
anagogical
analogical
anamorphic
anatomical
anchoretic
anchoritic
anchorless
anchorring
androecium
androgenic
anemograph
anemometer
anemometry
anemophily
angiosperm
anglomania
anglophile
anglophobe
anglophone
AngloSaxon
anisotropy
aphrodisia
apologetic
approvable
approvably
aragonitic
asafoetida
astrologer
astrologic
astronomer
astronomic
audiometer
audiometry
audiophile
authorship
ballooning
balloonist
bardolatry
bassoonist
batfowling
batholitic
bathometer
benzocaine
bestowment
bigmouthed
biological
biomorphic
blazonment
borborygmi
bottomless
bottommost
buffoonery
buttonball
buttonbush
buttondown
buttonhole
buttonhook
buttonless
buttonwood
callowness
cannonball
cantonment
canzonetta
carbonnade
carboxylic
cartomancy
cartoonist
cassolette
catholicon
catholicos
cellophane
censorious
censorship
chatoyance
chemotaxis
chiromancy
cismontane
cispontine
citronella
clinometer
clinometry
cnidoblast
coenobitic
coenobytic
cognominal
coleoptera
coleoptile
coleorhiza
collocutor
colloquial
colloquise
colloquist
colloquium
colportage
colporteur
commodious
commonable
commonalty
commonness
commonroom
commonweal
composedly
compositor
compotator
compounder
concoction
concoctive
concordant
condolence
conformism
conformist
conformity
confounded
conjointly
consociate
consolable
consonance
consonancy
consortium
contortion
contortive
convoluted
coproducer
coprolitic
corporally
corporator
corporeity
corroboree
cosmogonic
cosmopolis
cosmoramic
cottoncake
cottonseed
cottontail
cottonweed
cottonwood
cottonwool
coulometry
crinolette
crocoisite
ctenophore
cuckoopint
cuckoospit
custommade
cyclograph
cyclometer
cyclopedia
cyclopedic
cyclostome
cyclostyle
cystoscope
cystoscopy
deaconship
deflowerer
deodoriser
deplorable
deplorably
deployment
despondent
diabolical
diagonally
diplodocus
diplomatic
dipsomania
discobolus
discomfort
discommend
discommode
discompose
disconcert
disconfirm
disconnect
discontent
discophile
discordant
discounter
discourage
discourser
discoverer
dishonesty
disjointed
disloyally
disloyalty
disposable
dispossess
dissociate
dissoluble
dissolvent
dissonance
dissonancy
distortion
doctorship
draconites
dragonhead
dragonnade
dragontree
drosophila
dumfounder
ecological
economical
economiser
editorship
effloresce
effrontery
elaborator
embroidery
employable
employment
encroacher
engrossing
episodical
erotogenic
erotomania
ethnologic
eudiometer
eudiometry
euphonious
evaporable
evaporator
exploitage
exploitive
exprobrate
factorship
fallowness
fantoccini
fathomable
fathomless
fellowship
festoonery
fibrositis
FinnoUgric
flavourful
flavouring
foreordain
frigorific
frivolling
gadrooning
galloglass
Gallomania
Gallophile
Gallophobe
gambolling
gasconader
geological
geoponical
Glagolitic
glycolyses
glycolysis
glycosuria
glycosuric
goniometer
goniometry
Gorgonzola
gramophone
granophyre
GrecoRoman
gymnosophy
gymnosperm
gypsophila
haemolysis
haemolytic
hagiolatry
hagiologic
hagioscope
harbourage
harmonical
harmonious
harmoniser
hebdomadal
hectograph
hectolitre
hectometre
heliograph
heliolater
heliolatry
heliometer
heliophyte
helioscope
heliotaxis
heliotrope
heliotropy
hierocracy
hieroglyph
hierograph
hierolatry
hierophant
highoctane
hippocampi
Hippocrene
hippodrome
hippogriff
hippogryph
hippomanes
hippophagy
histologic
histolysis
histolytic
historical
hobnobbing
holloweyed
hollowness
hollowware
homeopathy
homoousian
hormonally
hyaloplasm
hydrologic
hydrolysis
hydrolytic
hydromancy
hydrometer
hydrometry
hydropathy
hydrophane
hydrophily
hydrophone
hydrophyte
hydroplane
hydroscope
hydrotaxis
hygrograph
hygrometer
hygrometry
hygrophyte
hygroscope
hypnotiser
hypsometer
hypsometry
iatrogenic
iconoclasm
iconolater
iconolatry
iconomachy
iconometer
iconometry
iconoscope
improbable
improbably
improperly
improvable
improvably
improviser
inchoately
inchoation
inchoative
ineloquent
inexorable
inexorably
inglorious
introducer
introrsely
introspect
inviolable
inviolably
iridosmine
isomorphic
Italophile
jargonelle
jimsonweed
jingoistic
karyoplasm
keyboarder
labiovelar
lampoonery
lampoonist
landocracy
landowning
leucocytic
leucoplast
leukocytic
lissomness
lithoglyph
lithograph
lithologic
lithophane
lithophyte
lithotrity
logrolling
lophophore
macrophage
macrospore
maisonette
malcontent
mangosteen
Mariolater
Mariolatry
marionette
marrowbone
marrowless
Massoretic
matronhood
matronship
matronymic
meadowland
meadowlark
mediocrity
meliorator
mellowness
mentorship
meteoritic
methodical
metronomic
metronymic
metropolis
microbiota
microcline
microfarad
microfiche
micrograph
microlitic
micrometer
micrometry
microphone
microphyte
micropylar
microscope
microscopy
microseism
microspore
midmorning
mignonette
mimeograph
misconduct
misfortune
misjoinder
misnomered
miswording
motionless
mumbojumbo
muttonhead
myological
mythologer
mythologic
mythomania
mythopoeia
mythopoeic
narcolepsy
narrowness
nationally
nationhood
nationless
nationwide
Neapolitan
necrolater
necrolatry
necromancy
necrophile
necrophily
necropolis
necroscopy
negrophile
negrophobe
neological
nephograph
nephoscope
neurolemma
neuropathy
neuroplasm
neurotoxin
nincompoop
nitrochalk
nitrogroup
noncontent
nonjoinder
nonlogical
nostologic
notionally

ochl**o**cracy
olig**o**clase
olig**o**psony
ombr**o**meter
ophi**o**later
ophi**o**latry
ophi**o**logic
opis**o**meter
oppr**o**brium
opti**o**nally
orat**o**rical
orol**o**gical
orth**o**clase
orth**o**doxly
orth**o**epist
orth**o**genic
orth**o**gonal
orth**o**pedic
orth**o**ptera
oste**o**blast
oste**o**clast
oste**o**pathy
oste**o**phyte
outp**o**uring
ovip**o**sitor
paed**o**gogue
paed**o**phile
pans**o**phist
pant**o**graph
pant**o**mimic
pard**o**nable
pard**o**nably
parr**o**tfish
pars**o**nbird
pars**o**nical
past**o**rally
past**o**rship
path**o**genic
path**o**logic
patr**o**lling
patr**o**nymic
peac**o**ckery
peac**o**ckish
perc**o**lator
perf**o**liate
perf**o**rator
perf**o**rming
peri**o**dical
peri**o**steal
peri**o**steum
pers**o**nable
pers**o**nally
pers**o**nalty
pers**o**nator
peti**o**lated
petr**o**glyph
petr**o**latum
petr**o**nella
phag**o**cytic
phen**o**cryst
phen**o**menal
phen**o**menon
phen**o**typic
pher**o**monal
phil**o**logen
phil**o**poena
phil**o**sophe
phil**o**sophy
phon**o**graph
phon**o**litic
phon**o**logic
phon**o**meter
phot**o**flood
phot**o**genic
phot**o**graph
phot**o**litho
phot**o**lysis
phot**o**lytic
phot**o**meter
phot**o**metry
phot**o**nasty
phot**o**phily
phot**o**phore
phot**o**print
phot**o**taxis
phot**o**trope
phyl**o**genic
phyt**o**genic
phyt**o**phagy
phyt**o**toxic
pian**o**forte
pict**o**graph
pict**o**rical
piez**o**meter
pige**o**nhole
pige**o**npair
pige**o**npost
pige**o**ntoed
pige**o**nwing
pill**o**wcase
pill**o**wlace
pill**o**wslip
pist**o**lling
pist**o**lshot
pist**o**lwhip
pist**o**nring
plan**o**meter
plec**o**ptera
plut**o**cracy
plut**o**latry
poly**o**nymic
porn**o**cracy
post**o**ffice
pozz**o**lanic
prec**o**cious
prec**o**ncert
prec**o**rdial
prem**o**nitor
prep**o**ssess
prep**o**tence
prep**o**tency
prim**o**rdial
prim**o**rdium
prof**o**undly
prol**o**cutor
prol**o**guise
prol**o**ngate
prom**o**ntory
pron**o**minal
pron**o**unced
pron**o**uncer
prop**o**rtion
prop**o**under
pros**o**dical
prot**o**phyta
prot**o**phyte
prot**o**plasm
prot**o**plast
prot**o**typal
prot**o**typic
prov**o**cator
psil**o**cybin
puls**o**meter
purp**o**seful
pycn**o**gonid
pycn**o**meter
pycn**o**style
pykn**o**meter
quat**o**rzain
quix**o**tical
radi**o**genic
radi**o**graph
radi**o**logic
radi**o**meter
radi**o**metry
radi**o**paque
radi**o**phone
radi**o**scopy
radi**o**sonde
rand**o**mness
rapp**o**rteur
rati**o**nally
reas**o**nable
reas**o**nably
reas**o**nless
rect**o**rship
regi**o**nally
renc**o**unter
repr**o**bance
repr**o**ducer
resp**o**ndent
resp**o**nsive
resp**o**nsory
rest**o**rable
retr**o**choir
retr**o**grade
retr**o**gress
retr**o**rsely
retr**o**spect
rhet**o**rical
rhin**o**ceros
rhin**o**scope
rhin**o**scopy
rhiz**o**genic
rhiz**o**morph
rhiz**o**phore
rhod**o**phane
ribb**o**nfish
ribb**o**nworm
ripr**o**aring
Russ**o**phile
Russ**o**phobe
sacr**o**iliac
sacr**o**sanct
sail**o**rless
sall**o**wness
salm**o**nella
salm**o**nleap
sapr**o**genic
sapr**o**phyte
sarc**o**lemma
sarc**o**phagi
sarc**o**phagy
sarc**o**plasm
sawt**o**othed
scho**o**lable
scho**o**lbook
scho**o**ldays
scho**o**lgirl
scho**o**lmaam
scho**o**lmarm
scho**o**lmate
scho**o**lroom
scho**o**ltime
scho**o**lwork
seas**o**nable
seas**o**nably
seas**o**nally
semi**o**paque
semi**o**tical
Serb**o**Croat
seri**o**comic
serm**o**niser
serv**o**motor
shad**o**wless
silh**o**uette
skib**o**bbing
slav**o**cracy
Slav**o**phile
Slav**o**phobe
snob**o**cracy
soci**o**logic
soci**o**metry
somn**o**lence
somn**o**lency
soph**o**moric
Sorb**o**nnist
spir**o**graph
spir**o**meter
spir**o**metry
spod**o**mancy
spor**o**phore
spor**o**phyll
spor**o**phyte
stat**o**scope
sten**o**graph
stom**o**daeum
styl**o**graph
subc**o**rdate
subm**o**ntane
subr**o**utine
summ**o**nable
supp**o**rtive
supp**o**sable
supp**o**sably
supp**o**sedly
syll**o**giser
symb**o**lical
symb**o**liser
symp**o**siast
sync**o**pated
sync**o**pator
tach**o**meter
tach**o**metry
tail**o**rbird
tail**o**rmade
tamb**o**urine
taur**o**machy
taut**o**meric
taut**o**phony
teet**o**tally
tele**o**logic
tele**o**stean
temp**o**rally
temp**o**ralty
temp**o**riser
terr**o**rless
thix**o**tropy
thor**o**ughly
ticp**o**longa
tomf**o**olery
tram**o**ntana
tram**o**ntane
trem**o**litic
trib**o**meter
trif**o**liate
trig**o**nally
trim**o**nthly
trim**o**rphic
trom**o**meter
trop**o**logic
trop**o**pause
trop**o**phyte
unbr**o**kenly
uncl**o**ister
unec**o**nomic
ungr**o**unded
unif**o**rmity
unil**o**cular
univ**o**cally
unkn**o**wable
unpr**o**voked
unsp**o**rting
untr**o**ubled
uran**o**metry
vari**o**litic
vari**o**meter
vect**o**graph
Vict**o**riana
vict**o**rious
vide**o**phone
visc**o**meter
visc**o**untcy
visi**o**nally
visi**o**nless
wagg**o**nette
want**o**nness
weap**o**nless
will**o**wherb
wind**o**wless
wind**o**wpane
wind**o**wseat
wind**o**wshop
wind**o**wsill
xiph**o**suran
yarb**o**rough
yell**o**wback
yell**o**wbird
yell**o**wness
yell**o**wwood
zinc**o**graph
zool**o**gical
zoom**o**rphic
abru**p**tness
acar**p**elous
acce**p**table
acce**p**tably
acce**p**tance
acce**p**tedly
acro**p**hobia
aero**p**hobia
allo**p**athic
allo**p**honic
anal**p**habet
anci**p**itous
ante**p**endia
ante**p**enult
anti**p**athic
anti**p**honal
anti**p**odean
anti**p**roton
aqua**p**laner
arch**p**riest
Areo**p**agite
asym**p**totic
auto**p**lasty
benz**p**yrene
bill**p**oster
blas**p**hemer
blue**p**encil
Caer**p**hilly
caes**p**itose
caly**p**trate
card**p**layer
cata**p**hract
cato**p**trics
cham**p**ignon
chea**p**ishly
chea**p**skate
chim**p**anzee
clas**p**knife
cons**p**ectus
cons**p**iracy
cons**p**irant
cory**p**haeus
cree**p**iness
crip**p**ledom
cris**p**ation
cris**p**bread
deca**p**itate
deca**p**odous
dece**p**tible
depo**p**ulate
desi**p**ience
dila**p**idate
disa**p**point
disa**p**prove
droo**p**ingly
elli**p**tical
ence**p**halic
ence**p**halon
endo**p**hytic
endo**p**odite
equi**p**otent
esca**p**ement
esca**p**ology
eury**p**terid
exas**p**erate
exos**p**heric
fels**p**athic
fire**p**olicy
flip**p**antly
flop**p**iness
four**p**oster
fowl**p**lague
golo**p**tious
golu**p**tious
gras**p**ingly
grum**p**iness
halo**p**hytic
hand**p**icked
head**p**hones
hemi**p**legia
hemi**p**legic
hemi**p**teran
holo**p**hrase
holo**p**hytic
homo**p**honic
hypo**p**hyses
hypo**p**hysis
idio**p**athic
inap**p**etent
inap**p**osite
inca**p**acity
inci**p**ience
inci**p**iency
inex**p**ertly
inex**p**iable
inex**p**iably
inex**p**licit
insi**p**idity
isos**p**orous
kens**p**eckle
long**p**rimer
lyco**p**odium
mala**p**ertly
mala**p**ropos
mani**p**ulate
meno**p**ausal
meso**p**hytic
meta**p**horic
meta**p**hrase
meta**p**hysic
meta**p**lasia
mono**p**honic
mono**p**odial
mono**p**odium
mono**p**olise
mono**p**olist
myco**p**lasma
nail**p**olish
noso**p**hobia
occu**p**ation
occu**p**ative
octo**p**odous
oeso**p**hagus
omni**p**otent
over**p**raise
pano**p**ticon
para**p**hrase
para**p**hrast
para**p**legia
para**p**legic
para**p**odium
peri**p**eteia
peri**p**heral
peri**p**teral
phos**p**hatic
phos**p**horic
phos**p**horus
pick**p**ocket
poly**p**hasic
poly**p**honic
poly**p**loidy

postpartum
pourparler
promptbook
promptness
prospector
prospectus
prosperity
prosperous
puerperium
puffpastry
pupiparous
pyrophoric
reappraise
receptacle
receptible
recipiency
reciprocal
recuperate
repopulate
resupinate
rockpigeon
schipperke
scrapmetal
scriptoria
scriptural
scrupulous
sculptress
sculptural
sculptured
seedpotato
selfparody
selfpoised
selfpraise
selfprofit
sharpnosed
sheepishly
sheeplouse
sheepshank
sheepshead
sitophobia
skimpiness
sleepiness
sleepyhead
slipperily
slitpocket
sloppiness
snappishly
snowplough
stepparent
striptease
stumpiness
subspecies
sweepingly
sweepstake
sycophancy
synoptical
telepathic
telephoner
telephonic
theophanic
theophoric
theopneust
thruppence
tocopherol
toxiphobia
trampoline
trappiness
trespasser
unemphatic
unemployed
unexpected
unexplored
unimproved
unripeness
usurpation
vestpocket
vituperate
viviparity
viviparous
voluptuary
voluptuous
wallpepper
whispering
wirepuller
woodpecker
woodpigeon
workpeople
xenophobia
xerophytic
xylophonic
antiquated
blanquette
brusquerie
deliquesce
lansquenet
obsequious
semiquaver
subaquatic
subaqueous
tranquilly
unrequited
aberrantly
aberration
abhorrence
abjuration
abnormally
absorbable
absorbance
absorbedly
absorbency
absorption
absorptive
abstracted
abstracter
abstractly
abstractor
abstrusely
abstrusity
absurdness
accordance
accurately
accursedly
adherently
adjuration
adjuratory
admiration
admiringly
adsorbable
adsorption
adsorptive
advertence
advertency
advertiser
afferently
affirmable
affordable
afterbirth
aftergrass
afterimage
afterlight
afterpains
aftershave
aftertaste
afterwards
aldermanic
aldermanry
allergenic
allurement
altarpiece
alteration
alterative
alternance
alternator
anadromous
anatropous
aneurismal
aneurysmal
anteriorly
anthracene
anthracite
anthracoid
anthropoid
aphoristic
apocryphal
apotropaic
apparelled
apparently
apparition
apperceive
arboreally
arborvitae
armorially
arterially
arteriolar
arthralgia
arthralgic
arthromere
ascariasis
asparagine
aspergilla
aspiration
assortment
asteriated
asteroidal
attornment
Australian
autarkical
babiroussa
balbriggan
bankruptcy
beforehand
beforetime
Belgravian
bellringer
besprinkle
bestridden
bichromate
biographer
biographic
biparietal
bipartisan
bizarrerie
bleariness
blearyeyed
blueribbon
blurringly
bullroarer
bushranger
camerlengo
camerlingo
canorously
castration
catarrhine
centralise
centralism
centralist
centrality
centreback
centrefold
centrehalf
centricity
centrifuge
centromere
centrosome
chairwoman
cheerfully
cheeriness
chevrotain
chlorinate
chloroform
Ciceronian
cinerarium
clearstory
coherently
coloration
coloratura
compradore
comprehend
compressed
compressor
compromise
concretely
concretion
concretise
concretism
concretist
congregant
congregate
congruence
congruency
contraband
contrabass
contractor
contradict
contraprop
contrarily
contravene
contribute
contritely
contrition
controlled
controller
controvert
coparcener
copartnery
Copernican
copyreader
covariance
coweringly
cribriform
cumbrously
cybernetic
daydreamer
deaeration
decoration
decorative
decorously
deeprooted
deferrable
deforciant
demoralise
demureness
demurrable
dendriform
dendrology
department
deportment
depuration
depurative
descriptor
deservedly
desirously
desorption
destructor
detergency
determined
deterrence
dextrality
dextrously
diagraphic
diarrhoeal
diarrhoeic
diatropism
dichroitic
dichromate
dimorphism
dimorphous
disarrange
discreetly
discrepant
discretely
discretion
disgruntle
disordered
disorderly
dispraiser
distracted
distrainer
distrainor
distraught
distressed
distribute
distringas
divaricate
divergence
divergency
dolorously
dreariness
dysgraphia
dysprosium
dystrophic
eartrumpet
effervesce
effortless
elderberry
elutriator
embarkment
emigration
emigratory
emparadise
emphractic
empiricism
empiricist
endorsable
endproduct
enduringly
enharmonic
enterolith
enterotomy
enterprise
enthralled
entireness
epeirogeny
ephorality
epigrapher
epigraphic
escarpment
ethereally
eucaryotic
excerption
execration
execrative
execratory
experience
experiment
expertness
expiration
expiratory
exportable
expurgator
exteriorly
externally
extirpator
federalise
federalism
federalist
federation
federative
feverishly
figuration
figurative
figurehead
filariasis
filtration
fimbriated
fireraiser
flagrantly
fleeringly
floorboard
floorcloth
fluoridate
fluorinate
fluorotype
forerunner
foudroyant
fragrantly
fratricide
funereally
futureless
futuristic
futurology
gangrenous
gastrology
gastronome
gastronomy
generalise
generalist
generality
generation
generative
generatrix
generosity
generously
geographer
geographic
geotropism
governable
governance
governessy
government
hairraiser
heparinise
heterodont
heterodoxy
heterodyne
heterogamy
heterogeny
heterogony
heterology
heteronomy
heterotaxy
hibernacle
histrionic
honorarium
hornrimmed
hoverplane
hovertrain
humoresque
humoristic
humorously
hungriness
hyperaemia
hyperaemic
hyperbaric
hyperbaton
hyperbolae
hyperbolas
hyperbolic
hyperdulia
hypergolic
hypersonic
icebreaker
ignorantly
immoralist
immorality
immortally
immortelle
immurement
imparadise
impartible
impartment
imperative
imperially
imperilled
impersonal
impervious
importable
importance
importuner
impureness
incurrable
indirectly
induration
indurative

infarction
inferiorly
infernally
inferrable
informally
inharmonic
inherently
inheritrix
innerrably
instructor
instrument
insurgence
insurgency
interbreed
interceder
intercross
interested
interferer
interferon
intergrade
interiorly
interleave
interloper
interlunar
intermarry
intermezzi
intermezzo
internally
internment
internodal
internship
interphase
interplant
interplead
interposal
interposer
interregna
interspace
interstate
interstice
intertidal
intertrigo
intertwine
intertwist
interurban
intervener
intervenor
intervolve
interweave
interwound
interwoven
interzonal
invariable
invariably
invariance
inveracity
inwardness
jackrabbit
jawbreaker
laboratory
laceration
lacerative
lachrymose
Lamarckian
Lamarckism
lambrequin
laparotomy
laterality
lawbreaker
lederhosen
liberalise
liberalism
liberalist
liberality
liberation
literalise
literalism
literalist
literality
literarily
literation
literature
liturgical
logorrhoea
lowerclass
lowprofile
Lupercalia
lustration
lustreless
lustrously
luxuriance
maceration
mandragora
manorhouse
margravate
margravine
materially
maternally
maturation
maturative
matureness
meagreness
membranous
memorandum
mineralise
mineralogy
miscreance
misericord
misprision
mithridate
moderately
moderation
moderatism
moderniser
modernness
monarchial
Monarchian
monarchism
monarchist
mongrelise
mongrelism
monorhymed
motorcycle
mycorrhiza
naturalise
naturalism
naturalist
naturopath
nephralgia
nephridium
nephrology
neutralise
neutralism
neutralist
neutrality
nevernever
newsreader
nondrinker
notarially
numeration
numerology
numerosity
numerously
nutcracker
obdurately
observable
observably
observance
obstructor
obturation
occurrence
oneirology
orneriness
orographic
osmiridium
otherwhere
otherwhile
otherworld
otterboard
ottershrew
outerspace
overrefine
overridden
overriding
paltriness
pancratium
pancreatic
pancreatin
pantrymaid
paperchase
paperknife
papermaker
papyrology
pastrycook
paternally
pederastic
pejoration
pejorative
peroration
picaresque
pilgrimage
piperidine
pityriasis
pokerfaced
Pomeranian
powerfully
powerhouse
prairiedog
prearrange
prefrontal
procreator
procrypsis
procryptic
programmer
propraetor
proprietor
protracted
protractor
protreptic
protrusile
protrusion
protrusive
puberulent
quadrangle
quadrantal
quadratics
quadrature
quadrennia
quadriceps
quadrireme
quadrivial
quadrivium
quadrumana
quadrumane
quadrumvir
quadruplet
quadruplex
quadrupole
quarrelled
quarreller
quarrender
quatrefoil
rackrenter
railroader
razorblade
razorshell
rechristen
recordable
recurrence
referendum
reformable
regardless
remarkable
remarkably
remarriage
remorseful
reparation
reparative
repertoire
reportable
reportedly
repurchase
reservedly
resorcinol
resorption
resorptive
restrained
restrainer
resurgence
retirement
retiringly
returnable
reverencer
reverently
reversible
revertible
rewardable
rewardless
rigorously
ritardando
ritornelli
ritornello
riverhorse
roadrunner
rockrabbit
rockribbed
sacerdotal
samarskite
saturation
saturnalia
satyriasis
sauerkraut
scabrously
scherzando
scleroderm
sclerotium
sclerotomy
scurrility
scurrilous
seborrhoea
secernment
securement
secureness
securiform
selfraised
selfregard
selfrising
selfruling
separately
separation
separatism
separatist
separative
separatory
severeness
shearwater
shiprigged
siderolite
siderostat
skywriting
smorrebrod
sneeringly
sobersided
sobersides
sombreness
somersault
sonorously
sororicide
soubriquet
speargrass
sperrylite
sphericity
spheroidal
spherulite
squareness
squaresail
squaretoed
squaretoes
squirarchy
squirearch
squirehood
squireling
squireship
starriness
starryeyed
staurolite
stirrupcup
suborbital
subordinal
subtrahend
suffragist
sugardaddy
sugarhouse
sugariness
sugarmaple
sultriness
superacute
superaltar
superation
superbness
supercargo
superduper
supergiant
superhuman
superiorly
superlunar
supernally
supernovae
superorder
superpower
supersonic
superstore
supertonic
supervisor
suppressor
surprising
suzerainty
sybaritism
syncretise
syncretism
syncretist
synergetic
tabernacle
taperecord
taperingly
tawdriness
teatrolley
tendrillar
tendrilled
theoretics
theurgical
thwartship
thwartwise
timbrology
timorously
tolerantly
toleration
towardness
toweringly
tribrachic
trierarchy
tubercular
tuberculin
tuberosity
tularaemia
tularaemic
tutorially
ulceration
ulcerative
ulotrichan
ulteriorly
umpireship
unabridged
underbelly
underbrush
undercliff
undercover
undercroft
underdress
underfloor
underglaze
underlease
underlinen
underlying
underminer
underneath
underpants
underproof
underquote
underscore
undersense
undersexed
undershirt
undershoot
undershrub
undersized
underskirt
underslung
understand
understate
understeer
understock
understood
understudy
undertaken
undertaker
undertrick
undervalue
underwater
underworld
underwrite
underwrote
unerringly
unforeseen
unmerciful
unmorality
unmortised
unscramble
unscreened
unscripted
unstrained
unstressed
unwariness
unworkable
unworthily
upperclass
upwardness
valorously
vaporiform
vaporously
veneration
ventricose
ventriculi
veterinary
viceregent
vigorously
viperiform
viperously
waterborne
waterbrash
waterclock
watercraft
watercress
waterflood
waterfront
waterglass
wateriness
watermelon
waterpower
waterproof
waterskier
waterspout
watertight
waterwheel

waterworks
waveringly
wintriness
wolframite
wondrously
abrasively
accessible
accessibly
accusation
accusative
accusatory
accusingly
accustomed
acoustical
adhesively
adjustable
adjustment
admissible
advisement
aerostatic
allosteric
allusively
altostrati
ambassador
ambushment
ancestress
antiSemite
antisepsis
antiseptic
antisocial
antistatic
appositely
apposition
appositive
arrestment
asbestosis
assessable
assessment
assistance
atmosphere
augustness
autostrada
autostrade
averseness
aversively
babysitter
backsheesh
backslider
backstairs
backstitch
backstroke
balustrade
banishment
barysphere
bemusement
bestseller
bimestrial
birdspider
birdstrike
blissfully
bluishness
bonesetter
boneshaker
bookseller
bootstraps
boyishness
brassiness
breastbone
breastwall
breastwork
bressummer
calcsinter
catastasis
cheesecake
cheesiness
chersonese
chessboard
Christhood
Christlike
chrysolite
chrysotile
cicisbeism
classicise
classicism
classicist
classified
classifier
cloistered
clumsiness
coarseness
cocksurely
cohesively
colossally
comestible
copesettic
cornstarch
counselled
counsellor
crassitude
crisscross
crossbench
crossbones
crossbreed
crosscheck
crossgrain
crosshatch
crossindex
crosslight
crosspatch
crosspiece
crossrefer
crossroads
crosstrees
cryoscopic
debasement
decisively
deepseated
dehiscence
delusional
delusively
depositary
deposition
depository
derestrict
derisively
desistance
detestable
detestably
digestible
disastrous
divestment
divisional
divisively
downstairs
downstream
downstroke
drawstring
dressiness
dressmaker
drowsihead
drowsiness
dumbstruck
effusively
egoistical
Eleusinian
embossment
emissivity
emulsifier
encasement
encashment
encystment
endoscopic
endosmosis
endosmotic
enlistment
enmeshment
equestrian
ergosterol
excusatory
exposition
expositive
expository
facesaving
fairspoken
famishment
fearsomely
fenestella
fenestrate
firescreen
flimsiness
folksiness
folksinger
foreshadow
foresheets
foursquare
fourstroke
freesoiler
freespeech
freespoken
garishness
gladsomely
glasscloth
glassfibre
glasshouse
glassiness
glasspaper
glassworks
glossarial
glossarist
glossiness
glossology
goatsbeard
goatsucker
grasscloth
grassroots
grasssnake
greasewood
greasiness
gressorial
gruesomely
gyroscopic
hairspring
hairstreak
hairstroke
handselled
handsomely
handspring
harassment
haruspices
headspring
headsquare
headstream
headstrong
heatstroke
hemisphere
heresiarch
highstrung
hoarseness
hocuspocus
holosteric
holusbolus
homosexual
horoscopic
hypostasis
hypostatic
illusional
illusively
illusorily
illustrate
immiscible
immiscibly
impassable
impassably
impassible
impassibly
impishness
imposingly
imposition
impossible
impossibly
imposthume
incasement
incessancy
incestuous
incisively
indiscreet
indiscrete
indisposed
indistinct
industrial
infusorial
infusorian
ingestible
insistence
insistency
intestinal
investment
ionisation
ionosphere
irresolute
Janusfaced
Jewishness
jocoseness
Johnsonese
johnsonian
juristical
lacustrine
landscaper
latescence
lavishment
lavishness
legislator
lifesaving
lockstitch
locustbean
logistical
lonesomely
longshanks
lotuseater
lumpsucker
lutestring
magistracy
magistrate
mainspring
mainstream
majestical
majuscular
manuscript
maraschino
markswoman
meerschaum
megascopic
melismatic
mesoscaphe
mesosphere
metastable
metastases
metastasis
metastatic
micaschist
millstream
minestrone
ministrant
minuscular
modishness
monistical
moonshiner
moonstruck
mopishness
moroseness
mosasaurus
mousseline
mulishness
nanisation
nanosecond
numismatic
oafishness
obfuscated
obtuseness
occasional
omniscient
opposeless
oppositely
opposition
otioseness
overshadow
overslaugh
overspread
overstride
overstrung
oversubtle
oversupply
owlishness
pacesetter
packsaddle
palisander
PalmSunday
papistical
paraselene
parasitism
parasitoid
patisserie
pedestrian
pentstemon
periscopic
perishable
pheasantry
phrasebook
picosecond
pleasantly
pleasantry
pleasingly
poinsettia
polysemous
porismatic
postscript
praesidium
pressagent
pressingly
pressurise
priesthood
priestling
prissiness
pubescence
puissantly
punishable
punishment
puristical
queasiness
quiescence
quiescency
rakishness
ravishment
reassemble
reassembly
redescribe
rediscover
registered
registrant
reissuable
relishable
remissible
remissness
renascence
reposition
repository
resistance
resistible
resistless
revisional
rhapsodise
rhapsodist
robustious
robustness
roodscreen
rotisserie
salesclerk
saleswoman
satisfying
scansorial
schismatic
Scotswoman
seamstress
seersucker
selfseeker
selfstyled
semestrial
sempstress
senescence
shoestring
shopsoiled
sidesaddle
sidestreet
sidestroke
silkscreen
sinisterly
sinistrous
sinusoidal
slipstitch
slipstream
softspoken
songstress
sparseness
Spenserian
splashback
splashdown
sponsorial
starstream
stepsister
stressless
synostosis
talismanic
tapestried
telescopic
theistical
themselves
theosopher
thousandth
timesaving
timeserver
tiresomely
toilsomely
townswoman
transactor
transcribe
transcript
transducer
transeptal
transferee
transferor
transfuser
transgress
transience
transiency
transistor
transition
transitive
transitory
translator
translucid
translunar
transmuter
transplant
transposal
transposer
transshape
transvalue
transverse
treasonous
Trotskyism
Trotskyist
Trotskyite
trousseaux
tumescence

typescript
typesetter
unassisted
unassuming
unbesought
uncustomed
undeserved
undesigned
undesirous
uneasiness
unhistoric
unjustness
unreserved
unresolved
uppishness
veldschoen
virescence
vivisector
wellspoken
wellspring
whatsoever
whensoever
whipstitch
WhitSunday
whomsoever
widespread
windscreen
windshield
windsleeve
wingspread
woolsorter
yourselves
abacterial
abortively
acroterion
acroterium
adaptation
adaptively
additional
admittable
admittance
admittedly
adoptively
adulterant
adulterate
adulteress
adulterine
adulterous
affettuoso
alliterate
allotropic
amputation
anaptyctic
anastigmat
anastomose
anastrophe
annotation
antitheism
antitheist
antitheses
antithesis
antithetic
apostatise
apostolate
apostrophe
appetising
appetitive
arbitrable
arbitrager
arbitrator
aristocrat
asceticism
astuteness
auditorial
auditorium
avantgarde
aventurine
aviatrices
azeotropic
beautician
beautifier
bewitchery
bimetallic
bipetalous
blastemata
blastocyst
blastoderm
blastomere
blastopore
bleatingly
blistering
blottesque
bluethroat
bluetongue
blusterous
boastfully
boisterous
brantgoose
bratticing
breathable
breathless
brentgoose
caoutchouc
capitalise
capitalism
capitalist
capitation
Capitoline
capitulary
capitulate
carotenoid
carotinoid
causticity
cavitation
chartreuse
chartulary
chasteness
chatterbox
chattiness
cicatrices
coaptation
coastguard
coastwards
cogitation
cogitative
colatitude
comstocker
constantan
Constantia
constantly
constipate
constitute
constraint
constringe
cooptation
cooptative
counteract
countryish
countryman
courthouse
covetingly
covetously
craftguild
craftiness
creatinine
creatively
creativity
creaturely
crustacean
crustation
crustiness
cryptogamy
cryptogram
cryptology
cunctation
cunctative
curatorial
daintiness
deactivate
debatement
demotivate
denaturant
denotation
denotative
deontology
deputation
devitalise
devotement
devotional
diastemata
digitalise
digitately
digitation
digitiform
dilatation
dilatorily
dilettante
dilettanti
diluteness
diphtheria
diphtheric
disutility
dogstongue
doubtfully
doubtingly
drafthorse
dubitation
dubitative
edentulous
effeteness
Egyptology
eighteenmo
eighteenth
elasticise
elasticity
electively
electorate
electrical
electronic
empathetic
enantiosis
endothelia
endstopped
epentheses
epenthesis
epenthetic
episternum
epistolary
epistrophe
equational
equatorial
equitation
erectility
eructation
eruptively
escutcheon
eventually
exactitude
exaltation
excitation
excitative
excitatory
excitement
excitingly
exenterate
expatriate
exultantly
exultation
exultingly
faintheart
fanaticise
fanaticism
faultiness
finiteness
firstclass
firstnight
flattering
fleetingly
flintiness
flirtation
floatation
floatboard
floatingly
floatplane
floatstone
foreteller
fourteener
fourteenth
fractional
frictional
frontbench
frontwards
frostiness
fruitarian
fruitfully
fugitively
functional
gametangia
gaultheria
gauntleted
gelatinise
gelatinous
geneticist
ghastfully
glottology
gluttonise
gluttonous
gnosticism
goaltender
gobstopper
graptolite
greatniece
greatuncle
grittiness
guesthouse
guestnight
guiltiness
gyrational
habitation
habitually
hauntingly
haustellum
haustorium
heartblock
heartblood
heartbreak
heartiness
heartsease
heartthrob
heartwhole
hebetation
henotheism
henotheist
heortology
hepatology
hereticate
heretofore
hesitantly
hesitation
hesitative
hipsterism
hylotheism
hypotactic
hypotenuse
hypotheses
hypothesis
ideational
illatively
illiteracy
illiterate
illstarred
immaterial
immaturely
immaturity
impatience
impotently
imputation
imputative
inactivate
inactively
inactivity
inaptitude
inartistic
incitation
incitement
inditement
ineptitude
infatuated
innateness
insatiable
insatiably
inveteracy
inveterate
invitation
invitatory
invitingly
irrational
irritation
irritative
isentropic
isopterous
janitorial
jauntiness
keratinise
keratinous
kineticist
knottiness
lavatorial
lawntennis
legateship
legitimacy
legitimate
legitimise
legitimism
legitimist
lengthways
lengthwise
levitation
lieutenant
lighterage
lighterman
lightfaced
lighthouse
lightingup
lightproof
limitation
limitative
limitrophe
lobsterpot
Lusitanian
maintainer
meditation
meditative
menstruate
menstruous
mesothorax
metatarsal
metatarsus
metatheses
metathesis
metathetic
metathorax
mightiness
militantly
militarily
militarise
militarism
militarist
militiaman
minstrelsy
minutebook
minutehand
minuteness
moisturise
monetarily
monetarism
monetarist
monitorial
monotheism
monotheist
monotonous
monstrance
moratorium
mountebank
moustached
moustachio
Mousterian
myasthenia
naphthenic
natatorial
natatorium
negatively
negativism
negativist
negativity
negotiable
negotiator
nematocyst
nicotinism
nightdress
nightglass
nightlight
nightshade
nightshift
nightshirt
nightstick
nightwatch
nineteenth
nomothetic
nonstarter
nutational
oblateness
obliterate
odontalgia
odontology
ommatidium
optatively
ornateness
oscitation
osmeterium
outstation
outstretch
overthrown
overthrust
overtopped
packthread
paintbrush
palatalise
palatinate
paratactic
paratroops
penetrable
penetrably
penetralia
penetrance
penetrator
penitently
perithecia
peritoneal
peritoneum
petiteness
petitioner
phantasise
phantasmal
phantasmic
phantastic
phantastry
pigsticker
pilothouse
pilotlight
pilotwhale
pinstriped
plantation
plantlouse

plasticise
plasticity
pointblank
politeness
politician
politicise
polytheism
polytheist
polytocous
positional
positively
positivism
positivist
positivity
practician
practising
praetorial
praetorian
presternum
prettiness
proctorage
proctorial
proctorise
prosthesis
prosthetic
prostitute
prostomial
prostomium
psalterium
psittacine
punctation
punctually
punctuator
punctulate
punitively
puritanise
puritanism
putatively
pyretology
pyrotechny
quantifier
quantitive
quartation
quarterage
quarterday
quartering
quartzitic
questioner
quintuplet
reactivate
reactively
reactivity
rebuttable
recitalist
recitation
recitative
recitativo
reentrance
refutation
relational
relatively
relativise
relativism
relativist
relativity
remittance
remoteness
repatriate
repetiteur
repetition
repetitive
reputation
revitalise
rheotropic
rightangle
rightfully
rightwards
ringtailed
roistering
roisterous
rotational
roustabout
rubythroat
safetybelt
sagittally
salutarily
salutation
salutatory
sanatorium
sanctifier
sanctimony
sanctitude
sanitarian
sanitarily
sanitarium
sanitation
scantiness
scattergun
scattering
scattiness
scepticism
Scotticise
Scotticism
scratchily
scratchwig
scrutineer
scrutinise
sedateness
selftaught
senatorial
serotinous
shantytown
sheathbill
sheathless
shiftiness
shirtfront
shirtwaist
shortbread
shortcrust
shortdated
shortening
shortlived
shortrange
shuttering
skirtdance
skittishly
slantingly
slatternly
sluttishly
smartmoney
smattering
smoothbore
smoothness
smuttiness
snootiness
solitarily
solstitial
somatology
somatotype
songthrush
Spartacist
spasticity
spectacled
spectacles
spectrally
splitlevel
splutterer
sportfully
sportiness
sportingly
sportively
sportswear
spottiness
squeteague
stentorian
stertorous
strategist
strathspey
stratiform
stratocrat
struthious
stypticity
substation
substitute
substratum
sudatorium
suretyship
sweatgland
sweatiness
sweatshirt
sweetbread
sweetbriar
sweetbrier
sweetening
sweetheart
sweltering
taciturnly
taleteller
tapotement
tauntingly
temptation
temptingly
teratogeny
teratology
teratomata
theatrical
thirteenth
thirtyfold
tinctorial
Tractarian
tractional
traitorous
troctolite
trustfully
trustiness
trustingly
tryptophan
unattached
unattended
unbuttoned
undeterred
unfathered
unfettered
unlettered
unorthodox
unsettling
vegetarian
vegetation
vegetative
velitation
velutinous
venational
visitation
visitorial
vocational
volatilise
volatility
volitional
vomitorium
waistcloth
wellturned
wheatstone
wiretapper
woodturner
wristwatch
yeastiness
zwitterion
accoucheur
accountant
accounting
adequately
affluently
agglutinin
aircushion
allpurpose
altruistic
amanuenses
amanuensis
apiculture
armourclad
armourless
artfulness
asexuality
assaultive
auscultate
aviculture
bijouterie
binaurally
bivouacked
calculable
calculably
calculator
camouflage
cappuccino
carbuncled
catburglar
cellularly
cellulitis
cellulosic
censurable
chequebook
cinquefoil
circuitous
circularly
circulator
circumcise
circumflex
circumfuse
circumvent
coagulable
coequality
colourable
colourably
colourfast
colourless
combustion
combustive
communally
communique
commutable
commutator
compulsion
compulsive
compulsory
computable
computator
concurrent
concurring
concussion
concussive
conduction
conductive
confusedly
conjugally
consuetude
consulship
consultant
consulting
consultive
consumable
consumedly
consummate
convulsant
convulsion
convulsive
cornucopia
corpulence
corpulency
corpuscule
corrugated
corrugator
corruption
corruptive
couturiere
cowpuncher
crapulence
craquelure
crenulated
crepuscule
culturally
curmudgeon
debauchery
debouchure
denouement
desquamate
devoutness
diffusible
disbudding
disburthen
discursive
discussant
discussion
discussive
discutient
disfurnish
disgustful
disputable
disputably
disqualify
disquieten
disquietly
disruption
disruptive
dissuasion
dissuasive
eloquently
embouchure
encourager
englutting
enthusiasm
enthusiast
euphuistic
evacuation
evacuative
evaluation
evaluative
excruciate
executable
exhaustion
exhaustive
factualism
factualist
factuality
famousness
favourable
favourably
fitfulness
flatulence
flatulency
flexuously
fortuitism
fortuitist
fortuitous
foxhunting
frequenter
frequently
globularly
gradualism
gradualist
graduation
granularly
granulator
granulitic
gratuitous
gunrunning
gutturally
Hindustani
honourable
honourably
honourless
humbuggery
humbugging
humourless
humoursome
illaudable
illaudably
imprudence
incautious
includible
ineducable
ineludible
inequality
iniquitous
inoculable
inoculator
insouciant
joyfulness
joyousness
kibbutznik
languisher
languorous
lawfulness
linguiform
linguistic
Lithuanian
manfulness
mansuetude
marguerite
marquisate
masquerade
mavourneen
measurable
measurably
measuredly
mensurable
Methuselah
molluscoid
molluscous
mosquitoes
muscularly
Mussulmans
nasturtium
nonnuclear
obituarist
obtruncate
odiousness
offputting
opaqueness
oracularly
orotundity
outgunning
outputting
outrunning
parturient
pasquinade
pasturable
pellucidly
penpushing
percussion
percussive
perdurable
perdurably
perjurious
permutable
perquisite
persuasion
persuasive
pincushion
pinnulated
plaguesome
porousness
Portuguese
postulator
pothunting
pozzuolana
precursory
prefulgent
prejudiced
presumable
presumably
presuppose
procumbent
procurable
procurance

procurator
producible
production
productive
profundity
promulgate
propulsion
propulsive
pursuivant
recoupment
recrudesce
redcurrant
resounding
ruefulness
rumrunning
sanguinary
sanguinely
sanguinity
savourless
secludedly
semiuncial
sensualise
sensualism
sensualist
sensuality
sensuously
Septuagint
shroudlaid
shroudless
sinfulness
singularly
skijumping
speculator
statuesque
statutable
statutably
stimulator
stipulator
subculture
subduction
subjugator
subnuclear
succulence
succulency
swanupping
Talmudical
Tartuffian
Tartuffism
textualist
texturally
throughout
throughput
throughway
tittupping
tongueless
tonguetied
tortuosity
tortuously
trifurcate
triquetrae
triquetral
triturable
triturator
truculence
truculency
turbulence
turbulency
ubiquitous
unblushing
unctuosity
unctuously
uneducated
unequalled
ungrudging
unhouseled
uniqueness
untruthful
usefulness
valvulitis
vanquisher
vascularly
victualled
victualler
virtuality
virtueless
virtuosity
virtuously
wampumpeag
wilfulness
woefulness
acervation
activation
activeness
alleviator
alloverish
ambivalent
asseverate
bedevilled
benevolent
biliverdin
cadaverous
caravaneer
caravanned
caravanner
chauvinism
chauvinist
decivilise
derivation
derivative
duumvirate
enervation
enervative
equivalent
equivocate
Eurovision
evolvement
excavation
grievously
halfvolley
Hanoverian
immoveable
impoverish
incivility
individual
innovation
innovative
innovatory
irreverent
Jehovistic
malevolent
monovalent
motivation
motiveless
nativeborn
nativeness
nativistic
newsvendor
nucivorous
omnivorous
Ordovician
papaverine
papaverous
polyvalent
rejuvenate
rejuvenise
relevantly
renovation
revivalism
revivalist
salivation
scurviness
seedvessel
sexivalent
shrivelled
Shrovetide
sleeveless
sleevelink
starvation
starveling
stopvolley
subaverage
televiewer
television
televisual
thievishly
titivation
trouvaille
twelvefold
twelvenote
twelvetone
unenviable
unravelled
unrivalled
unwavering
zollverein
aardwolves
backwardly
bejewelled
bellwether
bollweevil
cartwright
caseworker
codswallop
copywriter
cordwainer
deadweight
dishwasher
disownment
downwardly
dumbwaiter
duniwassal
embowelled
flagwaving
flyswatter
footwarmer
Glaswegian
halfwitted
handworked
headwaiter
highwayman
ironworker
longwinded
lukewarmly
makeweight
millwright
mineworker
newsworthy
newswriter
nonswimmer
noteworthy
outswinger
overweight
overwinter
periwigged
periwinkle
playwright
railwayman
roadworthy
ropewalker
rottweiler
sashwindow
screwplate
screwpress
selfwilled
semiweekly
shipwright
shopwalker
shopwindow
showwindow
shrewdness
shrewishly
shrewmouse
sidewinder
signwriter
slowwitted
songwriter
stalwartly
strawberry
strawboard
throwstick
tidewaiter
typewriter
unlawfully
untowardly
wainwright
wellwisher
werewolves
westwardly
wirewalker
wireworker
woodworker
annexation
bisexually
detoxicant
detoxicate
indexation
intoxicant
intoxicate
paroxysmal
paroxytone
peroxidise
preexilian
pyroxenite
relaxation
uniaxially
acotyledon
analysable
analytical
anchylosis
anchylotic
annoyingly
arrhythmia
arrhythmic
asphyxiant
asphyxiate
bathymeter
bathymetry
bathyscaph
bathyscope
bawdyhouse
bellyacher
bellydance
bellylaugh
biodynamic
bobbysocks
bobbysoxer
botryoidal
bradyseism
candyfloss
carryingon
chalybeate
cuttystool
daisychain
dialysable
dillydally
diphyletic
diphyodont
donnybrook
ecchymosis
ecchymotic
embryogeny
embryology
embryonate
emeryboard
emerypaper
emerywheel
epicycloid
essayistic
eurhythmic
everyplace
everything
everywhere
fairycycle
fiftyfifty
fortyniner
fuddyduddy
fuzzywuzzy
goodygoody
halfyearly
hankypanky
heavyarmed
hobbyhorse
hoitytoity
hokeypokey
honeyeater
honeyguide
honeysweet
hurdygurdy
hurlyburly
isodynamic
jerrybuilt
lacrymator
lardydardy
merrymaker
methylated
moneymaker
moneytaker
nambypamby
paddyfield
paddywagon
paddywhack
pastyfaced
pennyroyal
pennyworth
pharyngeal
picayunish
propylaeum
semiyearly
sillybilly
spagyrical
tachymeter
tachymetry
teenyweeny
topsyturvy
tricyclist
unicyclist
willynilly
willywilly
wishywashy
altazimuth
blitzkrieg
breezeless
breeziness
frenziedly
frizziness
homozygote
homozygous
horizontal
Lipizzaner
schizocarp
schizogony
scorzonera
seltzogene
sleaziness
sneezeweed
sneezewood
sneezewort
topazolite
wheeziness

---

abdication
aberrantly
aberration
abjuration
abnegation
Abrahamman
abrogation
abstracted
abstracter
abstractly
abstractor
abundantly
accurately
accusation
accusative
accusatory
acephalous
acervation
acrobatics
activation
adaptation
adequately
adjuration
adjuratory
admiration
adrenaline
Adullamite
advocation
advocatory
aerobatics
aeronautic
Africander
Africanise
Africanism
Africanist
Afrikander
algolagnia
algolagnic
alienation
allegation
allocation
allogamous
allopathic
almacanter
almucanter
alteration
alterative
amalgamate
ambivalent
ambulacral
ambulacrum
ambulation
ambulatory
amendatory
amputation
amygdaloid
anaplastic
angularity
annexation
annotation
annularity
annulation
anthracene
anthracite
anthracoid
antimasque
antimatter
antipathic
apostatise
aquamarine
araucarian
areolation
Areopagite
arrogantly
arrogation
arthralgia
arthralgic
asexuality
asparagine
aspiration
Athanasian
Australian
autogamous
automation
automatise
automatism
automatist
bacchantes
bacchantic
backgammon
backhanded
backhander
backwardly
bandmaster

barebacked
bedchamber
Belgravian
bellyacher
bemedalled
benefactor
Benthamism
Benthamite
bequeathal
bestialise
bestiality
bighearted
bilocation
bimetallic
biographer
biographic
bipetalous
bipolarity
bivouacked
blackamoor
blepharism
bluejacket
bookmaking
bookmarker
Brahmanism
breakables
Buchmanism
Buchmanite
burglarise
bushmaster
bushranger
cacciatore
cackhanded
cacodaemon
calamander
capitalise
capitalism
capitalist
capitation
caravaneer
caravanned
caravanner
cardialgia
caricature
caseharden
castration
catafalque
catenation
cavitation
centralise
centralism
centralist
centrality
chapfallen
chaplaincy
chiliastic
chimpanzee
choriambic
chromatics
chromatype
cinecamera
cinerarium
clawhammer
coadjacent
coaptation
coathanger
codswallop
coequality
cogitation
cogitative
coloration
coloratura
comicality
complacent
complainer
compradore
conflation
constantan
Constantia
constantly
contraband
contrabass
contractor
contradict
contraprop
contrarily
contravene
cooptation
cooptative
copulation
copulative
cordiality
cordwainer
corelation
corelative
coromandel
coronation
Corybantes
corybantic
covenanted
covenantee
covenanter
covenantor
crackajack
crispation
crustacean
crustation
cumulation
cumulative
cunctation
cunctative
datamation
deaeration
debonairly
decimalise
decimalism
decimation
decoration
decorative
dedication
dedicative
dedicatory
deescalate
defamation
defamatory
dehumanise
delegation
delicately
delocalise
demoralise
denegation
denotation
denotative
denudation
depilation
depilatory
depolarise
depuration
depurative
deputation
derivation
derivative
derogation
derogatory
desolately
desolation
desquamate
detonation
detonative
Devanagari
devitalise
devocalise
dextrality
diagraphic
diaphanous
digitalise
digitately
digitation
dilatation
discharger
disclaimer
disfeature
dishearten
dishwasher
dispraiser
disqualify
dissuasion
dissuasive
distracted
distrainer
distrainor
distraught
divagation
divination
divinatory
dominantly
domination
dominative
downfallen
downwardly
drophammer
dubitation
dubitative
dumbwaiter
duniwassal
dustjacket
dysgraphia
dysplastic
eczematous
efficacity
elongation
emaciation
emendation
emendatory
emigration
emigratory
emparadise
emphractic
encroacher
endogamous
enervation
enervative
enigmatise
enigmatist
enthralled
ephorality
epiblastic
epigrapher
epigraphic
equitation
equivalent
eructation
escalation
escheatage
Esculapian
estimation
estimative
eternalise
eternalist
ethicality
etiolation
evacuation
evacuative
evaluation
evaluative
evenhanded
exaltation
excavation
excitation
excitative
excitatory
excusatory
execration
execrative
execratory
exhalation
exhilarant
exhilarate
exhumation
expiration
expiratory
exultantly
exultation
exurbanite
exuviation
eyeglasses
faceharden
facesaving
factualism
factualist
factuality
fairhaired
fasciation
federalise
federalism
federalist
federation
federative
felspathic
feminality
figuration
figurative
filtration
finicality
fireraiser
fishcarver
flagrantly
flagwaving
fleamarket
flippantly
flirtation
floatation
floriation
fluviatile
flyswatter
footballer
footcandle
footwarmer
forecaster
forecastle
forefather
foregather
forehanded
forwearied
foundation
fourhanded
fragrantly
freehanded
freelancer
freemartin
fruitarian
fumigation
gaillardia
galimatias
galliambic
gametangia
gemination
generalise
generalist
generality
generation
generative
generatrix
geographer
geographic
glaciation
gladhander
glossarial
glossarist
Godfearing
gradualism
gradualist
graduation
grammarian
habitation
hackmatack
hairraiser
hamshackle
handbarrow
handgallop
handmaiden
hardhanded
headmaster
headwaiter
heavyarmed
hebetation
henhearted
hesitantly
hesitation
hesitative
highhanded
highjacker
highlander
highwayman
homemaking
homogamous
honorarium
houseagent
humpbacked
hyperaemia
hyperaemic
hypotactic
idiopathic
ignorantly
illegalise
illegality
illstarred
immolation
immoralist
immorality
impanation
imparadise
imperative
imputation
imputative
incapacity
inchoately
inchoation
inchoative
incitation
incubation
incubative
incubatory
incunabula
indagation
indexation
indication
indicative
indicatory
induration
indurative
inequality
inhalation
inhumanely
inhumanity
inhumation
initialise
initialled
initiation
initiative
initiatory
innovation
innovative
innovatory
insolation
insularism
insularity
insulation
intimately
intimation
intonation
intubation
inundation
inundatory
inurbanity
inveracity
invitation
invitatory
invocation
invocatory
iodination
ionisation
ironhanded
ironmaster
irrelative
irrigation
irritation
irritative
isoniazide
italianate
italianise
Italianism
jackhammer
jackrabbit
jocularity
journalese
journalise
journalism
journalist
jubilantly
jubilation
judicatory
judicature
Kantianism
keyboarder
kinematics
knockabout
laboratory
laceration
lacerative
laminarian
lamination
lanthanide
lapidarian
lapidarist
lapidation
laterality
laureation
lefthanded
lefthander
lesbianism
levigation
levitation
liberalise
liberalism
liberalist
liberality
liberation
lifejacket
lifesaving
limitation
limitative
lipomatous
lipreading
literalise
literalism
literalist
literality
literarily
literation
literature
Lithuanian
litigation
lobulation
logicality
longhaired
loudhailer
lovemaking
lukewarmly
Lusitanian
lustration
macadamise
maceration
maculation

maculature
mainlander
maintainer
maladapted
malefactor
malfeasant
mandragora
margravate
margravine
marshalled
marshaller
marshalsea
martialism
matriarchy
maturation
maturative
maximalist
medicament
medicaster
medication
medicative
meditation
meditative
membranous
memorandum
menopausal
messianism
metacarpal
metacarpus
metagalaxy
metatarsal
metatarsus
militantly
militarily
militarise
militarism
militarist
mineralise
mineralogy
minimalism
minimalist
mintmaster
mischanter
mismeasure
misogamist
mitigation
mitigative
mitigatory
moderately
moderation
moderatism
modulation
monetarily
monetarism
monetarist
monocarpic
monogamist
monogamous
monomaniac
monovalent
mosasaurus
motivation
moustached
moustachio
musicality
muskmallow
mutilation
myxomatous
nanisation
naturalise
naturalism
naturalist
nauseating
navigation
neoclassic
neoplastic
nephralgia
neutralise
neutralism
neutralist
neutrality
newscaster
nodulation
nominalism
nominalist
nominately
nomination
nominative
nonchalant
nonplaying
nonstarter
nucleation
numeration
nunciature
nuptiality
nutcracker
obdurately
obituarist
obligation
obligatory
obturation
occupation
occupative
oceanarium
ocellation
octonarian
odontalgia
oedematose
oedematous
omophagous
openhanded
ophthalmia
ophthalmic
oppilation
optimalise
ordinarily
ordination
orographic
oscitation
osculation
osculatory
outmeasure
outstation
overhanded
overlander
overlapped
overmanned
overmantel
overmaster
packsaddle
paediatric
pagination
palatalise
palisander
palliation
palliative
palliatory
Panamanian
pancratium
paratactic
parliament
partiality
pastmaster
patination
patriality
patriarchy
peculation
pederastic
pejoration
pejorative
permeation
permeative
peroration
persuasion
persuasive
petulantly
phantasise
phantasmal
phantasmic
phantastic
phantastry
pharmacist
pheasantry
pinecarpet
pinfeather
plagiarise
plagiarism
plagiarist
plantation
pleasantly
pleasantry
pleonastic
pneumatics
pockmarked
polydactyl
polygamist
polygamous
polymathic
polyvalent
Pomeranian
popularise
popularity
population
postmaster
postpartum
pourparler
pragmatise
pragmatism
pragmatist
preadamite
preglacial
pregnantly
pressagent
proclaimer
prognathic
programmer
propraetor
prothallia
prothallus
protracted
protractor
psittacine
puffpastry
puissantly
punctation
pupilarity
pupiparous
puritanise
puritanism
pyracantha
pyrogallol
pyromaniac
pyromantic
quadrangle
quadrantal
quadratics
quadrature
quartation
quizmaster
Rachmanism
radicalise
radicalism
radication
railwayman
rainmaking
ramshackle
razzmatazz
rearmament
recitalist
recitation
recitative
recitativo
recreantly
recreation
recreative
refutation
regelation
regularise
regularity
regulation
regulative
regulatory
relaxation
relegation
relevantly
relocation
renovation
reorganise
reparation
reparative
reputation
resonantly
restrained
restrainer
retinacula
revelation
revelatory
revitalise
revivalism
revivalist
revocation
revocatory
rheumatics
rheumatism
rheumatoid
rightangle
ringmaster
ringtailed
riproaring
rockbadger
rockgarden
rockrabbit
roofgarden
ropedancer
ropeladder
ropewalker
rosemallow
roundabout
rouseabout
roustabout
ruffianism
ruminantly
rumination
ruminative
Russianise
saccharate
saccharide
saccharify
saccharine
saccharoid
saccharose
sagination
salamander
salivation
salutarily
salutation
salutatory
sandbagger
sandcastle
sandmartin
sanitarian
sanitarily
sanitarium
sanitation
saturation
scandalise
scandalous
scarlatina
schematise
schematism
scholastic
secularise
secularism
secularist
secularity
selfparody
selfraised
selftaught
seminarian
seminarist
semination
sensualise
sensualism
sensualist
sensuality
separately
separation
separatism
separatist
separative
separatory
Septuagint
sergeantcy
serjeantcy
sexivalent
shellacked
shipmaster
shopwalker
sibilation
sidesaddle
similarity
simulacrum
simulation
simulative
simulatory
Singhalese
sluggardly
snickasnee
snowcapped
solidarism
solidarist
solidarity
solitarily
spallation
Spartacist
spatiality
specialise
specialism
specialist
speciality
speciation
spectacled
spectacles
spermaceti
spoliation
spoliative
spoliatory
squamation
squirarchy
stagnantly
stagnation
stalwartly
stargazing
starvation
stepfather
stephanite
stepladder
stepparent
stigmatise
stigmatism
stigmatist
stochastic
Stroganoff
stromatous
subclavian
subdeanery
subglacial
subheading
substation
subtrahend
suffragist
sunglasses
superacute
superaltar
superation
supination
supplanter
surrealism
surrealist
suzerainty
swanmaiden
swaybacked
tabularise
tabulation
taskmaster
taxidancer
teaplanter
telecamera
telecaster
telepathic
temptation
tepidarium
textualist
thereabout
thereafter
thereanent
thornapple
thousandth
tidewaiter
tilthammer
timesaving
titivation
titubation
tolerantly
toleration
topicality
tourmaline
tournament
toxication
trabeation
Tractarian
transactor
traumatism
trespasser
tribrachic
trierarchy
triphammer
trivialise
trivialism
triviality
trochanter
troubadour
trouvaille
truncately
truncation
tularaemia
tularaemic
typicality
ulceration
ulcerative
ultimately
unattached
unbalanced
undulation
undulatory
unequalled
unmorality
unpleasant
unpleasing
unremarked
unrivalled
unscramble
unsteadily
unstrained
untowardly
urticarial
urtication
ustulation
usurpation
utopianism
validation
Vaticanism
Vaticanist
vegetarian

vegetation
vegetative
velitation
veneration
vesication
vesicatory
victualled
victualler
Vietnamese
vigilantly
vinegarish
virtuality
visitation
viviparity
viviparous
westwardly
whereabout
windjammer
wirehaired
wiretapper
wirewalker
wolframite
woodcarver
woodlander
woolgather
workbasket
Wykehamist
yardmaster
zoophagous
zygodactyl
aboveboard
absorbable
absorbance
absorbedly
absorbency
acetabular
acetabulum
adsorbable
afterbirth
alphabetic
amphibious
amphibrach
ascribable
assemblage
bargeboard
beribboned
blackberry
blackboard
blockboard
brakeblock
breadboard
chalkboard
chalybeate
chessboard
childbirth
chokeberry
cicisbeism
clarabella
cloudberry
cloudburst
cnidoblast
coachbuilt
coenobitic
coenobytic
columbaria
confabbing
coralberry
corroboree
crackbrain
crispbread
crossbench
crossbones
crossbreed
Decembrist
deshabille
discobolus
disembogue
disembosom
disembowel
disembroil
dishabille
donnybrook
earthbound
elderberry
emeryboard
enjambment
entombment
exprobrate
fibreboard
flashboard
floatboard
floorboard
floribunda
frontbench
goatsbeard
gooseberry
hartebeest
heartblock
heartblood
heartbreak
hereabouts
hobnobbing
holusbolus
housebound
hullabaloo
hurlyburly
hyperbaric
hyperbaton
hyperbolae
hyperbolas
hyperbolic
improbable
improbably
incumbency
interbreed
jerrybuilt
knifeboard
kookaburra
loganberry
Maccabaean
mandibular
matchboard
microbiota
mouldboard
muliebrity
northbound
notchboard
opprobrium
osteoblast
otterboard
overabound
paintbrush
pasteboard
pitchblack
pointblank
prohibiter
prohibitor
punchboard
razorblade
recumbency
reprobance
resemblant
rockabilly
rowanberry
scaleboard
scarabaeid
scarabaeus
scoreboard
scribbling
shortbread
sillybilly
skateboard
skibobbing
soundboard
southbound
spadebeard
spellbound
stillbirth
stoneblind
stoneborer
stonebrash
stormbound
strawberry
strawboard
suborbital
superbness
sweetbread
sweetbriar
sweetbrier
syllabaria
thromboses
thrombosis
thrombotic
toothbrush
treadboard
ultrabasic
underbelly
underbrush
unnumbered
usquebaugh
vertebrate
vestibular
vestibulum
waterborne
waterbrash
whitebeard
wildebeest
youngberry
abreaction
accoucheur
adenectomy
adjunction
adjunctive
aerenchyma
affliction
afflictive
alliaceous
amphictyon
amylaceous
annunciate
anonaceous
apperceive
applicable
applicably
applicator
appreciate
arenaceous
atomically
attractant
attraction
attractive
atypically
auspicious
avaricious
Barmecidal
barracouta
batrachian
benzocaine
bewitchery
biblically
brainchild
breadcrumb
broadcloth
byelection
byssaceous
caoutchouc
cappuccino
capricious
caruncular
charactery
chelicerae
chemically
chiffchaff
clavichord
clavicular
clerically
clinically
coelacanth
collection
collective
collocutor
comanchero
compaction
concoction
concoctive
conduction
conductive
confection
conjecture
connection
connective
consecrate
consectary
consociate
convection
convective
conviction
convictive
coparcener
corbiculae
coriaceous
cornucopia
correction
corrective
corticated
cosmically
cretaceous
crisscross
critically
crosscheck
cryoscopic
curricular
curriculum
curvaceous
curvacious
cyclically
daisychain
debauchery
debouchure
defalcator
deflection
deflective
deforciant
dehiscence
denunciate
depreciate
desiccator
despicable
despicably
detraction
detractive
dielectric
difficulty
disenchant
disincline
dissection
dissociate
distichous
drupaceous
duodecimal
duplicator
embouchure
endoscopic
epicycloid
eradicable
eradicator
ericaceous
erotically
escutcheon
ethnically
excruciate
exotically
explicable
explicitly
expunction
extinction
extinctive
extractant
extraction
extractive
extricable
fabricator
fairycycle
fallacious
fantoccini
farcically
fascicular
fasciculus
firescreen
firstclass
fisticuffs
floorcloth
foliaceous
follicular
fornicator
frolicking
frolicsome
fungicidal
furuncular
gemmaceous
germicidal
glasscloth
glumaceous
gothically
gramicidin
grandchild
grasscloth
greencloth
gyroscopic
handicraft
hectically
heliacally
hendecagon
heptachord
herbaceous
heroically
heroicness
heroicomic
hierocracy
highoctane
hippocampi
Hippocrene
homunculus
horoscopic
horsecloth
horsecoper
housecraft
hydrically
iconoclasm
immiscible
immiscibly
impeccable
impeccably
impeccancy
implacable
implacably
implicitly
inculcator
indiscreet
indiscrete
ineducable
infarction
inflection
inflective
infliction
inflictive
infraction
inimically
injunction
injunctive
insouciant
inspection
inspective
interceder
intercross
intinction
invincible
invincibly
iridaceous
ironically
jinricksha
justiciary
Lamarckian
Lamarckism
landocracy
landscaper
larvicidal
latescence
lauraceous
lenticular
leprechaun
leucocytic
leukocytic
liliaceous
loosecover
loquacious
lowerclass
lubricator
lubricious
Lupercalia
majuscular
malvaceous
maniacally
manuscript
maraschino
mastectomy
masticable
masticator
matricidal
mediocrity
meerschaum
megascopic
melancholy
mendacious
mendicancy
mesoscaphe
metrically
micaschist
microcline
minuscular
monarchial
Monarchian
monarchism
monarchist
monoecious
mordacious
mosaically
mosaicking
motorcycle
myopically
myrtaceous
mystically
mythically
mythiciser
nautically
neglectful
nitpicking
nitrochalk
nonfiction
nonnuclear
obfuscated
ochlocracy
officence
oleraceous
oligoclase
olivaceous
omniscient
orthoclase
osteoclast
overactive
palmaceous
paperchase
parenchyma
parricidal

participle
particular
patriciate
patricidal
peacockery
peacockish
peduncular
pellicular
pellucidly
pennaceous
pentachord
perfection
perfective
periscopic
pernicious
pernickety
persecutor
pesticidal
phagocytic
phenacetin
phenocryst
phonically
phylactery
physically
physicking
pichiciago
picnicking
plainchant
playacting
plutocracy
poetically
pornocracy
porraceous
postscript
precocious
predacious
predecease
predicable
prediction
predictive
prefecture
prelection
prepackage
producible
production
productive
proficient
projectile
projection
projective
prolicidal
prolocutor
prosecutor
protection
protective
protectory
protectrix
provocator
psilocybin
pubescence
pugnacious
quiescence
quiescency
quinacrine
ranunculus
reconciler
redescribe
rediscover
reelection
reflection
reflective
refraction
refractive
refractory
rejoicings
renascence
repurchase
resorcinol
respectful
respecting
respective
retractile
retraction
retractive
retrochoir
revanchism
revanchist
rhinoceros
rollicking
roodscreen
rubrically
rubricator
rustically
salesclerk
sarracenia
scenically
scratchily
scratchwig
screechowl
selfacting
selfaction
senescence
septically
sepulchral
sequacious
SerboCroat
seriocomic
serviceman
shortcrust
silkscreen
skyjacking
slavocracy
snobocracy
spacecraft
spadiceous
spiracular
spiraculum
splanchnic
stagecoach
stagecraft
stalactite
statecraft
statically
steamchest
stomachful
stormcloud
subduction
subjectify
subjection
subjective
subnuclear
subsection
sufficient
supercargo
surfactant
surgically
suspicious
swordcraft
syndicator
synoecious
tablecloth
tactically
tarmacadam
telescopic
tentacular
terracotta
testaceous
tetrachord
thalecress
thirdclass
trabeculae
trabecular
tragacanth
tragically
tragicomic
trajection
trajectory
transcribe
transcript
tricyclist
trioecious
trisection
tropically
tubercular
tuberculin
tuffaceous
tumescence
typescript
undercliff
undercover
undercroft
uneducated
ungraceful
ungracious
unicyclist
unilocular
univocally
unmerciful
upperclass
uxoricidal
valleculae
vallecular
vasoactive
veldschoen
vermicelli
vermicidal
vermicular
vernacular
versicular
vertically
vibraculum
vindicable
vindicator
vindictive
violaceous
virescence
vortically
vorticella
vorticular
waistcloth
waterclock
watercraft
watercress
wheelchair
windscreen
witchcraft
worldclass
absurdness
accordance
accredited
achondrite
affordable
almondeyed
animadvert
aphrodisia
appendices
appendixes
ascendable
ascendance
ascendancy
ascendence
ascendency
ascendible
attendance
beechdrops
behindhand
belladonna
bellydance
candidness
commodious
confidante
confidence
considered
coproducer
curmudgeon
cursedness
cuspidated
cussedness
cylindered
cylindroid
defendable
degradable
degradedly
demandable
deoxidiser
dependable
dependably
dependence
dependency
depredator
diapedesis
diapedetic
diffidence
dillydally
diplodocus
disbudding
disordered
disorderly
dissidence
doggedness
eisteddfod
elatedness
elucidator
episodical
expandable
expendable
extendedly
extendible
fastidious
fervidness
floridness
foetidness
forbidding
formidable
formidably
friendless
friendlily
friendship
frigidness
fuddyduddy
gerundival
gesundheit
granadilla
granddaddy
grandducal
grenadilla
groundbait
groundless
groundling
groundmass
groundplan
groundrent
groundsman
groundwork
gynandrous
handedness
hippodrome
hookedness
hornedness
horridness
hybridiser
hyperdulia
illaudable
illaudably
impendence
impendency
imprudence
incandesce
incendiary
includible
incredible
incredibly
ineludible
ingredient
intendance
intendment
introducer
inwardness
jaggedness
lardydardy
limpidness
liquidator
liquidiser
liquidness
lopsidedly
methodical
mindedness
molendinar
molybdenum
monandrous
morbidezza
morbidness
nightdress
octandrian
octandrous
onesidedly
orthodoxly
outbidding
palindrome
palladious
pallidness
pearldiver
peccadillo
perfidious
periodical
phagedaena
phagedenic
placidness
precedence
precedency
prejudiced
premedical
presidency
presidiary
procedural
prosodical
providence
punchdrunk
putridness
raggedness
rancidness
recordable
recrudesce
redundance
redundancy
refundable
refundment
regardless
reproducer
rewardable
rewardless
ritardando
rootedness
ruggedness
sacerdotal
sacredness
scaredycat
secludedly
secondbest
secondhand
secondment
secondrate
seguidilla
sensedatum
serradilla
shieldless
shortdated
shouldered
shrewdness
shroudlaid
shroudless
skirtdance
smokedried
snakedance
sordidness
splendidly
spoondrift
squanderer
stolidness
stomodaeum
stupidness
submediant
subordinal
subsidence
subsidiary
succedanea
sugardaddy
suicidally
superduper
sworddance
synecdoche
Talmudical
threadbare
threadfish
threadmark
threadworm
toroidally
torpidness
torridness
towardness
transducer
triandrous
turbidness
turgidness
unbiddable
underdress
ungrudging
unhandsome
unkindness
unreadable
upwardness
verandahed
vivandiere
wickedness
wontedness
wrongdoing
abacterial
abducentes
aberdevine
abiogenist
acarpelous
accelerate
accidental
acrogenous
acromegaly
acroterion
acroterium
activeness
adherently
adjacently
adrenergic
adulterant
adulterate
adulteress
adulterine
adulterous
advisement
aesthetics
aesthetism
afferently
affluently
Albigenses
alliterate
alloverish
allurement
altogether
amanuenses
amanuensis
ambidexter
amercement
anapaestic
androecium
anopheline
antebellum

antecedent
antecessor
antependia
antepenult
antiheroic
antiSemite
antisepsis
antiseptic
aplacental
apoplectic
apothecary
apothecial
apothecium
apotheoses
apotheosis
apparelled
apparently
aquiferous
arbalester
arboreally
archdeacon
argumentum
Armageddon
armigerous
arytaenoid
asafoetida
assafetida
asseverate
astuteness
asymmetric
attunement
auriferous
autogenous
averseness
babblement
bafflement
baldheaded
bareheaded
barelegged
barometric
baronetage
battledore
battlement
battleship
beadleship
beekeeping
beforehand
beforetime
bejewelled
bellwether
bemusement
bestseller
biliverdin
biochemist
bladdernut
blanketing
blastemata
blistering
blitheness
blithering
blithesome
blottesque
bluepencil
blusterous
boisterous
bollweevil
bolometric
bolshevise
bolshevism
bolshevist
boneheaded
bonesetter
bookkeeper
bookseller
bootlegger
bootlessly
bottlefeed
bottleneck
bottletree
bowdlerise
bowdlerism
breezeless
bridgeable
bridgehead
bridgeless
bridgework
bridlepath
browbeaten
bufflehead
bullheaded
cacogenics
cadaverous
cajolement
candlefish
candletree
candlewick
candlewood
caramelise
carelessly
carotenoid
catalectic
cataleptic
cattlegrid
centreback
centrefold
centrehalf
cerebellum
chalcedony
challenger
chamaeleon
chamberpot
chancellor
chandelier
changeable
changeably
changeless
changeling
changeover
channelise
channelled
chargeable
chargehand
Charleston
chasteness
chatterbox
cheesecake
chequebook
chickenpox
childermas
chimneypot
choiceness
chuckerout
cinquefoil
clothesbag
clothespeg
clothespin
coarseness
cochleated
cockneyish
cockneyism
coffeemill
coherently
complected
complement
completely
completion
completive
complexion
complexity
comprehend
compressed
compressor
concretely
concretion
concretise
concretism
concretist
congregant
congregate
coniferous
conspectus
consuetude
coolheaded
copesettic
copyreader
cordierite
counselled
counsellor
counteract
couplement
covalently
cradlesong
craquelure
crescentic
crowkeeper
cryogenics
cuddlesome
cuttlebone
cuttlefish
damageable
dapplegrey
daydreamer
dazzlement
deadweight
debasement
debatement
decadently
decahedral
decahedron
decelerate
deepseated
defacement
defilement
definement
degeneracy
degenerate
deliberate
delineator
demonetise
demureness
denouement
desiderata
desiderate
devotement
diastemata
diathermal
diathermic
diligently
diluteness
discreetly
discrepant
discretely
discretion
distressed
divineness
documental
doorkeeper
dosimetric
doublebass
doubleness
doublepark
doubletalk
doubletime
dumbledore
dungbeetle
ectodermal
ectodermic
ectogenous
edibleness
effaceable
effacement
effeteness
eighteenmo
eighteenth
eloquently
embowelled
empanelled
encasement
endodermal
endodermis
endogenous
energetics
enfacement
engagement
engineroom
enlacement
enticement
entireness
ephemerous
episternum
epithelial
epithelium
escapement
ethereally
euhemerise
euhemerism
euhemerist
evangelise
evangelism
evangelist
eviscerate
evolvement
exaggerate
exasperate
excitement
exenterate
exothermal
exothermic
exulcerate
facileness
fadelessly
fairleader
fearlessly
featherbed
feathering
fecklessly
feebleness
femaleness
fickleness
fiddleback
fiddlehead
fiddlewood
fierceness
figurehead
finiteness
fishkettle
flannelled
flattering
flawlessly
fledgeling
flunkeydom
flunkeyism
folkmemory
foreteller
formlessly
founderous
Fourierism
fourleaved
fourteener
fourteenth
fragmental
frequenter
frequently
fringeless
fulllength
funereally
futureless
gamekeeper
gangrenous
garnierite
gatekeeper
gatelegged
gaucheness
genteelism
gentlefolk
gentleness
geochemist
geothermal
geothermic
Glaswegian
glauberite
glimmering
goalkeeper
goaltender
goggleeyed
goldbeater
grangerise
grangerism
graphemics
greasewood
greyheaded
halflength
halfnelson
halfyearly
halogenate
halogenous
handselled
Hanoverian
hardheaded
harmlessly
haustellum
heathendom
heathenise
heathenish
heathenism
heedlessly
hellbender
helplessly
hemihedral
hemihedron
hempnettle
hexahedral
hexahedron
hexamerous
hexametric
hipsterism
hoarseness
holohedral
homiletics
homocercal
homogenise
homogenous
homosexual
honeyeater
hopelessly
hucklebone
humaneness
humbleness
humoresque
hypodermal
hypodermic
hypodermis
hypotenuse
icebreaker
illiteracy
illiterate
immaterial
imminently
immoderacy
immoderate
immodestly
immoveable
immurement
impalement
impanelled
impotently
impoverish
impudently
impureness
inappetent
inbreeding
incasement
incidental
incinerate
incitement
incoherent
indecently
indigenous
indigested
indirectly
inditement
indolently
Indonesian
inducement
inexpertly
infidelity
inherently
innateness
innocently
innumeracy
innumerate
innumerous
inquietude
insaneness
insolently
intenerate
interested
intolerant
inveteracy
inveterate
irrelevant
irreverent
Ishmaelite
isopterous
isothermal
Japanesque
jawbreaker
jejuneness
jocoseness
journeyman
Kafkaesque
kenspeckle
kettledrum
knobkerrie
lambrequin
lawbreaker
lawntennis
legateship
lieutenant
lifelessly
ligamental
lighterage
lighterman
listlessly
littleness
lobsterpot
lockkeeper
longaevous
longheaded
longlegged
lossleader
lotuseater
loungesuit
lovelessly
loveletter
luciferase
luciferous
luculently
lustreless
macebearer
makeweight
malapertly
malleebird
malleefowl
manageable
manageably
management
manageress
managerial
manifestly
manifestos
manometric
mansuetude
marguerite

masquerade
matureness
meagreness
mealbeetle
meddlesome
Melanesian
mesomerism
metacentre
metalepsis
metamerism
mettlesome
Michaelmas
middleaged
middlebrow
middlemost
mindlessly
minutebook
minutehand
minuteness
miscreance
mockheroic
mongrelise
mongrelism
monogenism
monumental
moroseness
morphemics
motiveless
mountebank
mousseline
Mousterian
movelessly
muciferous
namelessly
nanosecond
nativeborn
nativeness
needlebath
needlebook
needlecord
needlefish
needlessly
needlework
nettlerash
newsletter
newsreader
newsvendor
nimbleness
nineteenth
nipplewort
northerner
noticeable
noticeably
notonectal
nubiferous
nuciferous
obediently
oblateness
obliterate
obtuseness
occidental
octahedral
octahedron
octamerous
octodecimo
oecumenism
oleiferous
omnigenous
oncogenous
opaqueness
openhearth
opposeless
orangepeel
orangewood
ornamental
ornateness
orthoepist
osmeterium
otioseness
outfielder
overrefine
overweight
pacesetter
paddleboat
painlessly
pallbearer
pancreatic
pancreatin
papaverine
papaverous
paramecium
parametric
paraselene
pebbledash
pedimental
pedimented
peerlessly
penitently
peridermal
perihelion
peripeteia
perplexity
petiteness
phrasebook
picaresque
picosecond
piliferous
pinebeauty
pitcherful
pitilessly
plaguesome
plangently
playfellow
plunderage
plunderous
poinsettia
politeness
polygenism
polygenist
polygenous
polyhedral
polyhedric
polyhedron
polymerise
polymerism
polymerous
Polynesian
polysemous
pomiferous
postbellum
pouncetbox
presternum
princeling
princeship
proceeding
procreator
prophesier
prophetess
proscenium
prospector
prospectus
prosperity
prosperous
protreptic
pruriently
psalterium
puerperium
purulently
puzzlement
pyrogenous
pyrometric
pyrotechny
pyroxenite
quadrennia
quarrelled
quarreller
quarrender
quarterage
quarterday
quartering
quatrefoil
rabblement
rackrenter
rattlehead
rattlepate
rattletrap
reassemble
reassembly
recklessly
recuperate
redolently
referendum
refinement
regalement
regeneracy
regenerate
regimental
rejuvenate
rejuvenise
remodelled
remonetise
remoteness
remunerate
requiescat
restlessly
reticently
retirement
reverencer
reverently
revilement
ringleader
ringnecked
ripplemark
roistering
roisterous
Romanesque
rontgenise
rottweiler
rovebeetle
rudimental
ruthlessly
saddleback
saddlefast
saddletree
saliferous
saltcellar
savageness
scarceness
scatheless
scattergun
scattering
seaanemone
securement
secureness
sedateness
seducement
seedvessel
selfdeceit
selfdenial
selffeeder
selflessly
selfregard
selfseeker
semiweekly
semiyearly
sentiently
sereneness
settlement
severeness
sexagenary
Sexagesima
shillelagh
shopkeeper
shortening
shrivelled
Shrovetide
shuttering
sicklebill
simpleness
singlefoot
singleness
singletree
slanderous
slatternly
sleeveless
sleevelink
slenderise
slipperily
sluicegate
slumberful
slumberous
smattering
smorrebrod
sneezeweed
sneezewood
sneezewort
softheaded
solacement
sombreness
soullessly
sourcebook
southerner
southernly
sparseness
Spencerian
Spenserian
sphalerite
spongecake
spongewood
spoonerism
spotlessly
sprucebeer
spruceness
squareness
squaresail
squaretoed
squaretoes
squeteague
squirearch
squirehood
squireling
squireship
stablemate
stableness
stagbeetle
staggering
starveling
statuesque
stiffening
stiflebone
strategist
stridently
subaverage
subspecies
subtleness
supineness
supplejack
supplement
suppleness
suppletion
suppletive
suppletory
suppressor
swaggering
sweetening
sweltering
syncretise
syncretism
syncretist
synthesise
synthesist
synthetise
synthetist
tactlessly
talebearer
taleteller
tanglement
taperecord
tapotement
tattletale
taxidermal
taxidermic
tearjerker
tearlessly
technetium
tegumental
telemetric
telpherage
tenemental
themselves
theoretics
thickening
thirteenth
throneless
thunderbox
thundering
thunderous
timekeeper
timelessly
timeserver
tirelessly
titanesque
toffeenose
tonelessly
tongueless
tonguetied
tortfeasor
tracheated
tracheitis
trammelled
trancelike
transeptal
trawlerman
triacetate
triggerman
triquetrae
triquetral
triskelion
trolleybus
tropaeolum
tumbledown
tumblerful
tumbleweed
tunelessly
turtleback
turtledove
turtleneck
twelvefold
twelvenote
twelvetone
twowheeler
typesetter
Tyrrhenian
umpireship
unaccented
unaffected
unattended
undefended
undeserved
undeterred
undigested
unexcelled
unexpected
unforeseen
unfriended
unfriendly
ungenerous
uniqueness
unlabelled
unlikeness
unnameable
unravelled
unredeemed
unreserved
unripeness
unscreened
unselected
unstressed
unwavering
vehemently
vicegerent
viceregent
viewlessly
virtueless
virulently
vituperate
vivisector
vociferant
vociferate
vociferous
volumetric
voyageable
waffleiron
wallpepper
wattlebird
wavelength
weatherbox
weathering
weatherman
wellheeled
wentletrap
Wertherian
Wertherism
whispering
Winchester
woodpecker
wordlessly
workpeople
yokefellow
yourselves
zollverein
zwitterion
blackfaced
blamefully
blissfully
boastfully
breadfruit
brickfield
calciferol
camouflage
candyfloss
chaudfroid
chauffeuse
cheerfully
dentifrice
doubtfully
doughfaced
dreadfully
engulfment
faithfully
fancifully
febrifugal
fiftyfifty
flashflood
forcefully
fruitfully
ghastfully
glassfibre
gooseflesh
gracefully
grapefruit
gratefully
gratifying
greenfinch
guilefully
henceforth
horseflesh
insufflate
interferer
interferon
Janusfaced
lightfaced
magnifical
magnificat

magnifying
mercifully
microfarad
microfiche
millefiori
mirthfully
mournfully
multifaced
paddyfield
paraffinic
pastyfaced
peacefully
permafrost
persiflage
photoflood
pianoforte
piscifauna
pokerfaced
pontifical
pontifices
postoffice
powerfully
pridefully
prizefight
proudflesh
rightfully
sacrificer
satisfying
scornfully
shamefaced
shamefully
sheriffdom
shirtfront
sideeffect
slothfully
smockfrock
spitefully
sportfully
stonefruit
swinefever
Tartuffian
Tartuffism
tastefully
thankfully
transferee
transferor
transfuser
trustfully
truthfully
underfloor
unedifying
unlawfully
vengefully
wastefully
watchfully
waterflood
waterfront
wearifully
whitefaced
wrathfully
wrongfully
Wycliffite
youthfully
aboriginal
abridgment
adjudgment
aftergrass
allergenic
amphigouri
anagogical
analogical
androgenic
anemograph
apologetic
aspergilla
astragalus
avantgarde
bedraggled
belongings
biodegrade
biological
blackguard
bloodguilt
brantgoose
brentgoose
bridegroom
bromegrass
bunchgrass
carmagnole
carragheen
centigrade
chinagraph
coastguard
collegiate
conjugally
contagious
contiguity
contiguous
corrigenda
corrigible
corrugated
corrugator
cosmogonic
couchgrass
courageous
craftguild
crossgrain
cyclograph
deflagrate
detergency
diningroom
disengaged
ditriglyph
divergence
divergency
divulgence
dorsigrade
earwigging
ecological
effulgence
ensanguine
epexegeses
epexegesis
epexegetic
erotogenic
expurgator
exsanguine
extinguish
farsighted
fastigiate
fibreglass
fieldglass
foreignism
galloglass
gaslighter
geological
goodygoody
goosegrass
gunfighter
hectograph
heliograph
heptagonal
hieroglyph
hierograph
hippogriff
hippogryph
honeyguide
houseguest
humbuggery
humbugging
hurdygurdy
hygrograph
hypergolic
hypnagogic
iatrogenic
impregnant
impregnate
indulgence
inelegance
ineligible
ineligibly
instigator
insurgence
insurgency
intangible
intangibly
intergrade
intrigante
intriguant
laryngitic
laryngitis
lemongrass
lentigines
lithoglyph
lithograph
liturgical
livingroom
lovingness
malingerer
Malpighian
meningioma
meningitis
micrograph
mimeograph
monsignori
Montagnard
mulligrubs
myological
mystagogic
mystagogue
negligence
negligible
negligibly
neological
nephograph
newsagency
nightglass
nitrogroup
nonlogical
oceangoing
orological
orthogenic
orthogonal
outrageous
outrightly
paedagogic
paedogogue
pantograph
passageway
pathogenic
pellagrous
pentagonal
petroglyph
phonograph
photogenic
photograph
phylogenic
phytogenic
pictograph
piecegoods
planigraph
Portuguese
presageful
presignify
prodigally
prodigious
prologuise
propagable
propaganda
propagator
pycnogonid
quickgrass
radiogenic
radiograph
rampageous
reeligible
refulgence
resurgence
retrograde
retrogress
revengeful
rhizogenic
salmagundi
saltigrade
saprogenic
satyagraha
scapegrace
sialagogic
sialagogue
smaragdine
smaragdite
speargrass
spirograph
springhalt
springhead
springless
springlike
springtail
springtide
springtime
springwood
stalagmite
stenograph
sterigmata
straighten
straightly
strengthen
stringbean
stringency
stringendo
stringhalt
stringless
stronghold
strongroom
stylograph
subjugator
supergiant
sweatgland
swordgrass
syllogiser
synergetic
syntagmata
takingness
tardigrade
termagancy
tetragonal
theurgical
throughout
throughput
throughway
tiringroom
toboggańer
transgress
triangular
twilighted
umbrageous
underglaze
unflagging
variegated
vectograph
watchglass
watchguard
waterglass
zigzagging
zincograph
zoological
acrophobia
aerophobia
allophonic
ambushment
analphabet
anarchical
antechapel
Antichrist
antiphonal
antitheism
antitheist
antitheses
antithesis
antithetic
asynchrony
attachable
attachment
autochthon
avouchment
backsheesh
banishment
bawdyhouse
blackheart
blasphemer
bleachable
blockhouse
bloodhound
bluethroat
bluishness
boneshaker
boyishness
branchiate
breathable
breathless
breechless
bronchiole
bronchitic
bronchitis
Caerphilly
cataphract
catechesis
catechetic
catechiser
catechumen
chinchilla
churchgoer
churchyard
clovehitch
coachhouse
cockchafer
coryphaeus
courthouse
crosshatch
cytochrome
delightful
detachable
detachedly
detachment
diarrhoeal
diarrhoeic
diphtheria
diphtheric
disinherit
drafthorse
empathetic
encashment
encephalic
encephalon
endophytic
endothelia
enmeshment
enrichment
epentheses
epenthesis
epenthetic
exospheric
faintheart
famishment
fianchetto
foreshadow
foresheets
fourchette
franchiser
freightage
Frenchness
garishness
gaultheria
glasshouse
greenheart
greenhouse
guardhouse
guesthouse
halophytic
headcheese
headphones
henotheism
henotheist
Herrnhuter
hitchhiker
hobbyhorse
holophrase
holophytic
homophonic
hylotheism
hypophyses
hypophysis
hypotheses
hypothesis
impishness
infighting
infrahuman
insightful
Jewishness
ladychapel
lavishment
lavishness
lederhosen
lengthways
lengthwise
lighthouse
longshanks
Manichaean
Manicheism
manorhouse
mesophytic
mesothorax
metaphoric
metaphrase
metaphysic
metatheses
metathesis
metathetic
metathorax
modishness
monochasia
monochrome
monophonic
monorhymed
monotheism
monotheist
moonshiner
mopishness
mulishness
myasthenia
naphthenic
nomothetic
nosophobia
oafishness
oesophagus
overcharge
overshadow
overthrown
overthrust
owlishness
packthread
paraphrase
paraphrast
peripheral
perishable
perithecia
phosphatic
phosphoric
phosphorus
pilothouse
planchette
pleochroic
ploughable
ploughland

polychaete
polychrest
polychrome
polyphasic
polyphonic
polytheism
polytheist
postchaise
powerhouse
preachment
prosthesis
prosthetic
punishable
punishment
pyrophoric
quenchable
quenchless
rakishness
ravishment
relishable
riverhorse
rosechafer
roughhouse
roundhouse
rubythroat
searchable
searchless
semichorus
shanghaier
sheathbill
sheathless
shirehorse
sitophobia
sketchable
sketchbook
sleighbell
smokehouse
smoothbore
smoothness
songthrush
spatchcock
speechless
spitchcock
splashback
splashdown
sprightful
stanchless
stanchness
steakhouse
stenchtrap
stitchwort
storehouse
strathspey
struthious
strychnine
strychnism
sugarhouse
superhuman
sweetheart
switchback
switchover
sycophancy
telephoner
telephonic
tetrahedra
theophanic
theophoric
thillhorse
thoughtful
tocopherol
toxiphobia
trenchancy
unemphatic
unfathered
unorthodox
uppishness
wheelhorse
wheelhouse
whorehouse
windshield
witchhazel
wretchedly
xenophobia
xerophytic
xylophonic
abdominous
abortively
abrasively
accusingly
adaptively
additional
adhesively
adhibition
adjudicate
administer
admiringly
admonition
admonitive
admonitory
adoptively
aerobiosis
aerobiotic
aeruginous
affability
affiliated
afterimage
alarmingly
albuminoid
albuminous
alkalinity
allegiance
alleviator
allusively
almsgiving
altazimuth
altruistic
amerciable
amiability
ammoniacal
ammoniated
ammunition
anastigmat
ancipitous
aneurismal
annalistic
annihilate
annoyingly
anteriorly
antibiosis
antibiotic
anticipant
anticipate
aphoristic
apodeictic
Apollinian
apparition
appetising
appetitive
appositely
apposition
appositive
aquilinity
arbalister
archaistic
archbishop
armorially
arterially
arteriolar
artificial
ascariasis
asceticism
aspidistra
assibilate
assimilate
associable
asteriated
ateleiosis
audibility
autodidact
aversively
babysitter
backbiting
bafflingly
balbriggan
battailous
beautician
beautifier
becomingly
bedevilled
bellringer
benedicite
Benedictus
beneficent
beneficial
besprinkle
bestridden
biennially
bioscience
biparietal
bitchiness
bituminise
bituminous
bleariness
bleatingly
blindingly
blockishly
bloodiness
blueribbon
blurringly
blushingly
bookbinder
bootlicker
bouncingly
brachiator
brachiopod
Brahminism
braininess
brassiness
bratticing
brawniness
breeziness
brilliance
brilliancy
broodiness
broodingly
Buddhistic
bumblingly
bumpkinish
bunglingly
bustlingly
cabalistic
cacomistle
caespitose
cajolingly
calamitous
calcsinter
caliginous
calyciform
campaigner
canaliculi
canonicals
canonicate
canonicity
capability
capacitate
capacitive
carabineer
carabinier
carotinoid
carryingon
causticity
cavalierly
centricity
centrifuge
ceruminous
champignon
charmingly
chattiness
chauvinism
chauvinist
cheapishly
cheekiness
cheeriness
cheesiness
childishly
chilliness
chlorinate
chronicity
chronicler
chubbiness
churlishly
circuitous
clamminess
clannishly
classicise
classicism
classicist
classified
classifier
cloudiness
clownishly
clumsiness
coercively
cohabitant
cohesively
coincident
colatitude
colchicine
colonially
comedienne
comehither
comeliness
compliance
compliancy
complicacy
complicate
complicity
compliment
conjointly
conscience
conspiracy
conspirant
constipate
constitute
contribute
contritely
contrition
coordinate
coradicate
costliness
councillor
councilman
covariance
covetingly
coweringly
craftiness
cragginess
crankiness
crassitude
creaminess
creatinine
creatively
creativity
creepiness
cribriform
crocoisite
crossindex
crustiness
cumuliform
curability
daintiness
damagingly
dauphiness
dazzlingly
deactivate
deadliness
debilitate
decapitate
decisively
decivilise
defeminise
deficiency
definienda
definitely
definition
definitive
definitude
defoliator
dehumidify
delaminate
delimitate
delphinium
delphinoid
delusional
delusively
demobilise
demolition
demoniacal
demotivate
dendriform
denominate
depositary
deposition
depository
deracinate
deridingly
derisively
desalinate
descriptor
desipience
detoxicant
detoxicate
devilishly
devotional
dickcissel
digitiform
dilapidate
diminished
disability
disdainful
disjointed
disquieten
disquietly
distribute
distringas
disutility
divaricate
divisional
divisively
dolomitise
doubtingly
drawlingly
dreaminess
dreariness
dressiness
droopingly
drowsihead
drowsiness
drudgingly
durability
duumvirate
dwarfishly
dynamistic
earthiness
ebullience
ebulliency
ebullition
effeminacy
effeminate
efficiency
effusively
elasticise
elasticity
electively
Eleusinian
elutriator
emancipate
emancipist
emarginate
embodiment
embolismic
embroidery
emissivity
emollition
empiricism
empiricist
emulsifier
enantiosis
endemicity
enduringly
engagingly
enregister
enrigiment
enticingly
enunciable
enunciator
epideictic
equability
equanimity
equational
equilibria
erectility
erethismic
ergodicity
eruptively
especially
essayistic
eugenicist
eulogistic
euphuistic
Eurovision
everliving
evilminded
exactitude
excitingly
excogitate
exhibition
exhibitory
exorbitant
expedience
expediency
expedition
experience
experiment
exploitage
exploitive
exposition
expositive
expository
exteriorly
exultingly
facilitate
fairminded
familiarly
fanaticise
fanaticism
fatalistic
faultiness
felicitate
felicitous
femininely
femininity
fetchingly
feverishly
fiducially
fiendishly
filariasis
filthiness
fimbriated
fivefinger
flabbiness
flaccidity
flashiness
fleabitten

fleacircus
fleeringly
fleetingly
fleshiness
flimsiness
flintiness
floatingly
floppiness
fluffiness
fluoridate
fluorinate
folksiness
folksinger
footlights
foraminous
forefinger
forfeiture
fortuitism
fortuitist
fortuitous
fractional
Franciscan
frangipane
frangipani
fratricide
freakiness
freakishly
freeliving
frenziedly
friability
frictional
frilliness
friskiness
frizziness
frostiness
frothiness
frowningly
fugitively
fuliginous
fumblingly
functional
fusibility
futuristic
gadolinite
gadolinium
gaingiving
ganglionic
gelatinise
gelatinous
geneticist
glancingly
glassiness
gloominess
glossiness
gnosticism
golddigger
goodliness
graphitise
graspingly
gratuitous
greasiness
greediness
grindingly
grisliness
grittiness
grogginess
growlingly
grubbiness
grudgingly
grumpiness
guiltiness
gunslinger
gyrational
habiliment
habilitate
halfwitted
handpicked
hardbilled
hardbitten
hardfisted
harelipped
hauntingly
heartiness
Hebraistic
hedonistic
heparinise
hereditary
heresiarch
hereticate
highbinder
highminded
hirudinean
histrionic
homeliness
hornrimmed
hourcircle
humanistic
humanities
humidifier
humoristic
hungriness
hypolimnia
idealistic
ideational
ignobility
ilangilang
illatively
illuminant
illuminate
illuminati
illuminism
illuminist
illusional
illusively
imbecilely
imbecility
imbibition
immobilise
immobility
impatience
impediment
impenitent
imperially
imperilled
impolitely
imposingly
imposition
impudicity
inactivate
inactively
inactivity
inaptitude
inartistic
incipience
incipiency
incisively
incivility
incogitant
indecision
indecisive
indefinite
indelicacy
indelicate
individual
indocility
inefficacy
ineptitude
inexpiable
inexpiably
infelicity
inferiorly
infinitely
infinitive
infinitude
ingeminate
inhabitant
inheritrix
inhibition
inhibitory
iniquitous
inkslinger
innominate
inordinate
insanitary
insatiable
insatiably
inseminate
insipidity
insociable
interiorly
intimidate
intoxicant
intoxicate
invaginate
invalidate
invalidism
invalidity
invariable
invariably
invariance
invigilate
invitingly
irradiance
irradicate
irrational
irreligion
isoseismal
jacobinise
Jacobinism
Jacobitism
jauntiness
Jehovistic
jingoistic
judicially
juvenility
keratinise
keratinous
kerchieves
kindliness
kineticist
kingfisher
kingliness
knopkierie
knottiness
laconicism
ladyfinger
ladykiller
languisher
lanuginose
lanuginous
laughingly
lawabiding
legalistic
legibility
legitimacy
legitimate
legitimise
legitimism
legitimist
leguminous
Leibnizian
libidinous
lifegiving
lightingup
likelihood
likeliness
likeminded
limaciform
linguiform
linguistic
livelihood
liveliness
loneliness
longwinded
lordliness
loveliness
luxuriance
lyophilise
maleficent
manchineel
manumitted
marquisate
marshiness
materially
measliness
megalithic
melanistic
menacingly
meridional
Mesolithic
middlingly
midshipman
mightiness
migrainous
militiaman
misaligned
misericord
misjoinder
misprision
mithridate
modifiable
moniliasis
moniliform
monolithic
moralistic
morphinism
mosquitoes
mouldiness
movability
mudskipper
mudslinger
munificent
musicianly
mutability
natalitial
nativistic
negatively
negativism
negativist
negativity
negotiable
negotiator
nephridium
nicotinism
nidificate
nihilistic
nonaligned
nondrinker
nonjoinder
nonswimmer
notability
notarially
notifiable
novelistic
nutational
obligingly
obnubilate
occasional
officially
oldmaidish
oleaginous
ommatidium
openminded
oppositely
opposition
optatively
optimistic
Ordovician
organicism
organicist
organismal
orneriness
osmiridium
outswinger
overnicety
overridden
overriding
overwinter
pacifiable
pacificate
pacificism
pacificist
painkiller
palatinate
paltriness
parabiosis
parabiotic
paradisaic
paradisean
paradisiac
paradisian
paralipsis
parasitism
parasitoid
pasquinade
patchiness
pathfinder
peculiarly
pemphigoid
pemphigous
penicillin
periwigged
periwinkle
peroxidise
perquisite
petitioner
phallicism
phlogistic
phlogiston
Phoenician
piercingly
pigsticker
pilgrimage
piperidine
pityriasis
plasticise
plasticity
pleadingly
pleasingly
pliability
ploddingly
pluckiness
polemicist
politician
politicise
polydipsia
polyhistor
populistic
portliness
positional
positively
positivism
positivist
positivity
postliminy
potability
practician
practising
praesidium
prairiedog
prancingly
prednisone
preeminent
preexilian
prescience
pressingly
prettiness
prevailing
priggishly
principate
principial
principium
principled
prissiness
proclivity
profligacy
profligate
proprietor
prosaicism
prosciutto
prostitute
proteiform
proteinous
psychiatry
psychicism
psychicist
pugilistic
punitively
purblindly
pursuivant
putatively
quadriceps
quadrireme
quadrivial
quadrivium
qualmishly
quantifier
quantitive
queasiness
quercitron
questioner
quirkiness
ramblingly
ratability
reactivate
reactively
reactivity
rechristen
recidivism
recidivist
recipiency
relational
relatively
relativise
relativism
relativist
relativity
remediable
remedially
remediless
repetiteur
repetition
repetitive
reposition
repository
repudiator
resilience
resiliency
resupinate
retiringly
retraining
revalidate
revisional
ringfinger
risibility
rockpigeon
rockribbed
Romanistic
rosaniline
roselipped
rotational
rubiginous
sacroiliac
salability
salicional
sanctifier
sanctimony
sanctitude
sanguinary
sanguinely
sanguinity
sapphirine
sashwindow
satyriasis

scantiness
scathingly
scattiness
scepticism
sciolistic
scoffingly
Scotticise
Scotticism
scrutineer
scrutinise
scurrility
scurrilous
scurviness
scyphiform
securiform
seemliness
seismicity
selfbinder
selfrising
selfwilled
semicircle
semidivine
semifitted
semiliquid
serotinous
shabbiness
shagginess
sheepishly
shiftiness
shipfitter
shiprigged
shockingly
shoddiness
shoplifter
shopwindow
showwindow
shrewishly
sickliness
sidewinder
similitude
simoniacal
simplicity
simplifier
simplistic
skimpiness
skindiving
skinniness
skirmisher
skittishly
skywriting
slanginess
slantingly
sleaziness
sleepiness
sloppiness
slowwitted
sluggishly
sluttishly
smelliness
smudginess
smuttiness
snappishly
sneakiness
sneakingly
sneeringly
sniffiness
snobbishly
snootiness
snubbingly
snuffiness
softbilled
softfinned
solecistic
solicitant
solicitous
solicitude
solifidian
solstitial
solubilise
solubility
soothingly
sororicide
soubriquet
soundingly
sowthistle
spankingly
spasticity
speediness
spermicide
sphericity
spiflicate
spillikins
spongiform
sponginess
spookiness
sportiness
sportingly
sportively
spottiness
spunkiness
squalidity
starriness
steadiness
steaminess
steeliness
stelliform
stencilled
stenciller
stepsister
stickiness
stiflingly
stillicide
stinginess
stingingly
stinkingly
stockiness
stodginess
storminess
strabismal
strabismic
strabismus
stratiform
strikingly
stubbiness
stuffiness
stumpiness
stunningly
sturdiness
stypticity
subacidity
substitute
sugariness
sultriness
superiorly
suppliance
supplicant
supplicate
surprising
sustaining
sweatiness
sweepingly
swimmingly
swingingly
sybaritism
tamability
taperingly
taradiddle
tauntingly
tawdriness
taxability
technician
technicist
televiewer
television
televisual
temptingly
tenability
tendrillar
tendrilled
tetchiness
theodicean
thermionic
thermistor
thievishly
thinkingly
thorniness
ticklishly
timeliness
toothiness
totemistic
touchiness
touchingly
tourbillon
tourniquet
toweringly
tractional
trafficked
trafficker
transience
transiency
transistor
transition
transitive
transitory
trappiness
trashiness
trendiness
trichiasis
trichinise
trichinous
trickiness
trickishly
triclinium
triflingly
trillionth
triplicate
triplicity
trustiness
trustingly
tutorially
ubiquitous
ulotrichan
ulteriorly
umbilicate
umbiliform
unabridged
unassisted
unavailing
unbeliever
uncloister
undeniable
undeniably
undesigned
undesirous
uneasiness
unendingly
unenviable
unerringly
unfadingly
unfamiliar
unfeminine
unfilially
unfinished
unholiness
uniaxially
unionistic
unofficial
unreliable
unrelieved
unruliness
unscripted
unsociable
unsociably
unsocially
untidiness
unwariness
upbraiding
vanadinite
vanquisher
vaporiform
vaticinate
velocipede
velutinous
venational
ventricose
ventriculi
verifiable
veterinary
viewfinder
villainage
villainess
villainous
villeinage
viperiform
viraginous
visibility
vitalistic
vitaminise
vitiligate
vocational
volatilise
volatility
volitional
volubility
voluminous
wassailing
wateriness
waveringly
weakliness
weakminded
weedkiller
wellwisher
wharfinger
wheeziness
whiskified
winebibber
wintriness
witchingly
wobbliness
womanishly
woodpigeon
woolliness
worshipful
worshipped
worshipper
worthiness
wrathiness
yearningly
yeastiness
yieldingly
zoophilous
mumbojumbo
touchjudge
attackable
autarkical
blitzkrieg
claspknife
dislikable
embankment
embarkment
hakenkreuz
jinrikisha
kinnikinic
knickknack
knockkneed
Lysenkoism
mistakable
mistakenly
paperknife
remarkable
remarkably
sauerkraut
shrinkable
shrinkwrap
sprinkling
Trotskyism
Trotskyist
Trotskyite
unbrokenly
unworkable
acatalepsy
acotyledon
aetiologic
afterlight
anacolutha
anchylosis
anchylotic
animalcula
animalcule
anticlimax
anticlinal
apiculture
apocalypse
appealable
aquaplaner
artfulness
assailable
assaultive
assoilment
astrologer
astrologic
auscultate
autoplasty
aviculture
backblocks
backslider
ballflower
barbellate
bardolatry
barrelling
batholitic
bellflower
bellylaugh
Berkeleian
Boswellian
Boswellise
Boswellism
brakelight
brazilwood
bricklayer
calculable
calculably
calculator
camerlengo
camerlingo
cancellate
cancelling
cancellous
candelabra
cannelloni
cantaloupe
cantilever
cantillate
cardplayer
carnallite
carpellary
cassolette
casualness
catholicon
catholicos
cellularly
cellulitis
cellulosic
centilitre
centillion
cephalopod
chatelaine
chiselling
chivalrous
circularly
circulator
coagulable
cockalorum
compelling
compulsion
compulsive
compulsory
conciliary
conciliate
condolence
consolable
consulship
consultant
consulting
consultive
convalesce
convoluted
convulsant
convulsion
convulsive
coprolitic
corbelling
cordillera
cornflakes
cornflower
corpulence
corpulency
crapulence
crenellate
crenulated
crewelwork
crinolette
crippledom
crosslight
cucullated
cudgelling
derailleur
derailment
diabolical
diphyletic
disbelieve
dismalness
dispelling
dissilient
dissoluble
dissolvent
distilland
distillate
distillery
distilling
disyllabic
disyllable
drivelling
drysaltery
earthlight
enamelling
enamellist
encyclical
entailment
escallonia
ethnologic
everglades
excellence
excellency
fertiliser
feuilleton
fibrillary
fibrillate
fibrillose
fireblight
fitfulness
flabellate
flagellant
flagellate
flashlight
flatulence
flatulency
floodlight
florilegia
flugelhorn
foamflower
fowlplague
fritillary
frivolling

fulfilling
fulfilment
funnelling
gambolling
gauntleted
genialness
gentilesse
Ghibelline
Glagolitic
globularly
glycolyses
glycolysis
goldilocks
granularly
granulator
granulitic
grovelling
haemolysis
haemolytic
hagiolatry
hagiologic
hallelujah
hangglider
hanselling
hectolitre
heliolater
heliolatry
hemiplegia
hemiplegic
hierolatry
highflying
histologic
histolysis
histolytic
hornblende
horselaugh
horseleech
hostelling
houselling
hydrologic
hydrolysis
hydrolytic
iconolater
iconolatry
inexplicit
infallible
infallibly
inoculable
inoculator
instalment
instilling
interleave
interloper
interlunar
inviolable
inviolably
jaywalking
joyfulness
kennelling
kieselguhr
laurelling
lavalliere
lawfulness
legislator
lithologic
logrolling
mamillated
manfulness
manteltree
maquillage
Mariolater
Mariolatry
marvelling
marvellous
maxilliped
medullated
metallurgy
metaplasia
methylated
microlitic
millilitre
misbelieve
miscellany
monoclinal
monoclinic
moonflower
multiloquy
muscularly
Mussulmans
mycoplasma
mythologer
mythologic
narcolepsy
Neapolitan
necrolater
necrolatry
neurilemma
neurolemma
nickelling
nightlight
nostologic
nyctalopia
nyctalopic
ophicleide
ophiolater
ophiolatry
ophiologic
oracularly
oscillator
outbalance
overblouse
overflight
overslaugh
paraplegia
paraplegic
parcelling
pastellist
pathologic
patrilocal
patrolling
pencilling
pennillion
perchloric
percolator
perfoliate
periclinal
pestilence
petiolated
petrolatum
philologen
phonolitic
phonologic
photolitho
photolysis
photolytic
piccalilli
pilotlight
pinnulated
pistillary
pistillate
pistolling
pistolshot
pistolwhip
pixillated
plantlouse
platelayer
plutolatry
polyclinic
polyploidy
postillion
postulator
potbellied
pozzolanic
prefulgent
prevalence
privileged
promulgate
propellant
propellent
propelling
propulsion
propulsive
propylaeum
prosilient
pummelling
radiologic
rebellious
recallable
recyclable
refillable
refuelling
repealable
repellance
repellancy
repellence
repellency
republican
revealable
revealment
riboflavin
roquelaure
ruefulness
safeblower
sandalwood
sarcolemma
satellitic
schoolable
schoolbook
schooldays
schoolgirl
schoolmaam
schoolmarm
schoolmate
schoolroom
schooltime
schoolwork
scrollwork
scutellate
selfglazed
septillion
sextillion
sheeplouse
shoreleave
shortlived
shovelhead
shovelling
shrillness
sideglance
signalling
sinfulness
singularly
snafflebit
snivelling
snowplough
soapflakes
socialiser
sociologic
somniloquy
somnolence
somnolency
speculator
speedlimit
spiralling
splitlevel
stabiliser
steriliser
stimulator
stipellate
stipulator
subculture
subsellium
succulence
succulency
superlunar
swinglebar
swiveleyed
swivelling
symbolical
symboliser
syphilitic
tablelinen
tantaliser
tasselling
teleologic
tessellate
testflight
thimbleful
thimblerig
ticpolonga
tinselling
tirailleur
topgallant
torchlight
tortellini
translator
translucid
translunar
travelling
travelogue
tremolitic
trifoliate
tropologic
trowelling
trucklebed
truculence
truculency
trundlebed
tunnelling
turbulence
turbulency
umbellifer
umbrellaed
unbiblical
underlease
underlinen
underlying
unemployed
unexplored
unhallowed
unscalable
unwieldily
unyielding
usefulness
valvulitis
variolitic
vascularly
venialness
ventilator
verbaliser
visualiser
wallflower
wilfulness
windflower
windsleeve
woefulness
zabaglione
abnormally
abstemious
academical
achromatic
acidimeter
acidimetry
affirmable
alchemical
aldermanic
aldermanry
alphameric
amphimacer
amphimixes
amphimixis
anatomical
anemometer
anemometry
anglomania
aposematic
arithmetic
astigmatic
audiometer
audiometry
autoimmune
barramunda
barramundi
bathometer
bathymeter
bathymetry
blancmange
bloodmoney
bottomless
bottommost
burramundi
cartomancy
centimetre
chiromancy
circumcise
circumflex
circumfuse
circumvent
clinometer
clinometry
coatimundi
cognominal
collembola
collimator
consumable
consumedly
consummate
coulometry
custommade
cyclometer
densimeter
determined
dilemmatic
diplomatic
dipsomania
discomfort
discommend
discommode
discompose
dissembler
dissimilar
dressmaker
ecchymosis
ecchymotic
economical
economiser
elecampane
embalmment
emblematic
emblements
endosmosis
endosmotic
enharmonic
epidemical
epilimnion
episematic
erotomania
eudiometer
eudiometry
extramural
fathomable
fathomless
fieldmouse
Gallomania
goniometer
goniometry
grandmamma
gravimeter
gravimetry
hebdomadal
hectometre
heliometer
Heptameron
heptameter
hippomanes
hydromancy
hydrometer
hydrometry
hygrometer
hygrometry
hypsometer
hypsometry
iconomachy
iconometer
iconometry
imprimatur
inclemency
informally
inharmonic
intermarry
intermezzi
intermezzo
intramural
judgematic
kerygmatic
lacrimator
lacrymator
lissomness
Mahommedan
matchmaker
mathematic
melismatic
merrymaker
micrometer
micrometry
millimetre
mischmetal
misnomered
mixedmedia
Mohammedan
moneymaker
moviemaker
Muhammadan
Muhammedan
multimedia
mythomania
necromancy
nincompoop
noisemaker
numismatic
ombrometer
opisometer
pantomimic
papermaker
parramatta
peacemaker
pentameter
pentimento
phenomenal
phenomenon
pheromonal
phlegmatic
phonematic
phonometer
photometer
photometry
piezometer
planimeter
planimetry
planometer
porismatic
portamento
presumable
presumably
procumbent
pronominal
proximally
Ptolemaist
pulsimeter
pulsometer
pycnometer
pyknometer
radiometer
radiometry
randomness

recommence
redeemable
reformable
rhizomorph
rhythmical
scaramouch
schismatic
scrapmetal
scrimmager
servomotor
sexlimited
shellmound
shrewmouse
skijumping
smartmoney
sociometry
sophomoric
spirometer
spirometry
spodomancy
stonemason
streamless
streamline
sublimable
subliminal
sugarmaple
systematic
systemless
tachometer
tachometry
tachymeter
tachymetry
talismanic
tantamount
tauromachy
tautomeric
tetrameter
tetramorph
transmuter
tribometer
trigeminal
tromometer
uncommonly
underminer
unexampled
unicameral
uranometry
variometer
victimiser
viscometer
voltameter
wampumpeag
watchmaker
watermelon
abominable
abominably
abominator
abstention
abstinence
abstinency
accountant
accounting
actionable
actionably
adamantine
aeroengine
agapanthus
aggrandise
airmanship
alcyonaria
alexanders
alimentary
alternance
alternator
Amerindian
angwantibo
appointive
apprentice
aragonitic
Ashkenazim
assignable
assignment
astringent
astronomer
astronomic
attainable
attainment
attornment
austenitic
autumnally
barkentine
barrenness
barrenwort
Bedlington
benignancy
biodynamic
biogenesis
biogenetic
blazonment
bobbinlace
brazenness
brigandage
brigandine
brigandism
brigantine
brokendown
brokenness
buccinator
burdensome
buttonball
buttonbush
buttondown
buttonhole
buttonhook
buttonless
buttonwood
byssinosis
cachinnate
calumniate
calumnious
cannonball
cantonment
canzonetta
carbonnade
carbuncled
carcinogen
carcinosis
centennial
cismontane
cispontine
citronella
Clarenceux
clementine
coetaneous
colonnaded
commandant
commandeer
commandery
commanding
commandoes
commentary
commentate
commonable
commonalty
commonness
commonroom
commonweal
communally
communique
compendium
compensate
concentric
concinnity
condensate
condensery
congeneric
congenital
consensual
consonance
consonancy
contendent
contention
continence
contingent
continuant
continuate
continuity
continuous
convenable
convenance
convenient
convention
conventual
convincing
coolingoff
Copernican
cottoncake
cottonseed
cottontail
cottonweed
cottonwood
cottonwool
cousinhood
cousinship
cowpuncher
cravenness
credential
criminally
cybernetic
dampingoff
deaconship
declension
declinable
descendant
descendent
descension
designator
designedly
designment
despondent
detainment
diagonally
Dickensian
diesinking
disconcert
disconfirm
disconnect
discontent
dishonesty
disownment
dispensary
dissension
dissonance
dissonancy
distensile
distension
distention
distinctly
draconites
dragonhead
dragonnade
dragontree
drawingpin
duodenitis
ecumenical
effrontery
egocentric
elementary
elevenplus
eliminable
eliminator
enchanting
enjoinment
entrancing
epicentral
epigenesis
epigenetic
euphonious
euthanasia
evidential
examinable
externally
extraneity
extraneous
Fahrenheit
fallingoff
fandangoes
fascinator
fescennine
fibrinogen
firstnight
flamingoes
florentine
fontanelle
fortyniner
fourinhand
foxhunting
fraxinella
fricandeau
fustanella
galvaniser
gargantuan
gasconader
geocentric
geoponical
germinally
goldenness
goldenseal
Gorgonzola
gormandise
governable
governance
governessy
government
gramineous
grandniece
greatniece
guestnight
gunrunning
harmonical
harmonious
harmoniser
heavenborn
heavensent
heavenward
helianthus
helminthic
herrenvolk
heulandite
hibernacle
hootenanny
hormonally
horrendous
husbandage
husbandman
hyphenated
imaginable
imaginably
imprinting
impugnable
impugnment
inclinable
infernally
innuendoes
inspanning
internally
internment
internodal
internship
isodynamic
isogenetic
jackanapes
jackknives
jardiniere
jargonelle
jimsonweed
Krishnaism
Kuomintang
landingnet
lawrencium
Lawrentian
leadenness
leafinsect
machinator
machinegun
mackintosh
maidenhair
maidenhead
maidenhood
maidenlike
maisonette
malcontent
malignance
malignancy
mallenders
manzanilla
marginalia
marginally
marginated
marionette
martensite
martingale
maternally
matronhood
matronship
matronymic
mayonnaise
meaningful
mechanical
meltingpot
mercantile
metronomic
metronymic
mignonette
millennial
millennium
misconduct
misventure
mizzenmast
mizzensail
moderniser
modernness
morganatic
motionless
muffinbell
muttonhead
nationally
nationhood
nationless
nationwide
nevernever
newfangled
noncontent
noogenesis
notionally
nullanulla
nyctinasty
obtainable
obtainment
obtruncate
oldfangled
oppugnancy
optionally
ordainment
ordonnance
originally
originator
orogenesis
orogenetic
orotundity
orphanhood
outgeneral
outgunning
outlandish
outrunning
oxygenator
packingbox
pangenesis
pangenetic
panhandler
panjandrum
paragnosis
paramnesia
pardonable
pardonably
parsonbird
parsonical
paternally
patronymic
pectinated
pendentive
penmanship
pennanular
percentage
percentile
permanence
permanency
personable
personally
personalty
personator
pertinence
pertinency
petronella
phalangeal
pharyngeal
photonasty
piccaninny
pickaninny
pigeonhole
pigeonpair
pigeonpost
pigeontoed
pigeonwing
pigmentary
pistonring
pollenosis
pollinator
polyandric
polyanthus
polyonymic
portentous
pothunting
pratincole
prebendary
preconcert
prehensile
prehension
premonitor
prepensely
presentday
presentive
pretendant
pretendent
pretension
prevenancy
prevenient
prevention
preventive
profundity
progenitor
prolongate
promenader
prominence
promontory
propensity
protanopic
protensive
provenance
provincial
prudential
pulvinated
purtenance
quarantine

rabbinical
rationally
reasonable
reasonably
reasonless
refringent
regionally
repugnance
repugnancy
resignedly
resounding
respondent
responsive
responsory
retainable
returnable
ribbonfish
ribbonworm
ritornelli
ritornello
rollingpin
roseengine
rottenness
rumrunning
salientian
sallenders
salmonella
salmonleap
salpingian
sapiential
sappanwood
sarmentose
sarmentous
saturnalia
scavengery
screenings
screenplay
sealingwax
seamanlike
seamanship
seasonable
seasonably
seasonally
secernment
segmentary
semiannual
semiuncial
sentential
septenarii
septennial
septennium
sequential
sermoniser
serpentine
sharpnosed
shenanigan
soddenness
soldanella
solemnness
Sorbonnist
spleenwort
sporangial
sporangium
staffnurse
strainedly
stupendous
subcentral
subkingdom
sublingual
submontane
subtenancy
subvention
succinctly
suddenness
sullenness
sultanship
summonable
supernally
supernovae
suspenders
suspension
suspensive
suspensoid
suspensory
sustenance
sustention
sustentive
syngenesis
tabernacle
tangential
tankengine
tendinitis
terminable
terminably
terminally
terminator
theopneust
torrential
tramontana
tramontane
trecentist
tremendous
trepanning
Tridentine
trigonally
trilingual
trimonthly
turpentine
tympanites
tympanitic
tympanitis
tyrannical
unblenched
unblinking
unbonneted
unchanging
underneath
uneconomic
unevenness
uneventful
unguentary
unilingual
unmannerly
unthinking
unwrinkled
upbringing
upstanding
vaccinator
villanelle
virginally
virginhood
visionally
visionless
vulcaniser
waggonette
Waldensian
wantonness
wappenshaw
wardenship
warmingpan
weaponless
wellington
willynilly
woodenhead
woodenness
workingman
aardwolves
ablebodied
acoelomate
actinolite
actinozoan
aerologist
aeronomist
Aethiopian
aficionado
agrologist
agronomist
aircooling
alcoholise
alcoholism
algologist
allegorise
allegorist
ameliorate
amoebocyte
ampelopsis
anadromous
anastomose
anatropous
anecdotage
anecdotist
antagonise
antagonism
antagonist
antemortem
anthropoid
antimonial
antimonite
antinomian
antipodean
antisocial
Apollonian
apostolate
apotropaic
aquafortis
aristocrat
arthromere
asteroidal
auctioneer
auditorial
auditorium
autecology
autologous
automobile
automotive
autonomist
autonomous
axiologist
babiroussa
Babylonian
ballooning
balloonist
balneology
barefooted
bassoonist
Beaujolais
bedclothes
benevolent
bibliology
bibliopegy
bibliophil
bibliopole
bibliopoly
bibliotics
bibulously
bichromate
bigamously
billposter
bioecology
blastocyst
blastoderm
blastomere
blastopore
bluebonnet
bluebottle
bluecollar
bluetongue
bondholder
boondoggle
botryoidal
bourbonism
bourbonist
bryologist
buffoonery
bullroarer
calceolate
Caledonian
camelopard
camphorate
canorously
Capitoline
captiously
cardiogram
cardiology
carphology
cartoonist
caseworker
catabolism
cataloguer
categorise
cautionary
cautiously
centromere
centrosome
ceremonial
certiorari
cessionary
charioteer
chersonese
chevrotain
chiffonier
chloroform
chromosome
chronogram
chronology
chrysolite
chrysotile
Ciceronian
cinchonine
clangorous
clodhopper
clubfooted
comicopera
complotted
compromise
comstocker
conchoidal
conchology
conglobate
controlled
controller
controvert
copyholder
corncockle
covetously
craniology
cryptogamy
cryptogram
cryptology
cuckoopint
cuckoospit
cumbrously
curatorial
cytologist
dampcourse
decapodous
decolonise
decolorant
decolorise
decorously
deeprooted
deerforest
deltiology
demagogism
demonology
dendrology
deontology
desirously
dextrously
diagnostic
diatropism
dichroitic
dichromate
dictionary
dilatorily
diphyodont
disclosure
diseconomy
divebomber
dogstongue
dolorously
dovecolour
dysprosium
dystrophic
echinoderm
edulcorate
Egyptology
electorate
embryogeny
embryology
embryonate
endopodite
endproduct
endstopped
enormously
enterolith
enterotomy
entomology
enzymology
eosinophil
epeirogeny
epiglottal
epiglottic
epiglottis
episcopacy
episcopate
epistolary
equatorial
equipotent
equivocate
ergonomics
ergonomist
escapology
ethologist
eudemonism
eudemonist
Eurodollar
exobiology
fabulously
factiously
fearnought
fearsomely
fellmonger
festoonery
fictioneer
fictionist
firepolicy
fishmonger
flamboyant
flapdoodle
flatfooted
flexuously
fluorotype
fluxionary
folklorist
foreboding
forecourse
foudroyant
fourfooted
fourposter
framboesia
Francophil
freebooter
freeholder
freeloader
freesoiler
froghopper
fullbodied
fullbottom
futurology
gadrooning
gastrology
gastronome
gastronomy
generosity
generously
geognostic
geotropism
glaciology
gladsomely
glauconite
gloriously
glossology
glottology
gluttonise
gluttonous
gobemouche
gobstopper
golfcourse
goodlooker
gorgeously
graciosity
graciously
graphology
graptolite
gressorial
grievously
gruesomely
guillotine
gyrocopter
halfcocked
halfdollar
halfvolley
handsomely
handworked
hardboiled
haustorium
Heliconian
helicopter
heortology
hepatology
heretofore
heterodont
heterodoxy
heterodyne
heterogamy
heterogeny
heterogony
heterology
heteronomy
heterotaxy
homecoming
homoeopath
homologate
homologise
homologous
horizontal
horologist
hotblooded
humorously
hypocorism
ideologist
illusorily
immemorial
immunology
inapposite
indecorous
infamously
infusorial
infusorian
invigorate
ironmonger
ironworker
irresolute
isoglossal
isosporous
janitorial
Johnsonese
johnsonian
katabolism
lampoonery
lampoonist
lanceolate
landholder

landlocked
languorous
laparotomy
lavatorial
leafhopper
lectionary
lepidolite
lexicology
locomotion
locomotive
locomotory
lonesomely
lowprofile
luminosity
luminously
lusciously
lustrously
lycopodium
lymphocyte
lymphomata
malacoderm
malacology
malevolent
malodorous
manifoldly
Marcionite
mayblossom
megalosaur
mesomorphy
metabolise
metabolism
metabolite
mineworker
misologist
missionary
missionise
misthought
monitorial
monologise
monologist
monopodial
monopodium
monopolise
monopolist
monotonous
moratorium
morphogeny
morphology
mouthorgan
musicology
mutinously
mycologist
nailpolish
natatorial
natatorium
naturopath
nauseously
nebulosity
nebulously
nematocyst
nephrology
newsmonger
newsworthy
nidicolous
nomologist
nonviolent
nosologist
noteworthy
nucivorous
nucleonics
nucleoside
nucleotide
numerology
numerosity
numerously
nympholept
oceanology
octopodous
odontology
oecologist
oenologist
omnipotent
omnivorous
oncologist
oneirology
ontologist
opinionist
oreologist
ovariotomy
overbought
overcommit
overcooked
overlooker
overtopped
Palaeocene
Palaeogene
palaeolith
palaeotype
Palaeozoic
palagonite
palynology
papyrology
parabolise
paraboloid
paradoxure
paralogise
paralogism
paranormal
parapodium
passionary
passionate
Passionist
patriotism
patulously
peashooter
pedagogics
pedalorgan
pedologist
penologist
pensionary
perilously
peritoneal
peritoneum
phelloderm
phlebotomy
phlogopite
phrenology
phyllotaxy
phylloxera
physiocrat
physiology
pickpocket
plasmodesm
plasmodium
plasmogamy
plasmolyse
plesiosaur
pogonology
pogonotomy
polemonium
polynomial
polytocous
pomologist
populously
postmortem
potamology
pozzuolana
praecocial
praetorial
praetorian
preciosity
preciously
prefrontal
previously
prismoidal
proctorage
proctorial
proctorise
proglottis
prognostic
propionate
prostomial
prostomium
proteolyse
psalmodise
psalmodist
psephology
pseudocarp
psychology
psychopath
pyretology
pyridoxine
Pyrrhonian
Pyrrhonism
Pyrrhonist
pyrrhotite
racecourse
railroader
ravenously
reafforest
reallocate
recolonise
redblooded
redecorate
reredorter
reunionism
reunionist
revalorise
rhapsodise
rhapsodist
rheologist
rhomboidal
rhomboidei
ricinoleic
rigorously
ripsnorter
roadworthy
rockbottom
rockhopper
rollcollar
rupicoline
rupicolous
sanatorium
sandhopper
satanology
sawtoothed
saxicoline
saxicolous
scabrously
scaffolder
scansorial
schemozzle
schizocarp
schizogony
Scillonian
scleroderm
sclerotium
sclerotomy
scorzonera
scyphozoan
sedulously
seedpotato
seignorage
seignorial
seismogram
seismology
selenodont
selenology
selfcolour
selfloving
selfmotion
selfpoised
seltzogene
semeiology
semeiotics
semidouble
senatorial
senseorgan
sensuously
serologist
sexologist
shibboleth
shopsoiled
sideboards
siderolite
siderostat
silkcotton
sinologist
sinusoidal
sixshooter
slitpocket
slowfooted
slowmotion
snowmobile
soapboiler
softboiled
solenoidal
somatology
somatotype
sonorously
spaciously
speciology
speciosity
speciously
speleology
sphenodone
sphenogram
sphenoidal
spheroidal
spongology
sponsorial
spuriously
stadholder
stationary
stationery
staurolite
stentorian
stepmother
stereobate
stereogram
stereopsis
stereotype
stereotypy
stertorous
stopvolley
strabotomy
stramonium
stratocrat
stubbornly
studiously
sudatorium
sulphonate
superorder
surefooted
symphonion
symphonist
synaloepha
synecology
taxonomist
teatrolley
technocrat
technology
teratogeny
teratology
teratomata
theodolite
theogonist
theologian
theologise
theologist
theosopher
thermogram
thermophil
thermopile
thermostat
threnodial
threnodist
timbrology
timorously
tinctorial
tiresomely
toilsomely
tomfoolery
topazolite
topologist
tortiously
tortuosity
tortuously
toxicology
traitorous
trampoline
treasonous
trichology
trichotomy
trochoidal
troctolite
troglodyte
trollopish
trombonist
trophology
tryptophan
tuberosity
tubicolous
tuitionary
typologist
unbecoming
unbesought
unctuosity
unctuously
uninformed
unresolved
unschooled
urbanology
urochordal
usuriously
uxoriously
valorously
vaporously
varicocele
varicosity
venomously
vestpocket
viceconsul
vigorously
viperously
virologist
virtuosity
virtuously
Visigothic
visitorial
vitriolise
vomitorium
werewolves
whatsoever
whensoever
WhitMonday
whomsoever
wildfowler
winebottle
wingcollar
wingfooted
wireworker
withholder
wondrously
woodworker
woolsorter
wrongously
zygomorphy
absorption
absorptive
accomplice
accomplish
acidophile
addlepated
adsorption
adsorptive
afterpains
altarpiece
anabaptism
anabaptist
anemophily
anglophile
anglophobe
anglophone
ascription
assumption
assumptive
atmosphere
audiophile
barysphere
birdspider
birthplace
bisulphate
bisulphide
bisulphite
brainpower
breakpoint
catchpenny
cellophane
checkpoint
childproof
coleoptera
coleoptile
conception
conceptive
conceptual
conniption
corruption
corruptive
cosmopolis
crosspatch
crosspiece
ctenophore
cyclopedia
cyclopedic
decampment
decompound
decompress
desorption
dimorphism
dimorphous
disappoint
disapprove
discipline
discophile
disruption
disruptive
dissipated
disulphate
disulphide
drosophila
embonpoint
emerypaper
encampment
enterprise
entrapment
enwrapping
erysipelas
escarpment
everyplace
excerption
extemporal
extirpator
fairspoken
fieldpiece
fixedpoint
flameproof
flashpoint
floatplane
forcipated
fortepiano
freespeech
freespoken
Gallophile

Gallophobe
glasspaper
gramophone
granophyre
gypsophila
hairspring
handspring
hankypanky
haruspices
headspring
heliophyte
hemisphere
hierophant
hippophagy
hocuspocus
hodgepodge
hokeypokey
homeopathy
horsepower
hotchpotch
houseplant
houseproud
hoverplane
hyaloplasm
hydropathy
hydrophane
hydrophily
hydrophone
hydrophyte
hydroplane
hygrophyte
impalpable
impalpably
improperly
incomplete
inculpable
indisposed
interphase
interplant
interplead
interposal
interposer
intrepidly
ionosphere
Italophile
karyoplasm
kidnapping
leucoplast
lightproof
lithophane
lithophyte
lophophore
macrophage
madreporic
mainspring
mesosphere
metempiric
metropolis
microphone
microphyte
micropylar
mouthpiece
multiphase
multiplier
multipolar
musicpaper
mythopoeia
mythopoeic
nambypamby
necrophile
necrophily
necropolis
negrophile
negrophobe
neuropathy
neuroplasm
oligopsony
orthopedic
orthoptera

osteopathy
osteophyte
overspread
paedophile
palimpsest
pansophist
pedalpoint
perception
perceptive
perceptual
percipient
peremptory
philippina
philippine
philopoena
photophily
photophore
photoprint
phytophagy
pinchpenny
plecoptera
preceptive
preceptory
precipitin
preemption
preemptive
presuppose
primiparae
protophyta
protophyte
protoplasm
protoplast
purseproud
radiopaque
radiophone
recompense
recoupment
redemption
redemptive
redemptory
reshipment
resorption
resorptive
resumption
resumptive
rhizophore
rhodophane
ridgepiece
Russophile
Russophobe
saprophyte
sarcophagi
sarcophagy
sarcoplasm
schipperke
screwplate
screwpress
seacaptain
semiopaque
shellproof
shockproof
sincipital
Slavophile
Slavophobe
smokeplant
smokeproof
snailpaced
softspoken
soundproof
sousaphone
sporophore
sporophyll
sporophyte
standpoint
stockpiler
stockproof
stormproof
subreption
superpower

susceptive
swanupping
swashplate
syncopated
syncopator
tautophony
terneplate
terreplein
tetrapolis
thinkpiece
thirdparty
thornproof
threepence
threepenny
threepiece
thruppence
thumbprint
tittupping
toothpaste
touchpaper
transplant
transposal
transposer
triumphant
tropopause
tropophyte
underpants
underproof
unprepared
usucaption
vibraphone
videophone
voiceprint
wastepaper
waterpower
waterproof
wellspoken
wellspring
widespread
wingspread
Algonquian
colloquial
colloquise
colloquist
colloquium
consequent
delinquent
earthquake
foursquare
headsquare
inadequacy
inadequate
ineloquent
infrequent
relinquish
subsequent
underquote
abhorrence
abstergent
abstersion
abstersive
acquirable
aerogramme
aerography
affeerment
algebraist
allegretto
allotropic
allpurpose
anamorphic
anastrophe
anchoretic
anchoritic
anchorless
anchorring
answerable
answerably
antheridia
antifreeze

antiproton
aphaereses
aphaeresis
apocarpous
apochromat
apostrophe
appearance
arbitrable
arbitrager
arbitrator
archerfish
archpriest
armourclad
armourless
artycrafty
authorship
autocratic
autoerotic
autography
aviatrices
azeotropic
background
badderlock
balderdash
banderilla
barbershop
barcarolle
bastardise
bestirring
betterment
binaurally
biomorphic
birthright
bitterling
bitterness
bitterroot
bitterwood
bizarrerie
bombardier
borborygmi
bordereaux
borderland
borderless
borderline
bothersome
budgerigar
bursarship
butterball
butterbean
butterfish
buttermilk
butterwort
cacography
calcareous
calibrator
cankerworm
canterbury
cartwright
cascarilla
catarrhine
catburglar
cavalryman
celebrated
celebrator
censorious
censorship
censurable
cerography
chaparajos
chaparejos
chartreuse
chimerical
chondritic
cicatrices
Cinderella
Cistercian
cleverness
cloverleaf
coacervate

coeternity
coleorhiza
collarbeam
collarbone
collarette
collarless
collarstud
colourable
colourably
colourfast
colourless
colportage
colporteur
commercial
comparable
comparably
comparator
comparison
concerning
concertina
concertino
concordant
concurrent
concurring
conference
conferment
conferring
confervoid
confirmand
conformism
conformist
conformity
consortium
constraint
constringe
contortion
contortive
convergent
conversant
conversely
conversion
cooperator
copperhead
copywriter
cornerwise
corporally
corporator
corporeity
cosmoramic
countryish
countryman
couturiere
couverture
cowparsley
crossrefer
crossroads
culturally
cumbersome
cummerbund
decagramme
decigramme
declarable
deepfreeze
deepfrozen
deferrable
democratic
demography
demurrable
denigrator
deodoriser
deplorable
deplorably
desecrater
desecrator
desperados
deterrence
diachronic
didgeridoo
difference

dinnerless
disarrange
disbarring
disburthen
discerning
discordant
discursive
disfurnish
disharmony
disparager
disparates
dispersant
dispersion
dispersive
dispersoid
dispirited
dissertate
disservice
distortion
doctorship
doxography
drawbridge
driverless
dunderhead
easterling
Eastertide
editorship
effloresce
elaborator
electrical
electronic
encourager
endearment
endocrinal
enumerable
enumerator
epidermoid
epistrophe
escadrille
escharotic
espadrille
evaporable
evaporator
exoterical
expatriate
exuberance
eyeservice
factorship
fairground
fatherhood
fatherland
fatherless
fatherlike
fathership
favourable
favourably
fetterlock
filterable
fingerbowl
fingerless
fingerling
fingermark
fingernail
fingerpost
fisherfolk
flowergirl
flowerless
footbridge
foreground
foreordain
forthright
forwarding
fosterling
fraternise
fraternity
frigorific
gaspereaux
gasteropod
Gilbertian

gingerbeer
gingersnap
girlfriend
glomerular
glomerulus
grassroots
GrecoRoman
gregarious
gutturally
gynocratic
halberdier
hammerbeam
hammerhead
hammerless
hammerlock
hammerpond
Hansardise
hawserlaid
henharrier
heptarchic
hierarchal
hierarchic
hinterland
historical
hithermost
hitherward
holography
homebrewed
honourable
honourably
honourless
humourless
humoursome
hysteresis
hysteretic
hysterical
ideography
impairment
incurrable
inexorable
inexorably
inferrable
inglorious
innerrably
inoperable
insobriety
inspirator
integrable
integrally
integrator
interregna
introrsely
isentropic
isochronal
isomorphic
itinerancy
jaguarundi
jasperware
jeopardise
jobbernowl
jolterhead
juggernaut
kaisership
kilogramme
kimberlite
Krugerrand
ladderback
lanternfly
lattermost
laundryman
leaderless
leadership
ledgerbait
ledgerline
leopardess
letterbomb
letterbook
lettercard
letterhead
letterless
lexigraphy
limitrophe
lipography
lipservice
litterlout
lockerroom
loggerhead
logography
logorrhoea
Lollardism
longprimer
loxodromic
lucubrator
lugubrious
lumberjack
lumberroom
lumbersome
lumberyard
malapropos
manservant
Massoretic
masterhand
masterhood
masterless
mastermind
mastership
masterwork
mavourneen
measurable
measurably
measuredly
meliorator
membership
menstruate
menstruous
mensurable
mentorship
mesmeriser
meteoritic
midmorning
millwright
minstrelsy
misfortune
miswording
mobocratic
monocratic
monstrance
montbretia
motherhood
motherland
motherless
mothership
motherwort
mozzarella
mycorrhiza
myocardium
mysterious
nasturtium
natterjack
nectareous
nethermost
newswriter
nomography
nonferrous
nosography
nudibranch
numberless
nurseryman
occurrence
oleography
oligarchic
oratorical
orchardist
orchardman
oreography
outstretch
overground
overgrowth
overpraise
oysterfarm
paederasty
palmerworm
paratroops
parturient
pastorally
pastorship
pasturable
pawnbroker
penetrable
penetrably
penetralia
penetrance
penetrator
pennyroyal
peppercorn
peppermill
peppermint
pepperwort
perdurable
perdurably
perforator
performing
perjurious
perversely
perversion
perversity
perversive
phanerogam
pictorical
piledriver
pilgarlick
pincerlike
pinstriped
playground
playwright
pluperfect
polygraphy
ponderable
powderhorn
powderpuff
prayerbook
prearrange
precarious
precordial
precursory
preferable
preferably
preference
preferment
preferring
premarital
preparator
preparedly
prescriber
primordial
primordium
procurable
procurance
procurator
properness
propertied
proportion
proscriber
proverbial
pulveriser
pursership
pyrography
quaternary
quaternate
quaternion
quaternity
quatorzain
rapporteur
readership
reappraise
reciprocal
rectorship
recurrence
redcurrant
reentrance
reiterance
remarriage
renderable
repairable
repatriate
researcher
respirable
respirator
restorable
retrorsely
rheotropic
rhetorical
rinderpest
roughrider
rubberneck
rudderfish
rudderless
runnerbean
runthrough
sailorless
saltarello
salubrious
sanderling
Sanskritic
savourless
sciagraphy
seaserpent
seborrhoea
seethrough
selfpraise
selfprofit
semidrying
serigraphy
sestertium
sestertius
setterwort
sexpartite
shandrydan
sherardise
shipbroker
shipwright
shortrange
showerbath
signwriter
silverbath
silverfish
silverside
silverware
silverweed
sisterhood
skewbridge
skiagraphy
skyscraper
snapdragon
snowgrouse
songwriter
souterrain
spagyrical
spectrally
spidercrab
spiderline
spiderwort
stewardess
stockrider
subcordate
submariner
submersion
subscriber
subshrubby
substratum
subterfuge
subversion
subversive
sufferable
sufferably
sufferance
summerlike
summertime
sunderance
sunparlour
supperless
supportive
suprarenal
synaeresis
syncarpous
synchronal
synchronic
tackdriver
tailorbird
tailormade
telegraphy
tellership
temperable
temperance
temperedly
temporally
temporalty
temporiser
tenderfoot
tenderloin
tenderness
tenebrific
tenebrious
tenterhook
terrorless
tetrarchic
tetterwort
texturally
theatrical
theocratic
tickertape
timberhead
timberline
timbertoes
timberwolf
timberwork
timocratic
tollbridge
tomography
topography
travertine
trichroism
trichromat
trifurcate
trimorphic
tripartite
triternate
triturable
triturator
typewriter
typography
unAmerican
unbearable
unbearably
unfairness
uniformity
unimproved
unipartite
university
unsporting
unswerving
uproarious
urethritis
vesperbell
vespertine
Victoriana
victorious
viscerally
viziership
vulnerable
vulnerably
wainwright
wanderings
wanderlust
wanderplug
weaverbird
weimaraner
westernise
wickerwork
wilderment
wilderness
winegrower
wintertide
wintertime
wiredrawer
withdrawal
withdrawer
wonderland
wonderment
wonderwork
woolgrower
wraparound
wunderkind
xerography
xylography
yarborough
yesteryear
zoomorphic
abscission
accessible
accessibly
accrescent
accursedly
admissible
adolescent
aftershave
aggression
aggressive
aircushion
alongshore
alpenstock
ambassador
analysable
angiosperm
Anglistics
AngloSaxon
appeasable
assessable
assessment
ballistics
baptistery
bathyscaph
bathyscope
birthstone
Blackshirt
blacksmith
bloodstain
bloodstock
bloodstone
bobbysocks
bobbysoxer
bradyseism
brainstorm
breadstick
breadstuff
bridesmaid
Britishism
broadsheet
broadsword
broomstick
brownshirt
brownstone
caddisworm
campestral
candescent
canvasback
canvaswork
carnassial
centesimal
chainsmoke
chalkstone
charismata
cheapskate
chemisette

Circassian
clearstory
clerestory
clingstone
clinkstone
closestool
Clydesdale
coalescent
coexistent
cognisable
cognisably
cognisance
colossally
combustion
combustive
commissary
commission
commissure
compassion
compasssaw
composedly
compositor
concession
concessive
concussion
concussive
condescend
confession
confiscate
confusedly
congestion
congestive
consistent
consistory
contestant
coralsnake
corpuscule
correspond
cranesbill
crankshaft
crepuscule
cuirassier
cuttystool
cyclostome
cyclostyle
cystoscope
cystoscopy
declassify
decrescent
defeasance
defeasible
defensible
defensibly
degressive
demoiselle
depressant
depression
depressive
despisable
dialysable
diecasting
diffusible
digression
digressive
discussant
discussion
discussive
disgustful
dismission
dismissive
dispassion
disposable
dispossess
disrespect
earthshine
ecclesiast
embossment
endorsable
Englishman
engrossing
enthusiasm
enthusiast
epigastric
erubescent
evanescent
excrescent
exhaustion
exhaustive
expansible
expressage
expression
expressive
expressway
extensible
famousness
fantastico
fibrositis
fieldstone
fireescape
flavescent
floatstone
florescent
floristics
flyfishing
fortissimi
fortissimo
fricasseed
frutescent
garnishing
glycosuria
glycosuric
grandstand
grapesugar
grasssnake
gravestone
greenshank
greenstick
greenstone
greenstuff
greensward
grindstone
gymnastics
gymnosophy
gymnosperm
hagioscope
harassment
harvestman
heartsease
helioscope
heuristics
Hindustani
honeysweet
horseshoer
hydroscope
hygroscope
hypersonic
iconoscope
impassable
impassably
impassible
impassibly
impersonal
impossible
impossibly
impresario
impression
impressive
impuissant
incessancy
inconstant
incrassate
increscent
inexistent
infeasible
infrasonic
ingression
inquisitor
insensible
insensibly
inspissate
interspace
interstate
interstice
introspect
iridescent
iridosmine
jackassery
joyousness
kriegspiel
lactescent
Lammastide
largescale
lebensraum
lemniscate
licensable
liquescent
loganstone
macrospore
mangosteen
marcescent
matchstick
mediastina
Methuselah
microscope
microscopy
microseism
microspore
millesimal
molluscoid
molluscous
morrispike
multistage
musicstand
musicstool
narcissism
narcissist
necroscopy
nephoscope
nightshade
nightshift
nightshirt
nightstick
nigrescent
nourishing
odiousness
opalescent
oppression
oppressive
orchestics
orchestral
ostensible
ostensibly
ottershrew
outerspace
outgassing
ovipositor
oxidisable
Parnassian
patisserie
patristics
peninsular
penpushing
pentastich
percussion
percussive
periosteal
periosteum
permission
permissive
persistent
pharisaism
philistine
philosophe
philosophy
phthisical
pianissimo
pincushion
pitchstone
plebiscite
plumassier
porousness
possession
possessive
possessory
precession
predestine
predispose
prehistory
prepossess
procession
profession
promissory
proofsheet
protestant
provisions
publishing
purposeful
purseseine
putrescent
putrescine
pycnostyle
radioscopy
radiosonde
razorshell
realisable
reconsider
refreshing
regression
regressive
reichsmark
releasable
remissible
remissness
remorseful
repression
repressive
rescission
rescissory
retrospect
reversible
rhinestone
rhinoscope
rhinoscopy
rodfishing
rotisserie
sacrosanct
samarskite
sargassoes
scoresheet
scrimshank
seabiscuit
selfesteem
sequestrum
sheepshank
sheepshead
shellshock
skrimshank
smallscale
smallsword
smokestack
snakestone
sobersided
sobersides
solidstate
somersault
soothsayer
spinescent
spoilsport
spokeshave
sportswear
spumescent
standstill
statistics
statoscope
stavesacre
stinkstone
stockstill
stonesnipe
storksbill
stressless
stylistics
submission
submissive
subsistent
successful
succession
successive
suggestion
suggestive
supersonic
superstore
supposable
supposably
supposedly
surmisable
swarmspore
sweatshirt
sweepstake
swordstick
symposiast
tablespoon
teleostean
tetrastich
tetrastyle
threescore
throwstick
thumbscrew
thumbstall
toothshell
touchstone
transshape
trousseaux
turgescent
ultrasonic
ultrasound
unblushing
unchastity
underscore
undersense
undersexed
undershirt
undershoot
undershrub
undersized
underskirt
underslung
understand
understate
understeer
understock
understood
understudy
unhouseled
unmeasured
unseasoned
upholstery
utilisable
vernissage
vitrescent
waterskier
waterspout
whaleshark
wheatstone
whitesmith
wholesaler
witnessbox
xiphosuran
abjectness
abruptness
accentuate
acceptable
acceptably
acceptance
acceptedly
accustomed
acoustical
acquitting
adjectival
adjustable
adjustment
admittable
admittance
admittedly
adroitness
adventurer
advertence
advertency
advertiser
aeolotropy
aerostatic
affectedly
affectless
affettuoso
aftertaste
agglutinin
agitatedly
alightment
allosteric
altostrati
amphoteric
analytical
ancestress
animatedly
anisotropy
anointment
antistatic
apolitical
apophthegm
archetypal
architrave
arrestment
arrhythmia
arrhythmic
asbestosis
assentient
assistance
assortment
asymptotic
augustness
autostrada
autostrade
backstairs
backstitch
backstroke
balustrade
barbituric
barratrous
basketball
basketwork
bassethorn
belletrist
bicultural
bijouterie
billetdoux
bimestrial
biometrics
bipartisan
birdstrike
blackthorn
bootstraps
breastbone
breastwall
breastwork
brevetting
brightness
brightwork
brocatelle
bucketshop
bullethead
calyptrate
cantatrice
carpetweed
caryatides
catastasis

catoptrics
charitable
charitably
chauntress
chemotaxis
Christhood
Christlike
clientship
cloistered
closetplay
cockatrice
collatable
collateral
comestible
commitment
committing
commutable
commutator
compatible
compatibly
compatriot
competence
competency
competitor
compotator
computable
computator
concettism
connatural
copartnery
coquettish
Corinthian
cornettist
cornstarch
corsetiere
cosentient
cowcatcher
creditable
creditably
crematoria
crosstrees
curvetting
daughterly
deceptible
deductible
dejectedly
delectable
delectably
dementedly
department
deportment
derestrict
dermatitis
dermatogen
desistance
despatcher
despiteful
despiteous
detectable
detestable
detestably
devoutness
dictatress
didactical
digestible
dilettante
dilettanti
directness
directoire
directress
disastrous
discutient
disenthral
disentitle
disentwine
dispatcher
dispiteous
disputable
disputably
dissatisfy
divestment
dogmatical
dogmatiser
downstairs
downstream
downstroke
dramatical
dramaturge
dramaturgy
drawstring
dumbstruck
dysenteric
earwitness
effectuate
effortless
egoistical
elliptical
Emmentaler
encystment
englutting
enlistment
equestrian
eremitical
ergosterol
escritoire
eurhythmic
eurypterid
everything
executable
exegetical
expectance
expectancy
expectedly
expertness
exportable
eyewitness
factitious
farfetched
fenestella
fenestrate
fictitious
flagitious
flightdeck
flightless
flightpath
flycatcher
forgetting
formatting
fourstroke
geodetical
geometrise
geriatrics
geriatrist
goloptious
goluptious
groceteria
haematosis
haematuria
hairstreak
hairstroke
headstream
headstrong
heartthrob
heatstroke
heliotaxis
heliotrope
heliotropy
hemipteran
Heptateuch
heptatonic
hermetical
hermitcrab
highstrung
hoitytoity
holosteric
hospitable
hospitably
housetrain
hovertrain
hydrotaxis
hypaethral
hypanthium
hypnotiser
hypostasis
hypostatic
idolatress
idolatrous
illnatured
illustrate
immortally
immortelle
impartible
impartment
importable
importance
importuner
imposthume
incantator
incautious
incestuous
indictable
indictment
indistinct
inductance
industrial
inevitable
inevitably
infectious
infiltrate
inflatable
ingestible
ingratiate
inimitable
inimitably
insentient
insistence
insistency
institutor
intactness
intentness
intertidal
intertrigo
intertwine
intertwist
intestinal
inventress
investment
isolatable
isometrics
jesuitical
juristical
kibbutznik
knighthood
lacustrine
lamentable
lamentably
lamentedly
librettist
licentiate
licentious
lithotrity
lockstitch
locustbean
logistical
lowpitched
lutestring
magistracy
magistrate
magnetiser
mainstream
majestical
malentendu
marketable
markethall
markettown
mediatress
mesenteric
mesenteron
metastable
metastases
metastasis
metastatic
millstream
minestrone
ministrant
mishitting
mismatched
moneytaker
monistical
moonstruck
nepenthean
neurotoxin
nonnatural
nutritious
objectival
objectless
obstetrics
offputting
offsetting
oftentimes
operettist
orientally
outfitting
outpatient
outputting
outsitting
outwitting
overstride
overstrung
palmatifid
panopticon
papistical
parentally
parenteral
parenthood
parrotfish
patentable
pathetical
pedestrian
pegmatitic
pentathlon
pentatomic
pentatonic
pentstemon
peripteral
permitting
permutable
perpetrate
perpetuate
perpetuity
phenotypic
philatelic
phototaxis
phototrope
phytotoxic
picketline
pinnatifid
planetable
planetaria
planktonic
pliantness
pocketable
pocketbook
pocketsize
podiatrist
polyatamic
potentiate
potentilla
prelatical
prepotence
prepotency
priesthood
priestling
profitable
profitably
profitless
promethium
promptbook
promptness
propitiate
propitious
prototypal
prototypic
provitamin
pulsatilla
puristical
quaintness
quickthorn
quixotical
ratcatcher
rebuttable
recentness
receptacle
receptible
regentship
registered
registrant
regretting
rejectable
relentless
reluctance
reluctancy
remittance
repeatable
repeatedly
repentance
repertoire
reportable
reportedly
resentment
resistance
resistible
resistless
resultless
revertible
rickettsia
robustious
robustness
sabbatical
sabretache
sabretooth
sagittally
scientific
scriptoria
scriptural
sculptress
sculptural
sculptured
seamstress
secretaire
seductress
selectness
selfstyled
semestrial
semiotical
sempstress
sensitiser
seventieth
shoestring
sidestreet
sidestroke
siegetrain
silentness
sinisterly
sinistrous
slavetrade
slightness
slipstitch
slipstream
sneakthief
societally
songstress
soundtrack
spiritedly
spiritless
spirituous
splintbone
splintcoal
splutterer
squinteyed
starstream
statutable
statutably
stealthily
steamtight
stilettoes
stomatitis
stomatopod
straitness
streetdoor
streetward
strictness
striptease
structural
structured
subletting
submitting
summitless
supertonic
symmetrise
sympathise
synanthous
synoptical
synostosis
talentless
tapestried
tarantella
tarantelle
teetotally
tenantable
tenantless
termitaria
theistical
thixotropy
threatener
thriftless
throatwort
thwartship
thwartwise
topsyturvy
trilateral
triliteral
triphthong
tumultuary
tumultuous
unbeatable
unbeatably
unbuttoned
uncritical
uncustomed
undertaken
undertaker
undertrick
unfaithful
unfettered
ungrateful
unhistoric
unilateral
uninitiate
unjustness
unlettered
unmeetness
unmortised
unsettling
unsuitable
untruthful
unwontedly
unworthily
varietally
vignettist
voluptuary
voluptuous
watchtower
watertight

weightless
whipstitch
whitethorn
absolutely
absolution
absolutism
absolutist
absolutory
abstrusely
abstrusity
accumulate
allocution
allrounder
altocumuli
amateurish
amateurism
Andalusian
andalusite
antiquated
apolaustic
articulate
attenuated
attenuator
auriculate
aventurine
bankruptcy
beefburger
biannually
bigmouthed
binoculars
bisexually
blanquette
bressummer
brusquerie
bureaucrat
capitulary
capitulate
Carthusian
chartulary
coalbunker
cocksurely
compounder
conclusion
conclusive
conclusory
confluence
confounded
congruence
congruency
creaturely
deliquesce
denaturant
depopulate
destructor
devolution
diminuendo
diminution
diminutive
discounter
discourage
discourser
disgruntle
dumfounder
eartrumpet
edentulous
emasculate
eventually
extenuator
fatiguable
filibuster
FinnoUgric
flavourful
flavouring
flocculate
flocculent
flosculous
forerunner
fraudulent
fussbudget
geniculate
goatsucker
granduncle
greatuncle
habitually
hackbuteer
halieutics
harbourage
headhunter
homoousian
hydraulics
immaculacy
immaculate
immaturely
immaturity
inaccuracy
inaccurate
inaugurate
infatuated
inosculate
insecurely
insecurity
insinuator
instructor
instrument
integument
interurban
intraurban
invaluable
invaluably
involucral
involucrum
involution
lacklustre
landhunger
landlubber
lansquenet
latifundia
leafcutter
limeburner
lionhunter
lucifugous
lumpsucker
Malthusian
manicurist
manipulate
manoeuvrer
manoeuvres
meticulous
miraculous
moisturise
mossbunker
nidifugous
nonplussed
novaculite
obsequious
obstructor
operculate
outpouring
overburden
oversubtle
oversupply
palmbutter
PalmSunday
paniculate
parimutuel
pasteurise
pasteurism
pediculate
pediculous
pedicurist
phillumeny
picayunish
portcullis
posthumous
praemunire
precaution
preclusion
preclusive
pressurise
profoundly
pronounced
pronouncer
propounder
protrusile
protrusion
protrusive
puberulent
punctually
punctuator
punctulate
pushbutton
pyrolusite
quadrumana
quadrumane
quadrumvir
quadruplet
quadruplex
quadrupole
quintuplet
ragamuffin
reissuable
rencounter
repopulate
resolutely
resolution
resolutive
restaurant
reticulate
revolution
ridiculous
roadrunner
scrofulous
scrupulous
seersucker
selfguided
selfmurder
selfruling
semilunate
semiquaver
sheabutter
shoebuckle
showjumper
silhouette
sinecurism
sinecurist
soapbubble
spathulate
spherulite
stirrupcup
stridulant
stridulate
stridulous
subaquatic
subaqueous
subroutine
sulphurate
sulphurise
sulphurous
surplusage
taciturnly
tambourine
thereunder
thoroughly
tranquilly
tufthunter
turnbuckle
unarguable
unassuming
ungrounded
unoccupied
unrequited
untroubled
vesiculate
viscountcy
vocabulary
wellturned
WhitSunday
wirepuller
woodcutter
woodturner
abbreviate
achievable
approvable
approvably
arborvitae
believable
bidonville
bivalvular
connivance
corrivalry
cultivable
cultivator
czarevitch
deceivable
decemviral
depravedly
deprivable
deservedly
discoverer
disenviron
effervesce
eigenvalue
forgivable
forgivably
gingivitis
illadvised
impervious
improvable
improvably
improviser
insolvable
insolvency
intervener
intervenor
intervolve
labiovelar
lascivious
medievally
misgivings
multivocal
observable
observably
observance
primevally
receivable
relievable
reservedly
resolvable
resolvedly
shrievalty
slidevalve
supervisor
survivance
transvalue
transverse
triumviral
tsarevitch
undervalue
unprovoked
vaudeville
wagonvault
ZendAvesta
afterwards
batfowling
bestowment
bilgewater
blackwater
breakwater
callowness
chairwoman
chuckwagon
coastwards
deathwatch
deflowerer
dreamworld
earthwards
emerywheel
everywhere
fallowness
fellowship
fleshwound
floodwater
freedwoman
freshwater
frontwards
fuzzywuzzy
glassworks
heartwhole
holloweyed
hollowness
hollowware
horsewoman
housewives
interweave
interwound
interwoven
Irishwoman
landowning
markswoman
marrowbone
marrowless
meadowland
meadowlark
mellowness
narrowness
nightwatch
noblewoman
northwards
otherwhere
otherwhile
otherworld
paddywagon
paddywhack
pennyworth
pilliwinks
pillowcase
pillowlace
pillowslip
pilotwhale
reviewable
rightwards
saleswoman
sallowness
Scotswoman
shadowless
shearwater
shirtwaist
shorewards
smallwares
snailwheel
southwards
spacewoman
steelworks
sternwards
teenyweeny
townswoman
treadwheel
underwater
underworld
underwrite
underwrote
unknowable
waterwheel
waterworks
Welshwoman
willowherb
willywilly
windowless
windowpane
windowseat
windowshop
windowsill
wishywashy
wongawonga
worldweary
worthwhile
wristwatch
yellowback
yellowbird
yellowness
yellowwood
asphyxiant
asphyxiate
bissextile
carboxylic
commixture
contextual
contexture
inflexible
inflexibly
overexcite
overexpose
postexilic
prefixture
premaxilla
reflexible
acronychal
anaglyphic
anaptyctic
aneurysmal
antonymous
apocryphal
ascomycete
barleybree
barleybroo
barleycorn
benzpyrene
biophysics
blearyeyed
brachylogy
brachyural
brachyuran
brandyball
brandysnap
bubblyjock
chatoyance
conveyable
conveyance
defrayable
defrayment
deployment
disloyally
disloyalty
donkeywork
employable
employment
epiphytism
eucalyptol
eucalyptus
eucaryotic
galleywest
geophysics
greedyguts
hemicyclic
homonymous
homozygote
homozygous
hypabyssal
hypogynous
ichthyosis
johnnycake
kerseymere
lachrymose
misogynist
misogynous
mixolydian
monkeysuit
monocyclic
monogynian
monogynous
monohybrid
monohydric
myxomycete
nonpayment

panegyrise
panegyrist
pantrymaid
paronymous
paroxysmal
paroxytone
pastrycook
pericyclic
perigynous
playbyplay
polycyclic
polygynous
prepayable
prepayment
presbyopia
presbyopic
presbytery
procrypsis
procryptic
purveyance
safetybelt
salicylate
shandygaff
shantytown
sleepyhead
sperrylite
staphyline
starryeyed
suretyship
symphylous
symphyseal
symphysial
synonymist
synonymity
synonymous
thirtyfold
tiddlywink
triglyphic
turkeycock
volleyball
whirlybird
winceyette
ylangylang
emblazoner
emblazonry
interzonal
Lipizzaner
Lippizaner
quartzitic
rendezvous
scherzando
squeezable
squeezebox

---

abnormally
abominable
abominably
abominator
absorbable
absorbance
acceptable
acceptably
acceptance
accordance
achievable
achromatic
acquirable
actionable
actionably
addlepated
adjustable
admittable
admittance
adsorbable
aerogramme
aerography
aerostatic
affiliated
affirmable
affordable
afterpains
aftertaste
afterwards
alcyonaria
aldermanic
aldermanry
algebraist
allegiance
alleviator
alternance
alternator
ambassador
amerciable
ammoniacal
ammoniated
amphimacer
analphabet
analysable
anglomania
AngloSaxon
answerable
answerably
antechapel
antiquated
antistatic
aposematic
appealable
appearance
appeasable
applicable
applicably
applicator
approvable
approvably
aquaplaner
arbitrable
arbitrager
arbitrator
arboreally
archdeacon
armorially
arterially
artycrafty
ascariasis
ascendable
ascendance
ascendancy
ascribable
Ashkenazim
assailable
assessable
assignable
assistance
associable
asteriated
astigmatic
astragalus
atomically
attachable
attackable
attainable
attendance
attenuated
attenuator
atypically
autocratic
autography
autoplasty
autumnally
avantgarde
backstairs
baldheaded
bardolatry
bareheaded
believable
bellydance
bellylaugh
benignancy
benzocaine
biannually
biblically
biennially
bilgewater
binaurally
biodynamic
bisexually
blackfaced
blackwater
blancmange
bleachable
boneheaded
boneshaker
brachiator
breakwater
breathable
bricklayer
bridgeable
brilliance
brilliancy
browbeaten
buccinator
bullheaded
bullroarer
cacography
calculable
calculably
calculator
calibrator
candelabra
cardplayer
cartomancy
catastasis
celebrated
celebrator
cellularly
censurable
cerography
changeable
changeably
chaparajos
chargeable
charitable
charitably
chatelaine
chatoyance
chemically
chemotaxis
chiromancy
chuckwagon
circularly
circulator
clerically
clinically
coagulable
coastwards
cochleated
cockchafer
coelacanth
cognisable
cognisably
cognisance
collatable
collimator
colonially
colonnaded
colossally
colourable
colourably
columbaria
commonable
commonalty
communally
commutable
commutator
comparable
comparably
comparator
compliance
compliancy
compotator
computable
computator
confidante
conjugally
connivance
consolable
consonance
consonancy
constraint
consumable
convenable
convenance
conveyable
conveyance
coolheaded
cooperator
copyreader
cornflakes
cornstarch
corporally
corporator
corrivalry
corrugated
corrugator
corticated
coryphaeus
cosmically
cosmoramic
covariance
creditable
creditably
crenulated
criminally
critically
crosshatch
crosspatch
cucullated
cultivable
cultivator
culturally
cuspidated
cyclically
damageable
daydreamer
deathwatch
decagramme
deceivable
decigramme
declarable
declinable
deepseated
defalcator
defeasance
defendable
deferrable
defoliator
defrayable
degradable
delectable
delectably
delineator
demandable
democratic
demography
demoniacal
demurrable
denigrator
dependable
dependably
deplorable
deplorably
depredator
deprivable
desecrater
desecrator
desiccator
designator
desistance
desperados
despicable
despicably
despisable
detachable
detectable
detestable
detestably
diagonally
dialysable
dilemmatic
dilettante
dilettanti
dillydally
diplomatic
dipsomania
disarrange
disengaged
dislikable
disloyally
disloyalty
disparager
disparates
disposable
disputable
disputably
dissipated
dissonance
dissonancy
disyllabic
disyllable
doughfaced
downstairs
doxography
dressmaker
duplicator
earthwards
effaceable
eigenvalue
elaborator
eliminable
eliminator
elucidator
elutriator
emblematic
emerypaper
Emmentaler
employable
encephalic
encephalon
encourager
endorsable
enumerable
enumerator
enunciable
enunciator
episematic
eradicable
eradicator
erotically
erotomania
especially
ethereally
ethnically
euthanasia
evaporable
evaporator
eventually
everglades
examinable
executable
exotically
expandable
expectance
expectancy
expendable
explicable
exportable
expurgator
extenuator
externally
extirpator
extricable
exuberance
fabricator
fairleader
familiarly
farcically
fascinator
fathomable
fatiguable
favourable
favourably
fiducially
filariasis
filterable
fimbriated
floodwater
forcipated
foreshadow
forgivable
forgivably
formidable
formidably
fornicator
fourleaved
fowlplague
freeloader
freshwater
frontwards
funereally
Gallomania
gasconader
germinally
glasspaper
globularly
goldbeater
gothically
governable
governance
granddaddy
grandmamma
granularly
granulator
greyheaded
gutturally
gynocratic
habitually
hagiolatry
halfyearly
hankypanky
hardheaded
hebdomadal
hectically
heliacally
heliolater
heliolatry
heliotaxis
hendecagon
heresiarch
heroically
hibernacle
hierolatry
hippocampi
hippomanes
holography
homeopathy
honeyeater
honourable
honourably
hootenanny
hormonally
horselaugh
hospitable
hospitably
hullabaloo

hydrically
hydromancy
hydropathy
hydrotaxis
hyperbaric
hyperbaton
hyphenated
hypostasis
hypostatic
icebreaker
iconolater
iconolatry
iconomachy
ideography
illaudable
illaudably
imaginable
imaginably
immortally
immoveable
impalpable
impalpably
impassable
impassably
impeccable
impeccably
impeccancy
imperially
implacable
implacably
importable
importance
impresario
imprimatur
improbable
improbably
improvable
improvably
impugnable
incantator
incessancy
inclinable
inculcator
inculpable
incurrable
indictable
inductance
ineducable
inelegance
inevitable
inevitably
inexorable
inexorably
inexpiable
inexpiably
infatuated
infernally
inferrable
inflatable
informally
inimically
inimitable
inimitably
innerrably
inoculable
inoculator
inoperable
insatiable
insatiably
insinuator
insociable
insolvable
inspirator
instigator
integrable
integrally
integrator
intendance
intermarry
internally
intrigante
invaluable
invaluably
invariable
invariably
invariance
inviolable
inviolably
ironically
irradiance
isodynamic
isolatable
itinerancy
jackanapes
Janusfaced
jawbreaker
judgematic
judicially
kerygmatic
kilogramme
Krishnaism
lacrimator
lacrymator
ladychapel
lamentable
lamentably
landscaper
lardydardy
lawbreaker
legislator
lexigraphy
licensable
lightfaced
Lipizzaner
lipography
Lippizaner
liquidator
logography
longheaded
longshanks
lossleader
lotuseater
lubricator
lucubrator
Lupercalia
luxuriance
Maccabaean
macebearer
machinator
malignance
malignancy
mamillated
manageable
manageably
maniacally
Manichaean
marginalia
marginally
marginated
Mariolater
Mariolatry
marketable
masticable
masticator
matchmaker
materially
maternally
mathematic
mayonnaise
measurable
measurably
medievally
medullated
meliorator
melismatic
mendicancy
mensurable
merrymaker
mesoscaphe
metaplasia
metastable
metastases
metastasis
metastatic
methylated
metrically
microfarad
middleaged
militiaman
miscreance
mistakable
mobocratic
modifiable
moneymaker
moneytaker
moniliasis
monochasia
monocratic
monstrance
morganatic
mosaically
moviemaker
Muhammadan
multifaced
muscularly
musicianly
musicpaper
mycoplasma
myopically
mystically
mythically
mythomania
nambypamby
nationally
nautically
necrolater
necrolatry
necromancy
negotiable
negotiator
neuropathy
newsreader
nightwatch
noisemaker
nomography
northwards
nosography
notarially
noticeable
noticeably
notifiable
notionally
nudibranch
numismatic
nyctinasty
obfuscated
observable
observably
observance
obtainable
oesophagus
officially
oleography
openhearth
ophiolater
ophiolatry
oppugnancy
optionally
oracularly
ordonnance
oreography
orientally
originally
originator
oscillator
osteopathy
outbalance
overcharge
overpraise
overshadow
overslaugh
oxidisable
oxygenator
pacifiable
paddywagon
paederasty
pallbearer
pancreatic
pancreatin
papermaker
pardonable
pardonably
parentally
parramatta
pastorally
pasturable
pastyfaced
patentable
paternally
peacemaker
pectinated
peculiarly
penetrable
penetrably
penetralia
penetrance
penetrator
percolator
perdurable
perdurably
perforator
perishable
permutable
personable
personally
personalty
personator
petiolated
petrolatum
phagedaena
pharisaism
phlegmatic
phonematic
phonically
phosphatic
photonasty
phototaxis
physically
pinebeauty
pinnulated
piscifauna
pityriasis
pixillated
planetable
planetaria
platelayer
ploughable
plutolatry
pocketable
poetically
pokerfaced
pollinator
polyatamic
polychaete
polygraphy
polyphasic
ponderable
porismatic
postchaise
postulator
pozzolanic
prearrange
predicable
preferable
preferably
preparator
prepayable
presumable
presumably
prevenancy
primevally
primiparae
procreator
procurable
procurance
procurator
prodigally
profitable
profitably
promenader
propagable
propaganda
propagator
propylaeum
provenance
provitamin
provocator
proximally
psychiatry
Ptolemaist
pulvinated
punctually
punctuator
punishable
purtenance
purveyance
pyrography
quenchable
radiopaque
railroader
rationally
realisable
reappraise
reasonable
reasonably
rebuttable
recallable
receivable
receptacle
recordable
recyclable
redeemable
redundance
redundancy
reentrance
refillable
reformable
refundable
regionally
reissuable
reiterance
rejectable
releasable
relievable
relishable
reluctance
reluctancy
remarkable
remarkably
remediable
remedially
remittance
renderable
repairable
repealable
repeatable
repellance
repellancy
repentance
reportable
reprobance
repudiator
repugnance
repugnancy
resistance
resolvable
respirable
respirator
restorable
retainable
returnable
revealable
reviewable
rewardable
riboflavin
rightwards
ringleader
ritardando
roquelaure
rosechafer
rubrically
rubricator
rustically
sabretache
sacrosanct
sagittally
saturnalia
satyriasis
scarabaeid
scarabaeus
scenically
scherzando
schismatic
schoolable
sciagraphy
scrimmager
searchable
seasonable
seasonably
seasonally
secretaire
selfglazed
selfpraise
semiopaque
semiquaver
semiyearly
sensedatum
septenarii
septically
serigraphy
shamefaced
shanghaier
shearwater
shirtwaist
shorewards
shortdated
shortrange
shrievalty
shrinkable
sideboards
sideglance
simoniacal
singularly
sketchable
skiagraphy
skirtdance
skyscraper
slidevalve
smallwares
snailpaced
snakedance
snapdragon
soapflakes
societally
softheaded
somersault
soothsayer
southwards
spectrally
speculator
spodomancy
squeezable
squeteague
squirearch

statically
statutable
statutably
stavesacre
sternwards
stimulator
stipulator
stomodaeum
stonemason
subaquatic
subjugator
sublimable
substratum
subtenancy
succedanea
sufferable
sufferably
sufferance
sugardaddy
sugarmaple
suicidally
summonable
sunderance
supercargo
supernally
suppliance
supposable
supposably
surgically
surmisable
survivance
sustenance
sworddance
sycophancy
syllabaria
syncopated
syncopator
syndicator
systematic
tabernacle
tactically
talebearer
talismanic
tarmacadam
tauromachy
teetotally
telegraphy
temperable
temperance
temporally
temporalty
tenantable
termagancy
terminable
terminably
terminally
terminator
termitaria
texturally
theocratic
theophanic
thirdparty
timocratic
tobogganer
tomography
toothpaste
topography
toroidally
tortfeasor
touchpaper
tracheated
tragacanth
tragically
translator
transvalue
trenchancy
trichiasis
trigonally
triturable
triturator
tropically
tropopause
tutorially
typography
ultrabasic
unarguable
unbearable
unbearably
unbeatable
unbeatably
unbiddable
undeniable
undeniably
underpants
undertaken
undertaker
undervalue
underwater
uneducated
unemphatic
unenviable
unfilially
uniaxially
univocally
unknowable
unnameable
unprepared
unreadable
unreliable
unscalable
unsociable
unsociably
unsocially
unsuitable
unworkable
usquebaugh
utilisable
vaccinator
variegated
varietally
vascularly
ventilator
verandahed
verifiable
vertically
vindicable
vindicator
virginally
viscerally
visionally
vortically
voyageable
vulnerable
vulnerably
wagonvault
wastepaper
watchmaker
weimaraner
whitefaced
wholesaler
wiredrawer
wishywashy
witchhazel
withdrawal
withdrawer
wristwatch
xerography
xylography
automobile
barleybree
barleybroo
basketball
blueribbon
brandyball
breakables
breastbone
butterball
butterbean
buttonball
buttonbush
cannonball
canterbury
canvasback
centreback
chequebook
collarbeam
collarbone
collembola
confabbing
conglobate
contraband
contrabass
contribute
cranesbill
cummerbund
cuttlebone
dissembler
distribute
doublebass
equilibria
fiddleback
fingerbowl
gingerbeer
groundbait
hammerbeam
heavenborn
hobnobbing
hucklebone
incunabula
jackrabbit
knockabout
ladderback
landlubber
ledgerbait
letterbomb
letterbook
locustbean
malleebird
marrowbone
middlebrow
minutebook
monohybrid
mountebank
muffinbell
nativeborn
needlebath
needlebook
oversubtle
paddleboat
parsonbird
phrasebook
pocketbook
prayerbook
procumbent
promptbook
proverbial
rockrabbit
rockribbed
roundabout
rouseabout
roustabout
runnerbean
saddleback
safetybelt
schoolbook
secondbest
sheathbill
showerbath
sicklebill
silverbath
sketchbook
skibobbing
sleighbell
smoothbore
smorrebrod
snowmobile
soapbubble
sourcebook
splashback
splintbone
sprucebeer
stereobate
stiflebone
storksbill
stringbean
switchback
tailorbird
thereabout
threadbare
turtleback
untroubled
vesperbell
volleyball
wattlebird
weaverbird
whereabout
whirlybird
winebibber
yellowback
yellowbird
abstracted
abstracter
abstractly
abstractor
accrescent
acronychal
adjudicate
adolescent
ambulacral
ambulacrum
amoebocyte
anaptyctic
androecium
animalcula
animalcule
anthracene
anthracite
anthracoid
antisocial
apodeictic
apoplectic
apothecary
apothecial
apothecium
aristocrat
armourclad
artificial
asceticism
ascomycete
barebacked
barleycorn
bathyscaph
bathyscope
beautician
bellyacher
benedicite
Benedictus
benefactor
beneficent
beneficial
bivouacked
blastocyst
bluejacket
bootlicker
bratticing
bureaucrat
canaliculi
candescent
canonicals
canonicate
canonicity
cappuccino
carbuncled
catalectic
causticity
centricity
cheesecake
chronicity
chronicler
circumcise
Cistercian
Clarenceux
classicise
classicism
classicist
coadjacent
coalescent
colchicine
commercial
complacent
complected
complicacy
complicate
complicity
comstocker
condescend
confiscate
conspectus
contractor
convincing
coradicate
corncockle
corpuscule
cottoncake
cowcatcher
cowpuncher
crepuscule
crustacean
cystoscope
cystoscopy
decrescent
despatcher
destructor
detoxicant
detoxicate
disconcert
dispatcher
distinctly
distracted
divaricate
dustjacket
efficacity
elasticise
elasticity
emphractic
empiricism
empiricist
encroacher
endemicity
entrancing
epideictic
equivocate
ergodicity
erubescent
eugenicist
evanescent
excrescent
fanaticise
fanaticism
fantoccini
farfetched
fireescape
flavescent
florescent
flycatcher
fratricide
frutescent
geneticist
gnosticism
goatsucker
hagioscope
halfcocked
hamshackle
handpicked
helioscope
hemicyclic
heptarchic
hereticate
hermitcrab
hierarchal
hierarchic
highjacker
humpbacked
hydroscope
hygroscope
hypotactic
iconoscope
impudicity
incapacity
increscent
indelicacy
indelicate
indirectly
inefficacy
infelicity
instructor
intoxicant
intoxicate
inveracity
involucral
involucrum
iridescent
irradicate
johnnycake
kenspeckle
kineticist
laconicism
lactescent
landlocked
largescale
lawrencium
lemniscate
lettercard
lifejacket
liquescent
lowpitched
lumpsucker
lymphocyte
malefactor
maleficent
marcescent
microscope
microscopy
misericord
mismatched
molluscoid
molluscous
monocyclic
moustached
moustachio
munificent
myxomycete
nanosecond
necroscopy
needlecord
nematocyst
nephoscope
nidificate
nigrescent
notonectal
nutcracker
obstructor
obtruncate
octodecimo
oligarchic
opalescent
Ordovician
organicism
organicist
overexcite
overnicety
pacificate
pacificism
pacificist

Palaeocene
paramecium
paratactic
pastrycook
peppercorn
pericyclic
phallicism
pharmacist
Phoenician
physiocrat
pickpocket
picosecond
pigsticker
pillowcase
plasticise
plasticity
plebiscite
polemicist
politician
politicise
polycyclic
polydactyl
polytocous
practician
praecocial
pratincole
preconcert
preglacial
prosaicism
prospector
prospectus
protracted
protractor
provincial
pseudocarp
psittacine
psychicism
psychicist
putrescent
putrescine
pyrotechny
quadriceps
radioscopy
ramshackle
ratcatcher
reallocate
researcher
retinacula
rhinoscope
rhinoscopy
ringnecked
scepticism
schizocarp
Scotticise
Scotticism
seabiscuit
seersucker
seismicity
selfdeceit
semiuncial
shellacked
shoebuckle
simplicity
simulacrum
slitpocket
smallscale
sororicide
Spartacist
spasticity
spatchcock
spectacled
spectacles
spermaceti
spermicide
sphericity
spidercrab
spiflicate
spinescent
spitchcock

splintcoal
spongecake
spumescent
statoscope
stillicide
stratocrat
stypticity
subglacial
subspecies
succinctly
superacute
supplicant
supplicate
swaybacked
taperecord
technician
technicist
technocrat
tetrarchic
theodicean
threescore
thumbscrew
trafficked
trafficker
transactor
tribrachic
trifurcate
triplicate
triplicity
turgescent
turkeycock
turnbuckle
ulotrichan
umbilicate
unaffected
unattached
unblenched
underscore
unexpected
unofficial
unselected
varicocele
ventricose
ventriculi
vestpocket
vitrescent
vivisector
woodpecker
zygodactyl
ablebodied
aggrandise
alexanders
Amerindian
antecedent
antipodean
Armageddon
autodidact
balderdash
bastardise
battledore
bestridden
billetdoux
blastoderm
bombardier
brigandage
brigandine
brigandism
brokendown
buttondown
chalcedony
Clydesdale
coincident
commandant
commandeer
commandery
commanding
commandoes
compendium
compradore

concordant
contendent
contradict
decahedral
decahedron
decapodous
dehumidify
descendant
descendent
despondent
dilapidate
diphyodont
disbudding
discordant
dumbledore
echinoderm
eisteddfod
embroidery
emparadise
endopodite
endproduct
flaccidity
flightdeck
fluoridate
forbidding
foreboding
foreordain
forwarding
fricandeau
fullbodied
fussbudget
gormandise
halberdier
Hansardise
hemihedral
hemihedron
heterodont
heterodoxy
heterodyne
heulandite
hexahedral
hexahedron
holohedral
horrendous
husbandage
husbandman
imparadise
inbreeding
individual
innuendoes
insipidity
intimidate
invalidate
invalidism
invalidity
jeopardise
kettledrum
lawabiding
leopardess
lipreading
Lollardism
lycopodium
malacoderm
mallenders
misconduct
miswording
mithridate
mixolydian
monohydric
monopodial
monopodium
myocardium
nephridium
octahedral
octahedron
octopodous
oldmaidish
ommatidium
orchardist

orchardman
orotundity
osmiridium
outbidding
outlandish
overridden
overriding
packsaddle
panhandler
panjandrum
parapodium
pebbledash
peroxidise
phelloderm
piperidine
plasmodesm
plasmodium
polyandric
polyhedral
polyhedric
polyhedron
praesidium
prebendary
precordial
pretendant
pretendent
primordial
primordium
proceeding
profundity
psalmodise
psalmodist
resounding
respondent
revalidate
rhapsodise
rhapsodist
rockbadger
ropeladder
sallenders
schooldays
scleroderm
selenodont
sherardise
sidesaddle
smaragdine
smaragdite
solifidian
sphenodone
splashdown
squalidity
stepladder
stewardess
streetdoor
stupendous
subacidity
subcordate
subheading
suspenders
taradiddle
threnodial
threnodist
tremendous
troglodyte
troubadour
tumbledown
turtledove
unabridged
unsteadily
unwieldily
unyielding
upbraiding
upstanding
abhorrence
absorbedly
absorbency
abstinence
abstinency
acatalepsy

acceptedly
accursedly
acidimeter
acidimetry
acotyledon
admittedly
advertence
advertency
affectedly
agitatedly
allegretto
allergenic
alliaceous
allosteric
almondeyed
alphabetic
alphameric
amphoteric
amylaceous
anchoretic
androgenic
anemometer
anemometry
animatedly
anonaceous
antifreeze
antitheism
antitheist
antitheses
antithesis
antithetic
aphaereses
aphaeresis
apologetic
apperceive
arenaceous
arithmetic
ascendence
ascendency
audiometer
audiometry
backsheesh
bathometer
bathymeter
bathymetry
Berkeleian
bijouterie
biogenesis
biogenetic
bioscience
biparietal
bizarrerie
blackberry
blackheart
blanquette
blasphemer
blearyeyed
bollweevil
bookkeeper
bordereaux
bradyseism
brocatelle
brusquerie
byssaceous
cacodaemon
calcareous
calciferol
camerlengo
cantilever
canzonetta
cassolette
catchpenny
catechesis
catechetic
cavalierly
centimetre
chalybeate
chaparejos
chartreuse

chauffeuse
chelicerae
chemisette
chokeberry
cicisbeism
Cinderella
citronella
clarabella
clinometer
clinometry
cloistered
cloudberry
coetaneous
collarette
collateral
comedienne
competence
competency
composedly
condolence
conference
confidence
confluence
confusedly
congeneric
congruence
congruency
conscience
considered
consumedly
continence
convalesce
coparcener
coralberry
coriaceous
corporeity
corpulence
corpulency
corrigenda
coulometry
courageous
crapulence
cretaceous
crinolette
crippledom
crossbench
crossrefer
crowkeeper
curvaceous
cybernetic
cyclometer
cyclopedia
cyclopedic
cylindered
daughterly
deepfreeze
deficiency
definienda
deflowerer
degradedly
dehiscence
dejectedly
deliquesce
dementedly
demoiselle
densimeter
dependence
dependency
depravedly
deservedly
designedly
desipience
despiteful
despiteous
detachedly
detergency
deterrence
diapedesis
diapedetic

difference
diffidence
diminuendo
diphtheria
diphtheric
diphyletic
discoverer
discreetly
dishonesty
disinherit
disordered
disorderly
dispiteous
disquieten
disquietly
dissidence
divergence
divergency
divulgence
doorkeeper
drupaceous
dungbeetle
dysenteric
ebullience
ebulliency
effervesce
efficiency
effloresce
effulgence
eighteenmo
eighteenth
elderberry
emblements
empathetic
endothelia
epentheses
epenthesis
epenthetic
epexegeses
epexegesis
epexegetic
epigenesis
epigenetic
ergosterol
ericaceous
erotogenic
erysipelas
eudiometer
eudiometry
eurypterid
excellence
excellency
exospheric
expectedly
expedience
expediency
experience
extendedly
extraneity
extraneous
faintheart
fenestella
feuilleton
fianchetto
flatulence
flatulency
florilegia
foliaceous
fontanelle
foresheets
fourchette
fourteener
fourteenth
framboesia
fraxinella
freespeech
frenziedly
frontbench
fustanella
gamekeeper
gaspereaux
gatekeeper
gaultheria
gauntleted
gemmaceous
gentilesse
glumaceous
goalkeeper
goatsbeard
goggleeyed
goniometer
goniometry
gooseberry
governessy
gramineous
gravimeter
gravimetry
greenheart
groceteria
hartebeest
headcheese
heartsease
hectometre
heliometer
hemiplegia
hemiplegic
hemipteran
henotheism
henotheist
Heptameron
heptameter
Heptateuch
herbaceous
holloweyed
holosteric
homebrewed
hornblende
horseleech
hydrometer
hydrometry
hygrometer
hygrometry
hylotheism
hyperaemia
hyperaemic
hypotheses
hypothesis
hypsometer
hypsometry
hysteresis
hysteretic
iatrogenic
iconometer
iconometry
immortelle
impatience
impendence
impendency
improperly
imprudence
incandesce
incipience
incipiency
inclemency
incumbency
indulgence
insistence
insistency
insolvency
insurgence
insurgency
interceder
interferer
interferon
interleave
intermezzi
intermezzo
interregna
intervener
intervenor
interweave
iridaceous
isogenetic
jargonelle
kerchieves
knopkierie
labiovelar
lamentedly
lansquenet
latescence
lauraceous
liliaceous
lockkeeper
loganberry
lopsidedly
machinegun
Mahommedan
maisonette
malentendu
malingerer
malvaceous
Manicheism
marionette
Massoretic
mealbeetle
measuredly
mesenteric
mesenteron
metatheses
metathesis
metathetic
Methuselah
micrometer
micrometry
microseism
mignonette
millimetre
minstrelsy
mischmetal
misnomered
mistakenly
mixedmedia
Mohammedan
molybdenum
monotheism
monotheist
montbretia
morbidezza
mozzarella
Muhammedan
multimedia
myasthenia
myrtaceous
naphthenic
narcolepsy
nectareous
negligence
neurilemma
neurolemma
nevernever
newsagency
nineteenth
nomothetic
noogenesis
occurrence
offlicence
oleraceous
olivaceous
ombrometer
onesidedly
ophicleide
opisometer
orogenesis
orogenetic
orthogenic
orthopedic
outgeneral
outrageous
outstretch
palmaceous
pangenesis
pangenetic
paramnesia
paraplegia
paraplegic
parenteral
passageway
pathogenic
patisserie
pennaceous
pentameter
pentimento
pentstemon
peripheral
peripteral
perithecia
permanence
permanency
pertinence
pertinency
pestilence
petronella
phagedenic
phenacetin
phenomenal
phenomenon
philatelic
phonometer
photogenic
photometer
photometry
phylogenic
phytogenic
piezometer
pinchpenny
planchette
planimeter
planimetry
planometer
polytheism
polytheist
porraceous
portamento
prairiedog
precedence
precedency
predecease
preference
preparedly
prepotence
prepotency
presageful
prescience
presidency
prevalence
privileged
prominence
propraetor
proprietor
prosthesis
prosthetic
providence
pubescence
pulsimeter
pulsometer
purposeful
purseseine
pycnometer
pyknometer
quiescence
quiescency
radiogenic
radiometer
radiometry
rampageous
recipiency
recommence
recompense
recrudesce
recumbency
recurrence
refulgence
registered
remorseful
renascence
repeatedly
repellence
repellency
reportedly
reservedly
resignedly
resilience
resiliency
resolvedly
resurgence
revengeful
rhinoceros
rhizogenic
ritornelli
ritornello
rotisserie
rovebeetle
rowanberry
salmonella
saltarello
saprogenic
sarcolemma
sarracenia
schipperke
scrapmetal
secludedly
selffeeder
selfseeker
semiweekly
senescence
serviceman
shopkeeper
shoreleave
shouldered
silhouette
sinisterly
snafflebit
sociometry
soldanella
somnolence
somnolency
spadebeard
spadiceous
spiritedly
spirometer
spirometry
splitlevel
splutterer
squanderer
squeezebox
squinteyed
stagbeetle
starryeyed
strainedly
strawberry
stringency
stringendo
striptease
subaqueous
subsidence
succulence
succulency
supposedly
suprarenal
sweetheart
swinefever
swinglebar
swiveleyed
synaeresis
synaloepha
synergetic
syngenesis
tachometer
tachometry
tachymeter
tachymetry
tarantella
tarantelle
tautomeric
teenyweeny
televiewer
temperedly
testaceous
tetrahedra
tetrameter
theopneust
thimbleful
thimblerig
thirteenth
threatener
threepence
threepenny
thruppence
timekeeper
tocopherol
transferee
transferor
transience
transiency
transverse
tribometer
trilateral
triliteral
tromometer
trousseaux
trucklebed
truculence
truculency
trundlebed
tuffaceous
tularaemia
tularaemic
tumescence
turbulence
turbulency
twowheeler
umbrageous
unbeliever
unbonneted
unbrokenly
underbelly
underlease
underneath
undersense
undersexed
unfathered
unfettered
ungraceful
ungrateful
unhouseled
unicameral
unilateral
unlettered
unmannerly
unnumbered
unredeemed
unrelieved
unscreened
unwontedly
uranometry
variometer
vermicelli
villanelle
violaceous
virescence
viscometer
voltameter
vorticella
waggonette

watermelon
wellheeled
whatsoever
whensoever
whitebeard
whomsoever
wildebeest
winceyette
windsleeve
worldweary
wretchedly
youngberry
ZendAvesta
archerfish
beautifier
bottlefeed
butterfish
calyciform
candlefish
centrefold
centrifuge
chloroform
cinquefoil
circumflex
circumfuse
classified
classifier
colourfast
cribriform
cumuliform
cuttlefish
dendriform
digitiform
discomfort
disconfirm
emulsifier
fisherfolk
gentlefolk
heretofore
humidifier
limaciform
linguiform
lowprofile
malleefowl
moniliform
needlefish
overrefine
oysterfarm
parrotfish
pluperfect
postoffice
proteiform
quantifier
quatrefoil
ragamuffin
ribbonfish
rudderfish
saddlefast
sanctifier
scyphiform
securiform
sheriffdom
shoplifter
sideeffect
silverfish
simplifier
singlefoot
spongiform
stelliform
stratiform
subterfuge
Tartuffian
Tartuffism
tenderfoot
thereafter
thirtyfold
threadfish
twelvefold
umbiliform

vaporiform
viperiform
whiskified
Wycliffite
abstergent
acromegaly
aeroengine
aerologist
agrologist
algolagnia
algolagnic
algologist
anastigmat
Areopagite
asparagine
astringent
autologous
axiologist
balbriggan
barelegged
Bedlington
bedraggled
boondoggle
bootlegger
bryologist
campaigner
cardiogram
cataloguer
catburglar
cattlegrid
champignon
chronogram
churchgoer
congregant
congregate
contingent
convergent
coolingoff
cryptogamy
cryptogram
curmudgeon
cytologist
dampingoff
dapplegrey
demagogism
Devanagari
drawingpin
earwigging
embryogeny
epeirogeny
ethologist
fallingoff
fandangoes
FinnoUgric
flamingoes
flowergirl
footlights
gatelegged
Glaswegian
golddigger
greedyguts
heterogamy
heterogeny
heterogony
homologate
homologise
homologous
homozygote
homozygous
horologist
houseagent
humbuggery
humbugging
ideologist
irreligion
kieselguhr
landingnet
longlegged
lucifugous

mandragora
martingale
meaningful
meltingpot
misaligned
misologist
monologise
monologist
morphogeny
mycologist
newfangled
nidifugous
nomologist
nonaligned
nosologist
oecologist
oenologist
oldfangled
omophagous
oncologist
ontologist
oreologist
packingbox
Palaeogene
paralogise
paralogism
pedagogics
pedologist
pemphigoid
pemphigous
penologist
periwigged
phalangeal
pharyngeal
plasmogamy
pomologist
prefulgent
pressagent
profligacy
profligate
prolongate
promulgate
refringent
rheologist
rockpigeon
rollingpin
roseengine
salpingian
sandbagger
scavengery
schizogony
schoolgirl
sealingwax
seismogram
selfregard
seltzogene
Septuagint
serologist
sexologist
shandygaff
shiprigged
sinologist
sluicegate
sphenogram
sporangial
sporangium
stereogram
strategist
subkingdom
sublingual
suffragist
tankengine
teratogeny
theologian
theologise
theologist
thermogram
thoroughly
topologist

trilingual
typologist
unchanging
undesigned
unflagging
ungrudging
unilingual
upbringing
viceregent
virologist
vitiligate
warmingpan
wellington
woodpigeon
workingman
zigzagging
zoophagous
accoucheur
acidophile
aerenchyma
aftershave
aircushion
alongshore
anemophily
anglophile
anglophobe
anglophone
apophthegm
arrhythmia
arrhythmic
atmosphere
audiophile
barysphere
bassethorn
batrachian
beforehand
behindhand
bewitchery
bisulphate
bisulphide
bisulphite
Blackshirt
blackthorn
brainchild
bridgehead
Britishism
broadsheet
brownshirt
bufflehead
bullethead
buttonhole
buttonhook
caoutchouc
carragheen
catarrhine
cellophane
centrehalf
chargehand
chiffchaff
Christhood
clavichord
coleorhiza
comanchero
comprehend
copperhead
Corinthian
cousinhood
crankshaft
crosscheck
ctenophore
daisychain
debauchery
debouchure
dimorphism
dimorphous
discophile
disenchant
disenthral
distichous

disulphate
disulphide
dragonhead
drosophila
drowsihead
dunderhead
earthshine
embouchure
emerywheel
Englishman
escutcheon
eurhythmic
everything
everywhere
Fahrenheit
farsighted
fatherhood
fiddlehead
figurehead
flugelhorn
flyfishing
fourinhand
Gallophile
Gallophobe
garnishing
gaslighter
gesundheit
gramophone
grandchild
granophyre
greenshank
gunfighter
gypsophila
hammerhead
heartthrob
heartwhole
heliophyte
hemisphere
heptachord
hierophant
hippophagy
horseshoer
hydrophane
hydrophily
hydrophone
hydrophyte
hygrophyte
hypaethral
hypanthium
imposthume
interphase
ionosphere
Italophile
jolterhead
knighthood
leprechaun
letterhead
likelihood
lithophane
lithophyte
livelihood
loggerhead
logorrhoea
lophophore
macrophage
maidenhair
maidenhead
maidenhood
Malpighian
maraschino
markethall
masterhand
masterhood
matronhood
meerschaum
melancholy
mesosphere
micaschist
microphone

microphyte
minutehand
monarchial
Monarchian
monarchism
monarchist
motherhood
multiphase
muttonhead
mycorrhiza
nationhood
necrophile
necrophily
negrophile
negrophobe
nepenthean
nightshade
nightshift
nightshirt
nitrochalk
nourishing
orphanhood
osteophyte
otherwhere
otherwhile
ottershrew
outrightly
paddywhack
paedophile
pansophist
paperchase
parenchyma
parenthood
penpushing
pentachord
pentathlon
photophily
photophore
phytophagy
pigeonhole
pilotwhale
pincushion
plainchant
powderhorn
priesthood
promethium
proofsheet
protophyta
protophyte
publishing
quickthorn
radiophone
rattlehead
razorshell
refreshing
repurchase
retrochoir
revanchism
revanchist
rhizophore
rhodophane
rodfishing
Russophile
Russophobe
saprophyte
sarcophagi
sarcophagy
scoresheet
scratchily
scratchwig
screechowl
scrimshank
seborrhoea
secondhand
sepulchral
sheepshank
sheepshead
shellshock
shovelhead

sisterhood
skrimshank
Slavophile
Slavophobe
sleepyhead
snailwheel
sneakthief
sousaphone
splanchnic
spokeshave
sporophore
sporophyll
sporophyte
springhalt
springhead
squirehood
stealthily
steamchest
stomachful
straighten
straightly
stringhalt
stronghold
subtrahend
sweatshirt
sympathise
synanthous
tautophony
tenterhook
tetrachord
throughout
throughput
throughway
timberhead
toothshell
transshape
treadwheel
triphthong
triumphant
tropophyte
twilighted
unblushing
undershirt
undershoot
undershrub
unfaithful
untruthful
unworthily
veldschoen
vibraphone
videophone
virginhood
waterwheel
whaleshark
wheelchair
whitethorn
willowherb
woodenhead
worthwhile
abbreviate
aboriginal
abstemious
academical
accessible
accessibly
accredited
acoustical
adjectival
admissible
advertiser
afterbirth
afterlight
agglutinin
alchemical
altarpiece
amphibious
amphimixes
amphimixis
anagogical
analogical
analytical
anarchical
anatomical
anchoritic
annunciate
antheridia
anticlimax
anticlinal
aphrodisia
apolitical
appendices
appendixes
appreciate
aragonitic
arborvitae
archpriest
ascendible
aspergilla
asphyxiant
asphyxiate
assentient
asteroidal
auspicious
austenitic
autarkical
avaricious
aviatrices
backslider
backstitch
banderilla
Barmecidal
batholitic
belongings
bidonville
biological
bipartisan
birdspider
birthright
botryoidal
brakelight
branchiate
brickfield
bronchiole
bronchitic
bronchitis
budgerigar
Caerphilly
calumniate
calumnious
camerlingo
capricious
cartwright
caryatides
cascarilla
catechiser
catholicon
catholicos
cellulitis
censorious
centesimal
centilitre
chaplaincy
childbirth
chimerical
chinchilla
chondritic
cicatrices
clovehitch
coenobitic
cognominal
collegiate
comestible
commodious
communique
comparison
compatible
compatibly
competitor
complainer
compositor
conchoidal
conciliary
conciliate
congenital
consociate
constringe
contagious
convenient
Copernican
coprolitic
copywriter
cordwainer
corrigible
corsetiere
cosentient
couturiere
crosslight
crosspiece
curvacious
czarevitch
deadweight
debonairly
decemviral
deceptible
deductible
defeasible
defensible
defensibly
deforciant
denunciate
deodoriser
deoxidiser
depreciate
dermatitis
deshabille
determined
diabolical
dichroitic
didactical
didgeridoo
diffusible
digestible
disbelieve
disclaimer
discutient
disentitle
disenviron
dishabille
dispirited
dispraiser
dissatisfy
dissilient
dissimilar
dissociate
distrainer
distrainor
dogmatical
dogmatiser
draconites
dramatical
drawbridge
dumbwaiter
duodecimal
duodenitis
earthlight
ecclesiast
ecological
economical
economiser
ecumenical
egoistical
electrical
elliptical
encyclical
endocrinal
enthusiasm
enthusiast
epidemical
episodical
eremitical
escadrille
espadrille
euphonious
excruciate
exegetical
exoterical
expansible
expatriate
explicitly
extendible
extensible
factitious
fairhaired
fallacious
fastidious
fastigiate
fertiliser
fibrositis
fictitious
fieldpiece
fiftyfifty
fireblight
fireraiser
firstnight
flagitious
flashlight
floodlight
footbridge
fortepiano
forthright
fortyniner
franchiser
freesoiler
frigorific
fungicidal
galvaniser
geodetical
geological
geoponical
germicidal
gerundival
gingivitis
girlfriend
Glagolitic
glassfibre
goloptious
goluptious
gramicidin
granadilla
grandniece
granulitic
greatniece
greenfinch
gregarious
grenadilla
guestnight
hairraiser
handmaiden
hangglider
hardboiled
harmonical
harmonious
harmoniser
haruspices
headwaiter
hectolitre
hermetical
historical
hitchhiker
housewives
hybridiser
hypnotiser
hysterical
illadvised
immiscible
immiscibly
impartible
impassible
impassibly
impervious
implicitly
impossible
impossibly
improviser
incautious
incendiary
includible
incredible
incredibly
indistinct
ineligible
ineligibly
ineludible
inexplicit
infallible
infallibly
infeasible
infectious
inflexible
inflexibly
ingestible
inglorious
ingratiate
ingredient
inquisitor
insensible
insensibly
insentient
insobriety
insouciant
intangible
intangibly
intertidal
intestinal
intrepidly
invincible
invincibly
jackknives
jardiniere
jesuitical
jinrikisha
juristical
justiciary
kinnikinic
larvicidal
laryngitic
laryngitis
lascivious
lavalliere
lentigines
licentiate
licentious
liquidiser
liturgical
lockstitch
logistical
longhaired
longprimer
loquacious
loudhailer
lubricious
lugubrious
magnetiser
magnifical
magnificat
maintainer
majestical
makeweight
manzanilla
matricidal
maxilliped
mechanical
mendacious
meningioma
meningitis
mesmeriser
metempiric
meteoritic
methodical
microbiota
microfiche
microlitic
millefiori
millesimal
millilitre
millwright
misbelieve
misgivings
moderniser
molendinar
monistical
monoclinal
monoclinic
monoecious
moonshiner
mordacious
mouthpiece
myological
mysterious
mythiciser
Neapolitan
negligible
negligibly
neological
newswriter
nightlight
nonlogical
nutritious
objectival
obsequious
oftentimes
omniscient
oratorical
orological
ostensible
ostensibly
outpatient
overflight
overweight
ovipositor
paddyfield
palladious
palmatifid
panopticon
pantomimic
papistical
paraffinic
parricidal
parsonical
participle
parturient
pathetical
patriciate
patricidal
pearldiver
peccadillo
pegmatitic
pellucidly
percipient
perfidious
perfoliate
periclinal
periodical
perjurious
pernicious
pesticidal
phonolitic
photolitho
phthisical
piccalilli
piccaninny
pichiciago
pickaninny
pictorical

piledriver
pilliwinks
pilotlight
pinnatifid
pinstriped
playwright
polyclinic
pontifical
pontifices
postexilic
potentiate
potentilla
precarious
precipitin
precocious
predacious
prejudiced
prelatical
premarital
premaxilla
premedical
premonitor
prescriber
presidiary
prevenient
prismoidal
prizefight
proclaimer
prodigious
producible
proficient
progenitor
prohibiter
prohibitor
prolicidal
pronominal
propitiate
propitious
proscriber
prosilient
prosodical
provisions
pugnacious
pulsatilla
pulveriser
puristical
quartzitic
quixotical
rabbinical
rebellious
receptible
reconciler
reconsider
reeligible
reflexible
rejoicings
remarriage
remissible
repatriate
republican
resistible
resorcinol
restrained
restrainer
reversible
revertible
rhetorical
rhomboidal
rhomboidei
rhythmical
ridgepiece
ringtailed
robustious
rockabilly
rottweiler
roughrider
sabbatical
sacrificer
salubrious
Sanskritic
satellitic
scientific
screenings
seguidilla
selfguided
selfpoised
selfraised
semiotical
sensitiser
sequacious
sermoniser
serradilla
seventieth
sexlimited
shenanigan
shipwright
shopsoiled
shortlived
signwriter
sillybilly
sincipital
sinusoidal
skewbridge
slipstitch
soapboiler
sobersided
sobersides
socialiser
softboiled
solenoidal
songwriter
spagyrical
speedlimit
sphenoidal
spheroidal
splendidly
stabiliser
steamtight
steriliser
stillbirth
stockpiler
stockrider
stomatitis
struthious
subliminal
submariner
submediant
suborbital
subordinal
subscriber
subsidiary
sufficient
supergiant
supervisor
suspicious
suzerainty
swanmaiden
syllogiser
symbolical
symboliser
symposiast
synoecious
synoptical
syphilitic
tablelinen
tackdriver
Talmudical
tantaliser
temporiser
tendinitis
tenebrific
tenebrious
testflight
theatrical
theistical
theurgical
thinkpiece
threepiece
tidewaiter
tollbridge
torchlight
tracheitis
tranquilly
tremolitic
trifoliate
trigeminal
trioecious
triumviral
trochoidal
trouvaille
tsarevitch
tympanites
tympanitic
tympanitis
typewriter
tyrannical
umbellifer
unAmerican
unbiblical
uncritical
underlinen
underminer
undersized
ungracious
uninitiate
unmerciful
unmortised
unrequited
unstrained
uproarious
urethritis
uxoricidal
valvulitis
variolitic
vaudeville
verbaliser
vermicidal
victimiser
Victoriana
victorious
visualiser
vivandiere
vulcaniser
waffleiron
wainwright
wanderings
watertight
whipstitch
willynilly
willywilly
windshield
wirehaired
zabaglione
zoological
bubblyjock
crackajack
lumberjack
natterjack
supplejack
bookmaking
cheapskate
diesinking
frolicking
homemaking
jaywalking
jinricksha
Lamarckian
Lamarckism
lovemaking
mosaicking
nitpicking
peacockery
peacockish
pernickety
physicking
picnicking
prepackage
rainmaking
rollicking
samarskite
skyjacking
spillikins
unblinking
underskirt
unthinking
unwrinkled
waterskier
wunderkind
aardwolves
acarpelous
accomplice
accomplish
accumulate
acephalous
actinolite
adrenaline
affability
affectless
aircooling
alcoholise
alcoholism
ambivalent
amiability
amygdaloid
anchorless
annihilate
anopheline
antebellum
apostolate
apparelled
armourless
arthralgia
arthralgic
articulate
asexuality
assemblage
assibilate
assimilate
audibility
auriculate
Australian
autecology
badderlock
balneology
barbellate
barrelling
batfowling
battailous
Beaujolais
bedevilled
bejewelled
bemedalled
benevolent
bestialise
bestiality
bestseller
bibliology
bimetallic
binoculars
bioecology
bipetalous
birthplace
bitterling
bluecollar
bobbinlace
bondholder
bookseller
borderland
borderless
borderline
Boswellian
Boswellise
Boswellism
bottomless
brachylogy
brakeblock
breathless
breechless
breezeless
bridgeless
broadcloth
buttonless
calceolate
camouflage
cancellate
cancelling
cancellous
candyfloss
cannelloni
cantillate
capability
capitalise
capitalism
capitalist
Capitoline
capitulary
capitulate
caramelise
cardialgia
cardiology
carnallite
carpellary
carphology
catabolism
catafalque
centillion
centralise
centralism
centralist
centrality
cerebellum
chamaeleon
chancellor
chandelier
changeless
changeling
channelise
channelled
chapfallen
chartulary
chiselling
Christlike
chronology
chrysolite
cloverleaf
cnidoblast
codswallop
coequality
collarless
colourless
comicality
compelling
conchology
controlled
controller
copyholder
corbelling
cordiality
cordillera
councillor
councilman
counselled
counsellor
craniology
craquelure
crenellate
cryptology
cudgelling
curability
decimalise
decimalism
decivilise
deescalate
delocalise
deltiology
demobilise
demonology
demoralise
dendrology
deontology
depopulate
derailleur
devitalise
devocalise
dextrality
digitalise
dinnerless
disability
discipline
disincline
dispelling
disqualify
distilland
distillate
distillery
distilling
disutility
ditriglyph
dovecolour
downfallen
drivelling
driverless
durability
easterling
edentulous
effortless
Egyptology
emasculate
embowelled
embryology
empanelled
enamelling
enamellist
enterolith
enthralled
entomology
enzymology
ephorality
epicycloid
epistolary
epithelial
epithelium
equability
equivalent
erectility
escapology
eternalise
eternalist
ethicality
Eurodollar
evangelise
evangelism
evangelist
everyplace
exobiology
factualism
factualist
factuality
fatherland
fatherless
fatherlike
fathomless
federalise
federalism
federalist
feminality
fetterlock
fibreglass
fibrillary
fibrillate
fibrillose
fieldglass
fingerless
fingerling

finicality
firepolicy
firstclass
flabellate
flagellant
flagellate
flannelled
flashflood
fledgeling
flightless
floatplane
flocculate
flocculent
floorcloth
flosculous
flowerless
footballer
foreteller
fosterling
fraudulent
freeholder
friability
friendless
friendlily
fringeless
fritillary
frivolling
fulfilling
funnelling
fusibility
futureless
futurology
galloglass
gambolling
gastrology
generalise
generalist
generality
geniculate
genteelism
Ghibelline
glaciology
glasscloth
glossology
glottology
gooseflesh
gradualism
gradualist
graphology
graptolite
grasscloth
greencloth
groundless
groundling
grovelling
halfdollar
halfnelson
halfvolley
hammerless
hammerlock
handgallop
handselled
hanselling
hardbilled
haustellum
hawserlaid
heartblock
heartblood
heortology
hepatology
heterology
hieroglyph
hinterland
honourless
horsecloth
horseflesh
hostelling
houselling
houseplant
hoverplane
humourless
hyaloplasm
hydraulics
hydroplane
iconoclasm
ignobility
ilangilang
illegalise
illegality
imbecilely
imbecility
immaculacy
immaculate
immobilise
immobility
immoralist
immorality
immunology
impanelled
imperilled
incivility
incomplete
indocility
inequality
infidelity
initialise
initialled
inosculate
instilling
insufflate
interplant
interplead
invigilate
irresolute
Ishmaelite
journalese
journalise
journalism
journalist
juvenility
karyoplasm
katabolism
kennelling
kimberlite
ladykiller
lanceolate
landholder
laterality
laurelling
leaderless
ledgerline
legibility
lepidolite
letterless
leucoplast
lexicology
liberalise
liberalism
liberalist
liberality
literalise
literalism
literalist
literality
lithoglyph
litterlout
logicality
logrolling
lowerclass
lustreless
lyophilise
maidenlike
malacology
malevolent
manifoldly
manipulate
maquillage
marrowless
marshalled
marshaller
marshalsea
martialism
marvelling
marvellous
masterless
maximalist
meadowland
meadowlark
metabolise
metabolism
metabolite
metagalaxy
meticulous
Michaelmas
microcline
mineralise
mineralogy
minimalism
minimalist
miraculous
miscellany
mongrelise
mongrelism
monopolise
monopolist
monovalent
morphology
motherland
motherless
motionless
motiveless
mousseline
movability
multiplier
musicality
musicology
muskmallow
mutability
nailpolish
nationless
naturalise
naturalism
naturalist
nephralgia
nephrology
neuroplasm
neutralise
neutralism
neutralist
neutrality
nickelling
nidicolous
nightglass
nominalism
nominalist
nonchalant
nonnuclear
nonviolent
notability
novaculite
numberless
numerology
nuptiality
nympholept
objectless
obnubilate
oceanology
odontalgia
odontology
oligoclase
oneirology
operculate
ophthalmia
ophthalmic
opposeless
optimalise
orthoclase
osteoblast
osteoclast
outfielder
painkiller
palaeolith
palatalise
palynology
paniculate
papyrology
parabolise
paraboloid
paraselene
parcelling
partiality
pastellist
patriality
patrolling
pediculate
pediculous
pencilling
penicillin
pennillion
perihelion
persiflage
petroglyph
photoflood
phrenology
physiology
picketline
pilgarlick
pillowlace
pincerlike
pistillary
pistillate
pistolling
pitchblack
plasmolyse
playfellow
pliability
ploughland
pogonology
pointblank
polyvalent
portcullis
postbellum
postillion
potability
potamology
potbellied
pozzuolana
preexilian
prevailing
priestling
princeling
profitless
propellant
propellent
propelling
proteolyse
prothallia
prothallus
protoplasm
protoplast
proudflesh
psephology
psychology
puberulent
pummelling
punctulate
pyretology
pyrogallol
quarrelled
quarreller
quenchless
radicalise
radicalism
ratability
razorblade
reasonless
recitalist
refuelling
regardless
relentless
remediless
remodelled
repopulate
resemblant
resistless
resultless
reticulate
revitalise
revivalism
revivalist
rewardless
ricinoleic
ridiculous
risibility
rollcollar
ropewalker
rosaniline
rosemallow
rudderless
rupicoline
rupicolous
sacroiliac
sailorless
salability
salesclerk
salicylate
salmonleap
saltcellar
sanderling
sarcoplasm
satanology
savourless
saxicoline
saxicolous
scaffolder
scandalise
scandalous
scatheless
screwplate
scribbling
scrofulous
scrupulous
scurrility
scurrilous
scutellate
seamanlike
searchless
seismology
selenology
selfcolour
selfruling
selfwilled
semeiology
sensualise
sensualism
sensualist
sensuality
septillion
sexivalent
sextillion
shadowless
sheathless
shibboleth
shieldless
shillelagh
shopwalker
shovelling
shrivelled
shroudlaid
shroudless
siderolite
signalling
Singhalese
sleeveless
sleevelink
smokeplant
snivelling
softbilled
solubilise
solubility
somatology
spathulate
spatiality
specialise
specialism
specialist
speciality
speciology
speechless
speleology
sperrylite
spherulite
spiderline
spiralling
spiritless
spongology
springless
springlike
sprinkling
squireling
stadholder
stanchless
staphyline
starveling
staurolite
stencilled
stenciller
stipellate
stoneblind
stopvolley
stormcloud
streamless
streamline
stressless
stridulant
stridulate
stridulous
stringless
subnuclear
subsellium
summerlike
summitless
sunparlour
superaltar
supperless
surrealism
surrealist
swashplate
sweatgland
swivelling
symphylous
synecology
systemless
tablecloth
talentless
taleteller
tamability
tasselling
taxability
teatrolley
technology
tenability
tenantless
tenderloin
tendrillar
tendrilled
teratology
terneplate
terreplein
terrorless
tessellate
textualist
themselves
theodolite

thirdclass
thriftless
throneless
timberline
timbrology
tinselling
tirailleur
tomfoolery
tongueless
topazolite
topgallant
topicality
tortellini
tourbillon
tourmaline
toxicology
trammelled
trampoline
trancelike
transplant
travelling
trichology
tricyclist
triskelion
trivialise
trivialism
triviality
troctolite
trophology
trowelling
tubicolous
tunnelling
typicality
umbrellaed
unavailing
undercliff
underfloor
underglaze
underslung
unequalled
unexcelled
unfamiliar
unicyclist
unlabelled
unmorality
unravelled
unresolved
unrivalled
unsettling
upperclass
urbanology
vesiculate
victualled
victualler
virtuality
virtueless
visibility
visionless
vitriolise
vocabulary
volatilise
volatility
volubility
waistcloth
wanderlust
wassailing
watchglass
waterclock
waterflood
waterglass
weaponless
weedkiller
weightless
werewolves
windowless
wingcollar
wirepuller
wirewalker
withholder

wonderland
worldclass
ylangylang
yokefellow
yourselves
zoophilous
Abrahamman
abridgment
acoelomate
adjudgment
adjustment
Adullamite
advisement
aeronomist
affeerment
afterimage
agronomist
alightment
allogamous
allurement
altazimuth
altocumuli
amalgamate
ambushment
amercement
anadromous
anastomose
anointment
antinomian
antiSemite
antonymous
arrestment
arthromere
assessment
assignment
assoilment
assortment
attachment
attainment
attornment
attunement
autogamous
autoimmune
autonomist
autonomous
avouchment
babblement
backgammon
bafflement
banishment
battlement
bedchamber
bemusement
Benthamism
Benthamite
bestowment
betterment
bichromate
biochemist
blackamoor
blacksmith
blastemata
blastomere
blazonment
bottommost
bressummer
bridesmaid
buttermilk
cajolement
cantonment
centromere
chainsmoke
charismata
choriambic
cinecamera
clawhammer
coffeemill
commitment
complement

compliment
compromise
conferment
confirmand
conformism
conformist
conformity
consummate
couplement
custommade
dazzlement
debasement
debatement
decampment
defacement
defilement
definement
defrayment
denouement
department
deployment
deportment
derailment
designment
desquamate
detachment
detainment
devotement
diastemata
dichromate
discommend
discommode
disharmony
disownment
divebomber
divestment
drophammer
eartrumpet
effacement
embalmment
embankment
embarkment
embodiment
embossment
employment
encampment
encasement
encashment
encystment
endearment
endogamous
enfacement
engagement
engulfment
enjambment
enjoinment
enlacement
enlistment
enmeshment
enrichment
enrigiment
entailment
enticement
entombment
entrapment
epidermoid
equanimity
ergonomics
ergonomist
escapement
escarpment
evolvement
excitement
experiment
famishment
fearsomely
fingermark
folkmemory
fulfilment

galliambic
geochemist
gladsomely
government
graphemics
groundmass
gruesomely
habiliment
handsomely
harassment
hithermost
homecoming
homogamous
homonymous
hornrimmed
hypolimnia
immurement
impairment
impalement
impartment
impediment
impugnment
incasement
incitement
indictment
inditement
inducement
instalment
instrument
integument
intendment
internment
investment
iridosmine
jackhammer
kerseymere
lachrymose
lattermost
lavishment
legitimacy
legitimate
legitimise
legitimism
legitimist
lonesomely
lymphomata
macadamise
management
mastermind
medicament
middlemost
misogamist
mizzenmast
monogamist
monogamous
morphemics
Mussulmans
nethermost
nonpayment
nonswimmer
obtainment
ordainment
overcommit
pantrymaid
parliament
paronymous
peppermill
peppermint
performing
phillumeny
pilgrimage
polygamist
polygamous
polynomial
polysemous
posthumous
postliminy
preachment
preadamite

preferment
prepayment
programmer
prostomial
prostomium
punishment
puzzlement
quadrumana
quadrumane
quadrumvir
rabblement
ravishment
rearmament
reassemble
reassembly
recoupment
refinement
refundment
regalement
reichsmark
resentment
reshipment
retirement
revealment
revilement
ripplemark
sanctimony
schoolmaam
schoolmarm
schoolmate
seaanemone
secernment
secondment
securement
seducement
settlement
showjumper
solacement
stablemate
stalagmite
sterigmata
supplement
synonymist
synonymity
synonymous
syntagmata
tailormade
tanglement
tapotement
taxonomist
telecamera
teratomata
threadmark
tilthammer
tiresomely
toilsomely
tournament
triphammer
unassuming
unbecoming
uniformity
unscramble
Vietnamese
whitesmith
wilderment
windjammer
wolframite
wonderment
Wykehamist
abdominous
abducentes
aberrantly
abiogenist
abjectness
abruptness
absurdness
abundantly
accidental
accusingly

acrogenous
activeness
adherently
adjacently
admiringly
adroitness
aeruginous
afferently
affluently
aficionado
Africander
Africanise
Africanism
Africanist
Afrikander
alarmingly
Albigenses
albuminoid
albuminous
alkalinity
allrounder
almacanter
almucanter
amanuenses
amanuensis
annoyingly
antagonise
antagonism
antagonist
antependia
antepenult
antimonial
antimonite
aplacental
Apollinian
Apollonian
apparently
aquilinity
argumentum
arrogantly
artfulness
arytaenoid
astuteness
auctioneer
augustness
autogenous
averseness
Babylonian
bacchantes
bacchantic
backhanded
backhander
bafflingly
ballooning
balloonist
barrenness
bassoonist
becomingly
bellringer
besprinkle
bitchiness
bitterness
bituminise
bituminous
bleariness
bleatingly
blindingly
blitheness
bloodiness
bluebonnet
bluepencil
bluetongue
bluishness
blurringly
blushingly
bookbinder
bottleneck
bouncingly
bourbonism

bourbonist
boyishness
Brahmanism
Brahminism
braininess
brassiness
brawniness
brazenness
breeziness
brightness
brokenness
broodiness
broodingly
Buchmanism
Buchmanite
buffoonery
bumblingly
bumpkinish
bunglingly
bushranger
bustlingly
cachinnate
cackhanded
cacogenics
cajolingly
calamander
calcsinter
Caledonian
caliginous
callowness
candidness
carabineer
carabinier
caravaneer
caravanned
caravanner
carbonnade
carmagnole
carotenoid
carotinoid
carryingon
cartoonist
casualness
cautionary
centennial
ceremonial
ceruminous
cessionary
challenger
charmingly
chasteness
chattiness
chauvinism
chauvinist
cheekiness
cheeriness
cheesiness
chersonese
chickenpox
chiffonier
chilliness
chimpanzee
chlorinate
choiceness
chubbiness
Ciceronian
cinchonine
clamminess
claspknife
cleverness
cloudiness
clumsiness
coalbunker
coarseness
coathanger
coeternity
coherently
comeliness
commonness
compounder
concerning
concinnity
confounded
conjointly
constantan
Constantia
constantly
coordinate
copartnery
coralsnake
coromandel
Corybantes
corybantic
costliness
covalently
covenanted
covenantee
covenanter
covenantor
covetingly
coweringly
craftiness
cragginess
crankiness
cravenness
creaminess
creatinine
creepiness
crescentic
crossindex
crustiness
cryogenics
cursedness
cussedness
daintiness
damagingly
dauphiness
dazzlingly
deadliness
decadently
decolonise
defeminise
dehumanise
delaminate
delphinium
delphinoid
demureness
denominate
deracinate
deridingly
desalinate
devoutness
diaphanous
dictionary
diligently
diluteness
directness
discerning
disconnect
discounter
disdainful
diseconomy
disfurnish
disgruntle
disjointed
dismalness
distringas
divineness
documental
doggedness
dogstongue
dominantly
doubleness
doubtingly
dragonnade
drawlingly
dreaminess
dreariness
dressiness
droopingly
drowsiness
drudgingly
dumfounder
earthiness
earwitness
ectogenous
edibleness
effeminacy
effeminate
effeteness
elatedness
Eleusinian
eloquently
emarginate
embryonate
endogenous
enduringly
engagingly
enticingly
entireness
epilimnion
eudemonism
eudemonist
evenhanded
evilminded
excitingly
expertness
exultantly
exultingly
exurbanite
eyewitness
facileness
fairminded
fallowness
famousness
faultiness
feebleness
fellmonger
femaleness
femininely
femininity
fervidness
fescennine
festoonery
fetchingly
fickleness
fictioneer
fictionist
fierceness
filthiness
fingernail
finiteness
fishmonger
fitfulness
fivefinger
flabbiness
flagrantly
flashiness
fleeringly
fleetingly
fleshiness
flimsiness
flintiness
flippantly
floatingly
floppiness
floridness
fluffiness
fluorinate
fluxionary
foetidness
folksiness
folksinger
footcandle
foraminous
forefinger
forehanded
foreignism
forerunner
fourhanded
fragmental
fragrantly
fraternise
fraternity
freakiness
freehanded
freelancer
Frenchness
frequenter
frequently
frigidness
frilliness
friskiness
frizziness
frostiness
frothiness
frowningly
fuliginous
fulllength
fumblingly
gadolinite
gadolinium
gadrooning
gametangia
gangrenous
garishness
gastronome
gastronomy
gaucheness
gelatinise
gelatinous
genialness
gentleness
gladhander
glancingly
glassiness
glauconite
gloominess
glossiness
gluttonise
gluttonous
goaltender
goldenness
goodliness
granduncle
graspingly
grasssnake
greasiness
greatuncle
greediness
grindingly
grisliness
grittiness
grogginess
growlingly
grubbiness
grudgingly
grumpiness
guiltiness
gunrunning
gunslinger
halflength
halogenate
halogenous
handedness
hardhanded
hauntingly
headhunter
heartiness
heathendom
heathenise
heathenish
heathenism
Heliconian
hellbender
heparinise
heroicness
hesitantly
heteronomy
highbinder
highhanded
highlander
highminded
hirudinean
hoarseness
hollowness
homeliness
homogenise
homogenous
hookedness
horizontal
hornedness
horridness
humaneness
humbleness
hungriness
hypogynous
hypotenuse
ignorantly
illuminant
illuminate
illuminati
illuminism
illuminist
imminently
impishness
imposingly
impotently
impregnant
impregnate
impudently
impureness
incidental
indecently
indefinite
indigenous
indolently
ingeminate
inherently
inhumanely
inhumanity
inkslinger
innateness
innocently
innominate
inordinate
insaneness
inseminate
insolently
inspanning
intactness
intentness
inurbanity
invaginate
invitingly
inwardness
ironhanded
ironmonger
italianate
italianise
Italianism
jacobinise
Jacobinism
jaggedness
jauntiness
jejuneness
Jewishness
jobbernowl
jocoseness
Johnsonese
johnsonian
joyfulness
joyousness
jubilantly
juggernaut
Kantianism
keratinise
keratinous
kindliness
kingliness
knickknack
knockkneed
knottiness
ladyfinger
lampoonery
lampoonist
landhunger
landowning
lanternfly
lanthanide
lanuginose
lanuginous
latifundia
laughingly
lavishness
lawfulness
lawntennis
leadenness
lectionary
lefthanded
lefthander
leguminous
lesbianism
libidinous
lieutenant
ligamental
lightingup
likeliness
likeminded
limpidness
lionhunter
liquidness
lissomness
Lithuanian
littleness
liveliness
loneliness
longwinded
lordliness
loveliness
lovingness
luculently
Lusitanian
mainlander
manchineel
manfulness
Marcionite
marshiness
matureness
mavourneen
meagreness
measliness
mellowness
membranous
memorandum
menacingly
messianism
metacentre
middlingly
midmorning
mightiness
migrainous
militantly
millennial
millennium
mindedness
minuteness
mischanter
misjoinder
misogynist
misogynous
missionary
missionise
modernness

modishness
monogenism
monogynian
monogynous
monomaniac
monotonous
monsignori
Montagnard
monumental
mopishness
morbidness
moroseness
morphinism
mossbunker
mouldiness
mudslinger
mulishness
narrowness
nativeness
newsmonger
newsvendor
nicotinism
nimbleness
nondrinker
nonjoinder
nucleonics
oafishness
obediently
oblateness
obligingly
obtuseness
occidental
odiousness
oecumenism
oleaginous
omnigenous
oncogenous
opaqueness
openhanded
openminded
opinionist
ornamental
ornateness
orneriness
otioseness
outgunning
outrunning
outswinger
overhanded
overlander
overmanned
overmantel
overwinter
owlishness
palagonite
palatinate
palisander
pallidness
PalmSunday
paltriness
Panamanian
paperknife
pasquinade
passionary
passionate
Passionist
patchiness
pathfinder
pedimental
pedimented
penitently
pensionary
perigynous
peritoneal
peritoneum
periwinkle
petiteness
petulantly
pheasantry
picayunish
piercingly
placidness
plangently
pleadingly
pleasantly
pleasantry
pleasingly
pliantness
ploddingly
pluckiness
polemonium
politeness
polygenism
polygenist
polygenous
polygynous
Pomeranian
porousness
portliness
praemunire
prancingly
preeminent
prefrontal
pregnantly
presignify
pressingly
prettiness
prissiness
profoundly
promptness
pronounced
pronouncer
properness
propionate
propounder
proscenium
proteinous
pruriently
puissantly
purblindly
puritanise
puritanism
purulently
putridness
pyracantha
pyrogenous
pyromaniac
pyromantic
pyroxenite
Pyrrhonian
Pyrrhonism
Pyrrhonist
quadrangle
quadrantal
quadrennia
quaintness
quarrender
quaternary
quaternate
quaternion
quaternity
queasiness
quirkiness
Rachmanism
rackrenter
raggedness
rakishness
ramblingly
rancidness
randomness
recentness
recolonise
recreantly
redolently
referendum
regimental
rejuvenate
rejuvenise
relevantly
remissness
remoteness
rencounter
reorganise
resonantly
resupinate
reticently
retiringly
retraining
reunionism
reunionist
reverencer
reverently
rightangle
ringfinger
roadrunner
robustness
rontgenise
rootedness
ropedancer
rottenness
rubberneck
rubiginous
rudimental
ruefulness
ruffianism
ruggedness
ruminantly
rumrunning
Russianise
sacredness
salamander
sallowness
sanguinary
sanguinely
sanguinity
sashwindow
savageness
scantiness
scarceness
scathingly
scattiness
Scillonian
scoffingly
scorzonera
scrutineer
scrutinise
scurviness
secureness
sedateness
seemliness
selectness
selfbinder
selfdenial
semiannual
semilunate
sentiently
septennial
septennium
sereneness
sergeantcy
serjeantcy
serotinous
severeness
sexagenary
shabbiness
shagginess
shiftiness
shockingly
shoddiness
shopwindow
shortening
showwindow
shrewdness
shrillness
sickliness
sidewinder
silentness
simpleness
sinfulness
singleness
skimpiness
skinniness
slanginess
slantingly
sleaziness
sleepiness
slightness
sloppiness
smelliness
smoothness
smudginess
smuttiness
sneakiness
sneakingly
sneeringly
sniffiness
snootiness
snubbingly
snuffiness
soddenness
softfinned
solemnness
sombreness
soothingly
Sorbonnist
sordidness
soundingly
spankingly
sparseness
speediness
sponginess
spookiness
sportiness
sportingly
spottiness
spruceness
spunkiness
squareness
stableness
stagnantly
stanchness
starriness
stationary
stationery
steadiness
steaminess
steeliness
stephanite
stickiness
stiffening
stiflingly
stinginess
stingingly
stinkingly
stockiness
stodginess
stolidness
stonesnipe
storminess
straitness
stramonium
strictness
stridently
strikingly
Stroganoff
strychnine
strychnism
stubbiness
stuffiness
stumpiness
stunningly
stupidness
sturdiness
subdeanery
subtleness
suddenness
sugariness
sullenness
sulphonate
sultriness
superbness
supineness
supplanter
suppleness
sustaining
sweatiness
sweepingly
sweetening
swimmingly
swingingly
symphonion
symphonist
takingness
taperingly
tauntingly
tawdriness
taxidancer
teaplanter
tegumental
temptingly
tenderness
tenemental
tetchiness
theogonist
thereanent
thereunder
thickening
thinkingly
thorniness
thousandth
timeliness
toffeenose
tolerantly
toothiness
torpidness
torridness
touchiness
touchingly
towardness
toweringly
trappiness
trashiness
treasonous
trendiness
trepanning
trichinise
trichinous
trickiness
triclinium
triflingly
triternate
trochanter
trombonist
trustiness
trustingly
tufthunter
tuitionary
turbidness
turgidness
turtleneck
twelvenote
Tyrrhenian
unaccented
unattended
unbalanced
undefended
uneasiness
unendingly
unerringly
unevenness
unfadingly
unfairness
unfeminine
unfriended
unfriendly
ungrounded
unholiness
uniqueness
unjustness
unkindness
unlikeness
unmeetness
unripeness
unruliness
untidiness
unwariness
uppishness
upwardness
usefulness
utopianism
vanadinite
Vaticanism
Vaticanist
vaticinate
vehemently
velutinous
venialness
veterinary
viceconsul
viewfinder
vigilantly
villainage
villainess
villainous
villeinage
viraginous
virulently
viscountcy
vitaminise
voluminous
wantonness
wateriness
wavelength
waveringly
weakliness
weakminded
westernise
wharfinger
wheeziness
WhitMonday
WhitSunday
wickedness
wilderness
wilfulness
wintriness
witchingly
wobbliness
woefulness
wontedness
woodenness
woodlander
woolliness
worthiness
wrathiness
yearningly
yeastiness
yellowness
yieldingly
aboveboard
accustomed
acrophobia
additional
aerobiosis
aerobiotic
aerophobia
aetiologic
allophonic
allotropic
amphigouri
anastrophe
anchylosis
anchylotic
anteriorly
antibiosis

antibiotic
antiphonal
antiproton
apochromat
apostrophe
apotheoses
apotheosis
arteriolar
asbestosis
astrologer
astrologic
astronomer
astronomic
asymptotic
ateleiosis
autoerotic
azeotropic
backblocks
background
ballflower
barcarolle
barefooted
bargeboard
barracouta
bawdyhouse
belladonna
bellflower
beribboned
blackboard
blockboard
blockhouse
bloodhound
bloodmoney
bobbysocks
bobbysoxer
brachiopod
brainpower
brantgoose
breadboard
breakpoint
brentgoose
byssinosis
cantaloupe
carcinogen
carcinosis
cellulosic
cephalopod
chairwoman
chalkboard
changeover
checkpoint
chessboard
clubfooted
coachhouse
cockalorum
cornflower
cornucopia
corroboree
cosmogonic
cosmopolis
courthouse
crematoria
crossbones
crossroads
cryoscopic
decompound
deepfrozen
deeprooted
delusional
dermatogen
devotional
diachronic
diarrhoeal
diarrhoeic
diplodocus
directoire
disappoint
discobolus
disembogue
disembosom
disembowel
divisional
drafthorse
dreamworld
earthbound
ecchymosis
ecchymotic
electronic
emblazoner
emblazonry
embonpoint
emeryboard
enantiosis
endoscopic
endosmosis
endosmotic
enharmonic
epistrophe
equational
escallonia
escharotic
escritoire
ethnologic
eucaryotic
extemporal
exteriorly
fairground
fairspoken
fibreboard
fibrinogen
fieldmouse
fixedpoint
flapdoodle
flashboard
flashpoint
flatfooted
fleshwound
floatboard
floorboard
foamflower
foreground
fourfooted
fractional
freebooter
freedwoman
freespoken
frictional
functional
ganglionic
gasteropod
glasshouse
glassworks
goldilocks
goodlooker
goodygoody
grassroots
GrecoRoman
greenhouse
guardhouse
guesthouse
gymnosophy
gyrational
gyroscopic
haematosis
hagiologic
headphones
henceforth
heptagonal
heptatonic
hereabouts
heroicomic
histologic
histrionic
hobbyhorse
hocuspocus
hodgepodge
hoitytoity
hokeypokey
holusbolus
homophonic
horoscopic
horsecoper
horsepower
horsewoman
hotblooded
hotchpotch
housebound
hydrologic
hyperbolae
hyperbolas
hyperbolic
hypergolic
hypersonic
hypnagogic
ichthyosis
ideational
illusional
impersonal
indisposed
inferiorly
infrasonic
inharmonic
interiorly
interloper
internodal
interposal
interposer
intervolve
interwound
interwoven
interzonal
Irishwoman
irrational
isentropic
isochronal
knifeboard
lederhosen
lighthouse
limitrophe
lithologic
loosecover
loxodromic
Lysenkoism
madreporic
malapropos
manorhouse
markswoman
matchboard
megascopic
meridional
mesothorax
metaphoric
metathorax
metronomic
metropolis
monophonic
moonflower
mouldboard
multiloquy
multipolar
multivocal
mystagogic
mystagogue
mythologer
mythologic
mythopoeia
mythopoeic
necropolis
neurotoxin
noblewoman
northbound
nosophobia
nostologic
notchboard
nutational
nyctalopia
nyctalopic
occasional
oceangoing
ophiologic
orthodoxly
orthogonal
otherworld
otterboard
overabound
overblouse
overcooked
overground
overgrowth
overlooker
paedagogic
paedogogue
parabiosis
parabiotic
paragnosis
paratroops
pasteboard
pathologic
patrilocal
pawnbroker
peashooter
pedalpoint
pennyroyal
pennyworth
pentagonal
pentatomic
pentatonic
perchloric
periscopic
petitioner
phanerogam
pheromonal
philologen
philopoena
philosophe
philosophy
phonologic
phosphoric
phosphorus
phytotoxic
pianoforte
piecegoods
pilothouse
planktonic
plantlouse
playground
pollenosis
polyphonic
polyploidy
positional
powerhouse
presbyopia
presbyopic
protanopic
punchboard
pycnogonid
pyrophoric
questioner
radiologic
radiosonde
reciprocal
redblooded
rediscover
relational
repertoire
revisional
rheotropic
rhizomorph
riverhorse
rotational
roughhouse
roundhouse
runthrough
sabretooth
sacerdotal
safeblower
saleswoman
salicional
scaleboard
scaramouch
scoreboard
Scotswoman
scriptoria
seethrough
selfprofit
semichorus
seriocomic
servomotor
sharpnosed
sheeplouse
shellmound
shipbroker
shirehorse
shrewmouse
sialagogic
sialagogue
sitophobia
sixshooter
skateboard
slowfooted
smartmoney
smokehouse
snowgrouse
snowplough
sociologic
softspoken
somniloquy
sophomoric
soundboard
southbound
spacewoman
spellbound
stagecoach
standpoint
steakhouse
steelworks
stomatopod
stoneborer
storehouse
stormbound
strawboard
sugarhouse
superiorly
supernovae
superpower
supersonic
supertonic
surefooted
switchover
synchronal
synchronic
synecdoche
synostosis
tantamount
teleologic
telephoner
telephonic
telescopic
terracotta
tetragonal
tetramorph
tetrapolis
theophoric
thermionic
thillhorse
thromboses
thrombosis
thrombotic
ticpolonga
townswoman
toxiphobia
tractional
tragicomic
transposal
transposer
travelogue
treadboard
trichroism
trichromat
trillionth
tropaeolum
tropologic
ulteriorly
ultrasonic
ultrasound
unbuttoned
uncommonly
uncustomed
undercover
underworld
uneconomic
unemployed
unexplored
unhallowed
unhistoric
unimproved
unorthodox
unprovoked
unschooled
unseasoned
venational
vocational
volitional
wallflower
watchtower
waterborne
waterpower
waterworks
wellspoken
Welshwoman
wheelhorse
wheelhouse
whorehouse
windflower
winegrower
wingfooted
wongawonga
woolgrower
workpeople
wraparound
wrongdoing
xenophobia
xylophonic
yarborough
Aethiopian
allpurpose
ampelopsis
anaglyphic
anamorphic
anatropous
angiosperm
anthropoid
anticipant
anticipate
antisepsis
antiseptic
apocarpous
apocryphal
apotropaic
bankruptcy
beekeeping
bibliopegy
bibliophil
bibliopole
bibliopoly
biographer
biographic
biomorphic
blastopore
bridlepath
camelopard
cataleptic
clodhopper
closetplay

comicopera
constipate
contraprop
correspond
cuckoopint
descriptor
diagraphic
diatropism
discompose
discrepant
disrespect
doublepark
dysgraphia
dystrophic
elecampane
elevenplus
emancipate
emancipist
endstopped
enwrapping
eosinophil
epigrapher
epigraphic
episcopacy
episcopate
Esculapian
eucalyptol
eucalyptus
fingerpost
flightpath
Francophil
frangipane
frangipani
froghopper
geographer
geographic
geotropism
gobstopper
groundplan
gymnosperm
gyrocopter
hammerpond
harelipped
helicopter
homoeopath
interspace
introspect
isomorphic
kidnapping
kriegspiel
leafhopper
macrospore
maladapted
metalepsis
microspore
midshipman
morrispike
mudskipper
naturopath
nincompoop
orangepeel
orographic
orthoepist
outerspace
overexpose
overlapped
oversupply
overtopped
paralipsis
philippina
philippine
phlogopite
pigeonpair
pigeonpost
playbyplay
polydipsia
powderpuff
predispose
presuppose
principate
principial
principium
principled
procrypsis
procryptic
protreptic
psychopath
quadruplet
quadruplex
quadrupole
quintuplet
rattlepate
retrospect
rinderpest
rockhopper
roselipped
sandhopper
screenplay
seaserpent
skijumping
snowcapped
spoilsport
stereopsis
stirrupcup
swanupping
swarmspore
syncarpous
tablespoon
theosopher
thermophil
thermopile
thornapple
tittupping
transeptal
triglyphic
trimorphic
trollopish
tryptophan
unexampled
unoccupied
unscripted
velocipede
wallpepper
wampumpeag
wanderplug
waterspout
windowpane
wiretapper
worshipful
worshipped
worshipper
zoomorphic
lambrequin
semiliquid
soubriquet
tourniquet
abacterial
accelerate
achondrite
acroterion
acroterium
adrenergic
adulterant
adulterate
adulteress
adulterine
adulterous
aeolotropy
aftergrass
allegorise
allegorist
alliterate
alloverish
altostrati
amateurish
amateurism
ameliorate
amphibrach
ancestress
anchorring
anemograph
angularity
anisotropy
annularity
antemortem
Antichrist
antiheroic
aquafortis
aquamarine
aquiferous
araucarian
architrave
armigerous
asseverate
asynchrony
auditorial
auditorium
auriferous
autostrada
autostrade
aventurine
backstroke
backwardly
balustrade
barratrous
beechdrops
beefburger
belletrist
benzpyrene
bestirring
bighearted
biliverdin
bimestrial
biodegrade
biometrics
bipolarity
birdstrike
bitterroot
bladdernut
blepharism
blistering
blithering
blitzkrieg
bluethroat
blusterous
boisterous
bookmarker
bootstraps
bowdlerise
bowdlerism
breadcrumb
breadfruit
bridegroom
bromegrass
bunchgrass
burglarise
cadaverous
calyptrate
camphorate
cantatrice
caseharden
caseworker
cataphract
categorise
catoptrics
centigrade
certiorari
chamberpot
chatterbox
chaudfroid
chauntress
childermas
childproof
chinagraph
chivalrous
chuckerout
cinerarium
clangorous
cockatrice
cocksurely
commonroom
compatriot
concurrent
concurring
conferring
coniferous
consecrate
conspiracy
conspirant
contrarily
cordierite
couchgrass
counteract
crackbrain
creaturely
crispbread
crisscross
crossbreed
crossgrain
crosstrees
curatorial
cyclograph
cylindroid
cytochrome
decelerate
Decembrist
decolorant
decolorise
decompress
deerforest
deflagrate
degeneracy
degenerate
deliberate
denaturant
dentifrice
depolarise
derestrict
desiderata
desiderate
diathermal
diathermic
dictatress
dilatorily
diningroom
directress
disapprove
disastrous
disbarring
discharger
discourage
discourser
disembroil
dishearten
donnybrook
dorsigrade
downstream
downstroke
downwardly
drawstring
dumbstruck
duumvirate
ectodermal
ectodermic
edulcorate
electorate
endodermal
endodermis
engineroom
enterprise
ephemerous
episternum
equatorial
equestrian
euhemerise
euhemerism
euhemerist
eviscerate
exaggerate
exasperate
exenterate
exhilarant
exhilarate
exothermal
exothermic
exprobrate
exulcerate
faceharden
featherbed
feathering
fenestrate
firescreen
fishcarver
flameproof
flattering
flavourful
flavouring
fleacircus
fleamarket
folklorist
footwarmer
forwearied
founderous
Fourierism
fourstroke
freemartin
fruitarian
gaillardia
garnierite
geometrise
geothermal
geothermic
geriatrics
geriatrist
glauberite
glimmering
glossarial
glossarist
Godfearing
goosegrass
grammarian
grangerise
grangerism
grapefruit
gressorial
groundrent
gynandrous
hairspring
hairstreak
hairstroke
hakenkreuz
handbarrow
handicraft
handspring
handworked
Hanoverian
harbourage
haustorium
headspring
headstream
headstrong
heartbreak
heatstroke
heavyarmed
hectograph
heliograph
heliotrope
heliotropy
henharrier
henhearted
hexamerous
hierocracy
hierograph
highstrung
Hippocrene
hippodrome
hippogriff
hippogryph
hipsterism
holophrase
homocercal
honorarium
hourcircle
housecraft
houseproud
housetrain
hovertrain
hygrograph
hypocorism
hypodermal
hypodermic
hypodermis
idolatress
idolatrous
illiteracy
illiterate
illstarred
illusorily
illustrate
immaterial
immaturely
immaturity
immemorial
immoderacy
immoderate
impoverish
inaccuracy
inaccurate
inaugurate
incinerate
incoherent
indecorous
indiscreet
indiscrete
industrial
inexpertly
infiltrate
infusorial
infusorian
innumeracy
innumerate
innumerous
insecurely
insecurity
insularism
insularity
intenerate
interbreed
intercross
intergrade
intertrigo
interurban
intolerant
intraurban
inventress
inveteracy
inveterate
invigorate
ironworker
irreverent
isometrics
isopterous
isosporous
isothermal
janitorial
jocularity
keyboarder
knobkerrie
Krugerrand
lacustrine
laminarian
landocracy
languorous
lapidarian

lapidarist
lavatorial
lebensraum
lemongrass
lighterage
lighterman
lightproof
limeburner
literarily
lithograph
lithotrity
livingroom
lobsterpot
lockerroom
luciferase
luciferous
lukewarmly
lumberroom
lutestring
magistracy
magistrate
mainspring
mainstream
malapertly
malodorous
manageress
managerial
manicurist
manuscript
marguerite
masquerade
matriarchy
mediatress
mediocrity
mesomerism
mesomorphy
metacarpal
metacarpus
metamerism
metaphrase
metatarsal
metatarsus
micrograph
militarily
militarise
militarism
militarist
millstream
mimeograph
minestrone
mineworker
ministrant
mockheroic
moisturise
monandrous
monetarily
monetarism
monetarist
monitorial
monocarpic
monochrome
moonstruck
moratorium
Mousterian
mouthorgan
muciferous
muliebrity
mulligrubs
natatorial
natatorium
nephograph
nettlerash
newsworthy
nightdress
nitrogroup
nonferrous
nonstarter
northerner
noteworthy
nubiferous
nuciferous
nucivorous
obituarist
obliterate
obstetrics
oceanarium
ochlocracy
octamerous
octandrian
octandrous
octonarian
oleiferous
omnivorous
opprobrium
ordinarily
osmeterium
outpouring
overburden
overspread
overstride
overstrung
overthrown
overthrust
packthread
paintbrush
palindrome
panegyrise
panegyrist
pantograph
papaverine
papaverous
paranormal
paraphrase
paraphrast
pasteurise
pasteurism
patriarchy
pedalorgan
pedestrian
pedicurist
pellagrous
peridermal
permafrost
perpetrate
phenocryst
phonograph
photograph
photoprint
phototrope
pictograph
piliferous
pinecarpet
pistonring
pitcherful
plagiarise
plagiarism
plagiarist
planigraph
pleochroic
plunderage
plunderous
plutocracy
pockmarked
podiatrist
polychrest
polychrome
polymerise
polymerism
polymerous
pomiferous
popularise
popularity
pornocracy
postmortem
postpartum
postscript
pourparler
praetorial
praetorian
preferring
pressurise
presternum
proctorage
proctorial
proctorise
prosperity
prosperous
psalterium
puerperium
punchdrunk
pupilarity
pupiparous
purseproud
quadrireme
quarterage
quarterday
quartering
quickgrass
quinacrine
radiograph
reafforest
recuperate
redcurrant
redecorate
redescribe
regeneracy
regenerate
registrant
regularise
regularity
remunerate
reredorter
restaurant
retrograde
retrogress
revalorise
riproaring
ripsnorter
roadworthy
rockgarden
roistering
roisterous
roodscreen
roofgarden
rubythroat
saccharate
saccharide
saccharify
saccharine
saccharoid
saccharose
saliferous
saltigrade
salutarily
sanatorium
sandmartin
sanitarian
sanitarily
sanitarium
sapphirine
satyagraha
sauerkraut
scansorial
scapegrace
scattergun
scattering
schoolroom
screwpress
sculptress
seamstress
secondrate
secularise
secularism
secularist
secularity
seductress
seignorage
seignorial
selfmurder
selfparody
semestrial
semicircle
seminarian
seminarist
sempstress
senatorial
senseorgan
SerboCroat
shellproof
shirtfront
shockproof
shoestring
shortbread
shortcrust
shuttering
sidestreet
sidestroke
siegetrain
silkscreen
similarity
sinecurism
sinecurist
sinistrous
slanderous
slatternly
slavetrade
slavocracy
slenderise
slipperily
slipstream
sluggardly
slumberful
slumberous
smattering
smockfrock
smokedried
smokeproof
snobocracy
solidarism
solidarist
solidarity
solitarily
songstress
songthrush
soundproof
soundtrack
souterrain
southerner
southernly
spacecraft
speargrass
Spencerian
Spenserian
sphalerite
spirograph
sponsorial
spoondrift
spoonerism
squirarchy
stagecraft
staggering
stalwartly
starstream
statecraft
stenograph
stentorian
stepparent
stertorous
stockproof
stonebrash
stonefruit
stormproof
strongroom
stubbornly
stylograph
subaverage
sudatorium
sulphurate
sulphurise
sulphurous
superorder
swaggering
sweetbread
sweetbriar
sweetbrier
sweltering
swordcraft
swordgrass
symmetrise
tabularise
taciturnly
tambourine
tapestried
tardigrade
taxidermal
taxidermic
tearjerker
telpherage
tepidarium
thalecress
thixotropy
thornproof
thumbprint
thunderbox
thundering
thunderous
timeserver
tinctorial
tiringroom
toothbrush
Tractarian
traitorous
transcribe
transcript
transgress
trawlerman
triandrous
trierarchy
triggerman
tumblerful
typescript
underbrush
undercroft
underdress
underproof
undertrick
underwrite
underwrote
undeserved
undesirous
undeterred
ungenerous
uninformed
unremarked
unreserved
untowardly
unwavering
urochordal
urticarial
vectograph
vegetarian
vertebrate
vicegerent
vinegarish
visitorial
vituperate
viviparity
viviparous
vociferant
vociferate
vociferous
voiceprint
vomitorium
waterbrash
watercraft
watercress
waterfront
waterproof
weatherbox
weathering
weatherman
wellspring
wellturned
Wertherian
Wertherism
westwardly
whispering
widespread
windscreen
wingspread
wireworker
witchcraft
woodcarver
woodturner
woodworker
woolsorter
zincograph
zollverein
zwitterion
zygomorphy
abscission
abstersion
abstersive
abstrusely
abstrusity
administer
aggression
aggressive
airmanship
altruistic
anapaestic
anaplastic
Andalusian
andalusite
aneurismal
aneurysmal
annalistic
antecessor
antimasque
aphoristic
apolaustic
appetising
arbalester
arbalister
archaistic
archbishop
aspidistra
Athanasian
authorship
bandmaster
barbershop
battleship
beadleship
billposter
biophysics
blithesome
blockishly
blottesque
bootlessly
bothersome
brandysnap
bucketshop
Buddhistic
burdensome
bursarship
bushmaster
cabalistic
cacomistle
carelessly
carnassial
Carthusian
censorship
centrosome
Charleston

cheapishly
childishly
chiliastic
chromosome
churlishly
Circassian
clannishly
clientship
clothesbag
clothespeg
clothespin
clownishly
collarstud
commissary
commission
commissure
compassion
compasssaw
compensate
compressed
compressor
compulsion
compulsive
compulsory
concession
concessive
conclusion
conclusive
conclusory
concussion
concussive
condensate
condensery
confession
consensual
consulship
conversant
conversely
conversion
convulsant
convulsion
convulsive
cottonseed
cousinship
cowparsley
cradlesong
crocoisite
cuckoospit
cuddlesome
cuirassier
cumbersome
deaconship
declassify
declension
degressive
depressant
depression
depressive
descension
devilishly
diagnostic
dickcissel
Dickensian
digression
digressive
diminished
disclosure
discursive
discussant
discussion
discussive
dishwasher
dismission
dismissive
dispassion
dispensary
dispersant
dispersion
dispersive
dispersoid
dispossess
dissension
dissuasion
dissuasive
distensile
distension
distressed
doctorship
duniwassal
dwarfishly
dynamistic
dysplastic
dysprosium
editorship
embolismic
engrossing
enregister
epiblastic
erethismic
essayistic
eulogistic
euphuistic
Eurovision
expressage
expression
expressive
expressway
eyeglasses
factorship
fadelessly
fatalistic
fathership
fearlessly
fecklessly
fellowship
feverishly
fiendishly
filibuster
flawlessly
forecaster
forecastle
formlessly
fortissimi
fortissimo
fourposter
Franciscan
freakishly
fricasseed
friendship
frolicsome
futuristic
generosity
geognostic
geophysics
gingersnap
goldenseal
graciosity
groundsman
hardfisted
harmlessly
headmaster
heavensent
Hebraistic
hedonistic
heedlessly
helplessly
homoousian
hopelessly
humanistic
humoresque
humoristic
humoursome
hypabyssal
idealistic
immodestly
impression
impressive
impuissant
inapposite
inartistic
incrassate
indecision
indecisive
indigested
Indonesian
ingression
inspissate
interested
internship
introrsely
ironmaster
isoglossal
isoseismal
jackassery
Japanesque
Jehovistic
jingoistic
Kafkaesque
kaisership
kingfisher
lacklustre
languisher
leadership
leafinsect
legalistic
legateship
lifelessly
linguistic
listlessly
loungesuit
lovelessly
lumbersome
luminosity
malfeasant
Malthusian
manifestly
manifestos
marquisate
martensite
mastership
matronship
mayblossom
meddlesome
medicaster
megalosaur
Melanesian
melanistic
membership
mentorship
mettlesome
mindlessly
mintmaster
mismeasure
misprision
mizzensail
monkeysuit
moralistic
mothership
movelessly
namelessly
narcissism
narcissist
nativistic
nebulosity
needlessly
neoclassic
neoplastic
newscaster
nihilistic
nonplussed
novelistic
nucleoside
numerosity
oligopsony
oppression
oppressive
optimistic
organismal
outgassing
outmeasure
overmaster
painlessly
palimpsest
paradisaic
paradisean
paradisiac
paradisian
Parnassian
paroxysmal
pastmaster
pastorship
pederastic
peerlessly
penmanship
percussion
percussive
permission
permissive
perquisite
persuasion
persuasive
perversely
perversion
perversity
perversive
phantasise
phantasmal
phantasmic
phantastic
phantastry
phlogistic
phlogiston
pianissimo
picaresque
pillowslip
pistolshot
pitilessly
plaguesome
pleonastic
plesiosaur
plumassier
pocketsize
polyhistor
Polynesian
populistic
possession
possessive
possessory
postmaster
practising
precession
preciosity
preclusion
preclusive
precursory
prednisone
prehensile
prehension
prepensely
prepossess
pretension
priggishly
princeship
procession
profession
prognostic
promissory
propensity
prophesier
propulsion
propulsive
protensive
protrusile
protrusion
protrusive
puffpastry
pugilistic
pursership
pyrolusite
qualmishly
quizmaster
readership
rechristen
recklessly
rectorship
regentship
regression
regressive
repression
repressive
requiescat
rescission
rescissory
responsive
responsory
restlessly
retrorsely
ringmaster
Romanesque
Romanistic
ruthlessly
sandcastle
sargassoes
scholastic
sciolistic
seamanship
seedvessel
selflessly
selfrising
Sexagesima
sheepishly
shipmaster
shrewishly
siderostat
silverside
simplistic
skirmisher
skittishly
sluggishly
sluttishly
snappishly
snickasnee
snobbishly
solecistic
soullessly
sowthistle
speciosity
spotlessly
squaresail
squireship
statuesque
stepsister
stochastic
strabismal
strabismic
strabismus
strathspey
submersion
submission
submissive
subversion
subversive
successful
succession
successive
sultanship
sunglasses
suppressor
suretyship
surplusage
surprising
suspension
suspensive
suspensoid
suspensory
symphyseal
symphysial
synthesise
synthesist
tactlessly
taskmaster
tearlessly
telecaster
television
televisual
tellership
thermistor
thermostat
thievishly
thwartship
ticklishly
timelessly
tirelessly
titanesque
tonelessly
tortuosity
totemistic
transistor
trespasser
trickishly
tuberosity
tunelessly
umpireship
unassisted
uncloister
unctuosity
undigested
unfinished
unforeseen
unhandsome
unionistic
university
unpleasant
unpleasing
unstressed
vanquisher
varicosity
vernissage
viewlessly
virtuosity
vitalistic
viziership
Waldensian
wappenshaw
wardenship
wellwisher
Winchester
windowseat
windowshop
windowsill
witnessbox
womanishly
wordlessly
workbasket
yardmaster
abdication
aberration
abjuration
abnegation
abreaction
abrogation
absolutely
absolution
absolutism
absolutist
absolutory
absorption
absorptive
abstention
accountant
accounting
accurately
accusation
accusative

accusatory
acervation
acquitting
acrobatics
activation
adamantine
adaptation
adenectomy
adequately
adhibition
adjunction
adjunctive
adjuration
adjuratory
admiration
admonition
admonitive
admonitory
adsorption
adsorptive
advocation
advocatory
aerobatics
aesthetics
aesthetism
affliction
afflictive
agapanthus
alienation
alimentary
allegation
allocation
allocution
allopathic
alpenstock
alteration
alterative
altogether
ambulation
ambulatory
amendatory
ammunition
amphictyon
amputation
anabaptism
anabaptist
ancipitous
anecdotage
anecdotist
Anglistics
angwantibo
annexation
annotation
annulation
antimatter
antipathic
apiculture
apostatise
apparition
appetitive
appointive
appositely
apposition
appositive
apprentice
areolation
arrogation
asafoetida
ascription
aspiration
assafetida
assaultive
assumption
assumptive
asymmetric
attractant
attraction
attractive
auscultate
autochthon
automation
automatise
automatism
automatist
automotive
aviculture
babysitter
backbiting
ballistics
baptistery
barkentine
barometric
baronetage
bedclothes
beforetime
bellwether
bequeathal
bibliotics
bigmouthed
bilocation
birthstone
bissextile
blanketing
bloodstain
bloodstock
bloodstone
bluebottle
bolometric
bonesetter
bottletree
brainstorm
breadstick
breadstuff
brevetting
brigantine
broomstick
brownstone
byelection
cacciatore
caespitose
calamitous
campestral
candletree
capacitate
capacitive
capitation
caricature
castration
catenation
cavitation
chalkstone
charactery
charioteer
chevrotain
chromatics
chromatype
chrysotile
circuitous
cismontane
cispontine
clearstory
clementine
clerestory
clingstone
clinkstone
closestool
coaptation
coexistent
cogitation
cogitative
cohabitant
colatitude
coleoptera
coleoptile
collection
collective
coloration
coloratura
colportage
colporteur
combustion
combustive
comehither
commentary
commentate
committing
commixture
compaction
completely
completion
completive
complotted
concentric
conception
conceptive
conceptual
concertina
concertino
concettism
concoction
concoctive
concretely
concretion
concretise
concretism
concretist
conduction
conductive
confection
conflation
congestion
congestive
conjecture
connection
connective
conniption
consectary
consistent
consistory
consortium
constitute
consuetude
consultant
consulting
consultive
contention
contestant
contextual
contexture
contortion
contortive
contritely
contrition
convection
convective
convention
conventual
conviction
convictive
cooptation
cooptative
copesettic
copulation
copulative
coquettish
corelation
corelative
cornettist
coronation
correction
corrective
corruption
corruptive
cottontail
couverture
crassitude
credential
crispation
crustation
cumulation
cumulative
cunctation
cunctative
curvetting
cuttystool
cyclostome
cyclostyle
datamation
deaeration
debilitate
decapitate
decimation
decoration
decorative
dedication
dedicative
dedicatory
defamation
defamatory
definitely
definition
definitive
definitude
deflection
deflective
delegation
delicately
delightful
delimitate
demolition
demonetise
denegation
denotation
denotative
denudation
depilation
depilatory
depositary
deposition
depository
depuration
depurative
deputation
derivation
derivative
derogation
derogatory
desolately
desolation
desorption
detonation
detonative
detraction
detractive
devolution
diecasting
dielectric
digitately
digitation
dilatation
diminution
diminutive
disburthen
discontent
discretely
discretion
disfeature
disgustful
disruption
disruptive
dissection
dissertate
distention
distortion
divagation
divination
divinatory
dolomitise
domination
dominative
dosimetric
doubletalk
doubletime
dragontree
drysaltery
dubitation
dubitative
Eastertide
ebullition
eczematous
effrontery
egocentric
elementary
elongation
emaciation
emendation
emendatory
emigration
emigratory
emollition
enchanting
energetics
enervation
enervative
englutting
enigmatise
enigmatist
enterotomy
epicentral
epigastric
epiglottal
epiglottic
epiglottis
epiphytism
equipotent
equitation
eructation
escalation
escheatage
estimation
estimative
etiolation
evacuation
evacuative
evaluation
evaluative
evidential
exactitude
exaltation
excavation
excerption
excitation
excitative
excitatory
excogitate
excusatory
execration
execrative
execratory
exhalation
exhaustion
exhaustive
exhibition
exhibitory
exhumation
exorbitant
expedition
expiration
expiratory
exploitage
exploitive
exposition
expositive
expository
expunction
extinction
extinctive
extractant
extraction
extractive
exultation
exuviation
facilitate
fantastico
fasciation
federation
federative
felicitate
felicitous
felspathic
fieldstone
figuration
figurative
filtration
fishkettle
fleabitten
flirtation
floatation
floatstone
florentine
floriation
floristics
fluorotype
fluviatile
flyswatter
forefather
foregather
forfeiture
forgetting
formatting
fortuitism
fortuitist
fortuitous
foundation
foxhunting
freightage
fullbottom
fumigation
galimatias
gargantuan
gemination
generation
generative
generatrix
geocentric
Gilbertian
glaciation
graduation
grandstand
graphitise
gratuitous
gravestone
greenstick
greenstone
greenstuff
grindstone
guillotine
gymnastics
habilitate
habitation
hackbuteer
hackmatack
halfwitted
halieutics
hardbitten
harvestman
hebetation
helianthus
helminthic
hempnettle
hereditary
hesitation
hesitative
heterotaxy

heuristics
hexametric
highoctane
Hindustani
homiletics
humanities
idiopathic
imbibition
immolation
impanation
impenitent
imperative
impolitely
imposition
imprinting
imputation
imputative
inappetent
inaptitude
inchoately
inchoation
inchoative
incitation
incogitant
inconstant
incubation
incubative
incubatory
indagation
indexation
indication
indicative
indicatory
induration
indurative
ineptitude
inexistent
infarction
infighting
infinitely
infinitive
infinitude
inflection
inflective
infliction
inflictive
infraction
inhabitant
inhalation
inheritrix
inhibition
inhibitory
inhumation
iniquitous
initiation
initiative
initiatory
injunction
injunctive
innovation
innovative
innovatory
inquietude
insanitary
insightful
insolation
inspection
inspective
insulation
interstate
interstice
intimately
intimation
intinction
intonation
intubation
inundation
inundatory
invitation
invitatory
invocation
invocatory
involution
iodination
ionisation
irrelative
irrigation
irritation
irritative
Jacobitism
jubilation
judicatory
judicature
kinematics
Kuomintang
laboratory
laceration
lacerative
lamination
Lammastide
laparotomy
lapidation
laureation
Lawrentian
leafcutter
levigation
levitation
liberation
librettist
limitation
limitative
lipomatous
literation
literature
litigation
lobulation
locomotion
locomotive
locomotory
loganstone
loveletter
lustration
maceration
mackintosh
maculation
maculature
malcontent
mangosteen
manometric
mansuetude
manteltree
manumitted
markettown
mastectomy
matchstick
maturation
maturative
mediastina
medication
medicative
meditation
meditative
megalithic
mercantile
Mesolithic
misfortune
mishitting
misventure
mitigation
mitigative
mitigatory
moderately
moderation
moderatism
modulation
monolithic
mosquitoes
motivation
multistage
musicstand
musicstool
mutilation
myxomatous
nanisation
nasturtium
natalitial
nauseating
navigation
neglectful
newsletter
nightstick
nodulation
nominately
nomination
nominative
noncontent
nonfiction
nucleation
nucleotide
numeration
nunciature
obdurately
obligation
obligatory
obturation
occupation
occupative
ocellation
oedematose
oedematous
offputting
offsetting
omnipotent
operettist
oppilation
oppositely
opposition
orchestics
orchestral
ordination
orthoptera
oscitation
osculation
osculatory
outfitting
outputting
outsitting
outstation
outwitting
ovariotomy
overactive
pacesetter
paediatric
pagination
palaeotype
palliation
palliative
palliatory
palmbutter
pancratium
parametric
parasitism
parasitoid
parimutuel
paroxytone
patination
patriotism
patristics
peculation
pejoration
pejorative
pendentive
pentastich
percentage
percentile
perception
perceptive
perceptual
peremptory
perfection
perfective
periosteal
periosteum
peripeteia
permeation
permeative
permitting
peroration
persistent
philistine
phlebotomy
phylactery
phyllotaxy
pigeontoed
pigmentary
pinfeather
pitchstone
plantation
playacting
plecoptera
pneumatics
pogonotomy
poinsettia
polyanthus
polymathic
population
portentous
pothunting
pouncetbox
pragmatise
pragmatism
pragmatist
precaution
preceptive
preceptory
predestine
prediction
predictive
preemption
preemptive
prefecture
prefixture
prehistory
prelection
presbytery
presentday
presentive
prevention
preventive
production
productive
proglottis
prognathic
projectile
projection
projective
promontory
propertied
prophetess
proportion
prostitute
protection
protective
protectory
protectrix
protestant
prudential
punctation
pushbutton
pycnostyle
pyrometric
pyrrhotite
quadratics
quadrature
quantitive
quarantine
quartation
quercitron
radication
rapporteur
rattletrap
razzmatazz
recitation
recitative
recitativo
recreation
recreative
redemption
redemptive
redemptory
reelection
reflection
reflective
refraction
refractive
refractory
refutation
regelation
regretting
regulation
regulative
regulatory
relaxation
relegation
relocation
remonetise
renovation
reparation
reparative
repetiteur
repetition
repetitive
reposition
repository
reputation
resolutely
resolution
resolutive
resorption
resorptive
respectful
respecting
respective
resumption
resumptive
retractile
retraction
retractive
revelation
revelatory
revocation
revocatory
revolution
rheumatics
rheumatism
rheumatoid
rhinestone
rickettsia
rockbottom
rumination
ruminative
saddletree
sagination
salientian
salivation
salutation
salutatory
sanctitude
sanitation
sapiential
sarmentose
sarmentous
saturation
sawtoothed
scarlatina
schematise
schematism
schooltime
sclerotium
sclerotomy
seacaptain
seedpotato
segmentary
selfacting
selfaction
selfesteem
selfmotion
semeiotics
semifitted
semination
sentential
separately
separation
separatism
separatist
separative
separatory
sequential
sequestrum
serpentine
sestertium
sestertius
sexpartite
shantytown
sheabutter
shipfitter
Shrovetide
sibilation
silkcotton
similitude
simulation
simulative
simulatory
singletree
skywriting
slowmotion
slowwitted
smokestack
snakestone
solicitant
solicitous
solicitude
solidstate
solstitial
somatotype
spallation
speciation
spoliation
spoliative
spoliatory
sprightful
springtail
springtide
springtime
squamation
squaretoed
squaretoes
stagnation
stalactite
standstill
starvation
statistics
stenchtrap
stepfather
stepmother
stereotype
stereotypy
stigmatise
stigmatism
stigmatist
stilettoes
stinkstone
stockstill
strabotomy

strengthen
stromatous
stylistics
subcentral
subculture
subduction
subjectify
subjection
subjective
subletting
submitting
submontane
subreption
subroutine
subsection
subsistent
substation
substitute
subvention
suggestion
suggestive
summertime
superation
superstore
supination
suppletion
suppletive
suppletory
supportive
surfactant
susceptive
sustention
sustentive
sweepstake
swordstick
sybaritism
syncretise
syncretism
syncretist
synthetise
synthetist
tabulation
tangential
tattletale
technetium
telemetric
teleostean
telepathic
temptation
tetrastich
tetrastyle
theoretics
thoughtful
throwstick
thumbstall
tickertape
timbertoes
titivation
titubation
toleration
tonguetied
torrential
touchstone
toxication
trabeation
trajection
trajectory
tramontana
tramontane
transition
transitive
transitory
traumatism
travertine
trecentist
triacetate
trichotomy
Tridentine
trimonthly

tripartite
triquetrae
triquetral
trisection
truncately
truncation
turpentine
twelvetone
typesetter
ubiquitous
ulceration
ulcerative
ultimately
unchastity
understand
understate
understeer
understock
understood
understudy
undulation
undulatory
uneventful
unguentary
unipartite
unsporting
upholstery
urtication
ustulation
usucaption
usurpation
validation
vasoactive
vegetation
vegetative
velitation
veneration
vesication
vesicatory
vespertine
vignettist
vindictive
Visigothic
visitation
volumetric
wentletrap
wheatstone
winebottle
wintertide
wintertime
woodcutter
woolgather
accentuate
acetabular
acetabulum
adventurer
aeronautic
affettuoso
Algonquian
anacolutha
babiroussa
barbituric
barramunda
barramundi
bibulously
bicultural
bigamously
bivalvular
blackguard
blamefully
blissfully
bloodguilt
boastfully
brachyural
brachyuran
burramundi
canorously
captiously
caruncular

catechumen
cautiously
cheerfully
clavicular
cloudburst
coachbuilt
coastguard
coatimundi
collocutor
colloquial
colloquise
colloquist
colloquium
connatural
consequent
contiguity
contiguous
continuant
continuate
continuity
continuous
convoluted
coproducer
corbiculae
covetously
craftguild
cumbrously
curricular
curriculum
dampcourse
decorously
delinquent
desirously
dextrously
difficulty
dissoluble
distraught
dolorously
doubtfully
dramaturge
dramaturgy
dreadfully
earthquake
effectuate
enormously
ensanguine
exsanguine
extinguish
extramural
fabulously
factiously
faithfully
fancifully
fascicular
fasciculus
fearnought
febrifugal
fisticuffs
flexuously
floribunda
follicular
forcefully
forecourse
foursquare
fruitfully
fuddyduddy
furuncular
fuzzywuzzy
generously
ghastfully
glomerular
glomerulus
gloriously
glycosuria
glycosuric
gobemouche
golfcourse
gorgeously
gracefully

graciously
grandducal
grapesugar
gratefully
grievously
guilefully
haematuria
hallelujah
headsquare
Herrnhuter
homunculus
honeyguide
houseguest
humorously
hurdygurdy
hurlyburly
hyperdulia
illnatured
importuner
inadequacy
inadequate
incestuous
ineloquent
infamously
infrahuman
infrequent
institutor
interlunar
intramural
intriguant
introducer
jaguarundi
jerrybuilt
kookaburra
lenticular
luminously
lusciously
lustrously
majuscular
mandibular
menopausal
menstruate
menstruous
mercifully
metallurgy
minuscular
mirthfully
misthought
mosasaurus
mournfully
mumbojumbo
mutinously
nauseously
nebulously
nonnatural
nullanulla
numerously
overbought
particular
patulously
peacefully
peduncular
pellicular
peninsular
pennanular
perilously
perpetuate
perpetuity
persecutor
populously
Portuguese
powerfully
preciously
previously
pridefully
procedural
prolocutor
prologuise
prosciutto

prosecutor
racecourse
ranunculus
ravenously
relinquish
reproducer
rightfully
rigorously
salmagundi
scabrously
scornfully
scriptural
sculptural
sculptured
sedulously
selftaught
semidouble
sensuously
shamefully
slothfully
sonorously
spaciously
speciously
spiracular
spiraculum
spirituous
spitefully
sportfully
spuriously
staffnurse
structural
structured
studiously
subsequent
subshrubby
superduper
superhuman
superlunar
tastefully
tentacular
thankfully
timorously
topsyturvy
tortiously
tortuously
touchjudge
trabeculae
trabecular
transducer
transfuser
translucid
translunar
transmuter
triangular
trustfully
truthfully
tubercular
tuberculin
tumultuary
tumultuous
unbesought
unctuously
underquote
unilocular
unlawfully
unmeasured
usuriously
uxoriously
valleculae
vallecular
valorously
vaporously
vengefully
venomously
vermicular
vernacular
versicular
vestibular
vestibulum

vibraculum
vigorously
viperously
virtuously
voluptuary
voluptuous
vorticular
wastefully
watchfully
watchguard
wearifully
wondrously
wrathfully
wrongfully
wrongously
xiphosuran
youthfully
aberdevine
abortively
abrasively
adaptively
adhesively
adoptively
allusively
almsgiving
animadvert
aversively
Belgravian
bolshevise
bolshevism
bolshevist
circumvent
coacervate
coercively
cohesively
confervoid
contravene
controvert
creatively
creativity
deactivate
decisively
delusively
demotivate
derisively
disservice
dissolvent
divisively
effusively
electively
emissivity
eruptively
everliving
eyeservice
facesaving
flagwaving
freeliving
fugitively
gaingiving
herrenvolk
illatively
illusively
inactivate
inactively
inactivity
incisively
irrelevant
lifegiving
lifesaving
lipservice
longaevous
manoeuvrer
manoeuvres
manservant
margravate
margravine
negatively
negativism
negativist

negativity
optatively
positively
positivism
positivist
positivity
proclivity
punitively
pursuivant
putatively
quadrivial
quadrivium
reactivate
reactively
reactivity
recidivism
recidivist
relatively
relativise
relativism
relativist
relativity
rendezvous
selfloving
semidivine
skindiving
sportively
subclavian
timesaving
unswerving
barrenwort
basketwork
bitterwood
brazilwood
breastwall
breastwork
bridgework
brightwork
broadsword
butterwort
buttonwood
caddisworm
candlewick
candlewood
cankerworm
canvaswork
carpetweed
commonweal
cornerwise
cottonweed
cottonwood
cottonwool
crewelwork
disentwine
donkeywork
fiddlewood
galleywest
greasewood
greensward
groundwork
heavenward
hitherward
hollowware
honeysweet
intertwine
intertwist
jasperware
jimsonweed
lengthways
lengthwise
masterwork
motherwort
nationwide
needlework
nipplewort
orangewood
palmerworm
pepperwort
pigeonwing

pistolwhip
ribbonworm
sandalwood
sappanwood
schoolwork
scrollwork
setterwort
shrinkwrap
silverware
silverweed
smallsword
sneezeweed
sneezewood
sneezewort
spiderwort
spleenwort
spongewood
sportswear
springwood
stitchwort
streetward
tetterwort
threadworm
throatwort
thwartwise
tiddlywink
timberwolf
timberwork
tumbleweed
wickerwork
wildfowler
wonderwork
yellowwood
ambidexter
complexion
complexity
homosexual
paradoxure
perplexity
phylloxera
pyridoxine
apocalypse
archetypal
borborygmi
carboxylic
cavalryman
chimneypot
churchyard
cockneyish
cockneyism
coenobytic
countryish
countryman
endophytic
fairycycle
flamboyant
flunkeydom
flunkeyism
foudroyant
glycolyses
glycolysis
gratifying
haemolysis
haemolytic
halophytic
highflying
highwayman
histolysis
histolytic
holophytic
hydrolysis
hydrolytic
hypophyses
hypophysis
journeyman
laundryman
leucocytic
leukocytic
lumberyard

magnifying
matronymic
mesophytic
metaphysic
metronymic
micropylar
monorhymed
motorcycle
nonplaying
nurseryman
patronymic
phagocytic
phenotypic
photolysis
photolytic
polyonymic
prototypal
prototypic
psilocybin
railwayman
satisfying
scaredycat
selfstyled
semidrying
shandrydan
trolleybus
Trotskyism
Trotskyist
Trotskyite
underlying
unedifying
xerophytic
yesteryear
actinozoan
Gorgonzola
isoniazide
kibbutznik
Leibnizian
Palaeozoic
quatorzain
schemozzle
scyphozoan
stargazing

---

abbreviate
aboveboard
accelerate
accentuate
accountant
accumulate
acoelomate
acromegaly
adjudicate
adulterant
adulterate
aficionado
aftergrass
afterimage
aftershave
alimentary
alliterate
altostrati
amalgamate
ameliorate
amphibrach
anecdotage
anemograph
annihilate
annunciate
anticipant
anticipate
apostolate
apothecary
apotropaic
appreciate
architrave
articulate
asphyxiant
asphyxiate

assemblage
asseverate
assibilate
assimilate
attractant
auriculate
auscultate
autodidact
autostrada
autostrade
balderdash
balustrade
barbellate
bargeboard
baronetage
basketball
bathyscaph
Beaujolais
beforehand
behindhand
bichromate
binoculars
biodegrade
birthplace
bisulphate
blackboard
blackguard
blackheart
blastemata
blockboard
bloodstain
bobbinlace
bootstraps
bordereaux
borderland
branchiate
brandyball
breadboard
breastwall
bridesmaid
bridlepath
brigandage
bromegrass
bunchgrass
butterball
buttonball
cachinnate
calceolate
calumniate
calyptrate
camelopard
camouflage
camphorate
cancellate
cannonball
canonicals
canonicate
cantillate
canvasback
capacitate
capitulary
capitulate
carbonnade
carpellary
cataphract
cautionary
cellophane
centigrade
centreback
centrehalf
certiorari
cessionary
chalkboard
chalybeate
chargehand
charismata
chartulary
cheapskate
cheesecake

chessboard
chevrotain
chiffchaff
chinagraph
chlorinate
churchyard
cismontane
Clydesdale
cnidoblast
coacervate
coastguard
cohabitant
collegiate
colourfast
colportage
commandant
commentary
commentate
commissary
compensate
complicacy
complicate
conciliary
conciliate
concordant
condensate
confirmand
confiscate
conglobate
congregant
congregate
consecrate
consectary
consociate
conspiracy
conspirant
constipate
consultant
consummate
contestant
continuant
continuate
contraband
contrabass
conversant
convulsant
coordinate
coradicate
coralsnake
cottoncake
cottontail
couchgrass
counteract
crackajack
crackbrain
crankshaft
crenellate
crossgrain
crossroads
cryptogamy
custommade
cyclograph
daisychain
deactivate
debilitate
decapitate
decelerate
decolorant
deescalate
deflagrate
deforciant
degeneracy
degenerate
delaminate
deliberate
delimitate
demotivate
denaturant
denominate

denunciate
depopulate
depositary
depreciate
depressant
deracinate
desalinate
descendant
desiderata
desiderate
desquamate
detoxicant
detoxicate
Devanagari
diastemata
dichromate
dictionary
dilapidate
discordant
discourage
discrepant
discussant
disenchant
dispensary
dispersant
dissertate
dissociate
distilland
distillate
disulphate
divaricate
dorsigrade
doublebass
doublepark
doubletalk
dragonnade
duumvirate
earthquake
ecclesiast
edulcorate
effectuate
effeminacy
effeminate
elecampane
electorate
elementary
emancipate
emarginate
emasculate
embryonate
emeryboard
enthusiasm
enthusiast
episcopacy
episcopate
epistolary
equivocate
escheatage
everyplace
eviscerate
exaggerate
exasperate
excogitate
excruciate
exenterate
exhilarant
exhilarate
exorbitant
expatriate
exploitage
expressage
exprobrate
extractant
exulcerate
facilitate
faintheart
fastigiate
fatherland
felicitate

fenestrate
fibreboard
fibreglass
fibrillary
fibrillate
fiddleback
fieldglass
fingermark
fingernail
fireescape
firstclass
flabellate
flagellant
flagellate
flamboyant
flashboard
flightpath
floatboard
floatplane
flocculate
floorboard
fluoridate
fluorinate
fluxionary
foreordain
fortepiano
foudroyant
fourinhand
foursquare
frangipane
frangipani
freightage
fritillary
galloglass
gaspereaux
geniculate
goatsbeard
goosegrass
grandstand
grasssnake
greenheart
greenshank
greensward
groundbait
groundmass
habilitate
hackmatack
halogenate
handicraft
harbourage
hawserlaid
headsquare
heartsease
heavenward
hectograph
heliograph
hereditary
hereticate
heterogamy
heterotaxy
hierocracy
hierograph
hierophant
highoctane
Hindustani
hinterland
hippophagy
hitherward
hollowware
holophrase
homoeopath
homologate
housecraft
houseplant
housetrain
hoverplane
hovertrain
husbandage
hyaloplasm

hydrophane
hydroplane
hygrograph
iconoclasm
ilangilang
illiteracy
illiterate
illuminant
illuminate
illuminati
illustrate
immaculacy
immaculate
immoderacy
immoderate
impregnant
impregnate
impuissant
inaccuracy
inaccurate
inactivate
inadequacy
inadequate
inaugurate
incendiary
incinerate
incogitant
inconstant
incrassate
indelicacy
indelicate
inefficacy
infiltrate
ingeminate
ingratiate
inhabitant
innominate
innumeracy
innumerate
inordinate
inosculate
insanitary
inseminate
insouciant
inspissate
insufflate
intenerate
intergrade
interleave
interphase
interplant
interspace
interstate
interweave
intimidate
intolerant
intoxicant
intoxicate
intriguant
invaginate
invalidate
inveteracy
inveterate
invigilate
invigorate
irradicate
irrelevant
italianate
jasperware
johnnycake
juggernaut
justiciary
karyoplasm
knickknack
knifeboard
Krugerrand
Kuomintang
ladderback
lanceolate

landocracy
largescale
lebensraum
lectionary
ledgerbait
legitimacy
legitimate
lemniscate
lemongrass
lengthways
leprechaun
lettercard
leucoplast
licentiate
lieutenant
lighterage
lithograph
lithophane
lowerclass
luciferase
lumberjack
lumberyard
lymphomata
macrophage
magistracy
magistrate
maidenhair
malfeasant
manipulate
manservant
maquillage
margravate
markethall
marquisate
martingale
masquerade
masterhand
matchboard
meadowland
meadowlark
meerschaum
megalosaur
menstruate
metagalaxy
metaphrase
micrograph
mimeograph
ministrant
minutehand
miscellany
missionary
mithridate
mizzenmast
mizzensail
Montagnard
motherland
mouldboard
mountebank
multiphase
multistage
musicstand
Mussulmans
natterjack
naturopath
needlebath
nephograph
nettlerash
neuroplasm
nidificate
nightglass
nightshade
nitrochalk
nonchalant
notchboard
obliterate
obnubilate
obtruncate
ochlocracy
oligoclase

operculate
orthoclase
osteoblast
osteoclast
otterboard
outerspace
oysterfarm
pacificate
paddywhack
palatinate
paniculate
pantograph
pantrymaid
paperchase
paradisaic
paraphrase
paraphrast
pasquinade
passionary
passionate
pasteboard
patriciate
pebbledash
pediculate
pensionary
percentage
perfoliate
perpetrate
perpetuate
persiflage
phonograph
photograph
phyllotaxy
phytophagy
pichiciago
pictograph
pigeonpair
pigmentary
pilgrimage
pillowcase
pillowlace
pilotwhale
pistillary
pistillate
pitchblack
plainchant
planigraph
plasmogamy
plesiosaur
ploughland
plunderage
plutocracy
pointblank
pornocracy
potentiate
pozzuolana
prebendary
predecease
prepackage
presidiary
pretendant
principate
proctorage
profligacy
profligate
prolongate
promulgate
propellant
propionate
propitiate
protestant
protoplasm
protoplast
pseudocarp
psychopath
punchboard
punctulate
pursuivant
quadrumana

quadrumane
quarterage
quaternary
quaternate
quatorzain
quickgrass
radiograph
rattlepate
razorblade
razzmatazz
reactivate
reallocate
recuperate
redcurrant
redecorate
regeneracy
regenerate
registrant
reichsmark
rejuvenate
remarriage
remunerate
repatriate
repopulate
repurchase
resemblant
restaurant
resupinate
reticulate
retrograde
revalidate
rhodophane
ripplemark
saccharate
saddleback
saddlefast
salicylate
saltigrade
sanguinary
sarcophagi
sarcophagy
sarcoplasm
satyagraha
sauerkraut
scaleboard
scapegrace
schizocarp
schooldays
schoolmaam
schoolmarm
schoolmate
scoreboard
screwplate
scrimshank
scutellate
seacaptain
secondhand
secondrate
seedpotato
segmentary
seignorage
selfregard
semilunate
sexagenary
shandygaff
sheepshank
shillelagh
shoreleave
showerbath
shroudlaid
siegetrain
silverbath
silverware
skateboard
skrimshank
slavetrade
slavocracy
sluicegate
smallscale

smokeplant
smokestack
snobocracy
solicitant
solidstate
soundboard
soundtrack
souterrain
spacecraft
spadebeard
spathulate
speargrass
spiflicate
spirograph
splashback
spokeshave
spongecake
springhalt
springtail
squaresail
stablemate
stagecoach
stagecraft
statecraft
stationary
stenograph
stereobate
sterigmata
stipellate
stonebrash
strawboard
streetward
stridulant
stridulate
stringhalt
striptease
stylograph
subaverage
subcordate
submediant
submontane
subsidiary
sulphonate
sulphurate
supergiant
supplejack
supplicant
supplicate
surfactant
surplusage
swashplate
sweatgland
sweepstake
sweetheart
switchback
swordcraft
swordgrass
symposiast
syntagmata
tailormade
tardigrade
tattletale
telpherage
teratomata
terneplate
tessellate
thirdclass
threadbare
threadmark
thumbstall
tickertape
topgallant
tramontana
tramontane
transplant
transshape
treadboard
triacetate
trifoliate

trifurcate
triplicate
triternate
triumphant
trousseaux
tuitionary
tumultuary
turtleback
umbilicate
umbrellaed
underglaze
underlease
underneath
understand
understate
unguentary
uninitiate
unpleasant
upperclass
vaticinate
vectograph
vernissage
vertebrate
vesiculate
veterinary
Victoriana
villainage
villeinage
vitiligate
vituperate
vocabulary
vociferant
vociferate
volleyball
voluptuary
watchglass
watchguard
waterbrash
watercraft
waterglass
whaleshark
wheelchair
whitebeard
windowpane
witchcraft
wonderland
worldclass
worldweary
yellowback
ylangylang
zincograph
abominable
abominably
absorbable
acceptable
acceptably
accessible
accessibly
achievable
acquirable
acrophobia
actionable
actionably
adjustable
admissible
admittable
adsorbable
aerophobia
affirmable
affordable
amerciable
analphabet
analysable
answerable
answerably
appealable
appeasable
applicable
applicably
approvable
approvably
arbitrable
ascendable
ascendible
ascribable
assailable
assessable
assignable
associable
attachable
attackable
attainable
bedchamber
believable
bleachable
blueribbon
breathable
bridgeable
calculable
calculably
candelabra
censurable
changeable
changeably
chargeable
charitable
charitably
chatterbox
choriambic
clothesbag
coagulable
cognisable
cognisably
collatable
colourable
colourably
comestible
commonable
commutable
comparable
comparably
compatible
compatibly
computable
consolable
consumable
convenable
conveyable
corrigible
creditable
creditably
cultivable
damageable
deceivable
deceptible
declarable
declinable
deductible
defeasible
defendable
defensible
defensibly
deferrable
defrayable
degradable
delectable
delectably
demandable
demurrable
dependable
dependably
deplorable
deplorably
deprivable
despicable
despicably
despisable
detachable
detectable
detestable
detestably
dialysable
diffusible
digestible
dislikable
disposable
disputable
disputably
dissoluble
disyllabic
disyllable
divebomber
effaceable
eliminable
employable
endorsable
enumerable
enunciable
eradicable
evaporable
examinable
executable
expandable
expansible
expendable
explicable
exportable
extendible
extensible
extricable
fathomable
fatiguable
favourable
favourably
featherbed
filterable
forgivable
forgivably
formidable
formidably
galliambic
glassfibre
governable
honourable
honourably
hospitable
hospitably
illaudable
illaudably
imaginable
imaginably
immiscible
immiscibly
immoveable
impalpable
impalpably
impartible
impassable
impassably
impassible
impassibly
impeccable
impeccably
implacable
implacably
importable
impossible
impossibly
improbable
improbably
improvable
improvably
impugnable
inclinable
includible
incredible
incredibly
inculpable
incurrable
indictable
ineducable
ineligible
ineligibly
ineludible
inevitable
inevitably
inexorable
inexorably
inexpiable
inexpiably
infallible
infallibly
infeasible
inferrable
inflatable
inflexible
inflexibly
ingestible
inimitable
inimitably
innerrably
inoculable
inoperable
insatiable
insatiably
insensible
insensibly
insociable
insolvable
intangible
intangibly
integrable
interurban
intraurban
invaluable
invaluably
invariable
invariably
invincible
invincibly
inviolable
inviolably
isolatable
jackrabbit
lamentable
lamentably
landlubber
licensable
manageable
manageably
marketable
masticable
measurable
measurably
mensurable
metastable
mistakable
modifiable
negligible
negligibly
negotiable
nosophobia
noticeable
noticeably
notifiable
observable
observably
obtainable
ostensible
ostensibly
oxidisable
pacifiable
packingbox
pardonable
pardonably
pasturable
patentable
penetrable
penetrably
perdurable
perdurably
perishable
permutable
personable
planetable
ploughable
pocketable
ponderable
pouncetbox
predicable
preferable
preferably
prepayable
prescriber
presumable
presumably
procurable
producible
profitable
profitably
propagable
proscriber
psilocybin
punishable
quenchable
realisable
reasonable
reasonably
reassemble
reassembly
rebuttable
recallable
receivable
receptible
recordable
recyclable
redeemable
reeligible
refillable
reflexible
reformable
refundable
reissuable
rejectable
releasable
relievable
relishable
remarkable
remarkably
remediable
remissible
renderable
repairable
repealable
repeatable
reportable
resistible
resolvable
respirable
restorable
retainable
returnable
revealable
reversible
revertible
reviewable
rewardable
rockrabbit
rockribbed
schoolable
searchable
seasonable
seasonably
semidouble
shrinkable
sitophobia
sketchable
snafflebit
soapbubble
squeezable
squeezebox
statutable
statutably
sublimable
subscriber
subshrubby
sufferable
sufferably
summonable
supposable
supposably
surmisable
swinglebar
temperable
tenantable
terminable
terminably
thunderbox
toxiphobia
triturable
trolleybus
trucklebed
trundlebed
unarguable
unbearable
unbearably
unbeatable
unbeatably
unbiddable
undeniable
undeniably
unenviable
unknowable
unnameable
unreadable
unreliable
unscalable
unscramble
unsociable
unsociably
unsuitable
unworkable
utilisable
verifiable
vindicable
voyageable
vulnerable
vulnerably
weatherbox
winebibber
witnessbox
xenophobia
academical
acoustical
alchemical
ammoniacal
amphimacer
anagogical
analogical
analytical
anarchical
anatomical
apolitical
appendices
archdeacon
autarkical
aviatrices
backblocks
biological
blackfaced
bluepencil
bobbysocks
catholicon
catholicos

chimerical
cicatrices
Copernican
coproducer
demoniacal
diabolical
didactical
diplodocus
dogmatical
doughfaced
dramatical
ecological
economical
ecumenical
egoistical
electrical
elliptical
encyclical
epidemical
episodical
eremitical
exegetical
exoterical
fairycycle
fleacircus
Franciscan
freelancer
geodetical
geological
geoponical
gobemouche
goldilocks
grandducal
granduncle
greatuncle
harmonical
haruspices
hermetical
hibernacle
historical
hocuspocus
homocercal
hourcircle
hysterical
iconomachy
inexplicit
introducer
Janusfaced
jesuitical
juristical
lightfaced
liturgical
logistical
magnifical
magnificat
majestical
matriarchy
mechanical
methodical
microfiche
monistical
motorcycle
multifaced
multivocal
myological
neological
nonlogical
oratorical
orological
panopticon
papistical
parsonical
pastyfaced
pathetical
patriarchy
patrilocal
periodical
perithecia
phthisical
pictorical
pokerfaced
pontifical
pontifices
prejudiced
prelatical
premedical
pronounced
pronouncer
prosodical
puristical
quixotical
rabbinical
receptacle
reciprocal
reproducer
republican
requiescat
reverencer
rhetorical
rhythmical
ropedancer
sabbatical
sabretache
sacrificer
scaredycat
semicircle
semiotical
shamefaced
simoniacal
snailpaced
spagyrical
squirarchy
stavesacre
stirrupcup
symbolical
synecdoche
synoptical
tabernacle
Talmudical
tauromachy
taxidancer
theatrical
theistical
theurgical
transducer
translucid
trierarchy
tyrannical
unAmerican
unbalanced
unbiblical
uncritical
whitefaced
zoological
absorbedly
acceptedly
accursedly
acotyledon
admittedly
affectedly
Africander
Afrikander
agitatedly
allrounder
ambassador
animatedly
antependia
antheridia
Armageddon
asteroidal
backhanded
backhander
backslider
backwardly
baldheaded
bareheaded
Barmecidal
bestridden
biliverdin
birdspider
bondholder
boneheaded
bookbinder
botryoidal
bullheaded
cackhanded
calamander
caryatides
caseharden
colonnaded
composedly
compounder
conchoidal
confounded
confusedly
consumedly
coolheaded
copyholder
copyreader
coromandel
crippledom
crossindex
cyclopedia
cyclopedic
degradedly
dejectedly
dementedly
depravedly
deservedly
designedly
desperados
detachedly
didgeridoo
downwardly
drawbridge
dumfounder
evenhanded
everglades
evilminded
expectedly
extendedly
faceharden
fairleader
fairminded
flapdoodle
flunkeydom
footbridge
footcandle
forehanded
foreshadow
fourhanded
freehanded
freeholder
freeloader
frenziedly
fuddyduddy
fungicidal
gaillardia
gasconader
germicidal
gladhander
goaltender
gramicidin
granddaddy
greyheaded
handmaiden
hangglider
hardhanded
hardheaded
heathendom
hebdomadal
hellbender
highbinder
highhanded
highlander
highminded
hodgepodge
hotblooded
interceder
internodal
intertidal
intrepidly
ironhanded
keyboarder
lamentedly
landholder
larvicidal
latifundia
lefthanded
lefthander
likeminded
longheaded
longwinded
lopsidedly
lossleader
Mahommedan
mainlander
manifoldly
matricidal
measuredly
memorandum
misjoinder
mixedmedia
Mohammedan
Muhammadan
Muhammedan
multimedia
newsreader
newsvendor
nonjoinder
onesidedly
openhanded
openminded
orthopedic
outfielder
overburden
overhanded
overlander
overridden
overshadow
packsaddle
palisander
PalmSunday
parricidal
pathfinder
patricidal
pellucidly
pesticidal
prairiedog
preparedly
presentday
prismoidal
profoundly
prolicidal
promenader
propounder
purblindly
quarrender
quarterday
railroader
reconsider
redblooded
referendum
repeatedly
reportedly
reservedly
resignedly
resolvedly
rhomboidal
rhomboidei
ringleader
rockgarden
roofgarden
ropeladder
roughrider
salamander
sashwindow
scaffolder
secludedly
selfbinder
selffeeder
selfguided
selfmurder
shandrydan
sheriffdom
shopwindow
showwindow
sidesaddle
sidewinder
sinusoidal
skewbridge
sluggardly
sobersided
sobersides
softheaded
solenoidal
sphenoidal
spheroidal
spiritedly
splendidly
stadholder
stepladder
stockrider
strainedly
subkingdom
sugardaddy
superorder
supposedly
swanmaiden
taradiddle
tarmacadam
temperedly
tetrahedra
thereunder
thousandth
tollbridge
touchjudge
trochoidal
unattended
undefended
unfriended
unfriendly
ungrounded
unorthodox
untowardly
unwontedly
urochordal
uxoricidal
vermicidal
viewfinder
weakminded
westwardly
WhitMonday
WhitSunday
withholder
woodlander
wretchedly
abjectness
abortively
abrasively
abridgment
abruptness
absolutely
abstergent
abstrusely
absurdness
accoucheur
accrescent
accurately
activeness
adaptively
adequately
adhesively
adjudgment
adjustment
adolescent
adoptively
adroitness
adulteress
advisement
affectless
affeerment
alexanders
alightment
allurement
allusively
altarpiece
ambivalent
ambushment
amercement
ancestress
anchorless
angiosperm
animadvert
anointment
antecedent
anthracene
antifreeze
antipodean
apophthegm
appositely
archpriest
armourless
arrestment
artfulness
arthromere
ascomycete
assentient
assessment
assignment
assoilment
assortment
astringent
astuteness
atmosphere
attachment
attainment
attornment
attunement
auctioneer
augustness
averseness
aversively
avouchment
babblement
backsheesh
bafflement
banishment
baptistery
barrenness
barysphere
battlement
bemusement
beneficent
benevolent
benzpyrene
bestowment
betterment
bewitchery
bibliopegy
bitchiness
bitterness
blastoderm
blastomere
blazonment
bleariness
blitheness
bloodiness
bluishness
borderless
bottlefeed
bottleneck
bottomless
boyishness

braininess
brassiness
brawniness
brazenness
breathless
breechless
breezeless
breeziness
brickfield
bridgehead
bridgeless
brightness
broadsheet
brokenness
broodiness
bufflehead
buffoonery
bullethead
butterbean
buttonless
cajolement
callowness
candescent
candidness
cantonment
carabineer
caravaneer
carpetweed
carragheen
casualness
centromere
chamaeleon
changeless
charactery
charioteer
chasteness
chattiness
chauntress
cheekiness
cheeriness
cheesiness
chersonese
chilliness
choiceness
chubbiness
cinecamera
circumvent
clamminess
Clarenceux
cleverness
cloudiness
cloverleaf
clumsiness
coadjacent
coalescent
coarseness
cocksurely
coercively
coexistent
cohesively
coincident
coleoptera
collarbeam
collarless
colourless
colporteur
comanchero
comeliness
comicopera
commandeer
commandery
commitment
commonness
commonweal
complacent
complement
completely
compliment
comprehend
concretely
concurrent
condensery
condescend
conferment
consequent
consistent
contendent
contingent
contravene
contritely
controvert
convenient
convergent
conversely
copartnery
copperhead
cordillera
corsetiere
coryphaeus
cosentient
costliness
cottonseed
cottonweed
couplement
couturiere
craftiness
cragginess
crankiness
cravenness
creaminess
creatively
creaturely
creepiness
crispbread
crossbreed
crosscheck
crosspiece
crosstrees
crustacean
crustiness
curmudgeon
cursedness
cussedness
daintiness
dauphiness
dazzlement
deadliness
debasement
debatement
debauchery
decampment
decisively
decompress
decrescent
deepfreeze
deerforest
defacement
defilement
definement
definitely
defrayment
delicately
delinquent
delusively
demureness
denouement
department
deployment
deportment
derailleur
derailment
derisively
descendent
designment
desolately
despondent
detachment
detainment
devotement
devoutness
diarrhoeal
diarrhoeic
dictatress
digitately
diluteness
dinnerless
directness
directress
disbelieve
discommend
disconcert
disconnect
discontent
discretely
discutient
dismalness
disownment
dispossess
disrespect
dissilient
dissolvent
distillery
divestment
divineness
divisively
doggedness
doubleness
downstream
dragonhead
dreaminess
dreariness
dressiness
driverless
drowsihead
drowsiness
drysaltery
dunderhead
earthiness
earwitness
echinoderm
edibleness
effacement
effeteness
effortless
effrontery
effusively
elatedness
electively
embalmment
embankment
embarkment
embodiment
embossment
embroidery
embryogeny
emerywheel
employment
encampment
encasement
encashment
encystment
endearment
enfacement
engagement
engulfment
enjambment
enjoinment
enlacement
enlistment
enmeshment
enrichment
enrigiment
entailment
enticement
entireness
entombment
entrapment
epeirogeny
equipotent
equivalent
erubescent
eruptively
escapement
escarpment
escutcheon
evanescent
everywhere
evolvement
excitement
excrescent
experiment
expertness
eyewitness
facileness
Fahrenheit
fallowness
famishment
famousness
fatherless
fathomless
faultiness
fearsomely
feebleness
femaleness
femininely
fervidness
festoonery
fickleness
fictioneer
fiddlehead
fieldpiece
fierceness
figurehead
filthiness
fingerless
finiteness
firescreen
fitfulness
flabbiness
flashiness
flavescent
fleshiness
flightdeck
flightless
flimsiness
flintiness
flocculent
floppiness
florescent
floridness
flowerless
fluffiness
foetidness
folksiness
foresheets
fraudulent
freakiness
freespeech
Frenchness
fricandeau
fricasseed
friendless
frigidness
frilliness
fringeless
friskiness
frizziness
frostiness
frothiness
frutescent
fugitively
fulfilment
futureless
galleywest
garishness
gaucheness
genialness
gentleness
gesundheit
gingerbeer
girlfriend
gladsomely
glassiness
gloominess
glossiness
goldenness
goldenseal
goodliness
gooseflesh
government
grandniece
greasiness
greatniece
greediness
grisliness
grittiness
grogginess
groundless
groundrent
grubbiness
gruesomely
grumpiness
guiltiness
gymnosperm
habiliment
hackbuteer
hairstreak
hakenkreuz
hammerbeam
hammerhead
hammerless
handedness
handsomely
harassment
hartebeest
headcheese
headstream
heartbreak
heartiness
heavensent
hemisphere
heroicness
heterogeny
Hippocrene
hirudinean
hoarseness
hollowness
homeliness
honeysweet
honourless
hookedness
hornedness
horridness
horseflesh
horseleech
houseagent
houseguest
humaneness
humbleness
humbuggery
humourless
hungriness
idolatress
illatively
illusively
imbecilely
immaturely
immurement
impairment
impalement
impartment
impediment
impenitent
impishness
impolitely
impugnment
impureness
inactively
inappetent
incasement
inchoately
incisively
incitement
incoherent
incomplete
increscent
indictment
indiscreet
indiscrete
inditement
inducement
ineloquent
inexistent
infinitely
infrequent
ingredient
inhumanely
innateness
insaneness
insecurely
insentient
insobriety
instalment
instrument
intactness
integument
intendment
intentness
interbreed
internment
interplead
intimately
introrsely
introspect
inventress
investment
inwardness
ionosphere
iridescent
irreverent
jackassery
jaggedness
jardiniere
jauntiness
jejuneness
Jewishness
jimsonweed
jocoseness
Johnsonese
jolterhead
journalese
joyfulness
joyousness
kerseymere
kindliness
kingliness
knockkneed
knottiness
lactescent
lampoonery
lavalliere
lavishment
lavishness
lawfulness
leadenness
leaderless
leafinsect
leopardess
letterhead
letterless
likeliness
limpidness
liquescent
liquidness

lissomness
littleness
liveliness
locustbean
loggerhead
loneliness
lonesomely
lordliness
loveliness
lovingness
lustreless
Maccabaean
maidenhead
mainstream
malacoderm
malcontent
maleficent
malevolent
mallenders
management
manageress
manchineel
manfulness
mangosteen
Manichaean
marcescent
marrowless
marshiness
masterless
matureness
mavourneen
meagreness
measliness
mediatress
medicament
mellowness
mesosphere
mightiness
millstream
mindedness
minuteness
misbelieve
moderately
modernness
modishness
monovalent
mopishness
morbidness
moroseness
morphogeny
motherless
motionless
motiveless
mouldiness
mouthpiece
muffinbell
mulishness
munificent
muttonhead
mythopoeia
mythopoeic
myxomycete
narrowness
nationless
nativeness
negatively
nepenthean
nightdress
nigrescent
nimbleness
nominately
noncontent
nonnuclear
nonpayment
nonviolent
numberless
nympholept
oafishness
obdurately
objectless
oblateness
obtainment
obtuseness
odiousness
omnipotent
omniscient
opalescent
opaqueness
opposeless
oppositely
optatively
orangepeel
ordainment
ornateness
orneriness
orthoptera
otherwhere
otioseness
outpatient
overnicety
overspread
owlishness
packthread
paddyfield
Palaeocene
Palaeogene
palimpsest
pallidness
paltriness
paradisean
paraselene
parliament
parturient
patchiness
peacockery
percipient
periosteal
periosteum
peripeteia
peritoneal
peritoneum
pernickety
persistent
perversely
petiteness
phagedaena
phalangeal
pharyngeal
phelloderm
phillumeny
philopoena
phylactery
phylloxera
placidness
plasmodesm
plecoptera
pliantness
pluckiness
pluperfect
politeness
polychaete
polychrest
polyvalent
porousness
portliness
Portuguese
positively
preachment
preconcert
preeminent
preferment
prefulgent
prepayment
prepensely
prepossess
presbytery
pressagent
pretendent
prettiness
prevenient
prissiness
procumbent
proficient
profitless
promptness
proofsheet
propellent
properness
prophetess
propylaeum
prosilient
proudflesh
puberulent
punishment
punitively
putatively
putrescent
putridness
puzzlement
quadriceps
quadrireme
quaintness
queasiness
quenchless
quirkiness
rabblement
raggedness
rakishness
rancidness
randomness
rapporteur
rattlehead
ravishment
razorshell
reactively
reafforest
rearmament
reasonless
recentness
recoupment
refinement
refringent
refundment
regalement
regardless
relatively
relentless
remediless
remissness
remoteness
repetiteur
resentment
reshipment
resistless
resolutely
respondent
resultless
retirement
retrogress
retrorsely
retrospect
revealment
revilement
rewardless
ricinoleic
ridgepiece
rinderpest
robustness
rockpigeon
roodscreen
rootedness
rottenness
rubberneck
rudderless
ruefulness
ruggedness
runnerbean
sacredness
safetybelt
sailorless
salesclerk
sallenders
sallowness
salmonleap
sanguinely
savageness
savourless
scantiness
scarabaeid
scarabaeus
scarceness
scatheless
scattiness
scavengery
scleroderm
scoresheet
scorzonera
screwpress
scrutineer
sculptress
scurviness
seamstress
searchless
seaserpent
secernment
secondbest
secondment
securement
secureness
sedateness
seducement
seductress
seemliness
selectness
selfdeceit
selfesteem
seltzogene
sempstress
separately
sereneness
settlement
seventieth
severeness
sexivalent
shabbiness
shadowless
shagginess
sheathless
sheepshead
shibboleth
shieldless
shiftiness
shoddiness
shortbread
shovelhead
shrewdness
shrillness
shroudless
sickliness
sideeffect
sidestreet
silentness
silkscreen
silverweed
simpleness
sinfulness
Singhalese
singleness
skimpiness
skinniness
slanginess
sleaziness
sleepiness
sleepyhead
sleeveless
sleighbell
slightness
slipstream
sloppiness
smelliness
smoothness
smudginess
smuttiness
snailwheel
sneakiness
sneezeweed
sniffiness
snootiness
snuffiness
soddenness
solacement
solemnness
sombreness
songstress
sordidness
sparseness
speechless
speediness
spermaceti
spinescent
spiritless
sponginess
spookiness
sportiness
sportively
sportswear
spottiness
springhead
springless
sprucebeer
spruceness
spumescent
spunkiness
squareness
stableness
stanchless
stanchness
starriness
starstream
stationery
steadiness
steamchest
steaminess
steeliness
stepparent
stewardess
stickiness
stinginess
stockiness
stodginess
stolidness
stomodaeum
storminess
straitness
streamless
stressless
strictness
stringbean
stringless
stubbiness
stuffiness
stumpiness
stupidness
sturdiness
subdeanery
subnuclear
subsequent
subsistent
subtleness
subtrahend
suddenness
sufficient
sugariness
sullenness
sultriness
summitless
superbness
supineness
supperless
supplement
suppleness
suspenders
sweatiness
sweetbread
symphyseal
systemless
takingness
talentless
tanglement
tapotement
tawdriness
teenyweeny
telecamera
teleostean
tenantless
tenderness
teratogeny
terreplein
terrorless
tetchiness
thalecress
theodicean
thereanent
thinkpiece
thorniness
threepiece
thriftless
throneless
timberhead
timeliness
tirailleur
tiresomely
toilsomely
tomfoolery
tongueless
toothiness
toothshell
torpidness
torridness
touchiness
tournament
towardness
transgress
trappiness
trashiness
treadwheel
trendiness
trickiness
truncately
trustiness
tumbleweed
turbidness
turgescent
turgidness
turtleneck
ultimately
underdress
understeer
uneasiness
unevenness
unfairness
unforeseen
unholiness
uniqueness
unjustness
unkindness
unlikeness
unmeetness
unripeness
unruliness
untidiness
unwariness
upholstery
uppishness

upwardness
usefulness
varicocele
velocipede
venialness
vesperbell
vicegerent
viceregent
Vietnamese
villainess
virtueless
visionless
vitrescent
vivandiere
wampumpeag
wantonness
watercress
wateriness
waterwheel
weakliness
weaponless
weightless
wheeziness
wickedness
widespread
wildebeest
wilderment
wilderness
wilfulness
willowherb
windowless
windowseat
windscreen
windshield
windsleeve
wingspread
wintriness
wobbliness
woefulness
wonderment
wontedness
woodenhead
woodenness
woodpigeon
woolliness
worthiness
wrathiness
yeastiness
yellowness
yesteryear
zollverein
artycrafty
cockchafer
crossrefer
delightful
despiteful
disdainful
disgustful
eisteddfod
fiftyfifty
fisticuffs
flavourful
frigorific
insightful
lanternfly
meaningful
neglectful
palmatifid
pinnatifid
pitcherful
presageful
purposeful
ragamuffin
remorseful
respectful
revengeful
rosechafer
scientific
selfprofit

slumberful
sprightful
stomachful
successful
tenebrific
thimbleful
thoughtful
tumblerful
umbellifer
uneventful
unfaithful
ungraceful
ungrateful
unmerciful
untruthful
worshipful
accusingly
admiringly
adrenergic
aetiologic
afterlight
alarmingly
annoyingly
arbitrager
arthralgia
arthralgic
astrologer
astrologic
bafflingly
balbriggan
barelegged
becomingly
beefburger
bellringer
birthright
bleatingly
blindingly
bluetongue
blurringly
blushingly
boondoggle
bootlegger
borborygmi
bouncingly
brakelight
broodingly
budgerigar
bumblingly
bunglingly
bushranger
bustlingly
cajolingly
carcinogen
cardialgia
carryingon
cartwright
challenger
charmingly
chuckwagon
coathanger
covetingly
coweringly
crosslight
damagingly
dazzlingly
deadweight
deridingly
dermatogen
discharger
disembogue
disengaged
disparager
distraught
distringas
dogstongue
doubtingly
drawlingly
droopingly
drudgingly

earthlight
encourager
enduringly
engagingly
enticingly
ethnologic
excitingly
exultingly
fearnought
febrifugal
fellmonger
fetchingly
fibrinogen
fireblight
firstnight
fishmonger
fivefinger
flashlight
fleeringly
fleetingly
floatingly
floodlight
florilegia
folksinger
forefinger
forthright
fowlplague
frowningly
fulllength
fumblingly
fussbudget
gametangia
gatelegged
glancingly
golddigger
grapesugar
graspingly
grindingly
growlingly
grudgingly
guestnight
gunslinger
hagiologic
halflength
hauntingly
hemiplegia
hemiplegic
hendecagon
histologic
hydrologic
hypnagogic
imposingly
inkslinger
interregna
invitingly
ironmonger
ladyfinger
landhunger
laughingly
lightingup
lithologic
longlegged
machinegun
makeweight
menacingly
middleaged
middlingly
millwright
misthought
mouthorgan
mudslinger
mystagogic
mystagogue
mythologer
mythologic
nephralgia
newsmonger
nightlight
nostologic

obligingly
odontalgia
oesophagus
ophiologic
outswinger
overbought
overflight
overweight
paddywagon
paedagogic
paedogogue
paraplegia
paraplegic
pathologic
pedalorgan
periwigged
phanerogam
philologen
phonologic
piercingly
pilotlight
playwright
pleadingly
pleasingly
ploddingly
prancingly
pressingly
privileged
prizefight
quadrangle
radiologic
ramblingly
retiringly
rightangle
ringfinger
rockbadger
sandbagger
scathingly
scattergun
scoffingly
scrimmager
selftaught
senseorgan
shenanigan
shiprigged
shipwright
shockingly
sialagogic
sialagogue
slantingly
snapdragon
sneakingly
sneeringly
snubbingly
sociologic
soothingly
soundingly
spankingly
sportingly
squeteague
steamtight
stiflingly
stingingly
stinkingly
strikingly
stunningly
sweepingly
swimmingly
swingingly
taperingly
tauntingly
teleologic
temptingly
testflight
thinkingly
torchlight
touchingly
toweringly
travelogue

triflingly
tropologic
trustingly
unabridged
unbesought
unendingly
unerringly
unfadingly
wainwright
watertight
wavelength
waveringly
wharfinger
witchingly
yearningly
yieldingly
acronychal
agapanthus
airmanship
allopathic
altogether
anaglyphic
anamorphic
antipathic
apocryphal
archbishop
authorship
autochthon
barbershop
battleship
beadleship
bedclothes
bellwether
bellyacher
bequeathal
bibliophil
bigmouthed
biographer
biographic
biomorphic
blockishly
bucketshop
bursarship
censorship
cheapishly
childishly
churlishly
clannishly
clientship
clownishly
comehither
consulship
cousinship
cowcatcher
cowpuncher
deaconship
despatcher
devilishly
diagraphic
diminished
disburthen
dishwasher
dispatcher
doctorship
dwarfishly
dysgraphia
dystrophic
editorship
encroacher
eosinophil
epigrapher
epigraphic
factorship
farfetched
fathership
fellowship
felspathic
feverishly
fiendishly

flycatcher
footlights
forefather
foregather
Francophil
freakishly
friendship
geographer
geographic
helianthus
helminthic
heptarchic
hierarchal
hierarchic
idiopathic
internship
isomorphic
kaisership
kingfisher
languisher
leadership
legateship
lowpitched
mastership
matronship
megalithic
membership
mentorship
Mesolithic
mismatched
monolithic
mothership
moustached
moustachio
oligarchic
orographic
pastorship
penmanship
pinfeather
pistolshot
pistolwhip
polyanthus
polymathic
priggishly
princeship
prognathic
pursership
pyrotechny
qualmishly
ratcatcher
readership
rectorship
regentship
researcher
sawtoothed
seamanship
sheepishly
shrewishly
skirmisher
skittishly
sluggishly
sluttishly
snappishly
snobbishly
squireship
stepfather
stepmother
strengthen
sultanship
suretyship
telepathic
tellership
tetrarchic
theosopher
thermophil
thievishly
thoroughly
thwartship
ticklishly

tribrachic
trickishly
triglyphic
trimonthly
trimorphic
tryptophan
ulotrichan
umpireship
unattached
unblenched
unfinished
vanquisher
verandahed
Visigothic
viziership
wappenshaw
wardenship
wellwisher
windowshop
womanishly
woolgather
zoomorphic
abacterial
abdication
aberdevine
aberration
abiogenist
abjuration
ablebodied
abnegation
abreaction
abrogation
abscission
absolution
absolutism
absolutist
absorption
absorptive
abstention
abstersion
abstersive
abstrusity
accomplice
accomplish
accounting
accusation
accusative
acervation
achondrite
acidophile
acquitting
acrobatics
acroterion
acroterium
actinolite
activation
adamantine
adaptation
adhibition
adjunction
adjunctive
adjuration
admiration
admonition
admonitive
adrenaline
adsorption
adsorptive
Adullamite
adulterine
advocation
aerobatics
aeroengine
aerologist
aeronomist
aesthetics
aesthetism
Aethiopian
affability
affliction
afflictive
Africanise
Africanism
Africanist
afterpains
aggrandise
aggression
aggressive
agrologist
agronomist
aircooling
aircushion
alcoholise
alcoholism
algebraist
algologist
Algonquian
alienation
alkalinity
allegation
allegorise
allegorist
allocation
allocution
alloverish
almsgiving
alteration
alterative
amateurish
amateurism
ambulation
Amerindian
amiability
ammunition
amputation
anabaptism
anabaptist
anchorring
Andalusian
andalusite
androecium
anecdotist
anemophily
Anglistics
anglophile
angularity
angwantibo
annexation
annotation
annularity
annulation
anopheline
antagonise
antagonism
antagonist
anthracite
Antichrist
antimonial
antimonite
antinomian
antiSemite
antisocial
antitheism
antitheist
Apollinian
Apollonian
apostatise
apothecial
apothecium
apparition
apperceive
appetising
appetitive
appointive
apposition
appositive
apprentice
aquamarine
aquilinity
araucarian
archerfish
areolation
Areopagite
arrogation
artificial
asafoetida
asceticism
ascription
asexuality
asparagine
aspiration
assafetida
assaultive
assumption
assumptive
Athanasian
attraction
attractive
audibility
audiophile
auditorial
auditorium
Australian
automation
automatise
automatism
automatist
automobile
automotive
autonomist
aventurine
axiologist
Babylonian
backbiting
backstairs
ballistics
ballooning
balloonist
barkentine
barrelling
bassoonist
bastardise
batfowling
batrachian
beautician
beautifier
beekeeping
beforetime
Belgravian
belletrist
benedicite
beneficial
Benthamism
Benthamite
benzocaine
Berkeleian
bestialise
bestiality
bestirring
bibliotics
bilocation
bimestrial
biochemist
biometrics
biophysics
bipolarity
birdstrike
bissextile
bisulphide
bisulphite
bitterling
bituminise
Blackshirt
blacksmith
blanketing
blepharism
blistering
blithering
blitzkrieg
bloodguilt
bolshevise
bolshevism
bolshevist
bombardier
bookmaking
borderline
Boswellian
Boswellise
Boswellism
bourbonism
bourbonist
bowdlerise
bowdlerism
bradyseism
Brahmanism
Brahminism
brainchild
bratticing
breadstick
breakpoint
brevetting
brigandine
brigandism
brigantine
Britishism
broomstick
brownshirt
bryologist
Buchmanism
Buchmanite
bumpkinish
burglarise
butterfish
buttermilk
byelection
cacogenics
Caledonian
cancelling
candlefish
candlewick
canonicity
cantatrice
capability
capacitive
capitalise
capitalism
capitalist
capitation
Capitoline
cappuccino
carabinier
caramelise
carnallite
carnassial
Carthusian
cartoonist
castration
catabolism
catarrhine
categorise
catenation
catoptrics
causticity
cavitation
centennial
centillion
centralise
centralism
centralist
centrality
centricity
ceremonial
chandelier
changeling
channelise
chatelaine
chauvinism
chauvinist
checkpoint
chiffonier
chiselling
Christlike
chromatics
chronicity
chrysolite
chrysotile
Ciceronian
cicisbeism
cinchonine
cinerarium
Circassian
circumcise
cispontine
Cistercian
claspknife
classicise
classicism
classicist
classified
classifier
clementine
coachbuilt
coaptation
cockatrice
cockneyish
cockneyism
coequality
coeternity
coffeemill
cogitation
cogitative
colchicine
coleoptile
coleorhiza
collection
collective
colloquial
colloquise
colloquist
colloquium
coloration
combustion
combustive
comicality
commanding
commercial
commission
committing
compaction
compassion
compatriot
compelling
compendium
completion
completive
complexion
complexity
complicity
compromise
compulsion
compulsive
conception
conceptive
concerning
concertina
concertino
concession
concessive
concettism
concinnity
conclusion
conclusive
concoction
concoctive
concretion
concretise
concretism
concretist
concurring
concussion
concussive
conduction
conductive
confabbing
confection
conferring
confession
conflation
conformism
conformist
conformity
congestion
congestive
connection
connective
conniption
consortium
constraint
consulting
consultive
contention
contiguity
continuity
contortion
contortive
contradict
contrarily
contrition
convection
convective
convention
conversion
conviction
convictive
convincing
convulsion
convulsive
cooptation
cooptative
copulation
copulative
coquettish
corbelling
cordiality
cordierite
corelation
corelative
Corinthian
cornerwise
cornettist
coronation
corporeity
correction
corrective
corruption
corruptive
countryish
craftguild
cranesbill
creatinine
creativity
credential
crispation
crocoisite
crustation
cryogenics
cuckoopint
cudgelling
cuirassier
cumulation
cumulative
cunctation
cunctative
curability

curatorial
curvetting
cuttlefish
cytologist
datamation
deaeration
Decembrist
decimalise
decimalism
decimation
decivilise
declassify
declension
decolonise
decolorise
decoration
decorative
dedication
dedicative
defamation
defeminise
definition
definitive
deflection
deflective
degressive
dehumanise
dehumidify
delegation
delocalise
delphinium
demagogism
demobilise
demolition
demonetise
demoralise
denegation
denotation
denotative
dentifrice
denudation
depilation
depolarise
deposition
depression
depressive
depuration
depurative
deputation
derestrict
derivation
derivative
derogation
descension
desolation
desorption
detonation
detonative
detraction
detractive
devitalise
devocalise
devolution
dextrality
diatropism
Dickensian
diecasting
diesinking
digitalise
digitation
digression
digressive
dilatation
dilatorily
diminution
diminutive
dimorphism
directoire
disability
disappoint
disbarring
disbudding
discerning
discipline
disconfirm
discophile
discretion
discursive
discussion
discussive
disentwine
disfurnish
disincline
dismission
dismissive
dispassion
dispelling
dispersion
dispersive
disqualify
disruption
disruptive
dissection
dissension
disservice
dissuasion
dissuasive
distensile
distension
distention
distilling
distortion
disulphide
disutility
divagation
divination
dolomitise
domination
dominative
doubletime
downstairs
drawstring
drivelling
drosophila
dubitation
dubitative
durability
dysprosium
earthshine
earwigging
easterling
Eastertide
ebullition
efficacity
elasticise
elasticity
Eleusinian
elongation
emaciation
emancipist
embonpoint
emendation
emigration
emissivity
emollition
emparadise
empiricism
empiricist
emulsifier
enamelling
enamellist
enchanting
endemicity
endopodite
energetics
enervation
enervative
englutting
engrossing
enigmatise
enigmatist
ensanguine
enterolith
enterprise
entrancing
enwrapping
ephorality
epilimnion
epiphytism
epithelial
epithelium
equability
equanimity
equatorial
equestrian
equitation
erectility
ergodicity
ergonomics
ergonomist
eructation
escalation
escritoire
Esculapian
estimation
estimative
eternalise
eternalist
ethicality
ethologist
etiolation
eudemonism
eudemonist
eugenicist
euhemerise
euhemerism
euhemerist
Eurovision
evacuation
evacuative
evaluation
evaluative
evangelise
evangelism
evangelist
everliving
everything
evidential
exaltation
excavation
excerption
excitation
excitative
execration
execrative
exhalation
exhaustion
exhaustive
exhibition
exhumation
expedition
expiration
exploitive
exposition
expositive
expression
expressive
expunction
exsanguine
extinction
extinctive
extinguish
extraction
extractive
extraneity
exultation
exurbanite
exuviation
eyeservice
facesaving
factualism
factualist
factuality
fanaticise
fanaticism
fantastico
fantoccini
fasciation
fatherlike
feathering
federalise
federalism
federalist
federation
federative
feminality
femininity
fescennine
fictionist
figuration
figurative
filtration
fingerling
finicality
firepolicy
fixedpoint
flaccidity
flagwaving
flashpoint
flattering
flavouring
fledgeling
flirtation
floatation
florentine
floriation
floristics
flowergirl
flunkeyism
fluviatile
flyfishing
folklorist
forbidding
foreboding
foreignism
forgetting
formatting
fortissimi
fortissimo
fortuitism
fortuitist
forwarding
forwearied
fosterling
foundation
Fourierism
foxhunting
fraternise
fraternity
fratricide
freeliving
friability
friendlily
frivolling
frolicking
fruitarian
fulfilling
fullbodied
fumigation
funnelling
fusibility
gadolinite
gadolinium
gadrooning
gaingiving
galimatias
Gallophile
gambolling
garnierite
garnishing
gelatinise
gemination
generalise
generalist
generality
generation
generative
generosity
geneticist
genteelism
geochemist
geometrise
geophysics
geotropism
geriatrics
geriatrist
Ghibelline
Gilbertian
glaciation
Glaswegian
glauberite
glauconite
glimmering
glossarial
glossarist
gluttonise
gnosticism
Godfearing
gormandise
graciosity
gradualism
gradualist
graduation
grammarian
grandchild
grangerise
grangerism
graphemics
graphitise
graptolite
gratifying
greenstick
gressorial
groundling
grovelling
guillotine
gunrunning
gymnastics
gypsophila
habitation
hairspring
halberdier
halieutics
handspring
Hanoverian
Hansardise
hanselling
haustorium
headspring
heathenise
heathenish
heathenism
hebetation
Heliconian
henharrier
henotheism
henotheist
heparinise
hesitation
hesitative
heulandite
heuristics
highflying
hippogriff
hipsterism
hobnobbing
hoitytoity
homecoming
homemaking
homiletics
homogenise
homologise
homoousian
honeyguide
honorarium
horologist
hostelling
houselling
humanities
humbugging
humidifier
hydraulics
hydrophily
hylotheism
hypanthium
hypocorism
ideologist
ignobility
illegalise
illegality
illuminism
illuminist
illusorily
imbecility
imbibition
immaterial
immaturity
immemorial
immobilise
immobility
immolation
immoralist
immorality
impanation
imparadise
imperative
imposition
impoverish
impression
impressive
imprinting
impudicity
imputation
imputative
inactivity
inapposite
inbreeding
incapacity
inchoation
inchoative
incitation
incivility
incubation
incubative
indagation
indecision
indecisive
indefinite
indexation
indication
indicative
indocility
Indonesian
induration
indurative
industrial
inequality
infarction
infelicity
infidelity
infighting
infinitive
inflection
inflective

infliction
inflictive
infraction
infusorial
infusorian
ingression
inhalation
inhibition
inhumanity
inhumation
initialise
initiation
initiative
injunction
injunctive
innovation
innovative
insecurity
insipidity
insolation
inspanning
inspection
inspective
instilling
insularism
insularity
insulation
interstice
intertrigo
intertwine
intertwist
intimation
intinction
intonation
intubation
inundation
inurbanity
invalidism
invalidity
inveracity
invitation
invocation
involution
iodination
ionisation
iridosmine
irrelative
irreligion
irrigation
irritation
irritative
Ishmaelite
isometrics
isoniazide
italianise
Italianism
Italophile
jacobinise
Jacobinism
Jacobitism
janitorial
jaywalking
jeopardise
jerrybuilt
jocularity
johnsonian
journalise
journalism
journalist
jubilation
juvenility
Kantianism
katabolism
kennelling
keratinise
kidnapping
kimberlite
kinematics
kineticist
kriegspiel
Krishnaism
laceration
lacerative
laconicism
lacustrine
Lamarckian
Lamarckism
laminarian
lamination
Lammastide
lampoonist
landowning
lanthanide
lapidarian
lapidarist
lapidation
laterality
laureation
laurelling
lavatorial
lawabiding
lawrencium
Lawrentian
ledgerline
legibility
legitimise
legitimism
legitimist
Leibnizian
lengthwise
lepidolite
lesbianism
levigation
levitation
liberalise
liberalism
liberalist
liberality
liberation
librettist
lifegiving
lifesaving
limitation
limitative
lipreading
lipservice
literalise
literalism
literalist
literality
literarily
literation
lithotrity
Lithuanian
litigation
lobulation
locomotion
locomotive
logicality
logrolling
Lollardism
lovemaking
lowprofile
luminosity
Lusitanian
lustration
lutestring
lycopodium
lyophilise
Lysenkoism
macadamise
maceration
maculation
magnifying
maidenlike
mainspring
malleebird
Malpighian
Malthusian
managerial
Manicheism
manicurist
manuscript
maraschino
Marcionite
margravine
marguerite
martensite
martialism
marvelling
mastermind
matchstick
maturation
maturative
maximalist
mayonnaise
mediastina
medication
medicative
mediocrity
meditation
meditative
Melanesian
mercantile
mesomerism
messianism
metabolise
metabolism
metabolite
metamerism
micaschist
microcline
microseism
midmorning
militarily
militarise
militarism
militarist
millennial
millennium
mineralise
minimalism
minimalist
mishitting
misogamist
misogynist
misologist
misprision
missionise
miswording
mitigation
mitigative
mixolydian
moderation
moderatism
modulation
moisturise
monarchial
Monarchian
monarchism
monarchist
monetarily
monetarism
monetarist
mongrelise
mongrelism
monitorial
monogamist
monogenism
monogynian
monologise
monologist
monomaniac
monopodial
monopodium
monopolise
monopolist
monotheism
monotheist
moratorium
morphemics
morphinism
morrispike
mosaicking
motivation
mousseline
Mousterian
movability
muliebrity
multiplier
musicality
mutability
mutilation
mycologist
mycorrhiza
myocardium
nailpolish
nanisation
narcissism
narcissist
nasturtium
natalitial
natatorial
natatorium
nationwide
naturalise
naturalism
naturalist
nauseating
navigation
nebulosity
necrophile
necrophily
needlefish
negativism
negativist
negativity
negrophile
nephridium
neutralise
neutralism
neutralist
neutrality
nickelling
nicotinism
nightshift
nightshirt
nightstick
nitpicking
nodulation
nominalism
nominalist
nomination
nominative
nomologist
nonfiction
nonplaying
nosologist
notability
nourishing
novaculite
nucleation
nucleonics
nucleoside
nucleotide
numeration
numerosity
nuptiality
obituarist
obligation
obstetrics
obturation
occupation
occupative
oceanarium
oceangoing
ocellation
octandrian
octodecimo
octonarian
oecologist
oecumenism
oenologist
offputting
offsetting
oldmaidish
ommatidium
oncologist
ontologist
operettist
ophicleide
opinionist
oppilation
opposition
oppression
oppressive
opprobrium
optimalise
orchardist
orchestics
ordinarily
ordination
Ordovician
oreologist
organicism
organicist
orotundity
orthoepist
oscitation
osculation
osmeterium
osmiridium
otherwhile
outbidding
outfitting
outgassing
outgunning
outlandish
outpouring
outputting
outrunning
outsitting
outstation
outwitting
overactive
overexcite
overpraise
overrefine
overriding
overstride
pacificism
pacificist
paedophile
pagination
palaeolith
palagonite
palatalise
palliation
palliative
Panamanian
pancratium
panegyrise
panegyrist
pansophist
papaverine
paperknife
parabolise
paradisiac
paradisian
paralogise
paralogism
paramecium
parapodium
parasitism
parcelling
Parnassian
parrotfish
parsonbird
partiality
Passionist
pastellist
pasteurise
pasteurism
patination
patriality
patriotism
patristics
patrolling
peacockish
peculation
pedagogics
pedalpoint
pedestrian
pedicurist
pedologist
pejoration
pejorative
pencilling
pendentive
pennillion
penologist
penpushing
pentastich
peppermill
peppermint
percentile
perception
perceptive
percussion
percussive
perfection
perfective
performing
perihelion
permeation
permeative
permission
permissive
permitting
peroration
peroxidise
perpetuity
perplexity
perquisite
persuasion
persuasive
perversion
perversity
perversive
phallicism
phantasise
pharisaism
pharmacist
philippina
philippine
philistine
phlogopite
Phoenician
photophily
photoprint
physicking
pianissimo
picayunish
picketline
picnicking
pigeonwing
pilgarlick
pincerlike
pincushion
piperidine
pistolling
pistonring
plagiarise
plagiarism

plagiarist
plantation
plasmodium
plasticise
plasticity
playacting
plebiscite
pliability
plumassier
pneumatics
pocketsize
podiatrist
polemicist
polemonium
politician
politicise
polygamist
polygenism
polygenist
polymerise
polymerism
Polynesian
polynomial
polyploidy
polytheism
polytheist
Pomeranian
pomologist
popularise
popularity
population
positivism
positivist
positivity
possession
possessive
postchaise
postillion
postliminy
postoffice
postscript
potability
potbellied
pothunting
practician
practising
praecocial
praemunire
praesidium
praetorial
praetorian
pragmatise
pragmatism
pragmatist
preadamite
precaution
preceptive
precession
preciosity
preclusion
preclusive
precordial
predestine
prediction
predictive
preemption
preemptive
preexilian
preferring
preglacial
prehensile
prehension
prelection
presentive
presignify
pressurise
pretension
prevailing
prevention
preventive
priestling
primordial
primordium
princeling
principial
principium
proceeding
procession
proclivity
proctorial
proctorise
production
productive
profession
profundity
projectile
projection
projective
prologuise
promethium
propelling
propensity
propertied
prophesier
proportion
propulsion
propulsive
prosaicism
proscenium
prosperity
prostomial
prostomium
protection
protective
protensive
protrusile
protrusion
protrusive
proverbial
provincial
prudential
psalmodise
psalmodist
psalterium
psittacine
psychicism
psychicist
Ptolemaist
publishing
puerperium
pummelling
punctation
pupilarity
puritanise
puritanism
purseseine
putrescine
pyridoxine
pyrolusite
pyromaniac
pyroxenite
Pyrrhonian
Pyrrhonism
Pyrrhonist
pyrrhotite
quadratics
quadrivial
quadrivium
quantifier
quantitive
quarantine
quartation
quartering
quaternion
quaternity
quinacrine
Rachmanism
radicalise
radicalism
radication
rainmaking
ratability
reactivity
reappraise
recidivism
recidivist
recitalist
recitation
recitative
recitativo
recolonise
recreation
recreative
redemption
redemptive
redescribe
reelection
reflection
reflective
refraction
refractive
refreshing
refuelling
refutation
regelation
regression
regressive
regretting
regularise
regularity
regulation
regulative
rejuvenise
relativise
relativism
relativist
relativity
relaxation
relegation
relinquish
relocation
remonetise
renovation
reorganise
reparation
reparative
repertoire
repetition
repetitive
reposition
repression
repressive
reputation
rescission
resolution
resolutive
resorption
resorptive
resounding
respecting
respective
responsive
resumption
resumptive
retractile
retraction
retractive
retraining
reunionism
reunionist
revalorise
revanchism
revanchist
revelation
revitalise
revivalism
revivalist
revocation
revolution
rhapsodise
rhapsodist
rheologist
rheumatics
rheumatism
ribbonfish
riproaring
risibility
rodfishing
roistering
rollicking
rontgenise
rosaniline
roseengine
rudderfish
ruffianism
rumination
ruminative
rumrunning
rupicoline
Russianise
Russophile
saccharide
saccharify
saccharine
sacroiliac
sagination
salability
salientian
salivation
salpingian
salutarily
salutation
samarskite
sanatorium
sanctifier
sanderling
sanguinity
sanitarian
sanitarily
sanitarium
sanitation
sapiential
sapphirine
satisfying
saturation
saxicoline
scandalise
scansorial
scarlatina
scattering
scepticism
schematise
schematism
schoolgirl
schooltime
Scillonian
sclerotium
Scotticise
Scotticism
scratchily
scribbling
scrutinise
scurrility
seamanlike
secretaire
secularise
secularism
secularist
secularity
seignorial
seismicity
selfacting
selfaction
selfdenial
selfloving
selfmotion
selfpraise
selfrising
selfruling
semeiotics
semestrial
semidivine
semidrying
seminarian
seminarist
semination
semiuncial
senatorial
sensualise
sensualism
sensualist
sensuality
sentential
separation
separatism
separatist
separative
septennial
septennium
septillion
Septuagint
sequential
serologist
serpentine
sestertium
sestertius
Sexagesima
sexologist
sexpartite
sextillion
shanghaier
sheathbill
sherardise
shirtwaist
shoestring
shortening
shovelling
Shrovetide
shuttering
sibilation
sicklebill
siderolite
signalling
silverfish
silverside
similarity
simplicity
simplifier
simulation
simulative
sinecurism
sinecurist
sinologist
skibobbing
skijumping
skindiving
skyjacking
skywriting
Slavophile
sleevelink
slenderise
slipperily
slowmotion
smaragdine
smaragdite
smattering
smokedried
sneakthief
snivelling
snowmobile
solidarism
solidarist
solidarity
solifidian
solitarily
solstitial
solubilise
solubility
Sorbonnist
sororicide
spallation
Spartacist
spasticity
spatiality
specialise
specialism
specialist
speciality
speciation
speciosity
Spencerian
Spenserian
spermicide
sperrylite
sphalerite
sphericity
spherulite
spiderline
spillikins
spiralling
spoliation
spoliative
sponsorial
spoondrift
spoonerism
sporangial
sporangium
springlike
springtide
springtime
sprinkling
squalidity
squamation
squireling
staggering
stagnation
stalactite
stalagmite
standpoint
standstill
staphyline
stargazing
starvation
starveling
statistics
staurolite
stealthily
stentorian
stephanite
stiffening
stigmatise
stigmatism
stigmatist
stillicide
stockstill
stoneblind
stonesnipe
storksbill
stramonium
strategist
streamline
strychnine
strychnism
stylistics
stypticity
subacidity
subclavian
subduction
subglacial
subheading
subjectify
subjection
subjective
subletting

submersion
submission
submissive
submitting
subreption
subroutine
subsection
subsellium
subspecies
substation
subvention
subversion
subversive
succession
successive
sudatorium
suffragist
suggestion
suggestive
sulphurise
summerlike
summertime
superation
supination
suppletion
suppletive
supportive
surprising
surrealism
surrealist
susceptive
suspension
suspensive
sustaining
sustention
sustentive
swaggering
swanupping
sweatshirt
sweetbriar
sweetbrier
sweetening
sweltering
swivelling
swordstick
sybaritism
symmetrise
sympathise
symphonion
symphonist
symphysial
syncretise
syncretism
syncretist
synonymist
synonymity
synthesise
synthesist
synthetise
synthetist
tabularise
tabulation
tailorbird
tamability
tambourine
tangential
tankengine
tapestried
Tartuffian
Tartuffism
tasselling
taxability
taxonomist
technetium
technician
technicist
television
temptation
tenability
tepidarium
tetrastich
textualist
theodolite
theogonist
theologian
theologise
theologist
theoretics
thermopile
thickening
threadfish
threnodial
threnodist
throwstick
thumbprint
thundering
thwartwise
tiddlywink
timberline
timesaving
tinctorial
tinselling
titivation
tittupping
titubation
toleration
tonguetied
topazolite
topicality
topologist
torrential
tortellini
tortuosity
tourmaline
toxication
trabeation
Tractarian
trajection
trampoline
trancelike
transcribe
transcript
transition
transitive
traumatism
travelling
travertine
trecentist
trepanning
trichinise
trichroism
triclinium
tricyclist
Tridentine
tripartite
triplicity
trisection
triskelion
trivialise
trivialism
triviality
troctolite
trollopish
trombonist
Trotskyism
Trotskyist
Trotskyite
trowelling
truncation
tuberosity
tunnelling
turpentine
typescript
typicality
typologist
Tyrrhenian
ulceration
ulcerative
unassuming
unavailing
unbecoming
unblinking
unblushing
unchanging
unchastity
unctuosity
undercliff
underlying
undershirt
underskirt
undertrick
underwrite
undulation
unedifying
unfamiliar
unfeminine
unflagging
ungrudging
unicyclist
uniformity
unipartite
university
unmorality
unoccupied
unofficial
unpleasing
unsettling
unsporting
unsteadily
unswerving
unthinking
unwavering
unwieldily
unworthily
unyielding
upbraiding
upbringing
upstanding
urticarial
urtication
ustulation
usucaption
usurpation
utopianism
validation
vanadinite
varicosity
vasoactive
Vaticanism
Vaticanist
vegetarian
vegetation
vegetative
velitation
veneration
vesication
vespertine
vignettist
vindictive
vinegarish
virologist
virtuality
virtuosity
visibility
visitation
visitorial
vitaminise
vitriolise
viviparity
voiceprint
volatilise
volatility
volubility
vomitorium
Waldensian
wassailing
waterskier
wattlebird
weathering
weaverbird
wellspring
Wertherian
Wertherism
westernise
whirlybird
whiskified
whispering
whitesmith
windowsill
wintertide
wintertime
wolframite
worthwhile
wrongdoing
wunderkind
Wycliffite
Wykehamist
yellowbird
zigzagging
zwitterion
chaparajos
chaparejos
hallelujah
barebacked
besprinkle
bivouacked
bluejacket
boneshaker
bookmarker
bootlicker
caseworker
coalbunker
comstocker
corncockle
cornflakes
dressmaker
dustjacket
fairspoken
fleamarket
freespoken
goatsucker
goodlooker
halfcocked
hamshackle
handpicked
handworked
highjacker
hitchhiker
hokeypokey
humpbacked
icebreaker
ironworker
jawbreaker
kenspeckle
landlocked
lawbreaker
lifejacket
lumpsucker
matchmaker
merrymaker
mineworker
moneymaker
moneytaker
mossbunker
moviemaker
noisemaker
nondrinker
nutcracker
overcooked
overlooker
papermaker
pawnbroker
peacemaker
periwinkle
pickpocket
pigsticker
pockmarked
ramshackle
ringnecked
ropewalker
seersucker
selfseeker
semiweekly
shellacked
shipbroker
shoebuckle
shopwalker
slitpocket
soapflakes
softspoken
swaybacked
tearjerker
trafficked
trafficker
turnbuckle
undertaken
undertaker
unprovoked
unremarked
vestpocket
watchmaker
wellspoken
wirewalker
wireworker
woodpecker
woodworker
workbasket
abnormally
acetabular
acetabulum
antebellum
apparelled
arboreally
armorially
armourclad
arterially
arteriolar
aspergilla
astragalus
atomically
atypically
autumnally
banderilla
barcarolle
bedevilled
bedraggled
bejewelled
bemedalled
bestseller
biannually
biblically
bidonville
biennially
bimetallic
binaurally
bisexually
bivalvular
blamefully
blissfully
bluecollar
boastfully
bookseller
breakables
brocatelle
Caerphilly
carboxylic
carbuncled
caruncular
cascarilla
catburglar
cerebellum
chancellor
channelled
chapfallen
cheerfully
chemically
chinchilla
chronicler
Cinderella
circumflex
citronella
clarabella
clavicular
clerically
clinically
closetplay
codswallop
colonially
colossally
commonalty
communally
conjugally
controlled
controller
corbiculae
corporally
corrivalry
cosmically
cosmopolis
councillor
counselled
counsellor
cowparsley
criminally
critically
culturally
curricular
curriculum
cyclically
demoiselle
deshabille
diagonally
difficulty
dillydally
discobolus
dishabille
disloyally
disloyalty
dissembler
dissimilar
doubtfully
downfallen
dreadfully
eigenvalue
elevenplus
embowelled
Emmentaler
empanelled
encephalic
encephalon
endothelia
enthralled
erotically
erysipelas
escadrille
espadrille
especially
ethereally
ethnically
Eurodollar
eventually
exotically
externally
faithfully
fancifully
farcically
fascicular
fasciculus
fenestella
fiducially
flannelled
follicular
fontanelle
footballer

forcefully
foreteller
fraxinella
freesoiler
fruitfully
funereally
furuncular
fustanella
germinally
ghastfully
glomerular
glomerulus
gothically
gracefully
granadilla
gratefully
grenadilla
groundplan
guilefully
gutturally
habitually
halfdollar
halfvolley
handgallop
handselled
hardbilled
hardboiled
haustellum
hectically
heliacally
hemicyclic
heroically
holusbolus
homunculus
hormonally
hullabaloo
hydrically
hyperbolae
hyperbolas
hyperbolic
hyperdulia
hypergolic
immortally
immortelle
impanelled
imperially
imperilled
infernally
informally
inimically
initialled
integrally
internally
intervolve
ironically
jargonelle
judicially
labiovelar
ladykiller
lenticular
loudhailer
Lupercalia
majuscular
mandibular
maniacally
manzanilla
marginalia
marginally
marshalled
marshaller
materially
maternally
medievally
mercifully
Methuselah
metrically
metropolis
micropylar
minstrelsy
minuscular
mirthfully
monocyclic
mosaically
mournfully
mozzarella
multipolar
muskmallow
myopically
mystically
mythically
nationally
nautically
necropolis
newfangled
notarially
notionally
nullanulla
officially
oldfangled
optionally
orientally
originally
painkiller
panhandler
parentally
particular
pastorally
paternally
peacefully
peccadillo
peduncular
pellicular
penetralia
penicillin
peninsular
pennanular
pentathlon
pericyclic
personally
personalty
petronella
philatelic
phonically
physically
piccalilli
pillowslip
playbyplay
playfellow
poetically
polycyclic
portcullis
postbellum
postexilic
potentilla
pourparler
powerfully
premaxilla
pridefully
primevally
principled
prodigally
prothallia
prothallus
proximally
pulsatilla
punctually
pyrogallol
quadruplet
quadruplex
quarrelled
quarreller
quintuplet
ranunculus
rationally
reconciler
regionally
remedially
remodelled
rightfully
ringtailed
ritornelli
ritornello
rockabilly
rollcollar
rosemallow
rottweiler
rubrically
rustically
sagittally
salmonella
saltarello
saltcellar
saturnalia
scenically
scornfully
screenplay
seasonally
seguidilla
selfstyled
selfwilled
septically
serradilla
shamefully
shopsoiled
shrievalty
shrivelled
sillybilly
slidevalve
slothfully
soapboiler
societally
softbilled
softboiled
soldanella
spectacled
spectacles
spectrally
spiracular
spiraculum
spitefully
sportfully
statically
stencilled
stenciller
stockpiler
stopvolley
suicidally
supernally
surgically
tactically
taleteller
tarantella
tarantelle
tastefully
teatrolley
teetotally
temporally
temporalty
tendrillar
tendrilled
tentacular
terminally
tetrapolis
texturally
thankfully
toroidally
tourbillon
trabeculae
trabecular
tragically
trammelled
tranquilly
transvalue
triangular
trigonally
tropaeolum
tropically
trouvaille
trustfully
truthfully
tubercular
tuberculin
tutorially
twowheeler
underbelly
undervalue
unequalled
unexampled
unexcelled
unfilially
unhouseled
uniaxially
unilocular
univocally
unlabelled
unlawfully
unravelled
unrivalled
unschooled
unsocially
untroubled
unwrinkled
valleculae
vallecular
varietally
vaudeville
vengefully
vermicelli
vermicular
vernacular
versicular
vertically
vestibular
vestibulum
vibraculum
victualled
victualler
villanelle
virginally
viscerally
visionally
vortically
vorticella
vorticular
wanderplug
wastefully
watchfully
watermelon
wearifully
weedkiller
wellheeled
wholesaler
wildfowler
willynilly
willywilly
wingcollar
wirepuller
wrathfully
wrongfully
yokefellow
youthfully
Abrahamman
accustomed
aerogramme
anastigmat
aneurismal
aneurysmal
anticlimax
apochromat
arrhythmia
arrhythmic
astronomer
astronomic
backgammon
biodynamic
blasphemer
bressummer
cacodaemon
catechumen
cavalryman
centesimal
chairwoman
childermas
clawhammer
cosmoramic
councilman
countryman
daydreamer
decagramme
decigramme
diathermal
diathermic
disclaimer
drophammer
duodecimal
ectodermal
ectodermic
embolismic
endodermal
endodermis
Englishman
erethismic
eurhythmic
exothermal
exothermic
footwarmer
freedwoman
geothermal
geothermic
grandmamma
GrecoRoman
groundsman
harvestman
heavyarmed
heroicomic
highwayman
hippocampi
hornrimmed
horsewoman
husbandman
hyperaemia
hyperaemic
hypodermal
hypodermic
hypodermis
infrahuman
Irishwoman
isodynamic
isoseismal
isothermal
jackhammer
journeyman
kilogramme
laundryman
lighterman
longprimer
loxodromic
lukewarmly
markswoman
matronymic
metronomic
metronymic
Michaelmas
midshipman
militiaman
millesimal
monorhymed
mumbojumbo
nambypamby
neurilemma
neurolemma
noblewoman
nonswimmer
nurseryman
oftentimes
ophthalmia
ophthalmic
orchardman
organismal
overcommit
pantomimic
paranormal
paroxysmal
patronymic
pentatomic
pentstemon
peridermal
phantasmal
phantasmic
polyatamic
polyonymic
proclaimer
programmer
provitamin
railwayman
saleswoman
sarcolemma
Scotswoman
seriocomic
serviceman
spacewoman
speedlimit
strabismal
strabismic
strabismus
superhuman
taxidermal
taxidermic
tilthammer
townswoman
tragicomic
trawlerman
trichromat
triggerman
triphammer
tularaemia
tularaemic
uncustomed
uneconomic
uninformed
unredeemed
weatherman
Welshwoman
windjammer
workingman
abhorrence
aboriginal
absorbance
absorbency
abstinence
abstinency
acceptance
accordance
additional
admittance
advertence
advertency
agglutinin
aldermanic
aldermanry
algolagnia
algolagnic
allegiance
allergenic
allophonic
alternance
androgenic
anglomania
anticlinal
antiphonal
appearance
aquaplaner
ascendance
ascendancy

ascendence
ascendency
assistance
attendance
barramunda
barramundi
belladonna
bellydance
belongings
benignancy
beribboned
bioscience
bladdernut
blancmange
bloodmoney
bluebonnet
brandysnap
brilliance
brilliancy
burramundi
camerlengo
camerlingo
campaigner
caravanned
caravanner
cartomancy
catchpenny
champignon
chaplaincy
chatoyance
chiromancy
coatimundi
coelacanth
cognisance
cognominal
comedienne
competence
competency
complainer
compliance
compliancy
condolence
conference
confidante
confidence
confluence
congruence
congruency
connivance
conscience
consonance
consonancy
constringe
continence
convenance
conveyance
coparcener
cordwainer
corpulence
corpulency
corrigenda
cosmogonic
covariance
crapulence
crossbench
crossbones
defeasance
deficiency
definienda
dehiscence
delusional
dependence
dependency
desipience
desistance
detergency
determined
deterrence
devotional
diachronic
difference
diffidence
dilettante
dilettanti
diminuendo
dipsomania
disarrange
dissidence
dissonance
dissonancy
distrainer
distrainor
divergence
divergency
divisional
divulgence
ebullience
ebulliency
efficiency
effulgence
eighteenmo
eighteenth
electronic
emblazoner
emblazonry
emblements
endocrinal
enharmonic
episternum
equational
erotogenic
erotomania
escallonia
excellence
excellency
expectance
expectancy
expedience
expediency
experience
exuberance
flatulence
flatulency
floribunda
forerunner
fortyniner
fourteener
fourteenth
fractional
frictional
frontbench
functional
Gallomania
ganglionic
gingersnap
governance
greenfinch
gyrational
hankypanky
headphones
heptagonal
heptatonic
hippomanes
histrionic
homophonic
hootenanny
hornblende
hydromancy
hypersonic
hypolimnia
iatrogenic
ideational
illusional
impatience
impeccancy
impendence
impendency
impersonal
importance
importuner
imprudence
incessancy
incipience
incipiency
inclemency
incumbency
indistinct
inductance
indulgence
inelegance
infrasonic
inharmonic
insistence
insistency
insolvency
insurgence
insurgency
intendance
interlunar
intervener
intervenor
interzonal
intestinal
intrigante
invariance
irradiance
irrational
isochronal
itinerancy
jaguarundi
kibbutznik
kinnikinic
landingnet
lansquenet
latescence
lawntennis
lentigines
limeburner
Lipizzaner
Lippizaner
longshanks
luxuriance
maintainer
malentendu
malignance
malignancy
mendicancy
meridional
misaligned
miscreance
misgivings
mistakenly
molendinar
molybdenum
monoclinal
monoclinic
monophonic
monstrance
moonshiner
musicianly
myasthenia
mythomania
naphthenic
necromancy
negligence
newsagency
nineteenth
nonaligned
northerner
nudibranch
nutational
observance
occasional
occurrence
offlicence
oppugnancy
ordonnance
orthogenic
orthogonal
outbalance
overmanned
paraffinic
pathogenic
penetrance
pentagonal
pentatonic
pentimento
periclinal
permanence
permanency
pertinence
pertinency
pestilence
petitioner
phagedenic
phenomenal
phenomenon
pheromonal
photogenic
phylogenic
phytogenic
piccaninny
pickaninny
pilliwinks
pinchpenny
planktonic
polyclinic
polyphonic
portamento
positional
pozzolanic
prearrange
precedence
precedency
preference
prepotence
prepotency
prescience
presidency
presternum
prevalence
prevenancy
procurance
prominence
pronominal
propaganda
provenance
providence
pubescence
purtenance
purveyance
pycnogonid
quadrennia
questioner
quiescence
quiescency
radiogenic
radiosonde
recipiency
recommence
recompense
recumbency
recurrence
redundance
redundancy
reentrance
refulgence
reiterance
rejoicings
relational
reluctance
reluctancy
remittance
renascence
repellance
repellancy
repellence
repellency
repentance
reprobance
repugnance
repugnancy
resilience
resiliency
resistance
resorcinol
restrained
restrainer
resurgence
revisional
rhizogenic
ritardando
roadrunner
rotational
sacrosanct
salicional
salmagundi
saprogenic
sarracenia
scherzando
screenings
senescence
shortrange
sideglance
skirtdance
slatternly
smartmoney
snakedance
snickasnee
softfinned
somnolence
somnolency
southerner
southernly
splanchnic
spodomancy
stringency
stringendo
stubbornly
subliminal
submariner
subordinal
subsidence
subtenancy
succedanea
succulence
succulency
sufferance
sunderance
superlunar
supersonic
supertonic
suppliance
suprarenal
survivance
sustenance
suzerainty
sworddance
sycophancy
synchronal
synchronic
tablelinen
taciturnly
talismanic
telephoner
telephonic
temperance
termagancy
tetragonal
theophanic
thermionic
thirteenth
threatener
threepence
threepenny
thruppence
ticpolonga
tobogganer
tractional
tragacanth
transience
transiency
translunar
trenchancy
trigeminal
trillionth
truculence
truculency
tumescence
turbulence
turbulency
ultrasonic
unbrokenly
unbuttoned
uncommonly
underlinen
underminer
underpants
undersense
undesigned
unscreened
unseasoned
unstrained
venational
virescence
vocational
volitional
wanderings
weimaraner
wellturned
wongawonga
woodturner
xylophonic
abdominous
absolutory
abstemious
acarpelous
accusatory
acephalous
acrogenous
actinozoan
adenectomy
adjuratory
admonitory
adulterous
advocatory
aeolotropy
aeruginous
affettuoso
albuminoid
albuminous
alliaceous
allogamous
allpurpose
alongshore
alpenstock
ambulatory
amendatory
amphibious
amygdaloid
amylaceous
anadromous
anastomose
anatropous
ancipitous
anglophobe
anglophone
anisotropy
anonaceous
anthracoid
anthropoid
antiheroic
antonymous
apocarpous

aquiferous
arenaceous
armigerous
arytaenoid
asynchrony
auriferous
auspicious
autecology
autogamous
autogenous
autologous
autonomous
avaricious
backstroke
badderlock
balneology
barleycorn
barratrous
barrenwort
basketwork
bassethorn
bathyscope
battailous
battledore
beechdrops
bibliology
bibliopole
bibliopoly
billetdoux
bioecology
bipetalous
birthstone
bitterroot
bitterwood
bituminous
blackamoor
blackthorn
blastopore
blithesome
bloodstock
bloodstone
bluethroat
blusterous
boisterous
bothersome
bottommost
brachylogy
brainstorm
brakeblock
brantgoose
brazilwood
breastbone
breastwork
brentgoose
bridegroom
bridgework
brightwork
broadcloth
broadsword
brokendown
bronchiole
brownstone
bubblyjock
burdensome
butterwort
buttondown
buttonhole
buttonhook
buttonwood
byssaceous
cacciatore
cadaverous
caddisworm
caespitose
calamitous
calcareous
caliginous
calumnious
calyciform
cancellous
candlewood
candyfloss
cankerworm
cannelloni
canvaswork
caoutchouc
capricious
cardiology
carmagnole
carotenoid
carotinoid
carphology
censorious
centrefold
centrosome
ceruminous
chainsmoke
chalcedony
chalkstone
chaudfroid
chequebook
childproof
chivalrous
chloroform
Christhood
chromosome
chronology
chuckerout
churchgoer
cinquefoil
circuitous
clangorous
clavichord
clearstory
clerestory
clingstone
clinkstone
closestool
coetaneous
collarbone
collembola
commandoes
commodious
commonroom
compradore
compulsory
conchology
conclusory
confervoid
coniferous
consistory
contagious
contiguous
continuous
coolingoff
coriaceous
correspond
cottonwood
cottonwool
courageous
cousinhood
cradlesong
craniology
cretaceous
crewelwork
cribriform
crisscross
cryptology
ctenophore
cuddlesome
cumbersome
cumuliform
curvaceous
curvacious
cuttlebone
cuttystool
cyclostome
cylindroid
cystoscope
cystoscopy
cytochrome
dampingoff
decapodous
dedicatory
defamatory
delphinoid
deltiology
demonology
dendriform
dendrology
deontology
depilatory
depository
derogatory
despiteous
diaphanous
digitiform
dimorphous
diningroom
diphyodont
disapprove
disastrous
discomfort
discommode
discompose
diseconomy
disembroil
disharmony
dispersoid
dispiteous
distichous
divinatory
donkeywork
donnybrook
dovecolour
downstroke
drupaceous
dumbledore
ectogenous
eczematous
edentulous
Egyptology
embryology
emendatory
emigratory
endogamous
endogenous
engineroom
enterotomy
entomology
enzymology
ephemerous
epicycloid
epidermoid
ericaceous
escapology
euphonious
excitatory
excusatory
execratory
exhibitory
exobiology
expiratory
expository
extraneous
factitious
fallacious
fallingoff
fandangoes
fastidious
fatherhood
felicitous
fetterlock
fibrillose
fictitious
fiddlewood
fieldstone
fingerbowl
fingerpost
fisherfolk
flagitious
flameproof
flamingoes
flashflood
floatstone
floorcloth
flosculous
flugelhorn
foliaceous
folkmemory
foraminous
fortuitous
founderous
fourstroke
frolicsome
fuliginous
futurology
Gallophobe
gangrenous
gastrology
gastronome
gastronomy
gelatinous
gemmaceous
gentlefolk
glaciology
glasscloth
glossology
glottology
glumaceous
gluttonous
goloptious
goluptious
goodygoody
Gorgonzola
gramineous
gramophone
graphology
grasscloth
grassroots
gratuitous
gravestone
greasewood
greencloth
greenstone
gregarious
grindstone
groundwork
gynandrous
hagioscope
hairstroke
halogenous
hammerlock
hammerpond
harmonious
headstrong
heartblock
heartblood
heartwhole
heatstroke
heavenborn
helioscope
heliotrope
heliotropy
heortology
hepatology
heptachord
herbaceous
heretofore
herrenvolk
heterodont
heterodoxy
heterogony
heterology
heteronomy
hexamerous
hippodrome
hithermost
homogamous
homogenous
homologous
homonymous
homozygote
homozygous
horrendous
horsecloth
horseshoer
houseproud
hucklebone
humoursome
hydrophone
hydroscope
hygroscope
hypogynous
iconoscope
idolatrous
immunology
impervious
incautious
incestuous
incubatory
indecorous
indicatory
indigenous
infectious
inglorious
inhibitory
iniquitous
initiatory
innovatory
innuendoes
innumerous
intercross
inundatory
invitatory
invocatory
iridaceous
isopterous
isosporous
jobbernowl
judicatory
keratinous
knighthood
knockabout
laboratory
lachrymose
languorous
lanuginose
lanuginous
laparotomy
lascivious
lattermost
lauraceous
leguminous
letterbomb
letterbook
lexicology
libidinous
licentious
lightproof
likelihood
liliaceous
limaciform
linguiform
lipomatous
litterlout
livelihood
livingroom
lockerroom
locomotory
loganstone
logorrhoea
longaevous
lophophore
loquacious
lubricious
luciferous
lucifugous
lugubrious
lumberroom
lumbersome
mackintosh
macrospore
maidenhood
malacology
malleefowl
malodorous
malvaceous
mandragora
markettown
marrowbone
marvellous
mastectomy
masterhood
masterwork
matronhood
meddlesome
melancholy
membranous
mendacious
meningioma
menstruous
meticulous
mettlesome
microbiota
microphone
microscope
microscopy
microspore
middlemost
migrainous
millefiori
mineralogy
minestrone
minutebook
miraculous
misericord
misogynous
mitigatory
mockheroic
molluscoid
molluscous
monandrous
moniliform
monochrome
monoecious
monogamous
monogynous
monotonous
monsignori
mordacious
morphology
mosquitoes
motherhood
motherwort
muciferous
musicology
musicstool
myrtaceous
mysterious
myxomatous
nanosecond
nationhood
nativeborn
necroscopy
nectareous
needlebook
needlecord
needlework
negrophobe
nephoscope
nephrology
nethermost
nidicolous

nidifugous
nincompoop
nipplewort
nitrogroup
nonferrous
nubiferous
nuciferous
nucivorous
numerology
nutritious
obligatory
obsequious
oceanology
octamerous
octandrous
octopodous
odontology
oedematose
oedematous
oleaginous
oleiferous
oleraceous
oligopsony
olivaceous
omnigenous
omnivorous
omophagous
oncogenous
oneirology
orangewood
orphanhood
osculatory
outrageous
ovariotomy
overexpose
overthrown
paddleboat
Palaeozoic
palindrome
palladious
palliatory
palmaceous
palmerworm
palynology
papaverous
papyrology
paraboloid
parasitoid
paratroops
parenthood
paronymous
paroxytone
pastrycook
pediculous
pellagrous
pemphigoid
pemphigous
pennaceous
pentachord
peppercorn
pepperwort
peremptory
perfidious
perigynous
perjurious
permafrost
pernicious
phlebotomy
photoflood
photophore
phototrope
phrasebook
phrenology
physiology
picosecond
piecegoods
pigeonhole
pigeonpost
pigeontoed
piliferous
pitchstone
plaguesome
pleochroic
plunderous
pocketbook
pogonology
pogonotomy
polychrome
polygamous
polygenous
polygynous
polymerous
polysemous
polytocous
pomiferous
porraceous
portentous
possessory
posthumous
potamology
powderhorn
pratincole
prayerbook
precarious
preceptory
precocious
precursory
predacious
predispose
prednisone
prehistory
presuppose
priesthood
prodigious
promissory
promontory
promptbook
propitious
prosperous
protectory
proteiform
proteinous
provisions
psephology
psychology
pugnacious
pupiparous
purseproud
pyretology
pyrogenous
quadrupole
quatrefoil
quickthorn
radiophone
radioscopy
rampageous
rebellious
redemptory
refractory
regulatory
rendezvous
repository
rescissory
responsory
retrochoir
revelatory
revocatory
rheumatoid
rhinestone
rhinoscope
rhinoscopy
rhizophore
ribbonworm
ridiculous
robustious
roisterous
roundabout
rouseabout
roustabout
rubiginous
rubythroat
rupicolous
Russophobe
sabretooth
saccharoid
saccharose
saliferous
salubrious
salutatory
sanctimony
sandalwood
sappanwood
sargassoes
sarmentose
sarmentous
satanology
saxicolous
scandalous
schizogony
schoolbook
schoolroom
schoolwork
sclerotomy
screechowl
scrofulous
scrollwork
scrupulous
scurrilous
scyphiform
scyphozoan
seaanemone
seborrhoea
securiform
seismology
selenodont
selenology
selfcolour
selfparody
semeiology
separatory
sequacious
SerboCroat
serotinous
setterwort
shantytown
shellproof
shellshock
shirtfront
shockproof
sidestroke
simulatory
singlefoot
sinistrous
sisterhood
sketchbook
slanderous
Slavophobe
slumberous
smallsword
smockfrock
smokeproof
smoothbore
snakestone
sneezewood
sneezewort
solicitous
somatology
soundproof
sourcebook
sousaphone
spadiceous
spatchcock
speciology
speleology
sphenodone
spiderwort
spirituous
spitchcock
splashdown
spleenwort
splintbone
splintcoal
spoilsport
spoliatory
spongewood
spongiform
spongology
sporophore
springwood
squaretoed
squaretoes
squirehood
statoscope
stelliform
stertorous
stiflebone
stilettoes
stinkstone
stitchwort
stockproof
stormcloud
stormproof
strabotomy
stratiform
streetdoor
stridulous
Stroganoff
stromatous
stronghold
strongroom
struthious
stupendous
subaqueous
sulphurous
sunparlour
superstore
suppletory
suspensoid
suspensory
suspicious
swarmspore
symphylous
synanthous
syncarpous
synecology
synoecious
synonymous
tablecloth
tablespoon
taperecord
tautophony
technology
tenderfoot
tenderloin
tenebrious
tenterhook
teratology
testaceous
tetrachord
tetterwort
thereabout
thirtyfold
thixotropy
thornproof
threadworm
threescore
throatwort
throughout
thunderous
timbertoes
timberwolf
timberwork
timbrology
tiringroom
toffeenose
touchstone
toxicology
traitorous
trajectory
transitory
treasonous
tremendous
triandrous
trichinous
trichology
trichotomy
trioecious
triphthong
trophology
troubadour
tubicolous
tuffaceous
tumbledown
tumultuous
turkeycock
turtledove
twelvefold
twelvenote
twelvetone
ubiquitous
umbiliform
umbrageous
undercroft
underfloor
underproof
underquote
underscore
undershoot
understock
understood
underwrote
undesirous
undulatory
ungenerous
ungracious
unhandsome
uproarious
urbanology
vaporiform
veldschoen
velutinous
ventricose
vesicatory
vibraphone
victorious
videophone
villainous
violaceous
viperiform
viraginous
virginhood
viviparous
vociferous
voluminous
voluptuous
waistcloth
waterclock
waterflood
waterfront
waterproof
waterspout
wheatstone
whereabout
whitethorn
wickerwork
wonderwork
yellowwood
zabaglione
zoophagous
zoophilous
acatalepsy
aerography
allotropic
anastrophe
antechapel
apocalypse
apostrophe
archetypal
autography
azeotropic
bookkeeper
brachiopod
cacography
cephalopod
cerography
chamberpot
chickenpox
chimneypot
clodhopper
clothespeg
clothespin
cornucopia
crowkeeper
cryoscopic
cuckoospit
demography
doorkeeper
doxography
drawingpin
eartrumpet
emerypaper
endoscopic
endstopped
epistrophe
froghopper
gamekeeper
gasteropod
gatekeeper
glasspaper
goalkeeper
gobstopper
gymnosophy
gyroscopic
harelipped
holography
horoscopic
horsecoper
ideography
interloper
isentropic
jackanapes
ladychapel
landscaper
leafhopper
lexigraphy
limitrophe
lipography
lobsterpot
lockkeeper
logography
malapropos
maxilliped
megascopic
meltingpot
mesomorphy
mesoscaphe
metacarpal
metacarpus
monocarpic
mudskipper
musicpaper
narcolepsy
nomography
nosography
nyctalopia
nyctalopic
oleography
oreography
overlapped
oversupply
overtopped
participle
periscopic
phenotypic

philosophe
philosophy
pinecarpet
pinstriped
polygraphy
presbyopia
presbyopic
protanopic
prototypal
prototypic
pyrography
rheotropic
rockhopper
rollingpin
roselipped
sandhopper
sciagraphy
serigraphy
shopkeeper
showjumper
skiagraphy
skyscraper
snowcapped
stomatopod
strathspey
sugarmaple
superduper
synaloepha
telegraphy
telescopic
thornapple
throughput
timekeeper
tomography
topography
touchpaper
typography
wallpepper
warmingpan
wastepaper
wiretapper
workpeople
worshipped
worshipper
xerography
xylography
zygomorphy
antimasque
blottesque
catafalque
communique
humoresque
Japanesque
Kafkaesque
multiloquy
picaresque
radiopaque
Romanesque
semiopaque
somniloquy
statuesque
titanesque
adventurer
afterbirth
afterwards
alcyonaria
allosteric
alphameric
ambulacral
ambulacrum
amphoteric
anteriorly
aristocrat
asymmetric
avantgarde
barbituric
barleybree
barleybroo
barometric
bicultural
bijouterie
bizarrerie
blackberry
bolometric
bottletree
brachyural
brachyuran
brusquerie
bullroarer
bureaucrat
calciferol
campestral
candletree
cardiogram
cattlegrid
cavalierly
cellularly
chelicerae
childbirth
chokeberry
chronogram
circularly
cloistered
cloudberry
cloudburst
coastwards
cockalorum
collateral
columbaria
concentric
congeneric
connatural
considered
contraprop
coralberry
cornstarch
corroboree
crematoria
cryptogram
cylindered
dampcourse
dapplegrey
daughterly
debonairly
decahedral
decahedron
decemviral
deflowerer
dielectric
diphtheria
diphtheric
discoverer
disenthral
disenviron
disinherit
disordered
disorderly
dosimetric
drafthorse
dragontree
dramaturge
dramaturgy
dreamworld
dysenteric
earthwards
egocentric
elderberry
epicentral
epigastric
equilibria
ergosterol
eurypterid
exospheric
extemporal
exteriorly
extramural
fairhaired
familiarly
FinnoUgric
forecourse
frontwards
gaultheria
generatrix
geocentric
glassworks
globularly
glycosuria
glycosuric
golfcourse
gooseberry
granularly
groceteria
haematuria
halfyearly
handbarrow
heartthrob
hemihedral
hemihedron
hemipteran
henceforth
Heptameron
heresiarch
hermitcrab
hexahedral
hexahedron
hexametric
hobbyhorse
holohedral
holosteric
hurdygurdy
hurlyburly
hypaethral
hyperbaric
illnatured
illstarred
impresario
improperly
inferiorly
inheritrix
interferer
interferon
interiorly
intermarry
intramural
involucral
involucrum
kettledrum
knobkerrie
knopkierie
kookaburra
lardydardy
loganberry
longhaired
macebearer
madreporic
malingerer
manoeuvrer
manoeuvres
manometric
manteltree
mesenteric
mesenteron
mesothorax
metallurgy
metaphoric
metathorax
metempiric
microfarad
middlebrow
misnomered
monohybrid
monohydric
mosasaurus
muscularly
nonnatural
northwards
octahedral
octahedron
openhearth
oracularly
orchestral
otherworld
ottershrew
outgeneral
overcharge
paediatric
pallbearer
panjandrum
parametric
parenteral
patisserie
peculiarly
pennyworth
perchloric
peripheral
peripteral
phosphoric
phosphorus
physiocrat
pianoforte
planetaria
polyandric
polyhedral
polyhedric
polyhedron
primiparae
procedural
protectrix
pyrometric
pyrophoric
quercitron
racecourse
rattletrap
registered
rhinoceros
rhizomorph
rightwards
riverhorse
rotisserie
rowanberry
saddletree
schipperke
scriptoria
scriptural
sculptural
sculptured
seismogram
semichorus
semiyearly
septenarii
sepulchral
sequestrum
shirehorse
shorewards
shouldered
shrinkwrap
sideboards
simulacrum
singletree
singularly
sinisterly
smallwares
smorrebrod
sophomoric
southwards
sphenogram
spidercrab
splutterer
squanderer
squirearch
staffnurse
steelworks
stenchtrap
stereogram
sternwards
stillbirth
stoneborer
stratocrat
strawberry
structural
structured
subcentral
supercargo
superiorly
syllabaria
talebearer
tautomeric
technocrat
telemetric
termitaria
tetramorph
theophoric
thermogram
thillhorse
thimblerig
thirdparty
thumbscrew
tocopherol
topsyturvy
transferee
transferor
transverse
trilateral
triliteral
triquetrae
triquetral
triumviral
ulteriorly
undershrub
underworld
undeterred
unexplored
unfathered
unfettered
unhistoric
unicameral
unilateral
unlettered
unmannerly
unmeasured
unnumbered
unprepared
vascularly
volumetric
waffleiron
waterborne
waterworks
wentletrap
wheelhorse
wirehaired
xiphosuran
youngberry
advertiser
aerobiosis
aftertaste
Albigenses
amanuenses
amanuensis
ampelopsis
anchylosis
antecessor
antibiosis
antisepsis
antitheses
antithesis
aphaereses
aphaeresis
aphrodisia
apotheoses
apotheosis
asbestosis
ascariasis
ateleiosis
autoplasty
babiroussa
bibulously
bigamously
biogenesis
bipartisan
bootlessly
byssinosis
canorously
captiously
carcinosis
carelessly
catastasis
catechesis
catechiser
cautiously
cellulosic
comparison
compasssaw
compressed
compressor
convalesce
covetously
cumbrously
decorously
deliquesce
deodoriser
deoxidiser
desirously
dextrously
diapedesis
dickcissel
discourser
disembosom
dishonesty
dispraiser
dissatisfy
distressed
dogmatiser
dolorously
duniwassal
ecchymosis
economiser
effervesce
effloresce
enantiosis
endosmosis
enormously
epentheses
epenthesis
epexegeses
epexegesis
epigenesis
euthanasia
eyeglasses
fabulously
factiously
fadelessly
fearlessly
fecklessly
fertiliser
filariasis
fireraiser
flawlessly
flexuously
formlessly
framboesia
franchiser
galvaniser
generously
gentilesse
gloriously
glycolyses
glycolysis
gorgeously
governessy
graciously
grievously
haematosis
haemolysis
hairraiser

halfnelson
harmlessly
harmoniser
heedlessly
helplessly
histolysis
hopelessly
humorously
hybridiser
hydrolysis
hypabyssal
hypnotiser
hypophyses
hypophysis
hypostasis
hypotheses
hypothesis
hysteresis
ichthyosis
illadvised
improviser
incandesce
indisposed
infamously
interposal
interposer
isoglossal
jinricksha
jinrikisha
lederhosen
lifelessly
liquidiser
listlessly
lovelessly
luminously
lusciously
lustrously
magnetiser
marshalsea
mayblossom
menopausal
mesmeriser
metalepsis
metaphysic
metaplasia
metastases
metastasis
metatarsal
metatarsus
metatheses
metathesis
mindlessly
moderniser
moniliasis
monochasia
movelessly
mutinously
mycoplasma
mythiciser
namelessly
nauseously
nebulously
needlessly
neoclassic
nonplussed
noogenesis
numerously
nyctinasty
orogenesis
paederasty
painlessly
pangenesis
parabiosis
paragnosis
paralipsis
paramnesia
patulously
peerlessly
perilously
photolysis
photonasty
pitilessly
pityriasis
pollenosis
polydipsia
polyphasic
populously
preciously
previously
procrypsis
prosthesis
pulveriser
ravenously
recklessly
recrudesce
restlessly
rickettsia
rigorously
ruthlessly
satyriasis
scabrously
sedulously
seedvessel
selflessly
selfpoised
selfraised
sensitiser
sensuously
sermoniser
sharpnosed
socialiser
sonorously
soullessly
spaciously
speciously
spotlessly
spuriously
stabiliser
stereopsis
steriliser
stonemason
studiously
sunglasses
supervisor
suppressor
syllogiser
symboliser
synaeresis
syngenesis
synostosis
tactlessly
tantaliser
tearlessly
temporiser
thromboses
thrombosis
timelessly
timorously
tirelessly
tonelessly
toothpaste
tortfeasor
tortiously
tortuously
transfuser
transposal
transposer
trespasser
trichiasis
tunelessly
ultrabasic
unctuously
unmortised
unstressed
usuriously
uxoriously
valorously
vaporously
venomously
verbaliser
viceconsul
victimiser
viewlessly
vigorously
viperously
virtuously
visualiser
vulcaniser
wishywashy
wondrously
wordlessly
wrongously
ZendAvesta
abducentes
aberrantly
abominator
abstracted
abstracter
abstractly
abstractor
abundantly
accidental
accredited
achromatic
acidimeter
acidimetry
addlepated
adherently
adjacently
administer
aerobiotic
aeronautic
aerostatic
afferently
affiliated
affluently
allegretto
alleviator
almacanter
almucanter
alphabetic
alternator
altruistic
ambidexter
ammoniated
anacolutha
anapaestic
anaplastic
anaptyctic
anchoretic
anchoritic
anchylotic
anemometer
anemometry
annalistic
antemortem
antibiotic
antimatter
antiproton
antiquated
antiseptic
antistatic
antithetic
aphoristic
aplacental
apodeictic
apolaustic
apologetic
apoplectic
aposematic
apparently
applicator
aquafortis
aragonitic
arbalester
arbalister
arbitrator
arborvitae
archaistic
argumentum
arithmetic
arrogantly
aspidistra
asteriated
astigmatic
asymptotic
attenuated
attenuator
audiometer
audiometry
austenitic
autocratic
autoerotic
babysitter
bacchantes
bacchantic
backstitch
bandmaster
bankruptcy
bardolatry
barefooted
batholitic
bathometer
bathymeter
bathymetry
Bedlington
Benedictus
benefactor
bighearted
bilgewater
billposter
biogenetic
biparietal
blackwater
blanquette
bluebottle
bonesetter
brachiator
breakwater
bronchitic
bronchitis
browbeaten
buccinator
Buddhistic
bushmaster
cabalistic
cacomistle
calcsinter
calculator
calibrator
canzonetta
cassolette
catalectic
cataleptic
catechetic
celebrated
celebrator
cellulitis
centilitre
centimetre
Charleston
chemisette
chiliastic
chondritic
circulator
clinometer
clinometry
clovehitch
clubfooted
cochleated
coenobitic
coenobytic
coherently
collarette
collarstud
collimator
collocutor
commutator
comparator
competitor
complected
complotted
compositor
compotator
computator
congenital
conjointly
conspectus
constantan
Constantia
constantly
contractor
convoluted
cooperator
copesettic
coprolitic
copywriter
corporator
corrugated
corrugator
corticated
Corybantes
corybantic
coulometry
covalently
covenanted
covenantee
covenanter
covenantor
crenulated
crescentic
crinolette
crosshatch
crosspatch
cucullated
cultivator
cuspidated
cybernetic
cyclometer
czarevitch
deathwatch
decadently
deeprooted
deepseated
defalcator
defoliator
delineator
democratic
denigrator
densimeter
depredator
dermatitis
descriptor
desecrater
desecrator
desiccator
designator
destructor
diagnostic
diapedetic
dichroitic
dilemmatic
diligently
diphyletic
diplomatic
discounter
discreetly
disentitle
disgruntle
dishearten
disjointed
disparates
dispirited
disquieten
disquietly
dissipated
distinctly
distracted
documental
dominantly
draconites
dumbwaiter
dungbeetle
duodenitis
duplicator
dynamistic
dysplastic
ecchymotic
elaborator
eliminator
eloquently
elucidator
elutriator
emblematic
empathetic
emphractic
endophytic
endosmotic
enregister
enumerator
enunciator
epenthetic
epexegetic
epiblastic
epideictic
epigenetic
epiglottal
epiglottic
epiglottis
episematic
eradicator
escharotic
essayistic
eucalyptol
eucalyptus
eucaryotic
eudiometer
eudiometry
eulogistic
euphuistic
evaporator
explicitly
expurgator
extenuator
extirpator
exultantly
fabricator
farsighted
fascinator
fatalistic
feuilleton
fianchetto
fibrositis
filibuster
fimbriated
fishkettle
flagrantly
flatfooted
fleabitten
flippantly
floodwater
flyswatter
forcipated
forecaster
forecastle
fornicator
fourchette
fourfooted
fourposter
fragmental
fragrantly
freebooter
freemartin
frequenter

frequently
freshwater
fullbottom
futuristic
gaslighter
gauntleted
geognostic
gingivitis
Glagolitic
goldbeater
goniometer
goniometry
granulator
granulitic
gravimeter
gravimetry
gunfighter
gynocratic
gyrocopter
haemolytic
hagiolatry
halfwitted
halophytic
hardbitten
hardfisted
headhunter
headmaster
headwaiter
Hebraistic
hectolitre
hectometre
hedonistic
helicopter
heliolater
heliolatry
heliometer
hempnettle
henhearted
heptameter
Herrnhuter
hesitantly
hierolatry
histolytic
holophytic
homeopathy
honeyeater
horizontal
hotchpotch
humanistic
humoristic
hydrolytic
hydrometer
hydrometry
hydropathy
hygrometer
hygrometry
hyperbaton
hyphenated
hypostatic
hypotactic
hypsometer
hypsometry
hysteretic
iconolater
iconolatry
iconometer
iconometry
idealistic
ignorantly
imminently
immodestly
implicitly
impotently
imprimatur
impudently
inartistic
incantator
incidental
inculcator
indecently
indigested
indirectly
indolently
inexpertly
infatuated
inherently
innocently
inoculator
inquisitor
insinuator
insolently
inspirator
instigator
institutor
instructor
integrator
interested
ironmaster
isogenetic
Jehovistic
jingoistic
jubilantly
judgematic
kerygmatic
lacklustre
lacrimator
lacrymator
laryngitic
laryngitis
leafcutter
legalistic
legislator
leucocytic
leukocytic
ligamental
linguistic
lionhunter
liquidator
lockstitch
lotuseater
loveletter
lubricator
lucubrator
luculently
machinator
maisonette
maladapted
malapertly
malefactor
mamillated
manifestly
manifestos
manumitted
marginated
Mariolater
Mariolatry
marionette
Massoretic
masticator
mathematic
mealbeetle
medicaster
medullated
melanistic
meliorator
melismatic
meningitis
mesophytic
metacentre
metastatic
metathetic
meteoritic
methylated
microlitic
micrometer
micrometry
mignonette
militantly
millilitre
millimetre
mintmaster
mischanter
mischmetal
mobocratic
monocratic
montbretia
monumental
moralistic
morganatic
nativistic
Neapolitan
necrolater
necrolatry
negotiator
neoplastic
neuropathy
newscaster
newsletter
newsworthy
newswriter
nightwatch
nihilistic
nomothetic
nonstarter
noteworthy
notonectal
novelistic
numismatic
obediently
obfuscated
obstructor
occidental
ombrometer
ophiolater
ophiolatry
opisometer
optimistic
originator
ornamental
orogenetic
oscillator
osteopathy
outrightly
outstretch
overmantel
overmaster
oversubtle
overwinter
ovipositor
oxygenator
pacesetter
palmbutter
pancreatic
pancreatin
pangenetic
parabiotic
paratactic
parramatta
pastmaster
peashooter
pectinated
pederastic
pedimental
pedimented
pegmatitic
penetrator
penitently
pentameter
percolator
perforator
persecutor
personator
petiolated
petrolatum
petulantly
phagocytic
phantastic
phantastry
pheasantry
phenacetin
phlegmatic
phlogistic
phlogiston
phonematic
phonolitic
phonometer
phosphatic
photolitho
photolytic
photometer
photometry
piezometer
pinnulated
pixillated
planchette
plangently
planimeter
planimetry
planometer
pleasantly
pleasantry
pleonastic
plutolatry
poinsettia
pollinator
polydactyl
polyhistor
populistic
porismatic
postmaster
postmortem
postpartum
postulator
precipitin
prefrontal
pregnantly
premarital
premonitor
preparator
procreator
procryptic
procurator
progenitor
proglottis
prognostic
prohibiter
prohibitor
prolocutor
propagator
propraetor
proprietor
prosciutto
prosecutor
prospector
prospectus
prosthetic
protracted
protractor
protreptic
provocator
pruriently
psychiatry
puffpastry
pugilistic
puissantly
pulsimeter
pulsometer
pulvinated
punctuator
purulently
pushbutton
pycnometer
pyknometer
pyracantha
pyromantic
quadrantal
quartzitic
quizmaster
rackrenter
radiometer
radiometry
rechristen
recreantly
redolently
regimental
relevantly
rencounter
repudiator
reredorter
resonantly
respirator
reticently
reverently
ringmaster
ripsnorter
roadworthy
rockbottom
Romanistic
rovebeetle
rubricator
rudimental
ruminantly
sacerdotal
sandcastle
sandmartin
Sanskritic
satellitic
schismatic
scholastic
sciolistic
scrapmetal
semifitted
sensedatum
sentiently
sergeantcy
serjeantcy
servomotor
sexlimited
sheabutter
shearwater
shipfitter
shipmaster
shoplifter
shortdated
siderostat
signwriter
silhouette
silkcotton
simplistic
sincipital
sixshooter
slipstitch
slowfooted
slowwitted
sociometry
solecistic
songwriter
sowthistle
speculator
spirometer
spirometry
stagbeetle
stagnantly
stalwartly
stepsister
stimulator
stipulator
stochastic
stomatitis
straighten
straightly
stridently
subaquatic
subjugator
suborbital
substratum
succinctly
superaltar
supplanter
surefooted
syncopated
syncopator
syndicator
synergetic
syphilitic
systematic
tachometer
tachometry
tachymeter
tachymetry
taskmaster
teaplanter
tegumental
telecaster
tendinitis
tenemental
terminator
terracotta
tetrameter
theocratic
thereafter
thermistor
thermostat
thrombotic
tidewaiter
timocratic
tolerantly
totemistic
tracheated
tracheitis
transactor
transeptal
transistor
translator
transmuter
tremolitic
tribometer
triturator
trochanter
tromometer
tsarevitch
tufthunter
twilighted
tympanites
tympanitic
tympanitis
typesetter
typewriter
unaccented
unaffected
unassisted
unbonneted
uncloister
underwater
undigested
uneducated
unemphatic
unexpected
unionistic
unrequited
unscripted
unselected
uranometry
urethritis
vaccinator
valvulitis
variegated
variolitic
variometer
vehemently
ventilator
vigilantly
vindicator
virulently

viscometer
viscountcy
vitalistic
vivisector
voltameter
waggonette
wellington
whipstitch
winceyette
Winchester
winebottle
wingfooted
woodcutter
woolsorter
wristwatch
xerophytic
yardmaster
zygodactyl
altazimuth
altocumuli
amphigouri
animalcula
animalcule
antepenult
apiculture
autoimmune
aviculture
background
barracouta
bawdyhouse
bellylaugh
blockhouse
bloodhound
breadcrumb
breadfruit
breadstuff
buttonbush
canaliculi
cantaloupe
canterbury
caricature
cataloguer
centrifuge
chartreuse
chauffeuse
circumfuse
coachhouse
colatitude
coloratura
commissure
commixture
conceptual
conjecture
consensual
constitute
consuetude
contextual
contexture
contribute
conventual
corpuscule
courthouse
couverture
craquelure
crassitude
crepuscule
cummerbund
debouchure
decompound
definitude
disclosure
disfeature
distribute
dumbstruck
earthbound
embouchure
endproduct
exactitude
fairground

fieldmouse
fleshwound
foreground
forfeiture
gargantuan
glasshouse
grapefruit
greedyguts
greenhouse
greenstuff
guardhouse
guesthouse
Heptateuch
hereabouts
highstrung
homosexual
horselaugh
housebound
hypotenuse
imposthume
inaptitude
incunabula
individual
ineptitude
infinitude
inquietude
interwound
irresolute
judicature
kieselguhr
lambrequin
lighthouse
literature
loungesuit
maculature
manorhouse
mansuetude
misconduct
misfortune
mismeasure
misventure
monkeysuit
moonstruck
mulligrubs
northbound
nunciature
outmeasure
overabound
overblouse
overground
overslaugh
overstrung
overthrust
paintbrush
paradoxure
parimutuel
perceptual
pilothouse
pinebeauty
piscifauna
plantlouse
playground
powderpuff
powerhouse
prefecture
prefixture
prostitute
punchdrunk
quadrature
retinacula
roquelaure
roughhouse
roundhouse
runthrough
sanctitude
scaramouch
seabiscuit
seethrough
semiannual

semiliquid
sheeplouse
shellmound
shortcrust
shrewmouse
similitude
smokehouse
snowgrouse
snowplough
solicitude
somersault
songthrush
soubriquet
southbound
spellbound
steakhouse
stonefruit
storehouse
stormbound
subculture
sublingual
substitute
subterfuge
sugarhouse
superacute
tantamount
televisual
theopneust
toothbrush
tourniquet
trilingual
tropopause
ultrasound
underbrush
underslung
understudy
unilingual
usquebaugh
ventriculi
wagonvault
wanderlust
wheelhouse
whorehouse
wraparound
yarborough
aardwolves
adjectival
bollweevil
cantilever
changeover
fishcarver
fourleaved
gerundival
housewives
interwoven
jackknives
kerchieves
loosecover
nevernever
objectival
pearldiver
piledriver
quadrumvir
rediscover
riboflavin
semiquaver
shortlived
splitlevel
supernovae
swinefever
switchover
tackdriver
themselves
timeserver
unbeliever
undercover
undeserved
unimproved
unrelieved

unreserved
unresolved
werewolves
whatsoever
whensoever
whomsoever
woodcarver
yourselves
ballflower
bellflower
brainpower
cornflower
disembowel
expressway
foamflower
homebrewed
horsepower
moonflower
overgrowth
passageway
safeblower
scratchwig
sealingwax
superpower
televiewer
throughway
unhallowed
wallflower
watchtower
waterpower
windflower
winegrower
wiredrawer
withdrawal
withdrawer
woolgrower
amphimixes
amphimixis
AngloSaxon
appendixes
bobbysoxer
chemotaxis
heliotaxis
hydrotaxis
neurotoxin
orthodoxly
phototaxis
phytotoxic
undersexed
aerenchyma
almondeyed
amoebocyte
amphictyon
blastocyst
blearyeyed
bricklayer
cardplayer
chromatype
cyclostyle
ditriglyph
fluorotype
goggleeyed
granophyre
heliophyte
heterodyne
hieroglyph
hippogryph
holloweyed
hydrophyte
hygrophyte
lithoglyph
lithophyte
lymphocyte
microphyte
nematocyst
osteophyte
palaeotype
parenchyma
pennyroyal

petroglyph
phenocryst
plasmolyse
platelayer
proteolyse
protophyta
protophyte
pycnostyle
saprophyte
somatotype
soothsayer
sporophyll
sporophyte
squinteyed
starryeyed
stereotype
stereotypy
swiveleyed
tetrastyle
troglodyte
tropophyte
unemployed
Ashkenazim
chimpanzee
deepfrozen
fuzzywuzzy
intermezzi
intermezzo
morbidezza
schemozzle
selfglazed
undersized
witchhazel

---

abacterial
aboriginal
Abrahamman
academical
accidental
acetabular
acoustical
acronychal
actinozoan
additional
adjectival
Aethiopian
alchemical
Algonquian
ambulacral
Amerindian
ammoniacal
anagogical
analogical
analytical
anarchical
anastigmat
anatomical
Andalusian
aneurismal
aneurysmal
anticlimax
anticlinal
antimonial
antinomian
antiphonal
antipodean
antisocial
aplacental
apochromat
apocryphal
apolitical
Apollinian
Apollonian
apothecial
araucarian
arborvitae
archetypal
aristocrat
armourclad

arteriolar
artificial
asteroidal
Athanasian
auditorial
Australian
autarkical
Babylonian
balbriggan
Barmecidal
batrachian
beautician
Belgravian
beneficial
bequeathal
Berkeleian
bicultural
bimestrial
biological
biparietal
bipartisan
bivalvular
bluecollar
bluethroat
Boswellian
botryoidal
brachyural
brachyuran
brandysnap
bridgehead
budgerigar
bufflehead
bullethead
bureaucrat
butterbean
Caledonian
campestral
cardiogram
carnassial
Carthusian
caruncular
catburglar
cavalryman
centennial
centesimal
ceremonial
chairwoman
chelicerae
childermas
chimerical
chronogram
Ciceronian
Circassian
Cistercian
clavicular
closetplay
clothesbag
cloverleaf
cognominal
collarbeam
collateral
colloquial
commercial
commonweal
compasssaw
conceptual
conchoidal
congenital
connatural
consensual
constantan
contextual
conventual
Copernican
copperhead
corbiculae
Corinthian
councilman
countryman

credential
crispbread
crustacean
cryptogram
curatorial
curricular
decahedral
decemviral
delusional
demoniacal
devotional
diabolical
diarrhoeal
diathermal
Dickensian
didactical
disenthral
dissimilar
distringas
divisional
documental
dogmatical
downstream
dragonhead
dramatical
drowsihead
dunderhead
duniwassal
duodecimal
ecological
economical
ectodermal
ecumenical
egoistical
electrical
Eleusinian
elliptical
encyclical
endocrinal
endodermal
Englishman
epicentral
epidemical
epiglottal
episodical
epithelial
equational
equatorial
equestrian
eremitical
erysipelas
Esculapian
Eurodollar
evidential
exegetical
exoterical
exothermal
expressway
extemporal
extramural
fascicular
febrifugal
fiddlehead
figurehead
follicular
fractional
fragmental
Franciscan
freedwoman
fricandeau
frictional
fruitarian
functional
fungicidal
furuncular
galimatias
gargantuan
geodetical
geological
geoponical
geothermal
germicidal
gerundival
Gilbertian
gingersnap
Glaswegian
glomerular
glossarial
goldenseal
grammarian
grandducal
grapesugar
GrecoRoman
gressorial
groundplan
groundsman
gyrational
hairstreak
halfdollar
hallelujah
hammerbeam
hammerhead
Hanoverian
harmonical
harvestman
headstream
heartbreak
hebdomadal
Heliconian
hemihedral
hemipteran
heptagonal
hermetical
hermitcrab
hexahedral
hierarchal
highwayman
hirudinean
historical
holohedral
homocercal
homoousian
homosexual
horizontal
horsewoman
husbandman
hypabyssal
hypaethral
hyperbolae
hyperbolas
hypodermal
hysterical
ideational
illusional
immaterial
immemorial
impersonal
incidental
individual
Indonesian
industrial
infrahuman
infusorial
infusorian
interlunar
internodal
interplead
interposal
intertidal
interurban
interzonal
intestinal
intramural
intraurban
involucral
Irishwoman
irrational
isochronal
isoglossal
isoseismal
isothermal
janitorial
jesuitical
johnsonian
jolterhead
journeyman
juristical
labiovelar
Lamarckian
laminarian
lapidarian
larvicidal
laundryman
lavatorial
Lawrentian
Leibnizian
lenticular
letterhead
ligamental
lighterman
Lithuanian
liturgical
locustbean
loggerhead
logistical
Lusitanian
Maccabaean
magnifical
magnificat
Mahommedan
maidenhead
mainstream
majestical
majuscular
Malpighian
Malthusian
managerial
mandibular
Manichaean
markswoman
matricidal
mechanical
Melanesian
menopausal
meridional
mesothorax
metacarpal
metatarsal
metathorax
methodical
Methuselah
Michaelmas
microfarad
micropylar
midshipman
militiaman
millennial
millesimal
millstream
minuscular
mischmetal
mixolydian
Mohammedan
molendinar
monarchial
Monarchian
monistical
monitorial
monoclinal
monogynian
monomaniac
monopodial
monumental
Mousterian
mouthorgan
Muhammadan
Muhammedan
multipolar
multivocal
muttonhead
myological
natalitial
natatorial
Neapolitan
neological
nepenthean
noblewoman
nonlogical
nonnatural
nonnuclear
notonectal
nurseryman
nutational
objectival
occasional
occidental
octahedral
octandrian
octonarian
oratorical
orchardman
orchestral
Ordovician
organismal
ornamental
orological
orthogonal
outgeneral
overspread
packthread
paddleboat
PalmSunday
Panamanian
papistical
paradisean
paradisiac
paradisian
paranormal
parenteral
Parnassian
paroxysmal
parricidal
parsonical
particular
passageway
pathetical
patricidal
patrilocal
pedalorgan
pedestrian
pedimental
peduncular
pellicular
peninsular
pennanular
pennyroyal
pentagonal
perceptual
periclinal
peridermal
periodical
periosteal
peripheral
peripteral
peritoneal
pesticidal
phalangeal
phanerogam
phantasmal
pharyngeal
phenomenal
pheromonal
Phoenician
phthisical
physiocrat
pictorical
playbyplay
politician
polyhedral
Polynesian
polynomial
Pomeranian
pontifical
positional
practician
praecocial
praetorial
praetorian
precordial
preexilian
prefrontal
preglacial
prelatical
premarital
premedical
presentday
primiparae
primordial
principial
prismoidal
procedural
proctorial
prolicidal
pronominal
prosodical
prostomial
prototypal
proverbial
provincial
prudential
puristical
pyromaniac
Pyrrhonian
quadrantal
quadrivial
quarterday
quixotical
rabbinical
railwayman
rattlehead
rattletrap
reciprocal
regimental
relational
republican
requiescat
revisional
rhetorical
rhomboidal
rhythmical
rollcollar
rotational
rubythroat
rudimental
runnerbean
sabbatical
sacerdotal
sacroiliac
saleswoman
salicional
salientian
salmonleap
salpingian
saltcellar
sanitarian
sapiential
scansorial
scaredycat
schoolmaam
Scillonian
Scotswoman
scrapmetal
screenplay
scriptural
sculptural
scyphozoan
sealingwax
seignorial
seismogram
selfdenial
semestrial
semiannual
seminarian
semiotical
semiuncial
senatorial
senseorgan
sentential
septennial
sepulchral
sequential
SerboCroat
serviceman
shandrydan
sheepshead
shenanigan
shortbread
shovelhead
shrinkwrap
siderostat
simoniacal
sincipital
sinusoidal
sleepyhead
slipstream
solenoidal
solifidian
solstitial
spacewoman
spagyrical
Spencerian
Spenserian
sphenogram
sphenoidal
spheroidal
spidercrab
spiracular
splintcoal
sponsorial
sporangial
sportswear
springhead
starstream
stenchtrap
stentorian
stereogram
strabismal
stratocrat
stringbean
structural
subcentral
subclavian
subglacial
subliminal
sublingual
subnuclear
suborbital
subordinal
superaltar
superhuman
superlunar
supernovae
suprarenal
sweetbread
sweetbriar
swinglebar
symbolical
symphyseal
symphysial
synchronal
synoptical
Talmudical
tangential
tarmacadam

Tartuffian
taxidermal
technician
technocrat
tegumental
teleostean
televisual
tendrillar
tenemental
tentacular
tetragonal
theatrical
theistical
theodicean
theologian
thermogram
thermostat
theurgical
threnodial
throughway
timberhead
tinctorial
torrential
townswoman
trabeculae
trabecular
Tractarian
tractional
transeptal
translunar
transposal
trawlerman
triangular
trichromat
trigeminal
triggerman
trilateral
trilingual
triliteral
triquetrae
triquetral
triumviral
trochoidal
tryptophan
tubercular
tyrannical
Tyrrhenian
ulotrichan
unAmerican
unbiblical
uncritical
unfamiliar
unicameral
unilateral
unilingual
unilocular
unofficial
urochordal
urticarial
uxoricidal
valleculae
vallecular
vegetarian
venational
vermicidal
vermicular
vernacular
versicular
vestibular
visitorial
vocational
volitional
vorticular
Waldensian
wampumpeag
wappenshaw
warmingpan
weatherman
Welshwoman
wentletrap
Wertherian
WhitMonday
WhitSunday
widespread
windowseat
wingcollar
wingspread
withdrawal
woodenhead
workingman
xiphosuran
yesteryear
zoological
anglophobe
angwantibo
Gallophobe
mulligrubs
mumbojumbo
nambypamby
negrophobe
redescribe
Russophobe
Slavophobe
subshrubby
transcribe
abhorrence
absorbance
absorbency
abstinence
abstinency
acceptance
accomplice
accordance
acrobatics
admittance
advertence
advertency
aerobatics
aesthetics
allegiance
alpenstock
altarpiece
alternance
amphibrach
Anglistics
appearance
apprentice
ascendance
ascendancy
ascendence
ascendency
assistance
attendance
autodidact
backstitch
badderlock
ballistics
bankruptcy
bellydance
benignancy
bibliotics
biometrics
biophysics
bioscience
birthplace
bloodstock
bobbinlace
bottleneck
brakeblock
breadstick
brilliance
brilliancy
broomstick
bubblyjock
cacogenics
candlewick
cantatrice
canvasback
cartomancy
cataphract
catoptrics
centreback
chaplaincy
chatoyance
chiromancy
chromatics
clovehitch
cockatrice
cognisance
competence
competency
compliance
compliancy
complicacy
condolence
conference
confidence
confluence
congruence
congruency
connivance
conscience
consonance
consonancy
conspiracy
continence
contradict
convalesce
convenance
conveyance
cornstarch
corpulence
corpulency
counteract
covariance
crackajack
crapulence
crossbench
crosscheck
crosshatch
crosspatch
crosspiece
cryogenics
czarevitch
deathwatch
defeasance
deficiency
degeneracy
dehiscence
deliquesce
dentifrice
dependence
dependency
derestrict
desipience
desistance
detergency
deterrence
difference
diffidence
disconnect
disrespect
disservice
dissidence
dissonance
dissonancy
divergence
divergency
divulgence
dumbstruck
ebullience
ebulliency
effeminacy
effervesce
efficiency
effloresce
effulgence
endproduct
energetics
episcopacy
ergonomics
everyplace
excellence
excellency
expectance
expectancy
expedience
expediency
experience
exuberance
eyeservice
fantastico
fetterlock
fiddleback
fieldpiece
firepolicy
flatulence
flatulency
flightdeck
floristics
freespeech
frontbench
geophysics
geriatrics
governance
grandniece
graphemics
greatniece
greenfinch
greenstick
gymnastics
hackmatack
halieutics
hammerlock
heartblock
Heptateuch
heresiarch
heuristics
hierocracy
homiletics
horseleech
hotchpotch
hydraulics
hydromancy
illiteracy
immaculacy
immoderacy
impatience
impeccancy
impendence
impendency
importance
imprudence
inaccuracy
inadequacy
incandesce
incessancy
incipience
incipiency
inclemency
incumbency
indelicacy
indistinct
inductance
indulgence
inefficacy
inelegance
innumeracy
insistence
insistency
insolvency
insurgence
insurgency
intendance
interspace
interstice
introspect
invariance
inveteracy
irradiance
isometrics
itinerancy
kinematics
knickknack
ladderback
landocracy
latescence
leafinsect
legitimacy
lipservice
lockstitch
lumberjack
luxuriance
magistracy
malignance
malignancy
matchstick
mendicancy
misconduct
miscreance
monstrance
moonstruck
morphemics
mouthpiece
natterjack
necromancy
negligence
newsagency
nightstick
nightwatch
nucleonics
nudibranch
observance
obstetrics
occurrence
ochlocracy
offlicence
oppugnancy
orchestics
ordonnance
outbalance
outerspace
outstretch
paddywhack
patristics
pedagogics
penetrance
pentastich
permanence
permanency
pertinence
pertinency
pestilence
pilgarlick
pillowlace
pitchblack
pluperfect
plutocracy
pneumatics
pornocracy
postoffice
precedence
precedency
preference
prepotence
prepotency
prescience
presidency
prevalence
prevenancy
procurance
profligacy
prominence
provenance
providence
pubescence
purtenance
purveyance
quadratics
quiescence
quiescency
recipiency
recommence
recrudesce
recumbency
recurrence
redundance
redundancy
reentrance
refulgence
regeneracy
reiterance
reluctance
reluctancy
remittance
renascence
repellance
repellancy
repellence
repellency
repentance
reprobance
repugnance
repugnancy
resilience
resiliency
resistance
resurgence
retrospect
rheumatics
ridgepiece
rubberneck
sacrosanct
saddleback
scapegrace
scaramouch
semeiotics
senescence
sergeantcy
serjeantcy
shellshock
sideeffect
sideglance
skirtdance
slavocracy
slipstitch
smockfrock
smokestack
snakedance
snobocracy
somnolence
somnolency
soundtrack
spatchcock
spitchcock
splashback
spodomancy
squirearch
stagecoach
statistics
stringency
stylistics
subsidence
subtenancy
succulence
succulency
sufferance
sunderance
supplejack
suppliance
survivance
sustenance
switchback
sworddance

swordstick
sycophancy
temperance
termagancy
tetrastich
theoretics
thinkpiece
threepence
threepiece
throwstick
thruppence
transience
transiency
trenchancy
truculence
truculency
tsarevitch
tumescence
turbulence
turbulency
turkeycock
turtleback
turtleneck
understock
undertrick
virescence
viscountcy
waterclock
whipstitch
wristwatch
yellowback
aficionado
afterwards
asafoetida
assafetida
autostrada
autostrade
avantgarde
balustrade
barramunda
barramundi
biodegrade
bisulphide
burramundi
carbonnade
centigrade
coastwards
coatimundi
colatitude
consuetude
corrigenda
crassitude
crossroads
custommade
definienda
definitude
diminuendo
discommode
disulphide
dorsigrade
dragonnade
earthwards
Eastertide
exactitude
floribunda
fratricide
frontwards
fuddyduddy
goodygoody
granddaddy
honeyguide
hornblende
hurdygurdy
inaptitude
ineptitude
infinitude
inquietude
intergrade
isoniazide
jaguarundi
Lammastide
lanthanide
lardydardy
malentendu
mansuetude
masquerade
nationwide
nightshade
northwards
nucleoside
nucleotide
ophicleide
overstride
pasquinade
piecegoods
polyploidy
propaganda
radiosonde
razorblade
retrograde
rightwards
ritardando
saccharide
salmagundi
saltigrade
sanctitude
scherzando
selfparody
shorewards
Shrovetide
sideboards
silverside
similitude
slavetrade
solicitude
sororicide
southwards
spermicide
springtide
sternwards
stillicide
stringendo
sugardaddy
tailormade
tardigrade
understudy
velocipede
wintertide
aardwolves
abducentes
ablebodied
abstracted
abstracter
accredited
accustomed
acidimeter
addlepated
administer
adventurer
advertiser
affiliated
Africander
Afrikander
Albigenses
allrounder
almacanter
almondeyed
almucanter
altogether
amanuenses
ambidexter
ammoniated
amphimacer
amphimixes
analphabet
anemometer
antechapel
antemortem
antimatter
antiquated
antitheses
aphaereses
apotheoses
apparelled
appendices
appendixes
aquaplaner
arbalester
arbalister
arbitrager
asteriated
astrologer
astronomer
attenuated
auctioneer
audiometer
aviatrices
babysitter
bacchantes
backhanded
backhander
backslider
baldheaded
ballflower
bandmaster
barebacked
barefooted
bareheaded
barelegged
barleybree
bathometer
bathymeter
beautifier
bedchamber
bedclothes
bedevilled
bedraggled
beefburger
bejewelled
bellflower
bellringer
bellwether
bellyacher
bemedalled
beribboned
bestridden
bestseller
bighearted
bigmouthed
bilgewater
billposter
biographer
birdspider
bivouacked
blackfaced
blackwater
blasphemer
blearyeyed
blitzkrieg
bloodmoney
bluebonnet
bluejacket
bobbysoxer
bombardier
bondholder
boneheaded
bonesetter
boneshaker
bookbinder
bookkeeper
bookmarker
bookseller
bootlegger
bootlicker
bottlefeed
bottletree
brainpower
breakables
breakwater
bressummer
bricklayer
broadsheet
browbeaten
bullheaded
bullroarer
bushmaster
bushranger
cackhanded
calamander
calcsinter
campaigner
candletree
cantilever
carabineer
carabinier
caravaneer
caravanned
caravanner
carbuncled
carcinogen
cardplayer
carpetweed
carragheen
caryatides
caseharden
caseworker
cataloguer
catechiser
catechumen
celebrated
challenger
chandelier
changeover
channelled
chapfallen
charioteer
chiffonier
chimpanzee
chronicler
churchgoer
cicatrices
circumflex
classified
classifier
clawhammer
clinometer
clodhopper
cloistered
clothespeg
clubfooted
coalbunker
coathanger
cochleated
cockchafer
colonnaded
comehither
commandeer
commandoes
complainer
complected
complotted
compounder
compressed
comstocker
confounded
considered
controlled
controller
convoluted
coolheaded
coparcener
coproducer
copyholder
copyreader
copywriter
cordwainer
cornflakes
cornflower
coromandel
corroboree
corrugated
corticated
Corybantes
cottonseed
cottonweed
counselled
covenanted
covenantee
covenanter
cowcatcher
cowparsley
cowpuncher
crenulated
crossbones
crossbreed
crossindex
crossrefer
crosstrees
crowkeeper
cucullated
cuirassier
cuspidated
cyclometer
cylindered
dapplegrey
daydreamer
deepfrozen
deeprooted
deepseated
deflowerer
densimeter
deodoriser
deoxidiser
dermatogen
desecrater
despatcher
determined
dickcissel
diminished
disburthen
discharger
disclaimer
discounter
discourser
discoverer
disembowel
disengaged
dishearten
dishwasher
disjointed
disordered
disparager
disparates
dispatcher
dispirited
dispraiser
disquieten
dissembler
dissipated
distracted
distrainer
distressed
divebomber
dogmatiser
doorkeeper
doughfaced
downfallen
draconites
dragontree
dressmaker
drophammer
dumbwaiter
dumfounder
dustjacket
eartrumpet
economiser
emblazoner
embowelled
emerypaper
emerywheel
Emmentaler
empanelled
emulsifier
encourager
encroacher
endstopped
enregister
enthralled
epentheses
epexegeses
epigrapher
eudiometer
evenhanded
everglades
evilminded
eyeglasses
faceharden
fairhaired
fairleader
fairminded
fairspoken
fandangoes
farfetched
farsighted
featherbed
fellmonger
fertiliser
fibrinogen
fictioneer
filibuster
fimbriated
fireraiser
firescreen
fishcarver
fishmonger
fivefinger
flamingoes
flannelled
flatfooted
fleabitten
fleamarket
floodwater
flycatcher
flyswatter
foamflower
folksinger
footballer
footwarmer
forcipated
forecaster
forefather
forefinger
foregather
forehanded
forerunner
foreteller
fortyniner
forwearied
fourfooted
fourhanded
fourleaved
fourposter
fourteener
franchiser
freebooter
freehanded
freeholder
freelancer
freeloader
freesoiler
freespoken
frequenter
freshwater
fricasseed

froghopper
fullbodied
fussbudget
galvaniser
gamekeeper
gasconader
gaslighter
gatekeeper
gatelegged
gauntleted
geographer
gingerbeer
gladhander
glasspaper
glycolyses
goalkeeper
goaltender
goatsucker
gobstopper
goggleeyed
goldbeater
golddigger
goniometer
goodlooker
gravimeter
greyheaded
gunfighter
gunslinger
gyrocopter
hackbuteer
hairraiser
halberdier
halfcocked
halfvolley
halfwitted
handmaiden
handpicked
handselled
handworked
hangglider
hardbilled
hardbitten
hardboiled
hardfisted
hardhanded
hardheaded
harelipped
harmoniser
haruspices
headhunter
headmaster
headphones
headwaiter
heavyarmed
helicopter
heliolater
heliometer
hellbender
henharrier
henhearted
heptameter
Herrnhuter
highbinder
highhanded
highjacker
highlander
highminded
hippomanes
hitchhiker
hokeypokey
holloweyed
homebrewed
honeyeater
honeysweet
hornrimmed
horsecoper
horsepower
horseshoer
hotblooded
housewives
humanities
humidifier
humpbacked
hybridiser
hydrometer
hygrometer
hyphenated
hypnotiser
hypophyses
hypotheses
hypsometer
icebreaker
iconolater
iconometer
illadvised
illnatured
illstarred
impanelled
imperilled
importuner
improviser
indigested
indiscreet
indisposed
infatuated
initialled
inkslinger
innuendoes
interbreed
interceder
interested
interferer
interloper
interposer
intervener
interwoven
introducer
ironhanded
ironmaster
ironmonger
ironworker
jackanapes
jackhammer
jackknives
Janusfaced
jawbreaker
jimsonweed
kerchieves
keyboarder
kingfisher
knockkneed
kriegspiel
ladychapel
ladyfinger
ladykiller
landholder
landhunger
landingnet
landlocked
landlubber
landscaper
languisher
lansquenet
lawbreaker
leafcutter
leafhopper
lederhosen
lefthanded
lefthander
lentigines
lifejacket
lightfaced
likeminded
limeburner
lionhunter
Lipizzaner
Lippizaner
liquidiser
lockkeeper
logorrhoea
longhaired
longheaded
longlegged
longprimer
longwinded
loosecover
lossleader
lotuseater
loudhailer
loveletter
lowpitched
lumpsucker
macebearer
magnetiser
mainlander
maintainer
maladapted
malingerer
mamillated
manchineel
mangosteen
manoeuvrer
manoeuvres
manteltree
manumitted
marginated
Mariolater
marshalled
marshaller
marshalsea
matchmaker
mavourneen
maxilliped
medicaster
medullated
merrymaker
mesmeriser
metastases
metatheses
methylated
micrometer
middleaged
mineworker
mintmaster
misaligned
mischanter
misjoinder
mismatched
misnomered
moderniser
moneymaker
moneytaker
monorhymed
moonflower
moonshiner
mosquitoes
mossbunker
moustached
moviemaker
mudskipper
mudslinger
multifaced
multiplier
musicpaper
mythiciser
mythologer
necrolater
nevernever
newfangled
newscaster
newsletter
newsmonger
newsreader
newswriter
noisemaker
nonaligned
nondrinker
nonjoinder
nonplussed
nonstarter
nonswimmer
northerner
nutcracker
obfuscated
oftentimes
oldfangled
ombrometer
openhanded
openminded
ophiolater
opisometer
orangepeel
ottershrew
outfielder
outswinger
overburden
overcooked
overhanded
overlander
overlapped
overlooker
overmanned
overmantel
overmaster
overridden
overtopped
overwinter
pacesetter
painkiller
palisander
pallbearer
palmbutter
panhandler
papermaker
parimutuel
pastmaster
pastyfaced
pathfinder
pawnbroker
peacemaker
pearldiver
peashooter
pectinated
pedimented
pentameter
periwigged
petiolated
petitioner
philologen
phonometer
photometer
pickpocket
piezometer
pigeontoed
pigsticker
piledriver
pinecarpet
pinfeather
pinnulated
pinstriped
pixillated
planimeter
planometer
platelayer
plumassier
pockmarked
pokerfaced
pontifices
postmaster
postmortem
potbellied
pourparler
prejudiced
prescriber
principled
privileged
proclaimer
programmer
prohibiter
promenader
pronounced
pronouncer
proofsheet
propertied
prophesier
propounder
proscriber
protracted
pulsimeter
pulsometer
pulveriser
pulvinated
pycnometer
pyknometer
quadruplet
quadruplex
quantifier
quarrelled
quarreller
quarrender
questioner
quintuplet
quizmaster
rackrenter
radiometer
railroader
ratcatcher
rechristen
reconciler
reconsider
redblooded
rediscover
registered
remodelled
rencounter
reproducer
reredorter
researcher
restrained
restrainer
reverencer
rhomboidei
ringfinger
ringleader
ringmaster
ringnecked
ringtailed
ripsnorter
roadrunner
rockbadger
rockgarden
rockhopper
rockribbed
roodscreen
roofgarden
ropedancer
ropeladder
ropewalker
rosechafer
roselipped
rottweiler
roughrider
sacrificer
saddletree
safeblower
salamander
sanctifier
sandbagger
sandhopper
sargassoes
sawtoothed
scaffolder
scoresheet
scrimmager
scrutineer
sculptured
seborrhoea
seedvessel
seersucker
selfbinder
selfesteem
selffeeder
selfglazed
selfguided
selfmurder
selfpoised
selfraised
selfseeker
selfstyled
selfwilled
semifitted
semiquaver
sensitiser
sermoniser
sexlimited
shamefaced
shanghaier
sharpnosed
sheabutter
shearwater
shellacked
shipbroker
shipfitter
shipmaster
shiprigged
shopkeeper
shoplifter
shopsoiled
shopwalker
shortdated
shortlived
shouldered
showjumper
shrivelled
sidestreet
sidewinder
signwriter
silkscreen
silverweed
simplifier
singletree
sixshooter
skirmisher
skyscraper
slitpocket
slowfooted
slowwitted
smallwares
smartmoney
smokedried
snailpaced
snailwheel
sneakthief
sneezeweed
snickasnee
snowcapped
soapboiler
soapflakes
sobersided
sobersides
socialiser
softbilled
softboiled
softfinned
softheaded
softspoken
songwriter
soothsayer
soubriquet
southerner
spectacled
spectacles
spirometer
splitlevel

splutterer
sprucebeer
squanderer
squaretoed
squaretoes
squinteyed
stabiliser
stadholder
starryeyed
stencilled
stenciller
stepfather
stepladder
stepmother
stepsister
steriliser
stilettoes
stockpiler
stockrider
stoneborer
stopvolley
straighten
strathspey
strengthen
structured
submariner
subscriber
subspecies
succedanea
sunglasses
superduper
superorder
superpower
supplanter
surefooted
swanmaiden
swaybacked
sweetbrier
swinefever
switchover
swiveleyed
syllogiser
symboliser
syncopated
tablelinen
tachometer
tachymeter
tackdriver
talebearer
taleteller
tantaliser
tapestried
taskmaster
taxidancer
teaplanter
tearjerker
teatrolley
telecaster
telephoner
televiewer
temporiser
tendrilled
tetrameter
themselves
theosopher
thereafter
thereunder
threatener
thromboses
thumbscrew
tidewaiter
tilthammer
timbertoes
timekeeper
timeserver
tobogganer
tonguetied
touchpaper
tourniquet
tracheated
trafficked
trafficker
trammelled
transducer
transferee
transfuser
transmuter
transposer
treadwheel
trespasser
tribometer
triphammer
trochanter
tromometer
trucklebed
trundlebed
tufthunter
tumbleweed
twilighted
twowheeler
tympanites
typesetter
typewriter
umbellifer
umbrellaed
unabridged
unaccented
unaffected
unassisted
unattached
unattended
unbalanced
unbeliever
unblenched
unbonneted
unbuttoned
uncloister
uncustomed
undefended
undercover
underlinen
underminer
undersexed
undersized
understeer
undertaken
undertaker
underwater
undeserved
undesigned
undeterred
undigested
uneducated
unemployed
unequalled
unexampled
unexcelled
unexpected
unexplored
unfathered
unfettered
unfinished
unforeseen
unfriended
ungrounded
unhallowed
unhouseled
unimproved
uninformed
unlabelled
unlettered
unmeasured
unmortised
unnumbered
unoccupied
unprepared
unprovoked
unravelled
unredeemed
unrelieved
unremarked
unrequited
unreserved
unresolved
unrivalled
unschooled
unscreened
unscripted
unseasoned
unselected
unstrained
unstressed
untroubled
unwrinkled
vanquisher
variegated
variometer
veldschoen
verandahed
verbaliser
vestpocket
victimiser
victualled
victualler
viewfinder
viscometer
visualiser
voltameter
vulcaniser
wallflower
wallpepper
wastepaper
watchmaker
watchtower
waterpower
waterskier
waterwheel
weakminded
weedkiller
weimaraner
wellheeled
wellspoken
wellturned
wellwisher
werewolves
wharfinger
whatsoever
whensoever
whiskified
whitefaced
wholesaler
whomsoever
wildfowler
Winchester
windflower
windjammer
windscreen
winebibber
winegrower
wingfooted
wiredrawer
wirehaired
wirepuller
wiretapper
wirewalker
wireworker
witchhazel
withdrawer
withholder
woodcarver
woodcutter
woodlander
woodpecker
woodturner
woodworker
woolgather
woolgrower
woolsorter
workbasket
worshipped
worshipper
yardmaster
yourselves
breadstuff
chiffchaff
claspknife
coolingoff
crankshaft
dampingoff
declassify
dehumidify
disqualify
dissatisfy
fallingoff
fisticuffs
greenstuff
handicraft
hippogriff
housecraft
nightshift
paperknife
powderpuff
presignify
saccharify
shandygaff
spacecraft
spoondrift
stagecraft
statecraft
Stroganoff
subjectify
swordcraft
undercliff
undercroft
watercraft
witchcraft
afterimage
anecdotage
apophthegm
assemblage
autecology
balneology
baronetage
bellylaugh
belongings
bibliology
bibliopegy
bioecology
blancmange
brachylogy
brigandage
camerlengo
camerlingo
camouflage
cardiology
carphology
centrifuge
chronology
colportage
conchology
constringe
craniology
cryptology
deltiology
demonology
dendrology
deontology
disarrange
discourage
dramaturge
dramaturgy
drawbridge
Egyptology
embryology
entomology
enzymology
escapology
escheatage
exobiology
exploitage
expressage
footbridge
freightage
futurology
gastrology
glaciology
glossology
glottology
graphology
harbourage
heortology
hepatology
heterology
hippophagy
hodgepodge
horselaugh
husbandage
immunology
intertrigo
lexicology
lighterage
macrophage
malacology
maquillage
metallurgy
mineralogy
misgivings
morphology
multistage
musicology
nephrology
numerology
oceanology
odontology
oneirology
overcharge
overslaugh
palynology
papyrology
percentage
persiflage
phrenology
physiology
phytophagy
pichiciago
pilgrimage
plunderage
pogonology
potamology
prearrange
prepackage
proctorage
psephology
psychology
pyretology
quarterage
rejoicings
remarriage
runthrough
sarcophagi
sarcophagy
satanology
screenings
seethrough
seignorage
seismology
selenology
semeiology
shillelagh
shortrange
skewbridge
snowplough
somatology
speciology
speleology
spongology
subaverage
subterfuge
supercargo
surplusage
synecology
technology
telpherage
teratology
ticpolonga
timbrology
tollbridge
touchjudge
toxicology
trichology
trophology
urbanology
usquebaugh
vernissage
villainage
villeinage
wanderings
wongawonga
yarborough
aerography
afterlight
anacolutha
anastrophe
apostrophe
autography
birthright
brakelight
cacography
cartwright
cerography
crosslight
deadweight
demography
distraught
doxography
earthlight
epistrophe
fearnought
fireblight
firstnight
flashlight
floodlight
forthright
gobemouche
guestnight
gymnosophy
holography
homeopathy
hydropathy
iconomachy
ideography
jinricksha
jinrikisha
kieselguhr
lexigraphy
limitrophe
lipography
logography
makeweight
matriarchy
mesomorphy
mesoscaphe
microfiche
millwright
misthought
neuropathy
newsworthy
nightlight
nomography
nosography
noteworthy
oleography
oreography
osteopathy

overbought
overflight
overweight
patriarchy
philosophe
philosophy
photolitho
pilotlight
playwright
polygraphy
prizefight
pyracantha
pyrography
roadworthy
sabretache
satyagraha
sciagraphy
selftaught
serigraphy
shipwright
skiagraphy
squirarchy
steamtight
synaloepha
synecdoche
tauromachy
telegraphy
testflight
tomography
topography
torchlight
trierarchy
typography
unbesought
wainwright
watertight
wishywashy
xerography
xylography
zygomorphy
achromatic
acrophobia
adrenergic
aerobiosis
aerobiotic
aeronautic
aerophobia
aerostatic
aetiologic
agglutinin
airmanship
albuminoid
alcyonaria
aldermanic
algolagnia
algolagnic
allergenic
allopathic
allophonic
allosteric
allotropic
alphabetic
alphameric
altruistic
amanuensis
ampelopsis
amphimixis
amphoteric
amygdaloid
anaglyphic
anamorphic
anapaestic
anaplastic
anaptyctic
anchoretic
anchoritic
anchylosis
anchylotic
androgenic
anglomania
annalistic
antependia
antheridia
anthracoid
anthropoid
antibiosis
antibiotic
antiheroic
antipathic
antisepsis
antiseptic
antistatic
antithesis
antithetic
aphaeresis
aphoristic
aphrodisia
apodeictic
apolaustic
apologetic
apoplectic
aposematic
apotheosis
apotropaic
aquafortis
aragonitic
archaistic
arithmetic
arrhythmia
arrhythmic
arthralgia
arthralgic
arytaenoid
asbestosis
ascariasis
Ashkenazim
astigmatic
astrologic
astronomic
asymmetric
asymptotic
ateleiosis
austenitic
authorship
autocratic
autoerotic
azeotropic
bacchantic
barbituric
barometric
batholitic
battleship
beadleship
Beaujolais
bibliophil
bijouterie
biliverdin
bimetallic
biodynamic
biogenesis
biogenetic
biographic
biomorphic
bizarrerie
bloodstain
bluepencil
bollweevil
bolometric
breadfruit
bridesmaid
bronchitic
bronchitis
brusquerie
Buddhistic
bursarship
byssinosis
cabalistic
carboxylic
carcinosis
cardialgia
carotenoid
carotinoid
catalectic
cataleptic
catastasis
catechesis
catechetic
cattlegrid
cellulitis
cellulosic
censorship
chaudfroid
chemotaxis
chevrotain
chiliastic
chondritic
choriambic
cinquefoil
clientship
clothespin
coenobitic
coenobytic
columbaria
concentric
confervoid
congeneric
Constantia
consulship
copesettic
coprolitic
cornucopia
corybantic
cosmogonic
cosmopolis
cosmoramic
cottontail
cousinship
crackbrain
crematoria
crescentic
crossgrain
cryoscopic
cuckoospit
cybernetic
cyclopedia
cyclopedic
cylindroid
daisychain
deaconship
delphinoid
democratic
dermatitis
diachronic
diagnostic
diagraphic
diapedesis
diapedetic
diarrhoeic
diathermic
dichroitic
dielectric
dilemmatic
diphtheria
diphtheric
diphyletic
diplomatic
dipsomania
disembroil
disinherit
dispersoid
disyllabic
doctorship
dosimetric
drawingpin
duodenitis
dynamistic
dysenteric
dysgraphia
dysplastic
dystrophic
ecchymosis
ecchymotic
ectodermic
editorship
egocentric
electronic
emblematic
embolismic
empathetic
emphractic
enantiosis
encephalic
endodermis
endophytic
endoscopic
endosmosis
endosmotic
endothelia
enharmonic
eosinophil
epenthesis
epenthetic
epexegesis
epexegetic
epiblastic
epicycloid
epideictic
epidermoid
epigastric
epigenesis
epigenetic
epiglottic
epiglottis
epigraphic
episematic
equilibria
erethismic
erotogenic
erotomania
escallonia
escharotic
essayistic
ethnologic
eucaryotic
eulogistic
euphuistic
eurhythmic
eurypterid
euthanasia
exospheric
exothermic
factorship
Fahrenheit
fatalistic
fathership
fellowship
felspathic
fibrositis
filariasis
fingernail
FinnoUgric
florilegia
foreordain
framboesia
Francophil
freemartin
friendship
frigorific
futuristic
gaillardia
galliambic
Gallomania
gametangia
ganglionic
gaultheria
generatrix
geocentric
geognostic
geographic
geothermic
gesundheit
gingivitis
Glagolitic
glycolysis
glycosuria
glycosuric
gramicidin
granulitic
grapefruit
groceteria
groundbait
gynocratic
gyroscopic
haematosis
haematuria
haemolysis
haemolytic
hagiologic
halophytic
hawserlaid
Hebraistic
hedonistic
heliotaxis
helminthic
hemicyclic
hemiplegia
hemiplegic
heptarchic
heptatonic
heroicomic
hexametric
hierarchic
histologic
histolysis
histolytic
histrionic
holophytic
holosteric
homophonic
horoscopic
housetrain
hovertrain
humanistic
humoristic
hydrologic
hydrolysis
hydrolytic
hydrotaxis
hyperaemia
hyperaemic
hyperbaric
hyperbolic
hyperdulia
hypergolic
hypersonic
hypnagogic
hypodermic
hypodermis
hypolimnia
hypophysis
hypostasis
hypostatic
hypotactic
hypothesis
hysteresis
hysteretic
iatrogenic
ichthyosis
idealistic
idiopathic
impresario
inartistic
inexplicit
infrasonic
inharmonic
inheritrix
internship
isentropic
isodynamic
isogenetic
isomorphic
jackrabbit
Jehovistic
jingoistic
judgematic
kaisership
kerygmatic
kibbutznik
kinnikinic
knobkerrie
knopkierie
lambrequin
laryngitic
laryngitis
latifundia
lawntennis
leadership
ledgerbait
legalistic
legateship
leucocytic
leukocytic
linguistic
lithologic
loungesuit
loxodromic
Lupercalia
madreporic
maidenhair
manometric
marginalia
Massoretic
mastership
mathematic
matronship
matronymic
megalithic
megascopic
melanistic
melismatic
membership
meningitis
mentorship
mesenteric
Mesolithic
mesophytic
metalepsis
metaphoric
metaphysic
metaplasia
metastasis
metastatic
metathesis
metathetic
metempiric
meteoritic
metronomic
metronymic
metropolis
microlitic
mixedmedia
mizzensail
mobocratic
mockheroic
molluscoid
moniliasis
monkeysuit
monocarpic
monochasia
monoclinic
monocratic
monocyclic
monohybrid
monohydric

monolithic
monophonic
montbretia
moralistic
morganatic
mothership
moustachio
multimedia
myasthenia
mystagogic
mythologic
mythomania
mythopoeia
mythopoeic
naphthenic
nativistic
necropolis
neoclassic
neoplastic
nephralgia
neurotoxin
nihilistic
nomothetic
noogenesis
nosophobia
nostologic
novelistic
numismatic
nyctalopia
nyctalopic
odontalgia
oligarchic
ophiologic
ophthalmia
ophthalmic
optimistic
orogenesis
orogenetic
orographic
orthogenic
orthopedic
overcommit
paedagogic
paediatric
Palaeozoic
palmatifid
pancreatic
pancreatin
pangenesis
pangenetic
pantomimic
pantrymaid
parabiosis
parabiotic
paraboloid
paradisaic
paraffinic
paragnosis
paralipsis
parametric
paramnesia
paraplegia
paraplegic
parasitoid
paratactic
pastorship
pathogenic
pathologic
patisserie
patronymic
pederastic
pegmatitic
pemphigoid
penetralia
penicillin
penmanship
pentatomic
pentatonic
perchloric
pericyclic
peripeteia
periscopic
perithecia
phagedenic
phagocytic
phantasmic
phantastic
phenacetin
phenotypic
philatelic
phlegmatic
phlogistic
phonematic
phonolitic
phonologic
phosphatic
phosphoric
photogenic
photolysis
photolytic
phototaxis
phylogenic
phytogenic
phytotoxic
pigeonpair
pillowslip
pinnatifid
pistolwhip
pityriasis
planetaria
planktonic
pleochroic
pleonastic
poinsettia
pollenosis
polyandric
polyatamic
polyclinic
polycyclic
polydipsia
polyhedric
polymathic
polyonymic
polyphasic
polyphonic
populistic
porismatic
portcullis
postexilic
pozzolanic
precipitin
presbyopia
presbyopic
princeship
procrypsis
procryptic
proglottis
prognathic
prognostic
prosthesis
prosthetic
protanopic
protectrix
prothallia
prototypic
protreptic
provitamin
psilocybin
pugilistic
pursership
pycnogonid
pyromantic
pyrometric
pyrophoric
quadrennia
quadrumvir
quartzitic
quatorzain
quatrefoil
radiogenic
radiologic
ragamuffin
readership
rectorship
regentship
retrochoir
rheotropic
rheumatoid
rhizogenic
riboflavin
ricinoleic
rickettsia
rockrabbit
rollingpin
Romanistic
rotisserie
saccharoid
sandmartin
Sanskritic
saprogenic
sarracenia
satellitic
saturnalia
satyriasis
scarabaeid
schismatic
scholastic
scientific
sciolistic
scratchwig
scriptoria
seabiscuit
seacaptain
seamanship
selfdeceit
selfprofit
semiliquid
septenarii
seriocomic
shroudlaid
sialagogic
siegetrain
simplistic
sitophobia
snafflebit
sociologic
solecistic
sophomoric
souterrain
speedlimit
splanchnic
springtail
squaresail
squireship
stereopsis
stochastic
stomatitis
stonefruit
strabismic
subaquatic
sultanship
supersonic
supertonic
suretyship
suspensoid
syllabaria
synaeresis
synchronic
synergetic
syngenesis
synostosis
syphilitic
systematic
talismanic
tautomeric
taxidermic
telemetric
teleologic
telepathic
telephonic
telescopic
tellership
tenderloin
tendinitis
tenebrific
termitaria
terreplein
tetrapolis
tetrarchic
theocratic
theophanic
theophoric
thermionic
thermophil
thimblerig
thrombosis
thrombotic
thwartship
timocratic
totemistic
toxiphobia
tracheitis
tragicomic
translucid
tremolitic
tribrachic
trichiasis
triglyphic
trimorphic
tropologic
tuberculin
tularaemia
tularaemic
tympanitic
tympanitis
ultrabasic
ultrasonic
umpireship
uneconomic
unemphatic
unhistoric
unionistic
urethritis
valvulitis
variolitic
Visigothic
vitalistic
viziership
volumetric
wardenship
wheelchair
xenophobia
xerophytic
xylophonic
zollverein
zoomorphic
backblocks
backstroke
birdstrike
bobbysocks
chainsmoke
cheesecake
Christlike
coralsnake
cottoncake
downstroke
earthquake
fatherlike
fourstroke
glassworks
goldilocks
grasssnake
hairstroke
hankypanky
heatstroke
johnnycake
longshanks
maidenlike
morrispike
pilliwinks
pincerlike
schipperke
seamanlike
sidestroke
spongecake
springlike
steelworks
summerlike
sweepstake
trancelike
waterworks
aberrantly
abnormally
abominable
abominably
abortively
abrasively
absolutely
absorbable
absorbedly
abstractly
abstrusely
abundantly
acceptable
acceptably
acceptedly
accessible
accessibly
accurately
accursedly
accusingly
achievable
acidophile
acquirable
acromegaly
actionable
actionably
adaptively
adequately
adherently
adhesively
adjacently
adjustable
admiringly
admissible
admittable
admittedly
adoptively
adsorbable
affectedly
afferently
affirmable
affluently
affordable
agitatedly
alarmingly
allusively
altocumuli
amerciable
analysable
anemophily
anglophile
animalcula
animalcule
animatedly
annoyingly
answerable
answerably
antepenult
anteriorly
apparently
appealable
appeasable
applicable
applicably
appositely
approvable
approvably
arbitrable
arboreally
armorially
arrogantly
arterially
ascendable
ascendible
ascribable
aspergilla
assailable
assessable
assignable
associable
atomically
attachable
attackable
attainable
atypically
audiophile
automobile
autumnally
aversively
backwardly
bafflingly
banderilla
barcarolle
basketball
becomingly
believable
besprinkle
biannually
biblically
bibliopole
bibliopoly
bibulously
bidonville
biennially
bigamously
binaurally
bisexually
bissextile
blamefully
bleachable
bleatingly
blindingly
blissfully
blockishly
bloodguilt
bluebottle
blurringly
blushingly
boastfully
boondoggle
bootlessly
bouncingly
brainchild
brandyball
breastwall
breathable
brickfield
bridgeable
brocatelle
bronchiole
broodingly
bumblingly
bunglingly
bustlingly
butterball
buttermilk
buttonball
buttonhole
cacomistle
Caerphilly
cajolingly
calculable
calculably

canaliculi
cannonball
canonicals
canorously
captiously
carelessly
carmagnole
cascarilla
cautiously
cavalierly
cellularly
censurable
centrefold
centrehalf
changeable
changeably
chargeable
charitable
charitably
charmingly
cheapishly
cheerfully
chemically
childishly
chinchilla
chrysotile
churlishly
Cinderella
circularly
citronella
clannishly
clarabella
clerically
clinically
clownishly
Clydesdale
coachbuilt
coagulable
cocksurely
coercively
coffeemill
cognisable
cognisably
coherently
cohesively
coleoptile
collatable
collembola
colonially
colossally
colourable
colourably
comestible
commonable
communally
commutable
comparable
comparably
compatible
compatibly
completely
composedly
computable
concretely
confusedly
conjointly
conjugally
consolable
constantly
consumable
consumedly
contrarily
contritely
convenable
conversely
conveyable
corncockle
corporally
corpuscule
corrigible
cosmically
covalently
covetingly
covetously
coweringly
craftguild
cranesbill
creatively
creaturely
creditable
creditably
crepuscule
criminally
critically
cultivable
culturally
cumbrously
cyclically
cyclostyle
damageable
damagingly
daughterly
dazzlingly
debonairly
decadently
deceivable
deceptible
decisively
declarable
declinable
decorously
deductible
defeasible
defendable
defensible
defensibly
deferrable
definitely
defrayable
degradable
degradedly
dejectedly
delectable
delectably
delicately
delusively
demandable
dementedly
demoiselle
demurrable
dependable
dependably
deplorable
deplorably
depravedly
deprivable
deridingly
derisively
deservedly
deshabille
designedly
desirously
desolately
despicable
despicably
despisable
detachable
detachedly
detectable
detestable
detestably
devilishly
dextrously
diagonally
dialysable
diffusible
digestible
digitately
dilatorily
diligently
dillydally
discophile
discreetly
discretely
disentitle
disgruntle
dishabille
dislikable
disloyally
disorderly
disposable
disputable
disputably
disquietly
dissoluble
distensile
distinctly
disyllable
divisively
dolorously
dominantly
doubletalk
doubtfully
doubtingly
downwardly
drawlingly
dreadfully
dreamworld
droopingly
drosophila
drudgingly
dungbeetle
dwarfishly
effaceable
effusively
electively
eliminable
eloquently
employable
endorsable
enduringly
engagingly
enormously
enticingly
enumerable
enunciable
eradicable
erotically
eruptively
escadrille
espadrille
especially
ethereally
ethnically
evaporable
eventually
examinable
excitingly
executable
exotically
expandable
expansible
expectedly
expendable
explicable
explicitly
exportable
extendedly
extendible
extensible
exteriorly
externally
extricable
exultantly
exultingly
fabulously
factiously
fadelessly
fairycycle
faithfully
familiarly
fancifully
farcically
fathomable
fatiguable
favourable
favourably
fearlessly
fearsomely
fecklessly
femininely
fenestella
fetchingly
feverishly
fiducially
fiendishly
filterable
fisherfolk
fishkettle
flagrantly
flapdoodle
flawlessly
fleeringly
fleetingly
flexuously
flippantly
floatingly
fluviatile
fontanelle
footcandle
forcefully
forecastle
forgivable
forgivably
formidable
formidably
formlessly
fragrantly
fraxinella
freakishly
frenziedly
frequently
friendlily
frowningly
fruitfully
fugitively
fumblingly
funereally
fustanella
Gallophile
generously
gentlefolk
germinally
ghastfully
gladsomely
glancingly
globularly
gloriously
gorgeously
Gorgonzola
gothically
governable
gracefully
graciously
granadilla
grandchild
granduncle
granularly
graspingly
gratefully
greatuncle
grenadilla
grievously
grindingly
growlingly
grudgingly
gruesomely
guilefully
gutturally
gypsophila
habitually
halfyearly
hamshackle
handsomely
harmlessly
hauntingly
heartwhole
hectically
heedlessly
heliacally
helplessly
hempnettle
heroically
herrenvolk
hesitantly
hibernacle
honourable
honourably
hopelessly
hormonally
hospitable
hospitably
hourcircle
humorously
hurlyburly
hydrically
hydrophily
ignorantly
illatively
illaudable
illaudably
illusively
illusorily
imaginable
imaginably
imbecilely
immaturely
imminently
immiscible
immiscibly
immodestly
immortally
immortelle
immoveable
impalpable
impalpably
impartible
impassable
impassably
impassible
impassibly
impeccable
impeccably
imperially
implacable
implacably
implicitly
impolitely
importable
imposingly
impossible
impossibly
impotently
improbable
improbably
improperly
improvable
improvably
impudently
impugnable
inactively
inchoately
incisively
inclinable
includible
incredible
incredibly
inculpable
incunabula
incurrable
indecently
indictable
indirectly
indolently
ineducable
ineligible
ineligibly
ineludible
inevitable
inevitably
inexorable
inexorably
inexpertly
inexpiable
inexpiably
infallible
infallibly
infamously
infeasible
inferiorly
infernally
inferrable
infinitely
inflatable
inflexible
inflexibly
informally
ingestible
inherently
inhumanely
inimically
inimitable
inimitably
innerrably
innocently
inoculable
inoperable
insatiable
insatiably
insecurely
insensible
insensibly
insociable
insolently
insolvable
intangible
intangibly
integrable
integrally
interiorly
internally
intimately
intrepidly
introrsely
invaluable
invaluably
invariable
invariably
invincible
invincibly
inviolable
inviolably
invitingly
ironically
isolatable
Italophile
jargonelle
jerrybuilt
jubilantly
judicially
kenspeckle
lamentable
lamentably
lamentedly

lanternfly
largescale
laughingly
licensable
lifelessly
listlessly
literarily
lonesomely
lopsidedly
lovelessly
lowprofile
luculently
lukewarmly
luminously
lusciously
lustrously
malapertly
manageable
manageably
maniacally
manifestly
manifoldly
manzanilla
marginally
marketable
markethall
martingale
masticable
materially
maternally
mealbeetle
measurable
measurably
measuredly
medievally
melancholy
menacingly
mensurable
mercantile
mercifully
metastable
metrically
middlingly
militantly
militarily
mindlessly
mirthfully
mistakable
mistakenly
moderately
modifiable
monetarily
mosaically
motorcycle
mournfully
movelessly
mozzarella
muffinbell
muscularly
musicianly
mutinously
myopically
mystically
mythically
namelessly
nationally
nauseously
nautically
nebulously
necrophile
necrophily
needlessly
negatively
negligible
negligibly
negotiable
negrophile
nitrochalk
nominately
notarially
noticeable
noticeably
notifiable
notionally
nullanulla
numerously
obdurately
obediently
obligingly
observable
observably
obtainable
officially
onesidedly
oppositely
optatively
optionally
oracularly
ordinarily
orientally
originally
orthodoxly
ostensible
ostensibly
otherwhile
otherworld
outrightly
oversubtle
oversupply
oxidisable
pacifiable
packsaddle
paddyfield
paedophile
painlessly
pardonable
pardonably
parentally
participle
pastorally
pasturable
patentable
paternally
patulously
peacefully
peccadillo
peculiarly
peerlessly
pellucidly
penetrable
penetrably
penitently
peppermill
percentile
perdurable
perdurably
perilously
perishable
periwinkle
permutable
personable
personally
perversely
petronella
petulantly
phonically
photophily
physically
piccalilli
piercingly
pigeonhole
pilotwhale
pitilessly
planetable
plangently
pleadingly
pleasantly
pleasingly
ploddingly
ploughable
pocketable
poetically
ponderable
populously
positively
potentilla
powerfully
prancingly
pratincole
preciously
predicable
preferable
preferably
pregnantly
prehensile
premaxilla
preparedly
prepayable
prepensely
pressingly
presumable
presumably
previously
pridefully
priggishly
primevally
procurable
prodigally
producible
profitable
profitably
profoundly
projectile
propagable
protrusile
proximally
pruriently
puissantly
pulsatilla
punctually
punishable
punitively
purblindly
purulently
putatively
pycnostyle
quadrangle
quadrupole
qualmishly
quenchable
ramblingly
ramshackle
rationally
ravenously
razorshell
reactively
realisable
reasonable
reasonably
reassemble
reassembly
rebuttable
recallable
receivable
receptacle
receptible
recklessly
recordable
recreantly
recyclable
redeemable
redolently
reeligible
refillable
reflexible
reformable
refundable
regionally
reissuable
rejectable
relatively
releasable
relevantly
relievable
relishable
remarkable
remarkably
remediable
remedially
remissible
renderable
repairable
repealable
repeatable
repeatedly
reportable
reportedly
reservedly
resignedly
resistible
resolutely
resolvable
resolvedly
resonantly
respirable
restlessly
restorable
retainable
reticently
retinacula
retiringly
retractile
retrorsely
returnable
revealable
reverently
reversible
revertible
reviewable
rewardable
rightangle
rightfully
rigorously
ritornelli
ritornello
rockabilly
rovebeetle
rubrically
ruminantly
Russophile
rustically
ruthlessly
safetybelt
sagittally
salmonella
saltarello
salutarily
sandcastle
sanguinely
sanitarily
scabrously
scathingly
scenically
schemozzle
schoolable
scoffingly
scornfully
scratchily
searchable
seasonable
seasonably
seasonally
secludedly
sedulously
seguidilla
selflessly
semicircle
semidouble
semiweekly
semiyearly
sensuously
sentiently
separately
septically
serradilla
shamefully
sheathbill
sheepishly
shockingly
shoebuckle
shrewishly
shrinkable
sicklebill
sidesaddle
sillybilly
singularly
sinisterly
sketchable
skittishly
slantingly
slatternly
Slavophile
sleighbell
slipperily
slothfully
sluggardly
sluggishly
sluttishly
smallscale
snappishly
sneakingly
sneeringly
snobbishly
snowmobile
snubbingly
soapbubble
societally
soldanella
solitarily
somersault
sonorously
soothingly
soullessly
soundingly
southernly
sowthistle
spaciously
spankingly
speciously
spectrally
spiritedly
spitefully
splendidly
sporophyll
sportfully
sportingly
sportively
spotlessly
springhalt
spuriously
squeezable
stagbeetle
stagnantly
stalwartly
standstill
statically
statutable
statutably
stealthily
stiflingly
stingingly
stinkingly
stockstill
storksbill
straightly
strainedly
stridently
strikingly
stringhalt
stronghold
stubbornly
studiously
stunningly
sublimable
succinctly
sufferable
sufferably
sugarmaple
suicidally
summonable
superiorly
supernally
supposable
supposably
supposedly
surgically
surmisable
sweepingly
swimmingly
swingingly
tabernacle
taciturnly
tactically
tactlessly
taperingly
taradiddle
tarantella
tarantelle
tastefully
tattletale
tauntingly
tearlessly
teetotally
temperable
temperedly
temporally
temptingly
tenantable
terminable
terminably
terminally
tetrastyle
texturally
thankfully
thermopile
thievishly
thinkingly
thirtyfold
thornapple
thoroughly
thumbstall
ticklishly
timberwolf
timelessly
timorously
tirelessly
tiresomely
toilsomely
tolerantly
tonelessly
toothshell
toroidally
tortiously
tortuously
touchingly
toweringly
tragically
tranquilly
trickishly
triflingly
trigonally
trimonthly
triturable
tropically

trouvaille vortically pianissimo beforehand conferring dispersant
truncately vorticella plaguesome behindhand confirmand dissilient
trustfully voyageable plasmogamy belladonna congregant dissolvent
trustingly vulnerable pogonotomy bemusement consequent distilland
truthfully vulnerably polychrome beneficent consistent distilling
tunelessly wagonvault quadrireme benevolent conspirant divestment
turnbuckle wastefully sarcolemma benzocaine constraint drawstring
tutorially watchfully schooltime benzpyrene consultant drivelling
twelvefold waveringly sclerotomy bestirring consulting earthbound
ulteriorly wearifully Sexagesima bestowment contendent earthshine
ultimately westwardly springtime betterment contestant earwigging
unarguable willynilly strabotomy birthstone contingent easterling
unbearable willywilly summertime bitterling continuant effacement
unbearably windowsill trichotomy blanketing contraband elecampane
unbeatable windshield unhandsome blazonment contravene embalmment
unbeatably winebottle wintertime blistering convenient embankment
unbiddable witchingly aberdevine blithering convergent embarkment
unbrokenly womanishly abridgment bloodhound conversant embodiment
uncommonly wondrously abstergent bloodstone convincing embonpoint
unctuously wordlessly accountant bookmaking convulsant embossment
undeniable workpeople accounting borderland corbelling embryogeny
undeniably worthwhile accrescent borderline correspond employment
underbelly wrathfully acquitting bratticing cosentient enamelling
underworld wretchedly adamantine breakpoint couplement encampment
unendingly wrongfully adjudgment breastbone cradlesong encasement
unenviable wrongously adjustment brevetting creatinine encashment
unerringly yearningly adolescent brigandine cuckoopint enchanting
unfadingly yieldingly adrenaline brigantine cudgelling encystment
unfilially youthfully adulterant brownstone cummerbund endearment
unfriendly adenectomy adulterine cajolement curvetting enfacement
uniaxially aerenchyma advisement cancelling cuttlebone engagement
univocally aerogramme aeroengine candescent dazzlement englutting
unknowable beforetime affeerment cannelloni debasement engrossing
unlawfully blithesome afterpains cantonment debatement engulfment
unmannerly borborygmi aircooling Capitoline decampment enjambment
unnameable bothersome alightment cappuccino decolorant enjoinment
unreadable breadcrumb allurement catarrhine decompound enlacement
unreliable burdensome almsgiving catchpenny decrescent enlistment
unscalable centrosome ambivalent cellophane defacement enmeshment
unscramble chromosome ambushment chalcedony defilement enrichment
unsociable cryptogamy amercement chalkstone definement enrigiment
unsociably cuddlesome anchorring changeling deforciant ensanguine
unsocially cumbersome anglophone chargehand defrayment entailment
unsteadily cyclostome anointment chatelaine delinquent enticement
unsuitable cytochrome anopheline checkpoint denaturant entombment
untowardly decagramme antecedent chiselling denouement entrancing
unwieldily decigramme anthracene cinchonine department entrapment
unwontedly diseconomy anticipant circumvent deployment enwrapping
unworkable doubletime appetising cismontane deportment epeirogeny
unworthily eighteenmo aquamarine cispontine depressant equipotent
usuriously enterotomy arrestment clementine derailment equivalent
utilisable fortissimi asparagine clingstone descendant erubescent
uxoriously fortissimo asphyxiant clinkstone descendent escapement
valorously frolicsome assentient coadjacent designment escarpment
vaporously gastronome assessment coalescent despondent evanescent
varicocele gastronomy assignment coexistent detachment everliving
varietally grandmamma assoilment cohabitant detainment everything
vascularly heterogamy assortment coincident detoxicant evolvement
vaudeville heteronomy astringent colchicine devotement excitement
vehemently hippodrome asynchrony collarbone diecasting excrescent
vengefully humoursome attachment comedienne diesinking exhilarant
venomously imposthume attainment commandant diphyodont exorbitant
ventriculi kilogramme attornment commanding disappoint experiment
verifiable laparotomy attractant commitment disbarring exsanguine
vermicelli letterbomb attunement committing disbudding extractant
vertically lumbersome autoimmune compelling discerning facesaving
vesperbell mastectomy aventurine complacent discipline fairground
viewlessly meddlesome avouchment complement discommend famishment
vigilantly meningioma babblement compliment discontent fantoccini
vigorously mettlesome backbiting comprehend discordant fatherland
villanelle monochrome background concerning discrepant feathering
vindicable mycoplasma bafflement concertina discussant fescennine
viperously neurilemma ballooning concertino discutient fieldstone
virginally neurolemma banishment concordant disenchant fingerling
virtuously octodecimo barkentine concurrent disentwine fixedpoint
virulently ovariotomy barrelling concurring disharmony flagellant
viscerally palindrome batfowling condescend disincline flagwaving
visionally parenchyma battlement confabbing disownment flamboyant
volleyball phlebotomy beekeeping conferment dispelling flashpoint

flattering
flavescent
flavouring
fledgeling
fleshwound
floatplane
floatstone
flocculent
florentine
florescent
flyfishing
forbidding
foreboding
foreground
forgetting
formatting
fortepiano
forwarding
fosterling
foudroyant
fourinhand
foxhunting
frangipane
frangipani
fraudulent
freeliving
frivolling
frolicking
frutescent
fulfilling
fulfilment
funnelling
gadrooning
gaingiving
gambolling
garnishing
Ghibelline
girlfriend
glimmering
Godfearing
government
gramophone
grandstand
gratifying
gravestone
greenshank
greenstone
grindstone
groundling
groundrent
grovelling
guillotine
gunrunning
habiliment
hairspring
hammerpond
handspring
hanselling
harassment
headspring
headstrong
heavensent
heterodont
heterodyne
heterogeny
heterogony
hierophant
highflying
highoctane
highstrung
Hindustani
hinterland
Hippocrene
hobnobbing
homecoming
homemaking
hootenanny
hostelling
houseagent
housebound
houselling
houseplant
hoverplane
hucklebone
humbugging
hydrophane
hydrophone
hydroplane
ilangilang
illuminant
immurement
impairment
impalement
impartment
impediment
impenitent
impregnant
imprinting
impugnment
impuissant
inappetent
inbreeding
incasement
incitement
incogitant
incoherent
inconstant
increscent
indictment
inditement
inducement
ineloquent
inexistent
infighting
infrequent
ingredient
inhabitant
insentient
insouciant
inspanning
instalment
instilling
instrument
integument
intendment
internment
interplant
interregna
intertwine
interwound
intolerant
intoxicant
intriguant
investment
iridescent
iridosmine
irrelevant
irreverent
jaywalking
kennelling
kidnapping
Krugerrand
Kuomintang
lactescent
lacustrine
landowning
laurelling
lavishment
lawabiding
ledgerline
lieutenant
lifegiving
lifesaving
lipreading
liquescent
lithophane
loganstone
logrolling
lovemaking
lutestring
magnifying
mainspring
malcontent
maleficent
malevolent
malfeasant
management
manservant
maraschino
marcescent
margravine
marrowbone
marvelling
masterhand
mastermind
meadowland
mediastina
medicament
microcline
microphone
midmorning
minestrone
ministrant
minutehand
miscellany
misfortune
mishitting
miswording
monovalent
morphogeny
mosaicking
motherland
mountebank
mousseline
munificent
musicstand
Mussulmans
nanosecond
nauseating
nickelling
nigrescent
nitpicking
nonchalant
noncontent
nonpayment
nonplaying
nonviolent
northbound
nourishing
obtainment
oceangoing
offputting
offsetting
oligopsony
omnipotent
omniscient
opalescent
ordainment
outbidding
outfitting
outgassing
outgunning
outpatient
outpouring
outputting
outrunning
outsitting
outwitting
overabound
overground
overrefine
overriding
overstrung
Palaeocene
Palaeogene
papaverine
paraselene
parcelling
parliament
paroxytone
parturient
patrolling
pedalpoint
pencilling
penpushing
peppermint
percipient
performing
permitting
persistent
phagedaena
philippina
philippine
philistine
phillumeny
philopoena
photoprint
physicking
piccaninny
pickaninny
picketline
picnicking
picosecond
pigeonwing
pinchpenny
piperidine
piscifauna
pistolling
pistonring
pitchstone
plainchant
playacting
playground
ploughland
pointblank
polyvalent
postliminy
pothunting
pozzuolana
practising
preachment
predestine
prednisone
preeminent
preferment
preferring
prefulgent
prepayment
pressagent
pretendant
pretendent
prevailing
prevenient
priestling
princeling
proceeding
procumbent
proficient
propellant
propellent
propelling
prosilient
protestant
provisions
psittacine
puberulent
publishing
pummelling
punchdrunk
punishment
purseseine
pursuivant
putrescent
putrescine
puzzlement
pyridoxine
pyrotechny
quadrumana
quadrumane
quarantine
quartering
quinacrine
rabblement
radiophone
rainmaking
ravishment
rearmament
recoupment
redcurrant
refinement
refreshing
refringent
refuelling
refundment
regalement
registrant
regretting
resemblant
resentment
reshipment
resounding
respecting
respondent
restaurant
retirement
retraining
revealment
revilement
rhinestone
rhodophane
riproaring
rodfishing
roistering
rollicking
rosaniline
roseengine
rumrunning
rupicoline
saccharine
sanctimony
sanderling
sapphirine
satisfying
saxicoline
scarlatina
scattering
schizogony
scribbling
scrimshank
seaanemone
seaserpent
secernment
secondhand
secondment
securement
seducement
selenodont
selfacting
selfloving
selfrising
selfruling
seltzogene
semidivine
semidrying
Septuagint
serpentine
settlement
sexivalent
sheepshank
shellmound
shirtfront
shoestring
shortening
shovelling
shuttering
signalling
skibobbing
skijumping
skindiving
skrimshank
skyjacking
skywriting
sleevelink
smaragdine
smattering
smokeplant
snakestone
snivelling
solacement
solicitant
sousaphone
southbound
spellbound
sphenodone
spiderline
spillikins
spinescent
spiralling
splintbone
sprinkling
spumescent
squireling
staggering
standpoint
staphyline
stargazing
starveling
stepparent
stiffening
stiflebone
stinkstone
stoneblind
stormbound
streamline
stridulant
strychnine
subheading
subletting
submediant
submitting
submontane
subroutine
subsequent
subsistent
subtrahend
sufficient
supergiant
supplement
supplicant
surfactant
surprising
sustaining
swaggering
swanupping
sweatgland
sweetening
sweltering
swivelling
tambourine
tanglement
tankengine
tantamount
tapotement
tasselling
tautophony
teenyweeny
teratogeny
thereanent
thickening
threepenny
thumbprint
thundering
tiddlywink
timberline

timesaving
tinselling
tittupping
topgallant
tortellini
touchstone
tourmaline
tournament
tramontana
tramontane
trampoline
transplant
travelling
travertine
trepanning
Tridentine
triphthong
triumphant
trowelling
tunnelling
turgescent
turpentine
twelvetone
ultrasound
unassuming
unavailing
unbecoming
unblinking
unblushing
unchanging
underlying
underslung
understand
unedifying
unfeminine
unflagging
ungrudging
unpleasant
unpleasing
unsettling
unsporting
unswerving
unthinking
unwavering
unyielding
upbraiding
upbringing
upstanding
vespertine
vibraphone
vicegerent
viceregent
Victoriana
videophone
vitrescent
vociferant
voiceprint
wassailing
waterborne
waterfront
weathering
wellspring
wheatstone
whispering
wilderment
windowpane
wonderland
wonderment
wraparound
wrongdoing
wunderkind
ylangylang
zabaglione
zigzagging
abdication
aberration
abjuration
abnegation
abominator
abreaction
abrogation
abscission
absolution
absorption
abstention
abstersion
abstractor
accusation
acervation
acotyledon
acroterion
activation
adaptation
adhibition
adjunction
adjuration
admiration
admonition
adsorption
advocation
affliction
aggression
aircushion
alienation
allegation
alleviator
allocation
allocution
alteration
alternator
ambassador
ambulation
ammunition
amphictyon
amputation
AngloSaxon
annexation
annotation
annulation
antecessor
antiproton
apparition
applicator
apposition
arbitrator
archbishop
archdeacon
areolation
Armageddon
arrogation
ascription
aspiration
assumption
attenuator
attraction
autochthon
automation
backgammon
barbershop
barleybroo
Bedlington
benefactor
bilocation
bitterroot
bitterwood
blackamoor
blueribbon
brachiator
brachiopod
brazilwood
bridegroom
buccinator
bucketshop
buttonhook
buttonwood
byelection
cacodaemon
calciferol
calculator
calibrator
candlewood
capitation
carryingon
castration
catenation
catholicon
catholicos
cavitation
celebrator
centillion
cephalopod
chamaeleon
chamberpot
champignon
chancellor
chaparajos
chaparejos
Charleston
chatterbox
chequebook
chickenpox
childproof
chimneypot
Christhood
chuckwagon
circulator
closestool
coaptation
codswallop
cogitation
collection
collimator
collocutor
coloration
combustion
commission
commonroom
commutator
compaction
comparator
comparison
compassion
compatriot
competitor
completion
complexion
compositor
compotator
compressor
compulsion
computator
conception
concession
conclusion
concoction
concretion
concussion
conduction
confection
confession
conflation
congestion
connection
conniption
contention
contortion
contractor
contraprop
contrition
convection
convention
conversion
conviction
convulsion
cooperator
cooptation
copulation
corelation
coronation
corporator
correction
corrugator
corruption
cottonwood
cottonwool
councillor
counsellor
cousinhood
covenantor
crippledom
crispation
crustation
cultivator
cumulation
cunctation
curmudgeon
cuttystool
datamation
deaeration
decahedron
decimation
declension
decoration
dedication
defalcator
defamation
definition
deflection
defoliator
delegation
delineator
demolition
denegation
denigrator
denotation
denudation
depilation
deposition
depredator
depression
depuration
deputation
derivation
derogation
descension
descriptor
desecrator
desiccator
designator
desolation
desorption
desperados
destructor
detonation
detraction
devolution
didgeridoo
digitation
digression
dilatation
diminution
diningroom
discretion
discussion
disembosom
disenviron
dismission
dispassion
dispersion
disruption
dissection
dissension
dissuasion
distension
distention
distortion
distrainor
divagation
divination
domination
donnybrook
dubitation
duplicator
ebullition
eisteddfod
elaborator
eliminator
elongation
elucidator
elutriator
emaciation
emendation
emigration
emollition
encephalon
enervation
engineroom
enumerator
enunciator
epilimnion
equitation
eradicator
ergosterol
eructation
escalation
escutcheon
estimation
etiolation
eucalyptol
Eurovision
evacuation
evaluation
evaporator
exaltation
excavation
excerption
excitation
execration
exhalation
exhaustion
exhibition
exhumation
expedition
expiration
exposition
expression
expunction
expurgator
extenuator
extinction
extirpator
extraction
exultation
exuviation
fabricator
fasciation
fascinator
fatherhood
federation
feuilleton
fiddlewood
figuration
filtration
flameproof
flashflood
flirtation
floatation
floriation
flunkeydom
foreshadow
fornicator
foundation
fullbottom
fumigation
gasteropod
gemination
generation
glaciation
graduation
granulator
greasewood
habitation
halfnelson
handbarrow
handgallop
heartblood
heartthrob
heathendom
hebetation
hemihedron
hendecagon
Heptameron
hesitation
hexahedron
hullabaloo
hyperbaton
imbibition
immolation
impanation
imposition
impression
imputation
incantator
inchoation
incitation
incubation
inculcator
indagation
indecision
indexation
indication
induration
infarction
inflection
infliction
infraction
ingression
inhalation
inhibition
inhumation
initiation
injunction
innovation
inoculator
inquisitor
insinuator
insolation
inspection
inspirator
instigator
institutor
instructor
insulation
integrator
interferon
intervenor
intimation
intinction
intonation
intubation
inundation
invitation
invocation
involution
iodination
ionisation
irreligion
irrigation
irritation
jubilation
knighthood
laceration
lacrimator
lacrymator

lamination
lapidation
laureation
legislator
letterbook
levigation
levitation
liberation
lightproof
likelihood
limitation
liquidator
literation
litigation
livelihood
livingroom
lobsterpot
lobulation
lockerroom
locomotion
lubricator
lucubrator
lumberroom
lustration
maceration
machinator
maculation
maidenhood
malapropos
malefactor
manifestos
masterhood
masticator
matronhood
maturation
mayblossom
medication
meditation
meliorator
meltingpot
mesenteron
middlebrow
minutebook
misprision
mitigation
moderation
modulation
motherhood
motivation
musicstool
muskmallow
mutilation
nanisation
nationhood
navigation
needlebook
negotiator
newsvendor
nincompoop
nodulation
nomination
nonfiction
nucleation
numeration
obligation
obstructor
obturation
occupation
ocellation
octahedron
oppilation
opposition
oppression
orangewood
ordination
originator
orphanhood
oscillator
oscitation
osculation
outstation
overshadow
ovipositor
oxygenator
packingbox
paddywagon
pagination
palliation
panopticon
parenthood
pastrycook
patination
peculation
pejoration
penetrator
pennillion
pentathlon
pentstemon
perception
percolator
percussion
perfection
perforator
perihelion
permeation
permission
peroration
persecutor
personator
persuasion
perversion
phenomenon
phlogiston
photoflood
phrasebook
pincushion
pistolshot
plantation
playfellow
pocketbook
pollinator
polyhedron
polyhistor
population
possession
postillion
postulator
pouncetbox
prairiedog
prayerbook
precaution
precession
preclusion
prediction
preemption
prehension
prelection
premonitor
preparator
pretension
prevention
priesthood
procession
procreator
procurator
production
profession
progenitor
prohibitor
projection
prolocutor
promptbook
propagator
proportion
propraetor
proprietor
propulsion
prosecutor
prospector
protection
protractor
protrusion
provocator
punctation
punctuator
pushbutton
pyrogallol
quartation
quaternion
quercitron
radication
recitation
recreation
redemption
reelection
reflection
refraction
refutation
regelation
regression
regulation
relaxation
relegation
relocation
renovation
reparation
repetition
reposition
repression
repudiator
reputation
rescission
resolution
resorcinol
resorption
respirator
resumption
retraction
revelation
revocation
revolution
rhinoceros
rockbottom
rockpigeon
rosemallow
rubricator
rumination
sagination
salivation
salutation
sandalwood
sanitation
sappanwood
sashwindow
saturation
schoolbook
schoolroom
selfaction
selfmotion
semination
separation
septillion
servomotor
sextillion
shellproof
sheriffdom
shockproof
shopwindow
showwindow
sibilation
silkcotton
simulation
singlefoot
sisterhood
sketchbook
slowmotion
smokeproof
smorrebrod
snapdragon
sneezewood
soundproof
sourcebook
spallation
speciation
speculator
spoliation
spongewood
springwood
squamation
squeezebox
squirehood
stagnation
starvation
stimulator
stipulator
stockproof
stomatopod
stonemason
stormproof
streetdoor
strongroom
subduction
subjection
subjugator
subkingdom
submersion
submission
subreption
subsection
substation
subvention
subversion
succession
suggestion
superation
supervisor
supination
suppletion
suppressor
suspension
sustention
symphonion
syncopator
syndicator
tablespoon
tabulation
television
temptation
tenderfoot
tenterhook
terminator
thermistor
thornproof
thunderbox
tiringroom
titivation
titubation
tocopherol
toleration
tortfeasor
tourbillon
toxication
trabeation
trajection
transactor
transferor
transistor
transition
translator
trisection
triskelion
triturator
truncation
ulceration
underfloor
underproof
undershoot
understood
undulation
unorthodox
urtication
ustulation
usucaption
usurpation
vaccinator
validation
vegetation
velitation
veneration
ventilator
vesication
vindicator
virginhood
visitation
vivisector
waffleiron
waterflood
watermelon
waterproof
weatherbox
wellington
windowshop
witnessbox
woodpigeon
yellowwood
yokefellow
zwitterion
aeolotropy
anemograph
anisotropy
bathyscaph
bathyscope
beechdrops
bootstraps
cantaloupe
chinagraph
chromatype
cyclograph
cystoscope
cystoscopy
ditriglyph
fireescape
fluorotype
hagioscope
hectograph
heliograph
helioscope
heliotrope
heliotropy
hieroglyph
hierograph
hippocampi
hippogryph
hydroscope
hygrograph
hygroscope
iconoscope
lithoglyph
lithograph
manuscript
micrograph
microscope
microscopy
mimeograph
necroscopy
nephograph
nephoscope
nympholept
palaeotype
pantograph
paratroops
petroglyph
phonograph
photograph
phototrope
pictograph
planigraph
postscript
quadriceps
radiograph
radioscopy
rhinoscope
rhinoscopy
rhizomorph
somatotype
spirograph
statoscope
stenograph
stereotype
stereotypy
stonesnipe
stylograph
tetramorph
thixotropy
tickertape
transcript
transshape
typescript
vectograph
zincograph
aboveboard
absolutory
accusatory
acidimetry
adjuratory
admonitory
advocatory
aldermanry
alexanders
alimentary
alongshore
ambulatory
amendatory
amphigouri
anemometry
angiosperm
animadvert
apiculture
apothecary
arthromere
aspidistra
atmosphere
audiometry
aviculture
backstairs
baptistery
bardolatry
bargeboard
barleycorn
barrenwort
barysphere
basketwork
bassethorn
bathymetry
battledore
bewitchery
binoculars
blackberry
blackboard
blackguard
blackheart
Blackshirt
blackthorn
blastoderm
blastomere
blastopore
blockboard
brainstorm
breadboard
breastwork
bridgework
brightwork
broadsword
brownshirt

buffoonery
butterwort
cacciatore
caddisworm
calyciform
camelopard
candelabra
cankerworm
canterbury
canvaswork
capitulary
caricature
carpellary
cautionary
centilitre
centimetre
centromere
certiorari
cessionary
chalkboard
charactery
chartulary
chessboard
chloroform
chokeberry
churchyard
cinecamera
clavichord
clearstory
clerestory
clinometry
cloudberry
coastguard
coleoptera
coloratura
comanchero
comicopera
commandery
commentary
commissary
commissure
commixture
compradore
compulsory
conciliary
conclusory
condensery
conjecture
consectary
consistory
contexture
controvert
copartnery
coralberry
cordillera
corrivalry
corsetiere
coulometry
couturiere
couverture
craquelure
crewelwork
cribriform
ctenophore
cumuliform
debauchery
debouchure
dedicatory
defamatory
dendriform
depilatory
depositary
depository
derogatory
Devanagari
dictionary
digitiform
directoire
disclosure
discomfort
disconcert
disconfirm
disfeature
dispensary
distillery
divinatory
donkeywork
doublepark
downstairs
drysaltery
dumbledore
echinoderm
effrontery
elderberry
elementary
emblazonry
embouchure
embroidery
emendatory
emeryboard
emigratory
epistolary
escritoire
eudiometry
everywhere
excitatory
excusatory
execratory
exhibitory
expiratory
expository
faintheart
festoonery
fibreboard
fibrillary
fingermark
flashboard
floatboard
floorboard
flowergirl
flugelhorn
fluxionary
folkmemory
forfeiture
foursquare
fritillary
glassfibre
goatsbeard
goniometry
gooseberry
granophyre
gravimetry
greenheart
greensward
groundwork
gymnosperm
hagiolatry
headsquare
heavenborn
heavenward
hectolitre
hectometre
heliolatry
hemisphere
heptachord
hereditary
heretofore
hierolatry
hitherward
hollowware
humbuggery
hydrometry
hygrometry
hypsometry
iconolatry
iconometry
incendiary
incubatory
indicatory
inhibitory
initiatory
innovatory
insanitary
intermarry
inundatory
invitatory
invocatory
ionosphere
jackassery
jardiniere
jasperware
judicatory
judicature
justiciary
kerseymere
knifeboard
kookaburra
laboratory
lacklustre
lampoonery
lavalliere
lectionary
lettercard
limaciform
linguiform
literature
locomotory
loganberry
lophophore
lumberyard
macrospore
maculature
malacoderm
malleebird
mallenders
mandragora
Mariolatry
masterwork
matchboard
meadowlark
mesosphere
metacentre
micrometry
microspore
millefiori
millilitre
millimetre
misericord
mismeasure
missionary
misventure
mitigatory
moniliform
monsignori
Montagnard
motherwort
mouldboard
nativeborn
necrolatry
needlecord
needlework
nightshirt
nipplewort
notchboard
nunciature
obligatory
ophiolatry
orthoptera
osculatory
otherwhere
otterboard
outmeasure
oysterfarm
palliatory
palmerworm
paradoxure
parsonbird
passionary
pasteboard
peacockery
pensionary
pentachord
peppercorn
pepperwort
peremptory
phantastry
pheasantry
phelloderm
photometry
photophore
phylactery
phylloxera
pigmentary
pistillary
planimetry
pleasantry
plecoptera
plutolatry
possessory
powderhorn
praemunire
prebendary
preceptory
preconcert
precursory
prefecture
prefixture
prehistory
presbytery
presidiary
promissory
promontory
protectory
proteiform
pseudocarp
psychiatry
puffpastry
punchboard
quadrature
quaternary
quickthorn
radiometry
redemptory
refractory
regulatory
reichsmark
repertoire
repository
rescissory
responsory
revelatory
revocatory
rhizophore
ribbonworm
ripplemark
roquelaure
rowanberry
salesclerk
sallenders
salutatory
sanguinary
scaleboard
scavengery
schizocarp
schoolgirl
schoolmarm
schoolwork
scleroderm
scoreboard
scorzonera
scrollwork
scyphiform
secretaire
securiform
segmentary
selfregard
separatory
setterwort
sexagenary
silverware
simulatory
skateboard
smallsword
smoothbore
sneezewort
sociometry
soundboard
spadebeard
spiderwort
spirometry
spleenwort
spoilsport
spoliatory
spongiform
sporophore
stationary
stationery
stavesacre
stelliform
stitchwort
stratiform
strawberry
strawboard
streetward
subculture
subdeanery
subsidiary
superstore
suppletory
suspenders
suspensory
swarmspore
sweatshirt
sweetheart
tachometry
tachymetry
tailorbird
taperecord
telecamera
tetrachord
tetrahedra
tetterwort
threadbare
threadmark
threadworm
threescore
throatwort
timberwork
tomfoolery
trajectory
transitory
treadboard
tuitionary
tumultuary
umbiliform
underscore
undershirt
underskirt
undulatory
unguentary
upholstery
uranometry
vaporiform
vesicatory
veterinary
viperiform
vivandiere
vocabulary
voluptuary
watchguard
wattlebird
weaverbird
whaleshark
whirlybird
whitebeard
whitethorn
wickerwork
willowherb
wonderwork
worldweary
yellowbird
youngberry
abiogenist
abjectness
abruptness
absolutism
absolutist
absurdness
acatalepsy
accomplish
activeness
adroitness
adulteress
aerologist
aeronomist
aesthetism
affectless
affettuoso
Africanise
Africanism
Africanist
aftergrass
aggrandise
agrologist
agronomist
alcoholise
alcoholism
algebraist
algologist
allegorise
allegorist
alloverish
allpurpose
amateurish
amateurism
anabaptism
anabaptist
anastomose
ancestress
anchorless
anecdotist
antagonise
antagonism
antagonist
Antichrist
antitheism
antitheist
apocalypse
apostatise
archerfish
archpriest
armourless
artfulness
asceticism
astuteness
augustness
automatise
automatism
automatist
autonomist
averseness
axiologist
babiroussa
backsheesh
balderdash
balloonist
barrenness
bassoonist
bastardise
bawdyhouse
belletrist
Benthamism
bestialise
biochemist

bitchiness
bitterness
bituminise
blastocyst
bleariness
blepharism
blitheness
blockhouse
bloodiness
bluishness
bolshevise
bolshevism
bolshevist
borderless
Boswellise
Boswellism
bottomless
bottommost
bourbonism
bourbonist
bowdlerise
bowdlerism
boyishness
bradyseism
Brahmanism
Brahminism
braininess
brantgoose
brassiness
brawniness
brazenness
breathless
breechless
breezeless
breeziness
brentgoose
bridgeless
brigandism
brightness
Britishism
brokenness
bromegrass
broodiness
bryologist
Buchmanism
bumpkinish
bunchgrass
burglarise
butterfish
buttonbush
buttonless
caespitose
callowness
candidness
candlefish
candyfloss
capitalise
capitalism
capitalist
caramelise
cartoonist
casualness
catabolism
categorise
centralise
centralism
centralist
changeless
channelise
chartreuse
chasteness
chattiness
chauffeuse
chauntress
chauvinism
chauvinist
cheekiness
cheeriness
cheesiness
chersonese
chilliness
choiceness
chubbiness
cicisbeism
circumcise
circumfuse
clamminess
classicise
classicism
classicist
cleverness
cloudburst
cloudiness
clumsiness
cnidoblast
coachhouse
coarseness
cockneyish
cockneyism
collarless
colloquise
colloquist
colourfast
colourless
comeliness
commonness
compromise
concettism
concretise
concretism
concretist
conformism
conformist
contrabass
coquettish
cornerwise
cornettist
costliness
couchgrass
countryish
courthouse
craftiness
cragginess
crankiness
cravenness
creaminess
creepiness
crisscross
crustiness
cursedness
cussedness
cuttlefish
cytologist
daintiness
dampcourse
dauphiness
deadliness
Decembrist
decimalise
decimalism
decivilise
decolonise
decolorise
decompress
deerforest
defeminise
dehumanise
delocalise
demagogism
demobilise
demonetise
demoralise
demureness
depolarise
devitalise
devocalise
devoutness
diatropism
dictatress
digitalise
diluteness
dimorphism
dinnerless
directness
directress
discompose
disfurnish
dismalness
dispossess
divineness
doggedness
dolomitise
doublebass
doubleness
drafthorse
dreaminess
dreariness
dressiness
driverless
drowsiness
earthiness
earwitness
ecclesiast
edibleness
effeteness
effortless
elasticise
elatedness
emancipist
emparadise
empiricism
empiricist
enamellist
enigmatise
enigmatist
enterprise
enthusiasm
enthusiast
entireness
epiphytism
ergonomist
eternalise
eternalist
ethologist
eudemonism
eudemonist
eugenicist
euhemerise
euhemerism
euhemerist
evangelise
evangelism
evangelist
expertness
extinguish
eyewitness
facileness
factualism
factualist
fallowness
famousness
fanaticise
fanaticism
fatherless
fathomless
faultiness
federalise
federalism
federalist
feebleness
femaleness
fervidness
fibreglass
fibrillose
fickleness
fictionist
fieldglass
fieldmouse
fierceness
filthiness
fingerless
fingerpost
finiteness
firstclass
fitfulness
flabbiness
flashiness
fleshiness
flightless
flimsiness
flintiness
floppiness
floridness
flowerless
fluffiness
flunkeyism
foetidness
folklorist
folksiness
forecourse
foreignism
fortuitism
fortuitist
Fourierism
fraternise
freakiness
Frenchness
friendless
frigidness
frilliness
fringeless
friskiness
frizziness
frostiness
frothiness
futureless
galleywest
galloglass
garishness
gaucheness
gelatinise
generalise
generalist
geneticist
genialness
genteelism
gentilesse
gentleness
geochemist
geometrise
geotropism
geriatrist
glasshouse
glassiness
gloominess
glossarist
glossiness
gluttonise
gnosticism
goldenness
golfcourse
goodliness
gooseflesh
goosegrass
gormandise
governessy
gradualism
gradualist
grangerise
grangerism
graphitise
greasiness
greediness
greenhouse
grisliness
grittiness
grogginess
groundless
groundmass
grubbiness
grumpiness
guardhouse
guesthouse
guiltiness
hammerless
handedness
Hansardise
hartebeest
headcheese
heartiness
heartsease
heathenise
heathenish
heathenism
henotheism
henotheist
heparinise
heroicness
hipsterism
hithermost
hoarseness
hobbyhorse
hollowness
holophrase
homeliness
homogenise
homologise
honourless
hookedness
hornedness
horologist
horridness
horseflesh
houseguest
humaneness
humbleness
humourless
hungriness
hyaloplasm
hylotheism
hypocorism
hypotenuse
iconoclasm
ideologist
idolatress
illegalise
illuminism
illuminist
immobilise
immoralist
imparadise
impishness
impoverish
impureness
initialise
innateness
insaneness
insularism
intactness
intentness
intercross
interphase
intertwist
invalidism
inventress
inwardness
italianise
Italianism
jacobinise
Jacobinism
Jacobitism
jaggedness
jauntiness
jejuneness
jeopardise
Jewishness
jocoseness
Johnsonese
journalese
journalise
journalism
journalist
joyfulness
joyousness
Kantianism
karyoplasm
katabolism
keratinise
kindliness
kineticist
kingliness
knottiness
Krishnaism
lachrymose
laconicism
Lamarckism
lampoonist
lanuginose
lapidarist
lattermost
lavishness
lawfulness
leadenness
leaderless
legitimise
legitimism
legitimist
lemongrass
lengthwise
leopardess
lesbianism
letterless
leucoplast
liberalise
liberalism
liberalist
librettist
lighthouse
likeliness
limpidness
liquidness
lissomness
literalise
literalism
literalist
littleness
liveliness
Lollardism
loneliness
lordliness
loveliness
lovingness
lowerclass
luciferase
lustreless
lyophilise
Lysenkoism
macadamise
mackintosh
manageress
manfulness
Manicheism
manicurist
manorhouse
marrowless
marshiness
martialism
masterless
matureness
maximalist
mayonnaise
meagreness
measliness
mediatress

mellowness
mesomerism
messianism
metabolise
metabolism
metamerism
metaphrase
micaschist
microseism
middlemost
mightiness
militarise
militarism
militarist
mindedness
mineralise
minimalism
minimalist
minstrelsy
minuteness
misogamist
misogynist
misologist
missionise
mizzenmast
moderatism
modernness
modishness
moisturise
monarchism
monarchist
monetarism
monetarist
mongrelise
mongrelism
monogamist
monogenism
monologise
monologist
monopolise
monopolist
monotheism
monotheist
mopishness
morbidness
moroseness
morphinism
motherless
motionless
motiveless
mouldiness
mulishness
multiphase
mycologist
nailpolish
narcissism
narcissist
narcolepsy
narrowness
nationless
nativeness
naturalise
naturalism
naturalist
needlefish
negativism
negativist
nematocyst
nethermost
nettlerash
neuroplasm
neutralise
neutralism
neutralist
nicotinism
nightdress
nightglass
nimbleness
nominalism

nominalist
nomologist
nosologist
numberless
oafishness
obituarist
objectless
oblateness
obtuseness
odiousness
oecologist
oecumenism
oedematose
oenologist
oldmaidish
oligoclase
oncologist
ontologist
opaqueness
operettist
opinionist
opposeless
optimalise
orchardist
oreologist
organicism
organicist
ornateness
orneriness
orthoclase
orthoepist
osteoblast
osteoclast
otioseness
outlandish
overblouse
overexpose
overpraise
overthrust
owlishness
pacificism
pacificist
paintbrush
palatalise
palimpsest
pallidness
paltriness
panegyrise
panegyrist
pansophist
paperchase
parabolise
paralogise
paralogism
paraphrase
paraphrast
parasitism
parrotfish
Passionist
pastellist
pasteurise
pasteurism
patchiness
patriotism
peacockish
pebbledash
pedicurist
pedologist
penologist
permafrost
peroxidise
petiteness
phallicism
phantasise
pharisaism
pharmacist
phenocryst
picayunish
pigeonpost

pillowcase
pilothouse
placidness
plagiarise
plagiarism
plagiarist
plantlouse
plasmodesm
plasmolyse
plasticise
pliantness
pluckiness
podiatrist
polemicist
politeness
politicise
polychrest
polygamist
polygenism
polygenist
polymerise
polymerism
polytheism
polytheist
pomologist
popularise
porousness
portliness
Portuguese
positivism
positivist
postchaise
powerhouse
pragmatise
pragmatism
pragmatist
predecease
predispose
prepossess
pressurise
presuppose
prettiness
prissiness
proctorise
profitless
prologuise
promptness
properness
prophetess
prosaicism
proteolyse
protoplasm
protoplast
proudflesh
psalmodise
psalmodist
psychicism
psychicist
Ptolemaist
puritanise
puritanism
putridness
Pyrrhonism
Pyrrhonist
quaintness
queasiness
quenchless
quickgrass
quirkiness
racecourse
Rachmanism
radicalise
radicalism
raggedness
rakishness
rancidness
randomness
reafforest
reappraise

reasonless
recentness
recidivism
recidivist
recitalist
recolonise
recompense
regardless
regularise
rejuvenise
relativise
relativism
relativist
relentless
relinquish
remediless
remissness
remonetise
remoteness
reorganise
repurchase
resistless
resultless
retrogress
reunionism
reunionist
revalorise
revanchism
revanchist
revitalise
revivalism
revivalist
rewardless
rhapsodise
rhapsodist
rheologist
rheumatism
ribbonfish
rinderpest
riverhorse
robustness
rontgenise
rootedness
rottenness
roughhouse
roundhouse
rudderfish
rudderless
ruefulness
ruffianism
ruggedness
Russianise
saccharose
sacredness
saddlefast
sailorless
sallowness
sarcoplasm
sarmentose
savageness
savourless
scandalise
scantiness
scarceness
scatheless
scattiness
scepticism
schematise
schematism
Scotticise
Scotticism
screwpress
scrutinise
sculptress
scurviness
seamstress
searchless
secondbest
secularise

secularism
secularist
secureness
sedateness
seductress
seemliness
selectness
selfpraise
seminarist
sempstress
sensualise
sensualism
sensualist
separatism
separatist
sereneness
serologist
severeness
sexologist
shabbiness
shadowless
shagginess
sheathless
sheeplouse
sherardise
shieldless
shiftiness
shirehorse
shirtwaist
shoddiness
shortcrust
shrewdness
shrewmouse
shrillness
shroudless
sickliness
silentness
silverfish
simpleness
sinecurism
sinecurist
sinfulness
Singhalese
singleness
sinologist
skimpiness
skinniness
slanginess
sleaziness
sleepiness
sleeveless
slenderise
slightness
sloppiness
smelliness
smokehouse
smoothness
smudginess
smuttiness
sneakiness
sniffiness
snootiness
snowgrouse
snuffiness
soddenness
solemnness
solidarism
solidarist
solubilise
sombreness
songstress
songthrush
Sorbonnist
sordidness
sparseness
Spartacist
speargrass
specialise
specialism

specialist
speechless
speediness
spiritless
sponginess
spookiness
spoonerism
sportiness
spottiness
springless
spruceness
spunkiness
squareness
stableness
staffnurse
stanchless
stanchness
starriness
steadiness
steakhouse
steamchest
steaminess
steeliness
stewardess
stickiness
stigmatise
stigmatism
stigmatist
stinginess
stockiness
stodginess
stolidness
stonebrash
storehouse
storminess
straitness
strategist
streamless
stressless
strictness
stringless
striptease
strychnism
stubbiness
stuffiness
stumpiness
stupidness
sturdiness
subtleness
suddenness
suffragist
sugarhouse
sugariness
sullenness
sulphurise
sultriness
summitless
superbness
supineness
supperless
suppleness
surrealism
surrealist
sweatiness
swordgrass
sybaritism
symmetrise
sympathise
symphonist
symposiast
syncretise
syncretism
syncretist
synonymist
synthesise
synthesist
synthetise
synthetist
systemless

tabularise
takingness
talentless
Tartuffism
tawdriness
taxonomist
technicist
tenantless
tenderness
terrorless
tetchiness
textualist
thalecress
theogonist
theologise
theologist
theopneust
thillhorse
thirdclass
thorniness
threadfish
threnodist
thriftless
throneless
thwartwise
timeliness
toffeenose
tongueless
toothbrush
toothiness
topologist
torpidness
torridness
touchiness
towardness
transgress
transverse
trappiness
trashiness
traumatism
trecentist
trendiness
trichinise
trichroism
trickiness
tricyclist
trivialise
trivialism
trollopish
trombonist
tropopause
Trotskyism
Trotskyist
trustiness
turbidness
turgidness
typologist
underbrush
underdress
underlease
undersense
uneasiness
unevenness
unfairness
unholiness
unicyclist
uniqueness
unjustness
unkindness
unlikeness
unmeetness
unripeness
unruliness
untidiness
unwariness
upperclass
uppishness
upwardness
usefulness
utopianism
Vaticanism
Vaticanist
venialness
ventricose
Vietnamese
vignettist
villainess
vinegarish
virologist
virtueless
visionless
vitaminise
vitriolise
volatilise
wanderlust
wantonness
watchglass
waterbrash
watercress
waterglass
wateriness
weakliness
weaponless
weightless
Wertherism
westernise
wheelhorse
wheelhouse
wheeziness
whorehouse
wickedness
wildebeest
wilderness
wilfulness
windowless
wintriness
wobbliness
woefulness
wontedness
woodenness
woolliness
worldclass
worthiness
wrathiness
Wykehamist
yeastiness
yellowness
abbreviate
abstrusity
accelerate
accentuate
accumulate
achondrite
acoelomate
actinolite
adjudicate
Adullamite
adulterate
affability
afterbirth
aftertaste
alkalinity
allegretto
alliterate
altazimuth
altostrati
amalgamate
ameliorate
amiability
amoebocyte
andalusite
angularity
annihilate
annularity
annunciate
anthracite
anticipate
antimonite
antiSemite
apostolate
appreciate
aquilinity
Areopagite
articulate
artycrafty
ascomycete
asexuality
asphyxiate
asseverate
assibilate
assimilate
audibility
auriculate
auscultate
autoplasty
barbellate
barracouta
benedicite
Benthamite
bestiality
bichromate
bipolarity
bisulphate
bisulphite
blacksmith
blanquette
blastemata
branchiate
bridlepath
broadcloth
Buchmanite
cachinnate
calceolate
calumniate
calyptrate
camphorate
cancellate
canonicate
canonicity
cantillate
canzonetta
capability
capacitate
capitulate
carnallite
cassolette
causticity
centrality
centricity
chalybeate
charismata
cheapskate
chemisette
childbirth
chlorinate
chronicity
chrysolite
coacervate
coelacanth
coequality
coeternity
collarette
collegiate
comicality
commentate
commonalty
compensate
complexity
complicate
complicity
conciliate
concinnity
condensate
confidante
confiscate
conformity
conglobate
congregate
consecrate
consociate
constipate
constitute
consummate
contiguity
continuate
continuity
contribute
coordinate
coradicate
cordiality
cordierite
corporeity
creativity
crenellate
crinolette
crocoisite
curability
deactivate
debilitate
decapitate
decelerate
deescalate
deflagrate
degenerate
delaminate
deliberate
delimitate
demotivate
denominate
denunciate
depopulate
depreciate
deracinate
desalinate
desiderata
desiderate
desquamate
detoxicate
dextrality
diastemata
dichromate
difficulty
dilapidate
dilettante
dilettanti
disability
dishonesty
disloyalty
dissertate
dissociate
distillate
distribute
disulphate
disutility
divaricate
durability
duumvirate
edulcorate
effectuate
effeminate
efficacity
eighteenth
elasticity
electorate
emancipate
emarginate
emasculate
emblements
embryonate
emissivity
endemicity
endopodite
enterolith
ephorality
episcopate
equability
equanimity
equivocate
erectility
ergodicity
ethicality
eviscerate
exaggerate
exasperate
excogitate
excruciate
exenterate
exhilarate
expatriate
exprobrate
extraneity
exulcerate
exurbanite
facilitate
factuality
fastigiate
felicitate
feminality
femininity
fenestrate
fianchetto
fibrillate
fiftyfifty
finicality
flabellate
flaccidity
flagellate
flightpath
flocculate
floorcloth
fluoridate
fluorinate
footlights
foresheets
fourchette
fourteenth
fraternity
friability
fulllength
fusibility
gadolinite
garnierite
generality
generosity
geniculate
glasscloth
glauberite
glauconite
graciosity
graptolite
grasscloth
grassroots
greedyguts
greencloth
habilitate
halflength
halogenate
heliophyte
henceforth
hereabouts
hereticate
heulandite
hoitytoity
homoeopath
homologate
homozygote
horsecloth
hydrophyte
hygrophyte
ignobility
illegality
illiterate
illuminate
illuminati
illustrate
imbecility
immaculate
immaturity
immobility
immoderate
immorality
impregnate
impudicity
inaccurate
inactivate
inactivity
inadequate
inapposite
inaugurate
incapacity
incinerate
incivility
incomplete
incrassate
indefinite
indelicate
indiscrete
indocility
inequality
infelicity
infidelity
infiltrate
ingeminate
ingratiate
inhumanity
innominate
innumerate
inordinate
inosculate
insecurity
inseminate
insipidity
insobriety
inspissate
insufflate
insularity
intenerate
interstate
intimidate
intoxicate
intrigante
inurbanity
invaginate
invalidate
invalidity
inveracity
inveterate
invigilate
invigorate
irradicate
irresolute
Ishmaelite
italianate
jocularity
juvenility
kimberlite
lanceolate
laterality
legibility
legitimate
lemniscate
lepidolite
liberality
licentiate
literality
lithophyte
lithotrity
logicality
luminosity
lymphocyte
lymphomata
magistrate
maisonette
manipulate

Marcionite
margravate
marguerite
marionette
marquisate
martensite
mediocrity
menstruate
metabolite
microbiota
microphyte
mignonette
mithridate
movability
muliebrity
musicality
mutability
myxomycete
naturopath
nebulosity
needlebath
negativity
neutrality
nidificate
nineteenth
notability
novaculite
numerosity
nuptiality
nyctinasty
obliterate
obnubilate
obtruncate
openhearth
operculate
orotundity
osteophyte
overexcite
overgrowth
overnicety
pacificate
paederasty
palaeolith
palagonite
palatinate
paniculate
parramatta
partiality
passionate
patriality
patriciate
pediculate
pennyworth
pentimento
perfoliate
pernickety
perpetrate
perpetuate
perpetuity
perplexity
perquisite
personalty
perversity
phlogopite
photonasty
pianoforte
pinebeauty
pistillate
planchette
plasticity
plebiscite
pliability
polychaete
popularity
portamento
positivity
potability
potentiate
preadamite
preciosity
principate
proclivity
profligate
profundity
prolongate
promulgate
propensity
propionate
propitiate
prosciutto
prosperity
prostitute
protophyta
protophyte
psychopath
punctulate
pupilarity
pyrolusite
pyroxenite
pyrrhotite
quaternate
quaternity
ratability
rattlepate
reactivate
reactivity
reallocate
recuperate
redecorate
regenerate
regularity
rejuvenate
relativity
remunerate
repatriate
repopulate
resupinate
reticulate
revalidate
risibility
sabretooth
saccharate
salability
salicylate
samarskite
sanguinity
saprophyte
schoolmate
screwplate
scurrility
scutellate
secondrate
secularity
seedpotato
seismicity
semilunate
sensuality
seventieth
sexpartite
shibboleth
showerbath
shrievalty
siderolite
silhouette
silverbath
similarity
simplicity
sluicegate
smaragdite
solidarity
solidstate
solubility
spasticity
spathulate
spatiality
speciality
speciosity
spermaceti
sperrylite
sphalerite
sphericity
spherulite
spiflicate
sporophyte
squalidity
stablemate
stalactite
stalagmite
staurolite
stephanite
stereobate
sterigmata
stillbirth
stipellate
stridulate
stypticity
subacidity
subcordate
substitute
sulphonate
sulphurate
superacute
supplicate
suzerainty
swashplate
synonymity
syntagmata
tablecloth
tamability
taxability
temporalty
tenability
teratomata
terneplate
terracotta
tessellate
theodolite
thirdparty
thirteenth
thousandth
toothpaste
topazolite
topicality
tortuosity
tragacanth
triacetate
trifoliate
trifurcate
trillionth
tripartite
triplicate
triplicity
triternate
triviality
troctolite
troglodyte
tropophyte
Trotskyite
tuberosity
twelvenote
typicality
umbilicate
unchastity
unctuosity
underneath
underpants
underquote
understate
underwrite
underwrote
uniformity
uninitiate
unipartite
university
unmorality
vanadinite
varicosity
vaticinate
vertebrate
vesiculate
virtuality
virtuosity
visibility
vitiligate
vituperate
viviparity
vociferate
volatility
volubility
waggonette
waistcloth
wavelength
whitesmith
winceyette
wolframite
Wycliffite
ZendAvesta
abdominous
abstemious
acarpelous
accoucheur
acephalous
acetabulum
acrogenous
acroterium
adulterous
aeruginous
agapanthus
albuminous
alliaceous
allogamous
ambulacrum
amphibious
amylaceous
anadromous
anatropous
ancipitous
androecium
anonaceous
antebellum
antimasque
antonymous
apocarpous
apothecium
aquiferous
arenaceous
argumentum
armigerous
astragalus
auditorium
auriferous
auspicious
autogamous
autogenous
autologous
autonomous
avaricious
barratrous
battailous
Benedictus
billetdoux
bipetalous
bituminous
bladdernut
blottesque
bluetongue
blusterous
boisterous
bordereaux
byssaceous
cadaverous
calamitous
calcareous
caliginous
calumnious
cancellous
caoutchouc
capricious
catafalque
censorious
cerebellum
ceruminous
chivalrous
chuckerout
cinerarium
circuitous
clangorous
Clarenceux
cockalorum
coetaneous
collarstud
colloquium
colporteur
commodious
communique
compendium
coniferous
consortium
conspectus
contagious
contiguous
continuous
coriaceous
coryphaeus
courageous
cretaceous
curriculum
curvaceous
curvacious
decapodous
delightful
delphinium
derailleur
despiteful
despiteous
diaphanous
dimorphous
diplodocus
disastrous
discobolus
disdainful
disembogue
disgustful
dispiteous
distichous
dogstongue
dovecolour
drupaceous
dysprosium
ectogenous
eczematous
edentulous
eigenvalue
elevenplus
endogamous
endogenous
ephemerous
episternum
epithelium
ericaceous
eucalyptus
euphonious
extraneous
factitious
fallacious
fasciculus
fastidious
felicitous
fictitious
flagitious
flavourful
fleacircus
flosculous
foliaceous
foraminous
fortuitous
founderous
fowlplague
fuliginous
gadolinium
gangrenous
gaspereaux
gelatinous
gemmaceous
glomerulus
glumaceous
gluttonous
goloptious
goluptious
gramineous
gratuitous
gregarious
gynandrous
hakenkreuz
halogenous
harmonious
haustellum
haustorium
helianthus
herbaceous
hexamerous
hocuspocus
holusbolus
homogamous
homogenous
homologous
homonymous
homozygous
homunculus
honorarium
horrendous
houseproud
humoresque
hypanthium
hypogynous
idolatrous
impervious
imprimatur
incautious
incestuous
indecorous
indigenous
infectious
inglorious
iniquitous
innumerous
insightful
involucrum
iridaceous
isopterous
isosporous
Japanesque
juggernaut
Kafkaesque
keratinous
kettledrum
knockabout
languorous
lanuginous
lascivious
lauraceous
lawrencium
lebensraum
leguminous
leprechaun
libidinous
licentious
lightingup
liliaceous
lipomatous
litterlout
longaevous
loquacious
lubricious

luciferous
lucifugous
lugubrious
lycopodium
machinegun
malodorous
malvaceous
marvellous
meaningful
meerschaum
megalosaur
membranous
memorandum
mendacious
menstruous
metacarpus
metatarsus
meticulous
migrainous
millennium
miraculous
misogynous
molluscous
molybdenum
monandrous
monoecious
monogamous
monogynous
monopodium
monotonous
moratorium
mordacious
mosasaurus
muciferous
multiloquy
myocardium
myrtaceous
mystagogue
mysterious
myxomatous
nasturtium
natatorium
nectareous
neglectful
nephridium
nidicolous
nidifugous
nitrogroup
nonferrous
nubiferous
nuciferous
nucivorous
nutritious
obsequious
oceanarium
octamerous
octandrous
octopodous
oedematous
oesophagus
oleaginous
oleiferous
oleraceous
olivaceous
ommatidium
omnigenous
omnivorous
omophagous
oncogenous
opprobrium
osmeterium
osmiridium
outrageous
paedogogue
palladious
palmaceous
pancratium
panjandrum
papaverous
paramecium
parapodium
paronymous
pediculous
pellagrous
pemphigous
pennaceous
perfidious
perigynous
periosteum
peritoneum
perjurious
pernicious
petrolatum
phosphorus
picaresque
piliferous
pitcherful
plasmodium
plesiosaur
plunderous
polemonium
polyanthus
polygamous
polygenous
polygynous
polymerous
polysemous
polytocous
pomiferous
porraceous
portentous
postbellum
posthumous
postpartum
praesidium
precarious
precocious
predacious
presageful
presternum
primordium
principium
prodigious
promethium
propitious
propylaeum
proscenium
prospectus
prosperous
prostomium
proteinous
prothallus
psalterium
puerperium
pugnacious
pupiparous
purposeful
purseproud
pyrogenous
quadrivium
radiopaque
rampageous
ranunculus
rapporteur
rebellious
referendum
remorseful
rendezvous
repetiteur
respectful
revengeful
ridiculous
robustious
roisterous
Romanesque
roundabout
rouseabout
roustabout
rubiginous
rupicolous
saliferous
salubrious
sanatorium
sanitarium
sarmentous
sauerkraut
saxicolous
scandalous
scarabaeus
scattergun
sclerotium
scrofulous
scrupulous
scurrilous
selfcolour
semichorus
semiopaque
sensedatum
septennium
sequacious
sequestrum
serotinous
sestertium
sestertius
sialagogue
simulacrum
sinistrous
slanderous
slumberful
slumberous
solicitous
somniloquy
spadiceous
spiraculum
spirituous
sporangium
sprightful
squeteague
statuesque
stertorous
stirrupcup
stomachful
stomodaeum
stormcloud
strabismus
stramonium
stridulous
stromatous
struthious
stupendous
subaqueous
subsellium
substratum
successful
sudatorium
sulphurous
sunparlour
suspicious
symphylous
synanthous
syncarpous
synoecious
synonymous
technetium
tenebrious
tepidarium
testaceous
thereabout
thimbleful
thoughtful
throughout
throughput
thunderous
tirailleur
titanesque
traitorous
transvalue
travelogue
treasonous
tremendous
triandrous
trichinous
triclinium
trioecious
trolleybus
tropaeolum
troubadour
trousseaux
tubicolous
tuffaceous
tumblerful
tumultuous
ubiquitous
umbrageous
undershrub
undervalue
undesirous
uneventful
unfaithful
ungenerous
ungraceful
ungracious
ungrateful
unmerciful
untruthful
uproarious
velutinous
vestibulum
vibraculum
viceconsul
victorious
villainous
violaceous
viraginous
viviparous
vociferous
voluminous
voluptuous
vomitorium
wanderplug
waterspout
whereabout
worshipful
zoophagous
zoophilous
absorptive
abstersive
accusative
adjunctive
admonitive
adsorptive
afflictive
aftershave
aggressive
alterative
apperceive
appetitive
appointive
appositive
architrave
assaultive
assumptive
attractive
automotive
capacitive
cogitative
collective
combustive
completive
compulsive
conceptive
concessive
conclusive
concoctive
concussive
conductive
congestive
connective
consultive
contortive
convective
convictive
convulsive
cooptative
copulative
corelative
corrective
corruptive
cumulative
cunctative
decorative
dedicative
definitive
deflective
degressive
denotative
depressive
depurative
derivative
detonative
detractive
digressive
diminutive
disapprove
disbelieve
discursive
discussive
dismissive
dispersive
disruptive
dissuasive
dominative
dubitative
enervative
estimative
evacuative
evaluative
excitative
execrative
exhaustive
exploitive
expositive
expressive
extinctive
extractive
federative
figurative
generative
hesitative
imperative
impressive
imputative
inchoative
incubative
indecisive
indicative
indurative
infinitive
inflective
inflictive
initiative
injunctive
innovative
inspective
interleave
intervolve
interweave
irrelative
irritative
lacerative
limitative
locomotive
maturative
medicative
meditative
misbelieve
mitigative
nominative
occupative
oppressive
overactive
palliative
pejorative
pendentive
perceptive
percussive
perfective
permeative
permissive
persuasive
perversive
possessive
preceptive
preclusive
predictive
preemptive
presentive
preventive
productive
projective
propulsive
protective
protensive
protrusive
quantitive
recitative
recitativo
recreative
redemptive
reflective
refractive
regressive
regulative
reparative
repetitive
repressive
resolutive
resorptive
respective
responsive
resumptive
retractive
ruminative
separative
shoreleave
simulative
slidevalve
spokeshave
spoliative
subjective
submissive
subversive
successive
suggestive
suppletive
supportive
susceptive
suspensive
sustentive
topsyturvy
transitive
turtledove
ulcerative
vasoactive
vegetative
vindictive
windsleeve
brokendown
buttondown
fingerbowl
jobbernowl
malleefowl
markettown
overthrown

screechowl
shantytown
splashdown
tumbledown
heterodoxy
heterotaxy
metagalaxy
phyllotaxy
lengthways
polydactyl
schooldays
zygodactyl
antifreeze
coleorhiza
deepfreeze
fuzzywuzzy
intermezzi
intermezzo
morbidezza
mycorrhiza
pocketsize
razzmatazz
underglaze

---

acrophobia
aerenchyma
aerophobia
alcyonaria
algolagnia
anacolutha
anglomania
animalcula
antependia
antheridia
aphrodisia
arrhythmia
arthralgia
asafoetida
aspergilla
aspidistra
assafetida
autostrada
babiroussa
banderilla
barracouta
barramunda
belladonna
blastemata
candelabra
canzonetta
cardialgia
cascarilla
charismata
chinchilla
Cinderella
cinecamera
citronella
clarabella
coleoptera
coleorhiza
collembola
coloratura
columbaria
comicopera
concertina
Constantia
cordillera
cornucopia
corrigenda
crematoria
cyclopedia
definienda
desiderata
diastemata
diphtheria
dipsomania
drosophila
dysgraphia
endothelia

equilibria
erotomania
escallonia
euthanasia
fenestella
floribunda
florilegia
framboesia
fraxinella
fustanella
gaillardia
Gallomania
gametangia
gaultheria
glycosuria
Gorgonzola
granadilla
grandmamma
grenadilla
groceteria
gypsophila
haematuria
hemiplegia
hyperaemia
hyperdulia
hypolimnia
incunabula
interregna
jinricksha
jinrikisha
kookaburra
latifundia
logorrhoea
Lupercalia
lymphomata
mandragora
manzanilla
marginalia
marshalsea
mediastina
meningioma
metaplasia
microbiota
mixedmedia
monochasia
montbretia
morbidezza
mozzarella
multimedia
myasthenia
mycoplasma
mycorrhiza
mythomania
mythopoeia
nephralgia
neurilemma
neurolemma
nosophobia
nullanulla
nyctalopia
odontalgia
ophthalmia
orthoptera
paramnesia
paraplegia
parenchyma
parramatta
penetralia
peripeteia
perithecia
petronella
phagedaena
philippina
philopoena
phylloxera
piscifauna
planetaria
plecoptera
poinsettia

polydipsia
potentilla
pozzuolana
premaxilla
presbyopia
propaganda
prothallia
protophyta
pulsatilla
pyracantha
quadrennia
quadrumana
retinacula
rickettsia
salmonella
sarcolemma
sarracenia
saturnalia
satyagraha
scarlatina
scorzonera
scriptoria
seborrhoea
seguidilla
serradilla
Sexagesima
sitophobia
soldanella
sterigmata
succedanea
syllabaria
synaloepha
syntagmata
tarantella
telecamera
teratomata
termitaria
terracotta
tetrahedra
ticpolonga
toxiphobia
tramontana
tularaemia
Victoriana
vorticella
wongawonga
xenophobia
ZendAvesta
breadcrumb
heartthrob
hermitcrab
letterbomb
spidercrab
undershrub
willowherb
achromatic
adrenergic
aerobiotic
aeronautic
aerostatic
aetiologic
aldermanic
algolagnic
allergenic
allopathic
allophonic
allosteric
allotropic
alphabetic
alphameric
altruistic
amphoteric
anaglyphic
anamorphic
anapaestic
anaplastic
anaptyctic
anchoretic
anchoritic

anchylotic
androgenic
annalistic
antibiotic
antiheroic
antipathic
antiseptic
antistatic
antithetic
aphoristic
apodeictic
apolaustic
apologetic
apoplectic
aposematic
apotropaic
aragonitic
archaistic
arithmetic
arrhythmic
arthralgic
astigmatic
astrologic
astronomic
asymmetric
asymptotic
austenitic
autocratic
autoerotic
azeotropic
bacchantic
barbituric
barometric
batholitic
bimetallic
biodynamic
biogenetic
biographic
biomorphic
bolometric
bronchitic
Buddhistic
cabalistic
caoutchouc
carboxylic
catalectic
cataleptic
catechetic
cellulosic
chiliastic
chondritic
choriambic
coenobitic
coenobytic
concentric
congeneric
copesettic
coprolitic
corybantic
cosmogonic
cosmoramic
crescentic
cryoscopic
cybernetic
cyclopedic
democratic
diachronic
diagnostic
diagraphic
diapedetic
diarrhoeic
diathermic
dichroitic
dielectric
dilemmatic
diphtheric
diphyletic
diplomatic
disyllabic

dosimetric
dynamistic
dysenteric
dysplastic
dystrophic
ecchymotic
ectodermic
egocentric
electronic
emblematic
embolismic
empathetic
emphractic
encephalic
endophytic
endoscopic
endosmotic
enharmonic
epenthetic
epexegetic
epiblastic
epideictic
epigastric
epigenetic
epiglottic
epigraphic
episematic
erethismic
erotogenic
escharotic
essayistic
ethnologic
eucaryotic
eulogistic
euphuistic
eurhythmic
exospheric
exothermic
fatalistic
felspathic
FinnoUgric
frigorific
futuristic
galliambic
ganglionic
geocentric
geognostic
geographic
geothermic
Glagolitic
glycosuric
granulitic
gynocratic
gyroscopic
haemolytic
hagiologic
halophytic
Hebraistic
hedonistic
helminthic
hemicyclic
hemiplegic
heptarchic
heptatonic
heroicomic
hexametric
hierarchic
histologic
histolytic
histrionic
holophytic
holosteric
homophonic
horoscopic
humanistic
humoristic
hydrologic
hydrolytic
hyperaemic

hyperbaric
hyperbolic
hypergolic
hypersonic
hypnagogic
hypodermic
hypostatic
hypotactic
hysteretic
iatrogenic
idealistic
idiopathic
inartistic
infrasonic
inharmonic
isentropic
isodynamic
isogenetic
isomorphic
Jehovistic
jingoistic
judgematic
kerygmatic
kinnikinic
laryngitic
legalistic
leucocytic
leukocytic
linguistic
lithologic
loxodromic
madreporic
manometric
Massoretic
mathematic
matronymic
megalithic
megascopic
melanistic
melismatic
mesenteric
Mesolithic
mesophytic
metaphoric
metaphysic
metastatic
metathetic
metempiric
meteoritic
metronomic
metronymic
microlitic
mobocratic
mockheroic
monocarpic
monoclinic
monocratic
monocyclic
monohydric
monolithic
monomaniac
monophonic
moralistic
morganatic
mystagogic
mythologic
mythopoeic
naphthenic
nativistic
neoclassic
neoplastic
nihilistic
nomothetic
nostologic
novelistic
numismatic
nyctalopic
oligarchic
ophiologic

ophthalmic
optimistic
orogenetic
orographic
orthogenic
orthopedic
paedagogic
paediatric
Palaeozoic
pancreatic
pangenetic
pantomimic
parabiotic
paradisaic
paradisiac
paraffinic
parametric
paraplegic
paratactic
pathogenic
pathologic
patronymic
pederastic
pegmatitic
pentatomic
pentatonic
perchloric
pericyclic
periscopic
phagedenic
phagocytic
phantasmic
phantastic
phenotypic
philatelic
phlegmatic
phlogistic
phonematic
phonolitic
phonologic
phosphatic
phosphoric
photogenic
photolytic
phylogenic
phytogenic
phytotoxic
planktonic
pleochroic
pleonastic
polyandric
polyatamic
polyclinic
polycyclic
polyhedric
polymathic
polyonymic
polyphasic
polyphonic
populistic
porismatic
postexilic
pozzolanic
presbyopic
procryptic
prognathic
prognostic
prosthetic
protanopic
prototypic
protreptic
pugilistic
pyromaniac
pyromantic
pyrometric
pyrophoric
quartzitic
radiogenic
radiologic
rheotropic
rhizogenic
ricinoleic
Romanistic
sacroiliac
Sanskritic
saprogenic
satellitic
schismatic
scholastic
scientific
sciolistic
seriocomic
sialagogic
simplistic
sociologic
solecistic
sophomoric
splanchnic
stochastic
strabismic
subaquatic
supersonic
supertonic
synchronic
synergetic
syphilitic
systematic
talismanic
tautomeric
taxidermic
telemetric
teleologic
telepathic
telephonic
telescopic
tenebrific
tetrarchic
theocratic
theophanic
theophoric
thermionic
thrombotic
timocratic
totemistic
tragicomic
tremolitic
tribrachic
triglyphic
trimorphic
tropologic
tularaemic
tympanitic
ultrabasic
ultrasonic
uneconomic
unemphatic
unhistoric
unionistic
variolitic
Visigothic
vitalistic
volumetric
xerophytic
xylophonic
zoomorphic
ablebodied
aboveboard
abstracted
accredited
accustomed
addlepated
affiliated
albuminoid
almondeyed
ammoniated
amygdaloid
anthracoid
anthropoid
antiquated
apparelled
armourclad
arytaenoid
asteriated
attenuated
background
backhanded
baldheaded
barebacked
barefooted
bareheaded
barelegged
bargeboard
bedevilled
bedraggled
beforehand
behindhand
bejewelled
bemedalled
beribboned
bighearted
bigmouthed
bitterwood
bivouacked
blackboard
blackfaced
blackguard
blearyeyed
blockboard
bloodhound
boneheaded
borderland
bottlefeed
brachiopod
brainchild
brazilwood
breadboard
brickfield
bridesmaid
bridgehead
broadsword
bufflehead
bullethead
bullheaded
buttonwood
cackhanded
camelopard
candlewood
caravanned
carbuncled
carotenoid
carotinoid
carpetweed
cattlegrid
celebrated
centrefold
cephalopod
chalkboard
channelled
chargehand
chaudfroid
chessboard
Christhood
churchyard
classified
clavichord
cloistered
clubfooted
coastguard
cochleated
collarstud
colonnaded
complected
complotted
comprehend
compressed
condescend
confervoid
confirmand
confounded
considered
contraband
controlled
convoluted
coolheaded
copperhead
correspond
corrugated
corticated
cottonseed
cottonweed
cottonwood
counselled
cousinhood
covenanted
craftguild
crenulated
crispbread
crossbreed
cucullated
cummerbund
cuspidated
cylindered
cylindroid
decompound
deeprooted
deepseated
delphinoid
determined
diminished
discommend
disengaged
disjointed
disordered
dispersoid
dispirited
dissipated
distilland
distracted
distressed
doughfaced
dragonhead
dreamworld
drowsihead
dunderhead
earthbound
eisteddfod
embowelled
emeryboard
empanelled
endstopped
enthralled
epicycloid
epidermoid
eurypterid
evenhanded
evilminded
fairground
fairhaired
fairminded
farfetched
farsighted
fatherhood
fatherland
featherbed
fibreboard
fiddlehead
fiddlewood
figurehead
fimbriated
flannelled
flashboard
flashflood
flatfooted
fleshwound
floatboard
floorboard
forcipated
foreground
forehanded
forwearied
fourfooted
fourhanded
fourinhand
fourleaved
freehanded
fricasseed
fullbodied
gasteropod
gatelegged
gauntleted
girlfriend
goatsbeard
goggleeyed
grandchild
grandstand
greasewood
greensward
greyheaded
halfcocked
halfwitted
hammerhead
hammerpond
handpicked
handselled
handworked
hardbilled
hardboiled
hardfisted
hardhanded
hardheaded
harelipped
hawserlaid
heartblood
heavenward
heavyarmed
henhearted
heptachord
highhanded
highminded
hinterland
hitherward
holloweyed
homebrewed
hornrimmed
hotblooded
housebound
houseproud
humpbacked
hyphenated
illadvised
illnatured
illstarred
impanelled
imperilled
indigested
indisposed
infatuated
initialled
interbreed
interested
interplead
interwound
ironhanded
Janusfaced
jimsonweed
jolterhead
knifeboard
knighthood
knockkneed
Krugerrand
landlocked
lefthanded
lettercard
letterhead
lightfaced
likelihood
likeminded
livelihood
loggerhead
longhaired
longheaded
longlegged
longwinded
lowpitched
lumberyard
maidenhead
maidenhood
maladapted
malleebird
mamillated
manumitted
marginated
marshalled
masterhand
masterhood
mastermind
matchboard
matronhood
maxilliped
meadowland
medullated
methylated
microfarad
middleaged
minutehand
misaligned
misericord
mismatched
misnomered
molluscoid
monohybrid
monorhymed
Montagnard
motherhood
motherland
mouldboard
moustached
multifaced
musicstand
muttonhead
nanosecond
nationhood
needlecord
newfangled
nonaligned
nonplussed
northbound
notchboard
obfuscated
oldfangled
openhanded
openminded
orangewood
orphanhood
otherworld
otterboard
overabound
overcooked
overground
overhanded
overlapped
overmanned
overspread
overtopped
packthread
paddyfield
palmatifid
pantrymaid
paraboloid
parasitoid
parenthood
parsonbird
pasteboard
pastyfaced

pectinated
pedimented
pemphigoid
pentachord
periwigged
petiolated
photoflood
picosecond
pigeontoed
pinnatifid
pinnulated
pinstriped
pixillated
playground
ploughland
pockmarked
pokerfaced
potbellied
prejudiced
priesthood
principled
privileged
pronounced
propertied
protracted
pulvinated
punchboard
purseproud
pycnogonid
quarrelled
rattlehead
redblooded
registered
remodelled
restrained
rheumatoid
ringnecked
ringtailed
rockribbed
roselipped
saccharoid
sandalwood
sappanwood
sawtoothed
scaleboard
scarabaeid
scoreboard
sculptured
secondhand
selfglazed
selfguided
selfpoised
selfraised
selfregard
selfstyled
selfwilled
semifitted
semiliquid
sexlimited
shamefaced
sharpnosed
sheepshead
shellacked
shellmound
shiprigged
shopsoiled
shortbread
shortdated
shortlived
shouldered
shovelhead
shrivelled
shroudlaid
silverweed
sisterhood
skateboard
sleepyhead
slowfooted
slowwitted
smallsword
smokedried
smorrebrod
snailpaced
sneezeweed
sneezewood
snowcapped
sobersided
softbilled
softboiled
softfinned
softheaded
soundboard
southbound
spadebeard
spectacled
spellbound
spongewood
springhead
springwood
squaretoed
squinteyed
squirehood
starryeyed
stencilled
stomatopod
stoneblind
stormbound
stormcloud
strawboard
streetward
stronghold
structured
subtrahend
surefooted
suspensoid
swaybacked
sweatgland
sweetbread
swiveleyed
syncopated
tailorbird
taperecord
tapestried
tendrilled
tetrachord
thirtyfold
timberhead
tonguetied
tracheated
trafficked
trammelled
translucid
treadboard
trucklebed
trundlebed
tumbleweed
twelvefold
twilighted
ultrasound
umbrellaed
unabridged
unaccented
unaffected
unassisted
unattached
unattended
unbalanced
unblenched
unbonneted
unbuttoned
uncustomed
undefended
undersexed
undersized
understand
understood
underworld
undeserved
undesigned
undeterred
undigested
uneducated
unemployed
unequalled
unexampled
unexcelled
unexpected
unexplored
unfathered
unfettered
unfinished
unfriended
ungrounded
unhallowed
unhouseled
unimproved
uninformed
unlabelled
unlettered
unmeasured
unmortised
unnumbered
unoccupied
unprepared
unprovoked
unravelled
unredeemed
unrelieved
unremarked
unrequited
unreserved
unresolved
unrivalled
unschooled
unscreened
unscripted
unseasoned
unselected
unstrained
unstressed
untroubled
unwrinkled
variegated
verandahed
victualled
virginhood
watchguard
waterflood
wattlebird
weakminded
weaverbird
wellheeled
wellturned
whirlybird
whiskified
whitebeard
whitefaced
widespread
windshield
wingfooted
wingspread
wirehaired
wonderland
woodenhead
worshipped
wraparound
wunderkind
yellowbird
yellowwood
abbreviate
aberdevine
abhorrence
abominable
absorbable
absorbance
absorptive
abstersive
abstinence
accelerate
accentuate
acceptable
acceptance
accessible
accomplice
accordance
accumulate
accusative
achievable
achondrite
acidophile
acoelomate
acquirable
actinolite
actionable
adamantine
adjudicate
adjunctive
adjustable
admissible
admittable
admittance
admonitive
adrenaline
adsorbable
adsorptive
Adullamite
adulterate
adulterine
advertence
aeroengine
aerogramme
affirmable
afflictive
affordable
Africanise
afterimage
aftershave
aftertaste
aggrandise
aggressive
alcoholise
allegiance
allegorise
alliterate
allpurpose
alongshore
altarpiece
alterative
alternance
amalgamate
ameliorate
amerciable
amoebocyte
analysable
anastomose
anastrophe
andalusite
anecdotage
anglophile
anglophobe
anglophone
animalcule
annihilate
annunciate
anopheline
answerable
antagonise
anthracene
anthracite
anticipate
antifreeze
antimasque
antimonite
antiSemite
apiculture
apocalypse
apostatise
apostolate
apostrophe
appealable
appearance
appeasable
apperceive
appetitive
applicable
appointive
appositive
appreciate
apprentice
approvable
aquamarine
arbitrable
arborvitae
architrave
Areopagite
arthromere
articulate
ascendable
ascendance
ascendence
ascendible
ascomycete
ascribable
asparagine
asphyxiate
assailable
assaultive
assemblage
assessable
asseverate
assibilate
assignable
assimilate
assistance
associable
assumptive
atmosphere
attachable
attackable
attainable
attendance
attractive
audiophile
auriculate
auscultate
autoimmune
automatise
automobile
automotive
autostrade
avantgarde
aventurine
aviculture
backstroke
balustrade
barbellate
barcarolle
barkentine
barleybree
baronetage
barysphere
bastardise
bathyscope
battledore
bawdyhouse
beforetime
believable
bellydance
benedicite
Benthamite
benzocaine
benzpyrene
besprinkle
bestialise
bibliopole
bichromate
bidonville
bijouterie
biodegrade
bioscience
birdstrike
birthplace
birthstone
bissextile
bisulphate
bisulphide
bisulphite
bituminise
bizarrerie
blancmange
blanquette
blastomere
blastopore
bleachable
blithesome
blockhouse
bloodstone
blottesque
bluebottle
bluetongue
bobbinlace
bolshevise
boondoggle
borderline
Boswellise
bothersome
bottletree
bowdlerise
branchiate
brantgoose
breastbone
breathable
brentgoose
bridgeable
brigandage
brigandine
brigantine
brilliance
brocatelle
bronchiole
brownstone
brusquerie
Buchmanite
burdensome
burglarise
buttonhole
cacciatore
cachinnate
cacomistle
caespitose
calceolate
calculable
calumniate
calyptrate
camouflage
camphorate
cancellate
candletree
canonicate
cantaloupe
cantatrice
cantillate
capacitate
capacitive
capitalise
Capitoline
capitulate
caramelise
carbonnade
caricature
carmagnole
carnallite
cassolette
catafalque

catarrhine
categorise
cellophane
censurable
centigrade
centilitre
centimetre
centralise
centrifuge
centromere
centrosome
chainsmoke
chalkstone
chalybeate
changeable
channelise
chargeable
charitable
chartreuse
chatelaine
chatoyance
chauffeuse
cheapskate
cheesecake
chelicerae
chemisette
chersonese
chimpanzee
chlorinate
Christlike
chromatype
chromosome
chrysolite
chrysotile
cinchonine
circumcise
circumfuse
cismontane
cispontine
claspknife
classicise
clementine
clingstone
clinkstone
Clydesdale
coacervate
coachhouse
coagulable
cockatrice
cogitative
cognisable
cognisance
colatitude
colchicine
coleoptile
collarbone
collarette
collatable
collective
collegiate
colloquise
colourable
colportage
combustive
comedienne
comestible
commentate
commissure
commixture
commonable
communique
commutable
comparable
compatible
compensate
competence
completive
compliance
complicate
compradore
compromise
compulsive
computable
conceptive
concessive
conciliate
conclusive
concoctive
concretise
concussive
condensate
condolence
conductive
conference
confidante
confidence
confiscate
confluence
congestive
conglobate
congregate
congruence
conjecture
connective
connivance
conscience
consecrate
consociate
consolable
consonance
constipate
constitute
constringe
consuetude
consultive
consumable
consummate
contexture
continence
continuate
contortive
contravene
contribute
convalesce
convective
convenable
convenance
conveyable
conveyance
convictive
convulsive
cooptative
coordinate
copulative
coradicate
coralsnake
corbiculae
cordierite
corelative
corncockle
cornerwise
corpulence
corpuscule
corrective
corrigible
corroboree
corruptive
corsetiere
cottoncake
courthouse
couturiere
couverture
covariance
covenantee
crapulence
craquelure
crassitude
creatinine
creditable
crenellate
crepuscule
crinolette
crocoisite
crosspiece
ctenophore
cuddlesome
cultivable
cumbersome
cumulative
cunctative
custommade
cuttlebone
cyclostome
cyclostyle
cystoscope
cytochrome
damageable
dampcourse
deactivate
debilitate
debouchure
decagramme
decapitate
deceivable
decelerate
deceptible
decigramme
decimalise
decivilise
declarable
declinable
decolonise
decolorise
decorative
dedicative
deductible
deepfreeze
deescalate
defeasance
defeasible
defeminise
defendable
defensible
deferrable
definitive
definitude
deflagrate
deflective
defrayable
degenerate
degradable
degressive
dehiscence
dehumanise
delaminate
delectable
deliberate
delimitate
deliquesce
delocalise
demandable
demobilise
demoiselle
demonetise
demoralise
demotivate
demurrable
denominate
denotative
dentifrice
denunciate
dependable
dependence
deplorable
depolarise
depopulate
depreciate
depressive
deprivable
depurative
deracinate
derivative
desalinate
deshabille
desiderate
desipience
desistance
despicable
despisable
desquamate
detachable
detectable
deterrence
detestable
detonative
detoxicate
detractive
devitalise
devocalise
dialysable
dichromate
difference
diffidence
diffusible
digestible
digitalise
digressive
dilapidate
dilettante
diminutive
directoire
disapprove
disarrange
disbelieve
discipline
disclosure
discommode
discompose
discophile
discourage
discursive
discussive
disembogue
disentitle
disentwine
disfeature
disgruntle
dishabille
disincline
dislikable
dismissive
dispersive
disposable
disputable
disruptive
dissertate
disservice
dissidence
dissociate
dissoluble
dissonance
dissuasive
distensile
distillate
distribute
disulphate
disulphide
disyllable
divaricate
divergence
divulgence
dogstongue
dolomitise
dominative
dorsigrade
doubletime
downstroke
drafthorse
dragonnade
dragontree
dramaturge
drawbridge
dubitative
dumbledore
dungbeetle
duumvirate
earthquake
earthshine
Eastertide
ebullience
edulcorate
effaceable
effectuate
effeminate
effervesce
effloresce
effulgence
eigenvalue
elasticise
elecampane
electorate
eliminable
emancipate
emarginate
emasculate
embouchure
embryonate
emparadise
employable
endopodite
endorsable
enervative
enigmatise
ensanguine
enterprise
enumerable
enunciable
episcopate
epistrophe
equivocate
eradicable
escadrille
escheatage
escritoire
espadrille
estimative
eternalise
euhemerise
evacuative
evaluative
evangelise
evaporable
everyplace
everywhere
eviscerate
exactitude
exaggerate
examinable
exasperate
excellence
excitative
excogitate
excruciate
execrative
executable
exenterate
exhaustive
exhilarate
expandable
expansible
expatriate
expectance
expedience
expendable
experience
explicable
exploitage
exploitive
exportable
expositive
expressage
expressive
exprobrate
exsanguine
extendible
extensible
extinctive
extractive
extricable
exuberance
exulcerate
exurbanite
eyeservice
facilitate
fairycycle
fanaticise
fastigiate
fatherlike
fathomable
fatiguable
favourable
federalise
federative
felicitate
fenestrate
fescennine
fibrillate
fibrillose
fieldmouse
fieldpiece
fieldstone
figurative
filterable
fireescape
fishkettle
flabellate
flagellate
flapdoodle
flatulence
floatplane
floatstone
flocculate
florentine
fluoridate
fluorinate
fluorotype
fluviatile
fontanelle
footbridge
footcandle
forecastle
forecourse
forfeiture
forgivable
formidable
fourchette
foursquare
fourstroke
fowlplague
frangipane
fraternise
fratricide
freightage
frolicsome
gadolinite
Gallophile
Gallophobe
garnierite
gastronome
gelatinise
generalise
generative
geniculate
gentilesse

geometrise
Ghibelline
glassfibre
glasshouse
glauberite
glauconite
gluttonise
gobemouche
golfcourse
gormandise
governable
governance
gramophone
grandniece
granduncle
grangerise
granophyre
graphitise
graptolite
grasssnake
gravestone
greatniece
greatuncle
greenhouse
greenstone
grindstone
guardhouse
guesthouse
guillotine
habilitate
hagioscope
hairstroke
halogenate
hamshackle
Hansardise
harbourage
headcheese
headsquare
heartsease
heartwhole
heathenise
heatstroke
hectolitre
hectometre
heliophyte
helioscope
heliotrope
hemisphere
hempnettle
heparinise
hereticate
heretofore
hesitative
heterodyne
heulandite
hibernacle
highoctane
Hippocrene
hippodrome
hobbyhorse
hodgepodge
hollowware
holophrase
homogenise
homologate
homologise
homozygote
honeyguide
honourable
hornblende
hospitable
hourcircle
hoverplane
hucklebone
humoresque
humoursome
husbandage
hydrophane
hydrophone
hydrophyte
hydroplane
hydroscope
hygrophyte
hygroscope
hyperbolae
hypotenuse
iconoscope
illaudable
illegalise
illiterate
illuminate
illustrate
imaginable
immaculate
immiscible
immobilise
immoderate
immortelle
immoveable
impalpable
imparadise
impartible
impassable
impassible
impatience
impeccable
impendence
imperative
implacable
importable
importance
impossible
imposthume
impregnate
impressive
improbable
improvable
imprudence
impugnable
imputative
inaccurate
inactivate
inadequate
inapposite
inaptitude
inaugurate
incandesce
inchoative
incinerate
incipience
inclinable
includible
incomplete
incrassate
incredible
incubative
inculpable
incurrable
indecisive
indefinite
indelicate
indicative
indictable
indiscrete
inductance
indulgence
indurative
ineducable
inelegance
ineligible
ineludible
ineptitude
inevitable
inexorable
inexpiable
infallible
infeasible
inferrable
infiltrate
infinitive
infinitude
inflatable
inflective
inflexible
inflictive
ingeminate
ingestible
ingratiate
inimitable
initialise
initiative
injunctive
innominate
innovative
innumerate
inoculable
inoperable
inordinate
inosculate
inquietude
insatiable
inseminate
insensible
insistence
insociable
insolvable
inspective
inspissate
insufflate
insurgence
intangible
integrable
intendance
intenerate
intergrade
interleave
interphase
interspace
interstate
interstice
intertwine
intervolve
interweave
intimidate
intoxicate
intrigante
invaginate
invalidate
invaluable
invariable
invariance
inveterate
invigilate
invigorate
invincible
inviolable
ionosphere
iridosmine
irradiance
irradicate
irrelative
irresolute
irritative
Ishmaelite
isolatable
isoniazide
italianate
italianise
Italophile
jacobinise
Japanesque
jardiniere
jargonelle
jasperware
jeopardise
johnnycake
Johnsonese
journalese
journalise
judicature
Kafkaesque
kenspeckle
keratinise
kerseymere
kilogramme
kimberlite
knobkerrie
knopkierie
lacerative
lachrymose
lacklustre
lacustrine
lamentable
Lammastide
lanceolate
lanthanide
lanuginose
largescale
latescence
lavalliere
ledgerline
legitimate
legitimise
lemniscate
lengthwise
lepidolite
liberalise
licensable
licentiate
lighterage
lighthouse
limitative
limitrophe
lipservice
literalise
literature
lithophane
lithophyte
locomotive
loganstone
lophophore
lowprofile
luciferase
lumbersome
luxuriance
lymphocyte
lyophilise
macadamise
macrophage
macrospore
maculature
magistrate
maidenlike
maisonette
malignance
manageable
manipulate
manorhouse
mansuetude
manteltree
maquillage
Marcionite
margravate
margravine
marguerite
marionette
marketable
marquisate
marrowbone
martensite
martingale
masquerade
masticable
maturative
mayonnaise
mealbeetle
measurable
meddlesome
medicative
meditative
menstruate
mensurable
mercantile
mesoscaphe
mesosphere
metabolise
metabolite
metacentre
metaphrase
metastable
mettlesome
microcline
microfiche
microphone
microphyte
microscope
microspore
mignonette
militarise
millilitre
millimetre
mineralise
minestrone
misbelieve
miscreance
misfortune
mismeasure
missionise
mistakable
misventure
mithridate
mitigative
modifiable
moisturise
mongrelise
monochrome
monologise
monopolise
monstrance
morrispike
motorcycle
mousseline
mouthpiece
multiphase
multistage
mystagogue
myxomycete
nationwide
naturalise
necrophile
negligence
negligible
negotiable
negrophile
negrophobe
nephoscope
neutralise
nidificate
nightshade
nominative
noticeable
notifiable
novaculite
nucleoside
nucleotide
nunciature
obliterate
obnubilate
observable
observance
obtainable
obtruncate
occupative
occurrence
oedematose
offlicence
oligoclase
operculate
ophicleide
oppressive
optimalise
ordonnance
orthoclase
ostensible
osteophyte
otherwhere
otherwhile
outbalance
outerspace
outmeasure
overactive
overblouse
overcharge
overexcite
overexpose
overpraise
overrefine
overstride
oversubtle
oxidisable
pacifiable
pacificate
packsaddle
paedogogue
paedophile
Palaeocene
Palaeogene
palaeotype
palagonite
palatalise
palatinate
palindrome
palliative
panegyrise
paniculate
papaverine
paperchase
paperknife
parabolise
paradoxure
paralogise
paraphrase
paraselene
pardonable
paroxytone
participle
pasquinade
passionate
pasteurise
pasturable
patentable
patisserie
patriciate
pediculate
pejorative
pendentive
penetrable
penetrance
percentage
percentile
perceptive
percussive
perdurable
perfective
perfoliate
perishable
periwinkle
permanence
permeative
permissive
permutable
peroxidise
perpetrate
perpetuate

perquisite
persiflage
personable
persuasive
pertinence
perversive
pestilence
phantasise
philippine
philistine
philosophe
phlogopite
photophore
phototrope
pianoforte
picaresque
picketline
pigeonhole
pilgrimage
pillowcase
pillowlace
pilothouse
pilotwhale
pincerlike
piperidine
pistillate
pitchstone
plagiarise
plaguesome
planchette
planetable
plantlouse
plasmolyse
plasticise
plebiscite
ploughable
plunderage
pocketable
pocketsize
politicise
polychaete
polychrome
polymerise
ponderable
popularise
Portuguese
possessive
postchaise
postoffice
potentiate
powerhouse
praemunire
pragmatise
pratincole
preadamite
prearrange
precedence
preceptive
preclusive
predecease
predestine
predicable
predictive
predispose
prednisone
preemptive
prefecture
preferable
preference
prefixture
prehensile
prepackage
prepayable
prepotence
prescience
presentive
pressurise
presumable
presuppose
prevalence
preventive
primiparae
principate
proctorage
proctorise
procurable
procurance
producible
productive
profitable
profligate
projectile
projective
prologuise
prolongate
prominence
promulgate
propagable
propionate
propitiate
propulsive
prostitute
protective
protensive
proteolyse
protophyte
protrusile
protrusive
provenance
providence
psalmodise
psittacine
pubescence
punctulate
punishable
puritanise
purseseine
purtenance
purveyance
putrescine
pycnostyle
pyridoxine
pyrolusite
pyroxenite
pyrrhotite
quadrangle
quadrature
quadrireme
quadrumane
quadrupole
quantitive
quarantine
quarterage
quaternate
quenchable
quiescence
quinacrine
racecourse
radicalise
radiopaque
radiophone
radiosonde
ramshackle
rattlepate
razorblade
reactivate
realisable
reallocate
reappraise
reasonable
reassemble
rebuttable
recallable
receivable
receptacle
receptible
recitative
recolonise
recommence
recompense
recordable
recreative
recrudesce
recuperate
recurrence
recyclable
redecorate
redeemable
redemptive
redescribe
redundance
reeligible
reentrance
refillable
reflective
reflexible
reformable
refractive
refulgence
refundable
regenerate
regressive
regularise
regulative
reissuable
reiterance
rejectable
rejuvenate
rejuvenise
relativise
releasable
relievable
relishable
reluctance
remarkable
remarriage
remediable
remissible
remittance
remonetise
remunerate
renascence
renderable
reorganise
repairable
reparative
repatriate
repealable
repeatable
repellance
repellence
repentance
repertoire
repetitive
repopulate
reportable
repressive
reprobance
repugnance
repurchase
resilience
resistance
resistible
resolutive
resolvable
resorptive
respective
respirable
responsive
restorable
resumptive
resupinate
resurgence
retainable
reticulate
retractile
retractive
retrograde
returnable
revalidate
revalorise
revealable
reversible
revertible
reviewable
revitalise
rewardable
rhapsodise
rhinestone
rhinoscope
rhizophore
rhodophane
ridgepiece
rightangle
riverhorse
Romanesque
rontgenise
roquelaure
rosaniline
roseengine
rotisserie
roughhouse
roundhouse
rovebeetle
ruminative
rupicoline
Russianise
Russophile
Russophobe
sabretache
saccharate
saccharide
saccharine
saccharose
saddletree
salicylate
saltigrade
samarskite
sanctitude
sandcastle
sapphirine
saprophyte
sarmentose
saxicoline
scandalise
scapegrace
schematise
schemozzle
schipperke
schoolable
schoolmate
schooltime
Scotticise
screwplate
scrutinise
scutellate
seaanemone
seamanlike
searchable
seasonable
secondrate
secretaire
secularise
seignorage
selfpraise
seltzogene
semicircle
semidivine
semidouble
semilunate
semiopaque
senescence
sensualise
separative
serpentine
sexpartite
sheeplouse
sherardise
shirehorse
shoebuckle
shoreleave
shortrange
shrewmouse
shrinkable
Shrovetide
sialagogue
sideglance
siderolite
sidesaddle
sidestroke
silhouette
silverside
silverware
similitude
simulative
Singhalese
singletree
sketchable
skewbridge
skirtdance
slavetrade
Slavophile
Slavophobe
slenderise
slidevalve
sluicegate
smallscale
smaragdine
smaragdite
smokehouse
smoothbore
snakedance
snakestone
snickasnee
snowgrouse
snowmobile
soapbubble
solicitude
solidstate
solubilise
somatotype
somnolence
sororicide
sousaphone
sowthistle
spathulate
specialise
spermicide
sperrylite
sphalerite
sphenodone
spherulite
spiderline
spiflicate
splintbone
spokeshave
spoliative
spongecake
sporophore
sporophyte
springlike
springtide
springtime
squeezable
squeteague
stablemate
staffnurse
stagbeetle
stalactite
stalagmite
staphyline
statoscope
statuesque
statutable
staurolite
stavesacre
steakhouse
stephanite
stereobate
stereotype
stiflebone
stigmatise
stillicide
stinkstone
stipellate
stonesnipe
storehouse
streamline
stridulate
striptease
strychnine
subaverage
subcordate
subculture
subjective
sublimable
submissive
submontane
subroutine
subsidence
substitute
subterfuge
subversive
successive
succulence
sufferable
sufferance
sugarhouse
sugarmaple
suggestive
sulphonate
sulphurate
sulphurise
summerlike
summertime
summonable
sunderance
superacute
supernovae
superstore
suppletive
suppliance
supplicate
supportive
supposable
surmisable
surplusage
survivance
susceptive
suspensive
sustenance
sustentive
swarmspore
swashplate
sweepstake
sworddance
symmetrise
sympathise
syncretise
synecdoche
synthesise
synthetise
tabernacle
tabularise
tailormade
tambourine
tankengine
taradiddle
tarantelle
tardigrade
tattletale
telpherage
temperable
temperance

tenantable
terminable
terneplate
tessellate
tetrastyle
theodolite
theologise
thermopile
thillhorse
thinkpiece
thornapple
threadbare
threepence
threepiece
threescore
thruppence
thwartwise
tickertape
timberline
titanesque
toffeenose
tollbridge
toothpaste
topazolite
touchjudge
touchstone
tourmaline
trabeculae
tramontane
trampoline
trancelike
transcribe
transferee
transience
transitive
transshape
transvalue
transverse
travelogue
travertine
triacetate
trichinise
Tridentine
trifoliate
trifurcate
tripartite
triplicate
triquetrae
triternate
triturable
trivialise
troctolite
troglodyte
tropopause
tropophyte
Trotskyite
trouvaille
truculence
tumescence
turbulence
turnbuckle
turpentine
turtledove
twelvenote
twelvetone
ulcerative
umbilicate
unarguable
unbearable
unbeatable
unbiddable
undeniable
underglaze
underlease
underquote
underscore
undersense
understate
undervalue
underwrite
underwrote
unenviable
unfeminine
unhandsome
uninitiate
unipartite
unknowable
unnameable
unreadable
unreliable
unscalable
unscramble
unsociable
unsuitable
unworkable
utilisable
valleculae
vanadinite
varicocele
vasoactive
vaticinate
vaudeville
vegetative
velocipede
ventricose
verifiable
vernissage
vertebrate
vesiculate
vespertine
vibraphone
videophone
Vietnamese
villainage
villanelle
villeinage
vindicable
vindictive
virescence
vitaminise
vitiligate
vitriolise
vituperate
vivandiere
vociferate
volatilise
voyageable
vulnerable
waggonette
waterborne
westernise
wheatstone
wheelhorse
wheelhouse
whorehouse
winceyette
windowpane
windsleeve
winebottle
wintertide
wintertime
wolframite
workpeople
worthwhile
Wycliffite
zabaglione
breadstuff
centrehalf
chiffchaff
childproof
cloverleaf
coolingoff
dampingoff
fallingoff
flameproof
greenstuff
hippogriff
lightproof
powderpuff
shandygaff
shellproof
shockproof
smokeproof
sneakthief
soundproof
stockproof
stormproof
Stroganoff
thornproof
timberwolf
undercliff
underproof
waterproof
accounting
acquitting
aircooling
almsgiving
anchorring
appetising
backbiting
ballooning
barrelling
batfowling
beekeeping
bestirring
bitterling
blanketing
blistering
blithering
blitzkrieg
bookmaking
bratticing
brevetting
cancelling
changeling
chiselling
clothesbag
clothespeg
commanding
committing
compelling
concerning
concurring
confabbing
conferring
consulting
convincing
corbelling
cradlesong
cudgelling
curvetting
diecasting
diesinking
disbarring
disbudding
discerning
dispelling
distilling
drawstring
drivelling
earwigging
easterling
enamelling
enchanting
englutting
engrossing
entrancing
enwrapping
everliving
everything
facesaving
feathering
fingerling
flagwaving
flattering
flavouring
fledgeling
flyfishing
forbidding
foreboding
forgetting
formatting
forwarding
fosterling
foxhunting
freeliving
frivolling
frolicking
fulfilling
funnelling
gadrooning
gaingiving
gambolling
garnishing
glimmering
Godfearing
gratifying
groundling
grovelling
gunrunning
hairspring
handspring
hanselling
headspring
headstrong
highflying
highstrung
hobnobbing
homecoming
homemaking
hostelling
houselling
humbugging
ilangilang
imprinting
inbreeding
infighting
inspanning
instilling
jaywalking
kennelling
kidnapping
Kuomintang
landowning
laurelling
lawabiding
lifegiving
lifesaving
lipreading
logrolling
lovemaking
lutestring
magnifying
mainspring
marvelling
midmorning
mishitting
miswording
mosaicking
nauseating
nickelling
nitpicking
nonplaying
nourishing
oceangoing
offputting
offsetting
outbidding
outfitting
outgassing
outgunning
outpouring
outputting
outrunning
outsitting
outwitting
overriding
overstrung
parcelling
patrolling
pencilling
penpushing
performing
permitting
physicking
picnicking
pigeonwing
pistolling
pistonring
playacting
pothunting
practising
prairiedog
preferring
prevailing
priestling
princeling
proceeding
propelling
publishing
pummelling
quartering
rainmaking
refreshing
refuelling
regretting
resounding
respecting
retraining
riproaring
rodfishing
roistering
rollicking
rumrunning
sanderling
satisfying
scattering
scratchwig
scribbling
selfacting
selfloving
selfrising
selfruling
semidrying
shoestring
shortening
shovelling
shuttering
signalling
skibobbing
skijumping
skindiving
skyjacking
skywriting
smattering
snivelling
spiralling
sprinkling
squireling
staggering
stargazing
starveling
stiffening
subheading
subletting
submitting
surprising
sustaining
swaggering
swanupping
sweetening
sweltering
swivelling
tasselling
thickening
thimblerig
thundering
timesaving
tinselling
tittupping
travelling
trepanning
triphthong
trowelling
tunnelling
unassuming
unavailing
unbecoming
unblinking
unblushing
unchanging
underlying
underslung
unedifying
unflagging
ungrudging
unpleasing
unsettling
unsporting
unswerving
unthinking
unwavering
unyielding
upbraiding
upbringing
upstanding
wampumpeag
wanderplug
wassailing
weathering
wellspring
whispering
wrongdoing
ylangylang
zigzagging
accomplish
afterbirth
alloverish
altazimuth
amateurish
amphibrach
anemograph
archerfish
backsheesh
backstitch
balderdash
bathyscaph
bellylaugh
blacksmith
bridlepath
broadcloth
bumpkinish
butterfish
buttonbush
candlefish
childbirth
chinagraph
clovehitch
cockneyish
coelacanth
coquettish
cornstarch
countryish
crossbench
crosshatch
crosspatch
cuttlefish
cyclograph
czarevitch
deathwatch
disfurnish
ditriglyph
eighteenth
enterolith

extinguish
flightpath
floorcloth
fourteenth
freespeech
frontbench
fulllength
glasscloth
gooseflesh
grasscloth
greencloth
greenfinch
halflength
hallelujah
heathenish
hectograph
heliograph
henceforth
Heptateuch
heresiarch
hieroglyph
hierograph
hippogryph
homoeopath
horsecloth
horseflesh
horselaugh
horseleech
hotchpotch
hygrograph
impoverish
lithoglyph
lithograph
lockstitch
mackintosh
Methuselah
micrograph
mimeograph
nailpolish
naturopath
needlebath
needlefish
nephograph
nettlerash
nightwatch
nineteenth
nudibranch
oldmaidish
openhearth
outlandish
outstretch
overgrowth
overslaugh
paintbrush
palaeolith
pantograph
parrotfish
peacockish
pebbledash
pennyworth
pentastich
petroglyph
phonograph
photograph
picayunish
pictograph
planigraph
proudflesh
psychopath
radiograph
relinquish
rhizomorph
ribbonfish
rudderfish
runthrough
sabretooth
scaramouch
seethrough
seventieth
shibboleth
shillelagh
showerbath
silverbath
silverfish
slipstitch
snowplough
songthrush
spirograph
squirearch
stagecoach
stenograph
stillbirth
stonebrash
stylograph
tablecloth
tetramorph
tetrastich
thirteenth
thousandth
threadfish
toothbrush
tragacanth
trillionth
trollopish
tsarevitch
underbrush
underneath
usquebaugh
vectograph
vinegarish
waistcloth
waterbrash
wavelength
whipstitch
whitesmith
wristwatch
yarborough
zincograph
altocumuli
altostrati
amphigouri
barramundi
borborygmi
burramundi
canaliculi
cannelloni
certiorari
coatimundi
Devanagari
dilettanti
fantoccini
fortissimi
frangipani
Hindustani
hippocampi
illuminati
intermezzi
jaguarundi
millefiori
monsignori
piccalilli
rhomboidei
ritornelli
salmagundi
sarcophagi
septenarii
spermaceti
tortellini
ventriculi
vermicelli
alpenstock
badderlock
basketwork
bloodstock
bottleneck
brakeblock
breadstick
breastwork
bridgework
brightwork
broomstick
bubblyjock
buttermilk
buttonhook
candlewick
canvasback
canvaswork
centreback
chequebook
crackajack
crewelwork
crosscheck
donkeywork
donnybrook
doublepark
doubletalk
dumbstruck
fetterlock
fiddleback
fingermark
fisherfolk
flightdeck
gentlefolk
greenshank
greenstick
groundwork
hackmatack
hairstreak
hammerlock
heartblock
heartbreak
herrenvolk
kibbutznik
knickknack
ladderback
letterbook
lumberjack
masterwork
matchstick
meadowlark
minutebook
moonstruck
mountebank
natterjack
needlebook
needlework
nightstick
nitrochalk
paddywhack
pastrycook
phrasebook
pilgarlick
pitchblack
pocketbook
pointblank
prayerbook
promptbook
punchdrunk
reichsmark
ripplemark
rubberneck
saddleback
salesclerk
schoolbook
schoolwork
scrimshank
scrollwork
sheepshank
shellshock
sketchbook
skrimshank
sleevelink
smockfrock
smokestack
soundtrack
sourcebook
spatchcock
spitchcock
splashback
supplejack
switchback
swordstick
tenterhook
threadmark
throwstick
tiddlywink
timberwork
turkeycock
turtleback
turtleneck
understock
undertrick
waterclock
whaleshark
wickerwork
wonderwork
yellowback
abacterial
aboriginal
academical
accidental
acoustical
acronychal
additional
adjectival
alchemical
ambulacral
ammoniacal
anagogical
analogical
analytical
anarchical
anatomical
aneurismal
aneurysmal
antechapel
anticlinal
antimonial
antiphonal
antisocial
aplacental
apocryphal
apolitical
apothecial
archetypal
artificial
asteroidal
auditorial
autarkical
Barmecidal
basketball
beneficial
bequeathal
bibliophil
bicultural
bimestrial
biological
biparietal
bluepencil
bollweevil
botryoidal
brachyural
brandyball
breastwall
butterball
buttonball
calciferol
campestral
cannonball
carnassial
centennial
centesimal
ceremonial
chimerical
cinquefoil
closestool
coffeemill
cognominal
collateral
colloquial
commercial
commonweal
conceptual
conchoidal
congenital
connatural
consensual
contextual
conventual
coromandel
cottontail
cottonwool
cranesbill
credential
curatorial
cuttystool
decahedral
decemviral
delightful
delusional
demoniacal
despiteful
devotional
diabolical
diarrhoeal
diathermal
dickcissel
didactical
disdainful
disembowel
disembroil
disenthral
disgustful
divisional
documental
dogmatical
dramatical
duniwassal
duodecimal
ecological
economical
ectodermal
ecumenical
egoistical
electrical
elliptical
emerywheel
encyclical
endocrinal
endodermal
eosinophil
epicentral
epidemical
epiglottal
episodical
epithelial
equational
equatorial
eremitical
ergosterol
eucalyptol
evidential
exegetical
exoterical
exothermal
extemporal
extramural
febrifugal
fingerbowl
fingernail
flavourful
flowergirl
fractional
fragmental
Francophil
frictional
functional
fungicidal
geodetical
geological
geoponical
geothermal
germicidal
gerundival
glossarial
goldenseal
grandducal
gressorial
gyrational
harmonical
hebdomadal
hemihedral
heptagonal
hermetical
hexahedral
hierarchal
historical
holohedral
homocercal
homosexual
horizontal
hypabyssal
hypaethral
hypodermal
hysterical
ideational
illusional
immaterial
immemorial
impersonal
incidental
individual
industrial
infusorial
insightful
internodal
interposal
intertidal
interzonal
intestinal
intramural
involucral
irrational
isochronal
isoglossal
isoseismal
isothermal
janitorial
jesuitical
jobbernowl
juristical
kriegspiel
ladychapel
larvicidal
lavatorial
ligamental
liturgical
logistical
magnifical
majestical
malleefowl
managerial
manchineel
markethall
matricidal
meaningful
mechanical
menopausal
meridional
metacarpal
metatarsal
methodical
millennial
millesimal

mischmetal
mizzensail
monarchial
monistical
monitorial
monoclinal
monopodial
monumental
muffinbell
multivocal
musicstool
myological
natalitial
natatorial
neglectful
neological
nonlogical
nonnatural
notonectal
nutational
objectival
occasional
occidental
octahedral
orangepeel
oratorical
orchestral
organismal
ornamental
orological
orthogonal
outgeneral
overmantel
papistical
paranormal
parenteral
parimutuel
paroxysmal
parricidal
parsonical
pathetical
patricidal
patrilocal
pedimental
pennyroyal
pentagonal
peppermill
perceptual
periclinal
peridermal
periodical
periosteal
peripheral
peripteral
peritoneal
pesticidal
phalangeal
phantasmal
pharyngeal
phenomenal
pheromonal
phthisical
pictorical
pitcherful
polydactyl
polyhedral
polynomial
pontifical
positional
praecocial
praetorial
precordial
prefrontal
preglacial
prelatical
premarital
premedical
presageful
primordial

principial
prismoidal
procedural
proctorial
prolicidal
pronominal
prosodical
prostomial
prototypal
proverbial
provincial
prudential
puristical
purposeful
pyrogallol
quadrantal
quadrivial
quatrefoil
quixotical
rabbinical
razorshell
reciprocal
regimental
relational
remorseful
resorcinol
respectful
revengeful
revisional
rhetorical
rhomboidal
rhythmical
rotational
rudimental
sabbatical
sacerdotal
salicional
sapiential
scansorial
schoolgirl
scrapmetal
screechowl
scriptural
sculptural
seedvessel
seignorial
selfdenial
semestrial
semiannual
semiotical
semiuncial
senatorial
sentential
septennial
sepulchral
sequential
sheathbill
sicklebill
simoniacal
sincipital
sinusoidal
sleighbell
slumberful
snailwheel
solenoidal
solstitial
spagyrical
sphenoidal
spheroidal
splintcoal
splitlevel
sponsorial
sporangial
sporophyll
sprightful
springtail
squaresail
standstill
stockstill

stomachful
storksbill
strabismal
structural
subcentral
subglacial
subliminal
sublingual
suborbital
subordinal
successful
suprarenal
symbolical
symphyseal
symphysial
synchronal
synoptical
Talmudical
tangential
taxidermal
tegumental
televisual
tenemental
tetragonal
theatrical
theistical
thermophil
theurgical
thimbleful
thoughtful
threnodial
thumbstall
tinctorial
tocopherol
toothshell
torrential
tractional
transeptal
transposal
treadwheel
trigeminal
trilateral
trilingual
triliteral
triquetral
triumviral
trochoidal
tumblerful
tyrannical
unbiblical
uncritical
uneventful
unfaithful
ungraceful
ungrateful
unicameral
unilateral
unilingual
unmerciful
unofficial
untruthful
urochordal
urticarial
uxoricidal
venational
vermicidal
vesperbell
viceconsul
visitorial
vocational
volitional
volleyball
waterwheel
windowsill
witchhazel
withdrawal
worshipful
zoological
zygodactyl

absolutism
acetabulum
acroterium
aesthetism
Africanism
alcoholism
amateurism
ambulacrum
anabaptism
androecium
angiosperm
antagonism
antebellum
antemortem
antitheism
apophthegm
apothecium
argumentum
asceticism
Ashkenazim
auditorium
automatism
Benthamism
blastoderm
blepharism
bolshevism
Boswellism
bourbonism
bowdlerism
bradyseism
Brahmanism
Brahminism
brainstorm
bridegroom
brigandism
Britishism
Buchmanism
caddisworm
calyciform
cankerworm
capitalism
cardiogram
catabolism
centralism
cerebellum
chauvinism
chloroform
chronogram
cicisbeism
cinerarium
classicism
cockalorum
cockneyism
collarbeam
colloquium
commonroom
compendium
concettism
concretism
conformism
consortium
cribriform
crippledom
cryptogram
cumuliform
curriculum
decimalism
delphinium
demagogism
dendriform
diatropism
digitiform
dimorphism
diningroom
disconfirm
disembosom
downstream
dysprosium
echinoderm

empiricism
engineroom
enthusiasm
epiphytism
episternum
epithelium
eudemonism
euhemerism
evangelism
factualism
fanaticism
federalism
flunkeydom
flunkeyism
foreignism
fortuitism
Fourierism
fullbottom
gadolinium
genteelism
geotropism
gnosticism
gradualism
grangerism
gymnosperm
hammerbeam
haustellum
haustorium
headstream
heathendom
heathenism
henotheism
hipsterism
honorarium
hyaloplasm
hylotheism
hypanthium
hypocorism
iconoclasm
illuminism
insularism
invalidism
involucrum
Italianism
Jacobinism
Jacobitism
journalism
Kantianism
karyoplasm
katabolism
kettledrum
Krishnaism
laconicism
Lamarckism
lawrencium
lebensraum
legitimism
lesbianism
liberalism
limaciform
linguiform
literalism
livingroom
lockerroom
Lollardism
lumberroom
lycopodium
Lysenkoism
mainstream
malacoderm
Manicheism
martialism
mayblossom
meerschaum
memorandum
mesomerism
messianism
metabolism
metamerism

microseism
militarism
millennium
millstream
minimalism
moderatism
molybdenum
monarchism
monetarism
mongrelism
moniliform
monogenism
monopodium
monotheism
moratorium
morphinism
myocardium
narcissism
nasturtium
natatorium
naturalism
negativism
nephridium
neuroplasm
neutralism
nicotinism
nominalism
oceanarium
oecumenism
ommatidium
opprobrium
organicism
osmeterium
osmiridium
oysterfarm
pacificism
palmerworm
pancratium
panjandrum
paralogism
paramecium
parapodium
parasitism
pasteurism
patriotism
periosteum
peritoneum
petrolatum
phallicism
phanerogam
pharisaism
phelloderm
plagiarism
plasmodesm
plasmodium
polemonium
polygenism
polymerism
polytheism
positivism
postbellum
postmortem
postpartum
praesidium
pragmatism
presternum
primordium
principium
promethium
propylaeum
prosaicism
proscenium
prostomium
proteiform
protoplasm
psalterium
psychicism
puerperium
puritanism

Pyrrhonism
quadrivium
Rachmanism
radicalism
recidivism
referendum
relativism
reunionism
revanchism
revivalism
rheumatism
ribbonworm
rockbottom
ruffianism
sanatorium
sanitarium
sarcoplasm
scepticism
schematism
schoolmaam
schoolmarm
schoolroom
scleroderm
sclerotium
Scotticism
scyphiform
secularism
securiform
seismogram
selfesteem
sensedatum
sensualism
separatism
septennium
sequestrum
sestertium
sheriffdom
simulacrum
sinecurism
slipstream
solidarism
specialism
sphenogram
spiraculum
spongiform
spoonerism
sporangium
starstream
stelliform
stereogram
stigmatism
stomodaeum
stramonium
stratiform
strongroom
strychnism
subkingdom
subsellium
substratum
sudatorium
surrealism
sybaritism
syncretism
tarmacadam
Tartuffism
technetium
tepidarium
thermogram
threadworm
tiringroom
traumatism
trichroism
triclinium
trivialism
tropaeolum
Trotskyism
umbiliform
utopianism
vaporiform
Vaticanism
vestibulum
vibraculum
viperiform
vomitorium
Wertherism
abdication
aberration
abjuration
abnegation
Abrahamman
abreaction
abrogation
abscission
absolution
absorption
abstention
abstersion
accusation
acervation
acotyledon
acroterion
actinozoan
activation
adaptation
adhibition
adjunction
adjuration
admiration
admonition
adsorption
advocation
Aethiopian
affliction
agglutinin
aggression
aircushion
Algonquian
alienation
allegation
allocation
allocution
alteration
ambulation
Amerindian
ammunition
amphictyon
amputation
Andalusian
AngloSaxon
annexation
annotation
annulation
antinomian
antipodean
antiproton
Apollinian
Apollonian
apparition
apposition
araucarian
archdeacon
areolation
Armageddon
arrogation
ascription
aspiration
assumption
Athanasian
attraction
Australian
autochthon
automation
Babylonian
backgammon
balbriggan
barleycorn
bassethorn
batrachian
beautician
Bedlington
Belgravian
Berkeleian
bestridden
biliverdin
bilocation
bipartisan
blackthorn
bloodstain
blueribbon
Boswellian
brachyuran
brokendown
browbeaten
butterbean
buttondown
byelection
cacodaemon
Caledonian
capitation
carcinogen
carragheen
carryingon
Carthusian
caseharden
castration
catechumen
catenation
catholicon
cavalryman
cavitation
centillion
chairwoman
chamaeleon
champignon
chapfallen
Charleston
chevrotain
chuckwagon
Ciceronian
Circassian
Cistercian
clothespin
coaptation
cogitation
collection
coloration
combustion
commission
compaction
comparison
compassion
completion
complexion
compulsion
conception
concession
conclusion
concoction
concretion
concussion
conduction
confection
confession
conflation
congestion
connection
conniption
constantan
contention
contortion
contrition
convection
convention
conversion
conviction
convulsion
cooptation
Copernican
copulation
corelation
Corinthian
coronation
correction
corruption
councilman
countryman
crackbrain
crispation
crossgrain
crustacean
crustation
cumulation
cunctation
curmudgeon
daisychain
datamation
deaeration
decahedron
decimation
declension
decoration
dedication
deepfrozen
defamation
definition
deflection
delegation
demolition
denegation
denotation
denudation
depilation
deposition
depression
depuration
deputation
derivation
dermatogen
derogation
descension
desolation
desorption
detonation
detraction
devolution
Dickensian
digitation
digression
dilatation
diminution
disburthen
discretion
discussion
disenviron
dishearten
dismission
dispassion
dispersion
disquieten
disruption
dissection
dissension
dissuasion
distension
distention
distortion
divagation
divination
domination
downfallen
drawingpin
dubitation
ebullition
Eleusinian
elongation
emaciation
emendation
emigration
emollition
encephalon
enervation
Englishman
epilimnion
equestrian
equitation
eructation
escalation
Esculapian
escutcheon
estimation
etiolation
Eurovision
evacuation
evaluation
exaltation
excavation
excerption
excitation
execration
exhalation
exhaustion
exhibition
exhumation
expedition
expiration
exposition
expression
expunction
extinction
extraction
exultation
exuviation
faceharden
fairspoken
fasciation
federation
feuilleton
fibrinogen
figuration
filtration
firescreen
fleabitten
flirtation
floatation
floriation
flugelhorn
foreordain
foundation
Franciscan
freedwoman
freemartin
freespoken
fruitarian
fumigation
gargantuan
gemination
generation
Gilbertian
glaciation
Glaswegian
graduation
gramicidin
grammarian
GrecoRoman
groundplan
groundsman
habitation
halfnelson
handmaiden
Hanoverian
hardbitten
harvestman
heavenborn
hebetation
Heliconian
hemihedron
hemipteran
hendecagon
Heptameron
hesitation
hexahedron
highwayman
hirudinean
homoousian
horsewoman
housetrain
hovertrain
husbandman
hyperbaton
imbibition
immolation
impanation
imposition
impression
imputation
inchoation
incitation
incubation
indagation
indecision
indexation
indication
Indonesian
induration
infarction
inflection
infliction
infraction
infrahuman
infusorian
ingression
inhalation
inhibition
inhumation
initiation
injunction
innovation
insolation
inspection
insulation
interferon
interurban
interwoven
intimation
intinction
intonation
intraurban
intubation
inundation
invitation
invocation
involution
iodination
ionisation
Irishwoman
irreligion
irrigation
irritation
johnsonian
journeyman
jubilation
laceration
Lamarckian
lambrequin
laminarian
lamination
lapidarian
lapidation
laundryman
laureation
Lawrentian
lederhosen
Leibnizian
leprechaun

levigation
levitation
liberation
lighterman
limitation
literation
Lithuanian
litigation
lobulation
locomotion
locustbean
Lusitanian
lustration
Maccabaean
maceration
machinegun
maculation
Mahommedan
Malpighian
Malthusian
mangosteen
Manichaean
markettown
markswoman
maturation
mavourneen
medication
meditation
Melanesian
mesenteron
midshipman
militiaman
misprision
mitigation
mixolydian
moderation
modulation
Mohammedan
Monarchian
monogynian
motivation
Mousterian
mouthorgan
Muhammadan
Muhammedan
mutilation
nanisation
nativeborn
navigation
Neapolitan
nepenthean
neurotoxin
noblewoman
nodulation
nomination
nonfiction
nucleation
numeration
nurseryman
obligation
obturation
occupation
ocellation
octahedron
octandrian
octonarian
oppilation
opposition
oppression
orchardman
ordination
Ordovician
oscitation
osculation
outstation
overburden
overridden
overthrown
paddywagon
pagination
palliation
Panamanian
pancreatin
panopticon
paradisean
paradisian
Parnassian
patination
peculation
pedalorgan
pedestrian
pejoration
penicillin
pennillion
pentathlon
pentstemon
peppercorn
perception
percussion
perfection
perihelion
permeation
permission
peroration
persuasion
perversion
phenacetin
phenomenon
philologen
phlogiston
Phoenician
pincushion
plantation
politician
polyhedron
Polynesian
Pomeranian
population
possession
postillion
powderhorn
practician
praetorian
precaution
precession
precipitin
preclusion
prediction
preemption
preexilian
prehension
prelection
pretension
prevention
procession
production
profession
projection
proportion
propulsion
protection
protrusion
provitamin
psilocybin
punctation
pushbutton
Pyrrhonian
quartation
quaternion
quatorzain
quercitron
quickthorn
radication
ragamuffin
railwayman
rechristen
recitation
recreation
redemption
reelection
reflection
refraction
refutation
regelation
regression
regulation
relaxation
relegation
relocation
renovation
reparation
repetition
reposition
repression
republican
reputation
rescission
resolution
resorption
resumption
retraction
revelation
revocation
revolution
riboflavin
rockgarden
rockpigeon
rollingpin
roodscreen
roofgarden
rumination
runnerbean
sagination
saleswoman
salientian
salivation
salpingian
salutation
sandmartin
sanitarian
sanitation
saturation
scattergun
Scillonian
Scotswoman
scyphozoan
seacaptain
selfaction
selfmotion
seminarian
semination
senseorgan
separation
septillion
serviceman
sextillion
shandrydan
shantytown
shenanigan
sibilation
siegetrain
silkcotton
silkscreen
simulation
slowmotion
snapdragon
softspoken
solifidian
souterrain
spacewoman
spallation
speciation
Spencerian
Spenserian
splashdown
spoliation
squamation
stagnation
starvation
stentorian
stonemason
straighten
strengthen
stringbean
subclavian
subduction
subjection
submersion
submission
subreption
subsection
substation
subvention
subversion
succession
suggestion
superation
superhuman
supination
suppletion
suspension
sustention
swanmaiden
symphonion
tablelinen
tablespoon
tabulation
Tartuffian
technician
teleostean
television
temptation
tenderloin
terreplein
theodicean
theologian
titivation
titubation
toleration
tourbillon
townswoman
toxication
trabeation
Tractarian
trajection
transition
trawlerman
triggerman
trisection
triskelion
truncation
tryptophan
tuberculin
tumbledown
Tyrrhenian
ulceration
ulotrichan
unAmerican
underlinen
undertaken
undulation
unforeseen
urtication
ustulation
usucaption
usurpation
validation
vegetarian
vegetation
veldschoen
velitation
veneration
vesication
visitation
waffleiron
Waldensian
warmingpan
watermelon
weatherman
wellington
wellspoken
Welshwoman
Wertherian
whitethorn
windscreen
woodpigeon
workingman
xiphosuran
zollverein
zwitterion
affettuoso
aficionado
allegretto
angwantibo
barleybroo
camerlengo
camerlingo
cappuccino
comanchero
concertino
didgeridoo
diminuendo
eighteenmo
fantastico
fianchetto
fortepiano
fortissimo
hullabaloo
impresario
intermezzo
intertrigo
maraschino
moustachio
mumbojumbo
octodecimo
peccadillo
pentimento
photolitho
pianissimo
pichiciago
portamento
prosciutto
recitativo
ritardando
ritornello
saltarello
scherzando
seedpotato
stringendo
supercargo
airmanship
archbishop
authorship
barbershop
battleship
beadleship
brandysnap
bucketshop
bursarship
censorship
clientship
codswallop
consulship
contraprop
cousinship
deaconship
doctorship
editorship
factorship
fathership
fellowship
friendship
gingersnap
handgallop
internship
kaisership
leadership
legateship
lightingup
mastership
matronship
membership
mentorship
mothership
nincompoop
nitrogroup
pastorship
penmanship
pillowslip
pistolwhip
princeship
pseudocarp
pursership
rattletrap
readership
rectorship
regentship
salmonleap
schizocarp
seamanship
shrinkwrap
squireship
stenchtrap
stirrupcup
sultanship
suretyship
tellership
thwartship
umpireship
viziership
wardenship
wentletrap
windowshop
abominator
abstracter
abstractor
accoucheur
acetabular
acidimeter
administer
adventurer
advertiser
Africander
Afrikander
alleviator
allrounder
almacanter
almucanter
alternator
altogether
ambassador
ambidexter
amphimacer
anemometer
antecessor
antimatter
applicator
aquaplaner
arbalester
arbalister
arbitrager
arbitrator
arteriolar
astrologer
astronomer
attenuator
auctioneer
audiometer
babysitter
backhander
backslider
ballflower
bandmaster
bathometer

bathymeter
beautifier
bedchamber
beefburger
bellflower
bellringer
bellwether
bellyacher
benefactor
bestseller
bilgewater
billposter
biographer
birdspider
bivalvular
blackamoor
blackwater
blasphemer
bluecollar
bobbysoxer
bombardier
bondholder
bonesetter
boneshaker
bookbinder
bookkeeper
bookmarker
bookseller
bootlegger
bootlicker
brachiator
brainpower
breakwater
bressummer
bricklayer
buccinator
budgerigar
bullroarer
bushmaster
bushranger
calamander
calcsinter
calculator
calibrator
campaigner
cantilever
carabineer
carabinier
caravaneer
caravanner
cardplayer
caruncular
caseworker
cataloguer
catburglar
catechiser
celebrator
challenger
chancellor
chandelier
changeover
charioteer
chiffonier
chronicler
churchgoer
circulator
classifier
clavicular
clawhammer
clinometer
clodhopper
coalbunker
coathanger
cockchafer
collimator
collocutor
colporteur
comehither
commandeer
commutator
comparator
competitor
complainer
compositor
compotator
compounder
compressor
computator
comstocker
contractor
controller
cooperator
coparcener
coproducer
copyholder
copyreader
copywriter
cordwainer
cornflower
corporator
corrugator
councillor
counsellor
covenanter
covenantor
cowcatcher
cowpuncher
crossrefer
crowkeeper
cuirassier
cultivator
curricular
cyclometer
daydreamer
defalcator
deflowerer
defoliator
delineator
denigrator
densimeter
deodoriser
deoxidiser
depredator
derailleur
descriptor
desecrater
desecrator
desiccator
designator
despatcher
destructor
discharger
disclaimer
discounter
discourser
discoverer
dishwasher
disparager
dispatcher
dispraiser
dissembler
dissimilar
distrainer
distrainor
divebomber
dogmatiser
doorkeeper
dovecolour
dressmaker
drophammer
dumbwaiter
dumfounder
duplicator
economiser
elaborator
eliminator
elucidator
elutriator
emblazoner
emerypaper
Emmentaler
emulsifier
encourager
encroacher
enregister
enumerator
enunciator
epigrapher
eradicator
eudiometer
Eurodollar
evaporator
expurgator
extenuator
extirpator
fabricator
fairleader
fascicular
fascinator
fellmonger
fertiliser
fictioneer
filibuster
fireraiser
fishcarver
fishmonger
fivefinger
floodwater
flycatcher
flyswatter
foamflower
folksinger
follicular
footballer
footwarmer
forecaster
forefather
forefinger
foregather
forerunner
foreteller
fornicator
fortyniner
fourposter
fourteener
franchiser
freebooter
freeholder
freelancer
freeloader
freesoiler
frequenter
freshwater
froghopper
furuncular
galvaniser
gamekeeper
gasconader
gaslighter
gatekeeper
geographer
gingerbeer
gladhander
glasspaper
glomerular
goalkeeper
goaltender
goatsucker
gobstopper
goldbeater
golddigger
goniometer
goodlooker
granulator
grapesugar
gravimeter
gunfighter
gunslinger
gyrocopter
hackbuteer
hairraiser
halberdier
halfdollar
hangglider
harmoniser
headhunter
headmaster
headwaiter
helicopter
heliolater
heliometer
hellbender
henharrier
heptameter
Herrnhuter
highbinder
highjacker
highlander
hitchhiker
honeyeater
horsecoper
horsepower
horseshoer
humidifier
hybridiser
hydrometer
hygrometer
hypnotiser
hypsometer
icebreaker
iconolater
iconometer
importuner
imprimatur
improviser
incantator
inculcator
inkslinger
inoculator
inquisitor
insinuator
inspirator
instigator
institutor
instructor
integrator
interceder
interferer
interloper
interlunar
interposer
intervener
intervenor
introducer
ironmaster
ironmonger
ironworker
jackhammer
jawbreaker
keyboarder
kieselguhr
kingfisher
labiovelar
lacrimator
lacrymator
ladyfinger
ladykiller
landholder
landhunger
landlubber
landscaper
languisher
lawbreaker
leafcutter
leafhopper
lefthander
legislator
lenticular
limeburner
lionhunter
Lipizzaner
Lippizaner
liquidator
liquidiser
lockkeeper
longprimer
loosecover
lossleader
lotuseater
loudhailer
loveletter
lubricator
lucubrator
lumpsucker
macebearer
machinator
magnetiser
maidenhair
mainlander
maintainer
majuscular
malefactor
malingerer
mandibular
manoeuvrer
Mariolater
marshaller
masticator
matchmaker
medicaster
megalosaur
meliorator
merrymaker
mesmeriser
micrometer
micropylar
mineworker
mintmaster
minuscular
mischanter
misjoinder
moderniser
molendinar
moneymaker
moneytaker
moonflower
moonshiner
mossbunker
moviemaker
mudskipper
mudslinger
multiplier
multipolar
musicpaper
mythiciser
mythologer
necrolater
negotiator
nevernever
newscaster
newsletter
newsmonger
newsreader
newsvendor
newswriter
noisemaker
nondrinker
nonjoinder
nonnuclear
nonstarter
nonswimmer
northerner
nutcracker
obstructor
ombrometer
ophiolater
opisometer
originator
oscillator
outfielder
outswinger
overlander
overlooker
overmaster
overwinter
ovipositor
oxygenator
pacesetter
painkiller
palisander
pallbearer
palmbutter
panhandler
papermaker
particular
pastmaster
pathfinder
pawnbroker
peacemaker
pearldiver
peashooter
peduncular
pellicular
penetrator
peninsular
pennanular
pentameter
percolator
perforator
persecutor
personator
petitioner
phonometer
photometer
piezometer
pigeonpair
pigsticker
piledriver
pinfeather
planimeter
planometer
platelayer
plesiosaur
plumassier
pollinator
polyhistor
postmaster
postulator
pourparler
premonitor
preparator
prescriber
proclaimer
procreator
procurator
progenitor
programmer
prohibiter
prohibitor
prolocutor
promenader
pronouncer
propagator
prophesier
propounder
propraetor
proprietor
proscriber
prosecutor
prospector
protractor
provocator
pulsimeter
pulsometer

pulveriser
punctuator
pycnometer
pyknometer
quadrumvir
quantifier
quarreller
quarrender
questioner
quizmaster
rackrenter
radiometer
railroader
rapporteur
ratcatcher
reconciler
reconsider
rediscover
rencounter
repetiteur
reproducer
repudiator
reredorter
researcher
respirator
restrainer
retrochoir
reverencer
ringfinger
ringleader
ringmaster
ripsnorter
roadrunner
rockbadger
rockhopper
rollcollar
ropedancer
ropeladder
ropewalker
rosechafer
rottweiler
roughrider
rubricator
sacrificer
safeblower
salamander
saltcellar
sanctifier
sandbagger
sandhopper
scaffolder
scrimmager
scrutineer
seersucker
selfbinder
selfcolour
selffeeder
selfmurder
selfseeker
semiquaver
sensitiser
sermoniser
servomotor
shanghaier
sheabutter
shearwater
shipbroker
shipfitter
shipmaster
shopkeeper
shoplifter
shopwalker
showjumper
sidewinder
signwriter
simplifier
sixshooter
skirmisher
skyscraper
soapboiler
socialiser
songwriter
soothsayer
southerner
speculator
spiracular
spirometer
splutterer
sportswear
sprucebeer
squanderer
stabiliser
stadholder
stenciller
stepfather
stepladder
stepmother
stepsister
steriliser
stimulator
stipulator
stockpiler
stockrider
stoneborer
streetdoor
subjugator
submariner
subnuclear
subscriber
sunparlour
superaltar
superduper
superlunar
superorder
superpower
supervisor
supplanter
suppressor
sweetbriar
sweetbrier
swinefever
swinglebar
switchover
syllogiser
symboliser
syncopator
syndicator
tachometer
tachymeter
tackdriver
talebearer
taleteller
tantaliser
taskmaster
taxidancer
teaplanter
tearjerker
telecaster
telephoner
televiewer
temporiser
tendrillar
tentacular
terminator
tetrameter
theosopher
thereafter
thereunder
thermistor
threatener
tidewaiter
tilthammer
timekeeper
timeserver
tirailleur
tobogganer
tortfeasor
touchpaper
trabecular
trafficker
transactor
transducer
transferor
transfuser
transistor
translator
translunar
transmuter
transposer
trespasser
triangular
tribometer
triphammer
triturator
trochanter
tromometer
troubadour
tubercular
tufthunter
twowheeler
typesetter
typewriter
umbellifer
unbeliever
uncloister
undercover
underfloor
underminer
understeer
undertaker
underwater
unfamiliar
unilocular
vaccinator
vallecular
vanquisher
variometer
ventilator
verbaliser
vermicular
vernacular
versicular
vestibular
victimiser
victualler
viewfinder
vindicator
viscometer
visualiser
vivisector
voltameter
vorticular
vulcaniser
wallflower
wallpepper
wastepaper
watchmaker
watchtower
waterpower
waterskier
weedkiller
weimaraner
wellwisher
wharfinger
whatsoever
wheelchair
whensoever
wholesaler
whomsoever
wildfowler
Winchester
windflower
windjammer
winebibber
winegrower
wingcollar
wiredrawer
wirepuller
wiretapper
wirewalker
wireworker
withdrawer
withholder
woodcarver
woodcutter
woodlander
woodpecker
woodturner
woodworker
woolgather
woolgrower
woolsorter
worshipper
yardmaster
yesteryear
aardwolves
abdominous
abducentes
abjectness
abruptness
abstemious
absurdness
acarpelous
acephalous
acrobatics
acrogenous
activeness
adroitness
adulteress
adulterous
aerobatics
aerobiosis
aeruginous
aesthetics
affectless
aftergrass
afterpains
afterwards
agapanthus
Albigenses
albuminous
alexanders
alliaceous
allogamous
amanuenses
amanuensis
ampelopsis
amphibious
amphimixes
amphimixis
amylaceous
anadromous
anatropous
ancestress
anchorless
anchylosis
ancipitous
Anglistics
anonaceous
antibiosis
antisepsis
antitheses
antithesis
antonymous
aphaereses
aphaeresis
apocarpous
apotheoses
apotheosis
appendices
appendixes
aquafortis
aquiferous
arenaceous
armigerous
armourless
artfulness
asbestosis
ascariasis
astragalus
astuteness
ateleiosis
augustness
auriferous
auspicious
autogamous
autogenous
autologous
autonomous
avaricious
averseness
aviatrices
bacchantes
backblocks
backstairs
ballistics
barratrous
barrenness
battailous
Beaujolais
bedclothes
beechdrops
belongings
Benedictus
bibliotics
binoculars
biogenesis
biometrics
biophysics
bipetalous
bitchiness
bitterness
bituminous
bleariness
blitheness
bloodiness
bluishness
blusterous
bobbysocks
boisterous
bootstraps
borderless
bottomless
boyishness
braininess
brassiness
brawniness
brazenness
breakables
breathless
breechless
breezeless
breeziness
bridgeless
brightness
brokenness
bromegrass
bronchitis
broodiness
bunchgrass
buttonless
byssaceous
byssinosis
cacogenics
cadaverous
calamitous
calcareous
caliginous
callowness
calumnious
cancellous
candidness
candyfloss
canonicals
capricious
carcinosis
caryatides
casualness
catastasis
catechesis
catholicos
catoptrics
cellulitis
censorious
ceruminous
changeless
chaparajos
chaparejos
chasteness
chattiness
chauntress
cheekiness
cheeriness
cheesiness
chemotaxis
childermas
chilliness
chivalrous
choiceness
chromatics
chubbiness
cicatrices
circuitous
clamminess
clangorous
cleverness
cloudiness
clumsiness
coarseness
coastwards
coetaneous
collarless
colourless
comeliness
commandoes
commodious
commonness
coniferous
conspectus
contagious
contiguous
continuous
contrabass
coriaceous
cornflakes
Corybantes
coryphaeus
cosmopolis
costliness
couchgrass
courageous
craftiness
cragginess
crankiness
cravenness
creaminess
creepiness
cretaceous
crisscross
crossbones
crossroads
crosstrees
crustiness
cryogenics
cursedness
curvaceous
curvacious
cussedness
daintiness
dauphiness
deadliness
decapodous
decompress
demureness

dermatitis
desperados
despiteous
devoutness
diapedesis
diaphanous
dictatress
diluteness
dimorphous
dinnerless
diplodocus
directness
directress
disastrous
discobolus
dismalness
disparates
dispiteous
dispossess
distichous
distringas
divineness
doggedness
doublebass
doubleness
downstairs
draconites
dreaminess
dreariness
dressiness
driverless
drowsiness
drupaceous
duodenitis
earthiness
earthwards
earwitness
ecchymosis
ectogenous
eczematous
edentulous
edibleness
effeteness
effortless
elatedness
elevenplus
emblements
enantiosis
endodermis
endogamous
endogenous
endosmosis
energetics
entireness
epentheses
epenthesis
epexegeses
epexegesis
ephemerous
epigenesis
epiglottis
ergonomics
ericaceous
erysipelas
eucalyptus
euphonious
everglades
expertness
extraneous
eyeglasses
eyewitness
facileness
factitious
fallacious
fallowness
famousness
fandangoes
fasciculus
fastidious
fatherless
fathomless
faultiness
feebleness
felicitous
femaleness
fervidness
fibreglass
fibrositis
fickleness
fictitious
fieldglass
fierceness
filariasis
filthiness
fingerless
finiteness
firstclass
fisticuffs
fitfulness
flabbiness
flagitious
flamingoes
flashiness
fleacircus
fleshiness
flightless
flimsiness
flintiness
floppiness
floridness
floristics
flosculous
flowerless
fluffiness
foetidness
foliaceous
folksiness
footlights
foraminous
foresheets
fortuitous
founderous
freakiness
Frenchness
friendless
frigidness
frilliness
fringeless
friskiness
frizziness
frontwards
frostiness
frothiness
fuliginous
futureless
galimatias
galloglass
gangrenous
garishness
gaucheness
gelatinous
gemmaceous
genialness
gentleness
geophysics
geriatrics
gingivitis
glassiness
glassworks
glomerulus
gloominess
glossiness
glumaceous
gluttonous
glycolyses
glycolysis
goldenness
goldilocks
goloptious
goluptious
goodliness
goosegrass
gramineous
graphemics
grassroots
gratuitous
greasiness
greediness
greedyguts
gregarious
grisliness
grittiness
grogginess
groundless
groundmass
grubbiness
grumpiness
guiltiness
gymnastics
gynandrous
haematosis
haemolysis
halieutics
halogenous
hammerless
handedness
harmonious
haruspices
headphones
heartiness
helianthus
heliotaxis
herbaceous
hereabouts
heroicness
heuristics
hexamerous
hippomanes
histolysis
hoarseness
hocuspocus
hollowness
holusbolus
homeliness
homiletics
homogamous
homogenous
homologous
homonymous
homozygous
homunculus
honourless
hookedness
hornedness
horrendous
horridness
housewives
humaneness
humanities
humbleness
humourless
hungriness
hydraulics
hydrolysis
hydrotaxis
hyperbolas
hypodermis
hypogynous
hypophyses
hypophysis
hypostasis
hypotheses
hypothesis
hysteresis
ichthyosis
idolatress
idolatrous
impervious
impishness
impureness
incautious
incestuous
indecorous
indigenous
infectious
inglorious
iniquitous
innateness
innuendoes
innumerous
insaneness
intactness
intentness
intercross
inventress
inwardness
iridaceous
isometrics
isopterous
isosporous
jackanapes
jackknives
jaggedness
jauntiness
jejuneness
Jewishness
jocoseness
joyfulness
joyousness
keratinous
kerchieves
kindliness
kinematics
kingliness
knottiness
languorous
lanuginous
laryngitis
lascivious
lauraceous
lavishness
lawfulness
lawntennis
leadenness
leaderless
leguminous
lemongrass
lengthways
lentigines
leopardess
letterless
libidinous
licentious
likeliness
liliaceous
limpidness
lipomatous
liquidness
lissomness
littleness
liveliness
loneliness
longaevous
longshanks
loquacious
lordliness
loveliness
lovingness
lowerclass
lubricious
luciferous
lucifugous
lugubrious
lustreless
malapropos
mallenders
malodorous
malvaceous
manageress
manfulness
manifestos
manoeuvres
marrowless
marshiness
marvellous
masterless
matureness
meagreness
measliness
mediatress
mellowness
membranous
mendacious
meningitis
menstruous
metacarpus
metalepsis
metastases
metastasis
metatarsus
metatheses
metathesis
meticulous
metropolis
Michaelmas
mightiness
migrainous
mindedness
minuteness
miraculous
misgivings
misogynous
modernness
modishness
molluscous
monandrous
moniliasis
monoecious
monogamous
monogynous
monotonous
mopishness
morbidness
mordacious
moroseness
morphemics
mosasaurus
mosquitoes
motherless
motionless
motiveless
mouldiness
muciferous
mulishness
mulligrubs
Mussulmans
myrtaceous
mysterious
myxomatous
narrowness
nationless
nativeness
necropolis
nectareous
nidicolous
nidifugous
nightdress
nightglass
nimbleness
nonferrous
noogenesis
northwards
nubiferous
nuciferous
nucivorous
nucleonics
numberless
nutritious
oafishness
objectless
oblateness
obsequious
obstetrics
obtuseness
octamerous
octandrous
octopodous
odiousness
oedematous
oesophagus
oftentimes
oleaginous
oleiferous
oleraceous
olivaceous
omnigenous
omnivorous
omophagous
oncogenous
opaqueness
opposeless
orchestics
ornateness
orneriness
orogenesis
otioseness
outrageous
owlishness
palladious
pallidness
palmaceous
paltriness
pangenesis
papaverous
parabiosis
paragnosis
paralipsis
paratroops
paronymous
patchiness
patristics
pedagogics
pediculous
pellagrous
pemphigous
pennaceous
perfidious
perigynous
perjurious
pernicious
petiteness
phosphorus
photolysis
phototaxis
piecegoods
piliferous
pilliwinks
pityriasis
placidness
pliantness
pluckiness
plunderous
pneumatics
politeness
pollenosis
polyanthus
polygamous
polygenous
polygynous
polymerous
polysemous
polytocous
pomiferous
pontifices

porousness
porraceous
portcullis
portentous
portliness
posthumous
precarious
precocious
predacious
prepossess
prettiness
prissiness
procrypsis
prodigious
profitless
proglottis
promptness
properness
prophetess
propitious
prospectus
prosperous
prosthesis
proteinous
prothallus
provisions
pugnacious
pupiparous
putridness
pyrogenous
quadratics
quadriceps
quaintness
queasiness
quenchless
quickgrass
quirkiness
raggedness
rakishness
rampageous
rancidness
randomness
ranunculus
reasonless
rebellious
recentness
regardless
rejoicings
relentless
remediless
remissness
remoteness
rendezvous
resistless
resultless
retrogress
rewardless
rheumatics
rhinoceros
ridiculous
rightwards
robustious
robustness
roisterous
rootedness
rottenness
rubiginous
rudderless
ruefulness
ruggedness
rupicolous
sacredness
sailorless
saliferous
sallenders
sallowness
salubrious
sargassoes
sarmentous
satyriasis
savageness
savourless
saxicolous
scandalous
scantiness
scarabaeus
scarceness
scatheless
scattiness
schooldays
screenings
screwpress
scrofulous
scrupulous
sculptress
scurrilous
scurviness
seamstress
searchless
secureness
sedateness
seductress
seemliness
selectness
semeiotics
semichorus
sempstress
sequacious
sereneness
serotinous
sestertius
severeness
shabbiness
shadowless
shagginess
sheathless
shieldless
shiftiness
shoddiness
shorewards
shrewdness
shrillness
shroudless
sickliness
sideboards
silentness
simpleness
sinfulness
singleness
sinistrous
skimpiness
skinniness
slanderous
slanginess
sleaziness
sleepiness
sleeveless
slightness
sloppiness
slumberous
smallwares
smelliness
smoothness
smudginess
smuttiness
sneakiness
sniffiness
snootiness
snuffiness
soapflakes
sobersides
soddenness
solemnness
solicitous
sombreness
songstress
sordidness
southwards
spadiceous
sparseness
speargrass
spectacles
speechless
speediness
spillikins
spiritless
spirituous
sponginess
spookiness
sportiness
spottiness
springless
spruceness
spunkiness
squareness
squaretoes
stableness
stanchless
stanchness
starriness
statistics
steadiness
steaminess
steeliness
steelworks
stereopsis
sternwards
stertorous
stewardess
stickiness
stilettoes
stinginess
stockiness
stodginess
stolidness
stomatitis
storminess
strabismus
straitness
streamless
stressless
strictness
stridulous
stringless
stromatous
struthious
stubbiness
stuffiness
stumpiness
stupendous
stupidness
sturdiness
stylistics
subaqueous
subspecies
subtleness
suddenness
sugariness
sullenness
sulphurous
sultriness
summitless
sunglasses
superbness
supineness
supperless
suppleness
suspenders
suspicious
sweatiness
swordgrass
symphylous
synaeresis
synanthous
syncarpous
syngenesis
synoecious
synonymous
synostosis
systemless
takingness
talentless
tawdriness
tenantless
tenderness
tendinitis
tenebrious
terrorless
testaceous
tetchiness
tetrapolis
thalecress
themselves
theoretics
thirdclass
thorniness
thriftless
thromboses
thrombosis
throneless
thunderous
timbertoes
timeliness
tongueless
toothiness
torpidness
torridness
touchiness
towardness
tracheitis
traitorous
transgress
trappiness
trashiness
treasonous
tremendous
trendiness
triandrous
trichiasis
trichinous
trickiness
trioecious
trolleybus
trustiness
tubicolous
tuffaceous
tumultuous
turbidness
turgidness
tympanites
tympanitis
ubiquitous
umbrageous
underdress
underpants
undesirous
uneasiness
unevenness
unfairness
ungenerous
ungracious
unholiness
uniqueness
unjustness
unkindness
unlikeness
unmeetness
unripeness
unruliness
untidiness
unwariness
upperclass
uppishness
uproarious
upwardness
urethritis
usefulness
valvulitis
velutinous
venialness
victorious
villainess
villainous
violaceous
viraginous
virtueless
visionless
viviparous
vociferous
voluminous
voluptuous
wanderings
wantonness
watchglass
watercress
waterglass
wateriness
waterworks
weakliness
weaponless
weightless
werewolves
wheeziness
wickedness
wilderness
wilfulness
windowless
wintriness
wobbliness
woefulness
wontedness
woodenness
woolliness
worldclass
worthiness
wrathiness
yeastiness
yellowness
yourselves
zoophagous
zoophilous
abiogenist
abridgment
absolutist
abstergent
accountant
accrescent
adjudgment
adjustment
adolescent
adulterant
advisement
aerologist
aeronomist
affeerment
Africanist
afterlight
agrologist
agronomist
algebraist
algologist
alightment
allegorist
allurement
ambivalent
ambushment
amercement
anabaptist
analphabet
anastigmat
anecdotist
animadvert
anointment
antagonist
antecedent
antepenult
Antichrist
anticipant
antitheist
apochromat
archpriest
aristocrat
arrestment
asphyxiant
assentient
assessment
assignment
assoilment
assortment
astringent
attachment
attainment
attornment
attractant
attunement
autodidact
automatist
autonomist
avouchment
axiologist
babblement
bafflement
balloonist
banishment
barrenwort
bassoonist
battlement
belletrist
bemusement
beneficent
benevolent
bestowment
betterment
biochemist
birthright
bitterroot
blackheart
Blackshirt
bladdernut
blastocyst
blazonment
bloodguilt
bluebonnet
bluejacket
bluethroat
bolshevist
bottommost
bourbonist
brakelight
breadfruit
breakpoint
broadsheet
brownshirt
bryologist
bureaucrat
butterwort
cajolement
candescent
cantonment
capitalist
cartoonist
cartwright
cataphract
centralist
chamberpot
chauvinist
checkpoint
chimneypot
chuckerout
circumvent
classicist
cloudburst
cnidoblast
coachbuilt

coadjacent
coalescent
coexistent
cohabitant
coincident
colloquist
colourfast
commandant
commitment
compatriot
complacent
complement
compliment
concordant
concretist
concurrent
conferment
conformist
congregant
consequent
consistent
conspirant
constraint
consultant
contendent
contestant
contingent
continuant
contradict
controvert
convenient
convergent
conversant
convulsant
cornettist
cosentient
counteract
couplement
crankshaft
crosslight
cuckoopint
cuckoospit
cytologist
dazzlement
deadweight
debasement
debatement
decampment
Decembrist
decolorant
decrescent
deerforest
defacement
defilement
definement
deforciant
defrayment
delinquent
denaturant
denouement
department
deployment
deportment
depressant
derailment
derestrict
descendant
descendent
designment
despondent
detachment
detainment
detoxicant
devotement
diphyodont
disappoint
discomfort
disconcert
disconnect
discontent
discordant
discrepant
discussant
discutient
disenchant
disinherit
disownment
dispersant
disrespect
dissilient
dissolvent
distraught
divestment
dustjacket
earthlight
eartrumpet
ecclesiast
effacement
emancipist
embalmment
embankment
embarkment
embodiment
embonpoint
embossment
empiricist
employment
enamellist
encampment
encasement
encashment
encystment
endearment
endproduct
enfacement
engagement
engulfment
enigmatist
enjambment
enjoinment
enlacement
enlistment
enmeshment
enrichment
enrigiment
entailment
enthusiast
enticement
entombment
entrapment
equipotent
equivalent
ergonomist
erubescent
escapement
escarpment
eternalist
ethologist
eudemonist
eugenicist
euhemerist
evanescent
evangelist
evolvement
excitement
excrescent
exhilarant
exorbitant
experiment
extractant
factualist
Fahrenheit
faintheart
famishment
fearnought
federalist
fictionist
fingerpost
fireblight
firstnight
fixedpoint
flagellant
flamboyant
flashlight
flashpoint
flavescent
fleamarket
flocculent
floodlight
florescent
folklorist
forthright
fortuitist
foudroyant
fraudulent
frutescent
fulfilment
fussbudget
galleywest
generalist
geneticist
geochemist
geriatrist
gesundheit
glossarist
government
gradualist
grapefruit
greenheart
groundbait
groundrent
guestnight
habiliment
handicraft
harassment
hartebeest
heavensent
henotheist
heterodont
hierophant
hithermost
honeysweet
horologist
houseagent
housecraft
houseguest
houseplant
ideologist
illuminant
illuminist
immoralist
immurement
impairment
impalement
impartment
impediment
impenitent
impregnant
impugnment
impuissant
inappetent
incasement
incitement
incogitant
incoherent
inconstant
increscent
indictment
indiscreet
indistinct
inditement
inducement
ineloquent
inexistent
inexplicit
infrequent
ingredient
inhabitant
insentient
insouciant
instalment
instrument
integument
intendment
internment
interplant
intertwist
intolerant
intoxicant
intriguant
introspect
investment
iridescent
irrelevant
irreverent
jackrabbit
jerrybuilt
journalist
juggernaut
kineticist
knockabout
lactescent
lampoonist
landingnet
lansquenet
lapidarist
lattermost
lavishment
leafinsect
ledgerbait
legitimist
leucoplast
liberalist
librettist
lieutenant
lifejacket
liquescent
literalist
litterlout
lobsterpot
loungesuit
magnificat
makeweight
malcontent
maleficent
malevolent
malfeasant
management
manicurist
manservant
manuscript
marcescent
maximalist
medicament
meltingpot
micaschist
middlemost
militarist
millwright
minimalist
ministrant
misconduct
misogamist
misogynist
misologist
misthought
mizzenmast
monarchist
monetarist
monkeysuit
monogamist
monologist
monopolist
monotheist
monovalent
motherwort
munificent
mycologist
narcissist
naturalist
negativist
nematocyst
nethermost
neutralist
nightlight
nightshift
nightshirt
nigrescent
nipplewort
nominalist
nomologist
nonchalant
noncontent
nonpayment
nonviolent
nosologist
nympholept
obituarist
obtainment
oecologist
oenologist
omnipotent
omniscient
oncologist
ontologist
opalescent
operettist
opinionist
orchardist
ordainment
oreologist
organicist
orthoepist
osteoblast
osteoclast
outpatient
overbought
overcommit
overflight
overthrust
overweight
pacificist
paddleboat
palimpsest
panegyrist
pansophist
paraphrast
parliament
parturient
Passionist
pastellist
pedalpoint
pedicurist
pedologist
penologist
peppermint
pepperwort
percipient
permafrost
persistent
pharmacist
phenocryst
photoprint
physiocrat
pickpocket
pigeonpost
pilotlight
pinecarpet
pistolshot
plagiarist
plainchant
playwright
pluperfect
podiatrist
polemicist
polychrest
polygamist
polygenist
polytheist
polyvalent
pomologist
positivist
postscript
pragmatist
preachment
preconcert
preeminent
preferment
prefulgent
prepayment
pressagent
pretendant
pretendent
prevenient
prizefight
procumbent
proficient
proofsheet
propellant
propellent
prosilient
protestant
protoplast
psalmodist
psychicist
Ptolemaist
puberulent
punishment
pursuivant
putrescent
puzzlement
Pyrrhonist
quadruplet
quintuplet
rabblement
ravishment
reafforest
rearmament
recidivist
recitalist
recoupment
redcurrant
refinement
refringent
refundment
regalement
registrant
relativist
requiescat
resemblant
resentment
reshipment
respondent
restaurant
retirement
retrospect
reunionist
revanchist
revealment
revilement
revivalist
rhapsodist
rheologist
rinderpest
rockrabbit
roundabout
rouseabout
roustabout
rubythroat
sacrosanct
saddlefast
safetybelt
sauerkraut
scaredycat

scoresheet
seabiscuit
seaserpent
secernment
secondbest
secondment
secularist
securement
seducement
selenodont
selfdeceit
selfprofit
selftaught
seminarist
sensualist
separatist
Septuagint
SerboCroat
serologist
setterwort
settlement
sexivalent
sexologist
shipwright
shirtfront
shirtwaist
shortcrust
sideeffect
siderostat
sidestreet
sinecurist
singlefoot
sinologist
slitpocket
smokeplant
snafflebit
sneezewort
solacement
solicitant
solidarist
somersault
Sorbonnist
soubriquet
spacecraft
Spartacist
specialist
speedlimit
spiderwort
spinescent
spleenwort
spoilsport
spoondrift
springhalt
spumescent
stagecraft
standpoint
statecraft
steamchest
steamtight
stepparent
stigmatist
stitchwort
stonefruit
strategist
stratocrat
stridulant
stringhalt
submediant
subsequent
subsistent
sufficient
suffragist
supergiant
supplement
supplicant
surfactant
surrealist
sweatshirt
sweetheart
swordcraft
symphonist
symposiast
syncretist
synonymist
synthesist
synthetist
tanglement
tantamount
tapotement
taxonomist
technicist
technocrat
tenderfoot
testflight
tetterwort
textualist
theogonist
theologist
theopneust
thereabout
thereanent
thermostat
threnodist
throatwort
throughout
throughput
thumbprint
topgallant
topologist
torchlight
tournament
tourniquet
transcript
transplant
trecentist
trichromat
tricyclist
triumphant
trombonist
Trotskyist
turgescent
typescript
typologist
unbesought
undercroft
undershirt
undershoot
underskirt
unicyclist
unpleasant
Vaticanist
vestpocket
vicegerent
viceregent
vignettist
virologist
vitrescent
vociferant
voiceprint
wagonvault
wainwright
wanderlust
watercraft
waterfront
waterspout
watertight
whereabout
wildebeest
wilderment
windowseat
witchcraft
wonderment
workbasket
Wykehamist
fricandeau
malentendu
compasssaw
foreshadow
handbarrow
middlebrow
muskmallow
ottershrew
overshadow
playfellow
rosemallow
sashwindow
shopwindow
showwindow
thumbscrew
wappenshaw
yokefellow
anticlimax
billetdoux
bordereaux
chatterbox
chickenpox
circumflex
Clarenceux
crossindex
gaspereaux
generatrix
inheritrix
mesothorax
metathorax
packingbox
pouncetbox
protectrix
quadruplex
sealingwax
squeezebox
thunderbox
trousseaux
unorthodox
weatherbox
witnessbox
aberrantly
abnormally
abominably
abortively
abrasively
absolutely
absolutory
absorbedly
absorbency
abstinency
abstractly
abstrusely
abstrusity
abundantly
acatalepsy
acceptably
acceptedly
accessibly
accurately
accursedly
accusatory
accusingly
acidimetry
acromegaly
actionably
adaptively
adenectomy
adequately
adherently
adhesively
adjacently
adjuratory
admiringly
admittedly
admonitory
adoptively
advertency
advocatory
aeolotropy
aerography
affability
affectedly
afferently
affluently
agitatedly
alarmingly
aldermanry
alimentary
alkalinity
allusively
ambulatory
amendatory
amiability
anemometry
anemophily
angularity
animatedly
anisotropy
annoyingly
annularity
answerably
anteriorly
apothecary
apparently
applicably
appositely
approvably
aquilinity
arboreally
armorially
arrogantly
arterially
artycrafty
ascendancy
ascendency
asexuality
asynchrony
atomically
atypically
audibility
audiometry
autecology
autography
autoplasty
autumnally
aversively
backwardly
bafflingly
balneology
bankruptcy
baptistery
bardolatry
bathymetry
becomingly
benignancy
bestiality
bewitchery
biannually
biblically
bibliology
bibliopegy
bibliopoly
bibulously
biennially
bigamously
binaurally
bioecology
bipolarity
bisexually
blackberry
blamefully
bleatingly
blindingly
blissfully
blockishly
bloodmoney
blurringly
blushingly
boastfully
bootlessly
bouncingly
brachylogy
brilliancy
broodingly
buffoonery
bumblingly
bunglingly
bustlingly
cacography
Caerphilly
cajolingly
calculably
canonicity
canorously
canterbury
capability
capitulary
captiously
cardiology
carelessly
carpellary
carphology
cartomancy
catchpenny
causticity
cautionary
cautiously
cavalierly
cellularly
centrality
centricity
cerography
cessionary
chalcedony
changeably
chaplaincy
charactery
charitably
charmingly
chartulary
cheapishly
cheerfully
chemically
childishly
chiromancy
chokeberry
chronicity
chronology
churlishly
circularly
clannishly
clearstory
clerestory
clerically
clinically
clinometry
closetplay
cloudberry
clownishly
cocksurely
coequality
coercively
coeternity
cognisably
coherently
cohesively
colonially
colossally
colourably
comicality
commandery
commentary
commissary
commonalty
communally
comparably
compatibly
competency
completely
complexity
compliancy
complicacy
complicity
composedly
compulsory
conchology
conciliary
concinnity
conclusory
concretely
condensery
conformity
confusedly
congruency
conjointly
conjugally
consectary
consistory
consonancy
conspiracy
constantly
consumedly
contiguity
continuity
contrarily
contritely
conversely
copartnery
coralberry
cordiality
corporally
corporeity
corpulency
corrivalry
cosmically
coulometry
covalently
covetingly
covetously
coweringly
cowparsley
craniology
creatively
creativity
creaturely
creditably
criminally
critically
cryptogamy
cryptology
culturally
cumbrously
curability
cyclically
cystoscopy
damagingly
dapplegrey
daughterly
dazzlingly
debauchery
debonairly
decadently
decisively
declassify
decorously
dedicatory
defamatory
defensibly
deficiency
definitely
degeneracy
degradedly
dehumidify
dejectedly
delectably
delicately
deltiology
delusively
dementedly

demography
demonology
dendrology
deontology
dependably
dependency
depilatory
deplorably
depositary
depository
depravedly
deridingly
derisively
derogatory
deservedly
designedly
desirously
desolately
despicably
detachedly
detergency
detestably
devilishly
dextrality
dextrously
diagonally
dictionary
difficulty
digitately
dilatorily
diligently
dillydally
disability
discreetly
discretely
diseconomy
disharmony
dishonesty
disloyally
disloyalty
disorderly
dispensary
disputably
disqualify
disquietly
dissatisfy
dissonancy
distillery
distinctly
disutility
divergency
divinatory
divisively
dolorously
dominantly
doubtfully
doubtingly
downwardly
doxography
dramaturgy
drawlingly
dreadfully
droopingly
drudgingly
drysaltery
durability
dwarfishly
ebulliency
effeminacy
efficacity
efficiency
effrontery
effusively
Egyptology
elasticity
elderberry
electively
elementary
eloquently
emblazonry
embroidery
embryogeny
embryology
emendatory
emigratory
emissivity
endemicity
enduringly
engagingly
enormously
enterotomy
enticingly
entomology
enzymology
epeirogeny
ephorality
episcopacy
epistolary
equability
equanimity
erectility
ergodicity
erotically
eruptively
escapology
especially
ethereally
ethicality
ethnically
eudiometry
eventually
excellency
excitatory
excitingly
excusatory
execratory
exhibitory
exobiology
exotically
expectancy
expectedly
expediency
expiratory
explicitly
expository
expressway
extendedly
exteriorly
externally
extraneity
exultantly
exultingly
fabulously
factiously
factuality
fadelessly
faithfully
familiarly
fancifully
farcically
favourably
fearlessly
fearsomely
fecklessly
feminality
femininely
femininity
festoonery
fetchingly
feverishly
fibrillary
fiducially
fiendishly
fiftyfifty
finicality
firepolicy
flaccidity
flagrantly
flatulency
flawlessly
fleeringly
fleetingly
flexuously
flippantly
floatingly
fluxionary
folkmemory
forcefully
forgivably
formidably
formlessly
fragrantly
fraternity
freakishly
frenziedly
frequently
friability
friendlily
fritillary
frowningly
fruitfully
fuddyduddy
fugitively
fumblingly
funereally
fusibility
futurology
fuzzywuzzy
gastrology
gastronomy
generality
generosity
generously
germinally
ghastfully
glaciology
gladsomely
glancingly
globularly
gloriously
glossology
glottology
goniometry
goodygoody
gooseberry
gorgeously
gothically
governessy
gracefully
graciosity
graciously
granddaddy
granularly
graphology
graspingly
gratefully
gravimetry
grievously
grindingly
growlingly
grudgingly
gruesomely
guilefully
gutturally
gymnosophy
habitually
hagiolatry
halfvolley
halfyearly
handsomely
hankypanky
harmlessly
hauntingly
hectically
heedlessly
heliacally
heliolatry
heliotropy
helplessly
heortology
hepatology
hereditary
heroically
hesitantly
heterodoxy
heterogamy
heterogeny
heterogony
heterology
heteronomy
heterotaxy
hierocracy
hierolatry
hippophagy
hoitytoity
hokeypokey
holography
homeopathy
honourably
hootenanny
hopelessly
hormonally
hospitably
humbuggery
humorously
hurdygurdy
hurlyburly
hydrically
hydromancy
hydrometry
hydropathy
hydrophily
hygrometry
hypsometry
iconolatry
iconomachy
iconometry
ideography
ignobility
ignorantly
illatively
illaudably
illegality
illiteracy
illusively
illusorily
imaginably
imbecilely
imbecility
immaculacy
immaturely
immaturity
imminently
immiscibly
immobility
immoderacy
immodestly
immorality
immortally
immunology
impalpably
impassably
impassibly
impeccably
impeccancy
impendency
imperially
implacably
implicitly
impolitely
imposingly
impossibly
impotently
improbably
improperly
improvably
impudently
impudicity
inaccuracy
inactively
inactivity
inadequacy
incapacity
incendiary
incessancy
inchoately
incipiency
incisively
incivility
inclemency
incredibly
incubatory
incumbency
indecently
indelicacy
indicatory
indirectly
indocility
indolently
inefficacy
ineligibly
inequality
inevitably
inexorably
inexpertly
inexpiably
infallibly
infamously
infelicity
inferiorly
infernally
infidelity
infinitely
inflexibly
informally
inherently
inhibitory
inhumanely
inhumanity
inimically
inimitably
initiatory
innerrably
innocently
innovatory
innumeracy
insanitary
insatiably
insecurely
insecurity
insensibly
insipidity
insistency
insobriety
insolently
insolvency
insularity
insurgency
intangibly
integrally
interiorly
intermarry
internally
intimately
intrepidly
introrsely
inundatory
inurbanity
invalidity
invaluably
invariably
inveracity
inveteracy
invincibly
inviolably
invitatory
invitingly
invocatory
ironically
itinerancy
jackassery
jocularity
jubilantly
judicatory
judicially
justiciary
juvenility
laboratory
lamentably
lamentedly
lampoonery
landocracy
lanternfly
laparotomy
lardydardy
laterality
laughingly
lectionary
legibility
legitimacy
lexicology
lexigraphy
liberality
lifelessly
lipography
listlessly
literality
literarily
lithotrity
locomotory
loganberry
logicality
logography
lonesomely
lopsidedly
lovelessly
luculently
lukewarmly
luminosity
luminously
lusciously
lustrously
magistracy
malacology
malapertly
malignancy
manageably
maniacally
manifestly
manifoldly
marginally
Mariolatry
mastectomy
materially
maternally
matriarchy
measurably
measuredly
medievally
mediocrity
melancholy
menacingly
mendicancy
mercifully
mesomorphy
metagalaxy
metallurgy
metrically
micrometry
microscopy
middlingly
militantly
militarily
mindlessly

mineralogy
minstrelsy
mirthfully
miscellany
missionary
mistakenly
mitigatory
moderately
monetarily
morphogeny
morphology
mosaically
mournfully
movability
movelessly
muliebrity
multiloquy
muscularly
musicality
musicianly
musicology
mutability
mutinously
myopically
mystically
mythically
nambypamby
namelessly
narcolepsy
nationally
nauseously
nautically
nebulosity
nebulously
necrolatry
necromancy
necrophily
necroscopy
needlessly
negatively
negativity
negligibly
nephrology
neuropathy
neutrality
newsagency
newsworthy
nominately
nomography
nosography
notability
notarially
noteworthy
noticeably
notionally
numerology
numerosity
numerously
nuptiality
nyctinasty
obdurately
obediently
obligatory
obligingly
observably
oceanology
ochlocracy
odontology
officially
oleography
oligopsony
oneirology
onesidedly
ophiolatry
oppositely
oppugnancy
optatively
optionally
oracularly
ordinarily
oreography
orientally
originally
orotundity
orthodoxly
osculatory
ostensibly
osteopathy
outrightly
ovariotomy
overnicety
oversupply
paederasty
painlessly
palliatory
PalmSunday
palynology
papyrology
pardonably
parentally
partiality
passageway
passionary
pastorally
paternally
patriality
patriarchy
patulously
peacefully
peacockery
peculiarly
peerlessly
pellucidly
penetrably
penitently
pensionary
perdurably
peremptory
perilously
permanency
pernickety
perpetuity
perplexity
personally
personalty
pertinency
perversely
perversity
petulantly
phantastry
pheasantry
phillumeny
philosophy
phlebotomy
phonically
photometry
photonasty
photophily
phrenology
phylactery
phyllotaxy
physically
physiology
phytophagy
piccaninny
pickaninny
piercingly
pigmentary
pinchpenny
pinebeauty
pistillary
pitilessly
plangently
planimetry
plasmogamy
plasticity
playbyplay
pleadingly
pleasantly
pleasantry
pleasingly
pliability
ploddingly
plutocracy
plutolatry
poetically
pogonology
pogonotomy
polygraphy
polyploidy
popularity
populously
pornocracy
positively
positivity
possessory
postliminy
potability
potamology
powerfully
prancingly
prebendary
precedency
preceptory
preciosity
preciously
precursory
preferably
pregnantly
prehistory
preparedly
prepensely
prepotency
presbytery
presentday
presidency
presidiary
presignify
pressingly
presumably
prevenancy
previously
pridefully
priggishly
primevally
proclivity
prodigally
profitably
profligacy
profoundly
profundity
promissory
promontory
propensity
prosperity
protectory
proximally
pruriently
psephology
psychiatry
psychology
puffpastry
puissantly
punctually
punitively
pupilarity
purblindly
purulently
putatively
pyretology
pyrography
pyrotechny
qualmishly
quarterday
quaternary
quaternity
quiescency
radiometry
radioscopy
ramblingly
ratability
rationally
ravenously
reactively
reactivity
reasonably
reassembly
recipiency
recklessly
recreantly
recumbency
redemptory
redolently
redundancy
refractory
regeneracy
regionally
regularity
regulatory
relatively
relativity
relevantly
reluctancy
remarkably
remedially
repeatedly
repellancy
repellency
reportedly
repository
repugnancy
rescissory
reservedly
resignedly
resiliency
resolutely
resolvedly
resonantly
responsory
restlessly
reticently
retiringly
retrorsely
revelatory
reverently
revocatory
rhinoscopy
rightfully
rigorously
risibility
roadworthy
rockabilly
rowanberry
rubrically
ruminantly
rustically
ruthlessly
saccharify
sagittally
salability
salutarily
salutatory
sanctimony
sanguinary
sanguinely
sanguinity
sanitarily
sarcophagy
satanology
scabrously
scathingly
scavengery
scenically
schizogony
sciagraphy
sclerotomy
scoffingly
scornfully
scratchily
screenplay
scurrility
seasonably
seasonally
secludedly
secularity
sedulously
segmentary
seismicity
seismology
selenology
selflessly
selfparody
semeiology
semiweekly
semiyearly
sensuality
sensuously
sentiently
separately
separatory
septically
sergeantcy
serigraphy
serjeantcy
sexagenary
shamefully
sheepishly
shockingly
shrewishly
shrievalty
sillybilly
similarity
simplicity
simulatory
singularly
sinisterly
skiagraphy
skittishly
slantingly
slatternly
slavocracy
slipperily
slothfully
sluggardly
sluggishly
sluttishly
smartmoney
snappishly
sneakingly
sneeringly
snobbishly
snobocracy
snubbingly
societally
sociometry
solidarity
solitarily
solubility
somatology
somniloquy
somnolency
sonorously
soothingly
soullessly
soundingly
southernly
spaciously
spankingly
spasticity
spatiality
speciality
speciology
speciosity
speciously
spectrally
speleology
sphericity
spiritedly
spirometry
spitefully
splendidly
spodomancy
spoliatory
spongology
sportfully
sportingly
sportively
spotlessly
spuriously
squalidity
squirarchy
stagnantly
stalwartly
statically
stationary
stationery
statutably
stealthily
stereotypy
stiflingly
stingingly
stinkingly
stopvolley
strabotomy
straightly
strainedly
strathspey
strawberry
stridently
strikingly
stringency
stubbornly
studiously
stunningly
stypticity
subacidity
subdeanery
subjectify
subshrubby
subsidiary
subtenancy
succinctly
succulency
sufferably
sugardaddy
suicidally
superiorly
supernally
suppletory
supposably
supposedly
surgically
suspensory
suzerainty
sweepingly
swimmingly
swingingly
sycophancy
synecology
synonymity
tachometry
tachymetry
taciturnly
tactically
tactlessly
tamability
taperingly
tastefully
tauntingly
tauromachy
tautophony
taxability
tearlessly
teatrolley

technology
teenyweeny
teetotally
telegraphy
temperedly
temporally
temporalty
temptingly
tenability
teratogeny
teratology
termagancy
terminably
terminally
texturally
thankfully
thievishly
thinkingly
thirdparty
thixotropy
thoroughly
threepenny
throughway
ticklishly
timbrology
timelessly
timorously
tirelessly
tiresomely
toilsomely
tolerantly
tomfoolery
tomography
tonelessly
topicality
topography
topsyturvy
toroidally
tortiously
tortuosity
tortuously
touchingly
toweringly
toxicology
tragically
trajectory
tranquilly
transiency
transitory
trenchancy
trichology
trichotomy
trickishly
trierarchy
triflingly
trigonally
trimonthly
triplicity
triviality
trophology
tropically
truculency
truncately
trustfully
trustingly
truthfully
tuberosity
tuitionary
tumultuary
tunelessly
turbulency
tutorially
typicality
typography
ulteriorly
ultimately
unbearably
unbeatably
unbrokenly
unchastity
uncommonly
unctuosity
unctuously
undeniably
underbelly
understudy
undulatory
unendingly
unerringly
unfadingly
unfilially
unfriendly
unguentary
uniaxially
uniformity
university
univocally
unlawfully
unmannerly
unmorality
unsociably
unsocially
unsteadily
untowardly
unwieldily
unwontedly
unworthily
upholstery
uranometry
urbanology
usuriously
uxoriously
valorously
vaporously
varicosity
varietally
vascularly
vehemently
vengefully
venomously
vertically
vesicatory
veterinary
viewlessly
vigilantly
vigorously
viperously
virginally
virtuality
virtuosity
virtuously
virulently
viscerally
viscountcy
visibility
visionally
viviparity
vocabulary
volatility
volubility
voluptuary
vortically
vulnerably
wastefully
watchfully
waveringly
wearifully
westwardly
WhitMonday
WhitSunday
willynilly
willywilly
wishywashy
witchingly
womanishly
wondrously
wordlessly
worldweary
wrathfully
wretchedly
wrongfully
wrongously
xerography
xylography
yearningly
yieldingly
youngberry
youthfully
zygomorphy
hakenkreuz
razzmatazz

11 letter words

abandonment
Abbevillian
abbreviator
abdominally
abecedarian
abhorrently
abiogeneses
abiogenesis
abiogenetic
abiological
abiotically
ablutionary
abnormality
abolishable
abolishment
abomination
abortionist
aboutsledge
aboveground
abracadabra
abranchiate
abridgement
absenteeism
absorbingly
absorptance
abstentious
abstinently
abstraction
abstractive
abstriction
abusiveness
academicals
academician
academicism
acarpellous
acatalectic
acaulescent
accelerando
accelerator
accentually
acceptation
acceptingly
accessorial
accessorise
accipitrine
acclamation
acclamatory
acclimation
acclimatise
acclivitous
accommodate
accompanist
accordantly
accordingly
accoucheuse
accountable
accountably
accountancy
accrescence
acculturate
accumulator
accusatival
acetylation
achievement
achondritic
achromatise
achromatism
acidifiable
acidophilic
acidulation
acinaciform
acknowledge
acoustician
acquiescent
acquirement
acquisition
acquisitive
acquittance
acriflavine
acrimonious
acropetally
actinometer
actinomyces
actinomycin
acumination
acupuncture
adenomatous
adiaphorism
adjectively
adjournment
adjudgement
adjudicator
adminicular
admiralship
adolescence
adoptianism
adoptianist
adoptionism
adoptionist
adulterator
adumbration
adumbrative
advancement
adventuress
adventurism
adventurist
adventurous
adverbially
adversative
adverseness
advertently
advertising
advisedness
Aeneolithic
aeolotropic
aerobically
aerobiology
aerodynamic
aerographer
aerological
aeronautics
aeronomical
aerostatics
aerostation
Aesculapian
aesthetical
aestivation
affectation
affectingly
affectional
affectioned
affectively
affectivity
afficionado
affiliation
affirmation
affirmative
affirmatory
affranchise
affrication
affricative
AfroAsiatic
afterburner
aftereffect
agglomerate
agglutinate
aggravation
aggregately
aggregation
aggregative
aggrievedly
agnatically
agnosticism
agonisingly
agonistical
agoraphobia
agoraphobic
agrarianism
agriculture
agrobiology
agrological
agronomical
ahistorical
aiguillette
ailurophile
ailurophobe
aimlessness
aircraftman
airlessness
airsickness
alabastrine
Albigensian
albuminuria
alcyonarian
alembicated
Alexandrian
alexandrine
alexandrite
algological
algorithmic
alkalescent
alkalimeter
alkalimetry
allAmerican
allantoides
allegorical
allelomorph
alleviation
alleviative
alleviatory
allocatable
allomorphic
allopathist
alphabetise
altercation
alternately
alternation
alternative
altitudinal
altocumulus
altorelievo
altorilievo
altostratus
amaranthine
amativeness
amazonstone
ambiguously
ambitiously
ambivalence
ambivalency
ambiversion
ameliorator
amenability
amenorrhoea
amentaceous
Americanise
Americanism
Americanist
amethystine
amiableness
amicability
amontillado
amorousness
amorphously
amphetamine
amphibolite
amphibology
amphictyony
amphimictic
amphisbaena
amplexicaul
anachronism
anachronous
anacoluthon
anacreontic
anadiplosis
anaesthesia
anaesthetic
anagnorisis
analogously
anaphylaxis
anarchistic
anastomoses
anastomosis
anastomotic
ancientness
androgynous
anecdotical
anemometric
anencephaly
anfractuous
angelically
angiography
Anglicanism
AngloFrench
AngloIndian
anglomaniac
AngloNorman
anglophobia
anglophobic
animalcular
anisotropic
annabergite
annihilator

anniversary
annunciator
anomalistic
anomalously
anonymously
antecedence
antechamber
antemundane
antenuptial
antependium
anteriority
antheridium
anthocyanin
anthologise
anthologist
anthracitic
anthropical
anticathode
anticipator
anticyclone
antifouling
antigravity
antiJacobin
antimonious
antineutron
antioxidant
antiphonary
antiphrasis
antipyretic
antiquarian
antiquation
antirrhinum
antiSemitic
antistrophe
antitypical
antivitamin
antonomasia
anxiousness
apartmental
aphrodisiac
apocalyptic
Apollinaris
apologetics
apomorphine
aponeuroses
aponeurosis
aponeurotic
apophyllite
aposiopesis
apostleship
apostolical
apostrophic
apotheosise
appallingly
apparatchik
apparelling
appealingly
appeasement
appellation
appellative
applaudable
application
applicative
applicatory
appogiatura
appointment
appreciable
appreciably
appreciator
approbation
approbatory
appropriate
approvingly
approximate
appurtenant
aquaculture
aquarellist
aquatically
aquiculture
arbitrageur
arbitrament
arbitrarily
arbitration
arbitrative
arbitratrix
arboraceous
arborescent
archaeology
archaeornis
archaically
archangelic
archdiocese
archduchess
archdukedom
Archimedean
archipelago
arduousness
arenicolous
Areopagitic
arglebargle
argumentive
aristocracy
Arminianism
armtwisting
aromaticity
arraignment
arrangement
arrestingly
arterialise
arthrospore
articulable
articulated
articulator
artillerist
artiodactyl
artlessness
ascensional
ascetically
ascomycetes
aseptically
aspergillum
aspergillus
aspersorium
asphyxiator
assafoetida
assassinate
assemblyman
assentation
assertively
assessorial
assiduously
assignation
assimilable
assimilator
association
associative
assortative
assuagement
assuredness
Assyriology
astigmatism
astringency
atheistical
athleticism
atmospheric
atomisation
atrabilious
atrociously
attemptable
attentively
attenuation
attestation
attitudinal
attractable
attribution
attributive
attritional
audaciously
audibleness
audiologist
audiometric
audiovisual
augmentable
Augustinian
auricularly
Aurignacian
austereness
autarchical
autochthony
autoerotism
autographic
automatable
autoplastic
autotrophic
auxanometer
avoirdupois
awesomeness
awestricken
awkwardness
axiological
azotobacter
babysitting
bacchanalia
bacciferous
bacilliform
backbencher
backcountry
bactericide
balefulness
ballbearing
balletomane
balmcricket
BaltoSlavic
bandylegged
banteringly
baptismally
barbarously
barbastelle
barbiturate
barefacedly
barleybroth
barnstormer
barquentine
barrelhouse
barrelorgan
bashfulness
bashibazouk
basipetally
basketchair
bassethound
bathingsuit
batholithic
bathymetric
bathyscaphe
bathysphere
battledress
battlefield
beachcomber
bearbaiting
bearishness
beastliness
beauteously
beautifully
beaverboard
bedevilment
bedizenment
beechmarten
befittingly
beguilement
beguilingly
behavioural
belatedness
bellbottoms
bellfounder
bellheather
bellicosity
belligerent
bellringing
Belorussian
Benedictine
benediction
benedictory
benefaction
beneficence
beneficiary
beneficiate
benevolence
benightedly
benightment
benignantly
bereavement
bergamasque
bergschrund
bersaglieri
bestselling
betweenmaid
betweenness
betweentime
bewhiskered
bewitchment
bibliolater
bibliolatry
bibliomancy
bibliomania
bibliopegic
bibliophile
bibliophily
bibliopolic
bibliotheca
bicarbonate
bicentenary
bicephalous
bicorporate
bicuspidate
biddability
biedermeier
bifurcation
bilaterally
biliousness
billetsdoux
billionaire
billposting
billsticker
bimetallism
bimetallist
bimillenary
bimillenium
binocularly
biochemical
biocoenoses
biocoenosis
biocoenotic
biofeedback
biometrical
biophysical
bipartition
biquadratic
birdbrained
birdfancier
birdwatcher
bisexuality
bitterapple
bittercress
bittersweet
bivouacking
blackavised
blackbeetle
blackbirder
blackcoated
blackfellow
blackgrouse
blackmailer
blackmarket
bladderwort
blamelessly
blameworthy
blasphemous
blastogenic
blepharitis
blessedness
blockbuster
bloodguilty
bloodlessly
bloodstream
bloodsucker
bloodvessel
blotchiness
blunderbuss
boardschool
Bodhisattva
bodybuilder
bodyservant
bohemianism
boilermaker
bombardment
bombilation
bombination
Bonapartean
Bonapartism
Bonapartist
bonbonniere
bondservant
bondservice
bondwashing
bookbinding
bookinghall
bookishness
bookkeeping
booklearned
bookselling
bookshelves
boorishness
bootlegging
borborygmus
botanically
botheration
bottleglass
bottlegreen
bottlenosed
bounteously
bountifully
bourgeoisie
boutonniere
bowdleriser
boysenberry
brachiation
brachyurous
bracteolate
bradycardia
braggadocio
Brahmanical
brahmaputra
Brahminical
brainlessly
brainsickly
brainteaser
branchiopod
brankursine
brazenfaced
breadbasket
breadcrumbs
breadthways
breadthwise
breadwinner
breastplate
breastwheel
breathalyse
breechblock
breezeblock
bricklaying
bridgeboard
brilliantly
bristletail
bristleworm
bristliness
Britishness
brittleness
broadcaster
broadleaved
broadminded
brotherhood
brucellosis
brusqueness
brutishness
bryozoology
bucolically
buffalorobe
bullbaiting
bulletproof
bullfighter
bullishness
bullterrier
bumblepuppy
bumptiously
bureaucracy
burglarious
burgomaster
bushmanship
bushwhacker
businessman
butcherbird
butterflies
butteriness
butyraceous
byeelection
Byronically
Byzantinism
Byzantinist
cabbagepalm
cabbagerose
cabbagetree
cabbageworm
cabbalistic
cacographic
cacophonous
caddishness
calceolaria
calcicolous
calciferous
calcifugous
calcination
calculating
calculation
calculative
calefacient
calefactory
calendrical
calibration
californium
calisthenic
calligraphy
callousness
calorimeter
calorimetry
calumniator
Calvinistic
calyptrogen
camaraderie
campanology
campanulate
campmeeting
canalicular
canaliculus
cancellated
candelabrum
candescence
candidature
candleberry
candlelight
candlepower
candlestick
cannibalise
cannibalism
canonically

cantharides
cantharidic
capableness
capaciously
capacitance
capillarity
captainship
captionless
captivation
carabiniere
carabinieri
caravanning
caravansary
carbocyclic
carbonation
carbuncular
carburetion
carburetted
carburetter
carburettor
carcinomata
cardinalate
cardiograph
cardsharper
carefulness
caressingly
caricatural
carminative
carnivorous
Carolingian
carpetsnake
carrageenan
carrageenin
carriageway
cartography
caruncuIate
carvelbuilt
caryopsides
cassiterite
castellated
castigation
casuistical
catachreses
catachresis
cataclysmic
catadromous
cataplectic
catastrophe
catchphrase
catechismal
catechistic
categorical
catercousin
caterpillar
catheterise
catholicise
Catholicism
catholicity
catswhisker
cauliflower
causatively
caustically
cavalierism
cavedweller
cavernously
ceaselessly
celebration
celebratory
celestially
cellularity
cementation
centenarian
centigramme
centreboard
centrepiece
centrifugal
centripetal
cerebration
ceremonious
ceroplastic
certifiable
certifiably
certificate
cesarevitch
cesarewitch
chaetognath
chafingdish
chainarmour
chainletter
chainsmoker
chainstitch
chalcedonic
challenging
chamaephyte
chamberlain
chambermaid
chameleonic
champertous
chancellery
chancellory
changefully
channelling
chansonnier
chanterelle
chanticleer
chaotically
chaperonage
charcuterie
chargesheet
charismatic
charlatanry
chartaceous
chaulmoogra
cheerleader
cheerlessly
cheesecloth
cheiromancy
chemotactic
chevalglass
chiaroscuro
chickenfeed
chickenwire
chieftaincy
childminder
chimaerical
chinoiserie
Chippendale
chirography
chiropodist
chiropteran
chitterling
chlorophyll
chloroplast
chloroprene
chockablock
choirmaster
chokecherry
cholesterol
choreograph
chorography
Christendom
christening
christiania
Christianly
Christmassy
Christology
chrominance
chromoplast
chromosomal
chronically
chronograph
chronologer
chronologic
chronometer
chronometry
chronoscope
chrysalides
chrysalises
chrysarobin
chrysoberyl
chrysoprase
chucklehead
churchgoing
churchiness
churchwoman
cicatricial
cinnabarine
cinquecento
circularise
circularity
circulation
circulative
circulatory
circumlunar
circumpolar
circumsolar
circumspect
circumvolve
cisatlantic
citizenship
cityslicker
civilianise
civilisable
clairschach
clairvoyant
clamorously
clandestine
clapperclaw
Clarencieux
classically
cleanlimbed
cleanliness
cleanshaven
clearheaded
cleistogamy
clericalism
clericalist
cliffhanger
climacteric
climatology
clinometric
clodhopping
closefisted
closehauled
clostridium
clothesline
clothesmoth
clothesprop
cloudcastle
coadunation
coagulation
coalescence
coarctation
cobblestone
coccidiosis
cochinchina
cockaleekie
cockleshell
cockyleekie
coconscious
codefendant
codicillary
coeducation
coefficient
coessential
coeternally
coexistence
coextension
coextensive
coffeehouse
coffeetable
cognateness
cognitional
cognitively
cognitivity
cognoscente
cognoscenti
cognoscible
coincidence
coinheritor
coinsurance
coldblooded
coldhearted
coleorrhiza
collaborate
collapsible
collectable
collectanea
collectedly
collectible
collenchyma
colligation
colligative
collimation
collinearly
collisional
collocation
collusively
colonelship
colonialism
colonialist
colorimeter
colorimetry
colouration
colourblind
colourfully
columbarium
columniated
combatively
combination
combinative
combinatory
combustible
comestibles
comeuppance
comfortable
comfortably
comfortless
commandment
commemorate
commendable
commendably
commendator
commensally
commentator
commination
comminatory
comminution
commiserate
commissural
committable
commonality
commonplace
commonsense
communalise
communalism
communalist
communicant
communicate
communistic
commutation
commutative
compactness
compaginate
comparatist
comparative
compartment
compassable
compellable
compendious
compensator
competently
competition
competitive
compilation
compilement
complacence
complacency
complainant
complaisant
complexness
compliantly
complicated
complotting
comportment
compositely
composition
compositive
compossible
compotation
compotatory
compression
compressive
comprisable
comptroller
compunction
compurgator
computation
computerise
comradeship
comstockery
concatenate
concealable
concealment
conceitedly
conceivable
conceivably
concentrate
conceptacle
concernment
concertedly
concertgoer
conciliator
conciseness
concomitant
concordance
concrescent
concubinage
concubinary
concubitant
concurrence
condemnable
condensable
conditional
conditioner
condolatory
condominium
condonation
condottiere
condottieri
conductance
conductible
conductress
condylomata
confabulate
confederacy
confederate
conferrable
confessedly
confidently
confidingly
confinement
confirmable
confiscable
confiscator
conflagrant
conflagrate
confliction
conflictive
conformable
conformably
conformally
conformance
confusingly
confutation
confutative
congealable
congealment
congelation
congenerous
congenially
congressman
congruently
congruously
conjectural
conjugality
conjugation
conjugative
conjunction
conjunctiva
conjunctive
conjuncture
conjuration
connectable
connectedly
connectible
connoisseur
connotation
connotative
connubially
conquerable
consanguine
consciously
consecrator
consecution
consecutive
consentient
consequence
conservable
conservancy
conservator
considerate
considering
consignable
consignment
consistence
consistency
consolation
consolatory
consolidate
consolingly
consonantal
consonantly
conspecific
conspicuity
conspicuous
conspirator
constellate
consternate
constituent
constitutor
constrictor
construable
constructor
consultancy
consumerism
consumingly
consummator
consumption
consumptive
containable
containment
contaminant
contaminate
contemplate
contentedly
contentious
contentment
conterminal
contestable
continental
continently
contingence
contingency

continuable
continually
continuance
continuator
contorniate
contrabasso
contractile
contraction
contractive
contractual
contracture
contradance
contraption
contrariety
contrarious
contrastive
contretemps
contributor
contrivable
contrivance
controlling
controlment
controversy
conurbation
convenances
convenience
conveniency
conventicle
convergence
convergency
conversable
conversance
conversancy
convertible
convertibly
conveyancer
convincible
convivially
convocation
convolution
convolvulus
cookgeneral
cooperation
cooperative
coordinator
coparcenary
copingstone
copiousness
coplanarity
copperplate
coppersmith
coralloidal
corbiculate
corbiesteps
cordialness
corecipient
cornerstone
cornhusking
corniferous
cornucopian
coronagraph
coronograph
corporality
corporately
corporation
corporatism
corporative
corporeally
corpulently
corpuscular
correctable
correctness
correlation
correlative
corrigendum
corroborant
corroborate
corrosively
corrugation
corruptible
corruptibly
corruptness
coruscation
cosignatory
cosmetician
cosmetology
cosmogonist
cosmography
cosmologist
cosmopolite
costbenefit
costiveness
cotemporary
coterminous
cotoneaster
cottongrass
cottonmouth
coulometric
counselling
countenance
counterblow
counterbond
counterfeit
counterfoil
counterfort
countermand
countermark
countermine
countermove
countermure
counterpane
counterpart
counterplan
counterplea
counterplot
countersign
countersink
countersunk
counterturn
countervail
counterview
counterwork
countlessly
countrified
countryfied
countryseat
countryside
countrywide
courteously
courtliness
coxcombical
crabbedness
crackerjack
craftswoman
craniometry
creationism
creationist
credentials
credibility
credulously
crematorium
crenellated
crenulation
crepitation
crepuscular
crestfallen
criminalist
criminality
crimination
criminative
criminatory
criminology
criticality
criticaster
crocidolite
crocodilian
crookbacked
crookedness
crossbearer
crossbowman
crossgarnet
crosslegged
crossstitch
crotcheteer
cruciferous
crucifixion
crucigerous
crunchiness
crustaceous
cryobiology
cryosurgery
cryotherapy
cryptically
cryptogamic
cryptograph
cryptomeria
crystalline
crystallise
crystallite
crystalloid
ctenophoran
culmination
culpability
cultivation
cunningness
cupellation
cupriferous
cupronickel
curableness
curatorship
curiousness
currentness
currishness
cursiveness
cursoriness
curtailment
curvilineal
curvilinear
customarily
custombuilt
customhouse
cybernation
cybernetics
cyclopaedia
cyclopaedic
cycloserine
cyclothymia
cyclothymic
cylindrical
cypripedium
cysticercus
cytogenesis
cytokinesis
cytological
dactylogram
dactylology
daisycutter
dangerously
dauntlessly
deactivator
deathrattle
debarkation
debauchment
debouchment
decantation
decarbonate
decarbonise
decarburise
deceitfully
deceivingly
decelerator
decemvirate
decennially
deceptively
decerebrate
declamation
declamatory
declaration
declarative
declaratory
declination
declivitous
decollation
decolletage
decolourise
decorticate
decrepitate
decrepitude
decrescendo
decussately
decussation
dedicatedly
deductively
deemphasise
deerstalker
defalcation
defectively
defenceless
defensively
deferential
defibrinate
deficiently
definiendum
deflagrator
defloration
defoliation
deforcement
deformation
defraudment
deglutition
degradation
degradingly
degustation
dehydration
deification
deistically
delectation
deleterious
deliciously
delightedly
delightsome
delineation
delinquency
deliriously
delitescent
deliverable
deliverance
deliveryman
demagnetise
demagogical
demagoguery
demagoguism
demandingly
demarcation
demarkation
demigoddess
democratise
democratism
demographer
demographic
demonolatry
demonstrate
demountable
dendritical
denigration
denigratory
denizenship
denominator
denticulate
dentigerous
denumerable
denunciator
deoxidation
deoxygenate
deoxyribose
depauperate
depauperise
dependently
deploringly
depopulator
deportation
depravation
depravement
deprecation
deprecative
deprecatory
depreciator
depredation
depredatory
depressible
deprivation
depthcharge
derangement
dereliction
dermatology
desalinator
descendable
descendible
describable
description
descriptive
desecration
desegregate
desensitise
deservingly
desexualise
desiccation
desiccative
desideratum
designation
desperadoes
desperately
desperation
despoilment
despondence
despondency
destination
destitution
destruction
destructive
desultorily
deteriorate
determinacy
determinant
determinate
determinism
determinist
detestation
detrainment
detribalise
detrimental
deuteration
deuterogamy
Deuteronomy
devaluation
devastation
developable
development
deviousness
devotedness
dexiotropic
dexterously
diachronism
diacritical
diadelphous
diagnostics
dialectally
dialectical
dialogistic
diamagnetic
diametrical
diamondback
diaphaneity
diaphoresis
diaphoretic
diapophysis
diapositive
diarthrosis
diastematic
diastrophic
diatessaron
dicephalous
dichogamous
dichotomise
dichotomist
dichotomous
dichromatic
dicotyledon
dictatorial
didacticism
differentia
differently
difficultly
diffidently
diffraction
diffuseness
diffusively
digestively
digitigrade
dilapidated
dilapidator
diluvialist
dimensional
dimwittedly
diningtable
dinnerdance
dinnertable
dinnerwagon
dinosaurian
Diophantine
diphtherial
diphtheroid
diphthongal
diphycercal
diplococcus
diplomatise
diplomatist
dipsomaniac
dipterocarp
directional
directivity
directorate
directorial
directrices
disablement
disaccustom
disaffected
disafforest
disannulled
disapproval
disarmament
disarmingly
disassemble
disassembly
disbandment
disbeliever
discalceate
discardable
discernible
discernibly
discernment
discerption
disciplinal
discipliner
discography
discontinue
discordance
discordancy
discotheque
discourtesy
discrepancy
discussable
discussible
disencumber

disentangle
disenthrall
disfunction
disgraceful
disgruntled
disguisedly
disgustedly
disharmonic
dishevelled
dishonestly
dishonourer
disillusion
disinclined
disinfector
disinterest
disinterred
disjunction
disjunctive
disjuncture
dislikeable
dislocation
dislodgment
dismayingly
disobedient
disobliging
disorganise
disparaging
disparately
dispensable
dispersedly
displeasure
disportment
disposition
dispositive
disputation
disquieting
disquietude
disremember
disseminate
disseminule
dissentient
dissepiment
dissertator
dissimilate
dissimulate
dissipation
dissipative
dissociable
dissolutely
dissolution
dissolvable
dissonantly
dissyllable
dissymmetry
distasteful
distempered
distensible
distinction
distinctive
distinguish
distraction
distractive
distressful
distribuend
distributor
distrustful
disturbance
disunionist
dithyrambic
dittography
divergently
diverticula
divestiture
divisionary
divisionism
divorcement
divulgation
divulgement
doctrinaire
doctrinally
documentary
dodecaphony
doggishness
dolefulness
dollishness
doltishness
domesticate
domesticity
domiciliary
domiciliate
domineering
donnishness
doorknocker
doublecheck
doublecross
doubleDutch
doubleedged
doubleender
doubleentry
doublefaced
doublequick
doublespeak
doublethink
doubtlessly
doughtiness
douroucouli
downdraught
downhearted
downtrodden
doxographer
draggletail
dramaturgic
drastically
draughtsman
drawingroom
dreadnought
dreamlessly
dresscircle
dressmaking
drillmaster
dropcurtain
dropforging
drouthiness
drunkenness
dualcontrol
dualpurpose
dubiousness
dumbfounder
dundrearies
duniewassal
duplication
duplicative
duplicitous
durableness
dutifulness
dynamically
dynamometer
dynamometry
dysfunction
dyslogistic
earnestness
earpiercing
earthcloset
earthenware
earthliness
easternmost
ebulliently
echosounder
eclecticism
econometric
ectoblastic
ectogenesis
ectogenetic
ectomorphic
ectoplasmic
ectotrophic
ecumenicism
ecumenicity
edification
edificatory
editorially
educability
educational
effectively
effectually
efficacious
efficiently
effulgently
egalitarian
egotistical
egregiously
einsteinium
ejaculation
ejaculatory
elaborately
elaboration
elaborative
elastically
elasticated
elastomeric
elbowgrease
elderliness
electioneer
electrician
electricity
electrocute
electrolier
electrology
electrolyse
electrolyte
electronics
electrotype
elementally
elephantine
elephantoid
elicitation
eligibility
elimination
eliminative
Elizabethan
ellipsoidal
ellipticity
elucidation
elucidative
elucidatory
elusiveness
elutriation
emancipator
emasculator
embarkation
embellisher
emblematise
emblematist
embowelling
embowerment
embraceable
embracement
embracingly
embrocation
embroiderer
embroilment
embryologic
embryonated
emmenagogue
Emmenthaler
emotionally
emotionless
empanelling
emperorship
empirically
emplacement
emptyhanded
emptyheaded
emulousness
emulsionise
enarthrosis
encapsulate
enchainment
enchantment
enchantress
enchiridion
encomiastic
encrustment
encumbrance
encystation
endearingly
endemically
endlessness
endocardiac
endocardial
endocardium
endometrium
endomorphic
endophagous
endoplasmic
endorsement
endoskelton
endothelial
endothelium
endothermal
endothermic
endotrophic
enfeoffment
enforceable
enforcement
enfranchise
engineering
engorgement
engrossment
enhancement
enigmatical
enjambement
enlargeable
enlargement
enlightened
enlivenment
enneahedron
ennoblement
enquiringly
ensanguined
enslavement
entablature
entablement
enterostomy
enterovirus
enterpriser
entertainer
enthralling
enthralment
entitlement
entomophily
entrainment
entreatment
entrustment
enucleation
enumeration
enumerative
enunciation
enunciative
envelopment
enviousness
environment
epeirogenic
ephemerides
epidiascope
epigastrium
epigraphist
epinephrine
epipetalous
episcopally
epithalamia
epithalamic
epithelioma
epochmaking
equableness
equiangular
equidistant
equilateral
equilibrate
equilibrist
equilibrium
equinoctial
equipollent
equivalence
equivalency
equivocally
equivocator
eradication
eradicative
Erastianism
ergatocracy
erotogenous
erotomaniac
erratically
erroneously
erubescence
erythrocyte
eschatology
escheatable
escheatment
esemplastic
esotericism
Esperantist
essentially
establisher
etherealise
ethereality
ethnography
ethnologist
ethological
Etruscology
etymologise
etymologist
eucalyptole
Eucharistic
euchologion
eudaemonism
eudaemonist
eudiometric
eugenically
euphemistic
eurhythmics
Europeanise
eurypteroid
evagination
evanescence
evangelical
evanishment
evaporation
evaporative
evasiveness
eveningstar
eventualise
eventuality
everlasting
evidentiary
evolutional
exaggerator
examination
exanthemata
exarcerbate
exceedingly
excellently
exceptional
excessively
exclamation
exclamatory
exclusively
exclusivity
excoriation
excremental
excrescence
excrescency
exculpation
exculpatory
excursively
exdirectory
executioner
executorial
executrices
executrixes
exemplarily
exemplarity
exercisable
exfoliation
exfoliative
exhaustible
exhaustless
exhortation
exhortative
exhortatory
existential
exogenously
exoneration
exonerative
exorbitance
exoskeletal
exoskeleton
exotericism
expansional
expansively
expansivity
expatiation
expatiative
expatiatory
expectantly
expectation
expectative
expectorant
expectorate
expediently
expeditious
expenditure
expensively
experienced
explainable
explanation
explanatory
explication
explicative
explicatory
exploitable
exploration
explorative
exploratory
explosively
exponential
exportation
expostulate
expressible
expropriate
expurgation
expurgatory
exquisitely
exsiccation
exstipulate
extemporary
extemporise
extensional
extensively
extenuation
extenuatory
exteriorise
exteriority
exterminate
externalise
externalism
externality
extirpation
extirpatory
extortioner
extractable
extradition
extrapolate

extravagant fimbriation forgetmenot furthersome glassblower gutlessness
extravagate financially forgettable furtiveness glasscutter guttapercha
extravasate fingerboard forgiveness furunculous glassmaking guttersnipe
extraverted fingerglass forlornness fusillation glauconitic gutturalise
extremeness fingerplate formalistic fustigation globeflower gutturalism
extrication fingerprint formational gafftopsail globigerina gymnospermy
extroverted fingerstall formication gainfulness globularity gynaecocrat
exuberantly finicalness formularise gallantness glomeration gynaecology
eyecatching FinnoUgrian formulation gallbladder glossolalia gypsiferous
fabrication firecracker fornication galleyslave glutinously gyrocompass
facelifting firefighter forthcoming Gallicanism gnotobiosis haberdasher
facetiously fireraising fortifiable gallimaufry gnotobiotic habiliments
facsimilist firewalking fortnightly Gallophobia godchildren habituation
factfinding firewatcher fortunately gallowsbird goddaughter haematocele
factionally firmamental forwardness gallowstree godforsaken haematocrit
factualness firstfruits foulmouthed gametangium godlessness haematology
facultative fissionable fourflusher gametophyte goldbeating haemocyanin
faddishness fissiparity fourpounder gamogenesis golddigging haemoglobin
fairweather fissiparous fourwheeler gangsterism goldenberry haemophilia
faithhealer flabbergast fractionary gardemanger gonfalonier haemophilic
faithlessly flaccidness fractionate garnishment goniometric haemoptysis
faithworthy flagcaptain fractionise garrulously goodhearted haemorrhage
fallibility flagellator fractiously gartersnake goodlooking haemorrhoid
Falstaffian flagofficer fragmentary gaseousness goodnatured haemostasis
falteringly flagwagging Francomania gasfittings gormandiser haemostatic
familiarise flamboyance Francophile gastrectomy gourmandise haggadistic
familiarity flamboyancy Francophobe gastronomic gourmandism haggardness
fanatically flamboyante francophone gastroscope gracelessly Hagiographa
fanfaronade flannelette franctireur gatecrasher gracileness hagiography
fantastical flannelling frankfurter geanticline gradational hagiologist
farawayness flatulently franklinite gegenschein gradiometer hagioscopic
farcicality flauntingly frankpledge gemmiferous gradualness hairbreadth
farinaceous flavourless frantically gemmiparous GraecoRoman hairdresser
farraginous flavoursome franticness gemmologist grammalogue hairraising
farreaching fleshliness fraternally gemmulation grammatical hairstyling
farthermost flexibility fraterniser gendarmerie gramophonic hairstylist
farthingale flightiness fratricidal genealogise grandfather hairtrigger
fasciaboard flimflammer fraudulence genealogist grandiflora halfbinding
fasciculate flirtatious freebooting generaliser grandiosely halfblooded
fascinating flocculence freehearted generalship grandiosity halfhearted
fascination floorwalker freemasonry generically grandmother halfholiday
fashionable florescence freethinker genetically grandnephew halflanding
fashionably floriferous freethought geniculated grandparent halfmeasure
fatefulness florilegium freezedried genitivally grangeriser hallucinate
fatiguingly floweriness frenchified genteelness granivorous halophilous
fatuousness fluctuation Frenchwoman gentianella granolithic halterbreak
faultfinder fluorescein fretfulness gentilitial granophyric Hamiltonian
faultlessly fluorescent friableness gentlemanly granularity handbreadth
favouritism fluoroscope fricandeaux gentlewoman granulation handfasting
fearfulness fluoroscopy frightfully genuflexion granulocyte handgrenade
feasibility folliculate frigidarium genuineness graphically handicapped
featheredge fomentation frivolously geochemical graphicness handicapper
featherhead foolishness frontrunner geomagnetic grasshopper handknitted
featherless footpoundal frostbitten geometrical gratulation handpainted
featureless footslogger frothhopper geophysical gratulatory handselling
fecundation footsoldier frowardness geopolitics gravedigger handwriting
feelingness foppishness frowstiness geostrophic gravelblind handwritten
feldspathic foraminated fructuation geosyncline gravimetric handwrought
feloniously foraminifer frugivorous geotectonic gravitation haphazardly
felspathoid forbearance fruitlessly Germanophil gravitative haplessness
fenestrated forbiddance frustration germination greasepaint haplography
fermentable foreclosure fulguration germinative greaseproof harbourless
ferociously foreignness fullblooded gerontology greatnephew hardhearted
ferriferous forequarter fullfledged gerrymander greengrocer hardhitting
ferruginous forerunning fullhearted gestatorial greenkeeper hardmouthed
festinately foreseeable fullmouthed gesticulate greenockite hardworking
festschrift foreshorten fulminating gettogether gristliness harebrained
fetichistic foresighted fulmination ghastliness grotesquely harmfulness
fetishistic forestaller fulminatory ghostliness grotesquery harmonistic
feudalistic forestation fulsomeness ghostwriter grouchiness harpsichord
fiddlestick forethinker funambulate giantpowder groundsheet harumscarum
fidgetiness forethought funambulist gibberellin groundwater harvesthome
fieldcornet foretopmast functionary gibbousness grumblingly hatefulness
fieldworker foretopsail functionate gigantesque guardedness haughtiness
filamentary forevermore fundamental gillyflower guesstimate haustellate
filamentous foreverness furnishings gimcrackery guilelessly hazardously
filmography forewarning furtherance gingerbread guiltlessly headborough
filmsetting forfeitable furthermore girlishness gullibility headhunting
filterpaper forgetfully furthermost glaringness gurgitation healthfully

healthiness
heartbroken
hearthstone
heartlessly
heartsblood
heartstring
heavenwards
heavyfooted
heavyhanded
heavyweight
hebephrenia
hebephrenic
Hebraically
hedgehopped
hedgepriest
hedgeschool
heedfulness
Hegelianism
heinousness
heldentenor
heliochrome
heliography
heliometric
heliotropic
helleborine
Hellenistic
hellishness
helminthoid
helpfulness
hemeralopia
hemianopsia
hemimorphic
hemipterous
hemispheric
hepatectomy
Hepplewhite
heptamerous
heptarchist
Heracleidan
herbivorous
hereditable
hereinafter
heresiology
heretically
hermeneutic
hermeticism
heroworship
herpetology
herringbone
herringgull
hesperidium
heteroclite
heteroecism
heterograft
heterophony
heteroploid
heteropolar
heterospory
heterotaxis
heterotroph
heterotypic
hexadecimal
hexametrist
hibernacula
hibernation
Hibernicism
hideousness
hierarchism
highbrowism
highfalutin
highpitched
highpowered
highranking
highstepper
highwrought
hilariously
Hindoostani
hippocampus
Hippocratic
hippopotami
hirsuteness
Hispanicise
Hispanicism
Hispanicist
histologist
historiated
historicise
historicism
historicist
historicity
histrionics
histrionism
hitherwards
hobbledehoy
hoggishness
hollandaise
holoblastic
holographic
holothurian
homeopathic
homeostasis
homeostatic
homesteader
homestretch
homiletical
homocentric
homoeopathy
homoestatic
homogeneity
homogeneous
homogenetic
homogeniser
homoiousian
homological
homomorphic
homophonous
homoplastic
homopterous
homosporous
homothallic
homozygosis
honeybadger
honeymooner
honeysuckle
hooliganism
hopefulness
hornswoggle
horological
horripilate
horsecollar
horsedoctor
horseradish
hospitalise
hospitality
hospitaller
housefather
householder
housekeeper
houselights
housemaster
housemother
housewifely
housewifery
huckleberry
Hudibrastic
hugeousness
humiliation
humiliatory
hummingbird
hunchbacked
hundredfold
hurriedness
hurryscurry
hurryskurry
hurtfulness
husbandlike
hyacinthine
hydraheaded
hydrobromic
hydrocarbon
hydrocyanic
hydrogenate
hydrogenous
hydrography
hydrologist
hydromedusa
hydrometeor
hydrometric
hydropathic
hydrophilic
hydrophobia
hydrophobic
hydrophytic
hydroponics
hydrosphere
hydrostatic
hydrotactic
hydrothorax
hydrotropic
hygrometric
hygrophytic
hygroscopic
hylogenesis
hylozoistic
hymenoptera
hymnography
hyoscyamine
hyperactive
hyperbolise
hyperboloid
hyperborean
hypercharge
hypercritic
hypermarket
hypermetric
hyperphagia
hyperplasia
hypersthene
hypertrophy
hyphenation
hypnopaedia
hypnopompic
hypoblastic
hypocycloid
hypogastric
hypoglossal
hypolimnion
hypophyseal
hypophysial
hypostatise
hypotension
hypothecate
hypothenuse
hypothermia
hypothesise
hypotyposis
hypsography
hypsometric
hypsophobia
ichnography
ichthyology
ichthyornis
ichthyosaur
iconography
iconostases
iconostasis
icosahedral
icosahedron
identically
ideographic
ideological
idiographic
idiomorphic
idiotically
idolisation
idyllically
ignobleness
ignominious
illaffected
illbreeding
illdisposed
illfavoured
illhumoured
illiberally
illimitable
illimitably
illiquidity
illmannered
illogically
illtempered
illuminable
illuminance
illuminator
illusionism
illusionist
illustrator
illustrious
imaginarily
imagination
imaginative
imbrication
imitatively
immanentism
immanentist
immarginate
immediately
immedicable
immenseness
immigration
immitigable
immitigably
immortalise
immortality
immoveables
immunologic
impanelling
imparkation
impartation
impartially
impassioned
impassively
impassivity
impatiently
impeachable
impeachment
impecunious
impedimenta
impenetrate
impenitence
impenitency
imperfectly
imperforate
imperialise
imperialism
imperialist
imperilling
imperilment
imperiously
impermanent
impermeable
impermeably
impersonate
impertinent
imperviable
impetration
impetratory
impetuosity
impetuously
impingement
implausible
implausibly
implemental
implication
implicative
imploringly
impolitical
impoliticly
importantly
importation
importunate
importunely
importunity
impoundment
impractical
imprecation
imprecatory
imprecisely
imprecision
impregnable
impregnably
impressible
impressment
impropriate
impropriety
improvement
improvident
imprudently
impuissance
impulsively
inadaptable
inadvertent
inadvisable
inalienable
inalienably
inalterable
inalterably
inanimately
inanimation
inappetence
inattention
inattentive
inaugurator
incalescent
incantation
incantatory
incarcerate
incardinate
incarnadine
incarnation
incertitude
incessantly
incinerator
incipiently
inclemently
inclination
inclusively
incoercible
incognisant
incoherence
incoherency
incommodity
incompetent
incompliant
incongruent
incongruity
incongruous
inconscient
inconsonant
inconstancy
incontinent
incorporate
incorporeal
incorrectly
incorruptly
increasable
incredulity
incredulous
incremental
incriminate
inculcation
inculpation
inculpatory
incunabulum
incuriosity
incuriously
incurvation
incurvature
indeciduous
indefinable
indefinably
indehiscent
indentation
independent
indifferent
indigestion
indigestive
indignantly
indignation
indirection
individuate
indivisible
indivisibly
IndoChinese
IndoIranian
indomitable
indomitably
indorsement
indubitable
indubitably
inductively
indulgently
industrious
inebriation
inedibility
ineffective
ineffectual
inefficient
inelegantly
ineloquence
ineluctable
ineluctably
inequitable
inequitably
inescapable
inessential
inestimable
inestimably
inexactness
inexcusable
inexcusably
inexistence
inexpedient
inexpensive
infanticide
infantilism
infantryman
infatuation
inferential
inferiority
infertility
infestation
infeudation
infiltrator
infinitival
infirmarian
inflammable
inflammably
inflexional
influential
informality
information
informative
informatory
infrangible
infrequence
infrequency
ingathering
ingeniously
ingenuously
ingrainedly
ingratitude
ingurgitate
inhabitable
inhabitancy

inheritable
inheritance
inheritress
initialling
injudicious
injuriously
innavigable
innervation
innocuously
innoxiously
innumerable
innumerably
innutrition
inobservant
inoculation
inoculative
inoffensive
inofficious
inoperative
inopportune
inquilinous
inquiringly
inquisition
inquisitive
insalubrity
inscribable
inscription
inscriptive
inscrutable
inscrutably
insectarium
insecticide
insectifuge
insectivore
insectology
inseminator
insensately
insensitive
inseparable
inseparably
insessorial
insidiously
insincerely
insincerity
insinuation
insinuative
insipidness
insistently
insouciance
inspiration
inspiratory
instability
installment
instigation
instigative
instillment
instinctive
instinctual
institution
instruction
instructive
insufflator
insultingly
insuperable
insuperably
intagliated
integrality
integration
integrative
intelligent
intemperate
intenseness
intensifier
intensional
intensively
intentional
intentioned
interactant
interaction
interactive
interallied
interatomic
interbedded
intercalary
intercalate
intercensal
intercepter
interceptor
intercessor
interchange
intercostal
intercourse
intercrural
interdental
interdepend
interesting
interfacial
interfacing
interfluent
interfusion
intergrowth
interiorise
interiority
interjacent
interleaves
interlinear
Interlingua
interlining
interlocker
interlunary
intermeddle
intermedium
intermingle
intermitted
internalise
internality
internecine
internuncio
interosseus
interplayed
interpolate
interpreter
interracial
interregnum
interrelate
interrogate
interrupter
interruptor
interseptal
intersexual
intersperse
interspinal
intertangle
intertribal
intervallic
interviewee
interviewer
intimidator
intolerable
intolerably
intolerance
intractable
intractably
intravenous
intrepidity
intricately
intriguante
intromitted
intromitter
introverted
intrusively
intuitional
intuitively
intuitivism
intumescent
invalidness
invectively
inventively
inventorial
investigate
investiture
inviability
invidiously
invigilator
invigorator
inviolately
involucrate
involuntary
involvement
invultation
ionospheric
ipecacuanha
ipsilateral
iridescence
irksomeness
ironhearted
ironmongery
irradiation
irradiative
irrecusable
irrecusably
irredentism
irredentist
irreducible
irreducibly
irrefutable
irrefutably
irregularly
irrelevance
irrelevancy
irreligious
irremissive
irremovable
irremovably
irreparable
irreparably
irresoluble
irretention
irretentive
irreverence
irrevocable
irrevocably
irruptively
isochronism
isochronous
isoelectric
isogeotherm
isometrical
isomorphism
isomorphous
itacolumite
ithyphallic
itinerantly
itineration
jabberwocky
Jacobinical
Jacobitical
jactitation
Jansenistic
jargonistic
jauntingcar
jealousness
jerrymander
journeywork
joylessness
Judaisation
judgmatical
judiciously
jumpingbean
jumpingjack
juridically
justiciable
justifiable
justifiably
juvenescent
kickstarter
kilocalorie
kindhearted
kinematical
kinesiology
kinetograph
kinetoscope
kitchenette
kitchensink
kitchenware
kleptomania
knavishness
knowingness
knownothing
knucklebone
Kulturkampf
kwashiorkor
kymographic
labefaction
labiodental
laboriously
lachrymator
laciniation
laconically
lacrimation
lacrimatory
lacrimosely
lacrymation
lacrymatory
lacrymosely
lactescence
lactiferous
laicisation
lakedweller
lamellicorn
lamelliform
lamentation
lammergeier
lammergeyer
lamplighter
Lancastrian
lancinating
lancination
landaulette
landgrabber
landgravine
landholding
landingbeam
landinggear
landlordism
languidness
larcenously
largeminded
laryngology
laryngotomy
lastingness
latchstring
lateritious
latifundium
latitudinal
latticework
laudability
laughinggas
launderette
laurustinus
lawlessness
lawmerchant
leapfrogged
learnedness
leaseholder
leatherback
leatherhead
leatherneck
leavetaking
lecherously
lectureship
legerdemain
legionnaire
legislation
legislative
legislature
Leibnitzian
lengthiness
lentiginous
lepidoptera
leprosarium
leptodactyl
lesemajesty
letterpress
levelheaded
leviratical
libertarian
liberticide
libertinage
libertinism
lichenology
lickerishly
lickspittle
lieutenancy
lifemanship
ligamentary
ligamentous
lightfooted
lighthanded
lightheaded
lightminded
lightsomely
lightweight
lilylivered
limitedness
limitlessly
limnologist
linedrawing
linefishing
linendraper
lineprinter
lingeringly
linguistics
lionhearted
liquefiable
liquescence
liquidambar
liquidation
lissomeness
literalness
lithography
lithophytic
lithosphere
lithotomise
lithotomist
lithotripsy
litigiously
litterateur
lixiviation
loathliness
loathsomely
loculicidal
logarithmic
loggerheads
logicalness
logographer
logographic
logomachist
longanimity
longplaying
longsighted
looselimbed
loosestrife
lophobranch
loudmouthed
loudspeaker
loutishness
louverboard
louvreboard
lovableness
lowpressure
lowspirited
loxodromics
lubrication
lubricative
lucratively
lucubration
ludicrously
luminescent
lumpishness
lustfulness
Lutheranism
luxuriantly
luxuriation
luxuriously
lycanthrope
lycanthropy
machicolate
machination
machinemade
mackerelsky
macrobiotic
macrocosmic
macrogamete
macroscopic
maddeningly
madreporite
madrigalian
madrigalist
magazinegun
magdalenian
magisterial
magisterium
magistratic
Maglemosian
magnanimity
magnanimous
magnificent
maidservant
mailcarrier
maintenance
maintopmast
maintopsail
maisonnette
makebelieve
maladaptive
maladjusted
maladroitly
malapropism
malariology
malediction
maledictory
malefaction
maleficence
malevolence
malfeasance
malfunction
maliciously
malignantly
malposition
malpractice
mammalogist
managership
mandarinate
mandibulate
mandolinist
manducation
manducatory
Manichaeism
manifestant
manifestoes
manipulable
manipulator
manneristic
mannishness
mansardroof
mantelpiece
mantelshelf
mantuamaker
manufactory
manufacture
manumission
manumitting
marcescence

marcescible
marchioness
marconigram
marginalise
marginality
margraviate
marketplace
marketvalue
marlinspike
marquessate
marqueterie
marquisette
marriagebed
marshalling
marshalship
marshmallow
martyrology
masculinely
masculinise
masculinity
masochistic
masquerader
massiveness
massproduce
masterfully
masterpiece
mastication
masticatory
mastodontic
mastoiditis
matchlessly
matchmaking
materialise
materialism
materialist
materiality
mathematics
matriarchal
matriculate
matrilineal
matrilinear
matrimonial
mawkishness
maxillipede
McCarthyism
meadowgrass
meadowsweet
meaningless
measureless
measurement
mechanician
mechanistic
mediaevally
mediastinal
mediastinum
mediateness
mediatorial
mediatrices
medicinable
medicinally
medicolegal
medievalism
medievalist
mediumistic
megalomania
megalopolis
megatherium
melancholia
melancholic
melanochroi
melanophore
melioration
meliorative
meliphagous
melliferous
mellifluent
mellifluous
melodiously
membraneous
memorabilia
memorialise
memorialist
mendelevium
meningocele
menservants
mensuration
mentholated
mentionable
meprobamate
mercenarily
merchandise
merchantman
mercilessly
mercurially
meritocracy
meritorious
meroblastic
merogenesis
Merovingian
merryandrew
merrymaking
mesalliance
mesoblastic
mesomorphic
messiahship
metacentric
metachrosis
metagenesis
metagenetic
metalloidal
metallurgic
metalworker
metamorphic
metaphysics
metaplastic
metapsychic
metasomatic
metastasise
meteoritics
meteoroidal
meteorology
Methodistic
methodology
methylamine
methylation
metonymical
metoposcopy
metrication
Micawberish
Micawberism
micrococcal
micrococcus
microcosmic
microgamete
micrography
microgroove
microlithic
micrometric
Micronesian
microphonic
microphytic
microscopic
microsecond
micturition
middleclass
middlesized
millenarian
milliampere
millionaire
millisecond
mimetically
mindbending
mindblowing
mindfulness
mindreading
mineraliser
minesweeper
miniaturise
miniaturist
ministerial
minnesinger
minuteglass
mirthlessly
misalliance
misanthrope
misanthropy
misbegotten
miscarriage
miscegenate
miscellanea
mischievous
miscibility
misconceive
misconstrue
miscreation
misericorde
miserliness
misestimate
misfeasance
misguidance
misguidedly
misjudgment
mismarriage
misremember
misspelling
mistrustful
mithridatic
mitrailleur
mockingbird
moderations
modernistic
moisturiser
molecricket
molecularly
molendinary
molestation
mollycoddle
molybdenite
momentarily
momentously
monarchical
monasterial
monasticism
moneylender
moneymaking
moneymarket
moneyspider
monitorship
monkeybread
monkeyshine
monocarpous
monochasial
monochasium
monochromat
monochromic
monoclinous
monoculture
monogenesis
monogenetic
monogrammed
monographer
monographic
monolingual
monological
monologuise
monologuist
monomorphic
mononuclear
monophagous
monophthong
Monophysite
monopoliser
monopterous
Monothelite
monozygotic
monseigneur
monstrosity
monstrously
moonlighter
mooringmast
morbiferous
moribundity
morningroom
moronically
morrisdance
mortarboard
mosstrooper
mothercraft
mothernaked
motherright
motivepower
mountaineer
mountainous
mountaintop
movableness
moveability
mudslinging
multangular
multicolour
multilinear
multinomial
multiparous
multiracial
multistorey
multivalent
mundaneness
municipally
munificence
murderously
murmuration
murmurously
musclebound
muscularity
musculation
musculature
musicalness
muskthistle
mustachioed
mutableness
muttonchops
mycological
mycophagist
mycorrhizae
mycorrhizal
myelomatous
myocarditis
myrmecology
mythography
mythologise
mythologist
mythomaniac
mythopoeist
mythopoetic
myxomatosis
myxomycetes
nailvarnish
namecalling
namedropper
naphthalene
narcoleptic
narratively
nasofrontal
nationalise
nationalism
nationalist
nationality
nationstate
naturalness
naturopathy
naughtiness
Neanderthal
nearsighted
necessarian
necessarily
necessitate
necessitous
neckerchief
necrobiosis
necrologist
necromancer
necromantic
necrophilia
necrophilic
necropoleis
needfulness
needlecraft
needlepoint
needlewoman
nefariously
negationist
negligently
negotiation
negotiatory
negotiatrix
negrophobia
neighbourly
neologistic
Neoplatonic
Neotropical
nephelinite
nephrectomy
nervelessly
nervousness
netherworld
nettlecloth
neurologist
neuropathic
neuroticism
neurotropic
neutraliser
nickelplate
nictitation
nightingale
nightmarish
nightporter
nightwalker
nigrescence
ninnyhammer
nitrogenise
nitrogenous
nittygritty
noctilucent
noctivagant
noctivagous
nocturnally
noiselessly
noisemaking
noisomeness
nomadically
nomenclator
nominatival
nomographer
nomographic
nomological
nonchalance
nondelivery
nondescript
nonetheless
nonexistent
nonfeasance
nonmatching
nonmetallic
nonpartisan
nonplussing
nonresident
nonsensical
nonsequitur
nonspecific
nonunionist
nonviolence
nonvolatile
northeaster
northwester
noseyparker
nosographer
nosographic
nosological
notableness
nothingness
noticeboard
notionalist
notoriously
nourishment
novelettish
noxiousness
nullifidian
nulliparity
nulliparous
numerically
numismatics
numismatist
nuncupation
nuncupative
nurserymaid
nutcrackers
nutrimental
nutritional
nutritively
nyctitropic
nyctophobia
nympholepsy
nymphomania
oarsmanship
obfuscation
obfuscatory
objectively
objectivism
objectivist
objectivity
objurgation
objurgatory
obliqueness
obliviously
obmutescent
obnoxiously
obscuration
obscureness
obsecration
observantly
observation
observatory
observingly
obsessional
obsessively
obsolescent
obstetrical
obstinately
obstruction
obstructive
obtestation
obtrusively
obviousness
occipitally
occultation
ochlocratic
octachordal
octagonally
octingenary
odoriferous
odorousness
oecological
oecumenical
oenological
oenophilist
oesophageal
oestrogenic
offenceless
offensively
offhandedly
officialdom
officialese
officialism
officiation
officinally

officiously
oilpainting
oldwomanish
olfactology
oligochaete
oligomerous
ominousness
ommatophore
omnifarious
omnipotence
omnipresent
omniscience
oncological
oneiromancy
onerousness
ontogenesis
ontogenetic
ontological
opalescence
opencircuit
openhearted
openmouthed
operational
operatively
operculated
operoseness
ophidiarium
ophiologist
opinionated
opportunely
opportunism
opportunist
opportunity
opprobrious
oppugnation
optometrist
oracularity
orangoutang
orbicularly
orchestrate
orchidology
orderliness
oreographic
oreological
organically
organisable
organscreen
orientalise
orientalism
orientalist
orientation
originality
origination
originative
ornithology
ornithopter
ornithosaur
orthocentre
orthodontia
orthodontic
orthoepical
orthography
orthopaedic
orthopedics
orthopedist
orthopteran
orthoscopic
orthotropic
oscillation
oscillatory
oscillogram
osmotically
ostensively
ostentation
osteography
osteologist
osteopathic
osteophytic
osteoplasty
ostracoderm
Ostrogothic
otherwhiles
outbreeding
outbuilding
outcropping
outdistance
outfighting
outrivalled
outspokenly
outstanding
outstripped
outwardness
ovariectomy
overanxious
overbalance
overbearing
overbidding
overcropped
overdevelop
overgarment
overindulge
overlapping
overmanning
overmeasure
overpayment
overproduce
overrunning
oversailing
oversetting
overstepped
overstretch
overstuffed
overtopping
overweening
overwritten
overwrought
oviposition
oxygenation
oxyhydrogen
oysterplant
ozoniferous
ozonisation
ozonosphere
pachydermal
pacifically
pacificator
packingcase
paddleboard
paddlewheel
paederastic
paediatrics
paediatrist
paedophilia
painfulness
painkilling
painstaking
Palaearctic
palaeotypic
Palestinian
palindromic
palmcabbage
palpability
palpitation
palsgravine
pamphleteer
pandemonium
panegyrical
Panglossian
panhellenic
panicmonger
pantalettes
pantheistic
pantomimist
pantothenic
paperhanger
papermaking
paperweight
papiermache
papyraceous
parachutist
paradisical
paradoxical
paragrapher
paragraphic
paraldehyde
paraleipsis
parallactic
parallelism
parallelled
paramedical
parametrise
paramoecium
paramorphic
paramountcy
paramountly
paraphraser
paraplectic
paraselenae
parasitical
parasitosis
parathyroid
paratrooper
paratyphoid
parentheses
parenthesis
parenthetic
parheliacal
parishioner
parochially
paronomasia
participant
participate
participial
particulate
partitioned
partitioner
partitively
partnership
parturition
passacaglia
passeriform
passibility
Passiontide
passivation
passiveness
pasteuriser
pastoralism
pastoralist
pastureland
patelliform
paternalism
paternalist
paternoster
pathologist
patriarchal
patrilineal
patrimonial
patristical
patronising
patternshop
paunchiness
pawnbroking
peacemaking
pearlescent
pearlfisher
peccability
peccadillos
pectination
peculiarity
pecuniarily
pedagogical
pedestalled
pedicellate
pediculosis
pedological
pedunculate
peevishness
Pelagianism
pelargonium
pellucidity
pendulously
penetrating
penetration
penetrative
penicillate
penicillium
peninsulate
penitential
pennyweight
penological
pensionable
pensionless
pensiveness
pentadactyl
pentagynous
pentahedron
pentamerous
pentandrous
pentathlete
pentavalent
pentazocine
Pentecostal
pentlandite
penultimate
penuriously
peptisation
perambulate
perceivable
perceivably
perceptible
perceptibly
perchlorate
percipience
percolation
peregrinate
perennation
perennially
perfectible
perfectness
perforation
perforative
performable
performance
perfunctory
pericardiac
pericardial
pericardium
pericranial
pericranium
perineurium
periodicity
periodontal
periostitis
peripatetic
periphrases
periphrasis
perishables
perishingly
perispermic
peristalith
peristalsis
peristaltic
peristomial
perithecium
peritonitis
permanently
permissible
permissibly
permutation
perpetrator
perpetually
perpetuance
perpetuator
perplexedly
persecution
perseverate
persistence
persistency
personalise
personalism
personalist
personality
personation
personative
personifier
perspective
perspicuity
perspicuous
persuadable
persuasible
pertinacity
pertinently
perturbable
pervasively
pervertedly
pessimistic
pestiferous
pestilently
pestologist
petitionary
petrography
petrologist
petticoated
pettifogger
pettishness
phagedaenic
phagocytise
phagocytose
phalanstery
phantasiast
phantasmata
pharisaical
phariseeism
pharyngitis
phenologist
philanderer
philatelist
philhellene
philologian
philologist
philosopher
philosophic
phonetician
phonography
phonologist
phosphonium
phosphorate
phosphorism
phosphorite
phosphorous
photoactive
photocopier
photofinish
photography
photometric
photooffset
photoperiod
photophilic
photophobia
photophobic
photosphere
phototactic
phototropic
phrasemaker
phraseogram
phraseology
phthiriasis
phycocyanin
phycologist
phylloclade
phyllotaxis
phylogynist
physicality
physiocracy
physiognomy
physiologic
phytography
phytologist
phytosterol
phytotomist
Pickwickian
pictography
pictorially
picturebook
picturecard
picturegoer
picturesque
pieceworker
pietistical
pigeonchest
piggishness
pigheadedly
pigsticking
pillowfight
pilocarpine
pilotburner
pinkishness
pinnatisect
pipecleaner
piperaceous
pipistrelle
piratically
piscatorial
piscivorous
pitchblende
piteousness
pitifulness
pivotbridge
placability
plagiariser
plagioclase
plagiostome
plainspoken
plaintively
planetarium
planetoidal
planimetric
planisphere
planoconvex
plantigrade
plasmolysis
plasmolytic
plasterwork
plasticiser
platearmour
plateresque
platforming
platinotype
platyrrhine
playerpiano
playfulness
playingcard
pleasurable
pleasurably
plebeianise
plebeianism
plectoptera
pleinairist
pleiotropic
Pleistocene
plenipotent
plenteously
plentifully
pleochroism
pleomorphic
pleurodynia
pliableness
plicateness
ploughshare
ploughstaff
pluralistic
plutocratic
pluviometer
pneumonitis

pocketknife
pocketmoney
pocketsized
pococurante
podophyllin
pointdevice
pointedness
pointillism
pointillist
pointlessly
poisonously
polarimeter
polarimetry
polarisable
polariscope
polemically
polevaulter
policewoman
politically
politicking
pollination
poltergeist
poltroonery
polyandrous
polycarpous
polychromic
polycrystal
polygenesis
polygenetic
polyglottal
polyglottic
polygonally
polygraphic
polymorphic
polyonymous
polypeptide
polyphagous
polyphonous
polystyrene
polytechnic
polyzoarium
pomegranate
pomiculture
pomological
pompousness
ponderation
ponderosity
ponderously
pontificals
pontificate
populariser
pornography
porphyritic
portability
porterhouse
portionless
portmanteau
portraitist
portraiture
positronium
posological
possibility
postclassic
posteriorly
postexilian
postglacial
postnuptial
postulation
potentially
potteringly
pourparlers
powderflask
powerlessly
practicable
practicably
practically
praetorship
pragmatical
prattlingly
prayerwheel
preachiness
preaudience
Precambrian
precautious
precedented
precedently
precentress
preceptress
precipitant
precipitate
precipitous
preciseness
preconceive
precontract
predatorily
predecessor
predicament
predication
predicative
predicatory
predictable
predictably
predominant
predominate
preelection
preeminence
preexistent
prefatorial
prefatorily
prefectural
prehistoric
preignition
prejudgment
prejudicial
prelibation
preliminary
prelusively
prelusorily
prematurely
prematurity
premeditate
premiership
premonition
premonitory
prenominate
preoccupied
preparation
preparative
preparatory
preposition
prepositive
preprandial
prerogative
presanctify
presbyteral
presciently
preselector
presentable
presentably
presentient
presentment
preservable
pressagency
prestigious
prestissimo
prestressed
presumingly
presumption
presumptive
pretendedly
pretentious
preterhuman
preterition
prevalently
prevaricate
preventable
preventible
previsional
prickliness
priestcraft
primaevally
primateship
primatology
primigenial
primiparous
primitively
primitivism
principally
privateness
privatively
prizewinner
probabilism
probabilist
probability
probational
probationer
problematic
proceedings
procephalic
prochronism
proconsular
procreation
procreative
procrustean
proctorship
procuration
procuratory
procurement
prodigalise
prodigality
profanation
profanatory
profaneness
professedly
proficiency
profiterole
profuseness
progenitrix
progeniture
progestogen
prognathism
prognathous
progression
progressism
progressist
progressive
prohibition
prohibitive
prohibitory
prolegomena
proletarian
proletariat
proliferate
proliferous
prolificacy
prolificity
prolocutrix
prominently
promiscuity
promiscuous
promisingly
promotional
promptitude
promulgator
proofreader
propagation
propagative
prophethood
prophetical
prophetship
prophylaxis
propinquity
propitiable
propitiator
proportions
proposition
proprietary
prorogation
prosaically
prosaicness
prosecution
prosecutrix
proselytise
proselytism
prosenchyma
prospective
prosthetics
prostitutor
prostration
protagonist
protectoral
protectress
proteolysis
proteolytic
Proterozoic
prothalamia
prothallial
prothallium
prothoracic
protomartyr
protonotary
protophytic
protractile
protraction
protractive
protrudable
protrusible
protuberant
provenience
providently
provisional
provisorily
provocateur
provocation
provocative
provokingly
provostship
proximately
prudishness
pruriginous
Prussianise
Prussianism
pseudograph
pseudomonas
pseudomorph
pseudopodia
psittacosis
psychedelia
psychedelic
psychiatric
psychically
psychodrama
psychogenic
psychograph
psychologic
psychometry
psychomotor
psychopathy
pteridology
pterodactyl
publication
publishable
publishment
pulchritude
pullthrough
pullulation
pulverulent
pumicestone
punchinello
punctilious
punctuality
punctuation
pupillarity
purchasable
pureblooded
purgatorial
purificator
puritanical
purportedly
purposeless
purposively
purpresture
pushfulness
pussyfooter
pussywillow
pustulation
putrescence
putrescible
pyramidally
pyramidical
pyrargyrite
pyroclastic
pyrotechnic
Pythagorean
Pythagorism
quacksalver
quadraphony
quadratical
quadrennial
quadrennium
quadrillion
quadrupedal
quaestorial
qualifiable
qualitative
quarrelling
quarrelsome
quarterback
quarterdeck
quartertone
quaternloaf
queenliness
querulously
questionary
quickchange
quickfiring
quickfreeze
quickfrozen
quicksilver
quickwitted
quiescently
quilldriver
quincuncial
quinquennia
quinquereme
quintillion
quitchgrass
quizzically
Rabelaisian
racemeeting
racketpress
radicalness
radioactive
radiocarbon
radiography
radiolarian
radiologist
radiometric
radiophonic
raffishness
rallentando
rancorously
rangefinder
rapaciously
rapscallion
rapturously
rarefaction
rarefactive
Rastafarian
ratatouille
rateability
ratiocinate
rationalise
rationalism
rationalist
rationality
rattlebrain
rattlepated
rattlesnake
raucousness
raunchiness
ravishingly
reachmedown
reactionary
reactionist
readability
readywitted
realignment
realisation
realpolitik
reanimation
reapportion
reappraisal
rearadmiral
reassertion
reassurance
reawakening
rebarbative
recalculate
recantation
receptacula
receptively
receptivity
recessional
recessively
reciprocate
reciprocity
reclaimable
reclamation
recognition
recognitive
recognitory
recommender
recommittal
recondition
reconnoitre
reconstruct
recoverable
recriminate
recruitment
rectangular
rectifiable
rectilineal
rectilinear
recumbently
recurrently
redactional
reddishness
redetermine
redirection
rediscovery
redoubtable
redundantly
reduplicate
reedbunting
reeducation
reedwarbler
reemergence
reenactment
reestablish
referential
reflectance
reflexively
reflexology
reformation
reformative
reformatory
refrangible
refreshment
refrigerant
refrigerate
refringency
regardfully
regenerable

regenerator
regimentals
regionalise
regionalism
regionalist
registrable
regretfully
regrettable
regrettably
regurgitate
reification
reincarnate
reinsertion
reinsurance
reintegrate
reintroduce
reiteration
reiterative
rejoicingly
rejuvenator
rejuvenesce
relatedness
relationism
relationist
reliability
religionise
religionism
religionist
religiosity
religiously
reluctantly
reluctation
remembrance
reminiscent
remonstrant
remonstrate
remorseless
remunerator
renaissance
renegotiate
reorientate
repartition
repellantly
repellently
repentantly
repetitious
replaceable
replacement
replenisher
repleteness
repleviable
replication
reportorial
reposefully
representer
repressible
repressibly
reproachful
reprobation
reprobative
reprobatory
reprogramme
reprography
reprovingly
repudiation
repugnantly
repulsively
requirement
requisition
resemblance
resentfully
reservation
residential
resignation
resiliently
resipiscent
resistively
resistivity
resourceful
respectable
respectably
respiration
respiratory
resplendent
respondence
respondency
responsible
responsibly
restatement
restfulness
restitution
restiveness
restoration
restorative
restriction
restrictive
restructure
resuscitate
retaliation
retaliative
retaliatory
retardation
retardative
retardatory
retentively
retentivity
retinacular
retinaculum
retinoscopy
retiredness
retraceable
retractable
retranslate
retribution
retributive
retributory
retrievable
retroaction
retroactive
retrocedent
retroflexed
retrorocket
revaccinate
revaluation
revendicate
reverberant
reverberate
reverential
reversional
reversioner
revisionary
revisionism
revisionist
reviviscent
rhabdomancy
rhapsodical
rheological
rheotropism
rhetorician
rheumaticky
rhinologist
rhinoscopic
rhizanthous
rhizocarpic
rhizomatous
rhombohedra
rhomboideus
rhynchodont
ribbongrass
ribvaulting
rickettsial
ricochetted
rifacimenti
rifacimento
rightangled
righteously
righthanded
righthander
rightminded
rightwinger
ringstraked
riotousness
ritualistic
roadholding
rockcrystal
rodenticide
rodomontade
roentgenise
roguishness
romanticise
romanticism
romanticist
ropedancing
ropewalking
Rosicrucian
rotogravure
rottenstone
roughfooted
roughlegged
roundedness
rubberstamp
rubefacient
rubefaction
rubicundity
rubrication
rudimentary
ruinousness
rumbustious
ruridecanal
Russophobia
rustication
Sabbatarian
sacculation
sacramental
sacrificial
saddlecloth
saddlehorse
Sadduceeism
safebreaker
safeconduct
safecracker
safekeeping
safetyvalve
sagaciously
Sagittarius
saintliness
saintpaulia
salaciously
saleability
salesladies
salinometer
salmonberry
salpingitis
saltatorial
saltimbanco
salvageable
salvational
sandbagging
sandskipper
sanguinaria
sanguineous
sansculotte
Sanskritist
saplessness
saponaceous
saprobiotic
saprogenous
saprophytic
sarcomatous
sarcophagus
sartorially
satanically
satiability
satinstitch
satirically
satisfiable
saturnalian
saturninely
sauropodous
sausagemeat
savouriness
saxophonist
scaffolding
scalariform
scalearmour
scaleinsect
scalpriform
scarabaeoid
scaremonger
scattergood
scenography
sceptically
schismatise
schistosity
schistosome
schizanthus
scholarship
scholiastic
schoolboard
schoolchild
schoolhouse
schottische
schwarmerei
scientistic
scientology
scintillant
scintillate
scissorbill
scissortail
scleroderma
sclerometer
sclerophyll
sclerotitis
scopolamine
scorchingly
scoriaceous
scorpionfly
ScotchIrish
Scotchwoman
scoundrelly
scoutmaster
scragginess
scrappiness
scratchwork
screamingly
screwdriver
scribacious
scrimpiness
scriptorial
scriptorium
scruffiness
scrumptious
scrutiniser
sculduddery
sculduggery
scuppernong
scurvygrass
scuttlebutt
scyphistoma
searchingly
searchlight
seasickness
seborrhoeic
secondarily
secondclass
secondrater
secondsight
secretarial
secretariat
secretively
sectionally
sedentarily
sedimentary
seditionary
seditiously
seductively
segmentally
segregation
segregative
seigneurial
seigniorage
seigniorial
seismically
seismograph
seismometer
seismometry
seismoscope
selaginella
selectively
selectivity
selfassured
selfcentred
selfclosing
selfcocking
selfcommand
selfconceit
selfcontent
selfcontrol
selfcreated
selfculture
selfdefence
selfdenying
selfdespair
selfdevoted
selfdisplay
selfelected
selfevident
selffeeding
selffeeling
selffertile
selfimposed
selfinduced
selfinvited
selfishness
selflimited
selfloading
selflocking
selfmastery
selfopinion
selfpitying
selfraising
selfreliant
selfreproof
selfrespect
selfsealing
selfseeking
selfservice
selfserving
selfstarter
selfsterile
selfsupport
selftorture
selfwinding
selfworship
semanticist
semasiology
semeiotical
semidiurnal
semiellipse
semimonthly
semipalmate
semiskilled
semitrailer
sempiternal
senatorship
sensational
senselessly
sensibility
sensitively
sensitivity
sensorially
sententious
sentimental
sentinelled
Septembrist
septenarius
septentrion
septicaemia
septicaemic
septiferous
septifragal
sequestrate
serendipity
sericulture
serigrapher
seriousness
serological
serpiginous
serrulation
sertularian
serviceable
serviceably
servicebook
serviceline
seventeenth
seventyfold
severalfold
sexagesimal
sexlessness
sexological
sextodecimo
shacklebolt
shacklebone
shadowgraph
shadowiness
Shaksperean
Shaksperian
shallowness
shamanistic
shamelessly
shapeliness
shareholder
sharepusher
sharpwitted
sheathknife
sheepfarmer
sheepmaster
sheetanchor
shellacking
shelljacket
shelterbelt
shelterless
shepherdess
sheriffalty
sheriffship
shiftlessly
shipbreaker
shipbuilder
shirtsleeve
shockheaded
shocktroops
shoeleather
shoplifting
shopsteward
shortchange
shortcoming
shorthanded
shortspoken
shortwinded
shoulderbag
shoulderpad
shovelboard
showerproof
showjumping
showmanship
showstopper
shrinkingly
shrinkproof
shrivelling
shrubbiness
shutterless
shuttlecock
sickbenefit
sickeningly

sickishness
sideslipped
sidestepped
sidewheeler
sightlessly
sightliness
sightreader
sightscreen
sightseeing
sightworthy
sigmoidally
signifiable
significant
signpainter
sillimanite
silveriness
silverplate
silverpoint
silversmith
silverstick
simperingly
simpliciter
sincereness
sinfonietta
singlestick
singletrack
singularise
singularity
sinistrally
sinistrorse
sinlessness
sinological
sinuousness
sittingroom
situational
sizableness
skatingrink
skeletonise
sketchiness
skilfulness
skulduddery
skulduggery
slaughterer
slavedriver
slaveholder
slavemarket
slavishness
Slavonicise
sleepingbag
sleepingcar
sleeplessly
sleepwalker
sleeveboard
slenderness
sleuthhound
slickenside
slightingly
slotmachine
smallholder
smallminded
smilelessly
smithereens
smithsonite
smokescreen
smokingroom
smoothfaced
smorgasbord
snatchblock
snickersnee
snowbunting
snowgoggles
snowleopard
soapboiling
soberminded
sociability
socialistic
Socinianism
sociologist
sociometric
sociopathic
sockdolager
sockdologen
softhearted
softshelled
solanaceous
soldierlike
soldiership
solifluxion
soliloquise
soliloquist
solipsistic
solmisation
solutionist
solvability
somatically
somatogenic
somatologic
somatoplasm
somatotonia
somatotonic
somewhither
somnambular
somniculous
somniferous
somnolently
songfulness
songsparrow
sonofabitch
sophistical
Soroptimist
sorrowfully
soteriology
sottishness
soulfulness
soundlessly
soupkitchen
southeaster
Southernism
southwester
sovereignly
sovereignty
spaceflight
spaceheater
spacesaving
sparingness
sparrowbill
sparrowhawk
spasmodical
spastically
spathaceous
spatterdash
speakership
specifiable
specificity
spectacular
spectatress
spectrality
spectrogram
spectrology
speculation
speculative
speechifier
speedometer
spelaeology
spellbinder
spendthrift
spermaphyte
spermatozoa
spermicidal
spessartite
sphaeridium
sphagnology
spherically
spherometer
spherulitic
sphincteral
sphincteric
sphygmogram
spifflicate
spindlelegs
spindletree
spinelessly
spiniferous
Spinozistic
spinsterish
spiraculate
spiritistic
spiritlevel
spiritually
spiritualty
spirituelle
spirochaete
spirochetal
spirometric
splashboard
splayfooted
splendorous
splenectomy
splenetical
spokeswoman
spondulicks
spondylitis
spongecloth
sponsorship
spontaneity
spontaneous
sporogenous
sporogonium
sporophytic
sportswoman
sporulation
spreadeagle
springboard
springclean
springhouse
springiness
squalidness
squarebuilt
squarsonage
squashiness
squeakiness
squeamishly
squintingly
squirearchy
stadtholder
stagemanage
stagestruck
stagflation
stainlessly
staircarpet
stakeholder
stalactitic
stalagmitic
stallholder
stampoffice
standardise
standoffish
standpatter
starchiness
starcrossed
starstudded
startlingly
stateliness
statesmanly
statistical
statutebook
statutorily
staunchless
staunchness
staurolitic
steadfastly
steamboiler
steamroller
steatopygia
steelworker
steeplebush
steeplejack
steerageway
steganogram
stegosaurus
stellionate
stencilling
stenochromy
stenography
stenotypist
stepbrother
stephanotis
stereograph
stereometry
stereophony
stereoscope
stereoscopy
stereotyped
stereotyper
stereotypic
sternsheets
sternutator
stethoscope
stethoscopy
stevengraph
stewardship
stichometry
stickinsect
stickleback
stiffnecked
stiflejoint
stiltedness
stimulation
stimulative
stipendiary
stipulation
stipulatory
stirrupbone
stirruppump
stockbroker
stockholder
stockinette
stockjobber
stockmarket
stocktaking
stoicalness
stomachache
stomachpump
stomatology
stonecurlew
stonecutter
stoneground
stonemarten
stonewaller
stoolpigeon
storekeeper
stormcentre
stormtroops
storyteller
Stradivarii
straightcut
straightish
straightway
straitlaced
stramineous
strangeness
strangulate
straphanger
strategical
stratocracy
streakiness
streetlight
strenuosity
strenuously
stretchable
stridulator
strikebound
stringboard
stringently
stringiness
stringpiece
stringybark
stroboscope
strongpoint
studentship
studiedness
stumblingly
stuntedness
stylisation
stylishness
stylography
stylopodium
suasiveness
subaerially
subarration
subaudition
subaxillary
subbasement
subcategory
subclinical
subcontract
subcontrary
subcortical
subcritical
subcultural
subdivision
subdominant
subjugation
subjunctive
sublimation
sublimeness
sublittoral
submarginal
submergence
submersible
submissible
submultiple
subordinate
subornation
subregional
subrogation
subscapular
subsequence
subservient
subsistence
subspecific
substandard
substantial
substantive
substituent
subsumption
subsumptive
subterminal
subtraction
subtractive
subtropical
subumbrella
suburbanise
suburbanite
succedaneum
succourless
succulently
suckingfish
sufficiency
suffixation
suffocation
suffocative
suffragette
suffumigate
sugarcoated
suggestible
suitability
sulphureous
sulphurwort
summariness
summational
summerhouse
summersault
sumptuosity
sumptuously
sunlessness
superabound
supercharge
superfamily
superficial
superficies
superfluity
superfluous
superheater
superimpose
superinduce
superintend
superioress
superiority
superjacent
superlative
superlunary
supermarket
supernatant
supernormal
superscribe
superscript
supersedeas
supersedure
superstrata
supersubtle
supertanker
supervision
supervisory
suppliantly
supportable
supportably
supposition
suppositive
suppository
suppression
suppressive
suppuration
suppurative
supremacist
supremeness
surbasement
surfboarder
surficially
surgeonfish
surpassable
surrebuttal
surrebutter
surrogation
surveillant
susceptible
susceptibly
suspenseful
suspensible
suspiration
sustainable
sustainment
susurration
swallowable
swallowdive
swallowhole
swallowtail
swallowwort
swarthiness
sweepstakes
swellheaded
swiftfooted
swimbladder
swingletree
swinishness
switchblade
switchboard
swordbearer
sybaritical
sycophantic
sycophantry
syllabarium
syllabicity
syllogistic

symbolistic
symmetrical
sympathetic
sympathiser
sympetalous
symphonious
symposiarch
symptomatic
synagogical
synchromesh
synchronise
synchronism
synchronous
synchrotron
syncopation
syndesmosis
syndicalism
syndicalist
syndication
synergistic
synonymical
syntactical
synthesiser
synthetical
syssarcosis
systematics
systematise
systematism
systematist
tabefaction
tabernacled
tabletennis
tacheometer
tachycardia
tachygraphy
taciturnity
tagliatelle
tagliatelli
talebearing
talentscout
talkatively
tameability
tangibility
tankfarming
tantalising
tapemachine
tapemeasure
taratantara
tarnishable
tarradiddle
tastelessly
tautologise
tautologism
tautologous
tautomerism
tautonymous
taxidermist
taxonomical
teachership
tearfulness
tearstained
teaspoonful
technically
technocracy
technologic
tediousness
teenybopper
teeterboard
teetotalism
teetotaller
tegumentary
teknonymous
telegrammic
telegrapher
telegraphic
telekinesis
telekinetic
teleologism
teleologist
telepathise
telepathist
telephonist
teleprinter
temerarious
temperament
temperately
temperative
temperature
tempestuous
temporality
temporarily
tenableness
tenaciously
tendencious
tendentious
tenementary
tensibility
tentaculate
tentatively
tenterhooks
tentpegging
tenuousness
tephromancy
teratogenic
teratologic
termagantly
termination
terminative
terminology
termitarium
terraqueous
terrestrial
terricolous
terrigenous
territorial
tessellated
testability
testatrices
testimonial
tetanically
tetracyclic
tetradactyl
tetrahedral
tetrahedron
tetramerous
tetrapodous
tetrarchate
tetravalent
Teutonicism
textureless
thalidomide
thanatology
thanklessly
thanksgiver
thankworthy
thaumatrope
thaumaturge
thaumaturgy
theatregoer
theatricals
thenceforth
theobromine
theocentric
theodolitic
theological
theorematic
theoretical
theosophist
therapeutic
thereabouts
theretofore
therewithal
thermically
thermionics
thermoduric
thermograph
thermolysis
thermolytic
thermometer
thermometry
thermophile
thermoscope
thermotaxis
thickheaded
thickwitted
thimbleweed
thingumabob
thingumajig
thinskinned
thirstiness
thistledown
thitherward
thixotropic
thoroughpin
thoroughwax
thoughtless
thrasonical
threadiness
threadpaper
threecolour
threedecker
threehanded
threelegged
threemaster
thriftiness
thrillingly
throatiness
throatlatch
thrombocyte
thunderbird
thunderbolt
thunderclap
thunderhead
thunderless
thunderpeal
thuriferous
thwartships
thyroiditis
tiddlywinks
tightfisted
tightlipped
timebargain
timepleaser
timeserving
timesharing
titanically
Titianesque
titillation
titleholder
tittivation
toastmaster
tobacconist
tobogganing
tobogganist
toffeenosed
togglejoint
tolbutamide
tonsillitis
toothbilled
toothpowder
toothsomely
topdressing
toploftical
topographer
topographic
topological
torchbearer
torchsinger
torticollis
torturously
totalisator
totteringly
touchtyping
toughminded
tourbillion
townspeople
toxicomania
toxophilite
trabeculate
tracasserie
tracelessly
tracheotomy
trackwalker
traditional
traducement
trafficator
trafficking
trafficless
tragedienne
tragicomedy
trailblazer
trainbearer
trammelling
transaction
transalpine
transceiver
transcriber
transection
transferred
transferrer
transfigure
transfinite
transfixion
transformer
transfusion
transhumant
transiently
transilient
translation
translocate
translucent
translunary
transmarine
transmittal
transmitted
transmitter
transpadane
transparent
transpierce
transponder
transporter
transsexual
transuranic
transversal
trapeziform
trapezoidal
Trappistine
traversable
treacherous
treacliness
treasonable
treasonably
treecreeper
trelliswork
tremblement
tremblingly
tremulously
trenchantly
trencherman
trendsetter
trepanation
trepidation
trestletree
trestlework
triadically
triangulate
tribulation
tribuneship
tribunicial
tribunitial
tributarily
trichinosis
trichomonad
tricksiness
tricoloured
triennially
triggerfish
trimestrial
trimorphism
trimorphous
Trinitarian
tripetalous
triphibious
triphyllous
triquetrous
tristichous
trisyllabic
trisyllable
tritagonist
tritheistic
trituration
triumvirate
trivialness
troglodytic
trophoblast
troposphere
trothplight
troublesome
troublously
trouserless
trousersuit
truculently
truehearted
trundletail
trustbuster
trusteeship
trustworthy
tryingplane
trypanosome
tryptophane
tuberculate
tuberculise
tuberculose
tuberculous
tufthunting
tumbledrier
tumefaction
tunableness
tunefulness
turbination
turbulently
turgescence
turtleshell
tuttifrutti
twelvemonth
twelvepenny
typecasting
typefounder
typefoundry
typesetting
typewritten
typicalness
typographer
typographic
typological
tyrannicide
tyrannosaur
tyrannously
ulotrichous
ultramarine
ultramodern
ultrasonics
ultraviolet
unaccounted
unadvisedly
unalterable
unambiguous
unanimously
unappealing
unashamedly
unassertive
unavailable
unavoidable
unavoidably
unawareness
unbeknownst
unbelieving
unbendingly
unbeseeming
unboundedly
unbreakable
uncanniness
uncanonical
uncatchable
unceasingly
uncertainly
uncertainty
unchristian
uncivilised
uncleanness
unclimbable
uncluttered
uncommitted
unconcealed
unconcerned
uncongenial
unconnected
unconscious
uncontested
uncountable
uncouthness
uncrushable
underbidder
undercharge
underexpose
underground
undergrowth
underhanded
undermanned
underpinned
underseller
undersigned
understated
undertaking
undertenant
undervaluer
underweight
underwriter
undeserving
undesirable
undeveloped
undisguised
undisturbed
undoubtedly
undutifully
unemotional
unendurable
unendurably
unequivocal
unessential
unexploited
unexpressed
unfailingly
unfaltering
unfashioned
unfeelingly
unfeignedly
unflappable
unflinching
unforgiving
unfortunate
unfurnished
ungetatable
ungodliness
unguardedly
unguiculate
unhappiness
unhealthily
unhelpfully
unicellular
unicoloured
unification
uniformness
unigeniture

unimportant
uninhabited
uninhibited
uninucleate
unipersonal
unipolarity
unisexually
universally
unkennelled
unlimitedly
unmanliness
unmatchable
unmeaningly
unmemorable
unmemorably
unmitigated
unnaturally
unnecessary
unnervingly
unobtrusive
unorganized
unorthodoxy
unpalatable
unpolitical
unpossessed
unprintable
unpromising
unqualified
unquietness
unrealistic
unreasoning
unrelenting
unremitting
unrighteous
unsaturated
unselective
unshockable
unshrinking
unskilfully
unsmilingly
unsolicited
unsoundness
unsparingly
unspeakable
unspeakably
unstoppable
unteachable
unthinkable
unthinkably
untouchable
unusualness
unutterable
unutterably
unvarnished
unwarranted
unweetingly
unwholesome
unwillingly
unwinkingly
unwittingly
Upanishadic
upholsterer
uprightness
uranography
urochordate
urticaceous
urticarious
uselessness
utilisation
utilitarian
vacationist
vaccination
vacillation
vacuolation
vacuousness
vagabondage
vagabondise
vagabondish
vagabondism
vagariously
valediction
valedictory
valiantness
valleculate
valuational
vaporimeter
vaporisable
variability
variational
variegation
variousness
varnishtree
varsovienne
vascularise
vascularity
vasculiform
vasectomise
vasodilator
vasopressin
vasopressor
vaticinator
vehmgericht
velvetiness
venatically
vendibility
venereology
venesection
venisection
ventilation
ventilative
ventricular
ventriculus
ventriloquy
venturesome
venturously
veraciously
verbalistic
verboseness
verdantique
veridically
verisimilar
vermiculate
vermiculite
vermination
verminously
versatilely
versatility
verticality
vertiginous
vesicularly
vespertinal
vestigially
vestryclerk
vesuvianite
vexatiously
vexillology
vibratility
vibrational
vicariously
viceadmiral
vicegerency
viceregally
viceroyalty
viceroyship
vichyssoise
viciousness
vicissitude
victualless
victualling
vinaigrette
vincibility
vindication
vindicative
vindicatory
vinedresser
viniculture
violoncello
viridescent
virilescent
virological
viscountess
viscousness
visibleness
viticulture
vitrescence
vitrifiable
vituperator
vivaciously
vivisection
vociferance
vociferator
voguishness
voicelessly
volcanicity
volcanology
volitionary
volkslieder
voltametric
volubleness
volumometer
voluntarily
voluntarism
voluntarist
voodooistic
voortrekker
voraciously
vortiginous
vulcanicity
vulcanology
waggishness
wainscoting
wainscotted
waitinglist
waitingroom
wakefulness
wappenschaw
wapperjawed
warmblooded
warmhearted
warrantable
warrantably
washability
washerwoman
washleather
waspishness
waspwaisted
wastebasket
watchmaking
waterbottle
watercolour
watercooled
watercooler
watercourse
waterlogged
waterskiing
waywardness
weakhearted
wealthiness
wearilessly
wearisomely
weathercock
weatherwise
weatherworn
wedgeshaped
wedgetailed
weenybopper
weighbridge
weightiness
Weismannism
welcomeness
welladvised
wellbeloved
welldefined
wellfounded
wellgroomed
wellmeaning
wellordered
wellrounded
wellwishing
weltschmerz
Wensleydale
Wesleyanism
westernmost
Westminster
wheelbarrow
wheelwright
whereabouts
wheresoever
wherewithal
whichsoever
whiffletree
whigmaleery
whimsically
whippletree
whistlestop
Whitechapel
whitecollar
whiteheaded
whitethroat
whitewasher
whitherward
whitishness
whitleather
Whitsuntide
wholesomely
wholesouled
whoremaster
whoremonger
whosesoever
widdershins
widowerhood
wildcatting
wildfowling
willingness
windcheater
windlestraw
winegrowing
winetasting
winningness
winningpost
winsomeness
winterberry
wintergreen
wirenetting
wirepulling
wiretapping
wisecracker
wishfulness
wistfulness
witchdoctor
witchhunter
witenagemot
witheringly
withershins
witlessness
wolfwhistle
womanliness
wonderfully
woodcarving
woodcutting
workability
workmanlike
workmanship
worldbeater
worldliness
worldlywise
worrisomely
worshipable
worshipless
worshipping
worthlessly
wreckmaster
wrongheaded
xanthochroi
xanthophyll
xenophilous
xeranthemum
xerophilous
xylocarpous
xylographer
xylographic
xylophagous
xylophonist
yacketyyack
yellowbelly
Yugoslavian
zealousness
zestfulness
zincography
zoantharian
zoographist
zoomorphism
zooplankton
zootechnics
Zoroastrian
zygomorphic

---

babysitting
bacchanalia
bacciferous
bacilliform
backbencher
backcountry
bactericide
balefulness
ballbearing
balletomane
balmcricket
BaltoSlavic
bandylegged
banteringly
baptismally
barbarously
barbastelle
barbiturate
barefacedly
barleybroth
barnstormer
barquentine
barrelhouse
barrelorgan
bashfulness
bashibazouk
basipetally
basketchair
bassethound
bathingsuit
batholithic
bathymetric
bathyscaphe
bathysphere
battledress
battlefield
cabbagepalm
cabbagerose
cabbagetree
cabbageworm
cabbalistic
cacographic
cacophonous
caddishness
calceolaria
calcicolous
calciferous
calcifugous
calcination
calculating
calculation
calculative
calefacient
calefactory
calendrical
calibration
californium
calisthenic
calligraphy
callousness
calorimeter
calorimetry
calumniator
Calvinistic
calyptrogen
camaraderie
campanology
campanulate
campmeeting
canalicular
canaliculus
cancellated
candelabrum
candescence
candidature
candleberry
candlelight
candlepower
candlestick
cannibalise
cannibalism
canonically
cantharides
cantharidic
capableness
capaciously
capacitance
capillarity
captainship
captionless
captivation
carabiniere
carabinieri
caravanning
caravansary
carbocyclic
carbonation
carbuncular
carburetion
carburetted
carburetter
carburettor
carcinomata
cardinalate
cardiograph
cardsharper
carefulness
caressingly
caricatural
carminative
carnivorous
Carolingian
carpetsnake
carrageenan
carrageenin
carriageway
cartography
carunculate
carvelbuilt
caryopsides
cassiterite
castellated
castigation
casuistical
catachreses
catachresis
cataclysmic
catadromous
cataplectic
catastrophe
catchphrase
catechismal
catechistic
categorical
catercousin
caterpillar
catheterise

catholicise
Catholicism
catholicity
catswhisker
cauliflower
causatively
caustically
cavalierism
cavedweller
cavernously
dactylogram
dactylology
daisycutter
dangerously
dauntlessly
earnestness
earpiercing
earthcloset
earthenware
earthliness
easternmost
fabrication
facelifting
facetiously
facsimilist
factfinding
factionally
factualness
facultative
faddishness
fairweather
faithhealer
faithlessly
faithworthy
fallibility
Falstaffian
falteringly
familiarise
familiarity
fanatically
fanfaronade
fantastical
farawayness
farcicality
farinaceous
farraginous
farreaching
farthermost
farthingale
fasciaboard
fasciculate
fascinating
fascination
fashionable
fashionably
fatefulness
fatiguingly
fatuousness
faultfinder
faultlessly
favouritism
gafftopsail
gainfulness
gallantness
gallbladder
galleyslave
Gallicanism
gallimaufry
Gallophobia
gallowsbird
gallowstree
gametangium
gametophyte
gamogenesis
gangsterism
gardemanger
garnishment
garrulously
gartersnake
gaseousness
gasfittings
gastrectomy
gastronomic
gastroscope
gatecrasher
haberdasher
habiliments
habituation
haematocele
haematocrit
haematology
haemocyanin
haemoglobin
haemophilia
haemophilic
haemoptysis
haemorrhage
haemorrhoid
haemostasis
haemostatic
haggadistic
haggardness
Hagiographa
hagiography
hagiologist
hagioscopic
hairbreadth
hairdresser
hairraising
hairstyling
hairstylist
hairtrigger
halfbinding
halfblooded
halfhearted
halfholiday
halflanding
halfmeasure
hallucinate
halophilous
halterbreak
Hamiltonian
handbreadth
handfasting
handgrenade
handicapped
handicapper
handknitted
handpainted
handselling
handwriting
handwritten
handwrought
haphazardly
haplessness
haplography
harbourless
hardhearted
hardhitting
hardmouthed
hardworking
harebrained
harmfulness
harmonistic
harpsichord
harumscarum
harvesthome
hatefulness
haughtiness
haustellate
hazardously
jabberwocky
Jacobinical
Jacobitical
jactitation
Jansenistic
jargonistic
jauntingcar
labefaction
labiodental
laboriously
lachrymator
laciniation
laconically
lacrimation
lacrimatory
lacrimosely
lacrymation
lacrymatory
lacrymosely
lactescence
lactiferous
laicisation
lakedweller
lamellicorn
lamelliform
lamentation
lammergeier
lammergeyer
lamplighter
Lancastrian
lancinating
lancination
landaulette
landgrabber
landgravine
landholding
landingbeam
landinggear
landlordism
languidness
larcenously
largeminded
laryngology
laryngotomy
lastingness
latchstring
lateritious
latifundium
latitudinal
latticework
laudability
laughinggas
launderette
laurustinus
lawlessness
lawmerchant
machicolate
machination
machinemade
mackerelsky
macrobiotic
macrocosmic
macrogamete
macroscopic
maddeningly
madreporite
madrigalian
madrigalist
magazinegun
magdalenian
magisterial
magisterium
magistratic
Maglemosian
magnanimity
magnanimous
magnificent
maidservant
mailcarrier
maintenance
maintopmast
maintopsail
maisonnette
makebelieve
maladaptive
maladjusted
maladroitly
malapropism
malariology
malediction
maledictory
malefaction
maleficence
malevolence
malfeasance
malfunction
maliciously
malignantly
malposition
malpractice
mammalogist
managership
mandarinate
mandibulate
mandolinist
manducation
manducatory
Manichaeism
manifestant
manifestoes
manipulable
manipulator
manneristic
mannishness
mansardroof
mantelpiece
mantelshelf
mantuamaker
manufactory
manufacture
manumission
manumitting
marcescence
marcescible
marchioness
marconigram
marginalise
marginality
margraviate
marketplace
marketvalue
marlinspike
marquessate
marqueterie
marquisette
marriagebed
marshalling
marshalship
marshmallow
martyrology
masculinely
masculinise
masculinity
masochistic
masquerader
massiveness
massproduce
masterfully
masterpiece
mastication
masticatory
mastodontic
mastoiditis
matchlessly
matchmaking
materialise
materialism
materialist
materiality
mathematics
matriarchal
matriculate
matrilineal
matrilinear
matrimonial
mawkishness
maxillipede
nailvarnish
namecalling
namedropper
naphthalene
narcoleptic
narratively
nasofrontal
nationalise
nationalism
nationalist
nationality
nationstate
naturalness
naturopathy
naughtiness
oarsmanship
pachydermal
pacifically
pacificator
packingcase
paddleboard
paddlewheel
paederastic
paediatrics
paediatrist
paedophilia
painfulness
painkilling
painstaking
Palaearctic
palaeotypic
Palestinian
palindromic
palmcabbage
palpability
palpitation
palsgravine
pamphleteer
pandemonium
panegyrical
Panglossian
panhellenic
panicmonger
pantalettes
pantheistic
pantomimist
pantothenic
paperhanger
papermaking
paperweight
papiermache
papyraceous
parachutist
paradisical
paradoxical
paragrapher
paragraphic
paraldehyde
paraleipsis
parallactic
parallelism
parallelled
paramedical
parametrise
paramoecium
paramorphic
paramountcy
paramountly
paraphraser
paraplectic
paraselenae
parasitical
parasitosis
parathyroid
paratrooper
paratyphoid
parentheses
parenthesis
parenthetic
parheliacal
parishioner
parochially
paronomasia
participant
participate
participial
particulate
partitioned
partitioner
partitively
partnership
parturition
passacaglia
passeriform
passibility
Passiontide
passivation
passiveness
pasteuriser
pastoralism
pastoralist
pastureland
patelliform
paternalism
paternalist
paternoster
pathologist
patriarchal
patrilineal
patrimonial
patristical
patronising
patternshop
paunchiness
pawnbroking
Rabelaisian
racemeeting
racketpress
radicalness
radioactive
radiocarbon
radiography
radiolarian
radiologist
radiometric
radiophonic
raffishness
rallentando
rancorously
rangefinder
rapaciously
rapscallion
rapturously
rarefaction
rarefactive
Rastafarian
ratatouille
rateability
ratiocinate
rationalise
rationalism
rationalist
rationality
rattlebrain
rattlepated
rattlesnake
raucousness
raunchiness
ravishingly
Sabbatarian
sacculation
sacramental
sacrificial
saddlecloth
saddlehorse
Sadduceeism

safebreaker
safeconduct
safecracker
safekeeping
safetyvalve
sagaciously
Sagittarius
saintliness
saintpaulia
salaciously
saleability
salesladies
salinometer
salmonberry
salpingitis
saltatorial
saltimbanco
salvageable
salvational
sandbagging
sandskipper
sanguinaria
sanguineous
sansculotte
Sanskritist
saplessness
saponaceous
saprobiotic
saprogenous
saprophytic
sarcomatous
sarcophagus
sartorially
satanically
satiability
satinstitch
satirically
satisfiable
saturnalian
saturninely
sauropodous
sausagemeat
savouriness
saxophonist
tabefaction
tabernacled
tabletennis
tacheometer
tachycardia
tachygraphy
taciturnity
tagliatelle
tagliatelli
talebearing
talentscout
talkatively
tameability
tangibility
tankfarming
tantalising
tapemachine
tapemeasure
taratantara
tarnishable
tarradiddle
tastelessly
tautologise
tautologism
tautologous
tautomerism
tautonymous
taxidermist
taxonomical
vacationist
vaccination
vacillation
vacuolation
vacuousness
vagabondage
vagabondise
vagabondish
vagabondism
vagariously
valediction
valedictory
valiantness
valleculate
valuational
vaporimeter
vaporisable
variability
variational
variegation
variousness
varnishtree
varsovienne
vascularise
vascularity
vasculiform
vasectomise
vasodilator
vasopressin
vasopressor
vaticinator
waggishness
wainscoting
wainscotted
waitinglist
waitingroom
wakefulness
wappenschaw
wapperjawed
warmblooded
warmhearted
warrantable
warrantably
washability
washerwoman
washleather
waspishness
waspwaisted
wastebasket
watchmaking
waterbottle
watercolour
watercooled
watercooler
watercourse
waterlogged
waterskiing
waywardness
xanthochroi
xanthophyll
yacketyyack
abandonment
Abbevillian
abbreviator
abdominally
abecedarian
abhorrently
abiogeneses
abiogenesis
abiogenetic
abiological
abiotically
ablutionary
abnormality
abolishable
abolishment
abomination
abortionist
aboutsledge
aboveground
abracadabra
abranchiate
abridgement
absenteeism
absorbingly
absorptance
abstentious
abstinently
abstraction
abstractive
abstriction
abusiveness
ebulliently
obfuscation
obfuscatory
objectively
objectivism
objectivist
objectivity
objurgation
objurgatory
obliqueness
obliviously
obmutescent
obnoxiously
obscuration
obscureness
obsecration
observantly
observation
observatory
observingly
obsessional
obsessively
obsolescent
obstetrical
obstinately
obstruction
obstructive
obtestation
obtrusively
obviousness
academicals
academician
academicism
acarpellous
acatalectic
acaulescent
accelerando
accelerator
accentually
acceptation
acceptingly
accessorial
accessorise
accipitrine
acclamation
acclamatory
acclimation
acclimatise
acclivitous
accommodate
accompanist
accordantly
accordingly
accoucheuse
accountable
accountably
accountancy
accrescence
acculturate
accumulator
accusatival
acetylation
achievement
achondritic
achromatise
achromatism
acidifiable
acidophilic
acidulation
acinaciform
acknowledge
acoustician
acquiescent
acquirement
acquisition
acquisitive
acquittance
acriflavine
acrimonious
acropetally
actinometer
actinomyces
actinomycin
acumination
acupuncture
echosounder
eclecticism
econometric
ectoblastic
ectogenesis
ectogenetic
ectomorphic
ectoplasmic
ectotrophic
ecumenicism
ecumenicity
ichnography
ichthyology
ichthyornis
ichthyosaur
iconography
iconostases
iconostasis
icosahedral
icosahedron
McCarthyism
occipitally
occultation
ochlocratic
octachordal
octagonally
octingenary
scaffolding
scalariform
scalearmour
scaleinsect
scalpriform
scarabaeoid
scaremonger
scattergood
scenography
sceptically
schismatise
schistosity
schistosome
schizanthus
scholarship
scholiastic
schoolboard
schoolchild
schoolhouse
schottische
schwarmerei
scientistic
scientology
scintillant
scintillate
scissorbill
scissortail
scleroderma
sclerometer
sclerophyll
sclerotitis
scopolamine
scorchingly
scoriaceous
scorpionfly
ScotchIrish
Scotchwoman
scoundrelly
scoutmaster
scragginess
scrappiness
scratchwork
screamingly
screwdriver
scribacious
scrimpiness
scriptorial
scriptorium
scruffiness
scrumptious
scrutiniser
sculduddery
sculduggery
scuppernong
scurvygrass
scuttlebutt
scyphistoma
adenomatous
adiaphorism
adjectively
adjournment
adjudgement
adjudicator
adminicular
admiralship
adolescence
adoptianism
adoptianist
adoptionism
adoptionist
adulterator
adumbration
adumbrative
advancement
adventuress
adventurism
adventurist
adventurous
adverbially
adversative
adverseness
advertently
advertising
advisedness
edification
edificatory
editorially
educability
educational
identically
ideographic
ideological
idiographic
idiomorphic
idiotically
idolisation
idyllically
odoriferous
odorousness
Aeneolithic
aeolotropic
aerobically
aerobiology
aerodynamic
aerographer
aerological
aeronautics
aeronomical
aerostatics
aerostation
Aesculapian
aesthetical
aestivation
beachcomber
bearbaiting
bearishness
beastliness
beauteously
beautifully
beaverboard
bedevilment
bedizenment
beechmarten
befittingly
beguilement
beguilingly
behavioural
belatedness
bellbottoms
bellfounder
bellheather
bellicosity
belligerent
bellringing
Belorussian
Benedictine
benediction
benedictory
benefaction
beneficence
beneficiary
beneficiate
benevolence
benightedly
benightment
benignantly
bereavement
bergamasque
bergschrund
bersaglieri
bestselling
betweenmaid
betweenness
betweentime
bewhiskered
bewitchment
ceaselessly
celebration
celebratory
celestially
cellularity
cementation
centenarian
centigramme
centreboard
centrepiece
centrifugal
centripetal
cerebration
ceremonious
ceroplastic
certifiable
certifiably
certificate
cesarevitch
cesarewitch
deactivator
deathrattle
debarkation
debauchment
debouchment
decantation
decarbonate
decarbonise
decarburise
deceitfully
deceivingly
decelerator
decemvirate
decennially
deceptively
decerebrate
declamation
declamatory
declaration
declarative
declaratory

declination
declivitous
decollation
decolletage
decolourise
decorticate
decrepitate
decrepitude
decrescendo
decussately
decussation
dedicatedly
deductively
deemphasise
deerstalker
defalcation
defectively
defenceless
defensively
deferential
defibrinate
deficiently
definiendum
deflagrator
defloration
defoliation
deforcement
deformation
defraudment
deglutition
degradation
degradingly
degustation
dehydration
deification
deistically
delectation
deleterious
deliciously
delightedly
delightsome
delineation
delinquency
deliriously
delitescent
deliverable
deliverance
deliveryman
demagnetise
demagogical
demagoguery
demagoguism
demandingly
demarcation
demarkation
demigoddess
democratise
democratism
demographer
demographic
demonolatry
demonstrate
demountable
dendritical
denigration
denigratory
denizenship
denominator
denticulate
dentigerous
denumerable
denunciator
deoxidation
deoxygenate
deoxyribose
depauperate
depauperise
dependently
deploringly
depopulator
deportation
depravation
depravement
deprecation
deprecative
deprecatory
depreciator
depredation
depredatory
depressible
deprivation
depthcharge
derangement
dereliction
dermatology
desalinator
descendable
descendible
describable
description
descriptive
desecration
desegregate
desensitise
deservingly
desexualise
desiccation
desiccative
desideratum
designation
desperadoes
desperately
desperation
despoilment
despondence
despondency
destination
destitution
destruction
destructive
desultorily
deteriorate
determinacy
determinant
determinate
determinism
determinist
detestation
detrainment
detribalise
detrimental
deuteration
deuterogamy
Deuteronomy
devaluation
devastation
developable
development
deviousness
devotedness
dexiotropic
dexterously
fearfulness
feasibility
featheredge
featherhead
featherless
featureless
fecundation
feelingness
feldspathic
feloniously
felspathoid
fenestrated
fermentable
ferociously
ferriferous
ferruginous
festinately
festschrift
fetichistic
fetishistic
feudalistic
geanticline
gegenschein
gemmiferous
gemmiparous
gemmologist
gemmulation
gendarmerie
genealogise
genealogist
generaliser
generalship
generically
genetically
geniculated
genitivally
genteelness
gentianella
gentilitial
gentlemanly
gentlewoman
genuflexion
genuineness
geochemical
geomagnetic
geometrical
geophysical
geopolitics
geostrophic
geosyncline
geotectonic
Germanophil
germination
germinative
gerontology
gerrymander
gestatorial
gesticulate
gettogether
headborough
headhunting
healthfully
healthiness
heartbroken
hearthstone
heartlessly
heartsblood
heartstring
heavenwards
heavyfooted
heavyhanded
heavyweight
hebephrenia
hebephrenic
Hebraically
hedgehopped
hedgepriest
hedgeschool
heedfulness
Hegelianism
heinousness
heldentenor
heliochrome
heliography
heliometric
heliotropic
helleborine
Hellenistic
hellishness
helminthoid
helpfulness
hemeralopia
hemianopsia
hemimorphic
hemipterous
hemispheric
hepatectomy
Hepplewhite
heptamerous
heptarchist
Heracleidan
herbivorous
hereditable
hereinafter
heresiology
heretically
hermeneutic
hermeticism
heroworship
herpetology
herringbone
herringgull
hesperidium
heteroclite
heteroecism
heterograft
heterophony
heteroploid
heteropolar
heterospory
heterotaxis
heterotroph
heterotypic
hexadecimal
hexametrist
jealousness
jerrymander
leapfrogged
learnedness
leaseholder
leatherback
leatherhead
leatherneck
leavetaking
lecherously
lectureship
legerdemain
legionnaire
legislation
legislative
legislature
Leibnitzian
lengthiness
lentiginous
lepidoptera
leprosarium
leptodactyl
lesemajesty
letterpress
levelheaded
leviratical
meadowgrass
meadowsweet
meaningless
measureless
measurement
mechanician
mechanistic
mediaevally
mediastinal
mediastinum
mediateness
mediatorial
mediatrices
medicinable
medicinally
medicolegal
medievalism
medievalist
mediumistic
megalomania
megalopolis
megatherium
melancholia
melancholic
melanochroi
melanophore
melioration
meliorative
meliphagous
melliferous
mellifluent
mellifluous
melodiously
membraneous
memorabilia
memorialise
memorialist
mendelevium
meningocele
menservants
mensuration
mentholated
mentionable
meprobamate
mercenarily
merchandise
merchantman
mercilessly
mercurially
meritocracy
meritorious
meroblastic
merogenesis
Merovingian
merryandrew
merrymaking
mesalliance
mesoblastic
mesomorphic
messiahship
metacentric
metachrosis
metagenesis
metagenetic
metalloidal
metallurgic
metalworker
metamorphic
metaphysics
metaplastic
metapsychic
metasomatic
metastasise
meteoritics
meteoroidal
meteorology
Methodistic
methodology
methylamine
methylation
metonymical
metoposcopy
metrication
Neanderthal
nearsighted
necessarian
necessarily
necessitate
necessitous
neckerchief
necrobiosis
necrologist
necromancer
necromantic
necrophilia
necrophilic
necropoleis
needfulness
needlecraft
needlepoint
needlewoman
nefariously
negationist
negligently
negotiation
negotiatory
negotiatrix
negrophobia
neighbourly
neologistic
Neoplatonic
Neotropical
nephelinite
nephrectomy
nervelessly
nervousness
netherworld
nettlecloth
neurologist
neuropathic
neuroticism
neurotropic
neutraliser
oecological
oecumenical
oenological
oenophilist
oesophageal
oestrogenic
peacemaking
pearlescent
pearlfisher
peccability
peccadillos
pectination
peculiarity
pecuniarily
pedagogical
pedestalled
pedicellate
pediculosis
pedological
pedunculate
peevishness
Pelagianism
pelargonium
pellucidity
pendulously
penetrating
penetration
penetrative
penicillate
penicillium
peninsulate
penitential
pennyweight
penological
pensionable
pensionless
pensiveness
pentadactyl
pentagynous
pentahedron
pentamerous
pentandrous
pentathlete
pentavalent
pentazocine
Pentecostal
pentlandite
penultimate
penuriously
peptisation
perambulate
perceivable
perceivably
perceptible
perceptibly
perchlorate
percipience
percolation

peregrinate
perennation
perennially
perfectible
perfectness
perforation
perforative
performable
performance
perfunctory
pericardiac
pericardial
pericardium
pericranial
pericranium
perineurium
periodicity
periodontal
periostitis
peripatetic
periphrases
periphrasis
perishables
perishingly
perispermic
peristalith
peristalsis
peristaltic
peristomial
perithecium
peritonitis
permanently
permissible
permissibly
permutation
perpetrator
perpetually
perpetuance
perpetuator
perplexedly
persecution
perseverate
persistence
persistency
personalise
personalism
personalist
personality
personation
personative
personifier
perspective
perspicuity
perspicuous
persuadable
persuasible
pertinacity
pertinently
perturbable
pervasively
pervertedly
pessimistic
pestiferous
pestilently
pestologist
petitionary
petrography
petrologist
petticoated
pettifogger
pettishness
reachmedown
reactionary
reactionist
readability
readywitted
realignment
realisation
realpolitik
reanimation
reapportion
reappraisal
rearadmiral
reassertion
reassurance
reawakening
rebarbative
recalculate
recantation
receptacula
receptively
receptivity
recessional
recessively
reciprocate
reciprocity
reclaimable
reclamation
recognition
recognitive
recognitory
recommender
recommittal
recondition
reconnoitre
reconstruct
recoverable
recriminate
recruitment
rectangular
rectifiable
rectilineal
rectilinear
recumbently
recurrently
redactional
reddishness
redetermine
redirection
rediscovery
redoubtable
redundantly
reduplicate
reedbunting
reeducation
reedwarbler
reemergence
reenactment
reestablish
referential
reflectance
reflexively
reflexology
reformation
reformative
reformatory
refrangible
refreshment
refrigerant
refrigerate
refringency
regardfully
regenerable
regenerator
regimentals
regionalise
regionalism
regionalist
registrable
regretfully
regrettable
regrettably
regurgitate
reification
reincarnate
reinsertion
reinsurance
reintegrate
reintroduce
reiteration
reiterative
rejoicingly
rejuvenator
rejuvenesce
relatedness
relationism
relationist
reliability
religionise
religionism
religionist
religiosity
religiously
reluctantly
reluctation
remembrance
reminiscent
remonstrant
remonstrate
remorseless
remunerator
renaissance
renegotiate
reorientate
repartition
repellantly
repellently
repentantly
repetitious
replaceable
replacement
replenisher
repleteness
repleviable
replication
reportorial
reposefully
representer
repressible
repressibly
reproachful
reprobation
reprobative
reprobatory
reprogramme
reprography
reprovingly
repudiation
repugnantly
repulsively
requirement
requisition
resemblance
resentfully
reservation
residential
resignation
resiliently
resipiscent
resistively
resistivity
resourceful
respectable
respectably
respiration
respiratory
resplendent
respondence
respondency
responsible
responsibly
restatement
restfulness
restitution
restiveness
restoration
restorative
restriction
restrictive
restructure
resuscitate
retaliation
retaliative
retaliatory
retardation
retardative
retardatory
retentively
retentivity
retinacular
retinaculum
retinoscopy
retiredness
retraceable
retractable
retranslate
retribution
retributive
retributory
retrievable
retroaction
retroactive
retrocedent
retroflexed
retrorocket
revaccinate
revaluation
revendicate
reverberant
reverberate
reverential
reversional
reversioner
revisionary
revisionism
revisionist
reviviscent
searchingly
searchlight
seasickness
seborrhoeic
secondarily
secondclass
secondrater
secondsight
secretarial
secretariat
secretively
sectionally
sedentarily
sedimentary
seditionary
seditiously
seductively
segmentally
segregation
segregative
seigneurial
seigniorage
seigniorial
seismically
seismograph
seismometer
seismometry
seismoscope
selaginella
selectively
selectivity
selfassured
selfcentred
selfclosing
selfcocking
selfcommand
selfconceit
selfcontent
selfcontrol
selfcreated
selfculture
selfdefence
selfdenying
selfdespair
selfdevoted
selfdisplay
selfelected
selfevident
selffeeding
selffeeling
selffertile
selfimposed
selfinduced
selfinvited
selfishness
selflimited
selfloading
selflocking
selfmastery
selfopinion
selfpitying
selfraising
selfreliant
selfreproof
selfrespect
selfsealing
selfseeking
selfservice
selfserving
selfstarter
selfsterile
selfsupport
selftorture
selfwinding
selfworship
semanticist
semasiology
semeiotical
semidiurnal
semiellipse
semimonthly
semipalmate
semiskilled
semitrailer
sempiternal
senatorship
sensational
senselessly
sensibility
sensitively
sensitivity
sensorially
sententious
sentimental
sentinelled
Septembrist
septenarius
septentrion
septicaemia
septicaemic
septiferous
septifragal
sequestrate
serendipity
sericulture
serigrapher
seriousness
serological
serpiginous
serrulation
sertularian
serviceable
serviceably
servicebook
serviceline
seventeenth
seventyfold
severalfold
sexagesimal
sexlessness
sexological
sextodecimo
teachership
tearfulness
tearstained
teaspoonful
technically
technocracy
technologic
tediousness
teenybopper
teeterboard
teetotalism
teetotaller
tegumentary
teknonymous
telegrammic
telegrapher
telegraphic
telekinesis
telekinetic
teleologism
teleologist
telepathise
telepathist
telephonist
teleprinter
temerarious
temperament
temperately
temperative
temperature
tempestuous
temporality
temporarily
tenableness
tenaciously
tendencious
tendentious
tenementary
tensibility
tentaculate
tentatively
tenterhooks
tentpegging
tenuousness
tephromancy
teratogenic
teratologic
termagantly
termination
terminative
terminology
termitarium
terraqueous
terrestrial
terricolous
terrigenous
territorial
tessellated
testability
testatrices
testimonial
tetanically
tetracyclic
tetradactyl
tetrahedral
tetrahedron
tetramerous
tetrapodous
tetrarchate
tetravalent
Teutonicism
textureless
vehmgericht
velvetiness
venatically

vendibility
venereology
venesection
venisection
ventilation
ventilative
ventricular
ventriculus
ventriloquy
venturesome
venturously
veraciously
verbalistic
verboseness
verdantique
veridically
verisimilar
vermiculate
vermiculite
vermination
verminously
versatilely
versatility
verticality
vertiginous
vesicularly
vespertinal
vestigially
vestryclerk
vesuvianite
vexatiously
vexillology
weakhearted
wealthiness
wearilessly
wearisomely
weathercock
weatherwise
weatherworn
wedgeshaped
wedgetailed
weenybopper
weighbridge
weightiness
Weismannism
welcomeness
welladvised
wellbeloved
welldefined
wellfounded
wellgroomed
wellmeaning
wellordered
wellrounded
wellwishing
weltschmerz
Wensleydale
Wesleyanism
westernmost
Westminster
xenophilous
xeranthemum
xerophilous
yellowbelly
zealousness
zestfulness
affectation
affectingly
affectional
affectioned
affectively
affectivity
afficionado
affiliation
affirmation
affirmative
affirmatory
affranchise
affrication
affricative
AfroAsiatic
afterburner
aftereffect
effectively
effectually
efficacious
efficiently
effulgently
offenceless
offensively
offhandedly
officialdom
officialese
officialism
officiation
officinally
officiously
agglomerate
agglutinate
aggravation
aggregately
aggregation
aggregative
aggrievedly
agnatically
agnosticism
agonisingly
agonistical
agoraphobia
agoraphobic
agrarianism
agriculture
agrobiology
agrological
agronomical
egalitarian
egotistical
egregiously
ignobleness
ignominious
ahistorical
chaetognath
chafingdish
chainarmour
chainletter
chainsmoker
chainstitch
chalcedonic
challenging
chamaephyte
chamberlain
chambermaid
chameleonic
champertous
chancellery
chancellory
changefully
channelling
chansonnier
chanterelle
chanticleer
chaotically
chaperonage
charcuterie
chargesheet
charismatic
charlatanry
chartaceous
chaulmoogra
cheerleader
cheerlessly
cheesecloth
cheiromancy
chemotactic
chevalglass
chiaroscuro
chickenfeed
chickenwire
chieftaincy
childminder
chimaerical
chinoiserie
Chippendale
chirography
chiropodist
chiropteran
chitterling
chlorophyll
chloroplast
chloroprene
chockablock
choirmaster
chokecherry
cholesterol
choreograph
chorography
Christendom
christening
christiania
Christianly
Christmassy
Christology
chrominance
chromoplast
chromosomal
chronically
chronograph
chronologer
chronologic
chronometer
chronometry
chronoscope
chrysalides
chrysalises
chrysarobin
chrysoberyl
chrysoprase
chucklehead
churchgoing
churchiness
churchwoman
ghastliness
ghostliness
ghostwriter
phagedaenic
phagocytise
phagocytose
phalanstery
phantasiast
phantasmata
pharisaical
phariseeism
pharyngitis
phenologist
philanderer
philatelist
philhellene
philologian
philologist
philosopher
philosophic
phonetician
phonography
phonologist
phosphonium
phosphorate
phosphorism
phosphorite
phosphorous
photoactive
photocopier
photofinish
photography
photometric
photooffset
photoperiod
photophilic
photophobia
photophobic
photosphere
phototactic
phototropic
phrasemaker
phraseogram
phraseology
phthiriasis
phycocyanin
phycologist
phylloclade
phyllotaxis
phylogynist
physicality
physiocracy
physiognomy
physiologic
phytography
phytologist
phytosterol
phytotomist
rhabdomancy
rhapsodical
rheological
rheotropism
rhetorician
rheumaticky
rhinologist
rhinoscopic
rhizanthous
rhizocarpic
rhizomatous
rhombohedra
rhomboideus
rhynchodont
shacklebolt
shacklebone
shadowgraph
shadowiness
Shaksperean
Shaksperian
shallowness
shamanistic
shamelessly
shapeliness
shareholder
sharepusher
sharpwitted
sheathknife
sheepfarmer
sheepmaster
sheetanchor
shellacking
shelljacket
shelterbelt
shelterless
shepherdess
sheriffalty
sheriffship
shiftlessly
shipbreaker
shipbuilder
shirtsleeve
shockheaded
shocktroops
shoeleather
shoplifting
shopsteward
shortchange
shortcoming
shorthanded
shortspoken
shortwinded
shoulderbag
shoulderpad
shovelboard
showerproof
showjumping
showmanship
showstopper
shrinkingly
shrinkproof
shrivelling
shrubbiness
shutterless
shuttlecock
thalidomide
thanatology
thanklessly
thanksgiver
thankworthy
thaumatrope
thaumaturge
thaumaturgy
theatregoer
theatricals
thenceforth
theobromine
theocentric
theodolitic
theological
theorematic
theoretical
theosophist
therapeutic
thereabouts
theretofore
therewithal
thermically
thermionics
thermoduric
thermograph
thermolysis
thermolytic
thermometer
thermometry
thermophile
thermoscope
thermotaxis
thickheaded
thickwitted
thimbleweed
thingumabob
thingumajig
thinskinned
thirstiness
thistledown
thitherward
thixotropic
thoroughpin
thoroughwax
thoughtless
thrasonical
threadiness
threadpaper
threecolour
threedecker
threehanded
threelegged
threemaster
thriftiness
thrillingly
throatiness
throatlatch
thrombocyte
thunderbird
thunderbolt
thunderclap
thunderhead
thunderless
thunderpeal
thuriferous
thwartships
thyroiditis
wheelbarrow
wheelwright
whereabouts
wheresoever
wherewithal
whichsoever
whiffletree
whigmaleery
whimsically
whippletree
whistlestop
Whitechapel
whitecollar
whiteheaded
whitethroat
whitewasher
whitherward
whitishness
whitleather
Whitsuntide
wholesomely
wholesouled
whoremaster
whoremonger
whosesoever
aiguillette
ailurophile
ailurophobe
aimlessness
aircraftman
airlessness
airsickness
bibliolater
bibliolatry
bibliomancy
bibliomania
bibliopegic
bibliophile
bibliophily
bibliopolic
bibliotheca
bicarbonate
bicentenary
bicephalous
bicorporate
bicuspidate
biddability
biedermeier
bifurcation
bilaterally
biliousness
billetsdoux
billionaire
billposting
billsticker
bimetallism
bimetallist
bimillenary
bimillenium
binocularly
biochemical
biocoenoses
biocoenosis
biocoenotic
biofeedback
biometrical
biophysical
bipartition
biquadratic
birdbrained
birdfancier
birdwatcher
bisexuality
bitterapple
bittercress
bittersweet
bivouacking
cicatricial
cinnabarine
cinquecento
circularise
circularity

circulation
circulative
circulatory
circumlunar
circumpolar
circumsolar
circumspect
circumvolve
cisatlantic
citizenship
cityslicker
civilianise
civilisable
diachronism
diacritical
diadelphous
diagnostics
dialectally
dialectical
dialogistic
diamagnetic
diametrical
diamondback
diaphaneity
diaphoresis
diaphoretic
diapophysis
diapositive
diarthrosis
diastematic
diastrophic
diatessaron
dicephalous
dichogamous
dichotomise
dichotomist
dichotomous
dichromatic
dicotyledon
dictatorial
didacticism
differentia
differently
difficultly
diffidently
diffraction
diffuseness
diffusively
digestively
digitigrade
dilapidated
dilapidator
diluvialist
dimensional
dimwittedly
diningtable
dinnerdance
dinnertable
dinnerwagon
dinosaurian
Diophantine
diphtherial
diphtheroid
diphthongal
diphycercal
diplococcus
diplomatise
diplomatist
dipsomaniac
dipterocarp
directional
directivity
directorate
directorial
directrices
disablement
disaccustom
disaffected
disafforest
disannulled
disapproval
disarmament
disarmingly
disassemble
disassembly
disbandment
disbeliever
discalceate
discardable
discernible
discernibly
discernment
discerption
disciplinal
discipliner
discography
discontinue
discordance
discordancy
discotheque
discourtesy
discrepancy
discussable
discussible
disencumber
disentangle
disenthrall
disfunction
disgraceful
disgruntled
disguisedly
disgustedly
disharmonic
dishevelled
dishonestly
dishonourer
disillusion
disinclined
disinfector
disinterest
disinterred
disjunction
disjunctive
disjuncture
dislikeable
dislocation
dislodgment
dismayingly
disobedient
disobliging
disorganise
disparaging
disparately
dispensable
dispersedly
displeasure
disportment
disposition
dispositive
disputation
disquieting
disquietude
disremember
disseminate
disseminule
dissentient
dissepiment
dissertator
dissimilate
dissimulate
dissipation
dissipative
dissociable
dissolutely
dissolution
dissolvable
dissonantly
dissyllable
dissymmetry
distasteful
distempered
distensible
distinction
distinctive
distinguish
distraction
distractive
distressful
distribuend
distributor
distrustful
disturbance
disunionist
dithyrambic
dittography
divergently
diverticula
divestiture
divisionary
divisionism
divorcement
divulgation
divulgement
einsteinium
fiddlestick
fidgetiness
fieldcornet
fieldworker
filamentary
filamentous
filmography
filmsetting
filterpaper
fimbriation
financially
fingerboard
fingerglass
fingerplate
fingerprint
fingerstall
finicalness
FinnoUgrian
firecracker
firefighter
fireraising
firewalking
firewatcher
firmamental
firstfruits
fissionable
fissiparity
fissiparous
giantpowder
gibberellin
gibbousness
gigantesque
gillyflower
gimcrackery
gingerbread
girlishness
hibernacula
hibernation
Hibernicism
hideousness
hierarchism
highbrowism
highfalutin
highpitched
highpowered
highranking
highstepper
highwrought
hilariously
Hindoostani
hippocampus
Hippocratic
hippopotami
hirsuteness
Hispanicise
Hispanicism
Hispanicist
histologist
historiated
historicise
historicism
historicist
historicity
histrionics
histrionism
hitherwards
kickstarter
kilocalorie
kindhearted
kinematical
kinesiology
kinetograph
kinetoscope
kitchenette
kitchensink
kitchenware
libertarian
liberticide
libertinage
libertinism
lichenology
lickerishly
lickspittle
lieutenancy
lifemanship
ligamentary
ligamentous
lightfooted
lighthanded
lightheaded
lightminded
lightsomely
lightweight
lilylivered
limitedness
limitlessly
limnologist
linedrawing
linefishing
linendraper
lineprinter
lingeringly
linguistics
lionhearted
liquefiable
liquescence
liquidambar
liquidation
lissomeness
literalness
lithography
lithophytic
lithosphere
lithotomise
lithotomist
lithotripsy
litigiously
litterateur
lixiviation
Micawberish
Micawberism
micrococcal
micrococcus
microcosmic
microgamete
micrography
microgroove
microlithic
micrometric
Micronesian
microphonic
microphytic
microscopic
microsecond
micturition
middleclass
middlesized
millenarian
milliampere
millionaire
millisecond
mimetically
mindbending
mindblowing
mindfulness
mindreading
mineraliser
minesweeper
miniaturise
miniaturist
ministerial
minnesinger
minuteglass
mirthlessly
misalliance
misanthrope
misanthropy
misbegotten
miscarriage
miscegenate
miscellanea
mischievous
miscibility
misconceive
misconstrue
miscreation
misericorde
miserliness
misestimate
misfeasance
misguidance
misguidedly
misjudgment
mismarriage
misremember
misspelling
mistrustful
mithridatic
mitrailleur
nickelplate
nictitation
nightingale
nightmarish
nightporter
nightwalker
nigrescence
ninnyhammer
nitrogenise
nitrogenous
nittygritty
oilpainting
Pickwickian
pictography
pictorially
picturebook
picturecard
picturegoer
picturesque
pieceworker
pietistical
pigeonchest
piggishness
pigheadedly
pigsticking
pillowfight
pilocarpine
pilotburner
pinkishness
pinnatisect
pipecleaner
piperaceous
pipistrelle
piratically
piscatorial
piscivorous
pitchblende
piteousness
pitifulness
pivotbridge
ribbongrass
ribvaulting
rickettsial
ricochetted
rifacimenti
rifacimento
rightangled
righteously
righthanded
righthander
rightminded
rightwinger
ringstraked
riotousness
ritualistic
sickbenefit
sickeningly
sickishness
sideslipped
sidestepped
sidewheeler
sightlessly
sightliness
sightreader
sightscreen
sightseeing
sightworthy
sigmoidally
signifiable
significant
signpainter
sillimanite
silveriness
silverplate
silverpoint
silversmith
silverstick
simperingly
simpliciter
sincereness
sinfonietta
singlestick
singletrack
singularise
singularity
sinistrally
sinistrorse
sinlessness
sinological
sinuousness
sittingroom
situational
sizableness
tiddlywinks
tightfisted
tightlipped
timebargain
timepleaser
timeserving
timesharing
titanically
Titianesque
titillation
titleholder
tittivation
vibratility
vibrational
vicariously
viceadmiral
vicegerency
viceregally

viceroyalty
viceroyship
vichyssoise
viciousness
vicissitude
victualless
victualling
vinaigrette
vincibility
vindication
vindicative
vindicatory
vinedresser
viniculture
violoncello
viridescent
virilescent
virological
viscountess
viscousness
visibleness
viticulture
vitrescence
vitrifiable
vituperator
vivaciously
vivisection
widdershins
widowerhood
wildcatting
wildfowling
willingness
windcheater
windlestraw
winegrowing
winetasting
winningness
winningpost
winsomeness
winterberry
wintergreen
wirenetting
wirepulling
wiretapping
wisecracker
wishfulness
wistfulness
witchdoctor
witchhunter
witenagemot
witheringly
withershins
witlessness
zincography
ejaculation
ejaculatory
skatingrink
skeletonise
sketchiness
skilfulness
skulduddery
skulduggery
alabastrine
Albigensian
albuminuria
alcyonarian
alembicated
Alexandrian
alexandrine
alexandrite
algological
algorithmic
alkalescent
alkalimeter
alkalimetry
allAmerican
allantoides
allegorical
allelomorph
alleviation
alleviative
alleviatory
allocatable
allomorphic
allopathist
alphabetise
altercation
alternately
alternation
alternative
altitudinal
altocumulus
altorelievo
altorilievo
altostratus
blackavised
blackbeetle
blackbirder
blackcoated
blackfellow
blackgrouse
blackmailer
blackmarket
bladderwort
blamelessly
blameworthy
blasphemous
blastogenic
blepharitis
blessedness
blockbuster
bloodguilty
bloodlessly
bloodstream
bloodsucker
bloodvessel
blotchiness
blunderbuss
clairschach
clairvoyant
clamorously
clandestine
clapperclaw
Clarencieux
classically
cleanlimbed
cleanliness
cleanshaven
clearheaded
cleistogamy
clericalism
clericalist
cliffhanger
climacteric
climatology
clinometric
clodhopping
closefisted
closehauled
clostridium
clothesline
clothesmoth
clothesprop
cloudcastle
elaborately
elaboration
elaborative
elastically
elasticated
elastomeric
elbowgrease
elderliness
electioneer
electrician
electricity
electrocute
electrolier
electrology
electrolyse
electrolyte
electronics
electrotype
elementally
elephantine
elephantoid
elicitation
eligibility
elimination
eliminative
Elizabethan
ellipsoidal
ellipticity
elucidation
elucidative
elucidatory
elusiveness
elutriation
flabbergast
flaccidness
flagcaptain
flagellator
flagofficer
flagwagging
flamboyance
flamboyancy
flamboyante
flannelette
flannelling
flatulently
flauntingly
flavourless
flavoursome
fleshliness
flexibility
flightiness
flimflammer
flirtatious
flocculence
floorwalker
florescence
floriferous
florilegium
floweriness
fluctuation
fluorescein
fluorescent
fluoroscope
fluoroscopy
glaringness
glassblower
glasscutter
glassmaking
glauconitic
globeflower
globigerina
globularity
glomeration
glossolalia
glutinously
illaffected
illbreeding
illdisposed
illfavoured
illhumoured
illiberally
illimitable
illimitably
illiquidity
illmannered
illogically
illtempered
illuminable
illuminance
illuminator
illusionism
illusionist
illustrator
illustrious
kleptomania
oldwomanish
olfactology
oligochaete
oligomerous
placability
plagiariser
plagioclase
plagiostome
plainspoken
plaintively
planetarium
planetoidal
planimetric
planisphere
planoconvex
plantigrade
plasmolysis
plasmolytic
plasterwork
plasticiser
platearmour
plateresque
platforming
platinotype
platyrrhine
playerpiano
playfulness
playingcard
pleasurable
pleasurably
plebeianise
plebeianism
plectoptera
pleinairist
pleiotropic
Pleistocene
plenipotent
plenteously
plentifully
pleochroism
pleomorphic
pleurodynia
pliableness
plicateness
ploughshare
ploughstaff
pluralistic
plutocratic
pluviometer
slaughterer
slavedriver
slaveholder
slavemarket
slavishness
Slavonicise
sleepingbag
sleepingcar
sleeplessly
sleepwalker
sleeveboard
slenderness
sleuthhound
slickenside
slightingly
slotmachine
ulotrichous
ultramarine
ultramodern
ultrasonics
ultraviolet
amaranthine
amativeness
amazonstone
ambiguously
ambitiously
ambivalence
ambivalency
ambiversion
ameliorator
amenability
amenorrhoea
amentaceous
Americanise
Americanism
Americanist
amethystine
amiableness
amicability
amontillado
amorousness
amorphously
amphetamine
amphibolite
amphibology
amphictyony
amphimictic
amphisbaena
amplexicaul
emancipator
emasculator
embarkation
embellisher
emblematise
emblematist
embowelling
embowerment
embraceable
embracement
embracingly
embrocation
embroiderer
embroilment
embryologic
embryonated
emmenagogue
Emmenthaler
emotionally
emotionless
empanelling
emperorship
empirically
emplacement
emptyhanded
emptyheaded
emulousness
emulsionise
imaginarily
imagination
imaginative
imbrication
imitatively
immanentism
immanentist
immarginate
immediately
immedicable
immenseness
immigration
immitigable
immitigably
immortalise
immortality
immoveables
immunologic
impanelling
imparkation
impartation
impartially
impassioned
impassively
impassivity
impatiently
impeachable
impeachment
impecunious
impedimenta
impenetrate
impenitence
impenitency
imperfectly
imperforate
imperialise
imperialism
imperialist
imperilling
imperilment
imperiously
impermanent
impermeable
impermeably
impersonate
impertinent
imperviable
impetration
impetratory
impetuosity
impetuously
impingement
implausible
implausibly
implemental
implication
implicative
imploringly
impolitical
impoliticly
importantly
importation
importunate
importunely
importunity
impoundment
impractical
imprecation
imprecatory
imprecisely
imprecision
impregnable
impregnably
impressible
impressment
impropriate
impropriety
improvement
improvident
imprudently
impuissance
impulsively
ominousness
ommatophore
omnifarious
omnipotence
omnipresent
omniscience
smallholder
smallminded
smilelessly
smithereens
smithsonite
smokescreen
smokingroom
smoothfaced
smorgasbord
anachronism
anachronous
anacoluthon
anacreontic
anadiplosis
anaesthesia
anaesthetic
anagnorisis
analogously
anaphylaxis
anarchistic
anastomoses

anastomosis
anastomotic
ancientness
androgynous
anecdotical
anemometric
anencephaly
anfractuous
angelically
angiography
Anglicanism
AngloFrench
AngloIndian
anglomaniac
AngloNorman
anglophobia
anglophobic
animalcular
anisotropic
annabergite
annihilator
anniversary
annunciator
anomalistic
anomalously
anonymously
antecedence
antechamber
antemundane
antenuptial
antependium
anteriority
antheridium
anthocyanin
anthologise
anthologist
anthracitic
anthropical
anticathode
anticipator
anticyclone
antifouling
antigravity
antiJacobin
antimonious
antineutron
antioxidant
antiphonary
antiphrasis
antipyretic
antiquarian
antiquation
antirrhinum
antiSemitic
antistrophe
antitypical
antivitamin
antonomasia
anxiousness
enarthrosis
encapsulate
enchainment
enchantment
enchantress
enchiridion
encomiastic
encrustment
encumbrance
encystation
endearingly
endemically
endlessness
endocardiac
endocardial
endocardium
endometrium
endomorphic
endophagous
endoplasmic

endorsement
endoskelton
endothelial
endothelium
endothermal
endothermic
endotrophic
enfeoffment
enforceable
enforcement
enfranchise
engineering
engorgement
engrossment
enhancement
enigmatical
enjambement
enlargeable
enlargement
enlightened
enlivenment
enneahedron
ennoblement
enquiringly
ensanguined
enslavement
entablature
entablement
enterostomy
enterovirus
enterpriser
entertainer
enthralling
enthralment
entitlement
entomophily
entrainment
entreatment
entrustment
enucleation
enumeration
enumerative
enunciation
enunciative
envelopment
enviousness
environment
gnotobiosis
gnotobiotic
inadaptable
inadvertent
inadvisable
inalienable
inalienably
inalterable
inalterably
inanimately
inanimation
inappetence
inattention
inattentive
inaugurator
incalescent
incantation
incantatory
incarcerate
incardinate
incarnadine
incarnation
incertitude
incessantly
incinerator
incipiently
inclemently
inclination
inclusively
incoercible
incognisant
incoherence

incoherency
incommodity
incompetent
incompliant
incongruent
incongruity
incongruous
inconscient
inconsonant
inconstancy
incontinent
incorporate
incorporeal
incorrectly
incorruptly
increasable
incredulity
incredulous
incremental
incriminate
inculcation
inculpation
inculpatory
incunabulum
incuriosity
incuriously
incurvation
incurvature
indeciduous
indefinable
indefinably
indehiscent
indentation
independent
indifferent
indigestion
indigestive
indignantly
indignation
indirection
individuate
indivisible
indivisibly
IndoChinese
IndoIranian
indomitable
indomitably
indorsement
indubitable
indubitably
inductively
indulgently
industrious
inebriation
inedibility
ineffective
ineffectual
inefficient
inelegantly
ineloquence
ineluctable
ineluctably
inequitable
inequitably
inescapable
inessential
inestimable
inestimably
inexactness
inexcusable
inexcusably
inexistence
inexpedient
inexpensive
infanticide
infantilism
infantryman
infatuation
inferential

inferiority
infertility
infestation
infeudation
infiltrator
infinitival
infirmarian
inflammable
inflammably
inflexional
influential
informality
information
informative
informatory
infrangible
infrequence
infrequency
ingathering
ingeniously
ingenuously
ingrainedly
ingratitude
ingurgitate
inhabitable
inhabitancy
inheritable
inheritance
inheritress
initialling
injudicious
injuriously
innavigable
innervation
innocuously
innoxiously
innumerable
innumerably
innutrition
inobservant
inoculation
inoculative
inoffensive
inofficious
inoperative
inopportune
inquilinous
inquiringly
inquisition
inquisitive
insalubrity
inscribable
inscription
inscriptive
inscrutable
inscrutably
insectarium
insecticide
insectifuge
insectivore
insectology
inseminator
insensately
insensitive
inseparable
inseparably
insessorial
insidiously
insincerely
insincerity
insinuation
insinuative
insipidness
insistently
insouciance
inspiration
inspiratory
instability
installment

instigation
instigative
instillment
instinctive
instinctual
institution
instruction
instructive
insufflator
insultingly
insuperable
insuperably
intagliated
integrality
integration
integrative
intelligent
intemperate
intenseness
intensifier
intensional
intensively
intentional
intentioned
interactant
interaction
interactive
interallied
interatomic
interbedded
intercalary
intercalate
intercensal
intercepter
interceptor
intercessor
interchange
intercostal
intercourse
intercrural
interdental
interdepend
interesting
interfacial
interfacing
interfluent
interfusion
intergrowth
interiorise
interiority
interjacent
interleaves
interlinear
Interlingua
interlining
interlocker
interlunary
intermeddle
intermedium
intermingle
intermitted
internalise
internality
internecine
internuncio
interosseus
interplayed
interpolate
interpreter
interracial
interregnum
interrelate
interrogate
interrupter
interruptor
interseptal
intersexual
intersperse
interspinal

intertangle
intertribal
intervallic
interviewee
interviewer
intimidator
intolerable
intolerably
intolerance
intractable
intractably
intravenous
intrepidity
intricately
intriguante
intromitted
intromitter
introverted
intrusively
intuitional
intuitively
intuitivism
intumescent
invalidness
invectively
inventively
inventorial
investigate
investiture
inviability
invidiously
invigilator
invigorator
inviolately
involucrate
involuntary
involvement
invultation
knavishness
knowingness
knownothing
knucklebone
oncological
oneiromancy
onerousness
ontogenesis
ontogenetic
ontological
pneumonitis
snatchblock
snickersnee
snowbunting
snowgoggles
snowleopard
unaccounted
unadvisedly
unalterable
unambiguous
unanimously
unappealing
unashamedly
unassertive
unavailable
unavoidable
unavoidably
unawareness
unbeknownst
unbelieving
unbendingly
unbeseeming
unboundedly
unbreakable
uncanniness
uncanonical
uncatchable
unceasingly
uncertainly
uncertainty
unchristian

uncivilised unmemorable bountifully commensally condensable consonantal
uncleanness unmemorably bourgeoisie commentator conditional consonantly
unclimbable unmitigated boutonniere commination conditioner conspecific
uncluttered unnaturally bowdleriser comminatory condolatory conspicuity
uncommitted unnecessary boysenberry comminution condominium conspicuous
unconcealed unnervingly coadunation commiserate condonation conspirator
unconcerned unobtrusive coagulation commissural condottiere constellate
uncongenial unorganized coalescence committable condottieri consternate
unconnected unorthodoxy coarctation commonality conductance constituent
unconscious unpalatable cobblestone commonplace conductible constitutor
uncontested unpolitical coccidiosis commonsense conductress constrictor
uncountable unpossessed cochinchina communalise condylomata construable
uncouthness unprintable cockaleekie communalism confabulate constructor
uncrushable unpromising cockleshell communalist confederacy consultancy
underbidder unqualified cockyleekie communicant confederate consumerism
undercharge unquietness coconscious communicate conferrable consumingly
underexpose unrealistic codefendant communistic confessedly consummator
underground unreasoning codicillary commutation confidently consumption
undergrowth unrelenting coeducation commutative confidingly consumptive
underhanded unremitting coefficient compactness confinement containable
undermanned unrighteous coessential compaginate confirmable containment
underpinned unsaturated coeternally comparatist confiscable contaminant
underseller unselective coexistence comparative confiscator contaminate
undersigned unshockable coextension compartment conflagrant contemplate
understated unshrinking coextensive compassable conflagrate contentedly
undertaking unskilfully coffeehouse compellable confliction contentious
undertenant unsmilingly coffeetable compendious conflictive contentment
undervaluer unsolicited cognateness compensator conformable conterminal
underweight unsoundness cognitional competently conformably contestable
underwriter unsparingly cognitively competition conformally continental
undeserving unspeakable cognitivity competitive conformance continently
undesirable unspeakably cognoscente compilation confusingly contingence
undeveloped unstoppable cognoscenti compilement confutation contingency
undisguised unteachable cognoscible complacence confutative continuable
undisturbed unthinkable coincidence complacency congealable continually
undoubtedly unthinkably coinheritor complainant congealment continuance
undutifully untouchable coinsurance complaisant congelation continuator
unemotional unusualness coldblooded complexness congenerous contorniate
unendurable unutterable coldhearted compliantly congenially contrabasso
unendurably unutterably coleorrhiza complicated congressman contractile
unequivocal unvarnished collaborate complotting congruently contraction
unessential unwarranted collapsible comportment congruously contractive
unexploited unweetingly collectable compositely conjectural contractual
unexpressed unwholesome collectanea composition conjugality contracture
unfailingly unwillingly collectedly compositive conjugation contradance
unfaltering unwinkingly collectible compossible conjugative contraption
unfashioned unwittingly collenchyma compotation conjunction contrariety
unfeelingly boardschool colligation compotatory conjunctiva contrarious
unfeignedly Bodhisattva colligative compression conjunctive contrastive
unflappable bodybuilder collimation compressive conjuncture contretemps
unflinching bodyservant collinearly comprisable conjuration contributor
unforgiving bohemianism collisional comptroller connectable contrivable
unfortunate boilermaker collocation compunction connectedly contrivance
unfurnished bombardment collusively compurgator connectible controlling
ungetatable bombilation colonelship computation connoisseur controlment
ungodliness bombination colonialism computerise connotation controversy
unguardedly Bonapartean colonialist comradeship connotative conurbation
unguiculate Bonapartism colorimeter comstockery connubially convenances
unhappiness Bonapartist colorimetry concatenate conquerable convenience
unhealthily bonbonniere colouration concealable consanguine conveniency
unhelpfully bondservant colourblind concealment consciously conventicle
unicellular bondservice colourfully conceitedly consecrator convergence
unicoloured bondwashing columbarium conceivable consecution convergency
unification bookbinding columniated conceivably consecutive conversable
uniformness bookinghall combatively concentrate consentient conversance
unigeniture bookishness combination conceptacle consequence conversancy
unimportant bookkeeping combinative concernment conservable convertible
uninhabited booklearned combinatory concertedly conservancy convertibly
uninhibited bookselling combustible concertgoer conservator conveyancer
uninucleate bookshelves comestibles conciliator considerate convincible
unipersonal boorishness comeuppance conciseness considering convivially
unipolarity bootlegging comfortable concomitant consignable convocation
unisexually borborygmus comfortably concordance consignment convolution
universally botanically comfortless concrescent consistence convolvulus
unkennelled botheration commandment concubinage consistency cookgeneral
unlimitedly bottleglass commemorate concubinary consolation cooperation
unmanliness bottlegreen commendable concubitant consolatory cooperative
unmatchable bottlenosed commendably concurrence consolidate coordinator
unmeaningly bounteously commendator condemnable consolingly coparcenary

copingstone
copiousness
coplanarity
copperplate
coppersmith
coralloidal
corbiculate
corbiesteps
cordialness
corecipient
cornerstone
cornhusking
corniferous
cornucopian
coronagraph
coronograph
corporality
corporately
corporation
corporatism
corporative
corporeally
corpulently
corpuscular
correctable
correctness
correlation
correlative
corrigendum
corroborant
corroborate
corrosively
corrugation
corruptible
corruptibly
corruptness
coruscation
cosignatory
cosmetician
cosmetology
cosmogonist
cosmography
cosmologist
cosmopolite
costbenefit
costiveness
cotemporary
coterminous
cotoneaster
cottongrass
cottonmouth
coulometric
counselling
countenance
counterblow
counterbond
counterfeit
counterfoil
counterfort
countermand
countermark
countermine
countermove
countermure
counterpane
counterpart
counterplan
counterplea
counterplot
countersign
countersink
countersunk
counterturn
countervail
counterview
counterwork
countlessly
countrified
countryfied
countryseat
countryside
countrywide
courteously
courtliness
coxcombical
doctrinaire
doctrinally
documentary
dodecaphony
doggishness
dolefulness
dollishness
doltishness
domesticate
domesticity
domiciliary
domiciliate
domineering
donnishness
doorknocker
doublecheck
doublecross
doubleDutch
doubleedged
doubleender
doubleentry
doublefaced
doublequick
doublespeak
doublethink
doubtlessly
doughtiness
douroucouli
downdraught
downhearted
downtrodden
doxographer
folliculate
fomentation
foolishness
footpoundal
footslogger
footsoldier
foppishness
foraminated
foraminifer
forbearance
forbiddance
foreclosure
foreignness
forequarter
forerunning
foreseeable
foreshorten
foresighted
forestaller
forestation
forethinker
forethought
foretopmast
foretopsail
forevermore
foreverness
forewarning
forfeitable
forgetfully
forgetmenot
forgettable
forgiveness
forlornness
formalistic
formational
formication
formularise
formulation
fornication
forthcoming
fortifiable
fortnightly
fortunately
forwardness
foulmouthed
fourflusher
fourpounder
fourwheeler
godchildren
goddaughter
godforsaken
godlessness
goldbeating
golddigging
goldenberry
gonfalonier
goniometric
goodhearted
goodlooking
goodnatured
gormandiser
gourmandise
gourmandism
hobbledehoy
hoggishness
hollandaise
holoblastic
holographic
holothurian
homeopathic
homeostasis
homeostatic
homesteader
homestretch
homiletical
homocentric
homoeopathy
homoestatic
homogeneity
homogeneous
homogenetic
homogeniser
homoiousian
homological
homomorphic
homophonous
homoplastic
homopterous
homosporous
homothallic
homozygosis
honeybadger
honeymooner
honeysuckle
hooliganism
hopefulness
hornswoggle
horological
horripilate
horsecollar
horsedoctor
horseradish
hospitalise
hospitality
hospitaller
housefather
householder
housekeeper
houselights
housemaster
housemother
housewifely
housewifery
ionospheric
journeywork
joylessness
loathliness
loathsomely
loculicidal
logarithmic
loggerheads
logicalness
logographer
logographic
logomachist
longanimity
longplaying
longsighted
looselimbed
loosestrife
lophobranch
loudmouthed
loudspeaker
loutishness
louverboard
louvreboard
lovableness
lowpressure
lowspirited
loxodromics
mockingbird
moderations
modernistic
moisturiser
molecricket
molecularly
molendinary
molestation
mollycoddle
molybdenite
momentarily
momentously
monarchical
monasterial
monasticism
moneylender
moneymaking
moneymarket
moneyspider
monitorship
monkeybread
monkeyshine
monocarpous
monochasial
monochasium
monochromat
monochromic
monoclinous
monoculture
monogenesis
monogenetic
monogrammed
monographer
monographic
monolingual
monological
monologuise
monologuist
monomorphic
mononuclear
monophagous
monophthong
Monophysite
monopoliser
monopterous
Monothelite
monozygotic
monseigneur
monstrosity
monstrously
moonlighter
mooringmast
morbiferous
moribundity
morningroom
moronically
morrisdance
mortarboard
mosstrooper
mothercraft
mothernaked
motherright
motivepower
mountaineer
mountainous
mountaintop
movableness
moveability
noctilucent
noctivagant
noctivagous
nocturnally
noiselessly
noisemaking
noisomeness
nomadically
nomenclator
nominatival
nomographer
nomographic
nomological
nonchalance
nondelivery
nondescript
nonetheless
nonexistent
nonfeasance
nonmatching
nonmetallic
nonpartisan
nonplussing
nonresident
nonsensical
nonsequitur
nonspecific
nonunionist
nonviolence
nonvolatile
northeaster
northwester
noseyparker
nosographer
nosographic
nosological
notableness
nothingness
noticeboard
notionalist
notoriously
nourishment
novelettish
noxiousness
pocketknife
pocketmoney
pocketsized
pococurante
podophyllin
pointdevice
pointedness
pointillism
pointillist
pointlessly
poisonously
polarimeter
polarimetry
polarisable
polariscope
polemically
polevaulter
policewoman
politically
politicking
pollination
poltergeist
poltroonery
polyandrous
polycarpous
polychromic
polycrystal
polygenesis
polygenetic
polyglottal
polyglottic
polygonally
polygraphic
polymorphic
polyonymous
polypeptide
polyphagous
polyphonous
polystyrene
polytechnic
polyzoarium
pomegranate
pomiculture
pomological
pompousness
ponderation
ponderosity
ponderously
pontificals
pontificate
populariser
pornography
porphyritic
portability
porterhouse
portionless
portmanteau
portraitist
portraiture
positronium
posological
possibility
postclassic
posteriorly
postexilian
postglacial
postnuptial
postulation
potentially
potteringly
pourparlers
powderflask
powerlessly
roadholding
rockcrystal
rodenticide
rodomontade
roentgenise
roguishness
romanticise
romanticism
romanticist
ropedancing
ropewalking
Rosicrucian
rotogravure
rottenstone
roughfooted
roughlegged
roundedness
soapboiling
soberminded
sociability
socialistic
Socinianism
sociologist
sociometric
sociopathic
sockdolager
sockdologen
softhearted
softshelled
solanaceous
soldierlike
soldiership

solifluxion
soliloquise
soliloquist
solipsistic
solmisation
solutionist
solvability
somatically
somatogenic
somatologic
somatoplasm
somatotonia
somatotonic
somewhither
somnambular
somniculous
somniferous
somnolently
songfulness
songsparrow
sonofabitch
sophistical
Soroptimist
sorrowfully
soteriology
sottishness
soulfulness
soundlessly
soupkitchen
southeaster
Southernism
southwester
sovereignly
sovereignty
toastmaster
tobacconist
tobogganing
tobogganist
toffeenosed
togglejoint
tolbutamide
tonsillitis
toothbilled
toothpowder
toothsomely
topdressing
toploftical
topographer
topographic
topological
torchbearer
torchsinger
torticollis
torturously
totalisator
totteringly
touchtyping
toughminded
tourbillion
townspeople
toxicomania
toxophilite
vociferance
vociferator
voguishness
voicelessly
volcanicity
volcanology
volitionary
volkslieder
voltametric
volubleness
volumometer
voluntarily
voluntarism
voluntarist
voodooistic
voortrekker
voraciously
vortiginous
wolfwhistle
womanliness
wonderfully
woodcarving
woodcutting
workability
workmanlike
workmanship
worldbeater
worldliness
worldlywise
worrisomely
worshipable
worshipless
worshipping
worthlessly
zoantharian
zoographist
zoomorphism
zooplankton
zootechnics
Zoroastrian
apartmental
aphrodisiac
apocalyptic
Apollinaris
apologetics
apomorphine
aponeuroses
aponeurosis
aponeurotic
apophyllite
aposiopesis
apostleship
apostolical
apostrophic
apotheosise
appallingly
apparatchik
apparelling
appealingly
appeasement
appellation
appellative
applaudable
application
applicative
applicatory
appogiatura
appointment
appreciable
appreciably
appreciator
approbation
approbatory
appropriate
approvingly
approximate
appurtenant
epeirogenic
ephemerides
epidiascope
epigastrium
epigraphist
epinephrine
epipetalous
episcopally
epithalamia
epithalamic
epithelioma
epochmaking
ipecacuanha
ipsilateral
opalescence
opencircuit
openhearted
openmouthed
operational
operatively
operculated
operoseness
ophidiarium
ophiologist
opinionated
opportunely
opportunism
opportunist
opportunity
opprobrious
oppugnation
optometrist
spaceflight
spaceheater
spacesaving
sparingness
sparrowbill
sparrowhawk
spasmodical
spastically
spathaceous
spatterdash
speakership
specifiable
specificity
spectacular
spectatress
spectrality
spectrogram
spectrology
speculation
speculative
speechifier
speedometer
spelaeology
spellbinder
spendthrift
spermaphyte
spermatozoa
spermicidal
spessartite
sphaeridium
sphagnology
spherically
spherometer
spherulitic
sphincteral
sphincteric
sphygmogram
spifflicate
spindlelegs
spindletree
spinelessly
spiniferous
Spinozistic
spinsterish
spiraculate
spiritistic
spiritlevel
spiritually
spiritualty
spirituelle
spirochaete
spirochetal
spirometric
splashboard
splayfooted
splendorous
splenectomy
splenetical
spokeswoman
spondulicks
spondylitis
spongecloth
sponsorship
spontaneity
spontaneous
sporogenous
sporogonium
sporophytic
sportswoman
sporulation
spreadeagle
springboard
springclean
springhouse
springiness
Upanishadic
upholsterer
uprightness
aquaculture
aquarellist
aquatically
aquiculture
equableness
equiangular
equidistant
equilateral
equilibrate
equilibrist
equilibrium
equinoctial
equipollent
equivalence
equivalency
equivocally
equivocator
squalidness
squarebuilt
squarsonage
squashiness
squeakiness
squeamishly
squintingly
squirearchy
arbitrageur
arbitrament
arbitrarily
arbitration
arbitrative
arbitratrix
arboraceous
arborescent
archaeology
archaeornis
archaically
archangelic
archdiocese
archduchess
archdukedom
Archimedean
archipelago
arduousness
arenicolous
Areopagitic
arglebargle
argumentive
aristocracy
Arminianism
armtwisting
aromaticity
arraignment
arrangement
arrestingly
arterialise
arthrospore
articulable
articulated
articulator
artillerist
artiodactyl
artlessness
brachiation
brachyurous
bracteolate
bradycardia
braggadocio
Brahmanical
brahmaputra
Brahminical
brainlessly
brainsickly
brainteaser
branchiopod
brankursine
brazenfaced
breadbasket
breadcrumbs
breadthways
breadthwise
breadwinner
breastplate
breastwheel
breathalyse
breechblock
breezeblock
bricklaying
bridgeboard
brilliantly
bristletail
bristleworm
bristliness
Britishness
brittleness
broadcaster
broadleaved
broadminded
brotherhood
brucellosis
brusqueness
brutishness
bryozoology
crabbedness
crackerjack
craftswoman
craniometry
creationism
creationist
credentials
credibility
credulously
crematorium
crenellated
crenulation
crepitation
crepuscular
crestfallen
criminalist
criminality
crimination
criminative
criminatory
criminology
criticality
criticaster
crocidolite
crocodilian
crookbacked
crookedness
crossbearer
crossbowman
crossgarnet
crosslegged
crossstitch
crotcheteer
cruciferous
crucifixion
crucigerous
crunchiness
crustaceous
cryobiology
cryosurgery
cryotherapy
cryptically
cryptogamic
cryptograph
cryptomeria
crystalline
crystallise
crystallite
crystalloid
draggletail
dramaturgic
drastically
draughtsman
drawingroom
dreadnought
dreamlessly
dresscircle
dressmaking
drillmaster
dropcurtain
dropforging
drouthiness
drunkenness
eradication
eradicative
Erastianism
ergatocracy
erotogenous
erotomaniac
erratically
erroneously
erubescence
erythrocyte
fractionary
fractionate
fractionise
fractiously
fragmentary
Francomania
Francophile
Francophobe
francophone
franctireur
frankfurter
franklinite
frankpledge
frantically
franticness
fraternally
fraterniser
fratricidal
fraudulence
freebooting
freehearted
freemasonry
freethinker
freethought
freezedried
frenchified
Frenchwoman
fretfulness
friableness
fricandeaux
frightfully
frigidarium
frivolously
frontrunner
frostbitten
frothhopper
frowardness
frowstiness
fructuation
frugivorous
fruitlessly
frustration
gracelessly
gracileness
gradational
gradiometer
gradualness
GraecoRoman
grammalogue
grammatical

gramophonic
grandfather
grandiflora
grandiosely
grandiosity
grandmother
grandnephew
grandparent
grangeriser
granivorous
granolithic
granophyric
granularity
granulation
granulocyte
graphically
graphicness
grasshopper
gratulation
gratulatory
gravedigger
gravelblind
gravimetric
gravitation
gravitative
greasepaint
greaseproof
greatnephew
greengrocer
greenkeeper
greenockite
gristliness
grotesquely
grotesquery
grouchiness
groundsheet
groundwater
grumblingly
iridescence
irksomeness
ironhearted
ironmongery
irradiation
irradiative
irrecusable
irrecusably
irredentism
irredentist
irreducible
irreducibly
irrefutable
irrefutably
irregularly
irrelevance
irrelevancy
irreligious
irremissive
irremovable
irremovably
irreparable
irreparably
irresoluble
irretention
irretentive
irreverence
irrevocable
irrevocably
irruptively
oracularity
orangoutang
orbicularly
orchestrate
orchidology
orderliness
oreographic
oreological
organically
organisable
organscreen
orientalise
orientalism
orientalist
orientation
originality
origination
originative
ornithology
ornithopter
ornithosaur
orthocentre
orthodontia
orthodontic
orthoepical
orthography
orthopaedic
orthopedics
orthopedist
orthopteran
orthoscopic
orthotropic
practicable
practicably
practically
praetorship
pragmatical
prattlingly
prayerwheel
preachiness
preaudience
Precambrian
precautious
precedented
precedently
precentress
preceptress
precipitant
precipitate
precipitous
preciseness
preconceive
precontract
predatorily
predecessor
predicament
predication
predicative
predicatory
predictable
predictably
predominant
predominate
preelection
preeminence
preexistent
prefatorial
prefatorily
prefectural
prehistoric
preignition
prejudgment
prejudicial
prelibation
preliminary
prelusively
prelusorily
prematurely
prematurity
premeditate
premiership
premonition
premonitory
prenominate
preoccupied
preparation
preparative
preparatory
preposition
prepositive
preprandial
prerogative
presanctify
presbyteral
presciently
preselector
presentable
presentably
presentient
presentment
preservable
pressagency
prestigious
prestissimo
prestressed
presumingly
presumption
presumptive
pretendedly
pretentious
preterhuman
preterition
prevalently
prevaricate
preventable
preventible
previsional
prickliness
priestcraft
primaevally
primateship
primatology
primigenial
primiparous
primitively
primitivism
principally
privateness
privatively
prizewinner
probabilism
probabilist
probability
probational
probationer
problematic
proceedings
procephalic
prochronism
proconsular
procreation
procreative
procrustean
proctorship
procuration
procuratory
procurement
prodigalise
prodigality
profanation
profanatory
profaneness
professedly
proficiency
profiterole
profuseness
progenitrix
progeniture
progestogen
prognathism
prognathous
progression
progressism
progressist
progressive
prohibition
prohibitive
prohibitory
prolegomena
proletarian
proletariat
proliferate
proliferous
prolificacy
prolificity
prolocutrix
prominently
promiscuity
promiscuous
promisingly
promotional
promptitude
promulgator
proofreader
propagation
propagative
prophethood
prophetical
prophetship
prophylaxis
propinquity
propitiable
propitiator
proportions
proposition
proprietary
prorogation
prosaically
prosaicness
prosecution
prosecutrix
proselytise
proselytism
prosenchyma
prospective
prosthetics
prostitutor
prostration
protagonist
protectoral
protectress
proteolysis
proteolytic
Proterozoic
prothalamia
prothallial
prothallium
prothoracic
protomartyr
protonotary
protophytic
protractile
protraction
protractive
protrudable
protrusible
protuberant
provenience
providently
provisional
provisorily
provocateur
provocation
provocative
provokingly
provostship
proximately
prudishness
pruriginous
Prussianise
Prussianism
trabeculate
tracasserie
tracelessly
tracheotomy
trackwalker
traditional
traducement
trafficator
trafficking
trafficless
tragedienne
tragicomedy
trailblazer
trainbearer
trammelling
transaction
transalpine
transceiver
transcriber
transection
transferred
transferrer
transfigure
transfinite
transfixion
transformer
transfusion
transhumant
transiently
transilient
translation
translocate
translucent
translunary
transmarine
transmittal
transmitted
transmitter
transpadane
transparent
transpierce
transponder
transporter
transsexual
transuranic
transversal
trapeziform
trapezoidal
Trappistine
traversable
treacherous
treacliness
treasonable
treasonably
treecreeper
trelliswork
tremblement
tremblingly
tremulously
trenchantly
trencherman
trendsetter
trepanation
trepidation
trestletree
trestlework
triadically
triangulate
tribulation
tribuneship
tribunicial
tribunitial
tributarily
trichinosis
trichomonad
tricksiness
tricoloured
triennially
triggerfish
trimestrial
trimorphism
trimorphous
Trinitarian
tripetalous
triphibious
triphyllous
triquetrous
tristichous
trisyllabic
trisyllable
tritagonist
tritheistic
trituration
triumvirate
trivialness
troglodytic
trophoblast
troposphere
trothplight
troublesome
troublously
trouserless
trousersuit
truculently
truehearted
trundletail
trustbuster
trusteeship
trustworthy
tryingplane
trypanosome
tryptophane
uranography
urochordate
urticaceous
urticarious
wreckmaster
wrongheaded
ascensional
ascetically
ascomycetes
aseptically
aspergillum
aspergillus
aspersorium
asphyxiator
assafoetida
assassinate
assemblyman
assentation
assertively
assessorial
assiduously
assignation
assimilable
assimilator
association
associative
assortative
assuagement
assuredness
Assyriology
astigmatism
astringency
eschatology
escheatable
escheatment
esemplastic
esotericism
Esperantist
essentially
establisher
isochronism
isochronous
isoelectric
isogeotherm
isometrical
isomorphism
isomorphous
oscillation
oscillatory
oscillogram
osmotically
ostensively
ostentation

osteography
osteologist
osteopathic
osteophytic
osteoplasty
ostracoderm
Ostrogothic
pseudograph
pseudomonas
pseudomorph
pseudopodia
psittacosis
psychedelia
psychedelic
psychiatric
psychically
psychodrama
psychogenic
psychograph
psychologic
psychometry
psychomotor
psychopathy
uselessness
atheistical
athleticism
atmospheric
atomisation
atrabilious
atrociously
attemptable
attentively
attenuation
attestation
attitudinal
attractable
attribution
attributive
attritional
ctenophoran
etherealise
ethereality
ethnography
ethnologist
ethological
Etruscology
etymologise
etymologist
itacolumite
ithyphallic
itinerantly
itineration
otherwhiles
pteridology
pterodactyl
stadtholder
stagemanage
stagestruck
stagflation
stainlessly
staircarpet
stakeholder
stalactitic
stalagmitic
stallholder
stampoffice
standardise
standoffish
standpatter
starchiness
starcrossed
starstudded
startlingly
stateliness
statesmanly
statistical
statutebook
statutorily
staunchless
staunchness
staurolitic
steadfastly
steamboiler
steamroller
steatopygia
steelworker
steeplebush
steeplejack
steerageway
steganogram
stegosaurus
stellionate
stencilling
stenochromy
stenography
stenotypist
stepbrother
stephanotis
stereograph
stereometry
stereophony
stereoscope
stereoscopy
stereotyped
stereotyper
stereotypic
sternsheets
sternutator
stethoscope
stethoscopy
stevengraph
stewardship
stichometry
stickinsect
stickleback
stiffnecked
stiflejoint
stiltedness
stimulation
stimulative
stipendiary
stipulation
stipulatory
stirrupbone
stirruppump
stockbroker
stockholder
stockinette
stockjobber
stockmarket
stocktaking
stoicalness
stomachache
stomachpump
stomatology
stonecurlew
stonecutter
stoneground
stonemarten
stonewaller
stoolpigeon
storekeeper
stormcentre
stormtroops
storyteller
Stradivarii
straightcut
straightish
straightway
straitlaced
stramineous
strangeness
strangulate
straphanger
strategical
stratocracy
streakiness
streetlight
strenuosity
strenuously
stretchable
stridulator
strikebound
stringboard
stringently
stringiness
stringpiece
stringybark
stroboscope
strongpoint
studentship
studiedness
stumblingly
stuntedness
stylisation
stylishness
stylography
stylopodium
utilisation
utilitarian
audaciously
audibleness
audiologist
audiometric
audiovisual
augmentable
Augustinian
auricularly
Aurignacian
austereness
autarchical
autochthony
autoerotism
autographic
automatable
autoplastic
autotrophic
auxanometer
bucolically
buffalorobe
bullbaiting
bulletproof
bullfighter
bullishness
bullterrier
bumblepuppy
bumptiously
bureaucracy
burglarious
burgomaster
bushmanship
bushwhacker
businessman
butcherbird
butterflies
butteriness
butyraceous
culmination
culpability
cultivation
cunningness
cupellation
cupriferous
cupronickel
curableness
curatorship
curiousness
currentness
currishness
cursiveness
cursoriness
curtailment
curvilineal
curvilinear
customarily
custombuilt
customhouse
dualcontrol
dualpurpose
dubiousness
dumbfounder
dundrearies
duniewassal
duplication
duplicative
duplicitous
durableness
dutifulness
eucalyptole
Eucharistic
euchologion
eudaemonism
eudaemonist
eudiometric
eugenically
euphemistic
eurhythmics
Europeanise
eurypteroid
fulguration
fullblooded
fullfledged
fullhearted
fullmouthed
fulminating
fulmination
fulminatory
fulsomeness
funambulate
funambulist
functionary
functionate
fundamental
furnishings
furtherance
furthermore
furthermost
furthersome
furtiveness
furunculous
fusillation
fustigation
guardedness
guesstimate
guilelessly
guiltlessly
gullibility
gurgitation
gutlessness
guttapercha
guttersnipe
gutturalise
gutturalism
huckleberry
Hudibrastic
hugeousness
humiliation
humiliatory
hummingbird
hunchbacked
hundredfold
hurriedness
hurryscurry
hurryskurry
hurtfulness
husbandlike
Judaisation
judgmatical
judiciously
jumpingbean
jumpingjack
juridically
justiciable
justifiable
justifiably
juvenescent
Kulturkampf
lubrication
lubricative
lucratively
lucubration
ludicrously
luminescent
lumpishness
lustfulness
Lutheranism
luxuriantly
luxuriation
luxuriously
mudslinging
multangular
multicolour
multilinear
multinomial
multiparous
multiracial
multistorey
multivalent
mundaneness
municipally
munificence
murderously
murmuration
murmurously
musclebound
muscularity
musculation
musculature
musicalness
muskthistle
mustachioed
mutableness
muttonchops
nullifidian
nulliparity
nulliparous
numerically
numismatics
numismatist
nuncupation
nuncupative
nurserymaid
nutcrackers
nutrimental
nutritional
nutritively
outbreeding
outbuilding
outcropping
outdistance
outfighting
outrivalled
outspokenly
outstanding
outstripped
outwardness
publication
publishable
publishment
pulchritude
pullthrough
pullulation
pulverulent
pumicestone
punchinello
punctilious
punctuality
punctuation
pupillarity
purchasable
pureblooded
purgatorial
purificator
puritanical
purportedly
purposeless
purposively
purpresture
pushfulness
pussyfooter
pussywillow
pustulation
putrescence
putrescible
quacksalver
quadraphony
quadratical
quadrennial
quadrennium
quadrillion
quadrupedal
quaestorial
qualifiable
qualitative
quarrelling
quarrelsome
quarterback
quarterdeck
quartertone
quaternloaf
queenliness
querulously
questionary
quickchange
quickfiring
quickfreeze
quickfrozen
quicksilver
quickwitted
quiescently
quilldriver
quincuncial
quinquennia
quinquereme
quintillion
quitchgrass
quizzically
rubberstamp
rubefacient
rubefaction
rubicundity
rubrication
rudimentary
ruinousness
rumbustious
ruridecanal
Russophobia
rustication
suasiveness
subaerially
subarration
subaudition
subaxillary
subbasement
subcategory
subclinical
subcontract
subcontrary
subcortical
subcritical
subcultural
subdivision
subdominant
subjugation
subjunctive
sublimation
sublimeness
sublittoral
submarginal
submergence
submersible
submissible
submultiple
subordinate

subornation
subregional
subrogation
subscapular
subsequence
subservient
subsistence
subspecific
substandard
substantial
substantive
substituent
subsumption
subsumptive
subterminal
subtraction
subtractive
subtropical
subumbrella
suburbanise
suburbanite
succedaneum
succourless
succulently
suckingfish
sufficiency
suffixation
suffocation
suffocative
suffragette
suffumigate
sugarcoated
suggestible
suitability
sulphureous
sulphurwort
summariness
summational
summerhouse
summersault
sumptuosity
sumptuously
sunlessness
superabound
supercharge
superfamily
superficial
superficies
superfluity
superfluous
superheater
superimpose
superinduce
superintend
superioress
superiority
superjacent
superlative
superlunary
supermarket
supernatant
supernormal
superscribe
superscript
supersedeas
supersedure
superstrata
supersubtle
supertanker
supervision
supervisory
suppliantly
supportable
supportably
supposition
suppositive
suppository
suppression
suppressive
suppuration
suppurative
supremacist
supremeness
surbasement
surfboarder
surficially
surgeonfish
surpassable
surrebuttal
surrebutter
surrogation
surveillant
susceptible
susceptibly
suspenseful
suspensible
suspiration
sustainable
sustainment
susurration
tuberculate
tuberculise
tuberculose
tuberculous
tufthunting
tumbledrier
tumefaction
tunableness
tunefulness
turbination
turbulently
turgescence
turtleshell
tuttifrutti
vulcanicity
vulcanology
Yugoslavian
avoirdupois
evagination
evanescence
evangelical
evanishment
evaporation
evaporative
evasiveness
eveningstar
eventualise
eventuality
everlasting
evidentiary
evolutional
ovariectomy
overanxious
overbalance
overbearing
overbidding
overcropped
overdevelop
overgarment
overindulge
overlapping
overmanning
overmeasure
overpayment
overproduce
overrunning
oversailing
oversetting
overstepped
overstretch
overstuffed
overtopping
overweening
overwritten
overwrought
oviposition
awesomeness
awestricken
awkwardness
kwashiorkor
swallowable
swallowdive
swallowhole
swallowtail
swallowwort
swarthiness
sweepstakes
swellheaded
swiftfooted
swimbladder
swingletree
swinishness
switchblade
switchboard
swordbearer
twelvemonth
twelvepenny
axiological
exaggerator
examination
exanthemata
exarcerbate
exceedingly
excellently
exceptional
excessively
exclamation
exclamatory
exclusively
exclusivity
excoriation
excremental
excrescence
excrescency
exculpation
exculpatory
excursively
exdirectory
executioner
executorial
executrices
executrixes
exemplarily
exemplarity
exercisable
exfoliation
exfoliative
exhaustible
exhaustless
exhortation
exhortative
exhortatory
existential
exogenously
exoneration
exonerative
exorbitance
exoskeletal
exoskeleton
exotericism
expansional
expansively
expansivity
expatiation
expatiative
expatiatory
expectantly
expectation
expectative
expectorant
expectorate
expediently
expeditious
expenditure
expensively
experienced
explainable
explanation
explanatory
explication
explicative
explicatory
exploitable
exploration
explorative
exploratory
explosively
exponential
exportation
expostulate
expressible
expropriate
expurgation
expurgatory
exquisitely
exsiccation
exstipulate
extemporary
extemporise
extensional
extensively
extenuation
extenuatory
exteriorise
exteriority
exterminate
externalise
externalism
externality
extirpation
extirpatory
extortioner
extractable
extradition
extrapolate
extravagant
extravagate
extravasate
extraverted
extremeness
extrication
extroverted
exuberantly
oxygenation
oxyhydrogen
byeelection
Byronically
Byzantinism
Byzantinist
cybernation
cybernetics
cyclopaedia
cyclopaedic
cycloserine
cyclothymia
cyclothymic
cylindrical
cypripedium
cysticercus
cytogenesis
cytokinesis
cytological
dynamically
dynamometer
dynamometry
dysfunction
dyslogistic
eyecatching
gymnospermy
gynaecocrat
gynaecology
gypsiferous
gyrocompass
hyacinthine
hydraheaded
hydrobromic
hydrocarbon
hydrocyanic
hydrogenate
hydrogenous
hydrography
hydrologist
hydromedusa
hydrometeor
hydrometric
hydropathic
hydrophilic
hydrophobia
hydrophobic
hydrophytic
hydroponics
hydrosphere
hydrostatic
hydrotactic
hydrothorax
hydrotropic
hygrometric
hygrophytic
hygroscopic
hylogenesis
hylozoistic
hymenoptera
hymnography
hyoscyamine
hyperactive
hyperbolise
hyperboloid
hyperborean
hypercharge
hypercritic
hypermarket
hypermetric
hyperphagia
hyperplasia
hypersthene
hypertrophy
hyphenation
hypnopaedia
hypnopompic
hypoblastic
hypocycloid
hypogastric
hypoglossal
hypolimnion
hypophyseal
hypophysial
hypostatise
hypotension
hypothecate
hypothenuse
hypothermia
hypothesise
hypotyposis
hypsography
hypsometric
hypsophobia
kymographic
lycanthrope
lycanthropy
mycological
mycophagist
mycorrhizae
mycorrhizal
myelomatous
myocarditis
myrmecology
mythography
mythologise
mythologist
mythomaniac
mythopoeist
mythopoetic
myxomatosis
myxomycetes
nyctitropic
nyctophobia
nympholepsy
nymphomania
oysterplant
pyramidally
pyramidical
pyrargyrite
pyroclastic
pyrotechnic
Pythagorean
Pythagorism
sybaritical
sycophantic
sycophantry
syllabarium
syllabicity
syllogistic
symbolistic
symmetrical
sympathetic
sympathiser
sympetalous
symphonious
symposiarch
symptomatic
synagogical
synchromesh
synchronise
synchronism
synchronous
synchrotron
syncopation
syndesmosis
syndicalism
syndicalist
syndication
synergistic
synonymical
syntactical
synthesiser
synthetical
syssarcosis
systematics
systematise
systematism
systematist
typecasting
typefounder
typefoundry
typesetting
typewritten
typicalness
typographer
typographic
typological
tyrannicide
tyrannosaur
tyrannously
xylocarpous
xylographer
xylographic
xylophagous
xylophonist
zygomorphic
azotobacter
ozoniferous
ozonisation
ozonosphere

---

abandonment
academicals
academician
academicism
acarpellous
acatalectic
acaulescent
alabastrine
amaranthine
amativeness

amazonstone
anachronism
anachronous
anacoluthon
anacreontic
anadiplosis
anaesthesia
anaesthetic
anagnorisis
analogously
anaphylaxis
anarchistic
anastomoses
anastomosis
anastomotic
apartmental
beachcomber
bearbaiting
bearishness
beastliness
beauteously
beautifully
beaverboard
blackavised
blackbeetle
blackbirder
blackcoated
blackfellow
blackgrouse
blackmailer
blackmarket
bladderwort
blamelessly
blameworthy
blasphemous
blastogenic
boardschool
brachiation
brachyurous
bracteolate
bradycardia
braggadocio
Brahmanical
brahmaputra
Brahminical
brainlessly
brainsickly
brainteaser
branchiopod
brankursine
brazenfaced
ceaselessly
chaetognath
chafingdish
chainarmour
chainletter
chainsmoker
chainstitch
chalcedonic
challenging
chamaephyte
chamberlain
chambermaid
chameleonic
champertous
chancellery
chancellory
changefully
channelling
chansonnier
chanterelle
chanticleer
chaotically
chaperonage
charcuterie
chargesheet
charismatic
charlatanry
chartaceous
chaulmoogra
clairschach
clairvoyant
clamorously
clandestine
clapperclaw
Clarencieux
classically
coadunation
coagulation
coalescence
coarctation
crabbedness
crackerjack
craftswoman
craniometry
deactivator
deathrattle
diachronism
diacritical
diadelphous
diagnostics
dialectally
dialectical
dialogistic
diamagnetic
diametrical
diamondback
diaphaneity
diaphoresis
diaphoretic
diapophysis
diapositive
diarthrosis
diastematic
diastrophic
diatessaron
draggletail
dramaturgic
drastically
draughtsman
drawingroom
dualcontrol
dualpurpose
egalitarian
ejaculation
ejaculatory
elaborately
elaboration
elaborative
elastically
elasticated
elastomeric
emancipator
emasculator
enarthrosis
eradication
eradicative
Erastianism
evagination
evanescence
evangelical
evanishment
evaporation
evaporative
evasiveness
exaggerator
examination
exanthemata
exarcerbate
fearfulness
feasibility
featheredge
featherhead
featherless
featureless
flabbergast
flaccidness
flagcaptain
flagellator
flagofficer
flagwagging
flamboyance
flamboyancy
flamboyante
flannelette
flannelling
flatulently
flauntingly
flavourless
flavoursome
fractionary
fractionate
fractionise
fractiously
fragmentary
Francomania
Francophile
Francophobe
francophone
franctireur
frankfurter
franklinite
frankpledge
frantically
franticness
fraternally
fraterniser
fratricidal
fraudulence
geanticline
ghastliness
giantpowder
glaringness
glassblower
glasscutter
glassmaking
glauconitic
gracelessly
gracileness
gradational
gradiometer
gradualness
GraecoRoman
grammalogue
grammatical
gramophonic
grandfather
grandiflora
grandiosely
grandiosity
grandmother
grandnephew
grandparent
grangeriser
granivorous
granolithic
granophyric
granularity
granulation
granulocyte
graphically
graphicness
grasshopper
gratulation
gratulatory
gravedigger
gravelblind
gravimetric
gravitation
gravitative
guardedness
headborough
headhunting
healthfully
healthiness
heartbroken
hearthstone
heartlessly
heartsblood
heartstring
heavenwards
heavyfooted
heavyhanded
heavyweight
hyacinthine
imaginarily
imagination
imaginative
inadaptable
inadvertent
inadvisable
inalienable
inalienably
inalterable
inalterably
inanimately
inanimation
inappetence
inattention
inattentive
inaugurator
itacolumite
jealousness
knavishness
kwashiorkor
leapfrogged
learnedness
leaseholder
leatherback
leatherhead
leatherneck
leavetaking
loathliness
loathsomely
meadowgrass
meadowsweet
meaningless
measureless
measurement
Neanderthal
nearsighted
opalescence
oracularity
orangoutang
ovariectomy
peacemaking
pearlescent
pearlfisher
phagedaenic
phagocytise
phagocytose
phalanstery
phantasiast
phantasmata
pharisaical
phariseeism
pharyngitis
placability
plagiariser
plagioclase
plagiostome
plainspoken
plaintively
planetarium
planetoidal
planimetric
planisphere
planoconvex
plantigrade
plasmolysis
plasmolytic
plasterwork
plasticiser
platearmour
plateresque
platforming
platinotype
platyrrhine
playerpiano
playfulness
playingcard
practicable
practicably
practically
praetorship
pragmatical
prattlingly
prayerwheel
quacksalver
quadraphony
quadratical
quadrennial
quadrennium
quadrillion
quadrupedal
quaestorial
qualifiable
qualitative
quarrelling
quarrelsome
quarterback
quarterdeck
quartertone
quaternloaf
reachmedown
reactionary
reactionist
readability
readywitted
realignment
realisation
realpolitik
reanimation
reapportion
reappraisal
rearadmiral
reassertion
reassurance
reawakening
rhabdomancy
rhapsodical
roadholding
scaffolding
scalariform
scalearmour
scaleinsect
scalpriform
scarabaeoid
scaremonger
scattergood
searchingly
searchlight
seasickness
shacklebolt
shacklebone
shadowgraph
shadowiness
Shaksperean
Shaksperian
shallowness
shamanistic
shamelessly
shapeliness
shareholder
sharepusher
sharpwitted
skatingrink
slaughterer
slavedriver
slaveholder
slavemarket
slavishness
Slavonicise
smallholder
smallminded
snatchblock
soapboiling
spaceflight
spaceheater
spacesaving
sparingness
sparrowbill
sparrowhawk
spasmodical
spastically
spathaceous
spatterdash
stadtholder
stagemanage
stagestruck
stagflation
stainlessly
staircarpet
stakeholder
stalactitic
stalagmitic
stallholder
stampoffice
standardise
standoffish
standpatter
starchiness
starcrossed
starstudded
startlingly
stateliness
statesmanly
statistical
statutebook
statutorily
staunchless
staunchness
staurolitic
suasiveness
swallowable
swallowdive
swallowhole
swallowtail
swallowwort
swarthiness
teachership
tearfulness
tearstained
teaspoonful
thalidomide
thanatology
thanklessly
thanksgiver
thankworthy
thaumatrope
thaumaturge
thaumaturgy
toastmaster
trabeculate
tracasserie
tracelessly
tracheotomy
trackwalker
traditional
traducement
trafficator
trafficking
trafficless
tragedienne
tragicomedy
trailblazer
trainbearer
trammelling
transaction
transalpine
transceiver
transcriber
transection
transferred

transferrer
transfigure
transfinite
transfixion
transformer
transfusion
transhumant
transiently
transilient
translation
translocate
translucent
translunary
transmarine
transmittal
transmitted
transmitter
transpadane
transparent
transpierce
transponder
transporter
transsexual
transuranic
transversal
trapeziform
trapezoidal
Trappistine
traversable
unaccounted
unadvisedly
unalterable
unambiguous
unanimously
unappealing
unashamedly
unassertive
unavailable
unavoidable
unavoidably
unawareness
Upanishadic
uranography
weakhearted
wealthiness
wearilessly
wearisomely
weathercock
weatherwise
weatherworn
zealousness
zoantharian
Abbevillian
abbreviator
Albigensian
albuminuria
ambiguously
ambitiously
ambivalence
ambivalency
ambiversion
arbitrageur
arbitrament
arbitrarily
arbitration
arbitrative
arbitratrix
arboraceous
arborescent
babysitting
bibliolater
bibliolatry
bibliomancy
bibliomania
bibliopegic
bibliophile
bibliophily
bibliopolic
bibliotheca

cabbagepalm
cabbagerose
cabbagetree
cabbageworm
cabbalistic
cobblestone
cybernation
cybernetics
debarkation
debauchment
debouchment
dubiousness
elbowgrease
embarkation
embellisher
emblematise
emblematist
embowelling
embowerment
embraceable
embracement
embracingly
embrocation
embroiderer
embroilment
embryologic
embryonated
fabrication
gibberellin
gibbousness
haberdasher
habiliments
habituation
hebephrenia
hebephrenic
Hebraically
hibernacula
hibernation
Hibernicism
hobbledehoy
imbrication
jabberwocky
labefaction
labiodental
laboriously
libertarian
liberticide
libertinage
libertinism
lubrication
lubricative
orbicularly
publication
publishable
publishment
Rabelaisian
rebarbative
ribbongrass
ribvaulting
rubberstamp
rubefacient
rubefaction
rubicundity
rubrication
Sabbatarian
seborrhoeic
soberminded
subaerially
subarration
subaudition
subaxillary
subbasement
subcategory
subclinical
subcontract
subcontrary
subcortical
subcritical
subcultural

subdivision
subdominant
subjugation
subjunctive
sublimation
sublimeness
sublittoral
submarginal
submergence
submersible
submissible
submultiple
subordinate
subornation
subregional
subrogation
subscapular
subsequence
subservient
subsistence
subspecific
substandard
substantial
substantive
substituent
subsumption
subsumptive
subterminal
subtraction
subtractive
subtropical
subumbrella
suburbanise
suburbanite
sybaritical
tabefaction
tabernacled
tabletennis
tobacconist
tobogganing
tobogganist
tuberculate
tuberculise
tuberculose
tuberculous
unbeknownst
unbelieving
unbendingly
unbeseeming
unboundedly
unbreakable
vibratility
vibrational
accelerando
accelerator
accentually
acceptation
acceptingly
accessorial
accessorise
accipitrine
acclamation
acclamatory
acclimation
acclimatise
acclivitous
accommodate
accompanist
accordantly
accordingly
accoucheuse
accountable
accountably
accountancy
accrescence
acculturate
accumulator
accusatival
alcyonarian

ancientness
archaeology
archaeornis
archaically
archangelic
archdiocese
archduchess
archdukedom
Archimedean
archipelago
ascensional
ascetically
ascomycetes
bacchanalia
bacciferous
bacilliform
backbencher
backcountry
bactericide
bicarbonate
bicentenary
bicephalous
bicorporate
bicuspidate
bucolically
cacographic
cacophonous
cicatricial
coccidiosis
cochinchina
cockaleekie
cockleshell
cockyleekie
coconscious
cyclopaedia
cyclopaedic
cycloserine
cyclothymia
cyclothymic
dactylogram
dactylology
decantation
decarbonate
decarbonise
decarburise
deceitfully
deceivingly
decelerator
decemvirate
decennially
deceptively
decerebrate
declamation
declamatory
declaration
declarative
declaratory
declination
declivitous
decollation
decolletage
decolourise
decorticate
decrepitate
decrepitude
decrescendo
decussately
decussation
dicephalous
dichogamous
dichotomise
dichotomist
dichotomous
dichromatic
dicotyledon
dictatorial
doctrinaire
doctrinally
documentary

encapsulate
enchainment
enchantment
enchantress
enchiridion
encomiastic
encrustment
encumbrance
encystation
eschatology
escheatable
escheatment
eucalyptole
Eucharistic
euchologion
exceedingly
excellently
exceptional
excessively
exclamation
exclamatory
exclusively
exclusivity
excoriation
excremental
excrescence
excrescency
exculpation
exculpatory
excursively
facelifting
facetiously
facsimilist
factfinding
factionally
factualness
facultative
fecundation
huckleberry
incalescent
incantation
incantatory
incarcerate
incardinate
incarnadine
incarnation
incertitude
incessantly
incinerator
incipiently
inclemently
inclination
inclusively
incoercible
incognisant
incoherence
incoherency
incommodity
incompetent
incompliant
incongruent
incongruity
incongruous
inconscient
inconsonant
inconstancy
incontinent
incorporate
incorporeal
incorrectly
incorruptly
increasable
incredulity
incredulous
incremental
incriminate
inculcation
inculpation
inculpatory

incunabulum
incuriosity
incuriously
incurvation
incurvature
Jacobinical
Jacobitical
jactitation
kickstarter
lachrymator
laciniation
laconically
lacrimation
lacrimatory
lacrimosely
lacrymation
lacrymatory
lacrymosely
lactescence
lactiferous
lecherously
lectureship
lichenology
lickerishly
lickspittle
loculicidal
lucratively
lucubration
lycanthrope
lycanthropy
machicolate
machination
machinemade
mackerelsky
macrobiotic
macrocosmic
macrogamete
macroscopic
McCarthyism
mechanician
mechanistic
Micawberish
Micawberism
micrococcal
micrococcus
microcosmic
microgamete
micrography
microgroove
microlithic
micrometric
Micronesian
microphonic
microphytic
microscopic
microsecond
micturition
mockingbird
mycological
mycophagist
mycorrhizae
mycorrhizal
necessarian
necessarily
necessitate
necessitous
neckerchief
necrobiosis
necrologist
necromancer
necromantic
necrophilia
necrophilic
necropoleis
nickelplate
nictitation
noctilucent
noctivagant
noctivagous

nocturnally
nyctitropic
nyctophobia
occipitally
occultation
oecological
oecumenical
oncological
orchestrate
orchidology
oscillation
oscillatory
oscillogram
pachydermal
pacifically
pacificator
packingcase
peccability
peccadillos
pectination
peculiarity
pecuniarily
Pickwickian
pictography
pictorially
picturebook
picturecard
picturegoer
picturesque
pocketknife
pocketmoney
pocketsized
pococurante
racemeeting
racketpress
recalculate
recantation
receptacula
receptively
receptivity
recessional
recessively
reciprocate
reciprocity
reclaimable
reclamation
recognition
recognitive
recognitory
recommender
recommittal
recondition
reconnoitre
reconstruct
recoverable
recriminate
recruitment
rectangular
rectifiable
rectilineal
rectilinear
recumbently
recurrently
rickettsial
ricochetted
rockcrystal
sacculation
sacramental
sacrificial
secondarily
secondclass
secondrater
secondsight
secretarial
secretariat
secretively
sectionally
sickbenefit
sickeningly
sickishness
sociability
socialistic
Socinianism
sociologist
sociometric
sociopathic
sockdolager
sockdologen
succedaneum
succourless
succulently
suckingfish
sycophantic
sycophantry
tacheometer
tachycardia
tachygraphy
taciturnity
technically
technocracy
technologic
uncanniness
uncanonical
uncatchable
unceasingly
uncertainly
uncertainty
unchristian
uncivilised
uncleanness
unclimbable
uncluttered
uncommitted
unconcealed
unconcerned
uncongenial
unconnected
unconscious
uncontested
uncountable
uncouthness
uncrushable
vacationist
vaccination
vacillation
vacuolation
vacuousness
vicariously
viceadmiral
vicegerency
viceregally
viceroyalty
viceroyship
vichyssoise
viciousness
vicissitude
victualless
victualling
vociferance
vociferator
yacketyyack
abdominally
androgynous
arduousness
audaciously
audibleness
audiologist
audiometric
audiovisual
bedevilment
bedizenment
biddability
Bodhisattva
bodybuilder
bodyservant
caddishness
codefendant
codicillary
dedicatedly
deductively
didacticism
dodecaphony
elderliness
endearingly
endemically
endlessness
endocardiac
endocardial
endocardium
endometrium
endomorphic
endophagous
endoplasmic
endorsement
endoskelton
endothelial
endothelium
endothermal
endothermic
endotrophic
eudaemonism
eudaemonist
eudiometric
exdirectory
faddishness
fiddlestick
fidgetiness
godchildren
goddaughter
godforsaken
godlessness
hedgehopped
hedgepriest
hedgeschool
hideousness
Hudibrastic
hydraheaded
hydrobromic
hydrocarbon
hydrocyanic
hydrogenate
hydrogenous
hydrography
hydrologist
hydromedusa
hydrometeor
hydrometric
hydropathic
hydrophilic
hydrophobia
hydrophobic
hydrophytic
hydroponics
hydrosphere
hydrostatic
hydrotactic
hydrothorax
hydrotropic
indeciduous
indefinable
indefinably
indehiscent
indentation
independent
indifferent
indigestion
indigestive
indignantly
indignation
indirection
individuate
indivisible
indivisibly
IndoChinese
IndoIranian
indomitable
indomitably
indorsement
indubitable
indubitably
inductively
indulgently
industrious
Judaisation
judgmatical
judiciously
ludicrously
maddeningly
madreporite
madrigalian
madrigalist
mediaevally
mediastinal
mediastinum
mediateness
mediatorial
mediatrices
medicinable
medicinally
medicolegal
medievalism
medievalist
mediumistic
middleclass
middlesized
moderations
modernistic
mudslinging
oldwomanish
orderliness
paddleboard
paddlewheel
pedagogical
pedestalled
pedicellate
pediculosis
pedological
pedunculate
podophyllin
radicalness
radioactive
radiocarbon
radiography
radiolarian
radiologist
radiometric
radiophonic
redactional
reddishness
redetermine
redirection
rediscovery
redoubtable
redundantly
reduplicate
rodenticide
rodomontade
rudimentary
saddlecloth
saddlehorse
Sadduceeism
sedentarily
sedimentary
seditionary
seditiously
seductively
sideslipped
sidestepped
sidewheeler
tediousness
tiddlywinks
underbidder
undercharge
underexpose
underground
undergrowth
underhanded
undermanned
underpinned
underseller
undersigned
understated
undertaking
undertenant
undervaluer
underweight
underwriter
undeserving
undesirable
undeveloped
undisguised
undisturbed
undoubtedly
undutifully
wedgeshaped
wedgetailed
widdershins
widowerhood
abecedarian
acetylation
adenomatous
alembicated
Alexandrian
alexandrine
alexandrite
ameliorator
amenability
amenorrhoea
amentaceous
Americanise
Americanism
Americanist
amethystine
anecdotical
anemometric
anencephaly
arenicolous
Areopagitic
aseptically
awesomeness
awestricken
beechmarten
biedermeier
blepharitis
blessedness
breadbasket
breadcrumbs
breadthways
breadthwise
breadwinner
breastplate
breastwheel
breathalyse
breechblock
breezeblock
byeelection
cheerleader
cheerlessly
cheesecloth
cheiromancy
chemotactic
chevalglass
cleanlimbed
cleanliness
cleanshaven
clearheaded
cleistogamy
clericalism
clericalist
coeducation
coefficient
coessential
coeternally
coexistence
coextension
coextensive
creationism
creationist
credentials
credibility
credulously
crematorium
crenellated
crenulation
crepitation
crepuscular
crestfallen
ctenophoran
deemphasise
deerstalker
dreadnought
dreamlessly
dresscircle
dressmaking
electioneer
electrician
electricity
electrocute
electrolier
electrology
electrolyse
electrolyte
electronics
electrotype
elementally
elephantine
elephantoid
epeirogenic
esemplastic
eveningstar
eventualise
eventuality
everlasting
executioner
executorial
executrices
executrixes
exemplarily
exemplarity
exercisable
eyecatching
feelingness
fieldcornet
fieldworker
fleshliness
flexibility
freebooting
freehearted
freemasonry
freethinker
freethought
freezedried
frenchified
Frenchwoman
fretfulness
greasepaint
greaseproof
greatnephew
greengrocer
greenkeeper
greenockite
guesstimate
haematocele
haematocrit
haematology
haemocyanin
haemoglobin
haemophilia
haemophilic
haemoptysis
haemorrhage
haemorrhoid
haemostasis
haemostatic

heedfulness
hierarchism
identically
ideographic
ideological
inebriation
inedibility
ineffective
ineffectual
inefficient
inelegantly
ineloquence
ineluctable
ineluctably
inequitable
inequitably
inescapable
inessential
inestimable
inestimably
inexactness
inexcusable
inexcusably
inexistence
inexpedient
inexpensive
ipecacuanha
kleptomania
lieutenancy
myelomatous
needfulness
needlecraft
needlepoint
needlewoman
oneiromancy
onerousness
opencircuit
openhearted
openmouthed
operational
operatively
operculated
operoseness
oreographic
oreological
overanxious
overbalance
overbearing
overbidding
overcropped
overdevelop
overgarment
overindulge
overlapping
overmanning
overmeasure
overpayment
overproduce
overrunning
oversailing
oversetting
overstepped
overstretch
overstuffed
overtopping
overweening
overwritten
overwrought
paederastic
paediatrics
paediatrist
paedophilia
peevishness
phenologist
pieceworker
pietistical
pleasurable
pleasurably
plebeianise
plebeianism
plectoptera
pleinairist
pleiotropic
Pleistocene
plenipotent
plenteously
plentifully
pleochroism
pleomorphic
pleurodynia
pneumonitis
preachiness
preaudience
Precambrian
precautious
precedented
precedently
precentress
preceptress
precipitant
precipitate
precipitous
preciseness
preconceive
precontract
predatorily
predecessor
predicament
predication
predicative
predicatory
predictable
predictably
predominant
predominate
preelection
preeminence
preexistent
prefatorial
prefatorily
prefectural
prehistoric
preignition
prejudgment
prejudicial
prelibation
preliminary
prelusively
prelusorily
prematurely
prematurity
premeditate
premiership
premonition
premonitory
prenominate
preoccupied
preparation
preparative
preparatory
preposition
prepositive
preprandial
prerogative
presanctify
presbyteral
presciently
preselector
presentable
presentably
presentient
presentment
preservable
pressagency
prestigious
prestissimo
prestressed
presumingly
presumption
presumptive
pretendedly
pretentious
preterhuman
preterition
prevalently
prevaricate
preventable
preventible
previsional
pseudograph
pseudomonas
pseudomorph
pseudopodia
pteridology
pterodactyl
queenliness
querulously
questionary
reedbunting
reeducation
reedwarbler
reemergence
reenactment
reestablish
rheological
rheotropism
rhetorician
rheumaticky
roentgenise
scenography
sceptically
sheathknife
sheepfarmer
sheepmaster
sheetanchor
shellacking
shelljacket
shelterbelt
shelterless
shepherdess
sheriffalty
sheriffship
skeletonise
sketchiness
sleepingbag
sleepingcar
sleeplessly
sleepwalker
sleeveboard
slenderness
sleuthhound
speakership
specifiable
specificity
spectacular
spectatress
spectrality
spectrogram
spectrology
speculation
speculative
speechifier
speedometer
spelaeology
spellbinder
spendthrift
spermaphyte
spermatozoa
spermicidal
spessartite
steadfastly
steamboiler
steamroller
steatopygia
steelworker
steeplebush
steeplejack
steerageway
steganogram
stegosaurus
stellionate
stencilling
stenochromy
stenography
stenotypist
stepbrother
stephanotis
stereograph
stereometry
stereophony
stereoscope
stereoscopy
stereotyped
stereotyper
stereotypic
sternsheets
sternutator
stethoscope
stethoscopy
stevengraph
stewardship
sweepstakes
swellheaded
teenybopper
teeterboard
teetotalism
teetotaller
theatregoer
theatricals
thenceforth
theobromine
theocentric
theodolitic
theological
theorematic
theoretical
theosophist
therapeutic
thereabouts
theretofore
therewithal
thermically
thermionics
thermoduric
thermograph
thermolysis
thermolytic
thermometer
thermometry
thermophile
thermoscope
thermotaxis
treacherous
treacliness
treasonable
treasonably
treecreeper
trelliswork
tremblement
tremblingly
tremulously
trenchantly
trencherman
trendsetter
trepanation
trepidation
trestletree
trestlework
twelvemonth
twelvepenny
unemotional
unendurable
unendurably
unequivocal
unessential
unexploited
unexpressed
uselessness
weenybopper
wheelbarrow
wheelwright
whereabouts
wheresoever
wherewithal
wreckmaster
affectation
affectingly
affectional
affectioned
affectively
affectivity
afficionado
affiliation
affirmation
affirmative
affirmatory
affranchise
affrication
affricative
anfractuous
befittingly
bifurcation
buffalorobe
coffeehouse
coffeetable
defalcation
defectively
defenceless
defensively
deferential
defibrinate
deficiently
definiendum
deflagrator
defloration
defoliation
deforcement
deformation
defraudment
differentia
differently
difficultly
diffidently
diffraction
diffuseness
diffusively
effectively
effectually
efficacious
efficiently
effulgently
enfeoffment
enforceable
enforcement
enfranchise
exfoliation
exfoliative
gafftopsail
infanticide
infantilism
infantryman
infatuation
inferential
inferiority
infertility
infestation
infeudation
infiltrator
infinitival
infirmarian
inflammable
inflammably
inflexional
influential
informality
information
informative
informatory
infrangible
infrequence
infrequency
lifemanship
nefariously
obfuscation
obfuscatory
offenceless
offensively
offhandedly
officialdom
officialese
officialism
officiation
officinally
officiously
olfactology
raffishness
referential
reflectance
reflexively
reflexology
reformation
reformative
reformatory
refrangible
refreshment
refrigerant
refrigerate
refringency
rifacimenti
rifacimento
safebreaker
safeconduct
safecracker
safekeeping
safetyvalve
softhearted
softshelled
sufficiency
suffixation
suffocation
suffocative
suffragette
suffumigate
toffeenosed
tufthunting
unfailingly
unfaltering
unfashioned
unfeelingly
unfeignedly
unflappable
unflinching
unforgiving
unfortunate
unfurnished
agglomerate
agglutinate
aggravation
aggregately
aggregation
aggregative
aggrievedly
aiguillette
algological
algorithmic
angelically
angiography
Anglicanism
AngloFrench
AngloIndian
anglomaniac
AngloNorman
anglophobia
anglophobic

arglebargle
argumentive
augmentable
Augustinian
beguilement
beguilingly
cognateness
cognitional
cognitively
cognitivity
cognoscente
cognoscenti
cognoscible
deglutition
degradation
degradingly
degustation
digestively
digitigrade
doggishness
engineering
engorgement
engrossment
ergatocracy
eugenically
gegenschein
gigantesque
haggadistic
haggardness
Hagiographa
hagiography
hagiologist
hagioscopic
Hegelianism
highbrowism
highfalutin
highpitched
highpowered
highranking
highstepper
highwrought
hoggishness
hugeousness
hygrometric
hygrophytic
hygroscopic
ingathering
ingeniously
ingenuously
ingrainedly
ingratitude
ingurgitate
legerdemain
legionnaire
legislation
legislative
legislature
ligamentary
ligamentous
lightfooted
lighthanded
lightheaded
lightminded
lightsomely
lightweight
logarithmic
loggerheads
logicalness
logographer
logographic
logomachist
magazinegun
magdalenian
magisterial
magisterium
magistratic
Maglemosian
magnanimity
magnanimous

magnificent
megalomania
megalopolis
megatherium
negationist
negligently
negotiation
negotiatory
negotiatrix
negrophobia
nightingale
nightmarish
nightporter
nightwalker
nigrescence
organically
organisable
organscreen
pigeonchest
piggishness
pigheadedly
pigsticking
regardfully
regenerable
regenerator
regimentals
regionalise
regionalism
regionalist
registrable
regretfully
regrettable
regrettably
regurgitate
rightangled
righteously
righthanded
righthander
rightminded
rightwinger
roguishness
sagaciously
Sagittarius
segmentally
segregation
segregative
sightlessly
sightliness
sightreader
sightscreen
sightseeing
sightworthy
sigmoidally
signifiable
significant
signpainter
sugarcoated
suggestible
tagliatelle
tagliatelli
tegumentary
tightfisted
tightlipped
togglejoint
ungetatable
ungodliness
unguardedly
unguiculate
vagabondage
vagabondise
vagabondish
vagabondism
vagariously
voguishness
waggishness
Yugoslavian
zygomorphic
abhorrently
achievement

achondritic
achromatise
achromatism
aphrodisiac
atheistical
athleticism
behavioural
bohemianism
dehydration
echosounder
enhancement
ephemerides
etherealise
ethereality
ethnography
ethnologist
ethological
exhaustible
exhaustless
exhortation
exhortative
exhortatory
ichnography
ichthyology
ichthyornis
ichthyosaur
inhabitable
inhabitancy
inheritable
inheritance
inheritress
ithyphallic
ochlocratic
ophidiarium
ophiologist
otherwhiles
schismatise
schistosity
schistosome
schizanthus
scholarship
scholiastic
schoolboard
schoolchild
schoolhouse
schottische
schwarmerei
sphaeridium
sphagnology
spherically
spherometer
spherulitic
sphincteral
sphincteric
sphygmogram
unhappiness
unhealthily
unhelpfully
upholsterer
vehmgericht
abiogeneses
abiogenesis
abiogenetic
abiological
abiotically
acidifiable
acidophilic
acidulation
acinaciform
adiaphorism
ahistorical
amiableness
amicability
animalcular
anisotropic
aristocracy
axiological
boilermaker
bricklaying

bridgeboard
brilliantly
bristletail
bristleworm
bristliness
Britishness
brittleness
chiaroscuro
chickenfeed
chickenwire
chieftaincy
childminder
chimaerical
chinoiserie
Chippendale
chirography
chiropodist
chiropteran
chitterling
cliffhanger
climacteric
climatology
clinometric
coincidence
coinheritor
coinsurance
criminalist
criminality
crimination
criminative
criminatory
criminology
criticality
criticaster
daisycutter
deification
deistically
drillmaster
edification
edificatory
editorially
elicitation
eligibility
elimination
eliminative
Elizabethan
enigmatical
epidiascope
epigastrium
epigraphist
epinephrine
epipetalous
episcopally
epithalamia
epithalamic
epithelioma
evidentiary
existential
fairweather
faithhealer
faithlessly
faithworthy
flightiness
flimflammer
flirtatious
friableness
fricandeaux
frightfully
frigidarium
frivolously
gainfulness
gristliness
guilelessly
guiltlessly
hairbreadth
hairdresser
hairraising
hairstyling
hairstylist

hairtrigger
heinousness
idiographic
idiomorphic
idiotically
imitatively
initialling
iridescence
itinerantly
itineration
laicisation
Leibnitzian
maidservant
mailcarrier
maintenance
maintopmast
maintopsail
maisonnette
moisturiser
nailvarnish
neighbourly
noiselessly
noisemaking
noisomeness
oligochaete
oligomerous
ominousness
opinionated
orientalise
orientalism
orientalist
orientation
originality
origination
originative
oviposition
painfulness
painkilling
painstaking
philanderer
philatelist
philhellene
philologian
philologist
philosopher
philosophic
pliableness
plicateness
pointdevice
pointedness
pointillism
pointillist
pointlessly
poisonously
prickliness
priestcraft
primaevally
primateship
primatology
primigenial
primiparous
primitively
primitivism
principally
privateness
privatively
prizewinner
psittacosis
quickchange
quickfiring
quickfreeze
quickfrozen
quicksilver
quickwitted
quiescently
quilldriver
quincuncial
quinquennia
quinquereme

quintillion
quitchgrass
quizzically
reification
reincarnate
reinsertion
reinsurance
reintegrate
reintroduce
reiteration
reiterative
rhinologist
rhinoscopic
rhizanthous
rhizocarpic
rhizomatous
ruinousness
saintliness
saintpaulia
scientistic
scientology
scintillant
scintillate
scissorbill
scissortail
seigneurial
seigniorage
seigniorial
seismically
seismograph
seismometer
seismometry
seismoscope
shiftlessly
shipbreaker
shipbuilder
shirtsleeve
skilfulness
slickenside
slightingly
smilelessly
smithereens
smithsonite
snickersnee
spifflicate
spindlelegs
spindletree
spinelessly
spiniferous
Spinozistic
spinsterish
spiraculate
spiritistic
spiritlevel
spiritually
spiritualty
spirituelle
spirochaete
spirochetal
spirometric
stichometry
stickinsect
stickleback
stiffnecked
stiflejoint
stiltedness
stimulation
stimulative
stipendiary
stipulation
stipulatory
stirrupbone
stirruppump
suitability
swiftfooted
swimbladder
swingletree
swinishness
switchblade

switchboard
thickheaded
thickwitted
thimbleweed
thingumabob
thingumajig
thinskinned
thirstiness
thistledown
thitherward
thixotropic
triadically
triangulate
tribulation
tribuneship
tribunicial
tribunitial
tributarily
trichinosis
trichomonad
tricksiness
tricoloured
triennially
triggerfish
trimestrial
trimorphism
trimorphous
Trinitarian
tripetalous
triphibious
triphyllous
triquetrous
tristichous
trisyllabic
trisyllable
tritagonist
tritheistic
trituration
triumvirate
trivialness
unicellular
unicoloured
unification
uniformness
unigeniture
unimportant
uninhabited
uninhibited
uninucleate
unipersonal
unipolarity
unisexually
universally
utilisation
utilitarian
voicelessly
wainscoting
wainscotted
waitinglist
waitingroom
weighbridge
weightiness
Weismannism
whichsoever
whiffletree
whigmaleery
whimsically
whippletree
whistlestop
Whitechapel
whitecollar
whiteheaded
whitethroat
whitewasher
whitherward
whitishness
whitleather
Whitsuntide
adjectively
adjournment
adjudgement
adjudicator
enjambement
injudicious
injuriously
objectively
objectivism
objectivist
objectivity
objurgation
objurgatory
rejoicingly
rejuvenator
rejuvenesce
acknowledge
alkalescent
alkalimeter
alkalimetry
awkwardness
irksomeness
lakedweller
makebelieve
teknonymous
unkennelled
wakefulness
ablutionary
ailurophile
ailurophobe
allAmerican
allantoides
allegorical
allelomorph
alleviation
alleviative
alleviatory
allocatable
allomorphic
allopathist
balefulness
ballbearing
balletomane
balmcricket
BaltoSlavic
belatedness
bellbottoms
bellfounder
bellheather
bellicosity
belligerent
bellringing
Belorussian
bilaterally
biliousness
billetsdoux
billionaire
billposting
billsticker
bullbaiting
bulletproof
bullfighter
bullishness
bullterrier
calceolaria
calcicolous
calciferous
calcifugous
calcination
calculating
calculation
calculative
calefacient
calefactory
calendrical
calibration
californium
calisthenic
calligraphy
callousness
calorimeter
calorimetry
calumniator
Calvinistic
calyptrogen
celebration
celebratory
celestially
cellularity
chlorophyll
chloroplast
chloroprene
coldblooded
coldhearted
coleorrhiza
collaborate
collapsible
collectable
collectanea
collectedly
collectible
collenchyma
colligation
colligative
collimation
collinearly
collisional
collocation
collusively
colonelship
colonialism
colonialist
colorimeter
colorimetry
colouration
colourblind
colourfully
columbarium
columniated
culmination
culpability
cultivation
cylindrical
delectation
deleterious
deliciously
delightedly
delightsome
delineation
delinquency
deliriously
delitescent
deliverable
deliverance
deliveryman
dilapidated
dilapidator
diluvialist
dolefulness
dollishness
doltishness
eclecticism
ellipsoidal
ellipticity
enlargeable
enlargement
enlightened
enlivenment
fallibility
Falstaffian
falteringly
feldspathic
feloniously
felspathoid
filamentary
filamentous
filmography
filmsetting
filterpaper
folliculate
fulguration
fullblooded
fullfledged
fullhearted
fullmouthed
fulminating
fulmination
fulminatory
fulsomeness
gallantness
gallbladder
galleyslave
Gallicanism
gallimaufry
Gallophobia
gallowsbird
gallowstree
gillyflower
goldbeating
golddigging
goldenberry
gullibility
halfbinding
halfblooded
halfhearted
halfholiday
halflanding
halfmeasure
hallucinate
halophilous
halterbreak
heldentenor
heliochrome
heliography
heliometric
heliotropic
helleborine
Hellenistic
hellishness
helminthoid
helpfulness
hilariously
hollandaise
holoblastic
holographic
holothurian
hylogenesis
hylozoistic
illaffected
illbreeding
illdisposed
illfavoured
illhumoured
illiberally
illimitable
illimitably
illiquidity
illmannered
illogically
illtempered
illuminable
illuminance
illuminator
illusionism
illusionist
illustrator
illustrious
kilocalorie
Kulturkampf
lilylivered
maladaptive
maladjusted
maladroitly
malapropism
malariology
malediction
maledictory
malefaction
maleficence
malevolence
malfeasance
malfunction
maliciously
malignantly
malposition
malpractice
melancholia
melancholic
melanochroi
melanophore
melioration
meliorative
meliphagous
melliferous
mellifluent
mellifluous
melodiously
millenarian
milliampere
millionaire
millisecond
molecricket
molecularly
molendinary
molestation
mollycoddle
molybdenite
multangular
multicolour
multilinear
multinomial
multiparous
multiracial
multistorey
multivalent
nullifidian
nulliparity
nulliparous
obliqueness
obliviously
oilpainting
Palaearctic
palaeotypic
Palestinian
palindromic
palmcabbage
palpability
palpitation
palsgravine
Pelagianism
pelargonium
pellucidity
pillowfight
pilocarpine
pilotburner
polarimeter
polarimetry
polarisable
polariscope
polemically
polevaulter
policewoman
politically
politicking
pollination
poltergeist
poltroonery
polyandrous
polycarpous
polychromic
polycrystal
polygenesis
polygenetic
polyglottal
polyglottic
polygonally
polygraphic
polymorphic
polyonymous
polypeptide
polyphagous
polyphonous
polystyrene
polytechnic
polyzoarium
pulchritude
pullthrough
pullulation
pulverulent
rallentando
relatedness
relationism
relationist
reliability
religionise
religionism
religionist
religiosity
religiously
reluctantly
reluctation
salaciously
saleability
salesladies
salinometer
salmonberry
salpingitis
saltatorial
saltimbanco
salvageable
salvational
scleroderma
sclerometer
sclerophyll
sclerotitis
selaginella
selectively
selectivity
selfassured
selfcentred
selfclosing
selfcocking
selfcommand
selfconceit
selfcontent
selfcontrol
selfcreated
selfculture
selfdefence
selfdenying
selfdespair
selfdevoted
selfdisplay
selfelected
selfevident
selffeeding
selffeeling
selffertile
selfimposed
selfinduced
selfinvited
selfishness
selflimited
selfloading
selflocking
selfmastery
selfopinion
selfpitying
selfraising
selfreliant
selfreproof
selfrespect
selfsealing
selfseeking
selfservice
selfserving

selfstarter
selfsterile
selfsupport
selftorture
selfwinding
selfworship
sillimanite
silveriness
silverplate
silverpoint
silversmith
silverstick
solanaceous
soldierlike
soldiership
solifluxion
soliloquise
soliloquist
solipsistic
solmisation
solutionist
solvability
splashboard
splayfooted
splendorous
splenectomy
splenetical
sulphureous
sulphurwort
syllabarium
syllabicity
syllogistic
talebearing
talentscout
talkatively
telegrammic
telegrapher
telegraphic
telekinesis
telekinetic
teleologism
teleologist
telepathise
telepathist
telephonist
teleprinter
tolbutamide
unlimitedly
valediction
valedictory
valiantness
valleculate
valuational
velvetiness
volcanicity
volcanology
volitionary
volkslieder
voltametric
volubleness
volumometer
voluntarily
voluntarism
voluntarist
vulcanicity
vulcanology
welcomeness
welladvised
wellbeloved
welldefined
wellfounded
wellgroomed
wellmeaning
wellordered
wellrounded
wellwishing
weltschmerz
wildcatting
wildfowling
willingness
wolfwhistle
xylocarpous
xylographer
xylographic
xylophagous
xylophonist
yellowbelly
adminicular
admiralship
aimlessness
Arminianism
armtwisting
atmospheric
bimetallism
bimetallist
bimillenary
bimillenium
bombardment
bombilation
bombination
bumblepuppy
bumptiously
camaraderie
campanology
campanulate
campmeeting
cementation
combatively
combination
combinative
combinatory
combustible
comestibles
comeuppance
comfortable
comfortably
comfortless
commandment
commemorate
commendable
commendably
commendator
commensally
commentator
commination
comminatory
comminution
commiserate
commissural
committable
commonality
commonplace
commonsense
communalise
communalism
communalist
communicant
communicate
communistic
commutation
commutative
compactness
compaginate
comparatist
comparative
compartment
compassable
compellable
compendious
compensator
competently
competition
competitive
compilation
compilement
complacence
complacency
complainant
complaisant
complexness
compliantly
complicated
complotting
comportment
compositely
composition
compositive
compossible
compotation
compotatory
compression
compressive
comprisable
comptroller
compunction
compurgator
computation
computerise
comradeship
comstockery
demagnetise
demagogical
demagoguery
demagoguism
demandingly
demarcation
demarkation
demigoddess
democratise
democratism
demographer
demographic
demonolatry
demonstrate
demountable
dimensional
dimwittedly
domesticate
domesticity
domiciliary
domiciliate
domineering
dumbfounder
emmenagogue
Emmenthaler
familiarise
familiarity
fimbriation
fomentation
gametangium
gametophyte
gamogenesis
gemmiferous
gemmiparous
gemmologist
gemmulation
gimcrackery
gymnospermy
Hamiltonian
hemeralopia
hemianopsia
hemimorphic
hemipterous
hemispheric
homeopathic
homeostasis
homeostatic
homesteader
homestretch
homiletical
homocentric
homoeopathy
homoestatic
homogeneity
homogeneous
homogenetic
homogeniser
homoiousian
homological
homomorphic
homophonous
homoplastic
homopterous
homosporous
homothallic
homozygosis
humiliation
humiliatory
hummingbird
hymenoptera
hymnography
immanentism
immanentist
immarginate
immediately
immedicable
immenseness
immigration
immitigable
immitigably
immortalise
immortality
immoveables
immunologic
jumpingbean
jumpingjack
kymographic
lamellicorn
lamelliform
lamentation
lammergeier
lammergeyer
lamplighter
limitedness
limitlessly
limnologist
luminescent
lumpishness
mammalogist
membraneous
memorabilia
memorialise
memorialist
mimetically
momentarily
momentously
namecalling
namedropper
nomadically
nomenclator
nominatival
nomographer
nomographic
nomological
numerically
numismatics
numismatist
nympholepsy
nymphomania
obmutescent
ommatophore
osmotically
pamphleteer
pomegranate
pomiculture
pomological
pompousness
pumicestone
remembrance
reminiscent
remonstrant
remonstrate
remorseless
remunerator
romanticise
romanticism
romanticist
rumbustious
semanticist
semasiology
semeiotical
semidiurnal
semiellipse
semimonthly
semipalmate
semiskilled
semitrailer
sempiternal
simperingly
simpliciter
somatically
somatogenic
somatologic
somatoplasm
somatotonia
somatotonic
somewhither
somnambular
somniculous
somniferous
somnolently
summariness
summational
summerhouse
summersault
sumptuosity
sumptuously
symbolistic
symmetrical
sympathetic
sympathiser
sympetalous
symphonious
symposiarch
symptomatic
tameability
temerarious
temperament
temperately
temperative
temperature
tempestuous
temporality
temporarily
timebargain
timepleaser
timeserving
timesharing
tumbledrier
tumefaction
unmanliness
unmatchable
unmeaningly
unmemorable
unmemorably
unmitigated
womanliness
abnormality
Aeneolithic
agnatically
agnosticism
annabergite
annihilator
anniversary
annunciator
bandylegged
banteringly
Benedictine
benediction
benedictory
benefaction
beneficence
beneficiary
beneficiate
benevolence
benightedly
benightment
benignantly
binocularly
Bonapartean
Bonapartism
Bonapartist
bonbonniere
bondservant
bondservice
bondwashing
canalicular
canaliculus
cancellated
candelabrum
candescence
candidature
candleberry
candlelight
candlepower
candlestick
cannibalise
cannibalism
canonically
cantharides
cantharidic
centenarian
centigramme
centreboard
centrepiece
centrifugal
centripetal
cinnabarine
cinquecento
concatenate
concealable
concealment
conceitedly
conceivable
conceivably
concentrate
conceptacle
concernment
concertedly
concertgoer
conciliator
conciseness
concomitant
concordance
concrescent
concubinage
concubinary
concubitant
concurrence
condemnable
condensable
conditional
conditioner
condolatory
condominium
condonation
condottiere
condottieri
conductance
conductible
conductress
condylomata
confabulate
confederacy
confederate
conferrable
confessedly
confidently
confidingly
confinement
confirmable
confiscable
confiscator
conflagrant

conflagrate
confliction
conflictive
conformable
conformably
conformally
conformance
confusingly
confutation
confutative
congealable
congealment
congelation
congenerous
congenially
congressman
congruently
congruously
conjectural
conjugality
conjugation
conjugative
conjunction
conjunctiva
conjunctive
conjuncture
conjuration
connectable
connectedly
connectible
connoisseur
connotation
connotative
connubially
conquerable
consanguine
consciously
consecrator
consecution
consecutive
consentient
consequence
conservable
conservancy
conservator
considerate
considering
consignable
consignment
consistence
consistency
consolation
consolatory
consolidate
consolingly
consonantal
consonantly
conspecific
conspicuity
conspicuous
conspirator
constellate
consternate
constituent
constitutor
constrictor
construable
constructor
consultancy
consumerism
consumingly
consummator
consumption
consumptive
containable
containment
contaminant
contaminate
contemplate
contentedly
contentious
contentment
conterminal
contestable
continental
continently
contingence
contingency
continuable
continually
continuance
continuator
contorniate
contrabasso
contractile
contraction
contractive
contractual
contracture
contradance
contraption
contrariety
contrarious
contrastive
contretemps
contributor
contrivable
contrivance
controlling
controlment
controversy
conurbation
convenances
convenience
conveniency
conventicle
convergence
convergency
conversable
conversance
conversancy
convertible
convertibly
conveyancer
convincible
convivially
convocation
convolution
convolvulus
cunningness
dangerously
dendritical
denigration
denigratory
denizenship
denominator
denticulate
dentigerous
denumerable
denunciator
diningtable
dinnerdance
dinnertable
dinnerwagon
dinosaurian
donnishness
dundrearies
duniewassal
dynamically
dynamometer
dynamometry
einsteinium
enneahedron
ennoblement
fanatically
fanfaronade
fantastical
fenestrated
financially
fingerboard
fingerglass
fingerplate
fingerprint
fingerstall
finicalness
FinnoUgrian
funambulate
funambulist
functionary
functionate
fundamental
gangsterism
gendarmerie
genealogise
genealogist
generaliser
generalship
generically
genetically
geniculated
genitivally
genteelness
gentianella
gentilitial
gentlemanly
gentlewoman
genuflexion
genuineness
gingerbread
gonfalonier
goniometric
gynaecocrat
gynaecology
handbreadth
handfasting
handgrenade
handicapped
handicapper
handknitted
handpainted
handselling
handwriting
handwritten
handwrought
Hindoostani
honeybadger
honeymooner
honeysuckle
hunchbacked
hundredfold
ignobleness
ignominious
innavigable
innervation
innocuously
innoxiously
innumerable
innumerably
innutrition
ionospheric
Jansenistic
kindhearted
kinematical
kinesiology
kinetograph
kinetoscope
Lancastrian
lancinating
lancination
landaulette
landgrabber
landgravine
landholding
landingbeam
landinggear
landlordism
languidness
lengthiness
lentiginous
linedrawing
linefishing
linendraper
lineprinter
lingeringly
linguistics
longanimity
longplaying
longsighted
managership
mandarinate
mandibulate
mandolinist
manducation
manducatory
Manichaeism
manifestant
manifestoes
manipulable
manipulator
manneristic
mannishness
mansardroof
mantelpiece
mantelshelf
mantuamaker
manufactory
manufacture
manumission
manumitting
mendelevium
meningocele
menservants
mensuration
mentholated
mentionable
mindbending
mindblowing
mindfulness
mindreading
mineraliser
minesweeper
miniaturise
miniaturist
ministerial
minnesinger
minuteglass
monarchical
monasterial
monasticism
moneylender
moneymaking
moneymarket
moneyspider
monitorship
monkeybread
monkeyshine
monocarpous
monochasial
monochasium
monochromat
monochromic
monoclinous
monoculture
monogenesis
monogenetic
monogrammed
monographer
monographic
monolingual
monological
monologuise
monologuist
monomorphic
mononuclear
monophagous
monophthong
Monophysite
monopoliser
monopterous
Monothelite
monozygotic
monseigneur
monstrosity
monstrously
mundaneness
municipally
munificence
ninnyhammer
nonchalance
nondelivery
nondescript
nonetheless
nonexistent
nonfeasance
nonmatching
nonmetallic
nonpartisan
nonplussing
nonresident
nonsensical
nonsequitur
nonspecific
nonunionist
nonviolence
nonvolatile
nuncupation
nuncupative
obnoxiously
oenological
oenophilist
omnifarious
omnipotence
omnipresent
omniscience
ornithology
ornithopter
ornithosaur
pandemonium
panegyrical
Panglossian
panhellenic
panicmonger
pantalettes
pantheistic
pantomimist
pantothenic
pendulously
penetrating
penetration
penetrative
penicillate
penicillium
peninsulate
penitential
pennyweight
penological
pensionable
pensionless
pensiveness
pentadactyl
pentagynous
pentahedron
pentamerous
pentandrous
pentathlete
pentavalent
pentazocine
Pentecostal
pentlandite
penultimate
penuriously
pinkishness
pinnatisect
ponderation
ponderosity
ponderously
pontificals
pontificate
punchinello
punctilious
punctuality
punctuation
rancorously
rangefinder
renaissance
renegotiate
ringstraked
sandbagging
sandskipper
sanguinaria
sanguineous
sansculotte
Sanskritist
senatorship
sensational
senselessly
sensibility
sensitively
sensitivity
sensorially
sententious
sentimental
sentinelled
sincereness
sinfonietta
singlestick
singletrack
singularise
singularity
sinistrally
sinistrorse
sinlessness
sinological
sinuousness
songfulness
songsparrow
sonofabitch
sunlessness
synagogical
synchromesh
synchronise
synchronism
synchronous
synchrotron
syncopation
syndesmosis
syndicalism
syndicalist
syndication
synergistic
synonymical
syntactical
synthesiser
synthetical
tangibility
tankfarming
tantalising
tenableness
tenaciously
tendencious
tendentious
tenementary
tensibility
tentaculate
tentatively
tenterhooks
tentpegging
tenuousness
tonsillitis
tunableness
tunefulness
unnaturally
unnecessary
unnervingly

venatically
vendibility
venereology
venesection
venisection
ventilation
ventilative
ventricular
ventriculus
ventriloquy
venturesome
venturously
vinaigrette
vincibility
vindication
vindicative
vindicatory
vinedresser
viniculture
Wensleydale
windcheater
windlestraw
winegrowing
winetasting
winningness
winningpost
winsomeness
winterberry
wintergreen
wonderfully
xanthochroi
xanthophyll
xenophilous
zincography
abolishable
abolishment
abomination
abortionist
aboutsledge
aboveground
acoustician
adolescence
adoptianism
adoptianist
adoptionism
adoptionist
aeolotropic
agonisingly
agonistical
agoraphobia
agoraphobic
amontillado
amorousness
amorphously
anomalistic
anomalously
anonymously
apocalyptic
Apollinaris
apologetics
apomorphine
aponeuroses
aponeurosis
aponeurotic
apophyllite
aposiopesis
apostleship
apostolical
apostrophic
apotheosise
aromaticity
atomisation
avoirdupois
azotobacter
biochemical
biocoenoses
biocoenosis
biocoenotic
biofeedback
biometrical
biophysical
blockbuster
bloodguilty
bloodlessly
bloodstream
bloodsucker
bloodvessel
blotchiness
bookbinding
bookinghall
bookishness
bookkeeping
booklearned
bookselling
bookshelves
boorishness
bootlegging
broadcaster
broadleaved
broadminded
brotherhood
chockablock
choirmaster
chokecherry
cholesterol
choreograph
chorography
clodhopping
closefisted
closehauled
clostridium
clothesline
clothesmoth
clothesprop
cloudcastle
cookgeneral
cooperation
cooperative
coordinator
crocidolite
crocodilian
crookbacked
crookedness
crossbearer
crossbowman
crossgarnet
crosslegged
crossstitch
crotcheteer
deoxidation
deoxygenate
deoxyribose
Diophantine
doorknocker
dropcurtain
dropforging
drouthiness
econometric
egotistical
emotionally
emotionless
epochmaking
erotogenous
erotomaniac
esotericism
evolutional
exogenously
exoneration
exonerative
exorbitance
exoskeletal
exoskeleton
exotericism
flocculence
floorwalker
florescence
floriferous
florilegium
floweriness
foolishness
footpoundal
footslogger
footsoldier
frontrunner
frostbitten
frothhopper
frowardness
frowstiness
geochemical
geomagnetic
geometrical
geophysical
geopolitics
geostrophic
geosyncline
geotectonic
ghostliness
ghostwriter
globeflower
globigerina
globularity
glomeration
glossolalia
gnotobiosis
gnotobiotic
goodhearted
goodlooking
goodnatured
grotesquely
grotesquery
grouchiness
groundsheet
groundwater
hooliganism
hyoscyamine
iconography
iconostases
iconostasis
icosahedral
icosahedron
idolisation
inobservant
inoculation
inoculative
inoffensive
inofficious
inoperative
inopportune
ironhearted
ironmongery
isochronism
isochronous
isoelectric
isogeotherm
isometrical
isomorphism
isomorphous
knowingness
knownothing
lionhearted
looselimbed
loosestrife
moonlighter
mooringmast
myocarditis
neologistic
Neoplatonic
Neotropical
odoriferous
odorousness
ozoniferous
ozonisation
ozonosphere
phonetician
phonography
phonologist
phosphonium
phosphorate
phosphorism
phosphorite
phosphorous
photoactive
photocopier
photofinish
photography
photometric
photooffset
photoperiod
photophilic
photophobia
photophobic
photosphere
phototactic
phototropic
ploughshare
ploughstaff
probabilism
probabilist
probability
probational
probationer
problematic
proceedings
procephalic
prochronism
proconsular
procreation
procreative
procrustean
proctorship
procuration
procuratory
procurement
prodigalise
prodigality
profanation
profanatory
profaneness
professedly
proficiency
profiterole
profuseness
progenitrix
progeniture
progestogen
prognathism
prognathous
progression
progressism
progressist
progressive
prohibition
prohibitive
prohibitory
prolegomena
proletarian
proletariat
proliferate
proliferous
prolificacy
prolificity
prolocutrix
prominently
promiscuity
promiscuous
promisingly
promotional
promptitude
promulgator
proofreader
propagation
propagative
prophethood
prophetical
prophetship
prophylaxis
propinquity
propitiable
propitiator
proportions
proposition
proprietary
prorogation
prosaically
prosaicness
prosecution
prosecutrix
proselytise
proselytism
prosenchyma
prospective
prosthetics
prostitutor
prostration
protagonist
protectoral
protectress
proteolysis
proteolytic
Proterozoic
prothalamia
prothallial
prothallium
prothoracic
protomartyr
protonotary
protophytic
protractile
protraction
protractive
protrudable
protrusible
protuberant
provenience
providently
provisional
provisorily
provocateur
provocation
provocative
provokingly
provostship
proximately
reorientate
rhombohedra
rhomboideus
riotousness
scopolamine
scorchingly
scoriaceous
scorpionfly
ScotchIrish
Scotchwoman
scoundrelly
scoutmaster
shockheaded
shocktroops
shoeleather
shoplifting
shopsteward
shortchange
shortcoming
shorthanded
shortspoken
shortwinded
shoulderbag
shoulderpad
shovelboard
showerproof
showjumping
showmanship
showstopper
slotmachine
smokescreen
smokingroom
smoothfaced
smorgasbord
snowbunting
snowgoggles
snowleopard
spokeswoman
spondulicks
spondylitis
spongecloth
sponsorship
spontaneity
spontaneous
sporogenous
sporogonium
sporophytic
sportswoman
sporulation
stockbroker
stockholder
stockinette
stockjobber
stockmarket
stocktaking
stoicalness
stomachache
stomachpump
stomatology
stonecurlew
stonecutter
stoneground
stonemarten
stonewaller
stoolpigeon
storekeeper
stormcentre
stormtroops
storyteller
swordbearer
thoroughpin
thoroughwax
thoughtless
toothbilled
toothpowder
toothsomely
troglodytic
trophoblast
troposphere
trothplight
troublesome
troublously
trouserless
trousersuit
ulotrichous
unobtrusive
unorganized
unorthodoxy
urochordate
violoncello
voodooistic
voortrekker
wholesomely
wholesouled
whoremaster
whoremonger
whosesoever
woodcarving
woodcutting
wrongheaded
zoographist
zoomorphism
zooplankton
zootechnics
alphabetise
amphetamine
amphibolite
amphibology
amphictyony
amphimictic
amphisbaena

amplexicaul
appallingly
apparatchik
apparelling
appealingly
appeasement
appellation
appellative
applaudable
application
applicative
applicatory
appogiatura
appointment
appreciable
appreciably
appreciator
approbation
approbatory
appropriate
approvingly
approximate
appurtenant
aspergillum
aspergillus
aspersorium
asphyxiator
baptismally
bipartition
capableness
capaciously
capacitance
capillarity
captainship
captionless
captivation
coparcenary
copingstone
copiousness
coplanarity
copperplate
coppersmith
cupellation
cupriferous
cupronickel
cypripedium
depauperate
depauperise
dependently
deploringly
depopulator
deportation
depravation
depravement
deprecation
deprecative
deprecatory
depreciator
depredation
depredatory
depressible
deprivation
depthcharge
diphtherial
diphtheroid
diphthongal
diphycercal
diplococcus
diplomatise
diplomatist
dipsomaniac
dipterocarp
duplication
duplicative
duplicitous
empanelling
emperorship
empirically
emplacement
emptyhanded
emptyheaded
Esperantist
euphemistic
expansional
expansively
expansivity
expatiation
expatiative
expatiatory
expectantly
expectation
expectative
expectorant
expectorate
expediently
expeditious
expenditure
expensively
experienced
explainable
explanation
explanatory
explication
explicative
explicatory
exploitable
exploration
explorative
exploratory
explosively
exponential
exportation
expostulate
expressible
expropriate
expurgation
expurgatory
foppishness
gypsiferous
haphazardly
haplessness
haplography
hepatectomy
Hepplewhite
heptamerous
heptarchist
hippocampus
Hippocratic
hippopotami
hopefulness
hyperactive
hyperbolise
hyperboloid
hyperborean
hypercharge
hypercritic
hypermarket
hypermetric
hyperphagia
hyperplasia
hypersthene
hypertrophy
hyphenation
hypnopaedia
hypnopompic
hypoblastic
hypocycloid
hypogastric
hypoglossal
hypolimnion
hypophyseal
hypophysial
hypostatise
hypotension
hypothecate
hypothenuse
hypothermia
hypothesise
hypotyposis
hypsography
hypsometric
hypsophobia
impanelling
imparkation
impartation
impartially
impassioned
impassively
impassivity
impatiently
impeachable
impeachment
impecunious
impedimenta
impenetrate
impenitence
impenitency
imperfectly
imperforate
imperialise
imperialism
imperialist
imperilling
imperilment
imperiously
impermanent
impermeable
impermeably
impersonate
impertinent
imperviable
impetration
impetratory
impetuosity
impetuously
impingement
implausible
implausibly
implemental
implication
implicative
imploringly
impolitical
impoliticly
importantly
importation
importunate
importunely
importunity
impoundment
impractical
imprecation
imprecatory
imprecisely
imprecision
impregnable
impregnably
impressible
impressment
impropriate
impropriety
improvement
improvident
imprudently
impuissance
impulsively
lepidoptera
leprosarium
leptodactyl
lophobranch
meprobamate
naphthalene
nephelinite
nephrectomy
opportunely
opportunism
opportunist
opportunity
opprobrious
oppugnation
paperhanger
papermaking
paperweight
papiermache
papyraceous
peptisation
pipecleaner
piperaceous
pipistrelle
populariser
pupillarity
rapaciously
rapscallion
rapturously
repartition
repellantly
repellently
repentantly
repetitious
replaceable
replacement
replenisher
repleteness
repleviable
replication
reportorial
reposefully
representer
repressible
repressibly
reproachful
reprobation
reprobative
reprobatory
reprogramme
reprography
reprovingly
repudiation
repugnantly
repulsively
ropedancing
ropewalking
saplessness
saponaceous
saprobiotic
saprogenous
saprophytic
Septembrist
septenarius
septentrion
septicaemia
septicaemic
septiferous
septifragal
sophistical
superabound
supercharge
superfamily
superficial
superficies
superfluity
superfluous
superheater
superimpose
superinduce
superintend
superioress
superiority
superjacent
superlative
superlunary
supermarket
supernatant
supernormal
superscribe
superscript
supersedeas
supersedure
superstrata
supersubtle
supertanker
supervision
supervisory
suppliantly
supportable
supportably
supposition
suppositive
suppository
suppression
suppressive
suppuration
suppurative
supremacist
supremeness
tapemachine
tapemeasure
tephromancy
topdressing
toploftical
topographer
topographic
topological
typecasting
typefounder
typefoundry
typesetting
typewritten
typicalness
typographer
typographic
typological
unpalatable
unpolitical
unpossessed
unprintable
unpromising
vaporimeter
vaporisable
wappenschaw
wapperjawed
acquiescent
acquirement
acquisition
acquisitive
acquittance
biquadratic
enquiringly
exquisitely
inquilinous
inquiringly
inquisition
inquisitive
liquefiable
liquescence
liquidambar
liquidation
requirement
requisition
sequestrate
unqualified
unquietness
abracadabra
abranchiate
abridgement
acriflavine
acrimonious
acropetally
aerobically
aerobiology
aerodynamic
aerographer
aerological
aeronautics
aeronomical
aerostatics
aerostation
AfroAsiatic
agrarianism
agriculture
agrobiology
agrological
agronomical
aircraftman
airlessness
airsickness
arraignment
arrangement
arrestingly
atrabilious
atrociously
auricularly
Aurignacian
barbarously
barbastelle
barbiturate
barefacedly
barleybroth
barnstormer
barquentine
barrelhouse
barrelorgan
bereavement
bergamasque
bergschrund
bersaglieri
birdbrained
birdfancier
birdwatcher
borborygmus
bureaucracy
burglarious
burgomaster
Byronically
carabiniere
carabinieri
caravanning
caravansary
carbocyclic
carbonation
carbuncular
carburetion
carburetted
carburetter
carburettor
carcinomata
cardinalate
cardiograph
cardsharper
carefulness
caressingly
caricatural
carminative
carnivorous
Carolingian
carpetsnake
carrageenan
carrageenin
carriageway
cartography
carunculate
carvelbuilt
caryopsides
cerebration
ceremonious
ceroplastic
certifiable
certifiably
certificate
Christendom
christening
christiania
Christianly
Christmassy

Christology
chrominance
chromoplast
chromosomal
chronically
chronograph
chronologer
chronologic
chronometer
chronometry
chronoscope
chrysalides
chrysalises
chrysarobin
chrysoberyl
chrysoprase
circularise
circularity
circulation
circulative
circulatory
circumlunar
circumpolar
circumsolar
circumspect
circumvolve
coralloidal
corbiculate
corbiesteps
cordialness
corecipient
cornerstone
cornhusking
corniferous
cornucopian
coronagraph
coronograph
corporality
corporately
corporation
corporatism
corporative
corporeally
corpulently
corpuscular
correctable
correctness
correlation
correlative
corrigendum
corroborant
corroborate
corrosively
corrugation
corruptible
corruptibly
corruptness
coruscation
curableness
curatorship
curiousness
currentness
currishness
cursiveness
cursoriness
curtailment
curvilineal
curvilinear
derangement
dereliction
dermatology
directional
directivity
directorate
directorial
directrices
durableness
earnestness
earpiercing
earthcloset
earthenware
earthliness
egregiously
erratically
erroneously
Etruscology
eurhythmics
Europeanise
eurypteroid
farawayness
farcicality
farinaceous
farraginous
farreaching
farthermost
farthingale
fermentable
ferociously
ferriferous
ferruginous
firecracker
firefighter
fireraising
firewalking
firewatcher
firmamental
firstfruits
foraminated
foraminifer
forbearance
forbiddance
foreclosure
foreignness
forequarter
forerunning
foreseeable
foreshorten
foresighted
forestaller
forestation
forethinker
forethought
foretopmast
foretopsail
forevermore
foreverness
forewarning
forfeitable
forgetfully
forgetmenot
forgettable
forgiveness
forlornness
formalistic
formational
formication
formularise
formulation
fornication
forthcoming
fortifiable
fortnightly
fortunately
forwardness
furnishings
furtherance
furthermore
furthermost
furthersome
furtiveness
furunculous
gardemanger
garnishment
garrulously
gartersnake
Germanophil
germination
germinative
gerontology
gerrymander
girlishness
gormandiser
gurgitation
gyrocompass
harbourless
hardhearted
hardhitting
hardmouthed
hardworking
harebrained
harmfulness
harmonistic
harpsichord
harumscarum
harvesthome
Heracleidan
herbivorous
hereditable
hereinafter
heresiology
heretically
hermeneutic
hermeticism
heroworship
herpetology
herringbone
herringgull
hirsuteness
hornswoggle
horological
horripilate
horsecollar
horsedoctor
horseradish
hurriedness
hurryscurry
hurryskurry
hurtfulness
irradiation
irradiative
irrecusable
irrecusably
irredentism
irredentist
irreducible
irreducibly
irrefutable
irrefutably
irregularly
irrelevance
irrelevancy
irreligious
irremissive
irremovable
irremovably
irreparable
irreparably
irresoluble
irretention
irretentive
irreverence
irrevocable
irrevocably
irruptively
jargonistic
jerrymander
juridically
larcenously
largeminded
laryngology
laryngotomy
marcescence
marcescible
marchioness
marconigram
marginalise
marginality
margraviate
marketplace
marketvalue
marlinspike
marquessate
marqueterie
marquisette
marriagebed
marshalling
marshalship
marshmallow
martyrology
mercenarily
merchandise
merchantman
mercilessly
mercurially
meritocracy
meritorious
meroblastic
merogenesis
Merovingian
merryandrew
merrymaking
mirthlessly
morbiferous
moribundity
morningroom
moronically
morrisdance
mortarboard
murderously
murmuration
murmurously
myrmecology
narcoleptic
narratively
nervelessly
nervousness
northeaster
northwester
nurserymaid
oarsmanship
parachutist
paradisical
paradoxical
paragrapher
paragraphic
paraldehyde
paraleipsis
parallactic
parallelism
parallelled
paramedical
parametrise
paramoecium
paramorphic
paramountcy
paramountly
paraphraser
paraplectic
paraselenae
parasitical
parasitosis
parathyroid
paratrooper
paratyphoid
parentheses
parenthesis
parenthetic
parheliacal
parishioner
parochially
paronomasia
participant
participate
participial
particulate
partitioned
partitioner
partitively
partnership
parturition
perambulate
perceivable
perceivably
perceptible
perceptibly
perchlorate
percipience
percolation
peregrinate
perennation
perennially
perfectible
perfectness
perforation
perforative
performable
performance
perfunctory
pericardiac
pericardial
pericardium
pericranial
pericranium
perineurium
periodicity
periodontal
periostitis
peripatetic
periphrases
periphrasis
perishables
perishingly
perispermic
peristalith
peristalsis
peristaltic
peristomial
perithecium
peritonitis
permanently
permissible
permissibly
permutation
perpetrator
perpetually
perpetuance
perpetuator
perplexedly
persecution
perseverate
persistence
persistency
personalise
personalism
personalist
personality
personation
personative
personifier
perspective
perspicuity
perspicuous
persuadable
persuasible
pertinacity
pertinently
perturbable
pervasively
pervertedly
phrasemaker
phraseogram
phraseology
piratically
pornography
porphyritic
portability
porterhouse
portionless
portmanteau
portraitist
portraiture
purchasable
pureblooded
purgatorial
purificator
puritanical
purportedly
purposeless
purposively
purpresture
pyramidally
pyramidical
pyrargyrite
pyroclastic
pyrotechnic
rarefaction
rarefactive
ruridecanal
sarcomatous
sarcophagus
sartorially
scragginess
scrappiness
scratchwork
screamingly
screwdriver
scribacious
scrimpiness
scriptorial
scriptorium
scruffiness
scrumptious
scrutiniser
serendipity
sericulture
serigrapher
seriousness
serological
serpiginous
serrulation
sertularian
serviceable
serviceably
servicebook
serviceline
shrinkingly
shrinkproof
shrivelling
shrubbiness
Soroptimist
sorrowfully
spreadeagle
springboard
springclean
springhouse
springiness
Stradivarii
straightcut
straightish
straightway
straitlaced
stramineous
strangeness
strangulate
straphanger
strategical
stratocracy
streakiness
streetlight
strenuosity
strenuously
stretchable
stridulator
strikebound

stringboard
stringently
stringiness
stringpiece
stringybark
stroboscope
strongpoint
surbasement
surfboarder
surficially
surgeonfish
surpassable
surrebuttal
surrebutter
surrogation
surveillant
taratantara
tarnishable
tarradiddle
teratogenic
teratologic
termagantly
termination
terminative
terminology
termitarium
terraqueous
terrestrial
terricolous
terrigenous
territorial
thrasonical
threadiness
threadpaper
threecolour
threedecker
threehanded
threelegged
threemaster
thriftiness
thrillingly
throatiness
throatlatch
thrombocyte
torchbearer
torchsinger
torticollis
torturously
turbination
turbulently
turgescence
turtleshell
tyrannicide
tyrannosaur
tyrannously
unrealistic
unreasoning
unrelenting
unremitting
unrighteous
uprightness
variability
variational
variegation
variousness
varnishtree
varsovienne
veraciously
verbalistic
verboseness
verdantique
veridically
verisimilar
vermiculate
vermiculite
vermination
verminously
versatilely
versatility
verticality
vertiginous
viridescent
virilescent
virological
voraciously
vortiginous
warmblooded
warmhearted
warrantable
warrantably
wirenetting
wirepulling
wiretapping
workability
workmanlike
workmanship
worldbeater
worldliness
worldlywise
worrisomely
worshipable
worshipless
worshipping
worthlessly
xeranthemum
xerophilous
Zoroastrian
absenteeism
absorbingly
absorptance
abstentious
abstinently
abstraction
abstractive
abstriction
Aesculapian
aesthetical
aestivation
assafoetida
assassinate
assemblyman
assentation
assertively
assessorial
assiduously
assignation
assimilable
assimilator
association
associative
assortative
assuagement
assuredness
Assyriology
austereness
bashfulness
bashibazouk
basipetally
basketchair
bassethound
bestselling
bisexuality
bushmanship
bushwhacker
businessman
cassiterite
castellated
castigation
casuistical
cesarevitch
cesarewitch
cisatlantic
cosignatory
cosmetician
cosmetology
cosmogonist
cosmography
cosmologist
cosmopolite
costbenefit
costiveness
customarily
custombuilt
customhouse
cysticercus
desalinator
descendable
descendible
describable
description
descriptive
desecration
desegregate
desensitise
deservingly
desexualise
desiccation
desiccative
desideratum
designation
desperadoes
desperately
desperation
despoilment
despondence
despondency
destination
destitution
destruction
destructive
desultorily
disablement
disaccustom
disaffected
disafforest
disannulled
disapproval
disarmament
disarmingly
disassemble
disassembly
disbandment
disbeliever
discalceate
discardable
discernible
discernibly
discernment
discerption
disciplinal
discipliner
discography
discontinue
discordance
discordancy
discotheque
discourtesy
discrepancy
discussable
discussible
disencumber
disentangle
disenthrall
disfunction
disgraceful
disgruntled
disguisedly
disgustedly
disharmonic
dishevelled
dishonestly
dishonourer
disillusion
disinclined
disinfector
disinterest
disinterred
disjunction
disjunctive
disjuncture
dislikeable
dislocation
dislodgment
dismayingly
disobedient
disobliging
disorganise
disparaging
disparately
dispensable
dispersedly
displeasure
disportment
disposition
dispositive
disputation
disquieting
disquietude
disremember
disseminate
disseminule
dissentient
dissepiment
dissertator
dissimilate
dissimulate
dissipation
dissipative
dissociable
dissolutely
dissolution
dissolvable
dissonantly
dissyllable
dissymmetry
distasteful
distempered
distensible
distinction
distinctive
distinguish
distraction
distractive
distressful
distribuend
distributor
distrustful
disturbance
disunionist
dysfunction
dyslogistic
easternmost
ensanguined
enslavement
essentially
exsiccation
exstipulate
fasciaboard
fasciculate
fascinating
fascination
fashionable
fashionably
festinately
festschrift
fissionable
fissiparity
fissiparous
fusillation
fustigation
gaseousness
gasfittings
gastrectomy
gastronomic
gastroscope
gestatorial
gesticulate
hesperidium
Hispanicise
Hispanicism
Hispanicist
histologist
historiated
historicise
historicism
historicist
historicity
histrionics
histrionism
hospitalise
hospitality
hospitaller
husbandlike
insalubrity
inscribable
inscription
inscriptive
inscrutable
inscrutably
insectarium
insecticide
insectifuge
insectivore
insectology
inseminator
insensately
insensitive
inseparable
inseparably
insessorial
insidiously
insincerely
insincerity
insinuation
insinuative
insipidness
insistently
insouciance
inspiration
inspiratory
instability
installment
instigation
instigative
instillment
instinctive
instinctual
institution
instruction
instructive
insufflator
insultingly
insuperable
insuperably
ipsilateral
justiciable
justifiable
justifiably
lastingness
lesemajesty
lissomeness
lustfulness
masculinely
masculinise
masculinity
masochistic
masquerader
massiveness
massproduce
masterfully
masterpiece
mastication
masticatory
mastodontic
mastoiditis
mesalliance
mesoblastic
mesomorphic
messiahship
misalliance
misanthrope
misanthropy
misbegotten
miscarriage
miscegenate
miscellanea
mischievous
miscibility
misconceive
misconstrue
miscreation
misericorde
miserliness
misestimate
misfeasance
misguidance
misguidedly
misjudgment
mismarriage
misremember
misspelling
mistrustful
mosstrooper
musclebound
muscularity
musculation
musculature
musicalness
muskthistle
mustachioed
nasofrontal
noseyparker
nosographer
nosographic
nosological
obscuration
obscureness
obsecration
observantly
observation
observatory
observingly
obsessional
obsessively
obsolescent
obstetrical
obstinately
obstruction
obstructive
oesophageal
oestrogenic
oysterplant
passacaglia
passeriform
passibility
Passiontide
passivation
passiveness
pasteuriser
pastoralism
pastoralist
pastureland
pessimistic
pestiferous
pestilently
pestologist
piscatorial
piscivorous
positronium
posological
possibility
postclassic
posteriorly
postexilian

postglacial
postnuptial
postulation
pushfulness
pussyfooter
pussywillow
pustulation
Rastafarian
resemblance
resentfully
reservation
residential
resignation
resiliently
resipiscent
resistively
resistivity
resourceful
respectable
respectably
respiration
respiratory
resplendent
respondence
respondency
responsible
responsibly
restatement
restfulness
restitution
restiveness
restoration
restorative
restriction
restrictive
restructure
resuscitate
Rosicrucian
Russophobia
rustication
susceptible
susceptibly
suspenseful
suspensible
suspiration
sustainable
sustainment
susurration
syssarcosis
systematics
systematise
systematism
systematist
tastelessly
tessellated
testability
testatrices
testimonial
unsaturated
unselective
unshockable
unshrinking
unskilfully
unsmilingly
unsolicited
unsoundness
unsparingly
unspeakable
unspeakably
unstoppable
vascularise
vascularity
vasculiform
vasectomise
vasodilator
vasopressin
vasopressor
vesicularly
vespertinal
vestigially
vestryclerk
vesuvianite
viscountess
viscousness
visibleness
washability
washerwoman
washleather
waspishness
waspwaisted
wastebasket
Wesleyanism
westernmost
Westminster
wisecracker
wishfulness
wistfulness
zestfulness
actinometer
actinomyces
actinomycin
afterburner
aftereffect
altercation
alternately
alternation
alternative
altitudinal
altocumulus
altorelievo
altorilievo
altostratus
antecedence
antechamber
antemundane
antenuptial
antependium
anteriority
antheridium
anthocyanin
anthologise
anthologist
anthracitic
anthropical
anticathode
anticipator
anticyclone
antifouling
antigravity
antiJacobin
antimonious
antineutron
antioxidant
antiphonary
antiphrasis
antipyretic
antiquarian
antiquation
antirrhinum
antiSemitic
antistrophe
antitypical
antivitamin
antonomasia
arterialise
arthrospore
articulable
articulated
articulator
artillerist
artiodactyl
artlessness
astigmatism
astringency
attemptable
attentively
attenuation
attestation
attitudinal
attractable
attribution
attributive
attritional
autarchical
autochthony
autoerotism
autographic
automatable
autoplastic
autotrophic
bathingsuit
batholithic
bathymetric
bathyscaphe
bathysphere
battledress
battlefield
betweenmaid
betweenness
betweentime
bitterapple
bittercress
bittersweet
botanically
botheration
bottleglass
bottlegreen
bottlenosed
butcherbird
butterflies
butteriness
butyraceous
catachreses
catachresis
cataclysmic
catadromous
cataplectic
catastrophe
catchphrase
catechismal
catechistic
categorical
catercousin
caterpillar
catheterise
catholicise
Catholicism
catholicity
catswhisker
citizenship
cityslicker
cotemporary
coterminous
cotoneaster
cottongrass
cottonmouth
cytogenesis
cytokinesis
cytological
deteriorate
determinacy
determinant
determinate
determinism
determinist
detestation
detrainment
detribalise
detrimental
dithyrambic
dittography
dutifulness
ectoblastic
ectogenesis
ectogenetic
ectomorphic
ectoplasmic
ectotrophic
entablature
entablement
enterostomy
enterovirus
enterpriser
entertainer
enthralling
enthralment
entitlement
entomophily
entrainment
entreatment
entrustment
establisher
extemporary
extemporise
extensional
extensively
extenuation
extenuatory
exteriorise
exteriority
exterminate
externalise
externalism
externality
extirpation
extirpatory
extortioner
extractable
extradition
extrapolate
extravagant
extravagate
extravasate
extraverted
extremeness
extrication
extroverted
fatefulness
fatiguingly
fatuousness
fetichistic
fetishistic
gatecrasher
gettogether
gutlessness
guttapercha
guttersnipe
gutturalise
gutturalism
hatefulness
heteroclite
heteroecism
heterograft
heterophony
heteroploid
heteropolar
heterospory
heterotaxis
heterotroph
heterotypic
hitherwards
intagliated
integrality
integration
integrative
intelligent
intemperate
intenseness
intensifier
intensional
intensively
intentional
intentioned
interactant
interaction
interactive
interallied
interatomic
interbedded
intercalary
intercalate
intercensal
intercepter
interceptor
intercessor
interchange
intercostal
intercourse
intercrural
interdental
interdepend
interesting
interfacial
interfacing
interfluent
interfusion
intergrowth
interiorise
interiority
interjacent
interleaves
interlinear
Interlingua
interlining
interlocker
interlunary
intermeddle
intermedium
intermingle
intermitted
internalise
internality
internecine
internuncio
interosseus
interplayed
interpolate
interpreter
interracial
interregnum
interrelate
interrogate
interrupter
interruptor
interseptal
intersexual
intersperse
interspinal
intertangle
intertribal
intervallic
interviewee
interviewer
intimidator
intolerable
intolerably
intolerance
intractable
intractably
intravenous
intrepidity
intricately
intriguante
intromitted
intromitter
introverted
intrusively
intuitional
intuitively
intuitivism
intumescent
kitchenette
kitchensink
kitchenware
latchstring
lateritious
latifundium
latitudinal
latticework
letterpress
literalness
lithography
lithophytic
lithosphere
lithotomise
lithotomist
lithotripsy
litigiously
litterateur
Lutheranism
matchlessly
matchmaking
materialise
materialism
materialist
materiality
mathematics
matriarchal
matriculate
matrilineal
matrilinear
matrimonial
metacentric
metachrosis
metagenesis
metagenetic
metalloidal
metallurgic
metalworker
metamorphic
metaphysics
metaplastic
metapsychic
metasomatic
metastasise
meteoritics
meteoroidal
meteorology
Methodistic
methodology
methylamine
methylation
metonymical
metoposcopy
metrication
mithridatic
mitrailleur
mothercraft
mothernaked
motherright
motivepower
mutableness
muttonchops
mythography
mythologise
mythologist
mythomaniac
mythopoeist
mythopoetic
nationalise
nationalism
nationalist
nationality
nationstate
naturalness
naturopathy
netherworld
nettlecloth
nitrogenise
nitrogenous
nittygritty
notableness
nothingness
noticeboard

notionalist
notoriously
nutcrackers
nutrimental
nutritional
nutritively
obtestation
obtrusively
octachordal
octagonally
octingenary
ontogenesis
ontogenetic
ontological
optometrist
orthocentre
orthodontia
orthodontic
orthoepical
orthography
orthopaedic
orthopedics
orthopedist
orthopteran
orthoscopic
orthotropic
ostensively
ostentation
osteography
osteologist
osteopathic
osteophytic
osteoplasty
ostracoderm
Ostrogothic
outbreeding
outbuilding
outcropping
outdistance
outfighting
outrivalled
outspokenly
outstanding
outstripped
outwardness
patelliform
paternalism
paternalist
paternoster
pathologist
patriarchal
patrilineal
patrimonial
patristical
patronising
patternshop
petitionary
petrography
petrologist
petticoated
pettifogger
pettishness
phthiriasis
pitchblende
piteousness
pitifulness
potentially
potteringly
putrescence
putrescible
Pythagorean
Pythagorism
ratatouille
rateability
ratiocinate
rationalise
rationalism
rationalist
rationality
rattlebrain
rattlepated
rattlesnake
retaliation
retaliative
retaliatory
retardation
retardative
retardatory
retentively
retentivity
retinacular
retinaculum
retinoscopy
retiredness
retraceable
retractable
retranslate
retribution
retributive
retributory
retrievable
retroaction
retroactive
retrocedent
retroflexed
retrorocket
ritualistic
rotogravure
rottenstone
satanically
satiability
satinstitch
satirically
satisfiable
saturnalian
saturninely
sittingroom
situational
soteriology
sottishness
tetanically
tetracyclic
tetradactyl
tetrahedral
tetrahedron
tetramerous
tetrapodous
tetrarchate
tetravalent
titanically
Titianesque
titillation
titleholder
tittivation
totalisator
totteringly
tuttifrutti
ultramarine
ultramodern
ultrasonics
ultraviolet
unteachable
unthinkable
unthinkably
untouchable
urticaceous
urticarious
vaticinator
viticulture
vitrescence
vitrifiable
vituperator
watchmaking
waterbottle
watercolour
watercooled
watercooler
watercourse
waterlogged
waterskiing
witchdoctor
witchhunter
witenagemot
witheringly
withershins
witlessness
abusiveness
acumination
acupuncture
adulterator
adumbration
adumbrative
aquaculture
aquarellist
aquatically
aquiculture
blunderbuss
bounteously
bountifully
bourgeoisie
boutonniere
brucellosis
brusqueness
brutishness
cauliflower
causatively
caustically
chucklehead
churchgoing
churchiness
churchwoman
coulometric
counselling
countenance
counterblow
counterbond
counterfeit
counterfoil
counterfort
countermand
countermark
countermine
countermove
countermure
counterpane
counterpart
counterplan
counterplea
counterplot
countersign
countersink
countersunk
counterturn
countervail
counterview
counterwork
countlessly
countrified
countryfied
countryseat
countryside
countrywide
courteously
courtliness
cruciferous
crucifixion
crucigerous
crunchiness
crustaceous
dauntlessly
deuteration
deuterogamy
Deuteronomy
doublecheck
doublecross
doubleDutch
doubleedged
doubleender
doubleentry
doublefaced
doublequick
doublespeak
doublethink
doubtlessly
doughtiness
douroucouli
drunkenness
ebulliently
ecumenicism
ecumenicity
educability
educational
elucidation
elucidative
elucidatory
elusiveness
elutriation
emulousness
emulsionise
enucleation
enumeration
enumerative
enunciation
enunciative
equableness
equiangular
equidistant
equilateral
equilibrate
equilibrist
equilibrium
equinoctial
equipollent
equivalence
equivalency
equivocally
equivocator
erubescence
exuberantly
faultfinder
faultlessly
feudalistic
fluctuation
fluorescein
fluorescent
fluoroscope
fluoroscopy
foulmouthed
fourflusher
fourpounder
fourwheeler
fructuation
frugivorous
fruitlessly
frustration
glutinously
gourmandise
gourmandism
grumblingly
haughtiness
haustellate
housefather
householder
housekeeper
houselights
housemaster
housemother
housewifely
housewifery
jauntingcar
journeywork
knucklebone
laudability
laughinggas
launderette
laurustinus
loudmouthed
loudspeaker
loutishness
louverboard
louvreboard
mountaineer
mountainous
mountaintop
naughtiness
neurologist
neuropathic
neuroticism
neurotropic
neutraliser
nourishment
paunchiness
pluralistic
plutocratic
pluviometer
pourparlers
prudishness
pruriginous
Prussianise
Prussianism
raucousness
raunchiness
roughfooted
roughlegged
roundedness
sauropodous
sausagemeat
sculduddery
sculduggery
scuppernong
scurvygrass
scuttlebutt
shutterless
shuttlecock
skulduddery
skulduggery
soulfulness
soundlessly
soupkitchen
southeaster
Southernism
southwester
squalidness
squarebuilt
squarsonage
squashiness
squeakiness
squeamishly
squintingly
squirearchy
studentship
studiedness
stumblingly
stuntedness
tautologise
tautologism
tautologous
tautomerism
tautonymous
Teutonicism
thunderbird
thunderbolt
thunderclap
thunderhead
thunderless
thunderpeal
thuriferous
touchtyping
toughminded
tourbillion
truculently
truehearted
trundletail
trustbuster
trusteeship
trustworthy
unusualness
unutterable
unutterably
advancement
adventuress
adventurism
adventurist
adventurous
adverbially
adversative
adverseness
advertently
advertising
advisedness
bivouacking
cavalierism
cavedweller
cavernously
civilianise
civilisable
devaluation
devastation
developable
development
deviousness
devotedness
divergently
diverticula
divestiture
divisionary
divisionism
divorcement
divulgation
divulgement
envelopment
enviousness
environment
favouritism
invalidness
invectively
inventively
inventorial
investigate
investiture
inviability
invidiously
invigilator
invigorator
inviolately
involucrate
involuntary
involvement
invultation
juvenescent
levelheaded
levirational
lovableness
movableness
moveability
novelettish
obviousness
pivotbridge
ravishingly
revaccinate
revaluation
revendicate
reverberant
reverberate
reverential
reversional
reversioner
revisionary
revisionism
revisionist
reviviscent
savouriness
seventeenth
seventyfold

severalfold
sovereignly
sovereignty
unvarnished
vivaciously
vivisection
bewhiskered
bewitchment
bowdleriser
downdraught
downhearted
downtrodden
lawlessness
lawmerchant
lowpressure
lowspirited
mawkishness
pawnbroking
powderflask
powerlessly
thwartships
townspeople
unwarranted
unweetingly
unwholesome
unwillingly
unwinkingly
unwittingly
anxiousness
auxanometer
coxcombical
dexiotropic
dexterously
doxographer
hexadecimal
hexametrist
lixiviation
loxodromics
luxuriantly
luxuriation
luxuriously
maxillipede
myxomatosis
myxomycetes
noxiousness
saxophonist
sexagesimal
sexlessness
sexological
sextodecimo
taxidermist
taxonomical
textureless
toxicomania
toxophilite
vexatiously
vexillology
boysenberry
bryozoology
cryobiology
cryosurgery
cryotherapy
cryptically
cryptogamic
cryptograph
cryptomeria
crystalline
crystallise
crystallite
crystalloid
erythrocyte
etymologise
etymologist
idyllically
joylessness
oxygenation
oxyhydrogen
phycocyanin
phycologist
phylloclade
phyllotaxis
phylogynist
physicality
physiocracy
physiognomy
physiologic
phytography
phytologist
phytosterol
phytotomist
psychedelia
psychedelic
psychiatric
psychically
psychodrama
psychogenic
psychograph
psychologic
psychometry
psychomotor
psychopathy
rhynchodont
scyphistoma
stylisation
stylishness
stylography
stylopodium
thyroiditis
tryingplane
trypanosome
tryptophane
waywardness
Byzantinism
Byzantinist
hazardously
sizableness

---

abracadabra
abranchiate
adiaphorism
advancement
agnatically
agrarianism
alkalescent
alkalimeter
alkalimetry
allAmerican
allantoides
amiableness
annabergite
appallingly
apparatchik
apparelling
aquaculture
aquarellist
aquatically
arraignment
arrangement
assafoetida
assassinate
atrabilious
audaciously
autarchical
auxanometer
behavioural
belatedness
bicarbonate
bilaterally
bipartition
Bonapartean
Bonapartism
Bonapartist
botanically
breadbasket
breadcrumbs
breadthways
breadthwise
breadwinner
breastplate
breastwheel
breathalyse
broadcaster
broadleaved
broadminded
Byzantinism
Byzantinist
camaraderie
canalicular
canaliculus
capableness
capaciously
capacitance
carabiniere
carabinieri
caravanning
caravansary
catachreses
catachresis
cataclysmic
catadromous
cataplectic
catastrophe
cavalierism
cesarevitch
cesarewitch
chiaroscuro
cicatricial
cisatlantic
cleanlimbed
cleanliness
cleanshaven
clearheaded
coparcenary
coralloidal
creationism
creationist
curableness
curatorship
debarkation
debauchment
decantation
decarbonate
decarbonise
decarburise
defalcation
demagnetise
demagogical
demagoguery
demagoguism
demandingly
demarcation
demarkation
depauperate
depauperise
derangement
desalinator
devaluation
devastation
didacticism
dilapidated
dilapidator
disablement
disaccustom
disaffected
disafforest
disannulled
disapproval
disarmament
disarmingly
disassemble
disassembly
dreadnought
dreamlessly
durableness
dynamically
dynamometer
dynamometry
embarkation
empanelling
encapsulate
enhancement
enjambement
enlargeable
enlargement
ensanguined
entablature
entablement
equableness
ergatocracy
erratically
establisher
eucalyptole
eudaemonism
eudaemonist
exhaustible
exhaustless
expansional
expansively
expansivity
expatiation
expatiative
expatiatory
fanatically
farawayness
filamentary
filamentous
financially
foraminated
foraminifer
friableness
funambulate
funambulist
gigantesque
greasepaint
greaseproof
greatnephew
gynaecocrat
gynaecology
hazardously
hepatectomy
Heracleidan
hexadecimal
hexametrist
hilariously
illaffected
immanentism
immanentist
immarginate
impanelling
imparkation
impartation
impartially
impassioned
impassively
impassivity
impatiently
incalescent
incantation
incantatory
incarcerate
incardinate
incarnadine
incarnation
infanticide
infantilism
infantryman
infatuation
ingathering
inhabitable
inhabitancy
innavigable
insalubrity
intagliated
invalidness
irradiation
irradiative
Judaisation
ligamentary
ligamentous
logarithmic
lovableness
lycanthrope
lycanthropy
magazinegun
maladaptive
maladjusted
maladroitly
malapropism
malariology
managership
McCarthyism
megalomania
megalopolis
megatherium
melancholia
melancholic
melanochroi
melanophore
mesalliance
metacentric
metachrosis
metagenesis
metagenetic
metalloidal
metallurgic
metalworker
metamorphic
metaphysics
metaplastic
metapsychic
metasomatic
metastasise
Micawberish
Micawberism
misalliance
misanthrope
misanthropy
monarchical
monasterial
monasticism
movableness
mutableness
nefariously
negationist
nomadically
notableness
octachordal
octagonally
olfactology
ommatophore
organically
organisable
organscreen
Palaearctic
palaeotypic
parachutist
paradisical
paradoxical
paragrapher
paragraphic
paraldehyde
paraleipsis
parallactic
parallelism
parallelled
paramedical
parametrise
paramoecium
paramorphic
paramountcy
paramountly
paraphraser
paraplectic
paraselenae
parasitical
parasitosis
parathyroid
paratrooper
paratyphoid
pedagogical
Pelagianism
pelargonium
perambulate
phrasemaker
phraseogram
phraseology
piratically
pleasurable
pleasurably
pliableness
polarimeter
polarimetry
polarisable
polariscope
preachiness
preaudience
pyramidally
pyramidical
pyrargyrite
rapaciously
ratatouille
rebarbative
recalculate
recantation
redactional
regardfully
relatedness
relationism
relationist
renaissance
repartition
retaliation
retaliative
retaliatory
retardation
retardative
retardatory
revaccinate
revaluation
rifacimenti
rifacimento
romanticise
romanticism
romanticist
sagaciously
salaciously
satanically
scragginess
scrappiness
scratchwork
selaginella
semanticist
semasiology
senatorship
sexagesimal
sheathknife
sizableness
solanaceous
somatically
somatogenic
somatologic
somatoplasm
somatotonia
somatotonic
speakership
sphaeridium
sphagnology
splashboard
splayfooted
squalidness
squarebuilt
squarsonage
squashiness
steadfastly

steamboiler
steamroller
steatopygia
Stradivarii
straightcut
straightish
straightway
straitlaced
stramineous
strangeness
strangulate
straphanger
strategical
stratocracy
subaerially
subarration
subaudition
subaxillary
sugarcoated
sybaritical
synagogical
taratantara
tenableness
tenaciously
teratogenic
teratologic
tetanically
theatregoer
theatricals
thrasonical
thwartships
titanically
tobacconist
totalisator
treacherous
treacliness
treasonable
treasonably
triadically
triangulate
tunableness
tyrannicide
tyrannosaur
tyrannously
uncanniness
uncanonical
uncatchable
unfailingly
unfaltering
unfashioned
unhappiness
unmanliness
unmatchable
unnaturally
unpalatable
unsaturated
unvarnished
unwarranted
vacationist
vagabondage
vagabondise
vagabondish
vagabondism
vagariously
venatically
veraciously
vexatiously
vicariously
vinaigrette
vivaciously
voraciously
womanliness
xeranthemum
alabastrine
barbarously
barbastelle
barbiturate
bombardment
bombilation
bombination
bonbonniere
borborygmus
bumblepuppy
cabbagepalm
cabbagerose
cabbagetree
cabbageworm
cabbalistic
carbocyclic
carbonation
carbuncular
carburetion
carburetted
carburetter
carburettor
cobblestone
combatively
combination
combinative
combinatory
combustible
corbiculate
corbiesteps
crabbedness
disbandment
disbeliever
doublecheck
doublecross
doubleDutch
doubleedged
doubleender
doubleentry
doublefaced
doublequick
doublespeak
doublethink
doubtlessly
dumbfounder
elaborately
elaboration
elaborative
erubescence
exuberantly
fimbriation
flabbergast
forbearance
forbiddance
gibberellin
gibbousness
globeflower
globigerina
globularity
harbourless
herbivorous
hobbledehoy
husbandlike
illbreeding
inebriation
inobservant
jabberwocky
Leibnitzian
membraneous
misbegotten
morbiferous
outbreeding
outbuilding
plebeianise
plebeianism
probabilism
probabilist
probability
probational
probationer
problematic
rhabdomancy
ribbongrass
rubberstamp
rumbustious
Sabbatarian
subbasement
surbasement
symbolistic
tolbutamide
trabeculate
tribulation
tribuneship
tribunicial
tribunitial
tributarily
tumbledrier
turbination
turbulently
unobtrusive
verbalistic
verboseness
abecedarian
Aesculapian
aircraftman
amicability
anachronism
anachronous
anacoluthon
anacreontic
anecdotical
apocalyptic
bacchanalia
bacciferous
beachcomber
beechmarten
biochemical
biocoenoses
biocoenosis
biocoenotic
blackavised
blackbeetle
blackbirder
blackcoated
blackfellow
blackgrouse
blackmailer
blackmarket
blockbuster
brachiation
brachyurous
bracteolate
bricklaying
brucellosis
butcherbird
calceolaria
calcicolous
calciferous
calcifugous
calcination
calculating
calculation
calculative
cancellated
carcinomata
catchphrase
chickenfeed
chickenwire
chockablock
chucklehead
circularise
circularity
circulation
circulative
circulatory
circumlunar
circumpolar
circumsolar
circumspect
circumvolve
coccidiosis
concatenate
concealable
concealment
conceitedly
conceivable
conceivably
concentrate
conceptacle
concernment
concertedly
concertgoer
conciliator
conciseness
concomitant
concordance
concrescent
concubinage
concubinary
concubitant
concurrence
coxcombical
crackerjack
crocidolite
crocodilian
cruciferous
crucifixion
crucigerous
deactivator
descendable
descendible
describable
description
descriptive
diachronism
diacritical
discalceate
discardable
discernible
discernibly
discernment
discerption
disciplinal
discipliner
discography
discontinue
discordance
discordancy
discotheque
discourtesy
discrepancy
discussable
discussible
educability
educational
ejaculation
ejaculatory
electioneer
electrician
electricity
electrocute
electrolier
electrology
electrolyse
electrolyte
electronics
electrotype
elicitation
elucidation
elucidative
elucidatory
enucleation
epochmaking
executioner
executorial
executrices
executrixes
eyecatching
farcicality
fasciaboard
fasciculate
fascinating
fascination
flaccidness
flocculence
fluctuation
fractionary
fractionate
fractionise
fractiously
fricandeaux
fructuation
functionary
functionate
geochemical
gimcrackery
godchildren
gracelessly
gracileness
hunchbacked
hyacinthine
inoculation
inoculative
inscribable
inscription
inscriptive
inscrutable
inscrutably
ipecacuanha
isochronism
isochronous
itacolumite
kitchenette
kitchensink
kitchenware
knucklebone
laicisation
Lancastrian
lancinating
lancination
larcenously
latchstring
marcescence
marcescible
marchioness
marconigram
masculinely
masculinise
masculinity
matchlessly
matchmaking
mercenarily
merchandise
merchantman
mercilessly
mercurially
miscarriage
miscegenate
miscellanea
mischievous
miscibility
misconceive
misconstrue
miscreation
musclebound
muscularity
musculation
musculature
myocarditis
narcoleptic
nonchalance
nuncupation
nuncupative
nutcrackers
obscuration
obscureness
oracularity
outcropping
peacemaking
peccability
peccadillos
perceivable
perceivably
perceptible
perceptibly
perchlorate
percipience
percolation
phycocyanin
phycologist
pieceworker
piscatorial
piscivorous
pitchblende
placability
plectoptera
plicateness
practicable
practicably
practically
Precambrian
precautious
precedented
precedently
precentress
preceptress
precipitant
precipitate
precipitous
preciseness
preconceive
precontract
prickliness
proceedings
procephalic
prochronism
proconsular
procreation
procreative
procrustean
proctorship
procuration
procuratory
procurement
psychedelia
psychedelic
psychiatric
psychically
psychodrama
psychogenic
psychograph
psychologic
psychometry
psychomotor
psychopathy
pulchritude
punchinello
punctilious
punctuality
punctuation
purchasable
quacksalver
quickchange
quickfiring
quickfreeze
quickfrozen
quicksilver
quickwitted
rancorously
raucousness
reachmedown
reactionary
reactionist
sacculation
sarcomatous
sarcophagus
shacklebolt
shacklebone
shockheaded
shocktroops
sincereness

slickenside
snickersnee
spaceflight
spaceheater
spacesaving
specifiable
specificity
spectacular
spectatress
spectrality
spectrogram
spectrology
speculation
speculative
stichometry
stickinsect
stickleback
stockbroker
stockholder
stockinette
stockjobber
stockmarket
stocktaking
subcategory
subclinical
subcontract
subcontrary
subcortical
subcritical
subcultural
succedaneum
succourless
succulently
susceptible
susceptibly
synchromesh
synchronise
synchronism
synchronous
synchrotron
syncopation
teachership
thickheaded
thickwitted
torchbearer
torchsinger
touchtyping
tracasserie
tracelessly
tracheotomy
trackwalker
trichinosis
trichomonad
tricksiness
tricoloured
truculently
unaccounted
unicellular
unicoloured
urochordate
vaccination
vascularise
vascularity
vasculiform
vincibility
viscountess
viscousness
voicelessly
volcanicity
volcanology
vulcanicity
vulcanology
watchmaking
welcomeness
whichsoever
witchdoctor
witchhunter
wreckmaster
zincography
academicals
academician
academicism
acidifiable
acidophilic
acidulation
anadiplosis
bandylegged
biddability
biedermeier
birdbrained
birdfancier
birdwatcher
bladderwort
bondservant
bondservice
bondwashing
bowdleriser
bradycardia
bridgeboard
caddishness
candelabrum
candescence
candidature
candleberry
candlelight
candlepower
candlestick
cardinalate
cardiograph
cardsharper
clodhopping
coadunation
coeducation
coldblooded
coldhearted
condemnable
condensable
conditional
conditioner
condolatory
condominium
condonation
condottiere
condottieri
conductance
conductible
conductress
condylomata
cordialness
credentials
credibility
credulously
dendritical
diadelphous
dundrearies
epidiascope
eradication
eradicative
evidentiary
faddishness
feldspathic
feudalistic
fiddlestick
fundamental
gardemanger
gendarmerie
goddaughter
goldbeating
golddigging
goldenberry
goodhearted
goodlooking
goodnatured
gradational
gradiometer
gradualness
handbreadth
handfasting
handgrenade
handicapped
handicapper
handknitted
handpainted
handselling
handwriting
handwritten
handwrought
hardhearted
hardhitting
hardmouthed
hardworking
headborough
headhunting
heedfulness
heldentenor
Hindoostani
hundredfold
illdisposed
inadaptable
inadvertent
inadvisable
inedibility
iridescence
kindhearted
landaulette
landgrabber
landgravine
landholding
landingbeam
landinggear
landlordism
laudability
loudmouthed
loudspeaker
maddeningly
magdalenian
maidservant
mandarinate
mandibulate
mandolinist
manducation
manducatory
meadowgrass
meadowsweet
mendelevium
middleclass
middlesized
mindbending
mindblowing
mindfulness
mindreading
mundaneness
murderously
needfulness
needlecraft
needlepoint
needlewoman
nondelivery
nondescript
outdistance
paddleboard
paddlewheel
paederastic
paediatrics
paediatrist
paedophilia
pandemonium
pendulously
ponderation
ponderosity
ponderously
powderflask
predatorily
predecessor
predicament
predication
predicative
predicatory
predictable
predictably
predominant
predominate
prodigalise
prodigality
prudishness
quadraphony
quadratical
quadrennial
quadrennium
quadrillion
quadrupedal
readability
readywitted
reddishness
reedbunting
reeducation
reedwarbler
roadholding
saddlecloth
saddlehorse
Sadduceeism
sandbagging
sandskipper
shadowgraph
shadowiness
soldierlike
soldiership
stadtholder
studentship
studiedness
subdivision
subdominant
syndesmosis
syndicalism
syndicalist
syndication
tendencious
tendentious
tiddlywinks
topdressing
traditional
traducement
unadvisedly
vendibility
verdantique
vindication
vindicative
vindicatory
voodooistic
widdershins
wildcatting
wildfowling
windcheater
windlestraw
wonderfully
woodcarving
woodcutting
Abbevillian
absenteeism
accelerando
accelerator
accentually
acceptation
acceptingly
accessorial
accessorise
adjectively
adventuress
adventurism
adventurist
adventurous
adverbially
adversative
adverseness
advertently
advertising
Aeneolithic
affectation
affectingly
affectional
affectioned
affectively
affectivity
afterburner
aftereffect
allegorical
allelomorph
alleviation
alleviative
alleviatory
altercation
alternately
alternation
alternative
anaesthesia
anaesthetic
angelically
antecedence
antechamber
antemundane
antenuptial
antependium
anteriority
appealingly
appeasement
appellation
appellative
arrestingly
arterialise
ascensional
ascetically
aspergillum
aspergillus
aspersorium
assemblyman
assentation
assertively
assessorial
atheistical
attemptable
attentively
attenuation
attestation
balefulness
barefacedly
bedevilment
Benedictine
benediction
benedictory
benefaction
beneficence
beneficiary
beneficiate
benevolence
bereavement
bicentenary
bicephalous
bimetallism
bimetallist
bisexuality
bohemianism
breechblock
breezeblock
bureaucracy
byeelection
calefacient
calefactory
calendrical
carefulness
caressingly
catechismal
catechistic
categorical
catercousin
caterpillar
cavedweller
cavernously
celebration
celebratory
celestially
cementation
cerebration
ceremonious
chaetognath
cheerleader
cheerlessly
cheesecloth
chieftaincy
codefendant
coleorrhiza
comestibles
comeuppance
corecipient
cotemporary
coterminous
cupellation
cybernation
cybernetics
deceitfully
deceivingly
decelerator
decemvirate
decennially
deceptively
decerebrate
defectively
defenceless
defensively
deferential
delectation
deleterious
dependently
dereliction
desecration
desegregate
desensitise
deservingly
desexualise
deteriorate
determinacy
determinant
determinate
determinism
determinist
detestation
developable
development
dicephalous
digestively
dimensional
directional
directivity
directorate
directorial
directrices
disencumber
disentangle
disenthrall
divergently
diverticula
divestiture
dodecaphony
dolefulness
domesticate
domesticity
eclecticism
effectively
effectually
egregiously
elderliness
embellisher
emmenagogue
Emmenthaler
emperorship

endearingly
endemically
enfeoffment
enneahedron
enterostomy
enterovirus
enterpriser
entertainer
envelopment
ephemerides
Esperantist
essentially
etherealise
ethereality
eugenically
exceedingly
excellently
exceptional
excessively
expectantly
expectation
expectative
expectorant
expectorate
expediently
expeditious
expenditure
expensively
experienced
extemporary
extemporise
extensional
extensively
extenuation
extenuatory
exteriorise
exteriority
exterminate
externalise
externalism
externality
facelifting
facetiously
fatefulness
fenestrated
firecracker
firefighter
fireraising
firewalking
firewatcher
fomentation
foreclosure
foreignness
forequarter
forerunning
foreseeable
foreshorten
foresighted
forestaller
forestation
forethinker
forethought
foretopmast
foretopsail
forevermore
foreverness
forewarning
freebooting
freehearted
freemasonry
freethinker
freethought
freezedried
gametangium
gametophyte
gaseousness
gatecrasher
gegenschein
genealogise
genealogist
generaliser
generalship
generically
genetically
GraecoRoman
greengrocer
greenkeeper
greenockite
haberdasher
harebrained
hatefulness
hebephrenia
hebephrenic
Hegelianism
hemeralopia
hereditable
hereinafter
heresiology
heretically
heteroclite
heteroecism
heterograft
heterophony
heteroploid
heteropolar
heterospory
heterotaxis
heterotroph
heterotypic
hibernacula
hibernation
Hibernicism
hideousness
homeopathic
homeostasis
homeostatic
homesteader
homestretch
honeybadger
honeymooner
honeysuckle
hopefulness
hugeousness
hymenoptera
hyperactive
hyperbolise
hyperboloid
hyperborean
hypercharge
hypercritic
hypermarket
hypermetric
hyperphagia
hyperplasia
hypersthene
hypertrophy
immediately
immedicable
immenseness
impeachable
impeachment
impecunious
impedimenta
impenetrate
impenitence
impenitency
imperfectly
imperforate
imperialise
imperialism
imperialist
imperilling
imperilment
imperiously
impermanent
impermeable
impermeably
impersonate
impertinent
imperviable
impetration
impetratory
impetuosity
impetuously
incertitude
incessantly
indeciduous
indefinable
indefinably
indehiscent
indentation
independent
inferential
inferiority
infertility
infestation
infeudation
ingeniously
ingenuously
inheritable
inheritance
inheritress
innervation
insectarium
insecticide
insectifuge
insectivore
insectology
inseminator
insensately
insensitive
inseparable
inseparably
insessorial
integrality
integration
integrative
intelligent
intemperate
intenseness
intensifier
intensional
intensively
intentional
intentioned
interactant
interaction
interactive
interallied
interatomic
interbedded
intercalary
intercalate
intercensal
intercepter
interceptor
intercessor
interchange
intercostal
intercourse
intercrural
interdental
interdepend
interesting
interfacial
interfacing
interfluent
interfusion
intergrowth
interiorise
interiority
interjacent
interleaves
interlinear
Interlingua
interlining
interlocker
interlunary
intermeddle
intermedium
intermingle
intermitted
internalise
internality
internecine
internuncio
interosseus
interplayed
interpolate
interpreter
interracial
interregnum
interrelate
interrogate
interrupter
interruptor
interseptal
intersexual
intersperse
interspinal
intertangle
intertribal
intervallic
interviewee
interviewer
invectively
inventively
inventorial
investigate
investiture
irrecusable
irrecusably
irredentism
irredentist
irreducible
irreducibly
irrefutable
irrefutably
irregularly
irrelevance
irrelevancy
irreligious
irremissive
irremovable
irremovably
irreparable
irreparably
irresoluble
irretention
irretentive
irreverence
irrevocable
irrevocably
isoelectric
juvenescent
kinematical
kinesiology
kinetograph
kinetoscope
labefaction
lakedweller
lamellicorn
lamelliform
lamentation
lateritious
legerdemain
lesemajesty
levelheaded
libertarian
liberticide
libertinage
libertinism
lifemanship
linedrawing
linefishing
linendraper
lineprinter
literalness
makebelieve
malediction
maledictory
malefaction
maleficence
malevolence
materialise
materialism
materialist
materiality
meteoritics
meteoroidal
meteorology
mimetically
mineraliser
minesweeper
misericorde
miserliness
misestimate
moderations
modernistic
molecricket
molecularly
molendinary
molestation
momentarily
momentously
moneylender
moneymaking
moneymarket
moneyspider
moveability
namecalling
namedropper
necessarian
necessarily
necessitate
necessitous
nomenclator
nonetheless
nonexistent
noseyparker
novelettish
numerically
objectively
objectivism
objectivist
objectivity
obsecration
observantly
observation
observatory
observingly
obsessional
obsessively
obtestation
offenceless
offensively
orderliness
orientalise
orientalism
orientalist
orientation
ostensively
ostentation
osteography
osteologist
osteopathic
osteophytic
osteoplasty
otherwhiles
Palestinian
panegyrical
paperhanger
papermaking
paperweight
parentheses
parenthesis
parenthetic
patelliform
paternalism
paternalist
paternoster
pedestalled
penetrating
penetration
penetrative
peregrinate
perennation
perennially
pigeonchest
pipecleaner
piperaceous
piteousness
polemically
polevaulter
pomegranate
potentially
powerlessly
praetorship
preelection
preeminence
preexistent
priestcraft
pureblooded
quaestorial
queenliness
quiescently
Rabelaisian
racemeeting
rarefaction
rarefactive
rateability
receptacula
receptively
receptivity
recessional
recessively
redetermine
referential
regenerable
regenerator
remembrance
renegotiate
repellantly
repellently
repentantly
repetitious
resemblance
resentfully
reservation
retentively
retentivity
revendicate
reverberant
reverberate
reverential
reversional
reversioner
rodenticide
ropedancing
ropewalking
rubefacient
rubefaction
safebreaker
safeconduct
safecracker
safekeeping
safetyvalve
saleability
salesladies
scientistic
scientology
scleroderma
sclerometer
sclerophyll

sclerotitis
screamingly
screwdriver
sedentarily
selectively
selectivity
semeiotical
serendipity
seventeenth
seventyfold
severalfold
sheepfarmer
sheepmaster
sheetanchor
shoeleather
sideslipped
sidestepped
sidewheeler
sleepingbag
sleepingcar
sleeplessly
sleepwalker
sleeveboard
soberminded
somewhither
soteriology
sovereignly
sovereignty
speechifier
speedometer
spherically
spherometer
spherulitic
splendorous
splenectomy
splenetical
spreadeagle
squeakiness
squeamishly
steelworker
steeplebush
steeplejack
steerageway
streakiness
streetlight
strenuosity
strenuously
stretchable
superabound
supercharge
superfamily
superficial
superficies
superfluity
superfluous
superheater
superimpose
superinduce
superintend
superioress
superiority
superjacent
superlative
superlunary
supermarket
supernatant
supernormal
superscribe
superscript
supersedeas
supersedure
superstrata
supersubtle
supertanker
supervision
supervisory
sweepstakes
synergistic
tabefaction
tabernacled
talebearing
talentscout
tameability
tapemachine
tapemeasure
telegrammic
telegrapher
telegraphic
telekinesis
telekinetic
teleologism
teleologist
telepathise
telepathist
telephonist
teleprinter
temerarious
tenementary
threadiness
threadpaper
threecolour
threedecker
threehanded
threelegged
threemaster
timebargain
timepleaser
timeserving
timesharing
treecreeper
triennially
truehearted
tuberculate
tuberculise
tuberculose
tuberculous
tumefaction
tunefulness
typecasting
typefounder
typefoundry
typesetting
typewritten
unbeknownst
unbelieving
unbendingly
unbeseeming
unceasingly
uncertainly
uncertainty
underbidder
undercharge
underexpose
underground
undergrowth
underhanded
undermanned
underpinned
underseller
undersigned
understated
undertaking
undertenant
undervaluer
underweight
underwriter
undeserving
undesirable
undeveloped
unfeelingly
unfeignedly
ungetatable
unhealthily
unhelpfully
unkennelled
unmeaningly
unmemorable
unmemorably
unnecessary
unnervingly
unrealistic
unreasoning
unrelenting
unremitting
unselective
unteachable
unweetingly
valediction
valedictory
vasectomise
venereology
venesection
viceadmiral
vicegerency
viceregally
viceroyalty
viceroyship
vinedresser
wakefulness
waterbottle
watercolour
watercooled
watercooler
watercourse
waterlogged
waterskiing
wheelbarrow
wheelwright
winegrowing
winetasting
wirenetting
wirepulling
wiretapping
wisecracker
witenagemot
biofeedback
buffalorobe
chafingdish
cliffhanger
coefficient
coffeehouse
coffeetable
comfortable
comfortably
comfortless
confabulate
confederacy
confederate
conferrable
confessedly
confidently
confidingly
confinement
confirmable
confiscable
confiscator
conflagrant
conflagrate
confliction
conflictive
conformable
conformably
conformally
conformance
confusingly
confutation
confutative
craftswoman
deification
differentia
differently
difficultly
diffidently
diffraction
diffuseness
diffusively
disfunction
dysfunction
edification
edificatory
fanfaronade
forfeitable
gafftopsail
gasfittings
godforsaken
gonfalonier
halfbinding
halfblooded
halfhearted
halfholiday
halflanding
halfmeasure
illfavoured
ineffective
ineffectual
inefficient
inoffensive
inofficious
malfeasance
malfunction
misfeasance
nonfeasance
outfighting
perfectible
perfectness
perforation
perforative
performable
performance
perfunctory
prefatorial
prefatorily
prefectural
profanation
profanatory
profaneness
professedly
proficiency
profiterole
profuseness
raffishness
reification
scaffolding
selfassured
selfcentred
selfclosing
selfcocking
selfcommand
selfconceit
selfcontent
selfcontrol
selfcreated
selfculture
selfdefence
selfdenying
selfdespair
selfdevoted
selfdisplay
selfelected
selfevident
selffeeding
selffeeling
selffertile
selfimposed
selfinduced
selfinvited
selfishness
selflimited
selfloading
selflocking
selfmastery
selfopinion
selfpitying
selfraising
selfreliant
selfreproof
selfrespect
selfsealing
selfseeking
selfservice
selfserving
selfstarter
selfsterile
selfsupport
selftorture
selfwinding
selfworship
shiftlessly
sinfonietta
spifflicate
stiffnecked
stiflejoint
sufficiency
suffixation
suffocation
suffocative
suffragette
suffumigate
surfboarder
surficially
swiftfooted
toffeenosed
trafficator
trafficking
trafficless
unification
uniformness
whiffletree
wolfwhistle
anagnorisis
bergamasque
bergschrund
braggadocio
burglarious
burgomaster
coagulation
congealable
congealment
congelation
congenerous
congenially
congressman
congruently
congruously
dangerously
diagnostics
disgraceful
disgruntled
disguisedly
disgustedly
doggishness
doughtiness
draggletail
eligibility
enigmatical
epigastrium
epigraphist
evagination
exaggerator
exogenously
fidgetiness
fingerboard
fingerglass
fingerplate
fingerprint
fingerstall
flagcaptain
flagellator
flagofficer
flagwagging
flightiness
forgetfully
forgetmenot
forgettable
forgiveness
fragmentary
frightfully
frigidarium
frugivorous
fulguration
gangsterism
gingerbread
gurgitation
haggadistic
haggardness
haughtiness
hedgehopped
hedgepriest
hedgeschool
hoggishness
imaginarily
imagination
imaginative
isogeotherm
jargonistic
judgmatical
languidness
largeminded
laughinggas
lengthiness
lingeringly
linguistics
loggerheads
longanimity
longplaying
longsighted
marginalise
marginality
margraviate
misguidance
misguidedly
naughtiness
neighbourly
oligochaete
oligomerous
originality
origination
originative
oxygenation
Panglossian
phagedaenic
phagocytise
phagocytose
piggishness
plagiariser
plagioclase
plagiostome
pragmatical
progenitrix
progeniture
progestogen
prognathism
prognathous
progression
progressism
progressist
progressive
purgatorial
rangefinder
ringstraked
roughfooted
roughlegged
sanguinaria
sanguineous
seigneurial
seigniorage
seigniorial
singlestick
singletrack
singularise
singularity
slightingly
songfulness
songsparrow

stagemanage
stagestruck
stagflation
steganogram
stegosaurus
suggestible
surgeonfish
tangibility
togglejoint
toughminded
tragedienne
tragicomedy
triggerfish
troglodytic
turgescence
unigeniture
waggishness
wedgeshaped
wedgetailed
weighbridge
weightiness
whigmaleery
zoographist
alphabetise
amphetamine
amphibolite
amphibology
amphictyony
amphimictic
amphisbaena
antheridium
anthocyanin
anthologise
anthologist
anthracitic
anthropical
archaeology
archaeornis
archaically
archangelic
archdiocese
archduchess
archdukedom
Archimedean
archipelago
arthrospore
asphyxiator
bashfulness
bashibazouk
bathingsuit
batholithic
bathymetric
bathyscaphe
bathysphere
bewhiskered
Bodhisattva
botheration
Brahmanical
brahmaputra
Brahminical
bushmanship
bushwhacker
catheterise
catholicise
Catholicism
catholicity
cochinchina
dichogamous
dichotomise
dichotomist
dichotomous
dichromatic
diphtherial
diphtheroid
diphthongal
diphycercal
disharmonic
dishevelled
dishonestly
dishonourer
dithyrambic
enchainment
enchantment
enchantress
enchiridion
enthralling
enthralment
eschatology
escheatable
escheatment
Eucharistic
euchologion
euphemistic
eurhythmics
fashionable
fashionably
haphazardly
highbrowism
highfalutin
highpitched
highpowered
highranking
highstepper
highwrought
hitherwards
hyphenation
illhumoured
lachrymator
lecherously
lichenology
lightfooted
lighthanded
lightheaded
lightminded
lightsomely
lightweight
lithography
lithophytic
lithosphere
lithotomise
lithotomist
lithotripsy
lophobranch
Lutheranism
machicolate
machination
machinemade
mathematics
mechanician
mechanistic
Methodistic
methodology
methylamine
methylation
mithridatic
mothercraft
mothernaked
motherright
mythography
mythologise
mythologist
mythomaniac
mythopoeist
mythopoetic
naphthalene
nephelinite
nephrectomy
netherworld
nightingale
nightmarish
nightporter
nightwalker
nothingness
offhandedly
orchestrate
orchidology
orthocentre
orthodontia
orthodontic
orthoepical
orthography
orthopaedic
orthopedics
orthopedist
orthopteran
orthoscopic
orthotropic
oxyhydrogen
pachydermal
panhellenic
parheliacal
pathologist
phthiriasis
pigheadedly
prehistoric
prohibition
prohibitive
prohibitory
pushfulness
Pythagorean
Pythagorism
rightangled
righteously
righthanded
righthander
rightminded
rightwinger
sightlessly
sightliness
sightreader
sightscreen
sightseeing
sightworthy
sophistical
tacheometer
tachycardia
tachygraphy
technically
technocracy
technologic
tephromancy
tightfisted
tightlipped
unchristian
unshockable
unshrinking
unthinkable
unthinkably
unwholesome
vichyssoise
washability
washerwoman
washleather
wishfulness
witheringly
withershins
abridgement
accipitrine
achievement
acriflavine
acrimonious
actinometer
actinomyces
actinomycin
adminicular
admiralship
advisedness
afficionado
affiliation
affirmation
affirmative
affirmatory
agriculture
Albigensian
altitudinal
ambiguously
ambitiously
ambivalence
ambivalency
ambiversion
ancientness
angiography
annihilator
anniversary
anticathode
anticipator
anticyclone
antifouling
antigravity
antiJacobin
antimonious
antineutron
antioxidant
antiphonary
antiphrasis
antipyretic
antiquarian
antiquation
antirrhinum
antiSemitic
antistrophe
antitypical
antivitamin
anxiousness
aquiculture
arbitrageur
arbitrament
arbitrarily
arbitration
arbitrative
arbitratrix
Arminianism
articulable
articulated
articulator
artillerist
artiodactyl
assiduously
assignation
assimilable
assimilator
astigmatism
attitudinal
audibleness
audiologist
audiometric
audiovisual
auricularly
Aurignacian
avoirdupois
bacilliform
basipetally
bedizenment
befittingly
benightedly
benightment
benignantly
bewitchment
biliousness
bimillenary
bimillenium
brainlessly
brainsickly
brainteaser
businessman
calibration
californium
calisthenic
capillarity
caricatural
chainarmour
chainletter
chainsmoker
chainstitch
cheiromancy
choirmaster
Christendom
christening
christiania
Christianly
Christmassy
Christology
citizenship
civilianise
civilisable
clairschach
clairvoyant
cleistogamy
codicillary
copingstone
copiousness
cosignatory
curiousness
cylindrical
dedicatedly
defibrinate
deficiently
definiendum
deliciously
delightedly
delightsome
delineation
delinquency
deliriously
delitescent
deliverable
deliverance
deliveryman
demigoddess
denigration
denigratory
denizenship
desiccation
desiccative
desideratum
designation
deviousness
dexiotropic
digitigrade
diningtable
disillusion
disinclined
disinfector
disinterest
disinterred
divisionary
divisionism
domiciliary
domiciliate
domineering
dubiousness
duniewassal
dutifulness
efficacious
efficiently
ellipsoidal
ellipticity
empirically
engineering
enlightened
enlivenment
entitlement
enviousness
environment
epeirogenic
equiangular
equidistant
equilateral
equilibrate
equilibrist
equilibrium
equinoctial
equipollent
equivalence
equivalency
equivocally
equivocator
eudiometric
exdirectory
exsiccation
extirpation
extirpatory
familiarise
familiarity
farinaceous
fatiguingly
fetichistic
fetishistic
finicalness
fruitlessly
fusillation
geniculated
genitivally
goniometric
habiliments
habituation
Hagiographa
hagiography
hagiologist
hagioscopic
Hamiltonian
heliochrome
heliography
heliometric
heliotropic
hemianopsia
hemimorphic
hemipterous
hemispheric
homiletical
Hudibrastic
humiliation
humiliatory
illiberally
illimitable
illimitably
illiquidity
immigration
immitigable
immitigably
impingement
incinerator
incipiently
indifferent
indigestion
indigestive
indignantly
indignation
indirection
individuate
indivisible
indivisibly
infiltrator
infinitival
infirmarian
insidiously
insincerely
insincerity
insinuation
insinuative
insipidness
insistently
intimidator
inviability
invidiously
invigilator
invigorator
inviolately
ipsilateral
judiciously
juridically
labiodental
laciniation
latifundium

latitudinal
legionnaire
legislation
legislative
legislature
lepidoptera
leviratical
limitedness
limitlessly
litigiously
lixiviation
logicalness
ludicrously
luminescent
magisterial
magisterium
magistratic
maliciously
malignantly
Manichaeism
manifestant
manifestoes
manipulable
manipulator
maxillipede
mediaevally
mediastinal
mediastinum
mediateness
mediatorial
mediatrices
medicinable
medicinally
medicolegal
medievalism
medievalist
mediumistic
melioration
meliorative
meliphagous
meningocele
meritocracy
meritorious
miniaturise
miniaturist
ministerial
monitorship
moribundity
motivepower
municipally
munificence
musicalness
nationalise
nationalism
nationalist
nationality
nationstate
nominatival
noticeboard
notionalist
noxiousness
numismatics
numismatist
obliqueness
obliviously
obviousness
occipitally
octingenary
officialdom
officialese
officialism
officiation
officinally
officiously
omnifarious
omnipotence
omnipresent
omniscience
oneiromancy
ophidiarium
ophiologist
orbicularly
ornithology
ornithopter
ornithosaur
oscillation
oscillatory
oscillogram
pacifically
pacificator
palindromic
panicmonger
papiermache
parishioner
pedicellate
pediculosis
penicillate
penicillium
peninsulate
penitential
pericardiac
pericardial
pericardium
pericranial
pericranium
perineurium
periodicity
periodontal
periostitis
peripatetic
periphrases
periphrasis
perishables
perishingly
perispermic
peristalith
peristalsis
peristaltic
peristomial
perithecium
peritonitis
petitionary
pipistrelle
pitifulness
plainspoken
plaintively
pleinairist
pleiotropic
Pleistocene
policewoman
politically
politicking
pomiculture
positronium
preignition
pumicestone
pupillarity
purificator
puritanical
radicalness
radioactive
radiocarbon
radiography
radiolarian
radiologist
radiometric
radiophonic
ratiocinate
rationalise
rationalism
rationalist
rationality
ravishingly
reciprocate
reciprocity
redirection
rediscovery
regimentals
regionalise
regionalism
regionalist
registrable
reliability
religionise
religionism
religionist
religiosity
religiously
reminiscent
residential
resignation
resiliently
resipiscent
resistively
resistivity
retinacular
retinaculum
retinoscopy
retiredness
revisionary
revisionism
revisionist
reviviscent
Rosicrucian
rubicundity
rudimentary
ruridecanal
Sagittarius
salinometer
satiability
satinstitch
satirically
satisfiable
schismatise
schistosity
schistosome
schizanthus
scribacious
scrimpiness
scriptorial
scriptorium
sedimentary
seditionary
seditiously
semidiurnal
semiellipse
semimonthly
semipalmate
semiskilled
semitrailer
sericulture
serigrapher
seriousness
shrinkingly
shrinkproof
shrivelling
sinistrally
sinistrorse
sociability
socialistic
Socinianism
sociologist
sociometric
sociopathic
solifluxion
soliloquise
soliloquist
solipsistic
sphincteral
sphincteric
springboard
springclean
springhouse
springiness
squintingly
squirearchy
stainlessly
staircarpet
stoicalness
stridulator
strikebound
stringboard
stringently
stringiness
stringpiece
stringybark
taciturnity
taxidermist
tediousness
thriftiness
thrillingly
Titianesque
titillation
toxicomania
trailblazer
trainbearer
tryingplane
typicalness
uncivilised
undisguised
undisturbed
unlimitedly
unmitigated
unrighteous
unwillingly
unwinkingly
unwittingly
uprightness
urticaceous
urticarious
vacillation
valiantness
variability
variational
variegation
variousness
vaticinator
venisection
veridically
verisimilar
vesicularly
vexillology
viciousness
vicissitude
viniculture
viridescent
virilescent
visibleness
viticulture
vivisection
vociferance
vociferator
volitionary
conjectural
conjugality
conjugation
conjugative
conjunction
conjunctiva
conjunctive
conjuncture
conjuration
disjunction
disjunctive
disjuncture
misjudgment
prejudgment
prejudicial
subjugation
subjunctive
backbencher
backcountry
basketchair
bookbinding
bookinghall
bookishness
bookkeeping
booklearned
bookselling
bookshelves
chokecherry
cockaleekie
cockleshell
cockyleekie
cookgeneral
huckleberry
kickstarter
lickerishly
lickspittle
mackerelsky
marketplace
marketvalue
mawkishness
mockingbird
monkeybread
monkeyshine
muskthistle
neckerchief
nickelplate
packingcase
Pickwickian
pinkishness
pocketknife
pocketmoney
pocketsized
racketpress
rickettsial
rockcrystal
Shaksperean
Shaksperian
sickbenefit
sickeningly
sickishness
smokescreen
smokingroom
sockdolager
sockdologen
spokeswoman
stakeholder
suckingfish
talkatively
tankfarming
unskilfully
volkslieder
weakhearted
workability
workmanlike
workmanship
yacketyyack
abolishable
abolishment
acclamation
acclamatory
acclimation
acclimatise
acclivitous
adolescence
adulterator
aeolotropic
agglomerate
agglutinate
aimlessness
airlessness
ameliorator
amplexicaul
analogously
Anglicanism
AngloFrench
AngloIndian
anglomaniac
AngloNorman
anglophobia
anglophobic
Apollinaris
apologetics
applaudable
application
applicative
applicatory
arglebargle
artlessness
athleticism
ballbearing
balletomane
barleybroth
bellbottoms
bellfounder
bellheather
bellicosity
belligerent
bellringing
bibliolater
bibliolatry
bibliomancy
bibliomania
bibliopegic
bibliophile
bibliophily
bibliopolic
bibliotheca
billetsdoux
billionaire
billposting
billsticker
boilermaker
brilliantly
bullbaiting
bulletproof
bullfighter
bullishness
bullterrier
calligraphy
callousness
cauliflower
cellularity
chalcedonic
challenging
childminder
cholesterol
coalescence
collaborate
collapsible
collectable
collectanea
collectedly
collectible
collenchyma
colligation
colligative
collimation
collinearly
collisional
collocation
collusively
coplanarity
coulometric
cyclopaedia
cyclopaedic
cycloserine
cyclothymia
cyclothymic
declamation
declamatory
declaration
declarative
declaratory
declination
declivitous
deflagrator
defloration
deglutition
deploringly
dialectally
dialectical

dialogistic
diplococcus
diplomatise
diplomatist
dislikeable
dislocation
dislodgment
dollishness
drillmaster
dualcontrol
dualpurpose
duplication
duplicative
duplicitous
dyslogistic
ebulliently
egalitarian
emblematise
emblematist
emplacement
emulousness
emulsionise
endlessness
enslavement
evolutional
exclamation
exclamatory
exclusively
exclusivity
explainable
explanation
explanatory
explication
explicative
explicatory
exploitable
exploration
explorative
exploratory
explosively
fallibility
faultfinder
faultlessly
feelingness
fieldcornet
fieldworker
folliculate
foolishness
forlornness
foulmouthed
fullblooded
fullfledged
fullhearted
fullmouthed
gallantness
gallbladder
galleyslave
Gallicanism
gallimaufry
Gallophobia
gallowsbird
gallowstree
gillyflower
girlishness
godlessness
guilelessly
guiltlessly
gullibility
gutlessness
hallucinate
haplessness
haplography
healthfully
healthiness
helleborine
Hellenistic
hellishness
hollandaise
hooliganism
idolisation
idyllically
implausible
implausibly
implemental
implication
implicative
imploringly
inalienable
inalienably
inalterable
inalterably
inclemently
inclination
inclusively
inelegantly
ineloquence
ineluctable
ineluctably
inflammable
inflammably
inflexional
influential
jealousness
joylessness
lawlessness
Maglemosian
mailcarrier
marlinspike
melliferous
mellifluent
mellifluous
millenarian
milliampere
millionaire
millisecond
mollycoddle
myelomatous
nailvarnish
negligently
neologistic
nullifidian
nulliparity
nulliparous
ochlocratic
opalescence
pellucidity
phalanstery
philanderer
philatelist
philhellene
philologian
philologist
philosopher
philosophic
phylloclade
phyllotaxis
phylogynist
pillowfight
pollination
prelibation
preliminary
prelusively
prelusorily
prolegomena
proletarian
proletariat
proliferate
proliferous
prolificacy
prolificity
prolocutrix
publication
publishable
publishment
pullthrough
pullulation
qualifiable
qualitative
quilldriver
rallentando
realignment
realisation
realpolitik
reclaimable
reclamation
reflectance
reflexively
reflexology
replaceable
replacement
replenisher
repleteness
repleviable
replication
saplessness
scalariform
scalearmour
scaleinsect
scalpriform
sculduddery
sculduggery
sexlessness
shallowness
shellacking
shelljacket
shelterbelt
shelterless
sillimanite
sinlessness
skeletonise
skilfulness
skulduddery
skulduggery
smallholder
smallminded
smilelessly
soulfulness
spelaeology
spellbinder
stalactitic
stalagmitic
stallholder
stellionate
stiltedness
stylisation
stylishness
stylography
stylopodium
sublimation
sublimeness
sublittoral
sunlessness
swallowable
swallowdive
swallowhole
swallowtail
swallowwort
swellheaded
syllabarium
syllabicity
syllogistic
tabletennis
tagliatelle
tagliatelli
thalidomide
titleholder
toploftical
trelliswork
twelvemonth
twelvepenny
unalterable
uncleanness
unclimbable
uncluttered
unflappable
unflinching
uselessness
utilisation
utilitarian
valleculate
violoncello
wealthiness
welladvised
wellbeloved
welldefined
wellfounded
wellgroomed
wellmeaning
wellordered
wellrounded
wellwishing
Wesleyanism
wholesomely
wholesouled
willingness
witlessness
worldbeater
worldliness
worldlywise
yellowbelly
zealousness
abomination
acumination
adumbration
adumbrative
alembicated
anemometric
animalcular
anomalistic
anomalously
apomorphine
aromaticity
atomisation
augmentable
balmcricket
biometrical
blamelessly
blameworthy
carminative
chamaephyte
chamberlain
chambermaid
chameleonic
champertous
chemotactic
chimaerical
clamorously
climacteric
climatology
commandment
commemorate
commendable
commendably
commendator
commensally
commentator
commination
comminatory
comminution
commiserate
commissural
committable
commonality
commonplace
commonsense
communalise
communalism
communalist
communicant
communicate
communistic
commutation
commutative
cosmetician
cosmetology
cosmogonist
cosmography
cosmologist
cosmopolite
crematorium
criminalist
criminality
crimination
criminative
criminatory
criminology
culmination
deemphasise
dermatology
diamagnetic
diametrical
diamondback
dismayingly
dramaturgic
ecumenicism
ecumenicity
elementally
elimination
eliminative
enumeration
enumerative
esemplastic
etymologise
etymologist
examination
exemplarily
exemplarity
fermentable
filmography
filmsetting
firmamental
flamboyance
flamboyancy
flamboyante
flimflammer
formalistic
formational
formication
formularise
formulation
fulminating
fulmination
fulminatory
gemmiferous
gemmiparous
gemmologist
gemmulation
geomagnetic
geometrical
Germanophil
germination
germinative
glomeration
gormandiser
grammalogue
grammatical
gramophonic
grumblingly
haematocele
haematocrit
haematology
haemocyanin
haemoglobin
haemophilia
haemophilic
haemoptysis
haemorrhage
haemorrhoid
haemostasis
haemostatic
harmfulness
harmonistic
helminthoid
hermeneutic
hermeticism
hummingbird
illmannered
isometrical
isomorphism
isomorphous
lammergeier
lammergeyer
lawmerchant
mammalogist
mismarriage
murmuration
murmurously
myrmecology
nonmatching
nonmetallic
palmcabbage
permanently
permissible
permissibly
permutation
prematurely
prematurity
premeditate
premiership
premonition
premonitory
primaevally
primateship
primatology
primigenial
primiparous
primitively
primitivism
prominently
promiscuity
promiscuous
promisingly
promotional
promptitude
promulgator
reemergence
rhombohedra
rhomboideus
salmonberry
segmentally
shamanistic
shamelessly
sigmoidally
solmisation
stampoffice
stimulation
stimulative
stomachache
stomachpump
stomatology
stumblingly
submarginal
submergence
submersible
submissible
submultiple
summariness
summational
summerhouse
summersault
swimbladder
symmetrical
termagantly
termination
terminative
terminology
termitarium
thimbleweed
trammelling
tremblement
tremblingly
tremulously
trimestrial
trimorphism

trimorphous
unambiguous
unemotional
unimportant
unsmilingly
vehmgericht
vermiculate
vermiculite
vermination
verminously
warmblooded
warmhearted
whimsically
zoomorphism
abandonment
acinaciform
acknowledge
adenomatous
agonisingly
agonistical
amenability
amenorrhoea
amentaceous
amontillado
anencephaly
anonymously
aponeuroses
aponeurosis
aponeurotic
arenicolous
barnstormer
blunderbuss
bounteously
bountifully
branchiopod
brankursine
cannibalise
cannibalism
carnivorous
chancellery
chancellory
changefully
channelling
chansonnier
chanterelle
chanticleer
chinoiserie
cinnabarine
clandestine
clinometric
cognateness
cognitional
cognitively
cognitivity
cognoscente
cognoscenti
cognoscible
coincidence
coinheritor
coinsurance
connectable
connectedly
connectible
connoisseur
connotation
connotative
connubially
cornerstone
cornhusking
corniferous
cornucopian
counselling
countenance
counterblow
counterbond
counterfeit
counterfoil
counterfort
countermand
countermark
countermine
countermove
countermure
counterpane
counterpart
counterplan
counterplea
counterplot
countersign
countersink
countersunk
counterturn
countervail
counterview
counterwork
countlessly
countrified
countryfied
countryseat
countryside
countrywide
craniometry
crenellated
crenulation
crunchiness
ctenophoran
cunningness
dauntlessly
dinnerdance
dinnertable
dinnerwagon
donnishness
downdraught
downhearted
downtrodden
drunkenness
earnestness
econometric
emancipator
enunciation
enunciative
epinephrine
ethnography
ethnologist
evanescence
evangelical
evanishment
eveningstar
eventualise
eventuality
exanthemata
exoneration
exonerative
FinnoUgrian
flannelette
flannelling
fornication
Francomania
Francophile
Francophobe
francophone
franctireur
frankfurter
franklinite
frankpledge
frantically
franticness
frenchified
Frenchwoman
frontrunner
furnishings
gainfulness
garnishment
geanticline
giantpowder
grandfather
grandiflora
grandiosely
grandiosity
grandmother
grandnephew
grandparent
grangeriser
granivorous
granolithic
granophyric
granularity
granulation
granulocyte
gymnospermy
heinousness
hornswoggle
hymnography
hypnopaedia
hypnopompic
ichnography
iconography
iconostases
iconostasis
identically
inanimately
inanimation
ironhearted
ironmongery
itinerantly
itineration
jauntingcar
launderette
limnologist
lionhearted
magnanimity
magnanimous
magnificent
maintenance
maintopmast
maintopsail
manneristic
mannishness
meaningless
minnesinger
moonlighter
morningroom
mountaineer
mountainous
mountaintop
Neanderthal
ninnyhammer
ominousness
opencircuit
openhearted
openmouthed
opinionated
orangoutang
ozoniferous
ozonisation
ozonosphere
painfulness
painkilling
painstaking
paunchiness
pawnbroking
pennyweight
phantasiast
phantasmata
phenologist
phonetician
phonography
phonologist
pinnatisect
planetarium
planetoidal
planimetric
planisphere
planoconvex
plantigrade
plenipotent
plenteously
plentifully
pointdevice
pointedness
pointillism
pointillist
pointlessly
pornography
prenominate
principally
quincuncial
quinquennia
quinquereme
quintillion
raunchiness
reanimation
reenactment
reincarnate
reinsertion
reinsurance
reintegrate
reintroduce
rhinologist
rhinoscopic
rhynchodont
roentgenise
roundedness
ruinousness
saintliness
saintpaulia
scenography
scintillant
scintillate
signifiable
significant
signpainter
slenderness
somnambular
somniculous
somniferous
somnolently
soundlessly
spendthrift
spindlelegs
spindletree
spinelessly
spiniferous
Spinozistic
spinsterish
spondulicks
spondylitis
spongecloth
sponsorship
spontaneity
spontaneous
standardise
standoffish
standpatter
stencilling
stenochromy
stenography
stenotypist
stonecurlew
stonecutter
stoneground
stonemarten
stonewaller
stuntedness
swingletree
swinishness
tarnishable
teenybopper
teknonymous
thanatology
thanklessly
thanksgiver
thankworthy
thenceforth
thingumabob
thingumajig
thinskinned
thunderbird
thunderbolt
thunderclap
thunderhead
thunderless
thunderpeal
townspeople
transaction
transalpine
transceiver
transcriber
transection
transferred
transferrer
transfigure
transfinite
transfixion
transformer
transfusion
transhumant
transiently
transilient
translation
translocate
translucent
translunary
transmarine
transmittal
transmitted
transmitter
transpadane
transparent
transpierce
transponder
transporter
transsexual
transuranic
transversal
trenchantly
trencherman
trendsetter
Trinitarian
trundletail
unanimously
unendurable
unendurably
uninhabited
uninhibited
uninucleate
Upanishadic
uranography
varnishtree
wainscoting
wainscotted
weenybopper
winningness
winningpost
wrongheaded
zoantharian
abdominally
abhorrently
abiogeneses
abiogenesis
abiogenetic
abiological
abiotically
abnormality
absorbingly
absorptance
accommodate
accompanist
accordantly
accordingly
accoucheuse
accountable
accountably
accountancy
achondritic
acropetally
adjournment
aerobically
aerobiology
aerodynamic
aerographer
aerological
aeronautics
aeronomical
aerostatics
aerostation
AfroAsiatic
agnosticism
agrobiology
agrological
agronomical
algological
algorithmic
allocatable
allomorphic
allopathist
altocumulus
altorelievo
altorilievo
altostratus
antonomasia
appogiatura
appointment
arboraceous
arborescent
Areopagitic
ascomycetes
association
associative
assortative
atmospheric
atrociously
autochthony
autoerotism
autographic
automatable
autoplastic
autotrophic
axiological
Belorussian
bicorporate
binocularly
bivouacking
bloodguilty
bloodlessly
bloodstream
bloodsucker
bloodvessel
bryozoology
bucolically
Byronically
cacographic
cacophonous
calorimeter
calorimetry
canonically
Carolingian
ceroplastic
chaotically
chlorophyll
chloroplast
chloroprene
chrominance
chromoplast
chromosomal
chronically
chronograph
chronologer
chronologic
chronometer
chronometry
chronoscope
coconscious
colonelship

colonialism
colonialist
colorimeter
colorimetry
colouration
colourblind
colourfully
coronagraph
coronograph
cotoneaster
crookbacked
crookedness
cryobiology
cryosurgery
cryotherapy
cytogenesis
cytokinesis
cytological
debouchment
decollation
decolletage
decolourise
decorticate
defoliation
deforcement
deformation
democratise
democratism
demographer
demographic
demonolatry
demonstrate
demountable
denominator
depopulator
deportation
devotedness
dicotyledon
dinosaurian
disobedient
disobliging
disorganise
divorcement
doxographer
echosounder
ectoblastic
ectogenesis
ectogenetic
ectomorphic
ectoplasmic
ectotrophic
elbowgrease
embowelling
embowerment
encomiastic
endocardiac
endocardial
endocardium
endometrium
endomorphic
endophagous
endoplasmic
endorsement
endoskelton
endothelial
endothelium
endothermal
endothermic
endotrophic
enforceable
enforcement
engorgement
ennoblement
entomophily
erroneously
ethological
Europeanise
excoriation
exfoliation
exfoliative
exhortation
exhortative
exhortatory
exponential
exportation
expostulate
extortioner
favouritism
feloniously
ferociously
floorwalker
fluorescein
fluorescent
fluoroscope
fluoroscopy
gamogenesis
gerontology
gyrocompass
halophilous
heroworship
holoblastic
holographic
holothurian
homocentric
homoeopathy
homoestatic
homogeneity
homogeneous
homogenetic
homogeniser
homoiousian
homological
homomorphic
homophonous
homoplastic
homopterous
homosporous
homothallic
homozygosis
horological
hylogenesis
hylozoistic
hypoblastic
hypocycloid
hypogastric
hypoglossal
hypolimnion
hypophyseal
hypophysial
hypostatise
hypotension
hypothecate
hypothenuse
hypothermia
hypothesise
hypotyposis
ideographic
ideological
idiographic
idiomorphic
idiotically
ignobleness
ignominious
illogically
immortalise
immortality
immoveables
impolitical
impoliticly
importantly
importation
importunate
importunely
importunity
impoundment
incoercible
incognisant
incoherence
incoherency
incommodity
incompetent
incompliant
incongruent
incongruity
incongruous
inconscient
inconsonant
inconstancy
incontinent
incorporate
incorporeal
incorrectly
incorruptly
IndoChinese
IndoIranian
indomitable
indomitably
indorsement
informality
information
informative
informatory
innocuously
innoxiously
insouciance
intolerable
intolerably
intolerance
involucrate
involuntary
involvement
ionospheric
Jacobinical
Jacobitical
kilocalorie
kymographic
laboriously
laconically
logographer
logographic
logomachist
loxodromics
masochistic
melodiously
memorabilia
memorialise
memorialist
meroblastic
merogenesis
Merovingian
mesoblastic
mesomorphic
metonymical
metoposcopy
monocarpous
monochasial
monochasium
monochromat
monochromic
monoclinous
monoculture
monogenesis
monogenetic
monogrammed
monographer
monographic
monolingual
monological
monologuise
monologuist
monomorphic
mononuclear
monophagous
monophthong
Monophysite
monopoliser
monopterous
Monothelite
monozygotic
moronically
mycological
mycophagist
mycorrhizae
mycorrhizal
myxomatosis
myxomycetes
nasofrontal
negotiation
negotiatory
negotiatrix
nomographer
nomographic
nomological
nosographer
nosographic
nosological
notoriously
obnoxiously
obsolescent
oecological
oenological
oenophilist
oesophageal
oncological
ontogenesis
ontogenetic
ontological
opportunely
opportunism
opportunist
opportunity
optometrist
oreographic
oreological
osmotically
parochially
paronomasia
pedological
penological
pilocarpine
pilotburner
pivotbridge
pleochroism
pleomorphic
pococurante
podophyllin
pomological
posological
preoccupied
proofreader
pyroclastic
pyrotechnic
recognition
recognitive
recognitory
recommender
recommittal
recondition
reconnoitre
reconstruct
recoverable
redoubtable
reformation
reformative
reformatory
rejoicingly
remonstrant
remonstrate
remorseless
reportorial
reposefully
resourceful
rheological
rheotropism
ricochetted
rodomontade
rotogravure
saponaceous
savouriness
saxophonist
scholarship
scholiastic
schoolboard
schoolchild
schoolhouse
schottische
seborrhoeic
secondarily
secondclass
secondrater
secondsight
serological
sexological
sinological
smoothfaced
sonofabitch
Soroptimist
stoolpigeon
stroboscope
strongpoint
subordinate
subornation
sycophantic
sycophantry
synonymical
taxonomical
theobromine
theocentric
theodolitic
theological
theorematic
theoretical
theosophist
throatiness
throatlatch
thrombocyte
tobogganing
tobogganist
topographer
topographic
topological
toxophilite
typographer
typographic
typological
unboundedly
uncommitted
unconcealed
unconcerned
uncongenial
unconnected
unconscious
uncontested
uncountable
uncouthness
undoubtedly
unforgiving
unfortunate
ungodliness
unpolitical
unpossessed
unsolicited
unsoundness
untouchable
upholsterer
vaporimeter
vaporisable
vasodilator
vasopressin
vasopressor
virological
widowerhood
xenophilous
xerophilous
xylocarpous
xylographer
xylographic
xylophagous
xylophonist
Yugoslavian
Zoroastrian
zygomorphic
acupuncture
adoptianism
adoptianist
adoptionism
adoptionist
anaphylaxis
apophyllite
aseptically
biophysical
blepharitis
bumptiously
campanology
campanulate
campmeeting
carpetsnake
chaperonage
Chippendale
clapperclaw
compactness
compaginate
comparatist
comparative
compartment
compassable
compellable
compendious
compensator
competently
competition
competitive
compilation
compilement
complacence
complacency
complainant
complaisant
complexness
compliantly
complicated
complotting
comportment
compositely
composition
compositive
compossible
compotation
compotatory
compression
compressive
comprisable
comptroller
compunction
compurgator
computation
computerise
cooperation
cooperative
copperplate
coppersmith
corporality
corporately
corporation
corporatism
corporative
corporeally
corpulently
corpuscular
crepitation
crepuscular
cryptically
cryptogamic
cryptograph

cryptomeria
culpability
desperadoes
desperately
desperation
despoilment
despondence
despondency
diaphaneity
diaphoresis
diaphoretic
diapophysis
diapositive
Diophantine
disparaging
disparately
dispensable
dispersedly
displeasure
disportment
disposition
dispositive
disputation
dropcurtain
dropforging
earpiercing
elephantine
elephantoid
epipetalous
evaporation
evaporative
foppishness
geophysical
geopolitics
graphically
graphicness
harpsichord
helpfulness
Hepplewhite
herpetology
hesperidium
hippocampus
Hippocratic
hippopotami
Hispanicise
Hispanicism
Hispanicist
hospitalise
hospitality
hospitaller
inappetence
inoperative
inopportune
inspiration
inspiratory
jumpingbean
jumpingjack
kleptomania
lamplighter
leapfrogged
lowpressure
lumpishness
malposition
malpractice
Neoplatonic
nonpartisan
nonplussing
nympholepsy
nymphomania
oilpainting
oviposition
palpability
palpitation
pamphleteer
perpetrator
perpetually
perpetuance
perpetuator
perplexedly
pompousness
porphyritic
preparation
preparative
preparatory
preposition
prepositive
preprandial
propagation
propagative
prophethood
prophetical
prophetship
prophylaxis
propinquity
propitiable
propitiator
proportions
proposition
proprietary
purportedly
purposeless
purposively
purpresture
reapportion
reappraisal
respectable
respectably
respiration
respiratory
resplendent
respondence
respondency
responsible
responsibly
rhapsodical
salpingitis
sceptically
scopolamine
scuppernong
scyphistoma
sempiternal
serpiginous
shapeliness
shepherdess
shipbreaker
shipbuilder
shoplifting
shopsteward
simperingly
simpliciter
soapboiling
soupkitchen
stepbrother
stephanotis
stipendiary
stipulation
stipulatory
sulphureous
sulphurwort
sumptuosity
sumptuously
suppliantly
supportable
supportably
supposition
suppositive
suppository
suppression
suppressive
suppuration
suppurative
surpassable
suspenseful
suspensible
suspiration
sympathetic
sympathiser
sympetalous
symphonious
symposiarch
symptomatic
temperament
temperately
temperative
temperature
tempestuous
temporality
temporarily
trapeziform
trapezoidal
Trappistine
trepanation
trepidation
tripetalous
triphibious
triphyllous
trophoblast
troposphere
trypanosome
tryptophane
unappealing
unipersonal
unipolarity
unsparingly
unspeakable
unspeakably
vespertinal
wappenschaw
wapperjawed
waspishness
waspwaisted
whippletree
zooplankton
barquentine
cinquecento
conquerable
disquieting
disquietude
inequitable
inequitably
marquessate
marqueterie
marquisette
masquerader
triquetrous
unequivocal
abbreviator
abortionist
acarpellous
accrescence
achromatise
achromatism
affranchise
affrication
affricative
aggravation
aggregately
aggregation
aggregative
aggrievedly
agoraphobia
agoraphobic
amaranthine
Americanise
Americanism
Americanist
amorousness
amorphously
anarchistic
androgynous
anfractuous
apartmental
aphrodisiac
appreciable
appreciably
appreciator
approbation
approbatory
appropriate
approvingly
approximate
astringency
attractable
attribution
attributive
attritional
barrelhouse
barrelorgan
bearbaiting
bearishness
boardschool
boorishness
bourgeoisie
carrageenan
carrageenin
carriageway
charcuterie
chargesheet
charismatic
charlatanry
chartaceous
chirography
chiropodist
chiropteran
choreograph
chorography
churchgoing
churchiness
churchwoman
Clarencieux
clericalism
clericalist
coarctation
comradeship
coordinator
correctable
correctness
correlation
correlative
corrigendum
corroborant
corroborate
corrosively
corrugation
corruptible
corruptibly
corruptness
courteously
courtliness
cupriferous
cupronickel
currentness
currishness
cypripedium
decrepitate
decrepitude
decrescendo
deerstalker
defraudment
degradation
degradingly
depravation
depravement
deprecation
deprecative
deprecatory
depreciator
depredation
depredatory
depressible
deprivation
detrainment
detribalise
detrimental
diarthrosis
disremember
doorknocker
dourouc ouli
embraceable
embracement
embracingly
embrocation
embroiderer
embroilment
embryologic
embryonated
enarthrosis
encrustment
enfranchise
engrossment
entrainment
entreatment
entrustment
everlasting
exarcerbate
excremental
excrescence
excrescency
exercisable
exorbitance
expressible
expropriate
extractable
extradition
extrapolate
extravagant
extravagate
extravasate
extraverted
extremeness
extrication
extroverted
fabrication
fairweather
farraginous
farreaching
fearfulness
ferriferous
ferruginous
flirtatious
florescence
floriferous
florilegium
fourflusher
fourpounder
fourwheeler
garrulously
gerrymander
glaringness
gourmandise
gourmandism
guardedness
hairbreadth
hairdresser
hairraising
hairstyling
hairstylist
hairtrigger
heartbroken
hearthstone
heartlessly
heartsblood
heartstring
Hebraically
herringbone
herringgull
hierarchism
horripilate
hurriedness
hurryscurry
hurryskurry
hydraheaded
hydrobromic
hydrocarbon
hydrocyanic
hydrogenate
hydrogenous
hydrography
hydrologist
hydromedusa
hydrometeor
hydrometric
hydropathic
hydrophilic
hydrophobia
hydrophobic
hydrophytic
hydroponics
hydrosphere
hydrostatic
hydrotactic
hydrothorax
hydrotropic
hygrometric
hygrophytic
hygroscopic
imbrication
impractical
imprecation
imprecatory
imprecisely
imprecision
impregnable
impregnably
impressible
impressment
impropriate
impropriety
improvement
improvident
imprudently
increasable
incredulity
incredulous
incremental
incriminate
infrangible
infrequence
infrequency
ingrainedly
ingratitude
intractable
intractably
intravenous
intrepidity
intricately
intriguante
intromitted
intromitter
introverted
intrusively
jerrymander
journeywork
lacrimation
lacrimatory
lacrimosely
lacrymation
lacrymatory
lacrymosely
laurustinus
learnedness
leprosarium
lubrication
lubricative
lucratively
macrobiotic
macrocosmic
macrogamete
macroscopic
madreporite
madrigalian
madrigalist
marriagebed
matriarchal

matriculate
matrilineal
matrilinear
matrimonial
meprobamate
merryandrew
merrymaking
metrication
micrococcal
micrococcus
microcosmic
microgamete
micrography
microgroove
microlithic
micrometric
Micronesian
microphonic
microphytic
microscopic
microsecond
misremember
mitrailleur
mooringmast
morrisdance
narratively
nearsighted
necrobiosis
necrologist
necromancer
necromantic
necrophilia
necrophilic
necropoleis
negrophobia
neurologist
neuropathic
neuroticism
neurotropic
nigrescence
nitrogenise
nitrogenous
nonresident
nourishment
nutrimental
nutritional
nutritively
obtrusively
odoriferous
odorousness
onerousness
operational
operatively
operculated
operoseness
opprobrious
ostracoderm
Ostrogothic
outrivalled
ovariectomy
overanxious
overbalance
overbearing
overbidding
overcropped
overdevelop
overgarment
overindulge
overlapping
overmanning
overmeasure
overpayment
overproduce
overrunning
oversailing
oversetting
overstepped
overstretch
overstuffed
overtopping
overweening
overwritten
overwrought
patriarchal
patrilineal
patrimonial
patristical
patronising
pearlescent
pearlfisher
petrography
petrologist
pharisaical
phariseeism
pharyngitis
pluralistic
pourparlers
prerogative
prorogation
pruriginous
pteridology
pterodactyl
putrescence
putrescible
quarrelling
quarrelsome
quarterback
quarterdeck
quartertone
querulously
rearadmiral
recriminate
recruitment
refrangible
refreshment
refrigerant
refrigerate
refringency
regretfully
regrettable
regrettably
reorientate
representer
repressible
repressibly
reproachful
reprobation
reprobative
reprobatory
reprogramme
reprography
reprovingly
retraceable
retractable
retranslate
retribution
retributive
retributory
retrievable
retroaction
retroactive
retrocedent
retroflexed
retrorocket
rubrication
sacramental
sacrificial
saprobiotic
saprogenous
saprophytic
sauropodous
scarabaeoid
scaremonger
scorchingly
scoriaceous
scorpionfly
scurvygrass
searchingly
searchlight
secretarial
secretariat
secretively
segregation
segregative
serrulation
shareholder
sharepusher
sharpwitted
sheriffalty
sheriffship
shirtsleeve
shortchange
shortcoming
shorthanded
shortspoken
shortwinded
smorgasbord
sorrowfully
sparingness
sparrowbill
sparrowhawk
spermaphyte
spermatozoa
spermicidal
spiraculate
spiritistic
spiritlevel
spiritually
spiritualty
spirituelle
spirochaete
spirochetal
spirometric
sporogenous
sporogonium
sporophytic
sportswoman
sporulation
starchiness
starcrossed
starstudded
startlingly
stereograph
stereometry
stereophony
stereoscope
stereoscopy
stereotyped
stereotyper
stereotypic
sternsheets
sternutator
stirrupbone
stirruppump
storekeeper
stormcentre
stormtroops
storyteller
subregional
subrogation
supremacist
supremeness
surrebuttal
surrebutter
surrogation
swarthiness
swordbearer
tarradiddle
tearfulness
tearstained
terraqueous
terrestrial
terricolous
terrigenous
territorial
tetracyclic
tetradactyl
tetrahedral
tetrahedron
tetramerous
tetrapodous
tetrarchate
tetravalent
therapeutic
thereabouts
theretofore
therewithal
thermically
thermionics
thermoduric
thermograph
thermolysis
thermolytic
thermometer
thermometry
thermophile
thermoscope
thermotaxis
thirstiness
thoroughpin
thoroughwax
thuriferous
thyroiditis
tourbillion
ultramarine
ultramodern
ultrasonics
ultraviolet
unbreakable
uncrushable
unorganized
unorthodoxy
unprintable
unpromising
vibratility
vibrational
vitrescence
vitrifiable
voortrekker
warrantable
warrantably
wearilessly
wearisomely
whereabouts
wheresoever
wherewithal
whoremaster
whoremonger
worrisomely
abusiveness
ahistorical
airsickness
anastomoses
anastomosis
anastomotic
anisotropic
aposiopesis
apostleship
apostolical
apostrophic
aristocracy
awesomeness
awestricken
bassethound
beastliness
bersaglieri
blasphemous
blastogenic
blessedness
boysenberry
bristletail
bristleworm
bristliness
brusqueness
cassiterite
catswhisker
causatively
caustically
ceaselessly
classically
closefisted
closehauled
clostridium
coessential
comstockery
consanguine
consciously
consecrator
consecution
consecutive
consentient
consequence
conservable
conservancy
conservator
considerate
considering
consignable
consignment
consistence
consistency
consolation
consolatory
consolidate
consolingly
consonantal
consonantly
conspecific
conspicuity
conspicuous
conspirator
constellate
consternate
constituent
constitutor
constrictor
construable
constructor
consultancy
consumerism
consumingly
consummator
consumption
consumptive
crestfallen
crossbearer
crossbowman
crossgarnet
crosslegged
crossstitch
crustaceous
crystalline
crystallise
crystallite
crystalloid
cursiveness
cursoriness
daisycutter
deistically
diastematic
diastrophic
dipsomaniac
disseminate
disseminule
dissentient
dissepiment
dissertator
dissimilate
dissimulate
dissipation
dissipative
dissociable
dissolutely
dissolution
dissolvable
dissonantly
dissyllable
dissymmetry
drastically
dresscircle
dressmaking
einsteinium
elastically
elasticated
elastomeric
elusiveness
emasculator
episcopally
Erastianism
evasiveness
existential
exoskeletal
exoskeleton
facsimilist
Falstaffian
feasibility
felspathoid
firstfruits
fissionable
fissiparity
fissiparous
fleshliness
frostbitten
frustration
fulsomeness
geostrophic
geosyncline
ghastliness
ghostliness
ghostwriter
glassblower
glasscutter
glassmaking
glossolalia
grasshopper
gristliness
guesstimate
gypsiferous
haustellate
hirsuteness
horsecollar
horsedoctor
horseradish
housefather
householder
housekeeper
houselights
housemaster
housemother
housewifely
housewifery
hyoscyamine
hypsography
hypsometric
hypsophobia
icosahedral
icosahedron
inescapable
inessential
inestimable
inestimably
irksomeness
Jansenistic
kwashiorkor
leaseholder
lissomeness
looselimbed
loosestrife
lowspirited
maisonnette
mansardroof
marshalling
marshalship
marshmallow

massiveness
massproduce
measureless
measurement
menservants
mensuration
messiahship
misspelling
moisturiser
monseigneur
monstrosity
monstrously
mosstrooper
mudslinging
noiselessly
noisemaking
noisomeness
nonsensical
nonsequitur
nonspecific
nurserymaid
oarsmanship
outspokenly
outstanding
outstripped
palsgravine
passacaglia
passeriform
passibility
Passiontide
passivation
passiveness
pensionable
pensionless
pensiveness
persecution
perseverate
persistence
persistency
personalise
personalism
personalist
personality
personation
personative
personifier
perspective
perspicuity
perspicuous
persuadable
persuasible
pessimistic
phosphonium
phosphorate
phosphorism
phosphorite
phosphorous
physicality
physiocracy
physiognomy
physiologic
pigsticking
plasmolysis
plasmolytic
plasterwork
plasticiser
poisonously
possibility
presanctify
presbyteral
presciently
preselector
presentable
presentably
presentient
presentment
preservable
pressagency
prestigious
prestissimo
prestressed
presumingly
presumption
presumptive
prosaically
prosaicness
prosecution
prosecutrix
proselytise
proselytism
prosenchyma
prospective
prosthetics
prostitutor
prostration
Prussianise
Prussianism
pussyfooter
pussywillow
questionary
rapscallion
reassertion
reassurance
reestablish
Russophobia
sansculotte
Sanskritist
sausagemeat
scissorbill
scissortail
seasickness
seismically
seismograph
seismometer
seismometry
seismoscope
sensational
senselessly
sensibility
sensitively
sensitivity
sensorially
spasmodical
spastically
spessartite
suasiveness
subscapular
subsequence
subservient
subsistence
subspecific
substandard
substantial
substantive
substituent
subsumption
subsumptive
syssarcosis
teaspoonful
tensibility
tessellated
thistledown
toastmaster
tonsillitis
trestletree
trestlework
tristichous
trisyllabic
trisyllable
trustbuster
trusteeship
trustworthy
unashamedly
unassertive
unessential
unisexually
unusualness
varsovienne
versatilely
versatility
Weismannism
Wensleydale
whistlestop
whosesoever
winsomeness
worshipable
worshipless
worshipping
abstentious
abstinently
abstraction
abstractive
abstriction
acatalectic
acetylation
aesthetical
aestivation
amativeness
amethystine
apotheosise
armtwisting
austereness
azotobacter
bactericide
BaltoSlavic
banteringly
baptismally
battledress
battlefield
bestselling
bitterapple
bittercress
bittersweet
blotchiness
bootlegging
bottleglass
bottlegreen
bottlenosed
boutonniere
Britishness
brittleness
brotherhood
brutishness
butterflies
butteriness
cantharides
cantharidic
captainship
captionless
captivation
cartography
castellated
castigation
centenarian
centigramme
centreboard
centrepiece
centrifugal
centripetal
certifiable
certifiably
certificate
chitterling
clothesline
clothesmoth
clothesprop
coeternally
containable
containment
contaminant
contaminate
contemplate
contentedly
contentious
contentment
conterminal
contestable
continental
continently
contingence
contingency
continuable
continually
continuance
continuator
contorniate
contrabasso
contractile
contraction
contractive
contractual
contracture
contradance
contraption
contrariety
contrarious
contrastive
contretemps
contributor
contrivable
contrivance
controlling
controlment
controversy
costbenefit
costiveness
cottongrass
cottonmouth
criticality
criticaster
crotcheteer
cultivation
curtailment
customarily
custombuilt
customhouse
cysticercus
dactylogram
dactylology
deathrattle
denticulate
dentigerous
depthcharge
destination
destitution
destruction
destructive
deuteration
deuterogamy
Deuteronomy
dexterously
diatessaron
dictatorial
dipterocarp
distasteful
distempered
distensible
distinction
distinctive
distinguish
distraction
distractive
distressful
distribuend
distributor
distrustful
disturbance
dittography
doctrinaire
doctrinally
doltishness
earthcloset
earthenware
earthliness
easternmost
editorially
egotistical
elutriation
emotionally
emotionless
emptyhanded
emptyheaded
epithalamia
epithalamic
epithelioma
erotogenous
erotomaniac
erythrocyte
esotericism
exotericism
exstipulate
factfinding
factionally
factualness
faithhealer
faithlessly
faithworthy
falteringly
fantastical
farthermost
farthingale
featheredge
featherhead
featherless
featureless
festinately
festschrift
filterpaper
flatulently
footpoundal
footslogger
footsoldier
forthcoming
fortifiable
fortnightly
fortunately
fraternally
fraterniser
fratricidal
fretfulness
frothhopper
furtherance
furthermore
furthermost
furthersome
furtiveness
fustigation
gartersnake
gastrectomy
gastronomic
gastroscope
genteelness
gentianella
gentilitial
gentlemanly
gentlewoman
geotectonic
gestatorial
gesticulate
gettogether
glutinously
gnotobiosis
gnotobiotic
gratulation
gratulatory
grotesquely
grotesquery
guttapercha
guttersnipe
gutturalise
gutturalism
halterbreak
heptamerous
heptarchist
histologist
historiated
historicise
historicism
historicist
historicity
histrionics
histrionism
hurtfulness
ichthyology
ichthyornis
ichthyosaur
illtempered
imitatively
inattention
inattentive
initialling
instability
installment
instigation
instigative
instillment
instinctive
instinctual
institution
instruction
instructive
jactitation
justiciable
justifiable
justifiably
Kulturkampf
lactescence
lactiferous
lastingness
latticework
leatherback
leatherhead
leatherneck
lectureship
lentiginous
leptodactyl
letterpress
litterateur
loathliness
loathsomely
loutishness
lustfulness
mantelpiece
mantelshelf
mantuamaker
martyrology
masterfully
masterpiece
mastication
masticatory
mastodontic
mastoiditis
mentholated
mentionable
micturition
mirthlessly
mistrustful
mortarboard
multangular
multicolour
multilinear
multinomial
multiparous
multiracial
multistorey
multivalent
mustachioed
muttonchops
Neotropical
nettlecloth
neutraliser
nictitation
nittygritty
noctilucent

noctivagant
noctivagous
nocturnally
northeaster
northwester
nyctitropic
nyctophobia
obstetrical
obstinately
obstruction
obstructive
oestrogenic
oysterplant
pantalettes
pantheistic
pantomimist
pantothenic
participant
participate
participial
particulate
partitioned
partitioner
partitively
partnership
parturition
pasteuriser
pastoralism
pastoralist
pastureland
patternshop
pectination
pentadactyl
pentagynous
pentahedron
pentamerous
pentandrous
pentathlete
pentavalent
pentazocine
Pentecostal
pentlandite
peptisation
pertinacity
pertinently
perturbable
pestiferous
pestilently
pestologist
petticoated
pettifogger
pettishness
photoactive
photocopier
photofinish
photography
photometric
photooffset
photoperiod
photophilic
photophobia
photophobic
photosphere
phototactic
phototropic
phytography
phytologist
phytosterol
phytotomist
pictography
pictorially
picturebook
picturecard
picturegoer
picturesque
pietistical
platearmour
plateresque
platforming
platinotype
platyrrhine
plutocratic
poltergeist
poltroonery
pontificals
pontificate
portability
porterhouse
portionless
portmanteau
portraitist
portraiture
postclassic
posteriorly
postexilian
postglacial
postnuptial
postulation
potteringly
prattlingly
pretendedly
pretentious
preterhuman
preterition
protagonist
protectoral
protectress
proteolysis
proteolytic
Proterozoic
prothalamia
prothallial
prothallium
prothoracic
protomartyr
protonotary
protophytic
protractile
protraction
protractive
protrudable
protrusible
protuberant
psittacosis
pustulation
quaternloaf
quitchgrass
rapturously
Rastafarian
rattlebrain
rattlepated
rattlesnake
rectangular
rectifiable
rectilineal
rectilinear
reiteration
reiterative
restatement
restfulness
restitution
restiveness
restoration
restorative
restriction
restrictive
restructure
rhetorician
riotousness
rottenstone
rustication
saltatorial
saltimbanco
sartorially
scattergood
ScotchIrish
Scotchwoman
scuttlebutt
sectionally
sententious
sentimental
sentinelled
Septembrist
septenarius
septentrion
septicaemia
septicaemic
septiferous
septifragal
sertularian
sextodecimo
shutterless
shuttlecock
sittingroom
skatingrink
sketchiness
slotmachine
smithereens
smithsonite
snatchblock
softhearted
softshelled
sottishness
southeaster
Southernism
southwester
spathaceous
spatterdash
stateliness
statesmanly
statistical
statutebook
statutorily
stethoscope
stethoscopy
subterminal
subtraction
subtractive
subtropical
suitability
sustainable
sustainment
switchblade
switchboard
syntactical
synthesiser
synthetical
systematics
systematise
systematism
systematist
tantalising
tastelessly
tautologise
tautologism
tautologous
tautomerism
tautonymous
teeterboard
teetotalism
teetotaller
tentaculate
tentatively
tenterhooks
tentpegging
testability
testatrices
testimonial
Teutonicism
textureless
thitherward
tittivation
toothbilled
toothpowder
toothsomely
torticollis
torturously
totteringly
tritagonist
tritheistic
trituration
trothplight
tufthunting
turtleshell
tuttifrutti
ulotrichous
unstoppable
unutterable
unutterably
ventilation
ventilative
ventricular
ventriculus
ventriloquy
venturesome
venturously
verticality
vertiginous
vestigially
vestryclerk
victualless
victualling
voltametric
vortiginous
waitinglist
waitingroom
wastebasket
weathercock
weatherwise
weatherworn
weltschmerz
westernmost
Westminster
Whitechapel
whitecollar
whiteheaded
whitethroat
whitewasher
whitherward
whitishness
whitleather
Whitsuntide
winterberry
wintergreen
wistfulness
worthlessly
xanthochroi
xanthophyll
zestfulness
zootechnics
ablutionary
aboutsledge
acaulescent
acculturate
accumulator
accusatival
acoustician
acquiescent
acquirement
acquisition
acquisitive
acquittance
adjudgement
adjudicator
aiguillette
ailurophile
ailurophobe
albuminuria
annunciator
appurtenant
arduousness
argumentive
assuagement
assuredness
Augustinian
beauteously
beautifully
beguilement
beguilingly
bicuspidate
bifurcation
biquadratic
calumniator
caruncula te
casuistical
chaulmoogra
cloudcastle
columbarium
columniated
conurbation
coruscation
decussately
decussation
deductively
degustation
denumerable
denunciator
desultorily
diluvialist
disunionist
divulgation
divulgement
documentary
draughtsman
drouthiness
effulgently
encumbrance
enquiringly
Etruscology
exculpation
exculpatory
excursively
expurgation
expurgatory
exquisitely
facultative
fatuousness
fecundation
flauntingly
fraudulence
furunculous
genuflexion
genuineness
glauconitic
grouchiness
groundsheet
groundwater
harumscarum
illuminable
illuminance
illuminator
illusionism
illusionist
illustrator
illustrious
immunologic
impuissance
impulsively
inaugurator
inculcation
inculpation
inculpatory
incunabulum
incuriosity
incuriously
incurvation
incurvature
indubitable
indubitably
inductively
indulgently
industrious
ingurgitate
injudicious
injuriously
innumerable
innumerably
innutrition
inquilinous
inquiringly
inquisition
inquisitive
insufflator
insultingly
insuperable
insuperably
intuitional
intuitively
intuitivism
intumescent
invultation
irruptively
lieutenancy
liquefiable
liquescence
liquidambar
liquidation
loculicidal
lucubration
luxuriantly
luxuriation
luxuriously
manufactory
manufacture
manumission
manumitting
minuteglass
naturalness
naturopathy
nonunionist
obfuscation
obfuscatory
objurgation
objurgatory
obmutescent
occultation
oecumenical
oppugnation
peculiarity
pecuniarily
pedunculate
penultimate
penuriously
pleurodynia
ploughshare
ploughstaff
pneumonitis
populariser
pseudograph
pseudomonas
pseudomorph
pseudopodia
recumbently
recurrently
redundantly
reduplicate
regurgitate
rejuvenator
rejuvenesce
reluctantly
reluctation
remunerator
repudiation
repugnantly
repulsively
requirement
requisition
resuscitate
rheumaticky
ritualistic
roguishness
saturnalian
saturninely
scoundrelly

scoutmaster
scruffiness
scrumptious
scrutiniser
seductively
sequestrate
shoulderbag
shoulderpad
shrubbiness
sinuousness
situational
slaughterer
sleuthhound
solutionist
staunchless
staunchness
staurolitic
subumbrella
suburbanise
suburbanite
susurration
tegumentary
tenuousness
thaumatrope
thaumaturge
thaumaturgy
thoughtless
triumvirate
troublesome
troublously
trouserless
trousersuit
undutifully
unfurnished
unguardedly
unguiculate
unqualified
unquietness
vacuolation
vacuousness
valuational
vesuvianite
vituperator
voguishness
volubleness
volumometer
voluntarily
voluntarism
voluntarist
aboveground
beaverboard
Calvinistic
carvelbuilt
chevalglass
convenances
convenience
conveniency
conventicle
convergence
convergency
conversable
conversance
conversancy
convertible
convertibly
conveyancer
convincible
convivially
convocation
convolution
convolvulus
curvilineal
curvilinear
flavourless
flavoursome
frivolously
gravedigger
gravelblind
gravimetric
gravitation
gravitative
harvesthome
heavenwards
heavyfooted
heavyhanded
heavyweight
knavishness
leavetaking
louverboard
louvreboard
nervelessly
nervousness
nonviolence
nonvolatile
peevishness
pervasively
pervertedly
pluviometer
prevalently
prevaricate
preventable
preventible
previsional
privateness
privatively
provenience
providently
provisional
provisorily
provocateur
provocation
provocative
provokingly
provostship
pulverulent
ribvaulting
salvageable
salvational
serviceable
serviceably
servicebook
serviceline
shovelboard
silveriness
silverplate
silverpoint
silversmith
silverstick
slavedriver
slaveholder
slavemarket
slavishness
Slavonicise
solvability
stevengraph
surveillant
traversable
trivialness
unavailable
unavoidable
unavoidably
universally
velvetiness
awkwardness
betweenmaid
betweenness
betweentime
dimwittedly
drawingroom
floweriness
forwardness
frowardness
frowstiness
knowingness
knownothing
oldwomanish
outwardness
reawakening
schwarmerei
showerproof
showjumping
showmanship
showstopper
snowbunting
snowgoggles
snowleopard
stewardship
unawareness
waywardness
Alexandrian
alexandrine
alexandrite
coexistence
coextension
coextensive
deoxidation
deoxygenate
deoxyribose
flexibility
inexactness
inexcusable
inexcusably
inexistence
inexpedient
inexpensive
proximately
thixotropic
unexploited
unexpressed
alcyonarian
Assyriology
babysitting
bodybuilder
bodyservant
butyraceous
calyptrogen
caryopsides
chrysalides
chrysalises
chrysarobin
chrysoberyl
chrysoprase
cityslicker
dehydration
encystation
eurypteroid
ithyphallic
laryngology
laryngotomy
lilylivered
molybdenite
papyraceous
playerpiano
playfulness
playingcard
polyandrous
polycarpous
polychromic
polycrystal
polygenesis
polygenetic
polyglottal
polyglottic
polygonally
polygraphic
polymorphic
polyonymous
polypeptide
polyphagous
polyphonous
polystyrene
polytechnic
polyzoarium
prayerwheel
sphygmogram
amazonstone
brazenfaced
Elizabethan
prizewinner
quizzically
rhizanthous
rhizocarpic
rhizomatous

---

acatalectic
acclamation
acclamatory
acinaciform
affranchise
AfroAsiatic
aggravation
agoraphobia
agoraphobic
alabastrine
Alexandrian
alexandrine
alexandrite
alphabetise
amaranthine
amenability
amicability
anfractuous
animalcular
anomalistic
anomalously
apocalyptic
appealingly
appeasement
applaudable
archaeology
archaeornis
archaically
archangelic
aromaticity
assuagement
attractable
awkwardness
barbarously
barbastelle
bereavement
bergamasque
bersaglieri
biddability
biquadratic
bombardment
buffalorobe
bureaucracy
cabbagepalm
cabbagerose
cabbagetree
cabbageworm
cabbalistic
campanology
campanulate
captainship
carrageenan
carrageenin
causatively
chamaephyte
chevalglass
chimaerical
cinnabarine
climacteric
climatology
cockaleekie
cognateness
collaborate
collapsible
combatively
commandment
compactness
compaginate
comparatist
comparative
compartment
compassable
comradeship
concatenate
confabulate
consanguine
containable
containment
contaminant
contaminate
coplanarity
crematorium
culpability
curtailment
declamation
declamatory
declaration
declarative
declaratory
deflagrator
defraudment
degradation
degradingly
depravation
depravement
dermatology
detrainment
diamagnetic
dictatorial
disbandment
discalceate
discardable
disharmonic
dismayingly
disparaging
disparately
distasteful
dramaturgic
educability
educational
Elizabethan
embraceable
embracement
embracingly
emplacement
enchainment
enchantment
enchantress
endearingly
enfranchise
enneahedron
enslavement
entrainment
epigastrium
equiangular
eschatology
Eucharistic
exclamation
exclamatory
explainable
explanation
explanatory
extractable
extradition
extrapolate
extravagant
extravagate
extravasate
extraverted
eyecatching
fanfaronade
fantastical
farraginous
feudalistic
firmamental
formalistic
formational
forwardness
fricandeaux
frowardness
fundamental
gallantness
gendarmerie
genealogise
genealogist
geomagnetic
Germanophil
gestatorial
goddaughter
gonfalonier
gormandiser
gradational
guttapercha
haematocele
haematocrit
haematology
haggadistic
haggardness
haphazardly
Hebraically
hemianopsia
heptamerous
heptarchist
hierarchism
Hispanicise
Hispanicism
Hispanicist
hollandaise
husbandlike
hydraheaded
icosahedral
icosahedron
illfavoured
illmannered
imitatively
impeachable
impeachment
implausible
implausibly
impractical
inadaptable
inexactness
inflammable
inflammably
infrangible
ingrainedly
ingratitude
instability
installment
intractable
intractably
intravenous
inviability
ipecacuanha
Lancastrian
landaulette
laudability
longanimity
lucratively
magdalenian
magnanimity
magnanimous
mammalogist
mandarinate
mansardroof
mechanician
mechanistic
mediaevally
mediastinal
mediastinum
mediateness
mediatorial
mediatrices
miniaturise
miniaturist
miscarriage
mismarriage
mitrailleur
mortarboard
moveability

multangular
mundaneness
mustachioed
myocarditis
narratively
nonmatching
nonpartisan
offhandedly
oilpainting
operational
operatively
ostracoderm
outwardness
overanxious
palpability
pantalettes
passacaglia
peccability
peccadillos
pentadactyl
pentagynous
pentahedron
pentamerous
pentandrous
pentathlete
pentavalent
pentazocine
permanently
pervasively
phalanstery
philanderer
philatelist
pinnatisect
piscatorial
placability
plicateness
pluralistic
polyandrous
portability
Precambrian
precautious
predatorily
prefatorial
prefatorily
prematurely
prematurity
preparation
preparative
preparatory
presanctify
prevalently
prevaricate
primaevally
primateship
primatology
privateness
privatively
probabilism
probabilist
probability
probational
probationer
profanation
profanatory
profaneness
propagation
propagative
prosaically
prosaicness
protagonist
purgatorial
Pythagorean
Pythagorism
Rastafarian
rateability
readability
rearadmiral
reawakening
reclaimable
reclamation
rectangular
reenactment
refrangible
reliability
replaceable
replacement
restatement
retraceable
retractable
retranslate
rhizanthous
ribvaulting
ritualistic
Sabbatarian
sacramental
saleability
saltatorial
salvageable
salvational
satiability
sausagemeat
scalariform
scarabaeoid
schwarmerei
screamingly
selfassured
sensational
shamanistic
situational
sociability
socialistic
solvability
somnambular
spelaeology
spiraculate
spreadeagle
squeakiness
squeamishly
stalactitic
stalagmitic
steganogram
stewardship
stomachache
stomachpump
stomatology
streakiness
subbasement
subcategory
submarginal
suitability
summariness
summational
surbasement
surpassable
sustainable
sustainment
syllabarium
syllabicity
sympathetic
sympathiser
syntactical
syssarcosis
talkatively
tameability
tantalising
tarradiddle
tentaculate
tentatively
termagantly
terraqueous
testability
testatrices
tetracyclic
tetradactyl
tetrahedral
tetrahedron
tetramerous
tetrapodous
tetrarchate
tetravalent
thanatology
therapeutic
threadiness
threadpaper
throatiness
throatlatch
Titianesque
tracasserie
trepanation
tritagonist
trypanosome
ultramarine
ultramodern
ultrasonics
ultraviolet
unavailable
unawareness
unceasingly
unflappable
unguardedly
unhealthily
unmeaningly
unqualified
unrealistic
unreasoning
unsparingly
unteachable
valiantness
valuational
variability
variational
verbalistic
verdantique
versatilely
versatility
vibratility
vibrational
viceadmiral
volcanicity
volcanology
voltametric
vulcanicity
vulcanology
warrantable
warrantably
washability
waywardness
welladvised
workability
Zoroastrian
adumbration
adumbrative
aerobically
aerobiology
agrobiology
alembicated
amiableness
annabergite
atrabilious
audibleness
backbencher
ballbearing
bearbaiting
bellbottoms
birdbrained
bodybuilder
bookbinding
bullbaiting
calibration
capableness
carabiniere
carabinieri
celebration
celebratory
cerebration
chamberlain
chambermaid
coldblooded
costbenefit
crabbedness
cryobiology
curableness
defibrinate
disablement
disobedient
disobliging
durableness
ectoblastic
ennoblement
entablature
entablement
equableness
establisher
exorbitance
flabbergast
flamboyance
flamboyancy
flamboyante
freebooting
friableness
fullblooded
gallbladder
goldbeating
grumblingly
hairbreadth
halfbinding
halfblooded
handbreadth
harebrained
headborough
highbrowism
holoblastic
Hudibrastic
hypoblastic
ignobleness
illiberally
indubitable
indubitably
inhabitable
inhabitancy
Jacobinical
Jacobitical
lovableness
lucubration
makebelieve
meroblastic
mesoblastic
mindbending
mindblowing
molybdenite
moribundity
movableness
mutableness
notableness
overbalance
overbearing
overbidding
pawnbroking
pliableness
presbyteral
pureblooded
reedbunting
rhombohedra
rhomboideus
safebreaker
sandbagging
scribacious
shipbreaker
shipbuilder
shrubbiness
sickbenefit
sizableness
snowbunting
soapboiling
stepbrother
stroboscope
stumblingly
surfboarder
swimbladder
talebearing
tenableness
theobromine
thimbleweed
timebargain
tourbillion
tremblement
tremblingly
troublesome
troublously
tunableness
unambiguous
vagabondage
vagabondise
vagabondish
vagabondism
visibleness
volubleness
warmblooded
wellbeloved
abracadabra
adjectively
affectation
affectingly
affectional
affectioned
affectively
affectivity
afficionado
agriculture
allocatable
altocumulus
anarchistic
anencephaly
antecedence
antechamber
anticathode
anticipator
anticyclone
aquaculture
aquiculture
articulable
articulated
articulator
association
associative
atrociously
audaciously
auricularly
autochthony
backcountry
balmcricket
binocularly
blotchiness
branchiopod
breechblock
capaciously
capacitance
caricatural
catachreses
catachresis
cataclysmic
catechismal
catechistic
chalcedonic
chancellery
chancellory
charcuterie
churchgoing
churchiness
churchwoman
coarctation
codicillary
coincidence
consciously
corecipient
crotcheteer
crunchiness
dedicatedly
deductively
defectively
deficiently
delectation
deliciously
democratise
democratism
desecration
desiccation
desiccative
didacticism
directional
directivity
directorate
directorial
directrices
disaccustom
dodecaphony
domiciliary
domiciliate
dropcurtain
dualcontrol
eclecticism
effectively
effectually
efficacious
efficiently
emancipator
emasculator
endocardiac
endocardial
endocardium
enunciation
enunciative
episcopally
exarcerbate
exercisable
expectantly
expectation
expectative
expectorant
expectorate
exsiccation
ferociously
fetichistic
finicalness
firecracker
flaccidness
flagcaptain
flocculence
foreclosure
Francomania
Francophile
Francophobe
francophone
franctireur
frenchified
Frenchwoman
gatecrasher
geniculated
glauconitic
GraecoRoman
grouchiness
gyrocompass
Heracleidan
homocentric
hyoscyamine
hypocycloid
impecunious
indeciduous
IndoChinese
inductively
inescapable
inexcusable
inexcusably
innocuously

insectarium
insecticide
insectifuge
insectivore
insectology
invectively
irrecusable
irrecusably
judiciously
kilocalorie
logicalness
ludicrously
mailcarrier
maliciously
Manichaeism
masochistic
medicinable
medicinally
medicolegal
metacentric
metachrosis
molecricket
molecularly
monocarpous
monochasial
monochasium
monochromat
monochromic
monoclinous
monoculture
municipally
musicalness
namecalling
noticeboard
objectively
objectivism
objectivist
objectivity
obsecration
octachordal
officialdom
officialese
officialism
officiation
officinally
officiously
olfactology
opencircuit
operculated
orbicularly
overcropped
palmcabbage
panicmonger
parachutist
parochially
paunchiness
pedicellate
pediculosis
penicillate
penicillium
pericardiac
pericardial
pericardium
pericranial
pericranium
pilocarpine
pipecleaner
pleochroism
pococurante
policewoman
polycarpous
polychromic
polycrystal
pomiculture
postclassic
preachiness
preoccupied
presciently
principally
pumicestone
pyroclastic
quincuncial
quitchgrass
radicalness
rapaciously
rapscallion
raunchiness
redactional
reincarnate
reluctantly
reluctation
revaccinate
rhynchodont
ricochetted
rifacimenti
rifacimento
rockcrystal
Rosicrucian
rubicundity
safeconduct
safecracker
sagaciously
salaciously
sansculotte
scorchingly
ScotchIrish
Scotchwoman
searchingly
searchlight
seductively
selectively
selectivity
selfcentred
selfclosing
selfcocking
selfcommand
selfconceit
selfcontent
selfcontrol
selfcreated
selfculture
sericulture
sketchiness
snatchblock
speechifier
starchiness
starcrossed
stencilling
stoicalness
subscapular
switchblade
switchboard
tenaciously
thenceforth
theocentric
tobacconist
toxicomania
treacherous
treacliness
treecreeper
trenchantly
trencherman
typecasting
typicalness
unaccounted
unnecessary
urticaceous
urticarious
vasectomise
vaticinator
veraciously
vesicularly
viniculture
viticulture
vivaciously
voraciously
wildcatting
windcheater
wisecracker
woodcarving
woodcutting
xylocarpous
abandonment
abridgement
adjudgement
adjudicator
aerodynamic
anecdotical
archdiocese
archduchess
archdukedom
assiduously
Benedictine
benediction
benedictory
bladderwort
bloodguilty
bloodlessly
bloodstream
bloodsucker
bloodvessel
blunderbuss
boardschool
breadbasket
breadcrumbs
breadthways
breadthwise
breadwinner
broadcaster
broadleaved
broadminded
catadromous
cavedweller
childminder
clandestine
cloudcastle
coordinator
dehydration
desideratum
downdraught
dreadnought
equidistant
expediently
expeditious
fieldcornet
fieldworker
fraudulence
golddigging
grandfather
grandiflora
grandiosely
grandiosity
grandmother
grandnephew
grandparent
guardedness
hairdresser
hereditable
hexadecimal
immediately
immedicable
impedimenta
injudicious
insidiously
invidiously
irradiation
irradiative
irredentism
irredentist
irreducible
irreducibly
juridically
lakedweller
launderette
lepidoptera
linedrawing
loxodromics
maladaptive
maladjusted
maladroitly
malediction
maledictory
melodiously
namedropper
Neanderthal
nomadically
ophidiarium
overdevelop
paradisical
paradoxical
pseudograph
pseudomonas
pseudomorph
pseudopodia
repudiation
residential
rhabdomancy
ropedancing
roundedness
ruridecanal
sculduddery
sculduggery
selfdefence
selfdenying
selfdespair
selfdevoted
selfdisplay
semidiurnal
skulduddery
skulduggery
slenderness
sockdolager
sockdologen
soundlessly
speedometer
spendthrift
spindlelegs
spindletree
spondulicks
spondylitis
standardise
standoffish
standpatter
steadfastly
Stradivarii
stridulator
swordbearer
taxidermist
theodolitic
thunderbird
thunderbolt
thunderclap
thunderhead
thunderless
thunderpeal
trendsetter
triadically
trundletail
unendurable
unendurably
ungodliness
valediction
valedictory
vasodilator
veridically
vinedresser
viridescent
welldefined
worldbeater
worldliness
worldlywise
abbreviator
abecedarian
aboveground
abstentious
academicals
academician
academicism
accrescence
achievement
adolescence
aggregately
aggregation
aggregative
aimlessness
airlessness
amphetamine
amplexicaul
ancientness
antheridium
aponeuroses
aponeurosis
aponeurotic
appreciable
appreciably
appreciator
arglebargle
artlessness
athleticism
augmentable
austereness
autoerotism
bactericide
balletomane
banteringly
barleybroth
barrelhouse
barrelorgan
basketchair
bassethound
beaverboard
betweenmaid
betweenness
betweentime
biedermeier
billetsdoux
biofeedback
biometrical
bitterapple
bittercress
bittersweet
blamelessly
blameworthy
boilermaker
botheration
boysenberry
brazenfaced
brucellosis
bulletproof
butterflies
butteriness
calceolaria
cancellated
candelabrum
candescence
carpetsnake
carvelbuilt
castellated
catheterise
ceaselessly
centenarian
chameleonic
chaperonage
chokecherry
cholesterol
choreograph
Clarencieux
closefisted
closehauled
coalescence
coeternally
coffeehouse
coffeetable
collectable
collectanea
collectedly
collectible
collenchyma
commemorate
commendable
commendably
commendator
commensally
commentator
compellable
compendious
compensator
competently
competition
competitive
concealable
concealment
conceitedly
conceivable
conceivably
concentrate
conceptacle
concernment
concertedly
concertgoer
condemnable
condensable
confederacy
confederate
conferrable
confessedly
congealable
congealment
congelation
congenerous
congenially
conjectural
connectable
connectedly
connectible
consecrator
consecution
consecutive
consentient
consequence
conservable
conservancy
conservator
contemplate
contentedly
contentious
contentment
conterminal
contestable
convenances
convenience
conveniency
conventicle
convergence
convergency
conversable
conversance
conversancy
convertible
convertibly
conveyancer
cooperation
cooperative
copperplate
coppersmith
cornerstone
correctable
correctness
correlation
correlative
cosmetician
cosmetology
credentials
crenellated

currentness
dangerously
decrepitate
decrepitude
decrescendo
deprecation
deprecative
deprecatory
depreciator
depredation
depredatory
depressible
descendable
descendible
desperadoes
desperately
desperation
deuteration
deuterogamy
Deuteronomy
dexterously
diadelphous
dialectally
dialectical
diametrical
diatessaron
differentia
differently
dinnerdance
dinnertable
dinnerwagon
dipterocarp
disbeliever
discernible
discernibly
discernment
discerption
dishevelled
dispensable
dispersedly
disremember
disseminate
disseminule
dissentient
dissepiment
dissertator
distempered
distensible
duniewassal
earnestness
easternmost
ecumenicism
ecumenicity
elementally
emblematise
emblematist
endlessness
entreatment
enumeration
enumerative
epinephrine
epipetalous
erubescence
escheatable
escheatment
esotericism
eudaemonism
eudaemonist
euphemistic
evanescence
evidentiary
exceedingly
excremental
excrescence
excrescency
exogenously
exoneration
exonerative
exotericism
expressible
extremeness
exuberantly
falteringly
farreaching
fermentable
fidgetiness
filterpaper
fingerboard
fingerglass
fingerplate
fingerprint
fingerstall
flagellator
florescence
floweriness
forbearance
forfeitable
forgetfully
forgetmenot
forgettable
fraternally
fraterniser
galleyslave
gardemanger
gartersnake
genteelness
geometrical
geotectonic
gibberellin
gingerbread
globeflower
glomeration
godlessness
goldenberry
gracelessly
gravedigger
gravelblind
grotesquely
grotesquery
guilelessly
gutlessness
guttersnipe
gynaecocrat
gynaecology
halterbreak
haplessness
harvesthome
heavenwards
hedgehopped
hedgepriest
hedgeschool
heldentenor
helleborine
Hellenistic
hermeneutic
hermeticism
herpetology
hesperidium
hitherwards
homoeopathy
homoestatic
horsecollar
horsedoctor
horseradish
housefather
householder
housekeeper
houselights
housemaster
housemother
housewifely
housewifery
hyphenation
illtempered
implemental
imprecation
imprecatory
imprecisely
imprecision
impregnable
impregnably
impressible
impressment
inclemently
incoercible
increasable
incredulity
incredulous
incremental
inelegantly
inflexional
infrequence
infrequency
inoperative
intrepidity
iridescence
isogeotherm
isometrical
itinerantly
itineration
jabberwocky
Jansenistic
joylessness
lactescence
lammergeier
lammergeyer
larcenously
largeminded
lawlessness
lawmerchant
leaseholder
leavetaking
lecherously
letterpress
lichenology
lickerishly
lingeringly
liquefiable
liquescence
litterateur
loggerheads
looselimbed
loosestrife
louverboard
Lutheranism
mackerelsky
maddeningly
madreporite
Maglemosian
malfeasance
manneristic
mantelpiece
mantelshelf
marcescence
marcescible
marketplace
marketvalue
masterfully
masterpiece
mathematics
medievalism
medievalist
mendelevium
menservants
mercenarily
millenarian
minnesinger
misbegotten
miscegenate
miscellanea
misfeasance
misremember
monkeybread
monkeyshine
monseigneur
mothercraft
mothernaked
motherright
murderously
myrmecology
neckerchief
nephelinite
nervelessly
netherworld
nickelplate
nigrescence
noiselessly
noisemaking
nondelivery
nondescript
nonfeasance
nonmetallic
nonresident
nonsensical
nonsequitur
nurserymaid
obstetrical
opalescence
orchestrate
oxygenation
oysterplant
paederastic
Palaearctic
palaeotypic
pandemonium
panhellenic
papiermache
parheliacal
passeriform
pasteuriser
patternshop
peacemaking
Pentecostal
perceivable
perceivably
perceptible
perceptibly
perfectible
perfectness
perpetrator
perpetually
perpetuance
perpetuator
persecution
perseverate
pervertedly
phagedaenic
phonetician
pieceworker
pigheadedly
planetarium
planetoidal
platearmour
plateresque
playerpiano
plebeianise
plebeianism
pocketknife
pocketmoney
pocketsized
poltergeist
ponderation
ponderosity
ponderously
porterhouse
posteriorly
postexilian
potteringly
powderflask
prayerwheel
precedented
precedently
precentress
preceptress
predecessor
prefectural
premeditate
preselector
presentable
presentably
presentient
presentment
preservable
pretendedly
pretentious
preterhuman
preterition
preventable
preventible
prizewinner
proceedings
procephalic
professedly
progenitrix
progeniture
progestogen
prolegomena
proletarian
proletariat
prosecution
prosecutrix
proselytise
proselytism
prosenchyma
protectoral
protectress
proteolysis
proteolytic
Proterozoic
provenience
pulverulent
putrescence
putrescible
quaternloaf
racketpress
rallentando
rangefinder
reemergence
reflectance
reflexively
reflexology
refreshment
regretfully
regrettable
regrettably
reiteration
reiterative
replenisher
repleteness
repleviable
representer
repressible
repressibly
respectable
respectably
rickettsial
rottenstone
rubberstamp
saplessness
scalearmour
scaleinsect
scaremonger
secretarial
secretariat
secretively
segmentally
segregation
segregative
selfelected
selfevident
semiellipse
senselessly
sententious
Septembrist
septenarius
septentrion
sequestrate
sexlessness
shamelessly
shapeliness
shareholder
sharepusher
shovelboard
showerproof
sickeningly
silveriness
silverplate
silverpoint
silversmith
silverstick
simperingly
sincereness
sinlessness
skeletonise
slavedriver
slaveholder
slavemarket
smilelessly
smokescreen
spaceflight
spaceheater
spacesaving
sphaeridium
spinelessly
spokeswoman
stagemanage
stagestruck
stakeholder
stateliness
statesmanly
stereograph
stereometry
stereophony
stereoscope
stereoscopy
stereotyped
stereotyper
stereotypic
stevengraph
stipendiary
stonecurlew
stonecutter
stoneground
stonemarten
stonewaller
storekeeper
streetlight
studentship
subaerially
submergence
submersible
subregional
subsequence
subservient
subterminal
succedaneum
suggestible
summerhouse
summersault
sunlessness
supremacist
supremeness
surgeonfish
surrebuttal
surrebutter
surveillant
susceptible
susceptibly
suspenseful
suspensible
symmetrical
sympetalous
syndesmosis
systematics

systematise
systematism
systematist
tabletennis
tacheometer
tastelessly
teeterboard
temperament
temperately
temperative
temperature
tempestuous
tendencious
tendentious
tenterhooks
terrestrial
tessellated
thereabouts
theretofore
therewithal
threecolour
threedecker
threehanded
threelegged
threemaster
titleholder
toffeenosed
totteringly
trabeculate
tracelessly
tragedienne
trapeziform
trapezoidal
traversable
trimestrial
tripetalous
turgescence
unbreakable
uncleanness
unfeelingly
unicellular
unigeniture
unipersonal
unisexually
universally
unspeakable
unspeakably
unweetingly
uselessness
valleculate
variegation
velvetiness
vespertinal
vitrescence
voicelessly
wappenschaw
wapperjawed
washerwoman
wastebasket
wedgeshaped
wedgetailed
Wesleyanism
westernmost
whereabouts
wheresoever
wherewithal
Whitechapel
whitecollar
whiteheaded
whitethroat
whitewasher
wholesomely
wholesouled
whoremaster
whoremonger
whosesoever
widdershins
winterberry
wintergreen
witheringly
withershins
witlessness
wonderfully
yacketyyack
zootechnics
acriflavine
antifouling
assafoetida
balefulness
barefacedly
bashfulness
bellfounder
benefaction
beneficence
beneficiary
beneficiate
birdfancier
bullfighter
calefacient
calefactory
californium
carefulness
chieftaincy
cliffhanger
codefendant
coefficient
disaffected
disafforest
dolefulness
dropforging
dumbfounder
dutifulness
factfinding
fatefulness
fearfulness
firefighter
flimflammer
fourflusher
fretfulness
fullfledged
gainfulness
genuflexion
handfasting
harmfulness
hatefulness
heedfulness
helpfulness
highfalutin
hopefulness
hurtfulness
illaffected
indefinable
indefinably
indifferent
ineffective
ineffectual
inefficient
inoffensive
inofficious
insufflator
irrefutable
irrefutably
labefaction
latifundium
leapfrogged
linefishing
lustfulness
malefaction
maleficence
manifestant
manifestoes
manufactory
manufacture
mindfulness
munificence
nasofrontal
needfulness
omnifarious
pacifically
pacificator
painfulness
pitifulness
platforming
playfulness
proofreader
purificator
pushfulness
rarefaction
rarefactive
restfulness
rubefacient
rubefaction
scaffolding
scruffiness
selffeeding
selffeeling
selffertile
skilfulness
solifluxion
songfulness
sonofabitch
soulfulness
spifflicate
stagflation
stiffnecked
tabefaction
tankfarming
tearfulness
thriftiness
trafficator
trafficking
trafficless
tumefaction
tunefulness
typefounder
typefoundry
vociferance
vociferator
wakefulness
wellfounded
whiffletree
wildfowling
wishfulness
wistfulness
zestfulness
abiogeneses
abiogenesis
abiogenetic
aerographer
Albigensian
allegorical
ambiguously
antigravity
appogiatura
assignation
astigmatism
Aurignacian
autographic
benightedly
benightment
benignantly
bourgeoisie
braggadocio
bridgeboard
cacographic
categorical
changefully
chargesheet
cookgeneral
cosignatory
cytogenesis
delightedly
delightsome
demagnetise
demagogical
demagoguery
demagoguism
demigoddess
demographer
demographic
denigration
denigratory
desegregate
designation
doxographer
draggletail
draughtsman
ectogenesis
ectogenetic
egregiously
enlightened
evangelical
exaggerator
fatiguingly
gamogenesis
grangeriser
handgrenade
holographic
homogeneity
homogeneous
homogenetic
homogeniser
hylogenesis
hypogastric
hypoglossal
ideographic
idiographic
illogically
immigration
inaugurator
incognisant
indigestion
indigestive
indignantly
indignation
intagliated
integrality
integration
integrative
invigilator
invigorator
irregularly
kymographic
landgrabber
landgravine
litigiously
logographer
logographic
malignantly
managership
merogenesis
metagenesis
metagenetic
monogenesis
monogenetic
monogrammed
monographer
monographic
nomographer
nomographic
nosographer
nosographic
octagonally
ontogenesis
ontogenetic
oppugnation
orangoutang
oreographic
overgarment
palsgravine
panegyrical
paragrapher
paragraphic
pedagogical
Pelagianism
peregrinate
ploughshare
ploughstaff
polygenesis
polygenetic
polyglottal
polyglottic
polygonally
polygraphic
pomegranate
postglacial
preignition
recognition
recognitive
recognitory
religionise
religionism
religionist
religiosity
religiously
renegotiate
repugnantly
resignation
rotogravure
scragginess
selaginella
serigrapher
sexagesimal
slaughterer
smorgasbord
snowgoggles
sphagnology
sphygmogram
spongecloth
swingletree
synagogical
telegrammic
telegrapher
telegraphic
thingumabob
thingumajig
thoughtless
tobogganing
tobogganist
topographer
topographic
triggerfish
typographer
typographic
unorganized
unrighteous
uprightness
vehmgericht
vicegerency
wellgroomed
winegrowing
wrongheaded
xylographer
xylographic
aesthetical
amethystine
anachronism
anachronous
anaphylaxis
annihilator
apophyllite
apotheosise
bacchanalia
beachcomber
beechmarten
bellheather
biochemical
biophysical
blepharitis
brachiation
brachyurous
brotherhood
butcherbird
cantharides
cantharidic
catchphrase
clodhopping
clothesline
clothesmoth
clothesprop
coinheritor
coldhearted
cornhusking
deathrattle
depthcharge
diachronism
diaphaneity
diaphoresis
diaphoretic
Diophantine
doughtiness
downhearted
earthcloset
earthenware
earthliness
elephantine
elephantoid
epithalamia
epithalamic
epithelioma
epochmaking
erythrocyte
faithhealer
faithlessly
faithworthy
farthermost
farthingale
featheredge
featherhead
featherless
fleshliness
flightiness
forthcoming
freehearted
frightfully
frothhopper
fullhearted
furtherance
furthermore
furthermost
furthersome
geochemical
geophysical
godchildren
goodhearted
graphically
graphicness
halfhearted
halfholiday
hardhearted
hardhitting
haughtiness
headhunting
hunchbacked
ichthyology
ichthyornis
ichthyosaur
incoherence
incoherency
indehiscent
ironhearted
isochronism
isochronous
kindhearted
kitchenette
kitchensink
kitchenware
kwashiorkor
landholding
latchstring
laughinggas
leatherback
leatherhead
leatherneck

lionhearted
loathliness
loathsomely
marchioness
marshalling
marshalship
marshmallow
matchlessly
matchmaking
mentholated
merchandise
merchantman
mirthlessly
mischievous
naughtiness
neighbourly
nonchalance
northeaster
northwester
nympholepsy
nymphomania
openhearted
pamphleteer
pantheistic
perchlorate
philhellene
pitchblende
porphyritic
prochronism
prophethood
prophetical
prophetship
prophylaxis
prothalamia
prothallial
prothallium
prothoracic
psychedelia
psychedelic
psychiatric
psychically
psychodrama
psychogenic
psychograph
psychologic
psychometry
psychomotor
psychopathy
pulchritude
punchinello
purchasable
reachmedown
roadholding
roughfooted
roughlegged
scyphistoma
shepherdess
slightingly
smithereens
smithsonite
softhearted
southeaster
Southernism
southwester
spathaceous
stephanotis
stethoscope
stethoscopy
stichometry
sulphureous
sulphurwort
symphonious
synchromesh
synchronise
synchronism
synchronous
synchrotron
synthesiser
synthetical
teachership
thitherward
toothbilled
toothpowder
toothsomely
torchbearer
torchsinger
touchtyping
toughminded
tracheotomy
trichinosis
trichomonad
triphibious
triphyllous
tritheistic
trophoblast
trothplight
truehearted
tufthunting
unashamedly
uninhabited
uninhibited
urochordate
warmhearted
watchmaking
weakhearted
weathercock
weatherwise
weatherworn
weighbridge
weightiness
whichsoever
whitherward
witchdoctor
witchhunter
worshipable
worshipless
worshipping
worthlessly
xanthochroi
xanthophyll
abolishable
abolishment
abomination
abstinently
abusiveness
acclimation
acclimatise
acclivitous
acidifiable
acquiescent
acquirement
acquisition
acquisitive
acquittance
acumination
aestivation
affrication
affricative
aggrievedly
agonisingly
agonistical
aiguillette
airsickness
amativeness
ameliorator
Americanise
Americanism
Americanist
amphibolite
amphibology
amphictyony
amphimictic
amphisbaena
anadiplosis
Anglicanism
aposiopesis
application
applicative
applicatory
appointment
Archimedean
archipelago
arenicolous
arraignment
astringency
atheistical
atomisation
attribution
attributive
attritional
bacciferous
baptismally
barbiturate
bashibazouk
bathingsuit
bearishness
beguilement
beguilingly
bellicosity
belligerent
bewhiskered
bibliolater
bibliolatry
bibliomancy
bibliomania
bibliopegic
bibliophile
bibliophily
bibliopolic
bibliotheca
billionaire
Bodhisattva
bombilation
bombination
bookinghall
bookishness
boorishness
Britishness
brutishness
bullishness
caddishness
calcicolous
calciferous
calcifugous
calcination
calligraphy
Calvinistic
candidature
cannibalise
cannibalism
captionless
captivation
carcinomata
cardinalate
cardiograph
carminative
carnivorous
carriageway
cassiterite
castigation
casuistical
cauliflower
centigramme
certifiable
certifiably
certificate
chafingdish
charismatic
clericalism
clericalist
coccidiosis
cochinchina
coexistence
cognitional
cognitively
cognitivity
colligation
colligative
collimation
collinearly
collisional
combination
combinative
combinatory
commination
comminatory
comminution
commiserate
commissural
committable
compilation
compilement
conciliator
conciseness
conditional
conditioner
confidently
confidingly
confinement
confirmable
confiscable
confiscator
considerate
considering
consignable
consignment
consistence
consistency
continental
continently
contingence
contingency
continuable
continually
continuance
continuator
convincible
convivially
corbiculate
corbiesteps
cordialness
corniferous
corrigendum
costiveness
craniometry
credibility
crepitation
criminalist
criminality
crimination
criminative
criminatory
criminology
criticality
criticaster
crocidolite
cruciferous
crucifixion
crucigerous
culmination
cultivation
cunningness
cupriferous
currishness
cursiveness
curvilineal
curvilinear
cypripedium
cysticercus
deceitfully
deceivingly
declination
declivitous
deification
denticulate
dentigerous
deoxidation
deprivation
destination
destitution
detribalise
detrimental
difficultly
diffidently
dimwittedly
disciplinal
discipliner
dislikeable
dissimilate
dissimulate
dissipation
dissipative
distinction
distinctive
distinguish
doggishness
dollishness
doltishness
donnishness
drawingroom
duplication
duplicative
duplicitous
earpiercing
edification
edificatory
egalitarian
egotistical
elicitation
eligibility
elimination
eliminative
elucidation
elucidative
elucidatory
elusiveness
emotionally
emotionless
enchiridion
enquiringly
epidiascope
eradication
eradicative
evagination
evanishment
evasiveness
eveningstar
examination
explication
explicative
explicatory
exquisitely
exstipulate
extrication
fabrication
facsimilist
factionally
faddishness
fallibility
farcicality
fasciaboard
fasciculate
fascinating
fascination
fashionable
fashionably
feasibility
feelingness
ferriferous
festinately
fissionable
fissiparity
fissiparous
flexibility
floriferous
florilegium
folliculate
foolishness
foppishness
forbiddance
foreignness
forgiveness
formication
fornication
fortifiable
frigidarium
frugivorous
fulminating
fulmination
fulminatory
furnishings
furtiveness
fustigation
Gallicanism
gallimaufry
garnishment
gasfittings
gemmiferous
gemmiparous
gentianella
gentilitial
genuineness
germination
germinative
gesticulate
girlishness
glaringness
globigerina
glutinously
gracileness
gradiometer
granivorous
gravimetric
gravitation
gravitative
gullibility
gurgitation
gypsiferous
handicapped
handicapper
hellishness
helminthoid
herbivorous
hereinafter
herringbone
herringgull
hoggishness
homoiousian
hooliganism
horripilate
hospitalise
hospitality
hospitaller
hummingbird
hurriedness
hyacinthine
idolisation
illdisposed
imaginarily
imagination
imaginative
imbrication
implication
implicative
impuissance
inalienable
inalienably
inanimately
inanimation
inclination
incriminate
IndoIranian
inedibility
inexistence

initialling
inquilinous
inquiringly
inquisition
inquisitive
inspiration
inspiratory
instigation
instigative
instillment
instinctive
instinctual
institution
intricately
intriguante
intuitional
intuitively
intuitivism
jactitation
Judaisation
jumpingbean
jumpingjack
justiciable
justifiable
justifiably
knavishness
knowingness
lacrimation
lacrimatory
lacrimosely
lactiferous
laicisation
lancinating
lancination
landingbeam
landinggear
lastingness
latticework
lentiginous
liquidambar
liquidation
loutishness
lubrication
lubricative
lumpishness
machicolate
machination
machinemade
madrigalian
madrigalist
magnificent
mandibulate
mannishness
marginalise
marginality
marlinspike
marriagebed
massiveness
mastication
masticatory
matriarchal
matriculate
matrilineal
matrilinear
matrimonial
mawkishness
meaningless
melliferous
mellifluent
mellifluous
mentionable
mercilessly
messiahship
metrication
milliampere
millionaire
millisecond
miscibility
mockingbird
mooringmast
morbiferous
morningroom
morrisdance
multicolour
multilinear
multinomial
multiparous
multiracial
multistorey
multivalent
negligently
nictitation
noctilucent
noctivagant
noctivagous
nonviolence
nothingness
nourishment
nullifidian
nulliparity
nulliparous
nutrimental
nutritional
nutritively
nyctitropic
obstinately
odoriferous
opinionated
orchidology
originality
origination
originative
outdistance
outfighting
outrivalled
ovariectomy
overindulge
ozoniferous
ozonisation
packingcase
paediatrics
paediatrist
palpitation
participant
participate
participial
particulate
partitioned
partitioner
partitively
passibility
Passiontide
passivation
passiveness
patriarchal
patrilineal
patrimonial
patristical
pectination
peevishness
pensionable
pensionless
pensiveness
peptisation
percipience
permissible
permissibly
persistence
persistency
pertinacity
pertinently
pessimistic
pestiferous
pestilently
petticoated
pettifogger
pettishness
pharisaical
phariseeism
phthiriasis
physicality
physiocracy
physiognomy
physiologic
pietistical
piggishness
pinkishness
piscivorous
plagiariser
plagioclase
plagiostome
planimetric
planisphere
platinotype
playingcard
plenipotent
pluviometer
pollination
pontificals
pontificate
portionless
possibility
precipitant
precipitate
precipitous
preciseness
predicament
predication
predicative
predicatory
predictable
predictably
prehistoric
prelibation
preliminary
premiership
previsional
primigenial
primiparous
primitively
primitivism
prodigalise
prodigality
proficiency
profiterole
prohibition
prohibitive
prohibitory
proliferate
proliferous
prolificacy
prolificity
prominently
promiscuity
promiscuous
promisingly
propinquity
propitiable
propitiator
providently
provisional
provisorily
proximately
prudishness
pruriginous
pteridology
publication
publishable
publishment
qualifiable
qualitative
raffishness
realignment
realisation
reanimation
recriminate
rectifiable
rectilineal
rectilinear
reddishness
refrigerant
refrigerate
refringency
reification
rejoicingly
renaissance
reorientate
replication
requirement
requisition
respiration
respiratory
restitution
restiveness
retribution
retributive
retributory
retrievable
roguishness
rubrication
rustication
sacrificial
salpingitis
saltimbanco
scoriaceous
seasickness
sectionally
selfimposed
selfinduced
selfinvited
selfishness
semeiotical
sempiternal
sensibility
sensitively
sensitivity
sentimental
sentinelled
septicaemia
septicaemic
septiferous
septifragal
serpiginous
serviceable
serviceably
servicebook
serviceline
sheriffalty
sheriffship
sickishness
signifiable
significant
sillimanite
sittingroom
skatingrink
slavishness
smokingroom
soldierlike
soldiership
solmisation
somniculous
somniferous
sophistical
sottishness
sparingness
specifiable
specificity
spiniferous
spiritistic
spiritlevel
spiritually
spiritualty
spirituelle
statistical
straightcut
straightish
straightway
straitlaced
studiedness
stylisation
stylishness
suasiveness
subdivision
sublimation
sublimeness
sublittoral
submissible
subsistence
suckingfish
sufficiency
suffixation
surficially
suspiration
swinishness
syndicalism
syndicalist
syndication
tagliatelle
tagliatelli
tangibility
tarnishable
tensibility
termination
terminative
terminology
termitarium
terricolous
terrigenous
territorial
testimonial
thalidomide
thuriferous
tittivation
tonsillitis
torticollis
traditional
tragicomedy
trepidation
Trinitarian
trivialness
turbination
tuttifrutti
unanimously
unclimbable
unfailingly
unfeignedly
unflinching
unguiculate
unification
unprintable
unquietness
unskilfully
unsmilingly
unthinkable
unthinkably
Upanishadic
utilisation
utilitarian
vaccination
varnishtree
vendibility
ventilation
ventilative
vermiculate
vermiculite
vermination
verminously
verticality
vertiginous
vestigially
vinaigrette
vincibility
vindication
vindicative
vindicatory
vitrifiable
voguishness
vortiginous
waggishness
waitinglist
waitingroom
waspishness
wearilessly
wearisomely
whitishness
willingness
winningness
winningpost
worrisomely
antiJacobin
showjumping
blackavised
blackbeetle
blackbirder
blackcoated
blackfellow
blackgrouse
blackmailer
blackmarket
blockbuster
bookkeeping
brankursine
bricklaying
chickenfeed
chickenwire
chockablock
chucklehead
crackerjack
crookbacked
crookedness
cytokinesis
doorknocker
drunkenness
exoskeletal
exoskeleton
frankfurter
franklinite
frankpledge
handknitted
knucklebone
painkilling
prickliness
quacksalver
quickchange
quickfiring
quickfreeze
quickfrozen
quicksilver
quickwitted
safekeeping
Sanskritist
shacklebolt
shacklebone
shockheaded
shocktroops
slickenside
snickersnee
soupkitchen
speakership
stickinsect
stickleback
stockbroker
stockholder
stockinette
stockjobber
stockmarket
stocktaking
strikebound
telekinesis
telekinetic
thanklessly
thanksgiver
thankworthy
thickheaded

thickwitted
trackwalker
tricksiness
unbeknownst
wreckmaster
abiological
acaulescent
accelerando
accelerator
acculturate
aerological
affiliation
agrological
algological
alkalescent
alkalimeter
alkalimetry
allelomorph
angelically
Apollinaris
appallingly
appellation
appellative
artillerist
axiological
bacilliform
battledress
battlefield
bimillenary
bimillenium
booklearned
bootlegging
bottleglass
bottlegreen
bottlenosed
bowdleriser
brilliantly
bucolically
bumblepuppy
burglarious
byeelection
canalicular
canaliculus
candleberry
candlelight
candlepower
candlestick
capillarity
Carolingian
cavalierism
challenging
charlatanry
chaulmoogra
civilianise
civilisable
cobblestone
cockleshell
complacence
complacency
complainant
complaisant
complexness
compliantly
complicated
complotting
conflagrant
conflagrate
confliction
conflictive
coralloidal
cupellation
cytological
decelerator
decollation
decolletage
decolourise
defalcation
defoliation
dereliction
desalinator
desultorily
devaluation
developable
development
disillusion
displeasure
divulgation
divulgement
doublecheck
doublecross
doubleDutch
doubleedged
doubleender
doubleentry
doublefaced
doublequick
doublespeak
doublethink
drillmaster
ebulliently
effulgently
embellisher
enucleation
envelopment
equilateral
equilibrate
equilibrist
equilibrium
ethological
eucalyptole
everlasting
excellently
exculpation
exculpatory
exfoliation
exfoliative
facelifting
facultative
familiarise
familiarity
fiddlestick
fusillation
gentlemanly
gentlewoman
goodlooking
habiliments
halflanding
Hamiltonian
Hegelianism
Hepplewhite
hobbledehoy
homiletical
homological
horological
huckleberry
humiliation
humiliatory
hypolimnion
ideological
idyllically
impolitical
impoliticly
impulsively
incalescent
inculcation
inculpation
inculpatory
indulgently
infiltrator
insalubrity
insultingly
intelligent
intolerable
intolerably
intolerance
invalidness
involucrate
involuntary
involvement
invultation
ipsilateral
irrelevance
irrelevancy
irreligious
isoelectric
lamellicorn
lamelliform
lamplighter
landlordism
levelheaded
lilylivered
loculicidal
maxillipede
megalomania
megalopolis
mesalliance
metalloidal
metallurgic
metalworker
middleclass
middlesized
misalliance
monolingual
monological
monologuise
monologuist
moonlighter
mudslinging
musclebound
mycological
needlecraft
needlepoint
needlewoman
Neoplatonic
nettlecloth
nomological
nonplussing
nosological
novelettish
obsolescent
occultation
oecological
oenological
oncological
ontological
oreological
oscillation
oscillatory
oscillogram
overlapping
paddleboard
paddlewheel
Panglossian
paraldehyde
paraleipsis
parallactic
parallelism
parallelled
patelliform
pearlescent
pearlfisher
peculiarity
pedological
penological
pentlandite
penultimate
perplexedly
phylloclade
phyllotaxis
pomological
populariser
posological
preelection
problematic
pupillarity
quilldriver
Rabelaisian
rattlebrain
rattlepated
rattlesnake
recalculate
repellantly
repellently
repulsively
resiliently
resplendent
retaliation
retaliative
retaliatory
revaluation
rheological
saddlecloth
saddlehorse
scholarship
scholiastic
selflimited
selfloading
selflocking
serological
sexological
shallowness
shellacking
shelljacket
shoeleather
shoplifting
shoulderbag
shoulderpad
simpliciter
singlestick
singletrack
sinological
smallholder
smallminded
snowleopard
soliloquise
soliloquist
spellbinder
squalidness
stallholder
steelworker
stellionate
stiflejoint
stoolpigeon
subclinical
suppliantly
swallowable
swallowdive
swallowhole
swallowtail
swallowwort
swellheaded
theological
thrillingly
tiddlywinks
titillation
togglejoint
topological
totalisator
trailblazer
trelliswork
troglodytic
tumbledrier
turtleshell
typological
unbelieving
unfaltering
unhelpfully
unpalatable
unpolitical
unrelenting
unselective
unsolicited
unwillingly
upholsterer
vacillation
vexillology
virilescent
virological
washleather
Wensleydale
wheelbarrow
wheelwright
whitleather
windlestraw
zooplankton
abdominally
accommodate
accompanist
accumulator
acrimonious
albuminuria
allAmerican
allomorphic
antemundane
antimonious
argumentive
ascomycetes
assemblyman
assimilable
assimilator
attemptable
automatable
bohemianism
Brahmanical
brahmaputra
Brahminical
bushmanship
calumniator
campmeeting
ceremonious
chrominance
chromoplast
chromosomal
columbarium
columniated
cotemporary
decemvirate
denominator
denumerable
documentary
dreamlessly
dynamically
dynamometer
dynamometry
ectomorphic
encomiastic
encumbrance
endemically
endometrium
endomorphic
enigmatical
enjambement
entomophily
ephemerides
extemporary
extemporise
filamentary
filamentous
foraminated
foraminifer
foulmouthed
fragmentary
freemasonry
fullmouthed
funambulate
funambulist
gourmandise
gourmandism
grammalogue
grammatical
halfmeasure
hardmouthed
harumscarum
hemimorphic
hexametrist
homomorphic
idiomorphic
ignominious
illimitable
illimitably
illuminable
illuminance
illuminator
incommodity
incompetent
incompliant
indomitable
indomitably
innumerable
innumerably
inseminator
intemperate
intimidator
intumescent
ironmongery
irremissive
irremovable
irremovably
judgmatical
kinematical
lesemajesty
lifemanship
ligamentary
ligamentous
logomachist
loudmouthed
manumission
manumitting
mesomorphic
metamorphic
monomorphic
myxomatosis
myxomycetes
oarsmanship
oecumenical
openmouthed
optometrist
overmanning
overmeasure
paramedical
parametrise
paramoecium
paramorphic
paramountcy
paramountly
perambulate
plasmolysis
plasmolytic
pleomorphic
pneumonitis
polemically
polymorphic
portmanteau
pragmatical
preeminence
pyramidally
pyramidical
racemeeting
recommender
recommittal
recumbently
regimentals
remembrance
resemblance
rheumaticky
rodomontade
rudimentary
scrimpiness
scrumptious
sedimentary
seismically
seismograph
seismometer
seismometry

seismoscope
selfmastery
semimonthly
showmanship
slotmachine
spasmodical
spermaphyte
spermatozoa
spermicidal
steamboiler
steamroller
stormcentre
stormtroops
stramineous
subumbrella
tapemachine
tapemeasure
tegumentary
tenementary
thaumatrope
thaumaturge
thaumaturgy
thermically
thermionics
thermoduric
thermograph
thermolysis
thermolytic
thermometer
thermometry
thermophile
thermoscope
thermotaxis
thrombocyte
trammelling
triumvirate
uncommitted
unlimitedly
unmemorable
unmemorably
unremitting
volumometer
Weismannism
wellmeaning
Westminster
whigmaleery
workmanlike
workmanship
zygomorphic
abranchiate
absenteeism
accentually
achondritic
actinometer
actinomyces
actinomycin
adminicular
advancement
adventuress
adventurism
adventurist
adventurous
aeronautics
aeronomical
agronomical
allantoides
anagnorisis
annunciator
antenuptial
antineutron
antonomasia
Arminianism
arrangement
ascensional
assentation
attentively
attenuation
auxanometer
bicentenary

botanically
brainlessly
brainsickly
brainteaser
businessman
Byronically
Byzantinism
Byzantinist
calendrical
canonically
carunculate
cementation
chainarmour
chainletter
chainsmoker
chainstitch
channelling
chronically
chronograph
chronologer
chronologic
chronometer
chronometry
chronoscope
cleanlimbed
cleanliness
cleanshaven
coconscious
colonelship
colonialism
colonialist
copingstone
coronagraph
coronograph
cotoneaster
cylindrical
decantation
decennially
defenceless
defensively
definiendum
delineation
delinquency
demandingly
demonolatry
demonstrate
denunciator
dependently
derangement
desensitise
diagnostics
dimensional
diningtable
disannulled
disencumber
disentangle
disenthrall
disinclined
disinfector
disinterest
disinterred
disunionist
domineering
emmenagogue
Emmenthaler
empanelling
engineering
enhancement
ensanguined
equinoctial
erroneously
essentially
eugenically
expansional
expansively
expansivity
expenditure
expensively
exponential

extensional
extensively
extenuation
extenuatory
farinaceous
fecundation
feloniously
financially
flannelette
flannelling
flauntingly
fomentation
fortnightly
furunculous
gegenschein
gerontology
gigantesque
goodnatured
greengrocer
greenkeeper
greenockite
groundsheet
groundwater
hymenoptera
immanentism
immanentist
immenseness
immunologic
impanelling
impenetrate
impenitence
impenitency
impingement
incantation
incantatory
incinerator
incongruent
incongruity
incongruous
inconscient
inconsonant
inconstancy
incontinent
incunabulum
indentation
infanticide
infantilism
infantryman
infinitival
ingeniously
ingenuously
insensately
insensitive
insincerely
insincerity
insinuation
insinuative
intenseness
intensifier
intensional
intensively
intentional
intentioned
inventively
inventorial
journeywork
juvenescent
knownothing
laciniation
laconically
lamentation
laryngology
laryngotomy
learnedness
Leibnitzian
linendraper
luminescent
lycanthrope
lycanthropy

melancholia
melancholic
melanochroi
melanophore
meningocele
metonymical
misanthrope
misanthropy
molendinary
momentarily
momentously
mononuclear
moronically
nomenclator
nominatival
nonunionist
octingenary
offenceless
offensively
organically
organisable
organscreen
orientalise
orientalism
orientalist
orientation
ostensively
ostentation
palindromic
parentheses
parenthesis
parenthetic
paronomasia
partnership
pecuniarily
pedunculate
peninsulate
perennation
perennially
perineurium
plainspoken
plaintively
pleinairist
postnuptial
potentially
prognathism
prognathous
queenliness
recantation
recondition
reconnoitre
reconstruct
redundantly
regenerable
regenerator
reminiscent
remonstrant
remonstrate
remunerator
repentantly
resentfully
retentively
retentivity
retinacular
retinaculum
retinoscopy
revendicate
rodenticide
romanticise
romanticism
romanticist
salinometer
saponaceous
satanically
satinstitch
scientistic
scientology
scoundrelly
secondarily

secondclass
secondrater
secondsight
sedentarily
seigneurial
seigniorage
seigniorial
semanticist
serendipity
seventeenth
seventyfold
shrinkingly
shrinkproof
Socinianism
solanaceous
sphincteral
sphincteric
splendorous
splenectomy
splenetical
springboard
springclean
springhouse
springiness
squintingly
stainlessly
staunchless
staunchness
sternsheets
sternutator
strangeness
strangulate
strenuosity
strenuously
stringboard
stringently
stringiness
stringpiece
stringybark
strongpoint
synonymical
talentscout
taxonomical
technically
technocracy
technologic
tetanically
titanically
trainbearer
triangulate
triennially
tryingplane
tyrannicide
tyrannosaur
tyrannously
unbendingly
uncanniness
uncanonical
unconcealed
unconcerned
uncongenial
unconnected
unconscious
uncontested
unkennelled
unmanliness
unwinkingly
voluntarily
voluntarism
voluntarist
wirenetting
witenagemot
womanliness
xeranthemum
achromatise
achromatism
acidophilic
acknowledge
adenomatous

Aeneolithic
aeolotropic
agglomerate
alcyonarian
amazonstone
amenorrhoea
amorousness
anacoluthon
analogously
androgynous
anemometric
angiography
AngloFrench
AngloIndian
anglomaniac
AngloNorman
anglophobia
anglophobic
anisotropic
anthocyanin
anthologise
anthologist
antioxidant
anxiousness
aphrodisiac
apologetics
apomorphine
approbation
approbatory
appropriate
approvingly
approximate
arduousness
artiodactyl
audiologist
audiometric
audiovisual
awesomeness
azotobacter
BaltoSlavic
batholithic
biliousness
biocoenoses
biocoenosis
biocoenotic
bonbonniere
borborygmus
boutonniere
burgomaster
callousness
carbocyclic
carbonation
cartography
caryopsides
catholicise
Catholicism
catholicity
chemotactic
chinoiserie
chirography
chiropodist
chiropteran
chorography
clamorously
clinometric
cognoscente
cognoscenti
cognoscible
coleorrhiza
collocation
comfortable
comfortably
comfortless
commonality
commonplace
commonsense
comportment
compositely
composition

compositive
compossible
compotation
compotatory
concomitant
concordance
condolatory
condominium
condonation
condottiere
condottieri
conformable
conformably
conformally
conformance
connoisseur
connotation
connotative
consolation
consolatory
consolidate
consolingly
consonantal
consonantly
contorniate
convocation
convolution
convolvulus
copiousness
corporality
corporately
corporation
corporatism
corporative
corporeally
corroborant
corroborate
corrosively
cosmogonist
cosmography
cosmologist
cosmopolite
cottongrass
cottonmouth
coulometric
coxcombical
crocodilian
ctenophoran
cupronickel
curiousness
cursoriness
customarily
custombuilt
customhouse
cyclopaedia
cyclopaedic
cycloserine
cyclothymia
cyclothymic
defloration
deploringly
despoilment
despondence
despondency
deviousness
dexiotropic
dialogistic
diamondback
diapophysis
diapositive
dichogamous
dichotomise
dichotomist
dichotomous
diplococcus
diplomatise
diplomatist
dipsomaniac
discography
discontinue
discordance
discordancy
discotheque
discourtesy
dishonestly
dishonourer
dislocation
dislodgment
disportment
disposition
dispositive
dissociable
dissolutely
dissolution
dissolvable
dissonantly
dittography
douroucouli
dubiousness
dyslogistic
econometric
editorially
elaborately
elaboration
elaborative
embrocation
embroiderer
embroilment
emulousness
enfeoffment
engrossment
enviousness
erotogenous
erotomaniac
ethnography
ethnologist
etymologise
etymologist
euchologion
eudiometric
evaporation
evaporative
exploitable
exploration
explorative
exploratory
explosively
expropriate
extroverted
fatuousness
filmography
FinnoUgrian
flagofficer
flavourless
flavoursome
forlornness
frivolously
fulsomeness
Gallophobia
gallowsbird
gallowstree
gaseousness
gemmologist
geopolitics
gettogether
gibbousness
gnotobiosis
gnotobiotic
godforsaken
goniometric
gramophonic
granolithic
granophyric
gymnospermy
haemocyanin
haemoglobin
haemophilia
haemophilic
haemoptysis
haemorrhage
haemorrhoid
haemostasis
haemostatic
Hagiographa
hagiography
hagiologist
hagioscopic
haplography
harbourless
harmonistic
heinousness
heliochrome
heliography
heliometric
heliotropic
hideousness
Hindoostani
hippocampus
Hippocratic
hippopotami
histologist
historiated
historicise
historicism
historicist
historicity
homeopathic
homeostasis
homeostatic
hugeousness
hydrobromic
hydrocarbon
hydrocyanic
hydrogenate
hydrogenous
hydrography
hydrologist
hydromedusa
hydrometeor
hydrometric
hydropathic
hydrophilic
hydrophobia
hydrophobic
hydrophytic
hydroponics
hydrosphere
hydrostatic
hydrotactic
hydrothorax
hydrotropic
hygrometric
hygrophytic
hygroscopic
hymnography
hypnopaedia
hypnopompic
hypsography
hypsometric
hypsophobia
ichnography
iconography
iconostases
iconostasis
imploringly
impropriate
impropriety
improvement
improvident
ineloquence
intromitted
intromitter
introverted
inviolately
irksomeness
isomorphism
isomorphous
itacolumite
jargonistic
jealousness
labiodental
legionnaire
leprosarium
leptodactyl
limnologist
lissomeness
lithography
lithophytic
lithosphere
lithotomise
lithotomist
lithotripsy
lophobranch
macrobiotic
macrocosmic
macrogamete
macroscopic
maisonnette
malposition
mandolinist
marconigram
mastodontic
mastoiditis
meadowgrass
meadowsweet
melioration
meliorative
meprobamate
meteoritics
meteoroidal
meteorology
Methodistic
methodology
micrococcal
micrococcus
microcosmic
microgamete
micrography
microgroove
microlithic
micrometric
Micronesian
microphonic
microphytic
microscopic
microsecond
misconceive
misconstrue
muttonchops
myelomatous
mythography
mythologise
mythologist
mythomaniac
mythopoeist
mythopoetic
narcoleptic
nationalise
nationalism
nationalist
nationality
nationstate
necrobiosis
necrologist
necromancer
necromantic
necrophilia
necrophilic
necropoleis
negrophobia
neologistic
nervousness
neurologist
neuropathic
neuroticism
neurotropic
nitrogenise
nitrogenous
noisomeness
nonvolatile
notionalist
noxiousness
nyctophobia
obviousness
ochlocratic
odorousness
oldwomanish
oligochaete
oligomerous
ominousness
onerousness
operoseness
ophiologist
opprobrious
orthocentre
orthodontia
orthodontic
orthoepical
orthography
orthopaedic
orthopedics
orthopedist
orthopteran
orthoscopic
orthotropic
osteography
osteologist
osteopathic
osteophytic
osteoplasty
Ostrogothic
oviposition
ozonosphere
paedophilia
pantomimist
pantothenic
pastoralism
pastoralist
pathologist
patronising
percolation
perforation
perforative
performable
performance
periodicity
periodontal
periostitis
personalise
personalism
personalist
personality
personation
personative
personifier
pestologist
petrography
petrologist
phagocytise
phagocytose
phenologist
philologian
philologist
philosopher
philosophic
phonography
phonologist
photoactive
photocopier
photofinish
photography
photometric
photooffset
photoperiod
photophilic
photophobia
photophobic
photosphere
phototactic
phototropic
phycocyanin
phycologist
phylogynist
phytography
phytologist
phytosterol
phytotomist
pictography
pictorially
pigeonchest
pillowfight
piteousness
planoconvex
pleiotropic
plutocratic
poisonously
polyonymous
pompousness
pornography
preconceive
precontract
predominant
predominate
premonition
premonitory
prenominate
preposition
prepositive
prerogative
proconsular
prolocutrix
promotional
proportions
proposition
prorogation
protomartyr
protonotary
protophytic
provocateur
provocation
provocative
provokingly
provostship
pterodactyl
purportedly
purposeless
purposively
radioactive
radiocarbon
radiography
radiolarian
radiologist
radiometric
radiophonic
rancorously
ratiocinate
rationalise
rationalism
rationalist
rationality
raucousness
regionalise
regionalism
regionalist
reproachful
reprobation
reprobative
reprobatory
reprogramme
reprography
reprovingly
respondence
respondency
responsible

resp**o**nsibly
rest**o**ration
rest**o**rative
retr**o**action
retr**o**active
retr**o**cedent
retr**o**flexed
retr**o**rocket
rhet**o**rician
rhin**o**logist
rhin**o**scopic
rhiz**o**carpic
rhiz**o**matous
ribb**o**ngrass
riot**o**usness
ruin**o**usness
Russ**o**phobia
salm**o**nberry
sapr**o**biotic
sapr**o**genous
sapr**o**phytic
sarc**o**matous
sarc**o**phagus
sart**o**rially
saur**o**podous
scen**o**graphy
scho**o**lboard
scho**o**lchild
scho**o**lhouse
scop**o**lamine
self**o**pinion
sens**o**rially
seri**o**usness
sext**o**decimo
shad**o**wgraph
shad**o**winess
sigm**o**idally
sinf**o**nietta
sinu**o**usness
Slav**o**nicise
soci**o**logist
soci**o**metric
soci**o**pathic
somn**o**lently
sorr**o**wfully
Spin**o**zistic
spir**o**chaete
spir**o**chetal
spir**o**metric
spor**o**genous
spor**o**gonium
spor**o**phytic
steg**o**saurus
sten**o**chromy
sten**o**graphy
sten**o**typist
styl**o**graphy
styl**o**podium
subc**o**ntract
subc**o**ntrary
subc**o**rtical
subd**o**minant
subr**o**gation
succ**o**urless
suff**o**cation
suff**o**cative
supp**o**rtable
supp**o**rtably
supp**o**sition
supp**o**sitive
supp**o**sitory
surr**o**gation
syll**o**gistic
symb**o**listic
symp**o**siarch
sync**o**pation
taut**o**logise
taut**o**logism
taut**o**logous
taut**o**merism
taut**o**nymous
tedi**o**usness
teet**o**talism
teet**o**taller
tekn**o**nymous
tele**o**logism
tele**o**logist
temp**o**rality
temp**o**rarily
tenu**o**usness
Teut**o**nicism
thix**o**tropic
thor**o**ughpin
thor**o**ughwax
thyr**o**iditis
topl**o**ftical
tric**o**loured
trim**o**rphism
trim**o**rphous
trop**o**sphere
unav**o**idable
unav**o**idably
unem**o**tional
unic**o**loured
unif**o**rmness
unip**o**larity
unpr**o**mising
unsh**o**ckable
unst**o**ppable
unwh**o**lesome
uran**o**graphy
vacu**o**lation
vacu**o**usness
vari**o**usness
vars**o**vienne
verb**o**seness
vici**o**usness
viol**o**ncello
visc**o**untess
visc**o**usness
vood**o**oistic
welc**o**meness
well**o**rdered
wins**o**meness
yell**o**wbelly
zeal**o**usness
zinc**o**graphy
zoom**o**rphism
acar**p**ellous
acce**p**tation
acce**p**tingly
acci**p**itrine
acro**p**etally
adia**p**horism
allo**p**athist
amor**p**hously
ante**p**endium
anti**p**honary
anti**p**hrasis
anti**p**yretic
Areo**p**agitic
auto**p**lastic
basi**p**etally
bice**p**halous
bill**p**osting
blas**p**hemous
Bona**p**artean
Bona**p**artism
Bona**p**artist
caco**p**honous
caly**p**trogen
cata**p**lectic
cero**p**lastic
cham**p**ertous
Chip**p**endale
clap**p**erclaw
cons**p**ecific
cons**p**icuity
cons**p**icuous
cons**p**irator
dece**p**tively
deem**p**hasise
depo**p**ulator
dice**p**halous
dila**p**idated
dila**p**idator
disa**p**proval
dual**p**urpose
ecto**p**lasmic
elli**p**soidal
elli**p**ticity
enca**p**sulate
endo**p**hagous
endo**p**lasmic
equi**p**ollent
esem**p**lastic
Euro**p**eanise
eury**p**teroid
exce**p**tional
exem**p**larily
exem**p**larity
fels**p**athoid
foot**p**oundal
four**p**ounder
halo**p**hilous
hand**p**ainted
hebe**p**hrenia
hebe**p**hrenic
hemi**p**terous
high**p**itched
high**p**owered
homo**p**honous
homo**p**lastic
homo**p**terous
hypo**p**hyseal
hypo**p**hysial
inap**p**etence
inci**p**iently
inde**p**endent
inex**p**edient
inex**p**ensive
inop**p**ortune
inse**p**arable
inse**p**arably
insi**p**idness
insu**p**erable
insu**p**erably
irre**p**arable
irre**p**arably
irru**p**tively
ithy**p**hallic
line**p**rinter
long**p**laying
lows**p**irited
mala**p**ropism
mani**p**ulable
mani**p**ulator
mass**p**roduce
meli**p**hagous
meta**p**hysics
meta**p**lastic
meta**p**sychic
meto**p**oscopy
miss**p**elling
mono**p**hagous
mono**p**hthong
Mono**p**hysite
mono**p**oliser
mono**p**terous
myco**p**hagist
nons**p**ecific
occi**p**itally
oeno**p**hilist
oeso**p**hageal
omni**p**otence
omni**p**resent
outs**p**okenly
over**p**ayment
over**p**roduce
para**p**hraser
para**p**lectic
peri**p**atetic
peri**p**hrases
peri**p**hrasis
pers**p**ective
pers**p**icuity
pers**p**icuous
phos**p**honium
phos**p**horate
phos**p**horism
phos**p**horite
phos**p**horous
podo**p**hyllin
poly**p**eptide
poly**p**hagous
poly**p**honous
pour**p**arlers
prom**p**titude
pros**p**ective
real**p**olitik
reap**p**ortion
reap**p**raisal
rece**p**tacula
rece**p**tively
rece**p**tivity
reci**p**rocate
reci**p**rocity
redu**p**licate
resi**p**iscent
saxo**p**honist
scal**p**riform
scor**p**ionfly
scra**p**piness
scri**p**torial
scri**p**torium
scup**p**ernong
self**p**itying
semi**p**almate
shar**p**witted
shee**p**farmer
shee**p**master
sign**p**ainter
slee**p**ingbag
slee**p**ingcar
slee**p**lessly
slee**p**walker
soli**p**sistic
Soro**p**timist
stam**p**office
stee**p**lebush
stee**p**lejack
stra**p**hanger
subs**p**ecific
swee**p**stakes
syco**p**hantic
syco**p**hantry
teas**p**oonful
tele**p**athise
tele**p**athist
tele**p**honist
tele**p**rinter
tent**p**egging
time**p**leaser
toxo**p**hilite
Trap**p**istine
unap**p**ealing
unex**p**loited
unex**p**ressed
unha**p**piness
unim**p**ortant
vaso**p**ressin
vaso**p**ressor
vitu**p**erator
whip**p**letree
wire**p**ulling
xeno**p**hilous
xero**p**hilous
xylo**p**hagous
xylo**p**honist
anti**q**uarian
anti**q**uation
brus**q**ueness
fore**q**uarter
illi**q**uidity
obli**q**ueness
quin**q**uennia
quin**q**uereme
abho**r**rently
abno**r**mality
abso**r**bingly
abso**r**ptance
abst**r**action
abst**r**active
abst**r**iction
acco**r**dantly
acco**r**dingly
admi**r**alship
adve**r**bially
adve**r**sative
adve**r**seness
adve**r**tently
adve**r**tising
affi**r**mation
affi**r**mative
affi**r**matory
afte**r**burner
afte**r**effect
agra**r**ianism
ailu**r**ophile
ailu**r**ophobe
airc**r**aftman
algo**r**ithmic
alte**r**cation
alte**r**nately
alte**r**nation
alte**r**native
alto**r**elievo
alto**r**ilievo
anac**r**eontic
ante**r**iority
anth**r**acitic
anth**r**opical
anti**r**rhinum
appa**r**atchik
appa**r**elling
appu**r**tenant
aqua**r**ellist
arbo**r**aceous
arbo**r**escent
arte**r**ialise
arth**r**ospore
aspe**r**gillum
aspe**r**gillus
aspe**r**sorium
asse**r**tively
asso**r**tative
assu**r**edness
Assy**r**iology
auta**r**chical
avoi**r**dupois
bell**r**inging
Belo**r**ussian
bica**r**bonate
bico**r**porate
bifu**r**cation
bipa**r**tition
buty**r**aceous
calo**r**imeter
calo**r**imetry
cama**r**aderie
cate**r**cousin
cate**r**pillar
cave**r**nously
cent**r**eboard
cent**r**epiece
cent**r**ifugal
cent**r**ipetal
cesa**r**evitch
cesa**r**ewitch
chee**r**leader
chee**r**lessly
chei**r**omancy
chia**r**oscuro
chlo**r**ophyll
chlo**r**oplast
chlo**r**oprene
choi**r**master
clai**r**schach
clai**r**voyant
clea**r**headed
colo**r**imeter
colo**r**imetry
comp**r**ession
comp**r**essive
comp**r**isable
conc**r**escent
cong**r**essman
cong**r**uently
cong**r**uously
cont**r**abasso
cont**r**actile
cont**r**action
cont**r**active
cont**r**actual
cont**r**acture
cont**r**adance
cont**r**aption
cont**r**ariety
cont**r**arious
cont**r**astive
cont**r**etemps
cont**r**ibutor
cont**r**ivable
cont**r**ivance
cont**r**olling
cont**r**olment
cont**r**oversy
conu**r**bation
copa**r**cenary
cote**r**minous
cybe**r**nation
cybe**r**netics
deba**r**kation
deca**r**bonate
deca**r**bonise
deca**r**burise
dece**r**ebrate
deco**r**ticate
defe**r**ential
defo**r**cement
defo**r**mation
deli**r**iously
dema**r**cation
dema**r**kation
dend**r**itical
depo**r**tation
desc**r**ibable
desc**r**iption
desc**r**iptive
dese**r**vingly
dest**r**uction
dest**r**uctive
dete**r**iorate
dete**r**minacy
dete**r**minant
dete**r**minate
dete**r**minism
dete**r**minist
diac**r**itical
dich**r**omatic
diff**r**action
disa**r**mament
disa**r**mingly
disc**r**epancy

disgraceful
disgruntled
disorganise
distraction
distractive
distressful
distribuend
distributor
distrustful
divergently
diverticula
divorcement
doctrinaire
doctrinally
dundrearies
elderliness
elutriation
embarkation
emperorship
empirically
endorsement
enforceable
enforcement
engorgement
enlargeable
enlargement
enterostomy
enterovirus
enterpriser
entertainer
enthralling
enthralment
environment
epeirogenic
epigraphist
Esperantist
etherealise
ethereality
excoriation
excursively
exdirectory
exhortation
exhortative
exhortatory
experienced
exportation
expurgation
expurgatory
exteriorise
exteriority
exterminate
externalise
externalism
externality
extirpation
extirpatory
extortioner
fimbriation
fireraising
floorwalker
fluorescein
fluorescent
fluoroscope
fluoroscopy
forerunning
fratricidal
gastrectomy
gastronomic
gastroscope
generaliser
generalship
generically
gimcrackery
haberdasher
hairraising
hazardously
hemeralopia
heteroclite
heteroecism
heterograft
heterophony
heteroploid
heteropolar
heterospory
heterotaxis
heterotroph
heterotypic
hibernacula
hibernation
Hibernicism
highranking
hilariously
histrionics
histrionism
hundredfold
hyperactive
hyperbolise
hyperboloid
hyperborean
hypercharge
hypercritic
hypermarket
hypermetric
hyperphagia
hyperplasia
hypersthene
hypertrophy
illbreeding
immarginate
immortalise
immortality
imparkation
impartation
impartially
imperfectly
imperforate
imperialise
imperialism
imperialist
imperilling
imperilment
imperiously
impermanent
impermeable
impermeably
impersonate
impertinent
imperviable
importantly
importation
importunate
importunely
importunity
incarcerate
incardinate
incarnadine
incarnation
incertitude
incorporate
incorporeal
incorrectly
incorruptly
incuriosity
incuriously
incurvation
incurvature
indirection
indorsement
inebriation
inferential
inferiority
infertility
infirmarian
informality
information
informative
informatory
ingurgitate
inheritable
inheritance
inheritress
injuriously
innervation
inscribable
inscription
inscriptive
inscrutable
inscrutably
instruction
instructive
interactant
interaction
interactive
interallied
interatomic
interbedded
intercalary
intercalate
intercensal
intercepter
interceptor
intercessor
interchange
intercostal
intercourse
intercrural
interdental
interdepend
interesting
interfacial
interfacing
interfluent
interfusion
intergrowth
interiorise
interiority
interjacent
interleaves
interlinear
Interlingua
interlining
interlocker
interlunary
intermeddle
intermedium
intermingle
intermitted
internalise
internality
internecine
internuncio
interosseus
interplayed
interpolate
interpreter
interracial
interregnum
interrelate
interrogate
interrupter
interruptor
interseptal
intersexual
intersperse
interspinal
intertangle
intertribal
intervallic
interviewee
interviewer
laboriously
lachrymator
lateritious
legerdemain
leviratical
libertarian
liberticide
libertinage
libertinism
literalness
logarithmic
louvreboard
lowpressure
luxuriantly
luxuriation
luxuriously
malariology
malpractice
margraviate
materialise
materialism
materialist
materiality
McCarthyism
membraneous
memorabilia
memorialise
memorialist
mindreading
mineraliser
miscreation
misericorde
miserliness
mistrustful
mithridatic
moderations
modernistic
monarchical
mycorrhizae
mycorrhizal
naturalness
naturopathy
nefariously
Neotropical
nephrectomy
neutraliser
notoriously
numerically
nutcrackers
objurgation
objurgatory
observantly
observation
observatory
observingly
obstruction
obstructive
oestrogenic
oneiromancy
opportunely
opportunism
opportunist
opportunity
orderliness
otherwhiles
outbreeding
outcropping
overrunning
paperhanger
papermaking
paperweight
papyraceous
paternalism
paternalist
paternoster
pelargonium
penuriously
piperaceous
pleurodynia
polarimeter
polarimetry
polarisable
polariscope
poltroonery
portraitist
portraiture
powerlessly
preprandial
procreation
procreative
procrustean
progression
progressism
progressist
progressive
proprietary
protractile
protraction
protractive
protrudable
protrusible
purpresture
pyrargyrite
quadraphony
quadratical
quadrennial
quadrennium
quadrillion
quadrupedal
quarrelling
quarrelsome
rebarbative
recurrently
redirection
referential
reformation
reformative
reformatory
regardfully
regurgitate
remorseless
repartition
reportorial
reservation
restriction
restrictive
restructure
retardation
retardative
retardatory
retiredness
reverberant
reverberate
reverential
reversional
reversioner
satirically
saturnalian
saturninely
scleroderma
sclerometer
sclerophyll
sclerotitis
seborrhoeic
selfraising
selfreliant
selfreproof
selfrespect
severalfold
soberminded
soteriology
sovereignly
sovereignty
sparrowbill
sparrowhawk
spherically
spherometer
spherulitic
squarebuilt
squarsonage
squirearchy
staircarpet
staurolitic
steerageway
stirrupbone
stirruppump
subarration
subcritical
subordinate
subornation
subtraction
subtractive
subtropical
suburbanise
suburbanite
suffragette
sugarcoated
superabound
supercharge
superfamily
superficial
superficies
superfluity
superfluous
superheater
superimpose
superinduce
superintend
superioress
superiority
superjacent
superlative
superlunary
supermarket
supernatant
supernormal
superscribe
superscript
supersedeas
supersedure
superstrata
supersubtle
supertanker
supervision
supervisory
suppression
suppressive
susurration
sybaritical
synergistic
tabernacled
temerarious
tephromancy
theorematic
theoretical
thwartships
topdressing
tuberculate
tuberculise
tuberculose
tuberculous
ulotrichous
uncertainly
uncertainty
unchristian
underbidder
undercharge
underexpose
underground
undergrowth
underhanded
undermanned
underpinned
underseller
undersigned
understated
undertaking
undertenant
undervaluer
underweight
underwriter
unforgiving
unfortunate
unfurnished

unnervingly
unshrinking
unvarnished
unwarranted
vagariously
vaporimeter
vaporisable
venereology
ventricular
ventriculus
ventriloquy
vestryclerk
vicariously
viceregally
viceroyalty
viceroyship
waterbottle
watercolour
watercooled
watercooler
watercourse
waterlogged
waterskiing
wellrounded
zoographist
accessorial
accessorise
accusatival
acoustician
advisedness
aerostatics
aerostation
agnosticism
altostratus
anaesthesia
anaesthetic
antiSemitic
antistrophe
arrestingly
assassinate
assessorial
atmospheric
attestation
Augustinian
babysitting
barnstormer
bergschrund
bestselling
bicuspidate
billsticker
blessedness
bodyservant
bondservant
bondservice
bookselling
bookshelves
breastplate
breastwheel
calisthenic
cardsharper
caressingly
catastrophe
celestially
chansonnier
cheesecloth
Christendom
christening
christiania
Christianly
Christmassy
Christology
chrysalides
chrysalises
chrysarobin
chrysoberyl
chrysoprase
cityslicker
classically
cleistogamy
coessential
coinsurance
comestibles
coruscation
counselling
crossbearer
crossbowman
crossgarnet
crosslegged
crossstitch
cryosurgery
decussately
decussation
deerstalker
degustation
detestation
devastation
digestively
dinosaurian
disassemble
disassembly
divestiture
divisionary
divisionism
domesticate
domesticity
dresscircle
dressmaking
echosounder
emulsionise
encystation
endoskelton
Etruscology
excessively
expostulate
feldspathic
fenestrated
festschrift
fetishistic
filmsetting
footslogger
footsoldier
foreseeable
foreshorten
foresighted
forestaller
forestation
frowstiness
gangsterism
glassblower
glasscutter
glassmaking
glossolalia
grasshopper
greasepaint
greaseproof
guesstimate
hairstyling
hairstylist
handselling
harpsichord
hemispheric
heresiology
highstepper
homesteader
homestretch
homosporous
hornswoggle
hypostatise
illusionism
illusionist
illustrator
illustrious
impassioned
impassively
impassivity
incessantly
industrious
inessential
infestation
inobservant
insessorial
insistently
investigate
investiture
ionospheric
irresoluble
kickstarter
kinesiology
legislation
legislative
legislature
lickspittle
longsighted
loudspeaker
magisterial
magisterium
magistratic
maidservant
metasomatic
metastasise
minesweeper
ministerial
misestimate
molestation
monasterial
monasticism
nearsighted
necessarian
necessarily
necessitate
necessitous
numismatics
numismatist
obfuscation
obfuscatory
obsessional
obsessively
obtestation
omniscience
oversailing
oversetting
overstepped
overstretch
overstuffed
painstaking
Palestinian
paraselenae
parasitical
parasitosis
parishioner
pedestalled
perishables
perishingly
perispermic
peristalith
peristalsis
peristaltic
peristomial
phrasemaker
phraseogram
phraseology
pipistrelle
pleasurable
pleasurably
Pleistocene
polystyrene
pressagency
priestcraft
Prussianise
Prussianism
quaestorial
quiescently
ravishingly
reassertion
reassurance
recessional
recessively
rediscovery
registrable
reinsertion
reinsurance
reposefully
resistively
resistivity
resuscitate
revisionary
revisionism
revisionist
rhapsodical
ringstraked
salesladies
sandskipper
satisfiable
schismatise
schistosity
schistosome
scissorbill
scissortail
selfsealing
selfseeking
selfservice
selfserving
selfstarter
selfsterile
selfsupport
semasiology
semiskilled
Shaksperean
Shaksperian
shopsteward
showstopper
sideslipped
sidestepped
sinistrally
sinistrorse
softshelled
songsparrow
spessartite
spinsterish
splashboard
sponsorship
squashiness
starstudded
tearstained
theosophist
thinskinned
thirstiness
thrasonical
timeserving
timesharing
townspeople
transaction
transalpine
transceiver
transcriber
transection
transferred
transferrer
transfigure
transfinite
transfixion
transformer
transfusion
transhumant
transiently
transilient
translation
translocate
translucent
translunary
transmarine
transmittal
transmitted
transmitter
transpadane
transparent
transpierce
transponder
transporter
transsexual
transuranic
transversal
treasonable
treasonably
trouserless
trousersuit
typesetting
unassertive
unbeseeming
undeserving
undesirable
undisguised
undisturbed
unessential
unfashioned
unpossessed
venesection
venisection
verisimilar
vicissitude
vivisection
volkslieder
wainscoting
wainscotted
weltschmerz
whimsically
Whitsuntide
Yugoslavian
abiotically
ablutionary
abortionist
aboutsledge
adoptianism
adoptianist
adoptionism
adoptionist
adulterator
agnatically
ahistorical
altitudinal
ambitiously
amentaceous
amontillado
anastomoses
anastomosis
anastomotic
antitypical
apartmental
apostleship
apostolical
apostrophic
aquatically
arbitrageur
arbitrament
arbitrarily
arbitration
arbitrative
arbitratrix
aristocracy
ascetically
aseptically
attitudinal
autotrophic
awestricken
beastliness
beauteously
beautifully
befittingly
belatedness
bewitchment
bilaterally
bimetallism
bimetallist
blastogenic
bounteously
bountifully
bracteolate
breathalyse
bristletail
bristleworm
bristliness
brittleness
bullterrier
bumptiously
caustically
chaetognath
chanterelle
chanticleer
chaotically
chartaceous
chitterling
cicatricial
cisatlantic
clostridium
coextension
coextensive
comptroller
comstockery
constellate
consternate
constituent
constitutor
constrictor
construable
constructor
countenance
counterblow
counterbond
counterfeit
counterfoil
counterfort
countermand
countermark
countermine
countermove
countermure
counterpane
counterpart
counterplan
counterplea
counterplot
countersign
countersink
countersunk
counterturn
countervail
counterview
counterwork
countlessly
countrified
countryfied
countryseat
countryside
countrywide
courteously
courtliness
craftswoman
creationism
creationist
crestfallen
crustaceous
cryotherapy
cryptically
cryptogamic
cryptograph
cryptomeria
crystalline
crystallise
crystallite
crystalloid
curatorship
dauntlessly
deactivator
deistically

deleterious
delitescent
devotedness
diarthrosis
diastematic
diastrophic
dicotyledon
digitigrade
diphtherial
diphtheroid
diphthongal
doubtlessly
downtrodden
drastically
drouthiness
ectotrophic
einsteinium
elastically
elasticated
elastomeric
electioneer
electrician
electricity
electrocute
electrolier
electrology
electrolyse
electrolyte
electronics
electrotype
enarthrosis
endothelial
endothelium
endothermal
endothermic
endotrophic
entitlement
Erastianism
ergatocracy
erratically
eventualise
eventuality
exanthemata
existential
expatiation
expatiative
expatiatory
facetiously
Falstaffian
fanatically
faultfinder
faultlessly
firstfruits
flirtatious
fluctuation
forethinker
forethought
foretopmast
foretopsail
fractionary
fractionate
fractionise
fractiously
frantically
franticness
freethinker
freethought
frontrunner
frostbitten
fructuation
fruitlessly
frustration
functionary
functionate
gafftopsail
gametangium
gametophyte
geanticline
genetically
genitivally
geostrophic
ghastliness
ghostliness
ghostwriter
giantpowder
greatnephew
gristliness
guiltlessly
habituation
hairtrigger
haustellate
healthfully
healthiness
heartbroken
hearthstone
heartlessly
heartsblood
heartstring
hepatectomy
heretically
holothurian
homothallic
hypotension
hypothecate
hypothenuse
hypothermia
hypothesise
hypotyposis
identically
idiotically
immitigable
immitigably
impatiently
impetration
impetratory
impetuosity
impetuously
inalterable
inalterably
inattention
inattentive
inestimable
inestimably
infatuation
ingathering
innutrition
irretention
irretentive
jauntingcar
kinetograph
kinetoscope
kleptomania
latitudinal
lengthiness
lieutenancy
lightfooted
lighthanded
lightheaded
lightminded
lightsomely
lightweight
limitedness
limitlessly
maintenance
maintopmast
maintopsail
megatherium
meritocracy
meritorious
mimetically
minuteglass
moisturiser
monitorship
Monothelite
monstrosity
monstrously
mosstrooper
mountaineer
mountainous
mountaintop
muskthistle
naphthalene
negationist
negotiation
negotiatory
negotiatrix
nightingale
nightmarish
nightporter
nightwalker
nonetheless
obmutescent
ommatophore
ornithology
ornithopter
ornithosaur
osmotically
outstanding
outstripped
overtopping
parathyroid
paratrooper
paratyphoid
penetrating
penetration
penetrative
penitential
perithecium
peritonitis
petitionary
phantasiast
phantasmata
pigsticking
pilotburner
piratically
pivotbridge
plantigrade
plasterwork
plasticiser
plectoptera
plenteously
plentifully
pointdevice
pointedness
pointillism
pointillist
pointlessly
politically
politicking
polytechnic
positronium
practicable
practicably
practically
praetorship
prattlingly
prestigious
prestissimo
prestressed
proctorship
prosthetics
prostitutor
prostration
psittacosis
pullthrough
punctilious
punctuality
punctuation
puritanical
pyrotechnic
quarterback
quarterdeck
quartertone
questionary
quintillion
ratatouille
reactionary
reactionist
redetermine
reestablish
reintegrate
reintroduce
relatedness
relationism
relationist
repetitious
rheotropism
rightangled
righteously
righthanded
righthander
rightminded
rightwinger
roentgenise
safetyvalve
Sagittarius
saintliness
saintpaulia
scattergood
sceptically
schottische
scintillant
scintillate
scoutmaster
scratchwork
scrutiniser
scuttlebutt
seditionary
seditiously
selftorture
semitrailer
senatorship
sheathknife
sheetanchor
shelterbelt
shelterless
shiftlessly
shirtsleeve
shortchange
shortcoming
shorthanded
shortspoken
shortwinded
shutterless
shuttlecock
sightlessly
sightliness
sightreader
sightscreen
sightseeing
sightworthy
sleuthhound
smoothfaced
solutionist
somatically
somatogenic
somatologic
somatoplasm
somatotonia
somatotonic
spastically
spatterdash
spectacular
spectatress
spectrality
spectrogram
spectrology
spontaneity
spontaneous
sportswoman
stadtholder
startlingly
steatopygia
stiltedness
strategical
stratocracy
stretchable
stuntedness
substandard
substantial
substantive
substituent
sumptuosity
sumptuously
swarthiness
swiftfooted
symptomatic
taciturnity
taratantara
teratogenic
teratologic
theatregoer
theatricals
thistledown
tightfisted
tightlipped
toastmaster
trestletree
trestlework
tristichous
trustbuster
trusteeship
trustworthy
tryptophane
unalterable
uncatchable
undutifully
ungetatable
unmatchable
unmitigated
unnaturally
unobtrusive
unorthodoxy
unsaturated
unutterable
unutterably
unwittingly
vacationist
venatically
vexatiously
volitionary
voortrekker
wealthiness
whistlestop
winetasting
wiretapping
zoantharian
accoucheuse
accountable
accountably
accountancy
acidulation
acupuncture
adjournment
Aesculapian
agglutinate
barquentine
bivouacking
calculating
calculation
calculative
carbuncular
carburetion
carburetted
carburetter
carburettor
cellularity
cinquecento
circularise
circularity
circulation
circulative
circulatory
circumlunar
circumpolar
circumsolar
circumspect
circumvolve
coadunation
coagulation
coeducation
collusively
colouration
colourblind
colourfully
combustible
comeuppance
communalise
communalism
communalist
communicant
communicate
communistic
commutation
commutative
compunction
compurgator
computation
computerise
concubinage
concubinary
concubitant
concurrence
conductance
conductible
conductress
confusingly
confutation
confutative
conjugality
conjugation
conjugative
conjunction
conjunctiva
conjunctive
conjuncture
conjuration
connubially
conquerable
consultancy
consumerism
consumingly
consummator
consumption
consumptive
cornucopian
corpulently
corpuscular
corrugation
corruptible
corruptibly
corruptness
credulously
crenulation
crepuscular
debauchment
debouchment
deglutition
demountable
depauperate
depauperise
diffuseness
diffusively
discussable
discussible
disfunction
disguisedly
disgustedly
disjunction
disjunctive
disjuncture
disputation
disquieting
disquietude

disturbance
dysfunction
ejaculation
ejaculatory
encrustment
entrustment
evolutional
exclusively
exclusivity
executioner
executorial
executrices
executrixes
exhaustible
exhaustless
factualness
favouritism
featureless
ferruginous
flatulently
formularise
formulation
fortunately
fulguration
garrulously
gemmulation
globularity
gradualness
granularity
granulation
granulocyte
gratulation
gratulatory
gutturalise
gutturalism
hallucinate
hirsuteness
illhumoured
impoundment
imprudently
inclusively
ineluctable
ineluctably
inequitable
inequitably
infeudation
influential
inoculation
inoculative
insouciance
intrusively
Kulturkampf
languidness
laurustinus
lectureship
linguistics
malfunction
manducation
manducatory
mantuamaker
marquessate
marqueterie
marquisette
masculinely
masculinise
masculinity
masquerader
measureless
measurement
mediumistic
mensuration
mercurially
micturition
misguidance
misguidedly
misjudgment
murmuration
murmurously
muscularity
musculation
musculature
nocturnally
nuncupation
nuncupative
obscuration
obscureness
obtrusively
oracularity
outbuilding
parturition
pastureland
pellucidity
pendulously
perfunctory
permutation
persuadable
persuasible
perturbable
picturebook
picturecard
picturegoer
picturesque
postulation
preaudience
prejudgment
prejudicial
prelusively
prelusorily
presumingly
presumption
presumptive
procuration
procuratory
procurement
profuseness
promulgator
protuberant
pullulation
pustulation
querulously
rapturously
recruitment
redoubtable
reeducation
resourceful
rumbustious
sacculation
Sadduceeism
sanguinaria
sanguineous
savouriness
serrulation
sertularian
singularise
singularity
speculation
speculative
sporulation
statutebook
statutorily
stimulation
stimulative
stipulation
stipulatory
subaudition
subcultural
subjugation
subjunctive
submultiple
subsumption
subsumptive
succulently
suffumigate
suppuration
suppurative
textureless
tolbutamide
torturously
traducement
tremulously
tribulation
tribuneship
tribunicial
tribunitial
tributarily
triquetrous
trituration
truculently
turbulently
unboundedly
uncluttered
uncountable
uncouthness
uncrushable
undoubtedly
unequivocal
uninucleate
unsoundness
untouchable
unusualness
vascularise
vascularity
vasculiform
venturesome
venturously
victualless
victualling
Abbevillian
alleviation
alleviative
alleviatory
ambivalence
ambivalency
ambiversion
anniversary
antivitamin
bedevilment
behavioural
benevolence
caravanning
caravansary
deliverable
deliverance
deliveryman
diluvialist
enlivenment
equivalence
equivalency
equivocally
equivocator
forevermore
foreverness
immoveables
inadvertent
inadvisable
individuate
indivisible
indivisibly
innavigable
irreverence
irrevocable
irrevocably
lixiviation
malevolence
Merovingian
motivepower
nailvarnish
obliviously
polevaulter
recoverable
rejuvenator
rejuvenesce
reviviscent
scurvygrass
shrivelling
sleeveboard
twelvemonth
twelvepenny
unadvisedly
uncivilised
undeveloped
vesuvianite
armtwisting
birdwatcher
bondwashing
bushwhacker
catswhisker
elbowgrease
embowelling
embowerment
fairweather
farawayness
firewalking
firewatcher
flagwagging
forewarning
fourwheeler
handwriting
handwritten
handwrought
hardworking
heroworship
highwrought
Micawberish
Micawberism
overweening
overwritten
overwrought
Pickwickian
reedwarbler
ropewalking
screwdriver
selfwinding
selfworship
sidewheeler
somewhither
typewritten
waspwaisted
wellwishing
widowerhood
wolfwhistle
bisexuality
desexualise
innoxiously
nonexistent
obnoxiously
preexistent
subaxillary
acetylation
anonymously
asphyxiator
bandylegged
bathymetric
bathyscaphe
bathysphere
bradycardia
cockyleekie
condylomata
dactylogram
dactylology
daisycutter
deoxygenate
deoxyribose
diphycercal
dissyllable
dissymmetry
dithyrambic
embryologic
embryonated
emptyhanded
emptyheaded
eurhythmics
geosyncline
gerrymander
gillyflower
heavyfooted
heavyhanded
heavyweight
honeybadger
honeymooner
honeysuckle
hurryscurry
hurryskurry
jerrymander
lacrymation
lacrymatory
lacrymosely
martyrology
merryandrew
merrymaking
methylamine
methylation
mollycoddle
moneylender
moneymaking
moneymarket
moneyspider
ninnyhammer
nittygritty
noseyparker
oxyhydrogen
pachydermal
pennyweight
pharyngitis
platyrrhine
pussyfooter
pussywillow
readywitted
splayfooted
storyteller
tachycardia
tachygraphy
teenybopper
trisyllabic
trisyllable
vichyssoise
weenybopper
bedizenment
breezeblock
bryozoology
citizenship
denizenship
freezedried
homozygosis
hylozoistic
magazinegun
monozygotic
polyzoarium
quizzically
schizanthus

---

abracadabra
abstraction
abstractive
accusatival
admiralship
aeronautics
aircraftman
allocatable
allopathist
ambivalence
ambivalency
amentaceous
anthracitic
anticathode
antiJacobin
apparatchik
arboraceous
Areopagitic
automatable
bacchanalia
barefacedly
bearbaiting
benefaction
bimetallism
bimetallist
birdfancier
birdwatcher
bivouacking
blackavised
blepharitis
Bonapartean
Bonapartism
Bonapartist
bondwashing
braggadocio
Brahmanical
brahmaputra
bullbaiting
burglarious
bushmanship
butyraceous
calefacient
calefactory
camaraderie
cantharides
cantharidic
caravanning
caravansary
caricatural
carriageway
chainarmour
charlatanry
chartaceous
chockablock
chrysalides
chrysalises
chrysarobin
complacence
complacency
complainant
complaisant
concealable
concealment
conflagrant
conflagrate
congealable
congealment
contrabasso
contractile
contraction
contractive
contractual
contracture
contradance
contraption
contrariety
contrarious
contrastive
cordialness
coronagraph
crustaceous
crystalline
crystallise
crystallite
crystalloid
dedicatedly
diaphaneity
diffraction
dinosaurian
Diophantine
disgraceful
distraction
distractive
dodecaphony
efficacious
elephantine
elephantoid
emmenagogue
endocardiac
endocardial
endocardium
enigmatical
enthralling

enthr**a**lment
entre**a**tment
epidi**a**scope
epigr**a**phist
epith**a**lamia
epith**a**lamic
equil**a**teral
equiv**a**lence
equiv**a**lency
esche**a**table
esche**a**tment
Esper**a**ntist
everl**a**sting
factu**a**lness
Falst**a**ffian
faraw**a**yness
farin**a**ceous
farre**a**ching
fasci**a**board
felsp**a**thoid
finic**a**lness
firer**a**ising
firew**a**lking
firew**a**tcher
flagc**a**ptain
flagw**a**gging
flirt**a**tious
forbe**a**rance
forew**a**rning
freem**a**sonry
gamet**a**ngium
gener**a**liser
gener**a**lship
genti**a**nella
gimcr**a**ckery
goodn**a**tured
gourm**a**ndise
gourm**a**ndism
gradu**a**lness
gramm**a**logue
gramm**a**tical
hairr**a**ising
halfl**a**nding
handf**a**sting
handp**a**inted
hemer**a**lopia
highf**a**lutin
highr**a**nking
hyper**a**ctive
hypog**a**stric
incre**a**sable
incun**a**bulum
inesc**a**pable
initi**a**lling
insep**a**rable
insep**a**rably
inter**a**ctant
inter**a**ction
inter**a**ctive
inter**a**llied
inter**a**tomic
ipsil**a**teral
irrep**a**rable
irrep**a**rably
judgm**a**tical
kiloc**a**lorie
kinem**a**tical
labef**a**ction
lesem**a**jesty
levir**a**tical
lifem**a**nship
liter**a**lness
logic**a**lness
logom**a**chist
mailc**a**rrier
malad**a**ptive
malef**a**ction
malfe**a**sance
malpr**a**ctice
mantu**a**maker
manuf**a**ctory
manuf**a**cture
margr**a**viate
marri**a**gebed
marsh**a**lling
marsh**a**lship
matri**a**rchal
membr**a**neous
memor**a**bilia
merch**a**ndise
merch**a**ntman
merry**a**ndrew
messi**a**hship
milli**a**mpere
miner**a**liser
misfe**a**sance
moder**a**tions
monoc**a**rpous
mount**a**ineer
mount**a**inous
mount**a**intop
music**a**lness
myxom**a**tosis
nailv**a**rnish
namec**a**lling
natur**a**lness
Neopl**a**tonic
neutr**a**liser
nomin**a**tival
nonch**a**lance
nonfe**a**sance
nutcr**a**ckers
oarsm**a**nship
omnif**a**rious
outst**a**nding
overb**a**lance
overg**a**rment
overl**a**pping
overm**a**nning
overp**a**yment
overs**a**iling
paedi**a**trics
paedi**a**trist
Palae**a**rctic
palmc**a**bbage
papyr**a**ceous
patri**a**rchal
pentl**a**ndite
peric**a**rdiac
peric**a**rdial
peric**a**rdium
perip**a**tetic
persu**a**dable
persu**a**sible
phant**a**siast
phant**a**smata
photo**a**ctive
pighe**a**dedly
piloc**a**rpine
piper**a**ceous
plagi**a**riser
plate**a**rmour
plein**a**irist
polev**a**ulter
polyc**a**rpous
popul**a**riser
portm**a**nteau
portr**a**itist
portr**a**iture
pourp**a**rlers
pragm**a**tical
prepr**a**ndial
press**a**gency
progn**a**thism
progn**a**thous
proth**a**lamia
proth**a**llial
proth**a**llium
protr**a**ctile
protr**a**ction
protr**a**ctive
psitt**a**cosis
purch**a**sable
purit**a**nical
quadr**a**phony
quadr**a**tical
Rabel**a**isian
radic**a**lness
radio**a**ctive
rapsc**a**llion
raref**a**ction
raref**a**ctive
reedw**a**rbler
reest**a**blish
reinc**a**rnate
repro**a**chful
retin**a**cular
retin**a**culum
retro**a**ction
retro**a**ctive
rheum**a**ticky
right**a**ngled
roped**a**ncing
ropew**a**lking
rubef**a**cient
rubef**a**ction
sandb**a**gging
sapon**a**ceous
scale**a**rmour
schiz**a**nthus
schol**a**rship
scori**a**ceous
scrib**a**cious
selfm**a**stery
selfr**a**ising
semip**a**lmate
sever**a**lfold
sheet**a**nchor
shell**a**cking
showm**a**nship
signp**a**inter
slotm**a**chine
smorg**a**sbord
solan**a**ceous
sonof**a**bitch
spath**a**ceous
spect**a**cular
spect**a**tress
sperm**a**phyte
sperm**a**tozoa
spess**a**rtite
spont**a**neity
spont**a**neous
stand**a**rdise
steer**a**geway
steph**a**notis
stoic**a**lness
subsc**a**pular
subst**a**ndard
subst**a**ntial
subst**a**ntive
subtr**a**ction
subtr**a**ctive
suffr**a**gette
super**a**bound
tabef**a**ction
tagli**a**telle
tagli**a**telli
tankf**a**rming
tapem**a**chine
tarat**a**ntara
telep**a**thise
telep**a**thist
temer**a**rious
thaum**a**trope
thaum**a**turge
thaum**a**turgy
there**a**bouts
timeb**a**rgain
trans**a**ction
trans**a**lpine
trivi**a**lness
tumef**a**ction
typec**a**sting
typic**a**lness
unash**a**medly
unbre**a**kable
uncle**a**nness
unget**a**table
uninh**a**bited
unorg**a**nized
unpal**a**table
unspe**a**kable
unspe**a**kably
unusu**a**lness
urtic**a**ceous
urtic**a**rious
victu**a**lless
victu**a**lling
waspw**a**isted
Weism**a**nnism
where**a**bouts
whigm**a**leery
wildc**a**tting
winet**a**sting
wiret**a**pping
witen**a**gemot
woodc**a**rving
workm**a**nlike
workm**a**nship
xyloc**a**rpous
zoogr**a**phist
zoopl**a**nkton
absor**b**ingly
adver**b**ially
after**b**urner
alpha**b**etise
amena**b**ility
amica**b**ility
amphi**b**olite
amphi**b**ology
appro**b**ation
appro**b**atory
argle**b**argle
assem**b**lyman
attri**b**ution
attri**b**utive
azoto**b**acter
bashi**b**azouk
bicar**b**onate
bidda**b**ility
black**b**eetle
black**b**irder
block**b**uster
bread**b**asket
canni**b**alise
canni**b**alism
cinna**b**arine
colla**b**orate
colum**b**arium
concu**b**inage
concu**b**inary
concu**b**itant
confa**b**ulate
connu**b**ially
conur**b**ation
corro**b**orant
corro**b**orate
credi**b**ility
crook**b**acked
cross**b**earer
cross**b**owman
culpa**b**ility
decar**b**onate
decar**b**onise
decar**b**urise
detri**b**alise
educa**b**ility
eligi**b**ility
Eliza**b**ethan
encum**b**rance
enjam**b**ement
falli**b**ility
feasi**b**ility
flexi**b**ility
frost**b**itten
funam**b**ulate
funam**b**ulist
glass**b**lower
gnoto**b**iosis
gnoto**b**iotic
gulli**b**ility
heart**b**roken
helle**b**orine
honey**b**adger
hunch**b**acked
hydro**b**romic
hyper**b**olise
hyper**b**oloid
hyper**b**orean
inedi**b**ility
insta**b**ility
inter**b**edded
invia**b**ility
lauda**b**ility
lopho**b**ranch
macro**b**iotic
mandi**b**ulate
mepro**b**amate
Micaw**b**erish
Micaw**b**erism
misci**b**ility
movea**b**ility
necro**b**iosis
neigh**b**ourly
oppro**b**rious
palpa**b**ility
passi**b**ility
pecca**b**ility
peram**b**ulate
pilot**b**urner
pitch**b**lende
pivot**b**ridge
placa**b**ility
porta**b**ility
possi**b**ility
preli**b**ation
proba**b**ilism
proba**b**ilist
proba**b**ility
prohi**b**ition
prohi**b**itive
prohi**b**itory
protu**b**erant
ratea**b**ility
reada**b**ility
rebar**b**ative
recum**b**ently
redou**b**table
relia**b**ility
remem**b**rance
repro**b**ation
repro**b**ative
repro**b**atory
resem**b**lance
retri**b**ution
retri**b**utive
retri**b**utory
rever**b**erant
rever**b**erate
salea**b**ility
sapro**b**iotic
satia**b**ility
scara**b**aeoid
sensi**b**ility
shrub**b**iness
socia**b**ility
solva**b**ility
spell**b**inder
steam**b**oiler
stock**b**roker
subum**b**rella
subur**b**anise
subur**b**anite
suita**b**ility
surre**b**uttal
surre**b**utter
sword**b**earer
sylla**b**arium
sylla**b**icity
tamea**b**ility
tangi**b**ility
teeny**b**opper
tensi**b**ility
testa**b**ility
throm**b**ocyte
tooth**b**illed
torch**b**earer
trail**b**lazer
train**b**earer
trust**b**uster
under**b**idder
undou**b**tedly
varia**b**ility
vendi**b**ility
vinci**b**ility
washa**b**ility
waste**b**asket
water**b**ottle
weeny**b**opper
weigh**b**ridge
wheel**b**arrow
worka**b**ility
world**b**eater
abran**c**hiate
accou**c**heuse
acina**c**iform
advan**c**ement
affri**c**ation
affri**c**ative
airsi**c**kness
alter**c**ation
Ameri**c**anise
Ameri**c**anism
Ameri**c**anist
amphi**c**tyony
anfra**c**tuous
Angli**c**anism
annun**c**iator
antho**c**yanin
appli**c**ation
appli**c**ative
appli**c**atory
appre**c**iable
appre**c**iably
appre**c**iator
areni**c**olous
attra**c**table
autar**c**hical
beach**c**omber
belli**c**osity
bergs**c**hrund
bewit**c**hment
bifur**c**ation
black**c**oated
brady**c**ardia
bread**c**rumbs
broad**c**aster
calci**c**olous
carbo**c**yclic
carun**c**ulate
cater**c**ousin
choke**c**herry
cleri**c**alism

clericalist
climacteric
cloudcastle
coeducation
collectable
collectanea
collectedly
collectible
collocation
compactness
conductance
conductible
conductress
conjectural
connectable
connectedly
connectible
consecrator
consecution
consecutive
convocation
coparcenary
corbiculate
cornucopian
correctable
correctness
coruscation
criticality
criticaster
cysticercus
daisycutter
debauchment
debouchment
defalcation
defenceless
deforcement
deification
demarcation
denticulate
denunciator
deprecation
deprecative
deprecatory
depreciator
depthcharge
desiccation
desiccative
dialectally
dialectical
difficultly
diphycercal
diplococcus
disaccustom
disencumber
disinclined
dislocation
dissociable
divorcement
dresscircle
duplication
duplicative
duplicitous
earthcloset
edification
edificatory
embraceable
embracement
embracingly
embrocation
emplacement
enforceable
enforcement
enhancement
eradication
eradicative
Etruscology
explication
explicative
explicatory
exsiccation
extractable
extrication
fabrication
farcicality
fasciculate
festschrift
fieldcornet
financially
folliculate
formication
fornication
forthcoming
furunculous
Gallicanism
geotectonic
gesticulate
glasscutter
gynaecocrat
gynaecology
haemocyanin
hallucinate
handicapped
handicapper
heliochrome
hippocampus
Hippocratic
horsecollar
hydrocarbon
hydrocyanic
hypercharge
hypercritic
imbrication
impeachable
impeachment
implication
implicative
impractical
imprecation
imprecatory
imprecisely
imprecision
incarcerate
inculcation
ineluctable
ineluctably
inexactness
insincerely
insincerity
insouciance
intercalary
intercalate
intercensal
intercepter
interceptor
intercessor
interchange
intercostal
intercourse
intercrural
intractable
intractably
intricately
ipecacuanha
justiciable
latticework
lubrication
lubricative
machicolate
macrocosmic
manducation
manducatory
mastication
masticatory
matriculate
melancholia
melancholic
metrication
micrococcal
micrococcus
microcosmic
mollycoddle
monarchical
multicolour
mustachioed
myrmecology
nomenclator
obfuscation
obfuscatory
ochlocratic
offenceless
oligochaete
omniscience
orthocentre
ostracoderm
participant
participate
participial
particulate
passacaglia
pedunculate
pellucidity
Pentecostal
perfectible
perfectness
persecution
petticoated
phagocytise
phagocytose
photocopier
phycocyanin
physicality
planoconvex
plutocratic
predecessor
predicament
predication
predicative
predicatory
predictable
predictably
prefectural
preoccupied
proficiency
prolocutrix
prosecution
prosecutrix
protectoral
protectress
provocateur
provocation
provocative
publication
quickchange
quiescently
radiocarbon
ratiocinate
recalculate
rediscovery
reeducation
reenactment
reflectance
reification
rejoicingly
replaceable
replacement
replication
respectable
respectably
resuscitate
retraceable
retractable
retrocedent
revaccinate
rhizocarpic
rubrication
rustication
Sadduceeism
scratchwork
seasickness
septicaemia
septicaemic
serviceable
serviceably
servicebook
serviceline
shortchange
shortcoming
somniculous
sphincteral
sphincteric
spiraculate
spirochaete
spirochetal
staircarpet
stalactitic
staunchless
staunchness
stenochromy
stomachache
stomachpump
stonecurlew
stonecutter
stormcentre
stretchable
sufficiency
suffocation
suffocative
sugarcoated
supercharge
surficially
syndicalism
syndicalist
syndication
syntactical
tachycardia
tentaculate
terricolous
tetracyclic
threecolour
tobacconist
torticollis
trabeculate
traducement
tragicomedy
transceiver
transcriber
tuberculate
tuberculise
tuberculose
tuberculous
uncatchable
unconcealed
unconcerned
undercharge
unguiculate
unification
uninucleate
unmatchable
unshockable
unteachable
untouchable
valleculate
vermiculate
vermiculite
verticality
vindication
vindicative
vindicatory
wainscoting
wainscotted
watercolour
watercooled
watercooler
watercourse
weltschmerz
Whitechapel
whitecollar
zootechnics
abecedarian
accordantly
accordingly
achondritic
aphrodisiac
artiodactyl
avoirdupois
biquadratic
calendrical
candidature
coccidiosis
comradeship
confederacy
confederate
confidently
confidingly
considerate
considering
crocidolite
crocodilian
cylindrical
degradation
degradingly
demandingly
deoxidation
dependently
depredation
depredatory
diffidently
dislodgment
elucidation
elucidative
elucidatory
exceedingly
expenditure
extradition
fecundation
forbiddance
frigidarium
gravedigger
groundsheet
groundwater
haberdasher
haggadistic
hazardously
horsedoctor
imprudently
incardinate
incredulity
incredulous
infeudation
interdental
interdepend
labiodental
legerdemain
leptodactyl
linendraper
liquidambar
liquidation
mastodontic
Methodistic
methodology
misjudgment
molendinary
molybdenite
orchidology
orthodontia
orthodontic
oxyhydrogen
pachydermal
palindromic
paraldehyde
peccadillos
pentadactyl
periodicity
periodontal
phagedaenic
pointdevice
preaudience
precedented
precedently
prejudgment
prejudicial
premeditate
providently
pteridology
pterodactyl
quilldriver
rearadmiral
recondition
redundantly
regardfully
retardation
retardative
retardatory
revendicate
scoundrelly
screwdriver
secondarily
secondclass
secondrater
secondsight
serendipity
sextodecimo
shoulderbag
shoulderpad
slavedriver
splendorous
spreadeagle
subaudition
subordinate
succedaneum
tarradiddle
tetradactyl
thalidomide
threadiness
threadpaper
threedecker
tragedienne
trepidation
unbendingly
viceadmiral
welladvised
witchdoctor
abiogeneses
abiogenesis
abiogenetic
acarpellous
acaulescent
accelerando
accelerator
acquiescent
acropetally
adulterator
advisedness
aesthetical
aftereffect
aggrievedly
Albigensian
alkalescent
allAmerican
altorelievo
ambiversion
anacreontic
anencephaly
annabergite
anniversary
antecedence
antependium
antineutron
antiSemitic
apotheosise
apparelling
aquarellist
arborescent
archaeology

archaeornis
argumentive
assuredness
backbencher
ballbearing
barquentine
basipetally
battledress
battlefield
beauteously
bedizenment
belatedness
bellheather
bestselling
betweenmaid
betweenness
betweentime
bilaterally
biochemical
biocoenoses
biocoenosis
biocoenotic
biofeedback
bladderwort
blessedness
blunderbuss
bodyservant
bondservant
bondservice
bookkeeping
booklearned
bookselling
bootlegging
bottleglass
bottlegreen
bottlenosed
bounteously
bourgeoisie
bowdleriser
bracteolate
breezeblock
bridgeboard
brotherhood
bullterrier
bumblepuppy
businessman
butcherbird
byeelection
campmeeting
candleberry
candlelight
candlepower
candlestick
centreboard
centrepiece
cesarevitch
cesarewitch
chalcedonic
challenging
chamaephyte
chamberlain
chambermaid
champertous
chancellery
chancellory
changefully
channelling
chanterelle
chargesheet
cheesecloth
chickenfeed
chickenwire
chimaerical
Chippendale
chitterling
cinquecento
citizenship
clandestine
clapperclaw
clothesline
clothesmoth
clothesprop
cobblestone
cockleshell
codefendant
coessential
coextension
coextensive
coffeehouse
coffeetable
coinheritor
coldhearted
colonelship
complexness
compression
compressive
concrescent
congressman
conquerable
conspecific
constellate
consternate
contretemps
cookgeneral
corbiesteps
costbenefit
cotoneaster
counselling
countenance
counterblow
counterbond
counterfeit
counterfoil
counterfort
countermand
countermark
countermine
countermove
countermure
counterpane
counterpart
counterplan
counterplea
counterplot
countersign
countersink
countersunk
counterturn
countervail
counterview
counterwork
courteously
crabbedness
crackerjack
crookedness
cytogenesis
decelerator
decerebrate
deferential
deleterious
delineation
delitescent
deliverable
deliverance
deliveryman
denizenship
denumerable
desideratum
devotedness
diastematic
discrepancy
disobedient
displeasure
distressful
documentary
domineering
doublecheck
doublecross
doubleDutch
doubleedged
doubleender
doubleentry
doublefaced
doublequick
doublespeak
doublethink
downhearted
drunkenness
dundrearies
earpiercing
earthenware
ectogenesis
ectogenetic
einsteinium
embowelling
embowerment
empanelling
endometrium
engineering
enlivenment
enucleation
ephemerides
epithelioma
erroneously
etherealise
ethereality
Europeanise
evangelical
exaggerator
exarcerbate
exdirectory
existential
exoskeletal
exoskeleton
exponential
fairweather
farthermost
featheredge
featherhead
featherless
fiddlestick
filamentary
filamentous
filmsetting
flabbergast
flannelette
flannelling
fluorescein
fluorescent
foreseeable
forevermore
foreverness
fragmentary
freehearted
freezedried
fullhearted
furtherance
furthermore
furthermost
furthersome
gamogenesis
gastrectomy
genteelness
gentlemanly
gentlewoman
geochemical
goldbeating
goodhearted
grangeriser
greasepaint
greaseproof
guardedness
halfhearted
halfmeasure
handselling
hardhearted
haustellate
hepatectomy
Hepplewhite
hexadecimal
hexametrist
hobbledehoy
homiletical
homocentric
homogeneity
homogeneous
homogenetic
homogeniser
huckleberry
hundredfold
hurriedness
hylogenesis
hypotension
illbreeding
illiberally
immanentism
immanentist
immoveables
impanelling
impenetrate
inadvertent
inalienable
inalienably
inalterable
inalterably
inappetence
inattention
inattentive
incalescent
incinerator
incoherence
incoherency
independent
indigestion
indigestive
indirection
ineffective
ineffectual
inessential
inexpedient
inexpensive
inferential
influential
innumerable
innumerably
inobservant
inoffensive
insuperable
insuperably
interesting
intolerable
intolerably
intolerance
intumescent
ironhearted
irredentism
irredentist
irrelevance
irrelevancy
irretention
irretentive
irreverence
isoelectric
journeywork
juvenescent
kindhearted
kitchenette
kitchensink
kitchenware
launderette
learnedness
leatherback
leatherhead
leatherneck
lieutenancy
ligamentary
ligamentous
limitedness
lionhearted
louvreboard
lowpressure
luminescent
maidservant
maintenance
makebelieve
managership
manifestant
manifestoes
marquessate
marqueterie
masquerader
mediaevally
merogenesis
metacentric
metagenesis
metagenetic
middleclass
middlesized
mindbending
mindreading
minuteglass
miscreation
misspelling
monogenesis
monogenetic
motivepower
musclebound
Neanderthal
needlecraft
needlepoint
needlewoman
nephrectomy
nettlecloth
nonspecific
northeaster
noticeboard
novelettish
obmutescent
obsolescent
oecumenical
ontogenesis
ontogenetic
openhearted
optometrist
orthoepical
outbreeding
ovariectomy
overbearing
overdevelop
overmeasure
oversetting
overweening
paddleboard
paddlewheel
pantheistic
paraleipsis
paramedical
parametrise
paraselenae
partnership
pearlescent
pedicellate
penitential
perineurium
perplexedly
perspective
philhellene
phrasemaker
phraseogram
phraseology
plasterwork
plenteously
pointedness
policewoman
polygenesis
polygenetic
polypeptide
polytechnic
preelection
premiership
primaevally
problematic
proceedings
procreation
procreative
progression
progressism
progressist
progressive
prophethood
prophetical
prophetship
prospective
psychedelia
psychedelic
pumicestone
purpresture
pyrotechnic
quadrennial
quadrennium
quarrelling
quarrelsome
quarterback
quarterdeck
quartertone
racemeeting
rattlebrain
rattlepated
rattlesnake
reassertion
recoverable
redetermine
redirection
referential
regenerable
regenerator
regimentals
reinsertion
reintegrate
rejuvenator
rejuvenesce
relatedness
remunerator
reorientate
reposefully
residential
resplendent
retiredness
retrievable
reverential
righteously
roundedness
rudimentary
ruridecanal
saddlecloth
saddlehorse
safekeeping
scattergood
scuppernong
sedimentary
seigneurial
selfcentred
selfdefence
selfdenying
selfdespair
selfdevoted
selffeeding
selffeeling
selffertile
selfreliant
selfreproof
selfrespect
selfsealing
selfseeking

selfservice	twelvepenny	imperforate	aggregation	haplography	roentgenise
selfserving	typesetting	indifferent	aggregative	heliography	salvageable
sexagesimal	unalterable	insufflator	analogously	hooliganism	saprogenous
shelterbelt	unappealing	interfacial	androgynous	hydrogenate	sausagemeat
shelterless	unassertive	interfacing	angiography	hydrogenous	scenography
shepherdess	unbeseeming	interfluent	apologetics	hydrography	scragginess
shoeleather	underexpose	interfusion	arraignment	hymnography	segregation
shrivelling	undeserving	justifiable	arrangement	hypsography	segregative
shutterless	undeveloped	justifiably	aspergillum	ichnography	serpiginous
sickbenefit	unessential	lactiferous	aspergillus	iconography	sporogenous
singlestick	unnecessary	lightfooted	assuagement	immarginate	sporogonium
singletrack	unquietness	liquefiable	belligerent	impingement	springboard
sleeveboard	unrelenting	magnificent	bersaglieri	impregnable	springclean
slenderness	unselective	melliferous	blackgrouse	impregnably	springhouse
slickenside	unutterable	mellifluent	bloodguilty	incongruent	springiness
smithereens	unutterably	mellifluous	cabbagepalm	incongruity	stalagmitic
snickersnee	vehmgericht	morbiferous	cabbagerose	incongruous	stenography
snowleopard	venereology	nullifidian	cabbagetree	indulgently	stoneground
softhearted	venesection	odoriferous	cabbageworm	inelegantly	straightcut
soldierlike	venisection	ozoniferous	calligraphy	ingurgitate	straightish
soldiership	vicegerency	pearlfisher	carrageenan	instigation	straightway
southeaster	viceregally	pestiferous	carrageenin	instigative	strangeness
Southernism	viridescent	pettifogger	cartography	intergrowth	strangulate
sovereignly	virilescent	photofinish	castigation	intriguante	stringboard
sovereignty	vituperator	pontificals	centigramme	laryngology	stringently
spatterdash	vivisection	pontificate	chirography	laryngotomy	stringiness
speakership	vociferance	proliferate	chorography	lentiginous	stringpiece
spelaeology	vociferator	proliferous	colligation	lithography	stringybark
splenectomy	warmhearted	prolificacy	colligative	macrogamete	strongpoint
splenetical	washleather	prolificity	compaginate	madrigalian	stylography
spongecloth	weakhearted	pussyfooter	conjugality	madrigalist	subjugation
squarebuilt	weathercock	qualifiable	conjugation	meningocele	subregional
squirearchy	weatherwise	quickfiring	conjugative	microgamete	subrogation
stiflejoint	weatherworn	quickfreeze	consignable	micrography	surrogation
stiltedness	wellbeloved	quickfrozen	consignment	microgroove	syllogistic
strategical	welldefined	rangefinder	copingstone	misbegotten	synergistic
strikebound	wellmeaning	Rastafarian	corrigendum	miscegenate	tachygraphy
studiedness	Wensleydale	rectifiable	corrugation	mythography	termagantly
stuntedness	whitherward	retroflexed	cosmogonist	negligently	terrigenous
subspecific	whitleather	roughfooted	cosmography	neologistic	tobogganing
suppression	widowerhood	sacrificial	crossgarnet	nitrogenise	tobogganist
suppressive	windlestraw	satisfiable	crucigerous	nitrogenous	triangulate
synthesiser	wirenetting	scruffiness	deflagrator	nittygritty	tritagonist
synthetical	acidifiable	septiferous	dentigerous	objurgation	tryingplane
talebearing	AngloFrench	septifragal	deoxygenate	objurgatory	uncongenial
tapemeasure	bacciferous	sheepfarmer	derangement	octingenary	underground
taxidermist	blackfellow	sheriffalty	dialogistic	orthography	undergrowth
teachership	calciferous	sheriffship	diamagnetic	osteography	undisguised
tegumentary	calcifugous	signifiable	dichogamous	Ostrogothic	unfeignedly
tenementary	cauliflower	significant	diningtable	outfighting	unforgiving
tentpegging	certifiable	somniferous	discography	pelargonium	uranography
thenceforth	certifiably	spaceflight	disorganise	pentagynous	variegation
theocentric	certificate	specifiable	dittography	petrography	vertiginous
theorematic	closefisted	specificity	divergently	phonography	vestigially
theoretical	corniferous	spiniferous	divulgation	photography	vinaigrette
thitherward	crestfallen	splayfooted	divulgement	phylogynist	vortiginous
thunderbird	cruciferous	steadfastly	dyslogistic	phytography	zincography
thunderbolt	crucifixion	superfamily	effulgently	pictography	adiaphorism
thunderclap	cupriferous	superficial	elbowgrease	pornography	amorphously
thunderhead	disaffected	superficies	engorgement	prerogative	anarchistic
thunderless	disafforest	superfluity	enlargeable	primigenial	antechamber
thunderpeal	disinfector	superfluous	enlargement	prodigalise	antiphonary
timeserving	enfeoffment	swiftfooted	ensanguined	prodigality	antiphrasis
toffeenosed	faultfinder	thuriferous	erotogenous	prolegomena	autochthony
togglejoint	ferriferous	tightfisted	ethnography	propagation	benightedly
topdressing	firstfruits	toploftical	expurgation	propagative	benightment
tracheotomy	flagofficer	transferred	expurgatory	prorogation	bicephalous
trammelling	floriferous	transferrer	farraginous	protagonist	blasphemous
transection	fortifiable	transfigure	ferruginous	pruriginous	blotchiness
triggerfish	frankfurter	transfinite	filmography	pyrargyrite	bookshelves
triquetrous	gemmiferous	transfixion	foreignness	Pythagorean	branchiopod
tritheistic	gillyflower	transformer	fustigation	Pythagorism	breathalyse
trouserless	globeflower	transfusion	geomagnetic	radiography	breechblock
trousersuit	grandfather	tuttifrutti	gettogether	realignment	bushwhacker
truehearted	gypsiferous	vitrifiable	globigerina	refrigerant	cacophonous
trusteeship	heavyfooted	aboveground	greengrocer	refrigerate	cardsharper
tumbledrier	housefather	abridgement	haemoglobin	regurgitate	catachreses
turtleshell	illaffected	adjudgement	Hagiographa	reprogramme	catachresis
twelvemonth	imperfectly	aggregately	hagiography	reprography	catechismal

catechistic
catswhisker
churchgoing
churchiness
churchwoman
clearheaded
cliffhanger
closehauled
crotcheteer
crunchiness
cryotherapy
deemphasise
delightedly
delightsome
diarthrosis
dicephalous
diphtherial
diphtheroid
diphthongal
draughtsman
drouthiness
emptyhanded
emptyheaded
enarthrosis
endophagous
endothelial
endothelium
endothermal
endothermic
enlightened
enneahedron
exanthemata
faithhealer
fetichistic
fetishistic
foreshorten
forethinker
forethought
fourwheeler
freethinker
freethought
frenchified
Frenchwoman
frothhopper
grasshopper
grouchiness
halophilous
healthfully
healthiness
hearthstone
heavyhanded
hebephrenia
hebephrenic
hedgehopped
holothurian
homophonous
homothallic
householder
hydraheaded
hypophyseal
hypophysial
hypothecate
hypothenuse
hypothermia
hypothesise
icosahedral
icosahedron
IndoChinese
ingathering
ithyphallic
leaseholder
lengthiness
levelheaded
lighthanded
lightheaded
Manichaeism
masochistic
megatherium
meliphagous
metachrosis
metaphysics
monochasial
monochasium
monochromat
monochromic
monophagous
monophthong
Monophysite
Monothelite
muskthistle
mycophagist
naphthalene
ninnyhammer
nonetheless
octachordal
oenophilist
oesophageal
ornithology
ornithopter
ornithosaur
paperhanger
parachutist
paraphraser
parathyroid
parishioner
parochially
paunchiness
pentahedron
periphrases
periphrasis
perishables
perishingly
perithecium
phosphonium
phosphorate
phosphorism
phosphorite
phosphorous
pleochroism
ploughshare
ploughstaff
podophyllin
polychromic
polyphagous
polyphonous
preachiness
prosthetics
pullthrough
quitchgrass
raunchiness
ravishingly
rhynchodont
ricochetted
righthanded
righthander
saxophonist
scorchingly
ScotchIrish
Scotchwoman
searchingly
searchlight
shareholder
sheathknife
shockheaded
shorthanded
sidewheeler
sketchiness
slaughterer
slaveholder
sleuthhound
smallholder
smoothfaced
snatchblock
softshelled
somewhither
spaceheater
speechifier
splashboard
squashiness
stadtholder
stakeholder
stallholder
starchiness
stockholder
straphanger
superheater
swarthiness
swellheaded
switchblade
switchboard
sycophantic
sycophantry
telephonist
tetrahedral
tetrahedron
thickheaded
thoughtless
threehanded
timesharing
titleholder
toxophilite
transhumant
treacherous
trenchantly
trencherman
underhanded
unfashioned
unorthodoxy
unrighteous
uprightness
wealthiness
whiteheaded
windcheater
witchhunter
wolfwhistle
wrongheaded
xenophilous
xerophilous
xylophagous
xylophonist
zoantharian
Abbevillian
abdominally
abiotically
ablutionary
abortionist
abstriction
accipitrine
adjudicator
adminicular
adoptianism
adoptianist
adoptionism
adoptionist
aerobically
aerobiology
afficionado
affiliation
agnatically
agrarianism
agrobiology
albuminuria
alembicated
algorithmic
alkalimeter
alkalimetry
alleviation
alleviative
alleviatory
altorilievo
ambitiously
amontillado
angelically
AngloIndian
annihilator
anteriority
anticipator
antivitamin
Apollinaris
appogiatura
aquatically
archaically
archdiocese
Arminianism
armtwisting
arterialise
ascetically
aseptically
assimilable
assimilator
association
associative
Assyriology
atrabilious
atrociously
audaciously
babysitting
beautifully
bedevilment
behavioural
bellringing
Benedictine
benediction
benedictory
beneficence
beneficiary
beneficiate
bohemianism
bookbinding
botanically
bountifully
brachiation
Brahminical
brilliantly
bucolically
bullfighter
bumptiously
Byronically
calorimeter
calorimetry
canalicular
canaliculus
canonically
capaciously
capacitance
captainship
carabiniere
carabinieri
Carolingian
caustically
cavalierism
centrifugal
centripetal
chanticleer
chaotically
chinoiserie
chrominance
chronically
civilianise
civilisable
classically
codicillary
coefficient
coincidence
colonialism
colonialist
colorimeter
colorimetry
compliantly
complicated
comprisable
conceitedly
conceivable
conceivably
confliction
conflictive
connoisseur
consciously
conspicuity
conspicuous
conspirator
constituent
constitutor
containable
containment
contributor
contrivable
contrivance
coordinator
corecipient
creationism
creationist
cryobiology
cryptically
curtailment
cytokinesis
deactivator
deficiently
definiendum
defoliation
deistically
deliciously
deliriously
dendritical
denominator
dereliction
desalinator
describable
description
descriptive
despoilment
deteriorate
detrainment
diacritical
digitigrade
dilapidated
dilapidator
diluvialist
disguisedly
disquieting
disquietude
distribuend
distributor
disunionist
divisionary
divisionism
doctrinaire
doctrinally
domiciliary
domiciliate
drastically
dynamically
ebulliently
efficiently
egregiously
elastically
elasticated
electioneer
elutriation
emancipator
embroiderer
embroilment
empirically
emulsionise
enchainment
encomiastic
endemically
entrainment
enunciation
enunciative
equidistant
equilibrate
equilibrist
equilibrium
Erastianism
erratically
eugenically
excoriation
exercisable
exfoliation
exfoliative
exorbitance
expatiation
expatiative
expatiatory
expediently
expeditious
experienced
explainable
exploitable
exteriorise
exteriority
facelifting
facetiously
factfinding
familiarise
familiarity
fanatically
farthingale
feloniously
ferociously
fimbriation
firefighter
flaccidness
foraminated
foraminifer
foresighted
forfeitable
fortnightly
fractionary
fractionate
fractionise
fractiously
frantically
franticness
fratricidal
functionary
functionate
geanticline
generically
genetically
genitivally
godchildren
golddigging
grandiflora
grandiosely
grandiosity
graphically
graphicness
habiliments
halfbinding
hardhitting
harpsichord
Hebraically
Hegelianism
hereditable
heresiology
heretically
highpitched
hilariously
histrionics
histrionism
humiliation
humiliatory
hypolimnion
identically
idiotically
idyllically
ignominious
illimitable
illimitably
illogically
illuminable
illuminance

illuminator
illusionism
illusionist
immediately
immedicable
immitigable
immitigably
impatiently
impedimenta
impenitence
impenitency
imperialise
imperialism
imperialist
imperilling
imperilment
imperiously
impolitical
impoliticly
inadvisable
incipiently
incuriosity
incuriously
indeciduous
indefinable
indefinably
indehiscent
individuate
indivisible
indivisibly
indomitable
indomitably
indubitable
indubitably
inebriation
inefficient
inequitable
inequitably
inestimable
inestimably
inferiority
infinitival
ingeniously
ingrainedly
inhabitable
inhabitancy
inheritable
inheritance
inheritress
injudicious
injuriously
innavigable
innoxiously
inofficious
inscribable
inscription
inscriptive
inseminator
insidiously
insipidness
interiorise
interiority
intimidator
invalidness
invidiously
invigilator
irradiation
irradiative
irreligious
irremissive
Jacobinical
Jacobitical
jauntingcar
judiciously
juridically
kinesiology
kwashiorkor
laboriously
laciniation
laconically
lamplighter
languidness
lateritious
laughinggas
Leibnitzian
lilylivered
linefishing
linguistics
litigiously
lixiviation
loculicidal
logarithmic
longsighted
lowspirited
luxuriantly
luxuriation
luxuriously
magazinegun
malariology
malediction
maledictory
maleficence
maliciously
manumission
manumitting
marchioness
marquisette
mastoiditis
materialise
materialism
materialist
materiality
medicinable
medicinally
melodiously
memorialise
memorialist
Merovingian
mimetically
mischievous
misericorde
misguidance
misguidedly
mithridatic
mitrailleur
monolingual
monseigneur
moonlighter
moronically
mudslinging
municipally
munificence
nearsighted
nefariously
negationist
negotiation
negotiatory
negotiatrix
nightingale
nomadically
nonexistent
nonunionist
notoriously
numerically
obliviously
obnoxiously
occipitally
officialdom
officialese
officialism
officiation
officinally
officiously
oilpainting
opencircuit
ophidiarium
organically
organisable
osmotically
outbuilding
overbidding
pacifically
pacificator
painkilling
paradisical
parasitical
parasitosis
peculiarity
pecuniarily
Pelagianism
penicillate
penicillium
penuriously
perceivable
perceivably
perspicuity
perspicuous
petitionary
Pickwickian
pigsticking
piratically
plantigrade
plasticiser
plebeianise
plebeianism
plentifully
pointillism
pointillist
polarimeter
polarimetry
polarisable
polariscope
polemically
politically
politicking
practicable
practicably
practically
preeminence
preexistent
presciently
prestigious
prestissimo
principally
proprietary
prosaically
prosaicness
prostitutor
Prussianise
Prussianism
psychiatric
psychically
punchinello
punctilious
purificator
pyramidally
pyramidical
quadrillion
questionary
quintillion
quizzically
rapaciously
reactionary
reactionist
reclaimable
recruitment
relationism
relationist
religionise
religionism
religionist
religiosity
religiously
reminiscent
repetitious
repudiation
resiliently
resipiscent
restriction
restrictive
retaliation
retaliative
retaliatory
revisionary
revisionism
revisionist
reviviscent
rifacimenti
rifacimento
sagaciously
salaciously
sanguinaria
sanguineous
satanically
satirically
scaleinsect
sceptically
scholiastic
scintillant
scintillate
scorpionfly
scrutiniser
scyphistoma
seditionary
seditiously
seigniorage
seigniorial
seismically
selaginella
selfdisplay
selflimited
selfpitying
selfwinding
semasiology
semidiurnal
shoplifting
sigmoidally
simpliciter
sleepingbag
sleepingcar
Socinianism
solutionist
somatically
soteriology
soupkitchen
spastically
spermicidal
spherically
squalidness
stellionate
stencilling
stickinsect
stockinette
Stradivarii
stramineous
subaxillary
subclinical
subcritical
substituent
superimpose
superinduce
superintend
superioress
superiority
suppliantly
surveillant
sustainable
sustainment
sybaritical
technically
telekinesis
telekinetic
tenaciously
tetanically
thermically
thermionics
thyroiditis
titanically
totalisator
tourbillion
trafficator
trafficking
trafficless
transiently
transilient
Trappistine
trelliswork
triadically
trichinosis
triphibious
tristichous
ulotrichous
unadvisedly
unambiguous
unavailable
unavoidable
unavoidably
unbelieving
unchristian
uncivilised
undesirable
undutifully
unequivocal
uninhibited
unlimitedly
unmitigated
unpolitical
unremitting
unshrinking
unsolicited
vacationist
vagariously
valediction
valedictory
vaporimeter
vaporisable
vasodilator
vaticinator
venatically
ventricular
ventriculus
ventriloquy
veraciously
veridically
verisimilar
vesuvianite
vexatiously
vicariously
vivaciously
volitionary
voraciously
wellwishing
Westminster
whimsically
worshipable
worshipless
worshipping
interjacent
maladjusted
shelljacket
stockjobber
superjacent
debarkation
demarkation
dislikeable
embarkation
endoskelton
greenkeeper
housekeeper
imparkation
provokingly
reawakening
sandskipper
semiskilled
shrinkingly
shrinkproof
squeakiness
storekeeper
streakiness
thinskinned
unwinkingly
acatalectic
acetylation
acidulation
acriflavine
Aeneolithic
Aesculapian
aiguillette
amiableness
anacoluthon
animalcular
anomalistic
anomalously
anthologise
anthologist
apocalyptic
apostleship
appallingly
appealingly
appellation
appellative
artillerist
audibleness
audiologist
autoplastic
bacilliform
bandylegged
barrelhouse
barrelorgan
batholithic
beastliness
beguilement
beguilingly
bimillenary
bimillenium
blamelessly
bloodlessly
bombilation
brainlessly
bricklaying
bristletail
bristleworm
bristliness
brittleness
broadleaved
brucellosis
buffalorobe
cabbalistic
calculating
calculation
calculative
cancellated
candelabrum
capableness
capillarity
carvelbuilt
castellated
cataclysmic
cataplectic
catholicise
Catholicism
catholicity
ceaselessly
cellularity
ceroplastic
chainletter
chameleonic
cheerleader
cheerlessly
chevalglass
chucklehead
circularise
circularity
circulation

circulative	exemplarity	legislative	pestologist	spindlelegs	vacuolation
circulatory	faithlessly	legislature	petrologist	spindletree	vascularise
cisatlantic	faultlessly	limitlessly	phenologist	spinelessly	vascularity
cityslicker	feudalistic	limnologist	philologian	sporulation	vasculiform
cleanlimbed	flagellator	loathliness	philologist	stagflation	ventilation
cleanliness	flatulently	longplaying	phonologist	stainlessly	ventilative
coagulation	fleshliness	looselimbed	phycologist	startlingly	verbalistic
cockaleekie	flimflammer	lovableness	phytologist	stateliness	vexillology
cockyleekie	florilegium	magdalenian	pipecleaner	steeplebush	visibleness
coldblooded	footslogger	mammalogist	pliableness	steeplejack	voicelessly
compellable	foreclosure	mandolinist	pluralistic	stickleback	volkslieder
compilation	formalistic	mantelpiece	pointlessly	stimulation	volubleness
compilement	formularise	mantelshelf	polyglottal	stimulative	warmblooded
conciliator	formulation	masculinely	polyglottic	stipulation	waterlogged
condolatory	fourflusher	masculinise	postclassic	stipulatory	wearilessly
condylomata	franklinite	masculinity	postglacial	stumblingly	whiffletree
congelation	friableness	matchlessly	postulation	subcultural	whippletree
consolation	frivolously	matrilineal	powerlessly	submultiple	whistlestop
consolatory	fruitlessly	matrilinear	prattlingly	succulently	womanliness
consolidate	fullblooded	maxillipede	preselector	superlative	worldliness
consolingly	fullfledged	mendelevium	prevalently	superlunary	worldlywise
consultancy	fusillation	mercilessly	prickliness	swimbladder	worthlessly
convolution	gallbladder	meroblastic	promulgator	swingletree	Yugoslavian
convolvulus	garrulously	mesalliance	proselytise	symbolistic	abnormality
coralloidal	gemmologist	mesoblastic	proselytism	tantalising	academicals
corpulently	gemmulation	metalloidal	pullulation	tastelessly	academician
correlation	genealogise	metallurgic	pupillarity	tautologise	academicism
correlative	genealogist	metaplastic	pureblooded	tautologism	acclamation
cosmologist	gentilitial	methylamine	pustulation	tautologous	acclamatory
countlessly	genuflexion	methylation	pyroclastic	teleologism	acclimation
courtliness	geopolitics	microlithic	queenliness	teleologist	acclimatise
credulously	ghastliness	mindblowing	querulously	tenableness	accommodate
crenellated	ghostliness	mirthlessly	radiolarian	tessellated	achromatise
crenulation	globularity	misalliance	radiologist	thanklessly	achromatism
crosslegged	gonfalonier	miscellanea	rectilineal	thimbleweed	adenomatous
cupellation	gracelessly	miserliness	rectilinear	thistledown	affirmation
curableness	gracileness	moneylender	reduplicate	threelegged	affirmative
curvilineal	granolithic	monoclinous	repellantly	thrillingly	affirmatory
curvilinear	granularity	movableness	repellently	tightlipped	agglomerate
dactylogram	granulation	multilinear	rhinologist	timepleaser	amphimictic
dactylology	granulocyte	muscularity	ritualistic	titillation	anemometric
dauntlessly	gratulation	musculation	roughlegged	tonsillitis	anglomaniac
decollation	gratulatory	musculature	sacculation	tracelessly	anonymously
decolletage	gravelblind	mutableness	saintliness	translation	apartmental
diadelphous	gristliness	mythologise	salesladies	translocate	Archimedean
disablement	grumblingly	mythologist	schoolboard	translucent	astigmatism
disbeliever	guilelessly	narcoleptic	schoolchild	translunary	audiometric
discalceate	guiltlessly	necrologist	schoolhouse	treacliness	awesomeness
disillusion	hagiologist	nephelinite	scopolamine	tremblement	bathymetric
disobliging	halfblooded	nervelessly	scuttlebutt	tremblingly	beechmarten
dissolutely	heartlessly	neurologist	selfclosing	tremulously	bergamasque
dissolution	Heracleidan	nickelplate	selfelected	trestletree	blackmailer
dissolvable	histologist	noctilucent	semiellipse	trestlework	blackmarket
dissyllable	holoblastic	noiselessly	senselessly	tribulation	broadminded
doubtlessly	homoplastic	nondelivery	serrulation	tricoloured	burgomaster
draggletail	houselights	nonvolatile	sertularian	trisyllabic	chaulmoogra
dreamlessly	hydrologist	notableness	shacklebolt	trisyllable	childminder
durableness	hypoblastic	ophiologist	shacklebone	troublesome	choirmaster
earthliness	hypoglossal	oracularity	shamelessly	troublously	circumlunar
ectoblastic	ignobleness	orderliness	shapeliness	truculently	circumpolar
ectoplasmic	inoculation	oscillation	shiftlessly	trundletail	circumsolar
ejaculation	inoculative	oscillatory	shovelboard	tunableness	circumspect
ejaculatory	inquilinous	oscillogram	shuttlecock	turbulently	circumvolve
elderliness	installment	osteologist	sideslipped	unexploited	clinometric
embellisher	instillment	pamphleteer	sightlessly	unfailingly	collimation
endoplasmic	intagliated	panhellenic	sightliness	unfeelingly	commemorate
ennoblement	intelligent	pantalettes	singularise	ungodliness	concomitant
entablature	interleaves	parallactic	singularity	unhealthily	condemnable
entablement	interlinear	parallelism	sizableness	unicellular	condominium
entitlement	Interlingua	parallelled	sleeplessly	unicoloured	consumerism
equableness	interlining	paraplectic	smilelessly	unipolarity	consumingly
esemplastic	interlocker	parheliacal	socialistic	unmanliness	consummator
establisher	interlunary	patelliform	sociologist	unqualified	consumption
ethnologist	inviolately	pathologist	solifluxion	unrealistic	consumptive
etymologise	itacolumite	patrilineal	somnolently	unskilfully	contaminant
etymologist	knucklebone	pendulously	soundlessly	unsmilingly	contaminate
euchologion	lamellicorn	perchlorate	speculation	unwholesome	contemplate
excellently	lamelliform	percolation	speculative	unwillingly	coterminous
exemplarily	legislation	pestilently	spifflicate	vacillation	coulometric

coxcombical
customarily
custombuilt
customhouse
declamation
declamatory
deformation
determinacy
determinant
determinate
determinism
determinist
detrimental
diplomatise
diplomatist
dipsomaniac
disarmament
disarmingly
disremember
disseminate
disseminule
dissimilate
dissimulate
dissymmetry
distempered
dressmaking
drillmaster
econometric
emblematise
emblematist
epochmaking
erotomaniac
eudaemonism
eudaemonist
eudiometric
euphemistic
exclamation
exclamatory
excremental
exterminate
extremeness
facsimilist
firmamental
fulsomeness
fundamental
gallimaufry
gardemanger
gerrymander
glassmaking
goniometric
grandmother
gravimetric
heliometric
heptamerous
honeymooner
housemaster
housemother
hydromedusa
hydrometeor
hydrometric
hygrometric
hypermarket
hypermetric
hypsometric
illhumoured
illtempered
impermanent
impermeable
impermeably
implemental
inanimately
inanimation
inclemently
incommodity
incremental
incriminate
infirmarian
inflammable
inflammably
informality
information
informative
informatory
intermeddle
intermedium
intermingle
intermitted
intromitted
intromitter
irksomeness
jerrymander
lacrimation
lacrimatory
lacrimosely
lacrymation
lacrymatory
lacrymosely
largeminded
lightminded
lissomeness
Maglemosian
marshmallow
matchmaking
mathematics
matrimonial
mediumistic
merrymaking
micrometric
misremember
moneymaking
moneymarket
myelomatous
mythomaniac
necromancer
necromantic
nightmarish
noisemaking
noisomeness
numismatics
numismatist
nutrimental
oldwomanish
oligomerous
pandemonium
panicmonger
pantomimist
papermaking
patrimonial
peacemaking
pentamerous
pessimistic
photometric
planimetric
Precambrian
predominant
predominate
preliminary
prenominate
presumingly
presumption
presumptive
protomartyr
proximately
radiometric
reachmedown
reanimation
reclamation
recommender
recommittal
recriminate
reformation
reformative
reformatory
rhizomatous
rightminded
sacramental
saltimbanco
sarcomatous
scaremonger
schismatise
scoutmaster
screamingly
selfimposed
sentimental
Septembrist
sheepmaster
sillimanite
slavemarket
smallminded
soberminded
sociometric
somnambular
sphygmogram
spirometric
squeamishly
stagemanage
stockmarket
stonemarten
subdominant
sublimation
sublimeness
subsumption
subsumptive
suffumigate
supermarket
supremacist
supremeness
systematics
systematise
systematism
systematist
tautomerism
testimonial
tetramerous
threemaster
toastmaster
toughminded
transmarine
transmittal
transmitted
transmitter
ultramarine
ultramodern
unanimously
unclimbable
uncommitted
undermanned
unpromising
voltametric
watchmaking
welcomeness
whoremaster
whoremonger
winsomeness
wreckmaster
abomination
abstentious
abstinently
accountable
accountably
accountancy
acumination
acupuncture
affranchise
alcyonarian
Alexandrian
alexandrine
alexandrite
alternately
alternation
alternative
amaranthine
amazonstone
ancientness
AngloNorman
appointment
archangelic
assignation
astringency
augmentable
Aurignacian
bathingsuit
benignantly
bombination
bonbonniere
bookinghall
boutonniere
boysenberry
brazenfaced
calcination
calumniator
Calvinistic
campanology
campanulate
carbonation
carbuncular
carcinomata
cardinalate
carminative
cavernously
centenarian
chafingdish
Clarencieux
coadunation
cochinchina
collenchyma
collinearly
columniated
combination
combinative
combinatory
commandment
commendable
commendably
commendator
commensally
commentator
commination
comminatory
comminution
commonality
commonplace
commonsense
communalise
communalism
communalist
communicant
communicate
communistic
compendious
compensator
compunction
concentrate
condensable
condonation
confinement
congenerous
congenially
conjunction
conjunctiva
conjunctive
conjuncture
consanguine
consentient
consonantal
consonantly
contentedly
contentious
contentment
continental
continently
contingence
contingency
continuable
continually
continuance
continuator
convenances
convenience
conveniency
conventicle
convincible
coplanarity
cosignatory
cottongrass
cottonmouth
credentials
criminalist
criminality
crimination
criminative
criminatory
criminology
culmination
cunningness
cupronickel
currentness
cybernation
cybernetics
decennially
declination
demagnetise
demountable
descendable
descendible
designation
despondence
despondency
destination
diamondback
disannulled
disbandment
discontinue
disfunction
dishonestly
dishonourer
disjunction
disjunctive
disjuncture
dispensable
dissentient
dissonantly
distensible
distinction
distinctive
distinguish
doorknocker
drawingroom
dreadnought
dysfunction
ecumenicism
ecumenicity
elementally
elimination
eliminative
enchantment
enchantress
enfranchise
equiangular
evagination
eveningstar
evidentiary
examination
exogenously
explanation
explanatory
externalise
externalism
externality
fascinating
fascination
feelingness
fermentable
festinately
fortunately
fricandeaux
fulminating
fulmination
fulminatory
gallantness
genuineness
geosyncline
Germanophil
germination
germinative
glaringness
glutinously
goldenberry
gormandiser
grandnephew
greatnephew
handknitted
harmonistic
heavenwards
heldentenor
Hellenistic
helminthoid
hemianopsia
hereinafter
hermeneutic
herringbone
herringgull
hibernacula
hibernation
Hibernicism
Hispanicise
Hispanicism
Hispanicist
hollandaise
hummingbird
husbandlike
hyacinthine
hyphenation
illmannered
imaginarily
imagination
imaginative
impoundment
incarnadine
incarnation
inclination
incognisant
indignantly
indignation
infrangible
instinctive
instinctual
internalise
internality
internecine
internuncio
Jansenistic
jargonistic
jumpingbean
jumpingjack
knowingness
lancinating
lancination
landingbeam
landinggear
larcenously
lastingness
legionnaire
lichenology
longanimity
machination
machinemade
maddeningly
magnanimity
magnanimous
maisonnette
malfunction
malignantly
marconigram

marginalise
marginality
marlinspike
meaningless
mechanician
mechanistic
mercenarily
Micronesian
millenarian
misconceive
misconstrue
mockingbird
modernistic
mooringmast
morningroom
multangular
multinomial
mundaneness
muttonchops
nationalise
nationalism
nationalist
nationality
nationstate
nonsensical
nothingness
notionalist
obstinately
offhandedly
oppugnation
originality
origination
originative
overanxious
overindulge
oxygenation
packingcase
paternalism
paternalist
paternoster
patronising
pectination
pentandrous
perennation
perennially
perfunctory
permanently
personalise
personalism
personalist
personality
personation
personative
personifier
pertinacity
pertinently
phalanstery
pharyngitis
philanderer
pigeonchest
platinotype
playingcard
poisonously
pollination
polyandrous
polyonymous
precentress
preconceive
precontract
preignition
premonition
premonitory
presanctify
presentable
presentably
presentient
presentment
pretendedly
pretentious
preventable
preventible
proconsular
profanation
profanatory
profaneness
progenitrix
progeniture
prominently
propinquity
prosenchyma
protonotary
provenience
rallentando
rationalise
rationalism
rationalist
rationality
recognition
recognitive
recognitory
reconnoitre
rectangular
refrangible
refringency
regionalise
regionalism
regionalist
replenisher
repugnantly
resignation
respondence
respondency
responsible
responsibly
retranslate
rhizanthous
ribbongrass
rottenstone
salmonberry
salpingitis
saturnalian
saturninely
segmentally
selfinduced
selfinvited
sententious
sentinelled
septenarius
septentrion
shamanistic
sickeningly
sinfonietta
sittingroom
skatingrink
Slavonicise
smokingroom
sparingness
sphagnology
steganogram
stevengraph
stiffnecked
stipendiary
studentship
subcontract
subcontrary
subjunctive
subornation
suckingfish
supernatant
supernormal
suspenseful
suspensible
tabernacled
tautonymous
teknonymous
tendencious
tendentious
termination
terminative
terminology
Teutonicism
Titianesque
trepanation
tribuneship
tribunicial
tribunitial
triennially
trypanosome
turbination
tyrannicide
tyrannosaur
tyrannously
unbeknownst
unboundedly
uncanniness
unconnected
uncountable
unflinching
unfurnished
unigeniture
unkennelled
unmeaningly
unprintable
unsoundness
unthinkable
unthinkably
unvarnished
vaccination
valiantness
verdantique
vermination
verminously
violoncello
volcanicity
volcanology
vulcanicity
vulcanology
waitinglist
waitingroom
wappenschaw
warrantable
warrantably
willingness
winningness
winningpost
abandonment
abiological
acrimonious
actinometer
actinomyces
actinomycin
aerological
aeronomical
agrological
agronomical
ahistorical
ailurophile
ailurophobe
algological
allegorical
allelomorph
allomorphic
ameliorator
anagnorisis
anastomoses
anastomosis
anastomotic
anecdotical
anthropical
antifouling
antimonious
antonomasia
aposiopesis
apostolical
aristocracy
arthrospore
assafoetida
auxanometer
axiological
backcountry
bellbottoms
bellfounder
benevolence
bibliolater
bibliolatry
bibliomancy
bibliomania
bibliopegic
bibliophile
bibliophily
bibliopolic
bibliotheca
billionaire
billposting
blastogenic
bryozoology
calceolaria
californium
captionless
cardiograph
categorical
ceremonious
chaetognath
chansonnier
cheiromancy
chiaroscuro
chlorophyll
chloroplast
chloroprene
choreograph
chromoplast
chromosomal
chronograph
chronologer
chronologic
chronometer
chronometry
chronoscope
chrysoberyl
chrysoprase
clodhopping
complotting
comstockery
controlling
controlment
controversy
coronograph
craniometry
cryptogamic
cryptograph
cryptomeria
curatorship
cytological
decolourise
demagogical
demagoguery
demagoguism
demigoddess
demonolatry
developable
development
diagnostics
diaphoresis
diaphoretic
dichromatic
dropforging
dualcontrol
dumbfounder
dynamometer
dynamometry
echosounder
ectomorphic
elastomeric
embryologic
embryonated
emotionally
emotionless
emperorship
endomorphic
enterostomy
enterovirus
entomophily
envelopment
environment
epeirogenic
episcopally
equinoctial
equipollent
equivocally
equivocator
ergatocracy
ethological
factionally
fashionable
fashionably
fissionable
flamboyance
flamboyancy
flamboyante
fluoroscope
fluoroscopy
footpoundal
footsoldier
foretopmast
foretopsail
foulmouthed
fourpounder
Francomania
Francophile
Francophobe
francophone
freebooting
fullmouthed
gafftopsail
gametophyte
gastronomic
gastroscope
glauconitic
glossolalia
goodlooking
gradiometer
GraecoRoman
greenockite
gyrocompass
halfholiday
hardmouthed
hardworking
headborough
hemimorphic
heroworship
heteroclite
heteroecism
heterograft
heterophony
heteroploid
heteropolar
heterospory
heterotaxis
heterotroph
heterotypic
highpowered
Hindoostani
homoeopathy
homoiousian
homological
homomorphic
horological
hylozoistic
hymenoptera
ideological
idiomorphic
immunologic
inopportune
interosseus
invigorator
ironmongery
irremovable
irremovably
irresoluble
irrevocable
irrevocably
isogeotherm
kinetograph
kinetoscope
kleptomania
knownothing
landholding
landlordism
lepidoptera
loudmouthed
maintopmast
maintopsail
malevolence
medicolegal
megalomania
megalopolis
melanochroi
melanophore
mentholated
mentionable
meritocracy
meritorious
mesomorphic
metamorphic
metasomatic
metoposcopy
millionaire
monitorship
monological
monologuise
monologuist
monomorphic
monopoliser
mycological
naturopathy
Neotropical
nomological
nonviolence
nosological
nympholepsy
nymphomania
octagonally
oecological
oenological
oestrogenic
ommatophore
omnipotence
oncological
oneiromancy
ontological
openmouthed
opinionated
orangoutang
oreological
outcropping
outspokenly
overtopping
palaeotypic
Panglossian
paradoxical
paramoecium
paramorphic
paramountcy
paramountly
paronomasia
Passiontide
pedagogical
pedological
penological
pensionable
pensionless
peritonitis
photooffset
phylloclade

phyllotaxis
physiocracy
physiognomy
physiologic
plagioclase
plagiostome
plasmolysis
plasmolytic
platforming
plectoptera
pleomorphic
pleurodynia
pluviometer
pneumonitis
poltroonery
polygonally
polymorphic
polyzoarium
pomological
portionless
posological
praetorship
proctorship
proteolysis
proteolytic
prothoracic
pseudograph
pseudomonas
pseudomorph
pseudopodia
psychodrama
psychogenic
psychograph
psychologic
psychometry
psychomotor
psychopathy
ratatouille
realpolitik
reapportion
renegotiate
retinoscopy
rhabdomancy
rhapsodical
rheological
rhombohedra
rhomboideus
roadholding
rodomontade
safeconduct
salinometer
scaffolding
scissorbill
scissortail
scleroderma
sclerometer
sclerophyll
sclerotitis
sectionally
seismograph
seismometer
seismometry
seismoscope
selfcocking
selfcommand
selfconceit
selfcontent
selfcontrol
selfloading
selflocking
selftorture
selfworship
semeiotical
semimonthly
senatorship
serological
sexological
shallowness
sinological
snowgoggles
soapboiling
sockdolager
sockdologen
soliloquise
soliloquist
somatogenic
somatologic
somatoplasm
somatotonia
somatotonic
sparrowbill
sparrowhawk
spasmodical
speedometer
spherometer
sponsorship
stampoffice
standoffish
staurolitic
steatopygia
stereograph
stereometry
stereophony
stereoscope
stereoscopy
stereotyped
stereotyper
stereotypic
stethoscope
stethoscopy
stichometry
stratocracy
stroboscope
subtropical
surfboarder
surgeonfish
swallowable
swallowdive
swallowhole
swallowtail
swallowwort
symphonious
symptomatic
synagogical
tacheometer
taxonomical
teaspoonful
technocracy
technologic
tephromancy
teratogenic
teratologic
theodolitic
theological
theosophist
thermoduric
thermograph
thermolysis
thermolytic
thermometer
thermometry
thermophile
thermoscope
thermotaxis
thrasonical
topological
toxicomania
treasonable
treasonably
trichomonad
troglodytic
trophoblast
tryptophane
typefounder
typefoundry
typological
unaccounted
uncanonical
unimportant
unmemorable
unmemorably
urochordate
vagabondage
vagabondise
vagabondish
vagabondism
viceroyalty
viceroyship
virological
volumometer
voodooistic
wellfounded
wellrounded
wildfowling
xanthochroi
xanthophyll
zygomorphic
absorptance
accompanist
acidophilic
agoraphobia
agoraphobic
anadiplosis
anglophobia
anglophobic
appropriate
archipelago
atmospheric
attemptable
bicorporate
bicuspidate
caryopsides
catchphrase
caterpillar
chiropodist
chiropteran
collapsible
comeuppance
conceptacle
corruptible
corruptibly
corruptness
cosmopolite
cotemporary
ctenophoran
cyclopaedia
cyclopaedic
cypripedium
decrepitate
decrepitude
depauperate
depauperise
diapophysis
disapproval
disciplinal
discipliner
dissepiment
dissipation
dissipative
enterpriser
epinephrine
exculpation
exculpatory
expropriate
exstipulate
extemporary
extemporise
extirpation
extirpatory
extrapolate
feldspathic
fissiparity
fissiparous
frankpledge
Gallophobia
gemmiparous
giantpowder
gramophonic
grandparent
granophyric
guttapercha
haemophilia
haemophilic
haemoptysis
hedgepriest
hemispheric
hippopotami
homeopathic
homosporous
horripilate
hydropathic
hydrophilic
hydrophobia
hydrophobic
hydrophytic
hydroponics
hygrophytic
hyperphagia
hyperplasia
hypnopaedia
hypnopompic
hypsophobia
impropriate
impropriety
inadaptable
incompetent
incompliant
incorporate
incorporeal
inculpation
inculpatory
intemperate
interplayed
interpolate
interpreter
intrepidity
ionospheric
lickspittle
lithophytic
loudspeaker
madreporite
microphonic
microphytic
multiparous
mythopoeist
mythopoetic
necrophilia
necrophilic
necropoleis
negrophobia
neuropathic
nightporter
noseyparker
nulliparity
nulliparous
nuncupation
nuncupative
nyctophobia
orthopaedic
orthopedics
orthopedist
orthopteran
osteopathic
osteophytic
osteoplasty
paedophilia
perceptible
perceptibly
percipience
perispermic
photoperiod
photophilic
photophobia
photophobic
plenipotent
preceptress
precipitant
precipitate
precipitous
primiparous
procephalic
protophytic
radiophonic
Russophobia
saintpaulia
saprophytic
sarcophagus
sauropodous
scrappiness
scrimpiness
scrumptious
selfopinion
Shaksperean
Shaksperian
sharepusher
sociopathic
songsparrow
sporophytic
standpatter
stoolpigeon
stylopodium
susceptible
susceptibly
syncopation
tetrapodous
therapeutic
toothpowder
townspeople
transpadane
transparent
transpierce
transponder
transporter
trothplight
underpinned
unflappable
unhappiness
unhelpfully
unstoppable
consequence
delinquency
ineloquence
infrequence
infrequency
nonsequitur
subsequence
terraqueous
abhorrently
acquirement
adjournment
adumbration
adumbrative
aerographer
amenorrhoea
anachronism
anachronous
antheridium
antigravity
antirrhinum
apomorphine
apostrophic
arbitrageur
arbitrament
arbitrarily
arbitration
arbitrative
arbitratrix
austereness
autoerotism
autographic
autotrophic
awestricken
awkwardness
bactericide
balmcricket
banteringly
barbarously
beaverboard
biedermeier
birdbrained
bitterapple
bittercress
bittersweet
boilermaker
bombardment
borborygmus
botheration
butterflies
butteriness
cacographic
calibration
carburetion
carburetted
carburetter
carburettor
catadromous
celebration
celebratory
cerebration
chaperonage
cicatricial
clamorously
clostridium
coeternally
coleorrhiza
colouration
colourblind
colourfully
comfortable
comfortably
comfortless
comparatist
comparative
compartment
comportment
comptroller
compurgator
concernment
concertedly
concertgoer
concordance
concurrence
conferrable
confirmable
conformable
conformably
conformally
conformance
conjuration
conservable
conservancy
conservator
constrictor
construable
constructor
conterminal
contorniate
convergence
convergency
conversable
conversance
conversancy
convertible
convertibly
cooperation
cooperative
copperplate
coppersmith
cornerstone
corporality
corporately
corporation
corporatism
corporative

corporeally
countrified
countryfied
countryseat
countryside
countrywide
cursoriness
dangerously
deathrattle
declaration
declarative
declaratory
defibrinate
defloration
dehydration
democratise
democratism
demographer
demographic
denigration
denigratory
deoxyribose
deploringly
desecration
desegregate
desperadoes
desperately
desperation
deuteration
deuterogamy
Deuteronomy
dexterously
diachronism
diastrophic
differentia
differently
dinnerdance
dinnertable
dinnerwagon
dipterocarp
discardable
discernible
discernibly
discernment
discerption
discordance
discordancy
disharmonic
disparaging
disparately
dispersedly
disportment
dissertator
disturbance
dithyrambic
downdraught
downtrodden
doxographer
easternmost
ectotrophic
editorially
elaborately
elaboration
elaborative
electrician
electricity
electrocute
electrolier
electrology
electrolyse
electrolyte
electronics
electrotype
enchiridion
endearingly
endotrophic
enquiringly
enumeration
enumerative
erythrocyte
esotericism
Eucharistic
evaporation
evaporative
exoneration
exonerative
exotericism
exploration
explorative
exploratory
exuberantly
falteringly
fanfaronade
favouritism
featureless
filterpaper
fingerboard
fingerglass
fingerplate
fingerprint
fingerstall
firecracker
floweriness
forlornness
forwardness
fraternally
fraterniser
frontrunner
frowardness
frustration
fulguration
gartersnake
gatecrasher
gendarmerie
geostrophic
gibberellin
gingerbread
glomeration
godforsaken
guttersnipe
gutturalise
gutturalism
haemorrhage
haemorrhoid
haggardness
hairbreadth
hairdresser
hairtrigger
halterbreak
handbreadth
handgrenade
handwriting
handwritten
handwrought
harebrained
heptarchist
hesperidium
hierarchism
highbrowism
highwrought
historiated
historicise
historicism
historicist
historicity
hitherwards
holographic
horseradish
Hudibrastic
ideographic
idiographic
immigration
impetration
impetratory
imploringly
incoercible
incorrectly
incorruptly
IndoIranian
innutrition
inoperative
inquiringly
inspiration
inspiratory
integrality
integration
integrative
interracial
interregnum
interrelate
interrogate
interrupter
interruptor
isochronism
isochronous
isomorphism
isomorphous
itinerantly
itineration
jabberwocky
Kulturkampf
kymographic
lammergeier
lammergeyer
landgrabber
landgravine
lawmerchant
leapfrogged
lecherously
lectureship
letterpress
lickerishly
linedrawing
lineprinter
lingeringly
litterateur
loggerheads
logographer
logographic
louverboard
loxodromics
lucubration
ludicrously
Lutheranism
mackerelsky
maladroitly
malapropism
mandarinate
manneristic
mansardroof
martyrology
massproduce
masterfully
masterpiece
measureless
measurement
melioration
meliorative
menservants
mensuration
mercurially
meteoritics
meteoroidal
meteorology
micturition
miscarriage
mismarriage
molecricket
monogrammed
monographer
monographic
monstrosity
monstrously
mortarboard
mosstrooper
mothercraft
mothernaked
motherright
multiracial
murderously
murmuration
murmurously
mycorrhizae
mycorrhizal
myocarditis
namedropper
nasofrontal
neckerchief
netherworld
nocturnally
nomographer
nomographic
nonpartisan
nosographer
nosographic
nurserymaid
obscuration
obscureness
obsecration
omnipresent
oreographic
outstripped
outwardness
overcropped
overproduce
overwritten
overwrought
oysterplant
paederastic
palsgravine
papiermache
paragrapher
paragraphic
paratrooper
parturition
passeriform
pastoralism
pastoralist
pastureland
patternshop
pawnbroking
penetrating
penetration
penetrative
peregrinate
perforation
perforative
performable
performance
pericranial
pericranium
perturbable
pervertedly
phthiriasis
pictorially
picturebook
picturecard
picturegoer
picturesque
plateresque
platyrrhine
playerpiano
poltergeist
polycrystal
polygraphic
pomegranate
ponderation
ponderosity
ponderously
porterhouse
positronium
posteriorly
potteringly
powderflask
prayerwheel
preparation
preparative
preparatory
preservable
prestressed
preterhuman
preterition
prevaricate
prochronism
procuration
procuratory
procurement
proofreader
proportions
prostration
Proterozoic
pulchritude
pulverulent
purportedly
quaternloaf
rancorously
rapturously
reappraisal
reciprocate
reciprocity
recurrently
reemergence
reintroduce
reiteration
reiterative
requirement
resourceful
respiration
respiratory
restoration
restorative
retrorocket
rheotropism
rhetorician
rockcrystal
Rosicrucian
rotogravure
rubberstamp
safebreaker
safecracker
Sanskritist
sartorially
savouriness
scalariform
scalpriform
schwarmerei
seborrhoeic
selfcreated
semitrailer
sensorially
serigrapher
shipbreaker
showerproof
sightreader
silveriness
silverplate
silverpoint
silversmith
silverstick
simperingly
sincereness
spectrality
spectrogram
spectrology
sphaeridium
starcrossed
steamroller
stepbrother
stewardship
subaerially
subarration
subcortical
submarginal
submergence
submersible
subservient
subterminal
summariness
summerhouse
summersault
supportable
supportably
suppuration
suppurative
suspiration
susurration
synchromesh
synchronise
synchronism
synchronous
synchrotron
syssarcosis
teeterboard
telegrammic
telegrapher
telegraphic
teleprinter
temperament
temperately
temperative
temperature
temporality
temporarily
tenterhooks
tetrarchate
textureless
theatregoer
theatricals
theobromine
topographer
topographic
torturously
totteringly
traversable
treecreeper
trimorphism
trimorphous
trituration
typewritten
typographer
typographic
unawareness
unexpressed
unguardedly
uniformness
unipersonal
universally
unobtrusive
unsparingly
unwarranted
vasopressin
vasopressor
venturesome
venturously
vespertinal
vinedresser
voortrekker
wapperjawed
washerwoman
waywardness
wellgroomed
wellordered
westernmost
widdershins
winegrowing
winterberry
wintergreen
wisecracker
witheringly
withershins
wonderfully
xylographer
xylographic
zoomorphism

abolishable
abolishment
aboutsledge
accessorial
accessorise
accrescence
acquisition
acquisitive
adolescence
adversative
adverseness
AfroAsiatic
agonisingly
agonistical
aimlessness
airlessness
alabastrine
amphisbaena
appeasement
artlessness
ascensional
aspersorium
assassinate
assessorial
atheistical
atomisation
BaltoSlavic
baptismally
barbastelle
bathyscaphe
bathysphere
bearishness
bewhiskered
bloodstream
bloodsucker
boardschool
Bodhisattva
bookishness
boorishness
brainsickly
Britishness
brutishness
bullishness
caddishness
candescence
caressingly
casuistical
chainsmoker
chainstitch
charismatic
cholesterol
clairschach
cleanshaven
coalescence
coconscious
coexistence
cognoscente
cognoscenti
cognoscible
collisional
collusively
combustible
commiserate
commissural
compassable
compositely
composition
compositive
compossible
conciseness
confessedly
confiscable
confiscator
confusingly
consistence
consistency
contestable
corpuscular
corrosively
craftswoman
crepuscular
crossstitch
currishness
cycloserine
decrescendo
decussately
decussation
defensively
demonstrate
depressible
desensitise
diapositive
diatessaron
diffuseness
diffusively
dimensional
disassemble
disassembly
discussable
discussible
disgustedly
disposition
dispositive
distasteful
doggishness
dollishness
doltishness
donnishness
earnestness
egotistical
ellipsoidal
encapsulate
encrustment
endlessness
endorsement
engrossment
entrustment
epigastrium
erubescence
evanescence
evanishment
excessively
exclusively
exclusivity
excrescence
excrescency
excursively
exhaustible
exhaustless
expansional
expansively
expansivity
expensively
explosively
expressible
exquisitely
extensional
extensively
faddishness
fantastical
florescence
foolishness
foppishness
furnishings
garnishment
gegenschein
girlishness
godlessness
grotesquely
grotesquery
gutlessness
gymnospermy
haemostasis
haemostatic
hagioscopic
haplessness
harumscarum
harvesthome
heartsblood
heartstring
hedgeschool
hellishness
hoggishness
homeostasis
homeostatic
homoestatic
honeysuckle
hurryscurry
hurryskurry
hydrosphere
hydrostatic
hygroscopic
hypersthene
iconostases
iconostasis
idolisation
illdisposed
immenseness
impassioned
impassively
impassivity
impersonate
impressible
impressment
impuissance
impulsively
incessantly
inclusively
inconscient
inconsonant
inconstancy
indorsement
inexistence
inquisition
inquisitive
insensately
insensitive
insessorial
intenseness
intensifier
intensional
intensively
interseptal
intersexual
intersperse
interspinal
intrusively
iridescence
joylessness
Judaisation
knavishness
lactescence
laicisation
Lancastrian
latchstring
laurustinus
lawlessness
leprosarium
lightsomely
liquescence
lithosphere
loathsomely
loosestrife
loutishness
lumpishness
macroscopic
malposition
mannishness
marcescence
marcescible
mawkishness
mediastinal
mediastinum
metapsychic
microscopic
microsecond
millisecond
minnesinger
moneyspider
morrisdance
multistorey
necessarian
necessarily
necessitate
necessitous
nigrescence
nondescript
nonresident
nourishment
obsessional
obsessively
obtrusively
offensively
opalescence
operoseness
orchestrate
organscreen
orthoscopic
ostensively
outdistance
oviposition
ozonisation
ozonosphere
patristical
peevishness
peninsulate
peptisation
periostitis
permissible
permissibly
persistence
persistency
pervasively
pettishness
pharisaical
phariseeism
philosopher
philosophic
photosphere
phytosterol
pietistical
piggishness
pinkishness
plainspoken
planisphere
preciseness
prehistoric
prelusively
prelusorily
preposition
prepositive
previsional
professedly
profuseness
progestogen
promiscuity
promiscuous
promisingly
proposition
provisional
provisorily
provostship
prudishness
publishable
publishment
purposeless
purposively
putrescence
putrescible
quacksalver
quicksilver
raffishness
realisation
recessional
recessively
reconstruct
reddishness
refreshment
remonstrant
remonstrate
remorseless
renaissance
representer
repressible
repressibly
repulsively
requisition
reversional
reversioner
rhinoscopic
roguishness
rumbustious
saplessness
satinstitch
selfassured
selfishness
sequestrate
sexlessness
shirtsleeve
shortspoken
sickishness
sightscreen
sightseeing
sinlessness
slavishness
smithsonite
smokescreen
solipsistic
solmisation
sophistical
sottishness
spacesaving
spokeswoman
sportswoman
squarsonage
stagestruck
statesmanly
statistical
stegosaurus
sternsheets
stylisation
stylishness
subbasement
submissible
subsistence
suggestible
sunlessness
superscribe
superscript
supersedeas
supersedure
superstrata
supersubtle
supposition
suppositive
suppository
surbasement
surpassable
sweepstakes
swinishness
symposiarch
syndesmosis
tarnishable
tempestuous
terrestrial
thanksgiver
toothsomely
torchsinger
tracasserie
transsexual
trendsetter
tricksiness
trimestrial
troposphere
turgescence
ultrasonics
unceasingly
unconscious
uncrushable
underseller
undersigned
understated
unpossessed
unreasoning
Upanishadic
upholsterer
uselessness
utilisation
varnishtree
verboseness
vichyssoise
vicissitude
vitrescence
voguishness
waggishness
waspishness
waterskiing
wearisomely
wedgeshaped
wheresoever
whichsoever
whitishness
wholesomely
wholesouled
whosesoever
witlessness
worrisomely
Zoroastrian
absenteeism
accentually
acceptation
acceptingly
acculturate
acoustician
acquittance
adjectively
adventuress
adventurism
adventurist
adventurous
advertently
advertising
aeolotropic
aerostatics
aerostation
affectation
affectingly
affectional
affectioned
affectively
affectivity
agglutinate
agnosticism
allantoides
altostratus
amphetamine
anaesthesia
anaesthetic
anisotropic
antistrophe
appurtenant
aromaticity
arrestingly
assentation
assertively
assortative
athleticism
attentively
attestation
attritional
Augustinian
balletomane
barbiturate
barnstormer

basketchair
bassethound
befittingly
bicentenary
billetsdoux
billsticker
biometrical
bipartition
brainteaser
breadthways
breadthwise
breastplate
breastwheel
bulletproof
Byzantinism
Byzantinist
calisthenic
calyptrogen
carpetsnake
cassiterite
catastrophe
catheterise
causatively
celestially
cementation
chemotactic
chieftaincy
Christendom
christening
christiania
Christianly
Christmassy
Christology
cleistogamy
climatology
coarctation
cognateness
cognitional
cognitively
cognitivity
combatively
comestibles
committable
commutation
commutative
competently
competition
competitive
compotation
compotatory
computation
computerise
concatenate
conditional
conditioner
condottiere
condottieri
confutation
confutative
connotation
connotative
cosmetician
cosmetology
crematorium
crepitation
cyclothymia
cyclothymic
decantation
deceitfully
deceptively
decorticate
deductively
deerstalker
defectively
deglutition
degustation
delectation
deportation
dermatology

destitution
desultorily
detestation
devastation
dexiotropic
diametrical
dichotomise
dichotomist
dichotomous
dictatorial
didacticism
digestively
dimwittedly
directional
directivity
directorate
directorial
directrices
discotheque
disentangle
disenthrall
disinterest
disinterred
disputation
diverticula
divestiture
domesticate
domesticity
doughtiness
dramaturgic
eclecticism
educational
effectively
effectually
egalitarian
elicitation
ellipticity
Emmenthaler
encystation
entertainer
epipetalous
eschatology
essentially
eurhythmics
eurypteroid
evolutional
exceptional
executioner
executorial
executrices
executrixes
exhortation
exhortative
exhortatory
expectantly
expectation
expectative
expectorant
expectorate
exportation
expostulate
extortioner
eyecatching
facultative
fenestrated
fidgetiness
flauntingly
flightiness
fomentation
forestaller
forestation
forgetfully
forgetmenot
forgettable
formational
franctireur
frightfully
frowstiness
gangsterism

gasfittings
geometrical
gerontology
gestatorial
gigantesque
gradational
gravitation
gravitative
guesstimate
gurgitation
haematocele
haematocrit
haematology
hairstyling
hairstylist
Hamiltonian
haughtiness
heliotropic
hemipterous
hermeticism
herpetology
highstepper
hirsuteness
homesteader
homestretch
homopterous
hospitalise
hospitality
hospitaller
hydrotactic
hydrothorax
hydrotropic
hypertrophy
hypostatise
illustrator
illustrious
imitatively
immortalise
immortality
impartation
impartially
impertinent
importantly
importation
importunate
importunely
importunity
incantation
incantatory
incertitude
incontinent
indentation
inductively
industrious
infanticide
infantilism
infantryman
infertility
infestation
infiltrator
ingratitude
insectarium
insecticide
insectifuge
insectivore
insectology
insistently
institution
insultingly
intentional
intentioned
intertangle
intertribal
intuitional
intuitively
intuitivism
invectively
inventively
inventorial

investigate
investiture
invultation
irruptively
isometrical
jactitation
kickstarter
lamentation
leavetaking
libertarian
liberticide
libertinage
libertinism
lithotomise
lithotomist
lithotripsy
lucratively
lycanthrope
lycanthropy
magisterial
magisterium
magistratic
marketplace
marketvalue
McCarthyism
mediateness
mediatorial
mediatrices
metastasise
miniaturise
miniaturist
ministerial
misanthrope
misanthropy
misestimate
molestation
momentarily
momentously
monasterial
monasticism
monopterous
narratively
naughtiness
neuroticism
neurotropic
nictitation
nonmatching
nonmetallic
nutritional
nutritively
nyctitropic
objectively
objectivism
objectivist
objectivity
obstetrical
obtestation
occultation
olfactology
operational
operatively
opportunely
opportunism
opportunist
opportunity
orientalise
orientalism
orientalist
orientation
orthotropic
ostentation
overstepped
overstretch
overstuffed
painstaking
Palestinian
palpitation
pantothenic
parentheses

parenthesis
parenthetic
partitioned
partitioner
partitively
pedestalled
pentathlete
penultimate
peristalith
peristalsis
peristaltic
peristomial
permutation
perpetrator
perpetually
perpetuance
perpetuator
philatelist
phonetician
phototactic
phototropic
phytotomist
pinnatisect
pipistrelle
piscatorial
plaintively
planetarium
planetoidal
pleiotropic
Pleistocene
plicateness
pocketknife
pocketmoney
pocketsized
polystyrene
potentially
predatorily
prefatorial
prefatorily
prematurely
prematurity
priestcraft
primateship
primatology
primitively
primitivism
privateness
privatively
probational
probationer
profiterole
proletarian
proletariat
promotional
promptitude
propitiable
propitiator
purgatorial
quaestorial
qualitative
racketpress
recantation
receptacula
receptively
receptivity
redactional
registrable
regretfully
regrettable
regrettably
reluctantly
reluctation
repartition
repentantly
repleteness
reportorial
resentfully
resistively
resistivity

restatement
restitution
retentively
retentivity
rickettsial
ringstraked
rodenticide
romanticise
romanticism
romanticist
Sabbatarian
Sagittarius
saltatorial
salvational
schistosity
schistosome
schottische
scientistic
scientology
scriptorial
scriptorium
secretarial
secretariat
secretively
sedentarily
seductively
selectively
selectivity
selfstarter
selfsterile
semanticist
sempiternal
sensational
sensitively
sensitivity
seventeenth
seventyfold
shocktroops
shopsteward
showstopper
sidestepped
sinistrally
sinistrorse
situational
skeletonise
slightingly
Soroptimist
spendthrift
spinsterish
spiritistic
spiritlevel
spiritually
spiritualty
spirituelle
squintingly
starstudded
statutebook
statutorily
stenotypist
stocktaking
stomatology
stormtroops
storyteller
straitlaced
streetlight
subcategory
sublittoral
summational
supertanker
symmetrical
sympathetic
sympathiser
sympetalous
tabletennis
talentscout
talkatively
tearstained
teetotalism
teetotaller

tentatively
termitarium
territorial
testatrices
thanatology
theretofore
thirstiness
thixotropic
thriftiness
throatiness
throatlatch
thwartships
tolbutamide
touchtyping
traditional
tributarily
Trinitarian
tripetalous
uncertainly
uncertainty
uncluttered
uncontested
uncouthness
undertaking
undertenant
undisturbed
unemotional
unfaltering
unfortunate
unweetingly
unwittingly
utilitarian
valuational
variational
vasectomise
velvetiness
versatilely
versatility
vibratility
vibrational
voluntarily
voluntarism
voluntarist
wedgetailed
weightiness
whitethroat
xeranthemum
yacketyyack
accumulator
agriculture
altitudinal
altocumulus
ambiguously
amorousness
antemundane
antenuptial
antiquarian
antiquation
anxiousness
aponeuroses
aponeurosis
aponeurotic
applaudable
aquaculture
aquiculture
archduchess
archdukedom
arduousness
articulable
articulated
articulator
assiduously
attenuation
attitudinal
auricularly
balefulness
bashfulness
Belorussian
biliousness
binocularly
bisexuality
bodybuilder
brankursine
brusqueness
bureaucracy
callousness
carefulness
charcuterie
coinsurance
congruently
congruously
copiousness
cornhusking
cryosurgery
curiousness
defraudment
depopulator
desexualise
destruction
destructive
devaluation
deviousness
discourtesy
disgruntled
distrustful
dolefulness
dourocoucouli
dropcurtain
dualpurpose
dubiousness
dutifulness
emasculator
emulousness
enviousness
eventualise
eventuality
extenuation
extenuatory
fatefulness
fatiguingly
fatuousness
fearfulness
FinnoUgrian
flavourless
flavoursome
flocculence
fluctuation
forequarter
forerunning
fraudulence
fretfulness
fructuation
gainfulness
gaseousness
geniculated
gibbousness
goddaughter
habituation
harbourless
harmfulness
hatefulness
headhunting
heedfulness
heinousness
helpfulness
hideousness
hopefulness
hugeousness
hurtfulness
illiquidity
impecunious
impetuosity
impetuously
implausible
implausibly
inaugurator
inexcusable
inexcusably
infatuation
ingenuously
innocuously
insalubrity
inscrutable
inscrutably
insinuation
insinuative
instruction
instructive
involucrate
involuntary
irrecusable
irrecusably
irreducible
irreducibly
irrefutable
irrefutably
irregularly
jealousness
landaulette
latifundium
latitudinal
lustfulness
manipulable
manipulator
mindfulness
mistrustful
moisturiser
molecularly
monoculture
mononuclear
moribundity
needfulness
nervousness
nonplussing
noxiousness
obliqueness
obstruction
obstructive
obviousness
odorousness
ominousness
onerousness
operculated
orbicularly
overrunning
painfulness
pasteuriser
pediculosis
piteousness
pitifulness
playfulness
pleasurable
pleasurably
pococurante
pomiculture
pompousness
postnuptial
precautious
procrustean
protrudable
protrusible
punctuality
punctuation
pushfulness
quadrupedal
quincuncial
quinquennia
quinquereme
raucousness
reassurance
reedbunting
reinsurance
restfulness
restructure
revaluation
ribvaulting
riotousness
rubicundity
ruinousness
sansculotte
sculduddery
sculduggery
selfculture
selfsupport
sericulture
seriousness
shipbuilder
showjumping
sinuousness
skilfulness
skulduddery
skulduggery
snowbunting
songfulness
soulfulness
spherulitic
spondulicks
sternutator
stirrupbone
stirruppump
strenuosity
strenuously
stridulator
succourless
sulphureous
sulphurwort
sumptuosity
sumptuously
taciturnity
tearfulness
tediousness
tenuousness
thingumabob
thingumajig
thoroughpin
thoroughwax
transuranic
tufthunting
tunefulness
unendurable
unendurably
unnaturally
unsaturated
vacuousness
variousness
vesicularly
viciousness
viniculture
viscountess
viscousness
viticulture
wakefulness
Whitsuntide
wirepulling
wishfulness
wistfulness
woodcutting
zealousness
zestfulness
abbreviator
abusiveness
acclivitous
achievement
aestivation
aggravation
amativeness
approvingly
audiovisual
bereavement
bloodvessel
captivation
carnivorous
clairvoyant
convivially
costiveness
cultivation
cursiveness
deceivingly
decemvirate
declivitous
depravation
depravement
deprivation
deservingly
dishevelled
elusiveness
enslavement
evasiveness
extravagant
extravagate
extravasate
extraverted
extroverted
forgiveness
frugivorous
furtiveness
granivorous
herbivorous
illfavoured
imperviable
improvement
improvident
incurvation
incurvature
innervation
intervallic
interviewee
interviewer
intravenous
introverted
involvement
massiveness
medievalism
medievalist
multivalent
noctivagant
noctivagous
observantly
observation
observatory
observingly
outrivalled
passivation
passiveness
pensiveness
pentavalent
perseverate
piscivorous
repleviable
reprovingly
reservation
restiveness
selfevident
suasiveness
subdivision
supervision
supervisory
tetravalent
tittivation
transversal
triumvirate
ultraviolet
undervaluer
unnervingly
varsovienne
acknowledge
blameworthy
breadwinner
cavedweller
duniewassal
faithworthy
fieldworker
floorwalker
gallowsbird
gallowstree
ghostwriter
heavyweight
hornswoggle
housewifely
housewifery
lakedweller
lightweight
meadowgrass
meadowsweet
metalworker
minesweeper
nightwalker
northwester
otherwhiles
paperweight
pennyweight
pieceworker
pillowfight
prizewinner
pussywillow
quickwitted
readywitted
rightwinger
shadowgraph
shadowiness
sharpwitted
shortwinded
sightworthy
sleepwalker
sorrowfully
southwester
steelworker
stonewaller
thankworthy
therewithal
thickwitted
trackwalker
trustworthy
underweight
underwriter
wheelwright
wherewithal
whitewasher
yellowbelly
amplexicaul
antioxidant
approximate
asphyxiator
inflexional
postexilian
reflexively
reflexology
suffixation
unisexually
aerodynamic
amethystine
anaphylaxis
anticyclone
antipyretic
antitypical
apophyllite
ascomycetes
barleybroth
biophysical
brachyurous
conveyancer
dicotyledon
dismayingly
eucalyptole
galleyslave
geophysical
homozygosis
hyoscyamine
hypocycloid
hypotyposis
ichthyology
ichthyornis
ichthyosaur
lachrymator

metonymical
monkeybread
monkeyshine
monozygotic
myxomycetes
panegyrical
paratyphoid
porphyritic
presbyteral
prophylaxis
safetyvalve
scurvygrass
spondylitis
synonymical
tiddlywinks
triphyllous
vestryclerk
Wesleyanism
haphazardly
pentazocine
Spinozistic
trapeziform
trapezoidal

---

abecedarian
abnormality
abomination
acceptation
acclamation
acclamatory
acclimation
acclimatise
accompanist
accordantly
acetylation
achromatise
achromatism
acidulation
acriflavine
acumination
adenomatous
adoptianism
adoptianist
adumbration
adumbrative
adversative
aerographer
aerostatics
aerostation
Aesculapian
aestivation
affectation
affiliation
affirmation
affirmative
affirmatory
affrication
affricative
aggravation
aggregately
aggregation
aggregative
agrarianism
alcyonarian
alleviation
alleviative
alleviatory
altercation
alternately
alternation
alternative
Americanise
Americanism
Americanist
amphetamine
Anglicanism
anglomaniac
antechamber
antigravity
antiquarian
antiquation
appellation
appellative
application
applicative
applicatory
appogiatura
approbation
approbatory
arbitrageur
arbitrament
arbitrarily
arbitration
arbitrative
arbitratrix
arglebargle
Arminianism
arterialise
artiodactyl
assentation
assignation
association
associative
assortative
astigmatism
atomisation
attenuation
attestation
Aurignacian
autographic
autoplastic
azotobacter
ballbearing
bashibazouk
beechmarten
bellheather
benignantly
bergamasque
bicephalous
bifurcation
birdbrained
bisexuality
bitterapple
blackmailer
blackmarket
Bodhisattva
bohemianism
bombilation
bombination
booklearned
botheration
brachiation
bradycardia
breadbasket
breathalyse
bricklaying
brilliantly
broadcaster
burgomaster
bushwhacker
cacographic
calcination
calculating
calculation
calculative
calibration
candelabrum
candidature
cannibalise
cannibalism
capillarity
captivation
carbonation
cardinalate
cardsharper
carminative
castigation
celebration
celebratory
cellularity
cementation
centenarian
cerebration
ceroplastic
chemotactic
chieftaincy
choirmaster
cinnabarine
circularise
circularity
circulation
circulative
circulatory
cisatlantic
civilianise
clericalism
clericalist
cliffhanger
closehauled
cloudcastle
coadunation
coagulation
coarctation
coeducation
coldhearted
colligation
colligative
collimation
collocation
colonialism
colonialist
colouration
columbarium
combination
combinative
combinatory
commination
comminatory
commonality
communalise
communalism
communalist
commutation
commutative
comparatist
comparative
compilation
compliantly
compotation
compotatory
computation
condolatory
condonation
confutation
confutative
congelation
conjugality
conjugation
conjugative
conjuration
connotation
connotative
consolation
consolatory
consonantal
consonantly
conurbation
convenances
conveyancer
convocation
cooperation
cooperative
coplanarity
corporality
corporately
corporation
corporatism
corporative
correlation
correlative
corrugation
coruscation
cosignatory
cotoneaster
crenulation
crepitation
crestfallen
criminalist
criminality
crimination
criminative
criminatory
criticality
criticaster
crookbacked
crossgarnet
culmination
cultivation
cupellation
customarily
cybernation
cyclopaedia
cyclopaedic
deathrattle
debarkation
decantation
declamation
declamatory
declaration
declarative
declaratory
declination
decollation
decussately
decussation
deemphasise
deerstalker
defalcation
defloration
defoliation
deformation
degradation
degustation
dehydration
deification
delectation
delineation
demarcation
demarkation
democratise
democratism
demographer
demographic
denigration
denigratory
deoxidation
deportation
depravation
deprecation
deprecative
deprecatory
depredation
depredatory
deprivation
desecration
desexualise
desiccation
desiccative
designation
desperadoes
desperately
desperation
destination
detestation
detribalise
deuteration
devaluation
devastation
dicephalous
dichogamous
diluvialist
diplomatise
diplomatist
dipsomaniac
disarmament
disentangle
dislocation
disorganise
disparaging
disparately
displeasure
disputation
dissipation
dissipative
dissonantly
dithyrambic
divulgation
downdraught
downhearted
doxographer
dressmaking
drillmaster
dundrearies
duniewassal
duplication
duplicative
ectoblastic
ectoplasmic
edification
edificatory
egalitarian
ejaculation
ejaculatory
elaborately
elaboration
elaborative
elicitation
elimination
eliminative
elucidation
elucidative
elucidatory
elutriation
embarkation
emblematise
emblematist
embrocation
emptyhanded
encomiastic
encystation
endophagous
endoplasmic
entablature
entertainer
enucleation
enumeration
enumerative
enunciation
enunciative
epipetalous
epochmaking
eradication
eradicative
Erastianism
erotomaniac
esemplastic
etherealise
ethereality
Europeanise
evagination
evaporation
evaporative
eventualise
eventuality
examination
exclamation
exclamatory
excoriation
exculpation
exculpatory
exemplarily
exemplarity
exfoliation
exfoliative
exhortation
exhortative
exhortatory
exoneration
exonerative
expatiation
expatiative
expatiatory
expectantly
expectation
expectative
explanation
explanatory
explication
explicative
explicatory
exploration
explorative
exploratory
exportation
expurgation
expurgatory
exsiccation
extenuation
extenuatory
externalise
externalism
externality
extirpation
extirpatory
extravagant
extravagate
extravasate
extrication
exuberantly
fabrication
facultative
fairweather
familiarise
familiarity
farcicality
fascinating
fascination
fecundation
feldspathic
festinately
fimbriation
firecracker
fissiparity
fissiparous
flimflammer
floorwalker
fluctuation
fomentation
forequarter
forestaller
forestation
formication
formularise
formulation
fornication
fortunately
freehearted
frigidarium
fructuation
frustration
fulguration
fullhearted
fulminating
fulmination

fulminatory
fusillation
fustigation
gallbladder
Gallicanism
gallimaufry
gardemanger
gatecrasher
gemmiparous
gemmulation
germination
germinative
gerrymander
glassmaking
globularity
glomeration
goldbeating
goodhearted
grandfather
grandparent
granularity
granulation
gratulation
gratulatory
gravitation
gravitative
gurgitation
gutturalise
gutturalism
haberdasher
habituation
halfhearted
halfmeasure
handicapped
handicapper
haphazardly
hardhearted
harebrained
heavyhanded
Hegelianism
hereinafter
hibernacula
hibernation
hippocampus
holoblastic
holographic
homeopathic
homoplastic
homothallic
honeybadger
hooliganism
horseradish
hospitalise
hospitality
hospitaller
housefather
housemaster
Hudibrastic
humiliation
humiliatory
hunchbacked
hydrocarbon
hydropathic
hydrotactic
hyoscyamine
hypermarket
hyphenation
hypnopaedia
hypoblastic
hypostatise
ideographic
idiographic
idolisation
imaginarily
imagination
imaginative
imbrication
immediately
immigration
immortalise
immortality
immoveables
imparkation
impartation
imperialise
imperialism
imperialist
impermanent
impetration
impetratory
implication
implicative
importantly
importation
imprecation
imprecatory
inanimately
inanimation
incantation
incantatory
incarnadine
incarnation
incessantly
inclination
inculcation
inculpation
inculpatory
incurvation
incurvature
indentation
indignantly
indignation
IndoIranian
inebriation
inelegantly
infatuation
infestation
infeudation
infirmarian
informality
information
informative
informatory
innervation
inoculation
inoculative
inoperative
insectarium
insensately
insinuation
insinuative
inspiration
inspiratory
instigation
instigative
integrality
integration
integrative
intercalary
intercalate
interfacial
interfacing
interjacent
internalise
internality
interracial
intertangle
intervallic
intricately
inviolately
invultation
ironhearted
irradiation
irradiative
ithyphallic
itinerantly
itineration
jactitation
jerrymander
Judaisation
kickstarter
kindhearted
kymographic
laciniation
lacrimation
lacrimatory
lacrymation
lacrymatory
laicisation
lamentation
lancinating
lancination
landgrabber
landgravine
leavetaking
legislation
legislative
legislature
leprosarium
leptodactyl
libertarian
lighthanded
linedrawing
lionhearted
liquidambar
liquidation
litterateur
lixiviation
logographer
logographic
longplaying
lubrication
lubricative
lucubration
Lutheranism
luxuriantly
luxuriation
machination
macrogamete
madrigalian
madrigalist
malignantly
manducation
manducatory
Manichaeism
marginalise
marginality
marshmallow
mastication
masticatory
matchmaking
materialise
materialism
materialist
materiality
mathematics
medievalism
medievalist
melioration
meliorative
meliphagous
memorialise
memorialist
mensuration
meprobamate
mercenarily
meroblastic
merrymaking
mesoblastic
metaplastic
metastasise
methylamine
methylation
metrication
microgamete
millenarian
mindreading
miscreation
molestation
momentarily
moneymaking
moneymarket
monochasial
monochasium
monogrammed
monographer
monographic
monophagous
multiparous
multiracial
multivalent
murmuration
muscularity
musculation
musculature
mycophagist
myelomatous
mythomaniac
naphthalene
nationalise
nationalism
nationalist
nationality
necessarian
necessarily
necromancer
necromantic
negotiation
negotiatory
negotiatrix
neuropathic
nictitation
nightmarish
nightwalker
ninnyhammer
noctivagant
noctivagous
noisemaking
nomographer
nomographic
nonmetallic
nonvolatile
northeaster
noseyparker
nosographer
nosographic
notionalist
nulliparity
nulliparous
numismatics
numismatist
nuncupation
nuncupative
obfuscation
obfuscatory
objurgation
objurgatory
obscuration
obsecration
observantly
observation
observatory
obstinately
obtestation
occultation
oesophageal
officialdom
officialese
officialism
officiation
oldwomanish
openhearted
ophidiarium
oppugnation
oracularity
oreographic
orientalise
orientalism
orientalist
orientation
originality
origination
originative
orthopaedic
oscillation
oscillatory
ostentation
osteopathic
outrivalled
overbearing
overmeasure
oxygenation
ozonisation
paederastic
painstaking
palpitation
palsgravine
paperhanger
papermaking
paragrapher
paragraphic
parallactic
passacaglia
passivation
pastoralism
pastoralist
paternalism
paternalist
peacemaking
pectination
peculiarity
pecuniarily
pedestalled
Pelagianism
penetrating
penetration
penetrative
pentadactyl
pentavalent
peptisation
percolation
perennation
perforation
perforative
pericranial
pericranium
perishables
peristalith
peristalsis
peristaltic
permutation
personalise
personalism
personalist
personality
personation
personative
pertinacity
phagedaenic
pharisaical
phototactic
physicality
planetarium
plebeianise
plebeianism
pollination
polygraphic
polyphagous
polyzoarium
pomegranate
ponderation
postclassic
postglacial
postulation
predicament
predication
predicative
predicatory
prelibation
preparation
preparative
preparatory
prerogative
primiparous
procreation
procreative
procuration
procuratory
prodigalise
prodigality
profanation
profanatory
proletarian
proletariat
propagation
propagative
prorogation
prostration
protomartyr
provocateur
provocation
provocative
proximately
Prussianise
Prussianism
psychiatric
pterodactyl
publication
pullulation
punctuality
punctuation
pupillarity
pustulation
pyroclastic
quacksalver
qualitative
radiocarbon
radiolarian
Rastafarian
rationalise
rationalism
rationalist
rationality
realisation
reanimation
reappraisal
rebarbative
recantation
receptacula
reclamation
redundantly
reeducation
reformation
reformative
reformatory
regionalise
regionalism
regionalist
reification
reiteration
reiterative
reluctantly
reluctation
repellantly
repentantly
replication
reprobation
reprobative
reprobatory
repudiation
repugnantly
reservation
resignation
respiration

respiratory
restoration
restorative
retaliation
retaliative
retaliatory
retardation
retardative
retardatory
revaluation
rhizocarpic
rhizomatous
righthanded
righthander
rotogravure
rubrication
rustication
Sabbatarian
sacculation
safecracker
Sagittarius
saintpaulia
salesladies
sarcomatous
saturnalian
scarabaeoid
schismatise
scholiastic
scopolamine
scoutmaster
secondarily
secretarial
secretariat
sedentarily
segregation
segregative
selfloading
selfsealing
selfstarter
semitrailer
septenarius
septicaemia
septicaemic
serigrapher
serrulation
sertularian
sheepfarmer
sheepmaster
shelljacket
shoeleather
shorthanded
sillimanite
singularise
singularity
slavemarket
sleepwalker
Socinianism
sociopathic
softhearted
solmisation
songsparrow
southeaster
spacesaving
spectrality
speculation
speculative
sporulation
squirearchy
stagemanage
stagflation
staircarpet
standpatter
steadfastly
stegosaurus
stimulation
stimulative
stipulation
stipulatory
stockmarket
stocktaking
stonemarten
stonewaller
straphanger
stylisation
subarration
subjugation
sublimation
subornation
subrogation
suburbanise
suburbanite
succedaneum
suffixation
suffocation
suffocative
superfamily
superjacent
superlative
supermarket
supernatant
supertanker
suppliantly
suppuration
suppurative
supremacist
surfboarder
surrogation
suspiration
susurration
swimbladder
sycophantic
sycophantry
syllabarium
sympetalous
syncopation
syndicalism
syndicalist
syndication
systematics
systematise
systematism
systematist
tabernacled
tachycardia
talebearing
tapemeasure
tearstained
teetotalism
teetotaller
telegrammic
telegrapher
telegraphic
temperament
temperately
temperative
temperature
temporality
temporarily
termagantly
termination
terminative
termitarium
tetradactyl
tetravalent
threehanded
threemaster
timesharing
titillation
tittivation
toastmaster
tobogganing
tobogganist
tolbutamide
topographer
topographic
trackwalker
translation
transmarine
transpadane
transparent
trenchantly
trepanation
trepidation
tribulation
tributarily
Trinitarian
tripetalous
trituration
truehearted
turbination
typographer
typographic
ultramarine
unappealing
uncertainly
uncertainty
underhanded
undermanned
undertaking
undervaluer
unification
unipolarity
unwarranted
utilisation
utilitarian
vaccination
vacillation
vacuolation
variegation
vascularise
vascularity
ventilation
ventilative
vermination
verticality
vesuvianite
vindication
vindicative
vindicatory
voluntarily
voluntarism
voluntarist
warmhearted
washleather
wastebasket
watchmaking
weakhearted
wedgetailed
wellmeaning
Wesleyanism
wheelbarrow
whitewasher
whitleather
whoremaster
wisecracker
wreckmaster
xylographer
xylographic
xylophagous
Yugoslavian
zoantharian
amphisbaena
barleybroth
beaverboard
boysenberry
breechblock
breezeblock
bridgeboard
candleberry
carvelbuilt
centreboard
chockablock
chrysoberyl
colourblind
contrabasso
contributor
coxcombical
custombuilt
decerebrate
describable
distribuend
distributor
disturbance
equilibrate
equilibrist
equilibrium
fasciaboard
fingerboard
gingerbread
goldenberry
gravelblind
halterbreak
heartsblood
huckleberry
incunabulum
insalubrity
inscribable
louverboard
louvreboard
memorabilia
monkeybread
mortarboard
musclebound
noticeboard
paddleboard
palmcabbage
perturbable
Precambrian
rattlebrain
reestablish
salmonberry
saltimbanco
schoolboard
Septembrist
shovelboard
sleeveboard
snatchblock
somnambular
sonofabitch
splashboard
springboard
squarebuilt
strikebound
stringboard
superabound
switchblade
switchboard
teeterboard
thereabouts
triphibious
trophoblast
unclimbable
uninhabited
uninhibited
whereabouts
winterberry
yellowbelly
abiotically
abstraction
abstractive
abstriction
accrescence
acupuncture
adjudicator
adminicular
adolescence
aerobically
affranchise
agnatically
alembicated
amentaceous
angelically
animalcular
anthracitic
anticyclone
antiJacobin
aquatically
arboraceous
archaically
archduchess
aristocracy
ascetically
ascomycetes
aseptically
barefacedly
basketchair
bathyscaphe
Benedictine
benediction
benedictory
benefaction
beneficence
beneficiary
beneficiate
bittercress
bivouacking
boardschool
botanically
bucolically
bureaucracy
butyraceous
byeelection
Byronically
calefacient
calefactory
canalicular
canaliculus
candescence
canonically
carbuncular
caustically
chanticleer
chaotically
chartaceous
cheesecloth
chronically
cinquecento
clairschach
Clarencieux
classically
coalescence
cochinchina
coconscious
coefficient
cognoscente
cognoscenti
cognoscible
collenchyma
complacence
complacency
complicated
compunction
comstockery
confiscable
confiscator
confliction
conflictive
conjunction
conjunctiva
conjunctive
conjuncture
conspecific
conspicuity
conspicuous
contractile
contraction
contractive
contractual
contracture
convincible
corpuscular
crepuscular
crustaceous
cryptically
decrescendo
deistically
dereliction
destruction
destructive
diffraction
discalceate
disfunction
disgraceful
disjunction
disjunctive
disjuncture
distinction
distinctive
distraction
distractive
doublecheck
doublecross
douroucouli
drastically
dynamically
dysfunction
efficacious
elastically
elasticated
empirically
endemically
enfranchise
equinoctial
equivocally
equivocator
ergatocracy
erratically
erubescence
eugenically
evanescence
excrescence
excrescency
exdirectory
eyecatching
fanatically
farinaceous
farreaching
florescence
frantically
franticness
fratricidal
gastrectomy
geanticline
gegenschein
generically
genetically
geosyncline
gimcrackery
graphically
graphicness
greenockite
hagioscopic
harpsichord
harumscarum
Hebraically
hedgeschool
hepatectomy
heptarchist
heretically
heteroclite
hexadecimal
hierarchism
hurryscurry
hygroscopic
hyperactive
hypocycloid
identically
idiotically
idyllically
illogically
immedicable
incoercible
inconscient
indirection

ineffective
ineffectual
inefficient
injudicious
inofficious
instinctive
instinctual
instruction
instructive
interactant
interaction
interactive
involucrate
iridescence
irreducible
irreducibly
irrevocable
irrevocably
isoelectric
juridically
labefaction
laconically
lactescence
lawmerchant
liquescence
loculicidal
logomachist
macroscopic
malediction
maledictory
malefaction
maleficence
malfunction
malpractice
manufactory
manufacture
marcescence
marcescible
melanochroi
meritocracy
microscopic
middleclass
mimetically
misconceive
misericorde
mononuclear
moronically
mothercraft
munificence
muttonchops
myxomycetes
neckerchief
needlecraft
nephrectomy
nettlecloth
nigrescence
nomadically
nondescript
nonmatching
nonspecific
numerically
nutcrackers
obstruction
obstructive
opalescence
organically
organscreen
orthoscopic
osmotically
ovariectomy
pacifically
pacificator
papyraceous
perfunctory
perspective
perspicuity
perspicuous
photoactive
phylloclade
physiocracy
Pickwickian
pigeonchest
pigsticking
piperaceous
piratically
plagioclase
plasticiser
polemically
politically
politicking
polytechnic
practicable
practicably
practically
preconceive
preelection
presanctify
priestcraft
promiscuity
promiscuous
prosaically
prosaicness
prosenchyma
prospective
protractile
protraction
protractive
psittacosis
psychically
purificator
putrescence
putrescible
pyrotechnic
quizzically
radioactive
rarefaction
rarefactive
redirection
reproachful
resourceful
restriction
restrictive
restructure
retinacular
retinaculum
retroaction
retroactive
rhinoscopic
rubefacient
rubefaction
ruridecanal
saddlecloth
saponaceous
satanically
satirically
sceptically
schoolchild
scoriaceous
scribacious
secondclass
seismically
selfcocking
selflocking
shellacking
sightscreen
simpliciter
slotmachine
smokescreen
solanaceous
somatically
spastically
spathaceous
spectacular
spermicidal
spherically
splenectomy
spongecloth
springclean
stratocracy
subjunctive
subspecific
subtraction
subtractive
superscribe
superscript
syssarcosis
tabefaction
tapemachine
technically
technocracy
tendencious
tetanically
tetrarchate
thermically
titanically
trafficator
trafficking
trafficless
transaction
transection
triadically
tristichous
tumefaction
turgescence
ulotrichous
unconscious
unflinching
unselective
unsolicited
urticaceous
valediction
valedictory
venatically
venesection
venisection
ventricular
ventriculus
veridically
vestryclerk
violoncello
vitrescence
vivisection
whimsically
xanthochroi
abracadabra
advisedness
Alexandrian
alexandrine
alexandrite
altitudinal
antecedence
applaudable
assuredness
attitudinal
awkwardness
battledress
belatedness
biofeedback
blessedness
bombardment
braggadocio
camaraderie
chalcedonic
coincidence
commandment
commendable
commendably
commendator
compendious
concordance
contradance
crabbedness
crookedness
defraudment
demigoddess
descendable
descendible
despondence
despondency
devotedness
diamondback
dilapidated
dilapidator
dinnerdance
disbandment
discardable
discordance
discordancy
disobedient
doubleDutch
embroiderer
flaccidness
forbiddance
forwardness
freezedried
fricandeaux
frowardness
gormandiser
guardedness
haggardness
hobbledehoy
hollandaise
hundredfold
hurriedness
husbandlike
impoundment
indeciduous
individuate
inexpedient
insipidness
intimidator
invalidness
languidness
latitudinal
learnedness
limitedness
mansardroof
mastoiditis
misguidance
misguidedly
mithridatic
morrisdance
myocarditis
offhandedly
outwardness
overbidding
overindulge
paramedical
pentandrous
persuadable
philanderer
pigheadedly
pleurodynia
pointedness
polyandrous
pretendedly
proceedings
protrudable
psychedelia
psychedelic
psychodrama
pyramidally
pyramidical
relatedness
respondence
respondency
retiredness
rhapsodical
roundedness
scleroderma
sculduddery
selfinduced
sigmoidally
skulduddery
spasmodical
squalidness
stewardship
stiltedness
stipendiary
studiedness
stuntedness
thermoduric
thyroiditis
troglodytic
tumbledrier
unavoidable
unavoidably
unboundedly
unguardedly
unsoundness
waywardness
wellordered
abhorrently
abridgement
absenteeism
abstinently
abusiveness
acatalectic
achievement
acquirement
adjudgement
advancement
adverseness
advertently
agglomerate
alphabetise
amativeness
amiableness
anemometric
apartmental
apologetics
apostleship
appeasement
appurtenant
Archimedean
archipelago
arrangement
artillerist
assafoetida
assuagement
audibleness
audiometric
austereness
awesomeness
bacciferous
bandylegged
bathymetric
beguilement
belligerent
bereavement
bicentenary
bimillenary
bimillenium
blackbeetle
blackfellow
blamelessly
blasphemous
bloodlessly
bloodvessel
bookkeeping
bookshelves
brainlessly
brainteaser
bristletail
bristleworm
brittleness
broadleaved
brusqueness
cabbagepalm
cabbagerose
cabbagetree
cabbageworm
calciferous
campmeeting
capableness
carburetion
carburetted
carburetter
carburettor
carrageenan
carrageenin
cassiterite
cataplectic
catheterise
cavalierism
cavedweller
ceaselessly
chainletter
chameleonic
cheerleader
cheerlessly
Christendom
christening
chucklehead
clearheaded
clinometric
cockaleekie
cockyleekie
cognateness
collinearly
commiserate
competently
compilement
computerise
comradeship
concatenate
conciseness
confederacy
confederate
confidently
confinement
congenerous
congruently
considerate
considering
consumerism
continental
continently
coparcenary
corniferous
corporeally
corpulently
corrigendum
costiveness
coulometric
countlessly
crossbearer
crosslegged
crotcheteer
cruciferous
crucigerous
cryotherapy
cupriferous
curableness
cursiveness
cybernetics
cycloserine
cypripedium
cysticercus
dauntlessly
decolletage
defenceless
deficiently
definiendum
deforcement
demagnetise
dentigerous
deoxygenate
depauperate
depauperise
dependently
depravement
derangement
desegregate

detrimental
differentia
differently
diffidently
diffuseness
diphtherial
diphtheroid
diphycercal
disablement
disaffected
disassemble
disassembly
dishevelled
dishonestly
disinfector
disinterest
disinterred
dislikeable
disquieting
disquietude
disremember
divergently
divorcement
divulgement
domineering
doubleedged
doubleender
doubleentry
doubtlessly
draggletail
dreamlessly
durableness
ebulliently
econometric
efficiently
effulgently
Elizabethan
elusiveness
embraceable
embracement
emplacement
emptyheaded
endorsement
endoskelton
endothelial
endothelium
endothermal
endothermic
enforceable
enforcement
engineering
engorgement
enhancement
enjambement
enlargeable
enlargement
enneahedron
ennoblement
enslavement
entablement
entitlement
equableness
erotogenous
eudiometric
eurypteroid
evasiveness
exanthemata
excellently
excremental
expediently
experienced
extraverted
extremeness
extroverted
faithhealer
faithlessly
faultlessly
featureless
ferriferous
firmamental
flatulently
floriferous
florilegium
foreseeable
forgiveness
fourwheeler
friableness
fruitlessly
fullfledged
fulsomeness
fundamental
furtiveness
gangsterism
gemmiferous
genuflexion
genuineness
gettogether
gibberellin
gigantesque
globigerina
goniometric
gracelessly
gracileness
grandnephew
gravimetric
greatnephew
greenkeeper
guilelessly
guiltlessly
guttapercha
gypsiferous
hairbreadth
hairdresser
handbreadth
handgrenade
heartlessly
heavyweight
heliometric
hemipterous
heptamerous
Heracleidan
hermeneutic
heteroecism
highstepper
hirsuteness
homesteader
homopterous
housekeeper
hydraheaded
hydrogenate
hydrogenous
hydromedusa
hydrometeor
hydrometric
hygrometric
hypermetric
hypothecate
hypothenuse
hypothermia
hypothesise
hypsometric
icosahedral
icosahedron
ignobleness
illaffected
illbreeding
immenseness
impatiently
imperfectly
impermeable
impermeably
impingement
implemental
improvement
imprudently
incarcerate
incipiently
inclemently
incompetent
incorrectly
incremental
indifferent
indorsement
indulgently
ingathering
insincerely
insincerity
insistently
intemperate
intenseness
interbedded
intercensal
intercepter
interceptor
intercessor
interdental
interdepend
interleaves
intermeddle
intermedium
internecine
interregnum
interrelate
interseptal
intersexual
intravenous
introverted
involvement
irksomeness
knucklebone
labiodental
lactiferous
lakedweller
latticework
lectureship
legerdemain
levelheaded
lightheaded
lightweight
limitlessly
lissomeness
loudspeaker
lovableness
machinemade
mackerelsky
magdalenian
magisterial
magisterium
massiveness
matchlessly
measureless
measurement
mediateness
megatherium
melliferous
mendelevium
mercilessly
Micawberish
Micawberism
micrometric
Micronesian
microsecond
millisecond
minesweeper
ministerial
mirthlessly
miscegenate
mischievous
misremember
molybdenite
monasterial
moneylender
monopterous
Monothelite
morbiferous
movableness
mundaneness
mutableness
narcoleptic
negligently
nervelessly
nitrogenise
nitrogenous
noiselessly
noisomeness
nonetheless
northwester
notableness
nutrimental
obliqueness
obscureness
octingenary
odoriferous
offenceless
oligomerous
omnipresent
operoseness
orthocentre
orthopedics
orthopedist
outbreeding
overstepped
overweening
ozoniferous
pachydermal
pamphleteer
pantalettes
paperweight
paraldehyde
parallelism
parallelled
paramoecium
paraplectic
passiveness
pastureland
pennyweight
pensiveness
pentahedron
pentamerous
perispermic
perithecium
permanently
perseverate
pertinently
pestiferous
pestilently
pharisееism
philatelist
photometric
photoperiod
picturebook
picturecard
picturegoer
picturesque
pipecleaner
planimetric
plateresque
pliableness
plicateness
pointdevice
pointlessly
powerlessly
precedented
precedently
preciseness
predecessor
presciently
preselector
prestressed
prevalently
primateship
primigenial
privateness
procurement
profaneness
profiterole
profuseness
proliferate
proliferous
prominently
proofreader
proprietary
prosthetics
protuberant
providently
purposeless
quiescently
quinquennia
quinquereme
racemeeting
radiometric
reachmedown
reawakening
recommender
recumbently
recurrently
refrigerant
refrigerate
remorseless
repellently
replaceable
replacement
repleteness
representer
requirement
resiliently
restatement
restiveness
retraceable
retrocedent
reverberant
reverberate
ricochetted
roentgenise
roughlegged
sacramental
Sadduceeism
safebreaker
safekeeping
salvageable
saprogenous
sausagemeat
scuttlebutt
selfcreated
selfelected
selffeeding
selffeeling
selfseeking
selfsterile
sempiternal
senselessly
sentimental
sentinelled
septiferous
serviceable
serviceably
servicebook
serviceline
seventeenth
sextodecimo
shacklebolt
shacklebone
Shaksperean
Shaksperian
shamelessly
shiftlessly
shipbreaker
shockheaded
shopsteward
shoulderbag
shoulderpad
shuttlecock
sidestepped
sidewheeler
sightlessly
sightreader
sightseeing
sincereness
sizableness
sleeplessly
smilelessly
sociometric
softshelled
somniferous
somnolently
soundlessly
southwester
spaceheater
spindlelegs
spindletree
spinelessly
spiniferous
spinsterish
spirometric
sporogenous
spreadeagle
stainlessly
statutebook
steeplebush
steeplejack
stickleback
stiffnecked
storekeeper
stormcentre
storyteller
strangeness
stringently
suasiveness
subbasement
subcategory
sublimeness
succulently
superheater
supersedeas
supersedure
supremeness
surbasement
swellheaded
swingletree
swordbearer
tabletennis
tastelessly
tautomerism
tenableness
terrigenous
tetrahedral
tetrahedron
tetramerous
textureless
thanklessly
theatregoer
therapeutic
thickheaded
thimbleweed
thistledown
threedecker
threelegged
thuriferous
timepleaser
Titianesque
torchbearer
townspeople
tracelessly
traducement
trainbearer
transceiver
transferred
transferrer
transiently
transsexual
transversal
treacherous
treecreeper
tremblement

trencherman
trendsetter
trestletree
trestlework
tribuneship
troublesome
truculently
trundletail
trusteeship
tunableness
turbulently
unawareness
unbelieving
unbeseeming
unconcealed
unconcerned
uncongenial
unconnected
uncontested
underseller
undertenant
underweight
unexpressed
unfaltering
unkennelled
unpossessed
unwholesome
vasopressin
vasopressor
venturesome
verboseness
vinedresser
visibleness
voicelessly
voltametric
volubleness
voortrekker
wearilessly
welcomeness
whiffletree
whippletree
whistlestop
whiteheaded
windcheater
winsomeness
worldbeater
worthlessly
wrongheaded
aftereffect
aircraftman
battlefield
beautifully
bountifully
brazenfaced
butterflies
centrifugal
changefully
colourfully
deceitfully
doublefaced
enfeoffment
facelifting
Falstaffian
flagofficer
forgetfully
frightfully
grandiflora
healthfully
masterfully
photooffset
pillowfight
plentifully
powderflask
regardfully
regretfully
reposefully
resentfully
selfdefence
sheriffalty
sheriffship
shoplifting
smoothfaced
sorrowfully
stampoffice
standoffish
thenceforth
undutifully
unhelpfully
unskilfully
welldefined
wonderfully
abiological
aerological
agrological
algological
archangelic
Areopagitic
astringency
axiological
bathingsuit
blastogenic
bookinghall
bootlegging
bottleglass
bottlegreen
bullfighter
cardiograph
carriageway
chaetognath
chafingdish
chevalglass
choreograph
chronograph
churchgoing
compurgator
conflagrant
conflagrate
consanguine
contingence
contingency
convergence
convergency
coronagraph
coronograph
cottongrass
cryptogamic
cryptograph
cunningness
cytological
demagogical
demagoguery
demagoguism
digitigrade
dislodgment
distinguish
drawingroom
emmenagogue
epeirogenic
equiangular
ethological
eveningstar
feelingness
fingerglass
FinnoUgrian
firefighter
flagwagging
foresighted
fortnightly
glaringness
goddaughter
golddigging
herringbone
herringgull
heterograft
homological
homozygosis
horological
hummingbird
ideological
immitigable
immitigably
infrangible
innavigable
irreligious
jumpingbean
jumpingjack
kinetograph
knowingness
lammergeier
lammergeyer
lamplighter
landingbeam
landinggear
lastingness
longsighted
marriagebed
meadowgrass
meaningless
minuteglass
misjudgment
mockingbird
monological
monologuise
monologuist
monozygotic
monseigneur
moonlighter
mooringmast
morningroom
multangular
mycological
nearsighted
nomological
nosological
nothingness
oecological
oenological
oestrogenic
oncological
ontological
oreological
packingcase
pedagogical
pedological
penological
pharyngitis
physiognomy
plantigrade
playingcard
poltergeist
pomological
posological
prejudgment
pressagency
prestigious
promulgator
pseudograph
psychogenic
psychograph
quitchgrass
rectangular
reemergence
refrangible
refringency
reintegrate
rheological
ribbongrass
salpingitis
sandbagging
sculduggery
scurvygrass
seismograph
serological
sexological
shadowgraph
sinological
sittingroom
skatingrink
skulduggery
smokingroom
snowgoggles
somatogenic
sparingness
steerageway
stereograph
stevengraph
strategical
submarginal
submergence
suckingfish
suffragette
synagogical
tentpegging
teratogenic
thanksgiver
theological
thermograph
thoroughpin
thoroughwax
topological
typological
unambiguous
unmitigated
viceregally
virological
waitinglist
waitingroom
willingness
winningness
winningpost
wintergreen
witenagemot
abolishable
abolishment
abranchiate
accoucheuse
acidophilic
agoraphobia
agoraphobic
anaesthesia
anaesthetic
anglophobia
anglophobic
antirrhinum
atmospheric
autarchical
barrelhouse
bassethound
bearishness
bergschrund
bewitchment
bookishness
boorishness
breadthways
breadthwise
Britishness
brutishness
bullishness
caddishness
calisthenic
catchphrase
chokecherry
cleanshaven
coffeehouse
ctenophoran
currishness
customhouse
cyclothymia
cyclothymic
debauchment
debouchment
depthcharge
diapophysis
discotheque
disenthrall
doggishness
dollishness
doltishness
donnishness
Emmenthaler
epinephrine
eurhythmics
evanishment
faddishness
festschrift
foolishness
foppishness
furnishings
Gallophobia
garnishment
girlishness
gramophonic
granophyric
haemophilia
haemophilic
heliochrome
hellishness
hemispheric
hoggishness
hydrophilic
hydrophobia
hydrophobic
hydrophytic
hydrothorax
hygrophytic
hypercharge
hyperphagia
hypsophobia
impeachable
impeachment
interchange
ionospheric
knavishness
lithophytic
loggerheads
loutishness
lumpishness
lycanthrope
lycanthropy
mannishness
mawkishness
McCarthyism
melancholia
melancholic
messiahship
microphonic
microphytic
misanthrope
misanthropy
monarchical
mustachioed
mycorrhizae
mycorrhizal
necrophilia
necrophilic
negrophobia
nourishment
nyctophobia
oligochaete
osteophytic
otherwhiles
outfighting
paedophilia
pantothenic
parentheses
parenthesis
parenthetic
peevishness
pentathlete
pettishness
photophilic
photophobia
photophobic
piggishness
pinkishness
porterhouse
preterhuman
procephalic
protophytic
prudishness
publishable
publishment
quickchange
radiophonic
raffishness
reddishness
refreshment
rhombohedra
roguishness
Russophobia
saddlehorse
saprophytic
sarcophagus
schoolhouse
scratchwork
seborrhoeic
selfishness
shortchange
sickishness
slavishness
sleuthhound
sottishness
spendthrift
spirochaete
spirochetal
sporophytic
springhouse
staunchless
staunchness
stenochromy
sternsheets
stomachache
stomachpump
straightcut
straightish
straightway
stretchable
stylishness
summerhouse
supercharge
swinishness
sympathetic
sympathiser
tarnishable
tenterhooks
uncatchable
uncouthness
uncrushable
undercharge
unmatchable
unteachable
untouchable
Upanishadic
varnishtree
voguishness
waggishness
waspishness
wedgeshaped
weltschmerz
Whitechapel
whitethroat
whitishness
xeranthemum
zootechnics
abbreviator
absorbingly
academicals
academician
academicism
acceptingly
acclivitous
accordingly
acidifiable
acinaciform

acoustician
acquisition
acquisitive
adjectively
adverbially
advertising
Aeneolithic
affectingly
affectional
affectioned
affectively
affectivity
AfroAsiatic
agglutinate
agnosticism
agonisingly
amenability
amicability
amphimictic
amplexicaul
anarchistic
annunciator
anomalistic
antheridium
antioxidant
aphrodisiac
appallingly
appealingly
appreciable
appreciably
appreciator
approvingly
approximate
aromaticity
arrestingly
ascensional
aspergillum
aspergillus
asphyxiator
assassinate
assertively
athleticism
attentively
attritional
audiovisual
Augustinian
awestricken
bacilliform
bactericide
balmcricket
banteringly
batholithic
bearbaiting
beastliness
befittingly
beguilingly
bicuspidate
biddability
billsticker
bipartition
blackbirder
blotchiness
bodybuilder
brainsickly
branchiopod
breadwinner
bristliness
broadminded
bullbaiting
butteriness
Byzantinism
Byzantinist
cabbalistic
calumniator
Calvinistic
caressingly
catechismal
catechistic
caterpillar
catholicise
Catholicism
catholicity
catswhisker
causatively
celestially
certifiable
certifiably
certificate
childminder
christiania
Christianly
churchiness
cicatricial
cityslicker
cleanlimbed
cleanliness
closefisted
clostridium
coccidiosis
cognitional
cognitively
cognitivity
collisional
collusively
columniated
combatively
comestibles
communicant
communicate
communistic
compaginate
competition
competitive
complainant
complaisant
compositely
composition
compositive
conciliator
concomitant
concubinage
concubinary
concubitant
conditional
conditioner
condominium
confidingly
confusingly
congenially
connubially
consolidate
consolingly
constrictor
consumingly
contaminant
contaminate
convenience
conveniency
convivially
corrosively
cosmetician
coterminous
countrified
courtliness
credibility
crocodilian
crucifixion
crunchiness
culpability
cupronickel
cursoriness
curvilineal
curvilinear
deceivingly
decemvirate
decennially
deceptively
declivitous
decorticate
decrepitate
decrepitude
deductively
defectively
defensively
defibrinate
deglutition
degradingly
demandingly
denunciator
deoxyribose
deploringly
depreciator
desensitise
deservingly
determinacy
determinant
determinate
determinism
determinist
dialogistic
diapositive
didacticism
diffusively
digestively
dimensional
directional
directivity
disarmingly
disbeliever
dismayingly
disobliging
disposition
dispositive
disseminate
disseminule
dissepiment
dissimilate
dissociable
diverticula
divestiture
domesticate
domesticity
doughtiness
dresscircle
drouthiness
duplicitous
dyslogistic
earthliness
eclecticism
ecumenicism
ecumenicity
editorially
educability
educational
effectively
einsteinium
elderliness
electrician
electricity
eligibility
ellipticity
embellisher
embracingly
enchiridion
endearingly
enquiringly
esotericism
essentially
establisher
Eucharistic
euphemistic
evolutional
exceedingly
exceptional
excessively
exclusively
exclusivity
excursively
executioner
exotericism
expansional
expansively
expansivity
expenditure
expensively
explosively
exquisitely
extensional
extensively
exterminate
extortioner
extradition
facsimilist
fallibility
falteringly
farraginous
fatiguingly
faultfinder
favouritism
feasibility
ferruginous
fetichistic
fetishistic
feudalistic
fidgetiness
financially
fireraising
flauntingly
fleshliness
flexibility
flightiness
floweriness
forethinker
formalistic
formational
fortifiable
franctireur
franklinite
freethinker
frenchified
frostbitten
frowstiness
gentilitial
geopolitics
ghastliness
ghostliness
gnotobiosis
gnotobiotic
gradational
granolithic
gravedigger
gristliness
grouchiness
grumblingly
guesstimate
gullibility
haggadistic
hairraising
hairtrigger
hallucinate
halophilous
handknitted
handpainted
handwriting
handwritten
harmonistic
haughtiness
healthiness
Hellenistic
hermeticism
hesperidium
Hibernicism
Hispanicise
Hispanicism
Hispanicist
historiated
historicise
historicism
historicist
historicity
horripilate
houselights
housewifely
housewifery
hylozoistic
illiquidity
imitatively
immarginate
impartially
impassioned
impassively
impassivity
impertinent
imperviable
imploringly
imprecisely
imprecision
improvident
impulsively
incardinate
incertitude
inclusively
incognisant
incontinent
incriminate
IndoChinese
inductively
inedibility
infanticide
infantilism
infertility
inflexional
ingratitude
ingurgitate
innutrition
inquilinous
inquiringly
inquisition
inquisitive
insecticide
insectifuge
insectivore
insensitive
insouciance
instability
insultingly
intagliated
intelligent
intensifier
intensional
intensively
intentional
intentioned
interlinear
Interlingua
interlining
intermingle
intermitted
interviewee
interviewer
intrepidity
intromitted
intromitter
intrusively
intuitional
intuitively
intuitivism
invectively
inventively
investigate
investiture
inviability
irruptively
Jansenistic
jargonistic
justiciable
justifiable
justifiably
lamellicorn
lamelliform
largeminded
laudability
lengthiness
lentiginous
liberticide
libertinage
libertinism
lickerishly
lickspittle
lightminded
lineprinter
lingeringly
liquefiable
loathliness
longanimity
looselimbed
lucratively
macrobiotic
maddeningly
magnanimity
magnanimous
magnificent
malposition
mandarinate
mandolinist
manneristic
marconigram
masculinely
masculinise
masculinity
masochistic
matrilineal
matrilinear
maxillipede
mechanician
mechanistic
mediumistic
mercurially
mesalliance
meteoritics
Methodistic
microlithic
micturition
minnesinger
misalliance
miscibility
miserliness
misestimate
modernistic
molecricket
molendinary
monasticism
monoclinous
mountaineer
mountainous
mountaintop
moveability
multilinear
muskthistle
narratively
naughtiness
necessitate
necessitous
necrobiosis
neologistic
nephelinite
neuroticism
nondelivery
nonresident
nullifidian
nutritional
nutritively
objectively
objectivism

objectivist
objectivity
observingly
obsessional
obsessively
obtrusively
oenophilist
offensively
omniscience
operational
operatively
orderliness
ostensively
outstripped
oversailing
overwritten
oviposition
Palestinian
palpability
pantheistic
pantomimist
paraleipsis
parheliacal
parishioner
parochially
participant
participate
participial
partitioned
partitioner
partitively
parturition
passeriform
passibility
patelliform
patrilineal
patronising
paunchiness
pearlfisher
peccability
peccadillos
pellucidity
penultimate
percipience
peregrinate
perennially
periodicity
perishingly
personifier
pervasively
pessimistic
phonetician
photofinish
phthiriasis
pictorially
pinnatisect
placability
plaintively
pleinairist
pluralistic
pontificals
pontificate
portability
portraitist
portraiture
possibility
posteriorly
postexilian
potentially
potteringly
prattlingly
preachiness
preaudience
precipitant
precipitate
precipitous
predominant
predominate
preignition
prejudicial
preliminary
prelusively
premeditate
premonition
premonitory
prenominate
preposition
prepositive
presumingly
preterition
prevaricate
previsional
prickliness
primitively
primitivism
privatively
prizewinner
probabilism
probabilist
probability
probational
probationer
proficiency
progenitrix
progeniture
prohibition
prohibitive
prohibitory
prolificacy
prolificity
promisingly
promotional
promptitude
propitiable
propitiator
proposition
provenience
provisional
provokingly
pruriginous
pulchritude
purposively
pussywillow
qualifiable
queenliness
quickfiring
quicksilver
quickwitted
Rabelaisian
rangefinder
rateability
ratiocinate
raunchiness
ravishingly
readability
readywitted
receptively
receptivity
recessional
recessively
recognition
recognitive
recognitory
recommittal
recondition
recriminate
rectifiable
rectilineal
rectilinear
redactional
reduplicate
reflexively
regurgitate
rejoicingly
reliability
repartition
replenisher
repleviable
reprovingly
repulsively
requisition
resistively
resistivity
resuscitate
retentively
retentivity
revaccinate
revendicate
reversional
reversioner
rhetorician
rhomboideus
rightminded
rightwinger
ritualistic
rodenticide
romanticise
romanticism
romanticist
sacrificial
saintliness
saleability
salvational
sandskipper
Sanskritist
saprobiotic
sartorially
satiability
satisfiable
saturninely
savouriness
scalariform
scalpriform
schottische
scientistic
scorchingly
ScotchIrish
scragginess
scrappiness
screamingly
scrimpiness
scruffiness
searchingly
secretively
seductively
selectively
selectivity
selfevident
selfopinion
selfraising
semanticist
semiskilled
sensational
sensibility
sensitively
sensitivity
sensorially
serendipity
serpiginous
shadowiness
shamanistic
shapeliness
sharpwitted
shipbuilder
shortwinded
shrinkingly
shrubbiness
sickeningly
sideslipped
sightliness
signifiable
significant
signpainter
silveriness
simperingly
sinfonietta
situational
sketchiness
Slavonicise
slightingly
smallminded
soapboiling
soberminded
sociability
socialistic
solipsistic
solvability
somewhither
Soroptimist
sovereignly
sovereignty
specifiable
specificity
speechifier
spellbinder
sphaeridium
spifflicate
Spinozistic
spiritistic
springiness
squashiness
squeakiness
squeamishly
squintingly
starchiness
startlingly
stateliness
stoolpigeon
streakiness
stringiness
stumblingly
subaerially
subaudition
subdivision
subdominant
subordinate
subregional
sufficiency
suffumigate
suitability
summariness
summational
superficial
superficies
supervision
supervisory
supposition
suppositive
suppository
surficially
swarthiness
syllabicity
syllogistic
symbolistic
symposiarch
synergistic
talkatively
tameability
tangibility
tantalising
tarradiddle
teleprinter
tensibility
tentatively
testability
Teutonicism
theatricals
therewithal
thickwitted
thinskinned
thirstiness
threadiness
thriftiness
thrillingly
throatiness
tightfisted
tightlipped
toothbilled
torchsinger
totteringly
toughminded
toxophilite
traditional
tragedienne
transfigure
transfinite
transfixion
transmittal
transmitted
transmitter
transpierce
trapeziform
treacliness
tremblingly
tribunicial
tribunitial
tricksiness
triennially
tritheistic
triumvirate
typewritten
tyrannicide
ultraviolet
unbendingly
uncanniness
unceasingly
uncommitted
underbidder
underpinned
undersigned
unemotional
unfailingly
unfashioned
unfeelingly
unforgiving
unfurnished
ungodliness
unhappiness
unigeniture
unmanliness
unmeaningly
unnervingly
unpromising
unqualified
unrealistic
unsmilingly
unsparingly
unvarnished
unweetingly
unwillingly
unwinkingly
unwittingly
valuational
variability
variational
varsovienne
vasculiform
velvetiness
vendibility
verbalistic
versatilely
versatility
vertiginous
vestigially
vibratility
vibrational
vicissitude
vincibility
vitrifiable
volcanicity
volkslieder
voodooistic
vortiginous
vulcanicity
washability
waspwaisted
wealthiness
weightiness
wherewithal
witheringly
wolfwhistle
womanliness
workability
worldliness
xenophilous
xerophilous
lesemajesty
stiflejoint
togglejoint
wapperjawed
airsickness
archdukedom
bewhiskered
hurryskurry
Kulturkampf
outspokenly
pocketknife
seasickness
sheathknife
unbreakable
unshockable
unspeakable
unspeakably
unthinkable
unthinkably
waterskiing
Abbevillian
aboutsledge
acarpellous
accumulator
acknowledge
admiralship
agriculture
aiguillette
altorelievo
altorilievo
ambivalence
ambivalency
amontillado
anadiplosis
anaphylaxis
annihilator
apophyllite
apostolical
apparelling
aquaculture
aquarellist
aquiculture
articulable
articulated
articulator
assemblyman
assimilable
assimilator
atrabilious
auricularly
balefulness
BaltoSlavic
bashfulness
bedevilment
benevolence
bersaglieri
bestselling
bibliolater
bibliolatry
bimetallism
bimetallist
binocularly
bookselling
brucellosis
calceolaria
cancellated
candlelight
carefulness

castellated
cauliflower
chancellery
chancellory
channelling
chronologer
chronologic
chrysalides
chrysalises
circumlunar
codicillary
colonelship
compellable
concealable
concealment
congealable
congealment
constellate
controlling
controlment
cordialness
counselling
crenellated
crystalline
crystallise
crystallite
crystalloid
curtailment
demonolatry
depopulator
despoilment
dicotyledon
disciplinal
discipliner
disinclined
dissyllable
dolefulness
domiciliary
domiciliate
dutifulness
earthcloset
emasculator
embowelling
embroilment
embryologic
empanelling
enthralling
enthralment
epithalamia
epithalamic
epithelioma
equipollent
equivalence
equivalency
evangelical
exoskeletal
exoskeleton
factualness
fatefulness
fearfulness
finicalness
firewalking
flagellator
flannelette
flannelling
flocculence
footsoldier
frankpledge
fraudulence
fretfulness
gainfulness
generaliser
generalship
geniculated
genteelness
gillyflower
glassblower
globeflower
glossolalia
godchildren
gradualness
grammalogue
haemoglobin
halfholiday
handselling
harmfulness
hatefulness
haustellate
heedfulness
helpfulness
hemeralopia
highfalutin
hopefulness
hurtfulness
hyperplasia
immunologic
impanelling
imperilling
imperilment
incompliant
initialling
installment
instillment
insufflator
interallied
interfluent
interplayed
invigilator
irregularly
irresoluble
kilocalorie
landaulette
landholding
literalness
logicalness
lustfulness
makebelieve
malevolence
manipulable
manipulator
marshalling
marshalship
medicolegal
mellifluent
mellifluous
mentholated
mindfulness
mineraliser
miscellanea
misspelling
mitrailleur
molecularly
monoculture
monopoliser
musicalness
namecalling
naturalness
needfulness
neutraliser
nomenclator
nonchalance
nonviolence
nympholepsy
operculated
orbicularly
osteoplasty
outbuilding
overbalance
painfulness
painkilling
panhellenic
paraselenae
pedicellate
pediculosis
penicillate
penicillium
philhellene
physiologic
pitchblende
pitifulness
plasmolysis
plasmolytic
playfulness
pointillism
pointillist
pomiculture
prophylaxis
proteolysis
proteolytic
prothalamia
prothallial
prothallium
psychologic
punctilious
pushfulness
quadrillion
quarrelling
quarrelsome
quintillion
radicalness
rapscallion
realpolitik
resemblance
restfulness
retroflexed
ribvaulting
roadholding
ropewalking
sansculotte
scaffolding
scintillant
scintillate
searchlight
selfculture
selfreliant
semiellipse
semipalmate
sericulture
severalfold
shirtsleeve
shrivelling
skilfulness
sockdolager
sockdologen
somatologic
songfulness
soulfulness
spaceflight
spherulitic
spiritlevel
spondulicks
spondylitis
staurolitic
stencilling
stoicalness
straitlaced
streetlight
stridulator
subaxillary
superfluity
superfluous
surveillant
tearfulness
technologic
teratologic
tessellated
theodolitic
thermolysis
thermolytic
throatlatch
tonsillitis
tourbillion
trailblazer
trammelling
transalpine
transilient
triphyllous
trisyllabic
trisyllable
trivialness
trothplight
tunefulness
typicalness
unavailable
uncivilised
undeveloped
unicellular
uninucleate
unusualness
vasodilator
ventriloquy
vesicularly
victualless
victualling
viniculture
viticulture
wakefulness
wellbeloved
whigmaleery
wirepulling
wishfulness
wistfulness
zestfulness
actinometer
actinomyces
actinomycin
aeronomical
agronomical
alkalimeter
alkalimetry
allelomorph
altocumulus
anastomoses
anastomosis
anastomotic
antiSemitic
antonomasia
auxanometer
baptismally
bibliomancy
bibliomania
biedermeier
biochemical
boilermaker
calorimeter
calorimetry
chainsmoker
charismatic
cheiromancy
Christmassy
chronometer
chronometry
colorimeter
colorimetry
confirmable
conformable
conformably
conformally
conformance
consummator
conterminal
cottonmouth
craniometry
cryptomeria
diastematic
dichromatic
disharmonic
dissymmetry
dynamometer
dynamometry
elastomeric
forgetmenot
Francomania
gendarmerie
gentlemanly
geochemical
gradiometer
gyrocompass
habiliments
hypolimnion
impedimenta
inestimable
inestimably
inflammable
inflammably
kleptomania
lachrymator
mantuamaker
megalomania
metasomatic
metonymical
milliampere
nymphomania
oneiromancy
papiermache
paronomasia
performable
performance
phrasemaker
pluviometer
pocketmoney
polarimeter
polarimetry
problematic
pseudomonas
pseudomorph
psychometry
psychomotor
rearadmiral
reclaimable
rhabdomancy
rifacimenti
rifacimento
salinometer
schwarmerei
sclerometer
seismometer
seismometry
selfcommand
selflimited
showjumping
speedometer
spherometer
stalagmitic
statesmanly
stereometry
stichometry
subterminal
superimpose
symptomatic
syndesmosis
synonymical
tacheometer
taxonomical
tephromancy
theorematic
thermometer
thermometry
thingumabob
thingumajig
toxicomania
trichomonad
twelvemonth
unashamedly
uniformness
vaporimeter
verisimilar
viceadmiral
volumometer
abandonment
abdominally
abiogeneses
abiogenesis
abiogenetic
acrimonious
adjournment
aerodynamic
Albigensian
albuminuria
AngloIndian
antemundane
antependium
antimonious
Apollinaris
argumentive
arraignment
bacchanalia
backbencher
barquentine
bedizenment
bellringing
betweenmaid
betweenness
betweentime
billionaire
biocoenoses
biocoenosis
biocoenotic
birdfancier
bonbonniere
bookbinding
bottlenosed
boutonniere
Brahmanical
Brahminical
bushmanship
captainship
captionless
carabiniere
carabinieri
caravanning
caravansary
Carolingian
ceremonious
challenging
chansonnier
chickenfeed
chickenwire
Chippendale
chrominance
citizenship
codefendant
coessential
coeternally
coextension
coextensive
concernment
condemnable
consignable
consignment
containable
containment
contorniate
cookgeneral
coordinator
costbenefit
countenance
cytogenesis
cytokinesis
deferential
denizenship
denominator
desalinator
detrainment
diamagnetic
diaphaneity
Diophantine
discernible
discernibly
discernment
disgruntled
doctrinaire
doctrinally
documentary

drunkenness
dualcontrol
earthenware
easternmost
ectogenesis
ectogenetic
elephantine
elephantoid
embryonated
emotionally
emotionless
enchainment
enlivenment
entrainment
environment
Esperantist
existential
explainable
exponential
factfinding
factionally
farthingale
fashionable
fashionably
filamentary
filamentous
fissionable
foraminated
foraminifer
foreignness
forerunning
forlornness
fragmentary
fraternally
fraterniser
gametangium
gamogenesis
gastronomic
gentianella
geomagnetic
glauconitic
gourmandise
gourmandism
halfbinding
halflanding
headhunting
highranking
homocentric
homogeneity
homogeneous
homogenetic
homogeniser
hylogenesis
hypotension
ignominious
illmannered
illuminable
illuminance
illuminator
immanentism
immanentist
impecunious
impregnable
impregnably
inalienable
inalienably
inattention
inattentive
indefinable
indefinably
independent
inessential
inexpensive
inferential
influential
ingrainedly
inoffensive
inseminator
involuntary
ironmongery
irredentism
irredentist
irretention
irretentive
Jacobinical
jauntingcar
kitchenette
kitchensink
kitchenware
latifundium
laughinggas
legionnaire
lieutenancy
lifemanship
ligamentary
ligamentous
magazinegun
maintenance
maisonnette
medicinable
medicinally
membraneous
mentionable
merchandise
merchantman
merogenesis
Merovingian
merryandrew
metacentric
metagenesis
metagenetic
millionaire
mindbending
monogenesis
monogenetic
monolingual
moribundity
mothernaked
mudslinging
nightingale
nocturnally
oarsmanship
octagonally
oecumenical
officinally
oilpainting
ontogenesis
ontogenetic
opinionated
outstanding
overmanning
overrunning
Passiontide
patternshop
penitential
pensionable
pensionless
pentlandite
peritonitis
pneumonitis
polygenesis
polygenetic
polygonally
portionless
portmanteau
preeminence
preprandial
punchinello
puritanical
quadrennial
quadrennium
quaternloaf
quincuncial
realignment
reedbunting
referential
regimentals
rejuvenator
rejuvenesce
reorientate
residential
resplendent
reverential
rightangled
rodomontade
ropedancing
rubicundity
rudimentary
safeconduct
sanguinaria
sanguineous
scaleinsect
schizanthus
scrutiniser
sectionally
sedimentary
selaginella
selfcentred
selfconceit
selfcontent
selfcontrol
selfdenying
selfwinding
semimonthly
sheetanchor
showmanship
sickbenefit
sleepingbag
sleepingcar
slickenside
snowbunting
spontaneity
spontaneous
stephanotis
stickinsect
stockinette
stramineous
subclinical
substandard
substantial
substantive
superinduce
superintend
surgeonfish
sustainable
sustainment
symphonious
taratantara
tegumentary
telekinesis
telekinetic
tenementary
theocentric
thrasonical
toffeenosed
treasonable
treasonably
trichinosis
tufthunting
uncanonical
uncleanness
unessential
unfeignedly
unorganized
unrelenting
unshrinking
vagabondage
vagabondise
vagabondish
vagabondism
vaticinator
viscountess
Weismannism
westernmost
Westminster
Whitsuntide
workmanlike
workmanship
zooplankton
ablutionary
abortionist
accessorial
accessorise
accommodate
adiaphorism
adoptionism
adoptionist
aerobiology
afficionado
agrobiology
allantoides
ambiguously
ambitiously
amorphously
amphibolite
amphibology
anachronism
anachronous
anacreontic
analogously
AngloNorman
anomalously
anonymously
anteriority
anthologise
anthologist
antiphonary
apostrophic
apotheosise
archaeology
archaeornis
archdiocese
arenicolous
aspersorium
assessorial
assiduously
Assyriology
atrociously
audaciously
audiologist
autoerotism
autotrophic
balletomane
barbarously
barnstormer
barrelorgan
beachcomber
beauteously
behavioural
bellicosity
bicarbonate
bicorporate
blackcoated
blameworthy
bounteously
bourgeoisie
bracteolate
bryozoology
buffalorobe
bumptiously
cacophonous
calcicolous
campanology
capaciously
carcinomata
carnivorous
catadromous
catercousin
cavernously
chaperonage
chaulmoogra
chiropodist
Christology
clairvoyant
clamorously
cleistogamy
climatology
coldblooded
collaborate
commemorate
comptroller
condylomata
congruously
consciously
coralloidal
cornucopian
corroborant
corroborate
cosmetology
cosmogonist
cosmologist
cosmopolite
cotemporary
courteously
creationism
creationist
credulously
crematorium
criminology
crocidolite
crossbowman
cryobiology
dactylogram
dactylology
dangerously
decarbonate
decarbonise
deliciously
deliriously
dermatology
desultorily
deteriorate
deuterogamy
Deuteronomy
dexterously
diachronism
diastrophic
dichotomise
dichotomist
dichotomous
dictatorial
diphthongal
diplococcus
dipterocarp
directorate
directorial
disafforest
dishonourer
disunionist
divisionary
divisionism
doorknocker
downtrodden
dreadnought
ectotrophic
egregiously
electioneer
electrocute
electrolier
electrology
electrolyse
electrolyte
electronics
electrotype
ellipsoidal
emulsionise
endotrophic
erroneously
erythrocyte
eschatology
ethnologist
Etruscology
etymologise
etymologist
euchologion
eudaemonism
eudaemonist
executorial
exogenously
expectorant
expectorate
extemporary
extemporise
exteriorise
exteriority
extrapolate
facetiously
faithworthy
fanfaronade
feloniously
ferociously
fieldcornet
fieldworker
footslogger
foreclosure
foreshorten
forethought
forthcoming
fractionary
fractionate
fractionise
fractiously
freebooting
freethought
frivolously
frothhopper
frugivorous
fullblooded
functionary
functionate
garrulously
gemmologist
genealogise
genealogist
geostrophic
Germanophil
gerontology
gestatorial
giantpowder
glutinously
gonfalonier
goodlooking
grandiosely
grandiosity
grandmother
granivorous
granulocyte
grasshopper
gynaecocrat
gynaecology
haematocele
haematocrit
haematology
hagiologist
halfblooded
Hamiltonian
handwrought
hazardously
heavyfooted
hedgehopped
helleborine
hemianopsia
herbivorous
heresiology
herpetology
highbrowism
highwrought
hilariously
hippopotami
histologist
histrionics
histrionism
homophonous
homosporous

honeymooner
hornswoggle
horsecollar
horsedoctor
householder
housemother
hydrologist
hydroponics
hyperbolise
hyperboloid
hyperborean
hypnopompic
hypoglossal
ichthyology
ichthyornis
ichthyosaur
illfavoured
illhumoured
illusionism
illusionist
imperforate
imperiously
impersonate
impetuosity
impetuously
incommodity
inconsonant
incorporate
incorporeal
incuriosity
incuriously
inferiority
ingeniously
ingenuously
injuriously
innocuously
innoxiously
insectology
insessorial
insidiously
intercostal
intercourse
interiorise
interiority
interlocker
interpolate
interrogate
inventorial
invidiously
isochronism
isochronous
judiciously
kinesiology
kwashiorkor
laboriously
lacrimosely
lacrymosely
larcenously
laryngology
laryngotomy
leapfrogged
leaseholder
lecherously
lichenology
lightfooted
lightsomely
limnologist
lithotomise
lithotomist
litigiously
loathsomely
loxodromics
ludicrously
luxuriously
machicolate
macrocosmic
madreporite
Maglemosian
maladroitly
malapropism
malariology
maliciously
mammalogist
marchioness
martyrology
massproduce
mastodontic
matrimonial
mediatorial
melodiously
meningocele
metalloidal
metalworker
meteoroidal
meteorology
methodology
micrococcal
micrococcus
microcosmic
mindblowing
misbegotten
mollycoddle
momentously
monstrosity
monstrously
mosstrooper
multicolour
multinomial
murderously
murmurously
myrmecology
mythologise
mythologist
mythopoeist
mythopoetic
namedropper
nasofrontal
necrologist
necropoleis
nefariously
negationist
neighbourly
neurologist
nightporter
nonunionist
notoriously
obliviously
obnoxiously
octachordal
officiously
olfactology
ophiologist
orchidology
ornithology
ornithopter
ornithosaur
orthodontia
orthodontic
oscillogram
osteologist
ostracoderm
Ostrogothic
overcropped
overproduce
overwrought
pandemonium
panicmonger
paratrooper
paternoster
pathologist
patrimonial
pawnbroking
pelargonium
pendulously
pentazocine
Pentecostal
penuriously
perchlorate
periodontal
peristomial
pestologist
petitionary
petrologist
petticoated
pettifogger
phenologist
philologian
philologist
philosopher
philosophic
phonologist
phosphonium
phosphorate
phosphorism
phosphorite
phosphorous
photocopier
phraseogram
phraseology
phycologist
phytologist
phytotomist
pieceworker
piscatorial
piscivorous
planetoidal
planoconvex
platinotype
Pleistocene
plenipotent
plenteously
poisonously
poltroonery
polyglottal
polyglottic
polyphonous
ponderosity
ponderously
positronium
predatorily
prefatorial
prefatorily
prelusorily
primatology
prochronism
prolegomena
protagonist
Proterozoic
protonotary
provisorily
pteridology
pureblooded
purgatorial
pussyfooter
Pythagorean
Pythagorism
quaestorial
querulously
questionary
radiologist
rancorously
rapaciously
rapturously
reactionary
reactionist
reciprocate
reciprocity
reconnoitre
rediscovery
reflexology
reintroduce
relationism
relationist
religionise
religionism
religionist
religiosity
religiously
reportorial
retrorocket
revisionary
revisionism
revisionist
rheotropism
rhinologist
rhynchodont
righteously
roughfooted
sagaciously
salaciously
saltatorial
sauropodous
saxophonist
scaremonger
schistosity
schistosome
scientology
scorpionfly
scriptorial
scriptorium
seditionary
seditiously
seigniorage
seigniorial
selfclosing
semasiology
shareholder
shortcoming
showstopper
sightworthy
skeletonise
slaveholder
smallholder
smithsonite
snowleopard
sociologist
solutionist
soteriology
spectrogram
spectrology
spelaeology
sphagnology
sphygmogram
splayfooted
splendorous
sporogonium
squarsonage
stadtholder
stakeholder
stallholder
starcrossed
statutorily
steamboiler
steamroller
steelworker
steganogram
stellionate
stepbrother
stockholder
stockjobber
stomatology
strenuosity
strenuously
stylopodium
sugarcoated
sumptuosity
sumptuously
superioress
superiority
supernormal
swiftfooted
synchromesh
synchronise
synchronism
synchronous
synchrotron
tautologise
tautologism
tautologous
teaspoonful
teenybopper
teleologism
teleologist
telephonist
tenaciously
terminology
terricolous
territorial
testimonial
tetrapodous
thalidomide
thanatology
thankworthy
theobromine
theretofore
thermionics
threecolour
thrombocyte
titleholder
tobacconist
toothpowder
toothsomely
torticollis
torturously
tracheotomy
tragicomedy
transformer
translocate
transponder
transporter
trapezoidal
tremulously
tricoloured
tritagonist
troublously
trustworthy
trypanosome
tyrannosaur
tyrannously
ultramodern
ultrasonics
unanimously
unbeknownst
unexploited
unicoloured
unorthodoxy
unreasoning
vacationist
vagariously
vasectomise
venereology
venturously
veraciously
verminously
vexatiously
vexillology
vicariously
vivaciously
volcanology
volitionary
voraciously
vulcanology
wainscoting
wainscotted
warmblooded
waterbottle
watercolour
watercooled
watercooler
watercourse
waterlogged
wearisomely
weenybopper
wellgroomed
wheresoever
whichsoever
whitecollar
wholesomely
wholesouled
whoremonger
whosesoever
winegrowing
witchdoctor
worrisomely
xylophonist
ailurophile
ailurophobe
anencephaly
antenuptial
anthropical
anticipator
antitypical
apomorphine
aposiopesis
bathysphere
bibliopegic
bibliophile
bibliophily
bibliopolic
brahmaputra
breastplate
bulletproof
bumblepuppy
candlepower
centrepiece
centripetal
chamaephyte
chlorophyll
chloroplast
chloroprene
chromoplast
chrysoprase
circumpolar
clodhopping
comeuppance
commonplace
consumption
consumptive
contemplate
contraption
copperplate
corecipient
description
descriptive
developable
development
diadelphous
discerption
discrepancy
distempered
dodecaphony
emancipator
entomophily
envelopment
epigraphist
episcopally
eucalyptole
filterpaper
fingerplate
fingerprint
flagcaptain
foretopmast
foretopsail
Francophile
Francophobe
francophone
gafftopsail
gametophyte
greasepaint
greaseproof
gymnospermy
heterophony
heteroploid
heteropolar

homoeopathy
hydrosphere
hymenoptera
hypotyposis
illdisposed
illtempered
inescapable
inscription
inscriptive
intersperse
interspinal
isomorphism
isomorphous
lepidoptera
letterpress
lithosphere
maintopmast
maintopsail
maladaptive
mantelpiece
marketplace
masterpiece
megalopolis
melanophore
moneyspider
motivepower
municipally
naturopathy
needlepoint
Neotropical
nickelplate
ommatophore
orthoepical
outcropping
overlapping
overtopping
oysterplant
ozonosphere
paratyphoid
photosphere
plainspoken
planisphere
playerpiano
plectoptera
polypeptide
postnuptial
presumption
presumptive
principally
pseudopodia
psychopathy
quadraphony
quadrupedal
racketpress
rattlepated
sclerophyll
selfimposed
selfreproof
selfsupport
shortspoken
showerproof
shrinkproof
silverplate
silverpoint
somatoplasm
spermaphyte
steatopygia
stereophony
stirrupbone
stirruppump
stringpiece
strongpoint
subscapular
subsumption
subsumptive
subtropical
theosophist
thermophile
threadpaper
trimorphism
trimorphous
troposphere
tryingplane
tryptophane
twelvepenny
unflappable
unstoppable
wiretapping
worshipable
worshipless
worshipping
xanthophyll
zoographist
zoomorphism
doublequick
grotesquely
grotesquery
propinquity
soliloquise
soliloquist
aboveground
accelerando
accelerator
achondritic
adulterator
aeolotropic
ahistorical
allAmerican
allegorical
allomorphic
altostratus
ambiversion
ameliorator
amenorrhoea
anagnorisis
angiography
AngloFrench
anisotropic
annabergite
anniversary
antiphrasis
antipyretic
antistrophe
aponeuroses
aponeurosis
aponeurotic
appropriate
bilaterally
biometrical
biquadratic
blackgrouse
bladderwort
blepharitis
blunderbuss
bodyservant
Bonapartean
Bonapartism
Bonapartist
bondservant
bondservice
bowdleriser
brankursine
breadcrumbs
brotherhood
bullterrier
burglarious
butcherbird
calendrical
californium
calligraphy
calyptrogen
cantharides
cantharidic
cartography
catachreses
catachresis
catastrophe
categorical
centigramme
chainarmour
chamberlain
chambermaid
champertous
chanterelle
chimaerical
chirography
chitterling
chorography
chrysarobin
clapperclaw
coinheritor
coinsurance
coleorrhiza
concurrence
conferrable
conquerable
consecrator
conspirator
consternate
contrariety
contrarious
cosmography
counterblow
counterbond
counterfeit
counterfoil
counterfort
countermand
countermark
countermine
countermove
countermure
counterpane
counterpart
counterplan
counterplea
counterplot
countersign
countersink
countersunk
counterturn
countervail
counterview
counterwork
crackerjack
cryosurgery
curatorship
cylindrical
decelerator
deflagrator
deleterious
deliverable
deliverance
deliveryman
denumerable
desideratum
dexiotropic
diametrical
diaphoresis
diaphoretic
diarthrosis
directrices
disapproval
discography
discourtesy
dittography
dropcurtain
dropforging
dualpurpose
earpiercing
ectomorphic
elbowgrease
embowerment
emperorship
enarthrosis
encumbrance
endocardiac
endocardial
endocardium
endomorphic
enterpriser
ephemerides
ethnography
exaggerator
exarcerbate
executrices
executrixes
expropriate
farthermost
featheredge
featherhead
featherless
fenestrated
filmography
firstfruits
flabbergast
flavourless
flavoursome
forbearance
forevermore
foreverness
forewarning
furtherance
furthermore
furthermost
furthersome
geometrical
ghostwriter
GraecoRoman
grangeriser
greengrocer
haemorrhage
haemorrhoid
Hagiographa
hagiography
haplography
harbourless
hardworking
headborough
heartbroken
hebephrenia
hebephrenic
hedgepriest
heliography
heliotropic
hemimorphic
heroworship
Hippocratic
homestretch
homomorphic
hydrobromic
hydrography
hydrotropic
hymnography
hypercritic
hypertrophy
hypsography
ichnography
iconography
idiomorphic
illiberally
illustrator
illustrious
impropriate
impropriety
inadvertent
inalterable
inalterably
inaugurator
incinerator
incoherence
incoherency
incongruent
incongruity
incongruous
industrious
infantryman
infiltrator
innumerable
innumerably
inobservant
inopportune
inseparable
inseparably
insuperable
insuperably
intercrural
intergrowth
interpreter
intertribal
intolerable
intolerably
intolerance
invigorator
irreparable
irreparably
irreverence
isometrical
landlordism
launderette
leatherback
leatherhead
leatherneck
linendraper
lithography
lithotripsy
lophobranch
lowspirited
magistratic
maidservant
mailcarrier
managership
masquerader
matriarchal
mediatrices
meritorious
mesomorphic
metachrosis
metamorphic
micrography
microgroove
miscarriage
mismarriage
moisturiser
monitorship
monocarpous
monochromat
monochromic
monomorphic
motherright
mythography
nailvarnish
Neanderthal
neurotropic
nittygritty
nyctitropic
obstetrical
ochlocratic
omnifarious
opencircuit
opprobrious
orthography
orthotropic
osteography
overgarment
overstretch
oxyhydrogen
Palaearctic
palindromic
panegyrical
paramorphic
paraphraser
partnership
pasteuriser
patriarchal
pericardiac
pericardial
pericardium
periphrases
periphrasis
perpetrator
petrography
phonography
photography
phototropic
phytography
pictography
pilocarpine
pipistrelle
pivotbridge
plagiariser
plasterwork
platearmour
platforming
platyrrhine
pleasurable
pleasurably
pleiotropic
pleochroism
pleomorphic
plutocratic
pococurante
polycarpous
polychromic
polymorphic
populariser
pornography
porphyritic
pourparlers
praetorship
premiership
proctorship
prothoracic
pullthrough
quarterback
quarterdeck
quartertone
quickfreeze
quickfrozen
quilldriver
radiography
reapportion
reassertion
reassurance
recoverable
redetermine
reedwarbler
regenerable
regenerator
registrable
reincarnate
reinsertion
reinsurance
remembrance
remunerator
reprogramme
reprography
ringstraked
scalearmour
scattergood
scenography
scholarship
scissorbill
scissortail
scoundrelly
screwdriver
scuppernong
secondrater
selffertile
selfservice
selfserving
selftorture
selfworship
senatorship

septifragal
shelterbelt
shelterless
shepherdess
shocktroops
shutterless
sinistrally
sinistrorse
slavedriver
slenderness
smithereens
snickersnee
soldierlike
soldiership
Southernism
spatterdash
speakership
spessartite
sponsorship
standardise
stenography
stockbroker
stoneground
stormtroops
stylography
subumbrella
succourless
sulphureous
sulphurwort
symmetrical
tachygraphy
taciturnity
tankfarming
taxidermist
teachership
temerarious
testatrices
thitherward
thixotropic
thunderbird
thunderbolt
thunderclap
thunderhead
thunderless
thunderpeal
timebargain
timeserving
transcriber
transuranic
triggerfish
trouserless
trousersuit
tuttifrutti
unalterable
unassertive
underground
undergrowth
underwriter
undeserving
undesirable
unendurable
unendurably
unimportant
unmemorable
unmemorably
unnaturally
unsaturated
unutterable
unutterably
uranography
urochordate
urticarious
vehmgericht
vicegerency
vinaigrette
vituperator
vociferance
vociferator
weathercock
weatherwise
weatherworn
weighbridge
wheelwright
whitherward
widowerhood
woodcarving
xylocarpous
zincography
zygomorphic
acaulescent
acquiescent
aimlessness
airlessness
alkalescent
amazonstone
amethystine
amorousness
anxiousness
arborescent
arduousness
armtwisting
arthrospore
artlessness
Belorussian
biliousness
billetsdoux
billposting
biophysical
bittersweet
bondwashing
businessman
callousness
candlestick
carpetsnake
caryopsides
chargesheet
chiaroscuro
chinoiserie
chromosomal
chronoscope
circumsolar
circumspect
civilisable
clandestine
clothesline
clothesmoth
clothesprop
cobblestone
cockleshell
collapsible
commensally
commissural
commonsense
compassable
compensator
compossible
compression
compressive
comprisable
concrescent
condensable
confessedly
congressman
connoisseur
contrastive
conversable
conversance
conversancy
copingstone
copiousness
coppersmith
corbiesteps
cornerstone
cornhusking
curiousness
delitescent
depressible
deviousness
diagnostics
diatessaron
discussable
discussible
disguisedly
dispensable
dispersedly
distensible
distressful
distrustful
doublespeak
dubiousness
emulousness
endlessness
engrossment
enterostomy
enviousness
epidiascope
equidistant
everlasting
exercisable
expressible
fatuousness
fiddlestick
fingerstall
fluorescein
fluorescent
fluoroscope
fluoroscopy
freemasonry
galleyslave
gallowsbird
gallowstree
gartersnake
gaseousness
gastroscope
geophysical
gibbousness
godforsaken
godlessness
groundsheet
gutlessness
guttersnipe
handfasting
haplessness
hearthstone
heinousness
heterospory
hideousness
Hindoostani
hugeousness
hypogastric
implausible
implausibly
impressible
impressment
impuissance
inadvisable
incalescent
increasable
indehiscent
indigestion
indigestive
indivisible
indivisibly
inexcusable
inexcusably
interesting
interosseus
intumescent
irrecusable
irrecusably
irremissive
jealousness
joylessness
juvenescent
kinetoscope
lawlessness
linefishing
linguistics
lowpressure
luminescent
malfeasance
manifestant
manifestoes
mantelshelf
manumission
marlinspike
marquessate
marquisette
meadowsweet
metoposcopy
middlesized
misconstrue
misfeasance
mistrustful
monkeyshine
nationstate
nervousness
nonexistent
nonfeasance
nonplussing
nonsensical
noxiousness
obmutescent
obsolescent
obviousness
odorousness
ominousness
onerousness
organisable
Panglossian
paradisical
pearlescent
permissible
permissibly
persuasible
phalanstery
phantasiast
phantasmata
piteousness
plagiostome
ploughshare
ploughstaff
pocketsized
polarisable
polariscope
pompousness
preexistent
prestissimo
proconsular
procrustean
professedly
progression
progressism
progressist
progressive
protrusible
pumicestone
purchasable
purpresture
rattlesnake
raucousness
reminiscent
renaissance
repressible
repressibly
resipiscent
responsible
responsibly
retinoscopy
retranslate
reviviscent
riotousness
rottenstone
rubberstamp
ruinousness
saplessness
scyphistoma
secondsight
seismoscope
selfassured
selfdespair
selfdisplay
selfmastery
selfrespect
seriousness
sexagesimal
sexlessness
silversmith
silverstick
singlestick
sinlessness
sinuousness
smorgasbord
stereoscope
stereoscopy
stethoscope
stethoscopy
stroboscope
submersible
submissible
summersault
sunlessness
suppression
suppressive
surpassable
suspenseful
suspensible
synthesiser
talentscout
tediousness
tenuousness
thermoscope
thwartships
topdressing
totalisator
tracasserie
Trappistine
traversable
trelliswork
turtleshell
typecasting
unadvisedly
unchristian
unipersonal
universally
unnecessary
uselessness
vacuousness
vaporisable
variousness
vichyssoise
viciousness
viridescent
virilescent
viscousness
wappenschaw
wellwishing
widdershins
windlestraw
winetasting
withershins
witlessness
zealousness
absorptance
abstentious
accipitrine
accountable
accountably
accountancy
accusatival
acquittance
acropetally
aesthetical
agonistical
alabastrine
algorithmic
allocatable
allopathist
amaranthine
amphictyony
ancientness
anecdotical
anfractuous
anticathode
antivitamin
apparatchik
appointment
atheistical
attemptable
attractable
augmentable
autochthony
automatable
babysitting
barbastelle
basipetally
bellbottoms
benightedly
benightment
bibliotheca
birdwatcher
bloodstream
capacitance
caricatural
casuistical
chainstitch
charcuterie
charlatanry
chiropteran
cholesterol
climacteric
coexistence
coffeetable
collectable
collectanea
collectedly
collectible
combustible
comfortable
comfortably
comfortless
commentator
committable
compactness
compartment
complotting
comportment
conceitedly
concentrate
conceptacle
concertedly
concertgoer
condottiere
condottieri
conductance
conductible
conductress
conjectural
connectable
connectedly
connectible
consentient
consistence
consistency
constituent
constitutor
consultancy
contentedly
contentious
contentment
contestable
contretemps
conventicle
convertible

convertibly
correctable
correctness
corruptible
corruptibly
corruptness
credentials
crossstitch
currentness
dedicatedly
delightedly
delightsome
demonstrate
demountable
dendritical
diacritical
dialectally
dialectical
dimwittedly
diningtable
dinnertable
discontinue
disgustedly
disportment
dissentient
dissertator
distasteful
doublethink
draughtsman
earnestness
egotistical
elementally
enchantment
enchantress
encrustment
endometrium
enigmatical
enlightened
entreatment
entrustment
epigastrium
equilateral
escheatable
escheatment
evidentiary
exhaustible
exhaustless
exorbitance
expeditious
exploitable
extractable
fantastical
felspathoid
fermentable
filmsetting
firewatcher
flirtatious
forfeitable
forgettable
gallantness
gasfittings
geotectonic
goodnatured
grammatical
haemoptysis
haemostasis
haemostatic
hardhitting
harvesthome
heartstring
heldentenor
helminthoid
hereditable
heterotaxis
heterotroph
heterotypic
hexametrist
highpitched
homeostasis

homeostatic
homiletical
homoestatic
hyacinthine
hydrostatic
hypersthene
iconostases
iconostasis
illimitable
illimitably
impenetrate
impenitence
impenitency
impolitical
impoliticly
impractical
inadaptable
inappetence
inconstancy
indomitable
indomitably
indubitable
indubitably
ineluctable
ineluctably
inequitable
inequitably
inexactness
inexistence
infinitival
inhabitable
inhabitancy
inheritable
inheritance
inheritress
inscrutable
inscrutably
interatomic
intractable
intractably
ipsilateral
irrefutable
irrefutably
isogeotherm
Jacobitical
judgmatical
kinematical
knownothing
Lancastrian
latchstring
lateritious
laurustinus
Leibnitzian
leviratical
logarithmic
loosestrife
manumitting
marqueterie
mediastinal
mediastinum
moderations
monophthong
multistorey
myxomatosis
Neoplatonic
nominatival
nonpartisan
novelettish
occipitally
omnipotence
optometrist
orchestrate
orthopteran
outdistance
oversetting
paediatrics
paediatrist
palaeotypic
parametrise

parasitical
parasitosis
patristical
perceptible
perceptibly
perfectible
perfectness
periostitis
peripatetic
persistence
persistency
pervertedly
phyllotaxis
phytosterol
pietistical
pragmatical
precautious
precentress
preceptress
precontract
predictable
predictably
prefectural
prehistoric
presbyteral
presentable
presentably
presentient
presentment
pretentious
preventable
preventible
progestogen
prognathism
prognathous
prophethood
prophetical
prophetship
proportions
prostitutor
protectoral
protectress
provostship
purportedly
quadratical
rallentando
reconstruct
recruitment
redoubtable
reenactment
reflectance
regrettable
regrettably
remonstrant
remonstrate
renegotiate
repetitious
respectable
respectably
retractable
rheumaticky
rhizanthous
rickettsial
rumbustious
satinstitch
sclerotitis
scrumptious
segmentally
selfpitying
semeiotical
sententious
septentrion
sequestrate
singletrack
slaughterer
somatotonia
somatotonic
sophistical
soupkitchen

spectatress
spermatozoa
sphincteral
sphincteric
splenetical
stagestruck
stalactitic
statistical
stereotyped
stereotyper
stereotypic
sternutator
studentship
subcontract
subcontrary
subcortical
subcritical
subcultural
sublittoral
submultiple
subsistence
substituent
suggestible
superstrata
supportable
supportably
susceptible
susceptibly
sweepstakes
sybaritical
syntactical
synthetical
tagliatelle
tagliatelli
telepathise
telepathist
tempestuous
tendentious
terrestrial
thaumatrope
thaumaturge
thaumaturgy
theoretical
thermotaxis
thoughtless
toploftical
trimestrial
triquetrous
typesetting
uncluttered
uncountable
understated
undoubtedly
ungetatable
unhealthily
unlimitedly
unpalatable
unpolitical
unprintable
unquietness
unremitting
unrighteous
upholsterer
uprightness
valiantness
verdantique
vespertinal
warrantable
warrantably
wildcatting
wirenetting
woodcutting
Zoroastrian
accentually
acculturate
adventuress
adventurism
adventurist
adventurous

aeronautics
afterburner
anacoluthon
antifouling
antineutron
attribution
attributive
avoirdupois
backcountry
barbiturate
bellfounder
blockbuster
bloodguilty
bloodsucker
brachyurous
calcifugous
campanulate
carunculate
comminution
confabulate
consecution
consecutive
consequence
construable
constructor
continuable
continually
continuance
continuator
convolution
corbiculate
daisycutter
decarburise
decolourise
delinquency
denticulate
destitution
difficultly
dinosaurian
disaccustom
disannulled
disencumber
disillusion
dissimulate
dissolutely
dissolution
dramaturgic
dumbfounder
echosounder
effectually
encapsulate
ensanguined
expostulate
exstipulate
fasciculate
folliculate
footpoundal
foulmouthed
fourflusher
fourpounder
frankfurter
frontrunner
fullmouthed
funambulate
funambulist
furunculous
gesticulate
glasscutter
hardmouthed
holothurian
homoiousian
honeysuckle
importunate
importunely
importunity
incorruptly
incredulity
incredulous
ineloquence

infrequence
infrequency
institution
interfusion
interlunary
internuncio
interrupter
interruptor
intriguante
ipecacuanha
itacolumite
loudmouthed
maladjusted
mandibulate
matriculate
metallurgic
miniaturise
miniaturist
noctilucent
nonsequitur
openmouthed
opportunely
opportunism
opportunist
opportunity
orangoutang
overstuffed
parachutist
paramountcy
paramountly
particulate
pedunculate
peninsulate
perambulate
perineurium
perpetually
perpetuance
perpetuator
persecution
pilotburner
polevaulter
prematurely
prematurity
preoccupied
prolocutrix
prosecution
prosecutrix
pulverulent
ratatouille
recalculate
restitution
retribution
retributive
retributory
Rosicrucian
seigneurial
semidiurnal
sharepusher
solifluxion
somniculous
spiraculate
spiritually
spiritualty
spirituelle
starstudded
stonecurlew
stonecutter
strangulate
subsequence
superlunary
supersubtle
surrebuttal
surrebutter
tentaculate
terraqueous
trabeculate
transfusion
transhumant
translucent

translunary
triangulate
trustbuster
tuberculate
tuberculise
tuberculose
tuberculous
typefounder
typefoundry
unaccounted
undisguised
undisturbed
unfortunate
unguiculate
unisexually
unobtrusive
valleculate
vermiculate
vermiculite
wellfounded
wellrounded
witchhunter
aggrievedly
blackavised
cesarevitch
circumvolve
conceivable
conceivably
conservable
conservancy
conservator
contrivable
contrivance
controversy
convolvulus
deactivator
dissolvable
enterovirus
genitivally
irrelevance
irrelevancy
irremovable
irremovably
lilylivered
margraviate
marketvalue
mediaevally
menservants
overdevelop
perceivable
perceivably
preservable
primaevally
retrievable
safetyvalve
selfdevoted
selfinvited
Stradivarii
subservient
unequivocal
welladvised
breastwheel
cesarewitch
churchwoman
craftswoman
dinnerwagon
Frenchwoman
gentlewoman
groundwater
heavenwards
Hepplewhite
highpowered
hitherwards
jabberwocky
needlewoman
netherworld
paddlewheel
policewoman
prayerwheel
Scotchwoman
shallowness
sparrowbill
sparrowhawk
spokeswoman
sportswoman
swallowable
swallowdive
swallowhole
swallowtail
swallowwort
tiddlywinks
washerwoman
wildfowling
complexness
overanxious
paradoxical
perplexedly
underexpose
androgynous
anthocyanin
apocalyptic
borborygmus
carbocyclic
cataclysmic
countryfied
countryseat
countryside
countrywide
farawayness
flamboyance
flamboyancy
flamboyante
haemocyanin
hairstyling
hairstylist
hydrocyanic
hypophyseal
hypophysial
journeywork
metaphysics
metapsychic
Monophysite
nurserymaid
overpayment
parathyroid
pentagynous
phagocytise
phagocytose
phycocyanin
phylogynist
podophyllin
polycrystal
polyonymous
polystyrene
proselytise
proselytism
pyrargyrite
rockcrystal
seventyfold
stenotypist
stringybark
tautonymous
teknonymous
tetracyclic
touchtyping
viceroyalty
viceroyship
Wensleydale
worldlywise
yacketyyack

---

abbreviator
abdominally
abiotically
abolishable
abracadabra
absorptance
accelerando
accelerator
accentually
accountable
accountably
accountancy
accumulator
acidifiable
acquittance
acropetally
adjudicator
adulterator
adverbially
aerobically
aerodynamic
AfroAsiatic
agnatically
alembicated
allocatable
altostratus
ameliorator
amphisbaena
anaphylaxis
angelically
angiography
annihilator
annunciator
anthocyanin
anticipator
antiphrasis
antivitamin
antonomasia
Apollinaris
applaudable
appreciable
appreciably
appreciator
aquatically
archaically
articulable
articulated
articulator
ascetically
aseptically
asphyxiator
assimilable
assimilator
attemptable
attractable
augmentable
auricularly
automatable
bacchanalia
BaltoSlavic
baptismally
basipetally
bathyscaphe
bibliolater
bibliolatry
bibliomancy
bibliomania
bilaterally
billionaire
binocularly
biquadratic
blackcoated
boilermaker
botanically
brainteaser
brazenfaced
broadleaved
bucolically
Byronically
calceolaria
calligraphy
calumniator
cancellated
canonically
capacitance
cartography
castellated
caustically
celestially
centigramme
certifiable
certifiably
chaotically
charismatic
charlatanry
cheerleader
cheiromancy
chirography
chorography
christiania
Christianly
Christmassy
chrominance
chronically
civilisable
classically
cleanshaven
clearheaded
coeternally
coffeetable
coinsurance
collectable
collectanea
collinearly
columniated
comeuppance
comfortable
comfortably
commendable
commendably
commendator
commensally
commentator
committable
compassable
compellable
compensator
complicated
comprisable
compurgator
concealable
conceivable
conceivably
conceptacle
conciliator
concordance
condemnable
condensable
conductance
conferrable
confirmable
confiscable
confiscator
conformable
conformably
conformally
conformance
congealable
congenially
connectable
connubially
conquerable
consecrator
conservable
conservancy
conservator
consignable
conspirator
construable
consultancy
consummator
containable
contestable
continuable
continually
continuance
continuator
contrabasso
contradance
contrivable
contrivance
conversable
conversance
conversancy
convivially
coordinator
corporeally
correctable
cosmography
countenance
crenellated
crossbearer
cryptically
cryptogamic
deactivator
decelerator
decennially
deflagrator
deistically
deliverable
deliverance
demonolatry
demountable
denominator
denumerable
denunciator
depopulator
depreciator
depthcharge
desalinator
descendable
describable
desideratum
developable
dialectally
diastematic
diatessaron
dichromatic
dilapidated
dilapidator
diningtable
dinnerdance
dinnertable
dinnerwagon
discardable
discography
discordance
discordancy
discrepancy
discussable
dislikeable
dispensable
dissertator
dissociable
dissolvable
dissyllable
disturbance
dittography
doctrinaire
doctrinally
doublefaced
drastically
dynamically
editorially
effectually
elastically
elasticated
elementally
emancipator
emasculator
embraceable
embryonated
Emmenthaler
emotionally
empirically
emptyheaded
encumbrance
endemically
enforceable
enlargeable
episcopally
epithalamia
epithalamic
equivocally
equivocator
erratically
escheatable
essentially
ethnography
eugenically
exaggerator
exercisable
exorbitance
explainable
exploitable
extractable
factionally
faithhealer
fanatically
fashionable
fashionably
fenestrated
fermentable
filmography
filterpaper
financially
fissionable
flagellator
flamboyance
flamboyancy
flamboyante
foraminated
forbearance
forbiddance
foreseeable
forfeitable
forgettable
fortifiable
Francomania
frantically
fraternally
furtherance
generically
genetically
geniculated
genitivally
gentlemanly
glossolalia
godforsaken
graphically
greasepaint
groundwater
haemocyanin
haemostasis
haemostatic
Hagiographa
hagiography
hairbreadth
handbreadth
haplography
harumscarum
heavenwards
Hebraically
heliography
hereditable
heretically
heterotaxis
Hippocratic
historiated
hitherwards
hollandaise
homeostasis
homeostatic

homesteader
homoeopathy
homoestatic
hydraheaded
hydrocyanic
hydrography
hydrostatic
hymnography
hypercharge
hyperphagia
hyperplasia
hypsography
ichnography
iconography
iconostases
iconostasis
identically
idiotically
idyllically
illiberally
illimitable
illimitably
illogically
illuminable
illuminance
illuminator
illustrator
immedicable
immitigable
immitigably
impartially
impeachable
impermeable
impermeably
imperviable
impregnable
impregnably
impuissance
inadaptable
inadvisable
inalienable
inalienably
inalterable
inalterably
inaugurator
incinerator
inconstancy
increasable
indefinable
indefinably
indomitable
indomitably
indubitable
indubitably
ineluctable
ineluctably
inequitable
inequitably
inescapable
inestimable
inestimably
inexcusable
inexcusably
infiltrator
inflammable
inflammably
inhabitable
inhabitancy
inheritable
inheritance
innavigable
innumerable
innumerably
inscribable
inscrutable
inscrutably
inseminator
inseparable
inseparably
insouciance
insufflator
insuperable
insuperably
intagliated
interchange
interleaves
interplayed
intimidator
intolerable
intolerably
intolerance
intractable
intractably
intriguante
invigilator
invigorator
ipecacuanha
irrecusable
irrecusably
irrefutable
irrefutably
irregularly
irrelevance
irrelevancy
irremovable
irremovably
irreparable
irreparably
irrevocable
irrevocably
juridically
justiciable
justifiable
justifiably
kleptomania
Kulturkampf
lachrymator
laconically
legionnaire
levelheaded
lieutenancy
lightheaded
linendraper
liquefiable
lithography
lophobranch
loudspeaker
magistratic
maintenance
malfeasance
manipulable
manipulator
mantuamaker
marketvalue
masquerader
mediaevally
medicinable
medicinally
megalomania
menservants
mentholated
mentionable
mercurially
mesalliance
metasomatic
micrography
millionaire
mimetically
misalliance
miscellanea
misfeasance
misguidance
mithridatic
molecularly
moronically
morrisdance
mothernaked
municipally
mythography
naturopathy
nocturnally
nomadically
nomenclator
nonchalance
nonfeasance
numerically
nymphomania
occipitally
ochlocratic
octagonally
officinally
oligochaete
oneiromancy
operculated
opinionated
orbicularly
organically
organisable
orthography
osmotically
osteography
osteoplasty
outdistance
overbalance
pacifically
pacificator
papiermache
paraphraser
parheliacal
parochially
paronomasia
pensionable
perceivable
perceivably
perennially
performable
performance
periphrases
periphrasis
perpetrator
perpetually
perpetuance
perpetuator
persuadable
perturbable
petrography
petticoated
phonography
photography
phrasemaker
phthiriasis
phycocyanin
phyllotaxis
phytography
pictography
pictorially
pipecleaner
piratically
pleasurable
pleasurably
plutocratic
pococurante
polarisable
polemically
politically
polygonally
pornography
potentially
practicable
practicably
practically
predictable
predictably
presentable
presentably
preservable
preventable
primaevally
principally
problematic
procephalic
promulgator
proofreader
prophylaxis
propitiable
propitiator
prosaically
prothalamia
prothoracic
protrudable
psychically
psychopathy
publishable
purchasable
purificator
pyramidally
qualifiable
quickchange
quizzically
radiography
rallentando
rattlepated
reassurance
reclaimable
recoverable
rectifiable
redoubtable
reflectance
regenerable
regenerator
registrable
regrettable
regrettably
reinsurance
rejuvenator
remembrance
remunerator
renaissance
replaceable
repleviable
reprogramme
reprography
resemblance
respectable
respectably
retraceable
retractable
retrievable
rhabdomancy
ringstraked
ruridecanal
safebreaker
safetyvalve
saltimbanco
salvageable
sanguinaria
sarcophagus
sartorially
satanically
satirically
satisfiable
scenography
sceptically
secondrater
sectionally
segmentally
seismically
selfcreated
sensorially
septifragal
serviceable
serviceably
sheriffalty
shipbreaker
shockheaded
shortchange
sightreader
sigmoidally
signifiable
sinistrally
smoothfaced
sockdolager
somatically
spaceheater
spastically
specifiable
spherically
spiritually
spiritualty
spirochaete
spreadeagle
statesmanly
stenography
sternutator
stomachache
Stradivarii
straitlaced
stretchable
stridulator
stylography
subaerially
sugarcoated
summersault
supercharge
superheater
supportable
supportably
surficially
surpassable
sustainable
swallowable
sweepstakes
swellheaded
swordbearer
symposiarch
symptomatic
tachygraphy
tarnishable
technically
tephromancy
tessellated
tetanically
theorematic
thermically
thermotaxis
thickheaded
thingumabob
thingumajig
threadpaper
throatlatch
timepleaser
titanically
torchbearer
totalisator
toxicomania
trafficator
trailblazer
trainbearer
transuranic
traversable
treasonable
treasonably
triadically
triennially
trisyllabic
trisyllable
unalterable
unavailable
unavoidable
unavoidably
unbreakable
uncatchable
unclimbable
unconcealed
uncountable
uncrushable
undercharge
understated
undesirable
unendurable
unendurably
unflappable
ungetatable
unisexually
universally
unmatchable
unmemorable
unmemorably
unmitigated
unnaturally
unpalatable
unprintable
unsaturated
unshockable
unspeakable
unspeakably
unstoppable
unteachable
unthinkable
unthinkably
untouchable
unutterable
unutterably
Upanishadic
uranography
vaporisable
vasodilator
vaticinator
venatically
veridically
vesicularly
vestigially
viceregally
viceroyalty
vitrifiable
vituperator
vociferance
vociferator
wapperjawed
warrantable
warrantably
wedgeshaped
whimsically
Whitechapel
whiteheaded
windcheater
worldbeater
worshipable
wrongheaded
zincography
biofeedback
blunderbuss
butcherbird
candelabrum
comestibles
counterblow
counterbond
deoxyribose
diamondback
exarcerbate
gallowsbird
herringbone
hummingbird
immoveables
jumpingbean
knucklebone
landgrabber
landingbeam
leatherback
mockingbird
palmcabbage
perishables
picturebook
quarterback

reedwarbler
scissorbill
scuttlebutt
servicebook
shacklebolt
shacklebone
shelterbelt
smorgasbord
sparrowbill
statutebook
steeplebush
stickleback
stirrupbone
stockjobber
stringybark
supersubtle
thunderbird
thunderbolt
academicals
academician
academicism
acatalectic
acaulescent
acoustician
acquiescent
agnosticism
alkalescent
amphimictic
amplexicaul
apparatchik
arborescent
archdiocese
aromaticity
artiodactyl
athleticism
Aurignacian
awestricken
azotobacter
backbencher
bactericide
balmcricket
billsticker
birdfancier
birdwatcher
bloodsucker
brainsickly
bushwhacker
carbocyclic
cataplectic
catholicise
Catholicism
catholicity
certificate
chemotactic
chiaroscuro
chronoscope
cicatricial
cityslicker
clapperclaw
communicant
communicate
concrescent
constrictor
constructor
cosmetician
crookbacked
cupronickel
decorticate
delitescent
didacticism
diplococcus
dipterocarp
disaffected
disinfector
diverticula
domesticate
domesticity
doorknocker
earpiercing
eclecticism
ecumenicism
ecumenicity
electrician
electricity
electrocute
ellipticity
epidiascope
erythrocyte
esotericism
exotericism
firecracker
firewatcher
fluorescein
fluorescent
fluoroscope
fluoroscopy
gastroscope
granulocyte
gynaecocrat
haematocele
haematocrit
hermeticism
heteroecism
hibernacula
Hibernicism
highpitched
Hispanicise
Hispanicism
Hispanicist
historicise
historicism
historicist
historicity
honeysuckle
horsedoctor
hunchbacked
hydrotactic
hypothecate
illaffected
imperfectly
incalescent
incorrectly
indehiscent
infanticide
insecticide
interfacial
interfacing
interjacent
interlocker
internecine
interracial
intumescent
juvenescent
kinetoscope
lamellicorn
leptodactyl
liberticide
luminescent
magnificent
matriarchal
mechanician
meningocele
metapsychic
metoposcopy
micrococcal
micrococcus
microsecond
millisecond
molecricket
monasticism
multiracial
neuroticism
noctilucent
obmutescent
obsolescent
opencircuit
packingcase
Palaearctic
parallactic
paramoecium
paraplectic
patriarchal
pearlescent
pentadactyl
pentazocine
periodicity
perithecium
pertinacity
phonetician
phototactic
picturecard
playingcard
Pleistocene
polariscope
pontificals
pontificate
postglacial
prejudicial
preselector
prevaricate
prolificacy
prolificity
pterodactyl
quincuncial
receptacula
reciprocate
reciprocity
reduplicate
reminiscent
resipiscent
retinoscopy
retrorocket
revendicate
reviviscent
rhetorician
rodenticide
romanticise
romanticism
romanticist
ropedancing
Rosicrucian
sacrificial
safecracker
seismoscope
selfconceit
selfelected
semanticist
sextodecimo
sheetanchor
shelljacket
shuttlecock
significant
Slavonicise
soupkitchen
specificity
spifflicate
stereoscope
stereoscopy
stethoscope
stethoscopy
stiffnecked
stroboscope
superficial
superficies
superjacent
supremacist
syllabicity
tabernacled
talentscout
tetracyclic
tetradactyl
Teutonicism
theatricals
thermoscope
threedecker
thrombocyte
thunderclap
translocate
translucent
tribunicial
tyrannicide
unconnected
viridescent
virilescent
volcanicity
vulcanicity
wappenschaw
weathercock
wisecracker
witchdoctor
accommodate
AngloIndian
antemundane
antependium
antheridium
antioxidant
Archimedean
bicuspidate
billetsdoux
bookbinding
chafingdish
Chippendale
chiropodist
clostridium
codefendant
consolidate
cypripedium
demigoddess
desperadoes
doubleedged
downtrodden
enchiridion
endocardiac
endocardial
endocardium
enneahedron
factfinding
footsoldier
fullfledged
gallbladder
godchildren
gourmandise
gourmandism
halfbinding
halflanding
hesperidium
honeybadger
horseradish
hydromedusa
icosahedral
icosahedron
illbreeding
illiquidity
improvident
incarnadine
incommodity
independent
interbedded
intermeddle
intermedium
intrepidity
landholding
landlordism
latifundium
massproduce
merchandise
merryandrew
mindbending
mindreading
mollycoddle
moribundity
nonresident
nullifidian
orthopedics
orthopedist
ostracoderm
outbreeding
outbuilding
outstanding
overbidding
overproduce
pellucidity
pentahedron
pentlandite
pericardiac
pericardial
pericardium
preprandial
quarterdeck
reachmedown
reintroduce
resplendent
retrocedent
rhomboideus
rhynchodont
roadholding
rubicundity
safeconduct
salesladies
sauropodous
scaffolding
sculduddery
selfevident
selffeeding
selfloading
selfwinding
shepherdess
skulduddery
spatterdash
sphaeridium
standardise
starstudded
stylopodium
substandard
superinduce
supersedeas
supersedure
swallowdive
swimbladder
tarradiddle
tetrahedral
tetrahedron
tetrapodous
thistledown
transpadane
ultramodern
underbidder
unorthodoxy
urochordate
vagabondage
vagabondise
vagabondish
vagabondism
Wensleydale
abiogeneses
abiogenesis
abiogenetic
aboutsledge
absenteeism
accoucheuse
accrescence
acknowledge
actinometer
adolescence
aggrievedly
aiguillette
alkalimeter
alkalimetry
ambivalence
ambivalency
amentaceous
anaesthesia
anaesthetic
AngloFrench
antecedence
antipyretic
aposiopesis
arboraceous
archangelic
archdukedom
ascomycetes
astringency
atmospheric
auxanometer
barbastelle
barefacedly
beneficence
benevolence
benightedly
bewhiskered
bibliopegic
biedermeier
blackbeetle
blastogenic
boysenberry
butyraceous
calisthenic
calorimeter
calorimetry
camaraderie
candescence
candleberry
carrageenan
carrageenin
carriageway
catachreses
catachresis
centripetal
chanterelle
charcuterie
chartaceous
chinoiserie
chiropteran
chokecherry
cholesterol
chronometer
chronometry
chrysoberyl
cinquecento
climacteric
coalescence
cockaleekie
cockyleekie
coexistence
cognoscente
cognoscenti
coincidence
collectedly
colorimeter
colorimetry
commonsense
complacence
complacency
conceitedly
concertedly
concurrence
confessedly
connectedly
consequence
consistence
consistency
contentedly
contingence
contingency
contretemps
controversy
convenience
conveniency
convergence
convergency
cookgeneral
costbenefit
craniometry
crustaceous

cryptomeria
cyclopaedia
cyclopaedic
cytogenesis
cytokinesis
decrescendo
dedicatedly
delightedly
delinquency
despondence
despondency
diamagnetic
diaphaneity
diaphoresis
diaphoretic
dicotyledon
dimwittedly
disbeliever
discalceate
discotheque
disgraceful
disguisedly
disgustedly
dispersedly
dissymmetry
distasteful
distempered
dynamometer
dynamometry
ectogenesis
ectogenetic
elastomeric
elbowgrease
embroiderer
enlightened
epeirogenic
equilateral
equivalence
equivalency
erubescence
evanescence
excrescence
excrescency
exoskeletal
exoskeleton
farinaceous
featheredge
flannelette
flocculence
florescence
forgetmenot
fourwheeler
frankpledge
fraudulence
fricandeaux
gamogenesis
gendarmerie
gentianella
geomagnetic
goldenberry
gradiometer
greenkeeper
gymnospermy
habiliments
hebephrenia
hebephrenic
heldentenor
hemispheric
highpowered
hobbledehoy
homestretch
homogeneity
homogeneous
homogenetic
housekeeper
huckleberry
hylogenesis
hypnopaedia
illmannered
illtempered
impedimenta
impenitence
impenitency
inappetence
incoherence
incoherency
ineloquence
inexistence
infrequence
infrequency
ingrainedly
interpreter
intersperse
interviewee
interviewer
ionospheric
ipsilateral
iridescence
irreverence
kitchenette
lactescence
lammergeier
lammergeyer
landaulette
launderette
lesemajesty
lilylivered
liquescence
loggerheads
magazinegun
maisonnette
maleficence
malevolence
Manichaeism
marcescence
marqueterie
marquisette
marriagebed
medicolegal
membraneous
merogenesis
metagenesis
metagenetic
minesweeper
misconceive
misguidedly
monogenesis
monogenetic
munificence
mythopoeist
mythopoetic
myxomycetes
nigrescence
nonviolence
nympholepsy
oestrogenic
offhandedly
omnipotence
omniscience
ontogenesis
ontogenetic
opalescence
orthopaedic
orthopteran
outspokenly
overdevelop
overstretch
panhellenic
pantothenic
papyraceous
paraselenae
parentheses
parenthesis
parenthetic
percipience
peripatetic
perplexedly
persistence
persistency
pervertedly
phagedaenic
phariseeism
philanderer
phytosterol
pigheadedly
piperaceous
pipistrelle
pitchblende
pluviometer
polarimeter
polarimetry
poltergeist
polygenesis
polygenetic
preaudience
preconceive
preeminence
presbyteral
pressagency
pretendedly
professedly
proficiency
provenience
psychedelia
psychedelic
psychogenic
psychometry
punchinello
purportedly
putrescence
quadrupedal
quickfreeze
reemergence
refringency
rejuvenesce
resourceful
respondence
respondency
retroflexed
rhombohedra
rifacimenti
rifacimento
Sadduceeism
salinometer
salmonberry
sanguineous
saponaceous
scarabaeoid
schwarmerei
scleroderma
sclerometer
scoriaceous
scoundrelly
seismometer
seismometry
selaginella
selfdefence
septicaemia
septicaemic
seventeenth
shirtsleeve
sickbenefit
sidewheeler
sightseeing
sinfonietta
slaughterer
smithereens
solanaceous
somatogenic
spathaceous
speedometer
spherometer
sphincteral
sphincteric
spiritlevel
spirituelle
spirochetal
spontaneity
spontaneous
steerageway
stereometry
sternsheets
stichometry
stockinette
storekeeper
stramineous
submergence
subsequence
subsistence
subumbrella
sufficiency
suffragette
sulphureous
suspenseful
sympathetic
tacheometer
tagliatelle
tagliatelli
telekinesis
telekinetic
teratogenic
terraqueous
thermometer
thermometry
tracasserie
tragedienne
transpierce
treecreeper
turgescence
twelvepenny
unadvisedly
unashamedly
unboundedly
uncluttered
undoubtedly
unfeignedly
unguardedly
uninucleate
unlimitedly
unrighteous
upholsterer
urticaceous
vaporimeter
varsovienne
vicegerency
vinaigrette
violoncello
vitrescence
volkslieder
volumometer
wellordered
wheresoever
whichsoever
whigmaleery
whosesoever
winterberry
witenagemot
xeranthemum
yellowbelly
acinaciform
aftereffect
bacilliform
chickenfeed
counterfeit
counterfoil
counterfort
countrified
countryfied
Falstaffian
frenchified
hereinafter
housewifely
housewifery
hundredfold
insectifuge
intensifier
lamelliform
overstuffed
passeriform
patelliform
personifier
photooffset
scalariform
scalpriform
seventyfold
severalfold
speechifier
stampoffice
standoffish
suckingfish
surgeonfish
theretofore
trapeziform
triggerfish
unqualified
vasculiform
annabergite
anthologise
anthologist
arbitrageur
audiologist
bandylegged
bellringing
bootlegging
borborygmus
calcifugous
Carolingian
challenging
cleistogamy
concertgoer
cosmologist
crosslegged
cryosurgery
dactylogram
desegregate
deuterogamy
disobliging
disparaging
dropforging
endophagous
ethnologist
etymologise
etymologist
euchologion
extravagant
extravagate
farthingale
flabbergast
flagwagging
florilegium
footslogger
gametangium
gemmologist
genealogise
genealogist
golddigging
gravedigger
hagiologist
hairtrigger
herringgull
histologist
hornswoggle
houselights
hydrologist
intelligent
interregnum
interrogate
investigate
ironmongery
jauntingcar
landinggear
laughinggas
leapfrogged
limnologist
mammalogist
marconigram
meliphagous
Merovingian
monolingual
monophagous
mudslinging
mycophagist
mythologise
mythologist
necrologist
neurologist
nightingale
noctivagant
noctivagous
oesophageal
ophiologist
oscillogram
osteologist
passacaglia
pathologist
pestologist
petrologist
pettifogger
phenologist
philologian
philologist
phonologist
phraseogram
phycologist
phytologist
picturegoer
polyphagous
radiologist
rhinologist
rightangled
roughlegged
sandbagging
scattergood
sculduggery
skulduggery
sleepingbag
sleepingcar
snowgoggles
sociologist
sovereignly
sovereignty
spectrogram
sphygmogram
steganogram
stoolpigeon
subcategory
suffumigate
tautologise
tautologism
tautologous
teleologism
teleologist
tentpegging
theatregoer
threelegged
timebargain
transfigure
undersigned
waterlogged
xylophagous
affranchise
ailurophile
ailurophobe
algorithmic
allopathist
amaranthine
amenorrhoea
anencephaly
anticathode
apomorphine
archduchess
autochthony
basketchair
bathysphere

bibliophile
bibliophily
bibliotheca
boardschool
bondwashing
bookinghall
breastwheel
brotherhood
bullfighter
chamaephyte
chargesheet
chlorophyll
chucklehead
clairschach
cochinchina
cockleshell
coleorrhiza
collenchyma
diadelphous
dodecaphony
doublecheck
doublethink
enfranchise
entomophily
epigraphist
eyecatching
farreaching
featherhead
felspathoid
firefighter
foresighted
fortnightly
Francophile
Francophobe
francophone
gametophyte
gegenschein
goddaughter
groundsheet
haemorrhage
haemorrhoid
harpsichord
harvesthome
hedgeschool
helminthoid
Hepplewhite
heptarchist
heterophony
hierarchism
hyacinthine
hydrosphere
hypersthene
isogeotherm
isomorphism
isomorphous
knownothing
lamplighter
lawmerchant
leatherhead
linefishing
lithosphere
logarithmic
logomachist
longsighted
mantelshelf
melanochroi
melanophore
monkeyshine
monophthong
moonlighter
muttonchops
nearsighted
neckerchief
nonmatching
ommatophore
ozonosphere
paddlewheel
paraldehyde
paratyphoid
photosphere
pigeonchest
planisphere
platyrrhine
ploughshare
polytechnic
prayerwheel
prognathism
prognathous
prophethood
prosenchyma
pyrotechnic
quadraphony
reproachful
rhizanthous
schoolchild
sclerophyll
slotmachine
sparrowhawk
spermaphyte
stereophony
swallowhole
tapemachine
telepathise
telepathist
tetrarchate
theosophist
thermophile
thoroughpin
thoroughwax
thunderhead
thwartships
trimorphism
trimorphous
tristichous
troposphere
tryptophane
turtleshell
ulotrichous
unflinching
unhealthily
wellwishing
widdershins
widowerhood
withershins
xanthochroi
xanthophyll
zoographist
zoomorphism
abiological
abranchiate
abstentious
accusatival
achondritic
acidophilic
acrimonious
aerological
aeronomical
aesthetical
agonistical
agrological
agronomical
ahistorical
algological
allAmerican
allantoides
allegorical
altitudinal
altorelievo
altorilievo
anagnorisis
anecdotical
anthracitic
anthropical
antimonious
antirrhinum
antiSemitic
antitypical
apostolical
appropriate
Areopagitic
atheistical
atrabilious
attitudinal
autarchical
axiological
battlefield
beneficiary
beneficiate
bersaglieri
biochemical
biometrical
biophysical
birdbrained
blackavised
blackmailer
blepharitis
bloodguilty
bonbonniere
bourgeoisie
boutonniere
bowdleriser
Brahmanical
Brahminical
burglarious
calefacient
calendrical
candlelight
cantharides
cantharidic
carabiniere
carabinieri
caryopsides
casuistical
categorical
centrepiece
ceremonious
cesarevitch
cesarewitch
chainstitch
chieftaincy
chimaerical
chrysalides
chrysalises
Clarencieux
coconscious
coefficient
cognoscible
coinheritor
collapsible
collectible
combustible
compendious
compossible
condottiere
condottieri
conductible
connectible
consentient
conspecific
contentious
conterminal
contorniate
contrariety
contrarious
conventicle
convertible
convertibly
convincible
coralloidal
corecipient
corruptible
corruptibly
coxcombical
credentials
crossstitch
cylindrical
cytological
deleterious
demagogical
dendritical
depressible
descendible
diacritical
dialectical
diametrical
directrices
discernible
discernibly
disciplinal
discipliner
discontinue
discussible
disinclined
disobedient
dissentient
distensible
domiciliary
domiciliate
efficacious
egotistical
ellipsoidal
enigmatical
ensanguined
enterovirus
enterpriser
entertainer
ephemerides
epithelioma
ethological
evangelical
evidentiary
executrices
executrixes
exhaustible
expeditious
expressible
expropriate
fantastical
flagofficer
flirtatious
foraminifer
fraterniser
fratricidal
furnishings
gasfittings
generaliser
geochemical
geometrical
geophysical
ghostwriter
glauconitic
gormandiser
grammatical
grangeriser
haemophilia
haemophilic
halfholiday
harebrained
heavyweight
hedgepriest
Heracleidan
hexadecimal
homiletical
homogeniser
homological
horological
hydrophilic
hypercritic
ideological
ignominious
illustrious
impecunious
implausible
implausibly
impolitical
impoliticly
impractical
impressible
impropriate
impropriety
incoercible
incompliant
inconscient
indivisible
indivisibly
industrious
inefficient
inexpedient
infinitival
infrangible
injudicious
inofficious
interspinal
intertribal
irreducible
irreducibly
irreligious
isometrical
Jacobinical
Jacobitical
judgmatical
kinematical
lateritious
latitudinal
laurustinus
leviratical
lightweight
lithotripsy
loculicidal
lowspirited
makebelieve
maladroitly
mantelpiece
marcescible
margraviate
masterpiece
mastoiditis
mediastinal
mediastinum
mediatrices
memorabilia
meritorious
metalloidal
meteoroidal
metonymical
middlesized
mineraliser
miscarriage
mismarriage
moderations
moisturiser
monarchical
moneyspider
monological
monopoliser
motherright
mustachioed
mycological
mycorrhizae
mycorrhizal
myocarditis
necrophilia
necrophilic
Neotropical
neutraliser
nittygritty
nominatival
nomological
nonpartisan
nonsensical
nonsequitur
nonspecific
nosological
obstetrical
oecological
oecumenical
oenological
omnifarious
oncological
ontological
opprobrious
oreological
orthoepical
otherwhiles
overanxious
paedophilia
panegyrical
paperweight
paradisical
paradoxical
paramedical
parasitical
pasteuriser
patristical
pedagogical
pedological
pennyweight
penological
perceptible
perceptibly
perfectible
periostitis
peritonitis
permissible
permissibly
persuasible
phantasiast
pharisaical
pharyngitis
photophilic
pietistical
pillowfight
pivotbridge
plagiariser
planetoidal
plasticiser
playerpiano
pneumonitis
pocketsized
pomological
populariser
porphyritic
posological
pragmatical
precautious
presentient
prestigious
pretentious
preventible
proceedings
prophetical
proportions
protrusible
punctilious
puritanical
putrescible
pyramidical
quadratical
quilldriver
ratatouille
realpolitik
reappraisal
rearadmiral
reconnoitre
refrangible
renegotiate
repetitious
repressible
repressibly
responsible
responsibly
rhapsodical
rheological
rheumaticky

rubefacient tonsillitis acarpellous controlling funambulate marginality
rumbustious toploftical aerobiology copperplate funambulist marketplace
salpingitis topological agrobiology corbiculate furunculous marshalling
satinstitch transceiver amenability corporality galleyslave marshmallow
sclerotitis transcriber amicability cosmetology geanticline martyrology
screwdriver transilient amontillado cosmopolite geosyncline materialise
scribacious trapezoidal amphibolite counselling gerontology materialism
scrumptious triphibious amphibology credibility gesticulate materialist
scrutiniser trothplight anticyclone crestfallen gibberellin materiality
searchlight typological antifouling criminalist grandiflora matriculate
secondsight uncanonical apophyllite criminality gravelblind meaningless
selfinvited uncertainly apparelling criminology gullibility measureless
selflimited uncertainty aquarellist criticality gutturalise medievalism
selfreliant uncivilised archaeology crocidolite gutturalism medievalist
semeiotical unconscious archipelago crocodilian gynaecology memorialise
semiellipse underweight arenicolous cryobiology haematology memorialist
semitrailer underwriter arterialise crystalline hairstyling meteorology
sententious undisguised aspergillum crystallise hairstylist methodology
serological unexploited aspergillus crystallite halophilous middleclass
sexagesimal uninhabited Assyriology crystalloid handselling minuteglass
sexological uninhibited bestselling culpability harbourless miscibility
simpliciter unorganized bicephalous dactylology haustellate misspelling
sinological unpolitical biddability deerstalker heartsblood mitrailleur
slavedriver unsolicited bimetallism defenceless heresiology mononuclear
sonofabitch urticarious bimetallist denticulate herpetology Monothelite
sophistical vehmgericht bisexuality dermatology heteroclite moveability
spaceflight verdantique blackfellow desexualise heteroploid multicolour
spasmodical verisimilar bodybuilder detribalise homothallic multivalent
spermicidal vespertinal bookselling dicephalous horripilate myrmecology
spherulitic viceadmiral bookshelves difficultly horsecollar namecalling
splenetical virological bottleglass diluvialist hospitalise naphthalene
spondulicks waterskiing bracteolate disannulled hospitality nationalise
spondylitis wedgetailed breastplate dishevelled hospitaller nationalism
stalactitic weighbridge breathalyse dissimilate householder nationalist
stalagmitic welladvised breechblock dissimulate husbandlike nationality
statistical welldefined breezeblock educability hyperbolise necropoleis
staurolitic wheelwright bryozoology electrolier hyperboloid nettlecloth
steamboiler crackerjack butterflies electrology hypocycloid nickelplate
stipendiary jumpingjack calcicolous electrolyse ichthyology nightwalker
strategical steeplejack campanology electrolyte immortalise nonetheless
streetlight bivouacking campanulate eligibility immortality nonmetallic
stringpiece comstockery cannibalise embowelling impanelling notionalist
subclinical cornhusking cannibalism emotionless imperialise oenophilist
subcortical dressmaking captionless empanelling imperialism offenceless
subcritical epochmaking cardinalate encapsulate imperialist officialdom
submarginal firewalking caruncuIate endoskelton imperilling officialese
submersible gimcrackery caterpillar endothelial incredulity officialism
submissible glassmaking cavedweller endothelium incredulous olfactology
submultiple goodlooking chamberlain enthralling inedibility orchidology
subservient greenockite chancellery epipetalous infantilism orientalise
subspecific hardworking chancellory equipollent infertility orientalism
subterminal highranking channelling eschatology informality orientalist
subtropical leavetaking chanticleer etherealise initialling originality
suggestible matchmaking cheesecloth ethereality insectology ornithology
susceptible merrymaking chevalglass Etruscology instability outrivalled
susceptibly moneymaking chitterling eventualise integrality oversailing
suspensible noisemaking chloroplast eventuality interallied oysterplant
sybaritical nutcrackers chockablock exhaustless intercalary painkilling
symmetrical painstaking Christology expostulate intercalate palpability
sympathiser papermaking chromoplast exstipulate internalise parallelism
symphonious pawnbroking clericalism externalise internality parallelled
synagogical peacemaking clericalist externalism interpolate particulate
synonymical Pickwickian climatology externality interrelate passibility
syntactical pigsticking clothesline extrapolate intervallic pastoralism
synthesiser politicking codicillary facsimilist inviability pastoralist
synthetical ropewalking colonialism fallibility ithyphallic pastureland
taxonomical selfcocking colonialist farcicality kinesiology paternalism
tearstained selflocking colourblind fasciculate lakedweller paternalist
temerarious selfseeking comfortless feasibility laryngology peccability
tendencious shellacking commonality featherless laudability peccadillos
tendentious stocktaking commonplace featureless leaseholder pedestalled
testatrices trafficking communalise fingerglass lichenology pedicellate
thanksgiver undertaking communalism fingerplate machicolate pedunculate
theodolitic unshrinking communalist flannelling mackerelsky penicillate
theological voortrekker comptroller flavourless madrigalian penicillium
theoretical watchmaking confabulate flexibility madrigalist peninsulate
thrasonical zooplankton conjugality floorwalker malariology pensionless
thyroiditis Abbevillian constellate folliculate mandibulate pentathlete
tiddlywinks abnormality contemplate forestaller marginalise pentavalent

perambulate
peristalith
peristalsis
peristaltic
personalise
personalism
personalist
personality
philatelist
philhellene
phraseology
phylloclade
physicality
placability
plagioclase
podophyllin
pointillism
pointillist
polevaulter
portability
portionless
possibility
postexilian
pourparlers
powderflask
primatology
probabilism
probabilist
probability
prodigalise
prodigality
prothallial
prothallium
pteridology
pulverulent
punctuality
purposeless
pussywillow
quacksalver
quadrillion
quarrelling
quaternloaf
quicksilver
quintillion
rapscallion
rateability
rationalise
rationalism
rationalist
rationality
readability
recalculate
reestablish
reflexology
regionalise
regionalism
regionalist
reliability
remorseless
retranslate
saddlecloth
saleability
satiability
saturnalian
scientology
scintillant
scintillate
secondclass
selffeeling
selfsealing
semasiology
semiskilled
sensibility
sentinelled
serviceline
shareholder
shelterless
shipbuilder
shrivelling
shutterless
silverplate
slaveholder
sleepwalker
smallholder
snatchblock
soapboiling
sociability
softshelled
soldierlike
solvability
somatoplasm
somniculous
soteriology
spectrality
spectrology
spelaeology
sphagnology
spindlelegs
spiraculate
spongecloth
springclean
stadtholder
stakeholder
stallholder
staunchless
steamroller
stencilling
stockholder
stomatology
stonewaller
storyteller
strangulate
subaxillary
succourless
suitability
surveillant
switchblade
sympetalous
syndicalism
syndicalist
tameability
tangibility
teetotalism
teetotaller
temporality
tensibility
tentaculate
terminology
terricolous
testability
tetravalent
textureless
thanatology
thoughtless
threecolour
thunderless
titleholder
toothbilled
torticollis
tourbillion
toxophilite
trabeculate
trackwalker
trafficless
trammelling
triangulate
tripetalous
triphyllous
trophoblast
trouserless
tryingplane
tuberculate
tuberculise
tuberculose
tuberculous
unappealing
underseller
undervaluer
unguiculate
unkennelled
valleculate
variability
vendibility
venereology
vermiculate
vermiculite
versatilely
versatility
verticality
vestryclerk
vexillology
vibratility
victualless
victualling
vincibility
volcanology
vulcanology
waitinglist
washability
watercolour
whitecollar
wildfowling
wirepulling
workability
workmanlike
worshipless
xenophilous
xerophilous
abandonment
abolishment
abridgement
achievement
acquirement
adjournment
adjudgement
advancement
amphetamine
antechamber
appeasement
appointment
approximate
arbitrament
arraignment
arrangement
assuagement
balletomane
beachcomber
bedevilment
bedizenment
beguilement
benightment
bereavement
betweenmaid
bewitchment
blasphemous
bombardment
carcinomata
catadromous
chainarmour
chambermaid
cleanlimbed
clothesmoth
commandment
compartment
compilement
comportment
concealment
concernment
condylomata
confinement
congealment
consignment
containment
contentment
controlment
coppersmith
countermand
countermark
countermine
countermove
countermure
curtailment
debauchment
debouchment
deforcement
defraudment
depravement
derangement
despoilment
detrainment
development
dichogamous
dichotomise
dichotomist
dichotomous
disablement
disarmament
disassemble
disassembly
disbandment
discernment
disencumber
dislodgment
disportment
disremember
dissepiment
dithyrambic
divorcement
divulgement
easternmost
embowerment
embracement
embroilment
emplacement
enchainment
enchantment
encrustment
endorsement
enfeoffment
enforcement
engorgement
engrossment
enhancement
enjambement
enlargement
enlivenment
ennoblement
enslavement
entablement
enthralment
entitlement
entrainment
entreatment
entrustment
envelopment
environment
escheatment
eurhythmics
evanishment
exanthemata
farthermost
flimflammer
foretopmast
forevermore
forthcoming
furthermore
furthermost
garnishment
guesstimate
hippocampus
hyoscyamine
hypnopompic
impeachment
imperilment
impingement
impoundment
impressment
improvement
indorsement
installment
instillment
involvement
itacolumite
legerdemain
lightsomely
liquidambar
lithotomise
lithotomist
loathsomely
longanimity
looselimbed
loxodromics
machinemade
macrogamete
magnanimity
magnanimous
maintopmast
measurement
meprobamate
methylamine
microgamete
misestimate
misjudgment
misremember
monogrammed
mooringmast
multinomial
ninnyhammer
nourishment
nurserymaid
overgarment
overpayment
pantomimist
penultimate
peristomial
phantasmata
phytotomist
platearmour
platforming
polyonymous
predicament
prejudgment
presentment
procurement
prolegomena
publishment
realignment
recruitment
redetermine
reenactment
refreshment
replacement
requirement
restatement
sausagemeat
scalearmour
scopolamine
selfcommand
semipalmate
shortcoming
silversmith
Soroptimist
subbasement
superfamily
surbasement
sustainment
synchromesh
tankfarming
tautonymous
taxidermist
teknonymous
telegrammic
temperament
thalidomide
theobromine
tolbutamide
toothsomely
traducement
tragicomedy
transhumant
tremblement
unbeseeming
vasectomise
wearisomely
weltschmerz
westernmost
wholesomely
worrisomely
abhorrently
ablutionary
abortionist
absorbingly
abstinently
abusiveness
acceptingly
accompanist
accordantly
accordingly
adoptianism
adoptianist
adoptionism
adoptionist
adverseness
advertently
advisedness
affectingly
afficionado
agglutinate
agonisingly
agrarianism
aimlessness
airlessness
airsickness
amativeness
Americanise
Americanism
Americanist
amiableness
amorousness
anachronism
anachronous
anacreontic
ancientness
androgynous
Anglicanism
anglomaniac
antiphonary
anxiousness
apartmental
appallingly
appealingly
approvingly
appurtenant
arduousness
Arminianism
arrestingly
artlessness
assassinate
assuredness
audibleness
Augustinian
austereness
awesomeness
awkwardness
backcountry
balefulness
banteringly
bashfulness
bearishness
beastliness
befittingly
beguilingly
belatedness
bellfounder

benignantly
betweenness
bicarbonate
bicentenary
biliousness
bimillenary
bimillenium
blessedness
blotchiness
bohemianism
bookishness
boorishness
breadwinner
brilliantly
bristliness
Britishness
brittleness
broadminded
brusqueness
brutishness
bullishness
butteriness
Byzantinism
Byzantinist
cacophonous
caddishness
californium
callousness
capableness
caravanning
carefulness
caressingly
carpetsnake
chaetognath
chansonnier
chaperonage
childminder
Christendom
christening
churchiness
cisatlantic
civilianise
cleanliness
cliffhanger
cognateness
compactness
compaginate
competently
complainant
complexness
compliantly
concatenate
conciseness
concubinage
concubinary
condominium
confidently
confidingly
confusingly
congruently
consolingly
consonantal
consonantly
consternate
consumingly
contaminant
contaminate
continental
continently
convenances
conveyancer
coparcenary
copiousness
cordialness
corpulently
correctness
corrigendum
corruptness
cosmogonist
costiveness
coterminous
courtliness
crabbedness
creationism
creationist
crookedness
crunchiness
cunningness
curableness
curiousness
currentness
currishness
cursiveness
cursoriness
curvilineal
curvilinear
decarbonate
decarbonise
deceivingly
defibrinate
deficiently
definiendum
degradingly
demandingly
deoxygenate
dependently
deploringly
deservingly
determinacy
determinant
determinate
determinism
determinist
detrimental
Deuteronomy
deviousness
devotedness
diachronism
differentia
differently
diffidently
diffuseness
diphthongal
dipsomaniac
disarmingly
disentangle
dismayingly
disorganise
disseminate
disseminule
dissonantly
disunionist
divergently
divisionary
divisionism
doggishness
dolefulness
dollishness
doltishness
donnishness
doubleender
doubleentry
doughtiness
drouthiness
drunkenness
dubiousness
dumbfounder
durableness
dutifulness
earnestness
earthliness
ebulliently
echosounder
efficiently
effulgently
einsteinium
elderliness
electioneer
electronics
elusiveness
embracingly
emptyhanded
emulousness
emulsionise
endearingly
endlessness
enquiringly
enviousness
equableness
Erastianism
erotogenous
erotomaniac
eudaemonism
eudaemonist
Europeanise
evasiveness
exceedingly
excellently
excremental
expectantly
expediently
experienced
exterminate
extremeness
exuberantly
factualness
faddishness
falteringly
fanfaronade
farawayness
farraginous
fatefulness
fatiguingly
fatuousness
faultfinder
fearfulness
feelingness
ferruginous
fidgetiness
finicalness
firmamental
flaccidness
flatulently
flauntingly
fleshliness
flightiness
floweriness
foolishness
footpoundal
foppishness
foreignness
forerunning
forethinker
foreverness
forewarning
forgiveness
forlornness
forwardness
fourpounder
fractionary
fractionate
fractionise
franklinite
franticness
freethinker
fretfulness
friableness
frontrunner
frowardness
frowstiness
fulsomeness
functionary
functionate
fundamental
furtiveness
gainfulness
gallantness
Gallicanism
gardemanger
gartersnake
gaseousness
genteelness
genuineness
gerrymander
ghastliness
ghostliness
gibbousness
girlishness
glaringness
godlessness
gonfalonier
gracileness
gradualness
graphicness
gristliness
grouchiness
grumblingly
guardedness
gutlessness
guttersnipe
haggardness
hallucinate
Hamiltonian
handgrenade
handpainted
haplessness
harmfulness
hatefulness
haughtiness
healthiness
heavyhanded
heedfulness
Hegelianism
heinousness
hellishness
helpfulness
hideousness
hirsuteness
histrionics
histrionism
hoggishness
homophonous
hooliganism
hopefulness
hugeousness
hurriedness
hurtfulness
hydrogenate
hydrogenous
hydroponics
hypolimnion
hypothenuse
ignobleness
illusionism
illusionist
immarginate
immenseness
impatiently
impermanent
impersonate
impertinent
implemental
imploringly
importantly
importunate
importunely
importunity
imprudently
incardinate
incessantly
incipiently
inclemently
inconsonant
incontinent
incremental
incriminate
indignantly
IndoChinese
IndoIranian
indulgently
inelegantly
inexactness
inquilinous
inquiringly
insipidness
insistently
insultingly
intenseness
intercensal
interdental
interlinear
Interlingua
interlining
interlunary
intermingle
internuncio
intertangle
intravenous
invalidness
irksomeness
isochronism
isochronous
itinerantly
jealousness
jerrymander
joylessness
knavishness
knowingness
labiodental
languidness
largeminded
lastingness
lawlessness
learnedness
leatherneck
lengthiness
lentiginous
libertinage
libertinism
lighthanded
lightminded
limitedness
lineprinter
lingeringly
lissomeness
literalness
loathliness
logicalness
loutishness
lovableness
lumpishness
lustfulness
Lutheranism
luxuriantly
maddeningly
magdalenian
malignantly
mandarinate
mandolinist
mannishness
marchioness
masculinely
masculinise
masculinity
massiveness
mastodontic
matrilineal
matrilinear
matrimonial
mawkishness
mediateness
mindfulness
minnesinger
miscegenate
miserliness
molendinary
molybdenite
moneylender
monoclinous
monseigneur
mountaineer
mountainous
mountaintop
movableness
multilinear
mundaneness
musicalness
mutableness
mythomaniac
nailvarnish
nasofrontal
naturalness
naughtiness
necromancer
necromantic
needfulness
negationist
negligently
nephelinite
nervousness
nitrogenise
nitrogenous
noisomeness
nonunionist
notableness
nothingness
noxiousness
nutrimental
obliqueness
obscureness
observantly
observingly
obviousness
octingenary
odorousness
oldwomanish
ominousness
onerousness
operoseness
opportunely
opportunism
opportunist
opportunity
orderliness
orthocentre
orthodontia
orthodontic
outwardness
overmanning
overrunning
overweening
painfulness
Palestinian
pandemonium
panicmonger
paperhanger
paramountcy
paramountly
passiveness
patrilineal
patrimonial
paunchiness
peevishness
Pelagianism
pelargonium
pensiveness
pentagynous
peregrinate
perfectness
pericranial
pericranium
periodontal
perishingly
permanently

pertinently
pestilently
petitionary
pettishness
phosphonium
photofinish
phylogynist
physiognomy
piggishness
pinkishness
piteousness
pitifulness
planoconvex
playfulness
plebeianise
plebeianism
pliableness
plicateness
pocketknife
pointedness
poltroonery
polyphonous
pomegranate
pompousness
positronium
potteringly
prattlingly
preachiness
precedented
precedently
preciseness
predominant
predominate
preliminary
prenominate
presciently
presumingly
prevalently
prickliness
primigenial
privateness
prizewinner
prochronism
profaneness
profuseness
prominently
promisingly
prosaicness
protagonist
providently
provokingly
prudishness
pruriginous
Prussianise
Prussianism
pushfulness
quadrennial
quadrennium
queenliness
questionary
quiescently
quinquennia
radicalness
raffishness
rangefinder
ratiocinate
rattlesnake
raucousness
raunchiness
ravishingly
reactionary
reactionist
reawakening
recommender
recriminate
rectilineal
rectilinear
recumbently
recurrently
reddishness
redundantly
reincarnate
rejoicingly
relatedness
relationism
relationist
religionise
religionism
religionist
reluctantly
repellantly
repellently
repentantly
repleteness
representer
reprovingly
repugnantly
resiliently
restfulness
restiveness
retiredness
revaccinate
revisionary
revisionism
revisionist
righthanded
righthander
rightminded
rightwinger
riotousness
roentgenise
roguishness
roundedness
ruinousness
sacramental
saintliness
saplessness
saprogenous
saturninely
savouriness
saxophonist
scaremonger
scorchingly
scorpionfly
scragginess
scrappiness
screamingly
scrimpiness
scruffiness
scuppernong
searchingly
seasickness
seditionary
selfishness
selfopinion
sentimental
seriousness
serpiginous
sexlessness
shadowiness
shallowness
shapeliness
sheathknife
shorthanded
shortwinded
shrinkingly
shrubbiness
sickeningly
sickishness
sightliness
signpainter
sillimanite
silveriness
simperingly
sincereness
sinlessness
sinuousness
sizableness
skeletonise
sketchiness
skilfulness
slavishness
slenderness
slightingly
smallminded
smithsonite
soberminded
Socinianism
solutionist
somnolently
songfulness
sottishness
soulfulness
Southernism
sparingness
spellbinder
sporogenous
sporogonium
springiness
squalidness
squarsonage
squashiness
squeakiness
squintingly
stagemanage
starchiness
startlingly
stateliness
staunchness
stellionate
stiltedness
stoicalness
stormcentre
strangeness
straphanger
streakiness
stringently
stringiness
studiedness
stumblingly
stuntedness
stylishness
suasiveness
subdominant
sublimeness
subordinate
suburbanise
suburbanite
succedaneum
succulently
summariness
sunlessness
superlunary
supertanker
suppliantly
supremeness
swarthiness
swinishness
sycophantic
sycophantry
synchronise
synchronism
synchronous
tabletennis
taciturnity
tearfulness
teaspoonful
tediousness
telephonist
teleprinter
tenableness
tenuousness
termagantly
terrigenous
testimonial
thermionics
thinskinned
thirstiness
threadiness
threehanded
thriftiness
thrillingly
throatiness
tobacconist
tobogganing
tobogganist
torchsinger
totteringly
toughminded
transfinite
transiently
translunary
transponder
treacliness
tremblingly
trenchantly
tricksiness
tritagonist
trivialness
truculently
tunableness
tunefulness
turbulently
typefounder
typefoundry
typicalness
ultrasonics
unaccounted
unawareness
unbendingly
uncanniness
unceasingly
uncleanness
uncongenial
uncouthness
underhanded
undermanned
underpinned
undertenant
unfailingly
unfeelingly
unfortunate
ungodliness
unhappiness
uniformness
unmanliness
unmeaningly
unnervingly
unquietness
unreasoning
unsmilingly
unsoundness
unsparingly
unusualness
unwarranted
unweetingly
unwillingly
unwinkingly
unwittingly
uprightness
uselessness
vacationist
vacuousness
valiantness
variousness
velvetiness
verboseness
vertiginous
vesuvianite
viciousness
viscousness
visibleness
voguishness
volitionary
volubleness
vortiginous
waggishness
wakefulness
waspishness
waywardness
wealthiness
weightiness
Weismannism
welcomeness
wellfounded
wellmeaning
wellrounded
Wesleyanism
whitishness
whoremonger
willingness
winningness
winsomeness
wishfulness
wistfulness
witchhunter
witheringly
witlessness
womanliness
worldliness
xylophonist
zealousness
zestfulness
zootechnics
aboveground
aeolotropic
affectional
affectioned
agoraphobia
agoraphobic
allelomorph
anadiplosis
anastomoses
anastomosis
anastomotic
anglophobia
anglophobic
anisotropic
antiJacobin
antistrophe
aponeuroses
aponeurosis
aponeurotic
ascensional
attritional
barrelhouse
bassethound
beaverboard
bibliopolic
biocoenoses
biocoenosis
biocoenotic
blackgrouse
bottlenosed
braggadocio
branchiopod
bridgeboard
brucellosis
calyptrogen
candlepower
catastrophe
cauliflower
centreboard
chainsmoker
chalcedonic
chameleonic
chaulmoogra
chromosomal
chronologer
chronologic
chrysarobin
churchgoing
churchwoman
circumpolar
circumsolar
circumvolve
coccidiosis
coffeehouse
cognitional
coldblooded
collisional
conditional
conditioner
cottonmouth
craftswoman
ctenophoran
customhouse
dexiotropic
diarthrosis
dimensional
directional
disapproval
disharmonic
douroucouli
earthcloset
educational
embryologic
emmenagogue
enarthrosis
evolutional
exceptional
executioner
expansional
extensional
extortioner
fasciaboard
fingerboard
formational
freemasonry
Frenchwoman
fullblooded
Gallophobia
gastronomic
gentlewoman
geotectonic
gillyflower
glassblower
globeflower
gnotobiosis
gnotobiotic
gradational
GraecoRoman
grammalogue
gramophonic
greengrocer
haemoglobin
hagioscopic
halfblooded
headborough
heartbroken
heavyfooted
heliotropic
hemeralopia
heteropolar
homozygosis
honeymooner
hydrobromic
hydrophobia
hydrophobic
hydrothorax
hydrotropic
hygroscopic
hypertrophy
hypotyposis
hypsophobia
illdisposed
immunologic
impassioned
inflexional
intensional
intentional
intentioned
interatomic
intergrowth

intuitional
jabberwocky
kilocalorie
lightfooted
louverboard
louvreboard
macrobiotic
macroscopic
megalopolis
melancholia
melancholic
metachrosis
microgroove
microphonic
microscopic
misericorde
monochromat
monochromic
monozygotic
mortarboard
mosstrooper
motivepower
multistorey
musclebound
myxomatosis
necrobiosis
needlepoint
needlewoman
negrophobia
Neoplatonic
netherworld
neurotropic
noticeboard
nutritional
nyctitropic
nyctophobia
obsessional
operational
orthoscopic
orthotropic
oxyhydrogen
paddleboard
palindromic
parasitosis
paratrooper
parishioner
partitioned
partitioner
pediculosis
photophobia
photophobic
phototropic
physiologic
plainspoken
pleiotropic
pleochroism
pocketmoney
policewoman
polychromic
porterhouse
posteriorly
prehistoric
previsional
probational
probationer
progestogen
promotional
protectoral
provisional
pseudomonas
pseudomorph
pseudopodia
psittacosis
psychologic
psychomotor
pullthrough
pureblooded
pussyfooter
quickfrozen
radiophonic
recessional
redactional
reversional
reversioner
rhinoscopic
roughfooted
Russophobia
saddlehorse
salvational
sansculotte
saprobiotic
schoolboard
schoolhouse
Scotchwoman
seborrhoeic
selfdevoted
selfimposed
sensational
shocktroops
shortspoken
shovelboard
silverpoint
sinistrorse
situational
sleeveboard
sleuthhound
sockdologen
somatologic
somatotonia
somatotonic
spermatozoa
splashboard
splayfooted
spokeswoman
sportswoman
springboard
springhouse
stephanotis
stiflejoint
stockbroker
stoneground
stormtroops
strikebound
stringboard
strongpoint
sublittoral
subregional
summational
summerhouse
superabound
swiftfooted
switchboard
syndesmosis
syssarcosis
technologic
teeterboard
tenterhooks
teratologic
thenceforth
thereabouts
thixotropic
toffeenosed
togglejoint
townspeople
traditional
trichinosis
trichomonad
twelvemonth
ultraviolet
underground
undergrowth
undeveloped
unemotional
unequivocal
unfashioned
unipersonal
valuational
variational
ventriloquy
vibrational
vichyssoise
warmblooded
washerwoman
watercooled
watercooler
wellbeloved
wellgroomed
whereabouts
aerographer
Aesculapian
allomorphic
apocalyptic
apostrophic
arthrospore
autographic
autotrophic
avoirdupois
bitterapple
bookkeeping
cabbagepalm
cacographic
circumspect
clodhopping
clothesprop
cornucopian
counterpane
counterpart
counterplan
counterplea
counterplot
demographer
demographic
diastrophic
doublespeak
doxographer
dualpurpose
ectomorphic
ectotrophic
endomorphic
endotrophic
frothhopper
geostrophic
Germanophil
grandnephew
grasshopper
greatnephew
gyrocompass
handicapped
handicapper
hedgehopped
hemianopsia
hemimorphic
heterospory
highstepper
holographic
homomorphic
ideographic
idiographic
idiomorphic
incorruptly
intercepter
interceptor
interdepend
interrupter
interruptor
interseptal
kymographic
logographer
logographic
malapropism
marlinspike
maxillipede
mesomorphic
metamorphic
milliampere
monocarpous
monographer
monographic
monomorphic
namedropper
narcoleptic
nomographer
nomographic
nosographer
nosographic
oreographic
ornithopter
outcropping
outstripped
overcropped
overlapping
overstepped
overtopping
paragrapher
paragraphic
paraleipsis
paramorphic
participant
participate
participial
philosopher
philosophic
photocopier
pilocarpine
pleomorphic
polycarpous
polygraphic
polymorphic
preoccupied
rheotropism
safekeeping
sandskipper
selfdespair
selfdisplay
selfrespect
selfsupport
serendipity
serigrapher
showjumping
showstopper
sideslipped
sidestepped
snowleopard
stenotypist
stirruppump
stomachpump
superimpose
teenybopper
telegrapher
telegraphic
thunderpeal
tightlipped
topographer
topographic
touchtyping
transalpine
typographer
typographic
underexpose
weenybopper
winningpost
wiretapping
worshipping
xylocarpous
xylographer
xylographic
zygomorphic
abecedarian
accessorial
accessorise
accipitrine
acculturate
adiaphorism
adventuress
adventurism
adventurist
adventurous
afterburner
agglomerate
alabastrine
alcyonarian
Alexandrian
alexandrine
alexandrite
AngloNorman
anteriority
antiquarian
arbitrarily
archaeornis
arglebargle
aristocracy
artillerist
aspersorium
assessorial
bacciferous
ballbearing
barbiturate
barleybroth
barnstormer
barrelorgan
battledress
beechmarten
belligerent
bergschrund
bicorporate
bittercress
blackbirder
blackmarket
blameworthy
bloodstream
booklearned
bottlegreen
brachyurous
bradycardia
buffalorobe
bulletproof
bullterrier
bureaucracy
cabbagerose
calciferous
capillarity
cardiograph
cardsharper
carnivorous
cassiterite
catchphrase
catheterise
cavalierism
cellularity
centenarian
chloroprene
choreograph
chronograph
chrysoprase
cinnabarine
circularise
circularity
coldhearted
collaborate
columbarium
commemorate
commiserate
computerise
concentrate
conductress
confederacy
confederate
conflagrant
conflagrate
congenerous
considerate
considering
consumerism
coplanarity
corniferous
coronagraph
coronograph
corroborant
corroborate
cotemporary
cottongrass
crematorium
crossgarnet
cruciferous
crucigerous
cryotherapy
cryptograph
cupriferous
customarily
cycloserine
cysticercus
decarburise
decemvirate
decerebrate
decolourise
demonstrate
dentigerous
depauperate
depauperise
desultorily
deteriorate
dictatorial
digitigrade
dinosaurian
diphtherial
diphtheroid
diphycercal
directorate
directorial
disafforest
disenthrall
disinterest
disinterred
domineering
doublecross
downhearted
dramaturgic
drawingroom
dresscircle
dundrearies
egalitarian
enchantress
endometrium
endothermal
endothermic
engineering
epigastrium
epinephrine
equilibrate
equilibrist
equilibrium
ergatocracy
eurypteroid
executorial
exemplarily
exemplarity
expectorant
expectorate
extemporary
extemporise
exteriorise
exteriority
extraverted
extroverted
faithworthy
familiarise
familiarity
ferriferous
festschrift
fieldcornet
fieldworker
fingerprint
FinnoUgrian
fissiparity

fissiparous
floriferous
forequarter
foreshorten
formularise
franctireur
frankfurter
freehearted
freezedried
frigidarium
frugivorous
fullhearted
gangsterism
gemmiferous
gemmiparous
gestatorial
gingerbread
globigerina
globularity
goodhearted
grandparent
granivorous
granularity
greaseproof
guttapercha
gypsiferous
halfhearted
halterbreak
haphazardly
hardhearted
heartstring
heliochrome
helleborine
hemipterous
heptamerous
herbivorous
heterograft
heterotroph
hexametrist
holothurian
homopterous
homosporous
hydrocarbon
hyperborean
hypermarket
hypothermia
ichthyornis
imaginarily
impenetrate
imperforate
incarcerate
incorporate
incorporeal
indifferent
inferiority
infirmarian
ingathering
inheritress
insalubrity
insectarium
insessorial
insincerely
insincerity
intemperate
interiorise
interiority
introverted
inventorial
involucrate
ironhearted
kickstarter
kindhearted
kinetograph
kwashiorkor
lactiferous
Lancastrian
latchstring
leprosarium
letterpress
libertarian
lionhearted
loosestrife
lycanthrope
lycanthropy
madreporite
magisterial
magisterium
mailcarrier
mansardroof
meadowgrass
mediatorial
megatherium
melliferous
mercenarily
meritocracy
metallurgic
metalworker
Micawberish
Micawberism
millenarian
miniaturise
miniaturist
ministerial
misanthrope
misanthropy
momentarily
monasterial
moneymarket
monkeybread
monopterous
morbiferous
morningroom
mothercraft
multiparous
muscularity
necessarian
necessarily
needlecraft
nightmarish
nightporter
nondescript
noseyparker
nulliparity
nulliparous
octachordal
odoriferous
oligomerous
openhearted
ophidiarium
optometrist
oracularity
orchestrate
organscreen
overbearing
ozoniferous
pachydermal
paediatrics
paediatrist
parametrise
parathyroid
peculiarity
pecuniarily
pentamerous
pentandrous
perchlorate
perineurium
perispermic
perseverate
pestiferous
phosphorate
phosphorism
phosphorite
phosphorous
photoperiod
physiocracy
pieceworker
pilotburner
piscatorial
piscivorous
planetarium
plantigrade
pleinairist
polyandrous
polystyrene
polyzoarium
Precambrian
precentress
preceptress
precontract
predatorily
prefatorial
prefatorily
prelusorily
prematurely
prematurity
priestcraft
primiparous
profiterole
proletarian
proletariat
proliferate
proliferous
protectress
protomartyr
protuberant
provisorily
pseudograph
psychodrama
psychograph
pupillarity
purgatorial
pyrargyrite
Pythagorean
Pythagorism
quaestorial
quickfiring
quinquereme
quitchgrass
racketpress
radiocarbon
radiolarian
Rastafarian
rattlebrain
reconstruct
refrigerant
refrigerate
reintegrate
remonstrant
remonstrate
reportorial
reverberant
reverberate
rhizocarpic
ribbongrass
Sabbatarian
Sagittarius
saltatorial
ScotchIrish
scriptorial
scriptorium
scurvygrass
secondarily
secretarial
secretariat
sedentarily
seigneurial
seigniorage
seigniorial
seismograph
selfreproof
selfstarter
selfsterile
semidiurnal
sempiternal
Septembrist
septenarius
septentrion
septiferous
sequestrate
sertularian
shadowgraph
Shaksperean
Shaksperian
sheepfarmer
shoulderbag
shoulderpad
showerproof
shrinkproof
sightscreen
sightworthy
singletrack
singularise
singularity
sittingroom
skatingrink
slavemarket
smokescreen
smokingroom
softhearted
somniferous
songsparrow
spectatress
spendthrift
spiniferous
spinsterish
splendorous
squirearchy
stagestruck
staircarpet
statutorily
steelworker
stenochromy
stereograph
stevengraph
stockmarket
stonecurlew
stonemarten
stratocracy
subcontract
subcontrary
superioress
superiority
supermarket
supernormal
superscribe
superscript
superstrata
surfboarder
syllabarium
tachycardia
talebearing
tautomerism
technocracy
temporarily
termitarium
terrestrial
territorial
tetramerous
thankworthy
thaumatrope
thermograph
thuriferous
timesharing
transferred
transferrer
transformer
transmarine
transparent
transporter
transversal
treacherous
trencherman
tributarily
trimestrial
Trinitarian
triquetrous
triumvirate
truehearted
trustworthy
tumbledrier
ultramarine
unconcerned
undisturbed
unfaltering
unipolarity
utilitarian
vascularise
vascularity
voluntarily
voluntarism
voluntarist
waitingroom
warmhearted
weakhearted
wheelbarrow
whitethroat
wintergreen
zoantharian
Zoroastrian
admiral**s**hip
adverti**s**ing
Albigen**s**ian
ambiver**s**ion
anarchi**s**tic
anniver**s**ary
anomali**s**tic
aphrodi**s**iac
apostle**s**hip
apotheo**s**ise
audiovi**s**ual
autopla**s**tic
bathing**s**uit
bellico**s**ity
Belorus**s**ian
bergama**s**que
blamele**s**sly
blockbu**s**ter
bloodle**s**sly
bloodve**s**sel
brainle**s**sly
brankur**s**ine
breadba**s**ket
broadca**s**ter
burgoma**s**ter
bushman**s**hip
busines**s**man
cabbali**s**tic
Calvini**s**tic
captain**s**hip
caravan**s**ary
catacly**s**mic
catechi**s**mal
catechi**s**tic
catswhi**s**ker
ceasele**s**sly
ceropla**s**tic
cheerle**s**sly
choirma**s**ter
citizen**s**hip
closefi**s**ted
cloudca**s**tle
coexten**s**ion
coexten**s**ive
colonel**s**hip
communi**s**tic
complai**s**ant
compres**s**ion
compres**s**ive
comrade**s**hip
congres**s**man
connois**s**eur
cotonea**s**ter
counter**s**ign
counter**s**ink
counter**s**unk
countle**s**sly
country**s**eat
country**s**ide
critica**s**ter
curator**s**hip
dauntle**s**sly
deempha**s**ise
delight**s**ome
denizen**s**hip
dialogi**s**tic
disaccu**s**tom
dishone**s**tly
disillu**s**ion
displea**s**ure
distres**s**ful
doubtle**s**sly
draught**s**man
dreamle**s**sly
drillma**s**ter
duniewa**s**sal
dyslogi**s**tic
ectobla**s**tic
ectopla**s**mic
embelli**s**her
emperor**s**hip
encomia**s**tic
endopla**s**mic
esempla**s**tic
establi**s**her
Euchari**s**tic
euphemi**s**tic
evening**s**tar
extrava**s**ate
faithle**s**sly
faultle**s**sly
fetichi**s**tic
fetishi**s**tic
feudali**s**tic
firerai**s**ing
flavour**s**ome
foreclo**s**ure
foretop**s**ail
formali**s**tic
fourflu**s**her
fruitle**s**sly
further**s**ome
gafftop**s**ail
gatecra**s**her
general**s**hip
gigante**s**que
gracele**s**sly
grandio**s**ely
grandio**s**ity
guilele**s**sly
guiltle**s**sly
haberda**s**her
haggadi**s**tic
hairdre**s**ser
hairrai**s**ing
halfmea**s**ure
harmoni**s**tic
heartle**s**sly
Helleni**s**tic
herowor**s**hip
holobla**s**tic
homoiou**s**ian
homopla**s**tic
housema**s**ter
Hudibra**s**tic
hylozoi**s**tic
hypobla**s**tic
hypoglo**s**sal
hypophy**s**eal
hypophy**s**ial
hypoten**s**ion
hypothe**s**ise
ichthyo**s**aur
impetuo**s**ity
impreci**s**ely

imprecision
incognisant
incuriosity
inexpensive
inoffensive
intercessor
intercostal
interfusion
interosseus
irremissive
Jansenistic
jargonistic
kitchensink
lacrimosely
lacrymosely
lectureship
lickerishly
lifemanship
limitlessly
lowpressure
macrocosmic
Maglemosian
maintopsail
maladjusted
managership
manneristic
manumission
marquessate
marshalship
masochistic
matchlessly
mechanistic
mediumistic
mercilessly
meroblastic
mesoblastic
messiahship
metaphysics
metaplastic
metastasise
Methodistic
microcosmic
Micronesian
mirthlessly
modernistic
monitorship
monochasial
monochasium
Monophysite
monstrosity
muskthistle
neologistic
nervelessly
noiselessly
nonplussing
northeaster
northwester
oarsmanship
omnipresent
ornithosaur
overmeasure
paederastic
Panglossian
pantheistic
partnership
paternoster
patronising
patternshop
pearlfisher
Pentecostal
pessimistic
picturesque
pinnatisect
plateresque
pluralistic
pointlessly
polycrystal
ponderosity
postclassic
powerlessly
praetorship
predecessor
premiership
prestissimo
prestressed
primateship
proctorship
progression
progressism
progressist
progressive
prophetship
provostship
pyroclastic
quarrelsome
Rabelaisian
religiosity
replenisher
rickettsial
ritualistic
rockcrystal
scaleinsect
schistosity
schistosome
scholarship
scholiastic
schottische
scientistic
scoutmaster
selfclosing
selfraising
selfworship
senatorship
senselessly
shamanistic
shamelessly
sharepusher
sheepmaster
sheriffship
shiftlessly
showmanship
sightlessly
sleeplessly
slickenside
smilelessly
snickersnee
socialistic
soldiership
solipsistic
soundlessly
southeaster
southwester
speakership
spinelessly
Spinozistic
spiritistic
sponsorship
squeamishly
stainlessly
starcrossed
steadfastly
stewardship
stickinsect
strenuosity
studentship
subdivision
sumptuosity
supervision
supervisory
suppression
suppressive
syllogistic
symbolistic
synergistic
tantalising
tapemeasure
tastelessly
teachership
thanklessly
threemaster
tightfisted
Titianesque
toastmaster
topdressing
tracelessly
transfusion
tribuneship
tritheistic
troublesome
trousersuit
trustbuster
trusteeship
trypanosome
tyrannosaur
uncontested
unexpressed
unfurnished
unnecessary
unobtrusive
unpossessed
unpromising
unrealistic
unvarnished
unwholesome
vasopressin
vasopressor
venturesome
verbalistic
viceroyship
vinedresser
voicelessly
voodooistic
waspwaisted
wastebasket
wearilessly
Westminster
whistlestop
whitewasher
whoremaster
wolfwhistle
workmanship
worthlessly
wreckmaster
abomination
abstraction
abstractive
abstriction
acceptation
acclamation
acclamatory
acclimation
acclimatise
acclivitous
acetylation
achromatise
achromatism
acidulation
acquisition
acquisitive
acumination
acupuncture
adenomatous
adumbration
adumbrative
adversative
Aeneolithic
aeronautics
aerostatics
aerostation
aestivation
affectation
affiliation
affirmation
affirmative
affirmatory
affrication
affricative
aggravation
aggregately
aggregation
aggregative
agriculture
aircraftman
alleviation
alleviative
alleviatory
alphabetise
altercation
alternately
alternation
alternative
amazonstone
amethystine
anacoluthon
anemometric
antenuptial
antineutron
antiquation
apologetics
appellation
appellative
application
applicative
applicatory
appogiatura
approbation
approbatory
aquaculture
aquiculture
arbitration
arbitrative
arbitratrix
argumentive
armtwisting
assafoetida
assentation
assignation
association
associative
assortative
astigmatism
atomisation
attenuation
attestation
attribution
attributive
audiometric
autoerotism
babysitting
barquentine
batholithic
bathymetric
bearbaiting
bellbottoms
bellheather
Benedictine
benediction
benedictory
benefaction
betweentime
bifurcation
billposting
bipartition
Bodhisattva
bombilation
bombination
Bonapartean
Bonapartism
Bonapartist
botheration
brachiation
bristletail
bullbaiting
byeelection
cabbagetree
calcination
calculating
calculation
calculative
calefactory
calibration
campmeeting
candidature
candlestick
captivation
carbonation
carburetion
carburetted
carburetter
carburettor
carminative
castigation
celebration
celebratory
cementation
cerebration
chainletter
champertous
circulation
circulative
circulatory
clandestine
clinometric
coadunation
coagulation
coarctation
cobblestone
coeducation
coessential
colligation
colligative
collimation
collocation
colouration
combination
combinative
combinatory
commination
comminatory
comminution
commutation
commutative
comparatist
comparative
competition
competitive
compilation
complotting
compositely
composition
compositive
compotation
compotatory
compunction
computation
concomitant
concubitant
condolatory
condonation
confliction
conflictive
confutation
confutative
congelation
conjugation
conjugative
conjunction
conjunctiva
conjunctive
conjuncture
conjuration
connotation
connotative
consecution
consecutive
consolation
consolatory
consumption
consumptive
contractile
contraction
contractive
contractual
contracture
contraption
contrastive
conurbation
convocation
convolution
cooperation
cooperative
copingstone
corbiesteps
cornerstone
corporately
corporation
corporatism
corporative
correlation
correlative
corrugation
coruscation
cosignatory
coulometric
counterturn
crenulation
crepitation
crimination
criminative
criminatory
crotcheteer
culmination
cultivation
cupellation
cybernation
cybernetics
daisycutter
deathrattle
debarkation
decantation
declamation
declamatory
declaration
declarative
declaratory
declination
declivitous
decollation
decolletage
decrepitate
decrepitude
decussately
decussation
defalcation
deferential
defloration
defoliation
deformation
deglutition
degradation
degustation
dehydration
deification
delectation
delineation
demagnetise
demarcation
demarkation
democratise
democratism
denigration
denigratory
deoxidation
deportation

depravation
deprecation
deprecative
deprecatory
depredation
depredatory
deprivation
dereliction
description
descriptive
desecration
desensitise
desiccation
desiccative
designation
desperately
desperation
destination
destitution
destruction
destructive
detestation
deuteration
devaluation
devastation
diagnostics
diapositive
diffraction
Diophantine
diplomatise
diplomatist
discerption
discourtesy
disfunction
disgruntled
disjunction
disjunctive
disjuncture
dislocation
disparately
disposition
dispositive
disputation
disquieting
disquietude
dissipation
dissipative
dissolutely
dissolution
distinction
distinctive
distraction
distractive
distrustful
divestiture
divulgation
documentary
draggletail
dropcurtain
dualcontrol
duplication
duplicative
duplicitous
dysfunction
econometric
edification
edificatory
ejaculation
ejaculatory
elaborately
elaboration
elaborative
electrotype
elephantine
elephantoid
elicitation
elimination
eliminative
Elizabethan
elucidation
elucidative
elucidatory
elutriation
embarkation
emblematise
emblematist
embrocation
encystation
entablature
enterostomy
enucleation
enumeration
enumerative
enunciation
enunciative
equidistant
equinoctial
eradication
eradicative
Esperantist
eucalyptole
eudiometric
evagination
evaporation
evaporative
everlasting
examination
exclamation
exclamatory
excoriation
exculpation
exculpatory
exdirectory
exfoliation
exfoliative
exhortation
exhortative
exhortatory
existential
exoneration
exonerative
expatiation
expatiative
expatiatory
expectation
expectative
expenditure
explanation
explanatory
explication
explicative
explicatory
exploration
explorative
exploratory
exponential
exportation
expurgation
expurgatory
exquisitely
exsiccation
extenuation
extenuatory
extirpation
extirpatory
extradition
extrication
fabrication
facelifting
facultative
fairweather
fascinating
fascination
favouritism
fecundation
feldspathic
festinately
fiddlestick
filamentary
filamentous
filmsetting
fimbriation
fingerstall
flagcaptain
fluctuation
fomentation
forestation
formication
formulation
fornication
fortunately
foulmouthed
fragmentary
freebooting
frostbitten
fructuation
frustration
fulguration
fullmouthed
fulminating
fulmination
fulminatory
fusillation
fustigation
gallowstree
gastrectomy
gemmulation
gentilitial
geopolitics
germination
germinative
gettogether
glasscutter
glomeration
goldbeating
goniometric
grandfather
grandmother
granolithic
granulation
gratulation
gratulatory
gravimetric
gravitation
gravitative
gurgitation
habituation
handfasting
handknitted
handwriting
handwritten
hardhitting
hardmouthed
headhunting
hearthstone
heliometric
hepatectomy
hibernation
Hindoostani
hippopotami
homeopathic
homocentric
housefather
housemother
humiliation
humiliatory
hydrometeor
hydrometric
hydropathic
hygrometric
hymenoptera
hyperactive
hypermetric
hyphenation
hypogastric
hypostatise
hypsometric
idolisation
imagination
imaginative
imbrication
immanentism
immanentist
immediately
immigration
imparkation
impartation
impetration
impetratory
implication
implicative
importation
imprecation
imprecatory
inadvertent
inanimately
inanimation
inattention
inattentive
incantation
incantatory
incarnation
incertitude
inclination
incompetent
inculcation
inculpation
inculpatory
incurvation
incurvature
indentation
indigestion
indigestive
indignation
indirection
inebriation
ineffective
ineffectual
inessential
infatuation
inferential
infestation
infeudation
influential
information
informative
informatory
ingratitude
ingurgitate
innervation
innutrition
inoculation
inoculative
inoperative
inopportune
inquisition
inquisitive
inscription
inscriptive
insensately
insensitive
insinuation
insinuative
inspiration
inspiratory
instigation
instigative
instinctive
instinctual
institution
instruction
instructive
integration
integrative
interactant
interaction
interactive
interesting
intermitted
intricately
intromitted
intromitter
investiture
inviolately
involuntary
invultation
irradiation
irradiative
irredentism
irredentist
irretention
irretentive
isoelectric
itineration
jactitation
Judaisation
labefaction
laciniation
lacrimation
lacrimatory
lacrymation
lacrymatory
laicisation
lamentation
lancinating
lancination
laryngotomy
legislation
legislative
legislature
lepidoptera
lickspittle
ligamentary
ligamentous
linguistics
liquidation
litterateur
lixiviation
loudmouthed
lubrication
lubricative
lucubration
luxuriation
machination
maladaptive
malediction
maledictory
malefaction
malfunction
malposition
malpractice
manducation
manducatory
manifestant
manifestoes
manufactory
manufacture
manumitting
mastication
masticatory
mathematics
melioration
meliorative
mensuration
merchantman
metacentric
meteoritics
methylation
metrication
microlithic
micrometric
micturition
misbegotten
misconstrue
miscreation
mistrustful
molestation
monoculture
murmuration
musculation
musculature
myelomatous
nationstate
Neanderthal
necessitate
necessitous
negotiation
negotiatory
negotiatrix
nephrectomy
neuropathic
nictitation
nonexistent
nonvolatile
novelettish
numismatics
numismatist
nuncupation
nuncupative
obfuscation
obfuscatory
objurgation
objurgatory
obscuration
obsecration
observation
observatory
obstinately
obstruction
obstructive
obtestation
occultation
officiation
oilpainting
openmouthed
oppugnation
orangoutang
orientation
origination
originative
oscillation
oscillatory
ostentation
osteopathic
Ostrogothic
outfighting
ovariectomy
oversetting
overwritten
oviposition
oxygenation
ozonisation
palpitation
pamphleteer
pantalettes
parachutist
parturition
Passiontide
passivation
pectination
penetrating
penetration
penetrative
penitential
peptisation
percolation
perennation
perforation
perforative
perfunctory
permutation
persecution
personation
personative

perspective
phagocytise
phagocytose
phalanstery
photoactive
photometric
plagiostome
planimetric
platinotype
plectoptera
plenipotent
ploughstaff
pollination
polyglottal
polyglottic
polypeptide
pomiculture
ponderation
portmanteau
portraitist
portraiture
postnuptial
postulation
precipitant
precipitate
precipitous
predication
predicative
predicatory
preelection
preexistent
preignition
prelibation
premeditate
premonition
premonitory
preparation
preparative
preparatory
preposition
prepositive
prerogative
presanctify
presumption
presumptive
preterition
procreation
procreative
procrustean
procuration
procuratory
profanation
profanatory
progenitrix
progeniture
prohibition
prohibitive
prohibitory
prolocutrix
promptitude
propagation
propagative
proposition
proprietary
prorogation
prosecution
prosecutrix
proselytise
proselytism
prospective
prosthetics
prostration
protonotary
protractile
protraction
protractive
provocateur
provocation
provocative
proximately
psychiatric
publication
pulchritude
pullulation
pumicestone
punctuation
purpresture
pustulation
qualitative
quartertone
quickwitted
racemeeting
radioactive
radiometric
rarefaction
rarefactive
readywitted
realisation
reanimation
reapportion
reassertion
rebarbative
recantation
reclamation
recognition
recognitive
recognitory
recommittal
recondition
redirection
reedbunting
reeducation
referential
reformation
reformative
reformatory
regimentals
regurgitate
reification
reinsertion
reiteration
reiterative
reluctation
reorientate
repartition
replication
reprobation
reprobative
reprobatory
repudiation
requisition
reservation
residential
resignation
respiration
respiratory
restitution
restoration
restorative
restriction
restrictive
restructure
resuscitate
retaliation
retaliative
retaliatory
retardation
retardative
retardatory
retribution
retributive
retributory
retroaction
retroactive
revaluation
reverential
rhizomatous
ribvaulting
ricochetted
rodomontade
rottenstone
rubberstamp
rubefaction
rubrication
rudimentary
rustication
sacculation
Sanskritist
sarcomatous
schismatise
schizanthus
scissortail
scyphistoma
sedimentary
segregation
segregative
selfcentred
selfcontent
selfcontrol
selfculture
selffertile
selfmastery
selftorture
semimonthly
sericulture
serrulation
sharpwitted
shoeleather
shoplifting
silverstick
singlestick
snowbunting
sociometric
sociopathic
solmisation
somewhither
speculation
speculative
spessartite
spindletree
spirometric
splenectomy
sporulation
stagflation
standpatter
stepbrother
stimulation
stimulative
stipulation
stipulatory
stonecutter
straightcut
straightish
straightway
stylisation
subarration
subaudition
subjugation
subjunctive
sublimation
subornation
subrogation
substantial
substantive
subsumption
subsumptive
subtraction
subtractive
suffixation
suffocation
suffocative
superintend
superlative
supernatant
supposition
suppositive
suppository
suppuration
suppurative
surrebuttal
surrebutter
surrogation
suspiration
susurration
swallowtail
swingletree
synchrotron
syncopation
syndication
systematics
systematise
systematism
systematist
tabefaction
taratantara
tegumentary
temperately
temperative
temperature
tenementary
termination
terminative
theocentric
therewithal
thickwitted
titillation
tittivation
tracheotomy
transaction
transection
translation
transmittal
transmitted
transmitter
Trappistine
trendsetter
trepanation
trepidation
trestletree
tribulation
tribunitial
trituration
trundletail
tufthunting
tumefaction
turbination
typecasting
typesetting
typewritten
unassertive
unchristian
uncommitted
unessential
unification
unigeniture
unimportant
unrelenting
unremitting
unselective
utilisation
vaccination
vacillation
vacuolation
valediction
valedictory
variegation
varnishtree
venesection
venisection
ventilation
ventilative
vermination
vicissitude
vindication
vindicative
vindicatory
viniculture
viscountess
viticulture
vivisection
voltametric
wainscoting
wainscotted
washleather
waterbottle
wherewithal
whiffletree
whippletree
whitleather
Whitsuntide
wildcatting
windlestraw
winetasting
wirenetting
woodcutting
adminicular
albuminuria
altocumulus
ambiguously
ambitiously
amorphously
analogously
anfractuous
animalcular
anomalously
anonymously
assiduously
atrociously
audaciously
barbarously
beauteously
beautifully
behavioural
bounteously
bountifully
brahmaputra
breadcrumbs
bumblepuppy
bumptiously
canalicular
canaliculus
capaciously
carbuncular
caricatural
carvelbuilt
catercousin
cavernously
centrifugal
changefully
circumlunar
clamorously
closehauled
colourfully
commissural
congruously
conjectural
consanguine
consciously
conspicuity
conspicuous
constituent
constitutor
contributor
convolvulus
corpuscular
courteously
credulously
crepuscular
custombuilt
dangerously
deceitfully
deliciously
deliriously
demagoguery
demagoguism
dexterously
dishonourer
distinguish
distribuend
distributor
doubleDutch
doublequick
downdraught
dreadnought
egregiously
equiangular
erroneously
exogenously
facetiously
feloniously
ferociously
firstfruits
forethought
forgetfully
fractiously
freethought
frightfully
frivolously
gallimaufry
garrulously
glutinously
goodnatured
grotesquely
grotesquery
handwrought
hazardously
healthfully
hermeneutic
highfalutin
highwrought
hilariously
hurryscurry
hurryskurry
illfavoured
illhumoured
imperiously
impetuously
incongruent
incongruity
incongruous
incunabulum
incuriously
indeciduous
individuate
ingeniously
ingenuously
injuriously
innocuously
innoxiously
insidiously
intercourse
intercrural
interfluent
invidiously
irresoluble
judiciously
laboriously
larcenously
lecherously
litigiously
ludicrously
luxuriously
maliciously
masterfully
mellifluent
mellifluous
melodiously
momentously
monologuise
monologuist
monstrously
multangular
murderously
murmurously

nefariously
neighbourly
notoriously
obliviously
obnoxiously
officiously
overindulge
overwrought
pendulously
penuriously
perspicuity
perspicuous
plenteously
plentifully
poisonously
ponderously
prefectural
preterhuman
proconsular
promiscuity
promiscuous
propinquity
prostitutor
querulously
rancorously
rapaciously
rapturously
rectangular
regardfully
regretfully
religiously
reposefully
resentfully
retinacular
retinaculum
righteously
sagaciously
saintpaulia
salaciously
seditiously
selfassured
selfinduced
soliloquise
soliloquist
somnambular
sorrowfully
spectacular
squarebuilt
stegosaurus
strenuously
subcultural
subscapular
substituent
sumptuously
superfluity
superfluous
tempestuous
tenaciously
thaumaturge
thaumaturgy
therapeutic
thermoduric
torturously
tremulously
tricoloured
troublously
tuttifrutti
tyrannously
unambiguous
unanimously
undutifully
unhelpfully
unicellular
unicoloured
unskilfully
vagariously
ventricular
ventriculus
venturously

veraciously
verminously
vexatiously
vicariously
vivaciously
voraciously
watercourse
wholesouled
wonderfully
acriflavine
adjectively
affectively
affectivity
antigravity
assertively
attentively
bodyservant
bondservant
bondservice
causatively
cognitively
cognitivity
collusively
combatively
corrosively
countervail
counterview
deceptively
deductively
defectively
defensively
diffusively
digestively
directivity
effectively
excessively
exclusively
exclusivity
excursively
expansively
expansivity
expensively
explosively
extensively
imitatively
impassively
impassivity
impulsively
inclusively
inductively
inobservant
insectivore
intensively
intrusively
intuitively
intuitivism
invectively
inventively
irruptively
landgravine
lucratively
maidservant
mendelevium
mischievous
narratively
nondelivery
nutritively
objectively
objectivism
objectivist
objectivity
obsessively
obtrusively
offensively
operatively
ostensively
palsgravine
partitively
pervasively

plaintively
pointdevice
prelusively
primitively
primitivism
privatively
purposively
receptively
receptivity
recessively
rediscovery
reflexively
repulsively
resistively
resistivity
retentively
retentivity
rotogravure
secretively
seductively
selectively
selectivity
selfservice
selfserving
sensitively
sensitivity
spacesaving
talkatively
tentatively
timeserving
unbelieving
undeserving
unforgiving
woodcarving
Yugoslavian
bittersweet
bladderwort
breadthways
breadthwise
bristleworm
cabbageworm
chickenwire
counterwork
countrywide
crossbowman
earthenware
giantpowder
highbrowism
journeywork
kitchenware
latticework
linedrawing
meadowsweet
mindblowing
plasterwork
scratchwork
shopsteward
sulphurwort
swallowwort
thimbleweed
thitherward
toothpowder
trelliswork
trestlework
unbeknownst
weatherwise
weatherworn
whitherward
winegrowing
worldlywise
crucifixion
genuflexion
intersexual
solifluxion
transfixion
transsexual
actinomyces
actinomycin
amphictyony

assemblyman
bricklaying
clairvoyant
cyclothymia
cyclothymic
deliveryman
diapophysis
granophyric
haemoptysis
heterotypic
hydrophytic
hygrophytic
infantryman
lithophytic
longplaying
McCarthyism
microphytic
osteophytic
palaeotypic
plasmolysis
plasmolytic
pleurodynia
proteolysis
proteolytic
protophytic
saprophytic
selfdenying
selfpitying
sporophytic
steatopygia
stereotyped
stereotyper
stereotypic
thermolysis
thermolytic
troglodytic
yacketyyack
bashibazouk
Leibnitzian
Proterozoic

---

ablutionary
abranchiate
academicals
accommodate
acculturate
afficionado
agglomerate
agglutinate
amontillado
amplexicaul
anencephaly
anniversary
antemundane
antioxidant
antiphonary
appropriate
approximate
appurtenant
archipelago
aristocracy
assassinate
balletomane
barbiturate
basketchair
beaverboard
beneficiary
beneficiate
betweenmaid
bicarbonate
bicentenary
bicorporate
bicuspidate
bimillenary
biofeedback
bodyservant
bondservant
bookinghall
bottleglass

bracteolate
breadthways
breastplate
bridgeboard
bristletail
bureaucracy
cabbagepalm
campanulate
caravansary
carcinomata
cardinalate
cardiograph
carpetsnake
carunculate
catchphrase
centreboard
certificate
chaetognath
chamberlain
chambermaid
chaperonage
chevalglass
Chippendale
chloroplast
choreograph
chromoplast
chronograph
chrysoprase
clairschach
clairvoyant
cleistogamy
codefendant
codicillary
collaborate
commemorate
commiserate
commonplace
communicant
communicate
compaginate
complainant
complaisant
concatenate
concentrate
concomitant
concubinage
concubinary
concubitant
condylomata
confabulate
confederacy
confederate
conflagrant
conflagrate
considerate
consolidate
constellate
consternate
contaminant
contaminate
contemplate
contorniate
coparcenary
copperplate
corbiculate
coronagraph
coronograph
corroborant
corroborate
cotemporary
cottongrass
countermand
countermark
counterpane
counterpart
countervail
crackerjack
credentials
cryotherapy

cryptograph
decarbonate
decemvirate
decerebrate
decolletage
decorticate
decrepitate
defibrinate
demonstrate
denticulate
deoxygenate
depauperate
desegregate
deteriorate
determinacy
determinant
determinate
deuterogamy
diamondback
digitigrade
dipterocarp
directorate
discalceate
disenthrall
disseminate
dissimilate
dissimulate
divisionary
documentary
domesticate
domiciliary
domiciliate
draggletail
dropcurtain
earthenware
elbowgrease
encapsulate
equidistant
equilibrate
ergatocracy
evidentiary
exanthemata
exarcerbate
expectorant
expectorate
expostulate
expropriate
exstipulate
extemporary
exterminate
extrapolate
extravagant
extravagate
extravasate
fanfaronade
farthingale
fasciaboard
fasciculate
filamentary
fingerboard
fingerglass
fingerplate
fingerstall
flabbergast
flagcaptain
folliculate
foretopmast
foretopsail
fractionary
fractionate
fragmentary
fricandeaux
funambulate
functionary
functionate
gafftopsail
galleyslave
gartersnake
gesticulate

guesstimate
gyrocompass
haemorrhage
hallucinate
handgrenade
haustellate
heterograft
Hindoostani
hippopotami
horripilate
hydrogenate
hypothecate
ichthyosaur
immarginate
impenetrate
imperforate
impersonate
importunate
impropriate
incarcerate
incardinate
incognisant
incompliant
inconsonant
incorporate
incriminate
individuate
ingurgitate
inobservant
intemperate
interactant
intercalary
intercalate
interlunary
interpolate
interrelate
interrogate
investigate
involucrate
involuntary
jumpingjack
kinetograph
kitchenware
lawmerchant
leatherback
legerdemain
libertinage
ligamentary
loggerheads
louverboard
louvreboard
machicolate
machinemade
maidservant
maintopmast
maintopsail
mandarinate
mandibulate
manifestant
margraviate
marketplace
marquessate
matriculate
meadowgrass
meprobamate
meritocracy
middleclass
minuteglass
miscarriage
miscegenate
misestimate
mismarriage
molendinary
mooringmast
mortarboard
mothercraft
nationstate
necessitate
needlecraft
nickelplate
nightingale
noctivagant
noticeboard
nurserymaid
octingenary
orangoutang
orchestrate
ornithosaur
oysterplant
packingcase
paddleboard
palmcabbage
participant
participate
particulate
pastureland
pedicellate
pedunculate
penicillate
peninsulate
penultimate
perambulate
perchlorate
peregrinate
perseverate
petitionary
phantasiast
phantasmata
phosphorate
phylloclade
physiocracy
picturecard
plagioclase
plantigrade
playerpiano
playingcard
ploughshare
ploughstaff
pomegranate
pontificals
pontificate
powderflask
precipitant
precipitate
precontract
predominant
predominate
preliminary
premeditate
prenominate
prevaricate
priestcraft
proliferate
prolificacy
proprietary
protonotary
protuberant
pseudograph
psychodrama
psychograph
quarterback
questionary
quitchgrass
ratiocinate
rattlebrain
rattlesnake
reactionary
recalculate
reciprocate
recriminate
reduplicate
refrigerant
refrigerate
regimentals
regurgitate
reincarnate
reintegrate
remonstrant
remonstrate
renegotiate
reorientate
resuscitate
retranslate
revaccinate
revendicate
reverberant
reverberate
revisionary
ribbongrass
rodomontade
rubberstamp
rudimentary
schoolboard
scintillant
scintillate
scissortail
scurvygrass
secondclass
sedimentary
seditionary
seigniorage
seismograph
selfcommand
selfdespair
selfreliant
semipalmate
sequestrate
shadowgraph
shopsteward
shovelboard
significant
silverplate
singletrack
sleeveboard
snowleopard
somatoplasm
sparrowhawk
spatterdash
spifflicate
spiraculate
splashboard
springboard
squarsonage
stagemanage
steeplejack
stellionate
stereograph
stevengraph
stickleback
stipendiary
strangulate
stratocracy
stringboard
stringybark
subaxillary
subcontract
subcontrary
subdominant
subordinate
substandard
suffumigate
superlunary
supernatant
superstrata
surveillant
swallowtail
switchblade
switchboard
taratantara
technocracy
teeterboard
tegumentary
tenementary
tentaculate
tetrarchate
theatricals
thermograph
thitherward
timebargain
trabeculate
transhumant
translocate
translunary
transpadane
triangulate
triumvirate
trophoblast
trundletail
tryingplane
tryptophane
tuberculate
tyrannosaur
undertenant
unfortunate
unguiculate
unimportant
uninucleate
unnecessary
urochordate
vagabondage
valleculate
vermiculate
volitionary
Wensleydale
whitherward
yacketyyack
abolishable
abracadabra
accountable
accountably
acidifiable
agoraphobia
agoraphobic
allocatable
anglophobia
anglophobic
antechamber
antiJacobin
applaudable
appreciable
appreciably
articulable
assimilable
attemptable
attractable
augmentable
automatable
beachcomber
certifiable
certifiably
chrysarobin
civilisable
cleanlimbed
coffeetable
cognoscible
collapsible
collectable
collectible
combustible
comfortable
comfortably
commendable
commendably
committable
compassable
compellable
compossible
comprisable
concealable
conceivable
conceivably
condemnable
condensable
conductible
conferrable
confirmable
confiscable
conformable
conformably
congealable
connectable
connectible
conquerable
conservable
consignable
construable
containable
contestable
continuable
contrivable
conversable
convertible
convertibly
convincible
correctable
corruptible
corruptibly
deliverable
demountable
denumerable
depressible
descendable
descendible
describable
developable
diningtable
dinnertable
disassemble
disassembly
discardable
discernible
discernibly
discussable
discussible
disencumber
dislikeable
dispensable
disremember
dissociable
dissolvable
dissyllable
distensible
dithyrambic
embraceable
enforceable
enlargeable
escheatable
exercisable
exhaustible
explainable
exploitable
expressible
extractable
fashionable
fashionably
fermentable
fissionable
foreseeable
forfeitable
forgettable
fortifiable
Gallophobia
haemoglobin
hereditable
hydrocarbon
hydrophobia
hydrophobic
hypsophobia
illimitable
illimitably
illuminable
immedicable
immitigable
immitigably
impeachable
impermeable
impermeably
imperviable
implausible
implausibly
impregnable
impregnably
impressible
inadaptable
inadvisable
inalienable
inalienably
inalterable
inalterably
incoercible
increasable
indefinable
indefinably
indivisible
indivisibly
indomitable
indomitably
indubitable
indubitably
ineluctable
ineluctably
inequitable
inequitably
inescapable
inestimable
inestimably
inexcusable
inexcusably
inflammable
inflammably
infrangible
inhabitable
inheritable
innavigable
innumerable
innumerably
inscribable
inscrutable
inscrutably
inseparable
inseparably
insuperable
insuperably
intertribal
intolerable
intolerably
intractable
intractably
irrecusable
irrecusably
irreducible
irreducibly
irrefutable
irrefutably
irremovable
irremovably
irreparable
irreparably
irresoluble
irrevocable
irrevocably
justiciable
justifiable
justifiably
landgrabber
liquefiable
liquidambar
looselimbed
manipulable
marcescible
marriagebed
medicinable
mentionable
misremember

negrophobia
nyctophobia
organisable
pensionable
perceivable
perceivably
perceptible
perceptibly
perfectible
performable
permissible
permissibly
persuadable
persuasible
perturbable
photophobia
photophobic
pleasurable
pleasurably
polarisable
practicable
practicably
predictable
predictably
presentable
presentably
preservable
preventable
preventible
propitiable
protrudable
protrusible
publishable
purchasable
putrescible
qualifiable
radiocarbon
reclaimable
recoverable
rectifiable
redoubtable
refrangible
regenerable
registrable
regrettable
regrettably
replaceable
repleviable
repressible
repressibly
respectable
respectably
responsible
responsibly
retraceable
retractable
retrievable
Russophobia
salvageable
satisfiable
serviceable
serviceably
shoulderbag
signifiable
sleepingbag
specifiable
stockjobber
stretchable
submersible
submissible
suggestible
supportable
supportably
surpassable
susceptible
susceptibly
suspensible
sustainable
swallowable
tarnishable
thingumabob
transcriber
traversable
treasonable
treasonably
trisyllabic
trisyllable
unalterable
unavailable
unavoidable
unavoidably
unbreakable
uncatchable
unclimbable
uncountable
uncrushable
undesirable
undisturbed
unendurable
unendurably
unflappable
ungetatable
unmatchable
unmemorable
unmemorably
unpalatable
unprintable
unshockable
unspeakable
unspeakably
unstoppable
unteachable
unthinkable
unthinkably
untouchable
unutterable
unutterably
vaporisable
vitrifiable
warrantable
warrantably
worshipable
abiological
actinomyces
actinomycin
aerological
aeronomical
aesthetical
agonistical
agrological
agronomical
ahistorical
algological
allAmerican
allegorical
anecdotical
anthropical
antitypical
apostolical
atheistical
autarchical
axiological
biochemical
biometrical
biophysical
braggadocio
Brahmanical
Brahminical
brazenfaced
calendrical
casuistical
categorical
chimaerical
conceptacle
convenances
conventicle
conveyancer
coxcombical
cylindrical
cysticercus
cytological
demagogical
dendritical
diacritical
dialectical
diametrical
diphycercal
diplococcus
directrices
doublefaced
dresscircle
egotistical
enigmatical
ethological
evangelical
executrices
experienced
fantastical
flagofficer
geochemical
geometrical
geophysical
grammatical
greengrocer
guttapercha
homiletical
homological
horological
ideological
impolitical
impoliticly
impractical
internuncio
isometrical
jabberwocky
Jacobinical
Jacobitical
jauntingcar
judgmatical
kinematical
leviratical
mediatrices
metonymical
micrococcal
micrococcus
monarchical
monological
mycological
necromancer
Neotropical
nomological
nonsensical
nosological
obstetrical
oecological
oecumenical
oenological
oncological
ontological
oreological
orthoepical
panegyrical
papiermache
paradisical
paradoxical
paramedical
parasitical
parheliacal
patristical
pedagogical
pedological
penological
pharisaical
pietistical
pomological
posological
pragmatical
prophetical
prothoracic
puritanical
pyramidical
quadratical
rhapsodical
rheological
rheumaticky
schottische
selfinduced
semeiotical
serological
sexological
sinological
sleepingcar
smoothfaced
sophistical
spasmodical
splenetical
spondulicks
squirearchy
statistical
stomachache
straightcut
straitlaced
strategical
subclinical
subcortical
subcritical
subtropical
sybaritical
symmetrical
synagogical
synonymical
syntactical
synthetical
taxonomical
testatrices
theological
theoretical
thrasonical
toploftical
topological
typological
uncanonical
unequivocal
unpolitical
vehmgericht
virological
aboutsledge
acknowledge
aggrievedly
allantoides
archdukedom
barefacedly
bellfounder
benightedly
blackbirder
bodybuilder
bradycardia
broadminded
cantharides
cantharidic
caryopsides
cheerleader
childminder
Christendom
chrysalides
clearheaded
coldblooded
collectedly
conceitedly
concertedly
confessedly
connectedly
contentedly
coralloidal
corrigendum
cyclopaedia
cyclopaedic
dedicatedly
definiendum
delightedly
dicotyledon
dimwittedly
disguisedly
disgustedly
dispersedly
doubleender
downtrodden
dumbfounder
echosounder
ellipsoidal
emptyhanded
emptyheaded
ephemerides
faultfinder
featheredge
footpoundal
fourpounder
frankpledge
fratricidal
fullblooded
gallbladder
gerrymander
giantpowder
hairbreadth
halfblooded
halfholiday
handbreadth
haphazardly
heavyhanded
Heracleidan
homesteader
householder
hydraheaded
hypnopaedia
ingrainedly
interbedded
intermeddle
jerrymander
largeminded
leaseholder
levelheaded
lighthanded
lightheaded
lightminded
loculicidal
masquerader
metalloidal
meteoroidal
misguidedly
mollycoddle
moneylender
moneyspider
octachordal
offhandedly
officialdom
orthopaedic
perplexedly
pervertedly
pigheadedly
pivotbridge
planetoidal
pretendedly
professedly
proofreader
pseudopodia
pureblooded
purportedly
quadrupedal
rangefinder
recommender
rhombohedra
righthanded
righthander
rightminded
shareholder
shipbuilder
shockheaded
shorthanded
shortwinded
sightreader
slaveholder
smallholder
smallminded
soberminded
spellbinder
spermicidal
stadtholder
stakeholder
stallholder
starstudded
stockholder
surfboarder
swellheaded
swimbladder
tachycardia
tarradiddle
thickheaded
threehanded
titleholder
toothpowder
toughminded
transponder
trapezoidal
typefounder
typefoundry
unadvisedly
unashamedly
unboundedly
underbidder
underhanded
undoubtedly
unfeignedly
unguardedly
unlimitedly
Upanishadic
volkslieder
warmblooded
weighbridge
wellfounded
wellrounded
whiteheaded
wrongheaded
abandonment
abolishment
abridgement
abusiveness
acaulescent
achievement
acquiescent
acquirement
adjectively
adjournment
adjudgement
advancement
adventuress
adverseness
advisedness
affectively
aftereffect
aggregately
aimlessness
airlessness
airsickness
alkalescent
alternately
altorelievo
altorilievo
amativeness
amiableness
amorousness
amphisbaena
ancientness
anxiousness
appeasement

appointment
arbitrageur
arbitrament
arborescent
archdiocese
archduchess
Archimedean
arduousness
arraignment
arrangement
artlessness
assertively
assuagement
assuredness
attentively
audibleness
austereness
awesomeness
awkwardness
balefulness
bashfulness
bathysphere
battledress
battlefield
bearishness
beastliness
bedevilment
bedizenment
beguilement
belatedness
belligerent
benightment
bereavement
bersaglieri
betweenness
bewitchment
bibliotheca
biliousness
bittercress
bittersweet
blessedness
bloodstream
blotchiness
bombardment
Bonapartean
bonbonniere
bookishness
boorishness
bottlegreen
boutonniere
breastwheel
bristliness
Britishness
brittleness
brusqueness
brutishness
bullishness
butteriness
caddishness
calefacient
callousness
capableness
captionless
carabiniere
carabinieri
carefulness
causatively
centrepiece
chancellery
chanticleer
chargesheet
chickenfeed
chloroprene
chucklehead
churchiness
circumspect
Clarencieux
cleanliness
cockleshell
coefficient
cognateness
cognitively
collusively
combatively
comfortless
commandment
compactness
compartment
compilement
complexness
comportment
compositely
comstockery
concealment
concernment
conciseness
concrescent
condottiere
condottieri
conductress
confinement
congealment
connoisseur
consentient
consignment
constituent
containment
contentment
contrariety
controlment
copiousness
corbiesteps
cordialness
corecipient
corporately
correctness
corrosively
corruptness
costiveness
counterfeit
countryseat
courtliness
crabbedness
crookedness
crotcheteer
crunchiness
cryosurgery
cunningness
curableness
curiousness
currentness
currishness
cursiveness
cursoriness
curtailment
curvilineal
curvilinear
debauchment
debouchment
deceptively
decussately
deductively
defectively
defenceless
defensively
deforcement
defraudment
delitescent
demagoguery
demigoddess
depravement
derangement
desperately
despoilment
detrainment
development
deviousness
devotedness
diffuseness
diffusively
digestively
disablement
disafforest
disarmament
disbandment
discernment
discourtesy
disinterest
dislodgment
disobedient
disparately
disportment
dissentient
dissepiment
dissolutely
distribuend
divorcement
divulgement
doggishness
dolefulness
dollishness
doltishness
donnishness
doublecheck
doublespeak
doughtiness
drouthiness
drunkenness
dubiousness
durableness
dutifulness
earnestness
earthliness
effectively
elaborately
elderliness
electioneer
elusiveness
embowerment
embracement
embroilment
emotionless
emplacement
emulousness
enchainment
enchantment
enchantress
encrustment
endlessness
endorsement
enfeoffment
enforcement
engorgement
engrossment
enhancement
enjambement
enlargement
enlivenment
ennoblement
enslavement
entablement
enthralment
entitlement
entrainment
entreatment
entrustment
envelopment
enviousness
environment
equableness
equipollent
escheatment
evanishment
evasiveness
excessively
exclusively
excursively
exhaustless
expansively
expensively
explosively
exquisitely
extensively
extremeness
factualness
faddishness
farawayness
fatefulness
fatuousness
fearfulness
featherhead
featherless
featureless
feelingness
festinately
fidgetiness
finicalness
flaccidness
flavourless
fleshliness
flightiness
floweriness
fluorescein
fluorescent
foolishness
foppishness
foreignness
foreverness
forgiveness
forlornness
fortunately
forwardness
franctireur
franticness
fretfulness
friableness
frowardness
frowstiness
fulsomeness
furtiveness
gainfulness
gallantness
garnishment
gaseousness
gegenschein
genteelness
genuineness
ghastliness
ghostliness
gibbousness
gimcrackery
gingerbread
girlishness
glaringness
godlessness
gracileness
gradualness
grandiosely
grandparent
graphicness
gristliness
grotesquely
grotesquery
grouchiness
groundsheet
guardedness
gutlessness
haematocele
haggardness
halterbreak
haplessness
harbourless
harmfulness
hatefulness
haughtiness
healthiness
hedgepriest
heedfulness
heinousness
hellishness
helpfulness
hideousness
hirsuteness
hoggishness
hopefulness
housewifely
housewifery
hugeousness
hurriedness
hurtfulness
hydrometeor
hydrosphere
hymenoptera
hyperborean
hypersthene
hypophyseal
ignobleness
imitatively
immediately
immenseness
impassively
impeachment
imperilment
impermanent
impertinent
impingement
importunely
impoundment
imprecisely
impressment
impropriety
improvement
improvident
impulsively
inadvertent
inanimately
incalescent
inclusively
incompetent
incongruent
inconscient
incontinent
incorporeal
indehiscent
independent
indifferent
IndoChinese
indorsement
inductively
inefficient
inexactness
inexpedient
inheritress
insensately
insincerely
insipidness
installment
instillment
intelligent
intenseness
intensively
interdepend
interfluent
interjacent
interlinear
interosseus
intricately
intrusively
intuitively
intumescent
invalidness
invectively
inventively
inviolately
involvement
irksomeness
ironmongery
irruptively
isogeotherm
jealousness
joylessness
jumpingbean
juvenescent
knavishness
knowingness
lacrimosely
lacrymosely
landingbeam
landinggear
languidness
lastingness
lawlessness
learnedness
leatherhead
leatherneck
lengthiness
lepidoptera
letterpress
lightsomely
limitedness
lissomeness
literalness
lithosphere
litterateur
loathliness
loathsomely
logicalness
loutishness
lovableness
lucratively
luminescent
lumpishness
lustfulness
macrogamete
magnificent
makebelieve
mannishness
mantelpiece
mantelshelf
marchioness
masculinely
massiveness
masterpiece
matrilineal
matrilinear
mawkishness
maxillipede
meadowsweet
meaningless
measureless
measurement
mediateness
mellifluent
meningocele
microgamete
milliampere
mindfulness
miserliness
misjudgment
mitrailleur
monkeybread
mononuclear
monseigneur
mountaineer
movableness
multilinear
multivalent
mundaneness
musicalness
mutableness
naphthalene
narratively
naturalness
naughtiness

necropoleis
needfulness
nervousness
noctilucent
noisomeness
nondelivery
nonetheless
nonexistent
nonresident
notableness
nothingness
nourishment
noxiousness
nutcrackers
nutritively
objectively
obliqueness
obmutescent
obscureness
obsessively
obsolescent
obstinately
obtrusively
obviousness
odorousness
oesophageal
offenceless
offensively
officialese
oligochaete
ominousness
omnipresent
onerousness
operatively
operoseness
opportunely
orderliness
organscreen
ostensively
ostracoderm
outwardness
overgarment
overpayment
ozonosphere
paddlewheel
painfulness
pamphleteer
partitively
passiveness
patrilineal
paunchiness
pearlescent
peevishness
pensionless
pensiveness
pentathlete
pentavalent
perfectness
pervasively
pettishness
phalanstery
philhellene
photosphere
pigeonchest
piggishness
pinkishness
pinnatisect
piteousness
pitifulness
plaintively
planisphere
playfulness
plectoptera
Pleistocene
plenipotent
pliableness
plicateness
pointedness
poltroonery

polystyrene
pompousness
portionless
portmanteau
pourparlers
prayerwheel
preachiness
precentress
preceptress
preciseness
predicament
preexistent
prejudgment
prelusively
prematurely
presentient
presentment
prickliness
primitively
privateness
privatively
procrustean
procurement
profaneness
profuseness
prolegomena
prosaicness
protectress
provocateur
proximately
prudishness
publishment
pulverulent
purposeless
purposively
pushfulness
Pythagorean
quarterdeck
queenliness
quickfreeze
quinquereme
racketpress
radicalness
raffishness
raucousness
raunchiness
realignment
receptively
recessively
recruitment
rectilineal
rectilinear
reddishness
rediscovery
reenactment
reflexively
refreshment
relatedness
reminiscent
remorseless
replacement
repleteness
repulsively
requirement
resipiscent
resistively
resplendent
restatement
restfulness
restiveness
retentively
retiredness
retrocedent
reviviscent
rhomboideus
riotousness
roguishness
roundedness
rubefacient

ruinousness
saintliness
saplessness
saturninely
sausagemeat
savouriness
scaleinsect
scragginess
scrappiness
scrimpiness
scruffiness
sculduddery
sculduggery
seasickness
seborrhoeic
secretively
seductively
selectively
selfconceit
selfcontent
selfevident
selfishness
selfmastery
selfrespect
sensitively
seriousness
sexlessness
shadowiness
Shaksperean
shallowness
shapeliness
shelterbelt
shelterless
shepherdess
shirtsleeve
shrubbiness
shutterless
sickishness
sightliness
sightscreen
silveriness
sincereness
sinlessness
sinuousness
sizableness
sketchiness
skilfulness
skulduddery
skulduggery
slavishness
slenderness
smithereens
smokescreen
songfulness
sottishness
soulfulness
sparingness
spectatress
spindlelegs
spirochaete
springclean
springiness
squalidness
squashiness
squeakiness
starchiness
stateliness
staunchless
staunchness
sternsheets
stickinsect
stiltedness
stoicalness
stoolpigeon
strangeness
streakiness
stringiness
stringpiece
studiedness

stuntedness
stylishness
suasiveness
subbasement
sublimeness
subservient
substituent
succedaneum
succourless
summariness
sunlessness
superintend
superioress
superjacent
supersedeas
supremeness
surbasement
sustainment
swarthiness
swinishness
synchromesh
talkatively
tearfulness
tediousness
temperament
temperately
tenableness
tentatively
tenuousness
tetravalent
textureless
thimbleweed
thirstiness
thoughtless
threadiness
thriftiness
throatiness
thunderhead
thunderless
thunderpeal
toothsomely
traducement
trafficless
tragicomedy
transilient
translucent
transparent
treacliness
tremblement
tricksiness
trivialness
troposphere
trouserless
tunableness
tunefulness
turtleshell
typicalness
ultramodern
unawareness
uncanniness
uncleanness
uncouthness
ungodliness
unhappiness
uniformness
unmanliness
unquietness
unsoundness
unusualness
uprightness
uselessness
vacuousness
valiantness
variousness
velvetiness
verboseness
versatilely
vestryclerk
viciousness

victualless
viridescent
virilescent
viscountess
viscousness
visibleness
voguishness
volubleness
waggishness
wakefulness
waspishness
waywardness
wealthiness
wearisomely
weightiness
welcomeness
weltschmerz
whigmaleery
whitishness
wholesomely
willingness
winningness
winsomeness
wintergreen
wishfulness
wistfulness
witlessness
womanliness
worldliness
worrisomely
worshipless
zealousness
zestfulness
conspecific
costbenefit
disgraceful
distasteful
distressful
distrustful
foraminifer
gallimaufry
mistrustful
nonspecific
overstuffed
reproachful
resourceful
scorpionfly
sickbenefit
subspecific
suspenseful
teaspoonful
absorbingly
acceptingly
accordingly
affectingly
agonisingly
appallingly
appealingly
approvingly
arglebargle
arrestingly
bandylegged
banteringly
barrelorgan
befittingly
beguilingly
bibliopegic
calyptrogen
candlelight
caressingly
centrifugal
chaulmoogra
chronologer
chronologic
cliffhanger
confidingly
confusingly
consolingly
consumingly

crosslegged
deceivingly
degradingly
demandingly
deploringly
deservingly
dinnerwagon
diphthongal
disarmingly
disentangle
dismayingly
doubleedged
downdraught
dramaturgic
dreadnought
embracingly
embryologic
emmenagogue
endearingly
enquiringly
exceedingly
falteringly
fatiguingly
flauntingly
footslogger
forethought
freethought
fullfledged
gardemanger
grammalogue
gravedigger
grumblingly
hairtrigger
handwrought
heavyweight
highwrought
honeybadger
hornswoggle
hyperphagia
immunologic
imploringly
inquiringly
insultingly
Interlingua
intermingle
intertangle
laughinggas
leapfrogged
lightweight
lingeringly
maddeningly
magazinegun
medicolegal
metallurgic
minnesinger
motherright
observingly
overwrought
oxyhydrogen
panicmonger
paperhanger
paperweight
pennyweight
perishingly
pettifogger
physiologic
pillowfight
potteringly
prattlingly
presumingly
progestogen
promisingly
provokingly
psychologic
ravishingly
rejoicingly
reprovingly
rightwinger
roughlegged

sarcophagus
scaremonger
scorchingly
screamingly
searchingly
searchlight
secondsight
septifragal
shrinkingly
sickeningly
simperingly
slightingly
sockdolager
sockdologen
somatologic
spaceflight
spreadeagle
squintingly
startlingly
steatopygia
straphanger
streetlight
stumblingly
technologic
teratologic
threelegged
thrillingly
torchsinger
totteringly
tremblingly
trothplight
unbendingly
unceasingly
underweight
unfailingly
unfeelingly
unmeaningly
unnervingly
unsmilingly
unsparingly
unweetingly
unwillingly
unwinkingly
unwittingly
waterlogged
wheelwright
whoremonger
witheringly
admiralship
Aeneolithic
aerographer
allomorphic
anacoluthon
apostleship
apostrophic
apparatchik
autographic
autotrophic
backbencher
batholithic
bellheather
birdwatcher
bushmanship
cacographic
captainship
citizenship
colonelship
comradeship
curatorship
demographer
demographic
denizenship
diastrophic
doxographer
ectomorphic
ectotrophic
Elizabethan
embellisher
emperorship
endomorphic
endotrophic
establisher
fairweather
feldspathic
firewatcher
foulmouthed
fourflusher
fullmouthed
gatecrasher
generalship
geostrophic
Germanophil
gettogether
grandfather
grandmother
grandnephew
granolithic
greatnephew
haberdasher
hardmouthed
hemimorphic
heroworship
highpitched
hobbledehoy
holographic
homeopathic
homomorphic
housefather
houselights
housemother
hydropathic
ideographic
idiographic
idiomorphic
kymographic
lectureship
lickerishly
lifemanship
logographer
logographic
loudmouthed
managership
marshalship
matriarchal
mesomorphic
messiahship
metamorphic
metapsychic
microlithic
monitorship
monographer
monographic
monomorphic
Neanderthal
neuropathic
nomographer
nomographic
nosographer
nosographic
oarsmanship
openmouthed
oreographic
osteopathic
Ostrogothic
paragrapher
paragraphic
paramorphic
partnership
patriarchal
patternshop
pearlfisher
philosopher
philosophic
pleomorphic
polygraphic
polymorphic
praetorship
premiership
primateship
proctorship
prophetship
provostship
replenisher
schizanthus
scholarship
selfworship
semimonthly
senatorship
serigrapher
sharepusher
sheetanchor
sheriffship
shoeleather
showmanship
sociopathic
soldiership
somewhither
soupkitchen
speakership
sponsorship
squeamishly
stepbrother
stewardship
studentship
teachership
telegrapher
telegraphic
therewithal
topographer
topographic
tribuneship
trusteeship
typographer
typographic
unfurnished
unvarnished
viceroyship
wappenschaw
washleather
wherewithal
whitewasher
whitleather
workmanship
xylographer
xylographic
zygomorphic
Abbevillian
abecedarian
abnormality
abomination
abortionist
absenteeism
abstraction
abstractive
abstriction
academician
academicism
acceptation
accessorial
accessorise
accipitrine
acclamation
acclimation
acclimatise
accompanist
acetylation
achromatise
achromatism
acidulation
acoustician
acquisition
acquisitive
acriflavine
acumination
adiaphorism
adoptianism
adoptianist
adoptionism
adoptionist
adumbration
adumbrative
adventurism
adventurist
adversative
advertising
aeronautics
aerostatics
aerostation
Aesculapian
aestivation
affectation
affectivity
affiliation
affirmation
affirmative
affranchise
affrication
affricative
aggravation
aggregation
aggregative
agnosticism
agrarianism
ailurophile
alabastrine
Albigensian
alcyonarian
Alexandrian
alexandrine
alexandrite
alleviation
alleviative
allopathist
alphabetise
altercation
alternation
alternative
amaranthine
ambiversion
amenability
Americanise
Americanism
Americanist
amethystine
amicability
amphetamine
amphibolite
anachronism
Anglicanism
AngloIndian
anglomaniac
annabergite
antenuptial
antependium
anteriority
antheridium
anthologise
anthologist
antifouling
antigravity
antiquarian
antiquation
aphrodisiac
apologetics
apomorphine
apophyllite
apotheosise
apparelling
appellation
appellative
application
applicative
approbation
aquarellist
arbitrarily
arbitration
arbitrative
argumentive
Arminianism
armtwisting
aromaticity
arterialise
artillerist
aspersorium
assafoetida
assentation
assessorial
assignation
association
associative
assortative
astigmatism
athleticism
atomisation
attenuation
attestation
attribution
attributive
audiologist
Augustinian
Aurignacian
autoerotism
babysitting
bactericide
ballbearing
barquentine
bearbaiting
bellicosity
bellringing
Belorussian
Benedictine
benediction
benefaction
bestselling
betweentime
bibliophile
bibliophily
biddability
biedermeier
bifurcation
billionaire
billposting
bimetallism
bimetallist
bimillenium
bipartition
birdfancier
bisexuality
bivouacking
bohemianism
bombilation
bombination
Bonapartism
Bonapartist
bondservice
bondwashing
bookbinding
bookkeeping
bookselling
bootlegging
botheration
brachiation
brankursine
breadthwise
bricklaying
bullbaiting
bullterrier
butcherbird
butterflies
byeelection
Byzantinism
Byzantinist
calcination
calculating
calculation
calculative
calibration
californium
campmeeting
candlestick
cannibalise
cannibalism
capillarity
captivation
caravanning
carbonation
carburetion
carminative
Carolingian
carvelbuilt
cassiterite
castigation
catheterise
catholicise
Catholicism
catholicity
cavalierism
celebration
cellularity
cementation
centenarian
cerebration
chafingdish
challenging
channelling
chansonnier
chickenwire
chiropodist
chitterling
christening
churchgoing
cicatricial
cinnabarine
circularise
circularity
circulation
circulative
civilianise
clandestine
clericalism
clericalist
clodhopping
clostridium
clothesline
coadunation
coagulation
coarctation
cochinchina
coeducation
coessential
coextension
coextensive
cognitivity
coleorrhiza
colligation
colligative
collimation
collocation
colonialism
colonialist
colouration
colourblind
columbarium
combination
combinative
commination
comminution
commonality
communalise
communalism
communalist
commutation
commutative
comparatist

comparative
competition
competitive
compilation
complotting
composition
compositive
compotation
compression
compressive
compunction
computation
computerise
condominium
condonation
confliction
conflictive
confutation
confutative
congelation
conjugality
conjugation
conjugative
conjunction
conjunctiva
conjunctive
conjuration
connotation
connotative
consanguine
consecution
consecutive
considering
consolation
conspicuity
consumerism
consumption
consumptive
contractile
contraction
contractive
contraption
contrastive
controlling
conurbation
convocation
convolution
cooperation
cooperative
coplanarity
coppersmith
cornhusking
cornucopian
corporality
corporation
corporatism
corporative
correlation
correlative
corrugation
coruscation
cosmetician
cosmogonist
cosmologist
cosmopolite
counselling
countermine
countersign
countersink
counterview
countrified
countryfied
countryside
countrywide
creationism
creationist
credibility
crematorium
crenulation
crepitation
criminalist
criminality
crimination
criminative
criticality
crocidolite
crocodilian
crucifixion
crystalline
crystallise
crystallite
culmination
culpability
cultivation
cupellation
customarily
custombuilt
cybernation
cybernetics
cycloserine
cypripedium
debarkation
decantation
decarbonise
decarburise
declamation
declaration
declarative
declination
decollation
decolourise
decussation
deemphasise
defalcation
deferential
defloration
defoliation
deformation
deglutition
degradation
degustation
dehydration
deification
delectation
delineation
demagnetise
demagoguism
demarcation
demarkation
democratise
democratism
denigration
deoxidation
depauperise
deportation
depravation
deprecation
deprecative
depredation
deprivation
dereliction
description
descriptive
desecration
desensitise
desexualise
desiccation
desiccative
designation
desperation
destination
destitution
destruction
destructive
desultorily
determinism
determinist
detestation
detribalise
deuteration
devaluation
devastation
diachronism
diagnostics
diaphaneity
diapositive
dichotomise
dichotomist
dictatorial
didacticism
diffraction
diluvialist
dinosaurian
Diophantine
diphtherial
diplomatise
diplomatist
dipsomaniac
directivity
directorial
discerption
disfunction
disillusion
disjunction
disjunctive
dislocation
disobliging
disorganise
disparaging
disposition
dispositive
disputation
disquieting
dissipation
dissipative
dissolution
distinction
distinctive
distinguish
distraction
distractive
disunionist
divisionism
divulgation
doctrinaire
domesticity
domineering
doublequick
doublethink
dressmaking
dropforging
dundrearies
duplication
duplicative
dysfunction
earpiercing
eclecticism
ecumenicism
ecumenicity
edification
educability
egalitarian
einsteinium
ejaculation
elaboration
elaborative
electrician
electricity
electrolier
electronics
elephantine
elicitation
eligibility
elimination
eliminative
ellipticity
elucidation
elucidative
elutriation
embarkation
emblematise
emblematist
embowelling
embrocation
empanelling
emulsionise
enchiridion
encystation
endocardiac
endocardial
endocardium
endometrium
endothelial
endothelium
enfranchise
engineering
enthralling
entomophily
enucleation
enumeration
enumerative
enunciation
enunciative
epigastrium
epigraphist
epinephrine
epochmaking
equilibrist
equilibrium
equinoctial
eradication
eradicative
Erastianism
erotomaniac
esotericism
Esperantist
etherealise
ethereality
ethnologist
etymologise
etymologist
euchologion
eudaemonism
eudaemonist
eurhythmics
Europeanise
evagination
evaporation
evaporative
eventualise
eventuality
everlasting
examination
exclamation
exclusivity
excoriation
exculpation
executorial
exemplarily
exemplarity
exfoliation
exfoliative
exhortation
exhortative
existential
exoneration
exonerative
exotericism
expansivity
expatiation
expatiative
expectation
expectative
explanation
explication
explicative
exploration
explorative
exponential
exportation
expurgation
exsiccation
extemporise
extenuation
exteriorise
exteriority
externalise
externalism
externality
extirpation
extradition
extrication
eyecatching
fabrication
facelifting
facsimilist
factfinding
facultative
fallibility
Falstaffian
familiarise
familiarity
farcicality
farreaching
fascinating
fascination
favouritism
feasibility
fecundation
festschrift
fiddlestick
filmsetting
fimbriation
fingerprint
FinnoUgrian
fireraising
firewalking
firstfruits
fissiparity
flagwagging
flannelling
flexibility
florilegium
fluctuation
fomentation
footsoldier
forerunning
forestation
forewarning
formication
formularise
formulation
fornication
forthcoming
fractionise
Francophile
franklinite
freebooting
freezedried
frenchified
frigidarium
fructuation
frustration
fulguration
fulminating
fulmination
funambulist
fusillation
fustigation
Gallicanism
gallowsbird
gametangium
gangsterism
geanticline
gemmologist
gemmulation
genealogise
genealogist
gentilitial
genuflexion
geopolitics
geosyncline
germination
germinative
gestatorial
glassmaking
globigerina
globularity
glomeration
goldbeating
golddigging
gonfalonier
goodlooking
gourmandise
gourmandism
grandiosity
granularity
granulation
gratulation
gravelblind
gravitation
gravitative
greasepaint
greenockite
gullibility
gurgitation
guttersnipe
gutturalise
gutturalism
habituation
hagiologist
hairraising
hairstyling
hairstylist
halfbinding
halflanding
Hamiltonian
handfasting
handselling
handwriting
hardhitting
hardworking
headhunting
heartstring
Hegelianism
helleborine
Hepplewhite
heptarchist
hermeticism
hesperidium
heteroclite
heteroecism
hexametrist
hibernation
Hibernicism
hierarchism
highbrowism
highranking
Hispanicise
Hispanicism
Hispanicist
histologist
historicise
historicism
historicist
historicity
histrionics
histrionism
hollandaise
holothurian
homogeneity
homoiousian
hooliganism
horseradish

hospitalise
hospitality
humiliation
hummingbird
husbandlike
hyacinthine
hydrologist
hydroponics
hyoscyamine
hyperactive
hyperbolise
hyphenation
hypolimnion
hypophysial
hypostatise
hypotension
hypothesise
idolisation
illbreeding
illiquidity
illusionism
illusionist
imaginarily
imagination
imaginative
imbrication
immanentism
immanentist
immigration
immortalise
immortality
impanelling
imparkation
impartation
impassivity
imperialise
imperialism
imperialist
imperilling
impetration
impetuosity
implication
implicative
importation
importunity
imprecation
imprecision
inanimation
inattention
inattentive
incantation
incarnadine
incarnation
inclination
incommodity
incongruity
incredulity
inculcation
inculpation
incuriosity
incurvation
indentation
indigestion
indigestive
indignation
indirection
IndoIranian
inebriation
inedibility
ineffective
inessential
inexpensive
infanticide
infantilism
infatuation
inferential
inferiority
infertility
infestation
infeudation
infirmarian
influential
informality
information
informative
ingathering
initialling
innervation
innutrition
inoculation
inoculative
inoffensive
inoperative
inquisition
inquisitive
insalubrity
inscription
inscriptive
insectarium
insecticide
insensitive
insessorial
insincerity
insinuation
insinuative
inspiration
instability
instigation
instigative
instinctive
institution
instruction
instructive
integrality
integration
integrative
intensifier
interaction
interactive
interallied
interesting
interfacial
interfacing
interfusion
interiorise
interiority
interlining
intermedium
internalise
internality
internecine
interracial
intrepidity
intuitivism
inventorial
inviability
invultation
irradiation
irradiative
irredentism
irredentist
irremissive
irretention
irretentive
isochronism
isomorphism
itacolumite
itineration
jactitation
Judaisation
kitchensink
knownothing
labefaction
laciniation
lacrimation
lacrymation
laicisation
lamentation
lammergeier
Lancastrian
lancinating
lancination
landgravine
landholding
landlordism
latchstring
latifundium
laudability
leavetaking
legionnaire
legislation
legislative
Leibnitzian
leprosarium
libertarian
liberticide
libertinism
limnologist
linedrawing
linefishing
linguistics
liquidation
lithotomise
lithotomist
lixiviation
logomachist
longanimity
longplaying
loosestrife
loxodromics
lubrication
lubricative
lucubration
Lutheranism
luxuriation
machination
madreporite
madrigalian
madrigalist
magdalenian
magisterial
magisterium
Maglemosian
magnanimity
mailcarrier
maladaptive
malapropism
malediction
malefaction
malfunction
malposition
malpractice
mammalogist
mandolinist
manducation
Manichaeism
manumission
manumitting
marginalise
marginality
marlinspike
marshalling
masculinise
masculinity
mastication
matchmaking
materialise
materialism
materialist
materiality
mathematics
matrimonial
McCarthyism
mechanician
mediatorial
medievalism
medievalist
megatherium
melioration
meliorative
memorialise
memorialist
mendelevium
mensuration
mercenarily
merchandise
Merovingian
merrymaking
metaphysics
metastasise
meteoritics
methylamine
methylation
metrication
Micawberish
Micawberism
Micronesian
micturition
millenarian
millionaire
mindbending
mindblowing
mindreading
miniaturise
miniaturist
ministerial
miscibility
misconceive
miscreation
misspelling
mockingbird
molestation
molybdenite
momentarily
monasterial
monasticism
moneymaking
monkeyshine
monochasial
monochasium
monologuise
monologuist
Monophysite
Monothelite
monstrosity
moribundity
moveability
mudslinging
multinomial
multiracial
murmuration
muscularity
musculation
mycophagist
mythologise
mythologist
mythomaniac
mythopoeist
nailvarnish
namecalling
nationalise
nationalism
nationalist
nationality
necessarian
necessarily
neckerchief
necrologist
needlepoint
negationist
negotiation
nephelinite
neurologist
neuroticism
nictitation
nightmarish
nitrogenise
noisemaking
nondescript
nonmatching
nonplussing
nonunionist
nonvolatile
notionalist
novelettish
nullifidian
nulliparity
numismatics
numismatist
nuncupation
nuncupative
obfuscation
objectivism
objectivist
objectivity
objurgation
obscuration
obsecration
observation
obstruction
obstructive
obtestation
occultation
oenophilist
officialism
officiation
oilpainting
oldwomanish
ophidiarium
ophiologist
opportunism
opportunist
opportunity
oppugnation
optometrist
oracularity
orientalise
orientalism
orientalist
orientation
originality
origination
originative
orthopedics
orthopedist
oscillation
ostentation
osteologist
outbreeding
outbuilding
outcropping
outfighting
outstanding
overbearing
overbidding
overlapping
overmanning
overrunning
oversailing
oversetting
overtopping
overweening
oviposition
oxygenation
ozonisation
paediatrics
paediatrist
painkilling
painstaking
Palestinian
palpability
palpitation
palsgravine
pandemonium
Panglossian
pantomimist
papermaking
parachutist
parallelism
parametrise
paramoecium
participial
parturition
passibility
Passiontide
passivation
pastoralism
pastoralist
paternalism
paternalist
pathologist
patrimonial
patronising
pawnbroking
peacemaking
peccability
pectination
peculiarity
pecuniarily
Pelagianism
pelargonium
pellucidity
penetrating
penetration
penetrative
penicillium
penitential
pentazocine
pentlandite
peptisation
percolation
perennation
perforation
perforative
pericardiac
pericardial
pericardium
pericranial
pericranium
perineurium
periodicity
peristalith
peristomial
perithecium
permutation
persecution
personalise
personalism
personalist
personality
personation
personative
personifier
perspective
perspicuity
pertinacity
pestologist
petrologist
phagocytise
phariseeism
phenologist
philatelist
philologian
philologist
phonetician
phonologist
phosphonium
phosphorism
phosphorite
photoactive
photocopier
photofinish
photoperiod
phycologist

phylogynist
physicality
phytologist
phytotomist
Pickwickian
pigsticking
pilocarpine
piscatorial
placability
planetarium
platforming
platyrrhine
plebeianise
plebeianism
pleinairist
pleochroism
pocketknife
pointdevice
pointillism
pointillist
politicking
pollination
poltergeist
polypeptide
polyzoarium
ponderation
ponderosity
portability
portraitist
positronium
possibility
postexilian
postglacial
postnuptial
postulation
Precambrian
preconceive
predatorily
predication
predicative
preelection
prefatorial
prefatorily
preignition
prejudicial
prelibation
prelusorily
prematurity
premonition
preoccupied
preparation
preparative
preposition
prepositive
preprandial
prerogative
presanctify
prestissimo
presumption
presumptive
preterition
primigenial
primitivism
probabilism
probabilist
probability
prochronism
procreation
procreative
procuration
prodigalise
prodigality
profanation
prognathism
progression
progressism
progressist
progressive
prohibition
prohibitive
proletarian
proletariat
prolificity
promiscuity
propagation
propagative
propinquity
proposition
prorogation
prosecution
proselytise
proselytism
prospective
prosthetics
prostration
protagonist
prothallial
prothallium
protractile
protraction
protractive
provisorily
provocation
provocative
Prussianise
Prussianism
publication
pullulation
punctuality
punctuation
pupillarity
purgatorial
pustulation
pyrargyrite
Pythagorism
quadrennial
quadrennium
quadrillion
quaestorial
qualitative
quarrelling
quickfiring
quincuncial
quintillion
Rabelaisian
racemeeting
radioactive
radiolarian
radiologist
rapscallion
rarefaction
rarefactive
Rastafarian
rateability
rationalise
rationalism
rationalist
rationality
reactionist
readability
realisation
reanimation
reapportion
reassertion
reawakening
rebarbative
recantation
receptivity
reciprocity
reclamation
recognition
recognitive
recondition
redetermine
redirection
reedbunting
reeducation
reestablish
referential
reformation
reformative
regionalise
regionalism
regionalist
reification
reinsertion
reiteration
reiterative
relationism
relationist
reliability
religionise
religionism
religionist
religiosity
reluctation
repartition
replication
reportorial
reprobation
reprobative
repudiation
requisition
reservation
residential
resignation
resistivity
respiration
restitution
restoration
restorative
restriction
restrictive
retaliation
retaliative
retardation
retardative
retentivity
retribution
retributive
retroaction
retroactive
revaluation
reverential
revisionism
revisionist
rheotropism
rhetorician
rhinologist
ribvaulting
rickettsial
roadholding
rodenticide
roentgenise
romanticise
romanticism
romanticist
ropedancing
ropewalking
Rosicrucian
rubefaction
rubicundity
rubrication
rustication
Sabbatarian
sacculation
sacrificial
Sadduceeism
safekeeping
Sagittarius
saleability
salesladies
saltatorial
sandbagging
Sanskritist
satiability
saturnalian
saxophonist
scaffolding
schismatise
schistosity
schoolchild
scissorbill
scopolamine
ScotchIrish
scriptorial
scriptorium
secondarily
secretarial
secretariat
sedentarily
segregation
segregative
seigneurial
seigniorial
selectivity
selfclosing
selfcocking
selfdenying
selffeeding
selffeeling
selffertile
selfloading
selflocking
selfopinion
selfpitying
selfraising
selfsealing
selfseeking
selfservice
selfserving
selfsterile
selfwinding
semanticist
sensibility
sensitivity
Septembrist
septenarius
septentrion
serendipity
serrulation
sertularian
serviceline
sextodecimo
Shaksperian
sheathknife
shellacking
shoplifting
shortcoming
showjumping
shrivelling
sightseeing
sillimanite
silverpoint
silversmith
silverstick
singlestick
singularise
singularity
skatingrink
skeletonise
Slavonicise
slickenside
slotmachine
smithsonite
snowbunting
soapboiling
sociability
Socinianism
sociologist
soldierlike
solifluxion
soliloquise
soliloquist
solmisation
solutionist
solvability
Soroptimist
Southernism
spacesaving
sparrowbill
specificity
spectrality
speculation
speculative
speechifier
spendthrift
spessartite
sphaeridium
spinsterish
spontaneity
sporogonium
sporulation
squarebuilt
stagflation
stampoffice
standardise
standoffish
statutorily
stencilling
stenotypist
stiflejoint
stimulation
stimulative
stipulation
stocktaking
straightish
strenuosity
strongpoint
stylisation
stylopodium
subarration
subaudition
subdivision
subjugation
subjunctive
sublimation
subornation
subrogation
substantial
substantive
subsumption
subsumptive
subtraction
subtractive
suburbanise
suburbanite
suckingfish
suffixation
suffocation
suffocative
suitability
sumptuosity
superfamily
superficial
superficies
superfluity
superiority
superlative
superscribe
superscript
supervision
supposition
suppositive
suppression
suppressive
suppuration
suppurative
supremacist
surgeonfish
surrogation
suspiration
susurration
swallowdive
syllabarium
syllabicity
synchronise
synchronism
syncopation
syndicalism
syndicalist
syndication
systematics
systematise
systematism
systematist
tabefaction
taciturnity
talebearing
tameability
tangibility
tankfarming
tantalising
tapemachine
tautologise
tautologism
tautomerism
taxidermist
teetotalism
teleologism
teleologist
telepathise
telepathist
telephonist
temperative
temporality
temporarily
tensibility
tentpegging
termination
terminative
termitarium
terrestrial
territorial
testability
testimonial
Teutonicism
thalidomide
theobromine
theosophist
thermionics
thermophile
thunderbird
thwartships
timeserving
timesharing
titillation
tittivation
tobacconist
tobogganing
tobogganist
togglejoint
tolbutamide
topdressing
touchtyping
tourbillion
toxophilite
trafficking
trammelling
transaction
transalpine
transection
transfinite
transfixion
transfusion
translation
transmarine
Trappistine
trepanation
trepidation
tribulation
tribunicial
tribunitial
tributarily

triggerfish
trimestrial
trimorphism
Trinitarian
tritagonist
trituration
tuberculise
tufthunting
tumbledrier
tumefaction
turbination
typecasting
typesetting
tyrannicide
ultramarine
ultrasonics
unappealing
unassertive
unbelieving
unbeseeming
unchristian
uncongenial
undertaking
undeserving
unessential
unfaltering
unflinching
unforgiving
unhealthily
unification
unipolarity
unobtrusive
unpromising
unqualified
unreasoning
unrelenting
unremitting
unselective
unshrinking
utilisation
utilitarian
vacationist
vaccination
vacillation
vacuolation
vagabondise
vagabondish
vagabondism
valediction
variability
variegation
vascularise
vascularity
vasectomise
vendibility
venesection
venisection
ventilation
ventilative
vermiculite
vermination
versatility
verticality
vesuvianite
vibratility
vichyssoise
victualling
vincibility
vindication
vindicative
vivisection
volcanicity
voluntarily
voluntarism
voluntarist
vulcanicity
wainscoting
waitinglist
washability
watchmaking
waterskiing
weatherwise
Weismannism
wellmeaning
wellwishing
Wesleyanism
Whitsuntide
widdershins
wildcatting
wildfowling
winegrowing
winetasting
wirenetting
wirepulling
wiretapping
withershins
woodcarving
woodcutting
workability
workmanlike
worldlywise
worshipping
xylophonist
Yugoslavian
zoantharian
zoographist
zoomorphism
zootechnics
Zoroastrian
thingumajig
awestricken
balmcricket
billsticker
blackmarket
bloodsucker
boilermaker
brainsickly
breadbasket
bushwhacker
catswhisker
chainsmoker
cityslicker
cockaleekie
cockyleekie
crookbacked
cupronickel
deerstalker
doorknocker
fieldworker
firecracker
floorwalker
forethinker
freethinker
godforsaken
heartbroken
honeysuckle
hunchbacked
hypermarket
interlocker
kwashiorkor
loudspeaker
mantuamaker
metalworker
molecricket
moneymarket
mothernaked
nightwalker
noseyparker
phrasemaker
pieceworker
plainspoken
retrorocket
ringstraked
safebreaker
safecracker
shelljacket
shipbreaker
shortspoken
slavemarket
sleepwalker
steelworker
stiffnecked
stockbroker
stockmarket
supermarket
supertanker
sweepstakes
threedecker
trackwalker
voortrekker
wastebasket
wisecracker
abdominally
abiotically
accentually
acidophilic
acropetally
adminicular
adverbially
aerobically
agnatically
altocumulus
angelically
animalcular
aquatically
archaically
archangelic
ascetically
aseptically
aspergillum
aspergillus
bacchanalia
baptismally
barbastelle
basipetally
beautifully
bibliopolic
bilaterally
blackfellow
blackmailer
bloodguilty
botanically
bountifully
bucolically
Byronically
canalicular
canaliculus
canonically
carbocyclic
carbuncular
caterpillar
caustically
cavedweller
celestially
changefully
chanterelle
chaotically
chronically
circumpolar
circumsolar
circumvolve
clapperclaw
classically
closehauled
coeternally
colourfully
comestibles
commensally
comptroller
conformally
congenially
connubially
continually
convivially
convolvulus
corporeally
corpuscular
counterblow
counterplan
counterplea
counterplot
crepuscular
crestfallen
cryptically
deceitfully
decennially
deistically
dialectally
disannulled
disgruntled
dishevelled
doctrinally
drastically
dynamically
editorially
effectually
elastically
elementally
Emmenthaler
emotionally
empirically
endemically
episcopally
equiangular
equivocally
erratically
essentially
eugenically
factionally
faithhealer
fanatically
financially
forestaller
forgetfully
fourwheeler
frantically
fraternally
frightfully
generically
genetically
genitivally
gentianella
gibberellin
glossolalia
graphically
haemophilia
haemophilic
healthfully
Hebraically
heretically
heteropolar
homothallic
horsecollar
hospitaller
hydrophilic
identically
idiotically
idyllically
illiberally
illogically
immoveables
impartially
incunabulum
intervallic
ithyphallic
juridically
laconically
lakedweller
marketvalue
marshmallow
masterfully
mediaevally
medicinally
megalopolis
melancholia
melancholic
memorabilia
mercurially
mimetically
moronically
multangular
municipally
necrophilia
necrophilic
nocturnally
nomadically
nonmetallic
numerically
occipitally
octagonally
officinally
organically
osmotically
otherwhiles
outrivalled
overdevelop
overindulge
pacifically
paedophilia
parallelled
parochially
passacaglia
peccadillos
pedestalled
perennially
perishables
perpetually
photophilic
pictorially
pipistrelle
piratically
plentifully
podophyllin
polemically
politically
polygonally
potentially
practically
primaevally
principally
procephalic
proconsular
prosaically
psychedelia
psychedelic
psychically
punchinello
pussywillow
pyramidally
quizzically
ratatouille
rectangular
reedwarbler
regardfully
regretfully
reposefully
resentfully
retinacular
retinaculum
rightangled
safetyvalve
saintpaulia
sartorially
satanically
satirically
sceptically
scoundrelly
sectionally
segmentally
seismically
selaginella
selfdisplay
semiskilled
semitrailer
sensorially
sentinelled
sheriffalty
sidewheeler
sigmoidally
sinistrally
snowgoggles
softshelled
somatically
somnambular
sorrowfully
spastically
spectacular
spherically
spiritually
spiritualty
spirituelle
steamboiler
steamroller
stonecurlew
stonewaller
storyteller
subaerially
subscapular
subumbrella
surficially
tabernacled
tagliatelle
tagliatelli
technically
teetotaller
tetanically
tetracyclic
thermically
thunderclap
titanically
toothbilled
torticollis
triadically
triennially
ultraviolet
unconcealed
underseller
undutifully
unhelpfully
unicellular
unisexually
universally
unkennelled
unnaturally
unskilfully
venatically
ventricular
ventriculus
veridically
verisimilar
vestigially
viceregally
viceroyalty
violoncello
watercooled
watercooler
wedgetailed
whimsically
whitecollar
wholesouled
wonderfully
yellowbelly
aerodynamic
aircraftman
algorithmic
AngloNorman
antivitamin
assemblyman
barnstormer
borborygmus
breadcrumbs
businessman
cataclysmic
catechismal

centigramme
chromosomal
churchwoman
congressman
contretemps
craftswoman
crossbowman
cryptogamic
cyclothymia
cyclothymic
deliveryman
draughtsman
ectoplasmic
endoplasmic
endothermal
endothermic
epithalamia
epithalamic
flimflammer
Frenchwoman
gastronomic
gentlewoman
GraecoRoman
hexadecimal
hydrobromic
hypothermia
infantryman
interatomic
Kulturkampf
logarithmic
macrocosmic
merchantman
microcosmic
monochromat
monochromic
monogrammed
needlewoman
ninnyhammer
pachydermal
palindromic
perispermic
policewoman
polychromic
preterhuman
prothalamia
reprogramme
Scotchwoman
septicaemia
septicaemic
sexagesimal
sheepfarmer
spokeswoman
sportswoman
supernormal
telegrammic
transformer
trencherman
washerwoman
wellgroomed
witenagemot
xeranthemum
absorptance
accelerando
accountancy
accrescence
acquittance
adolescence
affectional
affectioned
afterburner
altitudinal
ambivalence
ambivalency
AngloFrench
antecedence
anthocyanin
antirrhinum
archaeornis
ascensional
astringency
attitudinal
attritional
beneficence
benevolence
bibliomancy
bibliomania
birdbrained
blastogenic
booklearned
breadwinner
calisthenic
candescence
capacitance
carrageenan
carrageenin
chalcedonic
chameleonic
charlatanry
cheiromancy
chieftaincy
christiania
Christianly
chrominance
cinquecento
circumlunar
coalescence
coexistence
cognitional
cognoscente
cognoscenti
coincidence
coinsurance
collectanea
collisional
comeuppance
commonsense
complacence
complacency
concordance
concurrence
conditional
conditioner
conductance
conformance
consequence
conservancy
consistence
consistency
consultancy
conterminal
contingence
contingency
continuance
contradance
contrivance
convenience
conveniency
convergence
convergency
conversance
conversancy
countenance
crossgarnet
decrescendo
delinquency
deliverance
despondence
despondency
dimensional
dinnerdance
directional
disciplinal
discipliner
discontinue
discordance
discordancy
discrepancy
disharmonic
disinclined
disturbance
educational
encumbrance
enlightened
ensanguined
entertainer
epeirogenic
equivalence
equivalency
erubescence
evanescence
evolutional
exceptional
excrescence
excrescency
executioner
exorbitance
expansional
extensional
extortioner
fieldcornet
flamboyance
flamboyancy
flamboyante
flocculence
florescence
forbearance
forbiddance
forgetmenot
formational
Francomania
fraudulence
freemasonry
frontrunner
furnishings
furtherance
gasfittings
gentlemanly
geotectonic
gradational
gramophonic
habiliments
haemocyanin
harebrained
hebephrenia
hebephrenic
heldentenor
honeymooner
hydrocyanic
ichthyornis
illuminance
impassioned
impedimenta
impenitence
impenitency
impuissance
inappetence
incoherence
incoherency
inconstancy
ineloquence
inexistence
inflexional
infrequence
infrequency
inhabitancy
inheritance
insouciance
intensional
intentional
intentioned
interchange
interregnum
interspinal
intolerance
intriguante
intuitional
ipecacuanha
iridescence
irrelevance
irrelevancy
irreverence
kleptomania
lactescence
latitudinal
laurustinus
lieutenancy
liquescence
lophobranch
maintenance
maleficence
malevolence
malfeasance
marcescence
mediastinal
mediastinum
megalomania
menservants
mesalliance
microphonic
misalliance
miscellanea
misfeasance
misguidance
morrisdance
munificence
Neoplatonic
nigrescence
nonchalance
nonfeasance
nonviolence
nutritional
nymphomania
obsessional
oestrogenic
omnipotence
omniscience
oneiromancy
opalescence
operational
outdistance
outspokenly
overbalance
panhellenic
pantothenic
paraselenae
parishioner
partitioned
partitioner
percipience
performance
perpetuance
persistence
persistency
phagedaenic
phycocyanin
pilotburner
pipecleaner
pitchblende
pleurodynia
pocketmoney
pococurante
polytechnic
preaudience
preeminence
pressagency
previsional
prizewinner
probational
probationer
proceedings
proficiency
promotional
provenience
provisional
pseudomonas
psychogenic
putrescence
pyrotechnic
quickchange
quinquennia
radiophonic
rallentando
reassurance
recessional
redactional
reemergence
reflectance
refringency
reinsurance
remembrance
renaissance
resemblance
respondence
respondency
reversional
reversioner
rhabdomancy
rifacimenti
rifacimento
ruridecanal
saltimbanco
salvational
selfdefence
semidiurnal
sempiternal
sensational
seventeenth
shortchange
situational
snickersnee
somatogenic
somatotonia
somatotonic
sovereignly
sovereignty
statesmanly
submarginal
submergence
subregional
subsequence
subsistence
subterminal
sufficiency
summational
tabletennis
tearstained
tephromancy
teratogenic
thinskinned
tiddlywinks
toxicomania
traditional
tragedienne
transuranic
trichomonad
turgescence
twelvemonth
twelvepenny
unbeknownst
uncertainly
uncertainty
unconcerned
undermanned
underpinned
undersigned
unemotional
unfashioned
unipersonal
valuational
variational
varsovienne
vespertinal
vibrational
vicegerency
vitrescence
vociferance
welldefined
abstentious
acarpellous
acclamatory
acclivitous
acinaciform
acrimonious
adenomatous
adventurous
aerobiology
affirmatory
agrobiology
ailurophobe
alleviatory
amazonstone
amenorrhoea
amentaceous
amphibology
amphictyony
anachronous
androgynous
anfractuous
anticathode
anticyclone
antimonious
applicatory
approbatory
arboraceous
archaeology
arenicolous
arthrospore
Assyriology
atrabilious
autochthony
avoirdupois
bacciferous
bacilliform
barleybroth
bashibazouk
bellbottoms
benedictory
bicephalous
billetsdoux
bladderwort
blasphemous
boardschool
brachyurous
breechblock
breezeblock
bristleworm
brotherhood
bryozoology
buffalorobe
bulletproof
burglarious
butyraceous
cabbagerose
cabbageworm
cacophonous
calcicolous
calciferous
calcifugous
calefactory
campanology
carnivorous
catadromous
celebratory
ceremonious
chainarmour
champertous
chancellory
chartaceous
cheesecloth
chockablock
Christology
chronoscope
circulatory
climatology

clothesmoth
cobblestone
coconscious
combinatory
comminatory
compendious
compotatory
concertgoer
condolatory
congenerous
consolatory
conspicuous
contentious
contrarious
copingstone
cornerstone
corniferous
cosignatory
cosmetology
coterminous
counterbond
counterfoil
counterfort
countermove
counterwork
criminatory
criminology
cruciferous
crucigerous
crustaceous
cryobiology
crystalloid
cupriferous
dactylology
declamatory
declaratory
declivitous
deleterious
delightsome
denigratory
dentigerous
deoxyribose
deprecatory
depredatory
dermatology
desperadoes
Deuteronomy
diadelphous
dicephalous
dichogamous
dichotomous
diphtheroid
dodecaphony
doublecross
drawingroom
dualpurpose
duplicitous
easternmost
edificatory
efficacious
ejaculatory
electrology
elephantoid
elucidatory
endophagous
enterostomy
epidiascope
epipetalous
epithelioma
erotogenous
eschatology
Etruscology
eucalyptole
eurypteroid
exclamatory
exculpatory
exdirectory
exhortatory
expatiatory
expeditious
explanatory
explicatory
exploratory
expurgatory
extenuatory
extirpatory
farinaceous
farraginous
farthermost
felspathoid
ferriferous
ferruginous
filamentous
fissiparous
flavoursome
flirtatious
floriferous
fluoroscope
fluoroscopy
forevermore
Francophobe
francophone
frugivorous
fulminatory
furthermore
furthermost
furthersome
furunculous
gastrectomy
gastroscope
gemmiferous
gemmiparous
gerontology
grandiflora
granivorous
gratulatory
greaseproof
gynaecology
gypsiferous
haematology
haemorrhoid
halophilous
harpsichord
harvesthome
hearthstone
heartsblood
hedgeschool
heliochrome
helminthoid
hemipterous
hepatectomy
heptamerous
herbivorous
heresiology
herpetology
herringbone
heterophony
heteroploid
heterospory
heterotroph
homogeneous
homophonous
homopterous
homosporous
humiliatory
hundredfold
hydrogenous
hyperboloid
hypocycloid
ichthyology
ignominious
illustrious
impecunious
impetratory
imprecatory
incantatory
incongruous
incredulous
inculpatory
indeciduous
industrious
informatory
injudicious
inofficious
inquilinous
insectivore
insectology
inspiratory
intravenous
irreligious
isochronous
isomorphous
journeywork
kinesiology
kinetoscope
knucklebone
lacrimatory
lacrymatory
lactiferous
lamellicorn
lamelliform
laryngology
laryngotomy
lateritious
latticework
lentiginous
lichenology
ligamentous
lycanthrope
lycanthropy
magnanimous
malariology
maledictory
manducatory
manifestoes
mansardroof
manufactory
martyrology
masticatory
melanophore
meliphagous
melliferous
mellifluous
membraneous
meritorious
meteorology
methodology
metoposcopy
microgroove
microsecond
millisecond
misanthrope
misanthropy
mischievous
moderations
monocarpous
monoclinous
monophagous
monophthong
monopterous
morbiferous
morningroom
mountainous
multicolour
multiparous
mustachioed
muttonchops
myelomatous
myrmecology
necessitous
negotiatory
nephrectomy
nettlecloth
nitrogenous
noctivagous
nulliparous
obfuscatory
objurgatory
observatory
odoriferous
olfactology
oligomerous
ommatophore
omnifarious
opprobrious
orchidology
ornithology
oscillatory
ovariectomy
overanxious
ozoniferous
papyraceous
parathyroid
paratyphoid
passeriform
patelliform
pentagynous
pentamerous
pentandrous
perfunctory
perspicuous
pestiferous
phagocytose
phosphorous
phraseology
physiognomy
picturebook
picturegoer
piperaceous
piscivorous
plagiostome
plasterwork
platearmour
polariscope
polyandrous
polycarpous
polyonymous
polyphagous
polyphonous
precautious
precipitous
predicatory
premonitory
preparatory
prestigious
pretentious
primatology
primiparous
procuratory
profanatory
profiterole
prognathous
prohibitory
proliferous
promiscuous
prophethood
proportions
Proterozoic
pruriginous
pteridology
pumicestone
punctilious
quadraphony
quarrelsome
quartertone
quaternloaf
reachmedown
recognitory
reflexology
reformatory
repetitious
reprobatory
respiratory
retaliatory
retardatory
retinoscopy
retributory
rhizanthous
rhizomatous
rhynchodont
rottenstone
rumbustious
saddlecloth
sanguineous
saponaceous
saprogenous
sarcomatous
sauropodous
scalariform
scalearmour
scalpriform
scarabaeoid
scattergood
schistosome
scientology
scoriaceous
scratchwork
scribacious
scrumptious
scuppernong
scyphistoma
seismoscope
selfreproof
selfsupport
semasiology
sententious
septiferous
serpiginous
servicebook
seventyfold
severalfold
shacklebolt
shacklebone
shocktroops
showerproof
shrinkproof
shuttlecock
sittingroom
smokingroom
smorgasbord
snatchblock
solanaceous
somniculous
somniferous
soteriology
spathaceous
spectrology
spelaeology
sphagnology
spiniferous
splendorous
splenectomy
spongecloth
spontaneous
sporogenous
statutebook
stenochromy
stereophony
stereoscope
stereoscopy
stethoscope
stethoscopy
stipulatory
stirrupbone
stomatology
stormtroops
stramineous
stroboscope
subcategory
sulphureous
sulphurwort
superfluous
superimpose
supervisory
suppository
swallowhole
swallowwort
sympetalous
symphonious
synchronous
talentscout
tautologous
tautonymous
teknonymous
temerarious
tempestuous
tendencious
tendentious
tenterhooks
terminology
terraqueous
terricolous
terrigenous
tetramerous
tetrapodous
thanatology
thaumatrope
theatregoer
theretofore
thermoscope
thistledown
threecolour
thunderbolt
thuriferous
tracheotomy
trapeziform
treacherous
trelliswork
trestlework
trimorphous
tripetalous
triphibious
triphyllous
triquetrous
tristichous
troublesome
trypanosome
tuberculose
tuberculous
ulotrichous
unambiguous
unconscious
underexpose
unorthodoxy
unrighteous
unwholesome
urticaceous
urticarious
valedictory
vasculiform
venereology
venturesome
vertiginous
vexillology
vindicatory
volcanology
vortiginous
vulcanology
waitingroom
watercolour
weathercock
weatherworn
westernmost
whitethroat
widowerhood
winningpost
xenophilous
xerophilous
xylocarpous
xylophagous
aeolotropic
angiography
anisotropic
antistrophe

bathyscaphe
bitterapple
branchiopod
bumblepuppy
calligraphy
cardsharper
cartography
catastrophe
chirography
chorography
cosmography
dexiotropic
discography
dittography
ethnography
filmography
filterpaper
frothhopper
grasshopper
greenkeeper
Hagiographa
hagiography
hagioscopic
handicapped
handicapper
haplography
hedgehopped
heliography
heliotropic
hemeralopia
heterotypic
highstepper
hippocampus
housekeeper
hydrography
hydrotropic
hygroscopic
hymnography
hypertrophy
hypnopompic
hypsography
ichnography
iconography
linendraper
lithography
lithotripsy
macroscopic
micrography
microscopic
minesweeper
mosstrooper
mythography
namedropper
neurotropic
nyctitropic
nympholepsy
orthography
orthoscopic
orthotropic
osteography
outstripped
overcropped
overstepped
palaeotypic
paratrooper
petrography
phonography
photography
phototropic
phytography
pictography
pleiotropic
pornography
radiography
reprography
rhinoscopic
rhizocarpic
sandskipper
scenography
semiellipse
shoulderpad
showstopper
sideslipped
sidestepped
staircarpet
stenography
stereotyped
stereotyper
stereotypic
storekeeper
stylography
submultiple
tachygraphy
teenybopper
thixotropic
thoroughpin
threadpaper
tightlipped
townspeople
treecreeper
undeveloped
uranography
wedgeshaped
weenybopper
Whitechapel
zincography
bergamasque
discotheque
gigantesque
picturesque
plateresque
Titianesque
ventriloquy
verdantique
albuminuria
allelomorph
anemometric
antineutron
Apollinaris
arbitratrix
atmospheric
audiometric
auricularly
bathymetric
behavioural
bewhiskered
binocularly
boysenberry
cabbagetree
calceolaria
camaraderie
candelabrum
candleberry
caricatural
charcuterie
chinoiserie
chiropteran
chokecherry
cholesterol
chrysoberyl
climacteric
clinometric
clothesprop
collinearly
commissural
conjectural
controversy
cookgeneral
coulometric
crossbearer
cryptomeria
ctenophoran
dactylogram
depthcharge
diatessaron
dishonourer
disinterred
distempered
dualcontrol
econometric
elastomeric
embroiderer
enneahedron
enterovirus
equilateral
eudiometric
gallowstree
gendarmerie
godchildren
goldenberry
goniometric
goodnatured
granophyric
gravimetric
gymnospermy
gynaecocrat
haematocrit
harumscarum
heavenwards
heliometric
hemispheric
highpowered
hitherwards
homocentric
huckleberry
hurryscurry
hurryskurry
hydrometric
hydrothorax
hygrometric
hypercharge
hypermetric
hypogastric
hypsometric
icosahedral
icosahedron
illfavoured
illhumoured
illmannered
illtempered
intercourse
intercrural
intersperse
ionospheric
ipsilateral
irregularly
isoelectric
kilocalorie
lilylivered
marconigram
marqueterie
melanochroi
merryandrew
metacentric
micrometric
misconstrue
misericorde
molecularly
multistorey
negotiatrix
neighbourly
netherworld
orbicularly
orthopteran
oscillogram
pentahedron
philanderer
photometric
phraseogram
phytosterol
planimetric
posteriorly
prefectural
prehistoric
presbyteral
progenitrix
prolocutrix
prosecutrix
protectoral
pseudomorph
psychiatric
radiometric
rearadmiral
saddlehorse
salmonberry
sanguinaria
schwarmerei
scleroderma
selfassured
selfcentred
selfcontrol
sinistrorse
slaughterer
sociometric
songsparrow
spectrogram
sphincteral
sphincteric
sphygmogram
spindletree
spirometric
steganogram
stegosaurus
Stradivarii
subcultural
sublittoral
supercharge
swingletree
swordbearer
symposiarch
synchrotron
tetrahedral
tetrahedron
thaumaturge
thaumaturgy
thenceforth
theocentric
thermoduric
torchbearer
tracasserie
trainbearer
transferred
transferrer
transpierce
trestletree
tricoloured
uncluttered
undercharge
unicoloured
upholsterer
varnishtree
vesicularly
viceadmiral
voltametric
watercourse
wellordered
wheelbarrow
whiffletree
whippletree
windlestraw
winterberry
xanthochroi
abiogeneses
abiogenesis
ambiguously
ambitiously
amorphously
anadiplosis
anaesthesia
anagnorisis
analogously
anastomoses
anastomosis
anomalously
anonymously
antiphrasis
antonomasia
aponeuroses
aponeurosis
aposiopesis
assiduously
atrociously
audaciously
barbarously
beauteously
biocoenoses
biocoenosis
blackavised
blamelessly
bloodlessly
bloodvessel
bottlenosed
bounteously
bourgeoisie
bowdleriser
brainlessly
brainteaser
brucellosis
bumptiously
capaciously
catachreses
catachresis
catercousin
cavernously
ceaselessly
cheerlessly
Christmassy
chrysalises
clamorously
coccidiosis
congruously
consciously
contrabasso
countlessly
courteously
credulously
cytogenesis
cytokinesis
dangerously
dauntlessly
deliciously
deliriously
dexterously
diaphoresis
diapophysis
diarthrosis
doubtlessly
dreamlessly
duniewassal
earthcloset
ectogenesis
egregiously
enarthrosis
enterpriser
erroneously
exogenously
facetiously
faithlessly
faultlessly
feloniously
ferociously
fractiously
fraterniser
frivolously
fruitlessly
gamogenesis
garrulously
generaliser
glutinously
gnotobiosis
gormandiser
gracelessly
grangeriser
guilelessly
guiltlessly
haemoptysis
haemostasis
hairdresser
hazardously
heartlessly
hemianopsia
hilariously
homeostasis
homogeniser
homozygosis
hylogenesis
hyperplasia
hypoglossal
hypotyposis
iconostases
iconostasis
illdisposed
imperiously
impetuously
incuriously
ingeniously
ingenuously
injuriously
innocuously
innoxiously
insidiously
intercensal
intercessor
invidiously
judiciously
laboriously
larcenously
lecherously
lesemajesty
limitlessly
litigiously
ludicrously
luxuriously
mackerelsky
maliciously
matchlessly
melodiously
mercilessly
merogenesis
metachrosis
metagenesis
mineraliser
mirthlessly
moisturiser
momentously
monogenesis
monopoliser
monstrously
murderously
murmurously
myxomatosis
necrobiosis
nefariously
nervelessly
neutraliser
noiselessly
nonpartisan
notoriously
obliviously
obnoxiously
officiously
ontogenesis
osteoplasty
paraleipsis
paraphraser
parasitosis
parentheses
parenthesis
paronomasia
pasteuriser
pediculosis
pendulously
penuriously
periphrases

periphrasis
peristalsis
photooffset
phthiriasis
plagiariser
plasmolysis
plasticiser
plenteously
pointlessly
poisonously
polygenesis
ponderously
populariser
postclassic
powerlessly
predecessor
prestressed
proteolysis
psittacosis
querulously
rancorously
rapaciously
rapturously
reappraisal
rejuvenesce
religiously
righteously
sagaciously
salaciously
scrutiniser
seditiously
selfimposed
senselessly
shamelessly
shiftlessly
sightlessly
sleeplessly
smilelessly
soundlessly
spinelessly
stainlessly
starcrossed
strenuously
sumptuously
sympathiser
syndesmosis
synthesiser
syssarcosis
tastelessly
telekinesis
tenaciously
thanklessly
thermolysis
timepleaser
toffeenosed
torturously
tracelessly
transversal
tremulously
trichinosis
troublously
tyrannously
unanimously
uncivilised
undisguised
unexpressed
unpossessed
vagariously
vasopressin
vasopressor
venturously
veraciously
verminously
vexatiously
vicariously
vinedresser
vivaciously
voicelessly
voraciously
wearilessly
welladvised
worthlessly
abbreviator
abhorrently
abiogenetic
abstinently
acatalectic
accelerator
accordantly
accumulator
achondritic
actinometer
adjudicator
adulterator
advertently
AfroAsiatic
aiguillette
alembicated
alkalimeter
alkalimetry
altostratus
ameliorator
amphimictic
anacreontic
anaesthetic
anarchistic
anastomotic
annihilator
annunciator
anomalistic
anthracitic
anticipator
antipyretic
antiSemitic
apartmental
apocalyptic
aponeurotic
appreciator
Areopagitic
articulated
articulator
artiodactyl
ascomycetes
asphyxiator
assimilator
autoplastic
auxanometer
azotobacter
backcountry
beechmarten
benignantly
bibliolater
bibliolatry
biocoenotic
biquadratic
blackbeetle
blackcoated
blameworthy
blepharitis
blockbuster
Bodhisattva
brahmaputra
brilliantly
broadcaster
bullfighter
burgomaster
cabbalistic
calorimeter
calorimetry
calumniator
Calvinistic
cancellated
carburetted
carburetter
carburettor
castellated
cataplectic
catechistic
centripetal
ceroplastic
cesarevitch
cesarewitch
chainletter
chainstitch
charismatic
chemotactic
choirmaster
chronometer
chronometry
cisatlantic
closefisted
cloudcastle
coinheritor
coldhearted
colorimeter
colorimetry
columniated
commendator
commentator
communistic
compensator
competently
compliantly
complicated
compurgator
conciliator
confidently
confiscator
congruently
consecrator
conservator
consonantal
consonantly
conspirator
constitutor
constrictor
constructor
consummator
continental
continently
continuator
contributor
coordinator
corpulently
cotoneaster
craniometry
crenellated
criticaster
crossstitch
daisycutter
deactivator
deathrattle
decelerator
deficiently
deflagrator
demonolatry
denominator
denunciator
dependently
depopulator
depreciator
desalinator
desideratum
detrimental
dialogistic
diamagnetic
diaphoretic
diastematic
dichromatic
differentia
differently
difficultly
diffidently
dilapidated
dilapidator
disaccustom
disaffected
dishonestly
disinfector
dissertator
dissonantly
dissymmetry
distributor
divergently
doubleDutch
doubleentry
downhearted
drillmaster
dynamometer
dynamometry
dyslogistic
ebulliently
ectoblastic
ectogenetic
efficiently
effulgently
elasticated
emancipator
emasculator
embryonated
encomiastic
endoskelton
equivocator
esemplastic
Eucharistic
euphemistic
eveningstar
exaggerator
excellently
excremental
exoskeletal
exoskeleton
expectantly
expediently
extraverted
extroverted
exuberantly
faithworthy
fenestrated
fetichistic
fetishistic
feudalistic
firefighter
firmamental
flagellator
flannelette
flatulently
foraminated
forequarter
foreshorten
foresighted
formalistic
fortnightly
frankfurter
freehearted
frostbitten
fullhearted
fundamental
geniculated
geomagnetic
ghostwriter
glasscutter
glauconitic
gnotobiotic
goddaughter
goodhearted
gradiometer
groundwater
haemostatic
haggadistic
halfhearted
handknitted
handpainted
handwritten
hardhearted
harmonistic
heavyfooted
Hellenistic
hereinafter
hermeneutic
highfalutin
Hippocratic
historiated
holoblastic
homeostatic
homestretch
homoeopathy
homoestatic
homogenetic
homoplastic
horsedoctor
housemaster
Hudibrastic
hydrophytic
hydrostatic
hydrotactic
hygrophytic
hylozoistic
hypercritic
hypoblastic
illaffected
illuminator
illustrator
impatiently
imperfectly
implemental
importantly
imprudently
inaugurator
incessantly
incinerator
incipiently
inclemently
incorrectly
incorruptly
incremental
indignantly
indulgently
inelegantly
infiltrator
inseminator
insistently
insufflator
intagliated
intercepter
interceptor
intercostal
interdental
intermitted
interpreter
interrupter
interruptor
interseptal
intimidator
intromitted
intromitter
introverted
invigilator
invigorator
ironhearted
itinerantly
Jansenistic
jargonistic
kickstarter
kindhearted
kitchenette
labiodental
lachrymator
lamplighter
landaulette
launderette
leptodactyl
lickspittle
lightfooted
lineprinter
lionhearted
lithophytic
longsighted
lowspirited
luxuriantly
macrobiotic
magistratic
maisonnette
maladjusted
maladroitly
malignantly
manipulator
manneristic
marquisette
masochistic
mastodontic
mastoiditis
mechanistic
mediumistic
mentholated
meroblastic
mesoblastic
metagenetic
metaplastic
metasomatic
Methodistic
microphytic
misbegotten
mithridatic
modernistic
monogenetic
monozygotic
moonlighter
mountaintop
muskthistle
myocarditis
mythopoetic
myxomycetes
narcoleptic
nasofrontal
naturopathy
nearsighted
necromantic
negligently
neologistic
nightporter
nittygritty
nomenclator
nonsequitur
northeaster
northwester
nutrimental
observantly
ochlocratic
ontogenetic
openhearted
operculated
opinionated
ornithopter
orthocentre
orthodontia
orthodontic
osteophytic
overstretch
overwritten
pacificator
paederastic
Palaearctic
pantalettes
pantheistic
parallactic
paramountcy
paramountly
paraplectic
parenthetic
paternoster
pentadactyl
Pentecostal
periodontal

periostitis
peripatetic
peristaltic
peritonitis
permanently
perpetrator
perpetuator
pertinently
pessimistic
pestilently
petticoated
pharyngitis
phototactic
plasmolytic
pluralistic
plutocratic
pluviometer
pneumonitis
polarimeter
polarimetry
polevaulter
polycrystal
polygenetic
polyglottal
polyglottic
porphyritic
precedented
precedently
presciently
preselector
prevalently
problematic
prominently
promulgator
propitiator
prostitutor
proteolytic
protomartyr
protophytic
providently
psychometry
psychomotor
psychopathy
pterodactyl
purificator
pussyfooter
pyroclastic
quickwitted
quiescently
rattlepated
readywitted
realpolitik
recommittal
reconnoitre
recumbently
recurrently
redundantly
regenerator
rejuvenator
reluctantly
remunerator
repellantly
repellently
repentantly
representer
repugnantly
resiliently
ricochetted
ritualistic
rockcrystal
roughfooted
sacramental
salinometer
salpingitis
sansculotte
saprobiotic
saprophytic
satinstitch
scholiastic
scientistic
sclerometer
sclerotitis
scoutmaster
secondrater
seismometer
seismometry
selfcreated
selfdevoted
selfelected
selfinvited
selflimited
selfstarter
sentimental
shamanistic
sharpwitted
sheepmaster
sightworthy
signpainter
simpliciter
sinfonietta
socialistic
softhearted
solipsistic
somnolently
sonofabitch
southeaster
southwester
spaceheater
speedometer
spherometer
spherulitic
Spinozistic
spiritistic
spirochetal
splayfooted
spondylitis
sporophytic
stalactitic
stalagmitic
standpatter
staurolitic
steadfastly
stephanotis
stereometry
sternutator
stichometry
stockinette
stonecutter
stonemarten
stormcentre
stridulator
stringently
succulently
suffragette
sugarcoated
superheater
supersubtle
suppliantly
surrebuttal
surrebutter
swiftfooted
sycophantic
sycophantry
syllogistic
symbolistic
sympathetic
symptomatic
synergistic
tacheometer
telekinetic
teleprinter
termagantly
tessellated
tetradactyl
thankworthy
theodolitic
theorematic
therapeutic
thermolytic
thermometer
thermometry
thickwitted
threemaster
throatlatch
thyroiditis
tightfisted
toastmaster
tonsillitis
totalisator
trafficator
transiently
transmittal
transmitted
transmitter
transporter
trenchantly
trendsetter
tritheistic
troglodytic
truculently
truehearted
trustbuster
trustworthy
turbulently
tuttifrutti
typewritten
unaccounted
uncommitted
unconnected
uncontested
understated
underwriter
unexploited
uninhabited
uninhibited
unmitigated
unrealistic
unsaturated
unsolicited
unwarranted
vaporimeter
vasodilator
vaticinator
verbalistic
vinaigrette
vituperator
vociferator
volumometer
voodooistic
wainscotted
warmhearted
waspwaisted
waterbottle
weakhearted
Westminster
whistlestop
whoremaster
windcheater
witchdoctor
witchhunter
wolfwhistle
worldbeater
wreckmaster
zooplankton
aboveground
accoucheuse
acupuncture
agriculture
appogiatura
aquaculture
aquiculture
audiovisual
barrelhouse
bassethound
bathingsuit
bergschrund
blackgrouse
blunderbuss
candidature
chiaroscuro
coffeehouse
conjuncture
contractual
contracture
cottonmouth
countermure
countersunk
counterturn
customhouse
decrepitude
disjuncture
displeasure
disquietude
disseminule
diverticula
divestiture
douroucouli
electrocute
entablature
expenditure
foreclosure
halfmeasure
headborough
herringgull
hibernacula
hydromedusa
hypothenuse
incertitude
incurvature
ineffectual
ingratitude
inopportune
insectifuge
instinctual
intersexual
investiture
legislature
lowpressure
manufacture
massproduce
monoculture
monolingual
musclebound
musculature
opencircuit
overmeasure
overproduce
pomiculture
porterhouse
portraiture
progeniture
promptitude
pulchritude
pullthrough
purpresture
receptacula
reconstruct
reintroduce
restructure
rotogravure
safeconduct
schoolhouse
scuttlebutt
selfculture
selftorture
sericulture
sleuthhound
springhouse
stagestruck
steeplebush
stirruppump
stomachpump
stoneground
strikebound
summerhouse
summersault
superabound
superinduce
supersedure
tapemeasure
temperature
thereabouts
transfigure
transsexual
trousersuit
underground
undervaluer
unigeniture
vicissitude
viniculture
viticulture
whereabouts
accusatival
BaltoSlavic
bookshelves
broadleaved
cleanshaven
disapproval
disbeliever
infinitival
interleaves
nominatival
planoconvex
quacksalver
quicksilver
quilldriver
screwdriver
slavedriver
spiritlevel
thanksgiver
transceiver
wellbeloved
wheresoever
whichsoever
whosesoever
candlepower
carriageway
cauliflower
gillyflower
glassblower
globeflower
intergrowth
interviewee
interviewer
motivepower
steerageway
straightway
thoroughwax
undergrowth
wapperjawed
anaphylaxis
executrixes
heterotaxis
phyllotaxis
prophylaxis
retroflexed
thermotaxis
breathalyse
chamaephyte
chlorophyll
collenchyma
electrolyse
electrolyte
electrotype
erythrocyte
gametophyte
granulocyte
interplayed
lammergeyer
paraldehyde
platinotype
prosenchyma
sclerophyll
spermaphyte
thrombocyte
xanthophyll
middlesized
mycorrhizae
mycorrhizal
pocketsized
quickfrozen
spermatozoa
trailblazer
unorganized

Abbevillian
abecedarian
abiological
academician
accessorial
accusatival
acoustician
adminicular
aerological
aeronomical
Aesculapian
aesthetical
affectional
agonistical
agrological
agronomical
ahistorical
aircraftman
Albigensian
alcyonarian
Alexandrian
algological
allAmerican
allegorical
altitudinal
anecdotical
AngloIndian
anglomaniac
AngloNorman
animalcular
antenuptial
anthropical
antiquarian
antitypical
apartmental
aphrodisiac
apostolical
Archimedean
ascensional
assemblyman
assessorial
atheistical
attitudinal
attritional
audiovisual
Augustinian
Aurignacian
autarchical
axiological
barrelorgan
behavioural
Belorussian
biochemical
biometrical
biophysical
bloodstream
Bonapartean
Brahmanical
Brahminical
businessman
calendrical
canalicular
carbuncular
caricatural
Carolingian
carrageenan
carriageway
casuistical
catechismal

categorical
caterpillar
centenarian
centrifugal
centripetal
chimaerical
chiropteran
chromosomal
chucklehead
churchwoman
cicatricial
circumlunar
circumpolar
circumsolar
clapperclaw
coessential
cognitional
collisional
commissural
conditional
congressman
conjectural
consonantal
conterminal
continental
contractual
cookgeneral
coralloidal
cornucopian
corpuscular
cosmetician
counterplan
countryseat
coxcombical
craftswoman
crepuscular
crocodilian
crossbowman
ctenophoran
curvilineal
curvilinear
cylindrical
cytological
dactylogram
deferential
deliveryman
demagogical
dendritical
detrimental
diacritical
dialectical
diametrical
dictatorial
dimensional
dinosaurian
diphtherial
diphthongal
diphycercal
dipsomaniac
directional
directorial
disapproval
disciplinal
doublespeak
draughtsman
duniewassal
educational
egalitarian
egotistical
electrician
Elizabethan
ellipsoidal
endocardiac
endocardial
endothelial
endothermal
enigmatical
equiangular
equilateral
equinoctial
erotomaniac
ethological
evangelical
eveningstar
evolutional
exceptional
excremental
executorial
existential
exoskeletal
expansional
exponential
extensional
Falstaffian
fantastical
featherhead
FinnoUgrian
firmamental
footpoundal
formational
fratricidal
Frenchwoman
fundamental
gentilitial
gentlewoman
geochemical
geometrical
geophysical
gestatorial
gingerbread
gradational
GraecoRoman
grammatical
gynaecocrat
halfholiday
halterbreak
Hamiltonian
Heracleidan
heteropolar
hexadecimal
holothurian
homiletical
homoiousian
homological
horological
horsecollar
hydrothorax
hyperborean
hypoglossal
hypophyseal
hypophysial
icosahedral
ideological
implemental
impolitical
impractical
incorporeal
incremental
IndoIranian
ineffectual
inessential
infantryman
inferential
infinitival
infirmarian
inflexional
influential
insessorial
instinctual
intensional
intentional
intercensal
intercostal
intercrural
interdental
interfacial
interlinear
interracial
interseptal
intersexual
interspinal
intertribal
intuitional
inventorial
ipsilateral
isometrical
Jacobinical
Jacobitical
jauntingcar
judgmatical
jumpingbean
kinematical
labiodental
Lancastrian
landingbeam
landinggear
latitudinal
laughinggas
leatherhead
Leibnitzian
leviratical
libertarian
liquidambar
loculicidal
madrigalian
magdalenian
magisterial
Maglemosian
marconigram
matriarchal
matrilineal
matrilinear
matrimonial
mechanician
mediastinal
mediatorial
medicolegal
merchantman
Merovingian
metalloidal
meteoroidal
metonymical
micrococcal
Micronesian
millenarian
ministerial
monarchical
monasterial
monkeybread
monochasial
monochromat
monolingual
monological
mononuclear
multangular
multilinear
multinomial
multiracial
mycological
mycorrhizae
mycorrhizal
mythomaniac
nasofrontal
Neanderthal
necessarian
needlewoman
Neotropical
nominatival
nomological
nonpartisan
nonsensical
nosological
nullifidian
nutrimental
nutritional
obsessional
obstetrical
octachordal
oecological
oecumenical
oenological
oesophageal
oncological
ontological
operational
oreological
orthoepical
orthopteran
oscillogram
pachydermal
Palestinian
panegyrical
Panglossian
paradisical
paradoxical
paramedical
paraselenae
parasitical
parheliacal
participial
patriarchal
patrilineal
patrimonial
patristical
pedagogical
pedological
penitential
penological
Pentecostal
pericardiac
pericardial
pericranial
periodontal
peristomial
pharisaical
philologian
phonetician
phraseogram
Pickwickian
pietistical
piscatorial
planetoidal
policewoman
polycrystal
polyglottal
pomological
portmanteau
posological
postexilian
postglacial
postnuptial
pragmatical
Precambrian
prefatorial
prefectural
prejudicial
preprandial
presbyteral
preterhuman
previsional
primigenial
probational
proconsular
procrustean
proletarian
proletariat
promotional
prophetical
protectoral
prothallial
provisional
pseudomonas
purgatorial
puritanical
pyramidical
Pythagorean
quadratical
quadrennial
quadrupedal
quaestorial
quaternloaf
quincuncial
Rabelaisian
radiolarian
Rastafarian
reappraisal
rearadmiral
recessional
recommittal
rectangular
rectilineal
rectilinear
redactional
referential
reportorial
residential
retinacular
reverential
reversional
rhapsodical
rheological
rhetorician
rickettsial
rockcrystal
Rosicrucian
ruridecanal
Sabbatarian
sacramental
sacrificial
saltatorial
salvational
saturnalian
sausagemeat
Scotchwoman
scriptorial
secretarial
secretariat
seigneurial
seigniorial
selfdisplay
semeiotical
semidiurnal
sempiternal
sensational
sentimental
septifragal
serological
sertularian
sexagesimal
sexological
Shaksperean
Shaksperian
shoulderbag
shoulderpad
sinological
situational
sleepingbag
sleepingcar
somnambular
sophistical
spasmodical
spectacular
spectrogram
spermicidal
sphincteral
sphygmogram
spirochetal
splenetical
spokeswoman
sportswoman
springclean
statistical
steerageway
steganogram
straightway
strategical
subclinical
subcortical
subcritical
subcultural
sublittoral
submarginal
subregional
subscapular
substantial
subterminal
subtropical
summational
superficial
supernormal
supersedeas
surrebuttal
sybaritical
symmetrical
synagogical
synonymical
syntactical
synthetical
taxonomical
terrestrial
territorial
testimonial
tetrahedral
theological
theoretical
therewithal
thoroughwax
thrasonical
thunderclap
thunderhead
thunderpeal
toploftical
topological
traditional
transmittal
transsexual
transversal
trapezoidal
trencherman
tribunicial
tribunitial
trichomonad
trimestrial
Trinitarian
typological
uncanonical
unchristian
uncongenial
unemotional
unequivocal
unessential
unicellular
unipersonal
unpolitical
utilitarian
valuational
variational
ventricular
verisimilar
vespertinal
vibrational
viceadmiral
virological
wappenschaw
washerwoman
wherewithal
whitecollar
whitethroat
windlestraw
Yugoslavian
zoantharian
Zoroastrian
ailurophobe
breadcrumbs

buffalorobe
Francophobe
superscribe
absorptance
accountancy
accrescence
acquittance
adolescence
aeronautics
aerostatics
aftereffect
ambivalence
ambivalency
AngloFrench
antecedence
apologetics
aristocracy
astringency
beneficence
benevolence
bibliomancy
bibliotheca
biofeedback
bondservice
breechblock
breezeblock
bureaucracy
candescence
candlestick
capacitance
centrepiece
cesarevitch
cesarewitch
chainstitch
cheiromancy
chieftaincy
chockablock
chrominance
circumspect
clairschach
coalescence
coexistence
coincidence
coinsurance
comeuppance
commonplace
complacence
complacency
concordance
concurrence
conductance
confederacy
conformance
consequence
conservancy
consistence
consistency
consultancy
contingence
contingency
continuance
contradance
contrivance
convenience
conveniency
convergence
convergency
conversance
conversancy
countenance
crackerjack
crossstitch
cybernetics
delinquency
deliverance
despondence
despondency
determinacy
diagnostics
diamondback
dinnerdance
discordance
discordancy
discrepancy
disturbance
doublecheck
doubleDutch
doublequick
electronics
encumbrance
equivalence
equivalency
ergatocracy
erubescence
eurhythmics
evanescence
excrescence
excrescency
exorbitance
fiddlestick
flamboyance
flamboyancy
flocculence
florescence
forbearance
forbiddance
fraudulence
furtherance
geopolitics
histrionics
homestretch
hydroponics
illuminance
impenitence
impenitency
impuissance
inappetence
incoherence
incoherency
inconstancy
ineloquence
inexistence
infrequence
infrequency
inhabitancy
inheritance
insouciance
intolerance
iridescence
irrelevance
irrelevancy
irreverence
jumpingjack
lactescence
leatherback
leatherneck
lieutenancy
linguistics
liquescence
lophobranch
loxodromics
maintenance
maleficence
malevolence
malfeasance
malpractice
mantelpiece
marcescence
marketplace
massproduce
masterpiece
mathematics
meritocracy
mesalliance
metaphysics
meteoritics
misalliance
misfeasance
misguidance
morrisdance
munificence
nigrescence
nonchalance
nonfeasance
nonviolence
numismatics
omnipotence
omniscience
oneiromancy
opalescence
orthopedics
outdistance
overbalance
overproduce
overstretch
paediatrics
paramountcy
percipience
performance
perpetuance
persistence
persistency
physiocracy
pinnatisect
pointdevice
preaudience
precontract
preeminence
pressagency
proficiency
prolificacy
prosthetics
provenience
putrescence
quarterback
quarterdeck
reassurance
reconstruct
reemergence
reflectance
refringency
reinsurance
reintroduce
rejuvenesce
remembrance
renaissance
resemblance
respondence
respondency
rhabdomancy
safeconduct
saltimbanco
satinstitch
scaleinsect
selfdefence
selfrespect
selfservice
shuttlecock
silverstick
singlestick
singletrack
snatchblock
sonofabitch
stagestruck
stampoffice
steeplejack
stickinsect
stickleback
stratocracy
stringpiece
subcontract
submergence
subsequence
subsistence
sufficiency
superinduce
symposiarch
systematics
technocracy
tephromancy
thermionics
throatlatch
transpierce
turgescence
ultrasonics
vicegerency
vitrescence
vociferance
weathercock
yacketyyack
zootechnics
accelerando
afficionado
amontillado
anticathode
assafoetida
bactericide
countryside
countrywide
decrepitude
decrescendo
digitigrade
disquietude
fanfaronade
handgrenade
heavenwards
hitherwards
incertitude
infanticide
ingratitude
insecticide
liberticide
loggerheads
machinemade
maxillipede
misericorde
paraldehyde
Passiontide
phylloclade
pitchblende
plantigrade
polypeptide
promptitude
pulchritude
rallentando
rodenticide
rodomontade
slickenside
switchblade
thalidomide
tolbutamide
tragicomedy
tyrannicide
vicissitude
Whitsuntide
abiogeneses
actinometer
actinomyces
aerographer
affectioned
afterburner
alembicated
alkalimeter
allantoides
amenorrhoea
anastomoses
antechamber
aponeuroses
articulated
ascomycetes
auxanometer
awestricken
azotobacter
backbencher
balmcricket
bandylegged
barnstormer
beachcomber
beechmarten
bellfounder
bellheather
bewhiskered
bibliolater
biedermeier
billsticker
biocoenoses
birdbrained
birdfancier
birdwatcher
bittersweet
blackavised
blackbirder
blackcoated
blackmailer
blackmarket
blockbuster
bloodsucker
bloodvessel
bodybuilder
boilermaker
booklearned
bookshelves
bottlegreen
bottlenosed
bowdleriser
brainteaser
brazenfaced
breadbasket
breadwinner
breastwheel
broadcaster
broadleaved
broadminded
bullfighter
bullterrier
burgomaster
bushwhacker
butterflies
cabbagetree
calorimeter
calyptrogen
cancellated
candlepower
cantharides
carburetted
carburetter
cardsharper
caryopsides
castellated
catachreses
catswhisker
cauliflower
cavedweller
chainletter
chainsmoker
chansonnier
chanticleer
chargesheet
cheerleader
chickenfeed
childminder
choirmaster
chronologer
chronometer
chrysalides
chrysalises
cityslicker
cleanlimbed
cleanshaven
clearheaded
cliffhanger
closefisted
closehauled
coldblooded
coldhearted
collectanea
colorimeter
columniated
comestibles
complicated
comptroller
concertgoer
conditioner
convenances
conveyancer
cotoneaster
counterplea
counterview
countrified
countryfied
crenellated
crestfallen
criticaster
crookbacked
crossbearer
crossgarnet
crosslegged
crotcheteer
cupronickel
daisycutter
deerstalker
demographer
desperadoes
dilapidated
directrices
disaffected
disannulled
disbeliever
discipliner
disencumber
disgruntled
dishevelled
dishonourer
disinclined
disinterred
disremember
distempered
doorknocker
doubleedged
doubleender
doublefaced
downhearted
downtrodden
doxographer
drillmaster
dumbfounder
dundrearies
dynamometer
earthcloset
echosounder
elasticated
electioneer
electrolier
embellisher
embroiderer
embryonated
Emmenthaler
emptyhanded
emptyheaded
enlightened
ensanguined
enterpriser
entertainer
ephemerides
establisher
executioner
executrices
executrixes
experienced
extortioner
extraverted
extroverted
fairweather
faithhealer

faultfinder
fenestrated
fieldcornet
fieldworker
filterpaper
firecracker
firefighter
firewatcher
flagofficer
flimflammer
floorwalker
footslogger
footsoldier
foraminated
foraminifer
forequarter
foreshorten
foresighted
forestaller
forethinker
foulmouthed
fourflusher
fourpounder
fourwheeler
frankfurter
fraterniser
freehearted
freethinker
freezedried
frenchified
frontrunner
frostbitten
frothhopper
fullblooded
fullfledged
fullhearted
fullmouthed
gallbladder
gallowstree
gardemanger
gatecrasher
generaliser
geniculated
gerrymander
gettogether
ghostwriter
giantpowder
gillyflower
glassblower
glasscutter
globeflower
godchildren
goddaughter
godforsaken
gonfalonier
goodhearted
goodnatured
gormandiser
gradiometer
grandfather
grandmother
grandnephew
grangeriser
grasshopper
gravedigger
greatnephew
greengrocer
greenkeeper
groundsheet
groundwater
haberdasher
hairdresser
hairtrigger
halfblooded
halfhearted
handicapped
handicapper
handknitted
handpainted
handwritten
hardhearted
hardmouthed
harebrained
heartbroken
heavyfooted
heavyhanded
hedgehopped
hereinafter
highpitched
highpowered
highstepper
historiated
homesteader
homogeniser
honeybadger
honeymooner
hospitaller
housefather
householder
housekeeper
housemaster
housemother
hunchbacked
hydraheaded
hypermarket
iconostases
illaffected
illdisposed
illfavoured
illhumoured
illmannered
illtempered
immoveables
impassioned
intagliated
intensifier
intentioned
interallied
interbedded
intercepter
interleaves
interlocker
intermitted
interplayed
interpreter
interrupter
interviewee
interviewer
intromitted
intromitter
introverted
ironhearted
jerrymander
kickstarter
kindhearted
lakedweller
lammergeier
lammergeyer
lamplighter
landgrabber
largeminded
leapfrogged
leaseholder
levelheaded
lightfooted
lighthanded
lightheaded
lightminded
lilylivered
linendraper
lineprinter
lionhearted
logographer
longsighted
looselimbed
loudmouthed
loudspeaker
lowspirited
mailcarrier
maladjusted
manifestoes
mantuamaker
marriagebed
masquerader
meadowsweet
mediatrices
mentholated
merryandrew
metalworker
middlesized
mineraliser
minesweeper
minnesinger
misbegotten
miscellanea
misremember
moisturiser
molecricket
moneylender
moneymarket
moneyspider
monogrammed
monographer
monopoliser
moonlighter
mosstrooper
mothernaked
motivepower
mountaineer
multistorey
mustachioed
myxomycetes
namedropper
nearsighted
neckerchief
necromancer
neutraliser
nightporter
nightwalker
ninnyhammer
nomographer
northeaster
northwester
noseyparker
nosographer
openhearted
openmouthed
operculated
opinionated
organscreen
ornithopter
otherwhiles
outrivalled
outstripped
overcropped
overstepped
overstuffed
overwritten
oxyhydrogen
paddlewheel
pamphleteer
panicmonger
pantalettes
paperhanger
paragrapher
parallelled
paraphraser
paratrooper
parentheses
parishioner
partitioned
partitioner
pasteuriser
paternoster
pearlfisher
pedestalled
periphrases
perishables
personifier
petticoated
pettifogger
philanderer
philosopher
photocopier
photooffset
phrasemaker
picturegoer
pieceworker
pilotburner
pipecleaner
plagiariser
plainspoken
planoconvex
plasticiser
pluviometer
pocketmoney
pocketsized
polarimeter
polevaulter
populariser
prayerwheel
precedented
preoccupied
prestressed
prizewinner
probationer
progestogen
proofreader
pureblooded
pussyfooter
quacksalver
quickfrozen
quicksilver
quickwitted
quilldriver
rangefinder
rattlepated
readywitted
recommender
reedwarbler
replenisher
representer
retroflexed
retrorocket
reversioner
ricochetted
rightangled
righthanded
righthander
rightminded
rightwinger
ringstraked
roughfooted
roughlegged
safebreaker
safecracker
salesladies
salinometer
sandskipper
scaremonger
schwarmerei
sclerometer
scoutmaster
screwdriver
scrutiniser
secondrater
seismometer
selfassured
selfcentred
selfcreated
selfdevoted
selfelected
selfimposed
selfinduced
selfinvited
selflimited
selfstarter
semiskilled
semitrailer
sentinelled
serigrapher
shareholder
sharepusher
sharpwitted
sheepfarmer
sheepmaster
shelljacket
shipbreaker
shipbuilder
shockheaded
shoeleather
shorthanded
shortspoken
shortwinded
showstopper
sideslipped
sidestepped
sidewheeler
sightreader
sightscreen
signpainter
simpliciter
slaughterer
slavedriver
slaveholder
slavemarket
sleepwalker
smallholder
smallminded
smokescreen
smoothfaced
snickersnee
snowgoggles
soberminded
sockdolager
sockdologen
softhearted
softshelled
somewhither
soupkitchen
southeaster
southwester
spaceheater
speechifier
speedometer
spellbinder
spherometer
spindletree
spiritlevel
splayfooted
stadtholder
staircarpet
stakeholder
stallholder
standpatter
starcrossed
starstudded
steamboiler
steamroller
steelworker
stepbrother
stereotyped
stereotyper
stiffnecked
stockbroker
stockholder
stockjobber
stockmarket
stonecurlew
stonecutter
stonemarten
stonewaller
storekeeper
storyteller
straitlaced
straphanger
sugarcoated
superficies
superheater
supermarket
supertanker
surfboarder
surrebutter
sweepstakes
swellheaded
swiftfooted
swimbladder
swingletree
swordbearer
sympathiser
synthesiser
tabernacled
tacheometer
tearstained
teenybopper
teetotaller
telegrapher
teleprinter
tessellated
testatrices
thanksgiver
theatregoer
thermometer
thickheaded
thickwitted
thimbleweed
thinskinned
threadpaper
threedecker
threehanded
threelegged
threemaster
tightfisted
tightlipped
timepleaser
titleholder
toastmaster
toffeenosed
toothbilled
toothpowder
topographer
torchbearer
torchsinger
toughminded
trackwalker
trailblazer
trainbearer
transceiver
transcriber
transferred
transferrer
transformer
transmitted
transmitter
transponder
transporter
treecreeper
trendsetter
trestletree
tricoloured
truehearted
trustbuster
tumbledrier
typefounder
typewritten
typographer
ultraviolet
unaccounted
uncivilised
uncluttered
uncommitted
unconcealed
unconcerned
unconnected

uncontested
underbidder
underhanded
undermanned
underpinned
underseller
undersigned
understated
undervaluer
underwriter
undeveloped
undisguised
undisturbed
unexploited
unexpressed
unfashioned
unfurnished
unicoloured
uninhabited
uninhibited
unkennelled
unmitigated
unorganized
unpossessed
unqualified
unsaturated
unsolicited
unvarnished
unwarranted
upholsterer
vaporimeter
varnishtree
vinedresser
volkslieder
volumometer
voortrekker
wainscotted
wapperjawed
warmblooded
warmhearted
washleather
waspwaisted
wastebasket
watercooled
watercooler
waterlogged
weakhearted
wedgeshaped
wedgetailed
weenybopper
welladvised
wellbeloved
welldefined
wellfounded
wellgroomed
wellordered
wellrounded
Westminster
wheresoever
whichsoever
whiffletree
whippletree
Whitechapel
whiteheaded
whitewasher
whitleather
wholesouled
whoremaster
whoremonger
whosesoever
windcheater
wintergreen
wisecracker
witchhunter
worldbeater
wreckmaster
wrongheaded
xylographer
festschrift

heterograft
loosestrife
mothercraft
needlecraft
ploughstaff
pocketknife
presanctify
priestcraft
sheathknife
spendthrift
aboutsledge
acknowledge
aerobiology
agrobiology
amphibology
archaeology
archipelago
Assyriology
bryozoology
campanology
chaperonage
Christology
climatology
concubinage
cosmetology
countersign
criminology
cryobiology
dactylology
decolletage
depthcharge
dermatology
electrology
eschatology
Etruscology
featheredge
frankpledge
furnishings
gasfittings
gerontology
gynaecology
haematology
haemorrhage
headborough
heresiology
herpetology
hypercharge
ichthyology
insectifuge
insectology
interchange
kinesiology
laryngology
libertinage
lichenology
malariology
martyrology
meteorology
methodology
miscarriage
mismarriage
myrmecology
olfactology
orchidology
ornithology
overindulge
palmcabbage
phraseology
pivotbridge
primatology
proceedings
pteridology
pullthrough
quickchange
reflexology
scientology
seigniorage
semasiology
shortchange

soteriology
spectrology
spelaeology
sphagnology
spindlelegs
squarsonage
stagemanage
stomatology
supercharge
terminology
thanatology
thaumaturge
thaumaturgy
undercharge
vagabondage
venereology
vexillology
volcanology
vulcanology
weighbridge
angiography
antistrophe
bathyscaphe
blameworthy
calligraphy
candlelight
cartography
catastrophe
chirography
chorography
cosmography
discography
dittography
downdraught
dreadnought
ethnography
faithworthy
filmography
forethought
freethought
guttapercha
Hagiographa
hagiography
handwrought
haplography
heavyweight
heliography
highwrought
homoeopathy
hydrography
hymnography
hypertrophy
hypsography
ichnography
iconography
ipecacuanha
lightweight
lithography
micrography
motherright
mythography
naturopathy
orthography
osteography
overwrought
paperweight
papiermache
pennyweight
petrography
phonography
photography
phytography
pictography
pillowfight
pornography
psychopathy
radiography
reprography
scenography

schottische
searchlight
secondsight
sightworthy
spaceflight
squirearchy
stenography
stomachache
streetlight
stylography
tachygraphy
thankworthy
trothplight
trustworthy
underweight
uranography
vehmgericht
wheelwright
zincography
abiogenesis
abiogenetic
acatalectic
achondritic
acidophilic
actinomycin
admiralship
Aeneolithic
aeolotropic
aerodynamic
AfroAsiatic
agoraphobia
agoraphobic
albuminuria
algorithmic
allomorphic
amphimictic
anacreontic
anadiplosis
anaesthesia
anaesthetic
anagnorisis
anaphylaxis
anarchistic
anastomosis
anastomotic
anemometric
anglophobia
anglophobic
anisotropic
anomalistic
anthocyanin
anthracitic
antiJacobin
antiphrasis
antipyretic
antiSemitic
antivitamin
antonomasia
apocalyptic
Apollinaris
aponeurosis
aponeurotic
aposiopesis
apostleship
apostrophic
apparatchik
arbitratrix
archaeornis
archangelic
Areopagitic
atmospheric
audiometric
autographic
autoplastic
autotrophic
avoirdupois
bacchanalia
BaltoSlavic
basketchair

bathingsuit
batholithic
bathymetric
betweenmaid
bibliomania
bibliopegic
bibliopolic
biocoenosis
biocoenotic
biquadratic
blastogenic
blepharitis
bourgeoisie
bradycardia
braggadocio
bristletail
brucellosis
bushmanship
cabbalistic
cacographic
calceolaria
calisthenic
Calvinistic
camaraderie
cantharidic
captainship
carbocyclic
carrageenin
catachresis
cataclysmic
cataplectic
catechistic
catercousin
ceroplastic
chalcedonic
chamberlain
chambermaid
chameleonic
charcuterie
charismatic
chemotactic
chinoiserie
christiania
chronologic
chrysarobin
cisatlantic
citizenship
climacteric
clinometric
coccidiosis
cockaleekie
cockyleekie
colonelship
communistic
comradeship
conspecific
costbenefit
coulometric
counterfeit
counterfoil
countervail
cryptogamic
cryptomeria
crystalloid
curatorship
cyclopaedia
cyclopaedic
cyclothymia
cyclothymic
cytogenesis
cytokinesis
demographic
denizenship
dexiotropic
dialogistic
diamagnetic
diaphoresis
diaphoretic
diapophysis

diarthrosis
diastematic
diastrophic
dichromatic
differentia
diphtheroid
disharmonic
dithyrambic
draggletail
dramaturgic
dropcurtain
dyslogistic
econometric
ectoblastic
ectogenesis
ectogenetic
ectomorphic
ectoplasmic
ectotrophic
elastomeric
elephantoid
embryologic
emperorship
enarthrosis
encomiastic
endomorphic
endoplasmic
endothermic
endotrophic
epeirogenic
epithalamia
epithalamic
esemplastic
Eucharistic
eudiometric
euphemistic
eurypteroid
feldspathic
felspathoid
fetichistic
fetishistic
feudalistic
flagcaptain
fluorescein
foretopsail
formalistic
Francomania
gafftopsail
Gallophobia
gamogenesis
gastronomic
gegenschein
gendarmerie
generalship
geomagnetic
geostrophic
geotectonic
Germanophil
gibberellin
glauconitic
glossolalia
gnotobiosis
gnotobiotic
goniometric
gramophonic
granolithic
granophyric
gravimetric
haematocrit
haemocyanin
haemoglobin
haemophilia
haemophilic
haemoptysis
haemorrhoid
haemostasis
haemostatic
haggadistic
hagioscopic

harmonistic
hebephrenia
hebephrenic
heliometric
heliotropic
Hellenistic
helminthoid
hemeralopia
hemianopsia
hemimorphic
hemispheric
hermeneutic
heroworship
heteroploid
heterotaxis
heterotypic
highfalutin
Hippocratic
holoblastic
holographic
homeopathic
homeostasis
homeostatic
homocentric
homoestatic
homogenetic
homomorphic
homoplastic
homothallic
homozygosis
Hudibrastic
hydrobromic
hydrocyanic
hydrometric
hydropathic
hydrophilic
hydrophobia
hydrophobic
hydrophytic
hydrostatic
hydrotactic
hydrotropic
hygrometric
hygrophytic
hygroscopic
hylogenesis
hylozoistic
hyperboloid
hypercritic
hypermetric
hyperphagia
hyperplasia
hypnopaedia
hypnopompic
hypoblastic
hypocycloid
hypogastric
hypothermia
hypotyposis
hypsometric
hypsophobia
ichthyornis
iconostasis
ideographic
idiographic
idiomorphic
immunologic
interatomic
internuncio
intervallic
ionospheric
isoelectric
ithyphallic
Jansenistic
jargonistic
kilocalorie
kleptomania
kymographic
lectureship
legerdemain
lifemanship
lithophytic
logarithmic
logographic
macrobiotic
macrocosmic
macroscopic
magistratic
maintopsail
managership
manneristic
marqueterie
marshalship
masochistic
mastodontic
mastoiditis
mechanistic
mediumistic
megalomania
megalopolis
melancholia
melancholic
memorabilia
meroblastic
merogenesis
mesoblastic
mesomorphic
messiahship
metacentric
metachrosis
metagenesis
metagenetic
metallurgic
metamorphic
metaplastic
metapsychic
metasomatic
Methodistic
microcosmic
microlithic
micrometric
microphonic
microphytic
microscopic
mithridatic
modernistic
monitorship
monochromic
monogenesis
monogenetic
monographic
monomorphic
monozygotic
myocarditis
mythopoetic
myxomatosis
narcoleptic
necrobiosis
necromantic
necrophilia
necrophilic
necropoleis
negotiatrix
negrophobia
neologistic
Neoplatonic
neuropathic
neurotropic
nomographic
nonmetallic
nonspecific
nosographic
nurserymaid
nyctitropic
nyctophobia
nymphomania
oarsmanship
ochlocratic
oestrogenic
ontogenesis
ontogenetic
opencircuit
oreographic
orthodontia
orthodontic
orthopaedic
orthoscopic
orthotropic
osteopathic
osteophytic
Ostrogothic
paederastic
paedophilia
Palaearctic
palaeotypic
palindromic
panhellenic
pantheistic
pantothenic
paragraphic
paraleipsis
parallactic
paramorphic
paraplectic
parasitosis
parathyroid
paratyphoid
parenthesis
parenthetic
paronomasia
partnership
passacaglia
pediculosis
periostitis
peripatetic
periphrasis
perispermic
peristalsis
peristaltic
peritonitis
pessimistic
phagedaenic
pharyngitis
philosophic
photometric
photophilic
photophobia
photophobic
phototactic
phototropic
phthiriasis
phycocyanin
phyllotaxis
physiologic
planimetric
plasmolysis
plasmolytic
pleiotropic
pleomorphic
pleurodynia
pluralistic
plutocratic
pneumonitis
podophyllin
polychromic
polygenesis
polygenetic
polyglottic
polygraphic
polymorphic
polytechnic
porphyritic
postclassic
praetorship
prehistoric
premiership
primateship
problematic
procephalic
proctorship
progenitrix
prolocutrix
prophetship
prophylaxis
prosecutrix
proteolysis
proteolytic
Proterozoic
prothalamia
prothoracic
protophytic
provostship
pseudopodia
psittacosis
psychedelia
psychedelic
psychiatric
psychogenic
psychologic
pyroclastic
pyrotechnic
quinquennia
radiometric
radiophonic
rattlebrain
realpolitik
rhinoscopic
rhizocarpic
ritualistic
Russophobia
saintpaulia
salpingitis
sanguinaria
saprobiotic
saprophytic
scarabaeoid
scholarship
scholiastic
scientistic
scissortail
sclerotitis
seborrhoeic
selfconceit
selfdespair
selfworship
senatorship
septicaemia
septicaemic
shamanistic
sheriffship
showmanship
sickbenefit
socialistic
sociometric
sociopathic
soldiership
solipsistic
somatogenic
somatologic
somatotonia
somatotonic
speakership
spherulitic
sphincteric
Spinozistic
spiritistic
spirometric
spondylitis
sponsorship
sporophytic
stalactitic
stalagmitic
staurolitic
steatopygia
stephanotis
stereotypic
stewardship
Stradivarii
studentship
subspecific
swallowtail
sycophantic
syllogistic
symbolistic
sympathetic
symptomatic
syndesmosis
synergistic
syssarcosis
tabletennis
tachycardia
teachership
technologic
telegrammic
telegraphic
telekinesis
telekinetic
teratogenic
teratologic
tetracyclic
theocentric
theodolitic
theorematic
therapeutic
thermoduric
thermolysis
thermolytic
thermotaxis
thingumajig
thixotropic
thoroughpin
thyroiditis
timebargain
tonsillitis
topographic
torticollis
toxicomania
tracasserie
transuranic
tribuneship
trichinosis
trisyllabic
tritheistic
troglodytic
trousersuit
trundletail
trusteeship
typographic
unrealistic
Upanishadic
vasopressin
verbalistic
viceroyship
voltametric
voodooistic
workmanship
xylographic
zygomorphic
carpetsnake
gartersnake
husbandlike
jabberwocky
mackerelsky
marlinspike
rattlesnake
rheumaticky
soldierlike
spondulicks
tenterhooks
tiddlywinks
workmanlike
abdominally
abhorrently
abiotically
abolishable
absorbingly
abstinently
academicals
accentually
acceptingly
accordantly
accordingly
accountable
accountably
acidifiable
acropetally
adjectively
adverbially
advertently
aerobically
affectingly
affectively
aggregately
aggrievedly
agnatically
agonisingly
ailurophile
allocatable
alternately
ambiguously
ambitiously
amorphously
analogously
anencephaly
angelically
anomalously
anonymously
appallingly
appealingly
applaudable
appreciable
appreciably
approvingly
aquatically
arbitrarily
archaically
arglebargle
arrestingly
articulable
ascetically
aseptically
assertively
assiduously
assimilable
atrociously
attemptable
attentively
attractable
audaciously
augmentable
auricularly
automatable
banteringly
baptismally
barbarously
barbastelle
barefacedly
basipetally
battlefield
beauteously
beautifully
befittingly
beguilingly
benightedly
benignantly
bibliophile
bibliophily
bilaterally
binocularly
bitterapple
blackbeetle
blamelessly
bloodlessly
bookinghall

botanically
bounteously
bountifully
brainlessly
brainsickly
brilliantly
bucolically
bumptiously
Byronically
cabbagepalm
canonically
capaciously
caressingly
carvelbuilt
causatively
caustically
cavernously
ceaselessly
celestially
certifiable
certifiably
changefully
chanterelle
chaotically
cheerlessly
Chippendale
chlorophyll
Christianly
chronically
civilisable
clamorously
classically
cloudcastle
cockleshell
coeternally
coffeetable
cognitively
cognoscible
collapsible
collectable
collectedly
collectible
collinearly
collusively
colourfully
combatively
combustible
comfortable
comfortably
commendable
commendably
commensally
committable
compassable
compellable
competently
compliantly
compositely
compossible
comprisable
concealable
conceitedly
conceivable
conceivably
conceptacle
concertedly
condemnable
condensable
conductible
conferrable
confessedly
confidently
confidingly
confirmable
confiscable
conformable
conformably
conformally
confusingly
congealable
congenially
congruently
congruously
connectable
connectedly
connectible
connubially
conquerable
consciously
conservable
consignable
consolingly
consonantly
construable
consumingly
containable
contentedly
contestable
continently
continuable
continually
contractile
contrivable
conventicle
conversable
convertible
convertibly
convincible
convivially
corporately
corporeally
corpulently
correctable
corrosively
corruptible
corruptibly
countlessly
courteously
credentials
credulously
cryptically
customarily
custombuilt
dangerously
dauntlessly
deathrattle
deceitfully
deceivingly
decennially
deceptively
decussately
dedicatedly
deductively
defectively
defensively
deficiently
degradingly
deistically
deliciously
delightedly
deliriously
deliverable
demandingly
demountable
denumerable
dependently
deploringly
depressible
descendable
descendible
describable
deservingly
desperately
desultorily
developable
dexterously
dialectally
differently
difficultly
diffidently
diffusively
digestively
dimwittedly
diningtable
dinnertable
disarmingly
disassemble
disassembly
discardable
discernible
discernibly
discussable
discussible
disentangle
disenthrall
disguisedly
disgustedly
dishonestly
dislikeable
dismayingly
disparately
dispensable
dispersedly
disseminule
dissociable
dissolutely
dissolvable
dissonantly
dissyllable
distensible
divergently
diverticula
doctrinally
doubtlessly
douroucouli
drastically
dreamlessly
dresscircle
dynamically
ebulliently
editorially
effectively
effectually
efficiently
effulgently
egregiously
elaborately
elastically
elementally
embraceable
embracingly
emotionally
empirically
endearingly
endemically
enforceable
enlargeable
enquiringly
entomophily
episcopally
equivocally
erratically
erroneously
escheatable
essentially
eucalyptole
eugenically
exceedingly
excellently
excessively
exclusively
excursively
exemplarily
exercisable
exhaustible
exogenously
expansively
expectantly
expediently
expensively
explainable
exploitable
explosively
expressible
exquisitely
extensively
extractable
exuberantly
facetiously
factionally
faithlessly
falteringly
fanatically
farthingale
fashionable
fashionably
fatiguingly
faultlessly
feloniously
fermentable
ferociously
festinately
financially
fingerstall
fissionable
flatulently
flauntingly
foreseeable
forfeitable
forgetfully
forgettable
fortifiable
fortnightly
fortunately
fractiously
Francophile
frantically
fraternally
frightfully
frivolously
fruitlessly
garrulously
generically
genetically
genitivally
gentianella
gentlemanly
glutinously
gracelessly
grandiosely
graphically
grotesquely
grumblingly
guilelessly
guiltlessly
haematocele
haphazardly
hazardously
healthfully
heartlessly
Hebraically
hereditable
heretically
herringgull
hibernacula
hilariously
honeysuckle
hornswoggle
housewifely
hundredfold
identically
idiotically
idyllically
illiberally
illimitable
illimitably
illogically
illuminable
imaginarily
imitatively
immediately
immedicable
immitigable
immitigably
impartially
impassively
impatiently
impeachable
imperfectly
imperiously
impermeable
impermeably
imperviable
impetuously
implausible
implausibly
imploringly
impoliticly
importantly
importunely
imprecisely
impregnable
impregnably
impressible
imprudently
impulsively
inadaptable
inadvisable
inalienable
inalienably
inalterable
inalterably
inanimately
incessantly
incipiently
inclemently
inclusively
incoercible
incorrectly
incorruptly
increasable
incuriously
indefinable
indefinably
indignantly
indivisible
indivisibly
indomitable
indomitably
indubitable
indubitably
inductively
indulgently
inelegantly
ineluctable
ineluctably
inequitable
inequitably
inescapable
inestimable
inestimably
inexcusable
inexcusably
inflammable
inflammably
infrangible
ingeniously
ingenuously
ingrainedly
inhabitable
inheritable
injuriously
innavigable
innocuously
innoxiously
innumerable
innumerably
inquiringly
inscribable
inscrutable
inscrutably
insensately
inseparable
inseparably
insidiously
insincerely
insistently
insultingly
insuperable
insuperably
intensively
intermeddle
intermingle
intertangle
intolerable
intolerably
intractable
intractably
intricately
intrusively
intuitively
invectively
inventively
invidiously
inviolately
irrecusable
irrecusably
irreducible
irreducibly
irrefutable
irrefutably
irregularly
irremovable
irremovably
irreparable
irreparably
irresoluble
irrevocable
irrevocably
irruptively
itinerantly
judiciously
juridically
justiciable
justifiable
justifiably
laboriously
laconically
lacrimosely
lacrymosely
larcenously
lecherously
lickerishly
lickspittle
lightsomely
limitlessly
lingeringly
liquefiable
litigiously
loathsomely
lucratively
ludicrously
luxuriantly
luxuriously
maddeningly
maladroitly
maliciously
malignantly
manipulable
mantelshelf
marcescible
masculinely
masterfully
matchlessly

mediaevally
medicinable
medicinally
melodiously
meningocele
mentionable
mercenarily
mercilessly
mercurially
mimetically
mirthlessly
misguidedly
molecularly
mollycoddle
momentarily
momentously
monstrously
moronically
municipally
murderously
murmurously
muskthistle
narratively
necessarily
nefariously
negligently
neighbourly
nervelessly
netherworld
nightingale
nocturnally
noiselessly
nomadically
nonvolatile
notoriously
numerically
nutritively
objectively
obliviously
obnoxiously
observantly
observingly
obsessively
obstinately
obtrusively
occipitally
octagonally
offensively
offhandedly
officinally
officiously
operatively
opportunely
orbicularly
organically
organisable
osmotically
ostensively
outspokenly
pacifically
paramountly
parochially
partitively
pecuniarily
pendulously
pensionable
penuriously
perceivable
perceivably
perceptible
perceptibly
perennially
perfectible
performable
perishingly
permanently
permissible
permissibly
perpetually
perplexedly
persuadable
persuasible
pertinently
perturbable
pervasively
pervertedly
pestilently
pictorially
pigheadedly
pipistrelle
piratically
plaintively
pleasurable
pleasurably
plenteously
plentifully
pointlessly
poisonously
polarisable
polemically
politically
polygonally
ponderously
pontificals
posteriorly
potentially
potteringly
powerlessly
practicable
practicably
practically
prattlingly
precedently
predatorily
predictable
predictably
prefatorily
prelusively
prelusorily
prematurely
presciently
presentable
presentably
preservable
presumingly
pretendedly
prevalently
preventable
preventible
primaevally
primitively
principally
privatively
professedly
profiterole
prominently
promisingly
propitiable
prosaically
protractile
protrudable
protrusible
providently
provisorily
provokingly
proximately
psychically
publishable
punchinello
purchasable
purportedly
purposively
putrescible
pyramidally
qualifiable
querulously
quiescently
quizzically
rancorously
rapaciously
rapturously
ratatouille
ravishingly
receptacula
receptively
recessively
reclaimable
recoverable
rectifiable
recumbently
recurrently
redoubtable
redundantly
reflexively
refrangible
regardfully
regenerable
regimentals
registrable
regretfully
regrettable
regrettably
rejoicingly
religiously
reluctantly
repellantly
repellently
repentantly
replaceable
repleviable
reposefully
repressible
repressibly
reprovingly
repugnantly
repulsively
resentfully
resiliently
resistively
respectable
respectably
responsible
responsibly
retentively
retraceable
retractable
retrievable
righteously
sagaciously
salaciously
salvageable
sartorially
satanically
satirically
satisfiable
saturninely
sceptically
schoolchild
scissorbill
sclerophyll
scorchingly
scorpionfly
scoundrelly
screamingly
searchingly
secondarily
secretively
sectionally
sedentarily
seditiously
seductively
segmentally
seismically
selaginella
selectively
selffertile
selfsterile
semimonthly
senselessly
sensitively
sensorially
serviceable
serviceably
seventyfold
severalfold
shacklebolt
shamelessly
shelterbelt
shiftlessly
shrinkingly
sickeningly
sightlessly
sigmoidally
signifiable
simperingly
sinistrally
sleeplessly
slightingly
smilelessly
somatically
somnolently
sorrowfully
soundlessly
sovereignly
sparrowbill
spastically
specifiable
spherically
spinelessly
spiritually
spirituelle
spreadeagle
squarebuilt
squeamishly
squintingly
stainlessly
startlingly
statesmanly
statutorily
steadfastly
strenuously
stretchable
stringently
stumblingly
subaerially
submersible
submissible
submultiple
subumbrella
succulently
suggestible
summersault
sumptuously
superfamily
supersubtle
suppliantly
supportable
supportably
surficially
surpassable
susceptible
susceptibly
suspensible
sustainable
swallowable
swallowhole
tagliatelle
tagliatelli
talkatively
tarnishable
tarradiddle
tastelessly
technically
temperately
temporarily
tenaciously
tentatively
termagantly
tetanically
thanklessly
theatricals
thermically
thermophile
thrillingly
thunderbolt
titanically
toothsomely
torturously
totteringly
townspeople
tracelessly
transiently
traversable
treasonable
treasonably
tremblingly
tremulously
trenchantly
triadically
tributarily
triennially
trisyllable
troublously
truculently
turbulently
turtleshell
tyrannously
unadvisedly
unalterable
unanimously
unashamedly
unavailable
unavoidable
unavoidably
unbendingly
unboundedly
unbreakable
uncatchable
unceasingly
uncertainly
unclimbable
uncountable
uncrushable
undesirable
undoubtedly
undutifully
unendurable
unendurably
unfailingly
unfeelingly
unfeignedly
unflappable
ungetatable
unguardedly
unhealthily
unhelpfully
unisexually
universally
unlimitedly
unmatchable
unmeaningly
unmemorable
unmemorably
unnaturally
unnervingly
unpalatable
unprintable
unshockable
unskilfully
unsmilingly
unsparingly
unspeakable
unspeakably
unstoppable
unteachable
unthinkable
unthinkably
untouchable
unutterable
unutterably
unweetingly
unwillingly
unwinkingly
unwittingly
vagariously
vaporisable
venatically
venturously
veraciously
veridically
verminously
versatilely
vesicularly
vestigially
vexatiously
vicariously
viceregally
violoncello
vitrifiable
vivaciously
voicelessly
voluntarily
voraciously
warrantable
warrantably
waterbottle
wearilessly
wearisomely
Wensleydale
whimsically
wholesomely
witheringly
wolfwhistle
wonderfully
worrisomely
worshipable
worthlessly
xanthophyll
yellowbelly
bellbottoms
betweentime
centigramme
cleistogamy
collenchyma
delightsome
deuterogamy
Deuteronomy
enterostomy
epithelioma
flavoursome
furthersome
gastrectomy
gymnospermy
harvesthome
heliochrome
hepatectomy
hippopotami
laryngotomy
nephrectomy
ovariectomy
physiognomy
plagiostome
prestissimo
prosenchyma
psychodrama
quarrelsome
quinquereme
reprogramme
rubberstamp
schistosome
scleroderma
scyphistoma
sextodecimo
splenectomy

stenochromy
stirruppump
stomachpump
tracheotomy
troublesome
trypanosome
unwholesome
venturesome
abandonment
abolishment
aboveground
abridgement
acaulescent
accipitrine
achievement
acquiescent
acquirement
acriflavine
adjournment
adjudgement
advancement
advertising
alabastrine
alexandrine
alkalescent
amaranthine
amazonstone
amethystine
amphetamine
amphictyony
amphisbaena
antemundane
anticyclone
antifouling
antioxidant
apomorphine
apparelling
appeasement
appointment
appurtenant
arbitrament
arborescent
armtwisting
arraignment
arrangement
assuagement
autochthony
babysitting
ballbearing
balletomane
barquentine
bassethound
bearbaiting
bedevilment
bedizenment
beguilement
belligerent
bellringing
Benedictine
benightment
bereavement
bergschrund
bestselling
bewitchment
billposting
bivouacking
bodyservant
bombardment
bondservant
bondwashing
bookbinding
bookkeeping
bookselling
bootlegging
brankursine
bricklaying
bullbaiting
calculating
calefacient
campmeeting
caravanning
challenging
channelling
chitterling
chloroprene
christening
churchgoing
cinnabarine
clairvoyant
clandestine
clodhopping
clothesline
cobblestone
cochinchina
codefendant
coefficient
colourblind
commandment
communicant
compartment
compilement
complainant
complaisant
complotting
comportment
concealment
concernment
concomitant
concrescent
concubitant
confinement
conflagrant
congealment
consanguine
consentient
considering
consignment
constituent
containment
contaminant
contentment
controlling
controlment
copingstone
corecipient
cornerstone
cornhusking
corroborant
counselling
counterbond
countermand
countermine
counterpane
countersink
countersunk
crystalline
curtailment
cycloserine
debauchment
debouchment
deforcement
defraudment
delitescent
depravement
derangement
despoilment
determinant
detrainment
development
Diophantine
disablement
disarmament
disbandment
discernment
dislodgment
disobedient
disobliging
disparaging
disportment
disquieting
dissentient
dissepiment
distribuend
divorcement
divulgement
dodecaphony
domineering
doublethink
dressmaking
dropforging
earpiercing
elephantine
embowelling
embowerment
embracement
embroilment
empanelling
emplacement
enchainment
enchantment
encrustment
endorsement
enfeoffment
enforcement
engineering
engorgement
engrossment
enhancement
enjambement
enlargement
enlivenment
ennoblement
enslavement
entablement
enthralling
enthralment
entitlement
entrainment
entreatment
entrustment
envelopment
environment
epinephrine
epochmaking
equidistant
equipollent
escheatment
evanishment
everlasting
expectorant
extravagant
eyecatching
facelifting
factfinding
farreaching
fascinating
filmsetting
fingerprint
fireraising
firewalking
flagwagging
flannelling
fluorescent
forerunning
forewarning
forthcoming
francophone
freebooting
fulminating
garnishment
geanticline
geosyncline
glassmaking
globigerina
goldbeating
golddigging
goodlooking
grandparent
gravelblind
greasepaint
hairraising
hairstyling
halfbinding
halflanding
handfasting
handselling
handwriting
hardhitting
hardworking
headhunting
hearthstone
heartstring
helleborine
herringbone
heterophony
highranking
Hindoostani
hyacinthine
hyoscyamine
hypersthene
illbreeding
impanelling
impeachment
imperilling
imperilment
impermanent
impertinent
impingement
impoundment
impressment
improvement
improvident
inadvertent
incalescent
incarnadine
incognisant
incompetent
incompliant
incongruent
inconscient
inconsonant
incontinent
indehiscent
independent
indifferent
indorsement
inefficient
inexpedient
ingathering
initialling
inobservant
inopportune
installment
instillment
intelligent
interactant
interdepend
interesting
interfacing
interfluent
interjacent
interlining
internecine
intumescent
involvement
juvenescent
kitchensink
knownothing
knucklebone
lancinating
landgravine
landholding
latchstring
lawmerchant
leavetaking
linedrawing
linefishing
longplaying
luminescent
magnificent
maidservant
manifestant
manumitting
marshalling
matchmaking
measurement
mellifluent
merrymaking
methylamine
microsecond
millisecond
mindbending
mindblowing
mindreading
misjudgment
misspelling
moderations
moneymaking
monkeyshine
monophthong
mudslinging
multivalent
musclebound
namecalling
naphthalene
needlepoint
noctilucent
noctivagant
noisemaking
nonexistent
nonmatching
nonplussing
nonresident
nourishment
obmutescent
obsolescent
oilpainting
omnipresent
orangoutang
outbreeding
outbuilding
outcropping
outfighting
outstanding
overbearing
overbidding
overgarment
overlapping
overmanning
overpayment
overrunning
oversailing
oversetting
overtopping
overweening
oysterplant
painkilling
painstaking
palsgravine
papermaking
participant
pastureland
patronising
pawnbroking
peacemaking
pearlescent
penetrating
pentavalent
pentazocine
philhellene
pigsticking
pilocarpine
platforming
platyrrhine
playerpiano
Pleistocene
plenipotent
politicking
polystyrene
precipitant
predicament
predominant
preexistent
prejudgment
presentient
presentment
procurement
prolegomena
proportions
protuberant
publishment
pulverulent
pumicestone
quadraphony
quarrelling
quartertone
quickfiring
racemeeting
realignment
reawakening
recruitment
redetermine
reedbunting
reenactment
refreshment
refrigerant
reminiscent
remonstrant
replacement
requirement
resipiscent
resplendent
restatement
retrocedent
reverberant
reviviscent
rhynchodont
ribvaulting
roadholding
ropedancing
ropewalking
rottenstone
rubefacient
safekeeping
sandbagging
scaffolding
scintillant
scopolamine
scuppernong
selfclosing
selfcocking
selfcommand
selfcontent
selfdenying
selfevident
selffeeding
selffeeling
selfloading
selflocking
selfpitying
selfraising
selfreliant
selfsealing
selfseeking
selfserving
selfwinding
serviceline
shacklebone
shellacking
shoplifting
shortcoming
showjumping
shrivelling
sightseeing

significant
silverpoint
skatingrink
sleuthhound
slotmachine
smithereens
snowbunting
soapboiling
spacesaving
stencilling
stereophony
stiflejoint
stirrupbone
stocktaking
stoneground
strikebound
strongpoint
subbasement
subdominant
subservient
substituent
superabound
superintend
superjacent
supernatant
surbasement
surveillant
sustainment
talebearing
tankfarming
tantalising
tapemachine
temperament
tentpegging
tetravalent
theobromine
timeserving
timesharing
tobogganing
togglejoint
topdressing
touchtyping
traducement
trafficking
tragedienne
trammelling
transalpine
transhumant
transilient
translucent
transmarine
transpadane
transparent
Trappistine
tremblement
tryingplane
tryptophane
tufthunting
twelvepenny
typecasting
typesetting
ultramarine
unappealing
unbelieving
unbeseeming
underground
undertaking
undertenant
undeserving
unfaltering
unflinching
unforgiving
unimportant
unpromising
unreasoning
unrelenting
unremitting
unshrinking
varsovienne
victualling
viridescent
virilescent
wainscoting
watchmaking
waterskiing
wellmeaning
wellwishing
widdershins
wildcatting
wildfowling
winegrowing
winetasting
wirenetting
wirepulling
wiretapping
withershins
woodcarving
woodcutting
worshipping
abbreviator
abomination
abstraction
abstriction
accelerator
acceptation
acclamation
acclimation
accumulator
acetylation
acidulation
acquisition
acumination
adjudicator
adulterator
adumbration
aerostation
aestivation
affectation
affiliation
affirmation
affrication
aggravation
aggregation
alleviation
altercation
alternation
ambiversion
ameliorator
anacoluthon
annihilator
annunciator
anticipator
antineutron
antiquation
appellation
application
appreciator
approbation
arbitration
archdukedom
articulator
asphyxiator
assentation
assignation
assimilator
association
atomisation
attenuation
attestation
attribution
benediction
benefaction
bifurcation
bipartition
blackfellow
boardschool
bombilation
bombination
botheration
brachiation
branchiopod
brotherhood
bulletproof
byeelection
calcination
calculation
calibration
calumniator
captivation
carbonation
carburetion
carburettor
castigation
celebration
cementation
cerebration
cholesterol
Christendom
circulation
clothesprop
coadunation
coagulation
coarctation
coeducation
coextension
coinheritor
colligation
collimation
collocation
colouration
combination
commendator
commentator
commination
comminution
commutation
compensator
competition
compilation
composition
compotation
compression
compunction
compurgator
computation
conciliator
condonation
confiscator
confliction
confutation
congelation
conjugation
conjunction
conjuration
connotation
consecrator
consecution
conservator
consolation
conspirator
constitutor
constrictor
constructor
consummator
consumption
continuator
contraction
contraption
contributor
conurbation
convocation
convolution
cooperation
coordinator
corporation
correlation
corrugation
coruscation
counterblow
counterplot
crenulation
crepitation
crimination
crucifixion
culmination
cultivation
cupellation
cybernation
deactivator
debarkation
decantation
decelerator
declamation
declaration
declination
decollation
decussation
defalcation
deflagrator
defloration
defoliation
deformation
deglutition
degradation
degustation
dehydration
deification
delectation
delineation
demarcation
demarkation
denigration
denominator
denunciator
deoxidation
depopulator
deportation
depravation
deprecation
depreciator
depredation
deprivation
dereliction
desalinator
description
desecration
desiccation
designation
desperation
destination
destitution
destruction
detestation
deuteration
devaluation
devastation
diatessaron
dicotyledon
diffraction
dilapidator
dinnerwagon
disaccustom
discerption
disfunction
disillusion
disinfector
disjunction
dislocation
disposition
disputation
dissertator
dissipation
dissolution
distinction
distraction
distributor
divulgation
drawingroom
dualcontrol
duplication
dysfunction
edification
ejaculation
elaboration
elicitation
elimination
elucidation
elutriation
emancipator
emasculator
embarkation
embrocation
enchiridion
encystation
endoskelton
enneahedron
enucleation
enumeration
enunciation
equivocator
eradication
euchologion
evagination
evaporation
exaggerator
examination
exclamation
excoriation
exculpation
exfoliation
exhortation
exoneration
exoskeleton
expatiation
expectation
explanation
explication
exploration
exportation
expurgation
exsiccation
extenuation
extirpation
extradition
extrication
fabrication
fascination
fecundation
fimbriation
flagellator
fluctuation
fomentation
forestation
forgetmenot
formication
formulation
fornication
fructuation
frustration
fulguration
fulmination
fusillation
fustigation
gemmulation
genuflexion
germination
glomeration
granulation
gratulation
gravitation
greaseproof
gurgitation
habituation
heartsblood
hedgeschool
heldentenor
hibernation
hobbledehoy
horsedoctor
humiliation
hydrocarbon
hydrometeor
hyphenation
hypolimnion
hypotension
icosahedron
idolisation
illuminator
illustrator
imagination
imbrication
immigration
imparkation
impartation
impetration
implication
importation
imprecation
imprecision
inanimation
inattention
inaugurator
incantation
incarnation
incinerator
inclination
inculcation
inculpation
incurvation
indentation
indigestion
indignation
indirection
inebriation
infatuation
infestation
infeudation
infiltrator
information
innervation
innutrition
inoculation
inquisition
inscription
inseminator
insinuation
inspiration
instigation
institution
instruction
insufflator
integration
interaction
interceptor
intercessor
interfusion
interruptor
intimidator
invigilator
invigorator
invultation
irradiation
irretention
itineration
jactitation
Judaisation
kwashiorkor
labefaction
lachrymator
laciniation
lacrimation
lacrymation
laicisation
lamentation

lancination
legislation
liquidation
lixiviation
lubrication
lucubration
luxuriation
machination
malediction
malefaction
malfunction
malposition
manducation
manipulator
mansardroof
manumission
marshmallow
mastication
melanochroi
melioration
mensuration
methylation
metrication
micturition
miscreation
molestation
morningroom
mountaintop
murmuration
musculation
negotiation
nictitation
nomenclator
nuncupation
obfuscation
objurgation
obscuration
obsecration
observation
obstruction
obtestation
occultation
officialdom
officiation
oppugnation
orientation
origination
oscillation
ostentation
overdevelop
oviposition
oxygenation
ozonisation
pacificator
palpitation
parturition
passivation
patternshop
peccadillos
pectination
penetration
pentahedron
peptisation
percolation
perennation
perforation
permutation
perpetrator
perpetuator
persecution
personation
photoperiod
phytosterol
picturebook
pollination
ponderation
postulation
predecessor
predication
preelection
preignition
prelibation
premonition
preparation
preposition
preselector
presumption
preterition
procreation
procuration
profanation
progression
prohibition
promulgator
propagation
prophethood
propitiator
proposition
prorogation
prosecution
prostitutor
prostration
protraction
provocation
psychomotor
publication
pullulation
punctuation
purificator
pussywillow
pustulation
quadrillion
quintillion
radiocarbon
rapscallion
rarefaction
realisation
reanimation
reapportion
reassertion
recantation
reclamation
recognition
recondition
redirection
reeducation
reformation
regenerator
reification
reinsertion
reiteration
rejuvenator
reluctation
remunerator
repartition
replication
reprobation
repudiation
requisition
reservation
resignation
respiration
restitution
restoration
restriction
retaliation
retardation
retribution
retroaction
revaluation
rubefaction
rubrication
rustication
sacculation
scattergood
segregation
selfcontrol
selfopinion
selfreproof
septentrion
serrulation
servicebook
sheetanchor
showerproof
shrinkproof
sittingroom
smokingroom
solifluxion
solmisation
songsparrow
speculation
spermatozoa
sporulation
stagflation
statutebook
sternutator
stimulation
stipulation
stoolpigeon
stridulator
stylisation
subarration
subaudition
subdivision
subjugation
sublimation
subornation
subrogation
subsumption
subtraction
suffixation
suffocation
supervision
supposition
suppression
suppuration
surrogation
suspiration
susurration
synchrotron
syncopation
syndication
tabefaction
termination
tetrahedron
thingumabob
titillation
tittivation
totalisator
tourbillion
trafficator
transaction
transection
transfixion
transfusion
translation
trepanation
trepidation
tribulation
trituration
tumefaction
turbination
unification
utilisation
vaccination
vacillation
vacuolation
valediction
variegation
vasodilator
vasopressor
vaticinator
venesection
venisection
ventilation
vermination
vindication
vituperator
vivisection
vociferator
waitingroom
wheelbarrow
whistlestop
widowerhood
witchdoctor
witenagemot
xanthochroi
zooplankton
allelomorph
bumblepuppy
cardiograph
choreograph
chronograph
chronoscope
contretemps
corbiesteps
coronagraph
coronograph
cryotherapy
cryptograph
electrotype
epidiascope
fluoroscope
fluoroscopy
gastroscope
guttersnipe
heterotroph
kinetograph
kinetoscope
Kulturkampf
lycanthrope
lycanthropy
metoposcopy
misanthrope
misanthropy
muttonchops
nondescript
platinotype
polariscope
pseudograph
pseudomorph
psychograph
retinoscopy
seismograph
seismoscope
shadowgraph
shocktroops
stereograph
stereoscope
stereoscopy
stethoscope
stethoscopy
stevengraph
stormtroops
stroboscope
superscript
thaumatrope
thermograph
thermoscope
thwartships
ablutionary
abracadabra
acclamatory
acinaciform
acupuncture
affirmatory
agriculture
alkalimetry
alleviatory
anniversary
antiphonary
applicatory
appogiatura
approbatory
aquaculture
aquiculture
arthrospore
bacilliform
backcountry
bathysphere
beaverboard
benedictory
beneficiary
bersaglieri
bibliolatry
bicentenary
billionaire
bimillenary
bladderwort
bonbonniere
boutonniere
boysenberry
brahmaputra
bridgeboard
bristleworm
butcherbird
cabbageworm
calefactory
calorimetry
candidature
candleberry
carabiniere
carabinieri
caravansary
celebratory
centreboard
chancellery
chancellory
charlatanry
chaulmoogra
chiaroscuro
chickenwire
chokecherry
chronometry
circulatory
codicillary
colorimetry
combinatory
comminatory
compotatory
comstockery
concubinary
condolatory
condottiere
condottieri
conjuncture
consolatory
contracture
coparcenary
cosignatory
cotemporary
counterfort
countermark
countermure
counterpart
counterturn
counterwork
craniometry
criminatory
cryosurgery
declamatory
declaratory
demagoguery
demonolatry
denigratory
deprecatory
depredatory
dipterocarp
disjuncture
displeasure
dissymmetry
divestiture
divisionary
doctrinaire
documentary
domiciliary
doubleentry
dynamometry
earthenware
edificatory
ejaculatory
elucidatory
entablature
evidentiary
exclamatory
exculpatory
exdirectory
exhortatory
expatiatory
expenditure
explanatory
explicatory
exploratory
expurgatory
extemporary
extenuatory
extirpatory
fasciaboard
filamentary
fingerboard
foreclosure
forevermore
fractionary
fragmentary
freemasonry
fulminatory
functionary
furthermore
gallimaufry
gallowsbird
gimcrackery
goldenberry
grandiflora
gratulatory
grotesquery
halfmeasure
harpsichord
heterospory
housewifery
huckleberry
humiliatory
hummingbird
hurryscurry
hurryskurry
hydrosphere
hymenoptera
impetratory
imprecatory
incantatory
inculpatory
incurvature
informatory
insectivore
inspiratory
intercalary
interlunary
investiture
involuntary
ironmongery
isogeotherm
journeywork
kitchenware
lacrimatory
lacrymatory
lamellicorn
lamelliform
latticework
legionnaire
legislature
lepidoptera
ligamentary
lithosphere
louverboard
louvreboard

lowpressure
maledictory
manducatory
manufactory
manufacture
masticatory
melanophore
milliampere
millionaire
mockingbird
molendinary
monoculture
mortarboard
musculature
negotiatory
nondelivery
noticeboard
nutcrackers
obfuscatory
objurgatory
observatory
octingenary
ommatophore
orthocentre
oscillatory
ostracoderm
overmeasure
ozonosphere
paddleboard
passeriform
patelliform
perfunctory
petitionary
phalanstery
photosphere
picturecard
planisphere
plasterwork
playingcard
plectoptera
ploughshare
polarimetry
poltroonery
pomiculture
portraiture
pourparlers
predicatory
preliminary
premonitory
preparatory
procuratory
profanatory
progeniture
prohibitory
proprietary
protonotary
psychometry
purpresture
questionary
reactionary
recognitory
reconnoitre
rediscovery
reformatory
reprobatory
respiratory
restructure
retaliatory
retardatory
retributory
revisionary
rhombohedra
rotogravure
rudimentary
salmonberry
scalariform
scalpriform
schoolboard
scratchwork
sculduddery
sculduggery
sedimentary
seditionary
seismometry
selfculture
selfmastery
selfsupport
selftorture
sericulture
shopsteward
shovelboard
skulduddery
skulduggery
sleeveboard
smorgasbord
snowleopard
splashboard
springboard
stereometry
stichometry
stipendiary
stipulatory
stormcentre
stringboard
stringybark
subaxillary
subcategory
subcontrary
substandard
sulphurwort
superlunary
supersedure
supervisory
suppository
swallowwort
switchboard
sycophantry
tapemeasure
taratantara
teeterboard
tegumentary
temperature
tenementary
theretofore
thermometry
thitherward
thunderbird
transfigure
translunary
trapeziform
trelliswork
trestlework
troposphere
typefoundry
ultramodern
unigeniture
unnecessary
valedictory
vasculiform
vestryclerk
vindicatory
viniculture
viticulture
volitionary
weatherworn
weltschmerz
whigmaleery
whitherward
winterberry
abortionist
absenteeism
abusiveness
academicism
accessorise
acclimatise
accompanist
accoucheuse
achromatise
achromatism
adiaphorism
adoptianism
adoptianist
adoptionism
adoptionist
adventuress
adventurism
adventurist
adverseness
advisedness
affranchise
agnosticism
agrarianism
aimlessness
airlessness
airsickness
allopathist
alphabetise
amativeness
Americanise
Americanism
Americanist
amiableness
amorousness
anachronism
ancientness
Anglicanism
anthologise
anthologist
anxiousness
apotheosise
aquarellist
archdiocese
archduchess
arduousness
Arminianism
arterialise
artillerist
artlessness
assuredness
astigmatism
athleticism
audibleness
audiologist
austereness
autoerotism
awesomeness
awkwardness
balefulness
barrelhouse
bashfulness
battledress
bearishness
beastliness
belatedness
betweenness
biliousness
bimetallism
bimetallist
bittercress
blackgrouse
blessedness
blotchiness
blunderbuss
bohemianism
Bonapartism
Bonapartist
bookishness
boorishness
bottleglass
breadthwise
breathalyse
bristliness
Britishness
brittleness
brusqueness
brutishness
bullishness
butteriness
Byzantinism
Byzantinist
cabbagerose
caddishness
callousness
cannibalise
cannibalism
capableness
captionless
carefulness
catchphrase
catheterise
catholicise
Catholicism
cavalierism
chafingdish
chevalglass
chiropodist
chloroplast
Christmassy
chromoplast
chrysoprase
churchiness
circularise
civilianise
cleanliness
clericalism
clericalist
coffeehouse
cognateness
colonialism
colonialist
comfortless
commonsense
communalise
communalism
communalist
compactness
comparatist
complexness
computerise
conciseness
conductress
consumerism
contrabasso
controversy
copiousness
cordialness
corporatism
correctness
corruptness
cosmogonist
cosmologist
costiveness
cottongrass
courtliness
crabbedness
creationism
creationist
criminalist
crookedness
crunchiness
crystallise
cunningness
curableness
curiousness
currentness
currishness
cursiveness
cursoriness
customhouse
decarbonise
decarburise
decolourise
deemphasise
defenceless
demagnetise
demagoguism
demigoddess
democratise
democratism
deoxyribose
depauperise
desensitise
desexualise
determinism
determinist
detribalise
deviousness
devotedness
diachronism
dichotomise
dichotomist
didacticism
diffuseness
diluvialist
diplomatise
diplomatist
disafforest
discourtesy
disinterest
disorganise
distinguish
disunionist
divisionism
doggishness
dolefulness
dollishness
doltishness
donnishness
doublecross
doughtiness
drouthiness
drunkenness
dualpurpose
dubiousness
durableness
dutifulness
earnestness
earthliness
easternmost
eclecticism
ecumenicism
elbowgrease
elderliness
electrolyse
elusiveness
emblematise
emblematist
emotionless
emulousness
emulsionise
enchantress
endlessness
enfranchise
enviousness
epigraphist
equableness
equilibrist
Erastianism
esotericism
Esperantist
etherealise
ethnologist
etymologise
etymologist
eudaemonism
eudaemonist
Europeanise
evasiveness
eventualise
exhaustless
exotericism
extemporise
exteriorise
externalise
externalism
extremeness
facsimilist
factualness
faddishness
familiarise
farawayness
farthermost
fatefulness
fatuousness
favouritism
fearfulness
featherless
featureless
feelingness
fidgetiness
fingerglass
finicalness
flabbergast
flaccidness
flavourless
fleshliness
flightiness
floweriness
foolishness
foppishness
foreignness
foretopmast
foreverness
forgiveness
forlornness
formularise
forwardness
fractionise
franticness
fretfulness
friableness
frowardness
frowstiness
fulsomeness
funambulist
furthermost
furtiveness
gainfulness
gallantness
Gallicanism
gangsterism
gaseousness
gemmologist
genealogise
genealogist
genteelness
genuineness
ghastliness
ghostliness
gibbousness
girlishness
glaringness
godlessness
gourmandise
gourmandism
gracileness
gradualness
graphicness
gristliness
grouchiness
guardedness
gutlessness
gutturalise
gutturalism
gyrocompass
haggardness
hagiologist
hairstylist
haplessness
harbourless
harmfulness
hatefulness
haughtiness
healthiness

hedgepriest
heedfulness
Hegelianism
heinousness
hellishness
helpfulness
heptarchist
hermeticism
heteroecism
hexametrist
Hibernicism
hideousness
hierarchism
highbrowism
hirsuteness
Hispanicise
Hispanicism
Hispanicist
histologist
historicise
historicism
historicist
histrionism
hoggishness
hollandaise
hooliganism
hopefulness
horseradish
hospitalise
hugeousness
hurriedness
hurtfulness
hydrologist
hydromedusa
hyperbolise
hypostatise
hypothenuse
hypothesise
ignobleness
illusionism
illusionist
immanentism
immanentist
immenseness
immortalise
imperialise
imperialism
imperialist
IndoChinese
inexactness
infantilism
inheritress
insipidness
intenseness
intercourse
interiorise
internalise
intersperse
intuitivism
invalidness
irksomeness
irredentism
irredentist
isochronism
isomorphism
jealousness
joylessness
knavishness
knowingness
landlordism
languidness
lastingness
lawlessness
learnedness
lengthiness
letterpress
libertinism
limitedness
limnologist
lissomeness
literalness
lithotomise
lithotomist
lithotripsy
loathliness
logicalness
logomachist
loutishness
lovableness
lumpishness
lustfulness
Lutheranism
madrigalist
maintopmast
malapropism
mammalogist
mandolinist
Manichaeism
mannishness
marchioness
marginalise
masculinise
massiveness
materialise
materialism
materialist
mawkishness
McCarthyism
meadowgrass
meaningless
measureless
mediateness
medievalism
medievalist
memorialise
memorialist
merchandise
metastasise
Micawberish
Micawberism
middleclass
mindfulness
miniaturise
miniaturist
minuteglass
miserliness
monasticism
monologuise
monologuist
mooringmast
movableness
mundaneness
musicalness
mutableness
mycophagist
mythologise
mythologist
mythopoeist
nailvarnish
nationalise
nationalism
nationalist
naturalness
naughtiness
necrologist
needfulness
negationist
nervousness
neurologist
neuroticism
nightmarish
nitrogenise
noisomeness
nonetheless
nonunionist
notableness
nothingness
notionalist
novelettish
noxiousness
numismatist
nympholepsy
objectivism
objectivist
obliqueness
obscureness
obviousness
odorousness
oenophilist
offenceless
officialese
officialism
oldwomanish
ominousness
onerousness
operoseness
ophiologist
opportunism
opportunist
optometrist
orderliness
orientalise
orientalism
orientalist
orthopedist
osteologist
outwardness
packingcase
paediatrist
painfulness
pantomimist
parachutist
parallelism
parametrise
passiveness
pastoralism
pastoralist
paternalism
paternalist
pathologist
paunchiness
peevishness
Pelagianism
pensionless
pensiveness
perfectness
personalise
personalism
personalist
pestologist
petrologist
pettishness
phagocytise
phagocytose
phantasiast
phariseeism
phenologist
philatelist
philologist
phonologist
phosphorism
photofinish
phycologist
phylogynist
phytologist
phytotomist
pigeonchest
piggishness
pinkishness
piteousness
pitifulness
plagioclase
playfulness
plebeianise
plebeianism
pleinairist
pleochroism
pliableness
plicateness
pointedness
pointillism
pointillist
poltergeist
pompousness
porterhouse
portionless
portraitist
powderflask
preachiness
precentress
preceptress
preciseness
prickliness
primitivism
privateness
probabilism
probabilist
prochronism
prodigalise
profaneness
profuseness
prognathism
progressism
progressist
prosaicness
proselytise
proselytism
protagonist
protectress
prudishness
Prussianise
Prussianism
purposeless
pushfulness
Pythagorism
queenliness
quitchgrass
racketpress
radicalness
radiologist
raffishness
rationalise
rationalism
rationalist
raucousness
raunchiness
reactionist
reddishness
reestablish
regionalise
regionalism
regionalist
relatedness
relationism
relationist
religionise
religionism
religionist
remorseless
repleteness
restfulness
restiveness
retiredness
revisionism
revisionist
rheotropism
rhinologist
ribbongrass
riotousness
roentgenise
roguishness
romanticise
romanticism
romanticist
roundedness
ruinousness
saddlehorse
Sadduceeism
saintliness
Sanskritist
saplessness
savouriness
saxophonist
schismatise
schoolhouse
ScotchIrish
scragginess
scrappiness
scrimpiness
scruffiness
scurvygrass
seasickness
secondclass
selfishness
semanticist
semiellipse
Septembrist
seriousness
sexlessness
shadowiness
shallowness
shapeliness
shelterless
shepherdess
shrubbiness
shutterless
sickishness
sightliness
silveriness
sincereness
singularise
sinistrorse
sinlessness
sinuousness
sizableness
skeletonise
sketchiness
skilfulness
slavishness
Slavonicise
slenderness
Socinianism
sociologist
soliloquise
soliloquist
solutionist
somatoplasm
songfulness
Soroptimist
sottishness
soulfulness
Southernism
sparingness
spatterdash
spectatress
spinsterish
springhouse
springiness
squalidness
squashiness
squeakiness
standardise
standoffish
starchiness
stateliness
staunchless
staunchness
steeplebush
stenotypist
stiltedness
stoicalness
straightish
strangeness
streakiness
stringiness
studiedness
stuntedness
stylishness
suasiveness
sublimeness
suburbanise
succourless
suckingfish
summariness
summerhouse
sunlessness
superimpose
superioress
supremacist
supremeness
surgeonfish
swarthiness
swinishness
synchromesh
synchronise
synchronism
syndicalism
syndicalist
systematise
systematism
systematist
tautologise
tautologism
tautomerism
taxidermist
tearfulness
tediousness
teetotalism
teleologism
teleologist
telepathise
telepathist
telephonist
tenableness
tenuousness
Teutonicism
textureless
theosophist
thirstiness
thoughtless
threadiness
thriftiness
throatiness
thunderless
tobacconist
tobogganist
trafficless
treacliness
tricksiness
triggerfish
trimorphism
tritagonist
trivialness
trophoblast
trouserless
tuberculise
tuberculose
tunableness
tunefulness
typicalness
unawareness
unbeknownst
uncanniness
uncleanness
uncouthness
underexpose
ungodliness
unhappiness
uniformness
unmanliness
unquietness
unsoundness
unusualness
uprightness

uselessness
vacationist
vacuousness
vagabondise
vagabondish
vagabondism
valiantness
variousness
vascularise
vasectomise
velvetiness
verboseness
vichyssoise
viciousness
victualless
viscountess
viscousness
visibleness
voguishness
volubleness
voluntarism
voluntarist
waggishness
waitinglist
wakefulness
waspishness
watercourse
waywardness
wealthiness
weatherwise
weightiness
Weismannism
welcomeness
Wesleyanism
westernmost
whitishness
willingness
winningness
winningpost
winsomeness
wishfulness
wistfulness
witlessness
womanliness
worldliness
worldlywise
worshipless
xylophonist
zealousness
zestfulness
zoographist
zoomorphism
abnormality
abranchiate
accommodate
acculturate
affectivity
agglomerate
agglutinate
aiguillette
alexandrite
amenability
amicability
amphibolite
annabergite
anteriority
antigravity
apophyllite
appropriate
approximate
aromaticity
assassinate
barbiturate
barleybroth
bellicosity
beneficiate
bicarbonate
bicorporate
bicuspidate
biddability
bisexuality
bloodguilty
bracteolate
breastplate
campanulate
capillarity
carcinomata
cardinalate
caruncul ate
cassiterite
catholicity
cellularity
certificate
chaetognath
chamaephyte
cheesecloth
cinquecento
circularity
clothesmoth
cognitivity
cognoscente
cognoscenti
collaborate
commemorate
commiserate
commonality
communicate
compaginate
concatenate
concentrate
condylomata
confabulate
confederate
conflagrate
conjugality
considerate
consolidate
conspicuity
constellate
consternate
contaminate
contemplate
contorniate
contrariety
coplanarity
copperplate
coppersmith
corbiculate
corporality
corroborate
cosmopolite
cottonmouth
credibility
criminality
criticality
crocidolite
crystallite
culpability
decarbonate
decemvirate
decerebrate
decorticate
decrepitate
defibrinate
demonstrate
denticulate
deoxygenate
depauperate
desegregate
deteriorate
determinate
diaphaneity
directivity
directorate
discalceate
disseminate
dissimilate
dissimulate
domesticate
domesticity
domiciliate
ecumenicity
educability
electricity
electrocute
electrolyte
eligibility
ellipticity
encapsulate
equilibrate
erythrocyte
ethereality
eventuality
exanthemata
exarcerbate
exclusivity
exemplarity
expansivity
expectorate
expostulate
expropriate
exstipulate
exteriority
exterminate
externality
extrapolate
extravagate
extravasate
fallibility
familiarity
farcicality
fasciculate
feasibility
fingerplate
firstfruits
fissiparity
flamboyante
flannelette
flexibility
folliculate
fractionate
franklinite
funambulate
functionate
gametophyte
gesticulate
globularity
grandiosity
granularity
granulocyte
greenockite
guesstimate
gullibility
habiliments
hairbreadth
hallucinate
handbreadth
haustellate
Hepplewhite
heteroclite
historicity
homogeneity
horripilate
hospitality
houselights
hydrogenate
hypothecate
illiquidity
immarginate
immortality
impassivity
impedimenta
impenetrate
imperforate
impersonate
impetuosity
importunate
importunity
impropriate
impropriety
incarcerate
incardinate
incommodity
incongruity
incorporate
incredulity
incriminate
incuriosity
individuate
inedibility
inferiority
infertility
informality
ingurgitate
insalubrity
insincerity
instability
integrality
intemperate
intercalate
intergrowth
interiority
internality
interpolate
interrelate
interrogate
intrepidity
intriguante
investigate
inviability
involucrate
itacolumite
kitchenette
landaulette
laudability
launderette
lesemajesty
longanimity
machicolate
macrogamete
madreporite
magnanimity
maisonnette
mandarinate
mandibulate
marginality
margraviate
marquessate
marquisette
masculinity
materiality
matriculate
menservants
meprobamate
microgamete
miscegenate
miscibility
misestimate
molybdenite
Monophysite
Monothelite
monstrosity
moribundity
moveability
muscularity
nationality
nationstate
necessitate
nephelinite
nettlecloth
nickelplate
nittygritty
nulliparity
objectivity
oligochaete
opportunity
oracularity
orchestrate
originality
osteoplasty
palpability
participate
particulate
passibility
peccability
peculiarity
pedicellate
pedunculate
pellucidity
penicillate
peninsulate
pentathlete
pentlandite
penultimate
perambulate
perchlorate
peregrinate
periodicity
peristalith
perseverate
personality
perspicuity
pertinacity
phantasmata
phosphorate
phosphorite
physicality
placability
pococurante
pomegranate
ponderosity
pontificate
portability
possibility
precipitate
predominate
prematurity
premeditate
prenominate
prevaricate
probability
prodigality
proliferate
prolificity
promiscuity
propinquity
punctuality
pupillarity
pyrargyrite
rateability
ratiocinate
rationality
readability
recalculate
receptivity
reciprocate
reciprocity
recriminate
reduplicate
refrigerate
regurgitate
reincarnate
reintegrate
reliability
religiosity
remonstrate
renegotiate
reorientate
resistivity
resuscitate
retentivity
retranslate
revaccinate
revendicate
reverberate
rifacimenti
rifacimento
rubicundity
saddlecloth
saleability
sansculotte
satiability
schistosity
scintillate
scuttlebutt
selectivity
semipalmate
sensibility
sensitivity
sequestrate
serendipity
seventeenth
sheriffalty
sillimanite
silverplate
silversmith
sinfonietta
singularity
smithsonite
sociability
solvability
sovereignty
specificity
spectrality
spermaphyte
spessartite
spifflicate
spiraculate
spiritualty
spirochaete
spongecloth
spontaneity
stellionate
sternsheets
stockinette
strangulate
strenuosity
subordinate
suburbanite
suffragette
suffumigate
suitability
sumptuosity
superfluity
superiority
superstrata
syllabicity
taciturnity
tameability
tangibility
temporality
tensibility
tentaculate
testability
tetrarchate
thenceforth
thereabouts
thrombocyte
toxophilite
trabeculate
transfinite
translocate
triangulate
triumvirate
tuberculate
tuttifrutti
twelvemonth
uncertainty
undergrowth
unfortunate
unguiculate
uninucleate
unipolarity
urochordate

valleculate
variability
vascularity
vendibility
vermiculate
vermiculite
versatility
verticality
vesuvianite
vibratility
viceroyalty
vinaigrette
vincibility
volcanicity
vulcanicity
washability
whereabouts
workability
abstentious
acarpellous
acclivitous
acrimonious
adenomatous
adventurous
altocumulus
altostratus
amentaceous
amplexicaul
anachronous
androgynous
anfractuous
antependium
antheridium
antimonious
antirrhinum
arbitrageur
arboraceous
arenicolous
aspergillum
aspergillus
aspersorium
atrabilious
bacciferous
bashibazouk
bergamasque
bicephalous
billetsdoux
bimillenium
blasphemous
borborygmus
brachyurous
burglarious
butyraceous
cacophonous
calcicolous
calciferous
calcifugous
californium
canaliculus
candelabrum
carnivorous
catadromous
ceremonious
chainarmour
champertous
chartaceous
Clarencieux
clostridium
coconscious
columbarium
compendious
condominium
congenerous
connoisseur
conspicuous
contentious
contrarious
convolvulus
corniferous
corrigendum
coterminous
crematorium
cruciferous
crucigerous
crustaceous
cupriferous
cypripedium
cysticercus
declivitous
definiendum
deleterious
dentigerous
desideratum
diadelphous
dicephalous
dichogamous
dichotomous
diplococcus
discontinue
discotheque
disgraceful
distasteful
distressful
distrustful
duplicitous
efficacious
einsteinium
emmenagogue
endocardium
endometrium
endophagous
endothelium
enterovirus
epigastrium
epipetalous
equilibrium
erotogenous
expeditious
farinaceous
farraginous
ferriferous
ferruginous
filamentous
fissiparous
flirtatious
floriferous
florilegium
franctireur
fricandeaux
frigidarium
frugivorous
furunculous
gametangium
gemmiferous
gemmiparous
gigantesque
grammalogue
granivorous
gypsiferous
halophilous
harumscarum
hemipterous
heptamerous
herbivorous
hesperidium
hippocampus
homogeneous
homophonous
homopterous
homosporous
hydrogenous
ichthyosaur
ignominious
illustrious
impecunious
incongruous
incredulous
incunabulum
indeciduous
industrious
injudicious
inofficious
inquilinous
insectarium
Interlingua
intermedium
interosseus
interregnum
intravenous
irreligious
isochronous
isomorphous
lactiferous
lateritious
latifundium
laurustinus
lentiginous
leprosarium
ligamentous
litterateur
magazinegun
magisterium
magnanimous
marketvalue
mediastinum
megatherium
meliphagous
melliferous
mellifluous
membraneous
mendelevium
meritorious
micrococcus
mischievous
misconstrue
mistrustful
mitrailleur
monocarpous
monochasium
monoclinous
monophagous
monopterous
monseigneur
morbiferous
mountainous
multicolour
multiparous
myelomatous
necessitous
nitrogenous
noctivagous
nonsequitur
nulliparous
odoriferous
oligomerous
omnifarious
ophidiarium
opprobrious
ornithosaur
overanxious
ozoniferous
pandemonium
papyraceous
paramoecium
pelargonium
penicillium
pentagynous
pentamerous
pentandrous
pericardium
pericranium
perineurium
perithecium
perspicuous
pestiferous
phosphonium
phosphorous
picturesque
piperaceous
piscivorous
planetarium
platearmour
plateresque
polyandrous
polycarpous
polyonymous
polyphagous
polyphonous
polyzoarium
positronium
precautious
precipitous
prestigious
pretentious
primiparous
prognathous
proliferous
promiscuous
prothallium
provocateur
pruriginous
punctilious
quadrennium
repetitious
reproachful
resourceful
retinaculum
rhizanthous
rhizomatous
rhomboideus
rumbustious
Sagittarius
sanguineous
saponaceous
saprogenous
sarcomatous
sarcophagus
sauropodous
scalearmour
schizanthus
scoriaceous
scribacious
scriptorium
scrumptious
sententious
septenarius
septiferous
serpiginous
solanaceous
somniculous
somniferous
spathaceous
sphaeridium
spiniferous
splendorous
spontaneous
sporogenous
sporogonium
stegosaurus
straightcut
stramineous
stylopodium
succedaneum
sulphureous
superfluous
suspenseful
syllabarium
sympetalous
symphonious
synchronous
talentscout
tautologous
tautonymous
teaspoonful
teknonymous
temerarious
tempestuous
tendencious
tendentious
termitarium
terraqueous
terricolous
terrigenous
tetramerous
tetrapodous
threecolour
thuriferous
Titianesque
treacherous
trimorphous
tripetalous
triphibious
triphyllous
triquetrous
tristichous
tuberculous
tyrannosaur
ulotrichous
unambiguous
unconscious
unrighteous
urticaceous
urticarious
ventriculus
ventriloquy
verdantique
vertiginous
vortiginous
watercolour
xenophilous
xeranthemum
xerophilous
xylocarpous
xylophagous
abstractive
acquisitive
adumbrative
adversative
affirmative
affricative
aggregative
alleviative
alternative
altorelievo
altorilievo
appellative
applicative
arbitrative
argumentive
associative
assortative
attributive
Bodhisattva
calculative
carminative
circulative
circumvolve
coextensive
colligative
combinative
commutative
comparative
competitive
compositive
compressive
conflictive
confutative
conjugative
conjunctiva
conjunctive
connotative
consecutive
consumptive
contractive
contrastive
cooperative
corporative
correlative
countermove
criminative
declarative
deprecative
descriptive
desiccative
destructive
diapositive
disjunctive
dispositive
dissipative
distinctive
distractive
duplicative
elaborative
eliminative
elucidative
enumerative
enunciative
eradicative
evaporative
exfoliative
exhortative
exonerative
expatiative
expectative
explicative
explorative
facultative
galleyslave
germinative
gravitative
hyperactive
imaginative
implicative
inattentive
indigestive
ineffective
inexpensive
informative
inoculative
inoffensive
inoperative
inquisitive
inscriptive
insensitive
insinuative
instigative
instinctive
instructive
integrative
interactive
irradiative
irremissive
irretentive
legislative
lubricative
makebelieve
maladaptive
meliorative
microgroove
misconceive
nuncupative
obstructive
originative
penetrative
perforative
personative
perspective
photoactive
preconceive
predicative
preparative
prepositive
prerogative
presumptive

procreative
progressive
prohibitive
propagative
prospective
protractive
provocative
qualitative
radioactive
rarefactive
rebarbative
recognitive
reformative
reiterative
reprobative
restorative
restrictive
retaliative
retardative
retributive
retroactive
safetyvalve
segregative
shirtsleeve
speculative
stimulative
subjunctive
substantive
subsumptive
subtractive
suffocative
superlative
suppositive
suppressive
suppurative
swallowdive
temperative
terminative
unassertive
unobtrusive
unselective
ventilative
vindicative
reachmedown
sparrowhawk
thistledown
unorthodoxy
artiodactyl
breadthways
chrysoberyl
leptodactyl
pentadactyl
protomartyr
pterodactyl
tetradactyl
coleorrhiza
quickfreeze

---

abracadabra
agoraphobia
albuminuria
amenorrhoea
amphisbaena
anaesthesia
anglophobia
antonomasia
appogiatura
assafoetida
bacchanalia
bibliomania
bibliotheca
Bodhisattva
bradycardia
brahmaputra
calceolaria
carcinomata
chaulmoogra
christiania
cochinchina
coleorrhiza
collectanea
collenchyma
condylomata
conjunctiva
counterplea
cryptomeria
cyclopaedia
cyclothymia
differentia
diverticula
epithalamia
epithelioma
exanthemata
Francomania
Gallophobia
gentianella
globigerina
glossolalia
grandiflora
guttapercha
haemophilia
Hagiographa
hebephrenia
hemeralopia
hemianopsia
hibernacula
hydromedusa
hydrophobia
hymenoptera
hyperphagia
hyperplasia
hypnopaedia
hypothermia
hypsophobia
impedimenta
Interlingua
ipecacuanha
kleptomania
lepidoptera
megalomania
melancholia
memorabilia
miscellanea
necrophilia
negrophobia
nyctophobia
nymphomania
orthodontia
paedophilia
paronomasia
passacaglia
phantasmata
photophobia
plectoptera
pleurodynia
prolegomena
prosenchyma
prothalamia
pseudopodia
psychedelia
psychodrama
quinquennia
receptacula
rhombohedra
Russophobia
saintpaulia
sanguinaria
scleroderma
scyphistoma
selaginella
septicaemia
sinfonietta
somatotonia
spermatozoa
steatopygia
subumbrella
superstrata
tachycardia
taratantara
toxicomania
thingumabob
abiogenetic
acatalectic
achondritic
acidophilic
Aeneolithic
aeolotropic
aerodynamic
AfroAsiatic
agoraphobic
algorithmic
allomorphic
amphimictic
anacreontic
anaesthetic
anarchistic
anastomotic
anemometric
anglomaniac
anglophobic
anisotropic
anomalistic
anthracitic
antipyretic
antiSemitic
aphrodisiac
apocalyptic
aponeurotic
apostrophic
archangelic
Areopagitic
atmospheric
audiometric
autographic
autoplastic
autotrophic
BaltoSlavic
batholithic
bathymetric
bibliopegic
bibliopolic
biocoenotic
biquadratic
blastogenic
cabbalistic
cacographic
calisthenic
Calvinistic
cantharidic
carbocyclic
cataclysmic
cataplectic
catechistic
ceroplastic
chalcedonic
chameleonic
charismatic
chemotactic
chronologic
cisatlantic
climacteric
clinometric
communistic
conspecific
coulometric
cryptogamic
cyclopaedic
cyclothymic
demographic
dexiotropic
dialogistic
diamagnetic
diaphoretic
diastematic
diastrophic
dichromatic
dipsomaniac
disharmonic
dithyrambic
dramaturgic
dyslogistic
econometric
ectoblastic
ectogenetic
ectomorphic
ectoplasmic
ectotrophic
elastomeric
embryologic
encomiastic
endocardiac
endomorphic
endoplasmic
endothermic
endotrophic
epeirogenic
epithalamic
erotomaniac
esemplastic
Eucharistic
eudiometric
euphemistic
feldspathic
fetichistic
fetishistic
feudalistic
formalistic
gastronomic
geomagnetic
geostrophic
geotectonic
glauconitic
gnotobiotic
goniometric
gramophonic
granolithic
granophyric
gravimetric
haemophilic
haemostatic
haggadistic
hagioscopic
harmonistic
hebephrenic
heliometric
heliotropic
Hellenistic
hemimorphic
hemispheric
hermeneutic
heterotypic
Hippocratic
holoblastic
holographic
homeopathic
homeostatic
homocentric
homoestatic
homogenetic
homomorphic
homoplastic
homothallic
Hudibrastic
hydrobromic
hydrocyanic
hydrometric
hydropathic
hydrophilic
hydrophobic
hydrophytic
hydrostatic
hydrotactic
hydrotropic
hygrometric
hygrophytic
hygroscopic
hylozoistic
hypercritic
hypermetric
hypnopompic
hypoblastic
hypogastric
hypsometric
ideographic
idiographic
idiomorphic
immunologic
interatomic
intervallic
ionospheric
isoelectric
ithyphallic
Jansenistic
jargonistic
kymographic
lithophytic
logarithmic
logographic
macrobiotic
macrocosmic
macroscopic
magistratic
manneristic
masochistic
mastodontic
mechanistic
mediumistic
melancholic
meroblastic
mesoblastic
mesomorphic
metacentric
metagenetic
metallurgic
metamorphic
metaplastic
metapsychic
metasomatic
Methodistic
microcosmic
microlithic
micrometric
microphonic
microphytic
microscopic
mithridatic
modernistic
monochromic
monogenetic
monographic
monomorphic
monozygotic
mythomaniac
mythopoetic
narcoleptic
necromantic
necrophilic
neologistic
Neoplatonic
neuropathic
neurotropic
nomographic
nonmetallic
nonspecific
nosographic
nyctitropic
ochlocratic
oestrogenic
ontogenetic
oreographic
orthodontic
orthopaedic
orthoscopic
orthotropic
osteopathic
osteophytic
Ostrogothic
paederastic
Palaearctic
palaeotypic
palindromic
panhellenic
pantheistic
pantothenic
paragraphic
parallactic
paramorphic
paraplectic
parenthetic
pericardiac
peripatetic
perispermic
peristaltic
pessimistic
phagedaenic
philosophic
photometric
photophilic
photophobic
phototactic
phototropic
physiologic
planimetric
plasmolytic
pleiotropic
pleomorphic
pluralistic
plutocratic
polychromic
polygenetic
polyglottic
polygraphic
polymorphic
polytechnic
porphyritic
postclassic
prehistoric
problematic
procephalic
proteolytic
Proterozoic
prothoracic
protophytic
psychedelic
psychiatric
psychogenic
psychologic
pyroclastic
pyrotechnic
radiometric
radiophonic
rhinoscopic
rhizocarpic
ritualistic
saprobiotic
saprophytic
scholiastic
scientistic
seborrhoeic
septicaemic
shamanistic
socialistic
sociometric
sociopathic
solipsistic
somatogenic
somatologic
somatotonic
spherulitic
sphincteric
Spinozistic
spiritistic
spirometric
sporophytic

stalactitic countrified illhumoured rightangled transmitted adolescence
stalagmitic countryfied illmannered righthanded trichomonad adumbrative
staurolitic crenellated illtempered rightminded tricoloured adversative
stereotypic crookbacked impassioned ringstraked truehearted affirmative
subspecific crosslegged intagliated roughfooted unaccounted affranchise
sycophantic crystalloid intentioned roughlegged uncivilised affricative
syllogistic dilapidated interallied scarabaeoid uncluttered agglomerate
symbolistic diphtheroid interbedded scattergood uncommitted agglutinate
sympathetic disaffected interdepend schoolboard unconcealed aggregative
symptomatic disannulled intermitted schoolchild unconcerned agriculture
synergistic disgruntled interplayed selfassured unconnected aiguillette
technologic dishevelled intromitted selfcentred uncontested ailurophile
telegrammic disinclined introverted selfcommand underground ailurophobe
telegraphic disinterred ironhearted selfcreated underhanded alabastrine
telekinetic distempered kindhearted selfdevoted undermanned alexandrine
teratogenic distribuend largeminded selfelected underpinned alexandrite
teratologic doubleedged leapfrogged selfimposed undersigned alleviative
tetracyclic doublefaced leatherhead selfinduced understated allocatable
theocentric downhearted levelheaded selfinvited undeveloped alphabetise
theodolitic elasticated lightfooted selflimited undisguised alternative
theorematic elephantoid lighthanded semiskilled undisturbed amaranthine
therapeutic embryonated lightheaded sentinelled unexploited amazonstone
thermoduric emptyhanded lightminded seventyfold unexpressed ambivalence
thermolytic emptyheaded lilylivered severalfold unfashioned Americanise
thixotropic enlightened lionhearted sharpwitted unfurnished amethystine
topographic ensanguined longsighted shockheaded unicoloured amphetamine
transuranic eurypteroid looselimbed shopsteward uninhabited amphibolite
trisyllabic experienced loudmouthed shorthanded uninhibited annabergite
tritheistic extraverted louverboard shortwinded unkennelled antecedence
troglodytic extroverted louvreboard shoulderpad unmitigated antemundane
typographic fasciaboard lowspirited shovelboard unorganized anthologise
unrealistic featherhead maladjusted sideslipped unpossessed anticathode
Upanishadic felspathoid marriagebed sidestepped unqualified anticyclone
verbalistic fenestrated mentholated sleeveboard unsaturated antistrophe
voltametric fingerboard microsecond sleuthhound unsolicited apomorphine
voodooistic foraminated middlesized smallminded unvarnished apophyllite
xylographic foresighted millisecond smoothfaced unwarranted apotheosise
zygomorphic foulmouthed mockingbird smorgasbord wainscotted appellative
aboveground freehearted monkeybread snowleopard wapperjawed applaudable
affectioned freezedried monogrammed soberminded warmblooded applicative
alembicated frenchified mortarboard softhearted warmhearted appreciable
articulated fullblooded mothernaked softshelled waspwaisted appropriate
bandylegged fullfledged musclebound splashboard watercooled approximate
bassethound fullhearted mustachioed splayfooted waterlogged aquaculture
battlefield fullmouthed nearsighted springboard weakhearted aquiculture
beaverboard gallowsbird netherworld starcrossed wedgeshaped arbitrative
bergschrund geniculated noticeboard starstudded wedgetailed archdiocese
betweenmaid gingerbread nurserymaid stereotyped welladvised arglebargle
bewhiskered goodhearted openhearted stiffnecked wellbeloved argumentive
birdbrained goodnatured openmouthed stoneground welldefined arterialise
blackavised gravelblind operculated straitlaced wellfounded arthrospore
blackcoated haemorrhoid opinionated strikebound wellgroomed articulable
booklearned halfblooded outrivalled stringboard wellordered assassinate
bottlenosed halfhearted outstripped substandard wellrounded assimilable
branchiopod handicapped overcropped sugarcoated whiteheaded associative
brazenfaced handknitted overstepped superabound whitherward assortative
bridgeboard handpainted overstuffed superintend wholesouled attemptable
broadleaved hardhearted paddleboard swellheaded widowerhood attractable
broadminded hardmouthed parallelled swiftfooted wrongheaded attributive
brotherhood harebrained parathyroid switchboard abolishable augmentable
butcherbird harpsichord paratyphoid tabernacled aboutsledge automatable
cancellated heartsblood partitioned tearstained abranchiate bactericide
carburetted heavyfooted pastureland teeterboard absorptance balletomane
castellated heavyhanded pedestalled tessellated abstractive barbastelle
centreboard hedgehopped petticoated thickheaded accessorise barbiturate
chambermaid helminthoid photoperiod thickwitted accipitrine barquentine
chickenfeed heteroploid picturecard thimbleweed acclimatise barrelhouse
chucklehead highpitched playingcard thinskinned accommodate bathyscaphe
cleanlimbed highpowered pocketsized thitherward accoucheuse bathysphere
clearheaded historiated precedented threehanded accountable Benedictine
closefisted hummingbird preoccupied threelegged accrescence beneficence
closehauled hunchbacked prestressed thunderbird acculturate beneficiate
coldblooded hundredfold prophethood thunderhead achromatise benevolence
coldhearted hydraheaded pureblooded tightfisted acidifiable bergamasque
colourblind hyperboloid quickwitted tightlipped acknowledge betweentime
columniated hypocycloid rattlepated toffeenosed acquisitive bibliophile
complicated illaffected readywitted toothbilled acquittance bicarbonate
counterbond illdisposed retroflexed toughminded acriflavine bicorporate
countermand illfavoured ricochetted transferred acupuncture bicuspidate

billionaire
bitterapple
blackbeetle
blackgrouse
bonbonniere
bondservice
bourgeoisie
boutonniere
bracteolate
brankursine
breadthwise
breastplate
breathalyse
buffalorobe
cabbagerose
cabbagetree
calculative
camaraderie
campanulate
candescence
candidature
cannibalise
capacitance
carabiniere
cardinalate
carminative
carpetsnake
caruncluate
cassiterite
catastrophe
catchphrase
catheterise
catholicise
centigramme
centrepiece
certifiable
certificate
chamaephyte
chanterelle
chaperonage
charcuterie
chickenwire
chinoiserie
Chippendale
chloroprene
chrominance
chronoscope
chrysoprase
cinnabarine
circularise
circulative
circumvolve
civilianise
civilisable
clandestine
clothesline
cloudcastle
coalescence
cobblestone
cockaleekie
cockyleekie
coexistence
coextensive
coffeehouse
coffeetable
cognoscente
cognoscible
coincidence
coinsurance
collaborate
collapsible
collectable
collectible
colligative
combinative
combustible
comeuppance
comfortable
commemorate
commendable
commiserate
committable
commonplace
commonsense
communalise
communicate
commutative
compaginate
comparative
compassable
compellable
competitive
complacence
compositive
compossible
compressive
comprisable
computerise
concatenate
concealable
conceivable
concentrate
conceptacle
concordance
concubinage
concurrence
condemnable
condensable
condottiere
conductance
conductible
confabulate
confederate
conferrable
confirmable
confiscable
conflagrate
conflictive
conformable
conformance
confutative
congealable
conjugative
conjunctive
conjuncture
connectable
connectible
connotative
conquerable
consanguine
consecutive
consequence
conservable
considerate
consignable
consistence
consolidate
constellate
consternate
construable
consumptive
containable
contaminate
contemplate
contestable
contingence
continuable
continuance
contorniate
contractile
contractive
contracture
contradance
contrastive
contrivable
contrivance
convenience
conventicle
convergence
conversable
conversance
convertible
convincible
cooperative
copingstone
copperplate
corbiculate
cornerstone
corporative
correctable
correlative
corroborate
corruptible
cosmopolite
countenance
countermine
countermove
countermure
counterpane
countryside
countrywide
criminative
crocidolite
crystalline
crystallise
crystallite
customhouse
cycloserine
deathrattle
decarbonate
decarbonise
decarburise
decemvirate
decerebrate
declarative
decolletage
decolourise
decorticate
decrepitate
decrepitude
deemphasise
defibrinate
delightsome
deliverable
deliverance
demagnetise
democratise
demonstrate
demountable
denticulate
denumerable
deoxygenate
deoxyribose
depauperate
depauperise
deprecative
depressible
depthcharge
descendable
descendible
describable
descriptive
desegregate
desensitise
desexualise
desiccative
despondence
destructive
deteriorate
determinate
detribalise
developable
diapositive
dichotomise
digitigrade
diningtable
dinnerdance
dinnertable
Diophantine
diplomatise
directorate
disassemble
discalceate
discardable
discernible
discontinue
discordance
discotheque
discussable
discussible
disentangle
disjunctive
disjuncture
dislikeable
disorganise
dispensable
displeasure
dispositive
disquietude
disseminate
disseminule
dissimilate
dissimulate
dissipative
dissociable
dissolvable
dissyllable
distensible
distinctive
distractive
disturbance
divestiture
doctrinaire
domesticate
domiciliate
dresscircle
dualpurpose
duplicative
earthenware
elaborative
elbowgrease
electrocute
electrolyse
electrolyte
electrotype
elephantine
eliminative
elucidative
emblematise
embraceable
emmenagogue
emulsionise
encapsulate
encumbrance
enforceable
enfranchise
enlargeable
entablature
enumerative
enunciative
epidiascope
epinephrine
equilibrate
equivalence
eradicative
erubescence
erythrocyte
escheatable
etherealise
etymologise
eucalyptole
Europeanise
evanescence
evaporative
eventualise
exarcerbate
excrescence
exercisable
exfoliative
exhaustible
exhortative
exonerative
exorbitance
expatiative
expectative
expectorate
expenditure
explainable
explicative
exploitable
explorative
expostulate
expressible
expropriate
exstipulate
extemporise
exteriorise
exterminate
externalise
extractable
extrapolate
extravagate
extravasate
facultative
familiarise
fanfaronade
farthingale
fasciculate
fashionable
featheredge
fermentable
fingerplate
fissionable
flamboyance
flamboyante
flannelette
flavoursome
flocculence
florescence
fluoroscope
folliculate
forbearance
forbiddance
foreclosure
foreseeable
forevermore
forfeitable
forgettable
formularise
fortifiable
fractionate
fractionise
Francophile
Francophobe
francophone
franklinite
frankpledge
fraudulence
funambulate
functionate
furtherance
furthermore
furthersome
galleyslave
gallowstree
gametophyte
gartersnake
gastroscope
geanticline
gendarmerie
genealogise
geosyncline
germinative
gesticulate
gigantesque
gourmandise
grammalogue
granulocyte
gravitative
greenockite
guesstimate
guttersnipe
gutturalise
haematocele
haemorrhage
halfmeasure
hallucinate
handgrenade
harvesthome
haustellate
hearthstone
heliochrome
helleborine
Hepplewhite
hereditable
herringbone
heteroclite
Hispanicise
historicise
hollandaise
honeysuckle
hornswoggle
horripilate
hospitalise
husbandlike
hyacinthine
hydrogenate
hydrosphere
hyoscyamine
hyperactive
hyperbolise
hypercharge
hypersthene
hypostatise
hypothecate
hypothenuse
hypothesise
illimitable
illuminable
illuminance
imaginative
immarginate
immedicable
immitigable
immortalise
impeachable
impenetrate
impenitence
imperforate
imperialise
impermeable
impersonate
imperviable
implausible
implicative
importunate
impregnable
impressible
impropriate
impuissance
inadaptable
inadvisable
inalienable
inalterable
inappetence
inattentive
incarcerate
incardinate
incarnadine
incertitude
incoercible
incoherence
incorporate
increasable

incriminate
incurvature
indefinable
indigestive
individuate
indivisible
IndoChinese
indomitable
indubitable
ineffective
ineloquence
ineluctable
inequitable
inescapable
inestimable
inexcusable
inexistence
inexpensive
infanticide
inflammable
informative
infrangible
infrequence
ingratitude
ingurgitate
inhabitable
inheritable
inheritance
innavigable
innumerable
inoculative
inoffensive
inoperative
inopportune
inquisitive
inscribable
inscriptive
inscrutable
insecticide
insectifuge
insectivore
insensitive
inseparable
insinuative
insouciance
instigative
instinctive
instructive
insuperable
integrative
intemperate
interactive
intercalate
interchange
intercourse
interiorise
intermeddle
intermingle
internalise
internecine
interpolate
interrelate
interrogate
intersperse
intertangle
interviewee
intolerable
intolerance
intractable
intriguante
investigate
investiture
involucrate
iridescence
irradiative
irrecusable
irreducible
irrefutable
irrelevance

irremissive
irremovable
irreparable
irresoluble
irretentive
irreverence
irrevocable
itacolumite
justiciable
justifiable
kilocalorie
kinetoscope
kitchenette
kitchenware
knucklebone
lactescence
landaulette
landgravine
launderette
legionnaire
legislative
legislature
liberticide
libertinage
lickspittle
liquefiable
liquescence
lithosphere
lithotomise
loosestrife
lowpressure
lubricative
lycanthrope
machicolate
machinemade
macrogamete
madreporite
maintenance
maisonnette
makebelieve
maladaptive
maleficence
malevolence
malfeasance
malpractice
mandarinate
mandibulate
manipulable
mantelpiece
manufacture
marcescence
marcescible
marginalise
margraviate
marketplace
marketvalue
marlinspike
marquessate
marqueterie
marquisette
masculinise
massproduce
masterpiece
materialise
matriculate
maxillipede
medicinable
melanophore
meliorative
memorialise
meningocele
mentionable
meprobamate
merchandise
mesalliance
metastasise
methylamine
microgamete
microgroove

milliampere
millionaire
miniaturise
misalliance
misanthrope
miscarriage
miscegenate
misconceive
misconstrue
misericorde
misestimate
misfeasance
misguidance
mismarriage
mollycoddle
molybdenite
monkeyshine
monoculture
monologuise
Monophysite
Monothelite
morrisdance
munificence
musculature
muskthistle
mycorrhizae
mythologise
naphthalene
nationalise
nationstate
necessitate
nephelinite
nickelplate
nightingale
nigrescence
nitrogenise
nonchalance
nonfeasance
nonviolence
nonvolatile
nuncupative
obstructive
officialese
oligochaete
ommatophore
omnipotence
omniscience
opalescence
orchestrate
organisable
orientalise
originative
orthocentre
outdistance
overbalance
overindulge
overmeasure
overproduce
ozonosphere
packingcase
palmcabbage
palsgravine
papiermache
paraldehyde
parametrise
paraselenae
participate
particulate
Passiontide
pedicellate
pedunculate
penetrative
penicillate
peninsulate
pensionable
pentathlete
pentazocine
pentlandite
penultimate

perambulate
perceivable
perceptible
perchlorate
percipience
peregrinate
perfectible
perforative
performable
performance
permissible
perpetuance
perseverate
persistence
personalise
personative
perspective
persuadable
persuasible
perturbable
phagocytise
phagocytose
philhellene
phosphorate
phosphorite
photoactive
photosphere
phylloclade
picturesque
pilocarpine
pipistrelle
pitchblende
pivotbridge
plagioclase
plagiostome
planisphere
plantigrade
plateresque
platinotype
platyrrhine
pleasurable
plebeianise
Pleistocene
ploughshare
pocketknife
pococurante
pointdevice
polarisable
polariscope
polypeptide
polystyrene
pomegranate
pomiculture
pontificate
porterhouse
portraiture
practicable
preaudience
precipitate
preconceive
predicative
predictable
predominate
preeminence
premeditate
prenominate
preparative
prepositive
prerogative
presentable
preservable
presumptive
prevaricate
preventable
preventible
procreative
prodigalise
profiterole
progeniture

progressive
prohibitive
proliferate
promptitude
propagative
propitiable
proselytise
prospective
protractile
protractive
protrudable
protrusible
provenience
provocative
Prussianise
publishable
pulchritude
pumicestone
purchasable
purpresture
putrescence
putrescible
pyrargyrite
qualifiable
qualitative
quarrelsome
quartertone
quickchange
quickfreeze
quinquereme
radioactive
rarefactive
ratatouille
ratiocinate
rationalise
rattlesnake
reassurance
rebarbative
recalculate
reciprocate
reclaimable
recognitive
reconnoitre
recoverable
recriminate
rectifiable
redetermine
redoubtable
reduplicate
reemergence
reflectance
reformative
refrangible
refrigerate
regenerable
regionalise
registrable
regrettable
regurgitate
reincarnate
reinsurance
reintegrate
reintroduce
reiterative
rejuvenesce
religionise
remembrance
remonstrate
renaissance
renegotiate
reorientate
replaceable
repleviable
repressible
reprobative
reprogramme
resemblance
respectable
respondence

responsible
restorative
restrictive
restructure
resuscitate
retaliative
retardative
retraceable
retractable
retranslate
retributive
retrievable
retroactive
revaccinate
revendicate
reverberate
rodenticide
rodomontade
roentgenise
romanticise
rotogravure
rottenstone
saddlehorse
safetyvalve
salvageable
sansculotte
satisfiable
schismatise
schistosome
schoolhouse
schottische
scintillate
scopolamine
segregative
seigniorage
seismoscope
selfculture
selfdefence
selffertile
selfservice
selfsterile
selftorture
semiellipse
semipalmate
sequestrate
sericulture
serviceable
serviceline
shacklebone
sheathknife
shirtsleeve
shortchange
signifiable
sillimanite
silverplate
singularise
sinistrorse
skeletonise
Slavonicise
slickenside
slotmachine
smithsonite
snickersnee
soldierlike
soliloquise
specifiable
speculative
spermaphyte
spessartite
spifflicate
spindletree
spiraculate
spirituelle
spirochaete
spreadeagle
springhouse
squarsonage
stagemanage
stampoffice

standardise
stellionate
stereoscope
stethoscope
stimulative
stirrupbone
stockinette
stomachache
stormcentre
strangulate
stretchable
stringpiece
stroboscope
subjunctive
submergence
submersible
submissible
submultiple
subordinate
subsequence
subsistence
substantive
subsumptive
subtractive
suburbanise
suburbanite
suffocative
suffragette
suffumigate
suggestible
summerhouse
supercharge
superimpose
superinduce
superlative
superscribe
supersedure
supersubtle
supportable
suppositive
suppressive
suppurative
surpassable
susceptible
suspensible
sustainable
swallowable
swallowdive
swallowhole
swingletree
switchblade
synchronise
systematise
tagliatelle
tapemachine
tapemeasure
tarnishable
tarradiddle
tautologise
telepathise
temperative
temperature
tentaculate
terminative
tetrarchate
thalidomide
thaumatrope
thaumaturge
theobromine
theretofore
thermophile
thermoscope
thrombocyte
Titianesque
tolbutamide
townspeople
toxophilite
trabeculate
tracasserie
tragedienne
transalpine
transfigure
transfinite
translocate
transmarine
transpadane
transpierce
Trappistine
traversable
treasonable
trestletree
triangulate
trisyllable
triumvirate
troposphere
troublesome
tryingplane
trypanosome
tryptophane
tuberculate
tuberculise
tuberculose
turgescence
tyrannicide
ultramarine
unalterable
unassertive
unavailable
unavoidable
unbreakable
uncatchable
unclimbable
uncountable
uncrushable
undercharge
underexpose
undesirable
unendurable
unflappable
unfortunate
ungetatable
unguiculate
unigeniture
uninucleate
unmatchable
unmemorable
unobtrusive
unpalatable
unprintable
unselective
unshockable
unspeakable
unstoppable
unteachable
unthinkable
untouchable
unutterable
unwholesome
urochordate
vagabondage
vagabondise
valleculate
vaporisable
varnishtree
varsovienne
vascularise
vasectomise
ventilative
venturesome
verdantique
vermiculate
vermiculite
vesuvianite
vichyssoise
vicissitude
vinaigrette
vindicative
viniculture
viticulture
vitrescence
vitrifiable
vociferance
warrantable
waterbottle
watercourse
weatherwise
weighbridge
Wensleydale
whiffletree
whippletree
Whitsuntide
wolfwhistle
workmanlike
worldlywise
worshipable
bulletproof
greaseproof
Kulturkampf
mansardroof
mantelshelf
neckerchief
ploughstaff
quaternloaf
selfreproof
showerproof
shrinkproof
advertising
antifouling
apparelling
armtwisting
babysitting
ballbearing
bearbaiting
bellringing
bestselling
billposting
bivouacking
bondwashing
bookbinding
bookkeeping
bookselling
bootlegging
bricklaying
bullbaiting
calculating
campmeeting
caravanning
challenging
channelling
chitterling
christening
churchgoing
clodhopping
complotting
considering
controlling
cornhusking
counselling
disobliging
disparaging
disquieting
domineering
dressmaking
dropforging
earpiercing
embowelling
empanelling
engineering
enthralling
epochmaking
everlasting
eyecatching
facelifting
factfinding
farreaching
fascinating
filmsetting
fireraising
firewalking
flagwagging
flannelling
forerunning
forewarning
forthcoming
freebooting
fulminating
glassmaking
goldbeating
golddigging
goodlooking
hairraising
hairstyling
halfbinding
halflanding
handfasting
handselling
handwriting
hardhitting
hardworking
headhunting
heartstring
highranking
illbreeding
impanelling
imperilling
ingathering
initialling
interesting
interfacing
interlining
knownothing
lancinating
landholding
latchstring
leavetaking
linedrawing
linefishing
longplaying
manumitting
marshalling
matchmaking
merrymaking
mindbending
mindblowing
mindreading
misspelling
moneymaking
monophthong
mudslinging
namecalling
noisemaking
nonmatching
nonplussing
oilpainting
orangoutang
outbreeding
outbuilding
outcropping
outfighting
outstanding
overbearing
overbidding
overlapping
overmanning
overrunning
oversailing
oversetting
overtopping
overweening
painkilling
painstaking
papermaking
patronising
pawnbroking
peacemaking
penetrating
pigsticking
platforming
politicking
quarrelling
quickfiring
racemeeting
reawakening
reedbunting
ribvaulting
roadholding
ropedancing
ropewalking
safekeeping
sandbagging
scaffolding
scuppernong
selfclosing
selfcocking
selfdenying
selffeeding
selffeeling
selfloading
selflocking
selfpitying
selfraising
selfsealing
selfseeking
selfserving
selfwinding
shellacking
shoplifting
shortcoming
shoulderbag
showjumping
shrivelling
sightseeing
sleepingbag
snowbunting
soapboiling
spacesaving
stencilling
stocktaking
talebearing
tankfarming
tantalising
tentpegging
thingumajig
timeserving
timesharing
tobogganing
topdressing
touchtyping
trafficking
trammelling
tufthunting
typecasting
typesetting
unappealing
unbelieving
unbeseeming
undertaking
undeserving
unfaltering
unflinching
unforgiving
unpromising
unreasoning
unrelenting
unremitting
unshrinking
victualling
wainscoting
watchmaking
waterskiing
wellmeaning
wellwishing
wildcatting
wildfowling
winegrowing
winetasting
wirenetting
wirepulling
wiretapping
woodcarving
woodcutting
worshipping
allelomorph
AngloFrench
barleybroth
cardiograph
cesarevitch
cesarewitch
chaetognath
chafingdish
chainstitch
cheesecloth
choreograph
chronograph
clairschach
clothesmoth
coppersmith
coronagraph
coronograph
cottonmouth
crossstitch
cryptograph
distinguish
doubleDutch
hairbreadth
handbreadth
headborough
heterotroph
homestretch
horseradish
intergrowth
kinetograph
lophobranch
Micawberish
nailvarnish
nettlecloth
nightmarish
novelettish
oldwomanish
overstretch
peristalith
photofinish
pseudograph
pseudomorph
psychograph
pullthrough
reestablish
saddlecloth
satinstitch
ScotchIrish
seismograph
seventeenth
shadowgraph
silversmith
sonofabitch
spatterdash
spinsterish
spongecloth
standoffish
steeplebush
stereograph
stevengraph
straightish
suckingfish
surgeonfish
symposiarch
synchromesh
thenceforth
thermograph
throatlatch
triggerfish
twelvemonth
undergrowth
vagabondish

bersaglieri
carabinieri
cognoscenti
condottieri
douroucouli
Hindoostani
hippopotami
melanochroi
rifacimenti
schwarmerei
Stradivarii
tagliatelli
tuttifrutti
xanthochroi
apparatchik
bashibazouk
biofeedback
breechblock
breezeblock
candlestick
chockablock
countermark
countersink
countersunk
counterwork
crackerjack
diamondback
doublecheck
doublequick
doublespeak
doublethink
fiddlestick
halterbreak
journeywork
jumpingjack
kitchensink
latticework
leatherback
leatherneck
picturebook
plasterwork
powderflask
quarterback
quarterdeck
realpolitik
scratchwork
servicebook
shuttlecock
silverstick
singlestick
singletrack
skatingrink
snatchblock
sparrowhawk
stagestruck
statutebook
steeplejack
stickleback
stringybark
trelliswork
trestlework
vestryclerk
weathercock
yacketyyack
abiological
accessorial
accusatival
aerological
aeronomical
aesthetical
affectional
agonistical
agrological
agronomical
ahistorical
algological
allegorical
altitudinal
amplexicaul
anecdotical
antenuptial
anthropical
antitypical
apartmental
apostolical
artiodactyl
ascensional
assessorial
atheistical
attitudinal
attritional
audiovisual
autarchical
axiological
behavioural
biochemical
biometrical
biophysical
bloodvessel
boardschool
bookinghall
Brahmanical
Brahminical
breastwheel
bristletail
calendrical
caricatural
casuistical
catechismal
categorical
centrifugal
centripetal
chimaerical
chlorophyll
cholesterol
chromosomal
chrysoberyl
cicatricial
cockleshell
coessential
cognitional
collisional
commissural
conditional
conjectural
consonantal
conterminal
continental
contractual
cookgeneral
coralloidal
counterfoil
countervail
coxcombical
cupronickel
curvilineal
cylindrical
cytological
deferential
demagogical
dendritical
detrimental
diacritical
dialectical
diametrical
dictatorial
dimensional
diphtherial
diphthongal
diphycercal
directional
directorial
disapproval
disciplinal
disenthrall
disgraceful
distasteful
distressful
distrustful
draggletail
dualcontrol
duniewassal
educational
egotistical
ellipsoidal
endocardial
endothelial
endothermal
enigmatical
equilateral
equinoctial
ethological
evangelical
evolutional
exceptional
excremental
executorial
existential
exoskeletal
expansional
exponential
extensional
fantastical
fingerstall
firmamental
footpoundal
foretopsail
formational
fratricidal
fundamental
gafftopsail
gentilitial
geochemical
geometrical
geophysical
Germanophil
gestatorial
gradational
grammatical
hedgeschool
herringgull
hexadecimal
homiletical
homological
horological
hypoglossal
hypophyseal
hypophysial
icosahedral
ideological
implemental
impolitical
impractical
incorporeal
incremental
ineffectual
inessential
inferential
infinitival
inflexional
influential
insessorial
instinctual
intensional
intentional
intercensal
intercostal
intercrural
interdental
interfacial
interracial
interseptal
intersexual
interspinal
intertribal
intuitional
inventorial
ipsilateral
isometrical
Jacobinical
Jacobitical
judgmatical
kinematical
labiodental
latitudinal
leptodactyl
leviratical
loculicidal
magisterial
maintopsail
matriarchal
matrilineal
matrimonial
mediastinal
mediatorial
medicolegal
metalloidal
meteoroidal
metonymical
micrococcal
ministerial
mistrustful
monarchical
monasterial
monochasial
monolingual
monological
multinomial
multiracial
mycological
mycorrhizal
nasofrontal
Neanderthal
Neotropical
nominatival
nomological
nonsensical
nosological
nutrimental
nutritional
obsessional
obstetrical
octachordal
oecological
oecumenical
oenological
oesophageal
oncological
ontological
operational
oreological
orthoepical
pachydermal
paddlewheel
panegyrical
paradisical
paradoxical
paramedical
parasitical
parheliacal
participial
patriarchal
patrilineal
patrimonial
patristical
pedagogical
pedological
penitential
penological
pentadactyl
Pentecostal
pericardial
pericranial
periodontal
peristomial
pharisaical
phytosterol
pietistical
piscatorial
planetoidal
polycrystal
polyglottal
pomological
posological
postglacial
postnuptial
pragmatical
prayerwheel
prefatorial
prefectural
prejudicial
preprandial
presbyteral
previsional
primigenial
probational
promotional
prophetical
protectoral
prothallial
provisional
pterodactyl
purgatorial
puritanical
pyramidical
quadratical
quadrennial
quadrupedal
quaestorial
quincuncial
reappraisal
rearadmiral
recessional
recommittal
rectilineal
redactional
referential
reportorial
reproachful
residential
resourceful
reverential
reversional
rhapsodical
rheological
rickettsial
rockcrystal
ruridecanal
sacramental
sacrificial
saltatorial
salvational
scissorbill
scissortail
sclerophyll
scriptorial
secretarial
seigneurial
seigniorial
selfcontrol
semeiotical
semidiurnal
sempiternal
sensational
sentimental
septifragal
serological
sexagesimal
sexological
sinological
situational
sophistical
sparrowbill
spasmodical
spermicidal
sphincteral
spiritlevel
spirochetal
splenetical
statistical
strategical
subclinical
subcortical
subcritical
subcultural
sublittoral
submarginal
subregional
substantial
subterminal
subtropical
summational
superficial
supernormal
surrebuttal
suspenseful
swallowtail
sybaritical
symmetrical
synagogical
synonymical
syntactical
synthetical
taxonomical
teaspoonful
terrestrial
territorial
testimonial
tetradactyl
tetrahedral
theological
theoretical
therewithal
thrasonical
thunderpeal
toploftical
topological
traditional
transmittal
transsexual
transversal
trapezoidal
tribunicial
tribunitial
trimestrial
trundletail
turtleshell
typological
uncanonical
uncongenial
unemotional
unequivocal
unessential
unipersonal
unpolitical
valuational
variational
vespertinal
vibrational
viceadmiral
virological
wherewithal
Whitechapel
xanthophyll
absenteeism
academicism
achromatism
acinaciform
adiaphorism
adoptianism
adoptionism
adventurism
agnosticism
agrarianism

Americanism
anachronism
Anglicanism
antependium
antheridium
antirrhinum
archdukedom
Arminianism
aspergillum
aspersorium
astigmatism
athleticism
autoerotism
bacilliform
bimetallism
bimillenium
bloodstream
bohemianism
Bonapartism
bristleworm
Byzantinism
cabbagepalm
cabbageworm
californium
candelabrum
cannibalism
Catholicism
cavalierism
Christendom
clericalism
clostridium
colonialism
columbarium
communalism
condominium
consumerism
corporatism
corrigendum
creationism
crematorium
cypripedium
dactylogram
definiendum
demagoguism
democratism
desideratum
determinism
diachronism
didacticism
disaccustom
divisionism
drawingroom
eclecticism
ecumenicism
einsteinium
endocardium
endometrium
endothelium
epigastrium
equilibrium
Erastianism
esotericism
eudaemonism
exotericism
externalism
favouritism
florilegium
frigidarium
Gallicanism
gametangium
gangsterism
gourmandism
gutturalism
harumscarum
Hegelianism
hermeticism
hesperidium
heteroecism
Hibernicism
hierarchism
highbrowism
Hispanicism
historicism
histrionism
hooliganism
illusionism
immanentism
imperialism
incunabulum
infantilism
insectarium
intermedium
interregnum
intuitivism
irredentism
isochronism
isogeotherm
isomorphism
lamelliform
landingbeam
landlordism
latifundium
leprosarium
libertinism
Lutheranism
magisterium
malapropism
Manichaeism
marconigram
materialism
McCarthyism
mediastinum
medievalism
megatherium
mendelevium
Micawberism
monasticism
monochasium
morningroom
nationalism
neuroticism
objectivism
officialdom
officialism
ophidiarium
opportunism
orientalism
oscillogram
ostracoderm
pandemonium
parallelism
paramoecium
passeriform
pastoralism
patelliform
paternalism
Pelagianism
pelargonium
penicillium
pericardium
pericranium
perineurium
perithecium
personalism
phariseeism
phosphonium
phosphorism
phraseogram
planetarium
plebeianism
pleochroism
pointillism
polyzoarium
positronium
primitivism
probabilism
prochronism
prognathism
progressism
proselytism
prothallium
Prussianism
Pythagorism
quadrennium
rationalism
regionalism
relationism
religionism
retinaculum
revisionism
rheotropism
romanticism
Sadduceeism
scalariform
scalpriform
scriptorium
sittingroom
smokingroom
Socinianism
somatoplasm
Southernism
spectrogram
sphaeridium
sphygmogram
sporogonium
steganogram
stylopodium
succedaneum
syllabarium
synchronism
syndicalism
systematism
tautologism
tautomerism
teetotalism
teleologism
termitarium
Teutonicism
trapeziform
trimorphism
vagabondism
vasculiform
voluntarism
waitingroom
Weismannism
Wesleyanism
xeranthemum
zoomorphism
Abbevillian
abecedarian
abomination
abstraction
abstriction
academician
acceptation
acclamation
acclimation
acetylation
acidulation
acoustician
acquisition
actinomycin
acumination
adumbration
aerostation
Aesculapian
aestivation
affectation
affiliation
affirmation
affrication
aggravation
aggregation
aircraftman
Albigensian
alcyonarian
Alexandrian
allAmerican
alleviation
altercation
alternation
ambiversion
anacoluthon
AngloIndian
AngloNorman
anthocyanin
antiJacobin
antineutron
antiquarian
antiquation
antivitamin
appellation
application
approbation
arbitration
Archimedean
assemblyman
assentation
assignation
association
atomisation
attenuation
attestation
attribution
Augustinian
Aurignacian
awestricken
barrelorgan
beechmarten
Belorussian
benediction
benefaction
bifurcation
bipartition
bombilation
bombination
Bonapartean
botheration
bottlegreen
brachiation
businessman
byeelection
calcination
calculation
calibration
calyptrogen
captivation
carbonation
carburetion
Carolingian
carrageenan
carrageenin
castigation
catercousin
celebration
cementation
centenarian
cerebration
chamberlain
chiropteran
chrysarobin
churchwoman
circulation
cleanshaven
coadunation
coagulation
coarctation
coeducation
coextension
colligation
collimation
collocation
colouration
combination
commination
comminution
commutation
competition
compilation
composition
compotation
compression
compunction
computation
condonation
confliction
confutation
congelation
congressman
conjugation
conjunction
conjuration
connotation
consecution
consolation
consumption
contraction
contraption
conurbation
convocation
convolution
cooperation
cornucopian
corporation
correlation
corrugation
coruscation
cosmetician
counterplan
countersign
counterturn
craftswoman
crenulation
crepitation
crestfallen
crimination
crocodilian
crossbowman
crucifixion
ctenophoran
culmination
cultivation
cupellation
cybernation
debarkation
decantation
declamation
declaration
declination
decollation
decussation
defalcation
defloration
defoliation
deformation
deglutition
degradation
degustation
dehydration
deification
delectation
delineation
deliveryman
demarcation
demarkation
denigration
deoxidation
deportation
depravation
deprecation
depredation
deprivation
dereliction
description
desecration
desiccation
designation
desperation
destination
destitution
destruction
detestation
deuteration
devaluation
devastation
diatessaron
dicotyledon
diffraction
dinnerwagon
dinosaurian
discerption
disfunction
disillusion
disjunction
dislocation
disposition
disputation
dissipation
dissolution
distinction
distraction
divulgation
downtrodden
draughtsman
dropcurtain
duplication
dysfunction
edification
egalitarian
ejaculation
elaboration
electrician
elicitation
elimination
Elizabethan
elucidation
elutriation
embarkation
embrocation
enchiridion
encystation
endoskelton
enneahedron
enucleation
enumeration
enunciation
eradication
euchologion
evagination
evaporation
examination
exclamation
excoriation
exculpation
exfoliation
exhortation
exoneration
exoskeleton
expatiation
expectation
explanation
explication
exploration
exportation
expurgation
exsiccation
extenuation
extirpation
extradition
extrication
fabrication
Falstaffian
fascination
fecundation

fimbriation
FinnoUgrian
flagcaptain
fluctuation
fluorescein
fomentation
foreshorten
forestation
formication
formulation
fornication
Frenchwoman
frostbitten
fructuation
frustration
fulguration
fulmination
fusillation
fustigation
gegenschein
gemmulation
gentlewoman
genuflexion
germination
gibberellin
glomeration
godchildren
godforsaken
GraecoRoman
granulation
gratulation
gravitation
gurgitation
habituation
haemocyanin
haemoglobin
Hamiltonian
handwritten
heartbroken
Heracleidan
hibernation
highfalutin
holothurian
homoiousian
humiliation
hydrocarbon
hyperborean
hyphenation
hypolimnion
hypotension
icosahedron
idolisation
imagination
imbrication
immigration
imparkation
impartation
impetration
implication
importation
imprecation
imprecision
inanimation
inattention
incantation
incarnation
inclination
inculcation
inculpation
incurvation
indentation
indigestion
indignation
indirection
IndoIranian
inebriation
infantryman
infatuation
infestation
infeudation
infirmarian
information
innervation
innutrition
inoculation
inquisition
inscription
insinuation
inspiration
instigation
institution
instruction
integration
interaction
interfusion
invultation
irradiation
irretention
itineration
jactitation
Judaisation
jumpingbean
labefaction
laciniation
lacrimation
lacrymation
laicisation
lamellicorn
lamentation
Lancastrian
lancination
legerdemain
legislation
Leibnitzian
libertarian
liquidation
lixiviation
lubrication
lucubration
luxuriation
machination
madrigalian
magazinegun
magdalenian
Maglemosian
malediction
malefaction
malfunction
malposition
manducation
manumission
mastication
mechanician
melioration
mensuration
merchantman
Merovingian
methylation
metrication
Micronesian
micturition
millenarian
misbegotten
miscreation
molestation
murmuration
musculation
necessarian
needlewoman
negotiation
nictitation
nonpartisan
nullifidian
nuncupation
obfuscation
objurgation
obscuration
obsecration
observation
obstruction
obtestation
occultation
officiation
oppugnation
organscreen
orientation
origination
orthopteran
oscillation
ostentation
overwritten
oviposition
oxygenation
oxyhydrogen
ozonisation
Palestinian
palpitation
Panglossian
parturition
passivation
pectination
penetration
pentahedron
peptisation
percolation
perennation
perforation
permutation
persecution
personation
philologian
phonetician
phycocyanin
Pickwickian
plainspoken
podophyllin
policewoman
pollination
ponderation
postexilian
postulation
Precambrian
predication
preelection
preignition
prelibation
premonition
preparation
preposition
presumption
preterhuman
preterition
procreation
procrustean
procuration
profanation
progestogen
progression
prohibition
proletarian
propagation
proposition
prorogation
prosecution
prostration
protraction
provocation
publication
pullulation
punctuation
pustulation
Pythagorean
quadrillion
quickfrozen
quintillion
Rabelaisian
radiocarbon
radiolarian
rapscallion
rarefaction
Rastafarian
rattlebrain
reachmedown
realisation
reanimation
reapportion
reassertion
recantation
reclamation
recognition
recondition
redirection
reeducation
reformation
reification
reinsertion
reiteration
reluctation
repartition
replication
reprobation
repudiation
requisition
reservation
resignation
respiration
restitution
restoration
restriction
retaliation
retardation
retribution
retroaction
revaluation
rhetorician
Rosicrucian
rubefaction
rubrication
rustication
Sabbatarian
sacculation
saturnalian
Scotchwoman
segregation
selfopinion
septentrion
serrulation
sertularian
Shaksperean
Shaksperian
shortspoken
sightscreen
smokescreen
sockdologen
solifluxion
solmisation
soupkitchen
speculation
spokeswoman
sportswoman
sporulation
springclean
stagflation
stimulation
stipulation
stonemarten
stoolpigeon
stylisation
subarration
subaudition
subdivision
subjugation
sublimation
subornation
subrogation
subsumption
subtraction
suffixation
suffocation
supervision
supposition
suppression
suppuration
surrogation
suspiration
susurration
synchrotron
syncopation
syndication
tabefaction
termination
tetrahedron
thistledown
thoroughpin
timebargain
titillation
tittivation
tourbillion
transaction
transection
transfixion
transfusion
translation
trencherman
trepanation
trepidation
tribulation
Trinitarian
trituration
tumefaction
turbination
typewritten
ultramodern
unchristian
unification
utilisation
utilitarian
vaccination
vacillation
vacuolation
valediction
variegation
vasopressin
venesection
venisection
ventilation
vermination
vindication
vivisection
washerwoman
weatherworn
wintergreen
Yugoslavian
zoantharian
zooplankton
Zoroastrian
accelerando
afficionado
altorelievo
altorilievo
amontillado
archipelago
braggadocio
chiaroscuro
cinquecento
contrabasso
decrescendo
internuncio
playerpiano
prestissimo
punchinello
rallentando
rifacimento
saltimbanco
sextodecimo
violoncello
admiralship
apostleship
bushmanship
captainship
citizenship
clothesprop
colonelship
comradeship
curatorship
denizenship
dipterocarp
emperorship
generalship
heroworship
lectureship
lifemanship
managership
marshalship
messiahship
monitorship
mountaintop
oarsmanship
overdevelop
partnership
patternshop
praetorship
premiership
primateship
proctorship
prophetship
provostship
rubberstamp
scholarship
selfworship
senatorship
sheriffship
showmanship
soldiership
speakership
sponsorship
stewardship
stirruppump
stomachpump
studentship
teachership
thunderclap
tribuneship
trusteeship
viceroyship
whistlestop
workmanship
abbreviator
accelerator
accumulator
actinometer
adjudicator
adminicular
adulterator
aerographer
afterburner
alkalimeter
ameliorator
animalcular
annihilator
annunciator
antechamber
anticipator
appreciator
arbitrageur
articulator
asphyxiator
assimilator
auxanometer
azotobacter
backbencher
barnstormer
basketchair
beachcomber

bellfounder
bellheather
bibliolater
biedermeier
billsticker
birdfancier
birdwatcher
blackbirder
blackmailer
blockbuster
bloodsucker
bodybuilder
boilermaker
bowdleriser
brainteaser
breadwinner
broadcaster
bullfighter
bullterrier
burgomaster
bushwhacker
calorimeter
calumniator
canalicular
candlepower
carbuncular
carburetter
carburettor
cardsharper
caterpillar
catswhisker
cauliflower
cavedweller
chainarmour
chainletter
chainsmoker
chansonnier
chanticleer
cheerleader
childminder
choirmaster
chronologer
chronometer
circumlunar
circumpolar
circumsolar
cityslicker
cliffhanger
coinheritor
colorimeter
commendator
commentator
compensator
comptroller
compurgator
concertgoer
conciliator
conditioner
confiscator
connoisseur
consecrator
conservator
conspirator
constitutor
constrictor
constructor
consummator
continuator
contributor
conveyancer
coordinator
corpuscular
cotoneaster
crepuscular
criticaster
crossbearer
crotcheteer
curvilinear
daisycutter
deactivator
decelerator
deerstalker
deflagrator
demographer
denominator
denunciator
depopulator
depreciator
desalinator
dilapidator
disbeliever
discipliner
disencumber
dishonourer
disinfector
disremember
dissertator
distributor
doorknocker
doubleender
doxographer
drillmaster
dumbfounder
dynamometer
echosounder
electioneer
electrolier
emancipator
emasculator
embellisher
embroiderer
Emmenthaler
enterpriser
entertainer
equiangular
equivocator
establisher
eveningstar
exaggerator
executioner
extortioner
fairweather
faithhealer
faultfinder
fieldworker
filterpaper
firecracker
firefighter
firewatcher
flagellator
flagofficer
flimflammer
floorwalker
footslogger
footsoldier
foraminifer
forequarter
forestaller
forethinker
fourflusher
fourpounder
fourwheeler
franctireur
frankfurter
fraterniser
freethinker
frontrunner
frothhopper
gallbladder
gardemanger
gatecrasher
generaliser
gerrymander
gettogether
ghostwriter
giantpowder
gillyflower
glassblower
glasscutter
globeflower
goddaughter
gonfalonier
gormandiser
gradiometer
grandfather
grandmother
grangeriser
grasshopper
gravedigger
greengrocer
greenkeeper
groundwater
haberdasher
hairdresser
hairtrigger
handicapper
heldentenor
hereinafter
heteropolar
highstepper
homesteader
homogeniser
honeybadger
honeymooner
horsecollar
horsedoctor
hospitaller
housefather
householder
housekeeper
housemaster
housemother
hydrometeor
ichthyosaur
illuminator
illustrator
inaugurator
incinerator
infiltrator
inseminator
insufflator
intensifier
intercepter
interceptor
intercessor
interlinear
interlocker
interpreter
interrupter
interruptor
interviewer
intimidator
intromitter
invigilator
invigorator
jauntingcar
jerrymander
kickstarter
kwashiorkor
lachrymator
lakedweller
lammergeier
lammergeyer
lamplighter
landgrabber
landinggear
leaseholder
linendraper
lineprinter
liquidambar
litterateur
logographer
loudspeaker
mailcarrier
manipulator
mantuamaker
masquerader
matrilinear
metalworker
mineraliser
minesweeper
minnesinger
misremember
mitrailleur
moisturiser
moneylender
moneyspider
monographer
mononuclear
monopoliser
monseigneur
moonlighter
mosstrooper
motivepower
mountaineer
multangular
multicolour
multilinear
namedropper
necromancer
neutraliser
nightporter
nightwalker
ninnyhammer
nomenclator
nomographer
nonsequitur
northeaster
northwester
noseyparker
nosographer
ornithopter
ornithosaur
pacificator
pamphleteer
panicmonger
paperhanger
paragrapher
paraphraser
paratrooper
parishioner
partitioner
pasteuriser
paternoster
pearlfisher
perpetrator
perpetuator
personifier
pettifogger
philanderer
philosopher
photocopier
phrasemaker
picturegoer
pieceworker
pilotburner
pipecleaner
plagiariser
plasticiser
platearmour
pluviometer
polarimeter
polevaulter
populariser
predecessor
preselector
prizewinner
probationer
proconsular
promulgator
proofreader
propitiator
prostitutor
protomartyr
provocateur
psychomotor
purificator
pussyfooter
quacksalver
quicksilver
quilldriver
rangefinder
recommender
rectangular
rectilinear
reedwarbler
regenerator
rejuvenator
remunerator
replenisher
representer
retinacular
reversioner
righthander
rightwinger
safebreaker
safecracker
salinometer
sandskipper
scalearmour
scaremonger
sclerometer
scoutmaster
screwdriver
scrutiniser
secondrater
seismometer
selfdespair
selfstarter
semitrailer
serigrapher
shareholder
sharepusher
sheepfarmer
sheepmaster
sheetanchor
shipbreaker
shipbuilder
shoeleather
showstopper
sidewheeler
sightreader
signpainter
simpliciter
slaughterer
slavedriver
slaveholder
sleepingcar
sleepwalker
smallholder
sockdolager
somewhither
somnambular
southeaster
southwester
spaceheater
spectacular
speechifier
speedometer
spellbinder
spherometer
stadtholder
stakeholder
stallholder
standpatter
steamboiler
steamroller
steelworker
stepbrother
stereotyper
sternutator
stockbroker
stockholder
stockjobber
stonecutter
stonewaller
storekeeper
storyteller
straphanger
stridulator
subscapular
superheater
supertanker
surfboarder
surrebutter
swimbladder
swordbearer
sympathiser
synthesiser
tacheometer
teenybopper
teetotaller
telegrapher
teleprinter
thanksgiver
theatregoer
thermometer
threadpaper
threecolour
threedecker
threemaster
timepleaser
titleholder
toastmaster
toothpowder
topographer
torchbearer
torchsinger
totalisator
trackwalker
trafficator
trailblazer
trainbearer
transceiver
transcriber
transferrer
transformer
transmitter
transponder
transporter
treecreeper
trendsetter
trustbuster
tumbledrier
typefounder
typographer
tyrannosaur
underbidder
underseller
undervaluer
underwriter
unicellular
upholsterer
vaporimeter
vasodilator
vasopressor
vaticinator
ventricular
verisimilar
vinedresser
vituperator
vociferator
volkslieder
volumometer
voortrekker
washleather
watercolour
watercooler
weenybopper
Westminster
wheresoever
whichsoever
whitecollar
whitewasher

whitleather
whoremaster
whoremonger
whosesoever
windcheater
wisecracker
witchdoctor
witchhunter
worldbeater
wreckmaster
xylographer
abiogeneses
abiogenesis
abstentious
abusiveness
academicals
acarpellous
acclivitous
acrimonious
actinomyces
adenomatous
adventuress
adventurous
adverseness
advisedness
aeronautics
aerostatics
aimlessness
airlessness
airsickness
allantoides
altocumulus
altostratus
amativeness
amentaceous
amiableness
amorousness
anachronous
anadiplosis
anagnorisis
anaphylaxis
anastomoses
anastomosis
ancientness
androgynous
anfractuous
antimonious
antiphrasis
anxiousness
Apollinaris
apologetics
aponeuroses
aponeurosis
aposiopesis
arboraceous
archaeornis
archduchess
arduousness
arenicolous
artlessness
ascomycetes
aspergillus
assuredness
atrabilious
audibleness
austereness
avoirdupois
awesomeness
awkwardness
bacciferous
balefulness
bashfulness
battledress
bearishness
beastliness
belatedness
bellbottoms
betweenness
bicephalous
biliousness
biocoenoses
biocoenosis
bittercress
blasphemous
blepharitis
blessedness
blotchiness
blunderbuss
bookishness
bookshelves
boorishness
borborygmus
bottleglass
brachyurous
breadcrumbs
breadthways
bristliness
Britishness
brittleness
brucellosis
brusqueness
brutishness
bullishness
burglarious
butterflies
butteriness
butyraceous
cacophonous
caddishness
calcicolous
calciferous
calcifugous
callousness
canaliculus
cantharides
capableness
captionless
carefulness
carnivorous
caryopsides
catachreses
catachresis
catadromous
ceremonious
champertous
chartaceous
chevalglass
chrysalides
chrysalises
churchiness
cleanliness
coccidiosis
coconscious
cognateness
comestibles
comfortless
compactness
compendious
complexness
conciseness
conductress
congenerous
conspicuous
contentious
contrarious
contretemps
convenances
convolvulus
copiousness
corbiesteps
cordialness
corniferous
correctness
corruptness
costiveness
coterminous
cottongrass
courtliness
crabbedness
credentials
crookedness
cruciferous
crucigerous
crunchiness
crustaceous
cunningness
cupriferous
curableness
curiousness
currentness
currishness
cursiveness
cursoriness
cybernetics
cysticercus
cytogenesis
cytokinesis
declivitous
defenceless
deleterious
demigoddess
dentigerous
desperadoes
deviousness
devotedness
diadelphous
diagnostics
diaphoresis
diapophysis
diarthrosis
dicephalous
dichogamous
dichotomous
diffuseness
diplococcus
directrices
doggishness
dolefulness
dollishness
doltishness
donnishness
doublecross
doughtiness
drouthiness
drunkenness
dubiousness
dundrearies
duplicitous
durableness
dutifulness
earnestness
earthliness
ectogenesis
efficacious
elderliness
electronics
elusiveness
emotionless
emulousness
enarthrosis
enchantress
endlessness
endophagous
enterovirus
enviousness
ephemerides
epipetalous
equableness
erotogenous
eurhythmics
evasiveness
executrices
executrixes
exhaustless
expeditious
extremeness
factualness
faddishness
farawayness
farinaceous
farraginous
fatefulness
fatuousness
fearfulness
featherless
featureless
feelingness
ferriferous
ferruginous
fidgetiness
filamentous
fingerglass
finicalness
firstfruits
fissiparous
flaccidness
flavourless
fleshliness
flightiness
flirtatious
floriferous
floweriness
foolishness
foppishness
foreignness
foreverness
forgiveness
forlornness
forwardness
franticness
fretfulness
friableness
frowardness
frowstiness
frugivorous
fulsomeness
furnishings
furtiveness
furunculous
gainfulness
gallantness
gamogenesis
gaseousness
gasfittings
gemmiferous
gemmiparous
genteelness
genuineness
geopolitics
ghastliness
ghostliness
gibbousness
girlishness
glaringness
gnotobiosis
godlessness
gracileness
gradualness
granivorous
graphicness
gristliness
grouchiness
guardedness
gutlessness
gypsiferous
gyrocompass
habiliments
haemoptysis
haemostasis
haggardness
halophilous
haplessness
harbourless
harmfulness
hatefulness
haughtiness
healthiness
heavenwards
heedfulness
heinousness
hellishness
helpfulness
hemipterous
heptamerous
herbivorous
heterotaxis
hideousness
hippocampus
hirsuteness
histrionics
hitherwards
hoggishness
homeostasis
homogeneous
homophonous
homopterous
homosporous
homozygosis
hopefulness
houselights
hugeousness
hurriedness
hurtfulness
hydrogenous
hydroponics
hylogenesis
hypotyposis
ichthyornis
iconostases
iconostasis
ignobleness
ignominious
illustrious
immenseness
immoveables
impecunious
incongruous
incredulous
indeciduous
industrious
inexactness
inheritress
injudicious
inofficious
inquilinous
insipidness
intenseness
interleaves
interosseus
intravenous
invalidness
irksomeness
irreligious
isochronous
isomorphous
jealousness
joylessness
knavishness
knowingness
lactiferous
languidness
lastingness
lateritious
laughinggas
laurustinus
lawlessness
learnedness
lengthiness
lentiginous
letterpress
ligamentous
limitedness
linguistics
lissomeness
literalness
loathliness
loggerheads
logicalness
loutishness
lovableness
loxodromics
lumpishness
lustfulness
magnanimous
manifestoes
mannishness
marchioness
massiveness
mastoiditis
mathematics
mawkishness
meadowgrass
meaningless
measureless
mediateness
mediatrices
megalopolis
meliphagous
melliferous
mellifluous
membraneous
menservants
meritorious
merogenesis
metachrosis
metagenesis
metaphysics
meteoritics
micrococcus
middleclass
mindfulness
minuteglass
mischievous
miserliness
moderations
monocarpous
monoclinous
monogenesis
monophagous
monopterous
morbiferous
mountainous
movableness
multiparous
mundaneness
musicalness
mutableness
muttonchops
myelomatous
myocarditis
myxomatosis
myxomycetes
naturalness
naughtiness
necessitous
necrobiosis
necropoleis
needfulness
nervousness
nitrogenous
noctivagous
noisomeness
nonetheless
notableness
nothingness
noxiousness
nulliparous
numismatics
nutcrackers
obliqueness
obscureness
obviousness
odoriferous
odorousness

offenceless
oligomerous
ominousness
omnifarious
onerousness
ontogenesis
operoseness
opprobrious
orderliness
orthopedics
otherwhiles
outwardness
overanxious
ozoniferous
paediatrics
painfulness
pantalettes
papyraceous
paraleipsis
parasitosis
parentheses
parenthesis
passiveness
paunchiness
peccadillos
pediculosis
peevishness
pensionless
pensiveness
pentagynous
pentamerous
pentandrous
perfectness
periostitis
periphrases
periphrasis
perishables
peristalsis
peritonitis
perspicuous
pestiferous
pettishness
pharyngitis
phosphorous
phthiriasis
phyllotaxis
piggishness
pinkishness
piperaceous
piscivorous
piteousness
pitifulness
plasmolysis
playfulness
pliableness
plicateness
pneumonitis
pointedness
polyandrous
polycarpous
polygenesis
polyonymous
polyphagous
polyphonous
pompousness
pontificals
portionless
pourparlers
preachiness
precautious
precentress
preceptress
precipitous
preciseness
prestigious
pretentious
prickliness
primiparous
privateness
proceedings
profaneness
profuseness
prognathous
proliferous
promiscuous
prophylaxis
proportions
prosaicness
prosthetics
protectress
proteolysis
prudishness
pruriginous
pseudomonas
psittacosis
punctilious
purposeless
pushfulness
queenliness
quitchgrass
racketpress
radicalness
raffishness
raucousness
raunchiness
reddishness
regimentals
relatedness
remorseless
repetitious
repleteness
restfulness
restiveness
retiredness
rhizanthous
rhizomatous
rhomboideus
ribbongrass
riotousness
roguishness
roundedness
ruinousness
rumbustious
Sagittarius
saintliness
salesladies
salpingitis
sanguineous
saplessness
saponaceous
saprogenous
sarcomatous
sarcophagus
sauropodous
savouriness
schizanthus
sclerotitis
scoriaceous
scragginess
scrappiness
scribacious
scrimpiness
scruffiness
scrumptious
scurvygrass
seasickness
secondclass
selfishness
sententious
septenarius
septiferous
seriousness
serpiginous
sexlessness
shadowiness
shallowness
shapeliness
shelterless
shepherdess
shocktroops
shrubbiness
shutterless
sickishness
sightliness
silveriness
sincereness
sinlessness
sinuousness
sizableness
sketchiness
skilfulness
slavishness
slenderness
smithereens
snowgoggles
solanaceous
somniculous
somniferous
songfulness
sottishness
soulfulness
sparingness
spathaceous
spectatress
spindlelegs
spiniferous
splendorous
spondulicks
spondylitis
spontaneous
sporogenous
springiness
squalidness
squashiness
squeakiness
starchiness
stateliness
staunchless
staunchness
stegosaurus
stephanotis
sternsheets
stiltedness
stoicalness
stormtroops
stramineous
strangeness
streakiness
stringiness
studiedness
stuntedness
stylishness
suasiveness
sublimeness
succourless
sulphureous
summariness
sunlessness
superficies
superfluous
superioress
supersedeas
supremeness
swarthiness
sweepstakes
swinishness
sympetalous
symphonious
synchronous
syndesmosis
syssarcosis
systematics
tabletennis
tautologous
tautonymous
tearfulness
tediousness
teknonymous
telekinesis
temerarious
tempestuous
tenableness
tendencious
tendentious
tenterhooks
tenuousness
terraqueous
terricolous
terrigenous
testatrices
tetramerous
tetrapodous
textureless
theatricals
thereabouts
thermionics
thermolysis
thermotaxis
thirstiness
thoughtless
threadiness
thriftiness
throatiness
thunderless
thuriferous
thwartships
thyroiditis
tiddlywinks
tonsillitis
torticollis
trafficless
treacherous
treacliness
trichinosis
tricksiness
trimorphous
tripetalous
triphibious
triphyllous
triquetrous
tristichous
trivialness
trouserless
tuberculous
tunableness
tunefulness
typicalness
ulotrichous
ultrasonics
unambiguous
unawareness
uncanniness
uncleanness
unconscious
uncouthness
ungodliness
unhappiness
uniformness
unmanliness
unquietness
unrighteous
unsoundness
unusualness
uprightness
urticaceous
urticarious
uselessness
vacuousness
valiantness
variousness
velvetiness
ventriculus
verboseness
vertiginous
viciousness
victualless
viscountess
viscousness
visibleness
voguishness
volubleness
vortiginous
waggishness
wakefulness
waspishness
waywardness
wealthiness
weightiness
welcomeness
whereabouts
whitishness
widdershins
willingness
winningness
winsomeness
wishfulness
wistfulness
withershins
witlessness
womanliness
worldliness
worshipless
xenophilous
xerophilous
xylocarpous
xylophagous
zealousness
zestfulness
zootechnics
abandonment
abolishment
abortionist
abridgement
acaulescent
accompanist
achievement
acquiescent
acquirement
adjournment
adjudgement
adoptianist
adoptionist
advancement
adventurist
aftereffect
alkalescent
allopathist
Americanist
anthologist
antioxidant
appeasement
appointment
appurtenant
aquarellist
arbitrament
arborescent
arraignment
arrangement
artillerist
assuagement
audiologist
balmcricket
bathingsuit
bedevilment
bedizenment
beguilement
belligerent
benightment
bereavement
bewitchment
bimetallist
bittersweet
blackmarket
bladderwort
bodyservant
bombardment
Bonapartist
bondservant
breadbasket
Byzantinist
calefacient
candlelight
carvelbuilt
chargesheet
chiropodist
chloroplast
chromoplast
circumspect
clairvoyant
clericalist
codefendant
coefficient
colonialist
commandment
communalist
communicant
comparatist
compartment
compilement
complainant
complaisant
comportment
concealment
concernment
concomitant
concrescent
concubitant
confinement
conflagrant
congealment
consentient
consignment
constituent
containment
contaminant
contentment
controlment
corecipient
corroborant
cosmogonist
cosmologist
costbenefit
counterfeit
counterfort
counterpart
counterplot
countryseat
creationist
criminalist
crossgarnet
curtailment
custombuilt
debauchment
debouchment
deforcement
defraudment
delitescent
depravement
derangement
despoilment
determinant
determinist
detrainment
development
dichotomist
diluvialist
diplomatist
disablement
disafforest
disarmament
disbandment
discernment
disinterest
dislodgment

disobedient
disportment
dissentient
dissepiment
disunionist
divorcement
divulgement
downdraught
dreadnought
earthcloset
easternmost
emblematist
embowerment
embracement
embroilment
emplacement
enchainment
enchantment
encrustment
endorsement
enfeoffment
enforcement
engorgement
engrossment
enhancement
enjambement
enlargement
enlivenment
ennoblement
enslavement
entablement
enthralment
entitlement
entrainment
entreatment
entrustment
envelopment
environment
epigraphist
equidistant
equilibrist
equipollent
escheatment
Esperantist
ethnologist
etymologist
eudaemonist
evanishment
expectorant
extravagant
facsimilist
farthermost
festschrift
fieldcornet
fingerprint
flabbergast
fluorescent
forethought
foretopmast
forgetmenot
freethought
funambulist
furthermost
garnishment
gemmologist
genealogist
grandparent
greasepaint
groundsheet
gynaecocrat
haematocrit
hagiologist
hairstylist
handwrought
heavyweight
hedgepriest
heptarchist
heterograft
hexametrist
highwrought
Hispanicist
histologist
historicist
hydrologist
hypermarket
illusionist
immanentist
impeachment
imperialist
imperilment
impermanent
impertinent
impingement
impoundment
impressment
improvement
improvident
inadvertent
incalescent
incognisant
incompetent
incompliant
incongruent
inconscient
inconsonant
incontinent
indehiscent
independent
indifferent
indorsement
inefficient
inexpedient
inobservant
installment
instillment
intelligent
interactant
interfluent
interjacent
intumescent
involvement
irredentist
juvenescent
lawmerchant
lightweight
limnologist
lithotomist
logomachist
luminescent
madrigalist
magnificent
maidservant
maintopmast
mammalogist
mandolinist
manifestant
materialist
meadowsweet
measurement
medievalist
mellifluent
memorialist
miniaturist
misjudgment
molecricket
moneymarket
monochromat
monologuist
mooringmast
mothercraft
motherright
multivalent
mycophagist
mythologist
mythopoeist
nationalist
necrologist
needlecraft
needlepoint
negationist
neurologist
noctilucent
noctivagant
nondescript
nonexistent
nonresident
nonunionist
notionalist
nourishment
numismatist
objectivist
obmutescent
obsolescent
oenophilist
omnipresent
opencircuit
ophiologist
opportunist
optometrist
orientalist
orthopedist
osteologist
overgarment
overpayment
overwrought
oysterplant
paediatrist
pantomimist
paperweight
parachutist
participant
pastoralist
paternalist
pathologist
pearlescent
pennyweight
pentavalent
personalist
pestologist
petrologist
phantasiast
phenologist
philatelist
philologist
phonologist
photooffset
phycologist
phylogynist
phytologist
phytotomist
pigeonchest
pillowfight
pinnatisect
pleinairist
plenipotent
pointillist
poltergeist
portraitist
precipitant
precontract
predicament
predominant
preexistent
prejudgment
presentient
presentment
priestcraft
probabilist
procurement
progressist
proletariat
protagonist
protuberant
publishment
pulverulent
radiologist
rationalist
reactionist
realignment
reconstruct
recruitment
reenactment
refreshment
refrigerant
regionalist
relationist
religionist
reminiscent
remonstrant
replacement
requirement
resipiscent
resplendent
restatement
retrocedent
retrorocket
reverberant
revisionist
reviviscent
rhinologist
rhynchodont
romanticist
rubefacient
safeconduct
Sanskritist
sausagemeat
saxophonist
scaleinsect
scintillant
scuttlebutt
searchlight
secondsight
secretariat
selfconceit
selfcontent
selfevident
selfreliant
selfrespect
selfsupport
semanticist
Septembrist
shacklebolt
shelljacket
shelterbelt
sickbenefit
significant
silverpoint
slavemarket
sociologist
soliloquist
solutionist
Soroptimist
spaceflight
spendthrift
squarebuilt
staircarpet
stenotypist
stickinsect
stiflejoint
stockmarket
straightcut
streetlight
strongpoint
subbasement
subcontract
subdominant
subservient
substituent
sulphurwort
summersault
superjacent
supermarket
supernatant
superscript
supremacist
surbasement
surveillant
sustainment
swallowwort
syndicalist
systematist
talentscout
taxidermist
teleologist
telepathist
telephonist
temperament
tetravalent
theosophist
thunderbolt
tobacconist
tobogganist
togglejoint
traducement
transhumant
transilient
translucent
transparent
tremblement
tritagonist
trophoblast
trothplight
trousersuit
ultraviolet
unbeknownst
undertenant
underweight
unimportant
vacationist
vehmgericht
viridescent
virilescent
voluntarist
waitinglist
wastebasket
westernmost
wheelwright
whitethroat
winningpost
witenagemot
xylophonist
zoographist
portmanteau
blackfellow
clapperclaw
counterblow
counterview
grandnephew
greatnephew
marshmallow
merryandrew
pussywillow
songsparrow
stonecurlew
wappenschaw
wheelbarrow
windlestraw
arbitratrix
billetsdoux
Clarencieux
fricandeaux
hydrothorax
negotiatrix
planoconvex
progenitrix
prolocutrix
prosecutrix
thoroughwax
abdominally
abhorrently
abiotically
ablutionary
abnormality
absorbingly
abstinently
accentually
acceptingly
acclamatory
accordantly
accordingly
accountably
accountancy
acropetally
adjectively
adverbially
advertently
aerobically
aerobiology
affectingly
affectively
affectivity
affirmatory
aggregately
aggrievedly
agnatically
agonisingly
agrobiology
alkalimetry
alleviatory
alternately
ambiguously
ambitiously
ambivalency
amenability
amicability
amorphously
amphibology
amphictyony
analogously
anencephaly
angelically
angiography
anniversary
anomalously
anonymously
anteriority
antigravity
antiphonary
appallingly
appealingly
applicatory
appreciably
approbatory
approvingly
aquatically
arbitrarily
archaeology
archaically
aristocracy
aromaticity
arrestingly
ascetically
aseptically
assertively
assiduously
Assyriology
astringency
atrociously
attentively
audaciously
auricularly
autochthony
backcountry
banteringly
baptismally
barbarously
barefacedly
basipetally
beauteously
beautifully
befittingly
beguilingly
bellicosity
benedictory

beneficiary
benightedly
benignantly
bibliolatry
bibliomancy
bibliophily
bicentenary
biddability
bilaterally
bimillenary
binocularly
bisexuality
blamelessly
blameworthy
bloodguilty
bloodlessly
botanically
bounteously
bountifully
boysenberry
brainlessly
brainsickly
brilliantly
bryozoology
bucolically
bumblepuppy
bumptiously
bureaucracy
Byronically
calefactory
calligraphy
calorimetry
campanology
candleberry
canonically
capaciously
capillarity
caravansary
caressingly
carriageway
cartography
catholicity
causatively
caustically
cavernously
ceaselessly
celebratory
celestially
cellularity
certifiably
chancellery
chancellory
changefully
chaotically
charlatanry
cheerlessly
cheiromancy
chieftaincy
chirography
chokecherry
chorography
Christianly
Christmassy
Christology
chronically
chronometry
circularity
circulatory
clamorously
classically
cleistogamy
climatology
codicillary
coeternally
cognitively
cognitivity
collectedly
collinearly
collusively
colorimetry
colourfully
combatively
combinatory
comfortably
commendably
commensally
comminatory
commonality
competently
complacency
compliantly
compositely
compotatory
comstockery
conceitedly
conceivably
concertedly
concubinary
condolatory
confederacy
confessedly
confidently
confidingly
conformably
conformally
confusingly
congenially
congruently
congruously
conjugality
connectedly
connubially
consciously
conservancy
consistency
consolatory
consolingly
consonantly
conspicuity
consultancy
consumingly
contentedly
continently
contingency
continually
contrariety
controversy
conveniency
convergency
conversancy
convertibly
convivially
coparcenary
coplanarity
corporality
corporately
corporeally
corpulently
corrosively
corruptibly
cosignatory
cosmetology
cosmography
cotemporary
countlessly
courteously
craniometry
credibility
credulously
criminality
criminatory
criminology
criticality
cryobiology
cryosurgery
cryotherapy
cryptically
culpability
customarily
dactylology
dangerously
dauntlessly
deceitfully
deceivingly
decennially
deceptively
declamatory
declaratory
decussately
dedicatedly
deductively
defectively
defensively
deficiently
degradingly
deistically
deliciously
delightedly
delinquency
deliriously
demagoguery
demandingly
demonolatry
denigratory
dependently
deploringly
deprecatory
depredatory
dermatology
deservingly
desperately
despondency
desultorily
determinacy
deuterogamy
Deuteronomy
dexterously
dialectally
diaphaneity
differently
difficultly
diffidently
diffusively
digestively
dimwittedly
directivity
disarmingly
disassembly
discernibly
discography
discordancy
discourtesy
discrepancy
disguisedly
disgustedly
dishonestly
dismayingly
disparately
dispersedly
dissolutely
dissonantly
dissymmetry
dittography
divergently
divisionary
doctrinally
documentary
dodecaphony
domesticity
domiciliary
doubleentry
doubtlessly
drastically
dreamlessly
dynamically
dynamometry
ebulliently
ecumenicity
edificatory
editorially
educability
effectively
effectually
efficiently
effulgently
egregiously
ejaculatory
elaborately
elastically
electricity
electrology
elementally
eligibility
ellipticity
elucidatory
embracingly
emotionally
empirically
endearingly
endemically
enquiringly
enterostomy
entomophily
episcopally
equivalency
equivocally
ergatocracy
erratically
erroneously
eschatology
essentially
ethereality
ethnography
Etruscology
eugenically
eventuality
evidentiary
exceedingly
excellently
excessively
exclamatory
exclusively
exclusivity
excrescency
exculpatory
excursively
exdirectory
exemplarily
exemplarity
exhortatory
exogenously
expansively
expansivity
expatiatory
expectantly
expediently
expensively
explanatory
explicatory
exploratory
explosively
expurgatory
exquisitely
extemporary
extensively
extenuatory
exteriority
externality
extirpatory
exuberantly
facetiously
factionally
faithlessly
faithworthy
fallibility
falteringly
familiarity
fanatically
farcicality
fashionably
fatiguingly
faultlessly
feasibility
feloniously
ferociously
festinately
filamentary
filmography
financially
fissiparity
flamboyancy
flatulently
flauntingly
flexibility
fluoroscopy
forgetfully
fortnightly
fortunately
fractionary
fractiously
fragmentary
frantically
fraternally
freemasonry
frightfully
frivolously
fruitlessly
fulminatory
functionary
gallimaufry
garrulously
gastrectomy
generically
genetically
genitivally
gentlemanly
gerontology
gimcrackery
globularity
glutinously
goldenberry
gracelessly
grandiosely
grandiosity
granularity
graphically
gratulatory
grotesquely
grotesquery
grumblingly
guilelessly
guiltlessly
gullibility
gymnospermy
gynaecology
haematology
hagiography
halfholiday
haphazardly
haplography
hazardously
healthfully
heartlessly
Hebraically
heliography
hepatectomy
heresiology
heretically
herpetology
heterophony
heterospory
hilariously
historicity
hobbledehoy
homoeopathy
homogeneity
hospitality
housewifely
housewifery
huckleberry
humiliatory
hurryscurry
hurryskurry
hydrography
hymnography
hypertrophy
hypsography
ichnography
ichthyology
iconography
identically
idiotically
idyllically
illiberally
illimitably
illiquidity
illogically
imaginarily
imitatively
immediately
immitigably
immortality
impartially
impassively
impassivity
impatiently
impenitency
imperfectly
imperiously
impermeably
impetratory
impetuosity
impetuously
implausibly
imploringly
impoliticly
importantly
importunely
importunity
imprecatory
imprecisely
impregnably
impropriety
imprudently
impulsively
inalienably
inalterably
inanimately
incantatory
incessantly
incipiently
inclemently
inclusively
incoherency
incommodity
incongruity
inconstancy
incorrectly
incorruptly
incredulity
inculpatory
incuriosity
incuriously
indefinably
indignantly
indivisibly
indomitably
indubitably
inductively
indulgently
inedibility
inelegantly
ineluctably
inequitably

inestimably
inexcusably
inferiority
infertility
inflammably
informality
informatory
infrequency
ingeniously
ingenuously
ingrainedly
inhabitancy
injuriously
innocuously
innoxiously
innumerably
inquiringly
insalubrity
inscrutably
insectology
insensately
inseparably
insidiously
insincerely
insincerity
insistently
inspiratory
instability
insultingly
insuperably
integrality
intensively
intercalary
interiority
interlunary
internality
intolerably
intractably
intrepidity
intricately
intrusively
intuitively
invectively
inventively
inviability
invidiously
inviolately
involuntary
ironmongery
irrecusably
irreducibly
irrefutably
irregularly
irrelevancy
irremovably
irreparably
irrevocably
irruptively
itinerantly
jabberwocky
judiciously
juridically
justifiably
kinesiology
laboriously
laconically
lacrimatory
lacrimosely
lacrymatory
lacrymosely
larcenously
laryngology
laryngotomy
laudability
lecherously
lesemajesty
lichenology
lickerishly
lieutenancy

ligamentary
lightsomely
limitlessly
lingeringly
lithography
lithotripsy
litigiously
loathsomely
longanimity
lucratively
ludicrously
luxuriantly
luxuriously
lycanthropy
mackerelsky
maddeningly
magnanimity
maladroitly
malariology
maledictory
maliciously
malignantly
manducatory
manufactory
marginality
martyrology
masculinely
masculinity
masterfully
masticatory
matchlessly
materiality
mediaevally
medicinally
melodiously
mercenarily
mercilessly
mercurially
meritocracy
meteorology
methodology
metoposcopy
micrography
mimetically
mirthlessly
misanthropy
miscibility
misguidedly
molecularly
molendinary
momentarily
momentously
monstrosity
monstrously
moribundity
moronically
moveability
multistorey
municipally
murderously
murmurously
muscularity
myrmecology
mythography
narratively
nationality
naturopathy
necessarily
nefariously
negligently
negotiatory
neighbourly
nephrectomy
nervelessly
nittygritty
nocturnally
noiselessly
nomadically
nondelivery

notoriously
nulliparity
numerically
nutritively
nympholepsy
obfuscatory
objectively
objectivity
objurgatory
obliviously
obnoxiously
observantly
observatory
observingly
obsessively
obstinately
obtrusively
occipitally
octagonally
octingenary
offensively
offhandedly
officinally
officiously
olfactology
oneiromancy
operatively
opportunely
opportunity
oracularity
orbicularly
orchidology
organically
originality
ornithology
orthography
oscillatory
osmotically
ostensively
osteography
osteoplasty
outspokenly
ovariectomy
pacifically
palpability
paramountcy
paramountly
parochially
partitively
passibility
peccability
peculiarity
pecuniarily
pellucidity
pendulously
penuriously
perceivably
perceptibly
perennially
perfunctory
periodicity
perishingly
permanently
permissibly
perpetually
perplexedly
persistency
personality
perspicuity
pertinacity
pertinently
pervasively
pervertedly
pestilently
petitionary
petrography
phalanstery
phonography
photography

phraseology
physicality
physiocracy
physiognomy
phytography
pictography
pictorially
pigheadedly
piratically
placability
plaintively
pleasurably
plenteously
plentifully
pocketmoney
pointlessly
poisonously
polarimetry
polemically
politically
poltroonery
polygonally
ponderosity
ponderously
pornography
portability
possibility
posteriorly
potentially
potteringly
powerlessly
practicably
practically
prattlingly
precedently
predatorily
predicatory
predictably
prefatorily
preliminary
prelusively
prelusorily
prematurely
prematurity
premonitory
preparatory
presanctify
presciently
presentably
pressagency
presumingly
pretendedly
prevalently
primaevally
primatology
primitively
principally
privatively
probability
procuratory
prodigality
profanatory
professedly
proficiency
prohibitory
prolificacy
prolificity
prominently
promiscuity
promisingly
propinquity
proprietary
prosaically
protonotary
providently
provisorily
provokingly
proximately
psychically

psychometry
psychopathy
pteridology
punctuality
pupillarity
purportedly
purposively
pyramidally
quadraphony
querulously
questionary
quiescently
quizzically
radiography
rancorously
rapaciously
rapturously
rateability
rationality
ravishingly
reactionary
readability
receptively
receptivity
recessively
reciprocity
recognitory
recumbently
recurrently
rediscovery
redundantly
reflexively
reflexology
reformatory
refringency
regardfully
regretfully
regrettably
rejoicingly
reliability
religiosity
religiously
reluctantly
repellantly
repellently
repentantly
reposefully
repressibly
reprobatory
reprography
reprovingly
repugnantly
repulsively
resentfully
resiliently
resistively
resistivity
respectably
respiratory
respondency
responsibly
retaliatory
retardatory
retentively
retentivity
retinoscopy
retributory
revisionary
rhabdomancy
rheumaticky
righteously
rubicundity
rudimentary
sagaciously
salaciously
saleability
salmonberry
sartorially
satanically

satiability
satirically
saturninely
scenography
sceptically
schistosity
scientology
scorchingly
scorpionfly
scoundrelly
screamingly
sculduddery
sculduggery
searchingly
secondarily
secretively
sectionally
sedentarily
sedimentary
seditionary
seditiously
seductively
segmentally
seismically
seismometry
selectively
selectivity
selfdisplay
selfmastery
semasiology
semimonthly
senselessly
sensibility
sensitively
sensitivity
sensorially
serendipity
serviceably
shamelessly
sheriffalty
shiftlessly
shrinkingly
sickeningly
sightlessly
sightworthy
sigmoidally
simperingly
singularity
sinistrally
skulduddery
skulduggery
sleeplessly
slightingly
smilelessly
sociability
solvability
somatically
somnolently
sorrowfully
soteriology
soundlessly
sovereignly
sovereignty
spastically
specificity
spectrality
spectrology
spelaeology
sphagnology
spherically
spinelessly
spiritually
spiritualty
splenectomy
spontaneity
squeamishly
squintingly
squirearchy
stainlessly

startlingly
statesmanly
statutorily
steadfastly
steerageway
stenochromy
stenography
stereometry
stereophony
stereoscopy
stethoscopy
stichometry
stipendiary
stipulatory
stomatology
straightway
stratocracy
strenuosity
strenuously
stringently
stumblingly
stylography
subaerially
subaxillary
subcategory
subcontrary
succulently
sufficiency
suitability
sumptuosity
sumptuously
superfamily
superfluity
superiority
superlunary
supervisory
suppliantly
supportably
suppository
surficially
susceptibly
sycophantry
syllabicity
tachygraphy
taciturnity
talkatively
tameability
tangibility
tastelessly
technically
technocracy
tegumentary
temperately
temporality
temporarily
tenaciously
tenementary
tensibility
tentatively
tephromancy
termagantly
terminology
testability
tetanically
thanatology
thanklessly
thankworthy
thaumaturgy
thermically
thermometry
thrillingly
titanically
toothsomely
torturously
totteringly
tracelessly
tracheotomy
tragicomedy
transiently
translunary
treasonably
tremblingly
tremulously
trenchantly
triadically
tributarily
triennially
troublously
truculently
trustworthy
turbulently
twelvepenny
typefoundry
tyrannously
unadvisedly
unanimously
unashamedly
unavoidably
unbendingly
unboundedly
unceasingly
uncertainly
uncertainty
undoubtedly
undutifully
unendurably
unfailingly
unfeelingly
unfeignedly
unguardedly
unhealthily
unhelpfully
unipolarity
unisexually
universally
unlimitedly
unmeaningly
unmemorably
unnaturally
unnecessary
unnervingly
unorthodoxy
unskilfully
unsmilingly
unsparingly
unspeakably
unthinkably
unutterably
unweetingly
unwillingly
unwinkingly
unwittingly
uranography
vagariously
valedictory
variability
vascularity
venatically
vendibility
venereology
ventriloquy
venturously
veraciously
veridically
verminously
versatilely
versatility
verticality
vesicularly
vestigially
vexatiously
vexillology
vibratility
vicariously
vicegerency
viceregally
viceroyalty
vincibility
vindicatory
vivaciously
voicelessly
volcanicity
volcanology
volitionary
voluntarily
voraciously
vulcanicity
vulcanology
warrantably
washability
wearilessly
wearisomely
whigmaleery
whimsically
wholesomely
winterberry
witheringly
wonderfully
workability
worrisomely
worthlessly
yellowbelly
zincography
weltschmerz

12 letter words

abbreviation
abolitionary
abolitionism
abolitionist
aboriginally
abortiveness
abrasiveness
absentminded
absoluteness
absolutistic
absorptional
absorptivity
absquatulate
abstemiously
abstractable
abstractedly
abstractness
abstruseness
academically
acaulescence
acceleration
accelerative
accentuation
acciaccatura
accidentally
accommodator
accompanyist
accomplished
accordionist
accouchement
accoutrement
accretionary
accumulation
accumulative
accurateness
accursedness
accusatively
accusatorial
acetabularia
acetaldehyde
achlamydeous
acoustically
acquaintance
acquiescence
acronychally
actinomycete
adaptability
adaptiveness
additionally
adequateness
adhesiveness
adjectivally
adjudication
adjudicative
adjudicatory
administrant
administrate
admonishment
adorableness
adscititious
adulteration
adulterously
advantageous
adventitious
advisability
aerodynamics
aeroembolism
aeronautical
aeroneurosis
aerosiderite
aesthetician
aestheticism
aetiological
affectedness
affectionate
aforethought
AfroAmerican
afterthought
agamogenesis
agamogenetic
agentgeneral
agglutinogen
aggressively
agranulocyte
agribusiness
agricultural
ailurophobia
aircondition
aircraftsman
alexipharmic
Alhambresque
alimentation
alimentative
alkalescence
alliteration
alliterative
allomorphism
allusiveness
alphabetical
alphamerical
alphanumeric
alterability
altitudinous
amalgamation
amalgamative
amateurishly
ambassadress
ambidextrous
ambivalently
amelioration
ameliorative
amenableness
amentiferous
amicableness
amitotically
amortisation
amphibiously
amphibrachic
amphictyonic
amphisbaenic
amphitheatre
amphitropous
amygdaloidal
anaerobiosis
anaesthetise
anaesthetist
anagogically
anagrammatic
analogically
analphabetic
analytically
anamorphosis
anaphylactic
anastigmatic
anathematise
anatomically
anecdotalist
anemographic
anemophilous
angiocarpous
annihilation
annihilative
announcement
annunciation
anotherguess
antagonistic
antecedently
antediluvian
anteprandial
anthelmintic
anthropogeny
anthropoidal
anthropology
antiaircraft
anticipation
anticipative
anticipatory
anticlerical
anticyclonic
antigenicity
antigropelos
antimacassar
antimagnetic
antimalarial
antineutrino
antiparticle
antipathetic
antiperiodic
antiphonally
antirachitic
antiSemitism
antistrophic
antithetical
aperiodicity
apiculturist
apochromatic
apolitically
apostolicism
apostolicity
apostrophise
apothegmatic
apparatchiki
apparatchiks
apparentness
apparitional
appendectomy
appendicitis
appendicular
apperception
apperceptive
appetisingly
appositeness
appositional
appraisement
appraisingly
appreciation
appreciative
appreciatory
apprehension
apprehensive
approachable
appropriable
appropriator
appurtenance
aquicultural

arborescence
arborisation
archdeaconry
archdiocesan
archetypally
archetypical
archipelagic
architecture
argillaceous
aristocratic
Aristotelean
Aristotelian
arithmetical
aromatically
aromaticness
arrhythmical
articulately
articulation
articulatory
artificially
artilleryman
artistically
asphyxiation
assassinator
assibilation
assimilation
assimilative
assimilatory
astonishment
astoundingly
astringently
astrological
astronautics
astronomical
astrophysics
asymmetrical
asynchronism
asynchronous
atheromatous
athletically
atmospherics
attitudinise
attorneyship
attractively
attributable
augmentation
augmentative
auscultation
auscultatory
auspiciously
Australasian
authenticate
authenticity
autocatalyse
autochthones
autodidactic
autoimmunity
automaticity
automobilist
automorphism
autonomously
availability
avantgardism
avantgardist
avariciously
avitaminoses
avitaminosis
bacchanalian
bachelorhood
bachelorship
backbreaking
backpedalled
backslapping
backwardness
backwoodsman
bactericidal
bacteriology
bacteriostat
balladmonger
balletomania
ballottement
banderillero
bantamweight
barbarically
barometrical
baselessness
basidiospore
bassorelievo
bassorilievo
bathypelagic
battleground
battlemented
beachcombing
beatifically
bedazzlement
beggarliness
behaviourism
behaviourist
belittlement
bellbottomed
belletristic
belligerence
belligerency
bellylanding
benefactress
beneficently
beneficially
benevolently
benzaldehyde
bequeathment
berzelianite
beseechingly
bespectacled
bewilderedly
bewilderment
bewitchingly
bibliography
bibliologist
bibliomaniac
bibliopegist
bibliophilic
bibliopolist
bibliothecae
bicentennial
bilateralism
bilharziasis
bilharziosis
bilingualism
billingsgate
billsticking
biochemistry
biocoenology
bioecologist
biogeography
biographical
biologically
biometrician
biophysicist
bioscientist
biosynthesis
biosynthetic
birdsnesting
birdwatching
birefringent
blabbermouth
blackbirding
blackcurrant
blackguardly
bladderwrack
blamableness
blamefulness
blandishment
blastfurnace
blastosphere
blastulation
blatherskite
bletherskate
blissfulness
blisteringly
blithesomely
blockbusting
bloodbrother
bloodletting
bloodstained
bloodthirsty
bloodyminded
bluestocking
blunderingly
blusteringly
boastfulness
bobbydazzler
bodybuilding
bodysnatcher
bodystocking
boisterously
bombdisposal
bonnetmonkey
bonnyclabber
boogiewoogie
bookingclerk
booklearning
bootlessness
borosilicate
bottlewasher
boulevardier
bowcompasses
brachydactyl
brackishness
brainstormer
brainwashing
brambleberry
brassbounder
brassrubbing
breakthrough
breaststroke
breastsummer
breathalyser
breathlessly
breathtaking
breechloader
brickfielder
brilliantine
brinkmanship
brokenwinded
bronchoscope
broncobuster
brontosaurus
buccaneering
buccaneerish
buffalograss
bulletheaded
bullfighting
bullheadedly
bureaucratic
burglarproof
burningglass
businesslike
butterflynut
buttermuslin
butterscotch
Byelorussian
cabbagewhite
cabinetmaker
cachinnation
cachinnatory
calamitously
calcareously
calculatedly
calisthenics
calligrapher
calligraphic
callisthenic
calorescence
calorimetric
calumniation
calumniatory
calumniously
calycoideous
camiknickers
campfollower
campodeiform
canaliculate
canalisation
cancellation
candleholder
canonisation
canorousness
Cantabrigian
cantankerous
cantharidian
cantillation
capercaillie
capercailzie
capitalistic
capitulation
capriciously
captiousness
caravansarai
caravanserai
carbohydrate
carbonaceous
carburetting
carcinogenic
cardcarrying
cardinalship
cardiography
cardiologist
carelessness
caricaturist
carillonneur
Carlovingian
carpetbagger
carpetknight
carragheenin
carriageable
Cartesianism
cartographer
cartographic
cartological
cashandcarry
catachrestic
catamountain
cataphoresis
catastrophic
catechetical
caterwauling
catholically
catilinarian
cattlelifter
cautiousness
cementitious
censoriously
centesimally
centrespread
centrosphere
centuplicate
ceremonially
chairmanship
chalcolithic
chalcopyrite
championship
chancemedley
chaplainship
characterise
charlatanism
charnelhouse
charterhouse
charterparty
chastisement
chauvinistic
checkerberry
checkerboard
cheerfulness
cheeseburger
cheesecutter
cheesemonger
cheeseparing
cheirography
chemotherapy
chequerboard
cherubically
chesterfield
chieftainess
childbearing
childishness
chimneypiece
chiropractic
chiropractor
chitterlings
chivalrously
chlorination
chocolatebox
chondriosome
choreography
chorographic
chorological
chrematistic
chrestomathy
Christianise
Christianity
Christolatry
Christophany
chromaticism
chromaticity
chromatogram
chromatology
chromatopsia
chromosphere
chronography
chronologise
chronologist
chronometric
churchianity
churchwarden
churlishness
cinematheque
circuitously
circumcision
circumfluent
circumfusion
circumjacent
circumscribe
circumstance
cirrocumulus
cirrostratus
civilisation
clairaudient
clairvoyance
clangorously
clannishness
clapperboard
clarinettist
classicalism
classicalist
classicality
classifiable
clatteringly
claudication
clavicembalo
clearsighted
cleistogamic
cliffhanging
clinkerbuilt
closecropped
closegrained
closemouthed
clotheshorse
clothespress
clownishness
coacervation
coachbuilder
coalitionist
cockfighting
cocksureness
codification

coelenterate
coenobitical
coenobytical
coerciveness
coetaneously
cohabitation
cohesiveness
coincidental
coincidently
coldshoulder
coleopterist
coleopterous
collaborator
collaterally
collectively
collectivise
collectivism
collectivist
collectivity
collegialism
collegiality
collegiately
collinearity
colloquially
collywobbles
colonisation
coloquintida
colorimetric
colourlessly
columniation
combinations
comfortingly
commandingly
commemorator
commencement
commendation
commendatory
commensalism
commensalist
commensurate
commentation
commercially
commiserator
commissarial
commissariat
commissioner
committeeman
commodiously
commonwealth
communicable
communicably
communicator
companionate
companionway
compatriotic
compellation
compensation
compensative
compensatory
complacently
complaisance
complemental
completeness
complexional
complexioned
complication
composedness
compoundable
compressible
compulsively
compulsivity
compulsorily
compunctious
compurgation
compurgatory
concelebrant
concelebrate
concentrator
conceptional
conceptually
conchiferous
conchologist
conciliation
conciliative
conciliatory
conclusively
concomitance
concordantly
concrescence
concreteness
concubitancy
concupiscent
concurrently
condemnation
condemnatory
condensation
conductivity
conduplicate
confabulator
confectioner
conferential
confessional
confidential
confirmation
confirmative
confirmatory
confiscation
confiscatory
conformation
confoundedly
Confucianism
confusedness
congeniality
congenitally
conglobation
conglomerate
conglutinate
congratulant
congratulate
congregation
conidiophore
conidiospore
conjunctival
connaturally
connectional
connectively
conningtower
connubiality
conquistador
conscionable
conscription
consecration
consecratory
consensually
consentience
consentingly
consequently
conservation
conservatism
conservative
conservatory
considerable
considerably
consignation
consistently
consistorial
consociation
consolidator
conspiration
constabulary
constipation
constituency
constitution
constitutive
constriction
constrictive
constringent
construction
constructive
consultation
consultative
consummately
consummation
consummative
consummatory
contagionist
contagiously
containerise
contemplator
contemporary
contemporise
contemptible
contemptibly
contemptuous
conterminous
contestation
contextually
contiguously
contingently
continuation
continuative
continuously
contractable
contractedly
contractible
contradictor
contrapuntal
contrariness
contrariwise
contribution
contributive
contributory
contriteness
contrivement
controllable
contumacious
contumelious
convalescent
convectional
conveniently
conventicler
conventional
conversation
conveyancing
convincement
convincingly
conviviality
convulsively
coordinately
coordination
coordinative
copolymerise
copulatively
coquettishly
corelatively
corespondent
corporeality
correctional
correctitude
correctively
corroborator
cosmetically
cosmogonical
cosmographer
cosmographic
cosmological
cosmopolitan
cosmopolitic
costermonger
cottonocracy
cotyledonary
cotyledonous
councilwoman
countenancer
counteragent
counterblast
countercheck
counterclaim
counterforce
counterlight
countermarch
counterplead
counterpoint
counterpoise
counterproof
counterscarp
countershaft
countertenor
countrydance
countrywoman
courageously
courtmartial
courtplaster
cousingerman
covetousness
cowardliness
crackbrained
craftbrother
craniologist
crashlanding
creativeness
creepycrawly
crenellation
criticalness
crossbedding
crossbencher
crossbuttock
crosscountry
crosscurrent
crossexamine
crossgrained
crossheading
crossingover
crosspurpose
crosssection
cryptanalyst
cryptogamous
cryptography
cryptologist
crystalgazer
cuckingstool
cuckooflower
culpableness
cultivatable
cumbersomely
cumbrousness
cumulatively
cumulocirrus
cumulonimbus
cuprammonium
curlingirons
curlingtongs
curmudgeonly
curvicaudate
curvicostate
curvifoliate
curvirostral
customshouse
cynocephalus
cytogenetics
Czechoslovak
deactivation
deambulatory
debilitation
debonairness
decaffeinate
decalescence
decapitation
decasyllabic
decasyllable
deceleration
decentralise
decipherable
decipherment
decisiveness
declinometer
decomposable
decompressor
decongestant
decongestion
decongestive
deconsecrate
decontrolled
decoratively
decorousness
decreasingly
deescalation
definiteness
definitively
deflagration
deflationary
deflationist
defraudation
degenerately
degeneration
degenerative
deionisation
dejectedness
delamination
deliberately
deliberation
deliberative
delicatessen
delightfully
delimitation
delinquently
deliquescent
delitescence
delusiveness
demilitarise
demimondaine
demineralise
demodulation
demoniacally
demonstrable
demonstrably
demonstrator
denaturalise
denaturation
denomination
denominative
denouncement
densitometer
denticulated
dentilingual
denuclearise
denunciation
denunciative
denunciatory
deontologist
departmental
depoliticise
depopulation
depravedness
depreciation
depreciatory
depressingly
deputisation
deracination
derisiveness
derivational
derivatively
dermatophyte
derogatorily
desalination
desideration
desiderative
desirability
desirousness
desolateness
despairingly
despitefully
despoliation
despondently
despotically

desquamation
desquamative
desquamatory
dessertspoon
destructible
desulphurise
detachedness
determinable
determinably
determinedly
dethronement
detoxication
detumescence
Deuteronomic
deviationism
deviationist
dextrousness
diabolically
diageotropic
diagrammatic
dialectician
dialectology
diamagnetism
diamonddrill
diamondfield
diaphanously
diastrophism
diathermancy
diatomaceous
diatonically
dibranchiate
dichromatism
dictatorship
didactically
dietetically
differentiae
differential
digressional
digressively
dilapidation
dilatability
dilatoriness
dilettantish
dilettantism
diminishable
diminishment
diminutively
dinnerjacket
diphtheritic
diphthongise
directorship
disaccharide
disadvantage
disaffection
disaffiliate
disagreeable
disagreeably
disagreement
disallowance
disambiguate
disannulling
disannulment
disassociate
disastrously
disbursement
discerningly
discerptible
discipleship
disciplinary
disclamation
discographer
discomfiture
discommodity
discomposure
disconnected
disconnexion
disconsolate
discontented
discordantly
discountable
discouraging
discourteous
discoverable
discoverture
discreetness
discreteness
discretional
discriminant
discriminate
discursively
disdainfully
disembarrass
disenchanter
disendowment
disestablish
disfranchise
disgorgement
disguisement
disgustfully
disgustingly
disharmonise
dishevelment
disincentive
disinfectant
disinfection
disinflation
disingenuous
disintegrate
disinterment
disjointedly
dislodgement
disobedience
disorientate
dispensation
dispensatory
dispiritedly
displaceable
displacement
displeasedly
dispossessor
disputatious
disquisition
disregardful
disreputable
disreputably
dissatisfied
disseminator
dissentingly
dissertation
disseverance
disseverment
dissimilarly
dissimulator
dissocialise
dissociation
dissociative
dissuasively
dissymmetric
distemperate
distillation
distillatory
distinctness
distortional
distractedly
distrainable
distrainment
distributary
distribution
distributive
disturbingly
divarication
diversionary
diversionist
diverticular
diverticulum
divertimenti
divertimento
divisibility
divisiveness
dodecahedral
dodecahedron
dodecaphonic
dogmatically
dolorousness
domestically
domesticator
dorsiventral
doubleacting
doubledealer
doubledecked
doubledecker
doublelocked
doubtfulness
dovecoloured
downwardness
dramatically
dramaturgist
draughtboard
draughthorse
drawingboard
drawingpaper
dreadfulness
dressinggown
droughtiness
dubitatively
duckingstool
dunderheaded
duraluminium
dwarfishness
dynamometric
dynastically
earsplitting
earthshaking
eavesdropped
eavesdropper
eccentricity
ecclesiastic
ecclesiology
echinococcus
echolocation
echosounding
eclectically
ecologically
econometrics
economically
ecstatically
ectoparasite
editorialise
editorialist
educationist
edulcoration
effectuality
effectuation
effeminately
effervescent
efflorescent
effortlessly
effusiveness
Egyptologist
elasmobranch
electrically
electrolysis
electrolytic
electrometer
electronvolt
electroplate
electroscope
electroshock
electrotonic
electrotonus
electrotyper
eleemosynary
elementalism
elementarily
elliptically
elocutionary
elocutionist
elucubration
emancipation
emargination
emasculation
emasculatory
embattlement
embezzlement
embitterment
emblazonment
emblematical
embranchment
embryologist
emotionalise
emotionalism
emotionalist
emotionality
emphatically
empoisonment
empressement
emulsifiable
enantiomorph
encephalitic
encephalitis
enchantingly
encirclement
enclitically
encroachment
encrustation
encumberment
encumbrancer
encyclopedia
encyclopedic
endamagement
endangerment
endermically
endocarditis
endometritis
endoparasite
endoskeletal
enfeeblement
enginedriver
enginetuning
Englishwoman
enormousness
enshrinement
enswathement
entanglement
enterprising
entertaining
enthronement
enthusiastic
entomologise
entomologist
entrammelled
entrancement
entreatingly
entrenchment
entrepreneur
enviableness
envisagement
enzymologist
epexegetical
ephemerality
epicureanism
epicycloidal
epidemically
epidemiology
epigrammatic
epiphenomena
episcopalian
episodically
epistemology
epithalamion
epithalamium
equalisation
equalitarian
equationally
equestrienne
equidistance
equilibrator
equipollence
equipollency
equiprobable
equitability
equivalently
equivocation
equivocatory
eruptiveness
erythematous
erythroblast
erythromycin
escapologist
escutcheoned
esoterically
espagnolette
essentiality
estrangement
etherisation
ethnocentric
ethnographer
ethnographic
ethnological
etymological
etymologicon
euhemeristic
eunuchoidism
euphonically
euphoniously
EuroAmerican
evanescently
evangelistic
eveningdress
evidentially
evisceration
evolutionary
evolutionism
evolutionist
exacerbation
exaggeration
exaggerative
exaggeratory
exasperation
exchangeable
excitability
exclusionary
exclusionism
exclusionist
excogitation
excogitative
excruciating
excruciation
excursionist
executorship
exegetically
exenteration
exercitation
exhaustively
exhibitioner
exhilaration
exhilarative
exiguousness
exophthalmic
exophthalmos
exophthalmus
exorbitantly
exospherical
exoterically
expansionary
expansionism
expansionist
expatriation
expediential
experiential
experimental
experimenter
explantation
explicitness
exploitation

exploitative
expressional
expressively
expressivity
exprobration
exsanguinate
exsanguinous
exsufflicate
extensometer
exterminable
exterminator
extinguisher
extortionary
extortionate
extracranial
extraditable
extralimital
extramarital
extramundane
extraneously
extrasensory
extraspecial
extrauterine
extravagance
extravagancy
extravaganza
extraversion
extroversion
exulceration
fabulousness
facelessness
facilitation
factionalism
factiousness
factitiously
fainthearted
faintishness
faithfulness
faithhealing
falcongentil
falcongentle
fallaciously
fancifulness
fantasticate
fantasticism
farmsteading
farsightedly
fastidiously
fatherfigure
fatherliness
faultfinding
fearlessness
fearsomeness
featherbrain
featheriness
fecklessness
feebleminded
feldspathoid
felicitation
felicitously
feminineness
feminisation
fenestration
fermentation
fermentative
ferrugineous
fertilisable
feverishness
fibrillation
fibrinolysin
fictionalise
fictitiously
fiddlefaddle
fiddlesticks
fieldglasses
fiendishness
figuratively
filibusterer
filtrability
finalisation
firefighting
firstnighter
flabelliform
flagellation
flagellatory
flagitiously
flamboyantly
flamethrower
flammability
flatteringly
flavoprotein
flickeringly
flocculation
floodlighted
floriculture
fluidisation
fluorescence
fluoridation
fluorination
fluorocarbon
focalisation
folliculated
footplateman
foraminifera
forbiddingly
forcefulness
forcibleness
forebodement
forebodingly
forensically
foresightful
forestalment
formaldehyde
formlessness
forthrightly
fortuitously
fostermother
foundationer
fountainhead
fractionally
fractionator
FrancoGerman
frangibility
frankincense
fraudulently
freakishness
freestanding
freeswimming
freethinking
freewheeling
freightliner
frenchpolish
frenetically
frequentness
fricasseeing
frictionless
friendliness
frontbencher
frontiersman
frontispiece
fructiferous
fructivorous
fruitfulness
fugitiveness
fuliginosity
fullyfledged
functionally
functionless
furfuraceous
furunculosis
futilitarian
futurologist
galactogogue
galligaskins
gallinaceous
galvanically
galvanometer
galvanoscope
gamesmanship
gamesomeness
gametophytic
gamopetalous
gamophyllous
gamosepalous
ganglionated
gasification
gastronomist
gastropodous
geanticlinal
genealogical
generousness
genuflection
geochemistry
geographical
geologically
geomagnetism
geometrician
geophysicist
geopolitical
geosynclinal
geotectonics
geriatrician
Germanophile
Germanophobe
gerontocracy
gesellschaft
gesticulator
ghoulishness
gigantically
glaciologist
gladiatorial
gladsomeness
glassblowing
glaucescence
glaucomatous
glitteringly
globetrotter
glockenspiel
gloriousness
glossography
glossologist
gluttonously
glycogenesis
glycoprotein
glyphography
glyptography
gobbledegook
gobbledygook
gonadotropic
gonadotropin
goodhumoured
goodtempered
goosepimples
gorgeousness
governmental
governorship
gracefulness
graciousness
grallatorial
graminaceous
grammaticise
grammolecule
gramnegative
grampositive
granodiorite
graphologist
graspingness
gratefulness
gratifyingly
gratuitously
graveclothes
gravelelling
greathearted
greengrocery
greenishness
gregariously
grievousness
griseofulvin
grossularite
grotesquerie
groundcherry
groundlessly
grovellingly
gruesomeness
guaranteeing
guardianship
guestchamber
guilefulness
gymnosophist
gynaecocracy
gyromagnetic
haberdashery
habilitation
habitability
habitforming
habitualness
haematoblast
haematolysis
haematoxylon
haemophiliac
haemopoiesis
haemorrhagic
hagiographer
hagiographic
hagiological
hairdressing
hairsbreadth
hairsplitter
halftimbered
hallucinogen
hallucinosis
halogenation
halterbroken
handicapping
handkerchief
handsbreadth
handsomeness
happenstance
hardfavoured
hardfeatured
hardstanding
harlequinade
harmlessness
harmonically
harmoniously
harquebusier
headmistress
headquarters
headshrinker
heartburning
heartrending
heartstrings
heartwarming
heathenishly
heavenliness
heavyhearted
hebdomadally
hebetudinous
hectographic
hedgehopping
heedlessness
heliocentric
heliographer
heliographic
heliogravure
heliolatrous
heliotherapy
heliotropism
hellgrammite
helplessness
hemerocallis
hemichordate
hemimorphism
hemimorphite
hemiparasite
hemispheroid
henceforward
henotheistic
heortologist
heraldically
hereditament
hereditarily
hereinbefore
heritability
hermeneutics
hermetically
heroicalness
heroicomical
herpetologic
hesitatingly
hesperididia
heterocercal
heterocyclic
heteroecious
heterogamous
heterogenous
heterologous
heteromerous
heteronomous
heterophylly
heterosexual
heterozygote
heterozygous
hibernaculum
hierarchical
hieroglyphic
hierographer
hierophantic
highcoloured
highfaluting
highhandedly
highlystrung
highpressure
highsounding
highspirited
highstepping
hindquarters
hippocentaur
hippopotamus
hirepurchase
histogenesis
histogenetic
histological
historically
holidaymaker
homeomorphic
homeopathist
homesickness
homoeopathic
homoeostasis
homologation
homomorphism
homomorphous
homonymously
homosexually
homothallism
honeybuzzard
hoodmanblind
hopelessness
horizontally
horrendously
horribleness
horrifically
horrorstruck
horsebreaker
horsemanship
horsetrading
horsewhipped
horticulture
housebreaker
housekeeping
housetrained
housewarming
hubblebubble
hucklebacked

huggermugger
humanisation
humanitarian
humification
humorousness
humptydumpty
hybridisable
hydatidiform
hydrochloric
hydrodynamic
hydrofluoric
hydrographer
hydrographic
hydrokinetic
hydrological
hydrolysable
hydromedusae
hydromedusan
hydrophilous
hydroquinone
hydrostatics
hydrotherapy
hydrothermal
hydrotropism
hygienically
hygrophilous
hymenopteran
hymnographer
hyperacidity
hyperbolical
hyperplastic
hyperpyretic
hyperpyrexia
hypersthenia
hypersthenic
hypertension
hypertensive
hyperthermia
hypertrophic
hypnogenesis
hypnogenetic
hypnotherapy
hypnotically
hypnotisable
hypochlorite
hypochondria
hypocoristic
hypocritical
hypogastrium
hypognathous
hypophrygian
hypostatical
hyposulphite
hypothalamic
hypothalamus
hypothecator
hypothetical
hysterectomy
hysterically
hysteromania
ichthyocolla
ichthyolatry
ichthyophagy
iconoclastic
iconographer
idealisation
ideationally
identifiable
idiosyncrasy
idiothermous
idolatrously
illadvisedly
illegibility
illegitimacy
illegitimate
illiberality
illiterately
illnaturedly
illogicality
illtreatment
illumination
illuminative
illusiveness
illusoriness
illustration
illustrative
immaculately
immaterially
immatureness
immeasurable
immeasurably
immemorially
immensurable
immethodical
immoderately
immoderation
immovability
immunisation
immunologist
immutability
impartiality
impedimental
impenetrable
impenetrably
impenitently
imperatively
imperatorial
imperceptive
impercipient
imperfection
imperfective
imperishable
imperishably
impermanence
impermanency
impersonally
impersonator
impertinence
impertinency
imperviously
impetiginous
implantation
implicitness
impoliteness
imponderable
imponderably
impoverished
impregnation
impressively
imprisonment
impropriator
improvidence
improvisator
imputability
imputatively
inaccessible
inaccessibly
inaccurately
inactivation
inadequately
inadmissible
inadmissibly
inadvertence
inadvertency
inappeasable
inapplicable
inapplicably
inappositely
inarticulate
inartificial
inaudibility
inauguration
inauguratory
inauspicious
incalculable
incalculably
incalescence
incandescent
incapability
incapacitate
incatenation
incautiously
incendiarism
incestuously
incidentally
incineration
incisiveness
inclinometer
incognisable
incognisance
incognitable
incoherently
incommodious
incommutable
incommutably
incomparable
incomparably
incompatible
incompatibly
incompetence
incompetency
incompletely
incompliance
incomputable
inconcinnity
inconclusive
inconformity
inconsequent
inconsistent
inconsolable
inconsolably
inconsonance
inconstantly
inconsumable
inconsumably
incontiguous
incontinence
incontinency
inconvenient
incoordinate
incorporated
incorporator
incorporeity
incorrigible
incorrigibly
incorruption
increasingly
incrustation
incurability
indebtedness
indecisively
indeclinable
indecorously
indefeasible
indefeasibly
indefectible
indefensible
indefensibly
indefinitely
indehiscence
indelibility
indelicately
independence
independency
indicatively
indifference
indifferency
indigenously
indigestible
indirectness
indiscipline
indiscreetly
indiscretion
indisputable
indisputably
indissoluble
indissolubly
indistinctly
indivertible
indivertibly
individually
indoctrinate
IndoEuropean
IndoGermanic
industrially
ineffaceable
ineffaceably
inefficiency
inelasticity
ineradicable
ineradicably
inescutcheon
inexactitude
inexpedience
inexpediency
inexperience
inexpertness
inexplicable
inexplicably
inexpressive
inexpugnable
inexpugnably
inextensible
inextricable
inextricably
infanticidal
infectiously
infelicitous
infiniteness
infinitively
inflammation
inflammatory
inflationary
inflationism
inflationist
inflectional
infrequently
infringement
infundibular
infusibility
ingloriously
ingratiating
inhabitation
inharmonious
inhospitable
inhospitably
iniquitously
innutritious
inobservance
inoccupation
inoperculate
inordinately
inosculation
insalubrious
insecticidal
insemination
insolubilise
insolubility
inspectorate
inspectorial
inspissation
installation
instauration
instillation
instructress
instrumental
insufferable
insufferably
insufficient
insufflation
insurrection
integumental
intellection
intellective
intellectual
intelligence
intelligible
intelligibly
intemperance
inteneration
interbedding
interception
intercession
intercessory
interchanger
interconnect
intercropped
intercurrent
intercutting
interdiction
interdictive
interdictory
interdigital
interestedly
interfemoral
interference
interglacial
interjection
interjectory
interlobular
interlocutor
intermeddler
intermediacy
intermediary
intermediate
interminable
interminably
intermission
intermittent
intermitting
intermixture
intermundane
internuclear
internuncial
interoceanic
interoceptor
interpellate
interpleader
interpolator
interpretive
interrelated
interrogator
interruption
interruptive
intersection
interservice
interspinous
interstellar
interstitial
intertexture
intervenient
intervention
intervocalic
interwreathe
intimidation
intimidatory
intolerantly
intoxication
intracardiac
intracranial
intramundane
intransigent
intransitive
intrauterine
intrenchment
intriguingly
introduction
introductory
introjection
intromission
intromittent
intromitting
introversion
introversive
introvertive

intrusionist
intuitionism
intuitionist
intumescence
intussuscept
invagination
invalidation
inveiglement
invertebrate
investigator
inveterately
invigilation
invigoration
invisibility
involutional
invulnerable
invulnerably
irascibility
irrationally
irredeemable
irredeemably
irreflective
irreformable
irrefragable
irrefragably
irregardless
irregularity
irrelatively
irrelevantly
irremediable
irremediably
irremissible
irrepealable
irreprovable
irresistible
irresistibly
irresolutely
irresolution
irresolvable
irrespective
irrespirable
irresponsive
irreverently
irreversible
irreversibly
irritability
irritatingly
Ishmaelitish
isochromatic
isochronally
isodiametric
isolationism
isolationist
isothermally
jerrybuilder
jesuitically
jetpropelled
journalistic
judgematical
jurisconsult
jurisdiction
jurisprudent
juvenescence
kaleidoscope
karyokinesis
katzenjammer
Keynesianism
kilowatthour
kinaesthesia
kinaesthesis
kinaesthetic
kindergarten
kinnikinnick
kirschwasser
kissingcrust
kleptomaniac
klipspringer
knighterrant
knightliness
kremlinology
laboursaving
labyrinthian
labyrinthine
lachrymation
lachrymatory
lachrymosely
lacininiated
laisserfaire
laissezaller
laissezfaire
lakedwelling
landingcraft
landingfield
landingstage
landingstrip
landlubberly
languishment
languorously
lanternjawed
lanternslide
largehearted
laryngoscope
laryngoscopy
lasciviously
laterisation
laticiferous
latinisation
latitudinous
laudableness
laureateship
leapfrogging
leathercloth
ledgertackle
lefthandedly
legalisation
legitimately
legitimation
legitimatise
lepidopteran
leucocytosis
leukocytosis
levorotation
levorotatory
lexicography
lexicologist
liberalistic
libidinously
licentiously
licketysplit
lifelessness
lighthearted
limnological
linguistical
liquefacient
liquefaction
listlessness
literariness
lithographer
lithographic
lithological
lithospheric
lithotritist
liturgically
liturgiology
Liverpudlian
liverystable
localisation
lodginghouse
logistically
lonesomeness
longdistance
longitudinal
longshoreman
longstanding
longwindedly
lopsidedness
loquaciously
loungelizard
lovelessness
lovelornness
LowChurchman
lugubriously
lukewarmness
lumberjacket
luminescence
luminiferous
luminousness
lusciousness
lycanthropic
machicolated
macrocephaly
macropterous
mademoiselle
magistrature
magnetically
magnetisable
magnetograph
magnetometer
magnifically
magnificence
magniloquent
maidenliness
maidenstakes
maintainable
majestically
majorgeneral
malacologist
malapertness
malcontented
malevolently
malformation
malleability
malnutrition
maltreatment
malversation
mangelwurzel
Manicheanism
manifoldness
manipulation
manipulative
manipulatory
mannerliness
manoeuvrable
manometrical
mansionhouse
manslaughter
manufacturer
Marcionitism
marketgarden
marketsquare
marksmanship
marlinespike
marriageable
Marseillaise
marshharrier
marvellously
mastersinger
masterstroke
masterswitch
mastigophora
materialness
mathematical
matriarchate
maximisation
mealymouthed
meaningfully
mechanically
mediaevalism
mediaevalist
meditatively
meetinghouse
megalomaniac
melancholiac
melanochroic
melodramatic
meltingpoint
mendaciously
menstruation
mercantilism
mercantilist
merchantable
mercifulness
mercurialise
mercurialism
meretricious
meridionally
meristematic
merrythought
mesocephalic
mesothoracic
messeigneurs
metachronism
metagalactic
metalanguage
metallically
metallophone
metallurgist
metalworking
metamorphism
metamorphose
metaphorical
metaphrastic
metaphysical
metapsychics
metasomatism
metathetical
metathoracic
meteorically
meteorograph
methodically
meticulously
metrological
metropolitan
mezzorelievo
mezzosoprano
microanalyst
microbiology
microcapsule
microcephaly
microcircuit
microclimate
microcopying
microcrystal
micrographer
microphysics
microscopist
microseismic
microsurgery
middleweight
militaristic
millesimally
milliammeter
mindlessness
minedetector
mineralogist
minicomputer
minimisation
ministration
ministrative
miraculously
mirthfulness
misadventure
misalignment
misanthropic
misapprehend
misbehaviour
miscalculate
miscellanist
misdemeanant
misdemeanour
misdirection
miseducation
misinterpret
misjudgement
misknowledge
misplacement
mispronounce
misquotation
misrepresent
misselthrush
misstatement
mistakenness
mistranslate
mistreatment
mistressship
mithridatise
mithridatism
mitochondria
mitrailleuse
mnemotechnic
mobilisation
moderateness
modification
modificatory
moistureless
molecularity
monadelphous
monastically
monetisation
moneychanger
moneygrubber
moneyspinner
monitorially
monkeyflower
monkeyjacket
monkeypuzzle
monkeywrench
monochromate
monodramatic
monofilament
monographist
monomaniacal
monometallic
monomorphous
monopetalous
monophyletic
Monophysitic
monopodially
monopolistic
monostichous
monostrophic
monosyllabic
monosyllable
monotheistic
monotonously
monumentally
moralisation
mordaciously
morningdress
morphallaxis
morphologist
morrisdancer
mosstrooping
motherfigure
motherliness
mothertongue
motivational
motorcyclist
motorisation
mountainside
mournfulness
mourningband
mourningring
mouthbreeder
moveableness
movelessness
mucilaginous
muddleheaded
mulligatawny
multicentral
multidentate
multifarious
multiflorous
multifoliate
multiformity

multilateral
multilingual
multiloquous
multinuclear
multipartite
multipliable
multiplicand
multiplicate
multiplicity
multipurpose
multistoried
multivalence
multiversity
multungulate
municipalise
municipality
munificently
musicianship
musicologist
mutinousness
muttonheaded
muzzleloader
myrmecophily
mysteriously
mystifyingly
mythographer
mythological
mythologiser
nailscissors
namedropping
namelessness
nanoplankton
narcissistic
narcotically
narrowminded
naturalistic
naturopathic
nauseatingly
nauseousness
navigability
navigational
nebulisation
nebulousness
necrographer
necrological
necrophagous
necrophiliac
necrophilism
necrophilous
needlessness
negativeness
negativistic
neglectfully
negotiatress
negrophilism
negrophilist
neighbouring
neoclassical
neoDarwinian
neoDarwinism
neoDarwinist
Neohellenism
neonomianism
Neoplatonism
Neoplatonist
nephanalysis
nephelometer
nephelometry
nephrologist
nerveracking
Nestorianism
neurasthenia
neurasthenic
neuroanatomy
neurobiology
neurological
neuropterous
neuroscience
neurosurgeon
neurosurgery
neurotically
nevertheless
newfashioned
Newfoundland
newspaperman
nicotinamide
nidification
nightclothes
nimbostratus
niminypiminy
nitrobenzene
noctambulant
noctambulism
noctambulist
noctambulous
noctilucence
nomenclative
nomenclature
nominalistic
nonagenarian
nonalignment
nonchalantly
noncombatant
noncommittal
noncomplying
nonconductor
nonconformer
noneffective
nonefficient
nonessential
noneuclidean
nonexistence
nonflammable
nonflowering
nonidentical
nonobjective
nonresidence
nonresistant
noradrenalin
northeastern
northernmost
Northumbrian
northwestern
notification
novelisation
numerologist
numerousness
nutritionist
nutritiously
nychthemeral
nychthemeron
nyctitropism
nympholeptic
nymphomaniac
obdurateness
obedientiary
oblanceolate
obligatorily
obligingness
obliteration
obliterative
obmutescence
obnubilation
obscurantism
obscurantist
obsequiously
obsolescence
obsoleteness
obstetrician
obstreperous
occasionally
occidentally
occupational
oceanography
oceanologist
octogenarian
octosyllabic
octosyllable
odontologist
officeholder
offscourings
oldfashioned
oligarchical
omnipotently
omnipresence
omnisciently
omnivorously
oncorhynchus
oneirocritic
onesidedness
oneupmanship
onomatopoeia
onomatopoeic
openhandedly
openmindedly
operatically
ophiophagous
opinionative
opisthograph
opisthotonos
opposability
oppositeness
oppositional
oppressively
optimisation
orbicularity
orchestrator
orchidaceous
ordinariness
organgrinder
organisation
organography
organoleptic
orienteering
ornamentally
ornithomancy
ornithoscopy
orographical
orthodontics
orthodontist
orthogenesis
orthogenetic
orthographer
orthographic
orthopaedics
orthopaedist
orthopterist
orthopteroid
orthopterous
orthotropism
orthotropous
oscillograph
oscilloscope
ossification
ostentatious
osteogenesis
osteological
osteomalacia
osteoplastic
osteoporosis
otherworldly
outdatedness
outlandishly
outmanoeuvre
outpensioner
outrageously
outrivalling
outstretched
outstripping
outwardbound
overabundant
overachiever
overactivity
overcautious
overcritical
overcropping
overemphasis
overestimate
overexertion
overexposure
overlordship
overniceness
overpersuade
overpowering
overpressure
overreaction
oversimplify
overstepping
oxyacetylene
pacification
pacificatory
paedobaptism
paedogenesis
paedogenetic
paedomorphic
painlessness
palaeobotany
palaeography
Palaeolithic
palatability
paletteknife
palingenesia
palingenesis
palingenetic
Palladianism
palynologist
panchromatic
pancreatitis
panhellenism
panification
pantechnicon
pantisocracy
pantographic
papyrologist
paraboloidal
paradigmatic
paradisaical
paradisiacal
paraesthesia
paragraphist
parallelling
paralysation
paramagnetic
parametrical
paramilitary
paramorphism
paranormally
paraphrastic
parasiticide
parasitology
paratactical
parenthesise
parisyllabic
parkinsonism
parochialise
parochialism
parochiality
paronomastic
parsimonious
participator
particularly
partisanship
partitionist
pasqueflower
passepartout
passionately
passionfruit
pathetically
pathogenesis
pathogenetic
pathological
patriarchate
patternmaker
patulousness
peacefulness
pearlescence
peasepudding
peccadilloes
pedantically
pedicellaria
pedunculated
peerlessness
pejoratively
pellucidness
penalisation
penitentiary
pennypincher
pennywhistle
peradventure
perambulator
perceptively
perceptivity
perceptually
percussively
percutaneous
peregrinator
peremptorily
perfectively
perfervidity
perfidiously
perfoliation
performative
pericarditis
perilousness
periodically
periodontics
periodontist
periostracum
peripherally
periphrastic
perispomenon
peristeronic
peristomatic
perjuriously
permanganate
permeability
permissively
permittivity
perniciously
pernoctation
peroxidation
perpetration
perpetuation
perplexingly
perseverance
persistently
perspicacity
perspiration
perspiratory
persuasively
pertinacious
perturbation
perturbative
perverseness
perviousness
pestilential
pestological
petrifaction
petrographer
petrographic
petrological
pettifoggery
pettifogging
phagocytosis
phagocytotic
phanerogamic
pharmaceutic
pharmacology
phenological
phenomenally
phenotypical
philadelphus
philanthrope
philanthropy
philharmonic

philhellenic
philistinism
phillumenist
philodendron
philological
philosophise
phlebotomise
phlebotomist
phonasthenia
phonemically
phonetically
phonographer
phonographic
phonological
phosphoresce
photochromic
photofission
photogeology
photographer
photographic
photogravure
photokinesis
photokinetic
photomontage
photophilous
photosetting
photospheric
phototropism
phrasemonger
phraseograph
phreatophyte
phrenologist
phycological
phycomycetes
phyllotactic
phylogenesis
phylogenetic
physiognomic
physiography
physiologist
phytogenesis
phytogenetic
phytographer
phytological
phytophagous
pickerelweed
pictographic
pigeonbreast
pigmentation
pilotballoon
pinfeathered
pisciculture
pitcherplant
pitiableness
pitilessness
pitterpatter
placesetting
plainclothed
plainclothes
plaindealing
planetesimal
planetstruck
planispheric
planoconcave
plasterboard
platonically
Plattdeutsch
plausibility
playingfield
pleasantness
pleasingness
pleasureless
plebiscitary
plecopterous
plectognathi
pleiotropism
plenipotence
pleomorphism
plesiosaurus
plumbaginous
plumbiferous
plummerblock
pluriliteral
pluviometric
pneumaticity
pneumatology
pneumothorax
poikilotherm
pointilliste
polarimetric
polarisation
polarography
policyholder
polychaetous
polychromous
polyethylene
polyglottism
polyhistoric
polymorphism
polymorphous
polyneuritic
polyneuritis
polypetalous
polyphyletic
polysepalous
polysyllabic
polysyllable
polytheistic
polytonality
polyurethane
pontifically
pontificator
poorspirited
populousness
porcelainise
porcelainous
porcellanous
pornographer
pornographic
portentously
portmanteaus
portmanteaux
positiveness
positivistic
possessively
postdiluvian
postdoctoral
posteriority
postgraduate
posthumously
postmeridian
postmistress
postponement
postposition
postpositive
postprandial
potentiality
practicality
practitioner
pragmatistic
praiseworthy
pralltriller
praseodymium
precancelled
precariously
precedential
preceptorial
precessional
prechristian
preciousness
precipitable
precipitance
precipitancy
precipitator
precisianism
precisionist
preclassical
preclusively
precociously
precognition
precognitive
precondition
preconscious
predesignate
predestinate
predetermine
predictively
predigestion
predilection
predominance
predominancy
preeminently
preestablish
preexistence
prefabricate
prefectorial
preferential
preformation
preformative
prehensility
prehistorian
prelapsarian
premaxillary
premeditated
premeditator
premenstrual
prenticeship
preoccupancy
preparedness
preponderant
preponderate
preposterous
prerequisite
presbyterate
presbyterial
Presbyterian
prescription
prescriptive
preselection
preselective
presentation
presentative
presentiment
preservation
preservative
presidential
presumptuous
pretermitted
prevailingly
prevaricator
preventative
preventively
previousness
pricecutting
pridefulness
priestliness
priestridden
priggishness
primigravida
primogenital
primogenitor
primordially
princeliness
principality
printability
privatdocent
privatdozent
privateering
prizefighter
prizewinning
probationary
proboscidean
proboscidian
procathedral
processional
proclamation
proclamatory
proconsulate
prodigiously
productively
productivity
professional
professorate
professoress
professorial
proficiently
profiteering
profligately
profoundness
progenitress
progesterone
proglottides
programmable
programmatic
projectional
projectively
prolegomenon
prolifically
prolificness
prolongation
promulgation
pronominally
pronouncedly
proofreading
propaedeutic
propagandise
propagandism
propagandist
prophylactic
propitiation
propitiatory
propitiously
proportional
proportioned
proprietress
proscription
proscriptive
prosectorial
prosecutable
proselytiser
prosodically
prosopopoeia
prosperously
prostitution
protactinium
protectively
protectorate
protensively
protestation
prothalamion
prothalamium
prothonotary
protistology
protohistory
protoplasmic
protoplastic
prototypical
protozoology
protrusively
protuberance
proudhearted
proverbially
providential
provincially
provisionary
prudentially
psephologist
pseudocyesis
pseudonymity
pseudonymous
pseudopodium
psychiatrist
psychoactive
psychography
psychologise
psychologism
psychologist
psychometric
psychopathic
psychosexual
psychotropic
psychrometer
psychrometry
pteridophyte
pteridosperm
pterodactyle
publicspirit
puerperrally
pugnaciously
pulverisable
pumpernickel
punchingball
purblindness
purification
purificatory
purposebuilt
purposefully
pursestrings
putrefaction
putrefactive
pyroelectric
pyroligneous
pyromaniacal
pyromorphite
pyrotechnics
pyrotechnist
Quadragesima
quadrangular
quadraphonic
quadriennium
quadrinomial
quadriplegia
quadriplegic
quadrivalent
quadrumanous
quaestorship
qualmishness
quantifiable
quantisation
quantitative
quaquaversal
quarterbound
quarterfinal
quarterstaff
quattrocento
questionable
questionably
questionless
quinquennial
quinquennium
quintessence
quixotically
quizzicality
rabbinically
rabblerouser
racemisation
racketeering
radiobiology
radioelement
radiographer
radiographic
radioisotope
radiological
radionuclide
radiophonics
radiotherapy
rambunctious
ramification
rapprochment
ratification
ratiocinator
rattleheaded
ravenousness
razzledazzle
reactivation

reactiveness
readableness
readjustment
reallocation
reappearance
reassessment
reassignment
reassuringly
rebelliously
recalcitrant
recalcitrate
recalescence
recapitulate
receivership
receptaculum
receptionist
recessionary
rechargeable
reciprocally
reciprocator
recklessness
recognisable
recognisably
recognisance
recollection
recollective
recommitment
reconcilable
reconstitute
reconversion
reconveyance
recreational
recrudescent
recuperation
recuperative
redecoration
redemptioner
Redemptorist
redeployment
redintegrate
redistribute
reducibility
reductionism
reductionist
reflationary
reflectional
reflectively
reflectivity
refractivity
refractorily
refreshingly
refreshments
refrigerator
regardlessly
regeneration
regenerative
regimentally
registration
regressively
rehabilitate
reinvestment
reinvigorate
rejectamenta
rejuvenation
relationally
relationship
relativeness
relativistic
relentlessly
reliableness
rememberable
remembrancer
remilitarise
reminiscence
remonstrance
remonstrator
remorsefully
removability
remuneration
remunerative
remuneratory
renegotiable
renouncement
renunciation
renunciative
renunciatory
reoccupation
repatriation
repercussion
repercussive
repetitional
repetitively
repossession
reprehension
reprehensive
repressively
reproachable
reproachless
reproducible
reproduction
reproductive
reprographic
reservedness
resettlement
residentiary
residentship
resignedness
resiniferous
resipiscence
resistlessly
resoluteness
resolvedness
resoundingly
respectfully
respectively
resplendence
resplendency
responsively
responsorial
restaurateur
restlessness
restrainable
restrainedly
restrictedly
resupination
resurrection
resuscitator
reticulately
reticulation
reticulocyte
retiringness
retractation
retractility
retrenchment
retrocedence
retrocession
retrocessive
retroflexion
retropulsion
retroversion
reunionistic
revelational
revengefully
reverberator
reversionary
revictualled
revivalistic
reviviscence
rhetorically
rheumatology
rhinocerotic
rhinological
rhizocarpous
rhizogenetic
rhizophagous
rhododendron
rhombohedral
rhombohedron
rhynchophora
rhythmically
ribonuclease
ricochetting
ridiculously
rightfulness
rigorousness
risorgimento
robustiously
rollingstock
romanisation
romantically
rontgenogram
rontgenology
rootlessness
rosecoloured
rumbletumble
ruminatively
runningboard
ruralisation
ruthlessness
sabretoothed
saccharinity
saccharoidal
sacerdotally
sacrilegious
saddlebacked
sadistically
safecracking
salamandrian
salamandrine
salamandroid
salesmanship
salmonladder
salpiglossis
salubriously
salutariness
salutational
salutiferous
salvationism
salvationist
Samaritanism
sandyachting
sanguinarily
sanguineness
sanguinolent
sansculottic
saponifiable
saprophagous
sarcomatosis
sarcophagous
sardonically
sarrusophone
sarsaparilla
satisfaction
satisfactory
satisfyingly
scabbardfish
scabrousness
scandalously
Scandinavian
scareheading
scarificator
scatological
scatterbrain
scatteringly
scenepainter
sceneshifter
scenographic
schismatical
schizogonous
schizomycete
schizophrene
schizothymia
schizothymic
schoolfellow
schoolleaver
schoolmaster
schorlaceous
scintigraphy
scintillator
sclerenchyma
scornfulness
scorpionfish
scoundreldom
scoundrelism
scouringrush
scraperboard
scratchiness
screenwriter
scrimshanker
scripturally
scriptwriter
scrobiculate
scrupulosity
scrupulously
sculpturally
scurrilously
scutellation
secessionism
secessionist
seclusionist
secondstring
sectarianise
sectarianism
sectionalism
secularistic
sedgewarbler
sedulousness
segmentation
seismography
seismologist
seismometric
seismoscopic
selenography
selenologist
selfabsorbed
selfactivity
selfaffected
selfanalysis
selfapplause
selfapproval
selfbegotten
selfbetrayal
selfcatering
selfcoloured
selfcomposed
selfcontempt
selfcritical
selfdeceived
selfdeceiver
selfdelusion
selfdestruct
selfdevotion
selfdirected
selfdistrust
selfdoubting
selfeducated
selfeffacing
selfelective
selfemployed
selfevidence
selfexistent
selfflattery
selfhypnosis
selfidentity
selfignition
selfinterest
selfinvolved
selflessness
selflimiting
selfluminous
selfmurderer
selfpleasing
selfportrait
selfreliance
selfreproach
selfrighting
selfsameness
selfstarting
selfviolence
sellingplate
semantically
semiannually
semibasement
semicircular
semicylinder
semidarkness
semideponent
semidetached
semidiameter
semidomestic
semifinalist
semifinished
semiliterate
seminiferous
semiofficial
semiological
semiparasite
semiprecious
semitropical
sempiternity
sensibleness
sensitometer
sensualistic
sensuousness
sententially
separability
separateness
septennially
septilateral
septuagenary
Septuagesima
Septuagintal
sepulchrally
sequaciously
sequentially
sequestrator
seraphically
sergeantfish
sergeantship
sericultural
serjeantship
serpentiform
serpentinely
serviceberry
servicecourt
servicewoman
servitorship
servocontrol
sesquialtera
sexagenarian
sexcentenary
shadowboxing
Shakspereana
Shaksperiana
shamateurism
shamefacedly
shamefulness
sharecropper
sharpshooter
sharpsighted
shatterproof
sheepishness
sheepshearer
shillyshally
shipbuilding
shirtwaister
shootingiron
shortchanger
shortcircuit
shortpitched
shortsighted
shortsleeved
shortstaffed
shoulderbelt
shoulderknot

shouldernote	southernmost	stepdaughter	suberisation	susceptivity
shrewishness	southernwood	stereochromy	subinfeudate	suspensively
shuffleboard	southwestern	stereography	subjectively	suspiciously
sideslipping	spaciousness	stereoisomer	subjectivise	sustentation
sidestepping	sparkingplug	stereometric	subjectivism	sustentative
sidewhiskers	sparrowgrass	stereophonic	subjectivist	swaggeringly
sightreading	speakingtube	stereopticon	subjectivity	swaggerstick
significance	specialistic	stereoscopic	sublapsarian	swainishness
significancy	specifically	sterlingness	submaxillary	swashbuckler
silicicolous	specificness	sternutation	subminiature	sweepingness
siliciferous	speciousness	sternutative	submissively	sweetishness
silverglance	specktioneer	sternutatory	subnormality	swimmingbath
silviculture	spectrograph	sternwheeler	subsaturated	swimmingbell
simoniacally	spectrometer	stertorously	subscription	swimmingpool
simpleminded	spectrometry	stethoscopic	subsequently	swizzlestick
simultaneity	spectroscope	stichomythia	subservience	sycophantish
simultaneous	spectroscopy	stichomythic	subserviency	syllabically
Sinanthropus	speechlessly	stilboestrol	subsidiarily	sylviculture
singleacting	speedboating	stillhunting	subsonically	symbolically
singledecker	speleologist	stockbreeder	substantiate	synaesthesia
singlehanded	spermaphytic	stockbroking	substantival	synaesthetic
singleminded	spermathecal	stockingless	substitution	synarthrosis
singleseater	spermatocyte	stockjobbery	substitutive	synchronical
sinistrality	spermatozoid	stockjobbing	substruction	synchroniser
sinistrorsal	spermatozoon	stockraising	substructure	syncretistic
sinusoidally	spermogonium	stoneboiling	subtemperate	syndactylism
siphonophore	spheroidally	stonecutting	subterranean	syndactylous
siphonostele	sphragistics	stonedresser	subthreshold	syndetically
skateboarder	sphygmograph	stonemasonry	subversively	synonymously
skippingrope	spidermonkey	stonyhearted	succedaneous	synoptically
skittishness	spiegeleisen	stormtrooper	successfully	systematical
skrimshanker	spinsterhood	stouthearted	successional	systematiser
skullduggery	spiritedness	Stradivarius	successively	systemically
skunkcabbage	spiritlessly	straightaway	succinctness	taberdarship
slanderously	spiritualise	straightbred	sudoriferous	tabernacular
slaughterous	spiritualism	straightedge	sufficiently	tachygrapher
slaveholding	spiritualist	straightener	suggestively	tachygraphic
sledgehammer	spirituality	straightness	suitableness	tactlessness
sleepingpill	spitefulness	straitjacket	sulphonamide	tamelessness
sleepwalking	splendidness	stranglehold	sulphonation	tangentially
slipcarriage	spokesperson	straticulate	sulphuration	tangibleness
slipperiness	sporadically	stratigraphy	sulphuretted	taperecorder
slothfulness	sporogenesis	stratosphere	superannuate	taskmistress
slovenliness	sportfulness	streetwalker	supercharger	tastefulness
sluggishness	sportiveness	strengthener	superciliary	tautological
sluttishness	spotlessness	strengthless	supercilious	taxcollector
smallclothes	sprightfully	streptococci	supereminent	teachability
smallholding	spuriousness	streptomycin	supererogate	tearlessness
snaggletooth	squarerigged	stridulation	superhighway	technicality
snakecharmer	squattocracy	strikingness	superhumanly	technicolour
snapfastener	squirrelcage	stringcourse	supermundane	technocratic
snappishness	squirreltail	strobilation	supernaculum	technologist
snarlingiron	stablishment	stroboscopic	supernatural	tectonically
snobbishness	staffofficer	strongminded	superposable	teensyweensy
sociableness	staffsurgeon	strongylosis	supersedence	teetertotter
sociological	stagemanager	strontianite	supersensory	telaesthesia
sociometrist	staggeringly	strophanthin	supersession	telaesthetic
Socratically	Stakhanovism	structurally	superstition	telegraphese
sodafountain	Stakhanovite	strychninism	superstratum	telegraphist
softpedalled	stalactiform	stubbornness	supervenient	teleological
solarisation	stalwartness	studdingsail	supervention	televisional
solicitation	stammeringly	studiousness	supplemental	temptability
solicitously	standardbred	stupefacient	supplementer	teratologist
solifluction	standingroom	stupefaction	supplicantly	teratomatous
solitariness	stanniferous	stupefactive	supplication	tercentenary
somatopleure	starspangled	stupendously	supplicatory	terebinthine
somnambulant	stationhouse	stutteringly	suppositious	tergiversate
somnambulate	stationwagon	stylographic	suppressible	terribleness
somnambulism	statistician	subalternate	supramundane	terrifically
somnambulist	statuesquely	subalternity	supraorbital	terrifyingly
somniloquism	stealthiness	subapostolic	surefootedly	terrorstruck
somniloquist	steatopygous	subarrhation	surmountable	tessellation
sonorousness	steeplechase	subcelestial	surprisingly	testamentary
sophisticate	steganograph	subcommittee	surrealistic	testosterone
soporiferous	stellenbosch	subconscious	surrejoinder	testudineous
sorbefacient	stelliferous	subcontinent	surroundings	tetrachordal
soullessness	stenographer	subcutaneous	surveillance	tetragonally
soundingline	stenographic	subdivisible	surveyorship	tetrahedrite
southeastern	stepchildren	subeditorial	survivorship	tetramorphic

Teutonically
thankfulness
thanksgiving
thaumaturgic
theanthropic
theatregoing
theatrically
theistically
thematically
theocratical
theoretician
theosophical
therapeutics
therapeutist
thereinafter
thermocouple
thermography
thermolabile
thermometric
thermophilic
thermoscopic
thermosphere
thermostable
thermostatic
thermotactic
thermotropic
thickskinned
thickskulled
thievishness
thimbleberry
thirdborough
thitherwards
thoroughbass
thoroughbred
thoroughfare
thoroughness
thoughtfully
thousandfold
threequarter
threewheeler
thriftlessly
throughstone
thundercloud
thunderingly
thunderously
thunderstone
thunderstorm
ticklishness
tightmouthed
timehonoured
timelessness
timorousness
tintinnabula
tirelessness
tiresomeness
tittletattle
toastingfork
togetherness
toggleswitch
toilsomeness
tolerability
tonelessness
toploftiness
topsyturvily
torrefaction
torrentially
Torricellian
tortuousness
totalisation
totalitarian
touchingness
towardliness
toxicologist
toxicophobia
traceability
trachomatous
tractability
tradescantia
tradespeople
traditionary
traditionist
traducianism
traducianist
tragicomical
trainspotter
traitorously
trampolinist
tranquillise
tranquillity
transcendent
transduction
transferable
transference
transferring
transformism
transformist
transfusible
transgressor
transhipment
transhumance
transiliency
transitional
transitively
transitivity
transitorily
translatable
translucence
translucency
transmigrant
transmigrate
transmission
transmissive
transmitting
transmogrify
transmontane
transmutable
transoceanic
transpacific
transparency
transpirable
transplanter
transpontine
transposable
transshipped
transudation
transudatory
transversely
transvestism
transvestite
tremendously
trephination
trestletable
triangularly
tricentenary
trichologist
trichotomise
trichotomous
trichromatic
trickishness
tridactylous
trifurcation
triggerhappy
triglyphical
trigonometry
trinomialism
tripartitely
tripartition
triphthongal
triplication
triumphantly
trochanteric
troglodytism
trophallaxis
tropological
tropospheric
troublemaker
trumpetshell
trustfulness
truthfulness
tuberculated
tuberculosis
tumultuously
tunelessness
turbellarian
turriculated
turtlenecked
twentyfourmo
twitteringly
typefounding
typification
tyrannically
tyrannicidal
ubiquitarian
ubiquitously
ultramontane
ultramundane
umbrageously
unacceptable
unaccustomed
unaffectedly
unambivalent
unanswerable
unapologetic
unappeasable
unappetising
unassailable
unassumingly
unattractive
unauthorised
unbecomingly
unbelievable
unbelievably
unblinkingly
unblushingly
unbrokenness
uncalculated
uncelebrated
unchangeable
unchangeably
uncharitable
uncharitably
unchivalrous
unclassified
uncomeatable
uncommercial
uncommonness
unconformity
unconsidered
unconstraint
uncontrolled
unconvincing
uncritically
unctuousness
undemocratic
underachieve
underbidding
underclothes
undercoating
undercurrent
undercutting
underdevelop
undergarment
underinsured
underletting
undermanning
underpinning
underrunning
undersetting
understaffed
undersurface
undertenancy
underwritten
undetermined
undiplomatic
uneconomical
unemployable
unemployment
unencumbered
uneventfully
unexpectedly
unfaithfully
unfamiliarly
unfathomable
unfavourable
unfavourably
unflattering
unfrequented
ungainliness
ungovernable
ungracefully
ungraciously
ungratefully
unhesitating
unhistorical
unifoliolate
unilaterally
unimaginable
unimaginably
unimportance
uninterested
unionisation
unisexuality
unitarianism
universalise
universalism
universalist
universality
unkindliness
unlawfulness
unlikelihood
unlikeliness
unloveliness
unmanageable
unmercifully
unmistakable
unmistakably
unofficially
unparalleled
unpleasantly
unpopularity
unprejudiced
unpretending
unprincipled
unprofitable
unprofitably
unpronounced
unreasonable
unreasonably
unrecognised
unregenerate
unrepeatable
unreservedly
unresponsive
unrestrained
unscientific
unscriptural
unscrupulous
unsearchable
unseasonable
unsegregated
unsteadiness
unstructured
unsuccessful
unthinkingly
unthoughtful
untimeliness
untowardness
untruthfully
unwieldiness
unwontedness
unworldiness
unworthiness
unyieldingly
uproariously
urbanisation
urbanologist
usufructuary
usuriousness
uxoriousness
vainglorious
Valenciennes
valetudinary
valorisation
valuableness
vanquishable
vanquishment
vantagepoint
vaporisation
vaporousness
variableness
varicoloured
vasodilation
vasodilatory
vaticination
vauntcourier
vegetatively
venepuncture
venerability
vengefulness
venipuncture
venomousness
ventripotent
veridicality
verification
verificatory
vermiculated
vernacularly
vertebration
verticalness
verticillate
vesiculation
veterinarian
vibraphonist
vicargeneral
vicechairman
Victorianism
victoriously
vigorousness
vilification
villainously
vindictively
vinification
viridescence
virtuosoship
virtuousness
viscerotonic
viscosimeter
viscountship
visitational
visitatorial
vitalisation
vitiligation
vitreousness
vitrifaction
vituperation
vituperative
vituperatory
vivification
viviparously
vocabularian
vocalisation
vociferation
vociferously
voidableness
volatileness
volcanically
volitionally
volumetrical
voluminosity
voluminously
voluntaryism
voluntaryist
voluptuosity
voluptuously
vomiturition

wainscotting
waistcoating
walkietalkie
wallpainting
wallydraigle
warehouseman
wastefulness
watchfulness
watermanship
weatherboard
weatherbound
weatherglass
weatherhouse
weatherproof
welldisposed
wellfavoured
wellgrounded
Wellingtonia
welterweight
whencesoever
wherethrough
whigmaleerie
whimperingly
whimsicality
whippoorwill
whisperingly
whitelivered
whitewashing
whitherwards
wholehearted
whortleberry
wicketkeeper
williewaught
windingsheet
wineglassful
winklepicker
winterbourne
wollastonite
womanishness
wonderstruck
wonderworker
wondrousness
woodengraver
woodenheaded
woolgatherer
woollyheaded
workableness
workingclass
worshipfully
wrathfulness
wretchedness
wrongfulness
wunderkinder
xanthochroia
xiphisternum
YankeeDoodle
yellowhammer
youngberries
youthfulness
zoogeography
zygapophysis
zygomorphism
zygomorphous

---

bacchanalian
bachelorhood
bachelorship
backbreaking
backpedalled
backslapping
backwardness
backwoodsman
bactericidal
bacteriology
bacteriostat
balladmonger
balletomania
ballottement
banderillero
bantamweight
barbarically
barometrical
baselessness
basidiospore
bassorelievo
bassorilievo
bathypelagic
battleground
battlemented
cabbagewhite
cabinetmaker
cachinnation
cachinnatory
calamitously
calcareously
calculatedly
calisthenics
calligrapher
calligraphic
callisthenic
calorescence
calorimetric
calumniation
calumniatory
calumniously
calycoideous
camiknickers
campfollower
campodeiform
canaliculate
canalisation
cancellation
candleholder
canonisation
canorousness
Cantabrigian
cantankerous
cantharidian
cantillation
capercaillie
capercailzie
capitalistic
capitulation
capriciously
captiousness
caravansarai
caravanserai
carbohydrate
carbonaceous
carburetting
carcinogenic
cardcarrying
cardinalship
cardiography
cardiologist
carelessness
caricaturist
carillonneur
Carlovingian
carpetbagger
carpetknight
carragheenin
carriageable
Cartesianism
cartographer
cartographic
cartological
cashandcarry
catachrestic
catamountain
cataphoresis
catastrophic
catechetical
caterwauling
catholically
catilinarian
cattlelifter
cautiousness
earsplitting
earthshaking
eavesdropped
eavesdropper
fabulousness
facelessness
facilitation
factionalism
factiousness
factitiously
fainthearted
faintishness
faithfulness
faithhealing
falcongentil
falcongentle
fallaciously
fancifulness
fantasticate
fantasticism
farmsteading
farsightedly
fastidiously
fatherfigure
fatherliness
faultfinding
galactogogue
galligaskins
gallinaceous
galvanically
galvanometer
galvanoscope
gamesmanship
gamesomeness
gametophytic
gamopetalous
gamophyllous
gamosepalous
ganglionated
gasification
gastronomist
gastropodous
haberdashery
habilitation
habitability
habitforming
habitualness
haematoblast
haematolysis
haematoxylon
haemophiliac
haemopoiesis
haemorrhagic
hagiographer
hagiographic
hagiological
hairdressing
hairsbreadth
hairsplitter
halftimbered
hallucinogen
hallucinosis
halogenation
halterbroken
handicapping
handkerchief
handsbreadth
handsomeness
happenstance
hardfavoured
hardfeatured
hardstanding
harlequinade
harmlessness
harmonically
harmoniously
harquebusier
kaleidoscope
karyokinesis
katzenjammer
laboursaving
labyrinthian
labyrinthine
lachrymation
lachrymatory
lachrymosely
lacininiated
laisserfaire
laissezaller
laissezfaire
lakedwelling
landingcraft
landingfield
landingstage
landingstrip
landlubberly
languishment
languorously
lanternjawed
lanternslide
largehearted
laryngoscope
laryngoscopy
lasciviously
laterisation
laticiferous
latinisation
latitudinous
laudableness
laureateship
machicolated
macrocephaly
macropterous
mademoiselle
magistrature
magnetically
magnetisable
magnetograph
magnetometer
magnifically
magnificence
magniloquent
maidenliness
maidenstakes
maintainable
majestically
majorgeneral
malacologist
malapertness
malcontented
malevolently
malformation
malleability
malnutrition
maltreatment
malversation
mangelwurzel
Manicheanism
manifoldness
manipulation
manipulative
manipulatory
mannerliness
manoeuvrable
manometrical
mansionhouse
manslaughter
manufacturer
Marcionitism
marketgarden
marketsquare
marksmanship
marlinespike
marriageable
Marseillaise
marshharrier
marvellously
mastersinger
masterstroke
masterswitch
mastigophora
materialness
mathematical
matriarchate
maximisation
nailscissors
namedropping
namelessness
nanoplankton
narcissistic
narcotically
narrowminded
naturalistic
naturopathic
nauseatingly
nauseousness
navigability
navigational
pacification
pacificatory
paedobaptism
paedogenesis
paedogenetic
paedomorphic
painlessness
palaeobotany
palaeography
Palaeolithic
palatability
paletteknife
palingenesia
palingenesis
palingenetic
Palladianism
palynologist
panchromatic
pancreatitis
panhellenism
panification
pantechnicon
pantisocracy
pantographic
papyrologist
paraboloidal
paradigmatic
paradisaical
paradisiacal
paraesthesia
paragraphist
parallelling
paralysation
paramagnetic
parametrical
paramilitary
paramorphism
paranormally
paraphrastic
parasiticide
parasitology
paratactical
parenthesise
parisyllabic
parkinsonism
parochialise
parochialism
parochiality
paronomastic
parsimonious
participator
particularly
partisanship
partitionist
pasqueflower
passepartout
passionately
passionfruit
pathetically

pathogenesis
pathogenetic
pathological
patriarchate
patternmaker
patulousness
rabbinically
rabblerouser
racemisation
racketeering
radiobiology
radioelement
radiographer
radiographic
radioisotope
radiological
radionuclide
radiophonics
radiotherapy
rambunctious
ramification
rapprochment
ratification
ratiocinator
rattleheaded
ravenousness
razzledazzle
sabretoothed
saccharinity
saccharoidal
sacerdotally
sacrilegious
saddlebacked
sadistically
safecracking
salamandrian
salamandrine
salamandroid
salesmanship
salmonladder
salpiglossis
salubriously
salutariness
salutational
salutiferous
salvationism
salvationist
Samaritanism
sandyachting
sanguinarily
sanguineness
sanguinolent
sansculottic
saponifiable
saprophagous
sarcomatosis
sarcophagous
sardonically
sarrusophone
sarsaparilla
satisfaction
satisfactory
satisfyingly
taberdarship
tabernacular
tachygrapher
tachygraphic
tactlessness
tamelessness
tangentially
tangibleness
taperecorder
taskmistress
tastefulness
tautological
taxcollector
vainglorious
Valenciennes
valetudinary
valorisation
valuableness
vanquishable
vanquishment
vantagepoint
vaporisation
vaporousness
variableness
varicoloured
vasodilation
vasodilatory
vaticination
vauntcourier
wainscotting
waistcoating
walkietalkie
wallpainting
wallydraigle
warehouseman
wastefulness
watchfulness
watermanship
xanthochroia
YankeeDoodle
abbreviation
abolitionary
abolitionism
abolitionist
aboriginally
abortiveness
abrasiveness
absentminded
absoluteness
absolutistic
absorptional
absorptivity
absquatulate
abstemiously
abstractable
abstractedly
abstractness
abstruseness
obdurateness
obedientiary
oblanceolate
obligatorily
obligingness
obliteration
obliterative
obmutescence
obnubilation
obscurantism
obscurantist
obsequiously
obsolescence
obsoleteness
obstetrician
obstreperous
ubiquitarian
ubiquitously
academically
acaulescence
acceleration
accelerative
accentuation
acciaccatura
accidentally
accommodator
accompanyist
accomplished
accordionist
accouchement
accoutrement
accretionary
accumulation
accumulative
accurateness
accursedness
accusatively
accusatorial
acetabularia
acetaldehyde
achlamydeous
acoustically
acquaintance
acquiescence
acronychally
actinomycete
eccentricity
ecclesiastic
ecclesiology
echinococcus
echolocation
echosounding
eclectically
ecologically
econometrics
economically
ecstatically
ectoparasite
ichthyocolla
ichthyolatry
ichthyophagy
iconoclastic
iconographer
occasionally
occidentally
occupational
oceanography
oceanologist
octogenarian
octosyllabic
octosyllable
scabbardfish
scabrousness
scandalously
Scandinavian
scareheading
scarificator
scatological
scatterbrain
scatteringly
scenepainter
sceneshifter
scenographic
schismatical
schizogonous
schizomycete
schizophrene
schizothymia
schizothymic
schoolfellow
schoolleaver
schoolmaster
schorlaceous
scintigraphy
scintillator
sclerenchyma
scornfulness
scorpionfish
scoundreldom
scoundrelism
scouringrush
scraperboard
scratchiness
screenwriter
scrimshanker
scripturally
scriptwriter
scrobiculate
scrupulosity
scrupulously
sculpturally
scurrilously
scutellation
adaptability
adaptiveness
additionally
adequateness
adhesiveness
adjectivally
adjudication
adjudicative
adjudicatory
administrant
administrate
admonishment
adorableness
adscititious
adulteration
adulterously
advantageous
adventitious
advisability
editorialise
editorialist
educationist
edulcoration
idealisation
ideationally
identifiable
idiosyncrasy
idiothermous
idolatrously
odontologist
aerodynamics
aeroembolism
aeronautical
aeroneurosis
aerosiderite
aesthetician
aestheticism
aetiological
beachcombing
beatifically
bedazzlement
beggarliness
behaviourism
behaviourist
belittlement
bellbottomed
belletristic
belligerence
belligerency
bellylanding
benefactress
beneficently
beneficially
benevolently
benzaldehyde
bequeathment
berzelianite
beseechingly
bespectacled
bewilderedly
bewilderment
bewitchingly
cementitious
censoriously
centesimally
centrespread
centrosphere
centuplicate
ceremonially
deactivation
deambulatory
debilitation
debonairness
decaffeinate
decalescence
decapitation
decasyllabic
decasyllable
deceleration
decentralise
decipherable
decipherment
decisiveness
declinometer
decomposable
decompressor
decongestant
decongestion
decongestive
deconsecrate
decontrolled
decoratively
decorousness
decreasingly
deescalation
definiteness
definitively
deflagration
deflationary
deflationist
defraudation
degenerately
degeneration
degenerative
deionisation
dejectedness
delamination
deliberately
deliberation
deliberative
delicatessen
delightfully
delimitation
delinquently
deliquescent
delitescence
delusiveness
demilitarise
demimondaine
demineralise
demodulation
demoniacally
demonstrable
demonstrably
demonstrator
denaturalise
denaturation
denomination
denominative
denouncement
densitometer
denticulated
dentilingual
denuclearise
denunciation
denunciative
denunciatory
deontologist
departmental
depoliticise
depopulation
depravedness
depreciation
depreciatory
depressingly
deputisation
deracination
derisiveness
derivational
derivatively
dermatophyte
derogatorily
desalination
desideration
desiderative
desirability
desirousness
desolateness
despairingly
despitefully
despoliation

despondently
despotically
desquamation
desquamative
desquamatory
dessertspoon
destructible
desulphurise
detachedness
determinable
determinably
determinedly
dethronement
detoxication
detumescence
Deuteronomic
deviationism
deviationist
dextrousness
fearlessness
fearsomeness
featherbrain
featheriness
fecklessness
feebleminded
feldspathoid
felicitation
felicitously
feminineness
feminisation
fenestration
fermentation
fermentative
ferrugineous
fertilisable
feverishness
geanticlinal
genealogical
generousness
genuflection
geochemistry
geographical
geologically
geomagnetism
geometrician
geophysicist
geopolitical
geosynclinal
geotectonics
geriatrician
Germanophile
Germanophobe
gerontocracy
gesellschaft
gesticulator
headmistress
headquarters
headshrinker
heartburning
heartrending
heartstrings
heartwarming
heathenishly
heavenliness
heavyhearted
hebdomadally
hebetudinous
hectographic
hedgehopping
heedlessness
heliocentric
heliographer
heliographic
heliogravure
heliolatrous
heliotherapy
heliotropism
hellgrammite
helplessness
hemerocallis
hemichordate
hemimorphism
hemimorphite
hemiparasite
hemispheroid
henceforward
henotheistic
heortologist
heraldically
hereditament
hereditarily
hereinbefore
heritability
hermeneutics
hermetically
heroicalness
heroicomical
herpetologic
hesitatingly
hesperididia
heterocercal
heterocyclic
heteroecious
heterogamous
heterogenous
heterologous
heteromerous
heteronomous
heterophylly
heterosexual
heterozygote
heterozygous
jerrybuilder
jesuitically
jetpropelled
Keynesianism
leapfrogging
leathercloth
ledgertackle
lefthandedly
legalisation
legitimately
legitimation
legitimatise
lepidopteran
leucocytosis
leukocytosis
levorotation
levorotatory
lexicography
lexicologist
mealymouthed
meaningfully
mechanically
mediaevalism
mediaevalist
meditatively
meetinghouse
megalomaniac
melancholiac
melanochroic
melodramatic
meltingpoint
mendaciously
menstruation
mercantilism
mercantilist
merchantable
mercifulness
mercurialise
mercurialism
meretricious
meridionally
meristematic
merrythought
mesocephalic
mesothoracic
messeigneurs
metachronism
metagalactic
metalanguage
metallically
metallophone
metallurgist
metalworking
metamorphism
metamorphose
metaphorical
metaphrastic
metaphysical
metapsychics
metasomatism
metathetical
metathoracic
meteorically
meteorograph
methodically
meticulously
metrological
metropolitan
mezzorelievo
mezzosoprano
nebulisation
nebulousness
necrographer
necrological
necrophagous
necrophiliac
necrophilism
necrophilous
needlessness
negativeness
negativistic
neglectfully
negotiatress
negrophilism
negrophilist
neighbouring
neoclassical
neoDarwinian
neoDarwinism
neoDarwinist
Neohellenism
neonomianism
Neoplatonism
Neoplatonist
nephanalysis
nephelometer
nephelometry
nephrologist
nerveracking
Nestorianism
neurasthenia
neurasthenic
neuroanatomy
neurobiology
neurological
neuropterous
neuroscience
neurosurgeon
neurosurgery
neurotically
nevertheless
newfashioned
Newfoundland
newspaperman
peacefulness
pearlescence
peasepudding
peccadilloes
pedantically
pedicellaria
pedunculated
peerlessness
pejoratively
pellucidness
penalisation
penitentiary
pennypincher
pennywhistle
peradventure
perambulator
perceptively
perceptivity
perceptually
percussively
percutaneous
peregrinator
peremptorily
perfectively
perfervidity
perfidiously
perfoliation
performative
pericarditis
perilousness
periodically
periodontics
periodontist
periostracum
peripherally
periphrastic
perispomenon
peristeronic
peristomatic
perjuriously
permanganate
permeability
permissively
permittivity
perniciously
pernoctation
peroxidation
perpetration
perpetuation
perplexingly
perseverance
persistently
perspicacity
perspiration
perspiratory
persuasively
pertinacious
perturbation
perturbative
perverseness
perviousness
pestilential
pestological
petrifaction
petrographer
petrographic
petrological
pettifoggery
pettifogging
reactivation
reactiveness
readableness
readjustment
reallocation
reappearance
reassessment
reassignment
reassuringly
rebelliously
recalcitrant
recalcitrate
recalescence
recapitulate
receivership
receptaculum
receptionist
recessionary
rechargeable
reciprocally
reciprocator
recklessness
recognisable
recognisably
recognisance
recollection
recollective
recommitment
reconcilable
reconstitute
reconversion
reconveyance
recreational
recrudescent
recuperation
recuperative
redecoration
redemptioner
Redemptorist
redeployment
redintegrate
redistribute
reducibility
reductionism
reductionist
reflationary
reflectional
reflectively
reflectivity
refractivity
refractorily
refreshingly
refreshments
refrigerator
regardlessly
regeneration
regenerative
regimentally
registration
regressively
rehabilitate
reinvestment
reinvigorate
rejectamenta
rejuvenation
relationally
relationship
relativeness
relativistic
relentlessly
reliableness
rememberable
remembrancer
remilitarise
reminiscence
remonstrance
remonstrator
remorsefully
removability
remuneration
remunerative
remuneratory
renegotiable
renouncement
renunciation
renunciative
renunciatory
reoccupation
repatriation
repercussion
repercussive
repetitional
repetitively
repossession
reprehension
reprehensive
repressively
reproachable
reproachless
reproducible

reproduction
reproductive
reprographic
reservedness
resettlement
residentiary
residentship
resignedness
resiniferous
resipiscence
resistlessly
resoluteness
resolvedness
resoundingly
respectfully
respectively
resplendence
resplendency
responsively
responsorial
restaurateur
restlessness
restrainable
restrainedly
restrictedly
resupination
resurrection
resuscitator
reticulately
reticulation
reticulocyte
retiringness
retractation
retractility
retrenchment
retrocedence
retrocession
retrocessive
retroflexion
retropulsion
retroversion
reunionistic
revelational
revengefully
reverberator
reversionary
revictualled
revivalistic
reviviscence
secessionism
secessionist
seclusionist
secondstring
sectarianise
sectarianism
sectionalism
secularistic
sedgewarbler
sedulousness
segmentation
seismography
seismologist
seismometric
seismoscopic
selenography
selenologist
selfabsorbed
selfactivity
selfaffected
selfanalysis
selfapplause
selfapproval
selfbegotten
selfbetrayal
selfcatering
selfcoloured
selfcomposed
selfcontempt
selfcritical
selfdeceived
selfdeceiver
selfdelusion
selfdestruct
selfdevotion
selfdirected
selfdistrust
selfdoubting
selfeducated
selfeffacing
selfelective
selfemployed
selfevidence
selfexistent
selfflattery
selfhypnosis
selfidentity
selfignition
selfinterest
selfinvolved
selflessness
selflimiting
selfluminous
selfmurderer
selfpleasing
selfportrait
selfreliance
selfreproach
selfrighting
selfsameness
selfstarting
selfviolence
sellingplate
semantically
semiannually
semibasement
semicircular
semicylinder
semidarkness
semideponent
semidetached
semidiameter
semidomestic
semifinalist
semifinished
semiliterate
seminiferous
semiofficial
semiological
semiparasite
semiprecious
semitropical
sempiternity
sensibleness
sensitometer
sensualistic
sensuousness
sententially
separability
separateness
septennially
septilateral
septuagenary
Septuagesima
Septuagintal
sepulchrally
sequaciously
sequentially
sequestrator
seraphically
sergeantfish
sergeantship
sericultural
serjeantship
serpentiform
serpentinely
serviceberry
servicecourt
servicewoman
servitorship
servocontrol
sesquialtera
sexagenarian
sexcentenary
teachability
tearlessness
technicality
technicolour
technocratic
technologist
tectonically
teensyweensy
teetertotter
telaesthesia
telaesthetic
telegraphese
telegraphist
teleological
televisional
temptability
teratologist
teratomatous
tercentenary
terebinthine
tergiversate
terribleness
terrifically
terrifyingly
terrorstruck
tessellation
testamentary
testosterone
testudineous
tetrachordal
tetragonally
tetrahedrite
tetramorphic
Teutonically
vegetatively
venepuncture
venerability
vengefulness
venipuncture
venomousness
ventripotent
veridicality
verification
verificatory
vermiculated
vernacularly
vertebration
verticalness
verticillate
vesiculation
veterinarian
weatherboard
weatherbound
weatherglass
weatherhouse
weatherproof
welldisposed
wellfavoured
wellgrounded
Wellingtonia
welterweight
yellowhammer
affectedness
affectionate
aforethought
AfroAmerican
afterthought
effectuality
effectuation
effeminately
effervescent
efflorescent
effortlessly
effusiveness
officeholder
offscourings
agamogenesis
agamogenetic
agentgeneral
agglutinogen
aggressively
agranulocyte
agribusiness
agricultural
Egyptologist
chairmanship
chalcolithic
chalcopyrite
championship
chancemedley
chaplainship
characterise
charlatanism
charnelhouse
charterhouse
charterparty
chastisement
chauvinistic
checkerberry
checkerboard
cheerfulness
cheeseburger
cheesecutter
cheesemonger
cheeseparing
cheirography
chemotherapy
chequerboard
cherubically
chesterfield
chieftainess
childbearing
childishness
chimneypiece
chiropractic
chiropractor
chitterlings
chivalrously
chlorination
chocolatebox
chondriosome
choreography
chorographic
chorological
chrematistic
chrestomathy
Christianise
Christianity
Christolatry
Christophany
chromaticism
chromaticity
chromatogram
chromatology
chromatopsia
chromosphere
chronography
chronologise
chronologist
chronometric
churchianity
churchwarden
churlishness
ghoulishness
phagocytosis
phagocytotic
phanerogamic
pharmaceutic
pharmacology
phenological
phenomenally
phenotypical
philadelphus
philanthrope
philanthropy
philharmonic
philhellenic
philistinism
phillumenist
philodendron
philological
philosophise
phlebotomise
phlebotomist
phonasthenia
phonemically
phonetically
phonographer
phonographic
phonological
phosphoresce
photochromic
photofission
photogeology
photographer
photographic
photogravure
photokinesis
photokinetic
photomontage
photophilous
photosetting
photospheric
phototropism
phrasemonger
phraseograph
phreatophyte
phrenologist
phycological
phycomycetes
phyllotactic
phylogenesis
phylogenetic
physiognomic
physiography
physiologist
phytogenesis
phytogenetic
phytographer
phytological
phytophagous
rhetorically
rheumatology
rhinocerotic
rhinological
rhizocarpous
rhizogenetic
rhizophagous
rhododendron
rhombohedral
rhombohedron
rhynchophora
rhythmically
shadowboxing
Shakspereana
Shaksperiana
shamateurism
shamefacedly
shamefulness
sharecropper
sharpshooter
sharpsighted
shatterproof
sheepishness
sheepshearer
shillyshally
shipbuilding
shirtwaister
shootingiron
shortchanger
shortcircuit
shortpitched

shortsighted
shortsleeved
shortstaffed
shoulderbelt
shoulderknot
shouldernote
shrewishness
shuffleboard
thankfulness
thanksgiving
thaumaturgic
theanthropic
theatregoing
theatrically
theistically
thematically
theocratical
theoretician
theosophical
therapeutics
therapeutist
thereinafter
thermocouple
thermography
thermolabile
thermometric
thermophilic
thermoscopic
thermosphere
thermostable
thermostatic
thermotactic
thermotropic
thickskinned
thickskulled
thievishness
thimbleberry
thirdborough
thitherwards
thoroughbass
thoroughbred
thoroughfare
thoroughness
thoughtfully
thousandfold
threequarter
threewheeler
thriftlessly
throughstone
thundercloud
thunderingly
thunderously
thunderstone
thunderstorm
whencesoever
wherethrough
whigmaleerie
whimperingly
whimsicality
whippoorwill
whisperingly
whitelivered
whitewashing
whitherwards
wholehearted
whortleberry
ailurophobia
aircondition
aircraftsman
bibliography
bibliologist
bibliomaniac
bibliopegist
bibliophilic
bibliopolist
bibliothecae
bicentennial
bilateralism
bilharziasis
bilharziosis
bilingualism
billingsgate
billsticking
biochemistry
biocoenology
bioecologist
biogeography
biographical
biologically
biometrician
biophysicist
bioscientist
biosynthesis
biosynthetic
birdsnesting
birdwatching
birefringent
cinematheque
circuitously
circumcision
circumfluent
circumfusion
circumjacent
circumscribe
circumstance
cirrocumulus
cirrostratus
civilisation
diabolically
diageotropic
diagrammatic
dialectician
dialectology
diamagnetism
diamonddrill
diamondfield
diaphanously
diastrophism
diathermancy
diatomaceous
diatonically
dibranchiate
dichromatism
dictatorship
didactically
dietetically
differentiae
differential
digressional
digressively
dilapidation
dilatability
dilatoriness
dilettantish
dilettantism
diminishable
diminishment
diminutively
dinnerjacket
diphtheritic
diphthongise
directorship
disaccharide
disadvantage
disaffection
disaffiliate
disagreeable
disagreeably
disagreement
disallowance
disambiguate
disannulling
disannulment
disassociate
disastrously
disbursement
discerningly
discerptible
discipleship
disciplinary
disclamation
discographer
discomfiture
discommodity
discomposure
disconnected
disconnexion
disconsolate
discontented
discordantly
discountable
discouraging
discourteous
discoverable
discoverture
discreetness
discreteness
discretional
discriminant
discriminate
discursively
disdainfully
disembarrass
disenchanter
disendowment
disestablish
disfranchise
disgorgement
disguisement
disgustfully
disgustingly
disharmonise
dishevelment
disincentive
disinfectant
disinfection
disinflation
disingenuous
disintegrate
disinterment
disjointedly
dislodgement
disobedience
disorientate
dispensation
dispensatory
dispiritedly
displaceable
displacement
displeasedly
dispossessor
disputatious
disquisition
disregardful
disreputable
disreputably
dissatisfied
disseminator
dissentingly
dissertation
disseverance
disseverment
dissimilarly
dissimulator
dissocialise
dissociation
dissociative
dissuasively
dissymmetric
distemperate
distillation
distillatory
distinctness
distortional
distractedly
distrainable
distrainment
distributary
distribution
distributive
disturbingly
divarication
diversionary
diversionist
diverticular
diverticulum
divertimenti
divertimento
divisibility
divisiveness
fibrillation
fibrinolysin
fictionalise
fictitiously
fiddlefaddle
fiddlesticks
fieldglasses
fiendishness
figuratively
filibusterer
filtrability
finalisation
firefighting
firstnighter
gigantically
hibernaculum
hierarchical
hieroglyphic
hierographer
hierophantic
highcoloured
highfaluting
highhandedly
highlystrung
highpressure
highsounding
highspirited
highstepping
hindquarters
hippocentaur
hippopotamus
hirepurchase
histogenesis
histogenetic
histological
historically
kilowatthour
kinaesthesia
kinaesthesis
kinaesthetic
kindergarten
kinnikinnick
kirschwasser
kissingcrust
liberalistic
libidinously
licentiously
licketysplit
lifelessness
lighthearted
limnological
linguistical
liquefacient
liquefaction
listlessness
literariness
lithographer
lithographic
lithological
lithospheric
lithotritist
liturgically
liturgiology
Liverpudlian
liverystable
microanalyst
microbiology
microcapsule
microcephaly
microcircuit
microclimate
microcopying
microcrystal
micrographer
microphysics
microscopist
microseismic
microsurgery
middleweight
militaristic
millesimally
milliammeter
mindlessness
minedetector
mineralogist
minicomputer
minimisation
ministration
ministrative
miraculously
mirthfulness
misadventure
misalignment
misanthropic
misapprehend
misbehaviour
miscalculate
miscellanist
misdemeanant
misdemeanour
misdirection
miseducation
misinterpret
misjudgement
misknowledge
misplacement
mispronounce
misquotation
misrepresent
misselthrush
misstatement
mistakenness
mistranslate
mistreatment
mistressship
mithridatise
mithridatism
mitochondria
mitrailleuse
nicotinamide
nidification
nightclothes
nimbostratus
niminypiminy
nitrobenzene
pickerelweed
pictographic
pigeonbreast
pigmentation
pilotballoon
pinfeathered
pisciculture
pitcherplant
pitiableness
pitilessness
pitterpatter
ribonuclease
ricochetting
ridiculously
rightfulness
rigorousness
risorgimento
sideslipping
sidestepping
sidewhiskers

sightreading
significance
significancy
silicicolous
siliciferous
silverglance
silviculture
simoniacally
simpleminded
simultaneity
simultaneous
Sinanthropus
singleacting
singledecker
singlehanded
singleminded
singleseater
sinistrality
sinistrorsal
sinusoidally
siphonophore
siphonostele
ticklishness
tightmouthed
timehonoured
timelessness
timorousness
tintinnabula
tirelessness
tiresomeness
tittletattle
vibraphonist
vicargeneral
vicechairman
Victorianism
victoriously
vigorousness
vilification
villainously
vindictively
vinification
viridescence
virtuosoship
virtuousness
viscerotonic
viscosimeter
viscountship
visitational
visitatorial
vitalisation
vitiligation
vitreousness
vitrifaction
vituperation
vituperative
vituperatory
vivification
viviparously
wicketkeeper
williewaught
windingsheet
wineglassful
winklepicker
winterbourne
xiphisternum
skateboarder
skippingrope
skittishness
skrimshanker
skullduggery
skunkcabbage
alexipharmic
Alhambresque
alimentation
alimentative
alkalescence
alliteration
alliterative
allomorphism
allusiveness
alphabetical
alphamerical
alphanumeric
alterability
altitudinous
blabbermouth
blackbirding
blackcurrant
blackguardly
bladderwrack
blamableness
blamefulness
blandishment
blastfurnace
blastosphere
blastulation
blatherskite
bletherskate
blissfulness
blisteringly
blithesomely
blockbusting
bloodbrother
bloodletting
bloodstained
bloodthirsty
bloodyminded
bluestocking
blunderingly
blusteringly
clairaudient
clairvoyance
clangorously
clannishness
clapperboard
clarinettist
classicalism
classicalist
classicality
classifiable
clatteringly
claudication
clavicembalo
clearsighted
cleistogamic
cliffhanging
clinkerbuilt
closecropped
closegrained
closemouthed
clotheshorse
clothespress
clownishness
elasmobranch
electrically
electrolysis
electrolytic
electrometer
electronvolt
electroplate
electroscope
electroshock
electrotonic
electrotonus
electrotyper
eleemosynary
elementalism
elementarily
elliptically
elocutionary
elocutionist
elucubration
flabelliform
flagellation
flagellatory
flagitiously
flamboyantly
flamethrower
flammability
flatteringly
flavoprotein
flickeringly
flocculation
floodlighted
floriculture
fluidisation
fluorescence
fluoridation
fluorination
fluorocarbon
glaciologist
gladiatorial
gladsomeness
glassblowing
glaucescence
glaucomatous
glitteringly
globetrotter
glockenspiel
gloriousness
glossography
glossologist
gluttonously
glycogenesis
glycoprotein
glyphography
glyptography
illadvisedly
illegibility
illegitimacy
illegitimate
illiberality
illiterately
illnaturedly
illogicality
illtreatment
illumination
illuminative
illusiveness
illusoriness
illustration
illustrative
kleptomaniac
klipspringer
oldfashioned
oligarchical
placesetting
plainclothed
plainclothes
plaindealing
planetesimal
planetstruck
planispheric
planoconcave
plasterboard
platonically
Plattdeutsch
plausibility
playingfield
pleasantness
pleasingness
pleasureless
plebiscitary
plecopterous
plectognathi
pleiotropism
plenipotence
pleomorphism
plesiosaurus
plumbaginous
plumbiferous
plummerblock
pluriliteral
pluviometric
slanderously
slaughterous
slaveholding
sledgehammer
sleepingpill
sleepwalking
slipcarriage
slipperiness
slothfulness
slovenliness
sluggishness
sluttishness
ultramontane
ultramundane
amalgamation
amalgamative
amateurishly
ambassadress
ambidextrous
ambivalently
amelioration
ameliorative
amenableness
amentiferous
amicableness
amitotically
amortisation
amphibiously
amphibrachic
amphictyonic
amphisbaenic
amphitheatre
amphitropous
amygdaloidal
emancipation
emargination
emasculation
emasculatory
embattlement
embezzlement
embitterment
emblazonment
emblematical
embranchment
embryologist
emotionalise
emotionalism
emotionalist
emotionality
emphatically
empoisonment
empressement
emulsifiable
immaculately
immaterially
immatureness
immeasurable
immeasurably
immemorially
immensurable
immethodical
immoderately
immoderation
immovability
immunisation
immunologist
immutability
impartiality
impedimental
impenetrable
impenetrably
impenitently
imperatively
imperatorial
imperceptive
impercipient
imperfection
imperfective
imperishable
imperishably
impermanence
impermanency
impersonally
impersonator
impertinence
impertinency
imperviously
impetiginous
implantation
implicitness
impoliteness
imponderable
imponderably
impoverished
impregnation
impressively
imprisonment
impropriator
improvidence
improvisator
imputability
imputatively
omnipotently
omnipresence
omnisciently
omnivorously
smallclothes
smallholding
umbrageously
anaerobiosis
anaesthetise
anaesthetist
anagogically
anagrammatic
analogically
analphabetic
analytically
anamorphosis
anaphylactic
anastigmatic
anathematise
anatomically
anecdotalist
anemographic
anemophilous
angiocarpous
annihilation
annihilative
announcement
annunciation
anotherguess
antagonistic
antecedently
antediluvian
anteprandial
anthelmintic
anthropogeny
anthropoidal
anthropology
antiaircraft
anticipation
anticipative
anticipatory
anticlerical
anticyclonic
antigenicity
antigropelos
antimacassar
antimagnetic
antimalarial
antineutrino
antiparticle
antipathetic
antiperiodic
antiphonally
antirachitic
antiSemitism
antistrophic
antithetical
enantiomorph
encephalitic

encephalitis
enchantingly
encirclement
enclitically
encroachment
encrustation
encumberment
encumbrancer
encyclopedia
encyclopedic
endamagement
endangerment
endermically
endocarditis
endometritis
endoparasite
endoskeletal
enfeeblement
enginedriver
enginetuning
Englishwoman
enormousness
enshrinement
enswathement
entanglement
enterprising
entertaining
enthronement
enthusiastic
entomologise
entomologist
entrammelled
entrancement
entreatingly
entrenchment
entrepreneur
enviableness
envisagement
enzymologist
inaccessible
inaccessibly
inaccurately
inactivation
inadequately
inadmissible
inadmissibly
inadvertence
inadvertency
inappeasable
inapplicable
inapplicably
inappositely
inarticulate
inartificial
inaudibility
inauguration
inauguratory
inauspicious
incalculable
incalculably
incalescence
incandescent
incapability
incapacitate
incatenation
incautiously
incendiarism
incestuously
incidentally
incineration
incisiveness
inclinometer
incognisable
incognisance
incognitable
incoherently
incommodious
incommutable
incommutably
incomparable
incomparably
incompatible
incompatibly
incompetence
incompetency
incompletely
incompliance
incomputable
inconcinnity
inconclusive
inconformity
inconsequent
inconsistent
inconsolable
inconsolably
inconsonance
inconstantly
inconsumable
inconsumably
incontiguous
incontinence
incontinency
inconvenient
incoordinate
incorporated
incorporator
incorporeity
incorrigible
incorrigibly
incorruption
increasingly
incrustation
incurability
indebtedness
indecisively
indeclinable
indecorously
indefeasible
indefeasibly
indefectible
indefensible
indefensibly
indefinitely
indehiscence
indelibility
indelicately
independence
independency
indicatively
indifference
indifferency
indigenously
indigestible
indirectness
indiscipline
indiscreetly
indiscretion
indisputable
indisputably
indissoluble
indissolubly
indistinctly
indivertible
indivertibly
individually
indoctrinate
IndoEuropean
IndoGermanic
industrially
ineffaceable
ineffaceably
inefficiency
inelasticity
ineradicable
ineradicably
inescutcheon
inexactitude
inexpedience
inexpediency
inexperience
inexpertness
inexplicable
inexplicably
inexpressive
inexpugnable
inexpugnably
inextensible
inextricable
inextricably
infanticidal
infectiously
infelicitous
infiniteness
infinitively
inflammation
inflammatory
inflationary
inflationism
inflationist
inflectional
infrequently
infringement
infundibular
infusibility
ingloriously
ingratiating
inhabitation
inharmonious
inhospitable
inhospitably
iniquitously
innutritious
inobservance
inoccupation
inoperculate
inordinately
inosculation
insalubrious
insecticidal
insemination
insolubilise
insolubility
inspectorate
inspectorial
inspissation
installation
instauration
instillation
instructress
instrumental
insufferable
insufferably
insufficient
insufflation
insurrection
integumental
intellection
intellective
intellectual
intelligence
intelligible
intelligibly
intemperance
inteneration
interbedding
interception
intercession
intercessory
interchanger
interconnect
intercropped
intercurrent
intercutting
interdiction
interdictive
interdictory
interdigital
interestedly
interfemoral
interference
interglacial
interjection
interjectory
interlobular
interlocutor
intermeddler
intermediacy
intermediary
intermediate
interminable
interminably
intermission
intermittent
intermitting
intermixture
intermundane
internuclear
internuncial
interoceanic
interoceptor
interpellate
interpleader
interpolator
interpretive
interrelated
interrogator
interruption
interruptive
intersection
interservice
interspinous
interstellar
interstitial
intertexture
intervenient
intervention
intervocalic
interwreathe
intimidation
intimidatory
intolerantly
intoxication
intracardiac
intracranial
intramundane
intransigent
intransitive
intrauterine
intrenchment
intriguingly
introduction
introductory
introjection
intromission
intromittent
intromitting
introversion
introversive
introvertive
intrusionist
intuitionism
intuitionist
intumescence
intussuscept
invagination
invalidation
inveiglement
invertebrate
investigator
inveterately
invigilation
invigoration
invisibility
involutional
invulnerable
invulnerably
knighterrant
knightliness
mnemotechnic
oncorhynchus
oneirocritic
onesidedness
oneupmanship
onomatopoeia
onomatopoeic
pneumaticity
pneumatology
pneumothorax
snaggletooth
snakecharmer
snapfastener
snappishness
snarlingiron
snobbishness
unacceptable
unaccustomed
unaffectedly
unambivalent
unanswerable
unapologetic
unappeasable
unappetising
unassailable
unassumingly
unattractive
unauthorised
unbecomingly
unbelievable
unbelievably
unblinkingly
unblushingly
unbrokenness
uncalculated
uncelebrated
unchangeable
unchangeably
uncharitable
uncharitably
unchivalrous
unclassified
uncomeatable
uncommercial
uncommonness
unconformity
unconsidered
unconstraint
uncontrolled
unconvincing
uncritically
unctuousness
undemocratic
underachieve
underbidding
underclothes
undercoating
undercurrent
undercutting
underdevelop
undergarment
underinsured
underletting
undermanning
underpinning
underrunning
undersetting
understaffed
undersurface
undertenancy
underwritten
undetermined
undiplomatic
uneconomical
unemployable
unemployment
unencumbered

uneventfully
unexpectedly
unfaithfully
unfamiliarly
unfathomable
unfavourable
unfavourably
unflattering
unfrequented
ungainliness
ungovernable
ungracefully
ungraciously
ungratefully
unhesitating
unhistorical
unifoliolate
unilaterally
unimaginable
unimaginably
unimportance
uninterested
unionisation
unisexuality
unitarianism
universalise
universalism
universalist
universality
unkindliness
unlawfulness
unlikelihood
unlikeliness
unloveliness
unmanageable
unmercifully
unmistakable
unmistakably
unofficially
unparalleled
unpleasantly
unpopularity
unprejudiced
unpretending
unprincipled
unprofitable
unprofitably
unpronounced
unreasonable
unreasonably
unrecognised
unregenerate
unrepeatable
unreservedly
unresponsive
unrestrained
unscientific
unscriptural
unscrupulous
unsearchable
unseasonable
unsegregated
unsteadiness
unstructured
unsuccessful
unthinkingly
unthoughtful
untimeliness
untowardness
untruthfully
unwieldiness
unwontedness
unworldiness
unworthiness
unyieldingly
boastfulness
bobbydazzler
bodybuilding
bodysnatcher
bodystocking
boisterously
bombdisposal
bonnetmonkey
bonnyclabber
boogiewoogie
bookingclerk
booklearning
bootlessness
borosilicate
bottlewasher
boulevardier
bowcompasses
coacervation
coachbuilder
coalitionist
cockfighting
cocksureness
codification
coelenterate
coenobitical
coenobytical
coerciveness
coetaneously
cohabitation
cohesiveness
coincidental
coincidently
coldshoulder
coleopterist
coleopterous
collaborator
collaterally
collectively
collectivise
collectivism
collectivist
collectivity
collegialism
collegiality
collegiately
collinearity
colloquially
collywobbles
colonisation
coloquintida
colorimetric
colourlessly
columniation
combinations
comfortingly
commandingly
commemorator
commencement
commendation
commendatory
commensalism
commensalist
commensurate
commentation
commercially
commiserator
commissarial
commissariat
commissioner
committeeman
commodiously
commonwealth
communicable
communicably
communicator
companionate
companionway
compatriotic
compellation
compensation
compensative
compensatory
complacently
complaisance
complemental
completeness
complexional
complexioned
complication
composedness
compoundable
compressible
compulsively
compulsivity
compulsorily
compunctious
compurgation
compurgatory
concelebrant
concelebrate
concentrator
conceptional
conceptually
conchiferous
conchologist
conciliation
conciliative
conciliatory
conclusively
concomitance
concordantly
concrescence
concreteness
concubitancy
concupiscent
concurrently
condemnation
condemnatory
condensation
conductivity
conduplicate
confabulator
confectioner
conferential
confessional
confidential
confirmation
confirmative
confirmatory
confiscation
confiscatory
conformation
confoundedly
Confucianism
confusedness
congeniality
congenitally
conglobation
conglomerate
conglutinate
congratulant
congratulate
congregation
conidiophore
conidiospore
conjunctival
connaturally
connectional
connectively
conningtower
connubiality
conquistador
conscionable
conscription
consecration
consecratory
consensually
consentience
consentingly
consequently
conservation
conservatism
conservative
conservatory
considerable
considerably
consignation
consistently
consistorial
consociation
consolidator
conspiration
constabulary
constipation
constituency
constitution
constitutive
constriction
constrictive
constringent
construction
constructive
consultation
consultative
consummately
consummation
consummative
consummatory
contagionist
contagiously
containerise
contemplator
contemporary
contemporise
contemptible
contemptibly
contemptuous
conterminous
contestation
contextually
contiguously
contingently
continuation
continuative
continuously
contractable
contractedly
contractible
contradictor
contrapuntal
contrariness
contrariwise
contribution
contributive
contributory
contriteness
contrivement
controllable
contumacious
contumelious
convalescent
convectional
conveniently
conventicler
conventional
conversation
conveyancing
convincement
convincingly
conviviality
convulsively
coordinately
coordination
coordinative
copolymerise
copulatively
coquettishly
corelatively
corespondent
corporeality
correctional
correctitude
correctively
corroborator
cosmetically
cosmogonical
cosmographer
cosmographic
cosmological
cosmopolitan
cosmopolitic
costermonger
cottonocracy
cotyledonary
cotyledonous
councilwoman
countenancer
counteragent
counterblast
countercheck
counterclaim
counterforce
counterlight
countermarch
counterplead
counterpoint
counterpoise
counterproof
counterscarp
countershaft
countertenor
countrydance
countrywoman
courageously
courtmartial
courtplaster
cousingerman
covetousness
cowardliness
dodecahedral
dodecahedron
dodecaphonic
dogmatically
dolorousness
domestically
domesticator
dorsiventral
doubleacting
doubledealer
doubledecked
doubledecker
doublelocked
doubtfulness
dovecoloured
downwardness
focalisation
folliculated
footplateman
foraminifera
forbiddingly
forcefulness
forcibleness
forebodement
forebodingly
forensically
foresightful
forestalment
formaldehyde
formlessness
forthrightly
fortuitously
fostermother
foundationer
fountainhead
gobbledegook
gobbledygook
gonadotropic
gonadotropin
goodhumoured
goodtempered

goosepimples
gorgeousness
governmental
governorship
holidaymaker
homeomorphic
homeopathist
homesickness
homoeopathic
homoeostasis
homologation
homomorphism
homomorphous
homonymously
homosexually
homothallism
honeybuzzard
hoodmanblind
hopelessness
horizontally
horrendously
horribleness
horrifically
horrorstruck
horsebreaker
horsemanship
horsetrading
horsewhipped
horticulture
housebreaker
housekeeping
housetrained
housewarming
journalistic
localisation
lodginghouse
logistically
lonesomeness
longdistance
longitudinal
longshoreman
longstanding
longwindedly
lopsidedness
loquaciously
loungelizard
lovelessness
lovelornness
LowChurchman
mobilisation
moderateness
modification
modificatory
moistureless
molecularity
monadelphous
monastically
monetisation
moneychanger
moneygrubber
moneyspinner
monitorially
monkeyflower
monkeyjacket
monkeypuzzle
monkeywrench
monochromate
monodramatic
monofilament
monographist
monomaniacal
monometallic
monomorphous
monopetalous
monophyletic
Monophysitic
monopodially
monopolistic
monostichous
monostrophic
monosyllabic
monosyllable
monotheistic
monotonously
monumentally
moralisation
mordaciously
morningdress
morphallaxis
morphologist
morrisdancer
mosstrooping
motherfigure
motherliness
mothertongue
motivational
motorcyclist
motorisation
mountainside
mournfulness
mourningband
mourningring
mouthbreeder
moveableness
movelessness
noctambulant
noctambulism
noctambulist
noctambulous
noctilucence
nomenclative
nomenclature
nominalistic
nonagenarian
nonalignment
nonchalantly
noncombatant
noncommittal
noncomplying
nonconductor
nonconformer
noneffective
nonefficient
nonessential
noneuclidean
nonexistence
nonflammable
nonflowering
nonidentical
nonobjective
nonresidence
nonresistant
noradrenalin
northeastern
northernmost
Northumbrian
northwestern
notification
novelisation
poikilotherm
pointilliste
polarimetric
polarisation
polarography
policyholder
polychaetous
polychromous
polyethylene
polyglottism
polyhistoric
polymorphism
polymorphous
polyneuritic
polyneuritis
polypetalous
polyphyletic
polysepalous
polysyllabic
polysyllable
polytheistic
polytonality
polyurethane
pontifically
pontificator
poorspirited
populousness
porcelainise
porcelainous
porcellanous
pornographer
pornographic
portentously
portmanteaus
portmanteaux
positiveness
positivistic
possessively
postdiluvian
postdoctoral
posteriority
postgraduate
posthumously
postmeridian
postmistress
postponement
postposition
postpositive
postprandial
potentiality
robustiously
rollingstock
romanisation
romantically
rontgenogram
rontgenology
rootlessness
rosecoloured
sociableness
sociological
sociometrist
Socratically
sodafountain
softpedalled
solarisation
solicitation
solicitously
solifluction
solitariness
somatopleure
somnambulant
somnambulate
somnambulism
somnambulist
somniloquism
somniloquist
sonorousness
sophisticate
soporiferous
sorbefacient
soullessness
soundingline
southeastern
southernmost
southernwood
southwestern
toastingfork
togetherness
toggleswitch
toilsomeness
tolerability
tonelessness
toploftiness
topsyturvily
torrefaction
torrentially
Torricellian
tortuousness
totalisation
totalitarian
touchingness
towardliness
toxicologist
toxicophobia
vocabularian
vocalisation
vociferation
vociferously
voidableness
volatileness
volcanically
volitionally
volumetrical
voluminosity
voluminously
voluntaryism
voluntaryist
voluptuosity
voluptuously
vomiturition
wollastonite
womanishness
wonderstruck
wonderworker
wondrousness
woodengraver
woodenheaded
woolgatherer
woollyheaded
workableness
workingclass
worshipfully
youngberries
youthfulness
zoogeography
aperiodicity
apiculturist
apochromatic
apolitically
apostolicism
apostolicity
apostrophise
apothegmatic
apparatchiki
apparatchiks
apparentness
apparitional
appendectomy
appendicitis
appendicular
apperception
apperceptive
appetisingly
appositeness
appositional
appraisement
appraisingly
appreciation
appreciative
appreciatory
apprehension
apprehensive
approachable
appropriable
appropriator
appurtenance
epexegetical
ephemerality
epicureanism
epicycloidal
epidemically
epidemiology
epigrammatic
epiphenomena
episcopalian
episodically
epistemology
epithalamion
epithalamium
openhandedly
openmindedly
operatically
ophiophagous
opinionative
opisthograph
opisthotonos
opposability
oppositeness
oppositional
oppressively
optimisation
spaciousness
sparkingplug
sparrowgrass
speakingtube
specialistic
specifically
specificness
speciousness
specktioneer
spectrograph
spectrometer
spectrometry
spectroscope
spectroscopy
speechlessly
speedboating
speleologist
spermaphytic
spermathecal
spermatocyte
spermatozoid
spermatozoon
spermogonium
spheroidally
sphragistics
sphygmograph
spidermonkey
spiegeleisen
spinsterhood
spiritedness
spiritlessly
spiritualise
spiritualism
spiritualist
spirituality
spitefulness
splendidness
spokesperson
sporadically
sporogenesis
sportfulness
sportiveness
spotlessness
sprightfully
spuriousness
uproariously
aquicultural
equalisation
equalitarian
equationally
equestrienne
equidistance
equilibrator
equipollence
equipollency
equiprobable
equitability
equivalently
equivocation
equivocatory
squarerigged
squattocracy
squirrelcage
squirreltail
arborescence

arborisation
archdeaconry
archdiocesan
archetypally
archetypical
archipelagic
architecture
argillaceous
aristocratic
Aristotelean
Aristotelian
arithmetical
aromatically
aromaticness
arrhythmical
articulately
articulation
articulatory
artificially
artilleryman
artistically
brachydactyl
brackishness
brainstormer
brainwashing
brambleberry
brassbounder
brassrubbing
breakthrough
breaststroke
breastsummer
breathalyser
breathlessly
breathtaking
breechloader
brickfielder
brilliantine
brinkmanship
brokenwinded
bronchoscope
broncobuster
brontosaurus
crackbrained
craftbrother
craniologist
crashlanding
creativeness
creepycrawly
crenellation
criticalness
crossbedding
crossbencher
crossbuttock
crosscountry
crosscurrent
crossexamine
crossgrained
crossheading
crossingover
crosspurpose
crosssection
cryptanalyst
cryptogamous
cryptography
cryptologist
crystalgazer
dramatically
dramaturgist
draughtboard
draughthorse
drawingboard
drawingpaper
dreadfulness
dressinggown
droughtiness
eruptiveness
erythematous
erythroblast
erythromycin
fractionally
fractionator
FrancoGerman
frangibility
frankincense
fraudulently
freakishness
freestanding
freeswimming
freethinking
freewheeling
freightliner
frenchpolish
frenetically
frequentness
fricasseeing
frictionless
friendliness
frontbencher
frontiersman
frontispiece
fructiferous
fructivorous
fruitfulness
gracefulness
graciousness
grallatorial
graminaceous
grammaticise
grammolecule
gramnegative
grampositive
granodiorite
graphologist
graspingness
gratefulness
gratifyingly
gratuitously
graveclothes
gravelelling
greathearted
greengrocery
greenishness
gregariously
grievousness
griseofulvin
grossularite
grotesquerie
groundcherry
groundlessly
grovellingly
gruesomeness
irascibility
irrationally
irredeemable
irredeemably
irreflective
irreformable
irrefragable
irrefragably
irregardless
irregularity
irrelatively
irrelevantly
irremediable
irremediably
irremissible
irrepealable
irreprovable
irresistible
irresistibly
irresolutely
irresolution
irresolvable
irrespective
irrespirable
irresponsive
irreverently
irreversible
irreversibly
irritability
irritatingly
kremlinology
orbicularity
orchestrator
orchidaceous
ordinariness
organgrinder
organisation
organography
organoleptic
orienteering
ornamentally
ornithomancy
ornithoscopy
orographical
orthodontics
orthodontist
orthogenesis
orthogenetic
orthographer
orthographic
orthopaedics
orthopaedist
orthopterist
orthopteroid
orthopterous
orthotropism
orthotropous
practicality
practitioner
pragmatistic
praiseworthy
pralltriller
praseodymium
precancelled
precariously
precedential
preceptorial
precessional
prechristian
preciousness
precipitable
precipitance
precipitancy
precipitator
precisianism
precisionist
preclassical
preclusively
precociously
precognition
precognitive
precondition
preconscious
predesignate
predestinate
predetermine
predictively
predigestion
predilection
predominance
predominancy
preeminently
preestablish
preexistence
prefabricate
prefectorial
preferential
preformation
preformative
prehensility
prehistorian
prelapsarian
premaxillary
premeditated
premeditator
premenstrual
prenticeship
preoccupancy
preparedness
preponderant
preponderate
preposterous
prerequisite
presbyterate
presbyterial
Presbyterian
prescription
prescriptive
preselection
preselective
presentation
presentative
presentiment
preservation
preservative
presidential
presumptuous
pretermitted
prevailingly
prevaricator
preventative
preventively
previousness
pricecutting
pridefulness
priestliness
priestridden
priggishness
primigravida
primogenital
primogenitor
primordially
princeliness
principality
printability
privatdocent
privatdozent
privateering
prizefighter
prizewinning
probationary
proboscidean
proboscidian
procathedral
processional
proclamation
proclamatory
proconsulate
prodigiously
productively
productivity
professional
professorate
professoress
professorial
proficiently
profiteering
profligately
profoundness
progenitress
progesterone
proglottides
programmable
programmatic
projectional
projectively
prolegomenon
prolifically
prolificness
prolongation
promulgation
pronominally
pronouncedly
proofreading
propaedeutic
propagandise
propagandism
propagandist
prophylactic
propitiation
propitiatory
propitiously
proportional
proportioned
proprietress
proscription
proscriptive
prosectorial
prosecutable
proselytiser
prosodically
prosopopoeia
prosperously
prostitution
protactinium
protectively
protectorate
protensively
protestation
prothalamion
prothalamium
prothonotary
protistology
protohistory
protoplasmic
protoplastic
prototypical
protozoology
protrusively
protuberance
proudhearted
proverbially
providential
provincially
provisionary
prudentially
traceability
trachomatous
tractability
tradescantia
tradespeople
traditionary
traditionist
traducianism
traducianist
tragicomical
trainspotter
traitorously
trampolinist
tranquillise
tranquillity
transcendent
transduction
transferable
transference
transferring
transformism
transformist
transfusible
transgressor
transhipment
transhumance
transiliency
transitional
transitively
transitivity
transitorily
translatable
translucence
translucency
transmigrant
transmigrate
transmission
transmissive

transmitting
transmogrify
transmontane
transmutable
transoceanic
transpacific
transparency
transpirable
transplanter
transpontine
transposable
transshipped
transudation
transudatory
transversely
transvestism
transvestite
tremendously
trephination
trestletable
triangularly
tricentenary
trichologist
trichotomise
trichotomous
trichromatic
trickishness
tridactylous
trifurcation
triggerhappy
triglyphical
trigonometry
trinomialism
tripartitely
tripartition
triphthongal
triplication
triumphantly
trochanteric
troglodytism
trophallaxis
tropological
tropospheric
troublemaker
trumpetshell
trustfulness
truthfulness
urbanisation
urbanologist
wrathfulness
wretchedness
wrongfulness
asphyxiation
assassinator
assibilation
assimilation
assimilative
assimilatory
astonishment
astoundingly
astringently
astrological
astronautics
astronomical
astrophysics
asymmetrical
asynchronism
asynchronous
escapologist
escutcheoned
esoterically
espagnolette
essentiality
estrangement
Ishmaelitish
isochromatic
isochronally
isodiametric
isolationism
isolationist
isothermally
oscillograph
oscilloscope
ossification
ostentatious
osteogenesis
osteological
osteomalacia
osteoplastic
osteoporosis
psephologist
pseudocyesis
pseudonymity
pseudonymous
pseudopodium
psychiatrist
psychoactive
psychography
psychologise
psychologism
psychologist
psychometric
psychopathic
psychosexual
psychotropic
psychrometer
psychrometry
usufructuary
usuriousness
atheromatous
athletically
atmospherics
attitudinise
attorneyship
attractively
attributable
etherisation
ethnocentric
ethnographer
ethnographic
ethnological
etymological
etymologicon
otherworldly
pteridophyte
pteridosperm
pterodactyle
stablishment
staffofficer
staffsurgeon
stagemanager
staggeringly
Stakhanovism
Stakhanovite
stalactiform
stalwartness
stammeringly
standardbred
standingroom
stanniferous
starspangled
stationhouse
stationwagon
statistician
statuesquely
stealthiness
steatopygous
steeplechase
steganograph
stellenbosch
stelliferous
stenographer
stenographic
stepchildren
stepdaughter
stereochromy
stereography
stereoisomer
stereometric
stereophonic
stereopticon
stereoscopic
sterlingness
sternutation
sternutative
sternutatory
sternwheeler
stertorously
stethoscopic
stichomythia
stichomythic
stilboestrol
stillhunting
stockbreeder
stockbroking
stockingless
stockjobbery
stockjobbing
stockraising
stoneboiling
stonecutting
stonedresser
stonemasonry
stonyhearted
stormtrooper
stouthearted
Stradivarius
straightaway
straightbred
straightedge
straightener
straightness
straitjacket
stranglehold
straticulate
stratigraphy
stratosphere
streetwalker
strengthener
strengthless
streptococci
streptomycin
stridulation
strikingness
stringcourse
strobilation
stroboscopic
strongminded
strongylosis
strontianite
strophanthin
structurally
strychninism
stubbornness
studdingsail
studiousness
stupefacient
stupefaction
stupefactive
stupendously
stutteringly
stylographic
augmentation
augmentative
auscultation
auscultatory
auspiciously
Australasian
authenticate
authenticity
autocatalyse
autochthones
autodidactic
autoimmunity
automaticity
automobilist
automorphism
autonomously
buccaneering
buccaneerish
buffalograss
bulletheaded
bullfighting
bullheadedly
bureaucratic
burglarproof
burningglass
businesslike
butterflynut
buttermuslin
butterscotch
cuckingstool
cuckooflower
culpableness
cultivatable
cumbersomely
cumbrousness
cumulatively
cumulocirrus
cumulonimbus
cuprammonium
curlingirons
curlingtongs
curmudgeonly
curvicaudate
curvicostate
curvifoliate
curvirostral
customshouse
dubitatively
duckingstool
dunderheaded
duraluminium
euhemeristic
eunuchoidism
euphonically
euphoniously
EuroAmerican
fugitiveness
fuliginosity
fullyfledged
functionally
functionless
furfuraceous
furunculosis
futilitarian
futurologist
guaranteeing
guardianship
guestchamber
guilefulness
hubblebubble
hucklebacked
huggermugger
humanisation
humanitarian
humification
humorousness
humptydumpty
judgematical
jurisconsult
jurisdiction
jurisprudent
juvenescence
lugubriously
lukewarmness
lumberjacket
luminescence
luminiferous
luminousness
lusciousness
mucilaginous
muddleheaded
mulligatawny
multicentral
multidentate
multifarious
multiflorous
multifoliate
multiformity
multilateral
multilingual
multiloquous
multinuclear
multipartite
multipliable
multiplicand
multiplicate
multiplicity
multipurpose
multistoried
multivalence
multiversity
multungulate
municipalise
municipality
munificently
musicianship
musicologist
mutinousness
muttonheaded
muzzleloader
numerologist
numerousness
nutritionist
nutritiously
outdatedness
outlandishly
outmanoeuvre
outpensioner
outrageously
outrivalling
outstretched
outstripping
outwardbound
publicspirit
puerperrally
pugnaciously
pulverisable
pumpernickel
punchingball
purblindness
purification
purificatory
purposebuilt
purposefully
pursestrings
putrefaction
putrefactive
Quadragesima
quadrangular
quadraphonic
quadriennium
quadrinomial
quadriplegia
quadriplegic
quadrivalent
quadrumanous
quaestorship
qualmishness
quantifiable
quantisation
quantitative
quaquaversal
quarterbound
quarterfinal
quarterstaff
quattrocento
questionable
questionably
questionless
quinquennial
quinquennium
quintessence
quixotically

quizzicality
rumbletumble
ruminatively
runningboard
ruralisation
ruthlessness
subalternate
subalternity
subapostolic
subarrhation
subcelestial
subcommittee
subconscious
subcontinent
subcutaneous
subdivisible
subeditorial
suberisation
subinfeudate
subjectively
subjectivise
subjectivism
subjectivist
subjectivity
sublapsarian
submaxillary
subminiature
submissively
subnormality
subsaturated
subscription
subsequently
subservience
subserviency
subsidiarily
subsonically
substantiate
substantival
substitution
substitutive
substruction
substructure
subtemperate
subterranean
subthreshold
subversively
succedaneous
successfully
successional
successively
succinctness
sudoriferous
sufficiently
suggestively
suitableness
sulphonamide
sulphonation
sulphuration
sulphuretted
superannuate
supercharger
superciliary
supercilious
supereminent
supererogate
superhighway
superhumanly
supermundane
supernaculum
supernatural
superposable
supersedence
supersensory
supersession
superstition
superstratum
supervenient
supervention
supplemental
supplementer
supplicantly
supplication
supplicatory
suppositious
suppressible
supramundane
supraorbital
surefootedly
surmountable
surprisingly
surrealistic
surrejoinder
surroundings
surveillance
surveyorship
survivorship
susceptivity
suspensively
suspiciously
sustentation
sustentative
tuberculated
tuberculosis
tumultuously
tunelessness
turbellarian
turriculated
turtlenecked
wunderkinder
availability
avantgardism
avantgardist
avariciously
avitaminoses
avitaminosis
evanescently
evangelistic
eveningdress
evidentially
evisceration
evolutionary
evolutionism
evolutionist
overabundant
overachiever
overactivity
overcautious
overcritical
overcropping
overemphasis
overestimate
overexertion
overexposure
overlordship
overniceness
overpersuade
overpowering
overpressure
overreaction
oversimplify
overstepping
dwarfishness
swaggeringly
swaggerstick
swainishness
swashbuckler
sweepingness
sweetishness
swimmingbath
swimmingbell
swimmingpool
swizzlestick
twentyfourmo
twitteringly
exacerbation
exaggeration
exaggerative
exaggeratory
exasperation
exchangeable
excitability
exclusionary
exclusionism
exclusionist
excogitation
excogitative
excruciating
excruciation
excursionist
executorship
exegetically
exenteration
exercitation
exhaustively
exhibitioner
exhilaration
exhilarative
exiguousness
exophthalmic
exophthalmos
exophthalmus
exorbitantly
exospherical
exoterically
expansionary
expansionism
expansionist
expatriation
expediential
experiential
experimental
experimenter
explantation
explicitness
exploitation
exploitative
expressional
expressively
expressivity
exprobration
exsanguinate
exsanguinous
exsufflicate
extensometer
exterminable
exterminator
extinguisher
extortionary
extortionate
extracranial
extraditable
extralimital
extramarital
extramundane
extraneously
extrasensory
extraspecial
extrauterine
extravagance
extravagancy
extravaganza
extraversion
extroversion
exulceration
oxyacetylene
uxoriousness
Byelorussian
cynocephalus
cytogenetics
dynamometric
dynastically
gymnosophist
gynaecocracy
gyromagnetic
hybridisable
hydatidiform
hydrochloric
hydrodynamic
hydrofluoric
hydrographer
hydrographic
hydrokinetic
hydrological
hydrolysable
hydromedusae
hydromedusan
hydrophilous
hydroquinone
hydrostatics
hydrotherapy
hydrothermal
hydrotropism
hygienically
hygrophilous
hymenopteran
hymnographer
hyperacidity
hyperbolical
hyperplastic
hyperpyretic
hyperpyrexia
hypersthenia
hypersthenic
hypertension
hypertensive
hyperthermia
hypertrophic
hypnogenesis
hypnogenetic
hypnotherapy
hypnotically
hypnotisable
hypochlorite
hypochondria
hypocoristic
hypocritical
hypogastrium
hypognathous
hypophrygian
hypostatical
hyposulphite
hypothalamic
hypothalamus
hypothecator
hypothetical
hysterectomy
hysterically
hysteromania
lycanthropic
myrmecophily
mysteriously
mystifyingly
mythographer
mythological
mythologiser
nychthemeral
nychthemeron
nyctitropism
nympholeptic
nymphomaniac
pyroelectric
pyroligneous
pyromaniacal
pyromorphite
pyrotechnics
pyrotechnist
sycophantish
syllabically
sylviculture
symbolically
synaesthesia
synaesthetic
synarthrosis
synchronical
synchroniser
syncretistic
syndactylism
syndactylous
syndetically
synonymously
synoptically
systematical
systematiser
systemically
typefounding
typification
tyrannically
tyrannicidal
zygapophysis
zygomorphism
zygomorphous
Czechoslovak

---

academically
acaulescence
adaptability
adaptiveness
agamogenesis
agamogenetic
amalgamation
amalgamative
amateurishly
anaerobiosis
anaesthetise
anaesthetist
anagogically
anagrammatic
analogically
analphabetic
analytically
anamorphosis
anaphylactic
anastigmatic
anathematise
anatomically
availability
avantgardism
avantgardist
avariciously
beachcombing
beatifically
blabbermouth
blackbirding
blackcurrant
blackguardly
bladderwrack
blamableness
blamefulness
blandishment
blastfurnace
blastosphere
blastulation
blatherskite
boastfulness
brachydactyl
brackishness
brainstormer
brainwashing
brambleberry
brassbounder
brassrubbing
chairmanship
chalcolithic
chalcopyrite
championship
chancemedley
chaplainship
characterise
charlatanism
charnelhouse
charterhouse
charterparty
chastisement
chauvinistic
clairaudient

clairvoyance
clangorously
clannishness
clapperboard
clarinettist
classicalism
classicalist
classicality
classifiable
clatteringly
claudication
clavicembalo
coacervation
coachbuilder
coalitionist
crackbrained
craftbrother
craniologist
crashlanding
deactivation
deambulatory
diabolically
diageotropic
diagrammatic
dialectician
dialectology
diamagnetism
diamonddrill
diamondfield
diaphanously
diastrophism
diathermancy
diatomaceous
diatonically
dramatically
dramaturgist
draughtboard
draughthorse
drawingboard
drawingpaper
dwarfishness
elasmobranch
emancipation
emargination
emasculation
emasculatory
enantiomorph
evanescently
evangelistic
exacerbation
exaggeration
exaggerative
exaggeratory
exasperation
fearlessness
fearsomeness
featherbrain
featheriness
flabelliform
flagellation
flagellatory
flagitiously
flamboyantly
flamethrower
flammability
flatteringly
flavoprotein
fractionally
fractionator
FrancoGerman
frangibility
frankincense
fraudulently
geanticlinal
glaciologist
gladiatorial
gladsomeness
glassblowing
glaucescence
glaucomatous
gracefulness
graciousness
grallatorial
graminaceous
grammaticise
grammolecule
gramnegative
grampositive
granodiorite
graphologist
graspingness
gratefulness
gratifyingly
gratuitously
graveclothes
gravelelling
guaranteeing
guardianship
headmistress
headquarters
headshrinker
heartburning
heartrending
heartstrings
heartwarming
heathenishly
heavenliness
heavyhearted
inaccessible
inaccessibly
inaccurately
inactivation
inadequately
inadmissible
inadmissibly
inadvertence
inadvertency
inappeasable
inapplicable
inapplicably
inappositely
inarticulate
inartificial
inaudibility
inauguration
inauguratory
inauspicious
irascibility
leapfrogging
leathercloth
mealymouthed
meaningfully
peacefulness
pearlescence
peasepudding
phagocytosis
phagocytotic
phanerogamic
pharmaceutic
pharmacology
placesetting
plainclothed
plainclothes
plaindealing
planetesimal
planetstruck
planispheric
planoconcave
plasterboard
platonically
Plattdeutsch
plausibility
playingfield
practicality
practitioner
pragmatistic
praiseworthy
pralltriller
praseodymium
Quadragesima
quadrangular
quadraphonic
quadriennium
quadrinomial
quadriplegia
quadriplegic
quadrivalent
quadrumanous
quaestorship
qualmishness
quantifiable
quantisation
quantitative
quaquaversal
quarterbound
quarterfinal
quarterstaff
quattrocento
reactivation
reactiveness
readableness
readjustment
reallocation
reappearance
reassessment
reassignment
reassuringly
scabbardfish
scabrousness
scandalously
Scandinavian
scareheading
scarificator
scatological
scatterbrain
scatteringly
shadowboxing
Shakspereana
Shaksperiana
shamateurism
shamefacedly
shamefulness
sharecropper
sharpshooter
sharpsighted
shatterproof
skateboarder
slanderously
slaughterous
slaveholding
smallclothes
smallholding
snaggletooth
snakecharmer
snapfastener
snappishness
snarlingiron
spaciousness
sparkingplug
sparrowgrass
stablishment
staffofficer
staffsurgeon
stagemanager
staggeringly
Stakhanovism
Stakhanovite
stalactiform
stalwartness
stammeringly
standardbred
standingroom
stanniferous
starspangled
stationhouse
stationwagon
statistician
statuesquely
swaggeringly
swaggerstick
swainishness
swashbuckler
teachability
tearlessness
thankfulness
thanksgiving
thaumaturgic
toastingfork
traceability
trachomatous
tractability
tradescantia
tradespeople
traditionary
traditionist
traducianism
traducianist
tragicomical
trainspotter
traitorously
trampolinist
tranquillise
tranquillity
transcendent
transduction
transferable
transference
transferring
transformism
transformist
transfusible
transgressor
transhipment
transhumance
transiliency
transitional
transitively
transitivity
transitorily
translatable
translucence
translucency
transmigrant
transmigrate
transmission
transmissive
transmitting
transmogrify
transmontane
transmutable
transoceanic
transpacific
transparency
transpirable
transplanter
transpontine
transposable
transshipped
transudation
transudatory
transversely
transvestism
transvestite
unacceptable
unaccustomed
unaffectedly
unambivalent
unanswerable
unapologetic
unappeasable
unappetising
unassailable
unassumingly
unattractive
unauthorised
weatherboard
weatherbound
weatherglass
weatherhouse
weatherproof
wrathfulness
abbreviation
ambassadress
ambidextrous
ambivalently
arborescence
arborisation
bibliography
bibliologist
bibliomaniac
bibliopegist
bibliophilic
bibliopolist
bibliothecae
bobbydazzler
cabbagewhite
cabinetmaker
debilitation
debonairness
dibranchiate
dubitatively
embattlement
embezzlement
embitterment
emblazonment
emblematical
embranchment
embryologist
fabulousness
fibrillation
fibrinolysin
gobbledegook
gobbledygook
haberdashery
habilitation
habitability
habitforming
habitualness
hebdomadally
hebetudinous
hibernaculum
hubblebubble
hybridisable
laboursaving
labyrinthian
labyrinthine
liberalistic
libidinously
mobilisation
nebulisation
nebulousness
orbicularity
publicspirit
rabbinically
rabblerouser
rebelliously
ribonuclease
robustiously
sabretoothed
subalternate
subalternity
subapostolic
subarrhation
subcelestial
subcommittee
subconscious
subcontinent
subcutaneous
subdivisible
subeditorial
suberisation
subinfeudate
subjectively
subjectivise
subjectivism

subjectivist
subjectivity
sublapsarian
submaxillary
subminiature
submissively
subnormality
subsaturated
subscription
subsequently
subservience
subserviency
subsidiarily
subsonically
substantiate
substantival
substitution
substitutive
substruction
substructure
subtemperate
subterranean
subthreshold
subversively
taberdarship
tabernacular
tuberculated
tuberculosis
umbrageously
unbecomingly
unbelievable
unbelievably
unblinkingly
unblushingly
unbrokenness
urbanisation
urbanologist
vibraphonist
acceleration
accelerative
accentuation
acciaccatura
accidentally
accommodator
accompanyist
accomplished
accordionist
accouchement
accoutrement
accretionary
accumulation
accumulative
accurateness
accursedness
accusatively
accusatorial
archdeaconry
archdiocesan
archetypally
archetypical
archipelagic
architecture
bacchanalian
bachelorhood
bachelorship
backbreaking
backpedalled
backslapping
backwardness
backwoodsman
bactericidal
bacteriology
bacteriostat
bicentennial
buccaneering
buccaneerish
cachinnation
cachinnatory
cockfighting
cocksureness
cuckingstool
cuckooflower
decaffeinate
decalescence
decapitation
decasyllabic
decasyllable
deceleration
decentralise
decipherable
decipherment
decisiveness
declinometer
decomposable
decompressor
decongestant
decongestion
decongestive
deconsecrate
decontrolled
decoratively
decorousness
decreasingly
dichromatism
dictatorship
duckingstool
eccentricity
ecclesiastic
ecclesiology
encephalitic
encephalitis
enchantingly
encirclement
enclitically
encroachment
encrustation
encumberment
encumbrancer
encyclopedia
encyclopedic
escapologist
escutcheoned
exchangeable
excitability
exclusionary
exclusionism
exclusionist
excogitation
excogitative
excruciating
excruciation
excursionist
facelessness
facilitation
factionalism
factiousness
factitiously
fecklessness
fictionalise
fictitiously
focalisation
hectographic
hucklebacked
incalculable
incalculably
incalescence
incandescent
incapability
incapacitate
incatenation
incautiously
incendiarism
incestuously
incidentally
incineration
incisiveness
inclinometer
incognisable
incognisance
incognitable
incoherently
incommodious
incommutable
incommutably
incomparable
incomparably
incompatible
incompatibly
incompetence
incompetency
incompletely
incompliance
incomputable
inconcinnity
inconclusive
inconformity
inconsequent
inconsistent
inconsolable
inconsolably
inconsonance
inconstantly
inconsumable
inconsumably
incontiguous
incontinence
incontinency
inconvenient
incoordinate
incorporated
incorporator
incorporeity
incorrigible
incorrigibly
incorruption
increasingly
incrustation
incurability
lachrymation
lachrymatory
lachrymosely
lacininiated
licentiously
licketysplit
localisation
lycanthropic
machicolated
macrocephaly
macropterous
mechanically
microanalyst
microbiology
microcapsule
microcephaly
microcircuit
microclimate
microcopying
microcrystal
micrographer
microphysics
microscopist
microseismic
microsurgery
mucilaginous
necrographer
necrological
necrophagous
necrophiliac
necrophilism
necrophilous
nicotinamide
noctambulant
noctambulism
noctambulist
noctambulous
noctilucence
nychthemeral
nychthemeron
nyctitropism
occasionally
occidentally
occupational
oncorhynchus
orchestrator
orchidaceous
oscillograph
oscilloscope
pacification
pacificatory
peccadilloes
pickerelweed
pictographic
racemisation
racketeering
recalcitrant
recalcitrate
recalescence
recapitulate
receivership
receptaculum
receptionist
recessionary
rechargeable
reciprocally
reciprocator
recklessness
recognisable
recognisably
recognisance
recollection
recollective
recommitment
reconcilable
reconstitute
reconversion
reconveyance
recreational
recrudescent
recuperation
recuperative
ricochetting
saccharinity
saccharoidal
sacerdotally
sacrilegious
secessionism
secessionist
seclusionist
secondstring
sectarianise
sectarianism
sectionalism
secularistic
sociableness
sociological
sociometrist
Socratically
succedaneous
successfully
successional
successively
succinctness
sycophantish
tachygrapher
tachygraphic
tactlessness
technicality
technicolour
technocratic
technologist
tectonically
ticklishness
uncalculated
uncelebrated
unchangeable
unchangeably
uncharitable
uncharitably
unchivalrous
unclassified
uncomeatable
uncommercial
uncommonness
unconformity
unconsidered
unconstraint
uncontrolled
unconvincing
uncritically
unctuousness
vicargeneral
vicechairman
Victorianism
victoriously
vocabularian
vocalisation
vociferation
vociferously
wicketkeeper
additionally
bedazzlement
bodybuilding
bodysnatcher
bodystocking
codification
didactically
dodecahedral
dodecahedron
dodecaphonic
endamagement
endangerment
endermically
endocarditis
endometritis
endoparasite
endoskeletal
fiddlefaddle
fiddlesticks
hedgehopping
hydatidiform
hydrochloric
hydrodynamic
hydrofluoric
hydrographer
hydrographic
hydrokinetic
hydrological
hydrolysable
hydromedusae
hydromedusan
hydrophilous
hydroquinone
hydrostatics
hydrotherapy
hydrothermal
hydrotropism
indebtedness
indecisively
indeclinable
indecorously
indefeasible
indefeasibly
indefectible
indefensible
indefensibly
indefinitely
indehiscence
indelibility
indelicately
independence
independency
indicatively
indifference
indifferency
indigenously

indigestible
indirectness
indiscipline
indiscreetly
indiscretion
indisputable
indisputably
indissoluble
indissolubly
indistinctly
indivertible
indivertibly
individually
indoctrinate
IndoEuropean
IndoGermanic
industrially
judgematical
ledgertackle
lodginghouse
mademoiselle
mediaevalism
mediaevalist
meditatively
middleweight
moderateness
modification
modificatory
muddleheaded
nidification
obdurateness
oldfashioned
ordinariness
pedantically
pedicellaria
pedunculated
radiobiology
radioelement
radiographer
radiographic
radioisotope
radiological
radionuclide
radiophonics
radiotherapy
redecoration
redemptioner
Redemptorist
redeployment
redintegrate
redistribute
reducibility
reductionism
reductionist
ridiculously
saddlebacked
sadistically
sedgewarbler
sedulousness
sideslipping
sidestepping
sidewhiskers
sodafountain
sudoriferous
undemocratic
underachieve
underbidding
underclothes
undercoating
undercurrent
undercutting
underdevelop
undergarment
underinsured
underletting
undermanning
underpinning
underrunning
undersetting
understaffed
undersurface
undertenancy
underwritten
undetermined
undiplomatic
acetabularia
acetaldehyde
adequateness
agentgeneral
alexipharmic
amelioration
ameliorative
amenableness
amentiferous
anecdotalist
anemographic
anemophilous
aperiodicity
bletherskate
breakthrough
breaststroke
breastsummer
breathalyser
breathlessly
breathtaking
breechloader
Byelorussian
checkerberry
checkerboard
cheerfulness
cheeseburger
cheesecutter
cheesemonger
cheeseparing
cheirography
chemotherapy
chequerboard
cherubically
chesterfield
clearsighted
cleistogamic
coelenterate
coenobitical
coenobytical
coerciveness
coetaneously
creativeness
creepycrawly
crenellation
Czechoslovak
deescalation
dietetically
dreadfulness
dressinggown
electrically
electrolysis
electrolytic
electrometer
electronvolt
electroplate
electroscope
electroshock
electrotonic
electrotonus
electrotyper
eleemosynary
elementalism
elementarily
epexegetical
eveningdress
executorship
exegetically
exenteration
exercitation
feebleminded
fieldglasses
fiendishness
freakishness
freestanding
freeswimming
freethinking
freewheeling
freightliner
frenchpolish
frenetically
frequentness
greathearted
greengrocery
greenishness
gregariously
guestchamber
haematoblast
haematolysis
haematoxylon
haemophiliac
haemopoiesis
haemorrhagic
heedlessness
hierarchical
hieroglyphic
hierographer
hierophantic
idealisation
ideationally
identifiable
ineffaceable
ineffaceably
inefficiency
inelasticity
ineradicable
ineradicably
inescutcheon
inexactitude
inexpedience
inexpediency
inexperience
inexpertness
inexplicable
inexplicably
inexpressive
inexpugnable
inexpugnably
inextensible
inextricable
inextricably
kleptomaniac
kremlinology
meetinghouse
mnemotechnic
needlessness
obedientiary
oceanography
oceanologist
oneirocritic
onesidedness
oneupmanship
openhandedly
openmindedly
operatically
overabundant
overachiever
overactivity
overcautious
overcritical
overcropping
overemphasis
overestimate
overexertion
overexposure
overlordship
overniceness
overpersuade
overpowering
overpressure
overreaction
oversimplify
overstepping
paedobaptism
paedogenesis
paedogenetic
paedomorphic
peerlessness
phenological
phenomenally
phenotypical
pleasantness
pleasingness
pleasureless
plebiscitary
plecopterous
plectognathi
pleiotropism
plenipotence
pleomorphism
plesiosaurus
pneumaticity
pneumatology
pneumothorax
precancelled
precariously
precedential
preceptorial
precessional
prechristian
preciousness
precipitable
precipitance
precipitancy
precipitator
precisianism
precisionist
preclassical
preclusively
precociously
precognition
precognitive
precondition
preconscious
predesignate
predestinate
predetermine
predictively
predigestion
predilection
predominance
predominancy
preeminently
preestablish
preexistence
prefabricate
prefectorial
preferential
preformation
preformative
prehensility
prehistorian
prelapsarian
premaxillary
premeditated
premeditator
premenstrual
prenticeship
preoccupancy
preparedness
preponderant
preponderate
preposterous
prerequisite
presbyterate
presbyterial
Presbyterian
prescription
prescriptive
preselection
preselective
presentation
presentative
presentiment
preservation
preservative
presidential
presumptuous
pretermitted
prevailingly
prevaricator
preventative
preventively
previousness
psephologist
pseudocyesis
pseudonymity
pseudonymous
pseudopodium
pteridophyte
pteridosperm
pterodactyle
puerperrally
questionable
questionably
questionless
rhetorically
rheumatology
scenepainter
sceneshifter
scenographic
sheepishness
sheepshearer
sledgehammer
sleepingpill
sleepwalking
speakingtube
specialistic
specifically
specificness
speciousness
specktioneer
spectrograph
spectrometer
spectrometry
spectroscope
spectroscopy
speechlessly
speedboating
speleologist
spermaphytic
spermathecal
spermatocyte
spermatozoid
spermatozoon
spermogonium
stealthiness
steatopygous
steeplechase
steganograph
stellenbosch
stelliferous
stenographer
stenographic
stepchildren
stepdaughter
stereochromy
stereography
stereoisomer
stereometric
stereophonic
stereopticon
stereoscopic
sterlingness
sternutation
sternutative
sternutatory
sternwheeler
stertorously
stethoscopic
sweepingness

sweetishness
teensyweensy
teetertotter
theanthropic
theatregoing
theatrically
theistically
thematically
theocratical
theoretician
theosophical
therapeutics
therapeutist
thereinafter
thermocouple
thermography
thermolabile
thermometric
thermophilic
thermoscopic
thermosphere
thermostable
thermostatic
thermotactic
thermotropic
tremendously
trephination
trestletable
twentyfourmo
uneconomical
unemployable
unemployment
unencumbered
uneventfully
unexpectedly
whencesoever
wherethrough
wretchedness
affectedness
affectionate
buffalograss
definiteness
definitively
deflagration
deflationary
deflationist
defraudation
differentiae
differential
effectuality
effectuation
effeminately
effervescent
efflorescent
effortlessly
effusiveness
enfeeblement
infanticidal
infectiously
infelicitous
infiniteness
infinitively
inflammation
inflammatory
inflationary
inflationism
inflationist
inflectional
infrequently
infringement
infundibular
infusibility
lefthandedly
lifelessness
officeholder
offscourings
reflationary
reflectional
reflectively
reflectivity
refractivity
refractorily
refreshingly
refreshments
refrigerator
safecracking
softpedalled
sufficiently
unfaithfully
unfamiliarly
unfathomable
unfavourable
unfavourably
unflattering
unfrequented
agglutinogen
aggressively
angiocarpous
argillaceous
augmentation
augmentative
beggarliness
degenerately
degeneration
degenerative
digressional
digressively
dogmatically
enginedriver
enginetuning
Englishwoman
figuratively
fugitiveness
gigantically
hagiographer
hagiographic
hagiological
highcoloured
highfaluting
highhandedly
highlystrung
highpressure
highsounding
highspirited
highstepping
huggermugger
hygienically
hygrophilous
ingloriously
ingratiating
legalisation
legitimately
legitimation
legitimatise
lighthearted
logistically
lugubriously
magistrature
magnetically
magnetisable
magnetograph
magnetometer
magnifically
magnificence
magniloquent
megalomaniac
negativeness
negativistic
neglectfully
negotiatress
negrophilism
negrophilist
nightclothes
organgrinder
organisation
organography
organoleptic
pigeonbreast
pigmentation
pugnaciously
regardlessly
regeneration
regenerative
regimentally
registration
regressively
rightfulness
rigorousness
segmentation
sightreading
significance
significancy
suggestively
tightmouthed
togetherness
toggleswitch
ungainliness
ungovernable
ungracefully
ungraciously
ungratefully
vegetatively
vigorousness
zygapophysis
zygomorphism
zygomorphous
achlamydeous
adhesiveness
Alhambresque
atheromatous
athletically
behaviourism
behaviourist
cohabitation
cohesiveness
echinococcus
echolocation
echosounding
ephemerality
etherisation
ethnocentric
ethnographer
ethnographic
ethnological
euhemeristic
exhaustively
exhibitioner
exhilaration
exhilarative
ichthyocolla
ichthyolatry
ichthyophagy
inhabitation
inharmonious
inhospitable
inhospitably
Ishmaelitish
ophiophagous
otherworldly
rehabilitate
schismatical
schizogonous
schizomycete
schizophrene
schizothymia
schizothymic
schoolfellow
schoolleaver
schoolmaster
schorlaceous
spheroidally
sphragistics
sphygmograph
unhesitating
unhistorical
alimentation
alimentative
amicableness
amitotically
apiculturist
aristocratic
Aristotelean
Aristotelian
arithmetical
avitaminoses
avitaminosis
blissfulness
blisteringly
blithesomely
boisterously
brickfielder
brilliantine
brinkmanship
chieftainess
childbearing
childishness
chimneypiece
chiropractic
chiropractor
chitterlings
chivalrously
cliffhanging
clinkerbuilt
coincidental
coincidently
criticalness
deionisation
editorialise
editorialist
epicureanism
epicycloidal
epidemically
epidemiology
epigrammatic
epiphenomena
episcopalian
episodically
epistemology
epithalamion
epithalamium
evidentially
evisceration
exiguousness
fainthearted
faintishness
faithfulness
faithhealing
flickeringly
fricasseeing
frictionless
friendliness
glitteringly
grievousness
griseofulvin
guilefulness
hairdressing
hairsbreadth
hairsplitter
idiosyncrasy
idiothermous
iniquitously
klipspringer
knighterrant
knightliness
laisserfaire
laissezaller
laissezfaire
maidenliness
maidenstakes
maintainable
moistureless
nailscissors
neighbouring
oligarchical
opinionative
opisthograph
opisthotonos
orienteering
painlessness
philadelphus
philanthrope
philanthropy
philharmonic
philhellenic
philistinism
phillumenist
philodendron
philological
philosophise
poikilotherm
pointilliste
pricecutting
pridefulness
priestliness
priestridden
priggishness
primigravida
primogenital
primogenitor
primordially
princeliness
principality
printability
privatdocent
privatdozent
privateering
prizefighter
prizewinning
quinquennial
quinquennium
quintessence
quixotically
quizzicality
reinvestment
reinvigorate
rhinocerotic
rhinological
rhizocarpous
rhizogenetic
rhizophagous
scintigraphy
scintillator
seismography
seismologist
seismometric
seismoscopic
shillyshally
shipbuilding
shirtwaister
skippingrope
skittishness
slipcarriage
slipperiness
spidermonkey
spiegeleisen
spinsterhood
spiritedness
spiritlessly
spiritualise
spiritualism
spiritualist
spirituality
spitefulness
stichomythia
stichomythic
stilboestrol
stillhunting
suitableness
swimmingbath
swimmingbell
swimmingpool
swizzlestick
thickskinned
thickskulled
thievishness

thimbleberry
thirdborough
thitherwards
toilsomeness
triangularly
tricentenary
trichologist
trichotomise
trichotomous
trichromatic
trickishness
tridactylous
trifurcation
triggerhappy
triglyphical
trigonometry
trinomialism
tripartitely
tripartition
triphthongal
triplication
triumphantly
twitteringly
ubiquitarian
ubiquitously
unifoliolate
unilaterally
unimaginable
unimaginably
unimportance
uninterested
unionisation
unisexuality
unitarianism
universalise
universalism
universalist
universality
vainglorious
voidableness
wainscotting
waistcoating
whigmaleerie
whimperingly
whimsicality
whippoorwill
whisperingly
whitelivered
whitewashing
whitherwards
adjectivally
adjudication
adjudicative
adjudicatory
dejectedness
majestically
majorgeneral
pejoratively
rejectamenta
rejuvenation
alkalescence
lakedwelling
lukewarmness
unkindliness
ailurophobia
alliteration
alliterative
allomorphism
allusiveness
balladmonger
balletomania
ballottement
belittlement
bellbottomed
belletristic
belligerence
belligerency
bellylanding
bilateralism
bilharziasis
bilharziosis
bilingualism
billingsgate
billsticking
bulletheaded
bullfighting
bullheadedly
calamitously
calcareously
calculatedly
calisthenics
calligrapher
calligraphic
callisthenic
calorescence
calorimetric
calumniation
calumniatory
calumniously
calycoideous
chlorination
coldshoulder
coleopterist
coleopterous
collaborator
collaterally
collectively
collectivise
collectivism
collectivist
collectivity
collegialism
collegiality
collegiately
collinearity
colloquially
collywobbles
colonisation
coloquintida
colorimetric
colourlessly
columniation
culpableness
cultivatable
delamination
deliberately
deliberation
deliberative
delicatessen
delightfully
delimitation
delinquently
deliquescent
delitescence
delusiveness
dilapidation
dilatability
dilatoriness
dilettantish
dilettantism
dolorousness
eclectically
elliptically
falcongentil
falcongentle
fallaciously
feldspathoid
felicitation
felicitously
filibusterer
filtrability
folliculated
fuliginosity
fullyfledged
galactogogue
galligaskins
gallinaceous
galvanically
galvanometer
galvanoscope
halftimbered
hallucinogen
hallucinosis
halogenation
halterbroken
heliocentric
heliographer
heliographic
heliogravure
heliolatrous
heliotherapy
heliotropism
hellgrammite
helplessness
holidaymaker
illadvisedly
illegibility
illegitimacy
illegitimate
illiberality
illiterately
illnaturedly
illogicality
illtreatment
illumination
illuminative
illusiveness
illusoriness
illustration
illustrative
kaleidoscope
kilowatthour
malacologist
malapertness
malcontented
malevolently
malformation
malleability
malnutrition
maltreatment
malversation
melancholiac
melanochroic
melodramatic
meltingpoint
militaristic
millesimally
milliammeter
molecularity
mulligatawny
multicentral
multidentate
multifarious
multiflorous
multifoliate
multiformity
multilateral
multilingual
multiloquous
multinuclear
multipartite
multipliable
multiplicand
multiplicate
multiplicity
multipurpose
multistoried
multivalence
multiversity
multungulate
oblanceolate
obligatorily
obligingness
obliteration
obliterative
palaeobotany
palaeography
Palaeolithic
palatability
paletteknife
palingenesia
palingenesis
palingenetic
Palladianism
palynologist
pellucidness
phlebotomise
phlebotomist
pilotballoon
polarimetric
polarisation
polarography
policyholder
polychaetous
polychromous
polyethylene
polyglottism
polyhistoric
polymorphism
polymorphous
polyneuritic
polyneuritis
polypetalous
polyphyletic
polysepalous
polysyllabic
polysyllable
polytheistic
polytonality
polyurethane
pulverisable
relationally
relationship
relativeness
relativistic
relentlessly
reliableness
rollingstock
salamandrian
salamandrine
salamandroid
salesmanship
salmonladder
salpiglossis
salubriously
salutariness
salutational
salutiferous
salvationism
salvationist
sclerenchyma
selenography
selenologist
selfabsorbed
selfactivity
selfaffected
selfanalysis
selfapplause
selfapproval
selfbegotten
selfbetrayal
selfcatering
selfcoloured
selfcomposed
selfcontempt
selfcritical
selfdeceived
selfdeceiver
selfdelusion
selfdestruct
selfdevotion
selfdirected
selfdistrust
selfdoubting
selfeducated
selfeffacing
selfelective
selfemployed
selfevidence
selfexistent
selfflattery
selfhypnosis
selfidentity
selfignition
selfinterest
selfinvolved
selflessness
selflimiting
selfluminous
selfmurderer
selfpleasing
selfportrait
selfreliance
selfreproach
selfrighting
selfsameness
selfstarting
selfviolence
sellingplate
silicicolous
siliciferous
silverglance
silviculture
solarisation
solicitation
solicitously
solifluction
solitariness
splendidness
sulphonamide
sulphonation
sulphuration
sulphuretted
syllabically
sylviculture
telaesthesia
telaesthetic
telegraphese
telegraphist
teleological
televisional
tolerability
unlawfulness
unlikelihood
unlikeliness
unloveliness
Valenciennes
valetudinary
valorisation
valuableness
vilification
villainously
volatileness
volcanically
volitionally
volumetrical
voluminosity
voluminously
voluntaryism
voluntaryist
voluptuosity
voluptuously
walkietalkie
wallpainting
wallydraigle
welldisposed
wellfavoured
wellgrounded
Wellingtonia
welterweight
williewaught
wollastonite
yellowhammer
administrant
administrate

admonishment
atmospherics
bombdisposal
camiknickers
campfollower
campodeiform
cementitious
combinations
comfortingly
commandingly
commemorator
commencement
commendation
commendatory
commensalism
commensalist
commensurate
commentation
commercially
commiserator
commissarial
commissariat
commissioner
committeeman
commodiously
commonwealth
communicable
communicably
communicator
companionate
companionway
compatriotic
compellation
compensation
compensative
compensatory
complacently
complaisance
complemental
completeness
complexional
complexioned
complication
composedness
compoundable
compressible
compulsively
compulsivity
compulsorily
compunctious
compurgation
compurgatory
cumbersomely
cumbrousness
cumulatively
cumulocirrus
cumulonimbus
demilitarise
demimondaine
demineralise
demodulation
demoniacally
demonstrable
demonstrably
demonstrator
diminishable
diminishment
diminutively
domestically
domesticator
feminineness
feminisation
gamesmanship
gamesomeness
gametophytic
gamopetalous
gamophyllous
gamosepalous
gymnosophist
hemerocallis
hemichordate
hemimorphism
hemimorphite
hemiparasite
hemispheroid
homeomorphic
homeopathist
homesickness
homoeopathic
homoeostasis
homologation
homomorphism
homomorphous
homonymously
homosexually
homothallism
humanisation
humanitarian
humification
humorousness
humptydumpty
hymenopteran
hymnographer
immaculately
immaterially
immatureness
immeasurable
immeasurably
immemorially
immensurable
immethodical
immoderately
immoderation
immovability
immunisation
immunologist
immutability
limnological
lumberjacket
luminescence
luminiferous
luminousness
namedropping
namelessness
nimbostratus
niminypiminy
nomenclative
nomenclature
nominalistic
numerologist
numerousness
nympholeptic
nymphomaniac
obmutescence
pumpernickel
rambunctious
ramification
rememberable
remembrancer
remilitarise
reminiscence
remonstrance
remonstrator
remorsefully
removability
remuneration
remunerative
remuneratory
romanisation
romantically
rumbletumble
ruminatively
Samaritanism
semantically
semiannually
semibasement
semicircular
semicylinder
semidarkness
semideponent
semidetached
semidiameter
semidomestic
semifinalist
semifinished
semiliterate
seminiferous
semiofficial
semiological
semiparasite
semiprecious
semitropical
sempiternity
simoniacally
simpleminded
simultaneity
simultaneous
somatopleure
somnambulant
somnambulate
somnambulism
somnambulist
somniloquism
somniloquist
symbolically
tamelessness
temptability
timehonoured
timelessness
timorousness
tumultuously
unmanageable
unmercifully
unmistakable
unmistakably
vomiturition
womanishness
annihilation
annihilative
announcement
annunciation
banderillero
bantamweight
benefactress
beneficently
beneficially
benevolently
benzaldehyde
bonnetmonkey
bonnyclabber
canaliculate
canalisation
cancellation
candleholder
canonisation
canorousness
Cantabrigian
cantankerous
cantharidian
cantillation
censoriously
centesimally
centrespread
centrosphere
centuplicate
cinematheque
concelebrant
concelebrate
concentrator
conceptional
conceptually
conchiferous
conchologist
conciliation
conciliative
conciliatory
conclusively
concomitance
concordantly
concrescence
concreteness
concubitancy
concupiscent
concurrently
condemnation
condemnatory
condensation
conductivity
conduplicate
confabulator
confectioner
conferential
confessional
confidential
confirmation
confirmative
confirmatory
confiscation
confiscatory
conformation
confoundedly
Confucianism
confusedness
congeniality
congenitally
conglobation
conglomerate
conglutinate
congratulant
congratulate
congregation
conidiophore
conidiospore
conjunctival
connaturally
connectional
connectively
conningtower
connubiality
conquistador
conscionable
conscription
consecration
consecratory
consensually
consentience
consentingly
consequently
conservation
conservatism
conservative
conservatory
considerable
considerably
consignation
consistently
consistorial
consociation
consolidator
conspiration
constabulary
constipation
constituency
constitution
constitutive
constriction
constrictive
constringent
construction
constructive
consultation
consultative
consummately
consummation
consummative
consummatory
contagionist
contagiously
containerise
contemplator
contemporary
contemporise
contemptible
contemptibly
contemptuous
conterminous
contestation
contextually
contiguously
contingently
continuation
continuative
continuously
contractable
contractedly
contractible
contradictor
contrapuntal
contrariness
contrariwise
contribution
contributive
contributory
contriteness
contrivement
controllable
contumacious
contumelious
convalescent
convectional
conveniently
conventicler
conventional
conversation
conveyancing
convincement
convincingly
conviviality
convulsively
cynocephalus
denaturalise
denaturation
denomination
denominative
denouncement
densitometer
denticulated
dentilingual
denuclearise
denunciation
denunciative
denunciatory
dinnerjacket
dunderheaded
dynamometric
dynastically
eunuchoidism
fancifulness
fantasticate
fantasticism
fenestration
finalisation
functionally
functionless
ganglionated
genealogical
generousness
genuflection
gonadotropic
gonadotropin
gynaecocracy
handicapping
handkerchief
handsbreadth
handsomeness

henceforward
henotheistic
hindquarters
honeybuzzard
innutritious
kinaesthesia
kinaesthesis
kinaesthetic
kindergarten
kinnikinnick
landingcraft
landingfield
landingstage
landingstrip
landlubberly
languishment
languorously
lanternjawed
lanternslide
linguistical
lonesomeness
longdistance
longitudinal
longshoreman
longstanding
longwindedly
mangelwurzel
Manicheanism
manifoldness
manipulation
manipulative
manipulatory
mannerliness
manoeuvrable
manometrical
mansionhouse
manslaughter
manufacturer
mendaciously
menstruation
mindlessness
minedetector
mineralogist
minicomputer
minimisation
ministration
ministrative
monadelphous
monastically
monetisation
moneychanger
moneygrubber
moneyspinner
monitorially
monkeyflower
monkeyjacket
monkeypuzzle
monkeywrench
monochromate
monodramatic
monofilament
monographist
monomaniacal
monometallic
monomorphous
monopetalous
monophyletic
Monophysitic
monopodially
monopolistic
monostichous
monostrophic
monosyllabic
monosyllable
monotheistic
monotonously
monumentally
municipalise
municipality
munificently
nanoplankton
nonagenarian
nonalignment
nonchalantly
noncombatant
noncommittal
noncomplying
nonconductor
nonconformer
noneffective
nonefficient
nonessential
noneuclidean
nonexistence
nonflammable
nonflowering
nonidentical
nonobjective
nonresidence
nonresistant
obnubilation
omnipotently
omnipresence
omnisciently
omnivorously
ornamentally
ornithomancy
ornithoscopy
panchromatic
pancreatitis
panhellenism
panification
pantechnicon
pantisocracy
pantographic
penalisation
penitentiary
pennypincher
pennywhistle
pinfeathered
pontifically
pontificator
punchingball
renegotiable
renouncement
renunciation
renunciative
renunciatory
rontgenogram
rontgenology
runningboard
sandyachting
sanguinarily
sanguineness
sanguinolent
sansculottic
sensibleness
sensitometer
sensualistic
sensuousness
sententially
Sinanthropus
singleacting
singledecker
singlehanded
singleminded
singleseater
sinistrality
sinistrorsal
sinusoidally
sonorousness
synaesthesia
synaesthetic
synarthrosis
synchronical
synchroniser
syncretistic
syndactylism
syndactylous
syndetically
synonymously
synoptically
tangentially
tangibleness
tintinnabula
tonelessness
tunelessness
vanquishable
vanquishment
vantagepoint
venepuncture
venerability
vengefulness
venipuncture
venomousness
ventripotent
vindictively
vinification
windingsheet
wineglassful
winklepicker
winterbourne
wonderstruck
wonderworker
wondrousness
wunderkinder
xanthochroia
YankeeDoodle
abolitionary
abolitionism
abolitionist
aboriginally
abortiveness
acoustically
adorableness
aforethought
amortisation
anotherguess
apochromatic
apolitically
apostolicism
apostolicity
apostrophise
apothegmatic
aromatically
aromaticness
biochemistry
biocoenology
bioecologist
biogeography
biographical
biologically
biometrician
biophysicist
bioscientist
biosynthesis
biosynthetic
blockbusting
bloodbrother
bloodletting
bloodstained
bloodthirsty
bloodyminded
boogiewoogie
bookingclerk
booklearning
bootlessness
brokenwinded
bronchoscope
broncobuster
brontosaurus
chocolatebox
chondriosome
choreography
chorographic
chorological
closecropped
closegrained
closemouthed
clotheshorse
clothespress
clownishness
coordinately
coordination
coordinative
crossbedding
crossbencher
crossbuttock
crosscountry
crosscurrent
crossexamine
crossgrained
crossheading
crossingover
crosspurpose
crosssection
deontologist
droughtiness
ecologically
econometrics
economically
elocutionary
elocutionist
emotionalise
emotionalism
emotionalist
emotionality
enormousness
esoterically
evolutionary
evolutionism
evolutionist
exophthalmic
exophthalmos
exophthalmus
exorbitantly
exospherical
exoterically
flocculation
floodlighted
floriculture
footplateman
frontbencher
frontiersman
frontispiece
geochemistry
geographical
geologically
geomagnetism
geometrician
geophysicist
geopolitical
geosynclinal
geotectonics
ghoulishness
globetrotter
glockenspiel
gloriousness
glossography
glossologist
goodhumoured
goodtempered
goosepimples
grossularite
grotesquerie
groundcherry
groundlessly
grovellingly
heortologist
hoodmanblind
iconoclastic
iconographer
idolatrously
inobservance
inoccupation
inoperculate
inordinately
inosculation
isochromatic
isochronally
isodiametric
isolationism
isolationist
isothermally
neoclassical
neoDarwinian
neoDarwinism
neoDarwinist
Neohellenism
neonomianism
Neoplatonism
Neoplatonist
odontologist
onomatopoeia
onomatopoeic
orographical
phonasthenia
phonemically
phonetically
phonographer
phonographic
phonological
phosphoresce
photochromic
photofission
photogeology
photographer
photographic
photogravure
photokinesis
photokinetic
photomontage
photophilous
photosetting
photospheric
phototropism
poorspirited
probationary
proboscidean
proboscidian
procathedral
processional
proclamation
proclamatory
proconsulate
prodigiously
productively
productivity
professional
professorate
professoress
professorial
proficiently
profiteering
profligately
profoundness
progenitress
progesterone
proglottides
programmable
programmatic
projectional
projectively
prolegomenon
prolifically
prolificness
prolongation
promulgation
pronominally
pronouncedly
proofreading
propaedeutic
propagandise
propagandism
propagandist

prophylactic
propitiation
propitiatory
propitiously
proportional
proportioned
proprietress
proscription
proscriptive
prosectorial
prosecutable
proselytiser
prosodically
prosopopoeia
prosperously
prostitution
protactinium
protectively
protectorate
protensively
protestation
prothalamion
prothalamium
prothonotary
protistology
protohistory
protoplasmic
protoplastic
prototypical
protozoology
protrusively
protuberance
proudhearted
proverbially
providential
provincially
provisionary
reoccupation
rhododendron
rhombohedral
rhombohedron
rootlessness
scornfulness
scorpionfish
scoundreldom
scoundrelism
scouringrush
shootingiron
shortchanger
shortcircuit
shortpitched
shortsighted
shortsleeved
shortstaffed
shoulderbelt
shoulderknot
shouldernote
slothfulness
slovenliness
snobbishness
spokesperson
sporadically
sporogenesis
sportfulness
sportiveness
spotlessness
stockbreeder
stockbroking
stockingless
stockjobbery
stockjobbing
stockraising
stoneboiling
stonecutting
stonedresser
stonemasonry
stonyhearted
stormtrooper
stouthearted

thoroughbass
thoroughbred
thoroughfare
thoroughness
thoughtfully
thousandfold
trochanteric
troglodytism
trophallaxis
tropological
tropospheric
troublemaker
unofficially
uxoriousness
wholehearted
whortleberry
woodengraver
woodenheaded
woolgatherer
woollyheaded
wrongfulness
zoogeography
alphabetical
alphamerical
alphanumeric
amphibiously
amphibrachic
amphictyonic
amphisbaenic
amphitheatre
amphitropous
apparatchiki
apparatchiks
apparentness
apparitional
appendectomy
appendicitis
appendicular
apperception
apperceptive
appetisingly
appositeness
appositional
appraisement
appraisingly
appreciation
appreciative
appreciatory
apprehension
apprehensive
approachable
appropriable
appropriator
appurtenance
asphyxiation
capercaillie
capercailzie
capitalistic
capitulation
capriciously
captiousness
copolymerise
copulatively
cuprammonium
departmental
depoliticise
depopulation
depravedness
depreciation
depreciatory
depressingly
deputisation
diphtheritic
diphthongise
emphatically
empoisonment
empressement
espagnolette
euphonically

euphoniously
expansionary
expansionism
expansionist
expatriation
expediential
experiential
experimental
experimenter
explantation
explicitness
exploitation
exploitative
expressional
expressively
expressivity
exprobration
happenstance
hippocentaur
hippopotamus
hopelessness
hyperacidity
hyperbolical
hyperplastic
hyperpyretic
hyperpyrexia
hypersthenia
hypersthenic
hypertension
hypertensive
hyperthermia
hypertrophic
hypnogenesis
hypnogenetic
hypnotherapy
hypnotically
hypnotisable
hypochlorite
hypochondria
hypocoristic
hypocritical
hypogastrium
hypognathous
hypophrygian
hypostatical
hyposulphite
hypothalamic
hypothalamus
hypothecator
hypothetical
impartiality
impedimental
impenetrable
impenetrably
impenitently
imperatively
imperatorial
imperceptive
impercipient
imperfection
imperfective
imperishable
imperishably
impermanence
impermanency
impersonally
impersonator
impertinence
impertinency
imperviously
impetiginous
implantation
implicitness
impoliteness
imponderable
imponderably
impoverished
impregnation
impressively

imprisonment
impropriator
improvidence
improvisator
imputability
imputatively
lepidopteran
lopsidedness
nephanalysis
nephelometer
nephelometry
nephrologist
opposability
oppositeness
oppositional
oppressively
papyrologist
populousness
rapprochment
repatriation
repercussion
repercussive
repetitional
repetitively
repossession
reprehension
reprehensive
repressively
reproachable
reproachless
reproducible
reproduction
reproductive
reprographic
saponifiable
saprophagous
separability
separateness
septennially
septilateral
septuagenary
Septuagesima
Septuagintal
sepulchrally
siphonophore
siphonostele
sophisticate
soporiferous
superannuate
supercharger
superciliary
supercilious
supereminent
supererogate
superhighway
superhumanly
supermundane
supernaculum
supernatural
superposable
supersedence
supersensory
supersession
superstition
superstratum
supervenient
supervention
supplemental
supplementer
supplicantly
supplication
supplicatory
suppositious
suppressible
supramundane
supraorbital
taperecorder
toploftiness
topsyturvily

typefounding
typification
unparalleled
unpleasantly
unpopularity
unprejudiced
unpretending
unprincipled
unprofitable
unprofitably
unpronounced
vaporisation
vaporousness
xiphisternum
acquaintance
acquiescence
bequeathment
coquettishly
liquefacient
liquefaction
loquaciously
sequaciously
sequentially
sequestrator
abrasiveness
acronychally
aerodynamics
aeroembolism
aeronautical
aeroneurosis
aerosiderite
AfroAmerican
agranulocyte
agribusiness
agricultural
aircondition
aircraftsman
arrhythmical
barbarically
barometrical
berzelianite
birdsnesting
birdwatching
birefringent
borosilicate
bureaucratic
burglarproof
burningglass
caravansarai
caravanserai
carbohydrate
carbonaceous
carburetting
carcinogenic
cardcarrying
cardinalship
cardiography
cardiologist
carelessness
caricaturist
carillonneur
Carlovingian
carpetbagger
carpetknight
carragheenin
carriageable
Cartesianism
cartographer
cartographic
cartological
ceremonially
chrematistic
chrestomathy
Christianise
Christianity
Christolatry
Christophany
chromaticism
chromaticity

chromatogram
chromatology
chromatopsia
chromosphere
chronography
chronologise
chronologist
chronometric
circuitously
circumcision
circumfluent
circumfusion
circumjacent
circumscribe
circumstance
cirrocumulus
cirrostratus
corelatively
corespondent
corporeality
correctional
correctitude
correctively
corroborator
curlingirons
curlingtongs
curmudgeonly
curvicaudate
curvicostate
curvifoliate
curvirostral
deracination
derisiveness
derivational
derivatively
dermatophyte
derogatorily
directorship
dorsiventral
duraluminium
earsplitting
earthshaking
EuroAmerican
farmsteading
farsightedly
fermentation
fermentative
ferrugineous
fertilisable
firefighting
firstnighter
foraminifera
forbiddingly
forcefulness
forcibleness
forebodement
forebodingly
forensically
foresightful
forestalment
formaldehyde
formlessness
forthrightly
fortuitously
furfuraceous
furunculosis
geriatrician
Germanophile
Germanophobe
gerontocracy
gorgeousness
gyromagnetic
hardfavoured
hardfeatured
hardstanding
harlequinade
harmlessness
harmonically
harmoniously
harquebusier
heraldically
hereditament
hereditarily
hereinbefore
heritability
hermeneutics
hermetically
heroicalness
heroicomical
herpetologic
hirepurchase
horizontally
horrendously
horribleness
horrifically
horrorstruck
horsebreaker
horsemanship
horsetrading
horsewhipped
horticulture
irrationally
irredeemable
irredeemably
irreflective
irreformable
irrefragable
irrefragably
irregardless
irregularity
irrelatively
irrelevantly
irremediable
irremediably
irremissible
irrepealable
irreprovable
irresistible
irresistibly
irresolutely
irresolution
irresolvable
irrespective
irrespirable
irresponsive
irreverently
irreversible
irreversibly
irritability
irritatingly
jerrybuilder
jurisconsult
jurisdiction
jurisprudent
karyokinesis
kirschwasser
largehearted
laryngoscope
laryngoscopy
Marcionitism
marketgarden
marketsquare
marksmanship
marlinespike
marriageable
Marseillaise
marshharrier
marvellously
mercantilism
mercantilist
merchantable
mercifulness
mercurialise
mercurialism
meretricious
meridionally
meristematic
merrythought
miraculously
mirthfulness
moralisation
mordaciously
morningdress
morphallaxis
morphologist
morrisdancer
myrmecophily
narcissistic
narcotically
narrowminded
nerveracking
noradrenalin
northeastern
northernmost
Northumbrian
northwestern
paraboloidal
paradigmatic
paradisaical
paradisiacal
paraesthesia
paragraphist
parallelling
paralysation
paramagnetic
parametrical
paramilitary
paramorphism
paranormally
paraphrastic
parasiticide
parasitology
paratactical
parenthesise
parisyllabic
parkinsonism
parochialise
parochialism
parochiality
paronomastic
parsimonious
participator
particularly
partisanship
partitionist
peradventure
perambulator
perceptively
perceptivity
perceptually
percussively
percutaneous
peregrinator
peremptorily
perfectively
perfervidity
perfidiously
perfoliation
performative
pericarditis
perilousness
periodically
periodontics
periodontist
periostracum
peripherally
periphrastic
perispomenon
peristeronic
peristomatic
perjuriously
permanganate
permeability
permissively
permittivity
perniciously
pernoctation
peroxidation
perpetration
perpetuation
perplexingly
perseverance
persistently
perspicacity
perspiration
perspiratory
persuasively
pertinacious
perturbation
perturbative
perverseness
perviousness
phrasemonger
phraseograph
phreatophyte
phrenologist
porcelainise
porcelainous
porcellanous
pornographer
pornographic
portentously
portmanteaus
portmanteaux
purblindness
purification
purificatory
purposebuilt
purposefully
pursestrings
pyroelectric
pyroligneous
pyromaniacal
pyromorphite
pyrotechnics
pyrotechnist
ruralisation
sarcomatosis
sarcophagous
sardonically
sarrusophone
sarsaparilla
scraperboard
scratchiness
screenwriter
scrimshanker
scripturally
scriptwriter
scrobiculate
scrupulosity
scrupulously
seraphically
sergeantfish
sergeantship
sericultural
serjeantship
serpentiform
serpentinely
serviceberry
servicecourt
servicewoman
servitorship
servocontrol
shrewishness
skrimshanker
sorbefacient
sprightfully
Stradivarius
straightaway
straightbred
straightedge
straightener
straightness
straitjacket
stranglehold
straticulate
stratigraphy
stratosphere
streetwalker
strengthener
strengthless
streptococci
streptomycin
stridulation
strikingness
stringcourse
strobilation
stroboscopic
strongminded
strongylosis
strontianite
strophanthin
structurally
strychninism
surefootedly
surmountable
surprisingly
surrealistic
surrejoinder
surroundings
surveillance
surveyorship
survivorship
teratologist
teratomatous
tercentenary
terebinthine
tergiversate
terribleness
terrifically
terrifyingly
terrorstruck
threequarter
threewheeler
thriftlessly
throughstone
tirelessness
tiresomeness
torrefaction
torrentially
Torricellian
tortuousness
turbellarian
turriculated
turtlenecked
tyrannically
tyrannicidal
unreasonable
unreasonably
unrecognised
unregenerate
unrepeatable
unreservedly
unresponsive
unrestrained
uproariously
variableness
varicoloured
veridicality
verification
verificatory
vermiculated
vernacularly
vertebration
verticalness
verticillate
viridescence
virtuosoship
virtuousness
warehouseman
workableness
workingclass
worshipfully
absentminded
absoluteness

absolutistic
absorptional
absorptivity
absquatulate
abstemiously
abstractable
abstractedly
abstractness
abstruseness
adscititious
aesthetician
aestheticism
assassinator
assibilation
assimilation
assimilative
assimilatory
auscultation
auscultatory
auspiciously
Australasian
baselessness
basidiospore
bassorelievo
bassorilievo
beseechingly
bespectacled
businesslike
cashandcarry
cosmetically
cosmogonical
cosmographer
cosmographic
cosmological
cosmopolitan
cosmopolitic
costermonger
customshouse
desalination
desideration
desiderative
desirability
desirousness
desolateness
despairingly
despitefully
despoliation
despondently
despotically
desquamation
desquamative
desquamatory
dessertspoon
destructible
desulphurise
disaccharide
disadvantage
disaffection
disaffiliate
disagreeable
disagreeably
disagreement
disallowance
disambiguate
disannulling
disannulment
disassociate
disastrously
disbursement
discerningly
discerptible
discipleship
disciplinary
disclamation
discographer
discomfiture
discommodity
discomposure
disconnected
disconnexion
disconsolate
discontented
discordantly
discountable
discouraging
discourteous
discoverable
discoverture
discreetness
discreteness
discretional
discriminant
discriminate
discursively
disdainfully
disembarrass
disenchanter
disendowment
disestablish
disfranchise
disgorgement
disguisement
disgustfully
disgustingly
disharmonise
dishevelment
disincentive
disinfectant
disinfection
disinflation
disingenuous
disintegrate
disinterment
disjointedly
dislodgement
disobedience
disorientate
dispensation
dispensatory
dispiritedly
displaceable
displacement
displeasedly
dispossessor
disputatious
disquisition
disregardful
disreputable
disreputably
dissatisfied
disseminator
dissentingly
dissertation
disseverance
disseverment
dissimilarly
dissimulator
dissocialise
dissociation
dissociative
dissuasively
dissymmetric
distemperate
distillation
distillatory
distinctness
distortional
distractedly
distrainable
distrainment
distributary
distribution
distributive
disturbingly
ecstatically
enshrinement
enswathement
essentiality
exsanguinate
exsanguinous
exsufflicate
fastidiously
fostermother
gasification
gastronomist
gastropodous
gesellschaft
gesticulator
hesitatingly
hesperididia
histogenesis
histogenetic
histological
historically
hysterectomy
hysterically
hysteromania
insalubrious
insecticidal
insemination
insolubilise
insolubility
inspectorate
inspectorial
inspissation
installation
instauration
instillation
instructress
instrumental
insufferable
insufferably
insufficient
insufflation
insurrection
jesuitically
kissingcrust
lasciviously
listlessness
lusciousness
mastersinger
masterstroke
masterswitch
mastigophora
mesocephalic
mesothoracic
messeigneurs
misadventure
misalignment
misanthropic
misapprehend
misbehaviour
miscalculate
miscellanist
misdemeanant
misdemeanour
misdirection
miseducation
misinterpret
misjudgement
misknowledge
misplacement
mispronounce
misquotation
misrepresent
misselthrush
misstatement
mistakenness
mistranslate
mistreatment
mistressship
mosstrooping
musicianship
musicologist
mysteriously
mystifyingly
Nestorianism
obscurantism
obscurantist
obsequiously
obsolescence
obsoleteness
obstetrician
obstreperous
ossification
pasqueflower
passepartout
passionately
passionfruit
pestilential
pestological
pisciculture
positiveness
positivistic
possessively
postdiluvian
postdoctoral
posteriority
postgraduate
posthumously
postmeridian
postmistress
postponement
postposition
postpositive
postprandial
reservedness
resettlement
residentiary
residentship
resignedness
resiniferous
resipiscence
resistlessly
resoluteness
resolvedness
resoundingly
respectfully
respectively
resplendence
resplendency
responsively
responsorial
restaurateur
restlessness
restrainable
restrainedly
restrictedly
resupination
resurrection
resuscitator
risorgimento
rosecoloured
sesquialtera
susceptivity
suspensively
suspiciously
sustentation
sustentative
systematical
systematiser
systemically
taskmistress
tastefulness
tessellation
testamentary
testosterone
testudineous
unscientific
unscriptural
unscrupulous
unsearchable
unseasonable
unsegregated
unsteadiness
unstructured
unsuccessful
vasodilation
vasodilatory
vesiculation
viscerotonic
viscosimeter
viscountship
visitational
visitatorial
wastefulness
actinomycete
aetiological
afterthought
alterability
altitudinous
antagonistic
antecedently
antediluvian
anteprandial
anthelmintic
anthropogeny
anthropoidal
anthropology
antiaircraft
anticipation
anticipative
anticipatory
anticlerical
anticyclonic
antigenicity
antigropelos
antimacassar
antimagnetic
antimalarial
antineutrino
antiparticle
antipathetic
antiperiodic
antiphonally
antirachitic
antiSemitism
antistrophic
antithetical
articulately
articulation
articulatory
artificially
artilleryman
artistically
astonishment
astoundingly
astringently
astrological
astronautics
astronomical
astrophysics
attitudinise
attorneyship
attractively
attributable
authenticate
authenticity
autocatalyse
autochthones
autodidactic
autoimmunity
automaticity
automobilist
automorphism
autonomously
bathypelagic
battleground
battlemented
bottlewasher
butterflynut
buttermuslin
butterscotch
catachrestic
catamountain

cataphoresis
catastrophic
catechetical
caterwauling
catholically
catilinarian
cattlelifter
cottonocracy
cotyledonary
cotyledonous
cytogenetics
detachedness
determinable
determinably
determinedly
dethronement
detoxication
detumescence
ectoparasite
entanglement
enterprising
entertaining
enthronement
enthusiastic
entomologise
entomologist
entrammelled
entrancement
entreatingly
entrenchment
entrepreneur
estrangement
extensometer
exterminable
exterminator
extinguisher
extortionary
extortionate
extracranial
extraditable
extralimital
extramarital
extramundane
extraneously
extrasensory
extraspecial
extrauterine
extravagance
extravagancy
extravaganza
extraversion
extroversion
fatherfigure
fatherliness
futilitarian
futurologist
heterocercal
heterocyclic
heteroecious
heterogamous
heterogenous
heterologous
heteromerous
heteronomous
heterophylly
heterosexual
heterozygote
heterozygous
integumental
intellection
intellective
intellectual
intelligence
intelligible
intelligibly
intemperance
inteneration
interbedding
interception

intercession
intercessory
interchanger
interconnect
intercropped
intercurrent
intercutting
interdiction
interdictive
interdictory
interdigital
interestedly
interfemoral
interference
interglacial
interjection
interjectory
interlobular
interlocutor
intermeddler
intermediacy
intermediary
intermediate
interminable
interminably
intermission
intermittent
intermitting
intermixture
intermundane
internuclear
internuncial
interoceanic
interoceptor
interpellate
interpleader
interpolator
interpretive
interrelated
interrogator
interruption
interruptive
intersection
interservice
interspinous
interstellar
interstitial
intertexture
intervenient
intervention
intervocalic
interwreathe
intimidation
intimidatory
intolerantly
intoxication
intracardiac
intracranial
intramundane
intransigent
intransitive
intrauterine
intrenchment
intriguingly
introduction
introductory
introjection
intromission
intromittent
intromitting
introversion
introversive
introvertive
intrusionist
intuitionism
intuitionist
intumescence
intussuscept
jetpropelled

katzenjammer
laterisation
laticiferous
latinisation
latitudinous
literariness
lithographer
lithographic
lithological
lithospheric
lithotritist
liturgically
liturgiology
materialness
mathematical
matriarchate
metachronism
metagalactic
metalanguage
metallically
metallophone
metallurgist
metalworking
metamorphism
metamorphose
metaphorical
metaphrastic
metaphysical
metapsychics
metasomatism
metathetical
metathoracic
meteorically
meteorograph
methodically
meticulously
metrological
metropolitan
mithridatise
mithridatism
mitochondria
mitrailleuse
motherfigure
motherliness
mothertongue
motivational
motorcyclist
motorisation
mutinousness
muttonheaded
mythographer
mythological
mythologiser
naturalistic
naturopathic
nitrobenzene
notification
nutritionist
nutritiously
octogenarian
octosyllabic
octosyllable
optimisation
orthodontics
orthodontist
orthogenesis
orthogenetic
orthographer
orthographic
orthopaedics
orthopaedist
orthopterist
orthopteroid
orthopterous
orthotropism
orthotropous
ostentatious
osteogenesis
osteological

osteomalacia
osteoplastic
osteoporosis
outdatedness
outlandishly
outmanoeuvre
outpensioner
outrageously
outrivalling
outstretched
outstripping
outwardbound
pathetically
pathogenesis
pathogenetic
pathological
patriarchate
patternmaker
patulousness
petrifaction
petrographer
petrographic
petrological
pettifoggery
pettifogging
pitcherplant
pitiableness
pitilessness
pitterpatter
potentiality
putrefaction
putrefactive
ratification
ratiocinator
rattleheaded
reticulately
reticulation
reticulocyte
retiringness
retractation
retractility
retrenchment
retrocedence
retrocession
retrocessive
retroflexion
retropulsion
retroversion
ruthlessness
satisfaction
satisfactory
satisfyingly
tetrachordal
tetragonally
tetrahedrite
tetramorphic
tittletattle
totalisation
totalitarian
ultramontane
ultramundane
unthinkingly
unthoughtful
untimeliness
untowardness
untruthfully
vaticination
veterinarian
vitalisation
vitiligation
vitreousness
vitrifaction
vituperation
vituperative
vituperatory
watchfulness
watermanship
adulteration
adulterously

aquicultural
bluestocking
blunderingly
blusteringly
boulevardier
cautiousness
churchianity
churchwarden
churlishness
councilwoman
countenancer
counteragent
counterblast
countercheck
counterclaim
counterforce
counterlight
countermarch
counterplead
counterpoint
counterpoise
counterproof
counterscarp
countershaft
countertenor
countrydance
countrywoman
courageously
courtmartial
courtplaster
cousingerman
Deuteronomic
doubleacting
doubledealer
doubledecked
doubledecker
doublelocked
doubtfulness
educationist
edulcoration
elucubration
emulsifiable
equalisation
equalitarian
equationally
equestrienne
equidistance
equilibrator
equipollence
equipollency
equiprobable
equitability
equivalently
equivocation
equivocatory
eruptiveness
exulceration
faultfinding
fluidisation
fluorescence
fluoridation
fluorination
fluorocarbon
foundationer
fountainhead
fructiferous
fructivorous
fruitfulness
gluttonously
gruesomeness
housebreaker
housekeeping
housetrained
housewarming
journalistic
laudableness
laureateship
leucocytosis
leukocytosis

loungelizard
mountainside
mournfulness
mourningband
mourningring
mouthbreeder
nauseatingly
nauseousness
neurasthenia
neurasthenic
neuroanatomy
neurobiology
neurological
neuropterous
neuroscience
neurosurgeon
neurosurgery
neurotically
plumbaginous
plumbiferous
plummerblock
pluriliteral
pluviometric
prudentially
reunionistic
sculpturally
scurrilously
scutellation
shuffleboard
skullduggery
skunkcabbage
sluggishness
sluttishness
soullessness
soundingline
southeastern
southernmost
southernwood
southwestern
spuriousness
squarerigged
squattocracy
squirrelcage
squirreltail
stubbornness
studdingsail
studiousness
stupefacient
stupefaction
stupefactive
stupendously
stutteringly
tautological
Teutonically
thundercloud
thunderingly
thunderously
thunderstone
thunderstorm
touchingness
trumpetshell
trustfulness
truthfulness
usufructuary
usuriousness
vauntcourier
youngberries
youthfulness
advantageous
adventitious
advisability
civilisation
covetousness
deviationism
deviationist
divarication
diversionary
diversionist
diverticular

diverticulum
divertimenti
divertimento
divisibility
divisiveness
dovecoloured
eavesdropped
eavesdropper
enviableness
envisagement
feverishness
governmental
governorship
invagination
invalidation
inveiglement
invertebrate
investigator
inveterately
invigilation
invigoration
invisibility
involutional
invulnerable
invulnerably
juvenescence
levorotation
levorotatory
Liverpudlian
liverystable
lovelessness
lovelornness
moveableness
movelessness
navigability
navigational
nevertheless
novelisation
ravenousness
revelational
revengefully
reverberator
reversionary
revictualled
revivalistic
reviviscence
vivification
viviparously
bewilderedly
bewilderment
bewitchingly
bowcompasses
cowardliness
downwardness
LowChurchman
newfashioned
Newfoundland
newspaperman
towardliness
unwieldiness
unwontedness
unworldiness
unworthiness
dextrousness
lexicography
lexicologist
maximisation
sexagenarian
sexcentenary
taxcollector
toxicologist
toxicophobia
amygdaloidal
asymmetrical
asynchronism
asynchronous
cryptanalyst
cryptogamous
cryptography

cryptologist
crystalgazer
Egyptologist
erythematous
erythroblast
erythromycin
etymological
etymologicon
glycogenesis
glycoprotein
glyphography
glyptography
Keynesianism
oxyacetylene
phycological
phycomycetes
phyllotactic
phylogenesis
phylogenetic
physiognomic
physiography
physiologist
phytogenesis
phytogenetic
phytographer
phytological
phytophagous
psychiatrist
psychoactive
psychography
psychologise
psychologism
psychologist
psychometric
psychopathic
psychosexual
psychotropic
psychrometer
psychrometry
rhynchophora
rhythmically
stylographic
unyieldingly
enzymologist
mezzorelievo
mezzosoprano
muzzleloader
razzledazzle

abrasiveness
advantageous
agranulocyte
Alhambresque
alkalescence
ambassadress
antagonistic
apparatchiki
apparatchiks
apparentness
apparitional
assassinator
bedazzlement
behaviourism
behaviourist
bilateralism
breakthrough
breaststroke
breastsummer
breathalyser
breathlessly
breathtaking
calamitously
canaliculate
canalisation
caravansarai
caravanserai
catachrestic
catamountain
cataphoresis

catastrophic
clearsighted
cohabitation
cowardliness
creativeness
decaffeinate
decalescence
decapitation
decasyllabic
decasyllable
delamination
denaturalise
denaturation
departmental
deracination
desalination
detachedness
didactically
dilapidation
dilatability
dilatoriness
disaccharide
disadvantage
disaffection
disaffiliate
disagreeable
disagreeably
disagreement
disallowance
disambiguate
disannulling
disannulment
disassociate
disastrously
divarication
dreadfulness
duraluminium
dynamometric
dynastically
embattlement
endamagement
endangerment
entanglement
equalisation
equalitarian
equationally
escapologist
espagnolette
exhaustively
expansionary
expansionism
expansionist
expatriation
exsanguinate
exsanguinous
finalisation
focalisation
foraminifera
freakishness
galactogogue
gigantically
gonadotropic
gonadotropin
greathearted
gynaecocracy
heraldically
humanisation
humanitarian
hydatidiform
idealisation
ideationally
illadvisedly
immaculately
immaterially
immatureness
impartiality
incalculable
incalculably
incalescence

incandescent
incapability
incapacitate
incatenation
incautiously
infanticidal
inhabitation
inharmonious
insalubrious
invagination
invalidation
irrationally
kinaesthesia
kinaesthesis
kinaesthetic
legalisation
localisation
lycanthropic
malacologist
malapertness
megalomaniac
melancholiac
melanochroic
metachronism
metagalactic
metalanguage
metallically
metallophone
metallurgist
metalworking
metamorphism
metamorphose
metaphorical
metaphrastic
metaphysical
metapsychics
metasomatism
metathetical
metathoracic
miraculously
misadventure
misalignment
misanthropic
misapprehend
monadelphous
monastically
moralisation
negativeness
negativistic
nonagenarian
nonalignment
noradrenalin
oblanceolate
occasionally
oceanography
oceanologist
organgrinder
organisation
organography
organoleptic
ornamentally
oxyacetylene
palaeobotany
palaeography
Palaeolithic
palatability
paraboloidal
paradigmatic
paradisaical
paradisiacal
paraesthesia
paragraphist
parallelling
paralysation
paramagnetic
parametrical
paramilitary
paramorphism
paranormally

paraphrastic
parasiticide
parasitology
paratactical
pedantically
penalisation
peradventure
perambulator
phrasemonger
phraseograph
pleasantness
pleasingness
pleasureless
polarimetric
polarisation
polarography
recalcitrant
recalcitrate
recalescence
recapitulate
regardlessly
rehabilitate
relationally
relationship
relativeness
relativistic
repatriation
romanisation
romantically
ruralisation
salamandrian
salamandrine
salamandroid
Samaritanism
scraperboard
scratchiness
semantically
separability
separateness
seraphically
sexagenarian
Sinanthropus
sodafountain
solarisation
somatopleure
speakingtube
squarerigged
squattocracy
stealthiness
steatopygous
Stradivarius
straightaway
straightbred
straightedge
straightener
straightness
straitjacket
stranglehold
straticulate
stratigraphy
stratosphere
subalternate
subalternity
subapostolic
subarrhation
synaesthesia
synaesthetic
synarthrosis
telaesthesia
telaesthetic
teratologist
teratomatous
theanthropic
theatregoing
theatrically
totalisation
totalitarian
towardliness
triangularly

tyrannically
tyrannicidal
uncalculated
unfaithfully
unfamiliarly
unfathomable
unfavourable
unfavourably
ungainliness
unlawfulness
unmanageable
unparalleled
urbanisation
urbanologist
vicargeneral
vitalisation
vocabularian
vocalisation
volatileness
womanishness
zygapophysis
barbarically
blabbermouth
bobbydazzler
bombdisposal
cabbagewhite
carbohydrate
carbonaceous
carburetting
combinations
cumbersomely
cumbrousness
diabolically
disbursement
doubleacting
doubledealer
doubledecked
doubledecker
doublelocked
doubtfulness
feebleminded
flabelliform
forbiddingly
globetrotter
gobbledegook
gobbledygook
hubblebubble
inobservance
lumberjacket
misbehaviour
nimbostratus
plebiscitary
probationary
proboscidean
proboscidian
purblindness
rabbinically
rabblerouser
rambunctious
rumbletumble
scabbardfish
scabrousness
snobbishness
sorbefacient
stablishment
stubbornness
symbolically
turbellarian
adscititious
aircondition
aircraftsman
amicableness
anecdotalist
apiculturist
apochromatic
auscultation
auscultatory
bacchanalian
beachcombing

biochemistry
biocoenology
blackbirding
blackcurrant
blackguardly
blockbusting
bowcompasses
brachydactyl
brackishness
brickfielder
buccaneering
buccaneerish
calcareously
calculatedly
cancellation
carcinogenic
checkerberry
checkerboard
chocolatebox
circuitously
circumcision
circumfluent
circumfusion
circumjacent
circumscribe
circumstance
coacervation
coachbuilder
concelebrant
concelebrate
concentrator
conceptional
conceptually
conchiferous
conchologist
conciliation
conciliative
conciliatory
conclusively
concomitance
concordantly
concrescence
concreteness
concubitancy
concupiscent
concurrently
crackbrained
Czechoslovak
deactivation
discerningly
discerptible
discipleship
disciplinary
disclamation
discographer
discomfiture
discommodity
discomposure
disconnected
disconnexion
disconsolate
discontented
discordantly
discountable
discouraging
discourteous
discoverable
discoverture
discreetness
discreteness
discretional
discriminant
discriminate
discursively
educationist
electrically
electrolysis
electrolytic
electrometer

electronvolt
electroplate
electroscope
electroshock
electrotonic
electrotonus
electrotyper
elocutionary
elocutionist
elucubration
epicureanism
epicycloidal
exacerbation
executorship
falcongentil
falcongentle
fancifulness
flickeringly
flocculation
forcefulness
forcibleness
fractionally
fractionator
fricasseeing
frictionless
fructiferous
fructivorous
functionally
functionless
geochemistry
glaciologist
glockenspiel
glycogenesis
glycoprotein
gracefulness
graciousness
henceforward
inaccessible
inaccessibly
inaccurately
inactivation
inoccupation
isochromatic
isochronally
lasciviously
leucocytosis
LowChurchman
lusciousness
malcontented
Marcionitism
mercantilism
mercantilist
merchantable
mercifulness
mercurialise
mercurialism
miscalculate
miscellanist
narcissistic
narcotically
neoclassical
nonchalantly
noncombatant
noncommittal
noncomplying
nonconductor
nonconformer
obscurantism
obscurantist
panchromatic
pancreatitis
peacefulness
peccadilloes
perceptively
perceptivity
perceptually
percussively
percutaneous
phycological

phycomycetes
pisciculture
pitcherplant
placesetting
plecopterous
plectognathi
porcelainise
porcelainous
porcellanous
practicality
practitioner
precancelled
precariously
precedential
preceptorial
precessional
prechristian
preciousness
precipitable
precipitance
precipitancy
precipitator
precisianism
precisionist
preclassical
preclusively
precociously
precognition
precognitive
precondition
preconscious
pricecutting
procathedral
processional
proclamation
proclamatory
proconsulate
psychiatrist
psychoactive
psychography
psychologise
psychologism
psychologist
psychometric
psychopathic
psychosexual
psychotropic
psychrometer
psychrometry
punchingball
reactivation
reactiveness
reoccupation
saccharinity
saccharoidal
sarcomatosis
sarcophagous
sexcentenary
spaciousness
specialistic
specifically
specificness
speciousness
specktioneer
spectrograph
spectrometer
spectrometry
spectroscope
spectroscopy
stichomythia
stichomythic
stockbreeder
stockbroking
stockingless
stockjobbery
stockjobbing
stockraising
subcelestial
subcommittee

subconscious
subcontinent
subcutaneous
succedaneous
successfully
successional
successively
succinctness
susceptivity
synchronical
synchroniser
syncretistic
taxcollector
teachability
tercentenary
thickskinned
thickskulled
touchingness
traceability
trachomatous
tractability
tricentenary
trichologist
trichotomise
trichotomous
trichromatic
trickishness
trochanteric
unacceptable
unaccustomed
uneconomical
unscientific
unscriptural
unscrupulous
viscerotonic
viscosimeter
viscountship
volcanically
watchfulness
academically
banderillero
birdsnesting
birdwatching
bladderwrack
candleholder
cardcarrying
cardinalship
cardiography
cardiologist
coldshoulder
condemnation
condemnatory
condensation
conductivity
conduplicate
disdainfully
dunderheaded
epidemically
epidemiology
evidentially
feldspathoid
fiddlefaddle
fiddlesticks
gladiatorial
gladsomeness
goodhumoured
goodtempered
handicapping
handkerchief
handsbreadth
handsomeness
hardfavoured
hardfeatured
hardstanding
headmistress
headquarters
headshrinker
hebdomadally
heedlessness
hindquarters
hoodmanblind
inadequately
inadmissible
inadmissibly
inadvertence
inadvertency
isodiametric
kindergarten
landingcraft
landingfield
landingstage
landingstrip
landlubberly
laudableness
maidenliness
maidenstakes
mendaciously
middleweight
mindlessness
misdemeanant
misdemeanour
misdirection
mordaciously
muddleheaded
needlessness
neoDarwinian
neoDarwinism
neoDarwinist
obedientiary
outdatedness
paedobaptism
paedogenesis
paedogenetic
paedomorphic
predesignate
predestinate
predetermine
predictively
predigestion
predilection
predominance
predominancy
pridefulness
prodigiously
productively
productivity
prudentially
Quadragesima
quadrangular
quadraphonic
quadriennium
quadrinomial
quadriplegia
quadriplegic
quadrivalent
quadrumanous
readableness
readjustment
rhododendron
saddlebacked
sandyachting
sardonically
shadowboxing
sledgehammer
spidermonkey
studdingsail
studiousness
subdivisible
syndactylism
syndactylous
syndetically
tradescantia
tradespeople
traditionary
traditionist
traducianism
traducianist
tridactylous
vindictively
voidableness
windingsheet
wonderstruck
wonderworker
wondrousness
woodengraver
woodenheaded
wunderkinder
absentminded
acceleration
accelerative
accentuation
adhesiveness
adjectivally
adventitious
affectedness
affectionate
afterthought
alterability
anaerobiosis
anaesthetise
anaesthetist
antecedently
antediluvian
anteprandial
appendectomy
appendicitis
appendicular
apperception
apperceptive
appetisingly
atheromatous
baselessness
benefactress
beneficently
beneficially
benevolently
beseechingly
bicentennial
bioecologist
birefringent
bluestocking
breechloader
bureaucratic
capercaillie
capercailzie
carelessness
catechetical
caterwauling
cementitious
ceremonially
cheerfulness
cheeseburger
cheesecutter
cheesemonger
cheeseparing
chieftainess
chrematistic
chrestomathy
cinematheque
cohesiveness
coleopterist
coleopterous
corelatively
corespondent
covetousness
creepycrawly
deceleration
decentralise
degenerately
degeneration
degenerative
dejectedness
determinable
determinably
determinedly
dilettantish
dilettantism
directorship
disembarrass
disenchanter
disendowment
disestablish
diversionary
diversionist
diverticular
diverticulum
divertimenti
divertimento
dodecahedral
dodecahedron
dodecaphonic
domestically
domesticator
dovecoloured
eavesdropped
eavesdropper
eccentricity
eclectically
effectuality
effectuation
effeminately
effervescent
eleemosynary
embezzlement
encephalitic
encephalitis
endermically
enfeeblement
enterprising
entertaining
ephemerality
equestrienne
essentiality
etherisation
euhemeristic
expediential
experiential
experimental
experimenter
extensometer
exterminable
exterminator
facelessness
fenestration
feverishness
firefighting
forebodement
forebodingly
forensically
foresightful
forestalment
freestanding
freeswimming
freethinking
freewheeling
friendliness
gamesmanship
gamesomeness
gametophytic
genealogical
generousness
gesellschaft
governmental
governorship
greengrocery
greenishness
grievousness
gruesomeness
haberdashery
hebetudinous
hemerocallis
hereditament
hereditarily
hereinbefore
heterocercal
heterocyclic
heteroecious
heterogamous
heterogenous
heterologous
heteromerous
heteronomous
heterophylly
heterosexual
heterozygote
heterozygous
hibernaculum
hirepurchase
homeomorphic
homeopathist
homesickness
honeybuzzard
hopelessness
hymenopteran
hyperacidity
hyperbolical
hyperplastic
hyperpyretic
hyperpyrexia
hypersthenia
hypersthenic
hypertension
hypertensive
hyperthermia
hypertrophic
illegibility
illegitimacy
illegitimate
immeasurable
immeasurably
immemorially
immensurable
immethodical
impedimental
impenetrable
impenetrably
impenitently
imperatively
imperatorial
imperceptive
impercipient
imperfection
imperfective
imperishable
imperishably
impermanence
impermanency
impersonally
impersonator
impertinence
impertinency
imperviously
impetiginous
incendiarism
incestuously
indebtedness
indecisively
indeclinable
indecorously
indefeasible
indefeasibly
indefectible
indefensible
indefensibly
indefinitely
indehiscence
indelibility
indelicately
independence
independency
infectiously
infelicitous
insecticidal
insemination
integumental

intellection	irrepealable	preexistence	superstratum	confabulator
intellective	irreprovable	priestliness	supervenient	confectioner
intellectual	irresistible	priestridden	supervention	conferential
intelligence	irresistibly	quaestorship	surefootedly	confessional
intelligible	irresolutely	racemisation	sweepingness	confidential
intelligibly	irresolution	ravenousness	sweetishness	confirmation
intemperance	irresolvable	rebelliously	taberdarship	confirmative
inteneration	irrespective	receivership	tabernacular	confirmatory
interbedding	irrespirable	receptaculum	tamelessness	confiscation
interception	irresponsive	receptionist	taperecorder	confiscatory
intercession	irreverently	recessionary	telegraphese	conformation
intercessory	irreversible	redecoration	telegraphist	confoundedly
interchanger	irreversibly	redemptioner	teleological	Confucianism
interconnect	juvenescence	Redemptorist	televisional	confusedness
intercropped	kaleidoscope	redeployment	terebinthine	craftbrother
intercurrent	lakedwelling	regeneration	thievishness	differentiae
intercutting	laterisation	regenerative	threequarter	differential
interdiction	liberalistic	rejectamenta	threewheeler	disfranchise
interdictive	licentiously	relentlessly	timehonoured	furfuraceous
interdictory	lifelessness	rememberable	timelessness	halftimbered
interdigital	literariness	remembrancer	tirelessness	ineffaceable
interestedly	Liverpudlian	renegotiable	tiresomeness	ineffaceably
interfemoral	liverystable	repercussion	togetherness	inefficiency
interference	lonesomeness	repercussive	tolerability	malformation
interglacial	lovelessness	repetitional	tonelessness	newfashioned
interjection	lovelornness	repetitively	tuberculated	Newfoundland
interjectory	lukewarmness	reservedness	tuberculosis	nonflammable
interlobular	mademoiselle	resettlement	tunelessness	nonflowering
interlocutor	majestically	revelational	typefounding	oldfashioned
intermeddler	malevolently	revengefully	unbecomingly	perfectively
intermediacy	materialness	reverberator	unbelievable	perfervidity
intermediary	meretricious	reversionary	unbelievably	perfidiously
intermediate	meteorically	rosecoloured	uncelebrated	perfoliation
interminable	meteorograph	sacerdotally	undemocratic	performative
interminably	minedetector	safecracking	underachieve	pinfeathered
intermission	mineralogist	salesmanship	underbidding	prefabricate
intermittent	miseducation	sclerenchyma	underclothes	prefectorial
intermitting	moderateness	screenwriter	undercoating	preferential
intermixture	molecularity	secessionism	undercurrent	preformation
intermundane	monetisation	secessionist	undercutting	preformative
internuclear	moneychanger	selenography	underdevelop	professional
internuncial	moneygrubber	selenologist	undergarment	professorate
interoceanic	moneyspinner	sheepishness	underinsured	professoress
interoceptor	moveableness	sheepshearer	underletting	professorial
interpellate	movelessness	shrewishness	undermanning	proficiently
interpleader	namedropping	sideslipping	underpinning	profiteering
interpolator	namelessness	sidestepping	underrunning	profligately
interpretive	nevertheless	sidewhiskers	undersetting	profoundness
interrelated	nomenclative	sleepingpill	understaffed	selfabsorbed
interrogator	nomenclature	sleepwalking	undersurface	selfactivity
interruption	noneffective	speechlessly	undertenancy	selfaffected
interruptive	nonefficient	speedboating	underwritten	selfanalysis
intersection	nonessential	spheroidally	undetermined	selfapplause
interservice	noneuclidean	spiegeleisen	unhesitating	selfapproval
interspinous	nonexistence	splendidness	unmercifully	selfbegotten
interstellar	novelisation	steeplechase	unreasonable	selfbetrayal
interstitial	numerologist	streetwalker	unreasonably	selfcatering
intertexture	numerousness	strengthener	unrecognised	selfcoloured
intervenient	obsequiously	strengthless	unregenerate	selfcomposed
intervention	orienteering	streptococci	unrepeatable	selfcontempt
intervocalic	ostentatious	streptomycin	unreservedly	selfcritical
interwreathe	osteogenesis	subeditorial	unresponsive	selfdeceived
inveiglement	osteological	suberisation	unrestrained	selfdeceiver
invertebrate	osteomalacia	superannuate	unsearchable	selfdelusion
investigator	osteoplastic	supercharger	unseasonable	selfdestruct
inveterately	osteoporosis	superciliary	unsegregated	selfdevotion
irredeemable	otherworldly	supercilious	Valenciennes	selfdirected
irredeemably	paletteknife	supereminent	valetudinary	selfdistrust
irreflective	parenthesise	supererogate	vegetatively	selfdoubting
irreformable	peregrinator	superhighway	venepuncture	selfeducated
irrefragable	peremptorily	superhumanly	venerability	selfeffacing
irrefragably	phlebotomise	supermundane	veterinarian	selfelective
irregardless	phlebotomist	supernaculum	vicechairman	selfemployed
irregularity	phreatophyte	supernatural	warehouseman	selfevidence
irrelatively	phrenologist	superposable	watermanship	selfexistent
irrelevantly	pigeonbreast	supersedence	wineglassful	selfflattery
irremediable	potentiality	supersensory	buffalograss	selfhypnosis
irremediably	preeminently	supersession	cliffhanging	selfidentity
irremissible	preestablish	superstition	comfortingly	selfignition

selfinterest
selfinvolved
selflessness
selflimiting
selfluminous
selfmurderer
selfpleasing
selfportrait
selfreliance
selfreproach
selfrighting
selfsameness
selfstarting
selfviolence
shuffleboard
staffofficer
staffsurgeon
sufficiently
trifurcation
unaffectedly
unifoliolate
unofficially
usufructuary
amygdaloidal
anagogically
anagrammatic
beggarliness
biogeography
biographical
boogiewoogie
burglarproof
congeniality
congenitally
conglobation
conglomerate
conglutinate
congratulant
congratulate
congregation
diageotropic
diagrammatic
disgorgement
disguisement
disgustfully
disgustingly
epigrammatic
exaggeration
exaggerative
exaggeratory
exegetically
exiguousness
flagellation
flagellatory
flagitiously
ganglionated
geographical
gorgeousness
gregariously
hedgehopping
huggermugger
judgematical
knighterrant
knightliness
languishment
languorously
largehearted
ledgertackle
linguistical
lodginghouse
longdistance
longitudinal
longshoreman
longstanding
longwindedly
mangelwurzel
neighbouring
oligarchical
orographical
phagocytosis
phagocytotic
pragmatistic
priggishness
progenitress
progesterone
proglottides
programmable
programmatic
sanguinarily
sanguineness
sanguinolent
sedgewarbler
sergeantfish
sergeantship
singleacting
singledecker
singlehanded
singleminded
singleseater
sluggishness
snaggletooth
stagemanager
staggeringly
steganograph
suggestively
swaggeringly
swaggerstick
tangentially
tangibleness
tergiversate
toggleswitch
tragicomical
triggerhappy
triglyphical
trigonometry
troglodytism
vengefulness
whigmaleerie
zoogeography
alphabetical
alphamerical
alphanumeric
amphibiously
amphibrachic
amphictyonic
amphisbaenic
amphitheatre
amphitropous
anthelmintic
anthropogeny
anthropoidal
anthropology
archdeaconry
archdiocesan
archetypally
archetypical
archipelagic
architecture
arrhythmical
asphyxiation
authenticate
authenticity
bachelorhood
bachelorship
bathypelagic
bilharziasis
bilharziosis
cachinnation
cachinnatory
cashandcarry
catholically
dethronement
dichromatism
diphtheritic
diphthongise
disharmonise
dishevelment
emphatically
enchantingly
enshrinement
enthronement
enthusiastic
euphonically
euphoniously
exchangeable
fatherfigure
fatherliness
highcoloured
highfaluting
highhandedly
highlystrung
highpressure
highsounding
highspirited
highstepping
lachrymation
lachrymatory
lachrymosely
lighthearted
lithographer
lithographic
lithological
lithospheric
lithotritist
machicolated
mathematical
mechanically
methodically
mithridatise
mithridatism
motherfigure
motherliness
mothertongue
mythographer
mythological
mythologiser
Neohellenism
nephanalysis
nephelometer
nephelometry
nephrologist
nightclothes
nychthemeral
nychthemeron
orchestrator
orchidaceous
orthodontics
orthodontist
orthogenesis
orthogenetic
orthographer
orthographic
orthopaedics
orthopaedist
orthopterist
orthopteroid
orthopterous
orthotropism
orthotropous
panhellenism
pathetically
pathogenesis
pathogenetic
pathological
prehensility
prehistorian
rechargeable
rightfulness
ruthlessness
sightreading
siphonophore
siphonostele
sophisticate
tachygrapher
tachygraphic
technicality
technicolour
technocratic
technologist
tightmouthed
unchangeable
unchangeably
uncharitable
uncharitably
unchivalrous
unthinkingly
unthoughtful
xiphisternum
acciaccatura
accidentally
actinomycete
additionally
administrant
administrate
advisability
aetiological
agribusiness
agricultural
alliteration
alliterative
altitudinous
ambidextrous
ambivalently
angiocarpous
annihilation
annihilative
antiaircraft
anticipation
anticipative
anticipatory
anticlerical
anticyclonic
antigenicity
antigropelos
antimacassar
antimagnetic
antimalarial
antineutrino
antiparticle
antipathetic
antiperiodic
antiphonally
antirachitic
antiSemitism
antistrophic
antithetical
aquicultural
argillaceous
articulately
articulation
articulatory
artificially
artilleryman
artistically
assibilation
assimilation
assimilative
assimilatory
attitudinise
availability
basidiospore
belittlement
bewilderedly
bewilderment
bewitchingly
bilingualism
brainstormer
brainwashing
businesslike
cabinetmaker
calisthenics
camiknickers
capitalistic
capitulation
caricaturist
carillonneur
catilinarian
chairmanship
cheirography
Christianise
Christianity
Christolatry
Christophany
civilisation
clairaudient
clairvoyance
cleistogamic
codification
conidiophore
conidiospore
debilitation
decipherable
decipherment
decisiveness
definiteness
definitively
deliberately
deliberation
deliberative
delicatessen
delightfully
delimitation
delinquently
deliquescent
delitescence
demilitarise
demimondaine
demineralise
derisiveness
derivational
derivatively
desideration
desiderative
desirability
desirousness
deviationism
deviationist
diminishable
diminishment
diminutively
disincentive
disinfectant
disinfection
disinflation
disingenuous
disintegrate
disinterment
divisibility
divisiveness
dubitatively
echinococcus
elliptically
embitterment
encirclement
enginedriver
enginetuning
enviableness
envisagement
equidistance
equilibrator
equipollence
equipollency
equiprobable
equitability
equivalently
equivocation
equivocatory
excitability
exhibitioner
exhilaration
exhilarative
extinguisher
facilitation
felicitation
felicitously
feminineness

feminisation
filibusterer
fluidisation
freightliner
fruitfulness
fugitiveness
fuliginosity
futilitarian
gasification
geriatrician
habilitation
habitability
habitforming
habitualness
hagiographer
hagiographic
hagiological
heliocentric
heliographer
heliographic
heliogravure
heliolatrous
heliotherapy
heliotropism
hemichordate
hemimorphism
hemimorphite
hemiparasite
hemispheroid
heritability
hesitatingly
holidaymaker
horizontally
humification
hygienically
illiberality
illiterately
incidentally
incineration
incisiveness
indicatively
indifference
indifferency
indigenously
indigestible
indirectness
indiscipline
indiscreetly
indiscretion
indisputable
indisputably
indissoluble
indissolubly
indistinctly
indivertible
indivertibly
individually
infiniteness
infinitively
intimidation
intimidatory
invigilation
invigoration
invisibility
irritability
irritatingly
jurisconsult
jurisdiction
jurisprudent
lacininiated
laticiferous
latinisation
latitudinous
legitimately
legitimation
legitimatise
lepidopteran
lexicography
lexicologist
libidinously
logistically
luminescence
luminiferous
luminousness
magistrature
Manicheanism
manifoldness
manipulation
manipulative
manipulatory
maximisation
mediaevalism
mediaevalist
meditatively
meridionally
meristematic
meticulously
militaristic
minicomputer
minimisation
ministration
ministrative
misinterpret
mobilisation
modification
modificatory
monitorially
motivational
mucilaginous
municipalise
municipality
munificently
musicianship
musicologist
mutinousness
navigability
navigational
nidification
niminypiminy
nominalistic
nonidentical
notification
obligatorily
obligingness
obliteration
obliterative
occidentally
officeholder
omnipotently
omnipresence
omnisciently
omnivorously
oneirocritic
ophiophagous
optimisation
orbicularity
ordinariness
ornithomancy
ornithoscopy
oscillograph
oscilloscope
ossification
pacification
pacificatory
palingenesia
palingenesis
palingenetic
panification
parisyllabic
pedicellaria
penitentiary
pericarditis
perilousness
periodically
periodontics
periodontist
periostracum
peripherally
periphrastic
perispomenon
peristeronic
peristomatic
pitiableness
pitilessness
plainclothed
plainclothes
plaindealing
pleiotropism
policyholder
positiveness
positivistic
praiseworthy
purification
purificatory
radiobiology
radioelement
radiographer
radiographic
radioisotope
radiological
radionuclide
radiophonics
radiotherapy
ramification
ratification
ratiocinator
reciprocally
reciprocator
redintegrate
redistribute
regimentally
registration
reliableness
remilitarise
reminiscence
residentiary
residentship
resignedness
resiniferous
resipiscence
resistlessly
reticulately
reticulation
reticulocyte
retiringness
revictualled
revivalistic
reviviscence
ridiculously
ruminatively
sadistically
satisfaction
satisfactory
satisfyingly
schismatical
schizogonous
schizomycete
schizophrene
schizothymia
schizothymic
scrimshanker
scripturally
scriptwriter
semiannually
semibasement
semicircular
semicylinder
semidarkness
semideponent
semidetached
semidiameter
semidomestic
semifinalist
semifinished
semiliterate
seminiferous
semiofficial
semiological
semiparasite
semiprecious
semitropical
sericultural
silicicolous
siliciferous
sinistrality
sinistrorsal
skrimshanker
sociableness
sociological
sociometrist
solicitation
solicitously
solifluction
solitariness
sprightfully
squirrelcage
squirreltail
stridulation
strikingness
stringcourse
subinfeudate
swainishness
theistically
thriftlessly
toxicologist
toxicophobia
trainspotter
traitorously
typification
undiplomatic
unhistorical
unkindliness
unlikelihood
unlikeliness
unmistakable
unmistakably
untimeliness
unwieldiness
unyieldingly
variableness
varicoloured
vaticination
venipuncture
veridicality
verification
verificatory
vesiculation
vilification
vinification
viridescence
visitational
visitatorial
vitiligation
vivification
viviparously
vociferation
vociferously
volitionally
vomiturition
conjunctival
disjointedly
misjudgement
perjuriously
projectional
projectively
serjeantship
subjectively
subjectivise
subjectivism
subjectivist
subjectivity
backbreaking
backpedalled
backslapping
backwardness
backwoodsman
bookingclerk
booklearning
brokenwinded
cockfighting
cocksureness
cuckingstool
cuckooflower
duckingstool
fecklessness
hucklebacked
leukocytosis
licketysplit
marketgarden
marketsquare
marksmanship
misknowledge
monkeyflower
monkeyjacket
monkeypuzzle
monkeywrench
parkinsonism
pickerelweed
poikilotherm
racketeering
recklessness
Shakspereana
Shaksperiana
snakecharmer
spokesperson
Stakhanovism
Stakhanovite
taskmistress
ticklishness
walkietalkie
wicketkeeper
winklepicker
workableness
workingclass
YankeeDoodle
abolitionary
abolitionism
abolitionist
achlamydeous
adulteration
adulterously
agglutinogen
amalgamation
amalgamative
amelioration
ameliorative
analogically
analphabetic
analytically
apolitically
athletically
balladmonger
balletomania
ballottement
bellbottomed
belletristic
belligerence
belligerency
bellylanding
bibliography
bibliologist
bibliomaniac
bibliopegist
bibliophilic
bibliopolist
bibliothecae
billingsgate
billsticking
biologically
boulevardier
brilliantine
bulletheaded
bullfighting
bullheadedly
Byelorussian

calligrapher
calligraphic
callisthenic
Carlovingian
chalcolithic
chalcopyrite
childbearing
childishness
coalitionist
coelenterate
collaborator
collaterally
collectively
collectivise
collectivism
collectivist
collectivity
collegialism
collegiality
collegiately
collinearity
colloquially
collywobbles
curlingirons
curlingtongs
declinometer
deflagration
deflationary
deflationist
dialectician
dialectology
dislodgement
ecclesiastic
ecclesiology
ecologically
edulcoration
efflorescent
emblazonment
emblematical
emulsifiable
enclitically
Englishwoman
evolutionary
evolutionism
evolutionist
exclusionary
exclusionism
exclusionist
explantation
explicitness
exploitation
exploitative
exulceration
fallaciously
faultfinding
fieldglasses
folliculated
fullyfledged
galligaskins
gallinaceous
geologically
grallatorial
guilefulness
hallucinogen
hallucinosis
harlequinade
hellgrammite
idolatrously
implantation
implicitness
inclinometer
inelasticity
inflammation
inflammatory
inflationary
inflationism
inflationist
inflectional
ingloriously
isolationism
isolationist
malleability
marlinespike
mealymouthed
millesimally
milliammeter
mulligatawny
nailscissors
neglectfully
outlandishly
Palladianism
pellucidness
philadelphus
philanthrope
philanthropy
philharmonic
philhellenic
philistinism
phillumenist
philodendron
philological
philosophise
phyllotactic
phylogenesis
phylogenetic
pralltriller
prelapsarian
prolegomenon
prolifically
prolificness
prolongation
publicspirit
qualmishness
reallocation
reflationary
reflectional
reflectively
reflectivity
rollingstock
sculpturally
seclusionist
sellingplate
shillyshally
skullduggery
smallclothes
smallholding
soullessness
speleologist
stalactiform
stalwartness
stellenbosch
stelliferous
stilboestrol
stillhunting
stylographic
sublapsarian
syllabically
toilsomeness
toploftiness
unblinkingly
unblushingly
unclassified
unflattering
unilaterally
unpleasantly
villainously
wallpainting
wallydraigle
welldisposed
wellfavoured
wellgrounded
Wellingtonia
wholehearted
williewaught
wollastonite
woolgatherer
woollyheaded
yellowhammer
agamogenesis
agamogenetic
alimentation
alimentative
anamorphosis
anemographic
anemophilous
aromatically
aromaticness
asymmetrical
augmentation
augmentative
biometrician
blamableness
blamefulness
brambleberry
championship
chemotherapy
chimneypiece
commandingly
commemorator
commencement
commendation
commendatory
commensalism
commensalist
commensurate
commentation
commercially
commiserator
commissarial
commissariat
commissioner
committeeman
commodiously
commonwealth
communicable
communicably
communicator
cosmetically
cosmogonical
cosmographer
cosmographic
cosmological
cosmopolitan
cosmopolitic
curmudgeonly
deambulatory
dermatophyte
diamagnetism
diamonddrill
diamondfield
dogmatically
dramatically
dramaturgist
elementalism
elementarily
etymological
etymologicon
farmsteading
fermentation
fermentative
flamboyantly
flamethrower
flammability
formaldehyde
formlessness
geomagnetism
geometrician
Germanophile
Germanophobe
graminaceous
grammaticise
grammolecule
gramnegative
grampositive
haematoblast
haematolysis
haematoxylon
haemophiliac
haemopoiesis
haemorrhagic
harmlessness
harmonically
harmoniously
hermeneutics
hermetically
Ishmaelitish
kremlinology
mnemotechnic
myrmecophily
onomatopoeia
onomatopoeic
outmanoeuvre
permanganate
permeability
permissively
permittivity
pigmentation
plumbaginous
plumbiferous
plummerblock
premaxillary
premeditated
premeditator
premenstrual
primigravida
primogenital
primogenitor
primordially
promulgation
rhombohedral
rhombohedron
salmonladder
segmentation
shamateurism
shamefacedly
shamefulness
stammeringly
submaxillary
subminiature
submissively
surmountable
swimmingbath
swimmingbell
swimmingpool
thematically
thimbleberry
trampolinist
tremendously
trumpetshell
unambivalent
unemployable
unemployment
unimaginable
unimaginably
unimportance
vermiculated
whimperingly
whimsicality
agentgeneral
amenableness
amentiferous
asynchronism
asynchronous
avantgardism
avantgardist
blandishment
blunderingly
bonnetmonkey
bonnyclabber
brinkmanship
bronchoscope
broncobuster
brontosaurus
burningglass
chancemedley
chondriosome
clangorously
clannishness
clinkerbuilt
coenobitical
coenobytical
coincidental
coincidently
connaturally
connectional
connectively
conningtower
connubiality
councilwoman
countenancer
counteragent
counterblast
countercheck
counterclaim
counterforce
counterlight
countermarch
counterplead
counterpoint
counterpoise
counterproof
counterscarp
countershaft
countertenor
countrydance
countrywoman
craniologist
crenellation
deontologist
dinnerjacket
downwardness
econometrics
economically
emancipation
enantiomorph
ethnocentric
ethnographer
ethnographic
ethnological
evanescently
evangelistic
eveningdress
exenteration
fainthearted
faintishness
fiendishness
foundationer
fountainhead
FrancoGerman
frangibility
frankincense
frenchpolish
frenetically
frontbencher
frontiersman
frontispiece
geanticlinal
granodiorite
gymnosophist
hymnographer
hypnogenesis
hypnogenetic
hypnotherapy
hypnotically
hypnotisable
iconoclastic
iconographer
identifiable
illnaturedly
Keynesianism
kinnikinnick
limnological
loungelizard
magnetically
magnetisable

magnetograph
magnetometer
magnifically
magnificence
magniloquent
maintainable
malnutrition
mannerliness
meaningfully
morningdress
mountainside
neonomianism
odontologist
openhandedly
openmindedly
opinionative
painlessness
pennypincher
pennywhistle
perniciously
pernoctation
phanerogamic
phenological
phenomenally
phenotypical
phonasthenia
phonemically
phonetically
phonographer
phonographic
phonological
planetesimal
planetstruck
planispheric
planoconcave
plenipotence
pointilliste
pornographer
pornographic
prenticeship
princeliness
principality
printability
pronominally
pronouncedly
pugnaciously
quantifiable
quantisation
quantitative
quinquennial
quinquennium
quintessence
reinvestment
reinvigorate
reunionistic
rhinocerotic
rhinological
rhynchophora
runningboard
scandalously
Scandinavian
scenepainter
sceneshifter
scenographic
scintigraphy
scintillator
significance
significancy
skunkcabbage
slanderously
somnambulant
somnambulate
somnambulism
somnambulist
somniloquism
somniloquist
soundingline
spinsterhood
standardbred
standingroom
stanniferous
stenographer
stenographic
stoneboiling
stonecutting
stonedresser
stonemasonry
stonyhearted
subnormality
teensyweensy
thankfulness
thanksgiving
thundercloud
thunderingly
thunderously
thunderstone
thunderstorm
tranquillise
tranquillity
transcendent
transduction
transferable
transference
transferring
transformism
transformist
transfusible
transgressor
transhipment
transhumance
transiliency
transitional
transitively
transitivity
transitorily
translatable
translucence
translucency
transmigrant
transmigrate
transmission
transmissive
transmitting
transmogrify
transmontane
transmutable
transoceanic
transpacific
transparency
transpirable
transplanter
transpontine
transposable
transshipped
transudation
transudatory
transversely
transvestism
transvestite
trinomialism
twentyfourmo
unanswerable
unencumbered
uninterested
vainglorious
vauntcourier
vernacularly
wainscotting
whencesoever
wrongfulness
youngberries
absoluteness
absolutistic
absorptional
absorptivity
accommodator
accompanyist
accomplished
accordionist
accouchement
accoutrement
acronychally
admonishment
aerodynamics
aeroembolism
aeronautical
aeroneurosis
aerosiderite
AfroAmerican
allomorphism
announcement
appositeness
appositional
arborescence
arborisation
astonishment
astoundingly
atmospherics
attorneyship
autocatalyse
autochthones
autodidactic
autoimmunity
automaticity
automobilist
automorphism
autonomously
barometrical
bloodbrother
bloodletting
bloodstained
bloodthirsty
bloodyminded
borosilicate
calorescence
calorimetric
canonisation
canorousness
chlorination
chromaticism
chromaticity
chromatogram
chromatology
chromatopsia
chromosphere
chronography
chronologise
chronologist
chronometric
colonisation
coloquintida
colorimetric
colourlessly
copolymerise
cynocephalus
cytogenetics
debonairness
decomposable
decompressor
decongestant
decongestion
decongestive
deconsecrate
decontrolled
decoratively
decorousness
deionisation
demodulation
demoniacally
demonstrable
demonstrably
demonstrator
denomination
denominative
denouncement
depoliticise
depopulation
derogatorily
desolateness
detoxication
disobedience
disorientate
dolorousness
echolocation
echosounding
ectoparasite
effortlessly
empoisonment
endocarditis
endometritis
endoparasite
endoskeletal
entomologise
entomologist
EuroAmerican
excogitation
excogitative
extortionary
extortionate
floodlighted
fluorescence
fluoridation
fluorination
fluorocarbon
gamopetalous
gamophyllous
gamosepalous
gerontocracy
gyromagnetic
halogenation
henotheistic
heroicalness
heroicomical
homoeopathic
homoeostasis
homologation
homomorphism
homomorphous
homonymously
homosexually
homothallism
humorousness
hypochlorite
hypochondria
hypocoristic
hypocritical
hypogastrium
hypognathous
hypophrygian
hypostatical
hyposulphite
hypothalamic
hypothalamus
hypothecator
hypothetical
idiosyncrasy
idiothermous
illogicality
immoderately
immoderation
immovability
impoliteness
imponderable
imponderably
impoverished
incognisable
incognisance
incognitable
incoherently
incommodious
incommutable
incommutably
incomparable
incomparably
incompatible
incompatibly
incompetence
incompetency
incompletely
incompliance
incomputable
inconcinnity
inconclusive
inconformity
inconsequent
inconsistent
inconsolable
inconsolably
inconsonance
inconstantly
inconsumable
inconsumably
incontiguous
incontinence
incontinency
inconvenient
incoordinate
incorporated
incorporator
incorporeity
incorrigible
incorrigibly
incorruption
indoctrinate
IndoEuropean
IndoGermanic
inhospitable
inhospitably
insolubilise
insolubility
intolerantly
intoxication
involutional
kilowatthour
laboursaving
levorotation
levorotatory
majorgeneral
manoeuvrable
manometrical
melodramatic
mesocephalic
mesothoracic
mitochondria
monochromate
monodramatic
monofilament
monographist
monomaniacal
monometallic
monomorphous
monopetalous
monophyletic
Monophysitic
monopodially
monopolistic
monostichous
monostrophic
monosyllabic
monosyllable
monotheistic
monotonously
motorcyclist
motorisation
nanoplankton
negotiatress
nicotinamide
nonobjective
obsolescence
obsoleteness
octogenarian
octosyllabic
octosyllable
oncorhynchus
opposability

oppositeness
oppositional
parochialise
parochialism
parochiality
paronomastic
pejoratively
peroxidation
pilotballoon
pleomorphism
preoccupancy
proofreading
pyroelectric
pyroligneous
pyromaniacal
pyromorphite
pyrotechnics
pyrotechnist
recognisable
recognisably
recognisance
recollection
recollective
recommitment
reconcilable
reconstitute
reconversion
reconveyance
remonstrance
remonstrator
remorsefully
removability
renouncement
repossession
resoluteness
resolvedness
resoundingly
ribonuclease
ricochetting
rigorousness
risorgimento
saponifiable
schoolfellow
schoolleaver
schoolmaster
schorlaceous
scrobiculate
secondstring
shootingiron
simoniacally
sonorousness
soporiferous
strobilation
stroboscopic
strongminded
strongylosis
strontianite
strophanthin
sudoriferous
sycophantish
synonymously
synoptically
theocratical
theoretician
theosophical
throughstone
timorousness
uncomeatable
uncommercial
uncommonness
unconformity
unconsidered
unconstraint
uncontrolled
unconvincing
ungovernable
unionisation
unloveliness
unpopularity
untowardness
unwontedness
unworldiness
unworthiness
uproariously
valorisation
vaporisation
vaporousness
vasodilation
vasodilatory
venomousness
vigorousness
zygomorphism
zygomorphous
adaptability
adaptiveness
anaphylactic
auspiciously
bespectacled
biophysicist
campfollower
campodeiform
carpetbagger
carpetknight
chaplainship
clapperboard
companionate
companionway
compatriotic
compellation
compensation
compensative
compensatory
complacently
complaisance
complemental
completeness
complexional
complexioned
complication
composedness
compoundable
compressible
compulsively
compulsivity
compulsorily
compunctious
compurgation
compurgatory
corporeality
cryptanalyst
cryptogamous
cryptography
cryptologist
culpableness
despairingly
despitefully
despoliation
despondently
despotically
diaphanously
dispensation
dispensatory
dispiritedly
displaceable
displacement
displeasedly
dispossessor
disputatious
Egyptologist
epiphenomena
eruptiveness
exophthalmic
exophthalmos
exophthalmus
geophysicist
geopolitical
glyphography
glyptography
graphologist
happenstance
helplessness
herpetologic
hesperididia
hippocentaur
hippopotamus
humptydumpty
inappeasable
inapplicable
inapplicably
inappositely
inoperculate
inspectorate
inspectorial
inspissation
jetpropelled
kleptomaniac
klipspringer
leapfrogging
misplacement
mispronounce
morphallaxis
morphologist
Neoplatonism
Neoplatonist
nympholeptic
nymphomaniac
outpensioner
perpetration
perpetuation
perplexingly
preparedness
preponderant
preponderate
preposterous
propaedeutic
propagandise
propagandism
propagandist
prophylactic
propitiation
propitiatory
propitiously
proportional
proportioned
proprietress
psephologist
pumpernickel
purposebuilt
purposefully
rapprochment
reappearance
respectfully
respectively
resplendence
resplendency
responsively
responsorial
salpiglossis
sempiternity
serpentiform
serpentinely
shipbuilding
simpleminded
skippingrope
slipcarriage
slipperiness
snapfastener
snappishness
stepchildren
stepdaughter
stupefacient
stupefaction
stupefactive
stupendously
sulphonamide
sulphonation
sulphuration
sulphuretted
supplemental
supplementer
supplicantly
supplication
supplicatory
suppositious
suppressible
surprisingly
suspensively
suspiciously
temptability
trephination
tripartitely
tripartition
triphthongal
triplication
trophallaxis
tropological
tropospheric
unapologetic
unappeasable
unappetising
whippoorwill
absquatulate
adequateness
chequerboard
conquistador
desquamation
desquamative
desquamatory
disquisition
frequentness
harquebusier
iniquitously
misquotation
pasqueflower
quaquaversal
sesquialtera
ubiquitarian
ubiquitously
vanquishable
vanquishment
abbreviation
aboriginally
abortiveness
accretionary
adorableness
aforethought
aggressively
amortisation
aperiodicity
appraisement
appraisingly
appreciation
appreciative
appreciatory
apprehension
apprehensive
approachable
appropriable
appropriator
astringently
astrological
astronautics
astronomical
astrophysics
attractively
attributable
avariciously
capriciously
carragheenin
carriageable
characterise
charlatanism
charnelhouse
charterhouse
charterparty
cherubically
chiropractic
chiropractor
choreography
chorographic
chorological
churchianity
churchwarden
churlishness
cirrocumulus
cirrostratus
clarinettist
coerciveness
coordinately
coordination
coordinative
correctional
correctitude
correctively
corroborator
courageously
courtmartial
courtplaster
cuprammonium
decreasingly
defraudation
depravedness
depreciation
depreciatory
depressingly
dibranchiate
digressional
digressively
disregardful
disreputable
disreputably
dwarfishness
emargination
embranchment
embryologist
empressement
encroachment
encrustation
enormousness
entrammelled
entrancement
entreatingly
entrenchment
entrepreneur
estrangement
excruciating
excruciation
exercitation
exorbitantly
expressional
expressively
expressivity
exprobration
extracranial
extraditable
extralimital
extramarital
extramundane
extraneously
extrasensory
extraspecial
extrauterine
extravagance
extravagancy
extravaganza
extraversion
extroversion
fearlessness
fearsomeness
ferrugineous
fibrillation
fibrinolysin
floriculture
gloriousness
guaranteeing

guardianship
hairdressing
hairsbreadth
hairsplitter
heartburning
heartrending
heartstrings
heartwarming
heortologist
hierarchical
hieroglyphic
hierographer
hierophantic
horrendously
horribleness
horrifically
horrorstruck
hybridisable
hydrochloric
hydrodynamic
hydrofluoric
hydrographer
hydrographic
hydrokinetic
hydrological
hydrolysable
hydromedusae
hydromedusan
hydrophilous
hydroquinone
hydrostatics
hydrotherapy
hydrothermal
hydrotropism
hygrophilous
impregnation
impressively
imprisonment
impropriator
improvidence
improvisator
inarticulate
inartificial
increasingly
incrustation
ineradicable
ineradicably
infrequently
infringement
ingratiating
inordinately
intracardiac
intracranial
intramundane
intransigent
intransitive
intrauterine
intrenchment
intriguingly
introduction
introductory
introjection
intromission
intromittent
intromitting
introversion
introversive
introvertive
intrusionist
jerrybuilder
journalistic
laureateship
macrocephaly
macropterous
marriageable
matriarchate
merrythought
metrological
metropolitan
microanalyst
microbiology
microcapsule
microcephaly
microcircuit
microclimate
microcopying
microcrystal
micrographer
microphysics
microscopist
microseismic
microsurgery
misrepresent
mitrailleuse
morrisdancer
mournfulness
mourningband
mourningring
narrowminded
necrographer
necrological
necrophagous
necrophiliac
necrophilism
necrophilous
negrophilism
negrophilist
neurasthenia
neurasthenic
neuroanatomy
neurobiology
neurological
neuropterous
neuroscience
neurosurgeon
neurosurgery
neurotically
nitrobenzene
nonresidence
nonresistant
nutritionist
nutritiously
operatically
oppressively
outrageously
outrivalling
overabundant
overachiever
overactivity
overcautious
overcritical
overcropping
overemphasis
overestimate
overexertion
overexposure
overlordship
overniceness
overpersuade
overpowering
overpressure
overreaction
oversimplify
overstepping
patriarchate
pearlescence
peerlessness
petrifaction
petrographer
petrographic
petrological
pharmaceutic
pharmacology
pluriliteral
poorspirited
prerequisite
pteridophyte
pteridosperm
pterodactyle
puerperrally
putrefaction
putrefactive
quarterbound
quarterfinal
quarterstaff
recreational
recrudescent
refractivity
refractorily
refreshingly
refreshments
refrigerator
regressively
reprehension
reprehensive
repressively
reproachable
reproachless
reproducible
reproduction
reproductive
reprographic
retractation
retractility
retrenchment
retrocedence
retrocession
retrocessive
retroflexion
retropulsion
retroversion
sabretoothed
sacrilegious
saprophagous
sarrusophone
scareheading
scarificator
scornfulness
scorpionfish
scurrilously
sharecropper
sharpshooter
sharpsighted
shirtwaister
shortchanger
shortcircuit
shortpitched
shortsighted
shortsleeved
shortstaffed
snarlingiron
Socratically
sparkingplug
sparrowgrass
spermaphytic
spermathecal
spermatocyte
spermatozoid
spermatozoon
spermogonium
sphragistics
spiritedness
spiritlessly
spiritualise
spiritualism
spiritualist
spirituality
sporadically
sporogenesis
sportfulness
sportiveness
spuriousness
starspangled
stereochromy
stereography
stereoisomer
stereometric
stereophonic
stereopticon
stereoscopic
sterlingness
sternutation
sternutative
sternutatory
sternwheeler
stertorously
stormtrooper
supramundane
supraorbital
surrealistic
surrejoinder
surroundings
tearlessness
terribleness
terrifically
terrifyingly
terrorstruck
tetrachordal
tetragonally
tetrahedrite
tetramorphic
therapeutics
therapeutist
thereinafter
thermocouple
thermography
thermolabile
thermometric
thermophilic
thermoscopic
thermosphere
thermostable
thermostatic
thermotactic
thermotropic
thirdborough
thoroughbass
thoroughbred
thoroughfare
thoroughness
torrefaction
torrentially
Torricellian
turriculated
ultramontane
ultramundane
umbrageously
unbrokenness
uncritically
unfrequented
ungracefully
ungraciously
ungratefully
unprejudiced
unpretending
unprincipled
unprofitable
unprofitably
unpronounced
untruthfully
usuriousness
uxoriousness
vibraphonist
vitreousness
vitrifaction
wherethrough
whortleberry
anastigmatic
apostolicism
apostolicity
apostrophise
aristocratic
Aristotelean
Aristotelian
bassorelievo
bassorilievo
bioscientist
biosynthesis
biosynthetic
blastfurnace
blastosphere
blastulation
blissfulness
blisteringly
blusteringly
boastfulness
boisterously
brassbounder
brassrubbing
censoriously
chastisement
chesterfield
classicalism
classicalist
classicality
classifiable
closecropped
closegrained
closemouthed
conscionable
conscription
consecration
consecratory
consensually
consentience
consentingly
consequently
conservation
conservatism
conservative
conservatory
considerable
considerably
consignation
consistently
consistorial
consociation
consolidator
conspiration
constabulary
constipation
constituency
constitution
constitutive
constriction
constrictive
constringent
construction
constructive
consultation
consultative
consummately
consummation
consummative
consummatory
cousingerman
crashlanding
crossbedding
crossbencher
crossbuttock
crosscountry
crosscurrent
crossexamine
crossgrained
crossheading
crossingover
crosspurpose
crosssection
crystalgazer
deescalation
densitometer
dessertspoon
diastrophism
dissatisfied
disseminator

dissentingly
dissertation
disseverance
disseverment
dissimilarly
dissimulator
dissocialise
dissociation
dissociative
dissuasively
dissymmetric
dorsiventral
dressinggown
earsplitting
elasmobranch
emasculation
emasculatory
episcopalian
episodically
epistemology
evisceration
exasperation
exospherical
farsightedly
firstnighter
geosynclinal
glassblowing
glossography
glossologist
goosepimples
graspingness
griseofulvin
grossularite
guestchamber
horsebreaker
horsemanship
horsetrading
horsewhipped
housebreaker
housekeeping
housetrained
housewarming
inescutcheon
inosculation
irascibility
kirschwasser
kissingcrust
laisserfaire
laissezaller
laissezfaire
lopsidedness
mansionhouse
manslaughter
Marseillaise
marshharrier
menstruation
messeigneurs
misselthrush
misstatement
moistureless
mosstrooping
nauseatingly
nauseousness
newspaperman
offscourings
onesidedness
opisthograph
opisthotonos
outstretched
outstripping
parsimonious
passepartout
passionately
passionfruit
peasepudding
perseverance
persistently
perspicacity
perspiration
perspiratory
persuasively
phosphoresce
physiognomic
physiography
physiologist
plasterboard
plesiosaurus
possessively
praseodymium
presbyterate
presbyterial
Presbyterian
prescription
prescriptive
preselection
preselective
presentation
presentative
presentiment
preservation
preservative
presidential
presumptuous
proscription
proscriptive
prosectorial
prosecutable
proselytiser
prosodically
prosopopoeia
prosperously
prostitution
pursestrings
questionable
questionably
questionless
reassessment
reassignment
reassuringly
sansculottic
sarsaparilla
seismography
seismologist
seismometric
seismoscopic
sensibleness
sensitometer
sensualistic
sensuousness
subsaturated
subscription
subsequently
subservience
subserviency
subsidiarily
subsonically
substantiate
substantival
substitution
substitutive
substruction
substructure
swashbuckler
tessellation
toastingfork
topsyturvily
trestletable
trustfulness
unassailable
unassumingly
unisexuality
waistcoating
whisperingly
worshipfully
abstemiously
abstractable
abstractedly
abstractness
abstruseness
acetabularia
acetaldehyde
aesthetician
aestheticism
amateurishly
amitotically
anathematise
anatomically
anotherguess
apothegmatic
arithmetical
Australasian
avitaminoses
avitaminosis
bactericidal
bacteriology
bacteriostat
bantamweight
battleground
battlemented
beatifically
blatherskite
bletherskate
blithesomely
bootlessness
bottlewasher
butterflynut
buttermuslin
butterscotch
Cantabrigian
cantankerous
cantharidian
cantillation
captiousness
Cartesianism
cartographer
cartographic
cartological
cattlelifter
cautiousness
centesimally
centrespread
centrosphere
centuplicate
chitterlings
clatteringly
clotheshorse
clothespress
coetaneously
contagionist
contagiously
containerise
contemplator
contemporary
contemporise
contemptible
contemptibly
contemptuous
conterminous
contestation
contextually
contiguously
contingently
continuation
continuative
continuously
contractable
contractedly
contractible
contradictor
contrapuntal
contrariness
contrariwise
contribution
contributive
contributory
contriteness
contrivement
controllable
contumacious
contumelious
costermonger
cottonocracy
criticalness
cultivatable
customshouse
denticulated
dentilingual
destructible
Deuteronomic
dextrousness
diathermancy
diatomaceous
diatonically
dictatorship
dietetically
distemperate
distillation
distillatory
distinctness
distortional
distractedly
distrainable
distrainment
distributary
distribution
distributive
disturbingly
earthshaking
ecstatically
editorialise
editorialist
emotionalise
emotionalism
emotionalist
emotionality
epithalamion
epithalamium
erythematous
erythroblast
erythromycin
esoterically
exoterically
factionalism
factiousness
factitiously
faithfulness
faithhealing
fantasticate
fantasticism
fastidiously
featherbrain
featheriness
fertilisable
fictionalise
fictitiously
filtrability
flatteringly
footplateman
forthrightly
fortuitously
fostermother
gastronomist
gastropodous
geotectonics
gesticulator
glitteringly
gluttonously
gratefulness
gratifyingly
gratuitously
grotesquerie
halterbroken
heathenishly
hectographic
histogenesis
histogenetic
histological
historically
horticulture
hysterectomy
hysterically
hysteromania
ichthyocolla
ichthyolatry
ichthyophagy
illtreatment
installation
instauration
instillation
instructress
instrumental
isothermally
lanternjawed
lanternslide
leathercloth
lefthandedly
listlessness
maltreatment
mastersinger
masterstroke
masterswitch
mastigophora
meetinghouse
meltingpoint
mirthfulness
mistakenness
mistranslate
mistreatment
mistressship
mouthbreeder
multicentral
multidentate
multifarious
multiflorous
multifoliate
multiformity
multilateral
multilingual
multiloquous
multinuclear
multipartite
multipliable
multiplicand
multiplicate
multiplicity
multipurpose
multistoried
multivalence
multiversity
multungulate
muttonheaded
mysteriously
mystifyingly
Nestorianism
noctambulant
noctambulism
noctambulist
noctambulous
noctilucence
northeastern
northernmost
Northumbrian
northwestern
nyctitropism
obstetrician
obstreperous
pantechnicon
pantisocracy
pantographic
participator
particularly
partisanship
partitionist
patternmaker
pertinacious

perturbation
perturbative
pestilential
pestological
pettifoggery
pettifogging
photochromic
photofission
photogeology
photographer
photographic
photogravure
photokinesis
photokinetic
photomontage
photophilous
photosetting
photospheric
phototropism
phytogenesis
phytogenetic
phytographer
phytological
phytophagous
pictographic
pitterpatter
platonically
Plattdeutsch
pontifically
pontificator
portentously
portmanteaus
portmanteaux
postdiluvian
postdoctoral
posteriority
postgraduate
posthumously
postmeridian
postmistress
postponement
postposition
postpositive
postprandial
pretermitted
protactinium
protectively
protectorate
protensively
protestation
prothalamion
prothalamium
prothonotary
protistology
protohistory
protoplasmic
protoplastic
prototypical
protozoology
protrusively
protuberance
quattrocento
rattleheaded
restaurateur
restlessness
restrainable
restrainedly
restrictedly
rhetorically
rhythmically
rontgenogram
rontgenology
rootlessness
scatological
scatterbrain
scatteringly
scutellation
sectarianise
sectarianism
sectionalism
sententially
septennially
septilateral
septuagenary
Septuagesima
Septuagintal
shatterproof
skateboarder
skittishness
slothfulness
sluttishness
softpedalled
southeastern
southernmost
southernwood
southwestern
spitefulness
spotlessness
stationhouse
stationwagon
statistician
statuesquely
stethoscopic
stutteringly
subtemperate
subterranean
subthreshold
suitableness
sustentation
sustentative
systematical
systematiser
systemically
tactlessness
tastefulness
tautological
tectonically
teetertotter
testamentary
testosterone
testudineous
Teutonically
thitherwards
tintinnabula
tittletattle
tortuousness
truthfulness
turtlenecked
twitteringly
unattractive
unctuousness
unitarianism
unsteadiness
unstructured
vantagepoint
ventripotent
vertebration
verticalness
verticillate
Victorianism
victoriously
virtuosoship
virtuousness
wastefulness
weatherboard
weatherbound
weatherglass
weatherhouse
weatherproof
welterweight
whitelivered
whitewashing
whitherwards
winterbourne
wrathfulness
wretchedness
xanthochroia
youthfulness
acaulescence
accumulation
accumulative
accurateness
accursedness
accusatively
accusatorial
acoustically
acquaintance
acquiescence
adjudication
adjudicative
adjudicatory
ailurophobia
allusiveness
annunciation
appurtenance
bequeathment
calumniation
calumniatory
calumniously
chauvinistic
claudication
columniation
copulatively
coquettishly
cumulatively
cumulocirrus
cumulonimbus
delusiveness
denuclearise
denunciation
denunciative
denunciatory
deputisation
desulphurise
detumescence
draughtboard
draughthorse
droughtiness
effusiveness
encumberment
encumbrancer
escutcheoned
eunuchoidism
excursionist
exsufflicate
fabulousness
figuratively
fraudulently
furunculosis
futurologist
genuflection
ghoulishness
glaucescence
glaucomatous
groundcherry
groundlessly
illumination
illuminative
illusiveness
illusoriness
illustration
illustrative
immunisation
immunologist
immutability
imputability
imputatively
inaudibility
inauguration
inauguratory
inauspicious
incurability
industrially
infundibular
infusibility
innutritious
insufferable
insufferably
insufficient
insufflation
insurrection
intuitionism
intuitionist
intumescence
intussuscept
invulnerable
invulnerably
jesuitically
liquefacient
liquefaction
liturgically
liturgiology
loquaciously
lugubriously
manufacturer
monumentally
naturalistic
naturopathic
nebulisation
nebulousness
obdurateness
obmutescence
obnubilation
occupational
oneupmanship
patulousness
pedunculated
plausibility
pneumaticity
pneumatology
pneumothorax
populousness
proudhearted
pseudocyesis
pseudonymity
pseudonymous
pseudopodium
recuperation
recuperative
reducibility
reductionism
reductionist
rejuvenation
remuneration
remunerative
remuneratory
renunciation
renunciative
renunciatory
resupination
resurrection
resuscitator
rheumatology
robustiously
salubriously
salutariness
salutational
salutiferous
scoundreldom
scoundrelism
scouringrush
scrupulosity
scrupulously
secularistic
sedulousness
sepulchrally
sequaciously
sequentially
sequestrator
shoulderbelt
shoulderknot
shouldernote
simultaneity
simultaneous
sinusoidally
slaughterous
stouthearted
structurally
thaumaturgic
thoughtfully
thousandfold
triumphantly
troublemaker
tumultuously
unauthorised
unsuccessful
valuableness
vituperation
vituperative
vituperatory
volumetrical
voluminosity
voluminously
voluntaryism
voluntaryist
voluptuosity
voluptuously
chivalrously
clavicembalo
convalescent
convectional
conveniently
conventicler
conventional
conversation
conveyancing
convincement
convincingly
conviviality
convulsively
curvicaudate
curvicostate
curvifoliate
curvirostral
flavoprotein
galvanically
galvanometer
galvanoscope
graveclothes
gravelelling
grovellingly
heavenliness
heavyhearted
malversation
marvellously
nerveracking
perverseness
perviousness
pluviometric
prevailingly
prevaricator
preventative
preventively
previousness
privatdocent
privatdozent
privateering
proverbially
providential
provincially
provisionary
pulverisable
salvationism
salvationist
serviceberry
servicecourt
servicewoman
servitorship
servocontrol
silverglance
silviculture
slaveholding
slovenliness
subversively
surveillance

surveyorship
survivorship
sylviculture
uneventfully
universalise
universalism
universalist
universality
clownishness
drawingboard
drawingpaper
enswathement
outwardbound
alexipharmic
epexegetical
inexactitude
inexpedience
inexpediency
inexperience
inexpertness
inexplicable
inexplicably
inexpressive
inexpugnable
inexpugnably
inextensible
inextricable
inextricably
quixotically
unexpectedly
bodybuilding
bodysnatcher
bodystocking
calycoideous
cotyledonary
cotyledonous
encyclopedia
encyclopedic
enzymologist
karyokinesis
labyrinthian
labyrinthine
laryngoscope
laryngoscopy
palynologist
papyrologist
playingfield
polychaetous
polychromous
polyethylene
polyglottism
polyhistoric
polymorphism
polymorphous
polyneuritic
polyneuritis
polypetalous
polyphyletic
polysepalous
polysyllabic
polysyllable
polytheistic
polytonality
polyurethane
sphygmograph
strychninism
benzaldehyde
berzelianite
katzenjammer
mezzorelievo
mezzosoprano
muzzleloader
prizefighter
prizewinning
quizzicality
razzledazzle
rhizocarpous
rhizogenetic
rhizophagous
swizzlestick

---

acciaccatura
acetabularia
acetaldehyde
achlamydeous
acquaintance
adorableness
AfroAmerican
alphabetical
alphamerical
alphanumeric
amenableness
amicableness
antiaircraft
appraisement
appraisingly
aromatically
aromaticness
attractively
avitaminoses
avitaminosis
balladmonger
bantamweight
barbarically
beggarliness
benzaldehyde
bilharziasis
bilharziosis
blamableness
buccaneering
buccaneerish
buffalograss
bureaucratic
cabbagewhite
calcareously
Cantabrigian
cantankerous
carragheenin
cashandcarry
characterise
chivalrously
coetaneously
collaborator
collaterally
commandingly
companionate
companionway
compatriotic
confabulator
connaturally
contagionist
contagiously
containerise
convalescent
courageously
culpableness
cuprammonium
deflagration
deflationary
deflationist
defraudation
depravedness
dermatophyte
despairingly
deviationism
deviationist
diamagnetism
dibranchiate
dictatorship
disdainfully
disharmonise
dissatisfied
dogmatically
dramatically
dramaturgist
ecstatically
educationist
emblazonment
embranchment
emphatically
enchantingly
enswathement
entrammelled
entrancement
enviableness
estrangement
EuroAmerican
exchangeable
explantation
extracranial
extraditable
extralimital
extramarital
extramundane
extraneously
extrasensory
extraspecial
extrauterine
extravagance
extravagancy
extravaganza
extraversion
fallaciously
fantasticate
fantasticism
formaldehyde
fricasseeing
galvanically
galvanometer
galvanoscope
genealogical
geomagnetism
geriatrician
Germanophile
Germanophobe
gregariously
guaranteeing
haematoblast
haematolysis
haematoxylon
hierarchical
idolatrously
illnaturedly
immeasurable
immeasurably
implantation
inelasticity
ineradicable
ineradicably
inexactitude
inflammation
inflammatory
inflationary
inflationism
inflationist
ingratiating
installation
instauration
intracardiac
intracranial
intramundane
intransigent
intransitive
intrauterine
Ishmaelitish
isolationism
isolationist
laudableness
loquaciously
mechanically
mediaevalism
mediaevalist
mendaciously
mercantilism
mercantilist
miscalculate
mistakenness
mitrailleuse
mordaciously
moveableness
neoDarwinian
neoDarwinism
neoDarwinist
nephanalysis
neurasthenia
neurasthenic
newfashioned
noctambulant
noctambulism
noctambulist
noctambulous
oldfashioned
oligarchical
onomatopoeia
onomatopoeic
operatically
outdatedness
outlandishly
outmanoeuvre
outrageously
outwardbound
overabundant
overachiever
overactivity
Palladianism
peccadilloes
permanganate
philadelphus
philanthrope
philanthropy
phonasthenia
phreatophyte
pitiableness
precancelled
precariously
prefabricate
prelapsarian
premaxillary
preparedness
prevailingly
prevaricator
privatdocent
privatdozent
privateering
probationary
procathedral
propaedeutic
propagandise
propagandism
propagandist
protactinium
pugnaciously
readableness
rechargeable
reflationary
refractivity
refractorily
reliableness
restaurateur
retractation
retractility
salvationism
salvationist
sarsaparilla
sectarianise
sectarianism
selfabsorbed
selfactivity
selfaffected
selfanalysis
selfapplause
selfapproval
semiannually
sequaciously
shamateurism
sociableness
Socratically
somnambulant
somnambulate
somnambulism
somnambulist
sphragistics
sporadically
stalactiform
steganograph
sublapsarian
submaxillary
subsaturated
suitableness
supramundane
supraorbital
syllabically
syndactylism
syndactylous
testamentary
tetrachordal
tetragonally
tetrahedrite
tetramorphic
thematically
therapeutics
therapeutist
tridactylous
tripartitely
tripartition
ultramontane
ultramundane
umbrageously
unchangeable
unchangeably
uncharitable
uncharitably
unclassified
unflattering
ungracefully
ungraciously
ungratefully
unilaterally
unimaginable
unimaginably
unitarianism
unreasonable
unreasonably
unsearchable
unseasonable
uproariously
valuableness
vantagepoint
variableness
vernacularly
vibraphonist
villainously
voidableness
volcanically
wollastonite
workableness
agribusiness
assibilation
backbreaking
bellbottomed
blabbermouth
bodybuilding
brambleberry
cohabitation
deambulatory
deliberately
deliberation
deliberative
disobedience
exhibitioner
exorbitantly
filibusterer
flamboyantly
forebodement
forebodingly

illi**b**erality
inde**b**tedness
inha**b**itation
lugu**b**riously
nono**b**jective
obnu**b**ilation
para**b**oloidal
phle**b**otomise
phle**b**otomist
plum**b**aginous
plum**b**iferous
pres**b**yterate
pres**b**yterial
Pres**b**yterian
reha**b**ilitate
rhom**b**ohedral
rhom**b**ohedron
salu**b**riously
scab**b**ardfish
scro**b**iculate
self**b**egotten
self**b**etrayal
semi**b**asement
ship**b**uilding
snob**b**ishness
stil**b**oestrol
stro**b**ilation
stro**b**oscopic
stub**b**ornness
tere**b**inthine
thim**b**leberry
trou**b**lemaker
unam**b**ivalent
voca**b**ularian
adje**c**tivally
affe**c**tedness
affe**c**tionate
agri**c**ultural
ante**c**edently
anti**c**ipation
anti**c**ipative
anti**c**ipatory
anti**c**lerical
anti**c**yclonic
aqui**c**ultural
arti**c**ulately
arti**c**ulation
arti**c**ulatory
asyn**c**hronism
asyn**c**hronous
auto**c**atalyse
auto**c**hthones
bioe**c**ologist
bios**c**ientist
bree**c**hloader
bron**c**hoscope
bron**c**obuster
caly**c**oideous
card**c**arrying
cari**c**aturist
cata**c**hrestic
cate**c**hetical
chal**c**olithic
chal**c**opyrite
chan**c**emedley
chur**c**hianity
chur**c**hwarden
coer**c**iveness
coin**c**idental
coin**c**idently
cons**c**ionable
cons**c**ription
coun**c**ilwoman
cyno**c**ephalus
dees**c**alation
deje**c**tedness
deli**c**atessen
denu**c**learise
dera**c**ination
deta**c**hedness
dida**c**tically
dire**c**torship
disa**c**charide
dode**c**ahedral
dode**c**ahedron
dode**c**aphonic
dove**c**oloured
ecle**c**tically
edul**c**oration
effe**c**tuality
effe**c**tuation
eman**c**ipation
emas**c**ulation
emas**c**ulatory
ency**c**lopedia
ency**c**lopedic
endo**c**arditis
epis**c**opalian
eunu**c**hoidism
evis**c**eration
exer**c**itation
exul**c**eration
feli**c**itation
feli**c**itously
floc**c**ulation
Fran**c**oGerman
fren**c**hpolish
gala**c**togogue
glau**c**escence
glau**c**omatous
hemi**c**hordate
high**c**oloured
hypo**c**hlorite
hypo**c**hondria
hypo**c**oristic
hypo**c**ritical
imma**c**ulately
inac**c**essible
inac**c**essibly
inac**c**urately
inde**c**isively
inde**c**linable
inde**c**orously
indi**c**atively
indo**c**trinate
ines**c**utcheon
infe**c**tiously
inoc**c**upation
inos**c**ulation
inse**c**ticidal
iras**c**ibility
kirs**c**hwasser
lati**c**iferous
lexi**c**ography
lexi**c**ologist
mala**c**ologist
Mani**c**heanism
meso**c**ephalic
meta**c**hronism
meti**c**ulously
mini**c**omputer
mira**c**ulously
mito**c**hondria
mole**c**ularity
mono**c**hromate
muni**c**ipalise
muni**c**ipality
musi**c**ianship
musi**c**ologist
offi**c**eholder
offs**c**ourings
orbi**c**ularity
over**c**autious
over**c**ritical
over**c**ropping
oxya**c**etylene
paro**c**hialise
paro**c**hialism
paro**c**hiality
pedi**c**ellaria
peri**c**arditis
poli**c**yholder
poly**c**haetous
poly**c**hromous
preo**c**cupancy
pres**c**ription
pres**c**riptive
prin**c**eliness
prin**c**ipality
pros**c**ription
pros**c**riptive
rede**c**oration
redu**c**ibility
redu**c**tionism
redu**c**tionist
reje**c**tamenta
reo**c**cupation
reti**c**ulately
reti**c**ulation
reti**c**ulocyte
revi**c**tualled
rhyn**c**hophora
rico**c**hetting
ridi**c**ulously
rose**c**oloured
safe**c**racking
sans**c**ulottic
self**c**atering
self**c**oloured
self**c**omposed
self**c**ontempt
self**c**ritical
semi**c**ircular
semi**c**ylinder
seri**c**ultural
sili**c**icolous
sili**c**iferous
slip**c**arriage
soli**c**itation
soli**c**itously
spee**c**hlessly
step**c**hildren
stru**c**turally
stry**c**hninism
subs**c**ription
theo**c**ratical
toxi**c**ologist
toxi**c**ophobia
unac**c**eptable
unac**c**ustomed
unbe**c**omingly
unen**c**umbered
unre**c**ognised
unsu**c**cessful
vari**c**oloured
vati**c**ination
vesi**c**ulation
vice**c**hairman
when**c**esoever
wret**c**hedness
acci**d**entally
adju**d**ication
adju**d**icative
adju**d**icatory
aero**d**ynamics
ambi**d**extrous
amyg**d**aloidal
anec**d**otalist
ante**d**iluvian
arch**d**eaconry
arch**d**iocesan
auto**d**idactic
basi**d**iospore
blad**d**erwrack
blan**d**ishment
bloo**d**brother
bloo**d**letting
bloo**d**stained
bloo**d**thirsty
bloo**d**yminded
blun**d**eringly
bomb**d**isposal
chil**d**bearing
chil**d**ishness
chon**d**riosome
clau**d**ication
coni**d**iophore
coni**d**iospore
coor**d**inately
coor**d**ination
coor**d**inative
demo**d**ulation
desi**d**eration
desi**d**erative
disa**d**vantage
drea**d**fulness
equi**d**istance
expe**d**iential
fiel**d**glasses
fien**d**ishness
floo**d**lighted
flui**d**isation
foun**d**ationer
frau**d**ulently
gona**d**otropic
gona**d**otropin
guar**d**ianship
hair**d**ressing
here**d**itament
here**d**itarily
holi**d**aymaker
illa**d**visedly
immo**d**erately
immo**d**eration
impe**d**imental
inau**d**ibility
inci**d**entally
inor**d**inately
irre**d**eemable
irre**d**eemably
lake**d**welling
lepi**d**opteran
libi**d**inously
long**d**istance
melo**d**ramatic
meri**d**ionally
mine**d**etector
misa**d**venture
mise**d**ucation
mona**d**elphous
mono**d**ramatic
name**d**ropping
noni**d**entical
nora**d**renalin
occi**d**entally
para**d**igmatic
para**d**isaical
para**d**isiacal
pera**d**venture
post**d**iluvian
post**d**octoral
prou**d**hearted
pseu**d**ocyesis
pseu**d**onymity
pseu**d**onymous
pseu**d**opodium
resi**d**entiary
resi**d**entship
scan**d**alously
Scan**d**inavian
self**d**eceived
self**d**eceiver
self**d**elusion
self**d**estruct
self**d**evotion
self**d**irected
self**d**istrust
self**d**oubting
semi**d**arkness
semi**d**eponent
semi**d**etached
semi**d**iameter
semi**d**omestic
slan**d**erously
soun**d**ingline
spee**d**boating
stan**d**ardbred
stan**d**ingroom
step**d**aughter
Stra**d**ivarius
stri**d**ulation
stud**d**ingsail
sube**d**itorial
thir**d**borough
thun**d**ercloud
thun**d**eringly
thun**d**erously
thun**d**erstone
thun**d**erstorm
vaso**d**ilation
vaso**d**ilatory
veri**d**icality
viri**d**escence
well**d**isposed
abbr**e**viation
abst**e**miously
acad**e**mically
accr**e**tionary
aero**e**mbolism
afor**e**thought
aggr**e**ssively
alim**e**ntation
alim**e**ntative
amat**e**urishly
anth**e**lmintic
appr**e**ciation
appr**e**ciative
appr**e**ciatory
appr**e**hension
appr**e**hensive
arch**e**typally
arch**e**typical
athl**e**tically
augm**e**ntation
augm**e**ntative
auth**e**nticate
auth**e**nticity
bach**e**lorhood
bach**e**lorship
bact**e**ricidal
bact**e**riology
bact**e**riostat
ball**e**tomania
band**e**rillero
bell**e**tristic
bequ**e**athment
berz**e**lianite
bese**e**chingly
besp**e**ctacled
biog**e**ography
biom**e**trician
blam**e**fulness
bonn**e**tmonkey
boul**e**vardier
brok**e**nwinded
bull**e**theaded
butt**e**rflynut
butt**e**rmuslin
butt**e**rscotch
canc**e**llation
carp**e**tbagger
carp**e**tknight
Cart**e**sianism
cent**e**simally
chor**e**ography

closecropped
closegrained
closemouthed
coacervation
coelenterate
collectively
collectivise
collectivism
collectivist
collectivity
collegialism
collegiality
collegiately
commemorator
commencement
commendation
commendatory
commensalism
commensalist
commensurate
commentation
commercially
compellation
compensation
compensative
compensatory
concelebrant
concelebrate
concentrator
conceptional
conceptually
condemnation
condemnatory
condensation
confectioner
conferential
confessional
congeniality
congenitally
connectional
connectively
consecration
consecratory
consensually
consentience
consentingly
consequently
conservation
conservatism
conservative
conservatory
contemplator
contemporary
contemporise
contemptible
contemptibly
contemptuous
conterminous
contestation
contextually
convectional
conveniently
conventicler
conventional
conversation
conveyancing
coquettishly
correctional
correctitude
correctively
cosmetically
costermonger
crenellation
cumbersomely
decreasingly
depreciation
depreciatory
depressingly
dessertspoon
Deuteronomic
diageotropic
dialectician
dialectology
dietetically
differentiae
differential
digressional
digressively
dinnerjacket
discerningly
discerptible
dishevelment
dispensation
dispensatory
disregardful
disreputable
disreputably
disseminator
dissentingly
dissertation
disseverance
disseverment
distemperate
dunderheaded
ecclesiastic
ecclesiology
elementalism
elementarily
emblematical
empressement
enfeeblement
entreatingly
entrenchment
entrepreneur
epexegetical
epidemically
epidemiology
esoterically
evanescently
evidentially
exacerbation
exegetically
exoterically
expressional
expressively
expressivity
fatherfigure
fatherliness
fermentation
fermentative
flabelliform
flagellation
flagellatory
flamethrower
forcefulness
fostermother
frenetically
geometrician
geotectonics
globetrotter
goosepimples
gorgeousness
gracefulness
gratefulness
graveclothes
gravelelling
griseofulvin
grotesquerie
grovellingly
guilefulness
gynaecocracy
halterbroken
happenstance
harlequinade
heavenliness
hedgehopping
henceforward
hermeneutics
hermetically
herpetologic
hesperididia
homoeopathic
homoeostasis
horrendously
horsebreaker
horsemanship
horsetrading
horsewhipped
housebreaker
housekeeping
housetrained
housewarming
huggermugger
hygienically
hysterectomy
hysterically
hysteromania
impregnation
impressively
inadequately
increasingly
IndoEuropean
inflectional
infrequently
inoperculate
inspectorate
inspectorial
intrenchment
judgematical
katzenjammer
Keynesianism
kinaesthesia
kinaesthesis
kinaesthetic
kindergarten
lanternjawed
lanternslide
largehearted
laureateship
ledgertackle
licketysplit
liquefacient
liquefaction
lumberjacket
magnetically
magnetisable
magnetograph
magnetometer
maidenliness
maidenstakes
malleability
malversation
mangelwurzel
mannerliness
manoeuvrable
marketgarden
marketsquare
Marseillaise
marvellously
mastersinger
masterstroke
masterswitch
mathematical
messeigneurs
millesimally
misbehaviour
miscellanist
misdemeanant
misdemeanour
misrepresent
misselthrush
monkeyflower
monkeyjacket
monkeypuzzle
monkeywrench
motherfigure
motherliness
mothertongue
myrmecophily
mysteriously
nauseatingly
nauseousness
neglectfully
Neohellenism
nephelometer
nephelometry
nerveracking
nonresidence
nonresistant
obstetrician
oppressively
orchestrator
outpensioner
overemphasis
overestimate
overexertion
overexposure
palaeobotany
palaeography
Palaeolithic
panhellenism
pantechnicon
paraesthesia
passepartout
pathetically
patternmaker
peacefulness
peasepudding
perceptively
perceptivity
perceptually
perfectively
perfervidity
permeability
perpetration
perpetuation
perseverance
perverseness
phanerogamic
phonemically
phonetically
pickerelweed
pigmentation
pinfeathered
pitterpatter
placesetting
planetesimal
planetstruck
polyethylene
porcelainise
porcelainous
porcellanous
portentously
possessively
posteriority
praseodymium
precedential
preceptorial
precessional
predesignate
predestinate
predetermine
prefectorial
preferential
prehensility
premeditated
premeditator
premenstrual
prerequisite
preselection
preselective
presentation
presentative
presentiment
preservation
preservative
pretermitted
preventative
preventively
pricecutting
pridefulness
prizefighter
prizewinning
processional
professional
professorate
professoress
professorial
progenitress
progesterone
projectional
projectively
prolegomenon
prosectorial
prosecutable
proselytiser
protectively
protectorate
protensively
protestation
proverbially
prudentially
pulverisable
pumpernickel
pursestrings
putrefaction
putrefactive
pyroelectric
racketeering
recreational
reflectional
reflectively
reflectivity
refreshingly
refreshments
regressively
reprehension
reprehensive
repressively
respectfully
respectively
retrenchment
sabretoothed
scareheading
scenepainter
sceneshifter
screenwriter
scutellation
sedgewarbler
segmentation
selfeducated
selfeffacing
selfelective
selfemployed
selfevidence
selfexistent
sententially
septennially
sequentially
sequestrator
sergeantfish
sergeantship
serjeantship
serpentiform
serpentinely
sexcentenary
shamefacedly
shamefulness
sharecropper
silverglance
skateboarder
slaveholding
slovenliness
snakecharmer
sorbefacient

speleologist
spidermonkey
spitefulness
spokesperson
stagemanager
stereochromy
stereography
stereoisomer
stereometric
stereophonic
stereopticon
stereoscopic
stoneboiling
stonecutting
stonedresser
stonemasonry
streetwalker
stupefacient
stupefaction
stupefactive
stupendously
subcelestial
subjectively
subjectivise
subjectivism
subjectivist
subjectivity
subsequently
subservience
subserviency
subtemperate
subterranean
subversively
succedaneous
successfully
successional
successively
suggestively
surrealistic
surrejoinder
surveillance
surveyorship
susceptivity
suspensively
sustentation
sustentative
synaesthesia
synaesthetic
syndetically
systematical
systematiser
systemically
tangentially
tastefulness
teetertotter
telaesthesia
telaesthetic
tercentenary
tessellation
thereinafter
threequarter
threewheeler
torrefaction
torrentially
traceability
tradescantia
tradespeople
tremendously
tricentenary
turbellarian
uneventfully
unfrequented
unisexuality
universalise
universalism
universalist
universality
unpleasantly
unprejudiced
unpretending
unsteadiness
unwieldiness
unyieldingly
vengefulness
vertebration
viscerotonic
vitreousness
wastefulness
welterweight
wherethrough
whitelivered
whitewashing
wholehearted
wicketkeeper
winterbourne
wonderstruck
wonderworker
woodengraver
woodenheaded
wunderkinder
YankeeDoodle
zoogeography
artificially
benefactress
beneficently
beneficially
birefringent
bullfighting
campfollower
chieftainess
cliffhanging
cockfighting
codification
decaffeinate
disaffection
disaffiliate
dwarfishness
exsufflicate
firefighting
gasification
genuflection
hardfavoured
hardfeatured
highfaluting
humification
indefeasible
indefeasibly
indefectible
indefensible
indefensibly
indefinitely
indifference
indifferency
ineffaceable
ineffaceably
inefficiency
insufferable
insufferably
insufficient
insufflation
irreflective
irreformable
irrefragable
irrefragably
leapfrogging
manifoldness
manufacturer
modification
modificatory
monofilament
munificently
nidification
noneffective
nonefficient
notification
ossification
pacification
pacificatory
panification
proofreading
purification
purificatory
ramification
ratification
selfflattery
semifinalist
semifinished
shuffleboard
snapfastener
sodafountain
solifluction
staffofficer
staffsurgeon
surefootedly
thriftlessly
typefounding
typification
unaffectedly
unofficially
verification
verificatory
vilification
vinification
vivification
vociferation
vociferously
wellfavoured
amalgamation
amalgamative
antagonistic
antigenicity
antigropelos
clangorously
cytogenetics
delightfully
derogatorily
disagreeable
disagreeably
disagreement
draughtboard
draughthorse
droughtiness
emargination
espagnolette
evangelistic
exaggeration
exaggerative
exaggeratory
excogitation
excogitative
frangibility
freightliner
fuliginosity
halogenation
hellgrammite
hypogastrium
hypognathous
illegibility
illegitimacy
illegitimate
illogicality
inauguration
inauguratory
incognisable
incognisance
incognitable
indigenously
indigestible
IndoGermanic
integumental
invagination
invigilation
invigoration
irregardless
irregularity
loungelizard
metagalactic
monographist
navigability
navigational
nonagenarian
obligatorily
obligingness
octogenarian
paragraphist
peregrinator
polyglottism
postgraduate
priggishness
recognisable
recognisably
recognisance
renegotiable
resignedness
rontgenogram
rontgenology
sexagenarian
slaughterous
sledgehammer
sluggishness
snaggletooth
sphygmograph
spiegeleisen
sprightfully
staggeringly
swaggeringly
swaggerstick
telegraphese
telegraphist
thoughtfully
triggerhappy
unregenerate
unsegregated
vainglorious
wellgrounded
wineglassful
woolgatherer
wrongfulness
youngberries
aesthetician
aestheticism
anaphylactic
anathematise
annihilation
annihilative
anotherguess
apochromatic
apothegmatic
arithmetical
bacchanalian
beachcombing
biochemistry
biophysicist
blatherskite
bletherskate
blithesomely
brachydactyl
bullheadedly
cantharidian
clotheshorse
clothespress
coachbuilder
conchiferous
conchologist
crashlanding
Czechoslovak
diaphanously
diathermancy
earthshaking
epiphenomena
epithalamion
epithalamium
erythematous
erythroblast
erythromycin
exophthalmic
exophthalmos
exophthalmus
faithfulness
faithhealing
featherbrain
featheriness
forthrightly
geochemistry
geophysicist
glyphography
goodhumoured
graphologist
heathenishly
highhandedly
ichthyocolla
ichthyolatry
ichthyophagy
incoherently
indehiscence
isochromatic
isochronally
isothermally
knightterrant
knightliness
leathercloth
lefthandedly
LowChurchman
marshharrier
merchantable
mirthfulness
morphallaxis
morphologist
mouthbreeder
neighbouring
nonchalantly
northeastern
northernmost
Northumbrian
northwestern
nympholeptic
nymphomaniac
openhandedly
panchromatic
philharmonic
philhellenic
pitcherplant
polyhistoric
posthumously
prechristian
prophylactic
prothalamion
prothalamium
prothonotary
psephologist
psychiatrist
psychoactive
psychography
psychologise
psychologism
psychologist
psychometric
psychopathic
psychosexual
psychotropic
psychrometer
psychrometry
punchingball
rhythmically
saccharinity
saccharoidal
selfhypnosis
slothfulness
southeastern
southernmost
southernwood
southwestern
Stakhanovism
Stakhanovite
stethoscopic

stichomythia
stichomythic
subthreshold
sulphonamide
sulphonation
sulphuration
sulphuretted
swashbuckler
synchronical
synchroniser
teachability
thitherwards
timehonoured
touchingness
trachomatous
trephination
trichologist
trichotomise
trichotomous
trichromatic
triphthongal
trochanteric
trophallaxis
truthfulness
warehouseman
watchfulness
weatherboard
weatherbound
weatherglass
weatherhouse
weatherproof
whitherwards
worshipfully
wrathfulness
xanthochroia
youthfulness
abolitionary
abolitionism
abolitionist
aboriginally
acquiescence
adscititious
alexipharmic
amelioration
ameliorative
amphibiously
amphibrachic
amphictyonic
amphisbaenic
amphitheatre
amphitropous
aperiodicity
apolitically
archipelagic
architecture
astringently
attributable
auspiciously
autoimmunity
avariciously
beatifically
belligerence
belligerency
bibliography
bibliologist
bibliomaniac
bibliopegist
bibliophilic
bibliopolist
bibliothecae
billingsgate
boogiewoogie
bookingclerk
burningglass
cachinnation
cachinnatory
calligrapher
calligraphic
callisthenic
cantillation
capriciously
captiousness
carcinogenic
cardinalship
cardiography
cardiologist
carriageable
cautiousness
clarinettist
clavicembalo
coalitionist
collinearity
combinations
commiserator
commissarial
commissariat
commissioner
committeeman
conciliation
conciliative
conciliatory
confidential
confirmation
confirmative
confirmatory
confiscation
confiscatory
conningtower
considerable
considerably
consignation
consistently
consistorial
contiguously
contingently
continuation
continuative
continuously
convincement
convincingly
conviviality
cousingerman
craniologist
criticalness
cuckingstool
cultivatable
curlingirons
curlingtongs
curvicaudate
curvicostate
curvifoliate
curvirostral
declinometer
densitometer
denticulated
dentilingual
despitefully
discipleship
disciplinary
dispiritedly
dissimilarly
dissimulator
distillation
distillatory
distinctness
dorsiventral
drawingboard
drawingpaper
duckingstool
emotionalise
emotionalism
emotionalist
emotionality
empoisonment
enclitically
Englishwoman
eveningdress
explicitness
factionalism
factiousness
factitiously
fancifulness
farsightedly
fastidiously
fertilisable
fibrillation
fibrinolysin
fictionalise
fictitiously
flagitiously
floriculture
folliculated
forbiddingly
forcibleness
galligaskins
gallinaceous
gesticulator
glaciologist
gladiatorial
gloriousness
graciousness
graminaceous
gratifyingly
handicapping
hereinbefore
heroicalness
heroicomical
horribleness
horrifically
horticulture
hybridisable
implicitness
imprisonment
inclinometer
infringement
inspissation
instillation
intriguingly
intuitionism
intuitionist
inveiglement
isodiametric
jesuitically
kaleidoscope
kinnikinnick
kissingcrust
landingcraft
landingfield
landingstage
landingstrip
lasciviously
lodginghouse
longitudinal
lopsidedness
lusciousness
machicolated
magnifically
magnificence
magniloquent
mansionhouse
Marcionitism
marlinespike
marriageable
mastigophora
matriarchate
meaningfully
meetinghouse
meltingpoint
mercifulness
milliammeter
misdirection
morningdress
morrisdancer
mulligatawny
multicentral
multidentate
multifarious
multiflorous
multifoliate
multiformity
multilateral
multilingual
multiloquous
multinuclear
multipartite
multipliable
multiplicand
multiplicate
multiplicity
multipurpose
multistoried
multivalence
multiversity
mystifyingly
narcissistic
noctilucence
nutritionist
nutritiously
nyctitropism
obedientiary
onesidedness
opinionative
orchidaceous
outrivalling
pantisocracy
parkinsonism
parsimonious
participator
particularly
partisanship
partitionist
passionately
passionfruit
patriarchate
perfidiously
permissively
permittivity
perniciously
persistently
pertinacious
perviousness
pestilential
petrifaction
pettifoggery
pettifogging
philistinism
physiognomic
physiography
physiologist
pisciculture
planispheric
playingfield
plebiscitary
plenipotence
plesiosaurus
pluriliteral
pluviometric
poikilotherm
pontifically
pontificator
preciousness
precipitable
precipitance
precipitancy
precipitator
precisianism
precisionist
predictively
predigestion
predilection
prehistorian
presidential
previousness
primigravida
prodigiously
proficiently
profiteering
prolifically
prolificness
propitiation
propitiatory
propitiously
protistology
providential
provincially
provisionary
pteridophyte
pteridosperm
publicspirit
rabbinically
receivership
refrigerator
reunionistic
rollingstock
runningboard
sacrilegious
salpiglossis
scarificator
sectionalism
selfidentity
selfignition
selfinterest
selfinvolved
sellingplate
sempiternity
sensibleness
sensitometer
septilateral
serviceberry
servicecourt
servicewoman
servitorship
significance
significancy
silviculture
somniloquism
somniloquist
sophisticate
spaciousness
specialistic
specifically
specificness
speciousness
spiritedness
spiritlessly
spiritualise
spiritualism
spiritualist
spirituality
spuriousness
stationhouse
stationwagon
statistician
straightaway
straightbred
straightedge
straightener
straightness
straitjacket
studiousness
subdivisible
subminiature
submissively
subsidiarily
succinctness
sufficiently
survivorship
suspiciously
sylviculture
tangibleness
tergiversate
terribleness
terrifically
terrifyingly
tintinnabula

Torricellian
traditionary
traditionist
tragicomical
turriculated
unblinkingly
unchivalrous
uncritically
unfaithfully
ungainliness
unprincipled
unscientific
unthinkingly
usuriousness
uxoriousness
vermiculated
verticalness
verticillate
vindictively
vitrifaction
walkietalkie
Wellingtonia
williewaught
windingsheet
workingclass
xiphisternum
readjustment
blackbirding
blackcurrant
blackguardly
blockbusting
brackishness
breakthrough
brickfielder
brinkmanship
camiknickers
checkerberry
checkerboard
clinkerbuilt
crackbrained
flickeringly
frankincense
freakishness
glockenspiel
handkerchief
skunkcabbage
sparkingplug
speakingtube
specktioneer
stockbreeder
stockbroking
stockingless
stockjobbery
stockjobbing
stockraising
strikingness
thankfulness
thanksgiving
thickskinned
thickskulled
trickishness
unlikelihood
unlikeliness
absoluteness
absolutistic
acaulescence
acceleration
accelerative
alkalescence
argillaceous
artilleryman
availability
baselessness
battleground
battlemented
bewilderedly
bewilderment
booklearning
bootlessness
bottlewasher
brilliantine
burglarproof
canaliculate
canalisation
candleholder
carelessness
carillonneur
catilinarian
cattlelifter
chaplainship
charlatanism
churlishness
civilisation
complacently
complaisance
complemental
completeness
complexional
complexioned
complication
conclusively
conglobation
conglomerate
conglutinate
copolymerise
copulatively
corelatively
cotyledonary
cotyledonous
cumulatively
cumulocirrus
cumulonimbus
debilitation
decalescence
deceleration
demilitarise
depoliticise
desalination
desolateness
desulphurise
disallowance
disclamation
displaceable
displacement
displeasedly
doubleacting
doubledealer
doubledecked
doubledecker
doublelocked
duraluminium
echolocation
equalisation
equalitarian
equilibrator
exhilaration
exhilarative
fabulousness
facelessness
facilitation
fearlessness
fecklessness
feebleminded
fiddlefaddle
fiddlesticks
finalisation
focalisation
formlessness
futilitarian
ganglionated
gesellschaft
ghoulishness
gobbledegook
gobbledygook
grallatorial
habilitation
harmlessness
heedlessness
helplessness
heraldically
highlystrung
homologation
hopelessness
hubblebubble
hucklebacked
idealisation
impoliteness
incalculable
incalculably
incalescence
indelibility
indelicately
infelicitous
insalubrious
insolubilise
insolubility
intellection
intellective
intellectual
intelligence
intelligible
intelligibly
intolerantly
invalidation
involutional
invulnerable
invulnerably
irrelatively
irrelevantly
kremlinology
landlubberly
legalisation
lifelessness
listlessness
localisation
lovelessness
lovelornness
manslaughter
megalomaniac
metalanguage
metallically
metallophone
metallurgist
metalworking
middleweight
mindlessness
misalignment
misplacement
mobilisation
moralisation
movelessness
mucilaginous
muddleheaded
muzzleloader
namelessness
nebulisation
nebulousness
needlessness
neoclassical
Neoplatonism
Neoplatonist
nonalignment
nonflammable
nonflowering
novelisation
obsolescence
obsoleteness
oscillograph
oscilloscope
overlordship
painlessness
parallelling
paralysation
patulousness
pearlescence
peerlessness
penalisation
perilousness
perplexingly
phillumenist
phyllotactic
pitilessness
populousness
pralltriller
preclassical
preclusively
proclamation
proclamatory
profligately
proglottides
purblindness
pyroligneous
rabblerouser
rattleheaded
razzledazzle
reallocation
rebelliously
recalcitrant
recalcitrate
recalescence
recklessness
recollection
recollective
remilitarise
resoluteness
resolvedness
resplendence
resplendency
restlessness
revelational
rootlessness
rumbletumble
ruralisation
ruthlessness
saddlebacked
secularistic
sedulousness
selflessness
selflimiting
selfluminous
semiliterate
sepulchrally
shillyshally
shoulderbelt
shoulderknot
shouldernote
simpleminded
simultaneity
simultaneous
singleacting
singledecker
singlehanded
singleminded
singleseater
skullduggery
smallclothes
smallholding
snarlingiron
soullessness
spotlessness
stablishment
stealthiness
stellenbosch
stelliferous
sterlingness
stillhunting
subalternate
subalternity
supplemental
supplementer
supplicantly
supplication
supplicatory
tactlessness
tamelessness
tearlessness
ticklishness
timelessness
tirelessness
tittletattle
toggleswitch
tonelessness
totalisation
totalitarian
triglyphical
triplication
troglodytism
tumultuously
tunelessness
turtlenecked
unbelievable
unbelievably
uncalculated
uncelebrated
vitalisation
vitiligation
vocalisation
winklepicker
woollyheaded
accommodator
accompanyist
accomplished
accumulation
accumulative
Alhambresque
allomorphism
antimacassar
antimagnetic
antimalarial
assimilation
assimilative
assimilatory
asymmetrical
automaticity
automobilist
automorphism
barometrical
calamitously
calumniation
calumniatory
calumniously
catamountain
ceremonially
chrematistic
chromaticism
chromaticity
chromatogram
chromatology
chromatopsia
chromosphere
cinematheque
columniation
decomposable
decompressor
delamination
delimitation
demimondaine
denomination
denominative
detumescence
disambiguate
disembarrass
dynamometric
effeminately
elasmobranch
eleemosynary
encumberment
encumbrancer
endamagement
endometritis
enormousness
entomologise
entomologist
enzymologist
ephemerality

euhemeristic
flammability
foraminifera
grammaticise
grammolecule
gyromagnetic
headmistress
hemimorphism
hemimorphite
homomorphism
homomorphous
hoodmanblind
illumination
illuminative
immemorially
inadmissible
inadmissibly
incommodious
incommutable
incommutably
incomparable
incomparably
incompatible
incompatibly
incompetence
incompetency
incompletely
incompliance
incomputable
insemination
intemperance
intimidation
intimidatory
intumescence
irremediable
irremediably
irremissible
mademoiselle
manometrical
maximisation
metamorphism
metamorphose
minimisation
monomaniacal
monometallic
monomorphous
monumentally
openmindedly
optimisation
ornamentally
paramagnetic
parametrical
paramilitary
paramorphism
perambulator
peremptorily
pharmaceutic
pharmacology
pleomorphism
plummerblock
pneumaticity
pneumatology
pneumothorax
polymorphism
polymorphous
portmanteaus
portmanteaux
postmeridian
postmistress
pragmatistic
preeminently
pyromaniacal
pyromorphite
qualmishness
racemisation
recommitment
redemptioner
Redemptorist
regimentally
rememberable
remembrancer
rheumatology
salamandrian
salamandrine
salamandroid
scrimshanker
seismography
seismologist
seismometric
seismoscopic
selfmurderer
skrimshanker
spermaphytic
spermathecal
spermatocyte
spermatozoid
spermatozoon
spermogonium
stammeringly
stormtrooper
swimmingbath
swimmingbell
swimmingpool
taskmistress
thaumaturgic
thermocouple
thermography
thermolabile
thermometric
thermophilic
thermoscopic
thermosphere
thermostable
thermostatic
thermotactic
thermotropic
triumphantly
uncomeatable
uncommercial
uncommonness
undemocratic
unfamiliarly
untimeliness
venomousness
volumetrical
voluminosity
voluminously
whigmaleerie
zygomorphism
zygomorphous
absentminded
accentuation
acronychally
actinomycete
administrant
administrate
admonishment
advantageous
adventitious
aeronautical
aeroneurosis
agranulocyte
annunciation
antineutrino
appendectomy
appendicitis
appendicular
astonishment
autonomously
bicentennial
bilingualism
brainstormer
brainwashing
businesslike
cabinetmaker
canonisation
cementitious
charnelhouse
chimneypiece
chronography
chronologise
chronologist
chronometric
clannishness
clownishness
colonisation
debonairness
decentralise
decongestant
decongestion
decongestive
deconsecrate
decontrolled
definiteness
definitively
degenerately
degeneration
degenerative
deionisation
delinquently
demineralise
demoniacally
demonstrable
demonstrably
demonstrator
denunciation
denunciative
denunciatory
diminishable
diminishment
diminutively
disannulling
disannulment
disenchanter
disendowment
disincentive
disinfectant
disinfection
disinflation
disingenuous
disintegrate
disinterment
eccentricity
echinococcus
endangerment
enginedriver
enginetuning
entanglement
essentiality
expansionary
expansionism
expansionist
exsanguinate
exsanguinous
extensometer
extinguisher
feminineness
feminisation
forensically
friendliness
furunculosis
gerontocracy
gigantically
gramnegative
greengrocery
greenishness
groundcherry
groundlessly
homonymously
humanisation
humanitarian
hymenopteran
immensurable
immunisation
immunologist
impenetrable
impenetrably
impenitently
imponderable
imponderably
incandescent
incendiarism
incineration
inconcinnity
inconclusive
inconformity
inconsequent
inconsistent
inconsolable
inconsolably
inconsonance
inconstantly
inconsumable
inconsumably
incontiguous
incontinence
incontinency
inconvenient
infanticidal
infiniteness
infinitively
infundibular
inteneration
journalistic
juvenescence
lacininiated
laryngoscope
laryngoscopy
latinisation
licentiously
luminescence
luminiferous
luminousness
lycanthropic
melancholiac
melanochroic
misanthropic
misinterpret
misknowledge
mournfulness
mourningband
mourningring
mutinousness
niminypiminy
nomenclative
nomenclature
nominalistic
oblanceolate
oceanography
oceanologist
ordinariness
organgrinder
organisation
organography
organoleptic
orienteering
ostentatious
overniceness
palingenesia
palingenesis
palingenetic
palynologist
paranormally
parenthesise
paronomastic
pedantically
pedunculated
phrenologist
plainclothed
plainclothes
plaindealing
polyneuritic
polyneuritis
potentiality
ravenousness
reconcilable
reconstitute
reconversion
reconveyance
redintegrate
regeneration
regenerative
relentlessly
reminiscence
remonstrance
remonstrator
remuneration
remunerative
remuneratory
renunciation
renunciative
renunciatory
resiniferous
revengefully
ribonuclease
romanisation
romantically
ruminatively
saponifiable
scornfulness
scoundreldom
scoundrelism
secondstring
selenography
selenologist
semantically
seminiferous
simoniacally
Sinanthropus
splendidness
stanniferous
sternutation
sternutative
sternutatory
sternwheeler
stranglehold
strengthener
strengthless
stringcourse
strongminded
strongylosis
strontianite
subinfeudate
swainishness
synonymously
technicality
technicolour
technocratic
technologist
theanthropic
trainspotter
triangularly
tyrannically
tyrannicidal
unconformity
unconsidered
unconstraint
uncontrolled
unconvincing
unionisation
unkindliness
unmanageable
unwontedness
urbanisation
urbanologist
Valenciennes
voluntaryism
voluntaryist
womanishness
aetiological
agamogenesis
agamogenetic
aircondition
amitotically
anagogically

analogically
anamorphosis
anatomically
anemographic
anemophilous
angiocarpous
approachable
appropriable
appropriator
astrological
astronautics
astronomical
astrophysics
ballottement
bassorelievo
bassorilievo
biocoenology
biologically
bowcompasses
Byelorussian
campodeiform
carbohydrate
carbonaceous
Carlovingian
cartographer
cartographic
cartological
catholically
censoriously
chemotherapy
chiropractic
chiropractor
chocolatebox
chorographic
chorological
cirrocumulus
cirrostratus
coenobitical
coenobytical
coleopterist
coleopterous
colloquially
comfortingly
commodiously
commonwealth
composedness
compoundable
concomitance
concordantly
conformation
confoundedly
consociation
consolidator
corporeality
corroborator
cosmogonical
cosmographer
cosmographic
cosmological
cosmopolitan
cosmopolitic
cottonocracy
cuckooflower
customshouse
despoliation
despondently
despotically
diabolically
diamonddrill
diamondfield
diatomaceous
diatonically
discographer
discomfiture
discommodity
discomposure
disconnected
disconnexion
disconsolate
discontented
discordantly
discountable
discouraging
discourteous
discoverable
discoverture
disgorgement
disjointedly
dislodgement
dispossessor
dissocialise
dissociation
dissociative
distortional
ecologically
econometrics
economically
editorialise
editorialist
efflorescent
encroachment
episodically
ethnocentric
ethnographer
ethnographic
ethnological
etymological
etymologicon
euphonically
euphoniously
exploitation
exploitative
exprobration
extroversion
falcongentil
falcongentle
flavoprotein
geologically
geopolitical
glycogenesis
glycoprotein
granodiorite
gymnosophist
haemophiliac
haemopoiesis
haemorrhagic
hagiographer
hagiographic
hagiological
harmonically
harmoniously
hebdomadally
hectographic
heliocentric
heliographer
heliographic
heliogravure
heliolatrous
heliotherapy
heliotropism
hieroglyphic
hierographer
hierophantic
hippocentaur
hippopotamus
histogenesis
histogenetic
histological
historically
homeomorphic
homeopathist
horrorstruck
hydrochloric
hydrodynamic
hydrofluoric
hydrographer
hydrographic
hydrokinetic
hydrological
hydrolysable
hydromedusae
hydromedusan
hydrophilous
hydroquinone
hydrostatics
hydrotherapy
hydrothermal
hydrotropism
hygrophilous
hymnographer
hypnogenesis
hypnogenetic
hypnotherapy
hypnotically
hypnotisable
iconoclastic
iconographer
impropriator
improvidence
improvisator
incoordinate
ingloriously
introduction
introductory
introjection
intromission
intromittent
intromitting
introversion
introversive
introvertive
karyokinesis
leucocytosis
leukocytosis
limnological
lithographer
lithographic
lithological
lithospheric
lithotritist
macrocephaly
macropterous
malcontented
malformation
meteorically
meteorograph
methodically
metrological
metropolitan
mezzorelievo
mezzosoprano
microanalyst
microbiology
microcapsule
microcephaly
microcircuit
microclimate
microcopying
microcrystal
micrographer
microphysics
microscopist
microseismic
microsurgery
mnemotechnic
muttonheaded
mythographer
mythological
mythologiser
narcotically
narrowminded
necrographer
necrological
necrophagous
necrophiliac
necrophilism
necrophilous
negrophilism
negrophilist
neonomianism
Nestorianism
neuroanatomy
neurobiology
neurological
neuropterous
neuroscience
neurosurgeon
neurosurgery
neurotically
Newfoundland
nimbostratus
nitrobenzene
noncombatant
noncommittal
noncomplying
nonconductor
nonconformer
ophiophagous
orthodontics
orthodontist
orthogenesis
orthogenetic
orthographer
orthographic
orthopaedics
orthopaedist
orthopterist
orthopteroid
orthopterous
orthotropism
orthotropous
osteogenesis
osteological
osteomalacia
osteoplastic
osteoporosis
paedobaptism
paedogenesis
paedogenetic
paedomorphic
pantographic
pathogenesis
pathogenetic
pathological
perfoliation
performative
periodically
periodontics
periodontist
periostracum
pernoctation
pestological
petrographer
petrographic
petrological
phagocytosis
phagocytotic
phenological
phenomenally
phenotypical
philodendron
philological
philosophise
phonographer
phonographic
phonological
photochromic
photofission
photogeology
photographer
photographic
photogravure
photokinesis
photokinetic
photomontage
photophilous
photosetting
photospheric
phototropism
phycological
phycomycetes
phylogenesis
phylogenetic
phytogenesis
phytogenetic
phytographer
phytological
phytophagous
pictographic
pigeonbreast
planoconcave
platonically
plecopterous
pleiotropism
pornographer
pornographic
precociously
precognition
precognitive
precondition
preconscious
predominance
predominancy
preformation
preformative
preponderant
preponderate
preposterous
primogenital
primogenitor
primordially
proboscidean
proboscidian
proconsulate
profoundness
prolongation
pronominally
pronouncedly
proportional
proportioned
prosodically
prosopopoeia
protohistory
protoplasmic
protoplastic
prototypical
protozoology
pterodactyle
purposebuilt
purposefully
quixotically
radiobiology
radioelement
radiographer
radiographic
radioisotope
radiological
radionuclide
radiophonics
radiotherapy
ratiocinator
reproachable
reproachless
reproducible
reproduction
reproductive
reprographic
responsively
responsorial
retrocedence
retrocession
retrocessive
retroflexion
retropulsion
retroversion

rhetorically
rhinocerotic
rhinological
rhizocarpous
rhizogenetic
rhizophagous
rhododendron
salmonladder
saprophagous
sarcomatosis
sarcophagous
sardonically
scatological
scenographic
schoolfellow
schoolleaver
schoolmaster
semiofficial
semiological
servocontrol
shadowboxing
siphonophore
siphonostele
sociological
sociometrist
sporogenesis
stenographer
stenographic
stylographic
subcommittee
subconscious
subcontinent
subnormality
subsonically
supposititious
surmountable
surroundings
symbolically
tautological
taxcollector
tectonically
teleological
terrorstruck
testosterone
Teutonically
thoroughbass
thoroughbred
thoroughfare
thoroughness
toploftiness
trigonometry
trinomialism
tropological
tropospheric
unapologetic
unbrokenness
uneconomical
unifoliolate
unprofitable
unprofitably
unpronounced
unthoughtful
Victorianism
victoriously
viscosimeter
viscountship
yellowhammer
analphabetic
anteprandial
antiparticle
antipathetic
antiperiodic
antiphonally
backpedalled
cataphoresis
championship
clapperboard
conspiration
creepycrawly
decapitation
decipherable
decipherment
depopulation
dilapidation
earsplitting
ectoparasite
elliptically
encephalitic
encephalitis
endoparasite
equipollence
equipollency
equiprobable
escapologist
exasperation
exospherical
footplateman
gamopetalous
gamophyllous
grampositive
graspingness
hemiparasite
highpressure
hirepurchase
hypophrygian
inappeasable
inapplicable
inapplicably
inappositely
incapability
incapacitate
independence
independency
inexpedience
inexpediency
inexperience
inexpertness
inexplicable
inexplicably
inexpressive
inexpugnable
inexpugnably
irrepealable
irreprovable
malapertness
manipulation
manipulative
manipulatory
metaphorical
metaphrastic
metaphysical
metapsychics
misapprehend
monopetalous
monophyletic
Monophysitic
monopodially
monopolistic
nanoplankton
newspaperman
occupational
omnipotently
omnipresence
oneupmanship
overpersuade
overpowering
overpressure
paraphrastic
peripherally
periphrastic
perspicacity
perspiration
perspiratory
phosphoresce
polypetalous
polyphyletic
postponement
postposition
postpositive
postprandial
prosperously
puerperrally
reappearance
recapitulate
receptaculum
receptionist
reciprocally
reciprocator
recuperation
recuperative
redeployment
resipiscence
resupination
scorpionfish
scraperboard
scripturally
scriptwriter
scrupulosity
scrupulously
sculpturally
selfpleasing
selfportrait
semiparasite
semiprecious
seraphically
sharpshooter
sharpsighted
sheepishness
sheepshearer
skippingrope
sleepingpill
sleepwalking
slipperiness
snappishness
softpedalled
steeplechase
streptococci
streptomycin
strophanthin
subapostolic
sweepingness
sycophantish
synoptically
trampolinist
trumpetshell
unappeasable
unappetising
undiplomatic
unemployable
unemployment
unexpectedly
unimportance
unpopularity
unrepeatable
venepuncture
venipuncture
vituperation
vituperative
vituperatory
viviparously
voluptuosity
voluptuously
wallpainting
whimperingly
whippoorwill
whisperingly
zygapophysis
coloquintida
deliquescent
headquarters
hindquarters
obsequiously
quinquennial
quinquennium
tranquillise
tranquillity
absorptional
absorptivity
abstractable
abstractedly
abstractness
abstruseness
accordionist
accurateness
accursedness
afterthought
ailurophobia
aircraftsman
alterability
anaerobiosis
anagrammatic
anthropogeny
anthropoidal
anthropology
antirachitic
apparatchiki
apparatchiks
apparentness
apparitional
apperception
apperceptive
appurtenance
arborescence
arborisation
atheromatous
attorneyship
Australasian
biographical
calorescence
calorimetric
canorousness
capercaillie
capercailzie
caterwauling
centrespread
centrosphere
chairmanship
cheerfulness
cheirography
chlorination
clairaudient
clairvoyance
clearsighted
colorimetric
compressible
concrescence
concreteness
congratulant
congratulate
congregation
contractable
contractedly
contractible
contradictor
contrapuntal
contrariness
contrariwise
contribution
contributive
contributory
contriteness
contrivement
controllable
cowardliness
cumbrousness
decoratively
decorousness
departmental
desirability
desirousness
destructible
determinable
determinably
determinedly
dethronement
dextrousness
diagrammatic
dichromatism
discreetness
discreteness
discretional
discriminant
discriminate
disfranchise
disorientate
distractedly
distrainable
distrainment
distributary
distribution
distributive
divarication
diversionary
diversionist
diverticular
diverticulum
divertimenti
divertimento
dolorousness
effervescent
effortlessly
encirclement
endermically
enshrinement
enterprising
entertaining
enthronement
epigrammatic
etherisation
excursionist
experiential
experimental
experimenter
exterminable
exterminator
extortionary
extortionate
feverishness
figuratively
filtrability
fluorescence
fluoridation
fluorination
fluorocarbon
futurologist
gastronomist
gastropodous
generousness
geographical
governmental
governorship
haberdashery
hemerocallis
heterocercal
heterocyclic
heteroecious
heterogamous
heterogenous
heterologous
heteromerous
heteronomous
heterophylly
heterosexual
heterozygote
heterozygous
hibernaculum
humorousness
hyperacidity
hyperbolical
hyperplastic
hyperpyretic
hyperpyrexia
hypersthenia
hypersthenic
hypertension

hypertensive
hyperthermia
hypertrophic
illtreatment
impartiality
imperatively
imperatorial
imperceptive
impercipient
imperfection
imperfective
imperishable
imperishably
impermanence
impermanency
impersonally
impersonator
impertinence
impertinency
imperviously
incorporated
incorporator
incorporeity
incorrigible
incorrigibly
incorruption
incurability
indirectness
inharmonious
instructress
instrumental
insurrection
interbedding
interception
intercession
intercessory
interchanger
interconnect
intercropped
intercurrent
intercutting
interdiction
interdictive
interdictory
interdigital
interestedly
interfemoral
interference
interglacial
interjection
interjectory
interlobular
interlocutor
intermeddler
intermediacy
intermediary
intermediate
interminable
interminably
intermission
intermittent
intermitting
intermixture
intermundane
internuclear
internuncial
interoceanic
interoceptor
interpellate
interpleader
interpolator
interpretive
interrelated
interrogator
interruption
interruptive
intersection
interservice
interspinous
interstellar
interstitial
intertexture
intervenient
intervention
intervocalic
interwreathe
invertebrate
jetpropelled
labyrinthian
labyrinthine
lachrymation
lachrymatory
lachrymosely
laterisation
levorotation
levorotatory
liberalistic
literariness
liturgically
liturgiology
Liverpudlian
liverystable
majorgeneral
maltreatment
materialness
mineralogist
mispronounce
mistranslate
mistreatment
mistressship
mithridatise
mithridatism
moderateness
motorcyclist
motorisation
naturalistic
naturopathic
nephrologist
nevertheless
numerologist
numerousness
obdurateness
obstreperous
oncorhynchus
oneirocritic
orographical
otherworldly
overreaction
pancreatitis
papyrologist
pejoratively
polarimetric
polarisation
polarography
programmable
programmatic
proprietress
protrusively
Quadragesima
quadrangular
quadraphonic
quadriennium
quadrinomial
quadriplegia
quadriplegic
quadrivalent
quadrumanous
rapprochment
regardlessly
remorsefully
repercussion
repercussive
reservedness
restrainable
restrainedly
restrictedly
resurrection
retiringness
reverberator
reversionary
rigorousness
risorgimento
sacerdotally
Samaritanism
scabrousness
schorlaceous
sclerenchyma
scouringrush
scurrilously
selfreliance
selfreproach
selfrighting
separability
separateness
solarisation
sonorousness
soporiferous
sparrowgrass
spheroidally
squarerigged
squirrelcage
squirreltail
subarrhation
suberisation
sudoriferous
superannuate
supercharger
superciliary
supercilious
supereminent
supererogate
superhighway
superhumanly
supermundane
supernaculum
supernatural
superposable
supersedence
supersensory
supersession
superstition
superstratum
supervenient
supervention
suppressible
surprisingly
synarthrosis
syncretistic
taberdarship
tabernacular
taperecorder
theoretician
timorousness
tolerability
towardliness
tuberculated
tuberculosis
underachieve
underbidding
underclothes
undercoating
undercurrent
undercutting
underdevelop
undergarment
underinsured
underletting
undermanning
underpinning
underrunning
undersetting
understaffed
undersurface
undertenancy
underwritten
unmercifully
unparalleled
unscriptural
unscrupulous
unstructured
unworldiness
unworthiness
usufructuary
valorisation
vaporisation
vaporousness
venerability
ventripotent
veterinarian
vicargeneral
vigorousness
watermanship
wondrousness
abrasiveness
accusatively
accusatorial
acoustically
adhesiveness
advisability
aerosiderite
allusiveness
ambassadress
anaesthetise
anaesthetist
antiSemitism
antistrophic
appositeness
appositional
artistically
assassinator
atmospherics
backslapping
billsticking
birdsnesting
blissfulness
bluestocking
bodysnatcher
bodystocking
borosilicate
brassbounder
brassrubbing
breaststroke
breastsummer
calisthenics
catastrophic
cheeseburger
cheesecutter
cheesemonger
cheeseparing
chrestomathy
Christianise
Christianity
Christolatry
Christophany
classicalism
classicalist
classicality
classifiable
cleistogamic
cocksureness
cohesiveness
coldshoulder
corespondent
crossbedding
crossbencher
crossbuttock
crosscountry
crosscurrent
crossexamine
crossgrained
crossheading
crossingover
crosspurpose
crosssection
decasyllabic
decasyllable
decisiveness
delusiveness
derisiveness
disassociate
disastrously
disestablish
divisibility
divisiveness
domestically
domesticator
dressinggown
dynastically
eavesdropped
eavesdropper
echosounding
effusiveness
emulsifiable
endoskeletal
envisagement
equestrienne
farmsteading
fearsomeness
feldspathoid
fenestration
foresightful
forestalment
freestanding
freeswimming
gamesmanship
gamesomeness
gamosepalous
gladsomeness
glassblowing
glossography
glossologist
grossularite
gruesomeness
hairsbreadth
hairsplitter
handsbreadth
handsomeness
hardstanding
headshrinker
hemispheroid
highsounding
highspirited
highstepping
homesickness
homosexually
hypostatical
hyposulphite
idiosyncrasy
illusiveness
illusoriness
illustration
illustrative
inauspicious
incestuously
incisiveness
indiscipline
indiscreetly
indiscretion
indisputable
indisputably
indissoluble
indissolubly
indistinctly
industrially
infusibility
inhospitable
inhospitably
inobservance
intussuscept
investigator
invisibility
irresistible
irresistibly
irresolutely
irresolution

irresolvable
irrespective
irrespirable
irresponsive
jurisconsult
jurisdiction
jurisprudent
klipspringer
laisserfaire
laissezaller
laissezfaire
logistically
lonesomeness
longshoreman
longstanding
magistrature
majestically
marksmanship
meristematic
metasomatism
ministration
ministrative
monastically
monostichous
monostrophic
monosyllabic
monosyllable
nailscissors
nonessential
occasionally
octosyllabic
octosyllable
omnisciently
opposability
oppositeness
oppositional
oversimplify
overstepping
parasiticide
parasitology
parisyllabic
perispomenon
peristeronic
peristomatic
phrasemonger
phraseograph
plausibility
pleasantness
pleasingness
pleasureless
polysepalous
polysyllabic
polysyllable
poorspirited
praiseworthy
preestablish
priestliness
priestridden
quaestorship
reassessment
reassignment
reassuringly
recessionary
redistribute
registration
repossession
resistlessly
resuscitator
robustiously
sadistically
salesmanship
satisfaction
satisfactory
satisfyingly
schismatical
secessionism
secessionist
selfsameness
selfstarting
Shakspereana
Shaksperiana
sideslipping
sidestepping
sinistrality
sinistrorsal
sinusoidally
spinsterhood
starspangled
teensyweensy
theistically
theosophical
thousandfold
tiresomeness
toilsomeness
transcendent
transduction
transferable
transference
transferring
transformism
transformist
transfusible
transgressor
transhipment
transhumance
transiliency
transitional
transitively
transitivity
transitorily
translatable
translucence
translucency
transmigrant
transmigrate
transmission
transmissive
transmitting
transmogrify
transmontane
transmutable
transoceanic
transpacific
transparency
transpirable
transplanter
transpontine
transposable
transshipped
transudation
transudatory
transversely
transvestism
transvestite
unanswerable
unassailable
unassumingly
unhesitating
unhistorical
unmistakable
unmistakably
unreservedly
unresponsive
unrestrained
wainscotting
whimsicality
abortiveness
adaptability
adaptiveness
additionally
adulteration
adulterously
agentgeneral
alliteration
alliterative
altitudinous
amentiferous
amortisation
anastigmatic
antithetical
apostolicism
apostolicity
apostrophise
appetisingly
aristocratic
Aristotelean
Aristotelian
attitudinise
avantgardism
avantgardist
belittlement
bewitchingly
bilateralism
blastfurnace
blastosphere
blastulation
blisteringly
blusteringly
boastfulness
boisterously
breathalyser
breathlessly
breathtaking
brontosaurus
capitalistic
capitulation
charterhouse
charterparty
chastisement
chesterfield
chitterlings
clatteringly
constabulary
constipation
constituency
constitution
constitutive
constriction
constrictive
constringent
construction
constructive
countenancer
counteragent
counterblast
countercheck
counterclaim
counterforce
counterlight
countermarch
counterplead
counterpoint
counterpoise
counterproof
counterscarp
countershaft
countertenor
countrydance
countrywoman
courtmartial
courtplaster
covetousness
craftbrother
creativeness
cryptanalyst
cryptogamous
cryptography
cryptologist
crystalgazer
deactivation
delitescence
denaturalise
denaturation
deontologist
deputisation
diastrophism
dilatability
dilatoriness
dilettantish
dilettantism
diphtheritic
diphthongise
doubtfulness
dubitatively
Egyptologist
electrically
electrolysis
electrolytic
electrometer
electronvolt
electroplate
electroscope
electroshock
electrotonic
electrotonus
electrotyper
embattlement
embitterment
enantiomorph
epistemology
equationally
equitability
eruptiveness
escutcheoned
excitability
exenteration
expatriation
fainthearted
faintishness
faultfinding
firstnighter
flatteringly
fountainhead
fractionally
fractionator
freethinking
frictionless
frontbencher
frontiersman
frontispiece
fructiferous
fructivorous
fruitfulness
fugitiveness
functionally
functionless
gametophytic
geanticlinal
glitteringly
gluttonously
glyptography
goodtempered
greathearted
guestchamber
habitability
habitforming
habitualness
halftimbered
heartburning
heartrending
heartstrings
heartwarming
hebetudinous
henotheistic
heortologist
heritability
hesitatingly
homothallism
humptydumpty
hydatidiform
hypothalamic
hypothalamus
hypothecator
hypothetical
ideationally
identifiable
idiothermous
illiterately
immaterially
immatureness
immethodical
immutability
impetiginous
imputability
imputatively
inactivation
inarticulate
inartificial
incatenation
inextensible
inextricable
inextricably
innutritious
inveterately
irrationally
irritability
irritatingly
kleptomaniac
latitudinous
legitimately
legitimation
legitimatise
lighthearted
maintainable
meditatively
menstruation
meretricious
mesothoracic
metathetical
metathoracic
militaristic
misstatement
moistureless
monetisation
monitorially
monotheistic
monotonously
mosstrooping
mountainside
negativeness
negativistic
negotiatress
nicotinamide
nightclothes
nychthemeral
nychthemeron
obliteration
obliterative
obmutescence
odontologist
opisthograph
opisthotonos
ornithomancy
ornithoscopy
outstretched
outstripping
palatability
paletteknife
paratactical
penitentiary
pilotballoon
plasterboard
Plattdeutsch
plectognathi
pointilliste
polytheistic
polytonality
positiveness
positivistic
practicality
practitioner
prenticeship
printability
prostitution
pyrotechnics

pyrotechnist
quantifiable
quantisation
quantitative
quarterbound
quarterfinal
quarterstaff
quattrocento
questionable
questionably
questionless
quintessence
reactivation
reactiveness
relationally
relationship
relativeness
relativistic
repatriation
repetitional
repetitively
resettlement
rightfulness
salutariness
salutational
salutiferous
scatterbrain
scatteringly
scintigraphy
scintillator
scratchiness
semitropical
shatterproof
shirtwaister
shootingiron
shortchanger
shortcircuit
shortpitched
shortsighted
shortsleeved
shortstaffed
sightreading
skittishness
sluttishness
solitariness
somatopleure
spectrograph
spectrometer
spectrometry
spectroscope
spectroscopy
sportfulness
sportiveness
squattocracy
steatopygous
stertorously
stouthearted
straticulate
stratigraphy
stratosphere
stutteringly
substantiate
substantival
substitution
substitutive
substruction
substructure
sweetishness
temptability
teratologist
teratomatous
theatregoing
theatrically
tightmouthed
toastingfork
togetherness
tractability
traitorously
trestletable

trustfulness
twentyfourmo
twitteringly
unattractive
unauthorised
undetermined
unfathomable
uninterested
valetudinary
vauntcourier
vegetatively
visitational
visitatorial
volatileness
volitionally
vomiturition
waistcoating
whortleberry
absquatulate
accouchement
accoutrement
adequateness
agglutinogen
announcement
apiculturist
astoundingly
auscultation
auscultatory
calculatedly
carburetting
centuplicate
chequerboard
cherubically
circuitously
circumcision
circumfluent
circumfusion
circumjacent
circumscribe
circumstance
colourlessly
communicable
communicably
communicator
compulsively
compulsivity
compulsorily
compunctious
compurgation
compurgatory
concubitancy
concupiscent
concurrently
conductivity
conduplicate
Confucianism
confusedness
conjunctival
connubiality
conquistador
consultation
consultative
consummately
consummation
consummative
consummatory
contumacious
contumelious
convulsively
curmudgeonly
denouncement
desquamation
desquamative
desquamatory
disbursement
discursively
disguisement
disgustfully
disgustingly

disputatious
disquisition
dissuasively
disturbingly
elocutionary
elocutionist
elucubration
encrustation
enthusiastic
epicureanism
evolutionary
evolutionism
evolutionist
exclusionary
exclusionism
exclusionist
excruciating
excruciation
executorship
exhaustively
exiguousness
ferrugineous
fortuitously
frequentness
furfuraceous
gratuitously
hallucinogen
hallucinosis
harquebusier
incautiously
incrustation
iniquitously
intrusionist
laboursaving
languishment
languorously
linguistical
malnutrition
mercurialise
mercurialism
misjudgement
misquotation
multungulate
noneuclidean
obscurantism
obscurantist
pasqueflower
pellucidness
percussively
percutaneous
perjuriously
persuasively
perturbation
perturbative
polyurethane
presumptuous
productively
productivity
promulgation
protuberance
quaquaversal
rambunctious
recrudescent
renouncement
resoundingly
sanguinarily
sanguineness
sanguinolent
sarrusophone
seclusionist
sensualistic
sensuousness
septuagenary
Septuagesima
Septuagintal
sesquialtera
statuesquely
subcutaneous
testudineous

throughstone
tortuousness
traducianism
traducianist
trifurcation
ubiquitarian
ubiquitously
unblushingly
unctuousness
untruthfully
vanquishable
vanquishment
virtuosoship
virtuousness
ambivalently
behaviourism
behaviourist
benevolently
caravansarai
caravanserai
chauvinistic
derivational
derivatively
equivalently
equivocation
equivocatory
grievousness
immovability
impoverished
inadvertence
inadvertency
indivertible
indivertibly
individually
irreverently
irreversible
irreversibly
malevolently
motivational
omnivorously
reinvestment
reinvigorate
rejuvenation
removability
revivalistic
reviviscence
selfviolence
televisional
thievishness
unfavourable
unfavourably
ungovernable
unloveliness
backwardness
backwoodsman
birdwatching
downwardness
freewheeling
kilowatthour
longwindedly
lukewarmness
shrewishness
sidewhiskers
stalwartness
unlawfulness
untowardness
detoxication
intoxication
nonexistence
peroxidation
preexistence
analytically
arrhythmical
asphyxiation
bathypelagic
bellylanding
biosynthesis
biosynthetic
bobbydazzler

bonnyclabber
collywobbles
dissymmetric
embryologist
epicycloidal
fullyfledged
geosynclinal
heavyhearted
honeybuzzard
jerrybuilder
mealymouthed
merrythought
moneychanger
moneygrubber
moneyspinner
pennypincher
pennywhistle
sandyachting
stonyhearted
tachygrapher
tachygraphic
topsyturvily
wallydraigle
bedazzlement
embezzlement
horizontally
quizzicality
schizogonous
schizomycete
schizophrene
schizothymia
schizothymic
swizzlestick

---

absquatulate
abstractable
abstractedly
abstractness
accurateness
accusatively
accusatorial
adaptability
adequateness
advisability
aeronautical
aircraftsman
alterability
amalgamation
amalgamative
ambivalently
amygdaloidal
anagrammatic
antimacassar
antimagnetic
antimalarial
antiparticle
antipathetic
antirachitic
apparatchiki
apparatchiks
approachable
Australasian
autocatalyse
automaticity
availability
bacchanalian
backwardness
benefactress
bequeathment
biographical
birdwatching
burglarproof
cantharidian
capitalistic
caravansarai
caravanserai
cardcarrying
caricaturist
carriageable

chaplainship
charlatanism
chrematistic
chromaticism
chromaticity
chromatogram
chromatology
chromatopsia
cinematheque
clairaudient
complacently
complaisance
congratulant
congratulate
constabulary
contractable
contractedly
contractible
contradictor
contrapuntal
contrariness
contrariwise
copulatively
corelatively
cryptanalyst
crystalgazer
cumulatively
debonairness
decoratively
decreasingly
deescalation
delicatessen
derivational
derivatively
derogatorily
desirability
desolateness
desquamation
desquamative
desquamatory
diagrammatic
diaphanously
dilatability
disclamation
disfranchise
displaceable
displacement
dissuasively
distractedly
distrainable
distrainment
dodecahedral
dodecahedron
dodecaphonic
downwardness
dubitatively
ectoparasite
encroachment
endamagement
endocarditis
endoparasite
entreatingly
envisagement
epigrammatic
epithalamion
epithalamium
equitability
equivalently
excitability
exhilaration
exhilarative
figuratively
filtrability
flammability
foundationer
fountainhead
geographical
gladiatorial
grallatorial
grammaticise
gyromagnetic
habitability
hardfavoured
hemiparasite
heritability
hesitatingly
highfaluting
highhandedly
holidaymaker
hoodmanblind
hyperacidity
hypogastrium
immovability
immutability
imperatively
imperatorial
imputability
imputatively
incapability
incapacitate
increasingly
incurability
indicatively
ineffaceable
ineffaceably
irregardless
irrelatively
irritability
irritatingly
isodiametric
journalistic
kilowatthour
laureateship
lefthandedly
liberalistic
literariness
lukewarmness
maintainable
malleability
manslaughter
manufacturer
marriageable
matriarchate
meditatively
merchantable
metagalactic
metalanguage
microanalyst
militaristic
milliammeter
mineralogist
misplacement
misstatement
mistranslate
moderateness
monomaniacal
morphallaxis
motivational
mountainside
mucilaginous
naturalistic
nauseatingly
navigability
navigational
neoclassical
Neoplatonism
Neoplatonist
neuroanatomy
newspaperman
nominalistic
nonchalantly
nonflammable
obdurateness
obligatorily
occupational
openhandedly
opposability
ordinariness
orographical
overcautious
palatability
paramagnetic
paratactical
patriarchate
pejoratively
pericarditis
permeability
persuasively
pharmaceutic
pharmacology
philharmonic
pinfeathered
pleasantness
plumbaginous
pneumaticity
pneumatology
portmanteaus
portmanteaux
pragmatistic
preclassical
printability
proclamation
proclamatory
programmable
programmatic
prothalamion
prothalamium
pyromaniacal
Quadragesima
quadrangular
quadraphonic
quaquaversal
recreational
removability
reproachable
reproachless
restrainable
restrainedly
revelational
revivalistic
rheumatology
ruminatively
saccharinity
saccharoidal
salamandrian
salamandrine
salamandroid
salutariness
salutational
sandyachting
scabbardfish
scandalously
secularistic
selfcatering
selfsameness
semibasement
semidarkness
semiparasite
sensualistic
separability
separateness
septuagenary
Septuagesima
Septuagintal
sergeantfish
sergeantship
serjeantship
slipcarriage
snapfastener
solitariness
specialistic
spermaphytic
spermathecal
spermatocyte
spermatozoid
spermatozoon
Stakhanovism
Stakhanovite
stalwartness
standardbred
stepdaughter
substantiate
substantival
superannuate
surrealistic
teachability
temptability
thaumaturgic
thousandfold
tolerability
traceability
tractability
trochanteric
trophallaxis
unassailable
underachieve
unmanageable
unparalleled
unpleasantly
unsteadiness
untowardness
vegetatively
venerability
visitational
visitatorial
viviparously
wallpainting
wellfavoured
whigmaleerie
woolgatherer
acetabularia
adorableness
Alhambresque
alphabetical
amenableness
amicableness
amphibiously
amphibrachic
attributable
blackbirding
blamableness
blockbusting
bloodbrother
brassbounder
Cantabrigian
cherubically
childbearing
coachbuilder
coenobitical
coenobytical
collaborator
concubitancy
confabulator
connubiality
corroborator
crackbrained
craftbrother
crossbedding
crossbencher
crossbuttock
culpableness
disambiguate
disembarrass
elucubration
encumberment
encumbrancer
enfeeblement
enviableness
exprobration
forcibleness
frontbencher
glassblowing
hairsbreadth
handsbreadth
heartburning
honeybuzzard
horribleness
horsebreaker
housebreaker
hyperbolical
interbedding
jerrybuilder
laudableness
microbiology
mouthbreeder
moveableness
neighbouring
neurobiology
nitrobenzene
overabundant
paedobaptism
perambulator
pilotballoon
pitiableness
prefabricate
protuberance
radiobiology
readableness
reliableness
rememberable
remembrancer
reverberator
selfabsorbed
sensibleness
skateboarder
sociableness
speedboating
stockbreeder
stockbroking
stoneboiling
suitableness
swashbuckler
syllabically
tangibleness
terribleness
thirdborough
underbidding
valuableness
variableness
vertebration
voidableness
workableness
youngberries
acciaccatura
accouchement
amphictyonic
angiocarpous
annunciation
apperception
apperceptive
appreciation
appreciative
appreciatory
attractively
auspiciously
avariciously
beachcombing
beseechingly
bespectacled
bewitchingly
blackcurrant
bonnyclabber
capercaillie
capercailzie
capriciously
characterise
cirrocumulus
clavicembalo
closecropped
collectively
collectivise
collectivism
collectivist
collectivity
conductivity

confe**c**tioner
Confu**c**ianism
conne**c**tional
conne**c**tively
conse**c**ration
conse**c**ratory
conso**c**iation
conve**c**tional
corre**c**tional
corre**c**titude
corre**c**tively
criti**c**alness
cross**c**ountry
cross**c**urrent
curvi**c**audate
curvi**c**ostate
denti**c**ulated
denun**c**iation
denun**c**iative
denun**c**iatory
depre**c**iation
depre**c**iatory
diale**c**tician
diale**c**tology
disac**c**haride
disen**c**hanter
disin**c**entive
disso**c**ialise
disso**c**iation
disso**c**iative
encir**c**lement
epicy**c**loidal
escut**c**heoned
ethno**c**entric
excru**c**iating
excru**c**iation
expli**c**itness
extra**c**ranial
falla**c**iously
flori**c**ulture
folli**c**ulated
furun**c**ulosis
geote**c**tonics
gesti**c**ulator
grave**c**lothes
guest**c**hamber
gynae**c**ocracy
hallu**c**inogen
hallu**c**inosis
handi**c**apping
helio**c**entric
heroi**c**alness
heroi**c**omical
hippo**c**entaur
horti**c**ulture
hydro**c**hloric
icono**c**lastic
imper**c**eptive
imper**c**ipient
impli**c**itness
incal**c**ulable
incal**c**ulably
incon**c**innity
incon**c**lusive
indis**c**ipline
indis**c**reetly
indis**c**retion
inexa**c**titude
infle**c**tional
inspe**c**torate
inspe**c**torial
inter**c**eption
inter**c**ession
inter**c**essory
inter**c**hanger
inter**c**onnect
inter**c**ropped
inter**c**urrent
inter**c**utting
intra**c**ardiac
intra**c**ranial
juris**c**onsult
leuco**c**ytosis
leuko**c**ytosis
loqua**c**iously
machi**c**olated
macro**c**ephaly
melan**c**holiac
menda**c**iously
micro**c**apsule
micro**c**ephaly
micro**c**ircuit
micro**c**limate
micro**c**opying
micro**c**rystal
money**c**hanger
morda**c**iously
motor**c**yclist
multi**c**entral
myrme**c**ophily
nails**c**issors
negle**c**tfully
night**c**lothes
nomen**c**lative
nomen**c**lature
noneu**c**lidean
oblan**c**eolate
omnis**c**iently
overa**c**hiever
overa**c**tivity
pante**c**hnicon
parti**c**ipator
parti**c**ularly
pedun**c**ulated
pellu**c**idness
perfe**c**tively
perni**c**iously
perno**c**tation
phago**c**ytosis
phago**c**ytotic
photo**c**hromic
pisci**c**ulture
plain**c**lothed
plain**c**lothes
plano**c**oncave
preco**c**iously
predi**c**tively
prefe**c**torial
preoc**c**upancy
price**c**utting
produ**c**tively
produ**c**tivity
profi**c**iently
proje**c**tional
proje**c**tively
prose**c**torial
prose**c**utable
prota**c**tinium
prote**c**tively
prote**c**torate
publi**c**spirit
pugna**c**iously
ratio**c**inator
recal**c**itrant
recal**c**itrate
recon**c**ilable
refle**c**tional
refle**c**tively
refle**c**tivity
refra**c**tivity
refra**c**torily
renun**c**iation
renun**c**iative
renun**c**iatory
reper**c**ussion
reper**c**ussive
respe**c**tfully
respe**c**tively
resus**c**itator
retra**c**tation
retra**c**tility
retro**c**edence
retro**c**ession
retro**c**essive
rhino**c**erotic
rhizo**c**arpous
scrat**c**hiness
selfa**c**tivity
sepul**c**hrally
sequa**c**iously
servi**c**eberry
servi**c**ecourt
servi**c**ewoman
servo**c**ontrol
share**c**ropper
short**c**hanger
short**c**ircuit
silvi**c**ulture
skunk**c**abbage
small**c**lothes
snake**c**harmer
stala**c**tiform
stone**c**utting
subje**c**tively
subje**c**tivise
subje**c**tivism
subje**c**tivist
subje**c**tivity
suffi**c**iently
super**c**harger
super**c**iliary
super**c**ilious
suspi**c**iously
sylvi**c**ulture
synda**c**tylism
synda**c**tylous
tetra**c**hordal
Torri**c**ellian
tradu**c**ianism
tradu**c**ianist
tragi**c**omical
trans**c**endent
trida**c**tylous
tuber**c**ulated
tuber**c**ulosis
turri**c**ulated
uncal**c**ulated
under**c**lothes
under**c**oating
under**c**urrent
under**c**utting
ungra**c**efully
ungra**c**iously
unmer**c**ifully
unsuc**c**essful
Valen**c**iennes
vaunt**c**ourier
vermi**c**ulated
verna**c**ularly
verti**c**alness
verti**c**illate
vindi**c**tively
wains**c**otting
waist**c**oating
accor**d**ionist
appen**d**ectomy
appen**d**icitis
appen**d**icular
balla**d**monger
bewil**d**eredly
bewil**d**erment
bobby**d**azzler
campo**d**eiform
commo**d**iously
confi**d**ential
consi**d**erable
consi**d**erably
cowar**d**liness
curmu**d**geonly
disen**d**owment
dislo**d**gement
eaves**d**ropped
eaves**d**ropper
episo**d**ically
extra**d**itable
fasti**d**iously
forbi**d**dingly
frien**d**liness
grano**d**iorite
groun**d**cherry
groun**d**lessly
haber**d**ashery
heral**d**ically
hybri**d**isable
hydro**d**ynamic
impon**d**erable
impon**d**erably
incan**d**escent
incen**d**iarism
inera**d**icable
inera**d**icably
infun**d**ibular
inter**d**iction
inter**d**ictive
inter**d**ictory
inter**d**igital
intro**d**uction
intro**d**uctory
juris**d**iction
kalei**d**oscope
lopsi**d**edness
metho**d**ically
misju**d**gement
multi**d**entate
onesi**d**edness
orchi**d**aceous
ortho**d**ontics
ortho**d**ontist
Palla**d**ianism
pecca**d**illoes
perfi**d**iously
perio**d**ically
perio**d**ontics
perio**d**ontist
phila**d**elphus
philo**d**endron
plain**d**ealing
Platt**d**eutsch
prece**d**ential
preme**d**itated
preme**d**itator
presi**d**ential
proso**d**ically
provi**d**ential
pteri**d**ophyte
pteri**d**osperm
ptero**d**actyle
recru**d**escent
regar**d**lessly
repro**d**ucible
repro**d**uction
repro**d**uctive
rhodo**d**endron
sacer**d**otally
scoun**d**reldom
scoun**d**relism
secon**d**string
selfe**d**ucated
selfi**d**entity
shoul**d**erbelt
shoul**d**erknot
shoul**d**ernote
skull**d**uggery
splen**d**idness
spora**d**ically
stone**d**resser
subsi**d**iarily
succe**d**aneous
taber**d**arship
testu**d**ineous
towar**d**liness
trans**d**uction
under**d**evelop
unkin**d**liness
wally**d**raigle
acaul**e**scence
accel**e**ration
accel**e**rative
accid**e**ntally
acqui**e**scence
adult**e**ration
adult**e**rously
aeron**e**urosis
aesth**e**tician
aesth**e**ticism
alkal**e**scence
allit**e**ration
allit**e**rative
ambid**e**xtrous
anath**e**matise
anoth**e**rguess
antec**e**dently
antig**e**nicity
antin**e**utrino
antip**e**riodic
antiS**e**mitism
apoth**e**gmatic
appar**e**ntness
arbor**e**scence
archd**e**aconry
asymm**e**trical
backp**e**dalled
barom**e**trical
basel**e**ssness
battl**e**ground
battl**e**mented
bilat**e**ralism
bioch**e**mistry
bioco**e**nology
blabb**e**rmouth
bladd**e**rwrack
blath**e**rskite
bleth**e**rskate
blist**e**ringly
blith**e**somely
blund**e**ringly
blust**e**ringly
boist**e**rously
boogi**e**woogie
bookl**e**arning
bootl**e**ssness
bottl**e**washer
bullh**e**adedly
busin**e**sslike
cabin**e**tmaker
calor**e**scence
candl**e**holder
carel**e**ssness
cattl**e**lifter
centr**e**spread
chanc**e**medley
charn**e**lhouse
chart**e**rhouse
chart**e**rparty
check**e**rberry
check**e**rboard
chees**e**burger
chees**e**cutter
chees**e**monger
chees**e**paring
chequ**e**rboard
chest**e**rfield
chimn**e**ypiece
chitt**e**rlings
clapp**e**rboard

clatteringly
clinkerbuilt
clotheshorse
clothespress
complemental
completeness
complexional
complexioned
compressible
concrescence
concreteness
congregation
cotyledonary
cotyledonous
countenancer
counteragent
counterblast
countercheck
counterclaim
counterforce
counterlight
countermarch
counterplead
counterpoint
counterpoise
counterproof
counterscarp
countershaft
countertenor
crossexamine
cynocephalus
cytogenetics
decalescence
deceleration
degenerately
degeneration
degenerative
deliberately
deliberation
deliberative
delitescence
demineralise
desideration
desiderative
detumescence
diathermancy
discreetness
discreteness
discretional
disobedience
displeasedly
doubleacting
doubledealer
doubledecked
doubledecker
doublelocked
endometritis
enginedriver
enginetuning
ephemerality
epiphenomena
epistemology
erythematous
euhemeristic
evangelistic
evisceration
exaggeration
exaggerative
exaggeratory
exasperation
exenteration
exulceration
facelessness
fearlessness
featherbrain
featheriness
fecklessness
feebleminded
fiddlefaddle
fiddlesticks
flatteringly
flickeringly
fluorescence
formlessness
frequentness
gamopetalous
gamosepalous
geochemistry
glaucescence
glitteringly
glockenspiel
gobbledegook
gobbledygook
goodtempered
gramnegative
halogenation
handkerchief
hardfeatured
harmlessness
harquebusier
heathenishly
heedlessness
helplessness
homosexually
hopelessness
hubblebubble
hucklebacked
illiberality
illiterately
illtreatment
immaterially
immoderately
immoderation
impenetrable
impenetrably
impoverished
inaccessible
inaccessibly
inadvertence
inadvertency
inappeasable
incalescence
incatenation
incidentally
incineration
incoherently
indefeasible
indefeasibly
indefectible
indefensible
indefensibly
independence
independency
indigenously
indigestible
indirectness
indivertible
indivertibly
IndoGermanic
inexpedience
inexpediency
inexperience
inexpertness
inextensible
inobservance
inteneration
interestedly
intolerantly
intumescence
inveterately
irredeemable
irredeemably
irrelevantly
irremediable
irremediably
irrepealable
irreverently
irreversible
irreversibly
Ishmaelitish
isothermally
juvenescence
laisserfaire
laissezaller
laissezfaire
leathercloth
lifelessness
listlessness
loungelizard
lovelessness
luminescence
malapertness
maltreatment
manometrical
mediaevalism
mediaevalist
mesocephalic
middleweight
mindlessness
minedetector
mistreatment
mistressship
monadelphous
monometallic
monopetalous
monumentally
movelessness
muddleheaded
muzzleloader
namelessness
needlessness
nonagenarian
nonidentical
northeastern
northernmost
obedientiary
obliteration
obliterative
obmutescence
obsolescence
obsoleteness
obstreperous
occidentally
octogenarian
officeholder
ornamentally
overpersuade
overreaction
oxyacetylene
painlessness
pancreatitis
parametrical
pasqueflower
pearlescence
pedicellaria
peerlessness
penitentiary
perplexingly
philhellenic
phrasemonger
phraseograph
pitcherplant
pitilessness
plasterboard
plummerblock
polyneuritic
polyneuritis
polypetalous
polysepalous
postmeridian
praiseworthy
princeliness
propaedeutic
prosperously
puerperrally
pyrotechnics
pyrotechnist
quarterbound
quarterfinal
quarterstaff
quintessence
rabblerouser
radioelement
rattleheaded
razzledazzle
reappearance
reassessment
recalescence
recklessness
recuperation
recuperative
regeneration
regenerative
regimentally
reinvestment
rejuvenation
remuneration
remunerative
remuneratory
residentiary
residentship
resplendence
resplendency
restlessness
rontgenogram
rontgenology
rootlessness
rumbletumble
ruthlessness
saddlebacked
scatterbrain
scatteringly
sclerenchyma
scraperboard
selfbegotten
selfbetrayal
selfdeceived
selfdeceiver
selfdelusion
selfdestruct
selfdevotion
selflessness
selfreliance
selfreproach
semideponent
semidetached
sexagenarian
shatterproof
simpleminded
singleacting
singledecker
singlehanded
singleminded
singleseater
slanderously
sledgehammer
slipperiness
softpedalled
soullessness
southeastern
southernmost
southernwood
spiegeleisen
spotlessness
squarerigged
staggeringly
stammeringly
statuesquely
stellenbosch
stutteringly
supereminent
supererogate
supplemental
supplementer
suppressible
swaggeringly
swaggerstick
syncretistic
tactlessness
tamelessness
taperecorder
tearlessness
theoretician
thitherwards
thundercloud
thunderingly
thunderously
thunderstone
thunderstorm
timelessness
tirelessness
tittletattle
toggleswitch
tonelessness
triggerhappy
trumpetshell
tunelessness
turtlenecked
twitteringly
unacceptable
unaffectedly
unappeasable
unappetising
uncelebrated
uncomeatable
undetermined
unexpectedly
ungovernable
uninterested
unlikelihood
unlikeliness
unloveliness
unregenerate
unrepeatable
unreservedly
unscientific
untimeliness
viridescence
vituperation
vituperative
vituperatory
vociferation
vociferously
volumetrical
walkietalkie
weatherboard
weatherbound
weatherglass
weatherhouse
weatherproof
whencesoever
whimperingly
whisperingly
whitherwards
williewaught
winklepicker
YankeeDoodle
beatifically
blamefulness
blastfurnace
blissfulness
boastfulness
brickfielder
cheerfulness
curvifoliate
decaffeinate
disaffection
disaffiliate
disinfectant
disinfection
disinflation
doubtfulness
dreadfulness
exsufflicate
faithfulness

fancifulness
faultfinding
forcefulness
fruitfulness
fullyfledged
gracefulness
gratefulness
gratifyingly
guilefulness
habitforming
henceforward
horrifically
hydrofluoric
imperfection
imperfective
inconformity
indifference
indifferency
insufferable
insufferably
insufficient
insufflation
interfemoral
interference
liquefacient
liquefaction
magnifically
magnificence
mercifulness
mirthfulness
mournfulness
multifarious
multiflorous
multifoliate
multiformity
mystifyingly
noneffective
nonefficient
peacefulness
petrifaction
pettifoggery
pettifogging
photofission
pontifically
pontificator
pridefulness
prizefighter
prolifically
prolificness
putrefaction
putrefactive
retroflexion
rightfulness
satisfaction
satisfactory
satisfyingly
scarificator
scornfulness
selfaffected
selfeffacing
semiofficial
shamefacedly
shamefulness
significance
significancy
slothfulness
sorbefacient
specifically
specificness
spitefulness
sportfulness
stupefacient
stupefaction
stupefactive
subinfeudate
tastefulness
terrifically
terrifyingly
thankfulness
toploftiness
torrefaction
transferable
transference
transferring
transformism
transformist
transfusible
trustfulness
truthfulness
unconformity
unlawfulness
unprofitable
unprofitably
vengefulness
vitrifaction
wastefulness
watchfulness
wrathfulness
wrongfulness
youthfulness
aboriginally
agamogenesis
agamogenetic
agentgeneral
anagogically
analogically
anemographic
avantgardism
avantgardist
belligerence
belligerency
bilingualism
biologically
blackguardly
cabbagewhite
calligrapher
calligraphic
carragheenin
cartographer
cartographic
chorographic
closegrained
collegialism
collegiality
collegiately
consignation
contagionist
contagiously
contiguously
cosmogonical
cosmographer
cosmographic
courageously
crossgrained
decongestant
decongestion
decongestive
deflagration
diamagnetism
discographer
disingenuous
disregardful
ecologically
endangerment
entanglement
epexegetical
ethnographer
ethnographic
exsanguinate
exsanguinous
extinguisher
farsightedly
ferrugineous
fieldglasses
galligaskins
geologically
geomagnetism
glycogenesis
greengrocery
hagiographer
hagiographic
hectographic
heliographer
heliographic
heliogravure
hieroglyphic
hierographer
histogenesis
histogenetic
hydrographer
hydrographic
hymnographer
hypnogenesis
hypnogenetic
iconographer
impregnation
interglacial
intriguingly
inveiglement
laryngoscope
laryngoscopy
lithographer
lithographic
liturgically
liturgiology
majorgeneral
mastigophora
micrographer
moneygrubber
mulligatawny
mythographer
necrographer
organgrinder
orthogenesis
orthogenetic
orthographer
orthographic
osteogenesis
outrageously
paedogenesis
paedogenetic
palingenesia
palingenesis
palingenetic
pantographic
pathogenesis
pathogenetic
petrographer
petrographic
phonographer
phonographic
photogeology
photographer
photographic
photogravure
phylogenesis
phylogenetic
phytogenesis
phytogenetic
phytographer
pictographic
pornographer
pornographic
precognition
precognitive
predigestion
primigravida
primogenital
primogenitor
prodigiously
prolegomenon
propagandise
propagandism
propagandist
radiographer
radiographic
refrigerator
reprographic
revengefully
rhizogenetic
risorgimento
salpiglossis
scenographic
selfignition
sphragistics
sporogenesis
stenographer
stenographic
straightaway
straightbred
straightedge
straightener
straightness
stranglehold
strengthener
strengthless
stringcourse
strongminded
strongylosis
stylographic
tachygrapher
tachygraphic
tetragonally
throughstone
transgressor
triangularly
umbrageously
undergarment
unimaginable
unimaginably
vantagepoint
vicargeneral
analphabetic
antiphonally
antithetical
apprehension
apprehensive
asynchronism
asynchronous
autochthones
breathalyser
breathlessly
breathtaking
breechloader
bronchoscope
carbohydrate
catachrestic
cataphoresis
catechetical
churchianity
churchwarden
cliffhanging
coldshoulder
crossheading
decipherable
decipherment
delightfully
detachedness
diphtheritic
diphthongise
draughtboard
draughthorse
droughtiness
encephalitic
encephalitis
eunuchoidism
exospherical
fainthearted
faithhealing
freethinking
freewheeling
freightliner
frenchpolish
gamophyllous
greathearted
headshrinker
heavyhearted
hedgehopping
hemichordate
henotheistic
homothallism
hypochlorite
hypochondria
hypophrygian
hypothalamic
hypothalamus
hypothecator
hypothetical
idiothermous
immethodical
kirschwasser
largehearted
lighthearted
longshoreman
Manicheanism
marshharrier
mesothoracic
metachronism
metaphorical
metaphrastic
metaphysical
metathetical
metathoracic
misbehaviour
mitochondria
monochromate
monophyletic
Monophysitic
monotheistic
nychthemeral
nychthemeron
oncorhynchus
opisthograph
opisthotonos
ornithomancy
ornithoscopy
paraphrastic
parochialise
parochialism
parochiality
peripherally
periphrastic
phosphoresce
polychaetous
polychromous
polyphyletic
polytheistic
protohistory
proudhearted
reprehension
reprehensive
rhynchophora
ricochetting
scareheading
seraphically
sidewhiskers
slaughterous
slaveholding
smallholding
speechlessly
sprightfully
stepchildren
stillhunting
stonyhearted
stouthearted
strophanthin
strychninism
superhighway
superhumanly
sycophantish
tetrahedrite
thoughtfully
togetherness
transhipment
transhumance

unauthorised
unfathomable
vicechairman
wholehearted
wretchedness
abortiveness
abrasiveness
acquaintance
adaptiveness
additionally
adhesiveness
adjudication
adjudicative
adjudicatory
administrant
administrate
admonishment
aerosiderite
allusiveness
amentiferous
amortisation
anastigmatic
annihilation
annihilative
antediluvian
antiaircraft
anticipation
anticipative
anticipatory
apparitional
appetisingly
appositeness
appositional
appraisement
appraisingly
arborisation
archdiocesan
artificially
assibilation
assimilation
assimilative
assimilatory
astonishment
autodidactic
basidiospore
behaviourism
behaviourist
beneficently
beneficially
bioscientist
blandishment
bombdisposal
borosilicate
brackishness
brilliantine
bullfighting
calamitously
calorimetric
canaliculate
canalisation
canonisation
catilinarian
championship
chastisement
chauvinistic
childishness
chlorination
churlishness
circuitously
civilisation
clannishness
classicalism
classicalist
classicality
classifiable
claudication
clownishness
cockfighting
codification
coerciveness
cohabitation
cohesiveness
coincidental
coincidently
colonisation
colorimetric
complication
conchiferous
conidiophore
conidiospore
conquistador
conscionable
conspiration
constipation
constituency
constitution
constitutive
containerise
contribution
contributive
contributory
contriteness
contrivement
coordinately
coordination
coordinative
councilwoman
creativeness
crossingover
deactivation
debilitation
decapitation
decisiveness
definiteness
definitively
deionisation
delamination
delimitation
delusiveness
demilitarise
demoniacally
denomination
denominative
depoliticise
deputisation
deracination
derisiveness
desalination
despairingly
detoxication
dilapidation
diminishable
diminishment
discriminant
discriminate
disdainfully
disguisement
disjointedly
disorientate
disquisition
distributary
distribution
distributive
divarication
divisibility
divisiveness
dressinggown
dwarfishness
effeminately
effusiveness
emancipation
emargination
emulsifiable
enantiomorph
enshrinement
equalisation
equalitarian
equationally
equidistance
equilibrator
eruptiveness
etherisation
excogitation
excogitative
exercitation
exhibitioner
exorbitantly
expediential
experiential
experimental
experimenter
exploitation
exploitative
facilitation
faintishness
felicitation
felicitously
feminineness
feminisation
feverishness
fiendishness
finalisation
firefighting
fluidisation
fluoridation
fluorination
focalisation
foraminifera
foresightful
fortuitously
fractionally
fractionator
frangibility
frankincense
freakishness
frictionless
frontiersman
frontispiece
fructiferous
fructivorous
fugitiveness
fuliginosity
functionally
functionless
futilitarian
ganglionated
gasification
geanticlinal
ghoulishness
graspingness
gratuitously
greenishness
guardianship
habilitation
halftimbered
headmistress
hereditament
hereditarily
homesickness
humanisation
humanitarian
humification
hydatidiform
idealisation
ideationally
identifiable
illegibility
illegitimacy
illegitimate
illogicality
illumination
illuminative
illusiveness
immunisation
impedimental
impenitently
imperishable
imperishably
impetiginous
impoliteness
inactivation
inadmissible
inadmissibly
inarticulate
inartificial
inaudibility
incisiveness
indecisively
indefinitely
indehiscence
indelibility
indelicately
individually
inefficiency
infelicitous
infiniteness
infinitively
infusibility
inhabitation
iniquitously
inordinately
insemination
intimidation
intimidatory
intoxication
invagination
invalidation
invigilation
invisibility
irascibility
irrationally
irremissible
irresistible
irresistibly
kremlinology
labyrinthian
labyrinthine
lacininiated
languishment
laterisation
laticiferous
latinisation
legalisation
legitimately
legitimation
legitimatise
libidinously
linguistical
localisation
longdistance
longwindedly
luminiferous
Marseillaise
materialness
maximisation
meridionally
messeigneurs
minimisation
misalignment
mithridatise
mithridatism
mitrailleuse
mobilisation
modification
modificatory
monetisation
monofilament
moralisation
motorisation
mourningband
mourningring
municipalise
municipality
munificently
musicianship
nebulisation
negativeness
negativistic
negotiatress
nicotinamide
nidification
nonalignment
nonexistence
notification
novelisation
obligingness
obnubilation
occasionally
openmindedly
oppositeness
oppositional
optimisation
organisation
ossification
overniceness
oversimplify
pacification
pacificatory
panification
paradigmatic
paradisaical
paradisiacal
paramilitary
parasiticide
parasitology
penalisation
peroxidation
perspicacity
perspiration
perspiratory
plausibility
pleasingness
plumbiferous
pointilliste
polarimetric
polarisation
polyhistoric
positiveness
positivistic
postdiluvian
postmistress
practicality
practitioner
preeminently
preexistence
prenticeship
prevailingly
priggishness
principality
profligately
proprietress
prostitution
psychiatrist
punchingball
purblindness
purification
purificatory
pyroligneous
quadriennium
quadrinomial
quadriplegia
quadriplegic
quadrivalent
qualmishness
quantifiable
quantisation
quantitative
questionable
questionably
questionless
quizzicality
racemisation
radioisotope
ramification
ratification

reactivation
reactiveness
reassignment
recapitulate
reducibility
rehabilitate
reinvigorate
relationally
relationship
relativeness
relativistic
remilitarise
reminiscence
repetitional
repetitively
resiniferous
resipiscence
restrictedly
resupination
retiringness
reviviscence
romanisation
ruralisation
salutiferous
Samaritanism
sanguinarily
sanguineness
sanguinolent
saponifiable
Scandinavian
scintigraphy
scintillator
scorpionfish
scouringrush
scrobiculate
scurrilously
selfdirected
selfdistrust
selflimiting
selfrighting
selfviolence
semicircular
semidiameter
semifinalist
semifinished
semiliterate
seminiferous
sesquialtera
sheepishness
shootingiron
shrewishness
silicicolous
siliciferous
simoniacally
skippingrope
skittishness
sleepingpill
sluggishness
sluttishness
snappishness
snarlingiron
snobbishness
solarisation
solicitation
solicitously
soporiferous
soundingline
sparkingplug
speakingtube
sportiveness
stablishment
standingroom
stanniferous
stelliferous
sterlingness
stockingless
Stradivarius
straticulate
stratigraphy
strikingness
strobilation
studdingsail
subeditorial
suberisation
substitution
substitutive
sudoriferous
supplicantly
supplication
supplicatory
surprisingly
surveillance
swainishness
sweepingness
sweetishness
swimmingbath
swimmingbell
swimmingpool
taskmistress
technicality
technicolour
televisional
terebinthine
thereinafter
thievishness
ticklishness
toastingfork
totalisation
totalitarian
touchingness
transiliency
transitional
transitively
transitivity
transitorily
trephination
trickishness
triplication
typification
ubiquitarian
ubiquitously
unambivalent
unbelievable
unbelievably
underinsured
unfamiliarly
unhesitating
unionisation
unofficially
unscriptural
urbanisation
valorisation
vanquishable
vanquishment
vaporisation
vasodilation
vasodilatory
vaticination
ventripotent
veridicality
verification
verificatory
veterinarian
vilification
villainously
vinification
vitalisation
vitiligation
vivification
vocalisation
volatileness
volitionally
voluminosity
voluminously
welldisposed
whimsicality
womanishness
worshipfully
interjection
interjectory
introjection
nonobjective
stockjobbery
stockjobbing
surrejoinder
unprejudiced
endoskeletal
housekeeping
hydrokinetic
karyokinesis
kinnikinnick
mistakenness
photokinesis
photokinetic
unbrokenness
acetaldehyde
aetiological
anthelmintic
anticlerical
apiculturist
argillaceous
artilleryman
astrological
auscultation
auscultatory
bachelorhood
bachelorship
backslapping
bellylanding
benzaldehyde
berzelianite
bloodletting
brambleberry
buffalograss
calculatedly
cancellation
cantillation
carillonneur
cartological
catholically
chivalrously
chocolatebox
chorological
compellation
compulsively
compulsivity
compulsorily
concelebrant
concelebrate
conciliation
conciliative
conciliatory
consolidator
consultation
consultative
convalescent
convulsively
cosmological
crashlanding
crenellation
dentilingual
denuclearise
despoliation
diabolically
disallowance
distillation
distillatory
earsplitting
encyclopedia
encyclopedic
ethnological
etymological
etymologicon
extralimital
fertilisable
fibrillation
flabelliform
flagellation
flagellatory
floodlighted
footplateman
formaldehyde
genealogical
genuflection
geopolitical
gesellschaft
gravelelling
grovellingly
hagiological
heliolatrous
histological
hydrological
hydrolysable
inapplicable
inapplicably
indeclinable
inexplicable
inexplicably
installation
instillation
intellection
intellective
intellectual
intelligence
intelligible
intelligibly
interlobular
interlocutor
irreflective
limnological
lithological
magniloquent
mangelwurzel
marvellously
metallically
metallophone
metallurgist
metrological
miscalculate
miscellanist
misselthrush
multilateral
multilingual
multiloquous
mythological
mythologiser
nanoplankton
necrological
Neohellenism
nephelometer
nephelometry
neurological
noctilucence
oscillograph
oscilloscope
osteological
panhellenism
parallelling
pathological
perfoliation
pestilential
pestological
petrological
phenological
philological
phonological
phycological
phytological
pluriliteral
poikilotherm
polyglottism
porcelainise
porcelainous
porcellanous
predilection
preselection
preselective
promulgation
proselytiser
pyroelectric
radiological
rebelliously
recollection
recollective
redeployment
rhinological
sacrilegious
scatological
schoolfellow
schoolleaver
schoolmaster
schorlaceous
scutellation
selfelective
selfflattery
selfpleasing
semiological
septilateral
shuffleboard
sideslipping
snaggletooth
sociological
solifluction
somniloquism
somniloquist
steeplechase
subcelestial
swizzlestick
symbolically
tautological
taxcollector
teleological
tessellation
thimbleberry
translatable
translucence
translucency
trestletable
tropological
troublemaker
turbellarian
unapologetic
underletting
undiplomatic
unemployable
unemployment
unifoliolate
unwieldiness
unworldiness
unyieldingly
vainglorious
whitelivered
whortleberry
wineglassful
abstemiously
academically
accommodator
achlamydeous
aeroembolism
AfroAmerican
alphamerical
anatomically
arithmetical
autoimmunity
avitaminoses
avitaminosis
bantamweight
bowcompasses
brinkmanship
chairmanship
circumcision
circumfluent
circumfusion
circumjacent
circumscribe

circumstance
closemouthed
commemorator
concomitance
condemnation
condemnatory
consummately
consummation
consummative
consummatory
contemplator
contemporary
contemporise
contemptible
contemptibly
contemptuous
contumacious
contumelious
courtmartial
cuprammonium
customshouse
determinable
determinably
determinedly
diatomaceous
discomfiture
discommodity
discomposure
disseminator
dissimilarly
dissimulator
dissymmetric
distemperate
econometrics
economically
emblematical
endermically
entrammelled
epidemically
epidemiology
EuroAmerican
exterminable
exterminator
extramarital
extramundane
gamesmanship
hebdomadally
homeomorphic
horsemanship
hydromedusae
hydromedusan
impermanence
impermanency
incommodious
incommutable
incommutably
inflammation
inflammatory
inharmonious
intermeddler
intermediacy
intermediary
intermediate
interminable
interminably
intermission
intermittent
intermitting
intermixture
intermundane
intramundane
intromission
intromittent
intromitting
judgematical
marksmanship
mathematical
mealymouthed
misdemeanant
misdemeanour
neonomianism
noctambulant
noctambulism
noctambulist
noctambulous
noncombatant
noncommittal
noncomplying
oneupmanship
osteomalacia
overemphasis
paedomorphic
parsimonious
phenomenally
phonemically
photomontage
phycomycetes
predominance
predominancy
presumptuous
pronominally
recommitment
rhythmically
salesmanship
sarcomatosis
schismatical
selfemployed
sociometrist
somnambulant
somnambulate
somnambulism
somnambulist
sphygmograph
stagemanager
stonemasonry
subcommittee
subtemperate
supermundane
supramundane
systematical
systematiser
systemically
testamentary
tetramorphic
tightmouthed
transmigrant
transmigrate
transmission
transmissive
transmitting
transmogrify
transmontane
transmutable
trinomialism
ultramontane
ultramundane
uncommercial
uncommonness
undermanning
watermanship
aircondition
alimentation
alimentative
alphanumeric
announcement
astoundingly
astringently
astronautics
astronomical
attorneyship
augmentation
augmentative
authenticate
authenticity
billingsgate
biosynthesis
biosynthetic
birdsnesting
bodysnatcher
bookingclerk
brokenwinded
buccaneering
buccaneerish
burningglass
cachinnation
cachinnatory
calumniation
calumniatory
calumniously
camiknickers
cantankerous
carbonaceous
carcinogenic
cardinalship
cashandcarry
clarinettist
coelenterate
coetaneously
collinearity
columniation
combinations
commandingly
commencement
commendation
commendatory
commensalism
commensalist
commensurate
commentation
commonwealth
communicable
communicably
communicator
companionate
companionway
compensation
compensative
compensatory
compunctious
concentrator
condensation
congeniality
congenitally
conjunctival
conningtower
consensually
consentience
consentingly
contingently
continuation
continuative
continuously
conveniently
conventicler
conventional
convincement
convincingly
cottonocracy
cousingerman
cuckingstool
curlingirons
curlingtongs
declinometer
denouncement
despondently
diamonddrill
diamondfield
diatonically
dibranchiate
disannulling
disannulment
disconnected
disconnexion
disconsolate
discontented
dispensation
dispensatory
dissentingly
distinctness
drawingboard
drawingpaper
duckingstool
elementalism
elementarily
embranchment
enchantingly
entrancement
entrenchment
espagnolette
estrangement
euphonically
euphoniously
eveningdress
evidentially
exchangeable
explantation
extraneously
falcongentil
falcongentle
fermentation
fermentative
fibrinolysin
firstnighter
gallinaceous
galvanically
galvanometer
galvanoscope
geosynclinal
Germanophile
Germanophobe
governmental
governorship
graminaceous
guaranteeing
happenstance
harmonically
harmoniously
heavenliness
hereinbefore
hermeneutics
hibernaculum
horrendously
hygienically
hypognathous
implantation
inclinometer
incognisable
incognisance
incognitable
infringement
internuclear
internuncial
intransigent
intransitive
intrenchment
invulnerable
invulnerably
katzenjammer
kissingcrust
landingcraft
landingfield
landingstage
landingstrip
lodginghouse
maidenliness
maidenstakes
malcontented
marlinespike
meaningfully
mechanically
meetinghouse
meltingpoint
mercantilism
mercantilist
morningdress
multinuclear
multungulate
muttonheaded
nephanalysis
nonconductor
nonconformer
outlandishly
outmanoeuvre
outpensioner
parkinsonism
permanganate
pertinacious
philanthrope
philanthropy
pigeonbreast
pigmentation
platonically
playingfield
portentously
precancelled
precondition
preconscious
prehensility
premenstrual
preponderant
preponderate
presentation
presentative
presentiment
preventative
preventively
proconsulate
progenitress
prolongation
protensively
provincially
prudentially
rabbinically
radionuclide
rambunctious
recognisable
recognisably
recognisance
renouncement
resignedness
resoundingly
responsively
responsorial
retrenchment
rollingstock
runningboard
salmonladder
sardonically
screenwriter
segmentation
selfanalysis
selfinterest
selfinvolved
sellingplate
semiannually
sententially
septennially
sequentially
serpentiform
serpentinely
sexcentenary
siphonophore
siphonostele
slovenliness
steganograph
stupendously
subconscious
subcontinent
subminiature
subsonically
succinctness
supernaculum
supernatural
suspensively
sustentation

sustentative
tabernacular
tangentially
tectonically
tercentenary
Teutonically
tintinnabula
torrentially
tremendously
tricentenary
trigonometry
tyrannically
tyrannicidal
unblinkingly
unchangeable
unchangeably
uneconomical
uneventfully
ungainliness
unprincipled
unpronounced
unthinkingly
volcanically
Wellingtonia
windingsheet
woodengraver
woodenheaded
workingclass
actinomycete
ailurophobia
allomorphism
amelioration
ameliorative
anaerobiosis
anecdotalist
antagonistic
anthropogeny
anthropoidal
anthropology
aperiodicity
apostolicism
apostolicity
aristocratic
Aristotelean
Aristotelian
atheromatous
automobilist
automorphism
autonomously
backwoodsman
bellbottomed
benevolently
bibliography
bibliologist
bibliomaniac
bibliopegist
bibliophilic
bibliopolist
bibliothecae
bioecologist
biogeography
blastosphere
broncobuster
brontosaurus
calycoideous
campfollower
canorousness
captiousness
cardiography
cardiologist
catamountain
cautiousness
centrosphere
ceremonially
chalcolithic
chalcopyrite
cheirography
choreography
chromosphere
chronography
chronologise
chronologist
chronometric
clangorously
conchologist
conglobation
conglomerate
controllable
covetousness
craniologist
cryptogamous
cryptography
cryptologist
cuckooflower
cumbrousness
cumulocirrus
cumulonimbus
Czechoslovak
decorousness
demimondaine
deontologist
desirousness
dethronement
dextrousness
diageotropic
dichromatism
dilatoriness
dolorousness
dovecoloured
dynamometric
echinococcus
echolocation
echosounding
edulcoration
Egyptologist
elasmobranch
eleemosynary
embryologist
emotionalise
emotionalism
emotionalist
emotionality
enormousness
enthronement
entomologise
entomologist
enzymologist
episcopalian
equipollence
equipollency
equivocation
equivocatory
escapologist
exiguousness
fabulousness
factionalism
factiousness
fearsomeness
fictionalise
flamboyantly
fluorocarbon
forebodement
forebodingly
FrancoGerman
futurologist
gamesomeness
gametophytic
gastronomist
gastropodous
generousness
glaciologist
gladsomeness
glaucomatous
gloriousness
glossography
glossologist
gluttonously
glyphography
glyptography
gonadotropic
gonadotropin
gorgeousness
graciousness
grammolecule
grampositive
graphologist
grievousness
griseofulvin
gruesomeness
handsomeness
hemerocallis
hemimorphism
hemimorphite
heortologist
heterocercal
heterocyclic
heteroecious
heterogamous
heterogenous
heterologous
heteromerous
heteronomous
heterophylly
heterosexual
heterozygote
heterozygous
highcoloured
highsounding
homoeopathic
homoeostasis
homologation
homomorphism
homomorphous
horizontally
humorousness
hymenopteran
hypocoristic
illusoriness
immemorially
immunologist
inappositely
indecorously
interoceanic
interoceptor
invigoration
irreformable
irresolutely
irresolution
irresolvable
jetpropelled
kleptomaniac
languorously
lepidopteran
levorotation
levorotatory
lexicography
lexicologist
lonesomeness
lovelornness
luminousness
lusciousness
mademoiselle
malacologist
malevolently
manifoldness
mansionhouse
Marcionitism
megalomaniac
melanochroic
metamorphism
metamorphose
metasomatism
minicomputer
misknowledge
mispronounce
misquotation
monitorially
monomorphous
monopodially
monopolistic
monotonously
morphologist
musicologist
mutinousness
naturopathic
nauseousness
nebulousness
nephrologist
nonflowering
numerologist
numerousness
nympholeptic
nymphomaniac
oceanography
oceanologist
odontologist
offscourings
omnipotently
omnivorously
oneirocritic
opinionative
organography
organoleptic
overlordship
overpowering
palaeobotany
palaeography
Palaeolithic
palynologist
papyrologist
paraboloidal
paramorphism
paranormally
paronomastic
passionately
passionfruit
patulousness
perilousness
perviousness
phlebotomise
phlebotomist
phrenologist
phyllotactic
physiognomic
physiography
physiologist
plectognathi
pleomorphism
plesiosaurus
pluviometric
pneumothorax
polarography
polymorphism
polymorphous
polytonality
populousness
postdoctoral
postponement
postposition
postpositive
praseodymium
preciousness
previousness
proglottides
prothonotary
psephologist
pseudocyesis
pseudonymity
pseudonymous
pseudopodium
psychoactive
psychography
psychologise
psychologism
psychologist
psychometric
psychopathic
psychosexual
psychotropic
pyromorphite
rapprochment
ravenousness
reallocation
redecoration
renegotiable
reunionistic
rhombohedral
rhombohedron
rigorousness
rosecoloured
scabrousness
schizogonous
schizomycete
schizophrene
schizothymia
schizothymic
sectionalism
sedulousness
seismography
seismologist
seismometric
seismoscopic
selenography
selenologist
selfcoloured
selfcomposed
selfcontempt
selfdoubting
selfportrait
semidomestic
sensuousness
sinusoidally
sodafountain
somatopleure
sonorousness
spaciousness
sparrowgrass
speciousness
speleologist
spermogonium
spheroidally
spuriousness
staffofficer
stationhouse
stationwagon
steatopygous
stereochromy
stereography
stereoisomer
stereometric
stereophonic
stereopticon
stereoscopic
stertorously
stethoscopic
stichomythia
stichomythic
stilboestrol
stratosphere
stroboscopic
stubbornness
studiousness
subapostolic
sulphonamide
sulphonation
supraorbital
surefootedly
technocratic
technologist
teratologist
teratomatous
theosophical
thermocouple
thermography
thermolabile

thermometric
thermophilic
thermoscopic
thermosphere
thermostable
thermostatic
thermotactic
thermotropic
timehonoured
timorousness
tiresomeness
toilsomeness
tortuousness
toxicologist
toxicophobia
trachomatous
traitorously
trampolinist
transoceanic
trichologist
trichotomise
trichotomous
troglodytism
typefounding
unbecomingly
unctuousness
undemocratic
unfavourable
unfavourably
unimportance
unrecognised
urbanologist
usuriousness
uxoriousness
vaporousness
varicoloured
venomousness
vigorousness
virtuosoship
virtuousness
vitreousness
warehouseman
whippoorwill
wondrousness
xanthochroia
zoogeography
zygapophysis
zygomorphism
zygomorphous
absorptional
absorptivity
accompanyist
accomplished
alexipharmic
anemophilous
appropriable
appropriator
archipelagic
astrophysics
atmospherics
bathypelagic
centuplicate
chiropractic
chiropractor
coleopterist
coleopterous
conceptional
conceptually
concupiscent
conduplicate
corespondent
cosmopolitan
cosmopolitic
courtplaster
crosspurpose
decomposable
decompressor
desulphurise
discipleship
disciplinary
disreputable
disreputably
enterprising
entrepreneur
feldspathoid
flavoprotein
glycoprotein
goosepimples
haemophiliac
haemopoiesis
hairsplitter
hemispheroid
hierophantic
highspirited
hippopotamus
homeopathist
hydrophilous
hygrophilous
hyperplastic
hyperpyretic
hyperpyrexia
impropriator
inauspicious
incomparable
incomparably
incompatible
incompatibly
incompetence
incompetency
incompletely
incompliance
incomputable
incorporated
incorporator
incorporeity
indisputable
indisputably
inhospitable
inhospitably
intemperance
interpellate
interpleader
interpolator
interpretive
irrespective
irrespirable
irresponsive
jurisprudent
klipspringer
Liverpudlian
macropterous
metropolitan
microphysics
misapprehend
misrepresent
multipartite
multipliable
multiplicand
multiplicate
multiplicity
multipurpose
necrophagous
necrophiliac
necrophilism
necrophilous
negrophilism
negrophilist
neuropterous
ophiophagous
orthopaedics
orthopaedist
orthopterist
orthopteroid
orthopterous
osteoplastic
osteoporosis
passepartout
peasepudding
pennypincher
perceptively
perceptivity
perceptually
peremptorily
perispomenon
photophilous
phytophagous
plecopterous
plenipotence
poorspirited
preceptorial
precipitable
precipitance
precipitancy
precipitator
prelapsarian
prosopopoeia
protoplasmic
protoplastic
radiophonics
redemptioner
Redemptorist
retropulsion
rhizophagous
saprophagous
sarcophagous
sarsaparilla
scenepainter
selfapplause
selfapproval
Shakspereana
Shaksperiana
shortpitched
starspangled
sublapsarian
superposable
susceptivity
therapeutics
therapeutist
transpacific
transparency
transpirable
transplanter
transpontine
transposable
triumphantly
underpinning
unresponsive
vibraphonist
colloquially
consequently
delinquently
harlequinade
hydroquinone
inadequately
infrequently
prerequisite
subsequently
threequarter
unfrequented
anamorphosis
anteprandial
antigropelos
apochromatic
apostrophise
backbreaking
bactericidal
bacteriology
bacteriostat
banderillero
barbarically
bassorelievo
bassorilievo
beggarliness
bilharziasis
bilharziosis
birefringent
brassrubbing
butterflynut
buttermuslin
butterscotch
Byelorussian
calcareously
carburetting
censoriously
chondriosome
coacervation
colourlessly
comfortingly
commercially
compurgation
compurgatory
concordantly
concurrently
conferential
confirmation
confirmative
confirmatory
conformation
conscription
conservation
conservatism
conservative
conservatory
constriction
constrictive
constringent
construction
constructive
conterminous
conversation
corporeality
costermonger
countrydance
countrywoman
cumbersomely
curvirostral
dessertspoon
Deuteronomic
diastrophism
differentiae
differential
dinnerjacket
disagreeable
disagreeably
disagreement
disbursement
discerningly
discerptible
discordantly
discursively
disgorgement
disharmonise
dispiritedly
dissertation
distortional
disturbingly
dunderheaded
editorialise
editorialist
efflorescent
electrically
electrolysis
electrolytic
electrometer
electronvolt
electroplate
electroscope
electroshock
electrotonic
electrotonus
electrotyper
epicureanism
equiprobable
erythroblast
erythromycin
esoterically
exacerbation
exoterically
expatriation
fatherfigure
fatherliness
forthrightly
fostermother
furfuraceous
gregariously
haemorrhagic
hairdressing
halterbroken
heartrending
hellgrammite
hesperididia
hierarchical
highpressure
historically
horrorstruck
huggermugger
hypocritical
hysterectomy
hysterically
hysteromania
incoordinate
incorrigible
incorrigibly
incorruption
inexpressive
inextricable
inextricably
ingloriously
innutritious
inoperculate
insurrection
interrelated
interrogator
interruption
interruptive
irrefragable
irrefragably
irreprovable
isochromatic
isochronally
kindergarten
laboursaving
lanternjawed
lanternslide
leapfrogging
ledgertackle
lugubriously
lumberjacket
malformation
malversation
mannerliness
mastersinger
masterstroke
masterswitch
melodramatic
menstruation
mercurialise
mercurialism
meretricious
meteorically
meteorograph
mezzorelievo
misdirection
monodramatic
monographist
mosstrooping
motherfigure
motherliness
mothertongue
mysteriously
namedropping
neoDarwinian
neoDarwinism
neoDarwinist
nerveracking

Nestorianism
noradrenalin
obscurantism
obscurantist
oligarchical
omnipresence
outstretched
outstripping
outwardbound
overcritical
overcropping
overpressure
panchromatic
paragraphist
patternmaker
peregrinator
perfervidity
performative
perjuriously
perturbation
perturbative
perverseness
phanerogamic
pickerelweed
pitterpatter
polyurethane
posteriority
postgraduate
postprandial
precariously
prechristian
preferential
preformation
preformative
preparedness
prescription
prescriptive
preservation
preservative
pretermitted
prevaricator
primordially
proofreading
proportional
proportioned
proscription
proscriptive
proverbially
psychrometer
psychrometry
pulverisable
pumpernickel
quattrocento
rechargeable
reciprocally
reciprocator
repatriation
resurrection
rhetorically
safecracking
salubriously
sectarianise
sectarianism
selfcritical
semiprecious
semitropical
sightreading
silverglance
spectrograph
spectrometer
spectrometry
spectroscope
spectroscopy
spidermonkey
squirrelcage
squirreltail
stockraising
subarrhation
subnormality
subscription
subservience
subserviency
substruction
substructure
subterranean
subthreshold
subversively
synchronical
synchroniser
teetertotter
telegraphese
telegraphist
terrorstruck
theatregoing
theatrically
theocratical
trichromatic
trifurcation
tripartitely
tripartition
unattractive
uncharitable
uncharitably
underrunning
unitarianism
universalise
universalism
universalist
universality
unsearchable
unsegregated
uproariously
Victorianism
victoriously
viscerotonic
wellgrounded
welterweight
winterbourne
wonderstruck
wonderworker
wunderkinder
accursedness
aggressively
ambassadress
amphisbaenic
assassinator
bloodstained
brainstormer
callisthenic
Cartesianism
centesimally
cirrostratus
clearsighted
commiserator
commissarial
commissariat
commissioner
composedness
confessional
confiscation
confiscatory
confusedness
consistently
consistorial
contestation
crosssection
deconsecrate
demonstrable
demonstrably
demonstrator
depressingly
digressional
digressively
disassociate
disgustfully
disgustingly
dispossessor
diversionary
diversionist
earthshaking
ecclesiastic
ecclesiology
empoisonment
empressement
encrustation
Englishwoman
enthusiastic
evanescently
exclusionary
exclusionism
exclusionist
excursionist
exhaustively
expansionary
expansionism
expansionist
expressional
expressively
expressivity
extensometer
extrasensory
extraspecial
fantasticate
fantasticism
forensically
fricasseeing
grotesquerie
gymnosophist
heartstrings
hydrostatics
hypersthenia
hypersthenic
immeasurable
immeasurably
immensurable
impersonally
impersonator
impressively
imprisonment
inconsequent
inconsistent
inconsolable
inconsolably
inconsonance
inconstantly
inconsumable
inconsumably
incrustation
indissoluble
indissolubly
inelasticity
inspissation
intersection
interservice
interspinous
interstellar
interstitial
intrusionist
intussuscept
Keynesianism
kinaesthesia
kinaesthesis
kinaesthetic
lithospheric
metapsychics
mezzosoprano
microscopist
microseismic
microsurgery
millesimally
moneyspinner
morrisdancer
multistoried
narcissistic
neurasthenia
neurasthenic
neuroscience
neurosurgeon
neurosurgery
newfashioned
nimbostratus
nonessential
nonresidence
nonresistant
oldfashioned
oppressively
orchestrator
overestimate
pantisocracy
paraesthesia
partisanship
percussively
periostracum
permissively
persistently
philistinism
philosophise
phonasthenia
photosetting
photospheric
placesetting
planispheric
plebiscitary
possessively
precessional
precisianism
precisionist
predesignate
predestinate
prehistorian
preposterous
proboscidean
proboscidian
processional
professional
professorate
professoress
professorial
progesterone
protestation
protistology
provisionary
purposebuilt
purposefully
pursestrings
recessionary
reconstitute
refreshingly
refreshments
regressively
remonstrance
remonstrator
remorsefully
repossession
repressively
reversionary
sarrusophone
sceneshifter
scrimshanker
secessionism
secessionist
seclusionist
sequestrator
sharpshooter
sharpsighted
sheepshearer
shortsighted
shortsleeved
shortstaffed
skrimshanker
sophisticate
spokesperson
staffsurgeon
statistician
submissively
successfully
successional
successively
suggestively
supersedence
supersensory
supersession
superstition
superstratum
supposititious
synaesthesia
synaesthetic
telaesthesia
telaesthetic
testosterone
thanksgiving
thickskinned
thickskulled
tradescantia
tradespeople
trainspotter
transshipped
tropospheric
unblushingly
unclassified
unconsidered
unconstraint
undersetting
understaffed
undersurface
unreasonable
unreasonably
unseasonable
viscosimeter
wollastonite
xiphisternum
abolitionary
abolitionism
abolitionist
absentminded
accentuation
accoutrement
accretionary
acoustically
adjectivally
adscititious
advantageous
adventitious
affectedness
affectionate
aforethought
afterthought
agglutinogen
amitotically
amphitheatre
amphitropous
anaesthetise
anaesthetist
analytically
antistrophic
apolitically
appurtenance
archetypally
archetypical
architecture
aromatically
aromaticness
arrhythmical
artistically
athletically
balletomania
ballottement
belittlement
belletristic
bicentennial
billsticking
biometrician
bloodthirsty
bluestocking
bodystocking

bonnetmonkey
breakthrough
breaststroke
breastsummer
bulletheaded
calisthenics
carpetbagger
carpetknight
catastrophic
cementitious
chemotherapy
chieftainess
chrestomathy
Christianise
Christianity
Christolatry
Christophany
cleistogamic
coalitionist
collaterally
committeeman
compatriotic
connaturally
coquettishly
cosmetically
decentralise
decontrolled
deflationary
deflationist
dejectedness
densitometer
departmental
dermatophyte
despitefully
despotically
deviationism
deviationist
dictatorship
didactically
dietetically
dilettantish
dilettantism
directorship
disastrously
disestablish
disintegrate
disinterment
disputatious
dissatisfied
diverticular
diverticulum
divertimenti
divertimento
dogmatically
domestically
domesticator
dramatically
dramaturgist
dynastically
eccentricity
eclectically
ecstatically
educationist
effectuality
effectuation
effortlessly
elliptically
elocutionary
elocutionist
embattlement
embitterment
emphatically
enclitically
enswathement
entertaining
equestrienne
essentiality
evolutionary
evolutionism
evolutionist
executorship
exegetically
exophthalmic
exophthalmos
exophthalmus
extortionary
extortionate
factitiously
farmsteading
fenestration
fictitiously
flagitiously
flamethrower
forestalment
freestanding
frenetically
galactogogue
geometrician
geriatrician
gerontocracy
gigantically
globetrotter
haematoblast
haematolysis
haematoxylon
hardstanding
heliotherapy
heliotropism
hermetically
herpetologic
highstepping
horsetrading
housetrained
hydrotherapy
hydrothermal
hydrotropism
hypertension
hypertensive
hyperthermia
hypertrophic
hypnotherapy
hypnotically
hypnotisable
hypostatical
idolatrously
illnaturedly
illustration
illustrative
impartiality
impertinence
impertinency
incautiously
incestuously
incontiguous
incontinence
incontinency
indebtedness
indistinctly
indoctrinate
industrially
infanticidal
infectiously
inflationary
inflationism
inflationist
ingratiating
insecticidal
intertexture
intuitionism
intuitionist
invertebrate
investigator
isolationism
isolationist
jesuitically
knighterrant
knightliness
licentiously
licketysplit
lithotritist
logistically
longitudinal
longstanding
lycanthropic
magistrature
magnetically
magnetisable
magnetograph
magnetometer
majestically
malnutrition
marketgarden
marketsquare
meristematic
merrythought
ministration
ministrative
misanthropic
misinterpret
mnemotechnic
monastically
monostichous
monostrophic
narcotically
neurotically
nevertheless
nutritionist
nutritiously
nyctitropism
obstetrician
onomatopoeia
onomatopoeic
operatically
orienteering
orthotropism
orthotropous
ostentatious
outdatedness
overstepping
paletteknife
parenthesise
partitionist
pathetically
pedantically
percutaneous
peristeronic
peristomatic
permittivity
perpetration
perpetuation
phenotypical
phonetically
phototropism
phreatophyte
planetesimal
planetstruck
pleiotropism
polyethylene
potentiality
pralltriller
predetermine
preestablish
priestliness
priestridden
privatdocent
privatdozent
privateering
probationary
procathedral
profiteering
propitiation
propitiatory
propitiously
prototypical
quaestorship
quixotically
racketeering
radiotherapy
receptaculum
receptionist
redintegrate
redistribute
reductionism
reductionist
reflationary
registration
rejectamenta
relentlessly
resettlement
resistlessly
revictualled
robustiously
romantically
sabretoothed
sadistically
salvationism
salvationist
scripturally
scriptwriter
sculpturally
selfstarting
semantically
sempiternity
sensitometer
servitorship
shamateurism
sidestepping
simultaneity
simultaneous
Sinanthropus
sinistrality
sinistrorsal
Socratically
specktioneer
spinsterhood
spiritedness
spiritlessly
spiritualise
spiritualism
spiritualist
spirituality
squattocracy
stealthiness
stormtrooper
straitjacket
streetwalker
streptococci
streptomycin
strontianite
structurally
subalternate
subalternity
subcutaneous
subsaturated
synarthrosis
syndetically
synoptically
theanthropic
theistically
thematically
thriftlessly
topsyturvily
traditionary
traditionist
triphthongal
tumultuously
uncontrolled
uncritically
undertenancy
unfaithfully
unflattering
ungratefully
unhistorical
unilaterally
unmistakable
unmistakably
unpretending
unrestrained
untruthfully
unwontedness
unworthiness
voluntaryism
voluntaryist
voluptuosity
voluptuously
wherethrough
wicketkeeper
absoluteness
absolutistic
abstruseness
accumulation
accumulative
agranulocyte
agribusiness
agricultural
altitudinous
amateurishly
aquicultural
articulately
articulation
articulatory
attitudinise
blastulation
bodybuilding
bureaucratic
capitulation
cocksureness
coloquintida
compoundable
conclusively
confoundedly
conglutinate
deambulatory
defraudation
deliquescent
demodulation
denaturalise
denaturation
depopulation
destructible
diminutively
discountable
discouraging
discourteous
duraluminium
emasculation
emasculatory
extrauterine
filibusterer
flocculation
fraudulently
goodhumoured
grossularite
habitualness
headquarters
hebetudinous
hindquarters
hirepurchase
hyposulphite
immaculately
immatureness
inaccurately
inauguration
inauguratory
IndoEuropean
inescutcheon
inexpugnable
inexpugnably
inoccupation
inosculation
insalubrious
insolubilise
insolubility
instauration
instructress

instrumental
integumental
intrauterine
involutional
irregularity
landlubberly
latitudinous
LowChurchman
manipulation
manipulative
manipulatory
manoeuvrable
meticulously
miraculously
miseducation
moistureless
molecularity
Newfoundland
Northumbrian
obsequiously
orbicularity
phillumenist
pleasureless
posthumously
preclusively
profoundness
pronouncedly
protrusively
quadrumanous
quinquennial
quinquennium
readjustment
reassuringly
reoccupation
resoluteness
restaurateur
reticulately
reticulation
reticulocyte
ribonuclease
ridiculously
sansculottic
scrupulosity
scrupulously
selfluminous
selfmurderer
sericultural
shipbuilding
sternutation
sternutative
sternutatory
stridulation
sulphuration
sulphuretted
surmountable
surroundings
thoroughbass
thoroughbred
thoroughfare
thoroughness
tranquillise
tranquillity
transudation
transudatory
unaccustomed
unassumingly
unencumbered
unpopularity
unscrupulous
unstructured
unthoughtful
usufructuary
valetudinary
venepuncture
venipuncture
vesiculation
viscountship
vocabularian
vomiturition

abbreviation
boulevardier
Carlovingian
clairvoyance
conviviality
cultivatable
depravedness
disadvantage
discoverable
discoverture
dishevelment
disseverance
disseverment
dorsiventral
effervescent
extravagance
extravagancy
extravaganza
extraversion
extroversion
illadvisedly
imperviously
improvidence
improvisator
inconvenient
intervenient
intervention
intervocalic
introversion
introversive
introvertive
lasciviously
misadventure
multivalence
multiversity
outrivalling
peradventure
perseverance
receivership
reconversion
reconveyance
reservedness
resolvedness
retroversion
selfevidence
subdivisible
supervenient
supervention
survivorship
tergiversate
transversely
transvestism
transvestite
unchivalrous
unconvincing
brainwashing
caterwauling
collywobbles
freeswimming
heartwarming
horsewhipped
housewarming
interwreathe
lakedwelling
metalworking
narrowminded
northwestern
otherworldly
pennywhistle
prizewinning
sedgewarbler
shadowboxing
shirtwaister
sleepwalking
southwestern
sternwheeler
threewheeler
unanswerable
underwritten

whitewashing
yellowhammer
asphyxiation
contextually
overexertion
overexposure
premaxillary
selfexistent
submaxillary
unisexuality
acronychally
aerodynamics
anaphylactic
anticyclonic
biophysicist
bloodyminded
brachydactyl
conveyancing
copolymerise
creepycrawly
decasyllabic
decasyllable
geophysicist
highlystrung
homonymously
humptydumpty
ichthyocolla
ichthyolatry
ichthyophagy
idiosyncrasy
lachrymation
lachrymatory
lachrymosely
liverystable
monkeyflower
monkeyjacket
monkeypuzzle
monkeywrench
monosyllabic
monosyllable
niminypiminy
octosyllabic
octosyllable
paralysation
parisyllabic
policyholder
polysyllabic
polysyllable
presbyterate
presbyterial
Presbyterian
prophylactic
selfhypnosis
semicylinder
shillyshally
surveyorship
synonymously
teensyweensy
triglyphical
twentyfourmo
woollyheaded
bedazzlement
embezzlement
emblazonment
protozoology

---

accompanyist
advantageous
ambassadress
analphabetic
angiocarpous
anteprandial
archdeaconry
argillaceous
astronautics
avantgardism
avantgardist
backslapping
bellylanding

bobbydazzler
bodysnatcher
booklearning
boulevardier
brainwashing
breathalyser
brilliantine
brinkmanship
bullheadedly
calculatedly
capercaillie
capercailzie
carbonaceous
cardinalship
caterwauling
chairmanship
chieftainess
chocolatebox
cliffhanging
combinations
contumacious
conveyancing
courtmartial
crashlanding
criticalness
cultivatable
curvicaudate
demoniacally
diatomaceous
dilettantish
dilettantism
disadvantage
disembarrass
disestablish
displeasedly
disputatious
disregardful
doubleacting
emblematical
encephalitic
encephalitis
entertaining
extramarital
extravagance
extravagancy
extravaganza
feldspathoid
footplateman
forestalment
freestanding
furfuraceous
galligaskins
gallinaceous
gamesmanship
graminaceous
guardianship
haberdashery
habitualness
handicapping
hardfeatured
hardstanding
headquarters
heartwarming
hebdomadally
heliolatrous
hellgrammite
heroicalness
hibernaculum
hindquarters
homeopathist
homothallism
horsemanship
housewarming
hypognathous
hypostatical
hypothalamic
hypothalamus
illtreatment
impermanence

impermanency
inappeasable
incomparable
incomparably
incompatible
incompatibly
indefeasible
indefeasibly
intracardiac
irrefragable
irrefragably
irrepealable
judgematical
liquefacient
liquefaction
longstanding
maltreatment
marksmanship
marshharrier
materialness
mathematical
melodramatic
microcapsule
misbehaviour
mistreatment
monodramatic
monographist
mulligatawny
multifarious
multilateral
multipartite
multivalence
musicianship
nanoplankton
negotiatress
nephanalysis
nerveracking
northeastern
obscurantism
obscurantist
oneupmanship
orchidaceous
orthopaedics
orthopaedist
ostentatious
osteomalacia
outrivalling
overreaction
paedobaptism
pancreatitis
paragraphist
partisanship
passepartout
percutaneous
pertinacious
petrifaction
pilotballoon
polychaetous
porcelainise
porcelainous
postgraduate
postprandial
preestablish
propagandise
propagandism
propagandist
psychiatrist
psychoactive
pterodactyle
putrefaction
putrefactive
reappearance
receptaculum
rejectamenta
rhizocarpous
safecracking
salesmanship
sarcomatosis
sarsaparilla

satisfaction
satisfactory
scenepainter
schismatical
schorlaceous
sedgewarbler
selfanalysis
selfflattery
selfstarting
semidiameter
septilateral
sesquialtera
shamefacedly
shirtwaister
simoniacally
simultaneity
simultaneous
singleacting
skunkcabbage
sleepwalking
sorbefacient
southeastern
stagemanager
starspangled
stockraising
stonemasonry
strophanthin
stupefacient
stupefaction
stupefactive
subcutaneous
succedaneous
supernaculum
supernatural
sycophantish
systematical
systematiser
taberdarship
tabernacular
telegraphese
telegraphist
theocratical
torrefaction
translatable
transpacific
transparency
unappeasable
unattractive
unchivalrous
uncomeatable
undergarment
undermanning
unmistakable
unmistakably
unrepeatable
verticalness
vicechairman
vitrifaction
voluntaryism
voluntaryist
watermanship
whitewashing
wineglassful
adaptability
advisability
aeroembolism
alterability
amphisbaenic
anaerobiosis
automobilist
availability
broncobuster
carpetbagger
cheeseburger
conglobation
constabulary
contribution
contributive
contributory
desirability
dilatability
distributary
distribution
distributive
disturbingly
divisibility
elasmobranch
equilibrator
equitability
exacerbation
excitability
filtrability
flammability
frangibility
habitability
halterbroken
harquebusier
hereinbefore
heritability
hubblebubble
hucklebacked
illegibility
immovability
immutability
imputability
inaudibility
incapability
incurability
indelibility
infusibility
insalubrious
insolubilise
insolubility
invisibility
irascibility
irritability
landlubberly
malleability
navigability
noctambulant
noctambulism
noctambulist
noctambulous
noncombatant
opposability
palaeobotany
palatability
permeability
perturbation
perturbative
pigeonbreast
plausibility
printability
proverbially
reducibility
removability
saddlebacked
separability
shadowboxing
somnambulant
somnambulate
somnambulism
somnambulist
teachability
temptability
tolerability
traceability
tractability
uncelebrated
venerability
winterbourne
abstractable
abstractedly
abstractness
acciaccatura
acronychally
adjudication
adjudicative
adjudicatory
announcement
anticyclonic
antimacassar
antirachitic
approachable
aristocratic
artificially
benefactress
beneficently
beneficially
bureaucratic
canaliculate
cheesecutter
circumcision
classicalism
classicalist
classicality
claudication
codification
commencement
commercially
complacently
complication
compunctious
confiscation
confiscatory
conjunctival
contractable
contractedly
contractible
convincement
convincingly
creepycrawly
cumulocirrus
denouncement
destructible
detoxication
dibranchiate
displaceable
displacement
distinctness
distractedly
divarication
echinococcus
echolocation
embranchment
encroachment
entrancement
entrenchment
equivocation
equivocatory
evanescently
fluorocarbon
gasification
geanticlinal
geosynclinal
groundcherry
hemerocallis
heterocercal
heterocyclic
hierarchical
homesickness
humification
hyperacidity
illogicality
inarticulate
incapacitate
indefectible
indelicately
indirectness
ineffaceable
ineffaceably
inefficiency
infelicitous
inoperculate
instructress
interoceanic
interoceptor
intoxication
intrenchment
manufacturer
melanochroic
microscopist
miscalculate
miseducation
misplacement
modification
modificatory
munificently
neuroscience
nidification
notification
oligarchical
oneirocritic
ossification
overniceness
pacification
pacificatory
panification
paratactical
perspicacity
pharmaceutic
pharmacology
plebiscitary
postdoctoral
practicality
precancelled
prenticeship
proboscidean
proboscidian
provincially
pseudocyesis
purification
purificatory
pyrotechnics
pyrotechnist
quizzicality
rambunctious
ramification
rapprochment
ratification
reallocation
renouncement
reproachable
reproachless
restrictedly
retrenchment
ribonuclease
sandyachting
scrobiculate
selfdeceived
selfdeceiver
silicicolous
stereochromy
straticulate
stringcourse
succinctness
supplicantly
supplication
supplicatory
taperecorder
technicality
technicolour
technocratic
thermocouple
tradescantia
transoceanic
trifurcation
triplication
typification
unaffectedly
undemocratic
underachieve
unexpectedly
unofficially
unprincipled
unsearchable
unstructured
usufructuary
veridicality
verification
verificatory
vilification
vinification
vivification
whimsicality
xanthochroia
acetaldehyde
aerosiderite
aircondition
altitudinous
antecedently
aperiodicity
astoundingly
attitudinise
autodidactic
backpedalled
benzaldehyde
brachydactyl
cashandcarry
coincidental
coincidently
commandingly
commendation
commendatory
concordantly
contradictor
cotyledonary
cotyledonous
defraudation
despondently
diamonddrill
diamondfield
dilapidation
discordantly
disobedience
doubledealer
doubledecked
doubledecker
enginedriver
fluoridation
forbiddingly
forebodement
forebodingly
formaldehyde
gobbledegook
gobbledygook
hebetudinous
horrendously
humptydumpty
hydatidiform
incoordinate
individually
inexpedience
inexpediency
intimidation
intimidatory
invalidation
irremediable
irremediably
latitudinous
mithridatise
mithridatism
monopodially
morrisdancer
nonconductor
outlandishly
outwardbound
peroxidation
praseodymium
precondition
preponderant
preponderate
primordially
privatdocent
privatdozent

propaedeutic
razzledazzle
resoundingly
singledecker
softpedalled
stupendously
transudation
transudatory
tremendously
troglodytism
unsteadiness
unwieldiness
unworldiness
unyieldingly
valetudinary
YankeeDoodle
accursedness
affectedness
AfroAmerican
agamogenesis
agamogenetic
agentgeneral
alphabetical
alphamerical
anticlerical
antithetical
appendectomy
apperception
apperceptive
apprehension
apprehensive
appurtenance
archipelagic
architecture
arithmetical
artilleryman
attorneyship
backbreaking
bassorelievo
bathypelagic
belligerence
belligerency
bewilderedly
bewilderment
bicentennial
bioscientist
birdsnesting
bloodletting
brambleberry
buccaneering
buccaneerish
cabbagewhite
calcareously
campodeiform
carburetting
catechetical
childbearing
clarinettist
clavicembalo
coetaneously
collaterally
collinearity
commiserator
composedness
concelebrant
concelebrate
conferential
confidential
confusedness
considerable
considerably
contumelious
convalescent
corporeality
courageously
crossbedding
crossbencher
crossheading
crosssection
decaffeinate
decipherable
decipherment
decongestant
decongestion
decongestive
deconsecrate
dejectedness
deliquescent
denuclearise
depravedness
despitefully
detachedness
differentiae
differential
diphtheritic
disaffection
disagreeable
disagreeably
disagreement
discoverable
discoverture
discreetness
dishevelment
disincentive
disinfectant
disinfection
disingenuous
disintegrate
disinterment
disorientate
disseverance
disseverment
dorsiventral
econometrics
effervescent
efflorescent
embitterment
encumberment
endangerment
endoskeletal
epexegetical
epicureanism
ethnocentric
EuroAmerican
exospherical
expediential
experiential
extraneously
extrasensory
extraversion
extroversion
fainthearted
faithhealing
farmsteading
freewheeling
frontbencher
frontiersman
genuflection
glycogenesis
gravelelling
greathearted
hairdressing
heartrending
heavyhearted
heliocentric
henotheistic
hermeneutics
heteroecious
highpressure
highstepping
hippocentaur
histogenesis
histogenetic
housekeeping
hydromedusae
hydromedusan
hypertension
hypertensive
hypnogenesis
hypnogenetic
hypothecator
hypothetical
hysterectomy
idiothermous
imperceptive
imperfection
imperfective
imponderable
imponderably
incandescent
incompetence
incompetency
inconsequent
inconvenient
indebtedness
indifference
indifferency
inexpressive
insufferable
insufferably
insurrection
intellection
intellective
intellectual
intemperance
interbedding
interception
intercession
intercessory
interfemoral
interference
interjection
interjectory
intermeddler
intermediacy
intermediary
intermediate
interpellate
interrelated
intersection
interservice
intertexture
intervenient
intervention
introjection
introversion
introversive
introvertive
invertebrate
invulnerable
invulnerably
irredeemable
irredeemably
irreflective
irrespective
knighterrant
lakedwelling
largehearted
lighthearted
lopsidedness
macrocephaly
majorgeneral
Manicheanism
marlinespike
meristematic
metathetical
mezzorelievo
microcephaly
microseismic
misadventure
misdemeanant
misdemeanour
misdirection
misinterpret
mistakenness
mnemotechnic
monotheistic
multicentral
multidentate
multiversity
nitrobenzene
noneffective
nonessential
nonobjective
noradrenalin
northwestern
nychthemeral
nychthemeron
oblanceolate
omnipresence
onesidedness
orienteering
orthogenesis
orthogenetic
osteogenesis
outdatedness
outrageously
outstretched
overexertion
overpressure
overstepping
paedogenesis
paedogenetic
paletteknife
palingenesia
palingenesis
palingenetic
parallelling
pathogenesis
pathogenetic
peradventure
peripherally
peristeronic
perseverance
pestilential
phenomenally
philadelphus
philodendron
photogeology
photosetting
phylogenesis
phylogenetic
phytogenesis
phytogenetic
pickerelweed
placesetting
plaindealing
planetesimal
Plattdeutsch
polytheistic
polyurethane
precedential
predetermine
predigestion
predilection
preferential
preparedness
preselection
preselective
presidential
primogenital
primogenitor
privateering
profiteering
proofreading
proprietress
protuberance
proudhearted
providential
purposebuilt
purposefully
pyroelectric
quadriennium
quinquennial
quinquennium
racketeering
receivership
recollection
recollective
reconversion
reconveyance
recrudescent
redintegrate
refrigerator
rememberable
remorsefully
repossession
reprehension
reprehensive
reservedness
resignedness
resolvedness
resurrection
retrocedence
retrocession
retrocessive
retroversion
revengefully
reverberator
rhinocerotic
rhizogenetic
rhododendron
ricochetting
sacrilegious
scareheading
selfelective
selfidentity
selfpleasing
semiprecious
sempiternity
serviceberry
servicecourt
servicewoman
Shakspereana
Shaksperiana
shamateurism
shoulderbelt
shoulderknot
shouldernote
shuffleboard
sidestepping
sightreading
snaggletooth
sociometrist
southwestern
spinsterhood
spiritedness
sporogenesis
squirrelcage
squirreltail
steeplechase
stilboestrol
stonyhearted
stouthearted
subalternate
subalternity
subcelestial
subinfeudate
subthreshold
supersedence
supersensory
supersession
supervenient
supervention
swizzlestick
tergiversate
testamentary
tetrahedrite
theatregoing
therapeutics
therapeutist
thimbleberry
togetherness
Torricellian
transcendent

transferable
transference
transferring
transversely
transvestism
transvestite
trestletable
troublemaker
umbrageously
unanswerable
unbelievable
unbelievably
unbrokenness
uncommercial
underdevelop
underletting
undersetting
undertenancy
ungracefully
ungratefully
unilaterally
unpretending
unsegregated
unsuccessful
unwontedness
vantagepoint
vicargeneral
wholehearted
whortleberry
wretchedness
youngberries
aircraftsman
amentiferous
butterflynut
circumfluent
circumfusion
classifiable
conchiferous
cuckooflower
discomfiture
emulsifiable
fatherfigure
fiddlefaddle
fructiferous
griseofulvin
identifiable
inartificial
laticiferous
luminiferous
monkeyflower
motherfigure
nonconformer
pasqueflower
plumbiferous
quantifiable
resiniferous
salutiferous
saponifiable
schoolfellow
selfaffected
selfeffacing
seminiferous
semiofficial
siliciferous
soporiferous
staffofficer
stanniferous
stelliferous
sudoriferous
twentyfourmo
anastigmatic
antimagnetic
apothegmatic
astringently
battleground
bibliography
billingsgate
biogeography
bookingclerk
bullfighting
burningglass
cardiography
carriageable
cheirography
choreography
chronography
cockfighting
compurgation
compurgatory
congregation
conningtower
contingently
cousingerman
cryptogamous
cryptography
cuckingstool
curlingirons
curlingtongs
curmudgeonly
disgorgement
dislodgement
drawingboard
drawingpaper
duckingstool
endamagement
envisagement
estrangement
eveningdress
exchangeable
falcongentil
falcongentle
firefighting
foresightful
FrancoGerman
glossography
glyphography
glyptography
gramnegative
gyromagnetic
heterogamous
heterogenous
homologation
impetiginous
inexpugnable
inexpugnably
infringement
kindergarten
kissingcrust
landingcraft
landingfield
landingstage
landingstrip
lexicography
lodginghouse
marketgarden
marriageable
meaningfully
meetinghouse
meltingpoint
messeigneurs
misalignment
misjudgement
morningdress
mucilaginous
multungulate
nonalignment
oceanography
organography
palaeography
paradigmatic
paramagnetic
permanganate
physiognomic
physiography
playingfield
plectognathi
plumbaginous
polarography
profligately
prolongation
promulgation
psychography
pyroligneous
Quadragesima
reassignment
rechargeable
reinvigorate
rollingstock
runningboard
schizogonous
scintigraphy
seismography
selenography
selfbegotten
selfrighting
sellingplate
septuagenary
Septuagesima
Septuagintal
silverglance
spermogonium
stereography
stratigraphy
thanksgiving
thermography
thoroughbass
thoroughbred
thoroughfare
thoroughness
unchangeable
unchangeably
unmanageable
unrecognised
unthoughtful
vitiligation
Wellingtonia
windingsheet
woodengraver
workingclass
zoogeography
accouchement
aforethought
afterthought
alexipharmic
amphitheatre
anaesthetise
anaesthetist
anemophilous
arrhythmical
astrophysics
atmospherics
beseechingly
bewitchingly
bloodthirsty
breakthrough
bulletheaded
calisthenics
candleholder
carragheenin
chemotherapy
desulphurise
disaccharide
disenchanter
dodecahedral
dodecahedron
dunderheaded
earthshaking
Englishwoman
enswathement
escutcheoned
exophthalmic
exophthalmos
exophthalmus
farsightedly
flamethrower
guestchamber
haemophiliac
heliotherapy
hemispheroid
hierophantic
horsewhipped
hydrochloric
hydrophilous
hydrotherapy
hydrothermal
hygrophilous
hyperthermia
hypnotherapy
interchanger
lycanthropic
melancholiac
merrythought
microphysics
misanthropic
moneychanger
muddleheaded
muttonheaded
necrophagous
necrophiliac
necrophilism
necrophilous
negrophilism
negrophilist
nevertheless
newfashioned
officeholder
oldfashioned
ophiophagous
overachiever
pantechnicon
parenthesise
pennywhistle
photochromic
photophilous
phytophagous
policyholder
polyethylene
procathedral
radiophonics
radiotherapy
rattleheaded
refreshingly
refreshments
rhizophagous
rhombohedral
rhombohedron
saprophagous
sarcophagous
sceneshifter
scratchiness
scrimshanker
sepulchrally
sharpshooter
sheepshearer
shortchanger
Sinanthropus
singlehanded
skrimshanker
sledgehammer
snakecharmer
stealthiness
sternwheeler
straightaway
straightbred
straightedge
straightener
straightness
subarrhation
supercharger
synarthrosis
tetrachordal
theanthropic
threewheeler
throughstone
transshipped
triphthongal
triumphantly
unblushingly
unfaithfully
untruthfully
unworthiness
vibraphonist
wherethrough
woodenheaded
woollyheaded
yellowhammer
abbreviation
abolitionary
abolitionism
abolitionist
aboriginally
abstemiously
academically
accordionist
accretionary
acoustically
adjectivally
adscititious
adventitious
affectionate
agglutinogen
amitotically
amphibiously
anagogically
analogically
analytically
anatomically
annunciation
apolitically
appendicitis
appendicular
appreciation
appreciative
appreciatory
aromatically
aromaticness
artistically
asphyxiation
assassinator
athletically
auspiciously
avariciously
avitaminoses
avitaminosis
bactericidal
bacteriology
bacteriostat
banderillero
barbarically
bassorilievo
beatifically
berzelianite
billsticking
biologically
birefringent
blackbirding
bodybuilding
brickfielder
calumniation
calumniatory
calumniously
calycoideous
camiknickers
capriciously
Carlovingian
Cartesianism
catholically
cementitious
censoriously
centesimally
chaplainship
cherubically
chondriosome
Christianise
Christianity

churchianity
clearsighted
coalitionist
coenobitical
collegialism
collegiality
collegiately
coloquintida
columniation
commodiously
communicable
communicably
communicator
companionate
companionway
complaisance
conciliation
conciliative
conciliatory
concomitance
concubitancy
concupiscent
Confucianism
congeniality
congenitally
connubiality
conscription
consociation
consolidator
constriction
constrictive
constringent
contagionist
contagiously
conveniently
conviviality
cosmetically
debonairness
deflationary
deflationist
dentilingual
denunciation
denunciative
denunciatory
depreciation
depreciatory
despoliation
despotically
determinable
determinably
determinedly
deviationism
deviationist
diabolically
diatonically
didactically
dietetically
disaffiliate
disambiguate
dispiritedly
dissatisfied
disseminator
dissimilarly
dissocialise
dissociation
dissociative
distrainable
distrainment
diversionary
diversionist
diverticular
diverticulum
divertimenti
divertimento
dogmatically
domestically
domesticator
dramatically
dynastically
earsplitting
ecclesiastic
ecclesiology
eclectically
ecologically
economically
ecstatically
editorialise
editorialist
educationist
electrically
elliptically
elocutionary
elocutionist
emphatically
enclitically
endermically
enthusiastic
epidemically
epidemiology
episodically
esoterically
essentiality
euphonically
euphoniously
evolutionary
evolutionism
evolutionist
exclusionary
exclusionism
exclusionist
excruciating
excruciation
excursionist
exegetically
exoterically
expansionary
expansionism
expansionist
expatriation
explicitness
exterminable
exterminator
extortionary
extortionate
extraditable
extralimital
factitiously
fallaciously
fastidiously
faultfinding
ferrugineous
fertilisable
fictitiously
firstnighter
flagitiously
floodlighted
forensically
forthrightly
fountainhead
freeswimming
freethinking
frenetically
galvanically
geologically
geopolitical
gigantically
goosepimples
granodiorite
gregariously
hallucinogen
hallucinosis
harmonically
harmoniously
heraldically
hermetically
hesperididia
highspirited
historically
horrifically
hybridisable
hydrokinetic
hygienically
hypnotically
hypnotisable
hypocritical
hysterically
illadvisedly
impartiality
impercipient
impertinence
impertinency
imperviously
implicitness
improvidence
improvisator
inapplicable
inapplicably
inauspicious
incautiously
incendiarism
incognisable
incognisance
incognitable
inconcinnity
inconsistent
incontiguous
incontinence
incontinency
incorrigible
incorrigibly
indeclinable
indiscipline
indistinctly
ineradicable
ineradicably
inexplicable
inexplicably
inextricable
inextricably
infanticidal
infectiously
inflationary
inflationism
inflationist
infundibular
ingloriously
ingratiating
inhospitable
inhospitably
innutritious
insecticidal
insufficient
intelligence
intelligible
intelligibly
interdiction
interdictive
interdictory
interdigital
interminable
interminably
intermission
intermittent
intermitting
intermixture
intromission
intromittent
intromitting
intrusionist
intuitionism
intuitionist
investigator
irrespirable
isolationism
isolationist
jesuitically
jurisdiction
karyokinesis
Keynesianism
kinnikinnick
lasciviously
licentiously
liturgically
liturgiology
logistically
loquaciously
lugubriously
mademoiselle
magnetically
magnetisable
magnifically
magnificence
maintainable
majestically
mechanically
mendaciously
mercurialise
mercurialism
meretricious
metallically
meteorically
methodically
microbiology
microcircuit
millesimally
monastically
monostichous
mordaciously
mountainside
multilingual
mysteriously
nailscissors
narcotically
neonomianism
Nestorianism
neurobiology
neurotically
nonefficient
nonresidence
nonresistant
nutritionist
nutritiously
obsequiously
omnisciently
operatically
outstripping
overcritical
Palladianism
parochialise
parochialism
parochiality
participator
partitionist
pathetically
peccadilloes
pedantically
pellucidness
pennypincher
peregrinator
perfidiously
perfoliation
periodically
perjuriously
perniciously
phonemically
phonetically
photofission
photokinesis
photokinetic
platonically
pluriliteral
pontifically
pontificator
poorspirited
posteriority
potentiality
precariously
prechristian
precipitable
precipitance
precipitancy
precipitator
precisianism
precisionist
precociously
predesignate
predominance
predominancy
premaxillary
premeditated
premeditator
prescription
prescriptive
prevaricator
prizefighter
prizewinning
probationary
prodigiously
proficiently
progenitress
prolifically
prolificness
pronominally
propitiation
propitiatory
propitiously
proscription
proscriptive
prosodically
protohistory
provisionary
pugnaciously
pulverisable
quixotically
rabbinically
radiobiology
ratiocinator
rebelliously
recalcitrant
recalcitrate
receptionist
recessionary
recognisable
recognisably
recognisance
recommitment
reconcilable
reductionism
reductionist
reflationary
renunciation
renunciative
renunciatory
repatriation
restrainable
restrainedly
resuscitator
reversionary
rhetorically
rhythmically
risorgimento
robustiously
romantically
sadistically
salubriously
salvationism
salvationist
sardonically
scarificator
secessionism
secessionist
seclusionist
sectarianise
sectarianism
selfcritical

selfevidence
selfexistent
semantically
sequaciously
seraphically
sharpsighted
shipbuilding
shortcircuit
shortpitched
shortsighted
sideslipping
sidewhiskers
significance
significancy
sinusoidally
Socratically
specifically
specificness
specktioneer
spheroidally
sphragistics
splendidness
sporadically
stepchildren
stereoisomer
strontianite
subdivisible
submaxillary
subminiature
subscription
subsidiarily
subsonically
sufficiently
superciliary
supercilious
superhighway
suppositious
suspiciously
syllabically
symbolically
syndetically
synoptically
systemically
tectonically
terrifically
testudineous
Teutonically
theatrically
theistically
thematically
traditionary
traditionist
traducianism
traducianist
tranquillise
tranquillity
transhipment
transmigrant
transmigrate
transmission
transmissive
transmitting
transpirable
trinomialism
tyrannically
tyrannicidal
unassailable
uncharitable
uncharitably
unconsidered
unconvincing
uncritically
underbidding
underpinning
ungraciously
unifoliolate
unimaginable
unimaginably
unitarianism
unmercifully
unprofitable
unprofitably
uproariously
Valenciennes
verticillate
Victorianism
victoriously
viscosimeter
volcanically
wallpainting
whitelivered
circumjacent
dinnerjacket
katzenjammer
lumberjacket
monkeyjacket
straitjacket
cantankerous
carpetknight
thickskinned
thickskulled
unblinkingly
unthinkingly
wicketkeeper
wunderkinder
accomplished
accumulation
accumulative
adorableness
agranulocyte
agricultural
ambivalently
amenableness
amicableness
amygdaloidal
anaphylactic
annihilation
annihilative
antediluvian
antimalarial
apostolicism
apostolicity
aquicultural
articulately
articulation
articulatory
assibilation
assimilation
assimilative
assimilatory
Australasian
bedazzlement
beggarliness
belittlement
benevolently
bibliologist
bioecologist
blamableness
blastulation
bonnyclabber
borosilicate
breathlessly
breechloader
campfollower
cancellation
cantillation
capitalistic
capitulation
cardiologist
cattlelifter
centuplicate
chalcolithic
charnelhouse
chronologise
chronologist
colourlessly
compellation
conchologist
conduplicate
controllable
councilwoman
courtplaster
cowardliness
craniologist
crenellation
cryptologist
crystalgazer
culpableness
deambulatory
decasyllabic
decasyllable
deescalation
demodulation
deontologist
depopulation
discipleship
disciplinary
disinflation
distillation
distillatory
doublelocked
dovecoloured
effortlessly
Egyptologist
emasculation
emasculatory
embattlement
embezzlement
embryologist
encirclement
enfeeblement
entanglement
entomologise
entomologist
enviableness
enzymologist
epicycloidal
epithalamion
epithalamium
equipollence
equipollency
equivalently
escapologist
evangelistic
exsufflicate
fatherliness
fibrillation
fieldglasses
flabelliform
flagellation
flagellatory
flocculation
forcibleness
fraudulently
friendliness
fullyfledged
futurologist
glaciologist
glassblowing
glossologist
grammolecule
graphologist
graveclothes
grossularite
groundlessly
grovellingly
hairsplitter
heavenliness
heortologist
heterologous
hieroglyphic
highcoloured
highfaluting
horribleness
hydrofluoric
hyperplastic
hypochlorite
hyposulphite
iconoclastic
immaculately
immunologist
incompletely
incompliance
inconclusive
inosculation
installation
instillation
insufflation
interglacial
interpleader
inveiglement
invigilation
irregularity
irresolutely
irresolution
irresolvable
Ishmaelitish
journalistic
knightliness
laudableness
lexicologist
liberalistic
loungelizard
maidenliness
malacologist
malevolently
manifoldness
manipulation
manipulative
manipulatory
mannerliness
Marseillaise
marvellously
metagalactic
meticulously
microclimate
mineralogist
miraculously
miscellanist
mitrailleuse
molecularity
monadelphous
monofilament
monopolistic
monosyllabic
monosyllable
morphallaxis
morphologist
motherliness
moveableness
multiflorous
multipliable
multiplicand
multiplicate
multiplicity
musicologist
muzzleloader
naturalistic
Neohellenism
nephrologist
nightclothes
nomenclative
nomenclature
nominalistic
nonchalantly
noneuclidean
numerologist
nympholeptic
obnubilation
oceanologist
octosyllabic
octosyllable
odontologist
orbicularity
organoleptic
osteoplastic
Palaeolithic
palynologist
panhellenism
papyrologist
paraboloidal
paramilitary
parisyllabic
pedicellaria
philhellenic
phrenologist
physiologist
pitiableness
plainclothed
plainclothes
pointilliste
polysyllabic
polysyllable
porcellanous
postdiluvian
prevailingly
priestliness
princeliness
prophylactic
prothalamion
prothalamium
protoplasmic
protoplastic
psephologist
psychologise
psychologism
psychologist
radioelement
readableness
regardlessly
rehabilitate
relentlessly
reliableness
resettlement
resistlessly
reticulately
reticulation
reticulocyte
retroflexion
revivalistic
ridiculously
rosecoloured
salmonladder
salpiglossis
sansculottic
scandalously
schoolleaver
scintillator
scrupulosity
scrupulously
scurrilously
scutellation
seismologist
selenologist
selfcoloured
selfdelusion
selfreliance
semicylinder
sensibleness
sensualistic
sericultural
shortsleeved
slovenliness
smallclothes
sociableness
specialistic
speechlessly
speleologist
spiegeleisen
spiritlessly
stranglehold
stridulation
strobilation
suitableness
surrealistic

surveillance
tangibleness
taxcollector
technologist
teratologist
terribleness
tessellation
thermolabile
thriftlessly
towardliness
toxicologist
trampolinist
transiliency
transplanter
trichologist
trophallaxis
turbellarian
underclothes
unfamiliarly
ungainliness
unkindliness
unlikelihood
unlikeliness
unloveliness
unparalleled
unpopularity
untimeliness
urbanologist
valuableness
variableness
varicoloured
vasodilation
vasodilatory
vesiculation
vocabularian
voidableness
volatileness
whigmaleerie
workableness
absentminded
actinomycete
amalgamation
amalgamative
anagrammatic
anathematise
anthelmintic
antiSemitism
atheromatous
autoimmunity
autonomously
balladmonger
battlemented
bibliomaniac
biochemistry
bloodyminded
bonnetmonkey
buttermuslin
calorimetric
chancemedley
cheesemonger
chronometric
colorimetric
complemental
confirmation
confirmative
confirmatory
conformation
conglomerate
consummately
consummation
consummative
consummatory
conterminous
copolymerise
costermonger
cuprammonium
departmental
desquamation
desquamative
desquamatory
diagrammatic
dichromatism
disclamation
discommodity
discriminant
discriminate
disharmonise
dissymmetric
duraluminium
dynamometric
entrammelled
epigrammatic
epistemology
erythematous
experimental
experimenter
fearsomeness
feebleminded
fostermother
gamesomeness
geochemistry
gladsomeness
glaucomatous
goodhumoured
goodtempered
governmental
gruesomeness
halftimbered
handsomeness
heteromerous
homonymously
huggermugger
impedimental
inflammation
inflammatory
instrumental
integumental
isodiametric
kleptomaniac
lachrymation
lachrymatory
lachrymosely
legitimately
legitimation
legitimatise
lonesomeness
malformation
megalomaniac
metasomatism
milliammeter
minicomputer
narrowminded
noncommittal
nonflammable
Northumbrian
nymphomaniac
oversimplify
paronomastic
performative
phillumenist
phrasemonger
pluviometric
polarimetric
posthumously
preformation
preformative
pretermitted
proclamation
proclamatory
programmable
programmatic
psychometric
quadrumanous
schizomycete
schoolmaster
seismometric
selfcomposed
selflimiting
selfluminous
selfsameness
semidomestic
simpleminded
singleminded
spidermonkey
stereometric
stichomythia
stichomythic
strongminded
subcommittee
subnormality
supereminent
supplemental
supplementer
synonymously
teratomatous
thermometric
tiresomeness
toilsomeness
trachomatous
unassumingly
unbecomingly
unencumbered
accidentally
acquaintance
aerodynamics
antagonistic
antigenicity
apparentness
bacchanalian
biocoenology
cachinnation
cachinnatory
caravansarai
caravanserai
catilinarian
ceremonially
chauvinistic
chlorination
compoundable
condemnation
condemnatory
confoundedly
consignation
containerise
coordinately
coordination
coordinative
countenancer
crossingover
cryptanalyst
cumulonimbus
cytogenetics
delamination
demimondaine
denomination
denominative
deracination
desalination
dethronement
diamagnetism
diaphanously
discerningly
disconnected
disconnexion
discountable
disdainfully
disfranchise
disjointedly
dressinggown
effeminately
emargination
emotionalise
emotionalism
emotionalist
emotionality
enshrinement
enthronement
epiphenomena
factionalism
feminineness
fictionalise
fluorination
foraminifera
frankincense
frequentness
fuliginosity
gastronomist
geomagnetism
glockenspiel
gluttonously
graspingness
halogenation
heathenishly
heteronomous
highhandedly
hoodmanblind
horizontally
idiosyncrasy
illumination
illuminative
impregnation
incatenation
incidentally
indefensible
indefensibly
indefinitely
independence
independency
indigenously
inextensible
inordinately
insemination
invagination
kremlinology
labyrinthian
labyrinthine
lacininiated
lanternjawed
lanternslide
lefthandedly
libidinously
longwindedly
mansionhouse
Marcionitism
merchantable
metalanguage
microanalyst
mispronounce
mistranslate
monomaniacal
monotonously
monumentally
mourningband
mourningring
neuroanatomy
Newfoundland
nicotinamide
nonagenarian
nonidentical
obedientiary
obligingness
occidentally
octogenarian
openhandedly
openmindedly
opinionative
ornamentally
passionately
passionfruit
patternmaker
penitentiary
pleasantness
pleasingness
polytonality
portmanteaus
portmanteaux
postponement
precognition
precognitive
preeminently
profoundness
pronouncedly
prothonotary
pseudonymity
pseudonymous
pumpernickel
punchingball
purblindness
pyromaniacal
quadrangular
quadrinomial
regimentally
rejuvenation
residentiary
residentship
resplendence
resplendency
resupination
retiringness
reunionistic
rontgenogram
rontgenology
salamandrian
salamandrine
salamandroid
sanguinarily
sanguineness
sanguinolent
Scandinavian
sclerenchyma
scouringrush
sectionalism
selfcontempt
selfignition
semiannually
semifinalist
semifinished
septennially
sergeantfish
sergeantship
serjeantship
sexagenarian
shootingiron
skippingrope
sleepingpill
snarlingiron
soundingline
sparkingplug
speakingtube
Stakhanovism
Stakhanovite
standingroom
stationhouse
stationwagon
stellenbosch
sterlingness
stockingless
strikingness
strychninism
studdingsail
substantiate
substantival
sulphonamide
sulphonation
superannuate
surmountable
surroundings
sweepingness
swimmingbath
swimmingbell
swimmingpool
terebinthine
thereinafter
thousandfold
timehonoured

tintinnabula
toastingfork
touchingness
trephination
trochanteric
turtlenecked
underinsured
unregenerate
unscientific
vaticination
venepuncture
venipuncture
veterinarian
villainously
viscountship
voluminosity
voluminously
accommodator
additionally
aetiological
antigropelos
antiphonally
apochromatic
apostrophise
archdiocesan
astrological
astronomical
bachelorhood
bachelorship
backwoodsman
balletomania
basidiospore
beachcombing
behaviourism
behaviourist
bluestocking
bodystocking
brassbounder
bronchoscope
buffalograss
carcinogenic
carillonneur
cartological
cataphoresis
championship
chorological
chrestomathy
Christolatry
Christophany
clairvoyance
cleistogamic
closemouthed
coldshoulder
collaborator
collywobbles
commemorator
conidiophore
conidiospore
conscionable
corespondent
corroborator
cosmogonical
cosmological
cosmopolitan
cosmopolitic
cottonocracy
crosscountry
curvicostate
curvifoliate
curvirostral
declinometer
decomposable
densitometer
dermatophyte
Deuteronomic
diastrophism
dictatorship
diphthongise
directorship
disallowance
disassociate
disendowment
electrolysis
electrolytic
electrometer
electronvolt
electroplate
electroscope
electroshock
electrotonic
electrotonus
electrotyper
emblazonment
empoisonment
enantiomorph
encyclopedia
encyclopedic
equationally
equiprobable
erythroblast
erythromycin
espagnolette
ethnological
etymological
etymologicon
eunuchoidism
executorship
extensometer
fibrinolysin
fractionally
fractionator
frictionless
functionally
functionless
galactogogue
galvanometer
galvanoscope
ganglionated
genealogical
Germanophile
Germanophobe
gerontocracy
governorship
gymnosophist
gynaecocracy
habitforming
haematoblast
haematolysis
haematoxylon
haemopoiesis
hagiological
hedgehopping
hemichordate
henceforward
heroicomical
herpetologic
hippopotamus
histological
homeomorphic
hydrological
hyperbolical
hypochondria
hysteromania
ichthyocolla
ichthyolatry
ichthyophagy
ideationally
immethodical
impersonally
impersonator
imprisonment
inclinometer
incommodious
inconformity
inconsolable
inconsolably
inconsonance
incorporated
incorporator
incorporeity
indissoluble
indissolubly
inharmonious
interconnect
interlobular
interlocutor
interpolator
interrogator
intervocalic
irrationally
irreprovable
irresponsive
isochromatic
isochronally
jurisconsult
kaleidoscope
laryngoscope
laryngoscopy
leapfrogging
limnological
lithological
longshoreman
machicolated
magnetograph
magnetometer
magniloquent
mastigophora
mealymouthed
meridionally
mesothoracic
metallophone
metalworking
metaphorical
metathoracic
meteorograph
metrological
metropolitan
mezzosoprano
microcopying
mitochondria
mosstrooping
multifoliate
multiformity
multiloquous
myrmecophily
mythological
mythologiser
namedropping
necrological
neighbouring
nephelometer
nephelometry
neurological
occasionally
onomatopoeia
onomatopoeic
opisthograph
opisthotonos
ornithomancy
ornithoscopy
orthodontics
orthodontist
oscillograph
oscilloscope
osteological
osteoporosis
otherworldly
outmanoeuvre
overcropping
paedomorphic
panchromatic
pantisocracy
parsimonious
pathological
periodontics
periodontist
perispomenon
peristomatic
pestological
petrological
pettifoggery
pettifogging
phanerogamic
phenological
philological
philosophise
phonological
phosphoresce
photomontage
phraseograph
phreatophyte
phycological
phytological
planoconcave
plenipotence
poikilotherm
polyglottism
prolegomenon
prosopopoeia
protozoology
psychrometer
psychrometry
pteridophyte
pteridosperm
quaestorship
quattrocento
questionable
questionably
questionless
radiological
reciprocally
reciprocator
redeployment
relationally
relationship
rhinological
rhynchophora
sabretoothed
sacerdotally
sarrusophone
scatological
scorpionfish
selfviolence
semiological
semitropical
sensitometer
servitorship
servocontrol
siphonophore
siphonostele
skateboarder
slaveholding
smallholding
sociological
somniloquism
somniloquist
spectrograph
spectrometer
spectrometry
spectroscope
spectroscopy
speedboating
sphygmograph
squattocracy
steganograph
stockjobbery
stockjobbing
stoneboiling
streptococci
streptomycin
superposable
surefootedly
surrejoinder
surveyorship
survivorship
synchronical
synchroniser
tautological
teleological
tetragonally
tetramorphic
thirdborough
tightmouthed
tragicomical
transformism
transformist
transmogrify
transmontane
transpontine
transposable
trichromatic
trigonometry
tropological
ultramontane
unapologetic
unauthorised
uncommonness
unconformity
undercoating
undiplomatic
uneconomical
unemployable
unemployment
unfathomable
unhistorical
unpronounced
unreasonable
unreasonably
unresponsive
unseasonable
vainglorious
vauntcourier
viscerotonic
volitionally
wainscotting
waistcoating
wellgrounded
whippoorwill
ailurophobia
anamorphosis
anthropogeny
anthropoidal
anthropology
anticipation
anticipative
anticipatory
bibliopegist
bibliophilic
bibliopolist
biographical
bowcompasses
chalcopyrite
cheeseparing
constipation
contemplator
contemporary
contemporise
contemptible
contemptibly
contemptuous
contrapuntal
cynocephalus
discerptible
discomposure
distemperate
dodecaphonic
emancipation
episcopalian
extraspecial
frenchpolish
gametophytic
gamosepalous
gastropodous
geographical
heterophylly

homoeopathic
hymenopteran
inoccupation
interspinous
jetpropelled
lepidopteran
lithospheric
mesocephalic
moneyspinner
monkeypuzzle
municipalise
municipality
naturopathic
newspaperman
niminypiminy
noncomplying
obstreperous
orographical
overemphasis
overexposure
photospheric
pitterpatter
planispheric
polysepalous
presumptuous
principality
pseudopodium
psychopathic
quadraphonic
quadriplegia
quadriplegic
reoccupation
schizophrene
selfapplause
selfapproval
selfemployed
selfhypnosis
selfreproach
semideponent
somatopleure
spermaphytic
spokesperson
steatopygous
stereophonic
stereopticon
subtemperate
theosophical
thermophilic
toxicophobia
tradespeople
trainspotter
triglyphical
tropospheric
unacceptable
unscriptural
unscrupulous
ventripotent
winklepicker
worshipfully
zygapophysis
grotesquerie
acceleration
accelerative
accoutrement
adulteration
adulterously
Alhambresque
alliteration
alliterative
allomorphism
amateurishly
amelioration
ameliorative
amphibrachic
amphitropous
anemographic
anotherguess
antiaircraft
antiparticle
antiperiodic
antistrophic
appropriable
appropriator
asynchronism
asynchronous
automorphism
backwardness
belletristic
bilateralism
biometrician
blabbermouth
bladderwrack
blatherskite
bletherskate
blisteringly
bloodbrother
blunderingly
blusteringly
boisterously
burglarproof
calligrapher
calligraphic
Cantabrigian
cantharidian
cardcarrying
cartographer
cartographic
catachrestic
catastrophic
charterhouse
charterparty
checkerberry
checkerboard
chequerboard
chesterfield
chiropractic
chiropractor
chitterlings
chivalrously
chorographic
clangorously
clapperboard
clatteringly
clinkerbuilt
closecropped
closegrained
cocksureness
compatriotic
concurrently
consecration
consecratory
conspiration
contrariness
contrariwise
cosmographer
cosmographic
counteragent
counterblast
countercheck
counterclaim
counterforce
counterlight
countermarch
counterplead
counterpoint
counterpoise
counterproof
counterscarp
countershaft
countertenor
crackbrained
craftbrother
crossgrained
deceleration
decentralise
decompressor
decontrolled
deflagration
degenerately
degeneration
degenerative
deliberately
deliberation
deliberative
demineralise
denaturalise
denaturation
desideration
desiderative
despairingly
diathermancy
dilatoriness
disastrously
discographer
discouraging
discourteous
downwardness
eavesdropped
eavesdropper
eccentricity
ectoparasite
edulcoration
elucubration
encumbrancer
endocarditis
endoparasite
enterprising
entrepreneur
ephemerality
equestrienne
ethnographer
ethnographic
euhemeristic
evisceration
exaggeration
exaggerative
exaggeratory
exasperation
exenteration
exhilaration
exhilarative
exprobration
extracranial
exulceration
featherbrain
featheriness
fenestration
flatteringly
flavoprotein
flickeringly
geometrician
geriatrician
glitteringly
globetrotter
glycoprotein
greengrocery
haemorrhagic
hagiographer
hagiographic
hairsbreadth
handkerchief
handsbreadth
headshrinker
hectographic
heliographer
heliographic
heliogravure
heliotropism
hemimorphism
hemimorphite
hemiparasite
hierographer
hirepurchase
homomorphism
homomorphous
horsebreaker
horsetrading
housebreaker
housetrained
hydrographer
hydrographic
hydrotropism
hymnographer
hypertrophic
hypocoristic
hypophrygian
iconographer
idolatrously
illiberality
illiterately
illusoriness
illustration
illustrative
immaterially
immatureness
immemorially
immoderately
immoderation
impoverished
impropriator
inaccurately
inadvertence
inadvertency
inauguration
inauguratory
incineration
incoherently
indecorously
indiscreetly
indiscretion
indivertible
indivertibly
indoctrinate
IndoEuropean
IndoGermanic
industrially
inexperience
inexpertness
inobservance
instauration
inteneration
intercropped
interpretive
interwreathe
intolerantly
intracranial
inveterately
invigoration
irreformable
irregardless
irreverently
irreversible
irreversibly
isothermally
jurisprudent
klipspringer
laisserfaire
languorously
leathercloth
literariness
lithographer
lithographic
lithotritist
lovelornness
LowChurchman
lukewarmness
magistrature
malapertness
malnutrition
matriarchate
metachronism
metamorphism
metamorphose
metaphrastic
microcrystal
micrographer
militaristic
ministration
ministrative
misapprehend
misrepresent
moistureless
moneygrubber
monitorially
monochromate
monomorphous
monostrophic
mouthbreeder
mythographer
necrographer
northernmost
nyctitropism
obliteration
obliterative
obstetrician
omnivorously
ordinariness
organgrinder
orthographer
orthographic
orthotropism
orthotropous
overlordship
overpersuade
pantographic
paramorphism
paranormally
paraphrastic
patriarchate
pericarditis
periphrastic
perpetration
perspiration
perspiratory
petrographer
petrographic
philharmonic
phonographer
phonographic
photographer
photographic
photogravure
phototropism
phytographer
pictographic
pitcherplant
plasterboard
pleasureless
pleiotropism
pleomorphism
plummerblock
polychromous
polymorphism
polymorphous
pornographer
pornographic
postmeridian
pralltriller
prefabricate
priestridden
primigravida
prosperously
puerperrally
pyromorphite
quarterbound
quarterfinal
quarterstaff
rabblerouser
radiographer
radiographic
reassuringly
recuperation
recuperative
redecoration
redistribute

regeneration
regenerative
registration
remembrancer
remuneration
remunerative
remuneratory
reprographic
restaurateur
saccharinity
saccharoidal
salutariness
scabbardfish
scatterbrain
scatteringly
scenographic
scoundreldom
scoundrelism
scraperboard
secularistic
selfdirected
selfmurderer
selfportrait
semicircular
semidarkness
semiparasite
sharecropper
shatterproof
sinistrality
sinistrorsal
slanderously
slipcarriage
slipperiness
solitariness
southernmost
southernwood
squarerigged
staggeringly
stalwartness
stammeringly
standardbred
stenographer
stenographic
stertorously
stockbreeder
stockbroking
stonedresser
stormtrooper
stubbornness
stutteringly
stylographic
subterranean
sulphuration
sulphuretted
supererogate
supraorbital
swaggeringly
swaggerstick
tachygrapher
tachygraphic
thitherwards
thundercloud
thunderingly
thunderously
thunderstone
thunderstorm
traitorously
transgressor
triggerhappy
twitteringly
uncontrolled
underwritten
undetermined
ungovernable
unimportance
uninterested
unreservedly
unrestrained
untowardness
vertebration
vituperation
vituperative
vituperatory
viviparously
vociferation
vociferously
vomiturition
wallydraigle
weatherboard
weatherbound
weatherglass
weatherhouse
weatherproof
whimperingly
whisperingly
whitherwards
zygomorphism
zygomorphous
abstruseness
acaulescence
acquiescence
administrant
administrate
admonishment
aggressively
agribusiness
alkalescence
amortisation
appetisingly
appraisement
appraisingly
arborescence
arborisation
astonishment
baselessness
biophysicist
blandishment
blastosphere
blithesomely
bombdisposal
bootlessness
brackishness
breaststroke
breastsummer
brontosaurus
businesslike
butterscotch
calorescence
canalisation
canonisation
carelessness
centrespread
centrosphere
chastisement
childishness
chromosphere
churlishness
circumscribe
circumstance
civilisation
clannishness
clotheshorse
clothespress
clownishness
colonisation
commensalism
commensalist
commensurate
commissarial
commissariat
commissioner
compensation
compensative
compensatory
compressible
compulsively
compulsivity
compulsorily
conclusively
concrescence
condensation
confessional
conquistador
consensually
conversation
convulsively
cumbersomely
customshouse
Czechoslovak
decalescence
decreasingly
deionisation
delitescence
depressingly
deputisation
detumescence
digressional
digressively
diminishable
diminishment
disbursement
disconsolate
discursively
disguisement
dispensation
dispensatory
dispossessor
disquisition
dissuasively
dwarfishness
eleemosynary
empressement
equalisation
equidistance
etherisation
expressional
expressively
expressivity
facelessness
faintishness
fearlessness
fecklessness
feminisation
feverishness
fiddlesticks
fiendishness
filibusterer
finalisation
fluidisation
fluorescence
focalisation
formlessness
freakishness
fricasseeing
frontispiece
geophysicist
gesellschaft
ghoulishness
glaucescence
grampositive
greenishness
happenstance
harmlessness
headmistress
heedlessness
helplessness
heterosexual
highlystrung
homoeostasis
hopelessness
horrorstruck
humanisation
hypogastrium
idealisation
immunisation
imperishable
imperishably
impressively
inaccessible
inaccessibly
inadmissible
inadmissibly
inappositely
incalescence
increasingly
indecisively
indehiscence
indigestible
inspissation
interestedly
intransigent
intransitive
intumescence
irremissible
irresistible
irresistibly
juvenescence
laboursaving
languishment
laterisation
latinisation
legalisation
lifelessness
linguistical
listlessness
liverystable
localisation
longdistance
lovelessness
luminescence
maidenstakes
malversation
marketsquare
mastersinger
masterstroke
masterswitch
maximisation
mindlessness
minimisation
mistressship
mobilisation
monetisation
moralisation
motorisation
movelessness
namelessness
narcissistic
nebulisation
needlessness
neoclassical
nonexistence
novelisation
obmutescence
obsolescence
oppressively
optimisation
organisation
outpensioner
painlessness
paradisaical
paradisiacal
paralysation
parkinsonism
pearlescence
peerlessness
penalisation
percussively
permissively
persuasively
perverseness
pitilessness
planetstruck
plesiosaurus
polarisation
polyhistoric
possessively
postmistress
postposition
postpositive
precessional
preclassical
preclusively
preconscious
preexistence
prehensility
prelapsarian
premenstrual
priggishness
processional
proconsulate
professional
professorate
professoress
professorial
protensively
protrusively
psychosexual
publicspirit
qualmishness
quantisation
quintessence
racemisation
radioisotope
readjustment
reassessment
recalescence
recklessness
regressively
reinvestment
reminiscence
repressively
resipiscence
responsively
responsorial
restlessness
reviviscence
romanisation
rootlessness
ruralisation
ruthlessness
secondstring
seismoscopic
selfabsorbed
selfdestruct
selfdistrust
selflessness
semibasement
sheepishness
shillyshally
shrewishness
singleseater
skittishness
sluggishness
sluttishness
snapfastener
snappishness
snobbishness
solarisation
soullessness
spotlessness
stablishment
statuesquely
stereoscopic
stethoscopic
stratosphere
stroboscopic
subapostolic
subconscious
suberisation
sublapsarian
submissively
subversively
successfully
successional
successively

suppressible
surprisingly
suspensively
swainishness
sweetishness
tactlessness
tamelessness
taskmistress
tearlessness
televisional
terrorstruck
thermoscopic
thermosphere
thermostable
thermostatic
thievishness
ticklishness
timelessness
tirelessness
toggleswitch
tonelessness
totalisation
trickishness
tunelessness
unaccustomed
unclassified
unionisation
universalise
universalism
universalist
universality
unpleasantly
urbanisation
valorisation
vanquishable
vanquishment
vaporisation
viridescence
virtuosoship
vitalisation
vocalisation
welldisposed
whencesoever
womanishness
wonderstruck
absoluteness
absolutistic
absorptional
absorptivity
absquatulate
accurateness
accusatively
accusatorial
adequateness
aesthetician
aestheticism
alimentation
alimentative
amphictyonic
anecdotalist
antipathetic
apiculturist
apparatchiki
apparatchiks
apparitional
appositeness
appositional
Aristotelean
Aristotelian
asymmetrical
attractively
augmentation
augmentative
auscultation
auscultatory
authenticate
authenticity
autocatalyse
autochthones
automaticity
ballottement
barometrical
bellbottomed
bequeathment
bespectacled
bibliothecae
biosynthesis
biosynthetic
birdwatching
bloodstained
brainstormer
breathtaking
cabinetmaker
calamitously
callisthenic
caricaturist
characterise
charlatanism
chrematistic
chromaticism
chromaticity
chromatogram
chromatology
chromatopsia
cinematheque
circuitously
cirrostratus
coelenterate
cohabitation
coleopterist
coleopterous
collectively
collectivise
collectivism
collectivist
collectivity
comfortingly
commentation
committeeman
completeness
concentrator
conceptional
conceptually
concreteness
conductivity
confectioner
conglutinate
congratulant
congratulate
connectional
connectively
consentience
consentingly
consistently
consistorial
constituency
constitution
constitutive
consultation
consultative
contestation
contextually
contriteness
convectional
conventicler
conventional
copulatively
coquettishly
corelatively
correctional
correctitude
correctively
cumulatively
debilitation
decapitation
decoratively
definiteness
definitively
delicatessen
delightfully
delimitation
demilitarise
demonstrable
demonstrably
demonstrator
depoliticise
derivational
derivatively
derogatorily
desolateness
dessertspoon
diageotropic
dialectician
dialectology
diminutively
discontented
discreteness
discretional
disgustfully
disgustingly
dissentingly
dissertation
distortional
draughtboard
draughthorse
droughtiness
dubitatively
elementalism
elementarily
enchantingly
encrustation
endometritis
enginetuning
entreatingly
equalitarian
evidentially
excogitation
excogitative
exercitation
exhaustively
exhibitioner
exorbitantly
explantation
exploitation
exploitative
extrauterine
facilitation
fantasticate
fantasticism
felicitation
felicitously
fermentation
fermentative
figuratively
fortuitously
foundationer
freightliner
futilitarian
gamopetalous
geotectonics
gladiatorial
gonadotropic
gonadotropin
grallatorial
grammaticise
gratuitously
guaranteeing
habilitation
heartstrings
hereditament
hereditarily
hesitatingly
humanitarian
hydrostatics
hypersthenia
hypersthenic
illegitimacy
illegitimate
impenetrable
impenetrably
impenitently
imperatively
imperatorial
implantation
impoliteness
imputatively
inconstantly
incrustation
indicatively
inelasticity
inescutcheon
inexactitude
infiniteness
infinitively
inflectional
inhabitation
iniquitously
inspectorate
inspectorial
interstellar
interstitial
intrauterine
involutional
irrelatively
irritatingly
kilowatthour
kinaesthesia
kinaesthesis
kinaesthetic
laureateship
ledgertackle
levorotation
levorotatory
macropterous
malcontented
manometrical
meditatively
mercantilism
mercantilist
minedetector
misquotation
misselthrush
misstatement
moderateness
monometallic
monopetalous
mothertongue
motivational
multistoried
nauseatingly
navigational
neglectfully
Neoplatonism
Neoplatonist
neurasthenia
neurasthenic
neuropterous
nimbostratus
obdurateness
obligatorily
obsoleteness
occupational
omnipotently
oppositeness
oppositional
orchestrator
orthopterist
orthopteroid
orthopterous
overactivity
overestimate
oxyacetylene
paraesthesia
parametrical
parasiticide
parasitology
pejoratively
perceptively
perceptivity
perceptually
peremptorily
perfectively
periostracum
permittivity
pernoctation
persistently
philanthrope
philanthropy
philistinism
phlebotomise
phlebotomist
phonasthenia
phyllotactic
pigmentation
pinfeathered
plecopterous
pneumaticity
pneumatology
pneumothorax
polypetalous
portentously
practitioner
pragmatistic
preceptorial
predestinate
predictively
prefectorial
prehistorian
preposterous
presbyterate
presbyterial
Presbyterian
presentation
presentative
presentiment
preventative
preventively
productively
productivity
progesterone
proglottides
projectional
projectively
proportional
proportioned
prosectorial
prostitution
protactinium
protectively
protectorate
protestation
protistology
prudentially
psychotropic
pursestrings
quantitative
recapitulate
reconstitute
recreational
redemptioner
Redemptorist
reflectional
reflectively
reflectivity
refractivity
refractorily
remilitarise
remonstrance
remonstrator
renegotiable
repetitional
repetitively
resoluteness
respectfully
respectively

retractation
retractility
revelational
rheumatology
rumbletumble
ruminatively
salutational
Samaritanism
schizothymia
schizothymic
segmentation
selfactivity
selfbetrayal
selfcatering
selfinterest
semidetached
semiliterate
sententially
separateness
sequentially
sequestrator
serpentiform
serpentinely
sexcentenary
shortstaffed
slaughterous
solicitation
solicitously
sophisticate
spermathecal
spermatocyte
spermatozoid
spermatozoon
sprightfully
stalactiform
statistician
sternutation
sternutative
sternutatory
strengthener
strengthless
subcontinent
subeditorial
subjectively
subjectivise
subjectivism
subjectivist
subjectivity
substitution
substitutive
suggestively
superstition
superstratum
susceptivity
sustentation
sustentative
synaesthesia
synaesthetic
syncretistic
syndactylism
syndactylous
tangentially
teetertotter
telaesthesia
telaesthetic
tercentenary
testosterone
thaumaturgic
theoretician
thermotactic
thermotropic
thoughtfully
tittletattle
toploftiness
torrentially
totalitarian
transitional
transitively
transitivity

transitorily
tricentenary
trichotomise
trichotomous
tridactylous
tripartitely
tripartition
trumpetshell
ubiquitarian
ubiquitously
unappetising
unconstraint
understaffed
uneventfully
unflattering
unhesitating
vegetatively
vindictively
visitational
visitatorial
volumetrical
walkietalkie
wollastonite
woolgatherer
xiphisternum
accentuation
acetabularia
aeronautical
aeroneurosis
alphanumeric
antineutrino
attributable
bilingualism
blackcurrant
blackguardly
blamefulness
blastfurnace
blissfulness
blockbusting
boastfulness
brassrubbing
Byelorussian
canorousness
captiousness
catamountain
cautiousness
cheerfulness
cirrocumulus
clairaudient
coachbuilder
colloquially
confabulator
connaturally
consequently
construction
constructive
contiguously
continuation
continuative
continuously
covetousness
crossbuttock
crosscurrent
crosspurpose
cumbrousness
decorousness
delinquently
denticulated
desirousness
dextrousness
disannulling
disannulment
disreputable
disreputably
dissimulator
dolorousness
doubtfulness
dramaturgist
dreadfulness

echosounding
effectuality
effectuation
enormousness
exiguousness
exsanguinate
exsanguinous
extinguisher
extramundane
fabulousness
factiousness
faithfulness
fancifulness
floriculture
folliculated
forcefulness
fruitfulness
furunculosis
generousness
gesticulator
gloriousness
gorgeousness
gracefulness
graciousness
gratefulness
grievousness
guilefulness
harlequinade
heartburning
highsounding
honeybuzzard
horticulture
humorousness
hydroquinone
illnaturedly
immeasurable
immeasurably
immensurable
inadequately
incalculable
incalculably
incestuously
incommutable
incommutably
incomputable
inconsumable
inconsumably
incorruption
indisputable
indisputably
infrequently
intercurrent
intercutting
intermundane
internuclear
internuncial
interruption
interruptive
intramundane
intriguingly
introduction
introductory
intussuscept
jerrybuilder
Liverpudlian
longitudinal
luminousness
lusciousness
manslaughter
menstruation
mercifulness
metallurgist
microsurgery
mirthfulness
mournfulness
multinuclear
multipurpose
mutinousness
nauseousness

nebulousness
neurosurgeon
neurosurgery
noctilucence
numerousness
offscourings
overabundant
overcautious
particularly
patulousness
peacefulness
peasepudding
pedunculated
perambulator
perilousness
perpetuation
perviousness
pisciculture
polyneuritic
polyneuritis
populousness
preciousness
preoccupancy
prerequisite
previousness
pricecutting
pridefulness
prosecutable
radionuclide
ravenousness
repercussion
repercussive
reproducible
reproduction
reproductive
retropulsion
revictualled
rightfulness
rigorousness
scabrousness
scornfulness
scripturally
sculpturally
sedulousness
selfdoubting
selfeducated
sensuousness
shamefulness
silviculture
skullduggery
slothfulness
sodafountain
solifluction
sonorousness
spaciousness
speciousness
spiritualise
spiritualism
spiritualist
spirituality
spitefulness
sportfulness
spuriousness
staffsurgeon
stepdaughter
stillhunting
stonecutting
structurally
studiousness
subsaturated
subsequently
substruction
substructure
superhumanly
supermundane
supramundane
swashbuckler
sylviculture
tastefulness

thankfulness
threequarter
timorousness
topsyturvily
tortuousness
transduction
transfusible
transhumance
translucence
translucency
transmutable
triangularly
trustfulness
truthfulness
tuberculated
tuberculosis
tumultuously
turriculated
typefounding
ultramundane
uncalculated
unctuousness
undercurrent
undercutting
underrunning
undersurface
unfavourable
unfavourably
unfrequented
unisexuality
unlawfulness
unprejudiced
usuriousness
uxoriousness
vaporousness
vengefulness
venomousness
vermiculated
vernacularly
vigorousness
virtuousness
vitreousness
voluptuosity
voluptuously
warehouseman
wastefulness
watchfulness
wondrousness
wrathfulness
wrongfulness
youthfulness
abortiveness
abrasiveness
adaptiveness
adhesiveness
allusiveness
coacervation
coerciveness
cohesiveness
conservation
conservatism
conservative
conservatory
contrivement
creativeness
deactivation
decisiveness
delusiveness
derisiveness
divisiveness
effusiveness
eruptiveness
fructivorous
fugitiveness
hardfavoured
illusiveness
inactivation
incisiveness
irrelevantly

manoeuvrable
mediaevalism
mediaevalist
negativeness
negativistic
perfervidity
positiveness
positivistic
preservation
preservative
quadrivalent
quaquaversal
reactivation
reactiveness
relativeness
relativistic
selfdevotion
selfinvolved
sportiveness
Stradivarius
subservience
subserviency
unambivalent
wellfavoured
bantamweight
boogiewoogie
bottlewasher
brokenwinded
churchwarden
commonwealth
kirschwasser
mangelwurzel
middleweight
misknowledge
monkeywrench
neoDarwinian
neoDarwinism
neoDarwinist
nonflowering
overpowering
praiseworthy
screenwriter
scriptwriter
sparrowgrass
streetwalker
teensyweensy
welterweight
williewaught
wonderworker
ambidextrous
complexional
complexioned
crossexamine
homosexually
perplexingly
achlamydeous
archetypally
archetypical
carbohydrate
chimneypiece
coenobytical
countrydance
countrywoman
flamboyantly
gamophyllous
gratifyingly
holidaymaker
hydrodynamic
hydrolysable
hyperpyretic
hyperpyrexia
leucocytosis
leukocytosis
licketysplit
metaphysical
metapsychics
monophyletic
Monophysitic
motorcyclist

mystifyingly
oncorhynchus
phagocytosis
phagocytotic
phenotypical
phycomycetes
polyphyletic
proselytiser
prototypical
satisfyingly
strongylosis
terrifyingly
bilharziasis
bilharziosis
heterozygote
heterozygous
laissezaller
laissezfaire

---

abbreviation
acceleration
accelerative
accentuation
acciaccatura
accumulation
accumulative
adjudication
adjudicative
adjudicatory
adulteration
aerodynamics
alexipharmic
alimentation
alimentative
alliteration
alliterative
amalgamation
amalgamative
amelioration
ameliorative
amortisation
amphibrachic
amphisbaenic
anaphylactic
anathematise
anecdotalist
anemographic
annihilation
annihilative
annunciation
anticipation
anticipative
anticipatory
antimacassar
antimalarial
appreciation
appreciative
appreciatory
arborisation
articulately
articulation
articulatory
asphyxiation
assibilation
assimilation
assimilative
assimilatory
atheromatous
augmentation
augmentative
auscultation
auscultatory
Australasian
autocatalyse
autodidactic
bacchanalian
backbreaking
backpedalled
berzelianite

bespectacled
bibliomaniac
bilateralism
bilingualism
blackguardly
blastulation
bloodstained
bonnyclabber
bottlewasher
bowcompasses
brachydactyl
breathtaking
brontosaurus
cachinnation
cachinnatory
calligrapher
calligraphic
calumniation
calumniatory
canalisation
cancellation
canonisation
cantillation
capitulation
carpetbagger
Cartesianism
cartographer
cartographic
catilinarian
charlatanism
cheeseparing
childbearing
chiropractic
chiropractor
chlorination
chorographic
Christianise
Christianity
churchianity
churchwarden
circumjacent
civilisation
classicalism
classicalist
classicality
claudication
closegrained
coacervation
codification
cohabitation
collegialism
collegiality
collegiately
collinearity
colonisation
columniation
commendation
commendatory
commensalism
commensalist
commentation
commissarial
commissariat
compellation
compensation
compensative
compensatory
complication
compurgation
compurgatory
conciliation
conciliative
conciliatory
concordantly
condemnation
condemnatory
condensation
confirmation
confirmative

confirmatory
confiscation
confiscatory
conformation
Confucianism
congeniality
conglobation
congregation
connubiality
consecration
consecratory
conservation
conservatism
conservative
conservatory
consignation
consociation
conspiration
constipation
consultation
consultative
consummately
consummation
consummative
consummatory
contestation
continuation
continuative
conversation
conviviality
coordinately
coordination
coordinative
corporeality
cosmographer
cosmographic
countenancer
counteragent
courtplaster
crackbrained
crenellation
crossexamine
crossgrained
crossheading
cryptanalyst
cryptogamous
deactivation
deambulatory
debilitation
decapitation
deceleration
decentralise
deescalation
deflagration
defraudation
degenerately
degeneration
degenerative
deionisation
delamination
deliberately
deliberation
deliberative
delimitation
demilitarise
demineralise
demodulation
denaturalise
denaturation
denomination
denominative
denuclearise
denunciation
denunciative
denunciatory
depopulation
depreciation
depreciatory
deputisation

deracination
desalination
desideration
desiderative
despoliation
desquamation
desquamative
desquamatory
detoxication
dichromatism
dilapidation
dinnerjacket
disaccharide
disclamation
discographer
discordantly
discouraging
disenchanter
disinflation
dispensation
dispensatory
dissertation
dissocialise
dissociation
dissociative
distillation
distillatory
divarication
earthshaking
ecclesiastic
echolocation
ectoparasite
editorialise
editorialist
edulcoration
effectuality
effectuation
effeminately
elementalism
elementarily
elucubration
emancipation
emargination
emasculation
emasculatory
emotionalise
emotionalism
emotionalist
emotionality
encrustation
encumbrancer
endoparasite
enthusiastic
ephemerality
epicureanism
episcopalian
epithalamion
epithalamium
equalisation
equalitarian
equivocation
equivocatory
erythematous
essentiality
etherisation
ethnographer
ethnographic
evisceration
exacerbation
exaggeration
exaggerative
exaggeratory
exasperation
excogitation
excogitative
excruciating
excruciation
exenteration
exercitation

exhilaration	illiterately	Manicheanism	paralysation	racemisation
exhilarative	illogicality	manipulation	paraphrastic	radiographer
exophthalmic	illumination	manipulative	parochialise	radiographic
exophthalmos	illuminative	manipulatory	parochialism	ramification
exophthalmus	illustration	marketgarden	parochiality	ratification
exorbitantly	illustrative	maximisation	paronomastic	razzledazzle
expatriation	immaculately	mediaevalism	passionately	reactivation
explantation	immoderately	mediaevalist	penalisation	reallocation
exploitation	immoderation	megalomaniac	perfoliation	recuperation
exploitative	immunisation	menstruation	performative	recuperative
exprobration	impartiality	mercurialise	periphrastic	redecoration
extracranial	implantation	mercurialism	permanganate	regeneration
exulceration	impregnation	metagalactic	pernoctation	regenerative
facilitation	inaccurately	metaphrastic	peroxidation	registration
factionalism	inactivation	metasomatism	perpetration	rejuvenation
fainthearted	inadequately	microanalyst	perpetuation	remembrancer
faithhealing	inauguration	micrographer	perspicacity	remilitarise
farmsteading	inauguratory	minimisation	perspiration	remuneration
felicitation	incatenation	ministration	perspiratory	remunerative
feminisation	incendiarism	ministrative	perturbation	remuneratory
fenestration	incineration	miscellanist	perturbative	renunciation
fermentation	inconstantly	misdemeanant	petrographer	renunciative
fermentative	incrustation	misdemeanour	petrographic	renunciatory
fibrillation	indelicately	miseducation	phonographer	reoccupation
fictionalise	inflammation	misquotation	phonographic	repatriation
fiddlefaddle	inflammatory	mithridatise	photographer	reprographic
fieldglasses	ingratiating	mithridatism	photographic	restaurateur
finalisation	inhabitation	mobilisation	photogravure	resupination
flagellation	inoccupation	modification	phyllotactic	reticulately
flagellatory	inordinately	modificatory	phytographer	reticulation
flamboyantly	inosculation	molecularity	phytophagous	retractation
flocculation	insemination	monetisation	pictographic	revictualled
fluidisation	inspissation	moneychanger	pigmentation	rhizophagous
fluoridation	installation	monkeyjacket	pitterpatter	romanisation
fluorination	instauration	monofilament	plaindealing	ruralisation
fluorocarbon	instillation	monometallic	plesiosaurus	saddlebacked
focalisation	insufflation	monopetalous	polarisation	salmonladder
futilitarian	inteneration	moralisation	polypetalous	Samaritanism
gamopetalous	interchanger	morrisdancer	polysepalous	sanguinarily
gamosepalous	interglacial	motorisation	polytonality	saprophagous
gasification	intimidation	municipalise	porcellanous	sarcophagous
glaucomatous	intimidatory	municipality	pornographer	Scandinavian
gramnegative	intolerantly	mythographer	pornographic	scareheading
greathearted	intoxication	naturopathic	potentiality	scenographic
grossularite	intracranial	nebulisation	practicality	schoolmaster
guestchamber	invagination	necrographer	precisianism	scrimshanker
habilitation	invalidation	necrophagous	preformation	scutellation
hagiographer	inveterately	neonomianism	preformative	sectarianise
hagiographic	invigilation	Nestorianism	prelapsarian	sectarianism
halogenation	invigoration	neuroanatomy	presentation	sectionalism
heavyhearted	irregularity	nicotinamide	presentative	segmentation
hectographic	irrelevantly	nidification	preservation	selfeffacing
heliographer	katzenjammer	nomenclative	preservative	selfpleasing
heliographic	Keynesianism	nomenclature	preventative	semidetached
heliogravure	kindergarten	nonagenarian	primigravida	semifinalist
hemerocallis	kirschwasser	nonchalantly	principality	semiparasite
hemiparasite	kleptomaniac	noncombatant	proclamation	sexagenarian
hereditament	laboursaving	notification	proclamatory	shortchanger
hereditarily	lachrymation	novelisation	profligately	shortstaffed
heterogamous	lachrymatory	nymphomaniac	prolongation	sightreading
hierographer	laissezaller	obliteration	promulgation	singlehanded
hierophantic	largehearted	obliterative	proofreading	sinistrality
homoeopathic	laterisation	obnubilation	prophylactic	skateboarder
homologation	latinisation	octogenarian	propitiation	skrimshanker
horsetrading	ledgertackle	ophiophagous	propitiatory	sledgehammer
housetrained	legalisation	opinionative	protestation	snakecharmer
hucklebacked	legitimately	optimisation	prothalamion	softpedalled
humanisation	legitimation	orbicularity	prothalamium	solarisation
humanitarian	legitimatise	organisation	protoplasmic	solicitation
humification	levorotation	orthographer	protoplastic	speedboating
hydrographer	levorotatory	orthographic	proudhearted	spiritualise
hydrographic	lighthearted	ossification	psychopathic	spiritualism
hydrostatics	lithographer	osteoplastic	purification	spiritualist
hymnographer	lithographic	pacification	purificatory	spirituality
hyperplastic	localisation	pacificatory	quadrivalent	stenographer
iconoclastic	lumberjacket	Palladianism	quadrumanous	stenographic
iconographer	magistrature	panification	quantisation	sternutation
idealisation	malformation	pantographic	quantitative	sternutative
illiberality	malversation	paradisaical	quizzicality	sternutatory

stonyhearted
stouthearted
Stradivarius
straitjacket
streetwalker
stridulation
strobilation
strontianite
stylographic
subarrhation
suberisation
sublapsarian
subminiature
subnormality
subsidiarily
subterranean
sulphonamide
sulphonation
sulphuration
supercharger
supplicantly
supplication
supplicatory
sustentation
sustentative
tachygrapher
tachygraphic
technicality
teratomatous
tessellation
thereinafter
thermolabile
thermotactic
threequarter
tintinnabula
tittletattle
totalisation
totalitarian
trachomatous
tradescantia
traducianism
traducianist
transplanter
transudation
transudatory
trephination
trifurcation
trinomialism
triplication
triumphantly
turbellarian
typification
ubiquitarian
unambivalent
undercoating
understaffed
unhesitating
unionisation
unisexuality
unitarianism
universalise
universalism
universalist
universality
unpleasantly
unpopularity
unrestrained
urbanisation
valorisation
vaporisation
vasodilation
vasodilatory
vaticination
veridicality
verification
verificatory
vertebration
vesiculation
veterinarian
Victorianism
vilification
vinification
vitalisation
vitiligation
vituperation
vituperative
vituperatory
vivification
vocabularian
vocalisation
vociferation
waistcoating
walkietalkie
wallydraigle
whimsicality
wholehearted
williewaught
yellowhammer
analphabetic
brambleberry
brassrubbing
checkerberry
checkerboard
chequerboard
clapperboard
clinkerbuilt
collywobbles
concelebrant
concelebrate
counterblast
disestablish
draughtboard
drawingboard
equiprobable
erythroblast
featherbrain
haematoblast
halftimbered
hoodmanblind
infundibular
interlobular
invertebrate
landlubberly
Northumbrian
outwardbound
plasterboard
plummerblock
preestablish
purposebuilt
quarterbound
runningboard
scatterbrain
scraperboard
selfdoubting
serviceberry
shuffleboard
skunkcabbage
stellenbosch
stockjobbery
stockjobbing
supraorbital
thimbleberry
unencumbered
weatherboard
weatherbound
whortleberry
academically
acaulescence
acoustically
acquiescence
alkalescence
amitotically
anagogically
analogically
analytically
anatomically
antiaircraft
apolitically
apparatchiki
apparatchiks
appendectomy
appendicitis
appendicular
arborescence
archdeaconry
archdiocesan
architecture
argillaceous
aromatically
aromaticness
artistically
athletically
bactericidal
barbarically
beatifically
billsticking
biologically
birdwatching
bluestocking
bodystocking
bookingclerk
butterscotch
calorescence
camiknickers
carbonaceous
cashandcarry
catholically
cherubically
circumscribe
communicable
communicably
communicator
concrescence
constriction
constrictive
construction
constructive
contumacious
cosmetically
cottonocracy
countercheck
counterclaim
crosssection
decalescence
deconsecrate
delitescence
demoniacally
despotically
detumescence
diabolically
diatomaceous
diatonically
didactically
dietetically
disaffection
disassociate
disfranchise
disinfectant
disinfection
diverticular
diverticulum
dogmatically
domestically
domesticator
doubleacting
dramatically
dynastically
eclectically
ecologically
economically
ecstatically
electrically
elliptically
emphatically
enclitically
endermically
epidemically
episodically
esoterically
euphonically
exegetically
exoterically
fluorescence
forensically
frankincense
frenetically
furfuraceous
gallinaceous
galvanically
genuflection
geologically
gerontocracy
gesellschaft
gigantically
glaucescence
graminaceous
gynaecocracy
handkerchief
harmonically
heraldically
hermetically
heteroecious
hibernaculum
hirepurchase
historically
horrifically
hygienically
hypnotically
hypothecator
hysterectomy
hysterically
ichthyocolla
idiosyncrasy
imperfection
imperfective
inapplicable
inapplicably
inauspicious
incalescence
indehiscence
ineradicable
ineradicably
inescutcheon
inexplicable
inexplicably
inextricable
inextricably
infanticidal
insecticidal
insufficient
insurrection
intellection
intellective
intellectual
interdiction
interdictive
interdictory
interjection
interjectory
interlocutor
internuclear
intersection
intervocalic
introduction
introductory
introjection
intumescence
irreflective
irrespective
jesuitically
jurisdiction
juvenescence
kissingcrust
landingcraft
leathercloth
liquefacient
liquefaction
liturgically
logistically
LowChurchman
luminescence
magnetically
magnifically
magnificence
majestically
matriarchate
mechanically
meretricious
metallically
metapsychics
meteorically
methodically
misdirection
mnemotechnic
monastically
monostichous
motorcyclist
multinuclear
narcotically
nerveracking
neurotically
noctilucence
noneffective
nonefficient
nonobjective
obmutescence
obsolescence
operatically
orchidaceous
overreaction
pantisocracy
pathetically
patriarchate
pearlescence
pedantically
periodically
pertinacious
petrifaction
phonemically
phonetically
phycomycetes
platonically
pontifically
pontificator
preconscious
predilection
preselection
preselective
prevaricator
prolifically
prolificness
pronouncedly
prosodically
psychoactive
pterodactyle
putrefaction
putrefactive
pyroelectric
quattrocento
quixotically
rabbinically
radionuclide
recalescence
receptaculum
reciprocally
reciprocator
recollection
recollective
reminiscence
reproducible
reproduction
reproductive
resipiscence
resurrection
reviviscence

rhetorically
rhythmically
romantically
sadistically
safecracking
sardonically
satisfaction
satisfactory
scarificator
schorlaceous
sclerenchyma
seismoscopic
selfeducated
selfelective
semantically
semicircular
semiprecious
seraphically
servicecourt
shamefacedly
significance
significancy
simoniacally
singleacting
Socratically
solifluction
sorbefacient
specifically
specificness
sporadically
squattocracy
steeplechase
stereoscopic
stethoscopic
streptococci
stroboscopic
stupefacient
stupefaction
stupefactive
subconscious
subsonically
substruction
substructure
supernaculum
swashbuckler
syllabically
symbolically
syndetically
synoptically
systemically
tabernacular
tectonically
terrifically
Teutonically
theatrically
theistically
thematically
thermoscopic
thundercloud
torrefaction
transduction
translucence
translucency
transpacific
tyrannically
tyrannicidal
unattractive
uncritically
venepuncture
venipuncture
viridescence
vitrifaction
volcanically
workingclass
accommodator
accursedness
achlamydeous
affectedness
ambassadress

backwardness
backwoodsman
bullheadedly
calycoideous
carbohydrate
clairaudient
composedness
compoundable
confoundedly
confusedness
consolidator
countrydance
crossbedding
dejectedness
demimondaine
depravedness
detachedness
diamonddrill
downwardness
endocarditis
eveningdress
hebdomadally
hesperididia
highhandedly
hydromedusae
hydromedusan
immethodical
improvidence
incommodious
indebtedness
independence
independency
interbedding
intermeddler
intermediacy
intermediary
intermediate
irregardless
lefthandedly
Liverpudlian
longitudinal
longwindedly
lopsidedness
manifoldness
morningdress
Newfoundland
nonresidence
onesidedness
openhandedly
openmindedly
outdatedness
overlordship
peasepudding
pellucidness
pericarditis
postgraduate
preparedness
profoundness
purblindness
reservedness
resignedness
resolvedness
resplendence
resplendency
retrocedence
salamandrian
salamandrine
salamandroid
scabbardfish
selfevidence
selfmurderer
sinusoidally
spheroidally
spiritedness
splendidness
standardbred
supersedence
surroundings
tetrahedrite

thousandfold
unconsidered
underbidding
unprejudiced
untowardness
unwontedness
wretchedness
abortiveness
abrasiveness
absoluteness
abstruseness
accouchement
accoutrement
accurateness
acetaldehyde
adaptiveness
adequateness
adhesiveness
adorableness
aerosiderite
Alhambresque
allusiveness
ambivalently
amenableness
amentiferous
amicableness
amphitheatre
anaesthetise
anaesthetist
announcement
antecedently
appositeness
appraisement
Aristotelean
Aristotelian
astringently
atmospherics
ballottement
bantamweight
battlemented
bedazzlement
belittlement
beneficently
benevolently
benzaldehyde
bibliopegist
blamableness
breathlessly
brickfielder
buccaneering
buccaneerish
bulletheaded
calisthenics
calorimetric
cantankerous
carragheenin
carriageable
catachrestic
chancemedley
characterise
chastisement
chemotherapy
chronometric
cocksureness
coelenterate
coerciveness
cohesiveness
coincidental
coincidently
coleopterist
coleopterous
colorimetric
colourlessly
commencement
committeeman
commonwealth
complacently
complemental
completeness

conchiferous
concreteness
concurrently
conglomerate
consequently
consistently
containerise
contingently
contriteness
contrivement
conveniently
convincement
copolymerise
cousingerman
creativeness
culpableness
curmudgeonly
cytogenetics
decisiveness
decompressor
definiteness
delicatessen
delinquently
delusiveness
denouncement
departmental
derisiveness
desolateness
despondently
dethronement
diamagnetism
disagreeable
disagreeably
disagreement
disbursement
discipleship
disconnected
disconnexion
discontented
discreteness
disgorgement
disguisement
dislodgement
displaceable
displacement
dispossessor
dissymmetric
distemperate
divisiveness
dodecahedral
dodecahedron
doubledealer
doubledecked
doubledecker
dunderheaded
dynamometric
effortlessly
effusiveness
embattlement
embezzlement
empressement
encirclement
endamagement
enfeeblement
enshrinement
enswathement
entanglement
enthronement
entrammelled
entrancement
entrepreneur
enviableness
envisagement
equivalently
eruptiveness
escutcheoned
estrangement
evanescently
exchangeable

experimental
experimenter
extraspecial
extrauterine
falcongentil
falcongentle
fearsomeness
feminineness
forcibleness
forebodement
formaldehyde
FrancoGerman
fraudulently
freewheeling
fricasseeing
fructiferous
fugitiveness
fullyfledged
gamesomeness
geomagnetism
gladsomeness
gobbledegook
governmental
grammolecule
groundlessly
gruesomeness
guaranteeing
hairsbreadth
handsbreadth
handsomeness
heliotherapy
hemispheroid
hereinbefore
heterocercal
heterogenous
heteromerous
heterosexual
horribleness
horsebreaker
housebreaker
housekeeping
hydrotherapy
hydrothermal
hyperthermia
hypnotherapy
illusiveness
immatureness
impedimental
impenitently
impoliteness
incisiveness
incoherently
incompletely
indiscreetly
indiscretion
ineffaceable
ineffaceably
infiniteness
infrequently
infringement
instrumental
integumental
interoceanic
interoceptor
interpleader
interpretive
interstellar
interwreathe
intrauterine
inveiglement
irreverently
isodiametric
jetpropelled
laticiferous
laudableness
laureateship
lonesomeness
luminiferous
macropterous

malcontented
malevolently
marriageable
middleweight
minedetector
misapprehend
misjudgement
misplacement
misrepresent
misstatement
moderateness
moistureless
mouthbreeder
moveableness
muddleheaded
munificently
muttonheaded
negativeness
Neohellenism
neuropterous
nevertheless
newspaperman
nonflowering
nympholeptic
obdurateness
obsoleteness
obstreperous
omnipotently
omnisciently
oppositeness
organoleptic
orienteering
orthopaedics
orthopaedist
orthopterist
orthopteroid
orthopterous
outmanoeuvre
overniceness
overpowering
panhellenism
parenthesise
persistently
perverseness
pharmaceutic
phillumenist
pitiableness
pleasureless
plecopterous
plumbiferous
pluviometric
polarimetric
polychaetous
positiveness
postponement
precancelled
preeminently
prenticeship
preponderant
preponderate
preposterous
presbyterate
presbyterial
Presbyterian
privateering
procathedral
proficiently
profiteering
progesterone
propaedeutic
psychometric
psychosexual
Quadragesima
quaquaversal
racketeering
radioelement
radiotherapy
rattleheaded
reactiveness
readableness
rechargeable
regardlessly
relativeness
relentlessly
reliableness
renouncement
resettlement
resiniferous
resistlessly
resoluteness
retroflexion
rhombohedral
rhombohedron
salutiferous
sanguineness
schoolfellow
schoolleaver
scoundreldom
scoundrelism
seismometric
selfaffected
selfcatering
selfdeceived
selfdeceiver
selfdirected
selfinterest
selfsameness
semibasement
semidomestic
semiliterate
seminiferous
sensibleness
separateness
septuagenary
Septuagesima
sexcentenary
sheepshearer
shortsleeved
siliciferous
singledecker
singleseater
slaughterous
sociableness
soporiferous
speechlessly
spiegeleisen
spiritlessly
spokesperson
sportiveness
stanniferous
stelliferous
stereometric
sternwheeler
stockbreeder
stonedresser
stranglehold
subsequently
subtemperate
sudoriferous
sufficiently
suitableness
sulphuretted
supplemental
supplementer
tangibleness
taxcollector
teensyweensy
tercentenary
terribleness
testosterone
thermometric
threewheeler
thriftlessly
tiresomeness
toilsomeness
tradespeople
transgressor
transoceanic
tricentenary
turtlenecked
unchangeable
unchangeably
unflattering
unfrequented
uninterested
unmanageable
unregenerate
Valenciennes
valuableness
variableness
voidableness
volatileness
welterweight
whigmaleerie
wicketkeeper
woodenheaded
woollyheaded
workableness
xiphisternum
chesterfield
counterforce
delightfully
despitefully
diamondfield
disdainfully
disgustfully
laisserfaire
laissezfaire
landingfield
meaningfully
neglectfully
passionfruit
playingfield
purposefully
quarterfinal
remorsefully
respectfully
revengefully
sprightfully
staffofficer
successfully
thoughtfully
uneventfully
unfaithfully
ungracefully
ungratefully
unmercifully
untruthfully
worshipfully
advantageous
aetiological
anotherguess
astrological
buffalograss
burningglass
carcinogenic
cartological
chorological
clearsighted
cleistogamic
cosmological
crossingover
crystalgazer
disambiguate
disintegrate
dressinggown
ethnological
etymological
etymologicon
extravagance
extravagancy
extravaganza
firstnighter
floodlighted
forthrightly
galactogogue
genealogical
graspingness
hagiological
histological
hydrological
incontiguous
incorrigible
incorrigibly
intelligence
intelligible
intelligibly
interdigital
interrogator
investigator
irrefragable
irrefragably
leapfrogging
limnological
lithological
magnetograph
manslaughter
metalanguage
meteorograph
metrological
mourningband
mourningring
mythological
mythologiser
necrological
neurological
obligingness
opisthograph
oscillograph
osteological
pathological
pestological
petrological
pettifoggery
pettifogging
phanerogamic
phenological
philological
phonological
phraseograph
phycological
phytological
pleasingness
predesignate
prizefighter
punchingball
quadrangular
radiological
redintegrate
retiringness
rhinological
sacrilegious
scatological
scouringrush
semiological
sharpsighted
shootingiron
shortsighted
skippingrope
skullduggery
sleepingpill
snarlingiron
sociological
soundingline
sparkingplug
sparrowgrass
speakingtube
spectrograph
sphygmograph
standingroom
steganograph
stepdaughter
sterlingness
stockingless
strikingness
studdingsail
superhighway
sweepingness
swimmingbath
swimmingbell
swimmingpool
tautological
teleological
theatregoing
toastingfork
touchingness
transmigrant
transmigrate
transmogrify
tropological
unapologetic
unsegregated
weatherglass
acronychally
admonishment
ailurophobia
anamorphosis
antipathetic
antirachitic
approachable
astonishment
autochthones
bequeathment
bibliophilic
bibliothecae
biographical
biosynthesis
biosynthetic
blandishment
brackishness
bullfighting
callisthenic
charnelhouse
charterhouse
childishness
churlishness
cinematheque
clannishness
clotheshorse
clownishness
cockfighting
customshouse
cynocephalus
dibranchiate
diminishable
diminishment
dodecaphonic
draughthorse
dwarfishness
embranchment
encroachment
entrenchment
faintishness
feverishness
fiendishness
firefighting
foresightful
freakishness
gametophytic
geographical
ghoulishness
greenishness
groundcherry
haemorrhagic
heterophylly
hierarchical
hypersthenia
hypersthenic
imperishable
imperishably
intrenchment
kinaesthesia
kinaesthesis
kinaesthetic
languishment

lithospheric
lodginghouse
mansionhouse
meetinghouse
melanochroic
mesocephalic
misselthrush
neurasthenia
neurasthenic
oligarchical
orographical
overemphasis
paraesthesia
philanthrope
philanthropy
phonasthenia
photospheric
pinfeathered
planispheric
pneumothorax
priggishness
pyrotechnics
pyrotechnist
quadraphonic
qualmishness
rapprochment
reproachable
reproachless
retrenchment
sandyachting
schizophrene
schizothymia
schizothymic
selfrighting
sheepishness
shillyshally
shrewishness
skittishness
sluggishness
sluttishness
snappishness
snobbishness
spermaphytic
spermathecal
stablishment
stationhouse
stereochromy
stereophonic
strengthener
strengthless
swainishness
sweetishness
synaesthesia
synaesthetic
telaesthesia
telaesthetic
theosophical
thermophilic
thievishness
thoroughbass
thoroughbred
thoroughfare
thoroughness
ticklishness
toxicophobia
trickishness
triggerhappy
triglyphical
tropospheric
underachieve
unsearchable
unthoughtful
vanquishable
vanquishment
weatherhouse
womanishness
woolgatherer
xanthochroia
zygapophysis
absentminded
absolutistic
absorptional
absorptivity
accomplished
accusatively
adaptability
advisability
aesthetician
aestheticism
aggressively
agribusiness
aircondition
alterability
altitudinous
amateurishly
anaerobiosis
anemophilous
antagonistic
anthelmintic
antigenicity
antiperiodic
antiSemitism
aperiodicity
apostolicism
apostolicity
apparitional
appetisingly
appositional
appraisingly
appropriable
appropriator
artificially
astoundingly
attitudinise
attractively
authenticate
authenticity
automaticity
automobilist
availability
beggarliness
belletristic
beneficially
beseechingly
bewitchingly
bilharziasis
bilharziosis
biochemistry
biometrician
biophysicist
blisteringly
bloodthirsty
bloodyminded
blunderingly
blusteringly
borosilicate
brokenwinded
campodeiform
Cantabrigian
cantharidian
capercaillie
capercailzie
capitalistic
cattlelifter
centuplicate
ceremonially
chalcolithic
chauvinistic
chieftainess
chrematistic
chromaticism
chromaticity
circumcision
classifiable
clatteringly
coachbuilder
collectively
collectivise
collectivism
collectivist
collectivity
colloquially
comfortingly
commandingly
commercially
commissioner
compatriotic
complexional
complexioned
compulsively
compulsivity
conceptional
conclusively
conductivity
conduplicate
confectioner
confessional
conglutinate
connectional
connectively
consentience
consentingly
conterminous
contradictor
contrariness
contrariwise
convectional
conventicler
conventional
convincingly
convulsively
copulatively
coquettishly
corelatively
correctional
correctitude
correctively
cowardliness
cumulatively
cumulocirrus
cumulonimbus
curlingirons
decaffeinate
decoratively
decreasingly
definitively
depoliticise
depressingly
derivational
derivatively
desirability
despairingly
dialectician
digressional
digressively
dilatability
dilatoriness
diminutively
discerningly
disciplinary
discomfiture
discretional
discriminant
discriminate
discursively
disgustingly
disobedience
disquisition
dissentingly
dissuasively
distortional
disturbingly
divisibility
droughtiness
dubitatively
duraluminium
eccentricity
emulsifiable
enchantingly
enterprising
entertaining
entreatingly
equestrienne
equitability
euhemeristic
eunuchoidism
evangelistic
evidentially
excitability
exhaustively
exhibitioner
expressional
expressively
expressivity
exsanguinate
exsanguinous
exsufflicate
extinguisher
fantasticate
fantasticism
fatherfigure
fatherliness
featheriness
feebleminded
figuratively
filtrability
flabelliform
flammability
flatteringly
flickeringly
foraminifera
forbiddingly
forebodingly
foundationer
frangibility
friendliness
geochemistry
geometrician
geophysicist
geriatrician
glitteringly
grammaticise
grampositive
gratifyingly
grovellingly
habitability
haemophiliac
haemopoiesis
hairsplitter
harlequinade
headshrinker
heathenishly
heavenliness
hebetudinous
henotheistic
heritability
hesitatingly
horsewhipped
hydatidiform
hydrophilous
hydroquinone
hygrophilous
hyperacidity
hypocoristic
identifiable
illegibility
illegitimacy
illegitimate
illusoriness
immaterially
immemorially
immovability
immutability
imperatively
impetiginous
impoverished
impressively
impropriator
imputability
imputatively
inappositely
inartificial
inaudibility
incapability
incapacitate
incompliance
incoordinate
increasingly
incurability
indecisively
indefinitely
indelibility
indicatively
indoctrinate
industrially
inefficiency
inelasticity
inexactitude
inexpedience
inexpediency
inexperience
infelicitous
infinitively
inflectional
infusibility
insolubilise
insolubility
interspinous
interstitial
intransigent
intransitive
intriguingly
invisibility
involutional
irascibility
irrelatively
irremediable
irremediably
irritability
irritatingly
Ishmaelitish
jerrybuilder
journalistic
klipspringer
knightliness
lacininiated
latitudinous
liberalistic
literariness
lithotritist
loungelizard
maidenliness
malleability
malnutrition
mannerliness
Marcionitism
mastersinger
meditatively
mercantilism
mercantilist
microclimate
microseismic
militaristic
moneyspinner
monitorially
monomaniacal
monopodially
monopolistic
monotheistic
motherfigure
motherliness
motivational
mucilaginous
multipliable
multiplicand

multiplicate
multiplicity
mystifyingly
narcissistic
narrowminded
naturalistic
nauseatingly
navigability
navigational
necrophiliac
necrophilism
necrophilous
negativistic
negrophilism
negrophilist
neoDarwinian
neoDarwinism
neoDarwinist
neuroscience
newfashioned
niminypiminy
nominalistic
noncommittal
noneuclidean
obstetrician
occupational
oldfashioned
opposability
oppositional
oppressively
ordinariness
organgrinder
outlandishly
outpensioner
overachiever
overactivity
overestimate
Palaeolithic
palatability
paradisiacal
paramilitary
parasiticide
pejoratively
pennywhistle
perceptively
perceptivity
percussively
perfectively
perfervidity
permeability
permissively
permittivity
perplexingly
persuasively
philistinism
photophilous
plausibility
plebiscitary
plumbaginous
pneumaticity
polytheistic
porcelainise
porcelainous
positivistic
possessively
postmeridian
postposition
postpositive
practitioner
pragmatistic
pralltriller
precessional
preclusively
precognition
precognitive
precondition
predestinate
predictively
prefabricate
prehensility
prerequisite
presentiment
pretermitted
prevailingly
preventively
priestliness
priestridden
primordially
princeliness
printability
proboscidean
proboscidian
processional
productively
productivity
professional
projectional
projectively
proportional
proportioned
protactinium
protectively
protensively
protrusively
proverbially
provincially
prudentially
pumpernickel
pyromaniacal
quantifiable
reassuringly
reconstitute
recreational
redemptioner
redistribute
reducibility
reflectional
reflectively
reflectivity
refractivity
refreshingly
regressively
rehabilitate
relativistic
removability
renegotiable
repetitional
repetitively
repressively
resoundingly
respectively
responsively
retractility
reunionistic
revelational
revivalistic
ruminatively
saccharinity
salutariness
salutational
saponifiable
satisfyingly
scatteringly
scenepainter
sceneshifter
scratchiness
secularistic
selfactivity
selfignition
selflimiting
selfluminous
selfreliance
semicylinder
semifinished
semiofficial
sensualistic
sententially
separability
septennially
Septuagintal
sequentially
serpentiform
serpentinely
shirtwaister
simpleminded
singleminded
slipperiness
slovenliness
solitariness
sophisticate
specialistic
squarerigged
staggeringly
stalactiform
stammeringly
statistician
stealthiness
stockraising
stoneboiling
strongminded
strychninism
stutteringly
subcommittee
subcontinent
subjectively
subjectivise
subjectivism
subjectivist
subjectivity
submissively
subservience
subserviency
subversively
successional
successively
suggestively
supereminent
superstition
surprisingly
surrealistic
surrejoinder
susceptivity
suspensively
swaggeringly
syncretistic
tangentially
teachability
televisional
temptability
terrifyingly
thanksgiving
theoretician
thickskinned
thunderingly
tolerability
toploftiness
torrentially
towardliness
traceability
tractability
trampolinist
transiliency
transitional
transitively
transitivity
transshipped
tripartitely
tripartition
twitteringly
unappetising
unassumingly
unbecomingly
unblinkingly
unblushingly
unclassified
underwritten
unfamiliarly
ungainliness
unkindliness
unlikelihood
unlikeliness
unloveliness
unofficially
unprincipled
unsteadiness
unthinkingly
untimeliness
unwieldiness
unworldiness
unworthiness
unyieldingly
valetudinary
vegetatively
venerability
vicechairman
vindictively
visitational
vomiturition
whimperingly
whisperingly
winklepicker
wunderkinder
lanternjawed
homesickness
paletteknife
semidarkness
unmistakable
unmistakably
acetabularia
anticyclonic
archipelagic
banderillero
bassorelievo
bassorilievo
bathypelagic
blamefulness
blissfulness
boastfulness
bodybuilding
breathalyser
butterflynut
campfollower
cardinalship
cheerfulness
chitterlings
Christolatry
circumfluent
confabulator
contemplator
controllable
contumelious
cosmopolitan
cosmopolitic
counterlight
criticalness
cuckooflower
curvifoliate
Czechoslovak
decasyllabic
decasyllable
denticulated
disaffiliate
disannulling
disannulment
dishevelment
dissimilarly
dissimulator
doubtfulness
dreadfulness
electrolysis
electrolytic
encephalitic
encephalitis
endoskeletal
equipollence
equipollency
espagnolette
faithfulness
fancifulness
fibrinolysin
floriculture
folliculated
forcefulness
forestalment
freightliner
fruitfulness
furunculosis
gamophyllous
geanticlinal
geosynclinal
gesticulator
gracefulness
gratefulness
gravelelling
guilefulness
habitualness
haematolysis
heroicalness
herpetologic
homothallism
horticulture
hydrochloric
hyperbolical
hypothalamic
hypothalamus
ichthyolatry
incalculable
incalculably
inconsolable
inconsolably
indissoluble
indissolubly
interpellate
interpolator
interrelated
irrepealable
lakedwelling
machicolated
Marseillaise
materialness
mercifulness
metropolitan
mezzorelievo
mirthfulness
misknowledge
mitrailleuse
monkeyflower
monophyletic
monosyllabic
monosyllable
morphallaxis
mournfulness
multifoliate
multivalence
nephanalysis
noncomplying
octosyllabic
octosyllable
osteomalacia
outrivalling
parallelling
parisyllabic
particularly
pasqueflower
peacefulness
peccadilloes
pedicellaria
pedunculated
perambulator
philadelphus
philhellenic
pickerelweed
pilotballoon
pisciculture
pointilliste

polyphyletic
polysyllabic
polysyllable
premaxillary
pridefulness
quadriplegia
quadriplegic
reconcilable
retropulsion
ribonuclease
rightfulness
scintillator
scornfulness
selfanalysis
selfapplause
selfemployed
selfviolence
sesquialtera
shamefulness
shipbuilding
silverglance
silviculture
slaveholding
sleepwalking
slothfulness
smallholding
somatopleure
spitefulness
sportfulness
squirrelcage
squirreltail
stepchildren
strongylosis
submaxillary
superciliary
supercilious
surveillance
sylviculture
tastefulness
thankfulness
Torricellian
tranquillise
tranquillity
triangularly
trophallaxis
trustfulness
truthfulness
tuberculated
tuberculosis
turriculated
unassailable
uncalculated
unchivalrous
unlawfulness
unparalleled
vengefulness
vermiculated
vernacularly
verticalness
verticillate
wastefulness
watchfulness
wrathfulness
wrongfulness
youthfulness
alphanumeric
anagrammatic
anastigmatic
apochromatic
apothegmatic
arrhythmical
astronomical
balletomania
beachcombing
blabbermouth
cabinetmaker
centesimally
chrestomathy
cirrocumulus

clavicembalo
countermarch
declinometer
densitometer
diagrammatic
diathermancy
divertimenti
divertimento
electrometer
enantiomorph
epigrammatic
erythromycin
extensometer
extralimital
freeswimming
galvanometer
goosepimples
hellgrammite
heroicomical
holidaymaker
hysteromania
inclinometer
inconsumable
inconsumably
IndoGermanic
interfemoral
irredeemable
irredeemably
irreformable
isochromatic
isothermally
lukewarmness
magnetometer
melodramatic
meristematic
millesimally
milliammeter
monodramatic
nephelometer
nephelometry
nonflammable
nychthemeral
nychthemeron
ornithomancy
panchromatic
paradigmatic
paranormally
patternmaker
perispomenon
peristomatic
philharmonic
programmable
programmatic
prolegomenon
psychrometer
psychrometry
refreshments
rejectamenta
risorgimento
semidiameter
sensitometer
spectrometer
spectrometry
streptomycin
superhumanly
tragicomical
transhumance
trichromatic
trigonometry
troublemaker
undetermined
undiplomatic
uneconomical
unfathomable
viscosimeter
aboriginally
accompanyist
additionally
agamogenesis

agamogenetic
agentgeneral
agglutinogen
anteprandial
antimagnetic
antiphonally
apprehension
apprehensive
appurtenance
assassinator
avitaminoses
avitaminosis
bellylanding
bicentennial
bioscientist
birefringent
brilliantine
brinkmanship
carillonneur
Carlovingian
carpetknight
catamountain
chairmanship
championship
chaplainship
cliffhanging
coloquintida
conferential
confidential
conscionable
constringent
conveyancing
corespondent
cosmogonical
crashlanding
crossbencher
dentilingual
determinable
determinably
determinedly
Deuteronomic
differentiae
differential
dilettantish
dilettantism
diphthongise
disadvantage
disincentive
disingenuous
disorientate
disseminator
distrainable
distrainment
dorsiventral
echosounding
electronvolt
emblazonment
empoisonment
equationally
ethnocentric
expediential
experiential
exterminable
exterminator
extramundane
extrasensory
faultfinding
ferrugineous
fountainhead
fractionally
fractionator
freestanding
freethinking
frictionless
frontbencher
functionally
functionless
gamesmanship
ganglionated

glycogenesis
guardianship
gyromagnetic
hallucinogen
hallucinosis
hardstanding
heartrending
heliocentric
highsounding
hippocentaur
histogenesis
histogenetic
horsemanship
hydrodynamic
hydrokinetic
hypertension
hypertensive
hypnogenesis
hypnogenetic
hypochondria
ideationally
impermanence
impermanency
impersonally
impersonator
impertinence
impertinency
imprisonment
inconcinnity
inconsonance
incontinence
incontinency
inconvenient
indeclinable
indistinctly
inexpugnable
inexpugnably
inharmonious
interconnect
interminable
interminably
intermundane
internuncial
intervenient
intervention
intramundane
irrationally
irresponsive
isochronally
jurisconsult
karyokinesis
kinnikinnick
longstanding
lovelornness
maintainable
majorgeneral
marksmanship
meridionally
messeigneurs
misadventure
misalignment
mistakenness
mitochondria
mountainside
multicentral
multidentate
multilingual
musicianship
nanoplankton
nitrobenzene
nonalignment
nonessential
noradrenalin
northernmost
obscurantism
obscurantist
occasionally
oncorhynchus
oneupmanship

orthodontics
orthodontist
orthogenesis
orthogenetic
osteogenesis
overabundant
paedogenesis
paedogenetic
palingenesia
palingenesis
palingenetic
pantechnicon
paramagnetic
parsimonious
partisanship
pathogenesis
pathogenetic
pennypincher
peradventure
percutaneous
peregrinator
periodontics
periodontist
pestilential
phenomenally
philodendron
photokinesis
photokinetic
photomontage
phylogenesis
phylogenetic
physiognomic
phytogenesis
phytogenetic
planoconcave
plectognathi
postprandial
precedential
predominance
predominancy
preferential
presidential
primogenital
primogenitor
prizewinning
pronominally
propagandise
propagandism
propagandist
providential
pyroligneous
quadriennium
questionable
questionably
questionless
quinquennial
quinquennium
ratiocinator
reassignment
relationally
relationship
reprehension
reprehensive
restrainable
restrainedly
rhizogenetic
rhododendron
salesmanship
scorpionfish
selfhypnosis
selfidentity
servocontrol
simultaneity
simultaneous
sodafountain
southernmost
southernwood
sporogenesis
stagemanager

starspangled
stillhunting
strophanthin
stubbornness
subcutaneous
succedaneous
superannuate
supermundane
supersensory
supervenient
supervention
supramundane
sycophantish
synchronical
synchroniser
testamentary
testudineous
tetragonally
transcendent
transmontane
transpontine
typefounding
ultramontane
ultramundane
unbrokenness
uncommonness
unconvincing
undermanning
underpinning
underrunning
undertenancy
ungovernable
unimaginable
unimaginably
unpretending
unreasonable
unreasonably
unrecognised
unresponsive
unseasonable
vicargeneral
volitionally
wallpainting
watermanship
abolitionary
abolitionism
abolitionist
abstemiously
accordionist
accretionary
accusatorial
adulterously
aeroembolism
affectionate
aforethought
afterthought
agranulocyte
amphibiously
amphitropous
amygdaloidal
anthropogeny
anthropoidal
anthropology
antistrophic
asynchronism
asynchronous
auspiciously
autonomously
avariciously
bacteriology
bacteriostat
balladmonger
bibliologist
bibliopolist
biocoenology
bioecologist
blithesomely
bloodbrother
boisterously
bonnetmonkey
boogiewoogie
brainstormer
breechloader
calamitously
calcareously
calumniously
candleholder
capriciously
cardiologist
catastrophic
censoriously
cheesemonger
chivalrously
chondriosome
chromatogram
chromatology
chromatopsia
chronologise
chronologist
circuitously
clangorously
closecropped
coalitionist
coetaneously
commodiously
companionate
companionway
compulsorily
conchologist
consistorial
contagionist
contagiously
contemporary
contemporise
contiguously
continuously
costermonger
cotyledonary
cotyledonous
courageously
craftbrother
craniologist
cryptologist
cumbersomely
cuprammonium
decontrolled
deflationary
deflationist
deontologist
derogatorily
deviationism
deviationist
dialectology
diaphanously
disastrously
discommodity
discomposure
disconsolate
disharmonise
diversionary
diversionist
doublelocked
dovecoloured
eavesdropped
eavesdropper
ecclesiology
echinococcus
educationist
Egyptologist
elocutionary
elocutionist
embryologist
entomologise
entomologist
enzymologist
epicycloidal
epidemiology
epiphenomena
epistemology
escapologist
euphoniously
evolutionary
evolutionism
evolutionist
exclusionary
exclusionism
exclusionist
excursionist
expansionary
expansionism
expansionist
extortionary
extortionate
extraneously
factitiously
fallaciously
fastidiously
felicitously
fictitiously
flagitiously
flavoprotein
fortuitously
fostermother
frenchpolish
fructivorous
fuliginosity
futurologist
gastronomist
gastropodous
geotectonics
glaciologist
gladiatorial
glassblowing
globetrotter
glossologist
gluttonously
glycoprotein
goodhumoured
grallatorial
granodiorite
graphologist
gratuitously
graveclothes
greengrocery
gregariously
hardfavoured
harmoniously
heliotropism
heortologist
heterologous
heteronomous
highcoloured
homonymously
horrendously
hydrotropism
hypertrophic
hypochlorite
idolatrously
immunologist
imperatorial
imperviously
incautiously
incestuously
indecorously
indigenously
IndoEuropean
infectiously
inflationary
inflationism
inflationist
ingloriously
iniquitously
inspectorate
inspectorial
intercropped
intrusionist
intuitionism
intuitionist
isolationism
isolationist
kremlinology
lachrymosely
languorously
lasciviously
lexicologist
libidinously
licentiously
liturgiology
loquaciously
lugubriously
malacologist
marvellously
melancholiac
mendaciously
merrythought
metachronism
meticulously
microbiology
microscopist
mineralogist
miraculously
mispronounce
monochromate
monostrophic
monotonously
mordaciously
morphologist
mosstrooping
mothertongue
multiflorous
multistoried
musicologist
muzzleloader
mysteriously
Neoplatonism
Neoplatonist
nephrologist
neurobiology
nightclothes
nonconformer
numerologist
nutritionist
nutritiously
nyctitropism
oblanceolate
obligatorily
obsequiously
oceanologist
odontologist
officeholder
omnivorously
orthotropism
orthotropous
outrageously
overexposure
palaeobotany
palynologist
papyrologist
paraboloidal
parasitology
parkinsonism
partitionist
peremptorily
perfidiously
perjuriously
perniciously
pharmacology
phlebotomise
phlebotomist
photogeology
phototropism
phrasemonger
phrenologist
physiologist
plainclothed
plainclothes
pleiotropism
pneumatology
policyholder
polychromous
portentously
posteriority
posthumously
praiseworthy
precariously
preceptorial
precisionist
precociously
prefectorial
prehistorian
privatdocent
privatdozent
probationary
prodigiously
professorate
professoress
professorial
propitiously
prosectorial
prosperously
protectorate
prothonotary
protistology
protozoology
provisionary
psephologist
pseudopodium
psychologise
psychologism
psychologist
pugnaciously
quadrinomial
rabblerouser
radiobiology
radioisotope
radiophonics
rebelliously
receptionist
recessionary
Redemptorist
reductionism
reductionist
reflationary
refractorily
reinvigorate
responsorial
reticulocyte
reversionary
rheumatology
ridiculously
robustiously
rontgenogram
rontgenology
rosecoloured
sabretoothed
saccharoidal
salpiglossis
salubriously
salvationism
salvationist
sanguinolent
sansculottic
scandalously
schizogonous
scrupulosity
scrupulously
scurrilously
secessionism
secessionist
seclusionist
seismologist
selenologist
selfabsorbed
selfbegotten
selfcoloured

selfdevotion
selfinvolved
semideponent
sequaciously
shadowboxing
sharecropper
sharpshooter
silicicolous
sinistrorsal
slanderously
smallclothes
solicitously
specktioneer
speleologist
spermatocyte
spermatozoid
spermatozoon
spermogonium
spidermonkey
Stakhanovism
Stakhanovite
stertorously
stockbroking
stormtrooper
stringcourse
stupendously
subeditorial
supererogate
suspiciously
synonymously
taperecorder
technicolour
technologist
teetertotter
teratologist
tetrachordal
thermocouple
thunderously
timehonoured
toxicologist
traditionary
traditionist
trainspotter
traitorously
transitorily
tremendously
trichologist
trichotomise
trichotomous
triphthongal
tumultuously
twentyfourmo
ubiquitously
umbrageously
uncontrolled
underclothes
ungraciously
unifoliolate
uproariously
urbanologist
varicoloured
ventripotent
vibraphonist
victoriously
villainously
virtuosoship
visitatorial
viviparously
vociferously
voluminosity
voluminously
voluptuosity
voluptuously
wellfavoured
whencesoever
winterbourne
wollastonite
wonderworker
YankeeDoodle
allomorphism
antigropelos
apostrophise
apperception
apperceptive
archetypally
archetypical
automorphism
backslapping
blastosphere
bombdisposal
burglarproof
centrespread
centrosphere
charterparty
chimneypiece
Christophany
chromosphere
clothespress
conidiophore
conscription
counterplead
counterpoint
counterpoise
counterproof
dermatophyte
diastrophism
drawingpaper
electroplate
encyclopedia
encyclopedic
frontispiece
Germanophile
Germanophobe
goodtempered
gymnosophist
handicapping
hedgehopping
hemimorphism
hemimorphite
highstepping
homomorphism
homomorphous
hyposulphite
ichthyophagy
imperceptive
impercipient
incorruption
indiscipline
interception
interruption
interruptive
macrocephaly
mastigophora
meltingpoint
metallophone
metamorphism
metamorphose
mezzosoprano
microcapsule
microcephaly
microcopying
minicomputer
monadelphous
monographist
monomorphous
myrmecophily
namedropping
onomatopoeia
onomatopoeic
outstripping
overcropping
oversimplify
overstepping
paedobaptism
paragraphist
paramorphism
participator
phenotypical
philosophise
phreatophyte
pitcherplant
pleomorphism
polymorphism
polymorphous
preoccupancy
prescription
prescriptive
proscription
proscriptive
prosopopoeia
prototypical
pteridophyte
publicspirit
pyromorphite
rhynchophora
sarrusophone
selfcomposed
sellingplate
semitropical
shatterproof
sideslipping
sidestepping
siphonophore
stratosphere
subscription
telegraphese
telegraphist
thermosphere
transhipment
vantagepoint
weatherproof
welldisposed
zygomorphism
zygomorphous
inconsequent
magniloquent
marketsquare
multiloquous
somniloquism
somniloquist
statuesquely
aeroneurosis
AfroAmerican
alphamerical
angiocarpous
anticlerical
aristocratic
artilleryman
asymmetrical
avantgardism
avantgardist
bachelorhood
bachelorship
barometrical
battleground
belligerence
belligerency
bewilderedly
bewilderment
bibliography
biogeography
blackbirding
blackcurrant
blastfurnace
booklearning
boulevardier
breakthrough
bureaucratic
cardcarrying
cardiography
cataphoresis
cheirography
choreography
chronography
cirrostratus
collaborator
collaterally
commemorator
commiserator
concentrator
connaturally
considerable
considerably
corroborator
courtmartial
creepycrawly
crosscurrent
crosspurpose
cryptography
debonairness
decipherable
decipherment
demonstrable
demonstrably
demonstrator
diageotropic
dictatorship
diphtheritic
directorship
discoverable
discoverture
disembarrass
disinterment
disregardful
disseverance
disseverment
dramaturgist
elasmobranch
embitterment
encumberment
endangerment
endometritis
enginedriver
equilibrator
EuroAmerican
executorship
exospherical
extramarital
extraversion
extroversion
flamethrower
frontiersman
glossography
glyphography
glyptography
gonadotropic
gonadotropin
governorship
habitforming
halterbroken
headquarters
heartburning
heartstrings
heartwarming
hemichordate
henceforward
highspirited
hindquarters
homeomorphic
housewarming
hyperpyretic
hyperpyrexia
idiothermous
illnaturedly
immeasurable
immeasurably
immensurable
impenetrable
impenetrably
imponderable
imponderably
incomparable
incomparably
inconformity
incorporated
incorporator
incorporeity
indifference
indifferency
insalubrious
insufferable
insufferably
intemperance
intercurrent
interference
interservice
intracardiac
introversion
introversive
introvertive
invulnerable
invulnerably
irrespirable
knighterrant
lexicography
longshoreman
lycanthropic
manoeuvrable
manometrical
marshharrier
mesothoracic
metallurgist
metalworking
metaphorical
metathoracic
microcircuit
microsurgery
misanthropic
misinterpret
monkeywrench
multifarious
multiformity
multipartite
multipurpose
multiversity
neurosurgeon
neurosurgery
nimbostratus
oceanography
offscourings
oneirocritic
orchestrator
organography
osteoporosis
otherworldly
overexertion
paedomorphic
palaeography
parametrical
passepartout
periostracum
peripherally
peristeronic
perseverance
phosphoresce
photochromic
physiography
pigeonbreast
polarography
polyneuritic
polyneuritis
poorspirited
predetermine
protuberance
psychography
psychotropic
puerperrally
pursestrings
quaestorship
reappearance
receivership
reconversion
refrigerator
rememberable
remonstrance

remonstrator
retroversion
reverberator
rhinocerotic
rhizocarpous
sarsaparilla
scintigraphy
screenwriter
scripturally
scriptwriter
sculpturally
sedgewarbler
seismography
selenography
selfapproval
selfbetrayal
selfreproach
selfstarting
sempiternity
sepulchrally
sequestrator
servitorship
Shakspereana
Shaksperiana
shortcircuit
shoulderbelt
shoulderknot
shouldernote
Sinanthropus
slipcarriage
spinsterhood
staffsurgeon
stereography
stratigraphy
structurally
subalternate
subalternity
subsaturated
superstratum
surveyorship
survivorship
synarthrosis
taberdarship
technocratic
tergiversate
tetramorphic
theanthropic
thermography
thermotropic
thirdborough
togetherness
topsyturvily
transferable
transference
transferring
transformism
transformist
transparency
transpirable
transversely
unanswerable
unauthorised
uncelebrated
uncommercial
unconformity
unconstraint
undemocratic
undercurrent
undergarment
undersurface
unfavourable
unfavourably
unhistorical
unilaterally
vainglorious
volumetrical
voluntaryism
voluntaryist
wherethrough
whippoorwill
woodengraver
youngberries
zoogeography
baselessness
basidiospore
billingsgate
birdsnesting
blatherskite
bletherskate
blockbusting
bootlessness
brainwashing
bronchoscope
businesslike
Byelorussian
canorousness
captiousness
caravansarai
caravanserai
carelessness
cautiousness
complaisance
compressible
concupiscent
conidiospore
convalescent
counterscarp
countershaft
covetousness
cuckingstool
cumbrousness
curvicostate
curvirostral
decomposable
decongestant
decongestion
decongestive
decorousness
deliquescent
desirousness
dessertspoon
dextrousness
displeasedly
dissatisfied
dolorousness
duckingstool
effervescent
efflorescent
electroscope
electroshock
enormousness
exiguousness
fabulousness
facelessness
factiousness
fearlessness
fecklessness
fertilisable
formlessness
galligaskins
galvanoscope
generousness
glockenspiel
gloriousness
gorgeousness
graciousness
grievousness
haberdashery
hairdressing
harmlessness
heedlessness
helplessness
highpressure
hopelessness
humorousness
hybridisable
hydrolysable
hypnotisable
illadvisedly
improvisator
inaccessible
inaccessibly
inadmissible
inadmissibly
inappeasable
incandescent
incognisable
incognisance
inconsistent
indefeasible
indefeasibly
indefensible
indefensibly
inexpressive
inextensible
intercession
intercessory
intermission
intromission
intussuscept
irremissible
irreversible
irreversibly
kaleidoscope
landingstage
landingstrip
lanternslide
laryngoscope
laryngoscopy
licketysplit
lifelessness
listlessness
lovelessness
luminousness
lusciousness
mademoiselle
magnetisable
marlinespike
metaphysical
mindlessness
mistranslate
mistressship
Monophysitic
movelessness
mutinousness
nailscissors
namelessness
nauseousness
nebulousness
needlessness
neoclassical
nonresistant
northeastern
northwestern
numerousness
omnipresence
ornithoscopy
oscilloscope
overpersuade
overpressure
painlessness
patulousness
peerlessness
perilousness
perviousness
photofission
pitilessness
planetesimal
populousness
prechristian
preciousness
preclassical
predigestion
previousness
protohistory
pteridosperm
pulverisable
quarterstaff
quintessence
ravenousness
reassessment
recklessness
recognisable
recognisably
recognisance
recrudescent
repercussion
repercussive
repossession
restlessness
retrocession
retrocessive
rigorousness
rollingstock
rootlessness
ruthlessness
scabrousness
sedulousness
selfexistent
selflessness
sensuousness
sidewhiskers
siphonostele
sonorousness
soullessness
southeastern
southwestern
spaciousness
speciousness
spectroscope
spectroscopy
sphragistics
spotlessness
spuriousness
stereoisomer
stilboestrol
stonemasonry
studiousness
subcelestial
subdivisible
subthreshold
superposable
supersession
suppressible
swaggerstick
swizzlestick
tactlessness
tamelessness
tearlessness
throughstone
thunderstone
thunderstorm
timelessness
timorousness
tirelessness
tonelessness
tortuousness
transfusible
transmission
transmissive
transposable
transvestism
transvestite
trumpetshell
tunelessness
unappeasable
unctuousness
underinsured
unsuccessful
usuriousness
uxoriousness
vaporousness
venomousness
vigorousness
virtuousness
vitreousness
warehouseman
whitewashing
windingsheet
wineglassful
wondrousness
abstractable
abstractedly
abstractness
accidentally
acquaintance
administrant
administrate
adscititious
adventitious
aeronautical
agricultural
aircraftsman
alphabetical
ambidextrous
antineutrino
antiparticle
antithetical
apparentness
aquicultural
arithmetical
attributable
bellbottomed
benefactress
bloodletting
bodysnatcher
breaststroke
calculatedly
carburetting
catechetical
cementitious
chocolatebox
circumstance
clarinettist
coenobitical
coenobytical
combinations
compunctious
concomitance
concubitancy
congenitally
conjunctival
conningtower
conquistador
contemptible
contemptibly
contemptuous
contractable
contractedly
contractible
countertenor
crossbuttock
cultivatable
curlingtongs
destructible
discerptible
discountable
discourteous
discreetness
disjointedly
dispiritedly
disputatious
disreputable
disreputably
distinctness
distractedly
earsplitting
econometrics
electrotonic
electrotonus
electrotyper
emblematical
epexegetical
equidistance
explicitness

extraditable
farsightedly
feldspathoid
fiddlesticks
filibusterer
footplateman
frequentness
geopolitical
happenstance
hardfeatured
headmistress
heliolatrous
highlystrung
hippopotamus
homeopathist
homoeostasis
horizontally
horrorstruck
hymenopteran
hypocritical
hypogastrium
hypognathous
hypostatical
hypothetical
illtreatment
implicitness
inadvertence
inadvertency
incidentally
incognitable
incommutable
incommutably
incompatible
incompatibly
incompetence
incompetency
incomputable
indefectible
indigestible
indirectness
indisputable
indisputably
indivertible
indivertibly
inexpertness
inhospitable
inhospitably
innutritious
instructress
intercutting
interestedly
intermittent
intermitting
intromittent
intromitting
irresistible
irresistibly
judgematical
kilowatthour
labyrinthian
labyrinthine
lepidopteran
leucocytosis
leukocytosis
linguistical
liverystable
longdistance
maidenstakes
malapertness
maltreatment
manufacturer
masterstroke
mathematical
merchantable
metathetical
mistreatment
monumentally
mulligatawny
multilateral
negotiatress
nonexistence
nonidentical
obedientiary
occidentally
opisthotonos
ornamentally
ostentatious
outstretched
overcautious
overcritical
pancreatitis
paratactical
penitentiary
phagocytosis
phagocytotic
photosetting
placesetting
planetstruck
pleasantness
plenipotence
pluriliteral
poikilotherm
polyglottism
polyhistoric
polyurethane
portmanteaus
portmanteaux
postdoctoral
postmistress
precipitable
precipitance
precipitancy
precipitator
preexistence
premeditated
premeditator
premenstrual
presumptuous
pricecutting
progenitress
proglottides
proprietress
prosecutable
proselytiser
psychiatrist
rambunctious
readjustment
recalcitrant
recalcitrate
recommitment
regimentally
reinvestment
residentiary
residentship
restrictedly
resuscitator
ricochetting
sacerdotally
sarcomatosis
schismatical
secondstring
selfcontempt
selfcritical
selfdestruct
selfdistrust
selfflattery
selfportrait
septilateral
sergeantfish
sergeantship
sericultural
serjeantship
shortpitched
snaggletooth
snapfastener
sociometrist
stalwartness
stereopticon
stonecutting
straightaway
straightbred
straightedge
straightener
straightness
subapostolic
substantiate
substantival
succinctness
supernatural
supposititious
surefootedly
surmountable
systematical
systematiser
taskmistress
terebinthine
terrorstruck
theocratical
thermostable
thermostatic
translatable
transmitting
transmutable
trestletable
trochanteric
unacceptable
unaccustomed
unaffectedly
uncharitable
uncharitably
uncomeatable
undercutting
underletting
undersetting
unexpectedly
unimportance
unprofitable
unprofitably
unrepeatable
unscientific
unscriptural
unstructured
usufructuary
viscerotonic
viscountship
wainscotting
Wellingtonia
wonderstruck
absquatulate
antediluvian
apiculturist
astronautics
autoimmunity
behaviourism
behaviourist
brassbounder
breastsummer
broncobuster
buttermuslin
canaliculate
caricaturist
caterwauling
cheeseburger
cheesecutter
circumfusion
closemouthed
coldshoulder
commensurate
conceptually
congratulant
congratulate
consensually
constabulary
constituency
constitution
constitutive
contextually
contrapuntal
contribution
contributive
contributory
crosscountry
curvicaudate
desulphurise
distributary
distribution
distributive
enginetuning
griseofulvin
grotesquerie
harquebusier
hermeneutics
highfaluting
homosexually
hubblebubble
huggermugger
humptydumpty
hydrofluoric
inarticulate
inconclusive
individually
inoperculate
irresolutely
irresolution
jurisprudent
mangelwurzel
mealymouthed
miscalculate
moneygrubber
monkeypuzzle
multungulate
neighbouring
noctambulant
noctambulism
noctambulist
noctambulous
nonconductor
perceptually
Plattdeutsch
postdiluvian
proconsulate
prostitution
recapitulate
rumbletumble
scrobiculate
selfdelusion
semiannually
shamateurism
somnambulant
somnambulate
somnambulism
somnambulist
straticulate
subinfeudate
substitution
substitutive
thaumaturgic
therapeutics
therapeutist
thickskulled
tightmouthed
unpronounced
unscrupulous
vauntcourier
wellgrounded
adjectivally
inobservance
irreprovable
irresolvable
misbehaviour
unbelievable
unbelievably
underdevelop
unreservedly
whitelivered
bladderwrack
cabbagewhite
councilwoman
countrywoman
disallowance
disendowment
Englishwoman
masterswitch
servicewoman
stationwagon
thitherwards
toggleswitch
whitherwards
haematoxylon
intermixture
intertexture
actinomycete
amphictyonic
astrophysics
attorneyship
chalcopyrite
clairvoyance
eleemosynary
gobbledygook
heterocyclic
heterozygote
heterozygous
hieroglyphic
hypophrygian
microcrystal
microphysics
oxyacetylene
polyethylene
praseodymium
pseudocyesis
pseudonymity
pseudonymous
reconveyance
redeployment
schizomycete
steatopygous
stichomythia
stichomythic
syndactylism
syndactylous
tridactylous
troglodytism
unemployable
unemployment
bobbydazzler
honeybuzzard

---

aboriginally
abstractable
academically
accidentally
accommodator
acetabularia
acoustically
acquaintance
acronychally
additionally
adjectivally
amitotically
amphitheatre
anagogically
anagrammatic
analogically
analytically
anastigmatic
anatomically
antiphonally
apochromatic
apolitically
apothegmatic
approachable
appropriable
appropriator
appurtenance
archetypally

archipelagic
aristocratic
aromatically
artificially
artistically
assassinator
athletically
attributable
balletomania
barbarically
bathypelagic
beatifically
beneficially
bibliography
bilharziasis
biogeography
biologically
breechloader
bulletheaded
bureaucratic
cabinetmaker
caravansarai
cardiography
carriageable
cashandcarry
catholically
centesimally
ceremonially
charterparty
cheirography
cherubically
choreography
chrestomathy
Christolatry
chronography
circumstance
cirrostratus
clairvoyance
classifiable
cleistogamic
collaborator
collaterally
colloquially
commemorator
commercially
commiserator
commonwealth
communicable
communicably
communicator
complaisance
compoundable
concentrator
conceptually
concomitance
concubitancy
confabulator
congenitally
connaturally
conquistador
conscionable
consensually
considerable
considerably
consolidator
contemplator
contextually
contractable
controllable
corroborator
cosmetically
countermarch
countrydance
creepycrawly
cryptography
crystalgazer
cultivatable
cynocephalus
decasyllabic
decasyllable
decipherable
decomposable
demimondaine
demoniacally
demonstrable
demonstrably
demonstrator
denticulated
despotically
determinable
determinably
diabolically
diagrammatic
diathermancy
diatonically
didactically
dietetically
diminishable
disagreeable
disagreeably
disallowance
discountable
discoverable
displaceable
disreputable
disreputably
disseminator
disseverance
dissimilarly
dissimulator
distrainable
dogmatically
domestically
domesticator
doubledealer
dramatically
drawingpaper
dunderheaded
dynastically
eclectically
ecologically
economically
ecstatically
elasmobranch
electrically
elliptically
emphatically
emulsifiable
enclitically
endermically
epidemically
epigrammatic
episodically
equationally
equidistance
equilibrator
equiprobable
esoterically
euphonically
evidentially
exchangeable
exegetically
exoterically
exterminable
exterminator
extraditable
extravagance
extravagancy
extravaganza
fertilisable
folliculated
forensically
fractionally
fractionator
frenetically
functionally
galvanically
ganglionated
geologically
gesticulator
gigantically
glossography
glyphography
glyptography
haemorrhagic
hairsbreadth
handsbreadth
happenstance
harmonically
hebdomadally
heraldically
hermetically
hippopotamus
historically
holidaymaker
homoeostasis
homosexually
horizontally
horrifically
horsebreaker
housebreaker
hybridisable
hydrodynamic
hydrolysable
hygienically
hypnotically
hypnotisable
hypothalamic
hypothalamus
hypothecator
hysterically
hysteromania
ichthyolatry
ideationally
identifiable
immaterially
immeasurable
immeasurably
immemorially
immensurable
impenetrable
impenetrably
imperishable
imperishably
impersonally
impersonator
imponderable
imponderably
impropriator
improvisator
inappeasable
inapplicable
inapplicably
incalculable
incalculably
incidentally
incognisable
incognisance
incognitable
incommutable
incommutably
incomparable
incomparably
incompliance
incomputable
inconsolable
inconsolably
inconsonance
inconsumable
inconsumably
incorporated
incorporator
indeclinable
indisputable
indisputably
individually
IndoGermanic
industrially
ineffaceable
ineffaceably
ineradicable
ineradicably
inexplicable
inexplicably
inexpugnable
inexpugnably
inextricable
inextricably
inhospitable
inhospitably
inobservance
insufferable
insufferably
intemperance
interminable
interminably
interoceanic
interpleader
interpolator
interrelated
interrogator
intervocalic
interwreathe
investigator
invulnerable
invulnerably
irrationally
irredeemable
irredeemably
irreformable
irrefragable
irrefragably
irremediable
irremediably
irrepealable
irreprovable
irresolvable
irrespirable
isochromatic
isochronally
isothermally
jesuitically
lacininiated
laisserfaire
laissezfaire
lanternjawed
lexicography
liturgically
liverystable
logistically
longdistance
machicolated
magnetically
magnetisable
magnifically
maidenstakes
maintainable
majestically
manoeuvrable
marriageable
Marseillaise
mechanically
melodramatic
merchantable
meridionally
meristematic
mesocephalic
mesothoracic
metallically
metathoracic
meteorically
methodically
millesimally
monastically
monitorially
monodramatic
monomaniacal
monopodially
monosyllabic
monosyllable
monumentally
morphallaxis
muddleheaded
mulligatawny
multipliable
muttonheaded
muzzleloader
narcotically
neurotically
nimbostratus
nonflammable
noradrenalin
occasionally
occidentally
oceanography
octosyllabic
octosyllable
operatically
orchestrator
organography
ornamentally
ornithomancy
osteomalacia
overemphasis
palaeography
panchromatic
paradigmatic
paradisiacal
paranormally
parisyllabic
participator
particularly
pathetically
patternmaker
pedantically
pedicellaria
pedunculated
perambulator
perceptually
peregrinator
periodically
periostracum
peripherally
peristomatic
perseverance
phanerogamic
phenomenally
phonemically
phonetically
physiography
platonically
plectognathi
polarography
polysyllabic
polysyllable
pontifically
pontificator
precipitable
precipitance
precipitancy
precipitator
predominance
predominancy
premeditated
premeditator
preoccupancy
prevaricator
primordially
programmable
programmatic
prolifically
pronominally
prosecutable
prosodically
protuberance

proverbially
provincially
prudentially
psychography
puerperrally
pulverisable
pyromaniacal
quantifiable
questionable
questionably
quixotically
rabbinically
ratiocinator
rattleheaded
reappearance
rechargeable
reciprocally
reciprocator
recognisable
recognisably
recognisance
reconcilable
reconveyance
refrigerator
regimentally
relationally
rememberable
remonstrance
remonstrator
renegotiable
reproachable
restrainable
resuscitator
reverberator
rhetorically
rhythmically
romantically
sacerdotally
sadistically
saponifiable
sardonically
scarificator
schoolleaver
scintigraphy
scintillator
scripturally
sculpturally
seismography
selenography
selfapplause
selfbetrayal
selfeducated
selfreliance
semantically
semiannually
sententially
septennially
sepulchrally
sequentially
sequestrator
seraphically
sheepshearer
shillyshally
significance
significancy
silverglance
simoniacally
singleseater
sinusoidally
Socratically
specifically
spheroidally
sporadically
stagemanager
stationwagon
stereography
straightaway
stratigraphy
structurally

subsaturated
subsonically
superhumanly
superposable
superstratum
surmountable
surveillance
syllabically
symbolically
syndetically
synoptically
systemically
tangentially
technocratic
tectonically
terrifically
tetragonally
Teutonically
theatrically
theistically
thematically
thermography
thermostable
thermostatic
thitherwards
torrentially
transferable
transhumance
translatable
transmutable
transoceanic
transpirable
transposable
trestletable
triangularly
trichromatic
triggerhappy
trophallaxis
troublemaker
tuberculated
turriculated
tyrannically
unacceptable
unanswerable
unappeasable
unassailable
unbelievable
unbelievably
uncalculated
uncelebrated
unchangeable
unchangeably
uncharitable
uncharitably
uncomeatable
unconstraint
uncritically
undemocratic
undertenancy
undiplomatic
unemployable
unfamiliarly
unfathomable
unfavourable
unfavourably
ungovernable
unilaterally
unimaginable
unimaginably
unimportance
unmanageable
unmistakable
unmistakably
unofficially
unprofitable
unprofitably
unreasonable
unreasonably
unrepeatable

unsearchable
unseasonable
unsegregated
vanquishable
vermiculated
vernacularly
volcanically
volitionally
whitherwards
woodengraver
woodenheaded
woollyheaded
zoogeography
beachcombing
bonnyclabber
brassrubbing
clavicembalo
collywobbles
hubblebubble
moneygrubber
mourningband
punchingball
redistribute
sedgewarbler
shoulderbelt
skunkcabbage
standardbred
stockjobbery
stockjobbing
straightbred
swimmingbath
swimmingbell
thermolabile
thoroughbass
thoroughbred
tintinnabula
actinomycete
aesthetician
aestheticism
agranulocyte
amphibrachic
anaphylactic
antigenicity
aperiodicity
apostolicism
apostolicity
authenticate
authenticity
autodidactic
automaticity
bespectacled
biometrician
biophysicist
bodysnatcher
borosilicate
brachydactyl
bronchoscope
centuplicate
chiropractic
chiropractor
chromaticism
chromaticity
circumjacent
concupiscent
conduplicate
contradictor
convalescent
conventicler
conveyancing
counterscarp
crossbencher
deliquescent
depoliticise
dialectician
dinnerjacket
disconnected
doubledecked
doubledecker
doublelocked

eccentricity
echinococcus
effervescent
efflorescent
electroscope
exsufflicate
extraspecial
fantasticate
fantasticism
frontbencher
galvanoscope
geometrician
geophysicist
geriatrician
grammaticise
grammolecule
greengrocery
heterocyclic
hucklebacked
inartificial
incandescent
indistinctly
inelasticity
interglacial
internuncial
intussuscept
kaleidoscope
laryngoscope
laryngoscopy
ledgertackle
lumberjacket
metagalactic
microcircuit
minedetector
monkeyjacket
multiplicand
multiplicate
multiplicity
nonconductor
obstetrician
oncorhynchus
ornithoscopy
oscilloscope
outstretched
parasiticide
pennypincher
perspicacity
phyllotactic
planoconcave
pneumaticity
prefabricate
privatdocent
prophylactic
pumpernickel
recrudescent
reticulocyte
saddlebacked
schizomycete
selfaffected
selfdirected
selfeffacing
semidetached
semiofficial
shortcircuit
shortpitched
singledecker
sophisticate
spectroscope
spectroscopy
spermatocyte
squirrelcage
statistician
straitjacket
taxcollector
theoretician
thermotactic
turtlenecked
uncommercial
unconvincing

winklepicker
anteprandial
avantgardism
avantgardist
bellylanding
blackbirding
bodybuilding
boulevardier
cantharidian
chancemedley
corespondent
crashlanding
crossbedding
crossheading
curvicaudate
discommodity
disregardful
dodecahedral
dodecahedron
echosounding
eunuchoidism
extramundane
farmsteading
faultfinding
fiddlefaddle
freestanding
fullyfledged
gastropodous
hardstanding
heartrending
hemichordate
highsounding
horsetrading
hyperacidity
hypochondria
interbedding
intermeddler
intermundane
intracardiac
intramundane
jurisprudent
longstanding
mitochondria
noneuclidean
orthopaedics
orthopaedist
overabundant
peasepudding
perfervidity
philodendron
postmeridian
postprandial
priestridden
proboscidean
proboscidian
procathedral
proofreading
propagandise
propagandism
propagandist
pseudopodium
rhododendron
rhombohedral
rhombohedron
salmonladder
scareheading
shipbuilding
sightreading
slaveholding
smallholding
stepchildren
subinfeudate
supermundane
supramundane
transcendent
typefounding
ultramundane
underbidding
unpretending

abstractedly
acaulescence
achlamydeous
acquiescence
advantageous
agamogenesis
agamogenetic
agentgeneral
alkalescence
alphanumeric
amphisbaenic
analphabetic
antigropelos
antimagnetic
antipathetic
arborescence
archdiocesan
argillaceous
belligerence
belligerency
bewilderedly
bibliothecae
biosynthesis
biosynthetic
brambleberry
bullheadedly
calculatedly
callisthenic
calorescence
calycoideous
caravanserai
carbonaceous
carcinogenic
carragheenin
cataphoresis
checkerberry
chocolatebox
cinematheque
committeeman
concrescence
confoundedly
consentience
constituency
contractedly
countertenor
decalescence
declinometer
delitescence
densitometer
determinedly
detumescence
diatomaceous
discourteous
disjointedly
disobedience
dispiritedly
displeasedly
distractedly
divertimenti
divertimento
electrometer
encyclopedia
encyclopedic
endoskeletal
equestrienne
equipollence
equipollency
espagnolette
extensometer
farsightedly
ferrugineous
filibusterer
fluorescence
footplateman
frankincense
fricasseeing
furfuraceous
gallinaceous
galvanometer
glaucescence
glycogenesis
goodtempered
graminaceous
grotesquerie
groundcherry
guaranteeing
gyromagnetic
haemopoiesis
halftimbered
highhandedly
histogenesis
histogenetic
hydrokinetic
hymenopteran
hyperpyretic
hyperpyrexia
hypersthenia
hypersthenic
hypnogenesis
hypnogenetic
illadvisedly
illnaturedly
impermanence
impermanency
impertinence
impertinency
improvidence
inadvertence
inadvertency
incalescence
inclinometer
incompetence
incompetency
incontinence
incontinency
incorporeity
indehiscence
independence
independency
indifference
indifferency
indiscreetly
inefficiency
inexpedience
inexpediency
inexperience
intelligence
interestedly
interference
intumescence
juvenescence
karyokinesis
kinaesthesia
kinaesthesis
kinaesthetic
landlubberly
lefthandedly
lepidopteran
lithospheric
longshoreman
longwindedly
luminescence
mademoiselle
magnetometer
magnificence
majorgeneral
messeigneurs
milliammeter
misknowledge
mitrailleuse
monkeywrench
monophyletic
mouthbreeder
multilateral
multivalence
nephelometer
nephelometry
neurasthenia
neurasthenic
neuroscience
noctilucence
nonexistence
nonresidence
nychthemeral
nychthemeron
obmutescence
obsolescence
omnipresence
openhandedly
openmindedly
orchidaceous
orthogenesis
orthogenetic
osteogenesis
overachiever
paedogenesis
paedogenetic
palingenesia
palingenesis
palingenetic
paraesthesia
paramagnetic
pathogenesis
pathogenetic
pearlescence
percutaneous
perispomenon
philhellenic
phonasthenia
phosphoresce
photokinesis
photokinetic
photospheric
phycomycetes
phylogenesis
phylogenetic
phytogenesis
phytogenetic
pigeonbreast
pinfeathered
planispheric
plenipotence
pluriliteral
polyphyletic
portmanteaus
portmanteaux
preexistence
prolegomenon
pronouncedly
pseudocyesis
psychrometer
psychrometry
pyroligneous
quadriplegia
quadriplegic
quattrocento
quintessence
recalescence
refreshments
rejectamenta
reminiscence
resipiscence
resplendence
resplendency
restrainedly
restrictedly
retrocedence
reviviscence
rhizogenetic
ribonuclease
risorgimento
schorlaceous
selfcontempt
selfevidence
selfmurderer
selfviolence
semidiameter
sensitometer
septilateral
serviceberry
Shakspereana
shamefacedly
shortsleeved
simultaneity
simultaneous
snapfastener
somatopleure
spectrometer
spectrometry
spermathecal
sporogenesis
sternwheeler
stockbreeder
straightedge
straightener
strengthener
subcutaneous
subservience
subserviency
succedaneous
supersedence
surefootedly
synaesthesia
synaesthetic
teensyweensy
telaesthesia
telaesthetic
testudineous
thimbleberry
threewheeler
transference
transiliency
translucence
translucency
transparency
trigonometry
trochanteric
tropospheric
unaffectedly
unapologetic
unconsidered
underdevelop
unencumbered
unexpectedly
unparalleled
unreservedly
vicargeneral
viridescence
viscosimeter
warehouseman
whencesoever
whigmaleerie
whitelivered
whortleberry
wicketkeeper
woolgatherer
campodeiform
cattlelifter
dissatisfied
flabelliform
foraminifera
hereinbefore
hydatidiform
scabbardfish
sceneshifter
scorpionfish
sergeantfish
serpentiform
shortstaffed
stalactiform
thereinafter
thoroughfare
thousandfold
toastingfork
unclassified
understaffed
undersurface
anthropogeny
bibliologist
bibliopegist
billingsgate
bioecologist
birefringent
Cantabrigian
cardiologist
Carlovingian
carpetbagger
chromatogram
chronologise
chronologist
cliffhanging
conchologist
constringent
counteragent
craniologist
cryptologist
dentilingual
deontologist
diphthongise
discouraging
dramaturgist
dressinggown
Egyptologist
embryologist
entomologise
entomologist
enzymologist
escapologist
fatherfigure
futurologist
glaciologist
glossologist
gobbledegook
gobbledygook
graphologist
heortologist
heterologous
heterozygote
heterozygous
huggermugger
hypophrygian
immunologist
intransigent
leapfrogging
lexicologist
malacologist
metallurgist
microsurgery
mineralogist
morphologist
motherfigure
multilingual
musicologist
necrophagous
nephrologist
neurosurgeon
neurosurgery
numerologist
oceanologist
odontologist
ophiophagous
palynologist
papyrologist
pettifoggery
pettifogging
phrenologist
physiologist
phytophagous
psephologist
psychologise
psychologism
psychologist
rhizophagous
rontgenogram
saprophagous

sarcophagous
seismologist
selenologist
skullduggery
speleologist
squarerigged
staffsurgeon
starspangled
steatopygous
supererogate
technologist
teratologist
toxicologist
trichologist
urbanologist
acetaldehyde
allomorphism
apostrophise
apparatchiki
apparatchiks
automorphism
bachelorhood
benzaldehyde
birdwatching
blastosphere
brainwashing
cabbagewhite
centrosphere
Christophany
chromosphere
clearsighted
conidiophore
countercheck
countershaft
dermatophyte
diastrophism
disfranchise
electroshock
feldspathoid
firstnighter
floodlighted
formaldehyde
forthrightly
fountainhead
Germanophile
Germanophobe
gesellschaft
gymnosophist
haberdashery
handkerchief
hemimorphism
hemimorphite
hirepurchase
homeopathist
homomorphism
homomorphous
hypognathous
hyposulphite
ichthyophagy
inescutcheon
kilowatthour
labyrinthian
labyrinthine
LowChurchman
macrocephaly
manslaughter
mastigophora
matriarchate
metallophone
metamorphism
metamorphose
metapsychics
microcephaly
misapprehend
mnemotechnic
monadelphous
monographist
monomorphous
monostichous
myrmecophily
paragraphist
paramorphism
patriarchate
philosophise
phreatophyte
pleomorphism
poikilotherm
polymorphism
polymorphous
polyurethane
prizefighter
pteridophyte
pyromorphite
rhynchophora
sarrusophone
sclerenchyma
sharpsighted
shortsighted
siphonophore
spinsterhood
steeplechase
stepdaughter
stranglehold
stratosphere
subthreshold
superhighway
telegraphese
telegraphist
terebinthine
thermosphere
trumpetshell
unlikelihood
whitewashing
windingsheet
zygomorphism
zygomorphous
adscititious
adventitious
aeronautical
aetiological
AfroAmerican
alphabetical
alphamerical
amygdaloidal
anthropoidal
anticlerical
antiparticle
antirachitic
antithetical
appendicitis
archetypical
arithmetical
arrhythmical
astrological
astronomical
asymmetrical
bactericidal
bantamweight
barometrical
bassorelievo
bassorilievo
bibliophilic
biographical
bloodstained
carpetknight
cartological
catechetical
cementitious
chesterfield
chimneypiece
chitterlings
chorological
clairaudient
closegrained
coenobitical
coenobytical
combinations
compressible
compunctious
conjunctival
contemptible
contemptibly
contractible
contumacious
contumelious
cosmogonical
cosmological
cosmopolitan
cosmopolitic
counterlight
crackbrained
crossgrained
curvifoliate
destructible
diamondfield
dibranchiate
diphtheritic
disaffiliate
disassociate
discerptible
disputatious
emblematical
encephalitic
encephalitis
endocarditis
endometritis
enginedriver
epexegetical
epicycloidal
ethnological
etymological
etymologicon
EuroAmerican
exospherical
extralimital
extramarital
fiddlesticks
freightliner
frontispiece
geanticlinal
genealogical
geographical
geopolitical
geosynclinal
hagiological
heartstrings
heroicomical
hesperididia
heteroecious
hierarchical
highspirited
histological
housetrained
hydrological
hyperbolical
hypocritical
hypostatical
hypothetical
immethodical
impercipient
inaccessible
inaccessibly
inadmissible
inadmissibly
inauspicious
incommodious
incompatible
incompatibly
inconvenient
incorrigible
incorrigibly
indefeasible
indefeasibly
indefectible
indefensible
indefensibly
indigestible
indivertible
indivertibly
inextensible
infanticidal
inharmonious
innutritious
insalubrious
insecticidal
insufficient
intelligible
intelligibly
interdigital
intermediacy
intermediary
intermediate
intervenient
irremissible
irresistible
irresistibly
irreversible
irreversibly
judgematical
landingfield
limnological
linguistical
liquefacient
lithological
longitudinal
manometrical
masterswitch
mathematical
meretricious
metaphorical
metaphysical
metathetical
metrological
metropolitan
mezzorelievo
middleweight
misbehaviour
Monophysitic
multifarious
multifoliate
mythological
mythologiser
necrological
neoclassical
neurological
nonefficient
nonidentical
obedientiary
offscourings
oligarchical
oneirocritic
orographical
ostentatious
osteological
overcautious
overcritical
pancreatitis
pantechnicon
paraboloidal
paradisaical
parametrical
paratactical
parsimonious
pathological
penitentiary
pericarditis
pertinacious
pestological
petrological
phenological
phenotypical
philological
phonological
phycological
phytological
planetesimal
playingfield
pointilliste
polyneuritic
polyneuritis
poorspirited
preclassical
preconscious
primogenital
primogenitor
proglottides
proselytiser
prototypical
publicspirit
pursestrings
quarterfinal
radiological
rambunctious
reproducible
residentiary
rhinological
saccharoidal
sacrilegious
sarsaparilla
scatological
schismatical
screenwriter
scriptwriter
selfcritical
selfdeceived
selfdeceiver
semiological
semiprecious
semitropical
Shaksperiana
shootingiron
slipcarriage
snarlingiron
sociological
sorbefacient
spiegeleisen
staffofficer
stereopticon
stupefacient
subconscious
subdivisible
substantiate
substantival
superciliary
supercilious
supervenient
supposititious
suppressible
supraorbital
surroundings
synchronical
synchroniser
systematical
systematiser
tautological
teleological
theocratical
theosophical
thermophilic
toggleswitch
tragicomical
transfusible
transpacific
triglyphical
tropological
tyrannicidal
unauthorised
underachieve
undetermined
uneconomical
unhistorical
unprejudiced
unrecognised
unrestrained
unscientific

vainglorious
volumetrical
wallydraigle
welterweight
backbreaking
billsticking
blatherskite
bletherskate
bluestocking
bodystocking
breathtaking
camiknickers
earthshaking
freethinking
galligaskins
metalworking
nanoplankton
nerveracking
safecracking
shoulderknot
sidewhiskers
sleepwalking
stockbroking
swashbuckler
absquatulate
adaptability
advisability
aeroembolism
alterability
anecdotalist
anemophilous
anthropology
Aristotelean
Aristotelian
autocatalyse
automobilist
availability
bacchanalian
backpedalled
bacteriology
banderillero
bibliopolist
bilateralism
bilingualism
biocoenology
bookingclerk
brickfielder
burningglass
businesslike
canaliculate
candleholder
capercaillie
capercailzie
caterwauling
chromatology
classicalism
classicalist
classicality
coachbuilder
coldshoulder
collegialism
collegiality
commensalism
commensalist
congeniality
congratulant
congratulate
connubiality
constabulary
conviviality
corporeality
counterblast
counterclaim
counterplead
cryptanalyst
decentralise
decontrolled
demineralise
denaturalise
desirability
dialectology
dilatability
disannulling
disconsolate
disestablish
dissocialise
divisibility
ecclesiology
editorialise
editorialist
effectuality
electroplate
elementalism
emotionalise
emotionalism
emotionalist
emotionality
entrammelled
ephemerality
epidemiology
episcopalian
epistemology
equitability
erythroblast
essentiality
excitability
exophthalmic
exophthalmos
exophthalmus
factionalism
faithhealing
fictionalise
filtrability
flammability
frangibility
freewheeling
frenchpolish
frictionless
functionless
gamopetalous
gamophyllous
gamosepalous
gravelelling
griseofulvin
habitability
haematoblast
haemophiliac
hemerocallis
heritability
homothallism
hoodmanblind
hydrophilous
hygrophilous
illegibility
illiberality
illogicality
immovability
immutability
impartiality
imputability
inarticulate
inaudibility
incapability
incurability
indelibility
indiscipline
infusibility
inoperculate
insolubilise
insolubility
internuclear
interpellate
interstellar
invisibility
irascibility
irregardless
irritability
jerrybuilder
jetpropelled
kremlinology
laissezaller
lakedwelling
lanternslide
leathercloth
liturgiology
Liverpudlian
malleability
mediaevalism
mediaevalist
melancholiac
mercantilism
mercantilist
mercurialise
mercurialism
microanalyst
microbiology
miscalculate
mistranslate
moistureless
monometallic
monopetalous
motorcyclist
multinuclear
multungulate
municipalise
municipality
navigability
necrophiliac
necrophilism
necrophilous
negrophilism
negrophilist
neurobiology
nevertheless
Newfoundland
noctambulant
noctambulism
noctambulist
noctambulous
oblanceolate
officeholder
opposability
otherworldly
outrivalling
oversimplify
oxyacetylene
palatability
parallelling
parasitology
parochialise
parochialism
parochiality
peccadilloes
permeability
pharmacology
photogeology
photophilous
pilotballoon
pitcherplant
plaindealing
plausibility
pleasureless
plummerblock
pneumatology
policyholder
polyethylene
polypetalous
polysepalous
polytonality
potentiality
practicality
pralltriller
precancelled
preestablish
prehensility
premaxillary
principality
printability
proconsulate
protistology
protozoology
quadrivalent
questionless
quizzicality
radiobiology
radionuclide
recapitulate
reducibility
removability
reproachless
retractility
revictualled
rheumatology
rontgenology
sanguinolent
schoolfellow
scoundreldom
scoundrelism
scrobiculate
sectionalism
selfinvolved
sellingplate
semifinalist
separability
silicicolous
sinistrality
softpedalled
somnambulant
somnambulate
somnambulism
somnambulist
soundingline
spiritualise
spiritualism
spiritualist
spirituality
stockingless
stoneboiling
straticulate
streetwalker
strengthless
submaxillary
subnormality
syndactylism
syndactylous
teachability
technicality
technicolour
temptability
thickskulled
thundercloud
tolerability
Torricellian
traceability
tractability
tranquillise
tranquillity
tridactylous
trinomialism
unambivalent
uncontrolled
unifoliolate
unisexuality
universalise
universalism
universalist
universality
unscrupulous
venerability
veridicality
verticillate
walkietalkie
weatherglass
whimsicality
workingclass
accouchement
accoutrement
admonishment
aerodynamics
announcement
appraisement
astonishment
ballottement
bedazzlement
belittlement
bequeathment
bewilderment
blandishment
blithesomely
breastsummer
chastisement
commencement
contrivement
convincement
crossexamine
cryptogamous
cumbersomely
cumulonimbus
decipherment
denouncement
dethronement
diminishment
disagreement
disannulment
disbursement
disendowment
disgorgement
disguisement
dishevelment
disinterment
dislodgement
displacement
disseverment
distrainment
embattlement
embezzlement
embitterment
emblazonment
embranchment
empoisonment
empressement
encirclement
encroachment
encumberment
endamagement
endangerment
enfeeblement
enshrinement
enswathement
entanglement
enthronement
entrancement
entrenchment
envisagement
epiphenomena
epithalamion
epithalamium
estrangement
forebodement
forestalment
freeswimming
gastronomist
guestchamber
habitforming
heartwarming
hellgrammite
hereditament
heterogamous
heteronomous
housewarming
humptydumpty
idiothermous
illegitimacy
illegitimate
illtreatment

imprisonment
inconformity
infringement
intrenchment
inveiglement
katzenjammer
languishment
maltreatment
microclimate
misalignment
misjudgement
misplacement
misstatement
mistreatment
monochromate
monofilament
multiformity
nicotinamide
niminypiminy
nonalignment
northernmost
overestimate
phlebotomise
phlebotomist
polychromous
postponement
praseodymium
predetermine
presentiment
prothalamion
prothalamium
pseudonymity
pseudonymous
quadrinomial
radioelement
rapprochment
readjustment
reassessment
reassignment
recommitment
redeployment
reinvestment
renouncement
resettlement
retrenchment
rumbletumble
semibasement
sledgehammer
southernmost
stablishment
sulphonamide
transformism
transformist
transhipment
trichotomise
trichotomous
unconformity
undergarment
unemployment
vanquishment
yellowhammer
abolitionary
abolitionism
abolitionist
abortiveness
abrasiveness
absentminded
absoluteness
abstractness
abstruseness
accordionist
accretionary
accurateness
accursedness
adaptiveness
adequateness
adhesiveness
adorableness
affectedness
affectionate
agribusiness
allusiveness
altitudinous
ambivalently
amenableness
amicableness
antecedently
anthelmintic
apparentness
appetisingly
appositeness
appraisingly
aromaticness
astoundingly
astringently
asynchronism
asynchronous
attitudinise
autoimmunity
backwardness
balladmonger
baselessness
battlemented
beggarliness
beneficently
benevolently
berzelianite
beseechingly
bewitchingly
bibliomaniac
bicentennial
blamableness
blamefulness
blastfurnace
blissfulness
blisteringly
bloodyminded
blunderingly
blusteringly
boastfulness
bonnetmonkey
booklearning
bootlessness
brackishness
brassbounder
brokenwinded
calisthenics
canorousness
captiousness
carelessness
carillonneur
Cartesianism
cautiousness
charlatanism
cheerfulness
cheesemonger
chieftainess
childishness
Christianise
Christianity
churchianity
churlishness
clannishness
clatteringly
clownishness
coalitionist
cocksureness
coerciveness
cohesiveness
coincidental
coincidently
comfortingly
commandingly
companionate
companionway
complacently
complemental
completeness
composedness
concordantly
concreteness
concurrently
Confucianism
confusedness
conglutinate
consentingly
consequently
consistently
contagionist
conterminous
contingently
contrapuntal
contrariness
contriteness
conveniently
convincingly
costermonger
cotyledonary
cotyledonous
countenancer
covetousness
cowardliness
creativeness
criticalness
crosscountry
culpableness
cumbrousness
cuprammonium
debonairness
decaffeinate
decisiveness
decorousness
decreasingly
definiteness
deflationary
deflationist
dejectedness
delinquently
delusiveness
departmental
depravedness
depressingly
derisiveness
desirousness
desolateness
despairingly
despondently
detachedness
deviationism
deviationist
dextrousness
dilatoriness
discerningly
disciplinary
discontented
discordantly
discreetness
discreteness
discriminant
discriminate
disenchanter
disgustingly
disharmonise
dissentingly
distinctness
disturbingly
diversionary
diversionist
divisiveness
dolorousness
doubtfulness
downwardness
dreadfulness
droughtiness
duraluminium
dwarfishness
educationist
effusiveness
eleemosynary
elocutionary
elocutionist
enchantingly
encumbrancer
enginetuning
enormousness
entertaining
entreatingly
entrepreneur
enviableness
epicureanism
equivalently
eruptiveness
evanescently
evolutionary
evolutionism
evolutionist
exclusionary
exclusionism
exclusionist
excursionist
exiguousness
exorbitantly
expansionary
expansionism
expansionist
experimental
experimenter
explicitness
exsanguinate
exsanguinous
extortionary
extortionate
extracranial
fabulousness
facelessness
factiousness
faintishness
faithfulness
falcongentil
falcongentle
fancifulness
fatherliness
fearlessness
fearsomeness
featheriness
fecklessness
feebleminded
feminineness
feverishness
fiendishness
flamboyantly
flatteringly
flickeringly
forbiddingly
forcefulness
forcibleness
forebodingly
formlessness
fraudulently
freakishness
frequentness
friendliness
fruitfulness
fugitiveness
gamesomeness
generousness
geotectonics
ghoulishness
gladsomeness
glitteringly
gloriousness
gorgeousness
governmental
gracefulness
graciousness
graspingness
gratefulness
gratifyingly
greenishness
grievousness
grovellingly
gruesomeness
guilefulness
habitualness
handsomeness
harlequinade
harmlessness
headshrinker
heartburning
heavenliness
hebetudinous
heedlessness
helplessness
heroicalness
hesitatingly
heterogenous
hierophantic
homesickness
hopelessness
horribleness
humorousness
hydroquinone
illusiveness
illusoriness
immatureness
impedimental
impenitently
impetiginous
implicitness
impoliteness
incisiveness
incoherently
inconcinnity
inconstantly
incoordinate
increasingly
indebtedness
indirectness
indoctrinate
inexpertness
infiniteness
inflationary
inflationism
inflationist
infrequently
instrumental
integumental
interchanger
interconnect
interspinous
intolerantly
intracranial
intriguingly
intrusionist
intuitionism
intuitionist
irrelevantly
irreverently
irritatingly
isolationism
isolationist
Keynesianism
kinnikinnick
kleptomaniac
klipspringer
knightliness
latitudinous
laudableness
lifelessness
listlessness
literariness
lonesomeness
lopsidedness
lovelessness
lovelornness

lukewarmness
luminousness
lusciousness
maidenliness
malapertness
malcontented
malevolently
Manicheanism
manifoldness
mannerliness
mastersinger
materialness
megalomaniac
mercifulness
metachronism
mindlessness
mirthfulness
miscellanist
misdemeanant
misdemeanour
mistakenness
moderateness
moneychanger
moneyspinner
morrisdancer
motherliness
mothertongue
mournfulness
moveableness
movelessness
mucilaginous
munificently
mutinousness
mystifyingly
namelessness
narrowminded
nauseatingly
nauseousness
nebulousness
needlessness
negativeness
neoDarwinian
neoDarwinism
neoDarwinist
Neohellenism
neonomianism
Neoplatonism
Neoplatonist
Nestorianism
nonchalantly
numerousness
nutritionist
nymphomaniac
obdurateness
obligingness
obsoleteness
omnipotently
omnisciently
onesidedness
oppositeness
ordinariness
organgrinder
outdatedness
overniceness
painlessness
paletteknife
Palladianism
panhellenism
parkinsonism
partitionist
patulousness
peacefulness
peerlessness
pellucidness
perilousness
permanganate
perplexingly
persistently
perverseness
perviousness
philistinism
phillumenist
phrasemonger
pitiableness
pitilessness
pleasantness
pleasingness
plumbaginous
populousness
porcelainise
porcelainous
porcellanous
positiveness
preciousness
precisianism
precisionist
predesignate
predestinate
preeminently
preparedness
prevailingly
previousness
pridefulness
priestliness
priggishness
princeliness
prizewinning
probationary
proficiently
profoundness
prolificness
protactinium
provisionary
purblindness
pyrotechnics
pyrotechnist
quadriennium
quadrumanous
qualmishness
quinquennial
quinquennium
radiophonics
ravenousness
reactiveness
readableness
reassuringly
receptionist
recessionary
recklessness
reductionism
reductionist
reflationary
refreshingly
relativeness
reliableness
remembrancer
reservedness
resignedness
resoluteness
resolvedness
resoundingly
restlessness
retiringness
reversionary
rightfulness
rigorousness
rootlessness
ruthlessness
saccharinity
salutariness
salvationism
salvationist
Samaritanism
sanguineness
satisfyingly
scabrousness
scatteringly
scenepainter
schizogonous
scornfulness
scratchiness
scrimshanker
secessionism
secessionist
seclusionist
sectarianise
sectarianism
sedulousness
selflessness
selfluminous
selfsameness
semicylinder
semidarkness
semideponent
sempiternity
sensibleness
sensuousness
separateness
septuagenary
Septuagintal
serpentinely
sexcentenary
shamefulness
sheepishness
shortchanger
shouldernote
shrewishness
simpleminded
singlehanded
singleminded
skittishness
skrimshanker
slipperiness
slothfulness
slovenliness
sluggishness
sluttishness
snappishness
snobbishness
sociableness
solitariness
sonorousness
soullessness
spaciousness
specificness
speciousness
specktioneer
spermogonium
spidermonkey
spiritedness
spitefulness
splendidness
sportfulness
sportiveness
spotlessness
spuriousness
staggeringly
stalwartness
stammeringly
stealthiness
sterlingness
straightness
strikingness
strongminded
strontianite
strychninism
stubbornness
studiousness
stutteringly
subalternate
subalternity
subcontinent
subsequently
subterranean
succinctness
sufficiently
suitableness
supereminent
supplemental
supplementer
supplicantly
surprisingly
surrejoinder
swaggeringly
swainishness
sweepingness
sweetishness
tactlessness
tamelessness
tangibleness
tastefulness
tearlessness
tercentenary
terribleness
terrifyingly
thankfulness
thickskinned
thievishness
thoroughness
thunderingly
ticklishness
timelessness
timorousness
tirelessness
tiresomeness
togetherness
toilsomeness
tonelessness
toploftiness
tortuousness
touchingness
towardliness
tradescantia
traditionary
traditionist
traducianism
traducianist
trampolinist
transplanter
tricentenary
trickishness
triphthongal
triumphantly
trustfulness
truthfulness
tunelessness
twitteringly
unassumingly
unbecomingly
unblinkingly
unblushingly
unbrokenness
uncommonness
unctuousness
undermanning
underpinning
underrunning
unfrequented
ungainliness
unitarianism
unkindliness
unlawfulness
unlikeliness
unloveliness
unpleasantly
unpronounced
unsteadiness
unthinkingly
untimeliness
untowardness
unwieldiness
unwontedness
unworldiness
unworthiness
unyieldingly
usuriousness
uxoriousness
Valenciennes
valetudinary
valuableness
vaporousness
variableness
vengefulness
venomousness
verticalness
vibraphonist
Victorianism
vigorousness
virtuousness
vitreousness
voidableness
volatileness
wastefulness
watchfulness
wellgrounded
whimperingly
whisperingly
wollastonite
womanishness
wondrousness
workableness
wrathfulness
wretchedness
wrongfulness
wunderkinder
youthfulness
absorptional
aeroneurosis
agglutinogen
ailurophobia
amphictyonic
anaerobiosis
anamorphosis
anticyclonic
antiperiodic
apparitional
appositional
archdeaconry
autochthones
avitaminoses
avitaminosis
battleground
bellbottomed
bilharziosis
blabbermouth
bombdisposal
boogiewoogie
breakthrough
butterscotch
campfollower
charnelhouse
charterhouse
checkerboard
chequerboard
clapperboard
clotheshorse
commissioner
compatriotic
complexional
complexioned
conceptional
confectioner
confessional
connectional
conningtower
convectional
conventional
correctional
councilwoman
counterforce
counterpoint
counterpoise
countrywoman
crossingover
cuckooflower

curlingtongs
curmudgeonly
customshouse
Czechoslovak
derivational
Deuteronomic
diageotropic
digressional
discretional
distortional
dodecaphonic
draughtboard
draughthorse
drawingboard
electrotonic
electrotonus
enantiomorph
Englishwoman
escutcheoned
exhibitioner
expressional
flamethrower
foundationer
furunculosis
galactogogue
gonadotropic
gonadotropin
hallucinogen
hallucinosis
halterbroken
herpetologic
hydrochloric
hydrofluoric
ichthyocolla
inflectional
interfemoral
involutional
leucocytosis
leukocytosis
lodginghouse
lycanthropic
mansionhouse
meetinghouse
meltingpoint
misanthropic
monkeyflower
motivational
navigational
newfashioned
occupational
oldfashioned
onomatopoeia
onomatopoeic
opisthotonos
oppositional
osteoporosis
outpensioner
outwardbound
pasqueflower
peristeronic
phagocytosis
phagocytotic
philharmonic
photochromic
physiognomic
plasterboard
pneumothorax
polyhistoric
postdoctoral
practitioner
precessional
processional
professional
projectional
proportional
proportioned
prosopopoeia
psychotropic
quadraphonic
quarterbound
recreational
redemptioner
reflectional
repetitional
revelational
rhinocerotic
runningboard
salutational
sarcomatosis
scraperboard
seismoscopic
selfapproval
selfcomposed
selfemployed
selfhypnosis
selfreproach
servicecourt
servicewoman
sharpshooter
shuffleboard
Sinanthropus
snaggletooth
stationhouse
stellenbosch
stereoisomer
stereophonic
stereoscopic
stethoscopic
stonemasonry
stormtrooper
streptococci
stroboscopic
strongylosis
subapostolic
successional
synarthrosis
televisional
theanthropic
theatregoing
thermoscopic
thermotropic
thirdborough
toxicophobia
tradespeople
transitional
tuberculosis
unaccustomed
vantagepoint
viscerotonic
visitational
weatherboard
weatherbound
weatherhouse
welldisposed
Wellingtonia
wherethrough
YankeeDoodle
amphitropous
anemographic
angiocarpous
antistrophic
backslapping
basidiospore
calligrapher
calligraphic
cartographer
cartographic
catastrophic
chorographic
chromatopsia
closecropped
conidiospore
cosmographer
cosmographic
crosspurpose
dessertspoon
discographer
eavesdropped
eavesdropper
ethnographer
ethnographic
glockenspiel
goosepimples
hagiographer
hagiographic
handicapping
hectographic
hedgehopping
heliographer
heliographic
heliotropism
hieroglyphic
hierographer
highstepping
homeomorphic
horsewhipped
housekeeping
hydrographer
hydrographic
hydrotropism
hymnographer
hypertrophic
iconographer
IndoEuropean
intercropped
interoceptor
licketysplit
lithographer
lithographic
marlinespike
micrographer
microscopist
misinterpret
monostrophic
mosstrooping
multipurpose
mythographer
namedropping
necrographer
nyctitropism
nympholeptic
organoleptic
orthographer
orthographic
orthotropism
orthotropous
outstripping
overcropping
overstepping
paedomorphic
pantographic
petrographer
petrographic
philadelphus
phonographer
phonographic
photographer
photographic
phototropism
phytographer
pictographic
pleiotropism
pornographer
pornographic
pteridosperm
radiographer
radiographic
reprographic
rhizocarpous
scenographic
sharecropper
sideslipping
sidestepping
sleepingpill
sparkingplug
stenographer
stenographic
stylographic
swimmingpool
tachygrapher
tachygraphic
tetramorphic
transshipped
unprincipled
accusatorial
administrant
administrate
aerosiderite
alexipharmic
ambassadress
ambidextrous
amentiferous
antiaircraft
antimalarial
antineutrino
apiculturist
atmospherics
behaviourism
behaviourist
benefactress
blackcurrant
blackguardly
bladderwrack
bloodthirsty
brainstormer
breaststroke
buccaneering
buccaneerish
buffalograss
burglarproof
cantankerous
carbohydrate
caricaturist
catilinarian
centrespread
chalcopyrite
characterise
cheeseburger
cheeseparing
chemotherapy
childbearing
churchwarden
circumscribe
clothespress
coelenterate
coleopterist
coleopterous
collinearity
commensurate
commissarial
commissariat
compulsorily
concelebrant
concelebrate
conchiferous
conglomerate
consistorial
containerise
contemporary
contemporise
copolymerise
cottonocracy
counterproof
cousingerman
crosscurrent
cumulocirrus
curlingirons
deconsecrate
demilitarise
denuclearise
derogatorily
desulphurise
diamonddrill
disaccharide
disembarrass
disintegrate
distemperate
econometrics
elementarily
equalitarian
eveningdress
extrauterine
fainthearted
featherbrain
fluorocarbon
FrancoGerman
fructiferous
fructivorous
futilitarian
gerontocracy
gladiatorial
grallatorial
granodiorite
greathearted
grossularite
gynaecocracy
headmistress
heavyhearted
heliolatrous
heliotherapy
hemispheroid
hereditarily
heterocercal
heteromerous
highlystrung
horrorstruck
humanitarian
hydrotherapy
hydrothermal
hyperthermia
hypnotherapy
hypochlorite
hypogastrium
idiosyncrasy
imperatorial
incendiarism
inspectorate
inspectorial
instructress
intercurrent
intrauterine
invertebrate
irregularity
kindergarten
kissingcrust
knighterrant
landingcraft
largehearted
laticiferous
lighthearted
luminiferous
macropterous
magnetograph
mangelwurzel
marketgarden
marshharrier
masterstroke
melanochroic
meteorograph
mezzosoprano
misselthrush
molecularity
morningdress
mourningring
multiflorous
multistoried
negotiatress
neighbouring
neuropterous
newspaperman
nonagenarian
nonconformer
nonflowering
Northumbrian
obligatorily

obstreperous
octogenarian
opisthograph
orbicularity
orienteering
orthopterist
orthopteroid
orthopterous
oscillograph
overpowering
pantisocracy
passionfruit
peremptorily
philanthrope
philanthropy
phraseograph
planetstruck
plecopterous
plumbiferous
posteriority
postmistress
praiseworthy
preceptorial
prefectorial
prehistorian
prelapsarian
premenstrual
preponderant
preponderate
preposterous
presbyterate
presbyterial
Presbyterian
privateering
professorate
professoress
professorial
profiteering
progenitress
progesterone
proprietress
prosectorial
protectorate
proudhearted
psychiatrist
quaquaversal
racketeering
radiotherapy
recalcitrant
recalcitrate
Redemptorist
redintegrate
refractorily
reinvigorate
remilitarise
resiniferous
responsorial
salamandrian
salamandrine
salamandroid
salutiferous
sanguinarily
scatterbrain
schizophrene
scouringrush
secondstring
selfabsorbed
selfcatering
selfdestruct
selfdistrust
selfinterest
selfportrait
semiliterate
seminiferous
sexagenarian
shamateurism
shatterproof
siliciferous
sinistrorsal
skateboarder
skippingrope
slaughterous
snakecharmer
sociometrist
soporiferous
sparrowgrass
spectrograph
sphygmograph
spokesperson
squattocracy
standingroom
stanniferous
steganograph
stelliferous
stereochromy
stonyhearted
stouthearted
Stradivarius
subeditorial
sublapsarian
subsidiarily
subtemperate
sudoriferous
supercharger
taperecorder
taskmistress
terrorstruck
testosterone
tetrachordal
tetrahedrite
thaumaturgic
threequarter
totalitarian
transferring
transitorily
transmigrant
transmigrate
transmogrify
turbellarian
ubiquitarian
unchivalrous
undercurrent
unflattering
unpopularity
unregenerate
vauntcourier
veterinarian
vicechairman
visitatorial
vocabularian
weatherproof
wholehearted
wonderstruck
wonderworker
xanthochroia
xiphisternum
youngberries
absolutistic
accomplished
aircraftsman
Alhambresque
amateurishly
antagonistic
antimacassar
apprehension
apprehensive
astrophysics
attorneyship
Australasian
bachelorship
backwoodsman
bacteriostat
belletristic
biochemistry
bottlewasher
bowcompasses
breathlessly
brinkmanship
broncobuster
buttermuslin
Byelorussian
capitalistic
cardinalship
catachrestic
chairmanship
championship
chaplainship
chauvinistic
chondriosome
chrematistic
circumcision
circumfusion
colourlessly
coquettishly
courtplaster
decompressor
delicatessen
dictatorship
directorship
discipleship
discomposure
dispossessor
ecclesiastic
ectoparasite
effortlessly
endoparasite
enterprising
enthusiastic
euhemeristic
evangelistic
executorship
extinguisher
extrasensory
extraversion
extroversion
fieldglasses
frontiersman
fuliginosity
gamesmanship
geochemistry
governorship
groundlessly
guardianship
hairdressing
harquebusier
heathenishly
hemiparasite
henotheistic
highpressure
horsemanship
hyperplastic
hypertension
hypertensive
hypocoristic
iconoclastic
impoverished
inconclusive
inexpressive
intercession
intercessory
intermission
intromission
introversion
introversive
irresponsive
journalistic
jurisconsult
kirschwasser
lachrymosely
laureateship
liberalistic
marksmanship
metaphrastic
microcapsule
microcrystal
microphysics
microseismic
militaristic
misrepresent
mistressship
monopolistic
monotheistic
mountainside
multiversity
musicianship
nailscissors
narcissistic
naturalistic
negativistic
nominalistic
oneupmanship
osteoplastic
outlandishly
overexposure
overlordship
overpressure
paraphrastic
parenthesise
paronomastic
partisanship
pennywhistle
periphrastic
photofission
polytheistic
positivistic
pragmatistic
prenticeship
prerequisite
protoplasmic
protoplastic
Quadragesima
quaestorship
receivership
reconversion
regardlessly
relationship
relativistic
relentlessly
repercussion
repercussive
repossession
reprehension
reprehensive
residentship
resistlessly
retrocession
retrocessive
retropulsion
retroversion
reunionistic
revivalistic
salesmanship
salpiglossis
schoolmaster
scrupulosity
secularistic
selfdelusion
selfpleasing
semidomestic
semifinished
semiparasite
sensualistic
Septuagesima
sergeantship
serjeantship
servitorship
shirtwaister
specialistic
speechlessly
spiritlessly
stockraising
stonedresser
studdingsail
supersensory
supersession
surrealistic
surveyorship
survivorship
syncretistic
taberdarship
tergiversate
thriftlessly
transgressor
transmission
transmissive
transversely
unappetising
uninterested
unresponsive
unsuccessful
virtuosoship
viscountship
voluminosity
voluptuosity
watermanship
wineglassful
abbreviation
acceleration
accelerative
accentuation
acciaccatura
accumulation
accumulative
adjudication
adjudicative
adjudicatory
adulteration
aircondition
alimentation
alimentative
alliteration
alliterative
amalgamation
amalgamative
amelioration
ameliorative
amortisation
anaesthetise
anaesthetist
anathematise
annihilation
annihilative
annunciation
anticipation
anticipative
anticipatory
antiSemitism
appendectomy
apperception
apperceptive
appreciation
appreciative
appreciatory
arborisation
architecture
articulately
articulation
articulatory
asphyxiation
assibilation
assimilation
assimilative
assimilatory
astronautics
atheromatous
augmentation
augmentative
auscultation
auscultatory
bioscientist
birdsnesting
blastulation
blockbusting
bloodbrother
bloodletting

brilliantine
bullfighting
cachinnation
cachinnatory
calorimetric
calumniation
calumniatory
canalisation
cancellation
canonisation
cantillation
capitulation
carburetting
catamountain
chalcolithic
cheesecutter
chlorination
chronometric
civilisation
clarinettist
claudication
closemouthed
coacervation
cockfighting
codification
cohabitation
collegiately
colonisation
coloquintida
colorimetric
columniation
commendation
commendatory
commentation
compellation
compensation
compensative
compensatory
complication
compurgation
compurgatory
conciliation
conciliative
conciliatory
condemnation
condemnatory
condensation
conferential
confidential
confirmation
confirmative
confirmatory
confiscation
confiscatory
conformation
conglobation
congregation
conscription
consecration
consecratory
conservation
conservatism
conservative
conservatory
consignation
consociation
conspiration
constipation
constitution
constitutive
constriction
constrictive
construction
constructive
consultation
consultative
consummately
consummation
consummative
consummatory
contestation
continuation
continuative
contribution
contributive
contributory
conversation
coordinately
coordination
coordinative
correctitude
courtmartial
craftbrother
crenellation
crossbuttock
crosssection
cuckingstool
curvicostate
curvirostral
cytogenetics
deactivation
deambulatory
debilitation
decapitation
deceleration
decongestant
decongestion
decongestive
deescalation
deflagration
defraudation
degenerately
degeneration
degenerative
deionisation
delamination
deliberately
deliberation
deliberative
delimitation
demodulation
denaturation
denomination
denominative
denunciation
denunciative
denunciatory
depopulation
depreciation
depreciatory
deputisation
deracination
desalination
desideration
desiderative
despoliation
desquamation
desquamative
desquamatory
detoxication
diamagnetism
dichromatism
differentiae
differential
dilapidation
dilettantish
dilettantism
disadvantage
disaffection
disclamation
discomfiture
discoverture
disincentive
disinfectant
disinfection
disinflation
disorientate
dispensation
dispensatory
disquisition
dissertation
dissociation
dissociative
dissymmetric
distillation
distillatory
distributary
distribution
distributive
divarication
dorsiventral
doubleacting
duckingstool
dynamometric
earsplitting
echolocation
edulcoration
effectuation
effeminately
elucubration
emancipation
emargination
emasculation
emasculatory
encrustation
equalisation
equivocation
equivocatory
erythematous
etherisation
ethnocentric
evisceration
exacerbation
exaggeration
exaggerative
exaggeratory
exasperation
excogitation
excogitative
excruciating
excruciation
exenteration
exercitation
exhilaration
exhilarative
expatriation
expediential
experiential
explantation
exploitation
exploitative
exprobration
exulceration
facilitation
felicitation
feminisation
fenestration
fermentation
fermentative
fibrillation
finalisation
firefighting
flagellation
flagellatory
flavoprotein
flocculation
floriculture
fluidisation
fluoridation
fluorination
focalisation
foresightful
fostermother
gasification
genuflection
geomagnetism
glaucomatous
globetrotter
glycoprotein
gramnegative
grampositive
graveclothes
habilitation
hairsplitter
halogenation
headquarters
heliocentric
hermeneutics
highfaluting
hindquarters
hippocentaur
homoeopathic
homologation
horticulture
humanisation
humification
hydrostatics
hysterectomy
idealisation
illiterately
illumination
illuminative
illustration
illustrative
immaculately
immoderately
immoderation
immunisation
imperceptive
imperfection
imperfective
implantation
impregnation
inaccurately
inactivation
inadequately
inappositely
inauguration
inauguratory
incapacitate
incatenation
incineration
incompletely
inconsistent
incorruption
incrustation
indefinitely
indelicately
indiscretion
inexactitude
infelicitous
inflammation
inflammatory
ingratiating
inhabitation
inoccupation
inordinately
inosculation
insemination
inspissation
installation
instauration
instillation
insufflation
insurrection
intellection
intellective
intellectual
inteneration
interception
intercutting
interdiction
interdictive
interdictory
interjection
interjectory
intermittent
intermitting
intermixture
interpretive
interruption
interruptive
intersection
interstitial
intertexture
intervention
intimidation
intimidatory
intoxication
intransitive
introduction
introductory
introjection
intromittent
intromitting
introvertive
invagination
invalidation
inveterately
invigilation
invigoration
irreflective
irresolutely
irresolution
irrespective
Ishmaelitish
isodiametric
jurisdiction
lachrymation
lachrymatory
landingstage
landingstrip
laterisation
latinisation
legalisation
legitimately
legitimation
legitimatise
levorotation
levorotatory
liquefaction
lithotritist
localisation
magistrature
malformation
malnutrition
malversation
manipulation
manipulative
manipulatory
Marcionitism
maximisation
mealymouthed
menstruation
metasomatism
minimisation
ministration
ministrative
misadventure
misdirection
miseducation
misquotation
mithridatise
mithridatism
mobilisation
modification
modificatory
monetisation
moralisation
motorisation
multicentral
multidentate
multipartite
naturopathic
nebulisation

neuroanatomy
nidification
nightclothes
nomenclative
nomenclature
noncombatant
noncommittal
noneffective
nonessential
nonobjective
nonresistant
northeastern
northwestern
notification
novelisation
obliteration
obliterative
obnubilation
obscurantism
obscurantist
opinionative
optimisation
organisation
orthodontics
orthodontist
ossification
overexertion
overreaction
pacification
pacificatory
paedobaptism
palaeobotany
Palaeolithic
panification
paralysation
paramilitary
passepartout
passionately
penalisation
peradventure
perfoliation
performative
periodontics
periodontist
pernoctation
peroxidation
perpetration
perpetuation
perspiration
perspiratory
perturbation
perturbative
pestilential
petrifaction
photomontage
photosetting
pigmentation
pisciculture
pitterpatter
placesetting
plainclothed
plainclothes
Plattdeutsch
plebiscitary
pluviometric
polarimetric
polarisation
polychaetous
polyglottism
postposition
postpositive
precedential
prechristian
precognition
precognitive
precondition
predigestion
predilection
preferential
preformation
preformative
prescription
prescriptive
preselection
preselective
presentation
presentative
preservation
preservative
presidential
pretermitted
preventative
pricecutting
proclamation
proclamatory
profligately
prolongation
promulgation
propitiation
propitiatory
proscription
proscriptive
prostitution
protestation
prothonotary
protohistory
providential
psychoactive
psychometric
psychopathic
pterodactyle
purification
purificatory
putrefaction
putrefactive
pyroelectric
quantisation
quantitative
quarterstaff
racemisation
radioisotope
ramification
ratification
reactivation
reallocation
recollection
recollective
reconstitute
recuperation
recuperative
redecoration
regeneration
regenerative
registration
rehabilitate
rejuvenation
remuneration
remunerative
remuneratory
renunciation
renunciative
renunciatory
reoccupation
repatriation
reproduction
reproductive
restaurateur
resupination
resurrection
reticulately
reticulation
retractation
ricochetting
rollingstock
romanisation
ruralisation
sabretoothed
sandyachting
sansculottic
satisfaction
satisfactory
scutellation
segmentation
seismometric
selfbegotten
selfdevotion
selfdoubting
selfelective
selfexistent
selfflattery
selfidentity
selfignition
selflimiting
selfrighting
selfstarting
servocontrol
sesquialtera
silviculture
singleacting
siphonostele
smallclothes
sodafountain
solarisation
solicitation
solifluction
southeastern
southwestern
speakingtube
speedboating
sphragistics
squirreltail
stereometric
sternutation
sternutative
sternutatory
stichomythia
stichomythic
stilboestrol
stillhunting
stonecutting
stridulation
strobilation
strophanthin
stupefaction
stupefactive
subarrhation
subcelestial
subcommittee
suberisation
subminiature
subscription
substitution
substitutive
substruction
substructure
sulphonation
sulphuration
sulphuretted
superstition
supervention
supplication
supplicatory
sustentation
sustentative
swaggerstick
swizzlestick
sycophantish
sylviculture
teetertotter
teratomatous
tessellation
testamentary
therapeutics
therapeutist
thermometric
throughstone
thunderstone
thunderstorm
tightmouthed
tittletattle
torrefaction
totalisation
trachomatous
trainspotter
transduction
transmitting
transmontane
transpontine
transudation
transudatory
transvestism
transvestite
trephination
trifurcation
tripartitely
tripartition
triplication
troglodytism
typification
ultramontane
unattractive
underclothes
undercoating
undercutting
underletting
undersetting
underwritten
unhesitating
unionisation
unthoughtful
urbanisation
valorisation
vaporisation
vasodilation
vasodilatory
vaticination
venepuncture
venipuncture
ventripotent
verification
verificatory
vertebration
vesiculation
vilification
vinification
vitalisation
vitiligation
vitrifaction
vituperation
vituperative
vituperatory
vivification
vocalisation
vociferation
vomiturition
wainscotting
waistcoating
wallpainting
abstemiously
adulterously
aforethought
afterthought
agricultural
amphibiously
anotherguess
appendicular
aquicultural
auspiciously
autonomously
avariciously
boisterously
brontosaurus
calamitously
calcareously
calumniously
capriciously
censoriously
chivalrously
circuitously
circumfluent
cirrocumulus
clangorously
clinkerbuilt
coetaneously
commodiously
contagiously
contemptuous
contiguously
continuously
courageously
delightfully
despitefully
diaphanously
disambiguate
disastrously
disdainfully
disgustfully
disingenuous
diverticular
diverticulum
dovecoloured
euphoniously
extraneously
factitiously
fallaciously
fastidiously
felicitously
fictitiously
flagitiously
fortuitously
gluttonously
goodhumoured
gratuitously
gregariously
hardfavoured
hardfeatured
harmoniously
hibernaculum
highcoloured
homonymously
horrendously
hydromedusae
hydromedusan
idolatrously
imperviously
incautiously
incestuously
inconsequent
incontiguous
indecorously
indigenously
indissoluble
indissolubly
infectiously
infundibular
ingloriously
iniquitously
interlobular
interlocutor
languorously
lasciviously
libidinously
licentiously
loquaciously
lugubriously
magniloquent
manufacturer
marketsquare
marvellously
meaningfully
mendaciously
merrythought
metalanguage
meticulously
minicomputer

miraculously
mispronounce
monotonously
mordaciously
multiloquous
mysteriously
neglectfully
nutritiously
obsequiously
omnivorously
outmanoeuvre
outrageously
overpersuade
perfidiously
perjuriously
perniciously
pharmaceutic
plesiosaurus
portentously
postgraduate
posthumously
precariously
precociously
presumptuous
prodigiously
propaedeutic
propitiously
prosperously
pugnaciously
purposebuilt
purposefully
quadrangular
rabblerouser
rebelliously
receptaculum
remorsefully
respectfully
revengefully
ridiculously
robustiously
rosecoloured
salubriously
scandalously
scrupulously
scurrilously
selfcoloured
semicircular
sequaciously
sericultural
slanderously
solicitously
somniloquism
somniloquist
sprightfully
statuesquely
stertorously
stringcourse
stupendously
successfully
superannuate
supernaculum
supernatural
suspiciously
synonymously
tabernacular
thermocouple
thoughtfully
thunderously
timehonoured
traitorously
tremendously
tumultuously
twentyfourmo
ubiquitously
umbrageously
underinsured
uneventfully
unfaithfully
ungracefully

ungraciously
ungratefully
unmercifully
unscriptural
unstructured
untruthfully
uproariously
usufructuary
varicoloured
victoriously
villainously
viviparously
vociferously
voluminously
voluptuously
wellfavoured
williewaught
winterbourne
worshipfully
absorptivity
accusatively
aggressively
antediluvian
attractively
collectively
collectivise
collectivism
collectivist
collectivity
compulsively
compulsivity
conclusively
conductivity
connectively
convulsively
copulatively
corelatively
correctively
cumulatively
decoratively
definitively
derivatively
digressively
diminutively
discursively
dissuasively
dubitatively
electronvolt
exhaustively
expressively
expressivity
figuratively
heliogravure
imperatively
impressively
imputatively
indecisively
indicatively
infinitively
interservice
irrelatively
laboursaving
meditatively
oppressively
overactivity
pejoratively
perceptively
perceptivity
percussively
perfectively
permissively
permittivity
persuasively
photogravure
possessively
postdiluvian
preclusively
predictively
preventively

primigravida
productively
productivity
projectively
protectively
protensively
protrusively
reflectively
reflectivity
refractivity
regressively
repetitively
repressively
respectively
responsively
ruminatively
Scandinavian
selfactivity
Stakhanovism
Stakhanovite
subjectively
subjectivise
subjectivism
subjectivist
subjectivity
submissively
subversively
successively
suggestively
susceptivity
suspensively
thanksgiving
topsyturvily
transitively
transitivity
vegetatively
vindictively
contrariwise
glassblowing
henceforward
pickerelweed
southernwood
whippoorwill
disconnexion
heterosexual
psychosexual
retroflexion
shadowboxing
accompanyist
artilleryman
breathalyser
butterflynut
cardcarrying
electrolysis
electrolytic
electrotyper
erythromycin
fibrinolysin
gametophytic
haematolysis
haematoxylon
heterophylly
microcopying
nephanalysis
noncomplying
schizothymia
schizothymic
selfanalysis
spermaphytic
streptomycin
voluntaryism
voluntaryist
zygapophysis
bobbydazzler
honeybuzzard
loungelizard
monkeypuzzle
nitrobenzene
privatdozent

razzledazzle
spermatozoid
spermatozoon

---

abolitionary
absquatulate
accretionary
administrant
administrate
affectionate
antiaircraft
authenticate
billingsgate
blackcurrant
bladderwrack
blastfurnace
bletherskate
borosilicate
buffalograss
burningglass
canaliculate
carbohydrate
catamountain
centuplicate
checkerboard
chemotherapy
chequerboard
Christophany
clapperboard
clavicembalo
coelenterate
commensurate
companionate
concelebrant
concelebrate
conduplicate
conglomerate
conglutinate
congratulant
congratulate
constabulary
contemporary
cottonocracy
cotyledonary
counterblast
counterclaim
counterscarp
countershaft
curvicaudate
curvicostate
curvifoliate
decaffeinate
decongestant
deconsecrate
deflationary
dibranchiate
disadvantage
disaffiliate
disambiguate
disassociate
disciplinary
disconsolate
discriminant
discriminate
disembarrass
disinfectant
disintegrate
disorientate
distemperate
distributary
diversionary
draughtboard
drawingboard
electroplate
eleemosynary
elocutionary
erythroblast
evolutionary
exclusionary

expansionary
exsanguinate
exsufflicate
extortionary
extortionate
extramundane
fantasticate
featherbrain
gerontocracy
gesellschaft
gynaecocracy
haematoblast
harlequinade
heliotherapy
hemichordate
henceforward
hippocentaur
hirepurchase
honeybuzzard
hydrotherapy
hypnotherapy
ichthyophagy
idiosyncrasy
illegitimacy
illegitimate
inarticulate
incapacitate
incoordinate
indoctrinate
inflationary
inoperculate
inspectorate
intermediacy
intermediary
intermediate
intermundane
interpellate
intramundane
invertebrate
knighterrant
landingcraft
landingstage
loungelizard
macrocephaly
magnetograph
marketsquare
matriarchate
metalanguage
meteorograph
mezzosoprano
microcephaly
microclimate
miscalculate
misdemeanant
mistranslate
monochromate
mourningband
multidentate
multifoliate
multiplicand
multiplicate
multungulate
Newfoundland
noctambulant
noncombatant
nonresistant
obedientiary
oblanceolate
opisthograph
oscillograph
overabundant
overestimate
overpersuade
palaeobotany
pantisocracy
paramilitary
patriarchate
penitentiary
permanganate

photomontage
phraseograph
pigeonbreast
pitcherplant
planoconcave
plasterboard
plebiscitary
polyurethane
portmanteaus
portmanteaux
postgraduate
predesignate
predestinate
prefabricate
premaxillary
preponderant
preponderate
presbyterate
probationary
proconsulate
professorate
protectorate
prothonotary
provisionary
punchingball
quarterstaff
radiotherapy
recalcitrant
recalcitrate
recapitulate
recessionary
redintegrate
reflationary
rehabilitate
reinvigorate
residentiary
reversionary
ribonuclease
runningboard
scatterbrain
scraperboard
scrobiculate
selfportrait
selfreproach
sellingplate
semiliterate
septuagenary
sexcentenary
Shakspereana
Shaksperiana
shuffleboard
skunkcabbage
slipcarriage
sodafountain
somnambulant
somnambulate
sophisticate
sparrowgrass
spectrograph
sphygmograph
squattocracy
squirrelcage
squirreltail
steeplechase
steganograph
straticulate
studdingsail
subalternate
subinfeudate
submaxillary
substantiate
subtemperate
superannuate
superciliary
supererogate
supermundane
supramundane
swimmingbath
tercentenary
tergiversate
testamentary
thoroughbass
thoroughfare
traditionary
transmigrant
transmigrate
transmontane
tricentenary
ultramontane
ultramundane
undersurface
unifoliolate
unregenerate
usufructuary
valetudinary
verticillate
weatherboard
weatherglass
workingclass
abstractable
ailurophobia
approachable
appropriable
attributable
bonnyclabber
carriageable
chocolatebox
classifiable
communicable
communicably
compoundable
compressible
conscionable
considerable
considerably
contemptible
contemptibly
contractable
contractible
controllable
cultivatable
cumulonimbus
decasyllabic
decasyllable
decipherable
decomposable
demonstrable
demonstrably
destructible
determinable
determinably
diminishable
disagreeable
disagreeably
discerptible
discountable
discoverable
displaceable
disreputable
disreputably
distrainable
emulsifiable
equiprobable
exchangeable
exterminable
extraditable
fertilisable
fluorocarbon
guestchamber
hubblebubble
hybridisable
hydrolysable
hypnotisable
identifiable
immeasurable
immeasurably
immensurable
impenetrable
impenetrably
imperishable
imperishably
imponderable
imponderably
inaccessible
inaccessibly
inadmissible
inadmissibly
inappeasable
inapplicable
inapplicably
incalculable
incalculably
incognisable
incognitable
incommutable
incommutably
incomparable
incomparably
incompatible
incompatibly
incomputable
inconsolable
inconsolably
inconsumable
inconsumably
incorrigible
incorrigibly
indeclinable
indefeasible
indefeasibly
indefectible
indefensible
indefensibly
indigestible
indisputable
indisputably
indissoluble
indissolubly
indivertible
indivertibly
ineffaceable
ineffaceably
ineradicable
ineradicably
inexplicable
inexplicably
inexpugnable
inexpugnably
inextensible
inextricable
inextricably
inhospitable
inhospitably
insufferable
insufferably
intelligible
intelligibly
interminable
interminably
invulnerable
invulnerably
irredeemable
irredeemably
irreformable
irrefragable
irrefragably
irremediable
irremediably
irremissible
irrepealable
irreprovable
irresistible
irresistibly
irresolvable
irrespirable
irreversible
irreversibly
liverystable
magnetisable
maintainable
manoeuvrable
marriageable
merchantable
moneygrubber
monosyllabic
monosyllable
multipliable
nonflammable
octosyllabic
octosyllable
parisyllabic
polysyllabic
polysyllable
precipitable
programmable
prosecutable
pulverisable
quantifiable
questionable
questionably
rechargeable
recognisable
recognisably
reconcilable
rememberable
renegotiable
reproachable
reproducible
restrainable
rumbletumble
saponifiable
selfabsorbed
subdivisible
superposable
suppressible
surmountable
thermostable
toxicophobia
transferable
transfusible
translatable
transmutable
transpirable
transposable
trestletable
unacceptable
unanswerable
unappeasable
unassailable
unbelievable
unbelievably
unchangeable
unchangeably
uncharitable
uncharitably
uncomeatable
unemployable
unfathomable
unfavourable
unfavourably
ungovernable
unimaginable
unimaginably
unmanageable
unmistakable
unmistakably
unprofitable
unprofitably
unreasonable
unreasonably
unrepeatable
unsearchable
unseasonable
vanquishable
aeronautical
aetiological
AfroAmerican
alphabetical
alphamerical
anticlerical
antiparticle
antithetical
archetypical
arithmetical
arrhythmical
astrological
astronomical
asymmetrical
barometrical
bibliothecae
biographical
cartological
catechetical
chorological
coenobitical
coenobytical
cosmogonical
cosmological
countenancer
echinococcus
emblematical
encumbrancer
epexegetical
erythromycin
ethnological
etymological
etymologicon
EuroAmerican
exospherical
fiddlesticks
genealogical
geographical
geopolitical
hagiological
heroicomical
heterocercal
hierarchical
histological
hydrological
hyperbolical
hypocritical
hypostatical
hypothetical
immethodical
judgematical
limnological
linguistical
lithological
manometrical
mathematical
mesothoracic
metaphorical
metaphysical
metathetical
metathoracic
metrological
monomaniacal
morrisdancer
mythological
necrological
neoclassical
neurological
nonidentical
oligarchical
orographical
osteological
osteomalacia
overcritical
pantechnicon
paradisaical
paradisiacal
parametrical
paratactical
pathological
periostracum

pestological
petrological
phenological
phenotypical
philological
phonological
phycological
phytological
preclassical
prototypical
pyromaniacal
radiological
remembrancer
rhinological
scatological
schismatical
selfcritical
semiological
semitropical
sociological
spermatheeal
staffofficer
stereopticon
streptococci
streptomycin
synchronical
systematical
tautological
teleological
theocratical
theosophical
tragicomical
triglyphical
tropological
uneconomical
unhistorical
unprejudiced
unpronounced
volumetrical
absentminded
abstractedly
amygdaloidal
anthropoidal
antiperiodic
bactericidal
bewilderedly
blackguardly
bloodyminded
brassbounder
breechloader
brickfielder
brokenwinded
bulletheaded
bullheadedly
calculatedly
candleholder
churchwarden
coachbuilder
coldshoulder
confoundedly
conquistador
contractedly
determinedly
disjointedly
dispiritedly
displeasedly
distractedly
dunderheaded
encyclopedia
encyclopedic
epicycloidal
farsightedly
feebleminded
fiddlefaddle
hairsbreadth
handsbreadth
hesperididia
highhandedly
illadvisedly
illnaturedly
infanticidal
insecticidal
interestedly
interpleader
jerrybuilder
lefthandedly
longwindedly
marketgarden
misknowledge
mouthbreeder
muddleheaded
muttonheaded
muzzleloader
narrowminded
officeholder
openhandedly
openmindedly
organgrinder
otherworldly
paraboloidal
policyholder
priestridden
proglottides
pronouncedly
rattleheaded
restrainedly
restrictedly
saccharoidal
salmonladder
scoundreldom
semicylinder
shamefacedly
simpleminded
singlehanded
singleminded
skateboarder
stockbreeder
straightedge
strongminded
surefootedly
surrejoinder
taperecorder
tetrachordal
tyrannicidal
unaffectedly
unexpectedly
unreservedly
wellgrounded
woodenheaded
woollyheaded
wunderkinder
YankeeDoodle
abortiveness
abrasiveness
absoluteness
abstractness
abstruseness
accouchement
accoutrement
accurateness
accursedness
accusatively
actinomycete
adaptiveness
adequateness
adhesiveness
admonishment
adorableness
affectedness
aggressively
agribusiness
allusiveness
ambassadress
amenableness
amicableness
announcement
anotherguess
anthropogeny
apparentness
appositeness
appraisement
Aristotelean
aromaticness
articulately
astonishment
attractively
backwardness
ballottement
banderillero
baselessness
bassorelievo
bassorilievo
bedazzlement
beggarliness
belittlement
benefactress
bequeathment
bewilderment
birefringent
blamableness
blamefulness
blandishment
blastosphere
blissfulness
blithesomely
boastfulness
bookingclerk
bootlessness
brackishness
camiknickers
canorousness
captiousness
carelessness
carillonneur
cautiousness
centrespread
centrosphere
chastisement
cheerfulness
chesterfield
chieftainess
childishness
chimneypiece
chromosphere
churlishness
circumfluent
circumjacent
clairaudient
clannishness
clothespress
clownishness
cocksureness
coerciveness
cohesiveness
collectively
collegiately
commencement
completeness
composedness
compulsively
conclusively
concreteness
concupiscent
confusedness
connectively
constringent
consummately
contrariness
contriteness
contrivement
convalescent
convincement
convulsively
coordinately
copulatively
corelatively
corespondent
correctively
counteragent
countercheck
counterplead
covetousness
cowardliness
creativeness
criticalness
crosscurrent
culpableness
cumbersomely
cumbrousness
cumulatively
debonairness
decipherment
decisiveness
decoratively
decorousness
definiteness
definitively
degenerately
dejectedness
deliberately
deliquescent
delusiveness
denouncement
depravedness
derisiveness
derivatively
desirousness
desolateness
detachedness
dethronement
dextrousness
diamondfield
digressively
dilatoriness
diminishment
diminutively
disagreement
disannulment
disbursement
discreetness
discreteness
discursively
disendowment
disgorgement
disguisement
dishevelment
disinterment
dislodgement
displacement
disseverment
dissuasively
distinctness
distrainment
divisiveness
dolorousness
doubtfulness
downwardness
dreadfulness
droughtiness
dubitatively
dwarfishness
effeminately
effervescent
efflorescent
effusiveness
embattlement
embezzlement
embitterment
emblazonment
embranchment
empoisonment
empressement
encirclement
encroachment
encumberment
endamagement
endangerment
enfeeblement
enormousness
enshrinement
enswathement
entanglement
enthronement
entrancement
entrenchment
entrepreneur
enviableness
envisagement
epiphenomena
eruptiveness
estrangement
eveningdress
exhaustively
exiguousness
explicitness
expressively
fabulousness
facelessness
factiousness
faintishness
faithfulness
fancifulness
fatherliness
fearlessness
fearsomeness
featheriness
fecklessness
feminineness
feverishness
fiendishness
figuratively
flavoprotein
foraminifera
forcefulness
forcibleness
forebodement
forestalment
formlessness
fountainhead
freakishness
frequentness
frictionless
friendliness
frontispiece
fruitfulness
fugitiveness
functionless
gamesomeness
generousness
ghoulishness
gladsomeness
gloriousness
glycoprotein
gorgeousness
gracefulness
graciousness
graspingness
gratefulness
greengrocery
greenishness
grievousness
gruesomeness
guilefulness
haberdashery
habitualness
handsomeness
harmlessness
headmistress
headquarters
heavenliness
heedlessness
helplessness
hereditament
heroicalness
hindquarters

homesickness
hopelessness
horribleness
humorousness
illiterately
illtreatment
illusiveness
illusoriness
immaculately
immatureness
immoderately
imperatively
impercipient
implicitness
impoliteness
impressively
imprisonment
imputatively
inaccurately
inadequately
inappositely
incandescent
incisiveness
incompletely
inconsequent
inconsistent
inconvenient
indebtedness
indecisively
indefinitely
indelicately
indicatively
indirectness
IndoEuropean
inescutcheon
inexpertness
infiniteness
infinitively
infringement
inordinately
instructress
insufficient
interconnect
intercurrent
intermittent
internuclear
intervenient
intransigent
intrenchment
intromittent
intussuscept
inveiglement
inveterately
irregardless
irrelatively
irresolutely
jurisprudent
knightliness
lachrymosely
landingfield
languishment
laudableness
legitimately
lifelessness
liquefacient
listlessness
literariness
lonesomeness
lopsidedness
lovelessness
lovelornness
lukewarmness
luminousness
lusciousness
magniloquent
maidenliness
malapertness
maltreatment
manifoldness
mannerliness
materialness
meditatively
mercifulness
mezzorelievo
microsurgery
mindlessness
mirthfulness
misalignment
misapprehend
misjudgement
misplacement
misrepresent
misstatement
mistakenness
mistreatment
moderateness
moistureless
monofilament
morningdress
motherliness
mournfulness
moveableness
movelessness
multinuclear
mutinousness
namelessness
nauseousness
nebulousness
needlessness
negativeness
negotiatress
neurosurgeon
neurosurgery
nevertheless
nitrobenzene
nonalignment
nonefficient
noneuclidean
northeastern
northwestern
numerousness
obdurateness
obligingness
obsoleteness
onesidedness
onomatopoeia
onomatopoeic
oppositeness
oppressively
ordinariness
outdatedness
overniceness
oxyacetylene
painlessness
passionately
patulousness
peacefulness
peerlessness
pejoratively
pellucidness
perceptively
percussively
perfectively
perilousness
permissively
persuasively
perverseness
perviousness
pettifoggery
pickerelweed
pitiableness
pitilessness
playingfield
pleasantness
pleasingness
pleasureless
poikilotherm
polyethylene
populousness
positiveness
possessively
postmistress
postponement
preciousness
preclusively
predictively
preparedness
presentiment
preventively
previousness
pridefulness
priestliness
priggishness
princeliness
privatdocent
privatdozent
proboscidean
productively
professoress
profligately
profoundness
progenitress
projectively
prolificness
proprietress
prosopopoeia
protectively
protensively
protrusively
pteridosperm
purblindness
quadrivalent
qualmishness
questionless
radioelement
rapprochment
ravenousness
reactiveness
readableness
readjustment
reassessment
reassignment
recklessness
recommitment
recrudescent
redeployment
reflectively
regressively
reinvestment
relativeness
reliableness
renouncement
repetitively
repressively
reproachless
reservedness
resettlement
resignedness
resoluteness
resolvedness
respectively
responsively
restaurateur
restlessness
reticulately
retiringness
retrenchment
rightfulness
rigorousness
rootlessness
ruminatively
ruthlessness
salutariness
sanguineness
sanguinolent
scabrousness
schizomycete
schizophrene
scornfulness
scratchiness
sedulousness
selfexistent
selfflattery
selfinterest
selflessness
selfsameness
semibasement
semidarkness
semideponent
sensibleness
sensuousness
separateness
serpentinely
sesquialtera
shamefulness
sheepishness
shoulderbelt
shrewishness
sidewhiskers
siphonostele
skittishness
skullduggery
slipperiness
slothfulness
slovenliness
sluggishness
sluttishness
snappishness
snobbishness
sociableness
solitariness
sonorousness
sorbefacient
soullessness
southeastern
southwestern
spaciousness
specificness
speciousness
specktioneer
spiritedness
spitefulness
splendidness
sportfulness
sportiveness
spotlessness
spuriousness
stablishment
staffsurgeon
stalwartness
statuesquely
stealthiness
sterlingness
stockingless
stockjobbery
straightness
stratosphere
strengthless
strikingness
stubbornness
studiousness
stupefacient
subcontinent
subjectively
submissively
subterranean
subversively
successively
succinctness
suggestively
suitableness
supereminent
supervenient
suspensively
swainishness
sweepingness
sweetishness
swimmingbell
tactlessness
tamelessness
tangibleness
taskmistress
tastefulness
tearlessness
telegraphese
terribleness
thankfulness
thermosphere
thievishness
thoroughness
ticklishness
timelessness
timorousness
tirelessness
tiresomeness
togetherness
toilsomeness
tonelessness
toploftiness
tortuousness
touchingness
towardliness
transcendent
transhipment
transitively
transversely
trickishness
tripartitely
trumpetshell
trustfulness
truthfulness
tunelessness
unambivalent
unbrokenness
uncommonness
unctuousness
underachieve
undercurrent
undergarment
unemployment
ungainliness
unkindliness
unlawfulness
unlikeliness
unloveliness
unsteadiness
untimeliness
untowardness
unwieldiness
unwontedness
unworldiness
unworthiness
usuriousness
uxoriousness
valuableness
vanquishment
vaporousness
variableness
vegetatively
vengefulness
venomousness
ventripotent
verticalness
vigorousness
vindictively
virtuousness
vitreousness
voidableness
volatileness
wastefulness
watchfulness
windingsheet
womanishness
wondrousness
workableness

wrathfulness
wretchedness
wrongfulness
youthfulness
disregardful
foresightful
shortstaffed
transpacific
understaffed
unscientific
unsuccessful
unthoughtful
wineglassful
aforethought
afterthought
agglutinogen
appetisingly
appraisingly
archipelagic
astoundingly
balladmonger
bantamweight
bathypelagic
beseechingly
bewitchingly
blisteringly
blunderingly
blusteringly
boogiewoogie
carpetbagger
carpetknight
cheeseburger
cheesemonger
clatteringly
comfortingly
commandingly
consentingly
convincingly
costermonger
counterlight
decreasingly
depressingly
despairingly
discerningly
disgustingly
dissentingly
disturbingly
enchantingly
entreatingly
flatteringly
flickeringly
forbiddingly
forebodingly
fullyfledged
galactogogue
glitteringly
gratifyingly
grovellingly
haemorrhagic
hallucinogen
herpetologic
hesitatingly
huggermugger
increasingly
interchanger
intriguingly
irritatingly
klipspringer
mastersinger
merrythought
middleweight
moneychanger
mothertongue
mystifyingly
nauseatingly
perplexingly
phrasemonger
prevailingly
quadriplegia
quadriplegic
reassuringly
refreshingly
resoundingly
satisfyingly
scatteringly
shortchanger
squarerigged
stagemanager
staggeringly
stammeringly
stationwagon
stutteringly
supercharger
surprisingly
swaggeringly
terrifyingly
thaumaturgic
thunderingly
triphthongal
twitteringly
unassumingly
unbecomingly
unblinkingly
unblushingly
unthinkingly
unyieldingly
wallydraigle
welterweight
whimperingly
whisperingly
williewaught
accomplished
amateurishly
amphibrachic
anemographic
antistrophic
attorneyship
bachelorship
bloodbrother
bodysnatcher
bottlewasher
brinkmanship
calligrapher
calligraphic
cardinalship
cartographer
cartographic
catastrophic
chairmanship
chalcolithic
championship
chaplainship
chorographic
closemouthed
coquettishly
cosmographer
cosmographic
craftbrother
crossbencher
dictatorship
directorship
discipleship
discographer
ethnographer
ethnographic
executorship
extinguisher
fostermother
frontbencher
gamesmanship
governorship
graveclothes
guardianship
hagiographer
hagiographic
heathenishly
hectographic
heliographer
heliographic
hieroglyphic
hierographer
homeomorphic
homoeopathic
horsemanship
hydrographer
hydrographic
hymnographer
hypertrophic
iconographer
impoverished
laureateship
lithographer
lithographic
marksmanship
mealymouthed
micrographer
mistressship
monostrophic
musicianship
mythographer
naturopathic
necrographer
nightclothes
oncorhynchus
oneupmanship
orthographer
orthographic
outlandishly
outstretched
overlordship
paedomorphic
Palaeolithic
pantographic
partisanship
pennypincher
petrographer
petrographic
philadelphus
phonographer
phonographic
photographer
photographic
phytographer
pictographic
plainclothed
plainclothes
pornographer
pornographic
prenticeship
psychopathic
quaestorship
radiographer
radiographic
receivership
relationship
reprographic
residentship
sabretoothed
salesmanship
scenographic
semidetached
semifinished
sergeantship
serjeantship
servitorship
shortpitched
smallclothes
stenographer
stenographic
stichomythia
stichomythic
strophanthin
stylographic
surveyorship
survivorship
taberdarship
tachygrapher
tachygraphic
tetramorphic
tightmouthed
underclothes
virtuosoship
viscountship
watermanship
abbreviation
abolitionism
abolitionist
absorptivity
acceleration
accelerative
accentuation
accompanyist
accordionist
accumulation
accumulative
accusatorial
adaptability
adjudication
adjudicative
adulteration
advisability
aerodynamics
aeroembolism
aerosiderite
aesthetician
aestheticism
aircondition
alimentation
alimentative
alliteration
alliterative
allomorphism
alterability
amalgamation
amalgamative
amelioration
ameliorative
amortisation
anaesthetise
anaesthetist
anathematise
anecdotalist
annihilation
annihilative
annunciation
antediluvian
anteprandial
anticipation
anticipative
antigenicity
antimalarial
antineutrino
antiSemitism
aperiodicity
apiculturist
apostolicism
apostolicity
apostrophise
apparatchiki
apparatchiks
apperception
apperceptive
appreciation
appreciative
apprehension
apprehensive
arborisation
Aristotelian
articulation
asphyxiation
assibilation
assimilation
assimilative
astronautics
astrophysics
asynchronism
atmospherics
attitudinise
augmentation
augmentative
auscultation
Australasian
authenticity
autoimmunity
automaticity
automobilist
automorphism
availability
avantgardism
avantgardist
bacchanalian
backbreaking
backslapping
beachcombing
behaviourism
behaviourist
bellylanding
berzelianite
bibliologist
bibliomaniac
bibliopegist
bibliopolist
bicentennial
bilateralism
bilingualism
billsticking
bioecologist
biometrician
biophysicist
bioscientist
birdsnesting
birdwatching
blackbirding
blastulation
blatherskite
blockbusting
bloodletting
bluestocking
bodybuilding
bodystocking
booklearning
boulevardier
brainwashing
brassrubbing
breathtaking
brilliantine
buccaneering
buccaneerish
bullfighting
businesslike
Byelorussian
cabbagewhite
cachinnation
calisthenics
calumniation
canalisation
cancellation
canonisation
Cantabrigian
cantharidian
cantillation
capitulation
carburetting
cardcarrying
cardiologist
caricaturist
Carlovingian
Cartesianism
caterwauling
catilinarian
chalcopyrite
characterise
charlatanism
cheeseparing
childbearing

chlorination construction detoxication epicureanism futurologist
Christianise constructive deviationism episcopalian galligaskins
Christianity consultation deviationist epithalamion gasification
chromaticism consultative dialectician epithalamium gastronomist
chromaticity consummation diamagnetism equalisation genuflection
chronologise consummative diamonddrill equalitarian geomagnetism
chronologist contagionist diastrophism equitability geometrician
churchianity containerise dichromatism equivocation geophysicist
circumcision contemporise differentiae escapologist geotectonics
circumfusion contestation differential essentiality geriatrician
circumscribe continuation dilapidation etherisation Germanophile
civilisation continuative dilatability eunuchoidism glaciologist
clarinettist contrariwise dilettantish evisceration gladiatorial
classicalism contribution dilettantism evolutionism glassblowing
classicalist contributive diphthongise evolutionist glockenspiel
classicality conversation disaccharide exacerbation glossologist
claudication conveyancing disaffection exaggeration grallatorial
cliffhanging conviviality disannulling exaggerative grammaticise
clinkerbuilt coordination disclamation exasperation gramnegative
coacervation coordinative discommodity excitability grampositive
coalitionist copolymerise disconnexion exclusionism granodiorite
cockfighting corporeality discouraging exclusionist graphologist
codification counterpoint disestablish excogitation gravelelling
cohabitation counterpoise disfranchise excogitative grossularite
coleopterist courtmartial disharmonise excruciating guaranteeing
collectivise craniologist disincentive excruciation gymnosophist
collectivism crashlanding disinfection excursionist habilitation
collectivist crenellation disinflation exenteration habitability
collectivity crossbedding dispensation exercitation habitforming
collegialism crossexamine disquisition exhilaration haemophiliac
collegiality crossheading dissatisfied exhilarative hairdressing
collinearity crosssection dissertation expansionism halogenation
colonisation cryptologist dissocialise expansionist handicapping
coloquintida cuprammonium dissociation expatriation handkerchief
columniation cytogenetics dissociative expediential hardstanding
commendation deactivation distillation experiential harquebusier
commensalism debilitation distribution explantation heartburning
commensalist decapitation distributive exploitation heartrending
commentation deceleration divarication exploitative heartwarming
commissarial decentralise diversionist expressivity hedgehopping
commissariat decongestion divisibility exprobration heliotropism
compellation decongestive doubleacting extracranial hellgrammite
compensation deescalation dramaturgist extraspecial hemimorphism
compensative deflagration duraluminium extrauterine hemimorphite
complication deflationist earsplitting extraversion hemiparasite
compulsivity defraudation earthshaking extroversion heortologist
compulsorily degeneration eccentricity exulceration hereditarily
compurgation degenerative echolocation facilitation heritability
conchologist deionisation echosounding factionalism hermeneutics
conciliation delamination econometrics faithhealing highfaluting
conciliative deliberation ectoparasite fantasticism highsounding
condemnation deliberative editorialise farmsteading highstepping
condensation delimitation editorialist faultfinding homeopathist
conductivity demilitarise educationist felicitation homologation
conferential demimondaine edulcoration feminisation homomorphism
confidential demineralise effectuality fenestration homothallism
confirmation demodulation effectuation fermentation hoodmanblind
confirmative denaturalise Egyptologist fermentative horsetrading
confiscation denaturation elementalism fibrillation housekeeping
conformation denomination elementarily fictionalise housewarming
Confucianism denominative elocutionist filtrability humanisation
congeniality denuclearise elucubration finalisation humanitarian
conglobation denunciation emancipation firefighting humification
congregation denunciative emargination flagellation hydrostatics
connubiality deontologist emasculation flammability hydrotropism
conscription depoliticise embryologist flocculation hyperacidity
consecration depopulation emotionalise fluidisation hypertension
conservation depreciation emotionalism fluoridation hypertensive
conservatism deputisation emotionalist fluorination hypochlorite
conservative deracination emotionality focalisation hypogastrium
consignation derogatorily encrustation frangibility hypophrygian
consistorial desalination endoparasite freestanding hyposulphite
consociation desideration enginetuning freeswimming idealisation
conspiration desiderative enterprising freethinking illegibility
constipation desirability entertaining freewheeling illiberality
constitution despoliation entomologise frenchpolish illogicality
constitutive desquamation entomologist fricasseeing illumination
constriction desquamative enzymologist fuliginosity illuminative
constrictive desulphurise ephemerality futilitarian illustration

illustrative
immoderation
immovability
immunisation
immunologist
immutability
impartiality
imperatorial
imperceptive
imperfection
imperfective
implantation
impregnation
imputability
inactivation
inartificial
inaudibility
inauguration
incapability
incatenation
incendiarism
incineration
inconcinnity
inconclusive
inconformity
incorporeity
incorruption
incrustation
incurability
indelibility
indiscipline
indiscretion
inelasticity
inexpressive
inflammation
inflationism
inflationist
infusibility
ingratiating
inhabitation
inoccupation
inosculation
insemination
insolubilise
insolubility
inspectorial
inspissation
installation
instauration
instillation
insufflation
insurrection
intellection
intellective
inteneration
interbedding
interception
intercession
intercutting
interdiction
interdictive
interglacial
interjection
intermission
intermitting
internuncial
interpretive
interruption
interruptive
intersection
interservice
interstitial
intervention
intimidation
intoxication
intracardiac
intracranial
intransitive
intrauterine
introduction
introjection
intromission
intromitting
introversion
introversive
introvertive
intrusionist
intuitionism
intuitionist
invagination
invalidation
invigilation
invigoration
invisibility
irascibility
irreflective
irregularity
irresolution
irrespective
irresponsive
irritability
Ishmaelitish
isolationism
isolationist
jurisdiction
Keynesianism
kinnikinnick
kleptomaniac
laboursaving
labyrinthian
labyrinthine
lachrymation
laisserfaire
laissezfaire
lakedwelling
lanternslide
laterisation
latinisation
leapfrogging
legalisation
legitimation
legitimatise
levorotation
lexicologist
liquefaction
lithotritist
Liverpudlian
localisation
longstanding
malacologist
malformation
malleability
malnutrition
malversation
Manicheanism
manipulation
manipulative
Marcionitism
marlinespike
Marseillaise
marshharrier
maximisation
mediaevalism
mediaevalist
megalomaniac
melancholiac
meltingpoint
menstruation
mercantilism
mercantilist
mercurialise
mercurialism
metachronism
metallurgist
metalworking
metamorphism
metapsychics
metasomatism
microcopying
microphysics
microscopist
mineralogist
minimisation
ministration
ministrative
miscellanist
misdirection
miseducation
misquotation
mithridatise
mithridatism
mobilisation
modification
molecularity
monetisation
monographist
moralisation
morphologist
mosstrooping
motorcyclist
motorisation
mountainside
mourningring
multiformity
multipartite
multiplicity
multistoried
multiversity
municipalise
municipality
musicologist
myrmecophily
namedropping
navigability
nebulisation
necrophiliac
necrophilism
negrophilism
negrophilist
neighbouring
neoDarwinian
neoDarwinism
neoDarwinist
Neohellenism
neonomianism
Neoplatonism
Neoplatonist
nephrologist
nerveracking
Nestorianism
nicotinamide
nidification
niminypiminy
noctambulism
noctambulist
nomenclative
nonagenarian
noncomplying
noneffective
nonessential
nonflowering
nonobjective
Northumbrian
notification
novelisation
numerologist
nutritionist
nyctitropism
nymphomaniac
obligatorily
obliteration
obliterative
obnubilation
obscurantism
obscurantist
obstetrician
oceanologist
octogenarian
odontologist
opinionative
opposability
optimisation
orbicularity
organisation
orienteering
orthodontics
orthodontist
orthopaedics
orthopaedist
orthopterist
orthotropism
ossification
outrivalling
outstripping
overactivity
overcropping
overexertion
overpowering
overreaction
oversimplify
overstepping
pacification
paedobaptism
palatability
paletteknife
Palladianism
palynologist
panhellenism
panification
papyrologist
paragraphist
parallelling
paralysation
paramorphism
parasiticide
parenthesise
parkinsonism
parochialise
parochialism
parochiality
partitionist
peasepudding
penalisation
perceptivity
peremptorily
perfervidity
perfoliation
performative
periodontics
periodontist
permeability
permittivity
pernoctation
peroxidation
perpetration
perpetuation
perspicacity
perspiration
perturbation
perturbative
pestilential
petrifaction
pettifogging
philistinism
phillumenist
philosophise
phlebotomise
phlebotomist
photofission
photosetting
phototropism
phrenologist
physiologist
pigmentation
placesetting
plaindealing
plausibility
pleiotropism
pleomorphism
pneumaticity
polarisation
polyglottism
polymorphism
polytonality
porcelainise
postdiluvian
posteriority
postmeridian
postposition
postpositive
postprandial
potentiality
practicality
praseodymium
precedential
preceptorial
prechristian
precisianism
precisionist
precognition
precognitive
precondition
predetermine
predigestion
predilection
preestablish
prefectorial
preferential
preformation
preformative
prehensility
prehistorian
prelapsarian
prerequisite
presbyterial
Presbyterian
prescription
prescriptive
preselection
preselective
presentation
presentative
preservation
preservative
presidential
preventative
pricecutting
primigravida
principality
printability
privateering
prizewinning
proboscidian
proclamation
productivity
professorial
profiteering
prolongation
promulgation
proofreading
propagandise
propagandism
propagandist
propitiation
proscription
proscriptive
prosectorial
prostitution
protactinium
protestation
prothalamion
prothalamium
providential
psephologist
pseudonymity

pseudopodium
psychiatrist
psychoactive
psychologise
psychologism
psychologist
purification
purposebuilt
putrefaction
putrefactive
pyromorphite
pyrotechnics
pyrotechnist
Quadragesima
quadriennium
quadrinomial
quantisation
quantitative
quinquennial
quinquennium
quizzicality
racemisation
racketeering
radionuclide
radiophonics
ramification
ratification
reactivation
reallocation
receptionist
recollection
recollective
reconversion
recuperation
recuperative
redecoration
Redemptorist
reducibility
reductionism
reductionist
reflectivity
refractivity
refractorily
regeneration
regenerative
registration
rejuvenation
remilitarise
removability
remuneration
remunerative
renunciation
renunciative
reoccupation
repatriation
repercussion
repercussive
repossession
reprehension
reprehensive
reproduction
reproductive
responsorial
resupination
resurrection
reticulation
retractation
retractility
retrocession
retrocessive
retroflexion
retropulsion
retroversion
ricochetting
romanisation
ruralisation
saccharinity
safecracking
salamandrian
salamandrine
salvationism
salvationist
Samaritanism
sandyachting
sanguinarily
satisfaction
scabbardfish
Scandinavian
scareheading
scorpionfish
scoundrelism
scrupulosity
scutellation
secessionism
secessionist
seclusionist
secondstring
sectarianise
sectarianism
sectionalism
segmentation
seismologist
selenologist
selfactivity
selfcatering
selfdelusion
selfdevotion
selfdoubting
selfeffacing
selfelective
selfidentity
selfignition
selflimiting
selfpleasing
selfrighting
selfstarting
semifinalist
semiofficial
semiparasite
sempiternity
separability
Septuagesima
sergeantfish
sexagenarian
shadowboxing
shamateurism
shipbuilding
sideslipping
sidestepping
sightreading
simultaneity
singleacting
sinistrality
slaveholding
sleepingpill
sleepwalking
smallholding
sociometrist
solarisation
solicitation
solifluction
somnambulism
somnambulist
somniloquism
somniloquist
soundingline
speedboating
speleologist
spermogonium
sphragistics
spiritualise
spiritualism
spiritualist
spirituality
Stakhanovism
Stakhanovite
statistician
sternutation
sternutative
stillhunting
stockbroking
stockjobbing
stockraising
stoneboiling
stonecutting
Stradivarius
stridulation
strobilation
strontianite
strychninism
stupefaction
stupefactive
subalternity
subarrhation
subcelestial
subeditorial
suberisation
subjectivise
subjectivism
subjectivist
subjectivity
sublapsarian
subnormality
subscription
subsidiarily
substitution
substitutive
substruction
sulphonamide
sulphonation
sulphuration
supersession
superstition
supervention
supplication
susceptivity
sustentation
sustentative
swaggerstick
swizzlestick
sycophantish
syndactylism
teachability
technicality
technologist
telegraphist
temptability
teratologist
terebinthine
tessellation
tetrahedrite
thanksgiving
theatregoing
theoretician
therapeutics
therapeutist
thermolabile
tolerability
topsyturvily
torrefaction
Torricellian
totalisation
totalitarian
toxicologist
traceability
tractability
traditionist
traducianism
traducianist
trampolinist
tranquillise
tranquillity
transduction
transferring
transformism
transformist
transitivity
transitorily
transmission
transmissive
transmitting
transmogrify
transpontine
transudation
transvestism
transvestite
trephination
trichologist
trichotomise
trifurcation
trinomialism
tripartition
triplication
troglodytism
turbellarian
typefounding
typification
ubiquitarian
unappetising
unattractive
unclassified
uncommercial
unconformity
unconstraint
unconvincing
underbidding
undercoating
undercutting
underletting
undermanning
underpinning
underrunning
undersetting
unflattering
unhesitating
unionisation
unisexuality
unitarianism
universalise
universalism
universalist
universality
unpopularity
unpretending
unresponsive
urbanisation
urbanologist
valorisation
vantagepoint
vaporisation
vasodilation
vaticination
vauntcourier
venerability
veridicality
verification
vertebration
vesiculation
veterinarian
vibraphonist
Victorianism
vilification
vinification
visitatorial
vitalisation
vitiligation
vitrifaction
vituperation
vituperative
vivification
vocabularian
vocalisation
vociferation
voluminosity
voluntaryism
voluntaryist
voluptuosity
vomiturition
wainscotting
waistcoating
wallpainting
whimsicality
whippoorwill
whitewashing
wollastonite
youngberries
zygomorphism
bonnetmonkey
cabinetmaker
dinnerjacket
doubledecked
doubledecker
doublelocked
halterbroken
headshrinker
holidaymaker
horsebreaker
housebreaker
hucklebacked
ledgertackle
lumberjacket
maidenstakes
monkeyjacket
patternmaker
pumpernickel
saddlebacked
scrimshanker
singledecker
skrimshanker
spidermonkey
straitjacket
streetwalker
troublemaker
turtlenecked
walkietalkie
winklepicker
wonderworker
aboriginally
academically
accidentally
acoustically
acronychally
additionally
adjectivally
amitotically
anagogically
analogically
analytically
anatomically
antigropelos
antiphonally
apolitically
appendicular
archetypally
aromatically
artificially
artistically
athletically
backpedalled
barbarically
beatifically
beneficially
bespectacled
bibliophilic
biologically
bobbydazzler
buttermuslin
capercaillie
catholically
centesimally
ceremonially
chancemedley
cherubically
cirrocumulus
collaterally

colloquially
collywobbles
commercially
commonwealth
conceptually
congenitally
connaturally
consensually
contextually
conventicler
cosmetically
cynocephalus
decontrolled
delightfully
demoniacally
despitefully
despotically
diabolically
diatonically
didactically
dietetically
disdainfully
disgustfully
diverticular
diverticulum
dogmatically
domestically
doubledealer
dramatically
dynastically
eclectically
ecologically
economically
ecstatically
electrically
elliptically
emphatically
enclitically
endermically
entrammelled
epidemically
episodically
equationally
esoterically
euphonically
evidentially
exegetically
exoterically
forensically
fractionally
frenetically
functionally
galvanically
geologically
gigantically
goosepimples
haematoxylon
harmonically
hebdomadally
hemerocallis
heraldically
hermetically
heterocyclic
heterophylly
hibernaculum
historically
homosexually
horizontally
horrifically
hygienically
hypnotically
hysterically
ichthyocolla
ideationally
immaterially
immemorially
impersonally
incidentally
individually
industrially
infundibular
interlobular
intermeddler
interstellar
intervocalic
irrationally
isochronally
isothermally
jesuitically
jetpropelled
laissezaller
licketysplit
liturgically
logistically
mademoiselle
magnetically
magnifically
majestically
meaningfully
mechanically
meridionally
mesocephalic
metallically
meteorically
methodically
millesimally
monastically
monitorially
monometallic
monopodially
monumentally
narcotically
neglectfully
neurotically
noradrenalin
occasionally
occidentally
operatically
ornamentally
paranormally
pathetically
pedantically
perceptually
periodically
peripherally
phenomenally
phonemically
phonetically
platonically
pontifically
pralltriller
precancelled
primordially
prolifically
pronominally
prosodically
proverbially
provincially
prudentially
puerperrally
purposefully
quadrangular
quixotically
rabbinically
receptaculum
reciprocally
regimentally
relationally
remorsefully
respectfully
revengefully
revictualled
rhetorically
rhythmically
romantically
sacerdotally
sadistically
sardonically
sarsaparilla
schoolfellow
scripturally
sculpturally
sedgewarbler
semantically
semiannually
semicircular
sententially
septennially
sepulchrally
sequentially
seraphically
shillyshally
simoniacally
sinusoidally
Socratically
softpedalled
sparkingplug
specifically
spheroidally
sporadically
sprightfully
starspangled
sternwheeler
structurally
subapostolic
subsonically
successfully
supernaculum
swashbuckler
syllabically
symbolically
syndetically
synoptically
systemically
tabernacular
tangentially
tectonically
terrifically
tetragonally
Teutonically
theatrically
theistically
thematically
thermophilic
thickskulled
thoughtfully
threewheeler
torrentially
tyrannically
uncontrolled
uncritically
underdevelop
uneventfully
unfaithfully
ungracefully
ungratefully
unilaterally
unmercifully
unofficially
unparalleled
unprincipled
untruthfully
volcanically
volitionally
worshipfully
aircraftsman
alexipharmic
artilleryman
backwoodsman
bellbottomed
brainstormer
breastsummer
cleistogamic
committeeman
councilwoman
countrywoman
cousingerman
Deuteronomic
Englishwoman
exophthalmic
exophthalmos
exophthalmus
footplateman
FrancoGerman
frontiersman
hippopotamus
hydrodynamic
hydrothermal
hyperthermia
hypothalamic
hypothalamus
katzenjammer
longshoreman
LowChurchman
microseismic
newspaperman
nonconformer
phanerogamic
photochromic
physiognomic
planetesimal
protoplasmic
schizothymia
schizothymic
selfcontempt
servicewoman
sledgehammer
snakecharmer
stereoisomer
unaccustomed
vicechairman
warehouseman
yellowhammer
absorptional
acaulescence
acquaintance
acquiescence
alkalescence
amphictyonic
amphisbaenic
anticyclonic
apparitional
appositional
appurtenance
arborescence
archdeaconry
autochthones
balletomania
belligerence
belligerency
bloodstained
butterflynut
callisthenic
calorescence
carcinogenic
carragheenin
chitterlings
circumstance
clairvoyance
closegrained
commissioner
complaisance
complexional
complexioned
conceptional
concomitance
concrescence
concubitancy
confectioner
confessional
connectional
consentience
constituency
convectional
conventional
correctional
countertenor
countrydance
crackbrained
crossgrained
curlingtongs
curmudgeonly
decalescence
delitescence
derivational
detumescence
diathermancy
digressional
disallowance
discretional
disobedience
disseverance
distortional
divertimenti
divertimento
dodecaphonic
elasmobranch
electrotonic
electrotonus
equestrienne
equidistance
equipollence
equipollency
escutcheoned
exhibitioner
expressional
extravagance
extravagancy
extravaganza
fluorescence
foundationer
frankincense
freightliner
geanticlinal
geosynclinal
glaucescence
happenstance
heartstrings
housetrained
hypersthenia
hypersthenic
hysteromania
impermanence
impermanency
impertinence
impertinency
improvidence
inadvertence
inadvertency
incalescence
incognisance
incompetence
incompetency
incompliance
inconsonance
incontinence
incontinency
indehiscence
independence
independency
indifference
indifferency
IndoGermanic
inefficiency
inexpedience
inexpediency
inexperience
inflectional
inobservance
intelligence
intemperance
interference
interoceanic
intumescence
involutional

juvenescence
longdistance
longitudinal
luminescence
magnificence
mispronounce
mnemotechnic
moneyspinner
monkeywrench
motivational
multivalence
navigational
neurasthenia
neurasthenic
neuroscience
newfashioned
noctilucence
nonexistence
nonresidence
obmutescence
obsolescence
occupational
offscourings
oldfashioned
omnipresence
opisthotonos
oppositional
ornithomancy
outpensioner
pearlescence
perispomenon
peristeronic
perseverance
philharmonic
philhellenic
phonasthenia
plenipotence
practitioner
precessional
precipitance
precipitancy
predominance
predominancy
preexistence
preoccupancy
processional
professional
projectional
prolegomenon
proportional
proportioned
protuberance
pursestrings
quadraphonic
quarterfinal
quattrocento
quintessence
reappearance
recalescence
recognisance
reconveyance
recreational
redemptioner
reflectional
refreshments
rejectamenta
reminiscence
remonstrance
repetitional
resipiscence
resplendence
resplendency
retrocedence
revelational
reviviscence
risorgimento
salutational
selfevidence
selfreliance

selfviolence
shoulderknot
significance
significancy
silverglance
snapfastener
stereophonic
stonemasonry
straightener
strengthener
subservience
subserviency
successional
superhumanly
supersedence
surroundings
surveillance
teensyweensy
televisional
thickskinned
transference
transhumance
transiliency
transitional
translucence
translucency
transoceanic
transparency
undertenancy
undetermined
unimportance
unrestrained
Valenciennes
viridescence
viscerotonic
visitational
Wellingtonia
xiphisternum
achlamydeous
adjudicatory
adscititious
advantageous
adventitious
altitudinous
ambidextrous
amentiferous
amphitropous
anemophilous
angiocarpous
anthropology
anticipatory
appendectomy
appreciatory
argillaceous
articulatory
assimilatory
asynchronous
atheromatous
auscultatory
bachelorhood
bacteriology
basidiospore
biocoenology
breaststroke
bronchoscope
burglarproof
cachinnatory
calumniatory
calycoideous
campodeiform
cantankerous
carbonaceous
cementitious
chondriosome
chromatology
coleopterous
combinations
commendatory
compensatory

compunctious
compurgatory
conchiferous
conciliatory
condemnatory
confirmatory
confiscatory
conidiophore
conidiospore
consecratory
conservatory
consummatory
contemptuous
conterminous
contributory
contumacious
contumelious
cotyledonous
counterproof
crossbuttock
crosspurpose
cryptogamous
cuckingstool
curlingirons
deambulatory
denunciatory
depreciatory
desquamatory
dessertspoon
dialectology
diatomaceous
discourteous
disingenuous
dispensatory
disputatious
distillatory
dressinggown
duckingstool
ecclesiology
electronvolt
electroscope
electroshock
emasculatory
epidemiology
epistemology
equivocatory
erythematous
exaggeratory
exsanguinous
extrasensory
feldspathoid
ferrugineous
flabelliform
flagellatory
fructiferous
fructivorous
furfuraceous
gallinaceous
galvanoscope
gamopetalous
gamophyllous
gamosepalous
gastropodous
Germanophobe
glaucomatous
gobbledegook
gobbledygook
graminaceous
hebetudinous
heliolatrous
hemispheroid
hereinbefore
heteroecious
heterogamous
heterogenous
heterologous
heteromerous
heteronomous
heterozygote

heterozygous
homomorphous
hydatidiform
hydrophilous
hydroquinone
hygrophilous
hypognathous
hysterectomy
idiothermous
impetiginous
inauguratory
inauspicious
incommodious
incontiguous
infelicitous
inflammatory
inharmonious
innutritious
insalubrious
intercessory
interdictory
interjectory
interspinous
intimidatory
introductory
kaleidoscope
kilowatthour
kremlinology
lachrymatory
laryngoscope
laryngoscopy
laticiferous
latitudinous
leathercloth
levorotatory
liturgiology
luminiferous
macropterous
manipulatory
masterstroke
mastigophora
melanochroic
meretricious
metallophone
metamorphose
microbiology
misbehaviour
misdemeanour
modificatory
monadelphous
monomorphous
monopetalous
monostichous
mucilaginous
multifarious
multiflorous
multiloquous
multipurpose
nailscissors
necrophagous
necrophilous
neuroanatomy
neurobiology
neuropterous
noctambulous
northernmost
obstreperous
ophiophagous
orchidaceous
ornithoscopy
orthopteroid
orthopterous
orthotropous
oscilloscope
ostentatious
overcautious
pacificatory
parasitology
parsimonious

passepartout
peccadilloes
percutaneous
perspiratory
pertinacious
pharmacology
philanthrope
philanthropy
photogeology
photophilous
phytophagous
pilotballoon
plecopterous
plumbaginous
plumbiferous
plummerblock
pneumatology
polychaetous
polychromous
polymorphous
polypetalous
polysepalous
porcelainous
porcellanous
preconscious
preposterous
presumptuous
proclamatory
progesterone
propitiatory
protistology
protohistory
protozoology
pseudonymous
purificatory
pyroligneous
quadrumanous
radiobiology
radioisotope
rambunctious
remuneratory
renunciatory
resiniferous
rheumatology
rhizocarpous
rhizophagous
rhynchophora
rollingstock
rontgenology
sacrilegious
salamandroid
salutiferous
saprophagous
sarcophagous
sarrusophone
satisfactory
schizogonous
schorlaceous
selfluminous
seminiferous
semiprecious
serpentiform
shatterproof
shouldernote
silicicolous
siliciferous
simultaneous
siphonophore
skippingrope
slaughterous
snaggletooth
soporiferous
southernmost
southernwood
spectroscope
spectroscopy
spermatozoid
spermatozoon
spinsterhood

stalactiform
standingroom
stanniferous
steatopygous
stelliferous
stereochromy
sternutatory
stranglehold
subconscious
subcutaneous
subthreshold
succedaneous
sudoriferous
supercilious
supersensory
supplicatory
suppositious
swimmingpool
syndactylous
technicolour
teratomatous
testosterone
testudineous
thousandfold
throughstone
thundercloud
thunderstone
thunderstorm
toastingfork
trachomatous
transudatory
trichotomous
tridactylous
unchivalrous
unlikelihood
unscrupulous
vainglorious
vasodilatory
verificatory
vituperatory
weatherproof
xanthochroia
zygomorphous
bibliography
biogeography
cardiography
cheirography
choreography
chronography
closecropped
cryptography
diageotropic
drawingpaper
eavesdropped
eavesdropper
electrotyper
glossography
glyphography
glyptography
gonadotropic
gonadotropin
horsewhipped
humptydumpty
intercropped
lexicography
lycanthropic
misanthropic
oceanography
organography
palaeography
physiography
polarography
psychography
psychotropic
scintigraphy
seismography
seismoscopic
selenography
sharecropper
Sinanthropus
stereography
stereoscopic
stethoscopic
stormtrooper
stratigraphy
stroboscopic
theanthropic
thermocouple
thermography
thermoscopic
thermotropic
tradespeople
transshipped
triggerhappy
wicketkeeper
zoogeography
Alhambresque
cinematheque
acetabularia
agentgeneral
agricultural
alphanumeric
aquicultural
brambleberry
brontosaurus
calorimetric
caravansarai
caravanserai
cashandcarry
charterparty
checkerberry
chromatogram
chronometric
clotheshorse
colorimetric
counterforce
countermarch
cumulocirrus
curvirostral
dissimilarly
dissymmetric
dodecahedral
dodecahedron
dorsiventral
dovecoloured
draughthorse
dynamometric
enantiomorph
ethnocentric
filibusterer
goodhumoured
goodtempered
grotesquerie
groundcherry
halftimbered
hardfavoured
hardfeatured
heliocentric
highcoloured
hydrochloric
hydrofluoric
hymenopteran
hypochondria
interfemoral
isodiametric
landingstrip
landlubberly
lepidopteran
lithospheric
majorgeneral
manufacturer
misinterpret
mitochondria
multicentral
multilateral
nychthemeral
nychthemeron
particularly
pedicellaria
philodendron
photospheric
pinfeathered
planispheric
plesiosaurus
pluriliteral
pluviometric
pneumothorax
polarimetric
polyhistoric
postdoctoral
procathedral
psychometric
publicspirit
pyroelectric
rhododendron
rhombohedral
rhombohedron
rontgenogram
rosecoloured
seismometric
selfcoloured
selfmurderer
septilateral
sericultural
serviceberry
servocontrol
sheepshearer
shootingiron
snarlingiron
standardbred
stepchildren
stereometric
stilboestrol
straightbred
stringcourse
supernatural
thermometric
thimbleberry
thitherwards
thoroughbred
timehonoured
triangularly
trochanteric
tropospheric
twentyfourmo
unconsidered
underinsured
unencumbered
unfamiliarly
unscriptural
unstructured
varicoloured
vernacularly
vicargeneral
wellfavoured
whigmaleerie
whitelivered
whitherwards
whortleberry
winterbourne
woolgatherer
abstemiously
adulterously
aeroneurosis
agamogenesis
amphibiously
anaerobiosis
anamorphosis
antimacassar
archdiocesan
auspiciously
autonomously
avariciously
avitaminoses
avitaminosis
bilharziasis
bilharziosis
biosynthesis
bloodthirsty
boisterously
bombdisposal
bowcompasses
breathalyser
breathlessly
calamitously
calcareously
calumniously
capriciously
cataphoresis
censoriously
chivalrously
chromatopsia
circuitously
clangorously
coetaneously
colourlessly
commodiously
contagiously
contiguously
continuously
courageously
decompressor
delicatessen
diaphanously
disastrously
dispossessor
effortlessly
electrolysis
euphoniously
extraneously
factitiously
fallaciously
fastidiously
felicitously
fibrinolysin
fictitiously
fieldglasses
flagitiously
fortuitously
furunculosis
gluttonously
glycogenesis
gratuitously
gregariously
groundlessly
haematolysis
haemopoiesis
hallucinosis
harmoniously
histogenesis
homoeostasis
homonymously
horrendously
hydromedusae
hydromedusan
hypnogenesis
idolatrously
imperviously
incautiously
incestuously
indecorously
indigenously
infectiously
ingloriously
iniquitously
karyokinesis
kinaesthesia
kinaesthesis
kirschwasser
languorously
lasciviously
leucocytosis
leukocytosis
libidinously
licentiously
loquaciously
lugubriously
marvellously
mendaciously
meticulously
miraculously
monotonously
mordaciously
mysteriously
mythologiser
nephanalysis
nutritiously
obsequiously
omnivorously
orthogenesis
osteogenesis
osteoporosis
outrageously
overemphasis
paedogenesis
palingenesia
palingenesis
paraesthesia
pathogenesis
perfidiously
perjuriously
perniciously
phagocytosis
phosphoresce
photokinesis
phylogenesis
phytogenesis
Plattdeutsch
pointilliste
portentously
posthumously
precariously
precociously
prodigiously
propitiously
proselytiser
prosperously
pseudocyesis
pugnaciously
quaquaversal
rabblerouser
rebelliously
regardlessly
relentlessly
resistlessly
ridiculously
robustiously
salpiglossis
salubriously
sarcomatosis
scandalously
scrupulously
scurrilously
selfanalysis
selfcomposed
selfhypnosis
sequaciously
sinistrorsal
slanderously
solicitously
speechlessly
spiegeleisen
spiritlessly
spokesperson
sporogenesis
stellenbosch
stertorously
stonedresser
strongylosis
stupendously
suspiciously
synaesthesia
synarthrosis
synchroniser
synonymously

systematiser
telaesthesia
thriftlessly
thunderously
traitorously
transgressor
tremendously
tuberculosis
tumultuously
ubiquitously
umbrageously
unauthorised
ungraciously
unrecognised
uproariously
victoriously
villainously
viviparously
vociferously
voluminously
voluptuously
welldisposed
zygapophysis
absolutistic
accommodator
agamogenetic
ambivalently
amphitheatre
anagrammatic
analphabetic
anaphylactic
anastigmatic
antagonistic
antecedently
anthelmintic
antimagnetic
antipathetic
antirachitic
apochromatic
apothegmatic
appendicitis
appropriator
aristocratic
assassinator
astringently
autodidactic
bacteriostat
battlemented
belletristic
beneficently
benevolently
biochemistry
biosynthetic
brachydactyl
broncobuster
bureaucratic
butterscotch
capitalistic
catachrestic
cattlelifter
chauvinistic
cheesecutter
chiropractic
chiropractor
chrematistic
chrestomathy
Christolatry
cirrostratus
clearsighted
coincidental
coincidently
collaborator
commemorator
commiserator
communicator
compatriotic
complacently
complemental
concentrator
concordantly
concurrently
confabulator
consequently
consistently
consolidator
contemplator
contingently
contradictor
contrapuntal
conveniently
corroborator
cosmopolitan
cosmopolitic
courtplaster
crosscountry
declinometer
delinquently
demonstrator
densitometer
denticulated
departmental
despondently
diagrammatic
diphtheritic
disconnected
discontented
discordantly
disenchanter
disseminator
dissimulator
domesticator
ecclesiastic
electrolytic
electrometer
encephalitic
encephalitis
endocarditis
endometritis
endoskeletal
enthusiastic
epigrammatic
equilibrator
equivalently
espagnolette
euhemeristic
evanescently
evangelistic
exorbitantly
experimental
experimenter
extensometer
exterminator
extralimital
extramarital
fainthearted
falcongentil
falcongentle
firstnighter
flamboyantly
floodlighted
folliculated
forthrightly
fractionator
fraudulently
galvanometer
gametophytic
ganglionated
geochemistry
gesticulator
globetrotter
governmental
greathearted
gyromagnetic
hairsplitter
heavyhearted
henotheistic
hierophantic
highspirited
histogenetic
hydrokinetic
hyperplastic
hyperpyretic
hypnogenetic
hypocoristic
hypothecator
ichthyolatry
iconoclastic
impedimental
impenitently
impersonator
impropriator
improvisator
inclinometer
incoherently
inconstantly
incorporated
incorporator
indiscreetly
indistinctly
infrequently
instrumental
integumental
interdigital
interlocutor
interoceptor
interpolator
interrelated
interrogator
interwreathe
intolerantly
investigator
irrelevantly
irreverently
isochromatic
journalistic
kinaesthetic
kindergarten
lacininiated
largehearted
liberalistic
lighthearted
machicolated
magnetometer
malcontented
malevolently
manslaughter
masterswitch
melodramatic
meristematic
metagalactic
metaphrastic
metropolitan
microcrystal
militaristic
milliammeter
minedetector
minicomputer
monodramatic
monophyletic
Monophysitic
monopolistic
monotheistic
munificently
nanoplankton
narcissistic
naturalistic
negativistic
nephelometer
nephelometry
nimbostratus
nominalistic
nonchalantly
noncommittal
nonconductor
nympholeptic
omnipotently
omnisciently
oneirocritic
orchestrator
organoleptic
orthogenetic
osteoplastic
paedogenetic
palingenetic
panchromatic
pancreatitis
paradigmatic
paramagnetic
paraphrastic
paronomastic
participator
pathogenetic
pedunculated
pennywhistle
perambulator
peregrinator
pericarditis
periphrastic
peristomatic
persistently
phagocytotic
pharmaceutic
photokinetic
phycomycetes
phyllotactic
phylogenetic
phytogenetic
pitterpatter
plectognathi
polyneuritic
polyneuritis
polyphyletic
polytheistic
pontificator
poorspirited
positivistic
pragmatistic
praiseworthy
precipitator
preeminently
premeditated
premeditator
pretermitted
prevaricator
primogenital
primogenitor
prizefighter
proficiently
programmatic
propaedeutic
prophylactic
protoplastic
proudhearted
psychrometer
psychrometry
ratiocinator
reciprocator
refrigerator
relativistic
remonstrator
resuscitator
reunionistic
reverberator
revivalistic
rhinocerotic
rhizogenetic
sansculottic
scarificator
scenepainter
sceneshifter
schoolmaster
scintillator
screenwriter
scriptwriter
secularistic
selfaffected
selfbegotten
selfdirected
selfeducated
semidiameter
semidomestic
sensitometer
sensualistic
Septuagintal
sequestrator
sharpshooter
sharpsighted
shirtwaister
shortsighted
singleseater
specialistic
spectrometer
spectrometry
spermaphytic
stepdaughter
stonyhearted
stouthearted
subcommittee
subsaturated
subsequently
sufficiently
sulphuretted
superstratum
supplemental
supplementer
supplicantly
supraorbital
surrealistic
synaesthetic
syncretistic
taxcollector
technocratic
teetertotter
telaesthetic
thereinafter
thermostatic
thermotactic
threequarter
tittletattle
toggleswitch
tradescantia
trainspotter
transplanter
trichromatic
trigonometry
triumphantly
tuberculated
turriculated
unapologetic
uncalculated
uncelebrated
undemocratic
underwritten
undiplomatic
unfrequented
uninterested
unpleasantly
unsegregated
vermiculated
viscosimeter
wholehearted
acciaccatura
architecture
battleground
blabbermouth
breakthrough
charnelhouse
charterhouse
correctitude
customshouse
dentilingual
discomfiture
discomposure
discoverture
fatherfigure

floriculture
grammolecule
heliogravure
heterosexual
highlystrung
highpressure
horrorstruck
horticulture
inexactitude
intellectual
intermixture
intertexture
jurisconsult
kissingcrust
lodginghouse
magistrature
mansionhouse
meetinghouse
messeigneurs
microcapsule
microcircuit
misadventure
misselthrush
mitrailleuse
motherfigure
multilingual
nomenclature
outwardbound
overexposure
overpressure
passionfruit
peradventure
photogravure
pisciculture
planetstruck
premenstrual
psychosexual
quarterbound
reconstitute
redistribute
scouringrush
selfapplause
selfdestruct
selfdistrust
servicecourt
shortcircuit
silviculture
somatopleure
speakingtube
stationhouse
subminiature
substructure
sylviculture
terrorstruck
thirdborough
tintinnabula
venepuncture
venipuncture
weatherbound
weatherhouse
wherethrough
wonderstruck
conjunctival
crossingover
Czechoslovak
enginedriver
griseofulvin
outmanoeuvre
overachiever
schoolleaver
selfapproval
selfdeceived
selfdeceiver
selfinvolved
shortsleeved
substantival
whencesoever
woodengraver
campfollower

companionway
conningtower
creepycrawly
cuckooflower
flamethrower
lanternjawed
monkeyflower
mulligatawny
pasqueflower
straightaway
superhighway
hyperpyrexia
morphallaxis
trophallaxis
acetaldehyde
agranulocyte
autocatalyse
benzaldehyde
cryptanalyst
dermatophyte
formaldehyde
microanalyst
phreatophyte
pteridophyte
pterodactyle
reticulocyte
sclerenchyma
selfbetrayal
selfemployed
spermatocyte
capercailzie
crystalgazer
mangelwurzel
monkeypuzzle
razzledazzle

* * *

absorptional
accusatorial
aeronautical
aesthetician
aetiological
AfroAmerican
agentgeneral
agricultural
aircraftsman
alphabetical
alphamerical
amygdaloidal
antediluvian
anteprandial
anthropoidal
anticlerical
antimacassar
antimalarial
antithetical
apparitional
appendicular
appositional
aquicultural
archdiocesan
archetypical
Aristotelean
Aristotelian
arithmetical
arrhythmical
artilleryman
astrological
astronomical
asymmetrical
Australasian
bacchanalian
backwoodsman
bactericidal
bacteriostat
barometrical
bibliomaniac
bibliothecae
bicentennial
biographical

biometrician
bombdisposal
Byelorussian
Cantabrigian
cantharidian
caravansarai
caravanserai
Carlovingian
cartological
catechetical
catilinarian
centrespread
chorological
chromatogram
coenobitical
coenobytical
coincidental
commissarial
commissariat
committeeman
companionway
complemental
complexional
conceptional
conferential
confessional
confidential
conjunctival
connectional
consistorial
contrapuntal
convectional
conventional
correctional
cosmogonical
cosmological
cosmopolitan
councilwoman
counterplead
countrywoman
courtmartial
cousingerman
curvirostral
Czechoslovak
dentilingual
departmental
derivational
dialectician
differentiae
differential
digressional
discretional
distortional
diverticular
dodecahedral
dorsiventral
emblematical
endoskeletal
Englishwoman
epexegetical
epicycloidal
episcopalian
equalitarian
ethnological
etymological
EuroAmerican
exospherical
expediential
experiential
experimental
expressional
extracranial
extralimital
extramarital
extraspecial
footplateman
fountainhead
FrancoGerman
frontiersman

futilitarian
geanticlinal
genealogical
geographical
geometrician
geopolitical
geosynclinal
geriatrician
gladiatorial
governmental
grallatorial
haemophiliac
hagiological
heroicomical
heterocercal
heterosexual
hierarchical
histological
humanitarian
hydrological
hydromedusae
hydromedusan
hydrothermal
hymenopteran
hyperbolical
hypocritical
hypophrygian
hypostatical
hypothetical
immethodical
impedimental
imperatorial
inartificial
IndoEuropean
infanticidal
inflectional
infundibular
insecticidal
inspectorial
instrumental
integumental
intellectual
interdigital
interfemoral
interglacial
interlobular
internuclear
internuncial
interstellar
interstitial
intracardiac
intracranial
involutional
judgematical
kleptomaniac
labyrinthian
lepidopteran
limnological
linguistical
lithological
Liverpudlian
longitudinal
longshoreman
LowChurchman
majorgeneral
manometrical
mathematical
megalomaniac
melancholiac
metaphorical
metaphysical
metathetical
metrological
metropolitan
microcrystal
monomaniacal
motivational
multicentral
multilateral

multilingual
multinuclear
mythological
navigational
necrological
necrophiliac
neoclassical
neoDarwinian
neurological
newspaperman
nonagenarian
noncommittal
nonessential
noneuclidean
nonidentical
Northumbrian
nychthemeral
nymphomaniac
obstetrician
occupational
octogenarian
oligarchical
oppositional
orographical
osteological
overcritical
paraboloidal
paradisaical
paradisiacal
parametrical
paratactical
pathological
pestilential
pestological
petrological
phenological
phenotypical
philological
phonological
phycological
phytological
planetesimal
pluriliteral
pneumothorax
postdiluvian
postdoctoral
postmeridian
postprandial
precedential
preceptorial
precessional
prechristian
preclassical
prefectorial
preferential
prehistorian
prelapsarian
premenstrual
presbyterial
Presbyterian
presidential
primogenital
proboscidean
proboscidian
procathedral
processional
professional
professorial
projectional
proportional
prosectorial
prototypical
providential
psychosexual
pyromaniacal
quadrangular
quadrinomial
quaquaversal
quarterfinal

quinquennial
radiological
recreational
reflectional
repetitional
responsorial
revelational
rhinological
rhombohedral
rontgenogram
saccharoidal
salamandrian
salutational
Scandinavian
scatological
schismatical
selfapproval
selfbetrayal
selfcritical
semicircular
semiofficial
semiological
semitropical
septilateral
Septuagintal
sericultural
servicewoman
sexagenarian
sinistrorsal
sociological
spermathecal
statistician
straightaway
subcelestial
subeditorial
sublapsarian
substantival
subterranean
successional
superhighway
supernatural
supplemental
supraorbital
synchronical
systematical
tabernacular
tautological
teleological
televisional
tetrachordal
theocratical
theoretician
theosophical
Torricellian
totalitarian
tragicomical
transitional
triglyphical
triphthongal
tropological
turbellarian
tyrannicidal
ubiquitarian
uncommercial
uneconomical
unhistorical
unscriptural
veterinarian
vicargeneral
vicechairman
visitational
visitatorial
vocabularian
volumetrical
warehouseman
circumscribe
Germanophobe
speakingtube
acaulescence
acquaintance
acquiescence
aerodynamics
alkalescence
appurtenance
arborescence
astronautics
astrophysics
atmospherics
belligerence
belligerency
bladderwrack
blastfurnace
butterscotch
calisthenics
calorescence
chimneypiece
circumstance
clairvoyance
complaisance
concomitance
concrescence
concubitancy
consentience
constituency
cottonocracy
countercheck
counterforce
countermarch
countrydance
crossbuttock
cytogenetics
decalescence
delitescence
detumescence
diathermancy
disallowance
disobedience
disseverance
econometrics
elasmobranch
electroshock
equidistance
equipollence
equipollency
extravagance
extravagancy
fluorescence
frontispiece
geotectonics
gerontocracy
glaucescence
gynaecocracy
happenstance
hermeneutics
horrorstruck
hydrostatics
illegitimacy
impermanence
impermanency
impertinence
impertinency
improvidence
inadvertence
inadvertency
incalescence
incognisance
incompetence
incompetency
incompliance
inconsonance
incontinence
incontinency
indehiscence
independence
independency
indifference
indifferency
inefficiency
inexpedience
inexpediency
inexperience
inobservance
intelligence
intemperance
interconnect
interference
intermediacy
interservice
intumescence
juvenescence
kinnikinnick
longdistance
luminescence
magnificence
masterswitch
metapsychics
microphysics
mispronounce
monkeywrench
multivalence
neuroscience
noctilucence
nonexistence
nonresidence
obmutescence
obsolescence
omnipresence
ornithomancy
orthodontics
orthopaedics
pantisocracy
pearlescence
periodontics
perseverance
phosphoresce
planetstruck
Plattdeutsch
plenipotence
plummerblock
precipitance
precipitancy
predominance
predominancy
preexistence
preoccupancy
protuberance
pyrotechnics
quintessence
radiophonics
reappearance
recalescence
recognisance
reconveyance
reminiscence
remonstrance
resipiscence
resplendence
resplendency
retrocedence
reviviscence
rollingstock
selfdestruct
selfevidence
selfreliance
selfreproach
selfviolence
significance
significancy
silverglance
sphragistics
squattocracy
stellenbosch
streptococci
subservience
subserviency
supersedence
surveillance
swaggerstick
swizzlestick
terrorstruck
therapeutics
toggleswitch
transference
transhumance
transiliency
translucence
translucency
transparency
undersurface
undertenancy
unimportance
viridescence
wonderstruck
acetaldehyde
benzaldehyde
coloquintida
correctitude
disaccharide
formaldehyde
harlequinade
inexactitude
lanternslide
mountainside
nicotinamide
overpersuade
parasiticide
primigravida
radionuclide
sulphonamide
thitherwards
whitherwards
absentminded
accomplished
agglutinogen
autochthones
avitaminoses
backpedalled
balladmonger
battlemented
bellbottomed
bespectacled
bloodbrother
bloodstained
bloodyminded
bobbydazzler
bodysnatcher
bonnetmonkey
bonnyclabber
bottlewasher
boulevardier
bowcompasses
brainstormer
brassbounder
breastsummer
breathalyser
breechloader
brickfielder
brokenwinded
broncobuster
bulletheaded
cabinetmaker
calligrapher
campfollower
candleholder
carpetbagger
cartographer
cattlelifter
chancemedley
cheeseburger
cheesecutter
cheesemonger
churchwarden
clearsighted
closecropped
closegrained
closemouthed
coachbuilder
coldshoulder
collywobbles
commissioner
complexioned
confectioner
conningtower
conventicler
cosmographer
costermonger
countenancer
courtplaster
crackbrained
craftbrother
crossbencher
crossgrained
crossingover
crystalgazer
cuckooflower
declinometer
decontrolled
delicatessen
densitometer
denticulated
dinnerjacket
discographer
disconnected
discontented
disenchanter
dissatisfied
doubledealer
doubledecked
doubledecker
doublelocked
dovecoloured
drawingpaper
dunderheaded
eavesdropped
eavesdropper
electrometer
electrotyper
encumbrancer
enginedriver
entrammelled
escutcheoned
ethnographer
exhibitioner
experimenter
extensometer
extinguisher
fainthearted
feebleminded
fieldglasses
filibusterer
firstnighter
flamethrower
floodlighted
folliculated
fostermother
foundationer
freightliner
frontbencher
fullyfledged
galvanometer
ganglionated
globetrotter
glockenspiel
goodhumoured
goodtempered
goosepimples
graveclothes
greathearted
guestchamber
hagiographer
hairsplitter
halftimbered
hallucinogen
halterbroken
handkerchief

hardfavoured
hardfeatured
harquebusier
headshrinker
heavyhearted
heliographer
hierographer
highcoloured
highspirited
holidaymaker
horsebreaker
horsewhipped
housebreaker
housetrained
hucklebacked
huggermugger
hydrographer
hymnographer
iconographer
impoverished
inclinometer
incorporated
interchanger
intercropped
intermeddler
interpleader
interrelated
jerrybuilder
jetpropelled
katzenjammer
kindergarten
kirschwasser
klipspringer
lacininiated
laissezaller
lanternjawed
largehearted
lighthearted
lithographer
lumberjacket
machicolated
magnetometer
maidenstakes
malcontented
mangelwurzel
manslaughter
manufacturer
marketgarden
marshharrier
mastersinger
mealymouthed
micrographer
milliammeter
minicomputer
misinterpret
moneychanger
moneygrubber
moneyspinner
monkeyflower
monkeyjacket
morrisdancer
mouthbreeder
muddleheaded
multistoried
muttonheaded
muzzleloader
mythographer
mythologiser
narrowminded
necrographer
nephelometer
newfashioned
nightclothes
nonconformer
officeholder
oldfashioned
organgrinder
orthographer
outpensioner
outstretched
overachiever
pasqueflower
patternmaker
peccadilloes
pedunculated
pennypincher
petrographer
phonographer
photographer
phrasemonger
phycomycetes
phytographer
pickerelweed
pinfeathered
pitterpatter
plainclothed
plainclothes
policyholder
poorspirited
pornographer
practitioner
pralltriller
precancelled
premeditated
pretermitted
priestridden
prizefighter
proglottides
proportioned
proselytiser
proudhearted
psychrometer
pumpernickel
rabblerouser
radiographer
rattleheaded
redemptioner
remembrancer
revictualled
rosecoloured
sabretoothed
saddlebacked
salmonladder
scenepainter
sceneshifter
schoolleaver
schoolmaster
screenwriter
scrimshanker
scriptwriter
sedgewarbler
selfabsorbed
selfaffected
selfbegotten
selfcoloured
selfcomposed
selfdeceived
selfdeceiver
selfdirected
selfeducated
selfemployed
selfinvolved
selfmurderer
semicylinder
semidetached
semidiameter
semifinished
sensitometer
sharecropper
sharpshooter
sharpsighted
sheepshearer
shirtwaister
shortchanger
shortpitched
shortsighted
shortsleeved
shortstaffed
simpleminded
singledecker
singlehanded
singleminded
singleseater
skateboarder
skrimshanker
sledgehammer
smallclothes
snakecharmer
snapfastener
softpedalled
specktioneer
spectrometer
spidermonkey
spiegeleisen
squarerigged
staffofficer
stagemanager
standardbred
starspangled
stenographer
stepchildren
stepdaughter
stereoisomer
sternwheeler
stockbreeder
stonedresser
stonyhearted
stormtrooper
stouthearted
straightbred
straightener
straitjacket
streetwalker
strengthener
strongminded
subcommittee
subsaturated
sulphuretted
supercharger
supplementer
surrejoinder
swashbuckler
synchroniser
systematiser
tachygrapher
taperecorder
teetertotter
thereinafter
thickskinned
thickskulled
thoroughbred
threequarter
threewheeler
tightmouthed
timehonoured
trainspotter
transplanter
transshipped
troublemaker
tuberculated
turriculated
turtlenecked
unaccustomed
unauthorised
uncalculated
uncelebrated
unclassified
unconsidered
uncontrolled
underclothes
underinsured
understaffed
underwritten
undetermined
unencumbered
unfrequented
uninterested
unparalleled
unprejudiced
unprincipled
unpronounced
unrecognised
unrestrained
unsegregated
unstructured
Valenciennes
varicoloured
vauntcourier
vermiculated
viscosimeter
welldisposed
wellfavoured
wellgrounded
whencesoever
whitelivered
wholehearted
wicketkeeper
windingsheet
winklepicker
wonderworker
woodengraver
woodenheaded
woolgatherer
woollyheaded
wunderkinder
yellowhammer
youngberries
antiaircraft
countershaft
gesellschaft
landingcraft
oversimplify
paletteknife
quarterstaff
transmogrify
anthropology
bacteriology
biocoenology
breakthrough
chitterlings
chromatology
curlingtongs
dialectology
disadvantage
ecclesiology
epidemiology
epistemology
heartstrings
ichthyophagy
kremlinology
landingstage
liturgiology
metalanguage
microbiology
misknowledge
neurobiology
offscourings
parasitology
pharmacology
photogeology
photomontage
pneumatology
protistology
protozoology
pursestrings
radiobiology
rheumatology
rontgenology
skunkcabbage
slipcarriage
squirrelcage
straightedge
surroundings
thirdborough
wherethrough
aforethought
afterthought
bantamweight
bibliography
biogeography
cardiography
carpetknight
cheirography
choreography
chrestomathy
chronography
counterlight
cryptography
glossography
glyphography
glyptography
interwreathe
lexicography
merrythought
middleweight
oceanography
organography
palaeography
physiography
plectognathi
polarography
praiseworthy
psychography
scintigraphy
seismography
selenography
stereography
stratigraphy
thermography
welterweight
williewaught
zoogeography
absolutistic
acetabularia
aeroneurosis
agamogenesis
agamogenetic
ailurophobia
alexipharmic
alphanumeric
amphibrachic
amphictyonic
amphisbaenic
anaerobiosis
anagrammatic
analphabetic
anamorphosis
anaphylactic
anastigmatic
anemographic
antagonistic
anthelmintic
anticyclonic
antimagnetic
antipathetic
antiperiodic
antirachitic
antistrophic
apochromatic
apothegmatic
appendicitis
archipelagic
aristocratic
attorneyship
autodidactic
avitaminosis
bachelorship
balletomania
bathypelagic
belletristic
bibliophilic
bilharziasis
bilharziosis
biosynthesis
biosynthetic

boogiewoogie
brinkmanship
bureaucratic
buttermuslin
calligraphic
callisthenic
calorimetric
capercaillie
capercailzie
capitalistic
carcinogenic
cardinalship
carragheenin
cartographic
catachrestic
catamountain
cataphoresis
catastrophic
chairmanship
chalcolithic
championship
chaplainship
chauvinistic
chiropractic
chorographic
chrematistic
chromatopsia
chronometric
cleistogamic
colorimetric
compatriotic
cosmographic
cosmopolitic
counterclaim
decasyllabic
Deuteronomic
diageotropic
diagrammatic
dictatorship
diphtheritic
directorship
discipleship
dissymmetric
dodecaphonic
dynamometric
ecclesiastic
electrolysis
electrolytic
electrotonic
encephalitic
encephalitis
encyclopedia
encyclopedic
endocarditis
endometritis
enthusiastic
epigrammatic
erythromycin
ethnocentric
ethnographic
euhemeristic
evangelistic
executorship
exophthalmic
falcongentil
featherbrain
feldspathoid
fibrinolysin
flavoprotein
furunculosis
gamesmanship
gametophytic
glycogenesis
glycoprotein
gonadotropic
gonadotropin
governorship
griseofulvin
grotesquerie
guardianship
gyromagnetic
haematolysis
haemopoiesis
haemorrhagic
hagiographic
hallucinosis
hectographic
heliocentric
heliographic
hemerocallis
hemispheroid
henotheistic
herpetologic
hesperididia
heterocyclic
hieroglyphic
hierophantic
histogenesis
histogenetic
homeomorphic
homoeopathic
homoeostasis
horsemanship
hydrochloric
hydrodynamic
hydrofluoric
hydrographic
hydrokinetic
hyperplastic
hyperpyretic
hyperpyrexia
hypersthenia
hypersthenic
hyperthermia
hypertrophic
hypnogenesis
hypnogenetic
hypochondria
hypocoristic
hypothalamic
hysteromania
iconoclastic
IndoGermanic
interoceanic
intervocalic
isochromatic
isodiametric
journalistic
karyokinesis
kinaesthesia
kinaesthesis
kinaesthetic
landingstrip
laureateship
leucocytosis
leukocytosis
liberalistic
licketysplit
lithographic
lithospheric
lycanthropic
marksmanship
melanochroic
melodramatic
meristematic
mesocephalic
mesothoracic
metagalactic
metaphrastic
metathoracic
microcircuit
microseismic
militaristic
misanthropic
mistressship
mitochondria
mnemotechnic
monodramatic
monometallic
monophyletic
Monophysitic
monopolistic
monostrophic
monosyllabic
monotheistic
morphallaxis
musicianship
narcissistic
naturalistic
naturopathic
negativistic
nephanalysis
neurasthenia
neurasthenic
nominalistic
noradrenalin
nympholeptic
octosyllabic
oneirocritic
oneupmanship
onomatopoeia
onomatopoeic
organoleptic
orthogenesis
orthogenetic
orthographic
orthopteroid
osteogenesis
osteomalacia
osteoplastic
osteoporosis
overemphasis
overlordship
paedogenesis
paedogenetic
paedomorphic
Palaeolithic
palingenesia
palingenesis
palingenetic
panchromatic
pancreatitis
pantographic
paradigmatic
paraesthesia
paramagnetic
paraphrastic
parisyllabic
paronomastic
partisanship
passionfruit
pathogenesis
pathogenetic
pedicellaria
pericarditis
periphrastic
peristeronic
peristomatic
petrographic
phagocytosis
phagocytotic
phanerogamic
pharmaceutic
philharmonic
philhellenic
phonasthenia
phonographic
photochromic
photographic
photokinesis
photokinetic
photospheric
phyllotactic
phylogenesis
phylogenetic
physiognomic
phytogenesis
phytogenetic
pictographic
planispheric
pluviometric
polarimetric
polyhistoric
polyneuritic
polyneuritis
polyphyletic
polysyllabic
polytheistic
pornographic
positivistic
pragmatistic
prenticeship
programmatic
propaedeutic
prophylactic
prosopopoeia
protoplasmic
protoplastic
pseudocyesis
psychometric
psychopathic
psychotropic
publicspirit
pyroelectric
quadraphonic
quadriplegia
quadriplegic
quaestorship
radiographic
receivership
relationship
relativistic
reprographic
residentship
reunionistic
revivalistic
rhinocerotic
rhizogenetic
salamandroid
salesmanship
salpiglossis
sansculottic
sarcomatosis
scatterbrain
scenographic
schizothymia
schizothymic
secularistic
seismometric
seismoscopic
selfanalysis
selfhypnosis
selfportrait
semidomestic
sensualistic
sergeantship
serjeantship
servitorship
shortcircuit
sodafountain
specialistic
spermaphytic
spermatozoid
sporogenesis
squirreltail
stenographic
stereometric
stereophonic
stereoscopic
stethoscopic
stichomythia
stichomythic
streptomycin
stroboscopic
strongylosis
strophanthin
studdingsail
stylographic
subapostolic
surrealistic
surveyorship
survivorship
synaesthesia
synaesthetic
synarthrosis
syncretistic
taberdarship
tachygraphic
technocratic
telaesthesia
telaesthetic
tetramorphic
thaumaturgic
theanthropic
thermometric
thermophilic
thermoscopic
thermostatic
thermotactic
thermotropic
toxicophobia
tradescantia
transoceanic
transpacific
trichromatic
trochanteric
tropospheric
tuberculosis
unapologetic
undemocratic
undiplomatic
unscientific
virtuosoship
viscerotonic
viscountship
walkietalkie
watermanship
Wellingtonia
whigmaleerie
xanthochroia
zygapophysis
apparatchiki
apparatchiks
breaststroke
businesslike
fiddlesticks
marlinespike
masterstroke
aboriginally
abstemiously
abstractable
abstractedly
academically
accidentally
accusatively
acoustically
acronychally
additionally
adjectivally
adulterously
aggressively
amateurishly
ambivalently
amitotically
amphibiously
anagogically
analogically
analytically
anatomically
antecedently
antiparticle
antiphonally
apolitically
appetisingly

appraisingly
approachable
appropriable
archetypally
aromatically
articulately
artificially
artistically
astoundingly
astringently
athletically
attractively
attributable
auspiciously
autonomously
avariciously
barbarically
beatifically
beneficently
beneficially
benevolently
beseechingly
bewilderedly
bewitchingly
biologically
blackguardly
blisteringly
blithesomely
blunderingly
blusteringly
boisterously
breathlessly
bullheadedly
calamitously
calcareously
calculatedly
calumniously
capriciously
carriageable
catholically
censoriously
centesimally
ceremonially
cherubically
chesterfield
chivalrously
circuitously
clangorously
classifiable
clatteringly
clavicembalo
clinkerbuilt
coetaneously
coincidently
collaterally
collectively
collegiately
colloquially
colourlessly
comfortingly
commandingly
commercially
commodiously
communicable
communicably
complacently
compoundable
compressible
compulsively
compulsorily
conceptually
conclusively
concordantly
concurrently
confoundedly
congenitally
connaturally
connectively
conscionable
consensually
consentingly
consequently
considerable
considerably
consistently
consummately
contagiously
contemptible
contemptibly
contextually
contiguously
contingently
continuously
contractable
contractedly
contractible
controllable
conveniently
convincingly
convulsively
coordinately
copulatively
coquettishly
corelatively
correctively
cosmetically
courageously
creepycrawly
cultivatable
cumbersomely
cumulatively
curmudgeonly
decasyllable
decipherable
decomposable
decoratively
decreasingly
definitively
degenerately
deliberately
delightfully
delinquently
demoniacally
demonstrable
demonstrably
depressingly
derivatively
derogatorily
despairingly
despitefully
despondently
despotically
destructible
determinable
determinably
determinedly
diabolically
diamonddrill
diamondfield
diaphanously
diatonically
didactically
dietetically
digressively
diminishable
diminutively
disagreeable
disagreeably
disastrously
discerningly
discerptible
discordantly
discountable
discoverable
discursively
disdainfully
disgustfully
disgustingly
disjointedly
dispiritedly
displaceable
displeasedly
disreputable
disreputably
dissentingly
dissimilarly
dissuasively
distractedly
distrainable
disturbingly
dogmatically
domestically
dramatically
dubitatively
dynastically
eclectically
ecologically
economically
ecstatically
effeminately
effortlessly
electrically
electronvolt
elementarily
elliptically
emphatically
emulsifiable
enchantingly
enclitically
endermically
entreatingly
epidemically
episodically
equationally
equiprobable
equivalently
esoterically
euphonically
euphoniously
evanescently
evidentially
exchangeable
exegetically
exhaustively
exorbitantly
exoterically
expressively
exterminable
extraditable
extraneously
factitiously
falcongentle
fallaciously
farsightedly
fastidiously
felicitously
fertilisable
fictitiously
fiddlefaddle
figuratively
flagitiously
flamboyantly
flatteringly
flickeringly
forbiddingly
forebodingly
forensically
forthrightly
fortuitously
fractionally
fraudulently
frenetically
functionally
galvanically
geologically
Germanophile
gigantically
glitteringly
gluttonously
grammolecule
gratifyingly
gratuitously
gregariously
groundlessly
grovellingly
harmonically
harmoniously
heathenishly
hebdomadally
heraldically
hereditarily
hermetically
hesitatingly
heterophylly
highhandedly
historically
homonymously
homosexually
horizontally
horrendously
horrifically
hubblebubble
hybridisable
hydrolysable
hygienically
hypnotically
hypnotisable
hysterically
ichthyocolla
ideationally
identifiable
idolatrously
illadvisedly
illiterately
illnaturedly
immaculately
immaterially
immeasurable
immeasurably
immemorially
immensurable
immoderately
impenetrable
impenetrably
impenitently
imperatively
imperishable
imperishably
impersonally
imperviously
imponderable
imponderably
impressively
imputatively
inaccessible
inaccessibly
inaccurately
inadequately
inadmissible
inadmissibly
inappeasable
inapplicable
inapplicably
inappositely
incalculable
incalculably
incautiously
incestuously
incidentally
incognisable
incognitable
incoherently
incommutable
incommutably
incomparable
incomparably
incompatible
incompatibly
incompletely
incomputable
inconsolable
inconsolably
inconstantly
inconsumable
inconsumably
incorrigible
incorrigibly
increasingly
indecisively
indeclinable
indecorously
indefeasible
indefeasibly
indefectible
indefensible
indefensibly
indefinitely
indelicately
indicatively
indigenously
indigestible
indiscreetly
indisputable
indisputably
indissoluble
indissolubly
indistinctly
indivertible
indivertibly
individually
industrially
ineffaceable
ineffaceably
ineradicable
ineradicably
inexplicable
inexplicably
inexpugnable
inexpugnably
inextensible
inextricable
inextricably
infectiously
infinitively
infrequently
ingloriously
inhospitable
inhospitably
iniquitously
inordinately
insufferable
insufferably
intelligible
intelligibly
interestedly
interminable
interminably
intolerantly
intriguingly
inveterately
invulnerable
invulnerably
irrationally
irredeemable
irredeemably
irreformable
irrefragable
irrefragably
irrelatively
irrelevantly
irremediable
irremediably
irremissible
irrepealable
irreprovable

irresistible
irresistibly
irresolutely
irresolvable
irrespirable
irreverently
irreversible
irreversibly
irritatingly
isochronally
isothermally
jesuitically
jurisconsult
lachrymosely
landingfield
landlubberly
languorously
lasciviously
ledgertackle
lefthandedly
legitimately
libidinously
licentiously
liturgically
liverystable
logistically
longwindedly
loquaciously
lugubriously
macrocephaly
mademoiselle
magnetically
magnetisable
magnifically
maintainable
majestically
malevolently
manoeuvrable
marriageable
marvellously
meaningfully
mechanically
meditatively
mendaciously
merchantable
meridionally
metallically
meteorically
methodically
meticulously
microcapsule
microcephaly
millesimally
miraculously
monastically
monitorially
monkeypuzzle
monopodially
monosyllable
monotonously
monumentally
mordaciously
multipliable
munificently
myrmecophily
mysteriously
mystifyingly
narcotically
nauseatingly
neglectfully
neurotically
nonchalantly
nonflammable
nutritiously
obligatorily
obsequiously
occasionally
occidentally
octosyllable
omnipotently
omnisciently
omnivorously
openhandedly
openmindedly
operatically
oppressively
ornamentally
otherworldly
outlandishly
outrageously
paranormally
particularly
passionately
pathetically
pedantically
pejoratively
pennywhistle
perceptively
perceptually
percussively
peremptorily
perfectively
perfidiously
periodically
peripherally
perjuriously
permissively
perniciously
perplexingly
persistently
persuasively
phenomenally
phonemically
phonetically
platonically
playingfield
polysyllable
pontifically
portentously
possessively
posthumously
precariously
precipitable
preclusively
precociously
predictively
preeminently
prevailingly
preventively
primordially
prodigiously
productively
proficiently
profligately
programmable
projectively
prolifically
pronominally
pronouncedly
propitiously
prosecutable
prosodically
prosperously
protectively
protensively
protrusively
proverbially
provincially
prudentially
pterodactyle
puerperrally
pugnaciously
pulverisable
punchingball
purposebuilt
purposefully
quantifiable
questionable
questionably
quixotically
rabbinically
razzledazzle
reassuringly
rebelliously
rechargeable
reciprocally
recognisable
recognisably
reconcilable
reflectively
refractorily
refreshingly
regardlessly
regimentally
regressively
relationally
relentlessly
rememberable
remorsefully
renegotiable
repetitively
repressively
reproachable
reproducible
resistlessly
resoundingly
respectfully
respectively
responsively
restrainable
restrainedly
restrictedly
reticulately
revengefully
rhetorically
rhythmically
ridiculously
robustiously
romantically
rumbletumble
ruminatively
sacerdotally
sadistically
salubriously
sanguinarily
saponifiable
sardonically
sarsaparilla
satisfyingly
scandalously
scatteringly
scripturally
scrupulously
sculpturally
scurrilously
semantically
semiannually
sententially
septennially
sepulchrally
sequaciously
sequentially
seraphically
serpentinely
shamefacedly
shillyshally
shoulderbelt
simoniacally
sinusoidally
siphonostele
slanderously
sleepingpill
Socratically
solicitously
specifically
speechlessly
spheroidally
spiritlessly
sporadically
sprightfully
staggeringly
stammeringly
statuesquely
stertorously
stranglehold
structurally
stupendously
stutteringly
subdivisible
subjectively
submissively
subsequently
subsidiarily
subsonically
subthreshold
subversively
successfully
successively
sufficiently
suggestively
superhumanly
superposable
supplicantly
suppressible
surefootedly
surmountable
surprisingly
suspensively
suspiciously
swaggeringly
swimmingbell
syllabically
symbolically
syndetically
synonymously
synoptically
systemically
tangentially
tectonically
terrifically
terrifyingly
tetragonally
Teutonically
theatrically
theistically
thematically
thermocouple
thermolabile
thermostable
thoughtfully
thousandfold
thriftlessly
thunderingly
thunderously
tintinnabula
tittletattle
topsyturvily
torrentially
tradespeople
traitorously
transferable
transfusible
transitively
transitorily
translatable
transmutable
transpirable
transposable
transversely
tremendously
trestletable
triangularly
tripartitely
triumphantly
trumpetshell
tumultuously
twitteringly
tyrannically
ubiquitously
umbrageously
unacceptable
unaffectedly
unanswerable
unappeasable
unassailable
unassumingly
unbecomingly
unbelievable
unbelievably
unblinkingly
unblushingly
unchangeable
unchangeably
uncharitable
uncharitably
uncomeatable
uncritically
unemployable
uneventfully
unexpectedly
unfaithfully
unfamiliarly
unfathomable
unfavourable
unfavourably
ungovernable
ungracefully
ungraciously
ungratefully
unilaterally
unimaginable
unimaginably
unmanageable
unmercifully
unmistakable
unmistakably
unofficially
unpleasantly
unprofitable
unprofitably
unreasonable
unreasonably
unrepeatable
unreservedly
unsearchable
unseasonable
unthinkingly
untruthfully
unyieldingly
uproariously
vanquishable
vegetatively
vernacularly
victoriously
villainously
vindictively
viviparously
vociferously
volcanically
volitionally
voluminously
voluptuously
wallydraigle
whimperingly
whippoorwill
whisperingly
worshipfully
YankeeDoodle
appendectomy
chondriosome
hysterectomy
neuroanatomy
Quadragesima
sclerenchyma
Septuagesima

stereochromy
twentyfourmo
accouchement
accoutrement
administrant
admonishment
announcement
anthropogeny
antineutrino
appraisement
astonishment
backbreaking
backslapping
ballottement
battleground
beachcombing
bedazzlement
belittlement
bellylanding
bequeathment
bewilderment
billsticking
birdsnesting
birdwatching
birefringent
blackbirding
blackcurrant
blandishment
blockbusting
bloodletting
bluestocking
bodybuilding
bodystocking
booklearning
brainwashing
brassrubbing
breathtaking
brilliantine
buccaneering
bullfighting
carburetting
cardcarrying
caterwauling
chastisement
cheeseparing
childbearing
Christophany
circumfluent
circumjacent
clairaudient
cliffhanging
cockfighting
combinations
commencement
concelebrant
concupiscent
congratulant
constringent
contrivement
convalescent
conveyancing
convincement
corespondent
counteragent
counterpoint
crashlanding
crossbedding
crosscurrent
crossexamine
crossheading
curlingirons
decipherment
decongestant
deliquescent
demimondaine
denouncement
dethronement
diminishment
disagreement
disannulling
disannulment
disbursement
discouraging
discriminant
disendowment
disgorgement
disguisement
dishevelment
disinfectant
disinterment
dislodgement
displacement
disseverment
distrainment
doubleacting
earsplitting
earthshaking
echosounding
effervescent
efflorescent
embattlement
embezzlement
embitterment
emblazonment
embranchment
empoisonment
empressement
encirclement
encroachment
encumberment
endamagement
endangerment
enfeeblement
enginetuning
enshrinement
enswathement
entanglement
enterprising
entertaining
enthronement
entrancement
entrenchment
envisagement
epiphenomena
equestrienne
estrangement
excruciating
extramundane
extrauterine
faithhealing
farmsteading
faultfinding
firefighting
forebodement
forestalment
freestanding
freeswimming
freethinking
freewheeling
fricasseeing
galligaskins
glassblowing
gravelelling
guaranteeing
habitforming
hairdressing
handicapping
hardstanding
heartburning
heartrending
heartwarming
hedgehopping
hereditament
highfaluting
highlystrung
highsounding
highstepping
hoodmanblind
horsetrading
housekeeping
housewarming
hydroquinone
illtreatment
impercipient
imprisonment
incandescent
inconsequent
inconsistent
inconvenient
indiscipline
infringement
ingratiating
insufficient
interbedding
intercurrent
intercutting
intermittent
intermitting
intermundane
intervenient
intramundane
intransigent
intrauterine
intrenchment
intromittent
intromitting
inveiglement
jurisprudent
knighterrant
laboursaving
labyrinthine
lakedwelling
languishment
leapfrogging
liquefacient
longstanding
magniloquent
maltreatment
meltingpoint
metallophone
metalworking
mezzosoprano
microcopying
misalignment
misapprehend
misdemeanant
misjudgement
misplacement
misrepresent
misstatement
mistreatment
monofilament
mosstrooping
mourningband
mourningring
mulligatawny
multiplicand
namedropping
neighbouring
nerveracking
Newfoundland
niminypiminy
nitrobenzene
noctambulant
nonalignment
noncombatant
noncomplying
nonefficient
nonflowering
nonresistant
orienteering
outrivalling
outstripping
outwardbound
overabundant
overcropping
overpowering
overstepping
oxyacetylene
palaeobotany
parallelling
peasepudding
pettifogging
photosetting
pitcherplant
placesetting
plaindealing
polyethylene
polyurethane
postponement
predetermine
preponderant
presentiment
pricecutting
privatdocent
privatdozent
privateering
prizewinning
profiteering
progesterone
proofreading
quadrivalent
quarterbound
racketeering
radioelement
rapprochment
readjustment
reassessment
reassignment
recalcitrant
recommitment
recrudescent
redeployment
reinvestment
renouncement
resettlement
retrenchment
ricochetting
safecracking
salamandrine
sandyachting
sanguinolent
sarrusophone
scareheading
schizophrene
secondstring
selfcatering
selfdoubting
selfeffacing
selfexistent
selflimiting
selfpleasing
selfrighting
selfstarting
semibasement
semideponent
shadowboxing
Shakspereana
Shaksperiana
shipbuilding
sideslipping
sidestepping
sightreading
singleacting
slaveholding
sleepwalking
smallholding
somnambulant
sorbefacient
soundingline
speedboating
stablishment
stillhunting
stockbroking
stockjobbing
stockraising
stoneboiling
stonecutting
stupefacient
subcontinent
supereminent
supermundane
supervenient
supramundane
terebinthine
testosterone
thanksgiving
theatregoing
throughstone
thunderstone
transcendent
transferring
transhipment
transmigrant
transmitting
transmontane
transpontine
typefounding
ultramontane
ultramundane
unambivalent
unappetising
unconstraint
unconvincing
underbidding
undercoating
undercurrent
undercutting
undergarment
underletting
undermanning
underpinning
underrunning
undersetting
unemployment
unflattering
unhesitating
unpretending
vanquishment
vantagepoint
ventripotent
wainscotting
waistcoating
wallpainting
weatherbound
whitewashing
winterbourne
abbreviation
acceleration
accentuation
accommodator
accumulation
adjudication
adulteration
aircondition
alimentation
alliteration
amalgamation
amelioration
amortisation
annihilation
annunciation
anticipation
antigropelos
apperception
appreciation
apprehension
appropriator
arborisation
articulation
asphyxiation
assassinator
assibilation
assimilation
augmentation

auscultation
bachelorhood
blastulation
burglarproof
cachinnation
calumniation
canalisation
cancellation
canonisation
cantillation
capitulation
chiropractor
chlorination
chocolatebox
circumcision
circumfusion
civilisation
claudication
coacervation
codification
cohabitation
collaborator
colonisation
columniation
commemorator
commendation
commentation
commiserator
communicator
compellation
compensation
complication
compurgation
concentrator
conciliation
condemnation
condensation
confabulator
confirmation
confiscation
conformation
conglobation
congregation
conquistador
conscription
consecration
conservation
consignation
consociation
consolidator
conspiration
constipation
constitution
constriction
construction
consultation
consummation
contemplator
contestation
continuation
contradictor
contribution
conversation
coordination
corroborator
counterproof
countertenor
crenellation
crosssection
cuckingstool
deactivation
debilitation
decapitation
deceleration
decompressor
decongestion
deescalation
deflagration
defraudation
degeneration
deionisation
delamination
deliberation
delimitation
demodulation
demonstrator
denaturation
denomination
denunciation
depopulation
depreciation
deputisation
deracination
desalination
desideration
despoliation
desquamation
dessertspoon
detoxication
dilapidation
disaffection
disclamation
disconnexion
disinfection
disinflation
dispensation
dispossessor
disquisition
disseminator
dissertation
dissimulator
dissociation
distillation
distribution
divarication
dodecahedron
domesticator
duckingstool
echolocation
edulcoration
effectuation
elucubration
emancipation
emargination
emasculation
encrustation
epithalamion
equalisation
equilibrator
equivocation
etherisation
etymologicon
evisceration
exacerbation
exaggeration
exasperation
excogitation
excruciation
exenteration
exercitation
exhilaration
exophthalmos
expatriation
explantation
exploitation
exprobration
exterminator
extraversion
extroversion
exulceration
facilitation
felicitation
feminisation
fenestration
fermentation
fibrillation
finalisation
flagellation
flocculation
fluidisation
fluoridation
fluorination
fluorocarbon
focalisation
fractionator
gasification
genuflection
gesticulator
gobbledegook
gobbledygook
habilitation
haematoxylon
halogenation
homologation
humanisation
humification
hypertension
hypothecator
idealisation
illumination
illustration
immoderation
immunisation
imperfection
impersonator
implantation
impregnation
impropriator
improvisator
inactivation
inauguration
incatenation
incineration
incorporator
incorruption
incrustation
indiscretion
inescutcheon
inflammation
inhabitation
inoccupation
inosculation
insemination
inspissation
installation
instauration
instillation
insufflation
insurrection
intellection
inteneration
interception
intercession
interdiction
interjection
interlocutor
intermission
interoceptor
interpolator
interrogator
interruption
intersection
intervention
intimidation
intoxication
introduction
introjection
intromission
introversion
invagination
invalidation
investigator
invigilation
invigoration
irresolution
jurisdiction
lachrymation
laterisation
latinisation
legalisation
legitimation
levorotation
liquefaction
localisation
malformation
malnutrition
malversation
manipulation
maximisation
menstruation
minedetector
minimisation
ministration
misdirection
miseducation
misquotation
mobilisation
modification
monetisation
moralisation
motorisation
nanoplankton
nebulisation
neurosurgeon
nidification
nonconductor
notification
novelisation
nychthemeron
obliteration
obnubilation
opisthotonos
optimisation
orchestrator
organisation
ossification
overexertion
overreaction
pacification
panification
pantechnicon
paralysation
participator
penalisation
perambulator
peregrinator
perfoliation
perispomenon
pernoctation
peroxidation
perpetration
perpetuation
perspiration
perturbation
petrifaction
philodendron
photofission
pigmentation
pilotballoon
polarisation
pontificator
postposition
precipitator
precognition
precondition
predigestion
predilection
preformation
premeditator
prescription
preselection
presentation
preservation
prevaricator
primogenitor
proclamation
prolegomenon
prolongation
promulgation
propitiation
proscription
prostitution
protestation
prothalamion
purification
putrefaction
quantisation
racemisation
ramification
ratification
ratiocinator
reactivation
reallocation
reciprocator
recollection
reconversion
recuperation
redecoration
refrigerator
regeneration
registration
rejuvenation
remonstrator
remuneration
renunciation
reoccupation
repatriation
repercussion
repossession
reprehension
reproduction
resupination
resurrection
resuscitator
reticulation
retractation
retrocession
retroflexion
retropulsion
retroversion
reverberator
rhododendron
rhombohedron
romanisation
ruralisation
satisfaction
scarificator
schoolfellow
scintillator
scoundreldom
scutellation
segmentation
selfdelusion
selfdevotion
selfignition
sequestrator
servocontrol
shatterproof
shootingiron
shoulderknot
snarlingiron
solarisation
solicitation
solifluction
southernwood
spermatozoon
spinsterhood
spokesperson
staffsurgeon
standingroom
stationwagon
stereopticon
sternutation
stilboestrol
stridulation

strobilation
stupefaction
subarrhation
suberisation
subscription
substitution
substruction
sulphonation
sulphuration
supersession
superstition
supervention
supplication
sustentation
swimmingpool
taxcollector
tessellation
torrefaction
totalisation
transduction
transgressor
transmission
transudation
trephination
trifurcation
tripartition
triplication
typification
underdevelop
unionisation
unlikelihood
urbanisation
valorisation
vaporisation
vasodilation
vaticination
verification
vertebration
vesiculation
vilification
vinification
vitalisation
vitiligation
vitrifaction
vituperation
vivification
vocalisation
vociferation
vomiturition
weatherproof
bronchoscope
chemotherapy
electroscope
enantiomorph
galvanoscope
heliotherapy
hydrotherapy
hypnotherapy
intussuscept
kaleidoscope
laryngoscope
laryngoscopy
magnetograph
meteorograph
opisthograph
ornithoscopy
oscillograph
oscilloscope
philanthrope
philanthropy
phraseograph
radioisotope
radiotherapy
selfcontempt
skippingrope
spectrograph
spectroscope
spectroscopy
sphygmograph
steganograph
triggerhappy
abolitionary
acciaccatura
accretionary
adjudicatory
amphitheatre
anticipatory
appreciatory
archdeaconry
architecture
articulatory
assimilatory
auscultatory
banderillero
basidiospore
biochemistry
blastosphere
bookingclerk
brambleberry
cachinnatory
calumniatory
camiknickers
campodeiform
cashandcarry
centrosphere
checkerberry
checkerboard
chequerboard
Christolatry
chromosphere
clapperboard
commendatory
compensatory
compurgatory
conciliatory
condemnatory
confirmatory
confiscatory
conidiophore
conidiospore
consecratory
conservatory
constabulary
consummatory
contemporary
contributory
cotyledonary
counterscarp
crosscountry
deambulatory
deflationary
denunciatory
depreciatory
desquamatory
disciplinary
discomfiture
discomposure
discoverture
dispensatory
distillatory
distributary
diversionary
draughtboard
drawingboard
eleemosynary
elocutionary
emasculatory
equivocatory
evolutionary
exaggeratory
exclusionary
expansionary
extortionary
extrasensory
fatherfigure
flabelliform
flagellatory
floriculture
foraminifera
geochemistry
greengrocery
groundcherry
haberdashery
headquarters
heliogravure
henceforward
hereinbefore
highpressure
hindquarters
honeybuzzard
horticulture
hydatidiform
ichthyolatry
inauguratory
inflammatory
inflationary
intercessory
interdictory
interjectory
intermediary
intermixture
intertexture
intimidatory
introductory
lachrymatory
laisserfaire
laissezfaire
levorotatory
loungelizard
magistrature
manipulatory
marketsquare
mastigophora
messeigneurs
microsurgery
misadventure
modificatory
motherfigure
nailscissors
nephelometry
neurosurgery
nomenclature
northeastern
northwestern
obedientiary
outmanoeuvre
overexposure
overpressure
pacificatory
paramilitary
penitentiary
peradventure
perspiratory
pettifoggery
photogravure
pisciculture
plasterboard
plebiscitary
poikilotherm
premaxillary
probationary
proclamatory
propitiatory
prothonotary
protohistory
provisionary
psychrometry
pteridosperm
purificatory
recessionary
reflationary
remuneratory
renunciatory
residentiary
reversionary
rhynchophora
runningboard
satisfactory
scraperboard
selfflattery
septuagenary
serpentiform
serviceberry
servicecourt
sesquialtera
sexcentenary
shuffleboard
sidewhiskers
silviculture
siphonophore
skullduggery
somatopleure
southeastern
southwestern
spectrometry
stalactiform
sternutatory
stockjobbery
stonemasonry
stratosphere
submaxillary
subminiature
substructure
superciliary
supersensory
supplicatory
sylviculture
tercentenary
testamentary
thermosphere
thimbleberry
thoroughfare
thunderstorm
toastingfork
traditionary
transudatory
tricentenary
trigonometry
usufructuary
valetudinary
vasodilatory
venepuncture
venipuncture
verificatory
vituperatory
weatherboard
whortleberry
abolitionism
abolitionist
abortiveness
abrasiveness
absoluteness
abstractness
abstruseness
accompanyist
accordionist
accurateness
accursedness
adaptiveness
adequateness
adhesiveness
adorableness
aeroembolism
aestheticism
affectedness
agribusiness
allomorphism
allusiveness
ambassadress
amenableness
amicableness
anaesthetise
anaesthetist
anathematise
anecdotalist
anotherguess
antiSemitism
apiculturist
apostolicism
apostrophise
apparentness
appositeness
aromaticness
asynchronism
attitudinise
autocatalyse
automobilist
automorphism
avantgardism
avantgardist
backwardness
baselessness
beggarliness
behaviourism
behaviourist
benefactress
bibliologist
bibliopegist
bibliopolist
bilateralism
bilingualism
bioecologist
biophysicist
bioscientist
blamableness
blamefulness
blissfulness
boastfulness
bootlessness
brackishness
buccaneerish
buffalograss
burningglass
canorousness
captiousness
cardiologist
carelessness
caricaturist
Cartesianism
cautiousness
characterise
charlatanism
charnelhouse
charterhouse
cheerfulness
chieftainess
childishness
Christianise
chromaticism
chronologise
chronologist
churlishness
clannishness
clarinettist
classicalism
classicalist
clotheshorse
clothespress
clownishness
coalitionist
cocksureness
coerciveness
cohesiveness
coleopterist
collectivise
collectivism
collectivist
collegialism
commensalism
commensalist
completeness
composedness
conchologist
concreteness
Confucianism

confusedness
conservatism
contagionist
containerise
contemporise
contrariness
contrariwise
contriteness
copolymerise
counterblast
counterpoise
covetousness
cowardliness
craniologist
creativeness
criticalness
crosspurpose
cryptanalyst
cryptologist
culpableness
cumbrousness
customshouse
debonairness
decentralise
decisiveness
decorousness
definiteness
deflationist
dejectedness
delusiveness
demilitarise
demineralise
denaturalise
denuclearise
deontologist
depoliticise
depravedness
derisiveness
desirousness
desolateness
desulphurise
detachedness
deviationism
deviationist
dextrousness
diamagnetism
diastrophism
dichromatism
dilatoriness
dilettantish
dilettantism
diphthongise
discreetness
discreteness
disembarrass
disestablish
disfranchise
disharmonise
dissocialise
distinctness
diversionist
divisiveness
dolorousness
doubtfulness
downwardness
dramaturgist
draughthorse
dreadfulness
droughtiness
dwarfishness
editorialise
editorialist
educationist
effusiveness
Egyptologist
elementalism
elocutionist
embryologist
emotionalise
emotionalism
emotionalist
enormousness
entomologise
entomologist
enviableness
enzymologist
epicureanism
eruptiveness
erythroblast
escapologist
eunuchoidism
eveningdress
evolutionism
evolutionist
exclusionism
exclusionist
excursionist
exiguousness
expansionism
expansionist
explicitness
fabulousness
facelessness
factionalism
factiousness
faintishness
faithfulness
fancifulness
fantasticism
fatherliness
fearlessness
fearsomeness
featheriness
fecklessness
feminineness
feverishness
fictionalise
fiendishness
forcefulness
forcibleness
formlessness
frankincense
freakishness
frenchpolish
frequentness
frictionless
friendliness
fruitfulness
fugitiveness
functionless
futurologist
gamesomeness
gastronomist
generousness
geomagnetism
geophysicist
ghoulishness
glaciologist
gladsomeness
gloriousness
glossologist
gorgeousness
gracefulness
graciousness
grammaticise
graphologist
graspingness
gratefulness
greenishness
grievousness
gruesomeness
guilefulness
gymnosophist
habitualness
haematoblast
handsomeness
harmlessness
headmistress
heavenliness
heedlessness
heliotropism
helplessness
hemimorphism
heortologist
heroicalness
hirepurchase
homeopathist
homesickness
homomorphism
homothallism
hopelessness
horribleness
humorousness
hydrotropism
idiosyncrasy
illusiveness
illusoriness
immatureness
immunologist
implicitness
impoliteness
incendiarism
incisiveness
indebtedness
indirectness
inexpertness
infiniteness
inflationism
inflationist
insolubilise
instructress
intrusionist
intuitionism
intuitionist
irregardless
Ishmaelitish
isolationism
isolationist
Keynesianism
kissingcrust
knightliness
laudableness
legitimatise
lexicologist
lifelessness
listlessness
literariness
lithotritist
lodginghouse
lonesomeness
lopsidedness
lovelessness
lovelornness
lukewarmness
luminousness
lusciousness
maidenliness
malacologist
malapertness
Manicheanism
manifoldness
mannerliness
mansionhouse
Marcionitism
Marseillaise
materialness
mediaevalism
mediaevalist
meetinghouse
mercantilism
mercantilist
mercifulness
mercurialise
mercurialism
metachronism
metallurgist
metamorphism
metamorphose
metasomatism
microanalyst
microscopist
mindlessness
mineralogist
mirthfulness
miscellanist
misselthrush
mistakenness
mithridatise
mithridatism
mitrailleuse
moderateness
moistureless
monographist
morningdress
morphologist
motherliness
motorcyclist
mournfulness
moveableness
movelessness
multipurpose
municipalise
musicologist
mutinousness
namelessness
nauseousness
nebulousness
necrophilism
needlessness
negativeness
negotiatress
negrophilism
negrophilist
neoDarwinism
neoDarwinist
Neohellenism
neonomianism
Neoplatonism
Neoplatonist
nephrologist
Nestorianism
nevertheless
noctambulism
noctambulist
northernmost
numerologist
numerousness
nutritionist
nyctitropism
obdurateness
obligingness
obscurantism
obscurantist
obsoleteness
oceanologist
odontologist
onesidedness
oppositeness
ordinariness
orthodontist
orthopaedist
orthopterist
orthotropism
outdatedness
overniceness
paedobaptism
painlessness
Palladianism
palynologist
panhellenism
papyrologist
paragraphist
paramorphism
parenthesise
parkinsonism
parochialise
parochialism
partitionist
patulousness
peacefulness
peerlessness
pellucidness
perilousness
periodontist
perverseness
perviousness
philistinism
phillumenist
philosophise
phlebotomise
phlebotomist
phototropism
phrenologist
physiologist
pigeonbreast
pitiableness
pitilessness
pleasantness
pleasingness
pleasureless
pleiotropism
pleomorphism
polyglottism
polymorphism
populousness
porcelainise
positiveness
postmistress
preciousness
precisianism
precisionist
preestablish
preparedness
previousness
pridefulness
priestliness
priggishness
princeliness
professoress
profoundness
progenitress
prolificness
propagandise
propagandism
propagandist
proprietress
psephologist
psychiatrist
psychologise
psychologism
psychologist
purblindness
pyrotechnist
qualmishness
questionless
ravenousness
reactiveness
readableness
receptionist
recklessness
Redemptorist
reductionism
reductionist
relativeness
reliableness
remilitarise
reproachless
reservedness
resignedness
resoluteness
resolvedness
restlessness
retiringness
ribonuclease
rightfulness

rigorousness
rootlessness
ruthlessness
salutariness
salvationism
salvationist
Samaritanism
sanguineness
scabbardfish
scabrousness
scornfulness
scorpionfish
scoundrelism
scouringrush
scratchiness
secessionism
secessionist
seclusionist
sectarianise
sectarianism
sectionalism
sedulousness
seismologist
selenologist
selfapplause
selfdistrust
selfinterest
selflessness
selfsameness
semidarkness
semifinalist
sensibleness
sensuousness
separateness
sergeantfish
shamateurism
shamefulness
sheepishness
shrewishness
skittishness
slipperiness
slothfulness
slovenliness
sluggishness
sluttishness
snappishness
snobbishness
sociableness
sociometrist
solitariness
somnambulism
somnambulist
somniloquism
somniloquist
sonorousness
soullessness
southernmost
spaciousness
sparrowgrass
specificness
speciousness
speleologist
spiritedness
spiritualise
spiritualism
spiritualist
spitefulness
splendidness
sportfulness
sportiveness
spotlessness
spuriousness
Stakhanovism
stalwartness
stationhouse
stealthiness
steeplechase
sterlingness
stockingless
straightness
strengthless
strikingness
stringcourse
strychninism
stubbornness
studiousness
subjectivise
subjectivism
subjectivist
succinctness
suitableness
swainishness
sweepingness
sweetishness
sycophantish
syndactylism
tactlessness
tamelessness
tangibleness
taskmistress
tastefulness
tearlessness
technologist
teensyweensy
telegraphese
telegraphist
teratologist
terribleness
thankfulness
therapeutist
thievishness
thoroughbass
thoroughness
ticklishness
timelessness
timorousness
tirelessness
tiresomeness
togetherness
toilsomeness
tonelessness
toploftiness
tortuousness
touchingness
towardliness
toxicologist
traditionist
traducianism
traducianist
trampolinist
tranquillise
transformism
transformist
transvestism
trichologist
trichotomise
trickishness
trinomialism
troglodytism
trustfulness
truthfulness
tunelessness
unbrokenness
uncommonness
unctuousness
ungainliness
unitarianism
universalise
universalism
universalist
unkindliness
unlawfulness
unlikeliness
unloveliness
unsteadiness
untimeliness
untowardness
unwieldiness
unwontedness
unworldiness
unworthiness
urbanologist
usuriousness
uxoriousness
valuableness
vaporousness
variableness
vengefulness
venomousness
verticalness
vibraphonist
Victorianism
vigorousness
virtuousness
vitreousness
voidableness
volatileness
voluntaryism
voluntaryist
wastefulness
watchfulness
weatherglass
weatherhouse
womanishness
wondrousness
workableness
workingclass
wrathfulness
wretchedness
wrongfulness
youthfulness
zygomorphism
absorptivity
absquatulate
actinomycete
adaptability
administrate
advisability
aerosiderite
affectionate
agranulocyte
alterability
antigenicity
aperiodicity
apostolicity
authenticate
authenticity
autoimmunity
automaticity
availability
berzelianite
billingsgate
blabbermouth
blatherskite
bletherskate
bloodthirsty
borosilicate
cabbagewhite
canaliculate
carbohydrate
centuplicate
chalcopyrite
charterparty
Christianity
chromaticity
churchianity
classicality
coelenterate
collectivity
collegiality
collinearity
commensurate
commonwealth
companionate
compulsivity
concelebrate
conductivity
conduplicate
congeniality
conglomerate
conglutinate
congratulate
connubiality
conviviality
corporeality
curvicaudate
curvicostate
curvifoliate
decaffeinate
deconsecrate
dermatophyte
desirability
dibranchiate
dilatability
disaffiliate
disambiguate
disassociate
discommodity
disconsolate
discriminate
disintegrate
disorientate
distemperate
divertimenti
divertimento
divisibility
eccentricity
ectoparasite
effectuality
electroplate
emotionality
endoparasite
ephemerality
equitability
espagnolette
essentiality
excitability
expressivity
exsanguinate
exsufflicate
extortionate
fantasticate
filtrability
flammability
frangibility
fuliginosity
granodiorite
grossularite
habitability
hairsbreadth
handsbreadth
hellgrammite
hemichordate
hemimorphite
hemiparasite
heritability
heterozygote
humptydumpty
hyperacidity
hypochlorite
hyposulphite
illegibility
illegitimate
illiberality
illogicality
immovability
immutability
impartiality
imputability
inarticulate
inaudibility
incapability
incapacitate
inconcinnity
inconformity
incoordinate
incorporeity
incurability
indelibility
indoctrinate
inelasticity
infusibility
inoperculate
insolubility
inspectorate
intermediate
interpellate
invertebrate
invisibility
irascibility
irregularity
irritability
leathercloth
malleability
matriarchate
microclimate
miscalculate
mistranslate
molecularity
monochromate
multidentate
multifoliate
multiformity
multipartite
multiplicate
multiplicity
multiversity
multungulate
municipality
navigability
oblanceolate
opposability
orbicularity
overactivity
overestimate
palatability
parochiality
patriarchate
perceptivity
perfervidity
permanganate
permeability
permittivity
perspicacity
phreatophyte
plausibility
pneumaticity
pointilliste
polytonality
posteriority
postgraduate
potentiality
practicality
predesignate
predestinate
prefabricate
prehensility
preponderate
prerequisite
presbyterate
principality
printability
proconsulate
productivity
professorate
protectorate
pseudonymity
pteridophyte
pyromorphite
quattrocento
quizzicality
recalcitrate
recapitulate
reconstitute
redintegrate

redistribute
reducibility
reflectivity
refractivity
refreshments
rehabilitate
reinvigorate
rejectamenta
removability
reticulocyte
retractility
risorgimento
saccharinity
schizomycete
scrobiculate
scrupulosity
selfactivity
selfidentity
sellingplate
semiliterate
semiparasite
sempiternity
separability
shouldernote
simultaneity
sinistrality
snaggletooth
somnambulate
sophisticate
spermatocyte
spirituality
Stakhanovite
straticulate
strontianite
subalternate
subalternity
subinfeudate
subjectivity
subnormality
substantiate
subtemperate
superannuate
supererogate
susceptivity
swimmingbath
teachability
technicality
temptability
tergiversate
tetrahedrite
tolerability
traceability
tractability
tranquillity
transitivity
transmigrate
transvestite
unconformity
unifoliolate
unisexuality
universality
unpopularity
unregenerate
venerability
veridicality
verticillate
voluminosity
voluptuosity
whimsicality
wollastonite
achlamydeous
adscititious
advantageous
adventitious
Alhambresque
altitudinous
ambidextrous
amentiferous
amphitropous
anemophilous
angiocarpous
argillaceous
asynchronous
atheromatous
brontosaurus
butterflynut
calycoideous
cantankerous
carbonaceous
carillonneur
cementitious
cinematheque
cirrocumulus
cirrostratus
coleopterous
compunctious
conchiferous
contemptuous
conterminous
contumacious
contumelious
cotyledonous
cryptogamous
cumulocirrus
cumulonimbus
cuprammonium
cynocephalus
diatomaceous
discourteous
disingenuous
disputatious
disregardful
diverticulum
duraluminium
echinococcus
electrotonus
entrepreneur
epithalamium
erythematous
exophthalmus
exsanguinous
ferrugineous
foresightful
fructiferous
fructivorous
furfuraceous
galactogogue
gallinaceous
gamopetalous
gamophyllous
gamosepalous
gastropodous
glaucomatous
graminaceous
hebetudinous
heliolatrous
heteroecious
heterogamous
heterogenous
heterologous
heteromerous
heteronomous
heterozygous
hibernaculum
hippocentaur
hippopotamus
homomorphous
hydrophilous
hygrophilous
hypogastrium
hypognathous
hypothalamus
idiothermous
impetiginous
inauspicious
incommodious
incontiguous
infelicitous
inharmonious
innutritious
insalubrious
interspinous
kilowatthour
laticiferous
latitudinous
luminiferous
macropterous
meretricious
misbehaviour
misdemeanour
monadelphous
monomorphous
monopetalous
monostichous
mothertongue
mucilaginous
multifarious
multiflorous
multiloquous
necrophagous
necrophilous
neuropterous
nimbostratus
noctambulous
obstreperous
oncorhynchus
ophiophagous
orchidaceous
orthopterous
orthotropous
ostentatious
overcautious
parsimonious
passepartout
percutaneous
periostracum
pertinacious
philadelphus
photophilous
phytophagous
plecopterous
plesiosaurus
plumbaginous
plumbiferous
polychaetous
polychromous
polymorphous
polypetalous
polysepalous
porcelainous
porcellanous
portmanteaus
portmanteaux
praseodymium
preconscious
preposterous
presumptuous
protactinium
prothalamium
pseudonymous
pseudopodium
pyroligneous
quadriennium
quadrumanous
quinquennium
rambunctious
receptaculum
resiniferous
restaurateur
rhizocarpous
rhizophagous
sacrilegious
salutiferous
saprophagous
sarcophagous
schizogonous
schorlaceous
selfluminous
seminiferous
semiprecious
silicicolous
siliciferous
simultaneous
Sinanthropus
slaughterous
soporiferous
sparkingplug
spermogonium
stanniferous
steatopygous
stelliferous
Stradivarius
subconscious
subcutaneous
succedaneous
sudoriferous
supercilious
supernaculum
superstratum
supposititious
syndactylous
technicolour
teratomatous
testudineous
thundercloud
trachomatous
trichotomous
tridactylous
unchivalrous
unscrupulous
unsuccessful
unthoughtful
vainglorious
wineglassful
xiphisternum
zygomorphous
accelerative
accumulative
adjudicative
alimentative
alliterative
amalgamative
ameliorative
annihilative
anticipative
apperceptive
appreciative
apprehensive
assimilative
augmentative
bassorelievo
bassorilievo
compensative
conciliative
confirmative
conservative
constitutive
constrictive
constructive
consultative
consummative
continuative
contributive
coordinative
decongestive
degenerative
deliberative
denominative
denunciative
desiderative
desquamative
disincentive
dissociative
distributive
exaggerative
excogitative
exhilarative
exploitative
fermentative
gramnegative
grampositive
hypertensive
illuminative
illustrative
imperceptive
imperfective
inconclusive
inexpressive
intellective
interdictive
interpretive
interruptive
intransitive
introversive
introvertive
irreflective
irrespective
irresponsive
manipulative
mezzorelievo
ministrative
nomenclative
noneffective
nonobjective
obliterative
opinionative
performative
perturbative
planoconcave
postpositive
precognitive
preformative
prescriptive
preselective
presentative
preservative
preventative
proscriptive
psychoactive
putrefactive
quantitative
recollective
recuperative
regenerative
remunerative
renunciative
repercussive
reprehensive
reproductive
retrocessive
selfelective
sternutative
stupefactive
substitutive
sustentative
transmissive
unattractive
underachieve
unresponsive
vituperative
dressinggown
brachydactyl
extravaganza

---

acciaccatura
acetabularia
ailurophobia
balletomania
chromatopsia
coloquintida
encyclopedia
epiphenomena
extravaganza
foraminifera
hesperididia

hyperpyrexia
hypersthenia
hyperthermia
hypochondria
hysteromania
ichthyocolla
kinaesthesia
mastigophora
mitochondria
neurasthenia
onomatopoeia
osteomalacia
palingenesia
paraesthesia
pedicellaria
phonasthenia
primigravida
prosopopoeia
Quadragesima
quadriplegia
rejectamenta
rhynchophora
sarsaparilla
schizothymia
sclerenchyma
Septuagesima
sesquialtera
Shakspereana
Shaksperiana
stichomythia
synaesthesia
telaesthesia
tintinnabula
toxicophobia
tradescantia
Wellingtonia
xanthochroia
absolutistic
agamogenetic
alexipharmic
alphanumeric
amphibrachic
amphictyonic
amphisbaenic
anagrammatic
analphabetic
anaphylactic
anastigmatic
anemographic
antagonistic
anthelmintic
anticyclonic
antimagnetic
antipathetic
antiperiodic
antirachitic
antistrophic
apochromatic
apothegmatic
archipelagic
aristocratic
autodidactic
bathypelagic
belletristic
bibliomaniac
bibliophilic
biosynthetic
bureaucratic
calligraphic
callisthenic
calorimetric
capitalistic
carcinogenic
cartographic
catachrestic
catastrophic
chalcolithic
chauvinistic
chiropractic
chorographic
chrematistic
chronometric
cleistogamic
colorimetric
compatriotic
cosmographic
cosmopolitic
decasyllabic
Deuteronomic
diageotropic
diagrammatic
diphtheritic
dissymmetric
dodecaphonic
dynamometric
ecclesiastic
electrolytic
electrotonic
encephalitic
encyclopedic
enthusiastic
epigrammatic
ethnocentric
ethnographic
euhemeristic
evangelistic
exophthalmic
gametophytic
gonadotropic
gyromagnetic
haemophiliac
haemorrhagic
hagiographic
hectographic
heliocentric
heliographic
henotheistic
herpetologic
heterocyclic
hieroglyphic
hierophantic
histogenetic
homeomorphic
homoeopathic
hydrochloric
hydrodynamic
hydrofluoric
hydrographic
hydrokinetic
hyperplastic
hyperpyretic
hypersthenic
hypertrophic
hypnogenetic
hypocoristic
hypothalamic
iconoclastic
IndoGermanic
interoceanic
intervocalic
intracardiac
isochromatic
isodiametric
journalistic
kinaesthetic
kleptomaniac
liberalistic
lithographic
lithospheric
lycanthropic
megalomaniac
melancholiac
melanochroic
melodramatic
meristematic
mesocephalic
mesothoracic
metagalactic
metaphrastic
metathoracic
microseismic
militaristic
misanthropic
mnemotechnic
monodramatic
monometallic
monophyletic
Monophysitic
monopolistic
monostrophic
monosyllabic
monotheistic
narcissistic
naturalistic
naturopathic
necrophiliac
negativistic
neurasthenic
nominalistic
nympholeptic
nymphomaniac
octosyllabic
oneirocritic
onomatopoeic
organoleptic
orthogenetic
orthographic
osteoplastic
paedogenetic
paedomorphic
Palaeolithic
palingenetic
panchromatic
pantographic
paradigmatic
paramagnetic
paraphrastic
parisyllabic
paronomastic
pathogenetic
periphrastic
peristeronic
peristomatic
petrographic
phagocytotic
phanerogamic
pharmaceutic
philharmonic
philhellenic
phonographic
photochromic
photographic
photokinetic
photospheric
phyllotactic
phylogenetic
physiognomic
phytogenetic
pictographic
planispheric
pluviometric
polarimetric
polyhistoric
polyneuritic
polyphyletic
polysyllabic
polytheistic
pornographic
positivistic
pragmatistic
programmatic
propaedeutic
prophylactic
protoplasmic
protoplastic
psychometric
psychopathic
psychotropic
pyroelectric
quadraphonic
quadriplegic
radiographic
relativistic
reprographic
reunionistic
revivalistic
rhinocerotic
rhizogenetic
sansculottic
scenographic
schizothymic
secularistic
seismometric
seismoscopic
semidomestic
sensualistic
specialistic
spermaphytic
stenographic
stereometric
stereophonic
stereoscopic
stethoscopic
stichomythic
stroboscopic
stylographic
subapostolic
surrealistic
synaesthetic
syncretistic
tachygraphic
technocratic
telaesthetic
tetramorphic
thaumaturgic
theanthropic
thermometric
thermophilic
thermoscopic
thermostatic
thermotactic
thermotropic
transoceanic
transpacific
trichromatic
trochanteric
tropospheric
unapologetic
undemocratic
undiplomatic
unscientific
viscerotonic
absentminded
accomplished
bachelorhood
backpedalled
battleground
battlemented
bellbottomed
bespectacled
bloodstained
bloodyminded
brokenwinded
bulletheaded
centrespread
checkerboard
chequerboard
chesterfield
clapperboard
clearsighted
closecropped
closegrained
closemouthed
complexioned
counterplead
crackbrained
crossgrained
decontrolled
denticulated
diamondfield
disconnected
discontented
dissatisfied
doubledecked
doublelocked
dovecoloured
draughtboard
drawingboard
dunderheaded
eavesdropped
entrammelled
escutcheoned
fainthearted
feebleminded
feldspathoid
floodlighted
folliculated
fountainhead
fullyfledged
ganglionated
goodhumoured
goodtempered
greathearted
halftimbered
hardfavoured
hardfeatured
heavyhearted
hemispheroid
henceforward
highcoloured
highspirited
honeybuzzard
hoodmanblind
horsewhipped
housetrained
hucklebacked
impoverished
incorporated
intercropped
interrelated
jetpropelled
lacininiated
landingfield
lanternjawed
largehearted
lighthearted
loungelizard
machicolated
malcontented
mealymouthed
misapprehend
mourningband
muddleheaded
multiplicand
multistoried
muttonheaded
narrowminded
newfashioned
Newfoundland
oldfashioned
orthopteroid
outstretched
outwardbound
pedunculated
pickerelweed
pinfeathered
plainclothed
plasterboard
playingfield
poorspirited
precancelled
premeditated
pretermitted
proportioned
proudhearted

quarterbound
rattleheaded
revictualled
rosecoloured
runningboard
sabretoothed
saddlebacked
salamandroid
scraperboard
selfabsorbed
selfaffected
selfcoloured
selfcomposed
selfdeceived
selfdirected
selfeducated
selfemployed
selfinvolved
semidetached
semifinished
sharpsighted
shortpitched
shortsighted
shortsleeved
shortstaffed
shuffleboard
simpleminded
singlehanded
singleminded
softpedalled
southernwood
spermatozoid
spinsterhood
squarerigged
standardbred
starspangled
stonyhearted
stouthearted
straightbred
stranglehold
strongminded
subsaturated
subthreshold
sulphuretted
thickskinned
thickskulled
thoroughbred
thousandfold
thundercloud
tightmouthed
timehonoured
transshipped
tuberculated
turriculated
turtlenecked
unaccustomed
unauthorised
uncalculated
uncelebrated
unclassified
unconsidered
uncontrolled
underinsured
understaffed
undetermined
unencumbered
unfrequented
uninterested
unlikelihood
unparalleled
unprejudiced
unprincipled
unpronounced
unrecognised
unrestrained
unsegregated
unstructured
varicoloured
vermiculated
weatherboard
weatherbound
welldisposed
wellfavoured
wellgrounded
whitelivered
wholehearted
woodenheaded
woollyheaded
absquatulate
abstractable
acaulescence
accelerative
accumulative
acetaldehyde
acquaintance
acquiescence
actinomycete
adjudicative
administrate
aerosiderite
affectionate
agranulocyte
Alhambresque
alimentative
alkalescence
alliterative
amalgamative
ameliorative
amphitheatre
anaesthetise
anathematise
annihilative
anticipative
antiparticle
apostrophise
apperceptive
appreciative
apprehensive
approachable
appropriable
appurtenance
arborescence
architecture
assimilative
attitudinise
attributable
augmentative
authenticate
autocatalyse
basidiospore
belligerence
benzaldehyde
berzelianite
bibliothecae
billingsgate
blastfurnace
blastosphere
blatherskite
bletherskate
boogiewoogie
borosilicate
breaststroke
brilliantine
bronchoscope
businesslike
cabbagewhite
calorescence
canaliculate
capercaillie
capercailzie
carbohydrate
carriageable
centrosphere
centuplicate
chalcopyrite
characterise
charnelhouse
charterhouse
chimneypiece
chondriosome
Christianise
chromosphere
chronologise
cinematheque
circumscribe
circumstance
clairvoyance
classifiable
clotheshorse
coelenterate
collectivise
commensurate
communicable
companionate
compensative
complaisance
compoundable
compressible
concelebrate
conciliative
concomitance
concrescence
conduplicate
confirmative
conglomerate
conglutinate
congratulate
conidiophore
conidiospore
conscionable
consentience
conservative
considerable
constitutive
constrictive
constructive
consultative
consummative
containerise
contemporise
contemptible
continuative
contractable
contractible
contrariwise
contributive
controllable
coordinative
copolymerise
correctitude
counterforce
counterpoise
countrydance
crossexamine
crosspurpose
cultivatable
curvicaudate
curvicostate
curvifoliate
customshouse
decaffeinate
decalescence
decasyllable
decentralise
decipherable
decomposable
decongestive
deconsecrate
degenerative
deliberative
delitescence
demilitarise
demimondaine
demineralise
demonstrable
denaturalise
denominative
denuclearise
denunciative
depoliticise
dermatophyte
desiderative
desquamative
destructible
desulphurise
determinable
detumescence
dibranchiate
differentiae
diminishable
diphthongise
disaccharide
disadvantage
disaffiliate
disagreeable
disallowance
disambiguate
disassociate
discerptible
discomfiture
discomposure
disconsolate
discountable
discoverable
discoverture
discriminate
disfranchise
disharmonise
disincentive
disintegrate
disobedience
disorientate
displaceable
disreputable
disseverance
dissocialise
dissociative
distemperate
distrainable
distributive
draughthorse
ectoparasite
editorialise
electroplate
electroscope
emotionalise
emulsifiable
endoparasite
entomologise
equestrienne
equidistance
equipollence
equiprobable
espagnolette
exaggerative
exchangeable
excogitative
exhilarative
exploitative
exsanguinate
exsufflicate
exterminable
extortionate
extraditable
extramundane
extrauterine
extravagance
falcongentle
fantasticate
fatherfigure
fermentative
fertilisable
fictionalise
fiddlefaddle
floriculture
fluorescence
formaldehyde
frankincense
frontispiece
galactogogue
galvanoscope
Germanophile
Germanophobe
glaucescence
grammaticise
grammolecule
gramnegative
grampositive
granodiorite
grossularite
grotesquerie
happenstance
harlequinade
heliogravure
hellgrammite
hemichordate
hemimorphite
hemiparasite
hereinbefore
heterozygote
highpressure
hirepurchase
horticulture
hubblebubble
hybridisable
hydrolysable
hydromedusae
hydroquinone
hypertensive
hypnotisable
hypochlorite
hyposulphite
identifiable
illegitimate
illuminative
illustrative
immeasurable
immensurable
impenetrable
imperceptive
imperfective
imperishable
impermanence
impertinence
imponderable
improvidence
inaccessible
inadmissible
inadvertence
inappeasable
inapplicable
inarticulate
incalculable
incalescence
incapacitate
incognisable
incognisance
incognitable
incommutable
incomparable
incompatible
incompetence
incompliance
incomputable
inconclusive
inconsolable
inconsonance
inconsumable
incontinence
incoordinate
incorrigible
indeclinable
indefeasible
indefectible
indefensible

indehiscence magnetisable perturbative remonstrance supramundane
independence magnificence philanthrope remunerative surmountable
indifference maintainable philosophise renegotiable surveillance
indigestible manipulative phlebotomise renunciative sustentative
indiscipline manoeuvrable phosphoresce repercussive sylviculture
indisputable mansionhouse photogravure reprehensive telegraphese
indissoluble marketsquare photomontage reproachable terebinthine
indivertible marlinespike phreatophyte reproducible tergiversate
indoctrinate marriageable pisciculture reproductive testosterone
ineffaceable Marseillaise planoconcave resipiscence tetrahedrite
ineradicable masterstroke plenipotence resplendence thermocouple
inexactitude matriarchate pointilliste restrainable thermolabile
inexpedience meetinghouse polyethylene reticulocyte thermosphere
inexperience merchantable polysyllable retrocedence thermostable
inexplicable mercurialise polyurethane retrocessive thoroughfare
inexpressive metalanguage porcelainise reviviscence throughstone
inexpugnable metallophone postgraduate ribonuclease thunderstone
inextensible metamorphose postpositive rumbletumble tittletattle
inextricable microcapsule precipitable salamandrine tradespeople
inhospitable microclimate precipitance saponifiable tranquillise
inobservance ministrative precognitive sarrusophone transferable
inoperculate misadventure predesignate schizomycete transference
insolubilise miscalculate predestinate schizophrene transfusible
inspectorate misknowledge predetermine scrobiculate transhumance
insufferable mispronounce predominance sectarianise translatable
intellective mistranslate preexistence selfapplause translucence
intelligence mithridatise prefabricate selfelective transmigrate
intelligible mitrailleuse preformative selfevidence transmissive
intemperance monkeypuzzle preponderate selfreliance transmontane
interdictive monochromate prerequisite selfviolence transmutable
interference monosyllable presbyterate sellingplate transpirable
intermediate motherfigure prescriptive semiliterate transpontine
interminable mothertongue preselective semiparasite transposable
intermixture mountainside presentative shouldernote transvestite
intermundane multidentate preservative significance trestletable
interpellate multifoliate preventative silverglance trichotomise
interpretive multipartite proconsulate silviculture ultramontane
interruptive multipliable professorate siphonophore ultramundane
interservice multiplicate progesterone siphonostele unacceptable
intertexture multipurpose programmable skippingrope unanswerable
interwreathe multivalence propagandise skunkcabbage unappeasable
intramundane multungulate proscriptive slipcarriage unassailable
intransitive municipalise prosecutable somatopleure unattractive
intrauterine neuroscience protectorate somnambulate unbelievable
introversive nicotinamide protuberance sophisticate unchangeable
introvertive nitrobenzene psychoactive soundingline uncharitable
intumescence noctilucence psychologise speakingtube uncomeatable
invertebrate nomenclative pteridophyte spectroscope underachieve
invulnerable nomenclature pterodactyle spermatocyte undersurface
irredeemable noneffective pulverisable spiritualise unemployable
irreflective nonexistence putrefactive squirrelcage unfathomable
irreformable nonflammable pyromorphite Stakhanovite unfavourable
irrefragable nonobjective quantifiable stationhouse ungovernable
irremediable nonresidence quantitative steeplechase unifoliolate
irremissible oblanceolate questionable sternutative unimaginable
irrepealable obliterative quintessence straightedge unimportance
irreprovable obmutescence radioisotope straticulate universalise
irresistible obsolescence radionuclide stratosphere unmanageable
irresolvable octosyllable razzledazzle stringcourse unmistakable
irrespective omnipresence reappearance strontianite unprofitable
irrespirable opinionative recalcitrate stupefactive unreasonable
irresponsive oscilloscope recalescence subalternate unregenerate
irreversible outmanoeuvre recapitulate subcommittee unrepeatable
juvenescence overestimate rechargeable subdivisible unresponsive
kaleidoscope overexposure recognisable subinfeudate unsearchable
labyrinthine overpersuade recognisance subjectivise unseasonable
laisserfaire overpressure recollective subminiature vanquishable
laissezfaire oxyacetylene reconcilable subservience venepuncture
landingstage paletteknife reconstitute substantiate venipuncture
lanternslide parasiticide reconveyance substitutive verticillate
laryngoscope parenthesise recuperative substructure viridescence
ledgertackle parochialise redintegrate subtemperate vituperative
legitimatise patriarchate redistribute sulphonamide walkietalkie
liverystable pearlescence regenerative superannuate wallydraigle
lodginghouse pennywhistle rehabilitate supererogate weatherhouse
longdistance peradventure reinvigorate supermundane whigmaleerie
luminescence performative rememberable superposable winterbourne
mademoiselle permanganate remilitarise supersedence wollastonite
magistrature perseverance reminiscence suppressible YankeeDoodle

burglarproof
counterproof
handkerchief
quarterstaff
shatterproof
weatherproof
backbreaking
backslapping
beachcombing
bellylanding
billsticking
birdsnesting
birdwatching
blackbirding
blockbusting
bloodletting
bluestocking
bodybuilding
bodystocking
booklearning
brainwashing
brassrubbing
breathtaking
buccaneering
bullfighting
carburetting
cardcarrying
caterwauling
cheeseparing
childbearing
cliffhanging
cockfighting
conveyancing
crashlanding
crossbedding
crossheading
disannulling
discouraging
doubleacting
earsplitting
earthshaking
echosounding
enginetuning
enterprising
entertaining
excruciating
faithhealing
farmsteading
faultfinding
firefighting
freestanding
freeswimming
freethinking
freewheeling
fricasseeing
glassblowing
gravelelling
guaranteeing
habitforming
hairdressing
handicapping
hardstanding
heartburning
heartrending
heartwarming
hedgehopping
highfaluting
highlystrung
highsounding
highstepping
horsetrading
housekeeping
housewarming
ingratiating
interbedding
intercutting
intermitting
intromitting
laboursaving
lakedwelling
leapfrogging
longstanding
metalworking
microcopying
mosstrooping
mourningring
namedropping
neighbouring
nerveracking
noncomplying
nonflowering
orienteering
outrivalling
outstripping
overcropping
overpowering
overstepping
parallelling
peasepudding
pettifogging
photosetting
placesetting
plaindealing
pricecutting
privateering
prizewinning
profiteering
proofreading
racketeering
ricochetting
safecracking
sandyachting
scareheading
secondstring
selfcatering
selfdoubting
selfeffacing
selflimiting
selfpleasing
selfrighting
selfstarting
shadowboxing
shipbuilding
sideslipping
sidestepping
sightreading
singleacting
slaveholding
sleepwalking
smallholding
sparkingplug
speedboating
stillhunting
stockbroking
stockjobbing
stockraising
stoneboiling
stonecutting
thanksgiving
theatregoing
transferring
transmitting
typefounding
unappetising
unconvincing
underbidding
undercoating
undercutting
underletting
undermanning
underpinning
underrunning
undersetting
unflattering
unhesitating
unpretending
wainscotting
waistcoating
wallpainting
whitewashing
blabbermouth
breakthrough
buccaneerish
butterscotch
commonwealth
countermarch
dilettantish
disestablish
elasmobranch
enantiomorph
frenchpolish
hairsbreadth
handsbreadth
Ishmaelitish
leathercloth
magnetograph
masterswitch
meteorograph
misselthrush
monkeywrench
opisthograph
oscillograph
phraseograph
Plattdeutsch
preestablish
scabbardfish
scorpionfish
scouringrush
selfreproach
sergeantfish
snaggletooth
spectrograph
sphygmograph
steganograph
stellenbosch
swimmingbath
sycophantish
thirdborough
toggleswitch
wherethrough
apparatchiki
caravansarai
caravanserai
divertimenti
plectognathi
streptococci
bladderwrack
bookingclerk
countercheck
crossbuttock
Czechoslovak
electroshock
gobbledegook
gobbledygook
horrorstruck
kinnikinnick
planetstruck
plummerblock
rollingstock
swaggerstick
swizzlestick
terrorstruck
toastingfork
wonderstruck
absorptional
accusatorial
aeronautical
aetiological
agentgeneral
agricultural
alphabetical
alphamerical
amygdaloidal
anteprandial
anthropoidal
anticlerical
antimalarial
antithetical
apparitional
appositional
aquicultural
archetypical
arithmetical
arrhythmical
astrological
astronomical
asymmetrical
bactericidal
barometrical
bicentennial
biographical
bombdisposal
brachydactyl
cartological
catechetical
chorological
coenobitical
coenobytical
coincidental
commissarial
complemental
complexional
conceptional
conferential
confessional
confidential
conjunctival
connectional
consistorial
contrapuntal
convectional
conventional
correctional
cosmogonical
cosmological
courtmartial
cuckingstool
curvirostral
dentilingual
departmental
derivational
diamonddrill
differential
digressional
discretional
disregardful
distortional
dodecahedral
dorsiventral
duckingstool
emblematical
endoskeletal
epexegetical
epicycloidal
ethnological
etymological
exospherical
expediential
experiential
experimental
expressional
extracranial
extralimital
extramarital
extraspecial
falcongentil
foresightful
geanticlinal
genealogical
geographical
geopolitical
geosynclinal
gladiatorial
glockenspiel
governmental
grallatorial
hagiological
heroicomical
heterocercal
heterosexual
hierarchical
histological
hydrological
hydrothermal
hyperbolical
hypocritical
hypostatical
hypothetical
immethodical
impedimental
imperatorial
inartificial
infanticidal
inflectional
insecticidal
inspectorial
instrumental
integumental
intellectual
interdigital
interfemoral
interglacial
internuncial
interstitial
intracranial
involutional
judgematical
limnological
linguistical
lithological
longitudinal
majorgeneral
mangelwurzel
manometrical
mathematical
metaphorical
metaphysical
metathetical
metrological
microcrystal
monomaniacal
motivational
multicentral
multilateral
multilingual
mythological
navigational
necrological
neoclassical
neurological
noncommittal
nonessential
nonidentical
nychthemeral
occupational
oligarchical
oppositional
orographical
osteological
overcritical
paraboloidal
paradisaical
paradisiacal
parametrical
paratactical
pathological
pestilential
pestological
petrological
phenological
phenotypical
philological
phonological
phycological
phytological

planetesimal
pluriliteral
postdoctoral
postprandial
precedential
preceptorial
precessional
preclassical
prefectorial
preferential
premenstrual
presbyterial
presidential
primogenital
procathedral
processional
professional
professorial
projectional
proportional
prosectorial
prototypical
providential
psychosexual
pumpernickel
punchingball
pyromaniacal
quadrinomial
quaquaversal
quarterfinal
quinquennial
radiological
recreational
reflectional
repetitional
responsorial
revelational
rhinological
rhombohedral
saccharoidal
salutational
scatological
schismatical
selfapproval
selfbetrayal
selfcritical
semiofficial
semiological
semitropical
septilateral
Septuagintal
sericultural
servocontrol
sinistrorsal
sleepingpill
sociological
spermathecal
squirreltail
stilboestrol
studdingsail
subcelestial
subeditorial
substantival
successional
supernatural
supplemental
supraorbital
swimmingbell
swimmingpool
synchronical
systematical
tautological
teleological
televisional
tetrachordal
theocratical
theosophical
tragicomical
transitional
triglyphical
triphthongal
tropological
trumpetshell
tyrannicidal
uncommercial
uneconomical
unhistorical
unscriptural
unsuccessful
unthoughtful
vicargeneral
visitational
visitatorial
volumetrical
whippoorwill
wineglassful
abolitionism
aeroembolism
aestheticism
allomorphism
antiSemitism
apostolicism
asynchronism
automorphism
avantgardism
behaviourism
bilateralism
bilingualism
campodeiform
Cartesianism
charlatanism
chromaticism
chromatogram
classicalism
collectivism
collegialism
commensalism
Confucianism
conservatism
counterclaim
cuprammonium
deviationism
diamagnetism
diastrophism
dichromatism
dilettantism
diverticulum
duraluminium
elementalism
emotionalism
epicureanism
epithalamium
eunuchoidism
evolutionism
exclusionism
expansionism
factionalism
fantasticism
flabelliform
geomagnetism
heliotropism
hemimorphism
hibernaculum
homomorphism
homothallism
hydatidiform
hydrotropism
hypogastrium
incendiarism
inflationism
intuitionism
isolationism
Keynesianism
Manicheanism
Marcionitism
mediaevalism
mercantilism
mercurialism
metachronism
metamorphism
metasomatism
mithridatism
necrophilism
negrophilism
neoDarwinism
Neohellenism
neonomianism
Neoplatonism
Nestorianism
noctambulism
nyctitropism
obscurantism
orthotropism
paedobaptism
Palladianism
panhellenism
paramorphism
parkinsonism
parochialism
periostracum
philistinism
phototropism
pleiotropism
pleomorphism
poikilotherm
polyglottism
polymorphism
praseodymium
precisianism
propagandism
protactinium
prothalamium
pseudopodium
psychologism
pteridosperm
quadriennium
quinquennium
receptaculum
reductionism
rontgenogram
salvationism
Samaritanism
scoundreldom
scoundrelism
secessionism
sectarianism
sectionalism
serpentiform
shamateurism
somnambulism
somniloquism
spermogonium
spiritualism
Stakhanovism
stalactiform
standingroom
strychninism
subjectivism
supernaculum
superstratum
syndactylism
thunderstorm
traducianism
transformism
transvestism
trinomialism
troglodytism
unitarianism
universalism
Victorianism
voluntaryism
xiphisternum
zygomorphism
abbreviation
acceleration
accentuation
accumulation
adjudication
adulteration
aesthetician
AfroAmerican
agglutinogen
aircondition
aircraftsman
alimentation
alliteration
amalgamation
amelioration
amortisation
annihilation
annunciation
antediluvian
anticipation
apperception
appreciation
apprehension
arborisation
archdiocesan
Aristotelean
Aristotelian
articulation
artilleryman
asphyxiation
assibilation
assimilation
augmentation
auscultation
Australasian
bacchanalian
backwoodsman
biometrician
blastulation
buttermuslin
Byelorussian
cachinnation
calumniation
canalisation
cancellation
canonisation
Cantabrigian
cantharidian
cantillation
capitulation
Carlovingian
carragheenin
catamountain
catilinarian
chlorination
churchwarden
circumcision
circumfusion
civilisation
claudication
coacervation
codification
cohabitation
colonisation
columniation
commendation
commentation
committeeman
compellation
compensation
complication
compurgation
conciliation
condemnation
condensation
confirmation
confiscation
conformation
conglobation
congregation
conscription
consecration
conservation
consignation
consociation
conspiration
constipation
constitution
constriction
construction
consultation
consummation
contestation
continuation
contribution
conversation
coordination
cosmopolitan
councilwoman
countrywoman
cousingerman
crenellation
crosssection
deactivation
debilitation
decapitation
deceleration
decongestion
deescalation
deflagration
defraudation
degeneration
deionisation
delamination
deliberation
delicatessen
delimitation
demodulation
denaturation
denomination
denunciation
depopulation
depreciation
deputisation
deracination
desalination
desideration
despoliation
desquamation
dessertspoon
detoxication
dialectician
dilapidation
disaffection
disclamation
disconnexion
disinfection
disinflation
dispensation
disquisition
dissertation
dissociation
distillation
distribution
divarication
dodecahedron
dressinggown
echolocation
edulcoration
effectuation
elucubration
emancipation
emargination
emasculation
encrustation
Englishwoman
episcopalian
epithalamion
equalisation
equalitarian
equivocation
erythromycin

etherisation
etymologicon
EuroAmerican
evisceration
exacerbation
exaggeration
exasperation
excogitation
excruciation
exenteration
exercitation
exhilaration
expatriation
explantation
exploitation
exprobration
extraversion
extroversion
exulceration
facilitation
featherbrain
felicitation
feminisation
fenestration
fermentation
fibrillation
fibrinolysin
finalisation
flagellation
flavoprotein
flocculation
fluidisation
fluoridation
fluorination
fluorocarbon
focalisation
footplateman
FrancoGerman
frontiersman
futilitarian
gasification
genuflection
geometrician
geriatrician
glycoprotein
gonadotropin
griseofulvin
habilitation
haematoxylon
hallucinogen
halogenation
halterbroken
homologation
humanisation
humanitarian
humification
hydromedusan
hymenopteran
hypertension
hypophrygian
idealisation
illumination
illustration
immoderation
immunisation
imperfection
implantation
impregnation
inactivation
inauguration
incatenation
incineration
incorruption
incrustation
indiscretion
IndoEuropean
inescutcheon
inflammation
inhabitation

inoccupation
inosculation
insemination
inspissation
installation
instauration
instillation
insufflation
insurrection
intellection
inteneration
interception
intercession
interdiction
interjection
intermission
interruption
intersection
intervention
intimidation
intoxication
introduction
introjection
intromission
introversion
invagination
invalidation
invigilation
invigoration
irresolution
jurisdiction
kindergarten
labyrinthian
lachrymation
laterisation
latinisation
legalisation
legitimation
lepidopteran
levorotation
liquefaction
Liverpudlian
localisation
longshoreman
LowChurchman
malformation
malnutrition
malversation
manipulation
marketgarden
maximisation
menstruation
metropolitan
minimisation
ministration
misdirection
miseducation
misquotation
mobilisation
modification
monetisation
moralisation
motorisation
nanoplankton
nebulisation
neoDarwinian
neurosurgeon
newspaperman
nidification
nonagenarian
noneuclidean
noradrenalin
northeastern
Northumbrian
northwestern
notification
novelisation
nychthemeron
obliteration

obnubilation
obstetrician
octogenarian
optimisation
organisation
ossification
overexertion
overreaction
pacification
panification
pantechnicon
paralysation
penalisation
perfoliation
perispomenon
pernoctation
peroxidation
perpetration
perpetuation
perspiration
perturbation
petrifaction
philodendron
photofission
pigmentation
pilotballoon
polarisation
postdiluvian
postmeridian
postposition
prechristian
precognition
precondition
predigestion
predilection
preformation
prehistorian
prelapsarian
Presbyterian
prescription
preselection
presentation
preservation
priestridden
proboscidean
proboscidian
proclamation
prolegomenon
prolongation
promulgation
propitiation
proscription
prostitution
protestation
prothalamion
purification
putrefaction
quantisation
racemisation
ramification
ratification
reactivation
reallocation
recollection
reconversion
recuperation
redecoration
regeneration
registration
rejuvenation
remuneration
renunciation
reoccupation
repatriation
repercussion
repossession
reprehension
reproduction
resupination

resurrection
reticulation
retractation
retrocession
retroflexion
retropulsion
retroversion
rhododendron
rhombohedron
romanisation
ruralisation
salamandrian
satisfaction
Scandinavian
scatterbrain
scutellation
segmentation
selfbegotten
selfdelusion
selfdevotion
selfignition
servicewoman
sexagenarian
shootingiron
snarlingiron
sodafountain
solarisation
solicitation
solifluction
southeastern
southwestern
spermatozoon
spiegeleisen
spokesperson
staffsurgeon
stationwagon
statistician
stepchildren
stereopticon
sternutation
streptomycin
stridulation
strobilation
strophanthin
stupefaction
subarrhation
suberisation
sublapsarian
subscription
substitution
substruction
subterranean
sulphonation
sulphuration
supersession
superstition
supervention
supplication
sustentation
tessellation
theoretician
torrefaction
Torricellian
totalisation
totalitarian
transduction
transmission
transudation
trephination
trifurcation
tripartition
triplication
turbellarian
typification
ubiquitarian
underwritten
unionisation
urbanisation
valorisation

vaporisation
vasodilation
vaticination
verification
vertebration
vesiculation
veterinarian
vicechairman
vilification
vinification
vitalisation
vitiligation
vitrifaction
vituperation
vivification
vocabularian
vocalisation
vociferation
vomiturition
warehouseman
antineutrino
banderillero
bassorelievo
bassorilievo
clavicembalo
divertimento
mezzorelievo
mezzosoprano
quattrocento
risorgimento
twentyfourmo
attorneyship
bachelorship
brinkmanship
cardinalship
chairmanship
championship
chaplainship
counterscarp
dictatorship
directorship
discipleship
executorship
gamesmanship
governorship
guardianship
horsemanship
landingstrip
laureateship
marksmanship
mistressship
musicianship
oneupmanship
overlordship
partisanship
prenticeship
quaestorship
receivership
relationship
residentship
salesmanship
sergeantship
serjeantship
servitorship
surveyorship
survivorship
taberdarship
underdevelop
virtuosoship
viscountship
watermanship
accommodator
antimacassar
appendicular
appropriator
assassinator
balladmonger
bloodbrother
bobbydazzler

bodysnatcher
bonnyclabber
bottlewasher
boulevardier
brainstormer
brassbounder
breastsummer
breathalyser
breechloader
brickfielder
broncobuster
cabinetmaker
calligrapher
campfollower
candleholder
carillonneur
carpetbagger
cartographer
cattlelifter
cheeseburger
cheesecutter
cheesemonger
chiropractor
coachbuilder
coldshoulder
collaborator
commemorator
commiserator
commissioner
communicator
concentrator
confabulator
confectioner
conningtower
conquistador
consolidator
contemplator
contradictor
conventicler
corroborator
cosmographer
costermonger
countenancer
countertenor
courtplaster
craftbrother
crossbencher
crossingover
crystalgazer
cuckooflower
declinometer
decompressor
demonstrator
densitometer
discographer
disenchanter
dispossessor
disseminator
dissimulator
diverticular
domesticator
doubledealer
doubledecker
drawingpaper
eavesdropper
electrometer
electrotyper
encumbrancer
enginedriver
entrepreneur
equilibrator
ethnographer
exhibitioner
experimenter
extensometer
exterminator
extinguisher
filibusterer
firstnighter
flamethrower
fostermother
foundationer
fractionator
freightliner
frontbencher
galvanometer
gesticulator
globetrotter
guestchamber
hagiographer
hairsplitter
harquebusier
headshrinker
heliographer
hierographer
hippocentaur
holidaymaker
horsebreaker
housebreaker
huggermugger
hydrographer
hymnographer
hypothecator
iconographer
impersonator
impropriator
improvisator
inclinometer
incorporator
infundibular
interchanger
interlobular
interlocutor
intermeddler
internuclear
interoceptor
interpleader
interpolator
interrogator
interstellar
investigator
jerrybuilder
katzenjammer
kilowatthour
kirschwasser
klipspringer
laissezaller
lithographer
magnetometer
manslaughter
manufacturer
marshharrier
mastersinger
micrographer
milliammeter
minedetector
minicomputer
misbehaviour
misdemeanour
moneychanger
moneygrubber
moneyspinner
monkeyflower
morrisdancer
mouthbreeder
multinuclear
muzzleloader
mythographer
mythologiser
necrographer
nephelometer
nonconductor
nonconformer
officeholder
orchestrator
organgrinder
orthographer
outpensioner
overachiever
participator
pasqueflower
patternmaker
pennypincher
perambulator
peregrinator
petrographer
phonographer
photographer
phrasemonger
phytographer
pitterpatter
policyholder
pontificator
pornographer
practitioner
pralltriller
precipitator
premeditator
prevaricator
primogenitor
prizefighter
proselytiser
psychrometer
quadrangular
rabblerouser
radiographer
ratiocinator
reciprocator
redemptioner
refrigerator
remembrancer
remonstrator
restaurateur
resuscitator
reverberator
salmonladder
scarificator
scenepainter
sceneshifter
schoolleaver
schoolmaster
scintillator
screenwriter
scrimshanker
scriptwriter
sedgewarbler
selfdeceiver
selfmurderer
semicircular
semicylinder
semidiameter
sensitometer
sequestrator
sharecropper
sharpshooter
sheepshearer
shirtwaister
shortchanger
singledecker
singleseater
skateboarder
skrimshanker
sledgehammer
snakecharmer
snapfastener
specktioneer
spectrometer
staffofficer
stagemanager
stenographer
stepdaughter
stereoisomer
sternwheeler
stockbreeder
stonedresser
stormtrooper
straightener
streetwalker
strengthener
supercharger
supplementer
surrejoinder
swashbuckler
synchroniser
systematiser
tabernacular
tachygrapher
taperecorder
taxcollector
technicolour
teetertotter
thereinafter
threequarter
threewheeler
trainspotter
transgressor
transplanter
troublemaker
vauntcourier
viscosimeter
whencesoever
wicketkeeper
winklepicker
wonderworker
woodengraver
woolgatherer
wunderkinder
yellowhammer
abortiveness
abrasiveness
absoluteness
abstractness
abstruseness
accurateness
accursedness
achlamydeous
adaptiveness
adequateness
adhesiveness
adorableness
adscititious
advantageous
adventitious
aerodynamics
aeroneurosis
affectedness
agamogenesis
agribusiness
allusiveness
altitudinous
ambassadress
ambidextrous
amenableness
amentiferous
amicableness
amphitropous
anaerobiosis
anamorphosis
anemophilous
angiocarpous
anotherguess
antigropelos
apparatchiks
apparentness
appendicitis
appositeness
argillaceous
aromaticness
astronautics
astrophysics
asynchronous
atheromatous
atmospherics
autochthones
avitaminoses
avitaminosis
backwardness
baselessness
beggarliness
benefactress
bilharziasis
bilharziosis
biosynthesis
blamableness
blamefulness
blissfulness
boastfulness
bootlessness
bowcompasses
brackishness
brontosaurus
buffalograss
burningglass
calisthenics
calycoideous
camiknickers
canorousness
cantankerous
captiousness
carbonaceous
carelessness
cataphoresis
cautiousness
cementitious
cheerfulness
chieftainess
childishness
chitterlings
churlishness
cirrocumulus
cirrostratus
clannishness
clothespress
clownishness
cocksureness
coerciveness
cohesiveness
coleopterous
collywobbles
combinations
completeness
composedness
compunctious
conchiferous
concreteness
confusedness
contemptuous
conterminous
contrariness
contriteness
contumacious
contumelious
cotyledonous
covetousness
cowardliness
creativeness
criticalness
cryptogamous
culpableness
cumbrousness
cumulocirrus
cumulonimbus
curlingirons
curlingtongs
cynocephalus
cytogenetics
debonairness
decisiveness
decorousness
definiteness
dejectedness
delusiveness
depravedness
derisiveness
desirousness

desolateness
detachedness
dextrousness
diatomaceous
dilatoriness
discourteous
discreetness
discreteness
disembarrass
disingenuous
disputatious
distinctness
divisiveness
dolorousness
doubtfulness
downwardness
dreadfulness
droughtiness
dwarfishness
echinococcus
econometrics
effusiveness
electrolysis
electrotonus
encephalitis
endocarditis
endometritis
enormousness
enviableness
eruptiveness
erythematous
eveningdress
exiguousness
exophthalmos
exophthalmus
explicitness
exsanguinous
fabulousness
facelessness
factiousness
faintishness
faithfulness
fancifulness
fatherliness
fearlessness
fearsomeness
featheriness
fecklessness
feminineness
ferrugineous
feverishness
fiddlesticks
fieldglasses
fiendishness
forcefulness
forcibleness
formlessness
freakishness
frequentness
frictionless
friendliness
fructiferous
fructivorous
fruitfulness
fugitiveness
functionless
furfuraceous
furunculosis
galligaskins
gallinaceous
gamesomeness
gamopetalous
gamophyllous
gamosepalous
gastropodous
generousness
geotectonics
ghoulishness
gladsomeness
glaucomatous
gloriousness
glycogenesis
goosepimples
gorgeousness
gracefulness
graciousness
graminaceous
graspingness
gratefulness
graveclothes
greenishness
grievousness
gruesomeness
guilefulness
habitualness
haematolysis
haemopoiesis
hallucinosis
handsomeness
harmlessness
headmistress
headquarters
heartstrings
heavenliness
hebetudinous
heedlessness
heliolatrous
helplessness
hemerocallis
hermeneutics
heroicalness
heteroecious
heterogamous
heterogenous
heterologous
heteromerous
heteronomous
heterozygous
hindquarters
hippopotamus
histogenesis
homesickness
homoeostasis
homomorphous
hopelessness
horribleness
humorousness
hydrophilous
hydrostatics
hygrophilous
hypnogenesis
hypognathous
hypothalamus
idiothermous
illusiveness
illusoriness
immatureness
impetiginous
implicitness
impoliteness
inauspicious
incisiveness
incommodious
incontiguous
indebtedness
indirectness
inexpertness
infelicitous
infiniteness
inharmonious
innutritious
insalubrious
instructress
interspinous
irregardless
karyokinesis
kinaesthesis
knightliness
laticiferous
latitudinous
laudableness
leucocytosis
leukocytosis
lifelessness
listlessness
literariness
lonesomeness
lopsidedness
lovelessness
lovelornness
lukewarmness
luminiferous
luminousness
lusciousness
macropterous
maidenliness
maidenstakes
malapertness
manifoldness
mannerliness
materialness
mercifulness
meretricious
messeigneurs
metapsychics
microphysics
mindlessness
mirthfulness
mistakenness
moderateness
moistureless
monadelphous
monomorphous
monopetalous
monostichous
morningdress
morphallaxis
motherliness
mournfulness
moveableness
movelessness
mucilaginous
multifarious
multiflorous
multiloquous
mutinousness
nailscissors
namelessness
nauseousness
nebulousness
necrophagous
necrophilous
needlessness
negativeness
negotiatress
nephanalysis
neuropterous
nevertheless
nightclothes
nimbostratus
noctambulous
numerousness
obdurateness
obligingness
obsoleteness
obstreperous
offscourings
oncorhynchus
onesidedness
ophiophagous
opisthotonos
oppositeness
orchidaceous
ordinariness
orthodontics
orthogenesis
orthopaedics
orthopterous
orthotropous
ostentatious
osteogenesis
osteoporosis
outdatedness
overcautious
overemphasis
overniceness
paedogenesis
painlessness
palingenesis
pancreatitis
parsimonious
pathogenesis
patulousness
peacefulness
peccadilloes
peerlessness
pellucidness
percutaneous
pericarditis
perilousness
periodontics
pertinacious
perverseness
perviousness
phagocytosis
philadelphus
photokinesis
photophilous
phycomycetes
phylogenesis
phytogenesis
phytophagous
pitiableness
pitilessness
plainclothes
pleasantness
pleasingness
pleasureless
plecopterous
plesiosaurus
plumbaginous
plumbiferous
polychaetous
polychromous
polymorphous
polyneuritis
polypetalous
polysepalous
populousness
porcelainous
porcellanous
portmanteaus
positiveness
postmistress
preciousness
preconscious
preparedness
preposterous
presumptuous
previousness
pridefulness
priestliness
priggishness
princeliness
professoress
profoundness
progenitress
proglottides
prolificness
proprietress
pseudocyesis
pseudonymous
purblindness
pursestrings
pyroligneous
pyrotechnics
quadrumanous
qualmishness
questionless
radiophonics
rambunctious
ravenousness
reactiveness
readableness
recklessness
refreshments
relativeness
reliableness
reproachless
reservedness
resignedness
resiniferous
resoluteness
resolvedness
restlessness
retiringness
rhizocarpous
rhizophagous
rightfulness
rigorousness
rootlessness
ruthlessness
sacrilegious
salpiglossis
salutariness
salutiferous
sanguineness
saprophagous
sarcomatosis
sarcophagous
scabrousness
schizogonous
schorlaceous
scornfulness
scratchiness
sedulousness
selfanalysis
selfhypnosis
selflessness
selfluminous
selfsameness
semidarkness
seminiferous
semiprecious
sensibleness
sensuousness
separateness
shamefulness
sheepishness
shrewishness
sidewhiskers
silicicolous
siliciferous
simultaneous
Sinanthropus
skittishness
slaughterous
slipperiness
slothfulness
slovenliness
sluggishness
sluttishness
smallclothes
snappishness
snobbishness
sociableness
solitariness
sonorousness
soporiferous
soullessness
spaciousness
sparrowgrass
specificness
speciousness
sphragistics

spiritedness
spitefulness
splendidness
sporogenesis
sportfulness
sportiveness
spotlessness
spuriousness
stalwartness
stanniferous
stealthiness
steatopygous
stelliferous
sterlingness
stockingless
Stradivarius
straightness
strengthless
strikingness
strongylosis
stubbornness
studiousness
subconscious
subcutaneous
succedaneous
succinctness
sudoriferous
suitableness
supercilious
supposititious
surroundings
swainishness
sweepingness
sweetishness
synarthrosis
syndactylous
tactlessness
tamelessness
tangibleness
taskmistress
tastefulness
tearlessness
teratomatous
terribleness
testudineous
thankfulness
therapeutics
thievishness
thitherwards
thoroughbass
thoroughness
ticklishness
timelessness
timorousness
tirelessness
tiresomeness
togetherness
toilsomeness
tonelessness
toploftiness
tortuousness
touchingness
towardliness
trachomatous
trichotomous
trickishness
tridactylous
trophallaxis
trustfulness
truthfulness
tuberculosis
tunelessness
unbrokenness
unchivalrous
uncommonness
unctuousness
underclothes
ungainliness
unkindliness
unlawfulness
unlikeliness
unloveliness
unscrupulous
unsteadiness
untimeliness
untowardness
unwieldiness
unwontedness
unworldiness
unworthiness
usuriousness
uxoriousness
vainglorious
Valenciennes
valuableness
vaporousness
variableness
vengefulness
venomousness
verticalness
vigorousness
virtuousness
vitreousness
voidableness
volatileness
wastefulness
watchfulness
weatherglass
whitherwards
womanishness
wondrousness
workableness
workingclass
wrathfulness
wretchedness
wrongfulness
youngberries
youthfulness
zygapophysis
zygomorphous
abolitionist
accompanyist
accordionist
accouchement
accoutrement
administrant
admonishment
aforethought
afterthought
anaesthetist
anecdotalist
announcement
antiaircraft
apiculturist
appraisement
astonishment
automobilist
avantgardist
bacteriostat
ballottement
bantamweight
bedazzlement
behaviourist
belittlement
bequeathment
bewilderment
bibliologist
bibliopegist
bibliopolist
bioecologist
biophysicist
bioscientist
birefringent
blackcurrant
blandishment
butterflynut
cardiologist
caricaturist
carpetknight
chastisement
chronologist
circumfluent
circumjacent
clairaudient
clarinettist
classicalist
clinkerbuilt
coalitionist
coleopterist
collectivist
commencement
commensalist
commissariat
concelebrant
conchologist
concupiscent
congratulant
constringent
contagionist
contrivement
convalescent
convincement
corespondent
counteragent
counterblast
counterlight
counterpoint
countershaft
craniologist
crosscurrent
cryptanalyst
cryptologist
decipherment
decongestant
deflationist
deliquescent
denouncement
deontologist
dethronement
deviationist
diminishment
dinnerjacket
disagreement
disannulment
disbursement
discriminant
disendowment
disgorgement
disguisement
dishevelment
disinfectant
disinterment
dislodgement
displacement
disseverment
distrainment
diversionist
dramaturgist
editorialist
educationist
effervescent
efflorescent
Egyptologist
electronvolt
elocutionist
embattlement
embezzlement
embitterment
emblazonment
embranchment
embryologist
emotionalist
empoisonment
empressement
encirclement
encroachment
encumberment
endamagement
endangerment
enfeeblement
enshrinement
enswathement
entanglement
enthronement
entomologist
entrancement
entrenchment
envisagement
enzymologist
erythroblast
escapologist
estrangement
evolutionist
exclusionist
excursionist
expansionist
forebodement
forestalment
futurologist
gastronomist
geophysicist
gesellschaft
glaciologist
glossologist
graphologist
gymnosophist
haematoblast
heortologist
hereditament
homeopathist
illtreatment
immunologist
impercipient
imprisonment
incandescent
inconsequent
inconsistent
inconvenient
inflationist
infringement
insufficient
interconnect
intercurrent
intermittent
intervenient
intransigent
intrenchment
intromittent
intrusionist
intuitionist
intussuscept
inveiglement
isolationist
jurisconsult
jurisprudent
kissingcrust
knighterrant
landingcraft
languishment
lexicologist
licketysplit
liquefacient
lithotritist
lumberjacket
magniloquent
malacologist
maltreatment
mediaevalist
meltingpoint
mercantilist
merrythought
metallurgist
microanalyst
microcircuit
microscopist
middleweight
mineralogist
misalignment
miscellanist
misdemeanant
misinterpret
misjudgement
misplacement
misrepresent
misstatement
mistreatment
monkeyjacket
monofilament
monographist
morphologist
motorcyclist
musicologist
negrophilist
neoDarwinist
Neoplatonist
nephrologist
noctambulant
noctambulist
nonalignment
noncombatant
nonefficient
nonresistant
northernmost
numerologist
nutritionist
obscurantist
oceanologist
odontologist
orthodontist
orthopaedist
orthopterist
overabundant
palynologist
papyrologist
paragraphist
partitionist
passepartout
passionfruit
periodontist
phillumenist
phlebotomist
phrenologist
physiologist
pigeonbreast
pitcherplant
postponement
precisionist
preponderant
presentiment
privatdocent
privatdozent
propagandist
psephologist
psychiatrist
psychologist
publicspirit
purposebuilt
pyrotechnist
quadrivalent
radioelement
rapprochment
readjustment
reassessment
reassignment
recalcitrant
receptionist
recommitment
recrudescent
Redemptorist
redeployment
reductionist
reinvestment
renouncement
resettlement
retrenchment

salvationist
sanguinolent
secessionist
seclusionist
seismologist
selenologist
selfcontempt
selfdestruct
selfdistrust
selfexistent
selfinterest
selfportrait
semibasement
semideponent
semifinalist
servicecourt
shortcircuit
shoulderbelt
shoulderknot
sociometrist
somnambulant
somnambulist
somniloquist
sorbefacient
southernmost
speleologist
spiritualist
stablishment
straitjacket
stupefacient
subcontinent
subjectivist
supereminent
supervenient
technologist
telegraphist
teratologist
therapeutist
toxicologist
traditionist
traducianist
trampolinist
transcendent
transformist
transhipment
transmigrant
trichologist
unambivalent
unconstraint
undercurrent
undergarment
unemployment
universalist
urbanologist
vanquishment
vantagepoint
ventripotent
vibraphonist
voluntaryist
welterweight
williewaught
windingsheet
schoolfellow
chocolatebox
pneumothorax
portmanteaux
abolitionary
aboriginally
absorptivity
abstemiously
abstractedly
academically
accidentally
accretionary
accusatively
acoustically
acronychally
adaptability
additionally
adjectivally
adjudicatory
adulterously
advisability
aggressively
alterability
amateurishly
ambivalently
amitotically
amphibiously
anagogically
analogically
analytically
anatomically
antecedently
anthropogeny
anthropology
anticipatory
antigenicity
antiphonally
aperiodicity
apolitically
apostolicity
appendectomy
appetisingly
appraisingly
appreciatory
archdeaconry
archetypally
aromatically
articulately
articulatory
artificially
artistically
assimilatory
astoundingly
astringently
athletically
attractively
auscultatory
auspiciously
authenticity
autoimmunity
automaticity
autonomously
availability
avariciously
bacteriology
barbarically
beatifically
belligerency
beneficently
beneficially
benevolently
beseechingly
bewilderedly
bewitchingly
bibliography
biochemistry
biocoenology
biogeography
biologically
blackguardly
blisteringly
blithesomely
bloodthirsty
blunderingly
blusteringly
boisterously
bonnetmonkey
brambleberry
breathlessly
bullheadedly
cachinnatory
calamitously
calcareously
calculatedly
calumniatory
calumniously
capriciously
cardiography
cashandcarry
catholically
censoriously
centesimally
ceremonially
chancemedley
charterparty
checkerberry
cheirography
chemotherapy
cherubically
chivalrously
choreography
chrestomathy
Christianity
Christolatry
Christophany
chromaticity
chromatology
chronography
churchianity
circuitously
clangorously
classicality
clatteringly
coetaneously
coincidently
collaterally
collectively
collectivity
collegiality
collegiately
collinearity
colloquially
colourlessly
comfortingly
commandingly
commendatory
commercially
commodiously
communicably
companionway
compensatory
complacently
compulsively
compulsivity
compulsorily
compurgatory
conceptually
conciliatory
conclusively
concordantly
concubitancy
concurrently
condemnatory
conductivity
confirmatory
confiscatory
confoundedly
congeniality
congenitally
connaturally
connectively
connubiality
consecratory
consensually
consentingly
consequently
conservatory
considerably
consistently
constabulary
constituency
consummately
consummatory
contagiously
contemporary
contemptibly
contextually
contiguously
contingently
continuously
contractedly
contributory
conveniently
convincingly
conviviality
convulsively
coordinately
copulatively
coquettishly
corelatively
corporeality
correctively
cosmetically
cottonocracy
cotyledonary
courageously
creepycrawly
crosscountry
cryptography
cumbersomely
cumulatively
curmudgeonly
deambulatory
decoratively
decreasingly
definitively
deflationary
degenerately
deliberately
delightfully
delinquently
demoniacally
demonstrably
denunciatory
depreciatory
depressingly
derivatively
derogatorily
desirability
despairingly
despitefully
despondently
despotically
desquamatory
determinably
determinedly
diabolically
dialectology
diaphanously
diathermancy
diatonically
didactically
dietetically
digressively
dilatability
diminutively
disagreeably
disastrously
discerningly
disciplinary
discommodity
discordantly
discursively
disdainfully
disgustfully
disgustingly
disjointedly
dispensatory
dispiritedly
displeasedly
disreputably
dissentingly
dissimilarly
dissuasively
distillatory
distractedly
distributary
disturbingly
diversionary
divisibility
dogmatically
domestically
dramatically
dubitatively
dynastically
eccentricity
ecclesiology
eclectically
ecologically
economically
ecstatically
effectuality
effeminately
effortlessly
electrically
eleemosynary
elementarily
elliptically
elocutionary
emasculatory
emotionality
emphatically
enchantingly
enclitically
endermically
entreatingly
ephemerality
epidemically
epidemiology
episodically
epistemology
equationally
equipollency
equitability
equivalently
equivocatory
esoterically
essentiality
euphonically
euphoniously
evanescently
evidentially
evolutionary
exaggeratory
excitability
exclusionary
exegetically
exhaustively
exorbitantly
exoterically
expansionary
expressively
expressivity
extortionary
extraneously
extrasensory
extravagancy
factitiously
fallaciously
farsightedly
fastidiously
felicitously
fictitiously
figuratively
filtrability
flagellatory
flagitiously
flamboyantly
flammability
flatteringly
flickeringly
forbiddingly
forebodingly

forensically
forthrightly
fortuitously
fractionally
frangibility
fraudulently
frenetically
fuliginosity
functionally
galvanically
geochemistry
geologically
gerontocracy
gigantically
glitteringly
glossography
gluttonously
glyphography
glyptography
gratifyingly
gratuitously
greengrocery
gregariously
groundcherry
groundlessly
grovellingly
gynaecocracy
haberdashery
habitability
harmonically
harmoniously
heathenishly
hebdomadally
heliotherapy
heraldically
hereditarily
heritability
hermetically
hesitatingly
heterophylly
highhandedly
historically
homonymously
homosexually
horizontally
horrendously
horrifically
humptydumpty
hydrotherapy
hygienically
hyperacidity
hypnotherapy
hypnotically
hysterectomy
hysterically
ichthyolatry
ichthyophagy
ideationally
idiosyncrasy
idolatrously
illadvisedly
illegibility
illegitimacy
illiberality
illiterately
illnaturedly
illogicality
immaculately
immaterially
immeasurably
immemorially
immoderately
immovability
immutability
impartiality
impenetrably
impenitently
imperatively
imperishably
impermanency
impersonally
impertinency
imperviously
imponderably
impressively
imputability
imputatively
inaccessibly
inaccurately
inadequately
inadmissibly
inadvertency
inapplicably
inappositely
inaudibility
inauguratory
incalculably
incapability
incautiously
incestuously
incidentally
incoherently
incommutably
incomparably
incompatibly
incompetency
incompletely
inconcinnity
inconformity
inconsolably
inconstantly
inconsumably
incontinency
incorporeity
incorrigibly
increasingly
incurability
indecisively
indecorously
indefeasibly
indefensibly
indefinitely
indelibility
indelicately
independency
indicatively
indifferency
indigenously
indiscreetly
indisputably
indissolubly
indistinctly
indivertibly
individually
industrially
ineffaceably
inefficiency
inelasticity
ineradicably
inexpediency
inexplicably
inexpugnably
inextricably
infectiously
infinitively
inflammatory
inflationary
infrequently
infusibility
ingloriously
inhospitably
iniquitously
inordinately
insolubility
insufferably
intelligibly
intercessory
interdictory
interestedly
interjectory
intermediacy
intermediary
interminably
intimidatory
intolerantly
intriguingly
introductory
inveterately
invisibility
invulnerably
irascibility
irrationally
irredeemably
irrefragably
irregularity
irrelatively
irrelevantly
irremediably
irresistibly
irresolutely
irreverently
irreversibly
irritability
irritatingly
isochronally
isothermally
jesuitically
kremlinology
lachrymatory
lachrymosely
landlubberly
languorously
laryngoscopy
lasciviously
lefthandedly
legitimately
levorotatory
lexicography
libidinously
licentiously
liturgically
liturgiology
logistically
longwindedly
loquaciously
lugubriously
macrocephaly
magnetically
magnifically
majestically
malevolently
malleability
manipulatory
marvellously
meaningfully
mechanically
meditatively
mendaciously
meridionally
metallically
meteorically
methodically
meticulously
microbiology
microcephaly
microsurgery
millesimally
miraculously
modificatory
molecularity
monastically
monitorially
monopodially
monotonously
monumentally
mordaciously
mulligatawny
multiformity
multiplicity
multiversity
municipality
munificently
myrmecophily
mysteriously
mystifyingly
narcotically
nauseatingly
navigability
neglectfully
nephelometry
neuroanatomy
neurobiology
neurosurgery
neurotically
niminypiminy
nonchalantly
nutritiously
obedientiary
obligatorily
obsequiously
occasionally
occidentally
oceanography
omnipotently
omnisciently
omnivorously
openhandedly
openmindedly
operatically
opposability
oppressively
orbicularity
organography
ornamentally
ornithomancy
ornithoscopy
otherworldly
outlandishly
outrageously
overactivity
oversimplify
pacificatory
palaeobotany
palaeography
palatability
pantisocracy
paramilitary
paranormally
parasitology
parochiality
particularly
passionately
pathetically
pedantically
pejoratively
penitentiary
perceptively
perceptivity
perceptually
percussively
peremptorily
perfectively
perfervidity
perfidiously
periodically
peripherally
perjuriously
permeability
permissively
permittivity
perniciously
perplexingly
persistently
perspicacity
perspiratory
persuasively
pettifoggery
pharmacology
phenomenally
philanthropy
phonemically
phonetically
photogeology
physiography
platonically
plausibility
plebiscitary
pneumaticity
pneumatology
polarography
polytonality
pontifically
portentously
possessively
posteriority
posthumously
potentiality
practicality
praiseworthy
precariously
precipitancy
preclusively
precociously
predictively
predominancy
preeminently
prehensility
premaxillary
preoccupancy
prevailingly
preventively
primordially
principality
printability
probationary
proclamatory
prodigiously
productively
productivity
proficiently
profligately
projectively
prolifically
pronominally
pronouncedly
propitiatory
propitiously
prosodically
prosperously
protectively
protensively
prothonotary
protistology
protohistory
protozoology
protrusively
proverbially
provincially
provisionary
prudentially
pseudonymity
psychography
psychrometry
puerperrally
pugnaciously
purificatory
purposefully
questionably
quixotically
quizzicality
rabbinically
radiobiology
radiotherapy
reassuringly
rebelliously

recessionary
reciprocally
recognisably
reducibility
reflationary
reflectively
reflectivity
refractivity
refractorily
refreshingly
regardlessly
regimentally
regressively
relationally
relentlessly
remorsefully
removability
remuneratory
renunciatory
repetitively
repressively
residentiary
resistlessly
resoundingly
respectfully
respectively
resplendency
responsively
restrainedly
restrictedly
reticulately
retractility
revengefully
reversionary
rhetorically
rheumatology
rhythmically
ridiculously
robustiously
romantically
rontgenology
ruminatively
saccharinity
sacerdotally
sadistically
salubriously
sanguinarily
sardonically
satisfactory
satisfyingly
scandalously
scatteringly
scintigraphy
scripturally
scrupulosity
scrupulously
sculpturally
scurrilously
seismography
selenography
selfactivity
selfflattery
selfidentity
semantically
semiannually
sempiternity
sententially
separability
septennially
septuagenary
sepulchrally
sequaciously
sequentially
seraphically
serpentinely
serviceberry
sexcentenary
shamefacedly
shillyshally
significancy
simoniacally
simultaneity
sinistrality
sinusoidally
skullduggery
slanderously
Socratically
solicitously
specifically
spectrometry
spectroscopy
speechlessly
spheroidally
spidermonkey
spiritlessly
spirituality
sporadically
sprightfully
squattocracy
staggeringly
stammeringly
statuesquely
stereochromy
stereography
sternutatory
stertorously
stockjobbery
stonemasonry
straightaway
stratigraphy
structurally
stupendously
stutteringly
subalternity
subjectively
subjectivity
submaxillary
submissively
subnormality
subsequently
subserviency
subsidiarily
subsonically
subversively
successfully
successively
sufficiently
suggestively
superciliary
superhighway
superhumanly
supersensory
supplicantly
supplicatory
surefootedly
surprisingly
susceptivity
suspensively
suspiciously
swaggeringly
syllabically
symbolically
syndetically
synonymously
synoptically
systemically
tangentially
teachability
technicality
tectonically
teensyweensy
temptability
tercentenary
terrifically
terrifyingly
testamentary
tetragonally
Teutonically
theatrically
theistically
thematically
thermography
thimbleberry
thoughtfully
thriftlessly
thunderingly
thunderously
tolerability
topsyturvily
torrentially
traceability
tractability
traditionary
traitorously
tranquillity
transiliency
transitively
transitivity
transitorily
translucency
transmogrify
transparency
transudatory
transversely
tremendously
triangularly
tricentenary
triggerhappy
trigonometry
tripartitely
triumphantly
tumultuously
twitteringly
tyrannically
ubiquitously
umbrageously
unaffectedly
unassumingly
unbecomingly
unbelievably
unblinkingly
unblushingly
unchangeably
uncharitably
unconformity
uncritically
undertenancy
uneventfully
unexpectedly
unfaithfully
unfamiliarly
unfavourably
ungracefully
ungraciously
ungratefully
unilaterally
unimaginably
unisexuality
universality
unmercifully
unmistakably
unofficially
unpleasantly
unpopularity
unprofitably
unreasonably
unreservedly
unthinkingly
untruthfully
unyieldingly
uproariously
usufructuary
valetudinary
vasodilatory
vegetatively
venerability
veridicality
verificatory
vernacularly
victoriously
villainously
vindictively
vituperatory
viviparously
vociferously
volcanically
volitionally
voluminosity
voluminously
voluptuosity
voluptuously
whimperingly
whimsicality
whisperingly
whortleberry
worshipfully
zoogeography

13 letter words

abiologically
abortifacient
absorbability
abstractional
accelerometer
acceptability
accessibility
accidentalism
accidentprone
acclimatation
accommodating
accommodation
accommodative
accompaniment
accoutrements
accreditation
acculturation
acculturative
acetification
acetylcholine
achromaticity
acidification
acotyledonous
acquiescently
acquiescingly
acrimoniously
acrobatically
acrylonitrile
actinomorphic
actinomycetes
actinomycosis
actualisation
adiabatically
admeasurement
administrable
administrator
admirableness
admissibility
admonishingly
adventuresome
adventurously
adversatively
advertisement
advisableness
aerodynamical
aesthetically
affectionless
affenpinscher
affirmatively
afforestation
affreightment
aggiornamento
agglomeration
agglomerative
agglutination
agglutinative
aggravatingly
agonistically
agreeableness
agriculturist
aircraftwoman
airworthiness
alcoholically
alcoholometer
alcoholometry
algebraically
allegorically
allelomorphic
alternatively
aluminiferous
aluminisation
ambassadorial
ambidexterity
ambidexterous
ambiguousness
ambitiousness
amniocentesis
amorphousness
amphiprostyle
amplification
anachronistic
anachronously
anaerobically
anagrammatise
anagrammatism
analogousness
anaphrodisiac
anfractuosity
angiospermous
anglicisation
AngloAmerican
AngloCatholic
animadversion
animalisation
annexationist
anomalistical
anomalousness
anonymousness
answerability
anthelminthic

anthropogenic autocatalytic brotherliness circumvallate conceptualism
anthropometry autocephalous brutalisation circumvention conceptualist
anthropopathy autochthonism bumptiousness clairaudience concertmaster
anthropophagi autochthonous bureaucratise clandestinely concessionary
anthropophagy autoeroticism burglariously clarification conchological
anthroposophy automatically businesswoman clearheadedly concomitantly
Antichristian autonomically butterfingers clearinghouse concretionary
anticlimactic availableness butterflyfish cleistogamous concupiscence
anticlockwise axiomatically buttonthrough climactically concupiscible
anticoagulant baccalaureate cabinetmaking climatologist condescension
antihistamine backformation cacographical climbingframe conditionally
antilogarithm backpedalling calcification closedcircuit conduciveness
antinomianism backscratcher calculatingly clothesbasket conductorship
antipersonnel backwardation calligraphist coagulability condylomatous
antiscorbutic bacteriolysis callisthenics coarsegrained confabulation
apathetically bacteriolytic Calvinistical cobelligerent confabulatory
apheliotropic bacteriophage campanologist coeducational confectionary
apocalyptical balkanisation camphoraceous coenaesthesis confectionery
appellatively balsamiferous canaliculated coldbloodedly confederation
applicability BaltoSlavonic candlelighter coldheartedly confederative
applicatively bamboozlement candlesnuffer collaboration confessionary
apportionment barbarisation cannibalistic collaborative confidingness
apprehensible barbarousness capaciousness collaterality configuration
appropriately barefacedness caprification colleagueship conflagration
appropriation barrelchested carboniferous collectedness conflictingly
appropriative basidiomycete carbonisation collectorship confraternity
approximately bathymetrical carcinomatous colliesshangie confrontation
approximation battlecruiser cardiographer colloquialism conglomeratic
approximative beatification carnivorously colourfulness congratulator
arbitrariness beauteousness cartilaginous combativeness congressional
arbitrational beleaguerment catechisation combinatorial congresswoman
arboriculture belleslettres categorically commandership congruousness
archaeologist belligerently cauterisation commemoration conjecturable
archaeopteryx beneficiation centreforward commemorative conjecturally
archbishopric Berkeleianism centrifugally commemoratory conjugateness
archdeaconate betweenwhiles centripetally commensurable conjugational
archidiaconal bewilderingly cephalothorax commensurably conjunctional
archimandrite bibliographer cerebrospinal commercialise conjunctively
architectonic bibliographic ceremonialism commercialism connaturality
architectural bibliolatrist ceremonialist commercialist connectedness
argentiferous bibliolatrous ceremoniously commiseration consanguinity
argumentation bibliological certification commiserative conscientious
argumentative bibliophilism certificatory communication consciousness
arithmetician bibliophilist chalcoography communicative consecutively
aromatisation bildungsroman challengeable communicatory consenescence
arthritically biodegradable challengingly communisation consentaneity
artificiality bioenergetics changeability communitarian consentaneous
ascertainable biogeographer changefulness commutability consequential
ascertainment biotechnology characterless compagination conservatoire
assassination birefringence chateaubriand companionable considerately
assertiveness blackguardism cheerlessness companionably consideration
asserveration blameableness chemoreceptor companionless consolidation
assiduousness blamelessness chieftainship companionship consolidative
associateship blanketflower chinkerinchee comparability consolidatory
associativity blasphemously chlamydomonas comparatively conspicuously
Assyriologist blastogenesis chlamydospore compartmental constellation
asthenosphere bloodboltered choreographer compassionate constellatory
asthmatically bloodcurdling choreographic compatibility consternation
astonishingly bloodlessness chrematistics compendiously constrainable
astronautical bloodrelation Christmastide competitively constrainedly
astrophysical Bloomsburyite Christmastime complainingly constructable
atheistically boardinghouse chromatically complaisantly constructible
atlantosaurus bombastically chromatograph complementary consumptively
atmospherical bookingoffice chromatolytic complexedness containership
atomistically bouillabaisse chromatophore complicatedly contamination
atrociousness boundlessness chromospheric complimentary contaminative
attainability bounteousness chronographic compositeness contemplation
attentiveness bountifulness chronological compositional contemplative
attributively boustrophedon chrysanthemum comprehension contentedness
auctioneering brachycephaly chuckleheaded comprehensive contentiously
audaciousness brachydactyly churchmanship compressional continentally
Australianism brachypterous cicatrisation computational contortionist
authentically brainlessness cinematically concatenation contrabandist
authenticator brainstorming cinematograph concavoconvex contrabassoon
authorisation breechloading cinquecentist conceitedness contraception
authoritarian brilliantness circumambient concentration contraceptive
authoritative broadmindedly circumference concentrative contractility
autobiography broadspectrum circumfluence concentricity contractually
autocatalysis brokenhearted circumspectly conceptualise contradiction

contradictory
contrafagotto
contrapuntist
contrariously
contravention
controversial
convalescence
conventionary
conversazione
conversazioni
convertiplane
convexoconvex
convocational
convulsionary
cooperatively
copartnership
coreligionist
cornification
corporativism
correlatively
correlativity
correspondent
corresponsive
corrigibility
corroboration
corroborative
corroboratory
corrosiveness
corruptionist
corticotropic
corticotropin
cosmopolitise
cosmopolitism
costeffective
cottonpicking
counteraction
counteractive
counterattack
counterchange
countercharge
counterfeiter
counterstroke
counterweight
countinghouse
courteousness
courtsmartial
crackerbarrel
craftsmanship
craniological
credulousness
criminalistic
criminologist
crosscultural
crossgartered
crosshatching
crosspurposes
crossquestion
cruiserweight
cryobiologist
cryptanalysis
cryptanalytic
cryptographer
cryptographic
cryptological
crystalgazing
crystallinity
curvilinearly
customariness
cyberneticist
cylindrically
cytochemistry
daguerreotype
dangerousness
dastardliness
dauntlessness
deathlessness
deceitfulness
deceptiveness
decerebration
deciduousness
declaratively
decomposition
decompression
decontaminate
decontrolling
decortication
decrepitation
deductibility
defeasibility
defectiveness
defencelessly
defensibility
deferentially
defervescence
defibrination
deforestation
deformational
degranulation
deipnosophist
deleteriously
deliciousness
deliquescence
deliriousness
dematerialise
demonstration
demonstrative
demythologise
denationalise
dendritically
denticulation
deodorisation
deontological
dependability
depersonalise
deprecatingly
derequisition
derestriction
dermatologist
descriptively
desegregation
desirableness
desperateness
destructively
destructivity
desultoriness
deterioration
deteriorative
determinately
determination
determinative
deterministic
detrimentally
deuteragonist
Deuteronomist
devastatingly
developmental
devolutionary
devolutionist
dexterousness
diageotropism
diagnostician
diagrammatise
dialectically
diametrically
diaphragmatic
diathermanous
dichlamydeous
dichotomously
dictatorially
differentiate
diffusiveness
digestibility
dimensionally
dimensionless
disadvantaged
disaffectedly
disaffirmance
disappearance
disarticulate
disciplinable
discoloration
discommodious
disconcerting
disconcertion
disconformity
disconnection
discontinuity
discontinuous
discreditable
discreditably
discretionary
discriminator
disembodiment
disengagement
disfigurement
disgracefully
disharmonious
dishonourable
dishonourably
disintegrator
disinterested
disinvestment
disjunctively
dismantlement
dismemberment
disobediently
disparagement
disparagingly
disparateness
dispassionate
displantation
disposability
dispossession
dispraisingly
disproportion
disrespectful
dissemblingly
dissemination
disseminative
disseveration
dissimilarity
dissimilation
dissimilitude
dissimulation
dissolubility
dissoluteness
dissymetrical
distastefully
distinctively
distinguished
distressfully
distressingly
distributable
distrustfully
divertisement
doctrinairism
documentalist
documentation
dodecaphonist
domestication
domiciliation
doublecrosser
doubledealing
doubleglazing
doublejointed
doubletongued
doubtlessness
draftsmanship
draggletailed
dramatisation
dramaturgical
dreamlessness
dressimprover
dressingtable
dulcification
dysfunctional
eavesdropping
eccentrically
ecumenicalism
educationally
effectiveness
effervescence
effervescency
efficaciously
efflorescence
egocentricity
egregiousness
elaborateness
electioneerer
electrocution
electrologist
electromagnet
electrometric
electromotive
electrophorus
electroscopic
electrostatic
electrovalent
elephantiasis
embarrassment
embellishment
embranglement
embrittlement
embryogenesis
embryological
emphysematous
encapsulation
encephalogram
encompassment
encouragement
encouragingly
encyclopaedia
encyclopaedic
encyclopedism
encyclopedist
endocrinology
energetically
enigmatically
enjoyableness
enlightenment
entertainment
entomological
entomophagous
entomophilous
entomostracan
environmental
epeirogenesis
epigrammatise
epigrammatist
epiphenomenal
epiphenomenon
equestrianism
equidistantly
equilibration
equiponderant
equiponderate
equipotential
equivocalness
erroneousness
eschatologist
eschscholtzia
essentialness
establishment
ethnocentrism
Eucharistical
evangelically
everlastingly
evocativeness
examinational
examinatorial
exanthematous
exasperatedly
exceptionable
exceptionably
exceptionally
excessiveness
excitableness
exclusiveness
excommunicate
excrescential
excursiveness
excusableness
exemplariness
exhibitionism
exhibitionist
existentially
expansibility
expansiveness
expectoration
expeditionary
expeditiously
expensiveness
explanatorily
explorational
explosiveness
exponentially
expostulation
expostulatory
expressionism
expressionist
expropriation
expurgatorial
exquisiteness
extemporarily
extensibility
extensionally
extensiveness
extermination
exterminatory
exteroceptive
exterritorial
extracellular
extragalactic
extrajudicial
extraordinary
extraphysical
extrapolation
extratropical
extravagantly
extravasation
extravascular
extrinsically
facetiousness
facultatively
faithlessness
falsification
fantastically
fasciculation
fascinatingly
Fascistically
faultlessness
featherheaded
featherstitch
featherweight
felicitations
feloniousness
ferociousness
ferrimagnetic
ferroconcrete
ferroelectric
ferromagnetic
fertilisation
festschriften
feudalisation
feuilletonism
feuilletonist
fibrovascular
filterability
fissiparously
flagellantism
flirtatiously
floricultural
floristically
flourishingly
followthrough

foolhardiness
foraminiferal
foreknowledge
forementioned
foresightedly
forgetfulness
formalisation
formidability
formulisation
fortification
fortissississimo
fortunateness
fortunehunter
fortuneteller
fossiliferous
fossilisation
fractionalise
fractionation
fractiousness
fragmentarily
fragmentation
freeselection
frequentation
frequentative
frighteningly
frightfulness
frivolousness
frontogenesis
fruitlessness
frustratingly
fullfashioned
funambulation
functionalism
functionalist
fundamentally
galactosaemia
galvanisation
gametogenesis
garnetiferous
garrulousness
gasteropodous
gastrocnemius
gastroenteric
gastrological
gastronomical
generalisable
generalissimo
gentlemanlike
geocentricism
geochronology
geometrically
geomorphology
geostationary
geotropically
germanisation
gerontocratic
gerontologist
gesticulation
gesticulative
gesticulatory
glaciological
glamorisation
globetrotting
glorification
glossographer
glutinousness
gonadotrophic
gonadotrophin
goniometrical
goodnaturedly
gracelessness
graminivorous
grammatically
granddaughter
grandfatherly
grandiloquent
grandmotherly
graphological
gratification
gravitational
greensickness
grotesqueness
gubernatorial
guilelessness
guiltlessness
gymnastically
gymnospermous
gynaecocratic
gynaecologist
gynandromorph
habitableness
haematologist
hairsplitting
halfheartedly
halfsovereign
hallucination
hallucinative
hallucinatory
haphazardness
harbourmaster
hardheartedly
harmonisation
hazardousness
healthfulness
heartbreaking
heartlessness
heartsickness
heebiejeebies
helminthiasis
helminthology
helterskelter
hemicellulose
hemiparasitic
hemispherical
heptasyllabic
hermaphrodite
hermeneutical
herpetologist
heterogeneity
heterogeneous
heterogenesis
heterogenetic
heteromorphic
heteropterous
heterosporous
heterothallic
heterotrophic
hilariousness
histrionicism
hocuspocussed
hollowhearted
homeomorphism
homoeomorphic
homoeopathist
homogeneously
homoiothermal
homoiothermic
homosexuality
honorifically
horizontality
horripilation
horsechestnut
horsewhipping
horticultural
housebreaking
hundredweight
hybridisation
hydraulically
hydrocephalic
hydrocephalus
hydrochloride
hydrocracking
hydrodynamics
hydroelectric
hydrogenation
hydromedusoid
hydrometrical
hydrostatical
hydrosulphide
hydrosulphite
hydroxylamine
hymenopterous
hyperboloidal
hypercritical
hypermetrical
hypermetropia
hypermetropic
hyperphysical
hypertrophied
hypnoanalysis
hypnotisation
hypochondriac
hypoglycaemia
hypothecation
ichthyography
ichthyologist
ichthyosaurus
identicalness
ideographical
ideologically
idiomatically
idiosyncratic
ignominiously
illogicalness
illustriously
imaginatively
imitativeness
immarcescible
immaterialise
immaterialism
immaterialist
immateriality
immediateness
immiscibility
immovableness
immunological
immunotherapy
immutableness
impalpability
impartibility
impassability
impassibility
impassiveness
impeccability
impecuniosity
impenetration
imperceptible
imperceptibly
impercipience
imperfectness
imperialistic
imperiousness
impermissible
impersonalise
impersonality
impersonation
impertinently
imperturbable
imperturbably
impetuousness
implacability
implicatively
impolitically
imponderables
importunately
impossibility
impracticable
impracticably
impractically
impressionism
impressionist
improbability
impropriation
improvability
improvidently
improvisation
improvisatory
impulsiveness
inadvertently
inanimateness
inappreciable
inappreciably
inappropriate
inattentively
incandescence
incarceration
incardination
inclusiveness
incombustible
incommunicado
incompetently
inconceivable
inconceivably
incondensable
incongruously
inconsecutive
inconsequence
inconsiderate
inconsistence
inconsistency
inconspicuous
incontestable
incontestably
incontinently
inconvenience
inconveniency
inconvertible
inconvertibly
inconvincible
incorporation
incorporative
incorporeally
incorrectness
incorruptible
incorruptibly
incorruptness
incredibility
incredulously
incrementally
incriminatory
incurableness
incuriousness
indefatigable
indefatigably
independently
indescribable
indescribably
indeterminacy
indeterminate
indeterminism
indeterminist
indifferently
indiscernible
indiscernibly
indispensable
indispensably
indisposition
indissociable
indistinctive
individualise
individualism
individualist
individuality
individuation
indoctrinator
inductiveness
industrialise
industrialism
industrialist
industriously
ineducability
ineffableness
ineffectively
ineffectually
inefficacious
inefficiently
ineligibility
inevitability
inexhaustible
inexhaustibly
inexorability
inexpediently
inexpensively
inexperienced
inexpressible
inexpressibly
infallibilism
infallibilist
infallibility
infeasibility
inferentially
infinitesimal
inflexibility
inflexionless
inflorescence
influentially
informational
informatively
infundibulate
infuriatingly
ingeniousness
ingenuousness
ingurgitation
inhospitality
injudiciously
injuriousness
innocuousness
innoxiousness
inoffensively
inopportunely
inorganically
inquisitional
inquisitively
inquisitorial
insatiability
inscriptional
insectivorous
insensateness
insensibility
insensitively
insensitivity
insidiousness
insignificant
insinuatingly
insociability
insolubleness
inspectorship
inspirational
instantaneity
instantaneous
instinctively
institutional
instructional
instructively
insubordinate
insubstantial
insufficience
insufficiency
insupportable
insupportably
insusceptible
intangibility
integumentary
intelligencer
intelligently
intemperately
intensiveness
intentionally
intercalation
intercellular
intercolonial
intercolumnar
intercropping
intercultural
intercurrence

interdentally
interdigitate
interestingly
intergalactic
interjectural
interlacement
interlocution
interlocutory
interlocutrix
intermarriage
intermediator
intermittence
international
interoceptive
interosculate
interparietal
interpellator
interpersonal
interpolation
interpolative
interposition
interpretable
interpretress
interpunction
interrelation
interrogation
interrogative
interrogatory
interruptible
interspecific
interspersion
interstratify
intertropical
intraarterial
intracellular
intramuscular
intransigeant
intransigence
intrapersonal
intravenously
intricateness
intrinsically
introgression
introspection
introspective
introversible
intrusiveness
intuitiveness
invariability
inventiveness
inventorially
investigation
investigative
investigatory
invidiousness
invincibility
inviolability
inviolateness
invisibleness
involuntarily
irrationalise
irrationalism
irrationalist
irrationality
irreclaimable
irreclaimably
irrecoverable
irrecoverably
irrefrangible
irreligionist
irreligiously
irreplaceable
irrepressible
irrepressibly
irresponsible
irresponsibly
irretrievable
irretrievably
irreverential
irritableness
isochronously
isomerisation
isometrically
isostatically
italicisation
jerrybuilding
jiggerypokery
jollification
judgeadvocate
judgmatically
judiciousness
jurisprudence
justification
justificative
justificatory
juxtaposition
kaleidoscopic
kapellmeister
Kidderminster
kinematically
kinematograph
knickerbocker
knowledgeable
knowledgeably
knuckleduster
laboriousness
lackadaisical
laevorotation
laevorotatory
laissezpasser
lamellibranch
lancecorporal
lancesergeant
landownership
languishingly
laryngoscopic
laughableness
laughingstock
leadpoisoning
leatherjacket
lecherousness
legislatively
legislatorial
leishmaniasis
leisureliness
lepidopterist
lepidopterous
leptocephalic
leptospirosis
lethargically
letterperfect
levelcrossing
lexicographer
lexicographic
liberationist
librarianship
lickerishness
liebfraumilch
lifepreserver
lightfingered
lightheadedly
lightmindedly
lightsomeness
lignification
limitlessness
lineengraving
linseywoolsey
litigiousness
loathsomeness
longsuffering
lucrativeness
ludicrousness
luxuriousness
macaronically
Machiavellian
machicolation
machinegunner
mackerelshark
macrocephalic
macromolecule
Maginotminded
magisterially
magnanimously
magnetisation
magnetomotive
magnetosphere
magnification
magnificently
magniloquence
malacological
malacostracan
maladaptation
maladjustment
maladminister
maladroitness
malariologist
maliciousness
malleableness
Malthusianism
mammaliferous
manageability
manganiferous
mangoldwurzel
Manichaeanism
manifestation
manifestative
manipulatable
manneristical
martyrisation
martyrologist
masculineness
masterfulness
materfamilias
materialistic
mathematician
matriculation
matrilineally
meadowsaffron
mechanisation
mediatisation
mediterranean
megacephalous
megasporangia
meistersinger
mellifluously
melodiousness
melodramatics
melodramatise
melodramatist
membranaceous
mensurability
mercenariness
mercerisation
merchandising
mercilessness
meritoriously
mesencephalon
mesmerisation
metagrobolise
metalliferous
metallisation
metallography
metallurgical
metamorphoses
metamorphosis
metaphosphate
metaphysician
metastability
meteorologist
Methodistical
metonymically
metrification
microanalysis
microcephalic
micrococcocci
microdetector
micronutrient
microorganism
microphyllous
microscopical
microtonality
millefeuilles
millennialism
millionairess
mineralogical
ministerially
mirthlessness
misanthropist
miscegenation
miscellaneous
mischievously
miscomprehend
misconception
miserableness
misgovernment
mismanagement
mistrustfully
mistrustingly
misunderstand
misunderstood
mitochondrion
mnemotechnics
moderatorship
modernisation
Mohammedanism
mollification
momentariness
momentousness
Monarchianism
moneygrubbing
monochromatic
monocotyledon
monodactylous
monogrammatic
monometallism
monometallist
monomolecular
mononucleosis
monophthongal
Monophysitism
monosyllabism
monosymmetric
Monotheletism
monotrematous
monstrousness
monumentalise
morphogenesis
morphogenetic
morphological
mortification
mothercountry
mouldingboard
mountainously
mountebankery
mourningcloak
mourningpaper
mouthwatering
Muhammadanism
multicellular
multicoloured
multinational
multinucleate
multiplicable
multitudinous
mummification
musicological
mutagenically
mutualisation
myrmecologist
mystification
naphthylamine
nationalistic
navigableness
nearsightedly
necessitarian
necessitation
necessitously
nectariferous
nefariousness
negligibility
negotiability
neighbourhood
nemathelminth
neoclassicism
neoclassicist
neoplasticism
nephelometric
nervelessness
neurastheniac
neurovascular
nickeliferous
niggardliness
nightmarishly
nightwatchman
nitrification
nitrobacteria
nitrocompound
noiselessness
nomenclatural
nonaggression
nonappearance
nonattendance
noncollegiate
noncompliance
nonconducting
nonconforming
nonconformism
nonconformist
nonconformity
nondeductable
nonfigurative
nonforfeiting
nonfulfilment
nongovernment
nonproductive
nonresistance
nonreturnable
nonsensically
normalisation
northeasterly
northeastward
northwesterly
northwestward
nostalgically
notoriousness
nucleoprotein
nullification
numerological
numismatology
nutritionally
objectionable
objectionably
objectiveness
objectivistic
obliviousness
obnoxiousness
observational
obsessiveness
obstinateness
obstructively
obtrusiveness
occasionalism
occasionalist
occasionality
occidentalise
Occidentalism
Occidentalist
oceanographer
oceanographic
ochlocratical
octocentenary
odontoglossum
odontological
odoriferously
oecologically

offensiveness
offhandedness
officiousness
oleomargarine
omnicompetent
onomatopoetic
ontogenically
ontologically
openheartedly
operativeness
ophthalmology
opinionatedly
opisthobranch
opportuneness
opportunistic
oppositionist
opprobriously
orangeblossom
orchestration
oreographical
organogenesis
organotherapy
ornamentation
ornithologist
orthocephalic
orthognathism
orthognathous
osteomyelitis
ostreiculture
outgeneralled
outspokenness
outstandingly
overabundance
overbearingly
overconfident
overcredulous
overelaborate
overemphasise
overindulgent
overpopulated
overqualified
oversensitive
overstatement
oversubscribe
overvaluation
ovoviviparous
owneroccupier
oystercatcher
paddlesteamer
paediatrician
paedomorphism
painstakingly
painterliness
palaeographer
palaeographic
palaeontology
palaeozoology
palatableness
palletisation
palynological
panegyrically
panicstricken
pantagruelian
pantagruelism
pantagruelist
pantheistical
pantisocratic
papaveraceous
paperhangings
papillomatous
parabolically
paradoxically
parallelogram
paramagnetism
paranormality
paraphernalia
parasitically
parasiticidal
parasynthesis
parasynthetic
parenthetical
parliamentary
parthenocarpy
participation
participative
participatory
particoloured
particularise
particularism
particularist
particularity
partridgewood
passementerie
passionflower
paterfamilias
paternalistic
pathogenicity
pathognomonic
patriotically
patronisingly
peaceableness
pedagogically
pedestrianise
pedestrianism
pendulousness
penetrability
penetratingly
penetratively
penitentially
Pennsylvanian
pennyfarthing
pennypinching
penuriousness
peptonisation
perambulation
perambulatory
percussionist
perdurability
peregrination
perfectionism
perfectionist
perfunctorily
perichondrial
perichondrium
periodisation
perishability
perissodactyl
permutability
perpendicular
perseveration
perspectively
perspicacious
perspicuously
pervasiveness
pestiferously
petrification
petrochemical
petroliferous
phalansterian
phanerogamous
pharisaically
pharmaceutics
pharmaceutist
pharmacologic
pharmacopoeia
phenomenalise
phenomenalism
phenomenalist
phenomenology
phenylalanine
philanthropic
philhellenism
philhellenist
philosophical
philosophiser
phonautograph
phosphoretted
photochemical
photochromics
photochromism
photoelectric
photoelectron
photoemission
photoemissive
photoperiodic
photopositive
photoreceptor
phraseologist
phreatophytic
phrenetically
phrenological
phycoerythrin
phyllophagous
physiognomist
physiographer
physiographic
physiological
physiotherapy
phytoplankton
picturepalace
picturesquely
piezoelectric
pigeonchested
pigeonhearted
pigeonlivered
pigheadedness
piscicultural
plaintiveness
planimetrical
platiniferous
platitudinise
platitudinous
platyhelminth
plausibleness
plenitudinous
plenteousness
plentifulness
plethorically
pluralisation
pluripresence
pneumatically
pneumatolysis
pneumatolytic
pneumatometer
pneumatophore
pneumogastric
pneumonectomy
pococurantism
pointillistic
pointlessness
polarographic
poliomyelitis
polliniferous
polyadelphous
polycarbonate
polychromatic
polycotyledon
polydactylous
polyhistorian
polypropylene
polysynthesis
polysynthetic
ponderability
ponderousness
pontification
porcellaneous
postclassical
postcommunion
postoperative
postulational
potentiometer
powerlessness
practicalness
pragmatically
prairieoyster
prayermeeting
precautionary
precentorship
precipitantly
precipitately
precipitation
precipitative
precipitously
preconception
predatoriness
predestinator
predicability
predicamental
predicatively
predominantly
predomination
preengagement
preengineered
prefatorially
preferability
prefiguration
prefigurative
prefigurement
prehistorical
prejudicially
preliminarily
prematureness
premeditation
premeditative
premillennial
premonitorily
preoccupation
preordainment
preordination
preparatively
preparatorily
preponderance
preponderancy
prepositional
prepossessing
prepossession
prepreference
PreRaphaelite
prescientific
presidentship
prestigiously
presumptively
pretentiously
pretermission
pretermitting
preternatural
prevarication
pricelessness
primigravidae
primitiveness
primogenitary
primogenitive
primogeniture
primordiality
principalship
prismatically
prizefighting
probationally
problematical
processionary
processionist
proconsulship
procrastinate
procuratorial
professoriate
professorship
profitability
profitsharing
progenitorial
prognosticate
progressional
progressively
progressivism
prohibitively
projectionist
prolegomenary
prolegomenous
proliferation
proliferative
proliferously
prolification
promiscuously
pronounceable
pronouncement
pronunciation
proparoxytone
prophetically
proportionate
propositional
proprietorial
proprioceptor
prosopography
prospectively
prostaglandin
prosthodontia
protectionism
protectionist
protectorship
proteinaceous
Protestantism
protohistoric
protonotarial
protuberantly
provincialise
provincialism
provincialist
provinciality
provisionally
prudentialism
prudentialist
prudentiality
pseudoarchaic
pseudomorphic
pseudoscience
psilanthropic
psychasthenia
psychoanalyse
psychoanalyst
psychodynamic
psychogenesis
psychogenetic
psychokinesis
psychokinetic
psychological
psychometrics
psychometrist
psychophysics
psychosomatic
psychosurgery
psychotherapy
psychrometric
pteridologist
pulverisation
punctiliously
puritanically
purposelessly
purposiveness
pusillanimity
pusillanimous
pyrheliometer
pyrimethamine
pyrotechnical
quadragesimal
quadrennially
quadricipital
quadrilateral
quadrillionth
quadripartite
quadrumvirate
quadruplicate
quadruplicity
qualification
qualificatory
qualitatively
quarrelsomely

quartermaster
quartziferous
querulousness
questioningly
questionnaire
quicktempered
quickwittedly
quincentenary
quincuncially
quingentenary
quinquagenary
Quinquagesima
quinquevalent
quintillionth
quintuplicate
radioactivity
radiolocation
radiotelegram
randomisation
rapaciousness
rapturousness
ratiocination
ratiocinative
rationalistic
rattlebrained
reaffirmation
realistically
rearcommodore
rearrangement
recalcitrance
receptibility
receptiveness
recessiveness
reciprocality
reciprocation
reciprocative
recombination
recommendable
recomposition
reconcilement
reconsolidate
reconstructor
recrimination
recriminative
recriminatory
recrudescence
recrystallise
rectangularly
rectification
rectilinearly
redescription
redevelopment
reduplication
reduplicative
reembarkation
reexamination
referentially
reflexibility
reforestation
reformability
reformational
refractometer
refrigeration
regardfulness
regimentation
regretfulness
regurgitation
reimbursement
reincarnation
reinforcement
reinstatement
reintegration
reinvigorator
rejuvenescent
religiousness
reminiscently
remonstrantly
remonstration
remonstrative
remorselessly
removableness
renegotiation
reorientation
repetitionary
repetitiously
replenishment
reprehensible
reprehensibly
representable
reproachfully
reproachingly
republicanise
republicanism
republication
repulsiveness
requisiteness
resentfulness
resistibility
resolvability
resourcefully
resplendently
restoratively
restrictively
resuscitation
resuscitative
retentiveness
retranslation
retroactively
retroactivity
retrogression
retrogressive
retrospection
retrospective
revaccination
revelationist
revendication
reverberation
reverberative
reverberatory
reverentially
reversibility
revolutionary
revolutionise
revolutionism
revolutionist
rhadamanthine
RhaetoRomanic
rhapsodically
rheumatically
rhodochrosite
righteousness
righthandedly
ritualisation
roentgenogram
roentgenology
rollercoaster
rontgenoscopy
rudimentarily
runningstitch
Russification
sabrerattling
saccharimeter
saccharimetry
saccharometer
sacerdotalise
sacerdotalism
sacerdotalist
sacramentally
sacrificially
sacrosanctity
sadomasochism
sadomasochist
sagaciousness
salaciousness
salmonellosis
sanctimonious
sanitationist
sansculottism
sarcastically
scandalmonger
scarification
schadenfreude
schematically
schizocarpous
schizogenesis
schizophrenia
schizophrenic
scholarliness
scholasticism
schoolteacher
scientologist
scintillating
scintillation
scleroprotein
scolopendrium
scorbutically
scorification
scorpiongrass
scrapmerchant
scripturalism
scripturalist
scrumptiously
sculpturesque
searchwarrant
seaworthiness
secondariness
secretarybird
secretaryship
secretiveness
sedentariness
sedimentation
seditiousness
seductiveness
seismographer
seismographic
seismological
selectiveness
selenocentric
selenographer
selenographic
selenological
selfabasement
selfaddressed
selfadjusting
selfappointed
selfapproving
selfasserting
selfassertion
selfassertive
selfassurance
selfassuredly
selfawareness
selfcentredly
selfcollected
selfcommunion
selfconceited
selfcondemned
selfconfessed
selfconfident
selfconscious
selfconsuming
selfcontained
selfcontented
selfconvicted
selfcriticism
selfdeceiving
selfdeception
selfdeceptive
selfdefeating
selfdependent
selfdirecting
selfdirection
selfdiscovery
selfdispraise
selfeducation
selfevidently
selfexecuting
selfexistence
selffertility
selfforgetful
selfgenerated
selfgoverning
selfimportant
selfinduction
selfindulgent
selfinflicted
selfinsurance
selfknowledge
selfopinioned
selfpityingly
selfpollinate
selfpossessed
selfpropelled
selfrecording
selfregarding
selfreproving
selfrepugnant
selfrestraint
selfrevealing
selfrighteous
selfsacrifice
selfsatisfied
selfslaughter
selfsterility
selfsufficing
selfsupported
selfsurrender
selfsustained
selftormentor
semeiological
semiautomatic
semibarbarian
semibarbarism
semicivilised
semiconductor
semiconscious
semilogarithm
semiparasitic
semipermanent
semipermeable
semiporcelain
sensationally
senselessness
sensitisation
sensitiveness
sententiously
sentimentally
separableness
separationist
septentrional
sequentiality
sequestration
SerboCroatian
serendipitous
sergeantmajor
serialisation
sericulturist
seriousminded
serologically
sesquiplicate
sewingmachine
shabbygenteel
Shakespearean
Shakespearian
shamelessness
shapelessness
sharecropping
sharpshooting
sheepshearing
shiftlessness
shockabsorber
shootingbrake
shootingrange
shootingstick
shorttempered
shoulderblade
shoulderstrap
sicklefeather
sidesplitting
sightlessness
signalisation
significantly
signification
significative
silvertongued
singlehearted
skateboarding
slangingmatch
sleeplessness
smellingsalts
smokelessness
smoothingiron
sniftingvalve
snowblindness
sobermindness
socialisation
sociocultural
socioeconomic
softpedalling
solderingiron
solemnisation
solicitorship
solidungulate
somatological
somnambulator
somniloquence
sophistically
sophisticated
sorrowfulness
soulsearching
soundingboard
southeasterly
southeastward
southwesterly
southwestward
sovietologist
spasmodically
specification
spectacularly
spectrography
spectrometric
spectroscopic
speculatively
spelaeologist
speleological
Spencerianism
spermatoblast
spermatogenic
spermatophore
spermatophyte
spheroidicity
sphygmography
spindlelegged
spindleshanks
spinelessness
spinninghouse
spinningwheel
spiritualness
splendiferous
splenetically
spontaneously
sportsmanlike
sportsmanship
sprightliness
sprocketwheel
squandermania
squarebashing
squeamishness
squeezability
stabilisation
stainlessness
stalkinghorse
staminiferous
standoffishly
statelessness

statesmanlike
statesmanship
stationmaster
statistically
steadfastness
steeplechaser
steppingstone
stercoraceous
stereographic
stereoscopist
sterilisation
sternforemost
stickingplace
stigmatically
stirpiculture
stoichiometry
stoloniferous
stomatologist
strangulation
strategically
stratigraphic
stratocumulus
stratospheric
strawcoloured
streetwalking
strenuousness
streptococcal
streptococcus
strikebreaker
structuralism
structuralist
structureless
stylistically
subcontractor
subeditorship
subirrigation
sublieutenant
submachinegun
subordinately
subordination
subordinative
subpostmaster
subreptitious
subsaturation
subsequential
subserviently
substantially
substantively
substantivise
substitutable
substructural
subternatural
subterraneous
subtilisation
subversionary
suffocatingly
suffraganship
suffumigation
sulphureously
summarisation
sumptuousness
superabundant
superaddition
superannuable
supercalender
supercritical
superdominant
supereminence
superfamilies
superfetation
superficially
superfluidity
superfluously
superhumanity
superlatively
supernational
supernumerary
superordinate
superphysical
superposition
supersaturate
supersensible
superstitious
supersubtlety
supervenience
supplantation
supplementary
suppositional
supranational
surreptitious
surrogateship
swallowtailed
swashbuckling
Swedenborgian
swordsmanship
syllabication
symbiotically
symbolisation
symmetrically
symphonically
symphoniously
synallagmatic
synchronistic
synchronously
syntactically
synthetically
tablespoonful
tachistoscope
talkativeness
tantalisation
tantalisingly
taperecording
tastelessness
tautologously
taxonomically
teachableness
technicalness
technological
telegrammatic
telencephalon
teleportation
telerecording
televisionary
temerariously
temperamental
temperateness
tempestuously
temporalities
temporariness
temporisation
tenaciousness
tendentiously
tenderhearted
tentativeness
teratological
tercentennial
tergiversator
terminability
terminational
terminatively
terpsichorean
terrestrially
territorially
terrorisation
testification
tetrasyllable
thalassocracy
thanklessness
thaumaturgist
theanthropism
theatricalise
theatricalism
theatricality
thenceforward
theologically
theoretically
thereinbefore
theriomorphic
thermochemist
thermodynamic
thermogenesis
thermonuclear
thermophilous
thermoplastic
thermosetting
thermotropism
thigmotropism
thimblerigged
thimblerigger
thoroughbrace
thoroughgoing
thoroughpaced
thoughtlessly
thoughtreader
thrasonically
threateningly
threecornered
threequarters
thremmatology
thrillingness
thundershower
thunderstruck
thurification
tiddledywinks
timeconsuming
tintinnabular
tintinnabulum
titillatingly
toastmistress
tolerableness
tonguelashing
tonguetwister
tonsillectomy
toothsomeness
topographical
topologically
topsyturvydom
tortoiseshell
toxicological
toxoplasmosis
traceableness
tractableness
Tractarianism
traditionally
tranquilliser
transatlantic
transcendence
transcendency
transcription
transcriptive
transformable
transgression
transgressive
transistorise
transitionary
translational
transliterate
translocation
translucently
translucidity
transmigrator
transmissible
transmittable
transmutation
transmutative
transnational
transparently
transpiration
transpiratory
transportable
transposition
transshipment
transshipping
transversally
traumatically
treacherously
treasurership
tremulousness
triangularity
triangulation
tributariness
tricentennial
trichromatism
trigonometric
triliteralism
tritheistical
troglodytical
troublesomely
troublousness
trustworthily
tuberculation
turkeygobbler
typographical
typologically
tyrannosaurus
umbelliferous
unaccompanied
unaccountable
unaccountably
unadulterated
unambiguously
unanimousness
unanticipated
unarticulated
unbelievingly
unceremonious
uncertainness
uncircumcised
uncleanliness
uncomfortable
uncomfortably
uncompetitive
uncomplaining
uncomplicated
unconceivable
unconcernedly
unconditional
unconditioned
unconformable
unconquerable
unconsciously
unconstrained
uncoordinated
underachiever
undercarriage
underclothing
undereducated
underemphasis
underemployed
underestimate
underexposure
undergraduate
underhandedly
understanding
understrapper
underwhelming
undisciplined
unearthliness
unemotionally
unenlightened
unequivocally
unestablished
unexceptional
unfamiliarity
unfashionable
unfashionably
unfeelingness
unflinchingly
unforgettable
unforgettably
unforthcoming
unfortunately
ungrammatical
unhealthiness
unicameralism
unicameralist
unimpassioned
unimpeachable
uninformative
unintelligent
unintentional
uninterrupted
unmeaningness
unmentionable
unnaturalness
unnecessarily
unobtrusively
unprecedented
unpredictable
unpretentious
unpromisingly
unputdownable
unqualifiedly
unquestioning
unrelentingly
unremittingly
unrighteously
unselfishness
unsociability
unsubstantial
unsuitability
unsymmetrical
untrustworthy
unwarrantable
unwarrantably
unwholesomely
unwillingness
vacillatingly
valuelessness
vantageground
vapourishness
vegetarianism
venerableness
venereologist
ventriloquial
ventriloquise
ventriloquism
ventriloquist
venturesomely
venturousness
veraciousness
verbalisation
verbigeration
verifiability
verisimilarly
vermiculation
vernacularise
vernacularism
vernacularity
vernalisation
versicoloured
versification
vertiginously
vexatiousness
vicariousness
viceadmiralty
vicepresident
victimisation
villeggiatura
viniculturist
violoncellist
visionariness
visualisation
viticulturist
vitrification
vivaciousness
vivisectional
vocationalism
voicelessness
volatilisable
volcanologist
volumenometer
voluntariness
voluntaristic
voraciousness

vouchsafement
vulcanisation
vulcanologist
vulgarisation
vulnerability
waterproofing
wearisomeness
weatherbeaten
wellapPointed
wheelerdealer
whimsicalness
whithersoever
wholesomeness
windowshopper
winterberries
wonderfulness
wonderworking
woodengraving
woolgathering
worldlyminded
worrisomeness
worthlessness
wrongheadedly
xanthochroism
xylographical
Zarathustrian
zinjanthropus
zoogeographer
zoogeographic
zygodactylous

---

baccalaureate
backformation
backpedalling
backscratcher
backwardation
bacteriolysis
bacteriolytic
bacteriophage
balkanisation
balsamiferous
BaltoSlavonic
bamboozlement
barbarisation
barbarousness
barefacedness
barrelchested
basidiomycete
bathymetrical
battlecruiser
cabinetmaking
cacographical
calcification
calculatingly
calligraphist
callisthenics
Calvinistical
campanologist
camphoraceous
canaliculated
candlelighter
candlesnuffer
cannibalistic
capaciousness
caprification
carboniferous
carbonisation
carcinomatous
cardiographer
carnivorously
cartilaginous
catechisation
categorically
cauterisation
daguerreotype
dangerousness
dastardliness
dauntlessness
eavesdropping
facetiousness
facultatively
faithlessness
falsification
fantastically
fasciculation
fascinatingly
Fascistically
faultlessness
galactosaemia
galvanisation
gametogenesis
garnetiferous
garrulousness
gasteropodous
gastrocnemius
gastroenteric
gastrological
gastronomical
habitableness
haematologist
hairsplitting
halfheartedly
halfsovereign
hallucination
hallucinative
hallucinatory
haphazardness
harbourmaster
hardheartedly
harmonisation
hazardousness
kaleidoscopic
kapellmeister
laboriousness
lackadaisical
laevorotation
laevorotatory
laissezpasser
lamellibranch
lancecorporal
lancesergeant
landownership
languishingly
laryngoscopic
laughableness
laughingstock
macaronically
Machiavellian
machicolation
machinegunner
mackerelshark
macrocephalic
macromolecule
Maginotminded
magisterially
magnanimously
magnetisation
magnetomotive
magnetosphere
magnification
magnificently
magniloquence
malacological
malacostracan
maladaptation
maladjustment
maladminister
maladroitness
malariologist
maliciousness
malleableness
Malthusianism
mammaliferous
manageability
manganiferous
mangoldwurzel
Manichaeanism
manifestation
manifestative
manipulatable
manneristical
martyrisation
martyrologist
masculineness
masterfulness
materfamilias
materialistic
mathematician
matriculation
matrilineally
naphthylamine
nationalistic
navigableness
paddlesteamer
paediatrician
paedomorphism
painstakingly
painterliness
palaeographer
palaeographic
palaeontology
palaeozoology
palatableness
palletisation
palynological
panegyrically
panicstricken
pantagruelian
pantagruelism
pantagruelist
pantheistical
pantisocratic
papaveraceous
paperhangings
papillomatous
parabolically
paradoxically
parallelogram
paramagnetism
paranormality
paraphernalia
parasitically
parasiticidal
parasynthesis
parasynthetic
parenthetical
parliamentary
parthenocarpy
participation
participative
participatory
particoloured
particularise
particularism
particularist
particularity
partridgewood
passementerie
passionflower
paterfamilias
paternalistic
pathogenicity
pathognomonic
patriotically
patronisingly
radioactivity
radiolocation
radiotelegram
randomisation
rapaciousness
rapturousness
ratiocination
ratiocinative
rationalistic
rattlebrained
sabrerattling
saccharimeter
saccharimetry
saccharometer
sacerdotalise
sacerdotalism
sacerdotalist
sacramentally
sacrificially
sacrosanctity
sadomasochism
sadomasochist
sagaciousness
salaciousness
salmonellosis
sanctimonious
sanitationist
sansculottism
sarcastically
tablespoonful
tachistoscope
talkativeness
tantalisation
tantalisingly
taperecording
tastelessness
tautologously
taxonomically
vacillatingly
valuelessness
vantageground
vapourishness
waterproofing
xanthochroism
Zarathustrian
abiologically
abortifacient
absorbability
abstractional
objectionable
objectionably
objectiveness
objectivistic
obliviousness
obnoxiousness
observational
obsessiveness
obstinateness
obstructively
obtrusiveness
accelerometer
acceptability
accessibility
accidentalism
accidentprone
acclimatation
accommodating
accommodation
accommodative
accompaniment
accoutrements
accreditation
acculturation
acculturative
acetification
acetylcholine
achromaticity
acidification
acotyledonous
acquiescently
acquiescingly
acrimoniously
acrobatically
acrylonitrile
actinomorphic
actinomycetes
actinomycosis
actualisation
eccentrically
ecumenicalism
ichthyography
ichthyologist
ichthyosaurus
occasionalism
occasionalist
occasionality
occidentalise
Occidentalism
Occidentalist
oceanographer
oceanographic
ochlocratical
octocentenary
scandalmonger
scarification
schadenfreude
schematically
schizocarpous
schizogenesis
schizophrenia
schizophrenic
scholarliness
scholasticism
schoolteacher
scientologist
scintillating
scintillation
scleroprotein
scolopendrium
scorbutically
scorification
scorpiongrass
scrapmerchant
scripturalism
scripturalist
scrumptiously
sculpturesque
adiabatically
admeasurement
administrable
administrator
admirableness
admissibility
admonishingly
adventuresome
adventurously
adversatively
advertisement
advisableness
educationally
identicalness
ideographical
ideologically
idiomatically
idiosyncratic
odontoglossum
odontological
odoriferously
aerodynamical
aesthetically
beatification
beauteousness
beleaguerment
belleslettres
belligerently
beneficiation
Berkeleianism
betweenwhiles
bewilderingly
centreforward
centrifugally
centripetally
cephalothorax
cerebrospinal
ceremonialism
ceremonialist
ceremoniously
certification
certificatory
deathlessness

deceitfulness
deceptiveness
decerebration
deciduousness
declaratively
decomposition
decompression
decontaminate
decontrolling
decortication
decrepitation
deductibility
defeasibility
defectiveness
defencelessly
defensibility
deferentially
defervescence
defibrination
deforestation
deformational
degranulation
deipnosophist
deleteriously
deliciousness
deliquescence
deliriousness
dematerialise
demonstration
demonstrative
demythologise
denationalise
dendritically
denticulation
deodorisation
deontological
dependability
depersonalise
deprecatingly
derequisition
derestriction
dermatologist
descriptively
desegregation
desirableness
desperateness
destructively
destructivity
desultoriness
deterioration
deteriorative
determinately
determination
determinative
deterministic
detrimentally
deuteragonist
Deuteronomist
devastatingly
developmental
devolutionary
devolutionist
dexterousness
featherheaded
featherstitch
featherweight
felicitations
feloniousness
ferociousness
ferrimagnetic
ferroconcrete
ferroelectric
ferromagnetic
fertilisation
festschriften
feudalisation
feuilletonism
feuilletonist
generalisable
generalissimo
gentlemanlike
geocentricism
geochronology
geometrically
geomorphology
geostationary
geotropically
germanisation
gerontocratic
gerontologist
gesticulation
gesticulative
gesticulatory
healthfulness
heartbreaking
heartlessness
heartsickness
heebiejeebies
helminthiasis
helminthology
helterskelter
hemicellulose
hemiparasitic
hemispherical
heptasyllabic
hermaphrodite
hermeneutical
herpetologist
heterogeneity
heterogeneous
heterogenesis
heterogenetic
heteromorphic
heteropterous
heterosporous
heterothallic
heterotrophic
jerrybuilding
leadpoisoning
leatherjacket
lecherousness
legislatively
legislatorial
leishmaniasis
leisureliness
lepidopterist
lepidopterous
leptocephalic
leptospirosis
lethargically
letterperfect
levelcrossing
lexicographer
lexicographic
meadowsaffron
mechanisation
mediatisation
mediterranean
megacephalous
megasporangia
meistersinger
mellifluously
melodiousness
melodramatics
melodramatise
melodramatist
membranaceous
mensurability
mercenariness
mercerisation
merchandising
mercilessness
meritoriously
mesencephalon
mesmerisation
metagrobolise
metalliferous
metallisation
metallography
metallurgical
metamorphoses
metamorphosis
metaphosphate
metaphysician
metastability
meteorologist
Methodistical
metonymically
metrification
nearsightedly
necessitarian
necessitation
necessitously
nectariferous
nefariousness
negligibility
negotiability
neighbourhood
nemathelminth
neoclassicism
neoclassicist
neoplasticism
nephelometric
nervelessness
neurastheniac
neurovascular
oecologically
peaceableness
pedagogically
pedestrianise
pedestrianism
pendulousness
penetrability
penetratingly
penetratively
penitentially
Pennsylvanian
pennyfarthing
pennypinching
penuriousness
peptonisation
perambulation
perambulatory
percussionist
perdurability
peregrination
perfectionism
perfectionist
perfunctorily
perichondrial
perichondrium
periodisation
perishability
perissodactyl
permutability
perpendicular
perseveration
perspectively
perspicacious
perspicuously
pervasiveness
pestiferously
petrification
petrochemical
petroliferous
reaffirmation
realistically
rearcommodore
rearrangement
recalcitrance
receptibility
receptiveness
recessiveness
reciprocality
reciprocation
reciprocative
recombination
recommendable
recomposition
reconcilement
reconsolidate
reconstructor
recrimination
recriminative
recriminatory
recrudescence
recrystallise
rectangularly
rectification
rectilinearly
redescription
redevelopment
reduplication
reduplicative
reembarkation
reexamination
referentially
reflexibility
reforestation
reformability
reformational
refractometer
refrigeration
regardfulness
regimentation
regretfulness
regurgitation
reimbursement
reincarnation
reinforcement
reinstatement
reintegration
reinvigorator
rejuvenescent
religiousness
reminiscently
remonstrantly
remonstration
remonstrative
remorselessly
removableness
renegotiation
reorientation
repetitionary
repetitiously
replenishment
reprehensible
reprehensibly
representable
reproachfully
reproachingly
republicanise
republicanism
republication
repulsiveness
requisiteness
resentfulness
resistibility
resolvability
resourcefully
resplendently
restoratively
restrictively
resuscitation
resuscitative
retentiveness
retranslation
retroactively
retroactivity
retrogression
retrogressive
retrospection
retrospective
revaccination
revelationist
revendication
reverberation
reverberative
reverberatory
reverentially
reversibility
revolutionary
revolutionise
revolutionism
revolutionist
searchwarrant
seaworthiness
secondariness
secretarybird
secretaryship
secretiveness
sedentariness
sedimentation
seditiousness
seductiveness
seismographer
seismographic
seismological
selectiveness
selenocentric
selenographer
selenographic
selenological
selfabasement
selfaddressed
selfadjusting
selfappointed
selfapproving
selfasserting
selfassertion
selfassertive
selfassurance
selfassuredly
selfawareness
selfcentredly
selfcollected
selfcommunion
selfconceited
selfcondemned
selfconfessed
selfconfident
selfconscious
selfconsuming
selfcontained
selfcontented
selfconvicted
selfcriticism
selfdeceiving
selfdeception
selfdeceptive
selfdefeating
selfdependent
selfdirecting
selfdirection
selfdiscovery
selfdispraise
selfeducation
selfevidently
selfexecuting
selfexistence
selffertility
selfforgetful
selfgenerated
selfgoverning
selfimportant
selfinduction
selfindulgent
selfinflicted
selfinsurance
selfknowledge
selfopinioned
selfpityingly
selfpollinate
selfpossessed
selfpropelled

selfrecording
selfregarding
selfreproving
selfrepugnant
selfrestraint
selfrevealing
selfrighteous
selfsacrifice
selfsatisfied
selfslaughter
selfsterility
selfsufficing
selfsupported
selfsurrender
selfsustained
selftormentor
semeiological
semiautomatic
semibarbarian
semibarbarism
semicivilised
semiconductor
semiconscious
semilogarithm
semiparasitic
semipermanent
semipermeable
semiporcelain
sensationally
senselessness
sensitisation
sensitiveness
sententiously
sentimentally
separableness
separationist
septentrional
sequentiality
sequestration
SerboCroatian
serendipitous
sergeantmajor
serialisation
sericulturist
seriousminded
serologically
sesquiplicate
sewingmachine
teachableness
technicalness
technological
telegrammatic
telencephalon
teleportation
telerecording
televisionary
temerariously
temperamental
temperateness
tempestuously
temporalities
temporariness
temporisation
tenaciousness
tendentiously
tenderhearted
tentativeness
teratological
tercentennial
tergiversator
terminability
terminational
terminatively
terpsichorean
terrestrially
territorially
terrorisation
testification
tetrasyllable
vegetarianism
venerableness
venereologist
ventriloquial
ventriloquise
ventriloquism
ventriloquist
venturesomely
venturousness
veraciousness
verbalisation
verbigeration
verifiability
verisimilarly
vermiculation
vernacularise
vernacularism
vernacularity
vernalisation
versicoloured
versification
vertiginously
vexatiousness
wearisomeness
weatherbeaten
wellapPointed
affectionless
affenpinscher
affirmatively
afforestation
affreightment
effectiveness
effervescence
effervescency
efficaciously
efflorescence
offensiveness
offhandedness
officiousness
aggiornamento
agglomeration
agglomerative
agglutination
agglutinative
aggravatingly
agonistically
agreeableness
agriculturist
egocentricity
egregiousness
ignominiously
chalcoography
challengeable
challengingly
changeability
changefulness
characterless
chateaubriand
cheerlessness
chemoreceptor
chieftainship
chinkerinchee
chlamydomonas
chlamydospore
choreographer
choreographic
chrematistics
Christmastide
Christmastime
chromatically
chromatograph
chromatolytic
chromatophore
chromospheric
chronographic
chronological
chrysanthemum
chuckleheaded
churchmanship
phalansterian
phanerogamous
pharisaically
pharmaceutics
pharmaceutist
pharmacologic
pharmacopoeia
phenomenalise
phenomenalism
phenomenalist
phenomenology
phenylalanine
philanthropic
philhellenism
philhellenist
philosophical
philosophiser
phonautograph
phosphoretted
photochemical
photochromics
photochromism
photoelectric
photoelectron
photoemission
photoemissive
photoperiodic
photopositive
photoreceptor
phraseologist
phreatophytic
phrenetically
phrenological
phycoerythrin
phyllophagous
physiognomist
physiographer
physiographic
physiological
physiotherapy
phytoplankton
rhadamanthine
RhaetoRomanic
rhapsodically
rheumatically
rhodochrosite
shabbygenteel
Shakespearean
Shakespearian
shamelessness
shapelessness
sharecropping
sharpshooting
sheepshearing
shiftlessness
shockabsorber
shootingbrake
shootingrange
shootingstick
shorttempered
shoulderblade
shoulderstrap
thalassocracy
thanklessness
thaumaturgist
theanthropism
theatricalise
theatricalism
theatricality
thenceforward
theologically
theoretically
thereinbefore
theriomorphic
thermochemist
thermodynamic
thermogenesis
thermonuclear
thermophilous
thermoplastic
thermosetting
thermotropism
thigmotropism
thimblerigged
thimblerigger
thoroughbrace
thoroughgoing
thoroughpaced
thoughtlessly
thoughtreader
thrasonically
threateningly
threecornered
threequarters
thremmatology
thrillingness
thundershower
thunderstruck
thurification
wheelerdealer
whimsicalness
whithersoever
wholesomeness
aircraftwoman
airworthiness
bibliographer
bibliographic
bibliolatrist
bibliolatrous
bibliological
bibliophilism
bibliophilist
bildungsroman
biodegradable
bioenergetics
biogeographer
biotechnology
birefringence
cicatrisation
cinematically
cinematograph
cinquecentist
circumambient
circumference
circumfluence
circumspectly
circumvallate
circumvention
diageotropism
diagnostician
diagrammatise
dialectically
diametrically
diaphragmatic
diathermanous
dichlamydeous
dichotomously
dictatorially
differentiate
diffusiveness
digestibility
dimensionally
dimensionless
disadvantaged
disaffectedly
disaffirmance
disappearance
disarticulate
disciplinable
discoloration
discommodious
disconcerting
disconcertion
disconformity
disconnection
discontinuity
discontinuous
discreditable
discreditably
discretionary
discriminator
disembodiment
disengagement
disfigurement
disgracefully
disharmonious
dishonourable
dishonourably
disintegrator
disinterested
disinvestment
disjunctively
dismantlement
dismemberment
disobediently
disparagement
disparagingly
disparateness
dispassionate
displantation
disposability
dispossession
dispraisingly
disproportion
disrespectful
dissemblingly
dissemination
disseminative
disseveration
dissimilarity
dissimilation
dissimilitude
dissimulation
dissolubility
dissoluteness
dissymetrical
distastefully
distinctively
distinguished
distressfully
distressingly
distributable
distrustfully
divertisement
fibrovascular
filterability
fissiparously
hilariousness
histrionicism
jiggerypokery
Kidderminster
kinematically
kinematograph
liberationist
librarianship
lickerishness
liebfraumilch
lifepreserver
lightfingered
lightheadedly
lightmindedly
lightsomeness
lignification
limitlessness
lineengraving
linseywoolsey
litigiousness
microanalysis
microcephalic
micrococcocci
microdetector
micronutrient
microorganism
microphyllous
microscopical
microtonality
millefeuilles

millennialism
millionairess
mineralogical
ministerially
mirthlessness
misanthropist
miscegenation
miscellaneous
mischievously
miscomprehend
misconception
miserableness
misgovernment
mismanagement
mistrustfully
mistrustingly
misunderstand
misunderstood
mitochondrion
nickeliferous
niggardliness
nightmarishly
nightwatchman
nitrification
nitrobacteria
nitrocompound
picturepalace
picturesquely
piezoelectric
pigeonchested
pigeonhearted
pigeonlivered
pigheadedness
piscicultural
righteousness
righthandedly
ritualisation
sicklefeather
sidesplitting
sightlessness
signalisation
significantly
signification
significative
silvertongued
singlehearted
tiddledywinks
timeconsuming
tintinnabular
tintinnabulum
titillatingly
vicariousness
viceadmiralty
vicepresident
victimisation
villeggiatura
viniculturist
violoncellist
visionariness
visualisation
viticulturist
vitrification
vivaciousness
vivisectional
windowshopper
winterberries
zinjanthropus
skateboarding
alcoholically
alcoholometer
alcoholometry
algebraically
allegorically
allelomorphic
alternatively
aluminiferous
aluminisation
blackguardism
blameableness

blamelessness
blanketflower
blasphemously
blastogenesis
bloodboltered
bloodcurdling
bloodlessness
bloodrelation
Bloomsburyite
clairaudience
clandestinely
clarification
clearheadedly
clearinghouse
cleistogamous
climactically
climatologist
climbingframe
closedcircuit
clothesbasket
elaborateness
electioneerer
electrocution
electrologist
electromagnet
electrometric
electromotive
electrophorus
electroscopic
electrostatic
electrovalent
elephantiasis
flagellantism
flirtatiously
floricultural
floristically
flourishingly
glaciological
glamorisation
globetrotting
glorification
glossographer
glutinousness
illogicalness
illustriously
oleomargarine
plaintiveness
planimetrical
platiniferous
platitudinise
platitudinous
platyhelminth
plausibleness
plenitudinous
plenteousness
plentifulness
plethorically
pluralisation
pluripresence
slangingmatch
sleeplessness
ambassadorial
ambidexterity
ambidexterous
ambiguousness
ambitiousness
amniocentesis
amorphousness
amphiprostyle
amplification
embarrassment
embellishment
embranglement
embrittlement
embryogenesis
embryological
emphysematous
imaginatively
imitativeness

immarcescible
immaterialise
immaterialism
immaterialist
immateriality
immediateness
immiscibility
immovableness
immunological
immunotherapy
immutableness
impalpability
impartibility
impassability
impassibility
impassiveness
impeccability
impecuniosity
impenetration
imperceptible
imperceptibly
impercipience
imperfectness
imperialistic
imperiousness
impermissible
impersonalise
impersonality
impersonation
impertinently
imperturbable
imperturbably
impetuousness
implacability
implicatively
impolitically
imponderables
importunately
impossibility
impracticable
impracticably
impractically
impressionism
impressionist
improbability
impropriation
improvability
improvidently
improvisation
improvisatory
impulsiveness
omnicompetent
smellingsalts
smokelessness
smoothingiron
umbelliferous
anachronistic
anachronously
anaerobically
anagrammatise
anagrammatism
analogousness
anaphrodisiac
anfractuosity
angiospermous
anglicisation
AngloAmerican
AngloCatholic
animadversion
animalisation
annexationist
anomalistical
anomalousness
anonymousness
answerability
anthelminthic
anthropogenic
anthropometry
anthropopathy

anthropophagi
anthropophagy
anthroposophy
Antichristian
anticlimactic
anticlockwise
anticoagulant
antihistamine
antilogarithm
antinomianism
antipersonnel
antiscorbutic
encapsulation
encephalogram
encompassment
encouragement
encouragingly
encyclopaedia
encyclopaedic
encyclopedism
encyclopedist
endocrinology
energetically
enigmatically
enjoyableness
enlightenment
entertainment
entomological
entomophagous
entomophilous
entomostracan
environmental
inadvertently
inanimateness
inappreciable
inappreciably
inappropriate
inattentively
incandescence
incarceration
incardination
inclusiveness
incombustible
incommunicado
incompetently
inconceivable
inconceivably
incondensable
incongruously
inconsecutive
inconsequence
inconsiderate
inconsistence
inconsistency
inconspicuous
incontestable
incontestably
incontinently
inconvenience
inconveniency
inconvertible
inconvertibly
inconvincible
incorporation
incorporative
incorporeally
incorrectness
incorruptible
incorruptibly
incorruptness
incredibility
incredulously
incrementally
incriminatory
incurableness
incuriousness
indefatigable
indefatigably
independently

indescribable
indescribably
indeterminacy
indeterminate
indeterminism
indeterminist
indifferently
indiscernible
indiscernibly
indispensable
indispensably
indisposition
indissociable
indistinctive
individualise
individualism
individualist
individuality
individuation
indoctrinator
inductiveness
industrialise
industrialism
industrialist
industriously
ineducability
ineffableness
ineffectively
ineffectually
inefficacious
inefficiently
ineligibility
inevitability
inexhaustible
inexhaustibly
inexorability
inexpediently
inexpensively
inexperienced
inexpressible
inexpressibly
infallibilism
infallibilist
infallibility
infeasibility
inferentially
infinitesimal
inflexibility
inflexionless
inflorescence
influentially
informational
informatively
infundibulate
infuriatingly
ingeniousness
ingenuousness
ingurgitation
inhospitality
injudiciously
injuriousness
innocuousness
innoxiousness
inoffensively
inopportunely
inorganically
inquisitional
inquisitively
inquisitorial
insatiability
inscriptional
insectivorous
insensateness
insensibility
insensitively
insensitivity
insidiousness
insignificant
insinuatingly

insociability
insolubleness
inspectorship
inspirational
instantaneity
instantaneous
instinctively
institutional
instructional
instructively
insubordinate
insubstantial
insufficience
insufficiency
insupportable
insupportably
insusceptible
intangibility
integumentary
intelligencer
intelligently
intemperately
intensiveness
intentionally
intercalation
intercellular
intercolonial
intercolumnar
intercropping
intercultural
intercurrence
interdentally
interdigitate
interestingly
intergalactic
interjectural
interlacement
interlocution
interlocutory
interlocutrix
intermarriage
intermediator
intermittence
international
interoceptive
interosculate
interparietal
interpellator
interpersonal
interpolation
interpolative
interposition
interpretable
interpretress
interpunction
interrelation
interrogation
interrogative
interrogatory
interruptible
interspecific
interspersion
interstratify
intertropical
intraarterial
intracellular
intramuscular
intransigeant
intransigence
intrapersonal
intravenously
intricateness
intrinsically
introgression
introspection
introspective
introversible
intrusiveness
intuitiveness
invariability
inventiveness
inventorially
investigation
investigative
investigatory
invidiousness
invincibility
inviolability
inviolateness
invisibleness
involuntarily
knickerbocker
knowledgeable
knowledgeably
knuckleduster
mnemotechnics
onomatopoetic
ontogenically
ontologically
pneumatically
pneumatolysis
pneumatolytic
pneumatometer
pneumatophore
pneumogastric
pneumonectomy
sniftingvalve
snowblindness
unaccompanied
unaccountable
unaccountably
unadulterated
unambiguously
unanimousness
unanticipated
unarticulated
unbelievingly
unceremonious
uncertainness
uncircumcised
uncleanliness
uncomfortable
uncomfortably
uncompetitive
uncomplaining
uncomplicated
unconceivable
unconcernedly
unconditional
unconditioned
unconformable
unconquerable
unconsciously
unconstrained
uncoordinated
underachiever
undercarriage
underclothing
undereducated
underemphasis
underemployed
underestimate
underexposure
undergraduate
underhandedly
understanding
understrapper
underwhelming
undisciplined
unearthliness
unemotionally
unenlightened
unequivocally
unestablished
unexceptional
unfamiliarity
unfashionable
unfashionably
unfeelingness
unflinchingly
unforgettable
unforgettably
unforthcoming
unfortunately
ungrammatical
unhealthiness
unicameralism
unicameralist
unimpassioned
unimpeachable
uninformative
unintelligent
unintentional
uninterrupted
unmeaningness
unmentionable
unnaturalness
unnecessarily
unobtrusively
unprecedented
unpredictable
unpretentious
unpromisingly
unputdownable
unqualifiedly
unquestioning
unrelentingly
unremittingly
unrighteously
unselfishness
unsociability
unsubstantial
unsuitability
unsymmetrical
untrustworthy
unwarrantable
unwarrantably
unwholesomely
unwillingness
boardinghouse
bombastically
bookingoffice
bouillabaisse
boundlessness
bounteousness
bountifulness
boustrophedon
coagulability
coarsegrained
cobelligerent
coeducational
coenaesthesis
coldbloodedly
coldheartedly
collaboration
collaborative
collaterality
colleagueship
collectedness
collectorship
collieshangie
colloquialism
colourfulness
combativeness
combinatorial
commandership
commemoration
commemorative
commemoratory
commensurable
commensurably
commercialise
commercialism
commercialist
commiseration
commiserative
communication
communicative
communicatory
communisation
communitarian
commutability
compagination
companionable
companionably
companionless
companionship
comparability
comparatively
compartmental
compassionate
compatibility
compendiously
competitively
complainingly
complaisantly
complementary
complexedness
complicatedly
complimentary
compositeness
compositional
comprehension
comprehensive
compressional
computational
concatenation
concavoconvex
conceitedness
concentration
concentrative
concentricity
conceptualise
conceptualism
conceptualist
concertmaster
concessionary
conchological
concomitantly
concretionary
concupiscence
concupiscible
condescension
conditionally
conduciveness
conductorship
condylomatous
confabulation
confabulatory
confectionary
confectionery
confederation
confederative
confessionary
confidingness
configuration
conflagration
conflictingly
confraternity
confrontation
conglomeratic
congratulator
congressional
congresswoman
congruousness
conjecturable
conjecturally
conjugateness
conjugational
conjunctional
conjunctively
connaturality
connectedness
consanguinity
conscientious
consciousness
consecutively
consenescence
consentaneity
consentaneous
consequential
conservatoire
considerately
consideration
consolidation
consolidative
consolidatory
conspicuously
constellation
constellatory
consternation
constrainable
constrainedly
constructable
constructible
consumptively
containership
contamination
contaminative
contemplation
contemplative
contentedness
contentiously
continentally
contortionist
contrabandist
contrabassoon
contraception
contraceptive
contractility
contractually
contradiction
contradictory
contrafagotto
contrapuntist
contrariously
contravention
controversial
convalescence
conventionary
conversazione
conversazioni
convertiplane
convexoconvex
convocational
convulsionary
cooperatively
copartnership
coreligionist
cornification
corporativism
correlatively
correlativity
correspondent
corresponsive
corrigibility
corroboration
corroborative
corroboratory
corrosiveness
corruptionist
corticotropic
corticotropin
cosmopolitise
cosmopolitism
costeffective
cottonpicking
counteraction
counteractive
counterattack
counterchange
countercharge
counterfeiter
counterstroke
counterweight

countinghouse
courteousness
courtsmartial
doctrinairism
documentalist
documentation
dodecaphonist
domestication
domiciliation
doublecrosser
doubledealing
doubleglazing
doublejointed
doubletongued
doubtlessness
followthrough
foolhardiness
foraminiferal
foreknowledge
forementioned
foresightedly
forgetfulness
formalisation
formidability
formulisation
fortification
fortississimo
fortunateness
fortunehunter
fortuneteller
fossiliferous
fossilisation
gonadotrophic
gonadotrophin
goniometrical
goodnaturedly
hocuspocussed
hollowhearted
homeomorphism
homoeomorphic
homoeopathist
homogeneously
homoiothermal
homoiothermic
homosexuality
honorifically
horizontality
horripilation
horsechestnut
horsewhipping
horticultural
housebreaking
jollification
loathsomeness
longsuffering
moderatorship
modernisation
Mohammedanism
mollification
momentariness
momentousness
Monarchianism
moneygrubbing
monochromatic
monocotyledon
monodactylous
monogrammatic
monometallism
monometallist
monomolecular
mononucleosis
monophthongal
Monophysitism
monosyllabism
monosymmetric
Monotheletism
monotrematous
monstrousness
monumentalise
morphogenesis
morphogenetic
morphological
mortification
mothercountry
mouldingboard
mountainously
mountebankery
mourningcloak
mourningpaper
mouthwatering
noiselessness
nomenclatural
nonaggression
nonappearance
nonattendance
noncollegiate
noncompliance
nonconducting
nonconforming
nonconformism
nonconformist
nonconformity
nondeductable
nonfigurative
nonforfeiting
nonfulfilment
nongovernment
nonproductive
nonresistance
nonreturnable
nonsensically
normalisation
northeasterly
northeastward
northwesterly
northwestward
nostalgically
notoriousness
pococurantism
pointillistic
pointlessness
polarographic
poliomyelitis
polliniferous
polyadelphous
polycarbonate
polychromatic
polycotyledon
polydactylous
polyhistorian
polypropylene
polysynthesis
polysynthetic
ponderability
ponderousness
pontification
porcellaneous
postclassical
postcommunion
postoperative
postulational
potentiometer
powerlessness
roentgenogram
roentgenology
rollercoaster
rontgenoscopy
sobermindness
socialisation
sociocultural
socioeconomic
softpedalling
solderingiron
solemnisation
solicitorship
solidungulate
somatological
somnambulator
somniloquence
sophistically
sophisticated
sorrowfulness
soulsearching
soundingboard
southeasterly
southeastward
southwesterly
southwestward
sovietologist
toastmistress
tolerableness
tonguelashing
tonguetwister
tonsillectomy
toothsomeness
topographical
topologically
topsyturvydom
tortoiseshell
toxicological
toxoplasmosis
vocationalism
voicelessness
volatilisable
volcanologist
volumenometer
voluntariness
voluntaristic
voraciousness
vouchsafement
wonderfulness
wonderworking
woodengraving
woolgathering
worldlyminded
worrisomeness
worthlessness
zoogeographer
zoogeographic
apathetically
apheliotropic
apocalyptical
appellatively
applicability
applicatively
apportionment
apprehensible
appropriately
appropriation
appropriative
approximately
approximation
approximative
epeirogenesis
epigrammatise
epigrammatist
epiphenomenal
epiphenomenon
openheartedly
operativeness
ophthalmology
opinionatedly
opisthobranch
opportuneness
opportunistic
oppositionist
opprobriously
spasmodically
specification
spectacularly
spectrography
spectrometric
spectroscopic
speculatively
spelaeologist
speleological
Spencerianism
spermatoblast
spermatogenic
spermatophore
spermatophyte
spheroidicity
sphygmography
spindlelegged
spindleshanks
spinelessness
spinninghouse
spinningwheel
spiritualness
splendiferous
splenetically
spontaneously
sportsmanlike
sportsmanship
sprightliness
sprocketwheel
equestrianism
equidistantly
equilibration
equiponderant
equiponderate
equipotential
equivocalness
squandermania
squarebashing
squeamishness
squeezability
arbitrariness
arbitrational
arboriculture
archaeologist
archaeopteryx
archbishopric
archdeaconate
archidiaconal
archimandrite
architectonic
architectural
argentiferous
argumentation
argumentative
arithmetician
aromatisation
arthritically
artificiality
brachycephaly
brachydactyly
brachypterous
brainlessness
brainstorming
breechloading
brilliantness
broadmindedly
broadspectrum
brokenhearted
brotherliness
brutalisation
crackerbarrel
craftsmanship
craniological
credulousness
criminalistic
criminologist
crosscultural
crossgartered
crosshatching
crosspurposes
crossquestion
cruiserweight
cryobiologist
cryptanalysis
cryptanalytic
cryptographer
cryptographic
cryptological
crystalgazing
crystallinity
draftsmanship
draggletailed
dramatisation
dramaturgical
dreamlessness
dressimprover
dressingtable
erroneousness
fractionalise
fractionation
fractiousness
fragmentarily
fragmentation
freeselection
frequentation
frequentative
frighteningly
frightfulness
frivolousness
frontogenesis
fruitlessness
frustratingly
gracelessness
graminivorous
grammatically
granddaughter
grandfatherly
grandiloquent
grandmotherly
graphological
gratification
gravitational
greensickness
grotesqueness
irrationalise
irrationalism
irrationalist
irrationality
irreclaimable
irreclaimably
irrecoverable
irrecoverably
irrefrangible
irreligionist
irreligiously
irreplaceable
irrepressible
irrepressibly
irresponsible
irresponsibly
irretrievable
irretrievably
irreverential
irritableness
orangeblossom
orchestration
oreographical
organogenesis
organotherapy
ornamentation
ornithologist
orthocephalic
orthognathism
orthognathous
practicalness
pragmatically
prairieoyster
prayermeeting
precautionary
precentorship
precipitantly
precipitately
precipitation
precipitative
precipitously
preconception
predatoriness
predestinator

predicability
predicamental
predicatively
predominantly
predomination
preengagement
preengineered
prefatorially
preferability
prefiguration
prefigurative
prefigurement
prehistorical
prejudicially
preliminarily
prematureness
premeditation
premeditative
premillennial
premonitorily
preoccupation
preordainment
preordination
preparatively
preparatorily
preponderance
preponderancy
prepositional
prepossessing
prepossession
prepreference
PreRaphaelite
prescientific
presidentship
prestigiously
presumptively
pretentiously
pretermission
pretermitting
preternatural
prevarication
pricelessness
primigravidae
primitiveness
primogenitary
primogenitive
primogeniture
primordiality
principalship
prismatically
prizefighting
probationally
problematical
processionary
processionist
proconsulship
procrastinate
procuratorial
professoriate
professorship
profitability
profitsharing
progenitorial
prognosticate
progressional
progressively
progressivism
prohibitively
projectionist
prolegomenary
prolegomenous
proliferation
proliferative
proliferously
prolification
promiscuously
pronounceable
pronouncement
pronunciation
proparoxytone
prophetically
proportionate
propositional
proprietorial
proprioceptor
prosopography
prospectively
prostaglandin
prosthodontia
protectionism
protectionist
protectorship
proteinaceous
Protestantism
protohistoric
protonotarial
protuberantly
provincialise
provincialism
provincialist
provinciality
provisionally
prudentialism
prudentialist
prudentiality
traceableness
tractableness
Tractarianism
traditionally
tranquilliser
transatlantic
transcendence
transcendency
transcription
transcriptive
transformable
transgression
transgressive
transistorise
transitionary
translational
transliterate
translocation
translucently
translucidity
transmigrator
transmissible
transmittable
transmutation
transmutative
transnational
transparently
transpiration
transpiratory
transportable
transposition
transshipment
transshipping
transversally
traumatically
treacherously
treasurership
tremulousness
triangularity
triangulation
tributariness
tricentennial
trichromatism
trigonometric
triliteralism
tritheistical
troglodytical
troublesomely
troublousness
trustworthily
wrongheadedly
ascertainable
ascertainment
assassination
assertiveness
asserveration
assiduousness
associateship
associativity
Assyriologist
asthenosphere
asthmatically
astonishingly
astronautical
astrophysical
eschatologist
eschscholtzia
essentialness
establishment
isochronously
isomerisation
isometrically
isostatically
osteomyelitis
ostreiculture
pseudoarchaic
pseudomorphic
pseudoscience
psilanthropic
psychasthenia
psychoanalyse
psychoanalyst
psychodynamic
psychogenesis
psychogenetic
psychokinesis
psychokinetic
psychological
psychometrics
psychometrist
psychophysics
psychosomatic
psychosurgery
psychotherapy
psychrometric
atheistically
atlantosaurus
atmospherical
atomistically
atrociousness
attainability
attentiveness
attributively
ethnocentrism
italicisation
pteridologist
stabilisation
stainlessness
stalkinghorse
staminiferous
standoffishly
statelessness
statesmanlike
statesmanship
stationmaster
statistically
steadfastness
steeplechaser
steppingstone
stercoraceous
stereographic
stereoscopist
sterilisation
sternforemost
stickingplace
stigmatically
stirpiculture
stoichiometry
stoloniferous
stomatologist
strangulation
strategically
stratigraphic
stratocumulus
stratospheric
strawcoloured
streetwalking
strenuousness
streptococcal
streptococcus
strikebreaker
structuralism
structuralist
structureless
stylistically
auctioneering
audaciousness
Australianism
authentically
authenticator
authorisation
authoritarian
authoritative
autobiography
autocatalysis
autocatalytic
autocephalous
autochthonism
autochthonous
autoeroticism
automatically
autonomically
bumptiousness
bureaucratise
burglariously
businesswoman
butterfingers
butterflyfish
buttonthrough
curvilinearly
customariness
dulcification
Eucharistical
fullfashioned
funambulation
functionalism
functionalist
fundamentally
gubernatorial
guilelessness
guiltlessness
hundredweight
judgeadvocate
judgmatically
judiciousness
jurisprudence
justification
justificative
justificatory
juxtaposition
lucrativeness
ludicrousness
luxuriousness
Muhammadanism
multicellular
multicoloured
multinational
multinucleate
multiplicable
multitudinous
mummification
musicological
mutagenically
mutualisation
nucleoprotein
nullification
numerological
numismatology
nutritionally
outgeneralled
outspokenness
outstandingly
pulverisation
punctiliously
puritanically
purposelessly
purposiveness
pusillanimity
pusillanimous
quadragesimal
quadrennially
quadricipital
quadrilateral
quadrillionth
quadripartite
quadrumvirate
quadruplicate
quadruplicity
qualification
qualificatory
qualitatively
quarrelsomely
quartermaster
quartziferous
querulousness
questioningly
questionnaire
quicktempered
quickwittedly
quincentenary
quincuncially
quingentenary
quinquagenary
Quinquagesima
quinquevalent
quintillionth
quintuplicate
rudimentarily
runningstitch
Russification
subcontractor
subeditorship
subirrigation
sublieutenant
submachinegun
subordinately
subordination
subordinative
subpostmaster
subreptitious
subsaturation
subsequential
subserviently
substantially
substantively
substantivise
substitutable
substructural
subternatural
subterraneous
subtilisation
subversionary
suffocatingly
suffraganship
suffumigation
sulphureously
summarisation
sumptuousness
superabundant
superaddition
superannuable
supercalender
supercritical
superdominant
supereminence
superfamilies
superfetation
superficially
superfluidity
superfluously

superhumanity
superlatively
supernational
supernumerary
superordinate
superphysical
superposition
supersaturate
supersensible
superstitious
supersubtlety
supervenience
supplantation
supplementary
suppositional
supranational
surreptitious
surrogateship
tuberculation
turkeygobbler
vulcanisation
vulcanologist
vulgarisation
vulnerability
availableness
evangelically
everlastingly
evocativeness
overabundance
overbearingly
overconfident
overcredulous
overelaborate
overemphasise
overindulgent
overpopulated
overqualified
oversensitive
overstatement
oversubscribe
overvaluation
ovoviviparous
owneroccupier
swallowtailed
swashbuckling
Swedenborgian
swordsmanship
axiomatically
examinational
examinatorial
exanthematous
exasperatedly
exceptionable
exceptionably
exceptionally
excessiveness
excitableness
exclusiveness
excommunicate
excrescential
excursiveness
excusableness
exemplariness
exhibitionism
exhibitionist
existentially
expansibility
expansiveness
expectoration
expeditionary
expeditiously
expensiveness
explanatorily
explorational
explosiveness
exponentially
expostulation
expostulatory
expressionism
expressionist
expropriation
expurgatorial
exquisiteness
extemporarily
extensibility
extensionally
extensiveness
extermination
exterminatory
exteroceptive
exterritorial
extracellular
extragalactic
extrajudicial
extraordinary
extraphysical
extrapolation
extratropical
extravagantly
extravasation
extravascular
extrinsically
cyberneticist
cylindrically
cytochemistry
dysfunctional
gymnastically
gymnospermous
gynaecocratic
gynaecologist
gynandromorph
hybridisation
hydraulically
hydrocephalic
hydrocephalus
hydrochloride
hydrocracking
hydrodynamics
hydroelectric
hydrogenation
hydromedusoid
hydrometrical
hydrostatical
hydrosulphide
hydrosulphite
hydroxylamine
hymenopterous
hyperboloidal
hypercritical
hypermetrical
hypermetropia
hypermetropic
hyperphysical
hypertrophied
hypnoanalysis
hypnotisation
hypochondriac
hypoglycaemia
hypothecation
myrmecologist
mystification
oystercatcher
pyrheliometer
pyrimethamine
pyrotechnical
syllabication
symbiotically
symbolisation
symmetrically
symphonically
symphoniously
synallagmatic
synchronistic
synchronously
syntactically
synthetically
typographical
typologically
tyrannosaurus
xylographical
zygodactylous

---

anachronistic
anachronously
anaerobically
anagrammatise
anagrammatism
analogousness
anaphrodisiac
apathetically
availableness
beatification
beauteousness
blackguardism
blameableness
blamelessness
blanketflower
blasphemously
blastogenesis
boardinghouse
brachycephaly
brachydactyly
brachypterous
brainlessness
brainstorming
chalcoography
challengeable
challengingly
changeability
changefulness
characterless
chateaubriand
clairaudience
clandestinely
clarification
coagulability
coarsegrained
crackerbarrel
craftsmanship
craniological
deathlessness
diageotropism
diagnostician
diagrammatise
dialectically
diametrically
diaphragmatic
diathermanous
draftsmanship
draggletailed
dramatisation
dramaturgical
elaborateness
evangelically
examinational
examinatorial
exanthematous
exasperatedly
featherheaded
featherstitch
featherweight
flagellantism
fractionalise
fractionation
fractiousness
fragmentarily
fragmentation
glaciological
glamorisation
gracelessness
graminivorous
grammatically
granddaughter
grandfatherly
grandiloquent
grandmotherly
graphological
gratification
gravitational
healthfulness
heartbreaking
heartlessness
heartsickness
imaginatively
inadvertently
inanimateness
inappreciable
inappreciably
inappropriate
inattentively
italicisation
leadpoisoning
leatherjacket
loathsomeness
meadowsaffron
nearsightedly
orangeblossom
peaceableness
phalansterian
phanerogamous
pharisaically
pharmaceutics
pharmaceutist
pharmacologic
pharmacopoeia
plaintiveness
planimetrical
platiniferous
platitudinise
platitudinous
platyhelminth
plausibleness
practicalness
pragmatically
prairieoyster
prayermeeting
quadragesimal
quadrennially
quadricipital
quadrilateral
quadrillionth
quadripartite
quadrumvirate
quadruplicate
quadruplicity
qualification
qualificatory
qualitatively
quarrelsomely
quartermaster
quartziferous
reaffirmation
realistically
rearcommodore
rearrangement
rhadamanthine
RhaetoRomanic
rhapsodically
scandalmonger
scarification
searchwarrant
seaworthiness
shabbygenteel
Shakespearean
Shakespearian
shamelessness
shapelessness
sharecropping
sharpshooting
skateboarding
slangingmatch
spasmodically
stabilisation
stainlessness
stalkinghorse
staminiferous
standoffishly
statelessness
statesmanlike
statesmanship
stationmaster
statistically
swallowtailed
swashbuckling
teachableness
thalassocracy
thanklessness
thaumaturgist
toastmistress
traceableness
tractableness
Tractarianism
traditionally
tranquilliser
transatlantic
transcendence
transcendency
transcription
transcriptive
transformable
transgression
transgressive
transistorise
transitionary
translational
transliterate
translocation
translucently
translucidity
transmigrator
transmissible
transmittable
transmutation
transmutative
transnational
transparently
transpiration
transpiratory
transportable
transposition
transshipment
transshipping
transversally
traumatically
unaccompanied
unaccountable
unaccountably
unadulterated
unambiguously
unanimousness
unanticipated
unarticulated
wearisomeness
weatherbeaten
ambassadorial
ambidexterity
ambidexterous
ambiguousness
ambitiousness
arbitrariness
arbitrational
arboriculture
bibliographer
bibliographic
bibliolatrist
bibliolatrous
bibliological
bibliophilism
bibliophilist
cabinetmaking
cobelligerent
cyberneticist
embarrassment
embellishment
embranglement

embrittlement
embryogenesis
embryological
fibrovascular
gubernatorial
habitableness
hybridisation
laboriousness
liberationist
librarianship
sabrerattling
sobermindness
subcontractor
subeditorship
subirrigation
sublieutenant
submachinegun
subordinately
subordination
subordinative
subpostmaster
subreptitious
subsaturation
subsequential
subserviently
substantially
substantively
substantivise
substitutable
substructural
subternatural
subterraneous
subtilisation
subversionary
tablespoonful
tuberculation
umbelliferous
unbelievingly
accelerometer
acceptability
accessibility
accidentalism
accidentprone
acclimatation
accommodating
accommodation
accommodative
accompaniment
accoutrements
accreditation
acculturation
acculturative
alcoholically
alcoholometer
alcoholometry
archaeologist
archaeopteryx
archbishopric
archdeaconate
archidiaconal
archimandrite
architectonic
architectural
ascertainable
ascertainment
auctioneering
baccalaureate
backformation
backpedalling
backscratcher
backwardation
bacteriolysis
bacteriolytic
bacteriophage
cacographical
cicatrisation
deceitfulness
deceptiveness
decerebration
deciduousness
declaratively
decomposition
decompression
decontaminate
decontrolling
decortication
decrepitation
dichlamydeous
dichotomously
dictatorially
doctrinairism
documentalist
documentation
eccentrically
encapsulation
encephalogram
encompassment
encouragement
encouragingly
encyclopaedia
encyclopaedic
encyclopedism
encyclopedist
eschatologist
eschscholtzia
Eucharistical
exceptionable
exceptionably
exceptionally
excessiveness
excitableness
exclusiveness
excommunicate
excrescential
excursiveness
excusableness
facetiousness
facultatively
hocuspocussed
incandescence
incarceration
incardination
inclusiveness
incombustible
incommunicado
incompetently
inconceivable
inconceivably
incondensable
incongruously
inconsecutive
inconsequence
inconsiderate
inconsistence
inconsistency
inconspicuous
incontestable
incontestably
incontinently
inconvenience
inconveniency
inconvertible
inconvertibly
inconvincible
incorporation
incorporative
incorporeally
incorrectness
incorruptible
incorruptibly
incorruptness
incredibility
incredulously
incrementally
incriminatory
incurableness
incuriousness
lackadaisical
lecherousness
lickerishness
lucrativeness
macaronically
Machiavellian
machicolation
machinegunner
mackerelshark
macrocephalic
macromolecule
mechanisation
microanalysis
microcephalic
micrococcocci
microdetector
micronutrient
microorganism
microphyllous
microscopical
microtonality
necessitarian
necessitation
necessitously
nectariferous
nickeliferous
nucleoprotein
occasionalism
occasionalist
occasionality
occidentalise
Occidentalism
Occidentalist
oecologically
orchestration
picturepalace
picturesquely
pococurantism
recalcitrance
receptibility
receptiveness
recessiveness
reciprocality
reciprocation
reciprocative
recombination
recommendable
recomposition
reconcilement
reconsolidate
reconstructor
recrimination
recriminative
recriminatory
recrudescence
recrystallise
rectangularly
rectification
rectilinearly
saccharimeter
saccharimetry
saccharometer
sacerdotalise
sacerdotalism
sacerdotalist
sacramentally
sacrificially
sacrosanctity
secondariness
secretarybird
secretaryship
secretiveness
sicklefeather
socialisation
sociocultural
socioeconomic
tachistoscope
technicalness
technological
unceremonious
uncertainness
uncircumcised
uncleanliness
uncomfortable
uncomfortably
uncompetitive
uncomplaining
uncomplicated
unconceivable
unconcernedly
unconditional
unconditioned
unconformable
unconquerable
unconsciously
unconstrained
uncoordinated
vacillatingly
vicariousness
viceadmiralty
vicepresident
victimisation
vocationalism
audaciousness
deductibility
dodecaphonist
endocrinology
hydraulically
hydrocephalic
hydrocephalus
hydrochloride
hydrocracking
hydrodynamics
hydroelectric
hydrogenation
hydromedusoid
hydrometrical
hydrostatical
hydrosulphide
hydrosulphite
hydroxylamine
indefatigable
indefatigably
independently
indescribable
indescribably
indeterminacy
indeterminate
indeterminism
indeterminist
indifferently
indiscernible
indiscernibly
indispensable
indispensably
indisposition
indissociable
indistinctive
individualise
individualism
individualist
individuality
individuation
indoctrinator
inductiveness
industrialise
industrialism
industrialist
industriously
judgeadvocate
judgmatically
judiciousness
Kidderminster
ludicrousness
mediatisation
mediterranean
moderatorship
modernisation
paddlesteamer
pedagogically
pedestrianise
pedestrianism
radioactivity
radiolocation
radiotelegram
redescription
redevelopment
reduplication
reduplicative
rudimentarily
sadomasochism
sadomasochist
sedentariness
sedimentation
seditiousness
seductiveness
sidesplitting
tiddledywinks
underachiever
undercarriage
underclothing
undereducated
underemphasis
underemployed
underestimate
underexposure
undergraduate
underhandedly
understanding
understrapper
underwhelming
undisciplined
acetification
acetylcholine
breechloading
cheerlessness
chemoreceptor
clearheadedly
clearinghouse
cleistogamous
coeducational
coenaesthesis
credulousness
dreamlessness
dressimprover
dressingtable
electioneerer
electrocution
electrologist
electromagnet
electrometric
electromotive
electrophorus
electroscopic
electrostatic
electrovalent
elephantiasis
energetically
epeirogenesis
everlastingly
exemplariness
freeselection
frequentation
frequentative
greensickness
haematologist
heebiejeebies
identicalness
ideographical
ideologically
ineducability
ineffableness
ineffectively
ineffectually
inefficacious
inefficiently
ineligibility
inevitability

inexhaustible
inexhaustibly
inexorability
inexpediently
inexpensively
inexperienced
inexpressible
inexpressibly
laevorotation
laevorotatory
liebfraumilch
mnemotechnics
oceanographer
oceanographic
oleomargarine
openheartedly
operativeness
oreographical
overabundance
overbearingly
overconfident
overcredulous
overelaborate
overemphasise
overindulgent
overpopulated
overqualified
oversensitive
overstatement
oversubscribe
overvaluation
paediatrician
paedomorphism
phenomenalise
phenomenalism
phenomenalist
phenomenology
phenylalanine
piezoelectric
plenitudinous
plenteousness
plentifulness
plethorically
pneumatically
pneumatolysis
pneumatolytic
pneumatometer
pneumatophore
pneumogastric
pneumonectomy
precautionary
precentorship
precipitantly
precipitately
precipitation
precipitative
precipitously
preconception
predatoriness
predestinator
predicability
predicamental
predicatively
predominantly
predomination
preengagement
preengineered
prefatorially
preferability
prefiguration
prefigurative
prefigurement
prehistorical
prejudicially
preliminarily
prematureness
premeditation
premeditative
premillennial
premonitorily
preoccupation
preordainment
preordination
preparatively
preparatorily
preponderance
preponderancy
prepositional
prepossessing
prepossession
prepreference
PreRaphaelite
prescientific
presidentship
prestigiously
presumptively
pretentiously
pretermission
pretermitting
preternatural
prevarication
pseudoarchaic
pseudomorphic
pseudoscience
pteridologist
querulousness
questioningly
questionnaire
reembarkation
reexamination
rheumatically
roentgenogram
roentgenology
sheepshearing
sleeplessness
smellingsalts
specification
spectacularly
spectrography
spectrometric
spectroscopic
speculatively
spelaeologist
speleological
Spencerianism
spermatoblast
spermatogenic
spermatophore
spermatophyte
steadfastness
steeplechaser
steppingstone
stercoraceous
stereographic
stereoscopist
sterilisation
sternforemost
Swedenborgian
theanthropism
theatricalise
theatricalism
theatricality
thenceforward
theologically
theoretically
thereinbefore
theriomorphic
thermochemist
thermodynamic
thermogenesis
thermonuclear
thermophilous
thermoplastic
thermosetting
thermotropism
treacherously
treasurership
tremulousness
unearthliness
unemotionally
unenlightened
unequivocally
unestablished
unexceptional
wheelerdealer
affectionless
affenpinscher
affirmatively
afforestation
affreightment
anfractuosity
defeasibility
defectiveness
defencelessly
defensibility
deferentially
defervescence
defibrination
deforestation
deformational
differentiate
diffusiveness
effectiveness
effervescence
effervescency
efficaciously
efflorescence
infallibilism
infallibilist
infallibility
infeasibility
inferentially
infinitesimal
inflexibility
inflexionless
inflorescence
influentially
informational
informatively
infundibulate
infuriatingly
lifepreserver
nefariousness
offensiveness
offhandedness
officiousness
referentially
reflexibility
reforestation
reformability
reformational
refractometer
refrigeration
softpedalling
suffocatingly
suffraganship
suffumigation
unfamiliarity
unfashionable
unfashionably
unfeelingness
unflinchingly
unforgettable
unforgettably
unforthcoming
unfortunately
aggiornamento
agglomeration
agglomerative
agglutination
agglutinative
aggravatingly
algebraically
angiospermous
anglicisation
AngloAmerican
AngloCatholic
argentiferous
argumentation
argumentative
daguerreotype
degranulation
digestibility
ingeniousness
ingenuousness
ingurgitation
jiggerypokery
legislatively
legislatorial
lightfingered
lightheadedly
lightmindedly
lightsomeness
lignification
Maginotminded
magisterially
magnanimously
magnetisation
magnetomotive
magnetosphere
magnification
magnificently
magniloquence
megacephalous
megasporangia
negligibility
negotiability
niggardliness
nightmarishly
nightwatchman
organogenesis
organotherapy
pigeonchested
pigeonhearted
pigeonlivered
pigheadedness
regardfulness
regimentation
regretfulness
regurgitation
righteousness
righthandedly
sagaciousness
sightlessness
signalisation
significantly
signification
significative
ungrammatical
vegetarianism
zygodactylous
achromaticity
apheliotropic
atheistically
ethnocentrism
exhibitionism
exhibitionist
ichthyography
ichthyologist
ichthyosaurus
inhospitality
Mohammedanism
Muhammadanism
ochlocratical
ophthalmology
schadenfreude
schematically
schizocarpous
schizogenesis
schizophrenia
schizophrenic
scholarliness
scholasticism
schoolteacher
spheroidicity
sphygmography
unhealthiness
abiologically
acidification
adiabatically
animadversion
animalisation
arithmetician
axiomatically
brilliantness
chieftainship
chinkerinchee
climactically
climatologist
climbingframe
criminalistic
criminologist
deipnosophist
enigmatically
epigrammatise
epigrammatist
epiphenomenal
epiphenomenon
existentially
faithlessness
flirtatiously
frighteningly
frightfulness
frivolousness
guilelessness
guiltlessness
hairsplitting
idiomatically
idiosyncratic
imitativeness
knickerbocker
laissezpasser
leishmaniasis
leisureliness
meistersinger
neighbourhood
noiselessness
opinionatedly
opisthobranch
painstakingly
painterliness
philanthropic
philhellenism
philhellenist
philosophical
philosophiser
pointillistic
pointlessness
pricelessness
primigravidae
primitiveness
primogenitary
primogenitive
primogeniture
primordiality
principalship
prismatically
prizefighting
psilanthropic
quicktempered
quickwittedly
quincentenary
quincuncially
quingentenary
quinquagenary
Quinquagesima
quinquevalent
quintillionth
quintuplicate
reimbursement
reincarnation
reinforcement
reinstatement
reintegration
reinvigorator

scientologist
scintillating
scintillation
seismographer
seismographic
seismological
shiftlessness
sniftingvalve
spindlelegged
spindleshanks
spinelessness
spinninghouse
spinningwheel
spiritualness
stickingplace
stigmatically
stirpiculture
thigmotropism
thimblerigged
thimblerigger
triangularity
triangulation
tributariness
tricentennial
trichromatism
trigonometric
triliteralism
tritheistical
unicameralism
unicameralist
unimpassioned
unimpeachable
uninformative
unintelligent
unintentional
uninterrupted
voicelessness
whimsicalness
whithersoever
enjoyableness
injudiciously
injuriousness
objectionable
objectionably
objectiveness
objectivistic
rejuvenescent
allegorically
allelomorphic
atlantosaurus
balkanisation
balsamiferous
BaltoSlavonic
beleaguerment
belleslettres
belligerently
bildungsroman
calcification
calculatingly
calligraphist
callisthenics
Calvinistical
chlamydomonas
chlamydospore
coldbloodedly
coldheartedly
collaboration
collaborative
collaterality
colleagueship
collectedness
collectorship
collieshangie
colloquialism
colourfulness
cylindrically
deleteriously
deliciousness
deliquescence

deliriousness
dulcification
enlightenment
falsification
felicitations
feloniousness
filterability
followthrough
fullfashioned
galactosaemia
galvanisation
halfheartedly
halfsovereign
hallucination
hallucinative
hallucinatory
helminthiasis
helminthology
helterskelter
hilariousness
hollowhearted
illogicalness
illustriously
jollification
kaleidoscopic
malacological
malacostracan
maladaptation
maladjustment
maladminister
maladroitness
malariologist
maliciousness
malleableness
Malthusianism
mellifluously
melodiousness
melodramatics
melodramatise
melodramatist
millefeuilles
millennialism
millionairess
mollification
multicellular
multicoloured
multinational
multinucleate
multiplicable
multitudinous
nullification
obliviousness
palaeographer
palaeographic
palaeontology
palaeozoology
palatableness
palletisation
palynological
polarographic
poliomyelitis
polliniferous
polyadelphous
polycarbonate
polychromatic
polycotyledon
polydactylous
polyhistorian
polypropylene
polysynthesis
polysynthetic
pulverisation
religiousness
rollercoaster
salaciousness
salmonellosis
scleroprotein
selectiveness
selenocentric

selenographer
selenographic
selenological
selfabasement
selfaddressed
selfadjusting
selfappointed
selfapproving
selfasserting
selfassertion
selfassertive
selfassurance
selfassuredly
selfawareness
selfcentredly
selfcollected
selfcommunion
selfconceited
selfcondemned
selfconfessed
selfconfident
selfconscious
selfconsuming
selfcontained
selfcontented
selfconvicted
selfcriticism
selfdeceiving
selfdeception
selfdeceptive
selfdefeating
selfdependent
selfdirecting
selfdirection
selfdiscovery
selfdispraise
selfeducation
selfevidently
selfexecuting
selfexistence
selffertility
selfforgetful
selfgenerated
selfgoverning
selfimportant
selfinduction
selfindulgent
selfinflicted
selfinsurance
selfknowledge
selfopinioned
selfpityingly
selfpollinate
selfpossessed
selfpropelled
selfrecording
selfregarding
selfreproving
selfrepugnant
selfrestraint
selfrevealing
selfrighteous
selfsacrifice
selfsatisfied
selfslaughter
selfsterility
selfsufficing
selfsupported
selfsurrender
selfsustained
selftormentor
silvertongued
solderingiron
solemnisation
solicitorship
solidungulate
splendiferous
splenetically
sulphureously

syllabication
talkativeness
telegrammatic
telencephalon
teleportation
telerecording
televisionary
tolerableness
valuelessness
villeggiatura
volatilisable
volcanologist
volumenometer
voluntariness
voluntaristic
vulcanisation
vulcanologist
vulgarisation
vulnerability
wellapPointed
xylographical
admeasurement
administrable
administrator
admirableness
admissibility
admonishingly
atmospherical
bamboozlement
bombastically
bumptiousness
campanologist
camphoraceous
combativeness
combinatorial
commandership
commemoration
commemorative
commemoratory
commensurable
commensurably
commercialise
commercialism
commercialist
commiseration
commiserative
communication
communicative
communicatory
communisation
communitarian
commutability
compagination
companionable
companionably
companionless
companionship
comparability
comparatively
compartmental
compassionate
compatibility
compendiously
competitively
complainingly
complaisantly
complementary
complexedness
complicatedly
complimentary
compositeness
compositional
comprehension
comprehensive
compressional
computational
dematerialise
demonstration
demonstrative

demythologise
dimensionally
dimensionless
domestication
domiciliation
gametogenesis
gymnastically
gymnospermous
hemicellulose
hemiparasitic
hemispherical
homeomorphism
homoeomorphic
homoeopathist
homogeneously
homoiothermal
homoiothermic
homosexuality
hymenopterous
immarcescible
immaterialise
immaterialism
immaterialist
immateriality
immediateness
immiscibility
immovableness
immunological
immunotherapy
immutableness
lamellibranch
limitlessness
mammaliferous
membranaceous
momentariness
momentousness
mummification
nemathelminth
nomenclatural
numerological
numismatology
reminiscently
remonstrantly
remonstration
remonstrative
remorselessly
removableness
semeiological
semiautomatic
semibarbarian
semibarbarism
semicivilised
semiconductor
semiconscious
semilogarithm
semiparasitic
semipermanent
semipermeable
semiporcelain
somatological
somnambulator
somniloquence
summarisation
sumptuousness
symbiotically
symbolisation
symmetrically
symphonically
symphoniously
temerariously
temperamental
temperateness
tempestuously
temporalities
temporariness
temporisation
timeconsuming
unmeaningness
unmentionable

amniocentesis
annexationist
beneficiation
canaliculated
candlelighter
candlesnuffer
cannibalistic
centreforward
centrifugally
centripetally
cinematically
cinematograph
cinquecentist
concatenation
concavoconvex
conceitedness
concentration
concentrative
concentricity
conceptualise
conceptualism
conceptualist
concertmaster
concessionary
conchological
concomitantly
concretionary
concupiscence
concupiscible
condescension
conditionally
conduciveness
conductorship
condylomatous
confabulation
confabulatory
confectionary
confectionery
confederation
confederative
confessionary
confidingness
configuration
conflagration
conflictingly
confraternity
confrontation
conglomeratic
congratulator
congressional
congresswoman
congruousness
conjecturable
conjecturally
conjugateness
conjugational
conjunctional
conjunctively
connaturality
connectedness
consanguinity
conscientious
consciousness
consecutively
consenescence
consentaneity
consentaneous
consequential
conservatoire
considerately
consideration
consolidation
consolidative
consolidatory
conspicuously
constellation
constellatory
consternation
constrainable
constrainedly
constructable
constructible
consumptively
containership
contamination
contaminative
contemplation
contemplative
contentedness
contentiously
continentally
contortionist
contrabandist
contrabassoon
contraception
contraceptive
contractility
contractually
contradiction
contradictory
contrafagotto
contrapuntist
contrariously
contravention
controversial
convalescence
conventionary
conversazione
conversazioni
convertiplane
convexoconvex
convocational
convulsionary
dangerousness
denationalise
dendritically
denticulation
fantastically
funambulation
functionalism
functionalist
fundamentally
generalisable
generalissimo
gentlemanlike
gonadotrophic
gonadotrophin
goniometrical
gynaecocratic
gynaecologist
gynandromorph
honorifically
hundredweight
ignominiously
innocuousness
innoxiousness
kinematically
kinematograph
lancecorporal
lancesergeant
landownership
languishingly
lineengraving
linseywoolsey
longsuffering
manageability
manganiferous
mangoldwurzel
Manichaeanism
manifestation
manifestative
manipulatable
manneristical
mensurability
mineralogical
ministerially
Monarchianism
moneygrubbing
monochromatic
monocotyledon
monodactylous
monogrammatic
monometallism
monometallist
monomolecular
mononucleosis
monophthongal
Monophysitism
monosyllabism
monosymmetric
Monotheletism
monotrematous
monstrousness
monumentalise
nonaggression
nonappearance
nonattendance
noncollegiate
noncompliance
nonconducting
nonconforming
nonconformism
nonconformist
nonconformity
nondeductable
nonfigurative
nonforfeiting
nonfulfilment
nongovernment
nonproductive
nonresistance
nonreturnable
nonsensically
obnoxiousness
omnicompetent
ornamentation
ornithologist
owneroccupier
panegyrically
panicstricken
pantagruelian
pantagruelism
pantagruelist
pantheistical
pantisocratic
pendulousness
penetrability
penetratingly
penetratively
penitentially
Pennsylvanian
pennyfarthing
pennypinching
penuriousness
ponderability
ponderousness
pontification
punctiliously
randomisation
renegotiation
rontgenoscopy
runningstitch
sanctimonious
sanitationist
sansculottism
sensationally
senselessness
sensitisation
sensitiveness
sententiously
sentimentally
singlehearted
synallagmatic
synchronistic
synchronously
syntactically
synthetically
tantalisation
tantalisingly
tenaciousness
tendentiously
tenderhearted
tentativeness
tintinnabular
tintinnabulum
tonguelashing
tonguetwister
tonsillectomy
unnaturalness
unnecessarily
vantageground
venerableness
venereologist
ventriloquial
ventriloquise
ventriloquism
ventriloquist
venturesomely
venturousness
viniculturist
windowshopper
winterberries
wonderfulness
wonderworking
xanthochroism
zinjanthropus
abortifacient
acotyledonous
agonistically
amorphousness
anomalistical
anomalousness
anonymousness
apocalyptical
aromatisation
atomistically
biodegradable
bioenergetics
biogeographer
biotechnology
bloodboltered
bloodcurdling
bloodlessness
bloodrelation
Bloomsburyite
bookingoffice
broadmindedly
broadspectrum
brokenhearted
brotherliness
choreographer
choreographic
closedcircuit
clothesbasket
cooperatively
crosscultural
crossgartered
crosshatching
crosspurposes
crossquestion
deodorisation
deontological
egocentricity
evocativeness
floricultural
floristically
flourishingly
foolhardiness
frontogenesis
geocentricism
geochronology
geometrically
geomorphology
geostationary
geotropically
globetrotting
glorification
glossographer
goodnaturedly
grotesqueness
inoffensively
inopportunely
inorganically
isochronously
isomerisation
isometrically
isostatically
knowledgeable
knowledgeably
neoclassicism
neoclassicist
neoplasticism
odontoglossum
odontological
odoriferously
onomatopoetic
ovoviviparous
phonautograph
phosphoretted
photochemical
photochromics
photochromism
photoelectric
photoelectron
photoemission
photoemissive
photoperiodic
photopositive
photoreceptor
probationally
problematical
processionary
processionist
proconsulship
procrastinate
procuratorial
professoriate
professorship
profitability
profitsharing
progenitorial
prognosticate
progressional
progressively
progressivism
prohibitively
projectionist
prolegomenary
prolegomenous
proliferation
proliferative
proliferously
prolification
promiscuously
pronounceable
pronouncement
pronunciation
proparoxytone
prophetically
proportionate
propositional
proprietorial
proprioceptor
prosopography
prospectively
prostaglandin
prosthodontia
protectionism
protectionist
protectorship
proteinaceous
Protestantism
protohistoric
protonotarial
protuberantly

provincialise
provincialism
provincialist
provinciality
provisionally
reorientation
rhodochrosite
scolopendrium
scorbutically
scorification
scorpiongrass
shockabsorber
shootingbrake
shootingrange
shootingstick
shorttempered
shoulderblade
shoulderstrap
smokelessness
smoothingiron
snowblindness
spontaneously
sportsmanlike
sportsmanship
stoichiometry
stoloniferous
stomatologist
swordsmanship
thoroughbrace
thoroughgoing
thoroughpaced
thoughtlessly
thoughtreader
toothsomeness
troglodytical
troublesomely
troublousness
unobtrusively
violoncellist
wholesomeness
woodengraving
woolgathering
wrongheadedly
zoogeographer
zoogeographic
amphiprostyle
amplification
appellatively
applicability
applicatively
apportionment
apprehensible
appropriately
appropriation
appropriative
approximately
approximation
approximative
capaciousness
caprification
cephalothorax
copartnership
dependability
depersonalise
deprecatingly
emphysematous
expansibility
expansiveness
expectoration
expeditionary
expeditiously
expensiveness
explanatorily
explorational
explosiveness
exponentially
expostulation
expostulatory
expressionism
expressionist
expropriation
expurgatorial
haphazardness
heptasyllabic
hyperboloidal
hypercritical
hypermetrical
hypermetropia
hypermetropic
hyperphysical
hypertrophied
hypnoanalysis
hypnotisation
hypochondriac
hypoglycaemia
hypothecation
impalpability
impartibility
impassability
impassibility
impassiveness
impeccability
impecuniosity
impenetration
imperceptible
imperceptibly
impercipience
imperfectness
imperialistic
imperiousness
impermissible
impersonalise
impersonality
impersonation
impertinently
imperturbable
imperturbably
impetuousness
implacability
implicatively
impolitically
imponderables
importunately
impossibility
impracticable
impracticably
impractically
impressionism
impressionist
improbability
impropriation
improvability
improvidently
improvisation
improvisatory
impulsiveness
kapellmeister
lepidopterist
lepidopterous
leptocephalic
leptospirosis
naphthylamine
nephelometric
opportuneness
opportunistic
oppositionist
opprobriously
papaveraceous
paperhangings
papillomatous
peptonisation
rapaciousness
rapturousness
repetitionary
repetitiously
replenishment
reprehensible
reprehensibly
representable
reproachfully
reproachingly
republicanise
republicanism
republication
repulsiveness
separableness
separationist
septentrional
sophistically
sophisticated
superabundant
superaddition
superannuable
supercalender
supercritical
superdominant
supereminence
superfamilies
superfetation
superficially
superfluidity
superfluously
superhumanity
superlatively
supernational
supernumerary
superordinate
superphysical
superposition
supersaturate
supersensible
superstitious
supersubtlety
supervenience
supplantation
supplementary
suppositional
supranational
taperecording
topographical
topologically
topsyturvydom
typographical
typologically
unprecedented
unpredictable
unpretentious
unpromisingly
unputdownable
vapourishness
acquiescently
acquiescingly
exquisiteness
inquisitional
inquisitively
inquisitorial
requisiteness
sequentiality
sequestration
unqualifiedly
unquestioning
acrimoniously
acrobatically
acrylonitrile
aerodynamical
agreeableness
agriculturist
aircraftwoman
airworthiness
atrociousness
barbarisation
barbarousness
barefacedness
barrelchested
Berkeleianism
birefringence
bureaucratise
burglariously
carboniferous
carbonisation
carcinomatous
cardiographer
carnivorously
cartilaginous
cerebrospinal
ceremonialism
ceremonialist
ceremoniously
certification
certificatory
chrematistics
Christmastide
Christmastime
chromatically
chromatograph
chromatolytic
chromatophore
chromospheric
chronographic
chronological
chrysanthemum
circumambient
circumference
circumfluence
circumspectly
circumvallate
circumvention
coreligionist
cornification
corporativism
correlatively
correlativity
correspondent
corresponsive
corrigibility
corroboration
corroborative
corroboratory
corrosiveness
corruptionist
corticotropic
corticotropin
curvilinearly
derequisition
derestriction
dermatologist
egregiousness
erroneousness
ferociousness
ferrimagnetic
ferroconcrete
ferroelectric
ferromagnetic
fertilisation
foraminiferal
foreknowledge
forementioned
foresightedly
forgetfulness
formalisation
formidability
formulisation
fortification
fortississimo
fortunateness
fortunehunter
fortuneteller
garnetiferous
garrulousness
germanisation
gerontocratic
gerontologist
harbourmaster
hardheartedly
harmonisation
hermaphrodite
hermeneutical
herpetologist
horizontality
horripilation
horsechestnut
horsewhipping
horticultural
irrationalise
irrationalism
irrationalist
irrationality
irreclaimable
irreclaimably
irrecoverable
irrecoverably
irrefrangible
irreligionist
irreligiously
irreplaceable
irrepressible
irrepressibly
irresponsible
irresponsibly
irretrievable
irretrievably
irreverential
irritableness
jerrybuilding
jurisprudence
laryngoscopic
martyrisation
martyrologist
mercenariness
mercerisation
merchandising
mercilessness
meritoriously
mirthlessness
morphogenesis
morphogenetic
morphological
mortification
myrmecologist
nervelessness
normalisation
northeasterly
northeastward
northwesterly
northwestward
parabolically
paradoxically
parallelogram
paramagnetism
paranormality
paraphernalia
parasitically
parasiticidal
parasynthesis
parasynthetic
parenthetical
parliamentary
parthenocarpy
participation
participative
participatory
particoloured
particularise
particularism
particularist
particularity
partridgewood
perambulation
perambulatory
percussionist
perdurability
peregrination
perfectionism
perfectionist
perfunctorily

perichondrial verifiability dispossession misconception authorisation
perichondrium verisimilarly dispraisingly miserableness authoritarian
periodisation vermiculation disproportion misgovernment authoritative
perishability vernacularise disrespectful mismanagement autobiography
perissodactyl vernacularism dissemblingly mistrustfully autocatalysis
permutability vernacularity dissemination mistrustingly autocatalytic
perpendicular vernalisation disseminative misunderstand autocephalous
perseveration versicoloured disseveration misunderstood autochthonism
perspectively versification dissimilarity musicological autochthonous
perspicacious vertiginously dissimilation mystification autoeroticism
perspicuously voraciousness dissimilitude nostalgically automatically
pervasiveness worldlyminded dissimulation observational autonomically
phraseologist worrisomeness dissolubility obsessiveness bathymetrical
phreatophytic worthlessness dissoluteness obstinateness battlecruiser
phrenetically Zarathustrian dissymetrical obstructively betweenwhiles
phrenological absorbability distastefully oystercatcher butterfingers
porcellaneous abstractional distinctively passementerie butterflyfish
puritanically aesthetically distinguished passionflower buttonthrough
purposelessly answerability distressfully pestiferously catechisation
purposiveness assassination distressingly piscicultural categorically
pyrheliometer assertiveness distributable postclassical cottonpicking
pyrimethamine asserveration distrustfully postcommunion cytochemistry
pyrotechnical assiduousness dysfunctional postoperative deterioration
sarcastically associateship essentialness postulational deteriorative
scrapmerchant associativity fasciculation pusillanimity determinately
scripturalism Assyriologist fascinatingly pusillanimous determination
scripturalist Australianism Fascistically resentfulness determinative
scrumptiously basidiomycete festschriften resistibility deterministic
SerboCroatian businesswoman fissiparously resolvability detrimentally
serendipitous cosmopolitise fossiliferous resourcefully entertainment
sergeantmajor cosmopolitism fossilisation resplendently entomological
serialisation costeffective gasteropodous restoratively entomophagous
sericulturist customariness gastrocnemius restrictively entomophilous
seriousminded dastardliness gastroenteric resuscitation entomostracan
serologically descriptively gastrological resuscitative establishment
sorrowfulness desegregation gastronomical Russification extemporarily
sprightliness desirableness gesticulation sesquiplicate extensibility
sprocketwheel desperateness gesticulative tastelessness extensionally
strangulation destructively gesticulatory testification extensiveness
strategically destructivity histrionicism unselfishness extermination
stratigraphic desultoriness insatiability unsociability exterminatory
stratocumulus disadvantaged inscriptional unsubstantial exteroceptive
stratospheric disaffectedly insectivorous unsuitability exterritorial
strawcoloured disaffirmance insensateness unsymmetrical extracellular
streetwalking disappearance insensibility visionariness extragalactic
strenuousness disarticulate insensitively visualisation extrajudicial
streptococcal disciplinable insensitivity actinomorphic extraordinary
streptococcus discoloration insidiousness actinomycetes extraphysical
strikebreaker discommodious insignificant actinomycosis extrapolation
structuralism disconcerting insinuatingly actualisation extratropical
structuralist disconcertion insociability alternatively extravagantly
structureless disconformity insolubleness anthelminthic extravasation
surreptitious disconnection inspectorship anthropogenic extravascular
surrogateship discontinuity inspirational anthropometry extrinsically
teratological discontinuous instantaneity anthropopathy heterogeneity
tercentennial discreditable instantaneous anthropophagi heterogeneous
tergiversator discreditably instinctively anthropophagy heterogenesis
terminability discretionary institutional anthroposophy heterogenetic
terminational discriminator instructional Antichristian heteromorphic
terminatively disembodiment instructively anticlimactic heteropterous
terpsichorean disengagement insubordinate anticlockwise heterosporous
terrestrially disfigurement insubstantial anticoagulant heterothallic
territorially disgracefully insufficience antihistamine heterotrophic
terrorisation disharmonious insufficiency antilogarithm intangibility
thrasonically dishonourable insupportable antinomianism integumentary
threateningly dishonourably insupportably antipersonnel intelligencer
threecornered disintegrator insusceptible antiscorbutic intelligently
threequarters disinterested justification arthritically intemperately
thremmatology disinvestment justificative artificiality intensiveness
thrillingness disjunctively justificatory asthenosphere intentionally
tortoiseshell dismantlement masculineness asthmatically intercalation
turkeygobbler dismemberment masterfulness astonishingly intercellular
tyrannosaurus disobediently mesencephalon astronautical intercolonial
unrelentingly disparagement mesmerisation astrophysical intercolumnar
unremittingly disparagingly misanthropist attainability intercropping
unrighteously disparateness miscegenation attentiveness intercultural
veraciousness dispassionate miscellaneous attributively intercurrence
verbalisation displantation mischievously authentically interdentally
verbigeration disposability miscomprehend authenticator interdigitate

interestingly
intergalactic
interjectural
interlacement
interlocution
interlocutory
interlocutrix
intermarriage
intermediator
intermittence
international
interoceptive
interosculate
interparietal
interpellator
interpersonal
interpolation
interpolative
interposition
interpretable
interpretress
interpunction
interrelation
interrogation
interrogative
interrogatory
interruptible
interspecific
interspersion
interstratify
intertropical
intraarterial
intracellular
intramuscular
intransigeant
intransigence
intrapersonal
intravenously
intricateness
intrinsically
introgression
introspection
introspective
introversible
intrusiveness
intuitiveness
lethargically
letterperfect
litigiousness
materfamilias
materialistic
mathematician
matriculation
matrilineally
metagrobolise
metalliferous
metallisation
metallography
metallurgical
metamorphoses
metamorphosis
metaphosphate
metaphysician
metastability
meteorologist
Methodistical
metonymically
metrification
mitochondrion
mothercountry
mutagenically
mutualisation
nationalistic
nitrification
nitrobacteria
nitrocompound
notoriousness
nutritionally
obtrusiveness
octocentenary
ontogenically
ontologically
orthocephalic
orthognathism
orthognathous
osteomyelitis
ostreiculture
outgeneralled
outspokenness
outstandingly
paterfamilias
paternalistic
pathogenicity
pathognomonic
patriotically
patronisingly
petrification
petrochemical
petroliferous
potentiometer
ratiocination
ratiocinative
rationalistic
rattlebrained
retentiveness
retranslation
retroactively
retroactivity
retrogression
retrogressive
retrospection
retrospective
ritualisation
tetrasyllable
titillatingly
untrustworthy
viticulturist
vitrification
waterproofing
aluminiferous
aluminisation
bouillabaisse
boundlessness
bounteousness
bountifulness
boustrophedon
brutalisation
cauterisation
chuckleheaded
churchmanship
counteraction
counteractive
counterattack
counterchange
countercharge
counterfeiter
counterstroke
counterweight
countinghouse
courteousness
courtsmartial
cruiserweight
dauntlessness
deuteragonist
Deuteronomist
doublecrosser
doubledealing
doubleglazing
doublejointed
doubletongued
doubtlessness
ecumenicalism
educationally
equestrianism
equidistantly
equilibration
equiponderant
equiponderate
equipotential
equivocalness
faultlessness
feudalisation
feuilletonism
feuilletonist
fruitlessness
frustratingly
glutinousness
housebreaking
knuckleduster
laughableness
laughingstock
mouldingboard
mountainously
mountebankery
mourningcloak
mourningpaper
mouthwatering
neurastheniac
neurovascular
pluralisation
pluripresence
prudentialism
prudentialist
prudentiality
sculpturesque
soulsearching
soundingboard
southeasterly
southeastward
southwesterly
southwestward
squandermania
squarebashing
squeamishness
squeezability
tautologously
thundershower
thunderstruck
thurification
trustworthily
vouchsafement
adventuresome
adventurously
adversatively
advertisement
advisableness
devastatingly
developmental
devolutionary
devolutionist
divertisement
eavesdropping
environmental
invariability
inventiveness
inventorially
investigation
investigative
investigatory
invidiousness
invincibility
inviolability
inviolateness
invisibleness
involuntarily
levelcrossing
navigableness
revaccination
revelationist
revendication
reverberation
reverberative
reverberatory
reverentially
reversibility
revolutionary
revolutionise
revolutionism
revolutionist
sovietologist
vivaciousness
vivisectional
bewilderingly
powerlessness
sewingmachine
unwarrantable
unwarrantably
unwholesomely
unwillingness
dexterousness
juxtaposition
lexicographer
lexicographic
luxuriousness
taxonomically
toxicological
toxoplasmosis
vexatiousness
cryobiologist
cryptanalysis
cryptanalytic
cryptographer
cryptographic
cryptological
crystalgazing
crystallinity
phycoerythrin
phyllophagous
physiognomist
physiographer
physiographic
physiological
physiotherapy
phytoplankton
psychasthenia
psychoanalyse
psychoanalyst
psychodynamic
psychogenesis
psychogenetic
psychokinesis
psychokinetic
psychological
psychometrics
psychometrist
psychophysics
psychosomatic
psychosurgery
psychotherapy
psychrometric
stylistically
hazardousness

---

adiabatically
ambassadorial
assassination
atlantosaurus
attainability
audaciousness
broadmindedly
broadspectrum
canaliculated
capaciousness
chlamydomonas
chlamydospore
cicatrisation
clearheadedly
clearinghouse
copartnership
dematerialise
denationalise
devastatingly
disadvantaged
disaffectedly
disaffirmance
disappearance
disarticulate
dreamlessness
embarrassment
encapsulation
establishment
expansibility
expansiveness
foraminiferal
funambulation
galactosaemia
gonadotrophic
gonadotrophin
gynaecocratic
gynaecologist
gynandromorph
hazardousness
hilariousness
immarcescible
immaterialise
immaterialism
immaterialist
immateriality
impalpability
impartibility
impassability
impassibility
impassiveness
incandescence
incarceration
incardination
infallibilism
infallibilist
infallibility
insatiability
intangibility
invariability
irrationalise
irrationalism
irrationalist
irrationality
macaronically
malacological
malacostracan
maladaptation
maladjustment
maladminister
maladroitness
malariologist
manageability
megacephalous
megasporangia
metagrobolise
metalliferous
metallisation
metallography
metallurgical
metamorphoses
metamorphosis
metaphosphate
metaphysician
metastability
misanthropist
Mohammedanism
Monarchianism
Muhammadanism
mutagenically
nefariousness
nemathelminth
nonaggression
nonappearance
nonattendance
occasionalism
occasionalist
occasionality
oceanographer
oceanographic
organogenesis
organotherapy
ornamentation

palaeographer
palaeographic
palaeontology
palaeozoology
palatableness
papaveraceous
parabolically
paradoxically
parallelogram
paramagnetism
paranormality
paraphernalia
parasitically
parasiticidal
parasynthesis
parasynthetic
pedagogically
perambulation
perambulatory
phraseologist
polarographic
rapaciousness
recalcitrance
regardfulness
revaccination
sagaciousness
salaciousness
schadenfreude
scrapmerchant
separableness
separationist
somatological
squandermania
squarebashing
steadfastness
strangulation
strategically
stratigraphic
stratocumulus
stratospheric
strawcoloured
synallagmatic
tenaciousness
teratological
theanthropism
theatricalise
theatricalism
theatricality
thrasonically
treacherously
treasurership
triangularity
triangulation
tyrannosaurus
unearthliness
unfamiliarity
unfashionable
unfashionably
unnaturalness
unwarrantable
unwarrantably
veraciousness
vexatiousness
vicariousness
vivaciousness
vocationalism
volatilisable
voraciousness
Zarathustrian
bamboozlement
barbarisation
barbarousness
bombastically
carboniferous
carbonisation
combativeness
combinatorial
doublecrosser
doubledealing
doubleglazing
doublejointed
doubletongued
doubtlessness
elaborateness
globetrotting
harbourmaster
heebiejeebies
liebfraumilch
membranaceous
probationally
problematical
SerboCroatian
shabbygenteel
stabilisation
symbiotically
symbolisation
tributariness
unobtrusively
verbalisation
verbigeration
aircraftwoman
anachronistic
anachronously
apocalyptical
baccalaureate
blackguardism
brachycephaly
brachydactyly
brachypterous
calcification
calculatingly
carcinomatous
chuckleheaded
circumambient
circumference
circumfluence
circumspectly
circumvallate
circumvention
concatenation
concavoconvex
conceitedness
concentration
concentrative
concentricity
conceptualise
conceptualism
conceptualist
concertmaster
concessionary
conchological
concomitantly
concretionary
concupiscence
concupiscible
crackerbarrel
descriptively
disciplinable
discoloration
discommodious
disconcerting
disconcertion
disconformity
disconnection
discontinuity
discontinuous
discreditable
discreditably
discretionary
discriminator
dulcification
educationally
egocentricity
electioneerer
electrocution
electrologist
electromagnet
electrometric
electromotive
electrophorus
electroscopic
electrostatic
electrovalent
evocativeness
fasciculation
fascinatingly
Fascistically
fractionalise
fractionation
fractiousness
functionalism
functionalist
geocentricism
geochronology
glaciological
gracelessness
inscriptional
isochronously
knickerbocker
knuckleduster
lancecorporal
lancesergeant
masculineness
mercenariness
mercerisation
merchandising
mercilessness
miscegenation
miscellaneous
mischievously
miscomprehend
misconception
neoclassicism
neoclassicist
noncollegiate
noncompliance
nonconducting
nonconforming
nonconformism
nonconformist
nonconformity
peaceableness
percussionist
phycoerythrin
piscicultural
porcellaneous
practicalness
precautionary
precentorship
precipitantly
precipitately
precipitation
precipitative
precipitously
preconception
pricelessness
processionary
processionist
proconsulship
procrastinate
procuratorial
psychasthenia
psychoanalyse
psychoanalyst
psychodynamic
psychogenesis
psychogenetic
psychokinesis
psychokinetic
psychological
psychometrics
psychometrist
psychophysics
psychosomatic
psychosurgery
psychotherapy
psychrometric
punctiliously
quicktempered
quickwittedly
saccharimeter
saccharimetry
saccharometer
sanctimonious
sarcastically
shockabsorber
specification
spectacularly
spectrography
spectrometric
spectroscopic
speculatively
stickingplace
subcontractor
synchronistic
synchronously
teachableness
tercentennial
traceableness
tractableness
Tractarianism
tricentennial
trichromatism
unaccompanied
unaccountable
unaccountably
unicameralism
unicameralist
voicelessness
volcanologist
vouchsafement
vulcanisation
vulcanologist
acidification
bildungsroman
biodegradable
candlelighter
candlesnuffer
cardiographer
coeducational
coldbloodedly
coldheartedly
condescension
conditionally
conduciveness
conductorship
condylomatous
credulousness
dendritically
deodorisation
feudalisation
fundamentally
goodnaturedly
hardheartedly
hundredweight
inadvertently
ineducability
Kidderminster
landownership
leadpoisoning
meadowsaffron
nondeductable
paddlesteamer
paediatrician
paedomorphism
pendulousness
perdurability
ponderability
ponderousness
predatoriness
predestinator
predicability
predicamental
predicatively
predominantly
predomination
prudentialism
prudentialist
prudentiality
quadragesimal
quadrennially
quadricipital
quadrilateral
quadrillionth
quadripartite
quadrumvirate
quadruplicate
quadruplicity
randomisation
rhadamanthine
rhodochrosite
solderingiron
Swedenborgian
tendentiously
tenderhearted
tiddledywinks
traditionally
unadulterated
windowshopper
wonderfulness
wonderworking
woodengraving
accelerometer
acceptability
accessibility
admeasurement
adventuresome
adventurously
adversatively
advertisement
affectionless
affenpinscher
agreeableness
algebraically
allegorically
allelomorphic
alternatively
anaerobically
annexationist
apheliotropic
appellatively
argentiferous
ascertainable
ascertainment
assertiveness
asserveration
atheistically
attentiveness
barefacedness
beleaguerment
beneficiation
bioenergetics
birefringence
breechloading
bureaucratise
catechisation
categorically
cerebrospinal
ceremonialism
ceremonialist
ceremoniously
cheerlessness
chieftainship
chrematistics
cinematically
cinematograph
cobelligerent
coreligionist
cyberneticist
deceitfulness
deceptiveness
decerebration
defeasibility
defectiveness
defencelessly

defensibility
deferentially
defervescence
deleteriously
dependability
depersonalise
derequisition
derestriction
desegregation
deterioration
deteriorative
determinately
determination
determinative
deterministic
developmental
digestibility
dimensionally
dimensionless
disembodiment
disengagement
divertisement
dodecaphonist
domestication
eavesdropping
eccentrically
effectiveness
effervescence
effervescency
egregiousness
embellishment
encephalogram
entertainment
equestrianism
essentialness
exceptionable
exceptionably
exceptionally
excessiveness
expectoration
expeditionary
expeditiously
expensiveness
extemporarily
extensibility
extensionally
extensiveness
extermination
exterminatory
exteroceptive
exterritorial
facetiousness
foreknowledge
forementioned
foresightedly
freeselection
gametogenesis
generalisable
generalissimo
greensickness
gubernatorial
heterogeneity
heterogeneous
heterogenesis
heterogenetic
heteromorphic
heteropterous
heterosporous
heterothallic
heterotrophic
homeomorphism
hymenopterous
hyperboloidal
hypercritical
hypermetrical
hypermetropia
hypermetropic
hyperphysical
hypertrophied
immediateness
impeccability
impecuniosity
impenetration
imperceptible
imperceptibly
impercipience
imperfectness
imperialistic
imperiousness
impermissible
impersonalise
impersonality
impersonation
impertinently
imperturbable
imperturbably
impetuousness
indefatigable
indefatigably
independently
indescribable
indescribably
indeterminacy
indeterminate
indeterminism
indeterminist
infeasibility
inferentially
ingeniousness
ingenuousness
insectivorous
insensateness
insensibility
insensitively
insensitivity
integumentary
intelligencer
intelligently
intemperately
intensiveness
intentionally
intercalation
intercellular
intercolonial
intercolumnar
intercropping
intercultural
intercurrence
interdentally
interdigitate
interestingly
intergalactic
interjectural
interlacement
interlocution
interlocutory
interlocutrix
intermarriage
intermediator
intermittence
international
interoceptive
interosculate
interparietal
interpellator
interpersonal
interpolation
interpolative
interposition
interpretable
interpretress
interpunction
interrelation
interrogation
interrogative
interrogatory
interruptible
interspecific
interspersion
interstratify
intertropical
inventiveness
inventorially
investigation
investigative
investigatory
irreclaimable
irreclaimably
irrecoverable
irrecoverably
irrefrangible
irreligionist
irreligiously
irreplaceable
irrepressible
irrepressibly
irresponsible
irresponsibly
irretrievable
irretrievably
irreverential
kaleidoscopic
kapellmeister
kinematically
kinematograph
lamellibranch
levelcrossing
liberationist
lifepreserver
lineengraving
materfamilias
materialistic
mesencephalon
meteorologist
mineralogical
miserableness
moderatorship
modernisation
momentariness
momentousness
moneygrubbing
necessitarian
necessitation
necessitously
nomenclatural
numerological
objectionable
objectionably
objectiveness
objectivistic
observational
obsessiveness
offensiveness
osteomyelitis
owneroccupier
panegyrically
paperhangings
parenthetical
paterfamilias
paternalistic
pedestrianise
pedestrianism
penetrability
penetratingly
penetratively
peregrination
phreatophytic
phrenetically
phrenological
pigeonchested
pigeonhearted
pigeonlivered
potentiometer
powerlessness
preengagement
preengineered
receptibility
receptiveness
recessiveness
redescription
redevelopment
referentially
renegotiation
repetitionary
repetitiously
resentfulness
retentiveness
revelationist
revendication
reverberation
reverberative
reverberatory
reverentially
reversibility
RhaetoRomanic
sacerdotalise
sacerdotalism
sacerdotalist
schematically
scientologist
scleroprotein
sedentariness
selectiveness
selenocentric
selenographer
selenographic
selenological
semeiological
serendipitous
sheepshearing
sidesplitting
sleeplessness
sobermindness
solemnisation
spheroidicity
splendiferous
splenetically
squeamishness
squeezability
steeplechaser
streetwalking
strenuousness
streptococcal
streptococcus
subeditorship
superabundant
superaddition
superannuable
supercalender
supercritical
superdominant
supereminence
superfamilies
superfetation
superficially
superfluidity
superfluously
superhumanity
superlatively
supernational
supernumerary
superordinate
superphysical
superposition
supersaturate
supersensible
superstitious
supersubtlety
supervenience
taperecording
telegrammatic
telencephalon
teleportation
telerecording
televisionary
temerariously
threateningly
threecornered
threequarters
thremmatology
timeconsuming
tolerableness
tuberculation
umbelliferous
unbelievingly
unceremonious
uncertainness
underachiever
undercarriage
underclothing
undereducated
underemphasis
underemployed
underestimate
underexposure
undergraduate
underhandedly
understanding
understrapper
underwhelming
unfeelingness
unhealthiness
unmeaningness
unmentionable
unnecessarily
unrelentingly
unremittingly
unselfishness
vegetarianism
venerableness
venereologist
viceadmiralty
vicepresident
waterproofing
wheelerdealer
confabulation
confabulatory
confectionary
confectionery
confederation
confederative
confessionary
confidingness
configuration
conflagration
conflictingly
confraternity
confrontation
craftsmanship
differentiate
diffusiveness
disfigurement
draftsmanship
dysfunctional
halfheartedly
halfsovereign
ineffableness
ineffectively
ineffectually
inefficacious
inefficiently
inoffensively
nonfigurative
nonforfeiting
nonfulfilment
perfectionism
perfectionist
perfunctorily
prefatorially
preferability
prefiguration
prefigurative
prefigurement
professoriate
professorship

profitability
profitsharing
reaffirmation
selfabasement
selfaddressed
selfadjusting
selfappointed
selfapproving
selfasserting
selfassertion
selfassertive
selfassurance
selfassuredly
selfawareness
selfcentredly
selfcollected
selfcommunion
selfconceited
selfcondemned
selfconfessed
selfconfident
selfconscious
selfconsuming
selfcontained
selfcontented
selfconvicted
selfcriticism
selfdeceiving
selfdeception
selfdeceptive
selfdefeating
selfdependent
selfdirecting
selfdirection
selfdiscovery
selfdispraise
selfeducation
selfevidently
selfexecuting
selfexistence
selffertility
selfforgetful
selfgenerated
selfgoverning
selfimportant
selfinduction
selfindulgent
selfinflicted
selfinsurance
selfknowledge
selfopinioned
selfpityingly
selfpollinate
selfpossessed
selfpropelled
selfrecording
selfregarding
selfreproving
selfrepugnant
selfrestraint
selfrevealing
selfrighteous
selfsacrifice
selfsatisfied
selfslaughter
selfsterility
selfsufficing
selfsupported
selfsurrender
selfsustained
selftormentor
shiftlessness
sniftingvalve
suffocatingly
suffraganship
suffumigation
anagrammatise
anagrammatism
biogeographer
burglariously
coagulability
conglomeratic
congratulator
congressional
congresswoman
congruousness
dangerousness
diageotropism
diagnostician
diagrammatise
disgracefully
draggletailed
enigmatically
epigrammatise
epigrammatist
flagellantism
forgetfulness
fragmentarily
fragmentation
frighteningly
frightfulness
imaginatively
jiggerypokery
judgeadvocate
judgmatically
languishingly
laughableness
laughingstock
longsuffering
manganiferous
mangoldwurzel
misgovernment
neighbourhood
niggardliness
nongovernment
outgeneralled
pragmatically
progenitorial
prognosticate
progressional
progressively
progressivism
sergeantmajor
singlehearted
stigmatically
tergiversator
thigmotropism
tonguelashing
tonguetwister
trigonometric
troglodytical
vulgarisation
zoogeographer
zoogeographic
amphiprostyle
anthelminthic
anthropogenic
anthropometry
anthropopathy
anthropophagi
anthropophagy
anthroposophy
archaeologist
archaeopteryx
archbishopric
archdeaconate
archidiaconal
archimandrite
architectonic
architectural
arthritically
asthenosphere
asthmatically
authentically
authenticator
authorisation
authoritarian
authoritative
bathymetrical
cephalothorax
dichlamydeous
dichotomously
disharmonious
dishonourable
dishonourably
emphysematous
eschatologist
eschscholtzia
Eucharistical
haphazardness
lecherousness
lethargically
lightfingered
lightheadedly
lightmindedly
lightsomeness
Machiavellian
machicolation
machinegunner
mathematician
mechanisation
Methodistical
mothercountry
naphthylamine
nephelometric
nightmarishly
nightwatchman
offhandedness
orchestration
orthocephalic
orthognathism
orthognathous
pathogenicity
pathognomonic
pigheadedness
prehistorical
prohibitively
pyrheliometer
righteousness
righthandedly
sightlessness
sophistically
sophisticated
tachistoscope
technicalness
technological
unwholesomely
accidentalism
accidentprone
acrimoniously
actinomorphic
actinomycetes
actinomycosis
administrable
administrator
admirableness
admissibility
advisableness
affirmatively
aggiornamento
agriculturist
ambidexterity
ambidexterous
ambiguousness
ambitiousness
amniocentesis
angiospermous
Antichristian
anticlimactic
anticlockwise
anticoagulant
antihistamine
antilogarithm
antinomianism
antipersonnel
antiscorbutic
arbitrariness
arbitrational
artificiality
assiduousness
availableness
basidiomycete
bewilderingly
bouillabaisse
brainlessness
brainstorming
businesswoman
cabinetmaking
Christmastide
Christmastime
clairaudience
cleistogamous
cruiserweight
cylindrically
deciduousness
defibrination
deliciousness
deliquescence
deliriousness
desirableness
disintegrator
disinterested
disinvestment
domiciliation
efficaciously
enlightenment
environmental
epeirogenesis
equidistantly
equilibration
equiponderant
equiponderate
equipotential
equivocalness
excitableness
exhibitionism
exhibitionist
felicitations
feuilletonism
feuilletonist
fruitlessness
goniometrical
habitableness
hemicellulose
hemiparasitic
hemispherical
horizontality
immiscibility
indifferently
indiscernible
indiscernibly
indispensable
indispensably
indisposition
indissociable
indistinctive
individualise
individualism
individualist
individuality
individuation
infinitesimal
insidiousness
insignificant
insinuatingly
invidiousness
invincibility
inviolability
inviolateness
invisibleness
irritableness
judiciousness
jurisprudence
legislatively
legislatorial
lepidopterist
lepidopterous
lexicographer
lexicographic
limitlessness
litigiousness
ludicrousness
Maginotminded
magisterially
maliciousness
Manichaeanism
manifestation
manifestative
manipulatable
mediatisation
mediterranean
meritoriously
ministerially
musicological
nationalistic
navigableness
numismatology
obliviousness
occidentalise
Occidentalism
Occidentalist
officiousness
omnicompetent
ornithologist
panicstricken
papillomatous
penitentially
perichondrial
perichondrium
periodisation
perishability
perissodactyl
plaintiveness
poliomyelitis
prairieoyster
puritanically
pusillanimity
pusillanimous
pyrimethamine
radioactivity
radiolocation
radiotelegram
ratiocination
ratiocinative
rationalistic
reciprocality
reciprocation
reciprocative
regimentation
religiousness
reminiscently
resistibility
rudimentarily
sanitationist
schizocarpous
schizogenesis
schizophrenia
schizophrenic
scripturalism
scripturalist
sedimentation
seditiousness
semiautomatic
semibarbarian
semibarbarism
semicivilised
semiconductor
semiconscious
semilogarithm
semiparasitic
semipermanent
semipermeable
semiporcelain
serialisation
sericulturist

seriousminded
sewingmachine
socialisation
sociocultural
socioeconomic
solicitorship
solidungulate
sovietologist
sprightliness
stainlessness
stoichiometry
strikebreaker
subirrigation
thrillingness
titillatingly
toxicological
uncircumcised
undisciplined
unrighteously
unwillingness
vacillatingly
verifiability
verisimilarly
viniculturist
visionariness
viticulturist
vivisectional
conjecturable
conjecturally
conjugateness
conjugational
conjunctional
conjunctively
disjunctively
prejudicially
projectionist
zinjanthropus
backformation
backpedalling
backscratcher
backwardation
balkanisation
Berkeleianism
bookingoffice
brokenhearted
lackadaisical
lickerishness
mackerelshark
nickeliferous
Shakespearean
Shakespearian
sicklefeather
smokelessness
talkativeness
turkeygobbler
acclimatation
agglomeration
agglomerative
agglutination
agglutinative
amplification
analogousness
anglicisation
AngloAmerican
AngloCatholic
applicability
applicatively
belleslettres
belligerently
bibliographer
bibliographic
bibliolatrist
bibliolatrous
bibliological
bibliophilism
bibliophilist
brilliantness
calligraphist
callisthenics
chalcography
challengeable
challengingly
collaboration
collaborative
collaterality
colleagueship
collectedness
collectorship
collieshangie
colloquialism
declaratively
dialectically
efflorescence
exclusiveness
explanatorily
explorational
explosiveness
faultlessness
followthrough
foolhardiness
fullfashioned
guilelessness
guiltlessness
hallucination
hallucinative
hallucinatory
healthfulness
hollowhearted
implacability
implicatively
inclusiveness
ineligibility
inflexibility
inflexionless
inflorescence
influentially
italicisation
jollification
malleableness
mellifluously
millefeuilles
millennialism
millionairess
mollification
mouldingboard
negligibility
nucleoprotein
nullification
ochlocratical
palletisation
parliamentary
phalansterian
philanthropic
philhellenism
philhellenist
philosophical
philosophiser
phyllophagous
polliniferous
preliminarily
prolegomenary
prolegomenous
proliferation
proliferative
proliferously
prolification
psilanthropic
qualification
qualificatory
qualitatively
realistically
reflexibility
replenishment
rollercoaster
scolopendrium
sculpturesque
smellingsalts
soulsearching
spelaeologist
speleological
stalkinghorse
stoloniferous
stylistically
sublieutenant
swallowtailed
syllabication
tablespoonful
thalassocracy
triliteralism
uncleanliness
unflinchingly
villeggiatura
violoncellist
wellapPointed
wholesomeness
woolgathering
worldlyminded
aluminiferous
aluminisation
animadversion
animalisation
anomalistical
anomalousness
aromatisation
atomistically
blameableness
blamelessness
chemoreceptor
climactically
climatologist
climbingframe
commandership
commemoration
commemorative
commemoratory
commensurable
commensurably
commercialise
commercialism
commercialist
commiseration
commiserative
communication
communicative
communicatory
communisation
communitarian
commutability
cosmopolitise
cosmopolitism
criminalistic
criminologist
dermatologist
diametrically
dismantlement
dismemberment
dramatisation
dramaturgical
ecumenicalism
examinational
examinatorial
exemplariness
formalisation
formidability
formulisation
geometrically
geomorphology
germanisation
glamorisation
graminivorous
grammatically
haematologist
harmonisation
helminthiasis
helminthology
hermaphrodite
hermeneutical
isomerisation
isometrically
mammaliferous
mesmerisation
mismanagement
mnemotechnics
mummification
myrmecologist
normalisation
onomatopoetic
permutability
prematureness
premeditation
premeditative
premillennial
premonitorily
primigravidae
primitiveness
primogenitary
primogenitive
primogeniture
primordiality
promiscuously
reembarkation
reimbursement
salmonellosis
shamelessness
staminiferous
stomatologist
submachinegun
summarisation
symmetrically
terminability
terminational
terminatively
thimblerigged
thimblerigger
tremulousness
unambiguously
unemotionally
unimpassioned
unimpeachable
vermiculation
whimsicalness
agonistically
anonymousness
blanketflower
boundlessness
bounteousness
bountifulness
cannibalistic
carnivorously
changeability
changefulness
chinkerinchee
clandestinely
coenaesthesis
connaturality
connectedness
cornification
counteraction
counteractive
counterattack
counterchange
countercharge
counterfeiter
counterstroke
counterweight
countinghouse
craniological
dauntlessness
deontological
ethnocentrism
evangelically
exanthematous
frontogenesis
garnetiferous
granddaughter
grandfatherly
grandiloquent
grandmotherly
gymnastically
gymnospermous
hypnoanalysis
hypnotisation
identicalness
inanimateness
lignification
magnanimously
magnetisation
magnetomotive
magnetosphere
magnification
magnificently
magniloquence
manneristical
mountainously
mountebankery
odontoglossum
odontological
openheartedly
opinionatedly
orangeblossom
painstakingly
painterliness
Pennsylvanian
pennyfarthing
pennypinching
phanerogamous
phenomenalise
phenomenalism
phenomenalist
phenomenology
phenylalanine
phonautograph
planimetrical
plenitudinous
plenteousness
plentifulness
pointillistic
pointlessness
principalship
pronounceable
pronouncement
pronunciation
quincentenary
quincuncially
quingentenary
quinquagenary
Quinquagesima
quinquevalent
quintillionth
quintuplicate
reincarnation
reinforcement
reinstatement
reintegration
reinvigorator
roentgenogram
roentgenology
runningstitch
scandalmonger
scintillating
scintillation
signalisation
significantly
signification
significative
slangingmatch
somnambulator
somniloquence
soundingboard
Spencerianism
spindlelegged
spindleshanks
spinelessness
spinninghouse
spinningwheel

spontaneously
standoffishly
thanklessness
thenceforward
thundershower
thunderstruck
tranquilliser
transatlantic
transcendence
transcendency
transcription
transcriptive
transformable
transgression
transgressive
transistorise
transitionary
translational
transliterate
translocation
translucently
translucidity
transmigrator
transmissible
transmittable
transmutation
transmutative
transnational
transparently
transpiration
transpiratory
transportable
transposition
transshipment
transshipping
transversally
unanimousness
unanticipated
unenlightened
uninformative
unintelligent
unintentional
uninterrupted
vernacularise
vernacularism
vernacularity
vernalisation
vulnerability
wrongheadedly
abiologically
absorbability
accommodating
accommodation
accommodative
accompaniment
accoutrements
acrobatically
admonishingly
aerodynamical
afforestation
alcoholically
alcoholometer
alcoholometry
apportionment
arboriculture
associateship
associativity
astonishingly
atmospherical
atrociousness
autobiography
autocatalysis
autocatalytic
autocephalous
autochthonism
autochthonous
autoeroticism
automatically
autonomically
axiomatically
bloodboltered
bloodcurdling
bloodlessness
bloodrelation
Bloomsburyite
cacographical
chromatically
chromatograph
chromatolytic
chromatophore
chromospheric
chronographic
chronological
colourfulness
cryobiologist
cytochemistry
decomposition
decompression
decontaminate
decontrolling
decortication
deforestation
deformational
demonstration
demonstrative
devolutionary
devolutionist
disobediently
encompassment
encouragement
encouragingly
endocrinology
enjoyableness
entomological
entomophagous
entomophilous
entomostracan
erroneousness
excommunicate
exponentially
expostulation
expostulatory
feloniousness
ferociousness
gerontocratic
gerontologist
homoeomorphic
homoeopathist
homogeneously
homoiothermal
homoiothermic
homosexuality
honorifically
hypochondriac
hypoglycaemia
hypothecation
ideographical
ideologically
idiomatically
idiosyncratic
ignominiously
illogicalness
immovableness
impolitically
imponderables
importunately
impossibility
incombustible
incommunicado
incompetently
inconceivable
inconceivably
incondensable
incongruously
inconsecutive
inconsequence
inconsiderate
inconsistence
inconsistency
inconspicuous
incontestable
incontestably
incontinently
inconvenience
inconveniency
inconvertible
inconvertibly
inconvincible
incorporation
incorporative
incorporeally
incorrectness
incorruptible
incorruptibly
incorruptness
indoctrinator
informational
informatively
inhospitality
innocuousness
innoxiousness
insociability
insolubleness
involuntarily
laboriousness
melodiousness
melodramatics
melodramatise
melodramatist
metonymically
mitochondrion
monochromatic
monocotyledon
monodactylous
monogrammatic
monometallism
monometallist
monomolecular
mononucleosis
monophthongal
Monophysitism
monosyllabism
monosymmetric
Monotheletism
monotrematous
negotiability
notoriousness
obnoxiousness
octocentenary
oecologically
oleomargarine
ontogenically
ontologically
opportuneness
opportunistic
oppositionist
oreographical
pococurantism
preoccupation
preordainment
preordination
pyrotechnical
recombination
recommendable
recomposition
reconcilement
reconsolidate
reconstructor
reforestation
reformability
reformational
remonstrantly
remonstration
remonstrative
remorselessly
removableness
resolvability
resourcefully
revolutionary
revolutionise
revolutionism
revolutionist
sadomasochism
sadomasochist
scholarliness
scholasticism
schoolteacher
secondariness
serologically
shootingbrake
shootingrange
shootingstick
smoothingiron
sprocketwheel
subordinately
subordination
subordinative
taxonomically
theologically
theoretically
topographical
topologically
toxoplasmosis
typographical
typologically
uncomfortable
uncomfortably
uncompetitive
uncomplaining
uncomplicated
unconceivable
unconcernedly
unconditional
unconditioned
unconformable
unconquerable
unconsciously
unconstrained
uncoordinated
unforgettable
unforgettably
unforthcoming
unfortunately
unsociability
vapourishness
xylographical
zygodactylous
anaphrodisiac
bumptiousness
campanologist
camphoraceous
compagination
companionable
companionably
companionless
companionship
comparability
comparatively
compartmental
compassionate
compatibility
compendiously
competitively
complainingly
complaisantly
complementary
complexedness
complicatedly
complimentary
compositeness
compositional
comprehension
comprehensive
compressional
computational
cooperatively
corporativism
cryptanalysis
cryptanalytic
cryptographer
cryptographic
cryptological
deipnosophist
desperateness
diaphragmatic
disparagement
disparagingly
disparateness
dispassionate
displantation
disposability
dispossession
dispraisingly
disproportion
elephantiasis
epiphenomenal
epiphenomenon
graphological
herpetologist
inappreciable
inappreciably
inappropriate
inopportunely
inspectorship
inspirational
morphogenesis
morphogenetic
morphological
neoplasticism
nonproductive
perpendicular
preparatively
preparatorily
preponderance
preponderancy
prepositional
prepossessing
prepossession
prepreference
proparoxytone
prophetically
proportionate
propositional
proprietorial
proprioceptor
purposelessly
purposiveness
resplendently
rhapsodically
shapelessness
steppingstone
subpostmaster
sulphureously
sumptuousness
supplantation
supplementary
suppositional
symphonically
symphoniously
temperamental
temperateness
tempestuously
temporalities
temporariness
temporisation
terpsicnorean
cinquecentist
frequentation
frequentative
sesquiplicate
unequivocally
abortifacient
accreditation
achromaticity
affreightment

aggravatingly
amorphousness
anfractuosity
apprehensible
appropriately
appropriation
appropriative
approximately
approximation
approximative
astronautical
astrophysical
attributively
barrelchested
boardinghouse
caprification
characterless
choreographer
choreographic
churchmanship
clarification
coarsegrained
correlatively
correlativity
correspondent
corresponsive
corrigibility
corroboration
corroborative
corroboratory
corrosiveness
corruptionist
courteousness
courtsmartial
decrepitation
degranulation
deprecatingly
detrimentally
disrespectful
embranglement
embrittlement
embryogenesis
embryological
energetically
everlastingly
excrescential
expressionism
expressionist
expropriation
extracellular
extragalactic
extrajudicial
extraordinary
extraphysical
extrapolation
extratropical
extravagantly
extravasation
extravascular
extrinsically
ferrimagnetic
ferroconcrete
ferroelectric
ferromagnetic
fibrovascular
flirtatiously
floricultural
floristically
garrulousness
glorification
hairsplitting
heartbreaking
heartlessness
heartsickness
horripilation
hybridisation
hydraulically
hydrocephalic
hydrocephalus
hydrochloride
hydrocracking
hydrodynamics
hydroelectric
hydrogenation
hydromedusoid
hydrometrical
hydrostatical
hydrosulphide
hydrosulphite
hydroxylamine
impracticable
impracticably
impractically
impressionism
impressionist
improbability
impropriation
improvability
improvidently
improvisation
improvisatory
incredibility
incredulously
incrementally
incriminatory
inorganically
intraarterial
intracellular
intramuscular
intransigeant
intransigence
intrapersonal
intravenously
intricateness
intrinsically
introgression
introspection
introspective
introversible
intrusiveness
jerrybuilding
librarianship
lucrativeness
macrocephalic
macromolecule
matriculation
matrilineally
metrification
microanalysis
microcephalic
micrococcocci
microdetector
micronutrient
microorganism
microphyllous
microscopical
microtonality
mourningcloak
mourningpaper
nearsightedly
neurastheniac
neurovascular
nitrification
nitrobacteria
nitrocompound
nonresistance
nonreturnable
nutritionally
obtrusiveness
odoriferously
operativeness
opprobriously
ostreiculture
overabundance
overbearingly
overconfident
overcredulous
overelaborate
overemphasise
overindulgent
overpopulated
overqualified
oversensitive
overstatement
oversubscribe
overvaluation
patriotically
patronisingly
petrification
petrochemical
petroliferous
pharisaically
pharmaceutics
pharmaceutist
pharmacologic
pharmacopoeia
pluralisation
pluripresence
PreRaphaelite
pteridologist
quarrelsomely
quartermaster
quartziferous
querulousness
rearcommodore
rearrangement
recrimination
recriminative
recriminatory
recrudescence
recrystallise
refractometer
refrigeration
regretfulness
reorientation
reprehensible
reprehensibly
representable
reproachfully
reproachingly
retranslation
retroactively
retroactivity
retrogression
retrogressive
retrospection
retrospective
sabrerattling
sacramentally
sacrificially
sacrosanctity
scarification
scorbutically
scorification
scorpiongrass
searchwarrant
secretarybird
secretaryship
secretiveness
sharecropping
sharpshooting
shorttempered
sorrowfulness
spermatoblast
spermatogenic
spermatophore
spermatophyte
spiritualness
sportsmanlike
sportsmanship
stercoraceous
stereographic
stereoscopist
sterilisation
sternforemost
stirpiculture
subreptitious
supranational
surreptitious
surrogateship
swordsmanship
terrestrially
territorially
terrorisation
tetrasyllable
thereinbefore
theriomorphic
thermochemist
thermodynamic
thermogenesis
thermonuclear
thermophilous
thermoplastic
thermosetting
thermotropism
thoroughbrace
thoroughgoing
thoroughpaced
thurification
unarticulated
ungrammatical
unprecedented
unpredictable
unpretentious
unpromisingly
untrustworthy
vitrification
wearisomeness
worrisomeness
balsamiferous
blasphemously
blastogenesis
boustrophedon
closedcircuit
consanguinity
conscientious
consciousness
consecutively
consenescence
consentaneity
consentaneous
consequential
conservatoire
considerately
consideration
consolidation
consolidative
consolidatory
conspicuously
constellation
constellatory
consternation
constrainable
constrainedly
constructable
constructible
consumptively
crosscultural
crossgartered
crosshatching
crosspurposes
crossquestion
crystalgazing
crystallinity
dissemblingly
dissemination
disseminative
disseveration
dissimilarity
dissimilation
dissimilitude
dissimulation
dissolubility
dissoluteness
dissymetrical
dressimprover
dressingtable
exasperatedly
existentially
falsification
fissiparously
fossiliferous
fossilisation
frustratingly
geostationary
glossographer
horsechestnut
horsewhipping
housebreaking
isostatically
laissezpasser
leishmaniasis
leisureliness
linseywoolsey
meistersinger
mensurability
monstrousness
noiselessness
nonsensically
opisthobranch
outspokenness
outstandingly
passementerie
passionflower
perseveration
perspectively
perspicacious
perspicuously
phosphoretted
physiognomist
physiographer
physiographic
physiological
physiotherapy
prescientific
presidentship
prestigiously
presumptively
prismatically
prosopography
prospectively
prostaglandin
prosthodontia
questioningly
questionnaire
Russification
sansculottism
seismographer
seismographic
seismological
sensationally
senselessness
sensitisation
sensitiveness
spasmodically
subsaturation
subsequential
subserviently
substantially
substantively
substantivise
substitutable
substructural
swashbuckling
toastmistress
tonsillectomy
topsyturvydom
trustworthily
unestablished
versicoloured
versification
abstractional
acetification
acetylcholine
acotyledonous

aesthetically
apathetically
arithmetician
auctioneering
Australianism
bacteriolysis
bacteriolytic
bacteriophage
BaltoSlavonic
battlecruiser
beatification
biotechnology
brotherliness
brutalisation
butterfingers
butterflyfish
buttonthrough
cartilaginous
cauterisation
centreforward
centrifugally
centripetally
certification
certificatory
chateaubriand
clothesbasket
containership
contamination
contaminative
contemplation
contemplative
contentedness
contentiously
continentally
contortionist
contrabandist
contrabassoon
contraception
contraceptive
contractility
contractually
contradiction
contradictory
contrafagotto
contrapuntist
contrariously
contravention
controversial
corticotropic
corticotropin
costeffective
cottonpicking
customariness
dastardliness
deathlessness
denticulation
destructively
destructivity
deuteragonist
Deuteronomist
dexterousness
diathermanous
dictatorially
distastefully
distinctively
distinguished
distressfully
distressingly
distributable
distrustfully
doctrinairism
faithlessness
fantastically
featherheaded
featherstitch
featherweight
fertilisation
festschriften
filterability
fortification
fortississimo
fortunateness
fortunehunter
fortuneteller
gasteropodous
gastrocnemius
gastroenteric
gastrological
gastronomical
gentlemanlike
geotropically
gesticulation
gesticulative
gesticulatory
glutinousness
gratification
grotesqueness
helterskelter
heptasyllabic
histrionicism
horticultural
ichthyography
ichthyologist
ichthyosaurus
imitativeness
inattentively
instantaneity
instantaneous
instinctively
institutional
instructional
instructively
justification
justificative
justificatory
juxtaposition
leatherjacket
leptocephalic
leptospirosis
letterperfect
loathsomeness
Malthusianism
martyrisation
martyrologist
masterfulness
mirthlessness
mistrustfully
mistrustingly
mortification
mouthwatering
multicellular
multicoloured
multinational
multinucleate
multiplicable
multitudinous
mystification
nectariferous
northeasterly
northeastward
northwesterly
northwestward
nostalgically
obstinateness
obstructively
ophthalmology
oystercatcher
pantagruelian
pantagruelism
pantagruelist
pantheistical
pantisocratic
parthenocarpy
participation
participative
participatory
particoloured
particularise
particularism
particularist
particularity
partridgewood
peptonisation
pestiferously
photochemical
photochromics
photochromism
photoelectric
photoelectron
photoemission
photoemissive
photoperiodic
photopositive
photoreceptor
phytoplankton
picturepalace
picturesquely
platiniferous
platitudinise
platitudinous
platyhelminth
plethorically
pontification
postclassical
postcommunion
postoperative
postulational
pretentiously
pretermission
pretermitting
preternatural
protectionism
protectionist
protectorship
proteinaceous
Protestantism
protohistoric
protonotarial
protuberantly
rapturousness
rattlebrained
rectangularly
rectification
rectilinearly
restoratively
restrictively
rontgenoscopy
sententiously
sentimentally
septentrional
skateboarding
softpedalling
southeasterly
southeastward
southwesterly
southwestward
statelessness
statesmanlike
statesmanship
stationmaster
statistically
subternatural
subterraneous
subtilisation
syntactically
synthetically
tantalisation
tantalisingly
tastelessness
tautologously
tentativeness
testification
tintinnabular
tintinnabulum
toothsomeness
tortoiseshell
tritheistical
vantageground
ventriloquial
ventriloquise
ventriloquism
ventriloquist
venturesomely
venturousness
vertiginously
victimisation
weatherbeaten
whithersoever
winterberries
worthlessness
xanthochroism
acculturation
acculturative
acquiescently
acquiescingly
actualisation
argumentation
argumentative
beauteousness
daguerreotype
deductibility
desultoriness
documentalist
documentation
excursiveness
excusableness
expurgatorial
exquisiteness
facultatively
flourishingly
hocuspocussed
illustriously
immunological
immunotherapy
immutableness
impulsiveness
incurableness
incuriousness
inductiveness
industrialise
industrialism
industrialist
industriously
infundibulate
infuriatingly
ingurgitation
injudiciously
injuriousness
inquisitional
inquisitively
inquisitorial
insubordinate
insubstantial
insufficience
insufficiency
insupportable
insupportably
insusceptible
intuitiveness
luxuriousness
misunderstand
misunderstood
monumentalise
mutualisation
penuriousness
plausibleness
pneumatically
pneumatolysis
pneumatolytic
pneumatometer
pneumatophore
pneumogastric
pneumonectomy
pseudoarchaic
pseudomorphic
pseudoscience
reduplication
reduplicative
regurgitation
rejuvenescent
republicanise
republicanism
republication
repulsiveness
requisiteness
resuscitation
resuscitative
rheumatically
ritualisation
scrumptiously
seductiveness
sequentiality
sequestration
shoulderblade
shoulderstrap
structuralism
structuralist
structureless
thaumaturgist
thoughtlessly
thoughtreader
traumatically
troublesomely
troublousness
unputdownable
unqualifiedly
unquestioning
unsubstantial
unsuitability
valuelessness
visualisation
volumenometer
voluntariness
voluntaristic
Calvinistical
convalescence
conventionary
conversazione
conversazioni
convertiplane
convexoconvex
convocational
convulsionary
curvilinearly
frivolousness
galvanisation
gravitational
inevitability
laevorotation
laevorotatory
nervelessness
ovoviviparous
pervasiveness
prevarication
provincialise
provincialism
provincialist
provinciality
provisionally
pulverisation
silvertongued
subversionary
airworthiness
answerability
betweenwhiles
knowledgeable
knowledgeably
seaworthiness
snowblindness
inexhaustible
inexhaustibly
inexorability
inexpediently
inexpensively
inexperienced

inexpressible
inexpressibly
reexamination
unexceptional
acrylonitrile
Assyriologist
chrysanthemum
demythologise
encyclopaedia
encyclopaedic
encyclopedism
encyclopedist
laryngoscopic
palynological
polyadelphous
polycarbonate
polychromatic
polycotyledon
polydactylous
polyhistorian
polypropylene
polysynthesis
polysynthetic
prayermeeting
sphygmography
unsymmetrical
piezoelectric
prizefighting

---

actualisation
admeasurement
aggravatingly
anfractuosity
animadversion
animalisation
anomalistical
anomalousness
apocalyptical
archaeologist
archaeopteryx
aromatisation
baccalaureate
balkanisation
balsamiferous
barbarisation
barbarousness
beleaguerment
bombastically
brutalisation
bureaucratise
campanologist
cephalothorax
characterless
climactically
climatologist
coenaesthesis
collaboration
collaborative
collaterality
combativeness
commandership
compagination
companionable
companionably
companionless
companionship
comparability
comparatively
compartmental
compassionate
compatibility
concatenation
concavoconvex
confabulation
confabulatory
connaturality
consanguinity
containership
contamination

contaminative
convalescence
dastardliness
declaratively
defeasibility
degranulation
dermatologist
dictatorially
disharmonious
dismantlement
disparagement
disparagingly
disparateness
dispassionate
distastefully
dramatisation
dramaturgical
educationally
embranglement
eschatologist
Eucharistical
evocativeness
explanatorily
extracellular
extragalactic
extrajudicial
extraordinary
extraphysical
extrapolation
extratropical
extravagantly
extravasation
extravascular
fantastically
feudalisation
formalisation
fundamentally
galvanisation
germanisation
gymnastically
haematologist
haphazardness
heptasyllabic
hermaphrodite
hydraulically
imitativeness
implacability
impracticable
impracticably
impractically
infeasibility
instantaneity
instantaneous
intraarterial
intracellular
intramuscular
intransigeant
intransigence
intrapersonal
intravenously
juxtaposition
lackadaisical
lethargically
librarianship
lucrativeness
magnanimously
mammaliferous
manganiferous
mechanisation
mediatisation
mismanagement
mutualisation
nectariferous
neurastheniac
niggardliness
normalisation
nostalgically
offhandedness
onomatopoetic

operativeness
overabundance
pantagruelian
pantagruelism
pantagruelist
pervasiveness
phalansterian
philanthropic
phonautograph
phreatophytic
pluralisation
polyadelphous
precautionary
predatoriness
prefatorially
prematureness
preparatively
preparatorily
PreRaphaelite
prevarication
probationally
proparoxytone
psilanthropic
rectangularly
reexamination
refractometer
retranslation
rhadamanthine
ritualisation
sacramentally
sarcastically
selfabasement
selfaddressed
selfadjusting
selfappointed
selfapproving
selfasserting
selfassertion
selfassertive
selfassurance
selfassuredly
selfawareness
semiautomatic
sensationally
serialisation
signalisation
socialisation
somnambulator
spelaeologist
squeamishness
stomatologist
submachinegun
subsaturation
summarisation
supranational
syllabication
syntactically
talkativeness
tantalisation
tantalisingly
tentativeness
tetrasyllable
thalassocracy
threateningly
ungrammatical
unhealthiness
unicameralism
unicameralist
unmeaningness
unqualifiedly
vantageground
verbalisation
vernacularise
vernacularism
vernacularity
vernalisation
viceadmiralty
visualisation
volcanologist

vulcanisation
vulcanologist
vulgarisation
wellapPointed
zinjanthropus
acrobatically
adiabatically
algebraically
archbishopric
autobiography
cerebrospinal
climbingframe
coldbloodedly
cryobiologist
defibrination
disobediently
establishment
exhibitionism
exhibitionist
insubordinate
insubstantial
overbearingly
parabolically
reembarkation
reimbursement
republicanise
republicanism
republication
scorbutically
semibarbarian
semibarbarism
shabbygenteel
snowblindness
thimblerigged
thimblerigger
troublesomely
troublousness
unambiguously
unsubstantial
affectionless
agriculturist
Antichristian
anticlimactic
anticlockwise
anticoagulant
associateship
associativity
atrociousness
audaciousness
autocatalysis
autocatalytic
autocephalous
autochthonism
autochthonous
breechloading
capaciousness
catechisation
chalcoography
churchmanship
conscientious
consciousness
cytochemistry
deductibility
defectiveness
deliciousness
dodecaphonist
domiciliation
effectiveness
efficaciously
encyclopaedia
encyclopaedic
encyclopedism
encyclopedist
endocrinology
expectoration
felicitations
ferociousness
galactosaemia
hemicellulose

hypochondriac
impeccability
impecuniosity
indoctrinator
inductiveness
innocuousness
insectivorous
insociability
irreclaimable
irreclaimably
irrecoverable
irrecoverably
judiciousness
lexicographer
lexicographic
ludicrousness
malacological
malacostracan
maliciousness
Manichaeanism
megacephalous
mitochondrion
monochromatic
monocotyledon
musicological
objectionable
objectionably
objectiveness
objectivistic
octocentenary
officiousness
omnicompetent
overconfident
overcredulous
panicstricken
perichondrial
perichondrium
pococurantism
polycarbonate
polychromatic
polycotyledon
postclassical
postcommunion
preoccupation
prescientific
principalship
quincentenary
quincuncially
rapaciousness
rearcommodore
reincarnation
revaccination
sagaciousness
salaciousness
sansculottism
searchwarrant
seductiveness
selectiveness
selfcentredly
selfcollected
selfcommunion
selfconceited
selfcondemned
selfconfessed
selfconfident
selfconscious
selfconsuming
selfcontained
selfcontented
selfconvicted
selfcriticism
semicivilised
semiconductor
semiconscious
sericulturist
solicitorship
Spencerianism
sprocketwheel
stercoraceous

stoichiometry
structuralism
structuralist
structureless
tenaciousness
thenceforward
timeconsuming
toxicological
treacherously
unaccompanied
unaccountable
unaccountably
unexceptional
unnecessarily
unsociability
veraciousness
viniculturist
viticulturist
vivaciousness
voraciousness
accidentalism
accidentprone
aerodynamical
ambidexterity
ambidexterous
archdeaconate
assiduousness
basidiomycete
bloodboltered
bloodcurdling
bloodlessness
bloodrelation
boardinghouse
boundlessness
broadmindedly
broadspectrum
clandestinely
deciduousness
disadvantaged
equidistantly
expeditionary
expeditiously
gonadotrophic
gonadotrophin
granddaughter
grandfatherly
grandiloquent
grandmotherly
immediateness
injudiciously
insidiousness
invidiousness
lepidopterist
lepidopterous
maladaptation
maladjustment
maladminister
maladroitness
melodiousness
melodramatics
melodramatise
melodramatist
monodactylous
mouldingboard
occidentalise
Occidentalism
Occidentalist
paradoxically
polydactylous
pseudoarchaic
pseudomorphic
pseudoscience
scandalmonger
schadenfreude
selfdeceiving
selfdeception
selfdeceptive
selfdefeating
selfdependent

selfdirecting
selfdirection
selfdiscovery
selfdispraise
solidungulate
soundingboard
spindlelegged
spindleshanks
standoffishly
steadfastness
subeditorship
swordsmanship
thundershower
thunderstruck
worldlyminded
zygodactylous
accreditation
affreightment
agreeableness
answerability
anthelminthic
apprehensible
asthenosphere
authentically
authenticator
autoeroticism
bacteriolysis
bacteriolytic
bacteriophage
barrelchested
belleslettres
Berkeleianism
betweenwhiles
biodegradable
biogeographer
biotechnology
blameableness
blamelessness
brokenhearted
butterfingers
butterflyfish
cauterisation
chateaubriand
choreographer
choreographic
closedcircuit
colleagueship
collectedness
collectorship
commemoration
commemorative
commemoratory
commensurable
commensurably
commercialise
commercialism
commercialist
compendiously
competitively
conceitedness
concentration
concentrative
concentricity
conceptualise
conceptualism
conceptualist
concertmaster
concessionary
condescension
confectionary
confectionery
confederation
confederative
confessionary
conjecturable
conjecturally
connectedness
consecutively
consenescence

consentaneity
consentaneous
consequential
conservatoire
contemplation
contemplative
contentedness
contentiously
conventionary
conversazione
conversazioni
convertiplane
convexoconvex
cooperatively
correlatively
correlativity
correspondent
corresponsive
costeffective
daguerreotype
dangerousness
decrepitation
deprecatingly
desperateness
deuteragonist
Deuteronomist
dexterousness
diageotropism
dialectically
diametrically
differentiate
dismemberment
disrespectful
dissemblingly
dissemination
disseminative
disseveration
ecumenicalism
egocentricity
excrescential
expressionism
expressionist
filterability
flagellantism
forgetfulness
garnetiferous
gasteropodous
geocentricism
geometrically
globetrotting
gracelessness
grotesqueness
guilelessness
gynaecocratic
gynaecologist
helterskelter
hermeneutical
herpetologist
homoeomorphic
homoeopathist
horsechestnut
horsewhipping
housebreaking
impressionism
impressionist
incredibility
incredulously
incrementally
inflexibility
inflexionless
inspectorship
isomerisation
isometrically
jiggerypokery
judgeadvocate
Kidderminster
lancecorporal
lancesergeant
lecherousness

letterperfect
lickerishness
lineengraving
linseywoolsey
mackerelshark
magnetisation
magnetomotive
magnetosphere
malleableness
manneristical
masterfulness
mathematician
mercenariness
mercerisation
mesmerisation
millefeuilles
millennialism
miscegenation
miscellaneous
mothercountry
myrmecologist
nephelometric
nervelessness
nickeliferous
noiselessness
nondeductable
nonresistance
nonreturnable
nonsensically
nucleoprotein
orchestration
ostreiculture
outgeneralled
overelaborate
overemphasise
oystercatcher
palaeographer
palaeographic
palaeontology
palaeozoology
palletisation
passementerie
peaceableness
perfectionism
perfectionist
perpendicular
perseveration
phanerogamous
pigheadedness
ponderability
ponderousness
porcellaneous
prayermeeting
precentorship
predestinator
preferability
premeditation
premeditative
pretentiously
pretermission
pretermitting
preternatural
pricelessness
prizefighting
processionary
processionist
professoriate
professorship
progenitorial
projectionist
prolegomenary
prolegomenous
protectionism
protectionist
protectorship
proteinaceous
Protestantism
prudentialism
prudentialist

prudentiality
pulverisation
pyrheliometer
reflexibility
regretfulness
replenishment
reprehensible
reprehensibly
representable
rollercoaster
sabrerattling
secretarybird
secretaryship
secretiveness
selfeducation
selfevidently
selfexecuting
selfexistence
senselessness
sententiously
septentrional
sequentiality
sequestration
sergeantmajor
Shakespearean
Shakespearian
shamelessness
shapelessness
sharecropping
silvertongued
skateboarding
smokelessness
solderingiron
sovietologist
speleological
spinelessness
squeezability
statelessness
statesmanlike
statesmanship
stereographic
stereoscopist
streetwalking
subreptitious
subsequential
subserviently
subternatural
subterraneous
subversionary
surreptitious
Swedenborgian
symmetrically
tablespoonful
tastelessness
temperamental
temperateness
tempestuously
tendentiously
tenderhearted
tercentennial
terrestrially
thereinbefore
threecornered
threequarters
traceableness
tricentennial
turkeygobbler
uncleanliness
unfeelingness
unprecedented
unpredictable
unpretentious
unquestioning
valuelessness
villeggiatura
voicelessness
vulnerability
wholesomeness
winterberries

wonderfulness
wonderworking
woodengraving
zoogeographer
zoogeographic
artificiality
backformation
barefacedness
beneficiation
birefringence
chieftainship
disaffectedly
disaffirmance
fullfashioned
indefatigable
indefatigably
indifferently
ineffableness
ineffectively
ineffectually
inefficacious
inefficiently
inoffensively
insufficience
insufficiency
irrefrangible
liebfraumilch
manifestation
manifestative
reaffirmation
reinforcement
selffertility
selfforgetful
uninformative
verifiability
allegorically
ambiguousness
cacographical
categorically
changeability
changefulness
desegregation
draggletailed
egregiousness
energetically
enlightenment
evangelically
homogeneously
hypoglycaemia
ideographical
illogicalness
inorganically
insignificant
integumentary
litigiousness
manageability
metagrobolise
monogrammatic
mutagenically
navigableness
nonaggression
ontogenically
orangeblossom
oreographical
panegyrically
pedagogically
peregrination
quingentenary
religiousness
renegotiation
rontgenoscopy
selfgenerated
selfgoverning
slangingmatch
sphygmography
sprightliness
telegrammatic
thoughtlessly
thoughtreader
topographical
typographical
unrighteously
woolgathering
wrongheadedly
xylographical
aesthetically
alcoholically
alcoholometer
alcoholometry
anachronistic
anachronously
anaphrodisiac
antihistamine
apathetically
arithmetician
brachycephaly
brachydactyly
brachypterous
brotherliness
camphoraceous
clothesbasket
coldheartedly
conchological
deathlessness
diaphragmatic
diathermanous
elephantiasis
epiphenomenal
epiphenomenon
faithlessness
featherheaded
featherstitch
featherweight
foolhardiness
frighteningly
frightfulness
geochronology
graphological
halfheartedly
hardheartedly
ichthyography
ichthyologist
ichthyosaurus
inexhaustible
inexhaustibly
isochronously
laughableness
laughingstock
leatherjacket
leishmaniasis
loathsomeness
Malthusianism
merchandising
mirthlessness
mischievously
morphogenesis
morphogenetic
morphological
mouthwatering
neighbourhood
northeasterly
northeastward
northwesterly
northwestward
openheartedly
ophthalmology
pantheistical
parthenocarpy
philhellenism
philhellenist
plethorically
polyhistorian
prophetically
psychasthenia
psychoanalyse
psychoanalyst
psychodynamic
psychogenesis
psychogenetic
psychokinesis
psychokinetic
psychological
psychometrics
psychometrist
psychophysics
psychosomatic
psychosurgery
psychotherapy
psychrometric
saccharimeter
saccharimetry
saccharometer
southeasterly
southeastward
southwesterly
southwestward
sulphureously
swashbuckling
symphonically
symphoniously
synchronistic
synchronously
synthetically
teachableness
toothsomeness
trichromatism
tritheistical
vouchsafement
weatherbeaten
whithersoever
worthlessness
xanthochroism
acclimatation
acetification
acidification
acquiescently
acquiescingly
agonistically
aluminiferous
aluminisation
amphiprostyle
amplification
anglicisation
applicability
applicatively
archidiaconal
archimandrite
architectonic
architectural
atheistically
atomistically
attainability
attributively
auctioneering
beatification
belligerently
bibliographer
bibliographic
bibliolatrist
bibliolatrous
bibliological
bibliophilism
bibliophilist
bookingoffice
calcification
calligraphist
callisthenics
Calvinistical
cannibalistic
caprification
carcinomatous
cardiographer
carnivorously
cartilaginous
certification
certificatory
clarification
collieshangie
combinatorial
commiseration
commiserative
conditionally
confidingness
configuration
considerately
consideration
continentally
cornification
corrigibility
corticotropic
corticotropin
craniological
criminalistic
criminologist
curvilinearly
deceitfulness
denticulation
detrimentally
disciplinable
disfigurement
dissimilarity
dissimilation
dissimilitude
dissimulation
distinctively
distinguished
dulcification
embrittlement
examinational
examinatorial
exquisiteness
extrinsically
falsification
fasciculation
fascinatingly
Fascistically
ferrimagnetic
fertilisation
fissiparously
floricultural
floristically
formidability
fortification
fortississimo
fossiliferous
fossilisation
gesticulation
gesticulative
gesticulatory
glaciological
glorification
glutinousness
graminivorous
gratification
gravitational
heebiejeebies
helminthiasis
helminthology
homoiothermal
homoiothermic
horripilation
horticultural
hybridisation
imaginatively
implicatively
inanimateness
incriminatory
ineligibility
inevitability
inquisitional
inquisitively
inquisitorial
inspirational
instinctively
institutional
intricateness
intrinsically
intuitiveness
italicisation
jollification
justification
justificative
justificatory
kaleidoscopic
lignification
Machiavellian
machicolation
machinegunner
magnification
magnificently
magniloquence
matriculation
matrilineally
mellifluously
mercilessness
metrification
millionairess
mollification
mortification
multicellular
multicoloured
multinational
multinucleate
multiplicable
multitudinous
mummification
mystification
negligibility
nitrification
nonfigurative
nullification
nutritionally
obstinateness
odoriferously
opinionatedly
overindulgent
ovoviviparous
paediatrician
pantisocratic
parliamentary
participation
participative
participatory
particoloured
particularise
particularism
particularist
particularity
passionflower
patriotically
pestiferously
petrification
pharisaically
physiognomist
physiographer
physiographic
physiological
physiotherapy
piscicultural
planimetrical
platiniferous
platitudinise
platitudinous
plenitudinous
pluripresence
polliniferous
pontification
precipitantly
precipitately
precipitation
precipitative
precipitously
predicability
predicamental
predicatively

prefiguration
prefigurative
prefigurement
prehistorical
preliminarily
premillennial
presidentship
primigravidae
primitiveness
profitability
profitsharing
prohibitively
proliferation
proliferative
proliferously
prolification
promiscuously
provincialise
provincialism
provincialist
provinciality
provisionally
pteridologist
qualification
qualificatory
qualitatively
realistically
recrimination
recriminative
recriminatory
rectification
rectilinearly
refrigeration
reorientation
requisiteness
runningstitch
Russification
sacrificially
scarification
scorification
selfimportant
selfinduction
selfindulgent
selfinflicted
selfinsurance
semeiological
sensitisation
sensitiveness
sentimentally
significantly
signification
significative
somniloquence
sophistically
sophisticated
specification
spiritualness
stabilisation
staminiferous
stationmaster
statistically
sterilisation
stylistically
sublieutenant
subtilisation
symbiotically
tachistoscope
tergiversator
terminability
terminational
terminatively
territorially
testification
theriomorphic
thurification
tintinnabular
tintinnabulum
tonsillectomy
traditionally
triliteralism
unanimousness
unflinchingly
unsuitability
verbigeration
vermiculation
versicoloured
versification
vertiginously
victimisation
vitrification
wearisomeness
worrisomeness
blackguardism
blanketflower
chinkerinchee
chuckleheaded
crackerbarrel
foreknowledge
knickerbocker
knuckleduster
quicktempered
quickwittedly
selfknowledge
shockabsorber
stalkinghorse
stickingplace
strikebreaker
thanklessness
abiologically
accelerometer
acculturation
acculturative
acrylonitrile
allelomorphic
antilogarithm
apheliotropic
appellatively
availableness
battlecruiser
bewilderingly
bouillabaisse
brilliantness
burglariously
canaliculated
candlelighter
candlesnuffer
challengeable
challengingly
cobelligerent
complainingly
complaisantly
complementary
complexedness
complicatedly
complimentary
conflagration
conflictingly
conglomeratic
coreligionist
desultoriness
developmental
devolutionary
devolutionist
dichlamydeous
displantation
doublecrosser
doubledealing
doubleglazing
doublejointed
doubletongued
embellishment
equilibration
everlastingly
facultatively
feuilletonism
feuilletonist
gentlemanlike
ideologically
impalpability
impolitically
impulsiveness
infallibilism
infallibilist
infallibility
insolubleness
intelligencer
intelligently
involuntarily
irreligionist
irreligiously
kapellmeister
knowledgeable
knowledgeably
lamellibranch
levelcrossing
metalliferous
metallisation
metallography
metallurgical
neoclassicism
neoclassicist
neoplasticism
oecologically
ontologically
paddlesteamer
papillomatous
parallelogram
phyllophagous
problematical
pusillanimity
pusillanimous
rattlebrained
recalcitrance
repulsiveness
resolvability
resplendently
revelationist
revolutionary
revolutionise
revolutionism
revolutionist
scholarliness
scholasticism
semilogarithm
serologically
shoulderblade
shoulderstrap
sicklefeather
singlehearted
smellingsalts
supplantation
supplementary
swallowtailed
synallagmatic
theologically
thrillingness
tiddledywinks
titillatingly
topologically
troglodytical
typologically
umbelliferous
unbelievingly
unenlightened
unrelentingly
unselfishness
unwillingness
vacillatingly
wheelerdealer
accommodating
accommodation
accommodative
accompaniment
acrimoniously
argumentation
argumentative
asthmatically
automatically
axiomatically
Bloomsburyite
ceremonialism
ceremonialist
ceremoniously
chlamydomonas
chlamydospore
chrematistics
chromatically
chromatograph
chromatolytic
chromatophore
chromospheric
cinematically
cinematograph
decomposition
decompression
disembodiment
documentalist
documentation
dreamlessness
encompassment
enigmatically
entomological
entomophagous
entomophilous
entomostracan
excommunicate
extemporarily
foraminiferal
forementioned
fragmentarily
fragmentation
funambulation
grammatically
idiomatically
ignominiously
incombustible
incommunicado
incompetently
intemperately
judgmatically
kinematically
kinematograph
metamorphoses
metamorphosis
Mohammedanism
monometallism
monometallist
monomolecular
monumentalise
Muhammadanism
oleomargarine
ornamentation
paramagnetism
perambulation
perambulatory
pharmaceutics
pharmaceutist
pharmacologic
pharmacopoeia
pneumatically
pneumatolysis
pneumatolytic
pneumatometer
pneumatophore
pneumogastric
pneumonectomy
pragmatically
prismatically
pyrimethamine
recombination
recommendable
recomposition
regimentation
rheumatically
rudimentarily
sadomasochism
sadomasochist
schematically
scrumptiously
sedimentation
seismographer
seismographic
seismological
solemnisation
spasmodically
spermatoblast
spermatogenic
spermatophore
spermatophyte
stigmatically
thaumaturgist
thermochemist
thermodynamic
thermogenesis
thermonuclear
thermophilous
thermoplastic
thermosetting
thermotropism
thigmotropism
thremmatology
traumatically
uncomfortable
uncomfortably
uncompetitive
uncomplaining
uncomplicated
unfamiliarity
unremittingly
unsymmetrical
volumenometer
actinomorphic
actinomycetes
actinomycosis
administrable
administrator
admonishingly
adventuresome
adventurously
affenpinscher
antinomianism
argentiferous
astonishingly
atlantosaurus
attentiveness
autonomically
bioenergetics
brainlessness
brainstorming
businesswoman
cabinetmaking
chronographic
chronological
cylindrically
decontaminate
decontrolling
defencelessly
defensibility
deipnosophist
demonstration
demonstrative
dependability
diagnostician
dimensionally
dimensionless
disengagement
disintegrator
disinterested
disinvestment
eccentrically
erroneousness
essentialness
expansibility
expansiveness
expensiveness

exponentially
extensibility
extensionally
extensiveness
feloniousness
gerontocratic
gerontologist
goodnaturedly
greensickness
gynandromorph
hymenopterous
immunological
immunotherapy
impenetration
imponderables
incandescence
inconceivable
inconceivably
incondensable
incongruously
inconsecutive
inconsequence
inconsiderate
inconsistence
inconsistency
inconspicuous
incontestable
incontestably
incontinently
inconvenience
inconveniency
inconvertible
inconvertibly
inconvincible
infinitesimal
infundibulate
ingeniousness
ingenuousness
insensateness
insensibility
insensitively
insensitivity
insinuatingly
intangibility
intensiveness
intentionally
inventiveness
inventorially
invincibility
laryngoscopic
Maginotminded
mesencephalon
metonymically
misanthropist
misunderstand
misunderstood
momentariness
momentousness
mononucleosis
mourningcloak
mourningpaper
nomenclatural
oceanographer
oceanographic
offensiveness
organogenesis
organotherapy
palynological
paranormality
parenthetical
phrenetically
phrenological
plaintiveness
potentiometer
preengagement
preengineered
prognosticate
reconcilement
reconsolidate
reconstructor
reminiscently
remonstrantly
remonstration
remonstrative
resentfulness
retentiveness
revendication
scientologist
secondariness
sedentariness
selenocentric
selenographer
selenographic
selenological
serendipitous
sewingmachine
spinninghouse
spinningwheel
splendiferous
splenetically
squandermania
stainlessness
sternforemost
strangulation
strenuousness
taxonomically
technicalness
technological
telencephalon
theanthropism
triangularity
triangulation
tyrannosaurus
unconceivable
unconcernedly
unconditional
unconditioned
unconformable
unconquerable
unconsciously
unconstrained
unmentionable
voluntariness
voluntaristic
achromaticity
aggiornamento
agglomeration
agglomerative
airworthiness
amniocentesis
analogousness
angiospermous
AngloAmerican
AngloCatholic
appropriately
appropriation
appropriative
approximately
approximation
approximative
astronautical
astrophysical
authorisation
authoritarian
authoritative
BaltoSlavonic
bamboozlement
buttonthrough
carboniferous
carbonisation
chemoreceptor
colloquialism
compositeness
compositional
concomitantly
consolidation
consolidative
consolidatory
contortionist
convocational
corporativism
corroboration
corroborative
corroboratory
corrosiveness
cosmopolitise
cosmopolitism
cottonpicking
customariness
deodorisation
dichotomously
discoloration
discommodious
disconcerting
disconcertion
disconformity
disconnection
discontinuity
discontinuous
dishonourable
dishonourably
disposability
dispossession
dissolubility
dissoluteness
efflorescence
elaborateness
ethnocentrism
explorational
explosiveness
expropriation
ferroconcrete
ferroelectric
ferromagnetic
fibrovascular
followthrough
frivolousness
geomorphology
glamorisation
goniometrical
gymnospermous
harbourmaster
harmonisation
hollowhearted
homeomorphism
hydrocephalic
hydrocephalus
hydrochloride
hydrocracking
hydrodynamics
hydroelectric
hydrogenation
hydromedusoid
hydrometrical
hydrostatical
hydrosulphide
hydrosulphite
hydroxylamine
hypnoanalysis
hypnotisation
improbability
impropriation
improvability
improvidently
improvisation
improvisatory
inexorability
inflorescence
introgression
introspection
introspective
introversible
inviolability
inviolateness
laevorotation
laevorotatory
landownership
leptocephalic
leptospirosis
macrocephalic
macromolecule
mangoldwurzel
meadowsaffron
meteorologist
Methodistical
microanalysis
microcephalic
micrococcocci
microdetector
micronutrient
microorganism
microphyllous
microscopical
microtonality
miscomprehend
misconception
misgovernment
mnemotechnics
nationalistic
neurovascular
nitrobacteria
nitrocompound
noncollegiate
noncompliance
nonconducting
nonconforming
nonconformism
nonconformist
nonconformity
nonforfeiting
nongovernment
ochlocratical
opprobriously
orthocephalic
orthognathism
orthognathous
osteomyelitis
paedomorphism
pathogenicity
pathognomonic
patronisingly
peptonisation
periodisation
petrochemical
petroliferous
phenomenalise
phenomenalism
phenomenalist
phenomenology
philosophical
philosophiser
photochemical
photochromics
photochromism
photoelectric
photoelectron
photoemission
photoemissive
photoperiodic
photopositive
photoreceptor
phycoerythrin
phytoplankton
piezoelectric
pigeonchested
pigeonhearted
pigeonlivered
poliomyelitis
postoperative
preconception
predominantly
predomination
premonitorily
preponderance
preponderancy
prepositional
prepossessing
prepossession
primogenitary
primogenitive
primogeniture
primordiality
proconsulship
pronounceable
pronouncement
proportionate
propositional
prosopography
protohistoric
protonotarial
purposelessly
purposiveness
radioactivity
radiolocation
radiotelegram
randomisation
ratiocination
ratiocinative
rationalistic
reproachfully
reproachingly
restoratively
retroactively
retroactivity
retrogression
retrogressive
retrospection
retrospective
rhodochrosite
sacrosanctity
salmonellosis
schoolteacher
scolopendrium
seaworthiness
selfopinioned
SerboCroatian
seriousminded
sociocultural
socioeconomic
sorrowfulness
stoloniferous
subcontractor
subpostmaster
suffocatingly
suppositional
surrogateship
symbolisation
tautologously
temporalities
temporariness
temporisation
terrorisation
thoroughbrace
thoroughgoing
thoroughpaced
tortoiseshell
trigonometric
uncoordinated
unemotionally
unpromisingly
unwholesomely
violoncellist
visionariness
windowshopper
acceptability
amorphousness
antipersonnel
backpedalling
blasphemously
conspicuously
deceptiveness
disappearance
encapsulation
encephalogram
equiponderant

equiponderate
equipotential
exasperatedly
exceptionable
exceptionably
exceptionally
exemplariness
hemiparasitic
inappreciable
inappreciably
inappropriate
independently
inexpediently
inexpensively
inexperienced
inexpressible
inexpressibly
inopportunely
insupportable
insupportably
irreplaceable
irrepressible
irrepressibly
leadpoisoning
lifepreserver
manipulatable
metaphosphate
metaphysician
monophthongal
Monophysitism
nonappearance
outspokenness
overpopulated
paraphernalia
perspectively
perspicacious
perspicuously
phosphoretted
polypropylene
prospectively
receptibility
receptiveness
reciprocality
reciprocation
reciprocative
reduplication
reduplicative
scorpiongrass
scrapmerchant
scripturalism
scripturalist
sculpturesque
selfpityingly
selfpollinate
selfpossessed
selfpropelled
semiparasitic
semipermanent
semipermeable
semiporcelain
sharpshooting
sheepshearing
sleeplessness
softpedalling
steeplechaser
steppingstone
stirpiculture
streptococcal
streptococcus
teleportation
toxoplasmosis
unimpassioned
unimpeachable
vicepresident
deliquescence
derequisition
overqualified
quinquagenary
Quinquagesima
quinquevalent
tranquilliser
absorbability
abstractional
admirableness
adversatively
advertisement
affirmatively
afforestation
aircraftwoman
alternatively
anaerobically
anagrammatise
anagrammatism
anthropogenic
anthropometry
anthropopathy
anthropophagi
anthropophagy
anthroposophy
apportionment
arboriculture
arthritically
ascertainable
ascertainment
assertiveness
asserveration
Assyriologist
Australianism
centreforward
centrifugally
centripetally
cheerlessness
clairaudience
clearheadedly
clearinghouse
comprehension
comprehensive
compressional
concretionary
confraternity
confrontation
congratulator
congressional
congresswoman
congruousness
contrabandist
contrabassoon
contraception
contraceptive
contractility
contractually
contradiction
contradictory
contrafagotto
contrapuntist
contrariously
contravention
controversial
copartnership
cyberneticist
decerebration
decortication
deferentially
defervescence
deforestation
deformational
deliriousness
dendritically
depersonalise
descriptively
desirableness
destructively
destructivity
deterioration
deteriorative
determinately
determination
determinative
deterministic
diagrammatise
disarticulate
discreditable
discreditably
discretionary
discriminator
disgracefully
dispraisingly
disproportion
distressfully
distressingly
distributable
distrustfully
divertisement
doctrinairism
effervescence
effervescency
embarrassment
entertainment
environmental
epeirogenesis
epigrammatise
epigrammatist
excursiveness
expurgatorial
extermination
exterminatory
exteroceptive
exterritorial
flourishingly
gastrocnemius
gastroenteric
gastrological
gastronomical
generalisable
generalissimo
geotropically
gubernatorial
hazardousness
heterogeneity
heterogeneous
heterogenesis
heterogenetic
heteromorphic
heteropterous
heterosporous
heterothallic
heterotrophic
hilariousness
histrionicism
honorifically
hundredweight
hyperboloidal
hypercritical
hypermetrical
hypermetropia
hypermetropic
hyperphysical
hypertrophied
immarcescible
impartibility
imperceptible
imperceptibly
impercipience
imperfectness
imperialistic
imperiousness
impermissible
impersonalise
impersonality
impersonation
impertinently
imperturbable
imperturbably
importunately
incarceration
incardination
incorporation
incorporative
incorporeally
incorrectness
incorruptible
incorruptibly
incorruptness
incurableness
incuriousness
inferentially
informational
informatively
infuriatingly
ingurgitation
injuriousness
inscriptional
instructional
instructively
intercalation
intercellular
intercolonial
intercolumnar
intercropping
intercultural
intercurrence
interdentally
interdigitate
interestingly
intergalactic
interjectural
interlacement
interlocution
interlocutory
interlocutrix
intermarriage
intermediator
intermittence
international
interoceptive
interosculate
interparietal
interpellator
interpersonal
interpolation
interpolative
interposition
interpretable
interpretress
interpunction
interrelation
interrogation
interrogative
interrogatory
interruptible
interspecific
interspersion
interstratify
intertropical
invariability
laboriousness
liberationist
luxuriousness
macaronically
malariologist
materfamilias
materialistic
membranaceous
mineralogical
miserableness
mistrustfully
mistrustingly
moderatorship
modernisation
Monarchianism
nefariousness
nonproductive
notoriousness
numerological
observational
obstructively
opportuneness
opportunistic
owneroccupier
paperhangings
partridgewood
paterfamilias
paternalistic
penuriousness
polarographic
powerlessness
prairieoyster
preordainment
preordination
prepreference
procrastinate
progressional
progressively
progressivism
proprietorial
proprioceptor
quadragesimal
quadrennially
quadricipital
quadrilateral
quadrillionth
quadripartite
quadrumvirate
quadruplicate
quadruplicity
quarrelsomely
rearrangement
referentially
reforestation
reformability
reformational
regardfulness
regurgitation
remorselessly
restrictively
reverberation
reverberative
reverberatory
reverentially
reversibility
sacerdotalise
sacerdotalism
sacerdotalist
scleroprotein
selfrecording
selfregarding
selfreproving
selfrepugnant
selfrestraint
selfrevealing
selfrighteous
separableness
separationist
sobermindness
spheroidicity
squarebashing
subirrigation
subordinately
subordination
subordinative
suffraganship
superabundant
superaddition
superannuable
supercalender
supercritical
superdominant
supereminence
superfamilies
superfetation
superficially
superfluidity
superfluously
superhumanity
superlatively

supernational
supernumerary
superordinate
superphysical
superposition
supersaturate
supersensible
superstitious
supersubtlety
supervenience
taperecording
telerecording
temerariously
theoretically
tolerableness
tuberculation
unceremonious
uncertainness
uncircumcised
underachiever
undercarriage
underclothing
undereducated
underemphasis
underemployed
underestimate
underexposure
undergraduate
underhandedly
understanding
understrapper
underwhelming
unearthliness
unforgettable
unforgettably
unforthcoming
unfortunately
unwarrantable
unwarrantably
venerableness
venereologist
ventriloquial
ventriloquise
ventriloquism
ventriloquist
vicariousness
waterproofing
accessibility
admissibility
advisableness
ambassadorial
antiscorbutic
assassination
atmospherical
backscratcher
Christmastide
Christmastime
chrysanthemum
cleistogamous
coarsegrained
crosscultural
crossgartered
crosshatching
crosspurposes
crossquestion
cruiserweight
derestriction
devastatingly
digestibility
domestication
dressimprover
dressingtable
eavesdropping
equestrianism
eschscholtzia
excessiveness
excusableness
expostulation
expostulatory
festschriften
foresightedly
freeselection
glossographer
hairsplitting
halfsovereign
hemispherical
hocuspocussed
homosexuality
idiosyncratic
illustriously
immiscibility
impassability
impassibility
impassiveness
impossibility
indescribable
indescribably
indiscernible
indiscernibly
indispensable
indispensably
indisposition
indissociable
indistinctive
industrialise
industrialism
industrialist
industriously
inhospitality
insusceptible
investigation
investigative
investigatory
invisibleness
irresponsible
irresponsibly
jurisprudence
laissezpasser
legislatively
legislatorial
longsuffering
magisterially
megasporangia
metastability
ministerially
monosyllabism
monosymmetric
nearsightedly
necessitarian
necessitation
necessitously
numismatology
obsessiveness
occasionalism
occasionalist
occasionality
oppositionist
oversensitive
overstatement
oversubscribe
painstakingly
parasitically
parasiticidal
parasynthesis
parasynthetic
pedestrianise
pedestrianism
Pennsylvanian
perishability
perissodactyl
phraseologist
plausibleness
polysynthesis
polysynthetic
recessiveness
redescription
reinstatement
resistibility
resuscitation
resuscitative
rhapsodically
selfsacrifice
selfsatisfied
selfslaughter
selfsterility
selfsufficing
selfsupported
selfsurrender
selfsustained
sidesplitting
soulsearching
terpsichorean
thrasonically
transatlantic
transcendence
transcendency
transcription
transcriptive
transformable
transgression
transgressive
transistorise
transitionary
translational
transliterate
translocation
translucently
translucidity
transmigrator
transmissible
transmittable
transmutation
transmutative
transnational
transparently
transpiration
transpiratory
transportable
transposition
transshipment
transshipping
transversally
treasurership
undisciplined
unfashionable
unfashionably
verisimilarly
vivisectional
whimsicalness
abortifacient
ambitiousness
arbitrariness
arbitrational
beauteousness
blastogenesis
bounteousness
bountifulness
boustrophedon
bumptiousness
cicatrisation
constellation
constellatory
consternation
constrainable
constrainedly
constructable
constructible
counteraction
counteractive
counterattack
counterchange
countercharge
counterfeiter
counterstroke
counterweight
countinghouse
courteousness
courtsmartial
craftsmanship
cryptanalysis
cryptanalytic
cryptographer
cryptographic
cryptological
crystalgazing
crystallinity
dauntlessness
deleteriously
dematerialise
demythologise
denationalise
deontological
doubtlessness
draftsmanship
electioneerer
electrocution
electrologist
electromagnet
electrometric
electromotive
electrophorus
electroscopic
electrostatic
electrovalent
exanthematous
excitableness
existentially
facetiousness
faultlessness
flirtatiously
fractionalise
fractionation
fractiousness
frontogenesis
fruitlessness
frustratingly
functionalism
functionalist
gametogenesis
geostationary
guiltlessness
habitableness
healthfulness
heartbreaking
heartlessness
heartsickness
hypothecation
identicalness
immaterialise
immaterialism
immaterialist
immateriality
immutableness
impetuousness
inattentively
indeterminacy
indeterminate
indeterminism
indeterminist
insatiability
irrationalise
irrationalism
irrationalist
irrationality
irretrievable
irretrievably
irritableness
isostatically
lightfingered
lightheadedly
lightmindedly
lightsomeness
limitlessness
mediterranean
meistersinger
meritoriously
Monotheletism
monotrematous
monstrousness
mountainously
mountebankery
naphthylamine
negotiability
nemathelminth
nightmarishly
nightwatchman
nonattendance
odontoglossum
odontological
opisthobranch
ornithologist
outstandingly
painterliness
palatableness
penetrability
penetratingly
penetratively
penitentially
plenteousness
plentifulness
pointillistic
pointlessness
practicalness
prestigiously
prostaglandin
prosthodontia
punctiliously
puritanically
pyrotechnical
quartermaster
quartziferous
questioningly
questionnaire
quintillionth
quintuplicate
reintegration
repetitionary
repetitiously
RhaetoRomanic
righteousness
righthandedly
roentgenogram
roentgenology
sanctimonious
sanitationist
scintillating
scintillation
seditiousness
selftormentor
shiftlessness
shootingbrake
shootingrange
shootingstick
shorttempered
sightlessness
smoothingiron
sniftingvalve
somatological
spectacularly
spectrography
spectrometric
spectroscopic
spontaneously
sportsmanlike
sportsmanship
strategically
stratigraphic
stratocumulus
stratospheric
substantially
substantively
substantivise
substitutable
substructural
sumptuousness

teratological
theatricalise
theatricalism
theatricality
toastmistress
tractableness
Tractarianism
trustworthily
unanticipated
unarticulated
unestablished
unintelligent
unintentional
uninterrupted
unnaturalness
unobtrusively
unputdownable
vegetarianism
vexatiousness
vocationalism
volatilisable
Zarathustrian
accoutrements
agglutination
agglutinative
bildungsroman
calculatingly
cinquecentist
circumambient
circumference
circumfluence
circumspectly
circumvallate
circumvention
coagulability
coeducational
colourfulness
communication
communicative
communicatory
communisation
communitarian
commutability
computational
concupiscence
concupiscible
conduciveness
conductorship
conjugateness
conjugational
conjunctional
conjunctively
consumptively
convulsionary
corruptionist
credulousness
diffusiveness
disjunctively
dysfunctional
encouragement
encouragingly
exclusiveness
formulisation
fortunateness
fortunehunter
fortuneteller
frequentation
frequentative
garrulousness
hallucination
hallucinative
hallucinatory
inclusiveness
ineducability
influentially
intrusiveness
languishingly
leisureliness
masculineness
mensurability
nonfulfilment
obtrusiveness
pendulousness
percussionist
perdurability
perfunctorily
permutability
picturepalace
picturesquely
postulational
prejudicially
presumptively
procuratorial
pronunciation
protuberantly
querulousness
rapturousness
recrudescence
resourcefully
sesquiplicate
speculatively
suffumigation
tonguelashing
tonguetwister
tremulousness
tributariness
unadulterated
unequivocally
untrustworthy
vapourishness
venturesomely
venturousness
equivocalness
immovableness
inadvertently
individualise
individualism
individualist
individuality
individuation
irreverential
obliviousness
overvaluation
papaveraceous
redevelopment
reinvigorator
rejuvenescent
removableness
televisionary
backwardation
strawcoloured
annexationist
innoxiousness
obnoxiousness
acetylcholine
acotyledonous
anonymousness
bathymetrical
condylomatous
dissymetrical
embryogenesis
embryological
emphysematous
enjoyableness
jerrybuilding
martyrisation
martyrologist
moneygrubbing
pennyfarthing
pennypinching
phenylalanine
platyhelminth
recrystallise
topsyturvydom
horizontality
schizocarpous
schizogenesis
schizophrenia
schizophrenic

---

abstractional
acrobatically
adiabatically
admirableness
advisableness
agreeableness
aircraftwoman
anagrammatise
anagrammatism
AngloAmerican
annexationist
asthmatically
Australianism
autocatalysis
autocatalytic
automatically
availableness
axiomatically
backwardation
barefacedness
blameableness
burglariously
chateaubriand
chrematistics
chromatically
chromatograph
chromatolytic
chromatophore
chrysanthemum
cinematically
cinematograph
clairaudience
colleagueship
complainingly
complaisantly
conflagration
confraternity
congratulator
contrabandist
contrabassoon
contraception
contraceptive
contractility
contractually
contradiction
contradictory
contrafagotto
contrapuntist
contrariously
contravention
cryptanalysis
cryptanalytic
crystalgazing
crystallinity
desirableness
diagrammatise
dichlamydeous
disgracefully
displantation
dispraisingly
dodecaphonist
efficaciously
elephantiasis
enigmatically
enjoyableness
epigrammatise
epigrammatist
everlastingly
excitableness
excusableness
flirtatiously
foolhardiness
fullfashioned
generalisable
generalissimo
geostationary
goodnaturedly
grammatically
habitableness
hemiparasitic
hypnoanalysis
idiomatically
immovableness
immutableness
incurableness
indefatigable
indefatigably
ineffableness
inexhaustible
inexhaustibly
inorganically
intraarterial
irritableness
isostatically
judgeadvocate
judgmatically
kinematically
kinematograph
laughableness
liberationist
Machiavellian
maladaptation
malleableness
membranaceous
merchandising
microanalysis
mineralogical
miserableness
moderatorship
monodactylous
mountainously
navigableness
neoclassicism
neoclassicist
neoplasticism
oleomargarine
ophthalmology
outstandingly
overvaluation
paediatrician
palatableness
paramagnetism
parliamentary
peaceableness
pharmaceutics
pharmaceutist
pharmacologic
pharmacopoeia
pigheadedness
pneumatically
pneumatolysis
pneumatolytic
pneumatometer
pneumatophore
polycarbonate
polydactylous
pragmatically
prismatically
procrastinate
prostaglandin
psychasthenia
puritanically
quadragesimal
radioactivity
rearrangement
reembarkation
reincarnation
removableness
reproachfully
reproachingly
retroactively
retroactivity
revelationist
rheumatically
saccharimeter
saccharimetry
saccharometer
sadomasochism
sadomasochist
sanitationist
scandalmonger
schematically
scholarliness
scholasticism
selfsacrifice
selfsatisfied
semibarbarian
semibarbarism
semiparasitic
separableness
separationist
sergeantmajor
shockabsorber
spectacularly
spermatoblast
spermatogenic
spermatophore
spermatophyte
spontaneously
stigmatically
substantially
substantively
substantivise
suffraganship
superabundant
superaddition
superannuable
supplantation
teachableness
temerariously
thaumaturgist
tolerableness
traceableness
tractableness
Tractarianism
transatlantic
traumatically
uncleanliness
underachiever
unestablished
unimpassioned
vegetarianism
venerableness
woolgathering
zygodactylous
absorbability
attributively
bloodboltered
cannibalistic
collaboration
collaborative
confabulation
confabulatory
corroboration
corroborative
corroboratory
disembodiment
funambulation
heartbreaking
housebreaking
hyperboloidal
improbability
incombustible
jerrybuilding
neighbourhood
nitrobacteria
opprobriously
overabundance
perambulation
perambulatory
prohibitively
protuberantly
recombination
reverberation
reverberative

reverberatory
selfabasement
skateboarding
swashbuckling
syllabication
amniocentesis
anfractuosity
anglicisation
AngloCatholic
antiscorbutic
applicability
applicatively
backscratcher
biotechnology
bloodcurdling
characterless
climactically
coeducational
collectedness
collectorship
conduciveness
conductorship
confectionary
confectionery
conjecturable
conjecturally
connectedness
consecutively
convocational
corticotropic
corticotropin
crosscultural
defencelessly
denticulation
deprecatingly
dialectically
eschscholtzia
ethnocentrism
extracellular
fasciculation
ferroconcrete
festschriften
floricultural
gesticulation
gesticulative
gesticulatory
gynaecocratic
gynaecologist
hallucination
hallucinative
hallucinatory
horsechestnut
horticultural
hydrocephalic
hydrocephalus
hydrochloride
hydrocracking
hypercritical
immarcescible
immiscibility
impeccability
imperceptible
imperceptibly
impercipience
implacability
implicatively
impracticable
impracticably
impractically
incarceration
inconceivable
inconceivably
indescribable
indescribably
indiscernible
indiscernibly
ineducability
inspectorship
insusceptible
intercalation
intercellular
intercolonial
intercolumnar
intercropping
intercultural
intercurrence
intracellular
intricateness
invincibility
italicisation
lancecorporal
leptocephalic
levelcrossing
machicolation
macrocephalic
matriculation
mesencephalon
microcephalic
micrococcocci
Monarchianism
multicellular
multicoloured
myrmecologist
nitrocompound
nomenclatural
ochlocratical
orthocephalic
participation
participative
participatory
particoloured
particularise
particularism
particularist
particularity
perfectionism
perfectionist
petrochemical
photochemical
photochromics
photochromism
piscicultural
predicability
predicamental
predicatively
preoccupation
projectionist
protectionism
protectionist
protectorship
ratiocination
ratiocinative
recalcitrance
reconcilement
redescription
refractometer
resuscitation
resuscitative
revaccination
rhodochrosite
SerboCroatian
sharecropping
sociocultural
strawcoloured
submachinegun
suffocatingly
supercalender
supercritical
syntactically
telencephalon
threecornered
transcendence
transcendency
transcription
transcriptive
tuberculation
uncircumcised
unconceivable
unconcernedly
undercarriage
underclothing
undisciplined
unprecedented
vermiculation
vernacularise
vernacularism
vernacularity
versicoloured
accreditation
animadversion
archidiaconal
bewilderingly
closedcircuit
confederation
confederative
confidingness
considerately
consideration
cylindrically
dependability
eavesdropping
formidability
granddaughter
gynandromorph
hazardousness
hybridisation
hydrodynamics
imponderables
incandescence
incardination
incondensable
incredibility
incredulously
infundibulate
interdentally
interdigitate
kaleidoscopic
lackadaisical
Methodistical
microdetector
misunderstand
misunderstood
nondeductable
periodisation
polyadelphous
prejudicially
premeditation
premeditative
preordainment
preordination
presidentship
pteridologist
recrudescence
regardfulness
revendication
sacerdotalise
sacerdotalism
sacerdotalist
secondariness
selfaddressed
selfadjusting
selfeducation
serendipitous
shoulderblade
shoulderstrap
splendiferous
squandermania
subordinately
subordination
subordinative
superdominant
unconditional
unconditioned
unpredictable
unputdownable
viceadmiralty
accelerometer
accidentalism
accidentprone
acquiescently
acquiescingly
aesthetically
afforestation
ambidexterity
ambidexterous
antipersonnel
apathetically
archaeologist
archaeopteryx
archdeaconate
argumentation
argumentative
autocephalous
backpedalling
battlecruiser
beauteousness
betweenwhiles
bioenergetics
blanketflower
bounteousness
brotherliness
businesswoman
cabinetmaking
candlelighter
candlesnuffer
centreforward
challengeable
challengingly
changeability
changefulness
chinkerinchee
cinquecentist
clandestinely
clothesbasket
coarsegrained
coenaesthesis
coldheartedly
collieshangie
complementary
complexedness
comprehension
comprehensive
compressional
concretionary
congressional
congresswoman
constellation
constellatory
consternation
counteraction
counteractive
counterattack
counterchange
countercharge
counterfeiter
counterstroke
counterweight
courteousness
crackerbarrel
cruiserweight
decerebration
deferentially
deforestation
deleteriously
dematerialise
diathermanous
discreditable
discreditably
discretionary
disobediently
distressfully
distressingly
documentalist
documentation
doublecrosser
doubledealing
doubleglazing
doublejointed
doubletongued
energetically
epiphenomenal
epiphenomenon
erroneousness
evangelically
exasperatedly
existentially
exponentially
featherheaded
featherstitch
featherweight
ferroelectric
forementioned
fragmentarily
fragmentation
freeselection
frequentation
frequentative
gentlemanlike
halfheartedly
hardheartedly
heebiejeebies
hemicellulose
homogeneously
homosexuality
hundredweight
hydroelectric
immaterialise
immaterialism
immaterialist
immateriality
impenetration
inadvertently
inattentively
independently
indeterminacy
indeterminate
indeterminism
indeterminist
ineffectively
ineffectually
inexpediently
inexpensively
inexperienced
inferentially
influentially
inoffensively
interestingly
irreverential
knickerbocker
knowledgeable
knowledgeably
laissezpasser
leatherjacket
manageability
manifestation
manifestative
mediterranean
megacephalous
meistersinger
monometallism
monometallist
monumentalise
mountebankery
mutagenically
northeasterly
northeastward
occidentalise
Occidentalism
Occidentalist
octocentenary
ontogenically
openheartedly
orangeblossom
ornamentation
overbearingly

oversensitive
paddlesteamer
painterliness
pantheistical
papaveraceous
parthenocarpy
penitentially
perspectively
philhellenism
philhellenist
photoelectric
photoelectron
photoemission
photoemissive
phraseologist
phrenetically
phycoerythrin
piezoelectric
plenteousness
prepreference
problematical
progressional
progressively
progressivism
prophetically
prospectively
pyrimethamine
pyrotechnical
quadrennially
quarrelsomely
quartermaster
quincentenary
quingentenary
rattlebrained
redevelopment
referentially
reforestation
regimentation
reintegration
rejuvenescent
reorientation
resplendently
reverentially
righteousness
rontgenoscopy
rudimentarily
schadenfreude
sedimentation
selfcentredly
selfdeceiving
selfdeception
selfdeceptive
selfdefeating
selfdependent
selffertility
selfgenerated
selfrecording
selfregarding
selfreproving
selfrepugnant
selfrestraint
selfrevealing
semipermanent
semipermeable
sicklefeather
singlehearted
socioeconomic
softpedalling
soulsearching
southeasterly
southeastward
spelaeologist
Spencerianism
splenetically
squarebashing
strategically
strikebreaker
sublieutenant
supereminence
supplementary
synthetically
taperecording
telerecording
thenceforward
theoretically
thundershower
thunderstruck
tiddledywinks
tonguelashing
tonguetwister
tritheistical
unceremonious
undereducated
underemphasis
underemployed
underestimate
underexposure
unexceptional
unimpeachable
unintelligent
unintentional
uninterrupted
unnecessarily
unrelentingly
venereologist
vivisectional
volumenometer
weatherbeaten
wheelerdealer
whithersoever
acetification
acidification
amplification
beatification
calcification
caprification
certification
certificatory
clarification
cornification
costeffective
disaffectedly
disaffirmance
dulcification
falsification
fortification
glorification
grandfatherly
gratification
imperfectness
indifferently
insufficience
insufficiency
jollification
justification
justificative
justificatory
lightfingered
lignification
magnification
magnificently
materfamilias
mellifluously
metrification
millefeuilles
mollification
mortification
mummification
mystification
nitrification
nullification
odoriferously
paterfamilias
pennyfarthing
pestiferously
petrification
pontification
prizefighting
proliferation
proliferative
proliferously
prolification
qualification
qualificatory
rectification
Russification
sacrificially
scarification
scorification
significantly
signification
significative
specification
steadfastness
sternforemost
superfamilies
superfetation
superficially
superfluidity
superfluously
testification
thurification
transformable
uncomfortable
uncomfortably
unconformable
unselfishness
versification
vitrification
analogousness
beleaguerment
belligerently
biodegradable
blackguardism
calligraphist
compagination
configuration
conjugateness
conjugational
corrigibility
crossgartered
disengagement
disfigurement
expurgatorial
extragalactic
hydrogenation
incongruously
ineligibility
ingurgitation
intangibility
intergalactic
introgression
laryngoscopic
miscegenation
moneygrubbing
negligibility
nonaggression
nonfigurative
orthognathism
orthognathous
pantagruelian
pantagruelism
pantagruelist
pathogenicity
pathognomonic
preengagement
preengineered
prefiguration
prefigurative
prefigurement
primigravidae
primogenitary
primogenitive
primogeniture
prolegomenary
prolegomenous
refrigeration
regurgitation
retrogression
retrogressive
roentgenogram
roentgenology
sewingmachine
strangulation
surrogateship
transgression
transgressive
triangularity
triangulation
undergraduate
unforgettable
unforgettably
vantageground
verbigeration
vertiginously
villeggiatura
amorphousness
Antichristian
apprehensible
autochthonism
autochthonous
blasphemously
breechloading
catechisation
churchmanship
clearheadedly
crosshatching
cytochemistry
demythologise
encephalogram
enlightenment
exanthematous
healthfulness
hypochondriac
hypothecation
lightheadedly
Manichaeanism
metaphosphate
metaphysician
mitochondrion
monochromatic
monophthongal
Monophysitism
Monotheletism
naphthylamine
nemathelminth
opisthobranch
ornithologist
paperhangings
paraphernalia
perichondrial
perichondrium
perishability
phosphoretted
platyhelminth
polychromatic
prosthodontia
protohistoric
reprehensible
reprehensibly
righthandedly
searchwarrant
smoothingiron
sprightliness
stoichiometry
superhumanity
thoughtlessly
thoughtreader
treacherously
underhandedly
unfashionable
unfashionably
unrighteously
wrongheadedly
Zarathustrian
abortifacient
administrable
administrator
admonishingly
affreightment
ambitiousness
antihistamine
apheliotropic
arboriculture
archbishopric
arthritically
artificiality
associateship
associativity
Assyriologist
astonishingly
atrociousness
audaciousness
autobiography
basidiomycete
beneficiation
boardinghouse
bountifulness
brilliantness
bumptiousness
canaliculated
capaciousness
centrifugally
centripetally
clearinghouse
climbingframe
complicatedly
complimentary
conceitedness
conflictingly
conscientious
consciousness
conspicuously
containership
coreligionist
countinghouse
cryobiologist
deliciousness
deliriousness
denationalise
dendritically
descriptively
deterioration
deteriorative
discriminator
distributable
doctrinairism
domiciliation
dressimprover
dressingtable
egregiousness
electioneerer
equidistantly
equilibration
exhibitionism
exhibitionist
expeditionary
expeditiously
facetiousness
felicitations
feloniousness
ferociousness
flourishingly
foraminiferal
foresightedly
fractionalise
fractionation
fractiousness
functionalism
functionalist
grandiloquent
hilariousness
histrionicism
honorifically
identicalness

ignominiously
illogicalness
immediateness
imperialistic
imperiousness
impolitically
incuriousness
individualise
individualism
individualist
individuality
individuation
inefficacious
inefficiently
infinitesimal
infuriatingly
ingeniousness
injudiciously
injuriousness
innoxiousness
insatiability
inscriptional
insidiousness
insociability
invariability
invidiousness
invisibleness
irrationalise
irrationalism
irrationalist
irrationality
irreligionist
irreligiously
judiciousness
laboriousness
languishingly
laughingstock
litigiousness
luxuriousness
malariologist
maliciousness
materialistic
melodiousness
mischievously
mouldingboard
mourningcloak
mourningpaper
nearsightedly
nefariousness
negotiability
notoriousness
obliviousness
obnoxiousness
occasionalism
occasionalist
occasionality
officiousness
oppositionist
ostreiculture
parasitically
parasiticidal
partridgewood
penuriousness
perspicacious
perspicuously
plausibleness
plentifulness
pointillistic
polyhistorian
practicalness
prairieoyster
prescientific
prestigiously
principalship
proprietorial
proprioceptor
proteinaceous
punctiliously
quadricipital
quadrilateral
quadrillionth
quadripartite
questioningly
questionnaire
quintillionth
rapaciousness
reaffirmation
reinvigorator
religiousness
reminiscently
repetitionary
repetitiously
restrictively
sagaciousness
salaciousness
sanctimonious
scintillating
scintillation
scorpiongrass
seditiousness
selfdirecting
selfdirection
selfdiscovery
selfdispraise
selfpityingly
selfrighteous
semicivilised
sesquiplicate
shootingbrake
shootingrange
shootingstick
slangingmatch
smellingsalts
sniftingvalve
solicitorship
soundingboard
spinninghouse
spinningwheel
stalkinghorse
steppingstone
stickingplace
stirpiculture
stratigraphic
subeditorship
substitutable
technicalness
televisionary
tenaciousness
terpsichorean
thereinbefore
tortoiseshell
transistorise
transitionary
unambiguously
unanticipated
unarticulated
unbelievingly
unenlightened
unequivocally
unfamiliarity
unremittingly
unsociability
ventriloquial
ventriloquise
ventriloquism
ventriloquist
veraciousness
verifiability
verisimilarly
vexatiousness
vicariousness
vivaciousness
vocationalism
volatilisable
voraciousness
whimsicalness
extrajudicial
interjectural
maladjustment
sprocketwheel
acetylcholine
acotyledonous
actualisation
animalisation
anomalistical
anomalousness
anthelminthic
anticlimactic
anticlockwise
apocalyptical
appellatively
baccalaureate
barrelchested
Berkeleianism
blamelessness
bloodlessness
bouillabaisse
boundlessness
brainlessness
brutalisation
calculatingly
cartilaginous
cephalothorax
cheerlessness
chuckleheaded
coagulability
cobelligerent
coldbloodedly
condylomatous
consolidation
consolidative
consolidatory
convalescence
convulsionary
correlatively
correlativity
credulousness
curvilinearly
dauntlessness
deathlessness
discoloration
dissolubility
dissoluteness
doubtlessness
draggletailed
dreamlessness
embellishment
encyclopaedia
encyclopaedic
encyclopedism
encyclopedist
establishment
exemplariness
faithlessness
faultlessness
fertilisation
feudalisation
feuilletonism
feuilletonist
flagellantism
formalisation
formulisation
fossiliferous
fossilisation
frivolousness
fruitlessness
garrulousness
gracelessness
guilelessness
guiltlessness
heartlessness
hypoglycaemia
infallibilism
infallibilist
infallibility
intelligencer
intelligently
interlacement
interlocution
interlocutory
interlocutrix
inviolability
inviolateness
irreclaimable
irreclaimably
irreplaceable
kapellmeister
knuckleduster
lamellibranch
legislatively
legislatorial
limitlessness
magniloquence
mammaliferous
mangoldwurzel
masculineness
matrilineally
mercilessness
metalliferous
metallisation
metallography
metallurgical
mirthlessness
miscellaneous
mutualisation
nephelometric
nervelessness
nickeliferous
noiselessness
noncollegiate
nonfulfilment
normalisation
nostalgically
overelaborate
papillomatous
parallelogram
pendulousness
petroliferous
phenylalanine
pluralisation
pointlessness
porcellaneous
postclassical
postulational
powerlessness
premillennial
pricelessness
pusillanimity
pusillanimous
pyrheliometer
querulousness
radiolocation
rectilinearly
reduplication
reduplicative
republicanise
republicanism
republication
ritualisation
schoolteacher
selfslaughter
senselessness
serialisation
shamelessness
shapelessness
shiftlessness
sightlessness
signalisation
sleeplessness
smokelessness
snowblindness
socialisation
somniloquence
speculatively
spindlelegged
spindleshanks
spinelessness
stabilisation
stainlessness
statelessness
steeplechaser
sterilisation
subtilisation
superlatively
symbolisation
synallagmatic
tantalisation
tantalisingly
tastelessness
tautologously
thanklessness
thimblerigged
thimblerigger
thrillingness
titillatingly
tonsillectomy
toxoplasmosis
translational
transliterate
translocation
translucently
translucidity
tremulousness
troublesomely
troublousness
umbelliferous
unadulterated
unfeelingness
unhealthiness
unqualifiedly
unwholesomely
unwillingness
vacillatingly
valuelessness
verbalisation
vernalisation
visualisation
voicelessness
worldlyminded
worthlessness
acclimatation
accommodating
accommodation
accommodative
achromaticity
affirmatively
agglomeration
agglomerative
anonymousness
archimandrite
arithmetician
balsamiferous
bathymetrical
broadmindedly
circumambient
circumference
circumfluence
circumspectly
circumvallate
circumvention
commemoration
commemorative
commemoratory
concomitantly
consumptively
contamination
contaminative
contemplation
contemplative
customariness
deformational
determinately
determination
determinative
deterministic

detrimentally
discommodious
dismemberment
dissemblingly
dissemination
disseminative
dissimilarity
dissimilation
dissimilitude
dissimulation
dissymetrical
excommunicate
extermination
exterminatory
ferrimagnetic
ferromagnetic
fundamentally
goniometrical
grandmotherly
homeomorphism
hydromedusoid
hydrometrical
hypermetrical
hypermetropia
hypermetropic
impermissible
inanimateness
incommunicado
incrementally
incriminatory
informational
informatively
intermarriage
intermediator
intermittence
intramuscular
leishmaniasis
lightmindedly
macromolecule
maladminister
mathematician
miscomprehend
Mohammedanism
Muhammadanism
nightmarishly
noncompliance
numismatology
osteomyelitis
overemphasise
paedomorphism
passementerie
phenomenalise
phenomenalism
phenomenalist
phenomenology
planimetrical
poliomyelitis
predominantly
predomination
preliminarily
presumptively
randomisation
recommendable
recrimination
recriminative
recriminatory
reexamination
reformability
reformational
rhadamanthine
sacramentally
scrapmerchant
selfimportant
sentimentally
sobermindness
somnambulator
sphygmography
squeamishness
suffumigation
thremmatology
toastmistress
transmigrator
transmissible
transmittable
transmutation
transmutative
unanimousness
ungrammatical
unicameralism
unicameralist
unpromisingly
unsymmetrical
victimisation
alternatively
aluminiferous
aluminisation
asthenosphere
astronautical
attainability
authentically
authenticator
balkanisation
bildungsroman
bookingoffice
brokenhearted
buttonthrough
Calvinistical
campanologist
carboniferous
carbonisation
carcinomatous
combinatorial
commandership
commensurable
commensurably
communication
communicative
communicatory
communisation
communitarian
companionable
companionably
companionless
companionship
compendiously
concentration
concentrative
concentricity
conjunctional
conjunctively
consanguinity
consenescence
consentaneity
consentaneous
contentedness
contentiously
continentally
conventionary
cottonpicking
criminalistic
criminologist
cyberneticist
degranulation
disconcerting
disconcertion
disconformity
disconnection
discontinuity
discontinuous
dishonourable
dishonourably
disjunctively
dismantlement
distinctively
distinguished
dysfunctional
ecumenicalism
egocentricity
embranglement
examinational
examinatorial
explanatorily
extrinsically
fascinatingly
foreknowledge
fortunateness
fortunehunter
fortuneteller
galvanisation
geocentricism
germanisation
glutinousness
graminivorous
gubernatorial
harmonisation
helminthiasis
helminthology
hermeneutical
imaginatively
insignificant
instantaneity
instantaneous
instinctively
international
intransigeant
intransigence
intrinsically
lineengraving
machinegunner
magnanimously
manganiferous
mechanisation
mercenariness
micronutrient
millennialism
misconception
mismanagement
modernisation
multinational
multinucleate
nationalistic
nonconducting
nonconforming
nonconformism
nonconformist
nonconformity
nonsensically
obstinateness
offhandedness
outgeneralled
overindulgent
paternalistic
patronisingly
peptonisation
perfunctorily
perpendicular
phalansterian
philanthropic
pigeonchested
pigeonhearted
pigeonlivered
platiniferous
polliniferous
precentorship
preconception
premonitorily
preponderance
preponderancy
pretentiously
proconsulship
progenitorial
pronunciation
protonotarial
provincialise
provincialism
provincialist
provinciality
prudentialism
prudentialist
prudentiality
psilanthropic
rationalistic
rectangularly
replenishment
retranslation
runningstitch
salmonellosis
selfinduction
selfindulgent
selfinflicted
selfinsurance
selfknowledge
sententiously
septentrional
sequentiality
solemnisation
staminiferous
stoloniferous
subcontractor
supernational
supernumerary
supranational
Swedenborgian
tendentiously
tercentennial
terminability
terminational
terminatively
tintinnabular
tintinnabulum
transnational
tricentennial
trigonometric
tyrannosaurus
unflinchingly
unmeaningness
violoncellist
visionariness
volcanologist
vulcanisation
vulcanologist
woodengraving
zinjanthropus
abiologically
acrimoniously
acrylonitrile
actinomorphic
actinomycetes
actinomycosis
alcoholically
alcoholometer
alcoholometry
allegorically
allelomorphic
anaerobically
anthropogenic
anthropometry
anthropopathy
anthropophagi
anthropophagy
anthroposophy
anticoagulant
antilogarithm
antinomianism
auctioneering
autonomically
backformation
bamboozlement
bibliographer
bibliographic
bibliolatrist
bibliolatrous
bibliological
bibliophilism
bibliophilist
biogeographer
blastogenesis
camphoraceous
cardiographer
categorically
ceremonialism
ceremonialist
ceremoniously
chalcography
choreographer
choreographic
chromospheric
chronographic
chronological
conchological
confrontation
conglomeratic
controversial
craniological
cryptographer
cryptographic
cryptological
deipnosophist
deontological
developmental
diageotropism
diagnostician
disproportion
embryogenesis
embryological
entomological
entomophagous
entomophilous
entomostracan
environmental
epeirogenesis
equiponderant
equiponderate
equipotential
equivocalness
exteroceptive
extraordinary
frontogenesis
gametogenesis
gastrocnemius
gastroenteric
gastrological
gastronomical
geotropically
glaciological
glossographer
gonadotrophic
gonadotrophin
graphological
halfsovereign
heterogeneity
heterogeneous
heterogenesis
heterogenetic
heteromorphic
heteropterous
heterosporous
heterothallic
heterotrophic
homoeomorphic
homoeopathist
homoiothermal
homoiothermic
horizontality
hymenopterous
ideologically
immunological
immunotherapy
inopportunely
insubordinate
interoceptive
interosculate
irrecoverable
irrecoverably
leadpoisoning

lepidopterist
lepidopterous
lexicographer
lexicographic
macaronically
Maginotminded
malacological
malacostracan
meritoriously
metamorphoses
metamorphosis
microorganism
millionairess
monocotyledon
monomolecular
morphogenesis
morphogenetic
morphological
musicological
nonproductive
nucleoprotein
numerological
oceanographer
oceanographic
odontoglossum
odontological
oecologically
omnicompetent
ontologically
opinionatedly
organogenesis
organotherapy
outspokenness
overconfident
overpopulated
owneroccupier
palaeographer
palaeographic
palaeontology
palaeozoology
palynological
parabolically
paradoxically
paranormality
passionflower
patriotically
pedagogically
phrenological
phyllophagous
physiognomist
physiographer
physiographic
physiological
physiotherapy
plethorically
pneumogastric
pneumonectomy
polarographic
polycotyledon
postcommunion
prognosticate
pseudoarchaic
pseudomorphic
pseudoscience
psychoanalyse
psychoanalyst
psychodynamic
psychogenesis
psychogenetic
psychokinesis
psychokinetic
psychological
psychometrics
psychometrist
psychophysics
psychosomatic
psychosurgery
psychotherapy
rearcommodore
reinforcement
renegotiation
RhaetoRomanic
rhapsodically
schizocarpous
schizogenesis
schizophrenia
schizophrenic
scleroprotein
seismographer
seismographic
seismological
selenocentric
selenographer
selenographic
selenological
selfcollected
selfcommunion
selfconceited
selfcondemned
selfconfessed
selfconfident
selfconscious
selfconsuming
selfcontained
selfcontented
selfconvicted
selfforgetful
selfgoverning
selfpollinate
selfpossessed
selftormentor
semeiological
semiconductor
semiconscious
semilogarithm
semiporcelain
serologically
somatological
spasmodically
speleological
spheroidicity
standoffishly
stationmaster
stercoraceous
stereographic
stereoscopist
stratocumulus
stratospheric
superordinate
swallowtailed
symbiotically
symphonically
symphoniously
taxonomically
technological
teleportation
teratological
theologically
theriomorphic
thermochemist
thermodynamic
thermogenesis
thermonuclear
thermophilous
thermoplastic
thermosetting
thermotropism
thigmotropism
thrasonically
timeconsuming
topologically
toxicological
troglodytical
typologically
unaccompanied
unaccountable
unaccountably
uninformative
xanthochroism
zoogeographer
zoogeographic
accompaniment
affenpinscher
amphiprostyle
appropriately
appropriation
appropriative
astrophysical
atmospherical
conceptualise
conceptualism
conceptualist
concupiscence
concupiscible
corruptionist
cosmopolitise
cosmopolitism
crosspurposes
decomposition
decompression
decrepitation
disappearance
disciplinable
encompassment
expropriation
extemporarily
extraphysical
extrapolation
fissiparously
hairsplitting
hemispherical
hermaphrodite
hocuspocussed
horripilation
hyperphysical
impalpability
impropriation
incompetently
incorporation
incorporative
incorporeally
indispensable
indispensably
indisposition
inhospitality
insupportable
insupportably
intemperately
interparietal
interpellator
interpersonal
interpolation
interpolative
interposition
interpretable
interpretress
interpunction
intrapersonal
irresponsible
irresponsibly
jurisprudence
juxtaposition
megasporangia
microphyllous
multiplicable
nonappearance
pennypinching
photoperiodic
photopositive
phytoplankton
pluripresence
postoperative
precipitantly
precipitately
precipitation
precipitative
precipitously
PreRaphaelite
prosopography
recomposition
scolopendrium
scrumptiously
selfappointed
selfapproving
selfopinioned
sidesplitting
subreptitious
superphysical
superposition
surreptitious
transparently
transpiration
transpiratory
transportable
transposition
uncompetitive
uncomplaining
uncomplicated
waterproofing
wellapPointed
colloquialism
consequential
crossquestion
subsequential
threequarters
unconquerable
aggiornamento
airworthiness
algebraically
anachronistic
anachronously
anaphrodisiac
answerability
arbitrariness
arbitrational
authorisation
authoritarian
authoritative
autoeroticism
bacteriolysis
bacteriolytic
bacteriophage
barbarisation
barbarousness
birefringence
bloodrelation
boustrophedon
butterfingers
butterflyfish
cacographical
cauterisation
cerebrospinal
chemoreceptor
cicatrisation
colourfulness
commercialise
commercialism
commercialist
comparability
comparatively
compartmental
concertmaster
conservatoire
constrainable
constrainedly
constructable
constructible
contortionist
conversazione
conversazioni
convertiplane
cooperatively
corporativism
daguerreotype
dangerousness
dastardliness
declaratively
defibrination
deodorisation
desegregation
desperateness
deuteragonist
Deuteronomist
dexterousness
diaphragmatic
differentiate
disharmonious
disparagement
disparagingly
disparateness
efflorescence
elaborateness
electrocution
electrologist
electromagnet
electrometric
electromotive
electrophorus
electroscopic
electrostatic
electrovalent
embarrassment
encouragement
encouragingly
endocrinology
Eucharistical
explorational
exterritorial
filterability
frustratingly
gasteropodous
geochronology
geomorphology
glamorisation
helterskelter
ideographical
inappreciable
inappreciably
inappropriate
incorrectness
incorruptible
incorruptibly
incorruptness
inexorability
inexpressible
inexpressibly
inflorescence
inspirational
interrelation
interrogation
interrogative
interrogatory
interruptible
irrefrangible
irrepressible
irrepressibly
irretrievable
irretrievably
isochronously
isomerisation
jiggerypokery
Kidderminster
laevorotation
laevorotatory
lecherousness
leisureliness
lethargically
letterperfect
librarianship
lickerishness
liebfraumilch
lifepreserver
ludicrousness
mackerelshark
maladroitness

manneristical
martyrisation
martyrologist
masterfulness
melodramatics
melodramatise
melodramatist
mensurability
mercerisation
mesmerisation
metagrobolise
meteorologist
monogrammatic
monotrematous
monstrousness
mothercountry
nectariferous
niggardliness
nonforfeiting
oreographical
overcredulous
oystercatcher
penetrability
penetratingly
penetratively
perdurability
peregrination
phanerogamous
photoreceptor
picturepalace
picturesquely
polypropylene
ponderability
ponderousness
prayermeeting
preferability
preparatively
preparatorily
pretermission
pretermitting
preternatural
prevarication
primordiality
procuratorial
proparoxytone
proportionate
psychrometric
pulverisation
rapturousness
reciprocality
reciprocation
reciprocative
resourcefully
restoratively
rollercoaster
sabrerattling
seaworthiness
selfcriticism
selfpropelled
silvertongued
solderingiron
spectrography
spectrometric
spectroscopic
subirrigation
subserviently
substructural
subternatural
subterraneous
subversionary
summarisation
synchronistic
synchronously
telegrammatic
temperamental
temperateness
temporalities
temporariness
temporisation
tenderhearted
terrorisation
theatricalise
theatricalism
theatricality
topographical
trichromatism
typographical
uncoordinated
unobtrusively
unwarrantable
unwarrantably
vapourishness
venturesomely
venturousness
vicepresident
vulgarisation
vulnerability
winterberries
wonderfulness
wonderworking
xylographical
accessibility
admeasurement
admissibility
adversatively
agonistically
ambassadorial
angiospermous
assassination
atheistically
atomistically
BaltoSlavonic
belleslettres
Bloomsburyite
bombastically
brainstorming
broadspectrum
callisthenics
commiseration
commiserative
compassionate
compositeness
compositional
concessionary
condescension
confessionary
correspondent
corresponsive
corrosiveness
courtsmartial
craftsmanship
defeasibility
defensibility
demonstration
demonstrative
depersonalise
diffusiveness
dimensionally
dimensionless
dispassionate
disposability
dispossession
disrespectful
distastefully
draftsmanship
emphysematous
encapsulation
excessiveness
exclusiveness
excrescential
excursiveness
expansibility
expansiveness
expensiveness
explosiveness
expressionism
expressionist
exquisiteness
extensibility
extensionally
extensiveness
fantastically
Fascistically
floristically
fortississimo
greensickness
grotesqueness
gymnastically
gymnospermous
heartsickness
heptasyllabic
hydrostatical
hydrosulphide
hydrosulphite
impassability
impassibility
impassiveness
impersonalise
impersonality
impersonation
impossibility
impressionism
impressionist
impulsiveness
inclusiveness
inconsecutive
inconsequence
inconsiderate
inconsistence
inconsistency
inconspicuous
indissociable
infeasibility
inquisitional
inquisitively
inquisitorial
insensateness
insensibility
insensitively
insensitivity
insubstantial
intensiveness
interspecific
interspersion
interstratify
introspection
introspective
intrusiveness
lancesergeant
leptospirosis
lightsomeness
loathsomeness
microscopical
necessitarian
necessitation
necessitously
neurastheniac
nonresistance
obsessiveness
obtrusiveness
offensiveness
orchestration
panicstricken
pantisocratic
percussionist
perissodactyl
pervasiveness
pharisaically
philosophical
philosophiser
predestinator
prehistorical
prepositional
prepossessing
prepossession
processionary
processionist
professoriate
professorship
promiscuously
propositional
Protestantism
provisionally
purposelessly
purposiveness
realistically
recessiveness
reconsolidate
reconstructor
recrystallise
remonstrantly
remonstration
remonstrative
remorselessly
representable
repulsiveness
requisiteness
retrospection
retrospective
reversibility
sacrosanctity
sarcastically
selfasserting
selfassertion
selfassertive
selfassurance
selfassuredly
sequestration
Shakespearean
Shakespearian
sharpshooting
sheepshearing
sophistically
sophisticated
sportsmanlike
sportsmanship
statesmanlike
statesmanship
statistically
stylistically
subpostmaster
supersaturate
supersensible
superstitious
supersubtlety
suppositional
swordsmanship
tablespoonful
tachistoscope
tempestuously
terrestrially
tetrasyllable
thalassocracy
toothsomeness
transshipment
transshipping
unconsciously
unconstrained
understanding
understrapper
unquestioning
unsubstantial
untrustworthy
vouchsafement
wearisomeness
wholesomeness
worrisomeness
acceptability
accoutrements
acculturation
acculturative
adventuresome
adventurously
advertisement
affectionless
agglutination
agglutinative
apportionment
architectonic
architectural
argentiferous
aromatisation
ascertainable
ascertainment
assertiveness
atlantosaurus
attentiveness
chieftainship
Christmastide
Christmastime
cleistogamous
climatologist
collaterality
combativeness
commutability
compatibility
competitively
computational
concatenation
conditionally
connaturality
copartnership
deceitfulness
deceptiveness
decontaminate
decontrolling
decortication
deductibility
defectiveness
derestriction
dermatologist
desultoriness
devastatingly
diametrically
dichotomously
dictatorially
digestibility
disarticulate
disintegrator
disinterested
divertisement
domestication
dramatisation
dramaturgical
eccentrically
educationally
effectiveness
embrittlement
entertainment
equestrianism
eschatologist
essentialness
evocativeness
exceptionable
exceptionably
exceptionally
expectoration
expostulation
expostulatory
extratropical
facultatively
forgetfulness
frighteningly
frightfulness
galactosaemia
garnetiferous
geometrically
gerontocratic
gerontologist
globetrotting
gravitational
haematologist
herpetologist
hypertrophied
hypnotisation

illustriously
imitativeness
impartibility
impertinently
imperturbable
imperturbably
importunately
incontestable
incontestably
incontinently
indistinctive
indoctrinator
inductiveness
industrialise
industrialism
industrialist
industriously
inevitability
insectivorous
institutional
intentionally
intertropical
intuitiveness
inventiveness
inventorially
investigation
investigative
investigatory
isometrically
lucrativeness
magisterially
magnetisation
magnetomotive
magnetosphere
mediatisation
metastability
microtonality
ministerially
misanthropist
mnemotechnics
momentariness
momentousness
multitudinous
nonattendance
nonreturnable
nutritionally
objectionable
objectionably
objectiveness
objectivistic
onomatopoetic
operativeness
opportuneness
opportunistic
overstatement
painstakingly
palletisation
parenthetical
pedestrianise
pedestrianism
permutability
phreatophytic
plaintiveness
platitudinise
platitudinous
plenitudinous
potentiometer
predatoriness
prefatorially
prematureness
primitiveness
probationally
profitability
profitsharing
qualitatively
quicktempered
radiotelegram
receptibility
receptiveness
regretfulness
reinstatement
resentfulness
resistibility
retentiveness
scientologist
scripturalism
scripturalist
sculpturesque
secretarybird
secretaryship
secretiveness
sedentariness
seductiveness
selectiveness
selfsterility
sensationally
sensitisation
sensitiveness
shorttempered
sovietologist
spiritualness
stomatologist
streetwalking
streptococcal
streptococcus
structuralism
structuralist
structureless
subsaturation
symmetrically
talkativeness
tentativeness
territorially
theanthropism
threateningly
topsyturvydom
traditionally
tributariness
triliteralism
uncertainness
unearthliness
unemotionally
unforthcoming
unfortunately
unmentionable
unpretentious
unsuitability
voluntariness
voluntaristic
agriculturist
ambiguousness
assiduousness
bureaucratise
congruousness
deciduousness
deliquescence
derequisition
destructively
destructivity
devolutionary
devolutionist
distrustfully
harbourmaster
hydraulically
impecuniosity
impetuousness
ingenuousness
innocuousness
insinuatingly
insolubleness
instructional
instructively
integumentary
involuntarily
longsuffering
Malthusianism
manipulatable
mistrustfully
mistrustingly
mononucleosis
obstructively
overqualified
oversubscribe
phonautograph
pococurantism
precautionary
pronounceable
pronouncement
quadrumvirate
quadruplicate
quadruplicity
quincuncially
quinquagenary
Quinquagesima
quinquevalent
quintuplicate
reimbursement
revolutionary
revolutionise
revolutionism
revolutionist
sansculottism
scorbutically
selfsufficing
selfsupported
selfsurrender
selfsustained
semiautomatic
sericulturist
seriousminded
solidungulate
strenuousness
sulphureously
sumptuousness
thoroughbrace
thoroughgoing
thoroughpaced
tranquilliser
treasurership
unnaturalness
viniculturist
viticulturist
aggravatingly
asserveration
carnivorously
concavoconvex
defervescence
disadvantaged
disinvestment
disseveration
effervescence
effervescency
extravagantly
extravasation
extravascular
fibrovascular
improvability
improvidently
improvisation
improvisatory
inconvenience
inconveniency
inconvertible
inconvertibly
inconvincible
intravenously
introversible
misgovernment
neurovascular
nongovernment
observational
ovoviviparous
perseveration
resolvability
selfevidently
supervenience
tergiversator
transversally
followthrough
hollowhearted
horsewhipping
landownership
meadowsaffron
mouthwatering
nightwatchman
northwesterly
northwestward
quickwittedly
selfawareness
sorrowfulness
southwesterly
southwestward
trustworthily
underwhelming
windowshopper
approximately
approximation
approximative
convexoconvex
hydroxylamine
inflexibility
inflexionless
reflexibility
selfexecuting
selfexistence
aerodynamical
brachycephaly
brachydactyly
brachypterous
chlamydomonas
chlamydospore
ichthyography
ichthyologist
ichthyosaurus
idiosyncratic
linseywoolsey
metonymically
monosyllabism
monosymmetric
panegyrically
parasynthesis
parasynthetic
Pennsylvanian
polysynthesis
polysynthetic
shabbygenteel
turkeygobbler
haphazardness
quartziferous
squeezability

---

absorbability
acceptability
acclimatation
accompaniment
achromaticity
adversatively
affirmatively
aggravatingly
algebraically
alternatively
ambassadorial
AngloCatholic
answerability
anticoagulant
appellatively
applicability
applicatively
arbitrariness
arbitrational
archdeaconate
archimandrite
ascertainable
ascertainment
associateship
associativity
astronautical
attainability
baccalaureate
bouillabaisse
brilliantness
cacographical
calculatingly
cannibalistic
cartilaginous
changeability
chieftainship
circumambient
coagulability
coeducational
coldheartedly
combinatorial
commutability
comparability
comparatively
computational
conjugateness
conjugational
constrainable
constrainedly
convocational
cooperatively
corporativism
correlatively
correlativity
criminalistic
crossgartered
crosshatching
customariness
declaratively
decontaminate
deformational
dependability
deprecatingly
desperateness
deuteragonist
devastatingly
diaphragmatic
disadvantaged
disengagement
disparagement
disparagingly
disparateness
disposability
elaborateness
embarrassment
encephalogram
encompassment
encouragement
encouragingly
entertainment
examinational
examinatorial
exemplariness
explanatorily
explorational
expurgatorial
extragalactic
extravagantly
extravasation
extravascular
facultatively
fascinatingly
ferrimagnetic
ferromagnetic
fibrovascular
filterability
fissiparously
formidability
fortunateness
frustratingly
granddaughter
grandfatherly
gravitational
gubernatorial

halfheartedly
haphazardness
hardheartedly
ideographical
imaginatively
immediateness
impalpability
impassability
impeccability
imperialistic
implacability
implicatively
improbability
improvability
inanimateness
ineducability
inevitability
inexorability
informational
informatively
infuriatingly
insatiability
insensateness
insinuatingly
insociability
inspirational
intercalation
intergalactic
interlacement
intermarriage
international
interparietal
intricateness
invariability
inviolability
inviolateness
irreclaimable
irreclaimably
irrefrangible
irreplaceable
lackadaisical
legislatively
legislatorial
leishmaniasis
liebfraumilch
manageability
Manichaeanism
materfamilias
materialistic
mathematician
melodramatics
melodramatise
melodramatist
mensurability
mercenariness
metastability
mismanagement
momentariness
monogrammatic
mouthwatering
Muhammadanism
multinational
nationalistic
negotiability
neurovascular
nightmarishly
nightwatchman
nitrobacteria
northeasterly
northeastward
numismatology
observational
obstinateness
openheartedly
oreographical
overbearingly
overelaborate
overqualified
overstatement
painstakingly
paperhangings
paterfamilias
paternalistic
penetrability
penetratingly
penetratively
pennyfarthing
perdurability
perishability
permutability
pharisaically
phenylalanine
ponderability
postclassical
postulational
predicability
predicamental
predicatively
preengagement
preferability
preordainment
preparatively
preparatorily
procuratorial
profitability
pseudoarchaic
psychoanalyse
psychoanalyst
pusillanimity
pusillanimous
qualitatively
quinquagenary
Quinquagesima
rationalistic
reformability
reformational
reinstatement
resolvability
restoratively
rhadamanthine
righthandedly
sabrerattling
sacrosanctity
secondariness
secretarybird
secretaryship
sedentariness
selfabasement
selfawareness
selfslaughter
soulsearching
southeasterly
southeastward
speculatively
squeezability
steadfastness
suffocatingly
supercalender
superfamilies
superlatively
supernational
supersaturate
supranational
surrogateship
synallagmatic
telegrammatic
temperamental
temperateness
temporalities
temporariness
terminability
terminational
terminatively
thremmatology
titillatingly
topographical
toxoplasmosis
translational
transnational
transparently
tributariness
typographical
uncertainness
undercarriage
underhandedly
unimpeachable
unsociability
unsuitability
unwarrantable
unwarrantably
vacillatingly
verifiability
visionariness
voluntariness
voluntaristic
vouchsafement
vulnerability
xylographical
admirableness
advisableness
agreeableness
anaerobically
availableness
blameableness
Bloomsburyite
contrabandist
contrabassoon
decerebration
desirableness
dismemberment
dissemblingly
distributable
enjoyableness
equilibration
excitableness
excusableness
habitableness
immovableness
immutableness
incurableness
ineffableness
insolubleness
invisibleness
irritableness
laughableness
malleableness
miserableness
mountebankery
navigableness
orangeblossom
oversubscribe
palatableness
peaceableness
plausibleness
rattlebrained
removableness
separableness
shockabsorber
somnambulator
squarebashing
strikebreaker
superabundant
Swedenborgian
teachableness
tolerableness
traceableness
tractableness
unestablished
venerableness
winterberries
abstractional
acetylcholine
arboriculture
artificiality
barefacedness
barrelchested
battlecruiser
beneficiation
brachycephaly
bureaucratise
canaliculated
cinquecentist
closedcircuit
commercialise
commercialism
commercialist
complicatedly
condescension
conflictingly
conjunctional
conjunctively
conspicuously
contraception
contraceptive
contractility
contractually
destructively
destructivity
disconcerting
disconcertion
disgracefully
disjunctively
distinctively
doublecrosser
dysfunctional
efficaciously
equivocalness
excrescential
exteroceptive
gastrocnemius
identicalness
illogicalness
ineffectively
ineffectually
inefficacious
inefficiently
injudiciously
instinctively
instructional
instructively
interoceptive
microscopical
misconception
monodactylous
mononucleosis
mothercountry
obstructively
ostreiculture
owneroccupier
oystercatcher
perfunctorily
perspectively
perspicacious
perspicuously
pharmaceutics
pharmaceutist
pharmacologic
pharmacopoeia
pigeonchested
polydactylous
practicalness
preconception
promiscuously
pronunciation
prospectively
provincialise
provincialism
provincialist
provinciality
pyrotechnical
quadricipital
radioactivity
reproachfully
reproachingly
resourcefully
restrictively
retroactively
retroactivity
rollercoaster
schizocarpous
selenocentric
selfdeceiving
selfdeception
selfdeceptive
selfrecording
selfsacrifice
socioeconomic
spectacularly
stirpiculture
stratocumulus
taperecording
technicalness
telerecording
terpsichorean
thermochemist
unanticipated
unarticulated
unconsciously
underachiever
unflinchingly
violoncellist
vivisectional
whimsicalness
xanthochroism
zygodactylous
backpedalling
brachydactyly
chlamydomonas
chlamydospore
commandership
compendiously
contradiction
contradictory
dastardliness
discreditable
discreditably
disobediently
doubledealing
hundredweight
individualise
individualism
individualist
individuality
individuation
inexpediently
judgeadvocate
knowledgeable
knowledgeably
mangoldwurzel
niggardliness
nonconducting
nonproductive
offhandedness
overindulgent
partridgewood
perpendicular
pigheadedness
preponderance
preponderancy
primordiality
psychodynamic
rhapsodically
selfaddressed
selfinduction
selfindulgent
softpedalling
spasmodically
superaddition
thermodynamic
tiddledywinks
troglodytical
uncoordinated
undereducated
acotyledonous
agglomeration

agglomerative
amniocentesis
apprehensible
architectonic
architectural
arithmetician
asserveration
bathymetrical
belligerently
Berkeleianism
bewilderingly
blamelessness
blasphemously
bloodlessness
bloodrelation
boundlessness
brainlessness
cheerlessness
chemoreceptor
chuckleheaded
clearheadedly
collaterality
commiseration
commiserative
concatenation
confederation
confederative
conscientious
consenescence
considerately
consideration
continentally
convalescence
cyberneticist
cytochemistry
dauntlessness
deathlessness
defencelessly
defervescence
deliquescence
desegregation
detrimentally
differentiate
disaffectedly
disappearance
disintegrator
disinterested
disinvestment
disseveration
dissymetrical
doubtlessness
draggletailed
dreamlessness
effervescence
effervescency
efflorescence
emphysematous
ethnocentrism
exanthematous
extracellular
faithlessness
faultlessness
feuilletonism
feuilletonist
fortunehunter
fortuneteller
frighteningly
fruitlessness
fundamentally
gastroenteric
goniometrical
gracelessness
guilelessness
guiltlessness
heartlessness
hermeneutical
hydrocephalic
hydrocephalus
hydrogenation
hydromedusoid
hydrometrical
hypermetrical
hypermetropia
hypermetropic
hypothecation
immarcescible
imperceptible
imperceptibly
imperfectness
imponderables
inappreciable
inappreciably
incandescence
incarceration
incompetently
inconceivable
inconceivably
incondensable
inconsecutive
inconsequence
incontestable
incontestably
inconvenience
inconveniency
inconvertible
inconvertibly
incorrectness
incrementally
indifferently
indiscernible
indiscernibly
indispensable
indispensably
inexpressible
inexpressibly
inflorescence
insusceptible
intemperately
intercellular
interdentally
interjectural
intermediator
interpellator
interpersonal
interrelation
intracellular
intrapersonal
intravenously
introversible
irrepressible
irrepressibly
knuckleduster
lancesergeant
leisureliness
leptocephalic
lifepreserver
lightheadedly
limitlessness
machinegunner
mackerelshark
macrocephalic
magisterially
mercilessness
mesencephalon
microcephalic
microdetector
millefeuilles
ministerially
mirthlessness
miscegenation
mischievously
misgovernment
misunderstand
misunderstood
mnemotechnics
Mohammedanism
Monotheletism
monotrematous
multicellular
nemathelminth
nervelessness
noiselessness
nonappearance
nonattendance
nongovernment
northwesterly
northwestward
odoriferously
orthocephalic
outgeneralled
overcredulous
parallelogram
paraphernalia
passementerie
pathogenicity
perseveration
pestiferously
phenomenalise
phenomenalism
phenomenalist
phenomenology
photoperiodic
photoreceptor
picturepalace
picturesquely
planimetrical
platyhelminth
pointlessness
polyadelphous
postoperative
powerlessness
prairieoyster
prescientific
presidentship
pricelessness
primogenitary
primogenitive
primogeniture
proliferation
proliferative
proliferously
proprietorial
protuberantly
purposelessly
quicktempered
quinquevalent
radiotelegram
recommendable
recrudescence
refrigeration
remorselessly
reprehensible
reprehensibly
representable
reverberation
reverberative
reverberatory
roentgenogram
roentgenology
sacramentally
salmonellosis
scolopendrium
scrapmerchant
selfexecuting
selfsterility
senselessness
sentimentally
shamelessness
shapelessness
shiftlessness
shorttempered
shoulderblade
shoulderstrap
sightlessness
sleeplessness
smokelessness
southwesterly
southwestward
spindlelegged
spindleshanks
spinelessness
sprocketwheel
squandermania
stainlessness
statelessness
steeplechaser
superfetation
supersensible
supervenience
tastelessness
telencephalon
tergiversator
thanklessness
thimblerigged
thimblerigger
threateningly
transcendence
transcendency
transversally
treacherously
triliteralism
troublesomely
unbelievingly
uncompetitive
unconceivable
unconcernedly
unforgettable
unforgettably
unicameralism
unicameralist
unprecedented
unpretentious
unsymmetrical
unwholesomely
valuelessness
vantageground
venturesomely
verbigeration
vicepresident
voicelessness
worthlessness
wrongheadedly
abortifacient
aircraftwoman
bountifulness
butterfingers
butterflyfish
centreforward
centrifugally
changefulness
circumference
circumfluence
colourfulness
contrafagotto
costeffective
deceitfulness
disconformity
forgetfulness
frightfulness
healthfulness
honorifically
longsuffering
masterfulness
nonconforming
nonconformism
nonconformist
nonconformity
nonforfeiting
nonfulfilment
plentifulness
prepreference
regardfulness
regretfulness
resentfulness
selfdefeating
selfinflicted
selfsufficing
sicklefeather
sorrowfulness
standoffishly
thenceforward
wonderfulness
abiologically
affreightment
antilogarithm
bibliographer
bibliographic
bildungsroman
biogeographer
blastogenesis
bookingoffice
cardiographer
choreographer
choreographic
chronographic
coarsegrained
colleagueship
conflagration
consanguinity
coreligionist
cryptographer
cryptographic
distinguished
doubleglazing
embranglement
embryogenesis
epeirogenesis
foresightedly
frontogenesis
gametogenesis
glossographer
heterogeneity
heterogeneous
heterogenesis
heterogenetic
ideologically
irreligionist
irreligiously
lethargically
lexicographer
lexicographic
lineengraving
morphogenesis
morphogenetic
nearsightedly
nostalgically
oceanographer
oceanographic
odontoglossum
oecologically
ontologically
organogenesis
palaeographer
palaeographic
paramagnetism
pedagogically
physiognomist
physiographer
physiographic
pneumogastric
polarographic
prestigiously
prostaglandin
psychogenesis
psychogenetic
quadragesimal
rectangularly
reintegration
reinvigorator
runningstitch
schizogenesis
seismographer
seismographic
selenographer
selenographic

selfregarding
selfrighteous
semilogarithm
serologically
shabbygenteel
stereographic
strategically
stratigraphic
suffraganship
theologically
thermogenesis
thoroughbrace
thoroughgoing
thoroughpaced
topologically
turkeygobbler
typologically
unambiguously
unenlightened
villeggiatura
woodengraving
zoogeographer
zoogeographic
astrophysical
atmospherical
biotechnology
brokenhearted
comprehension
comprehensive
eschscholtzia
extraphysical
festschriften
hemispherical
hermaphrodite
hollowhearted
horsechestnut
horsewhipping
hydrochloride
hyperphysical
microphyllous
misanthropist
Monarchianism
parenthetical
petrochemical
photochemical
photochromics
photochromism
pigeonhearted
PreRaphaelite
rhodochrosite
sharpshooting
sheepshearing
singlehearted
submachinegun
superphysical
tenderhearted
theanthropism
transshipment
transshipping
underwhelming
unearthliness
unforthcoming
accessibility
accreditation
acetification
acidification
actualisation
admissibility
advertisement
affectionless
affenpinscher
agglutination
agglutinative
aluminiferous
aluminisation
amplification
anglicisation
animalisation
anomalistical
anticlimactic
apportionment
approximately
approximation
approximative
archidiaconal
argentiferous
aromatisation
assassination
assertiveness
attentiveness
authorisation
authoritarian
authoritative
bacteriolysis
bacteriolytic
bacteriophage
balkanisation
balsamiferous
barbarisation
beatification
birefringence
broadmindedly
brutalisation
calcification
Calvinistical
caprification
carboniferous
carbonisation
catechisation
cauterisation
certification
certificatory
cicatrisation
clarification
cobelligerent
combativeness
communication
communicative
communicatory
communisation
communitarian
compagination
companionable
companionably
companionless
companionship
compatibility
competitively
complainingly
complaisantly
compositeness
compositional
concomitantly
concupiscence
concupiscible
conditionally
conduciveness
confidingness
consolidation
consolidative
consolidatory
contamination
contaminative
cornification
corrigibility
corrosiveness
curvilinearly
deceptiveness
decortication
decrepitation
deductibility
defeasibility
defectiveness
defensibility
defibrination
deodorisation
derequisition
determinately
determination
determinative
deterministic
diffusiveness
digestibility
dimensionally
dimensionless
disaffirmance
disarticulate
dispraisingly
dissemination
disseminative
dissimilarity
dissimilation
dissimilitude
divertisement
domestication
dramatisation
dulcification
ecumenicalism
educationally
effectiveness
embellishment
endocrinology
essentialness
establishment
Eucharistical
evocativeness
exceptionable
exceptionably
exceptionally
excessiveness
exclusiveness
excursiveness
expansibility
expansiveness
expensiveness
explosiveness
exquisiteness
extensibility
extensionally
extensiveness
extermination
exterminatory
exterritorial
falsification
fertilisation
feudalisation
formalisation
formulisation
fortification
fossiliferous
fossilisation
galvanisation
garnetiferous
germanisation
glamorisation
glorification
graminivorous
gratification
greensickness
hallucination
hallucinative
hallucinatory
harmonisation
heartsickness
horripilation
hybridisation
hypnotisation
imitativeness
immiscibility
impartibility
impassibility
impassiveness
impercipience
impermissible
impertinently
impossibility
improvidently
improvisation
improvisatory
impulsiveness
incardination
inclusiveness
inconsiderate
inconsistence
inconsistency
incontinently
inconvincible
incredibility
incriminatory
indistinctive
inductiveness
ineligibility
infallibilism
infallibilist
infallibility
infeasibility
inflexibility
inflexionless
infundibulate
ingurgitation
inhospitality
inquisitional
inquisitively
inquisitorial
insectivorous
insensibility
insensitively
insensitivity
insignificant
insufficience
insufficiency
intangibility
intelligencer
intelligently
intensiveness
intentionally
interdigitate
intermittence
intrusiveness
intuitiveness
inventiveness
investigation
investigative
investigatory
invincibility
irretrievable
irretrievably
isomerisation
italicisation
jollification
justification
justificative
justificatory
lamellibranch
leadpoisoning
librarianship
lickerishness
lightfingered
lightmindedly
lignification
lucrativeness
magnanimously
magnetisation
magnification
magnificently
maladminister
mammaliferous
manganiferous
manneristical
martyrisation
masculineness
matrilineally
mechanisation
mediatisation
mercerisation
mesmerisation
metalliferous
metallisation
Methodistical
metrification
modernisation
mollification
mortification
mountainously
mummification
mutualisation
mystification
necessitarian
necessitation
necessitously
nectariferous
negligibility
nickeliferous
nitrification
nonresistance
normalisation
nullification
nutritionally
objectionable
objectionably
objectiveness
objectivistic
obsessiveness
obtrusiveness
offensiveness
operativeness
ovoviviparous
palletisation
pantheistical
participation
participative
participatory
patronisingly
pennypinching
peptonisation
peregrination
periodisation
pervasiveness
petrification
petroliferous
plaintiveness
platiniferous
pluralisation
polliniferous
pontification
potentiometer
precipitantly
precipitately
precipitation
precipitative
precipitously
predominantly
predomination
preengineered
prejudicially
preliminarily
premeditation
premeditative
premonitorily
preordination
prepositional
prevarication
primitiveness
prizefighting
probationally
progenitorial
prohibitively
prolification
propositional
protohistoric
provisionally
pulverisation
purposiveness
pyrheliometer
qualification

qualificatory
quartziferous
quickwittedly
randomisation
ratiocination
ratiocinative
recalcitrance
receptibility
receptiveness
recessiveness
recombination
reconcilement
recrimination
recriminative
recriminatory
rectification
rectilinearly
reduplication
reduplicative
reexamination
reflexibility
regurgitation
replenishment
republicanise
republicanism
republication
repulsiveness
requisiteness
resistibility
resuscitation
resuscitative
retentiveness
revaccination
revendication
reversibility
ritualisation
Russification
sacrificially
scarification
scorification
secretiveness
seductiveness
selectiveness
selfcriticism
selfevidently
selfexistence
selfopinioned
sensationally
sensitisation
sensitiveness
serendipitous
serialisation
signalisation
significantly
signification
significative
smoothingiron
snowblindness
sobermindness
socialisation
solderingiron
solemnisation
specification
spheroidicity
splendiferous
squeamishness
stabilisation
staminiferous
sterilisation
stoichiometry
stoloniferous
subirrigation
subordinately
subordination
subordinative
subtilisation
suffumigation
summarisation
superficially
suppositional
syllabication
symbolisation
talkativeness
tantalisation
tantalisingly
temporisation
tentativeness
terrorisation
testification
theatricalise
theatricalism
theatricality
thrillingness
thurification
toastmistress
traditionally
tranquilliser
transliterate
transmigrator
transmissible
transmittable
transpiration
transpiratory
tritheistical
umbelliferous
unconditional
unconditioned
undisciplined
unemotionally
unfashionable
unfashionably
unfeelingness
unmeaningness
unmentionable
unpredictable
unpromisingly
unqualifiedly
unselfishness
unwillingness
vapourishness
verbalisation
vernalisation
versification
vertiginously
victimisation
visualisation
vitrification
vulcanisation
vulgarisation
doublejointed
heebiejeebies
selfadjusting
outspokenness
psychokinesis
psychokinetic
agriculturist
alcoholically
alcoholometer
alcoholometry
Australianism
BaltoSlavonic
belleslettres
bibliolatrist
bibliolatrous
bibliological
breechloading
candlelighter
chronological
conchological
constellation
constellatory
craniological
cryptological
crystalgazing
crystallinity
deontological
disciplinable
domiciliation
embryological
entomological
evangelically
ferroelectric
flagellantism
freeselection
gastrological
generalisable
generalissimo
glaciological
grandiloquent
graphological
hairsplitting
hemicellulose
hydraulically
hydroelectric
immunological
malacological
manipulatable
mellifluously
mineralogical
miscellaneous
monomolecular
monosyllabism
morphological
multiplicable
musicological
nomenclatural
noncollegiate
numerological
odontological
ophthalmology
overvaluation
palynological
parabolically
Pennsylvanian
philhellenism
philhellenist
photoelectric
photoelectron
phrenological
physiological
phytoplankton
piezoelectric
pigeonlivered
pointillistic
porcellaneous
premillennial
psychological
punctiliously
quadrilateral
quadrillionth
quarrelsomely
quintillionth
redevelopment
sansculottism
scandalmonger
scintillating
scintillation
seismological
selenological
selfcollected
selfpollinate
semeiological
sericulturist
sidesplitting
somatological
speleological
superfluidity
superfluously
technological
teratological
tonguelashing
tonsillectomy
toxicological
uncomplaining
uncomplicated
underclothing
unfamiliarity
unintelligent
ventriloquial
ventriloquise
ventriloquism
ventriloquist
viniculturist
viticulturist
volatilisable
actinomorphic
actinomycetes
actinomycosis
allelomorphic
anagrammatise
anagrammatism
AngloAmerican
anthelminthic
antinomianism
autonomically
Christmastide
Christmastime
churchmanship
complementary
complimentary
conglomeratic
courtsmartial
craftsmanship
diagrammatise
dichlamydeous
discommodious
discriminator
disharmonious
draftsmanship
dressimprover
epigrammatise
epigrammatist
gentlemanlike
heteromorphic
homoeomorphic
integumentary
kapellmeister
Kidderminster
metonymically
monosymmetric
omnicompetent
parliamentary
photoemission
photoemissive
postcommunion
prayermeeting
pretermission
pretermitting
problematical
pseudomorphic
psychometrics
psychometrist
quadrumvirate
rearcommodore
sanctimonious
selfcommunion
sewingmachine
sportsmanlike
sportsmanship
statesmanlike
statesmanship
supereminence
supplementary
swordsmanship
taxonomically
theriomorphic
unaccompanied
unceremonious
underemphasis
underemployed
ungrammatical
verisimilarly
viceadmiralty
accidentalism
accidentprone
acrimoniously
acrylonitrile
aerodynamical
aggiornamento
argumentation
argumentative
auctioneering
betweenwhiles
boardinghouse
ceremonialism
ceremonialist
ceremoniously
challengeable
challengingly
chrysanthemum
clearinghouse
climbingframe
confrontation
containership
copartnership
countinghouse
cryptanalysis
cryptanalytic
deferentially
disconnection
displantation
doctrinairism
documentalist
documentation
dressingtable
elephantiasis
environmental
epiphenomenal
epiphenomenon
equiponderant
equiponderate
existentially
exponentially
foraminiferal
forementioned
fragmentarily
fragmentation
frequentation
frequentative
gastronomical
homogeneously
horizontality
hypnoanalysis
idiosyncratic
ignominiously
impecuniosity
inattentively
independently
inexpensively
inferentially
influentially
inoffensively
inorganically
involuntarily
landownership
laughingstock
macaronically
membranaceous
merchandising
microanalysis
millennialism
millionairess
monumentalise
mouldingboard
mourningcloak
mourningpaper
mutagenically
occidentalise
Occidentalism
Occidentalist
octocentenary
ontogenically
opinionatedly
ornamentation
orthognathism

orthognathous
outstandingly
overconfident
oversensitive
palaeontology
parasynthesis
parasynthetic
parthenocarpy
passionflower
pathognomonic
penitentially
pneumonectomy
polysynthesis
polysynthetic
preternatural
pronounceable
pronouncement
proteinaceous
puritanically
quadrennially
quincentenary
quincuncially
quingentenary
rearrangement
referentially
regimentation
rejuvenescent
reorientation
resplendently
reverentially
rontgenoscopy
rudimentarily
schadenfreude
sedimentation
selfcentredly
selfconceited
selfcondemned
selfconfessed
selfconfident
selfconscious
selfconsuming
selfcontained
selfcontented
selfconvicted
selfgenerated
semiconductor
semiconscious
sergeantmajor
shootingbrake
shootingrange
shootingstick
slangingmatch
smellingsalts
sniftingvalve
solidungulate
soundingboard
spinninghouse
spinningwheel
spontaneously
stalkinghorse
stationmaster
steppingstone
stickingplace
substantially
substantively
substantivise
subternatural
superannuable
supplantation
symphonically
symphoniously
thereinbefore
thermonuclear
thrasonically
timeconsuming
tintinnabular
tintinnabulum
uncleanliness
unintentional
unrelentingly
volumenometer
accommodating
accommodation
accommodative
ambiguousness
ambitiousness
amorphousness
anachronistic
anachronously
analogousness
anaphrodisiac
anomalousness
anonymousness
anticlockwise
antiscorbutic
apheliotropic
archaeologist
archaeopteryx
assiduousness
Assyriologist
asthenosphere
atlantosaurus
atrociousness
audaciousness
autobiography
autoeroticism
barbarousness
basidiomycete
beauteousness
bloodboltered
bounteousness
boustrophedon
bumptiousness
campanologist
capaciousness
carcinomatous
carnivorously
cephalothorax
cerebrospinal
chalcography
cleistogamous
climatologist
coldbloodedly
collaboration
collaborative
commemoration
commemorative
commemoratory
concavoconvex
condylomatous
congruousness
consciousness
convexoconvex
corroboration
corroborative
corroboratory
corticotropic
corticotropin
cosmopolitise
cosmopolitism
courteousness
credulousness
criminologist
cryobiologist
dangerousness
deciduousness
decomposition
deliciousness
deliriousness
demythologise
denationalise
depersonalise
dermatologist
desultoriness
deterioration
deteriorative
Deuteronomist
dexterousness
dichotomously
dictatorially
discoloration
disembodiment
dishonourable
dishonourably
egregiousness
electioneerer
electrocution
electrologist
electromagnet
electrometric
electromotive
electrophorus
electroscopic
electrostatic
electrovalent
encyclopaedia
encyclopaedic
encyclopedism
encyclopedist
erroneousness
eschatologist
expectoration
extemporarily
extrapolation
facetiousness
feloniousness
ferociousness
ferroconcrete
foreknowledge
fractionalise
fractionation
fractiousness
frivolousness
functionalism
functionalist
galactosaemia
garrulousness
gasteropodous
geochronology
gerontocratic
gerontologist
glutinousness
grandmotherly
gynaecocratic
gynaecologist
haematologist
hazardousness
herpetologist
hilariousness
histrionicism
hocuspocussed
homeomorphism
hyperboloidal
hypochondriac
ichthyography
ichthyologist
ichthyosaurus
imperiousness
impersonalise
impersonality
impersonation
impetuousness
inappropriate
incorporation
incorporative
incorporeally
incuriousness
indisposition
indissociable
ingeniousness
ingenuousness
injuriousness
innocuousness
innoxiousness
insidiousness
insupportable
insupportably
intercolonial
intercolumnar
interlocution
interlocutory
interlocutrix
interpolation
interpolative
interposition
interrogation
interrogative
interrogatory
inventorially
invidiousness
irrationalise
irrationalism
irrationalist
irrationality
irresponsible
irresponsibly
isochronously
judiciousness
juxtaposition
kaleidoscopic
laboriousness
laevorotation
laevorotatory
lancecorporal
laryngoscopic
lecherousness
lightsomeness
litigiousness
loathsomeness
ludicrousness
luxuriousness
machicolation
macromolecule
magnetomotive
magnetosphere
magniloquence
maladroitness
malariologist
maliciousness
martyrologist
megasporangia
melodiousness
metagrobolise
metallography
metaphosphate
meteorologist
micrococcocci
microtonality
mitochondrion
momentousness
monstrousness
multicoloured
myrmecologist
nefariousness
neighbourhood
nephelometric
nitrocompound
notoriousness
obliviousness
obnoxiousness
occasionalism
occasionalist
occasionality
officiousness
onomatopoetic
opisthobranch
ornithologist
paedomorphism
pantisocratic
papillomatous
particoloured
pendulousness
penuriousness
perichondrial
perichondrium
perissodactyl
phanerogamous
philosophical
philosophiser
phosphoretted
photopositive
phraseologist
phreatophytic
plenteousness
polypropylene
ponderousness
predatoriness
prefatorially
prolegomenary
prolegomenous
proparoxytone
proprioceptor
prosopography
prosthodontia
protonotarial
psychrometric
pteridologist
querulousness
questioningly
questionnaire
radiolocation
rapaciousness
rapturousness
reciprocality
reciprocation
reciprocative
recomposition
reconsolidate
religiousness
righteousness
sacerdotalise
sacerdotalism
sacerdotalist
sagaciousness
salaciousness
scientologist
scorpiongrass
seditiousness
selfknowledge
selfpropelled
skateboarding
somniloquence
sovietologist
spectrography
spectrometric
spectroscopic
spelaeologist
sphygmography
sternforemost
stomatologist
strawcoloured
strenuousness
streptococcal
streptococcus
sumptuousness
superdominant
superposition
synchronistic
synchronously
tautologously
tenaciousness
territorially
threecornered
toothsomeness
transformable
translocation
transportable
transposition
tremulousness
trichromatism
trigonometric
troublousness
trustworthily
tyrannosaurus
unanimousness

uncomfortable
uncomfortably
unconformable
unputdownable
venereologist
venturousness
veraciousness
versicoloured
vexatiousness
vicariousness
vivaciousness
vocationalism
volcanologist
voraciousness
vulcanologist
wearisomeness
wholesomeness
worrisomeness
angiospermous
anthropogenic
anthropometry
anthropopathy
anthropophagi
anthropophagy
anthroposophy
autocephalous
bibliophilism
bibliophilist
brachypterous
broadspectrum
centripetally
consumptively
contemplation
contemplative
contrapuntist
correspondent
corresponsive
cottonpicking
descriptively
developmental
disproportion
disrespectful
dodecaphonist
entomophagous
entomophilous
geomorphology
geotropically
gymnospermous
heteropterous
homoeopathist
hymenopterous
inconspicuous
inscriptional
interspecific
interspersion
introspection
introspective
lepidopterist
lepidopterous
leptospirosis
letterperfect
maladaptation
megacephalous
miscomprehend
noncompliance
nucleoprotein
overemphasise
overpopulated
phyllophagous
presumptively
principalship
psychophysics
quadripartite
quadruplicate
quadruplicity
quintuplicate
retrospection
retrospective
schizophrenia
schizophrenic
scleroprotein
selfappointed
selfapproving
selfdependent
selfimportant
selfreproving
selfrepugnant
selfsupported
sesquiplicate
Shakespearean
Shakespearian
tablespoonful
thermophilous
thermoplastic
unexceptional
wellapPointed
grotesqueness
accelerometer
accoutrements
allegorically
amphiprostyle
Antichristian
antipersonnel
appropriately
appropriation
appropriative
backformation
backscratcher
backwardation
biodegradable
bioenergetics
brotherliness
burglariously
calligraphist
camphoraceous
categorically
chinkerinchee
consternation
contrariously
counteraction
counteractive
counterattack
counterchange
countercharge
counterfeiter
counterstroke
counterweight
crackerbarrel
cruiserweight
cylindrically
daguerreotype
decompression
decontrolling
deleteriously
dematerialise
derestriction
diametrically
diathermanous
eavesdropping
eccentrically
equestrianism
exasperatedly
expropriation
extraordinary
extratropical
featherheaded
featherstitch
featherweight
foolhardiness
geometrically
globetrotting
gynandromorph
harbourmaster
heartbreaking
hemiparasitic
housebreaking
hydrocracking
hypercritical
hypertrophied
illustriously
immaterialise
immaterialism
immaterialist
immateriality
impropriation
inadvertently
incongruously
indescribable
indescribably
indeterminacy
indeterminate
indeterminism
indeterminist
indoctrinator
industrialise
industrialism
industrialist
industriously
inexperienced
inopportunely
insubordinate
intercropping
interpretable
interpretress
intertropical
intraarterial
introgression
irreverential
isometrically
jurisprudence
knickerbocker
leatherjacket
levelcrossing
mediterranean
meistersinger
meritoriously
metamorphoses
metamorphosis
microorganism
moneygrubbing
monochromatic
nonaggression
ochlocratical
oleomargarine
opprobriously
painterliness
panegyrically
pantagruelian
pantagruelism
pantagruelist
papaveraceous
paranormality
pedestrianise
pedestrianism
phycoerythrin
plethorically
pluripresence
pococurantism
polycarbonate
polychromatic
primigravidae
quartermaster
reaffirmation
redescription
reembarkation
reimbursement
reincarnation
reinforcement
retrogression
retrogressive
RhaetoRomanic
saccharimeter
saccharimetry
saccharometer
scholarliness
selfdirecting
selfdirection
selffertility
selfforgetful
selfsurrender
selftormentor
semibarbarian
semibarbarism
semiparasitic
semipermanent
semipermeable
semiporcelain
SerboCroatian
sharecropping
Spencerianism
stercoraceous
subterraneous
sulphureously
supercritical
superordinate
symmetrically
teleportation
temerariously
thundershower
thunderstruck
Tractarianism
transcription
transcriptive
transgression
transgressive
treasurership
undergraduate
uninformative
uninterrupted
unnaturalness
vegetarianism
waterproofing
weatherbeaten
wheelerdealer
whithersoever
acquiescently
acquiescingly
administrable
administrator
admonishingly
afforestation
antihistamine
archbishopric
astonishingly
businesswoman
candlesnuffer
chromospheric
circumspectly
clandestinely
clothesbasket
coenaesthesis
collieshangie
commensurable
commensurably
compassionate
compressional
concessionary
confessionary
congressional
congresswoman
conversazione
conversazioni
convulsionary
deforestation
deipnosophist
diagnostician
dispassionate
dispossession
distressfully
distressingly
distrustfully
entomostracan
equidistantly
everlastingly
expressionism
expressionist
extrinsically
flourishingly
fortissimo
fullfashioned
helterskelter
heterosporous
impressionism
impressionist
interestingly
interosculate
intransigeant
intransigence
intrinsically
languishingly
malacostracan
Malthusianism
manifestation
manifestative
meadowsaffron
mistrustfully
mistrustingly
neoclassicism
neoclassicist
neoplasticism
nonsensically
paddlesteamer
percussionist
phalansterian
polyhistorian
prepossessing
prepossession
processionary
processionist
proconsulship
procrastinate
professoriate
professorship
profitsharing
prognosticate
progressional
progressively
progressivism
pseudoscience
psychasthenia
psychosomatic
psychosurgery
reforestation
reminiscently
retranslation
sadomasochism
sadomasochist
scholasticism
selfasserting
selfassertion
selfassertive
selfassurance
selfassuredly
selfdiscovery
selfdispraise
selfinsurance
selfpossessed
selfrestraint
selfsustained
seriousminded
stereoscopist
stratospheric
subversionary
televisionary
thalassocracy
thermosetting
tortoiseshell
transistorise
underestimate
unimpassioned
unnecessarily
windowshopper
acrobatically
adiabatically
aesthetically

agonistically
airworthiness
anfractuosity
annexationist
apathetically
arthritically
asthmatically
atheistically
atomistically
authentically
authenticator
autocatalysis
autocatalytic
autochthonism
autochthonous
automatically
axiomatically
blanketflower
bombastically
brainstorming
buttonthrough
cabinetmaking
callisthenics
characterless
chrematistics
chromatically
chromatograph
chromatolytic
chromatophore
cinematically
cinematograph
climactically
collectedness
collectorship
compartmental
conceitedness
concentration
concentrative
concentricity
conceptualise
conceptualism
conceptualist
concertmaster
concretionary
conductorship
confectionary
confectionery
confraternity
congratulator
conjecturable
conjecturally
connectedness
consentaneity
consentaneous
contentedness
contentiously
contortionist
conventionary
convertiplane
corruptionist
demonstration
demonstrative
dendritically
devolutionary
devolutionist
diageotropism
dialectically
discontinuity
discontinuous
discretionary
dismantlement
distastefully
doubletongued
egocentricity
embrittlement
energetically
enigmatically
enlightenment
equipotential
exhibitionism
exhibitionist
expeditionary
expeditiously
fantastically
Fascistically
felicitations
flirtatiously
floristically
followthrough
geocentricism
geostationary
gonadotrophic
gonadotrophin
goodnaturedly
grammatically
gymnastically
helminthiasis
helminthology
heterothallic
heterotrophic
homoiothermal
homoiothermic
hydrostatical
idiomatically
immunotherapy
impenetration
impolitically
impracticable
impracticably
impractically
indefatigable
indefatigably
infinitesimal
inspectorship
instantaneity
instantaneous
insubstantial
interstratify
isostatically
judgmatically
kinematically
kinematograph
liberationist
Maginotminded
moderatorship
monocotyledon
monometallism
monometallist
monophthongal
neurastheniac
oppositionist
orchestration
organotherapy
paediatrician
panicstricken
parasitically
parasiticidal
patriotically
perfectionism
perfectionist
philanthropic
phonautograph
phrenetically
physiotherapy
pneumatically
pneumatolysis
pneumatolytic
pneumatometer
pneumatophore
polycotyledon
pragmatically
precautionary
precentorship
predestinator
prehistorical
pretentiously
prismatically
projectionist
prophetically
proportionate
protectionism
protectionist
protectorship
Protestantism
prudentialism
prudentialist
prudentiality
psilanthropic
psychotherapy
pyrimethamine
realistically
reconstructor
recrystallise
refractometer
remonstrantly
remonstration
remonstrative
renegotiation
repetitionary
repetitiously
revelationist
revolutionary
revolutionise
revolutionism
revolutionist
rheumatically
sanitationist
sarcastically
schematically
schoolteacher
scorbutically
scrumptiously
seaworthiness
selfpityingly
selfsatisfied
semiautomatic
sententiously
separationist
septentrional
sequentiality
sequestration
silvertongued
solicitorship
sophistically
sophisticated
spermatoblast
spermatogenic
spermatophore
spermatophyte
splenetically
sprightliness
statistically
stigmatically
stylistically
subcontractor
subeditorship
subpostmaster
subreptitious
substitutable
superstitious
surreptitious
symbiotically
syntactically
synthetically
tachistoscope
tempestuously
tendentiously
tercentennial
terrestrially
thaumaturgist
theoretically
thermotropism
thigmotropism
thoughtlessly
thoughtreader
tonguetwister
transatlantic
transitionary
traumatically
tricentennial
unadulterated
unconstrained
understanding
understrapper
unhealthiness
unquestioning
unremittingly
unrighteously
unsubstantial
untrustworthy
woolgathering
zinjanthropus
acculturation
acculturative
admeasurement
adventuresome
adventurously
attributively
beleaguerment
blackguardism
bloodcurdling
chateaubriand
clairaudience
colloquialism
confabulation
confabulatory
configuration
connaturality
consecutively
consequential
constructable
constructible
crosscultural
crosspurposes
crossquestion
degranulation
denticulation
disfigurement
dissimulation
dissolubility
dissoluteness
dramaturgical
encapsulation
excommunicate
expostulation
expostulatory
extrajudicial
fasciculation
floricultural
funambulation
gesticulation
gesticulative
gesticulatory
horticultural
hydrosulphide
hydrosulphite
imperturbable
imperturbably
importunately
incombustible
incommunicado
incorruptible
incorruptibly
incorruptness
incredulously
inexhaustible
inexhaustibly
institutional
intercultural
intercurrence
interpunction
interruptible
intramuscular
jerrybuilding
maladjustment
matriculation
metallurgical
micronutrient
multinucleate
multitudinous
nondeductable
nonfigurative
nonreturnable
opportuneness
opportunistic
overabundance
particularise
particularism
particularist
particularity
perambulation
perambulatory
piscicultural
platitudinise
platitudinous
plenitudinous
prefiguration
prefigurative
prefigurement
prematureness
preoccupation
scripturalism
scripturalist
sculpturesque
selfeducation
sociocultural
spiritualness
strangulation
structuralism
structuralist
structureless
sublieutenant
subsaturation
subsequential
substructural
superhumanity
supernumerary
supersubtlety
swashbuckling
threequarters
topsyturvydom
translucently
translucidity
transmutation
transmutative
triangularity
triangulation
tuberculation
unaccountable
unaccountably
uncircumcised
unconquerable
unfortunately
unobtrusively
vermiculation
vernacularise
vernacularism
vernacularity
Zarathustrian
animadversion
circumvallate
circumvention
conservatoire
contravention
controversial
halfsovereign
irrecoverable
irrecoverably
Machiavellian
selfgoverning
selfrevealing
semicivilised
subserviently
unequivocally
linseywoolsey

searchwarrant
streetwalking
swallowtailed
wonderworking
ambidexterity
ambidexterous
complexedness
homosexuality
paradoxically
underexposure
apocalyptical
heptasyllabic
hydrodynamics
hydroxylamine
hypoglycaemia
jiggerypokery
metaphysician
Monophysitism
naphthylamine
osteomyelitis
poliomyelitis
tetrasyllable
worldlyminded
bamboozlement
laissezpasser
palaeozoology

---

abortifacient
aerodynamical
aggiornamento
antilogarithm
archidiaconal
autocatalysis
autocatalytic
backpedalling
backscratcher
BaltoSlavonic
bibliolatrist
bibliolatrous
biodegradable
blackguardism
brachydactyly
calligraphist
camphoraceous
Christmastide
Christmastime
churchmanship
circumvallate
clearheadedly
complicatedly
consentaneity
consentaneous
conservatoire
contrabandist
contrabassoon
contrafagotto
conversazione
conversazioni
counteraction
counteractive
counterattack
courtsmartial
craftsmanship
cryptanalysis
cryptanalytic
disappearance
doctrinairism
draftsmanship
equivocalness
essentialness
exasperatedly
felicitations
flagellantism
gentlemanlike
hemiparasitic
homoeopathist
hydrocracking
hydrostatical
hypnoanalysis
identicalness
illogicalness
inefficacious
instantaneity
instantaneous
insubstantial
librarianship
lightheadedly
manipulatable
meadowsaffron
membranaceous
microanalysis
millionairess
miscellaneous
monometallism
monometallist
mountebankery
nomenclatural
nonappearance
ochlocratical
opinionatedly
orthognathism
orthognathous
oystercatcher
papaveraceous
perspicacious
phytoplankton
pneumogastric
pococurantism
porcellaneous
practicalness
PreRaphaelite
preternatural
primigravidae
principalship
problematical
proteinaceous
Protestantism
quadrilateral
quadripartite
recrystallise
schizocarpous
searchwarrant
selfregarding
semilogarithm
semiparasitic
sewingmachine
skateboarding
softpedalling
spiritualness
sportsmanlike
sportsmanship
squarebashing
statesmanlike
statesmanship
stercoraceous
streetwalking
subternatural
subterraneous
suffraganship
swordsmanship
technicalness
threequarters
tintinnabular
tintinnabulum
tonguelashing
uncomplaining
undergraduate
understanding
ungrammatical
unnaturalness
unsubstantial
whimsicalness
wrongheadedly
absorbability
acceptability
accessibility
admissibility
answerability
applicability
attainability
bouillabaisse
changeability
chateaubriand
clothesbasket
coagulability
commutability
comparability
compatibility
corrigibility
crackerbarrel
deductibility
defeasibility
defensibility
dependability
digestibility
disposability
dissolubility
expansibility
extensibility
filterability
formidability
immiscibility
impalpability
impartibility
impassability
impassibility
impeccability
implacability
impossibility
improbability
improvability
incredibility
ineducability
ineligibility
inevitability
inexorability
infallibilism
infallibilist
infallibility
infeasibility
inflexibility
infundibulate
insatiability
insensibility
insociability
intangibility
invariability
invincibility
inviolability
knickerbocker
lamellibranch
manageability
mensurability
metagrobolise
metastability
negligibility
negotiability
opisthobranch
overelaborate
penetrability
perdurability
perishability
permutability
polycarbonate
ponderability
predicability
preferability
profitability
receptibility
reflexibility
reformability
resistibility
resolvability
reversibility
semibarbarian
semibarbarism
squeezability
supersubtlety
terminability
thereinbefore
unsociability
unsuitability
verifiability
vulnerability
weatherbeaten
acetification
acidification
acquiescently
acquiescingly
amplification
anticlockwise
archdeaconate
architectonic
architectural
beatification
calcification
caprification
certification
certificatory
chemoreceptor
clarification
communication
communicative
communicatory
concavoconvex
constructable
constructible
convexoconvex
cornification
counterchange
countercharge
decortication
disaffectedly
disarticulate
domestication
dulcification
ecumenicalism
electrocution
falsification
fortification
gerontocratic
glorification
gratification
greensickness
gynaecocratic
heartsickness
hocuspocussed
hypoglycaemia
hypothecation
idiosyncratic
imperfectness
inappreciable
inappreciably
inconsecutive
incorrectness
indissociable
insufficience
insufficiency
interjectural
interlacement
interlocution
interlocutory
interlocutrix
interosculate
irreplaceable
jollification
justification
justificative
justificatory
lignification
magnification
magnificently
metrification
micrococcocci
mnemotechnics
mollification
mortification
multinucleate
mummification
mystification
nitrification
nitrobacteria
nondeductable
nullification
owneroccupier
pantisocratic
petrification
photoreceptor
pontification
prejudicially
prevarication
prolification
pronounceable
pronouncement
proprioceptor
pseudoscience
qualification
qualificatory
quincuncially
radiolocation
reciprocality
reciprocation
reciprocative
rectification
reduplication
reduplicative
reinforcement
reminiscently
republicanise
republicanism
republication
revendication
Russification
sacrificially
scarification
scorification
selfconceited
selfdiscovery
selfeducation
selfexecuting
semiporcelain
significantly
signification
significative
specification
steeplechaser
stereoscopist
streptococcal
streptococcus
substructural
superficially
swashbuckling
syllabication
testification
theatricalise
theatricalism
theatricality
thurification
translocation
translucently
translucidity
unforthcoming
unimpeachable
unpredictable
versification
vitrification
accommodating
accommodation
accommodative
acotyledonous
ambassadorial
anaphrodisiac
backwardation
clairaudience
consolidation

consolidative
consolidatory
disembodiment
equiponderant
equiponderate
extrajudicial
extraordinary
foolhardiness
hydromedusoid
improvidently
inconsiderate
independently
insubordinate
intermediator
knuckleduster
merchandising
Mohammedanism
Muhammadanism
multitudinous
outstandingly
overcredulous
perissodactyl
platitudinise
platitudinous
plenitudinous
prosthodontia
resplendently
selfcondemned
selfevidently
semiconductor
spheroidicity
superaddition
superordinate
unprecedented
wheelerdealer
accoutrements
angiospermous
AngloAmerican
animadversion
atmospherical
auctioneering
barefacedness
beleaguerment
belleslettres
blastogenesis
brachycephaly
broadspectrum
brokenhearted
centripetally
characterless
cinquecentist
circumference
circumvention
collectedness
commandership
complementary
complexedness
complimentary
comprehension
comprehensive
conceitedness
condescension
confraternity
conglomeratic
connectedness
consequential
containership
contentedness
contraception
contraceptive
contravention
controversial
copartnership
costeffective
crossquestion
daguerreotype
decompression
disconcerting
disconcertion
disconnection
disgracefully
dismemberment
dispossession
disrespectful
distastefully
doubledealing
embryogenesis
enlightenment
epeirogenesis
equipotential
excrescential
exteroceptive
ferroelectric
freeselection
frontogenesis
gametogenesis
gymnospermous
halfsovereign
heartbreaking
heebiejeebies
hemispherical
heterogeneity
heterogeneous
heterogenesis
heterogenetic
hollowhearted
homogeneously
horsechestnut
housebreaking
hydroelectric
infinitesimal
integumentary
interoceptive
interpretable
interpretress
interspecific
interspersion
introgression
introspection
introspective
irrecoverable
irrecoverably
irretrievable
irretrievably
irreverential
kapellmeister
landownership
letterperfect
Machiavellian
Manichaeanism
misconception
monomolecular
morphogenesis
morphogenetic
nonaggression
noncollegiate
nonforfeiting
offhandedness
organogenesis
osteomyelitis
outspokenness
parenthetical
parliamentary
petrochemical
pharmaceutics
pharmaceutist
photochemical
photoelectric
photoelectron
piezoelectric
pigeonhearted
pigheadedness
pluripresence
pneumonectomy
poliomyelitis
prayermeeting
preconception
premillennial
preponderance
preponderancy
prepossessing
prepossession
prepreference
psychogenesis
psychogenetic
psychometrics
psychometrist
quadragesimal
rejuvenescent
resourcefully
retrogression
retrogressive
retrospection
retrospective
schizogenesis
schoolteacher
selenocentric
selfasserting
selfassertion
selfassertive
selfdeceiving
selfdeception
selfdeceptive
selfdefeating
selfdependent
selfdirecting
selfdirection
selfgenerated
selfgoverning
selfrevealing
shabbygenteel
Shakespearean
Shakespearian
sheepshearing
sicklefeather
singlehearted
spontaneously
subsequential
sulphureously
supplementary
tenderhearted
tercentennial
thermogenesis
thermosetting
tonsillectomy
tortoiseshell
transgression
transgressive
treasurership
tricentennial
unadulterated
unconquerable
underwhelming
unrighteously
violoncellist
winterberries
aluminiferous
argentiferous
balsamiferous
blanketflower
carboniferous
counterfeiter
fossiliferous
garnetiferous
insignificant
longsuffering
mammaliferous
manganiferous
metalliferous
nectariferous
nickeliferous
overconfident
passionflower
petroliferous
platiniferous
polliniferous
quartziferous
schadenfreude
selfconfessed
selfconfident
selfsufficing
splendiferous
staminiferous
standoffishly
stoloniferous
umbelliferous
unqualifiedly
vouchsafement
anticoagulant
autobiography
bioenergetics
boardinghouse
cartilaginous
chalcoography
challengeable
challengingly
clearinghouse
cleistogamous
climbingframe
cobelligerent
countinghouse
crystalgazing
desegregation
deuteragonist
diaphragmatic
disengagement
disintegrator
disparagement
disparagingly
dressingtable
encouragement
encouragingly
extravagantly
ferrimagnetic
ferromagnetic
ichthyography
intelligencer
intelligently
interdigitate
interrogation
interrogative
interrogatory
investigation
investigative
investigatory
knowledgeable
knowledgeably
laughingstock
machinegunner
metallography
microorganism
mismanagement
mouldingboard
mourningcloak
mourningpaper
oleomargarine
partridgewood
phanerogamous
preengagement
prizefighting
prosopography
quinquagenary
Quinquagesima
rearrangement
selfforgetful
shootingbrake
shootingrange
shootingstick
slangingmatch
smellingsalts
sniftingvalve
solidungulate
soundingboard
spectrography
sphygmography
spinninghouse
spinningwheel
stalkinghorse
steppingstone
stickingplace
subirrigation
suffumigation
synallagmatic
tautologously
transmigrator
vantageground
acetylcholine
admonishingly
affreightment
airworthiness
archbishopric
astonishingly
autocephalous
autochthonism
autochthonous
barrelchested
bibliophilism
bibliophilist
buttonthrough
callisthenics
chuckleheaded
collieshangie
dodecaphonist
entomophagous
entomophilous
featherheaded
flourishingly
followthrough
foresightedly
fortunehunter
fullfashioned
geomorphology
helminthiasis
helminthology
heterothallic
homoiothermal
homoiothermic
immunotherapy
languishingly
megacephalous
monophthongal
nearsightedly
neurastheniac
organotherapy
overemphasise
philanthropic
phyllophagous
physiotherapy
pigeonchested
profitsharing
psilanthropic
psychophysics
psychotherapy
pyrimethamine
pyrotechnical
reproachfully
reproachingly
schizophrenia
schizophrenic
seaworthiness
selfrighteous
terpsichorean
thermochemist
thermophilous
thoroughbrace
thoroughgoing
thoroughpaced
underachiever
unenlightened
unflinchingly
unhealthiness
windowshopper
woolgathering
xanthochroism
zinjanthropus

abiologically
acrimoniously
acrobatically
acrylonitrile
adiabatically
aesthetically
agonistically
alcoholically
algebraically
allegorically
anaerobically
annexationist
anthelminthic
Antichristian
antinomianism
apathetically
appropriately
appropriation
appropriative
arthritically
artificiality
ascertainable
ascertainment
asthmatically
atheistically
atomistically
Australianism
authentically
authenticator
automatically
autonomically
axiomatically
beneficiation
Berkeleianism
bombastically
burglariously
butterfingers
candlelighter
categorically
ceremonialism
ceremonialist
ceremoniously
chieftainship
chinkerinchee
chrematistics
chromatically
cinematically
climactically
closedcircuit
colloquialism
commercialise
commercialism
commercialist
compassionate
compendiously
concessionary
concretionary
confectionary
confectionery
confessionary
constrainable
constrainedly
contentiously
contortionist
contradiction
contradictory
contrariously
conventionary
convertiplane
convulsionary
coreligionist
corruptionist
cottonpicking
cylindrically
deleteriously
dematerialise
dendritically
derestriction
devolutionary
devolutionist
dialectically
diametrically
disciplinable
discontinuity
discontinuous
discreditable
discreditably
discretionary
discriminator
disobediently
dispassionate
domiciliation
eccentrically
efficaciously
energetically
enigmatically
entertainment
equestrianism
evangelically
exhibitionism
exhibitionist
expeditionary
expeditiously
expressionism
expressionist
expropriation
extrinsically
fantastically
Fascistically
flirtatiously
floristically
foraminiferal
fortississimo
generalisable
generalissimo
geometrically
geostationary
geotropically
grammatically
gymnastically
hairsplitting
honorifically
horsewhipping
hydraulically
hypercritical
ideologically
idiomatically
ignominiously
illustriously
immaterialise
immaterialism
immaterialist
immateriality
impecuniosity
impolitically
impracticable
impracticably
impractically
impressionism
impressionist
impropriation
inconceivable
inconceivably
inconspicuous
indefatigable
indefatigably
indescribable
indescribably
indoctrinator
industrialise
industrialism
industrialist
industriously
inefficiently
inexpediently
inexperienced
injudiciously
inorganically
intransigeant
intransigence
intrinsically
irreclaimable
irreclaimably
irreligionist
irreligiously
isometrically
isostatically
jerrybuilding
judgmatically
Kidderminster
kinematically
lackadaisical
leptospirosis
lethargically
liberationist
macaronically
maladroitness
Malthusianism
meritoriously
metonymically
millennialism
Monarchianism
multiplicable
mutagenically
nonfulfilment
nonsensically
nostalgically
oecologically
ontogenically
ontologically
oppositionist
opprobriously
panegyrically
parabolically
paradoxically
parasitically
parasiticidal
patriotically
pedagogically
pedestrianise
pedestrianism
percussionist
perfectionism
perfectionist
perpendicular
pharisaically
photoemission
photoemissive
phrenetically
pigeonlivered
plethorically
pneumatically
pragmatically
precautionary
predestinator
preordainment
prestigiously
pretentiously
pretermission
pretermitting
primordiality
prismatically
processionary
processionist
projectionist
pronunciation
prophetically
proportionate
protectionism
protectionist
provincialise
provincialism
provincialist
provinciality
prudentialism
prudentialist
prudentiality
psychokinesis
psychokinetic
punctiliously
puritanically
quadricipital
realistically
redescription
renegotiation
repetitionary
repetitiously
revelationist
revolutionary
revolutionise
revolutionism
revolutionist
rhapsodically
rheumatically
saccharimeter
saccharimetry
sanitationist
sarcastically
schematically
scorbutically
scrumptiously
selfsatisfied
semicivilised
sententiously
separationist
sequentiality
serologically
sidesplitting
sophistically
sophisticated
spasmodically
Spencerianism
splenetically
statistically
stigmatically
strategically
stylistically
submachinegun
subreptitious
subserviently
subversionary
supercritical
supereminence
superstitious
surreptitious
symbiotically
symmetrically
symphonically
symphoniously
syntactically
synthetically
taxonomically
televisionary
temerariously
tendentiously
theologically
theoretically
thrasonically
topologically
Tractarianism
transcription
transcriptive
transitionary
transshipment
transshipping
traumatically
typologically
unanticipated
uncertainness
uncomplicated
unconceivable
unconsciously
uncoordinated
unfamiliarity
unquestioning
vegetarianism
verisimilarly
viceadmiralty
villeggiatura
volatilisable
leatherjacket
helterskelter
painstakingly
reembarkation
admirableness
advisableness
agreeableness
archaeologist
Assyriologist
availableness
bamboozlement
blameableness
bloodboltered
bloodrelation
brotherliness
butterflyfish
campanologist
cannibalistic
circumfluence
climatologist
confabulation
confabulatory
constellation
constellatory
contemplation
contemplative
cosmopolitise
cosmopolitism
criminalistic
criminologist
crosscultural
cryobiologist
crystallinity
dastardliness
defencelessly
degranulation
demythologise
denticulation
dermatologist
desirableness
dismantlement
dissemblingly
dissimilarity
dissimilation
dissimilitude
dissimulation
doubleglazing
electrologist
embranglement
embrittlement
encapsulation
encephalogram
enjoyableness
eschatologist
excitableness
excusableness
expostulation
expostulatory
extracellular
extragalactic
extrapolation
fasciculation
floricultural
funambulation
gerontologist
gesticulation
gesticulative
gesticulatory
gynaecologist
habitableness
haematologist
hemicellulose
heptasyllabic
herpetologist
horripilation

horticultural
hydrochloride
hydrosulphide
hydrosulphite
hydroxylamine
hyperboloidal
ichthyologist
immovableness
immutableness
imperialistic
incredulously
incurableness
ineffableness
insolubleness
intercalation
intercellular
intercolonial
intercolumnar
intercultural
intergalactic
interpellator
interpolation
interpolative
interrelation
intracellular
invisibleness
irritableness
laughableness
leisureliness
machicolation
mackerelshark
macromolecule
malariologist
malleableness
martyrologist
materialistic
matriculation
meteorologist
miserableness
mononucleosis
monosyllabism
Monotheletism
multicellular
multicoloured
myrmecologist
naphthylamine
nationalistic
navigableness
nemathelminth
niggardliness
noncompliance
odontoglossum
orangeblossom
ornithologist
overqualified
painterliness
palatableness
parallelogram
particoloured
particularise
particularism
particularist
particularity
paternalistic
peaceableness
perambulation
perambulatory
phenylalanine
philhellenism
philhellenist
phraseologist
piscicultural
platyhelminth
plausibleness
pointillistic
polyadelphous
prostaglandin
pteridologist
purposelessly
quadrillionth
quadruplicate
quadruplicity
quintillionth
quintuplicate
radiotelegram
rationalistic
reconcilement
reconsolidate
remorselessly
removableness
retranslation
salmonellosis
scholarliness
scientologist
scintillating
scintillation
selfcollected
selfinflicted
selfpollinate
separableness
sesquiplicate
sociocultural
sovietologist
spelaeologist
spindlelegged
sprightliness
stomatologist
strangulation
strawcoloured
supercalender
teachableness
temporalities
tetrasyllable
thermoplastic
thoughtlessly
tolerableness
traceableness
tractableness
tranquilliser
transatlantic
triangularity
triangulation
tuberculation
uncleanliness
unearthliness
unestablished
unintelligent
venerableness
venereologist
vermiculation
vernacularise
vernacularism
vernacularity
versicoloured
volcanologist
vulcanologist
anagrammatise
anagrammatism
anticlimactic
approximately
approximation
approximative
backformation
basidiomycete
blasphemously
cabinetmaking
carcinomatous
circumambient
compartmental
concertmaster
condylomatous
cytochemistry
decontaminate
developmental
diagrammatise
diathermanous
dichotomously
electromagnet
electrometric
electromotive
emphysematous
environmental
epigrammatise
epigrammatist
exanthematous
harbourmaster
indeterminacy
indeterminate
indeterminism
indeterminist
lightsomeness
loathsomeness
Maginotminded
magnanimously
magnetomotive
materfamilias
melodramatics
melodramatise
melodramatist
monogrammatic
monosymmetric
monotrematous
nephelometric
nitrocompound
ophthalmology
papillomatous
paranormality
paterfamilias
postcommunion
predicamental
prolegomenary
prolegomenous
psychrometric
quartermaster
quicktempered
reaffirmation
rearcommodore
scandalmonger
selfcommunion
selftormentor
semipermanent
semipermeable
seriousminded
shorttempered
spectrometric
stationmaster
subpostmaster
superdominant
superfamilies
superhumanity
supernumerary
telegrammatic
temperamental
toothsomeness
trichromatism
trigonometric
uncircumcised
uninformative
wearisomeness
wholesomeness
worldlyminded
worrisomeness
accompaniment
affenpinscher
agglutination
agglutinative
amniocentesis
anachronistic
anachronously
apprehensible
archimandrite
assassination
biotechnology
birefringence
brilliantness
broadmindedly
candlesnuffer
compagination
complainingly
concatenation
confidingness
conscientious
consternation
contamination
contaminative
continentally
curvilinearly
defibrination
denationalise
depersonalise
determinately
determination
determinative
deterministic
detrimentally
Deuteronomist
differentiate
disadvantaged
dissemination
disseminative
electioneerer
endocrinology
ethnocentrism
excommunicate
extermination
exterminatory
ferroconcrete
fractionalise
fractionation
frighteningly
functionalism
functionalist
fundamentally
gastrocnemius
gastroenteric
geochronology
hallucination
hallucinative
hallucinatory
histrionicism
hydrodynamics
hydrogenation
hypochondriac
impersonalise
impersonality
impersonation
impertinently
importunately
incardination
incommunicado
incondensable
incontinently
inconvenience
inconveniency
inconvincible
incrementally
incriminatory
indispensable
indispensably
indistinctive
interdentally
interpunction
intravenously
irrationalise
irrationalism
irrationalist
irrationality
irrefrangible
irresponsible
irresponsibly
isochronously
leishmaniasis
lightfingered
lightmindedly
maladminister
masculineness
matrilineally
microtonality
miscegenation
mitochondrion
mountainously
nonattendance
occasionalism
occasionalist
occasionality
opportuneness
opportunistic
overabundance
paperhangings
paramagnetism
passementerie
pathogenicity
pennypinching
peregrination
perichondrial
perichondrium
phenomenalise
phenomenalism
phenomenalist
phenomenology
physiognomist
predominantly
predomination
preengineered
preliminarily
preordination
prescientific
presidentship
primogenitary
primogenitive
primogeniture
psychoanalyse
psychoanalyst
pusillanimity
pusillanimous
quadrennially
questioningly
questionnaire
ratiocination
ratiocinative
recombination
recommendable
recrimination
recriminative
recriminatory
rectilinearly
reexamination
reincarnation
reprehensible
reprehensibly
representable
revaccination
rhadamanthine
righthandedly
roentgenogram
roentgenology
sacramentally
sacrosanctity
scolopendrium
scorpiongrass
selfopinioned
sentimentally
smoothingiron
snowblindness
sobermindness
solderingiron
subordinately
subordination
subordinative
superannuable
supersensible
supervenience
synchronistic
synchronously
threateningly

thrillingness
transcendence
transcendency
unaccountable
unaccountably
underhandedly
unfeelingness
unfortunately
unmeaningness
unpretentious
unwarrantable
unwarrantably
unwillingness
vertiginously
vocationalism
accelerometer
actinomorphic
affectionless
alcoholometer
alcoholometry
allelomorphic
amphiprostyle
anthropogenic
anthropometry
anthropopathy
anthropophagi
anthropophagy
anthroposophy
apportionment
bacteriolysis
bacteriolytic
bacteriophage
bibliological
bookingoffice
brainstorming
breechloading
centreforward
chlamydomonas
chlamydospore
chromatograph
chromatolytic
chromatophore
chronological
cinematograph
coldbloodedly
collectorship
companionable
companionably
companionless
companionship
conchological
conditionally
conductorship
correspondent
corresponsive
craniological
cryptological
decontrolling
deipnosophist
deontological
dimensionally
dimensionless
discommodious
disconformity
disharmonious
disproportion
doublejointed
doubletongued
eavesdropping
educationally
embryological
entomological
epiphenomenal
epiphenomenon
eschscholtzia
exceptionable
exceptionably
exceptionally
extensionally
extratropical
gastrological
gastronomical
glaciological
globetrotting
grandiloquent
graphological
gynandromorph
heteromorphic
homoeomorphic
hypertrophied
immunological
inflexionless
inspectorship
intentionally
intercropping
intertropical
kinematograph
levelcrossing
linseywoolsey
malacological
microscopical
mineralogical
moderatorship
monochromatic
morphological
mothercountry
musicological
nonconforming
nonconformism
nonconformist
nonconformity
numerological
nutritionally
objectionable
objectionably
odontological
palaeozoology
palynological
parthenocarpy
pathognomonic
pharmacologic
pharmacopoeia
phonautograph
phrenological
physiological
pneumatolysis
pneumatolytic
pneumatometer
pneumatophore
polychromatic
potentiometer
prairieoyster
precentorship
prehistorical
probationally
professoriate
professorship
protectorship
provisionally
pseudomorphic
psychological
psychosomatic
pyrheliometer
redevelopment
refractometer
reinvigorator
RhaetoRomanic
rollercoaster
rontgenoscopy
saccharometer
sadomasochism
sadomasochist
sanctimonious
sansculottism
seismological
selenological
selfappointed
selfimportant
selfrecording
semeiological
semiautomatic
sensationally
SerboCroatian
sharecropping
sharpshooting
silvertongued
socioeconomic
solicitorship
somatological
speleological
spermatoblast
spermatogenic
spermatophore
spermatophyte
stoichiometry
subeditorship
Swedenborgian
tablespoonful
tachistoscope
taperecording
technological
telerecording
teratological
thalassocracy
thenceforward
theriomorphic
toxicological
traditionally
turkeygobbler
unceremonious
underclothing
unemotionally
unequivocally
unfashionable
unfashionably
unmentionable
ventriloquial
ventriloquise
ventriloquism
ventriloquist
volumenometer
waterproofing
wellapPointed
wonderworking
apocalyptical
archaeopteryx
boustrophedon
cacographical
chromospheric
circumspectly
dressimprover
electrophorus
encyclopaedia
encyclopaedic
encyclopedism
encyclopedist
gasteropodous
heterosporous
hydrocephalic
hydrocephalus
ideographical
imperceptible
imperceptibly
impercipience
inappropriate
incorruptible
incorruptibly
incorruptness
insusceptible
interruptible
jiggerypokery
laissezpasser
leptocephalic
macrocephalic
mesencephalon
metamorphoses
metamorphosis
microcephalic
omnicompetent
onomatopoetic
oreographical
orthocephalic
ovoviviparous
participation
participative
participatory
philosophical
philosophiser
phreatophytic
picturepalace
polypropylene
preoccupation
selfdispraise
selfpropelled
selfsupported
serendipitous
stratospheric
telencephalon
topographical
typographical
unaccompanied
underemphasis
underemployed
underexposure
undisciplined
xylographical
inconsequence
magniloquence
somniloquence
acculturation
acculturative
admeasurement
adventuresome
adventurously
agglomeration
agglomerative
antiscorbutic
arbitrariness
asserveration
battlecruiser
belligerently
bewilderingly
bibliographer
bibliographic
biogeographer
bloodcurdling
bureaucratise
cardiographer
carnivorously
choreographer
choreographic
chronographic
coarsegrained
coldheartedly
collaboration
collaborative
collaterality
commemoration
commemorative
commemoratory
commiseration
commiserative
concentration
concentrative
concentricity
confederation
confederative
configuration
conflagration
connaturality
considerately
consideration
corroboration
corroborative
corroboratory
crossgartered
crosspurposes
cryptographer
cryptographic
customariness
decerebration
demonstration
demonstrative
desultoriness
deterioration
deteriorative
diageotropism
dictatorially
disaffirmance
discoloration
disfigurement
disinterested
disseveration
doublecrosser
dramaturgical
egocentricity
equilibration
exemplariness
expectoration
extemporarily
festschriften
fissiparously
geocentricism
glossographer
gonadotrophic
gonadotrophin
halfheartedly
haphazardness
hardheartedly
hermaphrodite
heterotrophic
homeomorphism
impenetration
imperturbable
imperturbably
imponderables
incarceration
inconvertible
inconvertibly
incorporation
incorporative
incorporeally
indifferently
indiscernible
indiscernibly
insupportable
insupportably
intemperately
intercurrence
intermarriage
interparietal
interpersonal
interstratify
intrapersonal
introversible
inventorially
lancecorporal
lancesergeant
lexicographer
lexicographic
lineengraving
magisterially
mediterranean
megasporangia
mercenariness
metallurgical
ministerially
misanthropist
miscomprehend
misgovernment
misunderstand
misunderstood
momentariness
nightmarishly
nonfigurative

nongovernment
nonreturnable
nucleoprotein
oceanographer
oceanographic
odoriferously
openheartedly
orchestration
outgeneralled
overbearingly
paediatrician
paedomorphism
palaeographer
palaeographic
panicstricken
paraphernalia
pennyfarthing
perseveration
pestiferously
phosphoretted
photochromics
photochromism
photoperiodic
physiographer
physiographic
polarographic
postoperative
predatoriness
prefatorially
prefiguration
prefigurative
prefigurement
prematureness
proliferation
proliferative
proliferously
protuberantly
pseudoarchaic
rattlebrained
reconstructor
refrigeration
reintegration
remonstrantly
remonstration
remonstrative
reverberation
reverberative
reverberatory
rhodochrosite
scleroprotein
scrapmerchant
scripturalism
scripturalist
sculpturesque
secondariness
secretarybird
secretaryship
sedentariness
seismographer
seismographic
selenographer
selenographic
selfaddressed
selfapproving
selfawareness
selfreproving
selfsacrifice
selfsterility
selfsurrender
septentrional
sequestration
shoulderblade
shoulderstrap
soulsearching
squandermania
stereographic
sternforemost
stratigraphic
strikebreaker
structuralism
structuralist
structureless
subcontractor
subsaturation
temporariness
tergiversator
terrestrially
territorially
theanthropism
thermotropism
thigmotropism
thimblerigged
thimblerigger
thoughtreader
threecornered
topsyturvydom
transformable
transparently
transpiration
transpiratory
transportable
transversally
treacherously
tributariness
triliteralism
trustworthily
uncomfortable
uncomfortably
unconcernedly
unconformable
unconstrained
undercarriage
understrapper
unicameralism
unicameralist
uninterrupted
verbigeration
visionariness
voluntariness
voluntaristic
woodengraving
zoogeographer
zoogeographic
actualisation
advertisement
aluminisation
anglicisation
animalisation
anomalistical
antipersonnel
aromatisation
asthenosphere
atlantosaurus
authorisation
balkanisation
barbarisation
bildungsroman
blamelessness
bloodlessness
boundlessness
brainlessness
brutalisation
businesswoman
Calvinistical
carbonisation
catechisation
cauterisation
cerebrospinal
cheerlessness
cicatrisation
communisation
complaisantly
compressional
concupiscence
concupiscible
congressional
congresswoman
consenescence
convalescence
counterstroke
dauntlessness
deathlessness
decomposition
defervescence
deliquescence
deodorisation
derequisition
disinvestment
dispraisingly
distressfully
distressingly
divertisement
doubtlessness
dramatisation
dreamlessness
effervescence
effervescency
efflorescence
electroscopic
electrostatic
embarrassment
embellishment
encompassment
establishment
Eucharistical
extravasation
extravascular
faithlessness
faultlessness
featherstitch
fertilisation
feudalisation
fibrovascular
formalisation
formulisation
fossilisation
fruitlessness
galactosaemia
galvanisation
germanisation
glamorisation
gracelessness
guilelessness
guiltlessness
harmonisation
heartlessness
hybridisation
hypnotisation
ichthyosaurus
immarcescible
impermissible
improvisation
improvisatory
incandescence
incombustible
inconsistence
inconsistency
incontestable
incontestably
indisposition
inexhaustible
inexhaustibly
inexpensively
inexpressible
inexpressibly
inflorescence
inoffensively
interposition
intramuscular
irrepressible
irrepressibly
isomerisation
italicisation
juxtaposition
kaleidoscopic
laryngoscopic
leadpoisoning
lickerishness
lifepreserver
limitlessness
magnetisation
magnetosphere
maladjustment
manneristical
martyrisation
mechanisation
mediatisation
meistersinger
mercerisation
mercilessness
mesmerisation
metallisation
metaphosphate
metaphysician
Methodistical
mirthlessness
modernisation
Monophysitism
mutualisation
neoclassicism
neoclassicist
nervelessness
neurovascular
noiselessness
nonresistance
normalisation
northeasterly
northeastward
northwesterly
northwestward
oversensitive
oversubscribe
palletisation
pantheistical
patronisingly
peptonisation
periodisation
photopositive
picturesquely
pluralisation
pointlessness
postclassical
powerlessness
pricelessness
progressional
progressively
progressivism
protohistoric
pulverisation
quarrelsomely
randomisation
recomposition
recrudescence
reimbursement
replenishment
ritualisation
runningstitch
selfabasement
selfconscious
selfconsuming
selfexistence
selfpossessed
semiconscious
senselessness
sensitisation
serialisation
shamelessness
shapelessness
shiftlessness
shockabsorber
sightlessness
signalisation
sleeplessness
smokelessness
socialisation
solemnisation
southeasterly
southeastward
southwesterly
southwestward
spectroscopic
spindleshanks
spinelessness
squeamishness
stabilisation
stainlessness
statelessness
steadfastness
sterilisation
subtilisation
summarisation
superposition
symbolisation
tantalisation
tantalisingly
tastelessness
temporisation
terrorisation
thanklessness
thundershower
thunderstruck
timeconsuming
toastmistress
toxoplasmosis
transmissible
transposition
tritheistical
troublesomely
tyrannosaurus
unimpassioned
unnecessarily
unobtrusively
unpromisingly
unselfishness
unwholesomely
valuelessness
vapourishness
venturesomely
verbalisation
vernalisation
vicepresident
victimisation
visualisatioh
voicelessness
vulcanisation
vulgarisation
whithersoever
worthlessness
Zarathustrian
abstractional
accidentalism
accidentprone
acclimatation
accreditation
achromaticity
administrable
administrator
adversatively
affirmatively
afforestation
aggravatingly
agriculturist
aircraftwoman
alternatively
ambidexterity
ambidexterous
AngloCatholic
antihistamine
apheliotropic
appellatively
applicatively
arbitrational
argumentation
argumentative
arithmetician

associateship
associativity
attributively
authoritarian
authoritative
autoeroticism
bathymetrical
brachypterous
calculatingly
cephalothorax
chrysanthemum
clandestinely
coeducational
coenaesthesis
combinatorial
communitarian
comparatively
competitively
compositeness
compositional
computational
concomitantly
conflictingly
confrontation
conjugateness
conjugational
conjunctional
conjunctively
consecutively
consumptively
contractility
contractually
convocational
cooperatively
corporativism
correlatively
correlativity
corticotropic
corticotropin
crosshatching
cyberneticist
declaratively
decrepitation
deferentially
deforestation
deformational
deprecatingly
descriptively
desperateness
destructively
destructivity
devastatingly
diagnostician
disjunctively
disparateness
displantation
dissoluteness
dissymetrical
distinctively
distrustfully
documentalist
documentation
draggletailed
dysfunctional
elaborateness
elephantiasis
entomostracan
equidistantly
everlastingly
examinational
examinatorial
existentially
explanatorily
explorational
exponentially
expurgatorial
exquisiteness
exterritorial
facultatively
fascinatingly
feuilletonism
feuilletonist
forementioned
fortunateness
fortuneteller
fragmentarily
fragmentation
frequentation
frequentative
frustratingly
goniometrical
grandfatherly
grandmotherly
gravitational
gubernatorial
heteropterous
horizontality
hydrometrical
hymenopterous
hypermetrical
hypermetropia
hypermetropic
imaginatively
immediateness
implicatively
inadvertently
inanimateness
inattentively
incompetently
ineffectively
ineffectually
inferentially
influentially
informational
informatively
infuriatingly
ingurgitation
inhospitality
inopportunely
inquisitional
inquisitively
inquisitorial
inscriptional
insensateness
insensitively
insensitivity
insinuatingly
inspirational
instinctively
institutional
instructional
instructively
interestingly
intermittence
international
intraarterial
intricateness
inviolateness
involuntarily
laevorotation
laevorotatory
legislatively
legislatorial
lepidopterist
lepidopterous
malacostracan
maladaptation
manifestation
manifestative
mathematician
microdetector
micronutrient
mistrustfully
mistrustingly
monodactylous
monumentalise
mouthwatering
multinational
necessitarian
necessitation
necessitously
neoplasticism
nightwatchman
numismatology
observational
obstinateness
obstructively
occidentalise
Occidentalism
Occidentalist
octocentenary
ornamentation
overstatement
paddlesteamer
palaeontology
parasynthesis
parasynthetic
penetratingly
penetratively
penitentially
perfunctorily
perspectively
phalansterian
planimetrical
polydactylous
polyhistorian
polysynthesis
polysynthetic
postulational
precipitantly
precipitately
precipitation
precipitative
precipitously
predicatively
premeditation
premeditative
premonitorily
preparatively
preparatorily
prepositional
presumptively
procrastinate
procuratorial
progenitorial
prognosticate
prohibitively
propositional
proprietorial
prospectively
protonotarial
psychasthenia
qualitatively
quickwittedly
quincentenary
quingentenary
radioactivity
recalcitrance
referentially
reforestation
reformational
regimentation
regurgitation
reinstatement
reorientation
requisiteness
restoratively
restrictively
resuscitation
resuscitative
retroactively
retroactivity
reverentially
rudimentarily
sabrerattling
sacerdotalise
sacerdotalism
sacerdotalist
scholasticism
sedimentation
selfcentredly
selfcontained
selfcontented
selfcriticism
selffertility
selfrestraint
selfsustained
sergeantmajor
sericulturist
speculatively
sprocketwheel
sublieutenant
substantially
substantively
substantivise
suffocatingly
superfetation
superlatively
supernational
supersaturate
supplantation
suppositional
supranational
surrogateship
swallowtailed
teleportation
temperateness
terminational
terminatively
thremmatology
titillatingly
transistorise
translational
transliterate
transmittable
transmutation
transmutative
transnational
uncompetitive
unconditional
unconditioned
underestimate
unexceptional
unforgettable
unforgettably
unintentional
unrelentingly
unremittingly
unsymmetrical
vacillatingly
viniculturist
viticulturist
vivisectional
zygodactylous
ambiguousness
ambitiousness
amorphousness
analogousness
anfractuosity
anomalousness
anonymousness
arboriculture
assiduousness
astronautical
atrociousness
audaciousness
baccalaureate
barbarousness
beauteousness
Bloomsburyite
bounteousness
bountifulness
bumptiousness
canaliculated
capaciousness
centrifugally
changefulness
colleagueship
colourfulness
commensurable
commensurably
conceptualise
conceptualism
conceptualist
congratulator
congruousness
conjecturable
conjecturally
consanguinity
consciousness
conspicuously
contrapuntist
courteousness
credulousness
dangerousness
deceitfulness
deciduousness
deliciousness
deliriousness
dexterousness
dishonourable
dishonourably
distinguished
distributable
egregiousness
erroneousness
facetiousness
feloniousness
ferociousness
forgetfulness
fractiousness
frightfulness
frivolousness
garrulousness
glutinousness
goodnaturedly
granddaughter
grotesqueness
hazardousness
healthfulness
hermeneutical
hilariousness
homosexuality
imperiousness
impetuousness
incongruously
incuriousness
individualise
individualism
individualist
individuality
individuation
ingeniousness
ingenuousness
injuriousness
innocuousness
innoxiousness
insidiousness
invidiousness
judiciousness
jurisprudence
laboriousness
lecherousness
liebfraumilch
litigiousness
ludicrousness
luxuriousness
maliciousness
masterfulness
mellifluously
melodiousness
millefeuilles
momentousness
moneygrubbing
monstrousness

nefariousness
neighbourhood
nonconducting
nonproductive
notoriousness
obliviousness
obnoxiousness
officiousness
ostreiculture
overindulgent
overpopulated
overvaluation
pantagruelian
pantagruelism
pantagruelist
pendulousness
penuriousness
perspicuously
plenteousness
plentifulness
ponderousness
proconsulship
promiscuously
psychosurgery
querulousness
rapaciousness
rapturousness
rectangularly
regardfulness
regretfulness
religiousness
resentfulness
righteousness
sagaciousness
salaciousness
seditiousness
selfadjusting
selfassurance
selfassuredly
selfinduction
selfindulgent
selfinsurance
selfrepugnant
selfslaughter
somnambulator
sorrowfulness
spectacularly
stirpiculture
stratocumulus
strenuousness
substitutable
sumptuousness
superabundant
superfluidity
superfluously
tempestuously
tenaciousness
thaumaturgist
thermonuclear
tremulousness
troublousness
unambiguously
unanimousness
unarticulated
undereducated
venturousness
veraciousness
vexatiousness
vicariousness
vivaciousness
voraciousness
wonderfulness
assertiveness
attentiveness
combativeness
conduciveness
corrosiveness
deceptiveness
defectiveness
diffusiveness
effectiveness
electrovalent
evocativeness
excessiveness
exclusiveness
excursiveness
expansiveness
expensiveness
explosiveness
extensiveness
graminivorous
imitativeness
impassiveness
impulsiveness
inclusiveness
inductiveness
insectivorous
intensiveness
intrusiveness
intuitiveness
inventiveness
judgeadvocate
lucrativeness
mischievously
objectiveness
objectivistic
obsessiveness
obtrusiveness
offensiveness
operativeness
Pennsylvanian
pervasiveness
plaintiveness
primitiveness
purposiveness
quadrumvirate
quinquevalent
receptiveness
recessiveness
repulsiveness
retentiveness
secretiveness
seductiveness
selectiveness
selfconvicted
sensitiveness
talkativeness
tentativeness
unbelievingly
betweenwhiles
counterweight
cruiserweight
featherweight
foreknowledge
hundredweight
mangoldwurzel
selfknowledge
tonguetwister
unputdownable
untrustworthy
proparoxytone
actinomycetes
actinomycosis
astrophysical
dichlamydeous
extraphysical
hyperphysical
microphyllous
monocotyledon
phycoerythrin
polycotyledon
psychodynamic
selfpityingly
superphysical
thermodynamic
tiddledywinks
troglodytical
accidentalism
acclimatation
accommodating
accommodation
accommodative
accreditation
acculturation
acculturative
acetification
acidification
actualisation
afforestation
agglomeration
agglomerative
agglutination
agglutinative
aluminisation
amplification
anagrammatise
anagrammatism
anglicisation
animalisation
anticlimactic
antihistamine
antinomianism
appropriately
appropriation
appropriative
approximately
approximation
approximative
argumentation
argumentative
aromatisation
artificiality
assassination
asserveration
atlantosaurus
Australianism
authorisation
authoritarian
authoritative
autocephalous
backformation
backwardation
balkanisation
barbarisation
beatification
beneficiation
Berkeleianism
bibliographer
bibliographic
biogeographer
bloodrelation
bouillabaisse
breechloading
brokenhearted
brutalisation
bureaucratise
cabinetmaking
calcification
caprification
carbonisation
carcinomatous
cardiographer
catechisation
cauterisation
ceremonialism
ceremonialist
certification
certificatory
choreographer
choreographic
chronographic
cicatrisation
clarification
cleistogamous
clothesbasket
coarsegrained
collaboration
collaborative
collaterality
collieshangie
colloquialism
commemoration
commemorative
commemoratory
commercialise
commercialism
commercialist
commiseration
commiserative
communication
communicative
communicatory
communisation
communitarian
compagination
complaisantly
concatenation
concentration
concentrative
conceptualise
conceptualism
conceptualist
concertmaster
concomitantly
condylomatous
confabulation
confabulatory
confederation
confederative
configuration
conflagration
confrontation
connaturality
considerately
consideration
consolidation
consolidative
consolidatory
constellation
constellatory
consternation
contamination
contaminative
contemplation
contemplative
cornification
corroboration
corroborative
corroboratory
crackerbarrel
cryptographer
cryptographic
crystalgazing
decerebration
decortication
decrepitation
defibrination
deforestation
degranulation
dematerialise
demonstration
demonstrative
denationalise
denticulation
deodorisation
depersonalise
desegregation
deterioration
deteriorative
determinately
determination
determinative
diagrammatise
diathermanous
discoloration
displantation
dissemination
disseminative
disseveration
dissimilarity
dissimilation
dissimulation
documentalist
documentation
domestication
domiciliation
doubledealing
doubleglazing
draggletailed
dramatisation
dulcification
ecumenicalism
electromagnet
electrovalent
emphysematous
encapsulation
encyclopaedia
encyclopaedic
entomophagous
epigrammatise
epigrammatist
equestrianism
equidistantly
equilibration
exanthematous
expectoration
expostulation
expostulatory
expropriation
extemporarily
extermination
exterminatory
extragalactic
extrapolation
extravagantly
extravasation
falsification
fasciculation
fertilisation
feudalisation
formalisation
formulisation
fortification
fossilisation
fractionalise
fractionation
fragmentarily
fragmentation
frequentation
frequentative
funambulation
functionalism
functionalist
galactosaemia
galvanisation
germanisation
gesticulation
gesticulative
gesticulatory
glamorisation
glorification
glossographer
gratification
hallucination
hallucinative
hallucinatory
harbourmaster
harmonisation
heartbreaking
heterothallic
hollowhearted
homosexuality
horizontality
horripilation

housebreaking
hybridisation
hydrodynamics
hydrogenation
hydroxylamine
hypnotisation
hypoglycaemia
hypothecation
ichthyosaurus
immaterialise
immaterialism
immaterialist
immateriality
impenetration
impersonalise
impersonality
impersonation
imponderables
importunately
impropriation
improvisation
improvisatory
incarceration
incardination
incorporation
incorporative
incriminatory
individualise
individualism
individualist
individuality
individuation
industrialise
industrialism
industrialist
ingurgitation
inhospitality
intemperately
intercalation
intergalactic
interpolation
interpolative
interrelation
interrogation
interrogative
interrogatory
interstratify
investigation
investigative
investigatory
involuntarily
irrationalise
irrationalism
irrationalist
irrationality
isomerisation
italicisation
jollification
justification
justificative
justificatory
laevorotation
laevorotatory
laissezpasser
leatherjacket
lexicographer
lexicographic
lignification
lineengraving
machicolation
magnetisation
magnification
maladaptation
Malthusianism
Manichaeanism
manifestation
manifestative
martyrisation
matriculation
mechanisation
mediatisation
mediterranean
megacephalous
megasporangia
melodramatics
melodramatise
melodramatist
mercerisation
mesmerisation
metallisation
metrification
microorganism
microtonality
millennialism
miscegenation
modernisation
Mohammedanism
mollification
Monarchianism
monosyllabism
monotrematous
monumentalise
mortification
Muhammadanism
mummification
mutualisation
mystification
naphthylamine
necessitarian
necessitation
nitrification
nonfigurative
normalisation
nullification
occasionalism
occasionalist
occasionality
occidentalise
Occidentalism
Occidentalist
oceanographer
oceanographic
oleomargarine
orchestration
ornamentation
outgeneralled
overemphasise
overvaluation
ovoviviparous
palaeographer
palaeographic
palletisation
papillomatous
paranormality
participation
participative
participatory
particularise
particularism
particularist
particularity
pedestrianise
pedestrianism
Pennsylvanian
peptonisation
perambulation
perambulatory
peregrination
periodisation
perissodactyl
perseveration
petrification
phanerogamous
phenomenalise
phenomenalism
phenomenalist
phenylalanine
phyllophagous
physiographer
physiographic
picturepalace
pigeonhearted
pluralisation
polarographic
pontification
postoperative
precipitantly
precipitately
precipitation
precipitative
predominantly
predomination
prefiguration
prefigurative
preliminarily
premeditation
premeditative
preoccupation
preordination
prevarication
primordiality
profitsharing
proliferation
proliferative
prolification
pronunciation
prostaglandin
protonotarial
protuberantly
provincialise
provincialism
provincialist
provinciality
prudentialism
prudentialist
prudentiality
psychoanalyse
psychoanalyst
pulverisation
pyrimethamine
qualification
qualificatory
quartermaster
quinquevalent
radiolocation
randomisation
ratiocination
ratiocinative
rattlebrained
reaffirmation
reciprocality
reciprocation
reciprocative
recombination
recrimination
recriminative
recriminatory
rectification
reduplication
reduplicative
reembarkation
reexamination
reforestation
refrigeration
regimentation
regurgitation
reincarnation
reintegration
remonstrantly
remonstration
remonstrative
renegotiation
reorientation
republicanise
republicanism
republication
resuscitation
resuscitative
retranslation
revaccination
revendication
reverberation
reverberative
reverberatory
ritualisation
rollercoaster
rudimentarily
Russification
sacerdotalise
sacerdotalism
sacerdotalist
scarification
schoolteacher
scintillating
scintillation
scorification
scripturalism
scripturalist
sedimentation
seismographer
seismographic
selenographer
selenographic
selfcontained
selfdefeating
selfeducation
selfrevealing
selfsustained
semibarbarian
semibarbarism
semipermanent
sensitisation
sequentiality
sequestration
SerboCroatian
serialisation
Shakespearean
Shakespearian
sheepshearing
sicklefeather
signalisation
significantly
signification
significative
singlehearted
socialisation
solemnisation
specification
Spencerianism
stabilisation
stationmaster
stereographic
sterilisation
strangulation
stratigraphic
structuralism
structuralist
subcontractor
subirrigation
subordinately
subordination
subordinative
subpostmaster
subsaturation
subtilisation
suffumigation
summarisation
superfetation
superhumanity
supplantation
swallowtailed
syllabication
symbolisation
tantalisation
teleportation
temporisation
tenderhearted
terrorisation
testification
theatricalise
theatricalism
theatricality
thermoplastic
thurification
Tractarianism
transatlantic
translocation
transmutation
transmutative
transpiration
transpiratory
triangularity
triangulation
trichromatism
triliteralism
tuberculation
tyrannosaurus
unaccompanied
unconstrained
understrapper
unfamiliarity
unfortunately
unicameralism
unicameralist
uninformative
unnecessarily
vegetarianism
verbalisation
verbigeration
vermiculation
vernacularise
vernacularism
vernacularity
vernalisation
versification
victimisation
villeggiatura
visualisation
vitrification
vocationalism
vulcanisation
vulgarisation
woodengraving
zoogeographer
zoogeographic
antiscorbutic
circumambient
imperturbable
imperturbably
indescribable
indescribably
moneygrubbing
mouldingboard
shootingbrake
shoulderblade
soundingboard
spermatoblast
thoroughbrace
tintinnabular
tintinnabulum
turkeygobbler
abiologically
abortifacient
acrobatically
actinomycetes
actinomycosis
adiabatically
aesthetically
agonistically
alcoholically
algebraically
allegorically
anaerobically
apathetically
archidiaconal

arthritically
asthmatically
atheistically
atomistically
authentically
authenticator
automatically
autonomically
axiomatically
bombastically
brachydactyly
broadspectrum
camphoraceous
categorically
chromatically
cinematically
climactically
concupiscence
concupiscible
consenescence
contradiction
contradictory
convalescence
costeffective
cottonpicking
counteraction
counteractive
crosshatching
cylindrically
defervescence
deliquescence
dendritically
derestriction
dialectically
diametrically
disconnection
disrespectful
eccentrically
effervescence
effervescency
efflorescence
electroscopic
energetically
enigmatically
evangelically
extravascular
extrinsically
fantastically
Fascistically
ferroconcrete
ferroelectric
fibrovascular
floristically
freeselection
geometrically
geotropically
grammatically
gymnastically
honorifically
hydraulically
hydrocracking
hydroelectric
ideologically
idiomatically
immarcescible
impolitically
impracticable
impracticably
impractically
incandescence
inconspicuous
inconvincible
indistinctive
inefficacious
inflorescence
inorganically
interpunction
interspecific
intramuscular
intrinsically
introspection
introspective
isometrically
isostatically
judgmatically
kaleidoscopic
kinematically
laryngoscopic
lethargically
macaronically
membranaceous
metonymically
micrococcocci
monomolecular
mourningcloak
multiplicable
mutagenically
neurovascular
nightwatchman
nonconducting
nonproductive
nonsensically
nostalgically
oecologically
ontogenically
ontologically
oversubscribe
panegyrically
papaveraceous
parabolically
paradoxically
parasitically
parasiticidal
parthenocarpy
patriotically
pedagogically
pennypinching
perpendicular
perspicacious
pharisaically
photoelectric
photoelectron
phrenetically
piezoelectric
plethorically
pneumatically
pneumonectomy
pragmatically
prismatically
prophetically
proteinaceous
pseudoarchaic
puritanically
realistically
recrudescence
retrospection
retrospective
rhapsodically
rheumatically
sacrosanctity
sadomasochism
sadomasochist
sarcastically
schematically
scorbutically
scrapmerchant
selfconscious
selfdirecting
selfdirection
selfinduction
semiconscious
serologically
sewingmachine
sophistically
sophisticated
soulsearching
spasmodically
spectroscopic
splenetically
statistically
stercoraceous
stigmatically
strategically
stylistically
symbiotically
symmetrically
symphonically
syntactically
synthetically
taxonomically
thalassocracy
theologically
theoretically
thermonuclear
thrasonically
tonsillectomy
topologically
traumatically
typologically
uncircumcised
uncomplicated
undereducated
unequivocally
archimandrite
barefacedness
biodegradable
bloodcurdling
broadmindedly
clearheadedly
coldbloodedly
collectedness
complexedness
conceitedness
connectedness
contentedness
dichlamydeous
discommodious
haphazardness
hypochondriac
jurisprudence
lightheadedly
lightmindedly
mitochondrion
nonattendance
offhandedness
overabundance
perichondrial
perichondrium
pigheadedness
recommendable
righthandedly
scolopendrium
snowblindness
sobermindness
transcendence
transcendency
undergraduate
underhandedly
wrongheadedly
acquiescently
admeasurement
admirableness
adventuresome
advertisement
advisableness
agreeableness
aluminiferous
ambidexterity
ambidexterous
argentiferous
assertiveness
associateship
attentiveness
auctioneering
availableness
balsamiferous
bamboozlement
barrelchested
belligerently
bioenergetics
blameableness
brachypterous
callisthenics
carboniferous
challengeable
chemoreceptor
chuckleheaded
circumspectly
cobelligerent
colleagueship
combativeness
compartmental
compositeness
conduciveness
conjugateness
corrosiveness
counterfeiter
counterweight
cruiserweight
curvilinearly
deceptiveness
defectiveness
defencelessly
desirableness
desperateness
developmental
diffusiveness
disengagement
disfigurement
disinterested
dismantlement
disobediently
disparagement
disparateness
dissoluteness
divertisement
effectiveness
elaborateness
electioneerer
electrometric
embranglement
embrittlement
encouragement
encyclopedism
encyclopedist
enjoyableness
environmental
equiponderant
equiponderate
evocativeness
excessiveness
excitableness
exclusiveness
excursiveness
excusableness
expansiveness
expensiveness
explosiveness
exquisiteness
extensiveness
featherheaded
featherweight
fortunateness
fortuneteller
fossiliferous
garnetiferous
gastrocnemius
grotesqueness
habitableness
heebiejeebies
helterskelter
heteropterous
homoiothermal
homoiothermic
hundredweight
hymenopterous
imitativeness
immediateness
immovableness
immunotherapy
immutableness
impassiveness
impertinently
improvidently
impulsiveness
inadvertently
inanimateness
inclusiveness
incompetently
inconsiderate
incontinently
incorporeally
incurableness
independently
indifferently
inductiveness
ineffableness
inefficiently
inexpediently
inexperienced
insensateness
insolubleness
intelligencer
intelligently
intensiveness
interlacement
intraarterial
intricateness
intrusiveness
intuitiveness
inventiveness
inviolateness
invisibleness
irreplaceable
irritableness
knowledgeable
knowledgeably
laughableness
lepidopterist
lepidopterous
lifepreserver
lightsomeness
loathsomeness
longsuffering
lucrativeness
macromolecule
magnificently
malleableness
mammaliferous
manganiferous
masculineness
matrilineally
metalliferous
microdetector
miscomprehend
miserableness
mismanagement
mononucleosis
monosymmetric
Monotheletism
mouthwatering
navigableness
nectariferous
nephelometric
neurastheniac
nickeliferous
objectiveness
obsessiveness
obstinateness
obtrusiveness
octocentenary
offensiveness
omnicompetent
operativeness
opportuneness

organotherapy
overstatement
paddlesteamer
palatableness
pantagruelian
pantagruelism
pantagruelist
paramagnetism
partridgewood
peaceableness
pervasiveness
petroliferous
phalansterian
philhellenism
philhellenist
phosphoretted
photoreceptor
physiotherapy
pigeonchested
plaintiveness
platiniferous
plausibleness
polliniferous
prayermeeting
predicamental
preengagement
preengineered
prefigurement
prematureness
PreRaphaelite
primitiveness
prolegomenary
prolegomenous
pronounceable
pronouncement
proprioceptor
psychotherapy
psychrometric
purposelessly
purposiveness
quartziferous
quincentenary
quingentenary
quinquagenary
Quinquagesima
radiotelegram
rearrangement
receptiveness
recessiveness
reconcilement
rectilinearly
reimbursement
reinforcement
reinstatement
reminiscently
remorselessly
removableness
repulsiveness
requisiteness
resplendently
retentiveness
sculpturesque
secretiveness
seductiveness
selectiveness
selfabasement
selfaddressed
selfawareness
selfcollected
selfconceited
selfcondemned
selfconfessed
selfcontented
selfevidently
selfforgetful
selfpossessed
selfpropelled
selfsurrender
selftormentor
semipermeable
semiporcelain
sensitiveness
separableness
spectrometric
spindlelegged
splendiferous
staminiferous
sternforemost
stoloniferous
strikebreaker
structureless
sublieutenant
subserviently
supercalender
supernumerary
surrogateship
talkativeness
teachableness
temperamental
temperateness
tentativeness
thereinbefore
thermochemist
thoughtlessly
thoughtreader
tolerableness
toothsomeness
traceableness
tractableness
transliterate
translucently
transparently
trigonometric
umbelliferous
unprecedented
venerableness
vouchsafement
wearisomeness
weatherbeaten
wheelerdealer
wholesomeness
woolgathering
worrisomeness
bookingoffice
climbingframe
disgracefully
distastefully
distressfully
distrustfully
foraminiferal
meadowsaffron
mistrustfully
reproachfully
resourcefully
anthropogenic
bibliological
birefringence
candlelighter
centrifugally
chromatograph
chronological
cinematograph
conchological
confidingness
contrafagotto
craniological
cryptological
deontological
dramaturgical
embryological
entomological
gastrological
glaciological
granddaughter
graphological
immunological
indefatigable
indefatigably
intransigeant
intransigence
irrefrangible
kinematograph
lancesergeant
lightfingered
malacological
metallurgical
mineralogical
morphological
musicological
noncollegiate
numerological
odontological
palynological
paperhangings
phonautograph
phrenological
physiological
psychological
scorpiongrass
seismological
selenological
selfrepugnant
selfslaughter
semeiological
smoothingiron
solderingiron
somatological
speleological
spermatogenic
technological
teratological
thoroughgoing
thrillingness
toxicological
unfeelingness
unmeaningness
unwillingness
AngloCatholic
betweenwhiles
boardinghouse
boustrophedon
cacographical
cephalothorax
chromospheric
chrysanthemum
clearinghouse
coenaesthesis
counterchange
countercharge
countinghouse
electrophorus
embellishment
establishment
grandfatherly
grandmotherly
hydrocephalic
hydrocephalus
ideographical
leptocephalic
lickerishness
macrocephalic
mesencephalon
metamorphoses
metamorphosis
microcephalic
mnemotechnics
oreographical
orthocephalic
parasynthesis
parasynthetic
philosophical
philosophiser
phreatophytic
polysynthesis
polysynthetic
prizefighting
psychasthenia
replenishment
spindleshanks
spinninghouse
squeamishness
stalkinghorse
steeplechaser
stratospheric
telencephalon
thundershower
topographical
typographical
underemphasis
unimpeachable
unselfishness
vapourishness
xylographical
absorbability
abstractional
acceptability
accessibility
accompaniment
achromaticity
acquiescingly
admissibility
admonishingly
adversatively
affirmatively
aggravatingly
airworthiness
alternatively
anachronistic
anaphrodisiac
answerability
appellatively
applicability
applicatively
arbitrariness
arbitrational
arithmetician
associativity
astonishingly
attainability
attributively
autoeroticism
bewilderingly
bibliophilism
bibliophilist
brotherliness
calculatingly
cannibalistic
cartilaginous
challengingly
changeability
clairaudience
clandestinely
coagulability
coeducational
commutability
comparability
comparatively
compatibility
competitively
complainingly
compositional
compressional
computational
concentricity
conflictingly
congressional
conjugational
conjunctional
conjunctively
consanguinity
consecutively
consumptively
contractility
convocational
cooperatively
corporativism
correlatively
correlativity
corrigibility
cosmopolitise
cosmopolitism
criminalistic
crystallinity
customariness
cyberneticist
cytochemistry
dastardliness
declaratively
decomposition
decontaminate
deductibility
defeasibility
defensibility
deferentially
deformational
dependability
deprecatingly
derequisition
descriptively
destructively
destructivity
desultoriness
deterministic
devastatingly
diagnostician
dictatorially
digestibility
disembodiment
disjunctively
disparagingly
disposability
dispraisingly
dissemblingly
dissimilitude
dissolubility
distinctively
distinguished
distressingly
doctrinairism
doublejointed
dysfunctional
egocentricity
elephantiasis
encouragingly
entomophilous
everlastingly
examinational
excommunicate
exemplariness
existentially
expansibility
explorational
exponentially
extensibility
extrajudicial
extraordinary
facultatively
fascinatingly
festschriften
filterability
flourishingly
foolhardiness
forementioned
formidability
frighteningly
frustratingly
fullfashioned
geocentricism
gravitational
helminthiasis
histrionicism
imaginatively
immiscibility
impalpability
impartibility

impassability
impassibility
impeccability
impercipience
imperialistic
implacability
implicatively
impossibility
improbability
improvability
inappreciable
inappreciably
inattentively
incommunicado
inconvenience
inconveniency
incredibility
indeterminacy
indeterminate
indeterminism
indeterminist
indisposition
indissociable
ineducability
ineffectively
ineligibility
inevitability
inexorability
inexpensively
infallibilism
infallibilist
infallibility
infeasibility
inferentially
inflexibility
influentially
informational
informatively
infuriatingly
inoffensively
inquisitional
inquisitively
insatiability
inscriptional
insensibility
insensitively
insensitivity
insignificant
insinuatingly
insociability
inspirational
instinctively
institutional
instructional
instructively
insubordinate
insufficience
insufficiency
intangibility
interdigitate
interestingly
intermediator
international
interparietal
interposition
invariability
inventorially
invincibility
inviolability
juxtaposition
kapellmeister
languishingly
legislatively
leishmaniasis
leisureliness
Maginotminded
magisterially
maladminister
manageability
materfamilias
materialistic
mathematician
meistersinger
mensurability
mercenariness
merchandising
metaphysician
metastability
millefeuilles
millionairess
ministerially
mistrustingly
momentariness
Monophysitism
multinational
multitudinous
nationalistic
negligibility
negotiability
neoclassicism
neoclassicist
neoplasticism
niggardliness
nightmarishly
noncompliance
nonforfeiting
objectivistic
observational
obstructively
opportunistic
outstandingly
overbearingly
overconfident
overqualified
oversensitive
paediatrician
painstakingly
painterliness
panicstricken
paterfamilias
paternalistic
pathogenicity
patronisingly
penetrability
penetratingly
penetratively
penitentially
perdurability
perishability
permutability
perspectively
photoperiodic
photopositive
platitudinise
platitudinous
plenitudinous
pointillistic
ponderability
postulational
predatoriness
predicability
predicatively
prefatorially
preferability
prejudicially
preparatively
prepositional
presumptively
primogenitary
primogenitive
primogeniture
procrastinate
profitability
prognosticate
progressional
progressively
progressivism
prohibitively
propositional
prospectively
pseudoscience
pusillanimity
pusillanimous
quadrennially
quadrillionth
quadrumvirate
quadruplicate
quadruplicity
qualitatively
questioningly
quincuncially
quintillionth
quintuplicate
radioactivity
rationalistic
receptibility
recomposition
reconsolidate
referentially
reflexibility
reformability
reformational
reproachingly
resistibility
resolvability
restoratively
restrictively
retroactively
retroactivity
reverentially
reversibility
sacrificially
scholarliness
scholasticism
seaworthiness
secondariness
sedentariness
selfappointed
selfconfident
selfconvicted
selfcriticism
selfdeceiving
selffertility
selfinflicted
selfopinioned
selfpityingly
selfpollinate
selfsacrifice
selfsterility
selfsufficing
septentrional
serendipitous
seriousminded
sesquiplicate
speculatively
spheroidicity
sprightliness
squeezability
standoffishly
substantially
substantively
substantivise
suffocatingly
superaddition
superdominant
superfamilies
superficially
superfluidity
superlatively
supernational
superordinate
superposition
supervenience
suppositional
supranational
synchronistic
tantalisingly
temporalities
temporariness
terminability
terminational
terminatively
terrestrially
territorially
thermophilous
thimblerigged
thimblerigger
threateningly
titillatingly
tonguetwister
translational
translucidity
transnational
transposition
tributariness
unbelievingly
uncleanliness
uncompetitive
uncomplaining
unconditional
unconditioned
underachiever
underestimate
unearthliness
unestablished
unexceptional
unflinchingly
unhealthiness
unimpassioned
unintelligent
unintentional
unobtrusively
unpromisingly
unqualifiedly
unrelentingly
unremittingly
unsociability
unsuitability
vacillatingly
verifiability
vicepresident
visionariness
vivisectional
voluntariness
voluntaristic
vulnerability
wellapPointed
worldlyminded
anticlockwise
greensickness
heartsickness
swashbuckling
arboriculture
autocatalysis
autocatalytic
backpedalling
bacteriolysis
bacteriolytic
blanketflower
bountifulness
canaliculated
changefulness
chromatolytic
circumvallate
colourfulness
congratulator
cryptanalysis
cryptanalytic
deceitfulness
decontrolling
equivocalness
eschscholtzia
essentialness
extracellular
foreknowledge
forgetfulness
frightfulness
healthfulness
heptasyllabic
hypnoanalysis
identicalness
illogicalness
intercellular
interpellator
intracellular
jerrybuilding
Machiavellian
masterfulness
microanalysis
microphyllous
monocotyledon
monometallism
monometallist
multicellular
multinucleate
nonfulfilment
osteomyelitis
ostreiculture
overindulgent
overpopulated
passionflower
pharmacologic
plentifulness
pneumatolysis
pneumatolytic
poliomyelitis
polycotyledon
practicalness
principalship
proconsulship
recrystallise
rectangularly
regardfulness
regretfulness
resentfulness
salmonellosis
selfindulgent
selfknowledge
semicivilised
softpedalling
somnambulator
sorrowfulness
spectacularly
spiritualness
stirpiculture
streetwalking
technicalness
tetrasyllable
tranquilliser
unarticulated
underemployed
underwhelming
undisciplined
unnaturalness
verisimilarly
violoncellist
whimsicalness
wonderfulness
accelerometer
accoutrements
aerodynamical
aggiornamento
alcoholometer
alcoholometry
anthropometry
chlamydomonas
diaphragmatic
disaffirmance
epiphenomenal
epiphenomenon
gastronomical
gynandromorph
irreclaimable
irreclaimably
liebfraumilch

monochromatic
monogrammatic
nemathelminth
pathognomonic
petrochemical
photochemical
platyhelminth
pneumatometer
polychromatic
potentiometer
psychosomatic
pyrheliometer
refractometer
RhaetoRomanic
saccharimeter
saccharimetry
saccharometer
semiautomatic
sergeantmajor
slangingmatch
squandermania
stoichiometry
stratocumulus
synallagmatic
telegrammatic
toxoplasmosis
transformable
unconformable
volumenometer
affectionless
anthelminthic
apportionment
ascertainable
ascertainment
blastogenesis
butterfingers
chieftainship
chinkerinchee
churchmanship
cinquecentist
circumvention
companionable
companionably
companionless
companionship
complementary
complimentary
comprehension
comprehensive
condescension
conditionally
consentaneity
consentaneous
consequential
constrainable
constrainedly
contrabandist
contrapuntist
contravention
correspondent
corresponsive
craftsmanship
dimensionally
dimensionless
disciplinable
discontinuity
discontinuous
discriminator
disharmonious
doubletongued
draftsmanship
educationally
embryogenesis
enlightenment
entertainment
epeirogenesis
equipotential
exceptionable
exceptionably
exceptionally
excrescential
extensionally
ferrimagnetic
ferromagnetic
flagellantism
frontogenesis
gametogenesis
gentlemanlike
heterogeneity
heterogeneous
heterogenesis
heterogenetic
indiscernible
indiscernibly
indoctrinator
inflexionless
instantaneity
instantaneous
insubstantial
integumentary
intentionally
irreverential
Kidderminster
librarianship
miscellaneous
misgovernment
morphogenesis
morphogenetic
mountebankery
nongovernment
nonreturnable
nutritionally
objectionable
objectionably
organogenesis
outspokenness
paraphernalia
parliamentary
phytoplankton
pococurantism
porcellaneous
predestinator
premillennial
preordainment
probationally
Protestantism
provisionally
psychodynamic
psychogenesis
psychogenetic
psychokinesis
psychokinetic
pyrotechnical
questionnaire
sanctimonious
schizogenesis
selenocentric
selfdependent
sensationally
shabbygenteel
silvertongued
socioeconomic
sportsmanlike
sportsmanship
statesmanlike
statesmanship
submachinegun
subsequential
subterraneous
suffraganship
superabundant
supereminence
supplementary
swordsmanship
tercentennial
thermodynamic
thermogenesis
threecornered
traditionally
tricentennial
unceremonious
uncertainness
unconcernedly
uncoordinated
understanding
unemotionally
unfashionable
unfashionably
unmentionable
unputdownable
unsubstantial
acetylcholine
acotyledonous
acrimoniously
adventurously
ambassadorial
anachronously
anfractuosity
annexationist
antipersonnel
archaeologist
archbishopric
archdeaconate
Assyriologist
autochthonism
autochthonous
biotechnology
blasphemously
burglariously
campanologist
carnivorously
ceremoniously
climatologist
combinatorial
compassionate
compendiously
concavoconvex
concessionary
concretionary
confectionary
confectionery
confessionary
conspicuously
contentiously
contortionist
contrariously
conventionary
convexoconvex
convulsionary
coreligionist
corruptionist
criminologist
cryobiologist
daguerreotype
deleteriously
demythologise
dermatologist
deuteragonist
Deuteronomist
devolutionary
devolutionist
diageotropism
dichotomously
discretionary
dispassionate
dodecaphonist
doublecrosser
efficaciously
electrologist
electromotive
encephalogram
endocrinology
eschatologist
examinatorial
exhibitionism
exhibitionist
expeditionary
expeditiously
explanatorily
expressionism
expressionist
expurgatorial
exterritorial
feuilletonism
feuilletonist
fissiparously
flirtatiously
gasteropodous
geochronology
geomorphology
geostationary
gerontologist
gonadotrophic
gonadotrophin
graminivorous
gubernatorial
gynaecologist
haematologist
helminthology
hermaphrodite
herpetologist
heterosporous
heterotrophic
homogeneously
hydrochloride
hyperboloidal
ichthyologist
ignominiously
illustriously
impecuniosity
impressionism
impressionist
incongruously
incredulously
industriously
injudiciously
inquisitorial
insectivorous
intercolonial
intravenously
irreligionist
irreligiously
isochronously
jiggerypokery
judgeadvocate
knickerbocker
leadpoisoning
legislatorial
liberationist
linseywoolsey
magnanimously
magnetomotive
malariologist
martyrologist
mellifluously
meritoriously
metagrobolise
meteorologist
misanthropist
mischievously
monophthongal
mountainously
multicoloured
myrmecologist
necessitously
nucleoprotein
numismatology
odontoglossum
odoriferously
onomatopoetic
ophthalmology
oppositionist
opprobriously
orangeblossom
ornithologist
overelaborate
palaeontology
palaeozoology
parallelogram
particoloured
percussionist
perfectionism
perfectionist
perfunctorily
perspicuously
pestiferously
phenomenology
photochromics
photochromism
phraseologist
physiognomist
polycarbonate
polyhistorian
precautionary
precipitously
premonitorily
preparatorily
prestigiously
pretentiously
processionary
processionist
procuratorial
progenitorial
projectionist
proliferously
promiscuously
proportionate
proprietorial
prosthodontia
protectionism
protectionist
pteridologist
punctiliously
quarrelsomely
rearcommodore
repetitionary
repetitiously
revelationist
revolutionary
revolutionise
revolutionism
revolutionist
rhodochrosite
roentgenogram
roentgenology
sanitationist
scandalmonger
scientologist
scleroprotein
scrumptiously
selfapproving
selfdiscovery
selfreproving
selfsupported
sententiously
separationist
sharpshooting
shockabsorber
sovietologist
spelaeologist
spontaneously
stereoscopist
stomatologist
strawcoloured
streptococcal
streptococcus
subversionary
sulphureously
superfluously
symphoniously
synchronously
tablespoonful
tautologously
televisionary
temerariously

tempestuously
tendentiously
terpsichorean
theanthropism
thermotropism
thigmotropism
thremmatology
transistorise
transitionary
treacherously
troublesomely
unambiguously
unconsciously
underexposure
unforthcoming
unquestioning
unrighteously
untrustworthy
unwholesomely
venereologist
venturesomely
versicoloured
vertiginously
volcanologist
vulcanologist
waterproofing
whithersoever
windowshopper
accidentprone
anthropopathy
anthropophagi
anthropophagy
asthenosphere
bacteriophage
brachycephaly
calligraphist
cerebrospinal
chromatophore
contraception
contraceptive
convertiplane
crosspurposes
deipnosophist
eavesdropping
exteroceptive
extratropical
homeomorphism
horsewhipping
hydrosulphide
hydrosulphite
hypertrophied
intercropping
interoceptive
intertropical
lancecorporal
magnetosphere
metaphosphate
microscopical
misconception
mourningpaper
nitrocompound
paedomorphism
pharmacopoeia
pneumatophore
polyadelphous
preconception
quadricipital
quicktempered
redescription
redevelopment
selfdeception
selfdeceptive
sharecropping
shorttempered
spermatophore
spermatophyte
stickingplace
thoroughpaced
transcription
transcriptive
transshipment
transshipping
unanticipated
grandiloquent
picturesquely
ventriloquial
ventriloquise
ventriloquism
ventriloquist
actinomorphic
administrable
administrator
allelomorphic
angiospermous
AngloAmerican
animadversion
antilogarithm
apheliotropic
atmospherical
autobiography
baccalaureate
bathymetrical
beleaguerment
bildungsroman
blackguardism
Bloomsburyite
brainstorming
buttonthrough
centreforward
chalcoography
characterless
chateaubriand
circumference
closedcircuit
collectorship
commandership
commensurable
commensurably
conductorship
confraternity
conglomeratic
conjecturable
conjecturally
containership
controversial
copartnership
corticotropic
corticotropin
courtsmartial
disappearance
disconcerting
disconcertion
disconformity
dishonourable
dishonourably
disintegrator
dismemberment
disproportion
dissymetrical
dressimprover
entomostracan
followthrough
gerontocratic
goniometrical
goodnaturedly
gymnospermous
gynaecocratic
halfsovereign
hemispherical
heteromorphic
homoeomorphic
hydrometrical
hypermetrical
hypermetropia
hypermetropic
ichthyography
idiosyncratic
inappropriate
inspectorship
intercurrence
intermarriage
interspersion
irrecoverable
irrecoverably
lamellibranch
landownership
leptospirosis
letterperfect
malacostracan
metallography
micronutrient
moderatorship
neighbourhood
nonappearance
nonconforming
nonconformism
nonconformist
nonconformity
opisthobranch
pantisocratic
philanthropic
planimetrical
precentorship
prehistorical
preponderance
preponderancy
prepreference
professoriate
professorship
prosopography
protectorship
pseudomorphic
psilanthropic
psychosurgery
quadripartite
recalcitrance
reinvigorator
schadenfreude
schizocarpous
schizophrenia
schizophrenic
searchwarrant
selfasserting
selfassertion
selfassertive
selfassurance
selfassuredly
selfcentredly
selfdispraise
selfgenerated
selfgoverning
selfimportant
selfinsurance
selfrecording
selfregarding
selfrestraint
semilogarithm
shootingrange
skateboarding
solicitorship
spectrography
sphygmography
subeditorship
Swedenborgian
taperecording
telerecording
thaumaturgist
thenceforward
theriomorphic
threequarters
transmigrator
treasurership
unadulterated
unconquerable
undercarriage
unsymmetrical
vantageground
viceadmiralty
winterberries
wonderworking
xanthochroism
zinjanthropus
affenpinscher
ambiguousness
ambitiousness
amorphousness
amphiprostyle
analogousness
anomalousness
anonymousness
anthroposophy
Antichristian
apprehensible
assiduousness
astrophysical
atrociousness
audaciousness
barbarousness
beauteousness
blamelessness
bloodlessness
boundlessness
bounteousness
brainlessness
bumptiousness
capaciousness
cheerlessness
chlamydospore
chrematistics
Christmastide
Christmastime
congruousness
consciousness
contrabassoon
courteousness
credulousness
crossquestion
dangerousness
dauntlessness
deathlessness
deciduousness
decompression
deliciousness
deliriousness
dexterousness
dispossession
doubtlessness
dreamlessness
egregiousness
embarrassment
encompassment
erroneousness
extraphysical
facetiousness
faithlessness
faultlessness
feloniousness
ferociousness
fortississimo
fractiousness
frivolousness
fruitlessness
garrulousness
generalisable
generalissimo
glutinousness
gracelessness
guilelessness
guiltlessness
hazardousness
heartlessness
hemiparasitic
hilariousness
horsechestnut
hyperphysical
imperiousness
impermissible
impetuousness
incondensable
incuriousness
indispensable
indispensably
inexpressible
inexpressibly
infinitesimal
ingeniousness
ingenuousness
injuriousness
innocuousness
innoxiousness
insidiousness
interpersonal
intrapersonal
introgression
introversible
invidiousness
irrepressible
irrepressibly
irresponsible
irresponsibly
judiciousness
laboriousness
lackadaisical
laughingstock
lecherousness
levelcrossing
limitlessness
litigiousness
ludicrousness
luxuriousness
mackerelshark
maliciousness
melodiousness
mercilessness
mirthlessness
misunderstand
misunderstood
momentousness
monstrousness
nefariousness
nervelessness
noiselessness
nonaggression
notoriousness
obliviousness
obnoxiousness
officiousness
pendulousness
penuriousness
photoemission
photoemissive
plenteousness
pluripresence
pneumogastric
pointlessness
ponderousness
postclassical
powerlessness
prepossessing
prepossession
pretermission
pricelessness
quadragesimal
querulousness
rapaciousness
rapturousness
rejuvenescent
religiousness
reprehensible
reprehensibly
retrogression
retrogressive
righteousness
rontgenoscopy
sagaciousness

salaciousness
seditiousness
selfadjusting
selfsatisfied
semiparasitic
senselessness
shamelessness
shapelessness
shiftlessness
shootingstick
shoulderstrap
sightlessness
sleeplessness
smellingsalts
smokelessness
spinelessness
squarebashing
stainlessness
statelessness
steppingstone
strenuousness
sumptuousness
superphysical
supersensible
tachistoscope
tastelessness
tenaciousness
tergiversator
thanklessness
tonguelashing
tortoiseshell
transgression
transgressive
transmissible
transversally
tremulousness
troublousness
unanimousness
valuelessness
venturousness
veraciousness
vexatiousness
vicariousness
vivaciousness
voicelessness
volatilisable
voraciousness
worthlessness
acrylonitrile
affreightment
amniocentesis
anomalistical
apocalyptical
archaeopteryx
architectonic
architectural
astronautical
backscratcher
belleslettres
bibliolatrist
bibliolatrous
bloodboltered
brilliantness
Calvinistical
centripetally
coldheartedly
complicatedly
conscientious
conservatoire
constructable
constructible
continentally
counterattack
counterstroke
crosscultural
crossgartered
detrimentally
differentiate
disadvantaged
disaffectedly
discreditable
discreditably
disinvestment
distributable
dressingtable
electrostatic
ethnocentrism
Eucharistical
exasperatedly
featherstitch
felicitations
floricultural
foresightedly
fundamentally
gastroenteric
globetrotting
hairsplitting
halfheartedly
hardheartedly
hermeneutical
homoeopathist
horticultural
hydrostatical
hypercritical
imperceptible
imperceptibly
imperfectness
incombustible
inconsistence
inconsistency
incontestable
incontestably
inconvertible
inconvertibly
incorrectness
incorruptible
incorruptibly
incorruptness
incrementally
inexhaustible
inexhaustibly
insupportable
insupportably
insusceptible
intercultural
interdentally
interjectural
intermittence
interpretable
interpretress
interruptible
maladjustment
maladroitness
manipulatable
manneristical
Methodistical
nearsightedly
nitrobacteria
nomenclatural
nondeductable
nonresistance
northeasterly
northeastward
northwesterly
northwestward
ochlocratical
openheartedly
opinionatedly
orthognathism
orthognathous
oystercatcher
pantheistical
parenthetical
passementerie
pennyfarthing
phycoerythrin
piscicultural
prescientific
presidentship
pretermitting
preternatural
problematical
protohistoric
psychometrics
psychometrist
quadrilateral
quickwittedly
representable
rhadamanthine
runningstitch
sabrerattling
sacramentally
sansculottism
selfexistence
selfrighteous
sentimentally
sidesplitting
sociocultural
southeasterly
southeastward
southwesterly
southwestward
steadfastness
subreptitious
substitutable
substructural
subternatural
supercritical
superstitious
supersubtlety
surreptitious
thermosetting
thunderstruck
toastmistress
transmittable
transportable
tritheistical
troglodytical
trustworthily
unaccountable
unaccountably
uncomfortable
uncomfortably
underclothing
unenlightened
unforgettable
unforgettably
ungrammatical
unpredictable
unpretentious
unwarrantable
unwarrantably
Zarathustrian
agriculturist
anticoagulant
battlecruiser
candlesnuffer
circumfluence
contractually
disarticulate
electrocution
fortunehunter
hemicellulose
hocuspocussed
hydromedusoid
inconsecutive
inconsequence
ineffectually
infundibulate
inopportunely
intercolumnar
interlocution
interlocutory
interlocutrix
interosculate
knuckleduster
machinegunner
magniloquence
mangoldwurzel
mothercountry
overcredulous
owneroccupier
pharmaceutics
pharmaceutist
postcommunion
reconstructor
selfcommunion
selfconsuming
selfexecuting
semiconductor
sericulturist
solidungulate
somniloquence
superannuable
supersaturate
timeconsuming
uninterrupted
viniculturist
viticulturist
BaltoSlavonic
inconceivable
inconceivably
irretrievable
irretrievably
pigeonlivered
primigravidae
sniftingvalve
topsyturvydom
unconceivable
aircraftwoman
businesswoman
congresswoman
spinningwheel
sprocketwheel
tiddledywinks
basidiomycete
butterflyfish
monodactylous
polydactylous
polypropylene
prairieoyster
proparoxytone
psychophysics
secretarybird
secretaryship
zygodactylous
conversazione
conversazioni

---

abiologically
acrobatically
adiabatically
administrable
administrator
aesthetically
agonistically
alcoholically
algebraically
allegorically
anaerobically
anthropopathy
apathetically
arthritically
ascertainable
asthmatically
atheistically
atomistically
authentically
authenticator
autobiography
automatically
autonomically
axiomatically
biodegradable
bombastically
canaliculated
categorically
centrifugally
centripetally
chalcography
challengeable
chromatically
chuckleheaded
cinematically
climactically
commensurable
commensurably
companionable
companionably
conditionally
conglomeratic
congratulator
conjecturable
conjecturally
constrainable
constructable
continentally
contractually
counterchange
countercharge
curvilinearly
cylindrically
deferentially
dendritically
detrimentally
dialectically
diametrically
diaphragmatic
dictatorially
dimensionally
disadvantaged
disaffirmance
disappearance
disciplinable
discreditable
discreditably
discriminator
dishonourable
dishonourably
disintegrator
distributable
dressingtable
eccentrically
educationally
electrostatic
elephantiasis
energetically
enigmatically
entomostracan
evangelically
exceptionable
exceptionably
exceptionally
existentially
exponentially
extensionally
extrinsically
fantastically
Fascistically
featherheaded
floristically
fundamentally
generalisable
geometrically
geotropically
gerontocratic
grammatically
gymnastically
gynaecocratic
helminthiasis
heptasyllabic
honorifically
hydraulically
hydrocephalic
hydrocephalus

ichthyography
ideologically
idiomatically
idiosyncratic
imperturbable
imperturbably
impolitically
impracticable
impracticably
impractically
inappreciable
inappreciably
inconceivable
inconceivably
incondensable
incontestable
incontestably
incorporeally
incrementally
indefatigable
indefatigably
indescribable
indescribably
indispensable
indispensably
indissociable
indoctrinator
ineffectually
inferentially
influentially
inorganically
insupportable
insupportably
intentionally
interdentally
intermediator
interpellator
interpretable
intrinsically
inventorially
irreclaimable
irreclaimably
irrecoverable
irrecoverably
irreplaceable
irretrievable
irretrievably
isometrically
isostatically
judgmatically
kinematically
knowledgeable
knowledgeably
lamellibranch
leishmaniasis
leptocephalic
lethargically
macaronically
macrocephalic
magisterially
malacostracan
manipulatable
matrilineally
mesencephalon
metallography
metonymically
microcephalic
ministerially
monochromatic
monogrammatic
mourningpaper
multiplicable
mutagenically
nonappearance
nonattendance
noncompliance
nondeductable
nonresistance
nonreturnable
nonsensically
nostalgically
nutritionally
objectionable
objectionably
oecologically
ontogenically
ontologically
opisthobranch
orthocephalic
overabundance
overpopulated
paddlesteamer
panegyrically
pantisocratic
parabolically
paradoxically
paraphernalia
parasitically
parthenocarpy
patriotically
pedagogically
penitentially
pharisaically
phrenetically
plethorically
pneumatically
polychromatic
pragmatically
predestinator
prefatorially
prejudicially
preponderance
preponderancy
prismatically
probationally
pronounceable
prophetically
prosopography
provisionally
psychodynamic
psychosomatic
puritanically
quadrennially
questionnaire
quincuncially
realistically
recalcitrance
recommendable
rectangularly
rectilinearly
referentially
reinvigorator
representable
reverentially
RhaetoRomanic
rhapsodically
rheumatically
sacramentally
sacrificially
sarcastically
schematically
scorbutically
selfassurance
selfdispraise
selfgenerated
selfinsurance
selfrestraint
semiautomatic
semipermeable
sensationally
sentimentally
sergeantmajor
serologically
shootingrange
slangingmatch
smellingsalts
sniftingvalve
somnambulator
sophistically
sophisticated
spasmodically
spectacularly
spectrography
sphygmography
spindleshanks
splenetically
squandermania
statistically
steeplechaser
stigmatically
strategically
strikebreaker
stylistically
substantially
substitutable
superannuable
superficially
symbiotically
symmetrically
symphonically
synallagmatic
syntactically
synthetically
taxonomically
telegrammatic
telencephalon
tergiversator
terrestrially
territorially
tetrasyllable
theologically
theoretically
thermodynamic
thoroughpaced
thoughtreader
thrasonically
topologically
traditionally
transformable
transmigrator
transmittable
transportable
transversally
traumatically
typologically
unaccountable
unaccountably
unadulterated
unanticipated
unarticulated
uncomfortable
uncomfortably
uncomplicated
unconceivable
unconformable
unconquerable
uncoordinated
undereducated
underemphasis
unemotionally
unequivocally
unfashionable
unfashionably
unforgettable
unforgettably
unimpeachable
unmentionable
unpredictable
unputdownable
unwarrantable
unwarrantably
verisimilarly
viceadmiralty
volatilisable
weatherbeaten
wheelerdealer
heebiejeebies
imponderables
moneygrubbing
monosyllabism
secretarybird
turkeygobbler
achromaticity
affenpinscher
anticlimactic
arithmetician
autoeroticism
backscratcher
basidiomycete
chinkerinchee
circumspectly
closedcircuit
concentricity
cyberneticist
diagnostician
egocentricity
excommunicate
extragalactic
extrajudicial
geocentricism
histrionicism
incommunicado
insignificant
intergalactic
judgeadvocate
knickerbocker
leatherjacket
macromolecule
mathematician
metaphysician
microdetector
neoclassicism
neoclassicist
neoplasticism
oystercatcher
paediatrician
panicstricken
pathogenicity
perissodactyl
prognosticate
quadruplicate
quadruplicity
quintuplicate
reconstructor
rejuvenescent
rontgenoscopy
scholasticism
schoolteacher
selfcollected
selfconvicted
selfcriticism
selfinflicted
selfsufficing
semiconductor
sesquiplicate
spheroidicity
streptococcal
streptococcus
subcontractor
tachistoscope
blackguardism
breechloading
contrabandist
correspondent
encyclopedism
encyclopedist
gasteropodous
hermaphrodite
jerrybuilding
overconfident
rearcommodore
reconsolidate
selfconfident
selfdependent
selfrecording
selfregarding
skateboarding
superabundant
superfluidity
taperecording
telerecording
translucidity
understanding
vicepresident
accelerometer
accoutrements
actinomycetes
aggiornamento
alcoholometer
alcoholometry
amniocentesis
anthropogenic
anthropometry
archaeopteryx
baccalaureate
birefringence
blastogenesis
bloodboltered
boustrophedon
broadmindedly
camphoraceous
chromospheric
chrysanthemum
circumference
circumfluence
clairaudience
clearheadedly
coenaesthesis
coldbloodedly
coldheartedly
complicatedly
concupiscence
consenescence
consentaneity
consentaneous
constrainedly
convalescence
crossgartered
defervescence
deliquescence
dichlamydeous
disaffectedly
effervescence
effervescency
efflorescence
electioneerer
embryogenesis
encyclopaedia
encyclopaedic
epeirogenesis
epiphenomenal
epiphenomenon
exasperatedly
ferrimagnetic
ferromagnetic
foraminiferal
foreknowledge
foresightedly
frontogenesis
galactosaemia
gametogenesis
gastroenteric
goodnaturedly
grandfatherly
grandmotherly
halfheartedly
halfsovereign
hardheartedly
heterogeneity
heterogeneous
heterogenesis
heterogenetic
hypoglycaemia
impercipience
incandescence

inconsequence
inconsistence
inconsistency
inconvenience
inconveniency
inflorescence
instantaneity
instantaneous
insufficience
insufficiency
intercurrence
intermittence
interparietal
intransigeant
intransigence
jurisprudence
lancesergeant
lightfingered
lightheadedly
lightmindedly
magniloquence
membranaceous
miscellaneous
monocotyledon
morphogenesis
morphogenetic
multinucleate
nearsightedly
nitrobacteria
northeasterly
northwesterly
onomatopoetic
openheartedly
opinionatedly
organogenesis
papaveraceous
parasynthesis
parasynthetic
passementerie
pigeonlivered
pluripresence
pneumatometer
polycotyledon
polysynthesis
polysynthetic
porcellaneous
potentiometer
preengineered
prepreference
proteinaceous
pseudoscience
psychasthenia
psychogenesis
psychogenetic
psychokinesis
psychokinetic
pyrheliometer
quadrilateral
quicktempered
quickwittedly
recrudescence
refractometer
righthandedly
saccharimeter
saccharimetry
saccharometer
schadenfreude
schizogenesis
schizophrenia
schizophrenic
selfassuredly
selfcentredly
selfexistence
selfknowledge
selfrighteous
shorttempered
somniloquence
southeasterly
southwesterly
spermatogenic
stercoraceous
stoichiometry
stratospheric
submachinegun
subterraneous
supereminence
supervenience
thermogenesis
threecornered
transcendence
transcendency
unconcernedly
underachiever
underhandedly
unenlightened
unqualifiedly
volumenometer
whithersoever
wrongheadedly
bookingoffice
butterflyfish
candlesnuffer
festschriften
letterperfect
meadowsaffron
overqualified
selfsacrifice
selfsatisfied
thereinbefore
waterproofing
archaeologist
Assyriologist
butterfingers
campanologist
climatologist
criminologist
cryobiologist
demythologise
dermatologist
doubletongued
electrologist
electromagnet
encephalogram
entomophagous
eschatologist
gerontologist
gynaecologist
haematologist
herpetologist
ichthyologist
malariologist
martyrologist
meteorologist
myrmecologist
ornithologist
overindulgent
parallelogram
phraseologist
phyllophagous
psychosurgery
pteridologist
radiotelegram
roentgenogram
scientologist
selfindulgent
silvertongued
sovietologist
spelaeologist
spindlelegged
stomatologist
Swedenborgian
thaumaturgist
thimblerigged
thimblerigger
unintelligent
venereologist
volcanologist
vulcanologist
anthropophagi
anthropophagy
asthenosphere
bacteriophage
brachycephaly
calligraphist
candlelighter
chromatophore
crosshatching
deipnosophist
granddaughter
homeomorphism
homoeopathist
hydrosulphide
hydrosulphite
hypertrophied
mackerelshark
magnetosphere
metaphosphate
miscomprehend
neighbourhood
nightwatchman
orthognathism
orthognathous
paedomorphism
pennyfarthing
pennypinching
phycoerythrin
pneumatophore
polyadelphous
pseudoarchaic
rhadamanthine
sadomasochism
sadomasochist
scrapmerchant
selfslaughter
sewingmachine
soulsearching
spermatophore
spermatophyte
spinningwheel
sprocketwheel
squarebashing
tonguelashing
tortoiseshell
trustworthily
underclothing
abortifacient
aerodynamical
AngloAmerican
anomalistical
antilogarithm
apocalyptical
apprehensible
astronautical
astrophysical
atmospherical
bathymetrical
battlecruiser
betweenwhiles
bibliological
bouillabaisse
cacographical
Calvinistical
cerebrospinal
chateaubriand
chronological
circumambient
coarsegrained
conchological
concupiscible
conscientious
constructible
conversazione
conversazioni
counterfeiter
counterweight
craniological
cruiserweight
cryptological
deontological
differentiate
discommodious
disharmonious
dissymetrical
draggletailed
dramaturgical
embryological
entomological
Eucharistical
extraphysical
extratropical
featherstitch
featherweight
felicitations
gastrological
gastronomical
glaciological
goniometrical
graphological
hemiparasitic
hemispherical
hermeneutical
hundredweight
hydrometrical
hydrostatical
hyperboloidal
hypercritical
hypermetrical
hyperphysical
ideographical
immarcescible
immunological
imperceptible
imperceptibly
impermissible
inappropriate
incombustible
inconvertible
inconvertibly
inconvincible
incorruptible
incorruptibly
indiscernible
indiscernibly
inefficacious
inexhaustible
inexhaustibly
inexpressible
inexpressibly
infinitesimal
insusceptible
intermarriage
interruptible
interspecific
intertropical
introversible
irrefrangible
irrepressible
irrepressibly
irresponsible
irresponsibly
lackadaisical
liebfraumilch
malacological
manneristical
metallurgical
Methodistical
micronutrient
microscopical
mineralogical
morphological
musicological
nemathelminth
noncollegiate
numerological
ochlocratical
odontological
oreographical
osteomyelitis
palynological
pantheistical
paperhangings
parasiticidal
parenthetical
perspicacious
petrochemical
philosophical
philosophiser
photochemical
phrenological
physiological
planimetrical
platyhelminth
poliomyelitis
postclassical
prehistorical
prescientific
primigravidae
problematical
professoriate
psychological
pyrotechnical
quadragesimal
quadricipital
rattlebrained
reprehensible
reprehensibly
runningstitch
sanctimonious
seismological
selenological
selfconceited
selfconscious
selfcontained
selfsustained
semeiological
semicivilised
semiconscious
semilogarithm
semiparasitic
smoothingiron
solderingiron
somatological
speleological
subreptitious
supercritical
superphysical
supersensible
superstitious
surreptitious
swallowtailed
technological
teratological
tiddledywinks
topographical
toxicological
tranquilliser
transmissible
tritheistical
troglodytical
typographical
unceremonious
uncircumcised
unconstrained
undercarriage
undisciplined
ungrammatical
unpretentious
unsymmetrical
xylographical
cabinetmaking
cottonpicking
heartbreaking
housebreaking
hydrocracking
jiggerypokery

mountebankery
phytoplankton
streetwalking
wonderworking
absorbability
acceptability
accessibility
accidentalism
acetylcholine
admissibility
affectionless
answerability
anticoagulant
applicability
artificiality
attainability
autocephalous
backpedalling
bibliophilism
bibliophilist
biotechnology
bloodcurdling
ceremonialism
ceremonialist
changeability
characterless
circumvallate
coagulability
collaterality
colloquialism
commercialise
commercialism
commercialist
commutability
companionless
comparability
compatibility
conceptualise
conceptualism
conceptualist
connaturality
contractility
convertiplane
corrigibility
decontrolling
deductibility
defeasibility
defensibility
dematerialise
denationalise
dependability
depersonalise
digestibility
dimensionless
disarticulate
disposability
dissolubility
documentalist
doubledealing
ecumenicalism
electrovalent
endocrinology
entomophilous
expansibility
extensibility
filterability
formidability
fortuneteller
fractionalise
functionalism
functionalist
gentlemanlike
geochronology
geomorphology
helminthology
helterskelter
hemicellulose
heterothallic
homosexuality
horizontality
immaterialise
immaterialism
immaterialist
immateriality
immiscibility
impalpability
impartibility
impassability
impassibility
impeccability
impersonalise
impersonality
implacability
impossibility
improbability
improvability
incredibility
individualise
individualism
individualist
individuality
industrialise
industrialism
industrialist
ineducability
ineligibility
inevitability
inexorability
infallibilism
infallibilist
infallibility
infeasibility
inflexibility
inflexionless
infundibulate
inhospitality
insatiability
insensibility
insociability
intangibility
interosculate
invariability
invincibility
inviolability
irrationalise
irrationalism
irrationalist
irrationality
linseywoolsey
Machiavellian
manageability
materfamilias
megacephalous
mensurability
metagrobolise
metastability
microphyllous
microtonality
millefeuilles
millennialism
monodactylous
monometallism
monometallist
monumentalise
mourningcloak
negligibility
negotiability
numismatology
occasionalism
occasionalist
occasionality
occidentalise
Occidentalism
Occidentalist
ophthalmology
outgeneralled
overcredulous
palaeontology
palaeozoology
pantagruelian
pantagruelism
pantagruelist
paranormality
paterfamilias
penetrability
perdurability
perishability
permutability
phenomenalise
phenomenalism
phenomenalist
phenomenology
picturepalace
polydactylous
polypropylene
ponderability
predicability
preferability
PreRaphaelite
primordiality
profitability
provincialise
provincialism
provincialist
provinciality
prudentialism
prudentialist
prudentiality
psychoanalyse
psychoanalyst
quinquevalent
receptibility
reciprocality
recrystallise
reflexibility
reformability
resistibility
resolvability
reversibility
roentgenology
sabrerattling
sacerdotalise
sacerdotalism
sacerdotalist
scripturalism
scripturalist
selffertility
selfpropelled
selfrevealing
selfsterility
semiporcelain
sequentiality
shoulderblade
softpedalling
solidungulate
spermatoblast
sportsmanlike
squeezability
statesmanlike
stickingplace
structuralism
structuralist
structureless
superfamilies
supersubtlety
swashbuckling
terminability
theatricalise
theatricalism
theatricality
thermonuclear
thermophilous
thremmatology
triliteralism
unicameralism
unicameralist
unsociability
unsuitability
verifiability
violoncellist
vocationalism
vulnerability
zygodactylous
accompaniment
admeasurement
advertisement
affreightment
angiospermous
antihistamine
apportionment
ascertainment
bamboozlement
beleaguerment
brainstorming
cleistogamous
Deuteronomist
disconformity
disembodiment
disengagement
disfigurement
disinvestment
dismantlement
dismemberment
disparagement
divertisement
embarrassment
embellishment
embranglement
embrittlement
encompassment
encouragement
enlightenment
entertainment
establishment
gastrocnemius
gymnospermous
hydrodynamics
hydroxylamine
intercolumnar
interlacement
maladjustment
misgovernment
mismanagement
naphthylamine
nonconforming
nonconformism
nonconformist
nonconformity
nonfulfilment
nongovernment
overstatement
phanerogamous
photochromics
photochromism
physiognomist
preengagement
prefigurement
preordainment
pronouncement
pusillanimity
pusillanimous
pyrimethamine
quarrelsomely
rearrangement
reconcilement
redevelopment
reimbursement
reinforcement
reinstatement
replenishment
selfabasement
selfcondemned
selfconsuming
sternforemost
thermochemist
timeconsuming
transshipment
troublesomely
underestimate
underwhelming
unforthcoming
unwholesomely
venturesomely
vouchsafement
acotyledonous
acquiescently
acquiescingly
admirableness
admonishingly
advisableness
aggravatingly
agreeableness
airworthiness
ambiguousness
ambitiousness
amorphousness
analogousness
annexationist
anomalousness
anonymousness
antinomianism
antipersonnel
arbitrariness
archdeaconate
assertiveness
assiduousness
astonishingly
atrociousness
attentiveness
audaciousness
Australianism
autochthonism
autochthonous
availableness
barbarousness
barefacedness
beauteousness
belligerently
Berkeleianism
bewilderingly
blameableness
blamelessness
bloodlessness
boundlessness
bounteousness
bountifulness
brainlessness
brilliantness
brotherliness
bumptiousness
calculatingly
callisthenics
capaciousness
cartilaginous
challengingly
changefulness
cheerlessness
clandestinely
collectedness
collieshangie
colourfulness
combativeness
compartmental
compassionate
complainingly
complaisantly
complexedness
compositeness
concavoconvex
conceitedness
concessionary
concomitantly
concretionary
conduciveness
confectionary

confectionery
confessionary
confidingness
conflictingly
confraternity
congruousness
conjugateness
connectedness
consanguinity
consciousness
contentedness
contortionist
conventionary
convexoconvex
convulsionary
coreligionist
corrosiveness
corruptionist
courteousness
credulousness
crystallinity
customariness
dangerousness
dastardliness
dauntlessness
deathlessness
deceitfulness
deceptiveness
deciduousness
decontaminate
defectiveness
deliciousness
deliriousness
deprecatingly
desirableness
desperateness
desultoriness
deuteragonist
devastatingly
developmental
devolutionary
devolutionist
dexterousness
diathermanous
diffusiveness
discretionary
disobediently
disparagingly
disparateness
dispassionate
dispraisingly
dissemblingly
dissoluteness
distressingly
dodecaphonist
doublejointed
doubtlessness
dreamlessness
effectiveness
egregiousness
elaborateness
encouragingly
enjoyableness
environmental
equestrianism
equidistantly
equivocalness
erroneousness
essentialness
everlastingly
evocativeness
excessiveness
excitableness
exclusiveness
excursiveness
excusableness
exemplariness
exhibitionism
exhibitionist
expansiveness
expeditionary
expensiveness
explosiveness
expressionism
expressionist
exquisiteness
extensiveness
extraordinary
extravagantly
facetiousness
faithlessness
fascinatingly
faultlessness
feloniousness
ferociousness
feuilletonism
feuilletonist
flourishingly
foolhardiness
forgetfulness
fortunateness
fortunehunter
fractiousness
frighteningly
frightfulness
frivolousness
fruitlessness
frustratingly
garrulousness
geostationary
glutinousness
gracelessness
greensickness
grotesqueness
guilelessness
guiltlessness
habitableness
haphazardness
hazardousness
healthfulness
heartlessness
heartsickness
hilariousness
identicalness
illogicalness
imitativeness
immediateness
immovableness
immutableness
impassiveness
imperfectness
imperiousness
impertinently
impetuousness
impressionism
impressionist
improvidently
impulsiveness
inadvertently
inanimateness
inclusiveness
incompetently
incontinently
incorrectness
incorruptness
incurableness
incuriousness
independently
indeterminacy
indeterminate
indeterminism
indeterminist
indifferently
inductiveness
ineffableness
inefficiently
inexpediently
inexperienced
infuriatingly
ingeniousness
ingenuousness
injuriousness
innocuousness
innoxiousness
inopportunely
insensateness
insidiousness
insinuatingly
insolubleness
insubordinate
intelligencer
intelligently
intensiveness
intercolonial
interestingly
intricateness
intrusiveness
intuitiveness
inventiveness
invidiousness
inviolateness
invisibleness
irreligionist
irritableness
judiciousness
laboriousness
languishingly
laughableness
leadpoisoning
lecherousness
leisureliness
liberationist
lickerishness
lightsomeness
limitlessness
litigiousness
loathsomeness
lucrativeness
ludicrousness
luxuriousness
machinegunner
Maginotminded
magnificently
maladroitness
maliciousness
malleableness
Malthusianism
Manichaeanism
masculineness
masterfulness
mediterranean
megasporangia
meistersinger
melodiousness
mercenariness
mercilessness
microorganism
mirthlessness
miserableness
mistrustingly
mnemotechnics
Mohammedanism
momentariness
momentousness
Monarchianism
monophthongal
monstrousness
mothercountry
Muhammadanism
multitudinous
navigableness
nefariousness
nervelessness
neurastheniac
niggardliness
noiselessness
notoriousness
objectiveness
obliviousness
obnoxiousness
obsessiveness
obstinateness
obtrusiveness
octocentenary
offensiveness
offhandedness
officiousness
operativeness
opportuneness
oppositionist
outspokenness
outstandingly
overbearingly
painstakingly
painterliness
palatableness
patronisingly
peaceableness
pedestrianise
pedestrianism
pendulousness
penetratingly
Pennsylvanian
penuriousness
percussionist
perfectionism
perfectionist
pervasiveness
phenylalanine
philhellenism
philhellenist
pigheadedness
plaintiveness
platitudinise
platitudinous
plausibleness
plenitudinous
plenteousness
plentifulness
pointlessness
polycarbonate
ponderousness
postcommunion
powerlessness
practicalness
precautionary
precipitantly
predatoriness
predicamental
predominantly
prematureness
premillennial
pricelessness
primitiveness
processionary
processionist
procrastinate
projectionist
prolegomenary
prolegomenous
proportionate
prostaglandin
prosthodontia
protectionism
protectionist
protuberantly
purposiveness
querulousness
questioningly
quincentenary
quingentenary
quinquagenary
rapaciousness
rapturousness
receptiveness
recessiveness
regardfulness
regretfulness
religiousness
reminiscently
remonstrantly
removableness
repetitionary
reproachingly
republicanise
republicanism
repulsiveness
requisiteness
resentfulness
resplendently
retentiveness
revelationist
revolutionary
revolutionise
revolutionism
revolutionist
righteousness
sagaciousness
salaciousness
sanitationist
scandalmonger
scholarliness
seaworthiness
secondariness
secretiveness
sedentariness
seditiousness
seductiveness
selectiveness
selfappointed
selfawareness
selfcommunion
selfcontented
selfevidently
selfgoverning
selfpityingly
selfpollinate
selfrepugnant
selfsurrender
selftormentor
semipermanent
senselessness
sensitiveness
separableness
separationist
seriousminded
shamelessness
shapelessness
shiftlessness
sightlessness
significantly
sleeplessness
smokelessness
snowblindness
sobermindness
sorrowfulness
Spencerianism
spinelessness
spiritualness
sprightliness
squeamishness
stainlessness
statelessness
steadfastness
strenuousness
sublieutenant
subserviently
subversionary
suffocatingly
sumptuousness
supercalender
superdominant
superhumanity
superordinate
tablespoonful

talkativeness
tantalisingly
tastelessness
teachableness
technicalness
televisionary
temperamental
temperateness
temporariness
tenaciousness
tentativeness
tercentennial
thanklessness
threateningly
thrillingness
titillatingly
tolerableness
toothsomeness
traceableness
tractableness
Tractarianism
transatlantic
transitionary
translucently
transparently
tremulousness
tributariness
tricentennial
troublousness
unaccompanied
unanimousness
unbelievingly
uncertainness
uncleanliness
uncomplaining
unearthliness
unfeelingness
unflinchingly
unhealthiness
unmeaningness
unnaturalness
unprecedented
unpromisingly
unquestioning
unrelentingly
unremittingly
unselfishness
unwillingness
vacillatingly
valuelessness
vapourishness
vegetarianism
venerableness
venturousness
veraciousness
vexatiousness
vicariousness
visionariness
vivaciousness
voicelessness
voluntariness
voraciousness
wearisomeness
wellapPointed
whimsicalness
wholesomeness
wonderfulness
worldlyminded
worrisomeness
worthlessness
abstractional
actinomycosis
aircraftwoman
AngloCatholic
anthroposophy
apheliotropic
arbitrational
archidiaconal
architectonic
BaltoSlavonic
bildungsroman
blanketflower
boardinghouse
businesswoman
buttonthrough
cephalothorax
chlamydomonas
clearinghouse
coeducational
compositional
compressional
computational
congressional
congresswoman
conjugational
conjunctional
conservatoire
contrafagotto
convocational
corticotropic
corticotropin
countinghouse
crosspurposes
deformational
dressimprover
dysfunctional
electrophorus
electroscopic
examinational
explorational
followthrough
forementioned
fullfashioned
gravitational
gynandromorph
hypermetropia
hypermetropic
informational
inquisitional
inscriptional
inspirational
institutional
instructional
international
interpersonal
intrapersonal
kaleidoscopic
lancecorporal
laryngoscopic
leptospirosis
metamorphoses
metamorphosis
micrococcocci
mononucleosis
mouldingboard
multinational
nitrocompound
observational
passionflower
pathognomonic
pharmacologic
pharmacopoeia
philanthropic
photoperiodic
postulational
prepositional
progressional
propositional
protohistoric
psilanthropic
quadrillionth
quintillionth
reformational
salmonellosis
selfopinioned
septentrional
socioeconomic
soundingboard
spectroscopic
spinninghouse
stalkinghorse
supernational
suppositional
supranational
terminational
thoroughgoing
thundershower
toxoplasmosis
translational
transnational
unconditional
unconditioned
underemployed
unexceptional
unimpassioned
unintentional
vantageground
vivisectional
xanthochroism
zinjanthropus
actinomorphic
allelomorphic
archbishopric
bibliographer
bibliographic
biogeographer
cardiographer
chemoreceptor
chlamydospore
choreographer
choreographic
chronographic
cryptographer
cryptographic
diageotropism
eavesdropping
glossographer
gonadotrophic
gonadotrophin
heteromorphic
heterotrophic
homoeomorphic
horsewhipping
intercropping
lexicographer
lexicographic
misanthropist
oceanographer
oceanographic
owneroccupier
palaeographer
palaeographic
photoreceptor
physiographer
physiographic
polarographic
proprioceptor
pseudomorphic
schizocarpous
seismographer
seismographic
selenographer
selenographic
sharecropping
stereographic
stereoscopist
stratigraphic
theanthropism
theriomorphic
thermotropism
thigmotropism
transshipping
understrapper
uninterrupted
windowshopper
zoogeographer
zoogeographic
accidentprone
acrylonitrile
agriculturist
aluminiferous
ambassadorial
ambidexterity
ambidexterous
archimandrite
argentiferous
auctioneering
authoritarian
balsamiferous
bibliolatrist
bibliolatrous
brachypterous
brokenhearted
carboniferous
chromatograph
cinematograph
climbingframe
cobelligerent
combinatorial
communitarian
counterstroke
crackerbarrel
dissimilarity
doctrinairism
equiponderant
equiponderate
ethnocentrism
examinatorial
explanatorily
expurgatorial
extemporarily
exterritorial
ferroconcrete
fossiliferous
fragmentarily
garnetiferous
graminivorous
gubernatorial
heteropterous
heterosporous
hollowhearted
homoiothermal
homoiothermic
hydrochloride
hymenopterous
hypochondriac
immunotherapy
inconsiderate
inquisitorial
insectivorous
interpretress
intraarterial
involuntarily
kinematograph
legislatorial
lepidopterist
lepidopterous
lifepreserver
longsuffering
mammaliferous
manganiferous
mangoldwurzel
metalliferous
millionairess
mitochondrion
mouthwatering
necessitarian
nectariferous
nickeliferous
oleomargarine
organotherapy
overelaborate
oversubscribe
ovoviviparous
particularise
particularism
particularist
particularity
perfunctorily
perichondrial
perichondrium
petroliferous
phalansterian
phonautograph
physiotherapy
pigeonhearted
platiniferous
polliniferous
polyhistorian
preliminarily
premonitorily
preparatorily
procuratorial
profitsharing
progenitorial
proprietorial
protonotarial
psychometrics
psychometrist
psychotherapy
quadrumvirate
quartziferous
rudimentarily
scolopendrium
scorpiongrass
searchwarrant
selfsupported
semibarbarian
semibarbarism
sericulturist
Shakespearean
Shakespearian
sheepshearing
shockabsorber
shootingbrake
singlehearted
splendiferous
staminiferous
stoloniferous
supernumerary
supersaturate
tenderhearted
terpsichorean
thalassocracy
thoroughbrace
thunderstruck
toastmistress
transistorise
transliterate
triangularity
umbelliferous
unfamiliarity
unnecessarily
untrustworthy
vernacularise
vernacularism
vernacularity
viniculturist
viticulturist
winterberries
woolgathering
Zarathustrian
adventuresome
anachronistic
anaphrodisiac
anfractuosity
animadversion
associateship
barrelchested
cannibalistic
chieftainship
churchmanship
clothesbasket
colleagueship
collectorship

commandership
companionship
comprehension
comprehensive
concertmaster
condescension
conductorship
containership
contrabassoon
controversial
copartnership
corresponsive
craftsmanship
criminalistic
cytochemistry
decompression
defencelessly
deterministic
disinterested
dispossession
distinguished
doublecrosser
draftsmanship
fortississimo
generalissimo
harbourmaster
hocuspocussed
hydromedusoid
impecuniosity
imperialistic
inspectorship
interspersion
introgression
kapellmeister
Kidderminster
knuckleduster
laissezpasser
landownership
levelcrossing
librarianship
maladminister
materialistic
merchandising
moderatorship
nationalistic
nightmarishly
nonaggression
objectivistic
odontoglossum
opportunistic
orangeblossom
overemphasise
paternalistic
photoemission
photoemissive
pigeonchested
pointillistic
prairieoyster
precentorship
prepossessing
prepossession
presidentship
pretermission
principalship
proconsulship
professorship
protectorship
psychophysics
purposelessly
quartermaster
Quinquagesima
rationalistic
remorselessly
retrogression
retrogressive
rhodochrosite
rollercoaster
sculpturesque
secretaryship
selfaddressed
selfconfessed
selfpossessed
solicitorship
sportsmanship
standoffishly
statesmanship
stationmaster
subeditorship
subpostmaster
suffraganship
surrogateship
swordsmanship
synchronistic
thermoplastic
thoughtlessly
tonguetwister
transgression
transgressive
treasurership
underexposure
unestablished
voluntaristic
acclimatation
accommodating
accommodation
accommodative
accreditation
acculturation
acculturative
acetification
acidification
actualisation
afforestation
agglomeration
agglomerative
agglutination
agglutinative
aluminisation
amphiprostyle
amplification
anagrammatise
anagrammatism
anglicisation
animalisation
anthelminthic
Antichristian
appropriately
appropriation
appropriative
approximately
approximation
approximative
arboriculture
argumentation
argumentative
aromatisation
assassination
asserveration
authorisation
authoritative
backformation
backwardation
balkanisation
barbarisation
beatification
belleslettres
beneficiation
bioenergetics
bloodrelation
brachydactyly
broadspectrum
brutalisation
bureaucratise
calcification
caprification
carbonisation
carcinomatous
catechisation
cauterisation
certification
certificatory
chrematistics
Christmastide
Christmastime
cicatrisation
cinquecentist
circumvention
clarification
collaboration
collaborative
commemoration
commemorative
commemoratory
commiseration
commiserative
communication
communicative
communicatory
communisation
compagination
complementary
complimentary
concatenation
concentration
concentrative
condylomatous
confabulation
confabulatory
confederation
confederative
configuration
conflagration
confrontation
consequential
considerately
consideration
consolidation
consolidative
consolidatory
constellation
constellatory
consternation
contamination
contaminative
contemplation
contemplative
contraception
contraceptive
contradiction
contradictory
contrapuntist
contravention
cornification
corroboration
corroborative
corroboratory
cosmopolitise
cosmopolitism
costeffective
counteraction
counteractive
counterattack
courtsmartial
crossquestion
daguerreotype
decerebration
decomposition
decortication
decrepitation
defibrination
deforestation
degranulation
demonstration
demonstrative
denticulation
deodorisation
derequisition
derestriction
desegregation
deterioration
deteriorative
determinately
determination
determinative
diagrammatise
discoloration
disconcerting
disconcertion
disconnection
displantation
disproportion
disrespectful
dissemination
disseminative
disseveration
dissimilation
dissimilitude
dissimulation
documentation
domestication
domiciliation
dramatisation
dulcification
electrocution
electrometric
electromotive
emphysematous
encapsulation
epigrammatise
epigrammatist
equilibration
equipotential
eschscholtzia
exanthematous
excrescential
expectoration
expostulation
expostulatory
expropriation
extermination
exterminatory
exteroceptive
extrapolation
extravasation
falsification
fasciculation
ferroelectric
fertilisation
feudalisation
flagellantism
formalisation
formulisation
fortification
fossilisation
fractionation
fragmentation
freeselection
frequentation
frequentative
funambulation
galvanisation
germanisation
gesticulation
gesticulative
gesticulatory
glamorisation
globetrotting
glorification
gratification
hairsplitting
hallucination
hallucinative
hallucinatory
harmonisation
horripilation
horsechestnut
hybridisation
hydroelectric
hydrogenation
hypnotisation
hypothecation
impenetration
impersonation
importunately
impropriation
improvisation
improvisatory
incarceration
incardination
inconsecutive
incorporation
incorporative
incriminatory
indisposition
indistinctive
individuation
ingurgitation
insubstantial
integumentary
intemperately
intercalation
interdigitate
interlocution
interlocutory
interlocutrix
interoceptive
interpolation
interpolative
interposition
interpunction
interrelation
interrogation
interrogative
interrogatory
interstratify
introspection
introspective
investigation
investigative
investigatory
irreverential
isomerisation
italicisation
jollification
justification
justificative
justificatory
juxtaposition
laevorotation
laevorotatory
laughingstock
lignification
machicolation
magnetisation
magnetomotive
magnification
maladaptation
manifestation
manifestative
martyrisation
matriculation
mechanisation
mediatisation
melodramatics
melodramatise
melodramatist
mercerisation
mesmerisation
metallisation
metrification
miscegenation
misconception
misunderstand
misunderstood
modernisation

mollification
Monophysitism
monosymmetric
Monotheletism
monotrematous
mortification
mummification
mutualisation
mystification
necessitation
nephelometric
nitrification
nonconducting
nonfigurative
nonforfeiting
nonproductive
normalisation
nucleoprotein
nullification
omnicompetent
orchestration
ornamentation
ostreiculture
oversensitive
overvaluation
palletisation
papillomatous
paramagnetism
parliamentary
participation
participative
participatory
peptonisation
perambulation
perambulatory
peregrination
periodisation
perseveration
petrification
pharmaceutics
pharmaceutist
phosphoretted
photoelectric
photoelectron
photopositive
piezoelectric
pluralisation
pneumogastric
pneumonectomy
pococurantism
pontification
postoperative
prayermeeting
precipitately
precipitation
precipitative
preconception
predomination
prefiguration
prefigurative
premeditation
premeditative
preoccupation
preordination
pretermitting
prevarication
primogenitary
primogenitive
primogeniture
prizefighting
proliferation
proliferative
prolification
pronunciation
proparoxytone
Protestantism
psychrometric
pulverisation
quadripartite
qualification
qualificatory
radiolocation
randomisation
ratiocination
ratiocinative
reaffirmation
reciprocation
reciprocative
recombination
recomposition
recrimination
recriminative
recriminatory
rectification
redescription
reduplication
reduplicative
reembarkation
reexamination
reforestation
refrigeration
regimentation
regurgitation
reincarnation
reintegration
remonstration
remonstrative
renegotiation
reorientation
republication
resuscitation
resuscitative
retranslation
retrospection
retrospective
revaccination
revendication
reverberation
reverberative
reverberatory
ritualisation
Russification
sacrosanctity
sansculottism
scarification
scintillating
scintillation
scleroprotein
scorification
sedimentation
selenocentric
selfadjusting
selfasserting
selfassertion
selfassertive
selfdeception
selfdeceptive
selfdefeating
selfdirecting
selfdirection
selfeducation
selfexecuting
selfforgetful
selfimportant
selfinduction
sensitisation
sequestration
SerboCroatian
serendipitous
serialisation
shabbygenteel
sharpshooting
shootingstick
shoulderstrap
sicklefeather
sidesplitting
signalisation
signification
significative
socialisation
solemnisation
specification
spectrometric
stabilisation
steppingstone
sterilisation
stirpiculture
strangulation
subirrigation
subordinately
subordination
subordinative
subsaturation
subsequential
subtilisation
suffumigation
summarisation
superaddition
superfetation
superposition
supplantation
supplementary
syllabication
symbolisation
tantalisation
teleportation
temporalities
temporisation
terrorisation
testification
thermosetting
threequarters
thurification
tonsillectomy
transcription
transcriptive
translocation
transmutation
transmutative
transpiration
transpiratory
transposition
triangulation
trichromatism
trigonometric
tuberculation
uncompetitive
unfortunately
uninformative
unsubstantial
verbalisation
verbigeration
vermiculation
vernalisation
versification
victimisation
villeggiatura
visualisation
vitrification
vulcanisation
vulgarisation
acrimoniously
adventurously
anachronously
antiscorbutic
architectural
atlantosaurus
blasphemously
burglariously
carnivorously
ceremoniously
compendiously
conspicuously
contentiously
contrariously
crosscultural
deleteriously
dichotomously
discontinuity
discontinuous
disgracefully
distastefully
distressfully
distrustfully
efficaciously
expeditiously
extracellular
extravascular
fibrovascular
fissiparously
flirtatiously
floricultural
grandiloquent
homogeneously
horticultural
ichthyosaurus
ignominiously
illustriously
incongruously
inconspicuous
incredulously
industriously
injudiciously
intercellular
intercultural
interjectural
intracellular
intramuscular
intravenously
irreligiously
isochronously
magnanimously
mellifluously
meritoriously
mischievously
mistrustfully
monomolecular
mountainously
multicellular
multicoloured
necessitously
neurovascular
nomenclatural
odoriferously
opprobriously
particoloured
perpendicular
perspicuously
pestiferously
picturesquely
piscicultural
precipitously
prestigiously
pretentiously
preternatural
proliferously
promiscuously
punctiliously
repetitiously
reproachfully
resourcefully
scrumptiously
sententiously
sociocultural
spontaneously
stratocumulus
strawcoloured
substructural
subternatural
sulphureously
superfluously
symphoniously
synchronously
tautologously
temerariously
tempestuously
tendentiously
tintinnabular
tintinnabulum
treacherously
tyrannosaurus
unambiguously
unconsciously
undergraduate
unrighteously
ventriloquial
ventriloquise
ventriloquism
ventriloquist
versicoloured
vertiginously
adversatively
affirmatively
alternatively
appellatively
applicatively
associativity
attributively
comparatively
competitively
conjunctively
consecutively
consumptively
cooperatively
corporativism
correlatively
correlativity
declaratively
descriptively
destructively
destructivity
disjunctively
distinctively
facultatively
imaginatively
implicatively
inattentively
ineffectively
inexpensively
informatively
inoffensively
inquisitively
insensitively
insensitivity
instinctively
instructively
legislatively
lineengraving
obstructively
penetratively
perspectively
predicatively
preparatively
presumptively
progressively
progressivism
prohibitively
prospectively
qualitatively
radioactivity
restoratively
restrictively
retroactively
retroactivity
selfapproving
selfdeceiving
selfdiscovery
selfreproving
speculatively
substantively
substantivise
superlatively
terminatively
unobtrusively
woodengraving

anticlockwise
centreforward
northeastward
northwestward
partridgewood
southeastward
southwestward
thenceforward
autocatalysis
autocatalytic
bacteriolysis
bacteriolytic
Bloomsburyite
chromatolytic
cryptanalysis
cryptanalytic
hypnoanalysis
microanalysis
phreatophytic
pneumatolysis
pneumatolytic
topsyturvydom
crystalgazing
doubleglazing

---

anthropophagi
anthropophagy
anticoagulant
archdeaconate
baccalaureate
bacteriophage
brachycephaly
centreforward
chateaubriand
chromatograph
cinematograph
circumvallate
climbingframe
compassionate
complementary
complimentary
concessionary
concretionary
confectionary
confessionary
conventionary
convertiplane
convulsionary
counterattack
decontaminate
devolutionary
differentiate
disarticulate
discretionary
dispassionate
equiponderant
equiponderate
excommunicate
expeditionary
extraordinary
geostationary
immunotherapy
inappropriate
incommunicado
inconsiderate
indeterminacy
indeterminate
infundibulate
insignificant
insubordinate
integumentary
interdigitate
intermarriage
interosculate
intransigeant
judgeadvocate
kinematograph
lancesergeant
mackerelshark

metaphosphate
misunderstand
mouldingboard
multinucleate
noncollegiate
northeastward
northwestward
octocentenary
organotherapy
overelaborate
parliamentary
phonautograph
physiotherapy
picturepalace
polycarbonate
precautionary
primogenitary
processionary
procrastinate
professoriate
prognosticate
prolegomenary
proportionate
pseudoarchaic
psychotherapy
quadrumvirate
quadruplicate
quincentenary
quingentenary
quinquagenary
quintuplicate
reconsolidate
repetitionary
revolutionary
scorpiongrass
scrapmerchant
searchwarrant
selfimportant
selfpollinate
selfrepugnant
semiporcelain
sesquiplicate
shootingbrake
shoulderblade
solidungulate
soundingboard
southeastward
southwestward
spermatoblast
stickingplace
sublieutenant
subversionary
superabundant
superdominant
supernumerary
superordinate
supersaturate
supplementary
televisionary
thalassocracy
thenceforward
thoroughbrace
transitionary
transliterate
undercarriage
underestimate
undergraduate
administrable
apprehensible
ascertainable
biodegradable
challengeable
commensurable
commensurably
companionable
companionably
concupiscible
conjecturable
constrainable

constructable
constructible
disciplinable
discreditable
discreditably
dishonourable
dishonourably
distributable
dressingtable
exceptionable
exceptionably
generalisable
heptasyllabic
immarcescible
imperceptible
imperceptibly
impermissible
imperturbable
imperturbably
impracticable
impracticably
inappreciable
inappreciably
incombustible
inconceivable
inconceivably
incondensable
incontestable
incontestably
inconvertible
inconvertibly
inconvincible
incorruptible
incorruptibly
indefatigable
indefatigably
indescribable
indescribably
indiscernible
indiscernibly
indispensable
indispensably
indissociable
inexhaustible
inexhaustibly
inexpressible
inexpressibly
insupportable
insupportably
insusceptible
interpretable
interruptible
introversible
irreclaimable
irreclaimably
irrecoverable
irrecoverably
irrefrangible
irreplaceable
irrepressible
irrepressibly
irresponsible
irresponsibly
irretrievable
irretrievably
knowledgeable
knowledgeably
manipulatable
multiplicable
nondeductable
nonreturnable
objectionable
objectionably
pronounceable
recommendable
reprehensible
reprehensibly
representable
semipermeable

shockabsorber
substitutable
superannuable
supersensible
tetrasyllable
transformable
transmissible
transmittable
transportable
unaccountable
unaccountably
uncomfortable
uncomfortably
unconceivable
unconformable
unconquerable
unfashionable
unfashionably
unforgettable
unforgettably
unimpeachable
unmentionable
unpredictable
unputdownable
unwarrantable
unwarrantably
volatilisable
aerodynamical
AngloAmerican
anomalistical
apocalyptical
astronautical
astrophysical
atmospherical
bathymetrical
bibliological
cacographical
Calvinistical
chronological
conchological
craniological
cryptological
deontological
dissymetrical
dramaturgical
embryological
entomological
entomostracan
Eucharistical
extraphysical
extratropical
gastrological
gastronomical
glaciological
goniometrical
graphological
hemispherical
hermeneutical
hydrometrical
hydrostatical
hypercritical
hypermetrical
hyperphysical
ideographical
immunological
inexperienced
intelligencer
intertropical
lackadaisical
malacological
malacostracan
manneristical
metallurgical
Methodistical
micrococcocci
microscopical
mineralogical
morphological
musicological

numerological
ochlocratical
odontological
oreographical
palynological
pantheistical
parenthetical
petrochemical
philosophical
photochemical
phrenological
physiological
planimetrical
postclassical
prehistorical
problematical
psychological
pyrotechnical
seismological
selenological
semeiological
somatological
speleological
streptococcal
streptococcus
supercritical
superphysical
technological
teratological
thoroughpaced
topographical
toxicological
tritheistical
troglodytical
typographical
ungrammatical
unsymmetrical
xylographical
boustrophedon
broadmindedly
chuckleheaded
clearheadedly
coldbloodedly
coldheartedly
complicatedly
constrainedly
disaffectedly
encyclopaedia
encyclopaedic
exasperatedly
featherheaded
foreknowledge
foresightedly
goodnaturedly
halfheartedly
hardheartedly
hyperboloidal
lightheadedly
lightmindedly
Maginotminded
monocotyledon
nearsightedly
openheartedly
opinionatedly
parasiticidal
photoperiodic
polycotyledon
primigravidae
prostaglandin
quickwittedly
righthandedly
selfassuredly
selfcentredly
selfknowledge
selfsurrender
seriousminded
supercalender
thoughtreader
topsyturvydom

unconcernedly
underhandedly
unqualifiedly
worldlyminded
wrongheadedly
abortifacient
accompaniment
admeasurement
admirableness
adversatively
advertisement
advisableness
affectionless
affirmatively
affreightment
agreeableness
airworthiness
alternatively
ambiguousness
ambitiousness
amorphousness
analogousness
anomalousness
anonymousness
appellatively
applicatively
apportionment
appropriately
approximately
arbitrariness
ascertainment
assertiveness
assiduousness
asthenosphere
atrociousness
attentiveness
attributively
audaciousness
availableness
bamboozlement
barbarousness
barefacedness
basidiomycete
beauteousness
beleaguerment
blameableness
blamelessness
bloodlessness
boundlessness
bounteousness
bountifulness
brainlessness
brilliantness
brotherliness
bumptiousness
butterfingers
capaciousness
changefulness
characterless
cheerlessness
circumambient
clandestinely
cobelligerent
collectedness
colourfulness
combativeness
companionless
comparatively
competitively
complexedness
compositeness
conceitedness
conduciveness
confectionery
confidingness
congruousness
conjugateness
conjunctively
connectedness
consciousness
consecutively
considerately
consumptively
contentedness
cooperatively
correlatively
correspondent
corrosiveness
courteousness
credulousness
customariness
dangerousness
dastardliness
dauntlessness
deathlessness
deceitfulness
deceptiveness
deciduousness
declaratively
defectiveness
deliciousness
deliriousness
descriptively
desirableness
desperateness
destructively
desultoriness
determinately
dexterousness
diffusiveness
dimensionless
disembodiment
disengagement
disfigurement
disinvestment
disjunctively
dismantlement
dismemberment
disparagement
disparateness
dissoluteness
distinctively
divertisement
doubtlessness
dreamlessness
effectiveness
egregiousness
elaborateness
electrovalent
embarrassment
embellishment
embranglement
embrittlement
encompassment
encouragement
enjoyableness
enlightenment
entertainment
equivocalness
erroneousness
essentialness
establishment
evocativeness
excessiveness
excitableness
exclusiveness
excursiveness
excusableness
exemplariness
expansiveness
expensiveness
explosiveness
exquisiteness
extensiveness
facetiousness
facultatively
faithlessness
faultlessness
feloniousness
ferociousness
ferroconcrete
foolhardiness
forgetfulness
fortunateness
fractiousness
frightfulness
frivolousness
fruitlessness
garrulousness
glutinousness
gracelessness
grandiloquent
greensickness
grotesqueness
guilelessness
guiltlessness
habitableness
haphazardness
hazardousness
healthfulness
heartlessness
heartsickness
hilariousness
identicalness
illogicalness
imaginatively
imitativeness
immediateness
immovableness
immutableness
impassiveness
imperfectness
imperiousness
impetuousness
implicatively
importunately
impulsiveness
inanimateness
inattentively
inclusiveness
incorrectness
incorruptness
incurableness
incuriousness
inductiveness
ineffableness
ineffectively
inexpensively
inflexionless
informatively
ingeniousness
ingenuousness
injuriousness
innocuousness
innoxiousness
inoffensively
inopportunely
inquisitively
insensateness
insensitively
insidiousness
insolubleness
instinctively
instructively
intemperately
intensiveness
interlacement
interpretress
intricateness
intrusiveness
intuitiveness
inventiveness
invidiousness
inviolateness
invisibleness
irritableness
jiggerypokery
judiciousness
laboriousness
laughableness
lecherousness
legislatively
leisureliness
letterperfect
lickerishness
lightsomeness
limitlessness
litigiousness
loathsomeness
lucrativeness
ludicrousness
luxuriousness
magnetosphere
maladjustment
maladroitness
maliciousness
malleableness
masculineness
masterfulness
mediterranean
melodiousness
mercenariness
mercilessness
micronutrient
millionairess
mirthlessness
miscomprehend
miserableness
misgovernment
mismanagement
momentariness
momentousness
monstrousness
mountebankery
navigableness
nefariousness
nervelessness
niggardliness
noiselessness
nonfulfilment
nongovernment
notoriousness
nucleoprotein
objectiveness
obliviousness
obnoxiousness
obsessiveness
obstinateness
obstructively
obtrusiveness
offensiveness
offhandedness
officiousness
omnicompetent
operativeness
opportuneness
outspokenness
overconfident
overindulgent
overstatement
painterliness
palatableness
peaceableness
pendulousness
penetratively
penuriousness
perspectively
pervasiveness
pharmacopoeia
picturesquely
pigheadedness
plaintiveness
plausibleness
plenteousness
plentifulness
pointlessness
polypropylene
ponderousness
powerlessness
practicalness
precipitately
predatoriness
predicatively
preengagement
prefigurement
prematureness
preordainment
preparatively
presumptively
pricelessness
primitiveness
progressively
prohibitively
pronouncement
prospectively
psychosurgery
purposiveness
qualitatively
quarrelsomely
querulousness
quinquevalent
rapaciousness
rapturousness
rearrangement
receptiveness
recessiveness
reconcilement
redevelopment
regardfulness
regretfulness
reimbursement
reinforcement
reinstatement
rejuvenescent
religiousness
removableness
replenishment
repulsiveness
requisiteness
resentfulness
restoratively
restrictively
retentiveness
retroactively
righteousness
sagaciousness
salaciousness
scholarliness
scleroprotein
seaworthiness
secondariness
secretiveness
sedentariness
seditiousness
seductiveness
selectiveness
selfabasement
selfawareness
selfconfident
selfdependent
selfdiscovery
selfindulgent
semipermanent
senselessness
sensitiveness
separableness
shabbygenteel
Shakespearean
shamelessness
shapelessness
shiftlessness
sightlessness
sleeplessness
smokelessness
snowblindness

sobermindness
sorrowfulness
speculatively
spinelessness
spinningwheel
spiritualness
sprightliness
sprocketwheel
squeamishness
stainlessness
statelessness
steadfastness
strenuousness
structureless
subordinately
substantively
sumptuousness
superlatively
supersubtlety
talkativeness
tastelessness
teachableness
technicalness
temperateness
temporariness
tenaciousness
tentativeness
terminatively
terpsichorean
thanklessness
thermonuclear
threequarters
thrillingness
toastmistress
tolerableness
toothsomeness
tortoiseshell
traceableness
tractableness
transshipment
tremulousness
tributariness
troublesomely
troublousness
unanimousness
uncertainness
uncleanliness
unearthliness
unfeelingness
unfortunately
unhealthiness
unintelligent
unmeaningness
unnaturalness
unobtrusively
unselfishness
unwholesomely
unwillingness
valuelessness
vapourishness
venerableness
venturesomely
venturousness
veraciousness
vexatiousness
vicariousness
vicepresident
visionariness
vivaciousness
voicelessness
voluntariness
voraciousness
vouchsafement
wearisomeness
whimsicalness
wholesomeness
wonderfulness
worrisomeness
worthlessness
candlesnuffer
disrespectful
interspecific
prescientific
selfforgetful
tablespoonful
acquiescingly
admonishingly
aggravatingly
astonishingly
bewilderingly
calculatingly
challengingly
collieshangie
complainingly
conflictingly
counterweight
cruiserweight
deprecatingly
devastatingly
disadvantaged
disparagingly
dispraisingly
dissemblingly
distressingly
encouragingly
everlastingly
fascinatingly
featherweight
flourishingly
frighteningly
frustratingly
hundredweight
infuriatingly
insinuatingly
interestingly
languishingly
megasporangia
meistersinger
mistrustingly
monophthongal
outstandingly
overbearingly
painstakingly
patronisingly
penetratingly
pharmacologic
questioningly
reproachingly
scandalmonger
selfpityingly
spindlelegged
submachinegun
suffocatingly
tantalisingly
thimblerigged
thimblerigger
threateningly
titillatingly
unbelievingly
unflinchingly
unpromisingly
unrelentingly
unremittingly
vacillatingly
actinomorphic
affenpinscher
allelomorphic
anthelminthic
associateship
backscratcher
bibliographer
bibliographic
biogeographer
cardiographer
chieftainship
chinkerinchee
choreographer
choreographic
chronographic
churchmanship
colleagueship
collectorship
commandership
companionship
conductorship
containership
copartnership
craftsmanship
cryptographer
cryptographic
distinguished
draftsmanship
glossographer
gonadotrophic
gonadotrophin
heteromorphic
heterotrophic
homoeomorphic
inspectorship
landownership
lexicographer
lexicographic
librarianship
moderatorship
nightmarishly
oceanographer
oceanographic
oystercatcher
palaeographer
palaeographic
physiographer
physiographic
polarographic
precentorship
presidentship
principalship
proconsulship
professorship
protectorship
pseudomorphic
schoolteacher
secretaryship
seismographer
seismographic
selenographer
selenographic
sicklefeather
solicitorship
sportsmanship
standoffishly
statesmanship
stereographic
stratigraphic
subeditorship
suffraganship
surrogateship
swordsmanship
theriomorphic
treasurership
unestablished
zoogeographer
zoogeographic
absorbability
acceptability
accessibility
accidentalism
acclimatation
accommodating
accommodation
accommodative
accreditation
acculturation
acculturative
acetification
acetylcholine
achromaticity
acidification
acrylonitrile
actualisation
admissibility
afforestation
agglomeration
agglomerative
agglutination
agglutinative
agriculturist
aluminisation
ambassadorial
ambidexterity
amplification
anagrammatise
anagrammatism
anaphrodisiac
anfractuosity
anglicisation
animadversion
animalisation
annexationist
answerability
Antichristian
anticlockwise
antihistamine
antinomianism
applicability
appropriation
appropriative
approximation
approximative
archaeologist
archimandrite
argumentation
argumentative
arithmetician
aromatisation
artificiality
assassination
asserveration
associativity
Assyriologist
attainability
auctioneering
Australianism
authorisation
authoritarian
authoritative
autochthonism
autoeroticism
backformation
backpedalling
backwardation
balkanisation
barbarisation
beatification
beneficiation
Berkeleianism
bibliolatrist
bibliophilism
bibliophilist
bioenergetics
blackguardism
bloodcurdling
bloodrelation
Bloomsburyite
bookingoffice
brainstorming
breechloading
brutalisation
bureaucratise
butterflyfish
cabinetmaking
calcification
calligraphist
callisthenics
campanologist
caprification
carbonisation
catechisation
cauterisation
ceremonialism
ceremonialist
certification
changeability
chrematistics
Christmastide
Christmastime
cicatrisation
cinquecentist
circumvention
clarification
climatologist
coagulability
collaboration
collaborative
collaterality
colloquialism
combinatorial
commemoration
commemorative
commercialise
commercialism
commercialist
commiseration
commiserative
communication
communicative
communisation
communitarian
commutability
compagination
comparability
compatibility
comprehension
comprehensive
concatenation
concentration
concentrative
concentricity
conceptualise
conceptualism
conceptualist
condescension
confabulation
confederation
confederative
configuration
conflagration
confraternity
confrontation
connaturality
consanguinity
consentaneity
consequential
conservatoire
consideration
consolidation
consolidative
constellation
consternation
contamination
contaminative
contemplation
contemplative
contortionist
contrabandist
contraception
contraceptive
contractility
contradiction
contrapuntist
contravention
controversial
coreligionist
cornification
corporativism
correlativity

corresponsive
corrigibility
corroboration
corroborative
corruptionist
cosmopolitise
cosmopolitism
costeffective
cottonpicking
counteraction
counteractive
courtsmartial
criminologist
crosshatching
crossquestion
cryobiologist
crystalgazing
crystallinity
cyberneticist
decerebration
decomposition
decompression
decontrolling
decortication
decrepitation
deductibility
defeasibility
defensibility
defibrination
deforestation
degranulation
deipnosophist
dematerialise
demonstration
demonstrative
demythologise
denationalise
denticulation
deodorisation
dependability
depersonalise
derequisition
derestriction
dermatologist
desegregation
destructivity
deterioration
deteriorative
determination
determinative
deuteragonist
Deuteronomist
devolutionist
diageotropism
diagnostician
diagrammatise
digestibility
discoloration
disconcerting
disconcertion
disconformity
disconnection
discontinuity
displantation
disposability
dispossession
disproportion
dissemination
disseminative
disseveration
dissimilarity
dissimilation
dissimulation
dissolubility
doctrinairism
documentalist
documentation
dodecaphonist
domestication
domiciliation
doubledealing
doubleglazing
dramatisation
dulcification
eavesdropping
ecumenicalism
egocentricity
electrocution
electrologist
electromotive
encapsulation
encyclopedism
encyclopedist
epigrammatise
epigrammatist
equestrianism
equilibration
equipotential
eschatologist
ethnocentrism
examinatorial
excrescential
exhibitionism
exhibitionist
expansibility
expectoration
explanatorily
expostulation
expressionism
expressionist
expropriation
expurgatorial
extemporarily
extensibility
extermination
exteroceptive
exterritorial
extrajudicial
extrapolation
extravasation
falsification
fasciculation
fertilisation
feudalisation
feuilletonism
feuilletonist
filterability
flagellantism
formalisation
formidability
formulisation
fortification
fortississimo
fossilisation
fractionalise
fractionation
fragmentarily
fragmentation
freeselection
frequentation
frequentative
funambulation
functionalism
functionalist
galvanisation
gastrocnemius
generalissimo
gentlemanlike
geocentricism
germanisation
gerontologist
gesticulation
gesticulative
glamorisation
globetrotting
glorification
gratification
gubernatorial
gynaecologist
haematologist
hairsplitting
halfsovereign
hallucination
hallucinative
harmonisation
heartbreaking
heebiejeebies
hermaphrodite
herpetologist
heterogeneity
histrionicism
homeomorphism
homoeopathist
homosexuality
horizontality
horripilation
horsewhipping
housebreaking
hybridisation
hydrochloride
hydrocracking
hydrodynamics
hydrogenation
hydrosulphide
hydrosulphite
hydroxylamine
hypertrophied
hypnotisation
hypochondriac
hypothecation
ichthyologist
immaterialise
immaterialism
immaterialist
immateriality
immiscibility
impalpability
impartibility
impassability
impassibility
impeccability
impecuniosity
impenetration
impersonalise
impersonality
impersonation
implacability
impossibility
impressionism
impressionist
improbability
impropriation
improvability
improvisation
incarceration
incardination
inconsecutive
incorporation
incorporative
incredibility
indeterminism
indeterminist
indisposition
indistinctive
individualise
individualism
individualist
individuality
individuation
industrialise
industrialism
industrialist
ineducability
ineligibility
inevitability
inexorability
infallibilism
infallibilist
infallibility
infeasibility
inflexibility
ingurgitation
inhospitality
inquisitorial
insatiability
insensibility
insensitivity
insociability
instantaneity
insubstantial
intangibility
intercalation
intercolonial
intercropping
interlocution
interoceptive
interpolation
interpolative
interposition
interpunction
interrelation
interrogation
interrogative
interspersion
interstratify
intraarterial
introgression
introspection
introspective
invariability
investigation
investigative
invincibility
inviolability
involuntarily
irrationalise
irrationalism
irrationalist
irrationality
irreligionist
irreverential
isomerisation
italicisation
jerrybuilding
jollification
justification
justificative
juxtaposition
laevorotation
leadpoisoning
legislatorial
lepidopterist
levelcrossing
liberationist
lignification
lineengraving
longsuffering
Machiavellian
machicolation
magnetisation
magnetomotive
magnification
maladaptation
malariologist
Malthusianism
manageability
Manichaeanism
manifestation
manifestative
martyrisation
martyrologist
materfamilias
mathematician
matriculation
mechanisation
mediatisation
melodramatics
melodramatise
melodramatist
mensurability
mercerisation
merchandising
mesmerisation
metagrobolise
metallisation
metaphysician
metastability
meteorologist
metrification
microorganism
microtonality
millennialism
misanthropist
miscegenation
misconception
mitochondrion
mnemotechnics
modernisation
Mohammedanism
mollification
Monarchianism
moneygrubbing
monometallism
monometallist
Monophysitism
monosyllabism
Monotheletism
monumentalise
mortification
mouthwatering
Muhammadanism
mummification
mutualisation
myrmecologist
mystification
naphthylamine
necessitarian
necessitation
negligibility
negotiability
neoclassicism
neoclassicist
neoplasticism
neurastheniac
nitrification
nonaggression
nonconducting
nonconforming
nonconformism
nonconformist
nonconformity
nonfigurative
nonforfeiting
nonproductive
normalisation
nullification
occasionalism
occasionalist
occasionality
occidentalise
Occidentalism
Occidentalist
oleomargarine
oppositionist
orchestration
ornamentation
ornithologist
orthognathism
overemphasise
overqualified
oversensitive
oversubscribe
overvaluation
owneroccupier
paediatrician

paedomorphism
palletisation
pantagruelian
pantagruelism
pantagruelist
paramagnetism
paranormality
participation
participative
particularise
particularism
particularist
particularity
paterfamilias
pathogenicity
pedestrianise
pedestrianism
penetrability
Pennsylvanian
pennyfarthing
pennypinching
peptonisation
perambulation
percussionist
perdurability
peregrination
perfectionism
perfectionist
perfunctorily
perichondrial
perichondrium
periodisation
perishability
permutability
perseveration
petrification
phalansterian
pharmaceutics
pharmaceutist
phenomenalise
phenomenalism
phenomenalist
phenylalanine
philhellenism
philhellenist
photochromics
photochromism
photoemission
photoemissive
photopositive
phraseologist
physiognomist
platitudinise
pluralisation
pococurantism
polyhistorian
ponderability
pontification
postcommunion
postoperative
prayermeeting
precipitation
precipitative
preconception
predicability
predomination
preferability
prefiguration
prefigurative
preliminarily
premeditation
premeditative
premillennial
premonitorily
preoccupation
preordination
preparatorily
prepossessing
prepossession
PreRaphaelite
pretermission
pretermitting
prevarication
primogenitive
primordiality
prizefighting
processionist
procuratorial
profitability
profitsharing
progenitorial
progressivism
projectionist
proliferation
proliferative
prolification
pronunciation
proprietorial
protectionism
protectionist
Protestantism
protonotarial
provincialise
provincialism
provincialist
provinciality
prudentialism
prudentialist
prudentiality
psychometrics
psychometrist
psychophysics
pteridologist
pulverisation
pusillanimity
pyrimethamine
quadripartite
quadruplicity
qualification
questionnaire
Quinquagesima
radioactivity
radiolocation
randomisation
ratiocination
ratiocinative
reaffirmation
receptibility
reciprocality
reciprocation
reciprocative
recombination
recomposition
recrimination
recriminative
recrystallise
rectification
redescription
reduplication
reduplicative
reembarkation
reexamination
reflexibility
reforestation
reformability
refrigeration
regimentation
regurgitation
reincarnation
reintegration
remonstration
remonstrative
renegotiation
reorientation
republicanise
republicanism
republication
resistibility
resolvability
resuscitation
resuscitative
retranslation
retroactivity
retrogression
retrogressive
retrospection
retrospective
revaccination
revelationist
revendication
reverberation
reverberative
reversibility
revolutionise
revolutionism
revolutionist
rhadamanthine
rhodochrosite
ritualisation
rudimentarily
Russification
sabrerattling
sacerdotalise
sacerdotalism
sacerdotalist
sacrosanctity
sadomasochism
sadomasochist
sanitationist
sansculottism
scarification
scholasticism
scientologist
scintillating
scintillation
scolopendrium
scorification
scripturalism
scripturalist
secretarybird
sedimentation
selfadjusting
selfapproving
selfasserting
selfassertion
selfassertive
selfcommunion
selfconsuming
selfcriticism
selfdeceiving
selfdeception
selfdeceptive
selfdefeating
selfdirecting
selfdirection
selfdispraise
selfeducation
selfexecuting
selffertility
selfgoverning
selfinduction
selfrecording
selfregarding
selfreproving
selfrestraint
selfrevealing
selfsacrifice
selfsatisfied
selfsterility
selfsufficing
semibarbarian
semibarbarism
sensitisation
separationist
sequentiality
sequestration
SerboCroatian
serialisation
sericulturist
sewingmachine
Shakespearian
sharecropping
sharpshooting
sheepshearing
shootingstick
sidesplitting
signalisation
signification
significative
skateboarding
socialisation
softpedalling
solemnisation
soulsearching
sovietologist
specification
spelaeologist
Spencerianism
spheroidicity
sportsmanlike
squarebashing
squeezability
stabilisation
statesmanlike
stereoscopist
sterilisation
stomatologist
strangulation
streetwalking
structuralism
structuralist
subirrigation
subordination
subordinative
subsaturation
subsequential
substantivise
subtilisation
suffumigation
summarisation
superaddition
superfamilies
superfetation
superfluidity
superhumanity
superposition
supplantation
swashbuckling
Swedenborgian
syllabication
symbolisation
tantalisation
taperecording
teleportation
telerecording
temporalities
temporisation
tercentennial
terminability
terrorisation
testification
thaumaturgist
theanthropism
theatricalise
theatricalism
theatricality
thermochemist
thermosetting
thermotropism
thigmotropism
thoroughgoing
thurification
timeconsuming
tonguelashing
Tractarianism
transcription
transcriptive
transgression
transgressive
transistorise
translocation
translucidity
transmutation
transmutative
transpiration
transposition
transshipping
triangularity
triangulation
tricentennial
trichromatism
triliteralism
trustworthily
tuberculation
unaccompanied
uncompetitive
uncomplaining
underclothing
understanding
underwhelming
unfamiliarity
unforthcoming
unicameralism
unicameralist
uninformative
unnecessarily
unquestioning
unsociability
unsubstantial
unsuitability
vegetarianism
venereologist
ventriloquial
ventriloquise
ventriloquism
ventriloquist
verbalisation
verbigeration
verifiability
vermiculation
vernacularise
vernacularism
vernacularity
vernalisation
versification
victimisation
viniculturist
violoncellist
visualisation
viticulturist
vitrification
vocationalism
volcanologist
vulcanisation
vulcanologist
vulgarisation
vulnerability
waterproofing
winterberries
wonderworking
woodengraving
woolgathering
xanthochroism
Zarathustrian
sergeantmajor
clothesbasket
knickerbocker
leatherjacket
panicstricken
strikebreaker
abiologically
acrobatically
adiabatically
aesthetically
agonistically

alcoholically
algebraically
allegorically
anaerobically
AngloCatholic
apathetically
arthritically
asthmatically
atheistically
atomistically
authentically
automatically
autonomically
axiomatically
betweenwhiles
bombastically
categorically
centrifugally
centripetally
chromatically
cinematically
climactically
conditionally
conjecturally
continentally
contractually
cylindrically
deferentially
dendritically
detrimentally
dialectically
diametrically
dictatorially
dimensionally
disgracefully
distastefully
distressfully
distrustfully
draggletailed
eccentrically
educationally
energetically
enigmatically
evangelically
exceptionally
existentially
exponentially
extensionally
extracellular
extravascular
extrinsically
fantastically
Fascistically
fibrovascular
floristically
fortuneteller
fundamentally
geometrically
geotropically
grammatically
gymnastically
heterothallic
honorifically
hydraulically
hydrocephalic
hydrocephalus
ideologically
idiomatically
impolitically
imponderables
impractically
incorporeally
incrementally
ineffectually
inferentially
influentially
inorganically
intentionally
intercellular
interdentally
intracellular
intramuscular
intrinsically
inventorially
isometrically
isostatically
judgmatically
kinematically
leptocephalic
lethargically
liebfraumilch
macaronically
macrocephalic
magisterially
matrilineally
mesencephalon
metonymically
microcephalic
millefeuilles
ministerially
mistrustfully
monomolecular
multicellular
mutagenically
neurovascular
nonsensically
nostalgically
nutritionally
oecologically
ontogenically
ontologically
orthocephalic
outgeneralled
panegyrically
parabolically
paradoxically
paraphernalia
parasitically
patriotically
pedagogically
penitentially
perpendicular
pharisaically
phrenetically
plethorically
pneumatically
pragmatically
prefatorially
prejudicially
prismatically
probationally
prophetically
provisionally
puritanically
quadrennially
quincuncially
realistically
referentially
reproachfully
resourcefully
reverentially
rhapsodically
rheumatically
sacramentally
sacrificially
sarcastically
schematically
scorbutically
selfpropelled
sensationally
sentimentally
serologically
smellingsalts
sniftingvalve
sophistically
spasmodically
splenetically
statistically
stigmatically
strategically
stratocumulus
stylistically
substantially
superficially
swallowtailed
symbiotically
symmetrically
symphonically
syntactically
synthetically
taxonomically
telencephalon
terrestrially
territorially
theologically
theoretically
thrasonically
tintinnabular
tintinnabulum
topologically
traditionally
transversally
traumatically
turkeygobbler
typologically
unemotionally
unequivocally
viceadmiralty
wheelerdealer
aircraftwoman
bildungsroman
businesswoman
chrysanthemum
congresswoman
galactosaemia
homoiothermal
homoiothermic
hypoglycaemia
infinitesimal
nightwatchman
paddlesteamer
psychodynamic
quadragesimal
socioeconomic
thermodynamic
abstractional
accoutrements
aggiornamento
anthropogenic
antipersonnel
arbitrational
archidiaconal
architectonic
BaltoSlavonic
birefringence
cerebrospinal
chlamydomonas
circumference
circumfluence
clairaudience
coarsegrained
coeducational
compositional
compressional
computational
concupiscence
congressional
conjugational
conjunctional
consenescence
convalescence
convocational
counterchange
defervescence
deformational
deliquescence
disaffirmance
disappearance
dysfunctional
effervescence
effervescency
efflorescence
electromagnet
epiphenomenal
epiphenomenon
examinational
explorational
forementioned
fullfashioned
gravitational
horsechestnut
impercipience
incandescence
inconsequence
inconsistence
inconsistency
inconvenience
inconveniency
inflorescence
informational
inquisitional
inscriptional
inspirational
institutional
instructional
insufficience
insufficiency
intercolumnar
intercurrence
intermittence
international
interpersonal
intransigence
intrapersonal
jurisprudence
lamellibranch
machinegunner
magniloquence
multinational
nemathelminth
nonappearance
nonattendance
noncompliance
nonresistance
observational
opisthobranch
overabundance
paperhangings
pathognomonic
platyhelminth
pluripresence
postulational
preponderance
preponderancy
prepositional
prepreference
progressional
propositional
pseudoscience
psychasthenia
quadrillionth
quintillionth
rattlebrained
recalcitrance
recrudescence
reformational
RhaetoRomanic
schizophrenia
schizophrenic
selfassurance
selfcondemned
selfcontained
selfexistence
selfinsurance
selfopinioned
selfsustained
septentrional
shootingrange
somniloquence
spermatogenic
spindleshanks
squandermania
supereminence
supernational
supervenience
suppositional
supranational
terminational
tiddledywinks
transcendence
transcendency
translational
transnational
unconditional
unconditioned
unconstrained
undisciplined
unenlightened
unexceptional
unimpassioned
unintentional
vivisectional
accidentprone
acotyledonous
adventuresome
aluminiferous
ambidexterous
angiospermous
argentiferous
autocephalous
autochthonous
balsamiferous
bibliolatrous
biotechnology
brachypterous
camphoraceous
carboniferous
carcinomatous
cartilaginous
certificatory
chlamydospore
chromatophore
cleistogamous
commemoratory
communicatory
condylomatous
confabulatory
conscientious
consentaneous
consolidatory
constellatory
contrabassoon
contradictory
conversazione
conversazioni
corroboratory
counterstroke
diathermanous
dichlamydeous
discommodious
discontinuous
disharmonious
emphysematous
endocrinology
entomophagous
entomophilous
exanthematous
expostulatory
exterminatory
felicitations
fossiliferous
garnetiferous
gasteropodous
geochronology
geomorphology

gesticulatory
graminivorous
gymnospermous
hallucinatory
helminthology
hemicellulose
heterogeneous
heteropterous
heterosporous
hydromedusoid
hymenopterous
improvisatory
inconspicuous
incriminatory
inefficacious
insectivorous
instantaneous
interlocutory
interrogatory
investigatory
justificatory
laevorotatory
laughingstock
lepidopterous
mammaliferous
manganiferous
megacephalous
membranaceous
metalliferous
microphyllous
miscellaneous
misunderstood
monodactylous
monotrematous
mourningcloak
multitudinous
nectariferous
neighbourhood
nickeliferous
numismatology
ophthalmology
orthognathous
overcredulous
ovoviviparous
palaeontology
palaeozoology
papaveraceous
papillomatous
participatory
partridgewood
perambulatory
perspicacious
petroliferous
phanerogamous
phenomenology
phyllophagous
platiniferous
platitudinous
plenitudinous
pneumatophore
pneumonectomy
polliniferous
polyadelphous
polydactylous
porcellaneous
prolegomenous
proparoxytone
proteinaceous
pusillanimous
qualificatory
quartziferous
rearcommodore
recriminatory
reverberatory
roentgenology
rontgenoscopy
sanctimonious
schizocarpous
selfconscious
selfrighteous
semiconscious
serendipitous
spermatophore
splendiferous
staminiferous
steppingstone
stercoraceous
sternforemost
stoloniferous
subreptitious
subterraneous
superstitious
surreptitious
tachistoscope
thereinbefore
thermophilous
thremmatology
tonsillectomy
transpiratory
umbelliferous
unceremonious
unpretentious
zygodactylous
anthroposophy
apheliotropic
autobiography
chalcoography
corticotropic
corticotropin
electroscopic
hypermetropia
hypermetropic
ichthyography
kaleidoscopic
laryngoscopic
metallography
mourningpaper
philanthropic
prosopography
psilanthropic
spectrography
spectroscopic
sphygmography
understrapper
windowshopper
zinjanthropus
sculpturesque
archaeopteryx
archbishopric
architectural
atlantosaurus
belleslettres
bloodboltered
broadspectrum
cephalothorax
chromospheric
countercharge
crackerbarrel
crosscultural
crossgartered
curvilinearly
electioneerer
electrometric
electrophorus
encephalogram
ferroelectric
floricultural
foraminiferal
gastroenteric
grandfatherly
grandmotherly
gynandromorph
horticultural
hydroelectric
ichthyosaurus
intercultural
interjectural
interlocutrix
lancecorporal
lightfingered
meadowsaffron
monosymmetric
multicoloured
nephelometric
nitrobacteria
nomenclatural
northeasterly
northwesterly
parallelogram
parthenocarpy
particoloured
passementerie
photoelectric
photoelectron
phycoerythrin
piezoelectric
pigeonlivered
piscicultural
pneumogastric
preengineered
preternatural
protohistoric
psychrometric
quadrilateral
quicktempered
radiotelegram
rectangularly
rectilinearly
roentgenogram
selenocentric
shorttempered
shoulderstrap
smoothingiron
sociocultural
solderingiron
southeasterly
southwesterly
spectacularly
spectrometric
stalkinghorse
stratospheric
strawcoloured
substructural
subternatural
threecornered
trigonometric
tyrannosaurus
verisimilarly
versicoloured
acrimoniously
actinomycosis
adventurously
amniocentesis
anachronously
autocatalysis
bacteriolysis
battlecruiser
blasphemously
blastogenesis
bouillabaisse
burglariously
carnivorously
ceremoniously
coenaesthesis
compendiously
conspicuously
contentiously
contrariously
crosspurposes
cryptanalysis
defencelessly
deleteriously
dichotomously
doublecrosser
efficaciously
elephantiasis
embryogenesis
epeirogenesis
expeditiously
fissiparously
flirtatiously
frontogenesis
gametogenesis
helminthiasis
heterogenesis
hocuspocussed
homogeneously
hypnoanalysis
ignominiously
illustriously
incongruously
incredulously
industriously
injudiciously
intravenously
irreligiously
isochronously
laissezpasser
leishmaniasis
leptospirosis
linseywoolsey
magnanimously
mellifluously
meritoriously
metamorphoses
metamorphosis
microanalysis
mischievously
mononucleosis
morphogenesis
mountainously
necessitously
odontoglossum
odoriferously
opprobriously
orangeblossom
organogenesis
parasynthesis
perspicuously
pestiferously
philosophiser
pneumatolysis
polysynthesis
precipitously
prestigiously
pretentiously
proliferously
promiscuously
psychogenesis
psychokinesis
punctiliously
purposelessly
remorselessly
repetitiously
salmonellosis
schizogenesis
scrumptiously
selfaddressed
selfconfessed
selfpossessed
semicivilised
sententiously
spontaneously
steeplechaser
sulphureously
superfluously
symphoniously
synchronously
tautologously
temerariously
tempestuously
tendentiously
thermogenesis
thoughtlessly
toxoplasmosis
tranquilliser
treacherously
unambiguously
uncircumcised
unconsciously
underemphasis
unrighteously
vertiginously
accelerometer
acquiescently
actinomycetes
administrator
alcoholometer
alcoholometry
anachronistic
anthropometry
anthropopathy
anticlimactic
antilogarithm
antiscorbutic
authenticator
autocatalytic
bacteriolytic
barrelchested
belligerently
brokenhearted
canaliculated
candlelighter
cannibalistic
chemoreceptor
chromatolytic
circumspectly
compartmental
complaisantly
concertmaster
concomitantly
conglomeratic
congratulator
contrafagotto
counterfeiter
criminalistic
cryptanalytic
cytochemistry
deterministic
developmental
diaphragmatic
discriminator
disintegrator
disinterested
disobediently
doublejointed
electrostatic
environmental
equidistantly
extragalactic
extravagantly
featherstitch
ferrimagnetic
ferromagnetic
festschriften
fortunehunter
gerontocratic
granddaughter
gynaecocratic
harbourmaster
helterskelter
hemiparasitic
heterogenetic
hollowhearted
idiosyncratic
imperialistic
impertinently
improvidently
inadvertently
incompetently
incontinently
independently
indifferently
indoctrinator
inefficiently

inexpediently
intelligently
intergalactic
intermediator
interparietal
interpellator
kapellmeister
Kidderminster
knuckleduster
magnificently
maladminister
materialistic
microdetector
monochromatic
monogrammatic
morphogenetic
mothercountry
nationalistic
objectivistic
onomatopoetic
opportunistic
osteomyelitis
overpopulated
pantisocratic
parasynthetic
paternalistic
perissodactyl
phosphoretted
photoreceptor
phreatophytic
phytoplankton
pigeonchested
pigeonhearted
pneumatolytic
pneumatometer
pointillistic
poliomyelitis
polychromatic
polysynthetic
potentiometer
prairieoyster
precipitantly
predestinator
predicamental
predominantly
proprioceptor
prosthodontia
protuberantly
psychogenetic
psychokinetic
psychosomatic
pyrheliometer
quadricipital
quartermaster
rationalistic
reconstructor
refractometer
reinvigorator
reminiscently
remonstrantly
resplendently
rollercoaster
runningstitch
saccharimeter
saccharimetry
saccharometer
selfappointed
selfcollected
selfconceited
selfcontented
selfconvicted
selfevidently
selfgenerated
selfinflicted
selfslaughter
selfsupported
selftormentor
semiautomatic
semiconductor

semilogarithm
semiparasitic
significantly
singlehearted
slangingmatch
somnambulator
sophisticated
stationmaster
stoichiometry
subcontractor
subpostmaster
subserviently
synallagmatic
synchronistic
telegrammatic
temperamental
tenderhearted
tergiversator
thermoplastic
tonguetwister
transatlantic
translucently
transmigrator
transparently
unadulterated
unanticipated
unarticulated
uncomplicated
uncoordinated
undereducated
uninterrupted
unprecedented
untrustworthy
volumenometer
voluntaristic
weatherbeaten
wellapPointed
arboriculture
boardinghouse
buttonthrough
clearinghouse
closedcircuit
countinghouse
dissimilitude
doubletongued
followthrough
macromolecule
nitrocompound
ostreiculture
primogeniture
schadenfreude
silvertongued
spinninghouse
stirpiculture
thunderstruck
underexposure
vantageground
villeggiatura
concavoconvex
convexoconvex
dressimprover
lifepreserver
underachiever
whithersoever
blanketflower
passionflower
thundershower
amphiprostyle
brachydactyly
daguerreotype
psychoanalyse
psychoanalyst
spermatophyte
underemployed
eschscholtzia
mangoldwurzel

---

abstractional
aerodynamical

aircraftwoman
ambassadorial
anaphrodisiac
AngloAmerican
anomalistical
Antichristian
apocalyptical
arbitrational
archidiaconal
architectural
arithmetician
astronautical
astrophysical
atmospherical
authoritarian
bathymetrical
bibliological
bildungsroman
businesswoman
cacographical
Calvinistical
cephalothorax
cerebrospinal
chlamydomonas
chronological
coeducational
combinatorial
communitarian
compartmental
compositional
compressional
computational
conchological
congressional
congresswoman
conjugational
conjunctional
consequential
controversial
convocational
courtsmartial
craniological
crosscultural
cryptological
deformational
deontological
developmental
diagnostician
dissymetrical
dramaturgical
dysfunctional
embryological
encephalogram
entomological
entomostracan
environmental
epiphenomenal
equipotential
Eucharistical
examinational
examinatorial
excrescential
explorational
expurgatorial
exterritorial
extracellular
extrajudicial
extraphysical
extratropical
extravascular
fibrovascular
floricultural
foraminiferal
gastrological
gastronomical
glaciological
goniometrical
graphological
gravitational

gubernatorial
hemispherical
hermeneutical
homoiothermal
horticultural
hydrometrical
hydrostatical
hyperboloidal
hypercritical
hypermetrical
hyperphysical
hypochondriac
ideographical
immunological
infinitesimal
informational
inquisitional
inquisitorial
inscriptional
inspirational
institutional
instructional
insubstantial
intercellular
intercolonial
intercolumnar
intercultural
interjectural
international
interparietal
interpersonal
intertropical
intraarterial
intracellular
intramuscular
intrapersonal
irreverential
lackadaisical
lancecorporal
legislatorial
Machiavellian
malacological
malacostracan
manneristical
materfamilias
mathematician
mediterranean
metallurgical
metaphysician
Methodistical
microscopical
mineralogical
monomolecular
monophthongal
morphological
mourningcloak
multicellular
multinational
musicological
necessitarian
neurastheniac
neurovascular
nightwatchman
nomenclatural
numerological
observational
ochlocratical
odontological
oreographical
paediatrician
palynological
pantagruelian
pantheistical
parallelogram
parasiticidal
parenthetical
paterfamilias
Pennsylvanian
perichondrial

perpendicular
petrochemical
phalansterian
philosophical
photochemical
phrenological
physiological
piscicultural
planimetrical
polyhistorian
postclassical
postulational
predicamental
prehistorical
premillennial
prepositional
preternatural
primigravidae
problematical
procuratorial
progenitorial
progressional
propositional
proprietorial
protonotarial
psychological
pyrotechnical
quadragesimal
quadricipital
quadrilateral
radiotelegram
reformational
roentgenogram
seismological
selenological
semeiological
semibarbarian
septentrional
SerboCroatian
Shakespearean
Shakespearian
shoulderstrap
sociocultural
somatological
speleological
streptococcal
subsequential
substructural
subternatural
supercritical
supernational
superphysical
suppositional
supranational
Swedenborgian
technological
temperamental
teratological
tercentennial
terminational
terpsichorean
thermonuclear
tintinnabular
topographical
toxicological
translational
transnational
tricentennial
tritheistical
troglodytical
typographical
unconditional
unexceptional
ungrammatical
unintentional
unsubstantial
unsymmetrical
ventriloquial
vivisectional

xylographical
Zarathustrian
oversubscribe
bioenergetics
birefringence
bookingoffice
callisthenics
chrematistics
circumference
circumfluence
clairaudience
concupiscence
consenescence
convalescence
counterattack
defervescence
deliquescence
disaffirmance
disappearance
effervescence
effervescency
efflorescence
featherstitch
hydrodynamics
impercipience
incandescence
inconsequence
inconsistence
inconsistency
inconvenience
inconveniency
indeterminacy
inflorescence
insufficience
insufficiency
intercurrence
intermittence
intransigence
jurisprudence
lamellibranch
laughingstock
letterperfect
liebfraumilch
magniloquence
melodramatics
micrococcocci
mnemotechnics
nonappearance
nonattendance
noncompliance
nonresistance
opisthobranch
overabundance
pharmaceutics
photochromics
picturepalace
pluripresence
preponderance
preponderancy
prepreference
pseudoscience
psychometrics
psychophysics
recalcitrance
recrudescence
runningstitch
selfassurance
selfexistence
selfinsurance
selfsacrifice
shootingstick
slangingmatch
somniloquence
stickingplace
supereminence
supervenience
thalassocracy
thoroughbrace
thunderstruck

transcendence
transcendency
Christmastide
dissimilitude
hydrochloride
hydrosulphide
incommunicado
schadenfreude
shoulderblade
accelerometer
actinomycetes
affenpinscher
alcoholometer
antipersonnel
backscratcher
barrelchested
battlecruiser
belleslettres
betweenwhiles
bibliographer
biogeographer
blanketflower
bloodboltered
brokenhearted
canaliculated
candlelighter
candlesnuffer
cardiographer
chinkerinchee
choreographer
chuckleheaded
clothesbasket
coarsegrained
concavoconvex
concertmaster
convexoconvex
counterfeiter
crackerbarrel
crossgartered
crosspurposes
cryptographer
disadvantaged
disinterested
distinguished
doublecrosser
doublejointed
doubletongued
draggletailed
dressimprover
electioneerer
electromagnet
featherheaded
festschriften
forementioned
fortunehunter
fortuneteller
fullfashioned
glossographer
granddaughter
harbourmaster
heebiejeebies
helterskelter
hocuspocussed
hollowhearted
hypertrophied
imponderables
inexperienced
intelligencer
kapellmeister
Kidderminster
knickerbocker
knuckleduster
laissezpasser
leatherjacket
lexicographer
lifepreserver
lightfingered
linseywoolsey
machinegunner

Maginotminded
maladminister
mangoldwurzel
meistersinger
metamorphoses
millefeuilles
mourningpaper
multicoloured
oceanographer
outgeneralled
overpopulated
overqualified
owneroccupier
oystercatcher
paddlesteamer
palaeographer
panicstricken
particoloured
passionflower
philosophiser
phosphoretted
physiographer
pigeonchested
pigeonhearted
pigeonlivered
pneumatometer
potentiometer
prairieoyster
preengineered
pyrheliometer
quartermaster
quicktempered
rattlebrained
refractometer
rollercoaster
saccharimeter
saccharometer
scandalmonger
schoolteacher
seismographer
selenographer
selfaddressed
selfappointed
selfcollected
selfconceited
selfcondemned
selfconfessed
selfcontained
selfcontented
selfconvicted
selfgenerated
selfinflicted
selfopinioned
selfpossessed
selfpropelled
selfsatisfied
selfslaughter
selfsupported
selfsurrender
selfsustained
semicivilised
seriousminded
shabbygenteel
shockabsorber
shorttempered
sicklefeather
silvertongued
singlehearted
sophisticated
spindlelegged
spinningwheel
sprocketwheel
stationmaster
steeplechaser
strawcoloured
strikebreaker
subpostmaster
supercalender
superfamilies

swallowtailed
temporalities
tenderhearted
thimblerigged
thimblerigger
thoroughpaced
thoughtreader
threecornered
thundershower
tonguetwister
tranquilliser
turkeygobbler
unaccompanied
unadulterated
unanticipated
unarticulated
uncircumcised
uncomplicated
unconditioned
unconstrained
uncoordinated
underachiever
undereducated
underemployed
understrapper
undisciplined
unenlightened
unestablished
unimpassioned
uninterrupted
unprecedented
versicoloured
volumenometer
weatherbeaten
wellapPointed
wheelerdealer
whithersoever
windowshopper
winterberries
worldlyminded
zoogeographer
interstratify
anthropophagi
anthropophagy
bacteriophage
biotechnology
buttonthrough
counterchange
countercharge
endocrinology
followthrough
foreknowledge
geochronology
geomorphology
halfsovereign
helminthology
intermarriage
numismatology
ophthalmology
palaeontology
palaeozoology
paperhangings
phenomenology
roentgenology
selfknowledge
shootingrange
thremmatology
undercarriage
anthropopathy
anthroposophy
antilogarithm
autobiography
chalcoography
counterweight
cruiserweight
featherweight
hundredweight
ichthyography
metallography

prosopography
semilogarithm
spectrography
sphygmography
untrustworthy
actinomorphic
actinomycosis
allelomorphic
amniocentesis
anachronistic
AngloCatholic
anthelminthic
anthropogenic
anticlimactic
antiscorbutic
apheliotropic
archbishopric
architectonic
associateship
autocatalysis
autocatalytic
bacteriolysis
bacteriolytic
BaltoSlavonic
bibliographic
blastogenesis
cannibalistic
chieftainship
choreographic
chromatolytic
chromospheric
chronographic
churchmanship
closedcircuit
coenaesthesis
colleagueship
collectorship
collieshangie
commandership
companionship
conductorship
conglomeratic
containership
copartnership
corticotropic
corticotropin
craftsmanship
criminalistic
cryptanalysis
cryptanalytic
cryptographic
deterministic
diaphragmatic
draftsmanship
electrometric
electroscopic
electrostatic
elephantiasis
embryogenesis
encyclopaedia
encyclopaedic
epeirogenesis
eschscholtzia
extragalactic
ferrimagnetic
ferroelectric
ferromagnetic
frontogenesis
galactosaemia
gametogenesis
gastroenteric
gerontocratic
gonadotrophic
gonadotrophin
gynaecocratic
helminthiasis
hemiparasitic
heptasyllabic
heterogenesis

heterogenetic
heteromorphic
heterothallic
heterotrophic
homoeomorphic
homoiothermic
hydrocephalic
hydroelectric
hydromedusoid
hypermetropia
hypermetropic
hypnoanalysis
hypoglycaemia
idiosyncratic
imperialistic
inspectorship
intergalactic
interlocutrix
interspecific
kaleidoscopic
landownership
laryngoscopic
leishmaniasis
leptocephalic
leptospirosis
lexicographic
librarianship
macrocephalic
materialistic
megasporangia
metamorphosis
microanalysis
microcephalic
moderatorship
monochromatic
monogrammatic
mononucleosis
monosymmetric
morphogenesis
morphogenetic
nationalistic
nephelometric
nitrobacteria
nucleoprotein
objectivistic
oceanographic
onomatopoetic
opportunistic
organogenesis
orthocephalic
osteomyelitis
palaeographic
pantisocratic
paraphernalia
parasynthesis
parasynthetic
passementerie
paternalistic
pathognomonic
pharmacologic
pharmacopoeia
philanthropic
photoelectric
photoperiodic
phreatophytic
phycoerythrin
physiographic
piezoelectric
pneumatolysis
pneumatolytic
pneumogastric
pointillistic
polarographic
poliomyelitis
polychromatic
polysynthesis
polysynthetic
precentorship
prescientific
presidentship
principalship
proconsulship
professorship
prostaglandin
prosthodontia
protectorship
protohistoric
pseudoarchaic
pseudomorphic
psilanthropic
psychasthenia
psychodynamic
psychogenesis
psychogenetic
psychokinesis
psychokinetic
psychosomatic
psychrometric
rationalistic
RhaetoRomanic
salmonellosis
schizogenesis
schizophrenia
schizophrenic
scleroprotein
secretaryship
seismographic
selenocentric
selenographic
semiautomatic
semiparasitic
semiporcelain
socioeconomic
solicitorship
spectrometric
spectroscopic
spermatogenic
sportsmanship
squandermania
statesmanship
stereographic
stratigraphic
stratospheric
subeditorship
suffraganship
surrogateship
swordsmanship
synallagmatic
synchronistic
telegrammatic
theriomorphic
thermodynamic
thermogenesis
thermoplastic
toxoplasmosis
transatlantic
treasurership
trigonometric
underemphasis
voluntaristic
zoogeographic
counterstroke
gentlemanlike
shootingbrake
spindleshanks
sportsmanlike
statesmanlike
tiddledywinks
abiologically
acquiescently
acquiescingly
acrimoniously
acrobatically
acrylonitrile
adiabatically
administrable
admonishingly
adventurously
adversatively
aesthetically
affirmatively
aggravatingly
agonistically
alcoholically
algebraically
allegorically
alternatively
amphiprostyle
anachronously
anaerobically
apathetically
appellatively
applicatively
apprehensible
appropriately
approximately
arthritically
ascertainable
asthmatically
astonishingly
atheistically
atomistically
attributively
authentically
automatically
autonomically
axiomatically
belligerently
bewilderingly
biodegradable
blasphemously
bombastically
brachycephaly
brachydactyly
broadmindedly
burglariously
calculatingly
carnivorously
categorically
centrifugally
centripetally
ceremoniously
challengeable
challengingly
chromatically
cinematically
circumspectly
clandestinely
clearheadedly
climactically
coldbloodedly
coldheartedly
commensurable
commensurably
companionable
companionably
comparatively
compendiously
competitively
complainingly
complaisantly
complicatedly
concomitantly
concupiscible
conditionally
conflictingly
conjecturable
conjecturally
conjunctively
consecutively
considerately
conspicuously
constrainable
constrainedly
constructable
constructible
consumptively
contentiously
continentally
contractually
contrariously
cooperatively
correlatively
curvilinearly
cylindrically
declaratively
defencelessly
deferentially
deleteriously
dendritically
deprecatingly
descriptively
destructively
determinately
detrimentally
devastatingly
dialectically
diametrically
dichotomously
dictatorially
dimensionally
disaffectedly
disciplinable
discreditable
discreditably
disgracefully
dishonourable
dishonourably
disjunctively
disobediently
disparagingly
dispraisingly
dissemblingly
distastefully
distinctively
distressfully
distressingly
distributable
distrustfully
dressingtable
eccentrically
educationally
efficaciously
encouragingly
energetically
enigmatically
equidistantly
evangelically
everlastingly
exasperatedly
exceptionable
exceptionably
exceptionally
existentially
expeditiously
explanatorily
exponentially
extemporarily
extensionally
extravagantly
extrinsically
facultatively
fantastically
fascinatingly
Fascistically
fissiparously
flirtatiously
floristically
flourishingly
foresightedly
fragmentarily
frighteningly
frustratingly
fundamentally
generalisable
geometrically
geotropically
goodnaturedly
grammatically
grandfatherly
grandmotherly
gymnastically
halfheartedly
hardheartedly
homogeneously
honorifically
hydraulically
ideologically
idiomatically
ignominiously
illustriously
imaginatively
immarcescible
imperceptible
imperceptibly
impermissible
impertinently
imperturbable
imperturbably
implicatively
impolitically
importunately
impracticable
impracticably
impractically
improvidently
inadvertently
inappreciable
inappreciably
inattentively
incombustible
incompetently
inconceivable
inconceivably
incondensable
incongruously
incontestable
incontestably
incontinently
inconvertible
inconvertibly
inconvincible
incorporeally
incorruptible
incorruptibly
incredulously
incrementally
indefatigable
indefatigably
independently
indescribable
indescribably
indifferently
indiscernible
indiscernibly
indispensable
indispensably
indissociable
industriously
ineffectively
ineffectually
inefficiently
inexhaustible
inexhaustibly
inexpediently
inexpensively
inexpressible
inexpressibly
inferentially
influentially
informatively
infuriatingly
injudiciously
inoffensively
inopportunely

inorganically
inquisitively
insensitively
insinuatingly
instinctively
instructively
insupportable
insupportably
insusceptible
intelligently
intemperately
intentionally
interdentally
interestingly
interpretable
interruptible
intravenously
intrinsically
introversible
inventorially
involuntarily
irreclaimable
irreclaimably
irrecoverable
irrecoverably
irrefrangible
irreligiously
irreplaceable
irrepressible
irrepressibly
irresponsible
irresponsibly
irretrievable
irretrievably
isochronously
isometrically
isostatically
judgmatically
kinematically
knowledgeable
knowledgeably
languishingly
legislatively
lethargically
lightheadedly
lightmindedly
macaronically
macromolecule
magisterially
magnanimously
magnificently
manipulatable
matrilineally
mellifluously
meritoriously
metonymically
ministerially
mischievously
mistrustfully
mistrustingly
mountainously
multiplicable
mutagenically
nearsightedly
necessitously
nightmarishly
nondeductable
nonreturnable
nonsensically
northeasterly
northwesterly
nostalgically
nutritionally
objectionable
objectionably
obstructively
odoriferously
oecologically
ontogenically
ontologically
openheartedly
opinionatedly
opprobriously
outstandingly
overbearingly
painstakingly
panegyrically
parabolically
paradoxically
parasitically
patriotically
patronisingly
pedagogically
penetratingly
penetratively
penitentially
perfunctorily
perspectively
perspicuously
pestiferously
pharisaically
phrenetically
picturesquely
plethorically
pneumatically
pragmatically
precipitantly
precipitately
precipitously
predicatively
predominantly
prefatorially
prejudicially
preliminarily
premonitorily
preparatively
preparatorily
prestigiously
presumptively
pretentiously
prismatically
probationally
progressively
prohibitively
proliferously
promiscuously
pronounceable
prophetically
prospectively
protuberantly
provisionally
punctiliously
puritanically
purposelessly
quadrennially
qualitatively
quarrelsomely
questioningly
quickwittedly
quincuncially
realistically
recommendable
rectangularly
rectilinearly
referentially
reminiscently
remonstrantly
remorselessly
repetitiously
reprehensible
reprehensibly
representable
reproachfully
reproachingly
resourcefully
resplendently
restoratively
restrictively
retroactively
reverentially
rhapsodically
rheumatically
righthandedly
rudimentarily
sacramentally
sacrificially
sarcastically
schematically
scorbutically
scrumptiously
selfassuredly
selfcentredly
selfevidently
selfpityingly
semipermeable
sensationally
sententiously
sentimentally
serologically
significantly
sophistically
southeasterly
southwesterly
spasmodically
spectacularly
speculatively
splenetically
spontaneously
standoffishly
statistically
stigmatically
strategically
stylistically
subordinately
subserviently
substantially
substantively
substitutable
suffocatingly
sulphureously
superannuable
superficially
superfluously
superlatively
supersensible
symbiotically
symmetrically
symphonically
symphoniously
synchronously
syntactically
synthetically
tantalisingly
tautologously
taxonomically
temerariously
tempestuously
tendentiously
terminatively
terrestrially
territorially
tetrasyllable
theologically
theoretically
thoughtlessly
thrasonically
threateningly
titillatingly
topologically
tortoiseshell
traditionally
transformable
translucently
transmissible
transmittable
transparently
transportable
transversally
traumatically
treacherously
troublesomely
trustworthily
typologically
unaccountable
unaccountably
unambiguously
unbelievingly
uncomfortable
uncomfortably
unconceivable
unconcernedly
unconformable
unconquerable
unconsciously
underhandedly
unemotionally
unequivocally
unfashionable
unfashionably
unflinchingly
unforgettable
unforgettably
unfortunately
unimpeachable
unmentionable
unnecessarily
unobtrusively
unpredictable
unpromisingly
unputdownable
unqualifiedly
unrelentingly
unremittingly
unrighteously
unwarrantable
unwarrantably
unwholesomely
vacillatingly
venturesomely
verisimilarly
vertiginously
volatilisable
wrongheadedly
adventuresome
Christmastime
climbingframe
fortississimo
generalissimo
pneumonectomy
Quinquagesima
tonsillectomy
abortifacient
accidentprone
accommodating
accompaniment
acetylcholine
admeasurement
advertisement
affreightment
anticoagulant
antihistamine
apportionment
ascertainment
auctioneering
backpedalling
bamboozlement
beleaguerment
bloodcurdling
brainstorming
breechloading
cabinetmaking
chateaubriand
circumambient
cobelligerent
conversazione
conversazioni
convertiplane
correspondent
cottonpicking
crosshatching
crystalgazing
decontrolling
disconcerting
disembodiment
disengagement
disfigurement
disinvestment
dismantlement
dismemberment
disparagement
divertisement
doubledealing
doubleglazing
eavesdropping
electrovalent
embarrassment
embellishment
embranglement
embrittlement
encompassment
encouragement
enlightenment
entertainment
equiponderant
establishment
felicitations
globetrotting
grandiloquent
hairsplitting
heartbreaking
horsewhipping
housebreaking
hydrocracking
hydroxylamine
insignificant
intercropping
interlacement
intransigeant
jerrybuilding
lancesergeant
leadpoisoning
levelcrossing
lineengraving
longsuffering
maladjustment
merchandising
micronutrient
miscomprehend
misgovernment
mismanagement
misunderstand
moneygrubbing
mouthwatering
naphthylamine
nitrocompound
nonconducting
nonconforming
nonforfeiting
nonfulfilment
nongovernment
oleomargarine
omnicompetent
overconfident
overindulgent
overstatement
pennyfarthing
pennypinching
phenylalanine
polypropylene
prayermeeting
preengagement
prefigurement
preordainment
prepossessing
pretermitting

prizefighting
profitsharing
pronouncement
proparoxytone
pyrimethamine
quinquevalent
rearrangement
reconcilement
redevelopment
reimbursement
reinforcement
reinstatement
rejuvenescent
replenishment
rhadamanthine
sabrerattling
scintillating
scrapmerchant
searchwarrant
selfabasement
selfadjusting
selfapproving
selfasserting
selfconfident
selfconsuming
selfdeceiving
selfdefeating
selfdependent
selfdirecting
selfexecuting
selfgoverning
selfimportant
selfindulgent
selfrecording
selfregarding
selfreproving
selfrepugnant
selfrestraint
selfrevealing
selfsufficing
semipermanent
sewingmachine
sharecropping
sharpshooting
sheepshearing
sidesplitting
skateboarding
softpedalling
soulsearching
squarebashing
steppingstone
streetwalking
sublieutenant
superabundant
superdominant
swashbuckling
taperecording
telerecording
thermosetting
thoroughgoing
timeconsuming
tonguelashing
transshipment
transshipping
uncomplaining
underclothing
understanding
underwhelming
unforthcoming
unintelligent
unquestioning
vantageground
vicepresident
vouchsafement
waterproofing
wonderworking
woodengraving
woolgathering
acclimatation
accommodation
accreditation
acculturation
acetification
acidification
actualisation
administrator
afforestation
agglomeration
agglutination
aluminisation
amplification
anglicisation
animadversion
animalisation
appropriation
approximation
argumentation
aromatisation
assassination
asserveration
authenticator
authorisation
backformation
backwardation
balkanisation
barbarisation
beatification
beneficiation
bloodrelation
boustrophedon
brutalisation
calcification
caprification
carbonisation
catechisation
cauterisation
certification
chemoreceptor
cicatrisation
circumvention
clarification
collaboration
commemoration
commiseration
communication
communisation
compagination
comprehension
concatenation
concentration
condescension
confabulation
confederation
configuration
conflagration
confrontation
congratulator
consideration
consolidation
constellation
consternation
contamination
contemplation
contrabassoon
contraception
contradiction
contravention
cornification
corroboration
counteraction
crossquestion
decerebration
decomposition
decompression
decortication
decrepitation
defibrination
deforestation
degranulation
demonstration
denticulation
deodorisation
derequisition
derestriction
desegregation
deterioration
determination
discoloration
disconcertion
disconnection
discriminator
disintegrator
displantation
dispossession
disproportion
dissemination
disseveration
dissimilation
dissimulation
documentation
domestication
domiciliation
dramatisation
dulcification
electrocution
encapsulation
epiphenomenon
equilibration
expectoration
expostulation
expropriation
extermination
extrapolation
extravasation
falsification
fasciculation
fertilisation
feudalisation
formalisation
formulisation
fortification
fossilisation
fractionation
fragmentation
freeselection
frequentation
funambulation
galvanisation
germanisation
gesticulation
glamorisation
glorification
gratification
hallucination
harmonisation
horripilation
hybridisation
hydrogenation
hypnotisation
hypothecation
impenetration
impersonation
impropriation
improvisation
incarceration
incardination
incorporation
indisposition
individuation
indoctrinator
ingurgitation
intercalation
interlocution
intermediator
interpellator
interpolation
interposition
interpunction
interrelation
interrogation
interspersion
introgression
introspection
investigation
isomerisation
italicisation
jollification
justification
juxtaposition
laevorotation
lignification
machicolation
magnetisation
magnification
maladaptation
manifestation
martyrisation
matriculation
meadowsaffron
mechanisation
mediatisation
mercerisation
mesencephalon
mesmerisation
metallisation
metrification
microdetector
miscegenation
misconception
misunderstood
mitochondrion
modernisation
mollification
monocotyledon
mortification
mummification
mutualisation
mystification
necessitation
neighbourhood
nitrification
nonaggression
normalisation
nullification
orangeblossom
orchestration
ornamentation
overvaluation
palletisation
participation
partridgewood
peptonisation
perambulation
peregrination
periodisation
perseveration
petrification
photoelectron
photoemission
photoreceptor
phytoplankton
pluralisation
polycotyledon
pontification
postcommunion
precipitation
preconception
predestinator
predomination
prefiguration
premeditation
preoccupation
preordination
prepossession
pretermission
prevarication
proliferation
prolification
pronunciation
proprioceptor
pulverisation
qualification
radiolocation
randomisation
ratiocination
reaffirmation
reciprocation
recombination
recomposition
reconstructor
recrimination
rectification
redescription
reduplication
reembarkation
reexamination
reforestation
refrigeration
regimentation
regurgitation
reincarnation
reintegration
reinvigorator
remonstration
renegotiation
reorientation
republication
resuscitation
retranslation
retrogression
retrospection
revaccination
revendication
reverberation
ritualisation
Russification
scarification
scintillation
scorification
sedimentation
selfassertion
selfcommunion
selfdeception
selfdirection
selfeducation
selfinduction
selftormentor
semiconductor
sensitisation
sequestration
sergeantmajor
serialisation
signalisation
signification
smoothingiron
socialisation
solderingiron
solemnisation
somnambulator
specification
stabilisation
sterilisation
strangulation
subcontractor
subirrigation
subordination
subsaturation
subtilisation
suffumigation
summarisation
superaddition
superfetation
superposition
supplantation
syllabication

symbolisation
tantalisation
telencephalon
teleportation
temporisation
tergiversator
terrorisation
testification
thurification
topsyturvydom
transcription
transgression
translocation
transmigrator
transmutation
transpiration
transposition
triangulation
tuberculation
verbalisation
verbigeration
vermiculation
vernalisation
versification
victimisation
visualisation
vitrification
vulcanisation
vulgarisation
chromatograph
cinematograph
daguerreotype
gynandromorph
immunotherapy
kinematograph
organotherapy
parthenocarpy
phonautograph
physiotherapy
psychotherapy
rontgenoscopy
tachistoscope
alcoholometry
anthropometry
arboriculture
asthenosphere
butterfingers
centreforward
certificatory
chlamydospore
chromatophore
commemoratory
communicatory
complementary
complimentary
concessionary
concretionary
confabulatory
confectionary
confectionery
confessionary
conservatoire
consolidatory
constellatory
contradictory
conventionary
convulsionary
corroboratory
cytochemistry
devolutionary
discretionary
expeditionary
expostulatory
exterminatory
extraordinary
geostationary
gesticulatory
hallucinatory
improvisatory

incriminatory
integumentary
interlocutory
interrogatory
investigatory
jiggerypokery
justificatory
laevorotatory
mackerelshark
magnetosphere
mothercountry
mouldingboard
mountebankery
northeastward
northwestward
octocentenary
ostreiculture
parliamentary
participatory
perambulatory
pneumatophore
precautionary
primogenitary
primogeniture
processionary
prolegomenary
psychosurgery
qualificatory
questionnaire
quincentenary
quingentenary
quinquagenary
rearcommodore
recriminatory
repetitionary
reverberatory
revolutionary
saccharimetry
secretarybird
selfdiscovery
soundingboard
southeastward
southwestward
spermatophore
stirpiculture
stoichiometry
subversionary
supernumerary
supplementary
televisionary
thenceforward
thereinbefore
threequarters
transitionary
transpiratory
underexposure
villeggiatura
accidentalism
admirableness
advisableness
affectionless
agreeableness
agriculturist
airworthiness
ambiguousness
ambitiousness
amorphousness
anagrammatise
anagrammatism
analogousness
annexationist
anomalousness
anonymousness
anticlockwise
antinomianism
arbitrariness
archaeologist
assertiveness
assiduousness

Assyriologist
atrociousness
attentiveness
audaciousness
Australianism
autochthonism
autoeroticism
availableness
barbarousness
barefacedness
beauteousness
Berkeleianism
bibliolatrist
bibliophilism
bibliophilist
blackguardism
blameableness
blamelessness
bloodlessness
boardinghouse
bouillabaisse
boundlessness
bounteousness
bountifulness
brainlessness
brilliantness
brotherliness
bumptiousness
bureaucratise
butterflyfish
calligraphist
campanologist
capaciousness
ceremonialism
ceremonialist
changefulness
characterless
cheerlessness
cinquecentist
clearinghouse
climatologist
collectedness
colloquialism
colourfulness
combativeness
commercialise
commercialism
commercialist
companionless
complexedness
compositeness
conceitedness
conceptualise
conceptualism
conceptualist
conduciveness
confidingness
congruousness
conjugateness
connectedness
consciousness
contentedness
contortionist
contrabandist
contrapuntist
coreligionist
corporativism
corrosiveness
corruptionist
cosmopolitise
cosmopolitism
countinghouse
courteousness
credulousness
criminologist
cryobiologist
customariness
cyberneticist
dangerousness

dastardliness
dauntlessness
deathlessness
deceitfulness
deceptiveness
deciduousness
defectiveness
deipnosophist
deliciousness
deliriousness
dematerialise
demythologise
denationalise
depersonalise
dermatologist
desirableness
desperateness
desultoriness
deuteragonist
Deuteronomist
devolutionist
dexterousness
diageotropism
diagrammatise
diffusiveness
dimensionless
disparateness
dissoluteness
doctrinairism
documentalist
dodecaphonist
doubtlessness
dreamlessness
ecumenicalism
effectiveness
egregiousness
elaborateness
electrologist
encyclopedism
encyclopedist
enjoyableness
epigrammatise
epigrammatist
equestrianism
equivocalness
erroneousness
eschatologist
essentialness
ethnocentrism
evocativeness
excessiveness
excitableness
exclusiveness
excursiveness
excusableness
exemplariness
exhibitionism
exhibitionist
expansiveness
expensiveness
explosiveness
expressionism
expressionist
exquisiteness
extensiveness
facetiousness
faithlessness
faultlessness
feloniousness
ferociousness
feuilletonism
feuilletonist
flagellantism
foolhardiness
forgetfulness
fortunateness
fractionalise
fractiousness
frightfulness

frivolousness
fruitlessness
functionalism
functionalist
garrulousness
geocentricism
gerontologist
glutinousness
gracelessness
greensickness
grotesqueness
guilelessness
guiltlessness
gynaecologist
habitableness
haematologist
haphazardness
hazardousness
healthfulness
heartlessness
heartsickness
hemicellulose
herpetologist
hilariousness
histrionicism
homeomorphism
homoeopathist
ichthyologist
identicalness
illogicalness
imitativeness
immaterialise
immaterialism
immaterialist
immediateness
immovableness
immutableness
impassiveness
imperfectness
imperiousness
impersonalise
impetuousness
impressionism
impressionist
impulsiveness
inanimateness
inclusiveness
incorrectness
incorruptness
incurableness
incuriousness
indeterminism
indeterminist
individualise
individualism
individualist
inductiveness
industrialise
industrialism
industrialist
ineffableness
infallibilism
infallibilist
inflexionless
ingeniousness
ingenuousness
injuriousness
innocuousness
innoxiousness
insensateness
insidiousness
insolubleness
intensiveness
interpretress
intricateness
intrusiveness
intuitiveness
inventiveness
invidiousness

inviolateness
invisibleness
irrationalise
irrationalism
irrationalist
irreligionist
irritableness
judiciousness
laboriousness
laughableness
lecherousness
leisureliness
lepidopterist
liberationist
lickerishness
lightsomeness
limitlessness
litigiousness
loathsomeness
lucrativeness
ludicrousness
luxuriousness
maladroitness
malariologist
maliciousness
malleableness
Malthusianism
Manichaeanism
martyrologist
masculineness
masterfulness
melodiousness
melodramatise
melodramatist
mercenariness
mercilessness
metagrobolise
meteorologist
microorganism
millennialism
millionairess
mirthlessness
misanthropist
miserableness
Mohammedanism
momentariness
momentousness
Monarchianism
monometallism
monometallist
Monophysitism
monosyllabism
Monotheletism
monstrousness
monumentalise
Muhammadanism
myrmecologist
navigableness
nefariousness
neoclassicism
neoclassicist
neoplasticism
nervelessness
niggardliness
noiselessness
nonconformism
nonconformist
notoriousness
objectiveness
obliviousness
obnoxiousness
obsessiveness
obstinateness
obtrusiveness
occasionalism
occasionalist
occidentalise
Occidentalism
Occidentalist
offensiveness
offhandedness
officiousness
operativeness
opportuneness
oppositionist
ornithologist
orthognathism
outspokenness
overemphasise
paedomorphism
painterliness
palatableness
pantagruelism
pantagruelist
paramagnetism
particularise
particularism
particularist
peaceableness
pedestrianise
pedestrianism
pendulousness
penuriousness
percussionist
perfectionism
perfectionist
pervasiveness
pharmaceutist
phenomenalise
phenomenalism
phenomenalist
philhellenism
philhellenist
photochromism
phraseologist
physiognomist
pigheadedness
plaintiveness
platitudinise
plausibleness
plenteousness
plentifulness
pococurantism
pointlessness
ponderousness
powerlessness
practicalness
predatoriness
prematureness
pricelessness
primitiveness
processionist
progressivism
projectionist
protectionism
protectionist
Protestantism
provincialise
provincialism
provincialist
prudentialism
prudentialist
psychoanalyse
psychoanalyst
psychometrist
pteridologist
purposiveness
querulousness
rapaciousness
rapturousness
receptiveness
recessiveness
recrystallise
regardfulness
regretfulness
religiousness
removableness
republicanise
republicanism
repulsiveness
requisiteness
resentfulness
retentiveness
revelationist
revolutionise
revolutionism
revolutionist
righteousness
sacerdotalise
sacerdotalism
sacerdotalist
sadomasochism
sadomasochist
sagaciousness
salaciousness
sanitationist
sansculottism
scholarliness
scholasticism
scientologist
scorpiongrass
scripturalism
scripturalist
seaworthiness
secondariness
secretiveness
sedentariness
seditiousness
seductiveness
selectiveness
selfawareness
selfcriticism
selfdispraise
semibarbarism
senselessness
sensitiveness
separableness
separationist
sericulturist
shamelessness
shapelessness
shiftlessness
sightlessness
sleeplessness
smokelessness
snowblindness
sobermindness
sorrowfulness
sovietologist
spelaeologist
Spencerianism
spermatoblast
spinelessness
spinninghouse
spiritualness
sprightliness
squeamishness
stainlessness
stalkinghorse
statelessness
steadfastness
stereoscopist
sternforemost
stomatologist
strenuousness
structuralism
structuralist
structureless
substantivise
sumptuousness
talkativeness
tastelessness
teachableness
technicalness
temperateness
temporariness
tenaciousness
tentativeness
thanklessness
thaumaturgist
theanthropism
theatricalise
theatricalism
thermochemist
thermotropism
thigmotropism
thrillingness
toastmistress
tolerableness
toothsomeness
traceableness
tractableness
Tractarianism
transistorise
tremulousness
tributariness
trichromatism
triliteralism
troublousness
unanimousness
uncertainness
uncleanliness
unearthliness
unfeelingness
unhealthiness
unicameralism
unicameralist
unmeaningness
unnaturalness
unselfishness
unwillingness
valuelessness
vapourishness
vegetarianism
venerableness
venereologist
ventriloquise
ventriloquism
ventriloquist
venturousness
veraciousness
vernacularise
vernacularism
vexatiousness
vicariousness
viniculturist
violoncellist
visionariness
viticulturist
vivaciousness
vocationalism
voicelessness
volcanologist
voluntariness
voraciousness
vulcanologist
wearisomeness
whimsicalness
wholesomeness
wonderfulness
worrisomeness
worthlessness
xanthochroism
absorbability
acceptability
accessibility
accoutrements
achromaticity
admissibility
aggiornamento
ambidexterity
anfractuosity
answerability
applicability
archdeaconate
archimandrite
artificiality
associativity
attainability
baccalaureate
basidiomycete
Bloomsburyite
changeability
circumvallate
coagulability
collaterality
commutability
comparability
compassionate
compatibility
concentricity
confraternity
connaturality
consanguinity
consentaneity
contractility
contrafagotto
correlativity
corrigibility
crystallinity
decontaminate
deductibility
defeasibility
defensibility
dependability
destructivity
differentiate
digestibility
disarticulate
disconformity
discontinuity
dispassionate
disposability
dissimilarity
dissolubility
egocentricity
equiponderate
excommunicate
expansibility
extensibility
ferroconcrete
filterability
formidability
hermaphrodite
heterogeneity
homosexuality
horizontality
hydrosulphite
immateriality
immiscibility
impalpability
impartibility
impassability
impassibility
impeccability
impecuniosity
impersonality
implacability
impossibility
improbability
improvability
inappropriate
inconsiderate
incredibility
indeterminate
individuality
ineducability
ineligibility
inevitability
inexorability
infallibility
infeasibility
inflexibility
infundibulate
inhospitality

insatiability
insensibility
insensitivity
insociability
instantaneity
insubordinate
intangibility
interdigitate
interosculate
invariability
invincibility
inviolability
irrationality
judgeadvocate
manageability
mensurability
metaphosphate
metastability
microtonality
multinucleate
negligibility
negotiability
nemathelminth
noncollegiate
nonconformity
occasionality
overelaborate
paranormality
particularity
pathogenicity
penetrability
perdurability
perishability
permutability
platyhelminth
polycarbonate
ponderability
predicability
preferability
PreRaphaelite
primordiality
procrastinate
professoriate
profitability
prognosticate
proportionate
provinciality
prudentiality
pusillanimity
quadrillionth
quadripartite
quadrumvirate
quadruplicate
quadruplicity
quintillionth
quintuplicate
radioactivity
receptibility
reciprocality
reconsolidate
reflexibility
reformability
resistibility
resolvability
retroactivity
reversibility
rhodochrosite
sacrosanctity
selffertility
selfpollinate
selfsterility
sequentiality
sesquiplicate
smellingsalts
solidungulate
spermatophyte
spheroidicity
squeezability
superfluidity
superhumanity
superordinate
supersaturate
supersubtlety
terminability
theatricality
transliterate
translucidity
triangularity
underestimate
undergraduate
unfamiliarity
unsociability
unsuitability
verifiability
vernacularity
viceadmiralty
vulnerability
acotyledonous
aluminiferous
ambidexterous
angiospermous
argentiferous
atlantosaurus
autocephalous
autochthonous
balsamiferous
bibliolatrous
brachypterous
broadspectrum
camphoraceous
carboniferous
carcinomatous
cartilaginous
chrysanthemum
cleistogamous
condylomatous
conscientious
consentaneous
diathermanous
dichlamydeous
discommodious
discontinuous
disharmonious
disrespectful
electrophorus
emphysematous
entomophagous
entomophilous
exanthematous
fossiliferous
garnetiferous
gasteropodous
gastrocnemius
graminivorous
gymnospermous
heterogeneous
heteropterous
heterosporous
horsechestnut
hydrocephalus
hymenopterous
ichthyosaurus
inconspicuous
inefficacious
insectivorous
instantaneous
lepidopterous
mammaliferous
manganiferous
megacephalous
membranaceous
metalliferous
microphyllous
miscellaneous
monodactylous
monotrematous
multitudinous
nectariferous
nickeliferous
odontoglossum
orthognathous
overcredulous
ovoviviparous
papaveraceous
papillomatous
perichondrium
perspicacious
petroliferous
phanerogamous
phyllophagous
platiniferous
platitudinous
plenitudinous
polliniferous
polyadelphous
polydactylous
porcellaneous
prolegomenous
proteinaceous
pusillanimous
quartziferous
sanctimonious
schizocarpous
scolopendrium
sculpturesque
selfconscious
selfforgetful
selfrighteous
semiconscious
serendipitous
splendiferous
staminiferous
stercoraceous
stoloniferous
stratocumulus
streptococcus
submachinegun
subreptitious
subterraneous
superstitious
surreptitious
tablespoonful
thermophilous
tintinnabulum
tyrannosaurus
umbelliferous
unceremonious
unpretentious
zinjanthropus
zygodactylous
accommodative
acculturative
agglomerative
agglutinative
appropriative
approximative
argumentative
authoritative
collaborative
commemorative
commiserative
communicative
comprehensive
concentrative
confederative
consolidative
contaminative
contemplative
contraceptive
corresponsive
corroborative
costeffective
counteractive
demonstrative
deteriorative
determinative
disseminative
electromotive
exteroceptive
frequentative
gesticulative
hallucinative
inconsecutive
incorporative
indistinctive
interoceptive
interpolative
interrogative
introspective
investigative
justificative
magnetomotive
manifestative
nonfigurative
nonproductive
oversensitive
participative
photoemissive
photopositive
postoperative
precipitative
prefigurative
premeditative
primogenitive
proliferative
ratiocinative
reciprocative
recriminative
reduplicative
remonstrative
resuscitative
retrogressive
retrospective
reverberative
selfassertive
selfdeceptive
significative
sniftingvalve
subordinative
transcriptive
transgressive
transmutative
uncompetitive
uninformative
archaeopteryx
perissodactyl

---

encyclopaedia
eschscholtzia
galactosaemia
hypermetropia
hypoglycaemia
megasporangia
nitrobacteria
paraphernalia
pharmacopoeia
prosthodontia
psychasthenia
Quinquagesima
schizophrenia
squandermania
villeggiatura
actinomorphic
allelomorphic
anachronistic
anaphrodisiac
AngloCatholic
anthelminthic
anthropogenic
anticlimactic
antiscorbutic
apheliotropic
archbishopric
architectonic
autocatalytic
bacteriolytic
BaltoSlavonic
bibliographic
cannibalistic
choreographic
chromatolytic
chromospheric
chronographic
conglomeratic
corticotropic
criminalistic
cryptanalytic
cryptographic
deterministic
diaphragmatic
electrometric
electroscopic
electrostatic
encyclopaedic
extragalactic
ferrimagnetic
ferroelectric
ferromagnetic
gastroenteric
gerontocratic
gonadotrophic
gynaecocratic
hemiparasitic
heptasyllabic
heterogenetic
heteromorphic
heterothallic
heterotrophic
homoeomorphic
homoiothermic
hydrocephalic
hydroelectric
hypermetropic
hypochondriac
idiosyncratic
imperialistic
intergalactic
interspecific
kaleidoscopic
laryngoscopic
leptocephalic
lexicographic
macrocephalic
materialistic
microcephalic
monochromatic
monogrammatic
monosymmetric
morphogenetic
nationalistic
nephelometric
neurastheniac
objectivistic
oceanographic
onomatopoetic
opportunistic
orthocephalic
palaeographic
pantisocratic
parasynthetic
paternalistic
pathognomonic
pharmacologic
philanthropic
photoelectric
photoperiodic
phreatophytic
physiographic
piezoelectric
pneumatolytic
pneumogastric
pointillistic
polarographic
polychromatic
polysynthetic

prescientific
protohistoric
pseudoarchaic
pseudomorphic
psilanthropic
psychodynamic
psychogenetic
psychokinetic
psychosomatic
psychrometric
rationalistic
RhaetoRomanic
schizophrenic
seismographic
selenocentric
selenographic
semiautomatic
semiparasitic
socioeconomic
spectrometric
spectroscopic
spermatogenic
stereographic
stratigraphic
stratospheric
synallagmatic
synchronistic
telegrammatic
theriomorphic
thermodynamic
thermoplastic
transatlantic
trigonometric
voluntaristic
zoogeographic
barrelchested
bloodboltered
brokenhearted
canaliculated
centreforward
chateaubriand
chuckleheaded
coarsegrained
crossgartered
disadvantaged
disinterested
distinguished
doublejointed
doubletongued
draggletailed
featherheaded
forementioned
fullfashioned
hocuspocussed
hollowhearted
hydromedusoid
hypertrophied
inexperienced
lightfingered
Maginotminded
miscomprehend
misunderstand
misunderstood
mouldingboard
multicoloured
neighbourhood
nitrocompound
northeastward
northwestward
outgeneralled
overpopulated
overqualified
particoloured
partridgewood
phosphoretted
pigeonchested
pigeonhearted
pigeonlivered
preengineered
quicktempered
rattlebrained
secretarybird
selfaddressed
selfappointed
selfcollected
selfconceited
selfcondemned
selfconfessed
selfcontained
selfcontented
selfconvicted
selfgenerated
selfinflicted
selfopinioned
selfpossessed
selfpropelled
selfsatisfied
selfsupported
selfsustained
semicivilised
seriousminded
shorttempered
silvertongued
singlehearted
sophisticated
soundingboard
southeastward
southwestward
spindlelegged
strawcoloured
swallowtailed
tenderhearted
thenceforward
thimblerigged
thoroughpaced
threecornered
unaccompanied
unadulterated
unanticipated
unarticulated
uncircumcised
uncomplicated
unconditioned
unconstrained
uncoordinated
undereducated
underemployed
undisciplined
unenlightened
unestablished
unimpassioned
uninterrupted
unprecedented
vantageground
versicoloured
wellapPointed
worldlyminded
accidentprone
accommodative
acculturative
acetylcholine
acrylonitrile
administrable
adventuresome
agglomerative
agglutinative
amphiprostyle
anagrammatise
anticlockwise
antihistamine
apprehensible
appropriative
approximative
arboriculture
archdeaconate
archimandrite
argumentative
ascertainable
asthenosphere
authoritative
baccalaureate
bacteriophage
basidiomycete
biodegradable
birefringence
Bloomsburyite
boardinghouse
bookingoffice
bouillabaisse
bureaucratise
challengeable
chinkerinchee
chlamydospore
Christmastide
Christmastime
chromatophore
circumference
circumfluence
circumvallate
clairaudience
clearinghouse
climbingframe
collaborative
collieshangie
commemorative
commensurable
commercialise
commiserative
communicative
companionable
compassionate
comprehensive
concentrative
conceptualise
concupiscence
concupiscible
confederative
conjecturable
consenescence
conservatoire
consolidative
constrainable
constructable
constructible
contaminative
contemplative
contraceptive
convalescence
conversazione
convertiplane
corresponsive
corroborative
cosmopolitise
costeffective
counteractive
counterchange
countercharge
counterstroke
countinghouse
daguerreotype
decontaminate
defervescence
deliquescence
dematerialise
demonstrative
demythologise
denationalise
depersonalise
deteriorative
determinative
diagrammatise
differentiate
disaffirmance
disappearance
disarticulate
disciplinable
discreditable
dishonourable
dispassionate
disseminative
dissimilitude
distributable
dressingtable
effervescence
efflorescence
electromotive
epigrammatise
equiponderate
exceptionable
excommunicate
exteroceptive
ferroconcrete
foreknowledge
fractionalise
frequentative
generalisable
gentlemanlike
gesticulative
hallucinative
hemicellulose
hermaphrodite
hydrochloride
hydrosulphide
hydrosulphite
hydroxylamine
immarcescible
immaterialise
imperceptible
impercipience
impermissible
impersonalise
imperturbable
impracticable
inappreciable
inappropriate
incandescence
incombustible
inconceivable
incondensable
inconsecutive
inconsequence
inconsiderate
inconsistence
incontestable
inconvenience
inconvertible
inconvincible
incorporative
incorruptible
indefatigable
indescribable
indeterminate
indiscernible
indispensable
indissociable
indistinctive
individualise
industrialise
inexhaustible
inexpressible
inflorescence
infundibulate
insubordinate
insufficience
insupportable
insusceptible
intercurrence
interdigitate
intermarriage
intermittence
interoceptive
interosculate
interpolative
interpretable
interrogative
interruptible
intransigence
introspective
introversible
investigative
irrationalise
irreclaimable
irrecoverable
irrefrangible
irreplaceable
irrepressible
irresponsible
irretrievable
judgeadvocate
jurisprudence
justificative
knowledgeable
macromolecule
magnetomotive
magnetosphere
magniloquence
manifestative
manipulatable
melodramatise
metagrobolise
metaphosphate
monumentalise
multinucleate
multiplicable
naphthylamine
nonappearance
nonattendance
noncollegiate
noncompliance
nondeductable
nonfigurative
nonproductive
nonresistance
nonreturnable
objectionable
occidentalise
oleomargarine
ostreiculture
overabundance
overelaborate
overemphasise
oversensitive
oversubscribe
participative
particularise
passementerie
pedestrianise
phenomenalise
phenylalanine
photoemissive
photopositive
picturepalace
platitudinise
pluripresence
pneumatophore
polycarbonate
polypropylene
postoperative
precipitative
prefigurative
premeditative
preponderance
prepreference
PreRaphaelite
primigravidae
primogenitive
primogeniture
procrastinate
professoriate
prognosticate
proliferative
pronounceable
proparoxytone
proportionate
provincialise

pseudoscience
psychoanalyse
pyrimethamine
quadripartite
quadrumvirate
quadruplicate
questionnaire
quintuplicate
ratiocinative
rearcommodore
recalcitrance
reciprocative
recommendable
reconsolidate
recriminative
recrudescence
recrystallise
reduplicative
remonstrative
reprehensible
representable
republicanise
resuscitative
retrogressive
retrospective
reverberative
revolutionise
rhadamanthine
rhodochrosite
sacerdotalise
schadenfreude
sculpturesque
selfassertive
selfassurance
selfdeceptive
selfdispraise
selfexistence
selfinsurance
selfknowledge
selfpollinate
selfsacrifice
semipermeable
sesquiplicate
sewingmachine
shootingbrake
shootingrange
shoulderblade
significative
sniftingvalve
solidungulate
somniloquence
spermatophore
spermatophyte
spinninghouse
sportsmanlike
stalkinghorse
statesmanlike
steppingstone
stickingplace
stirpiculture
subordinative
substantivise
substitutable
superannuable
supereminence
superordinate
supersaturate
supersensible
supervenience
tachistoscope
tetrasyllable
theatricalise
thereinbefore
thoroughbrace
transcendence
transcriptive
transformable
transgressive
transistorise
transliterate
transmissible
transmittable
transmutative
transportable
unaccountable
uncomfortable
uncompetitive
unconceivable
unconformable
unconquerable
undercarriage
underestimate
underexposure
undergraduate
unfashionable
unforgettable
unimpeachable
uninformative
unmentionable
unpredictable
unputdownable
unwarrantable
ventriloquise
vernacularise
volatilisable
accommodating
auctioneering
backpedalling
bloodcurdling
brainstorming
breechloading
cabinetmaking
cottonpicking
crosshatching
crystalgazing
decontrolling
disconcerting
doubledealing
doubleglazing
eavesdropping
globetrotting
hairsplitting
heartbreaking
horsewhipping
housebreaking
hydrocracking
intercropping
jerrybuilding
leadpoisoning
levelcrossing
lineengraving
longsuffering
merchandising
moneygrubbing
mouthwatering
nonconducting
nonconforming
nonforfeiting
pennyfarthing
pennypinching
prayermeeting
prepossessing
pretermitting
prizefighting
profitsharing
sabrerattling
scintillating
selfadjusting
selfapproving
selfasserting
selfconsuming
selfdeceiving
selfdefeating
selfdirecting
selfexecuting
selfgoverning
selfrecording
selfregarding
selfreproving
selfrevealing
selfsufficing
sharecropping
sharpshooting
sheepshearing
sidesplitting
skateboarding
softpedalling
soulsearching
squarebashing
streetwalking
swashbuckling
taperecording
telerecording
thermosetting
thoroughgoing
timeconsuming
tonguelashing
transshipping
uncomplaining
underclothing
understanding
underwhelming
unforthcoming
unquestioning
waterproofing
wonderworking
woodengraving
woolgathering
butterflyfish
buttonthrough
chromatograph
cinematograph
featherstitch
followthrough
gynandromorph
kinematograph
lamellibranch
liebfraumilch
nemathelminth
opisthobranch
phonautograph
platyhelminth
quadrillionth
quintillionth
runningstitch
slangingmatch
anthropophagi
conversazioni
micrococcocci
counterattack
laughingstock
mackerelshark
mourningcloak
shootingstick
thunderstruck
abstractional
aerodynamical
ambassadorial
anomalistical
antipersonnel
apocalyptical
arbitrational
archidiaconal
architectural
astronautical
astrophysical
atmospherical
bathymetrical
bibliological
cacographical
Calvinistical
cerebrospinal
chronological
coeducational
combinatorial
compartmental
compositional
compressional
computational
conchological
congressional
conjugational
conjunctional
consequential
controversial
convocational
courtsmartial
crackerbarrel
craniological
crosscultural
cryptological
deformational
deontological
developmental
disrespectful
dissymetrical
dramaturgical
dysfunctional
embryological
entomological
environmental
epiphenomenal
equipotential
Eucharistical
examinational
examinatorial
excrescential
explorational
expurgatorial
exterritorial
extrajudicial
extraphysical
extratropical
floricultural
foraminiferal
gastrological
gastronomical
glaciological
goniometrical
graphological
gravitational
gubernatorial
hemispherical
hermeneutical
homoiothermal
horticultural
hydrometrical
hydrostatical
hyperboloidal
hypercritical
hypermetrical
hyperphysical
ideographical
immunological
infinitesimal
informational
inquisitional
inquisitorial
inscriptional
inspirational
institutional
instructional
insubstantial
intercolonial
intercultural
interjectural
international
interparietal
interpersonal
intertropical
intraarterial
intrapersonal
irreverential
lackadaisical
lancecorporal
legislatorial
malacological
mangoldwurzel
manneristical
metallurgical
Methodistical
microscopical
mineralogical
monophthongal
morphological
multinational
musicological
nomenclatural
numerological
observational
ochlocratical
odontological
oreographical
palynological
pantheistical
parasiticidal
parenthetical
perichondrial
perissodactyl
petrochemical
philosophical
photochemical
phrenological
physiological
piscicultural
planimetrical
postclassical
postulational
predicamental
prehistorical
premillennial
prepositional
preternatural
problematical
procuratorial
progenitorial
progressional
propositional
proprietorial
protonotarial
psychological
pyrotechnical
quadragesimal
quadricipital
quadrilateral
reformational
seismological
selenological
selfforgetful
semeiological
septentrional
shabbygenteel
sociocultural
somatological
speleological
spinningwheel
sprocketwheel
streptococcal
subsequential
substructural
subternatural
supercritical
supernational
superphysical
suppositional
supranational
tablespoonful
technological
temperamental
teratological
tercentennial
terminational
topographical
tortoiseshell
toxicological

translational
transnational
tricentennial
tritheistical
troglodytical
typographical
unconditional
unexceptional
ungrammatical
unintentional
unsubstantial
unsymmetrical
ventriloquial
vivisectional
xylographical
accidentalism
anagrammatism
antilogarithm
antinomianism
Australianism
autochthonism
autoeroticism
Berkeleianism
bibliophilism
blackguardism
broadspectrum
ceremonialism
chrysanthemum
colloquialism
commercialism
conceptualism
corporativism
cosmopolitism
diageotropism
doctrinairism
ecumenicalism
encephalogram
encyclopedism
equestrianism
ethnocentrism
exhibitionism
expressionism
feuilletonism
flagellantism
functionalism
geocentricism
histrionicism
homeomorphism
immaterialism
impressionism
indeterminism
individualism
industrialism
infallibilism
irrationalism
Malthusianism
Manichaeanism
microorganism
millennialism
Mohammedanism
Monarchianism
monometallism
Monophysitism
monosyllabism
Monotheletism
Muhammadanism
neoclassicism
neoplasticism
nonconformism
occasionalism
Occidentalism
odontoglossum
orangeblossom
orthognathism
paedomorphism
pantagruelism
parallelogram
paramagnetism
particularism
pedestrianism
perfectionism
perichondrium
phenomenalism
philhellenism
photochromism
pococurantism
progressivism
protectionism
Protestantism
provincialism
prudentialism
radiotelegram
republicanism
revolutionism
roentgenogram
sacerdotalism
sadomasochism
sansculottism
scholasticism
scolopendrium
scripturalism
selfcriticism
semibarbarism
semilogarithm
Spencerianism
structuralism
theanthropism
theatricalism
thermotropism
thigmotropism
tintinnabulum
topsyturvydom
Tractarianism
trichromatism
triliteralism
unicameralism
vegetarianism
ventriloquism
vernacularism
vocationalism
xanthochroism
acclimatation
accommodation
accreditation
acculturation
acetification
acidification
actualisation
afforestation
agglomeration
agglutination
aircraftwoman
aluminisation
amplification
anglicisation
AngloAmerican
animadversion
animalisation
Antichristian
appropriation
approximation
argumentation
arithmetician
aromatisation
assassination
asserveration
authorisation
authoritarian
backformation
backwardation
balkanisation
barbarisation
beatification
beneficiation
bildungsroman
bloodrelation
boustrophedon
brutalisation
businesswoman
calcification
caprification
carbonisation
catechisation
cauterisation
certification
cicatrisation
circumvention
clarification
collaboration
commemoration
commiseration
communication
communisation
communitarian
compagination
comprehension
concatenation
concentration
condescension
confabulation
confederation
configuration
conflagration
confrontation
congresswoman
consideration
consolidation
constellation
consternation
contamination
contemplation
contrabassoon
contraception
contradiction
contravention
cornification
corroboration
corticotropin
counteraction
crossquestion
decerebration
decomposition
decompression
decortication
decrepitation
defibrination
deforestation
degranulation
demonstration
denticulation
deodorisation
derequisition
derestriction
desegregation
deterioration
determination
diagnostician
discoloration
disconcertion
disconnection
displantation
dispossession
disproportion
dissemination
disseveration
dissimilation
dissimulation
documentation
domestication
domiciliation
dramatisation
dulcification
electrocution
encapsulation
entomostracan
epiphenomenon
equilibration
expectoration
expostulation
expropriation
extermination
extrapolation
extravasation
falsification
fasciculation
fertilisation
festschriften
feudalisation
formalisation
formulisation
fortification
fossilisation
fractionation
fragmentation
freeselection
frequentation
funambulation
galvanisation
germanisation
gesticulation
glamorisation
glorification
gonadotrophin
gratification
halfsovereign
hallucination
harmonisation
horripilation
hybridisation
hydrogenation
hypnotisation
hypothecation
impenetration
impersonation
impropriation
improvisation
incarceration
incardination
incorporation
indisposition
individuation
ingurgitation
intercalation
interlocution
interpolation
interposition
interpunction
interrelation
interrogation
interspersion
introgression
introspection
investigation
isomerisation
italicisation
jollification
justification
juxtaposition
laevorotation
lignification
Machiavellian
machicolation
magnetisation
magnification
malacostracan
maladaptation
manifestation
martyrisation
mathematician
matriculation
meadowsaffron
mechanisation
mediatisation
mediterranean
mercerisation
mesencephalon
mesmerisation
metallisation
metaphysician
metrification
miscegenation
misconception
mitochondrion
modernisation
mollification
monocotyledon
mortification
mummification
mutualisation
mystification
necessitarian
necessitation
nightwatchman
nitrification
nonaggression
normalisation
nucleoprotein
nullification
orchestration
ornamentation
overvaluation
paediatrician
palletisation
panicstricken
pantagruelian
participation
Pennsylvanian
peptonisation
perambulation
peregrination
periodisation
perseveration
petrification
phalansterian
photoelectron
photoemission
phycoerythrin
phytoplankton
pluralisation
polycotyledon
polyhistorian
pontification
postcommunion
precipitation
preconception
predomination
prefiguration
premeditation
preoccupation
preordination
prepossession
pretermission
prevarication
proliferation
prolification
pronunciation
prostaglandin
pulverisation
qualification
radiolocation
randomisation
ratiocination
reaffirmation
reciprocation
recombination
recomposition
recrimination
rectification
redescription
reduplication
reembarkation
reexamination
reforestation
refrigeration
regimentation

regurgitation
reincarnation
reintegration
remonstration
renegotiation
reorientation
republication
resuscitation
retranslation
retrogression
retrospection
revaccination
revendication
reverberation
ritualisation
Russification
scarification
scintillation
scleroprotein
scorification
sedimentation
selfassertion
selfcommunion
selfdeception
selfdirection
selfeducation
selfinduction
semibarbarian
semiporcelain
sensitisation
sequestration
SerboCroatian
serialisation
Shakespearean
Shakespearian
signalisation
signification
smoothingiron
socialisation
solderingiron
solemnisation
specification
stabilisation
sterilisation
strangulation
subirrigation
submachinegun
subordination
subsaturation
subtilisation
suffumigation
summarisation
superaddition
superfetation
superposition
supplantation
Swedenborgian
syllabication
symbolisation
tantalisation
telencephalon
teleportation
temporisation
terpsichorean
terrorisation
testification
thurification
transcription
transgression
translocation
transmutation
transpiration
transposition
triangulation
tuberculation
verbalisation
verbigeration
vermiculation
vernalisation
versification
victimisation
visualisation
vitrification
vulcanisation
vulgarisation
weatherbeaten
Zarathustrian
aggiornamento
contrafagotto
fortississimo
generalissimo
incommunicado
associateship
chieftainship
churchmanship
colleagueship
collectorship
commandership
companionship
conductorship
containership
copartnership
craftsmanship
draftsmanship
inspectorship
landownership
librarianship
moderatorship
precentorship
presidentship
principalship
proconsulship
professorship
protectorship
secretaryship
shoulderstrap
solicitorship
sportsmanship
statesmanship
subeditorship
suffraganship
surrogateship
swordsmanship
treasurership
accelerometer
administrator
affenpinscher
alcoholometer
authenticator
backscratcher
battlecruiser
bibliographer
biogeographer
blanketflower
candlelighter
candlesnuffer
cardiographer
chemoreceptor
choreographer
concertmaster
congratulator
counterfeiter
cryptographer
discriminator
disintegrator
doublecrosser
dressimprover
electioneerer
extracellular
extravascular
fibrovascular
fortunehunter
fortuneteller
glossographer
granddaughter
harbourmaster
helterskelter
indoctrinator
intelligencer
intercellular
intercolumnar
intermediator
interpellator
intracellular
intramuscular
kapellmeister
Kidderminster
knickerbocker
knuckleduster
laissezpasser
lexicographer
lifepreserver
machinegunner
maladminister
meistersinger
microdetector
monomolecular
mourningpaper
multicellular
neurovascular
oceanographer
owneroccupier
oystercatcher
paddlesteamer
palaeographer
passionflower
perpendicular
philosophiser
photoreceptor
physiographer
pneumatometer
potentiometer
prairieoyster
predestinator
proprioceptor
pyrheliometer
quartermaster
reconstructor
refractometer
reinvigorator
rollercoaster
saccharimeter
saccharometer
scandalmonger
schoolteacher
seismographer
selenographer
selfslaughter
selfsurrender
selftormentor
semiconductor
sergeantmajor
shockabsorber
sicklefeather
somnambulator
stationmaster
steeplechaser
strikebreaker
subcontractor
subpostmaster
supercalender
tergiversator
thermonuclear
thimblerigger
thoughtreader
thundershower
tintinnabular
tonguetwister
tranquilliser
transmigrator
turkeygobbler
underachiever
understrapper
volumenometer
wheelerdealer
whithersoever
windowshopper
zoogeographer
accoutrements
acotyledonous
actinomycetes
actinomycosis
admirableness
advisableness
affectionless
agreeableness
airworthiness
aluminiferous
ambidexterous
ambiguousness
ambitiousness
amniocentesis
amorphousness
analogousness
angiospermous
anomalousness
anonymousness
arbitrariness
argentiferous
assertiveness
assiduousness
atlantosaurus
atrociousness
attentiveness
audaciousness
autocatalysis
autocephalous
autochthonous
availableness
bacteriolysis
balsamiferous
barbarousness
barefacedness
beauteousness
belleslettres
betweenwhiles
bibliolatrous
bioenergetics
blameableness
blamelessness
blastogenesis
bloodlessness
boundlessness
bounteousness
bountifulness
brachypterous
brainlessness
brilliantness
brotherliness
bumptiousness
butterfingers
callisthenics
camphoraceous
capaciousness
carboniferous
carcinomatous
cartilaginous
changefulness
characterless
cheerlessness
chlamydomonas
chrematistics
cleistogamous
coenaesthesis
collectedness
colourfulness
combativeness
companionless
complexedness
compositeness
conceitedness
conduciveness
condylomatous
confidingness
congruousness
conjugateness
connectedness
conscientious
consciousness
consentaneous
contentedness
corrosiveness
courteousness
credulousness
crosspurposes
cryptanalysis
customariness
dangerousness
dastardliness
dauntlessness
deathlessness
deceitfulness
deceptiveness
deciduousness
defectiveness
deliciousness
deliriousness
desirableness
desperateness
desultoriness
dexterousness
diathermanous
dichlamydeous
diffusiveness
dimensionless
discommodious
discontinuous
disharmonious
disparateness
dissoluteness
doubtlessness
dreamlessness
effectiveness
egregiousness
elaborateness
electrophorus
elephantiasis
embryogenesis
emphysematous
enjoyableness
entomophagous
entomophilous
epeirogenesis
equivocalness
erroneousness
essentialness
evocativeness
exanthematous
excessiveness
excitableness
exclusiveness
excursiveness
excusableness
exemplariness
expansiveness
expensiveness
explosiveness
exquisiteness
extensiveness
facetiousness
faithlessness
faultlessness
felicitations
feloniousness
ferociousness
foolhardiness
forgetfulness
fortunateness
fossiliferous
fractiousness
frightfulness
frivolousness
frontogenesis
fruitlessness
gametogenesis

garnetiferous
garrulousness
gasteropodous
gastrocnemius
glutinousness
gracelessness
graminivorous
greensickness
grotesqueness
guilelessness
guiltlessness
gymnospermous
habitableness
haphazardness
hazardousness
healthfulness
heartlessness
heartsickness
heebiejeebies
helminthiasis
heterogeneous
heterogenesis
heteropterous
heterosporous
hilariousness
hydrocephalus
hydrodynamics
hymenopterous
hypnoanalysis
ichthyosaurus
identicalness
illogicalness
imitativeness
immediateness
immovableness
immutableness
impassiveness
imperfectness
imperiousness
impetuousness
imponderables
impulsiveness
inanimateness
inclusiveness
inconspicuous
incorrectness
incorruptness
incurableness
incuriousness
inductiveness
ineffableness
inefficacious
inflexionless
ingeniousness
ingenuousness
injuriousness
innocuousness
innoxiousness
insectivorous
insensateness
insidiousness
insolubleness
instantaneous
intensiveness
interpretress
intricateness
intrusiveness
intuitiveness
inventiveness
invidiousness
inviolateness
invisibleness
irritableness
judiciousness
laboriousness
laughableness
lecherousness
leishmaniasis
leisureliness
lepidopterous
leptospirosis
lickerishness
lightsomeness
limitlessness
litigiousness
loathsomeness
lucrativeness
ludicrousness
luxuriousness
maladroitness
maliciousness
malleableness
mammaliferous
manganiferous
masculineness
masterfulness
materfamilias
megacephalous
melodiousness
melodramatics
membranaceous
mercenariness
mercilessness
metalliferous
metamorphoses
metamorphosis
microanalysis
microphyllous
millefeuilles
millionairess
mirthlessness
miscellaneous
miserableness
mnemotechnics
momentariness
momentousness
monodactylous
mononucleosis
monotrematous
monstrousness
morphogenesis
multitudinous
navigableness
nectariferous
nefariousness
nervelessness
nickeliferous
niggardliness
noiselessness
notoriousness
objectiveness
obliviousness
obnoxiousness
obsessiveness
obstinateness
obtrusiveness
offensiveness
offhandedness
officiousness
operativeness
opportuneness
organogenesis
orthognathous
osteomyelitis
outspokenness
overcredulous
ovoviviparous
painterliness
palatableness
papaveraceous
paperhangings
papillomatous
parasynthesis
paterfamilias
peaceableness
pendulousness
penuriousness
perspicacious
pervasiveness
petroliferous
phanerogamous
pharmaceutics
photochromics
phyllophagous
pigheadedness
plaintiveness
platiniferous
platitudinous
plausibleness
plenitudinous
plenteousness
plentifulness
pneumatolysis
pointlessness
poliomyelitis
polliniferous
polyadelphous
polydactylous
polysynthesis
ponderousness
porcellaneous
powerlessness
practicalness
predatoriness
prematureness
pricelessness
primitiveness
prolegomenous
proteinaceous
psychogenesis
psychokinesis
psychometrics
psychophysics
purposiveness
pusillanimous
quartziferous
querulousness
rapaciousness
rapturousness
receptiveness
recessiveness
regardfulness
regretfulness
religiousness
removableness
repulsiveness
requisiteness
resentfulness
retentiveness
righteousness
sagaciousness
salaciousness
salmonellosis
sanctimonious
schizocarpous
schizogenesis
scholarliness
scorpiongrass
seaworthiness
secondariness
secretiveness
sedentariness
seditiousness
seductiveness
selectiveness
selfawareness
selfconscious
selfrighteous
semiconscious
senselessness
sensitiveness
separableness
serendipitous
shamelessness
shapelessness
shiftlessness
sightlessness
sleeplessness
smellingsalts
smokelessness
snowblindness
sobermindness
sorrowfulness
spindleshanks
spinelessness
spiritualness
splendiferous
sprightliness
squeamishness
stainlessness
staminiferous
statelessness
steadfastness
stercoraceous
stoloniferous
stratocumulus
strenuousness
streptococcus
structureless
subreptitious
subterraneous
sumptuousness
superfamilies
superstitious
surreptitious
talkativeness
tastelessness
teachableness
technicalness
temperateness
temporalities
temporariness
tenaciousness
tentativeness
thanklessness
thermogenesis
thermophilous
threequarters
thrillingness
tiddledywinks
toastmistress
tolerableness
toothsomeness
toxoplasmosis
traceableness
tractableness
tremulousness
tributariness
troublousness
tyrannosaurus
umbelliferous
unanimousness
unceremonious
uncertainness
uncleanliness
underemphasis
unearthliness
unfeelingness
unhealthiness
unmeaningness
unnaturalness
unpretentious
unselfishness
unwillingness
valuelessness
vapourishness
venerableness
venturousness
veraciousness
vexatiousness
vicariousness
visionariness
vivaciousness
voicelessness
voluntariness
voraciousness
wearisomeness
whimsicalness
wholesomeness
winterberries
wonderfulness
worrisomeness
worthlessness
zinjanthropus
zygodactylous
abortifacient
accompaniment
admeasurement
advertisement
affreightment
agriculturist
annexationist
anticoagulant
apportionment
archaeologist
ascertainment
Assyriologist
bamboozlement
beleaguerment
bibliolatrist
bibliophilist
calligraphist
campanologist
ceremonialist
cinquecentist
circumambient
climatologist
closedcircuit
clothesbasket
cobelligerent
commercialist
conceptualist
contortionist
contrabandist
contrapuntist
coreligionist
correspondent
corruptionist
counterweight
criminologist
cruiserweight
cryobiologist
cyberneticist
deipnosophist
dermatologist
deuteragonist
Deuteronomist
devolutionist
disembodiment
disengagement
disfigurement
disinvestment
dismantlement
dismemberment
disparagement
divertisement
documentalist
dodecaphonist
electrologist
electromagnet
electrovalent
embarrassment
embellishment
embranglement
embrittlement
encompassment
encouragement
encyclopedist
enlightenment
entertainment
epigrammatist
equiponderant
eschatologist
establishment
exhibitionist

expressionist
featherweight
feuilletonist
functionalist
gerontologist
grandiloquent
gynaecologist
haematologist
herpetologist
homoeopathist
horsechestnut
hundredweight
ichthyologist
immaterialist
impressionist
indeterminist
individualist
industrialist
infallibilist
insignificant
interlacement
intransigeant
irrationalist
irreligionist
lancesergeant
leatherjacket
lepidopterist
letterperfect
liberationist
maladjustment
malariologist
martyrologist
melodramatist
meteorologist
micronutrient
misanthropist
misgovernment
mismanagement
monometallist
myrmecologist
neoclassicist
nonconformist
nonfulfilment
nongovernment
occasionalist
Occidentalist
omnicompetent
oppositionist
ornithologist
overconfident
overindulgent
overstatement
pantagruelist
particularist
percussionist
perfectionist
pharmaceutist
phenomenalist
philhellenist
phraseologist
physiognomist
preengagement
prefigurement
preordainment
processionist
projectionist
pronouncement
protectionist
provincialist
prudentialist
psychoanalyst
psychometrist
pteridologist
quinquevalent
rearrangement
reconcilement
redevelopment
reimbursement
reinforcement
reinstatement
rejuvenescent
replenishment
revelationist
revolutionist
sacerdotalist
sadomasochist
sanitationist
scientologist
scrapmerchant
scripturalist
searchwarrant
selfabasement
selfconfident
selfdependent
selfimportant
selfindulgent
selfrepugnant
selfrestraint
semipermanent
separationist
sericulturist
sovietologist
spelaeologist
spermatoblast
stereoscopist
sternforemost
stomatologist
structuralist
sublieutenant
superabundant
superdominant
thaumaturgist
thermochemist
transshipment
unicameralist
unintelligent
venereologist
ventriloquist
vicepresident
viniculturist
violoncellist
viticulturist
volcanologist
vouchsafement
vulcanologist
archaeopteryx
cephalothorax
concavoconvex
convexoconvex
interlocutrix
abiologically
absorbability
acceptability
accessibility
achromaticity
acquiescently
acquiescingly
acrimoniously
acrobatically
adiabatically
admissibility
admonishingly
adventurously
adversatively
aesthetically
affirmatively
aggravatingly
agonistically
alcoholically
alcoholometry
algebraically
allegorically
alternatively
ambidexterity
anachronously
anaerobically
anfractuosity
answerability
anthropometry
anthropopathy
anthropophagy
anthroposophy
apathetically
appellatively
applicability
applicatively
appropriately
approximately
arthritically
artificiality
associativity
asthmatically
astonishingly
atheistically
atomistically
attainability
attributively
authentically
autobiography
automatically
autonomically
axiomatically
belligerently
bewilderingly
biotechnology
blasphemously
bombastically
brachycephaly
brachydactyly
broadmindedly
burglariously
calculatingly
carnivorously
categorically
centrifugally
centripetally
ceremoniously
certificatory
chalcography
challengingly
changeability
chromatically
cinematically
circumspectly
clandestinely
clearheadedly
climactically
coagulability
coldbloodedly
coldheartedly
collaterality
commemoratory
commensurably
communicatory
commutability
companionably
comparability
comparatively
compatibility
compendiously
competitively
complainingly
complaisantly
complementary
complicatedly
complimentary
concentricity
concessionary
concomitantly
concretionary
conditionally
confabulatory
confectionary
confectionery
confessionary
conflictingly
confraternity
conjecturally
conjunctively
connaturality
consanguinity
consecutively
consentaneity
considerately
consolidatory
conspicuously
constellatory
constrainedly
consumptively
contentiously
continentally
contractility
contractually
contradictory
contrariously
conventionary
convulsionary
cooperatively
correlatively
correlativity
corrigibility
corroboratory
crystallinity
curvilinearly
cylindrically
cytochemistry
declaratively
deductibility
defeasibility
defencelessly
defensibility
deferentially
deleteriously
dendritically
dependability
deprecatingly
descriptively
destructively
destructivity
determinately
detrimentally
devastatingly
devolutionary
dialectically
diametrically
dichotomously
dictatorially
digestibility
dimensionally
disaffectedly
disconformity
discontinuity
discreditably
discretionary
disgracefully
dishonourably
disjunctively
disobediently
disparagingly
disposability
dispraisingly
dissemblingly
dissimilarity
dissolubility
distastefully
distinctively
distressfully
distressingly
distrustfully
eccentrically
educationally
effervescency
efficaciously
egocentricity
encouragingly
endocrinology
energetically
enigmatically
equidistantly
evangelically
everlastingly
exasperatedly
exceptionably
exceptionally
existentially
expansibility
expeditionary
expeditiously
explanatorily
exponentially
expostulatory
extemporarily
extensibility
extensionally
exterminatory
extraordinary
extravagantly
extrinsically
facultatively
fantastically
fascinatingly
Fascistically
filterability
fissiparously
flirtatiously
floristically
flourishingly
foresightedly
formidability
fragmentarily
frighteningly
frustratingly
fundamentally
geochronology
geometrically
geomorphology
geostationary
geotropically
gesticulatory
goodnaturedly
grammatically
grandfatherly
grandmotherly
gymnastically
halfheartedly
hallucinatory
hardheartedly
helminthology
heterogeneity
homogeneously
homosexuality
honorifically
horizontality
hydraulically
ichthyography
ideologically
idiomatically
ignominiously
illustriously
imaginatively
immateriality
immiscibility
immunotherapy
impalpability
impartibility
impassability
impassibility
impeccability
impecuniosity
imperceptibly
impersonality
impertinently
imperturbably
implacability
implicatively

impolitically
importunately
impossibility
impracticably
impractically
improbability
improvability
improvidently
improvisatory
inadvertently
inappreciably
inattentively
incompetently
inconceivably
incongruously
inconsistency
incontestably
incontinently
inconveniency
inconvertibly
incorporeally
incorruptibly
incredibility
incredulously
incrementally
incriminatory
indefatigably
independently
indescribably
indeterminacy
indifferently
indiscernibly
indispensably
individuality
industriously
ineducability
ineffectively
ineffectually
inefficiently
ineligibility
inevitability
inexhaustibly
inexorability
inexpediently
inexpensively
inexpressibly
infallibility
infeasibility
inferentially
inflexibility
influentially
informatively
infuriatingly
inhospitality
injudiciously
inoffensively
inopportunely
inorganically
inquisitively
insatiability
insensibility
insensitively
insensitivity
insinuatingly
insociability
instantaneity
instinctively
instructively
insufficiency
insupportably
intangibility
integumentary
intelligently
intemperately
intentionally
interdentally
interestingly
interlocutory
interrogatory
interstratify
intravenously
intrinsically
invariability
inventorially
investigatory
invincibility
inviolability
involuntarily
irrationality
irreclaimably
irrecoverably
irreligiously
irrepressibly
irresponsibly
irretrievably
isochronously
isometrically
isostatically
jiggerypokery
judgmatically
justificatory
kinematically
knowledgeably
laevorotatory
languishingly
legislatively
lethargically
lightheadedly
lightmindedly
linseywoolsey
macaronically
magisterially
magnanimously
magnificently
manageability
matrilineally
mellifluously
mensurability
meritoriously
metallography
metastability
metonymically
microtonality
ministerially
mischievously
mistrustfully
mistrustingly
mothercountry
mountainously
mountebankery
mutagenically
nearsightedly
necessitously
negligibility
negotiability
nightmarishly
nonconformity
nonsensically
northeasterly
northwesterly
nostalgically
numismatology
nutritionally
objectionably
obstructively
occasionality
octocentenary
odoriferously
oecologically
ontogenically
ontologically
openheartedly
ophthalmology
opinionatedly
opprobriously
organotherapy
outstandingly
overbearingly
painstakingly
palaeontology
palaeozoology
panegyrically
parabolically
paradoxically
paranormality
parasitically
parliamentary
parthenocarpy
participatory
particularity
pathogenicity
patriotically
patronisingly
pedagogically
penetrability
penetratingly
penetratively
penitentially
perambulatory
perdurability
perfunctorily
perishability
permutability
perspectively
perspicuously
pestiferously
pharisaically
phenomenology
phrenetically
physiotherapy
picturesquely
plethorically
pneumatically
pneumonectomy
ponderability
pragmatically
precautionary
precipitantly
precipitately
precipitously
predicability
predicatively
predominantly
prefatorially
preferability
prejudicially
preliminarily
premonitorily
preparatively
preparatorily
preponderancy
prestigiously
presumptively
pretentiously
primogenitary
primordiality
prismatically
probationally
processionary
profitability
progressively
prohibitively
prolegomenary
proliferously
promiscuously
prophetically
prosopography
prospectively
protuberantly
provinciality
provisionally
prudentiality
psychosurgery
psychotherapy
punctiliously
puritanically
purposelessly
pusillanimity
quadrennially
quadruplicity
qualificatory
qualitatively
quarrelsomely
questioningly
quickwittedly
quincentenary
quincuncially
quingentenary
quinquagenary
radioactivity
realistically
receptibility
reciprocality
recriminatory
rectangularly
rectilinearly
referentially
reflexibility
reformability
reminiscently
remonstrantly
remorselessly
repetitionary
repetitiously
reprehensibly
reproachfully
reproachingly
resistibility
resolvability
resourcefully
resplendently
restoratively
restrictively
retroactively
retroactivity
reverberatory
reverentially
reversibility
revolutionary
rhapsodically
rheumatically
righthandedly
roentgenology
rontgenoscopy
rudimentarily
saccharimetry
sacramentally
sacrificially
sacrosanctity
sarcastically
schematically
scorbutically
scrumptiously
selfassuredly
selfcentredly
selfdiscovery
selfevidently
selffertility
selfpityingly
selfsterility
sensationally
sententiously
sentimentally
sequentiality
serologically
significantly
sophistically
southeasterly
southwesterly
spasmodically
spectacularly
spectrography
speculatively
spheroidicity
sphygmography
splenetically
spontaneously
squeezability
standoffishly
statistically
stigmatically
stoichiometry
strategically
stylistically
subordinately
subserviently
substantially
substantively
subversionary
suffocatingly
sulphureously
superficially
superfluidity
superfluously
superhumanity
superlatively
supernumerary
supersubtlety
supplementary
symbiotically
symmetrically
symphonically
symphoniously
synchronously
syntactically
synthetically
tantalisingly
tautologously
taxonomically
televisionary
temerariously
tempestuously
tendentiously
terminability
terminatively
terrestrially
territorially
thalassocracy
theatricality
theologically
theoretically
thoughtlessly
thrasonically
threateningly
thremmatology
titillatingly
tonsillectomy
topologically
traditionally
transcendency
transitionary
translucently
translucidity
transparently
transpiratory
transversally
traumatically
treacherously
triangularity
troublesomely
trustworthily
typologically
unaccountably
unambiguously
unbelievingly
uncomfortably
unconcernedly
unconsciously
underhandedly
unemotionally
unequivocally
unfamiliarity
unfashionably
unflinchingly
unforgettably

unfortunately
unnecessarily
unobtrusively
unpromisingly
unqualifiedly
unrelentingly
unremittingly
unrighteously
unsociability
unsuitability
untrustworthy
unwarrantably
unwholesomely
vacillatingly
venturesomely
verifiability
verisimilarly
vernacularity
vertiginously
viceadmiralty
vulnerability
wrongheadedly

14 letter words

abovementioned
absentmindedly
absorptiveness
abstemiousness
abstractedness
abstractionism
abstractionist
acceleratingly
acceptableness
accomplishable
accomplishment
accountability
accumulatively
accustomedness
achondroplasia
achromatically
acknowledgment
administration
administrative
administratrix
advantageously
adventitiously
aerobiological
aerobiotically
aerodynamicist
aesthesiometer
aetiologically
affectionately
aforementioned
Africanisation
aggrandisement
aggressiveness
agrobiological
airconditioner
Albigensianism
allegorisation
allelomorphism
alphabetically
alphanumerical
altruistically
amateurishness
ambassadorship
ambidextrously
anagrammatical
anthropography
anthropologist
anthropometric
anticipatively
anticonvulsant
antidepressant
antifederalist
antiperspirant
antiphlogistic
antiquarianism
antiscriptural
antiseptically
antithetically
aphoristically
apologetically
apophthegmatic
apoplectically
apothegmatical
appendicectomy
apprehensively
apprenticeship
archaeological
archetypically
archidiaconate
archiepiscopal
architectonics
arithmetically
arrhythmically
arrondissement
articulateness
artificialness
associationism
astronomically
astrophysicist
asymmetrically
asymptotically
asynchronously
attainableness
attractiveness
audiofrequency
Augustinianism
auspiciousness
authentication
autobiographer
autobiographic
autocratically
autoradiograph
autosuggestion
avariciousness
backscattering
backscratching
bacteriologist
bacteriostasis
bacteriostatic
barometrically
basidiomycetes
bastardisation
bathingmachine
beautification
behaviouristic
beneficialness
bibliographise
bibliomaniacal
biodegradation
bioelectricity
bioengineering
biographically
bioluminescent
biosystematics
bituminisation
blackmarketeer
blockaderunner
bloodthirstily
boardingschool
boisterousness
boroughEnglish
bougainvillaea
bouleversement
bowdlerisation
brachycephalic
breathlessness
breathtakingly
bremsstrahlung
Brobdingnagian
bronchiectasis
bullheadedness
butterfingered
butterflyscrew
calamitousness
calcareousness
campanological
campylotropous
cantankerously
capitalisation
capriciousness
carcinogenesis
cardiovascular
cartographical
castrametation
catachrestical
catechetically
categorisation
censoriousness
centralisation
centrifugation
chancellorship
changeableness
characteristic
charitableness
chemoreception
chemoreceptive
chemosynthesis
chickenhearted
chickenlivered
chincherinchee
chivalrousness
Christological
chromatography
chronometrical
cinematography
circuitousness
circumambiency
circumambulate
circumbendibus
circumlittoral
circumlocution
circumlocutory
circumnavigate
circumspection
circumstantial
circumvolution
classconscious
classification
classificatory
claustrophobia
claustrophobic
clearsightedly
climatological
coessentiality
colourfastness
colourlessness
combustibility
commensurately
commensuration
commissaryship
commissionaire
committeewoman
commodiousness
commonsensical
communications
comparableness
compassionable
compatibleness
compensational
complexionless
compossibility
comprehensible
comprehensibly
compulsiveness
concavoconcave
conceivability
concelebration
concentrically
concessionaire
conclusiveness
concretisation
condescendence
conditionality
conductibility
confidentially
conformability
conglomeration
conglutination
conglutinative
congratulation
congratulative
congratulatory
congregational
conjunctivitis
conquistadores
consanguineous
conscienceless
conservational
conservatively
consociational
conspiratorial
constitutional
constitutively
constructional
constructively
constructivism
constructivist
consubstantial
consuetudinary
contagiousness
contemptuously
conterminously
contiguousness
continuousness
contractedness
contradictable
contradictious
contraindicate
contraposition
contrapositive
contrapuntally
controllership
controvertible
contumaciously
contumeliously
conventionally
conversational
convertibility
convexoconcave
convincingness
convulsiveness
coordinateness
copperbottomed
coquettishness
correspondence
correspondency
corruptibility
corticosteroid
corticosterone

corticotrophic
corticotrophin
cosmographical
cosmopolitical
cotemporaneous
councilchamber
councillorship
counsellorship
counterbalance
counterculture
countercurrent
countermeasure
counterplotted
countrydancing
courageousness
creditableness
crinkumcrankum
crossfertilise
crosspollinate
crossreference
cryptaesthesia
crystallisable
cucurbitaceous
cumbersomeness
cumulativeness
curvilinearity
cyanocobalamin
deceivableness
decimalisation
decolonisation
decolorisation
deconsecration
decorativeness
defenestration
definitiveness
degenerateness
dehumanisation
delectableness
deliberateness
deliberatively
delightfulness
delocalisation
demisemiquaver
demobilisation
democratically
demonetisation
demoralisation
denazification
denominational
denumerability
departmentally
dependableness
deplorableness
depolarisation
dermatological
despicableness
despiritualise
despitefulness
destructionist
determinedness
detestableness
detoxification
devitalisation
dextrorotation
dextrorotatory
diachronically
diagnostically
diagrammatical
dialectologist
diamantiferous
diamondiferous
diaphanousness
dicotyledonous
dieselelectric
differentiable
differentially
diffractometer
diminutiveness
dinoflagellate
diplomatically
disaffiliation
disaffirmation
disappointment
disapprobation
disapprobative
disapprobatory
disapprovingly
disarrangement
disassociation
disciplinarian
discolouration
discombobulate
discomfortable
discommendable
disconcertment
disconformable
disconnectedly
disconsolately
disconsolation
discontentedly
discontentment
discontinuance
discountenance
discouragement
discouragingly
discourteously
discriminating
discrimination
discriminative
discriminatory
discursiveness
disdainfulness
disembarkation
disembowelment
disenchantment
disenfranchise
disenthralment
disequilibrium
disfurnishment
disgruntlement
disheartenment
disinclination
disincorporate
disinfestation
disingenuously
disinheritance
disintegration
disintegrative
disjointedness
disorderliness
disorientation
dispensability
dispiritedness
disputatiously
disquisitional
disrespectable
dissertational
dissociability
distemperature
distensibility
distributional
distributively
diverticulitis
divertissement
dodecasyllable
dolichocephaly
dolomitisation
doublebreasted
ecclesiastical
ecclesiologist
econometrician
educationalist
effervescently
effortlessness
egalitarianism
eigenfrequency
electioneering
electrobiology
electrodeposit
electrodynamic
electrostatics
electrotherapy
electrothermal
electrothermic
electrovalency
elementariness
embarrassingly
emblematically
emulsification
enantiomorphic
encephalograph
encyclopaedism
encyclopaedist
endoradiosonde
endosmotically
enharmonically
enterprisingly
entertainingly
enthronisation
entomostracous
epexegetically
epidemiologist
epigrammatical
epistemologist
erythropoiesis
eschatological
esterification
ethnologically
etymologically
eulogistically
euphuistically
eutrophication
Evangelicalism
evangelisation
exasperatingly
exceptionality
exclaustration
excommunicable
excommunicator
excruciatingly
exhaustibility
exhaustiveness
exhilaratingly
existentialism
existentialist
experientially
experimentally
expressionless
expressiveness
extemporaneity
extemporaneous
extensionality
extinguishable
extinguishment
extracorporeal
extraneousness
extravehicular
factitiousness
faintheartedly
fallaciousness
fantasticality
farsightedness
fastidiousness
favourableness
featherbrained
ferrimagnetism
ferromagnesian
ferromagnetism
fictitiousness
figurativeness
flagitiousness
flatfootedness
floriculturist
foraminiferous
forbiddingness
foreordination
formidableness
forthrightness
fortuitousness
fortunetelling
forwardlooking
fraternisation
friendlessness
fructification
fullyfashioned
fundamentalism
fundamentalist
fundamentality
galactopoietic
gelatinisation
genealogically
generalisation
generalpurpose
geocentrically
geographically
gerontological
goodfellowship
goodhumouredly
goodtemperedly
gramineousness
grandiloquence
gratuitousness
gregariousness
groundlessness
gynaecological
gynandromorphy
gyrostabiliser
haematogenesis
hagiographical
halfpennyworth
hallucinogenic
handicraftsman
handkerchieves
harmoniousness
heartsearching
hebetudinosity
hereditariness
hermaphroditic
heroworshipper
heterochromous
heteromorphism
heteromorphous
heterophyllous
heterothallism
hierarchically
hieroglyphical
highhandedness
highmindedness
histochemistry
histopathology
historiography
histrionically
hobbledehoyish
hocuspocussing
holometabolism
holometabolous
homoeomorphism
homogenisation
homotransplant
honourableness
horrorstricken
horticulturist
humidification
hydrocoralline
hydrodynamical
hydrographical
hydromechanics
hygroscopicity
hyperbolically
hypercalcaemia
hypercatalexis
hypercriticise
hypercriticism
hyperglycaemia
hyperirritable
hypersensitive

hypersonically indecorousness intertwinement microcircuitry
hypocoristical indefiniteness intolerability microcomponent
hypocritically indemonstrable intractability microeconomics
hypodermically indestructible intramolecular microminiature
hypostatically indestructibly intransitively microprocessor
hypothetically indeterminable intrinsicality microsporangia
hypothyroidism indifferentism introductorily microstructure
hysterectomise indifferentist intuitionalism microtechnique
iatrochemistry indiscerptible intuitionalist militarisation
ichthyological indiscoverable invariableness millenarianism
ichthyophagous indiscreetness invincibleness mineralisation
ichthyosaurian indiscriminate inviolableness ministerialist
iconographical indistinctness irreconcilable miraculousness
idealistically indivisibility irreconcilably misapplication
identification indoctrination irreducibility misappropriate
idiopathically indubitability irrefutability miscalculation
illconditioned ineffectuality irremovability misinformation
illegitimately inevitableness irreproachable mistranslation
illimitability inexorableness irreproachably monkeybusiness
illiterateness inexpressively irreproducible monochromatism
illustrational infectiousness irresoluteness monopolisation
illustratively infelicitously irrespectively monosaccharide
imaginableness inflammability irrevocability monotonousness
immaculateness inflectionally Johannisberger morganatically
immethodically inflectionless judgematically mountaineering
immobilisation inflexibleness jurisdictional multifariously
immoderateness infralapsarian justifiability multilaterally
imparisyllabic infrangibility knickerbockers multinucleated
impassableness infrastructure knighterrantry multiplication
impassibleness ingloriousness kremlinologist multiplicative
imperativeness ingratiatingly lasciviousness myrmecological
impermeability inharmoniously latitudinarian myrmecophagous
imperviousness inheritability lefthandedness myrmecophilous
implacableness inimitableness legalistically mysteriousness
implausibility inordinateness legitimisation mythologically
implementation insatiableness liberalisation narrowmindedly
imponderabilia inscrutability libertarianism naturalisation
impoverishment insensibleness libidinousness necessarianism
impracticality inseparability licentiousness neglectfulness
impregnability insignificance lightheartedly neocolonialism
impressibility insignificancy linguistically neuroanatomist
impressionable instrumentally liturgiologist neurochemistry
impressiveness insufficiently longheadedness neuropathology
improvableness insuperability longitudinally neuroscientist
inadequateness insuppressible longwindedness neutralisation
inadvisability insurmountable loquaciousness newfangledness
inalienability insurmountably lovingkindness nightblindness
inalterability insurrectional lugubriousness nitrocellulose
inappositeness intangibleness lyophilisation nitroglycerine
inappreciation integrationist macrocephalous noctambulation
inappreciative intellectually macroeconomics nomenclatorial
inapproachable intelligential magniloquently nonbelligerent
inarticulately intelligentsia malappropriate noncommunicant
inarticulation intercessional malcontentedly nonconcurrence
inartistically intercessorial malodorousness noncooperation
inauspiciously intercommunion manageableness noninvolvement
incapacitation intercommunity marketgardener nonperformance
incautiousness interdependent martyrological nonrestrictive
incestuousness interferential marvellousness nonsensicality
incommensurate interferometer massproduction northeastwards
incommodiously interferometry mathematically northnortheast
incommunicable intergradation matriarchalism northnorthwest
incommunicably interjectional meddlesomeness northwestwards
incompleteness interlineation meditativeness noteworthiness
incompressible interlocutress megasporangium numismatically
incompressibly intermediately megasporophyll nutritiousness
inconclusively intermediation Mephistopheles obsequiousness
inconsequently intermigration meretriciously obstreperously
inconsiderable intermittently mesdemoiselles obstructionism
inconsiderably intermolecular metallographer obstructionist
inconsistently internationale metaphorically oecumenicalism
incontrollable interpellation metaphysically oleaginousness
inconveniently interpenetrate metapsychology omnivorousness
incoordination interplanetary metempsychosis oneirocritical
incorporeality interpretation meteorological openhandedness
incredibleness interpretative methodological openmindedness
indecipherable interpretively meticulousness ophthalmoscope
indecisiveness intersectional microbiologist ophthalmoscopy
indecomposable intersexuality microcephalous opinionatively

oppressiveness
optimistically
organisational
organometallic
ornithological
orthochromatic
orthographical
ostentatiously
osteoarthritis
outgeneralling
outlandishness
outrageousness
overabundantly
overcapitalise
overcommitment
overcompensate
overconfidence
overestimation
overexcitement
overindulgence
overpopulation
overpoweringly
overproduction
oversubscribed
overwhelmingly
oxyhaemoglobin
pachydermatous
palaeethnology
palaeobotanist
papilionaceous
paradoxicality
parallelepiped
parapsychology
parasitologist
paratactically
pardonableness
parenchymatous
parsimoniously
partridgeberry
passionateness
pasteurisation
pathogenically
pathologically
patresfamilias
penetrableness
perceptibility
perceptiveness
percutaneously
peremptoriness
perfectibility
perfidiousness
periodontology
peripateticism
perishableness
permissibility
permissiveness
perniciousness
personableness
persuasiveness
pertinaciously
perturbational
pestilentially
petrochemistry
petrographical
petrologically
phantasmagoria
phantasmagoric
pharmaceutical
pharmacologist
pharmacopoeial
phenobarbitone
phenylbutazone
philanthropise
philanthropist
philologically
phlegmatically
phosphorescent
photochemistry
photoperiodism
photosensitise
photosensitive
photosynthesis
photosynthetic
phototelegraph
phraseological
phthalocyanine
physiognomical
phytogeography
phytopathology
pianoaccordian
pigeonbreasted
pisciculturist
pistilliferous
planetstricken
pleasurability
pleonastically
pluviometrical
pneumatologist
pneumoconiosis
poikilothermal
poikilothermic
politicisation
polymerisation
polymorphously
polysaccharide
polytheistical
popularisation
portentousness
possessiveness
postmastership
postmillennial
postpositional
postpositively
potentiometric
practicability
pragmaticality
praiseworthily
prearrangement
precariousness
precociousness
predesignation
predestinarian
predestination
predeterminate
predictability
predisposition
prefabrication
preferentially
premeditatedly
premillenarian
preponderantly
preposterously
presbyterially
prescriptively
presentability
presentational
presentimental
presumptuously
presupposition
prettification
preventability
preventiveness
probabiliorism
probabiliorist
proceleusmatic
procrastinator
prodigiousness
productiveness
professionally
professorially
profitableness
progenitorship
prognosticator
progressionary
progressionism
progressionist
prohibitionism
prohibitionist
proletarianise
proletarianism
prolocutorship
propaedeutical
propagandistic
propitiatorily
propitiousness
proportionable
proportionably
proportionally
proprietorship
proprioceptive
proscriptively
prosencephalic
prosencephalon
prosperousness
protectiveness
prothonotarial
protozoologist
protrusiveness
providentially
pseudaesthesia
pseudepigrapha
pseudepigraphy
pseudomorphism
pseudomorphous
pseudonymously
psilanthropism
psilanthropist
psychoanalysis
psychoanalytic
psychochemical
psychodynamics
psychoneurosis
psychoneurotic
psychophysical
psychosomatics
psychosurgical
pteridological
publicspirited
pugnaciousness
purposefulness
pyrheliometric
Pythagoreanism
quadragenarian
quadrisyllabic
quadrisyllable
quantification
quantitatively
quarterbinding
quattrocentism
quattrocentist
quinquagesimal
quinquennially
quintessential
radicalisation
radioautograph
radiochemistry
radiosensitive
radiostrontium
radiotelegraph
radiotelephone
radiotelephony
radiotherapist
rambunctiously
rampageousness
reasonableness
rebelliousness
recapitulation
recapitulative
recapitulatory
recolonisation
recommencement
recommendation
recommendatory
reconciliation
reconciliatory
reconnaissance
reconstitution
reconstruction
reconstructive
recoverability
rectangularity
redintegration
redistribution
redistributive
reflectiveness
refractoriness
refrangibility
regardlessness
regeneratively
regressiveness
regularisation
rehabilitation
reintroduction
reinvigoration
rejuvenescence
relentlessness
relinquishment
remarkableness
reminiscential
remonetisation
remorsefulness
reorganisation
repetitiveness
representation
representative
reproductively
repudiationist
resinification
resistlessness
respectability
respectfulness
responsibility
responsiveness
restorationism
restorationist
restrictionist
resurrectional
retrogradation
revalorisation
revengefulness
revivification
rheumatologist
rhinencephalic
rhinencephalon
ridiculousness
rigidification
roadworthiness
robustiousness
roentgenoscopy
rontgenography
Rosicrucianism
roundaboutness
Russianisation
Sabbatarianism
sacramentalism
sacramentalist
sacramentarian
sacrilegiously
salubriousness
sanctification
sanguification
sanguinariness
saponification
satisfactorily
sauropterygian
scandalisation
scandalousness
scatterbrained
schematisation
schismatically
scholastically
schoolchildren
schoolmistress
scientifically
scintillometer
scrubbingbrush

scrupulousness
scurrilousness
seasonableness
secularisation
segregationist
selfabnegation
selfabsorption
selfaccusation
selfaccusatory
selfadjustment
selfadmiration
selfassumption
selfcomplacent
selfconfidence
selfconsequent
selfconsistent
selfcontrolled
selfcorrecting
selfdependence
selfdestroying
selfdetermined
selfdiscipline
selfeffacement
selfeffacingly
selfemployment
selfenergising
selfexplaining
selfexpression
selffertilised
selfflattering
selffulfilling
selfgovernment
selfimmolation
selfimportance
selfinductance
selfindulgence
selfinterested
selfpartiality
selfperception
selfpossession
selfpreserving
selfproclaimed
selfpropelling
selfpropulsion
selfprotection
selfregulating
selfrepression
selfrespectful
selfrespecting
selfrestrained
selfrevelation
selfsatisfying
selfsufficient
selfsuggestion
selfsupporting
selfsustaining
selftormenting
semicentennial
semiconducting
semielliptical
semiofficially
sensationalism
sensationalist
sensualisation
sentimentalise
sentimentalism
sentimentalist
sentimentality
septuagenarian
seriocomically
serviceability
servomechanism
sesquipedalian
Shakespeareana
Shakespeariana
shamefacedness
shortsightedly
shovehalfpenny
silicification
simplemindedly
simplification
simultaneously
singlebreasted
singlehandedly
singlemindedly
skimbleskamble
slanderousness
slatternliness
slaughterhouse
slaughterously
snaggletoothed
sociologically
sociopolitical
solicitousness
solidification
solitudinarian
solubilisation
somnambulation
somnambulistic
sophistication
soporiferously
soteriological
souldestroying
southeastwards
southwestwards
spatiotemporal
specialisation
spectrographic
spectroscopist
speechlessness
spermatogenous
spermatogonium
spermatophytic
sphaerocrystal
sphygmographic
spindleshanked
spinthariscope
spiritlessness
spiritualistic
spirituousness
spirochaetosis
sprightfulness
springcleaning
squadronleader
stadholdership
stampcollector
standardbearer
staphylococcus
stationariness
statuesqueness
steganographer
stertorousness
stigmatisation
stochastically
stoicheiometry
stoichiometric
stomatological
stoutheartedly
stratification
strikebreaking
strongmindedly
stultification
stumblingblock
stupendousness
subalternation
subconsciously
subcontinental
subcontrariety
subinfeudation
subjectiveness
sublieutenancy
submersibility
submicroscopic
submissiveness
substantialism
substantialist
substantiality
substantiation
substantivally
substitutional
substitutively
subversiveness
successfulness
successionally
successiveness
sufferableness
suggestibility
suggestiveness
sulphanilamide
superabundance
superannuation
superciliously
superconductor
superelevation
supereminently
supererogation
supererogatory
superficiality
superfoetation
superincumbent
superinduction
superintendent
supernaturally
superphosphate
superscription
supersensitive
supersonically
superstructure
superterranean
supervisorship
supposititious
supralapsarian
supramaxillary
suprasegmental
surefootedness
susceptibility
susceptiveness
suspensiveness
suspiciousness
swordswallower
sycophantishly
symmetrisation
symptomatology
synchronically
systematically
tachistoscopic
tachygraphical
tatterdemalion
tautologically
teleologically
telepathically
telephonically
telephotograph
telescopically
tergiversation
terminableness
terminological
territorialise
territorialism
territorialist
territoriality
terrorstricken
testimonialise
tetradactylous
tetragrammaton
thalassography
thanksoffering
theocratically
therianthropic
thermochemical
thermodynamics
thermoelectric
thimblerigging
thoughtfulness
thoughtreading
threadbareness
thriftlessness
thyrotoxicosis
tintinnabulary
tintinnabulate
tintinnabulous
topsyturviness
traditionalism
traditionalist
tragicomically
traitorousness
transcendental
transcendently
transformation
transformative
transitionally
transitiveness
transitoriness
transliterator
transmigration
transmigratory
transplantable
transportation
transsexualism
transvaluation
transversality
tremendousness
tridimensional
Trinitarianism
trivialisation
tropologically
troubleshooter
tumultuousness
twodimensional
tyrannicalness
ubiquitousness
ultimogeniture
ultramicrotome
ultramontanism
ultramontanist
ultrasonically
ultrastructure
umbrageousness
unaccommodated
unaccomplished
unacknowledged
unaffectedness
unappreciative
unapproachable
unattractively
unbecomingness
uncircumcision
uncommunicable
uncompromising
uncongeniality
unconscionable
uncontrollable
uncontrollably
uncontroverted
unconventional
unconvincingly
uncorroborated
underdeveloped
underemphasise
undergraduette
undermentioned
undernourished
understandable
understandably
understatement
undervaluation
undesirability
uneconomically
unemphatically
unenterprising
unenthusiastic
unexpectedness
unfaithfulness
unflatteringly
unfriendliness
ungraciousness

ungratefulness
unhesitatingly
unidimensional
unidirectional
uniformitarian
unintelligible
unintelligibly
universalistic
unmannerliness
unmentionables
unpalatability
unpleasantness
unpremeditated
unprofessional
unquestionable
unquestionably
unremunerative
unreservedness
unsatisfactory
unscrupulously
unsociableness
unsuccessfully
untruthfulness
uproariousness
utilitarianism
vaingloriously
valetudinarian
vasodilatation
vasodilatatory
vegetativeness
venereological
verisimilitude
verticillaster
vicechancellor
vicepresidency
victoriousness
villainousness
vindictiveness
vituperatively
viviparousness
vivisectionist
vociferousness
volatilisation
volcanological
volumetrically
voluminousness
voluptuousness
vulcanological
vulnerableness
watercolourist
watertightness
weakmindedness
weightlessness
weltanschauung
westernisation
whippersnapper
whortleberries
windowdressing
windowshopping
wonderstricken
worshipfulness
Zoroastrianism

---

backscattering
backscratching
bacteriologist
bacteriostasis
bacteriostatic
barometrically
basidiomycetes
bastardisation
bathingmachine
calamitousness
calcareousness
campanological
campylotropous
cantankerously
capitalisation
capriciousness
carcinogenesis
cardiovascular
cartographical
castrametation
catachrestical
catechetically
categorisation
factitiousness
faintheartedly
fallaciousness
fantasticality
farsightedness
fastidiousness
favourableness
galactopoietic
haematogenesis
hagiographical
halfpennyworth
hallucinogenic
handicraftsman
handkerchieves
harmoniousness
iatrochemistry
lasciviousness
latitudinarian
macrocephalous
macroeconomics
magniloquently
malappropriate
malcontentedly
malòdorousness
manageableness
marketgardener
martyrological
marvellousness
massproduction
mathematically
matriarchalism
narrowmindedly
naturalisation
pachydermatous
palaeethnology
palaeobotanist
papilionaceous
paradoxicality
parallelepiped
parapsychology
parasitologist
paratactically
pardonableness
parenchymatous
parsimoniously
partridgeberry
passionateness
pasteurisation
pathogenically
pathologically
patresfamilias
radicalisation
radioautograph
radiochemistry
radiosensitive
radiostrontium
radiotelegraph
radiotelephone
radiotelephony
radiotherapist
rambunctiously
rampageousness
Sabbatarianism
sacramentalism
sacramentalist
sacramentarian
sacrilegiously
salubriousness
sanctification
sanguification
sanguinariness
saponification
satisfactorily
sauropterygian
tachistoscopic
tachygraphical
tatterdemalion
tautologically
vaingloriously
valetudinarian
vasodilatation
vasodilatatory
watercolourist
watertightness
abovementioned
absentmindedly
absorptiveness
abstemiousness
abstractedness
abstractionism
abstractionist
obsequiousness
obstreperously
obstructionism
obstructionist
ubiquitousness
acceleratingly
acceptableness
accomplishable
accomplishment
accountability
accumulatively
accustomedness
achondroplasia
achromatically
acknowledgment
ecclesiastical
ecclesiologist
econometrician
ichthyological
ichthyophagous
ichthyosaurian
iconographical
scandalisation
scandalousness
scatterbrained
schematisation
schismatically
scholastically
schoolchildren
schoolmistress
scientifically
scintillometer
scrubbingbrush
scrupulousness
scurrilousness
administration
administrative
administratrix
advantageously
adventitiously
educationalist
idealistically
identification
idiopathically
aerobiological
aerobiotically
aerodynamicist
aesthesiometer
aetiologically
beautification
behaviouristic
beneficialness
censoriousness
centralisation
centrifugation
deceivableness
decimalisation
decolonisation
decolorisation
deconsecration
decorativeness
defenestration
definitiveness
degenerateness
dehumanisation
delectableness
deliberateness
deliberatively
delightfulness
delocalisation
demisemiquaver
demobilisation
democratically
demonetisation
demoralisation
denazification
denominational
denumerability
departmentally
dependableness
deplorableness
depolarisation
dermatological
despicableness
despiritualise
despitefulness
destructionist
determinedness
detestableness
detoxification
devitalisation
dextrorotation
dextrorotatory
featherbrained
ferrimagnetism
ferromagnesian
ferromagnetism
gelatinisation
genealogically
generalisation
generalpurpose
geocentrically
geographically
gerontological
heartsearching
hebetudinosity
hereditariness
hermaphroditic
heroworshipper
heterochromous
heteromorphism
heteromorphous
heterophyllous
heterothallism
lefthandedness
legalistically
legitimisation
meddlesomeness
meditativeness
megasporangium
megasporophyll
Mephistopheles
meretriciously
mesdemoiselles
metallographer
metaphorically
metaphysically
metapsychology
metempsychosis
meteorological
methodological
meticulousness
necessarianism
neglectfulness
neocolonialism
neuroanatomist
neurochemistry
neuropathology
neuroscientist

neutralisation
newfangledness
oecumenicalism
penetrableness
perceptibility
perceptiveness
percutaneously
peremptoriness
perfectibility
perfidiousness
periodontology
peripateticism
perishableness
permissibility
permissiveness
perniciousness
personableness
persuasiveness
pertinaciously
perturbational
pestilentially
petrochemistry
petrographical
petrologically
reasonableness
rebelliousness
recapitulation
recapitulative
recapitulatory
recolonisation
recommencement
recommendation
recommendatory
reconciliation
reconciliatory
reconnaissance
reconstitution
reconstruction
reconstructive
recoverability
rectangularity
redintegration
redistribution
redistributive
reflectiveness
refractoriness
refrangibility
regardlessness
regeneratively
regressiveness
regularisation
rehabilitation
reintroduction
reinvigoration
rejuvenescence
relentlessness
relinquishment
remarkableness
reminiscential
remonetisation
remorsefulness
reorganisation
repetitiveness
representation
representative
reproductively
repudiationist
resinification
resistlessness
respectability
respectfulness
responsibility
responsiveness
restorationism
restorationist
restrictionist
resurrectional
retrogradation
revalorisation
revengefulness
revivification
seasonableness
secularisation
segregationist
selfabnegation
selfabsorption
selfaccusation
selfaccusatory
selfadjustment
selfadmiration
selfassumption
selfcomplacent
selfconfidence
selfconsequent
selfconsistent
selfcontrolled
selfcorrecting
selfdependence
selfdestroying
selfdetermined
selfdiscipline
selfeffacement
selfeffacingly
selfemployment
selfenergising
selfexplaining
selfexpression
selffertilised
selfflattering
selffulfilling
selfgovernment
selfimmolation
selfimportance
selfinductance
selfindulgence
selfinterested
selfpartiality
selfperception
selfpossession
selfpreserving
selfproclaimed
selfpropelling
selfpropulsion
selfprotection
selfregulating
selfrepression
selfrespectful
selfrespecting
selfrestrained
selfrevelation
selfsatisfying
selfsufficient
selfsuggestion
selfsupporting
selfsustaining
selftormenting
semicentennial
semiconducting
semielliptical
semiofficially
sensationalism
sensationalist
sensualisation
sentimentalise
sentimentalism
sentimentalist
sentimentality
septuagenarian
seriocomically
serviceability
servomechanism
sesquipedalian
teleologically
telepathically
telephonically
telephotograph
telescopically
tergiversation
terminableness
terminological
territorialise
territorialism
territorialist
territoriality
terrorstricken
testimonialise
tetradactylous
tetragrammaton
vegetativeness
venereological
verisimilitude
verticillaster
weakmindedness
weightlessness
weltanschauung
westernisation
affectionately
aforementioned
Africanisation
effervescently
effortlessness
aggrandisement
aggressiveness
agrobiological
egalitarianism
chancellorship
changeableness
characteristic
charitableness
chemoreception
chemoreceptive
chemosynthesis
chickenhearted
chickenlivered
chincherinchee
chivalrousness
Christological
chromatography
chronometrical
phantasmagoria
phantasmagoric
pharmaceutical
pharmacologist
pharmacopoeial
phenobarbitone
phenylbutazone
philanthropise
philanthropist
philologically
phlegmatically
phosphorescent
photochemistry
photoperiodism
photosensitise
photosensitive
photosynthesis
photosynthetic
phototelegraph
phraseological
phthalocyanine
physiognomical
phytogeography
phytopathology
rheumatologist
rhinencephalic
rhinencephalon
Shakespeareana
Shakespeariana
shamefacedness
shortsightedly
shovehalfpenny
thalassography
thanksoffering
theocratically
therianthropic
thermochemical
thermodynamics
thermoelectric
thimblerigging
thoughtfulness
thoughtreading
threadbareness
thriftlessness
thyrotoxicosis
whippersnapper
whortleberries
airconditioner
bibliographise
bibliomaniacal
biodegradation
bioelectricity
bioengineering
biographically
bioluminescent
biosystematics
bituminisation
cinematography
circuitousness
circumambiency
circumambulate
circumbendibus
circumlittoral
circumlocution
circumlocutory
circumnavigate
circumspection
circumstantial
circumvolution
diachronically
diagnostically
diagrammatical
dialectologist
diamantiferous
diamondiferous
diaphanousness
dicotyledonous
dieselelectric
differentiable
differentially
diffractometer
diminutiveness
dinoflagellate
diplomatically
disaffiliation
disaffirmation
disappointment
disapprobation
disapprobative
disapprobatory
disapprovingly
disarrangement
disassociation
disciplinarian
discolouration
discombobulate
discomfortable
discommendable
disconcertment
disconformable
disconnectedly
disconsolately
disconsolation
discontentedly
discontentment
discontinuance
discountenance
discouragement
discouragingly
discourteously
discriminating
discrimination
discriminative
discriminatory
discursiveness
disdainfulness
disembarkation

disembowelment
disenchantment
disenfranchise
disenthralment
disequilibrium
disfurnishment
disgruntlement
disheartenment
disinclination
disincorporate
disinfestation
disingenuously
disinheritance
disintegration
disintegrative
disjointedness
disorderliness
disorientation
dispensability
dispiritedness
disputatiously
disquisitional
disrespectable
dissertational
dissociability
distemperature
distensibility
distributional
distributively
diverticulitis
divertissement
eigenfrequency
fictitiousness
figurativeness
hierarchically
hieroglyphical
highhandedness
highmindedness
histochemistry
histopathology
historiography
histrionically
liberalisation
libertarianism
libidinousness
licentiousness
lightheartedly
linguistically
liturgiologist
microbiologist
microcephalous
microcircuitry
microcomponent
microeconomics
microminiature
microprocessor
microsporangia
microstructure
microtechnique
militarisation
millenarianism
mineralisation
ministerialist
miraculousness
misapplication
misappropriate
miscalculation
misinformation
mistranslation
nightblindness
nitrocellulose
nitroglycerine
pianoaccordian
pigeonbreasted
pisciculturist
pistilliferous
ridiculousness
rigidification
silicification
simplemindedly
simplification
simultaneously
singlebreasted
singlehandedly
singlemindedly
tintinnabulary
tintinnabulate
tintinnabulous
vicechancellor
vicepresidency
victoriousness
villainousness
vindictiveness
vituperatively
viviparousness
vivisectionist
windowdressing
windowshopping
skimbleskamble
Albigensianism
allegorisation
allelomorphism
alphabetically
alphanumerical
altruistically
blackmarketeer
blockaderunner
bloodthirstily
classconscious
classification
classificatory
claustrophobia
claustrophobic
clearsightedly
climatological
electioneering
electrobiology
electrodeposit
electrodynamic
electrostatics
electrotherapy
electrothermal
electrothermic
electrovalency
elementariness
flagitiousness
flatfootedness
floriculturist
illconditioned
illegitimately
illimitability
illiterateness
illustrational
illustratively
oleaginousness
planetstricken
pleasurability
pleonastically
pluviometrical
slanderousness
slatternliness
slaughterhouse
slaughterously
ultimogeniture
ultramicrotome
ultramontanism
ultramontanist
ultrasonically
ultrastructure
amateurishness
ambassadorship
ambidextrously
embarrassingly
emblematically
emulsification
imaginableness
immaculateness
immethodically
immobilisation
immoderateness
imparisyllabic
impassableness
impassibleness
imperativeness
impermeability
imperviousness
implacableness
implausibility
implementation
imponderabilia
impoverishment
impracticality
impregnability
impressibility
impressionable
impressiveness
improvableness
omnivorousness
umbrageousness
anagrammatical
anthropography
anthropologist
anthropometric
anticipatively
anticonvulsant
antidepressant
antifederalist
antiperspirant
antiphlogistic
antiquarianism
antiscriptural
antiseptically
antithetically
enantiomorphic
encephalograph
encyclopaedism
encyclopaedist
endoradiosonde
endosmotically
enharmonically
enterprisingly
entertainingly
enthronisation
entomostracous
inadequateness
inadvisability
inalienability
inalterability
inappositeness
inappreciation
inappreciative
inapproachable
inarticulately
inarticulation
inartistically
inauspiciously
incapacitation
incautiousness
incestuousness
incommensurate
incommodiously
incommunicable
incommunicably
incompleteness
incompressible
incompressibly
inconclusively
inconsequently
inconsiderable
inconsiderably
inconsistently
incontrollable
inconveniently
incoordination
incorporeality
incredibleness
indecipherable
indecisiveness
indecomposable
indecorousness
indefiniteness
indemonstrable
indestructible
indestructibly
indeterminable
indifferentism
indifferentist
indiscerptible
indiscoverable
indiscreetness
indiscriminate
indistinctness
indivisibility
indoctrination
indubitability
ineffectuality
inevitableness
inexorableness
inexpressively
infectiousness
infelicitously
inflammability
inflectionally
inflectionless
inflexibleness
infralapsarian
infrangibility
infrastructure
ingloriousness
ingratiatingly
inharmoniously
inheritability
inimitableness
inordinateness
insatiableness
inscrutability
insensibleness
inseparability
insignificance
insignificancy
instrumentally
insufficiently
insuperability
insuppressible
insurmountable
insurmountably
insurrectional
intangibleness
integrationist
intellectually
intelligential
intelligentsia
intercessional
intercessorial
intercommunion
intercommunity
interdependent
interferential
interferometer
interferometry
intergradation
interjectional
interlineation
interlocutress
intermediately
intermediation
intermigration
intermittently
intermolecular
internationale
interpellation
interpenetrate
interplanetary
interpretation
interpretative
interpretively

intersectional unsuccessfully contumeliously northnortheast
intersexuality untruthfulness conventionally northnorthwest
intertwinement boardingschool conversational northwestwards
intolerability boisterousness convertibility noteworthiness
intractability boroughEnglish convexoconcave poikilothermal
intramolecular bougainvillaea convincingness poikilothermic
intransitively bouleversement convulsiveness politicisation
intrinsicality bowdlerisation coordinateness polymerisation
introductorily coessentiality copperbottomed polymorphously
intuitionalism colourfastness coquettishness polysaccharide
intuitionalist colourlessness correspondence polytheistical
invariableness combustibility correspondency popularisation
invincibleness commensurately corruptibility portentousness
inviolableness commensuration corticosteroid possessiveness
knickerbockers commissaryship corticosterone postmastership
knighterrantry commissionaire corticotrophic postmillennial
oneirocritical committeewoman corticotrophin postpositional
pneumatologist commodiousness cosmographical postpositively
pneumoconiosis commonsensical cosmopolitical potentiometric
snaggletoothed communications cotemporaneous roadworthiness
unaccommodated comparableness councilchamber robustiousness
unaccomplished compassionable councillorship roentgenoscopy
unacknowledged compatibleness counsellorship rontgenography
unaffectedness compensational counterbalance Rosicrucianism
unappreciative complexionless counterculture roundaboutness
unapproachable compossibility countercurrent sociologically
unattractively comprehensible countermeasure sociopolitical
unbecomingness comprehensibly counterplotted solicitousness
uncircumcision compulsiveness countrydancing solidification
uncommunicable concavoconcave courageousness solitudinarian
uncompromising conceivability dodecasyllable solubilisation
uncongeniality concelebration dolichocephaly somnambulation
unconscionable concentrically dolomitisation somnambulistic
uncontrollable concessionaire doublebreasted sophistication
uncontrollably conclusiveness foraminiferous soporiferously
uncontroverted concretisation forbiddingness soteriological
unconventional condescendence foreordination souldestroying
unconvincingly conditionality formidableness southeastwards
uncorroborated conductibility forthrightness southwestwards
underdeveloped confidentially fortuitousness topsyturviness
underemphasise conformability fortunetelling vociferousness
undergraduette conglomeration forwardlooking volatilisation
undermentioned conglutination goodfellowship volcanological
undernourished conglutinative goodhumouredly volumetrically
understandable congratulation goodtemperedly voluminousness
understandably congratulative hobbledehoyish voluptuousness
understatement congratulatory hocuspocussing wonderstricken
undervaluation congregational holometabolism worshipfulness
undesirability conjunctivitis holometabolous Zoroastrianism
uneconomically conquistadores homoeomorphism aphoristically
unemphatically consanguineous homogenisation apologetically
unenterprising conscienceless homotransplant apophthegmatic
unenthusiastic conservational honourableness apoplectically
unexpectedness conservatively horrorstricken apothegmatical
unfaithfulness consociational horticulturist appendicectomy
unflatteringly conspiratorial Johannisberger apprehensively
unfriendliness constitutional longheadedness apprenticeship
ungraciousness constitutively longitudinally epexegetically
ungratefulness constructional longwindedness epidemiologist
unhesitatingly constructively loquaciousness epigrammatical
unidimensional constructivism lovingkindness epistemologist
unidirectional constructivist monkeybusiness openhandedness
uniformitarian consubstantial monochromatism openmindedness
unintelligible consuetudinary monopolisation ophthalmoscope
unintelligibly contagiousness monosaccharide ophthalmoscopy
universalistic contemptuously monotonousness opinionatively
unmannerliness conterminously morganatically oppressiveness
unmentionables contiguousness mountaineering optimistically
unpalatability continuousness noctambulation spatiotemporal
unpleasantness contractedness nomenclatorial specialisation
unpremeditated contradictable nonbelligerent spectrographic
unprofessional contradictious noncommunicant spectroscopist
unquestionable contraindicate nonconcurrence speechlessness
unquestionably contraposition noncooperation spermatogenous
unremunerative contrapositive noninvolvement spermatogonium
unreservedness contrapuntally nonperformance spermatophytic
unsatisfactory controllership nonrestrictive sphaerocrystal
unscrupulously controvertible nonsensicality sphygmographic
unsociableness contumaciously northeastwards spindleshanked

spinthariscope	presentational	pseudaesthesia	outlandishness
spiritlessness	presentimental	pseudepigrapha	outrageousness
spiritualistic	presumptuously	pseudepigraphy	publicspirited
spirituousness	presupposition	pseudomorphism	pugnaciousness
spirochaetosis	prettification	pseudomorphous	purposefulness
sprightfulness	preventability	pseudonymously	quadragenarian
springcleaning	preventiveness	psilanthropism	quadrisyllabic
uproariousness	probabiliorism	psilanthropist	quadrisyllable
squadronleader	probabiliorist	psychoanalysis	quantification
archaeological	proceleusmatic	psychoanalytic	quantitatively
archetypically	procrastinator	psychochemical	quarterbinding
archidiaconate	prodigiousness	psychodynamics	quattrocentism
archiepiscopal	productiveness	psychoneurosis	quattrocentist
architectonics	professionally	psychoneurotic	quinquagesimal
arithmetically	professorially	psychophysical	quinquennially
arrhythmically	profitableness	psychosomatics	quintessential
arrondissement	progenitorship	psychosurgical	Russianisation
articulateness	prognosticator	attainableness	subalternation
artificialness	progressionary	attractiveness	subconsciously
brachycephalic	progressionism	ethnologically	subcontinental
breathlessness	progressionist	etymologically	subcontrariety
breathtakingly	prohibitionism	pteridological	subinfeudation
bremsstrahlung	prohibitionist	stadholdership	subjectiveness
Brobdingnagian	proletarianise	stampcollector	sublieutenancy
bronchiectasis	proletarianism	standardbearer	submersibility
creditableness	prolocutorship	staphylococcus	submicroscopic
crinkumcrankum	propaedeutical	stationariness	submissiveness
crossfertilise	propagandistic	statuesqueness	substantialism
crosspollinate	propitiatorily	steganographer	substantialist
crossreference	propitiousness	stertorousness	substantiality
cryptaesthesia	proportionable	stigmatisation	substantiation
crystallisable	proportionably	stochastically	substantivally
erythropoiesis	proportionally	stoicheiometry	substitutional
fraternisation	proprietorship	stoichiometric	substitutively
friendlessness	proprioceptive	stomatological	subversiveness
fructification	proscriptively	stoutheartedly	successfulness
gramineousness	prosencephalic	stratification	successionally
grandiloquence	prosencephalon	strikebreaking	successiveness
gratuitousness	prosperousness	strongmindedly	sufferableness
gregariousness	protectiveness	stultification	suggestibility
groundlessness	prothonotarial	stumblingblock	suggestiveness
irreconcilable	protozoologist	stupendousness	sulphanilamide
irreconcilably	protrusiveness	utilitarianism	superabundance
irreducibility	providentially	audiofrequency	superannuation
irrefutability	traditionalism	Augustinianism	superciliously
irremovability	traditionalist	auspiciousness	superconductor
irreproachable	tragicomically	authentication	superelevation
irreproachably	traitorousness	autobiographer	supereminently
irreproducible	transcendental	autobiographic	supererogation
irresoluteness	transcendently	autocratically	supererogatory
irrespectively	transformation	autoradiograph	superficiality
irrevocability	transformative	autosuggestion	superfoetation
kremlinologist	transitionally	bullheadedness	superincumbent
organisational	transitiveness	butterfingered	superinduction
organometallic	transitoriness	butterflyscrew	superintendent
ornithological	transliterator	cucurbitaceous	supernaturally
orthochromatic	transmigration	cumbersomeness	superphosphate
orthographical	transmigratory	cumulativeness	superscription
practicability	transplantable	curvilinearity	supersensitive
pragmaticality	transportation	eulogistically	supersonically
praiseworthily	transsexualism	euphuistically	superstructure
prearrangement	transvaluation	eutrophication	superterranean
precariousness	transversality	fullyfashioned	supervisorship
precociousness	tremendousness	fundamentalism	supposititious
predesignation	tridimensional	fundamentalist	supralapsarian
predestinarian	Trinitarianism	fundamentality	supramaxillary
predestination	trivialisation	humidification	suprasegmental
predeterminate	tropologically	judgematically	surefootedness
predictability	troubleshooter	jurisdictional	susceptibility
predisposition	associationism	justifiability	susceptiveness
prefabrication	astronomically	lugubriousness	suspensiveness
preferentially	astrophysicist	multifariously	suspiciousness
premeditatedly	asymmetrically	multilaterally	tumultuousness
premillenarian	asymptotically	multinucleated	vulcanological
preponderantly	asynchronously	multiplication	vulnerableness
preposterously	eschatological	multiplicative	avariciousness
presbyterially	esterification	numismatically	Evangelicalism
prescriptively	ostentatiously	nutritiousness	evangelisation
presentability	osteoarthritis	outgeneralling	overabundantly

overcapitalise
overcommitment
overcompensate
overconfidence
overestimation
overexcitement
overindulgence
overpopulation
overpoweringly
overproduction
oversubscribed
overwhelmingly
swordswallower
twodimensional
exasperatingly
exceptionality
exclaustration
excommunicable
excommunicator
excruciatingly
exhaustibility
exhaustiveness
exhilaratingly
existentialism
existentialist
experientially
experimentally
expressionless
expressiveness
extemporaneity
extemporaneous
extensionality
extinguishable
extinguishment
extracorporeal
extraneousness
extravehicular
oxyhaemoglobin
cyanocobalamin
gynaecological
gynandromorphy
gyrostabiliser
hydrocoralline
hydrodynamical
hydrographical
hydromechanics
hygroscopicity
hyperbolically
hypercalcaemia
hypercatalexis
hypercriticise
hypercriticism
hyperglycaemia
hyperirritable
hypersensitive
hypersonically
hypocoristical
hypocritically
hypodermically
hypostatically
hypothetically
hypothyroidism
hysterectomise
lyophilisation
myrmecological
myrmecophagous
myrmecophilous
mysteriousness
mythologically
pyrheliometric
Pythagoreanism
sycophantishly
symmetrisation
symptomatology
synchronically
systematically
tyrannicalness

---

amateurishness
anagrammatical
avariciousness
beautification
blackmarketeer
boardingschool
brachycephalic
chancellorship
changeableness
characteristic
charitableness
classconscious
classification
classificatory
claustrophobia
claustrophobic
cyanocobalamin
diachronically
diagnostically
diagrammatical
dialectologist
diamantiferous
diamondiferous
diaphanousness
egalitarianism
enantiomorphic
Evangelicalism
evangelisation
exasperatingly
featherbrained
flagitiousness
flatfootedness
fraternisation
gramineousness
grandiloquence
gratuitousness
heartsearching
imaginableness
inadequateness
inadvisability
inalienability
inalterability
inappositeness
inappreciation
inappreciative
inapproachable
inarticulately
inarticulation
inartistically
inauspiciously
phantasmagoria
phantasmagoric
pharmaceutical
pharmacologist
pharmacopoeial
pianoaccordian
planetstricken
practicability
pragmaticality
praiseworthily
quadragenarian
quadrisyllabic
quadrisyllable
quantification
quantitatively
quarterbinding
quattrocentism
quattrocentist
reasonableness
roadworthiness
scandalisation
scandalousness
scatterbrained
seasonableness
Shakespeareana
Shakespeariana
shamefacedness
slanderousness
slatternliness
slaughterhouse
slaughterously
snaggletoothed
spatiotemporal
stadholdership
stampcollector
standardbearer
staphylococcus
stationariness
statuesqueness
thalassography
thanksoffering
traditionalism
traditionalist
tragicomically
traitorousness
transcendental
transcendently
transformation
transformative
transitionally
transitiveness
transitoriness
transliterator
transmigration
transmigratory
transplantable
transportation
transsexualism
transvaluation
transversality
unaccommodated
unaccomplished
unacknowledged
unaffectedness
unappreciative
unapproachable
unattractively
weakmindedness
Albigensianism
ambassadorship
ambidextrously
bibliographise
bibliomaniacal
embarrassingly
emblematically
hebetudinosity
hobbledehoyish
liberalisation
libertarianism
libidinousness
publicspirited
rebelliousness
robustiousness
Sabbatarianism
subalternation
subconsciously
subcontinental
subcontrariety
subinfeudation
subjectiveness
sublieutenancy
submersibility
submicroscopic
submissiveness
substantialism
substantialist
substantiality
substantiation
substantivally
substitutional
substitutively
subversiveness
umbrageousness
unbecomingness
acceleratingly
acceptableness
accomplishable
accomplishment
accountability
accumulatively
accustomedness
archaeological
archetypically
archidiaconate
archiepiscopal
architectonics
backscattering
backscratching
bacteriologist
bacteriostasis
bacteriostatic
cucurbitaceous
deceivableness
decimalisation
decolonisation
decolorisation
deconsecration
decorativeness
dicotyledonous
ecclesiastical
ecclesiologist
encephalograph
encyclopaedism
encyclopaedist
eschatological
exceptionality
exclaustration
excommunicable
excommunicator
excruciatingly
factitiousness
fictitiousness
hocuspocussing
incapacitation
incautiousness
incestuousness
incommensurate
incommodiously
incommunicable
incommunicably
incompleteness
incompressible
incompressibly
inconclusively
inconsequently
inconsiderable
inconsiderably
inconsistently
incontrollable
inconveniently
incoordination
incorporeality
incredibleness
licentiousness
macrocephalous
macroeconomics
microbiologist
microcephalous
microcircuitry
microcomponent
microeconomics
microminiature
microprocessor
microsporangia
microstructure
microtechnique
necessarianism
noctambulation
oecumenicalism
pachydermatous
recapitulation
recapitulative
recapitulatory
recolonisation
recommencement
recommendation
recommendatory
reconciliation

reconciliatory
reconnaissance
reconstitution
reconstruction
reconstructive
recoverability
rectangularity
sacramentalism
sacramentalist
sacramentarian
sacrilegiously
secularisation
sociologically
sociopolitical
successfulness
successionally
successiveness
sycophantishly
tachistoscopic
tachygraphical
uncircumcision
uncommunicable
uncompromising
uncongeniality
unconscionable
uncontrollable
uncontrollably
uncontroverted
unconventional
unconvincingly
uncorroborated
vicechancellor
vicepresidency
victoriousness
vociferousness
audiofrequency
dodecasyllable
endoradiosonde
endosmotically
hydrocoralline
hydrodynamical
hydrographical
hydromechanics
indecipherable
indecisiveness
indecomposable
indecorousness
indefiniteness
indemonstrable
indestructible
indestructibly
indeterminable
indifferentism
indifferentist
indiscerptible
indiscoverable
indiscreetness
indiscriminate
indistinctness
indivisibility
indoctrination
indubitability
judgematically
meddlesomeness
meditativeness
radicalisation
radioautograph
radiochemistry
radiosensitive
radiostrontium
radiotelegraph
radiotelephone
radiotelephony
radiotherapist
redintegration
redistribution
redistributive
ridiculousness
underdeveloped
underemphasise
undergraduette
undermentioned
undernourished
understandable
understandably
understatement
undervaluation
undesirability
breathlessness
breathtakingly
bremsstrahlung
chemoreception
chemoreceptive
chemosynthesis
clearsightedly
coessentiality
creditableness
dieselelectric
electioneering
electrobiology
electrodeposit
electrodynamic
electrostatics
electrotherapy
electrothermal
electrothermic
electrovalency
elementariness
epexegetically
gregariousness
haematogenesis
hierarchically
hieroglyphical
idealistically
identification
ineffectuality
inevitableness
inexorableness
inexpressively
kremlinologist
oleaginousness
oneirocritical
openhandedness
openmindedness
overabundantly
overcapitalise
overcommitment
overcompensate
overconfidence
overestimation
overexcitement
overindulgence
overpopulation
overpoweringly
overproduction
oversubscribed
overwhelmingly
phenobarbitone
phenylbutazone
pleasurability
pleonastically
pneumatologist
pneumoconiosis
prearrangement
precariousness
precociousness
predesignation
predestinarian
predestination
predeterminate
predictability
predisposition
prefabrication
preferentially
premeditatedly
premillenarian
preponderantly
preposterously
presbyterially
prescriptively
presentability
presentational
presentimental
presumptuously
presupposition
prettification
preventability
preventiveness
pseudaesthesia
pseudepigrapha
pseudepigraphy
pseudomorphism
pseudomorphous
pseudonymously
pteridological
rheumatologist
roentgenoscopy
specialisation
spectrographic
spectroscopist
speechlessness
spermatogenous
spermatogonium
spermatophytic
steganographer
stertorousness
theocratically
therianthropic
thermochemical
thermodynamics
thermoelectric
tremendousness
uneconomically
unemphatically
unenterprising
unenthusiastic
unexpectedness
affectionately
defenestration
definitiveness
differentiable
differentially
diffractometer
effervescently
effortlessness
infectiousness
infelicitously
inflammability
inflectionally
inflectionless
inflexibleness
infralapsarian
infrangibility
infrastructure
lefthandedness
reflectiveness
refractoriness
refrangibility
sufferableness
unfaithfulness
unflatteringly
unfriendliness
aggrandisement
aggressiveness
Augustinianism
degenerateness
eigenfrequency
figurativeness
hagiographical
highhandedness
highmindedness
hygroscopicity
ingloriousness
ingratiatingly
legalistically
legitimisation
lightheartedly
lugubriousness
magniloquently
megasporangium
megasporophyll
neglectfulness
nightblindness
organisational
organometallic
pigeonbreasted
pugnaciousness
regardlessness
regeneratively
regressiveness
regularisation
rigidification
segregationist
suggestibility
suggestiveness
ungraciousness
ungratefulness
vegetativeness
achondroplasia
achromatically
aphoristically
behaviouristic
dehumanisation
enharmonically
ethnologically
exhaustibility
exhaustiveness
exhilaratingly
ichthyological
ichthyophagous
ichthyosaurian
inharmoniously
inheritability
Johannisberger
ophthalmoscope
ophthalmoscopy
rehabilitation
schematisation
schismatically
scholastically
schoolchildren
schoolmistress
sphaerocrystal
sphygmographic
unhesitatingly
arithmetically
boisterousness
chickenhearted
chickenlivered
chincherinchee
chivalrousness
climatological
crinkumcrankum
epidemiologist
epigrammatical
epistemologist
existentialism
existentialist
faintheartedly
friendlessness
idiopathically
inimitableness
knickerbockers
knighterrantry
opinionatively
philanthropise
philanthropist
philologically
poikilothermal
poikilothermic
psilanthropism
psilanthropist
quinquagesimal
quinquennially
quintessential
reintroduction

reinvigoration
rhinencephalic
rhinencephalon
scientifically
scintillometer
skimbleskamble
spindleshanked
spinthariscope
spiritlessness
spiritualistic
spirituousness
spirochaetosis
stigmatisation
thimblerigging
tridimensional
Trinitarianism
trivialisation
ubiquitousness
unidimensional
unidirectional
uniformitarian
unintelligible
unintelligibly
universalistic
utilitarianism
vaingloriously
weightlessness
whippersnapper
rejuvenescence
acknowledgment
allegorisation
allelomorphism
bullheadedness
calamitousness
calcareousness
colourfastness
colourlessness
delectableness
deliberateness
deliberatively
delightfulness
delocalisation
dolichocephaly
dolomitisation
eulogistically
fallaciousness
fullyfashioned
galactopoietic
gelatinisation
halfpennyworth
hallucinogenic
holometabolism
holometabolous
illconditioned
illegitimately
illimitability
illiterateness
illustrational
illustratively
malappropriate
malcontentedly
malodorousness
militarisation
millenarianism
multifariously
multilaterally
multinucleated
multiplication
multiplicative
palaeethnology
palaeobotanist
phlegmatically
politicisation
polymerisation
polymorphously
polysaccharide
polytheistical
relentlessness
relinquishment

salubriousness
selfabnegation
selfabsorption
selfaccusation
selfaccusatory
selfadjustment
selfadmiration
selfassumption
selfcomplacent
selfconfidence
selfconsequent
selfconsistent
selfcontrolled
selfcorrecting
selfdependence
selfdestroying
selfdetermined
selfdiscipline
selfeffacement
selfeffacingly
selfemployment
selfenergising
selfexplaining
selfexpression
selffertilised
selfflattering
selffulfilling
selfgovernment
selfimmolation
selfimportance
selfinductance
selfindulgence
selfinterested
selfpartiality
selfperception
selfpossession
selfpreserving
selfproclaimed
selfpropelling
selfpropulsion
selfprotection
selfregulating
selfrepression
selfrespectful
selfrespecting
selfrestrained
selfrevelation
selfsatisfying
selfsufficient
selfsuggestion
selfsupporting
selfsustaining
selftormenting
silicification
solicitousness
solidification
solitudinarian
solubilisation
sulphanilamide
teleologically
telepathically
telephonically
telephotograph
telescopically
valetudinarian
villainousness
volatilisation
volcanological
volumetrically
voluminousness
voluptuousness
vulcanological
vulnerableness
weltanschauung
administration
administrative
administratrix
campanological
campylotropous

combustibility
commensurately
commensuration
commissaryship
commissionaire
committeewoman
commodiousness
commonsensical
communications
comparableness
compassionable
compatibleness
compensational
complexionless
compossibility
comprehensible
comprehensibly
compulsiveness
cumbersomeness
cumulativeness
demisemiquaver
demobilisation
democratically
demonetisation
demoralisation
diminutiveness
homoeomorphism
homogenisation
homotransplant
humidification
immaculateness
immethodically
immobilisation
immoderateness
nomenclatorial
numismatically
rambunctiously
rampageousness
remarkableness
reminiscential
remonetisation
remorsefulness
semicentennial
semiconducting
semielliptical
semiofficially
simplemindedly
simplification
simultaneously
somnambulation
somnambulistic
symmetrisation
symptomatology
tumultuousness
unmannerliness
unmentionables
beneficialness
cantankerously
censoriousness
centralisation
centrifugation
cinematography
concavoconcave
conceivability
concelebration
concentrically
concessionaire
conclusiveness
concretisation
condescendence
conditionality
conductibility
confidentially
conformability
conglomeration
conglutination
conglutinative
congratulation
congratulative

congratulatory
congregational
conjunctivitis
conquistadores
consanguineous
conscienceless
conservational
conservatively
consociational
conspiratorial
constitutional
constitutively
constructional
constructively
constructivism
constructivist
consubstantial
consuetudinary
contagiousness
contemptuously
conterminously
contiguousness
continuousness
contractedness
contradictable
contradictious
contraindicate
contraposition
contrapositive
contrapuntally
controllership
controvertible
contumaciously
contumeliously
conventionally
conversational
convertibility
convexoconcave
convincingness
convulsiveness
denazification
denominational
denumerability
dinoflagellate
fantasticality
fundamentalism
fundamentalist
fundamentality
genealogically
generalisation
generalpurpose
gynaecological
gynandromorphy
handicraftsman
handkerchieves
honourableness
linguistically
longheadedness
longitudinally
longwindedness
manageableness
mineralisation
ministerialist
monkeybusiness
monochromatism
monopolisation
monosaccharide
monotonousness
nonbelligerent
noncommunicant
nonconcurrence
noncooperation
noninvolvement
nonperformance
nonrestrictive
nonsensicality
omnivorousness
ornithological
penetrableness

rontgenography
sanctification
sanguification
sanguinariness
sensationalism
sensationalist
sensualisation
sentimentalise
sentimentalism
sentimentalist
sentimentality
singlebreasted
singlehandedly
singlemindedly
synchronically
tintinnabulary
tintinnabulate
tintinnabulous
venereological
vindictiveness
windowdressing
windowshopping
wonderstricken
abovementioned
aforementioned
apologetically
apophthegmatic
apoplectically
apothegmatical
biodegradation
bioelectricity
bioengineering
biographically
bioluminescent
biosystematics
blockaderunner
bloodthirstily
Brobdingnagian
bronchiectasis
coordinateness
crossfertilise
crosspollinate
crossreference
econometrician
floriculturist
geocentrically
geographically
goodfellowship
goodhumouredly
goodtemperedly
groundlessness
iconographical
inordinateness
lyophilisation
neocolonialism
phosphorescent
photochemistry
photoperiodism
photosensitise
photosensitive
photosynthesis
photosynthetic
phototelegraph
probabiliorism
probabiliorist
proceleusmatic
procrastinator
prodigiousness
productiveness
professionally
professorially
profitableness
progenitorship
prognosticator
progressionary
progressionism
progressionist
prohibitionism
prohibitionist
proletarianise
proletarianism
prolocutorship
propaedeutical
propagandistic
propitiatorily
propitiousness
proportionable
proportionably
proportionally
proprietorship
proprioceptive
proscriptively
prosencephalic
prosencephalon
prosperousness
protectiveness
prothonotarial
protozoologist
protrusiveness
providentially
reorganisation
shortsightedly
shovehalfpenny
stochastically
stoicheiometry
stoichiometric
stomatological
stoutheartedly
swordswallower
thoughtfulness
thoughtreading
tropologically
troubleshooter
twodimensional
whortleberries
alphabetically
alphanumerical
appendicectomy
apprehensively
apprenticeship
capitalisation
capriciousness
copperbottomed
departmentally
dependableness
deplorableness
depolarisation
diplomatically
euphuistically
experientially
experimentally
expressionless
expressiveness
hyperbolically
hypercalcaemia
hypercatalexis
hypercriticise
hypercriticism
hyperglycaemia
hyperirritable
hypersensitive
hypersonically
hypocoristical
hypocritically
hypodermically
hypostatically
hypothetically
hypothyroidism
imparisyllabic
impassableness
impassibleness
imperativeness
impermeability
imperviousness
implacableness
implausibility
implementation
imponderabilia
impoverishment
impracticality
impregnability
impressibility
impressionable
impressiveness
improvableness
Mephistopheles
oppressiveness
papilionaceous
popularisation
repetitiveness
representation
representative
reproductively
repudiationist
saponification
septuagenarian
sophistication
soporiferously
superabundance
superannuation
superciliously
superconductor
superelevation
supereminently
supererogation
supererogatory
superficiality
superfoetation
superincumbent
superinduction
superintendent
supernaturally
superphosphate
superscription
supersensitive
supersonically
superstructure
superterranean
supervisorship
supposititious
supralapsarian
supramaxillary
suprasegmental
topsyturviness
unpalatability
unpleasantness
unpremeditated
unprofessional
coquettishness
loquaciousness
unquestionable
unquestionably
aerobiological
aerobiotically
aerodynamicist
Africanisation
agrobiological
airconditioner
arrhythmically
arrondissement
barometrically
boroughEnglish
carcinogenesis
cardiovascular
cartographical
Christological
chromatography
chronometrical
circuitousness
circumambiency
circumambulate
circumbendibus
circumlittoral
circumlocution
circumlocutory
circumnavigate
circumspection
circumstantial
circumvolution
correspondence
correspondency
corruptibility
corticosteroid
corticosterone
corticotrophic
corticotrophin
curvilinearity
dermatological
farsightedness
ferrimagnetism
ferromagnesian
ferromagnetism
foraminiferous
forbiddingness
foreordination
formidableness
forthrightness
fortuitousness
fortunetelling
forwardlooking
gerontological
gyrostabiliser
harmoniousness
hereditariness
hermaphroditic
heroworshipper
horrorstricken
horticulturist
irreconcilable
irreconcilably
irreducibility
irrefutability
irremovability
irreproachable
irreproachably
irreproducible
irresoluteness
irrespectively
irrevocability
jurisdictional
marketgardener
martyrological
marvellousness
meretriciously
miraculousness
morganatically
myrmecological
myrmecophagous
myrmecophilous
narrowmindedly
northeastwards
northnortheast
northnorthwest
northwestwards
paradoxicality
parallelepiped
parapsychology
parasitologist
paratactically
pardonableness
parenchymatous
parsimoniously
partridgeberry
perceptibility
perceptiveness
percutaneously
peremptoriness
perfectibility
perfidiousness
periodontology
peripateticism
perishableness
permissibility
permissiveness
perniciousness
personableness

persuasiveness
pertinaciously
perturbational
phraseological
portentousness
purposefulness
pyrheliometric
scrubbingbrush
scrupulousness
seriocomically
serviceability
servomechanism
sprightfulness
springcleaning
stratification
strikebreaking
strongmindedly
surefootedness
tergiversation
terminableness
terminological
territorialise
territorialism
territorialist
territoriality
terrorstricken
threadbareness
thriftlessness
tyrannicalness
unremunerative
unreservedness
uproariousness
verisimilitude
verticillaster
worshipfulness
Zoroastrianism
absentmindedly
absorptiveness
abstemiousness
abstractedness
abstractionism
abstractionist
aesthesiometer
associationism
auspiciousness
basidiomycetes
bastardisation
castrametation
cosmographical
cosmopolitical
despicableness
despiritualise
despitefulness
destructionist
disaffiliation
disaffirmation
disappointment
disapprobation
disapprobative
disapprobatory
disapprovingly
disarrangement
disassociation
disciplinarian
discolouration
discombobulate
discomfortable
discommendable
disconcertment
disconformable
disconnectedly
disconsolately
disconsolation
discontentedly
discontentment
discontinuance
discountenance
discouragement
discouragingly
discourteously
discriminating
discrimination
discriminative
discriminatory
discursiveness
disdainfulness
disembarkation
disembowelment
disenchantment
disenfranchise
disenthralment
disequilibrium
disfurnishment
disgruntlement
disheartenment
disinclination
disincorporate
disinfestation
disingenuously
disinheritance
disintegration
disintegrative
disjointedness
disorderliness
disorientation
dispensability
dispiritedness
disputatiously
disquisitional
disrespectable
dissertational
dissociability
distemperature
distensibility
distributional
distributively
fastidiousness
histochemistry
histopathology
historiography
histrionically
hysterectomise
insatiableness
inscrutability
insensibleness
inseparability
insignificance
insignificancy
instrumentally
insufficiently
insuperability
insuppressible
insurmountable
insurmountably
insurrectional
justifiability
lasciviousness
massproduction
mesdemoiselles
misapplication
misappropriate
miscalculation
misinformation
mistranslation
mysteriousness
obsequiousness
obstreperously
obstructionism
obstructionist
passionateness
pasteurisation
pestilentially
pisciculturist
pistilliferous
possessiveness
postmastership
postmillennial
postpositional
postpositively
resinification
resistlessness
respectability
respectfulness
responsibility
responsiveness
restorationism
restorationist
restrictionist
resurrectional
Rosicrucianism
Russianisation
sesquipedalian
susceptibility
susceptiveness
suspensiveness
suspiciousness
systematically
testimonialise
unsatisfactory
unscrupulously
unsociableness
unsuccessfully
vasodilatation
vasodilatatory
westernisation
aetiologically
altruistically
anthropography
anthropologist
anthropometric
anticipatively
anticonvulsant
antidepressant
antifederalist
antiperspirant
antiphlogistic
antiquarianism
antiscriptural
antiseptically
antithetically
articulateness
artificialness
astronomically
astrophysicist
attainableness
attractiveness
authentication
autobiographer
autobiographic
autocratically
autoradiograph
autosuggestion
bathingmachine
bituminisation
butterfingered
butterflyscrew
catachrestical
catechetically
categorisation
cotemporaneous
determinedness
detestableness
detoxification
enterprisingly
entertainingly
enthronisation
entomostracous
esterification
eutrophication
extemporaneity
extemporaneous
extensionality
extinguishable
extinguishment
extracorporeal
extraneousness
extravehicular
heterochromous
heteromorphism
heteromorphous
heterophyllous
heterothallism
iatrochemistry
intangibleness
integrationist
intellectually
intelligential
intelligentsia
intercessional
intercessorial
intercommunion
intercommunity
interdependent
interferential
interferometer
interferometry
intergradation
interjectional
interlineation
interlocutress
intermediately
intermediation
intermigration
intermittently
intermolecular
internationale
interpellation
interpenetrate
interplanetary
interpretation
interpretative
interpretively
intersectional
intersexuality
intertwinement
intolerability
intractability
intramolecular
intransitively
intrinsicality
introductorily
intuitionalism
intuitionalist
latitudinarian
liturgiologist
mathematically
matriarchalism
metallographer
metaphorically
metaphysically
metapsychology
metempsychosis
meteorological
methodological
meticulousness
mythologically
naturalisation
nitrocellulose
nitroglycerine
noteworthiness
nutritiousness
optimistically
orthochromatic
orthographical
ostentatiously
osteoarthritis
outgeneralling
outlandishness
outrageousness
pathogenically
pathologically
patresfamilias
petrochemistry
petrographical
petrologically
phthalocyanine

potentiometric
Pythagoreanism
retrogradation
satisfactorily
soteriological
tatterdemalion
tetradactylous
tetragrammaton
ultimogeniture
ultramicrotome
ultramontanism
ultramontanist
ultrasonically
ultrastructure
untruthfulness
vituperatively
watercolourist
watertightness
bougainvillaea
bouleversement
councilchamber
councillorship
counsellorship
counterbalance
counterculture
countercurrent
countermeasure
counterplotted
countrydancing
courageousness
doublebreasted
educationalist
emulsification
fructification
mountaineering
neuroanatomist
neurochemistry
neuropathology
neuroscientist
neutralisation
pluviometrical
roundaboutness
sauropterygian
scurrilousness
souldestroying
southeastwards
southwestwards
squadronleader
stultification
stumblingblock
stupendousness
tautologically
advantageously
adventitiously
devitalisation
diverticulitis
divertissement
favourableness
invariableness
invincibleness
inviolableness
lovingkindness
revalorisation
revengefulness
revivification
viviparousness
vivisectionist
bowdlerisation
newfangledness
dextrorotation
dextrorotatory
asymmetrically
asymptotically
asynchronously
cryptaesthesia
crystallisable
erythropoiesis
etymologically
oxyhaemoglobin

physiognomical
phytogeography
phytopathology
psychoanalysis
psychoanalytic
psychochemical
psychodynamics
psychoneurosis
psychoneurotic
psychophysical
psychosomatics
psychosurgical
thyrotoxicosis

---

advantageously
ambassadorship
attainableness
behaviouristic
breathlessness
breathtakingly
calamitousness
catachrestical
clearsightedly
denazification
departmentally
disaffiliation
disaffirmation
disappointment
disapprobation
disapprobative
disapprobatory
disapprovingly
disarrangement
disassociation
embarrassingly
enharmonically
exhaustibility
exhaustiveness
foraminiferous
galactopoietic
gelatinisation
gynaecological
gynandromorphy
idealistically
immaculateness
imparisyllabic
impassableness
impassibleness
incapacitation
incautiousness
inharmoniously
insatiableness
intangibleness
invariableness
Johannisberger
legalistically
malappropriate
manageableness
megasporangium
megasporophyll
metallographer
metaphorically
metaphysically
metapsychology
miraculousness
misapplication
misappropriate
oleaginousness
organisational
organometallic
palaeethnology
palaeobotanist
paradoxicality
parallelepiped
parapsychology
parasitologist
paratactically
phraseological
pleasurability

prearrangement
recapitulation
recapitulative
recapitulatory
regardlessness
rehabilitation
remarkableness
revalorisation
sphaerocrystal
squadronleader
stratification
subalternation
tyrannicalness
unfaithfulness
unmannerliness
unpalatability
unsatisfactory
volatilisation
Brobdingnagian
combustibility
cumbersomeness
doublebreasted
forbiddingness
hobbledehoyish
nonbelligerent
probabiliorism
probabiliorist
rambunctiously
Sabbatarianism
airconditioner
blackmarketeer
blockaderunner
brachycephalic
calcareousness
carcinogenesis
chickenhearted
chickenlivered
circuitousness
circumambiency
circumambulate
circumbendibus
circumlittoral
circumlocution
circumlocutory
circumnavigate
circumspection
circumstantial
circumvolution
concavoconcave
conceivability
concelebration
concentrically
concessionaire
conclusiveness
concretisation
diachronically
disciplinarian
discolouration
discombobulate
discomfortable
discommendable
disconcertment
disconformable
disconnectedly
disconsolately
disconsolation
discontentedly
discontentment
discontinuance
discountenance
discouragement
discouragingly
discourteously
discriminating
discrimination
discriminative
discriminatory
discursiveness
educationalist

electioneering
electrobiology
electrodeposit
electrodynamic
electrostatics
electrotherapy
electrothermal
electrothermic
electrovalency
fructification
geocentrically
illconditioned
inscrutability
knickerbockers
lasciviousness
malcontentedly
miscalculation
neocolonialism
noncommunicant
nonconcurrence
noncooperation
perceptibility
perceptiveness
percutaneously
pisciculturist
practicability
precariousness
precociousness
proceleusmatic
procrastinator
psychoanalysis
psychoanalytic
psychochemical
psychodynamics
psychoneurosis
psychoneurotic
psychophysical
psychosomatics
psychosurgical
sanctification
specialisation
spectrographic
spectroscopist
stochastically
subconsciously
subcontinental
subcontrariety
successfulness
successionally
successiveness
susceptibility
susceptiveness
synchronically
unaccommodated
unaccomplished
unacknowledged
uneconomically
unscrupulously
volcanological
vulcanological
biodegradation
bowdlerisation
cardiovascular
condescendence
conditionality
conductibility
creditableness
disdainfulness
epidemiologist
fundamentalism
fundamentalist
fundamentality
goodfellowship
goodhumouredly
goodtemperedly
handicraftsman
handkerchieves
inadequateness
inadvisability

med**d**lesomeness
mes**d**emoiselles
par**d**onableness
pre**d**esignation
pre**d**estinarian
pre**d**estination
pre**d**eterminate
pre**d**ictability
pre**d**isposition
pro**d**igiousness
pro**d**uctiveness
qua**d**ragenarian
qua**d**risyllabic
qua**d**risyllable
roa**d**worthiness
sta**d**holdership
tra**d**itionalism
tra**d**itionalist
tri**d**imensional
two**d**imensional
uni**d**imensional
uni**d**irectional
vin**d**ictiveness
win**d**owdressing
win**d**owshopping
won**d**erstricken
abs**e**ntmindedly
acc**e**leratingly
acc**e**ptableness
adv**e**ntitiously
aff**e**ctionately
all**e**gorisation
all**e**lomorphism
app**e**ndicectomy
ben**e**ficialness
bio**e**lectricity
bio**e**ngineering
cat**e**chetically
cat**e**gorisation
cin**e**matography
cot**e**mporaneous
dec**e**ivableness
def**e**nestration
deg**e**nerateness
del**e**ctableness
dep**e**ndableness
det**e**rminedness
det**e**stableness
dis**e**mbarkation
dis**e**mbowelment
dis**e**nchantment
dis**e**nfranchise
dis**e**nthralment
dis**e**quilibrium
div**e**rticulitis
div**e**rtissement
dod**e**casyllable
eff**e**rvescently
eig**e**nfrequency
enc**e**phalograph
ent**e**rprisingly
ent**e**rtainingly
est**e**rification
exc**e**ptionality
exp**e**rientially
exp**e**rimentally
ext**e**mporaneity
ext**e**mporaneous
ext**e**nsionality
for**e**ordination
fri**e**ndlessness
gen**e**alogically
gen**e**ralisation
gen**e**ralpurpose
heb**e**tudinosity
her**e**ditariness
het**e**rochromous
het**e**romorphism
het**e**romorphous
het**e**rophyllous
het**e**rothallism
hyp**e**rbolically
hyp**e**rcalcaemia
hyp**e**rcatalexis
hyp**e**rcriticise
hyp**e**rcriticism
hyp**e**rglycaemia
hyp**e**rirritable
hyp**e**rsensitive
hyp**e**rsonically
ill**e**gitimately
imm**e**thodically
imp**e**rativeness
imp**e**rmeability
imp**e**rviousness
inc**e**stuousness
ind**e**cipherable
ind**e**cisiveness
ind**e**composable
ind**e**corousness
ind**e**finiteness
ind**e**monstrable
ind**e**structible
ind**e**structibly
ind**e**terminable
inf**e**ctiousness
inf**e**licitously
inh**e**ritability
ins**e**nsibleness
ins**e**parability
int**e**grationist
int**e**llectually
int**e**lligential
int**e**lligentsia
int**e**rcessional
int**e**rcessorial
int**e**rcommunion
int**e**rcommunity
int**e**rdependent
int**e**rferential
int**e**rferometer
int**e**rferometry
int**e**rgradation
int**e**rjectional
int**e**rlineation
int**e**rlocutress
int**e**rmediately
int**e**rmediation
int**e**rmigration
int**e**rmittently
int**e**rmolecular
int**e**rnationale
int**e**rpellation
int**e**rpenetrate
int**e**rplanetary
int**e**rpretation
int**e**rpretative
int**e**rpretively
int**e**rsectional
int**e**rsexuality
int**e**rtwinement
irr**e**concilable
irr**e**concilably
irr**e**ducibility
irr**e**futability
irr**e**movability
irr**e**proachable
irr**e**proachably
irr**e**producible
irr**e**soluteness
irr**e**spectively
irr**e**vocability
lib**e**ralisation
lib**e**rtarianism
lic**e**ntiousness
mer**e**triciously
met**e**mpsychosis
met**e**orological
min**e**ralisation
nec**e**ssarianism
nom**e**nclatorial
not**e**worthiness
obs**e**quiousness
ost**e**ntatiously
ost**e**oarthritis
par**e**nchymatous
pen**e**trableness
per**e**mptoriness
phl**e**gmatically
pig**e**onbreasted
pot**e**ntiometric
reb**e**lliousness
reg**e**neratively
rel**e**ntlessness
rep**e**titiveness
rev**e**ngefulness
sch**e**matisation
sci**e**ntifically
sot**e**riological
spe**e**chlessness
sup**e**rabundance
sup**e**rannuation
sup**e**rciliously
sup**e**rconductor
sup**e**relevation
sup**e**reminently
sup**e**rerogation
sup**e**rerogatory
sup**e**rficiality
sup**e**rfoetation
sup**e**rincumbent
sup**e**rinduction
sup**e**rintendent
sup**e**rnaturally
sup**e**rphosphate
sup**e**rscription
sup**e**rsensitive
sup**e**rsonically
sup**e**rstructure
sup**e**rterranean
sup**e**rvisorship
sur**e**footedness
tel**e**ologically
tel**e**pathically
tel**e**phonically
tel**e**photograph
tel**e**scopically
thr**e**adbareness
unb**e**comingness
und**e**rdeveloped
und**e**remphasise
und**e**rgraduette
und**e**rmentioned
und**e**rnourished
und**e**rstandable
und**e**rstandably
und**e**rstatement
und**e**rvaluation
und**e**sirability
unh**e**sitatingly
unm**e**ntionables
unr**e**munerative
unr**e**servedness
val**e**tudinarian
veg**e**tativeness
ven**e**reological
vic**e**chancellor
vic**e**presidency
wat**e**rcolourist
wat**e**rtightness
con**f**identially
con**f**ormability
dif**f**erentiable
dif**f**erentially
dif**f**ractometer
dis**f**urnishment
hal**f**pennyworth
ine**f**fectuality
new**f**angledness
per**f**ectibility
per**f**idiousness
pre**f**abrication
pre**f**erentially
pro**f**essionally
pro**f**essorially
pro**f**itableness
sel**f**abnegation
sel**f**absorption
sel**f**accusation
sel**f**accusatory
sel**f**adjustment
sel**f**admiration
sel**f**assumption
sel**f**complacent
sel**f**confidence
sel**f**consequent
sel**f**consistent
sel**f**controlled
sel**f**correcting
sel**f**dependence
sel**f**destroying
sel**f**determined
sel**f**discipline
sel**f**effacement
sel**f**effacingly
sel**f**employment
sel**f**energising
sel**f**explaining
sel**f**expression
sel**f**fertilised
sel**f**flattering
sel**f**fulfilling
sel**f**government
sel**f**immolation
sel**f**importance
sel**f**inductance
sel**f**indulgence
sel**f**interested
sel**f**partiality
sel**f**perception
sel**f**possession
sel**f**preserving
sel**f**proclaimed
sel**f**propelling
sel**f**propulsion
sel**f**protection
sel**f**regulating
sel**f**repression
sel**f**respectful
sel**f**respecting
sel**f**restrained
sel**f**revelation
sel**f**satisfying
sel**f**sufficient
sel**f**suggestion
sel**f**supporting
sel**f**sustaining
sel**f**tormenting
suf**f**erableness
una**f**fectedness
uni**f**ormitarian
ana**g**rammatical
bio**g**raphically
bou**g**ainvillaea
con**g**lomeration
con**g**lutination
con**g**lutinative
con**g**ratulation
con**g**ratulative
con**g**ratulatory
con**g**regational
dia**g**nostically
dia**g**rammatical
dis**g**runtlement
epi**g**rammatical
fla**g**itiousness

geo**g**raphically
gre**g**ariousness
ima**g**inableness
jud**g**ematically
kni**g**hterrantry
lin**g**uistically
lon**g**headedness
lon**g**itudinally
lon**g**windedness
mor**g**anatically
out**g**eneralling
pra**g**maticality
pro**g**enitorship
pro**g**nosticator
pro**g**ressionary
pro**g**ressionism
pro**g**ressionist
san**g**uification
san**g**uinariness
sin**g**lebreasted
sin**g**lehandedly
sin**g**lemindedly
sna**g**gletoothed
ste**g**anographer
sti**g**matisation
sug**g**estibility
sug**g**estiveness
ter**g**iversation
tra**g**icomically
wei**g**htlessness
alp**h**abetically
alp**h**anumerical
ant**h**ropography
ant**h**ropologist
ant**h**ropometric
arc**h**aeological
arc**h**etypically
arc**h**idiaconate
arc**h**iepiscopal
arc**h**itectonics
arr**h**ythmically
aut**h**entication
bat**h**ingmachine
dis**h**eartenment
ent**h**ronisation
esc**h**atological
eup**h**uistically
hig**h**handedness
hig**h**mindedness
lig**h**theartedly
mat**h**ematically
Mep**h**istopheles
met**h**odological
myt**h**ologically
nig**h**tblindness
ort**h**ochromatic
ort**h**ographical
oxy**h**aemoglobin
pac**h**ydermatous
pat**h**ogenically
pat**h**ologically
pht**h**alocyanine
pro**h**ibitionism
pro**h**ibitionist
pyr**h**eliometric
Pyt**h**agoreanism
sop**h**istication
tac**h**istoscopic
tac**h**ygraphical
adm**i**nistration
adm**i**nistrative
adm**i**nistratrix
aet**i**ologically
Afr**i**canisation
Alb**i**gensianism
amb**i**dextrously
ant**i**cipatively
ant**i**convulsant
ant**i**depressant
ant**i**federalist
ant**i**perspirant
ant**i**phlogistic
ant**i**quarianism
ant**i**scriptural
ant**i**septically
ant**i**thetically
art**i**culateness
art**i**ficialness
aud**i**ofrequency
bas**i**diomycetes
cap**i**talisation
Chr**i**stological
dec**i**malisation
def**i**nitiveness
del**i**berateness
del**i**beratively
del**i**ghtfulness
dem**i**semiquaver
dev**i**talisation
dim**i**nutiveness
dis**i**nclination
dis**i**ncorporate
dis**i**nfestation
dis**i**ngenuously
dis**i**nheritance
dis**i**ntegration
dis**i**ntegrative
dol**i**chocephaly
exh**i**laratingly
ext**i**nguishable
ext**i**nguishment
hag**i**ographical
hum**i**dification
ill**i**mitability
ill**i**terateness
ind**i**fferentism
ind**i**fferentist
ind**i**scerptible
ind**i**scoverable
ind**i**screetness
ind**i**scriminate
ind**i**stinctness
ind**i**visibility
ins**i**gnificance
ins**i**gnificancy
inv**i**ncibleness
inv**i**olableness
jur**i**sdictional
lat**i**tudinarian
leg**i**timisation
lib**i**dinousness
lov**i**ngkindness
med**i**tativeness
met**i**culousness
mil**i**tarisation
min**i**sterialist
mis**i**nformation
non**i**nvolvement
num**i**smatically
omn**i**vorousness
one**i**rocritical
opt**i**mistically
orn**i**thological
pap**i**lionaceous
per**i**odontology
per**i**pateticism
per**i**shableness
pol**i**ticisation
pra**i**seworthily
rad**i**calisation
rad**i**oautograph
rad**i**ochemistry
rad**i**osensitive
rad**i**ostrontium
rad**i**otelegraph
rad**i**otelephone
rad**i**otelephony
rad**i**otherapist
red**i**ntegration
red**i**stribution
red**i**stributive
rel**i**nquishment
rem**i**niscential
res**i**nification
res**i**stlessness
rev**i**vification
rid**i**culousness
rig**i**dification
Ros**i**crucianism
sat**i**sfactorily
sch**i**smatically
sem**i**centennial
sem**i**conducting
sem**i**elliptical
sem**i**officially
ser**i**ocomically
sil**i**cification
soc**i**ologically
soc**i**opolitical
sol**i**citousness
sol**i**dification
sol**i**tudinarian
spr**i**ghtfulness
spr**i**ngcleaning
sto**i**cheiometry
sto**i**chiometric
str**i**kebreaking
sub**i**nfeudation
thr**i**ftlessness
tra**i**torousness
ult**i**mogeniture
unc**i**rcumcision
ver**i**similitude
viv**i**parousness
viv**i**sectionist
voc**i**ferousness
con**j**unctivitis
dis**j**ointedness
sub**j**ectiveness
bac**k**scattering
bac**k**scratching
mar**k**etgardener
mon**k**eybusiness
poi**k**ilothermal
poi**k**ilothermic
Sha**k**espeareana
Sha**k**espeariana
wea**k**mindedness
apo**l**ogetically
bib**l**iographise
bib**l**iomaniacal
bio**l**uminescent
bou**l**eversement
bul**l**headedness
dep**l**orableness
dia**l**ectologist
dip**l**omatically
ecc**l**esiastical
ecc**l**esiologist
ega**l**itarianism
emb**l**ematically
emu**l**sification
exc**l**austration
fal**l**aciousness
ful**l**yfashioned
hal**l**ucinogenic
imp**l**acableness
imp**l**ausibility
imp**l**ementation
ina**l**ienability
ina**l**terability
inf**l**ammability
inf**l**ectionally
inf**l**ectionless
inf**l**exibleness
ing**l**oriousness
mil**l**enarianism
neg**l**ectfulness
out**l**andishness
phi**l**anthropise
phi**l**anthropist
phi**l**ologically
pro**l**etarianise
pro**l**etarianism
pro**l**ocutorship
psi**l**anthropism
psi**l**anthropist
pub**l**icspirited
ref**l**ectiveness
sou**l**destroying
stu**l**tification
sub**l**ieutenancy
tha**l**assography
unf**l**atteringly
unp**l**easantness
uti**l**itarianism
vil**l**ainousness
asy**m**metrically
asy**m**ptotically
bre**m**sstrahlung
che**m**oreception
che**m**oreceptive
che**m**osynthesis
cli**m**atological
com**m**ensurately
com**m**ensuration
com**m**issaryship
com**m**issionaire
com**m**itteewoman
com**m**odiousness
com**m**onsensical
com**m**unications
cos**m**ographical
cos**m**opolitical
der**m**atological
dia**m**antiferous
dia**m**ondiferous
ele**m**entariness
ety**m**ologically
for**m**idableness
gra**m**ineousness
hae**m**atogenesis
har**m**oniousness
her**m**aphroditic
ini**m**itableness
kre**m**linologist
myr**m**ecological
myr**m**ecophagous
myr**m**ecophilous
per**m**issibility
per**m**issiveness
pre**m**editatedly
pre**m**illenarian
sha**m**efacedness
ski**m**bleskamble
sta**m**pcollector
sto**m**atological
stu**m**blingblock
sub**m**ersibility
sub**m**icroscopic
sub**m**issiveness
sym**m**etrisation
ter**m**inableness
ter**m**inological
thi**m**blerigging
tre**m**endousness
une**m**phatically
ack**n**owledgment
asy**n**chronously
bro**n**chiectasis
cha**n**cellorship
cha**n**geableness
chi**n**cherinchee
cou**n**cilchamber
cou**n**cillorship
cou**n**sellorship

counterbalance
counterculture
countercurrent
countermeasure
counterplotted
countrydancing
crinkumcrankum
cyanocobalamin
econometrician
enantiomorphic
ethnologically
Evangelicalism
evangelisation
fainteartedly
grandiloquence
iconographical
identification
magniloquently
mountaineering
openhandedness
openmindedness
opinionatively
perniciousness
phantasmagoria
phantasmagoric
phenobarbitone
phenylbutazone
pianoaccordian
planetstricken
pugnaciousness
quantification
quantitatively
quinquagesimal
quinquennially
quintessential
reintroduction
reinvigoration
rhinencephalic
rhinencephalon
roentgenoscopy
roundaboutness
scandalisation
scandalousness
scintillometer
slanderousness
somnambulation
somnambulistic
spindleshanked
spinthariscope
standardbearer
thanksoffering
transcendental
transcendently
transformation
transformative
transitionally
transitiveness
transitoriness
transliterator
transmigration
transmigratory
transplantable
transportation
transsexualism
transvaluation
transversality
Trinitarianism
unenterprising
unenthusiastic
unintelligible
unintelligibly
vaingloriously
vulnerableness
absorptiveness
accomplishable
accomplishment
accountability
achondroplasia
aerobiological
aerobiotically
aerodynamicist
agrobiological
aphoristically
arrondissement
associationism
autobiographer
autobiographic
autocratically
autoradiograph
autosuggestion
barometrically
bloodthirstily
boroughEnglish
chromatography
chronometrical
colourfastness
colourlessness
decolonisation
decolorisation
deconsecration
decorativeness
delocalisation
demobilisation
democratically
demonetisation
demoralisation
denominational
depolarisation
detoxification
dicotyledonous
dinoflagellate
disorderliness
disorientation
dolomitisation
effortlessness
endoradiosonde
endosmotically
entomostracous
eulogistically
excommunicable
excommunicator
favourableness
gerontological
gyrostabiliser
heroworshipper
holometabolism
holometabolous
homoeomorphism
homogenisation
homotransplant
honourableness
hypocoristical
hypocritically
hypodermically
hypostatically
hypothetically
hypothyroidism
idiopathically
immobilisation
immoderateness
imponderabilia
impoverishment
incommensurate
incommodiously
incommunicable
incommunicably
incompleteness
incompressible
incompressibly
inconclusively
inconsequently
inconsiderable
inconsiderably
inconsistently
incontrollable
inconveniently
incoordination
incorporeality
indoctrination
intolerability
malodorousness
monochromatism
monopolisation
monosaccharide
monotonousness
pleonastically
recolonisation
recommencement
recommendation
recommendatory
reconciliation
reconciliatory
reconnaissance
reconstitution
reconstruction
reconstructive
recoverability
remonetisation
remorsefulness
saponification
scholastically
schoolchildren
schoolmistress
soporiferously
strongmindedly
sycophantishly
theocratically
uncommunicable
uncompromising
uncongeniality
unconscionable
uncontrollable
uncontrollably
uncontroverted
unconventional
unconvincingly
uncorroborated
unsociableness
uproariousness
vasodilatation
vasodilatatory
Zoroastrianism
apophthegmatic
apoplectically
auspiciousness
campanological
campylotropous
comparableness
compassionable
compatibleness
compensational
complexionless
compossibility
comprehensible
comprehensibly
compulsiveness
copperbottomed
cryptaesthesia
despicableness
despiritualise
despitefulness
diaphanousness
dispensability
dispiritedness
disputatiously
inappositeness
inappreciation
inappreciative
inapproachable
lyophilisation
nonperformance
preponderantly
preposterously
propaedeutical
propagandistic
propitiatorily
propitiousness
proportionable
proportionably
proportionally
proprietorship
proprioceptive
purposefulness
rampageousness
respectability
respectfulness
responsibility
responsiveness
simplemindedly
simplification
staphylococcus
stupendousness
sulphanilamide
supposititious
suspensiveness
suspiciousness
symptomatology
tropologically
unappreciative
unapproachable
whippersnapper
conquistadores
disquisitional
sesquipedalian
ubiquitousness
achromatically
aforementioned
aggrandisement
aggressiveness
altruistically
apprehensively
apprenticeship
astronomically
astrophysicist
attractiveness
avariciousness
boardingschool
capriciousness
characteristic
charitableness
coordinateness
correspondence
correspondency
corruptibility
courageousness
disrespectable
eutrophication
excruciatingly
expressionless
expressiveness
extracorporeal
extraneousness
extravehicular
ferrimagnetism
ferromagnesian
ferromagnetism
floriculturist
heartsearching
hierarchically
hieroglyphical
horrorstricken
hydrocoralline
hydrodynamical
hydrographical
hydromechanics
hygroscopicity
iatrochemistry
impracticality
impregnability
impressibility
impressionable
impressiveness
improvableness
inarticulately
inarticulation
inartistically

incredibleness
infralapsarian
infrangibility
infrastructure
ingratiatingly
inordinateness
intractability
intramolecular
intransitively
intrinsicality
introductorily
macrocephalous
macroeconomics
matriarchalism
microbiologist
microcephalous
microcircuitry
microcomponent
microeconomics
microminiature
microprocessor
microsporangia
microstructure
microtechnique
narrowmindedly
neuroanatomist
neurochemistry
neuropathology
neuroscientist
nitrocellulose
nitroglycerine
nonrestrictive
nutritiousness
oppressiveness
outrageousness
overabundantly
overcapitalise
overcommitment
overcompensate
overconfidence
overestimation
overexcitement
overindulgence
overpopulation
overpoweringly
overproduction
oversubscribed
overwhelmingly
patresfamilias
petrochemistry
petrographical
petrologically
pharmaceutical
pharmacologist
pharmacopoeial
pteridological
quarterbinding
refractoriness
refrangibility
regressiveness
reorganisation
representation
representative
reproductively
retrogradation
sacramentalism
sacramentalist
sacramentarian
sacrilegiously
sauropterygian
scurrilousness
segregationist
shortsightedly
spermatogenous
spermatogonium
spermatophytic
spiritlessness
spiritualistic
spirituousness
spirochaetosis
stertorousness
supralapsarian
supramaxillary
suprasegmental
swordswallower
territorialise
territorialism
territorialist
territoriality
terrorstricken
tetradactylous
tetragrammaton
therianthropic
thermochemical
thermodynamics
thermoelectric
thyrotoxicosis
ultramicrotome
ultramontanism
ultramontanist
ultrasonically
ultrastructure
umbrageousness
unfriendliness
ungraciousness
ungratefulness
unpremeditated
unprofessional
untruthfulness
whortleberries
biosystematics
boisterousness
censoriousness
classconscious
classification
classificatory
coessentiality
consanguineous
conscienceless
conservational
conservatively
consociational
conspiratorial
constitutional
constitutively
constructional
constructively
constructivism
constructivist
consubstantial
consuetudinary
crossfertilise
crosspollinate
crossreference
crystallisable
dieselelectric
dissertational
dissociability
epistemologist
exasperatingly
existentialism
existentialist
farsightedness
massproduction
nonsensicality
parsimoniously
passionateness
personableness
persuasiveness
phosphorescent
physiognomical
possessiveness
presbyterially
prescriptively
presentability
presentational
presentimental
presumptuously
presupposition
proscriptively
prosencephalic
prosencephalon
prosperousness
reasonableness
Russianisation
seasonableness
sensationalism
sensationalist
sensualisation
substantialism
substantialist
substantiality
substantiation
substantivally
substitutional
substitutively
topsyturviness
worshipfulness
abstemiousness
abstractedness
abstractionism
abstractionist
aesthesiometer
amateurishness
apothegmatical
arithmetically
bacteriologist
bacteriostasis
bacteriostatic
bastardisation
butterfingered
butterflyscrew
cantankerously
cartographical
castrametation
centralisation
centrifugation
contagiousness
contemptuously
conterminously
contiguousness
continuousness
contractedness
contradictable
contradictious
contraindicate
contraposition
contrapositive
contrapuntally
controllership
controvertible
contumaciously
contumeliously
corticosteroid
corticosterone
corticotrophic
corticotrophin
destructionist
dextrorotation
dextrorotatory
distemperature
distensibility
distributional
distributively
erythropoiesis
factitiousness
fantasticality
fastidiousness
featherbrained
fictitiousness
flatfootedness
forthrightness
fortuitousness
fortunetelling
fraternisation
gratuitousness
histochemistry
histopathology
historiography
histrionically
horticulturist
hysterectomise
ichthyological
ichthyophagous
ichthyosaurian
instrumentally
justifiability
lefthandedness
martyrological
mistranslation
multifariously
multilaterally
multinucleated
multiplication
multiplicative
mysteriousness
neutralisation
noctambulation
northeastwards
northnortheast
northnorthwest
northwestwards
obstreperously
obstructionism
obstructionist
ophthalmoscope
ophthalmoscopy
partridgeberry
pasteurisation
pertinaciously
perturbational
pestilentially
photochemistry
photoperiodism
photosensitise
photosensitive
photosynthesis
photosynthetic
phototelegraph
phytogeography
phytopathology
pistilliferous
portentousness
postmastership
postmillennial
postpositional
postpositively
prettification
protectiveness
prothonotarial
protozoologist
protrusiveness
quattrocentism
quattrocentist
rectangularity
restorationism
restorationist
restrictionist
rontgenography
scatterbrained
sentimentalise
sentimentalism
sentimentalist
sentimentality
septuagenarian
slatternliness
southeastwards
southwestwards
spatiotemporal
stationariness
statuesqueness
systematically
tatterdemalion
tautologically
testimonialise
tintinnabulary

tintinnabulate
tintinnabulous
unattractively
verticillaster
victoriousness
weltanschauung
westernisation
accumulatively
accustomedness
Augustinianism
beautification
bituminisation
claustrophobia
claustrophobic
coquettishness
cucurbitaceous
cumulativeness
dehumanisation
denumerability
figurativeness
groundlessness
hocuspocussing
illustrational
illustratively
inauspiciously
indubitability
insufficiently
insuperability
insuppressible
insurmountable
insurmountably
insurrectional
intuitionalism
intuitionalist
liturgiologist
loquaciousness
lugubriousness
naturalisation
oecumenicalism
pneumatologist
pneumoconiosis
popularisation
pseudaesthesia
pseudepigrapha
pseudepigraphy
pseudomorphism
pseudomorphous
pseudonymously
regularisation
rejuvenescence
repudiationist
resurrectional
rheumatologist
robustiousness
salubriousness
scrubbingbrush
scrupulousness
secularisation
simultaneously
slaughterhouse
slaughterously
solubilisation
stoutheartedly
thoughtfulness
thoughtreading
troubleshooter
tumultuousness
unquestionable
unquestionably
unsuccessfully
vituperatively
volumetrically
voluminousness
voluptuousness
abovementioned
chivalrousness
conventionally
conversational
convertibility
convexoconcave
convincingness
convulsiveness
curvilinearity
inevitableness
marvellousness
pluviometrical
preventability
preventiveness
providentially
serviceability
servomechanism
shovehalfpenny
subversiveness
trivialisation
universalistic
forwardlooking
epexegetically
inexorableness
inexpressively
unexpectedness
encyclopaedism
encyclopaedist
polymerisation
polymorphously
polysaccharide
polytheistical
sphygmographic

---

aggrandisement
alphabetically
alphanumerical
archaeological
attractiveness
bastardisation
bougainvillaea
calcareousness
campanological
cantankerously
characteristic
chivalrousness
climatological
comparableness
compassionable
compatibleness
concavoconcave
consanguineous
contagiousness
courageousness
dermatological
diamantiferous
disdainfulness
educationalist
eschatological
exclaustration
extracorporeal
extraneousness
extravehicular
fallaciousness
fantasticality
forwardlooking
fundamentalism
fundamentalist
fundamentality
genealogically
gregariousness
haematogenesis
hermaphroditic
hierarchically
implacableness
implausibility
impracticality
inflammability
infralapsarian
infrangibility
infrastructure
ingratiatingly
intractability
intramolecular
intransitively
loquaciousness
miscalculation
morganatically
newfangledness
noctambulation
outlandishness
outrageousness
overabundantly
oxyhaemoglobin
philanthropise
philanthropist
phthalocyanine
precariousness
prefabrication
probabiliorism
probabiliorist
propaedeutical
propagandistic
psilanthropism
psilanthropist
pugnaciousness
Pythagoreanism
rampageousness
rectangularity
refractoriness
refrangibility
Sabbatarianism
sacramentalism
sacramentalist
sacramentarian
selfabnegation
selfabsorption
selfaccusation
selfaccusatory
selfadjustment
selfadmiration
selfassumption
sensationalism
sensationalist
somnambulation
somnambulistic
steganographer
stomatological
supralapsarian
supramaxillary
suprasegmental
tetradactylous
tetragrammaton
thalassography
threadbareness
ultramicrotome
ultramontanism
ultramontanist
ultrasonically
ultrastructure
umbrageousness
unflatteringly
ungraciousness
ungratefulness
uproariousness
villainousness
volcanological
vulcanological
weltanschauung
Zoroastrianism
aerobiological
aerobiotically
agrobiological
autobiographer
autobiographic
deliberateness
deliberatively
demobilisation
immobilisation
indubitability
lugubriousness
presbyterially
rehabilitation
salubriousness
scrubbingbrush
skimbleskamble
solubilisation
stumblingblock
thimblerigging
troubleshooter
affectionately
Africanisation
anticipatively
anticonvulsant
articulateness
associationism
asynchronously
autocratically
bronchiectasis
catachrestical
catechetically
chancellorship
chincherinchee
conscienceless
councilchamber
councillorship
delectableness
delocalisation
democratically
dodecasyllable
dolichocephaly
encyclopaedism
encyclopaedist
galactopoietic
hypocoristical
hypocritically
immaculateness
indecipherable
indecisiveness
indecomposable
indecorousness
indoctrination
infectiousness
irreconcilable
irreconcilably
meticulousness
miraculousness
monochromatism
overcapitalise
overcommitment
overcompensate
overconfidence
prescriptively
proscriptively
radicalisation
ridiculousness
Rosicrucianism
selfcomplacent
selfconfidence
selfconsequent
selfconsistent
selfcontrolled
selfcorrecting
semicentennial
semiconducting
silicification
solicitousness
speechlessness
stoicheiometry
stoichiometric
theocratically
unaccommodated
unaccomplished
unbecomingness
unsociableness
unsuccessfully
vicechancellor
aerodynamicist
ambidextrously
antidepressant
basidiomycetes
bloodthirstily

boardingschool
Brobdingnagian
coordinateness
grandiloquence
hereditariness
humidification
hypodermically
immoderateness
inordinateness
irreducibility
libidinousness
malodorousness
paradoxicality
pseudaesthesia
pseudepigrapha
pseudepigraphy
pseudomorphism
pseudomorphous
pseudonymously
repudiationist
rigidification
roundaboutness
scandalisation
scandalousness
selfdependence
selfdestroying
selfdetermined
selfdiscipline
slanderousness
solidification
souldestroying
spindleshanked
squadronleader
standardbearer
swordswallower
vasodilatation
vasodilatatory
abovementioned
abstemiousness
aforementioned
aggressiveness
amateurishness
apprehensively
apprenticeship
archetypically
authentication
bacteriologist
bacteriostasis
bacteriostatic
biodegradation
bouleversement
butterfingered
butterflyscrew
commensurately
commensuration
compensational
conceivability
concelebration
concentrically
concessionaire
condescendence
conservational
conservatively
contemptuously
conterminously
conventionally
conversational
convertibility
convexoconcave
copperbottomed
coquettishness
correspondence
correspondency
cumbersomeness
dialectologist
dieselelectric
differentiable
differentially
disheartenment
dispensability
disrespectable
dissertational
distemperature
distensibility
ecclesiastical
ecclesiologist
elementariness
emblematically
epexegetically
epidemiologist
expressionless
expressiveness
fraternisation
geocentrically
gynaecological
homoeomorphism
hysterectomise
implementation
impregnability
impressibility
impressionable
impressiveness
inadequateness
incredibleness
inflectionally
inflectionless
inflexibleness
judgematically
marketgardener
marvellousness
mathematically
mesdemoiselles
millenarianism
monkeybusiness
myrmecological
myrmecophagous
myrmecophilous
mysteriousness
neglectfulness
nonbelligerent
nonperformance
nonrestrictive
nonsensicality
oppressiveness
outgeneralling
overestimation
overexcitement
palaeethnology
palaeobotanist
pasteurisation
patresfamilias
perceptibility
perceptiveness
perfectibility
planetstricken
portentousness
possessiveness
predesignation
predestinarian
predestination
predeterminate
preferentially
premeditatedly
presentability
presentational
presentimental
preventability
preventiveness
proceleusmatic
professionally
professorially
progenitorship
proletarianise
proletarianism
prosencephalic
prosencephalon
protectiveness
pyrheliometric
reflectiveness
regressiveness
representation
representative
respectability
respectfulness
rhinencephalic
rhinencephalon
segregationist
selfeffacement
selfeffacingly
selfemployment
selfenergising
selfexplaining
selfexpression
semielliptical
Shakespeareana
Shakespeariana
shamefacedness
shovehalfpenny
sphaerocrystal
stupendousness
subjectiveness
submersibility
subversiveness
successfulness
successionally
successiveness
sufferableness
suggestibility
suggestiveness
susceptibility
susceptiveness
suspensiveness
symmetrisation
systematically
tatterdemalion
tremendousness
universalistic
unpleasantness
unpremeditated
unquestionable
unquestionably
vulnerableness
westernisation
wonderstricken
antifederalist
artificialness
beneficialness
dinoflagellate
disaffiliation
disaffirmation
flatfootedness
goodfellowship
indefiniteness
indifferentism
indifferentist
ineffectuality
insufficiently
irrefutability
selffertilised
selfflattering
selffulfilling
surefootedness
thriftlessness
unaffectedness
vociferousness
Albigensianism
allegorisation
categorisation
changeableness
delightfulness
eulogistically
Evangelicalism
evangelisation
homogenisation
illegitimately
insignificance
insignificancy
integrationist
manageableness
oleaginousness
phlegmatically
reorganisation
rontgenography
selfgovernment
slaughterhouse
slaughterously
snaggletoothed
sphygmographic
sprightfulness
thoughtfulness
thoughtreading
vaingloriously
aesthesiometer
apophthegmatic
apothegmatical
arithmetically
brachycephalic
bullheadedness
diachronically
diaphanousness
erythropoiesis
featherbrained
forthrightness
goodhumouredly
highhandedness
ichthyological
ichthyophagous
ichthyosaurian
knighterrantry
lefthandedness
longheadedness
lyophilisation
northeastwards
northnortheast
northnorthwest
northwestwards
openhandedness
ophthalmoscope
ophthalmoscopy
prothonotarial
psychoanalysis
psychoanalytic
psychochemical
psychodynamics
psychoneurosis
psychoneurotic
psychophysical
psychosomatics
psychosurgical
southeastwards
southwestwards
stadholdership
staphylococcus
stochastically
sulphanilamide
synchronically
weightlessness
worshipfulness
archidiaconate
archiepiscopal
architectonics
attainableness
auspiciousness
avariciousness
bathingmachine
bibliographise
bibliomaniacal
capriciousness
carcinogenesis
cardiovascular
charitableness
commissaryship
commissionaire
committeewoman
conditionality
confidentially

contiguousness
continuousness
convincingness
corticosteroid
corticosterone
corticotrophic
corticotrophin
creditableness
curvilinearity
deceivableness
despicableness
despiritualise
despitefulness
disciplinarian
dispiritedness
egalitarianism
factitiousness
farsightedness
fastidiousness
ferrimagnetism
fictitiousness
flagitiousness
floriculturist
forbiddingness
formidableness
gramineousness
handicraftsman
horticulturist
imaginableness
inalienability
inevitableness
inimitableness
intrinsicality
intuitionalism
intuitionalist
justifiability
lasciviousness
longitudinally
magniloquently
matriarchalism
Mephistopheles
multifariously
multilaterally
multinucleated
multiplication
multiplicative
nutritiousness
opinionatively
overindulgence
parsimoniously
passionateness
perfidiousness
permissibility
permissiveness
perniciousness
pertinaciously
pestilentially
physiognomical
pisciculturist
pistilliferous
pluviometrical
poikilothermal
poikilothermic
predictability
predisposition
premillenarian
prodigiousness
profitableness
prohibitionism
prohibitionist
propitiatorily
propitiousness
providentially
pteridological
publicspirited
Russianisation
sacrilegiously
selfimmolation
selfimportance
selfinductance
selfindulgence
selfinterested
sentimentalise
sentimentalism
sentimentalist
sentimentality
serviceability
sophistication
spatiotemporal
specialisation
spiritlessness
spiritualistic
spirituousness
stationariness
sublieutenancy
submicroscopic
submissiveness
suspiciousness
tachistoscopic
tergiversation
terminableness
terminological
territorialise
territorialism
territorialist
territoriality
testimonialise
therianthropic
tintinnabulary
tintinnabulate
tintinnabulous
traditionalism
traditionalist
tragicomically
tridimensional
Trinitarianism
trivialisation
twodimensional
unfaithfulness
unfriendliness
unidimensional
unidirectional
utilitarianism
verticillaster
vindictiveness
blackmarketeer
blockaderunner
chickenhearted
chickenlivered
crinkumcrankum
handkerchieves
knickerbockers
strikebreaking
thanksoffering
unacknowledged
acceleratingly
allelomorphism
apoplectically
bioelectricity
bowdlerisation
complexionless
conclusiveness
conglomeration
conglutination
conglutinative
cumulativeness
decolonisation
decolorisation
depolarisation
doublebreasted
exhilaratingly
hobbledehoyish
idealistically
infelicitously
intellectually
intelligential
intelligentsia
intolerability
kremlinologist
legalistically
meddlesomeness
metallographer
papilionaceous
parallelepiped
popularisation
rebelliousness
recolonisation
regularisation
revalorisation
scholastically
secularisation
simplemindedly
simplification
simultaneously
singlebreasted
singlehandedly
singlemindedly
subalternation
tumultuousness
unpalatability
accomplishable
accomplishment
accumulatively
asymmetrically
barometrically
bituminisation
calamitousness
chromatography
cinematography
cotemporaneous
decimalisation
dehumanisation
denominational
denumerability
disembarkation
disembowelment
dolomitisation
entomostracous
excommunicable
excommunicator
extemporaneity
extemporaneous
foraminiferous
highmindedness
holometabolism
holometabolous
illimitability
incommensurate
incommodiously
incommunicable
incommunicably
incompleteness
incompressible
incompressibly
indemonstrable
irremovability
metempsychosis
oecumenicalism
openmindedness
optimistically
peremptoriness
pharmaceutical
pharmacologist
pharmacopoeial
pneumatologist
pneumoconiosis
polymerisation
polymorphously
postmastership
postmillennial
pragmaticality
recommencement
recommendation
recommendatory
rheumatologist
schematisation
spermatogenous
spermatogonium
spermatophytic
stigmatisation
thermochemical
thermodynamics
thermoelectric
ultimogeniture
uncommunicable
uncompromising
unremunerative
volumetrically
voluminousness
weakmindedness
absentmindedly
achondroplasia
administration
administrative
administratrix
advantageously
adventitiously
appendicectomy
arrondissement
bioengineering
chronometrical
deconsecration
defenestration
definitiveness
degenerateness
demonetisation
dependableness
diagnostically
diminutiveness
disenchantment
disenfranchise
disenthralment
disinclination
disincorporate
disinfestation
disingenuously
disinheritance
disintegration
disintegrative
eigenfrequency
extensionality
extinguishable
extinguishment
friendlessness
gerontological
groundlessness
gynandromorphy
imponderabilia
inconclusively
inconsequently
inconsiderable
inconsiderably
inconsistently
incontrollable
inconveniently
insensibleness
intangibleness
invincibleness
Johannisberger
licentiousness
lovingkindness
misinformation
nomenclatorial
noninvolvement
organisational
organometallic
ostentatiously
parenchymatous
pleonastically
potentiometric
prognosticator
reconciliation
reconciliatory
reconnaissance
reconstitution
reconstruction

reco**n**structive
redi**n**tegration
rege**n**eratively
rele**n**tlessness
reli**n**quishment
remi**n**iscential
remo**n**etisation
resi**n**ification
reve**n**gefulness
sapo**n**ification
scie**n**tifically
spri**n**gcleaning
stro**n**gmindedly
subi**n**feudation
tyra**n**nicalness
unco**n**geniality
unco**n**scionable
unco**n**trollable
unco**n**trollably
unco**n**troverted
unco**n**ventional
unco**n**vincingly
unma**n**nerliness
unme**n**tionables
achr**o**matically
ackn**o**wledgment
aeti**o**logically
airc**o**nditioner
apol**o**getically
astr**o**nomically
astr**o**physicist
audi**o**frequency
cart**o**graphical
cens**o**riousness
chem**o**reception
chem**o**receptive
chem**o**synthesis
comm**o**diousness
comm**o**nsensical
comp**o**ssibility
conf**o**rmability
cons**o**ciational
cosm**o**graphical
cosm**o**political
cyan**o**cobalamin
depl**o**rableness
diam**o**ndiferous
dipl**o**matically
disc**o**louration
disc**o**mbobulate
disc**o**mfortable
disc**o**mmendable
disc**o**ncertment
disc**o**nformable
disc**o**nnectedly
disc**o**nsolately
disc**o**nsolation
disc**o**ntentedly
disc**o**ntentment
disc**o**ntinuance
disc**o**untenance
disc**o**uragement
disc**o**uragingly
disc**o**urteously
disj**o**intedness
diss**o**ciability
econ**o**metrician
ethn**o**logically
etym**o**logically
eutr**o**phication
ferr**o**magnesian
ferr**o**magnetism
fore**o**rdination
hagi**o**graphical
harm**o**niousness
hier**o**glyphical
hist**o**chemistry
hist**o**pathology
hist**o**riography
horr**o**rstricken
hydr**o**coralline
hydr**o**dynamical
hydr**o**graphical
hydr**o**mechanics
hygr**o**scopicity
iatr**o**chemistry
icon**o**graphical
illc**o**nditioned
impr**o**vableness
inco**o**rdination
inex**o**rableness
ingl**o**riousness
intr**o**ductorily
invi**o**lableness
macr**o**cephalous
macr**o**economics
malc**o**ntentedly
mete**o**rological
meth**o**dological
micr**o**biologist
micr**o**cephalous
micr**o**circuitry
micr**o**component
micr**o**economics
micr**o**miniature
micr**o**processor
micr**o**sporangia
micr**o**structure
micr**o**technique
myth**o**logically
narr**o**wmindedly
neoc**o**lonialism
neur**o**anatomist
neur**o**chemistry
neur**o**pathology
neur**o**scientist
nitr**o**cellulose
nitr**o**glycerine
nonc**o**mmunicant
nonc**o**ncurrence
nonc**o**operation
orth**o**chromatic
orth**o**graphical
oste**o**arthritis
pard**o**nableness
path**o**genically
path**o**logically
peri**o**dontology
pers**o**nableness
petr**o**chemistry
petr**o**graphical
petr**o**logically
phen**o**barbitone
phil**o**logically
phot**o**chemistry
phot**o**periodism
phot**o**sensitise
phot**o**sensitive
phot**o**synthesis
phot**o**synthetic
phot**o**telegraph
phyt**o**geography
phyt**o**pathology
pian**o**accordian
pige**o**nbreasted
prec**o**ciousness
prep**o**nderantly
prep**o**sterously
prol**o**cutorship
prop**o**rtionable
prop**o**rtionably
prop**o**rtionally
prot**o**zoologist
purp**o**sefulness
radi**o**autograph
radi**o**chemistry
radi**o**sensitive
radi**o**strontium
radi**o**telegraph
radi**o**telephone
radi**o**telephony
radi**o**therapist
reas**o**nableness
repr**o**ductively
resp**o**nsibility
resp**o**nsiveness
rest**o**rationism
rest**o**rationist
retr**o**gradation
saur**o**pterygian
scho**o**lchildren
scho**o**lmistress
seas**o**nableness
semi**o**fficially
seri**o**comically
serv**o**mechanism
soci**o**logically
soci**o**political
spir**o**chaetosis
subc**o**nsciously
subc**o**ntinental
subc**o**ntrariety
supp**o**sititious
taut**o**logically
tele**o**logically
terr**o**rstricken
thyr**o**toxicosis
trop**o**logically
unec**o**nomically
unif**o**rmitarian
unpr**o**fessional
vict**o**riousness
wind**o**wdressing
wind**o**wshopping
acce**p**tableness
anti**p**erspirant
anti**p**hlogistic
asym**p**totically
cons**p**iratorial
disa**p**pointment
disa**p**probation
disa**p**probative
disa**p**probatory
disa**p**provingly
ence**p**halograph
exas**p**eratingly
exce**p**tionality
half**p**ennyworth
idio**p**athically
inap**p**ositeness
inap**p**reciation
inap**p**reciative
inap**p**roachable
inca**p**acitation
inex**p**ressively
inse**p**arability
insu**p**erability
insu**p**pressible
irre**p**roachable
irre**p**roachably
irre**p**roducible
mala**p**propriate
mass**p**roduction
meta**p**horically
meta**p**hysically
meta**p**sychology
misa**p**plication
misa**p**propriate
mono**p**olisation
over**p**opulation
over**p**oweringly
over**p**roduction
para**p**sychology
peri**p**ateticism
phos**p**horescent
post**p**ositional
post**p**ositively
pros**p**erousness
reca**p**itulation
reca**p**itulative
reca**p**itulatory
scru**p**ulousness
self**p**artiality
self**p**erception
self**p**ossession
self**p**reserving
self**p**roclaimed
self**p**ropelling
self**p**ropulsion
self**p**rotection
stam**p**collector
syco**p**hantishly
tele**p**athically
tele**p**honically
tele**p**hotograph
unap**p**reciative
unap**p**roachable
unem**p**hatically
unex**p**ectedness
vice**p**residency
vitu**p**eratively
vivi**p**arousness
volu**p**tuousness
whip**p**ersnapper
anti**q**uarianism
dise**q**uilibrium
obse**q**uiousness
quin**q**uagesimal
quin**q**uennially
abso**r**ptiveness
abst**r**actedness
abst**r**actionism
abst**r**actionist
anag**r**ammatical
anth**r**opography
anth**r**opologist
anth**r**opometric
apho**r**istically
auto**r**adiograph
biog**r**aphically
cast**r**ametation
cent**r**alisation
cent**r**ifugation
clea**r**sightedly
comp**r**ehensible
comp**r**ehensibly
conc**r**etisation
cong**r**atulation
cong**r**atulative
cong**r**atulatory
cong**r**egational
cont**r**actedness
cont**r**adictable
cont**r**adictious
cont**r**aindicate
cont**r**aposition
cont**r**apositive
cont**r**apuntally
cont**r**ollership
cont**r**overtible
cucu**r**bitaceous
deco**r**ativeness
demo**r**alisation
depa**r**tmentally
dest**r**uctionist
dete**r**minedness
dext**r**orotation
dext**r**orotatory
diag**r**ammatical
diff**r**actometer
disa**r**rangement
disc**r**iminating
disc**r**imination
disc**r**iminative
disc**r**iminatory
disg**r**untlement

disorderliness
disorientation
distributional
distributively
diverticulitis
divertissement
effervescently
effortlessness
embarrassingly
endoradiosonde
enharmonically
enterprisingly
entertainingly
enthronisation
epigrammatical
esterification
experientially
experimentally
figurativeness
generalisation
generalpurpose
geographically
heterochromous
heteromorphism
heteromorphous
heterophyllous
heterothallism
histrionically
hyperbolically
hypercalcaemia
hypercatalexis
hypercriticise
hypercriticism
hyperglycaemia
hyperirritable
hypersensitive
hypersonically
imparisyllabic
imperativeness
impermeability
imperviousness
incorporeality
inharmoniously
inheritability
inscrutability
instrumentally
insurmountable
insurmountably
insurrectional
intercessional
intercessorial
intercommunion
intercommunity
interdependent
interferential
interferometer
interferometry
intergradation
interjectional
interlineation
interlocutress
intermediately
intermediation
intermigration
intermittently
intermolecular
internationale
interpellation
interpenetrate
interplanetary
interpretation
interpretative
interpretively
intersectional
intersexuality
intertwinement
invariableness
liberalisation
libertarianism
liturgiologist
mineralisation
mistranslation
naturalisation
neutralisation
obstreperously
obstructionism
obstructionist
oneirocritical
partridgeberry
prearrangement
procrastinator
progressionary
progressionism
progressionist
proprietorship
proprioceptive
protrusiveness
quadragenarian
quadrisyllabic
quadrisyllable
regardlessness
remarkableness
remorsefulness
restrictionist
resurrectional
scurrilousness
selfregulating
selfrepression
selfrespectful
selfrespecting
selfrestrained
selfrevelation
soporiferously
soteriological
superabundance
superannuation
superciliously
superconductor
superelevation
supereminently
supererogation
supererogatory
superficiality
superfoetation
superincumbent
superinduction
superintendent
supernaturally
superphosphate
superscription
supersensitive
supersonically
superstructure
superterranean
supervisorship
uncircumcision
uncorroborated
underdeveloped
underemphasise
undergraduette
undermentioned
undernourished
understandable
understandably
understatement
undervaluation
unscrupulously
venereological
watercolourist
watertightness
accustomedness
ambassadorship
antiscriptural
antiseptically
Augustinianism
autosuggestion
backscattering
backscratching
bremsstrahlung
Christological
classconscious
classification
classificatory
claustrophobia
claustrophobic
coessentiality
counsellorship
crossfertilise
crosspollinate
crossreference
demisemiquaver
detestableness
disassociation
emulsification
endosmotically
gyrostabiliser
hocuspocussing
hypostatically
illustrational
illustratively
impassableness
impassibleness
inauspiciously
incestuousness
indestructible
indestructibly
indiscerptible
indiscoverable
indiscreetness
indiscriminate
indistinctness
irresoluteness
irrespectively
jurisdictional
megasporangium
megasporophyll
ministerialist
monosaccharide
necessarianism
numismatically
oversubscribed
parasitologist
perishableness
phraseological
pleasurability
polysaccharide
praiseworthily
redistribution
redistributive
resistlessness
robustiousness
satisfactorily
schismatically
selfsatisfying
selfsufficient
selfsuggestion
selfsupporting
selfsustaining
telescopically
transcendental
transcendently
transformation
transformative
transitionally
transitiveness
transitoriness
transliterator
transmigration
transmigratory
transplantable
transportation
transsexualism
transvaluation
transversality
undesirability
unhesitatingly
unreservedness
verisimilitude
vivisectionist
antithetically
beautification
boisterousness
breathlessness
breathtakingly
capitalisation
constitutional
constitutively
constructional
constructively
constructivism
constructivist
counterbalance
counterculture
countercurrent
countermeasure
counterplotted
countrydancing
cryptaesthesia
crystallisable
devitalisation
dicotyledonous
electioneering
electrobiology
electrodeposit
electrodynamic
electrostatics
electrotherapy
electrothermal
electrothermic
electrovalency
enantiomorphic
epistemologist
existentialism
existentialist
faintheartedly
fructification
gelatinisation
goodtemperedly
heartsearching
hebetudinosity
homotransplant
hypothetically
hypothyroidism
identification
illiterateness
immethodically
inalterability
inarticulately
inarticulation
inartistically
indeterminable
insatiableness
latitudinarian
legitimisation
lightheartedly
meditativeness
meretriciously
militarisation
monotonousness
mountaineering
nightblindness
ornithological
paratactically
penetrableness
phantasmagoria
phantasmagoric
politicisation
polytheistical
practicability
prettification
quantification
quantitatively
quarterbinding
quattrocentism
quattrocentist
quintessential

reintroduction
repetitiveness
roentgenoscopy
sanctification
scatterbrained
scintillometer
selftormenting
shortsightedly
slatternliness
solitudinarian
spectrographic
spectroscopist
spinthariscope
stertorousness
stoutheartedly
stratification
stultification
substantialism
substantialist
substantiality
substantiation
substantivally
substitutional
substitutively
symptomatology
traitorousness
unattractively
unenterprising
unenthusiastic
unintelligible
unintelligibly
unsatisfactory
valetudinarian
vegetativeness
volatilisation
whortleberries
accountability
altruistically
bioluminescent
boroughEnglish
circuitousness
circumambiency
circumambulate
circumbendibus
circumlittoral
circumlocution
circumlocutory
circumnavigate
circumspection
circumstantial
circumvolution
colourfastness
colourlessness
combustibility
communications
compulsiveness
conductibility
conjunctivitis
conquistadores
consubstantial
consuetudinary
contumaciously
contumeliously
convulsiveness
corruptibility
discursiveness
disfurnishment
disputatiously
disquisitional
euphuistically
excruciatingly
exhaustibility
exhaustiveness
favourableness
fortuitousness
fortunetelling
gratuitousness
hallucinogenic
honourableness

incautiousness
linguistically
percutaneously
persuasiveness
perturbational
presumptuously
presupposition
productiveness
rambunctiously
sanguification
sanguinariness
sensualisation
septuagenarian
sesquipedalian
statuesqueness
ubiquitousness
untruthfulness
behaviouristic
impoverishment
inadvisability
indivisibility
irrevocability
omnivorousness
recoverability
reinvigoration
rejuvenescence
revivification
heroworshipper
longwindedness
noteworthiness
overwhelmingly
roadworthiness
detoxification
arrhythmically
biosystematics
campylotropous
fullyfashioned
martyrological
pachydermatous
phenylbutazone
tachygraphical
topsyturviness
denazification

---

abstractedness
abstractionism
abstractionist
Africanisation
anagrammatical
autoradiograph
biographically
blockaderunner
capitalisation
castrametation
centralisation
chromatography
cinematography
congratulation
congratulative
congratulatory
contractedness
contradictable
contradictious
contraindicate
contraposition
contrapositive
contrapuntally
cryptaesthesia
crystallisable
cumulativeness
decimalisation
decorativeness
dehumanisation
delocalisation
demoralisation
depolarisation
devitalisation
diagrammatical
diaphanousness

diffractometer
disheartenment
dodecasyllable
endoradiosonde
epigrammatical
exhilaratingly
figurativeness
generalisation
generalpurpose
geographically
highhandedness
idiopathically
imperativeness
incapacitation
inseparability
lefthandedness
liberalisation
matriarchalism
meditativeness
militarisation
mineralisation
mistranslation
monosaccharide
mountaineering
naturalisation
neuroanatomist
neutralisation
openhandedness
ophthalmoscope
ophthalmoscopy
osteoarthritis
overcapitalise
paratactically
peripateticism
persuasiveness
phantasmagoria
phantasmagoric
pharmaceutical
pharmacologist
pharmacopoeial
pianoaccordian
pleonastically
pneumatologist
polysaccharide
popularisation
postmastership
pragmaticality
procrastinator
pseudaesthesia
quadragenarian
radicalisation
radioautograph
regularisation
reorganisation
rheumatologist
roundaboutness
Russianisation
scandalisation
scandalousness
schematisation
scholastically
secularisation
selfpartiality
selfsatisfying
sensualisation
septuagenarian
specialisation
spermatogenous
spermatogonium
spermatophytic
standardbearer
stigmatisation
stochastically
substantialism
substantialist
substantiality
substantiation
substantivally
sulphanilamide

superabundance
superannuation
telepathically
therianthropic
trivialisation
unpalatability
unpleasantness
vegetativeness
viviparousness
alphabetically
consubstantial
cucurbitaceous
disembarkation
disembowelment
hyperbolically
microbiologist
nightblindness
overabundantly
phenobarbitone
prefabrication
probabiliorism
probabiliorist
prohibitionism
prohibitionist
scrubbingbrush
selfabnegation
selfabsorption
antiscriptural
attractiveness
auspiciousness
avariciousness
backscattering
backscratching
capriciousness
characteristic
classconscious
conductibility
consociational
corticosteroid
corticosterone
corticotrophic
corticotrophin
cyanocobalamin
despicableness
dialectologist
disenchantment
disinclination
disincorporate
dissociability
excruciatingly
extracorporeal
fallaciousness
floriculturist
gynaecological
hallucinogenic
handicraftsman
histochemistry
horticulturist
hydrocoralline
hypercalcaemia
hypercatalexis
hypercriticise
hypercriticism
iatrochemistry
implacableness
impracticality
inconclusively
indiscerptible
indiscoverable
indiscreetness
indiscriminate
inflectionally
inflectionless
intercessional
intercessorial
intercommunion
intercommunity
intractability
invincibleness

loquaciousness
macrocephalous
microcephalous
microcircuitry
microcomponent
myrmecological
myrmecophagous
myrmecophilous
neglectfulness
neurochemistry
nitrocellulose
nomenclatorial
orthochromatic
parenchymatous
perfectibility
perniciousness
petrochemistry
photochemistry
pisciculturist
precociousness
predictability
productiveness
prolocutorship
protectiveness
publicspirited
pugnaciousness
radiochemistry
reconciliation
reconciliatory
reflectiveness
refractoriness
respectability
respectfulness
selfaccusation
selfaccusatory
seriocomically
serviceability
spirochaetosis
stampcollector
subjectiveness
submicroscopic
superciliously
superconductor
suspiciousness
telescopically
tragicomically
transcendental
transcendently
uncircumcision
ungraciousness
unsuccessfully
verticillaster
vindictiveness
watercolourist
achondroplasia
appendicectomy
archidiaconate
arrondissement
commodiousness
confidentially
dependableness
disorderliness
fastidiousness
forbiddingness
formidableness
friendlessness
groundlessness
gynandromorphy
hydrodynamical
imponderabilia
incredibleness
interdependent
introductorily
jurisdictional
methodological
pachydermatous
perfidiousness
periodontology
premeditatedly
providentially
pteridological
regardlessness
reproductively
selfadjustment
selfadmiration
tetradactylous
threadbareness
underdeveloped
acceleratingly
aesthesiometer
Albigensianism
ambidextrously
antidepressant
antifederalist
antiperspirant
antiseptically
apoplectically
apothegmatical
archaeological
archiepiscopal
asymmetrically
barometrically
bioelectricity
boisterousness
bowdlerisation
bullheadedness
chancellorship
changeableness
chickenhearted
chickenlivered
coessentiality
complexionless
comprehensible
comprehensibly
concretisation
congregational
consuetudinary
counsellorship
counterbalance
counterculture
countercurrent
countermeasure
counterplotted
defenestration
degenerateness
deliberateness
deliberatively
demisemiquaver
demonetisation
denumerability
doublebreasted
epistemologist
Evangelicalism
evangelisation
exasperatingly
existentialism
existentialist
featherbrained
goodfellowship
goodtemperedly
halfpennyworth
handkerchieves
hobbledehoyish
holometabolism
holometabolous
homogenisation
hypodermically
illiterateness
immoderateness
impoverishment
inalienability
inalterability
indeterminable
ineffectuality
insuperability
intolerability
knickerbockers
longheadedness
macroeconomics
manageableness
meddlesomeness
microeconomics
northeastwards
obstreperously
oecumenicalism
oxyhaemoglobin
palaeethnology
phraseological
polymerisation
praiseworthily
progressionary
progressionism
progressionist
propaedeutical
prosperousness
pseudepigrapha
pseudepigraphy
quarterbinding
quintessential
recoverability
regeneratively
rejuvenescence
remonetisation
rontgenography
scatterbrained
selfdependence
selfdestroying
selfdetermined
selffertilised
selfperception
selfregulating
selfrepression
selfrespectful
selfrespecting
selfrestrained
selfrevelation
semicentennial
simplemindedly
singlebreasted
singlehandedly
singlemindedly
slanderousness
slatternliness
souldestroying
southeastwards
statuesqueness
strikebreaking
sublieutenancy
superelevation
supereminently
supererogation
supererogatory
unaffectedness
underemphasise
unenterprising
unexpectedness
unfriendliness
unintelligible
unintelligibly
unreservedness
venereological
vituperatively
vivisectionist
vociferousness
volumetrically
whippersnapper
audiofrequency
crossfertilise
disaffiliation
disaffirmation
disenfranchise
disinfestation
eigenfrequency
fullyfashioned
indifferentism
indifferentist
insufficiently
interferential
interferometer
interferometry
justifiability
misinformation
multifariously
satisfactorily
selfeffacement
selfeffacingly
semiofficially
shamefacedness
subinfeudation
superficiality
superfoetation
transformation
transformative
unprofessional
apologetically
biodegradation
bioengineering
boroughEnglish
cartographical
contagiousness
contiguousness
cosmographical
courageousness
disingenuously
epexegetically
extinguishable
extinguishment
farsightedness
hagiographical
hieroglyphical
hydrographical
hyperglycaemia
iconographical
impregnability
intangibleness
intergradation
liturgiologist
lovingkindness
nitroglycerine
orthographical
outrageousness
pathogenically
petrographical
phytogeography
prodigiousness
propagandistic
Pythagoreanism
rampageousness
retrogradation
revengefulness
roentgenoscopy
segregationist
springcleaning
strongmindedly
tachygraphical
tetragrammaton
umbrageousness
uncongeniality
undergraduette
antiphlogistic
antithetically
apprehensively
asynchronously
breathlessness
breathtakingly
bronchiectasis
catachrestical
catechetically
chincherinchee
delightfulness
disinheritance
dolichocephaly
encephalograph
faintheartedly
hypothetically
hypothyroidism

immethodically
lightheartedly
metaphorically
metaphysically
monochromatism
ornithological
overwhelmingly
perishableness
phosphorescent
polytheistical
shovehalfpenny
slaughterhouse
slaughterously
speechlessness
spinthariscope
sprightfulness
stoicheiometry
stoichiometric
stoutheartedly
sycophantishly
telephonically
telephotograph
thoughtfulness
thoughtreading
unemphatically
unenthusiastic
vicechancellor
administration
administrative
administratrix
aerobiological
aerobiotically
agrobiological
altruistically
anticipatively
aphoristically
artificialness
associationism
autobiographer
autobiographic
basidiomycetes
beautification
behaviouristic
beneficialness
bituminisation
boardingschool
bougainvillaea
Brobdingnagian
calamitousness
centrifugation
circuitousness
classification
classificatory
conceivability
conquistadores
conscienceless
conspiratorial
constitutional
constitutively
coordinateness
councilchamber
councillorship
definitiveness
demobilisation
denazification
denominational
detoxification
discriminating
discrimination
discriminative
discriminatory
disdainfulness
disjointedness
disorientation
disquisitional
distributional
distributively
dolomitisation
electioneering
emulsification
enantiomorphic
esterification
eulogistically
euphuistically
experientially
experimentally
foraminiferous
fortuitousness
fructification
gelatinisation
grandiloquence
gratuitousness
hereditariness
highmindedness
histrionically
humidification
hyperirritable
idealistically
identification
illegitimately
illimitability
immobilisation
imparisyllabic
inadvisability
inarticulately
inarticulation
inartistically
indecipherable
indecisiveness
indefiniteness
indivisibility
indubitability
infelicitously
inheritability
inordinateness
insatiableness
invariableness
kremlinologist
legalistically
legitimisation
libidinousness
linguistically
longwindedness
lyophilisation
oleaginousness
openmindedness
optimistically
organisational
papilionaceous
parasitologist
partridgeberry
politicisation
postmillennial
practicability
prettification
proprietorship
proprioceptive
quadrisyllabic
quadrisyllable
quantification
quantitatively
recapitulation
recapitulative
recapitulatory
rehabilitation
reinvigoration
reminiscential
repetitiveness
repudiationist
resinification
restrictionist
revivification
rigidification
sanctification
sanguification
sanguinariness
saponification
scintillometer
scurrilousness
selfdiscipline
sesquipedalian
silicification
simplification
solicitousness
solidification
solubilisation
soporiferously
soteriological
stratification
stultification
substitutional
substitutively
superincumbent
superinduction
superintendent
transitionally
transitiveness
transitoriness
ubiquitousness
undesirability
unhesitatingly
unsatisfactory
unsociableness
vasodilatation
vasodilatatory
verisimilitude
villainousness
volatilisation
voluminousness
weakmindedness
worshipfulness
interjectional
remarkableness
aetiologically
campylotropous
chivalrousness
compulsiveness
concelebration
convulsiveness
curvilinearity
dieselelectric
dinoflagellate
discolouration
encyclopaedism
encyclopaedist
ethnologically
etymologically
genealogically
infralapsarian
intellectually
intelligential
intelligentsia
interlineation
interlocutress
inviolableness
magniloquently
marvellousness
metallographer
miscalculation
multilaterally
mythologically
neocolonialism
nonbelligerent
parallelepiped
pathologically
pestilentially
petrologically
phenylbutazone
philologically
phthalocyanine
pistilliferous
poikilothermal
poikilothermic
premillenarian
proceleusmatic
pyrheliometric
rebelliousness
sacrilegiously
schoolchildren
schoolmistress
selfflattering
semielliptical
skimbleskamble
snaggletoothed
sociologically
spindleshanked
stumblingblock
supralapsarian
tautologically
teleologically
thimblerigging
transliterator
tropologically
troubleshooter
vaingloriously
whortleberries
abovementioned
abstemiousness
achromatically
aforementioned
arithmetically
bioluminescent
blackmarketeer
circumambiency
circumambulate
circumbendibus
circumlittoral
circumlocution
circumlocutory
circumnavigate
circumspection
circumstantial
circumvolution
contemptuously
contumaciously
contumeliously
determinedness
diplomatically
discombobulate
discomfortable
discommendable
distemperature
econometrician
emblematically
endosmotically
enharmonically
epidemiologist
excommunicable
excommunicator
ferrimagnetism
ferromagnesian
ferromagnetism
fundamentalism
fundamentalist
fundamentality
hydromechanics
impermeability
implementation
incommensurate
incommodiously
incommunicable
incommunicably
inflammability
inharmoniously
insurmountable
insurmountably
intermediately
intermediation
intermigration
intermittently
intermolecular
intramolecular
judgematically
mathematically
mesdemoiselles
microminiature

noctambulation
noncommunicant
numismatically
parsimoniously
phlegmatically
presumptuously
recommencement
recommendation
recommendatory
sacramentalism
sacramentalist
sacramentarian
schismatically
selfemployment
selfimmolation
selfimportance
sentimentalise
sentimentalism
sentimentalist
sentimentality
servomechanism
somnambulation
somnambulistic
sphygmographic
supramaxillary
systematically
testimonialise
transmigration
transmigratory
tridimensional
twodimensional
ultramicrotome
ultramontanism
ultramontanist
uncommunicable
undermentioned
unidimensional
unpremeditated
accountability
aggrandisement
airconditioner
alphanumerical
apprenticeship
astronomically
attainableness
authentication
bathingmachine
campanological
cantankerously
carcinogenesis
commensurately
commensuration
commonsensical
communications
compensational
concentrically
conjunctivitis
consanguineous
continuousness
conventionally
convincingness
diamantiferous
diamondiferous
disconcertment
disconformable
disconnectedly
disconsolately
disconsolation
discontentedly
discontentment
discontinuance
dispensability
distensibility
elementariness
extraneousness
fortunetelling
geocentrically
gramineousness
harmoniousness
illconditioned
imaginableness
infrangibility
insignificance
insignificancy
internationale
intransitively
intrinsicality
Johannisberger
malcontentedly
millenarianism
morganatically
multinucleated
newfangledness
nonconcurrence
nonsensicality
northnortheast
northnorthwest
outgeneralling
outlandishness
overindulgence
pardonableness
personableness
pertinaciously
philanthropise
philanthropist
pigeonbreasted
portentousness
preponderantly
presentability
presentational
presentimental
preventability
preventiveness
progenitorship
prosencephalic
prosencephalon
psilanthropism
psilanthropist
rambunctiously
reasonableness
reconnaissance
rectangularity
refrangibility
responsibility
responsiveness
rhinencephalic
rhinencephalon
seasonableness
selfenergising
selfinductance
selfindulgence
selfinterested
steganographer
stupendousness
subconsciously
subcontinental
subcontrariety
supernaturally
suspensiveness
terminableness
terminological
tintinnabulary
tintinnabulate
tintinnabulous
tremendousness
tyrannicalness
unacknowledged
undernourished
uneconomically
unmannerliness
volcanological
vulcanological
weltanschauung
allegorisation
allelomorphism
anthropography
anthropologist
anthropometric
anticonvulsant
bibliographise
bibliomaniacal
cardiovascular
categorisation
chronometrical
conglomeration
controllership
controvertible
decolonisation
decolorisation
dextrorotation
dextrorotatory
diagnostically
enthronisation
entomostracous
flatfootedness
heroworshipper
heterochromous
heteromorphism
heteromorphous
heterophyllous
heterothallism
homoeomorphism
hypocoristical
inappositeness
indecomposable
indecorousness
indemonstrable
irreconcilable
irreconcilably
irremovability
irresoluteness
irrevocability
malodorousness
monopolisation
monotonousness
noncooperation
noteworthiness
omnivorousness
oneirocritical
opinionatively
organometallic
overcommitment
overcompensate
overconfidence
overpopulation
overpoweringly
palaeobotanist
paradoxicality
passionateness
physiognomical
pluviometrical
pneumoconiosis
polymorphously
postpositional
postpositively
prognosticator
prothonotarial
pseudomorphism
pseudomorphous
pseudonymously
psychoanalysis
psychoanalytic
psychochemical
psychodynamics
psychoneurosis
psychoneurotic
psychophysical
psychosomatics
psychosurgical
recolonisation
revalorisation
roadworthiness
selfcomplacent
selfconfidence
selfconsequent
selfconsistent
selfcontrolled
selfcorrecting
selfgovernment
selfpossession
selftormenting
semiconducting
spatiotemporal
stadholdership
stationariness
stertorousness
surefootedness
symptomatology
thermochemical
thermodynamics
thermoelectric
traitorousness
ultimogeniture
unaccommodated
unaccomplished
unbecomingness
absorptiveness
accomplishable
accomplishment
astrophysicist
corruptibility
cosmopolitical
cotemporaneous
crosspollinate
disappointment
disapprobation
disapprobative
disapprobatory
disapprovingly
disciplinarian
enterprisingly
eutrophication
extemporaneity
extemporaneous
hermaphroditic
histopathology
hocuspocussing
inauspiciously
incompleteness
incompressible
incompressibly
incorporeality
insuppressible
interpellation
interpenetrate
interplanetary
interpretation
interpretative
interpretively
irrespectively
malappropriate
megasporangium
megasporophyll
metempsychosis
microprocessor
misapplication
misappropriate
multiplication
multiplicative
neuropathology
perceptibility
perceptiveness
peremptoriness
photoperiodism
phytopathology
presupposition
sauropterygian
sociopolitical
superphosphate
susceptibility
susceptiveness
transplantable
transportation
uncompromising
inadequateness
relinquishment

autocratically
bacteriologist
bacteriostasis
bacteriostatic
bastardisation
butterfingered
butterflyscrew
calcareousness
censoriousness
chemoreception
chemoreceptive
colourfastness
colourlessness
comparableness
conformability
conservational
conservatively
constructional
constructively
constructivism
constructivist
conterminously
conversational
convertibility
copperbottomed
countrydancing
crossreference
cumbersomeness
democratically
deplorableness
despiritualise
diachronically
differentiable
differentially
disarrangement
discursiveness
disfurnishment
dispiritedness
dissertational
electrobiology
electrodeposit
electrodynamic
electrostatics
electrotherapy
electrothermal
electrothermic
electrovalency
embarrassingly
erythropoiesis
favourableness
foreordination
forthrightness
forwardlooking
fraternisation
gregariousness
hierarchically
historiography
homotransplant
honourableness
horrorstricken
hypocritically
hysterectomise
inappreciation
inappreciative
inapproachable
incoordination
inexorableness
inexpressively
ingloriousness
insurrectional
integrationist
irreproachable
irreproachably
irreproducible
lugubriousness
martyrological
massproduction
meretriciously
meteorological
mysteriousness
nonperformance
overproduction
penetrableness
perturbational
prearrangement
precariousness
preferentially
prescriptively
proportionable
proportionably
proportionally
proscriptively
quattrocentism
quattrocentist
reintroduction
restorationism
restorationist
resurrectional
Rosicrucianism
salubriousness
selfpreserving
selfproclaimed
selfpropelling
selfpropulsion
selfprotection
spectrographic
spectroscopist
sphaerocrystal
squadronleader
submersibility
subversiveness
sufferableness
synchronically
tatterdemalion
terrorstricken
theocratically
unappreciative
unapproachable
unattractively
uncorroborated
unidirectional
uniformitarian
universalistic
uproariousness
vicepresidency
victoriousness
vulnerableness
westernisation
wonderstricken
aggressiveness
ambassadorship
biosystematics
bremsstrahlung
chemosynthesis
clearsightedly
combustibility
commissaryship
commissionaire
compassionable
compossibility
concessionaire
condescendence
correspondence
correspondency
deconsecration
disassociation
disrespectable
ecclesiastical
ecclesiologist
exhaustibility
exhaustiveness
expressionless
expressiveness
extensionality
fantasticality
heartsearching
hygroscopicity
hypersensitive
hypersonically
impassableness
impassibleness
impassibility
impressibility
impressionable
impressiveness
inconsequently
inconsiderable
inconsiderably
inconsistently
infrastructure
insensibleness
intersectional
intersexuality
Mephistopheles
metapsychology
microsporangia
microstructure
necessarianism
neuroscientist
nonrestrictive
oppressiveness
overestimation
parapsychology
patresfamilias
permissibility
permissiveness
photosensitise
photosensitive
photosynthesis
photosynthetic
possessiveness
predesignation
predestinarian
predestination
predisposition
preposterously
professionally
professorially
purposefulness
radiosensitive
radiostrontium
reconstitution
reconstruction
reconstructive
regressiveness
remorsefulness
representation
representative
selfassumption
Shakespeareana
Shakespeariana
shortsightedly
sophistication
submissiveness
successfulness
successionally
successiveness
suggestibility
suggestiveness
superscription
supersensitive
supersonically
superstructure
supposititious
suprasegmental
swordswallower
tachistoscopic
thalassography
thanksoffering
transsexualism
ultrasonically
ultrastructure
unconscionable
understandable
understandably
understatement
unquestionable
unquestionably
Zoroastrianism
absentmindedly
acceptableness
accustomedness
advantageously
adventitiously
affectionately
apophthegmatic
archetypically
architectonics
arrhythmically
asymptotically
Augustinianism
bloodthirstily
charitableness
Christological
claustrophobia
claustrophobic
climatological
committeewoman
compatibleness
conditionality
coquettishness
creditableness
delectableness
departmentally
dermatological
despitefulness
detestableness
disenthralment
disintegration
disintegrative
disputatiously
diverticulitis
divertissement
educationalist
effortlessness
egalitarianism
entertainingly
eschatological
exceptionality
factitiousness
fictitiousness
flagitiousness
galactopoietic
gerontological
gyrostabiliser
haematogenesis
hypostatically
illustrational
illustratively
incautiousness
incestuousness
incontrollable
indestructible
indestructibly
indistinctness
indoctrination
inevitableness
infectiousness
ingratiatingly
inimitableness
intertwinement
intuitionalism
intuitionalist
knighterrantry
libertarianism
licentiousness
longitudinally
marketgardener
microtechnique
ministerialist
nutritiousness
ostentatiously
percutaneously
phototelegraph
planetstricken
potentiometric
predeterminate

profitableness
proletarianise
proletarianism
propitiatorily
propitiousness
radiotelegraph
radiotelephone
radiotelephony
radiotherapist
redintegration
redistribution
redistributive
relentlessness
resistlessness
robustiousness
Sabbatarianism
scientifically
sensationalism
sensationalist
simultaneously
spiritlessness
spiritualistic
spirituousness
stomatological
subalternation
superterranean
symmetrisation
territorialise
territorialism
territorialist
territoriality
thriftlessness
thyrotoxicosis
topsyturviness
traditionalism
traditionalist
Trinitarianism
tumultuousness
uncontrollable
uncontrollably
uncontroverted
unfaithfulness
unflatteringly
ungratefulness
unmentionables
untruthfulness
utilitarianism
voluptuousness
watertightness
weightlessness
accumulatively
amateurishness
antiquarianism
articulateness
autosuggestion
conclusiveness
conglutination
conglutinative
crinkumcrankum
destructionist
diminutiveness
discountenance
discouragement
discouragingly
discourteously
disequilibrium
disgruntlement
exclaustration
goodhumouredly
hebetudinosity
immaculateness
implausibility
inscrutability
instrumentally
irreducibility
irrefutability
latitudinarian
meticulousness
miraculousness
obsequiousness
obstructionism
obstructionist
oversubscribed
pasteurisation
pleasurability
protrusiveness
quinquagesimal
quinquennially
ridiculousness
scrupulousness
selffulfilling
selfsufficient
selfsuggestion
selfsupporting
selfsustaining
solitudinarian
unremunerative
unscrupulously
valetudinarian
bouleversement
concavoconcave
deceivableness
effervescently
extravehicular
imperviousness
improvableness
inconveniently
lasciviousness
noninvolvement
supervisorship
tergiversation
transvaluation
transversality
unconventional
unconvincingly
undervaluation
acknowledgment
narrowmindedly
northwestwards
southwestwards
windowdressing
windowshopping
convexoconcave
inflexibleness
overexcitement
selfexplaining
selfexpression
aerodynamicist
brachycephalic
dicotyledonous
ichthyological
ichthyophagous
ichthyosaurian
monkeybusiness
presbyterially
staphylococcus
protozoologist

---

acceptableness
achromatically
advantageously
ambassadorship
antiquarianism
associationism
attainableness
autocratically
backscattering
blackmarketeer
bullheadedness
changeableness
charitableness
circumambiency
circumambulate
comparableness
contumaciously
creditableness
deceivableness
delectableness
democratically
dependableness
deplorableness
despicableness
detestableness
dinoflagellate
diplomatically
disarrangement
disembarkation
disputatiously
egalitarianism
embarrassingly
emblematically
encephalograph
entertainingly
favourableness
ferrimagnetism
ferromagnesian
ferromagnetism
formidableness
fullyfashioned
gyrostabiliser
histopathology
homotransplant
honourableness
hypercalcaemia
hypercatalexis
hypostatically
imaginableness
impassableness
implacableness
improvableness
inevitableness
inexorableness
infralapsarian
inimitableness
insatiableness
integrationist
internationale
invariableness
inviolableness
judgematically
libertarianism
longheadedness
manageableness
mathematically
millenarianism
morganatically
multifariously
multilaterally
necessarianism
neuropathology
northeastwards
numismatically
ostentatiously
pardonableness
penetrableness
percutaneously
perishableness
personableness
pertinaciously
phenobarbitone
phlegmatically
phytopathology
prearrangement
profitableness
proletarianise
proletarianism
propagandistic
psychoanalysis
psychoanalytic
quinquagesimal
reasonableness
reconnaissance
remarkableness
repudiationist
restorationism
restorationist
Sabbatarianism
satisfactorily
schismatically
seasonableness
segregationist
selfflattering
shamefacedness
shovehalfpenny
simultaneously
southeastwards
spinthariscope
sufferableness
supernaturally
supralapsarian
supramaxillary
sycophantishly
systematically
terminableness
tetradactylous
theocratically
transvaluation
Trinitarianism
unattractively
undervaluation
unemphatically
unsociableness
utilitarianism
vicechancellor
vulnerableness
circumbendibus
copperbottomed
discombobulate
distributional
distributively
doublebreasted
monkeybusiness
noctambulation
oversubscribed
palaeobotanist
perturbational
phenylbutazone
pigeonbreasted
roundaboutness
singlebreasted
somnambulation
somnambulistic
strikebreaking
superabundance
threadbareness
abstractedness
abstractionism
abstractionist
apoplectically
artificialness
beneficialness
bioelectricity
brachycephalic
condescendence
conjunctivitis
contractedness
convincingness
destructionist
diffractometer
disconcertment
heterochromous
hierarchically
hygroscopicity
inarticulately
inarticulation
incapacitation
ineffectuality
infelicitously
irreducibility
irrevocability
macroeconomics
microeconomics
miscalculation
monosaccharide
neuroscientist
nonconcurrence

obstructionism
obstructionist
oneirocritical
overexcitement
paratactically
pharmaceutical
pharmacologist
pharmacopoeial
pianoaccordian
pneumoconiosis
politicisation
polysaccharide
practicability
prosencephalic
prosencephalon
psychochemical
rambunctiously
restrictionist
rhinencephalic
rhinencephalon
schoolchildren
selfaccusation
selfaccusatory
springcleaning
superscription
thermochemical
unaffectedness
unconscionable
unexpectedness
vivisectionist
aggrandisement
airconditioner
antifederalist
autoradiograph
bastardisation
blockaderunner
contradictable
contradictious
diamondiferous
endoradiosonde
forbiddingness
foreordination
forwardlooking
hebetudinosity
hobbledehoyish
illconditioned
incoordination
latitudinarian
outlandishness
overindulgence
partridgeberry
preponderantly
propaedeutical
psychodynamics
selfinductance
selfindulgence
solitudinarian
stupendousness
tatterdemalion
thermodynamics
tremendousness
valetudinarian
windowdressing
abovementioned
aforementioned
alphabetically
antithetically
apologetically
apprehensively
architectonics
arithmetically
bouleversement
calcareousness
catechetically
chemoreception
chemoreceptive
chincherinchee
concelebration
confidentially
conscienceless
contumeliously
courageousness
crossfertilise
crossreference
cryptaesthesia
deconsecration
despitefulness
dieselelectric
differentiable
differentially
disinfestation
disingenuously
disinheritance
disintegration
disintegrative
disorderliness
disorientation
econometrician
effervescently
epexegetically
experientially
extraneousness
extravehicular
faintheartedly
fortunetelling
fundamentalism
fundamentalist
fundamentality
gramineousness
heartsearching
hydromechanics
hypersensitive
hypothetically
hysterectomise
impermeability
implementation
imponderabilia
inappreciation
inappreciative
incommensurate
inconsequently
inconveniently
indifferentism
indifferentist
indiscerptible
inexpressively
insurrectional
intellectually
intercessional
intercessorial
interdependent
interferential
interferometer
interferometry
interjectional
intermediately
intermediation
interpellation
interpenetrate
intersectional
intersexuality
irrespectively
knighterrantry
lightheartedly
macrocephalous
microcephalous
microtechnique
ministerialist
nitrocellulose
northwestwards
outgeneralling
outrageousness
overwhelmingly
pachydermatous
parallelepiped
pathogenically
pestilentially
photoperiodism
photosensitise
photosensitive
phototelegraph
phytogeography
polytheistical
predeterminate
preferentially
proceleusmatic
proprietorship
providentially
pseudaesthesia
purposefulness
quinquennially
radiosensitive
radiotelegraph
radiotelephone
radiotelephony
rampageousness
recommencement
recommendation
recommendatory
redintegration
remorsefulness
representation
representative
resurrectional
revengefulness
roentgenoscopy
sacramentalism
sacramentalist
sacramentarian
sacrilegiously
selfenergising
selfpreserving
sentimentalise
sentimentalism
sentimentalist
sentimentality
serviceability
servomechanism
skimbleskamble
snaggletoothed
southwestwards
spindleshanked
stoicheiometry
stoutheartedly
subalternation
subinfeudation
supersensitive
superterranean
suprasegmental
tergiversation
thermoelectric
thimblerigging
transcendental
transcendently
transsexualism
transversality
tridimensional
troubleshooter
twodimensional
umbrageousness
unappreciative
uncongeniality
unconventional
underdeveloped
undermentioned
ungratefulness
unidimensional
unidirectional
unmannerliness
unpremeditated
unprofessional
unsuccessfully
vicepresidency
whortleberries
beautification
butterfingered
butterflyscrew
centrifugation
classification
classificatory
colourfastness
denazification
detoxification
discomfortable
disconformable
emulsification
esterification
fructification
humidification
identification
nonperformance
patresfamilias
prettification
quantification
resinification
revivification
rigidification
sanctification
sanguification
saponification
selfeffacement
selfeffacingly
selfsufficient
semiofficially
silicification
simplification
solidification
soporiferously
stratification
stultification
apothegmatical
autosuggestion
bathingmachine
bibliographise
congregational
consanguineous
infrangibility
marketgardener
newfangledness
physiognomical
quadragenarian
rectangularity
refrangibility
reinvigoration
selfregulating
selfsuggestion
septuagenarian
ultimogeniture
apophthegmatic
arrhythmically
astrophysicist
bloodthirstily
boroughEnglish
comprehensible
comprehensibly
disenchantment
disenthralment
eutrophication
farsightedness
hermaphroditic
histochemistry
iatrochemistry
neurochemistry
orthochromatic
parenchymatous
petrochemistry
photochemistry
radiochemistry
radiotherapist
singlehandedly
spirochaetosis
superphosphate
unfaithfulness
untruthfulness
abstemiousness
adventitiously

affectionately
appendicectomy
archidiaconate
arrondissement
Augustinianism
auspiciousness
avariciousness
bacteriologist
bacteriostasis
bacteriostatic
bioengineering
bioluminescent
bronchiectasis
capriciousness
censoriousness
clearsightedly
commodiousness
communications
compatibleness
conditionality
consociational
contagiousness
contraindicate
cucurbitaceous
curvilinearity
despiritualise
determinedness
disaffiliation
disaffirmation
disequilibrium
dispiritedness
dissociability
diverticulitis
divertissement
ecclesiastical
ecclesiologist
educationalist
epidemiologist
exceptionality
excruciatingly
extensionality
factitiousness
fallaciousness
fastidiousness
fictitiousness
flagitiousness
forthrightness
gregariousness
hallucinogenic
harmoniousness
historiography
hypocritically
impassibleness
imperviousness
inauspiciously
incautiousness
inconsiderable
inconsiderably
inconsistently
incredibleness
indistinctness
infectiousness
inflexibleness
ingloriousness
ingratiatingly
insensibleness
insignificance
insignificancy
insufficiently
intangibleness
intelligential
intelligentsia
interlineation
intermigration
intermittently
intuitionalism
intuitionalist
invincibleness
Johannisberger
jurisdictional
justifiability
lasciviousness
licentiousness
liturgiologist
loquaciousness
lugubriousness
meretriciously
microbiologist
microcircuitry
microminiature
mountaineering
mysteriousness
nutritiousness
obsequiousness
perfidiousness
perniciousness
potentiometric
precariousness
precociousness
predesignation
premeditatedly
prescriptively
probabiliorism
probabiliorist
prodigiousness
progenitorship
prohibitionism
prohibitionist
propitiatorily
propitiousness
proscriptively
pugnaciousness
pyrheliometric
rebelliousness
reconciliation
reconciliatory
robustiousness
salubriousness
scientifically
scrubbingbrush
sensationalism
sensationalist
shortsightedly
stoichiometric
stumblingblock
superciliously
superficiality
supervisorship
supposititious
suspiciousness
traditionalism
traditionalist
transliterator
transmigration
transmigratory
tyrannicalness
ultramicrotome
unconvincingly
ungraciousness
unmentionables
uproariousness
verticillaster
victoriousness
watertightness
selfadjustment
cantankerously
lovingkindness
accomplishable
accomplishment
accumulatively
acknowledgment
antiphlogistic
articulateness
breathlessness
capitalisation
centralisation
chancellorship
circumlittoral
circumlocution
circumlocutory
colourlessness
controllership
councilchamber
councillorship
counsellorship
crystallisable
decimalisation
delocalisation
demobilisation
demoralisation
devitalisation
dicotyledonous
disciplinarian
disinclination
effortlessness
Evangelicalism
evangelisation
friendlessness
generalisation
generalpurpose
goodfellowship
grandiloquence
groundlessness
hieroglyphical
hyperglycaemia
immaculateness
immobilisation
incompleteness
inconclusively
interplanetary
irresoluteness
liberalisation
lyophilisation
marvellousness
meticulousness
mineralisation
miraculousness
misapplication
monopolisation
multiplication
multiplicative
naturalisation
neutralisation
nightblindness
nitroglycerine
nomenclatorial
nonbelligerent
ophthalmoscope
ophthalmoscopy
pistilliferous
postmillennial
premillenarian
radicalisation
regardlessness
rehabilitation
relentlessness
resistlessness
ridiculousness
scandalisation
scandalousness
scintillometer
scrupulousness
scurrilousness
selffulfilling
semielliptical
sensualisation
solubilisation
specialisation
speechlessness
spiritlessness
stadholdership
staphylococcus
superelevation
thriftlessness
transplantable
trivialisation
unintelligible
unintelligibly
vasodilatation
vasodilatatory
volatilisation
weightlessness
absentmindedly
allelomorphism
anagrammatical
bibliomaniacal
castrametation
chronometrical
conformability
conglomeration
conterminously
crinkumcrankum
demisemiquaver
departmentally
diagrammatical
discommendable
discriminating
discrimination
discriminative
discriminatory
epigrammatical
epistemologist
experimentally
goodhumouredly
goodtemperedly
heteromorphism
heteromorphous
homoeomorphism
indecomposable
inflammability
instrumentally
legitimisation
narrowmindedly
noncommunicant
organometallic
overcommitment
overcompensate
oxyhaemoglobin
pluviometrical
pseudomorphism
pseudomorphous
schoolmistress
selfadmiration
selfcomplacent
selfimmolation
simplemindedly
singlemindedly
strongmindedly
supereminently
symptomatology
unaccommodated
unaccomplished
unbecomingness
underemphasise
uniformitarian
verisimilitude
aerodynamicist
Africanisation
Albigensianism
anticonvulsant
bituminisation
boardingschool
bougainvillaea
Brobdingnagian
chickenhearted
chickenlivered
circumnavigate
coessentiality
coordinateness
decolonisation
dehumanisation
denominational
diaphanousness
disconnectedly
discountenance
disdainfulness

disfurnishment	asymptotically	irreproducible	tropologically
disgruntlement	autobiographer	magniloquently	ultramontanism
disjointedness	autobiographic	martyrological	ultramontanist
enthronisation	basidiomycetes	massproduction	ultrasonically
existentialism	behaviouristic	megasporangium	unacknowledged
existentialist	campanological	megasporophyll	unapproachable
foraminiferous	campylotropous	mesdemoiselles	uncorroborated
fraternisation	carcinogenesis	metallographer	undernourished
gelatinisation	Christological	metaphorically	uneconomically
halfpennyworth	classconscious	meteorological	vaingloriously
highhandedness	climatological	methodological	venereological
highmindedness	concavoconcave	microcomponent	volcanological
homogenisation	convexoconcave	misinformation	vulcanological
impregnability	corticosteroid	myrmecological	watercolourist
inalienability	corticosterone	myrmecophagous	anthropography
indefiniteness	corticotrophic	myrmecophilous	anthropologist
indemonstrable	corticotrophin	mythologically	anthropometric
inordinateness	cosmopolitical	neocolonialism	anticipatively
irreconcilable	cotemporaneous	noninvolvement	antidepressant
irreconcilably	crosspollinate	northnortheast	antiseptically
kremlinologist	cyanocobalamin	northnorthwest	archiepiscopal
lefthandedness	dermatological	ornithological	biographically
libidinousness	diachronically	overproduction	contemptuously
longwindedness	disappointment	papilionaceous	contraposition
mistranslation	disassociation	parsimoniously	contrapositive
monotonousness	discolouration	pathologically	contrapuntally
neuroanatomist	disembowelment	periodontology	correspondence
oecumenicalism	disincorporate	petrologically	correspondency
oleaginousness	dolichocephaly	philologically	disrespectable
openhandedness	electioneering	phosphorescent	distemperature
openmindedness	electrobiology	phraseological	geographically
opinionatively	electrodeposit	phthalocyanine	heterophyllous
overconfidence	electrodynamic	poikilothermal	indecipherable
passionateness	electrostatics	poikilothermic	microsporangia
prothonotarial	electrotherapy	proprioceptive	noncooperation
pseudonymously	electrothermal	protozoologist	obstreperously
psychoneurosis	electrothermic	pteridological	overcapitalise
psychoneurotic	electrovalency	Pythagoreanism	overpopulation
recolonisation	enantiomorphic	quattrocentism	predisposition
rejuvenescence	encyclopaedism	quattrocentist	presumptuously
reorganisation	encyclopaedist	reintroduction	presupposition
rontgenography	endosmotically	selfproclaimed	pseudepigrapha
Russianisation	enharmonically	selfpropelling	pseudepigraphy
sanguinariness	erythropoiesis	selfpropulsion	psychophysical
selfabnegation	eschatological	selfprotection	selfdependence
selfconfidence	ethnologically	seriocomically	selfemployment
selfconsequent	etymologically	sociologically	selfexplaining
selfconsistent	extemporaneity	sociopolitical	selfexpression
selfcontrolled	extemporaneous	soteriological	selfimportance
semicentennial	extracorporeal	spectrographic	selfrepression
semiconducting	flatfootedness	spectroscopist	selfsupporting
stationariness	galactopoietic	sphaerocrystal	sesquipedalian
substantialism	genealogically	sphygmographic	Shakespeareana
substantialist	gerontological	squadronleader	Shakespeariana
substantiality	gynaecological	stampcollector	unscrupulously
substantiation	haematogenesis	steganographer	worshipfulness
substantivally	histrionically	stomatological	acceleratingly
sulphanilamide	hocuspocussing	superconductor	achondroplasia
superannuation	hydrocoralline	superfoetation	allegorisation
superincumbent	hyperbolically	supersonically	amateurishness
superinduction	hypersonically	surefootedness	antiperspirant
superintendent	ichthyological	synchronically	antiscriptural
therianthropic	ichthyophagous	tautologically	asynchronously
tintinnabulary	ichthyosaurian	teleologically	audiofrequency
tintinnabulate	immethodically	telephonically	backscratching
tintinnabulous	inapproachable	telephotograph	biodegradation
unfriendliness	incommodiously	telescopically	boisterousness
unremunerative	incorporeality	terminological	bowdlerisation
villainousness	indiscoverable	territorialise	cartographical
voluminousness	inharmoniously	territorialism	catachrestical
weakmindedness	insurmountable	territorialist	categorisation
westernisation	insurmountably	territoriality	chivalrousness
accustomedness	intercommunion	testimonialise	claustrophobia
aerobiological	intercommunity	thanksoffering	claustrophobic
aerobiotically	interlocutress	thyrotoxicosis	conspiratorial
aetiologically	intermolecular	tragicomically	cosmographical
agrobiological	intramolecular	transformation	counterbalance
archaeological	irreproachable	transformative	counterculture
astronomically	irreproachably	transportation	countercurrent

countermeasure
counterplotted
decolorisation
degenerateness
deliberateness
deliberatively
denumerability
depolarisation
dextrorotation
dextrorotatory
disapprobation
disapprobative
disapprobatory
disapprovingly
discouragement
discouragingly
discourteously
disenfranchise
disheartenment
eigenfrequency
enterprisingly
exasperatingly
exhilaratingly
featherbrained
gynandromorphy
hagiographical
handicraftsman
handkerchieves
heroworshipper
hydrographical
hypercriticise
hypercriticism
hyperirritable
hypocoristical
hypodermically
iconographical
illiterateness
illustrational
illustratively
immoderateness
impoverishment
inalterability
incompressible
incompressibly
incontrollable
indecorousness
indestructible
indestructibly
indeterminable
indiscreetness
indiscriminate
indoctrination
inseparability
insuperability
insuppressible
intergradation
interpretation
interpretative
interpretively
intolerability
knickerbockers
malappropriate
malodorousness
matriarchalism
microprocessor
militarisation
misappropriate
monochromatism
noteworthiness
omnivorousness
orthographical
osteoarthritis
pasteurisation
petrographical
pleasurability
polymerisation
polymorphously
popularisation
prefabrication
prosperousness
quarterbinding
recoverability
redistribution
redistributive
regeneratively
regularisation
retrogradation
revalorisation
roadworthiness
scatterbrained
secularisation
selfcorrecting
selffertilised
selfpartiality
selfperception
selftormenting
slanderousness
slatternliness
standardbearer
stertorousness
submicroscopic
supererogation
supererogatory
symmetrisation
tachygraphical
tetragrammaton
traitorousness
uncompromising
uncontrollable
uncontrollably
uncontroverted
undergraduette
undesirability
unenterprising
unreservedness
vituperatively
viviparousness
vociferousness
whippersnapper
administration
administrative
administratrix
aesthesiometer
aggressiveness
altruistically
aphoristically
circumspection
circumstantial
commensurately
commensuration
commissaryship
commissionaire
commonsensical
compassionable
compensational
compossibility
compulsiveness
concessionaire
conclusiveness
conquistadores
consubstantial
conversational
convulsiveness
cumbersomeness
defenestration
diagnostically
disconsolately
disconsolation
discursiveness
dispensability
disquisitional
distensibility
dodecasyllable
entomostracous
eulogistically
euphuistically
exclaustration
expressionless
expressiveness
horrorstricken
idealistically
imparisyllabic
implausibility
impressibility
impressionable
impressiveness
inadvisability
inappositeness
inartistically
indecisiveness
indivisibility
intransitively
intrinsicality
legalistically
linguistically
meddlesomeness
metempsychosis
nonsensicality
oppressiveness
optimistically
organisational
permissibility
permissiveness
persuasiveness
phantasmagoria
phantasmagoric
planetstricken
pleonastically
possessiveness
postmastership
postpositional
postpositively
procrastinator
professionally
professorially
prognosticator
progressionary
progressionism
progressionist
protrusiveness
psychosomatics
psychosurgical
publicspirited
quadrisyllabic
quadrisyllable
quintessential
regressiveness
reminiscential
responsibility
responsiveness
scholastically
selfabsorption
selfassumption
selfdestroying
selfdiscipline
selfpossession
selfrespectful
selfrespecting
selfrestrained
selfsustaining
souldestroying
statuesqueness
stochastically
subconsciously
submersibility
submissiveness
subversiveness
successfulness
successionally
successiveness
suspensiveness
terrorstricken
thalassography
universalistic
unpleasantness
unsatisfactory
weltanschauung
windowshopping
wonderstricken
absorptiveness
accountability
apprenticeship
asymmetrically
attractiveness
authentication
barometrically
biosystematics
breathtakingly
bremsstrahlung
calamitousness
characteristic
chromatography
cinematography
circuitousness
combustibility
committeewoman
concentrically
concretisation
conductibility
conglutination
conglutinative
congratulation
congratulative
congratulatory
constitutional
constitutively
consuetudinary
conventionally
convertibility
coquettishness
corruptibility
cumulativeness
decorativeness
definitiveness
delightfulness
demonetisation
dialectologist
diamantiferous
diminutiveness
discontentedly
discontentment
discontinuance
dissertational
dolomitisation
elementariness
exhaustibility
exhaustiveness
fantasticality
figurativeness
fortuitousness
geocentrically
gratuitousness
hereditariness
heterothallism
holometabolism
holometabolous
idiopathically
illegitimately
illimitability
imperativeness
impracticality
indubitability
inflectionally
inflectionless
infrastructure
inheritability
inscrutability
intractability
irrefutability
malcontentedly
meditativeness
Mephistopheles
microstructure
neglectfulness
nonrestrictive
overestimation

palaeethnology
parasitologist
perceptibility
perceptiveness
peremptoriness
perfectibility
peripateticism
philanthropise
philanthropist
pneumatologist
portentousness
pragmaticality
predestinarian
predestination
predictability
preposterously
presbyterially
presentability
presentational
presentimental
preventability
preventiveness
productiveness
proportionable
proportionably
proportionally
protectiveness
psilanthropism
psilanthropist
quantitatively
radiostrontium
recapitulation
recapitulative
recapitulatory
reconstitution
reconstruction
reconstructive
reflectiveness
refractoriness
remonetisation
repetitiveness
respectability
respectfulness
rheumatologist
sauropterygian
schematisation
selfdetermined
selfinterested
selfsatisfying
slaughterhouse
slaughterously
solicitousness
sophistication
spatiotemporal
spermatogenous
spermatogonium
spermatophytic
sprightfulness
stigmatisation
subcontinental
subcontrariety
subjectiveness
substitutional
substitutively
suggestibility
suggestiveness
superstructure
susceptibility
susceptiveness
tachistoscopic
telepathically
thoughtfulness
thoughtreading
transitionally
transitiveness
transitoriness
ubiquitousness
ultrastructure
understandable
understandably
understatement
unflatteringly
unhesitatingly
unpalatability
unquestionable
unquestionably
vegetativeness
vindictiveness
volumetrically
Zoroastrianism
alphanumerical
constructional
constructively
constructivism
constructivist
contiguousness
continuousness
excommunicable
excommunicator
extinguishable
extinguishment
floriculturist
horticulturist
inadequateness
incestuousness
incommunicable
incommunicably
introductorily
longitudinally
multinucleated
overabundantly
pisciculturist
prolocutorship
radioautograph
relinquishment
reproductively
Rosicrucianism
spiritualistic
spirituousness
sublieutenancy
topsyturviness
tumultuousness
uncircumcision
uncommunicable
unenthusiastic
voluptuousness
cardiovascular
circumvolution
conceivability
conservational
conservatively
controvertible
irremovability
selfgovernment
selfrevelation
intertwinement
overpoweringly
praiseworthily
swordswallower
ambidextrously
complexionless
paradoxicality
archetypically
chemosynthesis
countrydancing
hydrodynamical
hypothyroidism
metaphysically
metapsychology
parapsychology
photosynthesis
photosynthetic

---

acceleratingly
accountability
accumulatively
aerodynamicist
anticipatively
archidiaconate
articulateness
backscratching
bibliomaniacal
biodegradation
breathtakingly
cardiovascular
cartographical
circumnavigate
colourfastness
commissaryship
compensational
conceivability
conformability
congregational
conservational
conservatively
consociational
conspiratorial
conversational
coordinateness
cosmographical
degenerateness
deliberateness
deliberatively
denominational
denumerability
discouragement
discouragingly
disenchantment
disenfranchise
dispensability
dissertational
dissociability
ecclesiastical
elementariness
exasperatingly
excruciatingly
exhilaratingly
faintheartedly
hagiographical
handicraftsman
heartsearching
hereditariness
holometabolism
holometabolous
hydrographical
iconographical
illimitability
illiterateness
illustrational
illustratively
immaculateness
immoderateness
impermeability
impregnability
inadequateness
inadvisability
inalienability
inalterability
inapproachable
indubitability
inflammability
ingratiatingly
inheritability
inordinateness
inscrutability
inseparability
insuperability
intergradation
interplanetary
intolerability
intractability
irrefutability
irremovability
irreproachable
irreproachably
irrevocability
justifiability
lightheartedly
marketgardener
neuroanatomist
nomenclatorial
opinionatively
organisational
orthographical
passionateness
patresfamilias
perturbational
petrographical
pleasurability
practicability
predictability
presentability
presentational
preventability
propitiatorily
quantitatively
recoverability
regeneratively
respectability
retrogradation
sanguinariness
selfeffacement
selfeffacingly
serviceability
singlehandedly
spiritualistic
spirochaetosis
stationariness
stoutheartedly
swordswallower
symptomatology
tachygraphical
tetragrammaton
threadbareness
tintinnabulary
tintinnabulate
tintinnabulous
transplantable
unapproachable
undergraduette
understandable
understandably
understatement
undesirability
unhesitatingly
universalistic
unpalatability
unpleasantness
vasodilatation
vasodilatatory
vituperatively
acceptableness
attainableness
changeableness
charitableness
comparableness
compatibleness
concelebration
counterbalance
creditableness
cyanocobalamin
deceivableness
delectableness
dependableness
deplorableness
despicableness
detestableness
electrobiology
favourableness
featherbrained
formidableness
gyrostabiliser
honourableness
imaginableness
impassableness
impassibleness

implacableness
improvableness
incredibleness
inevitableness
inexorableness
inflexibleness
inimitableness
insatiableness
insensibleness
intangibleness
invariableness
invincibleness
inviolableness
knickerbockers
manageableness
pardonableness
penetrableness
perishableness
personableness
profitableness
quarterbinding
reasonableness
remarkableness
scatterbrained
seasonableness
sufferableness
terminableness
uncorroborated
unsociableness
vulnerableness
whortleberries
appendicectomy
architectonics
chemoreception
chemoreceptive
communications
concavoconcave
constructional
constructively
constructivism
constructivist
contumaciously
convexoconcave
councilchamber
counterculture
countercurrent
crinkumcrankum
deconsecration
disassociation
diverticulitis
dolichocephaly
handkerchieves
hocuspocussing
hydromechanics
hysterectomise
inappreciation
inappreciative
inauspiciously
insufficiently
insurrectional
intellectually
interjectional
interlocutress
intersectional
introductorily
irreconcilable
irreconcilably
irrespectively
jurisdictional
matriarchalism
meretriciously
metapsychology
microtechnique
monosaccharide
multinucleated
parapsychology
pertinaciously
phthalocyanine
pianoaccordian

polysaccharide
proprioceptive
quattrocentism
quattrocentist
reminiscential
reproductively
resurrectional
Rosicrucianism
satisfactorily
selfdiscipline
selfperception
selfproclaimed
servomechanism
shamefacedness
sphaerocrystal
subconsciously
superficiality
superincumbent
tetradactylous
tyrannicalness
ultramicrotome
unappreciative
unattractively
unidirectional
weltanschauung
ambassadorship
bullheadedness
countrydancing
electrodeposit
electrodynamic
highhandedness
highmindedness
immethodically
incommodiously
inconsiderable
inconsiderably
intermediately
intermediation
irreproducible
lefthandedness
longheadedness
longitudinally
longwindedness
massproduction
openhandedness
openmindedness
overproduction
reintroduction
semiconducting
stadholdership
standardbearer
superinduction
unfriendliness
unpremeditated
weakmindedness
acknowledgment
antifederalist
apophthegmatic
audiofrequency
biosystematics
blockaderunner
boroughEnglish
brachycephalic
breathlessness
bronchiectasis
cantankerously
castrametation
catachrestical
characteristic
chronometrical
circumbendibus
colourlessness
committeewoman
commonsensical
comprehensible
comprehensibly
condescendence
conglomeration
controvertible

departmentally
dicotyledonous
discommendable
disconcertment
disconnectedly
discontentedly
discontentment
disrespectable
distemperature
effortlessness
eigenfrequency
experimentally
friendlessness
groundlessness
histochemistry
hobbledehoyish
iatrochemistry
incompleteness
incompressible
incompressibly
indiscreetness
instrumentally
insuppressible
interpretation
interpretative
interpretively
malcontentedly
neurochemistry
noncooperation
obstreperously
organometallic
overpoweringly
peripateticism
petrochemistry
pharmaceutical
photochemistry
pluviometrical
premillenarian
preponderantly
preposterously
presbyterially
propaedeutical
prosencephalic
prosencephalon
psychoneurosis
psychoneurotic
quadragenarian
radiochemistry
radiotherapist
regardlessness
rejuvenescence
relentlessness
resistlessness
rhinencephalic
rhinencephalon
sauropterygian
selfabnegation
selfdependence
selfdetermined
selfgovernment
selfinterested
selfrevelation
septuagenarian
sesquipedalian
Shakespeareana
Shakespeariana
slaughterhouse
slaughterously
soporiferously
spatiotemporal
speechlessness
spiritlessness
superelevation
superfoetation
tatterdemalion
thriftlessness
ultimogeniture
unflatteringly
unremunerative

weightlessness
crossreference
delightfulness
despitefulness
disdainfulness
insignificance
insignificancy
neglectfulness
overconfidence
purposefulness
remorsefulness
respectfulness
revengefulness
scientifically
selfconfidence
selffulfilling
selfsufficient
sprightfulness
successfulness
thanksoffering
thoughtfulness
unfaithfulness
ungratefulness
unsatisfactory
untruthfulness
worshipfulness
advantageously
aetiologically
autobiographer
autobiographic
autosuggestion
boardingschool
Brobdingnagian
carcinogenesis
clearsightedly
dinoflagellate
disintegration
disintegrative
ethnologically
etymologically
ferrimagnetism
ferromagnesian
ferromagnetism
forthrightness
genealogically
haematogenesis
intelligential
intelligentsia
intermigration
metallographer
mythologically
partridgeberry
pathologically
petrologically
philologically
predesignation
quinquagesimal
redintegration
sacrilegiously
selfsuggestion
shortsightedly
sociologically
spectrographic
sphygmographic
steganographer
suprasegmental
tautologically
teleologically
transmigration
transmigratory
tropologically
watertightness
biographically
chickenhearted
extravehicular
geographically
heterochromous
heterophyllous
heterothallism

hierarchically
idiopathically
indecipherable
palaeethnology
philanthropise
philanthropist
psilanthropism
psilanthropist
psychochemical
psychophysical
schoolchildren
telepathically
thermochemical
windowshopping
absentmindedly
absorptiveness
accomplishable
accomplishment
aesthesiometer
Africanisation
aggrandisement
aggressiveness
airconditioner
allegorisation
amateurishness
antiscriptural
apprenticeship
archiepiscopal
artificialness
attractiveness
authentication
autoradiograph
bastardisation
beautification
beneficialness
bituminisation
bloodthirstily
bowdlerisation
butterfingered
capitalisation
categorisation
centralisation
circumlittoral
classification
classificatory
combustibility
commissionaire
compassionable
complexionless
compossibility
compulsiveness
concessionaire
conclusiveness
concretisation
conductibility
conglutination
conglutinative
conterminously
contradictable
contradictious
conventionally
convertibility
convincingness
convulsiveness
coquettishness
corruptibility
cumulativeness
decimalisation
decolonisation
decolorisation
decorativeness
definitiveness
dehumanisation
delocalisation
demisemiquaver
demobilisation
demonetisation
demoralisation
denazification
depolarisation
detoxification
devitalisation
diamantiferous
diamondiferous
diminutiveness
disappointment
disciplinarian
discontinuance
discriminating
discrimination
discriminative
discriminatory
discursiveness
disfurnishment
disinclination
disquisitional
distensibility
dolomitisation
emulsification
endoradiosonde
enterprisingly
entertainingly
enthronisation
esterification
eutrophication
Evangelicalism
evangelisation
exhaustibility
exhaustiveness
expressionless
expressiveness
extinguishable
extinguishment
fantasticality
figurativeness
foraminiferous
forbiddingness
foreordination
fraternisation
fructification
gelatinisation
generalisation
hebetudinosity
homogenisation
humidification
hypercriticise
hypercriticism
hypocoristical
identification
illconditioned
illegitimately
immobilisation
imperativeness
implausibility
impoverishment
impracticality
impressibility
impressionable
impressiveness
inappositeness
incapacitation
incoordination
indecisiveness
indefiniteness
indiscriminate
indivisibility
indoctrination
infelicitously
inflectionally
inflectionless
infrangibility
intertwinement
intransitively
intrinsicality
irreducibility
latitudinarian
legitimisation
liberalisation
lovingkindness
lyophilisation
meditativeness
mesdemoiselles
militarisation
mineralisation
misapplication
monopolisation
multiplication
multiplicative
narrowmindedly
naturalisation
neuroscientist
neutralisation
nightblindness
nonbelligerent
nonsensicality
oecumenicalism
oppressiveness
outlandishness
overcapitalise
overestimation
overexcitement
paradoxicality
pasteurisation
perceptibility
perceptiveness
perfectibility
permissibility
permissiveness
persuasiveness
pistilliferous
politicisation
polymerisation
polytheistical
popularisation
possessiveness
postpositional
postpositively
pragmaticality
predestinarian
predestination
prefabrication
presentimental
prettification
preventiveness
productiveness
professionally
proportionable
proportionably
proportionally
protectiveness
protrusiveness
pseudepigrapha
pseudepigraphy
quantification
radicalisation
recolonisation
reconnaissance
reconstitution
redistribution
redistributive
reflectiveness
refrangibility
regressiveness
regularisation
rehabilitation
relinquishment
remonetisation
reorganisation
repetitiveness
resinification
responsibility
responsiveness
revalorisation
revivification
rigidification
Russianisation
sanctification
sanguification
saponification
scandalisation
schematisation
schoolmistress
secularisation
selfadmiration
selfsatisfying
semielliptical
semiofficially
sensualisation
silicification
simplemindedly
simplification
singlemindedly
solidification
solitudinarian
solubilisation
sophistication
specialisation
stigmatisation
stoicheiometry
stratification
strongmindedly
stultification
subcontinental
subjectiveness
submersibility
submissiveness
subversiveness
successionally
successiveness
suggestibility
suggestiveness
sulphanilamide
supereminently
susceptibility
susceptiveness
suspensiveness
symmetrisation
transitionally
transitiveness
trivialisation
unbecomingness
unconscionable
uniformitarian
unquestionable
unquestionably
valetudinarian
vegetativeness
verisimilitude
vindictiveness
volatilisation
westernisation
aerobiological
agrobiological
archaeological
butterflyscrew
campanological
chancellorship
chickenlivered
Christological
climatological
controllership
contumeliously
cosmopolitical
councillorship
counsellorship
crosspollinate
crystallisable
dermatological
dieselelectric
disaffiliation
disequilibrium
encephalograph
eschatological
floriculturist
forwardlooking
gerontological

goodfellowship
gynaecological
horticulturist
hyperbolically
hypercalcaemia
ichthyological
intermolecular
interpellation
intramolecular
martyrological
meteorological
methodological
myrmecological
newfangledness
nitrocellulose
noninvolvement
ornithological
overwhelmingly
parallelepiped
phototelegraph
phraseological
pisciculturist
postmillennial
probabiliorism
probabiliorist
pteridological
radiotelegraph
radiotelephone
radiotelephony
reconciliation
reconciliatory
scintillometer
selfemployment
selfexplaining
shovehalfpenny
sociopolitical
soteriological
springcleaning
stampcollector
stomatological
superciliously
terminological
thermoelectric
transvaluation
undervaluation
unintelligible
unintelligibly
venereological
verticillaster
volcanological
vulcanological
watercolourist
accustomedness
alphanumerical
anagrammatical
apothegmatical
arrhythmically
astronomically
basidiomycetes
bathingmachine
circumambiency
circumambulate
countermeasure
diagrammatical
enantiomorphic
epigrammatical
hypodermically
indeterminable
intercommunion
intercommunity
microcomponent
ophthalmoscope
ophthalmoscopy
overcommitment
phantasmagoria
phantasmagoric
selftormenting
seriocomically
tragicomically
unaccommodated
uncircumcision
uneconomically
abovementioned
aforementioned
apprehensively
Augustinianism
bioengineering
bioluminescent
chemosynthesis
classconscious
confidentially
conscienceless
contraindicate
curvilinearity
determinedness
diachronically
differentiable
differentially
disarrangement
disingenuously
disorientation
electioneering
enharmonically
excommunicable
excommunicator
experientially
fundamentalism
fundamentalist
fundamentality
halfpennyworth
hallucinogenic
histrionically
homotransplant
hydrodynamical
hypersensitive
hypersonically
implementation
incommensurate
incommunicable
incommunicably
inconveniently
indistinctness
inharmoniously
interlineation
interpenetrate
microminiature
mountaineering
neocolonialism
overabundantly
papilionaceous
parsimoniously
pathogenically
percutaneously
periodontology
pestilentially
photosensitise
photosensitive
photosynthesis
photosynthetic
physiognomical
prearrangement
preferentially
propagandistic
providentially
psychoanalysis
psychoanalytic
quinquennially
radiosensitive
recommencement
recommendation
recommendatory
representation
representative
roentgenoscopy
sacramentalism
sacramentalist
sacramentarian
scrubbingbrush
sentimentalise
sentimentalism
sentimentalist
sentimentality
simultaneously
slatternliness
squadronleader
stumblingblock
superannuation
superconductor
supersensitive
supersonically
sycophantishly
synchronically
telephonically
testimonialise
transcendental
transcendently
tridimensional
twodimensional
ultramontanism
ultramontanist
ultrasonically
uncommunicable
uncongeniality
unconventional
unconvincingly
undermentioned
unidimensional
vicechancellor
abstemiousness
achondroplasia
affectionately
allelomorphism
anthropography
anthropologist
anthropometric
antiphlogistic
asynchronously
auspiciousness
avariciousness
bacteriologist
bacteriostasis
bacteriostatic
boisterousness
calamitousness
calcareousness
capriciousness
censoriousness
chivalrousness
chromatography
cinematography
circuitousness
circumlocution
circumlocutory
circumvolution
claustrophobia
claustrophobic
commodiousness
conditionality
contagiousness
contiguousness
continuousness
contraposition
contrapositive
copperbottomed
correspondence
correspondency
courageousness
cumbersomeness
dextrorotation
dextrorotatory
dialectologist
diaphanousness
disapprobation
disapprobative
disapprobatory
disapprovingly
discombobulate
discomfortable
disconformable
disconsolately
disconsolation
ecclesiologist
educationalist
epidemiologist
epistemologist
exceptionality
extensionality
extraneousness
factitiousness
fallaciousness
fastidiousness
fictitiousness
flagitiousness
fortuitousness
goodhumouredly
gramineousness
grandiloquence
gratuitousness
gregariousness
gynandromorphy
harmoniousness
heteromorphism
heteromorphous
historiography
homoeomorphism
hygroscopicity
imperviousness
incautiousness
incestuousness
incontrollable
indecorousness
infectiousness
ingloriousness
intuitionalism
intuitionalist
kremlinologist
lasciviousness
libidinousness
licentiousness
liturgiologist
loquaciousness
lugubriousness
macroeconomics
malappropriate
malodorousness
marvellousness
meddlesomeness
Mephistopheles
meticulousness
microbiologist
microeconomics
microprocessor
microsporangia
miraculousness
misappropriate
monochromatism
monotonousness
mysteriousness
nonperformance
nutritiousness
obsequiousness
oleaginousness
omnivorousness
outrageousness
oxyhaemoglobin
palaeobotanist
parasitologist
peremptoriness
perfidiousness
perniciousness
pharmacologist
pharmacopoeial
phytogeography
pneumatologist
pneumoconiosis
portentousness

potentiometric
praiseworthily
precariousness
precociousness
predisposition
presupposition
prodigiousness
professorially
propitiousness
prosperousness
prothonotarial
protozoologist
pseudomorphism
pseudomorphous
psychosomatics
pugnaciousness
pyrheliometric
rampageousness
rebelliousness
refractoriness
reinvigoration
rheumatologist
ridiculousness
robustiousness
rontgenography
roundaboutness
salubriousness
scandalousness
scrupulousness
scurrilousness
selfabsorption
selfimmolation
selfimportance
sensationalism
sensationalist
slanderousness
solicitousness
spermatogenous
spermatogonium
spermatophytic
spirituousness
staphylococcus
stertorousness
stoichiometric
stupendousness
submicroscopic
supererogation
supererogatory
superphosphate
suspiciousness
tachistoscopic
thalassography
traditionalism
traditionalist
traitorousness
transitoriness
tremendousness
tumultuousness
ubiquitousness
umbrageousness
uncompromising
uncontrollable
uncontrollably
uncontroverted
ungraciousness
unmentionables
uproariousness
victoriousness
villainousness
viviparousness
vociferousness
voluminousness
voluptuousness
archetypically
circumspection
counterplotted
encyclopaedism
encyclopaedist
erythropoiesis
galactopoietic
generalpurpose
goodtemperedly
ichthyophagous
indecomposable
infralapsarian
interdependent
macrocephalous
microcephalous
myrmecophagous
myrmecophilous
overcompensate
polymorphously
prescriptively
proscriptively
publicspirited
selfcomplacent
selfpropelling
selfpropulsion
selfrespectful
selfrespecting
selfsupporting
supralapsarian
telescopically
unaccomplished
underemphasise
unenterprising
inconsequently
magniloquently
statuesqueness
antidepressant
antiquarianism
asymmetrically
barometrically
bibliographise
blackmarketeer
bouleversement
bremsstrahlung
chincherinchee
concentrically
cotemporaneous
crossfertilise
disaffirmation
disembarkation
disenthralment
disincorporate
disinheritance
disorderliness
doublebreasted
egalitarianism
extemporaneity
extemporaneous
extracorporeal
geocentrically
hermaphroditic
hydrocoralline
hyperirritable
hypothyroidism
imponderabilia
incorporeality
indifferentism
indifferentist
indiscerptible
infrastructure
interferential
interferometer
interferometry
knighterrantry
libertarianism
megasporangium
megasporophyll
metaphorically
microcircuitry
microstructure
millenarianism
ministerialist
misinformation
multifariously
necessarianism
nonrestrictive
northnortheast
northnorthwest
oneirocritical
orthochromatic
outgeneralling
pachydermatous
phenobarbitone
phosphorescent
photoperiodism
pigeonbreasted
predeterminate
proletarianise
proletarianism
Pythagoreanism
radiostrontium
reconstruction
reconstructive
Sabbatarianism
selfcorrecting
selfenergising
selfexpression
selfrepression
singlebreasted
spinthariscope
strikebreaking
subalternation
subcontrariety
superscription
superstructure
superterranean
tergiversation
territorialise
territorialism
territorialist
territoriality
thimblerigging
thoughtreading
topsyturviness
transformation
transformative
transportation
transversality
Trinitarianism
ultrastructure
unmannerliness
utilitarianism
vaingloriously
volumetrically
windowdressing
Zoroastrianism
Albigensianism
antiperspirant
arrondissement
corticosteroid
corticosterone
cryptaesthesia
disinfestation
divertissement
effervescently
electrostatics
embarrassingly
fullyfashioned
heroworshipper
ichthyosaurian
inconsistently
indemonstrable
inexpressively
intercessional
intercessorial
Johannisberger
metaphysically
mistranslation
northeastwards
northwestwards
oversubscribed
progressionary
progressionism
progressionist
pseudaesthesia
quintessential
selfconsequent
selfconsistent
selfpossession
selfpreserving
skimbleskamble
southeastwards
southwestwards
spectroscopist
spindleshanked
supervisorship
troubleshooter
unenthusiastic
unprofessional
unsuccessfully
vicepresidency
whippersnapper
abstractedness
abstractionism
abstractionist
achromatically
administration
administrative
administratrix
adventitiously
aerobiotically
alphabetically
altruistically
ambidextrously
antiseptically
antithetically
aphoristically
apologetically
apoplectically
arithmetically
associationism
asymptotically
autocratically
backscattering
bioelectricity
campylotropous
catechetically
circumstantial
coessentiality
conjunctivitis
conquistadores
consubstantial
contemptuously
contractedness
corticotrophic
corticotrophin
cucurbitaceous
defenestration
democratically
despiritualise
destructionist
diagnostically
diffractometer
diplomatically
discountenance
discourteously
disgruntlement
disheartenment
disjointedness
dispiritedness
disputatiously
econometrician
electrotherapy
electrothermal
electrothermic
emblematically
endosmotically
entomostracous
epexegetically
eulogistically
euphuistically
exclaustration
existentialism

existentialist
farsightedness
flatfootedness
fortunetelling
histopathology
horrorstricken
hypercatalexis
hypocritically
hypostatically
hypothetically
idealistically
inartistically
ineffectuality
integrationist
intermittently
internationale
judgematically
legalistically
linguistically
mathematically
morganatically
multilaterally
neuropathology
noteworthiness
numismatically
obstructionism
obstructionist
optimistically
ostentatiously
osteoarthritis
paratactically
phlegmatically
phytopathology
planetstricken
pleonastically
poikilothermal
poikilothermic
postmastership
premeditatedly
presumptuously
procrastinator
progenitorship
prognosticator
prohibitionism
prohibitionist
prolocutorship
proprietorship
radioautograph
rambunctiously
repudiationist
restorationism
restorationist
restrictionist
roadworthiness
schismatically
scholastically
segregationist
selfcontrolled
selfdestroying
selffertilised
selfflattering
selfpartiality
selfprotection
selfrestrained
selfsustaining
semicentennial
snaggletoothed
souldestroying
stochastically
sublieutenancy
substantialism
substantialist
substantiality
substantiation
substantivally
superintendent
supernaturally
supposititious
surefootedness
systematically
telephotograph
terrorstricken
theocratically
therianthropic
transliterator
unaffectedness
unemphatically
unexpectedness
vivisectionist
wonderstricken
behaviouristic
centrifugation
commensurately
commensuration
congratulation
congratulative
congratulatory
consanguineous
constitutional
constitutively
consuetudinary
contrapuntally
discolouration
distributional
distributively
inarticulately
inarticulation
inconclusively
indestructible
indestructibly
insurmountable
insurmountably
irresoluteness
miscalculation
monkeybusiness
noctambulation
noncommunicant
nonconcurrence
overindulgence
overpopulation
phenylbutazone
proceleusmatic
psychosurgical
recapitulation
recapitulative
recapitulatory
rectangularity
selfaccusation
selfaccusatory
selfadjustment
selfassumption
selfinductance
selfindulgence
selfregulating
somnambulation
somnambulistic
subinfeudation
substitutional
substitutively
superabundance
undernourished
unscrupulously
anticonvulsant
bougainvillaea
electrovalency
indiscoverable
underdeveloped
unreservedness
disembowelment
unacknowledged
intersexuality
supramaxillary
thyrotoxicosis
transsexualism
astrophysicist
dodecasyllable
hieroglyphical
hyperglycaemia
imparisyllabic
metempsychosis
nitroglycerine
parenchymatous
pseudonymously
psychodynamics
quadrisyllabic
quadrisyllable
thermodynamics

---

anagrammatical
apothegmatical
artificialness
bathingmachine
beneficialness
bibliographise
bremsstrahlung
circumstantial
communications
conquistadores
consubstantial
cotemporaneous
counterbalance
countrydancing
cucurbitaceous
cyanocobalamin
diagrammatical
disenthralment
electrovalency
encyclopaedism
encyclopaedist
epigrammatical
extemporaneity
extemporaneous
heterothallism
hydrocoralline
hydrodynamical
hypercatalexis
ichthyosaurian
imponderabilia
megasporangium
outgeneralling
papilionaceous
phantasmagoria
phantasmagoric
premeditatedly
psychoanalysis
psychoanalytic
selfexplaining
selfsustaining
Shakespeareana
Shakespeariana
subcontrariety
tyrannicalness
unsatisfactory
accountability
circumambiency
circumambulate
combustibility
compossibility
conceivability
conductibility
conformability
convertibility
corruptibility
denumerability
disapprobation
disapprobative
disapprobatory
discombobulate
dispensability
dissociability
distensibility
exhaustibility
holometabolism
holometabolous
illimitability
impermeability
implausibility
impregnability
impressibility
inadvisability
inalienability
inalterability
indivisibility
indubitability
inflammability
infrangibility
inheritability
inscrutability
inseparability
insuperability
intolerability
intractability
irreducibility
irrefutability
irremovability
irrevocability
Johannisberger
justifiability
perceptibility
perfectibility
permissibility
phenobarbitone
pleasurability
practicability
predictability
presentability
preventability
recoverability
redistribution
redistributive
refrangibility
respectability
responsibility
serviceability
standardbearer
submersibility
suggestibility
susceptibility
tintinnabulary
tintinnabulate
tintinnabulous
undesirability
unpalatability
apprenticeship
archidiaconate
authentication
beautification
bronchiectasis
circumlocution
circumlocutory
classification
classificatory
conscienceless
contradictable
contradictious
denazification
detoxification
disconnectedly
disrespectable
effervescently
emulsification
esterification
eutrophication
Evangelicalism
fantasticality
fructification
humidification
hypercalcaemia
hyperglycaemia
identification
impracticality
inapproachable
indestructible
indestructibly
indistinctness
intrinsicality

irreproachable
irreproachably
metempsychosis
microcircuitry
microprocessor
misapplication
multiplication
multiplicative
nitroglycerine
nonsensicality
oecumenicalism
oversubscribed
paradoxicality
pragmaticality
prefabrication
prettification
quantification
recommencement
resinification
revivification
rigidification
sanctification
sanguification
saponification
selfeffacement
selfeffacingly
selfinductance
semiofficially
silicification
simplification
solidification
sophistication
spectroscopist
staphylococcus
stratification
stultification
unapproachable
uncircumcision
unconvincingly
vicechancellor
acknowledgment
biodegradation
consuetudinary
contraindicate
dicotyledonous
intergradation
overabundantly
propagandistic
recommendation
recommendatory
retrogradation
sesquipedalian
subinfeudation
superconductor
transcendental
transcendently
undergraduette
abstractedness
accustomedness
advantageously
alphanumerical
antidepressant
appendicectomy
autosuggestion
bioengineering
bioluminescent
bullheadedness
carcinogenesis
chemoreception
chemoreceptive
chickenhearted
circumspection
committeewoman
contractedness
controllership
countermeasure
crossreference
curvilinearity
determinedness
dieselelectric
dinoflagellate
discountenance
discourteously
disembowelment
disheartenment
disjointedness
dispiritedness
dolichocephaly
doublebreasted
electioneering
electrodeposit
farsightedness
flatfootedness
fortunetelling
goodtemperedly
haematogenesis
highhandedness
highmindedness
inconsiderable
inconsiderably
incorporeality
indecipherable
indifferentism
indifferentist
indiscoverable
indiscreetness
intelligential
intelligentsia
interdependent
interferential
interlineation
intermolecular
interpenetrate
intramolecular
lefthandedness
longheadedness
longwindedness
mountaineering
multilaterally
neuroscientist
newfangledness
openhandedness
openmindedness
overcompensate
parallelepiped
partridgeberry
percutaneously
phosphorescent
phototelegraph
pigeonbreasted
postmastership
postmillennial
proprioceptive
psychochemical
Pythagoreanism
quattrocentism
quattrocentist
quinquagesimal
quintessential
radiotelegraph
radiotelephone
radiotelephony
reminiscential
selfconsequent
selfcorrecting
selfexpression
selfperception
selfpossession
selfpreserving
selfpropelling
selfprotection
selfrepression
selfrespectful
selfrespecting
selfsuggestion
selftormenting
semicentennial
shamefacedness
simultaneously
singlebreasted
spirochaetosis
springcleaning
stadholdership
strikebreaking
sublieutenancy
superintendent
surefootedness
thermochemical
thermoelectric
thoughtreading
transliterator
unaffectedness
underdeveloped
unexpectedness
unreservedness
weakmindedness
whortleberries
windowdressing
diamantiferous
diamondiferous
foraminiferous
handicraftsman
pistilliferous
shovehalfpenny
thanksoffering
anthropography
antiphlogistic
apophthegmatic
centrifugation
chromatography
cinematography
disarrangement
discouragement
discouragingly
historiography
nonbelligerent
oxyhaemoglobin
phytogeography
prearrangement
pseudepigrapha
pseudepigraphy
rontgenography
scrubbingbrush
selfabnegation
selfenergising
spermatogenous
spermatogonium
stumblingblock
supererogation
supererogatory
thalassography
clearsightedly
councilchamber
electrotherapy
electrothermal
electrothermic
forthrightness
fullyfashioned
handkerchieves
heroworshipper
histopathology
hobbledehoyish
hydromechanics
ichthyophagous
macrocephalous
matriarchalism
metapsychology
microcephalous
microtechnique
monosaccharide
myrmecophagous
myrmecophilous
neuropathology
noteworthiness
osteoarthritis
parapsychology
phytopathology
poikilothermal
poikilothermic
polymorphously
polysaccharide
roadworthiness
servomechanism
shortsightedly
spindleshanked
therianthropic
troubleshooter
underemphasise
watertightness
weltanschauung
abstractionism
abstractionist
achromatically
adventitiously
aerobiotically
aetiologically
Albigensianism
alphabetically
altruistically
antiquarianism
antiseptically
antithetically
aphoristically
apologetically
apoplectically
archetypically
arithmetically
arrhythmically
associationism
astronomically
asymmetrically
asymptotically
Augustinianism
autocratically
barometrically
biographically
bougainvillaea
catechetically
chickenlivered
chincherinchee
coessentiality
concentrically
conjunctivitis
consanguineous
contumaciously
contumeliously
cosmopolitical
crystallisable
democratically
destructionist
diachronically
diagnostically
diplomatically
disaffiliation
disassociation
disequilibrium
disinheritance
disputatiously
egalitarianism
electrobiology
emblematically
endosmotically
enharmonically
epexegetically
ethnologically
etymologically
eulogistically
euphuistically
excommunicable
excommunicator
existentialism
existentialist
extravehicular
genealogically
geocentrically
geographically

gyrostabiliser
hierarchically
histrionically
hyperbolically
hyperirritable
hypersonically
hypocritically
hypodermically
hypostatically
hypothetically
idealistically
idiopathically
immethodically
inappreciation
inappreciative
inartistically
inauspiciously
incommodiously
incommunicable
incommunicably
inconveniently
indeterminable
inharmoniously
insignificance
insignificancy
insufficiently
integrationist
intermediately
intermediation
internationale
irreconcilable
irreconcilably
judgematically
legalistically
libertarianism
linguistically
longitudinally
mathematically
meretriciously
metaphorically
metaphysically
microminiature
millenarianism
ministerialist
morganatically
multifariously
mythologically
necessarianism
neocolonialism
nonrestrictive
numismatically
obstructionism
obstructionist
oneirocritical
optimistically
ostentatiously
overcommitment
overconfidence
paratactically
parsimoniously
pathogenically
pathologically
pertinaciously
petrologically
philologically
phlegmatically
photoperiodism
pleonastically
probabiliorism
probabiliorist
procrastinator
prognosticator
progressionary
progressionism
progressionist
prohibitionism
prohibitionist
proletarianise
proletarianism
publicspirited
quarterbinding
rambunctiously
reconciliation
reconciliatory
repudiationist
restorationism
restorationist
restrictionist
Rosicrucianism
Sabbatarianism
sacrilegiously
schismatically
scholastically
schoolchildren
scientifically
segregationist
selfconfidence
selfconsistent
selfdiscipline
selffertilised
selffulfilling
selfpartiality
selfsufficient
seriocomically
sociologically
sociopolitical
spinthariscope
stochastically
subconsciously
substantialism
substantialist
substantiality
substantiation
substantivally
superciliously
superficiality
superscription
supersonically
supposititious
supramaxillary
synchronically
systematically
tautologically
teleologically
telepathically
telephonically
telescopically
territorialise
territorialism
territorialist
territoriality
testimonialise
theocratically
thimblerigging
thyrotoxicosis
tragicomically
Trinitarianism
tropologically
ultrasonically
unappreciative
uncommunicable
uncongeniality
uneconomically
unemphatically
unenthusiastic
unintelligible
unintelligibly
unpremeditated
utilitarianism
vaingloriously
vicepresidency
vivisectionist
volumetrically
Zoroastrianism
blackmarketeer
breathtakingly
disembarkation
skimbleskamble
acceptableness
anthropologist
attainableness
bacteriologist
changeableness
charitableness
circumvolution
comparableness
compatibleness
congratulation
congratulative
congratulatory
counterplotted
creditableness
crosspollinate
deceivableness
delectableness
dependableness
deplorableness
despicableness
detestableness
dialectologist
disconsolately
disconsolation
disgruntlement
disorderliness
dodecasyllable
ecclesiologist
epidemiologist
epistemologist
favourableness
formidableness
honourableness
imaginableness
imparisyllabic
impassableness
impassibleness
implacableness
improvableness
inarticulately
inarticulation
incontrollable
incredibleness
inevitableness
inexorableness
inflexibleness
inimitableness
insatiableness
insensibleness
intangibleness
interpellation
invariableness
invincibleness
inviolableness
kremlinologist
liturgiologist
manageableness
microbiologist
miscalculation
mistranslation
multinucleated
nitrocellulose
noctambulation
overindulgence
overpopulation
parasitologist
pardonableness
penetrableness
perishableness
personableness
pharmacologist
pneumatologist
profitableness
protozoologist
quadrisyllabic
quadrisyllable
reasonableness
recapitulation
recapitulative
recapitulatory
rectangularity
remarkableness
rheumatologist
seasonableness
selfcomplacent
selfimmolation
selfindulgence
selfproclaimed
selfregulating
selfrevelation
slatternliness
somnambulation
somnambulistic
spiritualistic
squadronleader
stampcollector
sufferableness
sulphanilamide
swordswallower
terminableness
unaccomplished
unacknowledged
uncontrollable
uncontrollably
unfriendliness
universalistic
unmannerliness
unscrupulously
unsociableness
verisimilitude
verticillaster
vulnerableness
aerodynamicist
anthropometric
biosystematics
cumbersomeness
disaffirmation
gynandromorphy
histochemistry
iatrochemistry
illegitimately
indiscriminate
intercommunion
intercommunity
meddlesomeness
misinformation
monochromatism
neurochemistry
overestimation
overwhelmingly
pachydermatous
parenchymatous
patresfamilias
petrochemistry
photochemistry
potentiometric
predeterminate
presentimental
pseudonymously
psychosomatics
pyrheliometric
radiochemistry
selfassumption
spatiotemporal
stoichiometric
suprasegmental
tatterdemalion
tetragrammaton
transformation
transformative
uncompromising
absentmindedly
affectionately
asynchronously
bibliomaniacal
boroughEnglish
Brobdingnagian
butterfingered

circumbendibus	traditionalist	snaggletoothed	discolouration
commonsensical	transplantable	soteriological	discomfortable
comprehensible	ultimogeniture	stoicheiometry	disconcertment
comprehensibly	unbecomingness	stomatological	disconformable
condescendence	understandable	successionally	disintegration
conditionality	understandably	supervisorship	disintegrative
conglutination	unmentionables	telephotograph	distemperature
conglutinative	unpleasantness	terminological	econometrician
conterminously	valetudinarian	transitionally	elementariness
contrapuntally	whippersnapper	unaccommodated	entomostracous
convincingness	aerobiological	unconscionable	exclaustration
correspondence	aesthesiometer	uncorroborated	faintheartedly
correspondency	agrobiological	unquestionable	featherbrained
departmentally	ambassadorship	unquestionably	heartsearching
disappointment	archaeological	venereological	hereditariness
disciplinarian	autoradiograph	volcanological	heterochromous
discommendable	campanological	vulcanological	heteromorphism
discontentedly	chancellorship	watercolourist	heteromorphous
discontentment	Christological	windowshopping	homoeomorphism
discontinuance	climatological	achondroplasia	horrorstricken
discriminating	commissionaire	antiperspirant	intermigration
discrimination	compassionable	antiscriptural	knighterrantry
discriminative	complexionless	brachycephalic	lightheartedly
discriminatory	concavoconcave	cartographical	marketgardener
disenchantment	concessionaire	claustrophobia	metallographer
disenfranchise	conventionally	claustrophobic	microsporangia
disinclination	convexoconcave	cosmographical	nonconcurrence
educationalist	councillorship	disincorporate	noncooperation
entertainingly	counsellorship	extracorporeal	nonperformance
exceptionality	dermatological	hagiographical	obstreperously
experimentally	diffractometer	hieroglyphical	overpoweringly
extensionality	enantiomorphic	hydrographical	peremptoriness
ferrimagnetism	encephalograph	hygroscopicity	philanthropise
ferromagnesian	endoradiosonde	iconographical	philanthropist
ferromagnetism	erythropoiesis	indiscerptible	planetstricken
forbiddingness	eschatological	malappropriate	praiseworthily
foreordination	expressionless	Mephistopheles	preponderantly
hebetudinosity	forwardlooking	microcomponent	preposterously
incoordination	galactopoietic	misappropriate	presbyterially
indoctrination	gerontological	orthographical	professorially
instrumentally	goodfellowship	petrographical	pseudomorphism
insurmountable	gynaecological	pharmacopoeial	pseudomorphous
insurmountably	hallucinogenic	prosencephalic	psilanthropism
interplanetary	hermaphroditic	prosencephalon	psilanthropist
intertwinement	hypothyroidism	rhinencephalic	psychosurgical
intuitionalism	ichthyological	rhinencephalon	radiotherapist
intuitionalist	impressionable	semielliptical	redintegration
latitudinarian	indecomposable	spermatophytic	refractoriness
lovingkindness	inflectionally	tachygraphical	reinvigoration
macroeconomics	inflectionless	audiofrequency	sanguinariness
malcontentedly	interferometer	demisemiquaver	sauropterygian
microeconomics	interferometry	eigenfrequency	scatterbrained
narrowmindedly	knickerbockers	grandiloquence	selfabsorption
nightblindness	martyrological	administration	selfadmiration
noncommunicant	megasporophyll	administrative	selfcontrolled
palaeethnology	meteorological	administratrix	selfdestroying
pneumoconiosis	methodological	allelomorphism	selfdetermined
predesignation	myrmecological	ambidextrously	selfgovernment
predestinarian	ophthalmoscope	antifederalist	selfimportance
predestination	ophthalmoscopy	autobiographer	selfinterested
premillenarian	ornithological	autobiographic	selfrestrained
psychodynamics	orthochromatic	behaviouristic	slaughterhouse
quadragenarian	phraseological	bioelectricity	slaughterously
quinquennially	physiognomical	blockaderunner	soporiferously
selfdependence	pianoaccordian	bloodthirstily	souldestroying
sensationalism	professionally	campylotropous	spectrographic
sensationalist	progenitorship	cantankerously	sphaerocrystal
septuagenarian	prolocutorship	characteristic	sphygmographic
simplemindedly	proportionable	commensurately	stationariness
singlehandedly	proportionably	commensuration	steganographer
singlemindedly	proportionally	commissaryship	stoutheartedly
solitudinarian	proprietorship	concelebration	superterranean
strongmindedly	pteridological	conglomeration	terrorstricken
subalternation	radioautograph	controvertible	threadbareness
subcontinental	radiostrontium	corticotrophic	transitoriness
superabundance	roentgenoscopy	corticotrophin	transmigration
supereminently	scintillometer	crinkumcrankum	transmigratory
thermodynamics	selfemployment	deconsecration	ultramicrotome
traditionalism	selfsupporting	defenestration	undernourished

unenterprising
unflatteringly
unremunerative
wonderstricken
accomplishable
accomplishment
Africanisation
aggrandisement
allegorisation
amateurishness
apprehensively
archiepiscopal
arrondissement
astrophysicist
bacteriostasis
bacteriostatic
bastardisation
bituminisation
boardingschool
bouleversement
bowdlerisation
breathlessness
capitalisation
cardiovascular
catachrestical
categorisation
centralisation
classconscious
colourfastness
colourlessness
concretisation
contraposition
contrapositive
coquettishness
decimalisation
decolonisation
decolorisation
dehumanisation
delocalisation
demobilisation
demonetisation
demoralisation
depolarisation
devitalisation
disfurnishment
divertissement
dolomitisation
ecclesiastical
effortlessness
embarrassingly
enterprisingly
enthronisation
evangelisation
extinguishable
extinguishment
fraternisation
friendlessness
gelatinisation
generalisation
groundlessness
homogenisation
homotransplant
hypersensitive
hypocoristical
immobilisation
impoverishment
incommensurate
incompressible
incompressibly
inconclusively
inexpressively
infralapsarian
insuppressible
intercessional
intercessorial
legitimisation
liberalisation
lyophilisation
mesdemoiselles
militarisation
mineralisation
monkeybusiness
monopolisation
naturalisation
neutralisation
outlandishness
pasteurisation
photosensitise
photosensitive
politicisation
polymerisation
polytheistical
popularisation
predisposition
presupposition
proceleusmatic
radicalisation
radiosensitive
recolonisation
reconnaissance
regardlessness
regularisation
rejuvenescence
relentlessness
relinquishment
remonetisation
reorganisation
resistlessness
revalorisation
Russianisation
scandalisation
schematisation
schoolmistress
secularisation
selfaccusation
selfaccusatory
selfadjustment
selfsatisfying
sensualisation
solubilisation
specialisation
speechlessness
spiritlessness
stigmatisation
submicroscopic
superphosphate
supersensitive
supralapsarian
symmetrisation
tachistoscopic
tergiversation
thriftlessness
transversality
tridimensional
trivialisation
twodimensional
unidimensional
unprofessional
unsuccessfully
volatilisation
weightlessness
westernisation
abovementioned
acceleratingly
accumulatively
aforementioned
airconditioner
anticipatively
architectonics
articulateness
backscattering
backscratching
castrametation
chemosynthesis
chronometrical
circumlittoral
compensational
confidentially
congregational
conservational
conservatively
consociational
conspiratorial
constitutional
constitutively
constructional
constructively
constructivism
constructivist
conversational
coordinateness
copperbottomed
corticosteroid
corticosterone
crossfertilise
cryptaesthesia
degenerateness
deliberateness
deliberatively
denominational
dextrorotation
dextrorotatory
differentiable
differentially
disinfestation
disorientation
disquisitional
dissertational
distributional
distributively
electrostatics
exasperatingly
excruciatingly
exhilaratingly
experientially
floriculturist
fundamentalism
fundamentalist
fundamentality
horticulturist
hypercriticise
hypercriticism
hysterectomise
illconditioned
illiterateness
illustrational
illustratively
immaculateness
immoderateness
implementation
inadequateness
inappositeness
incapacitation
incompleteness
inconsistently
indefiniteness
indemonstrable
infelicitously
ingratiatingly
inordinateness
insurrectional
intellectually
interjectional
intermittently
interpretation
interpretative
interpretively
intersectional
intransitively
introductorily
irresoluteness
irrespectively
jurisdictional
neuroanatomist
nomenclatorial
northeastwards
northnortheast
northnorthwest
northwestwards
opinionatively
organisational
organometallic
overcapitalise
overexcitement
palaeobotanist
passionateness
periodontology
peripateticism
perturbational
pestilentially
phenylbutazone
photosynthesis
photosynthetic
pisciculturist
pluviometrical
postpositional
postpositively
preferentially
prescriptively
presentational
propitiatorily
proscriptively
prothonotarial
providentially
pseudaesthesia
quantitatively
reconstitution
regeneratively
rehabilitation
representation
representative
reproductively
resurrectional
sacramentalism
sacramentalist
sacramentarian
satisfactorily
selfflattering
sentimentalise
sentimentalism
sentimentalist
sentimentality
southeastwards
southwestwards
substitutional
substitutively
superfoetation
sycophantishly
symptomatology
tetradactylous
transportation
ultramontanism
ultramontanist
unattractively
unconventional
undermentioned
understatement
unhesitatingly
unidirectional
uniformitarian
vasodilatation
vasodilatatory
vituperatively
abstemiousness
anticonvulsant
auspiciousness
avariciousness
boisterousness
calamitousness
calcareousness
capriciousness
censoriousness
chivalrousness
circuitousness
commodiousness
contagiousness

contemptuously
contiguousness
continuousness
counterculture
countercurrent
courageousness
delightfulness
despiritualise
despitefulness
diaphanousness
disdainfulness
disingenuously
diverticulitis
extraneousness
factitiousness
fallaciousness
fastidiousness
fictitiousness
flagitiousness
fortuitousness
generalpurpose
goodhumouredly
gramineousness
gratuitousness
gregariousness
harmoniousness
hocuspocussing
imperviousness
incautiousness
incestuousness
inconsequently
indecorousness
ineffectuality
infectiousness
infrastructure
ingloriousness
interlocutress
intersexuality
irreproducible
lasciviousness
libidinousness
licentiousness
loquaciousness
lugubriousness
magniloquently
malodorousness
marvellousness
massproduction
meticulousness
microstructure
miraculousness
monotonousness
mysteriousness
neglectfulness
nutritiousness
obsequiousness
oleaginousness
omnivorousness
outrageousness
overproduction
perfidiousness
perniciousness
pharmaceutical
portentousness
precariousness
precociousness
presumptuously
prodigiousness
propaedeutical
propitiousness
prosperousness
psychoneurosis
psychoneurotic
pugnaciousness
purposefulness
rampageousness
rebelliousness
reconstruction
reconstructive

reintroduction
remorsefulness
respectfulness
revengefulness
ridiculousness
robustiousness
roundaboutness
salubriousness
scandalousness
scrupulousness
scurrilousness
selfpropulsion
semiconducting
slanderousness
solicitousness
spirituousness
sprightfulness
statuesqueness
stertorousness
stupendousness
successfulness
superannuation
superincumbent
superinduction
supernaturally
superstructure
suspiciousness
thoughtfulness
traitorousness
transsexualism
transvaluation
tremendousness
tumultuousness
ubiquitousness
ultrastructure
umbrageousness
undervaluation
unfaithfulness
ungraciousness
ungratefulness
untruthfulness
uproariousness
victoriousness
villainousness
viviparousness
vociferousness
voluminousness
voluptuousness
worshipfulness
absorptiveness
aggressiveness
attractiveness
circumnavigate
compulsiveness
conclusiveness
convulsiveness
cumulativeness
decorativeness
definitiveness
diminutiveness
disapprovingly
discursiveness
exhaustiveness
expressiveness
figurativeness
imperativeness
impressiveness
indecisiveness
meditativeness
noninvolvement
oppressiveness
perceptiveness
permissiveness
persuasiveness
possessiveness
preventiveness
productiveness
protectiveness
protrusiveness

reflectiveness
regressiveness
repetitiveness
responsiveness
subjectiveness
submissiveness
subversiveness
successiveness
suggestiveness
superelevation
susceptiveness
suspensiveness
topsyturviness
transitiveness
uncontroverted
vegetativeness
vindictiveness
basidiomycetes
butterflyscrew
electrodynamic
halfpennyworth
heterophyllous
phthalocyanine
psychophysical

---

administration
administrative
administratrix
affectionately
Africanisation
Albigensianism
allegorisation
antifederalist
antiquarianism
Augustinianism
authentication
autobiographer
autobiographic
bastardisation
beautification
biodegradation
biosystematics
bituminisation
bowdlerisation
Brobdingnagian
capitalisation
castrametation
categorisation
centralisation
centrifugation
chickenhearted
classification
classificatory
coessentiality
commensurately
commensuration
concelebration
concretisation
conditionality
conglomeration
conglutination
conglutinative
congratulation
congratulative
congratulatory
councilchamber
countermeasure
crinkumcrankum
curvilinearity
decimalisation
decolonisation
decolorisation
deconsecration
defenestration
dehumanisation
delocalisation
demobilisation
demonetisation
demoralisation

denazification
depolarisation
despiritualise
detoxification
devitalisation
dextrorotation
dextrorotatory
disaffiliation
disaffirmation
disapprobation
disapprobative
disapprobatory
disassociation
disciplinarian
discolouration
disconsolately
disconsolation
discriminating
discrimination
discriminative
discriminatory
disembarkation
disinclination
disinfestation
disintegration
disintegrative
disorientation
distemperature
dolomitisation
doublebreasted
educationalist
egalitarianism
electrostatics
emulsification
enthronisation
entomostracous
esterification
eutrophication
Evangelicalism
evangelisation
exceptionality
exclaustration
existentialism
existentialist
extensionality
fantasticality
featherbrained
foreordination
fraternisation
fructification
fundamentalism
fundamentalist
fundamentality
gelatinisation
generalisation
homogenisation
humidification
hydromechanics
hypercalcaemia
hyperglycaemia
ichthyophagous
identification
illegitimately
immobilisation
implementation
impracticality
inappreciation
inappreciative
inarticulately
inarticulation
incapacitation
incoordination
incorporeality
indoctrination
ineffectuality
infralapsarian
intergradation
interlineation
intermediately

intermediation
intermigration
interpellation
interpretation
interpretative
intersexuality
intrinsicality
intuitionalism
intuitionalist
knighterrantry
latitudinarian
legitimisation
liberalisation
libertarianism
lyophilisation
macrocephalous
matriarchalism
metallographer
microcephalous
microminiature
microsporangia
militarisation
millenarianism
mineralisation
ministerialist
misapplication
miscalculation
misinformation
mistranslation
monochromatism
monopolisation
monosaccharide
multiplication
multiplicative
myrmecophagous
naturalisation
necessarianism
neocolonialism
neutralisation
noctambulation
noncooperation
nonsensicality
oecumenicalism
organometallic
overabundantly
overcapitalise
overestimation
overpopulation
pachydermatous
palaeobotanist
paradoxicality
parenchymatous
pasteurisation
phenylbutazone
phthalocyanine
pigeonbreasted
politicisation
polymerisation
polysaccharide
popularisation
pragmaticality
predesignation
predestinarian
predestination
prefabrication
premillenarian
preponderantly
prettification
proletarianise
proletarianism
prothonotarial
psychodynamics
psychosomatics
Pythagoreanism
quadragenarian
quantification
radicalisation
radiotherapist
recapitulation
recapitulative
recapitulatory
recolonisation
recommendation
recommendatory
reconciliation
reconciliatory
rectangularity
redintegration
regularisation
rehabilitation
reinvigoration
remonetisation
reorganisation
representation
representative
resinification
retrogradation
revalorisation
revivification
rigidification
Rosicrucianism
Russianisation
Sabbatarianism
sacramentalism
sacramentalist
sacramentarian
sanctification
sanguification
saponification
scandalisation
scatterbrained
schematisation
secularisation
selfabnegation
selfaccusation
selfaccusatory
selfadmiration
selfcomplacent
selfimmolation
selfpartiality
selfproclaimed
selfregulating
selfrestrained
selfrevelation
sensationalism
sensationalist
sensualisation
sentimentalise
sentimentalism
sentimentalist
sentimentality
septuagenarian
servomechanism
sesquipedalian
silicification
simplification
singlebreasted
skimbleskamble
solidification
solitudinarian
solubilisation
somnambulation
sophistication
specialisation
spectrographic
sphygmographic
spindleshanked
springcleaning
steganographer
stigmatisation
stratification
strikebreaking
stultification
subalternation
subinfeudation
substantialism
substantialist
substantiality
substantiation
sulphanilamide
superannuation
superelevation
supererogation
supererogatory
superficiality
superfoetation
superterranean
supralapsarian
symmetrisation
tatterdemalion
tergiversation
territorialise
territorialism
territorialist
territoriality
testimonialise
thermodynamics
thoughtreading
traditionalism
traditionalist
transformation
transformative
transmigration
transmigratory
transportation
transsexualism
transvaluation
transversality
Trinitarianism
trivialisation
ultramontanism
ultramontanist
unappreciative
uncongeniality
underemphasise
undervaluation
unenthusiastic
uniformitarian
unmentionables
unremunerative
utilitarianism
valetudinarian
vasodilatation
vasodilatatory
verticillaster
volatilisation
weltanschauung
westernisation
whippersnapper
Zoroastrianism
disequilibrium
imponderabilia
partridgeberry
scrubbingbrush
stumblingblock
achromatically
aerobiotically
aetiologically
alphabetically
altruistically
antiseptically
antithetically
aphoristically
apologetically
apoplectically
appendicectomy
archetypically
archiepiscopal
arithmetically
arrhythmically
astronomically
asymmetrically
asymptotically
autocratically
backscratching
barometrically
basidiomycetes
bathingmachine
biographically
boardingschool
cardiovascular
catechetically
circumspection
classconscious
concentrically
cucurbitaceous
democratically
diachronically
diagnostically
dieselelectric
diplomatically
disenfranchise
emblematically
endosmotically
enharmonically
epexegetically
ethnologically
etymologically
eulogistically
euphuistically
excommunicable
excommunicator
extravehicular
genealogically
geocentrically
geographically
heartsearching
hierarchically
histrionically
hyperbolically
hypersonically
hypocritically
hypodermically
hypostatically
hypothetically
idealistically
idiopathically
immethodically
inartistically
incommunicable
incommunicably
infrastructure
insignificance
insignificancy
intermolecular
intramolecular
irreproducible
judgematically
knickerbockers
legalistically
linguistically
massproduction
mathematically
metaphorically
metaphysically
microstructure
morganatically
mythologically
nonrestrictive
numismatically
optimistically
overproduction
papilionaceous
paratactically
pathogenically
pathologically
petrologically
philologically
phlegmatically
pleonastically
prognosticator
reconstruction
reconstructive
reintroduction
rejuvenescence
schismatically

nonperformance
orthochromatic
physiognomical
proceleusmatic
psychochemical
scintillometer
selfdetermined
stoicheiometry
superincumbent
tetragrammaton
thermochemical
carcinogenesis
chincherinchee
circumstantial
commissionaire
compassionable
complexionless
concavoconcave
concessionaire
consanguineous
consubstantial
conventionally
convexoconcave
cotemporaneous
countrydancing
discountenance
disheartenment
electrodynamic
expressionless
extemporaneity
extemporaneous
haematogenesis
impressionable
indeterminable
indifferentism
indifferentist
inflectionally
inflectionless
intelligential
intelligentsia
interdependent
interferential
longitudinally
megasporangium
microtechnique
neuroscientist
overcompensate
postmillennial
procrastinator
professionally
proportionable
proportionably
proportionally
quarterbinding
quattrocentism
quattrocentist
quintessential
radiostrontium
reminiscential
selfgovernment
selftormenting
semicentennial
sublieutenancy
successionally
superintendent
transitionally
unconscionable
unquestionable
unquestionably
abstractionism
abstractionist
advantageously
adventitiously
ambidextrously
anthropologist
archidiaconate
architectonics
associationism
asynchronously
bacteriologist
campylotropous
cantankerously
conspiratorial
contemptuously
conterminously
contumaciously
contumeliously
corticotrophic
corticotrophin
counterplotted
destructionist
dialectologist
dicotyledonous
discourteously
disincorporate
disingenuously
disputatiously
ecclesiologist
electrobiology
epidemiologist
epistemologist
extracorporeal
forwardlooking
gynandromorphy
hebetudinosity
heterochromous
histopathology
hobbledehoyish
holometabolism
holometabolous
hysterectomise
inauspiciously
incommodiously
infelicitously
inharmoniously
integrationist
intercessorial
internationale
introductorily
kremlinologist
liturgiologist
macroeconomics
meretriciously
metapsychology
microbiologist
microcomponent
microeconomics
multifariously
neuroanatomist
neuropathology
nomenclatorial
obstreperously
obstructionism
obstructionist
ostentatiously
palaeethnology
parapsychology
parasitologist
parsimoniously
percutaneously
periodontology
pertinaciously
pharmacologist
pharmacopoeial
philanthropise
philanthropist
photoperiodism
phytopathology
pneumatologist
polymorphously
preposterously
presumptuously
probabiliorism
probabiliorist
progressionary
progressionism
progressionist
prohibitionism
prohibitionist
propitiatorily
protozoologist
pseudonymously
psilanthropism
psilanthropist
rambunctiously
repudiationist
restorationism
restorationist
restrictionist
rheumatologist
sacrilegiously
satisfactorily
segregationist
selfcontrolled
selfdestroying
simultaneously
slaughterously
snaggletoothed
soporiferously
souldestroying
spectroscopist
spermatogonium
staphylococcus
subconsciously
superciliously
symptomatology
troubleshooter
ultramicrotome
unscrupulously
vaingloriously
vivisectionist
allelomorphism
bibliographise
chemoreception
chemoreceptive
dolichocephaly
electrodeposit
heteromorphism
heteromorphous
homoeomorphism
homotransplant
megasporophyll
parallelepiped
proprioceptive
pseudomorphism
pseudomorphous
radiotelephone
radiotelephony
selfabsorption
selfassumption
selfdiscipline
selfperception
shovehalfpenny
spatiotemporal
superphosphate
superscription
windowshopping
selfconsequent
alphanumerical
ambassadorship
anthropography
chancellorship
chromatography
chronometrical
cinematography
controllership
councillorship
counsellorship
countercurrent
crossreference
enantiomorphic
generalpurpose
goodhumouredly
goodtemperedly
historiography
inconsiderable
inconsiderably
indecipherable
indemonstrable
indiscoverable
malappropriate
misappropriate
multilaterally
nonconcurrence
osteoarthritis
oversubscribed
phytogeography
pianoaccordian
pluviometrical
postmastership
progenitorship
prolocutorship
proprietorship
pseudepigrapha
pseudepigraphy
psychoneurosis
psychoneurotic
publicspirited
rontgenography
selfpreserving
selfsupporting
Shakespeareana
Shakespeariana
stadholdership
subcontrariety
supernaturally
supervisorship
thalassography
therianthropic
transliterator
uncorroborated
whortleberries
abstemiousness
antidepressant
auspiciousness
autosuggestion
avariciousness
bioluminescent
bloodthirstily
boisterousness
breathlessness
butterflyscrew
calamitousness
calcareousness
capriciousness
censoriousness
chivalrousness
circuitousness
colourlessness
commodiousness
commonsensical
comprehensible
comprehensibly
contagiousness
contiguousness
continuousness
courageousness
crystallisable
diaphanousness
effortlessness
endoradiosonde
extraneousness
factitiousness
fallaciousness
fastidiousness
fictitiousness
flagitiousness
fortuitousness
friendlessness
gramineousness
gratuitousness
gregariousness
groundlessness
harmoniousness
hocuspocussing
imperviousness

incautiousness
incestuousness
incompressible
incompressibly
indecomposable
indecorousness
infectiousness
ingloriousness
insuppressible
lasciviousness
libidinousness
licentiousness
loquaciousness
lugubriousness
malodorousness
marvellousness
meticulousness
miraculousness
monotonousness
mysteriousness
nutritiousness
obsequiousness
oleaginousness
omnivorousness
ophthalmoscope
ophthalmoscopy
outrageousness
perfidiousness
perniciousness
phosphorescent
portentousness
precariousness
precociousness
prodigiousness
propitiousness
prosperousness
psychophysical
pugnaciousness
quinquagesimal
rampageousness
rebelliousness
reconnaissance
regardlessness
relentlessness
resistlessness
ridiculousness
robustiousness
roentgenoscopy
salubriousness
scandalousness
scrupulousness
scurrilousness
selfconsistent
selfexpression
selfpossession
selfrepression
selfsuggestion
slanderousness
solicitousness
speechlessness
spinthariscope
spiritlessness
spirituousness
stertorousness
stupendousness
suspiciousness
thriftlessness
traitorousness
tremendousness
tumultuousness
ubiquitousness
umbrageousness
ungraciousness
uproariousness
victoriousness
villainousness
viviparousness
vociferousness
voluminousness

voluptuousness
weightlessness
windowdressing
anagrammatical
antiscriptural
apothegmatical
bacteriostasis
bacteriostatic
bronchiectasis
catachrestical
circumlittoral
clearsightedly
colourfastness
communications
contradictable
contradictious
contrapuntally
controvertible
copperbottomed
cosmopolitical
departmentally
diagrammatical
disappointment
discomfortable
disconcertment
disconnectedly
discontentedly
discontentment
disenchantment
disinheritance
disrespectable
ecclesiastical
epigrammatical
experimentally
faintheartedly
forthrightness
handicraftsman
hyperirritable
hypocoristical
indestructible
indestructibly
indiscerptible
indiscreetness
indistinctness
instrumentally
insurmountable
insurmountably
interlocutress
interpenetrate
lightheartedly
malcontentedly
oneirocritical
overcommitment
pharmaceutical
polytheistical
praiseworthily
premeditatedly
propaedeutical
roundaboutness
schoolmistress
selfadjustment
selfimportance
selfinductance
semielliptical
shortsightedly
sociopolitical
spirochaetosis
stoutheartedly
supposititious
transplantable
unpleasantness
unpremeditated
watertightness
audiofrequency
blockaderunner
circumambulate
circumlocution
circumlocutory
circumvolution

demisemiquaver
discombobulate
discontinuance
eigenfrequency
floriculturist
grandiloquence
horticulturist
ichthyosaurian
incommensurate
intellectually
intercommunion
intercommunity
microcircuitry
nitrocellulose
pisciculturist
reconstitution
redistribution
redistributive
superconductor
tintinnabulary
tintinnabulate
tintinnabulous
undergraduette
watercolourist
chickenlivered
conjunctivitis
substantivally
committeewoman
goodfellowship
halfpennyworth
northeastwards
northwestwards
southeastwards
southwestwards
commissaryship
sauropterygian
selfemployment
sphaerocrystal
tetradactylous

---

accomplishable
achondroplasia
achromatically
aerobiotically
aetiologically
alphabetically
altruistically
anthropography
antiseptically
antithetically
aphoristically
apologetically
apophthegmatic
apoplectically
archetypically
arithmetically
arrhythmically
astronomically
asymmetrically
asymptotically
autocratically
bacteriostasis
bacteriostatic
barometrically
bibliomaniacal
biographically
brachycephalic
bronchiectasis
catechetically
chromatography
cinematography
commissionaire
compassionable
concentrically
concessionaire
confidentially
contradictable
contrapuntally
conventionally

counterbalance
crystallisable
cyanocobalamin
demisemiquaver
democratically
departmentally
diachronically
diagnostically
differentiable
differentially
diplomatically
discomfortable
discommendable
disconformable
discontinuance
discountenance
disinheritance
disrespectable
dodecasyllable
electrodynamic
emblematically
endosmotically
enharmonically
epexegetically
ethnologically
etymologically
eulogistically
euphuistically
excommunicable
excommunicator
experientially
experimentally
extinguishable
genealogically
geocentrically
geographically
hierarchically
historiography
histrionically
hyperbolically
hyperirritable
hypersonically
hypocritically
hypodermically
hypostatically
hypothetically
idealistically
idiopathically
immethodically
imparisyllabic
impressionable
inapproachable
inartistically
incommunicable
incommunicably
inconsiderable
inconsiderably
incontrollable
indecipherable
indecomposable
indemonstrable
indeterminable
indiscoverable
inflectionally
insignificance
insignificancy
instrumentally
insurmountable
insurmountably
intellectually
irreconcilable
irreconcilably
irreproachable
irreproachably
judgematically
legalistically
linguistically
longitudinally
mathematically

metaphorically
metaphysically
morganatically
multilaterally
multinucleated
mythologically
nonperformance
northeastwards
northwestwards
numismatically
optimistically
orthochromatic
paratactically
pathogenically
pathologically
pestilentially
petrologically
philologically
phlegmatically
phytogeography
pleonastically
preferentially
presbyterially
proceleusmatic
procrastinator
professionally
professorially
prognosticator
proportionable
proportionably
proportionally
prosencephalic
prosencephalon
providentially
pseudepigrapha
pseudepigraphy
quadrisyllabic
quadrisyllable
quinquennially
reconnaissance
rhinencephalic
rhinencephalon
rontgenography
schismatically
scholastically
scientifically
selfimportance
selfinductance
semiofficially
seriocomically
sociologically
southeastwards
southwestwards
squadronleader
standardbearer
stochastically
sublieutenancy
substantivally
successionally
superabundance
supernaturally
supersonically
synchronically
systematically
tautologically
teleologically
telepathically
telephonically
telescopically
tetragrammaton
thalassography
theocratically
tragicomically
transitionally
transliterator
transplantable
tropologically
ultrasonically
unaccommodated
unapproachable
uncommunicable
unconscionable
uncontrollable
uncontrollably
uncorroborated
understandable
understandably
uneconomically
unemphatically
unpremeditated
unquestionable
unquestionably
volumetrically
superincumbent
unmentionables
aerodynamicist
astrophysicist
bioelectricity
bioluminescent
butterflyscrew
chincherinchee
concavoconcave
contraindicate
convexoconcave
countrydancing
econometrician
entomostracous
horrorstricken
hygroscopicity
hypercriticise
hypercriticism
noncommunicant
ophthalmoscope
ophthalmoscopy
peripateticism
phosphorescent
planetstricken
roentgenoscopy
selfcomplacent
spinthariscope
stampcollector
staphylococcus
superconductor
terrorstricken
wonderstricken
encyclopaedism
encyclopaedist
hypothyroidism
interdependent
photoperiodism
pianoaccordian
quarterbinding
schoolchildren
superintendent
thoughtreading
unacknowledged
absentmindedly
aesthesiometer
audiofrequency
basidiomycetes
butterfingered
carcinogenesis
chemosynthesis
chickenlivered
circumambiency
clearsightedly
condescendence
consanguineous
correspondence
correspondency
cotemporaneous
crossreference
cryptaesthesia
cucurbitaceous
diffractometer
disconnectedly
discontentedly
eigenfrequency
electrovalency
erythropoiesis
extemporaneity
extemporaneous
faintheartedly
galactopoietic
goodhumouredly
goodtemperedly
grandiloquence
haematogenesis
hallucinogenic
handkerchieves
hypercalcaemia
hypercatalexis
hyperglycaemia
interferometer
interferometry
lightheartedly
malcontentedly
marketgardener
Mephistopheles
narrowmindedly
nonconcurrence
northnortheast
overconfidence
overindulgence
papilionaceous
partridgeberry
pharmacopoeial
photosynthesis
photosynthetic
premeditatedly
pseudaesthesia
rejuvenescence
scintillometer
selfconfidence
selfdependence
selfindulgence
Shakespeareana
shortsightedly
shovehalfpenny
simplemindedly
singlehandedly
singlemindedly
stoicheiometry
stoutheartedly
strongmindedly
undergraduette
vicepresidency
anthropologist
bacteriologist
Brobdingnagian
circumnavigate
dialectologist
ecclesiologist
epidemiologist
epistemologist
ichthyophagous
kremlinologist
liturgiologist
megasporangium
microbiologist
myrmecophagous
parasitologist
pharmacologist
pneumatologist
protozoologist
rheumatologist
sauropterygian
thimblerigging
allelomorphism
backscratching
bathingmachine
bibliographise
boardingschool
disenfranchise
dolichocephaly
heartsearching
heteromorphism
heteromorphous
homoeomorphism
megasporophyll
praiseworthily
pseudomorphism
pseudomorphous
radiotelephone
radiotelephony
superphosphate
aerobiological
agrobiological
alphanumerical
anagrammatical
apothegmatical
archaeological
campanological
cartographical
catachrestical
Christological
chronometrical
circumbendibus
classconscious
climatological
commonsensical
communications
comprehensible
comprehensibly
conjunctivitis
contradictious
controvertible
cosmographical
cosmopolitical
dermatological
diagrammatical
diverticulitis
ecclesiastical
epigrammatical
eschatological
featherbrained
gerontological
gynaecological
gyrostabiliser
hagiographical
hermaphroditic
hieroglyphical
hydrodynamical
hydrographical
hypocoristical
ichthyological
iconographical
imponderabilia
incompressible
incompressibly
indestructible
indestructibly
indiscerptible
insuppressible
irreproducible
malappropriate
martyrological
meteorological
methodological
microcircuitry
microtechnique
misappropriate
myrmecological
oneirocritical
ornithological
orthographical
osteoarthritis
oversubscribed
parallelepiped
petrographical
pharmaceutical
phraseological
physiognomical
pluviometrical
polytheistical
propaedeutical

psychochemical
psychophysical
psychosurgical
pteridological
publicspirited
quinquagesimal
scatterbrained
selfdetermined
selffertilised
selfproclaimed
selfrestrained
selfsufficient
semielliptical
Shakespeariana
sociopolitical
soteriological
stomatological
subcontrariety
supposititious
tachygraphical
terminological
thermochemical
unintelligible
unintelligibly
venereological
volcanological
vulcanological
forwardlooking
knickerbockers
strikebreaking
accountability
antifederalist
boroughEnglish
bougainvillaea
bremsstrahlung
circumambulate
coessentiality
combustibility
complexionless
compossibility
conceivability
conditionality
conductibility
conformability
conscienceless
convertibility
corruptibility
crossfertilise
denumerability
despiritualise
dinoflagellate
discombobulate
dispensability
dissociability
distensibility
educationalist
electrobiology
Evangelicalism
exceptionality
exhaustibility
existentialism
existentialist
expressionless
extensionality
fantasticality
fortunetelling
fundamentalism
fundamentalist
fundamentality
heterophyllous
heterothallism
histopathology
holometabolism
holometabolous
homotransplant
hydrocoralline
illimitability
impermeability
implausibility
impracticality
impregnability
impressibility
inadvisability
inalienability
inalterability
incorporeality
indivisibility
indubitability
ineffectuality
inflammability
inflectionless
infrangibility
inheritability
inscrutability
inseparability
insuperability
intersexuality
intolerability
intractability
intrinsicality
intuitionalism
intuitionalist
irreducibility
irrefutability
irremovability
irrevocability
justifiability
macrocephalous
matriarchalism
mesdemoiselles
metapsychology
microcephalous
ministerialist
myrmecophilous
neocolonialism
neuropathology
nitrocellulose
nonsensicality
oecumenicalism
organometallic
outgeneralling
overcapitalise
palaeethnology
paradoxicality
parapsychology
patresfamilias
perceptibility
perfectibility
periodontology
permissibility
phytopathology
pleasurability
practicability
pragmaticality
predictability
presentability
preventability
recoverability
refrangibility
respectability
responsibility
sacramentalism
sacramentalist
selfcontrolled
selfdiscipline
selffulfilling
selfpartiality
selfpropelling
sensationalism
sensationalist
sentimentalise
sentimentalism
sentimentalist
sentimentality
serviceability
sesquipedalian
stumblingblock
submersibility
substantialism
substantialist
substantiality
suggestibility
superficiality
supramaxillary
susceptibility
symptomatology
tatterdemalion
territorialise
territorialism
territorialist
territoriality
testimonialise
tetradactylous
tintinnabulary
tintinnabulate
tintinnabulous
traditionalism
traditionalist
transsexualism
transversality
uncongeniality
undesirability
unpalatability
vicechancellor
accomplishment
acknowledgment
aggrandisement
arrondissement
bouleversement
councilchamber
disappointment
disarrangement
disconcertment
discontentment
discouragement
disembowelment
disenchantment
disenthralment
disfurnishment
disgruntlement
disheartenment
divertissement
extinguishment
heterochromous
hysterectomise
impoverishment
intertwinement
macroeconomics
microeconomics
neuroanatomist
noninvolvement
overcommitment
overexcitement
prearrangement
psychodynamics
recommencement
relinquishment
selfadjustment
selfeffacement
selfemployment
selfgovernment
skimbleskamble
sulphanilamide
thermodynamics
understatement
absorptiveness
abstemiousness
abstractedness
abstractionism
abstractionist
acceleratingly
acceptableness
accustomedness
aggressiveness
Albigensianism
amateurishness
antiquarianism
archidiaconate
architectonics
articulateness
artificialness
associationism
attainableness
attractiveness
Augustinianism
auspiciousness
avariciousness
beneficialness
blockaderunner
boisterousness
breathlessness
breathtakingly
bullheadedness
calamitousness
calcareousness
capriciousness
censoriousness
changeableness
charitableness
chivalrousness
circuitousness
colourfastness
colourlessness
commodiousness
comparableness
compatibleness
compulsiveness
conclusiveness
consuetudinary
contagiousness
contiguousness
continuousness
contractedness
convincingness
convulsiveness
coordinateness
coquettishness
courageousness
creditableness
crinkumcrankum
crosspollinate
cumbersomeness
cumulativeness
deceivableness
decorativeness
definitiveness
degenerateness
delectableness
deliberateness
delightfulness
dependableness
deplorableness
despicableness
despitefulness
destructionist
determinedness
detestableness
diaphanousness
dicotyledonous
diminutiveness
disapprovingly
discouragingly
discursiveness
disdainfulness
disjointedness
disorderliness
dispiritedness
effervescently
effortlessness
egalitarianism
elementariness
embarrassingly
enterprisingly
entertainingly
exasperatingly
excruciatingly

exhaustiveness
exhilaratingly
expressiveness
extraneousness
factitiousness
fallaciousness
farsightedness
fastidiousness
favourableness
fictitiousness
figurativeness
flagitiousness
flatfootedness
forbiddingness
formidableness
forthrightness
fortuitousness
friendlessness
gramineousness
gratuitousness
gregariousness
groundlessness
harmoniousness
hereditariness
highhandedness
highmindedness
honourableness
hydromechanics
illiterateness
imaginableness
immaculateness
immoderateness
impassableness
impassibleness
imperativeness
imperviousness
implacableness
impressiveness
improvableness
inadequateness
inappositeness
incautiousness
incestuousness
incompleteness
inconsequently
inconsistently
inconveniently
incredibleness
indecisiveness
indecorousness
indefiniteness
indiscreetness
indiscriminate
indistinctness
inevitableness
inexorableness
infectiousness
inflexibleness
ingloriousness
ingratiatingly
inimitableness
inordinateness
insatiableness
insensibleness
insufficiently
intangibleness
integrationist
intercommunion
intercommunity
intermittently
internationale
invariableness
invincibleness
inviolableness
irresoluteness
knighterrantry
lasciviousness
lefthandedness
libertarianism
libidinousness
licentiousness
longheadedness
longwindedness
loquaciousness
lovingkindness
lugubriousness
magniloquently
malodorousness
manageableness
marvellousness
meddlesomeness
meditativeness
meticulousness
microcomponent
microsporangia
millenarianism
miraculousness
monkeybusiness
monotonousness
mysteriousness
necessarianism
neglectfulness
newfangledness
nightblindness
noteworthiness
nutritiousness
obsequiousness
obstructionism
obstructionist
oleaginousness
omnivorousness
openhandedness
openmindedness
oppressiveness
outlandishness
outrageousness
overabundantly
overpoweringly
overwhelmingly
palaeobotanist
pardonableness
passionateness
penetrableness
perceptiveness
peremptoriness
perfidiousness
perishableness
permissiveness
perniciousness
personableness
persuasiveness
phthalocyanine
portentousness
possessiveness
postmillennial
precariousness
precociousness
predeterminate
preponderantly
presentimental
preventiveness
prodigiousness
productiveness
profitableness
progressionary
progressionism
progressionist
prohibitionism
prohibitionist
proletarianise
proletarianism
propitiousness
prosperousness
protectiveness
protrusiveness
pugnaciousness
purposefulness
Pythagoreanism
rampageousness
reasonableness
rebelliousness
reflectiveness
refractoriness
regardlessness
regressiveness
relentlessness
remarkableness
remorsefulness
repetitiveness
repudiationist
resistlessness
respectfulness
responsiveness
restorationism
restorationist
restrictionist
revengefulness
ridiculousness
roadworthiness
robustiousness
Rosicrucianism
roundaboutness
Sabbatarianism
salubriousness
sanguinariness
scandalousness
scrupulousness
scurrilousness
seasonableness
segregationist
selfeffacingly
selfexplaining
selfsustaining
semicentennial
servomechanism
shamefacedness
slanderousness
slatternliness
solicitousness
speechlessness
spermatogenous
spermatogonium
spindleshanked
spiritlessness
spirituousness
sprightfulness
springcleaning
stationariness
statuesqueness
stertorousness
stupendousness
subcontinental
subjectiveness
submissiveness
subversiveness
successfulness
successiveness
sufferableness
suggestiveness
supereminently
superterranean
suprasegmental
surefootedness
susceptiveness
suspensiveness
suspiciousness
terminableness
thoughtfulness
threadbareness
thriftlessness
topsyturviness
traitorousness
transcendental
transcendently
transitiveness
transitoriness
tremendousness
Trinitarianism
tumultuousness
tyrannicalness
ubiquitousness
ultramontanism
ultramontanist
umbrageousness
unaffectedness
unbecomingness
unconvincingly
unexpectedness
unfaithfulness
unflatteringly
unfriendliness
ungraciousness
ungratefulness
unhesitatingly
unmannerliness
unpleasantness
unreservedness
unsociableness
untruthfulness
uproariousness
utilitarianism
vegetativeness
victoriousness
villainousness
vindictiveness
viviparousness
vivisectionist
vociferousness
voluminousness
voluptuousness
vulnerableness
watertightness
weakmindedness
weightlessness
worshipfulness
Zoroastrianism
abovementioned
aforementioned
airconditioner
archiepiscopal
circumlittoral
claustrophobia
claustrophobic
committeewoman
compensational
congregational
conquistadores
conservational
consociational
constitutional
constructional
conversational
copperbottomed
denominational
disquisitional
dissertational
distributional
electrodeposit
endoradiosonde
fullyfashioned
halfpennyworth
illconditioned
illustrational
insurrectional
intercessional
interjectional
intersectional
jurisdictional
metempsychosis
organisational
oxyhaemoglobin
perturbational
phantasmagoria
phantasmagoric
pneumoconiosis
postpositional

presentational
psychoneurosis
psychoneurotic
resurrectional
slaughterhouse
spatiotemporal
spirochaetosis
submicroscopic
substitutional
swordswallower
tachistoscopic
therianthropic
thyrotoxicosis
tridimensional
troubleshooter
twodimensional
unconventional
underdeveloped
undermentioned
unidimensional
unidirectional
unprofessional
autobiographer
autobiographic
campylotropous
corticotrophic
corticotrophin
enantiomorphic
generalpurpose
heroworshipper
metallographer
philanthropise
philanthropist
psilanthropism
psilanthropist
radiotherapist
spectrographic
spectroscopist
sphygmographic
steganographer
whippersnapper
windowshopping
antiperspirant
autoradiograph
backscattering
bioengineering
chickenhearted
conspiratorial
corticosteroid
corticosterone
countercurrent
curvilinearity
diamantiferous
diamondiferous
disciplinarian
disequilibrium
disincorporate
electioneering
electrotherapy
electrothermal
electrothermic
encephalograph
extracorporeal
floriculturist
foraminiferous
gynandromorphy
horticulturist
ichthyosaurian
incommensurate
infralapsarian
intercessorial
interlocutress
interpenetrate
introductorily
Johannisberger
latitudinarian
monosaccharide
mountaineering
nitroglycerine
nomenclatorial
nonbelligerent
phototelegraph
pisciculturist
pistilliferous
poikilothermal
poikilothermic
polysaccharide
predestinarian
premillenarian
probabiliorism
probabiliorist
propitiatorily
prothonotarial
quadragenarian
radioautograph
radiotelegraph
rectangularity
sacramentarian
satisfactorily
schoolmistress
scrubbingbrush
selfflattering
septuagenarian
solitudinarian
supralapsarian
telephotograph
thanksoffering
uncontroverted
uniformitarian
valetudinarian
watercolourist
whortleberries
ambassadorship
anticonvulsant
antidepressant
antiphlogistic
apprenticeship
behaviouristic
chancellorship
characteristic
commissaryship
controllership
councillorship
counsellorship
countermeasure
doublebreasted
ferromagnesian
goodfellowship
handicraftsman
hebetudinosity
histochemistry
hocuspocussing
iatrochemistry
microprocessor
neurochemistry
overcompensate
petrochemistry
photochemistry
pigeonbreasted
postmastership
progenitorship
prolocutorship
propagandistic
proprietorship
radiochemistry
selfenergising
selfexpression
selfinterested
selfpossession
selfpropulsion
selfrepression
singlebreasted
somnambulistic
sphaerocrystal
spiritualistic
stadholdership
supervisorship
sycophantishly
unaccomplished
uncircumcision
uncompromising
underemphasise
undernourished
unenterprising
unenthusiastic
universalistic
verticillaster
windowdressing
administration
administrative
administratrix
affectionately
Africanisation
allegorisation
anthropometric
appendicectomy
authentication
autosuggestion
bastardisation
beautification
biodegradation
biosystematics
bituminisation
blackmarketeer
bloodthirstily
bowdlerisation
capitalisation
castrametation
categorisation
centralisation
centrifugation
chemoreception
chemoreceptive
circumlocution
circumlocutory
circumspection
circumstantial
circumvolution
classification
classificatory
commensurately
commensuration
concelebration
concretisation
conglomeration
conglutination
conglutinative
congratulation
congratulative
congratulatory
consubstantial
contraposition
contrapositive
counterculture
counterplotted
decimalisation
decolonisation
decolorisation
deconsecration
defenestration
dehumanisation
delocalisation
demobilisation
demonetisation
demoralisation
denazification
depolarisation
detoxification
devitalisation
dextrorotation
dextrorotatory
dieselelectric
disaffiliation
disaffirmation
disapprobation
disapprobative
disapprobatory
disassociation
discolouration
disconsolately
disconsolation
discriminating
discrimination
discriminative
discriminatory
disembarkation
disinclination
disinfestation
disintegration
disintegrative
disorientation
distemperature
dolomitisation
electrostatics
emulsification
enthronisation
esterification
eutrophication
evangelisation
exclaustration
ferrimagnetism
ferromagnetism
foreordination
fraternisation
fructification
gelatinisation
generalisation
homogenisation
humidification
hypersensitive
identification
illegitimately
immobilisation
implementation
inappreciation
inappreciative
inarticulately
inarticulation
incapacitation
incoordination
indifferentism
indifferentist
indoctrination
infrastructure
intelligential
intelligentsia
interferential
intergradation
interlineation
intermediately
intermediation
intermigration
interpellation
interplanetary
interpretation
interpretative
legitimisation
liberalisation
lyophilisation
massproduction
microminiature
microstructure
militarisation
mineralisation
misapplication
miscalculation
misinformation
mistranslation
monochromatism
monopolisation
multiplication
multiplicative
naturalisation
neuroscientist
neutralisation
noctambulation

noncooperation
nonrestrictive
overestimation
overpopulation
overproduction
pachydermatous
parenchymatous
pasteurisation
phenobarbitone
photosensitise
photosensitive
politicisation
polymerisation
popularisation
potentiometric
predesignation
predestination
predisposition
prefabrication
presupposition
prettification
proprioceptive
psychosomatics
pyrheliometric
quantification
quattrocentism
quattrocentist
quintessential
radicalisation
radiosensitive
radiostrontium
recapitulation
recapitulative
recapitulatory
recolonisation
recommendation
recommendatory
reconciliation
reconciliatory
reconstitution
reconstruction
reconstructive
redintegration
redistribution
redistributive
regularisation
rehabilitation
reintroduction
reinvigoration
reminiscential
remonetisation
reorganisation
representation
representative
resinification
retrogradation
revalorisation
revivification
rigidification
Russianisation
sanctification
sanguification
saponification
scandalisation
schematisation
secularisation
selfabnegation
selfabsorption
selfaccusation
selfaccusatory
selfadmiration
selfassumption
selfconsistent
selfcorrecting
selfimmolation
selfperception
selfprotection
selfregulating
selfrespectful

selfrespecting
selfrevelation
selfsuggestion
selfsupporting
selftormenting
semiconducting
sensualisation
silicification
simplification
snaggletoothed
solidification
solubilisation
somnambulation
sophistication
specialisation
stigmatisation
stoichiometric
stratification
stultification
subalternation
subinfeudation
substantiation
superannuation
superelevation
supererogation
supererogatory
superfoetation
superinduction
superscription
supersensitive
superstructure
symmetrisation
tergiversation
thermoelectric
transformation
transformative
transmigration
transmigratory
transportation
transvaluation
trivialisation
ultimogeniture
ultramicrotome
ultrastructure
unappreciative
undervaluation
unremunerative
unsatisfactory
vasodilatation
vasodilatatory
verisimilitude
volatilisation
westernisation
advantageously
adventitiously
ambidextrously
antiscriptural
asynchronously
cantankerously
cardiovascular
contemptuously
conterminously
contumaciously
contumeliously
discourteously
disingenuously
disputatiously
extravehicular
inauspiciously
incommodiously
infelicitously
inharmoniously
intermolecular
intramolecular
meretriciously
multifariously
obstreperously
ostentatiously
parsimoniously

percutaneously
pertinaciously
polymorphously
preposterously
presumptuously
pseudonymously
rambunctiously
sacrilegiously
selfconsequent
simultaneously
slaughterously
soporiferously
subconsciously
superciliously
unscrupulously
unsuccessfully
vaingloriously
weltanschauung
accumulatively
anticipatively
apprehensively
conservatively
constitutively
constructively
constructivism
constructivist
deliberatively
distributively
illustratively
inconclusively
inexpressively
interpretively
intransitively
irrespectively
opinionatively
postpositively
prescriptively
proscriptively
quantitatively
regeneratively
reproductively
selfpreserving
substitutively
unattractively
vituperatively
northnorthwest
hobbledehoyish
psychoanalysis
psychoanalytic
selfdestroying
selfsatisfying
souldestroying
spermatophytic
phenylbutazone

---

anticonvulsant
antidepressant
antiperspirant
archidiaconate
autoradiograph
bougainvillaea
circumambulate
circumnavigate
concavoconcave
consuetudinary
contraindicate
convexoconcave
crosspollinate
dinoflagellate
discombobulate
disincorporate
dolichocephaly
electrotherapy
encephalograph
homotransplant
incommensurate
indiscriminate
internationale
interpenetrate

interplanetary
malappropriate
misappropriate
noncommunicant
northnortheast
overcompensate
phototelegraph
predeterminate
progressionary
radioautograph
radiotelegraph
Shakespeareana
Shakespeariana
superphosphate
supramaxillary
telephotograph
tintinnabulary
tintinnabulate
accomplishable
circumbendibus
claustrophobia
claustrophobic
compassionable
comprehensible
comprehensibly
contradictable
controvertible
councilchamber
crystallisable
differentiable
discomfortable
discommendable
disconformable
disrespectable
dodecasyllable
excommunicable
extinguishable
hyperirritable
imparisyllabic
impressionable
inapproachable
incommunicable
incommunicably
incompressible
incompressibly
inconsiderable
inconsiderably
incontrollable
indecipherable
indecomposable
indemonstrable
indestructible
indestructibly
indeterminable
indiscerptible
indiscoverable
insuppressible
insurmountable
insurmountably
irreconcilable
irreconcilably
irreproachable
irreproachably
irreproducible
oversubscribed
oxyhaemoglobin
proportionable
proportionably
quadrisyllabic
quadrisyllable
skimbleskamble
transplantable
unapproachable
uncommunicable
unconscionable
uncontrollable
uncontrollably
understandable
understandably

unintelligible
unintelligibly
unquestionable
unquestionably
aerobiological
agrobiological
alphanumerical
anagrammatical
apothegmatical
archaeological
bibliomaniacal
campanological
cartographical
catachrestical
Christological
chronometrical
climatological
commonsensical
cosmographical
cosmopolitical
dermatological
diagrammatical
ecclesiastical
epigrammatical
eschatological
gerontological
gynaecological
hagiographical
hieroglyphical
hydrodynamical
hydrographical
hypocoristical
ichthyological
iconographical
martyrological
meteorological
methodological
myrmecological
oneirocritical
ornithological
orthographical
petrographical
pharmaceutical
phraseological
physiognomical
pluviometrical
polytheistical
propaedeutical
psychochemical
psychophysical
psychosurgical
pteridological
semielliptical
sociopolitical
soteriological
staphylococcus
stomatological
tachygraphical
terminological
thermochemical
venereological
volcanological
vulcanological
absentmindedly
clearsightedly
disconnectedly
discontentedly
faintheartedly
goodhumouredly
goodtemperedly
lightheartedly
malcontentedly
narrowmindedly
premeditatedly
shortsightedly
simplemindedly
singlehandedly
singlemindedly
squadronleader
stoutheartedly
strongmindedly
absorptiveness
abstemiousness
abstractedness
acceptableness
accomplishment
accumulatively
accustomedness
acknowledgment
affectionately
aggrandisement
aggressiveness
amateurishness
anticipatively
apprehensively
arrondissement
articulateness
artificialness
attainableness
attractiveness
auspiciousness
avariciousness
beneficialness
bioluminescent
blackmarketeer
boisterousness
bouleversement
breathlessness
bullheadedness
calamitousness
calcareousness
capriciousness
censoriousness
changeableness
charitableness
chivalrousness
circuitousness
colourfastness
colourlessness
commensurately
commodiousness
comparableness
compatibleness
complexionless
compulsiveness
conclusiveness
conscienceless
conservatively
constitutively
constructively
contagiousness
contiguousness
continuousness
contractedness
convincingness
convulsiveness
coordinateness
coquettishness
countercurrent
courageousness
creditableness
cumbersomeness
cumulativeness
deceivableness
decorativeness
definitiveness
degenerateness
delectableness
deliberateness
deliberatively
delightfulness
dependableness
deplorableness
despicableness
despitefulness
determinedness
detestableness
diaphanousness
diminutiveness
disappointment
disarrangement
disconcertment
disconsolately
discontentment
discouragement
discursiveness
disdainfulness
disembowelment
disenchantment
disenthralment
disfurnishment
disgruntlement
disheartenment
disjointedness
disorderliness
dispiritedness
distributively
divertissement
effortlessness
elementariness
exhaustiveness
expressionless
expressiveness
extinguishment
extracorporeal
extraneousness
factitiousness
fallaciousness
farsightedness
fastidiousness
favourableness
fictitiousness
figurativeness
flagitiousness
flatfootedness
forbiddingness
formidableness
forthrightness
fortuitousness
friendlessness
gramineousness
gratuitousness
gregariousness
groundlessness
harmoniousness
hereditariness
highhandedness
highmindedness
honourableness
illegitimately
illiterateness
illustratively
imaginableness
immaculateness
immoderateness
impassableness
impassibleness
imperativeness
imperviousness
implacableness
impoverishment
impressiveness
improvableness
inadequateness
inappositeness
inarticulately
incautiousness
incestuousness
incompleteness
inconclusively
incredibleness
indecisiveness
indecorousness
indefiniteness
indiscreetness
indistinctness
inevitableness
inexorableness
inexpressively
infectiousness
inflectionless
inflexibleness
ingloriousness
inimitableness
inordinateness
insatiableness
insensibleness
intangibleness
interdependent
interlocutress
intermediately
interpretively
intertwinement
intransitively
invariableness
invincibleness
inviolableness
irresoluteness
irrespectively
knickerbockers
lasciviousness
lefthandedness
libidinousness
licentiousness
longheadedness
longwindedness
loquaciousness
lovingkindness
lugubriousness
malodorousness
manageableness
marvellousness
meddlesomeness
meditativeness
meticulousness
microcomponent
miraculousness
monkeybusiness
monotonousness
mysteriousness
neglectfulness
newfangledness
nightblindness
nonbelligerent
noninvolvement
northnorthwest
noteworthiness
nutritiousness
obsequiousness
oleaginousness
omnivorousness
openhandedness
openmindedness
opinionatively
oppressiveness
outlandishness
outrageousness
overcommitment
overexcitement
pardonableness
passionateness
penetrableness
perceptiveness
peremptoriness
perfidiousness
perishableness
permissiveness
perniciousness
personableness
persuasiveness
phosphorescent
portentousness
possessiveness
postpositively
prearrangement
precariousness

precociousness
prescriptively
preventiveness
prodigiousness
productiveness
profitableness
propitiousness
proscriptively
prosperousness
protectiveness
protrusiveness
pugnaciousness
purposefulness
quantitatively
rampageousness
reasonableness
rebelliousness
recommencement
reflectiveness
refractoriness
regardlessness
regeneratively
regressiveness
relentlessness
relinquishment
remarkableness
remorsefulness
repetitiveness
reproductively
resistlessness
respectfulness
responsiveness
revengefulness
ridiculousness
roadworthiness
robustiousness
roundaboutness
salubriousness
sanguinariness
scandalousness
schoolmistress
scrupulousness
scurrilousness
seasonableness
selfadjustment
selfcomplacent
selfconsequent
selfconsistent
selfeffacement
selfemployment
selfgovernment
selfsufficient
shamefacedness
slanderousness
slatternliness
solicitousness
speechlessness
spiritlessness
spirituousness
sprightfulness
stationariness
statuesqueness
stertorousness
stupendousness
subcontrariety
subjectiveness
submissiveness
substitutively
subversiveness
successfulness
successiveness
sufferableness
suggestiveness
superincumbent
superintendent
superterranean
surefootedness
susceptiveness
suspensiveness
suspiciousness
terminableness
thoughtfulness
threadbareness
thriftlessness
topsyturviness
traitorousness
transitiveness
transitoriness
tremendousness
tumultuousness
tyrannicalness
ubiquitousness
umbrageousness
unaffectedness
unattractively
unbecomingness
understatement
unexpectedness
unfaithfulness
unfriendliness
ungraciousness
ungratefulness
unmannerliness
unpleasantness
unreservedness
unsociableness
untruthfulness
uproariousness
vegetativeness
victoriousness
villainousness
vindictiveness
vituperatively
viviparousness
vociferousness
voluminousness
voluptuousness
vulnerableness
watertightness
weakmindedness
weightlessness
worshipfulness
selfrespectful
acceleratingly
breathtakingly
disapprovingly
discouragingly
embarrassingly
enterprisingly
entertainingly
exasperatingly
excruciatingly
exhilaratingly
ingratiatingly
Johannisberger
microsporangia
overpoweringly
overwhelmingly
selfeffacingly
unacknowledged
unconvincingly
unflatteringly
unhesitatingly
ambassadorship
apprenticeship
autobiographer
autobiographic
chancellorship
chincherinchee
commissaryship
controllership
corticotrophic
corticotrophin
councillorship
counsellorship
enantiomorphic
goodfellowship
metallographer
postmastership
progenitorship
prolocutorship
proprietorship
snaggletoothed
spectrographic
sphygmographic
stadholdership
steganographer
supervisorship
sycophantishly
unaccomplished
undernourished
abstractionism
abstractionist
accountability
administration
administrative
aerodynamicist
Africanisation
Albigensianism
allegorisation
allelomorphism
anthropologist
antifederalist
antiquarianism
architectonics
associationism
astrophysicist
Augustinianism
authentication
autosuggestion
backscattering
backscratching
bacteriologist
bastardisation
bathingmachine
beautification
bibliographise
biodegradation
bioelectricity
bioengineering
biosystematics
bituminisation
bloodthirstily
boroughEnglish
bowdlerisation
Brobdingnagian
capitalisation
castrametation
categorisation
centralisation
centrifugation
chemoreception
chemoreceptive
circumlocution
circumspection
circumstantial
circumvolution
classification
coessentiality
combustibility
commensuration
commissionaire
compossibility
conceivability
concelebration
concessionaire
concretisation
conditionality
conductibility
conformability
conglomeration
conglutination
conglutinative
congratulation
congratulative
conspiratorial
constructivism
constructivist
consubstantial
contraposition
contrapositive
convertibility
corruptibility
countrydancing
crossfertilise
curvilinearity
decimalisation
decolonisation
decolorisation
deconsecration
defenestration
dehumanisation
delocalisation
demobilisation
demonetisation
demoralisation
denazification
denumerability
depolarisation
despiritualise
destructionist
detoxification
devitalisation
dextrorotation
dialectologist
disaffiliation
disaffirmation
disapprobation
disapprobative
disassociation
disciplinarian
discolouration
disconsolation
discriminating
discrimination
discriminative
disembarkation
disenfranchise
disequilibrium
disinclination
disinfestation
disintegration
disintegrative
disorientation
dispensability
dissociability
distensibility
dolomitisation
ecclesiologist
econometrician
educationalist
egalitarianism
electioneering
electrostatics
emulsification
encyclopaedism
encyclopaedist
enthronisation
epidemiologist
epistemologist
esterification
eutrophication
Evangelicalism
evangelisation
exceptionality
exclaustration
exhaustibility
existentialism
existentialist
extemporaneity
extensionality
fantasticality
ferrimagnetism
ferromagnesian
ferromagnetism
floriculturist

foreordination
fortunetelling
forwardlooking
fraternisation
fructification
fundamentalism
fundamentalist
fundamentality
gelatinisation
generalisation
heartsearching
hebetudinosity
heteromorphism
heterothallism
hobbledehoyish
hocuspocussing
holometabolism
homoeomorphism
homogenisation
horticulturist
humidification
hydrocoralline
hydromechanics
hygroscopicity
hypercriticise
hypercriticism
hypersensitive
hypothyroidism
hysterectomise
ichthyosaurian
identification
illimitability
immobilisation
impermeability
implausibility
implementation
impracticality
impregnability
impressibility
inadvisability
inalienability
inalterability
inappreciation
inappreciative
inarticulation
incapacitation
incoordination
incorporeality
indifferentism
indifferentist
indivisibility
indoctrination
indubitability
ineffectuality
inflammability
infralapsarian
infrangibility
inheritability
inscrutability
inseparability
insuperability
integrationist
intelligential
intercessorial
intercommunion
intercommunity
interferential
intergradation
interlineation
intermediation
intermigration
interpellation
interpretation
interpretative
intersexuality
intolerability
intractability
intrinsicality
introductorily
intuitionalism
intuitionalist
irreducibility
irrefutability
irremovability
irrevocability
justifiability
kremlinologist
latitudinarian
legitimisation
liberalisation
libertarianism
liturgiologist
lyophilisation
macroeconomics
massproduction
matriarchalism
megasporangium
microbiologist
microeconomics
militarisation
millenarianism
mineralisation
ministerialist
misapplication
miscalculation
misinformation
mistranslation
monochromatism
monopolisation
monosaccharide
mountaineering
multiplication
multiplicative
naturalisation
necessarianism
neocolonialism
neuroanatomist
neuroscientist
neutralisation
nitroglycerine
noctambulation
nomenclatorial
noncooperation
nonrestrictive
nonsensicality
obstructionism
obstructionist
oecumenicalism
outgeneralling
overcapitalise
overestimation
overpopulation
overproduction
palaeobotanist
paradoxicality
parasitologist
pasteurisation
patresfamilias
perceptibility
perfectibility
peripateticism
permissibility
pharmacologist
pharmacopoeial
philanthropise
philanthropist
photoperiodism
photosensitise
photosensitive
phthalocyanine
pianoaccordian
pisciculturist
pleasurability
pneumatologist
politicisation
polymerisation
polysaccharide
popularisation
postmillennial
practicability
pragmaticality
praiseworthily
predesignation
predestinarian
predestination
predictability
predisposition
prefabrication
premillenarian
presentability
presupposition
prettification
preventability
probabiliorism
probabiliorist
progressionism
progressionist
prohibitionism
prohibitionist
proletarianise
proletarianism
propitiatorily
proprioceptive
prothonotarial
protozoologist
pseudomorphism
psilanthropism
psilanthropist
psychodynamics
psychosomatics
Pythagoreanism
quadragenarian
quantification
quarterbinding
quattrocentism
quattrocentist
quintessential
radicalisation
radiosensitive
radiostrontium
radiotherapist
recapitulation
recapitulative
recolonisation
recommendation
reconciliation
reconstitution
reconstruction
reconstructive
recoverability
rectangularity
redintegration
redistribution
redistributive
refrangibility
regularisation
rehabilitation
reintroduction
reinvigoration
reminiscential
remonetisation
reorganisation
representation
representative
repudiationist
resinification
respectability
responsibility
restorationism
restorationist
restrictionist
retrogradation
revalorisation
revivification
rheumatologist
rigidification
Rosicrucianism
Russianisation
Sabbatarianism
sacramentalism
sacramentalist
sacramentarian
sanctification
sanguification
saponification
satisfactorily
sauropterygian
scandalisation
schematisation
secularisation
segregationist
selfabnegation
selfabsorption
selfaccusation
selfadmiration
selfassumption
selfcorrecting
selfdestroying
selfdiscipline
selfenergising
selfexplaining
selfexpression
selfflattering
selffulfilling
selfimmolation
selfpartiality
selfperception
selfpossession
selfpreserving
selfpropelling
selfpropulsion
selfprotection
selfregulating
selfrepression
selfrespecting
selfrevelation
selfsatisfying
selfsuggestion
selfsupporting
selfsustaining
selftormenting
semicentennial
semiconducting
sensationalism
sensationalist
sensualisation
sentimentalise
sentimentalism
sentimentalist
sentimentality
septuagenarian
serviceability
servomechanism
sesquipedalian
silicification
simplification
solidification
solitudinarian
solubilisation
somnambulation
sophistication
souldestroying
specialisation
spectroscopist
spermatogonium
springcleaning
stigmatisation
stratification
strikebreaking
stultification
subalternation
subinfeudation
submersibility
substantialism
substantialist
substantiality

substantiation
suggestibility
sulphanilamide
superannuation
superelevation
supererogation
superficiality
superfoetation
superinduction
superscription
supersensitive
supralapsarian
susceptibility
symmetrisation
tatterdemalion
tergiversation
territorialise
territorialism
territorialist
territoriality
testimonialise
thanksoffering
thermodynamics
thimblerigging
thoughtreading
traditionalism
traditionalist
transformation
transformative
transmigration
transportation
transsexualism
transvaluation
transversality
Trinitarianism
trivialisation
ultramontanism
ultramontanist
unappreciative
uncircumcision
uncompromising
uncongeniality
underemphasise
undervaluation
undesirability
unenterprising
uniformitarian
unpalatability
unremunerative
utilitarianism
valetudinarian
vasodilatation
vivisectionist
volatilisation
watercolourist
westernisation
whortleberries
windowdressing
windowshopping
Zoroastrianism
crinkumcrankum
horrorstricken
planetstricken
spindleshanked
terrorstricken
wonderstricken
achromatically
aerobiotically
aetiologically
alphabetically
altruistically
antiseptically
antithetically
aphoristically
apologetically
apoplectically
archetypically
arithmetically
arrhythmically
astronomically
asymmetrically
asymptotically
autocratically
barometrically
biographically
brachycephalic
cardiovascular
catechetically
concentrically
confidentially
contrapuntally
conventionally
democratically
departmentally
diachronically
diagnostically
differentially
diplomatically
emblematically
endosmotically
enharmonically
epexegetically
ethnologically
etymologically
eulogistically
euphuistically
experientially
experimentally
extravehicular
genealogically
geocentrically
geographically
hierarchically
histrionically
hyperbolically
hypersonically
hypocritically
hypodermically
hypostatically
hypothetically
idealistically
idiopathically
immethodically
imponderabilia
inartistically
inflectionally
instrumentally
intellectually
intermolecular
intramolecular
judgematically
legalistically
linguistically
longitudinally
mathematically
Mephistopheles
mesdemoiselles
metaphorically
metaphysically
morganatically
multilaterally
mythologically
numismatically
optimistically
organometallic
paratactically
pathogenically
pathologically
pestilentially
petrologically
philologically
phlegmatically
pleonastically
preferentially
presbyterially
professionally
professorially
proportionally
prosencephalic
prosencephalon
providentially
quinquennially
rhinencephalic
rhinencephalon
schismatically
scholastically
scientifically
selfcontrolled
semiofficially
seriocomically
sociologically
stochastically
substantivally
successionally
supernaturally
supersonically
synchronically
systematically
tautologically
teleologically
telepathically
telephonically
telescopically
theocratically
tragicomically
transitionally
tropologically
ultrasonically
uneconomically
unemphatically
unmentionables
unsuccessfully
vicechancellor
volumetrically
committeewoman
copperbottomed
cyanocobalamin
electrodynamic
electrothermal
electrothermic
handicraftsman
hypercalcaemia
hyperglycaemia
poikilothermal
poikilothermic
quinquagesimal
selfproclaimed
abovementioned
aforementioned
airconditioner
audiofrequency
blockaderunner
circumambiency
compensational
condescendence
congregational
conservational
consociational
constitutional
constructional
conversational
correspondence
correspondency
counterbalance
crossreference
denominational
discontinuance
discountenance
disinheritance
disquisitional
dissertational
distributional
eigenfrequency
electrovalency
endoradiosonde
featherbrained
fullyfashioned
grandiloquence
hallucinogenic
illconditioned
illustrational
insignificance
insignificancy
insurrectional
intercessional
interjectional
intersectional
jurisdictional
marketgardener
nonconcurrence
nonperformance
organisational
overconfidence
overindulgence
perturbational
postpositional
presentational
reconnaissance
rejuvenescence
resurrectional
scatterbrained
selfconfidence
selfdependence
selfdetermined
selfimportance
selfinductance
selfindulgence
selfrestrained
shovehalfpenny
sublieutenancy
substitutional
superabundance
tridimensional
twodimensional
unconventional
undermentioned
unidimensional
unidirectional
unprofessional
vicepresidency
appendicectomy
boardingschool
campylotropous
circumlocutory
classconscious
classificatory
communications
congratulatory
consanguineous
contradictious
corticosteroid
corticosterone
cotemporaneous
cucurbitaceous
dextrorotatory
diamantiferous
diamondiferous
dicotyledonous
disapprobatory
discriminatory
electrobiology
entomostracous
extemporaneous
foraminiferous
generalpurpose
heterochromous
heteromorphous
heterophyllous
histopathology
holometabolous
ichthyophagous
macrocephalous
metapsychology
microcephalous
myrmecophagous
myrmecophilous

neuropathology
nitrocellulose
ophthalmoscope
ophthalmoscopy
pachydermatous
palaeethnology
papilionaceous
parapsychology
parenchymatous
periodontology
phenobarbitone
phenylbutazone
phytopathology
pistilliferous
pseudomorphous
radiotelephone
radiotelephony
recapitulatory
recommendatory
reconciliatory
roentgenoscopy
selfaccusatory
spermatogenous
spinthariscope
stumblingblock
supererogatory
supposititious
symptomatology
tetradactylous
tintinnabulous
transmigratory
ultramicrotome
unsatisfactory
vasodilatatory
anthropography
archiepiscopal
chromatography
cinematography
gynandromorphy
heroworshipper
historiography
parallelepiped
phytogeography
pseudepigrapha
pseudepigraphy
rontgenography
submicroscopic
tachistoscopic
thalassography
therianthropic
underdeveloped
whippersnapper
microtechnique
administratrix
anthropometric
antiscriptural
butterfingered
butterflyscrew
chickenlivered
circumlittoral
conquistadores
dieselelectric
halfpennyworth
northeastwards
northwestwards
partridgeberry
phantasmagoria
phantasmagoric
potentiometric
pyrheliometric
schoolchildren
southeastwards
southwestwards
spatiotemporal
standardbearer
stoichiometric
thermoelectric
achondroplasia
advantageously
adventitiously
ambidextrously
asynchronously
bacteriostasis
bronchiectasis
cantankerously
carcinogenesis
chemosynthesis
contemptuously
conterminously
contumaciously
contumeliously
cryptaesthesia
discourteously
disingenuously
disputatiously
electrodeposit
erythropoiesis
gyrostabiliser
haematogenesis
inauspiciously
incommodiously
infelicitously
inharmoniously
intelligentsia
meretriciously
metempsychosis
microprocessor
multifariously
obstreperously
ostentatiously
parsimoniously
percutaneously
pertinaciously
photosynthesis
pneumoconiosis
polymorphously
preposterously
presumptuously
pseudaesthesia
pseudonymously
psychoanalysis
psychoneurosis
rambunctiously
sacrilegiously
selffertilised
simultaneously
slaughterously
soporiferously
spirochaetosis
subconsciously
superciliously
thyrotoxicosis
unscrupulously
vaingloriously
aesthesiometer
antiphlogistic
apophthegmatic
bacteriostatic
basidiomycetes
behaviouristic
characteristic
chickenhearted
conjunctivitis
counterplotted
diffractometer
diverticulitis
doublebreasted
effervescently
excommunicator
galactopoietic
hermaphroditic
histochemistry
iatrochemistry
inconsequently
inconsistently
inconveniently
insufficiently
interferometer
interferometry
intermittently
knighterrantry
magniloquently
microcircuitry
multinucleated
neurochemistry
orthochromatic
osteoarthritis
overabundantly
petrochemistry
photochemistry
photosynthetic
pigeonbreasted
preponderantly
presentimental
proceleusmatic
procrastinator
prognosticator
propagandistic
psychoanalytic
psychoneurotic
publicspirited
radiochemistry
scintillometer
selfinterested
singlebreasted
somnambulistic
spermatophytic
sphaerocrystal
spiritualistic
stampcollector
stoicheiometry
subcontinental
superconductor
supereminently
suprasegmental
tetragrammaton
transcendental
transcendently
transliterator
troubleshooter
unaccommodated
uncontroverted
uncorroborated
undergraduette
unenthusiastic
universalistic
unpremeditated
verticillaster
bremsstrahlung
counterculture
countermeasure
distemperature
infrastructure
microminiature
microstructure
scrubbingbrush
slaughterhouse
superstructure
ultimogeniture
ultrastructure
verisimilitude
weltanschauung
demisemiquaver
handkerchieves
swordswallower
hypercatalexis
megasporophyll

---

aerobiological
agrobiological
alphanumerical
anagrammatical
antiscriptural
apothegmatical
archaeological
archiepiscopal
bibliomaniacal
Brobdingnagian
campanological
cardiovascular
cartographical
catachrestical
Christological
chronometrical
circumlittoral
circumstantial
climatological
committeewoman
commonsensical
compensational
congregational
conservational
consociational
conspiratorial
constitutional
constructional
consubstantial
conversational
cosmographical
cosmopolitical
denominational
dermatological
diagrammatical
disciplinarian
disquisitional
dissertational
distributional
ecclesiastical
econometrician
electrothermal
epigrammatical
eschatological
extracorporeal
extravehicular
ferromagnesian
gerontological
gynaecological
hagiographical
handicraftsman
hieroglyphical
hydrodynamical
hydrographical
hypocoristical
ichthyological
ichthyosaurian
iconographical
illustrational
infralapsarian
insurrectional
intelligential
intercessional
intercessorial
interferential
interjectional
intermolecular
intersectional
intramolecular
jurisdictional
latitudinarian
martyrological
meteorological
methodological
myrmecological
nomenclatorial
oneirocritical
organisational
ornithological
orthographical
patresfamilias
perturbational
petrographical
pharmaceutical
pharmacopoeial
phraseological
physiognomical
pianoaccordian

pluviometrical
poikilothermal
polytheistical
postmillennial
postpositional
predestinarian
premillenarian
presentational
presentimental
propaedeutical
prothonotarial
psychochemical
psychophysical
psychosurgical
pteridological
quadragenarian
quinquagesimal
quintessential
reminiscential
resurrectional
sacramentarian
sauropterygian
semicentennial
semielliptical
septuagenarian
sesquipedalian
sociopolitical
solitudinarian
soteriological
spatiotemporal
sphaerocrystal
stomatological
subcontinental
substitutional
superterranean
supralapsarian
suprasegmental
tachygraphical
terminological
thermochemical
transcendental
tridimensional
twodimensional
unconventional
unidimensional
unidirectional
uniformitarian
unprofessional
valetudinarian
venereological
volcanological
vulcanological
architectonics
audiofrequency
biosystematics
circumambiency
condescendence
correspondence
correspondency
counterbalance
crossreference
discontinuance
discountenance
disinheritance
eigenfrequency
electrostatics
electrovalency
grandiloquence
hydromechanics
insignificance
insignificancy
macroeconomics
microeconomics
nonconcurrence
nonperformance
overconfidence
overindulgence
psychodynamics
psychosomatics
reconnaissance
rejuvenescence
selfconfidence
selfdependence
selfimportance
selfinductance
selfindulgence
stumblingblock
sublieutenancy
superabundance
thermodynamics
vicepresidency
endoradiosonde
monosaccharide
northeastwards
northwestwards
polysaccharide
southeastwards
southwestwards
sulphanilamide
verisimilitude
abovementioned
aesthesiometer
aforementioned
airconditioner
autobiographer
basidiomycetes
blackmarketeer
blockaderunner
bougainvillaea
butterfingered
butterflyscrew
chickenhearted
chickenlivered
chincherinchee
conquistadores
copperbottomed
councilchamber
counterplotted
demisemiquaver
diffractometer
doublebreasted
featherbrained
fullyfashioned
gyrostabiliser
handkerchieves
heroworshipper
horrorstricken
illconditioned
interferometer
Johannisberger
marketgardener
Mephistopheles
mesdemoiselles
metallographer
multinucleated
oversubscribed
parallelepiped
pigeonbreasted
planetstricken
publicspirited
scatterbrained
schoolchildren
scintillometer
selfcontrolled
selfdetermined
selffertilised
selfinterested
selfproclaimed
selfrestrained
singlebreasted
snaggletoothed
spindleshanked
squadronleader
standardbearer
steganographer
swordswallower
terrorstricken
troubleshooter
unaccommodated
unaccomplished
unacknowledged
uncontroverted
uncorroborated
underdeveloped
undermentioned
undernourished
unmentionables
unpremeditated
verticillaster
whippersnapper
whortleberries
wonderstricken
electrobiology
histopathology
metapsychology
neuropathology
palaeethnology
parapsychology
periodontology
phytopathology
symptomatology
anthropography
chromatography
cinematography
gynandromorphy
historiography
phytogeography
pseudepigrapha
pseudepigraphy
rontgenography
thalassography
achondroplasia
administratrix
ambassadorship
anthropometric
antiphlogistic
apophthegmatic
apprenticeship
autobiographic
bacteriostasis
bacteriostatic
behaviouristic
brachycephalic
bronchiectasis
carcinogenesis
chancellorship
characteristic
chemosynthesis
claustrophobia
claustrophobic
commissaryship
conjunctivitis
controllership
corticosteroid
corticotrophic
corticotrophin
councillorship
counsellorship
cryptaesthesia
cyanocobalamin
dieselelectric
diverticulitis
electrodeposit
electrodynamic
electrothermic
enantiomorphic
erythropoiesis
galactopoietic
goodfellowship
haematogenesis
hallucinogenic
hermaphroditic
hypercalcaemia
hypercatalexis
hyperglycaemia
imparisyllabic
imponderabilia
intelligentsia
metempsychosis
microsporangia
organometallic
orthochromatic
osteoarthritis
oxyhaemoglobin
phantasmagoria
phantasmagoric
photosynthesis
photosynthetic
pneumoconiosis
poikilothermic
postmastership
potentiometric
proceleusmatic
progenitorship
prolocutorship
propagandistic
proprietorship
prosencephalic
pseudaesthesia
psychoanalysis
psychoanalytic
psychoneurosis
psychoneurotic
pyrheliometric
quadrisyllabic
rhinencephalic
somnambulistic
spectrographic
spermatophytic
sphygmographic
spiritualistic
spirochaetosis
stadholdership
stoichiometric
submicroscopic
supervisorship
tachistoscopic
therianthropic
thermoelectric
thyrotoxicosis
unenthusiastic
universalistic
absentmindedly
acceleratingly
accomplishable
accumulatively
achromatically
advantageously
adventitiously
aerobiotically
aetiologically
affectionately
alphabetically
altruistically
ambidextrously
anticipatively
antiseptically
antithetically
aphoristically
apologetically
apoplectically
apprehensively
archetypically
arithmetically
arrhythmically
astronomically
asymmetrically
asymptotically
asynchronously
autocratically
barometrically
biographically
bloodthirstily
breathtakingly
cantankerously
catechetically

clearsightedly
commensurately
compassionable
comprehensible
comprehensibly
concentrically
confidentially
conservatively
constitutively
constructively
contemptuously
conterminously
contradictable
contrapuntally
controvertible
contumaciously
contumeliously
conventionally
crystallisable
deliberatively
democratically
departmentally
diachronically
diagnostically
differentiable
differentially
diplomatically
disapprovingly
discomfortable
discommendable
disconformable
disconnectedly
disconsolately
discontentedly
discouragingly
discourteously
disingenuously
disputatiously
disrespectable
distributively
dodecasyllable
dolichocephaly
effervescently
embarrassingly
emblematically
endosmotically
enharmonically
enterprisingly
entertainingly
epexegetically
ethnologically
etymologically
eulogistically
euphuistically
exasperatingly
excommunicable
excruciatingly
exhilaratingly
experientially
experimentally
extinguishable
faintheartedly
genealogically
geocentrically
geographically
goodhumouredly
goodtemperedly
hierarchically
histrionically
hyperbolically
hyperirritable
hypersonically
hypocritically
hypodermically
hypostatically
hypothetically
idealistically
idiopathically
illegitimately
illustratively
immethodically
impressionable
inapproachable
inarticulately
inartistically
inauspiciously
incommodiously
incommunicable
incommunicably
incompressible
incompressibly
inconclusively
inconsequently
inconsiderable
inconsiderably
inconsistently
incontrollable
inconveniently
indecipherable
indecomposable
indemonstrable
indestructible
indestructibly
indeterminable
indiscerptible
indiscoverable
inexpressively
infelicitously
inflectionally
ingratiatingly
inharmoniously
instrumentally
insufficiently
insuppressible
insurmountable
insurmountably
intellectually
intermediately
intermittently
internationale
interpretively
intransitively
introductorily
irreconcilable
irreconcilably
irreproachable
irreproachably
irreproducible
irrespectively
judgematically
legalistically
lightheartedly
linguistically
longitudinally
magniloquently
malcontentedly
mathematically
megasporophyll
meretriciously
metaphorically
metaphysically
morganatically
multifariously
multilaterally
mythologically
narrowmindedly
numismatically
obstreperously
opinionatively
optimistically
ostentatiously
overabundantly
overpoweringly
overwhelmingly
paratactically
parsimoniously
pathogenically
pathologically
percutaneously
pertinaciously
pestilentially
petrologically
philologically
phlegmatically
pleonastically
polymorphously
postpositively
praiseworthily
preferentially
premeditatedly
preponderantly
preposterously
presbyterially
prescriptively
presumptuously
professionally
professorially
propitiatorily
proportionable
proportionably
proportionally
proscriptively
providentially
pseudonymously
quadrisyllable
quantitatively
quinquennially
rambunctiously
regeneratively
reproductively
sacrilegiously
satisfactorily
schismatically
scholastically
scientifically
selfeffacingly
semiofficially
seriocomically
shortsightedly
simplemindedly
simultaneously
singlehandedly
singlemindedly
skimbleskamble
slaughterously
sociologically
soporiferously
stochastically
stoutheartedly
strongmindedly
subconsciously
substantivally
substitutively
successionally
superciliously
supereminently
supernaturally
supersonically
sycophantishly
synchronically
systematically
tautologically
teleologically
telepathically
telephonically
telescopically
theocratically
tragicomically
transcendently
transitionally
transplantable
tropologically
ultrasonically
unapproachable
unattractively
uncommunicable
unconscionable
uncontrollable
uncontrollably
unconvincingly
understandable
understandably
uneconomically
unemphatically
unflatteringly
unhesitatingly
unintelligible
unintelligibly
unquestionable
unquestionably
unscrupulously
unsuccessfully
vaingloriously
vituperatively
volumetrically
appendicectomy
ultramicrotome
accomplishment
acknowledgment
aggrandisement
anticonvulsant
antidepressant
antiperspirant
arrondissement
backscattering
backscratching
bathingmachine
bioengineering
bioluminescent
bouleversement
bremsstrahlung
communications
corticosterone
countercurrent
countrydancing
disappointment
disarrangement
disconcertment
discontentment
discouragement
discriminating
disembowelment
disenchantment
disenthralment
disfurnishment
disgruntlement
disheartenment
divertissement
electioneering
extinguishment
fortunetelling
forwardlooking
heartsearching
hocuspocussing
homotransplant
hydrocoralline
impoverishment
interdependent
intertwinement
microcomponent
mountaineering
nitroglycerine
nonbelligerent
noncommunicant
noninvolvement
outgeneralling
overcommitment
overexcitement
phenobarbitone
phenylbutazone
phosphorescent
phthalocyanine
prearrangement
quarterbinding
radiotelephone
radiotelephony

recommencement
relinquishment
selfadjustment
selfcomplacent
selfconsequent
selfconsistent
selfcorrecting
selfdestroying
selfdiscipline
selfeffacement
selfemployment
selfenergising
selfexplaining
selfflattering
selffulfilling
selfgovernment
selfpreserving
selfpropelling
selfregulating
selfrespecting
selfsatisfying
selfsufficient
selfsupporting
selfsustaining
selftormenting
semiconducting
Shakespeareana
Shakespeariana
shovehalfpenny
souldestroying
springcleaning
strikebreaking
superincumbent
superintendent
thanksoffering
thimblerigging
thoughtreading
uncompromising
understatement
unenterprising
weltanschauung
windowdressing
windowshopping
administration
Africanisation
allegorisation
authentication
autosuggestion
bastardisation
beautification
biodegradation
bituminisation
boardingschool
bowdlerisation
capitalisation
castrametation
categorisation
centralisation
centrifugation
chemoreception
circumlocution
circumspection
circumvolution
classification
commensuration
concelebration
concretisation
conglomeration
conglutination
congratulation
contraposition
decimalisation
decolonisation
decolorisation
deconsecration
defenestration
dehumanisation
delocalisation
demobilisation
demonetisation
demoralisation
denazification
depolarisation
detoxification
devitalisation
dextrorotation
disaffiliation
disaffirmation
disapprobation
disassociation
discolouration
disconsolation
discrimination
disembarkation
disinclination
disinfestation
disintegration
disorientation
dolomitisation
emulsification
enthronisation
esterification
eutrophication
evangelisation
exclaustration
excommunicator
foreordination
fraternisation
fructification
gelatinisation
generalisation
homogenisation
humidification
identification
immobilisation
implementation
inappreciation
inarticulation
incapacitation
incoordination
indoctrination
intercommunion
intergradation
interlineation
intermediation
intermigration
interpellation
interpretation
legitimisation
liberalisation
lyophilisation
massproduction
microprocessor
militarisation
mineralisation
misapplication
miscalculation
misinformation
mistranslation
monopolisation
multiplication
naturalisation
neutralisation
noctambulation
noncooperation
overestimation
overpopulation
overproduction
pasteurisation
politicisation
polymerisation
popularisation
predesignation
predestination
predisposition
prefabrication
presupposition
prettification
procrastinator
prognosticator
prosencephalon
quantification
radicalisation
recapitulation
recolonisation
recommendation
reconciliation
reconstitution
reconstruction
redintegration
redistribution
regularisation
rehabilitation
reintroduction
reinvigoration
remonetisation
reorganisation
representation
resinification
retrogradation
revalorisation
revivification
rhinencephalon
rigidification
Russianisation
sanctification
sanguification
saponification
scandalisation
schematisation
secularisation
selfabnegation
selfabsorption
selfaccusation
selfadmiration
selfassumption
selfexpression
selfimmolation
selfperception
selfpossession
selfpropulsion
selfprotection
selfrepression
selfrevelation
selfsuggestion
sensualisation
silicification
simplification
solidification
solubilisation
somnambulation
sophistication
specialisation
stampcollector
stigmatisation
stratification
stultification
subalternation
subinfeudation
substantiation
superannuation
superconductor
superelevation
supererogation
superfoetation
superinduction
superscription
symmetrisation
tatterdemalion
tergiversation
tetragrammaton
transformation
transliterator
transmigration
transportation
transvaluation
trivialisation
uncircumcision
undervaluation
vasodilatation
vicechancellor
volatilisation
westernisation
autoradiograph
electrotherapy
encephalograph
ophthalmoscope
ophthalmoscopy
phototelegraph
radioautograph
radiotelegraph
roentgenoscopy
spinthariscope
telephotograph
circumlocutory
classificatory
commissionaire
concessionaire
congratulatory
consuetudinary
counterculture
countermeasure
dextrorotatory
disapprobatory
discriminatory
distemperature
histochemistry
iatrochemistry
infrastructure
interferometry
interplanetary
knickerbockers
knighterrantry
microcircuitry
microminiature
microstructure
neurochemistry
partridgeberry
petrochemistry
photochemistry
progressionary
radiochemistry
recapitulatory
recommendatory
reconciliatory
selfaccusatory
stoicheiometry
supererogatory
superstructure
supramaxillary
tintinnabulary
transmigratory
ultimogeniture
ultrastructure
unsatisfactory
vasodilatatory
absorptiveness
abstemiousness
abstractedness
abstractionism
abstractionist
acceptableness
accustomedness
aerodynamicist
aggressiveness
Albigensianism
allelomorphism
amateurishness
anthropologist
antifederalist
antiquarianism
articulateness
artificialness
associationism
astrophysicist
attainableness

attractivene**s**s
Augustinianis**m**
auspiciousne**s**s
avariciousne**s**s
bacteriologi**s**t
beneficialne**s**s
bibliographi**s**e
boisterousne**s**s
boroughEngli**s**h
breathlessne**s**s
bullheadedne**s**s
calamitousne**s**s
calcareousne**s**s
capriciousne**s**s
censoriousne**s**s
changeablene**s**s
charitablene**s**s
chivalrousne**s**s
circuitousne**s**s
colourfastne**s**s
colourlessne**s**s
commodiousne**s**s
comparablene**s**s
compatiblene**s**s
complexionle**s**s
compulsivene**s**s
conclusivene**s**s
consciencele**s**s
constructivi**s**m
constructivi**s**t
contagiousne**s**s
contiguousne**s**s
continuousne**s**s
contractedne**s**s
convincingne**s**s
convulsivene**s**s
coordinatene**s**s
coquettishne**s**s
courageousne**s**s
creditablene**s**s
crossfertili**s**e
cumbersomene**s**s
cumulativene**s**s
deceivablene**s**s
decorativene**s**s
definitivene**s**s
degeneratene**s**s
delectablene**s**s
deliberatene**s**s
delightfulne**s**s
dependablene**s**s
deplorablene**s**s
despicablene**s**s
despirituali**s**e
despitefulne**s**s
destructioni**s**t
determinedne**s**s
detestablene**s**s
dialectologi**s**t
diaphanousne**s**s
diminutivene**s**s
discursivene**s**s
disdainfulne**s**s
disenfranchi**s**e
disjointedne**s**s
disorderline**s**s
dispiritedne**s**s
ecclesiologi**s**t
educationali**s**t
effortlessne**s**s
egalitariani**s**m
elementarine**s**s
encyclopaedi**s**m
encyclopaedi**s**t
epidemiologi**s**t
epistemologi**s**t
Evangelicali**s**m
exhaustivene**s**s
existentiali**s**m
existentiali**s**t
expressionle**s**s
expressivene**s**s
extraneousne**s**s
factitiousne**s**s
fallaciousne**s**s
farsightedne**s**s
fastidiousne**s**s
favourablene**s**s
ferrimagneti**s**m
ferromagneti**s**m
fictitiousne**s**s
figurativene**s**s
flagitiousne**s**s
flatfootedne**s**s
floriculturi**s**t
forbiddingne**s**s
formidablene**s**s
forthrightne**s**s
fortuitousne**s**s
friendlessne**s**s
fundamentali**s**m
fundamentali**s**t
generalpurpo**s**e
gramineousne**s**s
gratuitousne**s**s
gregariousne**s**s
groundlessne**s**s
harmoniousne**s**s
hereditarine**s**s
heteromorphi**s**m
heterothalli**s**m
highhandedne**s**s
highmindedne**s**s
hobbledehoyi**s**h
holometaboli**s**m
homoeomorphi**s**m
honourablene**s**s
horticulturi**s**t
hypercritici**s**e
hypercritici**s**m
hypothyroidi**s**m
hysterectomi**s**e
illiteratene**s**s
imaginablene**s**s
immaculatene**s**s
immoderatene**s**s
impassablene**s**s
impassiblene**s**s
imperativene**s**s
imperviousne**s**s
implacablene**s**s
impressivene**s**s
improvablene**s**s
inadequatene**s**s
inappositene**s**s
incautiousne**s**s
incestuousne**s**s
incompletene**s**s
incrediblene**s**s
indecisivene**s**s
indecorousne**s**s
indefinitene**s**s
indifferenti**s**m
indifferenti**s**t
indiscreetne**s**s
indistinctne**s**s
inevitablene**s**s
inexorablene**s**s
infectiousne**s**s
inflectionle**s**s
inflexiblene**s**s
ingloriousne**s**s
inimitablene**s**s
inordinatene**s**s
insatiablene**s**s
insensiblene**s**s
intangiblene**s**s
integrationi**s**t
interlocutre**s**s
intuitionali**s**m
intuitionali**s**t
invariablene**s**s
invinciblene**s**s
inviolablene**s**s
irresolutene**s**s
kremlinologi**s**t
lasciviousne**s**s
lefthandedne**s**s
libertariani**s**m
libidinousne**s**s
licentiousne**s**s
liturgiologi**s**t
longheadedne**s**s
longwindedne**s**s
loquaciousne**s**s
lovingkindne**s**s
lugubriousne**s**s
malodorousne**s**s
manageablene**s**s
marvellousne**s**s
matriarchali**s**m
meddlesomene**s**s
meditativene**s**s
meticulousne**s**s
microbiologi**s**t
millenariani**s**m
ministeriali**s**t
miraculousne**s**s
monkeybusine**s**s
monochromati**s**m
monotonousne**s**s
mysteriousne**s**s
necessariani**s**m
neglectfulne**s**s
neocoloniali**s**m
neuroanatomi**s**t
neuroscienti**s**t
newfangledne**s**s
nightblindne**s**s
nitrocellulo**s**e
northnorthea**s**t
northnorthwe**s**t
noteworthine**s**s
nutritiousne**s**s
obsequiousne**s**s
obstructioni**s**m
obstructioni**s**t
oecumenicali**s**m
oleaginousne**s**s
omnivorousne**s**s
openhandedne**s**s
openmindedne**s**s
oppressivene**s**s
outlandishne**s**s
outrageousne**s**s
overcapitali**s**e
palaeobotani**s**t
parasitologi**s**t
pardonablene**s**s
passionatene**s**s
penetrablene**s**s
perceptivene**s**s
peremptorine**s**s
perfidiousne**s**s
peripatetici**s**m
perishablene**s**s
permissivene**s**s
perniciousne**s**s
personablene**s**s
persuasivene**s**s
pharmacologi**s**t
philanthropi**s**e
philanthropi**s**t
photoperiodi**s**m
photosensiti**s**e
pisciculturi**s**t
pneumatologi**s**t
portentousne**s**s
possessivene**s**s
precariousne**s**s
precociousne**s**s
preventivene**s**s
probabiliori**s**m
probabiliori**s**t
prodigiousne**s**s
productivene**s**s
profitablene**s**s
progressioni**s**m
progressioni**s**t
prohibitioni**s**m
prohibitioni**s**t
proletariani**s**e
proletariani**s**m
propitiousne**s**s
prosperousne**s**s
protectivene**s**s
protozoologi**s**t
protrusivene**s**s
pseudomorphi**s**m
psilanthropi**s**m
psilanthropi**s**t
pugnaciousne**s**s
purposefulne**s**s
Pythagoreani**s**m
quattrocenti**s**m
quattrocenti**s**t
radiotherapi**s**t
rampageousne**s**s
reasonablene**s**s
rebelliousne**s**s
reflectivene**s**s
refractorine**s**s
regardlessne**s**s
regressivene**s**s
relentlessne**s**s
remarkablene**s**s
remorsefulne**s**s
repetitivene**s**s
repudiationi**s**t
resistlessne**s**s
respectfulne**s**s
responsivene**s**s
restorationi**s**m
restorationi**s**t
restrictioni**s**t
revengefulne**s**s
rheumatologi**s**t
ridiculousne**s**s
roadworthine**s**s
robustiousne**s**s
Rosicruciani**s**m
roundaboutne**s**s
Sabbatariani**s**m
sacramentali**s**m
sacramentali**s**t
salubriousne**s**s
sanguinarine**s**s
scandalousne**s**s
schoolmistre**s**s
scrubbingbru**s**h
scrupulousne**s**s
scurrilousne**s**s
seasonablene**s**s
segregationi**s**t
sensationali**s**m
sensationali**s**t
sentimentali**s**e
sentimentali**s**m
sentimentali**s**t
servomechani**s**m
shamefacedne**s**s
slanderousne**s**s
slatternline**s**s
slaughterhou**s**e
solicitousne**s**s
spectroscopi**s**t

speechlessness
spiritlessness
spirituousness
sprightfulness
stationariness
statuesqueness
stertorousness
stupendousness
subjectiveness
submissiveness
substantialism
substantialist
subversiveness
successfulness
successiveness
sufferableness
suggestiveness
surefootedness
susceptiveness
suspensiveness
suspiciousness
terminableness
territorialise
territorialism
territorialist
testimonialise
thoughtfulness
threadbareness
thriftlessness
topsyturviness
traditionalism
traditionalist
traitorousness
transitiveness
transitoriness
transsexualism
tremendousness
Trinitarianism
tumultuousness
tyrannicalness
ubiquitousness
ultramontanism
ultramontanist
umbrageousness
unaffectedness
unbecomingness
underemphasise
unexpectedness
unfaithfulness
unfriendliness
ungraciousness
ungratefulness
unmannerliness
unpleasantness
unreservedness
unsociableness
untruthfulness
uproariousness
utilitarianism
vegetativeness
victoriousness
villainousness
vindictiveness
viviparousness
vivisectionist
vociferousness
voluminousness
voluptuousness
vulnerableness
watercolourist
watertightness
weakmindedness
weightlessness
worshipfulness
Zoroastrianism
accountability
archidiaconate
bioelectricity
circumambulate

circumnavigate
coessentiality
combustibility
compossibility
conceivability
conditionality
conductibility
conformability
contraindicate
convertibility
corruptibility
crosspollinate
curvilinearity
denumerability
dinoflagellate
discombobulate
disincorporate
dispensability
dissociability
distensibility
exceptionality
exhaustibility
extemporaneity
extensionality
fantasticality
fundamentality
halfpennyworth
hebetudinosity
hygroscopicity
illimitability
impermeability
implausibility
impracticality
impregnability
impressibility
inadvisability
inalienability
inalterability
incommensurate
incorporeality
indiscriminate
indivisibility
indubitability
ineffectuality
inflammability
infrangibility
inheritability
inscrutability
inseparability
insuperability
intercommunity
interpenetrate
intersexuality
intolerability
intractability
intrinsicality
irreducibility
irrefutability
irremovability
irrevocability
justifiability
malappropriate
misappropriate
nonsensicality
overcompensate
paradoxicality
perceptibility
perfectibility
permissibility
pleasurability
practicability
pragmaticality
predeterminate
predictability
presentability
preventability
recoverability
rectangularity
refrangibility

respectability
responsibility
selfpartiality
sentimentality
serviceability
subcontrariety
submersibility
substantiality
suggestibility
superficiality
superphosphate
susceptibility
territoriality
tintinnabulate
transversality
uncongeniality
undergraduette
undesirability
unpalatability
campylotropous
circumbendibus
classconscious
consanguineous
contradictious
cotemporaneous
crinkumcrankum
cucurbitaceous
diamantiferous
diamondiferous
dicotyledonous
disequilibrium
entomostracous
extemporaneous
foraminiferous
heterochromous
heteromorphous
heterophyllous
holometabolous
ichthyophagous
macrocephalous
megasporangium
microcephalous
microtechnique
myrmecophagous
myrmecophilous
pachydermatous
papilionaceous
parenchymatous
pistilliferous
pseudomorphous
radiostrontium
selfrespectful
spermatogenous
spermatogonium
staphylococcus
supposititious
tetradactylous
tintinnabulous
administrative
chemoreceptive
concavoconcave
conglutinative
congratulative
contrapositive
convexoconcave
disapprobative
discriminative
disintegrative
hypersensitive
inappreciative
interpretative
multiplicative
nonrestrictive
photosensitive
proprioceptive
radiosensitive
recapitulative
reconstructive
redistributive

representative
supersensitive
transformative
unappreciative
unremunerative

---

achondroplasia
bougainvillaea
claustrophobia
cryptaesthesia
hypercalcaemia
hyperglycaemia
imponderabilia
intelligentsia
microsporangia
phantasmagoria
pseudaesthesia
pseudepigrapha
Shakespeareana
Shakespeariana
anthropometric
antiphlogistic
apophthegmatic
autobiographic
bacteriostatic
behaviouristic
brachycephalic
characteristic
claustrophobic
corticotrophic
dieselelectric
electrodynamic
electrothermic
enantiomorphic
galactopoietic
hallucinogenic
hermaphroditic
imparisyllabic
organometallic
orthochromatic
phantasmagoric
photosynthetic
poikilothermic
potentiometric
proceleusmatic
propagandistic
prosencephalic
psychoanalytic
psychoneurotic
pyrheliometric
quadrisyllabic
rhinencephalic
somnambulistic
spectrographic
spermatophytic
sphygmographic
spiritualistic
stoichiometric
submicroscopic
tachistoscopic
therianthropic
thermoelectric
unenthusiastic
universalistic
abovementioned
aforementioned
butterfingered
chickenhearted
chickenlivered
copperbottomed
corticosteroid
counterplotted
doublebreasted
featherbrained
fullyfashioned
illconditioned
multinucleated
oversubscribed
parallelepiped

pigeonbreasted
publicspirited
scatterbrained
selfcontrolled
selfdetermined
selffertilised
selfinterested
selfproclaimed
selfrestrained
singlebreasted
snaggletoothed
spindleshanked
unaccommodated
unaccomplished
unacknowledged
uncontroverted
uncorroborated
underdeveloped
undermentioned
undernourished
unpremeditated
accomplishable
administrative
archidiaconate
bathingmachine
bibliographise
chemoreceptive
chincherinchee
circumambulate
circumnavigate
commissionaire
compassionable
comprehensible
concavoconcave
concessionaire
condescendence
conglutinative
congratulative
contradictable
contraindicate
contrapositive
controvertible
convexoconcave
correspondence
corticosterone
counterbalance
counterculture
countermeasure
crossfertilise
crosspollinate
crossreference
crystallisable
despiritualise
differentiable
dinoflagellate
disapprobative
discombobulate
discomfortable
discommendable
disconformable
discontinuance
discountenance
discriminative
disenfranchise
disincorporate
disinheritance
disintegrative
disrespectable
distemperature
dodecasyllable
endoradiosonde
excommunicable
extinguishable
generalpurpose
grandiloquence
hydrocoralline
hypercriticise
hyperirritable
hypersensitive

hysterectomise
impressionable
inappreciative
inapproachable
incommensurate
incommunicable
incompressible
inconsiderable
incontrollable
indecipherable
indecomposable
indemonstrable
indestructible
indeterminable
indiscerptible
indiscoverable
indiscriminate
infrastructure
insignificance
insuppressible
insurmountable
internationale
interpenetrate
interpretative
irreconcilable
irreproachable
irreproducible
malappropriate
microminiature
microstructure
microtechnique
misappropriate
monosaccharide
multiplicative
nitrocellulose
nitroglycerine
nonconcurrence
nonperformance
nonrestrictive
ophthalmoscope
overcapitalise
overcompensate
overconfidence
overindulgence
phenobarbitone
phenylbutazone
philanthropise
photosensitise
photosensitive
phthalocyanine
polysaccharide
predeterminate
proletarianise
proportionable
proprioceptive
quadrisyllable
radiosensitive
radiotelephone
recapitulative
reconnaissance
reconstructive
redistributive
rejuvenescence
representative
selfconfidence
selfdependence
selfdiscipline
selfimportance
selfinductance
selfindulgence
sentimentalise
skimbleskamble
slaughterhouse
spinthariscope
sulphanilamide
superabundance
superphosphate
supersensitive
superstructure

territorialise
testimonialise
tintinnabulate
transformative
transplantable
ultimogeniture
ultramicrotome
ultrastructure
unappreciative
unapproachable
uncommunicable
unconscionable
uncontrollable
underemphasise
undergraduette
understandable
unintelligible
unquestionable
unremunerative
verisimilitude
backscattering
backscratching
bioengineering
bremsstrahlung
countrydancing
discriminating
electioneering
fortunetelling
forwardlooking
heartsearching
hocuspocussing
mountaineering
outgeneralling
quarterbinding
selfcorrecting
selfdestroying
selfenergising
selfexplaining
selfflattering
selffulfilling
selfpreserving
selfpropelling
selfregulating
selfrespecting
selfsatisfying
selfsupporting
selfsustaining
selftormenting
semiconducting
souldestroying
springcleaning
strikebreaking
thanksoffering
thimblerigging
thoughtreading
uncompromising
unenterprising
weltanschauung
windowdressing
windowshopping
autoradiograph
boroughEnglish
encephalograph
halfpennyworth
hobbledehoyish
phototelegraph
radioautograph
radiotelegraph
scrubbingbrush
telephotograph
stumblingblock
aerobiological
agrobiological
alphanumerical
anagrammatical
antiscriptural
apothegmatical
archaeological
archiepiscopal

bibliomaniacal
boardingschool
campanological
cartographical
catachrestical
Christological
chronometrical
circumlittoral
circumstantial
climatological
commonsensical
compensational
congregational
conservational
consociational
conspiratorial
constitutional
constructional
consubstantial
conversational
cosmographical
cosmopolitical
denominational
dermatological
diagrammatical
disquisitional
dissertational
distributional
ecclesiastical
electrothermal
epigrammatical
eschatological
extracorporeal
gerontological
gynaecological
hagiographical
hieroglyphical
hydrodynamical
hydrographical
hypocoristical
ichthyological
iconographical
illustrational
insurrectional
intelligential
intercessional
intercessorial
interferential
interjectional
intersectional
jurisdictional
martyrological
megasporophyll
meteorological
methodological
myrmecological
nomenclatorial
oneirocritical
organisational
ornithological
orthographical
perturbational
petrographical
pharmaceutical
pharmacopoeial
phraseological
physiognomical
pluviometrical
poikilothermal
polytheistical
postmillennial
postpositional
presentational
presentimental
propaedeutical
prothonotarial
psychochemical
psychophysical
psychosurgical

pteridological
quinquagesimal
quintessential
reminiscential
resurrectional
selfrespectful
semicentennial
semielliptical
sociopolitical
soteriological
spatiotemporal
sphaerocrystal
stomatological
subcontinental
substitutional
suprasegmental
tachygraphical
terminological
thermochemical
transcendental
tridimensional
twodimensional
unconventional
unidimensional
unidirectional
unprofessional
venereological
volcanological
vulcanological
abstractionism
Albigensianism
allelomorphism
antiquarianism
associationism
Augustinianism
constructivism
crinkumcrankum
disequilibrium
egalitarianism
encyclopaedism
Evangelicalism
existentialism
ferrimagnetism
ferromagnetism
fundamentalism
heteromorphism
heterothallism
holometabolism
homoeomorphism
hypercriticism
hypothyroidism
indifferentism
intuitionalism
libertarianism
matriarchalism
megasporangium
millenarianism
monochromatism
necessarianism
neocolonialism
obstructionism
oecumenicalism
peripateticism
photoperiodism
probabiliorism
progressionism
prohibitionism
proletarianism
pseudomorphism
psilanthropism
Pythagoreanism
quattrocentism
radiostrontium
restorationism
Rosicrucianism
Sabbatarianism
sacramentalism
sensationalism
sentimentalism
servomechanism
spermatogonium
substantialism
territorialism
traditionalism
transsexualism
Trinitarianism
ultramontanism
utilitarianism
Zoroastrianism
administration
Africanisation
allegorisation
authentication
autosuggestion
bastardisation
beautification
biodegradation
bituminisation
bowdlerisation
Brobdingnagian
capitalisation
castrametation
categorisation
centralisation
centrifugation
chemoreception
circumlocution
circumspection
circumvolution
classification
commensuration
committeewoman
concelebration
concretisation
conglomeration
conglutination
congratulation
contraposition
corticotrophin
cyanocobalamin
decimalisation
decolonisation
decolorisation
deconsecration
defenestration
dehumanisation
delocalisation
demobilisation
demonetisation
demoralisation
denazification
depolarisation
detoxification
devitalisation
dextrorotation
disaffiliation
disaffirmation
disapprobation
disassociation
disciplinarian
discolouration
disconsolation
discrimination
disembarkation
disinclination
disinfestation
disintegration
disorientation
dolomitisation
econometrician
emulsification
enthronisation
esterification
eutrophication
evangelisation
exclaustration
ferromagnesian
foreordination
fraternisation
fructification
gelatinisation
generalisation
handicraftsman
homogenisation
horrorstricken
humidification
ichthyosaurian
identification
immobilisation
implementation
inappreciation
inarticulation
incapacitation
incoordination
indoctrination
infralapsarian
intercommunion
intergradation
interlineation
intermediation
intermigration
interpellation
interpretation
latitudinarian
legitimisation
liberalisation
lyophilisation
massproduction
militarisation
mineralisation
misapplication
miscalculation
misinformation
mistranslation
monopolisation
multiplication
naturalisation
neutralisation
noctambulation
noncooperation
overestimation
overpopulation
overproduction
oxyhaemoglobin
pasteurisation
pianoaccordian
planetstricken
politicisation
polymerisation
popularisation
predesignation
predestinarian
predestination
predisposition
prefabrication
premillenarian
presupposition
prettification
prosencephalon
quadragenarian
quantification
radicalisation
recapitulation
recolonisation
recommendation
reconciliation
reconstitution
reconstruction
redintegration
redistribution
regularisation
rehabilitation
reintroduction
reinvigoration
remonetisation
reorganisation
representation
resinification
retrogradation
revalorisation
revivification
rhinencephalon
rigidification
Russianisation
sacramentarian
sanctification
sanguification
saponification
sauropterygian
scandalisation
schematisation
schoolchildren
secularisation
selfabnegation
selfabsorption
selfaccusation
selfadmiration
selfassumption
selfexpression
selfimmolation
selfperception
selfpossession
selfpropulsion
selfprotection
selfrepression
selfrevelation
selfsuggestion
sensualisation
septuagenarian
sesquipedalian
silicification
simplification
solidification
solitudinarian
solubilisation
somnambulation
sophistication
specialisation
stigmatisation
stratification
stultification
subalternation
subinfeudation
substantiation
superannuation
superelevation
supererogation
superfoetation
superinduction
superscription
superterranean
supralapsarian
symmetrisation
tatterdemalion
tergiversation
terrorstricken
tetragrammaton
transformation
transmigration
transportation
transvaluation
trivialisation
uncircumcision
undervaluation
uniformitarian
valetudinarian
vasodilatation
volatilisation
westernisation
wonderstricken
ambassadorship
apprenticeship
chancellorship
commissaryship
controllership
councillorship

counsellorship commodiousness haematogenesis myrmecophilous
goodfellowship communications handkerchieves mysteriousness
postmastership comparableness harmoniousness neglectfulness
progenitorship compatibleness hereditariness newfangledness
prolocutorship complexionless heterochromous nightblindness
proprietorship compulsiveness heteromorphous northeastwards
stadholdership conclusiveness heterophyllous northwestwards
supervisorship conjunctivitis highhandedness noteworthiness
aesthesiometer conquistadores highmindedness nutritiousness
airconditioner consanguineous holometabolous obsequiousness
autobiographer conscienceless honourableness oleaginousness
blackmarketeer contagiousness hydromechanics omnivorousness
blockaderunner contiguousness hypercatalexis openhandedness
cardiovascular continuousness ichthyophagous openmindedness
councilchamber contractedness illiterateness oppressiveness
demisemiquaver contradictious imaginableness osteoarthritis
diffractometer convincingness immaculateness outlandishness
excommunicator convulsiveness immoderateness outrageousness
extravehicular coordinateness impassableness pachydermatous
gyrostabiliser coquettishness impassibleness papilionaceous
heroworshipper cotemporaneous imperativeness pardonableness
interferometer courageousness imperviousness parenchymatous
intermolecular creditableness implacableness passionateness
intramolecular cucurbitaceous impressiveness patresfamilias
Johannisberger cumbersomeness improvableness penetrableness
marketgardener cumulativeness inadequateness perceptiveness
metallographer deceivableness inappositeness peremptoriness
microprocessor decorativeness incautiousness perfidiousness
procrastinator definitiveness incestuousness perishableness
prognosticator degenerateness incompleteness permissiveness
scintillometer delectableness incredibleness perniciousness
squadronleader deliberateness indecisiveness personableness
stampcollector delightfulness indecorousness persuasiveness
standardbearer dependableness indefiniteness photosynthesis
steganographer deplorableness indiscreetness pistilliferous
superconductor despicableness indistinctness pneumoconiosis
swordswallower despitefulness inevitableness portentousness
transliterator determinedness inexorableness possessiveness
troubleshooter detestableness infectiousness precariousness
verticillaster diamantiferous inflectionless precociousness
vicechancellor diamondiferous inflexibleness preventiveness
whippersnapper diaphanousness ingloriousness prodigiousness
absorptiveness dicotyledonous inimitableness productiveness
abstemiousness diminutiveness inordinateness profitableness
abstractedness discursiveness insatiableness propitiousness
acceptableness disdainfulness insensibleness prosperousness
accustomedness disjointedness intangibleness protectiveness
aggressiveness disorderliness interlocutress protrusiveness
amateurishness dispiritedness invariableness pseudomorphous
architectonics diverticulitis invincibleness psychoanalysis
articulateness effortlessness inviolableness psychodynamics
artificialness electrostatics irresoluteness psychoneurosis
attainableness elementariness knickerbockers psychosomatics
attractiveness entomostracous lasciviousness pugnaciousness
auspiciousness erythropoiesis lefthandedness purposefulness
avariciousness exhaustiveness libidinousness rampageousness
bacteriostasis expressionless licentiousness reasonableness
basidiomycetes expressiveness longheadedness rebelliousness
beneficialness extemporaneous longwindedness reflectiveness
biosystematics extraneousness loquaciousness refractoriness
boisterousness factitiousness lovingkindness regardlessness
breathlessness fallaciousness lugubriousness regressiveness
bronchiectasis farsightedness macrocephalous relentlessness
bullheadedness fastidiousness macroeconomics remarkableness
calamitousness favourableness malodorousness remorsefulness
calcareousness fictitiousness manageableness repetitiveness
campylotropous figurativeness marvellousness resistlessness
capriciousness flagitiousness meddlesomeness respectfulness
carcinogenesis flatfootedness meditativeness responsiveness
censoriousness foraminiferous Mephistopheles revengefulness
changeableness forbiddingness mesdemoiselles ridiculousness
charitableness formidableness metempsychosis roadworthiness
chemosynthesis forthrightness meticulousness robustiousness
chivalrousness fortuitousness microcephalous roundaboutness
circuitousness friendlessness microeconomics salubriousness
circumbendibus gramineousness miraculousness sanguinariness
classconscious gratuitousness monkeybusiness scandalousness
colourfastness gregariousness monotonousness schoolmistress
colourlessness groundlessness myrmecophagous scrupulousness

scurrilousness
seasonableness
shamefacedness
slanderousness
slatternliness
solicitousness
southeastwards
southwestwards
speechlessness
spermatogenous
spiritlessness
spirituousness
spirochaetosis
sprightfulness
staphylococcus
stationariness
statuesqueness
stertorousness
stupendousness
subjectiveness
submissiveness
subversiveness
successfulness
successiveness
sufferableness
suggestiveness
supposititious
surefootedness
susceptiveness
suspensiveness
suspiciousness
terminableness
tetradactylous
thermodynamics
thoughtfulness
threadbareness
thriftlessness
thyrotoxicosis
tintinnabulous
topsyturviness
traitorousness
transitiveness
transitoriness
tremendousness
tumultuousness
tyrannicalness
ubiquitousness
umbrageousness
unaffectedness
unbecomingness
unexpectedness
unfaithfulness
unfriendliness
ungraciousness
ungratefulness
unmannerliness
unmentionables
unpleasantness
unreservedness
unsociableness
untruthfulness
uproariousness
vegetativeness
victoriousness
villainousness
vindictiveness
viviparousness
vociferousness
voluminousness
voluptuousness
vulnerableness
watertightness
weakmindedness
weightlessness
whortleberries
worshipfulness
abstractionist
accomplishment
acknowledgment
aerodynamicist
aggrandisement
anthropologist
anticonvulsant
antidepressant
antifederalist
antiperspirant
arrondissement
astrophysicist
bacteriologist
bioluminescent
bouleversement
constructivist
countercurrent
destructionist
dialectologist
disappointment
disarrangement
disconcertment
discontentment
discouragement
disembowelment
disenchantment
disenthralment
disfurnishment
disgruntlement
disheartenment
divertissement
ecclesiologist
educationalist
electrodeposit
encyclopaedist
epidemiologist
epistemologist
existentialist
extinguishment
floriculturist
fundamentalist
homotransplant
horticulturist
impoverishment
indifferentist
integrationist
interdependent
intertwinement
intuitionalist
kremlinologist
liturgiologist
microbiologist
microcomponent
ministerialist
neuroanatomist
neuroscientist
nonbelligerent
noncommunicant
noninvolvement
northnortheast
northnorthwest
obstructionist
overcommitment
overexcitement
palaeobotanist
parasitologist
pharmacologist
philanthropist
phosphorescent
pisciculturist
pneumatologist
prearrangement
probabiliorist
progressionist
prohibitionist
protozoologist
psilanthropist
quattrocentist
radiotherapist
recommencement
relinquishment
repudiationist
restorationist
restrictionist
rheumatologist
sacramentalist
segregationist
selfadjustment
selfcomplacent
selfconsequent
selfconsistent
selfeffacement
selfemployment
selfgovernment
selfsufficient
sensationalist
sentimentalist
spectroscopist
substantialist
superincumbent
superintendent
territorialist
traditionalist
ultramontanist
understatement
vivisectionist
watercolourist
butterflyscrew
administratrix
absentmindedly
acceleratingly
accountability
accumulatively
achromatically
advantageously
adventitiously
aerobiotically
aetiologically
affectionately
alphabetically
altruistically
ambidextrously
anthropography
anticipatively
antiseptically
antithetically
aphoristically
apologetically
apoplectically
appendicectomy
apprehensively
archetypically
arithmetically
arrhythmically
astronomically
asymmetrically
asymptotically
asynchronously
audiofrequency
autocratically
barometrically
bioelectricity
biographically
bloodthirstily
breathtakingly
cantankerously
catechetically
chromatography
cinematography
circumambiency
circumlocutory
classificatory
clearsightedly
coessentiality
combustibility
commensurately
compossibility
comprehensibly
conceivability
concentrically
conditionality
conductibility
confidentially
conformability
congratulatory
conservatively
constitutively
constructively
consuetudinary
contemptuously
conterminously
contrapuntally
contumaciously
contumeliously
conventionally
convertibility
correspondency
corruptibility
curvilinearity
deliberatively
democratically
denumerability
departmentally
dextrorotatory
diachronically
diagnostically
differentially
diplomatically
disapprobatory
disapprovingly
disconnectedly
disconsolately
discontentedly
discouragingly
discourteously
discriminatory
disingenuously
dispensability
disputatiously
dissociability
distensibility
distributively
dolichocephaly
effervescently
eigenfrequency
electrobiology
electrotherapy
electrovalency
embarrassingly
emblematically
endosmotically
enharmonically
enterprisingly
entertainingly
epexegetically
ethnologically
etymologically
eulogistically
euphuistically
exasperatingly
exceptionality
excruciatingly
exhaustibility
exhilaratingly
experientially
experimentally
extemporaneity
extensionality
faintheartedly
fantasticality
fundamentality
genealogically
geocentrically
geographically
goodhumouredly
goodtemperedly
gynandromorphy
hebetudinosity
hierarchically
histochemistry

histopathology
historiography
histrionically
hygroscopicity
hyperbolically
hypersonically
hypocritically
hypodermically
hypostatically
hypothetically
iatrochemistry
idealistically
idiopathically
illegitimately
illimitability
illustratively
immethodically
impermeability
implausibility
impracticality
impregnability
impressibility
inadvisability
inalienability
inalterability
inarticulately
inartistically
inauspiciously
incommodiously
incommunicably
incompressibly
inconclusively
inconsequently
inconsiderably
inconsistently
inconveniently
incorporeality
indestructibly
indivisibility
indubitability
ineffectuality
inexpressively
infelicitously
inflammability
inflectionally
infrangibility
ingratiatingly
inharmoniously
inheritability
inscrutability
inseparability
insignificancy
instrumentally
insufficiently
insuperability
insurmountably
intellectually
intercommunity
interferometry
intermediately
intermittently
interplanetary
interpretively
intersexuality
intolerability
intractability
intransitively
intrinsicality
introductorily
irreconcilably
irreducibility
irrefutability
irremovability
irreproachably
irrespectively
irrevocability
judgematically
justifiability
knighterrantry
legalistically
lightheartedly
linguistically
longitudinally
magniloquently
malcontentedly
mathematically
meretriciously
metaphorically
metaphysically
metapsychology
microcircuitry
morganatically
multifariously
multilaterally
mythologically
narrowmindedly
neurochemistry
neuropathology
nonsensicality
numismatically
obstreperously
ophthalmoscopy
opinionatively
optimistically
ostentatiously
overabundantly
overpoweringly
overwhelmingly
palaeethnology
paradoxicality
parapsychology
paratactically
parsimoniously
partridgeberry
pathogenically
pathologically
perceptibility
percutaneously
perfectibility
periodontology
permissibility
pertinaciously
pestilentially
petrochemistry
petrologically
philologically
phlegmatically
photochemistry
phytogeography
phytopathology
pleasurability
pleonastically
polymorphously
postpositively
practicability
pragmaticality
praiseworthily
predictability
preferentially
premeditatedly
preponderantly
preposterously
presbyterially
prescriptively
presentability
presumptuously
preventability
professionally
professorially
progressionary
propitiatorily
proportionably
proportionally
proscriptively
providentially
pseudepigraphy
pseudonymously
quantitatively
quinquennially
radiochemistry
radiotelephony
rambunctiously
recapitulatory
recommendatory
reconciliatory
recoverability
rectangularity
refrangibility
regeneratively
reproductively
respectability
responsibility
roentgenoscopy
rontgenography
sacrilegiously
satisfactorily
schismatically
scholastically
scientifically
selfaccusatory
selfeffacingly
selfpartiality
semiofficially
sentimentality
seriocomically
serviceability
shortsightedly
shovehalfpenny
simplemindedly
simultaneously
singlehandedly
singlemindedly
slaughterously
sociologically
soporiferously
stochastically
stoicheiometry
stoutheartedly
strongmindedly
subconsciously
subcontrariety
sublieutenancy
submersibility
substantiality
substantivally
substitutively
successionally
suggestibility
superciliously
supereminently
supererogatory
superficiality
supernaturally
supersonically
supramaxillary
susceptibility
sycophantishly
symptomatology
synchronically
systematically
tautologically
teleologically
telepathically
telephonically
telescopically
territoriality
thalassography
theocratically
tintinnabulary
tragicomically
transcendently
transitionally
transmigratory
transversality
tropologically
ultrasonically
unattractively
uncongeniality
uncontrollably
unconvincingly
understandably
undesirability
uneconomically
unemphatically
unflatteringly
unhesitatingly
unintelligibly
unpalatability
unquestionably
unsatisfactory
unscrupulously
unsuccessfully
vaingloriously
vasodilatatory
vicepresidency
vituperatively
volumetrically

15 letter words

abiogenetically
acanthocephalan
acclimatisation
accommodatingly
accountableness
achondroplastic
acknowledgeable
acknowledgement
acquisitiveness
adventurousness
aerodynamically
affranchisement
agriculturalist
airconditioning
alphabetisation
ambidexterously
Americanisation
amphitheatrical
anaesthesiology
anaesthetically
anisotropically
ankylostomiasis
annihilationism
antepenultimate

anthropocentric
anthropogenesis
anthropological
anthropomorphic
anthropopathism
anthropophagous
anticlericalism
antimonarchical
antisabbatarian
antitrinitarian
antivivisection
apocalyptically
approachability
appropriateness
approximatively
arboriculturist
archiepiscopate
architecturally
argumentatively
Aristotelianism
arterialisation
atherosclerosis
atherosclerotic
atmospherically
atrabiliousness
authoritatively
autographically
autoradiography
bacteriological
bibliographical
bioastronautics
biogeochemistry
biogeographical
bioluminescence
blameworthiness
bloodguiltiness
brachistochrone
brachycephalous
brachydactylous
broadmindedness
carnivorousness
cerebrovascular
ceremoniousness
chloramphenicol
Christadelphian
chromatographic
chronogrammatic
chronologically
churrigueresque
cinematographer
cinematographic
circumferential
circumnavigator
circumscription
circumspectness
circumstantiate
circumvallation
civilianisation
coconsciousness
coinstantaneous
coldbloodedness
coldheartedness
collenchymatous
commonplaceness
communalisation
communicability
communicatively
compartmentally
compassionately
compendiousness
competitiveness
complementarily
complementarity
complicatedness
compositionally
comprehensively
compressibility
computerisation
conceivableness
conceptualistic
condescendingly
confessionalism
confessionalist
confidentiality
configurational
congratulations
conjunctionally
connoisseurship
conscientiously
consecutiveness
consentaneously
consequentially
conservationist
considerateness
conspicuousness
constructionism
constructionist
consubstantiate
contemplatively
contemporaneity
contemporaneous
contemptibility
contentiousness
contractability
contractibility
contradictorily
contravallation
controversially
conventionalise
conventionalism
conventionalist
conventionality
conversationist
correspondingly
cosmopolitanism
counterapproach
counterattacker
counterirritant
countermovement
counterplotting
crossopterygian
cryptanalytical
cryptocommunist
crystallisation
crystallography
Czechoslovakian
decalcification
decarbonisation
decarburisation
decolourisation
decontamination
defencelessness
deleteriousness
demagnetisation
demonstrability
demonstrational
demonstratively
demystification
denitrification
departmentalise
departmentalism
dermatoglyphics
descriptiveness
desensitisation
desexualisation
dessertspoonful
destructibility
destructiveness
determinateness
detribalisation
developmentally
devitrification
differentiation
disadvantageous
disaffectedness
disagreeability
disappointingly
disarticulation
discommendation
disconcertingly
discontinuously
disenchantingly
disentanglement
disgracefulness
dishearteningly
disillusionment
disinflationary
disinterestedly
disorganisation
dispassionately
disproportional
disreputability
disrespectfully
dissatisfaction
dissatisfactory
distastefulness
distinctiveness
distinguishable
distinguishably
distrustfulness
dithyrambically
diversification
dolichocephalic
doublebarrelled
downheartedness
dramaturgically
dyslogistically
ecclesiasticism
ecclesiological
echinodermatous
eclaircissement
efficaciousness
electrification
electroanalysis
electrochemical
electrodynamics
electrokinetics
electromagnetic
electromyograph
electronegative
electrophoresis
electrophoretic
electropositive
emancipationist
enantiomorphism
enantiomorphous
encephalography
enfranchisement
entrepreneurial
episcopalianism
epistemological
epitheliomatous
equalitarianism
equiprobability
etherealisation
ethnocentricity
euphemistically
Europeanisation
everlastingness
exchangeability
excommunication
excommunicative
excommunicatory
exemplification
exhibitionistic
expeditiousness
experientialism
experientialist
experimentalise
experimentalism
experimentalist
experimentation
experimentative
expressionistic
extemporisation
exteriorisation
externalisation
extracurricular
extraillustrate
extraordinarily
familiarisation
fantasticalness
fashionableness
fissiparousness
flibbertigibbet
foresightedness
formularisation
fourdimensional
fragmentariness
frenchification
gastroenteritis
gentlemanliness
geochronologist
geomorphologist
gleichschaltung
governorgeneral
grandiloquently
greatgrandchild
gynandromorphic
halfheartedness
hardheartedness
heartbreakingly
heliotropically
Hellenistically
hendecasyllabic
hendecasyllable
hermaphroditism
hermeneutically
heterochromatic
heterodactyloos
heterogeneously
heterosexuality
historiographer
historiographic
hobbledehoyhood
homogeneousness
hospitalisation
humanitarianism
hydrodynamicist
hydropathically
hydrostatically
hypercatalectic
hypercritically
hyperthyroidism
ideographically
illimitableness
illustriousness
imaginativeness
immortalisation
immunochemistry
impenetrability
imperishability
impermeableness
imponderability
importunateness
impracticalness
imprescriptible
impressionistic
improvisatorial
inaccessibility
inadmissibility
inapplicability
inapprehensible
inappropriately
inattentiveness
incalculability
incommensurable
incommensurably
incommunicative
incomparability
incompatibility
incomprehension
incongruousness
inconsequential
inconsiderately
inconsideration

inconspicuously
incorrigibility
indefeasibility
indefensibility
indemnification
indeterminately
indetermination
indeterministic
indigestibility
indisciplinable
indissolubility
indistinctively
individualistic
indubitableness
ineffaceability
ineffectiveness
ineffectualness
inefficaciously
inexcusableness
inexpensiveness
inexplicability
infinitesimally
inflammableness
infrangibleness
infundibuliform
injudiciousness
innumerableness
inoffensiveness
inopportuneness
inquisitiveness
inquisitorially
inscrutableness
insensitiveness
inseparableness
insignificantly
instantaneously
instructiveness
instrumentalism
instrumentalist
instrumentality
instrumentation
insubordination
insurrectionary
insurrectionist
intellectualise
intellectualism
intellectualist
intellectuality
intelligibility
intemperateness
intensification
interchangeable
interchangeably
interclavicular
intercollegiate
interconnection
interdependence
interdependency
interdigitation
interfascicular
interferometric
interjectionary
internalisation
internationally
interpretership
interprovincial
interrogatively
interscholastic
interstratified
interventionism
interventionist
intolerableness
intractableness
introsusception
intussusception
intussusceptive
involuntariness
invulnerability
irrationalistic
irreparableness
irresistibility
irreversibility
irrevocableness
jurisprudential
kindheartedness
lackadaisically
levelheadedness
lexicographical
lightheadedness
lightmindedness
logarithmically
logographically
longsightedness
macroscopically
magnetoelectric
malacopterygian
maldistribution
malpractitioner
manicdepressive
manoeuvrability
margaritiferous
marketgardening
materialisation
mechanistically
mellifluousness
Mephistophelean
Mephistophelian
meritoriousness
meroblastically
metamathematics
methamphetamine
microanalytical
micromillimetre
microphotograph
microsporangium
microsporophyll
miniaturisation
misapprehension
misapprehensive
mischievousness
misconstruction
mistrustfulness
monosymmetrical
morphologically
multitudinously
nationalisation
nearsightedness
necessitousness
necromantically
neighbourliness
neurophysiology
neuropsychiatry
noncommissioned
noncontributory
nongovernmental
noninterference
nonintervention
nonprofessional
nonprofitmaking
nonsensicalness
northeastwardly
northwestwardly
notwithstanding
numismatologist
obstructiveness
oceanographical
odoriferousness
omnidirectional
ontogenetically
openheartedness
ophthalmologist
ophthalmoscopic
opinionatedness
opprobriousness
ornithorhynchus
orthopsychiatry
overconfidently
overdevelopment
palaeoanthropic
palaeobotanical
palaeogeography
palaeographical
palaeomagnetism
palaeontologist
pantheistically
paradoxicalness
parasympathetic
parenthetically
parliamentarian
parliamentarism
parthenogenesis
parthenogenetic
particularistic
penetrativeness
perfunctoriness
peripatetically
peristaltically
perpendicularly
personalisation
personification
perspicaciously
perspicuousness
pessimistically
pharisaicalness
pharmacological
phenomenalistic
phenomenologist
phenylketonuria
philanthropical
philosophically
phonautographic
phosphorescence
phosphorylation
photochemically
photoconducting
photoconductive
photoelectronic
photojournalism
photojournalist
photolithograph
photomechanical
photomicrograph
photosensitiser
photosynthesise
phototelegraphy
phrenologically
physicochemical
physiographical
physiologically
physiotherapist
phytogeographic
picturepostcard
picturesqueness
pithecanthropus
platitudinarian
pleasurableness
plenipotentiary
pleuropneumonia
plumbaginaceous
pneumatological
polycrystalline
polyunsaturated
postmillenarian
povertystricken
practicableness
precipitousness
predeterminable
prehistorically
prepositionally
prepossessingly
PreRaphaelitism
Presbyterianise
Presbyterianism
presentationism
presentationist
preservationist
prestidigitator
prestigiousness
pretentiousness
preternaturally
problematically
processionalist
procrastination
professionalise
professionalism
prognostication
prognosticative
progressiveness
prohibitiveness
properispomenon
proportionalist
proportionality
proportionately
prosenchymatous
protozoological
provocativeness
pseudepigraphic
psychologically
psychometrician
psychopathology
psychophysicist
psychotherapist
pulchritudinous
punctiliousness
purposelessness
pusillanimously
pyroelectricity
pyrotechnically
quadruplication
quarrelsomeness
quarterfinalist
quatercentenary
quickwittedness
quinquagenarian
quintuplication
radioautography
radiogoniometer
radiotelegraphy
rationalisation
reafforestation
reapportionment
reconcilability
reconsideration
reconsolidation
reestablishment
regionalisation
remonstratively
remorselessness
repetitiousness
reproachfulness
reproducibility
resourcefulness
respectableness
resurrectionism
resurrectionist
retrogressively
retrospectively
rhombencephalon
rhynchocephalia
righthandedness
rightmindedness
ritualistically
roentgenography
romanticisation
rontgenotherapy
rudimentariness
sadomasochistic
sanctimoniously
saprophytically
schistosomiasis
schoolmastering
selfabandonment
selfaffirmation
selfapprobation
selfcastigation
selfcentredness

selfcomplacency
selfconfidently
selfconsciously
selfconsequence
selfconsistency
selfconstituted
selfcontainment
selfdeprecating
selfdeprecatory
selfdestruction
selfdestructive
selfdetermining
selfdevelopment
selfdistrustful
selfexamination
selfexplanatory
selffertilising
selfforgetfully
selffulfillment
selfgratulation
selfhumiliation
selfimprovement
selfindulgently
selfopinionated
selfpollination
selfpropagating
selfrealisation
selfregistering
selfreplicating
selfreproachful
selfreprovingly
selfrighteously
selfsacrificing
selfsufficiency
semiconsciously
semicylindrical
semidocumentary
semiindependent
semitransparent
sententiousness
serviceableness
sesquicentenary
shootinggallery
shrinkresistant
significatively
singleheartedly
sleepingdraught
socialistically
sociolinguistic
softheartedness
sophisticatedly
speakingtrumpet
spectroscopical
speculativeness
speechification
spermatogenesis
spermatogenetic
splendiferously
spontaneousness
stadtholdership
stampcollecting
standardisation
standoffishness
stereochemistry
stereoisomerism
stoicheiometric
straightforward
stratigraphical
stretcherbearer
subordinateness
subpostmistress
substantialness
substantiveness
substitutionary
substratosphere
subterraneously
suburbanisation
sulphureousness
superabundantly
superconducting
superconductive
superficialness
superfluousness
superheterodyne
superimposition
superincumbence
superinducement
superintendence
superintendency
superlativeness
supernaturalise
supernaturalism
supernaturalist
supersaturation
superstitiously
superstructural
supplementarily
supplementation
supportableness
suppositionally
surreptitiously
susceptibleness
sycophantically
syllabification
syllogistically
symmetricalness
sympathetically
symptomatically
synchronisation
systematisation
technologically
telegraphically
telephotography
temperamentally
tempestuousness
tendentiousness
therapeutically
therianthropism
thermochemistry
thoughtlessness
thunderstricken
topographically
totalitarianism
transcriptional
transferability
transfiguration
transfigurement
transgressively
transilluminate
transliteration
transmutability
transparentness
transplantation
transpositional
treacherousness
treasonableness
trigonometrical
trinitrotoluene
trisyllabically
troublesomeness
trueheartedness
trustworthiness
trypanosomiasis
typographically
ultracentrifuge
ultramicroscope
unaccommodating
unceremoniously
unchallengeable
unchangeability
uncommunicative
uncomplainingly
uncomplimentary
uncomprehending
unconditionally
unconsciousness
undemonstrative
underemployment
underestimation
underprivileged
underproduction
understandingly
unexceptionable
unexceptionably
unexceptionally
unintelligently
unintentionally
unobjectionable
unparliamentary
unprecedentedly
unprepossessing
unpretentiously
unquestioningly
unrealistically
unrighteousness
unsophisticated
unsportsmanlike
unsubstantially
unsymmetrically
unwholesomeness
vasoconstrictor
ventriloquially
ventriloquistic
venturesomeness
vertiginousness
vicechamberlain
vicissitudinous
warmbloodedness
warmheartedness
warrantableness
weatherboarding
wellconditioned
wellintentioned
wrongheadedness
zoogeographical

---

bacteriological
carnivorousness
familiarisation
fantasticalness
fashionableness
gastroenteritis
halfheartedness
hardheartedness
lackadaisically
macroscopically
magnetoelectric
malacopterygian
maldistribution
malpractitioner
manicdepressive
manoeuvrability
margaritiferous
marketgardening
materialisation
nationalisation
palaeoanthropic
palaeobotanical
palaeogeography
palaeographical
palaeomagnetism
palaeontologist
pantheistically
paradoxicalness
parasympathetic
parenthetically
parliamentarian
parliamentarism
parthenogenesis
parthenogenetic
particularistic
radioautography
radiogoniometer
radiotelegraphy
rationalisation
sadomasochistic
sanctimoniously
saprophytically
vasoconstrictor
warmbloodedness
warmheartedness
warrantableness
abiogenetically
obstructiveness
acanthocephalan
acclimatisation
accommodatingly
accountableness
achondroplastic
acknowledgeable
acknowledgement
acquisitiveness
ecclesiasticism
ecclesiological
echinodermatous
eclaircissement
oceanographical
schistosomiasis
schoolmastering
adventurousness
ideographically
odoriferousness
aerodynamically
cerebrovascular
ceremoniousness
decalcification
decarbonisation
decarburisation
decolourisation
decontamination
defencelessness
deleteriousness
demagnetisation
demonstrability
demonstrational
demonstratively
demystification
denitrification
departmentalise
departmentalism
dermatoglyphics
descriptiveness
desensitisation
desexualisation
dessertspoonful
destructibility
destructiveness
determinateness
detribalisation
developmentally
devitrification
gentlemanliness
geochronologist
geomorphologist
heartbreakingly
heliotropically
Hellenistically
hendecasyllabic
hendecasyllable
hermaphroditism
hermeneutically
heterochromatic
heterodactyloos
heterogeneously
heterosexuality
levelheadedness
lexicographical
mechanistically
mellifluousness
Mephistophelean
Mephistophelian
meritoriousness
meroblastically
metamathematics
methamphetamine
nearsightedness

necessitousness
necromantically
neighbourliness
neurophysiology
neuropsychiatry
penetrativeness
perfunctoriness
peripatetically
peristaltically
perpendicularly
personalisation
personification
perspicaciously
perspicuousness
pessimistically
reafforestation
reapportionment
reconcilability
reconsideration
reconsolidation
reestablishment
regionalisation
remonstratively
remorselessness
repetitiousness
reproachfulness
reproducibility
resourcefulness
respectableness
resurrectionism
resurrectionist
retrogressively
retrospectively
selfabandonment
selfaffirmation
selfapprobation
selfcastigation
selfcentredness
selfcomplacency
selfconfidently
selfconsciously
selfconsequence
selfconsistency
selfconstituted
selfcontainment
selfdeprecating
selfdeprecatory
selfdestruction
selfdestructive
selfdetermining
selfdevelopment
selfdistrustful
selfexamination
selfexplanatory
selffertilising
selfforgetfully
selffulfillment
selfgratulation
selfhumiliation
selfimprovement
selfindulgently
selfopinionated
selfpollination
selfpropagating
selfrealisation
selfregistering
selfreplicating
selfreproachful
selfreprovingly
selfrighteously
selfsacrificing
selfsufficiency
semiconsciously
semicylindrical
semidocumentary
semiindependent
semitransparent
sententiousness
serviceableness
sesquicentenary
technologically
telegraphically
telephotography
temperamentally
tempestuousness
tendentiousness
ventriloquially
ventriloquistic
venturesomeness
vertiginousness
weatherboarding
wellconditioned
wellintentioned
affranchisement
efficaciousness
agriculturalist
chloramphenicol
Christadelphian
chromatographic
chronogrammatic
chronologically
churrigueresque
pharisaicalness
pharmacological
phenomenalistic
phenomenologist
phenylketonuria
philanthropical
philosophically
phonautographic
phosphorescence
phosphorylation
photochemically
photoconducting
photoconductive
photoelectronic
photojournalism
photojournalist
photolithograph
photomechanical
photomicrograph
photosensitiser
photosynthesise
phototelegraphy
phrenologically
physicochemical
physiographical
physiologically
physiotherapist
phytogeographic
rhombencephalon
rhynchocephalia
shootinggallery
shrinkresistant
therapeutically
therianthropism
thermochemistry
thoughtlessness
thunderstricken
airconditioning
bibliographical
bioastronautics
biogeochemistry
biogeographical
bioluminescence
cinematographer
cinematographic
circumferential
circumnavigator
circumscription
circumspectness
circumstantiate
circumvallation
civilianisation
differentiation
disadvantageous
disaffectedness
disagreeability
disappointingly
disarticulation
discommendation
disconcertingly
discontinuously
disenchantingly
disentanglement
disgracefulness
dishearteningly
disillusionment
disinflationary
disinterestedly
disorganisation
dispassionately
disproportional
disreputability
disrespectfully
dissatisfaction
dissatisfactory
distastefulness
distinctiveness
distinguishable
distinguishably
distrustfulness
dithyrambically
diversification
fissiparousness
historiographer
historiographic
kindheartedness
lightheadedness
lightmindedness
microanalytical
micromillimetre
microphotograph
microsporangium
microsporophyll
miniaturisation
misapprehension
misapprehensive
mischievousness
misconstruction
mistrustfulness
picturepostcard
picturesqueness
pithecanthropus
righthandedness
rightmindedness
ritualistically
significatively
singleheartedly
vicechamberlain
vicissitudinous
alphabetisation
blameworthiness
bloodguiltiness
electrification
electroanalysis
electrochemical
electrodynamics
electrokinetics
electromagnetic
electromyograph
electronegative
electrophoresis
electrophoretic
electropositive
flibbertigibbet
gleichschaltung
illimitableness
illustriousness
platitudinarian
pleasurableness
plenipotentiary
pleuropneumonia
plumbaginaceous
sleepingdraught
ultracentrifuge
ultramicroscope
ambidexterously
Americanisation
amphitheatrical
emancipationist
imaginativeness
immortalisation
immunochemistry
impenetrability
imperishability
impermeableness
imponderability
importunateness
impracticalness
imprescriptible
impressionistic
improvisatorial
omnidirectional
anaesthesiology
anaesthetically
anisotropically
ankylostomiasis
annihilationism
antepenultimate
anthropocentric
anthropogenesis
anthropological
anthropomorphic
anthropopathism
anthropophagous
anticlericalism
antimonarchical
antisabbatarian
antitrinitarian
antivivisection
enantiomorphism
enantiomorphous
encephalography
enfranchisement
entrepreneurial
inaccessibility
inadmissibility
inapplicability
inapprehensible
inappropriately
inattentiveness
incalculability
incommensurable
incommensurably
incommunicative
incomparability
incompatibility
incomprehension
incongruousness
inconsequential
inconsiderately
inconsideration
inconspicuously
incorrigibility
indefeasibility
indefensibility
indemnification
indeterminately
indetermination
indeterministic
indigestibility
indisciplinable
indissolubility
indistinctively
individualistic
indubitableness
ineffaceability
ineffectiveness
ineffectualness
inefficaciously
inexcusableness
inexpensiveness
inexplicability
infinitesimally
inflammableness

infrangibleness
infundibuliform
injudiciousness
innumerableness
inoffensiveness
inopportuneness
inquisitiveness
inquisitorially
inscrutableness
insensitiveness
inseparableness
insignificantly
instantaneously
instructiveness
instrumentalism
instrumentalist
instrumentality
instrumentation
insubordination
insurrectionary
insurrectionist
intellectualise
intellectualism
intellectualist
intellectuality
intelligibility
intemperateness
intensification
interchangeable
interchangeably
interclavicular
intercollegiate
interconnection
interdependence
interdependency
interdigitation
interfascicular
interferometric
interjectionary
internalisation
internationally
interpretership
interprovincial
interrogatively
interscholastic
interstratified
interventionism
interventionist
intolerableness
intractableness
introsusception
intussusception
intussusceptive
involuntariness
invulnerability
ontogenetically
pneumatological
unaccommodating
unceremoniously
unchallengeable
unchangeability
uncommunicative
uncomplainingly
uncomplimentary
uncomprehending
unconditionally
unconsciousness
undemonstrative
underemployment
underestimation
underprivileged
underproduction
understandingly
unexceptionable
unexceptionably
unexceptionally
unintelligently
unintentionally
unobjectionable
unparliamentary
unprecedentedly
unprepossessing
unpretentiously
unquestioningly
unrealistically
unrighteousness
unsophisticated
unsportsmanlike
unsubstantially
unsymmetrically
unwholesomeness
coconsciousness
coinstantaneous
coldbloodedness
coldheartedness
collenchymatous
commonplaceness
communalisation
communicability
communicatively
compartmentally
compassionately
compendiousness
competitiveness
complementarily
complementarity
complicatedness
compositionally
comprehensively
compressibility
computerisation
conceivableness
conceptualistic
condescendingly
confessionalism
confessionalist
confidentiality
configurational
congratulations
conjunctionally
connoisseurship
conscientiously
consecutiveness
consentaneously
consequentially
conservationist
considerateness
conspicuousness
constructionism
constructionist
consubstantiate
contemplatively
contemporaneity
contemporaneous
contemptibility
contentiousness
contractability
contractibility
contradictorily
contravallation
controversially
conventionalise
conventionalism
conventionalist
conventionality
conversationist
correspondingly
cosmopolitanism
counterapproach
counterattacker
counterirritant
countermovement
counterplotting
dolichocephalic
doublebarrelled
downheartedness
foresightedness
formularisation
fourdimensional
governorgeneral
hobbledehoyhood
homogeneousness
hospitalisation
logarithmically
logographically
longsightedness
monosymmetrical
morphologically
noncommissioned
noncontributory
nongovernmental
noninterference
nonintervention
nonprofessional
nonprofitmaking
nonsensicalness
northeastwardly
northwestwardly
notwithstanding
polycrystalline
polyunsaturated
postmillenarian
povertystricken
roentgenography
romanticisation
rontgenotherapy
socialistically
sociolinguistic
softheartedness
sophisticatedly
topographically
totalitarianism
zoogeographical
apocalyptically
approachability
appropriateness
approximatively
episcopalianism
epistemological
epitheliomatous
openheartedness
ophthalmologist
ophthalmoscopic
opinionatedness
opprobriousness
speakingtrumpet
spectroscopical
speculativeness
speechification
spermatogenesis
spermatogenetic
splendiferously
spontaneousness
equalitarianism
equiprobability
arboriculturist
archiepiscopate
architecturally
argumentatively
Aristotelianism
arterialisation
brachistochrone
brachycephalous
brachydactylous
broadmindedness
crossopterygian
cryptanalytical
cryptocommunist
crystallisation
crystallography
dramaturgically
fragmentariness
frenchification
grandiloquently
greatgrandchild
irrationalistic
irreparableness
irresistibility
irreversibility
irrevocableness
ornithorhynchus
orthopsychiatry
practicableness
precipitousness
predeterminable
prehistorically
prepositionally
prepossessingly
PreRaphaelitism
Presbyterianise
Presbyterianism
presentationism
presentationist
preservationist
prestidigitator
prestigiousness
pretentiousness
preternaturally
problematically
processionalist
procrastination
professionalise
professionalism
prognostication
prognosticative
progressiveness
prohibitiveness
properispomenon
proportionalist
proportionality
proportionately
prosenchymatous
protozoological
provocativeness
transcriptional
transferability
transfiguration
transfigurement
transgressively
transilluminate
transliteration
transmutability
transparentness
transplantation
transpositional
treacherousness
treasonableness
trigonometrical
trinitrotoluene
trisyllabically
troublesomeness
trueheartedness
trustworthiness
trypanosomiasis
wrongheadedness
pseudepigraphic
psychologically
psychometrician
psychopathology
psychophysicist
psychotherapist
atherosclerosis
atherosclerotic
atmospherically
atrabiliousness
etherealisation
ethnocentricity
stadtholdership
stampcollecting
standardisation
standoffishness
stereochemistry
stereoisomerism
stoicheiometric
straightforward
stratigraphical

stretcherbearer
authoritatively
autographically
autoradiography
euphemistically
Europeanisation
humanitarianism
jurisprudential
multitudinously
numismatologist
pulchritudinous
punctiliousness
purposelessness
pusillanimously
quadruplication
quarrelsomeness
quarterfinalist
quatercentenary
quickwittedness
quinquagenarian
quintuplication
rudimentariness
subordinateness
subpostmistress
substantialness
substantiveness
substitutionary
substratosphere
subterraneously
suburbanisation
sulphureousness
superabundantly
superconducting
superconductive
superficialness
superfluousness
superheterodyne
superimposition
superincumbence
superinducement
superintendence
superintendency
superlativeness
supernaturalise
supernaturalism
supernaturalist
supersaturation
superstitiously
superstructural
supplementarily
supplementation
supportableness
suppositionally
surreptitiously
susceptibleness
everlastingness
overconfidently
overdevelopment
exchangeability
excommunication
excommunicative
excommunicatory
exemplification
exhibitionistic
expeditiousness
experientialism
experientialist
experimentalise
experimentalism
experimentalist
experimentation
experimentative
expressionistic
extemporisation
exteriorisation
externalisation
extracurricular
extraillustrate
extraordinarily

dyslogistically
gynandromorphic
hydrodynamicist
hydropathically
hydrostatically
hypercatalectic
hypercritically
hyperthyroidism
pyroelectricity
pyrotechnically
sycophantically
syllabification
syllogistically
symmetricalness
sympathetically
symptomatically
synchronisation
systematisation
typographically
Czechoslovakian

---

acanthocephalan
anaesthesiology
anaesthetically
blameworthiness
brachistochrone
brachycephalous
brachydactylous
dramaturgically
emancipationist
enantiomorphism
enantiomorphous
fragmentariness
grandiloquently
heartbreakingly
imaginativeness
inaccessibility
inadmissibility
inapplicability
inapprehensible
inappropriately
inattentiveness
nearsightedness
pharisaicalness
pharmacological
platitudinarian
practicableness
quadruplication
quarrelsomeness
quarterfinalist
quatercentenary
reafforestation
reapportionment
stadtholdership
stampcollecting
standardisation
standoffishness
transcriptional
transferability
transfiguration
transfigurement
transgressively
transilluminate
transliteration
transmutability
transparentness
transplantation
transpositional
unaccommodating
weatherboarding
ambidexterously
arboriculturist
bibliographical
hobbledehoyhood
subordinateness
subpostmistress
substantialness
substantiveness
substitutionary

substratosphere
subterraneously
suburbanisation
acclimatisation
accommodatingly
accountableness
archiepiscopate
architecturally
bacteriological
coconsciousness
decalcification
decarbonisation
decarburisation
decolourisation
decontamination
ecclesiasticism
ecclesiological
encephalography
exchangeability
excommunication
excommunicative
excommunicatory
incalculability
incommensurable
incommensurably
incommunicative
incomparability
incompatibility
incomprehension
incongruousness
inconsequential
inconsiderately
inconsideration
inconspicuously
incorrigibility
lackadaisically
macroscopically
mechanistically
microanalytical
micromillimetre
microphotograph
microsporangium
microsporophyll
necessitousness
necromantically
picturepostcard
picturesqueness
reconcilability
reconsideration
reconsolidation
socialistically
sociolinguistic
sycophantically
technologically
unceremoniously
unchallengeable
unchangeability
uncommunicative
uncomplainingly
uncomplimentary
uncomprehending
unconditionally
unconsciousness
vicechamberlain
vicissitudinous
hydrodynamicist
hydropathically
hydrostatically
indefeasibility
indefensibility
indemnification
indeterminately
indetermination
indeterministic
indigestibility
indisciplinable
indissolubility
indistinctively
individualistic

indubitableness
radioautography
radiogoniometer
radiotelegraphy
rudimentariness
sadomasochistic
undemonstrative
underemployment
underestimation
underprivileged
underproduction
understandingly
Americanisation
Czechoslovakian
electrification
electroanalysis
electrochemical
electrodynamics
electrokinetics
electromagnetic
electromyograph
electronegative
electrophoresis
electrophoretic
electropositive
everlastingness
exemplification
frenchification
gleichschaltung
greatgrandchild
ideographically
ineffaceability
ineffectiveness
ineffectualness
inefficaciously
inexcusableness
inexpensiveness
inexplicability
oceanographical
openheartedness
overconfidently
overdevelopment
phenomenalistic
phenomenologist
phenylketonuria
pleasurableness
plenipotentiary
pleuropneumonia
pneumatological
precipitousness
predeterminable
prehistorically
prepositionally
prepossessingly
PreRaphaelitism
Presbyterianise
Presbyterianism
presentationism
presentationist
preservationist
prestidigitator
prestigiousness
pretentiousness
preternaturally
pseudepigraphic
reestablishment
roentgenography
sleepingdraught
speakingtrumpet
spectroscopical
speculativeness
speechification
spermatogenesis
spermatogenetic
stereochemistry
stereoisomerism
therapeutically
therianthropism
thermochemistry

treacherousness
treasonableness
unexceptionable
unexceptionably
unexceptionally
affranchisement
defencelessness
differentiation
efficaciousness
enfranchisement
infinitesimally
inflammableness
infrangibleness
infundibuliform
softheartedness
argumentatively
lightheadedness
lightmindedness
logarithmically
logographically
magnetoelectric
regionalisation
righthandedness
rightmindedness
significatively
achondroplastic
atherosclerosis
atherosclerotic
echinodermatous
etherealisation
ethnocentricity
exhibitionistic
ophthalmologist
ophthalmoscopic
schistosomiasis
schoolmastering
abiogenetically
anisotropically
Aristotelianism
coinstantaneous
episcopalianism
epistemological
epitheliomatous
flibbertigibbet
neighbourliness
opinionatedness
philanthropical
philosophically
quickwittedness
quinquagenarian
quintuplication
trigonometrical
trinitrotoluene
trisyllabically
unintelligently
unintentionally
injudiciousness
acknowledgeable
acknowledgement
ankylostomiasis
chloramphenicol
coldbloodedness
coldheartedness
collenchymatous
deleteriousness
dolichocephalic
eclaircissement
halfheartedness
heliotropically
Hellenistically
illimitableness
illustriousness
malacopterygian
maldistribution
malpractitioner
mellifluousness
multitudinously
palaeoanthropic
palaeobotanical
palaeogeography
palaeographical
palaeomagnetism
palaeontologist
polycrystalline
polyunsaturated
pulchritudinous
selfabandonment
selfaffirmation
selfapprobation
selfcastigation
selfcentredness
selfcomplacency
selfconfidently
selfconsciously
selfconsequence
selfconsistency
selfconstituted
selfcontainment
selfdeprecating
selfdeprecatory
selfdestruction
selfdestructive
selfdetermining
selfdevelopment
selfdistrustful
selfexamination
selfexplanatory
selffertilising
selfforgetfully
selffulfillment
selfgratulation
selfhumiliation
selfimprovement
selfindulgently
selfopinionated
selfpollination
selfpropagating
selfrealisation
selfregistering
selfreplicating
selfreproachful
selfreprovingly
selfrighteously
selfsacrificing
selfsufficiency
splendiferously
sulphureousness
syllabification
syllogistically
telegraphically
telephotography
wellconditioned
wellintentioned
atmospherically
commonplaceness
communalisation
communicability
communicatively
compartmentally
compassionately
compendiousness
competitiveness
complementarily
complementarity
complicatedness
compositionally
comprehensively
compressibility
computerisation
demagnetisation
demonstrability
demonstrational
demonstratively
demystification
familiarisation
homogeneousness
humanitarianism
immortalisation
immunochemistry
numismatologist
remonstratively
remorselessness
romanticisation
semiconsciously
semicylindrical
semidocumentary
semiindependent
semitransparent
symmetricalness
sympathetically
symptomatically
temperamentally
tempestuousness
annihilationism
cinematographer
cinematographic
conceivableness
conceptualistic
condescendingly
confessionalism
confessionalist
confidentiality
configurational
congratulations
conjunctionally
connoisseurship
conscientiously
consecutiveness
consentaneously
consequentially
conservationist
considerateness
conspicuousness
constructionism
constructionist
consubstantiate
contemplatively
contemporaneity
contemporaneous
contemptibility
contentiousness
contractability
contractibility
contradictorily
contravallation
controversially
conventionalise
conventionalism
conventionalist
conventionality
conversationist
denitrification
fantasticalness
gentlemanliness
gynandromorphic
hendecasyllabic
hendecasyllable
innumerableness
kindheartedness
longsightedness
manicdepressive
manoeuvrability
miniaturisation
monosymmetrical
noncommissioned
noncontributory
nongovernmental
noninterference
nonintervention
nonprofessional
nonprofitmaking
nonsensicalness
omnidirectional
ornithorhynchus
pantheistically
penetrativeness
punctiliousness
rontgenotherapy
sanctimoniously
sententiousness
singleheartedly
synchronisation
tendentiousness
ventriloquially
ventriloquistic
venturesomeness
apocalyptically
bioastronautics
biogeochemistry
biogeographical
bioluminescence
bloodguiltiness
broadmindedness
crossopterygian
geochronologist
geomorphologist
inoffensiveness
inopportuneness
odoriferousness
phonautographic
phosphorescence
phosphorylation
photochemically
photoconducting
photoconductive
photoelectronic
photojournalism
photojournalist
photolithograph
photomechanical
photomicrograph
photosensitiser
photosynthesise
phototelegraphy
problematically
processionalist
procrastination
professionalise
professionalism
prognostication
prognosticative
progressiveness
prohibitiveness
properispomenon
proportionalist
proportionality
proportionately
prosenchymatous
protozoological
provocativeness
rhombencephalon
shootinggallery
spontaneousness
stoicheiometric
thoughtlessness
troublesomeness
unobjectionable
wrongheadedness
zoogeographical
alphabetisation
amphitheatrical
approachability
appropriateness
approximatively
departmentalise
departmentalism
euphemistically
expeditiousness
experientialism
experientialist
experimentalise
experimentalism
experimentalist
experimentation
experimentative
expressionistic

hypercatalectic
hypercritically
hyperthyroidism
impenetrability
imperishability
impermeableness
imponderability
importunateness
impracticalness
imprescriptible
impressionistic
improvisatorial
Mephistophelean
Mephistophelian
opprobriousness
repetitiousness
reproachfulness
reproducibility
saprophytically
sophisticatedly
superabundantly
superconducting
superconductive
superficialness
superfluousness
superheterodyne
superimposition
superincumbence
superinducement
superintendence
superintendency
superlativeness
supernaturalise
supernaturalism
supernaturalist
supersaturation
superstitiously
superstructural
supplementarily
supplementation
supportableness
suppositionally
topographically
typographically
unparliamentary
unprecedentedly
unprepossessing
unpretentiously
acquisitiveness
inquisitiveness
inquisitorially
unquestioningly
aerodynamically
agriculturalist
airconditioning
atrabiliousness
carnivorousness
cerebrovascular
ceremoniousness
Christadelphian
chromatographic
chronogrammatic
chronologically
circumferential
circumnavigator
circumscription
circumspectness
circumstantiate
circumvallation
correspondingly
dermatoglyphics
Europeanisation
foresightedness
formularisation
hardheartedness
hermaphroditism
hermeneutically
irrationalistic
irreparableness
irresistibility
irreversibility
irrevocableness
jurisprudential
margaritiferous
marketgardening
meritoriousness
meroblastically
morphologically
northeastwardly
northwestwardly
paradoxicalness
parasympathetic
parenthetically
parliamentarian
parliamentarism
parthenogenesis
parthenogenetic
particularistic
perfunctoriness
peripatetically
peristaltically
perpendicularly
personalisation
personification
perspicaciously
perspicuousness
phrenologically
purposelessness
pyroelectricity
pyrotechnically
serviceableness
shrinkresistant
straightforward
stratigraphical
stretcherbearer
surreptitiously
unrealistically
unrighteousness
vertiginousness
warmbloodedness
warmheartedness
warrantableness
cosmopolitanism
descriptiveness
desensitisation
desexualisation
dessertspoonful
destructibility
destructiveness
disadvantageous
disaffectedness
disagreeability
disappointingly
disarticulation
discommendation
disconcertingly
discontinuously
disenchantingly
disentanglement
disgracefulness
dishearteningly
disillusionment
disinflationary
disinterestedly
disorganisation
dispassionately
disproportional
disreputability
disrespectfully
dissatisfaction
dissatisfactory
distastefulness
distinctiveness
distinguishable
distinguishably
distrustfulness
dyslogistically
fashionableness
fissiparousness
gastroenteritis
historiographer
historiographic
hospitalisation
inscrutableness
insensitiveness
inseparableness
insignificantly
instantaneously
instructiveness
instrumentalism
instrumentalist
instrumentality
instrumentation
insubordination
insurrectionary
insurrectionist
misapprehension
misapprehensive
mischievousness
misconstruction
mistrustfulness
obstructiveness
pessimistically
postmillenarian
pusillanimously
resourcefulness
respectableness
resurrectionism
resurrectionist
sesquicentenary
susceptibleness
systematisation
unsophisticated
unsportsmanlike
unsubstantially
unsymmetrically
vasoconstrictor
antepenultimate
anthropocentric
anthropogenesis
anthropological
anthropomorphic
anthropopathism
anthropophagous
anticlericalism
antimonarchical
antisabbatarian
antitrinitarian
antivivisection
arterialisation
authoritatively
autographically
autoradiography
determinateness
detribalisation
dithyrambically
entrepreneurial
extemporisation
exteriorisation
externalisation
extracurricular
extraillustrate
extraordinarily
heterochromatic
heterodactyloos
heterogeneously
heterosexuality
intellectualise
intellectualism
intellectualist
intellectuality
intelligibility
intemperateness
intensification
interchangeable
interchangeably
interclavicular
intercollegiate
interconnection
interdependence
interdependency
interdigitation
interfascicular
interferometric
interjectionary
internalisation
internationally
interpretership
interprovincial
interrogatively
interscholastic
interstratified
interventionism
interventionist
intolerableness
intractableness
introsusception
intussusception
intussusceptive
materialisation
metamathematics
methamphetamine
nationalisation
notwithstanding
ontogenetically
orthopsychiatry
pithecanthropus
rationalisation
retrogressively
retrospectively
ritualistically
totalitarianism
ultracentrifuge
ultramicroscope
churrigueresque
counterapproach
counterattacker
counterirritant
countermovement
counterplotting
doublebarrelled
equalitarianism
equiprobability
fourdimensional
neurophysiology
neuropsychiatry
plumbaginaceous
thunderstricken
trueheartedness
trustworthiness
adventurousness
civilianisation
developmentally
devitrification
diversification
governorgeneral
involuntariness
invulnerability
levelheadedness
povertystricken
downheartedness
unwholesomeness
lexicographical
cryptanalytical
cryptocommunist
crystallisation
crystallography
physicochemical
physiographical
physiologically
physiotherapist
phytogeographic
psychologically
psychometrician
psychopathology
psychophysicist

psychotherapist
rhynchocephalia
trypanosomiasis

---

atrabiliousness
bioastronautics
broadmindedness
decalcification
decarbonisation
decarburisation
demagnetisation
departmentalise
departmentalism
disadvantageous
disaffectedness
disagreeability
disappointingly
disarticulation
eclaircissement
equalitarianism
greatgrandchild
gynandromorphic
humanitarianism
incalculability
irrationalistic
logarithmically
malacopterygian
metamathematics
misapprehension
misapprehensive
oceanographical
palaeoanthropic
palaeobotanical
palaeogeography
palaeographical
palaeomagnetism
palaeontologist
paradoxicalness
parasympathetic
pleasurableness
romanticisation
speakingtrumpet
straightforward
stratigraphical
totalitarianism
treacherousness
treasonableness
unparliamentary
doublebarrelled
flibbertigibbet
hobbledehoyhood
problematically
unobjectionable
airconditioning
apocalyptically
brachistochrone
brachycephalous
brachydactylous
circumferential
circumnavigator
circumscription
circumspectness
circumstantiate
circumvallation
conceivableness
conceptualistic
Czechoslovakian
descriptiveness
discommendation
disconcertingly
discontinuously
electrification
electroanalysis
electrochemical
electrodynamics
electrokinetics
electromagnetic
electromyograph
electronegative
electrophoresis
electrophoretic
electropositive
geochronologist
inaccessibility
inscrutableness
mischievousness
misconstruction
noncommissioned
noncontributory
practicableness
precipitousness
processionalist
procrastination
psychologically
psychometrician
psychopathology
psychophysicist
psychotherapist
pulchritudinous
punctiliousness
quickwittedness
sanctimoniously
spectroscopical
speculativeness
susceptibleness
synchronisation
unaccommodating
coldbloodedness
coldheartedness
condescendingly
hardheartedness
hendecasyllabic
hendecasyllable
inadmissibility
kindheartedness
maldistribution
predeterminable
quadruplication
stadtholdership
tendentiousness
adventurousness
anaesthesiology
anaesthetically
antepenultimate
arterialisation
atherosclerosis
atherosclerotic
cerebrovascular
ceremoniousness
cinematographer
cinematographic
defencelessness
deleteriousness
desensitisation
desexualisation
determinateness
developmentally
disenchantingly
disentanglement
diversification
encephalography
etherealisation
expeditiousness
experientialism
experientialist
experimentalise
experimentalism
experimentalist
experimentation
experimentative
extemporisation
exteriorisation
externalisation
foresightedness
governorgeneral
heterochromatic
heterodactyloos
heterogeneously
heterosexuality
hypercatalectic
hypercritically
hyperthyroidism
impenetrability
imperishability
impermeableness
indefeasibility
indefensibility
indemnification
indeterminately
indetermination
indeterministic
insensitiveness
inseparableness
intellectualise
intellectualism
intellectualist
intellectuality
intelligibility
intemperateness
intensification
interchangeable
interchangeably
interclavicular
intercollegiate
interconnection
interdependence
interdependency
interdigitation
interfascicular
interferometric
interjectionary
internalisation
internationally
interpretership
interprovincial
interrogatively
interscholastic
interstratified
interventionism
interventionist
irreparableness
irresistibility
irreversibility
irrevocableness
levelheadedness
materialisation
necessitousness
parenthetically
penetrativeness
phrenologically
povertystricken
repetitiousness
sleepingdraught
speechification
splendiferously
stretcherbearer
superabundantly
superconducting
superconductive
superficialness
superfluousness
superheterodyne
superimposition
superincumbence
superinducement
superintendence
superintendency
superlativeness
supernaturalise
supernaturalism
supernaturalist
supersaturation
superstitiously
superstructural
telegraphically
telephotography
trueheartedness
unceremoniously
undemonstrative
underemployment
underestimation
underprivileged
underproduction
understandingly
unrealistically
vicechamberlain
confessionalism
confessionalist
confidentiality
configurational
differentiation
halfheartedness
ineffaceability
ineffectiveness
ineffectualness
inefficaciously
inoffensiveness
perfunctoriness
professionalise
professionalism
reafforestation
selfabandonment
selfaffirmation
selfapprobation
selfcastigation
selfcentredness
selfcomplacency
selfconfidently
selfconsciously
selfconsequence
selfconsistency
selfconstituted
selfcontainment
selfdeprecating
selfdeprecatory
selfdestruction
selfdestructive
selfdetermining
selfdevelopment
selfdistrustful
selfexamination
selfexplanatory
selffertilising
selfforgetfully
selffulfillment
selfgratulation
selfhumiliation
selfimprovement
selfindulgently
selfopinionated
selfpollination
selfpropagating
selfrealisation
selfregistering
selfreplicating
selfreproachful
selfreprovingly
selfrighteously
selfsacrificing
selfsufficiency
biogeochemistry
biogeographical
congratulations
disgracefulness
fragmentariness
imaginativeness
longsightedness
margaritiferous
neighbourliness
nongovernmental
prognostication
prognosticative
progressiveness
singleheartedly
trigonometrical
zoogeographical

alphabetisation
amphitheatrical
anthropocentric
anthropogenesis
anthropological
anthropomorphic
anthropopathism
anthropophagous
archiepiscopate
architecturally
authoritatively
dishearteningly
dithyrambically
euphemistically
exchangeability
fashionableness
lightheadedness
lightmindedness
mechanistically
Mephistophelean
Mephistophelian
methamphetamine
orthopsychiatry
pithecanthropus
prehistorically
prohibitiveness
righthandedness
rightmindedness
sophisticatedly
technologically
unchallengeable
unchangeability
unwholesomeness
agriculturalist
ambidexterously
annihilationism
anticlericalism
antimonarchical
antisabbatarian
antitrinitarian
antivivisection
Christadelphian
civilianisation
denitrification
devitrification
disillusionment
disinflationary
disinterestedly
dolichocephalic
echinodermatous
efficaciousness
equiprobability
exhibitionistic
familiarisation
gleichschaltung
heliotropically
illimitableness
indigestibility
indisciplinable
indissolubility
indistinctively
individualistic
infinitesimally
insignificantly
jurisprudential
lexicographical
manicdepressive
meritoriousness
miniaturisation
nationalisation
noninterference
nonintervention
numismatologist
omnidirectional
ornithorhynchus
peripatetically
peristaltically
pusillanimously
radioautography
radiogoniometer
radiotelegraphy
rationalisation
regionalisation
rudimentariness
schistosomiasis
semiconsciously
semicylindrical
semidocumentary
semiindependent
semitransparent
shrinkresistant
socialistically
sociolinguistic
stoicheiometric
unrighteousness
vicissitudinous
conjunctionally
lackadaisically
marketgardening
acclimatisation
bibliographical
bioluminescence
collenchymatous
dyslogistically
ecclesiasticism
ecclesiological
Hellenistically
inflammableness
mellifluousness
parliamentarian
parliamentarism
philanthropical
philosophically
syllabification
syllogistically
wellconditioned
wellintentioned
blameworthiness
commonplaceness
communalisation
communicability
communicatively
cosmopolitanism
dermatoglyphics
dramaturgically
exemplification
formularisation
geomorphologist
hermaphroditism
hermeneutically
plumbaginaceous
rhombencephalon
stampcollecting
symmetricalness
warmbloodedness
warmheartedness
acanthocephalan
acknowledgeable
acknowledgement
carnivorousness
coinstantaneous
connoisseurship
counterapproach
counterattacker
counterirritant
countermovement
counterplotting
downheartedness
emancipationist
enantiomorphism
enantiomorphous
ethnocentricity
frenchification
grandiloquently
magnetoelectric
openheartedness
opinionatedness
phenomenalistic
phenomenologist
phenylketonuria
phonautographic
plenipotentiary
quinquagenarian
quintuplication
rhynchocephalia
roentgenography
significatively
spontaneousness
standardisation
standoffishness
thunderstricken
transcriptional
transferability
transfiguration
transfigurement
transgressively
transilluminate
transliteration
transmutability
transparentness
transplantation
transpositional
trinitrotoluene
unintelligently
unintentionally
wrongheadedness
abiogenetically
accommodatingly
accountableness
achondroplastic
aerodynamically
arboriculturist
atmospherically
autographically
autoradiography
bloodguiltiness
chloramphenicol
chromatographic
chronogrammatic
chronologically
coconsciousness
decolourisation
decontamination
demonstrability
demonstrational
demonstratively
disorganisation
Europeanisation
excommunication
excommunicative
excommunicatory
homogeneousness
ideographically
immortalisation
imponderability
importunateness
incommensurable
incommensurably
incommunicative
incomparability
incompatibility
incomprehension
incongruousness
inconsequential
inconsiderately
inconsideration
inconspicuously
incorrigibility
intolerableness
involuntariness
logographically
manoeuvrability
meroblastically
monosymmetrical
ontogenetically
pyroelectricity
pyrotechnically
reconcilability
reconsideration
reconsolidation
remonstratively
remorselessness
resourcefulness
sadomasochistic
schoolmastering
shootinggallery
subordinateness
sycophantically
topographically
typographically
uncommunicative
uncomplainingly
uncomplimentary
uncomprehending
unconditionally
unconsciousness
unsophisticated
vasoconstrictor
compartmentally
compassionately
compendiousness
competitiveness
complementarily
complementarity
complicatedness
compositionally
comprehensively
compressibility
computerisation
cryptanalytical
cryptocommunist
dispassionately
disproportional
hospitalisation
inapplicability
inapprehensible
inappropriately
inopportuneness
malpractitioner
morphologically
nonprofessional
nonprofitmaking
perpendicularly
prepositionally
prepossessingly
properispomenon
proportionalist
proportionality
proportionately
purposelessness
reapportionment
respectableness
subpostmistress
sulphureousness
supplementarily
supplementation
supportableness
suppositionally
sympathetically
symptomatically
temperamentally
tempestuousness
trypanosomiasis
unsportsmanlike
sesquicentenary
affranchisement
Americanisation
approachability
appropriateness
approximatively
churrigueresque
correspondingly
detribalisation
disreputability
disrespectfully
enfranchisement

entrepreneurial
everlastingness
expressionistic
extracurricular
extraillustrate
extraordinarily
fourdimensional
heartbreakingly
hydrodynamicist
hydropathically
hydrostatically
impracticalness
imprescriptible
impressionistic
improvisatorial
infrangibleness
intractableness
introsusception
macroscopically
microanalytical
micromillimetre
microphotograph
microsporangium
microsporophyll
nearsightedness
necromantically
neurophysiology
neuropsychiatry
odoriferousness
opprobriousness
overconfidently
overdevelopment
pharisaicalness
pharmacological
PreRaphaelitism
quarrelsomeness
quarterfinalist
reproachfulness
reproducibility
retrogressively
retrospectively
saprophytically
spermatogenesis
spermatogenetic
stereochemistry
stereoisomerism
surreptitiously
therapeutically
therianthropism
thermochemistry
ultracentrifuge
ultramicroscope
unprecedentedly
unprepossessing
unpretentiously
warrantableness
anisotropically
Aristotelianism
conscientiously
consecutiveness
consentaneously
consequentially
conservationist
considerateness
conspicuousness
constructionism
constructionist
consubstantiate
crossopterygian
crystallisation
crystallography
dessertspoonful
dissatisfaction
dissatisfactory
episcopalianism
epistemological
fissiparousness
nonsensicalness
personalisation

personification
perspicaciously
perspicuousness
pessimistically
phosphorescence
phosphorylation
physicochemical
physiographical
physiologically
physiotherapist
Presbyterianise
Presbyterianism
presentationism
presentationist
preservationist
prestidigitator
prestigiousness
prosenchymatous
reestablishment
substantialness
substantiveness
substitutionary
substratosphere
trisyllabically
trustworthiness
bacteriological
contemplatively
contemporaneity
contemporaneous
contemptibility
contentiousness
contractability
contractibility
contradictorily
contravallation
controversially
destructibility
destructiveness
distastefulness
distinctiveness
distinguishable
distinguishably
distrustfulness
epitheliomatous
fantasticalness
gastroenteritis
gentlemanliness
historiographer
historiographic
inattentiveness
instantaneously
instructiveness
instrumentalism
instrumentalist
instrumentality
instrumentation
mistrustfulness
multitudinously
northeastwardly
northwestwardly
obstructiveness
ophthalmologist
ophthalmoscopic
pantheistically
parthenogenesis
parthenogenetic
particularistic
photochemically
photoconducting
photoconductive
photoelectronic
photojournalism
photojournalist
photolithograph
photomechanical
photomicrograph
photosensitiser
photosynthesise
phototelegraphy

phytogeographic
picturepostcard
picturesqueness
platitudinarian
postmillenarian
pretentiousness
preternaturally
protozoological
quatercentenary
rontgenotherapy
sententiousness
softheartedness
subterraneously
systematisation
ventriloquially
ventriloquistic
venturesomeness
vertiginousness
weatherboarding
acquisitiveness
argumentatively
illustriousness
immunochemistry
indubitableness
infundibuliform
injudiciousness
innumerableness
inquisitiveness
inquisitorially
insubordination
insurrectionary
insurrectionist
intussusception
intussusceptive
invulnerability
pleuropneumonia
pneumatological
pseudepigraphic
resurrectionism
resurrectionist
ritualistically
suburbanisation
thoughtlessness
troublesomeness
unquestioningly
unsubstantially
conventionalise
conventionalism
conventionalist
conventionality
conversationist
provocativeness
serviceableness
notwithstanding
inexcusableness
inexpensiveness
inexplicability
unexceptionable
unexceptionably
unexceptionally
ankylostomiasis
demystification
polycrystalline
polyunsaturated
unsymmetrically

---

affranchisement
alphabetisation
apocalyptically
compartmentally
compassionately
dermatoglyphics
dispassionately
dissatisfaction
dissatisfactory
distastefulness
dramaturgically
enfranchisement
exchangeability

extracurricular
extraillustrate
extraordinarily
fantasticalness
hermaphroditism
impracticalness
inflammableness
infrangibleness
instantaneously
intractableness
lackadaisically
margaritiferous
mechanistically
methamphetamine
miniaturisation
philanthropical
phonautographic
PreRaphaelitism
ritualistically
selfabandonment
selfaffirmation
selfapprobation
socialistically
syllabification
sympathetically
therapeutically
trypanosomiasis
ultracentrifuge
ultramicroscope
unchallengeable
unchangeability
unrealistically
warrantableness
atrabiliousness
cerebrovascular
coldbloodedness
exhibitionistic
flibbertigibbet
indubitableness
insubordination
meroblastically
plumbaginaceous
Presbyterianise
Presbyterianism
rhombencephalon
troublesomeness
unsubstantially
warmbloodedness
agriculturalist
anticlericalism
conscientiously
dolichocephalic
efficaciousness
emancipationist
episcopalianism
frenchification
gleichschaltung
inaccessibility
inexcusableness
lexicographical
malacopterygian
manicdepressive
overconfidently
polycrystalline
rhynchocephalia
selfcastigation
selfcentredness
selfcomplacency
selfconfidently
selfconsciously
selfconsequence
selfconsistency
selfconstituted
selfcontainment
semiconsciously
semicylindrical
speechification
stoicheiometric
treacherousness

unac**c**ommodating
unex**c**eptionable
unex**c**eptionably
unex**c**eptionally
vaso**c**onstrictor
vice**c**hamberlain
well**c**onditioned
aero**d**ynamically
ambi**d**exterously
bloo**d**guiltiness
broa**d**mindedness
disa**d**vantageous
expe**d**itiousness
four**d**imensional
gran**d**iloquently
inju**d**iciousness
omni**d**irectional
over**d**evelopment
para**d**oxicalness
pseu**d**epigraphic
self**d**eprecating
self**d**eprecatory
self**d**estruction
self**d**estructive
self**d**etermining
self**d**evelopment
self**d**istrustful
semi**d**ocumentary
stan**d**ardisation
stan**d**offishness
thun**d**erstricken
bact**e**riological
biog**e**ochemistry
biog**e**ographical
blam**e**worthiness
coll**e**nchymatous
comp**e**ndiousness
comp**e**titiveness
conc**e**ivableness
conc**e**ptualistic
cond**e**scendingly
conf**e**ssionalism
conf**e**ssionalist
cons**e**cutiveness
cons**e**ntaneously
cons**e**quentially
cons**e**rvationist
cont**e**mplatively
cont**e**mporaneity
cont**e**mporaneous
cont**e**mptibility
cont**e**ntiousness
conv**e**ntionalise
conv**e**ntionalism
conv**e**ntionalist
conv**e**ntionality
conv**e**rsationist
corr**e**spondingly
dess**e**rtspoonful
diff**e**rentiation
dish**e**arteningly
disr**e**putability
disr**e**spectfully
eccl**e**siasticism
eccl**e**siological
entr**e**preneurial
euph**e**mistically
expr**e**ssionistic
Hell**e**nistically
hend**e**casyllabic
hend**e**casyllable
herm**e**neutically
impr**e**scriptible
impr**e**ssionistic
magn**e**toelectric
mano**e**uvrability
mark**e**tgardening
nons**e**nsicalness
pala**e**oanthropic
pala**e**obotanical
pala**e**ogeography
pala**e**ographical
pala**e**omagnetism
pala**e**ontologist
perp**e**ndicularly
pith**e**canthropus
pred**e**terminable
pres**e**ntationism
pres**e**ntationist
pres**e**rvationist
pret**e**ntiousness
pret**e**rnaturally
proc**e**ssionalist
prof**e**ssionalise
prof**e**ssionalism
prop**e**rispomenon
pros**e**nchymatous
pyro**e**lectricity
quat**e**rcentenary
resp**e**ctableness
self**e**xamination
self**e**xplanatory
sent**e**ntiousness
ster**e**ochemistry
ster**e**oisomerism
subt**e**rraneously
surr**e**ptitiously
susc**e**ptibleness
symm**e**tricalness
syst**e**matisation
temp**e**ramentally
temp**e**stuousness
tend**e**ntiousness
unpr**e**cedentedly
unpr**e**possessing
unpr**e**tentiously
unqu**e**stioningly
zoog**e**ographical
disa**f**fectedness
inde**f**easibility
inde**f**ensibility
inef**f**aceability
inef**f**ectiveness
inef**f**ectualness
inef**f**icaciously
inof**f**ensiveness
reaf**f**orestation
self**f**ertilising
self**f**orgetfully
self**f**ulfillment
abio**g**enetically
auto**g**raphically
dema**g**netisation
disa**g**reeability
homo**g**eneousness
ideo**g**raphically
indi**g**estibility
insi**g**nificantly
logo**g**raphically
onto**g**enetically
ront**g**enotherapy
self**g**ratulation
tele**g**raphically
thou**g**htlessness
topo**g**raphically
typo**g**raphically
unri**g**hteousness
wron**g**headedness
anni**h**ilationism
brac**h**istochrone
brac**h**ycephalous
brac**h**ydactylous
cold**h**eartedness
Czec**h**oslovakian
down**h**eartedness
epit**h**eliomatous
geoc**h**ronologist
half**h**eartedness
hard**h**eartedness
kind**h**eartedness
misc**h**ievousness
morp**h**ologically
neig**h**bourliness
nort**h**eastwardly
nort**h**westwardly
open**h**eartedness
opht**h**almologist
opht**h**almoscopic
pant**h**eistically
part**h**enogenesis
part**h**enogenetic
psyc**h**ologically
psyc**h**ometrician
psyc**h**opathology
psyc**h**ophysicist
psyc**h**otherapist
pulc**h**ritudinous
self**h**umiliation
soft**h**eartedness
sulp**h**ureousness
sync**h**ronisation
true**h**eartedness
warm**h**eartedness
weat**h**erboarding
accl**i**matisation
acqu**i**sitiveness
Amer**i**canisation
amph**i**theatrical
arch**i**episcopate
arch**i**tecturally
bibl**i**ographical
carn**i**vorousness
conf**i**dentiality
conf**i**gurational
cons**i**derateness
detr**i**balisation
dist**i**nctiveness
dist**i**nguishable
dist**i**nguishably
ecla**i**rcissement
fash**i**onableness
fiss**i**parousness
hosp**i**talisation
imag**i**nativeness
inqu**i**sitiveness
inqu**i**sitorially
mald**i**stribution
mell**i**fluousness
Meph**i**stophelean
Meph**i**stophelian
mult**i**tudinously
notw**i**thstanding
odor**i**ferousness
opin**i**onatedness
parl**i**amentarian
parl**i**amentarism
part**i**cularistic
pess**i**mistically
phar**i**saicalness
phys**i**cochemical
phys**i**ographical
phys**i**ologically
phys**i**otherapist
plat**i**tudinarian
plen**i**potentiary
prec**i**pitousness
preh**i**storically
proh**i**bitiveness
self**i**mprovement
self**i**ndulgently
semi**i**ndependent
serv**i**ceableness
sign**i**ficatively
soph**i**sticatedly
stra**i**ghtforward
ther**i**anthropism
trin**i**trotoluene
vert**i**ginousness
well**i**ntentioned
unob**j**ectionable
quic**k**wittedness
spea**k**ingtrumpet
anky**l**ostomiasis
civi**l**ianisation
comp**l**ementarily
comp**l**ementarity
comp**l**icatedness
deca**l**cification
deco**l**ourisation
deve**l**opmentally
disi**l**lusionment
doub**l**ebarrelled
equa**l**itarianism
ever**l**astingness
fami**l**iarisation
gent**l**emanliness
hobb**l**edehoyhood
inca**l**culability
inte**l**lectualise
inte**l**lectualism
inte**l**lectualist
inte**l**lectuality
inte**l**ligibility
into**l**erableness
invo**l**untariness
invu**l**nerability
leve**l**headedness
prob**l**ematically
pusi**l**lanimously
sing**l**eheartedly
supp**l**ementarily
supp**l**ementation
tota**l**itarianism
acco**m**modatingly
anti**m**onarchical
argu**m**entatively
cere**m**oniousness
chro**m**atographic
cine**m**atographer
cine**m**atographic
exco**m**munication
exco**m**municative
exco**m**municatory
exte**m**porisation
frag**m**entariness
illi**m**itableness
inad**m**issibility
inco**m**mensurable
inco**m**mensurably
inco**m**municative
inco**m**parability
inco**m**patibility
inco**m**prehension
inde**m**nification
innu**m**erableness
inte**m**perateness
meta**m**athematics
phar**m**acological
pneu**m**atological
post**m**illenarian
rudi**m**entariness
sado**m**asochistic
sper**m**atogenesis
sper**m**atogenetic
ther**m**ochemistry
unco**m**municative
unco**m**plainingly
unco**m**plimentary
unco**m**prehending
unde**m**onstrative
unsy**m**metrically
acho**n**droplastic
adve**n**turousness
chro**n**ogrammatic
chro**n**ologically
coco**n**sciousness

decontamination
defencelessness
demonstrability
demonstrational
demonstratively
desensitisation
disenchantingly
disentanglement
disinflationary
disinterestedly
echinodermatous
gynandromorphic
humanitarianism
immunochemistry
impenetrability
imponderability
incongruousness
inconsequential
inconsiderately
inconsideration
inconspicuously
infinitesimally
infundibuliform
insensitiveness
intensification
noninterference
nonintervention
oceanographical
parenthetically
phrenologically
prognostication
prognosticative
reconcilability
reconsideration
reconsolidation
remonstratively
romanticisation
shrinkresistant
splendiferously
technologically
unconditionally
unconsciousness
acknowledgeable
acknowledgement
airconditioning
anisotropically
approachability
appropriateness
approximatively
authoritatively
commonplaceness
compositionally
connoisseurship
cosmopolitanism
discommendation
disconcertingly
discontinuously
dyslogistically
ethnocentricity
geomorphologist
heliotropically
historiographer
historiographic
hydrodynamicist
hydropathically
hydrostatically
improvisatorial
introsusception
macroscopically
microanalytical
micromillimetre
microphotograph
microsporangium
microsporophyll
misconstruction
nationalisation
necromantically
neurophysiology
neuropsychiatry
noncommissioned
noncontributory
nongovernmental
opprobriousness
orthopsychiatry
personalisation
personification
phenomenalistic
phenomenologist
philosophically
photochemically
photoconducting
photoconductive
photoelectronic
photojournalism
photojournalist
photolithograph
photomechanical
photomicrograph
photosensitiser
photosynthesise
phototelegraphy
phytogeographic
prepositionally
prepossessingly
proportionalist
proportionality
proportionately
protozoological
provocativeness
purposelessness
radioautography
radiogoniometer
radiotelegraphy
rationalisation
regionalisation
reproachfulness
reproducibility
retrogressively
retrospectively
saprophytically
schoolmastering
selfopinionated
sociolinguistic
subpostmistress
supportableness
suppositionally
syllogistically
trigonometrical
unsportsmanlike
unwholesomeness
antepenultimate
conspicuousness
disappointingly
encephalography
equiprobability
Europeanisation
exemplification
inapplicability
inapprehensible
inappropriately
inexpensiveness
inexplicability
inopportuneness
inseparableness
irreparableness
misapprehension
misapprehensive
peripatetically
perspicaciously
perspicuousness
phosphorescence
phosphorylation
reapportionment
selfpollination
selfpropagating
sleepingdraught
stampcollecting
sycophantically
telephotography
unsophisticated
quinquagenarian
anthropocentric
anthropogenesis
anthropological
anthropomorphic
anthropopathism
anthropophagous
arboriculturist
arterialisation
atherosclerosis
atherosclerotic
autoradiography
chloramphenicol
churrigueresque
comprehensively
compressibility
congratulations
contractability
contractibility
contradictorily
contravallation
controversially
decarbonisation
decarburisation
departmentalise
departmentalism
descriptiveness
destructibility
destructiveness
determinateness
disarticulation
disgracefulness
disorganisation
disproportional
distrustfulness
diversification
etherealisation
experientialism
experientialist
experimentalise
experimentalism
experimentalist
experimentation
experimentative
exteriorisation
externalisation
gastroenteritis
governorgeneral
heterochromatic
heterodactyloos
heterogeneously
heterosexuality
hypercatalectic
hypercritically
hyperthyroidism
immortalisation
imperishability
impermeableness
importunateness
incorrigibility
inscrutableness
instructiveness
instrumentalism
instrumentalist
instrumentality
instrumentation
insurrectionary
insurrectionist
interchangeable
interchangeably
interclavicular
intercollegiate
interconnection
interdependence
interdependency
interdigitation
interfascicular
interferometric
interjectionary
internalisation
internationally
interpretership
interprovincial
interrogatively
interscholastic
interstratified
interventionism
interventionist
logarithmically
malpractitioner
materialisation
mistrustfulness
nonprofessional
nonprofitmaking
obstructiveness
pleuropneumonia
povertystricken
procrastination
progressiveness
quadruplication
quarrelsomeness
remorselessness
resurrectionism
resurrectionist
selfrealisation
selfregistering
selfreplicating
selfreproachful
selfreprovingly
selfrighteously
subordinateness
suburbanisation
superabundantly
superconducting
superconductive
superficialness
superfluousness
superheterodyne
superimposition
superincumbence
superinducement
superintendence
superintendency
superlativeness
supernaturalise
supernaturalism
supernaturalist
supersaturation
superstitiously
superstructural
unceremoniously
underemployment
underestimation
underprivileged
underproduction
understandingly
unparliamentary
ventriloquially
ventriloquistic
anaesthesiology
anaesthetically
antisabbatarian
atmospherically
bioastronautics
Christadelphian
coinstantaneous
crossopterygian
demystification
foresightedness
illustriousness
indisciplinable
indissolubility
indistinctively
intussusception
intussusceptive
irresistibility

jurisprudential
longsightedness
monosymmetrical
nearsightedness
necessitousness
numismatologist
parasympathetic
peristaltically
pleasurableness
schistosomiasis
selfsacrificing
selfsufficiency
transcriptional
transferability
transfiguration
transfigurement
transgressively
transilluminate
transliteration
transmutability
transparentness
transplantation
transpositional
treasonableness
vicissitudinous
acanthocephalan
antitrinitarian
Aristotelianism
constructionism
constructionist
counterapproach
counterattacker
counterirritant
countermovement
counterplotting
cryptanalytical
cryptocommunist
crystallisation
crystallography
deleteriousness
denitrification
devitrification
electrification
electroanalysis
electrochemical
electrodynamics
electrokinetics
electromagnetic
electromyograph
electronegative
electrophoresis
electrophoretic
electropositive
enantiomorphism
enantiomorphous
epistemological
greatgrandchild
heartbreakingly
inattentiveness
indeterminately
indetermination
indeterministic
irrationalistic
lightheadedness
lightmindedness
meritoriousness
ornithorhynchus
penetrativeness
practicableness
prestidigitator
prestigiousness
punctiliousness
pyrotechnically
quarterfinalist
quintuplication
reestablishment
repetitiousness
righthandedness
rightmindedness
roentgenography
sanctimoniously
semitransparent
shootinggallery
spectroscopical
spontaneousness
stadtholdership
stratigraphical
stretcherbearer
substantialness
substantiveness
substitutionary
substratosphere
symptomatically
trustworthiness
unintelligently
unintentionally
accountableness
bioluminescence
circumferential
circumnavigator
circumscription
circumspectness
circumstantiate
circumvallation
communalisation
communicability
communicatively
computerisation
conjunctionally
consubstantiate
formularisation
perfunctoriness
picturepostcard
picturesqueness
polyunsaturated
resourcefulness
sesquicentenary
speculativeness
venturesomeness
antivivisection
individualistic
irreversibility
irrevocableness
desexualisation
dithyrambically
phenylketonuria
trisyllabically

---

antisabbatarian
approachability
autoradiography
chloramphenicol
chromatographic
cinematographer
cinematographic
congratulations
contractability
contractibility
contradictorily
contravallation
cryptanalytical
crystallisation
crystallography
disgracefulness
dishearteningly
efficaciousness
everlastingness
ineffaceability
inseparableness
irreparableness
malpractitioner
metamathematics
microanalytical
ophthalmologist
ophthalmoscopic
parliamentarian
parliamentarism
peripatetically
pharmacological
plumbaginaceous
pneumatological
procrastination
radioautography
reestablishment
reproachfulness
sadomasochistic
selfcastigation
selfsacrificing
spermatogenesis
spermatogenetic
spontaneousness
standardisation
substantialness
substantiveness
superabundantly
therianthropism
alphabetisation
consubstantiate
decarbonisation
decarburisation
detribalisation
heartbreakingly
neighbourliness
opprobriousness
prohibitiveness
selfabandonment
suburbanisation
syllabification
Americanisation
consecutiveness
decalcification
defencelessness
disenchantingly
ethnocentricity
extracurricular
hendecasyllabic
hendecasyllable
hypercatalectic
hypercritically
impracticalness
incalculability
indisciplinable
interchangeable
interchangeably
interclavicular
intercollegiate
interconnection
intractableness
particularistic
photochemically
photoconducting
photoconductive
physicochemical
pithecanthropus
provocativeness
reconcilability
respectableness
serviceableness
stampcollecting
stretcherbearer
superconducting
superconductive
transcriptional
ultracentrifuge
unprecedentedly
achondroplastic
confidentiality
considerateness
gynandromorphic
hydrodynamicist
imponderability
infundibuliform
interdependence
interdependency
interdigitation
lackadaisically
manicdepressive
reproducibility
splendiferously
subordinateness
unconditionally
abiogenetically
ambidexterously
antepenultimate
archiepiscopate
argumentatively
coldheartedness
complementarily
complementarity
comprehensively
compressibility
counterapproach
counterattacker
counterirritant
countermovement
counterplotting
deleteriousness
doublebarrelled
downheartedness
epistemological
epitheliomatous
etherealisation
Europeanisation
flibbertigibbet
fragmentariness
gentlemanliness
halfheartedness
hardheartedness
hobbledehoyhood
homogeneousness
impenetrability
inaccessibility
inattentiveness
indefeasibility
indefensibility
indeterminately
indetermination
indeterministic
indigestibility
ineffectiveness
ineffectualness
inexpensiveness
innumerableness
inoffensiveness
intolerableness
irreversibility
kindheartedness
northeastwardly
ontogenetically
openheartedness
overdevelopment
pantheistically
parthenogenesis
parthenogenetic
photoelectronic
problematically
progressiveness
pseudepigraphic
pyrotechnically
quarrelsomeness
quarterfinalist
rhombencephalon
rontgenotherapy
rudimentariness
selfcentredness
selfdeprecating
selfdeprecatory
selfdestruction
selfdestructive
selfdetermining
selfdevelopment
selffertilising
selfrealisation
selfregistering
selfreplicating
selfreproachful

selfreprovingly
singleheartedly
softheartedness
supplementarily
supplementation
thunderstricken
truehеartedness
unceremoniously
underemployment
underestimation
unexceptionable
unexceptionably
unexceptionally
unintelligently
unintentionally
unobjectionable
warmheartedness
weatherboarding
disaffectedness
disinflationary
interfascicular
interferometric
mellifluousness
odoriferousness
selfaffirmation
significatively
superficialness
superfluousness
transferability
transfiguration
transfigurement
bloodguiltiness
configurational
disorganisation
dyslogistically
greatgrandchild
incongruousness
phytogeographic
radiogoniometer
retrogressively
roentgenography
straightforward
syllogistically
transgressively
vertiginousness
acanthocephalan
dolichocephalic
encephalography
frenchification
gleichschaltung
levelheadedness
lightheadedness
ornithorhynchus
phosphorescence
phosphorylation
rhynchocephalia
righthandedness
speechification
stadtholdership
stoicheiometric
superheterodyne
sycophantically
telephotography
thoughtlessness
treacherousness
unrighteousness
unsophisticated
vicechamberlain
wrongheadedness
annihilationism
antivivisection
arboriculturist
arterialisation
atrabiliousness
brachistochrone
churrigueresque
civilianisation
complicatedness
conceivableness
connoisseurship
conscientiously
conspicuousness
descriptiveness
emancipationist
enantiomorphism
enantiomorphous
equalitarianism
exhibitionistic
expeditiousness
experientialism
experientialist
experimentalise
experimentalism
experimentalist
experimentation
experimentative
exteriorisation
extraillustrate
familiarisation
foresightedness
fourdimensional
grandiloquently
humanitarianism
illimitableness
imperishability
inadmissibility
individualistic
indubitableness
inefficaciously
infinitesimally
injudiciousness
irrationalistic
irresistibility
logarithmically
longsightedness
materialisation
mischievousness
nearsightedness
omnidirectional
perspicaciously
perspicuousness
postmillenarian
practicableness
prestidigitator
prestigiousness
punctiliousness
repetitiousness
sanctimoniously
selfdistrustful
selfrighteously
sesquicentenary
shootinggallery
sleepingdraught
speakingtrumpet
stratigraphical
substitutionary
superimposition
superincumbence
superinducement
superintendence
superintendency
totalitarianism
transilluminate
ventriloquially
ventriloquistic
interjectionary
photojournalism
photojournalist
shrinkresistant
anticlericalism
apocalyptically
coldbloodedness
disillusionment
exemplification
formularisation
inapplicability
inexplicability
intellectualise
intellectualism
intellectualist
intellectuality
intelligibility
meroblastically
phenylketonuria
photolithograph
pusillanimously
pyroelectricity
ritualistically
schoolmastering
socialistically
sociolinguistic
speculativeness
superlativeness
transliteration
trisyllabically
troublesomeness
unchallengeable
unparliamentary
unrealistically
unwholesomeness
warmbloodedness
acclimatisation
accommodatingly
bioluminescence
broadmindedness
circumferential
circumnavigator
circumscription
circumspectness
circumstantiate
circumvallation
contemplatively
contemporaneity
contemporaneous
contemptibility
determinateness
discommendation
euphemistically
excommunication
excommunicative
excommunicatory
impermeableness
incommensurable
incommensurably
incommunicative
inflammableness
lightmindedness
methamphetamine
micromillimetre
necromantically
noncommissioned
numismatologist
pessimistically
phenomenalistic
phenomenologist
photomechanical
photomicrograph
rightmindedness
selfimprovement
systematisation
transmutability
ultramicroscope
uncommunicative
unsymmetrically
accountableness
affranchisement
airconditioning
collenchymatous
commonplaceness
communalisation
communicability
communicatively
compendiousness
conjunctionally
consentaneously
contentiousness
conventionalise
conventionalism
conventionalist
conventionality
demagnetisation
disconcertingly
discontinuously
distinctiveness
distinguishable
distinguishably
enfranchisement
exchangeability
externalisation
governorgeneral
Hellenistically
hermeneutically
imaginativeness
indemnification
infrangibleness
insignificantly
instantaneously
internalisation
internationally
invulnerability
mechanistically
misconstruction
nationalisation
noncontributory
nonsensicalness
perfunctoriness
perpendicularly
personalisation
personification
philanthropical
polyunsaturated
presentationism
presentationist
pretentiousness
prosenchymatous
rationalisation
regionalisation
selfindulgently
semiindependent
sententiousness
supernaturalise
supernaturalism
supernaturalist
tendentiousness
trigonometrical
trypanosomiasis
unchangeability
warrantableness
wellintentioned
ankylostomiasis
anthropocentric
anthropogenesis
anthropological
anthropomorphic
anthropopathism
anthropophagous
antimonarchical
Aristotelianism
atherosclerosis
atherosclerotic
bibliographical
biogeochemistry
biogeographical
ceremoniousness
chronogrammatic
chronologically
controversially
crossopterygian
cryptocommunist
Czechoslovakian
decolourisation
developmentally
disproportional
echinodermatous
episcopalianism
extraordinarily

fashionableness
gastroenteritis
heterochromatic
heterodactyloos
heterogeneously
heterosexuality
immunochemistry
inopportuneness
insubordination
irrevocableness
lexicographical
malacopterygian
meritoriousness
morphologically
nonprofessional
nonprofitmaking
oceanographical
opinionatedness
overconfidently
palaeoanthropic
palaeobotanical
palaeogeography
palaeographical
palaeomagnetism
palaeontologist
paradoxicalness
phrenologically
physiographical
physiologically
physiotherapist
pleuropneumonia
prognostication
prognosticative
psychologically
psychometrician
psychopathology
psychophysicist
psychotherapist
reafforestation
reapportionment
selfcomplacency
selfconfidently
selfconsciously
selfconsequence
selfconsistency
selfconstituted
selfcontainment
selfforgetfully
selfpollination
semiconsciously
semidocumentary
standoffishness
stereochemistry
stereoisomerism
symptomatically
technologically
thermochemistry
treasonableness
unaccommodating
undemonstrative
vasoconstrictor
wellconditioned
zoogeographical
appropriateness
atmospherically
conceptualistic
cosmopolitanism
disappointingly
disreputability
entrepreneurial
extemporisation
fissiparousness
hermaphroditism
hydropathically
incomparability
incompatibility
incomprehension
intemperateness
interpretership
interprovincial
jurisprudential
microphotograph
misapprehension
misapprehensive
neurophysiology
neuropsychiatry
orthopsychiatry
plenipotentiary
precipitousness
PreRaphaelitism
saprophytically
selfapprobation
selfopinionated
surreptitiously
susceptibleness
therapeutically
transparentness
transplantation
transpositional
uncomplainingly
uncomplimentary
uncomprehending
underprivileged
underproduction
unprepossessing
consequentially
antitrinitarian
authoritatively
autographically
bacteriological
cerebrovascular
compartmentally
conservationist
constructionism
constructionist
conversationist
denitrification
dessertspoonful
devitrification
differentiation
disagreeability
dithyrambically
eclaircissement
electrification
electroanalysis
electrochemical
electrodynamics
electrokinetics
electromagnetic
electromyograph
electronegative
electrophoresis
electrophoretic
electropositive
equiprobability
geochronologist
geomorphologist
historiographer
historiographic
ideographically
inapprehensible
inappropriately
incorrigibility
insurrectionary
insurrectionist
interrogatively
logographically
margaritiferous
penetrativeness
picturepostcard
picturesqueness
polycrystalline
preservationist
preternaturally
properispomenon
proportionalist
proportionality
proportionately
pulchritudinous
quatercentenary
resourcefulness
resurrectionism
resurrectionist
selfgratulation
selfpropagating
semitransparent
spectroscopical
substratosphere
subterraneously
supportableness
synchronisation
telegraphically
temperamentally
topographically
typographically
unsportsmanlike
venturesomeness
acquisitiveness
coconsciousness
compassionately
compositionally
condescendingly
confessionalism
confessionalist
correspondingly
demonstrability
demonstrational
demonstratively
desensitisation
dispassionately
disrespectfully
distastefulness
diversification
ecclesiasticism
ecclesiological
expressionistic
fantasticalness
hydrostatically
imprescriptible
impressionistic
inconsequential
inconsiderately
inconsideration
inconspicuously
indissolubility
inquisitiveness
inquisitorially
insensitiveness
intensification
interscholastic
interstratified
introsusception
intussusception
intussusceptive
macroscopically
maldistribution
Mephistophelean
Mephistophelian
microsporangium
microsporophyll
necessitousness
pharisaicalness
philosophically
photosensitiser
photosynthesise
prehistorically
prepositionally
prepossessingly
processionalist
professionalise
professionalism
purposelessness
reconsideration
reconsolidation
remonstratively
remorselessness
retrospectively
sophisticatedly
subpostmistress
supersaturation
superstitiously
superstructural
suppositionally
tempestuousness
unconsciousness
understandingly
unquestioningly
unsubstantially
vicissitudinous
adventurousness
amphitheatrical
anaesthesiology
anaesthetically
anisotropically
architecturally
bioastronautics
Christadelphian
coinstantaneous
competitiveness
computerisation
decontamination
demystification
departmentalise
departmentalism
dermatoglyphics
disarticulation
disentanglement
disinterestedly
dissatisfaction
dissatisfactory
dramaturgically
heliotropically
hospitalisation
hyperthyroidism
illustriousness
immortalisation
importunateness
indistinctively
magnetoelectric
marketgardening
miniaturisation
multitudinously
noninterference
nonintervention
notwithstanding
parenthetically
peristaltically
phototelegraphy
platitudinarian
povertystricken
predeterminable
radiotelegraphy
romanticisation
schistosomiasis
symmetricalness
sympathetically
trinitrotoluene
unpretentiously
agriculturalist
desexualisation
destructibility
destructiveness
distrustfulness
inexcusableness
inscrutableness
instructiveness
instrumentalism
instrumentalist
instrumentality
instrumentation
involuntariness
manoeuvrability
mistrustfulness
obstructiveness
phonautographic
pleasurableness

quadruplication
quinquagenarian
quintuplication
selffulfillment
selfhumiliation
selfsufficiency
sulphureousness
carnivorousness
disadvantageous
improvisatorial
interventionism
interventionist
nongovernmental
acknowledgeable
acknowledgement
blameworthiness
northwestwardly
quickwittedness
trustworthiness
approximatively
selfexamination
selfexplanatory
aerodynamically
brachycephalous
brachydactylous
monosymmetrical
parasympathetic
Presbyterianise
Presbyterianism
semicylindrical
protozoological

---

acclimatisation
Americanisation
arterialisation
autographically
Christadelphian
civilianisation
coinstantaneous
coldheartedness
communalisation
decontamination
desexualisation
detribalisation
disadvantageous
disentanglement
disorganisation
dithyrambically
downheartedness
encephalography
etherealisation
Europeanisation
externalisation
familiarisation
fissiparousness
formularisation
halfheartedness
hardheartedness
hendecasyllabic
hendecasyllable
hospitalisation
hydropathically
hypercatalectic
ideographically
imaginativeness
immortalisation
incomparability
incompatibility
indefeasibility
interfascicular
internalisation
internationally
kindheartedness
lackadaisically
logographically
materialisation
meroblastically
nationalisation
necromantically
northeastwardly
numismatologist
openheartedness
palaeoanthropic
penetrativeness
peristaltically
personalisation
pharisaicalness
pithecanthropus
provocativeness
pusillanimously
quinquagenarian
rationalisation
regionalisation
righthandedness
selfabandonment
selfexamination
selfgratulation
selfrealisation
semitransparent
softheartedness
speculativeness
substratosphere
suburbanisation
superlativeness
supernaturalise
supernaturalism
supernaturalist
supersaturation
sycophantically
systematisation
telegraphically
temperamentally
topographically
transparentness
trueheartedness
typographically
vicechamberlain
warmheartedness
antisabbatarian
doublebarrelled
palaeobotanical
reestablishment
superabundantly
affranchisement
approachability
arboriculturist
biogeochemistry
brachycephalous
coconsciousness
collenchymatous
complicatedness
condescendingly
conjunctionally
conspicuousness
contractability
contractibility
cryptocommunist
destructibility
destructiveness
disconcertingly
disgracefulness
distinctiveness
eclaircissement
efficaciousness
enfranchisement
heterochromatic
immunochemistry
imprescriptible
ineffaceability
ineffectiveness
ineffectualness
inefficaciously
injudiciousness
instructiveness
interscholastic
irrevocableness
macroscopically
malpractitioner
obstructiveness
perfunctoriness
perspicaciously
perspicuousness
pharmacological
practicableness
prosenchymatous
pyrotechnically
quatercentenary
reproachfulness
resourcefulness
selfsacrificing
semidocumentary
sesquicentenary
stereochemistry
thermochemistry
unconsciousness
unobjectionable
airconditioning
autoradiography
brachydactylous
compendiousness
contradictorily
echinodermatous
heterodactyloos
hobbledehoyhood
individualistic
perpendicularly
prestidigitator
selfindulgently
semiindependent
alphabetisation
anticlericalism
architecturally
computerisation
confidentiality
conscientiously
considerateness
defencelessness
demagnetisation
differentiation
disaffectedness
disagreeability
disinterestedly
ethnocentricity
experientialism
experientialist
gastroenteritis
hermeneutically
impermeableness
imponderability
inapprehensible
incommensurable
incommensurably
inconsequential
insurrectionary
insurrectionist
intellectualise
intellectualism
intellectualist
intellectuality
intemperateness
interdependence
interdependency
interferometric
interjectionary
interventionism
interventionist
invulnerability
levelheadedness
lightheadedness
manicdepressive
mischievousness
nongovernmental
noninterference
nonintervention
northwestwardly
odoriferousness
phenomenalistic
phenomenologist
photomechanical
photosensitiser
phototelegraphy
phytogeographic
picturepostcard
picturesqueness
predeterminable
purposelessness
pyroelectricity
radiotelegraphy
remorselessness
resurrectionism
resurrectionist
roentgenography
serviceableness
stoicheiometric
superheterodyne
therapeutically
transferability
treacherousness
troublesomeness
ultracentrifuge
unprecedentedly
unpretentiously
unsymmetrically
unwholesomeness
venturesomeness
wrongheadedness
circumferential
nonprofessional
nonprofitmaking
selfaffirmation
selfsufficiency
standoffishness
bibliographical
biogeographical
chronogrammatic
churrigueresque
distinguishable
distinguishably
exchangeability
foresightedness
heterogeneously
infrangibleness
lexicographical
longsightedness
marketgardening
nearsightedness
oceanographical
palaeogeography
palaeographical
physiographical
plumbaginaceous
prestigiousness
selfregistering
selfrighteously
stratigraphical
unchangeability
zoogeographical
amphitheatrical
anaesthesiology
anaesthetically
atmospherically
comprehensively
disenchantingly
hermaphroditism
hyperthyroidism
interchangeable
interchangeably
microphotograph
neurophysiology
notwithstanding
parenthetically
photochemically
PreRaphaelitism
saprophytically
singleheartedly
straightforward

stretcherbearer
sympathetically
acquisitiveness
antitrinitarian
approximatively
authoritatively
bacteriological
bioluminescence
broadmindedness
communicability
communicatively
competitiveness
compositionally
decalcification
demystification
denitrification
desensitisation
determinateness
devitrification
disarticulation
dissatisfaction
dissatisfactory
diversification
dyslogistically
ecclesiasticism
ecclesiological
electrification
euphemistically
exemplification
frenchification
Hellenistically
historiographer
historiographic
improvisatorial
inapplicability
inconsiderately
inconsideration
incorrigibility
indemnification
indisciplinable
indistinctively
inexplicability
infundibuliform
inquisitiveness
inquisitorially
insensitiveness
insignificantly
intelligibility
intensification
interdigitation
lightmindedness
margaritiferous
mechanistically
micromillimetre
necessitousness
pantheistically
personification
pessimistically
photolithograph
photomicrograph
precipitousness
prepositionally
prohibitiveness
properispomenon
pulchritudinous
quickwittedness
reconcilability
reconsideration
rightmindedness
ritualistically
romanticisation
selfopinionated
significatively
socialistically
sociolinguistic
speechification
splendiferously
stereoisomerism
subordinateness
superficialness
suppositionally
syllabification
syllogistically
transfiguration
transfigurement
transliteration
ultramicroscope
unconditionally
unparliamentary
unrealistically
unsophisticated
vertiginousness
vicissitudinous
phenylketonuria
acknowledgeable
acknowledgement
agriculturalist
annihilationism
atrabiliousness
chronologically
crystallisation
crystallography
disinflationary
epitheliomatous
extraillustrate
grandiloquently
interclavicular
mellifluousness
morphologically
ophthalmologist
ophthalmoscopic
photoelectronic
phrenologically
physiologically
postmillenarian
psychologically
punctiliousness
quarrelsomeness
selffulfillment
selfpollination
semicylindrical
superfluousness
technologically
transilluminate
transplantation
trisyllabically
unchallengeable
uncomplainingly
uncomplimentary
unintelligently
ventriloquially
ventriloquistic
chloramphenicol
complementarily
complementarity
departmentalise
departmentalism
discommendation
epistemological
experimentalise
experimentalism
experimentalist
experimentation
experimentative
fourdimensional
gentlemanliness
inflammableness
instrumentalism
instrumentalist
instrumentality
instrumentation
monosymmetrical
noncommissioned
palaeomagnetism
parasympathetic
parliamentarian
parliamentarism
problematically
psychometrician
sanctimoniously
schoolmastering
selfcomplacency
selfhumiliation
superimposition
supplementarily
supplementation
symptomatically
unaccommodating
unceremoniously
underemployment
abiogenetically
aerodynamically
antepenultimate
antimonarchical
argumentatively
ceremoniousness
circumnavigator
cryptanalytical
fashionableness
fragmentariness
homogeneousness
inattentiveness
indefensibility
inexpensiveness
inoffensiveness
involuntariness
microanalytical
ontogenetically
opinionatedness
overconfidently
palaeontologist
parthenogenesis
parthenogenetic
preternaturally
rhombencephalon
rontgenotherapy
rudimentariness
selfcentredness
selfconfidently
selfconsciously
selfconsequence
selfconsistency
selfconstituted
selfcontainment
semiconsciously
shootinggallery
sleepingdraught
speakingtrumpet
spontaneousness
substantialness
substantiveness
superincumbence
superinducement
superintendence
superintendency
therianthropism
treasonableness
undemonstrative
unintentionally
vasoconstrictor
wellconditioned
acanthocephalan
accommodatingly
blameworthiness
carnivorousness
cerebrovascular
coldbloodedness
cosmopolitanism
decarbonisation
dermatoglyphics
disappointingly
dolichocephalic
electroanalysis
electrochemical
electrodynamics
electrokinetics
electromagnetic
electromyograph
electronegative
electrophoresis
electrophoretic
electropositive
enantiomorphism
enantiomorphous
equiprobability
extemporisation
exteriorisation
geochronologist
governorgeneral
inappropriately
indissolubility
intercollegiate
interconnection
interrogatively
irrationalistic
magnetoelectric
neighbourliness
ornithorhynchus
philosophically
phosphorescence
phosphorylation
photoconducting
photoconductive
photojournalism
photojournalist
physicochemical
plenipotentiary
protozoological
radiogoniometer
reconsolidation
rhynchocephalia
schistosomiasis
selfpropagating
spectroscopical
stadtholdership
stampcollecting
superconducting
superconductive
synchronisation
telephotography
transpositional
trigonometrical
trustworthiness
trypanosomiasis
unprepossessing
warmbloodedness
anthropocentric
anthropogenesis
anthropological
anthropomorphic
anthropopathism
anthropophagous
archiepiscopate
commonplaceness
contemplatively
contemporaneity
contemporaneous
contemptibility
correspondingly
crossopterygian
descriptiveness
developmentally
disproportional
disrespectfully
emancipationist
episcopalianism
geomorphologist
inconspicuously
malacopterygian
methamphetamine
microsporangium
microsporophyll
pleuropneumonia
pseudepigraphic
psychopathology
psychophysicist

quadruplication
quintuplication
retrospectively
selfapprobation
selfdeprecating
selfdeprecatory
selfexplanatory
selfimprovement
selfreplicating
selfreproachful
selfreprovingly
unexceptionable
unexceptionably
unexceptionally
achondroplastic
anisotropically
appropriateness
bioastronautics
counterapproach
counterattacker
counterirritant
countermovement
counterplotting
deleteriousness
dishearteningly
entrepreneurial
extraordinarily
flibbertigibbet
greatgrandchild
gynandromorphic
heartbreakingly
heliotropically
hypercritically
illustriousness
incomprehension
incongruousness
indeterminately
indetermination
indeterministic
innumerableness
inopportuneness
inseparableness
insubordination
interpretership
interprovincial
intolerableness
irreparableness
irreversibility
jurisprudential
meritoriousness
misapprehension
misapprehensive
omnidirectional
opprobriousness
pleasurableness
quarterfinalist
reafforestation
reapportionment
retrogressively
selffertilising
selfforgetfully
shrinkresistant
standardisation
subterraneously
sulphureousness
symmetricalness
thunderstricken
transcriptional
transgressively
trinitrotoluene
uncomprehending
underprivileged
underproduction
weatherboarding
ankylostomiasis
atherosclerosis
atherosclerotic
brachistochrone
circumscription

circumspectness
circumstantiate
compassionately
compressibility
confessionalism
confessionalist
connoisseurship
consubstantiate
conversationist
Czechoslovakian
dispassionately
distrustfulness
everlastingness
expressionistic
gleichschaltung
heterosexuality
imperishability
impressionistic
inaccessibility
inadmissibility
indigestibility
inexcusableness
irresistibility
misconstruction
mistrustfulness
neuropsychiatry
nonsensicalness
orthopsychiatry
polyunsaturated
prepossessingly
processionalist
procrastination
professionalise
professionalism
prognostication
prognosticative
progressiveness
sadomasochistic
selfcastigation
selfdestruction
selfdestructive
selfdistrustful
underestimation
accountableness
Aristotelianism
chromatographic
cinematographer
cinematographic
compartmentally
conceptualistic
congratulations
consentaneously
contentiousness
conventionalise
conventionalism
conventionalist
conventionality
demonstrability
demonstrational
demonstratively
dessertspoonful
discontinuously
distastefulness
equalitarianism
exhibitionistic
expeditiousness
fantasticalness
humanitarianism
hydrostatically
illimitableness
impenetrability
impracticalness
indubitableness
infinitesimally
inscrutableness
instantaneously
interstratified
intractableness
logarithmically

maldistribution
Mephistophelean
Mephistophelian
metamathematics
noncontributory
peripatetically
philanthropical
phonautographic
physiotherapist
pneumatological
prehistorically
Presbyterianise
Presbyterianism
presentationism
presentationist
pretentiousness
proportionalist
proportionality
proportionately
psychotherapist
remonstratively
repetitiousness
respectableness
selfdetermining
sententiousness
sophisticatedly
spermatogenesis
spermatogenetic
subpostmistress
substitutionary
superstitiously
superstructural
supportableness
surreptitiously
susceptibleness
tempestuousness
tendentiousness
thoughtlessness
totalitarianism
understandingly
unquestioningly
unrighteousness
unsportsmanlike
unsubstantially
warrantableness
wellintentioned
adventurousness
bloodguiltiness
configurational
consecutiveness
consequentially
constructionism
constructionist
decarburisation
decolourisation
disillusionment
disreputability
dramaturgically
excommunication
excommunicative
excommunicatory
extracurricular
importunateness
incalculability
incommunicative
introsusception
intussusception
intussusceptive
miniaturisation
multitudinously
particularistic
platitudinarian
radioautography
reproducibility
transmutability
uncommunicative
antivivisection
circumvallation
conceivableness

conservationist
contravallation
controversially
manoeuvrability
overdevelopment
preservationist
selfdevelopment
ambidexterously
paradoxicalness
apocalyptically
hydrodynamicist
photosynthesise
polycrystalline
povertystricken

---

accountableness
aerodynamically
annihilationism
antimonarchical
brachydactylous
circumnavigator
circumvallation
complicatedness
conceivableness
consentaneously
conservationist
contravallation
conversationist
counterapproach
counterattacker
cryptanalytical
disenchantingly
disinflationary
doublebarrelled
ecclesiasticism
electroanalysis
emancipationist
episcopalianism
equalitarianism
fashionableness
gentlemanliness
greatgrandchild
heterodactyloos
humanitarianism
hydrostatically
illimitableness
impermeableness
indubitableness
inefficaciously
inexcusableness
inflammableness
innumerableness
inscrutableness
inseparableness
instantaneously
interchangeable
interchangeably
interclavicular
intolerableness
intractableness
irreparableness
irrevocableness
levelheadedness
lightheadedness
marketgardening
microanalytical
opinionatedness
palaeomagnetism
perspicaciously
pleasurableness
polyunsaturated
practicableness
PreRaphaelitism
presentationism
presentationist
preservationist
preternaturally
problematically
psychopathology

respectableness
schoolmastering
serviceableness
subterraneously
supportableness
symptomatically
totalitarianism
transplantation
treasonableness
trisyllabically
uncomplainingly
understandingly
unparliamentary
unsubstantially
warrantableness
wrongheadedness
antisabbatarian
equiprobability
infundibuliform
weatherboarding
acanthocephalan
architecturally
atherosclerosis
atherosclerotic
circumscription
communicability
communicatively
constructionism
constructionist
disaffectedness
disarticulation
dolichocephalic
electrochemical
gleichschaltung
inapplicability
inexplicability
insurrectionary
insurrectionist
intellectualise
intellectualism
intellectualist
intellectuality
interjectionary
photomechanical
photomicrograph
physicochemical
pyroelectricity
reproducibility
resurrectionism
resurrectionist
rhombencephalon
rhynchocephalia
romanticisation
significatively
superficialness
superincumbence
ultramicroscope
accommodatingly
Christadelphian
electrodynamics
extraordinarily
inconsiderately
inconsideration
insubordination
multitudinously
platitudinarian
reconsideration
standardisation
superinducement
unprecedentedly
wellconditioned
abiogenetically
acknowledgeable
acknowledgement
amphitheatrical
anaesthesiology
anaesthetically
Aristotelianism
atmospherically
brachycephalous
circumferential
complementarily
complementarity
comprehensively
condescendingly
consequentially
controversially
departmentalise
departmentalism
disagreeability
discommendation
disconcertingly
disgracefulness
disrespectfully
distastefulness
echinodermatous
entrepreneurial
exchangeability
experimentalise
experimentalism
experimentalist
experimentation
experimentative
fourdimensional
heartbreakingly
heterogeneously
heterosexuality
hobbledehoyhood
homogeneousness
incomprehension
ineffaceability
infinitesimally
instrumentalism
instrumentalist
instrumentality
instrumentation
interpretership
magnetoelectric
misapprehension
misapprehensive
nonprofessional
omnidirectional
ontogenetically
overdevelopment
palaeogeography
parenthetically
parliamentarian
parliamentarism
peripatetically
phenylketonuria
photochemically
photoelectronic
prepossessingly
Presbyterianise
Presbyterianism
psychometrician
quatercentenary
reafforestation
resourcefulness
retrogressively
retrospectively
selfdetermining
selfdevelopment
semiindependent
sesquicentenary
shrinkresistant
singleheartedly
spontaneousness
stretcherbearer
sulphureousness
supplementarily
supplementation
sympathetically
transgressively
unchallengeable
unchangeability
uncomprehending
unrighteousness
wellintentioned
decalcification
demystification
denitrification
devitrification
diversification
electrification
exemplification
frenchification
indemnification
insignificantly
intensification
overconfidently
personification
quarterfinalist
selfconfidently
selffulfillment
selfsufficiency
speechification
splendiferously
standoffishness
syllabification
dermatoglyphics
incorrigibility
intelligibility
interdigitation
interrogatively
quinquagenarian
selfforgetfully
shootinggallery
sleepingdraught
speakingtrumpet
transfiguration
transfigurement
affranchisement
approachability
biogeochemistry
collenchymatous
enfranchisement
foresightedness
geomorphologist
heterochromatic
immunochemistry
imperishability
inapprehensible
interscholastic
logarithmically
longsightedness
metamathematics
methamphetamine
nearsightedness
philanthropical
physiotherapist
prosenchymatous
psychophysicist
psychotherapist
pyrotechnically
reproachfulness
selfrighteously
stereochemistry
thermochemistry
airconditioning
antivivisection
appropriateness
archiepiscopate
atrabiliousness
autoradiography
bloodguiltiness
ceremoniousness
coconsciousness
compassionately
compendiousness
confessionalism
confessionalist
contentiousness
contradictorily
conventionalise
conventionalism
conventionalist
conventionality
counterirritant
deleteriousness
disappointingly
discontinuously
dispassionately
eclaircissement
efficaciousness
epitheliomatous
exhibitionistic
expeditiousness
expressionistic
fantasticalness
hypercritically
illustriousness
impracticalness
impressionistic
inconspicuously
infrangibleness
injudiciousness
lackadaisically
meritoriousness
noncommissioned
nonprofitmaking
nonsensicalness
opprobriousness
paradoxicalness
perpendicularly
pharisaicalness
plumbaginaceous
prestidigitator
prestigiousness
pretentiousness
processionalist
professionalise
professionalism
proportionalist
proportionality
proportionately
pseudepigraphic
punctiliousness
repetitiousness
selfaffirmation
selfhumiliation
selfregistering
semicylindrical
sententiousness
sophisticatedly
stoicheiometric
superstitiously
surreptitiously
susceptibleness
symmetricalness
tendentiousness
transcriptional
uncomplimentary
unconsciousness
underprivileged
unquestioningly
electrokinetics
arterialisation
commonplaceness
communalisation
contemplatively
cosmopolitanism
crystallisation
crystallography
Czechoslovakian
defencelessness
desexualisation
detribalisation
encephalography
etherealisation
externalisation
extraillustrate
hospitalisation
immortalisation
incalculability
indissolubility

interco**l**legiate
interna**l**isation
materia**l**isation
micromi**l**limetre
nationa**l**isation
particu**l**aristic
perista**l**tically
persona**l**isation
photote**l**egraphy
postmil**l**enarian
purpose**l**essness
quadrup**l**ication
quintup**l**ication
radiote**l**egraphy
rationa**l**isation
reconci**l**ability
reconso**l**idation
reestab**l**ishment
regiona**l**isation
remorse**l**essness
selfexp**l**anatory
selfpol**l**ination
selfrea**l**isation
selfrep**l**icating
stadtho**l**dership
stampco**l**lecting
thought**l**essness
transil**l**uminate
unintel**l**igently
approxi**m**atively
compart**m**entally
counter**m**ovement
deconta**m**ination
develop**m**entally
dithyra**m**bically
electro**m**agnetic
electro**m**yograph
enantio**m**orphism
enantio**m**orphous
indeter**m**inately
indeter**m**ination
indeter**m**inistic
monosym**m**etrical
ophthal**m**ologist
ophthal**m**oscopic
selfexa**m**ination
subpost**m**istress
tempera**m**entally
trigono**m**etrical
unaccom**m**odating
vicecha**m**berlain
America**n**isation
antitri**n**itarian
biolumi**n**escence
broadmi**n**dedness
civilia**n**isation
coinsta**n**taneous
confide**n**tiality
conscie**n**tiously
decarbo**n**isation
determi**n**ateness
differe**n**tiation
disadva**n**tageous
disenta**n**glement
disorga**n**isation
electro**n**egative
ethnoce**n**tricity
Europea**n**isation
excommu**n**ication
excommu**n**icative
excommu**n**icatory
experie**n**tialism
experie**n**tialist
gastroe**n**teritis
geochro**n**ologist
hydrody**n**amicist
importu**n**ateness
incomme**n**surable
incomme**n**surably
incommu**n**icative
indisti**n**ctively
interco**n**nection
interve**n**tionism
interve**n**tionist
irratio**n**alistic
lightmi**n**dedness
necroma**n**tically
palaeoa**n**thropic
phenome**n**alistic
phenome**n**ologist
photoco**n**ducting
photoco**n**ductive
photose**n**sitiser
photosy**n**thesise
pitheca**n**thropus
pleurop**n**eumonia
pusilla**n**imously
radiogo**n**iometer
rightha**n**dedness
rightmi**n**dedness
roentge**n**ography
selfaba**n**donment
selfopi**n**ionated
semitra**n**sparent
socioli**n**guistic
subordi**n**ateness
suburba**n**isation
superco**n**ducting
superco**n**ductive
sycopha**n**tically
synchro**n**isation
ultrace**n**trifuge
uncommu**n**icative
unprete**n**tiously
vertigi**n**ousness
achondr**o**plastic
anisotr**o**pically
anthrop**o**centric
anthrop**o**genesis
anthrop**o**logical
anthrop**o**morphic
anthrop**o**pathism
anthrop**o**phagous
bacteri**o**logical
bioastr**o**nautics
chromat**o**graphic
chronol**o**gically
cinemat**o**grapher
cinemat**o**graphic
coldblo**o**dedness
contemp**o**raneity
contemp**o**raneous
corresp**o**ndingly
cryptoc**o**mmunist
disprop**o**rtional
ecclesi**o**logical
epistem**o**logical
grandil**o**quently
gynandr**o**morphic
heliotr**o**pically
histori**o**grapher
histori**o**graphic
interpr**o**vincial
macrosc**o**pically
Mephist**o**phelean
Mephist**o**phelian
microph**o**tograph
microsp**o**rangium
microsp**o**rophyll
morphol**o**gically
palaeob**o**tanical
parthen**o**genesis
parthen**o**genetic
pharmac**o**logical
phonaut**o**graphic
phrenol**o**gically
physiol**o**gically
phytoge**o**graphic
pneumat**o**logical
prehist**o**rically
protozo**o**logical
psychol**o**gically
rontgen**o**therapy
sadomas**o**chistic
sanctim**o**niously
spermat**o**genesis
spermat**o**genetic
technol**o**gically
trinitr**o**toluene
uncerem**o**niously
underpr**o**duction
ventril**o**quially
ventril**o**quistic
warmblo**o**dedness
apocaly**p**tically
autogra**p**hically
chloram**p**henicol
circums**p**ectness
counter**p**lotting
electro**p**horesis
electro**p**horetic
electro**p**ositive
ideogra**p**hically
inappro**p**riately
indisci**p**linable
interde**p**endence
interde**p**endency
logogra**p**hically
manicde**p**ressive
parasym**p**athetic
philoso**p**hically
picture**p**ostcard
selfcom**p**lacency
selfpro**p**agating
superim**p**osition
telegra**p**hically
topogra**p**hically
typogra**p**hically
underem**p**loyment
inconse**q**uential
adventu**r**ousness
anticle**r**icalism
bibliog**r**aphical
biogeog**r**aphical
blamewo**r**thiness
carnivo**r**ousness
chronog**r**ammatic
coldhea**r**tedness
compute**r**isation
configu**r**ational
conside**r**ateness
decarbu**r**isation
decolou**r**isation
demonst**r**ability
demonst**r**ational
demonst**r**atively
disinte**r**estedly
downhea**r**tedness
dramatu**r**gically
extempo**r**isation
exterio**r**isation
extracu**r**ricular
familia**r**isation
fissipa**r**ousness
formula**r**isation
governo**r**general
halfhea**r**tedness
hardhea**r**tedness
hermaph**r**oditism
impenet**r**ability
imponde**r**ability
impresc**r**iptible
incompa**r**ability
intempe**r**ateness
interfe**r**ometric
interst**r**atified
invulne**r**ability
kindhea**r**tedness
lexicog**r**aphical
maldist**r**ibution
manoeuv**r**ability
miniatu**r**isation
noncont**r**ibutory
nongove**r**nmental
noninte**r**ference
noninte**r**vention
oceanog**r**aphical
odorife**r**ousness
openhea**r**tedness
ornitho**r**hynchus
palaeog**r**aphical
phospho**r**escence
phospho**r**ylation
physiog**r**aphical
predete**r**minable
remonst**r**atively
selfapp**r**obation
selfdep**r**ecating
selfdep**r**ecatory
selfimp**r**ovement
selfrep**r**oachful
selfrep**r**ovingly
selfsac**r**ificing
softhea**r**tedness
stratig**r**aphical
superst**r**uctural
transfe**r**ability
transpa**r**entness
treache**r**ousness
truehea**r**tedness
trustwo**r**thiness
warmhea**r**tedness
zoogeog**r**aphical
compres**s**ibility
connois**s**eurship
dessert**s**poonful
disillu**s**ionment
dissati**s**faction
dissati**s**factory
dyslogi**s**tically
euphemi**s**tically
Helleni**s**tically
hendeca**s**yllabic
hendeca**s**yllable
improvi**s**atorial
inacces**s**ibility
inadmis**s**ibility
indefea**s**ibility
indefen**s**ibility
inexpen**s**iveness
inoffen**s**iveness
interfa**s**cicular
introsu**s**ception
intussu**s**ception
intussu**s**ceptive
irrever**s**ibility
mechani**s**tically
merobla**s**tically
northea**s**twardly
northwe**s**twardly
notwith**s**tanding
panthei**s**tically
pessimi**s**tically
picture**s**queness
polycry**s**talline
poverty**s**tricken
progres**s**iveness
properi**s**pomenon
quarrel**s**omeness
rituali**s**tically
schisto**s**omiasis
selfcon**s**ciously
selfcon**s**equence
selfcon**s**istency
selfcon**s**tituted
semicon**s**ciously

socialistically
spectroscopical
stereoisomerism
syllogistically
thunderstricken
transpositional
troublesomeness
trypanosomiasis
undemonstrative
unprepossessing
unrealistically
unsophisticated
unsportsmanlike
unwholesomeness
vasoconstrictor
venturesomeness
acclimatisation
acquisitiveness
agriculturalist
alphabetisation
ambidexterously
ankylostomiasis
argumentatively
authoritatively
brachistochrone
circumstantiate
competitiveness
compositionally
conjunctionally
consecutiveness
consubstantiate
contemptibility
contractability
contractibility
crossopterygian
demagnetisation
descriptiveness
desensitisation
destructibility
destructiveness
dishearteningly
disreputability
distinctiveness
distrustfulness
everlastingness
flibbertigibbet
fragmentariness
hydropathically
hypercatalectic
imaginativeness
inattentiveness
incompatibility
indigestibility
ineffectiveness
ineffectualness
inopportuneness
inquisitiveness
inquisitorially
insensitiveness
instructiveness
internationally
involuntariness
irresistibility
malacopterygian
malpractitioner
margaritiferous
misconstruction
mistrustfulness
necessitousness
numismatologist
obstructiveness
palaeontologist
penetrativeness
perfunctoriness
photolithograph
plenipotentiary
precipitousness
prepositionally
procrastination

prognostication
prognosticative
prohibitiveness
provocativeness
pulchritudinous
quickwittedness
radioautography
reapportionment
rudimentariness
selfcastigation
selfcentredness
selfcontainment
selfdestruction
selfdestructive
selfdistrustful
selffertilising
selfgratulation
speculativeness
straightforward
substantialness
substantiveness
substratosphere
superheterodyne
superintendence
superintendency
superlativeness
supernaturalise
supernaturalism
supernaturalist
supersaturation
suppositionally
systematisation
telephotography
therianthropism
transliteration
transmutability
unconditionally
underestimation
unexceptionable
unexceptionably
unexceptionally
unintentionally
unobjectionable
unsymmetrically
vicissitudinous
antepenultimate
arboriculturist
churrigueresque
conceptualistic
congratulations
conspicuousness
distinguishable
distinguishably
hermeneutically
incongruousness
individualistic
jurisprudential
mellifluousness
neighbourliness
perspicuousness
photojournalism
photojournalist
selfindulgently
semidocumentary
substitutionary
superabundantly
superfluousness
tempestuousness
therapeutically
cerebrovascular
mischievousness
hyperthyroidism
neurophysiology
neuropsychiatry
orthopsychiatry
saprophytically

---

accommodatingly
amphitheatrical

antisabbatarian
approachability
appropriateness
approximatively
argumentatively
authoritatively
bibliographical
biogeographical
cerebrovascular
chronogrammatic
circumstantiate
commonplaceness
communicability
communicatively
conceptualistic
configurational
considerateness
consubstantiate
contemplatively
contractability
demonstrability
demonstrational
demonstratively
determinateness
disagreeability
disreputability
electromagnetic
equiprobability
exchangeability
fragmentariness
heartbreakingly
hydrodynamicist
hypercatalectic
impenetrability
imperishability
imponderability
importunateness
improvisatorial
inapplicability
incalculability
incomparability
individualistic
ineffaceability
inexplicability
intemperateness
interrogatively
interstratified
involuntariness
invulnerability
irrationalistic
lexicographical
manoeuvrability
oceanographical
palaeographical
parasympathetic
particularistic
phenomenalistic
physiographical
reconcilability
remonstratively
rudimentariness
selfcontainment
selfexplanatory
selfpropagating
significatively
singleheartedly
stratigraphical
subordinateness
transferability
transmutability
unchangeability
zoogeographical
accountableness
conceivableness
dithyrambically
fashionableness
illimitableness
impermeableness
indubitableness

inexcusableness
inflammableness
infrangibleness
innumerableness
inscrutableness
inseparableness
intolerableness
intractableness
irreparableness
irrevocableness
pleasurableness
practicableness
respectableness
serviceableness
supportableness
susceptibleness
treasonableness
trisyllabically
vicechamberlain
warrantableness
anthropocentric
brachydactylous
contradictorily
disrespectfully
fantasticalness
heterodactyloos
impracticalness
inconspicuously
indistinctively
inefficaciously
interfascicular
introsusception
intussusception
intussusceptive
neuropsychiatry
nonsensicalness
omnidirectional
orthopsychiatry
paradoxicalness
perpendicularly
perspicaciously
pharisaicalness
photoelectronic
retrospectively
sadomasochistic
selfconsciously
semiconsciously
sophisticatedly
spectroscopical
symmetricalness
acknowledgeable
acknowledgement
broadmindedness
coldbloodedness
jurisprudential
levelheadedness
lightheadedness
lightmindedness
photoconducting
photoconductive
righthandedness
rightmindedness
selfabandonment
sleepingdraught
stadtholdership
superconducting
superconductive
underproduction
warmbloodedness
wrongheadedness
acanthocephalan
ambidexterously
biogeochemistry
bioluminescence
Christadelphian
churrigueresque
circumspectness
compartmentally
connoisseurship

crossopterygian
defencelessness
developmentally
dishearteningly
disinterestedly
dolichocephalic
electronegative
immunochemistry
inapprehensible
inconsiderately
inconsideration
interdependence
interdependency
malacopterygian
metamathematics
methamphetamine
monosymmetrical
phosphorescence
phototelegraphy
physiotherapist
plenipotentiary
pleuropneumonia
postmillenarian
PreRaphaelitism
psychotherapist
purposelessness
quinquagenarian
radiotelegraphy
reconsideration
remorselessness
rhombencephalon
rhynchocephalia
selfconsequence
selfdeprecating
selfdeprecatory
selfforgetfully
splendiferously
stereochemistry
superheterodyne
superintendence
superintendency
temperamentally
thermochemistry
thoughtlessness
transliteration
transparentness
trigonometrical
unprecedentedly
disgracefulness
dissatisfaction
dissatisfactory
distastefulness
distrustfulness
mistrustfulness
noninterference
reproachfulness
resourcefulness
straightforward
anthropogenesis
chromatographic
chronologically
cinematographer
cinematographic
disentanglement
dramaturgically
governorgeneral
historiographer
historiographic
morphologically
palaeomagnetism
parthenogenesis
parthenogenetic
phonautographic
phrenologically
physiologically
phytogeographic
prestidigitator
pseudepigraphic
psychologically
shootinggallery
sociolinguistic
spermatogenesis
spermatogenetic
technologically
autographically
chloramphenicol
electrochemical
electrophoresis
electrophoretic
gleichschaltung
hobbledehoyhood
hydropathically
ideographically
incomprehension
logographically
misapprehension
misapprehensive
ornithorhynchus
philosophically
photolithograph
photomechanical
physicochemical
telegraphically
therianthropism
topographically
typographically
uncomprehending
acclimatisation
acquisitiveness
affranchisement
alphabetisation
Americanisation
anticlericalism
antitrinitarian
arterialisation
civilianisation
communalisation
competitiveness
compositionally
compressibility
computerisation
conjunctionally
consecutiveness
contemptibility
contractibility
cosmopolitanism
crystallisation
decalcification
decarbonisation
decarburisation
decolourisation
decontamination
demagnetisation
demystification
denitrification
descriptiveness
desensitisation
desexualisation
destructibility
destructiveness
detribalisation
devitrification
disillusionment
disorganisation
distinctiveness
distinguishable
distinguishably
diversification
electrification
electrokinetics
enfranchisement
etherealisation
Europeanisation
everlastingness
excommunication
excommunicative
excommunicatory
exemplification
extemporisation
exteriorisation
externalisation
extraordinarily
familiarisation
flibbertigibbet
formularisation
frenchification
hospitalisation
imaginativeness
immortalisation
imprescriptible
inaccessibility
inadmissibility
inattentiveness
incommunicative
incompatibility
incorrigibility
indefeasibility
indefensibility
indemnification
indeterminately
indetermination
indeterministic
indigestibility
ineffectiveness
inexpensiveness
inoffensiveness
inquisitiveness
insensitiveness
insignificantly
instructiveness
insubordination
intelligibility
intensification
interdigitation
internalisation
internationally
irresistibility
irreversibility
maldistribution
malpractitioner
margaritiferous
materialisation
miniaturisation
multitudinously
nationalisation
noncontributory
obstructiveness
overconfidently
penetrativeness
personalisation
personification
platitudinarian
prepositionally
procrastination
prognostication
prognosticative
progressiveness
prohibitiveness
provocativeness
pusillanimously
quadruplication
quarterfinalist
quintuplication
radiogoniometer
rationalisation
reapportionment
reconsolidation
reestablishment
regionalisation
reproducibility
romanticisation
selfcastigation
selfconfidently
selfconsistency
selfexamination
selffertilising
selffulfillment
selfopinionated
selfpollination
selfrealisation
selfreplicating
selfsacrificing
selfsufficiency
speculativeness
speechification
standardisation
standoffishness
subpostmistress
substantialness
substantiveness
suburbanisation
superficialness
superlativeness
suppositionally
syllabification
synchronisation
systematisation
transpositional
uncommunicative
uncomplainingly
unconditionally
underestimation
unexceptionable
unexceptionably
unexceptionally
unintelligently
unintentionally
unobjectionable
wellconditioned
antepenultimate
anthropological
arboriculturist
Aristotelianism
atherosclerosis
atherosclerotic
bacteriological
bloodguiltiness
circumvallation
congratulations
contravallation
counterplotting
cryptanalytical
dermatoglyphics
ecclesiological
episcopalianism
epistemological
indisciplinable
intercollegiate
magnetoelectric
microanalytical
micromillimetre
overdevelopment
pharmacological
pneumatological
protozoological
selfcomplacency
selfdevelopment
selfhumiliation
selfindulgently
stampcollecting
underemployment
aerodynamically
anthropomorphic
cryptocommunist
gynandromorphic
logarithmically
photochemically
predeterminable
semidocumentary
uncomplimentary
unparliamentary
unsportsmanlike
bioastronautics
complementarily
complementarity
comprehensively

condescendingly
consentaneously
consequentially
correspondingly
departmentalise
departmentalism
disappointingly
discommendation
discontinuously
disenchantingly
electroanalysis
entrepreneurial
experimentalise
experimentalism
experimentalist
experimentation
experimentative
fourdimensional
gentlemanliness
greatgrandchild
heterogeneously
instantaneously
instrumentalism
instrumentalist
instrumentality
instrumentation
interchangeable
interchangeably
interconnection
nongovernmental
parliamentarian
parliamentarism
plumbaginaceous
pyrotechnically
quatercentenary
sanctimoniously
semicylindrical
sesquicentenary
subterraneously
superabundantly
supplementarily
supplementation
transplantation
unceremoniously
unchallengeable
understandingly
unsubstantially
wellintentioned
adventurousness
ankylostomiasis
atrabiliousness
autoradiography
brachistochrone
carnivorousness
ceremoniousness
coconsciousness
compassionately
compendiousness
confessionalism
confessionalist
conspicuousness
contentiousness
conventionalise
conventionalism
conventionalist
conventionality
countermovement
crystallography
Czechoslovakian
deleteriousness
dispassionately
efficaciousness
electropositive
enantiomorphism
enantiomorphous
encephalography
epitheliomatous
exhibitionistic
expeditiousness
expressionistic
fissiparousness
geochronologist
geomorphologist
hermaphroditism
homogeneousness
illustriousness
impressionistic
incongruousness
injudiciousness
inquisitorially
interferometric
interscholastic
mellifluousness
meritoriousness
mischievousness
necessitousness
numismatologist
odoriferousness
ophthalmologist
ophthalmoscopic
opprobriousness
palaeogeography
palaeontologist
perfunctoriness
perspicuousness
phenomenologist
picturepostcard
precipitousness
prestigiousness
pretentiousness
processionalist
professionalise
professionalism
proportionalist
proportionality
proportionately
punctiliousness
quarrelsomeness
radioautography
repetitiousness
roentgenography
schistosomiasis
selfapprobation
selfimprovement
selfreproachful
selfreprovingly
sententiousness
spontaneousness
stereoisomerism
stoicheiometric
substratosphere
sulphureousness
superfluousness
superimposition
telephotography
tempestuousness
tendentiousness
treacherousness
troublesomeness
trypanosomiasis
unaccommodating
unconsciousness
unquestioningly
unrighteousness
unwholesomeness
venturesomeness
vertiginousness
weatherboarding
achondroplastic
anisotropically
anthropopathism
anthropophagous
brachycephalous
counterapproach
dessertspoonful
heliotropically
macroscopically
Mephistophelean
Mephistophelian
properispomenon
semiindependent
transcriptional
grandiloquently
picturesqueness
ventriloquially
ventriloquistic
antimonarchical
atmospherically
circumferential
circumscription
contemporaneity
contemporaneous
controversially
counterirritant
disconcertingly
disproportional
doublebarrelled
echinodermatous
equalitarianism
extracurricular
heterochromatic
humanitarianism
hyperthyroidism
inappropriately
manicdepressive
marketgardening
microsporangium
microsporophyll
misconstruction
neighbourliness
philanthropical
photojournalism
photojournalist
photomicrograph
prehistorically
Presbyterianise
Presbyterianism
selfaffirmation
selfcentredness
selfdestruction
selfdestructive
selfdetermining
selfdistrustful
stretcherbearer
totalitarianism
ultramicroscope
unsymmetrically
anaesthesiology
antivivisection
archiepiscopate
ecclesiasticism
eclaircissement
incommensurable
incommensurably
infinitesimally
lackadaisically
neurophysiology
noncommissioned
nonprofessional
photosensitiser
prepossessingly
reafforestation
retrogressively
schoolmastering
selfregistering
semitransparent
shrinkresistant
transgressively
unprepossessing
abiogenetically
airconditioning
anaesthetically
annihilationism
apocalyptically
architecturally
blameworthiness
coinstantaneous
coldheartedness
complicatedness
confidentiality
conscientiously
conservationist
constructionism
constructionist
conversationist
counterattacker
differentiation
disadvantageous
disaffectedness
disinflationary
downheartedness
dyslogistically
emancipationist
ethnocentricity
euphemistically
experientialism
experientialist
foresightedness
gastroenteritis
halfheartedness
hardheartedness
Hellenistically
hermeneutically
hydrostatically
hypercritically
insurrectionary
insurrectionist
intellectualise
intellectualism
intellectualist
intellectuality
interjectionary
interpretership
interventionism
interventionist
kindheartedness
longsightedness
mechanistically
meroblastically
microphotograph
nearsightedness
necromantically
nonprofitmaking
northeastwardly
northwestwardly
notwithstanding
ontogenetically
openheartedness
opinionatedness
palaeoanthropic
palaeobotanical
pantheistically
parenthetically
peripatetically
peristaltically
pessimistically
phenylketonuria
photosynthesise
pithecanthropus
polycrystalline
polyunsaturated
povertystricken
presentationism
presentationist
preservationist
preternaturally
problematically
psychometrician
psychopathology
pyroelectricity
quickwittedness
resurrectionism
resurrectionist
ritualistically
rontgenotherapy
saprophytically

selfconstituted
selfrighteously
socialistically
softheartedness
speakingtrumpet
substitutionary
superstitiously
surreptitiously
sycophantically
syllogistically
sympathetically
symptomatically
therapeutically
thunderstricken
trinitrotoluene
trueheartedness
trustworthiness
ultracentrifuge
undemonstrative
unpretentiously
unrealistically
unsophisticated
vasoconstrictor
warmheartedness
agriculturalist
disarticulation
extraillustrate
inconsequential
indissolubility
ineffectualness
infundibuliform
inopportuneness
pulchritudinous
selfgratulation
superincumbence
superinducement
supernaturalise
supernaturalism
supernaturalist
supersaturation
superstructural
transfiguration
transfigurement
transilluminate
vicissitudinous
circumnavigator
interclavicular
interprovincial
nonintervention
underprivileged
heterosexuality
collenchymatous
electrodynamics
electromyograph
hendecasyllabic
hendecasyllable
phosphorylation
prosenchymatous
psychophysicist

---

anthropopathism
bioastronautics
coinstantaneous
congratulations
contemporaneity
contemporaneous
disadvantageous
dissatisfaction
dissatisfactory
electroanalysis
fantasticalness
gleichschaltung
impracticalness
ineffectualness
microsporangium
nonsensicalness
notwithstanding
palaeobotanical
paradoxicalness

pharisaicalness
photomechanical
plumbaginaceous
polycrystalline
selfcomplacency
selfreproachful
shootinggallery
sophisticatedly
substantialness
superficialness
symmetricalness
unsportsmanlike
weatherboarding
approachability
communicability
compressibility
contemptibility
contractability
contractibility
demonstrability
destructibility
disagreeability
disreputability
equiprobability
exchangeability
impenetrability
imperishability
imponderability
inaccessibility
inadmissibility
inapplicability
incalculability
incomparability
incompatibility
incorrigibility
indefeasibility
indefensibility
indigestibility
indissolubility
ineffaceability
inexplicability
intelligibility
invulnerability
irresistibility
irreversibility
maldistribution
manoeuvrability
noncontributory
reconcilability
reproducibility
selfapprobation
stretcherbearer
transferability
transmutability
unchangeability
anticlericalism
antimonarchical
archiepiscopate
brachistochrone
circumspectness
commonplaceness
decalcification
demystification
denitrification
devitrification
diversification
electrification
excommunication
excommunicative
excommunicatory
exemplification
frenchification
incommunicative
indemnification
insignificantly
intensification
personification
prognostication
prognosticative

quadruplication
quintuplication
selfdeprecating
selfdeprecatory
selfreplicating
selfsufficiency
speechification
superinducement
superstructural
syllabification
uncommunicative
condescendingly
correspondingly
discommendation
greatgrandchild
hermaphroditism
marketgardening
overconfidently
pulchritudinous
reconsolidation
selfconfidently
semicylindrical
superabundantly
unaccommodating
understandingly
vicissitudinous
anthropocentric
anthropogenesis
antivivisection
atherosclerosis
atherosclerotic
broadmindedness
chloramphenicol
circumferential
coldbloodedness
coldheartedness
complicatedness
consentaneously
disaffectedness
downheartedness
electrochemical
entrepreneurial
foresightedness
gastroenteritis
governorgeneral
halfheartedness
hardheartedness
heterogeneously
incomprehension
inconsequential
instantaneously
intercollegiate
interconnection
interpretership
introsusception
intussusception
intussusceptive
jurisprudential
kindheartedness
levelheadedness
lightheadedness
lightmindedness
longsightedness
magnetoelectric
manicdepressive
misapprehension
misapprehensive
nearsightedness
noninterference
nonintervention
openheartedness
opinionatedness
parthenogenesis
parthenogenetic
physicochemical
quickwittedness
righthandedness
rightmindedness
selfcentredness

selfrighteously
semidocumentary
semiindependent
softheartedness
spermatogenesis
spermatogenetic
stadtholdership
stampcollecting
subterraneously
trueheartedness
uncomplimentary
uncomprehending
unparliamentary
unprepossessing
vicechamberlain
warmbloodedness
warmheartedness
wrongheadedness
margaritiferous
selfsacrificing
acknowledgeable
acknowledgement
autoradiography
crystallography
electromagnetic
electronegative
encephalography
flibbertigibbet
interchangeable
interchangeably
palaeogeography
phototelegraphy
radioautography
radiotelegraphy
roentgenography
selfcastigation
selfindulgently
selfpropagating
telephotography
unchallengeable
unintelligently
anthropophagous
blameworthiness
brachycephalous
Mephistophelean
Mephistophelian
neuropsychiatry
orthopsychiatry
palaeoanthropic
photosynthesise
pithecanthropus
psychopathology
rontgenotherapy
sadomasochistic
trustworthiness
abiogenetically
aerodynamically
airconditioning
anaesthesiology
anaesthetically
anisotropically
annihilationism
apocalyptically
Aristotelianism
atmospherically
autographically
chronologically
circumnavigator
circumscription
confidentiality
conscientiously
conservationist
constructionism
constructionist
conversationist
differentiation
disinflationary
dithyrambically
dramaturgically

dyslogistically
emancipationist
episcopalianism
equalitarianism
euphemistically
experientialism
experientialist
extracurricular
heliotropically
Hellenistically
hermeneutically
humanitarianism
hydropathically
hydrostatically
hypercritically
ideographically
inappropriately
indisciplinable
inefficaciously
infinitesimally
insurrectionary
insurrectionist
interclavicular
interfascicular
interjectionary
interprovincial
interventionism
interventionist
lackadaisically
logarithmically
logographically
macroscopically
mechanistically
meroblastically
micromillimetre
morphologically
necromantically
neurophysiology
ontogenetically
pantheistically
parenthetically
peripatetically
peristaltically
perspicaciously
pessimistically
philosophically
photochemically
photosensitiser
phrenologically
physiologically
predeterminable
prehistorically
Presbyterianise
Presbyterianism
presentationism
presentationist
preservationist
prestidigitator
problematically
psychologically
pyrotechnically
resurrectionism
resurrectionist
ritualistically
sanctimoniously
saprophytically
selfconsciously
selfconstituted
selfcontainment
selfhumiliation
semiconsciously
shrinkresistant
socialistically
substitutionary
superstitiously
surreptitiously
sycophantically
syllogistically
sympathetically
symptomatically
technologically
telegraphically
therapeutically
topographically
totalitarianism
trisyllabically
typographically
unceremoniously
underprivileged
unpretentiously
unrealistically
unsophisticated
unsymmetrically
heartbreakingly
accountableness
achondroplastic
Christadelphian
circumvallation
conceivableness
conceptualistic
contravallation
disarticulation
disentanglement
fashionableness
gentlemanliness
geochronologist
geomorphologist
hendecasyllabic
hendecasyllable
hypercatalectic
illimitableness
impermeableness
individualistic
indubitableness
inexcusableness
inflammableness
infrangibleness
infundibuliform
innumerableness
inscrutableness
inseparableness
interscholastic
intolerableness
intractableness
irrationalistic
irreparableness
irrevocableness
neighbourliness
numismatologist
ophthalmologist
palaeontologist
phenomenalistic
phenomenologist
phosphorylation
pleasurableness
practicableness
PreRaphaelitism
respectableness
selffertilising
selffulfillment
selfgratulation
serviceableness
supportableness
susceptibleness
treasonableness
warrantableness
ankylostomiasis
biogeochemistry
chronogrammatic
collenchymatous
cryptocommunist
echinodermatous
epitheliomatous
hydrodynamicist
immunochemistry
interferometric
metamathematics
nongovernmental
nonprofitmaking
prosenchymatous
pusillanimously
quarrelsomeness
schistosomiasis
selfaffirmation
selfdetermining
stereochemistry
stereoisomerism
stoicheiometric
superincumbence
thermochemistry
transilluminate
troublesomeness
trypanosomiasis
underestimation
unwholesomeness
venturesomeness
circumstantiate
compartmentally
compassionately
confessionalism
confessionalist
consubstantiate
conventionalise
conventionalism
conventionalist
conventionality
decontamination
developmentally
dishearteningly
dispassionately
electrodynamics
electrokinetics
everlastingness
exhibitionistic
expressionistic
extraordinarily
impressionistic
inapprehensible
indeterminately
indetermination
indeterministic
inopportuneness
insubordination
interdependence
interdependency
multitudinously
palaeomagnetism
photojournalism
photojournalist
platitudinarian
plenipotentiary
postmillenarian
processionalist
procrastination
professionalise
professionalism
proportionalist
proportionality
proportionately
quarterfinalist
quinquagenarian
selfexamination
selfexplanatory
selfpollination
superintendence
superintendency
temperamentally
transparentness
uncomplainingly
unprecedentedly
unquestioningly
anthropological
anthropomorphic
bacteriological
compositionally
conjunctionally
counterplotting
dessertspoonful
disillusionment
ecclesiological
electromyograph
electrophoresis
electrophoretic
epistemological
gynandromorphic
heterochromatic
hobbledehoyhood
hyperthyroidism
internationally
microphotograph
microsporophyll
overdevelopment
pharmacological
phenylketonuria
philanthropical
photolithograph
photomicrograph
pneumatological
prepositionally
properispomenon
protozoological
radiogoniometer
reapportionment
selfabandonment
selfdevelopment
selfopinionated
spectroscopical
straightforward
suppositionally
trinitrotoluene
ultramicroscope
unconditionally
underemployment
unexceptionable
unexceptionably
unexceptionally
unintentionally
unobjectionable
acanthocephalan
bibliographical
biogeographical
counterapproach
dolichocephalic
imprescriptible
lexicographical
oceanographical
palaeographical
physiographical
rhombencephalon
rhynchocephalia
semitransparent
stratigraphical
zoogeographical
selfconsequence
agriculturalist
ambidexterously
chromatographic
churrigueresque
cinematographer
cinematographic
counterirritant
crossopterygian
doublebarrelled
enantiomorphism
enantiomorphous
ethnocentricity
fragmentariness
historiographer
historiographic
inconsiderately
inconsideration
inquisitorially
involuntariness
malacopterygian
particularistic
perfunctoriness

phonautographic
physiotherapist
phytogeographic
povertystricken
pseudepigraphic
psychometrician
psychotherapist
pyroelectricity
reconsideration
rudimentariness
singleheartedly
sleepingdraught
speakingtrumpet
splendiferously
superheterodyne
supernaturalise
supernaturalism
supernaturalist
supersaturation
therianthropism
thunderstricken
transfiguration
transfigurement
transliteration
ultracentrifuge
undemonstrative
vasoconstrictor
acclimatisation
affranchisement
alphabetisation
Americanisation
arterialisation
bioluminescence
cerebrovascular
civilianisation
communalisation
comprehensively
computerisation
controversially
crystallisation
decarbonisation
decarburisation
decolourisation
defencelessness
demagnetisation
desensitisation
desexualisation
detribalisation
disinterestedly
disorganisation
distinguishable
distinguishably
eclaircissement
electropositive
enfranchisement
etherealisation
Europeanisation
extemporisation
exteriorisation
externalisation
extraillustrate
familiarisation
formularisation
fourdimensional
hospitalisation
immortalisation
internalisation
materialisation
miniaturisation
nationalisation
noncommissioned
nonprofessional
ophthalmoscopic
personalisation
phosphorescence
picturepostcard
prepossessingly
psychophysicist
purposelessness
rationalisation
reestablishment
regionalisation
remorselessness
retrogressively
romanticisation
selfconsistency
selfrealisation
standardisation
standoffishness
subpostmistress
substratosphere
suburbanisation
superimposition
synchronisation
systematisation
thoughtlessness
transgressively
accommodatingly
amphitheatrical
antepenultimate
antisabbatarian
antitrinitarian
appropriateness
approximatively
arboriculturist
argumentatively
authoritatively
bloodguiltiness
brachydactylous
communicatively
complementarily
complementarity
configurational
consequentially
considerateness
contemplatively
contradictorily
cosmopolitanism
counterattacker
demonstrational
demonstratively
departmentalise
departmentalism
determinateness
disappointingly
disconcertingly
disenchantingly
disproportional
disrespectfully
ecclesiasticism
experimentalise
experimentalism
experimentalist
experimentation
experimentative
heterodactyloos
importunateness
improvisatorial
indistinctively
instrumentalism
instrumentalist
instrumentality
instrumentation
intemperateness
interdigitation
interrogatively
interstratified
malpractitioner
methamphetamine
monosymmetrical
omnidirectional
parasympathetic
parliamentarian
parliamentarism
photoelectronic
quatercentenary
reafforestation
remonstratively
retrospectively
schoolmastering
selfforgetfully
selfregistering
sesquicentenary
significatively
subordinateness
supplementarily
supplementation
transcriptional
transplantation
transpositional
trigonometrical
unsubstantially
wellconditioned
wellintentioned
adventurousness
architecturally
atrabiliousness
carnivorousness
ceremoniousness
coconsciousness
compendiousness
connoisseurship
conspicuousness
contentiousness
deleteriousness
discontinuously
disgracefulness
distastefulness
distrustfulness
efficaciousness
expeditiousness
fissiparousness
grandiloquently
heterosexuality
homogeneousness
illustriousness
incommensurable
incommensurably
incongruousness
inconspicuously
injudiciousness
intellectualise
intellectualism
intellectualist
intellectuality
mellifluousness
meritoriousness
mischievousness
misconstruction
mistrustfulness
necessitousness
odoriferousness
opprobriousness
perpendicularly
perspicuousness
photoconducting
photoconductive
picturesqueness
pleuropneumonia
polyunsaturated
precipitousness
prestigiousness
pretentiousness
preternaturally
punctiliousness
repetitiousness
reproachfulness
resourcefulness
selfdestruction
selfdestructive
selfdistrustful
sententiousness
sociolinguistic
spontaneousness
sulphureousness
superconducting
superconductive
superfluousness
tempestuousness
tendentiousness
treacherousness
unconsciousness
underproduction
unrighteousness
ventriloquially
ventriloquistic
vertiginousness
acquisitiveness
competitiveness
consecutiveness
countermovement
Czechoslovakian
descriptiveness
destructiveness
distinctiveness
imaginativeness
inattentiveness
ineffectiveness
inexpensiveness
inoffensiveness
inquisitiveness
insensitiveness
instructiveness
obstructiveness
penetrativeness
progressiveness
prohibitiveness
provocativeness
selfimprovement
selfreprovingly
speculativeness
substantiveness
superlativeness
northeastwardly
northwestwardly
cryptanalytical
dermatoglyphics
microanalytical
ornithorhynchus

---

acclimatisation
achondroplastic
agriculturalist
alphabetisation
Americanisation
anthropophagous
anticlericalism
antisabbatarian
antitrinitarian
Aristotelianism
arterialisation
brachycephalous
chromatographic
cinematographer
cinematographic
circumvallation
civilianisation
collenchymatous
communalisation
compassionately
complementarily
complementarity
computerisation
confessionalism
confessionalist
confidentiality
contravallation
conventionalise
conventionalism
conventionalist
conventionality
cosmopolitanism
counterattacker
crystallisation
Czechoslovakian
decalcification

decarbonisation
decarburisation
decolourisation
decontamination
demagnetisation
demystification
denitrification
departmentalise
departmentalism
desensitisation
desexualisation
detribalisation
devitrification
differentiation
disarticulation
discommendation
disorganisation
dispassionately
diversification
echinodermatous
electrification
electrodynamics
electronegative
episcopalianism
epitheliomatous
equalitarianism
etherealisation
Europeanisation
excommunication
excommunicative
excommunicatory
exemplification
experientialism
experientialist
experimentalise
experimentalism
experimentalist
experimentation
experimentative
extemporisation
exteriorisation
externalisation
extraordinarily
familiarisation
formularisation
frenchification
heterosexuality
historiographer
historiographic
hospitalisation
humanitarianism
immortalisation
inappropriately
incommunicative
inconsiderately
inconsideration
indemnification
indeterminately
indetermination
insignificantly
instrumentalism
instrumentalist
instrumentality
instrumentation
insubordination
intellectualise
intellectualism
intellectualist
intellectuality
intensification
interdigitation
internalisation
interscholastic
materialisation
metamathematics
methamphetamine
miniaturisation
nationalisation
nonprofitmaking
northeastwardly
northwestwardly
parliamentarian
parliamentarism
personalisation
personification
phonautographic
phosphorylation
photojournalism
photojournalist
physiotherapist
phytogeographic
platitudinarian
postmillenarian
Presbyterianise
Presbyterianism
processionalist
procrastination
professionalise
professionalism
prognostication
prognosticative
proportionalist
proportionality
proportionately
prosenchymatous
pseudepigraphic
psychotherapist
quadruplication
quarterfinalist
quinquagenarian
quintuplication
rationalisation
reafforestation
reconsideration
reconsolidation
regionalisation
romanticisation
selfaffirmation
selfapprobation
selfcastigation
selfdeprecating
selfdeprecatory
selfexamination
selfexplanatory
selfgratulation
selfhumiliation
selfpollination
selfpropagating
selfrealisation
selfreplicating
semitransparent
sleepingdraught
speechification
standardisation
suburbanisation
superabundantly
supernaturalise
supernaturalism
supernaturalist
supersaturation
supplementarily
supplementation
syllabification
synchronisation
systematisation
totalitarianism
transfiguration
transliteration
transplantation
unaccommodating
uncommunicative
undemonstrative
underestimation
superincumbence
abiogenetically
aerodynamically
anaesthetically
anisotropically
antivivisection
apocalyptically
atmospherically
autographically
bioluminescence
cerebrovascular
chronologically
dissatisfaction
dissatisfactory
dithyrambically
dramaturgically
dyslogistically
euphemistically
extracurricular
greatgrandchild
heliotropically
Hellenistically
hermeneutically
hydropathically
hydrostatically
hypercritically
ideographically
interclavicular
interconnection
interfascicular
lackadaisically
logarithmically
logographically
macroscopically
magnetoelectric
mechanistically
meroblastically
misconstruction
morphologically
necromantically
ontogenetically
ophthalmoscopic
pantheistically
parenthetically
peripatetically
peristaltically
pessimistically
philosophically
phosphorescence
photochemically
photoconducting
photoconductive
phrenologically
physiologically
plumbaginaceous
prehistorically
problematically
psychologically
pyrotechnically
ritualistically
saprophytically
selfcomplacency
selfdestruction
selfdestructive
selfreproachful
socialistically
stampcollecting
superconducting
superconductive
sycophantically
syllogistically
sympathetically
symptomatically
technologically
telegraphically
therapeutically
topographically
trisyllabically
typographically
underproduction
unrealistically
unsophisticated
unsymmetrically
broadmindedness
coldbloodedness
coldheartedness
complicatedness
disaffectedness
downheartedness
foresightedness
halfheartedness
hardheartedness
interdependence
interdependency
kindheartedness
levelheadedness
lightheadedness
lightmindedness
longsightedness
nearsightedness
openheartedness
opinionatedness
quickwittedness
righthandedness
rightmindedness
selfcentredness
softheartedness
superintendence
superintendency
trueheartedness
warmbloodedness
warmheartedness
wrongheadedness
accountableness
acknowledgeable
acknowledgement
acquisitiveness
affranchisement
appropriateness
churrigueresque
commonplaceness
competitiveness
conceivableness
consecutiveness
considerateness
countermovement
descriptiveness
destructiveness
determinateness
disentanglement
distinctiveness
doublebarrelled
eclaircissement
electrokinetics
enfranchisement
fashionableness
grandiloquently
hypercatalectic
illimitableness
imaginativeness
impermeableness
importunateness
inattentiveness
indubitableness
ineffectiveness
inexcusableness
inexpensiveness
inflammableness
infrangibleness
innumerableness
inoffensiveness
inopportuneness
inquisitiveness
inscrutableness
insensitiveness
inseparableness
instructiveness
intemperateness
interchangeable
interchangeably
interferometric
intolerableness
intractableness

irreparableness
irrevocableness
margaritiferous
marketgardening
Mephistophelean
Mephistophelian
nongovernmental
obstructiveness
overconfidently
palaeomagnetism
penetrativeness
photosynthesise
picturesqueness
pleasurableness
practicableness
progressiveness
prohibitiveness
provocativeness
quarrelsomeness
quatercentenary
respectableness
rontgenotherapy
schoolmastering
selfconfidently
selfimprovement
selfindulgently
selfregistering
serviceableness
sesquicentenary
speculativeness
stereoisomerism
stoicheiometric
stretcherbearer
subordinateness
substantiveness
superinducement
superlativeness
supportableness
susceptibleness
transfigurement
treasonableness
troublesomeness
unchallengeable
unintelligently
unwholesomeness
venturesomeness
warrantableness
disrespectfully
selfforgetfully
anthropological
bacteriological
circumnavigator
disadvantageous
ecclesiological
electromyograph
epistemological
everlastingness
intercollegiate
microphotograph
pharmacological
photolithograph
photomicrograph
pneumatological
protozoological
acanthocephalan
antimonarchical
bibliographical
biogeographical
brachistochrone
distinguishable
distinguishably
dolichocephalic
lexicographical
oceanographical
palaeographical
parasympathetic
physiographical
reestablishment
rhombencephalon
rhynchocephalia
standoffishness
stratigraphical
zoogeographical
accommodatingly
ankylostomiasis
antepenultimate
approachability
approximatively
argumentatively
authoritatively
biogeochemistry
blameworthiness
bloodguiltiness
communicability
communicatively
comprehensively
compressibility
conceptualistic
condescendingly
configurational
consequentially
contemplatively
contemptibility
contractability
contractibility
controversially
correspondingly
counterirritant
demonstrability
demonstrational
demonstratively
destructibility
disagreeability
disappointingly
disconcertingly
disenchantingly
dishearteningly
disproportional
disreputability
ecclesiasticism
electropositive
equiprobability
ethnocentricity
exchangeability
exhibitionistic
expressionistic
flibbertigibbet
fourdimensional
fragmentariness
gentlemanliness
heartbreakingly
hermaphroditism
hydrodynamicist
hyperthyroidism
immunochemistry
impenetrability
imperishability
imponderability
impressionistic
inaccessibility
inadmissibility
inapplicability
incalculability
incomparability
incompatibility
incorrigibility
indefeasibility
indefensibility
indeterministic
indigestibility
indissolubility
indistinctively
individualistic
ineffaceability
inexplicability
infundibuliform
inquisitorially
intelligibility
interrogatively
interstratified
involuntariness
invulnerability
irrationalistic
irresistibility
irreversibility
malpractitioner
manoeuvrability
neighbourliness
neuropsychiatry
noncommissioned
nonprofessional
omnidirectional
orthopsychiatry
particularistic
perfunctoriness
phenomenalistic
povertystricken
prepossessingly
PreRaphaelitism
psychometrician
psychophysicist
pulchritudinous
pyroelectricity
reconcilability
remonstratively
reproducibility
retrogressively
retrospectively
rudimentariness
sadomasochistic
schistosomiasis
selfdetermining
selffertilising
selfreprovingly
selfsacrificing
selfsufficiency
significatively
sociolinguistic
stereochemistry
superimposition
thermochemistry
thunderstricken
transcriptional
transferability
transgressively
transilluminate
transmutability
transpositional
trustworthiness
trypanosomiasis
ultracentrifuge
unchangeability
uncomplainingly
understandingly
unquestioningly
unsubstantially
vasoconstrictor
ventriloquially
ventriloquistic
vicissitudinous
wellconditioned
wellintentioned
disgracefulness
distastefulness
distrustfulness
electroanalysis
fantasticalness
gleichschaltung
hendecasyllabic
hendecasyllable
impracticalness
ineffectualness
mistrustfulness
nonsensicalness
paradoxicalness
perpendicularly
pharisaicalness
polycrystalline
reproachfulness
resourcefulness
selffulfillment
shootinggallery
substantialness
superficialness
symmetricalness
trinitrotoluene
underprivileged
chronogrammatic
electrochemical
heterochromatic
infinitesimally
micromillimetre
physicochemical
pleuropneumonia
properispomenon
radiogoniometer
anthropocentric
anthropogenesis
chloramphenicol
circumferential
coinstantaneous
compositionally
conjunctionally
contemporaneity
contemporaneous
disillusionment
electromagnetic
governorgeneral
incomprehension
inconsequential
indisciplinable
internationally
interprovincial
jurisprudential
microsporangium
misapprehension
misapprehensive
nonintervention
notwithstanding
ornithorhynchus
palaeobotanical
parthenogenesis
parthenogenetic
phenylketonuria
photomechanical
predeterminable
prepositionally
reapportionment
selfabandonment
selfcontainment
selfopinionated
semidocumentary
semiindependent
spermatogenesis
spermatogenetic
suppositionally
uncomplimentary
uncomprehending
unconditionally
unexceptionable
unexceptionably
unexceptionally
unintentionally
unobjectionable
unparliamentary
unsportsmanlike
airconditioning
ambidexterously
anaesthesiology
annihilationism
archiepiscopate
conscientiously
consentaneously
conservationist
constructionism
constructionist

contradictorily
conversationist
dessertspoonful
discontinuously
disinflationary
emancipationist
geochronologist
geomorphologist
heterogeneously
improvisatorial
inconspicuously
inefficaciously
instantaneously
insurrectionary
insurrectionist
interjectionary
interventionism
interventionist
multitudinously
neurophysiology
numismatologist
ophthalmologist
palaeontologist
perspicaciously
phenomenologist
presentationism
presentationist
preservationist
psychopathology
pusillanimously
resurrectionism
resurrectionist
sanctimoniously
selfconsciously
selfrighteously
semiconsciously
splendiferously
substitutionary
subterraneously
superheterodyne
superstitiously
surreptitiously
therianthropism
unceremoniously
unpretentiously
Christadelphian
circumscription
dermatoglyphics
enantiomorphism
enantiomorphous
introsusception
intussusception
intussusceptive
microsporophyll
overdevelopment
philanthropical
selfdevelopment
spectroscopical
substratosphere
amphitheatrical
anthropomorphic
architecturally
atherosclerosis
atherosclerotic
autoradiography
connoisseurship
counterapproach
crystallography
electrophoresis
electrophoretic
encephalography
gastroenteritis
gynandromorphic
incommensurable
incommensurably
interpretership
monosymmetrical
noninterference
palaeoanthropic

palaeogeography
photoelectronic
phototelegraphy
pithecanthropus
polyunsaturated
preternaturally
radioautography
radiotelegraphy
roentgenography
semicylindrical
stadtholdership
straightforward
telephotography
trigonometrical
vicechamberlain
weatherboarding
adventurousness
atrabiliousness
carnivorousness
ceremoniousness
coconsciousness
compendiousness
conspicuousness
contentiousness
defencelessness
deleteriousness
efficaciousness
expeditiousness
fissiparousness
homogeneousness
illustriousness
inapprehensible
incongruousness
injudiciousness
manicdepressive
mellifluousness
meritoriousness
mischievousness
necessitousness
odoriferousness
opprobriousness
perspicuousness
precipitousness
prestigiousness
pretentiousness
punctiliousness
purposelessness
remorselessness
repetitiousness
selfdistrustful
sententiousness
shrinkresistant
spontaneousness
sulphureousness
superfluousness
tempestuousness
tendentiousness
thoughtlessness
treacherousness
ultramicroscope
unconsciousness
unprepossessing
unrighteousness
vertiginousness
anthropopathism
circumspectness
circumstantiate
compartmentally
congratulations
consubstantiate
counterplotting
cryptanalytical
developmentally
disinterestedly
extraillustrate
imprescriptible
microanalytical
photosensitiser
picturepostcard

plenipotentiary
prestidigitator
selfconsistency
selfconstituted
singleheartedly
sophisticatedly
subpostmistress
superstructural
temperamentally
transparentness
unprecedentedly
arboriculturist
bioastronautics
cryptocommunist
entrepreneurial
maldistribution
noncontributory
selfconsequence
speakingtrumpet
brachydactylous
crossopterygian
heterodactyloos
hobbledehoyhood
malacopterygian
underemployment

---

abiogenetically
acanthocephalan
acknowledgeable
aerodynamically
anaesthetically
anisotropically
ankylostomiasis
apocalyptically
architecturally
atmospherically
autographically
autoradiography
chronogrammatic
chronologically
circumnavigator
compartmentally
compositionally
conjunctionally
consequentially
controversially
crystallography
developmentally
distinguishable
distinguishably
dithyrambically
dolichocephalic
dramaturgically
dyslogistically
encephalography
euphemistically
heliotropically
Hellenistically
hendecasyllabic
hendecasyllable
hermeneutically
heterochromatic
hydropathically
hydrostatically
hypercritically
ideographically
incommensurable
incommensurably
indisciplinable
infinitesimally
inquisitorially
interchangeable
interchangeably
internationally
lackadaisically
logarithmically
logographically
macroscopically
mechanistically

meroblastically
morphologically
necromantically
neuropsychiatry
ontogenetically
orthopsychiatry
palaeogeography
pantheistically
parenthetically
peripatetically
peristaltically
perpendicularly
pessimistically
philosophically
photochemically
phototelegraphy
phrenologically
physiologically
polyunsaturated
predeterminable
prehistorically
prepositionally
prestidigitator
preternaturally
problematically
psychologically
pyrotechnically
radioautography
radiotelegraphy
rhombencephalon
rhynchocephalia
ritualistically
roentgenography
saprophytically
schistosomiasis
selfopinionated
socialistically
stretcherbearer
suppositionally
sycophantically
syllogistically
sympathetically
symptomatically
technologically
telegraphically
telephotography
temperamentally
therapeutically
topographically
trisyllabically
trypanosomiasis
typographically
unchallengeable
unconditionally
unexceptionable
unexceptionably
unexceptionally
unintentionally
unobjectionable
unrealistically
unsophisticated
unsubstantially
unsymmetrically
ventriloquially
flibbertigibbet
counterattacker
ecclesiasticism
ethnocentricity
hydrodynamicist
hypercatalectic
interprovincial
ornithorhynchus
picturepostcard
povertystricken
psychometrician
psychophysicist
pyroelectricity
selfsacrificing
thunderstricken

ultramicroscope
vasoconstrictor
hyperthyroidism
notwithstanding
semiindependent
superheterodyne
uncomprehending
weatherboarding
anthropogenesis
bioluminescence
coinstantaneous
contemporaneity
contemporaneous
disadvantageous
disinterestedly
electromagnetic
electrcphoresis
electrophoretic
governorgeneral
interdependence
interdependency
micromillimetre
noninterference
parasympathetic
parthenogenesis
parthenogenetic
phosphorescence
plumbaginaceous
properispomenon
radiogoniometer
selfcomplacency
selfconsequence
selfconsistency
selfsufficiency
singleheartedly
sophisticatedly
spermatogenesis
spermatogenetic
superincumbence
superintendence
superintendency
underprivileged
unprecedentedly
infundibuliform
interstratified
ultracentrifuge
anthropophagous
crossopterygian
geochronologist
geomorphologist
malacopterygian
microsporangium
numismatologist
ophthalmologist
palaeontologist
phenomenologist
anthropopathism
Christadelphian
dermatoglyphics
enantiomorphism
enantiomorphous
greatgrandchild
hobbledehoyhood
microsporophyll
selfreproachful
substratosphere
amphitheatrical
anthropological
antimonarchical
bacteriological
bibliographical
biogeographical
chloramphenicol
circumstantiate
congratulations
consubstantiate
cryptanalytical
ecclesiological
electrochemical
epistemological
gastroenteritis
imprescriptible
inapprehensible
intercollegiate
lexicographical
microanalytical
monosymmetrical
oceanographical
palaeobotanical
palaeographical
pharmacological
philanthropical
photomechanical
photosensitiser
physicochemical
physiographical
plenipotentiary
pneumatological
protozoological
semicylindrical
spectroscopical
stratigraphical
trigonometrical
zoogeographical
Czechoslovakian
nonprofitmaking
agriculturalist
anaesthesiology
anticlericalism
approachability
brachycephalous
brachydactylous
communicability
compressibility
confessionalism
confessionalist
confidentiality
contemptibility
contractability
contractibility
conventionalise
conventionalism
conventionalist
conventionality
demonstrability
departmentalise
departmentalism
destructibility
disagreeability
disreputability
doublebarrelled
equiprobability
exchangeability
experientialism
experientialist
experimentalise
experimentalism
experimentalist
heterodactyloos
heterosexuality
impenetrability
imperishability
imponderability
inaccessibility
inadmissibility
inapplicability
incalculability
incomparability
incompatibility
incorrigibility
indefeasibility
indefensibility
indigestibility
indissolubility
ineffaceability
inexplicability
instrumentalism
instrumentalist
instrumentality
intellectualise
intellectualism
intellectualist
intellectuality
intelligibility
invulnerability
irresistibility
irreversibility
manoeuvrability
Mephistophelean
Mephistophelian
neurophysiology
photojournalism
photojournalist
polycrystalline
processionalist
professionalise
professionalism
proportionalist
proportionality
psychopathology
quarterfinalist
reconcilability
reproducibility
shootinggallery
supernaturalise
supernaturalism
supernaturalist
transferability
transmutability
unchangeability
unsportsmanlike
vicechamberlain
acknowledgement
affranchisement
antepenultimate
countermovement
disentanglement
disillusionment
eclaircissement
electrodynamics
enfranchisement
methamphetamine
overdevelopment
reapportionment
reestablishment
selfabandonment
selfcontainment
selfdevelopment
selffulfillment
selfimprovement
speakingtrumpet
superinducement
transfigurement
underemployment
accommodatingly
accountableness
acquisitiveness
adventurousness
airconditioning
annihilationism
appropriateness
Aristotelianism
atrabiliousness
blameworthiness
bloodguiltiness
broadmindedness
carnivorousness
ceremoniousness
circumspectness
coconsciousness
coldbloodedness
coldheartedness
commonplaceness
compendiousness
competitiveness
complicatedness
conceivableness
condescendingly
consecutiveness
conservationist
considerateness
conspicuousness
constructionism
constructionist
contentiousness
conversationist
correspondingly
cosmopolitanism
cryptocommunist
defencelessness
deleteriousness
descriptiveness
dessertspoonful
destructiveness
determinateness
disaffectedness
disappointingly
disconcertingly
disenchantingly
disgracefulness
dishearteningly
disinflationary
distastefulness
distinctiveness
distrustfulness
downheartedness
efficaciousness
emancipationist
episcopalianism
equalitarianism
everlastingness
expeditiousness
fantasticalness
fashionableness
fissiparousness
foresightedness
fragmentariness
gentlemanliness
grandiloquently
halfheartedness
hardheartedness
heartbreakingly
homogeneousness
humanitarianism
illimitableness
illustriousness
imaginativeness
impermeableness
importunateness
impracticalness
inattentiveness
incongruousness
indubitableness
ineffectiveness
ineffectualness
inexcusableness
inexpensiveness
inflammableness
infrangibleness
injudiciousness
innumerableness
inoffensiveness
inopportuneness
inquisitiveness
inscrutableness
insensitiveness
inseparableness
insignificantly
instructiveness
insurrectionary
insurrectionist
intemperateness
interjectionary
interventionism
interventionist
intolerableness

intractableness
involuntariness
irreparableness
irrevocableness
kindheartedness
levelheadedness
lightheadedness
lightmindedness
longsightedness
marketgardening
mellifluousness
meritoriousness
mischievousness
mistrustfulness
nearsightedness
necessitousness
neighbourliness
nongovernmental
nonsensicalness
obstructiveness
odoriferousness
openheartedness
opinionatedness
opprobriousness
overconfidently
paradoxicalness
penetrativeness
perfunctoriness
perspicuousness
pharisaicalness
picturesqueness
pleasurableness
practicableness
precipitousness
prepossessingly
Presbyterianise
Presbyterianism
presentationism
presentationist
preservationist
prestigiousness
pretentiousness
progressiveness
prohibitiveness
provocativeness
pulchritudinous
punctiliousness
purposelessness
quarrelsomeness
quatercentenary
quickwittedness
remorselessness
repetitiousness
reproachfulness
resourcefulness
respectableness
resurrectionism
resurrectionist
righthandedness
rightmindedness
rudimentariness
selfcentredness
selfconfidently
selfdetermining
selfindulgently
selfreprovingly
sententiousness
serviceableness
sesquicentenary
softheartedness
speculativeness
spontaneousness
standoffishness
subordinateness
substantialness
substantiveness
substitutionary
sulphureousness
superabundantly
superficialness
superfluousness
superlativeness
supportableness
susceptibleness
symmetricalness
tempestuousness
tendentiousness
thoughtlessness
totalitarianism
transilluminate
transparentness
treacherousness
treasonableness
troublesomeness
trueheartedness
trustworthiness
uncomplainingly
unconsciousness
understandingly
unintelligently
unquestioningly
unrighteousness
unwholesomeness
venturesomeness
vertiginousness
vicissitudinous
warmbloodedness
warmheartedness
warrantableness
wrongheadedness
atherosclerosis
atherosclerotic
configurational
counterapproach
demonstrational
disproportional
fourdimensional
malpractitioner
noncommissioned
nonprofessional
omnidirectional
ophthalmoscopic
palaeoanthropic
photoelectronic
pithecanthropus
pleuropneumonia
transcriptional
transpositional
wellconditioned
wellintentioned
anthropomorphic
archiepiscopate
chromatographic
cinematographer
cinematographic
gynandromorphic
historiographer
historiographic
phonautographic
physiotherapist
phytogeographic
pseudepigraphic
psychotherapist
therianthropism
antisabbatarian
antitrinitarian
arboriculturist
brachistochrone
complementarily
complementarity
contradictorily
electromyograph
entrepreneurial
extraillustrate
extraordinarily
improvisatorial
margaritiferous
microphotograph
northeastwardly
northwestwardly
parliamentarian
parliamentarism
photolithograph
photomicrograph
platitudinarian
postmillenarian
quinquagenarian
rontgenotherapy
schoolmastering
selfregistering
semitransparent
stereoisomerism
subpostmistress
supplementarily
achondroplastic
biogeochemistry
churrigueresque
conceptualistic
connoisseurship
exhibitionistic
expressionistic
immunochemistry
impressionistic
incomprehension
indeterministic
individualistic
interpretership
interscholastic
irrationalistic
manicdepressive
misapprehension
misapprehensive
particularistic
phenomenalistic
photosynthesise
sadomasochistic
selffertilising
sociolinguistic
stadtholdership
stereochemistry
thermochemistry
unprepossessing
ventriloquistic
acclimatisation
alphabetisation
Americanisation
anthropocentric
antivivisection
arterialisation
bioastronautics
circumferential
circumscription
circumvallation
civilianisation
collenchymatous
communalisation
compassionately
computerisation
contravallation
counterirritant
counterplotting
crystallisation
decalcification
decarbonisation
decarburisation
decolourisation
decontamination
demagnetisation
demystification
denitrification
desensitisation
desexualisation
detribalisation
devitrification
differentiation
disarticulation
discommendation
disorganisation
dispassionately
dissatisfaction
dissatisfactory
diversification
echinodermatous
electrification
electrokinetics
electronegative
electropositive
epitheliomatous
etherealisation
Europeanisation
excommunication
excommunicative
excommunicatory
exemplification
experimentation
experimentative
extemporisation
exteriorisation
externalisation
familiarisation
formularisation
frenchification
gleichschaltung
hermaphroditism
hospitalisation
immortalisation
inappropriately
incommunicative
inconsequential
inconsiderately
inconsideration
indemnification
indeterminately
indetermination
instrumentation
insubordination
intensification
interconnection
interdigitation
interferometric
internalisation
introsusception
intussusception
intussusceptive
jurisprudential
magnetoelectric
maldistribution
materialisation
metamathematics
miniaturisation
misconstruction
nationalisation
noncontributory
nonintervention
palaeomagnetism
personalisation
personification
phosphorylation
photoconducting
photoconductive
PreRaphaelitism
procrastination
prognostication
prognosticative
proportionately
prosenchymatous
quadruplication
quintuplication
rationalisation
reafforestation
reconsideration
reconsolidation
regionalisation
romanticisation
selfaffirmation
selfapprobation

selfcastigation
selfdeprecating
selfdeprecatory
selfdestruction
selfdestructive
selfdistrustful
selfexamination
selfexplanatory
selfgratulation
selfhumiliation
selfpollination
selfpropagating
selfrealisation
selfreplicating
semidocumentary
shrinkresistant
speechification
stampcollecting
standardisation
stoicheiometric
suburbanisation
superconducting
superconductive
superimposition
supersaturation
supplementation
syllabification
synchronisation
systematisation
transfiguration
transliteration
transplantation
unaccommodating
uncommunicative
uncomplimentary
undemonstrative
underestimation
underproduction
unparliamentary
ambidexterously
cerebrovascular
conscientiously
consentaneously
discontinuously
disrespectfully
extracurricular
heterogeneously
inconspicuously
inefficaciously
instantaneously
interclavicular
interfascicular
multitudinously
perspicaciously
phenylketonuria
pusillanimously
sanctimoniously
selfconsciously
selfconstituted
selfforgetfully
selfrighteously
semiconsciously
sleepingdraught
splendiferously
subterraneously
superstitiously
superstructural
surreptitiously
trinitrotoluene
unceremoniously
unpretentiously
approximatively
argumentatively
authoritatively
communicatively
comprehensively
contemplatively
demonstratively
indistinctively

interrogatively
remonstratively
retrogressively
retrospectively
significatively
transgressively
straightforward
electroanalysis

---

antepenultimate
archiepiscopate
circumstantiate
consubstantiate
counterapproach
counterirritant
disinflationary
electromyograph
extraillustrate
insurrectionary
intercollegiate
interjectionary
microphotograph
photolithograph
photomicrograph
picturepostcard
plenipotentiary
quatercentenary
rontgenotherapy
semidocumentary
sesquicentenary
shrinkresistant
straightforward
substitutionary
transilluminate
uncomplimentary
unparliamentary
vicechamberlain
acknowledgeable
distinguishable
distinguishably
flibbertigibbet
hendecasyllabic
hendecasyllable
imprescriptible
inapprehensible
incommensurable
incommensurably
indisciplinable
interchangeable
interchangeably
predeterminable
unchallengeable
unexceptionable
unexceptionably
unobjectionable
amphitheatrical
anthropological
antimonarchical
bacteriological
bibliographical
biogeographical
chloramphenicol
cryptanalytical
ecclesiological
electrochemical
epistemological
lexicographical
microanalytical
monosymmetrical
oceanographical
palaeobotanical
palaeographical
pharmacological
philanthropical
photomechanical
physicochemical
physiographical
pneumatological
protozoological

semicylindrical
spectroscopical
stratigraphical
trigonometrical
zoogeographical
disinterestedly
northeastwardly
northwestwardly
singleheartedly
sophisticatedly
unprecedentedly
accountableness
acknowledgement
acquisitiveness
adventurousness
affranchisement
appropriateness
approximatively
argumentatively
atrabiliousness
authoritatively
blameworthiness
bloodguiltiness
broadmindedness
carnivorousness
ceremoniousness
circumspectness
coconsciousness
coldbloodedness
coldheartedness
commonplaceness
communicatively
compassionately
compendiousness
competitiveness
complicatedness
comprehensively
conceivableness
consecutiveness
considerateness
conspicuousness
contemplatively
contentiousness
countermovement
defencelessness
deleteriousness
demonstratively
descriptiveness
destructiveness
determinateness
disaffectedness
disentanglement
disgracefulness
disillusionment
dispassionately
distastefulness
distinctiveness
distrustfulness
downheartedness
eclaircissement
efficaciousness
enfranchisement
everlastingness
expeditiousness
fantasticalness
fashionableness
fissiparousness
foresightedness
fragmentariness
gentlemanliness
halfheartedness
hardheartedness
homogeneousness
illimitableness
illustriousness
imaginativeness
impermeableness
importunateness
impracticalness

inappropriately
inattentiveness
incongruousness
inconsiderately
indeterminately
indistinctively
indubitableness
ineffectiveness
ineffectualness
inexcusableness
inexpensiveness
inflammableness
infrangibleness
injudiciousness
innumerableness
inoffensiveness
inopportuneness
inquisitiveness
inscrutableness
insensitiveness
inseparableness
instructiveness
intemperateness
interrogatively
intolerableness
intractableness
involuntariness
irreparableness
irrevocableness
kindheartedness
levelheadedness
lightheadedness
lightmindedness
longsightedness
mellifluousness
Mephistophelean
meritoriousness
mischievousness
mistrustfulness
nearsightedness
necessitousness
neighbourliness
nonsensicalness
obstructiveness
odoriferousness
openheartedness
opinionatedness
opprobriousness
overdevelopment
paradoxicalness
penetrativeness
perfunctoriness
perspicuousness
pharisaicalness
picturesqueness
pleasurableness
practicableness
precipitousness
prestigiousness
pretentiousness
progressiveness
prohibitiveness
proportionately
provocativeness
punctiliousness
purposelessness
quarrelsomeness
quickwittedness
reapportionment
reestablishment
remonstratively
remorselessness
repetitiousness
reproachfulness
resourcefulness
respectableness
retrogressively
retrospectively
righthandedness

rightmindedness
rudimentariness
selfabandonment
selfcentredness
selfcontainment
selfdevelopment
selffulfillment
selfimprovement
semiindependent
semitransparent
sententiousness
serviceableness
shootinggallery
significatively
softheartedness
speculativeness
spontaneousness
standoffishness
subordinateness
subpostmistress
substantialness
substantiveness
substratosphere
sulphureousness
superficialness
superfluousness
superinducement
superlativeness
supportableness
susceptibleness
symmetricalness
tempestuousness
tendentiousness
thoughtlessness
transfigurement
transgressively
transparentness
treacherousness
treasonableness
trinitrotoluene
troublesomeness
trueheartedness
trustworthiness
unconsciousness
underemployment
unrighteousness
unwholesomeness
venturesomeness
vertiginousness
warmbloodedness
warmheartedness
warrantableness
wrongheadedness
dessertspoonful
selfdistrustful
selfreproachful
accommodatingly
condescendingly
correspondingly
disappointingly
disconcertingly
disenchantingly
dishearteningly
heartbreakingly
prepossessingly
selfreprovingly
sleepingdraught
uncomplainingly
underprivileged
understandingly
unquestioningly
anthropomorphic
chromatographic
cinematographer
cinematographic
connoisseurship
gynandromorphic
historiographer
historiographic
interpretership
ornithorhynchus
phonautographic
phytogeographic
pseudepigraphic
stadtholdership
acclimatisation
agriculturalist
airconditioning
alphabetisation
Americanisation
annihilationism
anthropopathism
anticlericalism
antisabbatarian
antitrinitarian
antivivisection
approachability
arboriculturist
Aristotelianism
arterialisation
bioastronautics
Christadelphian
circumferential
circumscription
circumvallation
civilianisation
communalisation
communicability
complementarily
complementarity
compressibility
computerisation
confessionalism
confessionalist
confidentiality
conservationist
constructionism
constructionist
contemporaneity
contemptibility
contractability
contractibility
contradictorily
contravallation
conventionalise
conventionalism
conventionalist
conventionality
conversationist
cosmopolitanism
counterplotting
crossopterygian
cryptocommunist
crystallisation
Czechoslovakian
decalcification
decarbonisation
decarburisation
decolourisation
decontamination
demagnetisation
demonstrability
demystification
denitrification
departmentalise
departmentalism
dermatoglyphics
desensitisation
desexualisation
destructibility
detribalisation
devitrification
differentiation
disagreeability
disarticulation
discommendation
disorganisation
disreputability
dissatisfaction
diversification
ecclesiasticism
electrification
electrodynamics
electrokinetics
electronegative
electropositive
emancipationist
enantiomorphism
entrepreneurial
episcopalianism
equalitarianism
equiprobability
etherealisation
ethnocentricity
Europeanisation
exchangeability
excommunication
excommunicative
exemplification
experientialism
experientialist
experimentalise
experimentalism
experimentalist
experimentation
experimentative
extemporisation
exteriorisation
externalisation
extraordinarily
familiarisation
formularisation
frenchification
geochronologist
geomorphologist
greatgrandchild
hermaphroditism
heterosexuality
hospitalisation
humanitarianism
hydrodynamicist
hyperthyroidism
immortalisation
impenetrability
imperishability
imponderability
improvisatorial
inaccessibility
inadmissibility
inapplicability
incalculability
incommunicative
incomparability
incompatibility
incomprehension
inconsequential
inconsideration
incorrigibility
indefeasibility
indefensibility
indemnification
indetermination
indigestibility
indissolubility
ineffaceability
inexplicability
instrumentalism
instrumentalist
instrumentality
instrumentation
insubordination
insurrectionist
intellectualise
intellectualism
intellectualist
intellectuality
intelligibility
intensification
interconnection
interdigitation
internalisation
interprovincial
interstratified
interventionism
interventionist
introsusception
intussusception
intussusceptive
invulnerability
irresistibility
irreversibility
jurisprudential
malacopterygian
maldistribution
manicdepressive
manoeuvrability
marketgardening
materialisation
Mephistophelian
metamathematics
methamphetamine
microsporangium
miniaturisation
misapprehension
misapprehensive
misconstruction
nationalisation
nonintervention
nonprofitmaking
notwithstanding
numismatologist
ophthalmologist
palaeomagnetism
palaeontologist
parliamentarian
parliamentarism
personalisation
personification
phenomenologist
phosphorylation
photoconducting
photoconductive
photojournalism
photojournalist
photosynthesise
physiotherapist
platitudinarian
polycrystalline
postmillenarian
PreRaphaelitism
Presbyterianise
Presbyterianism
presentationism
presentationist
preservationist
processionalist
procrastination
professionalise
professionalism
prognostication
prognosticative
proportionalist
proportionality
psychometrician
psychophysicist
psychotherapist
pyroelectricity
quadruplication
quarterfinalist
quinquagenarian
quintuplication
rationalisation
reafforestation
reconcilability
reconsideration
reconsolidation

regionalisation
reproducibility
resurrectionism
resurrectionist
romanticisation
schoolmastering
selfaffirmation
selfapprobation
selfcastigation
selfdeprecating
selfdestruction
selfdestructive
selfdetermining
selfexamination
selffertilising
selfgratulation
selfhumiliation
selfpollination
selfpropagating
selfrealisation
selfregistering
selfreplicating
selfsacrificing
speechification
stampcollecting
standardisation
stereoisomerism
suburbanisation
superconducting
superconductive
superimposition
supernaturalise
supernaturalism
supernaturalist
supersaturation
supplementarily
supplementation
syllabification
synchronisation
systematisation
therianthropism
totalitarianism
transferability
transfiguration
transliteration
transmutability
transplantation
unaccommodating
unchangeability
uncommunicative
uncomprehending
undemonstrative
underestimation
underproduction
unprepossessing
unsportsmanlike
weatherboarding
counterattacker
povertystricken
thunderstricken
abiogenetically
acanthocephalan
aerodynamically
anaesthetically
anisotropically
apocalyptically
architecturally
atmospherically
autographically
cerebrovascular
chronologically
compartmentally
compositionally
conjunctionally
consequentially
controversially
developmentally
disrespectfully
dithyrambically
dolichocephalic
doublebarrelled
dramaturgically
dyslogistically
euphemistically
extracurricular
heliotropically
Hellenistically
hermeneutically
hydropathically
hydrostatically
hypercritically
ideographically
infinitesimally
inquisitorially
interclavicular
interfascicular
internationally
lackadaisically
logarithmically
logographically
macroscopically
mechanistically
meroblastically
morphologically
necromantically
ontogenetically
pantheistically
parenthetically
peripatetically
peristaltically
pessimistically
philosophically
photochemically
phrenologically
physiologically
prehistorically
prepositionally
preternaturally
problematically
psychologically
pyrotechnically
rhombencephalon
rhynchocephalia
ritualistically
saprophytically
selfforgetfully
socialistically
suppositionally
sycophantically
syllogistically
sympathetically
symptomatically
technologically
telegraphically
temperamentally
therapeutically
topographically
trisyllabically
typographically
unconditionally
unexceptionally
unintentionally
unrealistically
unsubstantially
unsymmetrically
ventriloquially
bioluminescence
configurational
demonstrational
disproportional
fourdimensional
interdependence
interdependency
malpractitioner
noncommissioned
noninterference
nonprofessional
omnidirectional
phosphorescence
photoelectronic
pleuropneumonia
properispomenon
selfcomplacency
selfconsequence
selfconsistency
selfsufficiency
superincumbence
superintendence
superintendency
transcriptional
transpositional
wellconditioned
wellintentioned
anaesthesiology
anthropophagous
brachistochrone
brachycephalous
brachydactylous
coinstantaneous
collenchymatous
congratulations
contemporaneous
disadvantageous
dissatisfactory
echinodermatous
enantiomorphous
epitheliomatous
excommunicatory
heterodactyloos
hobbledehoyhood
infundibuliform
margaritiferous
neurophysiology
noncontributory
plumbaginaceous
prosenchymatous
psychopathology
pulchritudinous
selfdeprecatory
selfexplanatory
ultramicroscope
vicissitudinous
autoradiography
crystallography
encephalography
ophthalmoscopic
palaeoanthropic
palaeogeography
phototelegraphy
pithecanthropus
radioautography
radiotelegraphy
roentgenography
speakingtrumpet
telephotography
churrigueresque
anthropocentric
governorgeneral
interferometric
magnetoelectric
perpendicularly
phenylketonuria
stoicheiometric
stretcherbearer
superstructural
ambidexterously
ankylostomiasis
anthropogenesis
atherosclerosis
conscientiously
consentaneously
discontinuously
electroanalysis
electrophoresis
heterogeneously
inconspicuously
inefficaciously
instantaneously
multitudinously
parthenogenesis
perspicaciously
photosensitiser
pusillanimously
sanctimoniously
schistosomiasis
selfconsciously
selfrighteously
semiconsciously
spermatogenesis
splendiferously
subterraneously
superstitiously
surreptitiously
trypanosomiasis
unceremoniously
unpretentiously
achondroplastic
atherosclerotic
biogeochemistry
chronogrammatic
circumnavigator
conceptualistic
electromagnetic
electrophoretic
exhibitionistic
expressionistic
gastroenteritis
grandiloquently
heterochromatic
hypercatalectic
immunochemistry
impressionistic
indeterministic
individualistic
insignificantly
interscholastic
irrationalistic
micromillimetre
neuropsychiatry
nongovernmental
orthopsychiatry
overconfidently
parasympathetic
parthenogenetic
particularistic
phenomenalistic
polyunsaturated
prestidigitator
radiogoniometer
sadomasochistic
selfconfidently
selfconstituted
selfindulgently
selfopinionated
sociolinguistic
spermatogenetic
stereochemistry
superabundantly
thermochemistry
unintelligently
unsophisticated
vasoconstrictor
ventriloquistic
gleichschaltung
ultracentrifuge
microsporophyll
superheterodyne

---

acanthocephalan
amphitheatrical
anthropological
antimonarchical
antisabbatarian
antitrinitarian
bacteriological
bibliographical

biogeographical
cerebrovascular
Christadelphian
circumferential
configurational
crossopterygian
cryptanalytical
Czechoslovakian
demonstrational
disproportional
ecclesiological
electrochemical
entrepreneurial
epistemological
extracurricular
fourdimensional
governorgeneral
improvisatorial
inconsequential
interclavicular
interfascicular
interprovincial
jurisprudential
lexicographical
malacopterygian
Mephistophelean
Mephistophelian
microanalytical
monosymmetrical
nongovernmental
nonprofessional
oceanographical
omnidirectional
palaeobotanical
palaeographical
parliamentarian
pharmacological
philanthropical
photomechanical
physicochemical
physiographical
platitudinarian
pneumatological
postmillenarian
protozoological
psychometrician
quinquagenarian
semicylindrical
spectroscopical
stratigraphical
superstructural
transcriptional
transpositional
trigonometrical
zoogeographical
bioastronautics
bioluminescence
counterapproach
dermatoglyphics
electrodynamics
electrokinetics
interdependence
interdependency
metamathematics
noninterference
phosphorescence
selfcomplacency
selfconsequence
selfconsistency
selfsufficiency
superincumbence
superintendence
superintendency
cinematographer
counterattacker
doublebarrelled
flibbertigibbet
historiographer
interstratified
malpractitioner
noncommissioned
photosensitiser
polyunsaturated
povertystricken
radiogoniometer
selfconstituted
selfopinionated
speakingtrumpet
stretcherbearer
thunderstricken
underprivileged
unsophisticated
wellconditioned
wellintentioned
anaesthesiology
neurophysiology
psychopathology
ultracentrifuge
autoradiography
crystallography
encephalography
palaeogeography
phototelegraphy
radioautography
radiotelegraphy
roentgenography
sleepingdraught
telephotography
achondroplastic
ankylostomiasis
anthropocentric
anthropogenesis
anthropomorphic
atherosclerosis
atherosclerotic
chromatographic
chronogrammatic
cinematographic
conceptualistic
connoisseurship
dolichocephalic
electroanalysis
electromagnetic
electrophoresis
electrophoretic
exhibitionistic
expressionistic
gastroenteritis
gynandromorphic
hendecasyllabic
heterochromatic
historiographic
hypercatalectic
impressionistic
indeterministic
individualistic
interferometric
interpretership
interscholastic
irrationalistic
magnetoelectric
ophthalmoscopic
palaeoanthropic
parasympathetic
parthenogenesis
parthenogenetic
particularistic
phenomenalistic
phenylketonuria
phonautographic
photoelectronic
phytogeographic
pleuropneumonia
pseudepigraphic
rhynchocephalia
sadomasochistic
schistosomiasis
sociolinguistic
spermatogenesis
spermatogenetic
stadtholdership
stoicheiometric
trypanosomiasis
ventriloquistic
vicechamberlain
unsportsmanlike
abiogenetically
accommodatingly
acknowledgeable
aerodynamically
ambidexterously
anaesthetically
anisotropically
apocalyptically
approximatively
architecturally
argumentatively
atmospherically
authoritatively
autographically
chronologically
communicatively
compartmentally
compassionately
complementarily
compositionally
comprehensively
condescendingly
conjunctionally
conscientiously
consentaneously
consequentially
contemplatively
contradictorily
controversially
correspondingly
demonstratively
developmentally
disappointingly
disconcertingly
discontinuously
disenchantingly
dishearteningly
disinterestedly
dispassionately
disrespectfully
distinguishable
distinguishably
dithyrambically
dramaturgically
dyslogistically
euphemistically
extraordinarily
grandiloquently
greatgrandchild
heartbreakingly
heliotropically
Hellenistically
hendecasyllable
hermeneutically
heterogeneously
hydropathically
hydrostatically
hypercritically
ideographically
imprescriptible
inapprehensible
inappropriately
incommensurable
incommensurably
inconsiderately
inconspicuously
indeterminately
indisciplinable
indistinctively
inefficaciously
infinitesimally
inquisitorially
insignificantly
instantaneously
interchangeable
interchangeably
internationally
interrogatively
lackadaisically
logarithmically
logographically
macroscopically
mechanistically
meroblastically
microsporophyll
morphologically
multitudinously
necromantically
northeastwardly
northwestwardly
ontogenetically
overconfidently
pantheistically
parenthetically
peripatetically
peristaltically
perpendicularly
perspicaciously
pessimistically
philosophically
photochemically
phrenologically
physiologically
predeterminable
prehistorically
prepositionally
prepossessingly
preternaturally
problematically
proportionately
psychologically
pusillanimously
pyrotechnically
remonstratively
retrogressively
retrospectively
ritualistically
sanctimoniously
saprophytically
selfconfidently
selfconsciously
selfforgetfully
selfindulgently
selfreprovingly
selfrighteously
semiconsciously
significatively
singleheartedly
socialistically
sophisticatedly
splendiferously
subterraneously
superabundantly
superstitiously
supplementarily
suppositionally
surreptitiously
sycophantically
syllogistically
sympathetically
symptomatically
technologically
telegraphically
temperamentally
therapeutically
topographically
transgressively
trisyllabically
typographically
unceremoniously

unchallengeable
uncomplainingly
unconditionally
understandingly
unexceptionable
unexceptionably
unexceptionally
unintelligently
unintentionally
unobjectionable
unprecedentedly
unpretentiously
unquestioningly
unrealistically
unsubstantially
unsymmetrically
ventriloquially
acknowledgement
affranchisement
airconditioning
brachistochrone
congratulations
counterirritant
countermovement
counterplotting
disentanglement
disillusionment
eclaircissement
enfranchisement
gleichschaltung
marketgardening
methamphetamine
nonprofitmaking
notwithstanding
overdevelopment
photoconducting
polycrystalline
reapportionment
reestablishment
schoolmastering
selfabandonment
selfcontainment
selfdeprecating
selfdetermining
selfdevelopment
selffertilising
selffulfillment
selfimprovement
selfpropagating
selfregistering
selfreplicating
selfsacrificing
semiindependent
semitransparent
shrinkresistant
stampcollecting
superconducting
superheterodyne
superinducement
transfigurement
trinitrotoluene
unaccommodating
uncomprehending
underemployment
unprepossessing
weatherboarding
acclimatisation
alphabetisation
Americanisation
antivivisection
arterialisation
chloramphenicol
circumnavigator
circumscription
circumvallation
civilianisation
communalisation
computerisation
contravallation
crystallisation
decalcification
decarbonisation
decarburisation
decolourisation
decontamination
demagnetisation
demystification
denitrification
desensitisation
desexualisation
detribalisation
devitrification
differentiation
disarticulation
discommendation
disorganisation
dissatisfaction
diversification
electrification
etherealisation
Europeanisation
excommunication
exemplification
experimentation
extemporisation
exteriorisation
externalisation
familiarisation
formularisation
frenchification
heterodactyloos
hobbledehoyhood
hospitalisation
immortalisation
incomprehension
inconsideration
indemnification
indetermination
instrumentation
insubordination
intensification
interconnection
interdigitation
internalisation
introsusception
intussusception
maldistribution
materialisation
miniaturisation
misapprehension
misconstruction
nationalisation
nonintervention
personalisation
personification
phosphorylation
prestidigitator
procrastination
prognostication
properispomenon
quadruplication
quintuplication
rationalisation
reafforestation
reconsideration
reconsolidation
regionalisation
rhombencephalon
romanticisation
selfaffirmation
selfapprobation
selfcastigation
selfdestruction
selfexamination
selfgratulation
selfhumiliation
selfpollination
selfrealisation
speechification
standardisation
suburbanisation
superimposition
supersaturation
supplementation
syllabification
synchronisation
systematisation
transfiguration
transliteration
transplantation
underestimation
underproduction
vasoconstrictor
electromyograph
microphotograph
photolithograph
photomicrograph
rontgenotherapy
ultramicroscope
biogeochemistry
disinflationary
dissatisfactory
excommunicatory
immunochemistry
infundibuliform
insurrectionary
interjectionary
micromillimetre
neuropsychiatry
noncontributory
orthopsychiatry
picturepostcard
plenipotentiary
quatercentenary
selfdeprecatory
selfexplanatory
semidocumentary
sesquicentenary
shootinggallery
stereochemistry
straightforward
substitutionary
substratosphere
thermochemistry
uncomplimentary
unparliamentary
accountableness
acquisitiveness
adventurousness
agriculturalist
annihilationism
anthropopathism
anticlericalism
appropriateness
arboriculturist
Aristotelianism
atrabiliousness
blameworthiness
bloodguiltiness
broadmindedness
carnivorousness
ceremoniousness
circumspectness
coconsciousness
coldbloodedness
coldheartedness
commonplaceness
compendiousness
competitiveness
complicatedness
conceivableness
confessionalism
confessionalist
consecutiveness
conservationist
considerateness
conspicuousness
constructionism
constructionist
contentiousness
conventionalise
conventionalism
conventionalist
conversationist
cosmopolitanism
cryptocommunist
defencelessness
deleteriousness
departmentalise
departmentalism
descriptiveness
destructiveness
determinateness
disaffectedness
disgracefulness
distastefulness
distinctiveness
distrustfulness
downheartedness
ecclesiasticism
efficaciousness
emancipationist
enantiomorphism
episcopalianism
equalitarianism
everlastingness
expeditiousness
experientialism
experientialist
experimentalise
experimentalism
experimentalist
fantasticalness
fashionableness
fissiparousness
foresightedness
fragmentariness
gentlemanliness
geochronologist
geomorphologist
halfheartedness
hardheartedness
hermaphroditism
homogeneousness
humanitarianism
hydrodynamicist
hyperthyroidism
illimitableness
illustriousness
imaginativeness
impermeableness
importunateness
impracticalness
inattentiveness
incongruousness
indubitableness
ineffectiveness
ineffectualness
inexcusableness
inexpensiveness
inflammableness
infrangibleness
injudiciousness
innumerableness
inoffensiveness
inopportuneness
inquisitiveness
inscrutableness
insensitiveness
inseparableness
instructiveness
instrumentalism
instrumentalist
insurrectionist
intellectualise
intellectualism

intellectualist
intemperateness
interventionism
interventionist
intolerableness
intractableness
involuntariness
irreparableness
irrevocableness
kindheartedness
levelheadedness
lightheadedness
lightmindedness
longsightedness
mellifluousness
meritoriousness
mischievousness
mistrustfulness
nearsightedness
necessitousness
neighbourliness
nonsensicalness
numismatologist
obstructiveness
odoriferousness
openheartedness
ophthalmologist
opinionatedness
opprobriousness
palaeomagnetism
palaeontologist
paradoxicalness
parliamentarism
penetrativeness
perfunctoriness
perspicuousness
pharisaicalness
phenomenologist
photojournalism
photojournalist
photosynthesise
physiotherapist
picturesqueness
pleasurableness
practicableness
precipitousness
PreRaphaelitism
Presbyterianise
Presbyterianism
presentationism
presentationist
preservationist
prestigiousness
pretentiousness
processionalist
professionalise
professionalism
progressiveness
prohibitiveness
proportionalist
provocativeness
psychophysicist
psychotherapist
punctiliousness
purposelessness
quarrelsomeness
quarterfinalist
quickwittedness
remorselessness
repetitiousness
reproachfulness
resourcefulness
respectableness
resurrectionism
resurrectionist
righthandedness
rightmindedness
rudimentariness
selfcentredness
sententiousness
serviceableness
softheartedness
speculativeness
spontaneousness
standoffishness
stereoisomerism
subordinateness
subpostmistress
substantialness
substantiveness
sulphureousness
superficialness
superfluousness
superlativeness
supernaturalise
supernaturalism
supernaturalist
supportableness
susceptibleness
symmetricalness
tempestuousness
tendentiousness
therianthropism
thoughtlessness
totalitarianism
transparentness
treacherousness
treasonableness
troublesomeness
trueheartedness
trustworthiness
unconsciousness
unrighteousness
unwholesomeness
venturesomeness
vertiginousness
warmbloodedness
warmheartedness
warrantableness
wrongheadedness
antepenultimate
approachability
archiepiscopate
circumstantiate
communicability
complementarity
compressibility
confidentiality
consubstantiate
contemporaneity
contemptibility
contractability
contractibility
conventionality
demonstrability
destructibility
disagreeability
disreputability
equiprobability
ethnocentricity
exchangeability
extraillustrate
heterosexuality
impenetrability
imperishability
imponderability
inaccessibility
inadmissibility
inapplicability
incalculability
incomparability
incompatibility
incorrigibility
indefeasibility
indefensibility
indigestibility
indissolubility
ineffaceability
inexplicability
instrumentality
intellectuality
intelligibility
intercollegiate
invulnerability
irresistibility
irreversibility
manoeuvrability
proportionality
pyroelectricity
reconcilability
reproducibility
transferability
transilluminate
transmutability
unchangeability
anthropophagous
brachycephalous
brachydactylous
churrigueresque
coinstantaneous
collenchymatous
contemporaneous
dessertspoonful
disadvantageous
echinodermatous
enantiomorphous
epitheliomatous
margaritiferous
microsporangium
ornithorhynchus
pithecanthropus
plumbaginaceous
prosenchymatous
pulchritudinous
selfdistrustful
selfreproachful
vicissitudinous
electronegative
electropositive
excommunicative
experimentative
incommunicative
intussusceptive
manicdepressive
misapprehensive
photoconductive
prognosticative
selfdestructive
superconductive
uncommunicative
undemonstrative

---

phenylketonuria
pleuropneumonia
rhynchocephalia
achondroplastic
anthropocentric
anthropomorphic
atherosclerotic
chromatographic
chronogrammatic
cinematographic
conceptualistic
dolichocephalic
electromagnetic
electrophoretic
exhibitionistic
expressionistic
gynandromorphic
hendecasyllabic
heterochromatic
historiographic
hypercatalectic
impressionistic
indeterministic
individualistic
interferometric
interscholastic
irrationalistic
magnetoelectric
ophthalmoscopic
palaeoanthropic
parasympathetic
parthenogenetic
particularistic
phenomenalistic
phonautographic
photoelectronic
phytogeographic
pseudepigraphic
sadomasochistic
sociolinguistic
spermatogenetic
stoicheiometric
ventriloquistic
doublebarrelled
greatgrandchild
hobbledehoyhood
interstratified
noncommissioned
picturepostcard
polyunsaturated
selfconstituted
selfopinionated
straightforward
underprivileged
unsophisticated
wellconditioned
wellintentioned
acknowledgeable
antepenultimate
archiepiscopate
bioluminescence
brachistochrone
churrigueresque
circumstantiate
consubstantiate
conventionalise
departmentalise
distinguishable
electronegative
electropositive
excommunicative
experimentalise
experimentative
extraillustrate
hendecasyllable
imprescriptible
inapprehensible
incommensurable
incommunicative
indisciplinable
intellectualise
interchangeable
intercollegiate
interdependence
intussusceptive
manicdepressive
methamphetamine
micromillimetre
misapprehensive
noninterference
phosphorescence
photoconductive
photosynthesise
polycrystalline
predeterminable
Presbyterianise
professionalise
prognosticative
selfconsequence
selfdestructive
substratosphere
superconductive
superheterodyne
superincumbence

superintendence
supernaturalise
transilluminate
trinitrotoluene
ultracentrifuge
ultramicroscope
unchallengeable
uncommunicative
undemonstrative
unexceptionable
unobjectionable
unsportsmanlike
airconditioning
counterplotting
gleichschaltung
marketgardening
nonprofitmaking
notwithstanding
photoconducting
schoolmastering
selfdeprecating
selfdetermining
selffertilising
selfpropagating
selfregistering
selfreplicating
selfsacrificing
stampcollecting
superconducting
unaccommodating
uncomprehending
unprepossessing
weatherboarding
counterapproach
electromyograph
microphotograph
photolithograph
photomicrograph
amphitheatrical
anthropological
antimonarchical
bacteriological
bibliographical
biogeographical
chloramphenicol
circumferential
configurational
cryptanalytical
demonstrational
dessertspoonful
disproportional
ecclesiological
electrochemical
entrepreneurial
epistemological
fourdimensional
governorgeneral
improvisatorial
inconsequential
interprovincial
jurisprudential
lexicographical
microanalytical
microsporophyll
monosymmetrical
nongovernmental
nonprofessional
oceanographical
omnidirectional
palaeobotanical
palaeographical
pharmacological
philanthropical
photomechanical
physicochemical
physiographical
pneumatological
protozoological
selfdistrustful
selfreproachful
semicylindrical
spectroscopical
stratigraphical
superstructural
transcriptional
transpositional
trigonometrical
zoogeographical
annihilationism
anthropopathism
anticlericalism
Aristotelianism
confessionalism
constructionism
conventionalism
cosmopolitanism
departmentalism
ecclesiasticism
enantiomorphism
episcopalianism
equalitarianism
experientialism
experimentalism
hermaphroditism
humanitarianism
hyperthyroidism
infundibuliform
instrumentalism
intellectualism
interventionism
microsporangium
palaeomagnetism
parliamentarism
photojournalism
PreRaphaelitism
Presbyterianism
presentationism
professionalism
resurrectionism
stereoisomerism
supernaturalism
therianthropism
totalitarianism
acanthocephalan
acclimatisation
alphabetisation
Americanisation
antisabbatarian
antitrinitarian
antivivisection
arterialisation
Christadelphian
circumscription
circumvallation
civilianisation
communalisation
computerisation
contravallation
crossopterygian
crystallisation
Czechoslovakian
decalcification
decarbonisation
decarburisation
decolourisation
decontamination
demagnetisation
demystification
denitrification
desensitisation
desexualisation
detribalisation
devitrification
differentiation
disarticulation
discommendation
disorganisation
dissatisfaction
diversification
electrification
etherealisation
Europeanisation
excommunication
exemplification
experimentation
extemporisation
exteriorisation
externalisation
familiarisation
formularisation
frenchification
hospitalisation
immortalisation
incomprehension
inconsideration
indemnification
indetermination
instrumentation
insubordination
intensification
interconnection
interdigitation
internalisation
introsusception
intussusception
malacopterygian
maldistribution
materialisation
Mephistophelean
Mephistophelian
miniaturisation
misapprehension
misconstruction
nationalisation
nonintervention
parliamentarian
personalisation
personification
phosphorylation
platitudinarian
postmillenarian
povertystricken
procrastination
prognostication
properispomenon
psychometrician
quadruplication
quinquagenarian
quintuplication
rationalisation
reafforestation
reconsideration
reconsolidation
regionalisation
rhombencephalon
romanticisation
selfaffirmation
selfapprobation
selfcastigation
selfdestruction
selfexamination
selfgratulation
selfhumiliation
selfpollination
selfrealisation
speechification
standardisation
suburbanisation
superimposition
supersaturation
supplementation
syllabification
synchronisation
systematisation
thunderstricken
transfiguration
transliteration
transplantation
underestimation
underproduction
vicechamberlain
connoisseurship
interpretership
stadtholdership
cerebrovascular
cinematographer
circumnavigator
counterattacker
extracurricular
historiographer
interclavicular
interfascicular
malpractitioner
photosensitiser
prestidigitator
radiogoniometer
stretcherbearer
vasoconstrictor
accountableness
acquisitiveness
adventurousness
ankylostomiasis
anthropogenesis
anthropophagous
appropriateness
atherosclerosis
atrabiliousness
bioastronautics
blameworthiness
bloodguiltiness
brachycephalous
brachydactylous
broadmindedness
carnivorousness
ceremoniousness
circumspectness
coconsciousness
coinstantaneous
coldbloodedness
coldheartedness
collenchymatous
commonplaceness
compendiousness
competitiveness
complicatedness
conceivableness
congratulations
consecutiveness
considerateness
conspicuousness
contemporaneous
contentiousness
defencelessness
deleteriousness
dermatoglyphics
descriptiveness
destructiveness
determinateness
disadvantageous
disaffectedness
disgracefulness
distastefulness
distinctiveness
distrustfulness
downheartedness
echinodermatous
efficaciousness
electroanalysis
electrodynamics
electrokinetics
electrophoresis
enantiomorphous
epitheliomatous
everlastingness
expeditiousness
fantasticalness

fashionableness
fissiparousness
foresightedness
fragmentariness
gastroenteritis
gentlemanliness
halfheartedness
hardheartedness
heterodactyloos
homogeneousness
illimitableness
illustriousness
imaginativeness
impermeableness
importunateness
impracticalness
inattentiveness
incongruousness
indubitableness
ineffectiveness
ineffectualness
inexcusableness
inexpensiveness
inflammableness
infrangibleness
injudiciousness
innumerableness
inoffensiveness
inopportuneness
inquisitiveness
inscrutableness
insensitiveness
inseparableness
instructiveness
intemperateness
intolerableness
intractableness
involuntariness
irreparableness
irrevocableness
kindheartedness
levelheadedness
lightheadedness
lightmindedness
longsightedness
margaritiferous
mellifluousness
meritoriousness
metamathematics
mischievousness
mistrustfulness
nearsightedness
necessitousness
neighbourliness
nonsensicalness
obstructiveness
odoriferousness
openheartedness
opinionatedness
opprobriousness
ornithorhynchus
paradoxicalness
parthenogenesis
penetrativeness
perfunctoriness
perspicuousness
pharisaicalness
picturesqueness
pithecanthropus
pleasurableness
plumbaginaceous
practicableness
precipitousness
prestigiousness
pretentiousness
progressiveness
prohibitiveness
prosenchymatous
provocativeness
pulchritudinous
punctiliousness
purposelessness
quarrelsomeness
quickwittedness
remorselessness
repetitiousness
reproachfulness
resourcefulness
respectableness
righthandedness
rightmindedness
rudimentariness
schistosomiasis
selfcentredness
sententiousness
serviceableness
softheartedness
speculativeness
spermatogenesis
spontaneousness
standoffishness
subordinateness
subpostmistress
substantialness
substantiveness
sulphureousness
superficialness
superfluousness
superlativeness
supportableness
susceptibleness
symmetricalness
tempestuousness
tendentiousness
thoughtlessness
transparentness
treacherousness
treasonableness
troublesomeness
trueheartedness
trustworthiness
trypanosomiasis
unconsciousness
unrighteousness
unwholesomeness
venturesomeness
vertiginousness
vicissitudinous
warmbloodedness
warmheartedness
warrantableness
wrongheadedness
acknowledgement
affranchisement
agriculturalist
arboriculturist
confessionalist
conservationist
constructionist
conventionalist
conversationist
counterirritant
countermovement
cryptocommunist
disentanglement
disillusionment
eclaircissement
emancipationist
enfranchisement
experientialist
experimentalist
flibbertigibbet
geochronologist
geomorphologist
hydrodynamicist
instrumentalist
insurrectionist
intellectualist
interventionist
numismatologist
ophthalmologist
overdevelopment
palaeontologist
phenomenologist
photojournalist
physiotherapist
presentationist
preservationist
processionalist
proportionalist
psychophysicist
psychotherapist
quarterfinalist
reapportionment
reestablishment
resurrectionist
selfabandonment
selfcontainment
selfdevelopment
selffulfillment
selfimprovement
semiindependent
semitransparent
shrinkresistant
sleepingdraught
speakingtrumpet
superinducement
supernaturalist
transfigurement
underemployment
abiogenetically
accommodatingly
aerodynamically
ambidexterously
anaesthesiology
anaesthetically
anisotropically
apocalyptically
approachability
approximatively
architecturally
argumentatively
atmospherically
authoritatively
autographically
autoradiography
biogeochemistry
chronologically
communicability
communicatively
compartmentally
compassionately
complementarily
complementarity
compositionally
comprehensively
compressibility
condescendingly
confidentiality
conjunctionally
conscientiously
consentaneously
consequentially
contemplatively
contemporaneity
contemptibility
contractability
contractibility
contradictorily
controversially
conventionality
correspondingly
crystallography
demonstrability
demonstratively
destructibility
developmentally
disagreeability
disappointingly
disconcertingly
discontinuously
disenchantingly
dishearteningly
disinflationary
disinterestedly
dispassionately
disreputability
disrespectfully
dissatisfactory
distinguishably
dithyrambically
dramaturgically
dyslogistically
encephalography
equiprobability
ethnocentricity
euphemistically
exchangeability
excommunicatory
extraordinarily
grandiloquently
heartbreakingly
heliotropically
Hellenistically
hermeneutically
heterogeneously
heterosexuality
hydropathically
hydrostatically
hypercritically
ideographically
immunochemistry
impenetrability
imperishability
imponderability
inaccessibility
inadmissibility
inapplicability
inappropriately
incalculability
incommensurably
incomparability
incompatibility
inconsiderately
inconspicuously
incorrigibility
indefeasibility
indefensibility
indeterminately
indigestibility
indissolubility
indistinctively
ineffaceability
inefficaciously
inexplicability
infinitesimally
inquisitorially
insignificantly
instantaneously
instrumentality
insurrectionary
intellectuality
intelligibility
interchangeably
interdependency
interjectionary
internationally
interrogatively
invulnerability
irresistibility
irreversibility
lackadaisically
logarithmically
logographically
macroscopically
manoeuvrability

mechanistically
meroblastically
morphologically
multitudinously
necromantically
neurophysiology
neuropsychiatry
noncontributory
northeastwardly
northwestwardly
ontogenetically
orthopsychiatry
overconfidently
palaeogeography
pantheistically
parenthetically
peripatetically
peristaltically
perpendicularly
perspicaciously
pessimistically
philosophically
photochemically
phototelegraphy
phrenologically
physiologically
plenipotentiary
prehistorically
prepositionally
prepossessingly
preternaturally
problematically
proportionality
proportionately
psychologically
psychopathology
pusillanimously
pyroelectricity
pyrotechnically
quatercentenary
radioautography
radiotelegraphy
reconcilability
remonstratively
reproducibility
retrogressively
retrospectively
ritualistically
roentgenography
rontgenotherapy
sanctimoniously
saprophytically
selfcomplacency
selfconfidently
selfconsciously
selfconsistency
selfdeprecatory
selfexplanatory
selfforgetfully
selfindulgently
selfreprovingly
selfrighteously
selfsufficiency
semiconsciously
semidocumentary
sesquicentenary
shootinggallery
significatively
singleheartedly
socialistically
sophisticatedly
splendiferously
stereochemistry
substitutionary
subterraneously
superabundantly
superintendency
superstitiously
supplementarily
suppositionally
surreptitiously
sycophantically
syllogistically
sympathetically
symptomatically
technologically
telegraphically
telephotography
temperamentally
therapeutically
thermochemistry
topographically
transferability
transgressively
transmutability
trisyllabically
typographically
unceremoniously
unchangeability
uncomplainingly
uncomplimentary
unconditionally
understandingly
unexceptionably
unexceptionally
unintelligently
unintentionally
unparliamentary
unprecedentedly
unpretentiously
unquestioningly
unrealistically
unsubstantially
unsymmetrically
ventriloquially